FOR BRAVERY IN THE FIELD

GREAT WAR BRITISH ARMY RECIPIENTS
OF THE MILITARY MEDAL 1914-1920

A REGISTER

FOR BRAVERY IN THE FIELD

GREAT WAR BRITISH ARMY RECIPIENTS
OF THE MILITARY MEDAL 1914-1920

A REGISTER

Peter Warrington

The Naval & Military Press Ltd

Published by

The Naval & Military Press Ltd
Unit 10 Ridgewood Industrial Park,
Uckfield, East Sussex,
TN22 5QE England

Tel: +44 (0) 1825 749494
Fax: +44 (0) 1825 765701

www.naval-military-press.com
www.nmarchive.com

© 2014 Peter Warrington. All rights reserved.
Printed and bound by CPI Group (UK) Ltd, Croydon, CR0 4YY

No part of this book may be reproduced, stored in a retrieval system, or transmitted by nay means without the express permission of the author.

Suffolk County Council	
30127 08371225 2	
Askews & Holts	Dec-2015
	£33.50

DEDICATED TO THE MILLIONS OF MEN AND WOMEN
WHO EXPERIENCED THE MOST CATASTROPHIC
EVENT IN RECORDED HUMAN HISTORY

IN ÆTURNUM NON OBLIVISCAR

INTRODUCTORY NOTES

The Military Medal was instituted by Royal Warrant in March 1916, for 'individual or associated acts of bravery', the details being published in a supplement to the *London Gazette*, number 29535, dated 4th April 1916. The decoration was originally restricted to non-commissioned officers and men in the army, but later extended to include Warrant Officers, women, and naval personnel engaged in action ashore.

For the first eighteen months of the Great War the only decoration available to be awarded for bravery to other ranks, apart from the Victoria Cross, was the Distinguished Conduct Medal, instituted in 1854. The DCM was a prestigious award which carried with it a bounty.

Various rationales have been put forward for the institution of the MM. It quickly became obvious that this war was not going to be 'all over by Christmas', a popular jingoistic belief in the early months of the conflict. War on an industrial scale produced thousands of individual acts of bravery, and in order to maintain the prestige of the award of the DCM, a lesser grade of decoration was deemed necessary, incidentally one which did not carry a bounty.

The MM was the lowest grade of reward for which a medal was given. Even so, it was a relative rarity. During the conflict a total of 5,704,416 men and women from the British Isles served in British uniform. Of these, only 88,529 were awarded the MM: this is only 1.55% of all serving personnel. Bars were awarded for subsequent acts of bravery. Four thousand and forty-four first bars were won, and 129 second bars. (These figures do not include Imperial troops or naval personnel).

In the register which follows, the rank given is that held by the recipient at the time of the award, except in the case of those people who were subsequently commissioned and who went on to win one or more of the 'officer' decorations, in which case the commissioned rank is given. Acting and temporary ranks have been ignored. Rank nomenclatures are those in contemporary use. Many of these changed during the later stages of the war, but for the sake of consistency the earlier nomenclatures are used. Many of the people in the register went on to be commissioned and some reached much higher rank and finished the war in command of companies/batteries/ squadrons or even battalions. A list of notable recipients is given separately.

Similarly, the regimental names given are the ones in official use at the time, and many of these changed shortly after the war. Thus, what was later to become the Black Watch is given the official name of Royal Highlanders, the Green Howards was the Yorkshire Regiment, the Buffs the East Kent Regiment, and so on. Despite officialdom, many regiments did use their unofficial titles during, and indeed, prior to the Great War.

It will be noted that some Mentions in Despatches (MID) and foreign decorations are given. These are by no means exhaustive, and are mentioned only because they were discovered during the research into the MM. To research all MM holders who were 'mentioned' or given foreign awards would be a whole new project in itself.

Surnames are in strict alphabetical order, with the exception of names beginning Mac or Mc, where the 'a' has been ignored. Thus John A. MacIntosh falls between John McIntosh and John T. McIntosh. As far as forenames are concerned, anyone looking for Irish relatives in the register will find only the anglicised version of the forename. In reality many of the Irish soldiers given the names John and James would have been Seán and Seámus. Apparently British Army record keepers did not recognise the Celtic versions.

Some of the abbreviations in the register are idiosyncratic in the effort to conserve space, and keep the book to a manageable size. Many of them are obvious, such as the county names. A list of the less obvious ones is given.

Finally, on a personal note, this has been a solo effort which has taken more than six years to complete. I could not have done it without the unqualified support of my 'significant other', Lynda, who has indulged my obsession in all it's manifestations.

There will inevitably be some mistakes. They are all mine.

ABBREVIATIONS

2nd Cpl	Second Corporal	EL	East Lancashire
A&SH	Argyll & Sutherland Highlanders	Eng	Engineer, Engineering
AASS	Anti-Aircraft Searchlight Section	ER	East Riding
AC Bn	Armoured Car Battalion	FA, Fd Amb	Field Ambulance
ACC	Army Cyclist Corps	FANY	First Aid Nursing Yeomanry
AE Coy	Area Employment Company	Fd Svy	Field Survey
AIF	Australian Imperial Force	FNU	First name unknown
Ammn Col	Ammunition Column	Ftr	Fitter
APM	Assistant Provost Marshal	Fus	Fusilier
Arm	Armourer, Armaments	Garr	Garrison
Arty	Artillery	GC Coy	Gun Carrier Company
ASC	Army Service Corps	GG, Gren Gds	Grenadier Guards
AT Coy	Army Troops Company	Gnr	Gunner
att	attached	H, Hldrs	Highlanders
Aux	Auxiliary	HAG	Heavy Artillery Group
BAC	Brigade Ammunition Column	HC	Home Counties
Bde	Brigade	Hld	Highland
Bdr	Bombardier	HLI	Highland Light Infantry
Bdsm	Bandsman	How	Howitzer
BG Op Coy	Broad Gauge Operating Company	Hrs, Huss	Hussars
Bn	Battalion	HT Coy	Horse Transport Company
BQMS	Battery Quarrtermaster Serjeant	HTMB, HTM Bty	Heavy Trench Mortar Battery
BRCS	British Red Cross Society	IWT	Inland Water Transport
BSM	Battery Serjeant Major	KAR	King's African Rifles
Bty	Battery	KEH	King Edward's Horse
Cab Sect	Cable Section	KOSB	King's Own Scottish Borderers
Capt	Captain	KRRC	King's Royal Rifle Corps
CCS	Casualty Clearing Section	L/Bdr	Lance Bombardier
CG(B)	Croix de Guerre (Belgium)	L/Cpl	Lance Corporal
CG(F)	Croix de Guerre (France)	L/Sjt	Lance Serjeant
CG(It)	Croce di Guerra (Italy)	L&BH	Lothians & Border Horse
CG, Coldm Gds	Coldstream Guards	Lab	Labour
Clk	Clerk	LACP	Light Armoured Car Patrol
Cmdt	Commandant	LAMB	Light Armoured Motor Battery
Cnty Lond Yeo	County of London Yeomanry	LF	Lancashire Fusiliers
CoH	Corporal of Horse	LI	Light Infantry
Conn Rgrs	Connaught Rangers	Lld	Lowland
Constr	Constuction	Lrs	Lancers
Coy	Company	LTMB	Light Trench Mortar Battery
Cpl	Corporal	MAC	Motor Ambulance Convoy
CQMS	Company Quartermaster Serjeant	MAG	Motor Ambulance Group
CRA	Commander Royal Artillery	Maj	Major
Cty Lond Yeo	City of London Yeomanry	MAS	Motor Air Line Section
DAC	Divisional Ammunition Column	MC(Gr)	Military Cross (Greece)
DCLI	Duke of Cornwall's Light Infantry	MCDR	Motor Cycle Despatch Rider
DEC	Divisional Employment Company	MdH(F)	Medaille d'Honneur (France)
DG, Dgn Gds	Dragoon Guards	MGC(HB)	Machine Gun Corps (Heavy Branch)
DLO Yeo	Duke of Lancaster's Own Yeomanry	MGC(HS)	Machine Gun Corps (Heavy Section)
DM(B)	Decoration Militaire (Belgium)		
Dmr	Drummer	MID	Mentioned in Despatches
Dns	Dragoons	MM(F)	Medaille Militaire(France)
DSC	Divisional Supply Column	MMV(It)	Medal for Military Valour(Italy)
DSC(US)	Distinguished Service Cross (United States)	Mob Wksp	Mobile Workshop
		MT	Mechanical Transport
Dvr	Driver	MTMB	Medium Trench Mortar Battery
E&M Coy	Electrical & Mechanical Company	Mtn Bty	Mountain Battery
EA	East Anglian	Nbld, Northbld	Northumberland

Nbrn	Northumbrian	SIH	South Irish Horse
NF	Northumberland Fusiliers	SJAB	St John's Ambulance Brigade
NIH	North Irish Horse	Sjt	Serjeant
NM	North Midland	SM	South Midland or Serjeant Major
N&DR	Nottinghamshire & Derbyshire Regiment	Som LI	Somerset Light Infantry
		Spec Coy	Special Company
OBLI	Oxfordshire & Buckinghamshire Light Infantry	Spr	Sapper
		SQMS	Squadron Quartermaster Serjeant
OLeo(B)	Order of Leopold (Belgium)	Sqn	Squadron
OStA(R)	Order of St Anne (Russia)	SR, Scot Rif	Scottish Rifles
OStG(R)	Order of St George (Russia)	SS	Shoeing Smith
Pte	Private	SSM	Squadron Serjeant Major
QAIMNS	Queen Alexandra's Imperial Military Nursing Service	Sub Cond	Sub-Conductor
		Svce	Service
QMS	Quartermaster Serjeant	SWB	South Wales Borderers
QMWAAC	Queen Mary's Womens' Auxiliary Army Corps	T&SC	Transport & Supply Column
		TC Coy	Tank Carrier Company
R Ir Rif	Royal Irish Rifles	Tfc Contr Coy	Traffic Control Company
RB, Rif Bde	Rifle Brigade	TFNS	Territorial Force Nursing Service
RDCC	Road Construction Company	Tk	Tank
RE	Royal Engineers	TM	Trench Mortar
Res Pk	Reserve Park	Tpr	Trooper
RF	Royal Fusiliers	Tpt	Transport
RFA	Royal Field Artillery	Tptr	Trumpeter
RGA	Royal Garrison Artillery	TS Coy	Tank Supply Company
RHA	Royal Horse Artillery	Tunn, Tunng Coy	Tunnelling Company
Rhd	Railhead	Tway Coy	Tramway Company
RLCC	Railway Construction Company	VAD	Voluntary Aid Detachment
Rly	Railway	VM(Rm)	Virtutea Militara (Rumania)
ROD	Railway Operating Division	WAFF	West African Frontier Force
RQMS	Regimental Quartermaster Serjeant	Wlr	Wheeler
RS	Royal Scots	WR, W Rid	West Riding
RSM	Regimental Serjeant Major	wrls	wireless
RWK	Royal West Kent	WRR	West Riding Regiment
SB, Sge Bty	Siege Battery	Wx	Wessex
SBAC	Siege Battery Ammunition Column	Y&LR	York & Lancaster Regiment
Sher Rgrs	Sherwood Rangers (Yeomanry)	Yeo	Yeomanry
Sig	Signal, Signals, Signaller	YLI	Yorkshire Light Infantry

SOME NOTABLE MILITARY MEDAL WINNERS

L/Cpl William Harold COLTMAN, VC, DCM & Bar, MM & Bar, Croix de Guerre (France), 1st/6th Bn North Staffordshire Regiment.

Major James Thomas Byford McCUDDEN, VC, DSO & Bar, MC & Bar, MM, Royal Flying Corps.
Died in a flying accident July 1917, aged 23.

CSM John Henry WILLIAMS, VC, DCM, MM & Bar, Medaille Militaire (France), 10th Bn South Wales Borderers.

Sjt William GREGG, VC, DCM, MM, 13th Bn Rifle Brigade.

Pte Henry TANDEY, VC, DCM, MM, 1st/5th Bn West Riding Regiment.

Sjt William McNALLY, VC, MM & Bar, 8th Bn Yorkshire Regiment.

Pte Hugh McIver, VC, MM & Bar, 2nd Bn Royal Scots.

Twenty-six other Victoria Cross winners also won single Military Medals.

L/Sjt Joseph J.HICKMAN, DCM & 2 Bars, MM & Bar, 2nd, 17th & 21st Bns Middlesex Regiment.

Sjt Stephen FORBES, DCM & Bar, MM & 2 Bars, Medal for Military Valour (Italy), 9th & 13th Bns York & Lancaster Regiment.

CSM William BIDDLE, MC, DCM & Bar, MM & Bar, 1st Bn Gloucestershire Regiment.

Eight other soldiers were awarded DCM & Bar, MM & Bar.

CSM James DONNELLY, MC, DCM & Bar, MM, Croix de Guerre (Belgium), 10th Bn Durham Light Infantry.

T/2Lt Edmund WEDGBURY, DSO, MC, DCM, MM, Gloucestershire Regiment attached to 1/8th Worcestershire Regiment.
Won the MM as a Serjeant with the Worcestershire Regiment. The only soldier to win all four of the main 'lesser' decorations.

T/2Lt Harold Everett HITCHIN, DSO, MC, MM & Bar, 18th Bn Durham Light Infantry.
Won the MM as Serjeant with the same battalion.

Capt Rupert Charles BAMBRIDGE, DSO, MC & Bar, MM, 10th Bn Royal Fusiliers.

Major Thomas HORTON, DSO, MC, MM, Royal Garrison Artillery. Won the MM as Corporal, 12 Siege Battery.

Six other DSO winners were awarded the MM.

CSM Charles William MUTTERS, MC, DCM, MM & Bar, 2nd Bn Manchester Regiment.

T/2Lt Frank Joseph POWELL, MC, DCM, MM & Bar, 8th Bn Royal Berkshire Regiment.
Won the MM with 5th Bn of the same regiment.

T/2Lt James SIDDONS, MC, DCM, MM & Bar, Cheshire Regiment. Won the MMs as a Serjeant in 4th Hussars.

T/2Lt Peter NOLAN, MC, DCM, MM & Bar, 16th Bn Royal Warwickshire Regiment.
Won the MMs as Pte then L/Sjt with the Irish Guards.

CSM Sidney PEARCE, MC, DCM, MM & Bar, Medaille Militaire (France), 1st & 2nd Bns Wiltshire Regiment.

T/2Lt Esau EDWARDS, MC & Bar, DCM, MM, 8th Bn Machine Gun Corps. Won the MM with 91 Coy of the same corps.

Capt Alexander GORDON, MC & Bar, DCM, MM, 2nd Bn Royal Scots. Won the MM as Lance Corporal with the Scots Guards.

T/2Lt Dan KEW, MC & Bar, DCM, MM, 1st Bn Bedfordshire Regiment attached to 1st/1st Bn Hertfordshire Regiment.
Won the MM as a L/Sjt with Royal Berkshire Regiment.

An apparently unique case was that of Sjt John W HAMMOND, MC, DCM, MM, who was initially serving as T/2Lt in the Lovat's Scouts, winning the Military Cross in the spring of 1917. He resigned his commission at war's end and re-enlisted as a Serjeant in 46th Bn Royal Fusiliers for service in North Russia, where he won the DCM and MM.

Another member of the same battalion was Pte Eustace Cameron MARRIOTT, formerly Captain, Royal Field Artillery, who resigned and re-enlisted, winning the MM in North Russia.

Finally, the strange case of Sjt Charles Edward COLLINS, MM, 17th RWF is worth mentioning. His real name was Coutart de Butts TAYLOR. In 1916, whilst serving as a Company Commander with the Royal Irish Rifles (he also held a commission in the Jersey Militia) in Salonika, he was accused of 'Conduct unbecoming an Officer & Gentleman' for drinking with NCOs in a house of ill repute. To escape the consequences he deserted and enlisted in the RWF in the name of COLLINS. He quickly gained promotion and in 1917/18 was wounded at least three times, being awarded the MM in Nov 1918. He was recommended for a field commission at this time but was severely wounded and died on Christmas Eve 1918. After an investigation his original commission was restored posthumously.

About the compiler

Peter Warrington served for 24 years in the British Army, the first twelve as an infantry grunt, before qualifying as a helicopter pilot. He is a keen amateur military historian with a Bachelor's degree in Modern History. After leaving the army he continued to fly helicopters for a living, mostly overseas, before returning to the UK and taking up a job in the archives of a well-respected English national newspaper. He is now completely retired and lives in south-east London with his partner Lynda.

A

AARON Harry MM L/Cpl 14/844 Royal Warwickshire Regt
AARON James MM Pte 19728 8th Yorkshire Light Infantry KIA 1.7.16.
AARONS Jack MM Sjt 11/832 11th East Yorkshire Regt
ABBA Archibald Clifford MM Sjt 10/697 East Yorkshire Regt
ABBA Walter MM Pte 1587 1/3rd (Northumbrian) Fd Amb RAMC
ABBERLEY Thomas Frederick MM L/Cpl 40791 8th North Staffordshire Regt KIA 20.9.17.
ABBERTON William MM Pte 68280 RAMC
ABBEY Thomas MM+Bar Sjt 596 1/5th Yorkshire Regt
ABBIE John MM Sjt 17065 Royal Highlanders
ABBISS Harry W. "DCM+Bar,MM" S/Sjt 45510 54 Fd Amb RAMC
ABBOT Fred MM Pte 1622 1/4th Northumberland Fusiliers
ABBOT Walter D. MM Pte S/14686 Arg & Suth Highlanders att MGC
ABBOTS James MM Pte 31114 10th Royal Welsh Fusiliers
ABBOTT Abraham MM Pte 240445 Yorkshire Light Infantry
ABBOTT Albert H. MM Cpl 173365 120 Bty 27 Bde RFA
ABBOTT Alexander C. MM Gnr 73657 RGA
ABBOTT Alfred H. MM Cpl 115218 RGA
ABBOTT B.E.J.C.P. MM Pte 22354 6th East Kent Regt
ABBOTT Charles MM Pte 13233 8th Lincolnshire Regt
ABBOTT Charles Henry MM Pte 235198 7th Yorkshire Regt KIA 12.5.17.
ABBOTT Cyril W. MM CSM 345169 16th Devonshire Regt
ABBOTT Frederick G. MM Sjt 16838 2nd Welsh Regt
ABBOTT George Henry MM Cpl 9/1730 9th Royal Munster Fusiliers
ABBOTT Halsey MM Sjt 54795 D/67 Bde RFA
ABBOTT Harold MM Cpl M/27418 Army Service Corps
ABBOTT Harry MM Cpl 68476 7th Royal West Surrey Regt
ABBOTT Henry S. MM Sjt 22374 2nd Royal West Surrey Regt
ABBOTT Herbert James MM Gnr Sig 159556 282 Siege Bty RGA
ABBOTT John MM Sjt 47303 A/160 Bde RFA
ABBOTT John Frederick MM L/Cpl 7418 2nd Worcestershire Regt
ABBOTT John Henry "MM,MID" Pte M2/114110 Army Service Corps
ABBOTT John T. MM Pte 81996 26th Royal Fusiliers
ABBOTT John Thomas MM Pte 22039 Northumberland Fusiliers
ABBOTT John Thomas MM Pte 2440 8th East Kent Regt
ABBOTT John W. MM Cpl 266995 10th Notts & Derby Regt
ABBOTT John W. MM Pte 11706 Cheshire Regt
ABBOTT John W. MM Pte 283570 4th London Regt
ABBOTT Joseph W. MM Sjt 200783 West Yorkshire Regt
ABBOTT P. MM L/Cpl 12516 9th Essex Regt
ABBOTT Percy "MM,MID" Sjt 9156 2nd Northamptonshire Regt
ABBOTT Percy George MM Pte 8264 2nd Worcestershire Regt
ABBOTT Percy H. MM Cpl 36222 8th Royal Berkshire Regt
ABBOTT Phillip H. MM Pte 12922 1/1st Duke of Lancaster's Own Yeomanry
ABBOTT R. MM CSM 5167 1st Essex Regt
ABBOTT Reginald MM Sjt 16000 46th Bn Machine Gun Corps
ABBOTT Richard MM Pte 23004 1st Lancashire Fusiliers
ABBOTT Richard C. MM Pte 301413 5/6th Royal Scots
ABBOTT Richard E. MM Pte 242360 5th York & Lancaster Regt
ABBOTT Richard O MM Cpl 9701 5th Middlesex Regt
ABBOTT Robert MM Pte 242226 2/5th East Lancashire Regt
ABBOTT Sidney J. MM.MID Sjt 8379 1st King's Own Scottish Borderers
ABBOTT Thomas MM Pte 67736 32nd Bn Machine Gun Corps
ABBOTT Thomas MM Pte 8359 1st Scots Guards
ABBOTT Walter J. MM CSM 8343 1st Hampshire Regt
ABBOTT William MM Cpl 58151 Machine Gun Corps
ABBOTT William E. MM Pte 24577 Royal West Kent Regt
ABBOTT William Henry MM Dvr 75116 C/77 Bde RFA
ABBOTT William N.J. MM Sjt L/298 16th Lancers
ABBOTT William W. MM Pte M2/073142 Army Service Corps
ABBOTTS William MM Cpl 46544 25 Bde RFA
ABBS George S. MM Pte 100632 92 Fd Amb RAMC
ABBS Thomas W. MM Sjt 70049 RAMC
ABDALE John MM Sjt T4/251823 Army Service Corps
A'BEAR Hedley John MM Sjt 2085 7th Royal West Surrey Regt KIA 10.7.17.
A'BEAR Thomas N. "DCM,MM" Pte 285169 1/1st Oxfordshire Yeomanry
ABEL Arthur MM L/Cpl 36763 RAMC
ABEL Bertie Henry MM Pte 38947 Essex Regt
ABEL Charles MM Sjt 92716 Tank Corps
ABEL Edward L. MM Pte 4619 1st London Regt
ABEL George Fowtrell MM Sjt 1449 Royal Fusiliers Died 20.6.18.
ABEL George W. MM Pte 15589 Royal Welsh Fusiliers
ABEL James MM Pte 301118 2/1st(Highland)Fd Amb RAMC
ABEL James D. MM Pte 201447 1/4th Gordon Highlanders
ABEL James W. MM Sjt 1633 1/5th Gloucestershire Regt
ABEL John W. MM Pte 43508 1st Essex Regt
ABELL Edward MM Sjt 10065 9th South Staffordshire Regt
ABELL Francis W. MM Pte 37210 South Staffordshire Regt
ABELL Frank Reginald MM Sgt 22817 Machine Gun Corps
ABELL Stanley MM Sjt 39814 Royal West Surrey Regt
ABERCROMBIE John MM Spr 94698 Royal Engineers
ABERCROMBIE John Fergus MM Pte 8764 1st Scots Guards KIA 27.9.18.
ABERCROMBIE Johnston MM Sjt 270007 1/1st Northumberland Yeo
ABERCROMBIE Robert H. MM Cpl 2262 RAMC
ABERDEIN Thomas MM Pte 303031 RAMC
ABERNETHY Frederick MM Cpl 163 20th Durham Light Infantry
ABERNETHY George A. "DCM,MM" Sjt 15383 17th Liverpool Regt
ABERNETHY S. MM+Bar L/Cpl 9524 2nd Scottish Rifles
ABERNETHY William MM Sjt 307440 2/1(Lowland)Hy Bty RGA
ABIGAIL Walter MM Gnr 8400 B/62 Bde RFA
ABLETT Arthur Charles MM+Bar CSM 16799 2nd Suffolk Regt
ABLIN John Goldin MM Cpl 3051 6th London Regt
ABLITT John "DCM,MM+Bar" Spr 97711 21 Div Sig Coy Royal Engineers
ABLOTT Frank MM Pte 10206 Coldstream Guards
ABNETT Thomas R. MM Cpl 88872 D/311 Bde RFA
ABOR Wilfrid Gaukroger MM Sjt 4073 2/1st HAC(Inf)
ABRAHAM David MM Sjt S/3546 12th Rifle Brigade
ABRAHAM Ernest W. MM Bdr L/27673 RFA
ABRAHAM Harold MM Cpl 432323 Royal Engineers
ABRAHAM James Harold MM Pte 2674 Oxf & Bucks Light Infantry
ABRAHAM John MM Pte 65924 RAMC
ABRAHAM John H. MM Pte 12186 Leicestershire Regt
ABRAHAM Maud Alice MM Sister F Civil Hospital Reserve
ABRAHAM Myles "DCM,MM,MID" Sjt L/41819 D/174 Bde RFA
ABRAHAM Robert "MC,MM" T/2Lt 9th Royal Inniskilling Fusiliers
ABRAHAMS Charles W. MM Pte 271492 1/1st Hertfordshire Regt
ABRAHAMS Edward MM Pte M2/098237 Army Service Corps att RAMC.
ABRAHAMS Edward F. MM Pte 10245 1st Duke of Cornwall's LI
ABRAHAMS John MM Pte 200329 Gloucestershire Regt
ABRAHAMS John W. MM Pte 201390 1/5th Manchester Regt
ABRAHAMS Joseph MM L/Cpl 1738 RAMC
ABRAHAMS Kenneth Duncan MM Sjt 1172 RFA
ABRAHAMS William G.L. MM L/Cpl 200077 Bedfordshire Regt
ABRAM James MM Pte 14826 12th Liverpool Regt
ABRATHAR Edward T. MM Fitter Cpl 36234 RFA
ABREY Arthur R. MM L/Cpl 683970 1/22nd London Regt
ABREY J.W. MM Cpl 11431 18th Middlesex Regt
ABSALOM Henry John MM L/Bdr 96724 267 Siege Bty RGA DOW 5.10.18.
ABSALOM W. MM Pte 60449 RAMC
ABSON Charles MM Pte 305102 15th Bn Tank Corps
ABURROW Edward R. MM Cpl 408532 Royal Engineers
ABY William MM Pte 305321 Notts & Derby Regt
ACCLETON Albert J. MM Cpl 65171 A/173 Bde RFA
ACCLETON Frederick Walter "DCM,MM" Cpl 37564 85 Bty 11 Bde RFA KIA 16.4.17.
ACHAM Ronald MM Spr 208082 Royal Engineers
ACHARD Alfred Ferdinand MM Bdr L/14491 D/157 Bde RFA Died 14.10.18.
ACHESON George A. MM Sjt 610023 RHA
ACHESON John MM Sjt 7/13817 6th Royal Dublin Fusiliers
ACKERLEY Sydney MM Pte 8046 17th Manchester Regt KIA 22.3.18.
ACKERMAN Albert MM Cpl 3422 11th Manchester Regt
ACKERMAN Alfred B. MM Pte 20570 4th Hampshire Regt
ACKERMAN Charles E. MM Pte G/61577 7th Middlesex Regt
ACKERS Richard MM Pte 267712 18th Liverpool Regt
ACKERS Thomas MM Cpl 98087 RGA
ACKLAM John MM Cpl 23521 Machine Gun Corps
ACKLAND Alfred R. "MM,MID" Sjt 59595 Royal Engineers
ACKLAND George H. MM L/Cpl 25610 Grenadier Guards
ACKLAND Henry J. MM Sjt 47872 RGA
ACKREL George H. MM Pte 57581 1st Lancashire Fusiliers
ACKROYD Abraham MM Dvr 196812 A/84 Bde RFA
ACKROYD Eli MM Bdr 283817 RGA
ACKROYD John A. MM+Bar L/Cpl 24726 5th West Riding Regt
ACKROYD Samuel MM S/Sjt Fitter 119 RFA

ACKROYD Thomas Hubert MM Gnr 1168 RFA
ACKROYD Tom H. MM Spr 83588 210 Fd Coy Royal Engineers
ACLAND Charles L. MM Pte 6531 Army Cyclist Corps
ACOCK A.J. MM Air Mech 2 12867 Royal Flying Corps
ACOCK Lawrence MM Pte 3/3800 2nd York & Lancaster Regt KIA 12.10.16.
ACOCK Reginald James MM Gnr 32037 12th Bn Tank Corps
ACOTT Thomas F.G. MM Sjt 105347 208 Siege Bty RGA
ACOTT William MM Pte G/640 6th Royal West Kent Regt
ACQUROFF Alexander MM Cpl 20671 55th Bn Machine Gun Corps DOW 22.3.18.
ACTON Ernest MM Pte 16592 6th Shropshire Light Infantry
ACTON Osmond T. MM+Bar Sjt 62849 Machine Gun Corps
ACTON T. MM+Bar Sjt 17295 2nd South Lancashire Regt
ACTON Thomas E. MM CQMS 200012 Lancashire Fusiliers
ADAIR Andrew MM L/Cpl 5509 18th Highland Light Infantry
ADAIR William "MM,MID" Sjt 6902 6th East Yorkshire Regt
ADAM Adam S. MM Pte 298089 4th London Regt
ADAM Francis MM Cpl 8531 1st Scottish Rifles
ADAM George MM Gnr(Sig) 227238 134 Bty 32 Bde RFA
ADAM Hyacinthe Alexander MM Bdr 89331 9 Div Ammn Col RFA
ADAM James MM Sjt 28425 120 Coy Machine Gun Corps
ADAM James P. MM BQMS 21767 11 Bde RFA
ADAM Robert MM Sjt 290477 1/7th Royal Highlanders
ADAM Robert MM L/Cpl 4698 Royal Highlanders
ADAM William MM Pte 265348 Seaforth Highlanders
ADAM William MM Pte 331828 1/9th Highland Light Infantry
ADAMS Albert MM Pte 295298 12th Somerset Light Infantry
ADAMS Albert MM Pte 38986 South Staffordshire Regt
ADAMS Albert MM L/Cpl 10391 Royal Inniskilling Fusiliers
ADAMS Albert J. MM Sjt 495012 RAMC
ADAMS Alexander MM Gnr 26952 38 Bde RFA
ADAMS Alfred MM Cpl 663290 C/211 Bde RFA
ADAMS Alfred MM L/Cpl 22552 Notts & Derby Regt
ADAMS Alfred MM Pte 24889 13th Yorkshire Regt
ADAMS Alfred E. MM Sjt 59399 8th Worcestershire Regt
ADAMS Alfred H. MM Cpl L/31616 RFA
ADAMS Alfred W. MM+Bar Spr 75270 Royal Engineers
ADAMS Andrew MM Pte 53276 4th Middlesex Regt
ADAMS Arthur MM L/Cpl 20023 15th Hampshire Regt
ADAMS Arthur E. MM Pte 7/15299 7th South Wales Borderers
ADAMS Arthur Frank MM Cpl 92199 4th Liverpool Regt DOW 13.10.18.
ADAMS Arthur Harry MM Pte 241063 1st North Staffordshire Regt DOW 13.5.18.
ADAMS Basil Archibald MM Pte 204693 15th Hampshire Regt
ADAMS Bert MM Gnr 59308 RFA
ADAMS Birket MM Sjt 19742 Machine Gun Corps
ADAMS C. MM Pte 305227 5th Bn Tank Corps
ADAMS C.W. MM L/Cpl 24094 Essex Regt
ADAMS Charles MM Pte 34052 6th West Riding Regt
ADAMS Charles MM L/Bdr 14273 RFA
ADAMS Charles A. MM BQMS 36743 34 Bde RFA
ADAMS E.A. MM Pte 43205 9th Essex Regt
ADAMS Edward MM Pte 386480 1/1st(Northumbrian)Fd Amb RAMC KIA 4.11.18.
ADAMS Edward MM Pte 37435 Royal Berkshire Regt
ADAMS Edwin J. MM Pte S/4108 Rifle Brigade
ADAMS Ernest Harry "MM+Bar,CG(B)" Sjt 87325 9 Div Sig Coy Royal Engineers
ADAMS Ernest J. MM Pte 14233 Notts & Derby Regt
ADAMS F.J.W. MM Air Mech 1 6642 Royal Flying Corps
ADAMS Francis Charles MM Sjt 27524 Hampshire Regt
ADAMS Frank MM Pte 9174 XIII Corps Cyclist Bn Army Cyclist Corps KIA 10.11.17.
ADAMS Frank MM L/Cpl 76458 Notts & Derby Regt
ADAMS Fred MM L/Cpl 14100 6th Oxf & Bucks Light Infantry KIA 26.9.16.
ADAMS Frederick MM L/Cpl 34360 8th York & Lancaster Regt KIA 30.9.17.
ADAMS Frederick MM Pte 38865 1/8th Hampshire Regt DOW 26.12.17.
ADAMS Frederick MM Pte 18717 1st Notts & Derby Regt Died 16.10.18.
ADAMS Frederick MM Sjt 8174 1st Lincolnshire Regt
ADAMS Frederick MM Pte 36599 South Wales Borderers
ADAMS Frederick G. MM Dvr 80728 Royal Engineers
ADAMS Frederick J. MM Pte 861181 33rd London Regt
ADAMS Frederick J. MM Pte 74870 RAMC
ADAMS Frederick W. MM Cpl 124057 RGA
ADAMS Frederick W. MM Cpl DM2/168450 Army Service Corps
ADAMS G. MM Pte 70840 Notts & Derby Regt
ADAMS G. MM Pte 50201 16th Royal Warwickshire Regt
ADAMS G. MM L/Sjt 3311 Middlesex Regt
ADAMS G. MM Pte 25002 Royal Irish Regt
ADAMS George MM Pte 37198 7th Norfolk Regt
ADAMS George "DCM,MM" Sjt 9007 1st Royal Berkshire Regt
ADAMS George MM Sjt 265931 1/1st Hertfordshire Regt
ADAMS George MM Sjt 1669 Royal Warwickshire Regt
ADAMS George "MM,MID" Sjt 7823 2nd King's Royal Rifle Corps
ADAMS George MM Pte 14856 Northamptonshire Regt
ADAMS George E. MM BSM 98060 RGA
ADAMS George J. MM Cpl CMT/3246 1 Div Train Army Service Corps
ADAMS H. MM Pte PS/2659 16th Middlesex Regt att Manmchester Regt
ADAMS Harry T. MM Sjt 3014 Royal Irish Regt
ADAMS Harry V. MM Pte 401325 RAMC
ADAMS Herbert MM Pte M/315976 Army Service Corps
ADAMS Herbert MM+Bar L/Sjt 11814 1st East Lancashire Regt
ADAMS Herbert L. MM Sjt 16531 GHQ Sig Coy Royal Engineers
ADAMS Hugh "DCM,MM" SSM 47249 20th Hussars
ADAMS Hugh "MM,MID" Sjt 44165 Royal Engineers
ADAMS Hugh M. MM CQMS S/10976 6th Cameron Highlanders KIA 23.8.17.
ADAMS Isaac T. MM Gnr 4385 RFA
ADAMS James MM Dvr 650979 376 Bty 169 Bde RFA
ADAMS James MM+Bar Sjt 292844 1/7th Royal Highlanders KIA 24.8.18.
ADAMS James "DCM,MM" RSM 1867 King's Royal Rifle Corps
ADAMS James MM Pte 7976 1st Hampshire Regt
ADAMS James MM Pte 240230 6th Royal Warwickshire Regt
ADAMS James Lewin MM L/Cpl 60529 9th Royal Fusiliers KIA 30.11.17.
ADAMS Jim MM Pte 8554 2nd Dorsetshire Regt
ADAMS John MM Pte 41126 Royal Scots
ADAMS John MM+Bar Sjt 13971 9th Royal Irish Fusiliers
ADAMS John MM L/Cpl 35021 109 Coy Machine Gun Corps
ADAMS John G. MM Gnr 206685 130 Hy Bty RGA
ADAMS John L. MM L/Cpl 240333 Notts & Derby Regt
ADAMS John W. MM Gnr Fitter 811060 RFA
ADAMS John William MM Pte 241171 1/5th Lincolnshire Regt
ADAMS Leslie B. MM Sjt 19390 2nd Grenadier Guards
ADAMS Reginald S. MM Pte 8895 2nd Hampshire Regt
ADAMS Reginald T. MM Pte 16353 2nd Coldstream Guards
ADAMS Robert MM Sjt 325120 1/1st Worcestershire Yeomanry
ADAMS Robert MM Pte 17122 12th Royal Irish Rifles
ADAMS Robert Harvey MM 2nd Cpl 253284 19 Div Sig Coy Royal Engineers
ADAMS Robert S. "MM,MSM" Sjt 15066 23rd Middlesex Regt
ADAMS Rufus "DCM+Bar,MM" CSM 9055 1st Northamptonshire Regt
ADAMS Samuel MM Sjt 7574 2nd Worcestershire Regt
ADAMS Sidney MM Pte 32554 East Surrey Regt
ADAMS Sidney J. MM Gnr Sig L/34938 D/83 Bde RFA
ADAMS Sidney J. MM Pte 50241 RAMC
ADAMS Stanley G. "DCM,MM" Sjt 49693 23 Div Sig Coy Royal Engineers
ADAMS Thomas MM Pte 273192 5/6th Royal Scots
ADAMS Thomas MM Pte 5117 Northumberland Fusiliers
ADAMS Thomas G. MM+Bar Pte G/9449 Royal Fusiliers
ADAMS Thomas W. MM L/Cpl 201630 4th Hampshire Regt
ADAMS Walter MM Spr 43787 Royal Engineers
ADAMS Walter MM Cpl 6225 37th Bn Machine Gun Corps
ADAMS Walter MM L/Cpl 19279 East Lancashire Regt
ADAMS Walter B. MM Cpl 492047 46 Div Sig Coy Royal Engineers
ADAMS Walter F. MM Sjt 74943 Royal Engineers
ADAMS Walter H. MM Cpl 40117 RFA
ADAMS Walter J. MM Pte 34370 9th Yorkshire Regt
ADAMS Walter R. MM Gnr 41745 RGA
ADAMS William MM L/Cpl 13917 1st Gloucestershire Regt
ADAMS William MM Pte 235721 1/1st Herefordshire Regt
ADAMS William MM Pnr 250429 Royal Engineers
ADAMS William MM L/Cpl 8247 Yorkshire Regt
ADAMS William MM Sjt 56737 32 Bde RFA
ADAMS William MM Gnr 635242 RFA
ADAMS William A. MM Dvr L/22647 D/156 Bde RFA
ADAMS William A. MM Pte 17953 2nd Border Regt
ADAMS William C. MM Gnr 60502 RFA
ADAMS William Ernest MM Bdr 39017 X48 TM Bty RGA KIA 29.7.17.

ADAMS William F. MM L/Cpl DM2/195053 Army Service Corps
ADAMS William G. MM Sjt 78780 RHA
ADAMS William H. MM Spr 45844 Royal Engineers
ADAMS William J. MM Pte 295256 12th Somerset Light Infantry KIA 6.11.17.
ADAMS William J. MM Pte 471112 12th London Regt
ADAMS William W.J. MM Cpl 44185 Royal Engineers
ADAMSON Alexander MM Cpl 332148 9th Highland Light Infantry
ADAMSON Andrew MM L/Cpl 12541 7th Royal Highlanders
ADAMSON Andrew MM Bdr 27093 RFA
ADAMSON Arnold MM Pte 307795 7th West Riding Regt
ADAMSON Arthur MM Cpl 6180 XIV Corps Cyclist Bn Army Cyclist Corps
ADAMSON Arthur R.H. MM Spr 482385 62 Div Sig Coy Royal Engineers
ADAMSON David "DCM,MM" L/Cpl 32988 1st Gloucestershire Regt
ADAMSON David MM L/Bdr 125685 527 Howitzer Bty RFA
ADAMSON David MM Pte 42040 2nd Bn Machine Gun Corps
ADAMSON David Catto MM Pte 92964 19 Fd Amb RAMC
ADAMSON Edmund MM Pte 20225 Cheshire Regt
ADAMSON Frederick MM Pte 20491 2/4th York & Lancaster Regt
ADAMSON George MM 2nd Cpl 21740 23 Fd Coy Royal Engineers
ADAMSON George MM Sjt 46452 37 Div Sig Coy Royal Engineers
ADAMSON Henry G. MM Gnr 60763 22 Bde RFA
ADAMSON James "DCM,MM+Bar" Sjt S/8084 7th Seaforth Highlanders
ADAMSON James MM L/Cpl 15330 6th Shropshire Light Infantry DOW 9.10.18.0
ADAMSON John MM Sjt T/11410 Att 19 Fd Amb RAMC Army Service Corps
ADAMSON John MM Cpl 17855 6th East Yorkshire Regt
ADAMSON John G. MM Sjt 25122 Durham Light Infantry
ADAMSON John W. MM Spr 312342 3 Div Sig Coy Royal Engineers
ADAMSON Joseph "DCM,MM,MID" Sjt 13964 7/8th King's Own Scottish Borderers
ADAMSON Percival MM Pte 18/471 18th Northumberland Fusiliers
ADAMSON Robert MM L/Cpl 91074 Royal Engineers
ADAMSON T. MM Pte 325758 Durham Light Infantry
ADAMSON Thomas MM Dvr 60533 RFA
ADAMSON Thomas W. MM L/Bdr 162224 RFA
ADAMSON William MM Pte S/14817 15th Arg & Suth Highlanders
ADAMSON William MM Pte 41271 9th Royal Irish Fusiliers
ADAMSON William R. MM Spr 43972 70 Fd Coy Royal Engineers
ADAWAY Albert MM Pte 12251 11th Hampshire Regt
ADAWAY Ernest MM Cpl 7738 3rd Rifle Brigade
ADCOCK Albert Herbert MM Pte 24022 Suffolk Regt KIA 11.8.18.
ADCOCK Charles MM Pte 27767 6th Lincolnshire Regt
ADCOCK John Stephen MM L/Bdr 127421 C/311 Bde RFA
ADCOCK John W. MM Spr 12865 54 Fd Coy Royal Engineers
ADCOCK Thomas William MM Gnr 89036 60 Heavy Bty RGA
ADCOCK Walter E. MM L/Cpl 33202 RAMC
ADCOCK William T. MM Pte 2446 North Staffordshire Regt
ADDAMS F. "MM,MID" Drummer 764 1st Northumberland Fusiliers
ADDERLEY Albert MM Pte 41152 South Wales Borderers
ADDERLEY Percy S. MM Sjt 15353 1st Grenadier Guards
ADDICOTT Edwin MM L/Cpl 4628 6th London Regt
ADDIS Thomas O. MM Sjt 3/8081 1st Dorsetshire Regt
ADDISON A. MM+Bar CSM 290138 1/7th Gordon Highlanders
ADDISON Albert R. MM Pte S/28624 Rifle Brigade
ADDISON Herbert MM Spr 471420 4 Div Sig Coy Royal Engineers
ADDISON John MM Cpl 55712 A/165 Bde RFA
ADDISON John T. MM Pte 14794 4th Coldstream Guards
ADDISON R.L. MM Sjt 84057 4th London Regt
ADDISON Thomas MM Sjt 4/8161 14th Durham Light Infantry KIA 18.9.16.
ADDISON Victor MM Bdr 73790 RFA
ADDISON Wallace MM Sjt 200626 1/4th Yorkshire Regt
ADDY Arthur MM Sjt L/5934 RFA
ADDY Harry E. MM Pte 43527 Manchester Regt
ADDY Henry James MM Cpl 15867 11th Northumberland Fusiliers DOW 27.10.18.
ADDY Herbert MM Cpl 44966 Machine Gun Corps
ADDY John W. MM Sjt DM2/112066 Army Service Corps
ADDY Reginald A. MM Cpl 200505 1/4th Norfolk Regt
ADDY W.H. MM Pte 3064 Yorkshire Light Infantry
ADDYMAN Arthur "MM,MSM" Cpl 7450 2nd Scots Guards
ADEONI Joseph MM Pte 377869 8th London Regt
ADEY Alfred MM Pte 14264 York & Lancaster Regt
ADEY William MM Pte 11483 4th Worcestershire Regt
ADIE Arthur MM Bdr 8480 RFA
ADIE Arthur A. "DCM,MM" Sgt 49106 47 Bty 41 Bde RFA
ADIE James MM Gnr 103769 64 Div Ammn Col RFA
ADKIN Ernest MM L/Cpl R/39600 King's Royal Rifle Corps
ADKIN Frederick Edward MM Sjt 15772 7th Northamptonshire Regt KIA 24.9.18.
ADKIN John E. MM Cpl 28750 West Yorkshire Regt
ADKIN Sidney Laurence Victor MM Cpl 5210 7th Royal West Kent Regt
ADKINS Charles MM L/Cpl 9064 3rd Coldstream Guards KIA 15.9.16.
ADKINS George William MM Cpl 2346 1/4th Oxf & Bucks Light Infantry
ADKINS Harry MM L/Sjt 240150 1/8th Worcestershire Regt KIA 27.8.17.
ADKINS William MM Gnr 77107 RFA
ADKINSON Robert MM Sjt 265375 1/6th Cheshire Regt
ADKINSON Walter MM Pte 71611 Machine Gun Corps
ADLAM Arthur Charles MM L/Cpl 9744 Scots Guards
ADLAM Frank MM Cpl 58396 RAMC
ADLAM H.A. MM Cpl 320517 1/1st Wiltshire Yeomanry
ADLAM Harold O. MM Pte 17738 2nd Hampshire Regt
ADLAM Thomas MM Pte 375037 10th London Regt
ADLARD Charles MM CSM 7082 1st Northumberland Fusiliers
ADLARD Harold MM Sjt 44084 6 Bty 40 Bde RFA
ADLARD Henry "DCM,MM" Sjt 63522 51 Bty 39 Bde RFA
ADLEM Herbert H. MM Pte 66595 RAMC
ADLER Philipp MM Sjt 7201 11th Royal Fusiliers KIA 17.2.17.
ADLINGTON Charles MM Pte 20090 9th Notts & Derby Regt
ADLINGTON George E. MM Spr 43701 Royal Engineers
ADLINGTON Stanley MM L/Cpl 536713 15th London Regt
ADLINGTON Thomas D. MM Sjt 17624 6th Liverpool Regt
ADMANS Albert MM L/Cpl 1579 1/4th Oxf & Bucks Light Infantry
ADMANS Sidney Austen MM L/Cpl 4217 1st East Kent Regt
ADNAMS William "MM,MID" L/Sjt 12340 1st Hampshire Regt
ADOLPHUS Benjamin MM Pte 5175 17th London Regt
ADOON Fred MM+Bar L/Cpl 9926 5th Northamptonshire Regt
ADSHEAD Arthur MM Pte 350336 Manchester Regt
ADSHEAD Thomas MM Pte 16113 12th Cheshire Regt
ADSHEAD Thomas MM Pte 45761 Cheshire Regt
AFFLECK Robert MM Pte 12521 Scots Guards
AFFLECK William MM Pte 22426 RAMC
AFFLEY William MM+Bar Sjt 56500 19th Welsh Regt
AFFORD Harold MM Spr 432338 Royal Engineers
AGAR Cecil R. MM L/Cpl 37334 West Yorkshire Regt
AGAR Ernest MM Pte 306189 2nd West Riding Regt
AGAR George MM Pnr 358730 Royal Engineers
AGAR Harold MM Sjt T4/039997 Army Service Corps
AGAR Hubert N. MM Cpl 206343 Royal West Kent Regt
AGAR Nicholas Raine MM Pte 31875 12th Durham Light Infantry KIA 20.9.17.
AGAR Thomas W. MM L/Cpl 265233 1/7th West Yorkshire Regt
AGATHE Louis H. MM+Bar Sjt 246853 D/110 Bde RFA
AGER Andrew MM Sjt 47017 1st Essex Regt KIA 9.10.18.
AGER Fred MM Pte H/10892 15th Hussars
AGER Harry Sydney MM L/Cpl 203471 1st London Regt
AGER Reginald Archibald MM L/Cpl 33310 8th Yorkshire Regt KIA 27.10.18.
AGER Richard H. MM Pte 46906 RAMC
AGER Walter Vivian MM Cpl 207634 63 Div Sig Coy Royal Engineers
AGER William H. MM Cpl 241026 Lincolnshire Regt
AGGETT James MM Cpl 9785 2nd Devonshire Regt
AGGETT Sidney MM Sjt 240473 1/5th D Coy Devonshire Regt KIA 30.9.18.
AGGLETON William Thomas MM Gnr 168929 2/3(Home Counties)Bde RFA
AGLAND W.E. MM Spr 358793 Royal Engineers
AGNEW Alexander MM Sjt S/3803 8th Royal Highlanders
AGNEW Gavin MM Cpl 16169 Royal Irish Rifles
AGNEW Thomas MM L/Cpl 6954 2nd Leinster Regt
AGNEW William "DCM,MM" L/Cpl 23169 4 Div Sig Coy Royal Engineers
AGNEW William Vans MM Pte 40234 Highland Light Infantry
AGUTTER George W. MM Pte 52075 12th Middlesex Regt
AGUTTER Tom MM Cpl 145885 1/1st Northamptonshire Yeomanry
AHERN James MM Cpl 840899 RFA
AHERN John "MM,MSM" Bdr 13136 49 Siege Bty RGA
AICKEN James MM+Bar Pte 18604 Machine Gun Corps
AIKEN Hugh J. MM Gnr 5560 RGA
AIKMAN David W. MM Pte 548 18th Northumberland Fusiliers

AIKMAN George MM Pte 251403 5/6th Royal Scots
AINGER Louis H. MM Cpl 340102 166 Siege Bty RGA
AINGER William MM Cpl 3473 2nd London Regt
AINGER William F. MM Cpl 62762 RFA
AINLEY F. MM Pte 32175 Machine Gun Corps
AINLEY Frank MM Cpl 1609 2/1(West Riding)Fd Coy Royal Engineers
AINLEY Joseph MM Pte 15981 8th West Riding Regt KIA 11.8.17.
AINLEY William MM Pte 11112 1st Royal Lancaster Regt
AINLEY William H. MM Pte 241352 5/6th Scottish Rifles
AINSCOUGH Thomas MM Pte 1147 North Lancashire Regt
AINSCOW Richard MM Pte 11034 15th Lancashire Fusiliers
AINSLEY E. MM Pte 7062 West Riding Regt
AINSLEY Henry R. MM Bdr 840742 D/241 Bde RFA
AINSLEY Thomas MM Pte 13306 Yorkshire Regt
AINSLEY William MM Pte 21/375 Durham Light Infantry
AINSLIE James MM Pte 6067 3rd Coldstream Guards
AINSLIE James MM L/Cpl 204259 Scottish Rifles
AINSLIE William James MM Sjt 6301 Worcestershire Regt
AINSWORTH Alfred MM L/Cpl 42026 2nd Royal Inniskilling Fusiliers
AINSWORTH Alfred MM Cpl 27914 1st Border Regt
AINSWORTH Alfred Ernest MM Sjt 13241 10th Essex Regt
AINSWORTH Arthur MM Pte 17849 11th Notts & Derby Regt
AINSWORTH Arthur MM Cpl 9065 B/150 Bde RFA KIA 9.4.18.
AINSWORTH David MM Pte 5339 Northumberland Fusiliers
AINSWORTH Ernest MM Pte 38535 2nd South Wales Borderers
AINSWORTH Frederick MM Pte 9470 12th Royal Fusiliers
AINSWORTH George MM Dvr 706671 RFA
AINSWORTH George MM Pte 32975 Cheshire Regt
AINSWORTH Harold MM Dvr 12022 RFA
AINSWORTH Henry E. MM 2nd Cpl 89313 Royal Engineers
AINSWORTH Herbert MM L/Cpl 40344 Royal Engineers KIA 8.8.18.
AINSWORTH James MM Pte 30451 Liverpool Regt
AINSWORTH John MM Sjt 242029 North Lancashire Regt
AINSWORTH John B. MM Sjt 10526 Welsh Regt
AINSWORTH John Edward MM Pte 13015 1st Norfolk Regt KIA 23.4.17.
AINSWORTH Nathaniel Angel "MM,MdH(F)" Cpl 20923 9th East Lancashire Regt
AINSWORTH Turnes MM Pte 32046 RAMC
AINSWORTH Walter MM L/Cpl 242858 5th York & Lancaster Regt
AINSWORTH Wilfred MM L/Cpl 164908 126 Fd Coy Royal Engineers
AIRD Alexander MM Pte 267281 1/5th Seaforth Highlanders
AIRD James MM Cpl 9167 A/71 Bde RFA
AIRD John W. MM Bdr 9169 RFA
AIRD Simpson MM Sjt 6940 6/7th Royal Scots Fusiliers
AIRD William P. MM Pte 39483 1st Scottish Rifles
AIRDRIE Robert MM Spr 425950 Royal Engineers
AIREY Alfred MM L/Bdr 800168 D/156 Bde RFA KIA 8.5.18.
AIREY Charles Thomas MM Sjt S/1583 7th Seaforth Highlanders KIA 12.10.17.
AIREY Ernest MM Pte 89018 2(Northumbrian)Fd Amb RAMC
AIREY Farnsworth MM Gnr 64157 RFA
AIREY George F. MM Pte 203106 East Lancashire Regt
AIREY Harry Charles MM Cpl 7507 B/160 Bde RFA
AIREY Herbert MM Pte 14094 4th Coldstream Guards
AIREY James MM Sjt 7721 18th Lancashire Fusiliers
AIREY James MM Pte 2783 1st Welsh Guards
AIREY James Walter J. "DCM,MM" Sjt 55137 RFA
AIREY Norman George MM L/Cpl 3091 West Yorkshire Regt
AIREY Percy MM Cpl 63964 Machine Gun Corps
AIREY Stanley Ernest MM Cpl Sig 840941 D/306 Bde RFA
AIREY Wilfred MM L/Cpl 6698 2nd Border Regt
AIRLIE James MM Gnr 80703 RFA
AISH Charles E.V. MM L/Cpl 595 7th Royal Sussex Regt
AISH Frederick MM L/Cpl 240956 Royal Warwickshire Regt
AITCHESON Thomas Charles "MM,MID" Cpl 17989 1 Fd Sqn Royal Engineers
AITCHISON Harry MM L/Cpl 331324 Highland Light Infantry
AITCHISON Harry MM L/Cpl 9303 2nd Royal Scots
AITCHISON James MM Pte 515289 14th London Regt
AITCHISON Peter MM+Bar Cpl 4109 2nd Dragoons
AITKEN Alexander B. MM L/Cpl 39262 5/6th Scottish Rifles
AITKEN Arthur H. "MM,MID" Sjt 14447 L Corps Sig Coy Royal Engineers
AITKEN David MM Pte 268240 Royal Warwickshire Regt
AITKEN David N. MM Pte 32228 2nd Royal Scots Fusiliers KIA 17.8.18.
AITKEN Donald R. MM Sjt S/9238 Gordon Highlanders
AITKEN H. MM+Bar Sjt S/4926 10th & 8/10th Gordon Highlanders
AITKEN Hector MM Sjt 23948 Highland Light Infantry
AITKEN J. MM L/Cpl 301308 RAMC
AITKEN James MM Sjt 645113 51 Div Ammn Col RFA
AITKEN James MM Pte 267075 Scottish Rifles
AITKEN James MM+Bar Cpl 22129 2nd King's Own Scottish Borderers
AITKEN James MM Sjt 19044 Manchester Regt
AITKEN John MM Gnr 631419 RFA
AITKEN Peter MM Cpl 276739 1/7th Arg & Suth Highlanders Died 27.8.18.
AITKEN Richard MM Pte 6195 2nd King's Own Scottish Borderers
AITKEN Robert MM Pte 5111 14th London Regt
AITKEN Robert MM+Bar Sjt 93350 219 Fd Coy Royal Engineers
AITKEN Thomas MM Pte 4/9119 10th Arg & Suth Highlanders DOW 24.8.18.
AITKEN William A. MM L/Cpl 12251 East Surrey Regt
AITKEN William B. MM Spr 39513 Royal Engineers
AITKEN William James MM Spr 166709 123 Fd Coy Royal Engineers
AITON Robert MM Pte 40289 Royal Scots
AKED Fred MM Pte 64653 100 Fd Amb RAMC
AKEHURST Arthur H. MM Pte 19049 Royal West Kent Regt
AKEHURST Leslie S.E. MM Pte G/27831 13th Royal Fusiliers
AKERMAN John R. MM L/Cpl 19342 2nd South Wales Borderers
AKEROYD Harry MM L/Cpl 269253 Notts & Derby Regt
AKERS Albert MM Pte 9180 2nd Bedfordshire Regt
AKERS Bernard J. MM L/Cpl 6556 East Kent Regt
AKERS J. MM L/Bdr 676707 RFA
AKERS Percy Newport MM L/Cpl 22865 42nd Bn Machine Gun Corps
AKERS Raymond MM Pte 13090 2nd Yorkshire Regt
AKERS Robert MM Gnr Fitter 193073 194 Siege Bty RGA
AKERS Thomas MM Sjt 242369 15/17th West Yorkshire Regt
AKERS Thomas MM Sjt M2/116557 Army Service Corps
AKESTER Addison MM Gnr 35281 RGA
AKHURST Frank G. MM Sjt 11922 A/74 Bde RFA
AKHURST Joseph L. MM Pte 74916 RAMC
AKITT Bernard MM Pte 75623 21 Fd Amb RAMC
ALBANY William MM Cpl 115 23rd Royal Fusiliers DOW 2.8.16.
ALBERT Alfred MM Pte 11789 2nd Highland Light Infantry
ALBERY William J. MM Sjt 207800 10th Royal West Surrey Regt
ALBIN Ernest Henry MM Dvr 16266 D/91 Bde RFA
ALBINSON Arthur "MC,MM(7786 Sjt R Fus)" T/2Lt Tank Corps
ALBON A.G. MM L/Cpl 28408 8th Royal Lancaster Regt
ALBON Edward MM Pte 17956 2nd Bedfordshire Regt
ALBON Frank MM Pte 57029 46th Bn Machine Gun Corps
ALBON John MM Sjt 200376 1/4th Suffolk Regt
ALBONE John MM Pte 60114 26th Royal Fusiliers KIA 20.9.17.
ALBRETHSON Ola MM BQMS 645585 255 Bde RFA
ALBROW Frederick W. MM Bdr 57491 29 Bty 42 Bde RFA
ALBURY H.W. MM Bdr L/31121 RFA
ALBUTT Frank MM Cpl B/2573 12th Rifle Brigade DOW 9.10.16.
ALBUTT George A. "MM+Bar,MID" Sjt Farrier 26259 58 Bty 35 Bde RFA
ALCOCK A.B. MM Sjt 50771 1st East Yorkshire Regt
ALCOCK Alick F.M. MM L/Cpl 17264 1st Coldstream Guards
ALCOCK Charles E. MM Gnr 78422 RFA
ALCOCK E.S. MM CSM 30847 10th Lancashire Fusiliers
ALCOCK Edward MM Pte 57866 1/5th York & Lancaster Regt
ALCOCK George MM 2nd Cpl 428358 423 Fd Coy Royal Engineers
ALCOCK George "MM,MIDx2" L/Cpl 10176 4th Worcestershire Regt
ALCOCK Harold R. MM Pte R/38805 2nd King's Royal Rifle Corps
ALCOCK Harry MM Gnr 25956 RFA
ALCOCK James S. MM Sjt 313251 1 Hy Bty RGA
ALCOCK John MM L/Sjt 6607 1st Coldstream Guards
ALCOCK John "MM,MSM" Pte M1/08235 381 Coy Army Service Corps
ALCOCK John B. MM Spr 89749 Royal Engineers
ALCOCK Michael H. MM CSM 51378 Lincolnshire Regt
ALCOCK Robert Frank "MM+Bar,MID" Sjt 72310 12 Bde RFA
ALCOCK T. MM Cpl Shoeing Smith 39003 15 Bde B Bty RHA
ALCOCK Walter MM Pte 16304 2nd East Lancashire Regt KIA 23.3.18.
ALCOCK William MM+Bar Sjt 9410 1st Royal Scots Fusiliers
ALCOCK William E. MM Pte 49394 Notts & Derby Regt
ALCOCK William P. MM Sjt 11728 21st Manchester Regt
ALCORN James MM Pte 300561 Arg & Suth Highlanders
ALCRAFT Benjamin Thomas MM Pte 25158 10th West Riding Regt
ALDEN Harry William MM Bdr 46140 25 Bde RFA

ALDEN William "MM,MSM" S/Sjt TT/0801 Army Veterinary Corps
ALDEN William E.J. MM Pte 25159 20th London Regt
ALDER Charles MM Pte 233042 2nd London Regt
ALDER Frank C. MM Pte 90800 RAMC
ALDER Frank J. MM Pte 94843 5th Bn Tank Corps
ALDER George MM L/Cpl 8186 1st Gloucestershire Regt
ALDER Harold H. MM Cpl 17635 Royal Engineers
ALDER Leonard MM Cpl 88159 55th Bn Machine Gun Corps
ALDER William Edward MM L/Cpl 71311 Royal Engineers
ALDERMAN Edgar MM Cpl 87355 Royal Engineers
ALDERMAN Fred MM Spr 140915 223 Fd Coy Royal Engineers
ALDERMAN Frederick George MM Pte 102008 Labour Corps
ALDERMAN Henry MM Cpl 15507 Royal Berkshire Regt
ALDERMAN Robert MM Sjt 12712 7th Royal West Kent Regt
ALDERMAN William R. MM Pte 25142 Welsh Regt
ALDERMAN William S. MM L/Cpl 500148 48 Div Sig Coy Royal Engineers
ALDERSON Alfred E. MM Pte 3174 Durham Light Infantry
ALDERSON Charles MM Sjt 5592 10th Hussars
ALDERSON Christopher Rowland "MC,MM(91843 Cpl)" T/2Lt Royal Engineers
ALDERSON George MM Gnr 58858 RGA
ALDERSON John Ernest Westgate MM Sjt 16187 7/8th King's Own Scottish Borderers
ALDERSON Ralph MM Pte 24371 3rd Grenadier Guards KIA 27.3.18.
ALDERSON Sidney MM L/Cpl 307391 8th West Yorkshire Regt
ALDERSON Thomas E. MM Sjt 307923 7th West Riding Regt
ALDERSON Thomas J. MM Sjt 16 RFA
ALDERSON Walker "MM+Bar,OLeo(B),MBC(Rm)" RSM 200084 1/4th Yorkshire Light Infantry
ALDERSON William MM Pte 20487 6th York & Lancaster Regt
ALDERSON William MM Pte 56702 Machine Gun Corps
ALDERTHAY William MM Pte 28030 13th Yorkshire Regt
ALDERTON Allan W. MM+Bar Cpl M2/052748 Army Service Corps
ALDHAM Benjamin MM Sjt 15086 Northamptonshire Regt
ALDHOUS Frank MM L/Cpl 16447 Suffolk Regt
ALDHURST George Reuben MM+Bar Sjt 18745 Machine Gun Corps
ALDIS George Stephen MM Pte 17/66 17th Northumberland Fusiliers
ALDOUS A. MM Pte 69537 6th Royal West Surrey Regt
ALDOUS A.L.J. MM Sjt 3991 6 Div Ammn Col. RFA
ALDOUS Albert E. MM Pte 232636 2nd London Regt
ALDOUS George A. MM BSM 34277 A/178 Bde RFA
ALDOUS William G. MM Dvr 43724 RFA
ALDRED Alfred B. MM L/Cpl G/21513 7th Royal West Kent Regt
ALDRED Archibald MM Pte 16629 7/8th King's Own Scottish Borderers
ALDRED Christopher MM Pte 3862 9th Lancashire Fusiliers
ALDRED George Bernard MM Sjt 77449 Royal Flying Corps
ALDRED James MM Sjt 276236 Manchester Regt
ALDRED William J. MM Sjt L/26974 RFA
ALDRICH Alexander W. MM Cpl 5399 Rifle Brigade
ALDRIDGE A.G. MM Pte 75694 1/1st Derbyshire Yeomanry
ALDRIDGE Alfred James MM Sjt G/11584 11th Royal West Kent Regt
ALDRIDGE Ernest "DCM,MM+Bar,MID" Sjt 358459 7 Div Sig Coy Royal Engineers
ALDRIDGE F.W. MM L/Cpl 470966 12th London Regt DOW 27.9.17.
ALDRIDGE Frederick MM+Bar Pte 265298 1/1st Hertfordshire Regt
ALDRIDGE Frederick George "DCM,MM" Sjt 106099 'N' Special Coy Royal Engineers DOW 3.4.18.
ALDRIDGE Harold Edward MM Gnr 122213 D/256 Bde RFA KIA 13.10.18.
ALDRIDGE Harry MM 2nd Cpl 74157 Royal Engineers
ALDRIDGE J. MM Pte 270002 Manchester Regt
ALDRIDGE John E. MM L/Sjt 435131 1/1st(South Midland)Fd Amb RAMC
ALDRIDGE Joseph F. MM L/Cpl 450524 1/11th London Regt
ALDRIDGE Nelson Joseph MM Pte 19635 6th Shropshire Light Infantry DOW 27.11.17.
ALDRIDGE Percy H. MM Cpl R/682 King's Royal Rifle Corps
ALDRIDGE Philip MM Bdr 76778 RFA
ALDRIDGE Reginald MM Pte 28259 1st Hampshire Regt
ALDRIDGE Reginald MM Sjt 440258 Royal Engineers
ALDRIDGE Richard MM L/Cpl 1723 7th Royal West Surrey Regt
ALDRIDGE Robert .N. MM Pte 138100 63rd Bn Machine Gun Corps
ALDRIDGE Thomas MM Sjt 280959 Lancashire Fusiliers
ALDRIDGE William MM Gnr 2005 MGC(Motors)
ALDRIDGE William F. MM Bdr 54196 18 Bde RFA
ALDWORTH John C. MM Sjt 2542 Royal Fusiliers
ALESWORTH Frederick W. MM Cpl 28653 Machine Gun Corps
ALEXANDER Albert MM CSM 138576 Rly Op Div Royal Engineers
ALEXANDER Andrew Y. MM Pte 241843 7th Gordon Highlanders
ALEXANDER Annie MM Sister F BRCS
ALEXANDER Archibald "MM,MID" Cpl 67698 RFA
ALEXANDER Charles MM Sjt 50871 MGC(Cav)
ALEXANDER Charles N. MM Pte C/12980 King's Royal Rifle Corps
ALEXANDER Christopher J. "DCM,MM+Bar" L/Cpl 8777 1st Hampshire Regt
ALEXANDER Claud MM Pte GS/4939 East Surrey Regt
ALEXANDER David MM+Bar CSM L/8907 6th East Kent Regt KIA 29.9.18.
ALEXANDER Douglas MM L/Cpl 2953 1/21st London Regt KIA 12.9.16.
ALEXANDER Frank Pryer MM+Bar Pte 15501 1st East Kent Regt
ALEXANDER George MM Spr 45920 63 Fd Coy Royal Engineers
ALEXANDER George A.J. MM Pte R/36639 13th King's Royal Rifle Corps
ALEXANDER H. MM Air Mech 1 6640 Royal Flying Corps
ALEXANDER Harold R. MM QMS 38001 54 Fd Amb RAMC
ALEXANDER Harry MM Pte 16/1524 16th West Yorkshire Regt
ALEXANDER Henry MM Dvr 45916 C/189 Bde RFA
ALEXANDER Henry W. MM+Bar Bdr 11765 RFA
ALEXANDER Hugh MM Sjt 112275 Royal Engineers
ALEXANDER James MM Pte 302973 1/7th Royal Scots
ALEXANDER James MM L/Sjt 1025 Royal Highlanders
ALEXANDER James Philip MM Pte 33788 15th Royal Warwickshire Regt DOW 29.6.18.
ALEXANDER John MM L/Sjt S/3168 Royal Highlanders
ALEXANDER John MM L/Cpl 164599 Royal Engineers
ALEXANDER John MM Sjt 4289 Machine Gun Corps
ALEXANDER Leonard J. MM+Bar L/Cpl 201823 7th Lincolnshire Regt
ALEXANDER Mark MM L/Cpl 20227 1st Border Regt
ALEXANDER P.F. MM Pte Machine Gun Corps
ALEXANDER Percy MM Pte 60815 Welsh Regt
ALEXANDER Ralph MM Bdr 17580 A/88 Bde RFA
ALEXANDER Robert MM Sjt S/26954 1/6th Seaforth Highlanders
ALEXANDER Robert MM Sjt 13394 2nd Grenadier Guards
ALEXANDER S.J. MM Sjt 415131 9th London Regt
ALEXANDER Samuel MM Sjt 202065 Liverpool Regt
ALEXANDER Soloman MM Pte 3948 Leicestershire Regt
ALEXANDER T. MM Pte 200494 London Regt
ALEXANDER Thomas MM Pte S/3615 Seaforth Highlanders
ALEXANDER Thomas MM Cpl 12475 6/7th Royal Scots Fusiliers
ALEXANDER W. MM Cpl 1022 1st Royal Highlanders
ALEXANDER Walter MM Pte 15171 Arg & Suth Highlanders
ALEXANDER Walter MM Cpl 51201 RHA KIA 24.8.18.
ALEXANDER Walter MM Cpl 2888 Gordon Highlanders
ALEXANDER William MM Pte 119433 61st Bn Machine Gun Corps
ALEXANDER William MM Pte 10702 2nd Royal Scots Fusiliers
ALEXANDER William MM Pte 14/17133 14th Royal Irish Rifles
ALEXANDER William MM Pte 201381 Suffolk Regt
ALEXANDER William I. MM Bdr 74233 119 Bty 27 Bde RFA
ALEXANDER William J. MM Sjt 21609 Machine Gun Corps
ALEY Alexander MM Sjt M2/101322 Att XI Corps HAG Army Service Corps
ALFIN William MM Cpl 43807 1st Middlesex Regt
ALFORD Charles MM Gnr 10574 C/58 Bde RFA
ALFORD Delbridge W. MM L/Sjt 2184 19th London Regt
ALFORD Henry Stephen MM Pte 4720 1st Coldstream Guards
ALFORD James MM Pte 50155 5th Highland Light Infantry
ALFORD Thomas MM Pte 8570 2nd Yorkshire Light Infantry
ALGAR John Charles Leopold Victor MM Pte 91013 RD Coy? Machine Gun Corps
ALGAR Percy MM Pte M/274471 Army Service Corps
ALGER Frank MM Bdr 44388 RFA
ALGIE John MM L/Cpl 809 Lancashire Fusiliers
ALINGTON Gervase Winford Stovin MM+Bar Cpl 766852 28th London Regt att 17th Lond Regt. KIA 9.11.18.
ALKER James Edward MM L/Cpl 12630 1st Lancashire Fusiliers
ALLABY Horice Frank "MM,MID" SQMS 3486 4th Dragoon Guards
ALLAM Bertram MM L/Cpl 4338 East Surrey Regt
ALLAM Edward MM Pte 11000 Lincolnshire Regt
ALLAM John Albert "MM,MSM" Sjt 66768 129 Fd Coy Royal Engineers
ALLAM S. MM Gnr 76545 RGA

ALLAN Alexander Stewart "MM,MM(F)" Sjt P/S4/236974 Royal Air Force
ALLAN Charles H. MM Saddler QMS 9880 28 Bde RFA
ALLAN D. MM Pte 44040 King's Own Scottish Borderers
ALLAN G. MM Cpl 524 Cheshire Fd Coy Royal Engineers
ALLAN George MM Bdr 78896 464 Bty 179 Bde RFA
ALLAN George MM Pte 3446 1st Middlesex Regt
ALLAN George MM Pte 40965 7th Cameron Highlanders
ALLAN Gordon MM Pte 250184 6th Manchester Regt
ALLAN Henry MM+Bar Sjt 11741 5th Cameron Highlanders
ALLAN Henry W. MM L/Cpl S/15627 13th Rifle Brigade
ALLAN Herbert MM L/Sjt 10415 1st North Lancashire Regt KIA 23.10.18.
ALLAN J. MM Cpl 40703 Scottish Rifles att MGC.
ALLAN J.B. MM Pte 315560 13th Royal Highlanders
ALLAN J.R. MM Pte 35283 16th Highland Light Infantry
ALLAN J.R. MM Cpl 402402 404 Fd Coy Royal Engineers
ALLAN James MM L/Cpl 251043 1/6th Arg & Suth Highlanders
ALLAN James MM Cpl 4/9753 Arg & Suth Highlanders
ALLAN James MM Sjt M2/184010 Army Service Corps
ALLAN James MM L/Cpl 134467 Royal Engineers
ALLAN James S. MM Pte 292507 Royal Highlanders
ALLAN John MM Cpl 295685 12th Royal Scots Fusiliers
ALLAN John MM Pte 10257 2nd Scottish Rifles
ALLAN John "MM,MID" BSM 38558 C/124 Bde RFA
ALLAN John MM Cpl 10825 6th Border Regt
ALLAN John MM Gnr 61694 MGC (Motors)
ALLAN John Calder MM Cpl 60575 D/112 Bde RFA
ALLAN John McPherson MM L/Cpl 10009 Scots Guards
ALLAN John R. MM Pte 130978 RAMC
ALLAN Lionel MM Spr 249420 18 Div Sig Coy Royal Engineers
ALLAN Nicol L. MM Cpl 18789 5/6th Royal Scots
ALLAN Norman B. MM+Bar Pte 19/740 Northumberland Fusiliers
ALLAN Percy MM Gnr 76212 RHA
ALLAN R.M. MM Pte 266870 Gordon Highlanders
ALLAN Reginald J. MM Dvr 841141 RFA
ALLAN Richard MM Pte 25269 Border Regt
ALLAN Robert MM Pte 76290 4th Bn Tank Corps
ALLAN Robert W. MM Pte 1585 Royal Highlanders
ALLAN Stewart MM Pte 17765 5th Cameron Highlanders
ALLAN T.C. MM Pte 45923 Durham Light Infantry
ALLAN Thomas MM+Bar Sjt 40652 13th & 1/6th Royal Highlanders
ALLAN Thomas MM L/Sjt 40002 13th Royal Scots
ALLAN Thomas MM Cpl 18391 7th Border Regt DOW 29.10.17.
ALLAN W. MM+Bar Pte 303026 RAMC
ALLAN W.H. MM Pte 403150 2/2nd(West Riding)Fd Amb RAMC
ALLAN Wilfred MM Pte 242450 Lincolnshire Regt
ALLAN William MM Gnr Sig 630338 255 Bde RFA
ALLAN William MM L/Sjt 352461 1/9th Royal Scots
ALLAN William W. MM L/Cpl 4029 Royal Scots
ALLANDES J. MM Spr 49685 Royal Engineers
ALLANSON Bertie MM Cpl 70370 B/175 Bde RFA
ALLANSON Stanley A. MM L/Cpl 1997 1/5th Yorkshire Regt
ALLANSON William MM L/Cpl 7377 2nd Dragoon Guards
ALLARD Harry R. MM L/Cpl 9230 2nd Oxf & Bucks Light Infantry
ALLARD John MM Sjt 20388 Royal Lancaster Regt
ALLARDYCE James "DSO+Bar,MM(3285 Cpl)" 2Lt 1/14th London Regt
ALLATT Frank G. MM Pte 1608 West Yorkshire Regt
ALLAWAY Charles W. "MM,CdiG(It)" Sjt 265114 1/1st Bucks Bn Oxf & Bucks Light Infantry
ALLBEURY Frank Le Boutilier "DCM,MM" Sjt 8334 1st Border Regt KIA 23.4.17.
ALLBRIGHT Thomas MM L/Cpl G/26624 6th East Kent Regt
ALLBRIGHTON Alfred MM Cpl 13294 11th West Yorkshire Regt KIA 20.9.17.
ALLBUTT James E. MM Pte 251202 3rd London Regt
ALLCHIN Charles David MM Dvr 1488 D/162 Bde RFA
ALLCHIN John Henry MM Pte 12586 8th Royal West Kent Regt KIA 20.8.16.
ALLCHORN Edward Walter MM Sjt SD/24 Royal Sussex Regt DOW 5.11.17.
ALLCHURCH W. MM Sjt 12803 1st South Staffordshire Regt DOW 10.10.17.
ALLCOAT Percy MM Sjt 15/52175 15th Royal Irish Rifles
ALLCOCK Albert Edward MM Dvr 71908 D/110 Bde RFA DOW 1.8.17.
ALLCOCK Alfred John MM L/Cpl 27736 7th Shropshire Light Infantry
ALLCOCK Benjamin MM Pte 9047 2nd South Staffordshire Regt
ALLCOCK David MM Gnr 83749 45 Bty 42 Bde RFA
ALLCOCK Ernest MM Cpl 306868 1/8th Lancashire Fusiliers
ALLCOCK Herbert S. MM Bdr 1661 RFA
ALLCOCK John MM Pte 33320 Devonshire Regt
ALLCOCK Leonard MM Pte 11519 15th Cheshire Regt
ALLCOCK Robert P. MM Cpl 341225 RAMC
ALLCOCK Samuel MM Sig 77931 149 Siege Bty RGA
ALLCOCK William MM Sjt 8380 2nd Notts & Derby Regt KIA 16.9.16.
ALLCORN Alfred MM Pte 27761 2nd Suffolk Regt DOW 23.8.18.
ALLCOTT Harold Benjamin MM Gnr 4678 D/251 Bde RFA KIA 18.4.18.
ALLCROFT P.L. MM Cpl 23173 8th Royal West Surrey Regt
ALLDAY Arthur Thomas MM Pte 57586 2nd Worcestershire Regt
ALLDER Arthur MM Sjt 40164 63 Fd Coy Royal Engineers
ALLDRED Arthur MM Cpl 228351 307 Road Construction Coy Royal Engineers
ALLEESON Albert MM Sjt 7652 1st Cheshire Regt KIA 23.10.18.
ALLEN A. MM Pte 308773 9th Bn Tank Corps
ALLEN A. "MM,MSM" CSM 315257 13th Royal Highlanders
ALLEN A. MM Pte 201502 4th Leicestershire Regt
ALLEN A. MM Cpl 203293 1/5th Notts & Derby Regt
ALLEN A. MM Pte 14661 13th Liverpool Regt
ALLEN A. MM Pte 14445 Gloucestershire Regt
ALLEN A. MM Pte 23435 Yorkshire Regt
ALLEN A. MM Pte 52483 Middlesex Regt
ALLEN A. MM Sjt 11187 Cheshire Regt
ALLEN A. MM S/Sjt Fitter 51867 181 Bde HQ RFA
ALLEN A.A. MM Gnr 74216 RFA
ALLEN A.A. MM Cpl 9153 Border Regt
ALLEN A.E. "DCM,MM" Pte 65177 5th Yorkshire Light Infantry
ALLEN A.E. MM L/Bdr 67046 B/110 Bde RFA
ALLEN A.E. MM Pte 42016 5th West Yorkshire Regt
ALLEN A.E. MM L/Bdr 69155 RFA
ALLEN A.E. MM Pte 3639 Royal Berkshire Regt
ALLEN A.J. MM Sjt 11948 RFA
ALLEN A.J. MM Pte 1817 1/5th West Yorkshire Regt
ALLEN A.P. MM Dvr 30735 5 Bde Ammn Col RFA
ALLEN A.V. MM Pte 35278 4th West Riding Regt
ALLEN A.W.H. MM L/Cpl 48424 Royal Engineers
ALLEN Albert Edward MM Gnr 103126 A/282 Bde RFA
ALLEN Andrew MM Dvr 215 A/86 Bde RFA
ALLEN Bertie MM Pte 65476 26th Royal Fusiliers
ALLEN C. MM Pte 8822 West Riding Regt
ALLEN Charles MM Sjt 36564 1st East Surrey Regt
ALLEN Charles MM L/Cpl 308812 Liverpool Regt
ALLEN Charles MM Sjt 330766 1/8th Hampshire Regt
ALLEN Charles H. MM L/Sjt 27623 6th South Wales Borderers
ALLEN Charles H. MM Sjt 5740 RFA
ALLEN Charles Lewis MM Pte 435075 RAMC
ALLEN Charles Randall MM Pte 2037 1st Gloucestershire Regt
ALLEN Charles Witter MM Pte 8528 2nd Bedfordshire Regt
ALLEN Cyril Fred MM Sjt STK/309 10th Royal Fusiliers
ALLEN Cyril L. MM Pte 332986 Liverpool Regt
ALLEN David MM L/Sjt 15944 9th Norfolk Regt
ALLEN David MM S/Sjt Fitter 57877 RGA
ALLEN David MM+Bar Sjt 63742 RGA
ALLEN Donald MM Spr 44727 Royal Engineers
ALLEN E.A. MM Pte G/13261 7th East Kent Regt
ALLEN Edmund MM Dvr 174732 RFA
ALLEN Edward MM Dvr 76831 A/78 Bde RFA
ALLEN Edward MM Cpl 797086 94 Bde RFA
ALLEN Ernest MM Gnr 61125 28 Bde RFA
ALLEN Ernest MM Gnr 797167 RFA
ALLEN Ernest MM Pte 25209 Notts & Derby Regt
ALLEN Ernest MM Spr 15262 1 Cav Div Sig Sqn Royal Engineers
ALLEN Ernest MM Pte 44107 Northumberland Fusiliers
ALLEN Francis MM Pte 266908 Oxf & Bucks Light Infantry
ALLEN Frank MM Pte R/12509 13th King's Royal Rifle Corps
ALLEN Frank MM Gnr 101970 D/160 Bde RFA
ALLEN Frank B. MM Gnr 106076 129 Siege Bty RGA
ALLEN Fred MM Pte 46814 61st Bn Machine Gun Corps DOW 25.10.18.
ALLEN Fred S. MM Spr 487979 Royal Engineers
ALLEN Frederick MM Cpl R/33718 13th King's Royal Rifle Corps
ALLEN Frederick MM Spr 1647 3/1(?)Fd Coy Royal Engineers
ALLEN Frederick MM Sjt 191072 RGA
ALLEN Frederick MM Cpl 42736 Durham Light Infantry
ALLEN Frederick "MM,MSM" Spr 313140 25 Div Sig Coy Royal Engineers

ALLEN Frederick A. MM L/Sjt 145409 1/1st Northamptonshire Yeomanry
ALLEN Frederick E. MM Pte 241113 Notts & Derby Regt
ALLEN Frederick J. MM L/Cpl 201562 2/4th Hampshire Regt
ALLEN Frederick J. MM Pte 10283 Royal Berkshire Regt
ALLEN G.A. MM Pte 435477 1 Fd Amb RAMC
ALLEN George MM L/Cpl 16500 5th Shropshire Light Infantry
ALLEN George MM Cpl 760045 C/250 Bde RFA
ALLEN George MM Sjt 351206 9th Manchester Regt
ALLEN George MM Gnr 54426 11 Bde RFA
ALLEN George "MM,MID" Pte 1141 1/1st Cambridgeshire Regt
ALLEN George MM Sjt 4844 C/241 Bde RFA
ALLEN George MM Pte 7584 2nd Border Regt
ALLEN George MM Gnr 5166 RFA
ALLEN George Albert MM L/Cpl 76275 1/4th London Regt KIA 21.9.18.
ALLEN George Albert MM L/Cpl 570147 17th London Regt
ALLEN George E. MM Pte S/26027 13th Rifle Brigade
ALLEN George E. MM Pte 2717 1st Welsh Guards
ALLEN George Ernest MM Pte 799 7th East Kent Regt
ALLEN George R. MM Pte 42815 8th West Yorkshire Regt
ALLEN George R. MM Pte 78757 Tank Corps
ALLEN George S. MM Pte 326159 1/1st Cambridgeshire Regt
ALLEN George Sharp "MM,MID" Pte 3321 1st Northumberland Fusiliers KIA 14.7.16.
ALLEN George W. MM Pte 9386 2nd Northamptonshire Regt
ALLEN H.J. MM Pte 12047 1/1st Hertfordshire Regt
ALLEN Harold MM L/Cpl 1216 Royal Fusiliers
ALLEN Harold Roscoe MM Bdr 109029 16 Heavy Bty RGA
ALLEN Harry MM L/Cpl 883 1/1st South Notts Hussars Yeo
ALLEN Harry MM Pte 10604 1/8th Worcestershire Regt KIA 27.8.17.
ALLEN Harry MM Pte 10693 Royal Fusiliers
ALLEN Harry Epworth MM Gnr 6149 150 Hy Bty RGA
ALLEN Henry MM Gnr 87420 190 Heavy Bty RGA
ALLEN Henry G. MM 2nd Cpl 9114 6 Div Sig Coy Royal Engineers
ALLEN Herbert MM CSM 6712 16th Manchester Regt
ALLEN Herbert A. MM Gnr Sig 318683 139 Hy Bty RGA
ALLEN Herbert A. MM Cpl 301309 11th Bn Tank Corps
ALLEN Herbert Charles MM Sjt 7416 6th Royal West Kent Regt
ALLEN Hildred MM Sjt 305544 2/7th West Riding Regt Died 18.5.18.
ALLEN J. MM L/Cpl 10/23200 South Wales Borderers
ALLEN J. "MM,MID" Cpl 84713 RFA
ALLEN Jack MM CSM 240202 1/8th Middlesex Regt
ALLEN James MM Cpl 139312 Royal Engineers
ALLEN James MM Sjt M2/204974 Army Service Corps
ALLEN James MM Pte 44354 South Wales Borderers
ALLEN James A. MM Sjt 39205 A Bty RHA
ALLEN James Trevor MM Pte 241484 1/5th Leicestershire Regt KIA 15.3.17.
ALLEN John MM Pte 25397 1st Shropshire Light Infantry
ALLEN John MM Sjt 9509 2nd Bedfordshire Regt
ALLEN John Henry MM Pte 27207 Royal Welsh Fusiliers
ALLEN John J. MM Cpl 64440 RGA
ALLEN John William MM Sjt 14048 D/107 Bde RFA
ALLEN Joseph MM L/Cpl 11376 1st Liverpool Regt
ALLEN Joseph MM Pte 12354 6th Oxf & Bucks Light Infantry KIA 10.8.17.
ALLEN Joseph H. MM Dvr 781327 RFA
ALLEN Josiah J. MM Sjt 137603 172 Tunnelling Coy Royal Engineers
ALLEN Mark MM Spr 22874 9 Fd Coy Royal Engineers
ALLEN Michael MM Pte 63457 Royal West Surrey Regt
ALLEN Norman MM Pnr 209610 Special Coy HQ 5th Army Royal Engineers
ALLEN R.T. MM Cpl 26591 7th East Kent Regt
ALLEN Ralph MM Pte 23182 1st Lancashire Fusiliers
ALLEN Reginald H. MM Sjt 11822 1st Dorsetshire Regt
ALLEN Reginald Osborne MM Pte 23656 8th Norfolk Regt DOW 1.11.16.
ALLEN Richard MM+Bar Cpl 1670 1 Motor Bde MGC(Motors)
ALLEN Richard MM Cpl 249750 Royal Engineers
ALLEN Robert MM Pte C/5655 18th Highland Light Infantry
ALLEN Robert MM Spr 486778 185 Tunnelling Coy Royal Engineers
ALLEN Robert Alexander MM+Bar Bdr 74863 C/104 Bde RFA
ALLEN Samuel MM Pte 31836 8th Northumberland Fusiliers
ALLEN Samuel "MM,MID" Sjt 62807 Machine Gun Corps
ALLEN Samuel MM Sjt 89266 9 Div Ammn Col RFA
ALLEN Sidney "DCM,MM" Sjt 1323 1/6th Seaforth Highlanders
ALLEN Stanley J. MM L/Cpl 17178 Machine Gun Corps
ALLEN Stephen MM Sjt 693 5th Connaught Rangers
ALLEN Ted MM L/Cpl 15225 South Staffordshire Regt
ALLEN Thomas MM Pte 78822 2nd Durham Light Infantry
ALLEN Thomas MM Pte 7140 1st Scots Guards
ALLEN Thomas MM Pte 39875 1st Northumberland Fusiliers
ALLEN Thomas MM Pte 245633 12th Manchester Regt KIA 4.11.18.
ALLEN Thomas MM Pte 48076 RAMC
ALLEN Thomas MM Sjt M2/077201 Army Service Corps DOW 7.8.17.
ALLEN Thomas E. MM Sjt 13802 7th Lincolnshire Regt
ALLEN Thomas Edward MM Cpl 28125 18th Liverpool Regt KIA 8.5.18.
ALLEN Thomas Joseph MM Pte 8/3978 8th Royal Irish Rifles KIA 2.7.16
ALLEN Thomas Leighton "DCM,MM" Cpl 41324 9 Div Sig Coy Royal Engineers DOW 13.10.16.
ALLEN Victor J. MM L/Cpl 7653 1st Royal Berkshire Regt
ALLEN Walter MM Pte 269562 2/7th Liverpool Regt
ALLEN Wilfred MM Pte 16810 8th Leicestershire Regt
ALLEN William MM Sjt G/38167 11th Royal Fusiliers
ALLEN William MM Pte 6395 Royal Berkshire Regt
ALLEN William MM Gnr 94092 RFA
ALLEN William MM Pte 31037 1st Northamptonshire Regt DOW 18.9.18.
ALLEN William MM L/Cpl 4166 7 Fd Amb RAMC
ALLEN William MM+Bar L/Cpl 10983 1st Middlesex Regt
ALLEN William Allan MM L/Cpl 266110 2/7th Royal Warwickshire Regt KIA 23.3.18.
ALLEN William B. MM+Bar Sjt 240157 5th West Riding Regt
ALLEN William C. MM Cpl 8362 1/4th Royal Berkshire Regt
ALLEN William C. MM Pte 374867 8th London Regt
ALLEN William E. MM Sjt 265307 7th Norfolk Regt
ALLEN William E. MM Pte 3489 Leicestershire Regt
ALLEN William H. MM Sjt 8/10979 8th Northumberland Fusiliers
ALLEN William Henry MM Cpl 92426 RGA
ALLEN William O. MM Bdr 71159 30 Bde RFA
ALLEN William R. MM Pte 42503 6th South Staffordshire Regt
ALLEN William Robert John MM Cpl 44018 RGA
ALLEN William T. MM Sjt 3/10591 1st Northamptonshire Regt
ALLENBY Agbert Oscar MM Cpl 801592 65 Bde RFA
ALLENBY Robert MM L/Cpl 16888 Northumberland Fusiliers
ALLENDER Thomas MM Gnr 20478 D/175 Bde RFA
ALLERY Frank J.A. MM Pte 19903 8th East Surrey Regt
ALLEWAY Ernest MM Cpl 12766 Northamptonshire Regt
ALLFORD Thomas MM Sjt 15138 1st Royal Munster Fusiliers
ALLIBONE Stephen "DCM,MM" Sjt 266629 1/1st Hertfordshire Regt
ALLIES Henry John "MM,MID" 2nd Cpl 103763 33 Div Sig Coy Royal Engineers
ALLINE Charles MM Pte 10897 2nd South Wales Borderers KIA 11.4.18.
ALLINGTON Leonard A. MM Pte 41862 6th Lincolnshire Regt
ALLINGTON William MM Sjt 129142 45th Royal Fusiliers
ALLINSON Alfred MM Pte 141149 51st Bn Machine Gun Corps
ALLINSON Charles W. MM L/Bdr 220157 X/30 Med TM Bty RFA
ALLINSON Ernest MM Pte M2/267829 Army Service Corps
ALLINSON George MM Pte 1685 5th Border Regt
ALLINSON Isaac W. MM Pte 250998 Durham Light Infantry
ALLINSON J.H. MM Pte 203486 West Yorkshire Regt
ALLINSON James MM Pte 21415 10th Northumberland Fusiliers
ALLINSON Walter B. MM Pte 241936 2/5th West Yorkshire Regt
ALLINSON Wilson MM Sjt 24514 10th West Riding Regt
ALLISON Charles MM Pte 326016 87 Fd Amb RAMC
ALLISON Frank MM L/Cpl 33199 1/5th Yorkshire Regt
ALLISON Frederick E. MM Pte G/11604 11th Royal West Surrey Regt
ALLISON George MM Pte M2/048871 Army Service Corps
ALLISON Harry MM CSM 7459 1st Bedfordshire Regt
ALLISON Harry MM Pte 34527 Durham Light Infantry
ALLISON J.S. MM L/Cpl 36010 9th Yorkshire Regt
ALLISON James MM Sjt 43118 16th Highland Light Infantry
ALLISON James MM Sjt 29253 Essex Regt
ALLISON James Duncan MM Pte 78051 16 Fd Amb RAMC
ALLISON John Edward MM Pte 11/802 11th East Yorkshire Regt KIA 12.4.18.
ALLISON John G. MM Gnr 242671 112 Bty 24 Bde RFA
ALLISON Joseph MM Pte 203075 West Riding Regt
ALLISON Matthew MM Pte 25224 52nd Bn Machine Gun Corps
ALLISON Reginald MM Pte 318354 5th London Regt
ALLISON Robert MM Pte 14978 7th Bedfordshire Regt
ALLISON Robert MM Bdr 104252 15 Bty 36 Bde RFA

ALLISON Robert MM Cpl 8704 2nd York & Lancaster Regt
ALLISON Thomas MM Sjt 28/386 Northumberland Fusiliers
ALLISON Walter O. MM Dvr 58123 41 Bty 42 Bde RFA
ALLISON William H. MM L/Cpl 241325 Yorkshire Regt
ALLISS Charles W. MM CQMS 60001 Labour Corps
ALLISTER David MM Pte 32193 8th East Lancashire Regt KIA 2.9.17.
ALLISTER Harry MM Pte 39226 18th King's Royal Rifle Corps KIA 3.10.18.
ALLISTON Albert MM Cpl 46183 Northumberland Fusiliers
ALLITT William MM Pte 722664 24th London Regt
ALLMAN George MM Gnr 805464 C/231 Bde RFA
ALLMAN John T. MM Pte 201156 North Staffordshire Regt
ALLMARK Daniel MM Cpl 102493 183 Tunnelling Coy Royal Engineers
ALLOM Arthur MM L/Bdr 27092 RFA
ALLON F.H. MM Gnr 222539 RFA
ALLOTT H. MM Pte 45803 33 Fd Amb RAMC
ALLOTT James MM Dvr T4/253892 62 Div Train Army Service Corps
ALLPORT Leopold MM L/Cpl 204563 1st Yorkshire Light Infantry
ALLPRESS W. MM Pnr 84472 Royal Engineers
ALLSEBROOK Frank J. "MM,MID" L/Sjt 6254 1st Dragoons
ALLSEBROOK John Lee MM Bdr 277373 323 Siege Bty RGA
ALLSEBROOK Percy MM Gnr 123064 RGA
ALLSFORD Ernest Harold MM Cpl 470725 2/12th London Regt
ALLSOP Beatrice Alice MM Sister F QAIMNS
ALLSOP Worthy W.J. MM Pte 35215 16th Royal Warwickshire Regt
ALLSOPP Alfred MM Pte 33838 7th West Riding Regt
ALLSOPP Cyril George MM Pte 634838 2/20th London Regt
ALLSOPP George E. MM Pte 201468 4th Leicestershire Regt
ALLSOPP James A. MM Pte 15035 West Yorkshire Regt
ALLSOPP John MM Cpl 75339 3rd (Light) Bn Tank Corps
ALLSOPP John MM Pte 8995 2nd York & Lancaster Regt
ALLSOPP Thomas MM L/Cpl 18128 3rd Coldstream Guards
ALLSOPP William MM Sjt 240928 Notts & Derby Regt
ALLSOPP William Frederick MM Pte 8684 2nd Middlesex Regt KIA 1.7.16.
ALLSWORTH Edward W. MM Pte 35804 Worcestershire Regt
ALLSWORTH Frederick Joseph MM Sjt 16387 1st A Coy Hampshire Regt KIA 1.7.16.
ALLSWORTH William MM L/Cpl 723406 24th London Regt
ALLTHORPE Leonard MM Pte 17141 7th Norfolk Regt
ALLTOFT Samuel MM Pte 201546 2nd Bedfordshire Regt
ALLTON Vincent James MM L/Cpl 32847 1st Northamptonshire Regt KIA 29.10.18.
ALLUM Albert MM Pte 5/6812 2nd Royal Munster Fusiliers DOW 9.10.18.
ALLUM Alfred MM Cpl 47193 Liverpool Regt
ALLUM Charles MM Sjt 85801 Labour Corps KIA 21.7.18.
ALLUM Horace St.Leger MM Cpl 95148 A/84 Bde RFA
ALLUM Thomas E. MM Pte 10708 1st East Surrey Regt att RFC
ALLWAY Henry MM+Bar Sjt 16352 1st Leicestershire Regt KIA 21.3.18.
ALLWOOD John O. MM+Bar Cpl 71745 21st Bn Machine Gun Corps
ALLWOOD Thomas MM Pte 47275 Notts & Derby Regt
ALLWOOD W. MM Cpl 24061 Liverpool Regt
ALLWRIGHT Charles L. MM Spr 311715 3 Div Sig Coy Royal Engineers
ALMEY George MM Pte 40694 Leicestershire Regt
ALMOND Christopher MM Bdr 102465 RHA att 29 Div Ammn Col.
ALMOND Donald MM Cpl 238190 5th West Riding Regt
ALMOND James H. MM Cpl 12161 RFA
ALMOND Peter MM Pte 15402 17th Lancashire Fusiliers
ALMOND William MM Pte 29980 1st Duke of Cornwall's LI
ALRED Eli MM Sjt 240788 2/6th West Yorkshire Regt
ALSING Hans MM L/Sjt 1088 7th East Kent Regt
ALSOP Thomas MM Sjt 23/691 23rd Northumberland Fusiliers KIA 29.4.17.
ALSTON Frank S. MM Sjt 30453 RFA
ALSTON Godfrey MM Sjt 2213 Royal Sussex Regt
ALSTON Guy S. MM Gnr 20728 RGA
ALSTON Percy MM Pte 11117 Royal Berkshire Regt
ALTHAM Wilfred MM Pte 202415 1/7th Manchester Regt
ALTHORPE Frederick MM+Bar Pte 10086 5th Northamptonshire Regt
ALTON Ernest MM Cpl 265487 West Riding Regt
ALTON James MM Sjt 10095 5th Oxf & Bucks Light Infantry
ALTON William MM Pte 19744 10th Notts & Derby Regt KIA 11.6.18.

ALTON William H. MM Pte 5828 55 Fd Amb RAMC
ALTY J. MM Pte 2710 Lancashire Fusiliers
ALTY Lewis MM Pte 9666 11th Lancashire Fusiliers
ALTY Richard MM+Bar L/Cpl 28616 1st West Yorkshire Regt
ALTY Robert MM Pte 16562 Liverpool Regt
ALTY William MM L/Cpl 1195 South Lancashire Regt
ALVES Alexander C. MM Pte P/804 2nd Rifle Brigade
ALVES James MM Pte 22960 1/7th West Riding Regt
ALWAY Arthur Daniel "MM,CStG(R)" Pte 201185 6th Bn Tank Corps
ALWAY William John MM Pte 6600 6th Royal West Surrey Regt
ALWYNNE William Annesley MM Pte 11256 4th Hussars Died 2.4.18.
AMATT Francis James MM Cpl 155803 173 Tunnelling Coy Royal Engineers KIA 15.4.16.
AMATT Harry John MM Pte 42063 1st Essex Regt
AMBERS F.D. MM L/Cpl G/9419 6th East Kent Regt
AMBLER Claude Bernard MM Sjt 23901 Liverpool Regt
AMBLER Frank MM+Bar Pte 242254 Gordon Highlanders
AMBLER George R. MM Sjt 82229 253 Tunnelling Coy Royal Engineers
AMBLER Percy MM Sjt 11969 Wiltshire Regt
AMBLER Robert MM Pte 26670 10th Cheshire Regt
AMBLIN Henry G. MM Cpl 33157 18 Bde Ammn Col RFA
AMBRIDGE George MM Sjt 253863 Royal Engineers
AMBROSE Henry James MM Sjt 116903 5 Labour Bn Royal Engineers
AMBROSE Isaac C. MM Pte 1905 1/1st Cambridgeshire Regt
AMBROSE James MM Sjt 4556 Royal Munster Fusiliers
AMBROSE John H. MM Sjt 211299 23 Div Sig Coy Royal Engineers
AMBROSE William MM Sjt 113557 Special Coy Royal Engineers
AMERY Harold MM Pte 40750 South Staffordshire Regt
AMERY Thomas John MM Sjt 7468 8th Somerset Light Infantry DOW 27.10.18.
AMES Albert J. MM Sjt 742781 25th London Regt
AMES Francis W. MM Pte 16590 2nd Scots Guards
AMES Fred M. MM Pte PS/2144 7th Middlesex Regt
AMES H.J.G. MM L/Cpl 41504 9th Essex Regt
AMES James B. MM L/Cpl 21393 Cheshire Regt
AMES James E. MM L/Sjt 290973 Middlesex Regt
AMES John MM Pte DM2/207646 Army Service Corps
AMES John MM L/Sjt 15402 Royal Welsh Fusiliers
AMES Oliver MM Dvr 785609 RFA
AMES Robert MM Pte R/21597 9th King's Royal Rifle Corps
AMES Samuel W. MM Pte 11826 4th Liverpool Regt
AMES William G. MM Cpl 267433 6th West Riding Regt
AMESBURY Thomas MM Dvr T3/027287 Army Service Corps
AMESS Charles MM Pte 4/7682 1st Royal Munster Fusiliers
AMEY Arthur C. MM Pte 45514 RAMC
AMEY Harry MM Pte 9873 5th Dorsetshire Regt KIA 3.10.18.
AMEY Henry James MM Pte 532034 15th London Regt DOW 5.4.17.
AMEY James G. MM Bugler 9261 1st Scottish Rifles
AMIS Edward A. MM Cpl 510176 Royal Engineers
AMIS Redmond H. MM L/Cpl 267242 Northumberland Fusiliers
AMISON Arthur B. MM Cpl 13352 South Staffordshire Regt
AMON Harry MM L/Cpl 151414 250 Tunnelling Coy Royal Engineers
AMOR Charles MM L/Cpl 236695 Royal Engineers
AMOR Edward H. MM Pte 30039 1st Hampshire Regt
AMOR Frederick MM L/Cpl 10363 Royal Berkshire Regt
AMOS Alexander "DCM,MM" Sjt 9/814 Royal Munster Fusiliers
AMOS Arthur MM Pte 241811 1/8th Worcestershire Regt KIA 4.3.17.
AMOS Arthur G. "DCM,MM" Sjt 729 East Surrey Regt
AMOS Edwin G. MM Pte 37005 5(Cav)Fd Amb RAMC
AMOS Francis Trehearne MM L/Cpl 49886 18th Royal Fusiliers
AMOS Harry R. MM Pte M/339006 Army Service Corps
AMOS Isaiah Francis William MM Cpl 13742 7th East Yorkshire Regt DOW 11.7.18.
AMOS James MM Cpl 21100 6th Cameron Highlanders
AMOS John MM Cpl 650289 RFA
AMOS Joseph MM L/Cpl 1975 5th South Lancashire Regt
AMOS Robert MM L/Cpl 17016 12th Royal Scots DOW 27.10.18.
AMOS Thomas MM Pte 14195 Welsh Regt
AMOS Walter Mart "MM,VM(Rm)" Bdr 910245 22 Bde RFA
AMOS William MM Cpl 86065 Royal Engineers
AMOS William MM Cpl 46185 8th Northumberland Fusiliers
AMOS William "MM,MSM" Sjt 430166 421 Fd Coy Royal Engineers
AMOS William MM Cpl 6589 Northumberland Fusiliers
AMOS William Bateman MM Pte 39793 2nd Welsh Regt KIA 8.9.16.
AMOS William J. MM Pte 50340 2/6th Royal Warwickshire Regt

AMSBRIDGE George H. MM Cpl G/18323 2nd Royal Sussex Regt
AMSBURY Joseph MM Pte G/19396 7th Royal Sussex Regt
AMSDEN Reginald MM Cpl 718284 1/23rd London Regt KIA 22.8.18.
AMSDEN Reginald A. MM Pte 353379 7th London Regt
AMSON James MM Cpl 492017 46 Div Sig Coy Royal Engineers
AMY Edward MM Gnr 114704 RFA
ANCLIFFE Arthur MM L/Cpl 7122 Coldstream Guards
ANCLIFFE William E. MM+Bar Pte 232558 2/2nd London Regt
ANDERSON Albert MM L/Cpl 65013 17 Div Sig Coy Royal Engineers
ANDERSON Albert Henry MM Sjt 276965 33 Siege Bty RGA
ANDERSON Albert M. MM Pte 2483 14th Royal West Surrey Regt
ANDERSON Alexander MM Pte 225015 10th Cameron Highlanders
ANDERSON Alexander MM Pte 307106 Royal Warwickshire Regt
ANDERSON Alexander MM Pte 35658 Royal Scots
ANDERSON Alexander MM L/Cpl 400527 Royal Engineers
ANDERSON Alexander MM Pte M2/052643 Army Service Corps
ANDERSON Alexander MM Pte 17367 26 Coy Machine Gun Corps KIA 9.4.17.
ANDERSON Alexander "MM+Bar,CG(F)" Pte S/18115 10th Cameron Highlanders
ANDERSON Alexander MM L/Sjt 3028 Royal Highlanders
ANDERSON Alexander MM Cpl 10408 1/8th Royal Highlanders
ANDERSON Alexander Buchan MM Gnr Sig 86783 277 Siege Bty RGA
ANDERSON Alexander McG. "DCM,MM+Bar,MID" CSM 13597 10th West Yorkshire Regt
ANDERSON Alfred MM Pte 88239 RAMC
ANDERSON Alfred MM Dvr L/4098 RFA
ANDERSON Alfred MM Sjt Farrier 34785 C/174 Bde RFA
ANDERSON Alfred MM Sjt 18387 1/4th North Lancashire Regt KIA 1.10.18.
ANDERSON Andrew MM Sjt 200150 1/5th Arg & Suth Highlanders
ANDERSON Andrew MM Gnr 110849 319 Siege Bty RGA
ANDERSON Angus K. MM Pte 3398 16th Highland Light Infantry
ANDERSON Archibald A. MM Sjt 18159 Royal Scots
ANDERSON Arthur MM Pte 240921 5/6th Scottish Rifles
ANDERSON Arthur MM Cpl 201173 Gordon Highlanders
ANDERSON Aubrey A. MM L/Cpl G/540 East Kent Regt
ANDERSON Bertram MM Pte 8343 Machine Gun Corps
ANDERSON Charles MM Pte 290076 7th Royal Highlanders
ANDERSON Charles MM Cpl 22573 32nd Bn Machine Gun Corps
ANDERSON Charles MM Sjt Piper 6349 2nd Gordon Highlanders
ANDERSON Charles MM Cpl 7168 1st Gordon Highlanders
ANDERSON Christopher MM Pte 18/422 18th Durham Light Infantry
ANDERSON Daniel MM Pte 46413 Royal Scots
ANDERSON David MM Pnr 421901 5 Div Sig Coy Royal Engineers
ANDERSON David MM Pte 35801 RAMC
ANDERSON David MM Sjt 19392 Durham Light Infantry
ANDERSON David MM Cpl 350219 1/9th Royal Scots
ANDERSON David MM CSM 5563 1st Cameron Highlanders Died 4.5.18.
ANDERSON David B. MM Gnr 5066 RFA
ANDERSON David B. MM Pte 46305 RAMC
ANDERSON David J. MM Gnr 6580 RFA
ANDERSON David R. MM Pte 44979 11th Essex Regt
ANDERSON David S. MM L/Cpl 40115 King's Own Scottish Borderers
ANDERSON Donald MM L/Cpl 1495 23rd Royal Fusiliers DOW 8.5.17.
ANDERSON Duncan MM RQMS 1 1/1st Lothian & Border Horse Yeo
ANDERSON Eben MM Dvr 88274 'P' Bty RHA
ANDERSON Ebenezer M. MM Pte 99620 Machine Gun Corps
ANDERSON Edmund MM Pte 20/247 20th Durham Light Infantry KIA 1.10.16.
ANDERSON Edward MM Cpl 8757 2nd Northamptonshire Regt
ANDERSON Edward MM L/Cpl 17758 Gloucestershire Regt
ANDERSON Edward MM Pte 9/5515 Royal Munster Fusiliers
ANDERSON Ewing W. MM Pte 37089 Highland Light Infantry
ANDERSON Francis MM Pte 4475 Labour Corps
ANDERSON Frank MM L/Cpl F/78 17th Middlesex Regt
ANDERSON Frank B. MM Pte 35704 28 Fd Amb RAMC
ANDERSON Fred MM Sjt 12390 Liverpool Regt
ANDERSON Fred MM Pte 12845 2nd Suffolk Regt
ANDERSON Frederick MM Pte 32508 16th Royal Warwickshire Regt
ANDERSON Frederick MM Pte 9876 1st Northamptonshire Regt
ANDERSON Frederick George MM Sjt SE5022 Att 74 Bde RFA Army Veterinary Corps
ANDERSON Frederick Sam "MM,MSM" Pte 45010 76 Coy Labour Corps
ANDERSON George MM L/Cpl 119475 35th Bn Machine Gun Corps
ANDERSON George MM Pte 200237 1/4th Gordon Highlanders
ANDERSON George MM Sjt 8845 1st Royal West Surrey Regt
ANDERSON George "MM,MSM" Sjt 5260 3rd Coldstream Guards
ANDERSON George MM Cpl 8836 Machine Gun Corps
ANDERSON George MM L/Cpl 22425 Hampshire Regt
ANDERSON George C. MM Spr 503836 51 Div Sig Coy Royal Engineers
ANDERSON George G. MM Pte 240953 Gordon Highlanders
ANDERSON George G. MM Pte 266245 Seaforth Highlanders
ANDERSON George Henry MM Pte 883 6th East Kent Regt
ANDERSON George P. MM Gnr 39813 RFA
ANDERSON George R. MM Sjt 1245 King Edward's Horse
ANDERSON George S MM Sjt 539 Royal Engineers
ANDERSON George Small MM Pte 23053 17th Highland Light Infantry DOW 2.4.17.
ANDERSON H. MM L/Cpl 15012 Royal Warwickshire Regt
ANDERSON Harry MM Sjt 13258 2nd Suffolk Regt
ANDERSON Harry MM Dvr 44588 RFA
ANDERSON Harry G. MM Pte G/31909 6th Royal West Kent Regt
ANDERSON Henry MM Bdr 68546 36 Bde RFA
ANDERSON Henry C. MM Cpl M2/149721 Army Service Corps
ANDERSON Henry J. MM Sjt 26602 1st Grenadier Guards
ANDERSON Herbert MM+Bar Sjt 18395 Machine Gun Corps
ANDERSON Hugh MM Cpl 30116 5/6th Scottish Rifles DOW 4.10.18.
ANDERSON Hugh MM Pte 290194 Royal Highlanders
ANDERSON Hugh MM L/Cpl 17/706 15th Royal Irish Rifles DOW 4.7.16.
ANDERSON Hugh MM Cpl 9292 2nd Royal Scots
ANDERSON Hugh A. MM L/Cpl 76039 Royal Engineers
ANDERSON Irving F. MM Pte 266273 Scottish Rifles
ANDERSON J. MM Pte 9019 2nd Scots Guards
ANDERSON James MM Pte 49974 9th Royal Irish Fusiliers
ANDERSON James MM Cpl 6205 RFA
ANDERSON James "DCM+Bar,MM" Sjt 179 2nd Seaforth Highlanders
ANDERSON James MM Gnr 307492 2/1(Lowland)Hy Bty RGA
ANDERSON James MM Pte 301383 1/7th Arg & Suth Highlanders
ANDERSON James MM Sjt 147140 Royal Engineers
ANDERSON James MM Gnr 126170 RFA
ANDERSON James MM Gnr 25747 110 Hy Bty RGA
ANDERSON James MM Sjt 67645 Machine Gun Corps
ANDERSON James MM Pte 39311 RAMC
ANDERSON James MM Cpl 56676 40 Bde RFA
ANDERSON James MM Pte 359184 Liverpool Regt
ANDERSON James A. MM Sjt 30207 Somerset Light Infantry
ANDERSON James Bruce MM Gnr 69068 7 Bty MGC (Motors)
ANDERSON James Douglas "MM+Bar,CG(B)" Pte 55403 88 Fd Amb RAMC
ANDERSON James F. "MM+Bar,MID" Sjt 66067 40 Bde RFA
ANDERSON James H. MM Pte 32605 14th Royal Warwickshire Regt
ANDERSON James I. "DCM,MM" Sjt 17831 9th Royal Inniskilling Fusiliers
ANDERSON James Lawrence MM Sjt 611039 19th London Regt
ANDERSON James Reginald MM Pte 1600 1(Northumbrian)Fd Amb RAMC
ANDERSON John "DCM,MM" Sjt 24803 13th Durham Light Infantry KIA 5.10.18.
ANDERSON John MM Pte 3292 1st Welsh Guards
ANDERSON John MM Pte S/24051 8th Royal Highlanders
ANDERSON John MM Pte 39350 15th Lancashire Fusiliers
ANDERSON John MM Pte 59222 201 Bn Machine Gun Corps
ANDERSON John MM Pte 6448 8th Royal Highlanders
ANDERSON John MM+Bar Sjt 54771 105 Fd Amb RAMC
ANDERSON John MM Pte 1335 Middlesex Regt
ANDERSON John MM Pte 195 4th Middlesex Regt
ANDERSON John MM L/Cpl 2050 1/7th West Yorkshire Regt
ANDERSON John "MM,MID" L/Cpl 21160 13th Durham Light Infantry
ANDERSON John MM Pte 8261 1st Scottish Rifles
ANDERSON John MM L/Cpl 38002 51 Fd Amb RAMC
ANDERSON John MM Spr 132957 Royal Engineers
ANDERSON John MM L/Cpl 265054 5th Seaforth Highlanders
ANDERSON John A. MM Sjt 243243 RFA
ANDERSON John C.M. MM Bdr 90509 RFA
ANDERSON John M. MM L/Cpl 27311 Durham Light Infantry

ANDERSON John McG. MM Cpl L/5418 16th Lancers
ANDERSON John William MM Cpl 31461 1st Bn Machine Gun Corps
ANDERSON Joseph MM Pte G/71053 4th London Regt
ANDERSON Joseph L. MM Pte 270855 1/1st Northumberland Yeo
ANDERSON M. MM Cpl 407063 RAMC
ANDERSON Matthew MM Pte 201960 Northumberland Fusiliers
ANDERSON Norman Louis MM Pte 260411 7th Border Regt KIA 9.10.18.
ANDERSON Peter Hendry MM L/Sjt 351240 1/9th Royal Scots KIA 23.4.17.
ANDERSON Robert MM Cpl 21433 2nd Northumberland Fusiliers
ANDERSON Robert MM Dvr 89448 71 Bty 36 Bde RFA
ANDERSON Robert MM Spr 151411 185 Tunnelling Coy Royal Engineers
ANDERSON Robert MM Pte 12863 10th Durham Light Infantry KIA 12.8.16.
ANDERSON Robert MM Pte 17/248 Royal Irish Rifles
ANDERSON Robert MM Sjt 7350 1st Cameron Highlanders
ANDERSON Robert MM+Bar Sjt 265215 6th Royal Highlanders
ANDERSON Robert H. MM Pte 278730 1/7th Arg & Suth Highlanders
ANDERSON Robert M MM CSM 12227 12th Royal Scots
ANDERSON Roderick J. MM L/Sjt S/5265 1st Royal Highlanders
ANDERSON Russell S. MM Pte 240608 6th Liverpool Regt
ANDERSON Samuel MM Spr 412073 409 Fd Coy Royal Engineers
ANDERSON Scott MM Pte M2/116016 Army Service Corps
ANDERSON T. MM Pte 204127 Northumberland Fusiliers
ANDERSON Thomas MM Pte S/41281 6th Cameron Highlanders
ANDERSON Thomas MM Pte 28242 2nd Royal Scots Fusiliers
ANDERSON Thomas MM Pnr 127112 Royal Engineers
ANDERSON Thomas MM Pte 16912 11th Royal Scots
ANDERSON Thomas E. MM Pte 203102 Yorkshire Regt
ANDERSON Thomas V. MM Pte 2943 Liverpool Regt
ANDERSON Thomas W. MM L/Bdr 52828 A/122 Bde RFA
ANDERSON Tom E. MM L/Cpl 10950 Wiltshire Regt
ANDERSON W. MM Pte 386283 RAMC
ANDERSON W. MM Pte 325211 Durham Light Infantry
ANDERSON W. MM Pte 40146 Royal Highlanders
ANDERSON W. MM Cpl 13231 Machine Gun Corps
ANDERSON W.H.C. MM Spr 46471 Royal Engineers
ANDERSON Wiliiam MM Pte 280251 1/7th Highland Light Infantry
ANDERSON William MM Bdr 760081 A/250 Bde RFA
ANDERSON William MM Cpl 200288 Royal Highlanders
ANDERSON William MM Pte 23182 Royal Highlanders
ANDERSON William "DCM,MM" Pte 242018 1/5th Seaforth Highlanders
ANDERSON William MM Pte H/270985 1/1st Northumberland Yeo
ANDERSON William "MM+Bar,MID." Sjt 200942 4th Gordon Highlanders
ANDERSON William MM Sjt 240535 1/6h Highland Light Infantry DOW 22.1.18.
ANDERSON William MM Pte 23294 10th Royal Inniskilling Fusiliers KIA 1.7.16.
ANDERSON William MM Bdr 55695 18 Bde RFA
ANDERSON William MM+Bar Cpl 7033 8th Highland Light Infantry
ANDERSON William MM Pte 4030 18th Bn Machine Gun Corps KIA 23.3.18.
ANDERSON William MM Pte 1719 Northumberland Fusiliers
ANDERSON William MM Pte 35709 RAMC
ANDERSON William MM L/Cpl R/23919 King's Royal Rifle Corps
ANDERSON William MM+Bar Pte 201515 Scottish Rifles
ANDERSON William MM Pte 331047 9th Highland Light Infantry KIA 13.4.18.
ANDERSON William J. MM Pte 15513 Royal Sussex Regt
ANDERSON William John MM Pte 4478 Seaforth Highlanders
ANDERSON William R. MM Cpl 1288 Royal Highlanders
ANDERSON William T. MM Cpl 110003 Tank Corps
ANDERSON William W. MM Gnr 179590 B/84 Bde RFA
ANDERSON Willwood S. MM Cpl 69093 15 Bde RFA
ANDERTON Cyril MM Cpl 92724 Royal Engineers
ANDERTON Thomas MM L/Cpl 356454 19th Liverpool Regt
ANDERTON Thomas W. MM Pte 1474 7th Royal West Surrey Regt
ANDERTON Walter MM Sjt 2403 5th South Lancashire Regt
ANDERTON William "DCM,MM+Bar" Sjt 12100 6th King's Own Scottish Borderers
ANDON J. MM Pte 10306 York & Lancaster Regt
ANDRE Albert Lewis MM Gnr Sig 955572 A/236 Bde RFA
ANDREOLI Ernest V.E. MM Pte 64001 7th Royal West Surrey Regt
ANDRESS John MM Pte 40908 RAMC

ANDREW Albert MM Cpl 350700 Royal Scots
ANDREW Alfred MM Pte 34936 Machine Gun Corps
ANDREW D.T. MM Pte 130857 Machine Gun Corps
ANDREW Fred MM Pte 11310 6th Yorkshire Regt KIA 30.3.18.
ANDREW George MM Pte 16096 East Yorkshire Regt
ANDREW George J. MM Pnr 209595 Royal Engineers
ANDREW Harry MM Gnr 76630 RGA
ANDREW John A. MM Pte S/18615 4th Gordon Highlanders
ANDREW John C. MM Sjt 21901 Duke of Cornwall's LI
ANDREW John E. MM Cpl 9130 2nd Dragoons
ANDREW Matthew MM SSM 810 1/1st Bedfordshire Yeomanry
ANDREW Richard E. MM Pte 26179 4th Leicestershire Regt
ANDREW Robert MM L/Cpl 27770 Royal Scots
ANDREW William MM Sjt 306251 2/8th West Yorkshire Regt
ANDREW William H. MM 2nd Cpl 176726 105 Fd Coy Royal Engineers
ANDREWS Albert E. MM Pte 6150 24th London Regt
ANDREWS Albert Edward MM Cpl 680474 1/22nd London Regt
ANDREWS Albert S. MM Pte 44769 12th Royal Irish Rifles
ANDREWS Albert W. MM L/Cpl 6218 East Surrey Regt
ANDREWS Alfred MM Sjt 26602 Machine Gun Corps
ANDREWS Alfred E. MM L/Cpl 505270 18th King's Royal Rifle Corps
ANDREWS Alfred Lawrence MM Dvr L/20954 C/64 Bde RFA
ANDREWS Arthur MM Cpl 16357 Royal Berkshire Regt
ANDREWS Arthur MM Pte 241446 Middlesex Regt
ANDREWS Charles MM Cpl 70783 54 Bty 39 Bde RFA KIA 24.7.16.
ANDREWS Charles MM Pte 8648 50th Bn Machine Gun Corps DOW 13.10.18.
ANDREWS Charles A. MM+Bar Sjt 44031 2nd Suffolk Regt
ANDREWS Charley "MM,MID" Sjt 19179 16th Royal Welsh Fusiliers
ANDREWS Charlie MM Pte 200471 4th West Riding Regt
ANDREWS Christopher "MM,CG(F)" 2nd Cpl 43407 Royal Engineers
ANDREWS David MM Pte 8816 2nd Hampshire Regt
ANDREWS David C. MM Pte 291107 24th Royal Welsh Fusiliers
ANDREWS E. MM Pte 267394 1/2nd Monmouthshire Regt
ANDREWS Edgar MM Pte 50436 Notts & Derby Regt
ANDREWS Edward MM Pte 12028 Shropshire Light Infantry
ANDREWS Eric George MM Cpl 345188 16th Devonshire Regt
ANDREWS F.W. MM Sjt R/14185 13th King's Royal Rifle Corps
ANDREWS Frank MM L/Cpl 166404 497 Fd Coy Royal Engineers
ANDREWS Frank MM Cpl 65874 138 Army Troops Coy Royal Engineers
ANDREWS Frank "MM,CG(B)" SM P/5212 Military Mounted Police
ANDREWS Frank MM Pte 11869 7th South Staffordshire Regt
ANDREWS Frank MM Pte 52107 Liverpool Regt
ANDREWS Frank George MM Cpl 67562 112 Siege Bty RGA
ANDREWS Fred MM Sjt 482229 Royal Engineers
ANDREWS Frederick MM Pte 39975 South Lancashire Regt
ANDREWS Frederick MM Pte 200152 1/5th Bedfordshire Regt
ANDREWS Frederick C.G. "MM,MID" 2nd Cpl 81746 Royal Engineers
ANDREWS Frederick George MM Sjt 656 Military Mounted Police
ANDREWS Frederick Walter MM Pte 17843 1st Coldstream Guards
ANDREWS G.E. MM Sjt 1/13527 South Wales Borderers
ANDREWS George Cyril Gibson MM L/Cpl 130 15th London Regt
ANDREWS George H. MM Pte 80610 4th London Regt
ANDREWS George Henry MM Gnr 113195 7 Div Ammn Col RFA
ANDREWS Henry MM Cpl 1689 1st Rifle Brigade
ANDREWS Henry MM Pte 3112 23rd Middlesex Regt KIA 25.3.18.
ANDREWS Henry Frederick MM Sjt 325895 1/1st Cambridgeshire Regt
ANDREWS Herbert MM Sjt 105469 213 Siege Bty RGA
ANDREWS Herbert Francis MM L/Cpl 6188 12th Middlesex Regt KIA 26.9.16.
ANDREWS Isaac MM Pte 52491 Lancashire Fusiliers
ANDREWS James "MM,MID" BSM 80514 56 Div Ammn Col RFA
ANDREWS James A. MM Spr 148384 63 Div Sig Coy Royal Engineers
ANDREWS James S. MM L/Sjt 330203 Royal Scots
ANDREWS John MM L/Sjt 13840 1st Scots Guards
ANDREWS John MM Gnr 148835 RFA
ANDREWS John A. MM Pte 39798 6th Northamptonshire Regt
ANDREWS John G. MM+Bar Pte 5310 Northumberland Fusiliers
ANDREWS John Leonard MM L/Cpl 1827 8th London Regt DOW 19.5.18.
ANDREWS Joseph MM L/Cpl 9234 1st West Yorkshire Regt
ANDREWS Joseph MM Pte 202304 York & Lancaster Regt
ANDREWS Joseph William MM Pte M2/080320 654 Coy Army Service Corps

ANDREWS Leonard W. MM Pte 33166 7th Norfolk Regt
ANDREWS Leslie W. MM Pte 301094 5th London Regt
ANDREWS Llewellyn MM L/Cpl 1814 1/3rd Monmouthshire Regt
ANDREWS Reginald E.G. MM Spr 147635 Royal Engineers
ANDREWS Richard "DCM,MM+Bar" CSM 241337 2/4th Yorkshire Light Infantry
ANDREWS Robert "DCM,MM" Sjt 86239 258 Tunnelling Coy Royal Engineers
ANDREWS Robert "MM,MSM" L/Cpl 8228 2nd York & Lancaster Regt
ANDREWS Roland MM BSM L/28115 A/72 Bde RFA
ANDREWS Sidney G. MM Sjt 18749 Royal Berkshire Regt
ANDREWS Stanley W. MM Cpl 3186 2nd Rifle Brigade
ANDREWS Sydney James MM Sjt 1335 1/3rd London Regt KIA 4.7.16.
ANDREWS Thomas MM Pte 5/12197 5th Royal Inniskilling Fusiliers
ANDREWS Thomas MM Pte 269882 2/7th Notts & Derby Regt DOW 22.3.18.
ANDREWS Thomas E. MM Bdr 41331 RFA
ANDREWS Thomas Henry MM Pte 241350 Leicestershire Regt
ANDREWS Thomas J.S. MM Pte 421426 10th London Regt
ANDREWS Vernon Harold MM+Bar Cpl 7533 3(Cav)Fd Amb RAMC DOW 24.3.18.
ANDREWS W.O. MM Gnr 91796 RHA
ANDREWS Walter MM L/Cpl 200971 West Yorkshire Regt
ANDREWS William "MM,MSM" Sjt 20819 109 Siege Bty RGA
ANDREWS William MM Pte 201860 2/7th Worcestershire Regt KIA 24.10.17.
ANDREWS William MM Cpl 12943 1st East Kent Regt
ANDREWS William A. MM Pte 16469 6th Lincolnshire Regt
ANDREWS William F. MM Dvr 109647 RFA
ANESS Arthur MM Gnr L/29065 D/160 Bde RFA
ANGEL Jack MM Pte J/1898 38th Royal Fusiliers
ANGEL James William MM Pte 26989 15th Hampshire Regt KIA 27.5.18.
ANGEL Robert L. MM Pte 548058 15th London Regt
ANGEL Thomas W. "DCM,MM" Sjt B/957 9th Rifle Brigade
ANGEL Wallace H. MM Pte 72600 4th Royal West Surrey Regt
ANGEL William "MC,MM(12512 L/Cpl)" T/2Lt 8th Royal Berkshire Regt
ANGELL Frederick MM Pnr 47304 Royal Engineers
ANGELL George A. MM Pte 251947 3rd London Regt
ANGELL John E. MM Pte G/6017 13th Royal Fusiliers
ANGELL Leonard George MM Cpl 48974 X/5 Med TM Bty RFA
ANGELL Richard Sidney MM Cpl 11543 5th Oxf & Bucks Light Infantry KIA 3.5.17.
ANGER Cecil A. MM Cpl 205037 4th Hampshire Regt
ANGLESEA Walter S. MM Dvr L/13585 RFA
ANGULATTA Connaught MM L/Cpl 18239 1st Grenadier Guards
ANGUS Alexander MM Pte 19796 1/7th Gordon Highlanders
ANGUS Alexander MM Pte 200604 1/4th King's Own Scottish Borderers
ANGUS Andrew MM L/Cpl 11688 1st Scots Guards
ANGUS G. MM Pte 320223 3 Fd Amb RAMC
ANGUS George MM Gnr 242752 A/18 Bde RFA
ANGUS George MM Cpl 266570 6th Gordon Highlanders
ANGUS George MM Pte 626 Gordon Highlanders
ANGUS James MM L/Cpl 3/2883 8th Royal Highlanders DOW 24.7.16.
ANGUS John MM+Bar L/Cpl 64518 36 Div Sig Coy Royal Engineers
ANGUS John R. MM Pte 19/826 Northumberland Fusiliers
ANGUS John W. MM Pte 265202 Northumberland Fusiliers
ANGUS Robert MM Pte 241521 Seaforth Highlanders
ANGUS W. MM Pte 276390 1/7th Arg & Suth Highlanders
ANGUS William MM L/Cpl 412304 412 Fd Coy Royal Engineers
ANGUS William MM L/Cpl 240127 Royal Lancaster Regt
ANKER Charles MM Pte 35423 Yorkshire Light Infantry
ANKERS Albert MM Pte M2/120455 659 Coy Army Service Corps
ANKERS Eli MM L/Cpl 12/7994 12th Lancashire Fusiliers
ANKERS Ernest MM L/Bdr 4837 B/56 Bde RFA
ANKERS Ernest MM L/Sjt 26730 1st Shropshire Light Infantry
ANKETELL Charles Edward MM Cpl 8076 8th East Surrey Regt Killed 11.5.18.
ANKETT William George "DCM,MM" CSM 2219 Royal Sussex Regt
ANNABEL Harold MM L/Cpl R/8055 8th King's Royal Rifle Corps
ANNABLE Joseph MM Pte 26593 Notts & Derby Regt
ANNABLE Joseph MM Cpl 13/306 East Yorkshire Regt
ANNABLE Maurice MM Pte 43084 1/9th Durham Light Infantry
ANNABLE Percy R. MM Pte 57592 Lancashire Fusiliers
ANNAN William M. MM Pte 200868 Royal Highlanders

ANNAND Dudley W.H. MM Cpl 200869 1/4th Gordon Highlanders
ANNAND George MM Cpl 66658 140 Fd Amb RAMC
ANNESS Henry MM Pte 30726 2nd Suffolk Regt KIA 21.3.18.
ANNETT Edward MM Sjt 201041 4th South Lancashire Regt
ANNETT Joseph MM L/Cpl 66246 10th Royal Scots
ANNETT William MM Pte M2/080811 Army Service Corps
ANNING Albert G. MM Dvr 950061 RFA
ANNING James A. MM Sjt 508288 Royal Engineers
ANNISON Alexander MM Sjt 3310 North Lancashire Regt
ANNISON Michael MM Pte 302875 Durham Light Infantry
ANNISON Reginald Clement MM Sjt 950611 A/15 Bde RFA
ANSCOMBE John F. MM Sjt 21538 Royal West Surrey Regt
ANSCOMBE William MM L/Cpl G2245 7th Royal West Surrey Regt
ANSELL Alfred MM Pte 45507 37 Fd Amb RAMC KIA 30.11.17.
ANSELL Alfred MM Pte 36227 6th Royal Berkshire Regt
ANSELL Clifford H. MM Pte 7563 22nd London Regt
ANSELL Frederick MM L/Cpl 38268 26 Fd Coy Royal Engineers
ANSELL Frederick MM Spr 100472 33 Div Sig Coy Royal Engineers
ANSELL Frederick Birkett "MM,CG(F)" CSM 6153 26th Royal Fusiliers
ANSELL Harry MM Pte C/1081 King's Royal Rifle Corps
ANSELL Isaac MM Cpl 86433 173 Tunnelling Coy. Royal Engineers
ANSELL J. MM Cpl 354131 3 Fd Amb RAMC
ANSELL John MM Pte 203283 23rd Middlesex Regt
ANSELL John MM Pte 16264 9th North Staffordshire Regt
ANSELL Percy MM Bdr 280008 RGA
ANSELL William MM Cpl 925373 A/280 Bde RFA
ANSELL William MM Cpl 10510 4th Middlesex Regt
ANSLOW W.J. MM Cpl 358383 RGA
ANSON Francis John MM Pte 3340 6th Bn Machine Gun Corps
ANSON John MM Cpl 9201 14th Arg & Suth Highlanders
ANSON John William "MM,CG(B)" L/Cpl 11/562 11th East Yorkshire Regt
ANSTEY Charles Ernest "DCM,MM" Sjt 7218 2nd Irish Guards
ANSTEY J. MM Pte 44158 9th Royal Inniskilling Fusiliers
ANSTEY John W. MM Cpl 14379 3rd Worcestershire Regt
ANSTEY Robert W. MM Spr 510250 Royal Engineers
ANSTEY Sidney MM Pte 33550 2nd Hampshire Regt
ANSTISS William MM+Bar Sjt 241250 8th Middlesex Regt
ANTCLIFFE Harold Edmund "DCM,MM,MMV(It)" Sjt 17957 11th Notts & Derby Regt
ANTELL Arthur MM Pte 17896 2nd Coldstream Guards
ANTELL Samuel Jonah MM Sjt 30782 D/74 Bde RFA
ANTHONY Alfred MM L/Cpl 15442 Notts & Derby Regt
ANTHONY Edward MM Spr 28915 Royal Engineers
ANTHONY Evan MM L/Cpl 14725 Dorsetshire Regt
ANTHONY Frederick MM L/Cpl 8532 2nd York & Lancaster Regt
ANTHONY Harold MM Gnr 239583 D/83 Bde RFA
ANTHONY Henry MM S/Sjt 36203 97 Fd Amb RAMC
ANTHONY John MM Gnr 184314 RFA
ANTHONY John T. MM+Bar Cpl 38094 Royal Welsh Fusiliers
ANTHONY W.F.B. MM L/Cpl 4013 3rd Dragoon Guards
ANTHONY William "DCM,MM" Sjt 17598 13th Royal Welsh Fusiliers
ANTRAM Arthur Edgar MM L/Sjt 372756 1/8th London Regt KIA 25.7.18.
ANTROBUS George MM L/Cpl MS/1107 1 Div MT Coy Army Service Corps
ANTROBUS George E. MM Cpl 356464 10th Liverpool Regt
ANTWIS Walter MM Sjt 1820 Welsh Regt
ANYAN John G. MM Pte 10801 2/1st HAC (Inf)
ANYON Cyril H. MM Pte 102091 Machine Gun Corps
APLIN A.C. MM Pte 53884 RAMC
APLIN Christopher MM Sjt 235446 1/1st Herefordshire Regt
APPERLEY Alfred MM Pte M2/032759 Army Service Corps
APPLEBY A.G. MM Pte 202982 Yorkshire Regt
APPLEBY Albert MM Dvr 34613 RFA
APPLEBY Arthur MM Sjt 760691 317 Bde RFA
APPLEBY Arthur Lumley MM Pte 205104 1/7th West Riding Regt KIA 11.10.18.
APPLEBY Charles H.D. MM Spr 45249 Royal Engineers
APPLEBY Cyril MM Pte 200852 1/7th Middlesex Regt
APPLEBY David MM Cpl 16074 Machine Gun Corps
APPLEBY E.H. MM Pte 42775 2nd Essex Regt
APPLEBY Ernest MM Pte 8974 36th Bn Machine Gun Corps
APPLEBY George Walter "MM,MID" Sjt 760690 317 Bde RFA
APPLEBY Harold F. MM L/Cpl C/3687 King's Royal Rifle Corps
APPLEBY James MM Pte 7374 2nd Oxf & Bucks Light Infantry
APPLEBY John MM L/Bdr Sig L/12381 A/175 Bde RFA
APPLEBY John William MM Pte 73515 21st Bn Machine Gun Corps
APPLEBY Johnson MM Dvr 69758 15 Div Ammn Col RFA

APPLEBY Joseph MM Sjt 325053 1/9th Durham Light Infantry
APPLEBY Percy MM Pte 20952 Bedfordshire Regt
APPLEBY Percy Frank MM L/Cpl 1273 2nd Royal Fusiliers KIA 29.9.18.
APPLEBY Robert MM Pte 18235 Manchester Regt
APPLEBY Robert George MM L/Cpl 592695 18th London Regt
APPLEBY Sydney MM Pte 300651 8th Durham Light Infantry
APPLEBY Sydney P. MM L/Cpl 202109 2/5th West Yorkshire Regt
APPLEBY William MM Cpl 60167 RFA
APPLEBY William MM Sjt 25/6 Northumberland Fusiliers
APPLEBY William E. MM Gnr 30518 RFA
APPLEFORD John D. MM Pte 4204 21st London Regt
APPLEGARTH John MM Bdr 72937 RFA
APPLEGATE Albert MM Cpl 27955 1st Devonshire Regt
APPLETON Arthur MM Cpl 200357 South Lancashire Regt
APPLETON Bertie MM Spr 84650 Royal Engineers
APPLETON Edward J. MM Pte 116833 7th Bn Machine Gun Corps
APPLETON John MM Sjt 280140 1/7th Lancashire Fusiliers KIA 22.8.18.
APPLETON John Parker MM Sjt 12361 8th Yorkshire Regt
APPLETON John W. MM Cpl 131426 234 Fd Coy Royal Engineers
APPLETON Leonard MM Pte 59030 13th Rifle Brigade
APPLETON W.J. MM Sjt 720635 London Regt
APPLEYARD A. MM Gnr 936066 RFA
APPLEYARD E. MM L/Cpl 15/30 West Yorkshire Regt
APPLEYARD Edmund "DCM,MM" Bdr Signaller 77970 253 Siege Bty RGA
APPLEYARD F. MM+Bar Sjt W/1761 B/121 Bde RFA
APPLEYARD Joseph H. MM Pte M2/080968 Army Service Corps
APPLEYARD Lionel MM Pte 204703 2/5th West Riding Regt KIA 23.7.18.
APPLEYARD Thomas MM Pte 34669 Northumberland Fusiliers
APPLEYARD Thomas W. MM Pte 102180 Machine Gun Corps
APPS Alfred Edward MM Pte 15/320 15th Royal Warwickshire Regt
APPS Charles MM Pte 22280 19 Fd Amb RAMC
APPS Frederick H. MM Cpl L/10622 8th Royal West Kent Regt
APPS Henry Arthur MM Bdr 125692 59 Siege Bty RGA
APPS Sam MM Pte 20398 10th Yorkshire Regt KIA 17.9.16.
APPS Samuel A. MM Pte 53147 36 Fd Amb RAMC
APPS Sidney G. MM Cpl 44207 10th South Wales Borderers
APPS William M. "DCM,MM" Sjt Farrier 952224 D/282 Bde RFA
APTED Robert MM Pte 3392 7th Royal West Surrey Regt
APTER Albert E. MM L/Cpl 5778 Machine Gun Corps
ARAH Robert MM Pte 57621 13th Liverpool Regt
ARANDLE George MM+Bar Pte 35936 North Lancashire Regt
ARBER Frederick MM Pte 17854 1st Essex Regt
ARBERY Ernest James MM Spr 61748 154 Fd Coy Royal Engineers
ARBERY Walter MM L/Sjt 25093 11th Oxf & Bucks Light Infantry
ARBIN Cecil Charles MM Pte 14684 8th Suffolk Regt
ARBLASTER Herbert MM L/Cpl 1 4th Bn GMGR
ARBLASTER John MM Pte 9132 7th South Staffordshire Regt
ARBON Edward MM Pte 240867 1/5th Norfolk Regt
ARBON George MM Gnr 71701 RFA
ARBON John W. "DCM,MM,MID" Sjt 26747 4 Siege Bty RGA
ARCH John G. MM Spr 268251 62 Div Sig Coy Royal Engineers
ARCH William MM Dvr 676836 B/285 Bde RFA
ARCH William Arthur MM Pte M2/164289 Army Service Corps
ARCHBOLD James H. MM Sjt 52286 154 Siege Bty RGA
ARCHBOLD Michael MM Pte 27247 9th Royal Dublin Fusiliers KIA 16.8.17.
ARCHBOLD Robert MM Dvr T4/249436 Army Service Corps
ARCHBOLD Walter MM Pte 14404 Northumberland Fusiliers
ARCHER Arnold G. MM Pte 1306 16th Middlesex Regt
ARCHER Arthur Alfred MM Gnr Sig 79495 180 Siege By RGA
ARCHER Arthur E. MM Cpl 16712 Machine Gun Corps
ARCHER Bertram C. MM Pte 47097 15th Lancashire Fusiliers
ARCHER Charles W. MM Pte 8916 6 Fd Amb RAMC
ARCHER Cyril MM Cpl 30787 7th South Staffordshire Regt
ARCHER Frank "MC+Bar,MM(8218 R Fus)" T/2Lt 25th att 2nd Lincs Regt Northumberland Fusiliers
ARCHER Frank "DCM,MM" Sjt 6576 1st Duke of Cornwall's LI
ARCHER Frederick MM Pte 3882 2nd Lancashire Fusiliers
ARCHER Frederick R.W. MM+Bar Cpl 64775 18 Div Sig Coy Royal Engineers
ARCHER George A. MM BQMS 31930 35 Bde RFA
ARCHER Harry "MM,MID" L/Sjt 7776 2nd West Yorkshire Regt
ARCHER Harry "MM+Bar,MID" Sjt 2063 1/8th West Yorkshire Regt
ARCHER Henry MM Sjt 293167 706 Coy Labour Corps
ARCHER James A. MM Pte 9997 8th Suffolk Regt
ARCHER John MM Sjt SE/17372 Army Veterinary Corps
ARCHER John T. MM L/Cpl 27504 Royal Welsh Fusiliers
ARCHER John W. MM Cpl S/7119 Army Ordnance Corps
ARCHER Joseph MM Cpl 3357 2/16th B Coy London Regt DOW 21.8.18.
ARCHER Joseph E.W. MM Cpl 9226 1st Coldstream Guards
ARCHER Joseph H. MM Pte 41501 RAMC
ARCHER Leonard C. MM Sjt 14271 2nd Scots Guards
ARCHER Reginald MM Pte 21927 118 Coy Machine Gun Corps KIA 14.10.16.
ARCHER Robert MM Pte 14322 24th Manchester Regt KIA 4.5.17.
ARCHER Robert Blair Buckle MM L/Cpl 10680 2nd Gordon Highlanders
ARCHER Robert Henry "DCM,MM" Cpl 265658 1/6th Northumberland Fusiliers KIA 14.4.18.
ARCHER Thomas "MM,MSM" Spr 492271 59 Div Sig Coy Royal Engineers
ARCHER William MM Spr 526149 3 Div Sig Coy Royal Engineers
ARCHER William H. MM Pte 240274 West Riding Regt
ARCHIBALD Donald Mcl. MM Cpl 250505 5/6th Royal Scots
ARCHIBALD Robert MM Sjt 35097 16th Highland Light Infantry
ARCHIBALD Robert F. MM Pte 15680 Gordon Highlanders
ARCHIBALD Thomas Malcolm MM L/Cpl 6576 2nd Scots Guards DOW 31.10.18.
ARCHIBALD Thomas R. MM Sjt 4373 1/8th Royal Scots
ARCHIBALD William MM Sjt 146823 RGA
ARCHMAN Samuel MM Dvr 93460 RFA
ARDEN Alfred M. MM Sjt 73936 18th Bn Machine Gun Corps
ARDEN James Arthur MM Gnr Sig 676006 2/1(W Lancs)Bde RFA
ARDEN James L. MM Sjt 84674 Machine Gun Corps
ARDERN Arthur W. MM Sjt 482006 49 Div Sig Coy Royal Engineers
ARDIE T. MM Pte 10284 King's Own Scottish Borderers
ARDRAN Alfred W. MM Pte 337453 RAMC
AREY John Hector MM L/Sjt 50712 1st East Yorkshire Regt
ARGEAT John R. MM Pte 18951 XIX Corps Cyclist Bn Army Cyclist Corps
ARGENT Bertie MM Pte 10717 XV Corps Cyclist Bn Army Cyclist Corps
ARGENT Charles B. MM+Bar CSM 240070 6th Liverpool Regt
ARGENT James MM Sjt 5781 2nd Suffolk Regt
ARGENT M. MM Pte 7685 Essex Regt
ARGENT Richard John MM Cpl 201470 2nd Suffolk Regt KIA 27.9.18.
ARGENT Walter W. MM CQMS 8638 2nd East Lancashire Regt
ARGILE Frank MM Dvr 95972 RFA
ARGYLE Frederick MM+Bar Sjt 9081 1st Hampshire Regt
ARGYLE Samuel MM Sjt 2847 7th Notts & Derby Regt
ARIES Wallace MM Sjt G/207954 11th Royal West Surrey Regt DOW 10.10.18.
ARIGHO Richard MM L/Cpl 33101 RAMC
ARIS Arthur MM Pte 53368 West Yorkshire Regt
ARIS J.J. MM Pte 423148 2/10th London Regt
ARIS Joseph MM Cpl 201235 2/4th Oxf & Bucks Light Infantry
ARKELL Cyril J. MM Pte 3086 Gloucestershire Regt
ARKELL William MM Cpl 277 Royal Warwickshire Regt
ARKILL Leonard W. MM Bdr 119843 RGA
ARKINSTALL John MM Pte R/11112 King's Royal Rifle Corps
ARKLAY Frederick MM+Bar Sjt 280465 4th London Regt
ARKLE Alfred MM L/Cpl 4126 10th Liverpool Regt
ARKLESS B. MM L/Cpl 19430 Royal Inniskilling Fusiliers
ARKLESS Frederick Frank MM Sjt 191449 'A' AA Bty RGA
ARKLESS J.G. MM Pte 35170 York & Lancaster Regt
ARKLESS John MM L/Cpl 1806 9th Durham Light Infantry
ARKLESS Mansfield G. MM Pte 235551 Northumberland Fusiliers
ARKSEY Albert MM+Bar Cpl 33399 11th East Yorkshire Regt KIA 6.9.18.
ARKWRIGHT Walter MM Pnr WR/26062 341 Rd Const Coy Royal Engineers
ARLISS George MM Pte 23033 1st Lincolnshire Regt
ARLISS George MM Sjt 240787 1/5th Lincolnshire Regt
ARMAN William Thomas MM Pte 12980 7th East Kent Regt
ARMER George MM Cpl 10396 2nd York & Lancaster Regt KIA 20.5.16.
ARMES Alfred Robert MM Cpl 475402 2/1st(Home Counties)Fd Amb RAMC
ARMFIELD Henry L. MM+Bar Pte 532890 15th London Regt
ARMIN Frank MM Spr 70990 Royal Engineers
ARMISTEAD M. MM Pte 235355 1st Lancashire Fusiliers
ARMITAGE Albert MM Cpl 269131 7th West Riding Regt
ARMITAGE Alfred MM Pte 3251 1/5th West Riding Regt

ARMITAGE Andrew MM Cpl 52654 RFA
ARMITAGE Daniel B. MM Cpl 17370 10th North Lancashire Regt
ARMITAGE George Oaks "MM,OStG(R)" Sjt Mechanic 77109 Workshop Detachment Tank Corps
ARMITAGE George T. MM Pte 201319 Yorkshire Light Infantry
ARMITAGE Harry MM Cpl 23478 Machine Gun Corps
ARMITAGE Herbert MM Pte 203562 5th West Riding Regt
ARMITAGE Joe MM L/Cpl 241549 5th West Riding Regt
ARMITAGE John MM Sjt 36164 A/256 Bde RFA
ARMITAGE John MM Pte 14886 Northumberland Fusiliers
ARMITAGE John James MM Gnr 73033 2 Bde RFA
ARMITAGE John William MM Sjt 30465 RAMC
ARMITAGE Percy Murray MM Pte 2218 1/9th London Regt
ARMITAGE Reuben MM Sjt 14440 11th Liverpool Regt
ARMITAGE T.W. MM Pte 18449 East Yorkshire Regt
ARMITAGE Thomas MM Gnr 66065 RGA
ARMITAGE Wilfred MM Spr 155136 Royal Engineers
ARMITAGE William MM Pte 50197 77 Fd Amb RAMC
ARMITAGE William MM Pte 308112 West Riding Regt
ARMITAGE Wright MM Pte 40879 5/6th Scottish Rifles
ARMITSTEAD Willis MM Gnr 700139 RFA
ARMITT James or Joseph MM Pte S/10045 Royal Highlanders
ARMOUR Albert V. MM L/Cpl 10254 7th East Surrey Regt
ARMOUR Alexander MM Spr 421004 Royal Engineers
ARMOUR Daniel C. MM Sjt 40231 Highland Light Infantry
ARMOUR David MM L/Cpl 9/13488 Royal Inniskilling Fusiliers
ARMOUR Hugh Weir MM L/Cpl 277400 1/7th Arg & Suth Highlanders
ARMOUR J.C. MM Pte 9739 1st Essex Regt
ARMOUR James Keith MM Pte 11463 14th Royal Highlanders
ARMOUR John L. MM Bdr 840385 RFA
ARMOUR Robert "DCM,MM" Sjt 10273 2nd Royal Scots
ARMOUR Thomas MM L/Cpl 8/12518 8th Royal Irish Rifles KIA 23.11.17.
ARMS Arthur MM Pte 200315 2nd South Staffordshire Regt
ARMSBY A. MM Pte 17721 Norfolk Regt att MGC.
ARMSDEN George S. MM L/Cpl 528015 54 Div Sig Coy Royal Engineers
ARMSON Charles MM Bdr 80240 RFA
ARMSON Percival James MM Pte 43558 12th Royal Irish Rifles
ARMSON Victor W. MM Cpl 675180 RFA
ARMSTEAD William MM Pte 52488 4th Liverpool Regt KIA 23.4.17.
ARMSTRONG Albert E. MM Pte 281994 Lancashire Fusiliers
ARMSTRONG Albert E. MM Pte C/6473 King's Royal Rifle Corps
ARMSTRONG Alexander Addison "MC,MM(18/855 Sjt)" T/2Lt 19th Northumberland Fusiliers
ARMSTRONG Alfred R. MM Pte M2/103839 Army Service Corps
ARMSTRONG Algernon Bennett MM Sjt 2866 1/24th London Regt
ARMSTRONG Andrew MM L/Cpl 9013 1/7th Royal Highlanders
ARMSTRONG Ben MM Cpl 10590 13th Royal Fusiliers
ARMSTRONG Charles MM Pte 5548 11th Middlesex Regt
ARMSTRONG Charles G. MM L/Cpl 13616 Durham Light Infantry
ARMSTRONG Edward MM Pte 13108 8th Yorkshire Regt
ARMSTRONG F. "MM,MID" Cpl L/12478 RFA
ARMSTRONG George MM Cpl 40126 Royal Engineers
ARMSTRONG George MM L/Sjt 281272 Highland Light Infantry
ARMSTRONG George MM Cpl 1453 Northumberland Fusiliers
ARMSTRONG George H. MM Pte 337499 RAMC
ARMSTRONG George N. MM Cpl 24795 20th Durham Light Infantry
ARMSTRONG George R. MM BQMS 30099 463 Bty 179 Bde RFA
ARMSTRONG George W. MM+Bar Pte 291114 1st Northumberland Fusiliers
ARMSTRONG Hamilton MM L/Cpl 371244 8th London Regt
ARMSTRONG Henry Charles "MM,CdiG(It)" Sjt 4002 2/1st HAC(Inf)
ARMSTRONG Herbert MM L/Cpl 2227 9th Highland Light Infantry
ARMSTRONG Hunter MM Cpl 63857 C/97 Bde RFA
ARMSTRONG Isaac MM+Bar Cpl 14/868 2nd York & Lancaster Regt
ARMSTRONG J. MM Pte 50249 RAMC
ARMSTRONG James "DCM,MM" Sjt 300337 1/8th Durham Light Infantry KIA 27.5.18.
ARMSTRONG James MM Pte 2580 Durham Light Infantry
ARMSTRONG James MM Pte 1504 1/6th Royal Highlanders KIA 13.11.16.
ARMSTRONG James MM L/Cpl 2636 1/6th Durham Light Infantry KIA 1.10.16.
ARMSTRONG James MM Cpl 830459 B/70 Bde RFA
ARMSTRONG James MM Sjt 4/4696 5th Connaught Rangers
ARMSTRONG James L. MM Sjt 350420 12th Highland Light Infantry
ARMSTRONG James S. MM Pte 530354 15th London Regt
ARMSTRONG James W. MM L/Cpl 128253 'B' Special Coy Royal Engineers
ARMSTRONG John MM 2nd Cpl 406461 51 Div Sig Coy Royal Engineers
ARMSTRONG John MM Cpl 39037 5th Royal Berkshire Regt
ARMSTRONG John MM Cpl 244397 RFA
ARMSTRONG John MM Gnr 36256 RFA
ARMSTRONG John MM Cpl 6594 25th Northumberland Fusiliers KIA 21.3.18.
ARMSTRONG John MM Pte 62606 RAMC
ARMSTRONG John A. MM Sjt 23489 Durham Light Infantry
ARMSTRONG John B. MM Gnr 149673 RFA
ARMSTRONG John George MM Sjt 12329 6th East Yorkshire Regt
ARMSTRONG John H. MM Pte 200346 1/4th East Yorkshire Regt
ARMSTRONG John Joseph MM L/Cpl 302062 1/8th Durham Light Infantry Died 22.8.18.
ARMSTRONG John Leslie MM Sjt 14/16175 14th Royal Irish Rifles KIA 16.8.17.
ARMSTRONG John R. MM Gnr 56686 RGA
ARMSTRONG John T. MM Cpl M/30509 1 Cav Div Supply Col Army Service Corps
ARMSTRONG John Thomas MM+Bar L/Cpl 35601 20th Liverpool Regt KIA 31.7.17.
ARMSTRONG John W. "MM,MSM" Cpl (MCDR) 149148 'G' Corps Sig Coy Royal Engineers
ARMSTRONG Johnston MM Cpl 71111 V Corps Cyclist Bn North Irish Horse
ARMSTRONG Jonathan MM L/Cpl 66293 106 Fd Coy Royal Engineers KIA 16.6.17.
ARMSTRONG Joseph Henry MM Cpl 85393 RGA
ARMSTRONG Leonard Frank MM L/Cpl 530145 1/15th London Regt
ARMSTRONG M.A. MM Pte 14922 16th Highland Light Infantry
ARMSTRONG Michael MM Pte 24046 12 Fd Amb RAMC
ARMSTRONG Norman MM Sjt 29661 1st Border Regt
ARMSTRONG Richard MM Sjt 32718 61st Bn Machine Gun Corps
ARMSTRONG Robert MM Pte 14123 Yorkshire Regt
ARMSTRONG Robert "MM,MSM" Sjt 11549 11th Royal Inniskilling Fusiliers
ARMSTRONG Robert MM Pte 2271 Manchester Regt
ARMSTRONG Robert MM L/Cpl DM2/206580 Army Service Corps
ARMSTRONG Robert E. MM Pte 13580 Border Regt
ARMSTRONG Thomas MM+Bar L/Sjt 24794 13th Durham Light Infantry
ARMSTRONG Thomas MM+Bar Pte 4297 6th Lancashire Fusiliers
ARMSTRONG Thomas MM Pte 18477 6th Yorkshire Regt
ARMSTRONG Thomas Gavin MM L/Cpl 333178 1/9th Highland Light Infantry
ARMSTRONG Thomas H. MM SM 1002 RAMC
ARMSTRONG Thomas H. MM Pte 38676 Durham Light Infantry
ARMSTRONG Thomas W. MM Sjt 24380 Yorkshire Light Infantry
ARMSTRONG William MM L/Cpl 202246 5th Lancashire Fusiliers
ARMSTRONG William MM Pte 60176 21st Manchester Regt
ARMSTRONG William MM Pte 59053 RAMC
ARMSTRONG William MM Pte 22981 7th Royal Inniskilling Fusiliers KIA 16.8.17.
ARMSTRONG William "MM,MID" CSM 3/7797 East Yorkshire Regt
ARMSTRONG William MM Dvr 20750 210 Bde RFA
ARMSTRONG William MM Sjt 9614 7/8th Royal Inniskilling Fusiliers
ARMSTRONG William MM+Bar Sjt 4284 5th Seaforth Highlanders
ARMSTRONG William MM Pte 6157 2nd Irish Guards KIA 3.5.18.
ARMSTRONG William C. MM Bdr 21218 31 Div Ammn Col RFA
ARMSTRONG William James "MM,Medaille Militaire(F)" Pte 15349 6th Dragoon Guards DOW 11.4.18.
ARNELL Frank E. MM Sjt 17550 47 Siege Bty RGA
ARNELL Frederick MM Sjt 69450 Tank Corps
ARNELL Ronald "MM,MID" Pte 204 Highland Cyclist Coy Army Cyclist Corps
ARNELL William R. MM Pte 9505 2nd East Lancashire Regt
ARNETT Francis Albert MM Dvr 118384 39 Div Ammn Col RFA
ARNEY George B.F. MM Sjt 700492 23rd London Regt
ARNFIELD George Rowland Hughes "MM,DM(B)" Sjt 75417 Royal Engineers
ARNFIELD Thomas MM L/Sjt 6207 16th Manchester Regt
ARNISON Joseph MM+Bar L/Cpl 27643 Border Regt
ARNISON Ralph Naters MM Sjt M2/132096 60 MT Coy Army Service Corps
ARNOLD A. MM Sjt 10354 2nd Scottish Rifles
ARNOLD Arthur MM Pte 44243 29th Bn Machine Gun Corps

ARNOLD Arthur MM Pte S/4527 13th Rifle Brigade
ARNOLD Arthur Edward "MC,MM(757 Cpl)" 2Lt 416 Fd Coy Royal Engineers KIA 13.10.18.
ARNOLD Bernard "DCM,MM" CQMS 16529 Lincolnshire Regt
ARNOLD Bernard P. MM Sjt 39310 49 Fd Amb RAMC
ARNOLD C.H MM Pte 200445 5th Notts & Derby Regt
ARNOLD Charles E. MM Sjt 207836 Royal Engineers
ARNOLD D. MM L/Cpl 403582 RAMC
ARNOLD Edmund MM Sjt R/4624 King's Royal Rifle Corps
ARNOLD Edward V. MM Pte 21674 Hampshire Regt
ARNOLD EdwardM. MM Pte 235994 4th York & Lancaster Regt
ARNOLD Edwin MM Pte 49683 6th Liverpool Regt
ARNOLD Esau W. MM Pte 15342 Suffolk Regt
ARNOLD Frank MM Pte 35896 1/1st Hertfordshire Regt
ARNOLD Frank S. MM Pte 43305 Machine Gun Corps
ARNOLD Frank T. MM Sjt 69972 Royal Engineers
ARNOLD Frederick MM Sjt 41158 Royal Irish Rifles
ARNOLD Frederick Arthur MM Cpl 47902 1/1(North Midland)Bde RGA DOW 7.7.17.
ARNOLD Frederick C. MM Cpl 90227 32nd Bn Machine Gun Corps
ARNOLD Frederick W. MM Pte M2/180779 30 Mot Amb Convoy Army Service Corps
ARNOLD Frederick W. MM Cpl 127581 Signal Service Royal Engineers
ARNOLD G. MM L/Cpl 491461 London Regt
ARNOLD George MM Sjt 1293 1/9th London Regt
ARNOLD George MM Pte 240130 1/5th Royal Sussex Regt
ARNOLD George C. MM L/Cpl 266411 2/7th West Yorkshire Regt
ARNOLD George H. MM L/Cpl 498464 Royal Engineers
ARNOLD George W. MM Pte R/21068 King's Royal Rifle Corps
ARNOLD Harold MM Pte 119595 Machine Gun Corps
ARNOLD Harry J. MM Cpl T1/1127 Army Service Corps
ARNOLD Henry A. MM Sjt M/33971 Army Service Corps
ARNOLD Herbert B. MM Pte 241233 Middlesex Regt
ARNOLD Horace MM Pte 682665 2/22nd London Regt
ARNOLD Hubert MM+Bar Sjt 40176 62 Fd Coy Royal Engineers
ARNOLD James MM Pte 20436 11th Suffolk Regt KIA 12.9.17.
ARNOLD James Henry MM Gnr 83748 178 Siege Bty RGA
ARNOLD John W. MM Pte S/733 10th Royal West Surrey Regt
ARNOLD John W. MM Pte R/12672 King's Royal Rifle Corps
ARNOLD Levi F. MM Cpl 31447 4th Hampshire Regt
ARNOLD Nigel Stephen MM 2nd Cpl 49574 Royal Engineers
ARNOLD Percy O. MM Pte 26698 South Wales Borderers
ARNOLD Philip MM Pte DM2/224296 91 Siege Bty Ammn Col Army Service Corps
ARNOLD Richard MM L/Cpl 8268 2nd (att 1st?) Worcestershire Regt
ARNOLD Richard Frederick MM Sjt 48765 2 Bde RFA
ARNOLD Richard J. MM L/Cpl 1148 7th Royal West Kent Regt
ARNOLD Robert MM Sjt 23452 Royal Berkshire Regt
ARNOLD Robert Henry MM Pte 25963 10th West Riding Regt
ARNOLD S. MM Pte 421292 RAMC
ARNOLD Stanley MM Sjt 531389 1/15th London Regt
ARNOLD Terry MM Pte 202288 Somerset Light Infantry
ARNOLD Victor A. MM Pte 242454 West Riding Regt
ARNOLD Walter "DCM,MM" Sjt 840329 D/240 Bde RFA
ARNOLD Walter MM Pte 35932 5th Border Regt
ARNOLD Walter E. MM Sjt 10403 6th Somerset Light Infantry
ARNOLD William MM Pte 130173 6th Bn Machine Gun Corps DOW 25.10.18.
ARNOLD William Arthur James MM Pte 200063 8th Norfolk Regt
ARNOLD William C. MM Sjt 014022 Army Ordnance Corps
ARNOLD William E. MM Pte 27780 Gloucestershire Regt
ARNOLD William H.W. MM Pte 40368 Seaforth Highlanders
ARNOLD William J. MM Sjt 10112 7th South Staffordshire Regt
ARNOLD William J. MM Pte 65313 RAMC
ARNOPP William G. MM Pte 4942 6th Royal Irish Rifles
ARNOTT James C. MM Pte 291827 1/7th Royal Highlanders
ARNOTT John MM Pte 87640 22nd Northumberland Fusiliers
ARNOTT John C. MM Cpl 19538 Royal Welsh Fusiliers
ARNOTT Robert MM Pte 73671 27 Fd Amb RAMC
ARNOTT Robert "MM,MID" Pte 3973 Scots Guards
ARNOTT Thomas Henry MM(1599 Cpl) Lt 5th Border Regt Died 18.3.21
ARNOTT William "MM,Oleo(B)" Sjt 15237 Machine Gun Corps
ARNOUP Alfred MM L/Cpl 10232 1st Northamptonshire Regt
ARNSBY Arthur Ernest MM Sjt 19885 11 Bde RFA
ARON Charles J. MM+Bar Pte G/49399 Royal Fusiliers
ARRAND Thomas William MM Dvr 81902 C/180 Bde RFA
ARRANDALE Jesse MM Pte 17353 Royal Lancaster Regt
ARRANDALE Samuel Richardson MM Sjt 7194 16th Manchester Regt
ARRIDGE Herbert Chadwick MM Pte 12/24 12th York & Lancaster Regt
ARRIS Robert MM Pte 17000 8th Northumberland Fusiliers
ARROW Thomas MM Pte 34852 1st Essex Regt
ARROWSMITH Donald MM Sjt 128158 RGA
ARROWSMITH Ernest MM Cpl 18360 7th East Lancashire Regt
ARROWSMITH Fred MM L/Sjt 9417 1st Manchester Regt
ARROWSMITH Jack Clifford MM Pte 16361 5th Shropshire Light Infantry DOW 8.9.17.
ARROWSMITH Joseph MM Pte 24679 2nd Grenadier Guards KIA 5.5.18.
ARROWSMITH Thomas MM Pte 72015 5th Devonshire Regt
ARSCOTT Harold W. MM CQMS 15083 8th Somerset Light Infantry
ARSCOTT Thomas MM Cpl R/703 12th King's Royal Rifle Corps
ARTER Alfred J. MM Gnr 166143 RGA
ARTER Charles R.McK. MM Sjt 3012 8th Gloucestershire Regt
ARTER Walter MM Pte 14507 Royal Berkshire Regt
ARTHEY William H. MM Sjt 51625 32 Bde RFA
ARTHOR Samuel R. MM Pte 8922 Irish Guards
ARTHUR Alexander "MC,MM(1730 Pte)" 2Lt 25th Northumberland Fusiliers DOW 1.10.18.
ARTHUR Alexander J.W. MM Sjt 32716 RGA
ARTHUR Geoffrey MM Cpl 157323 25th Bn Machine Gun Corps
ARTHUR George MM Pte 295469 12th Somerset Light Infantry
ARTHUR George H. MM Pte 89021 5 Fd Amb RAMC
ARTHUR John MM Dvr 82572 RFA
ARTHUR M. MM Sjt 98239 Royal Engineers
ARTHUR Philip N. MM Gnr 76797 RGA
ARTHUR Richard "DCM,MM" CQMS 4/12281 4th South Wales Borderers
ARTHUR Ronald JamesJ. MM Pte 530944 1/15th London Regt
ARTHUR William MM Pte 204973 2nd Seaforth Highlanders
ARTHUR William MM Pte 40911 RAMC
ARTHUR William Henry MM Cpl 17345 6th Yorkshire Regt
ARTHUR William J. MM Pte 12159 9th Scottish Rifles
ARTHURS Charles A. MM Pte 21292 4th Gloucestershire Regt
ARTHURS Frederick C. MM Gnr 69463 Tank Corps
ARTHURTON Reginald MM Sjt 84895 Royal Engineers
ARTHY Henry J. MM Pte 44236 7/8th Royal Inniskilling Fusiliers
ARTINGSTOLL Joseph MM+Bar L/Cpl 28634 Royal Engineers
ARTLEY Harold MM L/Cpl 40900 1st Norfolk Regt
ARUNDEL James MM+Bar Sjt S/3603 Royal Highlanders
ARUNDEL John W. MM Cpl 775939 Y/62 Med TM Bty RFA
ARUNDEL Tom MM Pte 20085 8th Yorkshire Light Infantry
ARUNDEL William MM Pte 14008 8th Royal Scots Fusiliers
ARUNDELL Albert Henry MM Pte 11229 1st Royal West Kent Regt DOW 18.4.18.
ASBRIDGE Charles MM Sjt 78734 32 Airline Section Royal Engineers
ASBURY Gilbert MM Cpl 44417 2 Fd Amb RAMC
ASBY Bert MM Sjt 9539 1st Yorkshire Light Infantry
ASCROFT Robert MM Pte 200692 North Lancashire Regt
ASH A. MM Cpl 1092 RFA
ASH Alfred MM Pte 8448 1st Scottish Rifles
ASH Ernest T. MM L/Cpl 10 GMGR
ASH Frank MM Gnr 48646 RGA
ASH Frederick MM Pte 2728 1/6th Gloucestershire Regt DOW 15.2.17.
ASH G. MM Pte Stk606 10th Royal Fusiliers
ASH George W. MM+Bar CSM 20236 Hampshire Regt
ASH Gilbert D. MM Cpl (MCDR) 74566 Royal Engineers
ASH Henry William MM Sjt 11686 1st Worcestershire Regt
ASH Horace William MM Cpl 245557 Royal Engineers
ASH J.C. MM Pte 241277 Notts & Derby Regt
ASH John MM Gnr 145351 D/36 Bde RFA
ASH Lionel M. MM Pte 11105 1st Scottish Rifles
ASH Robert MM Gnr 770011 D/250 Bde RFA
ASH Sidney MM Gnr L/23195 34 Div Ammn Col Royal Artillery
ASH Sidney Charles MM Pte 34718 2/4th West Riding Regt
ASH William MM L/Cpl 470939 Royal Engineers
ASHALL William MM Pte 147660 37th Bn Machine Gun Corps
ASHARD Frederick MM L/Cpl 325608 1/9th Durham Light Infantry
ASHARD George Leonard MM Gnr 10461 123 Bde RFA KIA 23.9.18.
ASHBEE Charles F. "MM,MSM" L/Sjt 53100 38 Fd Amb RAMC
ASHBOLT William E. MM Pte 4761 17th London Regt
ASHBRIDGE John MM Sjt 30129 RAMC
ASHBRIDGE John W. MM L/Cpl 240515 7th Border Regt

ASHBROOK Wilfred MM Pte 114938 86 Coy Machine Gun Corps Died 10.12.17.
ASHBROOK William Chrimes MM Sjt 10900 10th Cheshire Regt DOW 18.4.17.
ASHBURN Albert E. MM Pte 200437 1/4th Royal Lancaster Regt
ASHBY Alfred MM Pte 45429 Lancashire Fusiliers
ASHBY Arthur MM Sjt R/12922 King's Royal Rifle Corps
ASHBY Bertram George MM Sjt 12539 5th Northamptonshire Regt
ASHBY Charles L. MM Cpl 11712 16th King's Royal Rifle Corps
ASHBY Charles M. MM Gnr 755115 RFA
ASHBY Cybert T. MM Pte 14666 3rd Dragoon Guards
ASHBY Douglas F. MM L/Cpl 300430 5th London Regt
ASHBY Fred "DCM,MM" CSM G/15767 6th East Kent Regt
ASHBY Fred MM Pte 40813 2nd Bedfordshire Regt
ASHBY Frederick MM Pte 202745 2nd London Regt
ASHBY Herbert MM Pte 43003 Northamptonshire Regt
ASHBY Herbert MM Pte 1093 13th King's Royal Rifle Corps
ASHBY James MM Gnr 178930 A/230 Bde RFA
ASHBY John W. MM Pte 11099 Coldstream Guards
ASHBY John W. MM Gnr 65646 RGA
ASHBY Sydney MM 2nd Cpl 542167 457 Fd Coy Royal Engineers
ASHBY Sydney MM Sjt 506 Royal Flying Corps
ASHBY Thomas MM L/Cpl 9067 1st Royal Warwickshire Regt
ASHBY Walter John MM Spr 142229 First Army Sig Coy Royal Engineers
ASHCROFT Albert MM Bdr 53053 26 Bde RFA
ASHCROFT Edgar H. MM Sjt 15362 Liverpool Regt
ASHCROFT Ernest MM Sjt 351125 2nd Manchester Regt
ASHCROFT Frank MM Pte 29327 1st Royal Lancaster Regt
ASHCROFT George MM Pte 13711 1/5th North Lancashire Regt KIA 30.11.17.
ASHCROFT J. MM Sjt 16382 1st Grenadier Guards
ASHCROFT J. MM Pte 341059 64 Fd Amb RAMC
ASHCROFT James MM Cpl 25896 10th Royal Warwickshire Regt
ASHCROFT James MM Cpl 34775 8th York & Lancaster Regt KIA 18.9.17.
ASHCROFT John K. MM Dvr 690318 D/290 Bde RFA
ASHCROFT Joseph MM L/Cpl 242994 1/5th Royal Lancaster Regt KIA 20.9.17.
ASHCROFT Joseph J. MM Sjt 356346 10th Liverpool Regt
ASHCROFT Mark MM Spr 237675 25 Div Sig Coy Royal Engineers
ASHCROFT R. MM Pte 14531 Royal Lancaster Regt
ASHCROFT Richard MM Cpl 312090 39 Div Sig Coy Royal Engineers
ASHCROFT Samuel MM Cpl 50411 Labour Corps
ASHCROFT Thomas "MM,MMV(It)" Pte 201197 1/4th Gloucestershire Regt
ASHCROFT William MM L/Cpl 8835 2nd East Lancashire Regt
ASHDOWN Alfred E. MM Gnr 76206 MGC(Heavy Branch)
ASHDOWN Alfred George MM Pte 532275 15th London Regt
ASHDOWN Clifford MM Pte 5855 1st East Kent Regt
ASHDOWN Ernest A. MM L/Cpl 50978 1st Middlesex Regt
ASHDOWN Henry MM L/Cpl M/274442 Army Service Corps
ASHDOWN Herbert John MM+Bar Pte 31039 1st Northamptonshire Regt
ASHE Edward MM Pte 2254 1st Royal Irish Rifles
ASHE Henry MM Sjt 59956 D/87 Bde RFA
ASHE Robert MM Sjt 139732 Royal Engineers
ASHE William MM L/Sjt 23284 3rd Grenadier Guards
ASHELFORD T.E. MM L/Cpl 40128 10th Essex Regt
ASHENDEN Walter MM Sjt 17659 1st East Surrey Regt
ASHFIELD Joseph MM Gnr 170596 499 Siege Bty RGA
ASHFIELD Ralph MM L/Cpl 238048 9th West Riding Regt KIA 12.10.18.
ASHFIELD William Arthur MM Pte R/50040 16th King's Royal Rifle Corps KIA 12.10.18.
ASHFORD C. MM L/Cpl 8587 Essex Regt
ASHFORD Charles MM Pte 9337 Worcestershire Regt
ASHFORD Frederick H. MM Pte 143369 61st Bn Machine Gun Corps
ASHFORD George Henry MM Sjt 35098 194 Siege Bty RGA Real name Bashford.
ASHFORD Ralph MM Cpl 4197 13th Royal Sussex Regt
ASHFORD Thomas MM+Bar Sjt 11153 Royal Irish Fusiliers
ASHFORD Thomas H. MM Pte 40590 15th Royal Warwickshire Regt
ASHFORD Walter Augustus MM Sjt 138 11th Royal Sussex Regt KIA 3.4.18
ASHLEY Albert Edward "MM,MID" L/Sjt 13210 7th East Yorkshire Regt KIA 10.7.16.
ASHLEY Arthur MM Sjt Fitter 705841 B/102 Bde RFA Died 18.11.17.
ASHLEY Evelyn MM Sjt 95874 D/46 Bde RFA
ASHLEY Harry MM Pte 31964 1/4th Shropshire Light Infantry
ASHLEY Henry MM Pte 606 10th Cheshire Regt
ASHLEY Henry MM Sjt 92733 Royal Engineers
ASHLEY Horace MM Cpl 138509 19th Bn Machine Gun Corps
ASHLEY James MM Sjt 4996 Lancashire Fusiliers
ASHLEY James MM Pte 40932 10th Northumberland Fusiliers
ASHLEY James H. MM Sjt 305893 1/8th att 15th Lancashire Fusiliers
ASHLEY Jesse MM Cpl 7518 1st Leicestershire Regt
ASHLEY Peter MM Dvr 745423 15 Bde RHA
ASHLEY Thomas MM Pte 40576 Manchester Regt
ASHLEY William MM L/Cpl 15507 3rd Coldstream Guards
ASHLIN David George MM Cpl 2372 1/2(N Midland)Fd Amb RAMC
ASHMAN Charles J. MM Pte 33703 RAMC
ASHMAN Frank W. MM Cpl 29992 1st Worcestershire Regt
ASHMAN Gilbert Alfred MM Cpl 6424 9th Royal Fusiliers DOW 28.5.17.
ASHMAN James MM Pte 201483 2/7th Worcestershire Regt
ASHMAN W.F. MM Sjt TT/0192 Army Veterinary Corps
ASHMAN William H. MM L/Cpl 504448 Royal Engineers
ASHMENT Frederick MM Sjt M2/074398 Army Service Corps
ASHMOLE Walter MM L/Cpl 22623 2nd Worcestershire Regt
ASHMORE Arthur H. MM Pte 230256 2nd London Regt
ASHMORE George MM Cpl 9/14458 9th Leicestershire Regt KIA 25.9.16.
ASHMORE James MM Pte 245251 11th Manchester Regt
ASHMORE Richard MM Sjt 66917 RFA
ASHMORE Sidney MM Pte 45520 4th King's Royal Rifle Corps
ASHMORE Thomas "DCM,MM" Sjt 40508 48 Fd Amb RAMC
ASHMORE Thomas A. MM L/Cpl 3/3678 York & Lancaster Regt
ASHMORE Walter MM L/Cpl R/1738 King's Royal Rifle Corps
ASHMORE William MM Spr 854 456 Fd Coy Royal Engineers KIA 17.4.18.
ASHPLANT George MM L/Cpl 1938 Oxf & Bucks Light Infantry
ASHPOLE George W. MM Sjt 203413 6th Royal Warwickshire Regt
ASHTON Arthur W. MM Pte 72057 133 Fd Amb RAMC
ASHTON Benjamin MM Dvr 5389 RFA
ASHTON Bertram MM Gnr 997 RFA
ASHTON Charles MM Cpl 99915 7 Div Ammn Col RFA
ASHTON Charles L. MM Sjt 202561 2nd South Lancashire Regt
ASHTON Clarence H. MM Bdr 705414 RFA
ASHTON Ernest MM Sjt 50672 110 Bty 24 Bde RFA
ASHTON Evan W. MM Dvr 28782 RFA
ASHTON George MM L/Cpl 15781 King's Own Scottish Borderers
ASHTON Gilbert H.L. MM Pte 30274 1st Devonshire Regt
ASHTON Harold P. "DCM,MM" CSM 23133 18 Div Sig Coy Royal Engineers
ASHTON Harvey MM CSM 24821 10th Lancashire Fusiliers
ASHTON Jack MM Pte 25944 10th Royal West Surrey Regt
ASHTON James MM Pte 142316 Machine Gun Corps
ASHTON James MM Gnr Fitter 930011 B/281 Bde RFA
ASHTON James MM Pte 19410 11th Royal Scots KIA 12.10.17.
ASHTON John MM Pte S/27847 Rifle Brigade
ASHTON John H. "MM,MSM" Sjt 354180 1/3rd(East Lancashire)Fd Amb RAMC
ASHTON John H.W. MM Pnr 128351 Royal Engineers
ASHTON John Hubert MM Sjt P904 16th Rifle Brigade KIA 21.3.18.
ASHTON Mark Reginald MM Cpl 35295 15 Coy Machine Gun Corps
ASHTON Oswald MM Sjt 6003 1/5th East Kent Regt
ASHTON Percy MM Sjt 27190 Northamptonshire Regt
ASHTON Percy H. MM Sjt 42613 RFA
ASHTON R. MM L/Cpl P/14787 Military Foot Police
ASHTON R.F. MM Pte 240817 Lincolnshire Regt
ASHTON Reginald MM Sjt 432505 Royal Engineers
ASHTON Robert MM Gnr 40694 RFA
ASHTON Samuel MM Sjt 13564 D/77 Bde RFA
ASHTON Thomas MM Sjt 44932 15th Bn Machine Gun Corps
ASHTON Thomas MM L/Cpl 12669 7th North Lancashire Regt
ASHTON William MM Sjt 3582 7th Royal Lancaster Regt
ASHTON William MM Pte 106789 RAMC
ASHTON William MM Pte 10685 5th Shropshire Light Infantry
ASHTON William MM Pte 12896 20th Manchester Regt
ASHTON-SHARPE Francis R. MM+Bar L/Cpl 60086 Royal Fusiliers
ASHURST Ernest MM Pte 18943 19th Lancashire Fusiliers
ASHURST Robert MM+Bar Sjt 681911 RFA
ASHURST Thomas MM Bdr 34252 RFA
ASHURST William MM L/Bdr 50537 25 Hy Bty RGA
ASHURST William MM Pte 74577 10th Manchester Regt

ASHURST William Robert MM Pte 17865 7th North Lancashire Regt
ASHWELL James "DCM,MM" Sjt 24430 A/124 Bde RFA DOW 20.10.17.
ASHWELL William Edwin MM+Bar Sjt G/855 7th East Kent Regt
ASHWORTH Albert MM Pte 14902 Coldstream Guards
ASHWORTH Arthur MM Pte 36373 Lancashire Fusiliers
ASHWORTH Ben "MM,CG(F)" L/Bdr 18249 B/170 Bde RFA
ASHWORTH Bert MM Pte 350246 9th Manchester Regt
ASHWORTH Edward MM Cpl 22749 Machine Gun Corps
ASHWORTH Frank MM Cpl 54494 16th Royal Welsh Fusiliers
ASHWORTH Frank Martin MM Pte 10856 Shropshire Light Infantry
ASHWORTH Harry MM Sjt 280681 Lancashire Fusiliers
ASHWORTH Harry MM Pte 243859 1/5th North Lancashire Regt
ASHWORTH Henry T. MM Spr 72327 Royal Engineers
ASHWORTH James "DCM,MM" CSM 14051 24th Manchester Regt
ASHWORTH Jesse MM Pte 282241 15th Lancashire Fusiliers
ASHWORTH John MM L/Cpl 18748 Machine Gun Corps
ASHWORTH John MM Dvr 109928 RFA
ASHWORTH John MM Cpl 18070 RFA
ASHWORTH John MM Sjt 19489 2nd Lancashire Fusiliers
ASHWORTH John MM Sjt 7276 Middlesex Regt
ASHWORTH John I. MM L/Sjt 17825 2nd Grenadier Guards
ASHWORTH John S. MM L/Cpl 5689 2nd Suffolk Regt
ASHWORTH Jordan MM Cpl 440359 Royal Engineers
ASHWORTH Joseph MM Sjt 197882 47 Div Sig Coy Royal Engineers
ASHWORTH Joseph MM Pte 49947 Manchester Regt
ASHWORTH Norman "MM,MSM" Sjt 350097 RAMC
ASHWORTH Ralph MM Pte 36545 Lancashire Fusiliers
ASHWORTH Richard MM Pte 101396 RAMC
ASHWORTH Richard MM Dvr 188805 A/242 Bde RFA
ASHWORTH Richard H. "MM,MID" L/Cpl 20432 3rd Grenadier Guards
ASHWORTH Ronald MM Spr 442410 427 Fd Coy Royal Engineers
ASHWORTH Thomas B. MM Pte 7053 Royal Fusiliers
ASHWORTH Tom "DCM,MM" L/Sjt 17775 19th Liverpool Regt
ASHWORTH Walter "DCM,MM" Sjt 9743 1st Liverpool Regt
ASHWORTH Wilfred MM+Bar Sjt 241003 1st Lancashire Fusiliers
ASHWORTH William MM Cpl 66921 8th Lancashire Fusiliers
ASHWORTH William MM Dvr 750141 RFA
ASHWORTH William MM Sjt 240451 1/5th North Lancashire Regt DOW 21.2.18.
ASHWORTH William R. MM Sjt 43623 Manchester Regt
ASHWORTH William Walker MM Pte 269243 1/7th Liverpool Regt
ASKER John Henry MM Pte 201166 Royal Berkshire Regt
ASKEW A. MM Sjt 223 Royal Engineers
ASKEW Alfred MM Pte 43012 1st Bedfordshire Regt
ASKEW Arthur George MM L/Bdr 153189 283 Siege Bty RGA
ASKEW Frank L. MM Bdr 34151 236 Siege Bty RGA
ASKEW George MM Sjt 11084 2nd Notts & Derby Regt
ASKEW Harold MM Sjt P781 Military Mounted Police
ASKEW James MM Dvr 680503 RFA
ASKEW James W. MM Cpl 241181 7th Border Regt
ASKEW John MM Pte 18418 Grenadier Guards
ASKEW Joseph MM Sjt 21256 Durham Light Infantry
ASKEW Luther MM Cpl 713 247 Bde RFA
ASKEW Robert A. MM Pte M2/137215 Army Service Corps
ASKEW William MM Spr 132771 Royal Engineers
ASKEY Isaac MM+Bar Pte 21851 4th Grenadier Guards
ASKEY Thomas William MM Gnr 55123 22 Coy (sic) RGA
ASKEY William MM BSM 23030 120 Siege Bty RGA
ASKHAM Percy S. MM Sjt 200949 4th York & Lancaster Regt
ASKHAM William MM Sjt 19550 5th Dragoon Guards
ASKWITH Frank MM Pte 200494 Yorkshire Regt
ASLATT George Colson MM Pte 18057 10th att 13th Cheshire Regt DOW 17.1.17.
ASLATT Percy J. MM Pte 2245 RAMC
ASLETT Harry MM Pte 27590 Machine Gun Corps
ASLIN John Robert MM Pte Z/969 12th Rifle Brigade KIA 20.11.17.
ASLING Edward MM L/Cpl 94309 30th Bn Machine Gun Corps
ASPDEN Arthur MM Sjt R/34839 7th King's Royal Rifle Corps Died 21.3.18.
ASPDEN Harry MM Pte 16759 Border Regt Died 20.4.18.
ASPDEN James MM Sjt 202881 4th North Lancashire Regt
ASPDEN James MM Sjt 5/13241 7th South Wales Borderers
ASPDEN John Rawstorne MM Sjt 442360 432 Fd Coy Royal Engineers
ASPDEN John Richard MM Cpl 57207 8th Rifle Brigade KIA 3.10.16.
ASPDEN John T. MM Sjt 6546 7th Border Regt
ASPDEN Ronald William MM L/Cpl 2363 6th London Regt DOW 8.8.17.
ASPEY James MM L/Sjt 19979 12th Highland Light Infantry
ASPEY Percy MM CQMS 3/1028 2nd Yorkshire Light Infantry
ASPIN Joseph "MM,CG(F)" Cpl 42434 18th Durham Light Infantry
ASPIN Richard G. MM Pte 6876 Royal West Surrey Regt
ASPINALL Charles MM+Bar Bdr 776689 RFA
ASPINALL F. MM Pte 47494 Northumberland Fusiliers
ASPINALL Fred MM+Bar Sjt 1037 1st Welsh Guards
ASPINALL George R. MM Pte 18675 Shropshire Light Infantry
ASPINALL George R. MM Pte 27971 Machine Gun Corps
ASPINALL Giles MM Cpl 242532 4/5th North Lancashire Regt KIA 26.10.17.
ASPINALL Harry MM+Bar Pte 13802 15th Cheshire Regt
ASPINALL Herbert MM Dvr 232856 B/232 Bde RFA
ASPINALL Herbert MM+Bar Sjt 230471 2nd London Regt Died 15.2.19.
ASPINALL John MM Pte 32737 7th Border Regt
ASPINALL John MM Bdr L/8449 RFA
ASPINALL John C. MM Gnr 71518 RFA
ASPINALL Leonard MM Gnr 78016 9th Bn Tank Corps
ASPINALL Philip MM Cpl 11448 6th Border Regt
ASPINALL William MM Spr 360018 25 Div Sig Coy Royal Engineers
ASPINWALL James MM Sjt 16/916 16th Northumberland Fusiliers
ASPINWALL Reginald MM+Bar Cpl 265836 4th Liverpool Regt
ASPLAND William MM Pte 3563 1st King's Royal Rifle Corps
ASQUITH Ernest MM Gnr 776210 245 Bde RFA
ASQUITH Herbert O.K. MM Pte 241669 1/5th West Riding Regt
ASQUITH Horace MM Spr 100335 Royal Engineers
ASQUITH Horace Oswald. MM L/Cpl 15662 9th York & Lancaster Regt
ASQUITH Samuel MM Dvr 34429 RFA
ASQUITH Stanley MM Cpl 16221 Liverpool Regt
ASTBURY A. MM Pte 46636 North Staffordshire Regt
ASTBURY Arthur "MM,MID" Sjt 1169 1st Lancashire Fusiliers
ASTBURY James MM Pte R/13157 2nd King's Royal Rifle Corps Died 21.12.18.
ASTILL John MM Pte 40568 Leicestershire Regt
ASTILL Sydney E. MM Sjt 49142 Royal Engineers
ASTIN Albert "DCM,MM" CSM 7851 2nd & 13th Royal Welsh Fusiliers
ASTIN Hubert MM Pte 7338 East Lancashire Regt
ASTIN James A. MM Pte 203654 1st Lancashire Fusiliers
ASTINS Frank Edward MM Cpl 574377 1/17th London Regt
ASTLE Arthur Henry MM Pte 10688 1st Notts & Derby Regt
ASTLES John "MM,MIDx2" Sjt 11040 Worcestershire Regt
ASTLEY B. MM Pte 40200 Manchester Regt
ASTLEY Charles Raymond MM Sjt 10263 1st Welsh Regt
ASTLEY John S. "DCM,MM,MID" Pte 290188 1/7th Royal Welsh Fusiliers
ASTON Albert MM L/Cpl 240468 1/5th Devonshire Regt
ASTON Frederick Charles MM Cpl 200920 Worcestershire Regt
ASTON George MM Sjt Farrier 36533 35 Bty 22 Bde RFA
ASTON Harry MM Sjt 752 3 Bty 2(S Midland)Bde RFA
ASTON Howard M. MM Spr 74222 Royal Engineers
ASTON Samuel MM Sjt 13754 8th North Staffordshire Regt
ASTON T. MM Sjt 241388 North Lancashire Regt
ASTON Thomas MM Dvr 31956 RFA
ASTON Verney "DCM,MM" Sjt 240536 Northumberland Fusiliers
ASTON William H. MM Cpl 12817 1st Worcestershire Regt
ASTRIDGE Arthur Frederick "MM,CG(B)" Bdr 36923 405 Siege Bty RGA
ATACK Oscar "MM,MSM" Sjt 795438 49 Div Ammn Col RFA
ATACK William S. MM Pte 50221 RAMC
ATCHERLEY Eric G. MM+Bar Sjt 48160 Royal Engineers
ATCHISON Robert W. MM Pte 12024 Northumberland Fusiliers
ATHA Fred MM L/Cpl 305949 8th West Yorkshire Regt
ATHA Joseph A. MM Drummer 47900 2nd Welsh Regt
ATHAY George Henry MM Sjt 45592 2nd Bn Machine Gun Corps
ATHERTON Albert "MM,MID" Pte 15451 8th North Lancashire Regt
ATHERTON Albert MM L/Cpl 21132 South Lancashire Regt
ATHERTON Edward MM L/Cpl 251185 Manchester Regt
ATHERTON Henry MM Sjt 12906 77 Bde RFA DOW 13.7.17.
ATHERTON Henry P. MM Cpl 10076 1st Cheshire Regt
ATHERTON Hugh MM Pte 17094 2nd Lancashire Fusiliers
ATHERTON John MM Pte 582 2nd South Lancashire Regt
ATHERTON John MM Cpl 14489 9th North Lancashire Regt
ATHERTON John MM Pte 6/17111 6th South Wales Borderers
ATHERTON John MM Pte 10/12112 Border Regt
ATHERTON Joseph MM Sjt 350009 9th Manchester Regt

ATHERTON Joseph MM+Bar Cpl 200880 North Lancashire Regt
ATHERTON Luke MM Sjt 351092 15th Essex Regt
ATHERTON Moses MM Pte 63713 105 Fd Amb RAMC
ATHERTON Richard Constantine MM Sjt 7674 2nd Royal Welsh Fusiliers AKA Hargreaves.
ATHERTON Robert MM Pte 8519 1st Liverpool Regt
ATHERTON Sydney E. MM Pte 240391 1/5th Cheshire Regt
ATHERTON William MM+Bar Spr 432151 55 Div Sig Coy Royal Engineers
ATHEY John MM Pte 23/854 8th Northumberland Fusiliers
ATHORN James MM Sjt 3/10091 21st West Yorkshire Regt
ATHY Thomas MM Pte 4590 Leinster Regt
ATKEY W. "DCM,MM" CSM 9008 2nd Hampshire Regt
ATKIN Alfred MM Sjt 242073 1/5th Seaforth Highlanders KIA 12.10.18.
ATKIN Arnold F. MM Pte 21674 York & Lancaster Regt
ATKIN Frank MM Cpl 11682 2nd King's Own Scottish Borderers
ATKIN George MM Gnr 36375 RFA
ATKIN Herbert MM Pte 201560 East Yorkshire Regt
ATKIN James W. MM Cpl 22510 East Yorkshire Regt
ATKIN Joseph W. MM Pte 23034 9th Notts & Derby Regt
ATKIN Walter MM Pte 5327 Leinster Regt
ATKIN William Henry MM Sjt 43296 87 Fd Coy Royal Engineers DOW 5.4.18.
ATKINS Alfred MM Bdr 26145 RGA
ATKINS Alfred T. MM L/Cpl 22400 7th Norfolk Regt
ATKINS Archibald MM Cpl 204789 2nd London Regt
ATKINS Archie MM Spr 164445 Royal Engineers
ATKINS Arthur MM Pte 28083 Bedfordshire Regt
ATKINS Arthur S. MM+Bar Spr 554341 12 Fd Coy Royal Engineers
ATKINS Benjamin MM+Bar Bdr 42842 RFA
ATKINS Bertie MM L/Sjt 43461 9th Royal Irish Fusiliers
ATKINS Charles C. MM Sjt 3417 Gloucestershire Regt
ATKINS Charles E. MM Sjt 41850 Royal Engineers
ATKINS Dan "DCM,MM" Pte 22506 2/4th West Riding Regt
ATKINS Dennis MM Pte 43203 5 Fd Amb RAMC
ATKINS Edward MM Sjt 9488 2nd East Yorkshire Regt
ATKINS Ernest MM+Bar Sjt 207431 Signal Service Royal Engineers
ATKINS Ernest F. MM L/Cpl 18931 2nd Bedfordshire Regt
ATKINS F.A.V. MM Pte 11675 6th Duke of Cornwall's LI
ATKINS Frederick MM Pte 81717 25th Bn Machine Gun Corps
ATKINS Frederick H. MM L/Cpl 200790 Oxf & Bucks Light Infantry
ATKINS Frederick W. MM Pte R/16672 10th King's Royal Rifle Corps
ATKINS G.T. "MM,MID" Pte 8088 1st Essex Regt
ATKINS George "MM,MID" Pte 12905 2nd Worcestershire Regt
ATKINS George A. MM Pte 1994 RAMC
ATKINS James A. MM Pte 307691 West Riding Regt
ATKINS John MM Pte 51742 6th Liverpool Regt
ATKINS John Thomas Berridge MM Pte 11013 3rd Coldstream Guards
ATKINS Joseph MM Spr 71201 Royal Engineers
ATKINS Joseph H. MM Sjt 390890 1/9th London Regt
ATKINS Reginald MM Cpl 10047 2nd Bedfordshire Regt
ATKINS Richard Edward MM Pre 22815 12th Suffolk Regt KIA 12.4.18.
ATKINS Thomas MM Spr 83478 30 Div Sig Coy Royal Engineers
ATKINS Thomas MM Sjt 7630 1st North Staffordshire Regt
ATKINS Thomas MM Dvr 810173 RFA
ATKINS Thomas E. MM Pte 277133 9th Durham Light Infantry
ATKINS W. MM Sjt 8983 2nd Worcestershire Regt
ATKINS Walter MM L/Cpl 13388 8th Norfolk Regt
ATKINS William MM L/Cpl 492249 Royal Engineers
ATKINS William C. MM 2nd Cpl 140907 234 Fd Coy Royal Engineers
ATKINS William H. MM CSM 8749 1st Devonshire Regt
ATKINS William N. MM L/Sjt 11891 1st Middlesex Regt
ATKINSON Alexander B. MM L/Cpl 10330 8/10th Gordon Highlanders
ATKINSON Alfred MM L/Cpl 1603 1/4th Yorkshire Regt
ATKINSON Alfred P. MM Sjt 21287 1st Northumberland Fusiliers
ATKINSON Arthur MM Cpl 267604 23rd Cheshire Regt
ATKINSON Arthur Kenneth MM Spr 131400 206 Fd Coy Royal Engineers
ATKINSON Caleb MM Cpl 142280 19th Bn Machine Gun Corps DOW 30.5.18.
ATKINSON Charles MM Sjt 11269 Shropshire Light Infantry
ATKINSON Charles E. MM Cpl 16738 13th Cheshire Regt
ATKINSON Charles John "DCM,MM" Sjt 9522 1st Bedfordshire Regt
ATKINSON Ernest Thomas MM Pte 1513 6th East Kent Regt
ATKINSON Fred MM Cpl 48401 25th Bn Machine Gun Corps
ATKINSON Gardner MM Spr 470845 Royal Engineers
ATKINSON George MM Gnr 771476 B/250 Bde RFA
ATKINSON George MM Cpl 22498 26th Royal Fusiliers
ATKINSON George MM Dvr 751278 D/250 Bde RFA
ATKINSON George A. MM Pte PW/1726 19th Middlesex Regt
ATKINSON George Minto MM Cpl 27206 232 Army Bde RFA Sig Sub-section Royal Engineers
ATKINSON George T. MM L/Cpl 2210 Yorkshire Light Infantry
ATKINSON H. MM L/Cpl 265349 Yeomanry
ATKINSON H. MM L/Cpl 240941 North Lancashire Regt
ATKINSON Harold MM Cpl 96133 112 Bde RFA
ATKINSON Harold MM Pte 267313 2/7th West Yorkshire Regt
ATKINSON Harold Victor MM Pte 35736 15th Lancashire Fusiliers KIA 25.12.17.
ATKINSON Harry MM Pte 200896 15th Lancashire Fusiliers
ATKINSON Herbert MM Pte G/95143 4th London Regt
ATKINSON Herbert MM Pte 13/3 4th York & Lancaster Regt
ATKINSON Horace MM Pte 5966 11th Royal Sussex Regt KIA 26.9.17.
ATKINSON James MM Cpl 35740 19th Bn Machine Gun Corps
ATKINSON James MM Sjt 10817 Coldstream Guards
ATKINSON James G. MM Pte 32142 RAMC
ATKINSON John MM Pte 68768 95 Fd Amb RAMC
ATKINSON John MM L/Cpl 31902 2nd Manchester Regt
ATKINSON John MM L/Cpl 8072 4th Royal Fusiliers
ATKINSON John MM Pte 45655 15th Cheshire Regt KIA 13.10.18.
ATKINSON John MM+Bar Sjt 17093 7th Leicestershire Regt DOW 24.3.18.
ATKINSON John MM Pte 103705 29 Gen Hosp RAMC
ATKINSON John MM Sjt 204392 1/5th Durham Light Infantry
ATKINSON John A. MM Cpl 492521 Royal Engineers
ATKINSON John F. MM Sjt 243 1/4th Yorkshire Regt
ATKINSON John H. MM L/Bdr 74419 25 Heavy Bty RGA
ATKINSON John H. MM Pte 203414 1/4th West Riding Regt
ATKINSON John T. MM L/Cpl 41033 West Yorkshire Regt
ATKINSON John T. MM L/Sjt 15996 9th Gloucestershire Regt
ATKINSON John Thomas Noris MM L/Cpl 203501 1/4th West Riding Regt
ATKINSON John W. MM Gnr 180938 RFA
ATKINSON John W. MM Pte 13551 West Riding Regt
ATKINSON John William MM Pte 41245 26th Northumberland Fusiliers
ATKINSON Joseph MM Pte 24206 1st North Lancashire Regt
ATKINSON Joseph MM Pte 204010 1st East Surrey Regt
ATKINSON Joseph MM Pte 7795 Royal Irish Rifles
ATKINSON Joseph S. MM Spr 250777 Royal Engineers
ATKINSON Joseph Thomas Leslie MM Sjt 760238 RFA
ATKINSON Laurence Ralph MM Pte 1922 1/5th York & Lancaster Regt KIA 2.7.16.
ATKINSON Lionel MM Sjt 7 10th Lincolnshire Regt
ATKINSON Matthew MM L/Cpl 3615 10th York & Lancaster Regt
ATKINSON Reuben MM L/Cpl 322402 6th London Regt
ATKINSON Richard MM Sjt 21015 20th Durham Light Infantry
ATKINSON Richard MM Pte 2679 1/8th Durham Light Infantry
ATKINSON Robert MM Dvr 61155 7 Fd Coy Royal Engineers
ATKINSON Robert MM Pte 23377 15th Durham Light Infantry
ATKINSON Robert "DCM,MM+Bar" CSM 241001 1/8th Worcestershire Regt
ATKINSON Robert MM Cpl 58731 9th Bn Machine Gun Corps
ATKINSON Robert MM L/Cpl 390218 1/3rd(Northumbrian)Fd Amb RAMC KIA 27.5.18.
ATKINSON Robert Hird MM Pte 12821 9th West Riding Regt
ATKINSON Robert R. "DCM,MM,MIDx2" Sjt 13380 1st Norfolk Regt
ATKINSON Stranger MM Pte 23835 11th East Lancashire Regt KIA 12.9.18.
ATKINSON Thomas MM Sjt 201114 1/4th Royal Lancaster Regt
ATKINSON Thomas MM Cpl 200258 1/4th Northumberland Fusiliers
ATKINSON Thomas MM Pte 2596 1/5th Northumberland Fusiliers KIA 15.11.16.
ATKINSON Thomas MM Pte 33498 RAMC
ATKINSON Thomas A. MM Sjt 17410 Border Regt
ATKINSON Thomas G. MM Gnr 129988 A/86 Bde RFA
ATKINSON W.L. MM Pte 300455 London Regt
ATKINSON William MM Sjt 79238 2nd Durham Light Infantry
ATKINSON William "DCM,MM" Sjt 20898 Royal Engineers
ATKINSON William MM Bdr 70096 5 Bde RFA
ATKINSON William MM Bdsm 9183 2nd Seaforth Highlanders KIA 24.4.18.
ATKINSON William MM Sjt 200870 2/1st London Regt

ATKINSON William MM+Bar L/Cpl 15021 Northumberland Fusiliers
ATKINSON William B. MM Sjt 10745 Northumberland Fusiliers
ATKINSON William Bridger MM L/Cpl 66859 7 Fd Coy Royal Engineers Died 31.10.18.
ATKINSON William F. MM BQMS 705462 A/331 Bde RFA
ATKINSON William G. MM Cpl 29576 East Yorkshire Regt
ATLAY Alfred J. MM Pte R/25094 King's Royal Rifle Corps
ATLEE Douglas MM Cpl 490252 13th London Regt
ATTENBOROUGH Charles Donald MM Pte 18830 Machine Gun Corps
ATTENBOROUGH Fred K. MM Sjt G/30032 7th Royal West Kent Regt
ATTENBOROUGH Percy C. MM Sjt TT/0360 Army Veterinary Corps
ATTEWELL Gilbert John MM Pte 9478 2nd Royal Fusiliers KIA 13.4.18.
ATTEWELL Harry MM Pte 91867 Durham Light Infantry
ATTEY R.W. MM Sjt 41794 RFA
ATTFIELD Charles "MM,MID" Cpl 1078 1st Welsh Guards KIA 6.11.18.
ATTFIELD Ernest A. MM Cpl 7157 20th Hussars
ATTIKIN Sidney James MM Pte 4921 1/2nd London Regt KIA 2.5.17.
ATTIS George MM L/Cpl 16462 9th Devonshire Regt
ATTOE Thomas E. MM Cpl 423695 10th London Regt
ATTREE Alexander Cockburn MM L/Cpl 1919 1/22nd London Regt KIA 22.8.18.
ATTREE Edwin C. MM Sjt 6430 1/4th Royal Sussex Regt
ATTRELL Bert MM Pte 26768 21st Bn Machine Gun Corps
ATTWATER S. MM Cpl 2202 Royal Flying Corps
ATTWATER Walter H.H. MM Cpl M1/6280 Army Service Corps Att RAMC.
ATTWATERS Charles MM Sjt 2247 17th London Regt
ATTWELL George MM Pte 200188 Shropshire Light Infantry
ATTWELL Sidney MM Gnr 676834 315 Bde RFA DOW 31.7.18.
ATTWOOD Albert Benjamin MM Cpl 465 6th Royal West Kent Regt
ATTWOOD Arthur A. MM Pte 490073 13th London Regt
ATTWOOD David Charles MM Cpl 69450 138 Army Troops Coy Royal Engineers
ATTWOOD Harold E. MM CSM M/27400 4 Div Ammn Col Army Service Corps
ATTWOOD Sidney T. MM Pte 93036 2nd Durham Light Infantry
ATTWOOD William MM Cpl 235092 1/8th Royal Lancaster Regt
ATTY Richard William MM Sjt 41794 D/87 Bde RFA
AUBERTIN G.S. MM Pte 3452 Middlesex Regt
AUBREY David I. MM Pte 2328 1st Welsh Guards
AUBREY John MM Pte 14134 Devonshire Regt
AUBREY Oliver MM Dvr 32822 RFA
AUBURN William Edward MM Pte 30983 4th Bedfordshire Regt
AUCHTERLONIE William C. MM Sjt 635375 256 Bde RFA
AUCOTT Wilfred MM Pte Sig R/4773 13th King's Royal Rifle Corps
AUDEN Joseph "MM,Medaille d'Honneur(F)" Pte 30282 11th Worcestershire Regt
AUDSLEY Fred MM Sjt 305904 8th West Yorkshire Regt
AUDSLEY Harry MM L/Bdr 173933 RFA
AUGER Charles W. MM L/Cpl 3566 Oxf & Bucks Light Infantry
AUGER Herbert MM Sjt 8208 Machine Gun Corps
AUGHEY John MM Sjt 6/719 7th Leinster Regt
AUGHTON Richard MM Pte 51344 Liverpool Regt
AUKER Ralph MM L/Cpl 8552 1st Norfolk Regt
AUKER William J. "MM,MSM,MID" Sjt 8570 1st Norfolk Regt
AUKETT Arthur E. MM Cpl 1997 2nd King Edward's Horse Att KAR.
AUKETT Harold E. "MM,MID" Sjt L/36592 D/187 Bde RFA
AUKETT Herbert H.L. MM Cpl 3254 13th Hussars
AULD Andrew MM L/Cpl 13970 2nd Royal Irish Rifles
AULD Charles Smith MM Pte 301452 RAMC
AULD James MM Pte 10741 11th Northumberland Fusiliers KIA 27.10.18.
AULD Ninian MM Pte 55802 1/5th Highland Light Infantry
AULDJO William Jolly MM+Bar L/Cpl 38177 9th Northumberland Fusiliers
AULT Frank M. MM S/Sjt 42403 RAMC
AUNGIER H. MM+Bar Pte 6625 2nd Royal Sussex Regt
AUST Ceceil MM Pte 22719 2nd Grenadier Guards
AUST Edward D. MM Sjt M2/032548 Army Service Corps
AUST Ernest P. MM L/Cpl 57541 Machine Gun Corps
AUSTEN Albert E. "DCM,MM" Sjt 16249 32nd Bn Machine Gun Corps
AUSTEN Arthur C. MM+Bar L/Cpl 97878 18 Div Sig Coy Royal Engineers
AUSTEN Edward J. MM Gnr 78372 D/312 Bde RFA

AUSTEN George Alfred MM Pte 681127 2/22nd London Regt
AUSTEN P.W. MM Pte 651232 21st London Regt
AUSTIN Albert MM Cpl 67992 12 Bde RFA
AUSTIN Albert E. MM Pte 9453 2nd Royal Scots
AUSTIN Albert H. MM Cpl 11353 1st Worcestershire Regt
AUSTIN Alfred W. MM L/Cpl 49048 4th(ER) Bedfordshire Regt
AUSTIN Arthur MM Spr 100921 Royal Engineers
AUSTIN Arthur "MM,MID" Pte 8654 2nd Royal Scots
AUSTIN Arthur MM Dvr 96753 RFA
AUSTIN Arthur MM Sjt Z/1285 Rifle Brigade
AUSTIN Arthur Ewart MM Pte 40103 1/5th Seaforth Highlanders KIA 20.8.18.
AUSTIN Arthur H. MM L/Cpl 9294 2nd Royal Berkshire Regt
AUSTIN Arthur William MM Sjt 46523 RFA
AUSTIN Bertie MM Gnr 85103 D/83 Bde RFA
AUSTIN Bertie MM Gnr 75250 126 Bty 29 Bde RFA
AUSTIN Charles MM Sjt 10033 Royal Irish Fusiliers
AUSTIN Edwin MM Bdr 26444 Wiltshire Regt
AUSTIN Ernest J. MM L/Cpl 650916 21st London Regt
AUSTIN F.T. MM Gnr 283066 124 Hy Bty RGA
AUSTIN Frank "DCM,MM" Cpl 7038 1st North Staffordshire Regt
AUSTIN Frederick "MM,Medaille Militaire(F)" Bdr 81944 C/63 Bde RFA
AUSTIN Frederick Arthur MM SSM 3966 3rd Hussars
AUSTIN George MM Cpl 1325 17th Lancers
AUSTIN George MM L/Cpl 10256 1st Royal Welsh Fusiliers
AUSTIN George G. MM Gnr 177395 RFA
AUSTIN George Holland "MM,MID" Pte 8183 Scots Guards
AUSTIN George W. MM Pte 652135 21st London Regt
AUSTIN Harry MM+Bar Sjt 8308 2/4th Royal Berkshire Regt
AUSTIN Henry MM L/Cpl 40240 15/17th West Yorkshire Regt
AUSTIN Henry William MM Sjt 1738 A/236 Bde RFA
AUSTIN Herbert MM Pte 34466 20th Manchester Regt
AUSTIN Herbert O. MM Sjt 1321 Middlesex Regt
AUSTIN J. MM L/Cpl 12355 East Kent Regt
AUSTIN Jack MM Pte 14691 Cheshire Regt
AUSTIN James MM Pte 205041 2/4th Hampshire Regt
AUSTIN James MM+Bar Cpl 241271 1/5th Lincolnshire Regt KIA 2.5.18.
AUSTIN James Joseph MM Spr 66762 Royal Engineers
AUSTIN John MM Pte 266602 1/6th Gordon Highlanders
AUSTIN John "MM,MID" Pte 11734 6th Wiltshire Regt DOW 17.6.18.
AUSTIN John E. MM L/Cpl 7115 7th East Surrey Regt
AUSTIN John Edwin MM Sjt 60714 RFA
AUSTIN John W. MM Bdr 154153 RGA
AUSTIN John W. MM L/Sjt 33357 Royal Berkshire Regt
AUSTIN Joseph MM Gnr 82079 RFA
AUSTIN Joseph Richard MM Sjt 293078 138 Heavy Bty RGA
AUSTIN Leonard A. MM L/Cpl 29437 1st West Yorkshire Regt
AUSTIN Leonard Robert MM CQMS 11109 Royal West Surrey Regt
AUSTIN Oswald Kitson MM Pte 15190 3rd Grenadier Guards
AUSTIN Ralph MM Sjt 13240 Northamptonshire Regt
AUSTIN Reginald Jesse MM Sjt 91338 1st Liverpool Regt
AUSTIN Samuel MM Pte 7482 1st Royal West Kent Regt
AUSTIN Samuel Madge MM Cpl 280738 91 Siege Bty RGA KIA 13.9.18.
AUSTIN Stephen Burbidge MM Sjt 43012 Machine Gun Corps
AUSTIN Thomas MM Cpl 9011 1st South Staffordshire Regt
AUSTIN Thomas John MM Pte B/2857 8th Rifle Brigade KIA 16.5.17.
AUSTIN Tom D. MM Pte 28091 Yorkshire Light Infantry
AUSTIN William H. MM Pte 202129 7th Norfolk Regt
AUSTIN William H. MM Pte 14677 10th Hussars
AUSTIN William J. MM Spr 13232 12 Fd Coy Royal Engineers
AUSTIN William John MM+Bar Gnr 15226 17 Bty 41 Bde RFA DOW 2.4.18.
AUSTIN William Thomas "MM,MID" L/Sjt 11020 2nd Grenadier Guards
AUSTING George Arthur MM Pte 7199 2nd Worcestershire Regt
AUSTWICK George H. MM+Bar Sjt 482127 62 Div Sig Coy Royal Engineers
AUTON Charles W. MM Pte 242347 9th Highland Light Infantry
AUTON Thomas MM Pte 34515 5th West Riding Regt
AUTY Harold A. MM Pte 533197 15th London Regt
AUTY Joseph A. MM L/Cpl 20718 Yorkshire Light Infantry
AUTY Sydney MM L/Cpl 242911 York & Lancaster Regt
AVELING Frank MM Cpl 8717 1st Bedfordshire Regt
AVENELL Arthur Cecil MM Cpl 320069 1/1st Wiltshire Yeomanry
AVENELL Jesse MM Gnr 77698 RFA

AVENS Gerald William "MC,MM(1420 Sjt)" Lt 1/6th London Regt
AVENT Joseph MM Pte 293159 706 Coy Labour Corps
AVENT Lewis Thomas MM Cpl 439014 1/3(Northumbrian)Fd Amb RAMC
AVERALL William MM Cpl 50548 3 Div Ammn Col RFA
AVERELL Robert MM Pte 41534 9th Royal Irish Fusiliers
AVERILL Edward Thomas MM Spr 58357 18 Div Sig Coy Royal Engineers
AVERILL Fred MM Pte 26965 Royal Lancaster Regt
AVERILL John George MM Pte 2539 Royal Fusiliers
AVERN Henry MM Sjt 473250 12th London Regt
AVERY Albert MM Cpl 20706 10 Fd Amb RAMC
AVERY Alfred C. MM Pte S/27556 Rifle Brigade
AVERY Christopher MM Cpl 10856 5th Oxf & Bucks Light Infantry
AVERY Henry F. MM Pte M2/076675 Army Service Corps
AVERY James Herbert MM L/Cpl M2/136738 884 MT Coy Army Service Corps
AVERY Lewis W. MM Pte 17901 Gloucestershire Regt
AVERY Percy J. MM Sjt 11176 Wiltshire Regt
AVERY Sydney G. MM L/Cpl 62512 5th West Yorkshire Regt
AVERY Thomas A. MM CSM 265515 1/4th Oxf & Bucks Light Infantry
AVERY Walter MM L/Bdr 246659 29 Bde RFA
AVES Charles A. MM Pte 52004 5th West Yorkshire Regt
AVIS Clement MM Pte M2/099650 Fifth Army Railhead Coy Army Service Corps
AVIS Gordon John MM Pte 773 11th Royal Sussex Regt KIA 17.2.18.
AVIS L. MM Sjt 43510 9th Essex Regt
AVIS William MM Pte 12718 Hampshire Regt
AVRAMACHIS Victor "DCM,MM" Sjt 720598 1/24th London Regt
AWBERY W.G. MM L/Sjt 14273 South Lancashire Regt
AWCOCK George R. MM Pte L/9750 2nd Royal Sussex Regt
AWDE Herbert MM Sjt 43627 Royal Engineers
AXE Herbert MM Cpl 15973 10th West Riding Regt
AXELL Edward J. MM Cpl 54773 Machine Gun Corps
AXFORD Ernest William MM Pte 3914 1/15th London Regt
AXFORD Joseph MM Pte 267458 Royal Warwickshire Regt
AXON Charles MM Cpl 202052 8th Lancashire Fusiliers
AXON Charles MM L/Cpl 40436 Scottish Rifles
AXON James MM Spr 102377 172 Tunnelling Coy Royal Engineers
AXTELL Frank MM Cpl 6313 Middlesex Regt
AXTELL Sidney MM Cpl 265390 Oxf & Bucks Light Infantry
AXTEN Henry W. MM Cpl 202597 Y/57 Med TM Bty RFA
AXWORTHY Charles MM L/Cpl 9470 2nd Devonshire Regt
AXWORTHY Walter MM Pte 14549 14th Hampshire Regt
AYER Alexander MM L/Bdr Sig 180149 139 Hy Bty RGA
AYLESBURY P.E. MM Pte 372456 8th London Regt
AYLETT George Ernest MM Sjt Y/1568 2nd King's Royal Rifle Corps KIA 25.9.18.
AYLIEFF Edgar MM Pte 15767 Yorkshire Regt
AYLIFFE Ernest MM Pte 82376 26th Royal Welsh Fusiliers
AYLING Bertram A. MM Sjt 14883 RFA
AYLING Frederick Wilfrid MM Pte 532091 2/6th London Regt
AYLING Harry MM Cpl 57169 12th North Staffordshire Regt
AYLING Sidney C. MM Spr 26714 Royal Engineers
AYLING William MM Pte 242651 1/5th Royal Lancaster Regt DOW 19.3.18.
AYLOTT John MM Pte 18171 7th Bedfordshire Regt KIA 23.10.17.
AYLOTT Joseph MM L/Sjt 14021 Middlesex Regt
AYLWARD J.J. MM L/Cpl 26464 Royal Dublin Fusiliers
AYLWARD Reginald Walter MM+Bar L/Cpl 169480 MGC(Cavalry)
AYLWARD W.G. MM Air Mech 2 41142 Royal Air Force
AYLWIN Arthur John "MM,MID" Sjt 50767 9 Sqn Machine Gun Corps KIA 22.3.18.
AYLWIN B. MM Pte R/34572 2nd King's Royal Rifle Corps
AYNSLEY John MM Cpl 10/24456 10th Northumberland Fusiliers
AYNSLEY Thomas R. MM Pnr 220309 8 Div Sig Coy Royal Engineers
AYRE David MM L/Cpl 267475 6th Seaforth Highlanders KIA 25.3.18.
AYRE Edward S. MM Sjt 9040 2nd Devonshire Regt
AYRE Frederick G. MM L/Cpl 39734 Yorkshire Light Infantry
AYRE George A. MM Pte 241129 North Staffordshire Regt
AYRE Herbert Wilkinson MM Sjt 415 Lincolnshire Regt
AYRE Joseph MM Pte 86451 154 Coy Machine Gun Corps
AYRES Albert E. MM Pte 535226 15th London Regt
AYRES Arthur MM Gnr 106137 81 Bty RFA DOW 5.10.17.
AYRES Arthur James "DCM,MM,MID" Sjt G/6884 1st East Kent Regt KIA 18.9.18.
AYRES Arthur Llewellyn MM Spr 48713 22 Div Sig Coy Royal Engineers
AYRES Daniel MM Pte 16772 1/4th Royal Berkshire Regt
AYRES Ernest MM L/Cpl 201472 1/4th Oxf & Bucks Light Infantry
AYRES Ernest P. MM L/Cpl 18079 Royal Berkshire Regt
AYRES Frederik MM Pte 701971 23rd London Regt
AYRES George MM L/Cpl 13579 8th Norfolk Regt
AYRES George MM+Bar Cpl 54843 17th Royal Fusiliers
AYRES George R. MM Sjt 39830 102 Siege Bty RGA
AYRES James MM L/Cpl 19409 15th Hampshire Regt
AYRES James Oswald Thomas MM Pte 54248 9th Welsh Regt
AYRES P. MM Cpl 197908 Royal Engineers
AYRES Percy Thomas MM Sjt 76038 232 Bde RFA
AYRES Thomas H. MM Pte 89404 Machine Gun Corps
AYRES Walter MM Pte 15182 10th Hussars
AYRES William MM Sjt 55827 Royal Engineers
AYRES William MM+Bar Pte 52225 9th Cheshire Regt
AYRES William Arthur MM Pte 14328 8th Royal Berkshire Regt Died 22.7.18.
AYRIS George MM Pte 26363 5th Oxf & Bucks Light Infantry
AYSCOUGH Thomas L. MM Pte 65200 5th Yorkshire Light Infantry
AYSH John Dunning MM Sjt 8313 B/63 Bde RFA
AYTON Hugh MM Pte M2/148399 Army Service Corps

B

BABB Charles MM L/Cpl 25464 Duke of Cornwall's LI
BABB Charles William MM L/Cpl 500314 61 Div Sig Coy Royal Engineers DOW 2.5.18.
BABB G. MM Pte 15338 2nd Scots Guards
BABBAGE Herbert MM Spr 95682 Royal Engineers
BABBAYAN John MM Sjt 73592 9th Bn Machine Gun Corps
BABER Thomas E. MM Pte 56099 Machine Gun Corps
BABER William H. "MM,MID" 2nd Cpl 359 1(Home Counties)Fd Coy Royal Engineers
BABINGTON Frederick MM Pte 23097 11th Cheshire Regt KIA 28.5.18.
BACCHUS Harry Arthur MM Gnr 172424 106 Siege Bty RGA
BACH Ove "MM,MID" Spr 47186 Royal Engineers
BACHE Bert MM Dvr 101430 D/58 Bde RFA
BACHE George W. MM Cpl 840333 RFA
BACHE William Fernando MM Sjt 51119 Royal Engineers
BACHELL George Thomas MM L/Cpl 3826 1/15th London Regt
BACHER Percy MM L/Cpl 17301 5th Northamptonshire Regt
BACK Alfred J. MM Sjt 48553 94 Fd Coy Royal Engineers
BACK Ernest MM Sjt 28121 31 Hy Bty RGA
BACK George MM 2nd Cpl 48554 94 Fd Coy Royal Engineers
BACK Herbert MM Gnr 1603 RFA
BACK Herbert MM L/Cpl 20332 Royal Sussex Regt
BACK John MM+Bar Gnr L/5211 RFA
BACK Robert MM Bdr 16765 RFA
BACK Stanley MM L/Cpl 10249 5th Oxf & Bucks Light Infantry
BACKETT Harry MM L/Cpl 71733 9th Royal Fusiliers
BACKHOFF Harold Albert William MM Sjt 2516 12th London Regt
BACKHOUSE Frederick MM Gnr 681791 RFA
BACKHOUSE Harold MM Bdr 34239 RFA
BACKHOUSE Henry Edward MM Sjt 3/9998 8th Suffolk Regt KIA 12.10.17.
BACKHOUSE Robert Peter MM CSM 11646 17th Notts & Derby Regt DOW 22.9.17.
BACKHOUSE Walter MM Pte 32261 13th Liverpool Regt
BACKHOUSE William G. MM Sjt 301411 13th Bn Tank Corps
BACKHURST Walter A. MM Pte 12/17172 Notts & Derby Regt
BACKLOG William MM Pte 139380 37th Bn Machine Gun Corps
BACKMAN Victor MM L/Cpl 12736 Royal Berkshire Regt
BACKSHELL Edwin MM Pte 1548 Royal Sussex Regt
BACON Allan G. MM Dvr 74171 RFA
BACON Arthur MM Pte 1024 12th East Yorkshire Regt
BACON Douglas Alexander "MM,MSM" Pte 9/14507 6th Leicestershire Regt
BACON Edward John MM Gnr 75364 D/231 Bde RFA DOW 4.11.18.
BACON Frederick MM Pte 241355 6th York & Lancaster Regt
BACON George MM L/Cpl 29909 7/8th King's Own Scottish Borderers
BACON Henry George MM Sjt 86020 155 Siege Bty RGA
BACON James R. MM Gnr 98650 RFA
BACON John MM Cpl S/3788 13th Rifle Brigade
BACON John MM Sjt 9335 1st Royal Irish Rifles

BACON Norman Henry MM Sjt S/446 10th Rifle Brigade
BACON Reginald MM Pte 40828 Arg & Suth Highlanders
BACON Richard A. MM Cpl 201912 7th Royal West Surrey Regt
BACON Thomas Henry MM Pte 11213 2nd Lincolnshire Regt KIA 31.7.17.
BACON Thomas W. MM Sjt 18011 9th Norfolk Regt
BACON W.R. MM L/Cpl 2119 London Regt
BACON William MM L/Cpl 11/17581 Border Regt
BACON William MM Pte 201180 York & Lancaster Regt
BACON William A. MM Pte 372434 8th London Regt
BADAMS James B. MM Cpl 8321 1st Royal Welsh Fusiliers
BADBY Thomas F. MM Sjt 50781 MGC(Cavalry)
BADCOCK George MM CQMS 2612 Royal Sussex Regt
BADDAMS Henry J. MM Pte 426300 10th London Regt
BADDELEY Enoch MM L/Cpl 10655 2nd Royal West Surrey Regt KIA 26.10.17
BADDELEY Herbert MM L/Sjt 9967 2nd Coldstream Guards
BADDELEY Isaiah MM Gnr 19593 75 Bde RFA
BADDELEY Joseph MM Sjt 49448 Royal Engineers
BADDELEY Percy MM Pte 11392 North Staffordshire Regt
BADDELY George MM Dvr 80139 26 Bty 17 Bde RFA
BADDER Thomas W.S. MM Sjt 201505 6th Notts & Derby Regt
BADDON Roderick M. MM Pnr 282097 Royal Engineers
BADES Simon MM+Bar Pte 11329 6th North Lancashire Regt
BADGER Alfred Richard MM Sjt 202302 Oxf & Bucks Light Infantry
BADGER Frederick MM Sjt 250450 3rd London Regt
BADGER Joseph L. MM Cpl 30833 14th Bn Machine Gun Corps
BADGER Leslie MM Cpl(MCDR) 32336 15 Div Sig Coy Royal Engineers
BADGER Thomas Charles MM L/Sjt 4163 1/1st London Regt KIA 16.8.17.
BADGER William "MM,MID" Bdr 79577 RFA
BADHAM Albert MM Spr 195048 Royal Engineers
BADLAND A. MM Chief Mechanic 20954 Royal Air Force
BADLAND Thomas Renshaw MM+Bar Pte 203432 2/7th Worcestershire Regt
BADRICK William MM Sjt 45080 B/175 Bde RFA
BADROCK Wilfred MM Pte 26897 6th Shropshire Light Infantry KIA 1.4.18.
BAES Frederick MM Pte 6/1212 6th Leinster Regt
BAFF Charles MM Cpl 13840 10th D Coy Yorkshire Regt
BAGE George H. MM Spr 465098 Tyne Elect Engrs Royal Engineers
BAGG John J.E. "DCM,MM+2 Bars" Pte G/1565 East Surrey Regt
BAGG William MM Sjt 13956 Bedfordshire Regt Died 20.10.18.
BAGGALEY George H. MM Bdr 46827 RFA
BAGGALEY Harold MM Gnr 111912 32 Bty 33 Bde RFA
BAGGE Herbert MM Pte 8148 9th Royal Sussex Regt
BAGGETT Isaac T. MM Gnr 145732 RGA
BAGGLEY John MM Sjt 3388 1/4th Lincolnshire Regt
BAGGOTT Ernest MM Gnr 111353 10th Bn Tank Corps
BAGGOTT John MM+Bar Pte 26689 1st Grenadier Guards
BAGGOTT Richard MM+Bar Cpl L/12574 RFA
BAGGOTT Richard MM Pte 21285 8th Bedfordshire Regt
BAGLEE Isaac MM Sjt 85369 A/62 Bde RFA
BAGLEY Albert E. MM Pte 66633 Northumberland Fusiliers
BAGLEY Charles Edgar MM Cpl 8320 2nd South Staffordshire Regt
BAGLEY George MM Pte 25536 1st Grenadier Guards
BAGLEY Harry C. MM Pte 572851 17th London Regt
BAGLEY Harry C. MM Cpl 11056 11th Royal Warwickshire Regt
BAGLEY John MM Sjt 83912 RFA
BAGLEY Sidney Charles MM L/Cpl 151602 251 Tunnelling Coy Royal Engineers
BAGLEY William MM Dvr 604053 1(Shropshire)Bty RHA
BAGLEY William MM Gnr 122554 RFA
BAGNALL Andrew "DCM,MM+Bar" Sjt 13080 10th Northumberland Fusiliers
BAGNALL George Harry MM+Bar Pte 16767 6th Border Regt DOW 29.10.17.
BAGNALL Harold MM Pte 4/9833 South Staffordshire Regt
BAGNALL John MM Pte 20/157 Northumberland Fusiliers
BAGNALL John MM Pte 13/133 York & Lancaster Regt
BAGNALL John F. MM Spr 46563 Royal Engineers
BAGNALL Thomas MM Sjt 3/9230 6th West Yorkshire Regt
BAGNALL Thomas MM Cpl 24928 13th Royal Welsh Fusiliers
BAGNALL Victor MM+Bar Gnr 80452 C/47 Bde RFA
BAGNALL Willie "MM,CG(F)" Pte 45416 7th South Wales Borderers
BAGSHAW Albert MM Pte 35408 105 Fd Amb RAMC Died 11.9.18.
BAGSHAW Bernard MM Pte 201055 2/4th York & Lancaster Regt
BAGSHAW George P. "MM,MID" Sjt 240552 6th Notts & Derby Regt
BAGSHAW Reginald Henry MM Sjt 235829 9th West Yorkshire Regt
BAGSHAW Samuel MM Gnr 46945 RFA
BAGSTAFF William MM L/Cpl 325167 1/1st Cambridgeshire Regt att 2nd Suffolk Regt.
BAGULEY John MM Sjt 17989 19th Lancashire Fusiliers
BAGULEY William MM Cpl 79413 C/152 Bde RFA
BAGWELL George E. MM Sjt 38605 18 Div Ammn Col RFA
BAGWELL Herbert J. MM Sjt 10888 6th Somerset Light Infantry
BAIGENT Joseph MM L/Cpl 12935 2nd Royal West Surrey Regt
BAIGRIE James MM Sjt 18965 Royal Scots
BAIGRIE William MM Sjt 10350 1st Gordon Highlanders DOW 28.8.18.
BAIKIE Donald MM L/Cpl 240436 Seaforth Highlanders
BAILDHAM William MM Sjt 200483 1st Lincolnshire Regt
BAILES John W. MM Pte R/9205 13th King's Royal Rifle Corps
BAILEY Albert MM L/Cpl 23648 1st Royal Berkshire Regt
BAILEY Albert MM Pte 22372 4th West Riding Regt
BAILEY Albert MM Pte 10702 Royal Irish Fusiliers
BAILEY Albert MM Pte 2854 13th Royal Sussex Regt
BAILEY Albert Arthur MM Cpl 69665 149 Army Troops Coy Royal Engineers
BAILEY Albert Denis MM Pte 64420 213 Coy Machine Gun Corps
BAILEY Albert G. MM+Bar Pte 14681 7th Bedfordshire Regt
BAILEY Alfred MM Pte 15036 11th Royal Sussex Regt
BAILEY Alfred MM Pte 787 6th Royal West Surrey Regt
BAILEY Amos MM 2nd Cpl 546546 509 Fd Coy Royal Engineers
BAILEY Archibald Henry MM Pte 15025 Coldstream Guards
BAILEY Arthur E. MM Sjt 66290 Royal Engineers
BAILEY Arthur W. MM Pte 17539 Royal West Kent Regt
BAILEY Bertram MM Sjt 8763 9th Royal Fusiliers
BAILEY Charles MM Sjt 48691 Machine Gun Corps
BAILEY Charles MM Pte 141739 1st Bn Machine Gun Corps
BAILEY Charles MM Spr 85134 Royal Engineers
BAILEY Charles Amos MM L/Cpl 558267 56 Div Sig Coy Royal Engineers
BAILEY Charles F. MM Gnr Sig 115463 283 Siege Bty RGA
BAILEY Charles H. MM Cpl M2/078332 62 Div Train Army Service Corps
BAILEY Charles H. MM Sjt 211144 RGA
BAILEY Charles Harold MM L/Cpl 2674 1/24th London Regt
BAILEY Charles J. MM Pte M2/149248 Army Service Corps
BAILEY Charles J.W. MM Pte 9964 Royal West Surrey Regt
BAILEY Charles V. MM Dvr 1552 Royal Engineers
BAILEY Christopher MM L/Cpl 43717 9th Scottish Rifles
BAILEY Clifford MM Sjt 12620 9th West Riding Regt
BAILEY Cyril MM Gnr 19904 18 Div Ammn Col RFA
BAILEY E. MM Pte 19868 1st Essex Regt
BAILEY Edward MM Pte 9/1729 8th Royal Munster Fusiliers KIA 19.7.16.
BAILEY Edward MM Pte 26548 19th Manchester Regt KIA 8.9.18.
BAILEY Elphonso P. MM Pte 46538 North Staffordshire Regt
BAILEY Ernest MM Bdr 66206 RFA
BAILEY Ernest MM Pte 13865 West Yorkshire Regt
BAILEY Ernest Albert MM L/Cpl 4960 62 Coy Machine Gun Corps
BAILEY Ernest Charles MM Pte 13570 6th Northamptonshire Regt KIA 4.4.18.
BAILEY Ernest I. MM Pte 19604 Royal Welsh Fusiliers
BAILEY F. MM L/Cpl 265469 Oxf & Bucks Light Infantry
BAILEY F.S. MM L/Cpl 200317 South Staffordshire Regt
BAILEY Frank "DCM,MM" Sjt 8312 12th Gloucestershire Regt
BAILEY Frank MM Bdr 313312 RGA
BAILEY Frank MM Gnr 28923 D/160 Bde RFA
BAILEY Fred MM+Bar Pte 19013 Royal Berkshire Regt
BAILEY Frederick MM Cpl 253351 18 Div Sig Coy Royal Engineers
BAILEY Frederick "MM,MID" Sjt 387 RAMC
BAILEY Frederick MM Cpl 46064 Northumberland Fusiliers
BAILEY Frederick W. MM Sjt 1269 Army Cyclist Corps
BAILEY G.E. MM Cpl 1908 RFA
BAILEY George MM Spr 112566 185 Tunnelling Coy Royal Engineers
BAILEY George MM Gnr 56184 A/102 Bde RFA DOW 28.9.16.
BAILEY George MM Sjt 820022 RFA
BAILEY George MM+Bar Pte 21214 Grenadier Guards
BAILEY George A. MM Cpl 1605 West Riding Regt
BAILEY George H. MM Pte 171 14th Royal Warwickshire Regt
BAILEY H.W. MM Pte 46286 Worcestershire Regt
BAILEY Harold MM Sjt 145118 1/1st Northamptonshire Yeomanry
BAILEY Harold Glendenen MM Sjt 27134 14 Div Ammn Col RFA
BAILEY Harry MM Sjt 3/9879 Suffolk Regt
BAILEY Harry MM L/Cpl 25248 10th West Riding Regt

BAILEY Harry MM Pte 10652 2nd Worcestershire Regt
BAILEY Harry O. MM L/Cpl 12393 1st Grenadier Guards
BAILEY Harry W. MM Sjt 232973 2nd att 4th London Regt
BAILEY Hayden Weir MM Sjt 34854 82 Bde RFA DOW 27.8.17.
BAILEY Henry MM Sjt 780042 A/246 Bde RFA
BAILEY Henry Robert MM Cpl 13190 187 Bde RFA
BAILEY Horace E. MM L/Cpl 30635 1/1st Bedfordshire Yeomanry
BAILEY Hubert A. MM Cpl 200521 1/4th Gloucestershire Regt
BAILEY J. MM Cpl 71168 V Corps Cyclist Bn North Irish Horse
BAILEY Jack G.A. "DCM,MM" Sjt 3/6736 1st Dorsetshire Regt
BAILEY James MM Dvr 225205 B/75 Bde RFA
BAILEY James MM Pnr 147267 5 Mortar Bn Royal Engineers
BAILEY James MM Pte 479413 Labour Corps
BAILEY James MM Cpl 25437 84 Bde RGA
BAILEY James MM Pte 241469 2/6th Liverpool Regt
BAILEY James A. MM Pte 5720 1st Norfolk Regt
BAILEY James Alfred MM Sjt 7521 11th Royal Fusiliers KIA 17.2.17.
BAILEY James Arthur MM L/Cpl 311438 20 Div Sig Coy Royal Engineers att RFA.
BAILEY James George MM L/Cpl 32764 Royal Engineers
BAILEY James H. MM L/Cpl 5274 North Staffordshire Regt
BAILEY John MM+Bar Sjt 265851 1/6th West Riding Regt
BAILEY John MM Sjt 202 1st Lancashire Fusiliers
BAILEY John MM Pte 16212 1st Royal Irish Rifles
BAILEY John MM Sjt TT/01342 Army Veterinary Corps
BAILEY John MM Pte 26460 Border Regt
BAILEY John MM Pte 16212 13th Royal Irish Rifles
BAILEY John E. MM Bdr 26931 A/174 Bde RFA
BAILEY John Edmund MM Sjt 23854 1st Royal Welsh Fusiliers
BAILEY John W. MM L/Cpl A/202580 18th King's Royal Rifle Corps
BAILEY John W. MM Pte 240773 5th Leicestershire Regt
BAILEY John W. MM Pte 31023 South Lancashire Regt
BAILEY Joseph MM Sjt 34939 133 Fd Amb RAMC
BAILEY Joseph MM Cpl 13053 7th East Yorkshire Regt KIA 5.11.16.
BAILEY Joseph MM L/Cpl 10982 7th Gloucestershire Regt
BAILEY Joseph E. MM L/Cpl 281883 Lancashire Fusiliers
BAILEY Joseph T. MM Sjt 40583 2nd South Wales Borderers
BAILEY Joshua MM Sjt 9679 1st Royal Irish Regt
BAILEY Josias MM Cpl 3/11593 10th West Riding Regt
BAILEY Lewis MM Pte 11/538 East Yorkshire Regt
BAILEY Luther Llewellyn MM Cpl 12/16852 12th Notts & Derby Regt KIA 27.3.18.
BAILEY M. MM Pte M2/135961 Army Service Corps
BAILEY Matthew MM L/Cpl 350672 18th Highland Light Infantry
BAILEY P. MM Pte 512269 2 Fd Amb RAMC
BAILEY Percy E. MM Bdr 20445 9 Hy Arty Gp RGA
BAILEY Reginald B. MM L/Cpl 302671 6th Durham Light Infantry
BAILEY Robert MM Sjt A/768 18th King's Royal Rifle Corps
BAILEY Robert MM Sjt 197o7 1st Royal Lancaster Regt KIA 18.4.18.
BAILEY Robert C. MM Cpl C/3479 King's Royal Rifle Corps
BAILEY S. MM Pte 508243 RAMC
BAILEY Samuel MM Pte 9/1738 Royal Munster Fusiliers
BAILEY Samuel MM Gnr 143627 69 Siege Bty RGA
BAILEY Sidney MM L/Cpl 13336 6th Northamptonshire Regt KIA 4.11.18.
BAILEY Stanley MM Dvr 71700 RFA
BAILEY Stanley Claude "MM,CG(F)" Bdr 128455 X/30 Med TM Bty RFA
BAILEY Stanley E. MM Pte 300853 5th London Regt
BAILEY Sydney MM Pte 275726 7th Manchester Regt
BAILEY Sydney "MM+Bar,MID" Bdr 10772 D/49 Bde RFA
BAILEY Sydney MM L/Cpl 18440 Notts & Derby Regt
BAILEY Thomas MM L/Cpl 14724 1st Yorkshire Light Infantry
BAILEY Thomas MM Cpl 17042 7th Leicestershire Regt
BAILEY Thomas W. MM Cpl 20436 East Lancashire Regt
BAILEY Thomas William MM L/Cpl 107647 285 Army Troops Coy Royal Engineers Died 10.11.18.
BAILEY Tom MM Bdr 275468 109 Heavy Bty RGA
BAILEY Victor MM Pte S/6829 Middlesex Regt
BAILEY Wallace MM Pte 201722 North Staffordshire Regt
BAILEY Wallace E. MM Sjt 240831 Lancashire Fusiliers
BAILEY Walter MM CQMS 290170 Cheshire Regt
BAILEY Walter MM Pte 49430 9th Cheshire Regt
BAILEY Walter C. MM Cpl 372746 8th London Regt
BAILEY Walter E. MM Pte 7068 1st King's Royal Rifle Corps
BAILEY Wilfred James MM Pte 495466 2/2nd(Home Counties)Fd Amb RAMC
BAILEY William MM Pte 200970 1/4th Royal Welsh Fusiliers
BAILEY William MM Spr 166764 Royal Engineers
BAILEY William MM L/Cpl 63888 106 Fd Amb RAMC
BAILEY William MM Sjt 242141 7/8th King's Own Scottish Borderers
BAILEY William MM Pte 66640 101 Fd Amb. RAMC
BAILEY William MM Gnr 141457 285 Siege Bty RGA
BAILEY William MM Pte 20075 Manchester Regt
BAILEY William MM Bdr 34415 RFA
BAILEY William "MM,MSM" Sjt 480315 460 Fd Coy Royal Engineers
BAILEY William MM Pte 19729 Middlesex Regt
BAILEY William Bridger MM L/Sjt 6339 9th Royal Sussex Regt KIA 23.3.18.
BAILEY William C. MM Pte 1744 XVII Corps Cyclist Bn Army Cyclist Corps
BAILEY William H. MM Sjt 71428 RFA
BAILEY William J. MM Pte G2776 Royal Sussex Regt
BAILEY William Kilby MM Pte 40374 Worcestershire Regt
BAILEY William R. MM Pte 202191 Middlesex Regt
BAILEY Willie MM Pte 201943 7th West Riding Regt
BAILIE Hugh MM Pte 53361 108 Fd Amb RAMC
BAILIE Hugh MM Pte 331319 9th Liverpool Regt
BAILIE William MM Sjt 15/11871 Royal Irish Rifles
BAILIFF Thomas A. "DCM,MM" Pte 285063 1/1st Hertfordshire Regt
BAILLIE Charles MM Cpl 6705 8/10th Gordon Highlanders KIA 22.8.17.
BAILLIE George MM Pte S/9646 2nd Seaforth Highlanders
BAILLIE George MM Pte 40661 1st Scottish Rifles
BAILLIE George Robert MM Sjt 166194 RFA DOW 30.10.18.
BAILLIE John MM Spr 249115 350 Elect & Mech Coy Royal Engineers
BAILLIE Peter MM Sjt 19212 RGA
BAILLIE Robert G. MM L/Sjt 15264 1st Scots Guards
BAILLIE Samuel MM Sjt 276179 Royal Scots
BAILLIE William MM Pte 200734 King's Own Scottish Borderers
BAILY H. MM Bdr 357 RFA
BAILY J.C. MM Sjt 23963 14th Northumberland Fusiliers
BAIN Alexander MM Pte 250974 5/6th Royal Scots
BAIN Alexander MM Gnr 1216 MGC(Motors)
BAIN Alfred Angus MM Sjt 17813 20th Manchester Regt
BAIN Charles MM Pte 23233 1st Cameron Highlanders
BAIN Charles MM Sjt 2287 1/14th London Regt
BAIN Donald A. MM Pte 11466 1/4th Seaforth Highlanders
BAIN James MM Sjt 2034 9th Seaforth Highlanders
BAIN James MM Pte 18432 9 Coy (sic) Machine Gun Corps KIA 25.4.18.
BAIN James MM Sjt 22011 Machine Gun Corps
BAIN James Roderick MM Sjt 29038 112 Hy Bty RGA
BAIN John "DCM,MM" CSM 8710 2nd Seaforth Highlanders
BAIN John MM Pte 43492 2nd Royal Irish Rifles
BAIN John "MM,MID" Pte 8644 Royal Highlanders
BAIN John MM+Bar Sjt 23297 51st Bn Machine Gun Corps
BAIN Norman Grant MM Pte 53559 164 Coy Machine Gun Corps
BAIN Peter MM Sjt 7751 6th King's Own Scottish Borderers
BAIN Robert MM Sjt 9301 1st Royal Highlanders
BAIN Torquil MM Sjt 265024 Seaforth Highlanders
BAIN Walter MM L/Cpl 90174 18th Bn Machine Gun Corps
BAIN William MM Pte A/204083 13th King's Royal Rifle Corps
BAIN William MM Dvr 68968 RFA
BAINBRIDGE Fred MM Pte 43251 1st South Staffordshire Regt
BAINBRIDGE Harry "MM,MSM" Spr 26543 97 Fd Coy Royal Engineers
BAINBRIDGE James MM Spr 51886 102 Fd Coy Royal Engineers
BAINBRIDGE John G. MM Bdr 1161 RFA
BAINBRIDGE Oliver MM Pte 2357 1/6th Durham Light Infantry KIA 5.11.16.
BAINBRIDGE Richard MM Sjt 122507 1/1st(London)Heavy Bty RGA
BAINBRIDGE Thomas L. MM Sjt C/9121 King's Royal Rifle Corps
BAINBRIDGE Thomas Lawrence MM L/Cpl 200861 1/4th Yorkshire Regt KIA 23.4.17.
BAINBRIDGE William R. MM 2nd Cpl 105768 Royal Engineers
BAINES Bernard MM Gnr 112371 RFA
BAINES Cyril MM Gnr 124959 RGA
BAINES David MM Pte 3/6058 East Yorkshire Regt
BAINES Ernest S. MM Pte A/204084 13th King's Royal Rifle Corps
BAINES Henry MM Pte 13575 8th York & Lancaster Regt
BAINES James MM Gnr 710087 RFA
BAINES John MM Pte 241416 1/5th Royal Lancaster Regt DOW 8.8.18.
BAINES John MM Pte 4925 2nd Border Regt
BAINES John MM Pte 2479 2nd Manchester Regt
BAINES Joshua MM Pte 50568 Notts & Derby Regt

BAINES Michael MM L/Sjt 24412 20th Liverpool Regt
BAINES Richard MM L/Cpl 13886 10th North Lancashire Regt
BAINES Richard MM Sjt 1751 Lancashire Fusiliers
BAINES Thomas MM Dvr 146297 C/93 Bde RFA
BAINES Thomas MM Sjt 40833 Royal Irish Rifles
BAINES W. MM Pte 10950 East Kent Regt
BAINS George MM Pte 6828 Manchester Regt
BAIRD Charles McLean MM Pte 278918 Arg & Suth Highlanders
BAIRD David MM Pte 73851 RAMC
BAIRD Ernest W. MM L/Sjt 235168 1/1st Herefordshire Regt
BAIRD Gains Rogers MM Cpl 45947 D/88 Bde RFA
BAIRD George MM Pte 75300 Tank Corps
BAIRD James MM L/Cpl D/12904 2nd Dragoons
BAIRD James G.M. MM L/Cpl S/12297 6th Cameron Highlanders
BAIRD John MM Pte 24524 5th Cameron Highlanders KIA 14.12.17.
BAIRD John MM L/Cpl 15514 1st Scots Guards
BAIRD John MM Pte 41687 Gordon Highlanders
BAIRD John MM Cpl 17179 48 Div Train Army Service Corps
BAIRD Kenneth Mackay "MM+Bar,CG(F)(Medaille Militaire(F)" Sjt 350314 1/9th Royal Scots
BAIRD Richard MM CSM 39943 15th Cheshire Regt
BAIRD Robert MM+Bar Cpl 7755 C/77 Bde RFA KIA 20.4.18.
BAIRD Robert MM Pte 300812 1/7th Royal Scots
BAIRD Robert MM Cpl 17822 1/7th Royal Scots KIA 12.11.17.
BAIRD Thomas MM Sjt 250862 1/6th Arg & Suth Highlanders
BAIRD Thomas H. MM Sjt 5581 Royal Irish Fusiliers
BAIRD Walter MM Sjt 3926 Royal Highlanders
BAIRD William MM Pte S/43333 7th Seaforth Highlanders KIA 1.10.18.
BAIRD William MM Cpl 295039 12th Royal Scots Fusiliers
BAIRD William MM Sjt 7627 2nd Arg & Suth Highlanders
BAIRNE Tom MM+Bar Pte 11774 2nd West Riding Regt
BAIRSTOW Harry MM Pte 203204 Yorkshire Light Infantry
BAIRSTOW Pearson MM Pte 73416 61 Fd Amb RAMC
BAKER A.F. MM Pte 14357 Bedfordshire Regt
BAKER Albert MM S/Sjt 31803 RAMC
BAKER Albert MM Pte 19285 Machine Gun Corps
BAKER Albert MM Pte 20053 Leicestershire Regt
BAKER Albert MM Pte 25394 1st Somerset Light Infantry Died 7.12.18.
BAKER Albert E. "DCM,MM" Cpl 11398 1st Worcestershire Regt
BAKER Albert E. MM Pte 31965 49 Fd Amb RAMC
BAKER Albert E. MM Pte 14956 8th Suffolk Regt
BAKER Albert George MM L/Cpl 352481 7th London Regt KIA 22.8.18.
BAKER Albert L. MM Pte 858 56 Fd Amb RAMC
BAKER Albert V. MM Sjt 510021 RAMC
BAKER Albert William MM Pte 201471 1/4th Seaforth Highlanders KIA 21.3.18.
BAKER Alexander MM+Bar Pte 102665 1st Notts & Derby Regt
BAKER Alfred "MM,MID" Sjt 8237 2nd Suffolk Regt
BAKER Alfred MM Pte 45536 37 Fd Amb RAMC
BAKER Alfred MM Pte 18921 9th Cheshire Regt
BAKER Alfred Arthur MM Pte 4226 1/24th London Regt
BAKER Alfred Harold MM Gnr 83560 168 Siege Bty. RGA
BAKER Alfred W. MM Dvr 13097 33 Bde RFA
BAKER Arthur MM Sjt 265700 Liverpool Regt
BAKER Arthur MM Sjt 5696 2nd Suffolk Regt
BAKER Arthur MM Sjt 850126 62 Bde RFA
BAKER Arthur MM Dvr 26893 Royal Engineers
BAKER Arthur MM Cpl 7712 1st Royal Scots Fusiliers
BAKER Arthur MM Sjt 8015 1st Somerset Light Infantry
BAKER Arthur MM Gnr 10676 B/122 Bde RFA KIA 6.10.18.
BAKER Arthur "MM,MID,CG(F)" Cpl 3107 XVI Corps Cyclist Bn Army Cyclist Corps
BAKER Arthur MM Sjt 14120 C/241 Bde RFA
BAKER Arthur Charles MM Sjt 96451 RGA
BAKER Arthur G. MM Dvr 64092 C/47 Bde RFA
BAKER Arthur Leonard MM Spr 65507 106 Fd Coy Royal Engineers
BAKER Arthur W. MM L/Cpl 33197 Yorkshire Regt
BAKER Bert William MM Bdr 92551 C/51 Bde RFA
BAKER Bertram H. MM Cpl 62368 9th Welsh Regt
BAKER C.J. MM Pte 202312 Royal West Surrey Regt
BAKER Charles MM Sjt 14899 Devonshire Regt
BAKER Charles MM Sjt 419 GMGR
BAKER Charles MM Gnr 54827 B/105 Bde RFA
BAKER Charles MM Pte 47300 20th Hussars
BAKER Charles A. MM Pte P/1719 3rd Rifle Brigade
BAKER Charles Albert MM Pte 182 9th East Surrey Regt
BAKER Charles C. MM Cpl 48712 RFA
BAKER Charles F. MM Cpl 10485 RFA
BAKER Charles J. MM L/Cpl 4694 8th East Surrey Regt
BAKER Charles T. MM L/Cpl 8567 1st Suffolk Regt
BAKER Charles W. MM Bdr 960147 C/82 Bde RFA
BAKER Charles W. MM 2nd Cpl 506392 Royal Engineers
BAKER Charlie MM L/Sjt 9093 Irish Guards
BAKER Christopher MM Sjt 54288 B Bty RHA
BAKER Claud S. MM+Bar Pte G/67861 11th Royal West Surrey Regt
BAKER E.W. MM L/Cpl 23684 1st Royal West Surrey Regt
BAKER Edward MM Pte 60636 13th Welsh Regt
BAKER Edward MM Pte R30385 King's Royal Rifle Corps
BAKER Edward Andrew MM Pte 40515 2nd Bedfordshire Regt
BAKER Edwin MM Pte 14988 South Staffordshire Regt
BAKER Enoch MM Cpl 9623 2nd Yorkshire Regt
BAKER Eric MM 2nd Cpl 312773 30 Div Sig Coy Royal Engineers
BAKER Ernest MM Pte 1644 Yorkshire Regt
BAKER Ernest MM Cpl 2870 6th London Regt
BAKER Ernest G MM Sjt 908 21st London Regt
BAKER Ernest G. MM L/Cpl 6844 Royal West Surrey Regt
BAKER Ernest T. MM L/Cpl 5539 10th Hussars
BAKER F.G. MM Pte 512523 2/3rd(?)Fd Amb RAMC
BAKER F.G. MM Pte 8943 2nd East Kent Regt
BAKER Francis MM Pte 295371 12th Somerset Light Infantry
BAKER Francis W. MM Cpl 33143 7th Wiltshire Regt
BAKER Frank MM L/Cpl 102 10th East Yorkshire Regt
BAKER Frank MM Sjt 200642 1/4th York & Lancaster Regt
BAKER Frank A. MM Pte 11192 11th Hampshire Regt
BAKER Frank Alexander MM L/Cpl 2928 14th London Regt KIA 1.10.18.
BAKER Frank J. MM Cpl B/3150 Rifle Brigade
BAKER Frank Langley MM Pte 323262 6th London Regt
BAKER Frank T. MM Pte 1197 7th Royal Sussex Regt
BAKER Frederick MM L/Cpl 37181 2nd Manchester Regt
BAKER Frederick MM Sjt 13845 1st Royal Irish Fusiliers
BAKER Frederick MM Pte 238889 Shropshire Light Infantry
BAKER Frederick C. MM Cpl 151235 104th Bn Machine Gun Corps
BAKER Frederick C. MM BSM 4330 213 Siege Bty RGA
BAKER Frederick J. MM+Bar Pte 16191 8th Suffolk Regt
BAKER Frederick James MM Cpl 558086 56 Div Sig Coy Royal Engineers
BAKER George MM Pte 20380 Hampshire Regt
BAKER George "DCM,MM" Sjt 528095 54 Div Sig Coy Royal Engineers
BAKER George MM Gnr 85165 A/62 Bde RFA
BAKER George Alfred MM Pte 19718 Middlesex Regt
BAKER George C. MM Pte 3101 12th Middlesex Regt
BAKER George F. MM+Bar Pte M/296563 Army Service Corps
BAKER George H. MM Pnr 359683 12 Div Sig Coy Royal Engineers
BAKER George H. MM Cpl 14931 8th Suffolk Regt
BAKER George Henry "MC,MM" Cpl 129181 45th Royal Fusiliers
BAKER George W. MM Pte 44251 12th North Staffordshire Regt
BAKER George William MM Pte 419459 RAMC
BAKER Gordon G. MM Pte 304885 5th London Regt
BAKER H.E. MM Cpl 350276 1 Fd Amb RAMC
BAKER H.G. MM L/Cpl 43979 Royal Engineers
BAKER Harold E. MM Pte 31467 9th Devonshire Regt
BAKER Harold R. MM Gnr 348409 RGA
BAKER Harry MM Cpl 23003 1st Leicestershire Regt
BAKER Harry MM Pte 32363 1st East Surrey Regt
BAKER Harry MM L/Cpl 13717 Leicestershire Regt
BAKER Harry MM Dvr 61070 83 Fd Coy Royal Engineers
BAKER Harvey T. MM Pte 36235 Royal Berkshire Regt
BAKER Henry James MM L/Cpl 2365 Royal Sussex Regt
BAKER Henry Leonard MM CQMS 8074 9th Essex Regt DOW 20.3.18.
BAKER Herbert MM L/Cpl 28346 8th Somerset Light Infantry
BAKER Herbert MM Sjt 2482 9th Lancers
BAKER Herbert A. MM Cpl 353391 19th London Regt
BAKER Herbert Fullerton MM Cpl 554396 2/16th London Regt KIA 30.4.18.
BAKER Herbert G. MM 2nd Cpl 79755 Royal Engineers
BAKER Horace A.R. MM Pte 35874 11th Welsh Regt
BAKER Horace H. MM L/Cpl G/42193 13th Royal Fusiliers
BAKER Hyman MM Pte 33686 5/6th Scottish Rifles
BAKER J. MM Pte 33255 South Staffordshire Regt
BAKER James MM Pte 80513 7 Fd Amb RAMC Died 10.7.17.
BAKER James MM Gnr 32506 MGC (Motors)
BAKER James MM Gnr 72635 11 Bde RFA
BAKER James MM Pte 4646 1st Royal West Kent Regt

BAKER James MM Cpl 421219 10th London Regt
BAKER James Alexander MM L/Cpl 14208 12th East Surrey Regt KIA 27.9.17.
BAKER James E. MM Pte 1076 Royal West Surrey Regt
BAKER James Ernest MM Pte 6486 8th Royal West Surrey Regt
BAKER James W. MM Pte 10932 8th East Kent Regt
BAKER Jesse MM+Bar Sjt 31049 RGA
BAKER John MM L/Sjt 238089 1/4th Seaforth Highlanders
BAKER John MM Pte 206114 5th Devonshire Regt
BAKER John MM Cpl 35104 RAMC
BAKER John MM+Bar Sjt 102740 178 Tunnelling Coy Royal Engineers
BAKER John MM Pte L/10771 Royal West Surrey Regt
BAKER John MM Gnr 117219 230 Siege Bty RGA
BAKER John MM Gnr 275005 7 Siege Bty RGA
BAKER John A. MM Pte 21104 Duke of Cornwall's LI
BAKER John Denis MM Pte 6858 12th Lancers KIA 27.1.18.
BAKER John H. MM Pte 9604 17 Coy Labour Corps
BAKER John Henry MM L/Bdr Sig L/6172 B/256 Bde RFA
BAKER John Henry MM Pte 5256 1/6th South Staffordshire Regt
BAKER John Herbert MM Pte 6502 8th Royal West Kent Regt KIA 24.4.18.
BAKER John W. "MM,MID" Cpl 19583 13th Liverpool Regt
BAKER John W. MM Sjt T1/3985 Army Service Corps
BAKER Jonathan "DCM,MM+Bar" Sjt 201471 2/4th Yorkshire Light Infantry
BAKER Joseph MM Pte S/40333 1st Cameron Highlanders
BAKER Joseph MM Pte 28475 1st Grenadier Guards
BAKER Joseph E. MM Sjt 197838 Royal Engineers
BAKER Joseph Gilroy MM L/Bdr 45377 RFA
BAKER Joseph H. MM Pte 40805 Worcestershire Regt
BAKER Joseph Henry MM L/Sjt 61566 RAMC
BAKER Kenneth L. MM Pte 535528 15th London Regt
BAKER Lawrence H. MM Sjt 20968 Royal Engineers
BAKER Leonard MM Pte 43849 Notts & Derby Regt
BAKER Maurice "DCM,MM" Cpl 95318 152 Fd Coy Royal Engineers
BAKER Norman L. MM Pte 735011 24th London Regt
BAKER Patrick MM Pte 268 5th Connaught Rangers Att 5 R Mun Fus.
BAKER Percy H. MM CSM Y/1456 King's Royal Rifle Corps
BAKER Percy Willie MM Pte 41356 10th Essex Regt KIA 31.7.17.
BAKER Raymond MM Sjt 13609 4th Bedfordshire Regt
BAKER Reuben MM CSM 5394 1st Royal Welsh Fusiliers
BAKER Reuben MM Dvr 51814 26 Bde RFA
BAKER Richard MM L/Cpl 39687 South Wales Borderers
BAKER Richard MM Cpl 85534 Machine Gun Corps
BAKER Samuel MM Pte 202057 4th York & Lancaster Regt
BAKER Samuel MM Pte S/29724 2nd Rifle Brigade
BAKER Samuel MM L/Cpl 15733 West Yorkshire Regt
BAKER Samuel C. MM Pte 1830 Royal Sussex Regt
BAKER Septimus? W. MM Pte 59310 Royal Engineers
BAKER Sidney H. MM Gnr Fitter 211356 112 Bde RFA
BAKER Sydney MM Dvr 13063 3 Div Ammn Col RFA
BAKER Sydney MM Cpl 1421 16 Bty 6(London)Bde RFA
BAKER Sydney H. MM Pte 87433 14th Royal Welsh Fusiliers
BAKER Thomas "DCM,MM+Bar,MID" Cpl 29975 36 Bde RFA
BAKER Thomas MM Pte 2275 8th Liverpool Regt
BAKER Thomas MM Pte 25340 Liverpool Regt
BAKER Thomas MM Pte 242472 West Riding Regt
BAKER Thomas A. MM Sjt 6385 RGA
BAKER Thomas B. MM Pte 31638 Gloucestershire Regt
BAKER Thomas G. "MM,MID" Sjt Sig 30514 278 Siege Bty RGA
BAKER Thomas G. MM+Bar Cpl 10851 Royal Berkshire Regt
BAKER Victor J. MM+Bar Gnr 50090 RFA
BAKER W.L. MM Air Mech 2 63289 Royal Air Force
BAKER Walter MM Pte 201678 1/4th South Lancashire Regt
BAKER Walter MM Pte M2/032646 73 Coy Army Service Corps
BAKER Walter H. MM+Bar CQMS 14809 2nd Grenadier Guards
BAKER Walter J.T. MM Pte 76482 4th Royal Fusiliers
BAKER Walter W. MM Pte 7323 15th Hussars
BAKER William MM L/Cpl 16832 1st Grenadier Guards
BAKER William MM Pte 33506 York & Lancaster Regt
BAKER William MM Pte 49943 Machine Gun Corps
BAKER William MM Pte 538194 RAMC
BAKER William MM Cpl 1390 RAMC
BAKER William MM Sjt 8344 2nd Royal Sussex Regt
BAKER William MM Pte 307945 West Riding Regt
BAKER William MM Pte 23357 Liverpool Regt
BAKER William A. MM Pte 77826 17th Royal Fusiliers
BAKER William Alfred MM Sjt 2873 9th Lancers
BAKER William E. MM Pte 51114 Middlesex Regt
BAKER William G. MM Sjt 925538 C/290 Bde RFA
BAKER William G. MM Pte 471069 12th London Regt
BAKER William H. MM Cpl 2222 3 Fd Amb RAMC
BAKER William H. MM Sjt 11262 5tth Shropshire Light Infantry
BAKER William Hallam MM Pte R/16275 6th King's Royal Rifle Corps
BAKER William James MM Cpl F/521 17th Middlesex Regt KIA 22.10.16.
BAKER William M. MM+Bar Pte 351055 7th London Regt
BAKER William Thomas MM Pte 18149 2nd Bedfordshire Regt KIA 12.10.16.
BAKER Winton MM Cpl 250318 6th Manchester Regt
BAKES Harold MM Gnr 780737 311 Bde RFA
BAKEWELL Horace MM+Bar L/Cpl 23/444 23rd Northumberland Fusiliers Died 29.4.17.
BALCHIN Frederick Charles MM Spr 103125 32 Div Sig Coy Royal Engineers
BALCOMBE Alfred MM Bdr 61724 RFA
BALCOMBE Thomas MM Pte 3730 13th Royal Sussex Regt
BALCOMBE William H. MM Pte 12407 East Surrey Regt
BALDERSON Frederick Charles MM L/Cpl 31303 14th Gloucestershire Regt Died 22.10.17.
BALDERSON John MM Sjt 19382 North Lancashire Regt
BALDERSON Robert MM+Bar Cpl 14656 1st Lincolnshire Regt
BALDERSTON Jesse MM Pte 242399 Leicestershire Regt
BALDERSTON Joseph MM Pte 1922 1/4th Royal Lancaster Regt DOW 2.9.16.
BALDERSTON Thomas H. MM Cpl M/206398 Army Service Corps
BALDERSTONE William MM Pte B/635 Rifle Brigade
BALDING Marquis J. MM Pte 41279 7th Worcestershire Regt
BALDING William Ling MM Pte 40004 1st South Staffordshire Regt
BALDOCK Robert Nathaniel MM Sjt 2235 1/17th London Regt KIA 15.9.16.
BALDOCK William C. MM Pte 265472 1/1st Bucks Bn Oxf & Bucks Light Infantry
BALDOCK William T. MM L/Cpl 371291 8th London Regt
BALDREY Leonard MM Pte 6990 Royal West Surrey Regt att Yorks LI.KIA 4.10.17.
BALDREY William C. MM Sjt 1087 1/18th London Regt
BALDRY Alfred W. MM L/Sjt 19937 2nd Hampshire Regt
BALDRY Frederick MM Pte 63976 13th Yorkshire Regt
BALDRY Herbert MM Gnr 346025 RGA
BALDRY Percy William "MC,MM" CSM G/1851 East Kent Regt
BALDWIN Aaron J. MM Sjt 955664 RFA
BALDWIN Alexander MM Sjt 57324 RFA
BALDWIN Andrew MM BQMS 55490 135 Siege Bty RGA
BALDWIN Arthur MM Sjt 656 10th East Yorkshire Regt
BALDWIN Arthur Edward MM Cpl 473121 RAMC
BALDWIN Arthur J. MM Cpl 13190 Worcestershire Regt
BALDWIN Arthur Oliver MM Cpl (MCDR) 444241 42 Div Sig Coy Royal Engineers
BALDWIN C.F. MM Sjt 2158 Royal West Kent Regt
BALDWIN Charles MM L/Cpl G/9676 10th Royal West Kent Regt
BALDWIN Charles MM Cpl 2031 1/1st Bucks Bn Oxf & Bucks Light Infantry
BALDWIN Ernest MM Pte 241590 1/5th East Lancashire Regt KIA 8.11.18.
BALDWIN Francis MM L/Cpl 48396 Liverpool Regt
BALDWIN Fred MM Spr 27313 Royal Engineers
BALDWIN Frederick C. MM Spr 488605 Royal Engineers
BALDWIN Frederick T. MM Sjt 15098 Royal Engineers
BALDWIN Frederick W. MM Sjt 141780 296 Siege Bty RGA
BALDWIN George F. "DCM,MM" Pte 13830 10th Scottish Rifles
BALDWIN Gilbert MM Cpl M2/046883 178 Coy Army Service Corps
BALDWIN Herbert MM Dvr 785996 D/312 Bde RFA
BALDWIN Herbert Thomas Henry "MC,MM" CSM 4612 2nd Royal Welsh Fusiliers
BALDWIN Horace "DCM,MM" Cpl 201118 1/5th Bedfordshire Regt
BALDWIN Horace J. MM L/Sjt 225486 1st London Regt
BALDWIN Isaac Henshall MM Sjt 67498 56 Bty 44 Bde RFA
BALDWIN J. MM Pte 5742 Bedfordshire Regt
BALDWIN James P. MM Dvr L/40636 RFA
BALDWIN James William MM Sjt 1935 1/1st Buckinghamshire Oxf & Bucks Light Infantry
BALDWIN John MM Pte 1310 22nd Royal Fusiliers
BALDWIN John MM L/Cpl 35128 70 Coy Machine Gun Corps
BALDWIN John MM Pte 13869 Labour Corps
BALDWIN John G. MM Spr 153730 Royal Engineers
BALDWIN Leonard Macdonald MM Pte 28140 8th East Surrey Regt

BALDWIN Owen MM L/Sjt 265360 1/1st Buckinghamshire Oxf & Bucks Light Infantry
BALDWIN R.C. MM Sjt 203889 Lancashire Fusiliers
BALDWIN Rennie MM Sjt 986 Royal Engineers
BALDWIN Robert MM Pte 269091 5th West Riding Regt
BALDWIN Sidney T. MM Pte 1254 1st Welsh Guards
BALDWIN Stanley MM Pte 43126 Middlesex Regt
BALDWIN V.A. "MM,MID" Sjt 55101 RFA
BALDWIN William A. MM Bdr 8922 C/50 Bde RFA
BALDWIN William Frank MM Cpl 3346 24th London Regt
BALDWIN William G. MM Pte 15998 10th Hussars
BALDWIN William G.F. MM Sjt 18250 6th Bedfordshire Regt
BALDWIN William H. MM Pte 200887 1/5th Liverpool Regt
BALE Albert MM Pte 10355 Royal Berkshire Regt
BALE James MM Sjt 29633 118 Siege Bty RGA
BALE Percy H. MM Pte 26327 5th West Riding Regt
BALE Sidney MM Sjt 12485 Leicestershire Regt
BALE William J. MM Pte 232358 2nd London Regt
BALFE Joseph MM Sjt 4512 Irish Guards
BALFOUR Albert MM Air Mech 1 8575 Royal Flying Corps
BALFOUR Andrew "DCM,MM,MID" Bdr 844 B/263 Bde RFA
BALFOUR Arnold MM Cpl 306419 Liverpool Regt
BALFOUR C. MM L/Cpl P12933 Military Mounted Police
BALFOUR David MM Dvr 15224 86 Bty 35 Bde RFA
BALFOUR Francis J. MM Pte 13121 9th Border Regt
BALFOUR William MM L/Cpl 19351 VIII Corps Cyclist Bn Army Cyclist Corps
BALKWILL William B. MM Pte S/4620 13th Rifle Brigade
BALL Albert MM L/Cpl 17804 6th York & Lancaster Regt
BALL Albert J. MM L/Cpl 9977 5th Northamptonshire Regt
BALL Arthur Henry "DCM,MM" Gnr 78018 A/110 Bde RFA KIA 20.4.18.
BALL Bertram MM Pte 241396 2/5th Gloucestershire Regt
BALL Charles MM L/Cpl 1707 12th Royal Fusiliers KIA 8.10.16.
BALL Charles MM L/Cpl 10186 2nd Royal Welsh Fusiliers
BALL Charles MM Sjt 4318 1st Norfolk Regt
BALL Charles Edward MM L/Cpl 3521 13th Royal Sussex Regt KIA 3.9.16.
BALL Charles M. MM Gnr 832158 B/174 Bde RFA
BALL Cyril E. MM Gnr 40446 RGA
BALL Edgerton MM Sjt 281003 Lancashire Fusiliers
BALL Edward MM L/Cpl 240858 5th West Riding Regt
BALL Edward F. MM BQMS 905720 337 Bde RFA
BALL Edwin MM Pte 89458 136 Fd Amb RAMC
BALL Edwin F. MM Cpl 17324 Dorsetshire Regt
BALL Edwin P. MM Drummer L/13237 1st Royal Fusiliers
BALL Francis MM Dvr W/3686 RFA
BALL Frank MM L/Sjt 202083 1st London Regt
BALL Fred MM Pte 281811 Lancashire Fusiliers
BALL Fred H. MM Sjt 79206 RFA
BALL Frederick MM L/Cpl 39736 3 Squadron MGC (Cavalry)
BALL Frederick W. MM+Bar Sjt 240562 1/4th Royal Lancaster Regt
BALL George MM Pte 92124 14th Bn Tank Corps
BALL George MM Sjt 486268 Royal Engineers
BALL George MM+Bar L/Cpl 240369 1/5th South Lancashire Regt KIA 1.12.17.
BALL George MM Pte 31998 2nd Rifle Brigade
BALL George F. MM Cpl 40427 69 Fd Coy Royal Engineers
BALL George Henry MM Cpl 102818 177 Tunnelling Coy Royal Engineers
BALL George S. MM Pnr 322235 Royal Engineers
BALL Gerard MM+Bar Cpl 18342 10th Lancashire Fusiliers
BALL Harry MM Pte 29543 Yorkshire Regt
BALL Harry Harold MM Sjt 40445 Att 1st Bn Gordon H RAMC KIA 28.3.18.
BALL Henry MM Sjt L/31654 C/119 Bde RFA
BALL Henry MM Sjt 24806 Liverpool Regt
BALL Herbert MM L/Cpl 25976 17th Royal Welsh Fusiliers
BALL Herbert Alfred MM Sjt 38924 5 Div Ammn Col RFA
BALL Herbert Wallace MM Sjt 9023 Coldstream Guards
BALL J. MM L/Cpl 13281 11th Essex Regt
BALL Jacob E. MM Cpl 45125 Northumberland Fusiliers
BALL James MM Dvr 19713 B/75 Bde RFA
BALL James H. MM Pte 49027 7th Lancashire Fusiliers
BALL Joel J. MM Pte 20356 2nd Coldstream Guards
BALL John MM Dvr 88572 H Bty RHA
BALL John MM L/Cpl 307027 Royal Warwickshire Regt
BALL John MM Pte 29559 Yorkshire Regt
BALL John James MM Pte 282246 4th London Regt KIA 8.8.18.
BALL John R. MM Pte 13662 Machine Gun Corps
BALL John T. MM Pte 531134 15th London Regt
BALL John Thomas MM Spr 217132 2 Div Sig Coy Royal Engineers
BALL Leonard F. MM Cpl L/44955 RFA
BALL Nelson MM Cpl C/6868 King's Royal Rifle Corps
BALL Norbert J. MM Cpl 305591 13th Bn Tank Corps
BALL Richard MM Cpl 9887 Liverpool Regt
BALL Robert MM L/Cpl 308110 16th Bn Tank Corps
BALL Samuel MM Spr 47244 Royal Engineers
BALL Samuel MM Pte C/410 16th King's Royal Rifle Corps KIA 24.3.18.
BALL Samuel MM Pte 27483 1st Royal Warwickshire Regt
BALL T. "MM,MID" Sjt 330595 1/7th Liverpool Regt
BALL Thomas MM Pte 201812 Royal Scots Fusiliers
BALL Thomas MM Pte 240291 5th Devonshire Regt
BALL Thomas H. MM L/Cpl 309077 6th Bn Tank Corps
BALL Thomas James MM Sjt 32 Royal Sussex Regt att KAR.
BALL Thomas S. MM Gnr 2369 RFA
BALL Walter MM Dvr 84780 RFA
BALL Walter Albert MM Cpl 25520 2nd West Riding Regt
BALL Walter Harold MM Sjt G/211 9th Royal Fusiliers KIA 3.5.17.
BALL William "DCM,MM+Bar" Sjt 97474 154 Fd Coy Royal Engineers DOW 17.5.18.
BALL William MM Pte 33525 Cheshire Regt
BALL William MM Pte S/8092 9th Gordon Highlanders
BALL William MM Sjt 362249 RGA
BALL William Arthur MM+Bar Cpl 720879 1/24th London Regt
BALL William H. MM Pte 5621 VII Corps Cyclist Bn Army Cyclist Corps
BALL William Henry MM Pte 351916 13th Royal Scots
BALL William J. "DCM,MM" CSM 512830 14th London Regt
BALL William J. MM Pte 68890 RAMC
BALL William T. MM+Bar Pte G/13042 Royal Sussex Regt
BALL William W. MM Cpl 235567 8th York & Lancaster Regt
BALLAM Frank Mervin MM S/Sjt Fitter 90409 78 Bde RFA
BALLAM George Jackson MM Bdr 967 153 Bde RFA
BALLAM Kenneth MM Sjt 11808 70 Bty 34 Bde RFA KIA 28.4.17.
BALLAN Peter MM L/Cpl 23726 6th West Riding Regt
BALLANCE Margaret Hendebourck MM Sister F SJAB
BALLANCE Thomas J. MM Pte 37380 41st Bn Machine Gun Corps
BALLANTINE David MM Pte 97868 108 Coy Machine Gun Corps
BALLANTINE John H. MM Pnr 341195 21 Div Sig Coy Royal Engineers
BALLANTINE Louis MM Pte 14054 10th Royal Irish Rifles
BALLANTINE Thomas MM Cpl 84796 Royal Engineers
BALLANTINE William MM Pte 2005 8th London Regt
BALLANTYNE Ernest MM Gnr Fitter 760072 RFA
BALLANTYNE George M. MM L/Cpl 335114 8th Royal Scots
BALLANTYNE John MM Spr 134998 Royal Engineers
BALLANTYNE John C. MM Cpl 15150 8th Scottish Rifles
BALLANTYNE John M MM Pte 250313 5/6th Royal Scots
BALLANTYNE John T. MM+Bar Sjt 15760 Somerset Light Infantry
BALLANTYNE Walter MM Pte 8390 2nd Gordon Highlanders
BALLARD Albert MM Pte 6221 1st Royal Berkshire Regt
BALLARD B. MM Gnr 805469 RFA
BALLARD Charles MM Pte 202522 4th Worcestershire Regt
BALLARD Claude MM Pte 20035 5th Cameron Highlanders DOW 5.5.18.
BALLARD Frederick MM Gnr 750868 RFA
BALLARD Frederick MM Sjt 9717 Royal Berkshire Regt
BALLARD Frederick MM Gnr 61100 RFA
BALLARD George W. MM Cpl 405120 RAMC
BALLARD John Richard MM Pte 15175 10th Royal Welsh Fusiliers KIA 16.8.16.
BALLARD Richard W. MM Sjt 1835 2nd Dragoon Guards
BALLARD Samuel Louis MM L/Sjt 7849 2nd Coldstream Guards
BALLARD Thomas Henry MM Sjt 6362 3 Fd Amb RAMC
BALLARD Thomas Pearson MM Dvr 751323 A/250 Bde RFA
BALLARD Victor MM L/Cpl 24876 Machine Gun Corps
BALLETT Samuel MM Spr 29568 3 Div Sig Coy Royal Engineers
BALLINGALL Alexander MM Pte 998 10th Arg & Suth Highlanders
BALLINGALL David MM Pte 21330 17th Royal Scots
BALLINGALL John R. MM Cpl 291678 1/7th Royal Highlanders
BALLINGER Edward T. "DCM,MM" Sjt 8392 1st South Staffordshire Regt
BALLINGER George MM Sjt 93108 14th Bn Tank Corps
BALLINGER Percy "DCM,MM" Sjt 285819 151 Hy Bty RGA
BALLINGER Ralph MM L/Cpl 39689 12th Gloucestershire Regt
BALLOCH Peter MM L/Cpl 18531 13th Royal Scots
BALLS Albert MM Dvr 93534 C/46 Bde RFA
BALLS Albert E. MM BSM 940078 D/281 Bde RFA

BALLS Albert F. MM Sjt 35707 41 Siege Bty RGA
BALLS Charles William MM L/Cpl 325429 1/9th Durham Light Infantry
BALLS Ernest MM Gnr 156524 223 Siege Bty RGA
BALLS George W. MM CSM 7895 King's Royal Rifle Corps
BALLS Herbert MM Cpl 426 RFA
BALLS John E. MM L/Cpl 146185 19th Bn Machine Gun Corps
BALLS Robert W. MM L/Cpl 8921 Royal West Surrey Regt
BALLS Sydney H. MM Pte 723066 24th London Regt
BALLS William C. MM Cpl 18046 2nd Suffolk Regt
BALLS William H. MM L/Sjt 1808 7th Royal West Kent Regt
BALLSOM Herbert MM Dvr 70647 5 Bde RFA
BALMAIN Walter MM Cpl 2546 1st Royal Highlanders KIA 18.4.18.
BALMAN Charles MM+2 Bars Sjt R/23922 18th King's Royal Rifle Corps
BALMAN Richard MM Dvr 38717 D/82 Bde RFA
BALMER Arthur J. MM Gnr 28381 RFA
BALMER George MM Pte 301123 Arg & Suth Highlanders
BALMER George MM L/Cpl 72390 Machine Gun Corps Died 30.7.17
BALMER Herbert A. MM Pte 12589 3rd Royal Fusiliers
BALMER John Simpson MM Cpl 27217 8 Div Ammn Col RFA
BALMER Michael MM Cpl 267299 1st Notts & Derby Regt
BALMFORTH John F. MM Cpl 29357 29th Bn Machine Gun Corps
BALMFORTH Joseph MM Pte 308500 Liverpool Regt
BALMOND Harry MM Sjt 11433 Duke of Cornwall's LI
BALNAVES George Henry MM Dvr 66270 RFA
BALSHAW Reginald MM Gnr 244511 RFA
BALSHAW Thomas MM Cpl 9259 8/10th Gordon Highlanders
BALSOM Edward MM Sjt 760751 B/94 Bde RFA
BALSOM Harry Josiah MM L/Cpl 110667 Machine Gun Corps
BALSON Cyril M. MM Pte 1832 24 Fd Amb RAMC
BALSTER Alfred G. MM L/Cpl 370658 17th London Regt
BAMBER Edward MM L/Cpl 30002 8th Royal Lancaster Regt KIA 23.3.18.
BAMBER Frederick J. MM L/Cpl 20521 Welsh Regt
BAMBER Frederick William MM Sjt 53593 98 Fd Coy Royal Engineers Died 17.2.17.
BAMBER J.E. MM Spr 215746 Royal Engineers
BAMBER Jack W. MM 2nd Cpl 105289 Royal Engineers
BAMBER James MM L/Cpl 337 1/4th North Lancashire Regt
BAMBER Thomas MM Pte 62173 2nd Northumberland Fusiliers
BAMBER Thomas MM Pte 23228 12th Liverpool Regt KIA 7.10.16.
BAMBERGER Edward L. MM Sjt 8866 Royal Engineers "att 2nd Sappers & Miners, Indian Army"
BAMBLETT Charles Edward MM Pte 8588 10th Royal West Kent Regt
BAMBLETT William MM Cpl 2715 1st Rifle Brigade
BAMBOROUGH John George MM Pte 21549 12th Durham Light Infantry
BAMBOROUGH Thomas MM Pte 18077 12th Durham Light Infantry KIA 17.7.16.
BAMBRIDGE Albert MM Sjt 43697 Suffolk Regt
BAMBRIDGE Arthur R. MM Cpl 3785 7th Dragoon Guards
BAMBRIDGE Rupert Charles "DSO,MC+Bar,MM(STK/319 L/Sjt)" Capt 10th Royal Fusiliers DOW 23.5.18.
BAMFORD Alfred MM Pte 16560 12th Gloucestershire Regt
BAMFORD Ernest J. "MM,MSM" Dvr 9166 B/150 Bde RFA
BAMFORD Frank A. MM Sjt 17635 109 Siege Bty RGA
BAMFORD George MM+Bar Pte 202778 Liverpool Regt
BAMFORD Harold MM Cpl 860 1st Cyclist Coy Army Cyclist Corps
BAMFORD Henry J. MM Cpl(MCDR) 74956 19 Div Sig Coy Royal Engineers
BAMFORD J.H. MM Pte 241323 Lancashire Fusiliers
BAMFORD John J. MM Spr 107094 40 Div Sig Coy Royal Engineers
BAMFORD Norman S. MM Pte 30479 4th North Lancashire Regt
BAMFORD Thomas MM Pte 1170 2nd Manchester Regt
BAMFORTH Milton MM Pte 242692 West Riding Regt
BAMFORTH Walter MM Pte 241022 5th York & Lancaster Regt
BAMPFYLDE A.P. MM Spr 82553 Royal Engineers
BAMPING Jack MM Pte 30364 2nd Grenadier Guards
BAMPTON David G. MM Pte 17593 Hampshire Regt
BANAHAN Joseph MM Sjt 275782 Manchester Regt
BANBURY Douglas MM Pte 27463 1st Royal Dublin Fusiliers
BANCE Albert Edward MM Pte 230 13th East Surrey Regt KIA 26.11.17.
BANCE Charles MM L/Cpl 9685 1st Royal West Surrey Regt KIA 23.4.17.
BANCE George E. "MM,MSM" Sjt 19110 201st Bn? Machine Gun Corps
BANCROFT Arthur C. MM Sub Conductor 013017 Army Ordnance Corps
BANCROFT Fred MM Pte 13874 Labour Corps
BANCROFT Gilbert MM Dvr 312453 Royal Engineers
BANCROFT Harold MM Pte 306890 West Riding Regt
BANCROFT Harry O. MM L/Cpl 266604 Gordon Highlanders
BANCROFT Hudson MM+Bar 2nd Cpl 96923 Royal Engineers
BANCROFT James MM Pte 26573 4th Grenadier Guards
BANCROFT Joseph "DCM,MM" Sjt 200453 1/4th West Riding Regt KIA 4.5.18.
BANCROFT Thomas MM Pte 21241 Liverpool Regt
BAND Harry MM Pte 58216 Cheshire Regt
BAND Harry MM Pte 630095 20th London Regt
BANDEY Robert W. MM Pte 252820 3rd London Regt
BANDY Albert MM Pte R/4994 13th King's Royal Rifle Corps KIA 23.8.18.
BANE Henry MM L/Cpl 43522 Norfolk Regt
BANES Albert MM Pte 29349 Royal Fusiliers
BANES George H. MM Pte 13409 Yorkshire Regt
BANFORD Norman MM L/Cpl 43094 1st Scottish Rifles
BANFORD William MM Pte 17/1548 Royal Irish Rifles
BANGAY Herbert E. MM L/Cpl 66594 Royal Engineers
BANGS Hubert V. MM Cpl (MCDR) 77796 23 Div Sig Coy Royal Engineers
BANHAM A. MM+Bar Sjt 18600 19th Lancashire Fusiliers
BANHAM Charles Robert MM L/Bdr 54391 RHA
BANHAM E. MM Cpl 510446 2 Fd Amb RAMC
BANHAM Edward MM Sjt 16478 23 Fd Coy Royal Engineers
BANHAM F. MM Pte 11085 Essex Regt
BANHAM Frederick MM Sjt G/60304 26th Royal Fusiliers
BANHAM George W. MM Spr 43737 Royal Engineers
BANHAM John MM Cpl M2/055475 Att 45 Fd Amb Army Service Corps
BANHAM R. MM Cpl 5577 Lancashire Fusiliers
BANHAM Walter H. MM Cpl 54583 121 Heavy Bty RGA
BANISTER Frederick Charles. MM Pte 22639 3rd Grenadier Guards
BANISTER Herbert G. MM L/Cpl 42089 10th Royal Warwickshire Regt
BANKHEAD Hugh MM Gnr 64010 RFA
BANKHEAD William J. MM L/Cpl 79 1st Royal Irish Rifles
BANKIER Hugh H. MM Cpl 295595 12th Royal Scots Fusiliers
BANKS A. MM Pte 42515 Royal Irish Rifles
BANKS Bernard L. MM Sjt 48167 Royal Engineers
BANKS D. MM+Bar Pte 267557 Seaforth Highlanders
BANKS E. MM Sjt 362251 RGA
BANKS E.H. MM Pte S/27386 Rifle Brigade
BANKS E.W. MM Pte 302746 10th Bn Tank Corps
BANKS Ernest MM Pte 1719 Att 1/4(London)Fd Coy RE RAMC KIA 15.9.16.
BANKS Ernest J. MM.MID Pte 2382 Notts & Derby Regt
BANKS Ernest R. MM+Bar Sjt G/22 2nd Royal Sussex Regt
BANKS F.S. MM Pte 125746 Machine Gun Corps
BANKS Francis MM L/Cpl 2566 2nd B Coy Royal Irish Regt KIA 16.8.17.
BANKS G. MM Pte 34486 15th Royal Warwickshire Regt
BANKS G. MM Pte 203696 Liverpool Regt
BANKS George C. MM Pte 16098 5th Border Regt
BANKS H. MM L/Cpl 241816 York & Lancaster Regt
BANKS H.E. MM Cpl 200181 Northamptonshire Regt
BANKS H.F. MM L/Cpl 16133 Middlesex Regt
BANKS H.W.B. MM Pte 2891 Border Regt
BANKS Henry MM Sjt 1830 18th London Regt
BANKS Isaac MM L/Cpl 73057 24th Royal Welsh Fusiliers
BANKS James MM Cpl G/11173 13th Royal Fusiliers
BANKS James MM Sjt 101555 Royal Engineers
BANKS John MM Cpl 12/1485 1st East Yorkshire Regt
BANKS John MM Pte 325747 Arg & Suth Highlanders
BANKS John B. MM Cpl 715176 RFA
BANKS John H. MM Pte M2/106438 Army Service Corps
BANKS John W. MM Cpl 24239 Border Regt
BANKS Joseph MM Gnr Sig 680909 C/286 Bde RFA
BANKS Joseph MM+Bar L/Cpl 36233 Yorkshire Regt
BANKS Joseph W. "DCM,MM" Cpl 21588 East Yorkshire Regt
BANKS Joseph W. MM Pte 18447 Coldstream Guards
BANKS Nicholas L. MM Spr 47190 23 Div Sig Coy Royal Engineers
BANKS Percy Kenyon MM Spr 130909 Second Army Sig Coy Royal Engineers
BANKS Reginald W. MM Sjt 61934 RAMC
BANKS Sidney MM Pte 3336 24th Royal Fusiliers
BANKS Thomas MM Sjt 3766 18th Bn Machine Gun Corps

BANKS Thomas MM L/Cpl 282142 1st Lancashire Fusiliers KIA 11.4.18.
BANKS Walter MM Cpl 741561 5th London Regt
BANN James MM+Bar L/Cpl 12644 1st Scots Guards
BANNAN Joseph MM Pte 13832 11th Border Regt
BANNER Fred MM Pte 2476 South Lancashire Regt
BANNER Frederick William MM L/Cpl 19221 1st Lancashire Fusiliers
BANNER George MM Pte 241792 1/8th Worcestershire Regt KIA 4.3.17.
BANNER Robert MM Cpl 29750 Royal Scots
BANNERMAN David MM Pte 241396 Seaforth Highlanders
BANNERMAN Joseph MM Spr 9792 Royal Engineers
BANNING Charles R. MM L/Cpl 23358 5th Royal Lancaster Regt
BANNING Conward John MM Pte 201652 2/4th Hampshire Regt
BANNISTER Aalbert E. MM Pte 144767 37th Bn Machine Gun Corps
BANNISTER Arthur MM L/Cpl 43587 22nd Manchester Regt DOW 27.10.18.
BANNISTER Ernest MM Cpl 53356 12th Royal Scots
BANNISTER Ernie MM Pte 241116 East Lancashire Regt
BANNISTER F.C.D. MM Pte 1903 London Regt
BANNISTER George MM Sjt 266947 2nd Notts & Derby Regt
BANNISTER George W. MM Sjt 69898 Tank Corps
BANNISTER Hartley MM Pte 34794 5th East Lancashire Regt
BANNISTER James MM Gnr 66790 B/112 Bde RFA
BANNISTER James MM Pte 201716 7th Worcestershire Regt
BANNISTER John Henry Arthur MM Sjt 85277 143 Coy Labour Corps
BANNISTER Joseph MM Pte 236386 1/1st Herefordshire Regt
BANNISTER Maurice MM L/Cpl 9109 1st Royal Berkshire Regt
BANNISTER Richard MM Cpl 19833 18th Liverpool Regt
BANNISTER Sidney W. MM L/Bdr 266394 389 Bty 37 Bde RFA
BANNISTER Tom MM Pte 352168 1/2nd(East Lancashire)Fd Amb RAMC
BANNISTER Walter J. MM Pte 72737 17 Fd Amb RAMC
BANNISTER William MM Gnr 138404 RFA
BANNISTER William F. MM Pte 34406 23rd Bn Machine Gun Corps
BANNISTER William Henry MM Pte 14748 9th Cheshire Regt
BANNISTER William Walter MM Pte 17141 11th Suffolk Regt Died 4.12.17.
BANNON James MM Pte 4251 2nd Leinster Regt
BANNON Michael MM Cpl 304 23rd Cheshire Regt Died 6.11.18.
BANNON Peter MM Pte 8085 1st Royal Irish Fusiliers
BANNON T. MM Bdr 76743 99 Bty 20 Bde RFA
BANTHORPE Alfred V. MM Sjt 232245 2nd London Regt
BANTING George Ernest MM Sjt 720819 1/24th London Regt KIA 5.4.18.
BANTOCK George F. MM L/Cpl 29023 1st Duke of Cornwall's LI
BANTON Arthur MM Spr 45695 Royal Engineers
BANTON George MM Pte 7661 1st Shropshire Light Infantry
BANTON Joseph H. MM+Bar Cpl 23587 A/160 Bde RFA
BANTON William MM Pte 30005 Royal Welsh Fusiliers
BANWELL Walter J. MM Spr 42072 Royal Engineers
BANYARD Charles A. MM Cpl 4088 20 Fd Amb RAMC
BAPTIE A. MM Gnr T/2144 RGA
BAPTIE Charles MM Spr 156516 183 Tunnelling Coy Royal Engineers
BAPTIE David MM L/Bdr 129272 RGA
BAPTIST Henry MM Pte 70415 Machine Gun Corps
BAPTIST Matthew MM Pte 16274 1st Grenadier Guards
BAPTY William MM Pte 4/6974 West Yorkshire Regt
BARBER Albert Edward "MM,MIDx2" L/Cpl 9189 1st Essex Regt Died 3.6.16.
BARBER Alfred L. MM Spr 58842 Royal Engineers
BARBER Arthur MM Sjt M2/073045 Army Service Corps
BARBER Arthur MM Cpl 1583 1/7th Notts & Derby Regt
BARBER Arthur MM Pte 25810 Notts & Derby Regt
BARBER Arthur MM Pte 15409 Middlesex Regt
BARBER Bertram E. MM L/Cpl 301419 13th Bn Tank Corps
BARBER Christopher MM Dvr 25438 A/74 Bde RFA
BARBER Clifford H. MM 2nd Cpl 166570 82 Fd Coy Royal Engineers
BARBER Clive Richards MM Bdr 106199 255 Siege Bty RGA Died 20.11.18.
BARBER David Stephen MM Pte 22800 4th Grenadier Guards
BARBER Edward MM Pte 96140 17 Squadron MGC(Cavalry) Died 27.10.18.
BARBER Edwin MM Sjt 18301 Royal Engineers
BARBER Ernest MM Pte 20025 7th Shropshire Light Infantry KIA 23.8.18.
BARBER Frank MM Pte 13771 9th Cheshire Regt
BARBER Frank MM Spr 65283 154 Fd Coy Royal Engineers
BARBER Frank MM Sjt 39788 Manchester Regt
BARBER Frank "MM,MSM" Bdr 95642 A/47 Bde RFA
BARBER Fred MM Sjt 5653 2nd Dragoon Guards
BARBER Fred MM L/Cpl 6502 Machine Gun Corps
BARBER Frederick H. MM Sjt 17159 Machine Gun Corps
BARBER George S. MM L/Cpl 2414 7th Royal West Kent Regt
BARBER Harold Harcourt Rodwell MM Pte 16589 1st Norfolk Regt
BARBER Harry MM 2nd Cpl 52538 83 Fd Coy Royal Engineers
BARBER Harry T. MM Pte 1196 7th Royal Sussex Regt
BARBER Hayden A. MM Gnr L/1654 RHA
BARBER Herbert MM Sjt 9/12159 Cheshire Regt
BARBER Herbert R. MM Bdr 43832 26 Bde RFA
BARBER Herbert Stewart MM Pte 1950 8th London Regt
BARBER Horace W. MM Cpl 12427 7th Norfolk Regt
BARBER James MM L/Cpl 15817 Cheshire Regt
BARBER James Edward MM Spr 249174 IX Corps Heavy Artillery Sig Sect Royal Engineers
BARBER John J. MM Pte 40111 South Staffordshire Regt
BARBER Joshua MM Gnr 133435 405 Siege Bty RGA
BARBER Leonard R. MM Pte 25765 2nd Lancashire Fusiliers
BARBER Leslie A. MM Pte 262931 Middlesex Regt
BARBER Percy MM S/Sjt 18427 5 Gen Hosp RAMC
BARBER Percy B. MM Sjt L/24634 150 Bde RFA
BARBER Robert MM Sjt 51029 53 Siege Bty RGA
BARBER Robert F. MM Dvr T/30451 Att 9 Fd Amb RAMC Army Service Corps
BARBER Samuel MM Sjt 20009 Machine Gun Corps
BARBER Sydney G. MM L/Sjt 241072 5th Leicestershire Regt
BARBER V. MM Pte 201614 4th West Riding Regt
BARBER W.I. MM Bdr 1347 RFA
BARBER Wilfred MM Dvr 74189 C/110 Bde RFA
BARBER Wilfred Henry MM+Bar Pte 1066 2nd Scottish Rifles
BARBER William MM Pte 200348 1/4th Suffolk Regt
BARBER William George MM L/Cpl 26498 1/5th West Riding Regt
BARBER William H. MM L/Sjt 1048 1st Manchester Regt
BARBERY Charles W. MM Cpl 493833 13th London Regt
BARBET Charles William MM Gnr 98086 A/47 Bde RFA KIA 17.8.17.
BARBET Frederick James MM Gnr 40604 31 Hy Bty RGA
BARBITSKY Isaac MM Pte S/17775 Rifle Brigade
BARBOSSA Joseph MM Cpl 10557 15th Lancashire Fusiliers
BARBOUR Archibald MM Pte 280225 1/7th Highland Light Infantry
BARBOUR Graham MM Sjt 50510 Royal Scots
BARBOUR James MM CQMS 22288 2nd South Wales Borderers
BARBOUR R. MM Cpl 301080 2/1st(Highland)Fd Amb RAMC
BARBOUR R. MM L/Cpl P12495 Military Mounted Police
BARBOUR Robert MM Cpl 3255 1/6th Arg & Suth Highlanders
BARBOUR Thomas MM Spr 65104 105 Fd Coy Royal Engineers
BARBOUR Thomas MM Pte 15475 10th Scottish Rifles
BARBOUR Thomas MM L/Cpl 146527 'G' Special Coy Royal Engineers
BARBY Arthur A.L. MM Sjt 32812 23 Div Sig Coy Royal Engineers
BARBY K.E. MM Pte 17263 Northamptonshire Regt
BARCHARD Arthur MM Pte 14736 1st Lincolnshire Regt
BARCLAY Alexander MM Pte 43658 1/5th Gordon Highlanders
BARCLAY Alexander MM Gnr 87638 RGA
BARCLAY Archibald "DCM,MM" Gnr 49954 41 Bty 42 Bde RFA KIA 9.10.17.
BARCLAY Colin MM Pte 202844 Gordon Highlanders
BARCLAY Ernest C. "MM,MID" Sjt 290893 RGA
BARCLAY G. MM Pte 303179 28 Fd Amb RAMC
BARCLAY George MM Pte G/53857 19th London Regt
BARCLAY George MM Pte 1675 7th London Regt
BARCLAY James MM Pte 84919 8th Bn Machine Gun Corps
BARCLAY James MM Sjt 48350 9 Bde RFA
BARCLAY James S. MM Pte 5708 Gordon Highlanders
BARCLAY John MM Pte 203517 6th Royal Highlanders
BARCLAY John MM L/Cpl 248190 32 Div Sig Coy Royal Engineers
BARCLAY John MM Cpl 402671 491 Fd Coy Royal Engineers
BARCLAY John MM Pte 87907 13th Liverpool Regt
BARCLAY John MM Cpl 350366 9th Royal Scots
BARCLAY John MM Pte 122156 Machine Gun Corps
BARCLAY Joseph MM Pte 31032 1st Royal Scots
BARCLAY Percival J. MM L/Cpl 15888 4th Middlesex Regt
BARCLAY Robert MM Pte S/43124 6th Cameron Highlanders
BARCLAY Robert MM Pte 41861 12th Royal Scots
BARCLAY Robert MM Pte 43783 5/6th Royal Scots

BARCLAY Robert Powry MM L/Cpl 9279 2nd Scots Guards
BARCLAY Sydney G. MM L/Cpl 9255 Wiltshire Regt
BARCLAY Thomas MM Sjt 60229 45 Bde RFA
BARCLAY William MM L/Cpl 40751 Cameron Highlanders
BARCLAY William MM Pte 13255 Arg & Suth Highlanders
BARCLAY William C. MM L/Cpl 471575 406 Fd Coy Royal Engineers
BARCLAY William David MM Spr 57991 36 Div Sig Coy Royal Engineers
BARCLAY William F. MM Pte 20223 Machine Gun Corps
BARDELL Leonard MM+Bar Sjt 2624 Royal Warwickshire Regt
BARDEN Amos MM L/Cpl 5198 1st Scots Guards
BARDEN George MM Pte 756 6th Royal West Kent Regt
BARDEN H. MM Pte 1544 Royal West Kent Regt
BARDEN Harold J. MM Spr 541269 92 Fd Coy Royal Engineers
BARDEY Reginald MM Dvr 1438 5(London)Bde RFA
BARDILL Frank H. MM Cpl 4699 12th Manchester Regt
BARDILL Harry MM Gnr 200636 3rd Bn Tank Corps
BARDNER Harry MM Spr 166702 157 Fd Coy Royal Engineers
BARDOE Francis C. MM Spr 20672 54 Fd Coy Royal Engineers
BARDON James MM Pte 21018 Machine Gun Corps
BARDSLEY Ernest MM Pte 2342 8th Gloucestershire Regt
BARDSLEY John MM Pte 50430 4th Liverpool Regt
BARDSLEY Robert MM L/Cpl 13455 11th Manchester Regt
BARDWELL Frederick John MM Sjt 493628 1/13th London Regt
BAREFOOT David H. MM Gnr 280736 RGA
BAREHAM David MM Pte 50226 2nd Suffolk Regt KIA 18.6.17.
BAREHAM Frank MM Cpl 240580 2/4th York & Lancaster Regt
BAREHAM William MM Cpl 56444 23 Div Sig Coy Royal Engineers
BARELLA Cornelius MM Sjt 9287 2nd Durham Light Infantry
BARFIELD Henry G. MM Sjt 98292 C/84 Bde RFA
BARFIELD Thomas MM Pte 15104 Royal Sussex Regt
BARFOOT Leonard George MM Pte 11314 41st Bn Machine Gun Corps
BARFOOT Sidney MM Pte 202524 2/4th Hampshire Regt
BARFORD A.G. MM+Bar Sjt 71087 Machine Gun Corps
BARFORD John "MM,MM(F)" Pte 265798 Royal Sussex Regt
BARGE George MM Pte 6736 14th Gloucestershire Regt DOW 21.8.17.
BARGE J.A.E. MM L/Bdr 77135 71 Bty 36 Bde RFA
BARGE Leslie MM Pte 1780 8th East Kent Regt
BARGER George F. MM Dvr 54900 11 Bde RFA
BARGERY Harry MM Pte 40414 RAMC
BARGETON Patrick B. MM Sjt Z/251 Rifle Brigade
BARHAM Alfred MM L/Cpl 20125 East Kent Regt
BARHAM David MM L/Cpl 1594 1/4th Suffolk Regt
BARHAM Edward C. MM Cpl 60601 RFA
BARHAM Ernest G. MM Spr 126913 50 Div Sig Coy Royal Engineers Died 13.9.18.
BARHAM Frank MM Pte G/2691 Royal Sussex Regt
BARHAM Frederick MM Pte 201162 1/1st Cambridgeshire Regt KIA 22.8.18.
BARHAM Frederick S. MM Bdr 79971 RHA
BARHAM Harry MM L/Cpl 285140 1/6th Gloucestershire Regt
BARHAM Henry S. MM Pte 326374 1/1st Cambridgeshire Regt
BARHAM Henry W. MM Sjt S/2183 Rifle Brigade
BARK Francis MM Pte 24787 9th Notts & Derby Regt DOW 2.5.18.
BARK Harry MM Pte 252726 2nd Essex Regt
BARK Thomas MM Pte 9621 7th East Surrey Regt
BARKAS John MM Gnr 41736 RGA
BARKE Albert E. MM Pte 27442 Royal Berkshire Regt
BARKER Abraham MM Pte G/66874 26th Royal Fusiliers KIA 25.10.18.
BARKER Abraham MM Pte 570737 17th London Regt
BARKER Albert MM Dvr 110550 RFA
BARKER Albert "MM,MID" Sjt M/22987 1 Div Train Army Service Corps
BARKER Albert A. MM Pte 330812 Royal Warwickshire Regt
BARKER Alfred MM CSM 7770 2nd South Wales Borderers
BARKER Arthur E. MM Pte 71482 Notts & Derby Regt
BARKER Arthur Leslie MM Pte 44440 4th Bn Machine Gun Corps
BARKER Arthur S. MM Cpl 113645 RFA
BARKER C. MM Gnr 2495 35 Bde RFA
BARKER C. MM Pte 345079 RAMC
BARKER Charles MM Pte 25103 6th Northamptonshire Regt
BARKER Charles MM Sjt 23317 31st Bn Machine Gun Corps KIA 12.4.18.
BARKER Charles MM Pte 16946 13th Durham Light Infantry KIA 7.10.16.
BARKER Charles F. MM Pte 59379 Northumberland Fusiliers
BARKER Clarence E. MM Cpl 6450 18th Hussars
BARKER Clifford MM Pte 32992 Gloucestershire Regt
BARKER David MM Sjt 18444 12th Cheshire Regt
BARKER Edward MM Pte R/14253 7th King's Royal Rifle Corps KIA 25.8.16.
BARKER Ernest MM Pte 11546 10th West Yorkshire Regt
BARKER Ernest W. MM Pte G/6170 Middlesex Regt
BARKER Frank J. MM Cpl 304657 15th Bn Tank Corps
BARKER Frank James MM Sjt 652614 1/21st London Regt KIA 1.9.18.
BARKER Frank Waterhouse "MM,MID" Sjt 8369 Scots Guards
BARKER Frederick MM Pte R/7978 4th King's Royal Rifle Corps
BARKER Frederick H. MM Pte 241209 5th Lincolnshire Regt
BARKER Frederick W. MM Sjt 25699 24 Heavy Bty RGA
BARKER George MM+Bar L/Cpl 3187 Middlesex Regt
BARKER George F. MM Pte 10482 Leicestershire Regt
BARKER George R. MM Sjt 482182 Royal Engineers
BARKER H.A. MM Cpl 8794 Royal Air Force
BARKER H.B. MM Sjt 9577 East Kent Regt
BARKER H.W. MM Pte 723510 London Regt
BARKER Harold E. MM L/Cpl 4138 Machine Gun Corps
BARKER Harry MM Cpl 17242 9th Northumberland Fusiliers KIA 21.10.17.
BARKER Henry MM Gnr 96965 RFA
BARKER Henry MM L/Cpl 371206 1/8th London Regt
BARKER Henry MM Sjt 8474 2nd Welsh Regt
BARKER Henry Reginald MM Cpl 148061 32nd Bn Machine Gun Corps DOW 30.12.18.
BARKER Herbert MM Pte 52186 Rifle Brigade att 17 London.
BARKER Herbert "DCM,MM" Bdr 25082 A/59 Bde RFA
BARKER Hiram MM Pte 307908 8th Lancashire Fusiliers
BARKER Horace MM Pte 3923 6th A Coy York & Lancaster Regt
BARKER Horace G. MM Cpl 26681 16 Fd Amb RAMC
BARKER James MM+Bar Cpl 201748 1/5th Manchester Regt
BARKER James MM Spr 486945 Royal Engineers
BARKER James H. MM Gnr 142067 320 Siege Bty RGA
BARKER James Henry MM Pte 34706 Wiltshire Regt
BARKER Jesse MM Pte 24165 10th West Riding Regt
BARKER John MM Pte 555504 16th London Regt
BARKER John MM Pte 277104 1/7th Arg & Suth Highlanders
BARKER John H. MM Sjt 30325 RAMC
BARKER John R. MM L/Cpl 8129 1st Devonshire Regt
BARKER John W. MM Cpl 282588 2/5th Lancashire Fusiliers
BARKER John Williams MM QMS 281 1/5(London)Fd Amb RAMC Died 22.5.17.
BARKER Joseph MM Pte 21914 5th Royal Lancaster Regt
BARKER Lawrence MM Pte 24969 Leicestershire Regt
BARKER Lawrence MM L/Cpl 5743 11th Royal Sussex Regt KIA 3.4.18.
BARKER Leonard MM L/Cpl 11406 1st Worcestershire Regt
BARKER Leonard MM Sjt 1872 20th London Regt
BARKER Lord MM Pte 351425 2/9th Manchester Regt DOW 21.3.18.
BARKER Percy F. MM Cpl 43409 RAMC
BARKER Reginald G. MM Sjt 24107 Suffolk Regt
BARKER Robert E. MM Sjt 19173 11th Hampshire Regt
BARKER Robert George "MM,VM(Rm)" Cpl 24978 12th Cheshire Regt
BARKER Robert J. MM Pte 28203 Machine Gun Corps
BARKER S. MM+Bar Pte 405142 76 Fd Amb RAMC
BARKER Samuel MM Pte 307240 1/7th West Riding Regt
BARKER Samuel L. MM L/Cpl 18708 Grenadier Guards
BARKER Sidney MM Pte 15204 2nd Suffolk Regt
BARKER Sidney MM Cpl 427980 Royal Engineers
BARKER Sidney D. MM L/Cpl 368013 7th London Regt
BARKER Stanley MM+Bar L/Cpl 200096 1/4th West Riding Regt
BARKER Stephen T. MM Pte G/67162 13th Royal Fusiliers
BARKER Sydney D. MM Pte 36458 6th York & Lancaster Regt
BARKER T. MM L/Cpl P/3041 1 Traffic Control Coy Military Foot Police
BARKER Thomas MM Pte 11753 1st Notts & Derby Regt KIA 27.5.18.
BARKER Thomas MM Pte 11889 1st Notts & Derby Regt
BARKER Thomas MM Sjt 23613 Liverpool Regt
BARKER Thomas E. MM+Bar Sjt 38542 2nd Royal Fusiliers
BARKER Thomas Edward MM Spr 217540 49 Div Sig Coy Royal Engineers KIA 14.10.18.
BARKER Thomas H. MM Pte 243245 15th Hampshire Regt
BARKER Thomas H. "DCM,MM" Sjt 19117 2nd Royal Scots Fusiliers

BARKER Walter W. "DCM,MM" Sjt 266240 1st West Yorkshire Regt
BARKER Wilfred MM Sjt 13411 5th Dorsetshire Regt
BARKER Wilfred MM Sjt 12068 14th Leicestershire Regt
BARKER William MM Cpl 4/8046 9th West Yorkshire Regt
BARKER William MM Pte 45815 33 Fd Amb RAMC
BARKER William "DCM,MM" Sjt 67008 Royal Engineers
BARKER William "MM,MID" Pte 10090 East Surrey Regt
BARKER William MM Pte 250191 1/6th Manchester Regt
BARKER William MM Pte 6000 2nd Manchester Regt
BARKER William C. "MM,MSM" L/Cpl T/24692 63 Div Train Army Service Corps
BARKER William D. MM Cpl R/6986 King's Royal Rifle Corps
BARKER William H. MM Pte M2/194182 Army Service Corps
BARKER William R. MM Pte 45860 15th Suffolk Regt
BARKER Wilson MM+Bar Cpl 268800 5th West Riding Regt
BARKES Thomas William MM+Bar Sjt 25748 Notts & Derby Regt
BARKHAM George H. "DCM,MM" Sjt 590395 18th London Regt
BARKLEY Isaac MM Pre 331863 Liverpool Regt
BARKLEY William J. MM Pte 350309 9th Royal Scots
BARKMAN Sylvester MM Sjt 306925 8th Liverpool Regt
BARKS Frederick Henry MM L/Cpl 82571 3rd Bn Machine Gun Corps
BARKS Frederick James MM Gnr 891543 29 Bde RFA
BARKWAY Charles J. "DCM,MM" L/Cpl 205523 1/1st Buckinghamshire Yeo
BARKWORTH John MM Sjt 7658 Coldstream Guards
BARKWORTH John E. MM Pte 13/988 East Yorkshire Regt
BARLEY John E. MM Cpl 71060 Royal Engineers
BARLEY John S. MM Cpl 42146 Yorkshire Light Infantry
BARLEY Samuel MM+Bar Bdr 6637 109 Hy Bty RGA
BARLING Arthur Stanley MM Pte 493499 2/1st(Home Counties)Fd Amb RAMC
BARLING Lester MM Pte 43134 4th Middlesex Regt
BARLOW Albert MM Cpl 200936 2/5th Lancashire Fusiliers DOW 26.9.17.
BARLOW Albert J. MM Pte 51965 11th Royal Scots Fusiliers
BARLOW Albert M. MM Pnr 503997 61 Div Sig Coy Royal Engineers
BARLOW Alexander MM Sjt 608247 199 Coy Labour Corps
BARLOW Alfred MM Pte 202005 5th Lancashire Fusiliers
BARLOW Alfred H. MM Sjt 52221 2nd Lincolnshire Regt
BARLOW Alfred James MM Pte 128 1st Welsh Guards Died 11.11.18.
BARLOW Arthur MM Pte 26691 17th Lancashire Fusiliers
BARLOW Charles H. MM Pte 421218 RAMC
BARLOW Ernest MM Pte 14837 8th Lancashire Fusiliers
BARLOW Ernest "DCM,MM" Sjt 18427 8th Northumberland Fusiliers
BARLOW F. MM+Bar Cpl 534184 4 Fd Amb RAMC
BARLOW Frank MM Pte 235458 6th Leicestershire Regt
BARLOW Frank "MM,MID" Cpl 444030 Royal Engineers
BARLOW Frederick MM L/Cpl B/2764 Rifle Brigade
BARLOW George MM Sjt 11682 7th East Yorkshire Regt
BARLOW George MM L/Cpl 1658 Worcestershire Regt
BARLOW George Harold MM Sjt 17785 19th Liverpool Regt KIA 30.7.16.
BARLOW H. MM Sjt 66259 Royal Engineers
BARLOW Harold Howard MM Pte 64484 RAMC
BARLOW Harry MM L/Cpl 24025 6th North Lancashire Regt
BARLOW Harry Crosby "MM+Bar,CG(F)" L/Sjt 201368 2/4th Royal West Surrey Regt
BARLOW Harry M. MM Cpl 205558 10th Essex Regt
BARLOW Henry George MM Sjt 44443 91 Coy Machine Gun Corps
BARLOW Irvin MM Spr 209732 239 Light Railway Coy Royal Engineers
BARLOW James MM Dvr 74817 125 Bty 29 Bde RFA
BARLOW John MM 2nd Cpl 238162 Royal Engineers
BARLOW John MM CQMS 201247 Manchester Regt
BARLOW John MM Pte 52 8th Royal Fusiliers
BARLOW John MM Pte 8963 1st South Staffordshire Regt
BARLOW John MM Cpl 35954 Manchester Regt
BARLOW John Alfred MM+Bar Cpl 7537 35th Bn Machine Gun Corps
BARLOW John Leonard MM Pte 201641 8th Lincolnshire Regt
BARLOW Joseph MM 2nd Cpl 478333 459 Fd Coy Royal Engineers
BARLOW Joseph MM Pte 18406 Royal Munster Fusiliers
BARLOW Joseph MM L/Cpl S/5440 Rifle Brigade
BARLOW Leonard MM Pte M2/136886 Att 288 Army Troops Coy RE Army Service Corps
BARLOW Percy J. MM Sjt 9659 2nd Oxf & Bucks Light Infantry
BARLOW Reuben MM L/Cpl 422408 10th London Regt KIA 8.8.18.

BARLOW Samuel MM Sjt 13364 6/7th Royal Scots Fusiliers
BARLOW Sydney V. MM Pte 555263 16th London Regt
BARLOW Thomas MM Cpl 240805 1/5th Seaforth Highlanders KIA 10.4.18.
BARLOW Thomas H. MM Pte 3/6003 1st East Yorkshire Regt
BARLOW Thomas Pratt MM Sjt 1776 1/4th Oxf & Bucks Light Infantry KIA 23.7.16.
BARLOW Walter MM Pte 200164 5th South Staffordshire Regt
BARLOW William MM Pte 377978 1/8th Manchester Regt KIA 23.4.18.
BARLOW William G. MM Dvr 40498 2 Div Ammn Col RFA
BARLOW William H. MM Sjt 9217 9th Royal Fusiliers
BARLTROP Arthur MM Sjt 2909 2/1st HAC (Inf)
BARLTROP William J. "DCM,MM" L/Cpl C/3553 17th King's Royal Rifle Corps
BARMBY Frank MM Cpl 35967 4th Yorkshire Light Infantry
BARMES F. MM Sjt 27014 46 Coy Labour Corps
BARNABY Arthur MM Pte S/26328 Rifle Brigade
BARNACOTT Laurence MM Pte 1101 56 Fd Amb RAMC
BARNARD Albert MM L/Cpl M2/103870 Army Service Corps
BARNARD Albert Charles MM Spr 66459 105 Fd Coy Royal Engineers
BARNARD Alfred MM Bdr 46948 RFA
BARNARD Bruce MM L/Cpl 630967 1/20th London Regt KIA 1.9.18.
BARNARD Eric A. MM Cpl 310057 1/1st Warwickshire Yeomanry
BARNARD Francis MM Pte 2289 1/1st Surrey Yeomanry
BARNARD Francis F.G. MM Bdr 105476 RGA
BARNARD Frank N. MM Pte DM2/196282 Army Service Corps
BARNARD Frederick MM Sjt 2400 8th Royal West Surrey Regt KIA 21.8.16.
BARNARD G. MM Pte 36569 Essex Regt
BARNARD George "MM,MID" Cpl 12263 9th Essex Regt KIA 11.8.16.
BARNARD Horace MM Pte 14759 8th Lincolnshire Regt KIA 28.4.17.
BARNARD Hugh Frank MM Pte S/6701 2nd Rifle Brigade KIA 2.12.17.
BARNARD James MM Spr 107402 8 Div Sig Coy Royal Engineers
BARNARD Jesse MM Pte 103964 11 Fd Amb RAMC
BARNARD Joe MM Pte 64722 32nd Bn Machine Gun Corps
BARNARD John MM Pte M2/148158 Base MT Depot Army Service Corps
BARNARD John William MM Gnr 32505 RFA
BARNARD Sidney MM 2nd Cpl 252508 Royal Engineers
BARNARD Walter MM Gnr 124367 1 Div Ammn Col RFA
BARNARD William MM Sjt 200635 4th Essex Regt
BARNARD William MM Gnr 890626 RFA
BARNBROOK William MM Cpl 44355 Worcestershire Regt
BARNBY Walter A. "DCM,MM" Sjt 200343 1/4th East Yorkshire Regt
BARNED Harry P.T. MM Pte S/30361 Rifle Brigade
BARNES Albert MM Pte 27756 5th Yorkshire Light Infantry
BARNES Albert E. MM Pte S/30533 Rifle Brigade
BARNES Albert G. MM Cpl L/36221 C/180 Bde RFA
BARNES Albert H. MM Pte 61387 RAMC
BARNES Albert J. "DCM,MM" BSM 41034 134 Bty 32 Bde RFA
BARNES Albert W. MM L/Cpl 26767 15th Hampshire Regt
BARNES Alfred Edward MM Pte 14040 6th East Kent Regt
BARNES Alfred J. "DCM,MM" Sjt 421053 2/10th London Regt
BARNES Alfred J. "MM,MID" Sjt 2918 1/17th London Regt
BARNES Arthur MM Sjt 60678 7th Royal West Surrey Regt KIA 25.10.18.
BARNES Arthur MM S/Sjt Farrier 785038 312 Bde RFA
BARNES Arthur MM S/Sjt 19336 10 Fd Amb RAMC
BARNES Arthur MM Sjt 51113 41 Bde RFA
BARNES Arthur "MM,MID" Pte 10823 2nd Hampshire Regt
BARNES Arthur MM Cpl 3/193 2nd Wiltshire Regt KIA 26.8.17.
BARNES Arthur C. MM Pte 282029 4th London Regt
BARNES Arthur J. MM L/Cpl 107400 8 Div Sig Coy Royal Engineers
BARNES Arthur J. MM Cpl S/15104 1st Rifle Brigade
BARNES Bertie MM Gnr 86038 RFA
BARNES C. MM Sjt 13210 Norfolk Regt
BARNES Charles MM Pte 62007 91 Fd Amb RAMC
BARNES Charles MM Pte 5843 1st Royal West Surrey Regt
BARNES Charles MM+Bar Sjt 4337 6th Royal West Surrey Regt
BARNES Charles MM Pte 18215 15th Durham Light Infantry KIA 24.8.18.
BARNES Charles W.J. MM+Bar Pte 31493 15th Hampshire Regt
BARNES David MM+Bar Sjt 63350 N Bty RHA
BARNES David Arthur MM Pte 27536 1st Royal Welsh Fusiliers KIA 17.10.16.

BARNES David S. MM Pte 651400 21st London Regt
BARNES Douglas Arthur MM Cpl 20189 6th Royal Fusiliers
BARNES Edgar MM Pte 15759 6th Lincolnshire Regt
BARNES Edgar A.T. MM Pte M2/149226 Army Service Corps
BARNES Edward MM Cpl 8/12575 2nd Royal Irish Rifles KIA 28.9.18.
BARNES Edward G. MM 2nd Cpl 67193 Royal Engineers
BARNES Ernest MM L/Cpl 265978 Cheshire Regt
BARNES Ernest MM Gnr 93125 RGA DOW 12.6.17.
BARNES Ernest Edgar MM Pte 37505 9th Royal Fusiliers
BARNES F. MM Pte R/41811 18th King's Royal Rifle Corps
BARNES F. MM Cpl 201956 Dorsetshire Regt
BARNES F. MM Pte 5180 Middlesex Regt
BARNES F. MM Dvr L/22315 RFA
BARNES F. MM Sjt S/26580 Rifle Brigade
BARNES F. MM L/Cpl P6776 Military Foot Police
BARNES F.W. MM Pte 5453 London Regt
BARNES Frank MM(18417 L/Cpl Manch)+Bar Sjt 67656 21st Bn Machine Gun Corps KIA 21.3.18.
BARNES G. MM Pte 9983 5th Royal Berkshire Regt
BARNES G. MM Sjt 1771 RGA
BARNES G. MM Pte 13489 North Lancashire Regt
BARNES G. MM Pte 58091 Notts & Derby Regt
BARNES G. MM Spr 42632 Royal Engineers
BARNES G.B. MM CSM 9275 Scottish Rifles
BARNES G.F. MM Cpl 20755 RGA
BARNES G.H. MM Pte 16153 Royal Berkshire Regt
BARNES G.J. MM Sjt 56509 18th King's Royal Rifle Corps
BARNES G.P. MM 2nd Cpl 85545 Royal Engineers
BARNES George MM L/Cpl 8244 1st King's Royal Rifle Corps DOW 11.3.17.
BARNES George MM Pte 40635 57 Fd Amb RAMC Died 28.8.18.
BARNES George Anderson MM Sjt 9899 1st East Yorkshire Regt KIA 25.9.16.
BARNES H. MM Sjt 14178 Cheshire Regt
BARNES H. MM Sjt 5/14310 South Wales Borderers
BARNES H. MM Pte 33 4th GMGR
BARNES H.C. MM Sjt 240525 Gloucestershire Regt
BARNES H.H. MM Spr 474375 Royal Engineers
BARNES I. MM Pte S/40587 Gordon Highlanders
BARNES J. MM L/Cpl B/201790 8th London Regt
BARNES James "DCM,MM" CSM 8387 1st Royal Scots Fusiliers
BARNES James MM L/Sjt 225320 1st London Regt att 11th Royal Fusiliers.KIA 21.9.18.
BARNES James Henry MM Gnr 875638 B/272 Bde RFA
BARNES John MM Pte 56630 66 Fd Amb. RAMC
BARNES John MM Pte 15932 10th North Lancashire Regt KIA 28.4.17.
BARNES John MM Gnr 680565 RFA
BARNES John Garner MM Pte 7922 Essex Regt Died 18.3.18.
BARNES John J. MM Pte 22837 Notts & Derby Regt
BARNES John R. MM 2nd Cpl 137531 172 Tunnelling Coy Royal Engineers
BARNES John W. MM Cpl 204071 Lancashire Fusiliers
BARNES Joseph MM Pte 4088 8th Royal Irish Regt
BARNES Joseph MM Sjt 241625 Royal Lancaster Regt
BARNES Joseph MM Pte 1606 Liverpool Regt
BARNES Joseph S. MM Pte 18162 6th Wiltshire Regt
BARNES L.G. MM Gnr 681858 RFA
BARNES Percy R. MM Pte 26375 15th Notts & Derby Regt
BARNES Reginald John MM+Bar Cpl 531493 1/15th London Regt
BARNES Robert J. MM Pte M1/06284 Att 25 Fd Amb RAMC Army Service Corps
BARNES Samuel "DCM,MM" Pte 367870 2/10th Manchester Regt
BARNES T. MM Sjt 34283 58 Coy Labour Corps
BARNES Thomas MM Cpl 242865 Lancashire Fusiliers
BARNES Thomas MM Sjt 1229 Royal Engineers
BARNES Thomas MM+Bar Sjt 9832 2nd Scottish Rifles
BARNES Thomas MM Sjt 13337 10th Scottish Rifles
BARNES Thomas MM Sjt 11738 19th Manchester Regt
BARNES Thomas MM Sjt 15186 8th North Lancashire Regt
BARNES Thomas MM Pte 6141 12th Lancashire Fusiliers
BARNES Thomas A. MM L/Cpl 553062 16th London Regt
BARNES W. MM Spr 471654 147 Army Tps Coy Royal Engineers
BARNES Walter MM Pte 7952 1/5th South Staffordshire Regt
BARNES Walter Edward MM Pte 8209 2nd Yorkshire Regt KIA 23.7.16.
BARNES Walter Edward MM Sjt 88122 252 Siege Bty RGA
BARNES Walter T. MM Pte 235165 6th York & Lancaster Regt
BARNES William MM Sjt 306365 4th West Riding Regt
BARNES William MM Sjt 236452 10th West Yorkshire Regt
BARNES William MM L/Sjt 9264 2nd Royal Berkshire Regt KIA 17.8.16.
BARNES William MM Cpl 20768 Machine Gun Corps
BARNES William MM Pte SS/18792 Army Service Corps
BARNES William Enos John MM L/Cpl 5/3935 1st King's Royal Rifle Corps
BARNES William H. MM Cpl 34203 1st Devonshire Regt
BARNES William H. MM Pte 252445 6th Durham Light Infantry
BARNES William H. MM CQMS 14993 East Surrey Regt
BARNES William Henry "MM+Bar,CG(B)" Cpl 17276 19th Liverpool Regt KIA 22.3.18.
BARNES William J. MM 2nd Cpl 108680 156 Fd Coy Royal Engineers
BARNES William Robert MM Sjt 32651 116 Heavy Bty RGA
BARNET George D. MM Pte 10084 Coldstream Guards
BARNETT Alfred T. MM Pte Y/1529 King's Royal Rifle Corps
BARNETT Brian Max Joseph MM Pte 283813 1/4th London Regt KIA 28.3.18.
BARNETT Charles MM Bdr 27442 D/46 Bde RFA
BARNETT Charles H. MM L/Cpl 60703 8th West Yorkshire Regt
BARNETT Daniel MM Pte R/15461 4th King's Royal Rifle Corps
BARNETT Edmund H. MM L/Cpl 20009 7th Gloucestershire Regt
BARNETT Edward S. MM Pte 40146 Lincolnshire Regt
BARNETT Eli MM Pte 21030 1st Wiltshire Regt
BARNETT Ernest MM Sjt 10022 Cheshire Regt
BARNETT Ernest MM Sjt 7895 Coldstream Guards
BARNETT Frank MM L/Cpl 20595 10th Scottish Rifles KIA 23.7.18.
BARNETT Frederick W. MM Pte 51042 MGC(Cavalry)
BARNETT G.H. MM Pte 19249 Northamptonshire Regt
BARNETT George MM L/Cpl R/19846 King's Royal Rifle Corps
BARNETT Harold H. "DCM,MM" Sjt 50653 105 Bty 22 Bde RFA
BARNETT Harry MM Pte 24671 1st Devonshire Regt
BARNETT Henry Charles MM Sjt 12342 2nd D Coy Northamptonshire Regt
BARNETT Henry T. MM Cpl 15122 Royal Engineers
BARNETT James MM L/Cpl 55863 Machine Gun Corps
BARNETT John MM Spr 82450 Royal Engineers
BARNETT John "MM,MID" Sjt 37307 77 Fd Amb RAMC
BARNETT John MM Cpl 34362 York & Lancaster Regt
BARNETT John Bartholomew MM Pte 6707 18th A Coy King's Royal Rifle Corps KIA 21.9.17.
BARNETT John C. MM L/Cpl 3268 12th Middlesex Regt
BARNETT John R. MM Pte DM2/170797 Army Service Corps
BARNETT Lancelot H. MM Gnr 149731 RGA
BARNETT Lionel F. MM+Bar CSM 88017 50th Bn Machine Gun Corps
BARNETT Thomas MM Pte 633837 20th London Regt
BARNETT Thomas C. MM Pte 4621 Machine Gun Corps
BARNETT Tom MM Pte 322460 6th London Regt
BARNETT Walter MM Gnr 16906 RGA
BARNETT Walter MM Pte M2/032707 Army Service Corps
BARNETT William "MM,MSM" Sjt 26905 11th Lancashire Fusiliers
BARNETT William MM Sjt 9828 Royal Fusiliers
BARNETT William A. MM Sjt 1885 Yorkshire Regt
BARNETT William E. MM Pte 22954 Wiltshire Regt
BARNETT William Forbes "DCM,MM" Pte 266447 6th Gordon Highlanders KIA 11.4.18.
BARNETT William T. MM Cpl 55234 Machine Gun Corps
BARNEY Arthur MM CQMS 201152 2/4th Hampshire Regt
BARNEY George MM+Bar Pte 610511 1/19th London Regt
BARNFIELD George MM Sjt 201149 4th Gloucestershire Regt
BARNFIELD Henry John MM Pte 20082 12th Liverpool Regt KIA 16.8.17.
BARNFIELD Hubert Charles MM Pte 241134 2/5th Gloucestershire Regt KIA 15.11.17.
BARNHAM John William James MM+Bar Sjt 11243 11th Royal West Kent Regt KIA 1.12.17.
BARNHAM Thomas MM L/Cpl 6396 6th Royal West Kent Regt
BARNHILL David MM Cpl 11/14673 11th Royal Inniskilling Fusiliers KIA 1.7.16.
BARNICLE C. "DCM,MM" Sjt S/5691 9th Seaforth Highlanders
BARNICOAT Richard H. MM Pte 87801 49th Bn Machine Gun Corps
BARNIE William E. MM Cpl 106386 Royal Engineers
BARNLEY William Adolphus "DCM,MM,MID" CSM 453309 1/11th London Regt
BARNSDALE Frederick Herbert "DCM,MM" Sjt 41598 2nd Northamptonshire Regt
BARNSHAW Bertram Gwillim MM Pte 2907 10th Liverpool Regt

BARNSHAW H. MM L/Cpl 291323 Cheshire Regt
BARNSLEY Fred MM Pte 19324 8th East Lancashire Regt
BARNWELL Herbert E. MM Spr 74206 Royal Engineers
BARNWELL Walter Charles MM Pte 42691 7th Wiltshire Regt
BARNWELL William G. "DCM,MM" Cpl 2244 Oxf & Bucks Light Infantry
BARON Alfred MM Pte 300024 2/5th Lancashire Fusiliers
BARON James Ball "MM,CG(F)" Pte 20017 43 Coy Machine Gun Corps KIA 24.8.17.
BARON John Henry "MM,MID,CG(F)" SSM 4798 4th Hussars
BARON John Joseph MM Pte 6604 1st East Lancashire Regt DOW 23.3.18.
BARON Paul MM Pte 657 1st Manchester Regt
BARON Percy MM L/Cpl 25310 East Lancashire Regt
BARON Wilfred MM Pte 306908 West Riding Regt
BARONS Gerald MM Bdr 10916 RFA
BARR Adam J. MM Pte 42967 Worcestershire Regt
BARR Archibald MM Pte 332775 1/9th Highland Light Infantry
BARR Charles H. MM Gnr 49369 RFA
BARR Edward G. MM Pte P/1067 Rifle Brigade
BARR Harry George MM Pte A/2958 8th King's Royal Rifle Corps
BARR J. MM Pte 35980 Highland Light Infantry
BARR James MM Gnr 11994 88 Bty 14 Bde RFA
BARR James MM Pte 90152 9 Fd Amb RAMC
BARR James MM Sjt 64824 Machine Gun Corps
BARR James E. MM Pte 40917 RAMC
BARR John MM Gnr 126038 RFA
BARR John A. MM Spr 40475 Royal Engineers
BARR Matthew "DCM,MM" Sjt 588 C/106 Bde RFA
BARR Robert H. MM Pte 5757 Machine Gun Corps
BARR Thomas MM L/Cpl 8178 Royal Irish Rifles
BARR Thomas MM Pte 672 2nd Gordon Highlanders
BARR Thomas MM L/Cpl 81274 Royal Engineers
BARR Walter MM Sjt 5571 RFA
BARR William W. MM Pte 15117 Royal Fusiliers
BARRABLE Reginald.J. MM Dvr 237301 C/155 Bde RFA
BARRACK George MM Gnr 167366 47 Bty 41 Bde RFA
BARRACLOUGH Arthur MM Pte 41557 Northumberland Fusiliers
BARRACLOUGH B. MM L/Bdr Sig 89897 134 Bty 32 Bde RFA
BARRACLOUGH Edward MM Sjt 5415 1st Cameron Highlanders
BARRACLOUGH Harry MM Pte 18715 West Riding Regt
BARRACLOUGH Hubert MM Pte 21167 1st Coldstream Guards
BARRACLOUGH James MM L/Cpl 6321 1st West Yorkshire Regt KIA 29.4.18.
BARRACLOUGH Norman MM Spr 51270 9 Div Sig Coy Royal Engineers
BARRACLOUGH Percy MM L/Cpl 242525 Royal Lancaster Regt
BARRACLOUGH Ralph MM Dvr 27242 RFA
BARRACLOUGH Walter "DCM,MM" Sjt C/478 16th King's Royal Rifle Corps
BARRAJO B.C. MM Gnr 78088 RGA
BARRAND William MM Sjt 13498 4th Coldstream Guards
BARRAS James William "DCM+Bar,MM" L/Cpl 463025 50 Div Sig Coy Royal Engineers
BARRAS William MM Cpl 1929 Arg & Suth Highlanders DOW 25.3.18.
BARRAS William H. MM Pte 205269 Royal West Surrey Regt Att MGC.
BARRASS Cuthbert MM Pte 39815 Yorkshire Regt
BARRASS Thomas MM Sjt 1642 1/5th Northumberland Fusiliers KIA 14.11.16.
BARRASS Wilfred MM RSM 251866 Royal Engineers
BARRATT Albert H. MM Gnr 207227 355 Siege Bty RGA
BARRATT F. MM L/Cpl 10189 Royal Warwickshire Regt
BARRATT Fred MM L/Cpl 49773 Royal Engineers
BARRATT Frederick MM+Bar Sjt L/43303 RFA
BARRATT Frederick E. MM 2nd Cpl 134062 4 Div Sig Coy Royal Engineers
BARRATT George J. MM Pte 78431 Tank Corps
BARRATT Henry E. MM Sjt 47039 29 Bde RFA
BARRATT Henry Joseph MM Sjt 23486 D/161 Bde RFA KIA 26.9.18.
BARRATT J.E. MM L/Cpl P4963 Military Foot Police
BARRATT John MM Sjt 42407 59 Fd Amb RAMC
BARRATT John MM Cpl 19058 1st Suffolk Regt
BARRATT Thomas James MM Sjt 28079 58 Siege Bty RGA DOW 23.8.18.
BARRATT William MM Bdr 63808 42 Bde RFA
BARRATT William MM Bdr 820183 RFA
BARRATT Wilson MM L/Cpl 203711 2nd South Staffordshire Regt

BARRELL Edward MM L/Cpl M1/6244 First Army MT Coy Army Service Corps
BARRELL Henry MM Cpl 7977 54 Fd Coy Royal Engineers
BARRELL Robert J. MM L/Cpl 631138 2/20th London Regt
BARRELL Walter J. MM Sjt 77880 RFA
BARRETT Albert MM Sjt 307473 5th London Regt
BARRETT Albert MM Pte 267491 2/5th Gloucestershire Regt
BARRETT Albert A. MM L/Cpl 683204 22nd London Regt
BARRETT Alfred MM Sjt 18353 Royal Fusiliers
BARRETT Alfred F. MM 2nd Cpl 486089 Royal Engineers
BARRETT Alfred G. MM Sjt 2766 RAMC
BARRETT Archie James MM Sjt G/340 6th B Coy East Kent Regt KIA 13.9.16.
BARRETT Arthur E. MM Cpl 800480 C/230 Bde RFA
BARRETT Arthur E. MM+Bar Sjt 37769 18th Lancashire Fusiliers
BARRETT Arthur T. MM Pte 17631 Scottish Rifles
BARRETT Bartholomew MM Pte 9/3793 Royal Munster Fusiliers
BARRETT Benjamin MM Pte 306103 7th Liverpool Regt
BARRETT Bert MM Pte 203667 5th Notts & Derby Regt
BARRETT Bertie MM Cpl 78354 8th Bn Tank Corps
BARRETT Charles MM Bdr 66084 RGA
BARRETT Charles F MM Dvr T4/088882 Army Service Corps
BARRETT David MM+Bar Cpl 16573 Suffolk Regt
BARRETT Edward Joseph MM Sjt 56480 38 Bde RFA
BARRETT Ernest MM Pte 13364 2nd Worcestershire Regt
BARRETT Frank MM Cpl 40289 12th Bn Tank Corps
BARRETT Frank Robert MM L/Cpl 8343 7th East Kent Regt
BARRETT Frederick MM Pte 49353 5th East Lancashire Regt
BARRETT G.A. MM Bdr 20747 RFA
BARRETT G.H. MM Pte 13143 Dorsetshire Regt
BARRETT G.L. MM L/Cpl 325742 Cambridgeshire Regt
BARRETT George MM Cpl Shoeing Smith 26179 D/71 Bde RFA
BARRETT Harry MM+Bar Sjt 4825 34th Bn Machine Gun Corps
BARRETT Henry MM Cpl 52503 1st Liverpool Regt
BARRETT Henry A. MM+Bar L/Cpl 28253 East Surrey Regt
BARRETT Henry H.D. MM Pte 10788 Shropshire Light Infantry
BARRETT Herbert MM Pnr 255066 Royal Engineers Att RGA.
BARRETT Isaac R. MM Pte 4956 16th Lancers
BARRETT J.H. MM Cpl 800483 C/230 Bde RFA
BARRETT J.W.A. MM Pte S/1116 Rifle Brigade
BARRETT James MM Pte 25978 18th Welsh Regt KIA 9.4.18.
BARRETT James MM Pte 6272 1st West Yorkshire Regt
BARRETT James F. MM Pte 45545 38 Fd Amb RAMC
BARRETT John "DCM,MM" Cpl 14122 1/6th North Staffordshire Regt
BARRETT John MM Pte 1843 4th GMGR
BARRETT John MM Pte 18413 13th Welsh Regt
BARRETT John MM Sjt 5132 2nd Irish Guards
BARRETT John T. MM Bdr 66230 35 Bde RFA
BARRETT Joseph MM Cpl 42412 RAMC
BARRETT L. MM Pte 474405 London Regt
BARRETT Leonard W. "MM,MSM" Sjt 84193 211 Fd Coy Royal Engineers
BARRETT Louis F. "DCM,MM" RSM D/20040 4th Dragoon Guards
BARRETT N. MM Cpl 267489 West Riding Regt
BARRETT Patrick MM L/Cpl 4/7648 2nd Royal Munster Fusiliers KIA 10.11.17.
BARRETT Percy MM Sjt 75383 4th Bn Tank Corps
BARRETT Reuben Walter MM Sjt 2775 1/18th London Regt
BARRETT Robson J. MM Dvr 9863 5 Div Ammn Col RFA
BARRETT Stephen MM L/Bdr 62372 142 Siege Bty RGA
BARRETT Stephen John Rigaud MM L/Bdr 15456 D/251 Bde RFA
BARRETT Thomas MM Cpl 11942 49th Bn Machine Gun Corps
BARRETT Thomas MM Pte 201713 2/4th Oxf & Bucks Light Infantry
BARRETT Thomas MM Pte 32720 RAMC
BARRETT W. MM Gnr 92354 Tank Corps
BARRETT W.V. MM Sjt 3725 London Regt
BARRETT Walter MM Pte 202253 2/4th West Riding Regt
BARRETT William MM L/Cpl 2471 1/1st Cambridgeshire Regt
BARRETT William MM Pte 40892 1/6th Royal Highlanders
BARRETT William F. MM Dvr 720037 RFA
BARRETT William Henry MM Trumpeter 70494 H Bty RHA
BARRETT William Herbert MM L/Cpl 26532 Shropshire Light Infantry
BARRETT William J. MM Pte M2/053889 Army Service Corps
BARRETT William J. MM Sjt 7173 South Staffordshire Regt
BARRETT Willie MM Sjt 7703 1st West Yorkshire Regt
BARRIE Adam H. MM Gnr 200632 120 Bty 27 Bde RFA
BARRIE George MM Pte S/18502 Cameron Highlanders
BARRIE George A. MM(17916 Gordons)+Bar Pte 138438 26th Bn Machine Gun Corps

BARRIE Henry MM L/Cpl 240290 5/6th Scottish Rifles
BARRIE James MM Pte 18290 2nd Royal Scots Fusiliers
BARRINGER John "MM,MID" Sjt 8382 2nd Lincolnshire Regt
BARRINGTON George J. MM+Bar Sjt 13064 D/150 Bde RFA
BARRINGTON J. MM Pte 275519 1/9th Royal Scots
BARRINGTON James MM Cpl G5396 12th Royal Fusiliers KIA 2.9.16
BARRINGTON John MM Pte 2232 1/4th Gloucestershire Regt KIA 9.10.17.
BARRITT G. MM Gnr Sig 138298 280 Siege Bty RGA
BARRITT George E. MM CSM 53711 Durham Light Infantry
BARRON A. MM+Bar Pte 633050 20th London Regt
BARRON David MM Sjt 300213 Durham Light Infantry
BARRON Ernest A. MM Pte 372585 8th London Regt
BARRON Frederick MM Pte 6146 Coldstream Guards
BARRON George MM Pte 266126 Gordon Highlanders
BARRON George MM Pte 341025 3rd(West Lancashire)Fd Amb RAMC
BARRON Gibson MM Pte 333020 Highland Light Infantry
BARRON James MM L/Cpl 40112 Seaforth Highlanders
BARRON John MM Cpl 34850 9th Yorkshire Light Infantry
BARRON Lawrence MM Pte 15317 9th York & Lancaster Regt
BARRON Norman J. MM Cpl 20482 1st Gordon Highlanders
BARRON Richard MM Gnr 76053 3rd Bn Tank Corps
BARRON Thomas W. MM Sjt 18135 13th Durham Light Infantry
BARRON Ward MM Gnr 751623 RFA
BARRON William MM L/Cpl 241967 1/5th Gordon Highlanders
BARROS Joseph MM Cpl 41075 1 Squadron MGC(Cavalry)
BARROW Alan Dudley MM Pte M2/115657 Army Service Corps
BARROW Arthur Edmund MM Pte 8264 11th Royal West Kent Regt
BARROW Barnett MM L/Sjt 200921 1/5th Royal Lancaster Regt KIA 13.4.18.
BARROW Cornelius MM Pte 14161 7th Somerset Light Infantry
BARROW Edgar R. MM Pte 266575 9th Yorkshire Regt
BARROW Edward MM Pte M1/08248 Army Service Corps
BARROW Frederick J. MM Pte 9047 2nd Hampshire Regt
BARROW Frederick R.J. MM Pnr 358009 1 Div Sig Coy Royal Engineers
BARROW George W. MM+Bar Sjt 27/50 Northumberland Fusiliers
BARROW Horace MM L/Sjt 1795 1/7th West Riding Regt
BARROW Leonard MM L/Cpl 700539 1/23rd London Regt
BARROW Robert MM Pte 2143 1/16th London Regt
BARROW Thomas MM L/Cpl 97654 Royal Engineers
BARROW Thomas MM Sjt 17556 Liverpool Regt
BARROW William G. MM CQMS 8013 1st Cheshire Regt
BARROWCLIFFE Thomas MM Sjt 200527 1/4th East Lancashire Regt
BARROWCLIFFE William MM Sjt 28159 7th Duke of Cornwall's LI
BARROWS William MM Pte 5262 13th Northumberland Fusiliers KIA 1.7.16.
BARRS Walter William MM Gnr 86341 254 Siege Bty RGA
BARRY Arthur Patrick MM Pte 240400 6th Liverpool Regt
BARRY Denis MM Sjt 10542 Royal Irish Fusiliers
BARRY J. MM Cpl 12796 2nd South Lancashire Regt
BARRY J.B. MM Sjt 510480 RAMC
BARRY James MM L/Cpl 128684 Royal Engineers
BARRY James MM Cpl 27232 Durham Light Infantry
BARRY James MM Pte 302306 Manchester Regt
BARRY James G.H. MM Pte 54519 23rd Middlesex Regt
BARRY John "DCM,MM" Sjt D/20031 4th Dragoon Guards
BARRY John "MM,MSM" CSM T/23950 32 Div Train Army Service Corps
BARRY John MM Cpl 80519 X/29 Med TM Bty RFA
BARRY John MM Pte 3819 100 Fd Amb RAMC
BARRY John MM L/Sjt 3/5877 1st Dorsetshire Regt
BARRY John F. MM Pte 352640 7th London Regt
BARRY Joseph MM Pte 12007 6th Royal Dublin Fusiliers KIA 27.10.18.
BARRY Joseph MM Pte 2425 Middlesex Regt
BARRY Maurice MM Pnr 427942 Royal Engineers
BARRY Michael MM Bdr 30241 113 Hy Bty RGA
BARRY Patrick MM L/Cpl 6351 Irish Guards
BARRY Patrick "DCM,MM" Sjt 39017 5 Div Ammn Col RFA
BARRY Richard MM Pte 1983 7th Royal Irish Regt KIA 21.3.18.
BARRY Richard MM Sjt 10511 Machine Gun Corps
BARRY Thomas W. MM Cpl 59515 C/175 Bde RFA
BARRY Walter MM Gnr 905166 RFA
BARRY William J. MM Spr 551230 12 Div Sig Coy Royal Engineers
BARSBY Arthur B. MM Sjt 5995 16 Fd Amb RAMC
BARSBY George MM Pte 16616 1st Leicestershire Regt KIA 15.4.18.
BARSBY Harry MM Pte 28787 Notts & Derby Regt
BARSBY P. MM Sjt 14127 Leicestershire Regt
BARSBY Reginald S. MM Pte 5950 Middlesex Regt
BARSBY Walter MM L/Cpl 11072 Royal Scots Fusiliers
BARSDELL Ernest "DCM,MM" L/Cpl 4859 8th East Surrey Regt
BARSTON R.G. MM Dvr 80061 86 Bty 35 Bde RFA
BARSTOW Charles MM Pte 18273 1st Royal Warwickshire Regt
BARSTOW John MM Pte 16238 8th East Yorkshire Regt KIA 9.4.17.
BARSTOW Leonard MM Pte 16614 7th York & Lancaster Regt
BARTABY Ernest MM L/Cpl 4948 2nd Royal Irish Rifles
BARTEN Donald MM Pte 4724 8th Royal Fusiliers KIA 30.11.17.
BARTER Arthur C. MM Pte 11153 6th Dorsetshire Regt
BARTER John MM Cpl M/205252 Army Service Corps
BARTER Percy H. MM Gnr 66090 RGA
BARTER Stephen Raymond MM L/Cpl 9886 Royal Fusiliers
BARTER William MM Gnr 44746 A/103 Bde RFA KIA 24.7.26.
BARTHOLOMEW Charles MM L/Cpl L/7916 6th Royal West Kent Regt
BARTHOLOMEW Ernest MM Pte 11971 11th D Coy King's Royal Rifle Corps KIA 24.4.18.
BARTHOLOMEW Frank C. MM+Bar L/Cpl 8205 10th Royal Fusiliers
BARTHOLOMEW George E. MM Pte 5321 Royal Sussex Regt
BARTHOLOMEW Sandy MM Pte 17681 Royal Inniskilling Fusiliers
BARTHROP Jack MM Pte G3/9732 East Surrey Regt
BARTHROPP Marcus MM(202282 1st Lond)+Bar Sjt 238036 2nd South Staffordshire Regt
BARTLE Hyle H. MM+2 Bars Pte 41718 8th Lincolnshire Regt
BARTLE John Edward MM Pte 23192 2nd West Riding Regt
BARTLEMAN Frederick MM Pte 4011 1/12th London Regt KIA 19.9.16.
BARTLEMAN Henry MM Pte M2/147203 Army Service Corps
BARTLES John MM Pte 40899 Manchester Regt
BARTLETT Albert MM+Bar L/Cpl 5160 8th East Surrey Regt
BARTLETT Bernard M. MM Cpl 700724 23rd London Regt
BARTLETT Charles MM Pte 40270 Middlesex Regt
BARTLETT Charles MM L/Cpl 8004 2nd Northamptonshire Regt Died 8.11.18.
BARTLETT Charles MM Pte 10337 1st South Wales Borderers
BARTLETT Charles W.F. "MM,MID" Cpl 364 1st Welsh Guards
BARTLETT Chauncey Vivian MM Gnr 38911 6th Bn MGC (Motors)
BARTLETT Eric W. MM Pte 630607 20th London Regt
BARTLETT Ernest "DCM,MM" Bdr 25847 Y/23 Med TM Bty RFA KIA 13.4.17.Cardiff.
BARTLETT Ernest L. MM+Bar L/Cpl 24699 Royal Fusiliers
BARTLETT Ernest S. MM Pte 1279 10th Royal West Surrey Regt
BARTLETT Ernest William "MM,MdH(F)" Pte 15050 Welsh Regt
BARTLETT F.J. MM Pte 41811 6th Northamptonshire Regt
BARTLETT Felix MM Gnr 132918 319 Siege Bty RGA
BARTLETT Frederick J. MM Sjt 8794 2nd West Yorkshire Regt
BARTLETT Frederick John MM Dvr T3/030657 42 Div Train Army Service Corps
BARTLETT Frederick W. MM Pte 1189 East Surrey Regt
BARTLETT Geoffrey "MM,MMV(It)" Sjt 19387 26th Royal Fusiliers KIA 11.6.17.
BARTLETT George "DCM,MM" Sjt 45722 1st Devonshire Regt
BARTLETT George MM Sjt 117844 RFA
BARTLETT George MM Spr 402806 404 Fd Coy Royal Engineers Died 11.7.18.
BARTLETT George MM Sjt 240394 1/5th Seaforth Highlanders
BARTLETT George A. MM Dvr 115541 RFA
BARTLETT George H. MM Pte 85038 Machine Gun Corps
BARTLETT H.G. MM Cpl 457295 RAMC
BARTLETT Harry MM Pte 2236 1/20th London Regt
BARTLETT Harry Abel MM Pte 1229 13th Middlesex Regt KIA 10.10.18.
BARTLETT Henry MM Pte 12788 1st Worcestershire Regt
BARTLETT Henry G. MM Cpl 7454 1st Royal Berkshire Regt
BARTLETT Henry William Charles MM Pte 5132 2/1st HAC (Inf)
BARTLETT James T. MM Bdr 87879 RFA
BARTLETT John MM Gnr 51394 X/30 Med TM Bty RFA
BARTLETT John W. MM Spr 177820 Royal Engineers
BARTLETT Kenneth A.W. "MM,MSM" BSM 50320 C/76 Bde RFA
BARTLETT Leonard Owen MM Pte M2/222215 654 MT Coy Army Service Corps
BARTLETT Percy MM L/Cpl 207802 10th Royal West Surrey Regt
BARTLETT Percy M. MM Spr 151537 251 Tunnelling Coy Royal Engineers
BARTLETT Richard T. MM Pte 15064 7th Wiltshire Regt
BARTLETT Stanley Arthur MM Gnr 608341 Att 223 Bde RFA RHA
BARTLETT Thomas W. MM Cpl 292 7th East Surrey Regt

BARTLETT Thomas William MM Cpl 32509 1st South Staffordshire Regt
BARTLETT Wallace MM+Bar L/Cpl 18795 2nd Worcestershire Regt
BARTLETT Walter Martin "MM,MID" Bdr 10201 HQ 118 Bde RFA
BARTLETT William MM L/Sjt 11422 6th East Kent Regt
BARTLETT William MM Pte 143871 Machine Gun Corps
BARTLETT William MM Dvr 40940 D/58 Bde RFA DOW 19.10.18.
BARTLETT William C. "MM,MID" Spr 23825 Royal Engineers
BARTLETT William E. MM L/Sjt G/6986 11th Royal West Surrey Regt
BARTLETT William Frederick MM+Bar Sjt 5821 Machine Gun Corps
BARTLETT William J. MM Pte 21675 1st Coldstream Guards
BARTLEY John MM Pte 12240 East Yorkshire Regt
BARTLEY Roger MM L/Cpl 311440 Royal Engineers
BARTON Albert Edward MM Sjt 11738 9th West Yorkshire Regt
BARTON Alfred H. MM Cpl 2999 1/20th London Regt
BARTON Alfred M. MM Pte 54070 2nd King's Royal Rifle Corps
BARTON Archibald MM Pte S/3814 Seaforth Highlanders
BARTON Burland O. MM Sjt 235354 1/1st Gloucestershire Yeomanry
BARTON Charles MM Pte 47771 RAMC
BARTON Christopher MM+Bar L/Cpl 1036 7th East Kent Regt
BARTON Cyril MM Pte 16908 10th Scottish Rifles
BARTON Cyril Charles MM Pte 85964 154 Coy Machine Gun Corps
BARTON Edward H. MM Gnr Fitter 31068 RFA
BARTON Frederick MM Pte 4749 13th Royal Fusiliers
BARTON George MM Pte 21667 15th Hampshire Regt KIA 7.10.16.
BARTON George MM Sjt 43448 Suffolk Regt
BARTON George MM Pte 19782 Machine Gun Corps
BARTON George E. MM Pte 10576 1st Royal West Kent Regt
BARTON Henry Edward MM Sjt 242467 2/6th Royal Warwickshire Regt KIA 22.3.18.
BARTON Hugh MM+Bar Pte 6175 1st Royal Irish Fusiliers
BARTON James MM L/Cpl 43755 12th Royal Scots
BARTON James MM Pte 359705 Liverpool Regt
BARTON James MM Pte 16866 Hampshire Regt
BARTON James MM Sjt S/8646 8th Royal Highlanders KIA 12.10.17.
BARTON James Miles MM Pte 4066 2nd Rifle Brigade KIA 29.11.17.
BARTON John MM Sjt 241705 5th South Lancashire Regt
BARTON John MM Dvr 16101 C/165 Bde RFA
BARTON John MM+Bar Sjt 68107 107 Fd Amb RAMC
BARTON John Frederick MM Sjt 15298 Liverpool Regt
BARTON John R. MM Sjt 132662 Royal Engineers
BARTON Leonard MM Cpl 200900 4th Bn Tank Corps
BARTON Percy MM Cpl 265694 1/6th West Riding Regt KIA 4.5.18.
BARTON Percy Leonard MM Sjt 242369 2/6th Royal Warwickshire Regt KIA 27.9.17.
BARTON Robert C. "DCM,MM+Bar" Sjt 19057 15th Hampshire Regt
BARTON Sydney J. MM Pte 275132 3rd London Regt
BARTON Thomas MM+Bar Bdr 800451 C/230 Bde RFA
BARTON Thomas A. MM L/Cpl 12644 1st Worcestershire Regt
BARTON Thomas George MM Dvr 18320 RFA
BARTON Thomas W. MM Pte 203414 1/4th South Lancashire Regt
BARTON Walter MM Bdr 295387 207 Siege Bty RGA
BARTON Walter MM Pte 37264 16th Lancashire Fusiliers
BARTON Wilfred MM Cpl 40206 20th Manchester Regt
BARTON William MM Pte 16538 6th South Staffordshire Regt
BARTON William C. MM+Bar Pte 10646 1/1st Hertfordshire Regt
BARTON William R. MM L/Cpl 17150 Machine Gun Corps
BARTRAM Arthur William MM+Bar Sjt 522022 483 Fd Coy Royal Engineers
BARTRAM Ernest MM Cpl 241137 Leicestershire Regt
BARTRAM George William MM Pte 16/243 Northumberland Fusiliers
BARTRAM John T. MM L/Cpl S/18078 Rifle Brigade
BARTRAM Samuel MM Pte 19445 Durham Light Infantry
BARTRAM Sydney John MM Sjt 1524 1/6th Welsh Regt DOW 30.9.18.
BARTRICK Ernest F. MM Pte G/28709 7th Royal West Kent Regt
BARTUP A.T. MM Cpl 44348 Royal Engineers
BARTY Sidney John MM Pte 45336 2nd South Staffordshire Regt
BARWELL Edward MM Pte 82024 26th Royal Fusiliers
BARWELL Frederick C. MM+2 Bars CSM 14617 Lincolnshire Regt
BARWELL George MM Pte 22901 1st Border Regt KIA 28.9.18.
BARWELL George H. MM+Bar Sjt 722396 24th London Regt
BARWELL James MM Pte 11825 29th Bn Machine Gun Corps
BARWELL Wilfrid MM L/Cpl 30208 16th Royal Warwickshire Regt KIA 1.9.18.
BARWICK Edgar MM Spr 104620 106 Fd Coy Royal Engineers
BARWICK Frederick A. MM Sjt 17676 59 Fd Coy Royal Engineers
BARWICK G. MM Pte 235242 West Riding Regt
BARWICK James MM Sjt 8474 Royal Lancaster Regt
BARWICK William Rufus MM L/Cpl 6016 7th Royal Sussex Regt KIA 26.8.18.
BASCOMBE William Stanley MM Sjt 16483 Gloucestershire Regt
BASE G. MM Bdr 358069 RGA
BASELEY William MM Cpl 40729 RAMC
BASELEY William B. MM Cpl 66254 62nd Bn Machine Gun Corps
BASHAM Frederick MM Pte 452246 2/11th London Regt KIA 6.11.17.
BASHAM John MM Sjt 19457 11th Durham Light Infantry
BASHFORD James E. MM Pte 235598 5th West Riding Regt
BASHFORD John W. MM Pte 6272 East Surrey Regt
BASHFORD W.W.G. MM Pte 13118 9th Essex Regt
BASHFORTH John H.J. MM Cpl 67610 Machine Gun Corps
BASINGER Frederick S. MM Pte G/12198 19th Middlesex Regt
BASKEYFIELD John Alban MM Cpl 821018 B/87 Bde RFA
BASKOTT James Edward MM Bdr 43393 RGA DOW 11.12.17.
BASNETT Edward MM Sjt 15950 Royal Lancaster Regt
BASNETT Frank MM Pte 352292 1/2nd(East Lancashire)Fd Amb RAMC
BASNETT Percy MM Pte 235126 13th Liverpool Regt
BASQUIL John MM Pte 27048 Labour Corps
BASS C.J. MM Bdr 1994 RFA
BASS Charles Arthur MM Sjt 24093 2nd D Coy Royal Dublin Fusiliers DOW 11.11.18.
BASS Edward Thomas MM Pte 42705 2nd Essex Regt
BASS Ernest Robert Charles MM Gnr Wheeler 86931 C/63 Bde RFA
BASS Frank MM+Bar Pte C/653 16th King's Royal Rifle Corps
BASS George Herbert Cecil MM Pte 5137 8th London Regt
BASS George J. MM Pte 51990 24th Royal Fusiliers
BASS John MM L/Sjt 18751 1st Bedfordshire Regt KIA 2.9.18.
BASS Walter Edward MM Bdr 45517 V5 Hy TM Bty RGA DOW 3.4.17.
BASSADONA Sydney H. MM L/Sjt 1542 RAMC
BASSANT Thomas MM Pte 41832 4th Bedfordshire Regt
BASSETT F. MM Air Mech 2 6947 Royal Air Force
BASSETT Harry MM L/Cpl 260026 Royal Sussex Regt
BASSETT James MM Pte 15020 9th Royal Welsh Fusiliers KIA 22.3.18.
BASSETT James S. MM Pte 34242 9th Yorkshire Regt
BASSETT John MM Cpl 10550 Oxf & Bucks Light Infantry
BASSETT John A. MM L/Cpl 13/276 7th East Yorkshire Regt
BASSETT Rowland William MM Gnr 930018 281 Bde RFA
BASSETT William MM+Bar L/Cpl 6699 8th East Surrey Regt
BASSIL Percy MM L/Cpl 554109 511 Fd Coy Royal Engineers
BASSINGTHWAIGHT Henry J. MM Sjt 6501 Machine Gun Corps
BASTABLE George E. MM Pte 117386 9th Bn Machine Gun Corps
BASTABLE William MM Pte 45006 1st Royal Inniskilling Fusiliers
BASTARD Robert John Veal MM Pte 59840 9th Northumberland Fusiliers DOW 9.8.18.
BASTER Gerald Harry "MM,MID" Cpl 86907 A/62 Bde RFA
BASTER Stephen MM Dvr 36098 RFA
BASTERFIELD Henry MM Sjt 10673 1st Worcestershire Regt
BASTIN Ernest A. MM Cpl 1759 24 Fd Amb RAMC
BASTIN Leonard H. MM L/Bdr 8708 46 Bty 39 Bde RFA
BASTIN Wallace Hubert MM Spr 514509 568 Army Troops Coy Royal Engineers
BASTIN William George MM Sjt 15244 9th Royal Dublin Fusiliers
BASTOCK Samuel MM L/Cpl 11425 Leicestershire Regt
BASTON Ernest James MM Gnr 121159 350 Siege Bty RGA DOW 29.3.18.
BASTON James R. MM Pte 81219 15th Durham Light Infantry
BASTONE William J. MM S/Sjt 596 RAMC
BASTOW C. "DCM,MM" Sjt S/19290 16th Rifle Brigade
BASTOW Edward MM L/Cpl 530801 15th London Regt
BASTOW Harry MM Cpl 780738 RFA
BASTOW Herbert "DCM,MM" Sjt 56662 Att 81 Bde RGA Royal Engineers
BATCHELOR Albert MM Pte 41846 Manchester Regt
BATCHELOR Alfred J. MM Pte 510195 2nd(London)Fd Amb RAMC
BATCHELOR Arthur MM Pte 3831 1/7th Middlesex Regt KIA 16.9.16.
BATCHELOR Arthur Charles MM L/Cpl STK324 10th Royal Fusiliers DOW 4.5.17.
BATCHELOR Bertie MM Pte 44841 2/5th Manchester Regt KIA 21.3.18.

BATCHELOR Charles Clements "DCM,MM" Sjt G/3377 7th East Kent Regt
BATCHELOR Charles W. MM Spr 66492 Royal Engineers
BATCHELOR E. MM Pte 25939 Royal West Kent Regt
BATCHELOR Edward T. MM Pte 25614 1st Grenadier Guards
BATCHELOR Ernest L.J. MM Pte 29963 7th Royal West Kent Regt
BATCHELOR Frederick J. MM Pte 90503 RAMC
BATCHELOR George MM Sjt G/1373 8th East Kent Regt KIA 18.8.16.
BATCHELOR George V. "MM,MID" Sjt 17129 Royal Engineers
BATCHELOR Harry P. MM Dvr 92206 64 Fd Coy Royal Engineers
BATCHELOR Herbert John MM Pte 41622 6th Yorkshire Regt
BATCHELOR Jesse Albert MM Sjt 114 2nd Middlesex Regt
BATCHELOR Joseph MM Sjt 72715 2 Div Sig Coy Royal Engineers
BATCHELOR Percy "MM,MID" Pte 10179 RAMC
BATCHELOR Reginald Edwin MM Pte 4825 1/1st London Regt KIA 8.10.16.
BATCHELOR Stephen MM Sjt 327 2nd Royal West Surrey Regt
BATCHELOR Thomas MM Sjt 67203 Labour Corps
BATCHELOR Walter H. MM Cpl 114621 21st Bn Machine Gun Corps
BATCHELOR Walter Henry MM Sjt 16658 10th Welsh Regt KIA 2.8.17.
BATCHELOR William MM Sjt 8000 Highland Light Infantry
BATCHELOR William MM Cpl 14124 4th Bedfordshire Regt KIA 27.8.18.
BATCHELOR William George MM L/Cpl 13706 1st Royal West Surrey Regt KIA 3.3.18.
BATCHELOR William H. MM Cpl 2303 9th East Surrey Regt
BATCHELOR William J. MM Cpl 16013 8th Suffolk Regt
BATCHELOR William K. MM Sjt Farrier 30586 RFA
BATCHFORD William MM Pte 29836 11th Notts & Derby Regt Died 21.10.18.
BATCHLOR Samuel MM Cpl 22172 1st Royal Dublin Fusiliers
BATCUP A.E. MM Cpl G/22821 11th Royal West Surrey Regt
BATE Albert MM Cpl 795703 RFA Died 4.7.18.
BATE Arthur MM Cpl 13268 Worcestershire Regt
BATE George MM Sjt 2108 2nd King's Royal Rifle Corps KIA 30.3.18.
BATE James MM Pte 71923 9 Coy Machine Gun Corps KIA 3.5.17.
BATE R.W. MM Pte 10/43042 Royal Irish Rifles
BATE Thomas F. MM Pte 82231 23rd Royal Fusiliers
BATE W.H. MM L/Cpl P4518 Military Foot Police
BATE Walter C. MM Pte 139745 Machine Gun Corps
BATEASON John T. MM Dvr 87564 88 Bty 14 Bde RFA
BATEMAN Albert MM Pte 54258 5th Manchester Regt
BATEMAN Arthur E. MM Pte 47163 9th West Yorkshire Regt
BATEMAN Clarence MM Sjt 277346 Essex Regt
BATEMAN David Gwilym MM Pte M2/117245 Att 54 Fd Amb RAMC Army Service Corps
BATEMAN Edwin C. "DCM,MM" Sjt 36713 Royal Berkshire Regt
BATEMAN Eric Norman MM Pte 4608 1/12th B Coy London Regt
BATEMAN F.A. MM L/Cpl 680803 22nd London Regt
BATEMAN Harry MM Dvr 830928 B/306 Bde RFA
BATEMAN Henry MM Gnr 82302 RFA
BATEMAN John MM Pte 23097 6th Notts & Derby Regt
BATEMAN John MM Pte 3341 Machine Gun Corps
BATEMAN John S. MM Cpl 25647 17th Royal Welsh Fusiliers
BATEMAN John Saniglar MM Sjt 3712 9th Lancers
BATEMAN John William MM Pte 36340 2nd Yorkshire Regt
BATEMAN Ralph S. MM Pte 7100 Royal Fusiliers
BATEMAN Reginald MM Cpl 9702 2nd Leinster Regt
BATEMAN Roland "DCM,MM+Bar" Pte 12053 South Staffordshire Regt
BATEMAN Samuel MM Pte 12490 Royal Warwickshire Regt
BATEMAN Stephen Thomas "MC,MM(2365 L/Cpl)" 2Lt 7th att 1/8th Worcestershire Regt
BATEMAN Thomas MM Pte 352369 2nd Manchester Regt
BATEMAN Thomas E. MM Pte 200992 Royal Welsh Fusiliers
BATEMAN William MM Pte 87666 147 Labour Coy Labour Corps
BATEMAN William MM+Bar Pte 200195 1/4th Royal Sussex Regt
BATEMAN William MM Pte 241681 1/5th Lincolnshire Regt
BATEMAN William MM Pte 15569 1/7th West Yorkshire Regt Died 9.11.18.
BATEMAN William H. MM Cpl 201827 2/4th Royal Berkshire Regt
BATEMAN William Henry "MC,MM" 2Lt 1st Essex Regt
BATER R. MM Pte 341242 RAMC
BATER Samuel MM Pte 20007 8th Devonshire Regt DOW 6.9.16.
BATES A.J. MM+Bar L/Cpl 510338 RAMC
BATES Albert MM Cpl 4440 HAC
BATES Albert H. "MM,MID" Pte 2668 12th Lancers
BATES Alexander "MM,MC(G)" Pte 3/2082 9th Royal Lancaster Regt
BATES Alexander Arthur MM Bdr 69406 28 Bde RFA
BATES Arthur MM Pte 634846 20th London Regt
BATES Arthur C. MM Sjt 274 North Lancashire Regt
BATES Arthur George MM Sjt 106803 231 Fd Coy Royal Engineers
BATES Arthur J. MM Cpl 2717 8th Royal West Kent Regt
BATES Benjamin MM Pte 32329 2nd West Riding Regt
BATES Bennion MM Dvr 97341 17 Bty 41 Bde RFA
BATES Brian "MM,MM(F)" Pte 305582 15/17th West Yorkshire Regt
BATES Charles R. MM Pte 203009 1/5th Royal Warwickshire Regt
BATES Clement MM+Bar Pte 203504 2nd West Riding Regt
BATES Ernest MM Pte 18947 Machine Gun Corps
BATES F. MM Cpl 84062 Labour Corps
BATES Frederick MM Pte 200817 1/4th Royal Scots
BATES Frederick J. MM Spr 7830 2 Fd Coy Royal Engineers
BATES Frederick M. MM Pte 125583 29th Bn Machine Gun Corps
BATES George MM+Bar Pte 201952 Scottish Rifles
BATES George MM L/Sjt 20982 2nd Border Regt KIA 26.10.17.
BATES George A. MM L/Cpl 754 1/1st Bedfordshire Yeomanry
BATES George W. MM Pte 10863 Yorkshire Regt
BATES Gilbert MM Pte 27332 11th Notts & Derby Regt
BATES Harold E. MM Cpl 340089 RGA
BATES Harold John MM Cpl 135622 Inland Waterways Transport Royal Engineers
BATES Harold R. MM Pte 10713 Royal Fusiliers
BATES Harry MM L/Cpl 22204 1st Royal Dublin Fusiliers
BATES Henry MM L/Cpl 1812 16th Middlesex Regt
BATES Herbert MM Pte 26 11th East Yorkshire Regt
BATES Howard MM Pte 67275 1/5th Devonshire Regt
BATES James MM Dvr 266947 D/75 Bde RFA
BATES James MM Pte 200146 1/4th North Lancashire Regt
BATES James MM Sjt 24723 Machine Gun Corps
BATES James S. MM Pte 29050 2nd Lancashire Fusiliers
BATES Joe MM+Bar Pte 267064 2/4th West Riding Regt
BATES John MM Pte 18180 1st East Lancashire Regt
BATES John MM Cpl 24914 7 Fd Coy Royal Engineers
BATES John C. MM Sjt 34483 Yorkshire Light Infantry
BATES John William MM Pte 4627 Royal Warwickshire Regt
BATES Joseph G. MM S/Sjt SS/5284 Army Service Corps
BATES Joseph G.H. MM Bfr 75868 36 Bde RFA
BATES M.L. MM Cpl 36030 South Staffordshire Regt
BATES Percy MM Pte 266418 1/1st Hertfordshire Regt
BATES Robert MM L/Sjt 268034 1/6th Cheshire Regt
BATES Samuel MM Pte 14165 24th Manchester Regt
BATES Sydney MM Sjt 2492 17th London Regt
BATES T. MM Pte 26371 Worcestershire Regt
BATES Thomas MM Pte 3425 Durham Light Infantry
BATES Thomas MM Cpl 18813 8th South Lancashire Regt
BATES Thomas MM L/Cpl 51232 MGC(Cavalry)
BATES Thomas P. MM Sjt 9347 2nd Scottish Rifles
BATES Thomas William MM Sjt 374424 264 Siege Bty RGA
BATES Wilfred MM Bdr 45449 25 Bde RFA
BATES William MM Sjt 23/1415 Northumberland Fusiliers
BATES William E. MM Pte 10832 1st King's Own Scottish Borderers
BATES William Henry MM Pte 235459 Leicestershire Regt
BATES William J. MM Pte 555735 16th London Regt
BATESON Charles MM Cpl 61464 RAMC
BATESON Frderick L. MM Dvr 117980 RFA
BATESON Harry MM Cpl 43033 Seaforth Highlanders
BATESON John "MM,MID" Sjt 2002 West Riding Regt
BATESON Robert MM Pte 266966 2/6th West Riding Regt DOW 28.11.17.
BATESON William MM Cpl 14862 Border Regt
BATEUP E.D. MM Spr 107376 Royal Engineers
BATEY Lewis MM Pte 25255 10th West Riding Regt
BATEY Thomas MM Pte 18/1515 14th Durham Light Infantry
BATEY Thomas W. MM Pte 11/13899 Border Regt
BATEY Thomas W. MM L/Cpl 271023 1/1st Northumberland Yeo
BATEY William MM+Bar Pte 33925 Northumberland Fusiliers
BATH George MM Pte 13920 1st Lincolnshire Regt KIA 24.8.18.
BATH George S. MM Sjt 133 B/261 Bde RFA KIA 17.9.17.
BATH Hubert MM Pte 394181 2nd King's Royal Rifle Corps
BATH Walter H. MM CSM 25802 11th Oxf & Bucks Light Infantry
BATH William MM Pte 12041 6th Dorsetshire Regt
BATH William MM Pte 8311 2nd Hampshire Regt
BATHE Herbert MM L/Cpl 1807 1/4th York & Lancaster Regt
BATHER Hugh J. MM Pte 1439 1st Welsh Guards
BATHGATE John MM Pte S/30051 2nd Cameron Highlanders

BATHGATE Joseph MM Dvr 42990 6 Div Ammn Col RFA
BATHGATE Robbert K. MM Sjt 54976 RAMC
BATHO Charles H. MM Pte 18594 2nd Coldstream Guards
BATHURST Stanley East MM Sjt 2043 1/24th London Regt
BATKIN Horace C. MM Spr 2292 Royal Engineers
BATLEY Archie S. MM Cpl 7603 1st Norfolk Regt
BATLEY Benjamin MM+Bar L/Cpl 266607 6th Gordon Highlanders
BATLEY James MM Cpl 35562 9th North Lancashire Regt KIA 14.10.17.
BATLEY Joseph F. MM Pte 267901 West Riding Regt
BATLEY W. MM Pte 2565 1/8th Middlesex Regt
BATRICK William J. MM L/Bdr 52052 B/59 Bde RFA
BATSFORD Horace William MM Pte R/36726 2nd King's Royal Rifle Corps KIA 25.9.18.
BATSON D.G. "DCM,MM" BSM 20086 141 Hy Bty RGA
BATSON Frank S. MM Sjt 380970 Liverpool Regt
BATSON Frederick S. MM Sjt 20966 8th Norfolk Regt
BATSON Henry MM Pte A/3274 7th King's Royal Rifle Corps
BATSON Herbert MM Pte 11327 23rd Middlesex Regt
BATSON Percy MM L/Cpl 1940 21st Lancers
BATSON William MM Pte 9091 Royal Munster Fusiliers
BATSON William Archibald MM Pte 20005 2nd Royal Munster Fusiliers
BATSTONE Frederick H. MM Pte 11325 9th Lancers
BATSTONE Stephen MM Pte 26792 5th Royal Lancaster Regt
BATT Charles L. "DCM,MM" L/Cpl 232242 2/2nd London Regt
BATT Charles R. MM Gnr 147604 RGA
BATT Harry MM Pte 10332 Welsh Regt
BATT Henry John MM Bdr 68013 RFA
BATT William F. MM Pte 201537 9th Bn Tank Corps
BATTAM Harold MM Pte 29957 2nd Hampshire Regt
BATTAMS George MM Gnr 686493 C/277 Bde RFA
BATTAMS George MM+Bar Sjt 56520 39 Bde RFA
BATTAMS Henry MM Dvr 31180 B/177 Bde RFA
BATTAMS Walter MM+Bar Pte 17711 2nd Bedfordshire Regt
BATTEN Albert Edward MM Pte 1624 7th Royal West Kent Regt
BATTEN Albert H. MM Pte 14878 Hampshire Regt
BATTEN Ernest MM Pte 170727 57th Bn Machine Gun Corps
BATTEN George A. MM Sjt 21359 10th Lancashire Fusiliers
BATTEN Henry MM Cpl M2/077204 Army Service Corps Att RFA.
BATTEN Percy MM+Bar Sjt L/9813 1st Royal West Surrey Regt KIA 2.10.17.
BATTEN Ronald MM Cpl 20121 4 Div Sig Coy Royal Engineers
BATTEN W. MM Sjt 19213 Leicestershire Regt
BATTEN William MM Cpl 49226 61 Fd Coy Royal Engineers
BATTENSBY Frank R. MM Pte 51340 1st East Yorkshire Regt
BATTERHAM Ernest MM L/Cpl 14935 Lincolnshire Regt
BATTERS Alfred A. MM Pte 12850 2nd King's Royal Rifle Corps
BATTERSBY Charles MM Cpl 10225 1st Yorkshire Light Infantry
BATTERSBY Edward L. MM Pte 20829 East Lancashire Regt
BATTERSBY Fred MM Cpl 29008 Royal Welsh Fusiliers
BATTERSBY Frederick John MM Gnr 74224 A/61 Bde RFA
BATTERSBY George F. MM Pte 37278 2nd Welsh Regt
BATTERSBY Henry MM Gnr 48210 RGA
BATTERSBY James H. MM CSM 240891 5th Royal Lancaster Regt
BATTERSBY James L. MM L/Bdr Sig 67436 B/113 Bde RFA
BATTERSBY Robert L. MM Gnr 1202 RFA
BATTERSBY Simeon MM Cpl 58203 RAMC
BATTERSBY Wilfred Reed MM Pte 203250 11th Notts & Derby Regt
BATTERSHALL William A.G. MM Pte 280389 1/4th London Regt
BATTILAND Joseph "MC+Bar,MM(8146 CSM)" 2Lt 1/4th Yorkshire Light Infantry
BATTISON George MM Pte 20825 1st Royal Scots
BATTISON James M. MM L/Cpl Piper 2297 1/7th Arg & Suth Highlanders
BATTISON Thomas MM Sjt 8070 1st Northamptonshire Regt
BATTISTA Celesta MM Dvr 80305 RFA
BATTISTA Remegio MM Pte 32691 Northumberland Fusiliers
BATTLE Edgar Harry MM Sjt 9551 1st South Lancashire Regt Died 4.7.18.
BATTLE Harry MM Pte 12620 8th Yorkshire Regt
BATTLE Henry E. MM Spr 180218 54 Fd Coy Royal Engineers
BATTLE John Henry MM Pte 8722 2nd Worcestershire Regt DOW 8.11.16.
BATTLE Lancelot Percy MM Bdr 52661 A/38 Bde RFA Died 3.12.17.
BATTLE Stephen MM Pte 15848 West Yorkshire Regt
BATTRICK Owen MM CQMS 9774 Coldstream Guards
BATTS Bernard MM L/Cpl 200793 1/4th Oxf & Bucks Light Infantry
BATTS Frederick A. MM Pte 41359 1st Duke of Cornwall's LI
BATTY Frederick A. "MM,MID" Sjt 41062 RFA
BATTY John MM Pte 3270 20th London Regt
BATTY Joseph MM+Bar L/Sjt 4695 2nd East Lancashire Regt KIA 17.2.18.
BATTY Joseph MM Pte 48498 1/9th Manchester Regt
BATTY Lewis MM Sjt 785226 3 Bde RFA
BATTY Thomas MM Cpl 43269 288 Army Troops Coy Royal Engineers KIA 30.3.18.
BATTY Walter "MM,CG(B)" Sjt 21690 10th East Yorkshire Regt
BATTY William E. MM L/Cpl 86001 Middlesex Regt
BATTYE Harry MM L/Cpl 204034 West Riding Regt
BATTYE Herbert S. MM Bdr L/29364 C/174 Bde RFA
BAUGH William W.M. MM Sjt 16374 11th Notts & Derby Regt
BAUGHAM J. MM Sjt 12 Royal West Kent Regt
BAUGHN John MM L/Cpl 8888 1st Royal West Surrey Regt
BAUL Richard L. MM L/Cpl 23526 Machine Gun Corps
BAULCOMBE Charles MM Sjt 14040 49 Coy Machine Gun Corps
BAULKER W. MM Sjt 129230 45th Royal Fusiliers
BAUM Bertram MM Sjt 43440 9th Essex Regt
BAUM William MM Gnr 345553 213 Siege Bty RGA
BAUM Willie Harold MM Pte 10209 6th Leicestershire Regt
BAUMBROUGH William Herbert MM Sjt 548255 613 Fd Coy Royal Engineers
BAVIN Edward J. MM Cpl 27752 Postal Section Royal Engineers
BAVIN Frederick G. MM+Bar L/Cpl 202854 Essex Regt
BAVIN George MM Pte 2082 6th Lincolnshire Regt
BAWCUTT Edward MM Sjt 204476 10th Notts & Derby Regt
BAWDEN Frederick MM Pte 267367 2/5th Gloucestershire Regt
BAWDEN Samuel B. "DCM,MM" Sjt 5084 71 Fd Amb RAMC
BAWDEN Victor H. MM Pte 295421 12th Somerset Light Infantry
BAWN Alfred Samuel MM Bdr 796760 62 Div Ammn Col RFA
BAWN Robert MM Pte 14447 19th Durham Light Infantry
BAX Ernest H. MM Gnr 2801 MGC(Motors)
BAX Thomas "DCM,MM" Sjt 61162 17th Bn Machine Gun Corps
BAXENDALE A. MM Pte 19979 2nd Royal Scots Fusiliers
BAXENDALE Edwin MM+Bar Pte 35792 15th Lancashire Fusiliers
BAXENDALE John MM Sjt 19043 1st Border Regt
BAXENDALE Thomas MM Cpl 265904 Liverpool Regt
BAXENDALE William MM Cpl 52854 Durham Light Infantry
BAXTER Albert "MM,MID" Sjt 33592 3 Bde RHA
BAXTER Albert MM+Bar Dvr 30729 36 Div Ammn Col RFA
BAXTER Alfred A. MM Sjt M1/07662 Army Service Corps
BAXTER Alfred George MM Pte 44361 1st South Wales Borderers
BAXTER Alfred Judge MM L/Cpl 1755 6th London Regt
BAXTER Archibald MM Pte 302396 Arg & Suth Highlanders
BAXTER Arthur MM Pte 019922 Army Ordnance Corps
BAXTER Benjamin MM Cpl 5905 10th Hussars
BAXTER Charles MM+Bar 2nd Cpl 134178 Royal Engineers
BAXTER Charles MM Sjt 7070 C/82 Bde RFA
BAXTER Daniel MM Pte 10413 Arg & Suth Highlanders
BAXTER David MM Cpl 17672 7th Suffolk Regt
BAXTER Doctor? "MM,MSM" L/Cpl 121952 252 Tunnelling Coy Royal Engineers
BAXTER Ernest MM CSM 36513 5th East Lancashire Regt
BAXTER Ernest MM Spr 492145 46 Div Sig Coy Royal Engineers
BAXTER Frank H. MM Sjt 82381 RFA
BAXTER Fred MM Cpl 306015 1/7th West Riding Regt KIA 11.10.18.
BAXTER Frederick MM L/Cpl 306984 1/8th Notts & Derby Regt
BAXTER Frederick "MM,Medaille Militaire(F)" Sjt 8064 9th Essex Regt DOW 27.5.18.
BAXTER George MM Pte 12317 7th North Lancashire Regt DOW 14.11.16.
BAXTER George MM Pte 13/52 13th Royal Irish Rifles
BAXTER George MM Pte 53406 Notts & Derby Regt
BAXTER George MM Sjt 14025 8th Royal Scots Fusiliers
BAXTER George E. MM L/Cpl 12641 Lincolnshire Regt
BAXTER Gilbert MM Sjt 25749 45 Bde RFA
BAXTER Harold "DCM+Bar,MM" Sjt 15085 11th Essex Regt
BAXTER Harold MM Pte 117981 Machine Gun Corps
BAXTER Heber MM Pte 242518 Lancashire Fusiliers
BAXTER Henry MM Cpl 8474 Border Regt
BAXTER Henry C. MM+Bar L/Cpl 67675 3rd London Regt
BAXTER Henry J. MM L/Cpl 23179 Machine Gun Corps
BAXTER James MM L/Cpl 315061 13th Royal Highlanders
BAXTER James MM Pte 6613 7th Suffolk Regt
BAXTER James MM Gnr 92195 RFA
BAXTER James MM Pte 4325 6th Connaught Rangers
BAXTER James G. MM Pte 16151 13th Royal Scots
BAXTER James W. MM Sjt 19827 10 Fd Amb RAMC
BAXTER John MM L/Cpl 43763 4th North Staffordshire Regt

BAXTER John MM Pte 73071 11th Notts & Derby Regt KIA 17.10.17.
BAXTER John MM L/Bdr 200839 RGA
BAXTER John MM Pte 1597 12th Royal Irish Rifles
BAXTER John "MM,MID" CSM 6453 2nd Worcestershire Regt
BAXTER John H. MM 2nd Cpl 207469 63 Div Sig Coy Royal Engineers
BAXTER Peter MM Cpl 202524 Royal Scots
BAXTER Peter MM Pte 200539 1/4th Royal Scots
BAXTER Richard MM Pte 8046 2nd Dragoons
BAXTER Robert MM Sjt 393267 13th London Regt
BAXTER Robert MM Cpl 34373 53 Bty 2 Bde RFA
BAXTER Robert MM Sjt 10353 2nd Royal Scots Fusiliers KIA 19.7.18.
BAXTER Samuel MM L/Cpl 19/40 15th Royal Irish Rifles
BAXTER Samuel MM Cpl 8047 1st Royal Scots Fusiliers
BAXTER Samuel MM L/Cpl 32499 Notts & Derby Regt
BAXTER Samuel A. MM Sjt 9885 1st Bedfordshire Regt
BAXTER Thomas MM L/Cpl 10300 South Lancashire Regt
BAXTER Thomas MM L/Cpl 276231 1/7th Arg & Suth Highlanders
BAXTER Thomas MM Pte M2/045625 Army Service Corps
BAXTER Thomas MM Sjt 31040 Machine Gun Corps
BAXTER Walter MM Cpl 11057 Devonshire Regt
BAXTER William MM Pte 40855 1st Royal Irish Rifles
BAXTER William MM Pte 3860 Northumberland Fusiliers
BAYBUT Albert "DCM+Bar,MM" Sjt 355141 1/10th Liverpool Regt
BAYES Charles "MM,MID" Cpl 16529 55 Fd Coy Royal Engineers
BAYES Charles William MM Pte 6973 10th Duke of Cornwall's LI
BAYES Herbert C. MM L/Sjt 10231 Royal West Surrey Regt
BAYES Morgan G. MM L/Cpl 267597 Monmouthshire Regt
BAYES Walter James MM Gnr 830509 RFA
BAYFIELD John H. MM L/Cpl 10592 8th Royal West Surrey Regt
BAYFORD Frank William MM Sjt 15044 7th Bedfordshire Regt KIA 3.5.17.
BAYFORD John J. MM Pte S/2919 Rifle Brigade
BAYLES Amos MM Pte 34853 Yorkshire Light Infantry
BAYLES George MM Sjt 554027 511 Fd Coy Royal Engineers DOW 21.9.17.
BAYLES John MM Pte 4/9508 2nd Durham Light Infantry
BAYLES Robert William MM Cpl 200515 Yorkshire Regt
BAYLES W. MM Pte 14311 Durham Light Infantry
BAYLEY Alfred MM Pte 50159 11th Cheshire Regt
BAYLEY Arthur M. MM Sjt Fitter 14363 RFA
BAYLEY C. MM+Bar Pte 54945 Royal Fusiliers
BAYLEY Ernest W.C. MM L/Bdr 76018 RFA
BAYLEY George A. MM Sjt 1120 1/2(South Midland) Fd Coy Royal Engineers
BAYLEY George F. MM Sjt 945579 RFA
BAYLEY George J. "DCM,MM" CSM 610037 19th London Regt
BAYLEY James W. MM L/Cpl 10256 Royal Engineers
BAYLEY John MM Bdr 725936 158 Bde RFA
BAYLEY P.T. MM Sjt 265173 7th Royal Warwickshire Regt
BAYLEY Raymond MM L/Cpl 205696 1st Wiltshire Regt
BAYLEY Walter F. MM Pte 12235 Royal Fusiliers
BAYLEY William MM Spr 492417 Royal Engineers
BAYLEY William MM Cpl 111364 10th Bn Tank Corps
BAYLEY William H. MM L/Bdr 931398 337 Bde RFA
BAYLIE Frank MM Cpl 551981 47 Div Sig Coy Royal Engineers
BAYLIFF Albert MM Pte 12895 8th Border Regt
BAYLIFF Horry MM+Bar Pte 16022 16th Royal Welsh Fusiliers
BAYLIS Charles MM Pte R/8092 King's Royal Rifle Corps
BAYLIS Harry MM Pte 45963 4th Worcestershire Regt
BAYLIS Louis Gerald MM L/Sjt 203875 1/4th Royal Berkshire Regt
BAYLIS Sidney J. MM Pte 23900 Royal Warwickshire Regt
BAYLIS Thomas S. MM Sjt 8183 C/150 Bde RFA
BAYLIS William MM Bdr 281703 RGA
BAYLIS William H. MM Pte 38316 4th North Staffordshire Regt
BAYLISS Arthur Edward MM L/Cpl 240105 1/6th Royal Warwickshire Regt KIA 9.3.17.
BAYLISS Charles Thomas MM Cpl 240544 8th Middlesex Regt
BAYLISS Frank H. MM Cpl 11277 King's Royal Rifle Corps
BAYLISS Frank Y. MM Pte 306452 Royal Warwickshire Regt
BAYLISS Harry MM Sjt 20456 85 Bty 11 Bde RFA
BAYLISS J.F. "MM,MID" Sjt 51025 RAMC
BAYLISS James H. MM Pte 1119 Royal Warwickshire Regt
BAYLISS John J. MM L/Cpl 18310 11th Worcestershire Regt
BAYLISS R.A. MM Pte 266214 Hertfordshire Regt
BAYLISS Robert "DCM,MM" Cpl 34887 Gds Div Sig Coy Royal Engineers
BAYLISS Sidney A. MM Pte 202579 1st London Regt

BAYLISS William Joseph "MM,CG(B)" Sjt 32028 27 Fd Amb RAMC
BAYLY A.W. MM Sjt 497289 RAMC
BAYNE Adam MM Sjt 147742 Royal Engineers
BAYNES Albert Edward MM Pte 24836 37th Bn Machine Gun Corps KIA 28.9.18.
BAYNES William Henry MM Sjt 9265 2nd Royal West Surrey Regt Died 12.10.18.
BAYNHAM Benjamin V. MM L/Cpl 54660 Machine Gun Corps
BAYNHAM Frank Ernest "MM,CdeG(F)" Cpl 3388 XVI Corps Bn Army Cyclist Corps
BAYNON M. MM Trumpeter 68973 RFA
BAYNON W. MM Pte 320256 Welsh Regt
BAYNTON Arthur W. MM Sjt 680456 1/22nd London Regt
BAYNTON Harold MM Cpl 555 17th Royal Fusiliers
BAYS John MM Pte 35612 7 Fd Amb RAMC KIA 14.6.17.
BAYSON Charles E. MM Pte 55168 Royal Welsh Fusiliers
BAYTON Henry Thomas MM Pte 680818 1/22nd London Regt KIA 30.5.18.
BAZELEY Arthur MM L/Cpl 18495 2nd Oxf & Bucks Light Infantry
BAZELEY William MM Cpl 8863 7th Leicestershire Regt
BAZELY Alexander C. MM Gnr 51960 V Bty RHA
BAZIRE Alfred E. MM Pte 300795 5th London Regt
BAZLEY Henry MM Spr 42798 Royal Engineers
BEACH Bertie John MM Pte M/353753 304 MT Coy Army Service Corps
BEACH David MM Pte 4261 Yorkshire Regt
BEACH Frederick Jesse MM Cpl 948 1/3rd London Regt
BEACH George MM Pte 10/21147 10th South Wales Borderers
BEACH James MM Pte 32617 8th East Surrey Regt
BEACHALL H. MM Gnr 81204 RGA
BEACHAM Allen W. MM 2nd Cpl 28668 Royal Engineers
BEACOCK William MM Pte 13/1308 13th East Yorkshire Regt
BEADEN Frederick J. MM Pte 3/10126 Suffolk Regt
BEADEN William George "DCM,MM" Sjt 200231 15th & 1/4th Suffolk Regt
BEADLE Alfred Henry MM Sjt 76367 163 Siege Bty RGA KIA 27.9.18.
BEADLE Charles William "MC,MM(1863 Pte 15th Lond),MID" T/2Lt East Surrey Regt
BEADLE Ernest J. MM Pte 50532 4th Middlesex Regt
BEADLE Henry G. MM Pte 495022 728 Coy Labour Corps
BEADLE James MM Pte M2/175280 Army Service Corps
BEADLE Richard MM L/Sjt 2408 Manchester Regt
BEADLE Sidney George MM Pte 754 11th Middlesex Regt KIA 12.5.17.
BEADLES William Ewart MM L/Sjt 290228 1/7th Royal Welsh Fusiliers
BEADNELL Arnold W. MM Pte 34291 RAMC
BEADNELL Robert MM Gnr 1230 2(Northumb'ld)Bde RFA
BEADNELL W.E. MM Cpl 41835 10th Northumberland Fusiliers
BEAGAN Ellis MM L/Cpl 6728 1st Liverpool Regt DOW 16.9.18.
BEAGLES L.W. MM L/Cpl 40665 1st Essex Regt
BEAGLEY Edmund James MM L/Cpl 100509 33 Div Sig Coy Royal Engineers
BEAGRIE George MM Pte 17 10th Highland Light Infantry
BEAK Sidney MM L/Cpl 8086 2nd Wiltshire Regt
BEAKE Albert M. MM Spr 496395 204 Fd Coy Royal Engineers
BEAKE Walter H. MM Pte 7594 5 Fd Amb RAMC
BEAKE William Harold MM Sjt 19027 10th Royal West Kent Regt KIA 31.7.17.
BEAKHURST W. MM Pte 281725 2nd London Regt
BEAL Alma C. MM Pte 36214 RAMC
BEAL Edgar MM Spr 171712 51 Div Sig Coy Royal Engineers
BEAL Francis H. MM Pte M2/132512 Army Service Corps
BEAL Frederick MM L/Cpl 9862 5th Oxf & Bucks Light Infantry
BEAL Robert MM Pte 18421 10th Royal West Kent Regt KIA 29.9.18.
BEAL Robert George MM Sjt 45274 527 Siege Bty RGA DOW 30.9.18.
BEAL Stephen MM Pnr 251581 Royal Engineers
BEALE Albert MM Pte 1199 15th Royal Warwickshire Regt KIA 9.7.18.
BEALE Albert E. MM Cpl 14734 6th Bedfordshire Regt
BEALE Alfred G. MM Cpl 282916 4th London Regt
BEALE Alfred William "MM,MID" Sjt 931 7th Royal Sussex Regt KIA 9.4.17.
BEALE Arthur MM Cpl 202291 Notts & Derby Regt
BEALE Ernest R. MM L/Sjt 19107 15th Hampshire Regt
BEALE F.B. MM Pte 433076 RAMC
BEALE George MM L/Cpl 23597 16th Welsh Regt

BEALE James MM L/Cpl 6684 10th Royal West Kent Regt
BEALE Robert F. MM Spr 46434 Royal Engineers
BEALE Sidney H. MM L/Cpl 18501 Wiltshire Regt
BEALE Walter J. MM Cpl 56965 18 Div Sig Coy Royal Engineers
BEALE William C. MM Gnr 57302 RGA
BEALE William Ernest MM+Bar Sjt 23082 15th Durham Light Infantry KIA 10.11.18.
BEALES Harry E. MM Sjt 13550 2nd Suffolk Regt
BEALING George Roy MM L/Cpl 3/437 6th Wiltshire Regt
BEALING Leonard F. MM Pnr 23395 Hampshire Regt
BEALL Thomas Herman(Henman?) MM Pte 648 7th B Coy Royal Sussex Regt KIA 27.5.18.
BEAM C.H. MM Cpl 50798 Royal Engineers
BEAMAN Albert MM Pte 8221 1st Worcestershire Regt
BEAMENT Jack MM Pte C/12 King's Royal Rifle Corps
BEAMER Henry J. MM Pte 337641 RAMC
BEAMES William E. MM Pte 5372 2nd Leinster Regt DOW 1.11.18.
BEAMISH James MM Cpl 35181 RFA
BEAN Arthur W. MM 2nd Cpl 84954 207 Fd Coy Royal Engineers
BEAN Bernard MM L/Cpl 78970 RAMC
BEAN Frank Noel MM CSM 741594 2/10th London Regt
BEAN George C. MM L/Cpl 13137 8th Norfolk Regt
BEAN Hubert T. MM Pte 8042 2nd Hampshire Regt
BEAN James Reuben MM Sjt 12296 1st Royal Fusiliers
BEAN John MM Cpl 8864 East Lancashire Regt
BEAN John Thomas MM Cpl 104245 234 Fd Coy Royal Engineers
BEAN Joseph MM Gnr 84834 RFA
BEAN Robert "DCM,MM" Cpl 29807 Norfolk Regt
BEAN Robert MM Sjt 5603 RGA
BEAN Silvester MM+Bar Sjt 6738 9th King's Royal Rifle Corps
BEAN Thomas H. MM Sjt M2/049606 775 Coy Army Service Corps
BEAN Wilfred E. MM Pte 329279 1/1st Cambridgeshire Regt KIA 22.8.18.
BEANEY Ernest MM Cpl 21372 Y47 Med TM Bty RGA
BEANEY W.G. MM Spr 187783 Royal Engineers
BEANEY William MM Dvr 10353 C/78 Bde RFA
BEANLAND Norman MM Pte 204912 17th Liverpool Regt
BEANLAND Walter MM Pte 5207 Northumberland Fusiliers
BEAR Bertram MM SSM 4855 18th Hussars
BEAR Edward Adolph MM+Bar Pte 242448 1/5th Yorkshire Light Infantry
BEAR George MM Pte 5689 7th Dragoon Guards Att Cav Corps Sig Sqn.
BEAR Harry D. MM Cpl 372258 8th London Regt
BEAR Oliver Henry MM Sjt 13726 8th Norfolk Regt KIA 22.10.17.
BEARCHILL. Tom B. MM Pte 266492 Cheshire Regt
BEARCROFT Sidney J. MM L/Sjt 11329 8th Gloucestershire Regt
BEARCROFT Walter E. MM Pte 19620 4th Worcestershire Regt
BEARD A. MM Sjt 200626 9th North Staffordshire Regt
BEARD Alfred MM Pte 17177 6th South Wales Borderers
BEARD Arthur MM L/Cpl 2206 1/5th Cheshire Regt
BEARD Arthur Norman MM Cpl 281756 2/7th Lancashire Fusiliers DOW 19.4.18.
BEARD Charles E. MM+Bar Spr 500447 Royal Engineers
BEARD Donald MM Sjt 839 Royal Flying Corps
BEARD Ernest MM Cpl 305569 8th Royal Warwickshire Regt
BEARD Ernest F. MM Pte 34563 Middlesex Regt
BEARD F.T. MM Pte 497457 RAMC
BEARD Frank MM Pte 14085 8th Yorkshire Light Infantry
BEARD L. MM Sjt 5722 Liverpool Regt
BEARD R. MM L/Cpl 8813 Leicestershire Regt
BEARD R. MM Pte 41228 1st Royal Lancaster Regt
BEARD Randolph "DCM,MM,MSM,MID" CSM Drill Sjt 12909 2nd Grenadier Guards
BEARD Sydney MM L/Cpl S/31018 13th Rifle Brigade KIA 2.6.18.
BEARD W. MM Bdr 47452 C/148 Bde RFA
BEARDER F.N. MM S/Sjt Fitter 146464 210 Siege Bty RGA
BEARDMORE Edgar MM Cpl 226025 1st Monmouthshire Regt
BEARDMORE Ernest James MM Dvr T2/SR/02807 19 Div Train Army Service Corps
BEARDMORE Frederick W. MM Sjt 97265 Royal Engineers
BEARDMORE G.A. MM Air Mech 1 6509 Royal Flying Corps
BEARDMORE Harold MM Cpl 18248 2nd Royal Scots Fusiliers
BEARDMORE Harold MM Sjt 1768 Leicestershire Regt
BEARDMORE Sydney MM Pte 60724 12/13th Northumberland Fusiliers
BEARDMORE Thomas G. MM Pte 201271 7th Bn Tank Corps
BEARDMORE Tom S. MM Pte 50013 2nd Lancashire Fusiliers
BEARDMORE W. MM Dvr 29925 460 Bty 15 Bde RFA
BEARDOW William MM Pte 9712 1st Cheshire Regt

BEARDSALL George MM Pte 305863 9th Lancashire Fusiliers
BEARDSALL William MM Pte 306188 6th Notts & Derby Regt DOW 3.5.18.
BEARDSHALL William MM Pte 13/39 13th York & Lancaster Regt
BEARDSLEY Albert MM Pte 6486 1st Notts & Derby Regt
BEARDSLEY Amos MM Pte 95429 9th Bn Tank Corps
BEARDSLEY Charles T. MM Cpl 63264 4th Yorkshire Light Infantry
BEARDSLEY James H.R. MM Pte 99124 13th Royal Fusiliers
BEARDSLEY Percy MM+Bar Pte 242683 5th West Riding Regt
BEARDSLEY Richard D. MM Sjt 10257 Royal Engineers
BEARDSLEY Thomas MM Cpl 52966 21 Siege Bty RGA
BEARDSMORE Herbert MM CQMS 2570 North Staffordshire Regt
BEARDSWORTH James B. MM Gnr 140961 303 Siege Bty RGA
BEARDWOOD Allan MM Bdr L/16181 107 Bty 23 Bde RFA
BEARE Frederick C. MM L/Cpl 202092 Somerset Light Infantry
BEARNE Frank MM Pte 240370 1/5th Devonshire Regt
BEARRYMAN T.E.J. MM L/Cpl 9471 2nd North Lancashire Regt
BEARRYMAN Thomas E. MM CQMS PW/1813 19th Middlesex Regt
BEASANT Jack MM Cpl 51028 8th Worcestershire Regt
BEASANT Albert William MM Sjt 12 Royal Berkshire Regt KIA 14.8.16.
BEASLEY Alfred G. MM Pte R/2046 King's Royal Rifle Corps
BEASLEY Arthur P. MM Pte 350003 9th Liverpool Regt
BEASLEY Bertie T. MM Pte 10031 Wiltshire Regt
BEASLEY Frederick MM Pte 60326 RAMC
BEASLEY Harry MM Pte 1267 9th Royal Fusiliers
BEASLEY Henry MM Pnr 254153 Royal Engineers
BEASLEY John MM(58411 Gnr RFA)+Bar Spr 253056 Royal Engineers
BEASLEY Robert MM Pte 46872 19th Durham Light Infantry
BEASLEY Robert MM Pte 4692 King's Royal Rifle Corps
BEASLEY Samuel MM Cpl 40130 1st South Staffordshire Regt
BEASLEY W. MM Cpl 2205 Durham Light Infantry
BEASLEY Walter MM Gnr 139447 247 Siege Bty RGA
BEASLEY William MM Dvr 66775 39 Bde RFA
BEASLEY William MM Sjt 2100 Middlesex Regt
BEASLEY William MM Pte 9879 Northamptonshire Regt
BEASTALL Leslie MM Pte 242442 Notts & Derby Regt
BEASTALL Thomas E. MM Cpl 2759 Royal Warwickshire Regt
BEATON Alex MM Sjt 330307 9th Highland Light Infantry
BEATON Benjamin MM Pte 2556 Yorkshire Regt
BEATON Donald MM L/Cpl 3320 1/8th Arg & Suth Highlanders KIA 19.9.18.
BEATON Eric Barnaby. "MM+2 Bars,CG(B)" Spr 87321 Royal Engineers
BEATON Frederick MM Pte 19644 11th Highland Light Infantry
BEATON James MM L/Cpl 39535 17th Royal Scots
BEATON James MM L/Cpl 8331 2nd Highland Light Infantry
BEATON Kenneth MM Pte 18591 Grenadier Guards
BEATON William MM Sjt P/722 Rifle Brigade
BEATSON Albert MM Pne 479956 Royal Engineers
BEATSON John M. MM Sjt 72201 Machine Gun Corps
BEATSON William G. MM Pte 138222 63rd Bn Machine Gun Corps
BEATTIE Alexander MM Pte 28245 15th Hampshire Regt
BEATTIE Alexander MM Pte 6683 2nd Scots Guards
BEATTIE Andrew C. MM Cpl 291161 443 Bty RFA
BEATTIE Benjamin MM L/Cpl 13990 Royal Irish Rifles
BEATTIE Charles MM Pte 11324 2nd Scots Guards
BEATTIE Charles G. MM Dvr T4/241185 Army Service Corps
BEATTIE David MM Pte 44550 13th Durham Light Infantry
BEATTIE David MM Cpl Sig 902156 337 Bde RFA
BEATTIE David MM L/Cpl 46933 95 Fd Coy Royal Engineers
BEATTIE George E. MM L/Cpl 27/85 Northumberland Fusiliers
BEATTIE J. MM Sjt 20524 Machine Gun Corps
BEATTIE James "MM,MdH(F)" Pte 66246 12th Cheshire Regt
BEATTIE James "DCM,MM" Sjt 225620 1st Monmouthshire Regt
BEATTIE James MM Cpl 280474 1/7th Highland Light Infantry
BEATTIE James MM Pte S/43359 Royal Highlanders
BEATTIE James D. MM+Bar Sjt 63202 RGA
BEATTIE James M. MM Pte 32437 South Lancashire Regt
BEATTIE John MM Spr 412703 409 Fd Coy Royal Engineers
BEATTIE John MM L/Cpl 240856 8th Royal Highlanders
BEATTIE John MM Pte 751 1st Gordon Highlanders
BEATTIE John MM Sjt 43125 Royal Scots Fusiliers
BEATTIE Joseph MM Gnr 75580 C/76 Bde RFA
BEATTIE Richard B. MM Pte 240126 1/5th King's Own Scottish Borderers
BEATTIE Robert MM Pte 8344 1st Royal Highlanders KIA 13.7.16.
BEATTIE Robert MM Cpl M/273065 Army Service Corps

BEATTIE Robert MM L/Cpl 7682 1st Cameron Highlanders
BEATTIE Thomas MM Sjt G/16402 10th Royal West Kent Regt
BEATTIE Thomas MM+Bar Pte S/4794 Royal Highlanders
BEATTIE Thomas Leonard MM Bdr 35898 RGA
BEATTIE Victor MM L/Sjt 17240 Royal Irish Rifles
BEATTIE William MM Bdr 645790 51 Div Ammn Col RFA
BEATTIE William MM Pte 223015 1st Cameron Highlanders
BEATTIE William MM Cpl 20693 RGA
BEATTIE William MM L/Cpl 200794 1/4th Seaforth Highlanders KIA 20.7.18.
BEATTY John MM+Bar Cpl 17465 1st Royal Fusiliers
BEATTY John R. MM Pte 16828 Royal Inniskilling Fusiliers
BEATTY Thomas MM Pte 242555 Worcestershire Regt
BEATY Reginald MM Pte 2172 9th Yorkshire Light Infantry DOW 24.8.18.
BEAUCHAMP Joseph H. MM 2nd Cpl 19155 5 Div Sig Coy Royal Engineers
BEAUCHAMP Thomas John MM L/Cpl 64762 Guards Div Sig Coy Royal Engineers
BEAUCHAMP Walter S. MM L/Sjt 300666 1/28th London Regt
BEAUCHAMP William G. MM+2 Bars L/Cpl 15180 1st Coldstream Guards
BEAUFOY Harry MM Sjt 53390 38 Bde RFA
BEAUMONT Albert Edward Diamond MM L/Bdr L/29724 D/181 Bde RFA
BEAUMONT Arnold Chatterton MM L/Sjt 28627 Leicestershire Regt
BEAUMONT Arthur MM Pte 142616 Machine Gun Corps
BEAUMONT Bertie MM Spr 481983 Royal Engineers
BEAUMONT Charles George MM Dvr 36674 D/190 Bde RFA KIA 4.11.18.
BEAUMONT Fred MM Pte 20454 9th Northumberland Fusiliers
BEAUMONT Frederick MM Bdr 291311 RGA
BEAUMONT Frederick J. MM Bdr 317124 RGA
BEAUMONT George MM Pte 2531 7th East Kent Regt
BEAUMONT George Machin MM Pte 39941 6th York & Lancaster Regt Died 5.12.17.
BEAUMONT Harry MM Pte 17293 Royal Scots
BEAUMONT Henry Richard MM+Bar CSM R/18544 King's Royal Rifle Corps
BEAUMONT Herbert MM Cpl 478057 Royal Engineers
BEAUMONT Herbert W. MM+Bar Cpl 200119 Yorkshire Light Infantry
BEAUMONT John MM Sjt 27003 48 Hy Bty RGA
BEAUMONT Lewis A. "MM,MID" Sjt 51065 Royal Engineers
BEAUMONT Phineas MM Cpl 9919 Machine Gun Corps
BEAUMONT Thomas F. MM Pte 57624 Liverpool Regt
BEAUMONT Walter MM Sjt 300133 1/7th Royal Scots
BEAUTYMAN John William MM Sjt 1063 1/9th Durham Light Infantry
BEAVAN Frank G. MM Cpl 722858 24th London Regt
BEAVAN Frederick Leslie MM Pte 1375 23rd Royal Fusiliers KIA 17.2.17.
BEAVAN J.H. MM Air Mech 2 9272 Royal Flying Corps
BEAVAN R. MM L/Cpl 106388 Machine Gun Corps
BEAVAN Thomas J. MM Dvr 25503 B/75 Bde RFA
BEAVAN W.O. MM Sjt 56182 C/180 Bde RFA
BEAVAN William Henry MM Sjt 205664 1st Wiltshire Regt
BEAVER Alfred J. MM Pte 9586 South Staffordshire Regt
BEAVER Arthur MM Pte 240116 5th Leicestershire Regt
BEAVER Charles MM Dvr T3/028990 187 Coy Army Service Corps
BEAVER George Henry MM Sjt 6251 1st Somerset Light Infantry
BEAVER Harold "MM,MID,CG(F)" L/Cpl 13982 9th East Lancashire Regt
BEAVER James W. MM L/Sjt 10785 1st South Wales Borderers
BEAVER John W. MM Pte 13357 West Riding Regt
BEAVIN James MM L/Bdr 43989 5 Bde N Bty RHA
BEAVINS Samuel MM Pte 704055 21st London Regt
BEAVIS Benjamin R. MM Gnr 41491 RGA
BEAVIS Edward W. MM CSM 251946 Royal Engineers
BEAVIS William MM Pte 68276 10th Royal Fusiliers
BEAVON Thomas MM Pte 17899 1/7th Cheshire Regt
BEAZER Norman H.J. MM Pte 52107 Machine Gun Corps
BEAZER William C. MM Sjt 193 Welsh Guards
BEAZLEY Eric V. MM L/Sjt 23156 12th Highland Light Infantry
BEAZLEY Francis H. MM Sjt 86130 170 Tunnelling Coy Royal Engineers
BEAZLEY Richard John MM L/Cpl 2317 1/5th London Regt KIA 15.9.16.
BEAZOR Frank MM Sjt 12939 2nd Suffolk Regt
BEBB Frederick MM Pte 25928 Welsh Regt

BEBB John M. MM Pte 11570 6th Shropshire Light Infantry
BEBBINGTON Charles MM Sjt 5538 12th Manchester Regt KIA 7.7.16.
BEBELL Albert F. MM Pte 992 9th Royal Fusiliers
BEBELMAN John A. MM Pte 70135 RAMC
BECCONSALL John MM Pte 305774 8th Liverpool Regt
BECK Albert J. MM Pte 5383 8th East Surrey Regt
BECK Arthur Stanley MM L/Bdr 836705 110 Bty 24 Bde RFA
BECK Edward MM Cpl 14858 1st Hampshire Regt
BECK Edward George MM L/Cpl STK/23 10th Royal Fusiliers
BECK Edwin MM+Bar Sjt 9461 Army Cyclist Corps
BECK Ernest C. MM CSM 9493 1st Dorsetshire Regt
BECK Frederick "DCM,MM" Sjt 15911 9th Norfolk Regt
BECK George MM Pte C/12812 18th King's Royal Rifle Corps KIA 21.5.17.
BECK George MM Sjt 62647 7 Bde RHA
BECK George MM Cpl 51005 11 Bde RFA
BECK George MM Cpl 40245 RGA
BECK Harold MM Cpl 4171 Army Cyclist Corps
BECK James A. MM Pte 16021 1st Lincolnshire Regt
BECK James H. MM Pte 21308 22nd Manchester Regt
BECK Robert MM Pte 11682 7th Yorkshire Regt
BECK Stephen MM Sjt 33286 7th Border Regt
BECK Vincent MM Spr 520191 565 Army Tps Coy Royal Engineers
BECK William MM Bdr 680073 RFA
BECK William MM Cpl 251086 Essex Regt
BECK William MM Pte 10569 6th Lincolnshire Regt
BECKENSOLE Albert George MM Pte 40008 1st Royal West Surrey Regt KIA 13.4.18.
BECKER Archibald F MM Cpl L/40039 RFA
BECKER Christian MM Dvr 926288 D/290 Bde RFA
BECKER F.G. MM Spr 308094 Royal Engineers
BECKETT Arthur J.T. MM+Bar Sjt 85547 34 Div Sig Coy Royal Engineers
BECKETT Benjamin J. MM Sjt 2323 31 Army Tps Coy Royal Engineers
BECKETT Charles MM Cpl T/18582 6 Reserve Park Army Service Corps
BECKETT Charles MM Pte 10040 1st Shropshire Light Infantry
BECKETT Dick MM Pte 62995 13th Royal Fusiliers
BECKETT Ernest MM Bdr 35390 D/168 Bde RFA
BECKETT Ernest Edward MM 2nd Cpl 312621 1 Div Sig Coy Royal Engineers
BECKETT Ezra MM Pte 203632 South Lancashire Regt
BECKETT Frederick H. MM Sjt 500205 Royal Engineers
BECKETT Frederick W. MM Sjt 50216 Machine Gun Corps
BECKETT George MM Pte 71105 Notts & Derby Regt
BECKETT George W.H. "MM,MID" Cpl 35047 34 Bde RFA
BECKETT Harold MM Pte 27397 16th Royal Welsh Fusiliers
BECKETT L.V. MM Cpl 54288 Royal Engineers
BECKETT Percy "MM,MSM" Cpl G/2712 8th Royal Sussex Regt
BECKETT Percy Phillip MM Pte 43404 1st Northamptonshire Regt
BECKETT Reginald W. MM Pte 17746 Royal West Kent Regt
BECKETT Richard "MM,MSM,VM(Rm)" CSM 242370 1/5th North Lancashire Regt
BECKETT Richard Wright Webster MM Cpl 241012 1/5th Yorkshire Regt
BECKETT Thomas MM Pte 2923 12th King's Royal Rifle Corps
BECKETT Thomas MM Pte 116107 34th Bn Machine Gun Corps
BECKETT Walter "DCM,MM" Sjt 27029 11th East Lancashire Regt
BECKETT William MM Sjt 696092 57 Div Ammn Col RFA
BECKETT William MM Spr 552018 Royal Engineers
BECKETT William A. "MM+Bar,MID" SM 17794 18 Fd Amb RAMC
BECKETT William McD. MM Pte 17268 Liverpool Regt
BECKHAM James MM Sjt 44853 39 Bde RFA
BECKHAM John W. MM L/Sjt 270143 Manchester Regt
BECKHAM Sidney G. MM Pte P/4126 Rifle Brigade
BECKINGHAM Albert "MM,MID" Sjt B/53 7th B Coy Rifle Brigade DOW 16.4.17.
BECKINGHAM Frederick G. MM Spr 67168 Royal Engineers
BECKINGHAM Owen MM Pte 18016 2nd Leinster Regt
BECKLAKE W. MM L/Cpl 145346 1/1st Northamptonshire Yeomanry
BECKLEY Cecil R. MM L/Sjt 630386 20th London Regt
BECKLEY G. MM Pte 201704 Liverpool Regt
BECKS John W. MM Pte 48041 Royal Fusiliers
BECKWITH Edward MM Pte 721276 24th London Regt
BECKWITH Harold T. MM Pte 19578 Gloucestershire Regt
BECKWITH William MM Bdr 781831 RFA
BECKWITH William MM Pte 332169 9th Liverpool Regt KIA 28.3.18.
BEDBROOK Harry MM Sjt 26452 RGA

BEDDALL Harold MM Cpl 15529 7/8th King's Own Scottish Borderers KIA 31.7.17.
BEDDARD Arthur MM Sjt L/44146 B/175 Bde RFA
BEDDEN James W. MM Gnr 221107 RFA
BEDDIN Ralph Spencer MM Sjt 15668 1/2nd Monmouthshire Regt KIA 28.1.17.
BEDDING William Arthur "MM,MSM,MID" Staff SM T/17438 HQ I Corps Army Service Corps
BEDDOE David Thomas MM Pte 54195 9tth Royal Welsh Fusiliers KIA 22.3.18.
BEDDOE William A. MM Sjt 618423 RFA
BEDDOES Albert G. MM Pte 572198 17th London Regt
BEDDOES John MM Pte 240990 5th Yorkshire Light Infantry KIA 20.7.18.
BEDDOW Albert MM Pte 21051 Yorkshire Regt
BEDDOW William C. MM Sjt 5335 Machine Gun Corps
BEDDOWS Harry MM Pte 17573 24th Royal Welsh Fusiliers
BEDDOWS J.E. MM Cpl 2916 Royal Flying Corps
BEDDOWS Joseph MM Pte 15812 Gloucestershire Regt
BEDFORD Albert E. MM L/Cpl 240827 Notts & Derby Regt
BEDFORD Benjamin MM Pte 43413 1st Lincolnshire Regt
BEDFORD Bernard MM Pte 13/54 13th York & Lancaster Regt
BEDFORD E.L. MM L/Cpl 240227 Seaforth Highlanders
BEDFORD Fred MM Sjt TT/03214 Army Veterinary Corps
BEDFORD George F. MM L/Cpl 267592 1/2nd Monmouthshire Regt
BEDFORD George F. MM Pte 240314 5th Leicestershire Regt
BEDFORD George Henry MM Pte G/5687 7th Royal West Surrey Regt KIA 1.7.16.
BEDFORD H. MM L/Cpl 41113 11th West Yorkshire Regt
BEDFORD Harry MM Pte DM2/209111 51 Div Train Army Service Corps
BEDFORD Joseph Edward MM Sjt 25785 14th Worcestershire Regt
BEDFORD Joseph Thomas MM Cpl 150611 52 Bde RFA
BEDFORD Sidney Victor MM Pte G/14671 6th East Kent Regt
BEDFORD Sydney MM Pte 13/1356 13th York & Lancaster Regt
BEDFORD Thomas E. "MM,MID" Sjt 10280 1st Royal Inniskilling Fusiliers
BEDFORD William MM Sjt 13380 4th Royal Fusiliers KIA 31.8.18.
BEDINGFIELD Thomas MM+Bar Sjt 19410 19th Durham Light Infantry
BEDMAN William Arthur MM Gnr 127909 'B' AA Bty RGA
BEDWELL Arthur MM Pre 21041 Gloucestershire Regt
BEE Charles R. MM L/Sjt 720742 1/24th London Regt
BEE Ernest MM L/Cpl 49394 61st Bn Machine Gun Corps KIA 30.9.18.
BEE Ernest H. MM Spr 489935 46 Div Sig Coy Royal Engineers
BEE J. MM Pte 9698 RAMC
BEE J. MM+2 Bars Cpl 325086 Durham Light Infantry
BEE James MM Pte 3657 Lancashire Fusiliers
BEE John George MM Gnr 800479 C/230 Bde RFA
BEE Thomas MM Gnr 56662 C/112 Bde RFA KIA 13.10.16.
BEE William "DCM,MM" Sjt 48835 83 Fd Coy Royal Engineers
BEEBEE Richard Thomas MM Sjt L/23012 D/162 Bde RFA
BEEBY Frank George MM Sjt 70212 BX?Cable Section Royal Engineers
BEEBY Horace S. MM Cpl 17891 1st Northamptonshire Regt
BEEBY Walter S. MM Spr 236948 Royal Engineers
BEECH Charles MM Pte 21126 1st Hampshire Regt
BEECH Edward Charles MM Cpl L/25963 B/71 Bde RFA KIA 26.8.18.
BEECH Ernest L. "MM,MID" Spr 96661 30 Div Sig Coy Royal Engineers
BEECH Frederick MM Pte 15316 5th Royal Berkshire Regt
BEECH James MM Spr 492015 46 Div Sig Coy Royal Engineers
BEECH Joseph (or James) MM Pte 40408 43 Fd Amb RAMC KIA 21.3.18.
BEECH Joshua MM CSM 31474 East Lancashire Regt
BEECH Percy MM Sjt 14010 8th York & Lancaster Regt
BEECH Samuel "DCM,MM" Gnr 70099 48 Bty 36 Bde RFA KIA 19.10.17.
BEECH William MM Bdr 86419 B/68 Bde RFA
BEECH William Arthur MM Sjt 3/8862 1st South Staffordshire Regt KIA 26.10.17.
BEECHAM Frederick G. MM Sub-Conductor S/7511 Army Ordnance Corps
BEECHAM Richard MM Spr 164779 95 Fd Coy Royal Engineers
BEECHER Patrick MM Pte 22711 Royal Irish Fusiliers
BEECHEY A.E. MM Pte 23649 Norfolk Regt
BEECROFT Cecil MM Gnr Sig 232757 B/174 Bde RFA
BEECROFT Harry MM Gnr 122098 RGA
BEECROFT Henry MM Pte G/2744 8th Royal Sussex Regt
BEECROFT Herbert MM L/Cpl 9058 Northumberland Fusiliers
BEECROFT John Edward "MM,MID" Cpl 10049 1st East Yorkshire Regt
BEECROFT Leonard MM Sjt 6936 11th Notts & Derby Regt
BEEDELL William Edward MM Bdr 79463 C/73 Bde RFA
BEEDHAM William MM L/Sjt 15946 Lincolnshire Regt
BEEHOO Frederick MM Pte 3098 East Surrey Regt
BEEKS Leonard H. MM L/Cpl 263020 1/8th Middlesex Regt
BEELEY Arnold MM Spr 482269 Royal Engineers
BEELEY Harry MM Gnr 296878 RGA
BEELEY Joseph MM Pte 7776 9th Manchester Regt
BEELEY Phillip A. MM Cpl 97219 14th Bn Tank Corps
BEELS George Isaac MM Pte 53625 1st Bn Machine Gun Corps
BEENEY Arthur MM+Bar Pte 69262 6th Royal West Surrey Regt
BEENEY Joseph MM Pte 8522 9th Royal Sussex Regt
BEENY Arthur William John MM Pte 42126 1st Essex Regt
BEER Adolph George MM Sjt 18872 16 Coy Machine Gun Corps KIA 15.9.16.
BEER Arthur F. MM Sjt 146006 312 Siege Bty RGA
BEER Edgar K. MM Pte 37102 12th Somerset Light Infantry
BEER Edward W.J. MM Pnr 82034 25 Div Sig Coy Royal Engineers
BEER Ernest Henry MM Cpl 62380 23 Heavy Bty RGA
BEER Ernest Victor MM Sjt 46701 18 Div Sig Coy Royal Engineers
BEER Frank MM Pte 208838 6th Wiltshire Regt
BEER George "DCM,MM" CSM 108060 181 Coy Labour Corps Died 10.11.18.
BEER George Lewis MM Pte 72488 23 Coy Machine Gun Corps
BEER George R. MM L/Cpl 552291 Royal Engineers
BEER Harold MM Pte 300610 7th Essex Regt
BEER Henry MM Cpl 2254 1/1st Hertfordshire Regt
BEER John MM L/Cpl 16241 3rd Coldstream Guards
BEER Stanley F. "MM,MID" L/Cpl 12025 10th Devonshire Regt
BEER Thomas MM Pte S/9439 13th Rifle Brigade
BEER William MM S/Sjt 168 Army Veterinary Corps
BEER William H. MM L/Cpl 432496 57 Div Sig Coy Royal Engineers
BEERE Lewis J. MM Pte 2818 16th Lancers
BEERE William G. MM Pte 50580 14th Royal Warwickshire Regt
BEERS William MM Pte 5237 3rd Coldstream Guards
BEES Bertie MM Sjt 94884 Tank Corps
BEESLEY Alfred W. MM Pte 266726 Royal Warwickshire Regt
BEESLEY Arthur MM L/Cpl 60614 73 Fd Coy Royal Engineers
BEESLEY Charles H.J. MM Sjt 85912 21st Bn Machine Gun Corps
BEESLEY Henry T. MM Pte R/14515 16th King's Royal Rifle Corps
BEESLEY J. MM L/Cpl 16/62 8th West Yorkshire Regt
BEESLEY James MM Cpl 20792 18 Fd Amb RAMC
BEESLEY John MM Sjt 37877 18 Bde RFA
BEESLEY John MM Pte 2008 17th London Regt
BEESLEY Martin MM Dvr T/21302 Att 4 Fd Amb RAMC Army Service Corps
BEESLEY Robert P. MM Pte 205225 17th Armoured Car Bn Tank Corps
BEESLEY Victor MM L/Cpl 46131 1st Worcestershire Regt
BEESLEY William Arthur MM Pte 201122 1/5th Bedfordshire Regt KIA 22.12.17.
BEESON Arthur G. "MM,MIDx2" Spr 1189 1/1st London Div Sig Coy Royal Engineers
BEESON Ernest MM Cpl T/14558 2 Div Train Army Service Corps
BEESON Harold F. "MM,MSM,MID" Sjt 930021 Y/56 Med TM Bty RFA
BEESON Henry R. "MM,MID" Sjt 2403 9th Royal Fusiliers
BEESON John William Henry MM BSM 24137 34 Bde RFA
BEESTON Alfred MM Cpl 1323 Royal Engineers
BEESTON Ernest MM L/Sjt 2295 1/6th Liverpool Regt KIA 1.7.16.
BEESTON George MM+Bar Sjt 26223 Machine Gun Corps
BEESTON James MM Sjt 8463 Royal Warwickshire Regt
BEESTON William MM Pte 15593 South Staffordshire Regt
BEET Richard MM Pte 40537 9th Norfolk Regt
BEETHAM Harry MM Sjt 16481 Lancashire Fusiliers
BEETON Edward V. MM CSM 4496 2nd Royal West Surrey Regt
BEETON Titus R. MM CSM 15308 10th York & Lancaster Regt
BEEVER John William MM Pte 15482 9th York & Lancaster Regt
BEEVERS Charles MM Sjt 265534 West Yorkshire Regt
BEEVERS F. MM Dvr 46104 4 Div Ammn Col RFA att RGA
BEEVERS F. "DCM,MM" Sjt 401452 1/1(West Riding)Fd Amb RAMC
BEEVERS Frank W. MM Cpl 482055 Royal Engineers
BEEVERS John W. MM Cpl L/5647 RFA
BEEVERS William MM Pte 28086 2nd Grenadier Guards
BEEVOR William H. MM Pte 55691 4th York & Lancaster Regt

BEGBIE James A. MM L/Cpl S/26342 2nd Seaforth Highlanders
BEGG Alexander MM Pte S/15707 1/6th Seaforth Highlanders DOW 30.7.18.
BEGG David Wilson MM Gnr 167068 41 Div Ammn Col RFA
BEGG Granville MM Sjt 17016 1st Northumberland Fusiliers
BEGG James G. MM Pte S/2569 1st Gordon Highlanders
BEGG Louis MM Sjt 1327 Royal Highlanders
BEGG William MM L/Sjt S/3977 9th Seaforth Highlanders DOW 23.12.17.
BEGG William H. MM Pte 21804 4th Gordon Highlanders
BEGGS George A. MM Cpl 35753 11th Border Regt
BEGGS George Arthur "MC,MM(2040 Sjt)" T/Lt 1/13th London Regt
BEGLEY J. MM Spr 548637 Royal Engineers
BEHAN Thomas MM Cpl 16451 6th Royal Dublin Fusiliers
BEHAN Thomas MM Cpl 3344 21st Bn Machine Gun Corps
BEHARIE J.E. MM Spr 21593 5 Div Sig Coy Royal Engineers
BEIRNE John P. MM Sjt 205286 16th Royal Welsh Fusiliers
BEITH Edmund MM Sjt 76540 RFA
BELAND Charles MM Dvr 72122 22 Bde RFA
BELAND William John MM Sjt 12987 2nd Middlesex Regt
BELANN Thomas MM Sjt 58778 D/106 Bde RFA
BELBIN George Thomas MM L/Cpl 10216 Machine Gun Corps
BELBIN Harry MM Sjt 8539 2nd Hampshire Regt
BELCH William MM Pte 5550 Lancashire Fusiliers
BELCHER Francis MM+Bar Pte 12784 1st Royal Berkshire Regt
BELCHER Fred MM Cpl 17958 8th Royal Berkshire Regt
BELCHER G. MM Pte 202025 Oxf & Bucks Light Infantry
BELCHER James MM L/Cpl 16185 Durham Light Infantry
BELCHER James MM Cpl 66406 C/107 Bde RFA KIA 10.4.17.
BELCHER John MM L/Cpl 612208 19th London Regt
BELCHER Joseph MM Cpl 40777 1st Leicestershire Regt KIA 8.10.18.
BELCHER Leonard Jack MM Mech S/Sjt M2/106434 23 Army Fd Park Army Service Corps
BELCHER Richard MM Pte 40770 1/5th West Yorkshire Regt KIA 22.4.18.
BELCHER Sidney MM Sjt 472 C/237 Bde RFA
BELCHER Thomas MM L/Cpl 20912 4th Grenadier Guards
BELCHER William Sidney MM Gnr 198770 B/298 Bde RFA
BELDERSON George F. MM Pte 9982 1st Scottish Rifles
BELDING S. MM Gnr 32507 7 Bty MGC(Motors)
BELDING Wilmer MM+Bar Cpl Sig 38 C/46 Bde RFA
BELFIELD George Henry "DCM,MM" Cpl 20849 Machine Gun Corps
BELFIELD John W. MM Pte 3302 Northumberland Fusiliers
BELGER Alfred MM Bdr 925189 RFA
BELGER T. "MM,MID" Bdr 71675 36 Bde RFA
BELITHER Rowland MM Pte 18806 3rd Grenadier Guards
BELKIN Barnet MM Pte R/19738 16th King's Royal Rifle Corps
BELL Albert MM Spr 103858 Royal Engineers
BELL Albert A. MM Pte 23/965 Northumberland Fusiliers
BELL Albert W. MM Cpl 27188 14 Div Ammn Col RFA
BELL Alexander MM L/Cpl 85254 18th Bn Machine Gun Corps DOW 26.10.18.
BELL Alexander MM L/Cpl CMT/2536 5 Advance Park Army Service Corps
BELL Alexander MM Cpl 43141 8th Royal Scots KIA 23.7.18.
BELL Alexander MM L/Cpl 1899 Royal Highlanders
BELL Alonzo W. MM Pte 32/401 Northumberland Fusiliers
BELL Andrew MM Sjt 13579 1st Border Regt
BELL Andrew MM Pte 17369 Royal Scots Fusiliers
BELL Archibald "MM,MSM" Dvr 53354 2 Div Ammn Col RFA
BELL Arthur "MM,CG(F)" Pte 18849 1st Suffolk Regt
BELL Arthur MM Cpl 24823 31 Hy Bty RGA
BELL Arthur MM Sjt 16/757 1st West Yorkshire Regt
BELL Benjamin MM Pte 31498 East Yorkshire Regt
BELL Bert MM L/Cpl 87790 Royal Engineers
BELL Binning MM Sjt 345042 24th Royal Welsh Fusiliers
BELL Cecil MM Pte M2/078296 Army Service Corps
BELL Charles MM Cpl 43356 2nd Highland Light Infantry
BELL Charles MM Bdr 90852 RGA
BELL Charles E. MM 2nd Cpl 182446 Royal Engineers
BELL Charles Nursur MM Pte 386076 1/1st(Northumbrian)Fd Amb RAMC
BELL Charlie MM Cpl 241339 7th Lincolnshire Regt
BELL Christopher "DCM,MM+Bar" L/Cpl 21871 1st King's Own Scottish Borderers
BELL D. MM Pte 265514 Gordon Highlanders
BELL David MM Pte 5918 Royal Sussex Regt
BELL Douglas M. MM Pte 535034 15th London Regt
BELL Duncan D. MM Pte 53082 1st Royal Scots Fusiliers
BELL Edward MM Pte 37938 24th Northumberland Fusiliers DOW 31.10.17.
BELL Edward MM Pte 20/558 Durham Light Infantry
BELL Edward John MM Pte 7445 Machine Gun Corps
BELL Edward Robson MM+Bar Cpl 325389 1/9th Durham Light Infantry KIA 21.7.18.
BELL Edward W. MM L/Cpl 11277 Northumberland Fusiliers
BELL Edwin Charles MM L/Cpl 1215 18th Durham Light Infantry
BELL Edwin Isaac MM 2nd Cpl 63342 92 Fd Coy Royal Engineers
BELL Ernest MM Pte 90014 RAMC
BELL Ernest MM Cpl 113609 GHQ BEF Sig Coy Royal Engineers
BELL Ernest MM+Bar Cpl 53045 RFA
BELL Ernest E. MM+Bar Cpl 268495 5th West Riding Regt
BELL F.H. MM Pte 35106 RAMC
BELL Fergus MM Cpl 630069 RFA
BELL Frank A. MM L/Cpl 11/30147 Border Regt
BELL Fred MM Dvr 27430 A/46 Bde RFA
BELL Frederick "DCM,MM" Sjt 18830 11 Gen Hosp RAMC
BELL Frederick MM Sjt 9583 2nd Scottish Rifles
BELL Frederick MM CQMS 2/9721 South Wales Borderers
BELL G.H.A. MM Sjt 14161 London Regt
BELL George MM L/Sjt 24784 Railway Section Royal Engineers
BELL George MM Pte 13/1212 York & Lancaster Regt
BELL George MM Spr 42135 62 Fd Coy Royal Engineers KIA 12.12.16.
BELL George MM Sjt 357 8th London Regt
BELL George MM Pte 9085 2nd Lincolnshire Regt
BELL George MM Pte 13647 8th Lincolnshire Regt
BELL George B. MM Pte 26714 Durham Light Infantry
BELL George F. MM Sjt 116452 RFA
BELL George G. MM L/Cpl 201669 5/6th Scottish Rifles
BELL George Goudie "DCM,MM,MSM,MID" CSM 7748 32nd Bn Machine Gun Corps
BELL George H. MM Cpl 31751 Northumberland Fusiliers
BELL George H. MM Pte 300971 Arg & Suth Highlanders
BELL George Henry MM Pte 18916 2nd West Yorkshire Regt KIA 27.3.18.
BELL George R. MM Sjt 16040 7 Div Sig Coy Royal Engineers
BELL George T. MM Pte 200488 Worcestershire Regt
BELL Gilbert F. MM Cpl 8465 Border Regt
BELL H. MM Gnr Fitter 2351 A/148 Bde RFA
BELL Harold MM Pte 15737 East Lancashire Regt
BELL Harper MM CSM 16233 12th Royal Irish Rifles
BELL Harry MM Sjt 40570 1st Leicestershire Regt
BELL Harry MM Pte 83727 Machine Gun Corps
BELL Harvey MM L/Cpl 345004 1/9th Durham Light Infantry
BELL Henry MM Pte 516203 14th London Regt
BELL Henry C. MM SM 47037 RAMC
BELL Henry D. MM Spr 465873 Royal Engineers
BELL Henry G. MM L/Cpl C/6017 King's Royal Rifle Corps
BELL Herbert Sidney MM L/Cpl 43653 12th Yorkshire Light Infantry KIA 19.7.18.
BELL Hugh MM Pte 11584 Royal Inniskilling Fusiliers
BELL Hugh MM Sjt 201542 North Lancashire Regt
BELL I. MM L/Cpl 204578 Northumberland Fusiliers
BELL J. MM Pnr 121366 Royal Engineers
BELL J. MM Pte 16738 East Yorkshire Regt
BELL James MM Pte 62427 10th Royal Scots
BELL James "DCM,MM" Pte 240522 1/5th Royal Scots Fusiliers
BELL James MM Pte 14038 12th Cheshire Regt
BELL James MM Pte 203196 1st Northumberland Fusiliers
BELL James MM Pte 13513 8th Border Regt
BELL James MM+2 Bars Cpl 9583 2nd Royal Scots Fusiliers
BELL James MM Cpl 40583 Royal Scots Fusiliers
BELL James MM Gnr 77524 RHA
BELL James MM Cpl 20432 Devonshire Regt
BELL James MM Pte 15629 Notts & Derby Regt
BELL James MM L/Cpl 24702 Yorkshire Light Infantry
BELL James H. MM Cpl 45817 86 Fd Coy Royal Engineers
BELL James H. MM+Bar Cpl 695056 22nd London Regt
BELL James Henry MM Pte 202420 1/5th Lincolnshire Regt
BELL James Richard MM Gnr 951547 43 Bty 24 Bde RFA
BELL James W. MM Pte S/31069 5th Cameron Highlanders
BELL James W. MM+Bar Sjt 202467 5/6th Scottish Rifles
BELL James W. MM Pte 2762 2nd Royal Lancaster Regt
BELL James William MM Gnr 78758 24 Siege Bty RGA
BELL John MM Pte M2/148697 Army Service Corps
BELL John MM Cpl D/1481 2nd Dragoons
BELL John MM+Bar L/Cpl 242648 5th Yorkshire Light Infantry

BELL John MM Cpl 22838 2nd Royal Inniskilling Fusiliers
BELL John MM Sjt G/6345 2nd Royal Sussex Regt
BELL John MM Bdr 23879 12 Bde RFA
BELL John MM Sjt 19528 Northumberland Fusiliers
BELL John MM Pte 5107 1st Cameron Highlanders
BELL John Edward Thompson MM Sjt 27144 C/286 Bde RFA
BELL John H. "DCM,MM" Sjt 51385 2nd Royal Scots Fusiliers
BELL John J. MM Pte 250447 5/6th Royal Scots
BELL John L. MM L/Cpl 195946 Royal Engineers
BELL John William MM Cpl 253251 Railway Operating Division Royal Engineers
BELL Joseph MM CSM 39383 16th Lancashire Fusiliers
BELL Joseph MM Gnr 72436 126 Siege Bty RGA
BELL Joseph MM Cpl 15/593 15th Royal Irish Rifles
BELL Joseph MM Pte 25000 6th King's Own Scottish Borderers KIA 24.3.18.
BELL Joseph MM Pte 291088 Northumberland Fusiliers
BELL Joseph MM Pte 1279 1/9th Durham Light Infantry KIA 6.11.16.
BELL Joseph MM Pte 3/152 2nd Wiltshire Regt KIA 9.4.17.
BELL Joseph MM Cpl 2627 24th Royal Fusiliers
BELL Joseph MM Gnr 751101 A/124 Bde RFA DOW 29.9.18.
BELL Kenneth M. MM L/Cpl 23336 Royal Engineers
BELL Lancelot W. MM Sjt 1275 1/8th Notts & Derby Regt
BELL Laurence MM Pte 89036 59 Fd Amb RAMC
BELL Leonard MM+Bar Pte 9743 1st York & Lancaster Regt
BELL Leonard Waring MM Pte 24962 2nd West Riding Regt
BELL Leslie "MM,MIDx2" Sjt 200088 Northumberland Fusiliers
BELL Lewis MM L/Sjt 1080 Northumberland Fusiliers
BELL Martin MM Pte 11/15337 11th Border Regt
BELL Matthew MM Pte 235593 5th West Riding Regt
BELL Matthew MM Pte 3/8885 1st West Yorkshire Regt
BELL Maurice W. MM Pte 57664 141 Fd Amb RAMC
BELL Montague R.J. MM Bdr 147701 RGA
BELL Morris J. MM Pte 301829 5th London Regt
BELL Neil MM Cpl 76156 IV Corps Sig Coy Royal Engineers
BELL Nicholas MM Pte 18633 6th Yorkshire Regt
BELL Ninian MM Pte 386262 1/1st(Northumbrian)Fd Amb RAMC Died 17.9.18.
BELL Norman MM Pte 25947 East Surrey Regt
BELL Percy MM Pte 32746 13th Liverpool Regt
BELL Peter "DCM,MM" Sjt 50955 2nd Royal Scots
BELL Peter MM Cpl 1739 10th Arg & Suth Highlanders KIA 30.12.17.
BELL Ralph Ryan MM Gnr 96095 RGA
BELL Reginald MM Pte 241764 Notts & Derby Regt
BELL Reginald F. MM Cpl 58284 Northumberland Fusiliers
BELL Reginald J.H. MM Sjt 365539 10th Liverpool Regt
BELL Richard MM L/Cpl 15072 5 Fd Coy Royal Engineers
BELL Richard MM Cpl 23/49 Northumberland Fusiliers
BELL Robert MM Cpl 235805 9th Northumberland Fusiliers
BELL Robert "DCM,MM" CSM 265104 1/6th Royal Highlanders
BELL Robert MM Pte 13466 2nd King's Own Scottish Borderers
BELL Robert MM Spr 57975 36 Div Sig Coy Royal Engineers
BELL Robert MM Pte 18017 2nd King's Own Scottish Borderers
BELL Robert MM Pte 64844 22nd Northumberland Fusiliers
BELL Robert MM L/Cpl 276186 Arg & Suth Highlanders
BELL Robert MM Pte 28090 Durham Light Infantry
BELL Robert MM Pte S/18090 Cameron Highlanders
BELL Robert Fairley MM Sjt 14804 9th D Coy Northumberland Fusiliers KIA 17.4.18.
BELL Robert James MM Pte 26770 7th Shropshire Light Infantry DOW 12.4.18.
BELL Robert Joseph MM Sjt 250068 1/6th Durham Light Infantry
BELL Robert Morton MM Pte 3480 1/9th London Regt KIA 1.7.16.
BELL Samuel MM Pte 555 16th Royal Irish Rifles
BELL Septimus MM Bdr 99055 RFA
BELL Simpson D. MM Pte 11307 9th West Yorkshire Regt
BELL Theodore J. MM L/Cpl 438427 430 Fd Coy Royal Engineers
BELL Thomas "DCM,MM" Pte 27963 8th Border Regt
BELL Thomas MM Pte 260490 1st Border Regt
BELL Thomas MM L/Cpl 27582 8th West Yorkshire Regt
BELL Thomas MM Pte 240165 1/5th Border Regt
BELL Thomas MM Cpl 9171 Cameron Highlanders
BELL Thomas MM SM 299 Royal Flying Corps
BELL Thomas MM Pte 941 Northumberland Fusiliers
BELL Thomas MM L/Cpl 27810 2nd King's Own Scottish Borderers
BELL Thomas Frederick MM+Bar Pte 10084 1st Royal Berkshire Regt KIA 29.4.17.
BELL Thomas J. MM L/Cpl 46079 Durham Light Infantry
BELL Thomas M. MM Sjt 205554 2nd Northumberland Fusiliers
BELL Thomas S. MM+Bar Sjt 1657 23rd Royal Fusiliers
BELL Thomas W. MM Sjt 47092 27 Bde RFA
BELL Thomas William MM Pte 12124 Scots Guards
BELL Walter MM Cpl 5346 3rd Bn GMGR
BELL William MM Pte 18399 9th Bn Machine Gun Corps
BELL William MM Pte 34567 5th West Riding Regt
BELL William MM L/Cpl 203707 2nd Royal Scots Fusiliers DOW 14.10.18.
BELL William MM L/Cpl 251482 3rd London Regt
BELL William MM Pte 7146 Royal Fusiliers
BELL William MM Pte 200618 5th Cameron Highlanders
BELL William MM Pte 41165 2nd Royal Scots Fusiliers
BELL William MM Cpl 200107 1/4th King's Own Scottish Borderers
BELL William MM Cpl 200864 1/4th North Lancashire Regt
BELL William MM Pte 10470 2nd Gordon Highlanders
BELL William MM Sjt 106 1/5th Royal Lancaster Regt
BELL William MM Cpl 3119 1st Essex Regt
BELL William A. MM Sjt 10130 2nd Highland Light Infantry
BELL William H. MM Sjt 24782 4th Liverpool Regt
BELL William H. MM Gnr 88906 RGA
BELL William R. "MM,MID" Cpl 39687 7 Bde RHA
BELLAMY Charles H. MM Sjt 19430 15th Durham Light Infantry
BELLAMY Edmund Charles MM Gnr 145862 294 Siege Bty RGA KIA 25.5.18.
BELLAMY Ernest Edward MM Pte A/203 1st King's Royal Rifle Corps KIA 8.10.18
BELLAMY Frank P. MM Pte 424116 RAMC
BELLAMY Frederick John MM Cpl 9616 1st Northamptonshire Regt KIA 24.9.18.
BELLAMY Harry MM Pnr 443932 42 Div Sig Coy Royal Engineers
BELLAMY Henry MM SSM 45622 7th Hussars
BELLAMY Herbert MM Gnr 79123 A/123 Bde RFA
BELLAMY Horace MM Spr 2276 2/2nd(West Riding)Fd Coy Royal Engineers
BELLAMY John J. MM Cpl 204472 8th Royal West Kent Regt
BELLAMY John W. MM Pte 34172 7th Suffolk Regt
BELLAMY Thomas Epton "MM,MID" Sjt 1435 230 Bde RFA
BELLAMY Thomas S. MM Pte 122967 5th Bn Machine Gun Corps
BELLAMY William Alfred MM Sjt 212 280 Bde RFA
BELLARS Olentus William MM Pte 241953 1/6th South Staffordshire Regt
BELLARUS William MM Pte 631 2nd South Lancashire Regt
BELLCHAMBER F.J. MM+Bar Pte 8018 6th East Kent Regt
BELLCHAMBERS Sydney MM L/Cpl D/18313 1/1st Northamptonshire Yeomanry
BELLEINI Alfred Francis John MM Pte 27210 Grenadier Guards
BELLERBY Charles Henry MM Sjt 38111 20th Lancashire Fusiliers
BELLERBY Thomas MM+Bar Cpl 15384 Durham Light Infantry
BELLERBY Thomas V. MM Pte 29029 East Yorkshire Regt
BELLEW Thomas MM Gnr 66932 RFA
BELLFIELD Harry Henry MM Pte 16196 7th South Staffordshire Regt KIA 21.11.17.
BELLI Albert MM Cpl 265502 1/2nd Monmouthshire Regt
BELLIN William MM Pte 14/10 2nd York & Lancaster Regt
BELLINGER Alfred Ernest MM Drummer 1117 1/22nd London Regt
BELLINGER Norman William "DCM,MM" Cpl 17391 13th Essex Regt
BELLINGHAM Alfred MM L/Cpl 3340 7th Hussars
BELLINGHAM Frank Sidney MM L/Cpl 530889 1/15th London Regt KIA 22.3.18.
BELLINGHAM John G. MM Pte M2/166842 Army Service Corps
BELLINGHAM Robert MM Sjt 276177 Arg & Suth Highlanders
BELLINGHAM Walter H. MM Cpl 22127 Royal West Surrey Regt
BELLIS Albert MM Gnr L/3717 165 Bde att X/31 Med TM Bty RFA att X/31 MTM Bty. KIA 17.7.16.
BELLIS Arthur MM Pte 48916 Att 2/10th London Regt Rifle Brigade DOW 29.8.18.
BELLIS David P.W. MM Gnr 293320 RGA
BELLIS John MM Pte 240948 Cheshire Regt
BELLIS Thomas "DCM,MM" Sjt 550197 520 Fd Coy Royal Engineers
BELLIS Thomas MM Gnr 67474 C/112 Bde RFA
BELLMAN Charles John MM L/Cpl 4435 4th Royal Fusiliers
BELLOWS Sydney MM Cpl 29537 2nd Hampshire Regt
BELLOWS William J. MM Pte 20417 9th Welsh Regt
BELLWOOD John E. MM L/Cpl 5938 Rifle Brigade
BELLWORTHY William C. MM 2nd Cpl 58335 156 Fd Coy Royal Engineers
BELMONT William E. MM Sjt 26980 Royal Engineers
BELSEY Richard MM Sjt 156107 170 Tunnelling Coy Royal Engineers Died 19.11.16.

BELSHAM Ernest MM Pte 18826 1/1st Hertfordshire Regt
BELSHAM W.G. MM Pte 44193 9th Essex Regt
BELSON T.E. MM Dvr 800361 RFA
BELSTEN Reginald Stanley MM Cpl 92457 RFA
BELTON Henry Scott Butler MM Pte 1655 12th Royal Sussex Regt
BELTON John Thomas MM Pte 10729 2nd Royal Sussex Regt
BELTON Thomas S. MM Dvr 38480 RFA
BELTRAM John "DCM,MM" Sjt 550065 517 Fd Coy Royal Engineers
BELWOOD Harry MM Pte 220626 1st Royal Berkshire Regt
BEMAN Horace S. "MM,MID" Pte 10610 1st Middlesex Regt
BEMAN S. MM Pte 27765 16th Lancashire Fusiliers
BEMAND Harry MM L/Cpl 18032 11th Somerset Light Infantry
BEMMENT William G. MM L/Bdr 90876 RGA
BEMROSE Cyril C. MM Cpl 44535 8th Royal Berkshire Regt
BEMROSE Jane MM Sister F SJAB
BENBOW George Parkin "MM,MID" Sjt 1432 1/5th Liverpool Regt KIA 8.8.16.
BENBOW Walter Harrold MM Sjt Y/964 1st King's Royal Rifle Corps KIA 23.8.18.
BENBROOK Arthur R. "MM,MIDx2" S/Sjt Farrier 11158 37 Bde RFA
BENCE Paul Alfred MM Cpl 45387 95 Fd Coy Royal Engineers KIA 6.5.17.
BENCE Sidney Robert MM Sjt 2029 1/3rd London Regt KIA 17.2.17.
BENCH Arthur MM Pte 6887 Royal Warwickshire Regt
BENCH Frederick G. MM Cpl G/17394 6th Royal West Kent Regt
BENDA Percy MM Sjt 13575 Norfolk Regt
BENDALL Arthur John MM Pte 326855 1/1st Cambridgeshire Regt KIA 22.8.18.
BENDALL Reginald Charles MM Pte 19174 1st Coldstream Guards
BENDALL Sydney MM Cpl 2859 North Lancashire Regt
BENDER Henry James MM Sjt 276911 14 Hy Bty RGA
BENDING Albert MM L/Cpl 203633 1st London Regt
BENDON John W. MM Dvr 210611 92 Bty 17 Bde RFA
BENDORFFE Simeon MM Pte 19130 2nd South Wales Borderers
BENEDECTY Adolph MM Pte 281166 Lancashire Fusiliers
BENEY Lester MM Gnr 146192 RFA
BENFIELD Edward MM Cpl 21309 41 Bde RFA
BENFIELD Joseph MM+Bar Gnr 11015 C/124 Bde RFA
BENFIELD Sydney R. MM Gnr 110814 RFA
BENFORD Charles J. MM Gnr 720045 RFA
BENFORD Harry "MM,MID" Sjt 9234 2nd Oxf & Bucks Light Infantry
BENFORD Jesse L. MM Pte 353916 7th London Regt
BENGE Roger MM Pte 32020 5 Fd Amb RAMC
BENGE William H. MM Pte 230933 2nd London Regt
BENGER Frederick MM Pte 89459 RAMC
BENGER William J. MM Sjt 88288 Royal Flying Corps
BENHAM Charles John MM L/Cpl 3208 12th Middlesex Regt KIA 26.9.16.
BENHAM Frederick W. MM Sjt 352657 RGA
BENIAMS Henry "DCM,MM,MID" CSM 11788 1st Worcestershire Regt
BENINSON Robert "DCM,MM" L/Cpl G/6066 Royal West Surrey Regt
BENISTON William Henry MM L/Cpl 107076 231 Fd Coy Royal Engineers
BENJAFIELD Harry W.C. "MM,MID" Sjt S/16023 6 Div Train Army Service Corps
BENJAMIN Bernard MM Dvr 836809 25 Div Ammn Col RFA
BENJAMIN Ernest MM Gnr 24016 RFA
BENJAMIN Frank MM L/Bdr 88214 Z Bty RHA
BENJAMIN Henry MM Pte 26532 13th Welsh Regt KIA 1.12.17
BENJAMIN Horace MM Pte 32199 1st Gloucestershire Regt
BENJAMIN John H. MM Pte 642 7 Fd Amb RAMC
BENJAMIN Joseph MM Cpl 48517 Liverpool Regt
BENJAMIN William MM Pte 17112 2nd Grenadier Guards
BENN John H. MM Pte 33612 North Lancashire Regt
BENN Joseph A. MM L/Cpl 81585 15th Durham Light Infantry
BENN Leonard MM Pte 2901 24th Royal Fusiliers DOW 20.10.18.
BENN Sydney MM Pte 266005 1/1st Hertfordshire Regt
BENN William MM Pte 241211 1/6th West Yorkshire Regt
BENN William Robert MM Pte 1948 1/22nd London Regt
BENNALLACK Howard E. MM L/Cpl 184706 218 Fd Coy Royal Engineers
BENNELL George H. MM Pte 33475 2/4th West Riding Regt
BENNELLICK William E. MM Pte 74767 RAMC
BENNER A.T. MM Pte S/31336 2nd Rifle Brigade
BENNER William MM Pte 17614 9th Leicestershire Regt
BENNETS G. MM Pte 23852 10th Duke of Cornwall's LI
BENNETT Albert MM Pte 203838 1/4th York & Lancaster Regt
BENNETT Albert H. MM+Bar Sjt 7876 2nd Oxf & Bucks Light Infantry
BENNETT Albert V. MM Pte 15138 5th Dorsetshire Regt
BENNETT Alex MM Cpl 26973 9th Scottish Rifles
BENNETT Alexander MM+Bar Pte 240258 1/5th Royal Highlanders
BENNETT Alfred MM+Bar Pte 9549 1st Cheshire Regt
BENNETT Alfred MM Gnr 77392 Tank Corps
BENNETT Alfred Charles MM Pte 203409 Royal Warwickshire Regt
BENNETT Alfred E. MM Pte B/201060 10th London Regt
BENNETT Alfred W. MM Bdr 49042 RGA
BENNETT Archibald MM Sjt 2131 1/9th Highland Light Infantry
BENNETT Arthur MM Pte 140676 Machine Gun Corps
BENNETT Arthur MM Gnr 124213 RGA
BENNETT Arthur MM+Bar Cpl 129233 RFA
BENNETT Arthur M. MM Pte 63351 RAMC
BENNETT Aubrey W. "DCM,MM" Sjt 62 7th East Surrey Regt
BENNETT Bernard J. MM Dvr 140048 RHA
BENNETT C.E. MM Pte 13159 2nd Essex Regt
BENNETT Charles MM Sjt 22422 10th Duke of Cornwall's LI
BENNETT Charles MM L/Cpl 16331 1st Royal Berkshire Regt
BENNETT Charles MM Sjt 263167 1st Worcestershire Regt
BENNETT Charles A.S. MM Pte G/76899 3rd London Regt
BENNETT Charles G. MM L/Cpl 1671 Royal Engineers
BENNETT Charles George Frederick MM L/Cpl 16194 2nd Grenadier Guards
BENNETT Charles Gordon "MM,MSM" Staff SM S/18771 14 Div Train? Army Service Corps
BENNETT Clarence V. MM Pte R/33393 King's Royal Rifle Corps
BENNETT Cuthbert F. MM L/Cpl DM2/180185 Army Service Corps
BENNETT Daniel MM L/Cpl 49066 56 Fd Amb RAMC
BENNETT David "MM+Bar,MM(F)" Sjt 579 6th Royal West Kent Regt
BENNETT Douglas William MM L/Sjt 19112 1st Grenadier Guards DOW 19.11.18.
BENNETT E. MM+Bar L/Cpl 193287 Royal Engineers
BENNETT E.E. MM Sjt 309046 Royal Engineers
BENNETT Edward MM Sjt 48001 42nd Bn Machine Gun Corps
BENNETT Edward MM Pte G/4785 7th Royal West Surrey Regt KIA 28.9.16.
BENNETT Ernest Edward MM Spr 13305 218 Fd Coy Royal Engineers
BENNETT Frank MM Pte 12589 7th Leicestershire Regt
BENNETT Frank MM Cpl 2488 1/7th C Coy Middlesex Regt KIA 16.9.16.
BENNETT Frank E. MM Cpl G/2835 Royal Sussex Regt
BENNETT Fred MM L/Cpl 19117 5th Yorkshire Light Infantry
BENNETT Fred MM Pte 26318 West Riding Regt
BENNETT Frederick "MM,MID" Sjt 546513 512 Fd Coy Royal Engineers
BENNETT Frederick "MM,CdiG(It)" Sjt 825093 C/240 Bde RFA
BENNETT Frederick MM Pte 15968 8th Royal Lancaster Regt
BENNETT Frederick Claude MM Sjt 8785 Scots Guards
BENNETT Frederick H. MM Cpl 203006 1/5th Royal Warwickshire Regt
BENNETT Frederick W. MM Cpl 13579 9th East Lancashire Regt
BENNETT George MM Cpl 76571 RGA
BENNETT George MM Pte 3/9892 Northamptonshire Regt
BENNETT George MM Farrier QMS 88483 RFA
BENNETT George MM+Bar Sjt 10660 5th Royal Berkshire Regt
BENNETT George MM Cpl 26969 15th Hampshire Regt
BENNETT George MM Bdr 795842 246 Bde RFA
BENNETT George "DCM,MM" Sjt 34498 130 Bty 40 Bde RFA
BENNETT George A. "MM,MID" Bdr 39045 RFA
BENNETT George E. MM Pte 8214 1st Gloucestershire Regt
BENNETT George H. MM Pte 103169 35th Bn Machine Gun Corps
BENNETT George H. MM Gnr 690051 RFA
BENNETT George William MM L/Sjt 26469 16th Notts & Derby Regt KIA 16.4.18.
BENNETT Gordon MM Sjt 40754 RFA
BENNETT H. MM Cpl 75233 Tank Corps
BENNETT Harold MM L/Cpl 20/660 20th Durham Light Infantry
BENNETT Harry "MM,CdeG(F)" L/Cpl 14989 12th West Yorkshire Regt KIA 20.11.17.
BENNETT Harry MM Pte 2984 1/4th Leicestershire Regt
BENNETT Harry MM+Bar L/Cpl 10254 2nd West Riding Regt
BENNETT Harry L. MM Pte 40248 2nd Leicestershire Regt
BENNETT Harry W. MM Pte 7047 1st Border Regt
BENNETT Henry MM L/Sjt 21974 3rd Grenadier Guards
BENNETT Henry MM Pte 14087 9th South Staffordshire Regt
BENNETT Henry J. MM Sjt 19982 33rd Bn Machine Gun Corps

BENNETT Henry R. MM Bdr 117210 RFA
BENNETT Herbert MM Pte M2/032428 Army Service Corps
BENNETT Herbert Brookland MM Cpl 4377 1st Rifle Brigade
BENNETT Hervey MM Pte 26256 17th Manchester Regt
BENNETT Horace W. MM Pte 26670 1/4th Oxf & Bucks Light Infantry
BENNETT J. MM Sjt 44490 Manchester Regt
BENNETT J. MM Pte 8793 Worcestershire Regt
BENNETT J.A.C. MM Pte 512556 RAMC
BENNETT James MM L/Cpl 32360 1st East Surrey Regt
BENNETT James MM Pte 23159 Royal Inniskilling Fusiliers
BENNETT James J. MM Sjt 7547 1st Suffolk Regt
BENNETT James Paul MM Sjt 106224 2 Special Coy Royal Engineers Died 10.11.18.
BENNETT James T. MM Pte 130722 Machine Gun Corps
BENNETT Jesse MM L/Cpl 4/4964 2nd Bedfordshire Regt
BENNETT John MM Pte 43814 1/8th Middlesex Regt
BENNETT John MM Sjt 572 7th Royal West Surrey Regt
BENNETT John MM Spr 16459 79 Fd Coy Royal Engineers
BENNETT John MM Cpl 23691 1st Border Regt DOW 11.2.18.
BENNETT John MM L/Cpl 7421 Lancashire Fusiliers
BENNETT John MM L/Cpl 5921 Leicestershire Regt
BENNETT John MM Pte 12315 1st Coldstream Guards
BENNETT John MM Cpl 9384 2nd Royal Welsh Fusiliers Died 1.9.16.
BENNETT John MM L/Sjt 15632 13th Royal Scots
BENNETT John MM Sjt 5542 Royal Welsh Fusiliers
BENNETT John "MM,MID" Pte 4/9218 South Staffordshire Regt
BENNETT John MM Sjt 15209 8th Devonshire Regt
BENNETT John MM L/Cpl 45668 Royal Engineers
BENNETT John Edwin Francis Theodore MM Sjt 1694 Royal Warwickshire Regt KIA 24.7.16.
BENNETT John F. MM Sjt 191336 'P' AA Bty RGA
BENNETT John Frederick MM Pte 201160 1/4th Royal Lancaster Regt KIA 9.4.18.
BENNETT John J. MM+Bar Sjt 41132 Northumberland Fusiliers
BENNETT John James MM Sjt 200046 1/4th Duke of Cornwall's LI DOW 14.12.17.
BENNETT John Lewis MM Pte DM2/162879 594 MT Coy Army Service Corps
BENNETT John Walter MM+Bar Pte S/688 8th Rifle Brigade KIA 26.3.18.
BENNETT John William MM Pte 1729 5th Lancashire Fusiliers
BENNETT Joseph MM L/Cpl 133461 212 Fd Coy Royal Engineers
BENNETT Joseph MM Dvr 19838 RFA
BENNETT Joseph MM Sjt 3/8996 9th Royal Irish Rifles KIA 1.7.16.
BENNETT Joseph MM Pte 15752 Notts & Derby Regt
BENNETT Joseph MM Spr 442166 Royal Engineers
BENNETT Lancelot MM Cpl 59549 42 Bde RFA
BENNETT Michael MM Pte 12332 11th Liverpool Regt KIA 21.7.17.
BENNETT Oliver J. MM L/Sjt 29850 2nd Grenadier Guards
BENNETT Percy D. MM Cpl 733549 24th London Regt
BENNETT R. MM Dvr L/3041 D/187 Bde RFA
BENNETT Richard MM Pte 13243 9th Welsh Regt
BENNETT Richard B. MM Dvr 64632 RFA
BENNETT Robert William MM L/Cpl R/17846 1st King's Royal Rifle Corps KIA 23.3.18.
BENNETT Samuel MM Sjt C/6680 King's Royal Rifle Corps
BENNETT Samuel W. MM Gnr 62554 RGA
BENNETT Sidney MM Sjt 245440 2nd London Regt
BENNETT Sidney G. MM Sjt H/285199 1/1st Oxfordshire Yeomanry
BENNETT Stanley MM L/Sjt 8995 2nd Northamptonshire Regt
BENNETT Sydney MM Sjt 7964 2nd Essex Regt
BENNETT Thomas MM L/Cpl 46639 4th York & Lancaster Regt
BENNETT Thomas MM Pte 252395 1/6th Arg & Suth Highlanders
BENNETT Thomas MM+Bar Pte 99019 13th Royal Fusiliers
BENNETT Thomas MM Pte 4205 7th Royal West Kent Regt
BENNETT Thomas MM L/Cpl S/4340 2nd Gordon Highlanders
BENNETT Thomas MM Pte 45709 2nd Bn Machine Gun Corps
BENNETT Thomas V.R. MM Sjt 24752 Manchester Regt
BENNETT Tom MM Pte 37266 25th Northumberland Fusiliers Died 21.3.18.
BENNETT Victor MM Pte 201752 2/4th Hampshire Regt DOW 4.11.18.
BENNETT W.J. MM Gnr Sig 931051 C/291 Bde RFA
BENNETT Wallace MM Pte 12329 Royal West Surrey Regt
BENNETT Walter MM Sjt 44674 B/102 Bde RFA KIA 31.10.18.
BENNETT Walter MM Pte 55169 Royal Welsh Fusiliers
BENNETT William MM Cpl 240028 1/5th Leicestershire Regt
BENNETT William MM Sjt 5828 62nd Bn Machine Gun Corps
BENNETT William MM Sjt 32018 15 Bde RFA
BENNETT William MM Pte M2/167448 Army Service Corps
BENNETT William MM Sjt 7959 Machine Gun Corps
BENNETT William MM Pte 437002 RAMC
BENNETT William MM Pte 26649 Leicestershire Regt
BENNETT William MM Gnr 159800 232 Bde RFA
BENNETT William F.E.B. MM Cpl 1897 6th Dragoons
BENNETT William J. MM+Bar Cpl 7012 4th Middlesex Regt
BENNETT William J. MM+Bar Sjt 10422 8th Devonshire Regt
BENNETT William James MM Sjt 21865 18th Liverpool Regt KIA 9.4.17.
BENNETT William T. MM Bdr 37760 RFA
BENNETT William V. MM Cpl 512207 Royal Engineers
BENNETTO Edward MM Dvr 65872 5 Bde G Bty RHA
BENNETTON Albert Thomas MM Pte 44682 8th Royal Berkshire Regt KIA 23.9.18.
BENNETTS Richard MM L/Sjt F/198 Middlesex Regt
BENNETTS Thomas O. MM Pte 240402 Duke of Cornwall's LI
BENNEWORTH Cristopher C. MM Pte 71787 Notts & Derby Regt
BENNIE Alexander Stewart MM Cpl 40486 6th Cameron Highlanders
BENNIE Thomas MM L/Cpl 402089 Royal Engineers
BENNING Albert MM L/Cpl A/7749 2nd Scottish Rifles
BENNING Charles Casimir MM Cpl 9263 2nd Essex Regt
BENNING Ernest Henry MM Cpl 26858 174 Bde RFA
BENNING George H. MM Sjt 10595 RFA
BENNINGTON John William MM L/Cpl P3791 Mons Sub-area Military Mounted Police
BENNINGTON S.L. MM Air Mech 1 4909 Royal Flying Corps
BENNION Daniel MM Pte 201104 2nd Royal Welsh Fusiliers
BENNISON Arthur MM Pte 698123 22nd London Regt
BENNISON John C. MM Pte 23651 East Yorkshire Regt
BENNISON Smith MM+Bar Pte 23212 Liverpool Regt
BENNS Joseph N. MM Gnr 301627 Tank Corps
BENSEL Thomas MM Pte 14430 1st Dorsetshire Regt DOW 28.4.18.
BENSON Adam MM Gnr 1999 MGC (Motors)
BENSON Bernard MM Pte 22832 1/6th Durham Light Infantry
BENSON Charles J. MM L/Cpl 26255 7th Royal Irish Regt
BENSON Ernest MM Cpl 26346 Machine Gun Corps
BENSON Finlay Douglas "MM,MID" Sjt 7251 1st Coldstream Guards KIA 15.9.16.
BENSON Fred MM Gnr 113205 RGA
BENSON Frederick MM Sjt 22/466 22nd Durham Light Infantry
BENSON Frederick P. MM Cpl 47752 Lancashire Fusiliers
BENSON George MM+Bar Pte 40848 1/4th South Lancashire Regt
BENSON Harold MM Bdr 74164 C/110 Bde RFA KIA 22.10.18.
BENSON Harry MM L/Cpl R/30183 13th King's Royal Rifle Corps
BENSON Herbert MM Pte 241827 5th Yorkshire Light Infantry
BENSON J. MM Pte 73432 Machine Gun Corps
BENSON James "MM,MID" CQMS 355065 10th Liverpool Regt
BENSON James MM Sjt 11831 41st Bn Machine Gun Corps
BENSON John MM Pte 6/19403 6th Royal Inniskilling Fusiliers
BENSON John MM Gnr 166759 202 Siege Bty RGA
BENSON John MM Sjt 240672 Royal Lancaster Regt
BENSON John Kemp MM Sjt 6218 18th Royal Fusiliers
BENSON Percy MM L/Cpl 59886 Machine Gun Corps
BENSON R. MM Pte R/11294 King's Royal Rifle Corps
BENSON R. MM Pte 20001 Shropshire Light Infantry
BENSON Robert H. "DCM,MM" Sjt 27691 1st Royal Dublin Fusiliers
BENSON Stanley MM Pte 45115 7 Fd Amb RAMC DOW 3.5.17.
BENSON T. MM Pte 13127 2nd Coldstream Guards
BENSON Thomas MM Pte 3/3117 Yorkshire Light Infantry
BENSON Wilfred R. MM Pte 22339 1st Coldstream Guards
BENSON William MM L/Cpl R/6214 King's Royal Rifle Corps
BENSON William MM L/Cpl 4/7733 West Yorkshire Regt
BENSTEAD Arthur J. MM Pte 718338 23rd London Regt
BENSTEAD Charles MM Pte 13/498 East Yorkshire Regt
BENSTEAD Frank H. MM L/Cpl 25996 8th East Surrey Regt
BENSTEAD Leonard MM Pte 521079 15th London Regt
BENSTEAD Rufus MM Pte 14114 1st Grenadier Guards
BENSTEAD Walter W. MM Pte 43790 1/8th Middlesex Regt
BENSTED H. MM Pte 202587 Royal West Kent Regt
BENT Albert E. MM Pte 35937 1st East Surrey Regt
BENT Albert Henry MM Spr 46537 31 Div Sig Coy Royal Engineers
BENT Alfred George MM L/Cpl 24685 Royal Welsh Fusiliers
BENT George A. MM Cpl 1581 Leicestershire Regt
BENT Harold MM Cpl 56031 RGA
BENT Joseph MM Pte 20123 4th Grenadier Guards KIA 13.4.18.
BENT Wilfred MM Pte 13/1362 15th York & Lancaster Regt

BENTALL Arthur MM Bdr 340577 RGA
BENTALL F. MM+Bar L/Cpl 19788 1st Essex Regt
BENTHAM William MM L/Cpl 21525 1st North Lancashire Regt
BENTHAM William MM Bdr 187082 RGA
BENTHAM William MM Spr 139152 Royal Engineers
BENTLEY A.E. MM L/Cpl 571933 London Regt
BENTLEY Albert "MM,MID" Pte 1967 Lancashire Fusiliers
BENTLEY Allan C. MM Pte 18733 2nd Coldstream Guards
BENTLEY Arthur R. MM Sjt 5125 1/7th Middlesex Regt
BENTLEY Colin MM Sjt 72501 4th Royal Fusiliers
BENTLEY Eli MM Pte 38560 Lancashire Fusiliers
BENTLEY Ernest E. MM Dvr 1985 RFA
BENTLEY F.A. MM Pte 23313 1st Essex Regt
BENTLEY Frank MM Spr 32994 26 Fd Coy Royal Engineers
BENTLEY Frank J. MM Sjt 241387 16th North Staffordshire Regt
BENTLEY Frederick MM Pte 36747 East Yorkshire Regt
BENTLEY Frederick Charles MM+Bar L/Bdr 9739 C/291 Bde RFA
BENTLEY George MM Pte 23525 3rd Worcestershire Regt KIA 26.4.18.
BENTLEY George H. MM Bdr 64261 RFA
BENTLEY Harold MM Sjt 15089 Royal Lancaster Regt
BENTLEY Harry MM Pte 282087 1/7th Highland Light Infantry KIA 27.9.18.
BENTLEY Herbert "DCM,MM,MID" Sjt 700025 A/210 Bde RFA
BENTLEY J. MM Pte 323486 London Regt
BENTLEY James A. MM Sjt 775421 RFA
BENTLEY John MM Bdr 750923 RFA
BENTLEY John MM Pte 17149 2nd South Staffordshire Regt DOW 25.3.18.
BENTLEY Jonathan MM Pte 19370 Grenadier Guards
BENTLEY Louis "DCM,MM+Bar" L/Cpl 330606 9th Liverpool Regt
BENTLEY Oswald MM Cpl Z/1015 1st Rifle Brigade KIA 28.3.18.
BENTLEY Thomas "MM,CdeG(F)" L/Cpl 25401 Cheshire Regt
BENTLEY Thomas MM Pte 5/5871 2nd Royal Munster Fusiliers
BENTLEY Thomas M. "DCM,MM" Sjt 44793 32 Bty 33 Bde RFA
BENTLEY William MM L/Cpl PS/6917 Royal Fusiliers
BENTLEY William MM Pte 8244 Machine Gun Corps
BENTLEY William MM L/Cpl 24930 2nd South Wales Borderers KIA 21.11.17.
BENTON Arthur Samuel MM Dvr T/292556 667 Coy Army Service Corps
BENTON Arthur Victor MM Sjt 550995 1/16th London Regt
BENTON David MM Spr 1082 Royal Engineers
BENTON George Thomas MM Gnr 155601 D/52 Bde RFA
BENTON Harold G. MM Cpl 437106 RAMC
BENTON Harry Albert MM Gnr 926451 B/50 Bde RFA
BENTON John W. MM Pte 22788 2nd Grenadier Guards
BENTON John W. MM Cpl WR/22887 315 Rly Const Coy Royal Engineers
BENTON Richard F. MM Sjt 8883 4 Sig Troop Royal Engineers
BENTON Stephen MM Cpl 8902 RGA
BENZIE Andrew MM Cpl 1802 1 Fd Amb RAMC
BENZIE William MM Pte 69844 Tank Corps
BERE Henry G. MM Pte 14268 2nd Royal Fusiliers
BERESFORD Charles MM Pte 32025 RAMC
BERESFORD Daniel A.E. "DCM,MM+Bar" Sjt A/1856 16th King's Royal Rifle Corps
BERESFORD E.W. MM Pte 7622 North Staffordshire Regt
BERESFORD Harry T. MM Pte 46186 RAMC
BERESFORD Henry "DCM,MM" Pte 71286 2nd Notts & Derby Regt
BERESFORD Horace MM Pte 13177 1/8th Notts & Derby Regt
BERESFORD Isaac MM Pte 17428 11th Notts & Derby Regt
BERESFORD Joseph MM 2nd Cpl 50847 Royal Engineers
BERESFORD Joseph Henry MM Pte M2/106218 Army Service Corps
BERESFORD Thomas MM Pte 251509 Manchester Regt
BERESFORD Thomas Moss MM L/Cpl G/20203 8th East Kent Regt KIA 16.4.17.
BERG Charles Douglas MM Cpl 513811 1/14th London Regt
BERGENDORFF Otto MM L/Bdr 810282 RFA
BERGIN John MM Sjt 8303 Royal Irish Regt
BERGIN Joseph MM Pte 8092 8th Seaforth Highlanders
BERGIN Martin MM Pte 18983 2nd Lancashire Fusiliers
BERGIN Michael MM Sjt 9093 2nd Royal Irish Regt
BERGIN Michael MM Gnr 15986 RGA
BERGIN Richard T. MM Pte 10602 2nd Royal West Surrey Regt
BERGMAN Alfred MM Gnr 113307 RGA
BERMINGHAM David MM Pte 308935 Liverpool Regt
BERMINGHAM Thomas MM Spr 32228 Royal Engineers
BERNARD T. MM Gnr 32004 MGC(Motors)

BERNARD Thomas MM Cpl 20410 Machine Gun Corps
BERNARD Thomas Turnbull MM Pte 51814 Royal Scots
BERNASCONI Walter L.V.G. MM Cpl 160728 Royal Engineers
BERRIBALL Sidney MM L/Cpl 185 1st Dragoon Guards
BERRIDGE Ambrose MM Sjt 11420 1 Special Coy King's Royal Rifle Corps
BERRIDGE John T. MM Pte 203178 West Riding Regt
BERRIDGE William Alfred "MC,MM(1822 Sjt)" 2Lt 5th Leicestershire Regt Died 15.2.19.
BERRIE George Murray MM Cpl 14120 16th Highland Light Infantry
BERRIMAN George MM Cpl 20255 26 Fd Coy Royal Engineers
BERRIMAN Richard Bidby MM Pte 67016 Machine Gun Corps
BERRINGTON Robert William MM Cpl 14032 8th Leicestershire Regt KIA 25.9.16.
BERRISS A. MM L/Cpl 19935 Royal Berkshire Regt
BERROWS George Alfred Allen MM Pte S/4997 12th Rifle Brigade DOW 29.5.17.
BERRY A. MM L/Sjt 2611 1/4th Yorkshire Light Infantry
BERRY Albert MM Pte 6/16769 6th D Coy South Wales Borderers Died 23.9.18.
BERRY Albert MM L/Cpl 2694 South Lancashire Regt
BERRY Albert George "MM+Bar,MID" L/Cpl 9213 2nd Devonshire Regt
BERRY Albert S. MM+Bar Cpl L/22023 RFA
BERRY Alexander MM Cpl 1765 York & Lancaster Regt
BERRY Arthur MM Bdr 35105 RFA
BERRY Arthur MM Gnr 59314 X/38 TM Bty RGA KIA 22.9.17.
BERRY Arthur John MM Sjt 250959 1/6th Manchester Regt Died 22.4.18.
BERRY Arthur John MM Bdr 32092 49 Siege Bty RGA DOW 16.7.17.
BERRY Charles MM Pte 16/819 15/17th West Yorkshire Regt DOW 30.9.18.
BERRY Charles E. MM Pte 7693 1 Fd Amb RAMC
BERRY Charles F. MM Cpl 36794 111 Fd Amb RAMC
BERRY Clement N. MM L/Cpl 207425 63 Div Sig Coy Royal Engineers
BERRY Edgar MM Sjt 57639 2 Bde RFA
BERRY Edward MM Pte 241326 6th South Lancashire Regt
BERRY Ernest MM Gnr 4650 D/74 Bde RFA
BERRY Ernest MM Pte 8249 Machine Gun Corps
BERRY Ernest MM Sjt 301578 13th Bn Tank Corps
BERRY F.R. MM Air Mech 2 401789 Royal Air Force
BERRY F.T. MM Sjt 41232 Machine Gun Corps
BERRY Frank MM Gnr 163828 D/168 Bde RFA
BERRY Frank MM Sjt 266338 1/9th Middlesex Regt
BERRY Frank MM Pte 202913 5th Royal Berkshire Regt
BERRY Frank G.J. MM Gnr 172967 B/82 Bde RFA
BERRY Fred MM Sjt 242839 Lancashire Fusiliers
BERRY Frederick MM Dvr 67044 A/112 Bde RFA
BERRY Frederick R. MM L/Cpl 9575 2nd Royal Welsh Fusiliers
BERRY G.E. MM+Bar L/Cpl 3237 7th East Kent Regt
BERRY G.F.W. MM Sjt 13573 10th Essex Regt
BERRY Gavin MM Sjt 350191 1st Royal Highlanders
BERRY George MM L/Cpl 10628 2nd Bedfordshire Regt
BERRY George MM Sjt 40118 Scottish Rifles
BERRY George MM Pte 6325 King's Royal Rifle Corps
BERRY H.C. MM L/Cpl R/33924 King's Royal Rifle Corps
BERRY Harold MM Pte 115070 Machine Gun Corps
BERRY Harry MM L/Cpl 241996 1/5th East Lancashire Regt Died 14.6.18.
BERRY Harry Albert MM L/Cpl 1987 1/2nd London Regt KIA 16.8.17.
BERRY Harry Brewerton MM Dvr 781614 95 Bde RFA
BERRY Henry "DCM,MM" Sjt L/8263 11th Royal Fusiliers
BERRY Henry MM Sjt 200774 Leicestershire Regt
BERRY Jack MM Pte 4693 East Surrey Regt
BERRY James MM Sjt 635675 B/256 Bde RFA
BERRY James MM Gnr 46063 33 Siege Bty RGA
BERRY James MM+Bar Sjt 93116 Royal Engineers
BERRY James MM Pte 281572 1/7th Lancashire Fusiliers KIA 3.4.18.
BERRY James MM Pte S/19907 Rifle Brigade
BERRY James Joseph MM Gnr 55280 22 Heavy Bty RGA
BERRY James P. MM Pte 235935 1/1st Herefordshire Regt
BERRY James William MM Bdr 830291 RFA
BERRY John MM Pte 7860 2nd Arg & Suth Highlanders
BERRY John MM Pte 10/14544 10th Cheshire Regt KIA 11.8.17.
BERRY John W. MM Spr 45564 105 Fd Coy Royal Engineers
BERRY Joseph MM Pte 240283 1/7th West Riding Regt DOW 13.10.18.

BERRY Joseph MM L/Cpl 243312 1/5th North Lancashire Regt
BERRY Kenneth MM Cpl 200708 2/4th West Riding Regt
BERRY Leonard MM Spr 556371 Royal Engineers
BERRY Michael MM Pte 307730 15th Bn Tank Corps
BERRY Oscar MM Pte 6457 Royal Welsh Fusiliers
BERRY Ralph MM Gnr 935312 282 Bde RFA
BERRY Samuel Elijah MM Cpl 19962 2nd South Wales Borderers DOW 21.11.17.
BERRY Sidney E. MM Cpl 20614 3 Div Sig Coy Royal Engineers
BERRY Thomas MM Cpl 240919 1/5th York & Lancaster Regt KIA 22.9.18.
BERRY Thomas MM L/Cpl 6/3646 Royal Irish Regt
BERRY Thomas MM Pte 352386 12th Royal Scots
BERRY Thomas Alfred MM+Bar Sjt 15969 12 Bde RFA
BERRY W.G. MM Pte 28939 8th Royal Lancaster Regt
BERRY Walter MM Sjt 320017 1/5th Durham Light Infantry
BERRY Walter MM L/Cpl 27185 Notts & Derby Regt
BERRY Walter H. MM Pte 300991 5th London Regt
BERRY William MM Pte 19351 North Lancashire Regt
BERRY William MM L/Cpl 11402 15th Hussars KIA 8.8.18.
BERRY William E. MM L/Cpl 550295 Royal Engineers
BERRY William R. MM Sjt 394241 16th London Regt
BERRYMAN Charles A.J. MM Sjt 9381 2nd Lincolnshire Regt
BERRYMAN Harry T. "MM,MSM" Pte 7433 1 CCS RAMC
BERTENSHAW John MM Sjt 18779 Machine Gun Corps
BERTIE Ernest MM Cpl 14522 9th Royal Inniskilling Fusiliers
BERTRAM David MM Sjt 1359 18th Middlesex Regt
BERTRAM James MM L/Cpl 14573 5th Cameron Highlanders
BERTRAM James C. MM Spr 358046 21 Div Sig Coy Royal Engineers
BERTRAM Robert Arthur MM+Bar 2nd Cpl 51271 9 Div Sig Coy Royal Engineers
BERTRAM William MM Sjt 41793 Machine Gun Corps
BERTRAM William "MM+Bar,MMV(It)" CSM 5238 11th Northumberland Fusiliers
BERTWHISTLE Fred James MM Sjt 800248 B/230 Bde RFA
BERWICK John MM Pte 27449 14th Arg & Suth Highlanders
BERWICK William C. MM Pte 13297 8th Norfolk Regt
BESANT Charles MM Pte 11155 1st King's Royal Rifle Corps
BESANT Harold S. MM Pte R/8500 King's Royal Rifle Corps
BESANT William P. MM Sjt 95517 A/65 Bde RFA
BESCOBY Fred MM Gnr 5951 RFA
BESLEE Leonard MM Cpl 2649 7th East Kent Regt
BESLEY Ernest J. MM Sjt 52726 MGC(Cavalry)
BESSANT Ernest C. "MM,MID" Cpl 56680 RGA
BESSANT Thomas J. MM Pte 31551 4th Hampshire Regt
BESSELL Arthur "MM,MID" Sjt L/9008 2nd Royal West Surrey Regt
BESSLER Charles H. MM Sjt 33876 Labour Corps
BEST Alexander MM Pte 16229 7th East Yorkshire Regt
BEST Alfred MM Gnr 31392 15 Bde RFA
BEST Andrew MM Dvr 39595 D/160 Bde RFA
BEST Charles H. MM Sjt 608194 18th London Regt
BEST Clifford MM Cpl 15/1387 1st West Yorkshire Regt
BEST E.J. MM L/Cpl 87540 Royal Engineers
BEST Edward D. MM Pte 24086 2nd Manchester Regt
BEST Edwin MM Pte 28420 Durham Light Infantry
BEST Ernest MM Sjt 10/986 10th East Yorkshire Regt
BEST Ernest W. MM Pte 59109 29th Bn Machine Gun Corps
BEST Fred MM Sjt 23847 1st Duke of Cornwall's LI
BEST George Kenneth MM Cpl 207667 63 Div Sig Coy Royal Engineers
BEST Harold MM Cpl S/44199 7th Gordon Highlanders
BEST Harold MM L/Sjt 17890 10th West Riding Regt
BEST Harold MM Sjt 4890 16th Lancers
BEST James Henry MM Pte G/41092 9th Royal Fusiliers KIA 22.10.18.
BEST John William MM Cpl 12093 14th Arg & Suth Highlanders
BEST Robert MM Pte M2/081066 Army Service Corps att RAMC.
BEST Robert MM Pte 16396 2nd Manchester Regt
BEST Robert MM Gnr 92266 Tank Corps
BEST S.C. MM Sjt 700524 London Regt
BEST William MM Pte 242088 East Kent Regt
BEST William MM Gnr 128454 RGA
BEST William G. MM Cpl Fitter 65552 RFA
BEST William H. MM Cpl 265962 1/6th West Riding Regt
BESTALL Bertram W. MM Pte 14682 Lancashire Fusiliers
BESTILE Francis MM Pte 14438 7/8th King's Own Scottish Borderers
BESTLEY James MM Sjt 220500 2nd Royal Berkshire Regt
BESTON Frederick S. MM Pte 201838 Royal Berkshire Regt

BESTWICK Robert MM Cpl 22540 11th Hussars
BESWICK Arthur MM L/Cpl 18419 2nd Coldstream Guards
BESWICK C. MM Gnr 781130 RFA
BESWICK George MM Pte 14052 Army Cyclist Corps
BESWICK Peter MM Cpl 52061 Liverpool Regt
BESWICK R. "DCM,MM" Cpl 3907 Machine Gun Corps
BESWICK Robert MM Gnr 1394 MGC(Motors)
BESWICK Robert "MM,CG(F)" Bdr 84651 D/99 Bde RFA
BESWICK Walter MM Sjt 47707 D/311 Bde RFA
BESWICK William MM L/Cpl 266767 1/6th Cheshire Regt
BETCHLEY Joseph H. MM Sjt 225862 10th Royal Fusiliers
BETHEL John MM Pte 352336 2(East Lancs)Fd Amb RAMC
BETHELL Archibald Francis MM Bdr 40091 A/84 Bde RFA DOW 11.8.17.
BETHELL Arthur MM Pte 1677 7th East Kent Regt
BETHELL Clifford MM Pte 295291 12th Somerset Light Infantry
BETHELL Frederick MM Gnr 950272 RFA
BETHELL John MM CSM 240054 6th South Staffordshire Regt
BETHELL John MM Pte 17274 Liverpool Regt
BETHELL Sidney E. MM Pte 203145 4th East Yorkshire Regt
BETHELL Thomas J. MM Sjt 610195 2/19th London Regt
BETHLE Frank MM Pte 11608 RAMC DOW 25.6.17.
BETHUNE George MM+Bar Sjt 12602 Seaforth Highlanders
BETT Tom MM L/Cpl 7771 Lincolnshire Regt
BETTANEY H. MM Sjt 2040 RFA
BETTANY James Albert MM Pte 240029 Royal Lancaster Regt KIA 10.8.19
BETTERIDGE Charles Henry MM+Bar Pte 57539 8th Bn Machine Gun Corps Died 26.9.18.
BETTERIDGE George MM Sjt 15013 2nd Royal Fusiliers
BETTERIDGE Joseph H. MM Pnr 197181 Royal Engineers
BETTERIDGE William MM 2nd Cpl 171600 Royal Engineers
BETTESWORTH Charles Henry MM Pte 9926 3rd Coldstream Guards DOW 20.10.17.
BETTINSON Albert Nelson MM L/Cpl 43674 Essex Regt
BETTLES F. MM Pte 29151 Essex Regt
BETTLES Frank MM Dvr 209322 3 Pontoon Park Royal Engineers
BETTLES Richard MM Sjt 110348 6 Tank Carrier Coy Tank Corps
BETTLES William MM Sjt 225061 1/4th Northamptonshire Regt
BETTLEY Thomas MM Pte 8965 12th Highland Light Infantry
BETTLEY William Bertram "MM,MM(F)" Cpl 301 1/4th North Lancashire Regt DOW 10.10.16.
BETTRIDGE Arthur MM L/Cpl 254285 Royal Engineers
BETTRIDGE Harry J. MM Cpl 171603 Royal Engineers
BETTRIDGE J. MM Sjt 8798 2/4th Hampshire Regt
BETTRIDGE Joseph MM Pte 4/8000 Durham Light Infantry
BETTS Ernest "MM,CdeG(F)" Pte 11515 7th East Yorkshire Regt
BETTS Ernest W. MM Sjt 9324 3rd Coldstream Guards
BETTS Frederick J. MM Cpl M2/079856 Army Service Corps
BETTS George MM Sjt 3496 24th Northumberland Fusiliers KIA 9.4.17.
BETTS George E. MM Sjt 290760 RGA
BETTS Harold MM+Bar Sjt 61627 2nd Leicestershire Regt
BETTS Harold MM Pte 22869 2nd York & Lancaster Regt
BETTS Harold A. MM Pte 74123 1st Bn Machine Gun Corps
BETTS Harry MM Sjt 97406 35th Bn Machine Gun Corps
BETTS Henry Charles MM Pte 1385 1/7th London Regt
BETTS Herbert Edward MM Bdr Sig 52873 D/246 Bde RFA
BETTS Jesse Albert MM Pte G/10588 10th Royal West Kent Regt
BETTS Jim Roy MM Sjt 26175 RFA
BETTS John Percy MM Pte 270991 10th East Kent Regt KIA 6.8.18.
BETTS John William MM L/Cpl 11902 6th Leicestershire Regt
BETTS Laurence James MM Sjt 270760 10th East Kent Regt
BETTS Phillip MM Pte 13015 5th Northamptonshire Regt
BETTS Robert MM Bdr 68860 RGA
BETTS Sidney John "MM,CdeG" Cpl 250617 1/6th Durham Light Infantry
BETTS Sidney Walter MM Dvr 83952 A/131 Bde RFA
BETTS William MM L/Cpl 89864 76 Fd Coy Royal Engineers
BETTY John Richard MM Sjt 6621 3rd Coldstream Guards
BEVAN Albert E. MM L/Cpl 512405 3rd(London)Fd Amb RAMC
BEVAN Albert E. MM 2nd Cpl 251578 7 Div Sig Coy Royal Engineers
BEVAN Benjamin H. MM Gnr 371295 RGA
BEVAN David MM Sjt 7202 11th Royal Fusiliers
BEVAN Edward "MM,MID" Pte 10308 8th South Staffordshire Regt
BEVAN Edward J. MM Cpl 17190 Welsh Regt
BEVAN Elijah MM Cpl 18825 6th North Lancashire Regt
BEVAN George MM L/Cpl L/9364 1st East Kent Regt KIA 15.9.16.
BEVAN George Vinson MM Sjt SE27243 Army Veterinary Corps DOW 7.11.18.

BEVAN Harold Humphrey MM Pte 388575 2/2nd(Northumbrian)Fd Amb RAMC
BEVAN J.C. MM Pte 16827 Gloucestershire Regt
BEVAN James MM L/Sjt 350645 1/5th Manchester Regt
BEVAN John MM Pte 20841 South Wales Borderers
BEVAN Percy MM Sjt 659 King Edward's Horse
BEVAN Ralph Henry MM Pte 67218 2/2nd London Regt DOW 15.9.18.
BEVAN Randolph Arthur MM Spr 358768 Att 35 Bde RGA sigs Royal Engineers
BEVAN Richard MM Cpl 45950 2nd Welsh Regt KIA 15.9.18.
BEVAN Robert A. MM Sjt 4953 Royal Irish Rifles
BEVAN S.T. MM Gnr 82003 RGA
BEVAN Thomas S. MM L/Cpl 452034 Royal Engineers
BEVAN W. MM Pte 24723 8th Shropshire Light Infantry
BEVAN William J. MM Sjt 1823 1/6th Welsh Regt
BEVELL William H. MM L/Cpl 46805 Royal Engineers
BEVENS George H. "DCM,MM(42028 W Yorks)" Pte 65193 5th Yorkshire Light Infantry
BEVERIDGE Andrew Robbie MM Bdr Sig 660706 379 Bty 169 Bde RFA
BEVERIDGE David MM Pte 158989 9th Bn Machine Gun Corps
BEVERIDGE Henry MM L/Cpl 2942 8th Royal Highlanders
BEVERIDGE James MM Gnr Sig 141699 290 Siege Bty RGA
BEVERIDGE James MM Sjt 280109 7th Highland Light Infantry
BEVERIDGE James MM Pte 10363 1st Scottish Rifles KIA 18.8.16.
BEVERIDGE James MM Pte 4750 9th Royal Highlanders
BEVERIDGE John MM Sjt S/5367 Arg & Suth Highlanders
BEVERIDGE Richard MM+Bar Sjt 205019 13th Bn Tank Corps
BEVERIDGE Robert MM L/Cpl 40707 12th Royal Scots KIA 20.9.17.
BEVERIDGE William MM Pte 36975 11th Royal Scots
BEVERIDGE William MM L/Cpl S/6813 Seaforth Highlanders
BEVERIDGE William MM L/Cpl 45522 23 Div Sig Coy Royal Engineers
BEVERIDGE William MM Pte 20941 5th Cameron Highlanders
BEVERIDGE William N. MM Cpl 492 C/106 Bde RFA
BEVERLEY Arthur MM L/Cpl 200053 West Riding Regt
BEVERLEY George MM Sjt 200709 West Riding Regt
BEVERLEY Harold MM Cpl 150185 102nd Bn Machine Gun Corps
BEVERLEY Lawrence MM Cpl 478059 456 Fd Coy Royal Engineers
BEVERLEY William G. MM+Bar Cpl 94613 Y/37 Med TM Bty RFA
BEVERLY Maxwell G. MM L/Cpl S/43097 1st Royal Highlanders
BEVIN Stanley A. MM Sjt 15126 Machine Gun Corps
BEVINGTON Arthur H. MM Sjt 47952 A/230 Bde RFA
BEVINGTON Eli Clyde MM Gnr 41758 G Bty RHA KIA 27.8.18.
BEVINGTON George MM Sjt 241475 2/6th Royal Warwickshire Regt
BEVINGTON George MM L/Cpl 31244 2nd York & Lancaster Regt KIA 21.3.18.
BEVIS Severn P. MM CQMS 345429 24th Royal Welsh Fusiliers
BEW George S. MM Pte 203021 1st Middlesex Regt
BEWES John T. MM Spr 62903 38 Div Sig Coy Royal Engineers
BEWICK Ernest MM L/Sjt 27/60 8th Northumberland Fusiliers
BEWICK James MM Dvr 751627 A/250 Bde RFA
BEWICK Lloyd MM Bdr 40479 RGA
BEWICK P. MM Cpl 337929 RGA
BEWICKE Sydney MM 2nd Cpl 7856 Royal Engineers
BEWLEY H.F. MM Pte 252933 London Regt
BEWS George MM Pte 16954 13th Durham Light Infantry
BEWSEY Edward John MM L/Cpl 281390 4th London Regt
BEWSEY Frank Victor MM Sjt 47637 A/50 Bde RFA KIA 15.11.17.
BEWSEY Panalir Harry MM L/Cpl 10488 2nd Yorkshire Light Infantry KIA 18.2.18.
BEWSHEA Percy E. MM L/Cpl 266841 Gordon Highlanders
BEWSHER Stanley De M. MM Pte 18048 East Lancashire Regt
BEXON P. MM Dvr 88706 40 Bde RFA
BEXON William MM Cpl 9/15139 Leicestershire Regt
BEY Peter K. MM Gnr 242920 C/317 Bde RFA
BEYER Richard G. MM Pte 32527 34 Fd Amb RAMC
BEYNON Edwin J. MM Bdr 3249 A/110 Bde RFA
BEYNON Frank Warmington MM Sjt Wheeler 800101 A/230 Bde RFA
BEYNON Frederick C. MM Pte 23021 Wiltshire Regt
BEYNON Ivor O. MM Cpl 10823 2nd Welsh Regt
BIBBINS Henry MM Dvr L/27417 27 Bty 35 Bde RFA
BIBBY Alexander MM Pte 59521 Liverpool Regt
BIBBY Alfred MM Pte 16866 2nd King's Own Scottish Borderers
BIBBY Benjamin MM Pte 20421 1st Highland Light Infantry
BIBBY David MM L/Cpl 45349 4th Essex Regt
BIBBY George MM Pte 23636 East Lancashire Regt
BIBBY H. MM Pte 1715 4th West Riding Regt
BIBBY John MM Sjt 83379 Machine Gun Corps
BIBBY Thomas MM+Bar Pte 21822 North Lancashire Regt
BIBBY Tom MM Pte 12010 19th Manchester Regt
BIBBY William MM Pte R/8643 1st King's Royal Rifle Corps
BIBBY William MM Cpl 200707 North Lancashire Regt
BIBBY William MM Cpl 16544 RFA
BICHAN John MM Pte 267189 Seaforth Highlanders
BICHAN Robert MM Pte 55404 10th Royal Fusiliers
BICHENER Percy W. MM Pte 68572 Royal Fusiliers
BICK Harry MM Cpl H/7371 15th Hussars
BICK James MM Sjt Fitter 830050 B/241 Bde RFA
BICKELL Francis G. MM Pte 14138 1st Middlesex Regt
BICKELL Philip J. MM CQMS 64244 108 Coy Labour Corps
BICKENS Eugene MM Gnr 95489 66 Div Ammn Col RFA
BICKER David MM Pte 41570 7/8th Royal Inniskilling Fusiliers
BICKER William MM Pte 240468 1/5th Royal Scots Fusiliers
BICKERDIKE Fred MM Gnr 80463 244 Siege Bty RGA
BICKERS Edward C. MM Cpl 48546 Royal Berkshire Regt
BICKERS William Philip MM Pte 43494 9th Royal Irish Rifles DOW 23.3.18.
BICKERSTAFF Arthur MM Sjt S/13149 12th Rifle Brigade DOW 28.3.18.
BICKERSTAFF Charles Walter MM Cpl 10335 1st Middlesex Regt KIA 15.7.16.
BICKERSTAFF James MM Pte 25596 1st Grenadier Guards
BICKERSTAFFE Edmund J. MM Pte 2126 Yorkshire Light Infantry
BICKERSTAFFE Edwin MM Pte 44581 12th Manchester Regt DOW 8.9.18.
BICKERSTAFFE William MM L/Cpl 18/1360 West Yorkshire Regt
BICKERTON Charles MM Cpl 325981 9th Durham Light Infantry
BICKERTON Joseph MM Sjt 33632 RAMC
BICKERTON Robert MM Sjt 240459 5th Royal Lancaster Regt
BICKERTON William MM 2nd Cpl 52743 87 Fd Coy Royal Engineers
BICKFORD Arscott Fitzwilliam MM Pte 3/7184 9th Devonshire Regt
BICKFORD William C. MM Pte 21485 3rd Coldstream Guards
BICKLEY Arthur MM Gnr 544 132 Hy Bty RGA
BICKMORE E. MM Pte 18228 1st Essex Regt
BICKMORE William Edward "MM,MID" Sjt 98496 C/303 Bde RFA
BICKNELL Alfred MM+Bar Cpl 95153 D/63 Bde RFA KIA 5.9.18.
BICKNELL C.F. MM L/Cpl 497272 RAMC
BICKNELL Edward MM Pte 17922 Hampshire Regt
BICKNELL Fred MM Bdr 2967 B/241 Bde RFA
BICKNELL Oscar D. MM Sjt M2/020316 594 MT Coy Army Service Corps
BICKNELL Thomas M. MM Pte 40198 Royal West Surrey Regt
BICKNELL William C. MM Cpl 36921 1st Royal Welsh Fusiliers
BIDDISCOMBE Arthur MM Cpl 240259 Somerset Light Infantry
BIDDISCOMBE R. MM Pte 541 Royal Irish Regt
BIDDLE Albert Edmund MM Pte 85656 148 Coy Machine Gun Corps KIA 9.10.17.
BIDDLE Ernest Richard MM Cpl 118322 X/6 Med TM Bty RFA
BIDDLE George "DCM,MM" Sjt 510019 2/2nd(London)Fd Amb RAMC
BIDDLE George MM Pte 10800 2nd Essex Regt DOW 3.5.17.
BIDDLE Joseph MM Cpl S/2742 3rd Rifle Brigade
BIDDLE Percy Henry MM Gnr 84615 169 Siege Bty RGA
BIDDLE William "MC,DCM+Bar,MM+Bar" CSM 5820 1st Gloucestershire Regt
BIDDLE William Albert MM Sjt 12507 9th Devonshire Regt KIA 5.10.18.
BIDDLECOMBE George MM Pte 33636 Devonshire Regt
BIDDLECOMBE Thomas E. MM Pte 23394 Hampshire Regt
BIDDLES George T. MM Pte 202817 Highland Light Infantry
BIDDLES Thomas E. MM Bdr 159650 RFA
BIDDULPH Leonard James Edward MM Pte 1691 1st London Regt
BIDE Walter A. MM Cpl 12133 12th Somerset Light Infantry
BIDE William Henry MM Pte A/252 1st King's Royal Rifle Corps
BIDEWELL E.R. MM Cpl 7467 Royal Air Force
BIDWELL Arthur John MM Pte 16622 2nd Suffolk Regt KIA 21.8.18.
BIDWELL William B. MM Sjt M2/105461 Army Service Corps
BIELBY F. MM Gnr L/12373 RFA
BIERTON Herbert E. MM Sjt 19074 Machine Gun Corps
BIFFEN Arthur MM L/Cpl G/62300 9th Royal Fusiliers
BIFFEN Ernest MM Pte 241061 1st Royal West Kent Regt
BIFFIN Arthur MM Cpl 18294 Yorkshire Light Infantry
BIFFIN Sidney R. MM Pte S/10309 2nd Seaforth Highlanders
BIGG Arthur MM Pte 49528 1/4th Northamptonshire Regt
BIGG Charles Robert MM Pte R/35664 1st King's Royal Rifle Corps

BIGGADIKE Richard "MM,MID" L/Cpl 4884 2nd Dragoon Guards
BIGGAR George MM Pte 25922 12th Highland Light Infantry
BIGGAR Thomas MM Cpl 40126 12th Royal Scots KIA 16.7.18.
BIGGIN George H. MM Cpl 19700 9th Scottish Rifles
BIGGIN Thomas MM Pte 11671 1st Grenadier Guards
BIGGINS William H. MM L/Cpl 476748 Royal Engineers
BIGGLESTON Charles S. MM Gnr 119825 RGA
BIGGS Albert MM Sjt 5754 2nd Oxf & Bucks Light Infantry
BIGGS Alfred R. MM Bdr 4866 RGA
BIGGS Alphonsus MM Cpl 20355 10 Fd Amb RAMC
BIGGS Arthur MM Cpl 15820 9th West Yorkshire Regt
BIGGS Edwin MM Spr 132865 179 Tunnelling Coy Royal Engineers
BIGGS GeorgeA. MM Gnr 91476 8 Div Ammn Col RFA
BIGGS James MM Pte 18426 11th Notts & Derby Regt
BIGGS John J. MM Pte 19107 8th Somerset Light Infantry
BIGGS Joseph MM Sjt 45552 5 Bde RFA
BIGGS Mackay Heriot MM Pte 33785 14th Royal Warwickshire Regt
BIGGS Ralph MM Cpl 265852 2/1st Buckinghamshire Bn Oxf & Bucks Light Infantry
BIGGS Robert J. MM Pte 4515 4th Hussars
BIGGS Walter MM BSM 53008 64 Bty 5 Bde RFA
BIGGS William MM Cpl 34012 24th Royal Welsh Fusiliers
BIGGS William Edward MM Pte 206176 23rd Middlesex Regt
BIGLEY Reginald D. MM Cpl 76812 14th Royal Welsh Fusiliers
BIGLEY William MM Cpl 5724 1st East Yorkshire Regt
BIGMORE George P. MM Pte 23903 East Lancashire Regt
BIGNELL Charles MM Sjt 935284 RFA
BIGNELL Charles "MM,MID" Sjt 7570 5th Oxf & Bucks Light Infantry
BIGNELL Frank MM Pte 5263 8th East Kent Regt
BIGNELL Frank MM Pte 10966 1st Grenadier Guards
BIGNELL George F. MM Pte 10037 Leicestershire Regt
BIGNELL Walter MM Cpl 2453 Middlesex Regt
BIGRIGG Jonathan "MM+Bar,MID" Sjt 240485 1/5th Border Regt KIA 12.1.17.
BIGWOOD William E. MM Sjt 8506 Hampshire Regt
BILBY Henry MM Sjt 8298 6th Royal West Kent Regt
BILHAM J.E. MM L/Cpl 16213 Royal Sussex Regt
BILL H. MM L/Cpl 421054 3 Fd Amb RAMC
BILL Henry "DCM,MM" L/Cpl 2112 Leinster Regt
BILL John McC. MM L/Sjt 17/878 15th Royal Irish Rifles
BILLAM J.W.A. MM S/Sjt 508300 RAMC
BILLETT George MM Pte G/5723 9th Royal Fusiliers
BILLETT Sidney A. MM Sjt 71807 42 Bde RFA
BILLETT William C. MM Pte 242292 Middlesex Regt
BILLING Frederick H. "DCM,MM" Sjt 13029 4th Grenadier Guards
BILLING George MM Cpl 2672 2/1st London Regt
BILLING George "MM,MSM" Sjt 8649 9th West Yorkshire Regt
BILLING R.D. MM L/Cpl 6278 Royal Sussex Regt
BILLING Sidney MM Cpl 175125 1/1st Yorkshire Dragoons Yeo
BILLINGE Arthur "DCM,MM" Sjt 676452 D/285 Bde RFA
BILLINGHAM George John MM Cpl 593009 2/18th London Regt
BILLINGHAM Henry J. MM Pte 421588 10th London Regt
BILLINGHAM John E. MM Cpl 204028 8th Worcestershire Regt
BILLINGHAM Reginald S. MM Cpl 5445 HAC
BILLINGHAM Stanley MM Pte 70647 Notts & Derby Regt
BILLINGHURST Alfred Noel MM Sjt 28434 7th Shropshire Light Infantry
BILLINGHURST William J. MM Spr 134958 Royal Engineers
BILLINGS Alfred C. MM L/Cpl 17790 Royal Sussex Regt
BILLINGS Alfred J. MM Cpl 13655 Suffolk Regt
BILLINGS Charles G. MM Pte G/2411 8th Royal West Kent Regt
BILLINGS Harry MM Pte 40024 North Staffordshire Regt
BILLINGS Thomas MM Cpl 51570 West Yorkshire Regt
BILLINGTON Charles MM Sjt L/17597 A/170 Bde RFA
BILLINGTON Ernest MM Pte 34185 Royal Warwickshire Regt
BILLINGTON Frank MM Dvr 77387 31 Bde RFA
BILLINGTON Frederick MM Pte 21413 Wiltshire Regt
BILLINGTON Henry MM Bdr 745871 RFA
BILLINGTON J. MM Dvr 700075 80 Bty 15 Bde RFA
BILLINGTON James MM Pte 240022 1/5th York & Lancaster Regt
BILLINGTON Joseph MM Sjt 10743 6th Border Regt
BILLINGTON Louis W. MM Sjt 9921 1/5th London Regt
BILLINGTON Wilfred MM Gnr Sig L/15900 A/71 Bde RFA
BILLINGTON William MM Pte 35956 1st Bedfordshire Regt
BILLINGTON William MM Pte 18731 9th Leicestershire Regt
BILLINGTON William H.T. MM L/Cpl 13003 Shropshire Light Infantry
BILLMAN George MM Pte 27820 6th Royal Dublin Fusiliers
BILLMORE Charles MM Pte G/37516 11th Royal West Surrey Regt
BILLS Arthur MM Pte 267359 6th West Riding Regt
BILLS Ernest MM Bdr L/26538 D/155 Bde RFA
BILLS Thomas "DCM,MM,CdiG(It)" CSM 8479 1st South Staffordshire Regt
BILLSON Arthur C. MM Sjt 200077 7th Middlesex Regt
BILSBOROUGH Arthur MM Cpl 71741 135 Fd Amb RAMC
BILSBORROW William MM Cpl L/16277 B/149 Bde RFA DOW 2.5.18.
BILSON Albert MM Pte 16771 5th Notts & Derby Regt
BILSTON Henry Augustus Morris MM Cpl 40934 27 Siege Bty RGA
BILTON Ernest MM L/Sjt 305892 1/8th Notts & Derby Regt
BILTON Frank MM L/Cpl 1190 Lincolnshire Regt
BILTON Henry MM Pte M2/131351 Third Army Tpt & Sup Col Army Service Corps
BILTON Herbert MM Cpl 481804 62 Div Sig Coy Royal Engineers
BILTON Joseph F. MM Pnr 104110 Royal Engineers
BILTON Sidney P. MM L/Cpl 9007 1st South Wales Borderers
BILTON Stewart MM Pte 201431 1/4th Seaforth Highlanders KIA 26-29.10.18
BILTON Thomas MM L/Sjt 325356 Durham Light Infantry
BILTON William MM Bdr 151482 381 Siege Bty RGA
BILTON William "MM,MID" Cpl 41832 Royal Engineers
BIMPSON Harry MM Pte 10271 2nd South Lancashire Regt
BINCH Hugh MM Pte 206494 Labour Corps DOW 20.8.18.
BINDER Arthur Robert MM Sjt PS/1902 16th B Coy Middlesex Regt KIA 31.5.17.
BINDER John H. MM Sjt 147415 238 Army Tps Coy Royal Engineers
BINDLEY Frederick Thomas MM Pte 15988 1/5th Leicestershire Regt
BINDLEY Leonard Patrick MM Cpl 201504 1/4th Norfolk Regt
BINDLOSS Charles MM L/Sjt 50615 Middlesex Regt
BINDON Cuthbert J. MM Pte 70601 48th Bn Machine Gun Corps
BINDON W.W. MM Pte 695075 London Regt
BINEDELL J.H. MM Pte 339463 RAMC
BINES Jack "MM,MSM" Sjt 15615 288 Siege Bty RGA
BINFIELD Thomas MM Cpl 11563 16th Lancashire Fusiliers
BING Alfred MM Dvr 80540 A/63 Bde RFA KIA 17.8.18.
BING Frank J. MM Pte 513684 14th London Regt
BING Leonard MM Sjt G/707 6th East Kent Regt KIA 4.8.16.
BING Sydney H. "MM,MSM" L/Cpl 101633 Royal Engineers
BINGHAM Albert MM Sjt 242400 1/4th York & Lancaster Regt
BINGHAM Alexander MM Cpl 412059 Royal Engineers
BINGHAM Arthur David MM 2nd Cpl 40005 61 Fd Coy Royal Engineers
BINGHAM Britton C. MM Pte 16586 Royal Sussex Regt
BINGHAM Charles A. MM Bdr 54845 RFA
BINGHAM George MM Pte S/12885 8/10th Gordon Highlanders
BINGHAM George MM Pte 18036 Liverpool Regt
BINGHAM James MM Sjt 38741 35 Bde RFA
BINGHAM John R. MM Sjt 42492 Royal Engineers
BINGHAM Joseph MM Pte 21139 Royal Dublin Fusiliers
BINGHAM Melville MM Pte 20910 2nd Dragoon Guards
BINGHAM Tom MM Pte 202093 2/5th West Yorkshire Regt
BINGHAM William MM Sjt 12103 4th Worcestershire Regt
BINGHAM William MM L/Cpl 7785 Notts & Derby Regt
BINGHAM William Charles MM Cpl 1743 1st North Lancashire Regt KIA 17.8.16.
BINGHAM William J. MM Pte 17/1509 Royal Irish Rifles
BINGLEY Andrew MM Pte A/200156 3rd King's Royal Rifle Corps
BINGS Henry MM L/Cpl 34282 York & Lancaster Regt
BINION Charles E. MM Cpl 62873 RAMC
BINKS Albert MM+Bar Pte 240850 1/5th North Lancashire Regt
BINKS Alfred Ernest MM Cpl 10579 10th Essex Regt
BINKS Arthur MM Pte 33642 HMHS 'Britannic' RAMC Died 21.11.16.
BINKS Bernard Edward MM Pte 10768 7th Border Regt KIA 8.6.18.
BINKS Ernest MM Pte 77349 99 Fd Amb RAMC
BINKS Harry MM Pte 7556 Yorkshire Regt
BINKS Herbert MM L/Cpl 18187 8th Royal West Kent Regt
BINKS Robert MM L/Cpl 457401 Royal Engineers
BINKS Roland Charles MM Pte 22862 Lincolnshire Regt
BINKS Stanley J. MM Gnr L/36211 RFA
BINLY J.H. MM Gnr 69648 Tank Corps
BINNEE John MM Cpl 771081 RFA
BINNEY Edward MM Pte 35418 RAMC
BINNEY Ernest MM Sjt 1971 1/5th York & Lancaster Regt
BINNIE Alexander C. MM Gnr 243341 C/156 Bde RFA
BINNIE James Y. MM Pte 275239 1/4th Royal Scots
BINNIE John MM Pte M1/08903 1 Base MT Depot Army Service Corps
BINNIE Richard MM Pte 23074 2nd Royal Scots

BINNIE W. MM L/Cpl 3271 Arg & Suth Highlanders
BINNIE William "DCM,MM" Cpl 276041 1/7th Arg & Suth Highlanders
BINNS Albert MM Spr 6830 Royal Engineers
BINNS Arthur MM Pte 15/1137 15th West Yorkshire Regt
BINNS Charles MM Cpl 428376 Royal Engineers
BINNS David MM Pte 11569 8th Yorkshire Regt
BINNS George Edward MM Pte 24795 13th Royal Fusiliers DOW 6.3.18.
BINNS Harry G. MM Pte 15465 10th West Riding Regt
BINNS James H. MM Pte 81373 8th West Yorkshire Regt
BINNS James T. MM Gnr 686689 RFA
BINNS John MM Sjt R/5231 King's Royal Rifle Corps
BINNS Joseph MM Pte 24162 10th West Riding Regt DOW 22.9.17.
BINNS Leslie MM Sjt 12913 Yorkshire Light Infantry
BINNS Raymond M. MM Cpl 52517 Cheshire Regt
BINNS S. MM Pte 38101 9th Essex Regt
BINNS T. MM Pte 201586 Royal Lancaster Regt
BINSTEAD Charles MM Cpl 17886 15th Hampshire Regt
BINSTEAD Charles W. MM Spr 159032 Royal Engineers
BINSTEAD Ernest MM Pte 2432 1/4th Royal Sussex Regt
BINSTEAD Harold George MM Pte 42132 1st Essex Regt
BINYON Herbert C. MM Pte 589158 17th London Regt
BIRBECK John MM+Bar Cpl 63409 RFA
BIRBECK Joseph MM Pte 9547 5th West Yorkshire Regt
BIRBECK T.A. MM Pte 43454 15th Royal Irish Rifles
BIRCH A. "DCM,MM" L/Sjt SP/87828 17th Royal Fusiliers
BIRCH Arthur MM Sjt 293608 136 Hy Bty RGA
BIRCH C. MM Sjt 15/97 15th West Yorkshire Regt
BIRCH Charles MM L/Cpl 32509 Royal Lancaster Regt
BIRCH Charles Ralph MM Cpl 17021 Liverpool Regt
BIRCH Ernest Albert MM Bdr 19581 39 Bde RFA
BIRCH Ernest H. MM Gnr 72316 RFA
BIRCH Frank MM Pte 19223 2nd Bedfordshire Regt KIA 21.9.18.
BIRCH Frank MM Pte 1884 Worcestershire Regt
BIRCH Frank A. MM Pte 205869 2/4th Royal West Surrey Regt
BIRCH Frederick MM Sjt 2279 Royal Engineers
BIRCH Frederick MM L/Sjt 242394 Worcestershire Regt
BIRCH George MM Pte 11532 4th Royal Fusiliers
BIRCH George F. MM Spr 242782 157 Fd Coy Royal Engineers
BIRCH George H.E. MM Pte 65412 39th Bn Machine Gun Corps
BIRCH Harold MM L/Cpl 10712 4th Liverpool Regt Died 20.2.19.
BIRCH Henry MM Pte 85612 29th Durham Light Infantry
BIRCH Henry MM+Bar Pte 26742 13th Liverpool Regt
BIRCH Henry J. MM Cpl 57475 5th Lancashire Fusiliers
BIRCH Herbert MM Pte 37327 8th East Lancashire Regt
BIRCH James MM+Bar L/Cpl 171612 Royal Engineers
BIRCH John MM Cpl 14097 10th Royal Fusiliers
BIRCH John Fruman MM L/Cpl DM2/163281 562 MT Coy Army Service Corps
BIRCH John H. MM 2nd Cpl 42896 70 Fd Coy Royal Engineers
BIRCH John H. MM Dvr 71861 A/317 Bde RFA
BIRCH Laurence W. MM 2nd Cpl 103982 E Corps Sig Coy Royal Engineers
BIRCH Richard MM L/Sjt 43614 4th Bedfordshire Regt
BIRCH Robert MM Pte 2502 2nd Royal Munster Fusiliers
BIRCH Robert MM Pte 36961 4th South Staffordshire Regt
BIRCH Samuel G. MM L/Cpl 72426 Machine Gun Corps
BIRCH Samuel M. MM Pte 66600 Royal Fusiliers
BIRCH Thomas George MM CQMS 8440 1st Gloucestershire Regt DOW 11.11.17.
BIRCH W.J. MM Pte 266918 Royal Warwickshire Regt
BIRCH Walter MM Sjt 9689 17 Bty 41 Bde RFA KIA 9.4.18.
BIRCH William MM Pte 241734 6th South Staffordshire Regt
BIRCH William MM L/Cpl 7194 1st Wiltshire Regt
BIRCH William MM Bdr 38872 RFA
BIRCH William Henry MM L/Cpl 100665 20 Army Troops Coy Royal Engineers
BIRCH William Rider MM Pte 20974 22nd Manchester Regt
BIRCHALL Alfred MM Pte 4721 2nd Lancashire Fusiliers
BIRCHALL Arthur MM L/Cpl 3381 North Staffordshire Regt
BIRCHALL George MM Pte 8469 11th Lancashire Fusiliers
BIRCHALL George MM Pte 21176 King's Own Scottish Borderers
BIRCHALL J. MM Cpl 341050 RAMC
BIRCHALL James MM Gnr 685885 RFA
BIRCHALL James MM Pte 41385 RAMC
BIRCHALL James E. MM Pte 91004 1st Liverpool Regt
BIRCHALL Joseph MM Sjt 354064 3 Fd Amb RAMC
BIRCHALL William "DCM,MM" Sjt 8569 1st South Staffordshire Regt
BIRCHALL William MM Pte 26871 South Lancashire Regt
BIRCHALL William V. MM Pte 26600 10th Shropshire Light Infantry
BIRCHAM Joseph MM Spr 107096 40 Div Sig Coy Royal Engineers
BIRCHENALL Walter O. MM S/Sjt 513 Army Veterinary Corps
BIRCHENOUGH Joe MM Pte 201575 5th West Riding Regt
BIRCHLEY Jason MM Dvr 47053 RFA
BIRCUMSHAW J.H. MM L/Cpl 13385 4th Bn Machine Gun Corps
BIRD Albert MM Sjt 19100 Royal Fusiliers
BIRD Albert MM Sjt 8973 1st Coldstream Guards KIA 27.9.18.
BIRD Albert H. "DCM,MM" L/Sjt 14621 12th Gloucestershire Regt
BIRD Alfred MM Cpl 202016 1st Worcestershire Regt
BIRD Arthur B. MM Cpl 4858 Rifle Brigade
BIRD Arthur William MM Cpl M2/136331 Army Service Corps
BIRD Cecil MM Cpl 1142 20th London Regt
BIRD Charles MM Cpl 469 17th Lancers
BIRD Charles E. MM Pte 253455 1/3rd London Regt
BIRD Charles G. MM Sjt 46290 Royal Engineers
BIRD Charles Henry MM Pte 203138 1/6th North Staffordshire Regt
BIRD Charles K. MM Cpl 625426 HAC
BIRD Charles William MM Pte 89025 58 Fd Amb RAMC
BIRD Clifford J. MM Spr 8511 Royal Engineers
BIRD David MM Gnr 29719 115 Hy Bty RGA
BIRD Edward MM Dvr L/46311 B/190 Bde RFA
BIRD Edwin MM Sjt 5541 6th York & Lancaster Regt
BIRD Ernest F. MM QMS Armourer T/1389 Army Ordnance Corps
BIRD Frank Herbert MM Sjt T3/031325 21 Reserve Park Army Service Corps
BIRD Frank Sealey MM Pte M2/193464 Army Service Corps
BIRD Fred MM Bdr 56275 RFA
BIRD Frederick MM Pte 24835 23rd Middlesex Regt
BIRD Frederick MM Pte 9766 1st South Staffordshire Regt
BIRD Frederick MM Pte 8650 Royal Warwickshire Regt
BIRD Frederick C. MM+Bar Sjt 680181 74 Bde RFA
BIRD Frederick Edmund MM Cpl 9400 1st Lincolnshire Regt
BIRD G. MM Pte 33127 Essex Regt
BIRD George MM Spr 66576 Royal Engineers
BIRD George MM+Bar L/Bdr 43465 C/50 Bde RFA
BIRD George A. MM Pte 1727 10th Royal Warwickshire Regt
BIRD Harry MM Cpl 51483 1/6th Cheshire Regt
BIRD Henry G. MM Pte 439216 RAMC
BIRD Henry S. MM Gnr 127217 RGA
BIRD Henry Thomas MM Pte 8638 2/4th Royal West Surrey Regt
BIRD Herbert H. MM Spr 62190 105 Fd Coy Royal Engineers
BIRD J. MM Pte 720409 London Regt
BIRD James MM L/Cpl 5844 1st Wiltshire Regt
BIRD James MM Pte 2033 7th Royal Sussex Regt KIA 7.7.16.
BIRD Jesse MM Pte 17754 5th Northamptonshire Regt
BIRD John MM Pte 14047 24th Manchester Regt
BIRD John A. MM Pte 25182 Norfolk Regt
BIRD John M. MM Cpl 8914 5th South Staffordshire Regt
BIRD John V. MM Pte 13156 6th Dorsetshire Regt
BIRD John W. MM Pte 26808 Grenadier Guards
BIRD Joseph MM Pte 47539 7th Leicestershire Regt
BIRD Joseph MM+Bar Sjt 240047 North Staffordshire Regt
BIRD Lawrence A. MM Sjt 13021 1st East Surrey Regt
BIRD Norman I. MM Pte 28650 Machine Gun Corps
BIRD Percy MM Sjt 33474 RGA
BIRD Peter MM Cpl 265802 Gordon Highlanders
BIRD R. MM Cpl 18427 Royal West Kent Regt
BIRD Robert MM Pte 201347 Leicestershire Regt
BIRD Samuel MM Pte 58812 Machine Gun Corps
BIRD Samuel MM Pte 351550 1/9th Royal Scots
BIRD Stanley MM Pte 26327 1st East Surrey Regt
BIRD Stanley MM Pte 325444 1/1st Cambridgeshire Regt
BIRD Thomas MM Pte 34208 10th Shropshire Light Infantry
BIRD Thomas W. MM L/Cpl 18908 Oxf & Bucks Light Infantry
BIRD Walter MM Pte 43397 8th West Yorkshire Regt
BIRD William MM Pte 4228 7th East Surrey Regt DOW 26.7.16.
BIRD William MM+Bar Bdr 73096 8 Bde RFA
BIRD William MM Pte 19003 7th South Staffordshire Regt
BIRD William MM L/Cpl 8234 2nd Border Regt att RE.
BIRD William Alfred MM Sjt 1331 7th A Coy East Surrey Regt KIA 24.1.18.
BIRD William B. MM Sjt 18611 Northamptonshire Regt
BIRD William C. MM Sjt 281043 4th London Regt
BIRD William Charles MM L/Cpl 18291 Machine Gun Corps
BIRD William E. MM Cpl 202691 Somerset Light Infantry
BIRD William J. MM Cpl 99959 RFA
BIRDSALL Charles MM Cpl 14461 12th West Yorkshire Regt
BIRDSALL Dalton MM Sjt T3/026724 Army Service Corps
BIRDSALL Harold MM Gnr 96140 D/71 Bde RFA

BIRDSALL Walter MM Bdr 34352 A/123 Bde RFA
BIRDSEY William MM Cpl 220357 1st Royal Berkshire Regt
BIRKBY George E. MM Pte 66389 Machine Gun Corps
BIRKBY Linford MM Pte 22667 110 Fd Amb RAMC
BIRKETT Arthur Bolton "DCM,MM" Sjt 8931 1/4th Royal Lancaster Regt
BIRKETT Charley MM CSM 14/367 York & Lancaster Regt
BIRKETT James MM Pte 266338 6th West Riding Regt
BIRKETT Joseph MM Sjt 2277 Liverpool Regt
BIRKETT Lambert W. "DCM,MM" CSM 200010 3rd Worcestershire Regt
BIRKETT Matthew MM Sjt 8764 1st King's Royal Rifle Corps KIA 22.8.18.
BIRKETT Patrick MM Pte 16757 Royal Irish Fusiliers
BIRKIN Reginald "DCM,MM" Cpl Fitter 201597 275 Bde RFA DOW 18.4.18.
BIRKINSHAW George MM Cpl 201886 West Riding Regt
BIRKINSHAW Jesse MM L/Cpl 20450 Royal Highlanders
BIRKINSHAW Robert Smith "DCM,MM,MM(F),DSC(USA)" CSM 12077 1st West Yorkshire Regt
BIRKINSHAW Walter MM Cpl 13/146 York & Lancaster Regt
BIRKITT Arthur Bolton MM Sjt 8931 1st Royal Lancaster Regt
BIRKMYRE Joseph H. MM L/Cpl 17268 12th Royal Irish Rifles
BIRKS Frank A. MM L/Cpl 27955 1st Duke of Cornwall's LI
BIRKS George Joseph MM Pte 14618 North Staffordshire Regt
BIRKS Harry MM Pte 301177 2nd Manchester Regt
BIRKS John MM L/Cpl 40985 Northumberland Fusiliers
BIRKS William MM Pte 38706 6th York & Lancaster Regt
BIRLEY Alfred MM Sjt 6746 1st Gloucestershire Regt
BIRLEY William MM Cpl 13149 1st Yorkshire Light Infantry
BIRMINGHAM James MM Sjt 305273 1/8th Lancashire Fusiliers
BIRMINGHAM John MM Sjt 18314 Royal Munster Fusiliers
BIRMINGHAM Thomas MM Gnr 1652 23 Siege Bty RGA
BIRMINGHAM Walter William MM Sjt 9517 7th Royal West Surrey Regt KIA 25.10.18.
BIRNIE Alexander MM Pte 10525 2nd Scots Guards DOW 14.12.17.
BIRNIE Edward MM Cpl 200013 'A' Bn Tank Corps
BIRNIE James MM Pte 13681 15th Highland Light Infantry
BIRNIE John "DCM,MM" Sjt 48366 30 Bty 39 Bde RFA
BIRNIE Robert Charles MM Sjt Drummer 7893 12th Middlesex Regt KIA 6.8.17.
BIRNIE William MM Pte 452 10/11th Highland Light Infantry KIA 28.4.17.
BIRRELL Alexander MM Dvr T1/1217 3 Lab Coy Army Service Corps
BIRRELL David MM Dvr 46213 A/89 Bde RFA
BIRRELL George "DCM,MM" Sjt S/6579 8th Royal Highlanders
BIRRELL Robert MM Sjt 17351 Machine Gun Corps
BIRRELL Thomas Wilson Lushman MM Sjt 22656 King's Own Scottish Borderers
BIRRELL William MM L/Cpl 265071 7th Scottish Rifles KIA 20.5.18.
BIRRELL William MM L/Bdr 56270 366 Bty 117 Bde RFA
BIRSE John MM+Bar Pte 32146 RAMC
BIRSS Hugh MM Cpl 249561 51 Div Sig Coy Royal Engineers
BIRT Albert J. MM Cpl 832003 C/306 Bde RFA
BIRT Alfred W. MM L/Cpl 24829 2nd Hampshire Regt
BIRT Edgar MM Cpl 13255 A/87 Bde RFA
BIRT Oliver MM Gnr 145401 250 Siege Bty RGA
BIRTLES Frederick MM L/Cpl 235043 1st North Staffordshire Regt
BIRTLES Norman "DCM,MM" Sjt 36839 B/78 Bde RFA
BIRTLES Samuel MM Pte 11327 Liverpool Regt
BIRTLES William MM Pte 8797 1st Gordon Highlanders KIA 30.8.18.
BIRTWHISTLE Harry MM Pte 202175 6th Leicestershire Regt KIA 29.5.18.
BIRTWISTLE J.W. MM Cpl 5434 East Lancashire Regt
BIRTWISTLE John W. MM Pte 300028 Lancashire Fusiliers
BIRTWISTLE Robert H. MM Pte 101068 12 Fd Amb RAMC
BISBY Ernest MM Cpl 72497 Machine Gun Corps
BISCOE F.A. MM Air Mech 1 7443 Royal Flying Corps
BISCOE James William MM Bdr 71912 18 Bde RFA DOW 25.8.18.
BISGOOD Harold T. MM Sjt 3254 2nd London Regt
BISH Albert Charles MM Gnr 88744 13 Heavy Bty RGA
BISHOP Albert MM Pte 51301 RAMC
BISHOP Albert E. MM Bdr 11160 27 Bty 35 Bde RFA
BISHOP Albert Edwin MM Pte M2/074090 Att 76 Fd Amb Army Service Corps
BISHOP Alfred F. MM Pte 9132 10th Royal West Kent Regt
BISHOP Alfred MM Pte 26010 1/4th West Riding Regt
BISHOP Alfred C. MM Cpl 420726 10th London Regt
BISHOP Andrew MM Pte 201605 1/7th Worcestershire Regt KIA 16.8.17.
BISHOP Arthur MM+Bar Cpl 4314 Royal West Surrey Regt
BISHOP Bradley MM Cpl 6/17159 6th South Wales Borderers
BISHOP Charles MM Pte 201813 6th Bn Tank Corps
BISHOP Charles MM Pte 3002 7th Royal Sussex Regt
BISHOP Charles G. "DCM,MM,MID" Pte 12569 4th Royal Fusiliers
BISHOP Charles Harold MM Cpl 1270 15th London Regt
BISHOP Cyril MM Gnr 795825 RFA
BISHOP Edgar MM Pte 125658 18th Bn Machine Gun Corps
BISHOP Edgar H. MM CSM 13429 Army Cyclist Corps
BISHOP Edward B. MM Pte G/2961 Royal West Surrey Regt
BISHOP Edward C. MM Cpl 13806 3rd Royal Fusiliers
BISHOP Edwin MM Bdr 12671 28 Bde RFA
BISHOP Ernest MM Bdr 66365 A/107 Bde RFA
BISHOP Ernest C. MM Pte 6474 9 Gen Hosp RAMC
BISHOP Frederic William MM Sjt 56721 YY Cable Sect Royal Engineers
BISHOP Frederick MM Sjt 564 5th Royal Irish Regt
BISHOP Frederick MM Pte 50225 South Lancashire Regt
BISHOP Frederick MM Sjt 19074 15th Hampshire Regt
BISHOP Frederick C. "MM,MSM" Sjt 625566 Att 309 Siege Bty RGA HAC
BISHOP Frederick C. MM Cpl 60639 57 Bde RFA
BISHOP Frederick W. MM Cpl 9814 RAMC
BISHOP George MM S/Sjt Farrier 30751 38 Bde RFA
BISHOP George MM Sjt 89793 147 Army Tps Coy Royal Engineers
BISHOP George E. MM L/Cpl 17873 12th Royal Fusiliers
BISHOP George Robert MM L/Cpl 55962 296 Railway Coy Royal Engineers
BISHOP H.P. MM Dvr 28311 RFA
BISHOP Harold MM Sjt 20480 RFA
BISHOP Henry Charles MM CSM 10371 2nd Middlesex Regt
BISHOP Henry Robert MM Sjt 20616 Machine Gun Corps
BISHOP Henry W. MM Sjt 74510 52 Bty 15 Bde RFA
BISHOP James "DCM,MM" Cpl 8374 1st Gloucestershire Regt
BISHOP James MM Pte 400 11th Royal Sussex Regt DOW 23.10.16.
BISHOP James MM L/Cpl 21456 11th South Lancashire Regt
BISHOP John "DCM,MM,MSM" Sjt 12125 66 Div Sig Coy Royal Engineers
BISHOP John H. MM Sjt 52951 Royal Fusiliers
BISHOP John Richard MM Sjt 6744 2nd Royal Warwickshire Regt
BISHOP Joseph MM Pte 19113 Northamptonshire Regt
BISHOP Joseph MM L/Cpl 9293 2nd West Riding Regt
BISHOP Joseph MM L/Cpl 33304 Bedfordshire Regt
BISHOP L. MM Pte 31755 York & Lancaster Regt
BISHOP Langham MM Gnr 60578 221 Siege Bty RGA KIA 7.5.17.
BISHOP Leonard MM Cpl 9721 7th Royal Fusiliers
BISHOP Michael MM+Bar L/Cpl 11794 1st Irish Guards
BISHOP R. MM Pte 19091 Royal Irish Fusiliers
BISHOP Ralph Murdoch MM Cpl 20230 34th Bn Machine Gun Corps DOW 15.4.18.
BISHOP Reginald MM Sjt 8761 6th Dragoon Guards
BISHOP Samuel MM Cpl 7217 Machine Gun Corps
BISHOP Sidney Hollier MM Bdr 10385 84 Bty 11 Bde RFA
BISHOP Stanley G. "MM,MID" Sjt 8234 1st Royal West Kent Regt
BISHOP Thomas MM Cpl 13354 Machine Gun Corps
BISHOP Thomas W. MM Pte 4106 16th London Regt
BISHOP Victor MM Pte 204140 1st Dorsetshire Regt
BISHOP W.M. MM Pte 339377 RAMC
BISHOP Walter MM+Bar Sjt 7828 1st Dorsetshire Regt
BISHOP Walter H. MM S/Sjt 66149 RAMC
BISHOP Westley S. MM Pte 304745 5th London Regt
BISHOP William MM Sjt 53317 D/174 Bde RFA
BISHOP William G. MM Sjt 240055 Duke of Cornwall's LI
BISHOP William G. MM Cpl 86294 8th Bn Machine Gun Corps
BISHOP William H. MM Pte 201351 Northamptonshire Regt
BISHOP William Isaiah Dracon MM Pte 11428 1st Devonshire Regt
BISHOP Winterton Walter MM Pte 17089 1st Coldstream Guards
BISHOPP Stephen MM Pte 68461 17th Royal Fusiliers Died 7.5.18.
BISHORK A. "MM,MID" Sjt 13513 10th Essex Regt
BISHTON William MM Pte 30922 1st East Lancashire Regt
BISS Henry Charles MM CSM 9265 8th Somerset Light Infantry KIA 15.10.16.
BISS John MM Gnr 13838 B/152 Bde RFA
BISS Walter J. MM Sjt 29649 RGA
BISSEL Arthur MM Sjt 15495 2/4th York & Lancaster Regt
BISSELL Benjamin MM Gnr 76752 RFA
BISSENDEN W. MM Pte 2757 RAMC

BISSET Donald "DCM,MM" Sjt 3130 6th Royal Irish Regt
BISSET George MM L/Cpl 265371 1/6th Gordon Highlanders
BISSET John Henry MM L/Cpl 510805 1/14th London Regt
BISSET Thomas "DCM,MM" Sjt 240523 1/5th Gordon Highlanders
BISSETT Cecil C MM+Bar Gnr 650177 RFA
BISSETT Frank MM Pte G/26326 7th Royal Fusiliers
BISSETT James MM Pte 3607 Royal Highlanders
BISSETT P. MM Pte 4239 Royal Irish Rifles
BISSETT Thomas R.W. MM Pnr 406387 51 Div Sig Coy Royal Engineers
BISSETT William MM Pte 265453 Gordon Highlanders
BISSETT William MM Cpl 5932 5th Dragoon Guards
BISSETT William C. MM Pte 201891 Gordon Highlanders
BISSON Henry MM L/Cpl 6/3162 6th Royal Irish Regt KIA 9.9.16.
BISSUIRE William C. MM Pte 78400 RAMC
BITHELL Harold MM Pte 13452 9th Royal Welsh Fusiliers KIA 20.11.16.
BITHELL James William MM Pte 18170 5th Shropshire Light Infantry
BITHELL John MM Sjt 12189 11th Hampshire Regt
BITTLE William G. MM Sjt 57732 RGA
BITTLESTONE Lewis Alfred MM L/Sjt 2543 1/7th Durham Light Infantry DOW 5.10.18.
BITTON Barnet MM Sjt 2933 1st London Regt
BIZLEY Humphrey Arthur MM Pte 2201 Gloucestershire Regt
BIZLEY William E. "MM,MID" CSM 165 1/4th Gloucestershire Regt
BLABER Cecil E. MM Pte 11920 Royal West Surrey Regt
BLABER Lewis Victor MM Sjt 31786 208 Siege Bty RGA KIA 9.4.18.
BLABER William MM Cpl 2786 12th London Regt
BLACK A. MM Pte 7753 RAMC
BLACK Alexander "DCM,MM" L/Cpl S/16877 14th Royal Highlanders
BLACK Alexander MM Pte S/6618 Royal Highlanders
BLACK Alexander MM L/Sjt 6400 2nd Scots Guards Died 27.10.18.
BLACK Alfred "DCM,MM" Sjt 1994 MGC(Motors)
BLACK Arthur J. MM Sjt 200761 16th Bn Tank Corps
BLACK Ben MM Cpl 685109 RFA
BLACK Benjamin William MM Sjt 2983 1/8th Durham Light Infantry KIA 18.9.16.
BLACK C. MM Dvr 93139 RGA
BLACK Daniel MM Sjt 6276 1st Irish Guards
BLACK David "MM,MMV(It)" Pte 38157 1/4th Royal Berkshire Regt
BLACK David MM Gnr 228056 C/317 Bde RFA KIA 27.9.18.
BLACK David MM Pte 40633 Royal Scots Fusiliers
BLACK Donald MM Pte 292871 Royal Highlanders
BLACK Donald MM Pte 26440 5th Cameron Highlanders DOW 29.4.18.
BLACK Dugald MM Pte 4918 12th Arg & Suth Highlanders
BLACK Duncan MM Cpl 14042 2nd Royal Dublin Fusiliers KIA 21.3.18.
BLACK F.A. MM Pte 8946 8 CCS RAMC
BLACK Fred MM L/Cpl 42446 1/4th Leicestershire Regt
BLACK George "MM,MID" Gnr 52692 RGA
BLACK George H. "DCM,MM" Sjt 19378 1st Bn Machine Gun Corps
BLACK George M. MM Dvr 77240 5 Bde RHA
BLACK Henry W. MM Cpl 17130 RGA
BLACK Hugh L.S. MM Pte 59725 11th Royal Scots Fusiliers
BLACK J. MM Pte 276137 Arg & Suth Highlanders
BLACK James MM Cpl 9030 1st Northumberland Fusiliers
BLACK James MM Pte 516184 14th London Regt
BLACK James MM Sjt 47685 RFA
BLACK James MM L/Cpl 21010 2nd Royal Scots
BLACK James MM Pte M2/175954 Army Service Corps
BLACK James MM Sjt 201733 1/5th Highland Light Infantry DOW 1.12.17.
BLACK James MM Sjt 686744 RFA
BLACK James MM Sjt 346027 RGA
BLACK James MM Sjt 3222 11th Royal Scots
BLACK James MM Pte 14812 7th Border Regt
BLACK James Armstrong MM Gnr 15454 35 Bty 22 Bde RFA DOW 1.9.16.
BLACK James Joseph MM Cpl 14961 13th Liverpool Regt DOW 29.9.17.
BLACK Jeremiah MM 2nd Cpl 91973 185 Tunnelling Coy Royal Engineers
BLACK John MM Cpl 266463 11th Royal Scots Fusiliers
BLACK John MM Pte DM2/206586 Army Service Corps
BLACK John MM Pte 238095 5/6th Scottish Rifles KIA 22.9.18.
BLACK John MM Cpl 345749 14th Royal Highlanders
BLACK John MM Pte 5936 1st East Kent Regt
BLACK John MM Pte 8046 King's Own Scottish Borderers
BLACK John MM Spr 65552 126 Fd Coy Royal Engineers
BLACK John MM Cpl S/2880 Gordon Highlanders
BLACK John MM Pte 8899 12th Highland Light Infantry
BLACK John MM Gnr 7623 RFA
BLACK John MM Pte 30217 Border Regt
BLACK John A. MM Sjt 4430 6th Dragoons
BLACK Jonathan MM Dvr T4/251850 Army Service Corps
BLACK Max MM Pte 23007 17th Highland Light Infantry
BLACK Norman MM Pte S/11293 5th Cameron Highlanders
BLACK Robert MM Pte S/12571 10th Arg & Suth Highlanders
BLACK Robert MM L/Cpl 35596 56th Bn Machine Gun Corps
BLACK Robert MM+Bar Cpl 267426 9th Seaforth Highlanders
BLACK Robert MM Sjt 13441 15th Highland Light Infantry
BLACK Robert MM(270080 Manch)+Bar Pte 235838 2nd East Lancashire Regt
BLACK Samuel MM Sjt 240326 6th Devonshire Regt
BLACK Stewart Roger MM L/Cpl S/43415 Gordon Highlanders
BLACK Sydney MM L/Cpl 139661 Royal Engineers
BLACK Thomas MM Pte 113339 288 Coy Machine Gun Corps
BLACK Thomas MM Pte 325072 Lancashire Fusiliers
BLACK Thomas MM L/Cpl 6354 Northumberland Fusiliers
BLACK Tom MM L/Cpl 45064 7 Fd Coy Royal Engineers Died 12.10.18.
BLACK Walter Hugh Montgomery MM Pte 290625 1/8th Scottish Rifles DOW 29.10.18.
BLACK William MM Gnr 308315 RGA
BLACK William MM Pte 18798 Royal Scots
BLACK William MM Gnr 92791 RFA
BLACK William "MM,MSM" Sjt S2/9969 Army Service Corps
BLACK William MM Pte 27783 Liverpool Regt
BLACK William Christie "MM+Bar,CG(B)" Sjt 93842 41 Div Sig Coy Royal Engineers
BLACK William Hay MM Sjt 17834 Royal Scots
BLACK William J. MM Cpl 15/12566 15th Royal Irish Rifles
BLACK William James "MM,MIDx2" CSM 7846 2nd Coldstream Guards Died 9.2.18.
BLACKA James MM Spr 311451 Royal Engineers
BLACKA Sam MM Pte 202210 2/4th West Riding Regt
BLACKA William Tillotson MM Spr 217533 Fifth Army Sig Coy Royal Engineers
BLACKABY Ewart Walker MM Cpl 530217 2/15th London Regt
BLACKADDER Charles MM+Bar Sjt 15342 5 Fd Coy Royal Engineers
BLACKALL Frederick MM L/Bdr Sig 96779 263 Siege Bty RGA
BLACKBIRD Thomas S. MM Pte 20501 2nd York & Lancaster Regt
BLACKBOURN Ernest MM Dvr 14953 D/150 Bde RFA
BLACKBOURN Oliver H. MM Bdr 41349 RFA
BLACKBOURNE J.W. MM L/Cpl 40893 Lincolnshire Regt
BLACKBURN Adam MM Pte 39982 11th Lancashire Fusiliers
BLACKBURN Alfred MM Spr 268090 63 Div Sig Coy Royal Engineers
BLACKBURN Andrew Kennedy "MM,Medaille Militaire(F)" Pte S/13175 6th Cameron Highlanders KIA 1.8.17.
BLACKBURN Arthur Dean MM Sjt 266173 2/4th West Riding Regt KIA 30.8.18.
BLACKBURN Barnabas MM L/Sjt 240022 1st Royal West Kent Regt KIA 27.9.18.
BLACKBURN C. MM Cpl 23607 Royal Engineers
BLACKBURN Dennis MM Pte 572758 17th London Regt
BLACKBURN Edmund MM Pte 441 4th Bn GMGR
BLACKBURN Edward C. MM+Bar Sjt 13800 8th & 9th Norfolk Regt
BLACKBURN Edwin Duncan MM Pte 357915 10th Liverpool Regt KIA 30.11.17.
BLACKBURN Fred MM Pte 19/915 Northumberland Fusiliers
BLACKBURN Frederick MM+Bar Pte 34662 9th York & Lancaster Regt
BLACKBURN George MM CSM 238048 4th Gloucestershire Regt
BLACKBURN George W. MM Pte 1548 Lincolnshire Regt
BLACKBURN H. MM Sjt 7424 King's Royal Rifle Corps
BLACKBURN Harry MM L/Cpl 47545 1/5th Lancashire Fusiliers
BLACKBURN Harry MM L/Cpl B/21433 11th Highland Light Infantry
BLACKBURN Harry MM L/Sjt 2806 West Riding Regt
BLACKBURN J.T. MM Sjt 1258 Military Foot Police
BLACKBURN James MM Pte 13421 1st Lincolnshire Regt KIA 4.10.17.
BLACKBURN James MM Spr 97193 Royal Engineers
BLACKBURN John "DCM,MM+Bar" L/Cpl 106375 Royal Engineers
BLACKBURN John MM Gnr 59420 RGA
BLACKBURN John W. MM Sjt 935317 282 Bde RFA

BLACKBURN John William MM Pte 306327 10th West Yorkshire Regt KIA 15.8.18.
BLACKBURN Joseph MM L/Cpl 8233 11th Lancashire Fusiliers
BLACKBURN Richard MM Spr 37832 Royal Engineers
BLACKBURN Richard MM Pte 14/986 14th York & Lancaster Regt
BLACKBURN Robert "DCM,MM" Sjt 22949 2nd Grenadier Guards
BLACKBURN Thomas MM Pte 27952 Royal Inniskilling Fusiliers
BLACKBURN Thomas MM L/Bdr 8866 RFA
BLACKBURN Tom MM Pte 42628 Yorkshire Regt
BLACKBURN Wilfred MM L/Cpl 530 XV Corps Cyclist Bn Army Cyclist Corps
BLACKBURN William MM Cpl 65620 114 Siege Bty RGA
BLACKBURN William MM L/Bdr 66471 RFA
BLACKBURN William MM L/Cpl 1596 1/4th Northumberland Fusiliers
BLACKBURN William MM Pte 21679 East Lancashire Regt
BLACKEBY John W. MM Bdr 41519 RFA
BLACKER Harry MM Pte M/38380 Army Service Corps
BLACKER John MM Pte 3497 15th Royal Irish Rifles
BLACKETT Bertie W. MM L/Cpl 22293 11th Northumberland Fusiliers
BLACKETT John T. MM Pte 7208 5th Dorsetshire Regt
BLACKETT Norman MM Spr 281693 61 Div Sig Coy Royal Engineers
BLACKETT Robert MM Pte 16559 York & Lancaster Regt
BLACKETT Robert W. "MM,MID" Sjt 11722 Coldstream Guards
BLACKFORD George H. MM Cpl 46056 Royal Engineers
BLACKFORD John MM Sjt G/10975 6th Royal West Kent Regt
BLACKFORD John H. MM Pte G/14241 1st East Kent Regt
BLACKFORD Thomas MM Pte 235350 4th Middlesex Regt
BLACKHALL James MM Cpl 18592 5th Cameron Highlanders
BLACKHAM Frederick William MM L/Cpl G/14451 20th Middlesex Regt
BLACKHURST Samuel MM L/Cpl 241394 South Lancashire Regt
BLACKHURST William "DCM,MM" Cpl 82304 X/24 Med TM Bty RFA
BLACKIE George MM Cpl 59371 Royal Scots
BLACKIE James Scott MM Pte S/7185 11th Arg & Suth Highlanders KIA 26.8.17.
BLACKIE John MM Pte M1/09171 Army Service Corps
BLACKITH John de la H. MM L/Cpl 19669 Royal Fusiliers
BLACKLAW Duncan A. MM Pte 6717 1st Royal Scots Fusiliers
BLACKLEDGE Hugh MM Pte 33602 Lancashire Fusiliers
BLACKLEDGE J. MM Pte 73248 Notts & Derby Regt
BLACKLEDGE John "DCM,MM+Bar,MID,CG(F)" Sjt 27849 15th Lancashire Fusiliers
BLACKLER Reginald MM+Bar Sjt 5020 1st Duke of Cornwall's LI
BLACKLEY Robert MM L/Cpl 295090 12th Royal Scots Fusiliers Died 18.10.18.
BLACKLEY William "MC,MM(13010 Sjt 15th Bn)" T/2Lt 2nd Highland Light Infantry
BLACKLOCK John MM L/Cpl 20060 5th Shropshire Light Infantry
BLACKLOCK Thomas E. MM Sjt 14980 9th Border Regt
BLACKMAN Albert E. MM Pte 301428 13th Bn Tank Corps
BLACKMAN Edward D. "MM,MID" Sjt 1564 1/3rd London Regt
BLACKMAN Edward Miller MM Pte 1194 7th D Coy Royal West Kent Regt KIA 27.9.16.
BLACKMAN Frederick MM Pte 202880 Essex Regt
BLACKMAN G.F. MM Sjt 1484 1st Rifle Brigade
BLACKMAN Gilbert MM Pte D/2957 7th Dragoon Guards
BLACKMAN Lewis H. MM Pte 11281 2nd Royal Fusiliers
BLACKMAN W.J. MM L/Cpl 10176 Royal West Kent Regt
BLACKMAN William MM Pte R/32658 King's Royal Rifle Corps
BLACKMAN William T. MM Pte G/408 2nd Royal Sussex Regt
BLACKMOOR H.A. MM Pte 341597 RAMC att MGC.
BLACKMORE Arthur James MM L/Sjt 19731 1st Scottish Rifles KIA 24.10.18.
BLACKMORE Francis MM Cpl S/27421 9th Rifle Brigade
BLACKMORE Herbert MM Spr 46347 Royal Engineers
BLACKMORE Herbert MM Cpl 17273 12th Royal Irish Rifles DOW 7.6.18.
BLACKMORE John O. MM L/Cpl 341112 RAMC
BLACKMORE Joseph MM Pte 6810 Royal Irish Regt
BLACKMORE Percival G. MM Pte 49627 74th Bn Machine Gun Corps
BLACKMORE Robert MM Sjt 53134 157 Siege Bty RGA
BLACKMORE Robert R. MM Gnr 371343 RGA
BLACKMORE W.V. MM Pte 6481 Army Cyclist Corps
BLACKMUR William John MM Pte 26797 14th Royal Welsh Fusiliers

BLACKNELL Arthur Edward MM L/Cpl 11941 11th West Yorkshire Regt KIA 29.9.17.
BLACKSHAW Arthur H. MM Pte 21142 22nd Manchester Regt
BLACKSHAW Ben MM Pte 7564 East Kent Regt
BLACKSHAW E. MM L/Cpl P4850 Military Mounted Police
BLACKSHAW George MM Pte 290325 7th Cheshire Regt
BLACKSHAW Samuel MM Pte 200689 4th East Yorkshire Regt
BLACKSHAW William MM Pte 34419 Welsh Regt
BLACKSTAFFE Harold P. MM Sjt 560479 47 Div Sig Coy Royal Engineers
BLACKSTOCK John F.A. MM Pte 241214 Royal Scots Fusiliers
BLACKSTOCK John P. MM Cpl 71368 RFA
BLACKTIN Henry MM Bdr 785464 C/150 Bde RFA
BLACKWELL Arthur MM Pte 5137 16 Fd Amb RAMC
BLACKWELL Charles MM Pte 201227 1st Gloucestershire Regt
BLACKWELL Edward MM Spr 558512 Royal Engineers
BLACKWELL Frederick G. MM L/Bdr 64610 RFA
BLACKWELL Frederick Harry MM Sjt T/13470 1 Div Train Army Service Corps
BLACKWELL G.A. MM Pte 28257 6th Northamptonshire Regt
BLACKWELL George J. MM Pte M2/135999 52 Div Train Army Service Corps
BLACKWELL Harry MM Pte 63106 Machine Gun Corps
BLACKWELL Henry MM L/Cpl 45009 1st Royal Inniskilling Fusiliers
BLACKWELL Horace MM Pte A/2007 9th King's Royal Rifle Corps DOW 21.3.18.
BLACKWELL James Alexander MM Gnr 14463 D/71 Bde RFA
BLACKWELL James W. MM Dvr 57334 HQ 110 Bde RFA
BLACKWELL John H. "MM,MID,DM(B)" CQMS 11300 2nd Grenadier Guards
BLACKWELL John W. MM Cpl 56777 RFA
BLACKWELL Leonard MM Pte 266284 Cheshire Regt
BLACKWELL Reginald W. MM Pte 145212 1/1st Northamptonshire Yeomanry
BLACKWELL Sidney Albert MM Sjt M2/034889 345 Coy Army Service Corps
BLACKWELL Stanley G. MM Sjt 36094 253 Siege Bty RGA
BLACKWELL William MM Dvr 98108 RFA
BLACKWOOD Alfred MM Pte 735014 24th London Regt
BLACKWOOD David MM Sjt 325549 1/7th Arg & Suth Highlanders
BLACKWOOD David MM Pte 331192 Highland Light Infantry
BLACKWOOD James MM Pte 18845 7/8th King's Own Scottish Borderers
BLACKWOOD James MM Gnr 50440 RGA
BLACKWOOD John MM Cpl 252080 1/6th Arg & Suth Highlanders
BLACKWOOD William MM Pte 240157 1/5th Royal Scots Fusiliers
BLACOE John MM Pte 24288 9th North Lancashire Regt KIA 8.9.17.
BLADE E.H. MM Cpl 49174 Royal Engineers
BLADEN George Wilkinson "MC,MM(8175 Sjt 1st Bn)" 2Lt 11th East Yorkshire Regt
BLADEN James Samuel MM Pte 10228 2nd Royal Irish Regt KIA 21.3.18.
BLADES Alfred Fox MM+Bar Sjt 53418 40 Trench Bty(sic) RGA
BLADES F. MM Pte 138152 RAMC
BLADES James MM Sjt 29697 2nd Royal Dublin Fusiliers
BLADES Myles "MM,MID" Cpl 17/9126 17th Manchester Regt
BLADES Oswald MM Pte 2430 2nd Northumberland Fusiliers
BLADES S. MM Sjt 756 Military Mounted Police
BLADES Thomas MM L/Cpl 22074 15th Durham Light Infantry KIA 31.3.18.
BLADON James MM Pte 29316 8th Royal Lancaster Regt KIA 1.10.18.
BLAGBURN Fred MM Pte 3906 12th Manchester Regt
BLAGDEN Samuel MM Sjt 14673 12th Notts & Derby Regt
BLAGDON Frederick MM Dvr T4/070532 284 Coy Army Service Corps
BLAIKIE William MM Sjt 1 10th Arg & Suth Highlanders
BLAIKIE William MM Sjt S/12534 6th Cameron Highlanders
BLAIKIE William MM Pte 16161 Machine Gun Corps
BLAIN Alexander MM L/Cpl 240509 5th Royal Scots Fusiliers
BLAIN John MM Cpl 3/9100 1st Royal Irish Rifles
BLAIN Solomon MM Pte 2976 1st King's Royal Rifle Corps DOW 27.7.16.
BLAIR Donald MM+Bar L/Cpl S/10286 1st Gordon Highlanders
BLAIR Edward MM Cpl 10021 12th West Yorkshire Regt
BLAIR George A. MM Pte 1930 Army Cyclist Corps
BLAIR H. MM Air Mech 2 64937 Royal Flying Corps
BLAIR Henry MM Pte 303291 Arg & Suth Highlanders
BLAIR James MM+Bar Cpl 19857 9th Royal Inniskilling Fusiliers

BLAIR James F. MM Pte 68176 4th London Regt
BLAIR John MM L/Cpl 200861 1/4th Royal Scots Fusiliers
BLAIR Joseph MM+Bar L/Cpl 8/4399 8th Northumberland Fusiliers
BLAIR Mary Agnes Crawford MM Sister F QAIMNS
BLAIR Robert MM Gnr 21473 B/107 Bde RFA
BLAIR Robert C. MM Cpl 71512 1st North Irish Horse
BLAIR Samuel MM Pte 12/17184 Royal Irish Rifles
BLAIR Sidney MM Bdr 6927 A/82 Bde RFA
BLAIR Stanley MM Spr 479979 Royal Engineers
BLAIR Thomas "MM,MID" Sjt 2/9261 2nd South Wales Borderers
BLAIR William MM Pte 345446 14th Royal Highlanders
BLAKE Albert MM Pte 10055 Northamptonshire Regt
BLAKE Albert C. MM+Bar L/Cpl 9197 Middlesex Regt
BLAKE Albert Charles MM L/Sjt 31102 20th Machine Gun Corps KIA 1.4.18.
BLAKE Albert Edward MM Pte 15419 1st Middlesex Regt KIA 24.9.17.
BLAKE Arthur E. MM CSM 10325 Royal Berkshire Regt
BLAKE Basil Wilfrid "MM,MID" Gnr 77271 RHA
BLAKE C.A. MM Pte 12297 6th Duke of Cornwall's LI
BLAKE Charles MM Pte 6220 Royal Warwickshire Regt
BLAKE Charles S. MM Sjt 207857 Royal Engineers
BLAKE E.W. MM L/Cpl L/8588 6th East Kent Regt
BLAKE Edward "DCM,MM" Cpl 24768 10th Royal Inniskilling Fusiliers
BLAKE Edward C. MM L/Cpl 87616 42nd Bn Machine Gun Corps
BLAKE Eric T. MM+Bar Sjt 14554 2nd Bedfordshire Regt
BLAKE Francis Bertie MM Sjt 16434 Oxf & Bucks Light Infantry
BLAKE Frank MM Sjt 44625 32 Div Sig Coy Royal Engineers
BLAKE Frank MM Bdr 95548 RFA
BLAKE Frederick Charles MM Cpl 9860 2nd Wiltshire Regt
BLAKE Frederick W. MM Sjt 11045 2nd Wiltshire Regt
BLAKE Frederick W. MM Cpl 21745 3rd Hussars
BLAKE George MM Pte 5/6057 Royal Munster Fusiliers
BLAKE Harold V. MM Pte 18125 Wiltshire Regt
BLAKE Harry MM Sjt 5955 19th Hussars
BLAKE Harry J. MM Pte 18730 Royal Warwickshire Regt
BLAKE Henry MM Sjt 422117 416 Fd Coy Royal Engineers
BLAKE Henry J. MM Sjt TT/0197 Army Veterinary Corps
BLAKE Hermann Frank MM Pte 31180 12th Norfolk Regt
BLAKE Hubert MM Pte 58842 West Yorkshire Regt
BLAKE James MM Pte 339119 2nd(West Lancashire)Fd Amb RAMC
BLAKE James MM Sjt 44785 Machine Gun Corps
BLAKE John MM Pte 307712 Liverpool Regt
BLAKE John MM Pte 20223 7th Northamptonshire Regt AKA John George Langford.
BLAKE John MM Pte 27756 18th Welsh Regt Died 30.4.18.
BLAKE John H.B. MM Pte L/11361 8th East Surrey Regt
BLAKE Joseph MM Sjt 13688 15th Durham Light Infantry KIA 10.4.17.
BLAKE Louis MM Pte 25364 Gloucestershire Regt
BLAKE Percy MM Pte 49736 1st Cheshire Regt
BLAKE Reginald MM+Bar CSM 200890 1st att 2/2nd London Regt KIA 21.3.18.
BLAKE Sidney John MM Pte 205413 6th Royal West Surrey Regt KIA 24.4.18.
BLAKE Thomas A. MM Dvr 71107 40 Bde RFA
BLAKE Walter T. MM Pte 39848 Somerset Light Infantry
BLAKE Wilfred A. MM Pte 27146 13th West Riding Regt
BLAKE William MM Pte 5837 1st Royal Dublin Fusiliers
BLAKE William MM Staff SM T/16290 Att 8 Fd Amb RAMC Army Service Corps
BLAKE William MM Cpl 93783 RFA
BLAKE William Gladstone MM+Bar L/Sjt 20567 11th South Lancashire Regt KIA 23.3.18.
BLAKE William J. "MM,MID" L/Cpl 19376 Welsh Regt
BLAKEBOROUGH Donald MM Pte 24701 Yorkshire Regt
BLAKEBOROUGH George Ivor MM Cpl 24941 9th West Yorkshire Regt
BLAKEBROUGH Percy MM Pte 242136 1/5th West Riding Regt
BLAKELEY Arthur MM Pte 17564 Royal Scots
BLAKELEY H. MM Sjt 64520 RGA
BLAKELEY Harold MM Cpl 461484 RAMC
BLAKELEY James E. MM Sjt 305907 West Riding Regt
BLAKELEY John MM Pte 10436 6th Leinster Regt
BLAKELEY Joseph MM Bdr 686749 D/310 Bde RFA
BLAKEMAN Robert MM Gnr 121309 D/102 Bde RFA
BLAKEMORE George MM L/Sjt 2984 4th York & Lancaster Regt
BLAKEMORE Ralph F.C. "MM,MID" Sjt 51192 RHA

BLAKESLEY Edward MM Gnr 1736 RFA
BLAKESLEY Edward MM Cpl 2008 Worcestershire Regt
BLAKESLEY John B. MM Gnr 81112 133 Siege Bty RGA
BLAKEWAY Ralph MM Sjt 325280 1/1st Worcestershire Yeo
BLAKEWAY Thomas H. MM Gnr Shoeing Smith 146667 RGA
BLAKEWAY William MM Pte 35376 10th Worcestershire Regt
BLAKEY Arthur MM Pte 11/1229 11th East Yorkshire Regt
BLAKEY David Harkness MM Sjt 11/18634 11th Royal Inniskilling Fusiliers KIA 1.7.16.
BLAKEY Fred MM Pte 240624 Lincolnshire Regt
BLAKEY Fred MM Gnr 32492 A/78 Bde RFA
BLAKEY Frederick A. MM Pte 16/520 1st West Yorkshire Regt
BLAKEY James H. MM Spr 251745 5 Div Sig Coy Royal Engineers
BLAKEY John MM Spr 184394 150 Fd Coy Royal Engineers
BLAKEY John MM Cpl 15078 1st Middlesex Regt KIA 29.9.18
BLAKEY John Stanley "DCM,MM" Sjt 2104 1/4th Lincolnshire Regt
BLAKEY Thomas MM Cpl 29450 Highland Light Infantry
BLAKEY Thomas MM Pte 44767 8th Royal Berkshire Regt KIA 26.10.18.
BLAKEY Thomas MM L/Cpl 8712 9th Royal Highlanders
BLAKEY William MM Sjt 240182 5th Yorkshire Light Infantry KIA 10.6.18.
BLAKEY William MM Dvr 64310 RFA
BLAKEY William Elliott MM Sjt 17/265 Northumberland Fusiliers
BLAKLEY Andrew MM Sjt 265231 1/7th Scottish Rifles
BLAKLEY James F. MM Cpl 240405 Border Regt
BLAKLEY Thomas MM CSM 240416 1/5th Royal Scots Fusiliers
BLAMIRES Arthur MM Dvr 103762 RFA
BLAMIRES Seth MM Dvr 103763 19 Div Ammn Col RFA
BLAMPIED Lionel G. "DCM,MM+Bar" Sjt 13223 1st Middlesex Regt
BLANCH Frederick Walter MM QMS Wheeler 8335 25 Bde RFA
BLANCHARD Albert MM Gnr 84491 231 Siege Bty RGA
BLANCHARD Albert L. MM Pnr 71041 35 Div Sig Coy Royal Engineers
BLANCHARD Enoch MM L/Cpl 268 12th Yorkshire Light Infantry
BLANCHARD Joseph MM Pte 200670 West Yorkshire Regt
BLANCHARD Percy Walter MM Dvr Fitter 751340 B/350 Bde RFA DOW 27.4.18.
BLANCHARD Thomas Henry MM Pte 15091 7th Lincolnshire Regt
BLANCHE Charles Richard MM Bdr 94842 B/78 Bde RFA
BLANCHFLOWER Cecil MM L/Cpl Z/2840 3rd D Coy Rifle Brigade KIA 20.1.18.
BLANCHFLOWER John MM Gnr 680888 RFA
BLANCHFLOWER Percy Robert MM Pte 302183 1/8th Arg & Suth Highlanders KIA 10.10.18.
BLANCHFLOWER Victor G. MM Pte 678189 21st London Regt
BLAND Alfred MM Gnr 77681 A/95 Bde RFA
BLAND Arthur MM Pte M2/076963 Army Service Corps
BLAND Arthur MM Pnr 39593 58 Div Sig Coy Royal Engineers
BLAND Arthur Samuel MM Sjt 6097 1st Northamptonshire Regt
BLAND Charles B. MM Cpl 785989 RFA
BLAND Charles H. MM L/Cpl 432055 Royal Engineers att RFA.
BLAND Edward MM Pte 31513 3rd Grenadier Guards
BLAND Ernest MM Pte M2/047467 Army Service Corps att RAMC.
BLAND George A. MM Gnr 68275 50 Siege Bty RGA
BLAND George Henry MM Pte 3/7450 1st Bedfordshire Regt KIA 4.10.17.
BLAND Harry MM Pte 49069 74 Fd Amb RAMC
BLAND Henry MM Pte 354123 3rd(Easl Lancashire)Fd Amb RAMC
BLAND Henry R. MM Sjt 2129 23rd London Regt
BLAND James MM Pte 419028 9th London Regt att 16 KRRC.
BLAND Norman MM Dvr 780226 B/246 Bde RFA
BLAND Robert MM Pte 200946 West Yorkshire Regt
BLAND Robert MM Cpl 13240 10 Rly Const Coy Royal Engineers
BLAND Wilfred H. MM Pte 202766 2nd West Riding Regt
BLAND William MM Pte 307943 West Riding Regt
BLAND William S. MM L/Cpl 40787 Middlesex Regt
BLANDAMER Sidney A. MM Sjt 33688 Devonshire Regt
BLANDEN Frank H. MM Sjt 41897 RFA
BLANDFORD Alfred "DCM,MM" Sjt 27821 43 Fd Amb RAMC
BLANDFORD George Henry MM Pte 4108 7th Royal West Kent Regt
BLANE William MM Pte 240412 1/5th Royal Scots Fusiliers
BLANEY Andrew Patrick "MM+Bar,MID" Sjt M2/182722 Army Service Corps
BLANEY Daniel MM L/Cpl 52018 21 Div Sig Coy Royal Engineers
BLANK Frederick MM Pte 10741 5th Royal Berkshire Regt
BLANKLEY Ernest MM Pte 44150 Durham Light Infantry
BLANKLEY Ronald F. MM Pte 62991 Royal Fusiliers
BLANKS Ernest G. MM Pte 30484 2nd Grenadier Guards

BLANKS Harry MM Sjt 4766 2nd Suffolk Regt
BLANKS W. MM Bdr 68742 134 Bty 32 Bde RFA
BLANN Henry MM Bdr 940087 RFA
BLANNING George H. MM Pte 22673 Gloucestershire Regt
BLANSHARD Herbert MM Sjt 8581 Yorkshire Light Infantry
BLANTHORNE Edward H. MM Sjt 1921 RAMC
BLASDALE Percival James MM Pte 11896 Grenadier Guards
BLASDALE W.P. MM Bdr 750392 RFA
BLATCHER George A. MM Gnr 139459 14 Bde T Bty RHA
BLATCHFORD Walter F. MM Pte 40950 1st Royal Warwickshire Regt
BLATHERWICK George W.H. MM Pte 38198 Gloucestershire Regt
BLAXALL Isaac H. MM Gnr 87435 136 Hy Bty RGA
BLAY Norman F. MM Gnr Sig 214269 B/186 Bde RFA
BLAYDON Percy S. MM Cpl 56911 99 Siege Bty RGA
BLAYLOCK George MM Cpl 124556 Royal Engineers
BLAYLOCK John James MM L/Cpl R/26291 11th Border Regt KIA 2.12.17.
BLAYLOCK Joseph MM Tpr 3162 2nd Life Guards
BLAYLOCK Norman MM L/Cpl 142906 Royal Engineers
BLAYMIRE George Alfred MM L/Cpl 1757 1/8th West Yorkshire Regt
BLAYNEY George MM Pte 16907 2nd Royal Dublin Fusiliers
BLAYNEY Robert MM Sjt 301847 Durham Light Infantry
BLAZEY John MM Sjt 13971 Notts & Derby Regt
BLEAKLEY Daniel MM 2nd Cpl 56617 50 Div Sig Coy Royal Engineers
BLEAKLEY Henry C. MM Pte 254299 14th Arg & Suth Highlanders
BLEASBY A. MM L/Cpl 8743 Scottish Rifles
BLEASDALE Herbert MM L/Cpl 70381 166 Coy Machine Gun Corps
BLEASDALE James MM Pte 3457 Liverpool Regt
BLEASDALE James MM Dvr 680441 A/286 Bde RFA
BLEASDALE John William MM L/Cpl 8/15917 Border Regt
BLEASDALE Roy MM Spr 361910 Royal Engineers
BLEASDALE Tom MM Cpl 14727 1st Border Regt
BLEASE Emmanuel MM Pte 14524 1st Cheshire Regt DOW 27.10.17.
BLEASE James MM Pte 18241 2nd North Lancashire Regt
BLEASE William MM CSM 1976 Liverpool Regt
BLEESE J. MM L/Cpl 59323 1st Northamptonshire Regt
BLENCOWE Albert MM Sjt 49747 RGA
BLENCOWE M.J. MM Pte 235339 Northumberland Fusiliers
BLENDELL H.E. MM Dvr 800292 B/230 Bde RFA
BLENKEY John MM Pte 3110 1/4th Yorkshire Regt KIA 25.10.16.
BLENKHAM Allan MM Pte 241922 2/5th York & Lancaster Regt DOW 14.7.17.
BLENKINSHIP Albert MM Cpl 58798 3 Div Sig Coy Royal Engineers
BLENKINSOP Edward MM Pte 42296 2nd Suffolk Regt
BLENKINSOP James W. MM Sjt 27262 11th East Lancashire Regt
BLENKINSOP John MM Bdr 40718 RFA
BLENKINSOPP Thomas MM Pte 19315 Northamptonshire Regt
BLENKIRON Harold MM Sjt 71059 34th Bn Machine Gun Corps
BLENT Peter MM+Bar Sjt 8876 1st Rifle Brigade
BLEWITT Edward "MM,MID" L/Cpl 27196 D Cable Sect Royal Engineers
BLEWITT George MM Pte 56511 Lancashire Fusiliers
BLEWITT Seth MM QMS Wheeler 17116 11 Heavy Bty RGA Died 8.4.18.
BLEWITT Sidney MM Dvr 128894 B/74 Bde RFA
BLEZARD Harold MM Pte 28473 East Lancashire Regt
BLEZARD John "MM+Bar,MID" Bdr 57013 D/112 Bde RFA
BLIGHT Arthur MM Pte 240464 1/5th Devonshire Regt
BLIGHT Edwin MM Pte 465128 1 Fd Amb RAMC
BLIGHT Richard MM Gnr 8805 22 Bde RFA
BLINCKO Frederick W. MM L/Cpl 73048 24th Royal Fusiliers
BLINCOE Albert E. MM Dvr 66358 RHA
BLINCOW John "MM,MID" Pte S/4751 Gordon Highlanders
BLINKHORN Ellis MM Pte 87429 5th Liverpool Regt
BLINMAN Urban A. MM Spr 505921 3 Cav Div Sig Sqn 6 Tp Royal Engineers
BLINSTON Thomas MM Dvr 229280 B/246 Bde RFA
BLISS Charles James MM Cpl 5427 9th Royal Sussex Regt KIA 4.11.18.
BLISS G. MM Cpl 10146 20th Hussars
BLISS William Charles MM Sjt 1450 8th London Regt
BLISS William S. MM L/Cpl 787 King Edward's Horse
BLISSITT Charles MM CSM 254 17th Royal Fusiliers
BLOCK Isaac MM Pte 22909 Border Regt
BLOCK Thomas H. MM Pte 29399 6th Royal West Surrey Regt
BLOCKLEY George MM Pte 41207 12th Suffolk Regt KIA 5.9.18.
BLODWELL Edward MM L/Cpl 33978 North Lancashire Regt

BLOGG Ernest E. MM Dvr 930056 RFA
BLOGG Joseph Andrew Martin MM Pte 327898 1/1st Cambridgeshire Regt DOW 4.9.18.
BLOMEMEY Thomas MM Sjt 38437 Lancashire Fusiliers
BLOMFIELD J. MM Pte 1974 Liverpool Regt
BLOMLEY James MM Pte 60257 Royal Welsh Fusiliers
BLOMLEY James MM Pte 282229 Lancashire Fusiliers
BLOOD Bert MM 2nd Cpl 256515 Royal Engineers
BLOOD George W. MM Pte 36039 East Surrey Regt att London Regt.
BLOOD Joseph P. MM Cpl 16/774 Royal Warwickshire Regt
BLOOD William Joseph "MM,OstG(R)" Sjt 16104 11th Worcestershire Regt
BLOODWORTH Arthur E. MM Sjt 16802 Leicestershire Regt
BLOODWORTH Frederick J. MM Pte 241462 5th Leicestershire Regt
BLOODWORTH Robert MM Sjt 743 2nd Rifle Brigade
BLOODWORTH Walter MM L/Cpl 200540 3rd (Light) Bn Tank Corps
BLOODWORTH William Harry MM Dvr 26511 D/161 Bde RFA
BLOOM Harry MM Pte S/27982 Rifle Brigade
BLOOM Jack MM Sjt 41618 RAMC
BLOOM Jack MM Pte 204463 West Riding Regt
BLOOM Moses MM Cpl J/2581 38th Royal Fusiliers
BLOOMBERG Gerald MM L/Cpl 34249 8th York & Lancaster Regt
BLOOMER John MM Sjt S/3755 7th Seaforth Highlanders
BLOOMER Joseph MM Pte 15692 10th Worcestershire Regt KIA 3.7.16.
BLOOMER Joseph "MM,MID" Sjt 19282 Worcestershire Regt
BLOOMER Samuel MM Pte 52266 Worcestershire Regt
BLOOMER William John MM Pte 3617 4/5th Royal Highlanders KIA 1.4.18.
BLOOMFIELD Alfred MM L/Cpl 28271 Durham Light Infantry
BLOOMFIELD Arthur Frederick MM Cpl 8052 2nd Royal Lancaster Regt
BLOOMFIELD Charles MM L/Cpl 8300 2nd West Riding Regt
BLOOMFIELD Charles A. MM Gnr 142356 RGA
BLOOMFIELD George MM Sjt G/5462 13th Royal Fusiliers
BLOOMFIELD James MM Pte 6137 Notts & Derby Regt
BLOOMFIELD James MM+Bar Sjt 8917 6th East Kent Regt DOW 29.8.18.
BLOOMFIELD James MM Sjt 25707 RGA
BLOOMFIELD John J. MM Pte 32674 Durham Light Infantry att MGC.
BLOOMFIELD Joseph MM Gnr 23757 B/112 Bde RFA
BLOOMFIELD Sidney MM L/Bdr 889512 RFA
BLOOMFIELD Thomas A. MM Sjt 7789 1st Suffolk Regt
BLOOMFIELD W.R. MM Pte 2470 1st Rifle Brigade
BLOOMFIELD William Charles MM Pte 293346 2/10th Middlesex Regt
BLOOR Aaron MM Pte 201220 North Staffordshire Regt
BLOOR Albert Edward MM Sjt R/15224 2nd Rifle Brigade
BLOOR James M. MM Pte 240519 6th North Staffordshire Regt
BLOOR Joseph "MC,MM(3284 L/Sjt Gord H)" 2Lt 1/8th Notts & Derby Regt
BLOOR Norman MM Pte 66026 Royal Fusiliers
BLORE Vernon William MM Pte 15814 11th Northumberland Fusiliers
BLOSSE Walter MM Pte 6339 24 Coy Machine Gun Corps
BLOSTEIN Philip MM Pte 43172 2nd Royal Dublin Fusiliers DOW 5.8.17.
BLOUNT Henry D. MM Pte 52086 Royal Fusiliers
BLOUNT Henry Herbert MM+Bar Gnr 66993 9 Siege Bty RGA
BLOUNT Sidney V. MM S/Sjt 417003 1 Fd Amb RAMC
BLOW Frederick A. MM+Bar Sjt 22695 Border Regt
BLOW George S. MM Sjt 33747 RAMC
BLOW James N. MM Pte 71786 11th Notts & Derby Regt
BLOWER Frederick W. MM Sjt 494735 Royal Engineers
BLOWER Humphrey Douglas MM Pte 50803 Machine Gun Corps
BLOWER James MM Pte 9626 7th att 1st Shropshire Light Infantry KIA 18.9.16.
BLOWER Percy MM L/Bdr 297334 156 Hy Bty RGA
BLOWER Thomas MM L/Cpl 11608 Yorkshire Light Infantry
BLOWERS Andrew G. MM Gnr Sig 881573 RFA
BLOWES Charles W. MM Dvr 67858 C/159 Bde RFA
BLOWES Ernest J. MM Pte G/68677 24th Royal Fusiliers
BLOWFIELD Joseph MM L/Cpl 24598 2nd Oxf & Bucks Light Infantry
BLOWS Alfred Charles MM Cpl 31471 Machine Gun Corps
BLOWS Charles MM Pte 1542 17th London Regt DOW 3.2.17.
BLOWS Frank S. MM Pte 473453 1st(East Anglian)Fd Amb RAMC

BLOXAM William H. MM Sjt 43591 8th Lincolnshire Regt
BLOXHAM Albert MM Pte 13779 12th Hampshire Regt
BLOXHAM Arthur MM Pte 17020 7th Duke of Cornwall's LI
BLOXHAM Ernest MM Gnr 755767 B/251 Bde RFA
BLOXHAM Leslie W. MM Pte 720685 24th London Regt
BLOY Gerald Cronin MM L/Cpl 34673 11th Royal Welsh Fusiliers
BLUCK Harold MM Pte 1802 RAMC
BLUD John "MM,MID" Sjt 7527 1st Shropshire Light Infantry
BLUE Allan P. MM Sjt 113016 Royal Engineers
BLUE John MM+Bar Cpl 4/9407 2nd Arg & Suth Highlanders
BLUFF Frederick MM Bdr 45190 RFA
BLUMER Thomas S. "MM,MID" Sjt 104052 Royal Engineers
BLUMIRE E.J. MM L/Cpl G/3349 Middlesex Regt
BLUMIRE William MM Pte 324396 6th London Regt
BLUMSON W. MM Sjt S/5287 Rifle Brigade
BLUMSON W.J. MM L/Cpl 301548 5th London Regt
BLUMSON William C. MM Pte 28850 6th Royal Dublin Fusiliers
BLUNDELL Alfred George MM Pte 6677 7th East Surrey Regt
BLUNDELL Alfred Henry MM Cpl 97813 769 Area Empl Coy Labour Corps
BLUNDELL Arthur MM Cpl 13834 6th Northamptonshire Regt
BLUNDELL Harold J. MM L/Cpl 10580 15th Royal Warwickshire Regt
BLUNDELL Reginald Walter MM Sjt G/6615 Royal Fusiliers
BLUNDELL Robert MM Pte 12433 13th Liverpool Regt KIA 3.5.17.
BLUNDELL Robert MM Pte 265319 7th Liverpool Regt
BLUNDELL Tom Ludford MM Cpl 685 22nd Royal Fusiliers
BLUNDELL Wilfred MM Spr 41455 Royal Engineers
BLUNDEN Alfred E. MM Sjt 40632 18 Bde RFA
BLUNDEN Archibald W. MM Pte 203247 3rd London Regt
BLUNDEN Charles MM Bdr 9043 RFA
BLUNDEN Charles Henry MM Pte 15882 11tth Royal Sussex Regt KIA 3.4.18.
BLUNDEN Harold MM Cpl 250140 1/5th Essex Regt
BLUNDEN Herbert H. MM Dvr 246268 34 Bty 238 Bde RFA
BLUNDY Alfred Joseph MM Pte 9563 1st Lincolnshire Regt
BLUNDY Rowland E. MM L/Cpl 14603 Grenadier Guards
BLUNN Alfred MM Sjt 23955 Royal Welsh Fusiliers
BLUNN George Henry MM Cpl 53920 30 Siege Bty RGA
BLUNN John MM Pte 31737 2/4th Hampshire Regt
BLUNT Charles George MM Sjt B/3459 Rifle Brigade
BLUNT Charles T. "MM,MID" Sjt 2080 1/8th Notts & Derby Regt
BLUNT Frank W. MM L/Cpl 23845 5th Oxf & Bucks Light Infantry
BLUNT Harry MM Pte 3/10888 Northamptonshire Regt
BLUNT John MM Gnr Fitter 65005 30 Bty 39 Bde RFA KIA 29.3.18.
BLUNT John Edward Mackenzie MM Sjt 352346 1/8th Manchester Regt
BLUNT Joseph M. MM Pte 28230 Border Regt
BLUNT Norman MM Pte 25091 2nd Worcestershire Regt
BLUNT Robert MM Pte 10089 South Staffordshire Regt
BLUNT Robert James MM L/Cpl 10385 6th Leicestershire Regt KIA 21.3.18.
BLUNT Walter W. MM Pte M2/047185 Army Service Corps
BLUNT William MM(1130 R Warw)+Bar Sjt 11996 10th Royal West Surrey Regt
BLURTON Arthur "MM+Bar,CdeG(F)" Gnr 91791 Tank Corps
BLURTON Bernard J. MM Bdr 173941 C/315 Bde RFA
BLURTON John E. MM Spr 132803 Royal Engineers
BLURTON William MM Gnr 48779 RGA
BLYTH Alexander MM Pte 22/919 Northumberland Fusiliers
BLYTH Archibald MM Sjt 325003 1/8th Royal Scots KIA 21.3.18.
BLYTH Charles V. "DCM,MM" CSM 18335 7th Northamptonshire Regt
BLYTH David MM Pte S/24266 8th Royal Highlanders
BLYTH Ernest MM Sjt 10148 6th York & Lancaster Regt
BLYTH Frederick MM Spr 81679 Royal Engineers
BLYTH H. MM Pte 11666 7th Duke of Cornwall's LI
BLYTH James MM Pte 23034 Wiltshire Regt
BLYTH John "MM+Bar,MSM" L/Cpl 8601 1st Royal Scots Fusiliers
BLYTH Phillip MM Sjt 9713 11th Lancashire Fusiliers
BLYTH Robert MM Pte 8341 1st Highland Light Infantry
BLYTH Robert "MM,GMV(S)" Pte 50308 RAMC
BLYTH Robert J. MM Pte M2/050370 Army Service Corps
BLYTH Robert James MM Sjt 13857 1st Royal Dublin Fusiliers
BLYTH Sidney M. MM Pte 15738 9th Norfolk Regt
BLYTHE Arthur MM Sjt 116017 1/1st Duke of Lancaster's Own Yeomanry
BLYTHE Cyril MM Pte 101694 6th Durham Light Infantry
BLYTHE David M. MM Gnr L/12479 RFA
BLYTHE Douglas D. MM Cpl 52247 Royal Fusiliers
BLYTHE Enoch MM Sjt 200540 13th Cheshire Regt DOW 14.8.17.
BLYTHE Frederick MM+Bar Pte 31533 RAMC
BLYTHE Henry MM 2nd Cpl 85820 Royal Engineers
BLYTHE John "DCM,MM" Sjt 25/770 20th Northumberland Fusiliers
BLYTHE John MM Pte 18568 1st Notts & Derby Regt
BLYTHE John MM L/Cpl 13315 11th Border Regt
BLYTHE John Edward MM L/Sjt 15353 10th Northumberland Fusiliers KIA 25.9.16.
BLYTHE Josiah Edward MM Cpl 240827 1/6th South Staffordshire Regt
BLYTHE Phillip MM Pte 40951 5th South Wales Borderers
BLYTHE Thomas MM+Bar Pte 9154 4th West Riding Regt
BLYTHE Walter MM Pte 202170 1/5th Notts & Derby Regt
BLYTHE Walter Thomas MM Cpl 61793 80 Fd Coy Royal Engineers
BLYTHE Wilfred MM Pte 21006 1st Coldstream Guards
BLYTHE William MM Pnr 182444 7 Div Sig Coy Royal Engineers DOW 9.6.17.
BLYTHE William MM Sjt L/13353 8th Royal Fusiliers KIA 7.7.16.
BLYTHING Edwin MM Bdr 25977 RFA
BLYTHMAN Reginald MM Pte 512504 2/14th London Regt
BLYTON Alfred W. "MM,MID" Sjt 38189 RGA
BOA John MM Gnr 122259 251 Siege Bty RGA
BOA William A. MM L/Cpl 126691 Lovat's Scouts Yeomanry
BOAD George MM Pte MS/716 53 Coy Army Service Corps
BOAD Thomas B. MM L/Cpl 471343 Royal Engineers
BOAD Wilfred MM Sjt 22338 9th Scottish Rifles KIA 7.6.17.
BOAG George MM Pte R/32765 King's Royal Rifle Corps
BOAG Herbert M. "DCM,MM" CSM B/19945 26th Royal Fusiliers
BOAG John MM Pte 9509 1st Cameron Highlanders DOW 29.7.16.
BOAG Walter R. MM Sjt 10/735 East Yorkshire Regt
BOAG William MM Cpl 5413 2nd Dragoons
BOAGEY Robert MM Sjt 51618 248 Fd Coy Royal Engineers
BOAGEY Robert MM L/Sjt 17190 Durham Light Infantry
BOAKES Albert E. MM Pte A/204096 13th King's Royal Rifle Corps
BOAL John Edgar MM Pte 2074 1/7th Northumberland Fusiliers DOW 8.12.16.
BOAL Thomas MM Pte 200554 Durham Light Infantry
BOALCH Sydney C. MM Sjt 85814 Royal Engineers
BOALER Charles A. MM Gnr 622282 RHA
BOALER George W. MM Sjt 426012 RAMC
BOALER Lewis MM Pte 26719 16th Notts & Derby Regt
BOAM Harry MM Sjt 666 1/2(West Riding)Fd Coy Royal Engineers
BOAR Charles MM Cpl 3/2479 9th Essex Regt KIA 30.11.17.
BOARD Arthur L. MM Dvr 109449 RFA
BOARD Ernest V. MM+Bar Sjt 21072 Gloucestershire Regt
BOARD Frederick MM L/Cpl 16068 2nd Hampshire Regt KIA 3.9.18.
BOARD John A. MM L/Sjt 165 North Lancashire Regt
BOARD John E. MM Pte 371593 8th London Regt
BOARD William C. MM Sjt 1785 9th Highland Light Infantry KIA 20.5.17.
BOARDMAN Arthur MM Cpl 97705 D/50 Bde RFA
BOARDMAN Charles "MM+Bar,MID" Sjt 988 2nd Manchester Regt
BOARDMAN Charles MM L/Cpl 12014 7th South Staffordshire Regt
BOARDMAN Edward MM Sjt 300239 8th Manchester Regt
BOARDMAN Edwin MM CQMS 240021 5th South Lancashire Regt
BOARDMAN Frank MM Gnr Fitter 80935 RFA
BOARDMAN James MM Pte 240808 5th Seaforth Highlanders
BOARDMAN James A. MM+Bar Sjt 265123 1/6th Cheshire Regt
BOARDMAN James Edward MM Sjt 22588 18th Lancashire Fusiliers
BOARDMAN John A. MM Pte 5348 10th Lancashire Fusiliers
BOARDMAN John W.L. MM Pte 42081 2nd Suffolk Regt
BOARDMAN Joseph MM Pte 11205 6th Border Regt
BOARDMAN Percy MM Dvr 67224 B/112 Bde RFA
BOARDMAN S. MM Sjt 375347 Manchester Regt
BOARDMAN Stanley MM L/Cpl 15511 8th North Lancashire Regt
BOARDMAN Thomas H. MM Sjt 43059 Royal Engineers
BOARER Leonard J. MM Pte 24861 Machine Gun Corps
BOARER Walter MM Pte 21069 7th East Kent Regt DOW 21.6.18.
BOASE P. MM Pte 201328 Yorkshire Regt
BOAST A. MM Pte 538128 RAMC
BOAST George D. MM Gnr 706351 RFA
BOAST Henry MM L/Cpl C/73 King's Royal Rifle Corps
BOAST Robert James MM L/Cpl 22848 Machine Gun Corps
BOAST William H. MM L/Cpl 65809 Machine Gun Corps
BOATH David MM L/Cpl 20946 3 Div Sig Coy Royal Engineers
BOATMAN Edward J.W. MM Gnr 233532 421 Bty RFA
BOAZ William MM Sjt 422164 Royal Engineers
BOCKING Frederick MM Pte 66317 10th Royal Fusiliers KIA 8.10.18.

BOCKING Harold MM Cpl 393029 9th London Regt
BOCOCK Frank Ernest MM L/Cpl 40486 7th Norfolk Regt
BOCOCK Frederick J. MM Dvr 78881 RFA
BOCOCK William E. MM L/Cpl 200186 1st Bn Tank Corps
BODDEN Christopher G. MM Pte M2/097683 Army Service Corps
BODDINGTON Albert MM Cpl 1153 1/6th Royal Warwickshire Regt
BODDINGTON Arthur L. "MM,MID" Sjt 9300 Oxf & Bucks Light Infantry
BODDINGTON Edward E. MM L/Cpl 31172 Northamptonshire Regt
BODDINGTON Philip "MM+Bar,MID" L/Cpl 8519 2nd Northamptonshire Regt KIA 1.10.17.
BODDY Frederick C. MM+Bar Sjt 48771 92 Fd Coy Royal Engineers
BODDY Henry MM L/Cpl 40157 6th York & Lancaster Regt
BODDY Herbert L. MM Pte 2241 21st London Regt
BODDY John MM Cpl L/27644 B/51 Bde RFA
BODDY Victor S. MM Pte 490157 1/13th London Regt
BODDY William C. MM Gnr 49982 RGA
BODEN George MM Sjt 15525 1/4th Cheshire Regt KIA 7.10.18.
BODEN William MM Cpl 352105 1/2nd(East Lancashire)Fd Amb RAMC
BODGER Victor MM Gnr 54230 69 Siege Bty RGA
BODGER Walter C. MM Gnr 183248 D/162 Bde RFA
BODIE John A. MM Pte 484 1st Royal West Kent Regt
BODKIN Ernest A. MM Gnr 94857 RFA
BODLE George MM Sjt 21550 12th Suffolk Regt
BODLEY Alfred W. MM Gnr 179143 RFA
BODLEY J.H.W. MM Sjt 376815 5th London Regt
BODLEY William MM Gnr 34477 RGA
BODSWORTH Ernest George MM S/Sjt Armt T1216 Army Ordnance Corps
BODSWORTH James MM Pte 72602 104 Fd Amb RAMC
BODY Edward MM Pte 12817 6th Lincolnshire Regt
BODY W.T. MM Pte 4895 Worcestershire Regt
BODY William G. MM Cpl 95160 1st Bn Tank Corps
BOEG Joseph MM Spr 113811 Royal Engineers
BOEY Arthur J. MM L/Cpl 97555 21st Bn Machine Gun Corps
BOFF Charles MM Pte 40575 Leicestershire Regt
BOFFIN Harry G. MM Pte M2/047540 Army Service Corps
BOGAN Edward MM Gnr 87626 RGA
BOGARD Isaac MM Pte 263049 1/1st Monmouthshire Regt att 10th SWB
BOGG Mark MM Cpl 8559 1st West Yorkshire Regt DOW 26.1.17.
BOGGIS Alfred John MM Pte 18279 9th Norfolk Regt KIA 8.10.18.
BOGGIS James MM Pte 3/5994 2nd Royal Munster Fusiliers
BOGIE Andrew William "MM,MID" CQMS 149 1/4th Hampshire Regt Died 22.9.16.
BOGIE Hugh S. MM Pte 351822 1/8th Manchester Regt
BOGIE William MM Sjt 290206 1/7th Royal Highlanders KIA 17.9.17.
BOGLE Peter D. MM Pte S/15899 Royal Highlanders
BOGLE Robert H. MM Cpl 57915 RGA
BOGLE Thomas MM Spr 137665 178 Tunnelling Coy Royal Engineers
BOGUE John MM Pte 203715 Welsh Regt
BOGUE Robert MM Pte 56519 Machine Gun Corps
BOGUSZ Frank Rudolph MM Pte 34329 2/4th Oxf & Bucks Light Infantry
BOILING Frank L. MM Bdr 966020 D/44 Bde RFA
BOISSON James H. MM Sjt 69217 42 Bde RFA
BOISTON John "MM,MID" Pte 12147 2nd King's Own Scottish Borderers
BOLAM George MM Pte 22/366 9th Durham Light Infantry
BOLAM John MM Pte 3445 Northumberland Fusiliers
BOLAM Joseph MM Pte 26/775 Northumberland Fusiliers
BOLAM Richard E. MM Cpl 14656 6th Royal Inniskilling Fusiliers
BOLAM Thomas R. MM Cpl 106331 Royal Engineers
BOLAN Charles MM L/Cpl 15151 Gordon Highlanders
BOLAN W. "MM,MSM" L/Cpl 139393 252 Tunnelling Coy Royal Engineers
BOLAND Frederick Charles MM L/Cpl 14920 2nd Royal Dublin Fusiliers DOW 14.10.18.
BOLAND James Joseph MM Pte 278997 1/7th Arg & Suth Highlanders
BOLAND Maurice MM L/Sjt 747 2nd Royal Munster Fusiliers DOW 25.9.16.
BOLCH Llewellyn MM L/Cpl 11603 1st South Wales Borderers
BOLD Frank MM Pte 10/913 10th East Yorkshire Regt
BOLD William MM Dvr W/5437 RFA
BOLDEN Henry MM L/Sjt 1650 East Kent Regt
BOLDERSON Arthur MM L/Sjt 540 1/5th West Yorkshire Regt KIA 14.7.16.
BOLDERSON Charles "DCM,MM" Cpl 200794 1/5th West Yorkshire Regt
BOLDY Frank MM Pte 13/142 York & Lancaster Regt
BOLDY J. MM Pte 32204 York & Lancaster Regt
BOLE Thomas M. MM Pte S/14703 6th Cameron Highlanders
BOLGER James MM Cpl 72946 24 Bde RFA
BOLGER John MM Pte 32459 8th East Surrey Regt
BOLINGBROKE H.P. MM Sjt 293340 RGA
BOLINGBROKE Peter Edmund MM Pte 512311 RAMC
BOLITHO James A. MM L/Cpl 38930 1st Duke of Cornwall's LI
BOLLAND Adam MM L/Cpl 11792 10th Durham Light Infantry
BOLLAND Arthur MM Cpl 6453 Royal West Surrey Regt
BOLLAND Edwin MM Cpl 7806 XV Corps Cyclist Bn Army Cyclist Corps
BOLLAND Howard MM Sjt 12822 7th Lincolnshire Regt
BOLLAND W. MM Sjt 11640 Durham Light Infantry
BOLLARD Arthur Edward MM Gnr Sig 145861 294 Siege Bty RGA
BOLLEN Alfred MM Pte 352204 7th London Regt
BOLLER William H. MM Bdr 369 RFA
BOLSHAW John W. MM Tpr 5362 3rd Bn GMGR
BOLSON C. MM L/Sjt 7471 48th Bn Machine Gun Corps
BOLSTRIDGE Alex MM Bdr 1367 D/242 Bde RFA Died 2.3.17.
BOLT Albert MM Sjt 203336 1/4th West Riding Regt
BOLT Brinley MM Pte 12635 1st Devonshire Regt
BOLT E.E.F. MM Sjt 461108 RAMC
BOLT George H. MM Pte 018982 Army Ordnance Corps
BOLT William Maurice MM L/Cpl 203136 Devonshire Regt
BOLT William N. MM Pte 17/8409 Manchester Regt
BOLTMAN Pierre MM Sjt 8941 Yorkshire Regt
BOLTON A. MM L/Cpl 49693 1st Liverpool Regt
BOLTON Alexander J. MM+Bar L/Sjt 200602 Seaforth Highlanders
BOLTON Archibald MM Pte Y/341 9th King's Royal Rifle Corps DOW 5.4.18.
BOLTON Ben MM L/Sjt 11258 Leicestershire Regt
BOLTON Ben MM Cpl 15440 Yorkshire Light Infantry
BOLTON Claud MM L/Cpl 201893 1/4th West Riding Regt
BOLTON E. MM Pte 36679 Essex Regt
BOLTON Edgar "MM,MID" Pte 5461 1st East Lancashire Regt
BOLTON Ernest Edward MM L/Cpl 5157 12th East Surrey Regt KIA 13.8.17.
BOLTON Frank H.M. MM Pte 305333 5th London Regt
BOLTON George MM Sjt 43472 37th Bn Machine Gun Corps
BOLTON George MM Gnr 148698 401 Bty 4 Bde RFA KIA 5.9.18.
BOLTON George H. MM Sjt 780973 D/246 Bde RFA
BOLTON George Samuel MM Gnr 38715 C/85 Bde RFA
BOLTON Grimshaw MM Sjt 7144 Gordon Highlanders
BOLTON H. MM Pte 12816 1st Shropshire Light Infantry
BOLTON Harold MM Gnr L/28180 164 Bde RFA
BOLTON Harry MM Pte 57790 5th York & Lancaster Regt
BOLTON Harry MM Pte 403069 2/2nd(West Riding)Fd Amb RAMC
BOLTON Henry Charles MM+Bar Sjt 23563 20th Lancashire Fusiliers
BOLTON Henry Joseph MM+Bar Gnr 30133 RGA
BOLTON James MM L/Sjt 11163 Yorkshire Light Infantry
BOLTON Jason "MM,MID" L/Cpl 7210 1st Middlesex Regt
BOLTON John MM Cpl 96150 B/51 Bde RFA
BOLTON John MM L/Cpl 200782 2/5th Lancashire Fusiliers
BOLTON John C. MM Cpl 25039 7th Royal Irish Regt KIA 21.3.18.
BOLTON John Crayston MM L/Cpl 5441 8th Royal West Kent Regt KIA 27.6.17.
BOLTON John H. MM Cpl 100306 290 Army Tps Coy Royal Engineers
BOLTON John J. MM Pte 351845 5/6th Royal Scots
BOLTON John J. MM Cpl 16477 Machine Gun Corps
BOLTON Joseph MM L/Cpl 4310 8th Northumberland Fusiliers
BOLTON Richard MM+Bar Sjt 17222 East Yorkshire Regt
BOLTON Robert MM Sjt 42973 9th Yorkshire Light Infantry
BOLTON Robert Albert MM Sjt T3/027272 15 Div Train Army Service Corps
BOLTON Robert Edward MM Pte 403163 RAMC
BOLTON Robert Henry MM Sjt 305318 1/8th Notts & Derby Regt
BOLTON Walter John MM Sjt 27553 14th Hampshire Regt
BOLTON William MM Sjt 97464 RFA
BOLTON William MM Pte 10257 7th East Surrey Regt
BOLTON William MM CQMS 13517 7th Norfolk Regt
BOLTON William MM Cpl 44644 91 Fd Coy Royal Engineers KIA 26.7.17.
BOLTON William M. MM Sjt 25487 37th Bn Machine Gun Corps
BOLTON Willie MM Pte 15271 9th Yorkshire Light Infantry KIA 26.4.18.

BOLTWOOD Charles MM Dvr T4/086781 Army Service Corps
BOLWELL Alexander MM Sjt 14878 6th Somerset Light Infantry
BONAM Christopher MM Cpl 16938 1st Leicestershire Regt KIA 11.4.17.
BONAR Charles Alexander MM L/Sjt 761 1st Welsh Guards
BONAR Herbert S. MM L/Cpl 202865 1/4th Royal Scots Fusiliers
BONAS George W. MM+Bar Sjt 1289 11th East Yorkshire Regt
BOND Adam H. MM L/Cpl M2/180772 272 Coy Army Service Corps
BOND Albert MM Spr 62318 86 Fd Coy Royal Engineers
BOND Albert J. MM L/Cpl 200870 4th Bn Tank Corps
BOND Alfred Ernest MM Sjt 27302 A/46 Bde RFA
BOND Andrew T. MM Pte 20312 Arg & Suth Highlanders
BOND Arthur MM Pte 303160 6th Manchester Regt
BOND Arthur J. MM Cpl 21137 32nd Bn Machine Gun Corps
BOND Arthur T. MM Pte 445277 34 Coy Labour Corps
BOND Bernard MM Pte 16774 Grenadier Guards
BOND C.W. MM Sjt 13379 Suffolk Regt
BOND Charles H. MM Pte 113337 17th Bn(sic) Machine Gun Corps
BOND Charles Isaac MM 2nd Cpl 96343 41 Div Sig Coy Royal Engineers
BOND Charles J. MM Pte 5984 13th Royal Fusiliers
BOND Colin MM L/Cpl 21511 2nd York & Lancaster Regt DOW 4.6.17.
BOND Dennis MM Sjt 5947 1st Suffolk Regt
BOND E.M. MM Sjt G/6269 Royal Fusiliers
BOND Ernest G.S. MM L/Sjt 27321 1st Somerset Light Infantry
BOND F. MM Air Mech 2 28941 Royal Flying Corps
BOND Francis MM L/Cpl 26223 Royal Welsh Fusiliers
BOND Frank MM Pte 9468 2nd Royal Welsh Fusiliers
BOND Frank D. MM Dvr 60559 212 Fd Coy Royal Engineers
BOND Frank W. "DCM,MM+Bar" Cpl 10647 RAMC
BOND Frederick MM Sjt 8781 1st Royal Inniskilling Fusiliers DOW 20.5.17.
BOND Frederick James MM Pte 290956 9th Devonshire Regt
BOND G. MM Pte 27/824 27th Northumberland Fusiliers
BOND George MM Pte 359597 10th Liverpool Regt
BOND George MM Spr 154628 Royal Engineers
BOND George MM L/Cpl 4437 6th Connaught Rangers
BOND George MM Sjt 6433 Army Cyclist Corps
BOND George MM Cpl 241327 Liverpool Regt
BOND George H. "MM,MIDx2" L/Cpl 23621 2 Div Sig Coy Royal Engineers
BOND George H.J. MM+Bar Sjt 25538 37th Bn Machine Gun Corps
BOND Hannibal MM Sjt 830959 421 Bty RFA
BOND Harold E. MM Cpl M2/200901 Army Service Corps
BOND Harold P. MM Gnr 17555 1 Siege Bty RGA
BOND Harry MM Sjt 200147 1/5th South Staffordshire Regt
BOND Henry A. MM L/Cpl 55998 1st Northumberland Fusiliers
BOND Herbert E. MM Cpl 8201 Royal West Kent Regt
BOND James MM Pte G/30606 10th Royal West Kent Regt
BOND James William "DCM,MM" Sjt 265012 1/6th Welsh Regt
BOND John MM Pte 260334 13th Liverpool Regt
BOND John R. MM L/Bdr 192971 RFA
BOND Leonard Evelyn MM Cpl 2600 1/6th London Regt KIA 15.9.16.
BOND Mark MM Pte 8876 2nd Devonshire Regt
BOND Michael "MM+Bar,Cross of St George(R)" Sjt 27/827 19th Northumberland Fusiliers KIA 29.3.18.
BOND Reginald Edward MM+Bar Pte 350892 7th London Regt
BOND Richard MM Cpl 113654 Second Army Sig Coy Royal Engineers
BOND Richard H. MM Pte 36780 RAMC
BOND Robert Alfred MM L/Cpl 207754 247 Fd Coy Royal Engineers
BOND Sidney A. MM L/Sjt 275167 6th Essex Regt
BOND Stanley L. MM L/Cpl 35234 15th Royal Warwickshire Regt
BOND Wallace W. MM 2nd Cpl 41707 Royal Engineers
BOND Walter MM Pte 5538 Coldstream Guards att RE.
BOND Wilfred MM Pte 202735 Oxf & Bucks Light Infantry
BOND William MM Pte 5913 1st Dorsetshire Regt
BOND William MM Pte R/4814 16th King's Royal Rifle Corps DOW 13.4.18.
BOND William Ernest MM Pte 41614 Att 88 Bde (Bty?) RFA RAMC DOW 21.5.17.
BOND William Henry MM Pte 43392 13th Durham Light Infantry KIA 20.9.17.
BONE Albert "MM,MID" Pte 8589 Hampshire Regt
BONE Alfred MM L/Cpl 57360 82 Fd Coy Royal Engineers
BONE Alfred Philip "DCM,MM+Bar" Sjt 85640 34 Div Sig Coy Royal Engineers DOW 28.10.17.
BONE Aubrey Augustus MM Sjt 64542 41 Bde RFA

BONE C.A.J. MM L/Cpl L/11066 1st Royal Fusiliers
BONE Charles MM L/Sjt 43842 West Yorkshire Regt
BONE Charles Christie MM Sjt 229 22nd Royal Fusiliers
BONE George MM Pte 90015 137 Fd Amb RAMC
BONE George A. MM Sjt 450713 11th London Regt
BONE Harold J. MM Pte 12416 7th Royal Sussex Regt
BONE Henry J. MM Cpl 191161 RGA
BONE Henry W. MM Sjt 43999 Royal Engineers
BONE Herbert James MM Cpl 590666 2/18th London Regt
BONE Herbert W. MM L/Cpl C/12843 King's Royal Rifle Corps
BONE James MM Pte 21320 Arg & Suth Highlanders
BONE John MM Bdr 26171 RFA
BONE Percy W. MM Spr 166005 Royal Engineers
BONE Robert G. MM L/Cpl 302321 5th London Regt
BONE Stanley A. MM Sjt 96865 328 Siege Bty RGA
BONE Thomas "DCM,MM" Cpl S/19220 Rifle Brigade
BONE William MM Sjt 200613 2/4th Hampshire Regt
BONE William MM Bdr 21373 B/78 Bde RFA
BONE William A. MM Sjt 12/888 7th East Yorkshire Regt
BONE William Arthur MM Cpl G/4952 8th East Surrey Regt KIA 1.7.16.
BONE William J. MM Cpl 345938 16th Devonshire Regt
BONEHAM Cyril G. MM Pte 10171 Coldstream Guards
BONEHAM Harry MM L/Sjt 12411 1st Coldstream Guards
BONEHILL William MM Pte 9940 Royal Warwickshire Regt
BONELL William Frederick MM Cpl 735756 RFA
BONES Alfred J. MM Pte 72611 3rd Royal Fusiliers
BONES Harry MM Sjt 18677 7 Fd Coy Royal Engineers
BONES J.R. MM CSM L/8522 1st East Kent Regt
BONES William MM Cpl 15553 7th East Kent Regt KIA 22.8.18.
BONEWELL W. MM CSM 21742 7th East Yorkshire Regt
BONFIELD Jack MM Sjt 2271 MGC(Motors)
BONFIELD John MM Cpl G/6006 13th Royal Fusiliers
BONHAM Albert MM Spr 281990 31 Div Sig Coy Royal Engineers
BONHAM Alec MM Sjt B712 Rifle Brigade
BONHAM Joseph MM L/Cpl 6402 1st Irish Guards
BONIFACE Alfred E. MM L/Cpl M2/049226 Army Service Corps
BONIFACE George Horace MM Pte 38580 2/5th Lancashire Fusiliers
BONIFACE John F. MM L/Cpl 11528 7th Dragoon Guards
BONIFACE Walter MM Cpl 15888 13th Royal Sussex Regt
BONIFACE William MM Pte 18038 2nd Leinster Regt
BONNALLO Marshall MM Dvr 13320 49 Bty 40 Bde RFA
BONNAR James MM Pte 252405 1/6th Arg & Suth Highlanders
BONNAR Matthew C. MM Pte M2/052228 Army Service Corps
BONNAR William MM Pte 201087 1/5th Seaforth Highlanders
BONNELL Sarah MM Miss F First Aid Nursing Yeomanry
BONNER Cecil MM Pte 241565 2/5th West Riding Regt
BONNER Charles MM L/Cpl 11409 15th Hussars
BONNER Charles C. "MM,MID" L/Cpl 1451 Durham Light Infantry
BONNER Edward MM L/Cpl G/30560 17th Royal Sussex Regt
BONNER Edwin Charles MM Pte 9090 6th Royal West Kent Regt
BONNER George MM Sjt 60167 15/17th West Yorkshire Regt
BONNER George W. MM Pte 1878 24 Fd Amb RAMC
BONNER Harry Victor MM Sjt 41664 A/74 Bde RFA
BONNER Harry Victor MM Cpl 18/636 Northumberland Fusiliers
BONNER James A. MM Pte 68193 8th Royal West Surrey Regt
BONNER John W. MM Pte 235370 10th West Riding Regt
BONNER Joseph J. MM Pte 64436 102 Fd Amb RAMC KIA 16.10.17.
BONNER Robert MM Pte 18157 1st Royal Inniskilling Fusiliers
BONNER Samuel MM Bdr 27756 D/168 Bde RFA
BONNER Thomas MM Pte 25433 15th Hampshire Regt
BONNER Thomas H. MM Pte 15050 1 Special Coy Middlesex Regt
BONNER Walter H. MM Bdr 316374 RGA
BONNER William MM Pte 3877 15 Fd Amb RAMC
BONNER William I. MM Sjt 64916 Notts & Derby Regt
BONNER William J. MM Pte 51451 14th Welsh Regt
BONNET Harry L. MM L/Cpl G/95785 10th Royal Fusiliers
BONNEY John MM Sjt 685009 RFA
BONNEY Wilfred George MM Cpl 45643 RFA
BONNICK Thomas George "MM,MC(G)" Sjt 3570 4th Rifle Brigade
BONNINGTON Tom MM Pte 129992 18th Bn Machine Gun Corps
BONNON John MM Gnr 13444 C/160 Bde RFA
BONNY Robert G. MM Sjt 27914 'L' Bty RHA
BONSALL Frederick MM Pte 202299 Royal Lancaster Regt
BONSALL George MM Dvr L/8010 RFA
BONSALL Herbert MM Cpl 33463 9th Royal Welsh Fusiliers KIA 4.1.18.
BONSER Albert E. MM Sjt R/12832 King's Royal Rifle Corps

BONSER Alfred J. MM S/Sjt 8666 66 Fd Amb RAMC
BONSER Arthur MM Sjt R/9414 4th King's Royal Rifle Corps
BONSER Reginald MM Gnr 215200 A/83 Bde RFA
BONSEY Arthur G. MM Cpl 4480 2nd Royal Fusiliers
BONSEY Ernest MM Cpl 4421 1st Royal West Surrey Regt KIA 25.9.17.
BONSEY Frederick J. MM Pte 202988 1st London Regt
BONSOR Albert Edward MM Gnr 156321 157 Siege Bty RGA
BONTHRONE William MM L/Cpl 46080 Royal Engineers
BOOBYER Frederick MM L/Cpl 15071 Gloucestershire Regt
BOOBYER James MM L/Cpl 23431 South Wales Borderers
BOOCOCK Harry Anderson MM Pte 267015 West Riding Regt
BOOCOCK James MM Cpl 13/70 13th York & Lancaster Regt
BOOCOCK Joseph MM Pte 22849 7th Royal West Surrey Regt
BOOCOCK Richard MM L/Cpl 58728 170 Coy Machine Gun Corps
BOOCOCK W.H. MM Pte 201120 1/5th Welsh Regt
BOOD Ben MM Dvr 810353 B/232 Bde RFA
BOOKER Audsley MM Sjt 306674 8th West Yorkshire Regt
BOOKER Francis W. MM Pte 275039 7th Manchester Regt
BOOKER George A. MM Pte 16250 32nd Bn Machine Gun Corps
BOOKER George H. MM Dvr 624937 HAC att B/126 Bde RFA
BOOKER Harry MM Cpl 203541 Scottish Rifles
BOOKER Harry MM+Bar Pte A/650 King's Royal Rifle Corps
BOOKER J.H. MM Pte 403446 2 Fd Amb RAMC
BOOKER James E. MM Cpl 7274 6th Dragoon Guards
BOOKER Percy MM L/Cpl 2143 7th Royal Sussex Regt
BOOKER Richard Kirkby MM Pte 33876 16th Royal Warwickshire Regt
BOOKER Thomas MM Pte 10506 South Staffordshire Regt
BOOKER Young MM Spr 100186 226 Fd Coy Royal Engineers
BOOL Edwin W. MM Bdr 30855 RFA
BOOL Frank L. MM Dvr 476178 Royal Engineers
BOOL Victor C. MM Pte 633761 20th London Regt
BOOLE Harry MM Pte 53378 15/17th West Yorkshire Regt
BOOMER William H. MM Pte 23411 15th Hussars
BOOMSMA T. MM Pte 52017 10th West Yorkshire Regt
BOON Albert MM Cpl 67265 113 Coy Labour Corps
BOON Christopher MM Pte 34550 8th East Surrey Regt
BOON Cyril C. MM L/Cpl 12251 Machine Gun Corps
BOON Douglas MM Pte 243696 1/7th Cheshire Regt
BOON Elijah MM L/Cpl 13266 9th North Staffordshire Regt
BOON Horace Frederick Henry MM L/Cpl 10507 2nd Scots Guards
BOON Isaac MM Pte 201680 2/4th South Lancashire Regt
BOON John Rutherford MM Cpl 235446 9th York & Lancaster Regt
BOON John W. MM L/Cpl 283991 4th London Regt
BOON Robert MM Pte 5856 Army Cyclist Corps
BOON Sidney Charles MM Cpl 5058 9th Royal Fusiliers KIA 21.9.18.
BOON Walter A. MM Pte 50217 54th Bn Machine Gun Corps
BOON William "MM,MSM" CQMS 10464 Royal Dublin Fusiliers
BOORER Frederick MM Cpl 55779 16th Royal Welsh Fusiliers
BOORMAN Albert E. MM Pte 490244 1/13th London Regt
BOORMAN Alfred J. MM Gnr 68770 RFA
BOORMAN Arthur John MM Pte 25888 6th Royal West Kent Regt
BOORMAN Frederick MM Sjt 56094 25 Bde RFA
BOOST Thomas William "MM,MSM" Cpl 65749 36 Div Ammn Col RFA
BOOT Ernest MM Pte 16331 1st South Staffordshire Regt Sentenced to death Mar 1917.Commuted.
BOOTE Charles E. MM Pte S/21473 Rifle Brigade
BOOTH Arthur MM Pte 62185 RAMC
BOOTH Arthur MM Pte 281059 Lancashire Fusiliers
BOOTH Cecil B. MM Sjt 54060 19th Durham Light Infantry
BOOTH Charles Buchan "DCM,MM" Pte 200083 1/4th Gordon Highlanders
BOOTH Charles Henry "DCM,MM" Sjt 9894 2nd Coldstream Guards
BOOTH Charles L. MM L/Cpl 20442 8th West Yorkshire Regt
BOOTH Charles R. MM Sjt Fitter 687436 RFA
BOOTH Charles T. MM Cpl 11903 4th Royal Fusiliers
BOOTH Christopher William MM L/Cpl 22559 4th Grenadier Guards
BOOTH Edgar "DCM,MM" Cpl 202042 2/5th West Riding Regt DOW 8.11.18.
BOOTH Edward MM Pte 95 Middlesex Regt
BOOTH Edward O. MM Pte 55853 2/5th Highland Light Infantry KIA 24.8.18.
BOOTH Edwin J. MM S/Sjt Armt Art 58056 RGA
BOOTH Eli MM Cpl M2/116191 Att 74 Fd Amb RAMC Army Service Corps
BOOTH Ernest MM Spr 444484 Royal Engineers
BOOTH Ernest H. MM Cpl 50810 94 Fd Coy Royal Engineers
BOOTH Ernest Harry MM Gnr Sig 940464 D/48 Bde RFA
BOOTH Frank MM L/Sjt 37334 Machine Gun Corps
BOOTH Fred MM Cpl Shoeing Smith 61546 135 Bty 32 Bde RFA
BOOTH Fred MM Pte 21338 Grenadier Guards
BOOTH Frederick MM Sjt 41810 RAMC
BOOTH George MM Pte 14623 17th Lancashire Fusiliers
BOOTH George H. MM L/Cpl 68376 30th Bn Machine Gun Corps
BOOTH George Henry MM Pte M2/073198 15 Div Train Army Service Corps
BOOTH George W. MM Spr 72214 Royal Engineers
BOOTH George William MM Pte 3465 19th Middlesex Regt
BOOTH Gilbert R. MM Pte 26840 2/4th West Riding Regt
BOOTH Harold MM Gnr 25526 23 Div Ammn Col RFA
BOOTH Harold Guy Brooke MM L/Sjt 808 22nd Royal Fusiliers
BOOTH Harry MM Pte 20105 1st King's Own Scottish Borderers
BOOTH Henry E. MM Bdr 293279 140 Hy Bty RGA
BOOTH Herbert MM Cpl 307932 7th West Riding Regt
BOOTH Herbert MM+Bar Pte 300758 8th Durham Light Infantry
BOOTH James MM Sjt 65256 Northumberland Fusiliers
BOOTH James MM Pte 8338 22 Fd Amb RAMC
BOOTH James H. MM L/Bdr 292730 137 Hy Bty RGA
BOOTH James M. MM Cpl 676 Royal Engineers
BOOTH John "DCM,MM" L/Cpl 12141 7th Royal Lancaster Regt KIA 28.9.17.
BOOTH John MM Pte 14007 1st Middlesex Regt
BOOTH John MM Gne 100773 RFA
BOOTH John MM Pte 12354 2nd Notts & Derby Regt
BOOTH John MM L/Cpl 1028 GMGR
BOOTH John MM Bdr 776097 RFA
BOOTH John E. MM Pte 20039 15th Lancashire Fusiliers
BOOTH John E. MM Pte 224274 Labour Corps
BOOTH John T. MM Sjt 19218 Durham Light Infantry
BOOTH John W. MM Pte 39713 9th Yorkshire Light Infantry
BOOTH John William MM Sjt S/11458 Highland Light Infantry KIA 7.8.17.
BOOTH Joseph MM Gnr 190187 D/122 Bde RFA
BOOTH Joseph MM Cpl 19778 Border Regt
BOOTH Joseph E. MM Spr 440592 431 Fd Coy Royal Engineers KIA 25.3.18.
BOOTH Joseph H. MM Pte 36549 Lancashire Fusiliers
BOOTH Kenneth S. MM Dvr 144803 RFA
BOOTH Leonard MM Pte E/1639 17th Royal Fusiliers
BOOTH Leonard Alfred MM Sjt 203338 2nd Suffolk Regt KIA 27.9.18.
BOOTH Leonard Randolph Budworth MM Pte 48632 13th Liverpool Regt KIA 8.10.18.
BOOTH Maurice Evans MM Pte 12798 3rd Coldstream Guards
BOOTH Oliver MM Gnr 81917 120 Bty 27 Bde RFA KIA 24.7.16.
BOOTH Percy MM Pte 124004 Machine Gun Corps
BOOTH R.N. MM Air Mech 1 26216 Royal Flying Corps
BOOTH Robert MM Spr 57998 36 Div Sig Coy Royal Engineers
BOOTH Robert MM Pte 7548 20th Manchester Regt
BOOTH Samuel MM Pte L/17458 7th Royal Fusiliers
BOOTH Samuel MM Sjt 268683 9th West Riding Regt
BOOTH Thomas MM+Bar Sjt 56527 102 Fd Coy Royal Engineers
BOOTH Thomas MM Gnr 148416 RGA
BOOTH Thomas MM Sjt 352563 94 Fd Amb RAMC
BOOTH Thomas MM Dvr 23312 37 Bde RFA
BOOTH W. MM Cpl 305563 13th Bn Tank Corps
BOOTH Walter MM Pte 24294 Lancashire Fusiliers
BOOTH Walter MM+2 Bars Pte 70884 RAMC
BOOTH Wilfred MM Pte M2/073975 365 MT Coy Army Service Corps
BOOTH William MM+Bar Pte 48670 13th Liverpool Regt
BOOTH William MM Pte 202447 2nd Lincolnshire Regt
BOOTH William MM Pte 2759 Lancashire Fusiliers
BOOTH William A. MM L/Cpl 9992 1st Royal West Kent Regt
BOOTH William H. MM Pte 202378 Lancashire Fusiliers
BOOTH William Henry MM L/Cpl 17753 11th Notts & Derby Regt
BOOTH William Henry MM Cpl 17553 2nd South Lancashire Regt KIA 22.3.18.
BOOTH William Herbert MM CSM 7061 2nd Yorkshire Light Infantry
BOOTH William T. MM L/Cpl 390 Royal Sussex Regt
BOOTHBY A. MM Cpl 290332 7th Cheshire Regt
BOOTHBY Frederick T. MM Pte S/27483 Rifle Brigade
BOOTHMAN John James MM L/Cpl 3895 1/5th Liverpool Regt
BOOTHROYD Frank MM L/Cpl 89432 72 Fd Coy Royal Engineers
BOOTHROYD Gilbert MM Pte 24865 7th West Riding Regt
BOOTHWAY Edward MM Pte 41809 Royal Irish Rifles
BOOTON John Edward MM Cpl R/861 7th King's Royal Rifle Corps

BOOTREY Patrick MM Pte 1504 7th Leinster Regt
BORDER Alfred H. MM Pte 572705 17th London Regt
BORE William A. MM Gnr 58308 RFA
BOREHAM Alfred W. MM Pte R/2011 4th King's Royal Rifle Corps
BOREHAM Edward MM Pte 12649 1 Special Coy King's Royal Rifle Corps
BOREHAM George MM Sjt 8786 38th Bn Machine Gun Corps
BOREHAM Harry Edward "MM,MSM" CQMS 14774 11th Essex Regt
BOREHAM Victor MM Pte 16046 5th Northamptonshire Regt KIA 20.9.18.
BOREHAM William MM Sjt 1220 Royal Sussex Regt
BORELAND Charles MM Sjt 15/12557 15th Royal Irish Rifles
BORELAND Samuel Ernest MM L/Cpl 15/12556 15th Royal Irish Rifles
BORKETT Charles A. MM 2nd Cpl 253233 Royal Engineers
BORKETT William MM Sjt M1/7148 89 Coy Army Service Corps
BORLAND John MM L/Sjt 12861 2nd Royal Scots Fusiliers
BORLASE Charles MM Pte M2/055191 Army Service Corps
BORLEY Edward Arthur MM Sjt 721090 1/24th London Regt
BORLEY Rufus S. MM Sjt 12062 2nd Highland Light Infantry
BORLEY Victor G. MM Pte 200311 1/4th Suffolk Regt
BORRER Thomas H. MM L/Cpl 40928 Lancashire Fusiliers
BORRETT John H. MM Sjt 67568 43 Bty 24 Bde RFA
BORRETT William G. MM F/Sjt 897 Royal Flying Corps
BORRIE William A. MM Pte 391642 9th London Regt
BORROW Francis MM Cpl 9906 Hampshire Regt
BORROWS H.E. MM Gnr 1291 RFA
BORROWS J. MM Cpl 43158 Essex Regt
BORTHWICK J.R. MM Sjt 20138 2nd Manchester Regt
BORTHWICK Stephen MM Sjt 46865 D/94 Bde RFA Died 7.11.18.
BORTHWICK Thomas MM L/Cpl 7042 1st Royal Lancaster Regt DOW 1.7.16.
BORTHWICK Thomas D. MM L/Cpl 482419 62 Div Sig Coy Royal Engineers
BORTHWICK William MM Pte 331584 Highland Light Infantry
BOSBURY Tom "MM,MID" Sjt 51433 Machine Gun Corps
BOSCHI James Lawrence MM Pte 47070 15th Lancashire Fusiliers
BOSELEY Percy Henry MM Pte L/8229 7th East Kent Regt KIA 12.10.17.
BOSHELL A. MM Pte 403410 2 Fd Amb RAMC
BOSHER Alfred MM Spr 59345 Royal Engineers
BOSHER George MM Gnr 36571 421 Bty RFA
BOSHER William H.C. MM Pte 703342 23rd London Regt
BOSHIER Henry MM L/Cpl 16465 2nd King's Own Scottish Borderers
BOSLEY Cornelius "DCM,MM" Sjt 26408 D/83 Bde RFA
BOSLEY George MM+Bar Sjt 492043 46 Div Sig Coy Royal Engineers
BOSLEY Richard James MM Cpl 37040 1st Royal West Surrey Regt
BOSLEY William "MM,CG(F)" Pte 16594 11th Worcestershire Regt
BOSS John W. MM Sjt 44491 42nd Bn Machine Gun Corps
BOSSOM Percy Grantham MM Pte 27725 8th Gloucestershire Regt DOW 12.5.17.
BOSTOCK Albert MM Cpl 282580 Lancashire Fusiliers
BOSTOCK Edward York MM L/Cpl 204240 7th East Yorkshire Regt
BOSTOCK James "MM,MID" Cpl 16759 HQ 109 Bde RFA
BOSTOCK Joe MM Dvr 34568 40 Div Ammn Col RFA
BOSTOCK John MM Sjt R/11001 9th King's Royal Rifle Corps
BOSTOCK Joseph R. MM T/Cpl 28836 23 Fd Coy Royal Engineers
BOSTOCK Reginald T. MM L/Cpl 17326 Royal Welsh Fusiliers
BOSTOCK Richard MM Pte 9534 Liverpool Regt
BOSTOCK T. MM L/Cpl 52506 18th Gloucestershire Regt
BOSTOCK W. MM L/Cpl 10763 9th Cheshire Regt
BOSTOCK William MM+Bar 2nd Cpl 7030 Royal Engineers
BOSTON Arthur J. MM Sjt 12538 1st Bedfordshire Regt
BOSTON Ernest MM Pte 38215 15th Lancashire Fusiliers
BOSTWICK Albert H. MM Dvr 41283 RFA
BOSWARD Ernest A. MM Pte 63266 4th Yorkshire Light Infantry
BOSWELL A.D. MM 2nd Cpl 198900 Royal Engineers
BOSWELL Arthur E. MM Pte 200630 1/4th Royal Sussex Regt
BOSWELL Edward G. MM L/Cpl 208697 6th Dorsetshire Regt
BOSWELL Frederick Walter "DCM,MM,MID" L/Cpl 70059 1/1st Berkshire Yeomanry
BOSWELL George W. MM Pte M2/133876 Army Service Corps
BOSWELL John W. MM Pte 21064 Notts & Derby Regt
BOSWELL Thomas J. MM Cpl 130819 Royal Engineers
BOSWELL Thomas William MM Sjt 290738 124 Heavy Bty RGA
BOSWELL William MM S/Sjt 277 RAMC
BOSWELL William Albert MM Dvr 19287 D/64 Bde RFA

BOSWORTH Fred MM Gnr 840636 RFA
BOSWORTH Frederick A. MM+Bar Bdr 840058 RFA
BOSWORTH Joseph MM Sjt 10627 2nd Grenadier Guards KIA 1.12.17.
BOSWORTH Richard MM L/Cpl 14212 17th Lancashire Fusiliers
BOSWORTH William MM L/Cpl 32837 1 Div Sig Coy Royal Engineers
BOTHAM Frank MM L/Bdr 686084 RFA
BOTHAM John Charles Beardmore MM Bdr 134540 C/232 Bde RFA
BOTHAM John W. MM Pte 33110 2nd Welsh Regt
BOTHAM Thomas MM+Bar Cpl 10319 Leicestershire Regt
BOTHAM William E. MM Pte 276702 7th Manchester Regt
BOTHAMLEY John J. MM Pte 12235 6th Lincolnshire Regt
BOTHWELL Francis I. MM Pte 514842 14th London Regt
BOTHWELL Frank MM Pte 54676 4 Fd Amb RAMC KIA 27.9.18.
BOTHWELL John MM Sjt 9997 2nd Highland Light Infantry
BOTT Frederick MM Spr 146543 106 Fd Coy Royal Engineers
BOTT George A. MM Pte 548034 15th London Regt
BOTT Harry MM Sjt 17694 2nd Wiltshire Regt KIA 7.8.18.
BOTT J.H. MM L/Cpl 417420 RAMC
BOTT John E. MM Sjt M2/099492 Army Service Corps
BOTT Nelson MM Sjt T/29538 2 Div Train Army Service Corps
BOTT Norman Albert "DCM,MM" Sjt 19003 1st Suffolk Regt
BOTT Samuel MM Cpl 50283 RAMC
BOTTCHER William MM Pte 280 Welsh Guards
BOTTERELL George MM+Bar Cpl 240034 1/5th Devonshire Regt
BOTTERELL Thomas MM Bdr 71271 88 Bde RFA
BOTTERILL Archibald MM L/Sjt 8117 8th Hussars
BOTTERILL George A. MM Sjt 202009 1st Leicestershire Regt
BOTTING Arthur MM Pte 14491 7th Shropshire Light Infantry KIA 13.11.16.
BOTTING George MM Sjt 9917 1st Royal West Kent Regt
BOTTING Gerald Victor MM L/Cpl 200320 2nd Bn Tank Corps
BOTTING Herbert MM Sjt 757 GMGR
BOTTING J. MM Sjt 39732 36 Bde RFA
BOTTING John David MM L/Sjt S/15 8th Royal West Surrey Regt DOW 2.4.18.
BOTTING Ronald "DCM,MM" Cpl L/13678 1st Royal Fusiliers
BOTTOM George Arthur MM Cpl 20447 6th Royal West Kent Regt KIA 29.9.18.
BOTTOMLEY Arthur MM L/Cpl 201773 Seaforth Highlanders
BOTTOMLEY Eddie MM Cpl 242133 6th West Riding Regt
BOTTOMLEY Ernest MM Sjt 21429 6th York & Lancaster Regt
BOTTOMLEY Ernest MM Sjt 8543 2nd East Yorkshire Regt
BOTTOMLEY Fred MM Pte 242336 7th West Yorkshire Regt
BOTTOMLEY George MM CQMS 3/12126 8th West Riding Regt DOW 28.4.17.
BOTTOMLEY Harold E. MM Cpl 10159 2nd Royal Fusiliers
BOTTOMLEY J. MM Pte 305435 7th West Riding Regt
BOTTOMLEY James MM Pte 21781 1st Royal Lancaster Regt KIA 18.4.18.
BOTTOMLEY John MM Pte 14017 10th North Lancashire Regt DOW 6.4.18.
BOTTOMLEY John William MM Pte S/235 12th Rifle Brigade
BOTTOMLEY Robert MM Pte 403111 RAMC
BOTTOMLEY Samuel MM L/Cpl 18602 Yorkshire Light Infantry
BOTTOMLEY W. MM Gnr 18336 RFA
BOTTOMS Thomas MM Pte 18674 109 Coy Machine Gun Corps KIA 1.7.16.
BOTTOMS Wilfred MM Sjt 13899 Yorkshire Regt
BOTTRILL John T. MM Spr 478713 54 Fd Coy Royal Engineers
BOTTRILL Stephen Neil MM Cpl 2115 Liverpool Regt
BOTTWOOD N. MM Cpl 42666 Royal Engineers
BOTWRIGHT George MM Pte 13923 2nd Yorkshire Light Infantry
BOTWRIGHT John J. MM Pte 7297 Middlesex Regt
BOUCH C. MM Sjt 38685 Yorkshire Light Infantry
BOUCH Reg MM Gnr Sig 875997 A/223 Bde RFA
BOUCHER Bertram Jesse MM Gnr 98099 13 Bty 17 Bde RFA
BOUCHER Frederick J. MM Pte 33019 RAMC
BOUCHIER Frederick MM Pte 10467 1st King's Royal Rifle Corps
BOUCKLEY Reginald A. MM Pte 50290 RAMC
BOUGH Edward MM Pte 19554 Royal Sussex Regt
BOUGH Harry MM Pte 29358 8th Somerset Light Infantry
BOUGHEY Edgar MM+Bar Sjt 8461 5th Yorkshire Light Infantry
BOUGHEY Norman MM Pte G/8916 13th Royal Fusiliers
BOUGHTON Alfred "MM,MID" Sjt 650294 21st London Regt
BOUGHTON Ernest J. MM L/Cpl M2/050815 Army Service Corps
BOUGHTON Jack MM Dvr 114681 RFA
BOUGHTON John MM Pte 451471 11th London Regt
BOUGHTON William John MM Pte 110734 Machine Gun Corps

BOUL Thomas Arthur MM Bdr 72462 56 Bty 34 Bde RFA
BOULDEN Basil R. "MM,MSM" Cpl 915815 B/291 Bde RFA
BOULDEN George Lewis MM Bdr 47618 Y/37 Med TM Bty RGA
BOULDSTRIDGE Walter W. MM L/Cpl 283803 4th London Regt
BOULGER John Bradley MM Pte 16947 12th Durham Light Infantry
BOULSTRIDGE William MM Sjt 40090 Z Bty RHA
BOULT Arthur Frederick MM Sjt 1390 21st London Regt
BOULT John R. MM Pte 57492 2/5th West Yorkshire Regt
BOULTER A.C. MM Gnr 156686 RGA
BOULTER J. MM Pte 25378 10th West Riding Regt
BOULTER William Arthur MM Pte 37762 2nd Worcestershire Regt KIA 29.9.18.
BOULTER William F. MM Spr 66637 23 Div Sig Coy Royal Engineers DOW 9.10.16.
BOULTER William G. MM Cpl 45748 RFA
BOULTON Alfred MM Spr 496483 Royal Engineers
BOULTON Ben MM Gnr 313308 RGA
BOULTON Bertram Frederick MM Sjt 2878 North Staffordshire Regt
BOULTON David Grahame MM Dvr 190548 D/38 Bde RFA
BOULTON Edward MM+Bar Gnr 78909 B/70 Bde RFA
BOULTON Edward MM L/Sjt 28541 1st Royal Warwickshire Regt
BOULTON Frederick James MM Pte 20748 10th Royal West Kent Regt KIA 25.10.18.
BOULTON George MM Sjt 830039 RFA
BOULTON Harry MM L/Cpl 510456 RAMC
BOULTON Joseph Frederick MM Dvr 1003 47 Div Ammn Col RFA
BOULTON Mark H. MM Cpl 28537 252 Coy Machine Gun Corps
BOULTON Samuel MM L/Cpl 13628 1st Worcestershire Regt
BOULTON Thomas G. "DCM,MM" Cpl 18277 1st Gloucestershire Regt
BOULTON William Henry MM L/Cpl 83161 21st Bn Machine Gun Corps DOW 29.8.18.
BOULTON Wilson J. MM Pte R/19326 13th King's Royal Rifle Corps
BOUNDS Edward W. MM Pte L/14604 4th Royal Fusiliers
BOUNDY B.O. MM Air Mech 1 25272 Royal Flying Corps
BOUQUET Henry W. MM Gnr 60175 RFA
BOURDIN Henry Charles MM L/Cpl 41039 Middlesex Regt
BOURGOURD A.H. MM Pte 47353 11th Royal Fusiliers
BOURHILL Alexander MM Cpl 265309 Liverpool Regt
BOURHILL Richard C. MM Cpl 267449 7th Liverpool Regt
BOURKE Bernard "DCM,MM" Cpl M2/131363 13 Lt Armd Mot Bty Army Service Corps
BOURKE James B. MM+Bar Cpl 42839 Royal Engineers
BOURKE T. MM Pte 403358 2/2nd(West Riding)Fd Amb RAMC
BOURN Arthur W. MM Pte 43421 Suffolk Regt
BOURN Herbert J. MM Gnr 197204 125 Bty 29 Bde RFA
BOURNE Albert MM+Bar L/Cpl B/201668 12th Rifle Brigade
BOURNE Alfred A. MM Cpl 296245 99 Siege Bty RGA
BOURNE Arthur E. MM Pte 20272 1st Coldstream Guards
BOURNE Bertie MM Sjt 29189 6th Royal Warwickshire Regt
BOURNE Bertram MM Sjt 15458 7th Yorkshire Light Infantry
BOURNE E. MM Sjt 39179 B/175 Bde RFA
BOURNE Edward R. MM+Bar Sjt 21494 Machine Gun Corps
BOURNE Ernest George MM Sjt 70047 41 Bde RFA
BOURNE Frank MM L/Cpl 9771 1st Devonshire Regt
BOURNE Frederick H. MM Cpl 49163 D/310 Bde RFA
BOURNE George Herbert MM Bdr 102387 B/77 Bde RFA
BOURNE H. MM Sjt 265069 West Yorkshire Regt
BOURNE James MM Spr 30978 Royal Engineers
BOURNE John MM L/Cpl 266009 7th Liverpool Regt
BOURNE Joseph S. MM Pte 5212 9th Royal Sussex Regt
BOURNE Louis MM S/Sjt Farrier 15925 31 Hy Bty RGA
BOURNE Stephen F. MM Pte 65289 RAMC
BOURNE Vivian J. MM Cpl 104413 Labour Corps
BOURNE W.H. MM Pte 403165 RAMC
BOURNER Albert Edward MM Cpl S3/029811 17 Fd Bakery Army Service Corps
BOURNER George MM L/Cpl 8973 6th East Kent Regt
BOURNES Norman J. MM Sjt 19183 10th Yorkshire Regt
BOURTON Thomas MM L/Cpl 61505 39 Coy Machine Gun Corps
BOUSFIELD Edward MM L/Cpl C/12420 King's Royal Rifle Corps
BOUSFIELD John MM L/Cpl 3453 1/9th Durham Light Infantry
BOUSFIELD John A. MM Pte 22282 8th Royal Lancaster Regt
BOUSFIELD Joseph MM Pte 21352 15th Durham Light Infantry KIA 28.5.18.
BOUSHER Arthur G. MM Sjt 1860 24th London Regt
BOUSKILL David MM Dvr 84539 11 Bty 84 Bde RFA DOW 20.12.18.
BOUSTEAD Joseph H. MM Cpl 51890 23rd Middlesex Regt
BOUTFLOWER Ralph S. MM Sjt 1510 Durham Light Infantry
BOUTILIER Borden S. MM Pnr 197189 Royal Engineers
BOUTTELL Cecil MM Pte 77190 RAMC
BOUVERIE Charles MM Sjt 302078 5th London Regt
BOVELL William MM Pte S/10546 6th Cameron Highlanders
BOVILL Alfred P MM Pte 16759 Welsh Regt
BOVILLE Joseph MM Sjt 104015 227 Fd Coy Royal Engineers
BOVIN Alfred MM+Bar Pte 9369 1st Dorsetshire Regt
BOVINGDON Frederick H. MM BSM 45068 C/187 Bde RFA
BOVINGDON George H. MM+Bar L/Cpl 38197 Royal Fusiliers
BOVINGDON Thomas P. MM Pte 766504 1/28th London Regt
BOWCOCK Stanley MM Cpl 14998 1st Cheshire Regt
BOWCOCK William MM L/Cpl R/11561 King's Royal Rifle Corps
BOWCUTT John MM Sjt 830073 B/241 Bde RFA
BOWDEN Arthur Samuel MM Pte R/31774 18th King's Royal Rifle Corps
BOWDEN Charles MM Sjt 34512 1/6th Cheshire Regt
BOWDEN Charles MM Spr 28920 Royal Engineers
BOWDEN Edward C.S. MM Dvr 496450 Royal Engineers
BOWDEN Ernest "MM+Bar,MID" Sjt 20950 5 Fd Coy Royal Engineers
BOWDEN Ernest A. "MM,MID" Sjt 6825 2nd Devonshire Regt
BOWDEN Fred MM Sjt 7280 11th Notts & Derby Regt
BOWDEN Frederick W. MM L/Cpl 498272 Royal Engineers
BOWDEN Griffith MM L/Cpl 44424 15th Welsh Regt
BOWDEN James MM Cpl 14521 10th Cheshire Regt
BOWDEN John E. MM L/Cpl H/271037 1/1st Northumberland Yeo
BOWDEN John R. MM Sjt Wheeler 25918 1 Siege Bty RGA
BOWDEN Philip S. MM Gnr 39392 RFA
BOWDEN Samuel MM Pte 42025 Machine Gun Corps
BOWDEN Samuel Hollingworth MM Pte 19541 10th Yorkshire Regt
BOWDEN William MM Pte 38530 37 Fd Amb RAMC
BOWDEN William S. MM Pte 14/17196 15th Royal Irish Rifles
BOWDITCH Arthur Frederick MM Pte 39953 1st Wiltshire Regt KIA 15.9.18.
BOWDITCH D.A.H. MM Pte 512491 3 Fd Amb RAMC
BOWDITCH John H. MM Pte 104 Durham Light Infantry
BOWDLER Fred MM Pte 307976 15th Bn Tank Corps
BOWDLER John MM Pte 5582 1st Scots Guards
BOWDREY James F. MM Pte 31493 Suffolk Regt
BOWE Arthur MM L/Sjt 19219 8th Northumberland Fusiliers
BOWE Francis MM Pte 375979 19th Durham Light Infantry
BOWE James MM Pte 925 Lancashire Fusiliers
BOWE John G. MM Gnr 116315 RGA
BOWE William MM Pte 23474 12th Manchester Regt
BOWELL Thomas William MM Gnr 9752 Z/15 Med TM Bty RFA DOW 9.4.17.London SW.
BOWELS Albert E. MM Sjt 229620 26th Royal Fusiliers
BOWEN Arthur E. MM Sjt 57996 RGA
BOWEN Charles MM Sjt 7/24250 Royal Dublin Fusiliers
BOWEN E.J. MM Pnr 214673 Royal Engineers
BOWEN Edward MM Cpl A/2947 13th King's Royal Rifle Corps
BOWEN Edward MM L/Cpl 16764 13th Royal Welsh Fusiliers
BOWEN George A. MM Pte 46008 Welsh Regt
BOWEN George Aaron MM L/Sjt 241127 2/6th North Staffordshire Regt KIA 29.11.17.
BOWEN Godfrey W. MM Pte 203760 1st Lincolnshire Regt
BOWEN Griffith MM Pte 8/16671 8th South Wales Borderers
BOWEN Harold H. MM Gnr 1547 MGC(Motors)
BOWEN Herbert MM Cpl 5127 6th Notts & Derby Regt
BOWEN John MM Gnr 69279 2 Bde RFA
BOWEN John MM+Bar Pte 23508 Shropshire Light Infantry
BOWEN Robert MM L/Cpl 76062 Machine Gun Corps
BOWEN Stanley MM Cpl 60432 14 Bde RFA
BOWEN Stanley J. MM Pte 57201 99 Fd Amb RAMC
BOWEN Walter G. MM Sjt 2168 Monmouthshire Regt
BOWEN William "MM,MID" Sjt T4/174013 Army Service Corps
BOWER Albert MM Pte 17/9500 17th Manchester Regt
BOWER Alexander MM Cpl 15769 9th Yorkshire Regt
BOWER Ambrose MM L/Cpl 7584 2nd Yorkshire Regt KIA 26.0.17.
BOWER Andrew MM Pte 17692 12th Highland Light Infantry
BOWER Edwin A. MM Spr 191951 Royal Engineers
BOWER Ernest C. MM L/Cpl 200888 6th York & Lancaster Regt
BOWER Frank S. MM Sjt 12092 West Riding Regt
BOWER Frederick William MM Sjt 19371 17th Lancashire Fusiliers
BOWER H. MM Cpl 405247 RAMC
BOWER Harold MM Pte 242650 Yorkshire Light Infantry
BOWER Herbert MM Spr 17265 475 Fd Coy Royal Engineers
BOWER John A. MM Pte 64737 9th Northumberland Fusiliers
BOWER William MM Pte 20413 2nd West Riding Regt
BOWER William MM Pte 18968 9th Notts & Derby Regt

BOWER William R. MM L/Cpl 1895 1/1st Sherwood Rangers Yeo
BOWERBANK Vincent MM RQMS 18/663 Northumberland Fusiliers
BOWERBANK William MM Pte 49633 1st Liverpool Regt
BOWERMAN Thomas H. MM Sjt 82659 2nd London Regt
BOWERS Arthur "DCM,MM" CQMS 7372 3rd Coldstream Guards
BOWERS Cecil Charles "DCM,MM" L/Sjt 352483 1/7th London Regt KIA 2.12.17.
BOWERS Ernest MM Pte 2313 Royal Sussex Regt
BOWERS Frank MM Pte 2559 2nd East Surrey Regt
BOWERS Fred MM Sjt 71668 A/76 Bde RFA
BOWERS George MM Pte 27733 Hampshire Regt
BOWERS J. MM Pte 6595 West Riding Regt
BOWERS John MM Pte 352064 5th Manchester Regt
BOWERS Sidney MM Pte 2416 1/1st Hertfordshire Regt
BOWERS T. MM Gnr 106404 RFA
BOWERS Thomas W. MM Pte 80998 RAMC
BOWERS Tom Kitchen MM Sjt 12701 Machine Gun Corps
BOWERS W.H. MM Dvr 17034 Royal Engineers
BOWERY George "DCM,MM" Sjt 265791 1/1st Bucks Bn Oxf & Bucks Light Infantry
BOWERY Henry Arthur MM Pte 54305 1st Middlesex Regt KIA 23.10.18.
BOWES Charles H. MM Pte 16405 8th Northumberland Fusiliers
BOWES Edward MM+Bar Pte 11984 8th Royal West Kent Regt
BOWES Frederick MM Bdr 765525 RFA
BOWES George MM Sjt 2542 2nd Northumberland Fusiliers
BOWES George R. MM Pte 533014 2/15th London Regt
BOWES Glenniss MM Cpl 43 4th Bn GMGR
BOWES Oliver "MM,MID" Sjt 797 Military Mounted Police
BOWES Robert MM Pte 9158 Gordon Highlanders
BOWIE Andrew MM Pte S/22910 7th Royal Highlanders
BOWIE Charles Long MM Pte 327121 1/8th Arg & Suth Highlanders
BOWIE David MM Pte 7599 16th Manchester Regt
BOWIE Hamilton A.L.Y. MM Pte 22226 1st King's Own Scottish Borderers
BOWIE James MM+Bar Gnr 97114 C/162 Bde RFA
BOWIE Peter MM CQMS 6458 2nd Seaforth Highlanders
BOWIE Peter MM Pte 200915 Gordon Highlanders
BOWIE William MM Pte 24052 Royal Scots Fusiliers
BOWIE William John MM Sjt 7956 Middlesex Regt
BOWKER Arthur J. MM Sjt 240619 6th South Staffordshire Regt
BOWKER James "MM,MID" Sjt 354 Yorkshire Light Infantry
BOWKER John James MM Cpl 17205 32nd Bn Machine Gun Corps
BOWKER William MM Gnr 28490 8 Div Ammn Col RFA
BOWKER William MM Pte 1734 West Riding Regt
BOWKER William Henry MM F/Sjt 491 Royal Flying Corps
BOWKETT William MM L/Cpl 18288 8th Yorkshire Light Infantry
BOWLER Albert E. MM Sjt M/27701 1 Cav Div Supply Col Army Service Corps
BOWLER Alfred George MM L/Cpl 4686 1st East Surrey Regt
BOWLER Arthur E. MM Pte G/75127 17th Royal Fusiliers
BOWLER C.M. MM Cpl 12312 York & Lancaster Regt
BOWLER Charles "DCM,MM" Sjt 13960 2nd Notts & Derby Regt
BOWLER Charles MM Dvr 110862 B/50 Bde RFA
BOWLER Ernest MM Sjt 42359 1/1st Hertfordshire Regt KIA 4.11.18.
BOWLER George MM Pte 14188 2nd Scots Guards
BOWLER Leonard MM L/Cpl 242533 8th Worcestershire Regt
BOWLER P.J. MM Sjt 676442 RFA
BOWLER Thomas MM Pte 44748 39th Bn Machine Gun Corps
BOWLER Vernon J. MM Sjt 34603 RFA
BOWLER W.C. MM Sjt TT/03376 Army Veterinary Corps
BOWLES Alfred E. MM RSM 314 1/8th Middlesex Regt
BOWLES Cecil Oscar MM L/Sjt 403 1st Welsh Guards
BOWLES Charles A. MM Sjt 4228 1st Dragoons
BOWLES Frederick MM Pte 12120 6th Royal Berkshire Regt
BOWLES Frederick Arthur MM Sjt 320063 12th Norfolk Regt
BOWLES Henry MM Cpl G/51054 17th Royal Fusiliers
BOWLES Herbert MM Pte 16103 1/1st Hertfordshire Regt
BOWLES Herbert J. MM Cpl 292406 2nd Middlesex Regt
BOWLES Horace J. MM Pte 12257 Norfolk Regt
BOWLES John MM Cpl 426115 Royal Engineers
BOWLES John MM Cpl 2571 1/9th Liverpool Regt KIA 22.9.17.
BOWLES John H. MM Sjt 1430 RFA
BOWLES John J. MM Pte 33114 7th West Riding Regt
BOWLES Linda MM Sister F QAIMNS
BOWLES Noah MM Bdr 71610 41 Bde RFA
BOWLES Percy William "MC,MM(65311 Sjt L Bty RHA)" 2Lt C/219 Bde RFA KIA 10.9.18.
BOWLES Stanley Charles MM Pte 473012 1st(East Anglian)Fd Amb RAMC
BOWLES Wallace George MM L/Cpl 608632 1/18th London Regt
BOWLEY Gilbert George MM Pte 12713 2nd Worcestershire Regt KIA 24.6.18.
BOWLEY Reginald J. MM Pte 41248 North Staffordshire Regt
BOWLEY Tom "DCM,MM" CSM 10141 6th Royal Berkshire Regt
BOWLEY Walter MM Pte 23209 2nd Notts & Derby Regt
BOWLING Fred "DCM,MM" Cpl 293525 136 Hy Bty RGA
BOWLING Henry J. MM L/Cpl 11/13718 11th Border Regt
BOWLING Percy MM L/Cpl 682356 22nd London Regt
BOWMAN A.E. MM L/Cpl 204793 1/5th Notts & Derby Regt
BOWMAN Archibald MM Cpl 14426 15th Highland Light Infantry
BOWMAN Arthur J. MM L/Bdr 153211 185 Siege Bty RGA
BOWMAN Bruce MM Gnr 45155 B/117 Bde RFA
BOWMAN Charles MM Pte 200067 1/4th Northumberland Fusiliers DOW 28.5.18.
BOWMAN Charles J. MM Sjt 2303 8th London Regt
BOWMAN Charles W. MM+Bar Cpl Sig 53251 121 Siege Bty RGA
BOWMAN Edward MM Gnr 951102 112 Bty 24 Bde RFA
BOWMAN Ernest MM L/Cpl 51454 1/7th Cheshire Regt
BOWMAN George MM L/Sjt 265828 1/6th West Riding Regt KIA 12.10.18
BOWMAN H.T. MM Pte 23126 Machine Gun Corps
BOWMAN Harry A. MM Pte 1700 Royal Highlanders
BOWMAN Herbert MM Pte 32788 1st West Yorkshire Regt
BOWMAN Horace E. "DCM,MM" Sjt 530234 1/15th London Regt
BOWMAN J. MM L/Cpl P2880 Military Mounted Police
BOWMAN John MM Pte 275889 1/7th Manchester Regt
BOWMAN John C. "MM,MID" Bdsm 6366 2nd Scottish Rifles
BOWMAN Joseph MM L/Cpl 24772 13th Durham Light Infantry DOW 5.11.17.
BOWMAN Richard "MM,MID" Cpl 15959 7th South Lancashire Regt KIA 22.7.16.
BOWMAN Robert MM Pte 203040 Gordon Highlanders
BOWMAN Sidney MM Sjt 8173 1st Hampshire Regt
BOWMAN Stanley J. MM Sjt 240531 Suffolk Regt
BOWMAN Thomas MM Bdr 95727 B/44 Bde RFA
BOWMAN Thomas J. MM Dvr 36089 RFA
BOWMAN Thomas W. MM Dvr 463277 50 Div Sig Coy Royal Engineers
BOWMAN Thomas W. "DCM,MM" Sjt 19731 2/4th York & Lancaster Regt
BOWMAN Thomas Young MM Pte 21046 13th Durham Light Infantry KIA 5.10.18.
BOWMAN William MM Sjt 90394 124 Hy Bty RGA
BOWMAN William MM Bdr 85959 A/153 Bde RFA
BOWMAN William MM L/Cpl 203778 5th Lancashire Fusiliers
BOWMAN William MM Pte 722390 24th London Regt
BOWMAN William Edward MM Dvr 85442 B/46 Bde RFA
BOWMER Arthur MM Pte 30201 2nd Northumberland Fusiliers
BOWMER Claud MM Cpl 90334 RFA
BOWN Arthur MM Sjt 19180 22 Coy Machine Gun Corps DOW 29.8.16.
BOWN B. MM Sjt 9801 4th South Wales Borderers
BOWN Dugald McInnes MM Pte 14147 2nd Scots Guards KIA 11.10.18.
BOWN F.J. MM Sjt 48819 Royal Engineers
BOWN Harry G. MM CQMS T4/249014 Army Service Corps
BOWN John William MM Pte 13312 Leicestershire Regt
BOWN Norman MM Pte 60311 West Yorkshire Regt
BOWNESS Nicholas MM Sjt 2345 5th Border Regt KIA 22.3.18.
BOWNESS Sidney MM Cpl 1604 1/5th Lincolnshire Regt KIA 19.6.17.
BOWRING Frederick Brentford MM S/Sjt Farrier 99269 D/74 Bde RFA
BOWRING George MM Cpl 265829 7th Royal Warwickshire Regt
BOWRING Harry MM Pte 28671 Hampshire Regt
BOWRING Reuben William MM L/Cpl P/3107 Military Mounted Police
BOWRON Albert "MM,MSM" Sjt 250164 1/6th Durham Light Infantry
BOWRON William A. MM L/Cpl 17194 Durham Light Infantry
BOWSER Ernest MM Bdr 36449 189 Bde RFA
BOWSER Percy W. MM Pte 16487 Royal Fusiliers
BOWSER Richard T. MM Pte 270561 11th Royal Scots
BOWSHER Jesse MM Gnr Sig 243601 465 Bty 65 Bde RFA
BOWSHER Percy John Beckingham MM Cpl 65253 130 Fd Coy Royal Engineers KIA 17.4.18.
BOWSHER Thomas MM Pte 66333 12th Cheshire Regt
BOWSTEAD J.C. "DCM,MM" Cpl 8390 4th Hussars
BOWYER Amos MM Pte 8947 1st Cheshire Regt
BOWYER Charles MM Gnr 119659 MGC(Motors)

BOWYER E.E. MM L/Cpl 45512 5th Northamptonshire Regt
BOWYER Ernest MM Sjt 240907 Notts & Derby Regt
BOWYER George MM CSM 22364 118 MG Coy Machine Gun Corps
BOWYER George MM Bdr 1182 40 Siege Bty RGA
BOWYER Samuel MM+Bar Bdr 92432 180 Siege Bty RGA
BOWYER Walter James MM+Bar Sjt 61617 24th Royal Fusiliers
BOWYER William MM Gnr 172719 136 Siege Bty RGA
BOX Frederick T. MM L/Cpl 11480 Royal West Surrey Regt
BOX George Charles MM Pte 23896 41st Bn Machine Gun Corps
BOX Jack Graham MM Gnr 83811 A/47 Bde RFA
BOX James A. MM Pte 27928 2/4th Hampshire Regt
BOX John Arthur MM Pte 201681 2/4th York & Lancaster Regt DOW 5.9.18.
BOX John Henry Gilbert MM+Bar L/Cpl 301765 2/5th London Regt
BOX John W. MM+2 Bars CSM R/16956 13th King's Royal Rifle Corps
BOX Samuel MM Pte 21255 East Lancashire Regt
BOX Sidney Richard MM Cpl 240167 Royal Warwickshire Regt
BOX Thomas P. MM Pte 16154 Royal Irish Regt
BOX Walter MM Bdr 33974 RGA
BOX William MM L/Sjt 15877 Hampshire Regt
BOXALL Frederick George "MM,MSM" S/Sjt 30539 75 Fd Amb RAMC DOW 11.4.18.
BOXALL Frederick J. MM Pte 231552 2nd London Regt
BOXALL Harold Granville MM Pte 42326 10th Essex Regt
BOXALL John W. MM Pte 32965 Bedfordshire Regt
BOXALL William MM Cpl 32579 1st South Staffordshire Regt
BOXALL William R. MM Pte 83499 RAMC
BOYCE Albert MM Pte 20978 1st Essex Regt
BOYCE Alfred MM Pte 26689 16th Middlesex Regt KIA 1.12.17.
BOYCE Arthur C.K. MM Pte 36401 Notts & Derby Regt
BOYCE Edward MM Dvr 86547 RFA
BOYCE Ernest A. MM Sjt 570961 17th London Regt
BOYCE Ernest T. MM L/Bdr 956170 B/236 Bde RFA
BOYCE Frank N. MM Cpl 71446 18 Div Sig Coy Royal Engineers
BOYCE Frederick MM L/Cpl 9387 2nd Bedfordshire Regt KIA 11.8.16.
BOYCE Frederick Joseph "MM,MSM" CQMS 13726 11th West Yorkshire Regt
BOYCE Henry F. MM Spr 28685 Royal Engineers
BOYCE Joseph MM L/Cpl 21649 6th King's Own Scottish Borderers
BOYCE Patrick T. MM Cpl 7329 2nd Border Regt
BOYCE Percy E. MM Pte 24274 2nd Royal Dublin Fusiliers
BOYCE Robert E. MM Sjt 266292 2/6th Gloucestershire Regt
BOYCE Thomas Walker "MC,MM(16/291 Sjt R Iriish Rif)" Capt Royal Inniskilling Fusiliers
BOYCE William MM Cpl M2/168228 594 MT Coy Army Service Corps att RGA.
BOYCE William H. MM L/Cpl 306683 2 Tank Carrier Coy Tank Corps
BOYCE William J. MM Pte 202082 Royal Warwickshire Regt
BOYCK William MM Pte 78550 9th Bn Tank Corps
BOYCOTT Leonard MM Pte 23366 8th Yorkshire Regt KIA 8.6.17.
BOYD Alexander MM Bdr 92932 B/78 Bde RFA
BOYD Anna Georgina MM Sister F QAIMNS
BOYD Brian MM Sjt 17926 14th Royal Irish Rifles DOW 7.6.17.
BOYD Christy MM Pte 27382 9th Royal Inniskilling Fusiliers DOW 19.12.17.
BOYD Clarence Frederick MM Pte 40087 2/8th Worcestershire Regt KIA 15.5.18.
BOYD Emmanuel Lewis MM Pte 38471 1st Lancashire Fusiliers
BOYD George MM Pte 251411 1/6th Arg & Suth Highlanders
BOYD Hugh MM Dvr 631413 RFA
BOYD Humphrey MM+Bar SSM H/71014 North Irish Horse
BOYD James MM Pte 21746 1/5th Bedfordshire Regt
BOYD James "DCM,MM,MID" Sjt 6699 2nd Scots Guards
BOYD James MM Pte 12/17299 12th Royal Irish Rifles
BOYD James MM Cpl 10400 1st Royal Irish Fusiliers DOW 11.10.18.
BOYD James A. MM Sjt 14673 Yorkshire Light Infantry
BOYD James Burrows MM CSM 18884 10th Royal Irish Rifles
BOYD John MM Bdr 59015 5 Div Ammn Col RFA
BOYD John MM Sjt M2/188488 Army Service Corps
BOYD John MM Sjt 6209 1/7th Gordon Highlanders
BOYD John James MM L/Sjt 2/8747 Royal Irish Regt
BOYD John M. MM Sjt 19424 16th Royal Scots KIA 10.4.18.
BOYD John Martin MM Gnr 68991 123 Siege Bty RGA
BOYD Joseph MM Sjt 750416 275 Bde RFA
BOYD Patrick MM Pte 902 2nd Royal Irish Rifles
BOYD R. MM Cpl 14/17296 Royal Irish Rifles
BOYD R.N. MM L/Cpl 302899 Arg & Suth Highlanders
BOYD Robert MM Pte 26538 2nd Lancashire Fusiliers
BOYD Sidney Charles MM Sjt 721388 2/24th London Regt
BOYD Thomas MM L/Cpl 6546 2nd Seaforth Highlanders
BOYD Thomas MM Sjt 32276 RAMC
BOYD Thomas Allan "MM,CdeG(F)" Pte 33416 78 Coy Machine Gun Corps
BOYD W.H. "MM,MSM" Sjt P4645 Military Mounted Police
BOYD W.John McK. MM Cpl 13140 10th Arg & Suth Highlanders
BOYD Wallace MM Pte 13511 12th Royal Scots
BOYD Walter George MM Pte 1577 1/4th East Yorkshire Regt
BOYD Walter M. MM+Bar Pte 56157 1/2nd(Highland)Fd Amb RAMC
BOYD William MM Pte 33140 13th East Lancashire Regt KIA 8.9.18.
BOYD William MM Cpl 7317 King's Own Scottish Borderers
BOYD William MM Pte 8272 11th Lancashire Fusiliers
BOYD William MM L/Cpl 330163 1/7th Liverpool Regt
BOYD William Andus "MM,MID" Sjt 11240 1st Notts & Derby Regt
BOYD William B. MM Sjt 295993 RGA
BOYD William James MM Pte 15/11890 Royal Irish Rifles
BOYDE Edward F. MM Pte 2166 1/13th London Regt
BOYDE William MM Pte 10466 Royal Irish Fusiliers
BOYDELL J. MM Pte 276845 Manchester Regt
BOYDELL Jesse MM Pte 533933 15th London Regt
BOYDEN George Frederick MM Dvr 955763 A/236 Bde RFA
BOYDEN Henry T. MM L/Cpl S/7618 11th Middlesex Regt
BOYDEN Walter MM L/Cpl 50299 RAMC
BOYDEN William D. MM L/Cpl 28293 Notts & Derby Regt
BOYER Frank H. MM Pte 8691 RAMC
BOYER James MM Gnr 160828 479 Siege Bty RGA
BOYER Richard "MM,MID" CSM 7705 Leinster Regt
BOYER William MM Pte 241025 1/5th Yorkshire Light Infantry
BOYES Alfred MM Sjt 6423 71 Coy Machine Gun Corps
BOYES Alfred John MM Pte 17301 2/4th Hampshire Regt
BOYES Harry MM L/Cpl 72294 Royal Engineers
BOYES James MM Sjt 350982 9th Royal Scots
BOYES James W. MM Pte 23020 6th King's Own Scottish Borderers
BOYES Lewis MM Sjt 35321 RAMC
BOYES Thomas Francis MM Sjt 12253 A/161 Bde RFA
BOYLAN Charles MM Sjt 46855 C/59 Bde RFA
BOYLAN Grant S.P. MM L/Cpl 10535 Royal West Kent Regt
BOYLAN John MM Pte 37904 RAMC
BOYLAN John Joseph MM Pte 326016 Arg & Suth Highlanders Died 1.7.18.
BOYLAN Owen MM Pte 8143 4 Fd Amb RAMC
BOYLE Alexander MM L/Cpl 330961 Highland Light Infantry
BOYLE Arthur J. MM Pte 24930 Highland Light Infantry
BOYLE Charles S. MM CSM 402033 404 Fd Coy Royal Engineers
BOYLE Daniel MM Pte 2369 6th Royal Irish Regt
BOYLE Edward MM Cpl 12898 8th Yorkshire Regt
BOYLE Ernest MM L/Cpl 2478 1st Welsh Guards
BOYLE Ernest A. MM Cpl 200238 Gloucestershire Regt
BOYLE Farigle MM L/Cpl 6273 1st Irish Guards
BOYLE James MM Sjt 8601 2nd Royal Irish Regt
BOYLE James MM Dvr 7333 RFA
BOYLE James MM Pte 9723 1st Scots Guards KIA 15.9.16.
BOYLE James MM Spr 420031 Royal Engineers
BOYLE James G. MM L/Cpl 12249 2nd Highland Light Infantry
BOYLE John MM Gnr Sig 651070 C/180 Bde RFA
BOYLE John "MM,CG(F)" Pte R/27231 18th King's Royal Rifle Corps
BOYLE John MM Pte 20231 2nd Grenadier Guards
BOYLE John MM+Bar Bdr 33421 25 Bde RFA
BOYLE John MM Pte S/17792 6th Cameron Highlanders DOW 24.8.17.
BOYLE John MM Pte 23980 Royal Inniskilling Fusiliers
BOYLE John MM Pte 21633 Royal Irish Fusiliers
BOYLE John Joseph MM L/Cpl 207877 248 Fd Coy Royal Engineers
BOYLE Joseph "MM,MID" Pte 8/12211 8th Royal Irish Rifles
BOYLE Matthew MM Pte 23853 1st Scottish Rifles
BOYLE Patrick MM Pte 10732 1st Irish Guards
BOYLE Patrick MM Pte 15220 Northumberland Fusiliers
BOYLE Philip MM Pte 16330 Scottish Rifles
BOYLE Richard MM Pte 4132 6th Connaught Rangers
BOYLE William MM Pte S/4448 5th Gordon Highlanders
BOYLE William MM Sjt 7247 8th East Lancashire Regt
BOYLE William MM L/Cpl S/8832 Seaforth Highlanders

BOYLEN Patrick "MM,MSM,MID" Sjt 5682 1st Royal Scots Fusiliers
BOYLES Edwin MM CQMS 14220 1st Grenadier Guards
BOYLES Leslie MM Gnr 113749 RFA
BOYLE-THOMAS Samuel R.E. MM Pte 92715 London Regt
BOYNE Alexander J. MM Sjt 265050 1/6th Gordon Highlanders
BOYNE Arthur Robert MM L/Cpl 4989 1/2nd London Regt
BOYNE James A. MM Sjt 21508 2nd Durham Light Infantry
BOYNE Jasper MM Pte 51889 Royal Scots
BOYNES James Hunter Eastwood MM L/Bdr 49389 85 Bty 11 Bde RFA
BOYNTON Richard MM Pte 41104 Lancashire Fusiliers
BOYNTON Robert Barker MM L/Cpl 390082 RAMC
BOYNTON Thomas MM L/Cpl 16560 6th York & Lancaster Regt
BOYS Sampson MM L/Cpl 1270 Royal Sussex Regt
BOYS William MM Pte 62486 RAMC
BOYSON George T. MM Pte 77423 Tank Corps
BOYTER John MM 2nd Cpl 97916 156 Fd Coy Royal Engineers
BOYTON Robert MM+Bar Pte 7967 2nd Irish Guards KIA 23.4.18.
BOZIER Alfred W. MM Pte 11388 2nd Royal Fusiliers
BRABANT Leonard MM+Bar Pte 39714 15th Lancashire Fusiliers
BRABBAN Irving MM Sjt 200355 1/5th Durham Light Infantry
BRABBAN James William MM Sjt 751565 127 Bty 29 Bde RFA DOW 27.11.18.
BRABBEN Samuel Robert MM Pte 203177 1/4th West Riding Regt
BRABBIN William J. MM L/Cpl 85345 Royal Engineers
BRABBON Alfred J. MM L/Cpl 95667 Royal Engineers
BRABENDER William M. MM Pte 290134 1/8th Scottish Rifles
BRABHAM John MM L/Cpl 4851 King's Royal Rifle Corps
BRABIN Robert MM Pte 242879 4/5th North Lancashire Regt
BRABNER John H. MM Cpl 970291 RFA
BRABSTON Michael MM Pte 4751 1st Irish Guards
BRACE Ernest "MM,MID" L/Cpl P/1114 Military Foot Police
BRACE George MM Pte 1706 Lincolnshire Regt
BRACE George MM Pte 201140 5th South Staffordshire Regt
BRACE Henry Augustus MM Spr 55862 296 Fd Coy Royal Engineers
BRACE James MM Spr 1625 Royal Engineers
BRACE William MM Pte 56486 Machine Gun Corps
BRACE William MM Pte 72395 Machine Gun Corps
BRACEGIRDLE Charles M. MM Sjt 240452 Royal Welsh Fusiliers
BRACEGIRDLE James MM Pte 8377 12th Lancashire Fusiliers
BRACEWELL Joseph MM Pte 18438 1st King's Own Scottish Borderers KIA 11.4.18.
BRACEWELL Leonard MM Gnr 25493 A/93 Bde RFA
BRACEY George E. MM Spr 84932 34 Div Sig Coy Royal Engineers
BRACEY Henry James "MM,Medaille Militaire(F)" CQMS 2019 1st Northumberland Fusiliers KIA 11.4.17.
BRACEY Tom MM Cpl 1994 9th Royal Fusiliers
BRACKEN John W. MM Cpl 113519 17th Bn(sic) Machine Gun Corps
BRACKENBURY H.H. MM Pte 10428 Duke of Cornwall's LI
BRACKENBURY John MM Pte 202113 4th Lincolnshire Regt DOW 5.1.18.
BRACKFIELD Edward MM Cpl 68531 23 Bde RFA
BRACKPOOL Harry MM Pte 8355 7th Royal Sussex Regt
BRACKSTON Henry P. MM Pte 50263 RAMC
BRACKSTONE George F. MM+Bar L/Bdr 97807 5 Bde Ammn Col RFA
BRADBERRY John MM L/Cpl 554224 Royal Engineers
BRADBURY Albert MM Pte 242391 West Riding Regt
BRADBURY Alfred MM Cpl 25983 10th West Riding Regt
BRADBURY Arthur MM Pte 19630 10th York & Lancaster Regt
BRADBURY Arthur MM Gnr 96138 B/232 Bde RFA
BRADBURY Charles E. MM Pte 20053 Shropshire Light Infantry
BRADBURY Ernest MM L/Cpl 241658 Royal Lancaster Regt
BRADBURY Ernest MM Gnr 109856 10th Bn Tank Corps KIA 23.10.18.
BRADBURY Ernest MM Pte 5226 Northumberland Fusiliers
BRADBURY Fred MM+Bar Cpl 12582 1st Leicestershire Regt
BRADBURY George "MM,MID" Sjt 14455 6th Northamptonshire Regt
BRADBURY Harry "DCM,MM" Sjt 240144 5th Border Regt
BRADBURY Harry G.W. MM+Bar Sjt 6453 24th Royal Fusiliers
BRADBURY Henry MM Pte 19430 13th Liverpool Regt
BRADBURY Herbert "DCM,MM" Sjt 426099 Royal Engineers
BRADBURY John Shaw MM Dvr 805352 B/231 Bde RFA KIA 11.8.17.
BRADBURY John T. MM Pte 201739 Worcestershire Regt
BRADBURY John W. MM Sjt 14014 7th Leicestershire Regt
BRADBURY Joseph MM Dvr 71914 D/110 Bde RFA
BRADBURY Joseph MM Pte 23697 11th Manchester Regt
BRADBURY L. MM L/Cpl P13005 Military Foot Police
BRADBURY Lawrence MM Pte 22501 1st Royal Lancaster Regt
BRADBURY Maurice R. MM Sjt 375462 10th Manchester Regt
BRADBURY Samuel MM+Bar Cpl 241002 6th North Staffordshire Regt
BRADBURY Thomas MM Pte 18595 19th Lancashire Fusiliers
BRADBURY Tom MM Pte 28158 Duke of Cornwall's LI
BRADBURY Wilfred MM Sjt 40420 20th Manchester Regt
BRADBURY William MM Pte 14278 10th Cheshire Regt
BRADBURY William MM Pte 43061 9th Royal Inniskilling Fusiliers
BRADBURY William MM Cpl 242015 5th South Lancashire Regt
BRADBURY William G. MM Pte 30133 Somerset Light Infantry
BRADDICK Hubert Charles MM Pte 21691 1st Somerset Light Infantry KIA 3.9.16.
BRADDICK John MM+Bar Pte 401255 2/1st(West Riding)Fd Amb RAMC
BRADDOCK Frank P. MM Gnr 676842 B/285 RFA
BRADDOW Vallance MM Cpl 41216 1st Royal Lancaster Regt
BRADDY George J. MM Pte 25531 Scottish Rifles
BRADFIELD Alan Edwin MM+Bar Sjt 43435 Norfolk Regt
BRADFIELD Ernest E. MM Pte 26706 Somerset Light Infantry
BRADFIELD Ernest H. MM Spr 254288 2 Div Sig Coy Royal Engineers
BRADFIELD Henry Hugh Palmer "MM+Bar,CG(F),MM(F)" Spr 85012 Royal Engineers
BRADFIELD Horace MM Pte 327544 1/1st Cambridgeshire Regt
BRADFORD Albert MM+Bar Pte 32511 South Staffordshire Regt
BRADFORD Albert Edward MM Pte 11376 16th Lancashire Fusiliers KIA 2.7.16.
BRADFORD Alfred Harry "MM,MSM" Pte 030239 Army Ordnance Corps
BRADFORD Arthur MM Pte 33102 7th West Riding Regt
BRADFORD Arthur MM Gnr 99949 RGA
BRADFORD Charles MM Pte 355887 25th Royal Welsh Fusiliers
BRADFORD Charles "MM,MID" Cpl 10181 15th Hussars
BRADFORD Charles Henry MM L/Cpl 3/2991 8th York & Lancaster Regt KIA 1.7.16.
BRADFORD Charles William MM Sjt 787 1/5th London Regt KIA 20.7.16.
BRADFORD Cyril MM Pte 11611 2nd Royal Fusiliers
BRADFORD Edward W. MM Pte S/9902 Rifle Brigade
BRADFORD Edwin "MM,MID" Sjt 139225 250 Tunnelling Coy Royal Engineers
BRADFORD Frederick Thomas MM Bdr L/43192 RFA
BRADFORD H. MM Pte 497209 RAMC
BRADFORD Harry MM L/Cpl 6052 Suffolk Regt
BRADFORD John MM Cpl L/27590 D/168 Bde RFA
BRADFORD John MM Sjt 35186 19th Bn Machine Gun Corps
BRADFORD John MM Gnr 81490 35 Bty 22 Bde RFA
BRADFORD John E. MM L/Cpl 9293 3rd Coldstream Guards
BRADFORD Marcus E. MM L/Cpl 4220 15th London Regt
BRADFORD Thomas MM L/Cpl 34692 183 Coy Machine Gun Corps
BRADFORD Walter F. MM Pte 14106 4th Coldstream Guards
BRADFORD William MM Cpl 8955 2nd Royal West Surrey Regt
BRADING Cecil H. MM Pte 10080 Royal West Surrey Regt
BRADLEY A. MM Bdr 14023 RGA
BRADLEY Alan Frederick MM Pte 548061 15th London Regt
BRADLEY Albert MM Pte 88339 Machine Gun Corps
BRADLEY Albert MM L/Cpl A/1029 King's Royal Rifle Corps
BRADLEY Albert MM L/Cpl Y/1197 King's Royal Rifle Corps
BRADLEY Albert MM Pte 12024 5th Liverpool Regt
BRADLEY Albert E. MM CQMS 16/529 16th Royal Warwickshire Regt
BRADLEY Albion MM Sjt 8694 2nd Leinster Regt
BRADLEY Alexander MM Pte 9399 6th East Kent Regt
BRADLEY Alfred MM Pte S/13089 Gordon Highlanders
BRADLEY Alfred MM Sjt 35407 111 Heavy Bty RGA
BRADLEY Anthony MM Pte 78868 RAMC
BRADLEY Arthur MM Pte 32836 2/4th West Riding Regt
BRADLEY Arthur MM Sjt 1962 6th Yorkshire Light Infantry KIA 24.8.17.
BRADLEY Arthur "MM,MID" Sjt 7731 1st Northamptonshire Regt DOW 28.4.17.
BRADLEY Arthur MM Bdr 21577 128 Heavy Bty RGA KIA 22.8.18.
BRADLEY Arthur J. MM Dvr 83201 RFA
BRADLEY Arthur S. MM+Bar Sjt 60028 Royal Engineers
BRADLEY Charles MM Sjt 10229 Machine Gun Corps
BRADLEY Charles Frederick MM Gnr 830478 B/241 Bde RFA
BRADLEY Charles H. MM Pte 201540 2/4th York & Lancaster Regt

BRADLEY Clifford MM L/Cpl 16814 Dorsetshire Regt
BRADLEY Edgar Morris MM L/Cpl 12670 9th Suffolk Regt
BRADLEY Ernest MM Pte 2346 1/5th Yorkshire Regt
BRADLEY Ernest MM Pte R/1309 King's Royal Rifle Corps
BRADLEY Ernest Norman MM Pte 385 1/2nd(West Riding)Fd Amb RAMC DOW 28.4.18.
BRADLEY Francis MM Pte 37774 10th Gloucestershire Regt
BRADLEY Frank MM Pte 39666 20th Manchester Regt
BRADLEY Frank MM 2nd Cpl 492448 Royal Engineers
BRADLEY Frank MM Pte 6646 13th Rifle Brigade
BRADLEY Frank MM Cpl 18069 1st Bedfordshire Regt KIA 23.4.17.
BRADLEY Fred MM Pte 78219 5th Bn Tank Corps
BRADLEY Fred MM Pte 307688 2nd West Yorkshire Regt
BRADLEY Fred MM Pte 69314 RAMC
BRADLEY Fred MM L/Cpl 51646 Royal Fusiliers
BRADLEY Frederick MM Cpl 246769 Royal Engineers
BRADLEY Frederick G. MM Spr 203966 69 Fd Coy Royal Engineers
BRADLEY George MM Pte 29669 1st Border Regt
BRADLEY George MM Cpl 17709 D Bn MGC(Heavy Branch) DOW 3.5.17.
BRADLEY George Sidney MM L/Cpl 235872 9th West Yorkshire Regt
BRADLEY George W. MM L/Cpl 98629 223 Fd Coy Royal Engineers
BRADLEY George W.A. MM Cpl 67322 RHA
BRADLEY George William MM Dvr 11137 34 Div Ammn Col RFA
BRADLEY Greenwood MM Cpl 241764 1/6th West Yorkshire Regt KIA 25.4.18.
BRADLEY H. MM+Bar Pte 19430 Liverpool Regt
BRADLEY Harold MM Gnr 114161 RGA
BRADLEY Harold MM Pte 35553 Yorkshire Light Infantry
BRADLEY Headley Charles MM Pte 23022 Machine Gun Corps
BRADLEY Henry MM Dvr L/42403 RFA
BRADLEY Herbert MM Sjt 241043 1/8th Worcestershire Regt
BRADLEY Isaac MM L/Sjt 21/766 21st Northumberland Fusiliers KIA 9.4.17.
BRADLEY J. "MM,MID" Cpl 12790 Royal Welsh Fusiliers
BRADLEY Jacob MM Pte 203913 1st Liverpool Regt
BRADLEY James "DCM,MM" Sjt 9456 1st Royal Inniskilling Fusiliers
BRADLEY James MM Pte 23828 1st Border Regt
BRADLEY James MM Sjt 20496 Royal Inniskilling Fusiliers
BRADLEY James MM+Bar L/Cpl 201126 West Yorkshire Regt
BRADLEY James MM Cpl 6/4666 6th Connaught Rangers
BRADLEY Jim MM Pte 11950 East Yorkshire Regt
BRADLEY John MM Pte 41581 1/7th Royal Highlanders
BRADLEY John MM Spr 432204 Royal Engineers
BRADLEY John MM Dvr 10174 RFA
BRADLEY John A. MM Pte S/41970 1/5th Seaforth Highlanders
BRADLEY John Edward MM Pte 12153 8th Royal West Kent Regt
BRADLEY John H. MM Pte 45012 RAMC
BRADLEY Joseph MM Pte 2329 1/1st Sherwood Rangers Yeo
BRADLEY Joseph MM Pte 2249 1/6th West Riding Regt
BRADLEY Newton MM Cpl 24531 5 Div Sig Coy Royal Engineers
BRADLEY Norman MM+Bar Pte 202163 North Staffordshire Regt
BRADLEY Norman MM Spr 310793 Royal Engineers
BRADLEY R. MM Pte 201589 Royal Lancaster Regt
BRADLEY Robert "DCM,MM" Gnr L/9483 50 Bty 34 Bde RFA
BRADLEY Stanley Victor MM Pte 554122 16th London Regt KIA 30.11.17.
BRADLEY Thomas MM L/Cpl 13376 9th Cheshire Regt DOW 6.6.18.
BRADLEY Thomas MM(33012 Shrop LI)+Bar Pte 68635 6th Cheshire Regt
BRADLEY Thomas MM Pte 1756 1/6th West Yorkshire Regt KIA 3.9.16.
BRADLEY Thomas Brown MM Cpl 20/310 22nd Northumberland Fusiliers Died 10.4.18.
BRADLEY Walter MM Pnr 211650 Third Army Sig Coy Royal Engineers
BRADLEY Walter J. "DCM,MM" Sjt 5047 HAC
BRADLEY William MM Cpl 44532 3rd Bn Machine Gun Corps KIA 2.9.18.
BRADLEY William MM L/Cpl 95177 2/4th London Regt KIA 1.9.18.
BRADLEY William MM Sjt L/28995 D/236 Bde RFA
BRADLEY William Charles MM Cpl 17271 Oxf & Bucks Light Infantry
BRADLEY William D. MM Sjt 510369 14th London Regt
BRADLEY William E. MM L/Cpl 15291 Worcestershire Regt
BRADLEY William H. MM Pte 295040 Durham Light Infantry
BRADLEY William J. MM Sjt 5595 7th Border Regt
BRADLEY William James MM Pte 21683 2nd Royal Inniskilling Fusiliers
BRADMAN Alfred MM Sjt 33540 D/67 Bde RFA
BRADMAN Ernest MM CSM 7292 Royal West Kent Regt
BRADNOCK Ernest Joseph MM Sjt 10504 21st Middlesex Regt KIA 9.4.18.
BRADSHAW Allen "MM,MID" Pte 1722 London Fd Amb RAMC
BRADSHAW Arthur MM CSM 6698 1st Duke of Cornwall's LI
BRADSHAW Benjamin MM L/Bdr 67551 91 Siege Bty RGA
BRADSHAW C. MM L/Cpl 200127 Leicestershire Regt
BRADSHAW Charles Ernest MM Bdr 29199 D/160 Bde RFA
BRADSHAW Charles Lewis MM Pte M2/203550 Att 198 Siege Bty RGA Army Service Corps
BRADSHAW Claude MM Sjt 240990 Leicestershire Regt
BRADSHAW Donald Groves MM L/Cpl 531275 1/15th London Regt
BRADSHAW Edward MM Pte 2660 2nd York & Lancaster Regt KIA 1.12.17.
BRADSHAW George MM Cpl 300550 Manchester Regt
BRADSHAW George MM Cpl 4311 Machine Gun Corps
BRADSHAW George S. MM Spr 558430 Royal Engineers
BRADSHAW George Walter MM Pte 22550 11th Notts & Derby Regt KIA 19.10.17.
BRADSHAW Harold MM Pte 3428 Leicestershire Regt
BRADSHAW Harry MM L/Cpl 15836 Liverpool Regt
BRADSHAW Harry MM Sjt 81380 201 Fd Coy Royal Engineers
BRADSHAW Harry "MM,MID" Bdr 59870 38 Bde RFA
BRADSHAW Harry MM Cpl 201056 North Lancashire Regt
BRADSHAW Harry MM Pte 405114 RAMC
BRADSHAW Herbert Henry MM Sjt 30227 RAMC
BRADSHAW James MM Spr 492170 Royal Engineers
BRADSHAW James R. MM Cpl 265652 Royal Warwickshire Regt
BRADSHAW John MM L/Cpl 375386 10th Manchester Regt
BRADSHAW John MM Cpl 240438 1/5th North Lancashire Regt
BRADSHAW John Gilbert MM Gnr L/796 149 Bde RFA
BRADSHAW John H. MM L/Cpl 24949 14th Worcestershire Regt
BRADSHAW John J. MM Pte 19191 Lancashire Fusiliers
BRADSHAW Joseph MM Sjt 40351 Northumberland Fusiliers
BRADSHAW Joseph MM+Bar Pte 17363 17 Fd Amb RAMC
BRADSHAW Leonard MM Sjt 96046 RFA
BRADSHAW Lionel MM Sjt 720068 RFA
BRADSHAW Oliver MM Pte A/201881 2nd King's Royal Rifle Corps
BRADSHAW R.Herbert MM Pte 73503 Durham Light Infantry
BRADSHAW Robert MM Pte 2517 1/4th East Yorkshire Regt
BRADSHAW Robert MM Sjt 11125 8th West Riding Regt
BRADSHAW Robert H. MM L/Cpl 23875 1st Grenadier Guards
BRADSHAW Russell MM Cpl 15400 East Lancashire Regt
BRADSHAW Samuel MM Pte 200467 4th York & Lancaster Regt
BRADSHAW Sidney MM Pte 14955 7th Border Regt
BRADSHAW T. MM Cpl 10553 5th North Lancashire Regt
BRADSHAW Thomas MM Gnr 186281 X/4 Med TM Bty RFA
BRADSHAW Thomas A. MM S/Sjt Farrier 90562 A/282 Bde RFA
BRADSHAW Thomas R. MM CSM 1319 7th Liverpool Regt
BRADSHAW William MM Cpl 241042 11th Cheshire Regt KIA 1.6.18.
BRADSHAW William MM Pte 276327 7th Manchester Regt
BRADSHAW William D. MM Sjt 144703 Royal Engineers
BRADSHAW William Henry MM Pte 20995 12th Liverpool Regt
BRADSHAW William J. MM Pte 19329 16th Royal Welsh Fusiliers
BRADWELL Edgar MM Pte 19468 1/4th Northamptonshire Regt
BRADWELL H. MM L/Cpl 270413 Royal Engineers
BRADY Charles H. MM Cpl 2850 Yorkshire Regt
BRADY J.W. MM Pte 235167 South Lancashire Regt
BRADY James "MM,Oleo(B)" Sjt 11986 8th Royal Lancaster Regt DOW 26.3.18.
BRADY John MM L/Cpl 2386 York & Lancaster Regt
BRADY Matthew MM Pte 243399 15th Lancashire Fusiliers
BRADY Patrick MM L/Cpl 276 2nd Lincolnshire Regt
BRADY Patrick MM Pte 9242 48th Bn Machine Gun Corps
BRADY Robert MM Spr 44800 Royal Engineers
BRADY William MM Pte 41036 12th Highland Light Infantry
BRADY William Albert MM Pte 551086 2/16th London Regt KIA 18.10.18.
BRAGG Bertie Charles "DCM,MM" Sjt 10574 9th Essex Regt DOW 17.7.17.
BRAGG Charles MM Pte 9596 1st Royal Warwickshire Regt
BRAGG Edward MM Cpl 30128 124 Coy Machine Gun Corps DOW 11.10.16.
BRAGG Frederick Charles MM Cpl 46242 RGA
BRAGG Harry MM Cpl 498312 476 Fd Coy Royal Engineers
BRAGG Leslie H. MM L/Cpl 151226 104th Bn Machine Gun Corps

BRAGG Robert MM Cpl 30061 Border Regt
BRAGGINTON Percy MM Pte 612 9th Royal Fusiliers
BRAGGS A.B. MM Pte 19814 Royal West Kent Regt
BRAHAM Frank E. MM Gnr 95300 RFA
BRAHAM Herbert MM CQMS 305069 8th Royal Warwickshire Regt
BRAHAM Richard W. MM Cpl 42033 RFA
BRAID Andrew MM 2nd Cpl 50218 Royal Engineers
BRAID Henry MM Pte 358542 1/10th Liverpool Regt
BRAID John MM L/Cpl 18967 Royal Engineers
BRAID Thomas MM BQMS 52258 112 Bty 24 Bde RFA
BRAIDEN Edward "MM,MID" Cpl 11053 Y/48 Med TM Bty RGA att RFA
BRAIDEN Samuel T. MM Pnr 25466 1 Div Sig Coy Royal Engineers
BRAIG Frederick MM 2nd Cpl 357430 XIII Corps HQ Sig Sect Royal Engineers
BRAILEY Herbert "MM,CG(B)" Pte 23/399 18th Durham Light Infantry
BRAILSFORD Harry A. MM 2nd Cpl 311869 Royal Engineers
BRAIN Christopher B. MM Pte 235852 1/1st Herefordshire Regt
BRAIN Ernest MM Gnr Sig 781101 B/311 Bde RFA
BRAIN George MM Sjt 40683 D/282 Bde RFA KIA 4.7.17.
BRAIN Rosa MM Staff Nurse F TFNS
BRAIN Samuel J. MM Pte 266321 Gloucestershire Regt
BRAIN William "DCM+Bar,MM" Sjt 2141 1st Lancashire Fusiliers
BRAIN William MM Bdr 11791 A/87 Bde RFA
BRAINT Henry Edward MM Pte 6413 East Surrey Regt
BRAITHWAITE Arthur MM+Bar Cpl 281019 1st Lancashire Fusiliers
BRAITHWAITE Charles MM Cpl 898 RFA
BRAITHWAITE Clarence MM Gnr 68380 143 Siege Bty RGA
BRAITHWAITE Ernest MM Pte 1775 West Riding Regt
BRAITHWAITE George William MM L/Cpl 28378 11th Cheshire Regt KIA 15.3.18.
BRAITHWAITE Leonard MM Pte 30973 58th Bn Machine Gun Corps
BRAITHWAITE Sidney MM Sjt 7940 2nd Yorkshire Regt
BRAITHWAITE Thomas MM Pte 276418 Manchester Regt
BRAKENBURY William Horace MM Sjt C/9749 13th King's Royal Rifle Corps KIA 23.10.18
BRAKES John MM L/Sjt 22084 Notts & Derby Regt
BRAMAH Harry MM+Bar Sjt S/9079 Gordon Highlanders
BRAMALL Howard MM S/Sjt Fitter 51866 RFA
BRAMBLE D. MM Cpl 10882 Royal Dublin Fusiliers
BRAMBLE Treharne MM L/Cpl 10098 Machine Gun Corps
BRAME Luke MM Pte 8821 3rd Coldstream Guards
BRAME Wallace H. MM Bdr 54218 RFA
BRAMELD Herbert W. MM Sjt 149 Royal Engineers
BRAMHALL Henry MM L/Sjt 1531 Cheshire Regt
BRAMHALL John W. MM Sjt 470377 Royal Engineers
BRAMHALL Samuel MM Pte 240231 1/5th Cheshire Regt
BRAMHAM William MM Spr 76112 8 Div Sig Coy Royal Engineers
BRAMHILL John W. MM L/Cpl 75636 RAMC
BRAMHILL T. MM Pte 1323 Lancashire Fusiliers
BRAMLEY A.H. MM Cpl 50870 Machine Gun Corps
BRAMLEY Edward MM Bdr L/8347 B/150 Bde RFA
BRAMLEY Edwin A. "DCM,MM" Sjt 457183 Royal Engineers
BRAMLEY Frank MM Sjt 680034 A/70 Bde RFA
BRAMLEY George MM Cpl 5228 Royal Sussex Regt
BRAMLEY Jack MM Cpl 75596 115 Bty 25 Bde RFA
BRAMLEY Mellor MM+Bar L/Cpl 31481 1st Lancashire Fusiliers
BRAMLEY Norman MM Pte 22679 Leicestershire Regt
BRAMLEY Robert MM Pte 44869 2nd Yorkshire Regt
BRAMMA Charles E. MM Cpl 795210 RFA
BRAMMER George Henry MM CSM 16918 1st Essex Regt
BRAMMER John MM Sjt 12926 6th Shropshire Light Infantry
BRAMMER Lewis MM Pte 11033 1st North Staffordshire Regt KIA 31.5.16.
BRAMPTON George S. MM L/Cpl 3743 HAC(Inf)
BRAMPTON Winifred Addie MM Miss F BRCS
BRAMS Charles A.F. MM Cpl 40758 9th Essex Regt
BRAMWELL Ernest MM Cpl 97366 1st Notts & Derby Regt
BRAMWELL Ernest W. MM Spr 151281 250 Tunnelling Coy Royal Engineers
BRAMWELL Francis MM Cpl 3/10974 11th Liverpool Regt
BRAMWELL G. MM Pte 15467 York & Lancaster Regt
BRAMWELL Harry MM Pte 29306 8th East Surrey Regt
BRAMWELL J.R. MM Cpl 242527 Northumberland Fusiliers
BRAMWELL James MM Sjt 1/10371 1st Liverpool Regt
BRAMWELL Matthew MM Gnr 770013 C/250 Bde RFA
BRANAGAN William MM L/Cpl 590937 18th London Regt
BRANCH Albert W. MM Pte R/5793 2nd King's Royal Rifle Corps

BRANCH Cecil W.J. MM Pte 36811 RAMC
BRANCH Edmund D. MM Cpl 75550 RGA
BRANCH Frederick Albert MM Sjt 27499 2nd Royal Berkshire Regt KIA 27.4.18.
BRANCH George MM Pte 8687 10th Royal West Kent Regt
BRANCH Harold MM Pte 43318 RAMC
BRANCH James Frederick MM Sjt 8328 1st Scottish Rifles KIA 29.10.16.
BRANCH Laurie Haynes MM Pte 532613 2/15th London Regt
BRANCH Robert MM L/Cpl 498201 Royal Engineers
BRANCH Spencer O. MM L/Cpl 300103 2/5th London Regt
BRANCH Sydney E. MM L/Cpl 28269 1st Hampshire Regt
BRAND Albert MM Pte 27045 12th East Surrey Regt
BRAND Edward L. MM CQMS 591 8th London Regt
BRAND Ezra MM Cpl 13440 7th Duke of Cornwall's LI
BRAND Frederick MM Pte 423232 10th London Regt KIA 20.2.18.
BRAND Harold E. MM Gnr 16149 14 Bde RHA
BRAND Millenson C. MM Cpl 65077 32 Bde RFA
BRAND Richard Morris "DCM,MM" CSM 16176 7th Bedfordshire Regt KIA 3.5.17.
BRAND Robert A. MM Spr 411922 33 Light Railway Operating Coy Royal Engineers
BRAND Sidney MM Sjt 51594 28 Bde RFA
BRAND Sidney W. MM Bdr Sig 202606 169 Bde RFA
BRAND Thomas Harold MM Pte 17441 15th Notts & Derby Regt
BRAND Walter MM L/Cpl 300175 7th Essex Regt
BRANDER William MM Pte 018539 Army Ordnance Corps
BRANDER William MM Cpl 44683 60 Coy Machine Gun Corps
BRANDIE William MM Pte 6383 Gordon Highlanders
BRANDOM Sidney C. MM Sjt SE/10585 Army Veterinary Corps att RFA.
BRANDON Bert Victor MM Sjt 17664 6th Wiltshire Regt KIA 20.8.16.
BRANDON Joseph MM Gnr Sig 760510 B/317 Bde RFA
BRANDON Samuel V. MM Pte 201339 2/4th Hampshire Regt
BRANDON Thomas MM Cpl 470423 528 Fd Coy Royal Engineers
BRANDRETH Frank MM Pte 49943 11th Cheshire Regt Died 5.9.18.
BRANDRETH Harry MM Pte 17303 Royal Scots
BRANDRICK William J. MM Gnr 33427 RFA
BRANDUM Henry MM Pte 505293 13th London Regt KIA 24.8.18.
BRANEGAN Arthur G. MM Pte 26954 Royal West Kent Regt
BRANGAM John MM L/Sjt 15351 Royal Inniskilling Fusiliers
BRANIGAN Joseph A. MM Pte 69293 9 Fd Amb RAMC
BRANKSTON Henderson MM Pte 15340 13th Durham Light Infantry KIA 18.10.17.
BRANKSTON William MM Pte 21610 19th Durham Light Infantry
BRANN James MM Pte 42655 RAMC
BRANNAN James MM L/Cpl 276910 1/7th Arg & Suth Highlanders
BRANNAN James MM L/Cpl 9917 1st King's Own Scottish Borderers
BRANNAN John MM Dvr 4450 D/122 Bde RFA
BRANNAN John MM Pte 252645 1/8th Arg & Suth Highlanders DOW 31.7.18.
BRANNAN Matthew MM Pte 9905 9th York & Lancaster Regt
BRANNAN Michael MM Sjt 4684 B/123 Bde RFA
BRANNAN Michael MM Sjt 375057 2nd Royal Scots KIA 23.8.18.
BRANNON John T. MM Pte 17645 7th Duke of Cornwall's LI
BRANNON Patrick MM Pte 22434 6th Royal Dublin Fusiliers
BRANSON Arthur F. MM L/Cpl 200164 Royal Berkshire Regt
BRANSON George W. MM Gnr 211782 D/76 Bde RFA
BRANT George MM Sjt 88688 RFA
BRANT John MM CSM L/12558 1st Royal Fusiliers
BRANT John William MM L/Cpl 18375 2nd Lincolnshire Regt KIA 22.3.18.
BRANTER John MM Pte 13318 9th West Riding Regt
BRANTINGHAM Thomas Aloysius MM Sjt 21231 Manchester Regt
BRASH Charles MM Pte 8297 2nd Arg & Suth Highlanders
BRASH Foster E. MM Sjt 75721 MGC(Heavy Branch)
BRASH Frank MM L/Cpl 55153 Machine Gun Corps
BRASH Norval MM Cpl 42248 6th King's Own Scottish Borderers
BRASHER Ernest MM Dvr 36469 63 Fd Coy Royal Engineers
BRASIER Herbert Jack MM L/Cpl 10489 Machine Gun Corps KIA 21.3.18.
BRASIER Jabez MM Pte 64588 15th Yorkshire Light Infantry
BRASNETT Gurney MM L/Sjt 473168 RAMC
BRASSETT Frederick MM L/Cpl 27587 16th Royal Welsh Fusiliers
BRASSINGTON Harold MM Dvr Sig 705552 B/112 Bde RFA
BRASSINGTON William Henry MM Sjt 2618 West Riding Regt KIA 23.8.18.
BRASSLEAY Ernest MM Cpl 548724 513 Fd Coy Royal Engineers
BRATCHIE David MM Cpl 285011 Royal Highlanders

BRATCHIE Hugh MM Pte S/6330 11th Arg & Suth Highlanders
BRATCHIE James MM Sjt 2445 8/10th Gordon Highlanders
BRATT Charles M. MM Spr WR/281517 19 Lt Rly Op Coy Royal Engineers
BRAUND Arthur E. MM Dvr T3/025049 Army Service Corps
BRAUND Edward MM Cpl 232641 2nd London Regt
BRAUND Frederick D. MM+Bar 2nd Cpl 254312 5 Div Sig Coy Royal Engineers
BRAUND George MM L/Cpl 24060 1st Lancashire Fusiliers KIA 12.4.18.
BRAUNTON Frederick J. MM Bdr 63057 276 Siege Bty RGA
BRAVERY James A. MM Sjt 68786 32 Bde RFA
BRAVERY William MM BQMS 1181 520 Siege Bty RGA
BRAWN Alfred A. MM Pte 106232 RAMC
BRAWN Augustus E. MM+Bar Sjt H/256793 15th Hussars
BRAWN George W. MM Pte 106231 28 Fd Amb RAMC
BRAWN H. MM Pte 19155 Royal Scots
BRAWN Percy Cyril MM Pte 9036 2nd Northamptonshire Regt
BRAY Albert E. MM Pte 235410 Att 7ShropsLI Herefordshire Regt
BRAY Arthur MM Gnr 66629 306 Siege Bty RGA
BRAY Cecil MM Spr 92633 144 Army Troops Coy Royal Engineers
BRAY Charles MM Cpl 200314 Leicestershire Regt
BRAY Charles A. MM L/Cpl 145273 106 Fd Coy Royal Engineers
BRAY Charles Henry MM Pte L/11120 2nd Royal Sussex Regt
BRAY Charles W. MM Spr 551149 Royal Engineers
BRAY Edgar MM Pte 29542 Hampshire Regt
BRAY Edward R. MM Cpl 12902 1st Highland Light Infantry
BRAY Ernest MM Pte 11739 1st East Surrey Regt
BRAY Francis William MM L/Cpl 203133 8th Border Regt
BRAY Frederick C. MM Bdr 614501 2/1(Warwick)Bty RHA
BRAY George MM 2nd Cpl 160916 First Army Sig Coy Royal Engineers
BRAY George Dawson MM L/Cpl R/9008 13th King's Royal Rifle Corps
BRAY Harry MM L/Cpl 200333 1/4th Leicestershire Regt
BRAY Henry MM Pte 16131 18th Lancashire Fusiliers KIA 22.6.18.
BRAY Horace P. MM Cpl 112321 1 Gun Carrier Coy Tank Corps
BRAY James L. MM Pte 28501 10th Duke of Cornwall's LI
BRAY John A. MM Spr 966 Royal Engineers
BRAY John W. MM Sjt 29320 RGA
BRAY Leonard MM Pte 2847 24th Royal Fusiliers
BRAY Richard Harry MM Sjt 76385 'C' Bn Tank Corps
BRAY Samuel R. MM Pte R/32177 18th King's Royal Rifle Corps
BRAY Thomas V. MM Pte 385156 18th London Regt
BRAY Walter MM Pte 65098 6th Yorkshire Regt
BRAY Walter Luke "DCM,MM" Sjt 19264 3rd Grenadier Guards
BRAY Wilfred MM Cpl 152245 Royal Engineers
BRAY William H. MM L/Cpl 25483 10th Duke of Cornwall's LI
BRAYBROOK Francis William MM Pte 2406 Leicestershire Regt
BRAYDON Stanley R. MM Pte 3014 1/24th London Regt
BRAYFIELD Alfred E. MM Gnr 169024 RGA
BRAYLEY Fred MM Cpl 205192 1st Devonshire Regt
BRAYNE Albert V. MM Sjt 16077 54 Fd Coy Royal Engineers
BRAYSHAW Charles E. "MM+Bar,MID" Bdr 439 RFA
BRAYSHAW Edward Hutton "MM,MSM" Gnr 154904 C/52 Bde RFA
BRAYSHAW Thomas MM Cpl 72545 112 Bty 24 Bde RFA
BRAZELL Jeremiah MM Sjt 2437 1/6th Welsh Regt
BRAZIER Edward D. MM Bdsm 9539 2nd Arg & Suth Highlanders
BRAZIER Harold MM L/Bdr 71520 RFA
BRAZIER Henry MM Pte 22505 Hampshire Regt
BRAZIER Herbert Thomas MM L/Cpl B/203084 9th Rifle Brigade DOW 19.4.18.
BRAZIER Jack MM Pte 27871 2nd Worcestershire Regt
BRAZIER John MM L/Cpl 23953 Royal Engineers
BRAZIER L.F. MM Pte G/22060 6th East Kent Regt
BRAZIER Reginald MM Cpl 245788 2nd London Regt
BRAZIER Richard C. MM L/Cpl 2102 1st Royal West Kent Regt
BRAZIER Thomas David MM Cpl M2/106334 654 Coy Army Service Corps
BRAZIER William George MM Pte 21588 Royal West Surrey Regt
BRAZIER William Thomas MM Spr 177306 69 Fd Coy Royal Engineers
BRAZINGTON John MM Cpl 28935 6th Royal Dublin Fusiliers
BREACH William MM Gnr 29280 34 Siege Bty RGA
BREADMORE Frederick James MM Pte 201804 1/4th Royal Berkshire Regt
BREAKSPEAR Frederick "DCM,MM" L/Cpl 24739 5th Dorsetshire Regt
BREAKSPEAR William MM Sjt 37034 A/307 Bde RFA
BREAKSPEAR William MM Pte 11726 2nd A Coy Royal Berkshire Regt Died 1.5.18.
BREAKWELL Harry MM L/Sjt 10153 2nd Royal Welsh Fusiliers
BREALEY Ernest S. MM L/Cpl 510221 58 Div Sig Coy Royal Engineers
BREAR Frank MM Pte 2062 1/5th C Coy Royal Lancaster Regt KIA 18.9.16.
BREAR George W. MM L/Cpl 267154 2/5th West Yorkshire Regt
BREARLEY Ernest C. MM L/Cpl 21322 1st King's Own Scottish Borderers
BREARLEY Frank Arthur MM Pte 67370 2nd London Regt KIA 8.10.18.
BREARLEY Fred MM Gnr 2114 15 Bty MGC(Motors)
BREARLEY James MM Cpl 280158 10th Lancashire Fusiliers
BREARLEY John A. MM Dvr 63657 RFA
BREARLEY Sydney MM 2nd Cpl 89713 142 Army Troops Coy Royal Engineers
BREARS Bertram MM Bdr 786597 RFA
BREARTON Daniel MM L/Cpl 130612 Royal Engineers
BREATCLIFFE John MM+2 Bars Gnr 68559 94 Bty 18 Bde RFA
BREATHWICK John MM L/Sjt 13/147 12th York & Lancaster Regt
BREATHWICK Samuel J. "DCM,MM" Cpl 17231 5th Royal Berkshire Regt
BREBBER Alexander Harry Walker MM L/Cpl 290856 Gordon Highlanders
BREBBER George MM Pte 9095 2nd Highland Light Infantry
BREBNER William MM Pte 241293 1/4th Gordon Highlanders
BREBNER William MM Sjt 630893 255 Bde RFA
BRECHIN Andrew A. MM Pte 301304 2/1st(Highland)Fd Amb RAMC
BRECHIN John MM Pte 290184 7th Gordon Highlanders DOW 20.6.18.
BRECKENRIDGE Archibald A. MM Pte 40084 1st Royal Scots Fusiliers
BRECKIN Edward F. MM Sjt 15/84 15/17th West Yorkshire Regt
BRECKON Harry Walter MM Pte 533358 15th London Regt DOW 27.7.17.
BRECKON Henry MM Spr 474752 9 Div Sig Coy Royal Engineers att RFA
BREDIN F. MM Pte 386031 RAMC
BREE Clifford H. MM Pte 339466 RAMC
BREE Helier William "MM,CG(B)" CSM 31138 2nd Hampshire Regt
BREED Frederick C. MM Sjt 26070 Notts & Derby Regt
BREED Stephen MM Pte 1632 7th Royal West Kent Regt
BREEDEN James C. "DCM,MM" Sjt L/37717 A/180 Bde RFA
BREEDS Harry MM Pte 204659 7th Royal West Kent Regt
BREEDS William MM Pte 1703 6 Fd Amb RAMC
BREEN Charles E. MM Sjt 391554 16th London Regt
BREEN Christopher MM Pte 1377 2nd Lancashire Fusiliers
BREEN John MM Sjt 2931 1/22nd London Regt
BREEN Richard MM Sjt 14069 10th North Lancashire Regt
BREEN Robert MM Cpl 19/277 Royal Irish Rifles
BREESE Albert E. MM Cpl 592623 18th London Regt
BREESE Walter T. MM Dvr 116009 D/59 Bde RFA
BREESE William Lloyd MM Sjt Wheeler 705696 210 Bde RFA
BREEZE Albert MM+2 Bars L/Cpl 201564 1/7th Worcestershire Regt
BREEZE Cecil Herbert MM Dvr T4/059438 6 Div Train Army Service Corps
BREEZE David MM L/Sjt 18913 Machine Gun Corps
BREEZE H. MM Pte 20839 Essex Regt
BREEZE Harry "DCM,MM,MID" CSM 95926 106 Fd Coy Royal Engineers
BREEZE Hugh Reginald MM Pte 721046 1/24th London Regt
BREEZE John W. MM Spr 488210 466 Fd Coy Royal Engineers
BREEZE William MM Pte 41356 Royal Irish Rifles
BREHAUT Frederick T.Albert MM Sjt 450 1/9th London Regt
BREHAUT James MM Sjt 6/3141 Royal Irish Regt
BREHENEY James W. MM Sjt 23336 Yorkshire Regt
BREHENEY Joseph MM Sjt 3/617 2nd Yorkshire Light Infantry Died 31.10.18.
BREHENY James MM Pte 13548 8th Yorkshire Regt
BREITHAUPT George MM Pte 339208 RAMC
BREMNER Alexander MM Pte 241407 Seaforth Highlanders
BREMNER Alexander J. MM Pte 40088 Seaforth Highlanders
BREMNER Angus MM Sjt 8582 2nd Gordon Highlanders KIA 26.10.17.
BREMNER Archibald D. MM+Bar Sjt 81056 Royal Engineers
BREMNER Charles MM L/Cpl 235608 Gordon Highlanders
BREMNER Harry MM Sjt 2304 1/5th Gordon Highlanders KIA 15.11.16.
BREMNER James MM Bdr 42079 RFA

BREMNER James D. MM Dvr 630685 255 Bde RFA
BREMNER James F. MM Pte 3165 Gordon Highlanders
BREMNER Robert G. MM L/Cpl 511253 14th London Regt
BREMNER William MM Pte 1745 1st Royal Highlanders KIA 25.9.16.
BREMNER William MM Cpl 9546 1st Gordon Highlanders
BRENCHLEY George MM Pte 2652 7th East Kent Regt KIA 23.8.18.
BRENNAN Christopher MM+Bar CSM 27690 Machine Gun Corps
BRENNAN David MM Sjt 61084 252 Siege Bty RGA
BRENNAN Edward MM L/Cpl 2268 East Yorkshire Regt
BRENNAN Frank MM Pte 57108 5th Manchester Regt
BRENNAN Frederick MM L/Cpl 721727 1/24th London Regt
BRENNAN James MM Sjt 17583 19th Lancashire Fusiliers
BRENNAN James MM Pte 3565 2nd Royal Irish Regt DOW 6.11.18.
BRENNAN James MM Sjt 3/1882 Yorkshire Light Infantry
BRENNAN James MM Sjt 6332 2nd Irish Guards
BRENNAN James MM Sjt 14808 35 Bde RFA
BRENNAN John MM Cpl 28107 Royal Inniskilling Fusiliers
BRENNAN John MM Pte 42852 Royal Irish Rifles
BRENNAN John K. MM Pte 13539 14th Durham Light Infantry
BRENNAN Joseph MM L/Cpl 8047 1st North Staffordshire Regt KIA 26.3.18.
BRENNAN M. MM Pte 205693 1st Wiltshire Regt
BRENNAN Stanley J. MM+Bar Sjt 25976 3 Siege Bty RGA
BRENNAN Stephen MM Pte 7862 Royal Irish Regt
BRENNAN Thomas MM Cpl 2987 2nd Leinster Regt
BRENNAN Thomas MM L/Cpl 25489 Durham Light Infantry
BRENNAN Thomas "MM,MID" Pte 5610 Royal Dublin Fusiliers
BRENNAN Thomas MM Pte 3813 8th Royal Munster Fusiliers
BRENNAN Thomas MM L/Cpl 6/1048 16th King's Royal Rifle Corps Died 5.11.18.
BRENNAN Thomas Edward MM Pte M2/053441 402 Coy Army Service Corps
BRENNAN William "MM,MSM" L/Cpl 10054 54 Fd Coy Royal Engineers
BRENNAND Harry MM Gnr 161074 36 Bde RFA
BRENNAND Thomas MM L/Sjt 306161 Liverpool Regt
BRENNEN Edward W. MM Spr 402695 Royal Engineers
BRENT Frederick S. MM L/Cpl G/12094 19th Middlesex Regt
BRENT James MM Sjt 3540 Middlesex Regt
BRENTLEY Albert MM Cpl 8966 Yorkshire Light Infantry
BRENTNALL Alfred Charles MM Cpl 161627 21 Div Sig Coy Royal Engineers
BRENTON Alfred MM Cpl 25777 6 Siege Bty RGA
BRERETON Albert E. MM Cpl 3125 Oxf & Bucks Light Infantry
BRERETON Frank Allen MM+Bar L/Cpl 129162 'F' Special Coy Royal Engineers DOW 10.6.18.
BRERETON Norman MM Sjt 17834 20th Manchester Regt
BRERETON Percy E. MM Pte 11157 1st Middlesex Regt
BRERETON Robert G. MM Sjt 47185 RFA
BRERETON Thomas MM Gnr 319501 V/13 Heavy TM Bty RGA
BRESLAND John MM Pte 3893 2nd Royal Inniskilling Fusiliers
BRESQUAR Victor MM Cpl 14/19254 Liverpool Regt
BRESSER Kenneth MM Pte 242476 Notts & Derby Regt
BRESSEY Sydney Herbert MM L/Cpl 1489 1/15th London Regt KIA 21.9.18.
BRETHERTON James MM L/Cpl 55288 Machine Gun Corps
BRETHERTON William MM Sjt 341525 65 Fd Amb RAMC
BRETT Charles Frederick MM Gnr 28001 65 Bty 28 Bde RFA
BRETT Charles Henry MM Gnr 955597 236 Bde RFA
BRETT Charles John MM L/Cpl 320755 1/6th London Regt
BRETT Charles Thomas MM Pte R/33758 9th King's Royal Rifle Corps KIA 22.10.17.
BRETT Henry MM Pte 18267 7th Bedfordshire Regt
BRETT Henry J. MM L/Cpl 52178 7th Lincolnshire Regt
BRETT Leslie H. MM Pnr 129450 Royal Engineers
BRETT Richard MM+Bar Sjt L/30702 D/77 Bde RFA
BRETT Sydney C. MM Gnr 78278 RFA
BRETT Thomas MM Pte 390253 3rd(Northumbrian)Fd Amb RAMC
BRETT Thomas Henry MM Pte A/203410 1/12th London Regt
BRETT Walter MM Sjt 6341 4/5th Royal Highlanders KIA 25.9.17.
BRETT William MM L/Cpl 135547 118 Railway Coy Royal Engineers
BRETT William MM Pte 13926 Lincolnshire Regt
BRETT William MM Sjt 9741 1st Lancashire Fusiliers Died 15.10.18.
BRETT William G. MM Pte 32865 13th East Lancashire Regt
BRETTELL Charles W. "DCM,MM" BSM 61112 C/236 Bde RFA
BRETTELL Leslie MM Pte 240186 6th Royal Warwickshire Regt
BRETTELL William Joseph Harold MM Sjt 15996 RGA
BRETTON H.K. "MM,MID" L/Cpl 2028 1/1st City of London Yeo
BREWER Alfred E. MM+Bar Sjt 420589 10th London Regt

BREWER David MM Cpl G/14662 2nd Royal Sussex Regt
BREWER Frederick J. MM Sjt 322091 RGA
BREWER H. MM Pte 233486 London Regt
BREWER Harold MM Dvr 620319 RHA
BREWER Henry MM Pte 2080 5th Royal Lancaster Regt
BREWER Herbert D. MM Pte 12740 Dorsetshire Regt
BREWER James MM Sjt 200176 1/4th Royal Sussex Regt
BREWER John MM+Bar Pte 17490 1st North Lancashire Regt DOW 4.6.18.
BREWER John Garland Richards "DCM,MM+Bar,CG(It)" Sjt 58069 23 Div Sig Coy Royal Engineers
BREWER Victor "MM,MID" Sjt 13167 RGA Died 7.5.18.
BREWER William MM Pte 364372 RAMC
BREWER William Arthur MM L/Cpl 554523 16th London Regt DOW 7.4.18.
BREWIN Frederick MM Dvr 149383 C/255 Bde RFA
BREWIN James MM Cpl 7107 1st Leicestershire Regt
BREWIS Ralph MM Spr 51286 102 Fd Coy Royal Engineers
BREWIS Robert Ernest MM Pte 89034 58 Fd Amb RAMC KIA 6.6.18.
BREWIS Thomas L. MM Pte 78451 11th Northumberland Fusiliers
BREWIS William "DCM,MM" Sjt H/270443 1/1st Northumberland Yeo
BREWSTER Arthur Edward MM CQMS 8058 2nd Lincolnshire Regt
BREWSTER Charles MM Pte M2/147854 Army Service Corps
BREWSTER Charles Edward MM Cpl S2/016219 21 Div Train Army Service Corps
BREWSTER Ernest MM Sjt 86374 Royal Engineers
BREWSTER Ernest MM+Bar Gnr 1168 RFA
BREWSTER George MM Sjt L/11550 17th Royal Sussex Regt
BREWSTER George MM Spr 408302 504 Fd Coy Royal Engineers
BREWSTER Lawrence Sidney MM Pte 16585 1st South Wales Borderers KIA 26.9.18.
BREWSTER Samuel G. MM L/Cpl 38123 12th East Surrey Regt
BREWSTER Stanley W. MM Pte 235356 2nd South Staffordshire Regt
BREWSTER William J. "DCM,MM" Sjt 27706 10 Siege Bty RGA
BRIAN George MM Pte 13601 2nd Coldstream Guards
BRIAN George MM Cpl 27479 Highland Light Infantry
BRIAN Ivor Edgar MM Pte 32823 2nd Lincolnshire Regt Died 15.11.18.
BRIAN William H. MM BSM 69775 A/149 Bde RFA
BRIANCE Claude Henry MM Pte 32556 3 Bty MGC(Motors)
BRIANT Charles Edward MM Sjt 13470 6th Dorsetshire Regt Died 15.10.17.
BRIANT Herbert H. MM L/Cpl 60980 Machine Gun Corps
BRIARS James Danson MM Pte 27465 13th Cheshire Regt
BRICE Francis MM Sjt 22452 South Wales Borderers
BRICE George A. MM+Bar Pte 16027 4th Royal Fusiliers
BRICE Henry A. MM Pte 66809 9th Devonshire Regt
BRICKEL Sydney MM Pte 201879 Middlesex Regt
BRICKELL Ernest MM Gnr 3327 B/119 Bde RFA
BRICKELL Frederick J. MM Pte 53750 9th Welsh Regt
BRICKLEBANK Thomas MM Cpl 21614 2nd York & Lancaster Regt
BRICKNALL Arthur L. MM Cpl 5304 2nd Leinster Regt
BRICKNALL David MM Pte 43112 Royal Highlanders
BRICKNELL Edward MM Pte 302676 2nd Manchester Regt
BRICKNELL Edward MM Pte 10968 Oxf & Bucks Light Infantry
BRICKNELL Ernest Joseph MM Dvr 85348 36 Bde RFA
BRICKNELL George MM Sjt 8/10088 8th D Coy South Staffordshire Regt KIA 12.10.17.
BRICKNELL Harry F. MM Pte 8650 20th Hussars
BRICKNELL Henry MM Cpl 266889 1st Royal Warwickshire Regt
BRICKNELL Thomas MM Gnr 67641 135 Hy Bty RGA KIA 16.10.18.
BRICKWOOD George MM 2nd Cpl 96459 Royal Engineers
BRICKWOOD W.J. MM Pte 497518 RAMC
BRIDDOCK Albert MM Gnr 26628 RFA
BRIDDON Albert MM L/Cpl 3331 2nd Notts & Derby Regt
BRIDGE A.H. MM Pte 69303 92 Fd Amb RAMC
BRIDGE Albert E. MM Dvr T4/044534 Army Service Corps
BRIDGE Edward MM Sjt 14805 Liverpool Regt
BRIDGE Ernest MM Bdr 97689 RFA
BRIDGE Frederick W. MM Pte 9548 1st Somerset Light Infantry
BRIDGE James Thomas "MC,MM(2308 Sjt)" Capt 8th Royal Warwickshire Regt
BRIDGE John MM Pte 74581 10th Manchester Regt
BRIDGE John "MM,MID" Dvr 24128 123 Bty 28 Bde RFA
BRIDGE John H. MM Pte 30784 RAMC
BRIDGE Joseph MM Pte 12678 2nd Manchester Regt
BRIDGE Norman E. MM L/Cpl 251702 2nd Manchester Regt

BRIDGE Percival MM Sjt M2/115464 Army Service Corps
BRIDGE T.H. MM Pte 20712 RAMC
BRIDGE William MM L/Cpl 30413 Worcestershire Regt
BRIDGE William E. "MM,MID" Cpl 13926 Yorkshire Light Infantry
BRIDGEFORD Peter R. MM Sjt 290151 Gordon Highlanders
BRIDGEMAN Archibald G. MM Cpl 2106 Seaforth Highlanders
BRIDGEMAN G. MM Pte 32804 RAMC
BRIDGEMAN James MM Cpl 55934 14th Royal Welsh Fusiliers
BRIDGEMENT Fred MM Pte 17/641 West Yorkshire Regt
BRIDGEN Frank MM L/Cpl 306052 Royal Warwickshire Regt
BRIDGEN Harold E. MM L/Cpl 560327 Royal Engineers
BRIDGENS Francis H. MM+Bar Pte 93185 2nd Durham Light Infantry
BRIDGER Albert MM Pte G/17685 6th East Kent Regt KIA 27.3.18.
BRIDGER Albert G.C. "DCM,MM" L/Sjt 9331 Coldstream Guards
BRIDGER Bernard G. MM L/Cpl 34629 7th Norfolk Regt
BRIDGER C.E. MM Cpl G/475 9th Royal Sussex Regt
BRIDGER George Fred MM Gnr 65307 RHA
BRIDGER Harold MM Cpl 15513 Royal West Kent Regt
BRIDGER Harry MM Sjt 26891 RGA
BRIDGER Henry MM Pte 17171 Royal West Kent Regt
BRIDGER Jack MM Pte G/1759 8th Royal Sussex Regt
BRIDGER Percy William "MM,MID" Pte 4017 7th Royal Sussex Regt KIA 3.5.17.
BRIDGER Richard W. MM Pte 320124 Royal Sussex Regt
BRIDGES Edwin L. MM Pte 572454 17th London Regt
BRIDGES Frank "DCM,MM" CSM 202428 2nd Bn South Wales Borderers
BRIDGES Frederick MM L/Sjt 14525 Norfolk Regt
BRIDGES Frederick E. MM Sjt 603602 76 Coy Labour Corps
BRIDGES George MM Sjt 92998 6th Bn Tank Corps
BRIDGES Herbert E. MM Pte 18459 South Lancashire Regt
BRIDGES John MM Pte 241155 Worcestershire Regt
BRIDGES John F. "DCM,MM+Bar" Sjt 8963 1st Wiltshire Regt
BRIDGES John T. MM Sjt 10372 Royal Irish Fusiliers
BRIDGES Sidney C. MM L/Cpl 700341 23rd London Regt
BRIDGES Thomas MM Pte 36683 1st Somerset Light Infantry
BRIDGES Thomas MM L/Cpl 22088 Suffolk Regt
BRIDGES Thomas John MM Cpl 201978 2/7th Worcestershire Regt
BRIDGES William John "DCM,MM" Sjt 29486 93 Bde 35 Hy Bty RGA KIA 20.7.18.
BRIDGESTOCK Tom MM Pte 267117 Notts & Derby Regt
BRIDGETT Charles MM Sjt 34383 D/156 Bde RFA
BRIDGEWATER Arnold MM Pte 31196 York & Lancaster Regt
BRIDGEWATER Henry Ernest MM Cpl 2484 1/6th South Staffordshire Regt
BRIDGEWATER James MM Gnr 53014 352 Siege Bty RGA
BRIDGEWATER William MM L/Cpl 1502 2nd Rifle Brigade
BRIDGFORD William MM Pte 74626 17 Fd Amb RAMC DOW 29.4.18.
BRIDGMAN Alfred MM L/Cpl 240691 8th Gloucestershire Regt
BRIDGMAN William E. MM Cpl 307762 2nd Lancashire Fusiliers
BRIDGWATER George MM Bdr 88086 'O' Bty RHA
BRIDLE Charles W. MM L/Cpl G/1767 Royal Sussex Regt
BRIDLE Edwin E. MM Gnr 11303 RFA
BRIDLE Frederick MM Dvr 926161 C/290 Bde RFA
BRIDLE Joe MM Pte 9320 6th Royal West Kent Regt
BRIDLE William E. MM Pte 12659 Machine Gun Corps
BRIDSON Joseph MM Pte 50929 RAMC
BRIDSON Thomas Edward MM L/Cpl 9182 1st Royal Lancaster Regt KIA 19.5.18.
BRIEN Andrew MM Pte 7068 2nd Royal Irish Regt
BRIEN Charles MM Pte 10382 1st Royal Irish Fusiliers
BRIEN Edward MM+Bar L/Cpl 5336 2nd Royal Irish Regt DOW 27.3.18.
BRIEN John MM Pte 594 Royal West Surrey Regt
BRIEN Kieran MM Gnr 24664 1 Siege Bty RGA
BRIEN Martin MM Sjt 1115 5th Royal Irish Regt
BRIEN Patrick MM L/Cpl 6202 Irish Guards
BRIEN Robert MM Pte 6039 37th Bn Machine Gun Corps
BRIER Thomas W. MM Bdr 119072 RGA
BRIERLEY Abraham MM Pte 127453 19 Coy Machine Gun Corps KIA 18.4.18.
BRIERLEY Alfred MM Cpl 935166 RFA
BRIERLEY B. MM Pte 5022 Lancashire Fusiliers
BRIERLEY Charles E. MM Pte 252014 Manchester Regt
BRIERLEY Edward "DCM,MM" Sjt 45385 95 Fd Coy Royal Engineers
BRIERLEY Edward MM Pte 240104 6th East Lancashire Regt
BRIERLEY Edward MM Pte 20041 Royal Dublin Fusiliers
BRIERLEY Frank MM Sjt 11990 10th West Riding Regt KIA 27.10.18.
BRIERLEY Frank MM Cpl 15248 31st Bn Machine Gun Corps
BRIERLEY Harry MM Pte 59257 12th Manchester Regt
BRIERLEY James MM Gnr Sig L/45385 A/211 Bde RFA
BRIERLEY John MM Pte 61398 12th Manchester Regt
BRIERLEY John W. MM L/Cpl 62433 30th Bn Machine Gun Corps
BRIERLEY Mark MM Pte 24886 Machine Gun Corps
BRIERLEY Percy MM Pte 23981 2nd Grenadier Guards
BRIERLEY Samuel MM L/Cpl 52776 7th Lancashire Fusiliers
BRIERLY Thomas W. MM L/Cpl 53411 5th Lancashire Fusiliers
BRIERS John A. MM Sjt S4/248786 48 Div Train Army Service Corps
BRIERS Joseph MM L/Cpl 13622 9th Royal Welsh Fusiliers
BRIERS Leonard G. MM+Bar Pte 14718 17th Lancashire Fusiliers
BRIFFETT Frederick MM Pte G/18561 2nd Royal Sussex Regt
BRIGGS Albert MM Pte 4716 Middlesex Regt
BRIGGS Albert H. MM Cpl 23635 29th Bn Machine Gun Corps
BRIGGS Alexander MM Spr 132674 Royal Engineers
BRIGGS Arthur H. MM Pnr 254761 37 Div Sig Coy Royal Engineers
BRIGGS Burton "DCM,MM" Sjt 12604 22 Coy Labour Corps
BRIGGS Chris MM L/Bdr 805473 A/123 Bde RFA
BRIGGS Edgar MM+Bar Bdr 3144 A/246 Bde RFA
BRIGGS Ernest A. MM L/Cpl 3757 2nd Lancashire Fusiliers
BRIGGS Fred MM Dvr L/17715 RFA
BRIGGS Frederick Charles MM L/Cpl 42032 Yorkshire Regt
BRIGGS Frederick H. MM Pte 82223 RAMC
BRIGGS George MM Pte 242453 5th Lincolnshire Regt
BRIGGS George MM Sjt 4303 1st East Surrey Regt
BRIGGS George MM Pte 17663 7th Border Regt
BRIGGS George Alfred MM Pte 22158 15th Royal Welsh Fusiliers
BRIGGS George Edward MM Sjt 9055 7th East Yorkshire Regt
BRIGGS George K. MM Pte 700157 23rd London Regt
BRIGGS Gilbert MM Pte 202425 1/9th Royal Scots
BRIGGS Hadyn H. MM Pnr 72738 Royal Engineers
BRIGGS Harry MM BSM 676545 40 Bde RFA
BRIGGS Henry MM Pte 240106 1/8th Worcestershire Regt
BRIGGS Henry G. MM Pte STK/918 10th Royal Fusiliers
BRIGGS Horace G. MM Pte 31991 75 Fd Amb RAMC
BRIGGS J. MM Sjt 352195 2(East Lancs)Fd Amb RAMC
BRIGGS J. MM Pte 205336 Labour Corps
BRIGGS James "DCM,MM" Cpl 14439 2nd(DCM);8th(MM) Royal Scots Fusiliers
BRIGGS James MM Sjt 2082 1/10th Liverpool Regt
BRIGGS James MM Cpl 1511 Royal Horse Guards
BRIGGS James MM Pte 14/1464 8th York & Lancaster Regt
BRIGGS James A. MM Sjt 11054 East Surrey Regt
BRIGGS James T. MM Pte 45539 RAMC
BRIGGS John George MM Gnr 61695 123 Siege Bty RGA
BRIGGS John H. MM L/Sjt 23547 Yorkshire Regt
BRIGGS John William "DCM,MM" Sjt 13244 8th Leicestershire Regt KIA 17.10.17.
BRIGGS Joseph MM Dvr T4/161028 Att 66 Fd Amb RAMC Army Service Corps
BRIGGS Joseph William MM Pte 32467 10th North Lancashire Regt KIA 11.4.17.
BRIGGS Joshua "MM,Military Cross(Greece)" Gnr 134763 D/116 Bde RFA
BRIGGS R. MM Sjt P/4893 Military Mounted Police
BRIGGS Ralph Bonser MM Gnr 27132 A/46 Bde RFA
BRIGGS Robert E. MM Spr 48466 Royal Engineers
BRIGGS Squire MM Pte 63565 2nd West Yorkshire Regt
BRIGGS T.W. MM Pte 27718 Lancashire Fusiliers
BRIGGS Thomas MM CSM 1270 11th Manchester Regt
BRIGGS Thomas Herbert MM Pte 10513 2nd East Lancashire Regt KIA 31.7.17.
BRIGGS Walter MM L/Cpl 129323 Royal Engineers
BRIGGS Walter MM L/Cpl 405272 RAMC
BRIGGS Walter MM Bdr Sig 780112 A/246 Bde RFA
BRIGGS William MM Pte 201595 1/4th West Riding Regt
BRIGGS William R. MM Gnr 54188 18 Bde RFA
BRIGHAM Arthur MM Pte R/8720 King's Royal Rifle Corps
BRIGHAM Thomas MM Pte 24625 Machine Gun Corps
BRIGHT Albert B. MM Dvr 27110 RFA
BRIGHT Albert E. MM Sjt 15321 4th Worcestershire Regt
BRIGHT Albert Edward "DCM,MM" L/Sjt 10719 4th Coldstream Guards DOW 14.4.18.
BRIGHT Edward John MM Pte 495158 82 Fd Amb RAMC
BRIGHT F.T.J. MM L/Cpl 23726 Essex Regt
BRIGHT George MM Dvr 60923 154 Fd Coy Royal Engineers

BRIGHT Harry MM Dvr 141477 Royal Engineers
BRIGHT Henry Mark MM Spr 463113 50 Div Sig Coy Royal Engineers
BRIGHT John A. MM Pte 260390 1/1st County of London Yeomanry
BRIGHT John William MM L/Cpl 49493 160 Coy Machine Gun Corps
BRIGHT Lionel J. MM+Bar Sjt G/4800 12th Royal Fusiliers
BRIGHT Maurice MM Cpl 17677 Wiltshire Regt
BRIGHT Norman James MM L/Cpl 18642 1st East Yorkshire Regt
BRIGHT P.J. MM Sjt 10717 9th Essex Regt
BRIGHT Robert MM Cpl 641 RFA
BRIGHT William O. MM L/Sjt 17014 1st Grenadier Guards
BRIGHTMAN Arthur MM Pte 200698 1/5th Bedfordshire Regt
BRIGHTMAN Frank "DCM,MM" CSM 8561 2nd Northamptonshire Regt
BRIGHTMORE Edward J. MM Pte 6583 1st East Lancashire Regt
BRIGHTMORE Henry MM Sjt 11651 2nd Scots Guards KIA 4.7.17.
BRIGHTMORE Robert MM Cpl 442022 Royal Engineers
BRIGHTMORE Thomas William MM Pte 307404 2/8th Notts & Derby Regt
BRIGHTMORE William MM Bdr L/26405 C/245 Bde RFA
BRIGHTON Alfred MM+Bar Cpl 200527 2nd Worcestershire Regt
BRIGHTON Edmund L. MM L/Cpl 71243 Royal Engineers
BRIGHTON George MM CSM 13556 9th Norfolk Regt
BRIGHTON James MM Sjt 32511 2 Bty MGC(Motors)
BRIGHTON Samuel James MM+Bar Cpl 17101 2nd Suffolk Regt DOW 27.9.18.
BRIGHTWELL William A. MM+Bar Cpl 66254 26th Royal Fusiliers
BRIGHURST Frank R. MM Pte 90067 RAMC
BRIGNALL Herbert MM Spr 283974 50 Div Sig Coy Royal Engineers
BRIGNELL Albert E. MM Sjt 2385 Yorkshire Light Infantry
BRIGSTOCK Walter MM Gnr 45970 C/189 Bde RFA
BRIMBLE H.J. MM Sjt 43423 RFA
BRIMBLE Walter G. MM Pte 17674 8th Somerset Light Infantry
BRIMELOW Henry MM Sjt 19982 King's Own Scottish Borderers
BRIMELOW Joshua L. MM Pte 375446 Manchester Regt
BRIMER Frederick MM Pte 40052 1/5th Royal Scots Fusiliers
BRIMER William N. MM Pte 19302 Durham Light Infantry
BRIMFIELD Arthur MM Pte 27557 Liverpool Regt
BRIMICOMBE Percy W. MM Pte 48549 5th Royal Berkshire Regt
BRIMICOMBE Sydney James MM CSM 8200 2nd No.3 Coy Coldstream Guards KIA 16.9.16.
BRIMSON Frank G. MM Pte 94098 Liverpool Regt
BRIND Arthur MM L/Cpl 10/43039 15th Royal Irish Rifles
BRIND Francis S. MM Pte 13594 4th Coldstream Guards
BRINDLE George MM Pte 37338 South Lancashire Regt
BRINDLE Herbert MM Pte 42405 59 Fd Amb RAMC KIA 23.9.17.
BRINDLE J. MM Pte 15005 South Lancashire Regt
BRINDLE John Alfred MM L/Sjt 18/1390 10th West Yorkshire Regt DOW 11.10.18.
BRINDLE Robert MM Pte 446500 714 Coy Labour Corps
BRINDLE T. MM Sjt 240344 East Lancashire Regt
BRINDLEY Albert MM L/Cpl 12396 8th North Staffordshire Regt
BRINDLEY Arthur MM Cpl 774 RFA
BRINDLEY Harry MM Sjt 44694 17th Manchester Regt KIA 22.3.18.
BRINDLEY Thomas "DCM,MM" Cpl 4417 2nd Royal Warwickshire Regt KIA 9.10.17.
BRINDLEY Thomas C. MM Pte 11569 King's Royal Rifle Corps
BRINDLEY Tom MM Cpl 49007 1st Cheshire Regt DOW 9.8.17.
BRINDLEY William MM Sjt 14479 12th Liverpool Regt
BRINE Albert MM Cpl 55230 12th Manchester Regt
BRINE Robert "DCM,MM" Sjt 3802 1st Hampshire Regt
BRINKEY Thomas MM Cpl 60891 Royal Engineers
BRINKHURST John F. MM L/Cpl 6854 9th Royal Sussex Regt
BRINKWORTH George Arthur "MM,MID" Cpl 13646 Gloucestershire Regt
BRINSDEN William F. MM+Bar Sjt 9472 2nd Oxf & Bucks Light Infantry
BRINT Walter R. MM 2nd Cpl 34616 54 Fd Coy Royal Engineers
BRINTON Edgar "MC,MM(43366 Sjt RHA)" 2Lt D/174 Bde RFA
BRINTON Henry MM Dvr 825341 C/155 Bde RFA
BRION Albert T. MM Pte 10963 5th Royal Berkshire Regt
BRISBANE James MM L/Cpl 3085 Royal Highlanders
BRISBY Walter "DCM,MM" Sjt G/7733 11th Royal Fusiliers
BRISCOE Arthur MM Sjt 56540 11 Bde RFA
BRISCOE James MM Cpl 24920 9th Royal Welsh Fusiliers
BRISCOE James MM Spr 254372 Royal Engineers
BRISCOE Joseph MM Pte 200241 11th Manchester Regt
BRISCOE William MM Gnr 117217 RFA
BRISLEN Thomas MM Pte 14287 4th Liverpool Regt KIA 11.4.18.
BRISLEY Alfred Thomas MM Pte 270125 6th East Kent Regt
BRISLEY Phillip M. MM Sjt 41876 36 Bde RFA
BRISTOW Albert J. MM Sjt B/1866 Rifle Brigade
BRISTOW Duncan MM Sjt S/8443 1st Gordon Highlanders
BRISTOW Edward A. MM Cpl M2/176194 Army Service Corps
BRISTOW Frederick W. MM Sjt 35612 RGA
BRISTOW G. MM Cpl 551145 London Regt
BRISTOW George MM L/Cpl 16428 Royal Berkshire Regt
BRISTOW Henry MM L/Sjt 2081 1/1st Westmorland & Cumberland Yeomanry
BRISTOW Henry Gayen MM Sjt 37562 15 Siege Bty RGA KIA 30.8.16.
BRISTOW Henry Stanley MM Cpl 681135 1/22nd London Regt
BRISTOW John MM Sjt 12480 7th Somerset Light Infantry
BRISTOW John MM L/Sjt 10040 Leicestershire Regt
BRISTOW Marenza MM Pte 20766 2nd Bedfordshire Regt KIA 22.8.18.
BRISTOW Percy MM Sjt 29890 14th Royal Warwickshire Regt
BRISTOW Robert MM Pte 57701 RAMC
BRISTOW Sidney MM Sjt 36765 RAMC
BRISTOW Sidney V. MM L/Cpl 23621 7th Border Regt
BRISTOW Walter MM L/Cpl 486041 Royal Engineers
BRISTOWE Sydney MM Pte 41059 3rd Rifle Brigade
BRITCHER Albert MM Gnr 42200 RGA
BRITNELL John MM Cpl Fitter 291885 132 Heavy Bty RGA
BRITNELL William T. MM Spr 63189 Royal Engineers
BRITON James "DCM,MM" L/Cpl 280566 7th Highland Light Infantry
BRITT Albert H. MM Cpl 68686 57 Bty 45 Bde RFA
BRITT Alfred E. MM Dvr 68560 5 Bde RFA
BRITT Frederick MM Pte G/160 7th Royal Sussex Regt
BRITT James "DCM,MM" CSM 9402 6th Dorsetshire Regt
BRITT John MM Gnr 32601 81 Siege Bty RGA
BRITTAIN Alfred J. MM Pte S/21065 Rifle Brigade
BRITTAIN Charles H. MM Pte 18245 1st Bedfordshire Regt
BRITTAIN Charles N. MM Sjt 52168 7 Bde H Bty RHA
BRITTAIN Frank H. MM Pte 202938 7th Middlesex Regt
BRITTAIN George H. MM L/Sjt 7388 2nd South Staffordshire Regt
BRITTEN C.S. MM Air Mech 1 45211 Royal Flying Corps att RGA.
BRITTEN Frederick MM L/Cpl 8716 1st Wiltshire Regt
BRITTEN H.G. MM Sjt 331564 Hampshire Regt
BRITTEN Harry "MM,MID" Sjt 290 1/1st North Somerset Yeomanry
BRITTER John Joseph MM Bdr 71631 58 Bty 35 Bde RFA KIA 12.7.16.
BRITTIAN David T. MM Pte 94075 1st Liverpool Regt
BRITTLEBANK Arthur MM Sjt 43555 9 Hy Bty RGA
BRITTON Alexander MM Sjt 2033 1/3rd Monmouthshire Regt
BRITTON Andrew P. MM Sjt 11761 8th Lincolnshire Regt
BRITTON Arthur MM Pte F/271 16th Middlesex Regt
BRITTON Bertie G. MM Spr 84899 Royal Engineers
BRITTON Clifford MM Cpl 18642 8th Yorkshire Light Infantry KIA 23.1.17.
BRITTON Dennis MM+Bar Pte 246 10th Royal West Kent Regt
BRITTON Earl MM Pte 52118 1/5th Manchester Regt DOW 15.8.18.
BRITTON Edward "MM,MID" Pte 15582 14th Durham Light Infantry KIA 13.10.16.
BRITTON Frank MM Sjt 265858 4th West Riding Regt
BRITTON Frederick MM Cpl 240926 1st Royal West Kent Regt KIA 26.10.17.
BRITTON Frederick Maxwell MM+Bar Sjt 2677 1/6th Durham Light Infantry
BRITTON George E. MM L/Cpl 38909 Northumberland Fusiliers
BRITTON John A. MM L/Cpl 1524 Monmouthshire Regt
BRITTON N.L. MM Gnr 4726 RGA
BRITTON Percy George MM Pte 36566 41 Coy Machine Gun Corps
BRITTON R.H. MM+Bar Sjt 34461 2nd Essex Regt
BRITTON Renwick Stanley MM L/Cpl 28146 1st Somerset Light Infantry DOW 28.9.18.
BRITTON Robert MM L/Cpl 6296 11th Manchester Regt
BRITTON Robert Samuel MM L/Cpl 325972 1/9th Durham Light Infantry
BRITTON Samuel Small MM+Bar Sjt 6165 4th King's Royal Rifle Corps
BRITTON Sidney MM Dvr 74154 RFA
BRITTON Thomas Henry MM Sjt 8996 1st Devonshire Regt DOW 23.7.16.
BRITTON Walter H. MM Pte 15513 Notts & Derby Regt
BRIXEY Archibald C. MM Sjt 38932 A Bty RHA
BRIXEY Charles MM L/Cpl 68930 11th Royal Welsh Fusiliers
BRIXEY H.G. MM Pte 320605 London Regt

BRIXEY James W. MM Pte S/7100 Rifle Brigade
BRIXTON James MM Pte 11473 2nd Devonshire Regt
BRIXTON John A. MM Dvr 18266 54 Fd Coy Royal Engineers
BRIZELL Clarence H. MM Cpl 676585 RFA
BROAD Arthur S. MM Sjt 5053 5th Dragoon Guards
BROAD Charles MM Sjt 11492 Yorkshire Regt
BROAD Charles F. MM Gnr 93877 RFA
BROAD Edward MM+Bar L/Cpl 345368 16th Devonshire Regt
BROAD James MM Pte S/26301 Rifle Brigade
BROAD John J. MM Dvr 17148 B/50 Bde RFA
BROAD Joseph MM Pte S/5635 12th Rifle Brigade KIA 20.9.17.
BROAD W. MM Cpl 4290 10th Hussars
BROAD William George MM Pte 3248 Royal West Kent Regt DOW 29.3.18.
BROADBENT C. MM Pte 400051 RAMC
BROADBENT Frank MM Pte 337333 RAMC
BROADBENT George MM L/Cpl 202787 1/4th West Riding Regt
BROADBENT James Edward MM Pte 2564 2nd Manchester Regt DOW 30.12.17.
BROADBENT John E. MM Gnr 152816 D/189 Bde RFA
BROADBENT Thomas MM Pte 43068 8th Seaforth Highlanders
BROADBENT William Ivory MM L/Cpl P/6039 Military Mounted Police
BROADBRIDGE Arthur MM+Bar Sjt 95549 RFA
BROADBRIDGE Percival James MM L/Cpl 69192 91 Fd Amb RAMC
BROADFOOT James "DCM,MM" Pte 6176 Cameron Highlanders
BROADFOOT James F. MM Pte 20817 4th Grenadier Guards KIA 13.4.18.
BROADFOOT John MM Sjt 204036 5/6th Scottish Rifles
BROADFOOT John G. MM Gnr 750758 RFA
BROADFOOT John R. "MM,MID" Sjt 42663 Royal Engineers
BROADHEAD Alfred E. MM CSM 12731 11th Royal Fusiliers
BROADHEAD Cecil C. MM Sjt 30352 RGA
BROADHEAD Charles E. MM Pte 105129 11 Fd Amb RAMC
BROADHEAD Phillip H. MM Pte 82354 26th Royal Welsh Fusiliers
BROADHEAD Thomas MM Pte 241160 6th Notts & Derby Regt
BROADHEAD Thomas H. MM+Bar Sjt 13/48 11th East Yorkshire Regt
BROADHEAD Tom H. MM Pte 40779 7th East Yorkshire Regt
BROADHEAD Walter MM Bdr 5188 RFA
BROADHURST Arthur MM Pte 39592 125 Coy Machine Gun Corps
BROADHURST Frank MM Pte 290620 Cheshire Regt
BROADHURST George MM Pnr 259296 Royal Engineers
BROADHURST George T. MM Pte 151926 33rd Bn Machine Gun Corps
BROADHURST Harold "MM,MID" Pte 1160 9th Manchester Regt
BROADHURST John MM Pte G/14592 7th East Kent Regt
BROADHURST John T. MM Dvr L/4776 RFA
BROADHURST John Thomas MM L/Cpl 11468 8th South Staffordshire Regt
BROADHURST Reuben MM Sjt 1674 RFA
BROADHURST William MM Pte 9178 South Staffordshire Regt
BROADHURST William Albert James MM Gnr 651768 381 Bty RFA
BROADHURST William J. MM Sjt P/415 Military Mounted Police
BROADLEY Benjamin MM Pte 64626 15th Yorkshire Light Infantry
BROADLEY George T. MM Pte 860472 33rd London Regt
BROADLEY Thomas MM Gnr 74466 43 Bde RFA
BROADLEY William MM Cpl 356847 4th Hampshire Regt
BROADRICK George Frederick MM Sjt 761390 C/317 Bde RFA
BROADWAY John MM L/Cpl 43457 Lincolnshire Regt
BROADWAY Leonard J. MM L/Cpl 11408 Duke of Cornwall's LI
BROATCH David MM Pte 15850 Lancashire Fusiliers
BROATCH John MM Sjt 5773 3 Railway Coy Royal Engineers
BROCK Edwin MM+Bar L/Cpl 240660 York & Lancaster Regt
BROCK Francis MM Sjt 52680 5 Pontoon Park Royal Engineers
BROCK Frederick Albert MM Sjt 13353 10th Scottish Rifles
BROCK Hector J. MM Pte 7078 Army Cyclist Corps
BROCK Henry G. MM Sjt 15937 9 Fd Coy Royal Engineers
BROCK Herbert MM Gnr 116831 RFA
BROCK J.H. MM Cpl 1666 Royal Irish Rifles
BROCK Samuel MM Sjt 9314 1st Royal Irish Rifles
BROCK Samuel MM+Bar Pte 205247 1st Royal West Surrey Regt
BROCK William MM Pte 21550 11th Royal Scots
BROCK William MM L/Cpl 12600 Coldstream Guards
BROCKBANK Frances (sic) MM Sjt 470334 526 Fd Coy Royal Engineers
BROCKBANK George MM Pte 7092 7th Dragoon Guards
BROCKBANK Harry H. MM Cpl A/201882 2nd King's Royal Rifle Corps
BROCKBANK Robert Edward MM Sjt 8504 1st Royal Lancaster Regt KIA 12.10.17.
BROCKELBANK Charles MM Sjt 18592 20th Lancashire Fusiliers KIA 24.11.17.
BROCKHOUSE Arthur MM Pte 437448 2 Fd Amb RAMC
BROCKHURST Edward MM Cpl 7106 2nd South Staffordshire Regt
BROCKHURST Ernest MM Cpl 497133 13th London Regt
BROCKIE John MM L/Cpl 200384 1/4th Cheshire Regt KIA 30.7.18.
BROCKLAND Harry "DCM,MM+Bar" BSM 291927 132 Hy Bty RGA
BROCKLEBANK Bernard MM Sjt 193167 Royal Engineers
BROCKLEBANK John MM Pte 34786 8th York & Lancaster Regt
BROCKLEHURST Arthur MM L/Cpl 13265 1/6th North Staffordshire Regt KIA 3.10.18.
BROCKLEHURST Edmund William MM Pte 35203 11th Lancashire Fusiliers
BROCKLESBY Albert John MM+Bar Bdr 27259 149 Bde RFA
BROCKLESBY George MM Sjt Farrier 18454 RFA
BROCKLESS Ernest MM Pte 1859 Yorkshire Regt
BROCKMAN Alfred James MM Pte 20038 10 Fd Amb RAMC
BROCKS Henry A. MM Cpl 200216 1/4th Royal Berkshire Regt
BROCKWELL Augustus P. MM L/Cpl 1644 8th London Regt
BRODERICK Albert MM Pte 25468 East Surrey Regt
BRODERICK Michael MM Spr 95581 Royal Engineers
BRODERICK William MM Sjt 58312 34 Bde RFA
BRODIE Alexander "DCM,MM+Bar" Sjt 20122 51st Bn Machine Gun Corps
BRODIE James MM Dvr 12182 4 Div Ammn Col RFA
BRODIE James MM Sjt 276432 1/7th Arg & Suth Highlanders
BRODIE John MM Dvr 82549 92 Bty 17 Bde RFA
BRODIE Robert S. MM Spr 410306 1 Siege Coy R Monmouth RE
BRODIE Samuel MM L/Cpl 240595 1/6th Highland Light Infantry
BRODIE Thomas MM Pte 290606 7th Royal Highlanders
BRODIE W.C. MM L/Cpl 2046 1/8th Royal Warwickshire Regt
BRODIE William Gunning MM Sjt 48542 13th Liverpool Regt KIA 18.4.18.
BRODRICK Harold MM Pte 47822 2nd Northamptonshire Regt
BRODRICK John MM+Bar Pte 15994 1st Royal Scots Fusiliers
BRODRICK Martin MM Pte 15854 Yorkshire Light Infantry
BROE Thomas MM Sjt 281253 1/7th Lancashire Fusiliers
BROGAN Herbert MM Cpl 4323 Leinster Regt Awarded for 'Easter Rising'.
BROGAN J. MM L/Cpl 133288 46th Royal Fusiliers
BROGAN James MM Pte 5169 1st Royal Welsh Fusiliers
BROGAN James William MM Pte 44439 276 Coy Machine Gun Corps
BROGAN Philip "MM,MSM" Cpl 9368 14th Arg & Suth Highlanders
BROGAN Robert L. MM Pte 28156 4th North Lancashire Regt
BROGDEN Benjamin MM SSM 6592 18th Hussars
BROGDEN Edward G. MM Cpl 40896 2/4th Hampshire Regt
BROGDEN James MM Sjt 16646 8th East Lancashire Regt
BROKENSHA Leonard H. MM Gnr 75016 Tank Corps
BROLLY James MM L/Cpl 33905 1/1st Bucks Bn Oxf & Bucks Light Infantry
BROMAGE Arthur Benjamin MM Pte 36708 4th(ER)Bn South Staffordshire Regt
BROMAGE Frederick G. "MM,MID" Cpl 3941 RFA
BROMAN Alfred J. MM Cpl 44480 8th Somerset Light Infantry
BROME William MM Cpl 7047 D/82 Bde RFA
BROMFIELD James "MM,CG(F)" Pte 3/4844 1st York & Lancaster Regt
BROMFIELD John MM Pte 201906 2/5th West Yorkshire Regt
BROMFIELD Samuel MM Pte 713501 23rd London Regt
BROMHAM Albert Victor MM Cpl 13102 8th Norfolk Regt
BROMHEAD John Paul MM Pte 9848 8th Royal Fusiliers KIA 3.8.16.
BROMILEY James MM Pte 30296 5th Lancashire Fusiliers
BROMILEY Thomas H. MM Sjt 242694 5th North Lancashire Regt
BROMLEY Adam MM Sjt 18/1053 11th West Yorkshire Regt
BROMLEY Albert N. MM Cpl 432 GMGR
BROMLEY Arthur MM L/Cpl 1869 9th Royal Fusiliers
BROMLEY Bernard MM L/Bdr 123257 RGA
BROMLEY Charles MM Pte 39593 Machine Gun Corps
BROMLEY Edward MM Sjt 2105 6th Lancashire Fusiliers
BROMLEY Edward MM Cpl 45805 43 Bde RFA
BROMLEY George "DCM,MM,CG(B)" Sjt 3/4833 1st & 13th York & Lancaster Regt
BROMLEY George J. MM L/Cpl 13623 East Surrey Regt
BROMLEY Henry MM Pte 13626 11th West Yorkshire Regt
BROMLEY Herbert MM Sjt C/972 16th King's Royal Rifle Corps
BROMLEY James Albert MM Pte 8994 8th Shropshire Light Infantry KIA 31.8.17.

BROMLEY John Henry MM Sjt 51815 54 Bty 39 Bde RFA DOW 3.8.17.
BROMLEY Joseph MM Pte 12945 9th North Lancashire Regt KIA 27.5.18.
BROMLEY Lawrence F. MM Cpl 13692 7th North Lancashire Regt
BROMLEY Percival Arthur MM L/Sjt 26241 207 Coy Machine Gun Corps KIA 26.9.17.
BROMLEY Sidney H. MM Sjt 35102 RFA
BROMLEY Thomas MM CSM 13529 North Lancashire Regt
BROMLEY W. MM Bdr 16228 RFA
BROMLEY William Henry MM Cpl 4966 62 Coy Machine Gun Corps DOW 15.7.16.
BROMPTON Frederick MM Pte 240623 1/5th Yorkshire Light Infantry
BROMPTON Jack MM Gnr 148872 RFA
BROMWELL G.A. MM Dvr 2837 C/83 Bde RFA
BROMWICH John A. MM Pte 43846 1st Norfolk Regt
BROOK A. MM Sjt 259595 Royal Engineers
BROOK A. MM Sjt 220 West Riding Regt
BROOK Charles MM Pte 14280 Yorkshire Light Infantry
BROOK F. MM Pte S/8590 Seaforth Highlanders
BROOK George MM 2nd Cpl 69381 128 Fd Coy Royal Engineers
BROOK Herbert MM Pte 53417 14th Durham Light Infantry
BROOK Horace MM L/Cpl 27585 37th Bn Machine Gun Corps KIA 24.8.18.
BROOK Hubert MM+Bar Pte 242392 5th West Riding Regt
BROOK James MM Cpl 17/370 West Yorkshire Regt
BROOK James H. MM Sjt 129552 Royal Engineers
BROOK Joe Willie MM Pte 202410 1/4th West Riding Regt
BROOK John MM Bdr 40488 111 Bty 24 Bde RFA
BROOK Robert W. MM Cpl 11906 King's Royal Rifle Corps
BROOK Sam MM Pte 41301 East Yorkshire Regt
BROOK Thomas "MM,MID" Pte 3375 1/6th West Riding Regt
BROOK Thomas W. MM Pte 103077 19th Bn Machine Gun Corps
BROOK Thorpe MM Sjt 143011 'E' Special Coy Royal Engineers
BROOK West MM Pte 25986 13tth Cheshire Regt
BROOK William MM Dvr 93087 18 Bde Ammn Col RFA
BROOKE Arthur MM L/Cpl G/1920 8th Royal Sussex Regt Died 22.2.19.
BROOKE Charles J. MM Pte A/204402 13th King's Royal Rifle Corps
BROOKE Clifford S. MM Pte 201793 2nd Seaforth Highlanders
BROOKE George MM Pte 351988 7th London Regt
BROOKE James B. MM Pte 20784 Lancashire Fusiliers
BROOKE Jim MM Pte 16575 2nd Northumberland Fusiliers
BROOKE John P. MM Pte 282537 4th London Regt
BROOKE Stanley MM Pte 1361 Yorkshire Light Infantry
BROOKER Albert MM Sjt 9206 Royal Munster Fusiliers
BROOKER Alfred William MM Pte 19944 13th East Surrey Regt
BROOKER Charles MM Cpl 2425 9th Royal Fusiliers DOW 21.12.17.
BROOKER Charles Edward MM+Bar Sjt 38024 48 Fd Amb RAMC
BROOKER Charles W. MM Sjt 26953 Royal West Kent Regt
BROOKER Daniel MM 2nd Cpl 94256 4 Foreway Coy Royal Engineers
BROOKER Frank MM Pte 3095 12th Middlesex Regt
BROOKER Frederick MM L/Cpl Z/2737 Rifle Brigade
BROOKER Frederick James "MM,MID" CSM 3795 4th Rifle Brigade
BROOKER Henry W. MM Pte 251887 3rd London Regt
BROOKER Herbert MM+2 Bars Pte 63805 138 Fd Amb RAMC KIA 9.8.17.
BROOKER Herbert George MM Cpl 78549 'I' Bn Tank Corps
BROOKER James MM Sjt S/2954 Rifle Brigade
BROOKER John MM Sjt 19080 4 Div Ammn Col RFA
BROOKER Joseph A. MM Pte 7030 16 Fd Amb RAMC att Seaforth Hldrs
BROOKER Leslie Jesse "DCM,MM" CSM L/9567 1st Royal West Surrey Regt
BROOKER Merton R. MM Pte 266799 7th Royal West Kent Regt
BROOKER Percy W. MM Spr 49738 18 Div Sig Coy Royal Engineers
BROOKER Reuben MM Sjt 12035 3rd Coldstream Guards
BROOKER Roy L. MM Sjt 1765 9th East Surrey Regt
BROOKER William C. MM+Bar L/Cpl 874 East Surrey Regt
BROOKES Alexander MM L/Cpl 721961 1/24th London Regt
BROOKES Charles E. MM BSM 30638 191 Siege Bty RGA
BROOKES Charles G. MM L/Cpl 24289 Lancashire Fusiliers
BROOKES Charles W. MM Spr 48821 Royal Engineers
BROOKES Claudian W.T. MM Gnr 155497 RGA
BROOKES Cuthbert MM 2nd Cpl 87393 39 Div Sig Coy Royal Engineers DOW 20.11.17.
BROOKES F.C. MM Pte 628012 19th London Regt
BROOKES Fred MM Cpl 2349 South Staffordshire Regt
BROOKES Frederick C. MM Cpl 5686 90 Fd Amb RAMC
BROOKES George C. MM Pte 35319 2nd West Riding Regt
BROOKES George William MM Pte 12340 6th Shropshire Light Infantry DOW 30.6.16.
BROOKES Harry MM Pte 40446 Scottish Rifles
BROOKES Harry C. MM Spr 63182 Royal Engineers
BROOKES Horace MM Pte 20698 Bedfordshire Regt
BROOKES Oliver A. MM Pte 7114 Machine Gun Corps
BROOKES W. "DCM+Bar,MM" S/Sjt 339298 63 Fd Amb RAMC
BROOKES W. MM Sjt 248961 63 Div Sig Coy Royal Engineers
BROOKES W.A. MM L/Cpl P3528 Military Mounted Police
BROOKES W.B. MM Pte 201114 5th Royal Warwickshire Regt
BROOKES Walter MM Pte 12840 9th Cheshire Regt
BROOKES Wilfred da Cunha MM L/Cpl 38017 Machine Gun Corps Died 2.2.18.
BROOKES William MM Sjt 23095 Yorkshire Light Infantry
BROOKES William Francis MM+Bar Sjt 12043 2nd Worcestershire Regt KIA 1.11.16.
BROOKES William Henry MM+Bar Pte 6062 1st North Staffordshire Regt
BROOKES William J. MM Pte 73365 RAMC
BROOKFIELD Jeffery MM Pte 4819 Liverpool Regt
BROOKFIELD Robert MM Cpl 1080 9th Royal Fusiliers
BROOKFIELD William J. MM+Bar Dvr 197064 A/162 Bde RFA
BROOKIN Joseph J. "MM,MID" Pte 46074 Liverpool Regt
BROOKING Gilbert "MC,MM(M2/050989 CSM)" T/2Lt Army Service Corps
BROOKING L. "MM,MIDx2" Sjt 2623 A/159 Bde RFA
BROOKLAND William MM Pte S/31409 8th Rifle Brigade
BROOKLING Charles MM Pte 46014 RAMC
BROOKLING Stephen MM Pte 12171 11th Hampshire Regt
BROOKMAN Alfred Thomas MM Cpl 15503 1st East Kent Regt
BROOKMAN Bernard J. MM L/Cpl 265814 Gloucestershire Regt
BROOKMAN George H. MM Pte 20091 20 Fd Amb RAMC
BROOKMAN Walter H. MM Sjt 8488 2nd Royal West Kent Regt
BROOKS Albert "DCM,MM" CSM 200307 1st London Regt DOW 17.6.18.
BROOKS Alexander MM Gnr 837119 A/307 Bde RFA KIA 10.5.18.
BROOKS Alfred MM Cpl 341484 RAMC
BROOKS Alfred MM Sjt 750048 RFA
BROOKS Arnold E. MM L/Cpl 17073 15 Fd Coy Royal Engineers
BROOKS Arthur MM Sjt 240099 5th Yorkshire Light Infantry
BROOKS Arthur MM Pte 3928 West Yorkshire Regt
BROOKS Arthur MM Pte 31819 RAMC
BROOKS Arthur W. MM Pte 656062 21st London Regt
BROOKS Asa MM Pte 250236 Manchester Regt
BROOKS Benjamin J. MM Pte 15481 1st Royal Fusiliers
BROOKS Bernard MM Sjt 16230 8th East Lancashire Regt
BROOKS Charles MM L/Cpl 242590 North Lancashire Regt
BROOKS Charles H. MM Pte 33284 Manchester Regt
BROOKS David MM Pte 30556 2/5th Lancashire Fusiliers
BROOKS Edwin Harry MM 2nd Cpl 47039 24 Div Sig Coy Royal Engineers
BROOKS Elias MM Pte 7463 11th Royal Fusiliers
BROOKS Ernest G. MM Spr 496544 226 Fd Coy Royal Engineers
BROOKS Francis J. MM Pte 21799 1/4th Royal Berkshire Regt
BROOKS Frank MM Pte 251773 10th Manchester Regt
BROOKS Frank Edward MM+Bar Sjt 17838 Wiltshire Regt
BROOKS Frank H. MM Sjt 56613 24 Div Sig Coy Royal Engineers
BROOKS Frank O. MM Gnr 34736 8 Bde RFA
BROOKS Fred Victor MM Pte 82415 11th Royal Fusiliers KIA 30.8.18.
BROOKS Frederick Charles MM Pte M2/130948 62 Auxiliary Petrol Coy Army Service Corps
BROOKS Frederick G. "DCM,MM" Cpl 350366 1/7th London Regt
BROOKS Frederick J. MM Pte 33732 RAMC
BROOKS Frederick W. MM Spr 487991 Royal Engineers
BROOKS George MM L/Cpl 8087 Northumberland Fusiliers
BROOKS George MM Bdr 64072 RGA
BROOKS George MM Pte 232070 2nd London Regt
BROOKS George MM Sjt 265134 7th Scottish Rifles
BROOKS George MM Pte 258311 Labour Corps
BROOKS George J. MM L/Cpl 10736 Royal West Surrey Regt
BROOKS George Richard MM Pte G/8385 6th East Kent Regt DOW 6.10.17.
BROOKS H. MM Pte 22889 9 Fd Amb RAMC
BROOKS Harold MM Cpl 375718 10th Manchester Regt
BROOKS Harold Frank MM Pte C/750 16th King's Royal Rifle Corps KIA 20.5.17.

BROOKS Harold R. MM Pte 25531 Wiltshire Regt
BROOKS Harry MM Cpl 9/14477 Leicestershire Regt
BROOKS Harry MM Pte 15247 10th North Lancashire Regt
BROOKS Henry G. MM Pte 265154 Oxf & Bucks Light Infantry
BROOKS Henry Victor MM Gnr 846163 61 Div Ammn Col RFA
BROOKS Herbert H. MM CSM T/28977 Army Service Corps
BROOKS J.H. MM Sjt L/17980 RFA
BROOKS Jacob MM Sjt 490055 467 Fd Coy Royal Engineers KIA 21.3.18.
BROOKS James MM Pte 17216 Shropshire Light Infantry
BROOKS James H. MM Dvr 61982 61 Fd Coy Royal Engineers
BROOKS James W. MM L/Cpl 5296 Royal West Surrey Regt
BROOKS John MM CQMS 52117 15th Cheshire Regt
BROOKS John MM Pte 68676 95 Fd Amb RAMC KIA 12.4.18.
BROOKS John MM Pte 449511 826 Area Empl Coy Labour Corps
BROOKS John MM L/Cpl 201952 11th Royal Scots Fusiliers
BROOKS John MM Cpl 53940 Z/50 Med TM Bty RGA
BROOKS John MM Sjt 5008 1st Royal Dublin Fusiliers KIA 4.9.18.
BROOKS John Alfred MM Pte 20207 1st Royal West Kent Regt
BROOKS John T. MM Pte 14125 8th North Staffordshire Regt
BROOKS John W. MM+Bar L/Cpl 240416 1/8th Middlesex Regt
BROOKS John William "DCM,MM,MIDx2" Cpl 3630 1st Rifle Brigade
BROOKS Joseph MM Spr 79879 185 Tunnelling Coy Royal Engineers
BROOKS Joseph MM Dvr 750461 RFA
BROOKS Joseph T. MM Cpl 17522 1st Royal Welsh Fusiliers
BROOKS Joseph W. MM Cpl 75798 Royal Engineers
BROOKS Leslie J. MM Sjt 40047 RFA
BROOKS Oswald MM Cpl C/9381 20th King's Royal Rifle Corps
BROOKS Percy MM Cpl 2523 7th South Lancashire Regt
BROOKS Raymond John MM Pte 16025 2nd Coldstream Guards KIA 30.11.17.
BROOKS Reginald MM L/Cpl G/280 11th Middlesex Regt KIA 28.7.16.
BROOKS Richard J. MM Bdr 25812 RFA
BROOKS Robert MM Pte S/9738 Rifle Brigade
BROOKS Robert J. MM Pte 17096 1st Norfolk Regt
BROOKS Sidney MM Pte 67013 6 Fd Amb RAMC
BROOKS Sidney G. "MM,MID" Sjt 1219 2nd London Regt
BROOKS Sydney "MM,CG(B)" Sjt 20724 31st Bn Machine Gun Corps
BROOKS Thomas H. MM BSM 28480 124 Hy Bty RGA
BROOKS Thomas J. MM Pte R/24862 King's Royal Rifle Corps
BROOKS Thomas Richard MM Sjt 22161 Machine Gun Corps
BROOKS Tom D. MM Sjt 35263 RFA
BROOKS Walter James MM Pte 20748 32nd Royal Fusiliers DOW 20.4.18.
BROOKS William MM Pte 28752 18th Manchester Regt
BROOKS William A. MM Gnr 169461 C/50 Bde RFA
BROOKS William John MM Pte 42062 2nd Worcestershire Regt KIA 29.9.18.
BROOKSBANK Clifford S. MM Gnr 99465 59 Siege Bty RGA
BROOKSBANK Herbert MM Sjt 58 Yorkshire Regt
BROOKSBANK John Henry MM Dvr 25499 168 Bde RFA
BROOKSBANK Norman W. MM Pte 202579 4th West Riding Regt
BROOKSBANK Walter MM+Bar L/Cpl 7661 1st West Yorkshire Regt
BROOM Cecil Allen "DCM,MM,CdeG(F)" Pte DM2/153985 Att 87(W Lancs)Fd Amb Army Service Corps
BROOM Charles MM Pte 102765 1st Bn Machine Gun Corps
BROOM Evan MM Pte 47236 2nd Royal Welsh Fusiliers
BROOM Frederick H. MM Cpl 92039 6th Notts & Derby Regt
BROOM Frederick W. MM L/Cpl 41233 2nd Royal Scots Fusiliers KIA 16.9.17.
BROOM George MM Pte 13001 12th Royal Scots
BROOM Harold MM Pte 51619 6th Liverpool Regt DOW 5.10.18.
BROOM Harry C. MM Pte 37428 Suffolk Regt
BROOM Henry J. MM Sjt 19593 1st Dragoon Guards
BROOM Henry Reginald MM Dvr 42 14 Div Ammn Col RFA
BROOM James MM Sjt 8824 1st Devonshire Regt
BROOM John MM Dvr 52126 'U' Bty RHA
BROOM John MM Pte 1869 1st 3 Coy Welsh Guards KIA 1.12.17.
BROOM John W. MM Pte 42746 11th Suffolk Regt
BROOM Richard Alexander MM L/Cpl 38511 5 Fd Amb RAMC
BROOM Richard E. MM L/Cpl 15121 2nd Middlesex Regt
BROOM Robert MM Gnr 39812 RGA
BROOM Sidney William MM Pte 200784 1/4th Lincolnshire Regt
BROOM Thomas MM Sjt 32470 3rd Middlesex Regt
BROOM W. MM Pte 439352 RAMC
BROOME Alfred H. MM Pte 550791 16th London Regt
BROOME Alfred John MM Pte 26534 6th Shropshire Light Infantry
BROOME Edward Charles MM L/Cpl 9595 12th Suffolk Regt
BROOME Florence MM Sister F Civil Hospital Reserve
BROOME Gerald MM+Bar Sjt 200305 1/4th Shropshire Light Infantry
BROOME Henry MM Pte 2856 19th London Regt
BROOME John MM Pte 17767 South Lancashire Regt
BROOME John W. MM Pte 43936 12th North Staffordshire Regt
BROOME Reginald MM Pte 21375 Manchester Regt
BROOME Thomas MM Sjt 200561 North Staffordshire Regt
BROOME Timothy MM Pte 16994 Shropshire Light Infantry
BROOMFIELD Agnew Turnbull MM Cpl 120730 228 Fd Coy Royal Engineers
BROOMFIELD Edgar MM Pte 11616 10th Royal West Kent Regt KIA 2.10.18.
BROOMFIELD George MM Pte G/23087 2nd Royal West Kent Regt
BROOMFIELD George MM Pte S/14422 Rifle Brigade
BROOMHALL Edwin MM+2 Bars Sjt 53148 RAMC
BROOMHALL James MM Pte 8186 8th North Staffordshire Regt KIA 30.12.17.
BROOMHALL William C. MM Pte 10045 1st Royal Welsh Fusiliers
BROOMHEAD William MM Sjt 30237 5th Royal Lancaster Regt
BROPHY Francis William MM Sjt 711 1/8th Liverpool Regt KIA 9.11.16.
BROPHY J. MM Pte 341229 RAMC
BROPHY Peter "DCM,MM" Sjt 4907 1st Royal Dublin Fusiliers Awarded for 'Easter Rising'.
BROPHY William MM Sjt 428348 423 Fd Coy Royal Engineers
BROSTER Albert MM Sjt 27038 North Lancashire Regt
BROSTER Charles Raymond "DCM,MM" Sjt 12207 7th Dragoon Guards
BROSTER Harold MM Pte 46007 RAMC
BROSTER Robert MM Drummer 11422 2nd King's Own Scottish Borderers KIA 28.6.18.
BROSTER Thomas MM Pte 765 13th Cheshire Regt
BROSTER Walter MM L/Cpl 28741 1st Lancashire Fusiliers
BROSTER William Cropper "DCM,MM" Sjt 2061 1/6th Liverpool Regt DOW 26.9.16.
BROTHERS William Alfred MM L/Cpl 241416 1/6th South Staffordshire Regt
BROTHERSTON Arthur MM Pte 1298 1/8th Royal Scots
BROTHERSTONE David MM L/Sjt 12941 Royal Welsh Fusiliers
BROTHERTON Edward MM Pte 10654 7th South Staffordshire Regt
BROTHERTON Ernest MM Sjt 82217 23rd Royal Fusiliers
BROTHERTON Esme MM Sjt 203576 1st London Regt KIA 16.8.17.
BROTHERTON Tom MM Pte 240892 East Lancashire Regt
BROTHERWOOD Charles MM Bdr 10476 D/190 Bde RFA
BROTHWELL John T. "MM,MSM" Sjt 785624 A/312 Bde RFA
BROUGH A. MM Sjt S/12353 7th Royal Highlanders
BROUGH Albert MM L/Sjt R/3952 13th King's Royal Rifle Corps
BROUGH Alfred MM Gnr 810105 RFA
BROUGH Andrew MM+Bar L/Cpl 291706 5th Royal Highlanders
BROUGH Arnold H. MM Gnr 716 12 Bty MGC(Motors)
BROUGH D. MM L/Bdr 750 RFA
BROUGH David MM Gnr 93204 RFA
BROUGH Harry MM Sjt 785097 RFA
BROUGH Harry William MM Sjt 13730 D/180 Bde RFA
BROUGH Herbert MM Sjt 46661 RGA
BROUGH Jack MM Pte 350095 1/9th Liverpool Regt
BROUGH James MM Pte S/13548 4th Gordon Highlanders
BROUGH James MM Sjt 27249 20th Durham Light Infantry
BROUGH James MM L/Cpl 31911 Notts & Derby Regt
BROUGH Joseph T. MM Spr 71184 Royal Engineers
BROUGH Michael "DCM,MM+Bar" Sjt 17750 Durham Light Infantry
BROUGH Peter S. MM Pte 310082 1st Gordon Highlanders
BROUGH Robert MM+Bar Sjt 271223 2nd Royal Scots
BROUGH Robert H. MM Bdr 531 MGC(Motors)
BROUGH William MM Cpl 113603 GHQ BEF Sig Coy Royal Engineers
BROUGH William MM BSM 40495 RFA
BROUGHTON Albert MM Pte 2275 2/4th Oxf & Bucks Light Infantry KIA 28.9.16.
BROUGHTON Allan MM Pte 74416 7th Manchester Regt
BROUGHTON Arnold MM Cpl 276264 7th Manchester Regt
BROUGHTON Arthur "MM,MID" Cpl 240433 5th Lincolnshire Regt
BROUGHTON Arthur MM Pte 267774 2/4th West Riding Regt
BROUGHTON E. MM Pte 20411 Duke of Cornwall's LI
BROUGHTON Fred MM Dvr 17005 D/170 Bde RFA
BROUGHTON Frederick MM Dvr 931561 C/291 Bde RFA
BROUGHTON George W. MM Bdr 14657 5 Siege Bty RGA

BROUGHTON Gilbert MM Sjt 308185 4 Tank Supply Coy Tank Corps
BROUGHTON Henry G. MM Pte 265239 9th Middlesex Regt
BROUGHTON James William MM Sjt 16309 Machine Gun Corps
BROUGHTON John MM+Bar Sjt 90627 RFA
BROUGHTON John MM Cpl 2533 West Riding Regt
BROUGHTON John MM Cpl 26540 160 Siege Bty RGA
BROUGHTON Percy William MM L/Cpl 3734 1st Royal West Kent Regt DOW 26.2.18.
BROUGHTON Peter MM Pte 21962 17th Lancashire Fusiliers
BROUGHTON Thomas George MM Gnr 14755 D/95 Bde RFA DOW 27.9.17.
BROUGHTON Walter MM Sjt 1643 1/5th West Yorkshire Regt
BROUGHTON William MM Cpl 15562 9th North Lancashire Regt
BROW Robert F. MM Dvr 650194 RFA
BROWELL Arthur MM Pte 38525 10 Fd Amb RAMC
BROWELL John MM Cpl 869 RFA
BROWETT Alfred A. MM+Bar L/Cpl 661479 21st London Regt
BROWETT George MM Pte 28723 18th Hussars
BROWN A. MM Pte 40664 1st Royal Irish Rifles
BROWN A. MM Pte 7281 Royal Warwickshire Regt
BROWN A. MM L/Sjt 14157 14 Bde RHA
BROWN A. MM Pte 86202 Machine Gun Corps
BROWN Adam MM L/Cpl 290668 1st Royal Highlanders
BROWN Adam MM L/Cpl 25045 Highland Light Infantry
BROWN Adam W. MM Pte 37928 Machine Gun Corps
BROWN Albert MM L/Cpl 14994 11th Essex Regt
BROWN Albert MM Pte 43909 Royal Berkshire Regt
BROWN Albert MM Sjt 10118 1st East Lancashire Regt KIA 25.8.17.
BROWN Albert MM Cpl 8398 2nd Yorkshire Regt KIA 31.3.17.
BROWN Albert MM Gnr 27438 RFA
BROWN Albert A. MM Pte O/648 13th Rifle Brigade
BROWN Albert E. MM+2 Bars Sjt 16793 8th Lincolnshire Regt
BROWN Albert E. MM+Bar Spr 51100 Royal Engineers
BROWN Albert Edward MM Pte 18697 11th Royal West Kent Regt KIA 20.9.17.
BROWN Albert M. MM Bdr 33347 RGA
BROWN Albert S. MM Cpl 9/8238 Royal West Kent Regt
BROWN Albert W. MM Spr 518812 Royal Engineers
BROWN Alec MM Pte 68683 24th Royal Fusiliers
BROWN Alec MM Gnr 24956 B/91 Bde RFA
BROWN Alexander MM Dvr 103853 83 Bty 11 Bde RFA
BROWN Alexander MM Pte 66352 6th Durham Light Infantry
BROWN Alexander MM Pte 292409 8/10th Gordon Highlanders
BROWN Alexander MM+Bar Spr 23311 5 Div Sig Coy Royal Engineers
BROWN Alexander MM L/Cpl 51107 Royal Engineers
BROWN Alexander "DCM,MM" Cpl 6870 7th Seaforth Highlanders
BROWN Alexander C. MM Gnr 322790 RGA
BROWN Alfred MM Pte 44732 1st South Wales Borderers
BROWN Alfred MM Pte 20109 12th Liverpool Regt KIA 16.8.17.
BROWN Alfred Ernest MM Pte 18686 5th A Coy Royal Berkshire Regt KIA 5.4.18.
BROWN Alfred R. MM Pte 33468 13th Middlesex Regt
BROWN Alfred T.A. MM L/Cpl PS/10387 Royal Fusiliers
BROWN Alfred W. MM Pte 300047 8th Durham Light Infantry
BROWN Alfred William MM Cpl 205269 1 Gun Carrier Coy Tank Corps
BROWN Allan MM Pte 8356 Seaforth Highlanders
BROWN Allan F. MM Bdr 295797 RGA
BROWN Andrew MM Sjt 297 1/5th Gordon Highlanders KIA 31.7.16.
BROWN Andrew MM Cpl T4/241441 51 Div Train Army Service Corps
BROWN Andrew William Alston MM L/Sjt S/4295 9th Royal Highlanders KIA 24.5.16.
BROWN Archibald MM Pte 21304 5/6th Royal Scots
BROWN Archibald MM Sjt 685173 C/293 Bde RFA
BROWN Archibald MM Pte 42694 7th Gordon Highlanders
BROWN Archibald MM Pte 29225 East Yorkshire Regt
BROWN Arnold T. MM Cpl 42909 Royal Engineers
BROWN Arthur MM L/Cpl 159833 75 Fd Coy Royal Engineers
BROWN Arthur MM Sjt M2/077621 Army Service Corps
BROWN Arthur MM L/Cpl 52215 Liverpool Regt
BROWN Arthur MM Pte 38716 22nd Northumberland Fusiliers KIA 13.4.18.
BROWN Arthur MM Spr 504327 503 Fd Coy Royal Engineers
BROWN Arthur A. MM Cpl 81121 10th Royal Fusiliers
BROWN Arthur D. MM Spr 67158 406 Fd Coy Royal Engineers
BROWN Arthur Edward MM Sjt 291346 8th Scottish Rifles DOW 17.8.18.

BROWN Arthur G. MM Sjt 59441 Labour Corps
BROWN Arthur J. MM Bdr L/47223 41 Div Ammn Col RFA
BROWN Arthur R. MM Sjt L/42580 A/291 Bde RFA
BROWN Arthur S.B. MM Pte 34468 14th Royal Warwickshire Regt
BROWN Arthur W. MM L/Cpl 7309 18th Royal Fusiliers
BROWN Arthur William MM+Bar L/Cpl 266053 6th Notts & Derby Regt
BROWN Baxter G. MM Pte 63901 RAMC
BROWN Benjamin "MM,MID" Spr 79894 178 Tunnelling Coy Royal Engineers
BROWN Bernard Robert MM Cpl 1826 21st London Regt
BROWN Bert "DCM,MM" Sjt 9828 2nd A Coy Highland Light Infantry DOW 2.10.17.
BROWN Bert MM Cpl 30168 6th Royal Warwickshire Regt
BROWN Bert MM L/Cpl 10995 8th Devonshire Regt
BROWN Bertram MM Pte 1661 Army Cyclist Corps
BROWN Bertram H. "MM,MID" BSM 825327 B/240 Bde RFA
BROWN C. MM L/Cpl 9026 Lincolnshire Regt
BROWN C. MM Sjt 1863 Royal Flying Corps
BROWN C. "MM,MID" L/Cpl 2206 York & Lancaster Regt
BROWN C.W. MM Bdr 36089 'Z' Bty RHA
BROWN Cecil MM Gnr 211747 RGA
BROWN Cecil E. MM Pte 999 Royal Sussex Regt
BROWN Charles MM Pte 52805 Notts & Derby Regt
BROWN Charles MM Sjt 320197 1/6th London Regt
BROWN Charles MM L/Cpl 23152 4th Grenadier Guards KIA 1.12.17.
BROWN Charles MM Cpl 7152 1st Leicestershire Regt
BROWN Charles MM 2nd Cpl 45954 25 Div Sig Coy Royal Engineers DOW 2.5.18.
BROWN Charles MM Pte 316766 24th Royal Welsh Fusiliers
BROWN Charles A. MM Pte 38104 8th Lincolnshire Regt
BROWN Charles A. MM L/Sjt 2559 2nd Rifle Brigade
BROWN Charles A.R. MM Pte 138115 63rd Bn Machine Gun Corps
BROWN Charles Alfred MM Pte 41122 9th Northumberland Fusiliers DOW 7.5.18.
BROWN Charles Andrew MM Sjt 9224 111 Siege Bty RGA
BROWN Charles B. MM Pte 112224 12th Bn Tank Corps
BROWN Charles Francis MM L/Sjt 18249 1st Grenadier Guards
BROWN Charles J. MM Pte 72039 5th Devonshire Regt
BROWN Charles J. MM Bdr 88305 RGA
BROWN Charles Leonard MM L/Cpl M2/121306 Att 156 Siege Bty RGA Army Service Corps
BROWN Charles R. MM L/Cpl 20953 8th Royal West Kent Regt
BROWN Charles R. MM Sjt 14396 8th Yorkshire Light Infantry
BROWN Charles Reginald MM Spr 281754 50 Div Sig Coy Royal Engineers
BROWN Charles T. MM Cpl 546545 509 Fd Coy Royal Engineers
BROWN Charles William MM Gnr 39083 130 Heavy Bty RGA
BROWN Charley MM Pte 71021 10th Notts & Derby Regt DOW 25.10.18.
BROWN Charlie MM Cpl 45794 21st Bn Machine Gun Corps
BROWN Charlie MM Pte 29038 7th Bedfordshire Regt KIA 15.8.17.
BROWN Clement T. MM Pte 37392 Northumberland Fusiliers
BROWN Colin MM Pte 4213 2nd Border Regt
BROWN Daniel MM L/Cpl 21193 Royal Dublin Fusiliers
BROWN Daniel MM L/Cpl 13473 Royal West Surrey Regtt
BROWN David MM Pte 202301 5/6th Scottish Rifles
BROWN David MM L/Cpl 203532 6th Royal Highlanders
BROWN David MM Pte 8043 11th Royal Fusiliers KIA 10.8.17.
BROWN David "DCM,MM" Sjt 376329 1/10th Manchester Regt
BROWN David MM Sjt 28047 30 Siege Bty RGA KIA 7.10.17.
BROWN David "DCM,MM" Sjt 290769 1/7th Royal Highlanders
BROWN David MM Pte 2220 1st Welsh Guards
BROWN David MM L/Cpl 15/19873 Royal Irish Rifles
BROWN David MM Pte S/18202 5th Cameron Highlanders
BROWN David McI. MM Pte 51703 11th Royal Scots
BROWN David Scott MM Pte 352207 1/9th Royal Scots
BROWN David W. MM Bdr 165872 RGA
BROWN Donald "DCM,MM" Sjt 47859 Royal Engineers
BROWN Douglas MM Pte 205232 Lancashire Fusiliers
BROWN Duncan MM Pte 17536 2nd Cameron Highlanders
BROWN Duncan MM Pte 12465 Scots Guards
BROWN E.J. "MM,MID" Pte 320159 London Regt
BROWN Edgar W. MM Cpl 121682 47th Bn Machine Gun Corps
BROWN Edward MM Pte 22581 8th Royal Lancaster Regt
BROWN Edward MM L/Cpl 21245 1st Hampshire Regt
BROWN Edward MM Dvr 17737 45 Bde RFA
BROWN Edward MM Pte 6659 3rd Dragoon Guards
BROWN Edward MM Pte 60907 RAMC

BROWN Edward Charles MM Pte 35739 RAMC
BROWN Edward Ernest MM Pte M2/167499 Att 235 Siege Bty RGA Army Service Corps
BROWN Edward Felix MM Dvr 95685 D/92 Bde RFA
BROWN Edward J. MM Dvr 59290 RFA
BROWN Edward W. MM Pte 76061 RAMC
BROWN Edwin R. MM Pte 28680 5th Royal Lancaster Regt
BROWN Enos MM Bdr 85637 66 Div Ammn Col RFA
BROWN Eric T.F. MM Pte 18140 XIX Corps Cyclist Bn Army Cyclist Corps
BROWN Ernest MM Pte G/61445 26th Royal Fusiliers
BROWN Ernest MM Dvr 965448 RFA
BROWN Ernest MM Pte 4898 Machine Gun Corps
BROWN Ernest MM Pte 34185 12th Middlesex Regt KIA 9.11.18.
BROWN Ernest MM Pte 18199 Royal Lancaster Regt
BROWN Ernest MM Gnr L/197 C/64 Bde RFA
BROWN Ernest MM Pte 8671 6th West Yorkshire Regt
BROWN Ernest MM Sjt 10704 2nd Royal Irish Fusiliers
BROWN Ernest A. MM Pte 68412 10th Royal West Surrey Regt
BROWN Ernest C. MM Cpl 30400 RGA
BROWN Ernest H. MM Sjt 112226 Royal Engineers
BROWN Ernest J. "DCM,MM,DM(B)" Cpl 7922 2nd Royal Sussex Regt
BROWN Ernest J. MM Pte 200902 1/5th Bedfordshire Regt
BROWN Ernest James MM Pte 1157 11th Royal Sussex Regt KIA 12.10.16.
BROWN Ernest W. MM Bdr 43093 44 Bde RFA
BROWN F. MM Pte 22076 Yeomanry
BROWN F.J. MM Dvr 5637 40 Bde RFA
BROWN Francis M. MM Pte 23572 6th Gordon Highlanders
BROWN Frank MM Sjt M2/138741 Army Service Corps
BROWN Frank MM Cpl 10439 D/72 Bde RFA
BROWN Frank MM Pte 5/17640 5th South Wales Borderers
BROWN Frank Albert MM Cpl 38022 RAMC
BROWN Fred MM+Bar Cpl 16420 Yorkshire Light Infantry
BROWN Fred MM Pte 242594 West Riding Regt
BROWN Fred MM Cpl 2789 16th Manchester Regt
BROWN Fred MM Sjt 13287 8th Shropshire Light Infantry
BROWN Frederick MM Sjt 40452 1st Scottish Rifles
BROWN Frederick MM L/Cpl 235031 Royal Welsh Fusiliers
BROWN Frederick MM Pte 10852 2nd Royal Warwickshire Regt DOW 4.5.17.
BROWN Frederick MM Sjt 132501 276 Siege Bty RGA KIA 13.9.18.
BROWN Frederick MM Pte 535061 15th London Regt
BROWN Frederick MM Pte 203058 West Yorkshire Regt
BROWN Frederick MM Pte 1666 1/5th West Yorkshire Regt
BROWN Frederick "MM,MID" Bdr 94952 D/69 Bde RFA
BROWN Frederick MM Sjt 16441 2nd Bedfordshire Regt
BROWN Frederick MM Sjt 21359 Cheshire Regt
BROWN Frederick MM L/Cpl 201855 268 Railway Coy Royal Engineers
BROWN Frederick A. MM L/Cpl 242445 5th Lincolnshire Regt
BROWN Frederick A. MM Pte 93011 6th Bn Tank Corps
BROWN Frederick Arthur MM Pte 53647 167 Coy Machine Gun Corps
BROWN Frederick C. MM CQMS 17980 5th Bn Machine Gun Corps
BROWN Frederick E.F. MM S/Sjt 41610 RAMC
BROWN Frederick Edgar MM Spr 69225 35 Div Sig Coy Royal Engineers
BROWN Frederick George MM 2nd Cpl 20119 5 Fd Coy Royal Engineers Died 10.11.16.
BROWN Frederick J. "DCM,MM" Pte 289 6th Royal West Kent Regt
BROWN Frederick J. "DCM,MM" Sjt 200298 4th West Riding Regt
BROWN Frederick T. MM Sjt SE/3797 Army Veterinary Corps
BROWN G. MM Sjt 130679 46th Royal Fusiliers
BROWN G. MM Pte 11671 1st Liverpool Regt
BROWN G.H. MM Cpl 42378 West Yorkshire Regt
BROWN George MM+Bar L/Cpl 5097 2nd Lancashire Fusiliers
BROWN George "DCM,MM" Sjt 9832 2nd Highland Light Infantry
BROWN George "DCM,MM" L/Sjt 5162 East Surrey Regt
BROWN George MM L/Cpl Y/492 1st King's Royal Rifle Corps
BROWN George MM L/Cpl 300037 1/8th Arg & Suth Highlanders
BROWN George MM Sjt 20850 Machine Gun Corps
BROWN George MM L/Cpl 40125 7th Seaforth Highlanders KIA 12.4.18.
BROWN George MM+Bar Sjt 23276 C/231 Bde RFA
BROWN George MM Pte 9237 1st Royal Inniskilling Fusiliers DOW 21.11.16.
BROWN George MM Pte 4834 13th Middlesex Regt
BROWN George MM Spr 47349 Royal Engineers
BROWN George MM Pte 8177 1st West Yorkshire Regt att 69 Coy MGC.KIA 9.3.17.
BROWN George MM Pte 13232 Northumberland Fusiliers
BROWN George MM Pte A203070 King's Royal Rifle Corps
BROWN George MM L/Cpl 72383 Royal Engineers
BROWN George MM L/Sjt 5162 8th East Surrey Regt
BROWN George MM Sjt 935027 RFA
BROWN George A. MM Dvr 115297 RFA
BROWN George Arthur MM Sjt 250 1/4th York & Lancaster Regt KIA 8.9.16.
BROWN George E. MM L/Cpl 21686 1st Coldstream Guards
BROWN George Ethelbert MM Pte 35035 9th Cheshire Regt DOW 7.6.17.
BROWN George F. MM Pte 240582 1/6th Highland Light Infantry
BROWN George Frederick "MM,MID" Sjt 6092 1st East Surrey Regt KIA 29.7.16.
BROWN George Harry MM Pte 304897 15th Bn Tank Corps
BROWN George Henry MM Pte 41037 2nd West Yorkshire Regt KIA 24.4.18.
BROWN George Leopold MM Pte 17994 9th Essex Regt KIA 17.7.17.
BROWN George Leslie MM Sjt 530500 1/15th London Regt
BROWN George V. "DCM,MM" Sjt 242578 2nd Middlesex Regt
BROWN George W. MM Sjt 33574 A/86 Bde RFA
BROWN George W. MM Pte 325256 Durham Light Infantry
BROWN George William MM Gnr 123985 23 Siege Bty RGA DOW 7.10.17.
BROWN Gerald W. MM L/Cpl 39894 RAMC
BROWN Griffith Henry MM Pte 240345 2/5th South Lancashire Regt KIA 30.11.17.
BROWN H. MM Pte 63047 12th Suffolk Regt
BROWN H. MM Sjt 7258 Royal Flying Corps
BROWN H.D. MM Cpl 3529 Royal Warwickshire Regt
BROWN H.H. MM+Bar Sjt 22701 RGA
BROWN Harold MM Pte 24948 6th Royal West Surrey Regt
BROWN Harold MM Cpl 1015 RAMC
BROWN Harold A. MM Spr 430741 50 Div Sig Coy Royal Engineers
BROWN Harold E. MM Sjt 19604 18th Hussars
BROWN Harold J. MM Pte 17025 2nd Scots Guards
BROWN Harry MM Spr 66090 105 Fd Coy Royal Engineers
BROWN Harry MM L/Cpl 15319 1st Coldstream Guards KIA 8.11.18.
BROWN Harry MM Sjt 1/7408 1st Leinster Regt
BROWN Harry MM Pte 123228 Machine Gun Corps
BROWN Harry MM+Bar Pte R/24221 King's Royal Rifle Corps
BROWN Harry MM Bdr 109557 B/70 Bde RFA
BROWN Harry MM Pte 100192 24th Royal Fusiliers KIA 1.10.18.
BROWN Harry MM Pte 11787 19th Hussars
BROWN Harry MM Pte 18173 East Lancashire Regt
BROWN Harry A. MM Pte 16138 5th Northamptonshire Regt
BROWN Harry J. MM Sjt 27889 Machine Gun Corps
BROWN Harry R. MM L/Cpl 240171 Royal Highlanders
BROWN Harry William MM Dvr 622324 'I' Bty RHA
BROWN Henry MM Sjt 24179 99 Siege Bty RGA
BROWN Henry "MM,CG(B)" Pte 345795 Royal Welsh Fusiliers
BROWN Henry MM Pte M/37725 686 Coy? Army Service Corps
BROWN Henry MM Gnr 622090 RHA
BROWN Henry C. MM Sjt 20292 Devonshire Regt
BROWN Henry C. MM Sjt 6214 Machine Gun Corps
BROWN Henry J. MM Pte 6039 Royal West Kent Regt
BROWN Henry Thomson MM Sjt 14173 7/8th King's Own Scottish Borderers KIA 20.6.17.
BROWN Herbert MM Gnr 222915 466 Bty 65 Bde RFA
BROWN Herbert MM Pte G/22360 1st East Kent Regt
BROWN Herbert MM Gnr 45488 RGA
BROWN Herbert Edward MM Gnr 134744 329 Siege Bty RGA
BROWN Herbert H. MM Pte 241589 1st Lincolnshire Regt
BROWN Herbert Niertin MM SM 390017 3(Northumbrian)Fd Amb RAMC
BROWN Horace MM Cpl 72713 RFA
BROWN Horace A. MM Sjt L/46016 C/255 Bde RFA
BROWN Horace T. MM Sjt R/22828 16th King's Royal Rifle Corps
BROWN Hubert Ladd MM Pte 390530 2nd(Northumbrian)Fd Amb RAMC
BROWN Hugh MM Cpl 335176 Royal Scots
BROWN Hugh C. MM Pte 18355 7th Manchester Regt
BROWN Hugh Fletcher MM Cpl 3638 2nd Arg & Suth Highlanders DOW 10.10.18.
BROWN Isaiah MM Sjt 17108 9th South Staffordshire Regt
BROWN J. MM Pte 38391 1st Essex Regt

BROWN J. MM Cpl 967 Military Foot Police
BROWN J. MM Pte 351061 9th Manchester Regt
BROWN J. MM Pte 23754 Liverpool Regt
BROWN J. MM Cpl 22/1599 Northumberland Fusiliers
BROWN J. MM Sjt 19197 1st King's Own Scottish Borderers
BROWN J.T. "MM,MID" Cpl 68723 14 Bde RFA
BROWN Jack "DCM,MM" Sjt 26326 1/5th Notts & Derby Regt KIA 3.10.18.
BROWN Jack "MM,MID" Sjt 14349 Royal Berkshire Regt
BROWN Jack MM L/Cpl C/13 16th King's Royal Rifle Corps
BROWN James MM Pte 80125 7th Durham Light Infantry
BROWN James MM Pte 200442 4th Gordon Highlanders
BROWN James MM Pte S/22158 2nd Arg & Suth Highlanders
BROWN James MM L/Cpl 25134 1st Highland Light Infantry
BROWN James MM CSM S/3136 11th Rifle Brigade
BROWN James MM L/Cpl 72546 Notts & Derby Regt
BROWN James MM Sjt 30230 108 Bty 23 Bde RFA KIA 26.7.16.
BROWN James MM Cpl 154959 303 Siege Bty RGA
BROWN James MM Sjt 51170 1st Royal Scots Fusiliers
BROWN James MM Pte 10137 2nd North Lancashire Regt
BROWN James MM L/Cpl 243314 5th North Lancashire Regt
BROWN James MM Gnr 30406 RFA
BROWN James MM Cpl 422017 Royal Engineers
BROWN James MM Pte 265949 Gordon Highlanders
BROWN James MM Pte 5/12610 5th Royal Irish Fusiliers
BROWN James MM L/Sjt 200363 1/4th East Lancashire Regt
BROWN James MM Sjt L/9953 2nd Royal West Surrey Regt
BROWN James MM Pte 31792 RAMC
BROWN James MM Pte 9877 East Lancashire Regt
BROWN James MM CSM 541 Scottish Rifles
BROWN James MM L/Cpl 9727 2nd Bedfordshire Regt
BROWN James MM Sjt 19200 North Lancashire Regt
BROWN James MM Bdr 344323 RGA
BROWN James MM Cpl 16705 2nd King's Own Scottish Borderers
BROWN James Douglas MM 2nd Cpl 516 51 Div Sig Coy Royal Engineers DOW 4.5.18.
BROWN James H. MM Spr 224006 476 Fd Coy Royal Engineers
BROWN James J. MM(5193 R Fus)+Bar Pte 684429 22nd London Regt
BROWN James K. MM Pte 40121 6th King's Own Scottish Borderers KIA 30.9.18.
BROWN James N. MM Pte 22669 Army Cyclist Corps
BROWN James R. MM Sjt 121927 250 Tunnelling Coy Royal Engineers
BROWN James T. MM Pte A/204403 13th King's Royal Rifle Corps
BROWN James W. MM Pte G/28718 7th Royal West Kent Regt
BROWN James Walker MM Pte 7455 2nd Lincolnshire Regt KIA 1.7.16.
BROWN Jesse MM Pte M1/09161 59 Div MT Coy Army Service Corps
BROWN John MM Pte 275759 5/6th Royal Scots
BROWN John MM Pte 7813 12th Highland Light Infantry
BROWN John MM Cpl S/10411 8th Royal Highlanders
BROWN John MM Pte 76455 RAMC
BROWN John MM Sjt 246865 B/148 RFA KIA 24.4.18.
BROWN John MM Cpl 38342 13th Liverpool Regt
BROWN John MM Gnr 59900 RGA
BROWN John MM Pte 46857 Northumberland Fusiliers
BROWN John "MM,MID" Pte 4716 1st East Surrey Regt DOW 31.8.16.
BROWN John MM Pte 14125 Royal Irish Rifles
BROWN John MM Sjt 19159 14 Bde RHA
BROWN John MM L/Cpl 11067 2nd Royal Scots
BROWN John MM Cpl 7063 2nd Highland Light Infantry
BROWN John MM Pte 2562 2nd South Lancashire Regt
BROWN John MM Sjt 7408 2nd Scottish Rifles KIA 1.8.17.
BROWN John MM Pte 22263 Dorsetshire Regt
BROWN John MM Cpl 769723 28th London Regt
BROWN John MM Pte 23/1416 Northumberland Fusiliers
BROWN John MM L/Cpl 4077 Royal Welsh Fusiliers
BROWN John MM L/Cpl 11755 Hampshire Regt
BROWN John MM Pte 9243 Scots Guards
BROWN John A. MM L/Sjt 16620 1st Grenadier Guards
BROWN John David MM BSM 940004 D/312 Bde RFA DOW 4.11.18.
BROWN John E. MM+Bar Sjt 24638 8th Bn Machine Gun Corps
BROWN John E. MM Cpl 140693 Machine Gun Corps
BROWN John E. MM Gnr 113957 B/101 Bde RFA
BROWN John Edward MM L/Cpl 20278 36 Coy Machine Gun Corps
BROWN John G. DCM Pte 16418 Yorkshire Regt
BROWN John G. MM Sjt 23246 Durham Light Infantry
BROWN John Henry MM Gnr 12117 4 Div Ammn Col RFA
BROWN John Herbert "MM,MID" Sjt 29721 RGA
BROWN John Keith MM L/Cpl 515479 1/14th London Regt KIA 1.10.18.
BROWN John R. MM Sjt 13/1063 13th East Yorkshire Regt
BROWN John R. MM Pte 2454 5/6th Scottish Rifles
BROWN John R. MM Gnr 72464 RFA
BROWN John Robert MM+Bar L/Cpl 40635 7th Norfolk Regt DOW 17.10.18.
BROWN John Scholfield MM Dvr 44745 A/103 Bde RFA
BROWN John Thomas MM Cpl 2756 1/7th Durham Light Infantry
BROWN John Tweedie MM L/Cpl 267661 6th Royal Highlanders KIA 21.3.18.
BROWN John W. MM Sjt 12339 Durham Light Infantry
BROWN John W. MM L/Sjt 71467 Machine Gun Corps
BROWN John William MM L/Cpl 35665 23rd Manchester Regt
BROWN John William MM Sjt 736 10th Yorkshire Regt DOW 11.4.18.
BROWN John Wilson MM Pte 12896 8th Border Regt DOW 17.10.18.
BROWN Joseph MM L/Sjt 15509 18th Lancashire Fusiliers KIA 31.10.18
BROWN Joseph MM Gnr 32937 3 Bty 45 Bde RFA
BROWN Joseph MM Sjt T4/251787 Army Service Corps
BROWN Joseph MM Dvr 665080 RFA
BROWN Joseph "MM,MID" L/Cpl 23643 2 Div? Sig Coy Royal Engineers
BROWN Joseph MM L/Cpl 34159 North Lancashire Regt
BROWN Joseph Arthur MM Cpl 113443 'O' Special Coy Royal Engineers KIA 20.4.17.
BROWN Joseph Austin MM Pte 22/368 22nd Durham Light Infantry KIA 26.3.18.
BROWN Joseph H. MM Sjt 97368 RFA
BROWN Joseph S. MM Pte 58738 25th Bn Machine Gun Corps
BROWN Kenward G. MM Pte 204178 Royal West Kent Regt
BROWN L.S. MM Sjt 2687 Lancashire Fusiliers
BROWN Lancelot MM+Bar L/Cpl 12461 13th Liverpool Regt
BROWN Leonard MM Pte 201935 3rd Worcestershire Regt
BROWN Leonard MM Cpl 9047 15th Suffolk Regt
BROWN Leonard G. MM Pte MS/4571 Army Service Corps
BROWN Leonard George MM+Bar Sjt 8372 2nd Leicestershire Regt
BROWN Leslie MM Cpl 31950 RFA DOW 18.6.18.
BROWN Lewis MM Cpl 9742 2nd Oxf & Bucks Light Infantry
BROWN Lionel MM Pte K/1451 Royal Fusiliers
BROWN M. "DCM,MM" Pte 2918 2nd Royal Scots
BROWN Mary Agatha MM Sister F QAIMNS
BROWN Matthew MM Pte 35502 Yorkshire Light Infantry
BROWN Maurice MM Sjt 70417 RGA
BROWN Maurice C. MM Gnr 87133 RFA
BROWN Maurice H. MM L/Cpl 26576 Royal Engineers
BROWN Michael MM L/Cpl 275412 1/7th Arg & Suth Highlanders
BROWN Neil MM L/Cpl 235104 6th Seaforth Highlanders
BROWN Nicholas MM Pte 18150 Durham Light Infantry
BROWN Noel MM Gnr 45701 RFA
BROWN Norman MM Cpl 2471 1st Lancashire Fusiliers
BROWN Norman MM Pte 1537 5/6th Scottish Rifles
BROWN Norman Ernest MM Sjt 1312 Durham Light Infantry
BROWN Ogilvie S. MM Spr 256880 Royal Engineers
BROWN Patrick MM Cpl 82787 RFA
BROWN Patrick MM Pte 22505 7th Royal Inniskilling Fusiliers KIA 6.8.16.
BROWN Percival H. MM Sjt 240897 Gloucestershire Regt
BROWN Percy MM+Bar Sjt 8068 2nd Suffolk Regt
BROWN Percy MM Pte 295173 12th Somerset Light Infantry
BROWN Percy MM Spr 23569 1 Sig Troop Royal Engineers
BROWN Percy "MM,CG(B)" Pte 31663 2nd Hampshire Regt
BROWN Percy E. MM Pte 20716 6th King's Own Scottish Borderers
BROWN Percy T. MM CQMS 16119 10th Essex Regt
BROWN Percy V. MM Pte 40079 1st Bn Tank Corps
BROWN Peter "DCM,MM" Cpl 1132 VI Corps Cyclist Bn Army Cyclist Corps
BROWN Peter MM Spr 207556 Royal Engineers
BROWN Peter C. MM Sjt 23154 6 Div Sig Coy Royal Engineers
BROWN Philip H. MM Pte 203011 Royal Berkshire Regt
BROWN R. MM L/Cpl P2789 Military Foot Police
BROWN R.B. MM RSM 5 RAMC
BROWN Raymond MM Sjt 32739 Lincolnshire Regt
BROWN Richard MM L/Cpl 21135 14th Royal Welsh Fusiliers
BROWN Richard J. MM Dvr 217113 RFA

BROWN Richard Matthew MM Dvr 92141 66 Div Ammn Col RFA
BROWN Richard William MM Sjt 11979 2nd Middlesex Regt KIA 1.7.16.
BROWN Robert MM L/Cpl 240879 1/6th Highland Light Infantry
BROWN Robert "MM,MSM" Pte 764631 28th London Regt
BROWN Robert MM Sjt 9333 1st Worcestershire Regt KIA 25.4.18.
BROWN Robert MM Pte 128 RAMC
BROWN Robert MM L/Cpl S/4903 9th Royal Highlanders KIA 25.8.17.
BROWN Robert MM Pte 1810 Northumberland Fusiliers
BROWN Robert "MM+Bar,MID" Sjt 37310 22nd Northumberland Fusiliers
BROWN Robert MM Sjt 25252 1st Liverpool Regt
BROWN Robert MM Cpl 71253 Royal Engineers
BROWN Robert A. MM L/Bdr 184900 116 Hy Bty RGA
BROWN Robert F. MM Cpl 82502 Royal Engineers
BROWN Robert I. MM Gnr 347487 RGA
BROWN Robert John "MM3634, 1/4th R Hldrs)+Bar" Pte 88094 37 Coy Machine Gun Corps
BROWN Robert Rupert Harrison MM Sjt 412 RFA
BROWN Robert T. MM L/Cpl 152688 50th Bn Machine Gun Corps
BROWN Rufus MM 2nd Cpl 101740 Royal Engineers
BROWN S. MM Pte 437046 1/2nd(South Midland?)Fd Amb RAMC
BROWN Samuel MM Pte 16713 7th Royal Fusiliers
BROWN Samuel MM Sjt 37219 2nd Lancashire Fusiliers KIA 8.8.18.
BROWN Samuel MM L/Cpl 242031 Lancashire Fusiliers
BROWN Samuel H. MM Pte M2/021695 Army Service Corps
BROWN Samuel J. MM Dvr L/36650 D/187 Bde RFA
BROWN Samuel J. MM+Bar Sjt C/8039 18th King's Royal Rifle Corps
BROWN Samuel Joseph MM Pte 417374 1(North Midland)Fd Amb RAMC
BROWN Samuel P. MM Cpl 12081 North Staffordshire Regt
BROWN Sidney MM Pte 45975 2nd Welsh Regt
BROWN Sidney "MM,CG(B)" Pte 28091 11th East Yorkshire Regt KIA 8.9.18.
BROWN Sidney MM Pte 49590 9th Royal Fusiliers
BROWN Sidney MM CSM 6429 2nd Worcestershire Regt
BROWN Sidney MM Cpl 9079 Lancashire Fusiliers
BROWN Sidney Arthur MM Pte 53149 36 Fd Amb RAMC
BROWN Sidney C. MM Pte 46598 North Staffordshire Regt
BROWN Stanley MM Gnr 66793 RFA
BROWN Stephen MM Pte 332841 9th Highland Light Infantry
BROWN Stephen James MM Pte 18492 1st Liverpool Regt KIA 26.3.18.
BROWN Stewart MM Sjt 365957 67 Siege Bty RGA
BROWN Sydney MM Pte 24455 1st Royal West Surrey Regt
BROWN Sydney MM Cpl 1287 1/9th Durham Light Infantry
BROWN Sydney W. MM L/Cpl B/200956 Rifle Brigade
BROWN Sydney Walter James MM Dvr T4/036327 Att 1 Fd Svy Bn RE Army Service Corps
BROWN T. MM Sjt 8826 2nd Leinster Regt
BROWN T. MM Pte 12157 1st King's Own Scottish Borderers
BROWN Thomas MM Pte S/24033 7th Seaforth Highlanders
BROWN Thomas MM Pte 35894 9th Yorkshire Regt
BROWN Thomas MM L/Cpl S/17540 4th Gordon Highlanders
BROWN Thomas MM Pte 43567 Scottish Rifles
BROWN Thomas MM Pte S/12248 10th Arg & Suth Highlanders
BROWN Thomas MM Pte 30741 1st Royal Dublin Fusiliers DOW 30.9.18.
BROWN Thomas MM Pte 43646 11th West Yorkshire Regt
BROWN Thomas MM Pte 201860 Lancashire Fusiliers
BROWN Thomas MM Pte 14026 1st Notts & Derby Regt
BROWN Thomas MM Pte C/209 King's Royal Rifle Corps
BROWN Thomas MM Pte 9071 10th Durham Light Infantry
BROWN Thomas MM Sjt 265375 1/6th Seaforth Highlanders KIA 14.5.17.
BROWN Thomas MM Pte 18/1732 Royal Irish Rifles
BROWN Thomas MM Pte 119431 Machine Gun Corps KIA 15.4.18.
BROWN Thomas MM 2nd Cpl 36054 210 Fd Coy Royal Engineers DOW 23.6.18.
BROWN Thomas A. MM Pte 14523 Royal Inniskilling Fusiliers
BROWN Thomas B. MM Pte 38513 Northumberland Fusiliers
BROWN Thomas C. MM Gnr 1397 RFA
BROWN Thomas C. MM L/Cpl B/190 Rifle Brigade
BROWN Thomas David MM Cpl 151054 103rd Bn Machine Gun Corps
BROWN Thomas Ernest MM Sjt 66075 140 Fd Amb RAMC DOW 8.12.17.
BROWN Thomas H. MM Bdr 58543 RFA
BROWN Thomas H.A. MM Pte 253803 2nd London Regt
BROWN Thomas Luke MM Sjt 6930 1st Hampshire Regt KIA 1.7.16.
BROWN Thomas P. MM Sjt 41851 12th Highland Light Infantry DOW 24.8.17.
BROWN Thomas Richard MM L/Sjt 7156 1st Dorsetshire Regt KIA 3.10.18.
BROWN Thomas W. MM Cpl 200827 2/4th North Lancashire Regt
BROWN Thomas William MM Pte 51295 2nd Manchester Regt KIA 23.8.18.
BROWN Thomas William Walter MM L/Cpl 65904 129 Fd Coy Royal Engineers
BROWN Tom MM Cpl 56033 129 Fd Coy Royal Engineers
BROWN Tom MM+Bar Sjt L/29412 RFA
BROWN W. MM CSM 63819 5th Lancashire Fusiliers
BROWN W. MM Pte 39854 South Wales Borderers
BROWN W. MM Pte 9499 Royal Highlanders
BROWN W.J. "MM,MID" Sjt 37627 RFA
BROWN Walter MM Pte 231211 2/2nd London Regt KIA 26.10.17.
BROWN Walter MM Pte 17202 2nd Scots Guards
BROWN Walter MM Sjt 275243 5/6th Royal Scots
BROWN Walter MM Pte 2315 1/4th Gloucestershire Regt DOW 23.8.16.
BROWN Walter "MM,CG(F)" Sjt 9877 18th King's Royal Rifle Corps
BROWN Walter MM CQMS 221331 Royal Engineers
BROWN Walter MM Pte 18880 5th Wiltshire Regt
BROWN Walter D. MM Spr 332736 Royal Engineers
BROWN Walter Edward MM Pte 16013 4th Royal Fusiliers KIA 6.11.16.
BROWN Walter H. MM Pte 72360 7th Royal West Surrey Regt
BROWN Walter J. MM Farrier Sjt 14524 Royal Engineers
BROWN Walter J. MM Pte 28011 Welsh Regt
BROWN Wilfred MM Sjt 27675 17th Notts & Derby Regt
BROWN Wilfred Armitage MM 2nd Cpl 74145 'E' Corps Sig Coy Royal Engineers
BROWN William MM Pte 67532 15th Cheshire Regt
BROWN William MM Pte G/1411 7th East Kent Regt
BROWN William MM Gnr 966381 B/286 RFA
BROWN William MM L/Cpl 376637 2/10th Manchester Regt
BROWN William MM Pte 13376 1st Bedfordshire Regt
BROWN William MM Gnr 17637 109 Heavy Bty RGA
BROWN William MM Cpl 5316 18th Highland Light Infantry
BROWN William MM Sjt 71707 1st North Irish Horse
BROWN William "MM,MID" Sjt 721 15th Royal Irish Rifles
BROWN William MM Pte 13998 Army Cyclist Corps
BROWN William MM Cpl 8522 2nd Cameron Highlanders
BROWN William MM Cpl 23073 12th Highland Light Infantry
BROWN William MM Pte 22344 15th Durham Light Infantry
BROWN William MM Sjt 590884 18th London Regt
BROWN William MM Pte 252028 3rd London Regt
BROWN William MM Pte 27208 Highland Light Infantry
BROWN William MM Spr 413916 Royal Engineers
BROWN William MM Sjt 9765 Cameron Highlanders
BROWN William MM Sjt 16148 King's Own Scottish Borderers
BROWN William MM Pte 7893 2nd Suffolk Regt KIA 16.8.16.
BROWN William MM Dvr 58476 RFA
BROWN William MM Gnr 39516 36 Bde RFA
BROWN William MM+Bar Pte 290298 7th Royal Highlanders DOW 31.3.18.
BROWN William MM Pte 27464 King's Own Scottish Borderers
BROWN William "MM,MID" L/Cpl 13066 4th Royal Fusiliers
BROWN William MM Pte 292411 Gordon Highlanders
BROWN William MM Pte 422337 10th London Regt
BROWN William MM Pte 32970 1st Gloucestershire Regt
BROWN William MM+Bar Cpl 9051 Machine Gun Corps
BROWN William MM Pte 31487 East Yorkshire Regt
BROWN William MM Spr 499948 Royal Engineers
BROWN William A. MM Pte 236561 1/1st Herefordshire Regt
BROWN William Alfred MM Pte B/202119 16th Rifle Brigade
BROWN William C. MM Pte 33023 8th East Surrey Regt
BROWN William C. MM Pte 235187 Liverpool Regt
BROWN William C. MM Sjt 9447 Royal Irish Regt
BROWN William D. MM Cpl 16685 1st Norfolk Regt
BROWN William D.T. MM L/Cpl 7444 Middlesex Regt
BROWN William Dunsmuir MM 2nd Cpl 425906 4 Fd Svy Coy Royal Engineers DOW 20.4.18.
BROWN William E. MM Pte 17913 Gloucestershire Regt
BROWN William Ernest Adolphus MM Pte 27517 1st Royal Welsh Fusiliers KIA 2.11.16.
BROWN William Francis "MM,MID" Pte 13676 11th Essex Regt
BROWN William G. MM Cpl 36417 405 Siege Bty RGA

BROWN William H. MM Pte 9751 1st Devonshire Regt
BROWN William H. MM Pte 9849 1st Royal Highlanders
BROWN William H. MM Pte 13178 8th Lincolnshire Regt
BROWN William H. MM Pnr 482212 Royal Engineers
BROWN William Henry MM Pte S/7023 9th Seaforth Highlanders KIA 23.7.17.
BROWN William Henry MM Sjt 26715 30 Bty 39 Bde RFA DOW 24.7.16.
BROWN William Henry "MM,MID" Cpl 61926 81 Fd Coy Royal Engineers
BROWN William Henry MM Pte 240702 2/5th Yorkshire Light Infantry
BROWN William Henry MM Cpl 5266 7th Royal West Kent Regt KIA 23.2.17.
BROWN William J. MM Pte 8576 1st Scottish Rifles
BROWN William J. MM Pte 34719 Highland Light Infantry
BROWN William J. MM Gnr 169402 RGA
BROWN William J. MM Pte 27096 Welsh Regt
BROWN William J. MM Pte 24646 Labour Corps
BROWN William John MM Sjt 70269 C Cable Section Royal Engineers
BROWN William Lawson MM Pte S/4233 9th Gordon Highlanders KIA 24.8.17.
BROWN William N. MM L/Cpl 15/164 West Yorkshire Regt
BROWN William P. MM L/Cpl 201491 1st Royal Scots Fusiliers
BROWN William T. MM Pte 34631 1/5th Royal Warwickshire Regt
BROWN William W. MM L/Cpl 13466 Army Cyclist Corps
BROWN William Yates MM Pte 678001 21st London Regt
BROWN Wilson MM Sjt 242271 1/4th West Riding Regt DOW 15.10.18.
BROWNBILL Edward MM L/Cpl 90137 25th Bn Machine Gun Corps
BROWNE Arthur H. MM Cpl 25055 7th Royal Irish Regt
BROWNE Bernard Joseph "MC,MM(25579 Pte)" T/2Lt 25579 10th Royal Dublin Fusiliers
BROWNE Charles MM Sjt S/4060 Rifle Brigade
BROWNE Charlie MM Sjt 86717 B/71 Bde RFA
BROWNE Edmond Laidman MM Cpl 78592 'H' Bn Tank Corps
BROWNE George MM Cpl 8471 1st Royal Dublin Fusiliers
BROWNE George MM+Bar Sjt 3232 7th East Kent Regt
BROWNE John MM Sjt 519967 Labour Corps
BROWNE Louis J. MM Sjt 200724 5th Liverpool Regt
BROWNE Mark W. MM L/Sjt 6271 Irish Guards
BROWNE Norman MM Gnr 925165 RFA
BROWNE Philip M. MM Bdr 59124 RFA
BROWNE Stanley MM Sjt 46303 Machine Gun Corps
BROWNE Stanley MM L/Cpl 9142 8th Royal West Kent Regt
BROWNE Thomas MM Pte 11515 2nd Royal Dublin Fusiliers
BROWNE William MM Pte 4555 2nd Royal Irish Rifles KIA 18.8.18.
BROWNE William C. MM Pte 10762 Leicestershire Regt
BROWNELL Joseph MM Dvr 697413 RFA
BROWNHILL Ernest A. MM+Bar Sjt 903 RAMC
BROWNHILL Ernest H. MM Pte 38027 77 Fd Amb RAMC
BROWNHILL Frank MM Spr 431765 Royal Engineers
BROWNING Alfred MM Pte 959 6th East Kent Regt
BROWNING Charles C. MM Spr 312583 Royal Engineers
BROWNING Charles E. "DCM,MM" L/Sjt 20600 3rd Grenadier Guards
BROWNING Charles William MM L/Sjt 9424 2nd Royal West Surrey Regt
BROWNING Egbert J. MM Sjt SS/394 Army Service Corps
BROWNING Ernest J. MM Cpl 5822 Duke of Cornwall's LI
BROWNING Frank Edward MM Sjt 531574 1/15th London Regt
BROWNING Frederick MM L/Cpl 11589 11th Hampshire Regt KIA 23.3.18.
BROWNING George MM Sjt 9839 Coldstream Guards
BROWNING Harry MM+Bar Cpl 13610 1st Norfolk Regt Died 3.8.18.
BROWNING James MM Sjt 94707 RFA
BROWNING James "DCM,MM" L/Cpl 11319 2nd Devonshire Regt
BROWNING Percy MM Sjt 307891 16th Bn Tank Corps
BROWNING Sydney J. MM Pte 8081 York & Lancaster Regt
BROWNING Wilfred MM Pte 350730 19th London Regt
BROWNING William F. MM Pte 44928 2nd Hampshire Regt
BROWNJOHN Frank E. MM Sjt 490747 1/13th London Regt
BROWNJOHN Harry W. MM Sjt 34948 RFA
BROWNLEE John H. MM Pte 46806 RAMC
BROWNLEE John Thomas MM Pte 46350 9th Notts & Derby Regt
BROWNLEE William MM Pte 3233 1st Royal Inniskilling Fusiliers
BROWNLIE George MM Pte S/25862 2nd Arg & Suth Highlanders
BROWNLIE James MM Cpl 278710 Arg & Suth Highlanders
BROWNLIE William MM Pte 240232 5/6th Scottish Rifles
BROWNLOW Ernest C. MM Sjt 71164 1st Notts & Derby Regt
BROWNLOW Frederick C. MM Pte 11019 Royal Irish Regt
BROWNLOW James W. MM Pte R/10060 1st King's Royal Rifle Corps KIA 27.7.16.
BROWNLOW Thomas P. "DCM,MM,MID" CSM 6115 1st Scots Guards
BROWNRIDGE Harry MM Cpl 142083 2nd Bn Machine Gun Corps
BROWNRIDGE Herbert MM Sjt 21/34 West Yorkshire Regt
BROWNRIGG Ernest R.J. MM Sjt 10589 1st King's Royal Rifle Corps
BROWNRIGG Philip Donald MM Cpl 6593 1st East Kent Regt
BROWNSELL Albert F. MM Pte 3177 7th London Regt
BROWNSELL Walter Isaac MM L/Cpl 22264 4th Grenadier Guards
BROWNSETT John MM Pte 7750 North Staffordshire Regt
BROWNSWORD George MM L/Cpl 23676 2nd Worcestershire Regt
BROWNWOOD Edward MM Pte 352126 2/2nd(East Lancashire)Fd Amb RAMC
BROWRING Charles Walter Daniel MM L/Sjt 18352 13th Essex Regt
BROWSTER E. MM Dvr 28893 RFA
BROXHOLME Thomas MM Pte 27183 Royal Lancaster Regt
BROXSON Henry MM Sjt 10098 Durham Light Infantry
BROXUP Harry MM Spr 147524 Royal Engineers
BRUCASS John "MC,MM" CSM 1155 12th Middlesex Regt
BRUCE Albert E. MM Pte 61607 West Yorkshire Regt
BRUCE Alexander MM Pte S/43105 Gordon Highlanders
BRUCE Alexander MM Pte 29717 6th King's Own Scottish Borderers DOW 2.10.18.
BRUCE Alexander "MM,MSM" Arm QMS 839 Army Ordnance Corps
BRUCE Alexander MM Pte 308803 9th Bn Tank Corps
BRUCE Alexander James MM Bdr 58390 B/15 Bde RFA KIA 26.1.17.
BRUCE Archibald "MM,MID" Cpl M2/049895 Att 54 Fd Amb RAMC Army Service Corps
BRUCE Arthur S. MM+Bar L/Cpl 207405 Royal Engineers
BRUCE Clifford MM Pte 40746 9th Scottish Rifles DOW 26.12.18.
BRUCE David G. MM CSM 316462 13th Royal Highlanders
BRUCE Duff Morris MM Gnr 945451 14 Bde RFA
BRUCE George MM Cpl 635709 256 Bde RFA
BRUCE George B.S. MM Pte 241985 Seaforth Highlanders
BRUCE George W. MM Pte 19695 Northumberland Fusiliers
BRUCE Jack MM Cpl Fitter 36844 RFA
BRUCE James "MM,MID" Sjt 13543 7th Yorkshire Regt
BRUCE James MM Spr 406426 Royal Engineers
BRUCE James A. MM Pte 240822 Gordon Highlanders
BRUCE John MM Pte 291240 10th Royal Highlanders
BRUCE John MM Gnr Shoeing Smith 148702 1/1st(Highland)Heavy Bty RGA DOW 8.10.18.
BRUCE John MM L/Cpl 24371 2 Div Sig Coy Royal Engineers
BRUCE John E. MM Bdr 292270 RGA
BRUCE John H.H. MM Spr 266461 Royal Engineers
BRUCE Joseph MM S/Sjt 9798 Royal Engineers
BRUCE Percy MM Spr 362383 85 Bde RGA Sig Sect Royal Engineers
BRUCE Robert MM Sjt 7278 2nd Royal West Surrey Regt
BRUCE Robert MM Sjt 3864 Gordon Highlanders
BRUCE Thomas MM L/Sjt 241138 Seaforth Highlanders
BRUCE Thomas Ernest MM Pte 14/16274 15th Royal Irish Rifles DOW 20.10.18.
BRUCE William MM Pte 266582 Liverpool Regt
BRUCE William MM Pte 40147 1/7th Royal Scots
BRUCE William A. MM Pte 201657 1st London Regt
BRUCKSHAW Tom MM Sjt 16528 7/8th King's Own Scottish Borderers
BRUCKSHAW William MM Cpl Sig 33456 D/156 Bde RFA
BRUETON Gilbert H. MM Spr 207514 Royal Engineers
BRUETON William MM Cpl 9960 7th South Staffordshire Regt
BRUFFELL James MM Cpl 800257 RFA
BRUFORD Sidney MM L/Cpl 6952 2nd Coldstream Guards
BRUIN Frank MM L/Cpl 320101 6th London Regt
BRUINES Frederick "MM,MID" Sjt 480316 Royal Engineers
BRUMBY Bernard MM L/Cpl 10/691 East Yorkshire Regt
BRUMBY George MM L/Sjt 242518 9th Yorkshire Light Infantry
BRUMFITT Richard MM L/Cpl 225428 3rd London Regt
BRUMHAM Percy MM L/Cpl 852 Army Cyclist Corps
BRUMMELL William MM Pte 3533 Leinster Regt
BRUMMIT Senior MM Pte 24960 1/5th West Riding Regt
BRUMPTON C. "DCM,MM" Cpl 11120 1st Lincolnshire Regt
BRUNDISH W.A. MM Gnr 128540 RFA

BRUNDLE Arthur MM Pte 7871 1st Suffolk Regt
BRUNGER Jesse Thomas MM Pnr 252714 X Corps Sig Coy Royal Engineers
BRUNGER William Thomas MM Sjt 781 East Kent Regt
BRUNKER James MM Pte 3/12227 7th South Wales Borderers
BRUNNING Abraham Mason MM Pte 24954 7th Suffolk Regt
BRUNNING George MM Sjt 48479 4th North Staffordshire Regt
BRUNNING Reginald MM Pte R/12962 King's Royal Rifle Corps
BRUNT George MM Sjt 13538 Notts & Derby Regt
BRUNT Harold James MM Pte 43275 7th Bedfordshire Regt DOW 4.4.18.
BRUNT Reginald G. MM Sjt 200653 West Riding Regt
BRUNT William MM QMS 47982 R Corps Sig Coy Royal Engineers
BRUNT William H. MM Pte 202455 1st Northamptonshire Regt
BRUNTON Albert MM Pte 43218 7th Lincolnshire Regt
BRUNTON Edward W. MM Sjt 23850 5 Fd Coy Royal Engineers
BRUNTON Francis MM Sjt 13289 4th Hussars
BRUNTON George MM Pte 27907 Royal Dublin Fusiliers
BRUNTON J. "DCM,MM" L/Cpl 8836 2nd Scottish Rifles
BRUNTON Robert MM L/Cpl S/3633 8th Royal Highlanders
BRUNTON Robert William MM L/Cpl 3/5377 1st Cameron Highlanders
BRUNTON Thomas MM Dvr T3/026006 35 Div Train Army Service Corps
BRUNTON W.M. MM Bdr 1146 MGC(Motors)
BRUNWIN William Edgar MM Sjt 53756 Royal Engineers
BRUNYEE Alfred P. MM Pte 52183 Royal Fusiliers
BRUSH John MM Dvr T2/12440 Army Service Corps
BRUSH Willoughby J.D. MM Cpl 239295 Royal Engineers
BRUSHETT Albert V. MM Pte 392325 9th London Regt
BRUST Charles MM Pte 200119 1/7th Middlesex Regt
BRUTE P.J. MM Sjt 2046 XVII Corps Cyclist Bn Army Cyclist Corps
BRUTNELL Harry MM Sjt 200521 1st Lincolnshire Regt
BRUTON Patrick MM Pte 5115 Irish Guards
BRUTON Thomas Aloysius MM Sjt 691 Worcestershire Regt KIA 1.9.18.
BRYAN Albert E. MM L/Cpl 21679 6th York & Lancaster Regt
BRYAN Alfred MM L/Cpl 8950 1st Lincolnshire Regt KIA 21.3.18.
BRYAN Benjamin J. MM Pte 11273 6th Lincolnshire Regt
BRYAN Bernard J. MM Cpl 2400 Royal Warwickshire Regt
BRYAN Charles E. MM Bdr 190689 142 Siege Bty RGA
BRYAN Charles E. MM Cpl 1198 1/8th Notts & Derby Regt
BRYAN Charles Frederick MM Pnr 65713 XVII Corps Sig Coy Royal Engineers
BRYAN Edward MM Sjt 26246 7th Royal Irish Regt
BRYAN Edward MM Sjt 13982 3rd Royal Fusiliers
BRYAN Edward "MM,MID" Sjt Drummer 13197 6th Royal Dublin Fusiliers
BRYAN Edward MM L/Cpl 61401 6th Cheshire Regt
BRYAN Ernest MM Pte 41078 8th Royal Lancaster Regt
BRYAN Ernest Edward "MM,MSM,MID" Sjt 15755 17th Liverpool Regt
BRYAN Harold MM Cpl 93253 C/48 Bde RFA
BRYAN Harry "MM,MID" Gnr 28345 RFA
BRYAN James MM+Bar Sjt 72092 46th Bn Machine Gun Corps
BRYAN John MM Sjt 1952 2nd Lancashire Fusiliers
BRYAN Joshua F. MM Sjt 8006 Yorkshire Regt
BRYAN Richard H. MM Pte 295096 4th London Regt
BRYAN Robert H. MM L/Cpl 204457 1st Somerset Light Infantry
BRYAN Samuel MM Pte 43610 6th Royal Dublin Fusiliers
BRYAN Stanley A. MM Bdr 353220 RGA
BRYAN Thomas MM Pte 22872 Royal Scots Fusiliers
BRYAN Thomas MM Pte 18082 20th Manchester Regt KIA 1.7.16.
BRYAN Thomas H. MM Pte 14035 Northamptonshire Regt
BRYAN Walter K. MM L/Cpl 13494 Grenadier Guards
BRYAN William MM L/Cpl 8242 1st Scottish Rifles
BRYANS Hugh A. MM Pte 27599 Suffolk Regt
BRYANT A.F. "DCM,MM" Sjt 9393 East Lancashire Regt
BRYANT Alfred MM Pte 232477 2nd London Regt
BRYANT Alfred E. MM Sjt 9939 8th Royal West Surrey Regt
BRYANT Arthur Alfred MM Cpl 2084 20th London Regt
BRYANT Arthur G. MM+Bar Sjt 13011 2nd Suffolk Regt
BRYANT Charles MM Pte 25169 Norfolk Regt
BRYANT Charles Nicholson MM L/Cpl 325387 1/9th Durham Light Infantry
BRYANT Claude E. MM Pte 203630 West Yorkshire Regt
BRYANT Edward MM L/Cpl 14014 7th Shropshire Light Infantry
BRYANT Edward A. MM Sjt 6674 11th Norfolk Regt
BRYANT Ernest R. MM Pte 10946 1st King's Royal Rifle Corps
BRYANT Frank MM Sjt 200983 2/4th Lincolnshire Regt
BRYANT George MM+Bar Dvr 89345 22 Bde RFA
BRYANT George "MM,MID" Sjt 8178 3rd Coldstream Guards
BRYANT George A. MM Pte G/6576 2nd Royal Sussex Regt
BRYANT George Benjamin MM Pte 17629 7th Shropshire Light Infantry KIA 26.9.17.
BRYANT Harry MM Sjt SE/14097 Army Veterinary Corps
BRYANT Herbert H. MM Pte H/10028 4th Hussars
BRYANT J. MM Dvr 1047 35 Bde RFA
BRYANT James MM Pte 8386 2nd Royal Munster Fusiliers
BRYANT James MM Pte 4/4836 Royal Irish Regt
BRYANT James E. MM Gnr 182231 RFA
BRYANT John MM Cpl 108419 47 Bty 41 Bde RFA
BRYANT John MM+Bar Cpl 392118 9th London Regt
BRYANT Reuben MM Pte 233878 2/2nd London Regt KIA 21.3.18.
BRYANT Robert H.W. MM Cpl 240665 1/5th Royal Sussex Regt
BRYANT Roy MM Pte 145934 19th Bn Machine Gun Corps
BRYANT Walter Albert MM CQMS 420296 1/10th London Regt
BRYANT William A. MM Spr 25403 Royal Engineers
BRYANT William Henry MM Pte 22913 1st Border Regt DOW 24.10.18.
BRYANT William J. MM Sjt 730492 RFA
BRYANT William Robert MM CSM 9575 1st Worcestershire Regt KIA 31.7.17.
BRYANT William T.H. MM+Bar Pte 16400 2nd Grenadier Guards
BRYARS Charles MM Pte 205554 11th East Yorkshire Regt
BRYARS William Arthur MM Sjt 51280 102 Fd Coy Royal Engineers
BRYCE G. MM Cpl 290607 Royal Highlanders
BRYCE George MM Cpl 2456 12th Royal Scots
BRYCE George MM Sjt 55977 52nd Bn Machine Gun Corps
BRYCE James MM Sjt 123350 38 Coy Labour Corps
BRYCE John MM Sjt 306238 8th West Yorkshire Regt
BRYCE John MM Sjt 1863 8/10th Gordon Highlanders
BRYCE Robert MM Spr 193164 Royal Engineers
BRYCE Thomas MM L/Sjt 11635 2nd Scots Guards
BRYCE Thomas MM Pte 301603 1/7th Royal Scots
BRYCE William MM Pte 40690 Gordon Highlanders
BRYCESON Thomas G. MM Sjt 190 RFA
BRYDE William MM Sjt 17047 Liverpool Regt
BRYDEN David MM CSM 5023 2/4th Royal Berkshire Regt
BRYDEN Henry MM Pte 11453 9th Royal Inniskilling Fusiliers Died 23.2.18.
BRYDEN Herbert MM Cpl 265067 West Riding Regt
BRYDEN John MM Gnr 7777 RFA
BRYDEN Thomas MM L/Cpl 1278 23rd Royal Fusiliers
BRYDEN William MM Pte 332913 9th Highland Light Infantry
BRYDON George MM Sjt 4746 1st Royal West Kent Regt DOW 3.3.18. Real name Adam Brydon Veitch.
BRYDON Robert MM Pte 3/5778 1st Cameron Highlanders
BRYDONE Alexander MM Cpl 772 4th Bn GMGR
BRYER Charles MM Cpl 95212 Liverpool Regt
BRYNING Ernest MM Gnr L/10011 B/149 Bde RFA
BRYON Joseph MM Pte 9998 1st Yorkshire Light Infantry
BRYSON Alexander Clark MM Sjt S/9456 Arg & Suth Highlanders
BRYSON Andrew MM Cpl 20710 11th Royal Scots
BRYSON Frederick W. MM Sjt 21757 17th Royal Scots
BRYSON Frederick W. MM Pte 18130 Welsh Regt
BRYSON George MM+Bar Sjt 326455 RGA
BRYSON James MM Pte 12243 1st King's Own Scottish Borderers
BRYSON John MM Pte 326021 1/6th Arg & Suth Highlanders
BRYSON Robert MM Pte S/20788 8th Royal Highlanders
BRYSON William MM+Bar Pte 11587 9th Scottish Rifles
BUBB Percy R. MM Sjt 229693 13th Royal Fusiliers
BUBB William MM L/Cpl 27694 14th Royal Warwickshire Regt
BUCHAN Alexander MM CSM 240991 Gordon Highlanders
BUCHAN Alexander MM Cpl 26697 2nd Royal Scots KIA 12.4.18.
BUCHAN Charles MM Pte R/37870 King's Royal Rifle Corps
BUCHAN Charles J. MM Cpl 152708 9th Bn Machine Gun Corps
BUCHAN Charles Murray MM L/Sjt 24143 Grenadier Guards
BUCHAN David MM Pte S/6973 1/8th Arg & Suth Highlanders
BUCHAN George Douglas MM Pte 22278 45 Coy Machine Gun Corps KIA 16.7.17.
BUCHAN James MM Pte 1592 1/5th B Coy Gordon Highlanders DOW 15.11.16.
BUCHAN Robert MM Pte 301343 RAMC
BUCHAN Robert C. MM Sjt 25656 Scottish Rifles
BUCHAN Sidney John MM Gnr L/40768 B/189 Bde RFA KIA 21.3.18.
BUCHAN Walker MM L/Cpl 201025 4th Gordon Highlanders
BUCHANAN Alexander MM Spr 27293 Cavalry Sig Sqn Royal Engineers

BUCHANAN Alexander MM+2 Bars Sjt 275042 1/7th Arg & Suth Highlanders
BUCHANAN Archibald MM Sjt 75201 MGC(Heavy Branch)
BUCHANAN Charles MM Pte 395453 9th London Regt
BUCHANAN David MM Pte S/10399 Gordon Highlanders
BUCHANAN Duncan MM Pte 2245 9th Seaforth Highlanders
BUCHANAN Francis T.G. MM+Bar L/Sjt 36803 RAMC
BUCHANAN George H. MM Pte 38788 5/6th Royal Scots
BUCHANAN Harry B. MM Sjt 785292 RFA
BUCHANAN Henry MM Gnr 24299 C/70 Bde RFA
BUCHANAN Henry R. MM Pte 40992 1st Royal Scots Fusiliers
BUCHANAN James "DCM,MM,CdeG(F)" Pte 203285 5th King's Own Scottish Borderers
BUCHANAN James MM Cpl 310350 7th Gordon Highlanders
BUCHANAN James MM Bdr 36253 6 Div Ammn Col RFA
BUCHANAN James George MM Spr 87053 204 Fd Coy Royal Engineers
BUCHANAN John MM Bdr 89947 A/117 Bde RFA
BUCHANAN John MM Pte S/40006 10th Arg & Suth Highlanders
BUCHANAN John MM Pte 291326 1/7th Royal Highlanders
BUCHANAN John MM Pte 240315 5th Royal Scots Fusiliers
BUCHANAN John MM Pte 2576 1/7th Royal Highlanders KIA 25.4.17.
BUCHANAN John "MM+Bar,MID" Cpl 36377 RFA
BUCHANAN John Y.S. MM L/Cpl 111527 5th Bn Tank Corps
BUCHANAN Joseph Marshall MM L/Cpl 27418 9th Royal Inniskilling Fusiliers KIA 20.11.17.
BUCHANAN Richard MM Pte 50545 1/6th North Staffordshire Regt KIA 2.5.18.
BUCHANAN Thomas MM L/Cpl STK/922 10th Royal Fusiliers
BUCHANAN W. MM Sjt 325470 RGA
BUCHANAN William MM Pte 12618 6th King's Own Scottish Borderers
BUCHANAN William MM Pte 17665 1/7th Gordon Highlanders
BUCHANAN William MM+Bar Cpl 10417 Cameron Highlanders
BUCHANAN William Alexander MM+Bar Cpl 9022 14th Arg & Suth Highlanders
BUCK Alfred George MM Spr 39511 57 Div Sig Coy Royal Engineers
BUCK Alfred Richard MM Pte 2091 5th Gloucestershire Regt
BUCK Arthur MM L/Cpl 43495 Royal Irish Fusiliers
BUCK Cyril Alfred Spencer MM Pte 2740 18th London Regt KIA 26.10.17.
BUCK Edward MM Cpl 536010 Royal Engineers
BUCK Edward MM+Bar CSM 505309 13th London Regt
BUCK Ernest MM Pte 326322 1/1st Cambridgeshire Regt
BUCK G. MM 2nd Cpl 63622 Royal Engineers
BUCK G.E. MM L/Cpl P/906 Military Mounted Police
BUCK George MM Pte 22552 9th Scottish Rifles DOW 23.7.18.
BUCK George MM Pte 202995 9th Yorkshire Regt
BUCK George MM Pte 241189 5th Yorkshire Light Infantry
BUCK George MM Sjt 1330 Monmouthshire Regt
BUCK George T. MM Sjt 3713 8th Royal West Kent Regt
BUCK Harry MM L/Bdr 26504 C/59 Bde RFA
BUCK Henry G. MM Pte 1124 5th London Regt
BUCK John MM Pte 9456 Lincolnshire Regt
BUCK John MM Pte 68085 51st Bn Machine Gun Corps
BUCK John A. MM Pte 205047 16th Middlesex Regt att MGC
BUCK John Bertram Hampshire "MM,MID" Sjt S/3057 Rifle Brigade
BUCK R.A. MM Pte 24662 9th Essex Regt
BUCK Walter MM Cpl 1027 Military Foot Police
BUCK Walter Cyril MM Cpl 13296 7th Oxf & Bucks Light Infantry
BUCK Wilfred MM L/Cpl 24245 2/4th York & Lancaster Regt KIA 4.11.18.
BUCK William E. MM Pte 8680 2nd Suffolk Regt
BUCKBERRY Walter MM Dvr 15696 35 Div Ammn Col RFA
BUCKBY Thomas H. MM Sjt 22855 Royal Engineers
BUCKELL Arthur F. MM Sjt 37283 524 Siege Bty RGA
BUCKENHAM Arthur Henry "DCM,MM+Bar,MSM" BSM 50231 B/74 Bde RFA
BUCKENHAM John A. MM+Bar Sjt 698041 1/6th London Regt
BUCKENHAM John W. MM L/Sjt 17152 7th Norfolk Regt
BUCKENHAM William MM Pte 18741 7th Norfolk Regt
BUCKERFIELD Richard MM Sjt 200265 East Yorkshire Regt
BUCKERFIELD William MM Pte 9804 South Staffordshire Regt
BUCKETT Wallace MM Pte 205440 2/4th Hampshire Regt
BUCKHAM Edward MM Pte 75698 19th Durham Light Infantry
BUCKHAM George Hector MM Sjt 113109 'J' Special Coy Royal Engineers
BUCKHAM Robert MM L/Cpl 6650 1st Dragoons

BUCKHAM Thomas Rukin MM Sjt 26688 A/83 Bde RFA KIA 20.7.16.
BUCKINGHAM Charles W. MM Cpl 12595 West Yorkshire Regt
BUCKINGHAM George MM Sjt 19891 10th Hampshire Regt
BUCKINGHAM George MM Bdr 291855 RGA
BUCKINGHAM George MM Cpl 307462 Royal Warwickshire Regt
BUCKINGHAM George MM L/Cpl 3720 2nd Rifle Brigade
BUCKINGHAM George E. MM Cpl 43610 RGA
BUCKINGHAM Horace MM Cpl 98587 56 Div Ammn Col RFA
BUCKINGHAM James William MM CoH 14 Royal Horse Guards
BUCKINGHAM John MM Cpl 2708 6th Dragoon Guards
BUCKINGHAM Joseph MM Cpl 204156 1st London Regt
BUCKINGHAM Walter MM Pte 3662 1/4th London Regt
BUCKLAND Arthur Instone MM Sjt M2/052327 Army Service Corps
BUCKLAND Basil George "MM,CG(F)" Sjt 29723 65 Coy Machine Gun Corps Died 8.10.18.
BUCKLAND Francis G. MM BSM 83388 319 Siege Bty RGA
BUCKLAND Frederick C. MM Cpl M/34955 10 Pontoon Park Army Service Corps
BUCKLAND George MM Pte M2/204039 Army Service Corps
BUCKLAND Harry MM Pte 16047 Machine Gun Corps
BUCKLAND James "MM,MID" Cpl M2/081407 Army Service Corps
BUCKLAND Jesse MM Cpl M2/139049 Army Service Corps
BUCKLAND William C. MM Sjt 38375 RFA
BUCKLAND William J. MM Pte 200699 9th Royal Sussex Regt
BUCKLE Ernest MM Sjt 15494 4th Grenadier Guards KIA 13.4.18.
BUCKLE Harry D. MM L/Cpl 203127 2nd Suffolk Regt
BUCKLE Herbert MM+Bar Sjt 312039 RGA
BUCKLE James Johnson MM Pte 26321 9th Norfolk Regt
BUCKLE John MM Sjt 7737 1st West Yorkshire Regt
BUCKLE Olave E. MM Sjt 240096 1/8th Middlesex Regt
BUCKLE Richard MM L/Cpl 14906 Northumberland Fusiliers
BUCKLER Edmund Francis MM Cpl T4/243460 129 HT Coy Army Service Corps
BUCKLER Thomas MM Cpl 10271 Royal Warwickshire Regt
BUCKLER William MM L/Cpl 9606 1st Royal Warwickshire Regt
BUCKLES Gustave MM L/Cpl 321826 6th London Regt
BUCKLEY Abel MM Pte 8252 10 Fd Amb RAMC
BUCKLEY Albert MM Pte 241053 1/5th North Lancashire Regt KIA 30.11.17.
BUCKLEY Arthur MM Pte 9497 1st Cheshire Regt
BUCKLEY Arthur R. MM Pte 47354 MGC(Cavalry)
BUCKLEY Charles H. MM Pte 12407 8th North Staffordshire Regt
BUCKLEY Charles J. MM Sjt 9327 8th Lincolnshire Regt
BUCKLEY David Cornelius MM CSM 4665 Somerset Light Infantry
BUCKLEY Eric S. MM Pte 66123 RAMC
BUCKLEY Frank MM L/Cpl 15528 11th East Lancashire Regt
BUCKLEY Frank MM Bdr 706313 RFA
BUCKLEY Frank MM Cpl 48004 92 Fd Coy Royal Engineers
BUCKLEY Frederick MM Cpl 200646 5th Notts & Derby Regt
BUCKLEY G. MM Dvr 10072 RFA
BUCKLEY G.J. MM Pte 3983 London Regt
BUCKLEY George MM L/Sjt 14830 24th Manchester Regt
BUCKLEY Harold Ernest MM L/Cpl 13572 Liverpool Regt
BUCKLEY Harry "DCM,MM" Bdr 45479 39 Bde RFA
BUCKLEY Harry MM Bdr 87725 'H' Bty RHA DOW 10.10.18.
BUCKLEY J.C. MM Pte 512550 RAMC
BUCKLEY James MM Pte 243556 1/5th North Lancashire Regt
BUCKLEY James MM Sjt 14069 24th Manchester Regt
BUCKLEY James MM Pte 23529 Welsh Regt
BUCKLEY John MM L/Cpl 305073 5th West Riding Regt
BUCKLEY John MM L/Cpl 52706 Cheshire Regt
BUCKLEY John MM Sjt 72321 Royal Engineers
BUCKLEY John MM Pte 75021 12th Manchester Regt
BUCKLEY John MM Sjt 735909 RFA
BUCKLEY John MM Sjt 7116 Shropshire Light Infantry
BUCKLEY John H. MM Sjt 14619 9th Notts & Derby Regt
BUCKLEY John Robert MM Pte 8250 4 Fd Amb RAMC
BUCKLEY Joseph MM Pte M2/079122 HQ Fifth Army Army Service Corps
BUCKLEY Percy MM Pte 31731 6th West Riding Regt
BUCKLEY Peter MM Sjt 101403 170 Coy Labour Corps
BUCKLEY Robert MM Pte 14021 9th Royal Irish Fusiliers
BUCKLEY Robert MM+Bar Gnr L/10140 A/149 Bde RFA
BUCKLEY Stephen MM Pte 9632 1st Irish Guards
BUCKLEY Tom H. MM L/Cpl 13001 7th South Lancashire Regt
BUCKLEY William MM Cpl 8633 2nd Royal Munster Fusiliers
BUCKLEY William MM Pte 20056 Shropshire Light Infantry
BUCKLEY William MM+Bar L/Cpl 8436 1st Cheshire Regt
BUCKLEY William MM Pte 21921 1/5th Royal Lancaster Regt

BUCKLEY William MM Pte 29680 North Lancashire Regt
BUCKLEY William Alfred MM Cpl 7639 1st Lincolnshire Regt KIA 27.5.18.
BUCKLEY William R. MM Pte 4466 2nd Border Regt
BUCKLEY Willie MM Pte 203595 West Riding Regt
BUCKMAN Charles MM Pte 230538 2nd London Regt
BUCKMAN James Norman MM Pte 325837 1/1st Worcestershire Yeomanry
BUCKMAN Stephen A. MM+Bar L/Sjt 2237 2nd Royal Sussex Regt
BUCKMASTER George A. MM Pte 301878 14th Bn Tank Corps
BUCKNALL Thomas MM Sjt 117179 291 Siege Bty RGA
BUCKNELL Frederick C. MM Pte 242418 Royal West Surrey Regt
BUCKNELL John MM L/Cpl 80937 1/1st Essex Yeomanry
BUCKNELL Leonard Arthur MM Cpl B/203085 9th Rifle Brigade KIA 4.4.18.
BUCKROYD Joe MM L/Sjt 26285 1/5th West Yorkshire Regt
BUCKSEY Harold MM Pte 30679 RAMC
BUCKTHORPE Martin A. MM Spr 19108 5 Div Sig Coy Royal Engineers
BUCKTON Stephen MM Sjt 14876 Yorkshire Regt
BUCKTROUT George MM L/Cpl 17045 8th York & Lancaster Regt
BUCKTROUT Robert MM+Bar Sjt 7426 2nd York & Lancaster Regt
BUCKWELL E.V. MM Sjt S/358 Royal Sussex Regt
BUCKWELL James MM Sjt S/384 Royal Sussex Regt
BUDD A.E. MM Cpl 54141 Royal Engineers
BUDD Alexander "DCM,MM" Cpl 76687 3rd (Light) Bn Tank Corps
BUDD Arthur MM Sjt 200033 1/4th Royal Sussex Regt
BUDD Charles MM+Bar Cpl 41093 37 Bde RFA
BUDD Ernest W. MM Pte 30326 7th Norfolk Regt
BUDD Francis E. MM Pte 12718 5th Lancers
BUDD Frank MM Pte 26585 Wiltshire Regt
BUDD Frederick George "MC,MM(13206 Pte Devon Regt)" T/2Lt 16th King's Royal Rifle Corps DOW 15.10.18.
BUDD George F. MM Pte 324892 6th London Regt att KRRC
BUDD George F. MM Pte 9899 Devonshire Regt
BUDD George James MM+Bar Sjt M1/08687 1(North Midland)Fd Amb Army Service Corps
BUDD John T. MM L/Cpl 24463 Royal Welsh Fusiliers
BUDD Joseph Cecil MM Cpl 102133 Y/41 Med TM Bty RFA KIA 30.7.18.
BUDD Joseph Richard William MM Sjt 493353 2/1st(Home Counties)Fd Amb RAMC
BUDD Percy Edgar MM Gnr 69571 Tank Corps
BUDD Percy James MM Pte 14848 12th East Surrey Regt KIA 12.11.16.
BUDD Robert H. MM L/Cpl 40640 Norfolk Regt
BUDD William MM Sjt 5756 1st Devonshire Regt
BUDD William MM L/Cpl 7821 1st Devonshire Regt
BUDD William C. MM Sjt 675128 RFA
BUDDEN Frederick C. MM Pte 202836 4th Hampshire Regt
BUDGE Albert MM CSM M/22484 4 Div Train Army Service Corps
BUDGE Alexander MM Cpl 46036 Royal Engineers
BUDGE Bernard MM Sjt 2408 Labour Corps
BUDGE John P. MM Cpl 128416 21st Bn Machine Gun Corps
BUDGE William MM Cpl 13359 Scottish Rifles
BUDGEN Archibald H. MM Pte 19384 5th Royal Berkshire Regt
BUDGEN Fergus MM Gnr 41916 B/94 Bde RFA
BUDGETT Fred MM Pte 27049 14th Gloucestershire Regt Died 4.4.18.
BUERY Walter J. MM L/Cpl 61952 23rd Royal Fusiliers
BUFFHAM Leonard MM Pte 43945 5th Royal Berkshire Regt
BUFFIN Thomas MM Pte 3443 6th London Regt
BUFFREY Joseph William MM Sjt 19396 13th Gloucestershire Regt
BUFTON Herbert E. "DCM+Bar,MM" CSM 17229 5th Shropshire Light Infantry
BUFTON William C. MM CSM 355040 25th Royal Welsh Fusiliers
BUGG Charles F. MM Pte 39546 Yorkshire Light Infantry
BUGG Oscar W. MM Sjt 80101 1/1st Essex Yeomanry
BUGGINS Thomas E. MM Pte 267220 Oxf & Bucks Light Infantry
BUGGY Michael MM Pte 16108 2nd Royal Dublin Fusiliers
BUGLASS Alexander MM Pte 9908 1st Royal Scots
BUGLASS Joseph "DCM,MM" L/Cpl 10/11807 1st Northumberland Fusiliers
BUGLER Albert D. "MM,MID" L/Cpl 12792 Devonshire Regt
BUICK David MM Cpl 65295 126 Fd Coy Royal Engineers KIA 22.3.18.
BUICK George MM Sjt 120625 291 Siege Bty RGA KIA 24.4.18.
BUICK Henry "DCM,MM" Sjt 290137 1/8th Scottish Rifles
BUICK James MM L/Cpl 11/2204 Royal Irish Rifles
BUIE Alexander MM Cpl 203217 1/4th West Riding Regt KIA 11.10.18.

BUIST Alexander MM Pte 33361 Hampshire Regt
BUIST Thomas MM Pte 267069 Royal Highlanders
BULCRAIG Francis John MM Cpl 1543 1/23rd London Regt
BULFORD Robert Reginald MM+Bar L/Sjt 554485 16th London Regt
BULGER George Horace MM Gnr L/32943 177 Bde RFA
BULL A. MM L/Cpl 2808 10th Essex Regt
BULL Albert MM Pte C/6367 King's Royal Rifle Corps
BULL Albert E. MM Sjt 20771 RGA
BULL Albert George William MM 2nd Cpl 69538 138 Army Tps Coy Royal Engineers
BULL Albury MM Sjt 285224 1/1st Oxfordshire Yeomanry
BULL Arthur MM Pte 16169 Machine Gun Corps
BULL Arthur E. "DCM,MM" Sjt 58356 39 Bde RFA
BULL Arthur Henry John MM Pte 6813 West Riding Regt
BULL Arthur William MM Pte DM2/207734 Att 142 Fd Amb RAMC Army Service Corps
BULL Cephas MM Pte 242652 North Staffordshire Regt
BULL Charles MM Pte 20793 1st Hampshire Regt KIA 8.6.18.
BULL Charles MM Pte 30825 RAMC
BULL Charles MM BSM 614009 15 Bde RHA
BULL Charles H. MM Pte 32511 Oxf & Bucks Light Infantry
BULL Douglas MM Cpl 12085 7th Norfolk Regt
BULL Ernest G. MM Pte 285094 4th Oxf & Bucks Light Infantry
BULL Ernest James MM Bdr 68496 RFA
BULL G. "MM,MID" Cpl 89580 RFA
BULL Harold MM Pte 11362 Yorkshire Light Infantry
BULL Harry W. MM Pte 471684 12th London Regt
BULL Henry MM Sjt 20619 8th Gloucestershire Regt
BULL Henry George MM Cpl 781 12 Army Auxiliary HT Coy Army Service Corps
BULL Henry L. "DCM,MM" L/Cpl 16040 11th Royal Warwickshire Regt
BULL Henry R. "MM,MID" Sjt Z/154 Rifle Brigade
BULL James MM Gnr 91427 B/54 Bde RFA
BULL James Alfred MM Pte 15084 10th Royal Warwickshire Regt
BULL John W. MM Pte G/12072 7th Royal Sussex Regt
BULL John William Henry MM Pte 241713 1/5th Lincolnshire Regt
BULL Kenneth MM L/Cpl 24968 Leicestershire Regt
BULL Lawrence George MM Sjt 20236 South Wales Borderers
BULL Leslie S. "DCM,MM+Bar" Sjt 41231 2 Sqn MGC(Cavalry)
BULL Sydney MM Sjt 1857 Royal Flying Corps
BULL Thomas W. MM Pte 241401 6th North Staffordshire Regt
BULL Walter MM Pte SPTS/4502 23rd Royal Fusiliers
BULL William A. MM Pte 260098 Seaforth Highlanders
BULL William George MM Sjt 9136 1st Oxf & Bucks Light Infantry
BULLARD Frederick J.W. MM+Bar Pte R/37616 13th King's Royal Rifle Corps
BULLARD George H. MM Cpl 4938 Notts & Derby Regt
BULLARD Harry MM Pte 38057 8th East Surrey Regt
BULLARD Sidney Albert MM Pte 612057 1/19th London Regt
BULLAS Robert C. "MM,MID" Bdr 44699 33 Bde RFA
BULLEN Albert E. "MM,MID" 2nd Cpl 9236 237 Fd Coy Royal Engineers
BULLEN Cyril Leonard MM L/Cpl 512060 574 Army Troops Coy Royal Engineers
BULLEN Elliott T.P.E. "MM,MID" Sjt 16277 Royal Engineers
BULLEN Ernest G. MM Sjt 12034 12th Hampshire Regt
BULLEN Fred James MM Sjt 45291 4th Hussars
BULLEN Frederick W. MM Sjt H/27920 3rd Hussars
BULLEN George S. MM Pte 21227 7th East Kent Regt
BULLEN Henry W. MM Pte Z/971 Rifle Brigade
BULLEN James MM Pte 17038 9th York & Lancaster Regt
BULLEN John Henry MM Pte 240051 Leicestershire Regt
BULLEN John William MM Spr 426413 422 Fd Coy Royal Engineers
BULLEN Nelson MM Pte 36758 East Lancashire Regt
BULLEN Peter MM Pte 12/23710 South Wales Borderers
BULLER Horatio E. MM Cpl 951294 1 Div Ammn Col RFA
BULLER James C. MM Sjt 242623 6th Royal Warwickshire Regt
BULLEY Walter Edwin MM Cpl L/603 RFA
BULLICK William Packer MM Sjt 17339 12th Royal Irish Rifles
BULLIMORE Charles William MM Pte 9036 1st Lincolnshire Regt
BULLIMORE Thomas MM Gnr 104217 48 Bty 36 Bde RFA
BULLING Alfred Edgar MM Sjt 472098 12th London Regt DOW 5.11.18.
BULLING Harold M. MM Pte 87581 13th Liverpool Regt
BULLIVANT Fred MM Pte 50433 West Yorkshire Regt
BULLIVANT George MM Pte 8576 2nd Worcestershire Regt
BULLIVANT Thomas G. MM Sjt 82311 RGA
BULLMAN Edward MM Bdr 42222 RFA

BULLOCH Edmond MM Spr 93820 Royal Engineers
BULLOCK Alexander MM Pte 31352 1/5th Gloucestershire Regt
BULLOCK Alfred H. MM Pte 424017 10th London Regt
BULLOCK Arthur MM Pte 14856 9th Yorkshire Light Infantry KIA 9.4.17.
BULLOCK Benjamin MM Pte 200928 4th Worcestershire Regt
BULLOCK Charles Frederick MM Pte 533279 1/15th London Regt KIA 1.4.18.
BULLOCK David MM Pte 11633 Machine Gun Corps
BULLOCK Edward Charles MM Sjt 800064 A/230 Bde RFA
BULLOCK Ernest MM+Bar Pte 3/10055 7th Norfolk Regt KIA 30.11.17.
BULLOCK Ernest MM Cpl 494311 477 Fd Coy Royal Engineers
BULLOCK Frank MM L/Cpl 17/809 West Yorkshire Regt
BULLOCK Fred MM Pte 24886 10th Duke of Cornwall's LI
BULLOCK Frederick MM Pte 4028 1/6th London Regt KIA 15.9.16.
BULLOCK Frederick J. MM Spr 18035 Royal Engineers
BULLOCK George MM L/Cpl 9897 1st Border Regt
BULLOCK George Henry "DCM,MM+Bar" Sjt 16173 2nd South Staffordshire Regt
BULLOCK George Ramsden MM Pte 300192 18th Liverpool Regt
BULLOCK Herbert MM Sjt 18/992 West Yorkshire Regt
BULLOCK Herbert Charles Stuart MM SM 116 Royal Flying Corps
BULLOCK J. MM L/Cpl 139055 Royal Engineers
BULLOCK John MM Gnr 56641 A/102 Bde RFA DOW 27.7.16.
BULLOCK John T. MM Cpl 20529 10th South Wales Borderers
BULLOCK Joseph MM Sjt 65101 1st Northumberland Fusiliers
BULLOCK Leonard MM Bdr 16785 RFA
BULLOCK Rees Morris MM Cpl 2438 Middlesex Regt
BULLOCK Reuben MM Pte 1022 Royal Sussex Regt
BULLOCK Richard MM Pte 18736 9th Yorkshire Light Infantry KIA 7.11.18.
BULLOCK Robert MM Pte 11874 King's Own Scottish Borderers
BULLOCK Robert J. MM Pte 4964 6th Royal Irish Rifles
BULLOCK Robert R. MM Cpl 1590 16th Lancers
BULLOCK Robert W. MM Gnr 56607 RFA
BULLOCK Samuel Charles Watts MM Spr 463039 50 Div Sig Coy Royal Engineers
BULLOCK Sydney MM L/Cpl 15630 5th South Staffordshire Regt
BULLOCK W. MM Sjt 16024 East Yorkshire Regt
BULLOCK Walter T. MM L/Bdr 291429 128 Ht Bty RGA
BULLOCK William MM+Bar Pte 29888 8th North Staffordshire Regt
BULLOCK William MM Pte 26/73 26th Northumberland Fusiliers
BULLOCK William Jarvis "MM,CdeG(F)" Cpl 320250 1/1st Wiltshire Yeomanry
BULLOWS A. MM Pte 12377 Northumberland Fusiliers
BULMAN Alexander MM Pte 13276 8th East Yorkshire Regt
BULMAN George Reay MM L/Cpl 418042 52 Div Sig Coy Royal Engineers
BULMER Clarence MM Pte 62203 55 Fd Amb RAMC
BULMER Harry MM Sjt 178862 'C' AA Bty RGA
BULMER Percy Calvert Louis Hirst MM 2nd Cpl 62234 18 Div Sig Coy Royal Engineers
BULMER T. MM Pte CHT/227 Army Service Corps
BULMER Thomas H. MM+Bar Sjt Fitter 1691 A/251 Bde RFA
BULPIN William John "MM,MID" Sjt 23978 X9 Med TM Bty RGA
BULTER Albert MM Sjt 700448 23rd London Regt
BUMPHREY S.G. MM Pte 41361 Essex Regt
BUMPSTEAD William C. MM Pte 70176 Royal West Surrey Regt
BUMSTEAD Albert MM Pte 202236 4th West Riding Regt
BUMSTEAD Egbert "DCM,MM" Sjt 23855 55 Fd Coy Royal Engineers
BUMSTEAD George T. MM L/Cpl 6047 Wiltshire Regt
BUMSTEAD William G. MM+Bar Pte M2/182247 47 Div Train Army Service Corps
BUNCE A. MM Pte 44712 Manchester Regt
BUNCE Albert MM Pte 20715 14th Gloucestershire Regt KIA 3.4.18.
BUNCE Alfred MM+Bar Pte 19225 1st South Staffordshire Regt
BUNCE Charles E. MM Pte 16/267 Royal Warwickshire Regt
BUNCE Ernest C.A. MM Sjt 2489 8th Royal Sussex Regt
BUNCE Henry Frank MM Gnr 800664 D/230 Bde RFA
BUNCE James MM Dvr 144260 RFA
BUNCE Joseph H. MM+Bar CSM 9499 5th Royal Berkshire Regt
BUNCE T. MM L/Cpl P1041 Military Mounted Police
BUNCE Walter Robert MM Spr 62254 15 Div Sig Coy Royal Engineers
BUNCE William MM Pte G/68177 1/2nd London Regt
BUNCH Samuel MM Sjt 56886 108 Fd Coy Royal Engineers
BUNCHER Alonzo MM Sjt 12010 Leicestershire Regt
BUNCLARK Albert Victor MM+Bar L/Cpl 1296 1/22nd London Regt

BUNCLE Richard B. MM Sjt 8709 Worcestershire Regt
BUNDAY Frank MM Pte M2/119917 Army Service Corps
BUNDOCK Harry W. MM Cpl R/16910 King's Royal Rifle Corps
BUNDY George MM Sjt 7317 2nd South Staffordshire Regt
BUNGAY Charles J. MM Sjt 420921 10th London Regt
BUNKELL William MM Sjt 321832 2/6th London Regt
BUNKER Henry Gordon MM Pte 28333 Royal West Kent Regt
BUNKER Jack MM Pte G/1997 Royal Sussex Regt
BUNKER Spencer G. MM Pte 204710 15th Hampshire Regt
BUNN Albert MM Sjt 242742 6th Royal Warwickshire Regt
BUNN Albert J. MM Pte 182080 Royal Engineers
BUNN Arthur MM Gnr 106194 200 Siege Bty RGA
BUNN Clifford Charles MM Cpl 15426 9th Suffolk Regt KIA 21.3.18.
BUNN Frederick George MM Pte 235453 Leicestershire Regt
BUNN George W. MM L/Cpl 21741 24th Royal Welsh Fusiliers
BUNN Henry C. MM L/Cpl 4428 1/20th London Regt
BUNN Henry T. MM Cpl 1111 13th Middlesex Regt
BUNN Herbert C. MM Cpl 1362 1/21st London Regt
BUNN James MM Sjt 376106 10th Manchester Regt
BUNN Sydney George MM L/Cpl 202151 1/5th Notts & Derby Regt
BUNNAGE Edward Arthur MM Pte 680439 1/22nd London Regt
BUNNELL Wilfred "MM,MID" Pte 11570 Royal Welsh Fusiliers
BUNNETT Charles "DCM,MM(6414 3rd Huss)+Bar" Sjt 246308 D/121 Bde RFA
BUNNETT G. MM Cpl 17800 12th East Surrey Regt
BUNNING Alfred R. MM Pte 320519 12th Norfolk Regt
BUNNY Martin MM Sjt 8003 Duke of Cornwall's LI
BUNT A. MM Pte 421087 RAMC
BUNTER William MM Cpl 91570 RFA
BUNTING Arthur MM Pte 7305 Scots Guards
BUNTING Charles MM+Bar Pte 48105 4th Royal Fusiliers
BUNTING Charles W. MM Pte 9402 1/8th Arg & Suth Highlanders
BUNTING George Henry MM Pte 21646 2nd York & Lancaster Regt
BUNTING John J. MM RSM 37651 15th Notts & Derby Regt
BUNTING John William MM Pte 12998 7th Leicestershire Regt
BUNTING Phillip H. MM Cpl 392337 9th London Regt
BUNTING Samuel MM Sjt 16/50 Royal Irish Rifles
BUNTING Walter MM Pte 37544 26th Northumberland Fusiliers
BUNTON William H. MM Cpl 240625 8th Middlesex Regt
BUNYAN Eric Edward MM Cpl 14903 Northamptonshire Regt
BUNYAN Frank MM Pte 50957 2nd Royal Scots
BUNYAN George MM+Bar Pte 23352 Bedfordshire Regt
BUNYAN Henry MM Pte 33018 6th Leicestershire Regt KIA 26.4.18.
BUNYAN William MM Pte 200040 1/5th Bedfordshire Regt
BUNYAN William Joseph MM Sjt 3808 TM Bde Salonika B Bty RFA KIA 18.9.18.
BURBECK Fred MM BSM 614226 2/1(Warwick)Bty RHA
BURBERRY Henry Charles MM L/Sjt G11332 Royal West Surrey Regt
BURBIDGE John William MM+Bar Sjt 242577 5th Leicestershire Regt
BURBRIDGE George W. MM L/Cpl 18968 6th Royal West Kent Regt
BURBRIDGE Joseph MM L/Cpl 58336 RAMC
BURCH Alfred MM Dvr 5980 RFA
BURCH Alfred Frederick MM Cpl L/16353 8th Royal Fusiliers
BURCH Charles E. MM Pte 203172 Middlesex Regt
BURCH Charles P. MM Sjt 70660 Royal Engineers
BURCH Christopher A. MM Pte M/317381 Army Service Corps
BURCH Clarence R. MM Dvr 925344 A/280 Bde RFA
BURCH Ernest Sydney MM Sjt 80353 42 Bde RFA
BURCH Frank MM Pte 266610 1st Bedfordshire Regt KIA 27.9.18.
BURCH Henry MM L/Cpl 16578 2nd West Riding Regt DOW 13.10.16.
BURCH James MM Pte 21206 1st Middlesex Regt
BURCH Thomas MM Cpl 5925 1/4th Royal Sussex Regt
BURCH William G. MM Sjt 11312 11 Fd Coy Royal Engineers
BURCHALL Arthur MM 2nd Cpl 147206 Special Bde Royal Engineers
BURCHAM Josiah W. MM Cpl 43612 6th Northamptonshire Regt
BURCHELL H. MM L/Cpl 6040 7th Royal Sussex Regt
BURCHELL R.E. MM+Bar Sjt M1/07416 Army Service Corps
BURCHELL Richard MM L/Bdr 740283 RFA
BURCHELL Sidney MM Sjt 21302 1st Duke of Cornwall's LI
BURCHELL Tom MM Bdr 41993 25 Bde RFA
BURCHELL William MM Sjt 22540 RFA
BURCHELL William H. MM L/Cpl 538123 50 Div Sig Coy Royal Engineers
BURCHETT G.E. MM Pte 9650 East Kent Regt
BURCHETT Jack "MM,MID" L/Cpl 8716 19th Hussars

BURCHETT John G. MM Sjt 17810 1st Grenadier Guards
BURCHETT John Hilary Pyne MM Sjt 199864 61 Div Sig Coy Royal Engineers
BURCHILL William Patrick MM L/Cpl 85717 32nd Bn Machine Gun Corps KIA 30.9.18.
BURCHMORE Percy MM Pte 291793 Northumberland Fusiliers
BURCHMORE William MM Pte R/16334 King's Royal Rifle Corps
BURCOMBE Charles MM Pte 19952 Machine Gun Corps
BURD Vernon MM Pte 260198 Royal Warwickshire Regt
BURDASS William John MM L/Cpl 242506 1/5th Lincolnshire Regt
BURDEN C.C. MM Sjt 8220 1st East Kent Regt
BURDEN Charles W. MM Gnr 169937 59 Siege Bty RGA
BURDEN Frank MM L/Cpl 10412 2nd C Coy Welsh Regt KIA 8.9.16.
BURDEN Frederick MM Dvr 182933 48 Bty 36 Bde RFA
BURDEN Frederick MM Pte 7835 2nd Royal Sussex Regt
BURDEN Henry A. MM Sjt 201858 1/4th Oxf & Bucks Light Infantry
BURDEN Henry J. MM Bdr 59694 27 Bde RFA
BURDEN Herbert C. MM Pte 204990 15th Hampshire Regt
BURDEN J.L. MM 2nd Cpl 42491 Royal Engineers
BURDEN John MM Pte 235057 2nd Seaforth Highlanders
BURDEN Leonard MM Pte 45581 15th Hampshire Regt
BURDEN Samuel J. MM+Bar Sjt A/204073 13th King's Royal Rifle Corps
BURDEN Stanley Robert MM Sjt 1847 1/7th London Regt DOW 11.10.16.
BURDEN William MM Pte 31163 1st Devonshire Regt
BURDEN William R. MM Sjt 94959 47 Bty 41 Bde RFA
BURDESS George MM Bdr 760392 159 Bde RFA
BURDETT Albert Ernest MM Sjt 84627 207 Fd Coy Royal Engineers
BURDETT George MM+Bar L/Cpl 41733 2nd Yorkshire Regt
BURDETT George MM Cpl 67768 40 Bde RFA
BURDETT Harry MM Pte 43729 Essex Regt
BURDETT Thomas MM Cpl 42435 2/5th West Yorkshire Regt
BURDETT William B. MM Sjt 28790 3 Sig Sqn Royal Engineers
BURDGE George Cary "MC,MM(2817 Pte Leinster Regt)" T/2Lt 9th Royal Inniskilling Fusiliers
BURDISS Martin MM Cpl 597 Royal Engineers
BURDON Albert Edward MM Gnr 165803 RFA
BURDON George H. MM+Bar Cpl 61750 226 Fd Coy Royal Engineers
BURDON Henry MM Sjt 486688 470 Fd Coy Royal Engineers
BURDON John E. MM Pte M/22655 62 Div Train Army Service Corps
BURDON Oliver MM Sjt 18/314 18th Durham Light Infantry
BURDON Surtees MM Cpl 12652 Yorkshire Regt
BURFOOT Thomas MM Pte 203433 1/4th West Riding Regt
BURFOOT William MM Pte 205746 2nd Bn Tank Corps
BURFORD Arthur MM+Bar 2nd Cpl 144740 Railway Operating Division Royal Engineers
BURFORD George MM Pte 12295 Royal Berkshire Regt
BURFORD John T. MM Pte 240992 5th Northumberland Fusiliers
BURFORD Levi "DCM,MM" Cpl 240991 1/5th Northumberland Fusiliers
BURFORD William J. MM L/Cpl 16455 2nd Oxf & Bucks Light Infantry
BURGE George Joseph MM Pte SPTS/2626 24th Royal Fusiliers KIA 3.10.18.
BURGE Phillip Scott "MC,MM(1182 Pte 10th R Fus)" T/Capt Royal Air Force KIA 24.7.18.
BURGE Stanley J. MM Pte 78418 RAMC
BURGE William H. MM L/Bdr 63766 25 Bde RFA
BURGESS A.R. MM Pte 43432 Norfolk Regt
BURGESS Adolphus C. MM Gnr 319008 RGA
BURGESS Albert E.F. MM Pte 230233 2nd London Regt
BURGESS Alexander MM Cpl S/6871 Seaforth Highlanders
BURGESS Alfred MM+Bar Cpl 235206 19th Liverpool Regt
BURGESS Alfred Herbert MM L/Cpl 19745 14th Bn Machine Gun Corps KIA 21.3.18.
BURGESS Alfred W. MM Sjt 11813 6th Dorsetshire Regt
BURGESS Archibald F. MM Pte K/423 22nd Royal Fusiliers
BURGESS Arthur MM Pte 47044 77 Fd Amb RAMC
BURGESS Arthur MM L/Cpl 1442 21st London Regt
BURGESS Arthur A. MM Pte 2829 2nd Rifle Brigade
BURGESS Arthur J. MM L/Bdr 74078 42 Bde RFA
BURGESS Benjamin MM Sjt 14779 Royal Lancaster Regt
BURGESS Charles MM CQMS 375536 10th Manchester Regt
BURGESS Charles MM Sjt 9486 1st Northamptonshire Regt
BURGESS Charles MM Spr 210956 38 Div Sig Coy Royal Engineers
BURGESS Charles MM Pte 202696 Hampshire Regt
BURGESS Charles J. MM Sjt 78876 1st Royal West Surrey Regt
BURGESS Cyril MM Dvr 140138 'Z' Bty RHA Died 14.10.18.
BURGESS David MM 2nd Cpl 251960 Royal Engineers
BURGESS E. MM L/Bdr L/3180 C/150 Bde RFA
BURGESS Ernest Malcolm MM Pte 348022 6th London Regt KIA 10.9.18.
BURGESS F.H. MM Pte 39410 RAMC
BURGESS Francis MM Cpl 25857 Dorsetshire Regt
BURGESS Francis J. MM+Bar Sjt S/6381 Gordon Highlanders
BURGESS Frank MM Pte 37820 RAMC
BURGESS Frank E. MM Pte 52649 Durham Light Infantry
BURGESS Frederick MM Pte 231896 2nd London Regt
BURGESS Frederick MM CSM 14796 Durham Light Infantry
BURGESS Frederick "MM,MID" Cpl 201131 2nd Bedfordshire Regt
BURGESS Frederick Charles MM Cpl L/37419 X/40 Med TM Bty RFA
BURGESS Frederick G. "DCM,MM,MID" Sjt 12409 115 Hy Bty RGA
BURGESS Frederick J. MM Pte 3/6145 1st East Yorkshire Regt
BURGESS George MM Sjt 12032 1st Liverpool Regt DOW 30.8.18.
BURGESS George Alfred MM Spr 177218 105 Fd Coy Royal Engineers
BURGESS George Frederick "DCM,MM" Bdr 15519 RFA
BURGESS George H. MM Spr 519956 Royal Engineers
BURGESS George Henry MM Pte 239196 Labour Corps
BURGESS George T. MM Pte M2/137200 Army Service Corps
BURGESS Harold MM Pte M2/105298 Army Service Corps
BURGESS Harold MM Gnr 36853 RFA
BURGESS Harry MM Cpl 201823 1/5th South Staffordshire Regt DOW 3.10.18.
BURGESS Harry MM Pte 376259 Manchester Regt
BURGESS Harry Roger Moody MM Pte 38834 4th Liverpool Regt KIA 16.4.18.
BURGESS James MM Pte 53667 2nd Welsh Regt
BURGESS James F. MM Cpl 44504 Royal Engineers
BURGESS John MM Pte 60026 26th Royal Fusiliers KIA 1.4.18.
BURGESS John MM Pte 44380 Middlesex Regt
BURGESS John E. MM Pte 27264 7th Shropshire Light Infantry
BURGESS Joseph MM Pte 9892 1st Yorkshire Light Infantry
BURGESS Joseph MM Cpl 11790 Duke of Cornwall's LI
BURGESS Lionel MM L/Cpl 55134 Machine Gun Corps
BURGESS Percy W. MM Spr 313268 Royal Engineers
BURGESS Percy William MM L/Cpl 14473 South Staffordshire Regt
BURGESS Sidney Jenius MM L/Cpl 43048 112 Coy Machine Gun Corps KIA 23.4.17.
BURGESS Stanley MM Spr 193168 Royal Engineers
BURGESS Stanley "MM,MID" Sjt 6995 2nd Royal Sussex Regt
BURGESS Sydney MM Pte M2/131245 47 Div Train Army Service Corps
BURGESS Thomas MM Sjt A/200865 1st King's Royal Rifle Corps
BURGESS Thomas H. MM Pte 19662 6th Yorkshire Regt
BURGESS Walter Arthur MM Cpl 14223 4th Hussars DOW 27.3.18.
BURGESS Walter J. "DCM,MM" Sjt 81870 6th Bn Machine Gun Corps
BURGESS William MM Cpl 128430 200th Bn Machine Gun Corps
BURGESS William MM Cpl 8333 1st Scottish Rifles
BURGESS William MM Cpl 89296 Machine Gun Corps
BURGESS William E. MM Spr 19205 55 Fd Coy Royal Engineers
BURGESS William G. MM L/Sjt 240363 1/8th Middlesex Regt
BURGESS William H. MM Sjt 6918 13th Hussars
BURGESS William Young MM Gnr 85640 B/54 Bde RFA
BURGIN George W. MM L/Cpl 13/93 13th York & Lancaster Regt
BURGIN John W. MM Dvr 231775 RFA
BURGIN Reginald MM Sjt S4/144835 58 Rly Supply Depot Army Service Corps
BURGIN Reginald MM Pte 12/321 8th York & Lancaster Regt
BURGIN W. MM Sjt 11068 Machine Gun Corps
BURGIN Walter MM Pte 43033 Lincolnshire Regt
BURGOIN Laurence MM Sjt 8802 2nd Lincolnshire Regt
BURGOINE Charles MM Pte G/21174 2nd Royal Sussex Regt
BURGON Harold MM L/Cpl 2851 2/5th Lancashire Fusiliers
BURGOYNE James MM Cpl 250936 5/6th Royal Scots
BURGOYNE Richard MM Pte 54800 11th Manchester Regt
BURGOYNE William P. MM Pte 50355 2/6th Royal Warwickshire Regt
BURGOYNE Willie MM Pte 241025 9th West Yorkshire Regt
BURGUM Arthur MM Sjt 40519 20th Manchester Regt
BURHOUSE George R. MM L/Cpl C/7465 King's Royal Rifle Corps
BURKE Arthur MM Pte 19202 7th Border Regt
BURKE Arthur MM L/Cpl 17762 2nd Coldstream Guards
BURKE Arthur J. MM Sjt 2248 1/8th Liverpool Regt

BURKE Cornelius MM L/Cpl 1/8363 1st Royal Munster Fusiliers
BURKE Daniel MM Pte 64101 RAMC
BURKE Dennis MM Pte 67326 Cheshire Regt
BURKE Edmund Stanley MM Sjt 32428 14th Royal Warwickshire Regt
BURKE Hubert MM Pte 36487 8 Fd Amb RAMC
BURKE J. MM Pte 2258 2nd Leinster Regt
BURKE James MM Gnr 112868 RGA
BURKE James MM Sjt 8/17090 Royal Dublin Fusiliers
BURKE James MM Sjt 151370 Royal Engineers
BURKE John MM Pte 3224 19 Fd Amb RAMC
BURKE John MM L/Cpl 8503 6th Royal Irish Regt KIA 7.6.17.
BURKE John MM Pte 29471 1st Royal Irish Fusiliers
BURKE John "MM,MID" Pte 1811 2nd Royal Scots
BURKE John MM Spr 14000 38 Fd Coy Royal Engineers
BURKE John MM CQMS 10809 2nd Royal Dublin Fusiliers
BURKE John F. MM Pte 13753 8th North Staffordshire Regt
BURKE Kenneth MM Pte 4552 1/1st London Regt KIA 15.9.16.
BURKE Leonard MM Pte 24442 8th West Riding Regt
BURKE Michael MM Bdr 73908 RGA
BURKE Patrick MM Pte 2174 1st Gloucestershire Regt DOW 16.9.18.
BURKE Patrick MM Sjt 755788 RFA
BURKE Patrick Daniel "MM,MdH(F)" Sjt 9/14478 9th East Lancashire Regt
BURKE Robert E. MM Gnr Sig 243890 C/330 Bde RFA
BURKE Russel MM Sjt 4436 19 Coy Machine Gun Corps KIA 26.3.18.
BURKE S. MM Sjt 3855 Royal Lancaster Regt
BURKE Sidney H. MM Pte 39326 RAMC
BURKE Sydney MM Pte 5210 1 Gen Hosp RAMC
BURKE Thomas MM Pte 5910 6th Connaught Rangers
BURKE Thomas MM Pte 23108 Royal Irish Fusiliers
BURKE Thomas MM L/Sjt 17839 20th Manchester Regt
BURKE Thomas MM Pte 308978 1/6th Liverpool Regt KIA 30.11.17.
BURKE Thomas Peter MM 2nd Cpl 40785 33 Base Park Royal Engineers
BURKE Valentine MM Cpl 11203 2nd Grenadier Guards KIA 31.7.17.
BURKE Walter MM+Bar Sjt 16530 3rd Grenadier Guards
BURKE Walter MM Sjt 9879 2nd York & Lancaster Regt KIA 21.3.18.
BURKE Walter W. MM Pte 18044 1st Scots Guards
BURKE William MM Dvr 502156 50 Div Sig Coy Royal Engineers
BURKE William MM Gnr 22327 RFA
BURKE William MM Pte 12516 Durham Light Infantry
BURKE William MM Sjt 59608 Machine Gun Corps
BURKE William MM Cpl 24011 Royal Inniskilling Fusiliers
BURKE William S. MM Pte 203109 1st London Regt
BURKETT Charles E. MM Bdr 72544 27 Bde RFA
BURKETT William MM Cpl 10616 12th Manchester Regt
BURKEY Ernest MM Pte 10328 2nd Dragoon Guards
BURKHARDT George Albert MM Pte 31776 RAMC
BURKHILL Thomas "MM+Bar,MID" CSM 15248 9th West Yorkshire Regt
BURKILL Herbert MM Sjt 3882 Machine Gun Corps
BURKILL John MM Gnr 760111 C/72 Bde RFA
BURKILL Walter MM Pte 5532 Yorkshire Light Infantry
BURKIN H.M. MM Pte 11941 2nd King's Own Scottish Borderers
BURKIN John William MM Cpl 12235 8th Border Regt DOW 18.4.18.
BURKIN Walter MM Pte 205018 2nd Yorkshire Light Infantry
BURKINSHAW Ernest Victor MM Pte 27833 8th York & Lancaster Regt
BURKITT Arthur MM Sjt 79239 2nd Durham Light Infantry
BURKITT John MM Cpl 16761 1st Border Regt
BURKS George E. MM Pte 65913 Royal Fusiliers
BURKS Henry J. MM L/Cpl 15221 Middlesex Regt
BURLAND Harry MM Pnr 129909 Royal Engineers
BURLEIGH (Joseph Gordon) Foster MM Cpl 321902 'G' AA Bty RGA DOW 3.11.17.
BURLEIGH Charles MM Sjt 17736 15th Essex Regt
BURLEIGH George Edward MM Gnr 44356 84 Bty 11 Bde RFA KIA 7.11.17.
BURLEIGH George H. MM Sjt 244720 5 Fd Svy Bn Royal Engineers
BURLEIGH Thomas H.W. MM Pte 45829 44 Fd Amb RAMC
BURLES Leonard P. "DCM,MM" Sjt 65610 106 Fd Coy Royal Engineers

BURLEY Alfred MM+Bar Cpl R/3326 1st King's Royal Rifle Corps KIA 10.9.18.
BURLEY Charles E. MM L/Cpl 107407 Royal Engineers
BURLEY Edward MM L/Cpl 242042 5th Yorkshire Light Infantry
BURLEY Frederick P. MM Sjt 19098 5 Fd Amb RAMC
BURLEY H.R. MM Sjt 17554 19th Liverpool Regt
BURLEY John MM Pte 266187 1/7th Scottish Rifles
BURLEY John G. MM L/Cpl 16725 10th York & Lancaster Regt
BURLEY Stanley MM Pte 242121 1st Royal West Kent Regt
BURLEY W.G. "DCM,MM" Sjt 650234 1/21st London Regt
BURLEY Walter Herbert MM Cpl R/2955 7th King's Royal Rifle Corps
BURLING Alfred James MM Pte 68463 90 Fd Amb RAMC
BURLING James MM Cpl 22002 Royal West Surrey Regt
BURLINGHAM George W. MM+Bar L/Sjt 29777 Norfolk Regt
BURLINGHAM Harry MM CSM 88033 1st Liverpool Regt
BURLINSON William G. MM Pte 32065 Durham Light Infantry
BURLISON Thomas MM+Bar Sjt 147754 Royal Engineers
BURLOCK Alfred W. MM BSM 79 RGA
BURLONG P. "DCM,MM" Cpl 18694 1st Essex Regt
BURMAN George William MM L/Cpl 882 Welsh Guards
BURMAN Percy L. MM L/Cpl 8139 12th York & Lancaster Regt
BURMAN Roland MM Gnr 65344 RGA
BURN George Oriel "MM,MM(F)" Sjt 19855 Welsh Regt
BURN George William MM Pte 27280 Durham Light Infantry
BURN Henry T. MM Pte 7692 Royal Sussex Regt
BURN Jabez MM Pte 6/13614 6th Lincolnshire Regt DOW 1.5.18.
BURN Matthew William MM Pte 242687 1/5th York & Lancaster Regt
BURNAGE Ernest MM Pte 21413 29th Bn Machine Gun Corps
BURNAGE George A. MM Pte 49980 RAMC
BURNAND John MM Pte 82777 15th Durham Light Infantry
BURNAND Leonard John MM Pte 5302 1st Royal West Surrey Regt
BURNBY Matthew Bolden MM Sjt 12/1164 York & Lancaster Regt
BURNE T. MM+Bar Pte 11774 2nd West Riding Regt
BURNELL Francis G. MM Pte 35247 16th Royal Warwickshire Regt
BURNELL George MM Pte 56515 Lancashire Fusiliers
BURNELL Harold Adam MM Sjt 63704 145 Army Troops Coy Royal Engineers
BURNELL James W. MM+Bar Pnr 206781 33 Div Sig Coy Royal Engineers
BURNELL Ralph H. MM Cpl T4/241915 Army Service Corps
BURNET William J. MM Pte 265501 Monmouthshire Regt
BURNETT Albert MM Pte 7046 1st Devonshire Regt
BURNETT Albert G. MM Cpl 1873 Royal Engineers
BURNETT Alexander MM+Bar Sjt 330420 Royal Scots
BURNETT Alexander "DCM+Bar,MM" Cpl 18327 25th Bn Machine Gun Corps
BURNETT Andrew MM Pte 32712 2nd Highland Light Infantry
BURNETT Edison MM Pte 63626 Machine Gun Corps
BURNETT Froude MM L/Cpl 4917 Duke of Cornwall's LI
BURNETT George MM Sjt 273806 Royal Engineers
BURNETT George MM Sjt 5757 2/1st HAC (Inf)
BURNETT Herbert R. MM Cpl 106151 Royal Engineers
BURNETT James E MM Pte 154121 32nd Bn Machine Gun Corps
BURNETT John MM Gnr 796443 RFA
BURNETT John Charles MM Bdr 84728 46 Bde RFA
BURNETT Norman MM Bdr Sig 307274 2/1(Lowland)Hy Bty RGA DOW 1.10.18.
BURNETT Robert MM CSM 200545 1/4th Gordon Highlanders
BURNETT Septimus C. "DCM,MM" L/Cpl 22129 6th Royal West Surrey Regt
BURNETT Stanley J. MM L/Cpl 2851 Monmouthshire Regt
BURNETT Thomas MM Cpl 1408 1(Northumbrian)Bde RFA
BURNETT Thomas Edward MM L/Sjt 8441 2nd West Yorkshire Regt KIA 1.7.16.
BURNETT Tom MM L/Cpl 12860 6th East Lancashire Regt
BURNETT Walter MM Pte 240266 1/5th East Lancashire Regt
BURNETT William "DCM,MM" Pte S/11869 1st Cameron Highlanders
BURNETT William MM Pte 14978 1st Gordon Highlanders
BURNETT William J. MM Pte 457291 24 Fd Amb RAMC
BURNEY John MM Sjt 18189 Machine Gun Corps
BURNEY William J. MM Spr 414467 412 Fd Coy Royal Engineers
BURNHAM Albert MM Pte 13185 1st Northumberland Fusiliers DOW 22.3.18.
BURNHAM Albert MM Pte 2595 8th Royal Fusiliers
BURNHAM Horace MM Sjt 63516 192 Hy Bty RGA
BURNHAM Isaac Henry MM+Bar Gnr 71554 D/311 Bde RFA KIA 30.10.17.

BURNHAM James MM Pte 229578 1st London Regt
BURNHAM John Stainforth MM Pte 40288 12/13th Northumberland Fusiliers Died 27.5.18.
BURNHAM Sydney Walter MM Pnr 60145 14 Div Sig Coy Royal Engineers
BURNHAM W. MM Sjt 34872 9th Essex Regt
BURNHILL Howard V. MM CQMS 20151 Welsh Regt
BURNINGHAM Charles MM Pte 302668 5th London Regt
BURNISTON David MM Cpl 201946 Yorkshire Regt
BURNLEY Ernest MM Pte 76340 RAMC
BURNLEY Harold MM Gnr 96142 A/50 Bde RFA KIA 19.10.17.
BURNLEY Harry MM Cpl 1334 RFA
BURNLEY Herbert MM L/Cpl 266104 1/6th West Riding Regt
BURNS Alexander Fraser MM L/Cpl 755 GMGR
BURNS Alfred J. MM Cpl 835112 RFA
BURNS Alfred V. MM Pte 18309 Coldstream Guards
BURNS Arthur MM+Bar Cpl 133400 45th Royal Fusiliers
BURNS Arthur MM L/Cpl 699 1st Gordon Highlanders
BURNS Austin MM L/Cpl 14913 12th West Yorkshire Regt
BURNS Bernard MM Pte 21351 Durham Light Infantry
BURNS Charles MM Sjt 12837 13th Yorkshire Regt
BURNS Daniel MM Pte 241174 1/6th Highland Light Infantry
BURNS David MM Pte 152822 12th Bn Machine Gun Corps
BURNS David MM Sjt 202319 Royal Highlanders
BURNS David W. MM Pte 291123 1st Cambridgeshire Regt
BURNS Edward MM Sjt 6827 XV Corps Cyclist Bn Army Cyclist Corps
BURNS George MM+Bar Cpl 17020 North Lancashire Regt
BURNS George "MM,MSM" Sjt 78549 W6 Airline Sect Royal Engineers
BURNS George MM L/Cpl 18/430 18th Durham Light Infantry
BURNS Henry MM Sjt 9530 1st Northumberland Fusiliers
BURNS Herbert MM Sjt 52840 Durham Light Infantry
BURNS Hugh "DCM,MM" Sjt 8778 1st Scottish Rifles KIA 12.4.18.
BURNS J. MM Pte 2893 Durham Light Infantry
BURNS James MM Pte 295941 12th Royal Scots Fusiliers
BURNS James MM Spr 130960 253 Tunnelling Coy Royal Engineers
BURNS James MM Pnr 53351 Royal Engineers
BURNS James MM Pte 200291 1/4th King's Own Scottish Borderers
BURNS James MM L/Cpl 15299 10th Arg & Suth Highlanders
BURNS James MM Pte 51339 Liverpool Regt
BURNS James MM Cpl 22/366 22nd Northumberland Fusiliers
BURNS James MM+Bar Cpl Sig 33370 307 Siege Bty RGA
BURNS James F. MM Pte 41351 2nd Yorkshire Light Infantry
BURNS James P. MM Pte 235139 1st North Lancashire Regt
BURNS John MM Cpl 655227 B/77 Bde RFA
BURNS John MM Sjt 265598 1/6th West Riding Regt
BURNS John MM Dvr 104139 D/82 Bde RFA
BURNS John MM 2nd Cpl 428361 423 Fd Coy Royal Engineers
BURNS John MM Gnr 74900 RFA
BURNS John MM Pte S/12250 Arg & Suth Highlanders
BURNS John MM Sjt 8066 1st West Yorkshire Regt
BURNS John T. MM Pte 201421 North Lancashire Regt
BURNS Michael MM+Bar Cpl 40763 1st Northamptonshire Regt
BURNS Patrick MM Pte 4829 2nd Lancashire Fusiliers
BURNS Robert MM L/Cpl 14761 11th West Yorkshire Regt KIA 4.7.16.
BURNS Robert MM Dvr 56574 11 Bde RFA
BURNS Robert MM Pte S/16615 Rifle Brigade
BURNS Robert S. MM Pte 11511 Arg & Suth Highlanders
BURNS Stewart Cameron MM L/Cpl 352344 1/9th C Coy Royal Scots KIA 23.4.17.
BURNS Thomas MM Pte 52915 2 Squadron MGC(Cavalry)
BURNS Thomas MM Dvr 786639 RFA
BURNS Victor MM L/Cpl 2018 20th London Regt
BURNS W.D. MM Cpl 8387 Scottish Rifles
BURNS William MM L/Cpl 10658 11th Royal Warwickshire Regt KIA 16.7.16.
BURNS William MM Sjt 265720 2/7th West Yorkshire Regt
BURNS William MM Cpl 95105 13th Liverpool Regt KIA 21.8.18.
BURNS William J. MM Pte 26694 7th Liverpool Regt
BURNS William Reece MM Pnr 249448 38 Div Sig Coy Royal Engineers Died 30.6.18.
BURNS William W. MM Gnr 166266 RFA
BURNSIDE Albert MM Cpl 325647 1/9th Durham Light Infantry
BURNSIDE Andrew MM L/Bdr 98351 255 Siege Bty RGA
BURNSIDE James MM Spr 420328 459 Fd Coy Royal Engineers
BURNSIDE Mark E. MM Pte 19653 9th West Yorkshire Regt

BURNYEAT Martin MM Pte 15461 9th North Staffordshire Regt
BURR Alfred MM Cpl 156562 1 Special Coy Royal Engineers KIA 24.3.18.
BURR Walter J. MM Spr 25060 Royal Engineers
BURR William Charles MM Spr 96245 222 Fd Coy Royal Engineers
BURR William John "MM,MID" Sjt 2615 4th Royal Fusiliers
BURRAGE Charles Ernest MM Pnr 252611 'A' Corps Sig Coy Royal Engineers
BURRAGE Charles James MM 2nd Cpl 41190 12 Div Sig Coy Royal Engineers DOW 1.8.16.
BURRELL Charles H. MM Pte M2/032366 Army Service Corps
BURRELL Ernest MM Cpl 40209 20th Manchester Regt
BURRELL Ernest "DCM+Bar,MM,MID" CSM 9067 1st Lincolnshire Regt
BURRELL Francis J.P. MM Pte R/9683 King's Royal Rifle Corps
BURRELL Frank MM Dvr 789 1/1(North Midland)Bde RFA
BURRELL Frederick MM Pte 7317 East Surrey Regt
BURRELL George H. MM Cpl W/5530 X/38 Med TM Bty RFA
BURRELL Herbert C. "DCM,MM" L/Cpl S/7992 4th Royal Fusiliers
BURRELL Joseph MM L/Cpl 42875 4th North Staffordshire Regt
BURRELL Thomas MM Sjt 10691 East Lancashire Regt
BURRELL Thomas H. MM Pnr 195974 Royal Engineers
BURRELL Walter A. MM Gnr 233438 RFA
BURRELL William "MM,CG(B)" Cpl 17385 12th York & Lancaster Regt
BURRIDGE A. MM Pte 459037 RAMC
BURRIDGE Fred MM Sjt 16809 29th Bn Machine Gun Corps
BURRIDGE George W. MM Cpl 8095 2nd York & Lancaster Regt
BURRIDGE Harry Shortman Peter MM Cpl 27518 15th Hampshire Regt KIA 21.10.18.
BURRIDGE John MM Pte 7460 1st Somerset Light Infantry
BURRIDGE Reginald J. MM Cpl 40121 Bedfordshire Regt
BURRIDGE Samuel MM Pte 74885 RAMC
BURRIDGE William H. MM Pte 23013 8th Royal West Surrey Regt
BURROUGH James W. MM L/Cpl 200235 1/4th Gloucestershire Regt
BURROUGH Richard MM Cpl A/200252 11th King's Royal Rifle Corps
BURROUGHS John MM Cpl 570252 17th London Regt
BURROUGHS Walter MM Pte 29829 1st Wiltshire Regt
BURROW Alexander MM Pte 11766 Liverpool Regt
BURROW Edwin MM Gnr 56614 C Bty RHA
BURROW George "DCM,MM" Sjt 266035 5th West Riding Regt
BURROW Harry A. MM Spr 63001 Royal Engineers
BURROW John G. MM L/Sjt 15101 Northumberland Fusiliers
BURROW Joseph MM Gnr 675500 B/88 Bde RFA
BURROW William MM Gnr 715189 D/152 Bde RFA
BURROW William MM Sjt 76480 117 Bty 26 Bde RFA KIA 25.4.18.
BURROWS Albert W. MM L/Sjt 10382 11th Royal Fusiliers
BURROWS Alfred MM Pte 7891 Norfolk Regt
BURROWS Arthur MM Cpl 4969 Machine Gun Corps
BURROWS Benjamin MM L/Cpl 43461 1st Middlesex Regt KIA 23.10.18.
BURROWS Bertie J. MM BQMS 10983 2 Siege Bty RGA
BURROWS Charles W. MM Sjt 37926 RFA
BURROWS Edward MM Pte 18594 2nd Grenadier Guards
BURROWS Edward MM Pte 592235 2/18th London Regt
BURROWS Ernest H. MM Pte 200139 Royal Warwickshire Regt
BURROWS Ernest Revell MM Sjt 16839 2nd Suffolk Regt KIA 28.3.18.
BURROWS Francis W.J. MM Spr 107426 Guards Div Sig Coy Royal Engineers
BURROWS Frank MM Sjt 46768 D/11 Bde RFA
BURROWS Frederick MM Gnr 1840 235 Bde RFA
BURROWS George MM Bdr 28981 RFA
BURROWS George W. MM Sjt 36971 RAMC
BURROWS Harold MM 2nd Cpl 486319 468 Fd Coy Royal Engineers
BURROWS Harry MM Sjt 73839 Machine Gun Corps
BURROWS Henry MM L/Cpl 43539 5/6th Royal Scots
BURROWS James MM Pte 19582 13th Liverpool Regt KIA 16.8.16.
BURROWS John MM L/Sjt 17463 2nd Coldstream Guards
BURROWS John MM(20624 R Warw)+Bar Pte 50586 11th Somerset Light Infantry
BURROWS John Richard MM Cpl Shoeing Smith 1559 465 Bty 65 Bde RFA
BURROWS John Thomas MM Sjt 7759 1st West Yorkshire Regt KIA 27.5.18.
BURROWS Leonard MM Gnr 44126 RFA
BURROWS Robert H. MM Cpl 11682 8th East Surrey Regt

BURROWS Samuel Foster MM Pte 18551 4th B Coy Bedfordshire Regt KIA 11.2.17.
BURROWS Sidney MM Pte 497171 RAMC
BURROWS Stanley Napier MM L/Cpl 24768 3rd Grenadier Guards
BURROWS T. MM Pte 328846 Cambridgeshire Regt
BURROWS Thomas MM L/Sjt 21310 22nd Manchester Regt
BURROWS William MM Pte 37815 South Wales Borderers
BURROWS William "DCM,MM,MSM" BSM 78687 RFA
BURROWS William MM Sjt 57965 42 Bde RFA KIA 19.5.17.
BURROWS William MM Pte S/40329 1st Cameron Highlanders
BURROWS William T. MM Gnr 76030 23 Bde RFA
BURRY Charles Henry MM Cpl 682612 2/22nd London Regt KIA 30.2.18.
BURRY Ernest H. MM Pte 13616 5th Wiltshire Regt
BURRY Thomas MM Spr 249108 1 Water Boring Section Royal Engineers
BURRY William John MM PTE 21788 6th Royal West Surrey Regt
BURSLEM Albert MM Cpl 278202 56 Siege Bty RGA
BURSNALL Daniel MM Gnr 113551 RGA
BURSTON Frank MM Pte 6/17458 6th South Wales Borderers
BURSTON John MM Pte 306954 8th Liverpool Regt
BURT Alfred MM Sjt 3/9123 Royal Munster Fusiliers
BURT Alfred J. MM Pte 242623 1st East Surrey Regt
BURT Arthur MM Cpl 54063 Durham Light Infantry
BURT Ernest Charles MM Gnr 52560 17 Heavy Bty RGA
BURT George MM S/Sjt Farrier 20193 RGA
BURT Harold MM Pte 81710 RAMC
BURT James MM Sjt 240022 5/6th Scottish Rifles
BURT John MM Cpl 27727 13th Royal Scots
BURT John E. MM Spr 86184 170 Tunnelling Coy Royal Engineers
BURT John W. MM Sjt 590495 2/18th London Regt
BURT Julius MM Cpl 75774 36 Bde RFA
BURT Oscar MM L/Cpl 24762 2nd Royal West Surrey Regt
BURT Peter R. MM Cpl S/13355 5th Cameron Highlanders
BURT Sidney G. "MM,MID" CSM 43 Royal Engineers
BURT T.A. MM Gnr 565752 421 Bty RFA
BURT Thomas "MM,CG(B)" Sjt 78273 15th Notts & Derby Regt
BURT Walter Ernest MM Sjt 44883 9th Essex Regt
BURT William MM L/Cpl 8433 Dorsetshire Regt
BURT William George "MM,MSM,MID" SM(Arty Clk) 28936 RGA
BURTENSHAW George Albert MM Pte 613 1st Rifle Brigade KIA 31.1.18.
BURTENSHAW Herbert Stanley MM Bdr 950390 RFA
BURTENSHAW Richard J. MM Cpl R/12741 4th King's Royal Rifle Corps
BURTLE Thomas MM Pte 41961 3rd Worcestershire Regt
BURTMORE Blenheim Edward MM Pte 20695 13th Liverpool Regt KIA 23.7.16.
BURTOFT Thomas MM Sjt 240144 1/5th C Coy York & Lancaster Regt Died 18.8.17.
BURTON Albert W.S. MM Spr 152844 ? Div Sig Coy Royal Engineers
BURTON Alfred MM Cpl 42526 2nd Suffolk Regt KIA 30.8.18.
BURTON Alfred "MM,MC(G)" Cpl 18322 11th Worcestershire Regt
BURTON Alfred O. MM Pte 20874 Royal Welsh Fusiliers
BURTON Archie Clements MM Spr 65103 105 Fd Coy Royal Engineers
BURTON Arthur MM Spr 48316 Royal Engineers
BURTON Arthur Cecil MM Pte 18288 2nd Grenadier Guards
BURTON Arthur Torrens MM Sjt 54626 RAMC
BURTON B.B. MM Sjt 1109 RFA
BURTON Charles MM Pte 32055 RAMC
BURTON Charles H. MM L/Cpl 23010 1st Grenadier Guards
BURTON Charles J. MM Sjt 83393 444 Siege Bty RGA
BURTON Charles S. MM L/Cpl 538550 Royal Engineers
BURTON Clement MM Pte 201457 1/4th Yorkshire Light Infantry
BURTON Dan "MM,MSM,MID" Sjt SS/5291 Army Service Corps
BURTON Douglas MM Pte 41043 Seaforth Highlanders
BURTON Edwin "DCM,MM" Cpl 781506 X/62 Med TM Bty RFA
BURTON Ernest MM Dvr 63810 RFA
BURTON Ernest MM Pte 15942 9th Norfolk Regt
BURTON Ernest E. MM Sjt 41411 Royal Engineers
BURTON F. MM Sjt 200278 Worcestershire Regt
BURTON Frank MM+Bar Sjt 10580 Royal Berkshire Regt
BURTON Fred MM Pte 12570 6th Northamptonshire Regt
BURTON Frederick Charles MM Sjt 233170 1/2nd London Regt KIA 10.9.18.
BURTON Frederick J. MM Cpl 8995 1st Norfolk Regt
BURTON G.W. MM Cpl G/60303 26th Royal Fusiliers
BURTON George MM Gnr 88000 13 Bde RFA
BURTON George MM Pte 28348 Durham Light Infantry
BURTON George MM Sjt 12517 11th Hampshire Regt KIA 9.9.16.
BURTON George F. MM Cpl 397001 5 Fd Coy Royal Engineers
BURTON George F. "MM,MID" Spr 37816 7 Div Sig Coy Royal Engineers
BURTON Harold MM Pte 40754 West Yorkshire Regt
BURTON Harold MM Pte 78402 RAMC DOW 15.10.17.
BURTON Harry MM Pte 70555 42 Coy Machine Gun Corps
BURTON Harry F.J. MM Pte 36009 7th Wiltshire Regt
BURTON Henry MM Pte 6/484 Rifle Brigade
BURTON Herbert MM Pte 12213 North Lancashire Regt
BURTON Herbert William MM Sjt 325034 1/1st Cambridgeshire Regt
BURTON Horace O. MM Pte 2054 2nd Royal Munster Fusiliers
BURTON James MM L/Cpl 9291 York & Lancaster Regt
BURTON James MM Pte 28509 1st Royal West Kent Regt KIA 27.9.18.
BURTON James A. MM Bdr 69176 RGA
BURTON James H. MM Pte 242405 1st West Yorkshire Regt
BURTON James Henry MM Sjt 265100 Notts & Derby Regt
BURTON John MM Pte 26173 13th Royal Scots DOW 2.11.16.
BURTON John "MM,MID" Pte 56710 RAMC
BURTON John MM Gnr 63724 RGA
BURTON John G. MM Sjt 16386 6th Bn Machine Gun Corps
BURTON John Henry MM Sjt 1844 1/7th Liverpool Regt KIA 11.8.16.
BURTON Joseph Ashton MM Sjt 300417 2/5th London Regt
BURTON Leonard MM Pte 21488 Border Regt
BURTON Percy Charles MM Pte 22142 Leicestershire Regt
BURTON Richard MM Pte 356120 10th Liverpool Regt
BURTON Robert E. MM L/Cpl 40046 South Staffordshire Regt
BURTON Robert H. MM Sjt 28802 2nd King's Own Scottish Borderers
BURTON Sidney MM Cpl 2682 7th Rifle Brigade KIA 2.12.17.
BURTON Solomon MM L/Cpl 19779 9th Notts & Derby Regt DOW 24.7.17.
BURTON Stanley MM L/Sjt 10593 1st Grenadier Guards
BURTON Thomas A. MM L/Bdr 40860 RGA
BURTON Thomas Edward MM Spr 46207 21 Div Sig Coy Royal Engineers
BURTON Thomas H. MM Pte 376912 Manchester Regt
BURTON Timothy MM Pte 44670 9th Durham Light Infantry
BURTON W.G. MM Pte 42702 2nd Essex Regt
BURTON Walter MM+Bar Sjt 590600 18th London Regt
BURTON William C. MM Pte 589 1st Welsh Guards
BURTON William R. MM Pte 5436 2nd Leinster Regt
BURTONSHAW William H. MM Sjt 355632 25th Royal Welsh Fusiliers
BURVILLE Charles MM Pte 323203 6th London Regt
BURWELL John Bertie MM L/Cpl 43616 4th Bedfordshire Regt
BURY Albert G. MM Sjt 14310 Northamptonshire Regt
BURY Harry MM Cpl 15402 11th East Lancashire Regt
BURY James "DCM,MM,MID" Sjt 2308 1/6th West Riding Regt KIA 1.4.18.
BURY James MM Pte 242742 East Lancashire Regt
BURY James A. MM Pte 32147 RAMC
BURY James T. MM Pte 50329 South Lancashire Regt
BURY James William "MM,MID" Sjt 17505 9th D Coy Scottish Rifles KIA 14.7.16.
BURY Joseph MM Gnr 67046 13 Bty RFA DOW 24.4.17.
BURY Sidney MM Sjt 16786 38 Bde RFA
BURY Thomas MM Pte 6707 1st East Lancashire Regt
BUSBRIDGE Benjamin MM Cpl 8563 2nd Wiltshire Regt
BUSBY Alfred G.E. MM Sjt 9685 Royal West Surrey Regt
BUSBY Arthur MM Cpl 29382 14th Highland Light Infantry KIA 24.11.17.
BUSBY Cornelius Colin MM Pte 2875 1/1st Bucks Bn Oxf & Bucks Light Infantry KIA 23.8.16.
BUSBY E. MM Cpl 433083 RAMC
BUSBY George MM Pte 3552 1/5th North Staffordshire Regt
BUSBY Joseph MM Pte 16493 11th Notts & Derby Regt
BUSBY Lewis J. MM Cpl 323194 6th London Regt
BUSBY Sidney F. MM Spr 40962 59 Fd Coy Royal Engineers
BUSE Glanfrwyd MM Sjt 17834 Welsh Regt
BUSFIELD Fred MM Pte 13107 2nd East Lancashire Regt
BUSFIELD Herbert MM Cpl 17/303 9th West Yorkshire Regt
BUSFIELD Joseph MM Pte 241866 2/5th West Yorkshire Regt KIA 20.7.18.
BUSH Alfred MM Cpl 26089 16th Notts & Derby Regt KIA 20.9.17.
BUSH Charles W. MM L/Cpl 248077 12th Manchester Regt

BUSH Driver Poyntz (sic) MM Pte 70709 RAMC
BUSH Frank MM Pte 34873 1st Essex Regt KIA 5.3.18.
BUSH Frederick George MM+Bar Cpl 68200 13 Bty RFA KIA 3.9.16.
BUSH Frederick John MM Sjt 3/2340 10th Essex Regt KIA 26.9.16.
BUSH George F. MM Cpl 50533 Royal Engineers
BUSH Harold MM Sjt 4530 9th Lancers
BUSH Harry MM Spr 178317 Royal Engineers
BUSH John MM Sjt Farrier 20189 5th Dragoon Guards
BUSH John MM Sjt 56858 MGC(Cavalry)
BUSH John Horace MM Pte 11593 1st Hampshire Regt
BUSH Leslie C.J. MM Pte 38882 Gloucestershire Regt
BUSH Samuel James Ewens MM Sjt Fitter 3392 59 Bty 18 Bde RFA
BUSH Thomas MM Cpl 21801 1st South Wales Borderers
BUSH William J. MM Pte 5603 Royal West Kent Regt
BUSHBY Frederick MM Pte 201464 4th Hampshire Regt
BUSHBY James MM Pte 14293 Machine Gun Corps
BUSHBY John MM Cpl 241747 7th Seaforth Highlanders
BUSHBY William George MM Gnr 45467 D/123 Bde RFA KIA 27.9.18.
BUSHELL Albert MM Sjt 240441 1/5th Northumberland Fusiliers KIA 12.4.18.
BUSHELL Alfred MM Pte 354122 Middlesex Regt
BUSHELL Ernest A. "MM,MID" Sjt Drummer 1605 1st Coldstream Guards
BUSHELL Frederick Ernest Frank MM Pte 15564 7th East Kent Regt
BUSHELL George MM Pte 17942 Middlesex Regt
BUSHELL George W. MM Pte 202998 Yorkshire Regt
BUSHELL Herbert E. MM Sjt 28239 10th East Yorkshire Regt
BUSHELL John Bates MM Pte 27115 5th Royal Berkshire Regt Died 3.11.18.
BUSHELL Percival Charles MM Pte 2130 7th East Kent Regt
BUSHELL Robert Reginald MM Sjt 2294 1/1st Cambridgeshire Regt
BUSHELL Sidney MM+Bar Bdr 60158 RGA
BUSHELL Stanley N. MM Pte 11227 4th Hampshire Regt
BUSHELL William MM Pte 2236 RAMC
BUSHILL George MM Pte 290717 1st Gordon Highlanders KIA 23.10.18.
BUSHNELL Cyril MM Pte 201335 1/1st Bucks Bn Oxf & Bucks Light Infantry
BUSHNELL Ernest MM L/Cpl 18261 15th Hampshire Regt KIA 5.8.17.
BUSHNELL Horace G. MM Cpl 20089 Royal Welsh Fusiliers
BUSHNELL Joseph E. MM Pte 46249 Royal Welsh Fusiliers
BUSKELL Arthur E. MM CSM 240626 1/8th Middlesex Regt
BUSKELL John MM Sjt 601 6 Div Ammn Col RFA
BUSS Charles MM Pte 203075 13th Royal Sussex Regt
BUSS Charles E. MM Cpl 4845 1st Rifle Brigade
BUSS Fred MM Sjt 9981 East Kent Regt
BUSSELL C.W. MM L/Cpl 20197 East Kent Regt
BUSSELL Frederick R. "MM,MID" Sjt G/1379 8th Royal Sussex Regt
BUSSEY Frank T. MM Spr 84896 34 Div Sig Coy Royal Engineers
BUSSEY Thomas MM L/Cpl 42156 Yorkshire Light Infantry
BUSSINGHAM John E. MM Pte 202757 Royal Lancaster Regt
BUSSINGHAM John W. MM Pte 19738 1st Bedfordshire Regt
BUSTARD Ernest Albert MM Dvr 6403 RFA
BUSTEED John MM Spr 26254 1 Div Sig Coy Royal Engineers
BUSTIN Charles MM Cpl 79921 176 Tunnelling Coy Royal Engineers
BUSTIN Frederick MM L/Cpl 202396 11th Royal Sussex Regt
BUSTIN William Henry MM Pte 235061 16th Notts & Derby Regt KIA 21.3.18.
BUSWELL Albert MM Gnr 39582 D/160 Bde RFA
BUSWELL Percy E. MM+Bar Sjt 700959 23rd London Regt
BUSWELL Ralph MM Cpl 145392 1/1st Northamptonshire Yeomanry
BUSWELL Ted MM L/Cpl 40783 1st Leicestershire Regt
BUTCHART David R. MM Pte 43282 Seaforth Highlanders
BUTCHART James Greig MM Pte 13290 Scots Guards
BUTCHART Thomas MM Pte 76275 16th Notts & Derby Regt KIA 16.8.17.
BUTCHER A. "MM,MID" Pte 16738 1st Essex Regt
BUTCHER Albert MM Cpl G/145 6th Royal West Surrey Regt KIA 12.5.17.
BUTCHER Albert MM Gnr 142357 352 Siege Bty RGA
BUTCHER Arthur C. MM Dvr 63814 RFA
BUTCHER Bertram A. MM Cpl 87233 Y/12 Med TM Bty RFA
BUTCHER Charles MM Pte 12668 11th Suffolk Regt DOW 4.12.18.
BUTCHER Charles MM+Bar Spr 479981 Royal Engineers
BUTCHER Charles E. MM Sjt 390863 9th London Regt
BUTCHER Clarence Joseph "MM,MSM" Sjt 16160 L Sig Coy Royal Engineers
BUTCHER Daniel MM Pte 358455 Liverpool Regt
BUTCHER David J. MM Pte 5/18007 5th South Wales Borderers
BUTCHER Edwin G. MM+Bar Sjt 423400 10th London Regt
BUTCHER Frederick C. MM Pte 65242 8 Fd Amb RAMC
BUTCHER George MM Gnr 138853 RGA
BUTCHER George William MM Sjt 200084 2/4th Oxf & Bucks Light Infantry
BUTCHER H. MM Cpl 573085 17th London Regt
BUTCHER Harold H. MM Sjt GS/8010 11th Royal West Kent Regt
BUTCHER Harold W.T. MM Sjt 781817 D/312 Bde RFA
BUTCHER Harry MM Pte 18571 Royal Berkshire Regt
BUTCHER Henry H. MM Pte 60902 Royal Welsh Fusiliers
BUTCHER Henry J. MM Pte 65252 Machine Gun Corps
BUTCHER Herbert J. MM Sjt G/10826 11th Royal West Surrey Regt
BUTCHER Herbert Thomas MM Dvr 40276 D/83 Bde RFA DOW 29.7.17.
BUTCHER Horace G. MM Pte M2/113438 Army Service Corps att RAMC
BUTCHER James MM Pte 323618 6th London Regt
BUTCHER John E.H. MM L/Cpl 1856 17th Royal Fusiliers
BUTCHER John George "MM,MID" Pte M2/120788 Army Service Corps
BUTCHER Mark MM Pte 12100 9th Essex Regt
BUTCHER Noel E. MM Sjt 250506 1/3rd London Regt
BUTCHER Norman MM Pte 18629 1st Notts & Derby Regt KIA 5.3.17.
BUTCHER Percy MM Cpl 5488 2nd A Coy Rifle Brigade KIA 24.10.16.
BUTCHER Percy I. MM Cpl 1816 1/4th Suffolk Regt
BUTCHER Philip N. MM 2nd Cpl 42445 Royal Engineers
BUTCHER Randolph MM Pte R/11210 1st King's Royal Rifle Corps DOW 6.5.17.
BUTCHER Reginald MM Pte 18814 RAMC
BUTCHER Robert MM Sjt 2238 1/4th Royal Lancaster Regt
BUTCHER Stanley George MM Bdr 341159 521 Siege Bty RGA
BUTCHER Thomas MM Sjt L/11337 4th Royal Fusiliers
BUTCHER Wallace E. MM+Bar Gnr 208384 RFA
BUTCHER Walter MM Gnr 831647 C/306 Bde RFA
BUTCHER William MM Pte 243632 1/5th Royal West Surrey Regt
BUTCHER William MM Pte 61159 Royal Fusiliers
BUTCHER William MM Cpl 184 7th Royal Sussex Regt
BUTCHER William J. MM Pte 4905 13th Royal Fusiliers
BUTCHERS William MM Cpl 72001 8th Bn Machine Gun Corps
BUTLER Abraham MM Pte B/200663 7th Rifle Brigade DOW 29.9.17.
BUTLER Albert Edward MM Pte 10934 2nd Coldstream Guards
BUTLER Albert Henry MM Cpl 200186 2/4th Royal Berkshire Regt KIA 21.3.18.
BUTLER Alfred E. MM Bdr 66367 RGA
BUTLER Alfred Henry MM Pte 16913 10th Worcestershire Regt KIA 4.10.17.
BUTLER Alfred J. MM Sjt 56323 9 Div Sig Coy Royal Engineers
BUTLER Archibald J. MM Pte 13261 8th Royal Berkshire Regt
BUTLER Arthur MM Pte 5365 Rifle Brigade
BUTLER Arthur L. MM Pte C/9149 King's Royal Rifle Corps
BUTLER Arthur Leonard "DCM,MM" Sjt 612175 1/19th London Regt
BUTLER Arthur William MM CSM L/5613 1st D Coy Royal West Surrey Regt DOW 5.12.17.
BUTLER Benjamin MM Pte 20148 Royal Berkshire Regt
BUTLER Benjamin MM Pte 200771 1/5th West Yorkshire Regt DOW 18.2.19.
BUTLER C. MM+Bar Sjt 31695 RFA
BUTLER C.G. MM L/Cpl 1959 Middlesex Regt
BUTLER Cecil B. MM Sjt 151233 104th Bn Machine Gun Corps
BUTLER Charles MM Pte 26863 8th Royal Lancaster Regt
BUTLER Charles MM Bugler 1556 1/1st Cambridgeshire Regt
BUTLER Charles Herbert Thomlinson MM Pte 70673 13 Coy Machine Gun Corps
BUTLER Charles Samuel Frederick MM Pte 479417 144 Coy Labour Corps
BUTLER Charles W. MM Sjt 895281 A/64 Bde RFA
BUTLER Christopher MM Pte 5696 Royal Dublin Fusiliers
BUTLER David MM Cpl 21717 6th West Yorkshire Regt
BUTLER David MM Spr 7037 2 Field Squadron Royal Engineers
BUTLER Edgar MM Sjt 775073 C/245 Bde RFA DOW 13.9.17.
BUTLER Edgar H. MM Sjt 16981 10th Royal Warwickshire Regt
BUTLER Edgar Jesse MM Sjt 285062 Oxfordshire Yeomanry Died 5.11.18.

BUTLER Edward MM Gnr 50400 RGA
BUTLER Edward MM Pte 7509 11th Royal Fusiliers KIA 17.2.17.
BUTLER Edward MM BQMS 173693 479 Siege Bty RGA
BUTLER Edwin MM Sjt 57848 38th Bn Machine Gun Corps
BUTLER Emmanuel MM Pte 20974 7/8th King's Own Scottish Borderers KIA 31.7.17.
BUTLER Eric MM Pte 43720 8th Royal Berkshire Regt
BUTLER Eric C. MM Cpl 45229 1/1st Surrey Yeomanry
BUTLER Ernest MM L/Bdr 207535 D/150 Bde RFA
BUTLER Ernest MM Cpl 4569 1st Rifle Brigade
BUTLER F.E. MM L/Cpl S/1577 16th Rifle Brigade
BUTLER Frank MM Cpl 62244 51 Siege Bty RGA
BUTLER Frank MM L/Bdr 86409 276 Siege Bty RGA
BUTLER Frank MM Sjt 8367 1st Bedfordshire Regt
BUTLER Frank A. MM Pte 16066 East Surrey Regt
BUTLER Frank Percival MM Pte 49306 Bedfordshire Regt
BUTLER Frederick MM Pte 240907 6th North Staffordshire Regt
BUTLER Frederick MM Pte 10189 10th Royal West Surrey Regt KIA 26.3.18.
BUTLER Frederick George Talbot MM L/Cpl STK/630 10th Royal Fusiliers
BUTLER George MM Pte S/7691 1st Royal Highlanders
BUTLER George MM Gnr Sig 52564 164 Siege Bty RGA
BUTLER George MM+Bar Sjt 401484 1st Essex Regt
BUTLER George MM Cpl 504413 503 Fd Coy Royal Engineers
BUTLER George MM RSM 5697 2nd North Lancashire Regt
BUTLER George MM+Bar Cpl 51728 6th Liverpool Regt
BUTLER George MM Dvr 755264 RFA
BUTLER George William MM Cpl 107419 B/187 Bde RFA DOW 28.9.17.
BUTLER Harold MM Gnr 170001 170 Siege Bty RGA
BUTLER Harry MM L/Cpl 23468 150 Coy Machine Gun Corps KIA 23.4.17.
BUTLER Henry "DCM,MM,MID" S/Sjt 18566 3 Fd Amb RAMC
BUTLER Henry MM Pte 5620 2nd Scots Guards
BUTLER Henry MM L/Cpl 14468 Royal Lancaster Regt
BUTLER Herbert MM Cpl 99273 RFA
BUTLER Herbert J. MM Cpl 40750 Suffolk Regt
BUTLER Herbert W. MM Sjt 425656 10th London Regt
BUTLER Herman Seymour MM Sjt 13171 Gloucestershire Regt
BUTLER Jack MM Gnr 79120 29 Bty 126 Bde RFA KIA 29.3.18.
BUTLER James MM Pte 128552 3rd Bn Machine Gun Corps
BUTLER Jesse H. MM Pte 1974 GMGR
BUTLER Jesse J. MM Pte 76969 9th Royal Fusiliers
BUTLER John MM Pte 45478 Leicestershire Regt
BUTLER John MM L/Sjt 7803 2nd Leinster Regt
BUTLER John MM Gnr 49339 RGA KIA 27.9.18. Real name Buckley.
BUTLER John MM L/Cpl 20168 Royal Irish Fusiliers
BUTLER John MM Bdr 121147 156 Bde RFA
BUTLER John A. MM Pte 64630 15th Yorkshire Light Infantry
BUTLER John Francis "DCM,MM" Sjt 11420 Shropshire Light Infantry
BUTLER John S. MM Pte 18441 Notts & Derby Regt
BUTLER John T. MM Sjt 332095 Highland Light Infantry
BUTLER Joseph MM Bdr 21526 RGA
BUTLER Joseph MM Bdr 407 W/49 Med TM Bty RFA
BUTLER Joseph Henry MM Pte 8982 2nd Lincolnshire Regt
BUTLER Leonard MM Pte 511 2nd Leinster Regt
BUTLER Lewis Claude Cyril MM Cpl 768 Rifle Brigade Died 1.4.17.
BUTLER Lewis J. "MM,MID" Sjt 6912 2nd Worcestershire Regt
BUTLER Matthew MM Cpl 24330 Machine Gun Corps
BUTLER Maurice R. MM Pte 44866 1st King's Royal Rifle Corps
BUTLER Michael MM Gnr 100835 110 Bde RFA
BUTLER Michael P. MM Pte 131151 45th Royal Fusiliers
BUTLER Morris A. "DCM,MM,MID" QMS 1772 1 Fd Amb RAMC
BUTLER Pierce Francis "MM,MSM" Sjt 10845 Royal Engineers
BUTLER Reginald MM Bdr 29394 A/91 Bde RFA
BUTLER Richard MM Pte 13766 10th West Riding Regt
BUTLER Richard Henry MM Sjt 12871 8th Norfolk Regt
BUTLER Robert MM Cpl 1026 RFA
BUTLER Robert Alexander MM Pte 5199 2nd Royal Warwickshire Regt KIA 9.10.17.
BUTLER Roderick MM Cpl 1539 21st London Regt
BUTLER Stanley Reginald MM Sjt 9241 7th Somerset Light Infantry KIA 27.3.18.
BUTLER T. MM Pte 437157 RAMC
BUTLER Theodore MM+Bar L/Sjt 9243 Welsh Regt
BUTLER Thomas MM Cpl 10957 6th York & Lancaster Regt
BUTLER Thomas MM Sjt 13048 2nd Middlesex Regt KIA 1.7.16.
BUTLER Thomas MM Sjt 18557 Royal Engineers
BUTLER Thomas MM Pte 18631 1st Royal Dublin Fusiliers KIA 10.10.17.
BUTLER Thomas MM Pte 7784 Middlesex Regt
BUTLER Thomas A. MM Cpl 43911 3 Bde RHA
BUTLER Thomas Broadhurst MM Pte 356460 10th Liverpool Regt
BUTLER Thomas Henry "MM,MID" Cpl 2054 1st Dragoons KIA 3.3.18.
BUTLER W.(or J.W.) "DCM,MM" L/Cpl 7778 13th Royal Fusiliers
BUTLER W.G. MM Pte 44559 1st King's Royal Rifle Corps
BUTLER William MM Sjt 9484 109 Fd Amb RAMC
BUTLER William MM L/Cpl 40691 Gordon Highlanders
BUTLER William "DCM,MM+2 Bars,MID" Cpl G/1229 4th Middlesex Regt
BUTLER William "DCM,MM(15360 North Fus)" Sjt 50652 1st East Yorkshire Regt
BUTLER William MM L/Cpl 42440 8th West Yorkshire Regt
BUTLER William MM Cpl 15/12210 Liverpool Regt
BUTLER William H. MM Spr 217582 427 Fd Coy Royal Engineers
BUTLER William Henry MM Cpl 19444 2nd Royal Berkshire Regt KIA 2.4.18.
BUTLER William N. MM Pte 253165 3rd London Regt
BUTLER-DOWERS John Henry MM Pte 372183 3 Fd Amb RAMC
BUTLERS A. MM L/Cpl 43056 Royal Highlanders
BUTLIN Ernest G. MM Pte 253415 3rd London Regt
BUTLIN James L. MM Sjt 15872 6th Northamptonshire Regt
BUTLIN William Roland MM Spr 151581 182 Tunnelling Coy Royal Engineers
BUTLING Bert C. MM L/Cpl 11984 12th East Surrey Regt
BUTT Albert MM Sjt 566 2nd Middlesex Regt
BUTT Austin MM Cpl 7149 89 Coy Machine Gun Corps KIA 9.4.17.
BUTT Bernard F. MM Pte 9999 Royal West Surrey Regt
BUTT Berthold W.H. MM L/Cpl 4185 Suffolk Regt
BUTT Charles MM L/Cpl 40963 1/4th Royal Lancaster Regt
BUTT George MM Pte 738167 24th London Regt
BUTT Richard MM Cpl 241000 1/5th Gloucestershire Regt
BUTTALL Frederick A. MM Sjt 64030 17th Worcestershire Regt
BUTTEFIELD Albert MM Pte 43699 8th Worcestershire Regt
BUTTER Andrew James Moyes MM Sjt 106265 Royal Engineers
BUTTERFIELD Alexander MM Pte G/2546 12th Middlesex Regt DOW 6.1.18.
BUTTERFIELD Alfred Fallows MM Cpl 356348 1/10th Liverpool Regt KIA 30.11.17.
BUTTERFIELD Arthur H. MM L/Bdr L/4602 C/153 Bde RFA
BUTTERFIELD George Hartley MM Pte 31399 2nd York & Lancaster Regt
BUTTERFIELD Horace MM+Bar L/Cpl 16/1553 1/5th West Yorkshire Regt DOW 2.11.18.
BUTTERFIELD James MM Pte 265891 5th West Riding Regt
BUTTERFIELD James MM Pte 266671 1/1st Hertfordshire Regt KIA 23.8.18.
BUTTERFIELD Walter MM Pte 13731 2nd West Riding Regt
BUTTERFIELD Wilfred MM Sjt 16899 2nd Northumberland Fusiliers
BUTTERICK Charles MM Pte 26912 South Staffordshire Regt
BUTTERISS Walter George MM Pte 13234 Leicestershire Regt
BUTTERLY Thomas MM Pte 26205 8th Royal Inniskilling Fusiliers KIA 7.8.17.
BUTTERS Andrew MM L/Cpl 13062 9th Northumberland Fusiliers KIA 16.5.17.
BUTTERS Edward H. MM Pte 22200 Royal Fusiliers
BUTTERS Frederick Hall Robarts MM Pte 200256 5/6th Scottish Rifles
BUTTERS Sid MM Bdr 64674 2 Bde RFA
BUTTERS Thomas MM Pte 1576 1/4th Northumberland Fusiliers KIA 15.9.16.
BUTTERS Walter H. MM Bdr 28954 B/152 Bde RFA
BUTTERWICK Edgar MM Pte 21119 RAMC
BUTTERWOOD John "MM+Bar,MID" Sjt 3/6936 2nd Yorkshire Regt
BUTTERWORTH Albert "DCM,MM" L/Cpl 10235 18th Manchester Regt
BUTTERWORTH Archie MM L/Cpl 15/1574 11th West Yorkshire Regt KIA 20.9.17.
BUTTERWORTH Arthur MM+Bar Sjt 705376 RFA
BUTTERWORTH Edgar MM Sjt 250681 10th Manchester Regt
BUTTERWORTH Edmond MM Pte 580 2nd Arg & Suth Highlanders
BUTTERWORTH Edward MM Pte 200581 2/5th Lancashire Fusiliers
BUTTERWORTH Ernest MM Bdr 35712 RFA
BUTTERWORTH Ernest MM Pte 40071 1st Northumberland Fusiliers KIA 13.4.18.
BUTTERWORTH Fielden MM Gnr 149145 RFA

BUTTERWORTH Frank MM L/Cpl 201593 1/4th Royal Lancaster Regt
BUTTERWORTH Fred MM+Bar Sjt 7255 11th Royal Fusiliers KIA 4.11.18.
BUTTERWORTH H. MM L/Cpl C/778 King's Royal Rifle Corps
BUTTERWORTH Herbert MM Gnr 67453 RFA
BUTTERWORTH James MM Pte 1753 West Yorkshire Regt
BUTTERWORTH John MM Pte 6462 7th East Lancashire Regt DOW 31.7.16.
BUTTERWORTH John MM Bdr 36792 RFA
BUTTERWORTH John E. MM L/Cpl 87305 204 Fd Coy Royal Engineers
BUTTERWORTH M.A. MM Pte 21415 9th Essex Regt
BUTTERWORTH Samuel "MM,MID" Pte 15891 1/4th Shropshire Light Infantry
BUTTERWORTH Sydney MM Pte 251145 Manchester Regt
BUTTERWORTH Tom MM Gnr 47035 RFA
BUTTERWORTH Walter MM Sjt PS/7010 Royal Fusiliers
BUTTERWORTH William MM Gnr 202282 Royal Lancaster Regt
BUTTERY Harry MM+Bar Sjt 66952 174 Tunnelling Coy Royal Engineers
BUTTERY Harry "MM,MID" Gnr 38441 RFA
BUTTERY Herbert MM Dvr 45347 104 Bde RFA
BUTTERY Richard "DCM,MM" L/Sjt 15862 11th West Yorkshire Regt
BUTTERY Thomas Frederick MM Sjt 306795 8th West Yorkshire Regt KIA 28.7.18.
BUTTERY William G. MM+Bar Sjt 19873 Machine Gun Corps
BUTTERY William Thomas MM Pte 27729 2nd Bn Machine Gun Corps
BUTTLE Albert A. MM Gnr 645168 RFA
BUTTLE John MM Spr 444287 Royal Engineers
BUTTLE Thomas MM Pte 3/7300 6th Somerset Light Infantry
BUTTLE William H. MM Sjt 10361 2nd Welsh Regt
BUTTLING Herbert G. MM Pte 149693 Machine Gun Corps
BUTTON F. MM Pte 18833 Bedfordshire Regt
BUTTON Frederick Charles MM Pte 2945 1/6th North Staffordshire Regt
BUTTON Frederick W. MM Sjt 20874 18th Lancashire Fusiliers
BUTTON H. MM Cpl 9025 9th Essex Regt
BUTTON James "MM,MSM" Sjt 82225 257 Tunnelling Coy Royal Engineers
BUTTON John MM L/Cpl 22336 Liverpool Regt
BUTTON Robert N. "DCM,MM" CSM 7803 11th Northumberland Fusiliers
BUTTON Sydney Victor MM L/Cpl 12117 10th West Yorkshire Regt KIA 23.3.18.
BUTTON William J. "MM,MID" Sjt 134260 Royal Engineers
BUTTRESS Albert E. MM Gnr 16438 6th Northamptonshire Regt
BUTTWELL John MM Cpl 1421 7th Royal West Kent Regt KIA 24.4.18.
BUXTON Albert Edward MM Pte 19774 9th Notts & Derby Regt KIA 4.10.17.
BUXTON Albert Edward MM Spr 50007 20 Div Sig Coy Royal Engineers DOW 30.11.17.
BUXTON Arthur MM Bdr 30174 X/17 Med TM Bty RGA
BUXTON Cedric MM Sjt 99367 D/67 Bde RFA
BUXTON Charles E. MM Cpl 84560 Machine Gun Corps
BUXTON Charles F. MM Gnr L/39013 A/178 Bde RFA
BUXTON Edwin MM L/Sjt G/1243 6th East Kent Regt
BUXTON Ernest MM "MM,MID" Pte 890 1/1st North Somerset Yeomanry
BUXTON Ernest H. MM Pte 17305 9th Norfolk Regt
BUXTON Frederick MM Sjt 207453 Royal Engineers
BUXTON Harry MM 2nd Cpl 254283 Royal Engineers
BUXTON Horace MM Pte 16828 Leicestershire Regt
BUXTON James MM L/Cpl 10049 1st North Staffordshire Regt
BUXTON John MM Gnr 800477 B/231 Bde RFA
BUXTON John MM Pte 52810 7th Liverpool Regt
BUXTON Markham MM Pte 117149 7th Bn Machine Gun Corps
BUXTON Percy MM Pte 45136 1/5th London Regt DOW 11.12.18.
BUXTON Robert MM Cpl 6493 Royal Warwickshire Regt
BUXTON Steven "DCM,MM" Sjt 42497 156 Siege Bty RGA
BUXTON Thomas MM Pte 3205 Liverpool Regt
BUXTON William MM Sjt 7599 1st King's Royal Rifle Corps att MGC.
BUXTON William MM Cpl 40687 Bedfordshire Regt
BUZAN Charles Edward MM Pte 103662 1/3rd(Welsh)Fd Amb RAMC
BUZZARD Charles Herbert MM Pte 22763 1st Lancashire Fusiliers
BUZZARD John "MM,MID" L/Cpl 1838 8th East Kent Regt
BYARD Charles H. MM 2nd Cpl 388769 Royal Engineers

BYARS William MM Sjt 241268 1/7th Royal Highlanders KIA 27.3.18.
BYART Albert George MM Pte 698125 22nd London Regt KIA 10.10.18.
BYART Harry MM Cpl 70883 421 Bty RFA
BYDAWELL Francis MM Pte 9677 1st Shropshire Light Infantry KIA 8.9.17.
BYDE David MM L/Cpl 9502 2nd Royal Berkshire Regt KIA 16.11.16.
BYE Harry MM Pte 4042 Yorkshire Regt
BYE Henry J. MM Sjt M/32611 1 Cav Div Advanced Park Army Service Corps
BYE John Thomas D. MM Pte 205011 East Surrey Regt
BYE Robert MM Cpl 240432 1/8th Middlesex Regt
BYE Samuel MM Pte 7258 Middlesex Regt
BYE Wesley MM Cpl 64539 X/4 Med TM Bty RFA
BYERS Allan MM Cpl 112258 Royal Engineers
BYERS G.F. MM L/Cpl P13371 Military Mounted Police
BYERS John W. MM L/Cpl 42249 6th Leicestershire Regt
BYERS William MM Pte 295916 12th Royal Scots Fusiliers
BYERS William MM Pte 15325 11th Border Regt
BYFORD Albert E. MM Sjt 19247 Machine Gun Corps
BYFORD H. MM Cpl 570047 17th London Regt
BYFORD Percy MM Pte 251269 1/5th Essex Regt
BYGRAVE A. MM Pte 18251 Royal West Kent Regt
BYGRAVE Frank MM L/Cpl 60030 Royal Fusiliers
BYGRAVE William MM Pte 20748 1/1st Hertfordshire Regt
BYHAM Harry MM Sjt 24081 Duke of Cornwall's LI
BYHAM William Arthur MM Cpl A606 7th King's Royal Rifle Corps
BYLES Harry J. MM+Bar Sjt 8630 1st Royal Berkshire Regt
BYLES Herbert T. "DCM,MM" Sjt 139138 177 Tunnelling Coy Royal Engineers
BYNG E. "MM,MID" Sjt 1202 GMGR
BYNG G. MM 2nd Cpl 311095 10 Div Sig Coy Royal Engineers
BYNG Hubert MM Cpl 240072 1/8th Worcestershire Regt
BYOTT George V. MM Pte 698126 22nd London Regt
BYRD Bernard "MM,MID" Sjt 16517 Royal Dublin Fusiliers
BYRNE Augustine MM Sjt 14874 2nd Royal Dublin Fusiliers
BYRNE Cornelius MM Gnr 153550 RGA
BYRNE E.O. MM Pte 75661 Machine Gun Corps
BYRNE Ellen MM Sister F QAIMNS
BYRNE Frank MM Pte 201468 1/4th Cheshire Regt KIA 25.10.18.
BYRNE Frank MM Pte 325492 9th Durham Light Infantry
BYRNE Frederick MM Pte 251953 13th Durham Light Infantry
BYRNE George N. MM Pte 108185 Machine Gun Corps
BYRNE George W. MM Pte 14309 Northamptonshire Regt
BYRNE James MM Spr 664 Royal Engineers
BYRNE James MM Pte 8106 Irish Guards
BYRNE James MM Cpl 8692 North Lancashire Regt
BYRNE James Christopher MM Sjt 4535 1st Royal Welsh Fusiliers
BYRNE John MM Pte 24807 1st Royal Dublin Fusiliers
BYRNE John MM Gnr 84194 RFA
BYRNE John MM Pte 9590 Royal Dublin Fusiliers
BYRNE John G. MM Sjt 1730 2nd Irish Guards
BYRNE Joseph MM Pte 8868 1st Royal Dublin Fusiliers
BYRNE Laurence "DCM,MM" CQMS 8901 1st Royal Dublin Fusiliers
BYRNE Michael MM Sjt 16601 15th Cheshire Regt
BYRNE Michael "DCM,MM+Bar,CG(B)" Pte 6945 2nd Leinster Regt
BYRNE Michael "MM,MID" Sjt 11538 350 Siege Bty RGA
BYRNE Michael MM Pte 17366 Yorkshire Regt
BYRNE Michael MM Cpl 86516 Royal Engineers
BYRNE Michael MM Gnr 59532 RGA
BYRNE Patrick MM Pte 18057 1st Royal Munster Fusiliers
BYRNE Patrick MM Pte 2408 1/5th South Lancashire Regt
BYRNE Patrick MM Pte 3533 7th Leinster Regt KIA 9.9.16.
BYRNE Peter MM Pte 18213 1st Royal Dublin Fusiliers
BYRNE Ralph MM Sjt 5454 RFA
BYRNE Ralph Eugene MM Bdr 88732 C/180 Bde RFA KIA 4.4.18.
BYRNE Robert Henry MM Pte 9017 2nd Leinster Regt
BYRNE Thomas MM L/Cpl 8849 Royal Lancaster Regt
BYRNE Thomas MM Pte 202056 Liverpool Regt
BYRNE Thomas MM Pte 7596 2nd Leinster Regt
BYRNE Thomas MM Pte 5460 1st Royal Dublin Fusiliers Died 6.7.18.
BYRNE Walter MM Pte 11114 2nd East Surrey Regt
BYRNE William G. MM Spr 27236 Royal Engineers
BYRNES Patrick MM Pte 6186 1st Irish Guards
BYROM Thomas Harrop MM Pte 350381 9th Manchester Regt
BYROM William H. MM L/Sjt 10154 1st Cheshire Regt

BYRON Archibald L. MM Pte 11419 Duke of Cornwall's LI
BYRON David MM Cpl 13086 42 Army Troops Coy Royal Engineers
BYRON Frank MM Spr 22599 5 Fd Coy Royal Engineers
BYRON Harry MM Pte 702256 23rd London Regt
BYSOUTH Ernest MM Pte 23475 8th Bedfordshire Regt
BYTHEWAY Henry MM Pte 19550 1st South Staffordshire Regt
BYTHEWAY Joseph MM Pte 11210 Oxf & Bucks Light Infantry
BYWATER Harry MM L/Cpl 21886 10th West Yorkshire Regt
BYWATER William MM Pte 16639 8th South Wales Borderers

C

CABLE Alfred MM Sjt 124420 19th Bn Machine Gun Corps
CABLE Charles MM Cpl 722996 24th London Regt
CABLE Charles Windsor MM CSM 39650 13th Royal Scots
CABLE George MM Pte 33857 West Riding Regt
CABLE George "MM,MID" Pte 2/9532 1st South Wales Borderers
CABLE Joseph MM Pte 25/873 Northumberland Fusiliers
CABLE Leonard Colin MM Pte 6426 12th Royal Fusiliers KIA 15.6.17.
CABLE Samuel MM Cpl 4/6121 14th Durham Light Infantry KIA 23.4.17.
CABLE Victor J. MM Bdr 73207 5 Bde RFA
CABORN Frank. MM L/Cpl 11/246 East Yorkshire Regt
CACKETT Charles "MM,MIDx2" CQMS 69531 4 Fd Svy Coy Royal Engineers
CACKETT Harry MM Sjt 41270 Rifle Brigade att 1/28th London Regt
CACKETT Harry MM Sjt 41270 Rifle Brigade
CADAMY Charles W. MM Pte R/12325 13th King's Royal Rifle Corps
CADD Alfred "MM,MSM" Sjt L/17268 RFA
CADDEN Bernard MM Pte 201802 1/4th Cheshire Regt
CADDEN David MM Pte 60205 RAMC
CADDICK Joseph H. MM L/Cpl 321543 6th London Regt
CADDICK William MM Sjt 31399 RGA
CADDIS Robert MM Pte 9900 Arg & Suth Highlanders
CADDOO George MM Pte 16874 Royal Inniskilling Fusiliers
CADDOW William H. MM Spr 48599 Royal Engineers
CADDY A. MM Pte 30009 Dorsetshire Regt
CADE Albert MM Pte 12348 99 Fd Amb RAMC
CADE Herbert J. MM L/Sjt 25370 103 Fd Amb RAMC
CADMAN George MM Pte 15422 8th South Lancashire Regt
CADMAN Harold MM CQMS 17842 20th Manchester Regt
CADMAN Harry MM Pte 28464 11th Notts & Derby Regt
CADMAN John W. MM Pte 12292 10th Lancashire Fusiliers
CADWALLADER Arthur E. MM Pte 43554 5th South Staffordshire Regt
CADWALLADER John MM Spr 151480 171 Tunnelling Coy Royal Engineers
CADWALLADER William George "MM,MID,CG(B)" Spr 101635 Fourth Army HQ Sig Coy Royal Engineers DOW 2.8.18.
CADWELL John MM Sjt L/3421 D/149 Bde RFA
CADY David MM Pte 24679 Royal Fusiliers
CAESAR George "MM,MSM" Sjt G/2379 8th Royal Sussex Regt KIA 7.8.18.
CAESAR Henry MM Sjt 2419 1/1st Monmouthshire Regt
CAESAR William C. MM Pte 78169 4th Royal Fusiliers
CAFFERTY Cornelius MM Pte 24774 1/4th Royal Lancaster Regt KIA 15.1.19.
CAFFERY John MM Pte 38491 Durham Light Infantry
CAFFREY Charles MM Pte 14654 4th Liverpool Regt DOW 16.4.18.
CAFFREY James "MM,MID" Cpl 32098 38 Bde RFA
CAFFREY Joseph Edward MM Sjt 7157 Coldstream Guards
CAFFREY Martin MM Sjt 203098 East Yorkshire Regt
CAFFYN George W. MM L/Cpl 91085 130 Fd Coy Royal Engineers
CAGE Albert W. MM Gnr 915368 C/160 Bde RFA
CAGE Philip MM+Bar Pte 4724 8th East Surrey Regt KIA 1.9.18.
CAGILL Joseph MM Pte 148600 55th Bn Machine Gun Corps
CAHILL Bernard S. MM Sjt 49835 105 Fd Amb RAMC
CAHILL Christopher MM Pte 36697 South Lancashire Regt
CAHILL Edward MM Bdr 91639 RFA
CAHILL Edward MM Pte 5017 Royal West Kent Regt
CAHILL Edward Albert MM Pte 12/1277 1/4th York & Lancaster Regt
CAHILL James "MM,MID" Cpl 2400 1/5th Yorkshire Light Infantry
CAHILL James MM Pte 8168 1st Leinster Regt
CAHILL Joseph MM Sjt S/2403 17th Royal Sussex Regt
CAHILL Joseph "MM,MSM" Sjt 9829 2nd Royal Dublin Fusiliers
CAHILL Lawrence MM Pte 260137 2nd South Wales Borderers
CAHILL Michael MM Pte 3/19864 South Wales Borderers
CAHILL Patrick MM Pte 1/9244 1st Royal Munster Fusiliers
CAHILL Patrick MM Pte 7529 2nd Royal Munster Fusiliers
CAHILL Richard MM Gnr 80569 RFA
CAHILL Thomas Laurence MM Sjt 6457 2nd Irish Guards KIA 26.3.18.
CAHILL William MM Sjt 200159 5th South Staffordshire Regt
CAIGER Sidney T. MM Spr 26851 9 Div Sig Coy Royal Engineers
CAIL Thomas W. MM Dvr 47791 Royal Engineers
CAILES Albert J. MM 2nd Cpl 43463 Royal Engineers
CAIN Arthur Reginald MM Cpl 9760 1st Border Regt KIA 23.4.17.
CAIN Benjamin MM Pte 241834 2/4th North Lancashire Regt KIA 29.8.18.
CAIN George Thomas MM L/Cpl 8229 13th Cheshire Regt KIA 10.8.17.
CAIN James A. MM Sjt 240998 5th King's Own Scottish Borderers
CAIN James Edward MM Gnr L/25688 D/168 Bde RFA KIA 30.10.17.
CAIN John MM Sjt 5568 69 Coy Machine Gun Corps
CAIN John Charles MM L/Cpl G/2137 1st East Kent Regt
CAIN John Joseph MM Pte 22672 23rd Manchester Regt
CAIN Michael H. MM Pte 241679 1/5th East Lancashire Regt
CAIN Peter MM Pte 8027 12th Lancashire Fusiliers
CAIN T. MM Pte 241832 South Lancashire Regt
CAIN William MM L/Cpl 1463 16th Lancers
CAIN William MM Sjt 21/123 Northumberland Fusiliers
CAIN William R. MM Sjt 7154 2nd Royal Scots
CAINE Frederick MM L/Cpl 2380 1/5th West Riding Regt KIA 9.10.17.
CAINE John MM L/Cpl 19583 2nd East Lancashire Regt KIA 27.5.18.
CAINE Thomas Arthur MM Bdr 5549 D/86 Bde RFA
CAINE Victor MM Sjt 11309 1st South Staffordshire Regt KIA 26.10.17.
CAINE Walter MM Sjt 43484 Royal Engineers
CAINE William MM Spr 27230 III Corps Sig Coy Royal Engineers
CAINES Charles Benjamin MM Cpl 1714 17th Royal Fusiliers KIA 31.10.18.
CAINES Charles J. MM CSM 4938 48th Bn Machine Gun Corps
CAINEY Henry MM Gnr 676944 B/285 Bde RFA
CAINEY Henry MM L/Sjt 25196 1st Somerset Light Infantry
CAIRNEY Joseph MM Pte S/2359 Gordon Highlanders
CAIRNIE John MM L/Cpl 41675 5/6th Scottish Rifles
CAIRNIE Robert MM Pte 43107 Royal Highlanders
CAIRNIE Robert MM Pte 200966 Royal Highlanders
CAIRNS Alban MM Gnr 701089 RFA
CAIRNS Alexander MM Pte S/23651 5th Cameron Highlanders
CAIRNS David MM L/Cpl S/40873 5th Cameron Highlanders
CAIRNS David MM L/Cpl 20930 Royal Irish Fusiliers
CAIRNS Edward MM Cpl 203042 1/5th West Yorkshire Regt
CAIRNS George MM Cpl 27252 16th Highland Light Infantry
CAIRNS James I. MM Pte 42326 16th Highland Light Infantry
CAIRNS John MM Pte 19606 West Yorkshire Regt
CAIRNS John MM Bdr 656235 RFA
CAIRNS Joseph MM Cpl 1578 1/5th Royal Highlanders
CAIRNS Leo MM Pte 22346 Lancashire Fusiliers
CAIRNS Owen MM L/Cpl 24/1015 24th Northumberland Fusiliers
CAIRNS Robert MM+Bar Sjt 16711 11th Royal Scots
CAIRNS Robert MM Gnr 307164 RGA
CAIRNS Stanley J. MM L/Cpl 23390 2nd Royal West Surrey Regt
CAIRNS T. MM Sjt 139058 Royal Engineers
CAIRNS Thomas MM Cpl 7322 Northumberland Fusiliers
CAIRNS Thomas MM Sjt 14031 9th Royal Inniskilling Fusiliers KIA 29.3.18.
CAIRNS Thomas MM+Bar Pte 5064 2nd Scots Guards
CAIRNS W. "DCM,MM" Cpl 10362 1st Scottish Rifles
CAIRNS W.H. MM Sjt P1952 Military Foot Police
CAIRNS William MM+Bar Sjt 4/8030 2nd Arg & Suth Highlanders
CAIRNS William MM L/Cpl 18896 12th Royal Irish Rifles
CAIRNS William MM Pte 34053 Royal Scots
CAISLEY Charles G. MM Pte 81239 15th Durham Light Infantry
CAISLEY Nixon MM Dvr 27398 RFA
CAISLEY Robert MM Dvr T4/159914 Army Service Corps
CAITHNESS James Petrie MM Pte 40949 2nd Royal Irish Rifles KIA 23.3.18.
CAIZERGUES William H. MM Sjt 696852 55 Div Ammn Col RFA
CAKE Harry Frederick MM Pte 14732 2nd Hampshire Regt DOW 12.4.18.
CAKEBREAD Joseph MM Pte 29832 2nd Bedfordshire Regt KIA 4.11.18.

CALBREATH John Herbert MM L/Cpl A/731 13th King's Royal Rifle Corps KIA 25.8.18.
CALBREATH William H. "MM,MID" Sjt 500203 48 Div Sig Coy Royal Engineers
CALCOTT John William MM Gnr 137952 B/58 Bde RFA KIA 7.11.18.
CALCUTT Harold M. MM Cpl 512562 RAMC
CALCUTT Samuel MM Cpl T1/3056 8 Reserve Park Army Service Corps
CALDBECK William D. MM L/Cpl 202264 Liverpool Regt
CALDECOURT L.W. MM Gnr 78234 RFA
CALDER Alfred MM Pte S/9697 8/10th Gordon Highlanders
CALDER Andrew "MM,MID" Pte 10124 2nd Gordon Highlanders
CALDER Charles MM Pte 22487 4th Gordon Highlanders
CALDER Donald MM L/Cpl 12501 8th Seaforth Highlanders
CALDER Ernest B. MM Pte 301012 RAMC
CALDER Frank Maltman MM Sjt 9422 2/2(Highland)Fd Coy Royal Engineers DOW 4.12.16.
CALDER Gilbert MM Cpl M2/033755 Army Service Corps
CALDER Henry MM L/Sjt 17228 1st Grenadier Guards
CALDER Hugh MM Pte 27331 Highland Light Infantry
CALDER J. MM Pte 241989 1/4th Seaforth Highlanders
CALDER John MM Cpl S/5336 7th Seaforth Highlanders
CALDER John "DCM,MM" CSM 22964 2/8th Worcestershire Regt
CALDER John MM Sjt 10874 2nd Royal Scots
CALDER John MM Cpl 4/8592 1st West Yorkshire Regt KIA 23.10.18.
CALDER L.J. MM Pte 275797 1/7th Arg & Suth Highlanders
CALDER Robert "MM,MID" L/Cpl 275847 5/6th Royal Scots
CALDER William MM Dvr 945 Royal Engineers
CALDERBANK Joseph MM Cpl 225684 309 Road Constr Coy Royal Engineers KIA 8.10.17.
CALDICOTT George "DCM,MM" Sjt 7995 2nd South Lancashire Regt DOW 15.6.17.
CALDICOTT William MM Gnr 18073 C/71 Bde RFA
CALDOW David MM Pte 240140 5th Royal Scots Fusiliers
CALDWELL Alex "DCM,MM" Sjt 325266 1/9th Durham Light Infantry Died 14.6.17.
CALDWELL Alexander MM L/Cpl 8876 Seaforth Highlanders
CALDWELL Christopher MM Pte 42018 1/1st Hertfordshire Regt
CALDWELL James A. MM+Bar BSM 308107 RGA
CALDWELL Joseph MM Pte 5111 Royal Irish Rifles
CALDWELL Kenneth MM Pte 6770 6th East Kent Regt
CALDWELL Louis J. MM Sjt 56556 Machine Gun Corps
CALDWELL Samuel MM Pte 332395 9th Highland Light Infantry KIA 26.10.18.
CALDWELL Thomas MM Sjt 13050 Scots Guards
CALE Herbert MM+Bar Pte 14627 2/4th Royal Berkshire Regt
CALE S.A. MM L/Cpl 129939 45th Royal Fusiliers
CALEY Arthur J. MM Cpl 20684 16th Royal Warwickshire Regt
CALEY Bertie MM L/Sjt G/7949 1st East Kent Regt
CALEY Ernest H. MM Pte G/18890 2nd Royal Sussex Regt
CALEY Frederick MM Pte 28678 Royal Lancaster Regt
CALEY Robert H.F. MM L/Cpl 3720 17th Bn Machine Gun Corps
CALEY William Arthur MM Cpl 24182 44 Bde RFA
CALLAGHAN A.V. MM Sjt 8181 6th East Kent Regt
CALLAGHAN Albert V. MM Pte 43979 18th King's Royal Rifle Corps
CALLAGHAN Alfred MM Gnr 110658 RGA
CALLAGHAN Arthur Ernest "DCM,MM" Sjt 8748 1st Gloucestershire Regt
CALLAGHAN Charles MM Gnr 76614 30 Bde RFA
CALLAGHAN Charles "MM,MID" Sjt 45400 D/256 Bde RFA Died 30.12.17.
CALLAGHAN Edward MM Dvr 741044 266 Bde RFA Died 9.10.18.
CALLAGHAN Edward MM Dvr 84532 2 Bde RFA
CALLAGHAN Frank MM Pte 3702 2nd Northumberland Fusiliers
CALLAGHAN Hugh MM Cpl 240351 6th Highland Light Infantry
CALLAGHAN James MM Pte 12699 6th Royal Dublin Fusiliers
CALLAGHAN John MM Cpl 5121 2nd Royal Irish Regt DOW 28.8.18.
CALLAGHAN John MM Pte 351149 Royal Highlanders
CALLAGHAN John P. MM Pte 10335 Royal West Kent Regt
CALLAGHAN John W. MM Gnr 972 RFA
CALLAGHAN Patrick MM Pte 9309 2nd Irish Guards
CALLAGHAN R. MM Pte 21013 1st Essex Regt
CALLAGHAN T. MM Pte 40795 1st Northamptonshire Regt
CALLAGHAN T. MM+Bar Sjt 14959 62 Coy Machine Gun Corps DOW 7.10.17.
CALLAGHAN William MM L/Cpl 7436 York & Lancaster Regt
CALLAN Fred MM Sjt 23551 1st West Yorkshire Regt
CALLAN George MM Pte R/14228 2nd King's Royal Rifle Corps DOW 13.4.17.

CALLAN James W. MM Cpl 71674 Royal Engineers
CALLAN Peter MM L/Cpl 16259 1st Somerset Light Infantry
CALLANDER Alexander S. MM Sjt 17132 Machine Gun Corps
CALLANDER Elizabeth Beveridge MM Miss F First Aid Nursing Yeomanry
CALLANDER Leonard J. MM Dvr 508447 505 Fd Coy Royal Engineers
CALLANT William A. MM Pte 24886 16th Royal Warwickshire Regt
CALLARD Edmund C. MM Pte 74440 RAMC
CALLARD Edward J. MM+Bar Sjt 231011 10th Shropshire Light Infantry
CALLAWAY Alfred MM Gnr 88144 RFA AKA Alfred Mockford.
CALLAWAY Edward MM Dvr 109485 RFA
CALLAWAY Sydney A. MM Cpl 497601 RAMC
CALLCOTT John Herbert MM L/Cpl 12539 6th Royal Berkshire Regt
CALLEAR Richard Gabriel MM Sjt 9458 2nd Worcestershire Regt DOW 26/28.3.18.
CALLENDER W. MM 2nd Cpl 140031 Royal Engineers
CALLER Samuel J. MM Cpl 10451 5th Royal Berkshire Regt
CALLERY Thomas MM Pte 48438 13th Rifle Brigade
CALLEY Claude A. MM Gnr 10313 238 Siege Bty RGA
CALLIGAN John T. MM Pte 22235 1st Northumberland Fusiliers
CALLIGAN Peter MM Cpl 21812 23 Heavy Bty RGA DOW 16.8.16.
CALLIGAN Sidney MM Pte 31810 West Riding Regt
CALLINGHAM Albert J. MM Sjt 4823 East Surrey Regt
CALLINGHAM Ernest MM Sjt 52606 RFA
CALLISON Christopher MM Cpl 3455 12th Manchester Regt KIA 26.8.18.
CALLISTER Bertie R. MM Sjt 27078 Shropshire Light Infantry
CALLISTER Charles F.C. MM Gnr Fitter 362980 51 Siege Bty RGA
CALLOW C.W. "DCM,MM" Sjt 23043 110 Heavy Bty RGA
CALLOW Ernest James MM Sjt 15/868 15th Royal Warwickshire Regt
CALLOW Frederick William "MM,MSM,CdeG(F)" Sjt 34000 42 Bty 2 Bde RFA
CALLOW George H. MM Pte 34692 7th Royal Warwickshire Regt
CALLOW George W. MM Pte 33645 Gloucestershire Regt
CALLOW Gilbert "MM,MID" Sjt 1125 1/1st Hertfordshire Regt KIA 31.7.17.
CALLOW Harold E. MM Pte 33894 Middlesex Regt
CALLOW Robert K. MM Sjt 106110 Royal Engineers
CALLOWAY Frank MM Dvr 77624 RFA
CALMAN Richard H. MM Cpl 569 Royal Warwickshire Regt
CALMAN Timothy MM Sjt F/1088 Middlesex Regt
CALOW Joseph W. "MM,MID" Pte 7076 8th Royal West Kent Regt
CALTON Ernest MM Bdr 751333 A/315 Bde RFA
CALTON Ernest L. MM Cpl 69726 Tank Corps
CALVER Charles E. MM Cpl 15012 8th Suffolk Regt
CALVER Joseph W. MM Pte 106490 RAMC
CALVER Richard J. MM Sjt 14181 East Surrey Regt
CALVERLEY George Harry "DCM,MM" Sjt 40354 15/17th West Yorkshire Regt DOW 12.8.18.
CALVERLEY Herbert "MM,GMV(S)" Pte 63393 RAMC
CALVERLEY Stewart John MM Pte 88405 5th Bn Machine Gun Corps
CALVERT Albert MM Pte 39459 34 Coy Machine Gun Corps
CALVERT Francis MM Dvr 54790 41 Bde RFA
CALVERT George E. "DCM,MM" Sjt 265433 1/6th West Riding Regt
CALVERT Jim MM Sjt C/6589 18th King's Royal Rifle Corps
CALVERT John B. MM+Bar L/Sjt 15365 4th Coldstream Guards
CALVERT John George MM Pte 10469 9th Northumberland Fusiliers
CALVERT Joseph S. MM Spr 140468 80 Fd Coy Royal Engineers
CALVERT Laurence "VC,MM,MID,Oleo(B)" Sjt 240194 5th Yorkshire Light Infantry
CALVERT Robert William MM L/Cpl 21/781 21st Northumberland Fusiliers KIA 1.7.16.
CALVIN James MM L/Cpl 9239 2nd Worcestershire Regt
CAMBER Albert J. MM Pte 2002 7th Royal West Surrey Regt
CAMBER Henry J. MM Pte 3175 7th Royal West Surrey Regt
CAMBRAY Percy MM Cpl 12165 6th Oxf & Bucks Light Infantry
CAMBREY Charles W. MM Pte 6386 2nd Wiltshire Regt
CAMBREY William MM L/Cpl 355971 Royal Welsh Fusiliers
CAMBRIDGE Charles William MM Cpl 2027 137 Siege Bty RGA
CAMBRIDGE Denis MM Pte 6763 1st Royal Munster Fusiliers
CAMBURN George E. MM L/Cpl 571493 17th London Regt
CAMERON Alexander MM L/Cpl 12189 Arg & Suth Highlanders att Labour Corps
CAMERON Alexander MM Pte 12930 11th Arg & Suth Highlanders
CAMERON Alexander MM L/Cpl 325 1st Seaforth Highlanders

CAMERON Alexander P. MM L/Cpl S/24059 7th Seaforth Highlanders
CAMERON Alexander R. MM Pte 290650 1/7th Gordon Highlanders
CAMERON Allan MM Cpl 5113 2nd Cameron Highlanders
CAMERON Andrew MM Pte 1912 Durham Light Infantry
CAMERON Andrew Stuart MM Pte 72193 44 Coy Machine Gun Corps DOW 2.3.18.
CAMERON Angus MM L/Cpl S/40877 6th Royal Highlanders
CAMERON Angus "DCM,MM+Bar" L/Cpl 779 4th GMGR
CAMERON Archibald MM Cpl 315274 13th Royal Highlanders
CAMERON Archie MM Sjt 16964 King's Own Scottish Borderers KIA 11.4.18.
CAMERON Bernard MM Pte 42503 167 Coy Machine Gun Corps KIA 3.5.17.
CAMERON Charles MM Bdr 93136 A/50 Bde RFA
CAMERON Charles Hogg Chuthill MM Sjt 22102 32nd Royal Fusiliers
CAMERON Colin J.F. MM Pte 126777 Lovat's Scouts Yeomanry
CAMERON David MM L/Cpl S/43520 Gordon Highlanders
CAMERON Donald MM Pte 12108 5th Cameron Highlanders
CAMERON Donald MM L/Cpl 1024 1/5th Seaforth Highlanders KIA 14.11.16.
CAMERON Donald MM Pte 266216 Seaforth Highlanders
CAMERON Donald S. "DCM,MM" Sjt 11940 11th Royal Scots
CAMERON Duncan MM Pte 2699 2nd Dragoons
CAMERON Duncan MM Gnr 133680 D/190 Bde RFA
CAMERON Garnet Stewart MM+Bar Cpl 21379 42 Bty 2 Bde RFA
CAMERON George MM Pte 22/399 Northumberland Fusiliers
CAMERON Hamish I. MM Spr 207448 Royal Engineers
CAMERON Hazelton R. MM Spr 207472 Royal Engineers
CAMERON Herbert J. MM L/Cpl 984 King Edward's Horse
CAMERON Hugh MM Cpl 15928 6th Cameron Highlanders
CAMERON Hugh MM Pte 200738 1/4th Royal Scots Fusiliers
CAMERON Hugh MM Pte S/7896 2nd Arg & Suth Highlanders
CAMERON Hugh MM Cpl 11051 5th Cameron Highlanders
CAMERON Hugh MM Gnr 116350 RGA
CAMERON James MM L/Bdr 135528 299 Siege Bty RGA
CAMERON James MM+Bar Pte 315071 13th Royal Highlanders
CAMERON James MM Pte 266318 Royal Highlanders
CAMERON John MM Pte 300912 2nd Arg & Suth Highlanders Died 25.10.18.
CAMERON John MM Sjt R/15457 3rd King's Royal Rifle Corps
CAMERON John MM Pte 575985 Labour Corps
CAMERON John MM L/Cpl 40821 Gordon Highlanders
CAMERON John MM Cpl 14022 7th Cameron Highlanders
CAMERON John MM Pte S/5479 Seaforth Highlanders
CAMERON John MM Cpl 22665 8th Northumberland Fusiliers KIA 9.10.18.
CAMERON John Fletcher MM Cpl S/17596 Cameron Highlanders
CAMERON Kenneth MM Sjt 9008 2nd Seaforth Highlanders KIA 1.7.16.
CAMERON Murdoch MM Spr 89355 Royal Engineers
CAMERON Peter MM Pte 9563 6th Dragoons
CAMERON Peter MM Cpl 28986 Royal Engineers
CAMERON Robert J. MM Sjt S/18323 Cameron Highlanders
CAMERON Robert John "MM,MM(F)" Pte 335205 1/8th Royal Scots
CAMERON Robert Ramsey MM Sjt 93125 A/38 Bde RFA KIA 15.9.17.
CAMERON Ronald MM Pte 53548 1/9th Highland Light Infantry
CAMERON Samuel MM L/Cpl 9480 1/7th Arg & Suth Highlanders KIA 2.9.18.
CAMERON Thomas G. MM Bugler 136 1/9th Durham Light Infantry
CAMERON William MM Pte 43914 19th Bn Machine Gun Corps
CAMERON William MM Cpl 5836 9th Seaforth Highlanders
CAMERON William MM Pte 34798 North Staffordshire Regt
CAMERON William D. MM Dvr T4/241891 Army Service Corps
CAMERON William J. MM Spr 47858 Royal Engineers
CAMFIELD Frederick George MM L/Cpl 15292 Att TM Bty RGA Royal West Surrey Regt
CAMIDGE Arthur Robert MM Spr 161295 Signal Service Royal Engineers
CAMIS Ernest MM Cpl 57797 36 Bde RFA
CAMKIN David MM Pte G/72772 1/24th London Regt
CAMM Arthur C. "DCM,MM" Bdr 68740 9 Bty 41 Bde RFA
CAMM Harry MM Sjt M2/177616 Army Service Corps
CAMMACK William H. MM Pte 663 East Surrey Regt
CAMMACK Zacharia MM Bdr 800115 A/230 Bde RFA
CAMMIDGE Clement MM Pte 65323 4th Royal Fusiliers
CAMMISH Thomas R. MM Gnr L/12177 RFA
CAMMISS Harry MM Gnr 84591 RFA

CAMP Abel "DCM,MM+Bar" Cpl 71578 47 Bty 44 Bde RFA
CAMP Frederick MM L/Cpl R/18470 1st King's Royal Rifle Corps
CAMP Frederick George MM Cpl 81091 Y/36 Med TM Bty RFA
CAMP G. MM Cpl 26833 1st Essex Regt
CAMP George MM Sjt 631443 20th London Regt
CAMP George S. MM Pte 1080 22nd London Regt
CAMP John N. MM Pte M2/115811 Army Service Corps
CAMP Martin S. MM Bdr 35123 RFA
CAMP Sidney J. MM Sjt 50204 24 Bde RFA
CAMP Walter Charles MM Pte 15911 12th East Surrey Regt
CAMP Warwick F. MM Cpl 19726 Royal Engineers
CAMP William Alfred MM Sjt 8068 1st Leicestershire Regt
CAMPBELL A. MM Pte 345259 Royal Highlanders
CAMPBELL Alexander MM Cpl 366567 521 Siege Bty RGA
CAMPBELL Alexander MM Sjt 242358 1/6th Seaforth Highlanders
CAMPBELL Alexander MM Pte 235105 4th Yorkshire Light Infantry
CAMPBELL Alexander MM Sjt 15392 Royal Inniskilling Fusiliers
CAMPBELL Alexander "MM,MID" Sjt 41139 Royal Engineers
CAMPBELL Alexander MM Pte 3855 8th Seaforth Highlanders
CAMPBELL Alexander MM Cpl 12035 Gordon Highlanders
CAMPBELL Alexander J. MM Pte 44398 Royal Scots
CAMPBELL Alexander S. MM Pte 43355 16 Fd Amb RAMC
CAMPBELL Alfred MM Cpl 96482 A/91 Bde RFA
CAMPBELL Archibald MM L/Cpl 292872 1/7th Royal Highlanders
CAMPBELL Archibald MM Pte 303001 1/8th Arg & Suth Highlanders DOW 21.3.18.
CAMPBELL Archibald D. MM L/Cpl 315037 Royal Highlanders
CAMPBELL Archibald M. MM Spr 406026 Royal Engineers
CAMPBELL Arthur MM Sjt 3170 Lincolnshire Regt
CAMPBELL Arthur F. MM Pte 12551 Royal Inniskilling Fusiliers
CAMPBELL Bernard MM L/Cpl 3/7581 9th Royal Irish Rifles
CAMPBELL Colin MM Bdr 751236 RFA
CAMPBELL Colin MM Sjt Wheeler 631415 B/255 Bde RFA KIA 21.4.17.
CAMPBELL Daniel MM Pte 3383 Royal Highlanders
CAMPBELL Daniel MM Pte 70730 Machine Gun Corps DOW 21.9.18.
CAMPBELL Daniel Hugh MM Pte 267491 1/5th Seaforth Highlanders
CAMPBELL David MM Sjt 27337 10th Scottish Rifles
CAMPBELL David MM Spr 148601 Royal Engineers
CAMPBELL David MM+Bar Sjt 16438 6th King's Own Scottish Borderers
CAMPBELL David MM Sjt 1985 2nd Irish Guards
CAMPBELL David MM Bdr L/6525 C/83 Bde RFA
CAMPBELL David M. MM Pte 39262 12th Royal Scots Fusiliers
CAMPBELL David William MM Pte 6083 1st Royal Irish Fusiliers att 112 Light TM Bty
CAMPBELL Donald MM Cpl 10722 2nd Gordon Highlanders
CAMPBELL Donald MM Sjt 9545 1st Royal Scots
CAMPBELL Donald MM Cpl 270255 5/6th Royal Scots
CAMPBELL Dugald MM Pte 23263 Royal Scots
CAMPBELL Edward MM Pte 333946 1/9th Highland Light Infantry
CAMPBELL Edward Ralph MM L/Cpl 43550 22nd Manchester Regt
CAMPBELL Ernest MM Pte 14033 Royal Lancaster Regt
CAMPBELL Fairlie J. MM L/Cpl 290506 Royal Highlanders
CAMPBELL Fred MM Bdr 72269 RFA
CAMPBELL Fred MM Pte 38593 4th Hampshire Regt
CAMPBELL George MM Pte 46245 1/4th Royal Scots
CAMPBELL George MM Sjt 202534 1/4th Gordon Highlanders KIA 25.3.18.
CAMPBELL George MM L/Sjt 240646 1/5th Gordon Highlanders DOW 13.4.17.
CAMPBELL George MM Pte 64772 RAMC
CAMPBELL George A. MM Spr 1675 Royal Engineers
CAMPBELL George Edward MM Sjt 240845 Royal Lancaster Regt
CAMPBELL George G. MM Gnr 797075 RFA
CAMPBELL George Joseph MM Sjt 1489 2nd Middlesex Regt
CAMPBELL Henry MM Cpl 6210 RGA
CAMPBELL Henry E. MM Pte 2932 24th London Regt
CAMPBELL Henry J. MM Sjt M/340542 1018 Coy Army Service Corps
CAMPBELL Herbert MM L/Cpl 68322 16 Fd Amb RAMC
CAMPBELL Herbert MM Cpl 34404 Yorkshire Regt
CAMPBELL Hugh "DCM,MM" Pte 8591 8th Northumberland Fusiliers
CAMPBELL Hugh MM L/Cpl 46731 21 Div Sig Coy Royal Engineers
CAMPBELL Hugh MM L/Cpl 22367 Machine Gun Corps
CAMPBELL Ian McLaren MM Cpl 21713 19th Liverpool Regt KIA 30.3.18.

CAMPBELL James MM Sjt 13501 9th Royal Irish Fusiliers
CAMPBELL James MM Spr 496508 233 Fd Coy Royal Engineers DOW 9.8.18.
CAMPBELL James MM Dvr 64258 150 Fd Coy Royal Engineers
CAMPBELL James MM Pte 265791 2nd Seaforth Highlanders
CAMPBELL James MM Sjt 8/15473 8th Royal Dublin Fusiliers KIA 9.9.16.
CAMPBELL James MM Pte G/1304 Royal Irish Fusiliers
CAMPBELL James MM L/Cpl 47734 Royal Engineers
CAMPBELL James MM Cpl 48848 Royal Engineers
CAMPBELL James MM L/Cpl 1428 Royal Engineers
CAMPBELL James "MM,MID" Cpl S/16551 Cameron Highlanders
CAMPBELL James MM Pte 15/12230 Royal Irish Rifles
CAMPBELL James MM Sjt 76796 Signal Service Royal Engineers
CAMPBELL James Ferguson MM Sjt 21377 A/59 Bde RFA
CAMPBELL James H. MM Pte 34822 12th Manchester Regt
CAMPBELL James S. MM Sjt 316066 1 Fd Amb RAMC
CAMPBELL James T. MM L/Cpl 15092 Machine Gun Corps
CAMPBELL John MM L/Cpl 412845 409 Fd Coy Royal Engineers
CAMPBELL John "MM,MID" CSM 7288 1st Highland Light Infantry
CAMPBELL John MM L/Sjt 331272 Highland Light Infantry
CAMPBELL John MM Bdr 61090 Z/5 Med TM Bty RGA
CAMPBELL John MM Pte 57533 24th Welsh Regt
CAMPBELL John MM Cpl 307799 15th Bn Tank Corps KIA 27.9.18.
CAMPBELL John MM Pte 4334 15th Royal Irish Rifles
CAMPBELL John MM Pte 240411 1/5th Royal Scots Fusiliers
CAMPBELL John MM Pte 30753 91 Coy Machine Gun Corps
CAMPBELL John "MM,MID" Pte 12965 1/4th Cameron Highlanders
CAMPBELL John "DCM,MM" Sjt 17846 Royal Scots
CAMPBELL John MM 2nd Cpl 139413 252 Tunnelling Coy Royal Engineers DOW 18.4.17.
CAMPBELL John MM L/Cpl S/1876 2nd Arg & Suth Highlanders
CAMPBELL John MM Drummer 1602 1/8th Arg & Suth Highlanders
CAMPBELL John MM Pte 2/9089 2nd Manchester Regt
CAMPBELL John MM L/Cpl 2907 Royal Highlanders
CAMPBELL John MM Pte 315837 13th Royal Highlanders
CAMPBELL John MM Pte 34890 Royal Scots Fusiliers
CAMPBELL John MM Gnr 71253 D/330 Bde RFA
CAMPBELL John MM L/Cpl 41765 Highland Light Infantry
CAMPBELL John MM Cpl Shoeing Smith 6930 A/58 Bde RFA
CAMPBELL John MM L/Cpl 73957 RAMC
CAMPBELL John A. MM Pte S/12428 Gordon Highlanders
CAMPBELL John B. MM Spr 182418 Royal Engineers
CAMPBELL John G. MM Pte 242717 1st East Lancashire Regt
CAMPBELL John Keith MM Pte 12267 1st Scots Guards
CAMPBELL John Theodore MM Sjt 20/30 Northumberland Fusiliers
CAMPBELL John W. MM Sjt 1798 Durham Light Infantry
CAMPBELL John Waran MM Spr 402591 401 Fd Coy Royal Engineers KIA 8.12.17.
CAMPBELL Leo MM Sjt 16459 Cameron Highlanders
CAMPBELL Malcolm MM L/Cpl 7160 1st Seaforth Highlanders
CAMPBELL Mary Gwynnedd MM Nurse F BRCS
CAMPBELL Oswald MM L/Cpl 352105 1/9th Royal Scots
CAMPBELL Patrick MM Pte 23104 6th Royal Dublin Fusiliers
CAMPBELL Percy "DCM,MM" Sjt 95392 1st Liverpool Regt KIA 29.9.18.
CAMPBELL Peter MM Sjt 49322 13th Royal Fusiliers DOW 30.10.18.
CAMPBELL Peter MM+Bar Sjt 81065 Royal Engineers
CAMPBELL Peter MM Spr 420041 406 Fd Coy Royal Engineers DOW 25.2.18.
CAMPBELL Peter MM L/Sjt 2141 1/7th Royal Highlanders DOW 24.4.17.
CAMPBELL Peter MM Sjt 420037 406 Fd Coy Royal Engineers
CAMPBELL R. MM Pte 332791 14th Highland Light Infantry
CAMPBELL R.G. MM L/Cpl 2616 2nd Life Guards
CAMPBELL Reginald MM Cpl 22640 Liverpool Regt
CAMPBELL Robert MM Pte 44761 1st Bn Machine Gun Corps
CAMPBELL Robert MM Sjt 281845 RGA
CAMPBELL Robert MM Pte 20499 1st King's Own Scottish Borderers
CAMPBELL Robert MM CQMS 2349 1/14th London Regt
CAMPBELL Robert MM Pte 8909 7th Royal Fusiliers KIA 25.5.18.
CAMPBELL Robert MM Pte 3/12646 12th Durham Light Infantry
CAMPBELL Robert J. MM Pte 6771 RAMC
CAMPBELL Roderick J. MM Spr 171962 Royal Engineers
CAMPBELL Samuel MM Bdr 110505 RFA
CAMPBELL T. MM Pte 16409 Scottish Rifles
CAMPBELL Thomas "DCM,MM" Sjt 46459 82 Fd Coy Royal Engineers KIA 23.10.17.
CAMPBELL Thomas MM Pte 8697 1st Royal Lancaster Regt
CAMPBELL Thomas MM Bdr 22165 A/28 Bde RFA DOW 10.4.18.
CAMPBELL W. MM L/Cpl T4/086495 Army Service Corps
CAMPBELL W. MM Sjt 40775 Gordon Highlanders
CAMPBELL Walter C. MM L/Cpl G3/8708 East Surrey Regt
CAMPBELL Ward MM L/Sjt 24759 Highland Light Infantry
CAMPBELL William MM Cpl 295505 12th Royal Scots Fusiliers
CAMPBELL William MM Pte 14907 1st Royal Scots Fusiliers
CAMPBELL William MM Cpl 34872 2nd Royal Scots Fusiliers
CAMPBELL William MM Sjt 265185 1/6th Seaforth Highlanders
CAMPBELL William MM Dvr 92388 RFA
CAMPBELL William MM Gnr 169807 RFA
CAMPBELL William MM Dvr 57907 Royal Engineers
CAMPBELL William MM Gnr 56088 RFA
CAMPBELL William MM Pte S/9455 Arg & Suth Highlanders
CAMPBELL William L. MM Pte 8258 2nd Royal Scots Fusiliers
CAMPBELL William P. MM Pte 39964 21st London Regt
CAMPBELL William R. MM Pte 4303 11th Highland Light Infantry
CAMPBELTON Albert C. MM Sjt 16451 5 Div Sig Coy Royal Engineers
CAMPING Ernest W. MM Gnr 51683 A Bty RHA
CAMPING W.C. MM L/Cpl 26301 Royal Fusiliers
CAMPION Alfred E. MM Sjt 558 6th Royal West Surrey Regt
CAMPION Alfred H.O. MM S/Sjt 11734 11 Fd Amb RAMC
CAMPION Edward P. MM Pte 10537 2nd West Riding Regt
CAMPION Ernest MM Pte 514070 RAMC
CAMPION John MM Pte 2455 Middlesex Regt
CAMPION John W.F. MM Pte 295488 2nd London Regt
CAMPION Michael F. MM Gnr 73649 310 Bde RFA
CAMPION Walter MM Pte 21727 Highland Light Infantry
CAMPKIN James MM Bdr 110570 B/180 Bde RFA
CAMPLIN Ernest MM Cpl 3485 1st Royal West Kent Regt KIA 29.9.18.
CAMPLIN Walter MM Pte 17180 9th Royal Sussex Regt
CAMPLING Thomas MM Sjt 49072 8th Royal Welsh Fusiliers DOW 30.4.18.
CAMPS William F. MM Pte 23966 Duke of Cornwall's LI
CAMPSIE William MM L/Cpl 357503 Guards Div Sig Coy Royal Engineers
CANAVAN Alfred MM Sjt 15553 Liverpool Regt
CANCANNON Arthur MM Pte 10968 1st Notts & Derby Regt KIA 31.7.17.
CANDLER John Ernest MM+Bar L/Cpl 321066 6th London Regt
CANDLIN Frederick MM Pte 241088 Worcestershire Regt
CANDLIN William MM+Bar Gnr 92992 106 Bty 22 Bde RFA
CANDLISH Anthony G. MM Pte 203487 King's Own Scottish Borderers
CANDY Albert Henry John MM Sjt 33893 115 Heavy Bty RGA
CANDY William L. MM Pte 14182 Gordon Highlanders
CANE Albert MM Pte G/18575 2nd Royal Sussex Regt
CANE Alfred Reginald MM Gnr 126601 'U' AA Bty RGA
CANE David T. MM Sjt 7539 11th Royal Fusiliers
CANFIELD George William MM Pte S/36244 2nd Rifle Brigade DOW 25.4.18.
CANHAM Ernest "MM,CG(B)" Sjt 147098 Royal Engineers
CANHAM George MM L/Cpl 8495 2nd Lincolnshire Regt
CANHAM John "DCM,MM" Sjt 15247 1st Grenadier Guards
CANHAM John Thomas MM L/Cpl 47184 11th Notts & Derby Regt DOW 31.10.18.
CANHAM Spencer G. MM Pte 95452 1st Middlesex Regt
CANHAM Thomas O. MM Sjt 19912 Yorkshire Regt
CANHAM Walter R. MM Pte 13905 Suffolk Regt
CANN Ernest V. "DCM,MM" Sjt 439013 RAMC
CANN Fred MM Dvr 106887 RFA
CANNAN Leonard H. MM Pte 241872 4th North Staffordshire Regt
CANNELL Maurice MM Bdr 122138 RFA
CANNELL W. MM L/Cpl 129308 46th Royal Fusiliers
CANNING Joseph MM Bdr 22770 B/173 Bde RFA
CANNING William MM Bdr 32512 39 Bde RFA
CANNINGS Albert E. MM Cpl 315151 RGA
CANNINGS George F. MM+Bar Pte 8036 9th Yorkshire Regt
CANNON Albert MM Pte 43348 West Yorkshire Regt
CANNON Arthur W. "MM,MSM" CSM 203341 1/5th Royal Warwickshire Regt
CANNON Charles MM L/Cpl 16530 4th Middlesex Regt
CANNON Cornelius MM 2nd Cpl 147213 Royal Engineers
CANNON Edward MM Pte 302137 Manchester Regt
CANNON Frederick A. MM Pte G/4256 Royal West Kent Regt
CANNON Frederick Eli Samuel MM BSM 28810 B/123 Bde RFA
CANNON George MM Sjt 26174 2nd Welsh Regt KIA 23.7.18.

CANNON Henry F. MM Sjt 632883 20th London Regt
CANNON Herbert MM Sjt 680345 RFA
CANNON Herbert.S. MM Sjt 10926 6th Border Regt
CANNON John MM Pte 19672 1st East Lancashire Regt
CANNON John MM Pte 10112 5th Northamptonshire Regt
CANNON John MM Pte 80217 14th Royal Welsh Fusiliers
CANNON John MM Pnr 105357 Royal Engineers
CANNON John G. MM L/Cpl 51892 Machine Gun Corps
CANNON John J. "DCM,MM" Cpl 147129 19th Bn Machine Gun Corps
CANNON Lewis MM+Bar Sjt 558024 1 Div Sig Coy Royal Engineers
CANNON T.G. MM L/Cpl 683075 London Regt
CANNON Thomas MM L/Cpl 6729 1/21st London Regt KIA 6.11.16.
CANNON Walter MM Pte R/36760 13th King's Royal Rifle Corps DOW 16.12.18.
CANNON Willam MM Pte 17114 7th Wiltshire Regt
CANNOT Percy A. MM Pte 1337 Royal Fusiliers
CANNY Michael MM Pte 8/5414 8th Royal Munster Fusiliers
CANNY William M. MM Cpl 200362 7th Middlesex Regt
CANSFIELD Charlie MM Sjt 27491 B/46 Bde RFA
CANSFIELD John MM Pte 3/11474 West Riding Regt
CANT Bertie MM Cpl 5821 2nd Suffolk Regt KIA 24.3.18.
CANT E.J. MM Pte 41047 Middlesex Regt
CANTELLO Henry J. MM Cpl 19311 RAMC
CANTILLON Robert MM+Bar Pte 18613 Royal Dublin Fusiliers
CANTLE Bert Horace MM Dvr 950712 RFA
CANTLE Ernest John MM Cpl 43895 RFA
CANTLE James C. MM Cpl 720989 24th London Regt
CANTLE Leonard Laver MM Pte 2455 1/4th Gloucestershire Regt
CANTLEY George MM Pte 14382 Army Cyclist Corps
CANTWELL James MM Spr 23264 Royal Engineers
CANTY Charles Ernest MM Gnr 27349 A/173 Bde RFA
CANTY Thomas MM Dvr 11687 B/102 Bde RFA
CANWELL Albert MM Sjt 63061 41 Bty 42 Bde RFA
CANWELL Samuel James MM Pte 14988 10th Notts & Derby Regt
CAPE Edward Thomas MM L/Cpl 5292 1st Duke of Cornwall's LI
CAPE Jonathan F. MM Pte 202845 1/5th Border Regt
CAPE William P. "MM,MID" Gnr 57657 RGA
CAPEL Bertie MM Pte 47914 17 Squadron MGC(Cavalry) Died 17.10.18.
CAPEL Charles J. MM L/Cpl G/11246 Royal West Surrey Regt
CAPEL George MM Sjt 8223 2nd Oxf & Bucks Light Infantry
CAPEL James MM L/Cpl 29528 Middlesex Regt
CAPEL Thomas MM L/Cpl 13004 6th Bedfordshire Regt
CAPELL Richard MM L/Cpl 1798 RAMC
CAPELLA Albert MM Cpl 166186 32nd Bn Machine Gun Corps
CAPENHURST William G. MM Pte 38973 2nd Yorkshire Regt
CAPES George T. MM Gnr 57589 42 Bde RFA
CAPEWELL Albert MM Cpl 12564 1st Worcestershire Regt
CAPEWELL Albert MM Pte 73386 2nd Notts & Derby Regt
CAPEWELL Frederick MM L/Cpl 6/17086 6th South Wales Borderers
CAPEWELL Frederick H. MM Cpl 12717 2nd Worcestershire Regt
CAPEWELL Joseph MM Pte 7234 2nd South Staffordshire Regt
CAPLIN E.J. MM Gnr 618197 RHA
CAPON Arthur MM Pte 7364 1/4th Suffolk Regt DOW 25.5.17.
CAPON George W. MM+Bar Cpl 1841 Lancashire Fusiliers
CAPON H.F. MM Pte 202140 Royal West Surrey Regt
CAPON Harry MM Cpl 47033 14 Bde RHA
CAPON Herbert E. MM Cpl 42769 Royal Irish Rifles
CAPON Will F. MM Pte 3967 6th London Regt
CAPON William MM Sjt 67329 111 Siege Bty RGA
CAPP George MM Pte M2/099516 Army Service Corps
CAPP John MM Pte 205500 Royal West Surrey Regt
CAPPELL Robert Stewart MM Sjt 147105 Royal Engineers
CAPPELLA William MM Bdr 10545 C/77 Bde RFA
CAPPER Charles MM Gnr 604208 RHA
CAPPER Joe MM Pnr 252790 Royal Engineers
CAPPERAULD Andrew MM Pte 52817 1st Northumberland Fusiliers
CAPPS Robert W. MM Pte 21910 Lincolnshire Regt
CAPSTICK Herbert MM Pte 27872 South Lancashire Regt
CAPSTICK Walter MM Gnr 228344 RFA
CARAMELETIS Cosmo MM Pte 368037 RAMC
CARBERRY James MM Cpl 7609 2nd Royal Irish Regt KIA 21.8.18.
CARBERRY Michael MM+Bar L/Cpl 4435 1st Irish Guards
CARBONELL Edgar MM L/Cpl 13818 Suffolk Regt
CARBONI Bernard MM Pte 12038 6th York & Lancaster Regt DOW 2.10.18.
CARD Alfred MM Sjt 61167 129 Coy Machine Gun Corps
CARD Edgar J. MM L/Cpl 720584 24th London Regt

CARD Thomas MM Sjt 840632 D/307 Bde RFA
CARDEN Challion P. MM CQMS 102315 17th Bn Machine Gun Corps
CARDEN Charles W. MM L/Cpl 181424 Royal Engineers
CARDEN Harry MM Pte 723379 1/24th London Regt KIA 23.3.18.
CARDEN John MM Pte 34720 2/4th West Riding Regt
CARDEN M.J. MM L/Cpl G/26052 Middlesex Regt
CARDEN William MM Pte 1152 7th Royal West Surrey Regt
CARDER Alfred MM Sjt 12919 11th Essex Regt DOW 19.9.17.
CARDER James MM Sjt 56542 8 Bde RFA
CARDOW David MM Sjt 120616 306 Siege Bty RGA
CARDWELL John MM Pte 10793 6th Yorkshire Regt
CARDY Arthur C. "DCM,MM+Bar" Sjt 37128 49 Fd Amb RAMC
CARDY Frederick MM L/Cpl 23171 11th Essex Regt KIA 21.3.18.
CARDY Frederick MM+Bar Sjt 810211 AQ/232 Bde RFA
CARDY H. MM L/Cpl 12593 9th Essex Regt
CARE Arthur MM Pte 11206 8th Gloucestershire Regt Died 11.4.18.
CARE Charles MM Pte 718046 23rd London Regt
CARELESS Alfred W. MM Pte 96798 13th Liverpool Regt
CARELESS Cyril Harry "MM,MSM" Cpl 61329 103 Coy Labour Corps
CARESS Alfred F. MM Cpl 9570 2nd Bedfordshire Regt
CARESWELL John MM Cpl 20355 2nd York & Lancaster Regt
CARESWELL Robert Walter MM 2nd Cpl 129131 'N' Special Coy Royal Engineers DOW 15.11.17.
CAREY A.G. MM Sjt 556498 16th London Regt
CAREY Albert Victor MM Cpl 16837 8th Bedfordshire Regt KIA 21.3.18.
CAREY Alfred MM L/Cpl 266463 2/5th West Riding Regt KIA 6.11.18.
CAREY Arnold MM L/Cpl 18205 6th Wiltshire Regt
CAREY Arthur A. MM Pte 33878 1/1st Bucks Bn Oxf & Bucks Light Infantry
CAREY Edmund MM Pte 22681 Wiltshire Regt
CAREY Edward MM Pte 10863 6th Royal West Surrey Regt
CAREY Edward MM Pte 44423 41 Coy Machine Gun Corps
CAREY Frederick William "DCM,MM" L/Cpl 5800 1st East Kent Regt
CAREY Gerald MM Pte 7454 1st Scots Guards
CAREY James MM Pte 9692 2nd East Lancashire Regt
CAREY James H. MM Cpl 8859 2nd Gloucestershire Regt
CAREY Joseph MM Sjt 39396 24 Bde RFA
CAREY Leonard C. MM L/Bdr 745121 RFA
CAREY Robert George MM Bdr 26690 A/186 Bde RFA
CAREY Thomas MM Pte 51410 13th Liverpool Regt
CAREY Thomas J.H. MM Cpl 7076 HAC
CAREY William MM Cpl 5/18111 5th South Wales Borderers
CAREY William Henry MM L/Sjt 202761 2/4th Royal Berkshire Regt DOW 15.3.18.
CAREY William John MM Cpl Fitter 24700 A/59 Bde RFA
CAREY William T MM Sjt 36070 RFA
CARGILL Alexander MM Pte 20412 Machine Gun Corps
CARGILL David MM Gnr 675457 RFA
CARGILL James "MM,MMV(It)" Bdr 86879 168 Heavy Bty RGA
CARGILL John MM Sjt 200735 1/4th Royal Highlanders
CARGILL John M. MM Spr 139056 170 Tunnelling Coy Royal Engineers
CARGILL Reginald MM Pte 51897 Liverpool Regt
CARHART Ernest J. MM Pte 39173 1/9th Highland Light Infantry
CARL John Brown MM Pte S/11256 2nd Gordon Highlanders DOW 19.7.16.
CARLE George MM L/Cpl 300267 1/5th London Regt
CARLESS Frank MM Pte 8160 1/5th South Staffordshire Regt
CARLESS R. MM Pte 23237 2nd South Staffordshire Regt
CARLESS William MM Spr 360659 4 Div Sig Coy Royal Engineers
CARLEY Bertie MM Sjt R/3221 King's Royal Rifle Corps
CARLIC Frederick MM Cpl 6679 1st Gordon Highlanders KIA 30.4.18.
CARLILE Albert MM Pte 201846 1/4th Seaforth Highlanders
CARLILE Alfred MM Sjt 30590 30 Bde RFA
CARLILE Fred "DCM,MM" Sjt 13016 9th Notts & Derby Regt
CARLILE George MM Pte 241011 7th Seaforth Highlanders DOW 22.10.18.
CARLILE Harold C. MM Cpl 3528 13th London Regt
CARLILE James MM Cpl M1/5705 Army Service Corps
CARLILE William James "MC,MM(3006 Sjt 2nd Bn)" 2Lt 13th Rifle Brigade
CARLIN Duncan MM Pte 36891 Scottish Rifles
CARLIN J.H. MM Sjt 8800 Cameron Highlanders
CARLIN John MM Cpl L/10559 7th East Kent Regt KIA 30.9.18.
CARLIN Patrick MM Spr 474237 218 Fd Coy Royal Engineers

CARLIN Patrick MM L/Cpl 42269 12th Royal Scots
CARLINE George A. MM Sjt 121598 185 Tunnelling Coy Royal Engineers
CARLINE L. MM Dvr 781087 RFA
CARLING Cyril MM Sjt 55511 2nd Highland Light Infantry
CARLING Robert "DCM,MM" L/Cpl 388249 RAMC
CARLISLE David MM CQMS 3/9250 Royal Irish Rifles
CARLISLE David MM Pte 12/17413 12th Royal Irish Rifles
CARLISLE J. MM+Bar Pte 5/4534 King's Royal Rifle Corps
CARLISLE Thomas F.B. MM F/Sjt 351 1 Squadron Royal Flying Corps Died 8.7.16.
CARLISLE William S. MM L/Cpl 357964 Liverpool Regt
CARLOS William MM Pte 102400 Machine Gun Corps
CARLOW Charles MM Cpl 10337 Suffolk Regt
CARLOW Thomas MM Gnr 78856 158 Siege Bty RGA
CARLTON George P. MM Gnr 127164 RFA
CARLTON Joseph W. MM Pte C/1244 King's Royal Rifle Corps
CARLTON Samuel F. MM Pte 5678 Royal West Kent Regt
CARLYLE John MM Cpl 266522 1/4th Royal Scots Fusiliers
CARLYLE Robert A. MM Pte 29896 1/4th Leicestershire Regt
CARLYLE Walter MM Pte 17131 Cameron Highlanders
CARMAN A.P. MM Pte 67139 London Regt
CARMAN Thomas MM L/Cpl 61898 Machine Gun Corps
CARMICHAEL Archibald MM Dvr 936071 RFA
CARMICHAEL Charles MM Dvr 32415 117 Bty 26 Bde RFA
CARMICHAEL David MM Pte 90240 RAMC
CARMICHAEL David Colville MM L/Cpl 1358 23rd Royal Fusiliers
CARMICHAEL Duncan MM Pte 31126 Royal Scots
CARMICHAEL George MM L/Cpl 12003 2nd King's Own Scottish Borderers
CARMICHAEL Gordon MM 2nd Cpl 494671 479 Fd Coy Royal Engineers
CARMICHAEL Henry MM Gnr 188077 106 Bty 22 Bde RFA
CARMICHAEL J. MM L/Cpl 203131 Royal Scots Fusiliers
CARMICHAEL James MM Sjt 49779 52nd Bn Machine Gun Corps
CARMICHAEL James MM Sjt 72463 Machine Gun Corps
CARMICHAEL James MM CQMS 11123 4th Liverpool Regt KIA 25.9.17.
CARMICHAEL John MM Pte 301403 1/8th Arg & Suth Highlanders
CARMICHAEL John MM Sjt 30303 Scottish Rifles
CARMICHAEL John MM Pte M2/102437 Army Service Corps
CARMICHAEL John H. "DCM,MM" L/Cpl 58435 32nd Bn Machine Gun Corps
CARMICHAEL Mervin "DCM,MM+Bar" Pte 1211 2nd Arg & Suth Highlanders
CARMICHAEL Neil MM 2nd Cpl 181931 11 Div Sig Coy Royal Engineers
CARMICHAEL Neil MM Pte 376095 11th Royal Scots
CARMICHAEL Norman MM Sjt C/12026 21st King's Royal Rifle Corps
CARMICHAEL Peter MM Cpl S/8028 Arg & Suth Highlanders
CARMICHAEL R.J. MM SSM H/71419 North Irish Horse
CARMICHAEL Robert MM L/Cpl 325054 9th Durham Light Infantry
CARMICHAEL Victor MM Cpl 201196 Seaforth Highlanders
CARMICHAEL W. MM Gnr 3952 12 Bde RFA
CARMICHAEL William MM Pte 201254 Seaforth Highlanders
CARMICHAEL William Henry MM Sjt 60705 1st Northumberland Fusiliers KIA 27.9.18.
CARMICHAEL William Henry MM Gnr 80365 RFA
CARMONT James Henry MM Pte 28647 23rd Manchester Regt
CARN Alec Thomas MM Cpl 37336 Royal Engineers
CARNAGHAN R.J. MM Pte 96897 Middlesex Regt
CARNE W.H. MM Dvr 1968 25 Fd Amb RAMC
CARNEGIE J. MM L/Cpl P/15871 Military Foot Police
CARNEGIE Thomas MM Cpl 19435 Royal Scots
CARNELL Alfred Alexander MM Pte 1527 23rd Middlesex Regt
CARNELL Arthur MM Pte 12026 Yorkshire Light Infantry
CARNELL Henry MM Sjt 367 6th Royal West Kent Regt
CARNELL John F. "MM,MID" L/Cpl 10570 2nd Coldstream Guards
CARNELL Joseph MM Pnr 44765 Royal Engineers
CARNELL Oscar MM Pte 405104 3rd(West Riding)Fd Amb RAMC
CARNELLEY Thomas MM Pte 15474 York & Lancaster Regt
CARNELLY John H. MM Spr 155899 182 Tunnelling Coy Royal Engineers
CARNER William H. MM Sjt 15493 8th Royal Lancaster Regt
CARNES Edward H. MM+Bar Sjt 48122 2nd Welsh Regt
CARNEY Edward MM Sjt 701580 C/317 Bde RFA
CARNEY Edward MM L/Cpl 241315 Royal Lancaster Regt
CARNEY John MM L/Sjt 1525 19th Durham Light Infantry
CARNEY John MM L/Cpl 8171 8th West Yorkshire Regt
CARNEY John MM Cpl 12414 Oxf & Bucks Light Infantry
CARNEY John MM Spr 311702 Royal Engineers
CARNEY Lawrence MM Pte 23908 East Lancashire Regt
CARNEY Martin MM Spr 93217 Royal Engineers
CARNEY Michael MM Spr 151632 Royal Engineers
CARNEY Robert MM Pte 25048 Liverpool Regt
CARNEY Thomas MM Cpl 202721 West Yorkshire Regt
CARNEY Thomas MM L/Cpl 15109 Yorkshire Regt
CARNEY William MM L/Cpl 15813 8th York & Lancaster Regt
CARNLEY Cyril MM Pte 29692 7th Royal Warwickshire Regt
CARNON Reg MM L/Sjt 15743 Royal Lancaster Regt
CAROLAN Andrew J. MM+Bar Sjt 10736 1st Royal Irish Rifles
CARPENTER Albert V. MM Cpl 120498 RFA
CARPENTER Alfred MM Sjt 458 A/235 Bde RFA
CARPENTER C.C. MM Pte 43357 RAMC
CARPENTER Charles P. MM Pte 240619 2/8th Middlesex Regt
CARPENTER Christopher C. MM L/Cpl 121183 Royal Engineers
CARPENTER Christopher T. "DCM,MM" Sjt 13073 1st Coldstream Guards
CARPENTER Duncan A. MM+Bar L/Cpl 137929 Royal Engineers
CARPENTER Edward G. MM Pte 305186 5th London Regt
CARPENTER F. MM Sjt 235787 Yorkshire Light Infantry
CARPENTER Frederick MM L/Cpl G/5501 1st East Kent Regt
CARPENTER Frederick MM Pte 723373 24th London Regt
CARPENTER George MM Bdr 9813 RFA
CARPENTER George MM Pte 21551 Devonshire Regt
CARPENTER George W. MM L/Cpl 10769 4th Worcestershire Regt
Carpenter Harold Leslie "MM,CG(B)" Sjt 41788 4th Worcestershire Regt
CARPENTER Harry L. MM Cpl S/4004 Rifle Brigade
CARPENTER Henry J. MM Pte 282992 4th London Regt
CARPENTER Horace "MM,MID" Pte 3999 2nd Rifle Brigade
CARPENTER John W. MM Pte 3910 7th Royal Sussex Regt
CARPENTER John William MM Cpl 266016 2/7th Royal Warwickshire Regt
CARPENTER Percival MM Pte 474382 11th London Regt
CARPENTER Reginald G. MM L/Cpl M/32539 1 Cav Div Supply Col Army Service Corps
CARPENTER Reginald J. MM Cpl 14841 11 Fd Coy Royal Engineers
CARPENTER S.J. "MM,MID" Pte 12822 1st Grenadier Guards
CARPENTER Thomas MM QMS Wheeler 22121 29 Bde RFA
CARR A.S. MM L/Cpl P5921 Military Foot Police
CARR Albert MM Sjt 41020 1st Northumberland Fusiliers
CARR Alexander MM Cpl 4492 RFA
CARR Alexander Lisle MM L/Cpl 352133 1/9th Royal Scots
CARR Alfred Arthur "DCM,MM" L/Bdr 284241 100 Siege Bty RGA DOW 25.6.18.
CARR Anthony MM L/Cpl 241597 Leicestershire Regt
CARR Arthur MM Sjt 141149 Army Cyclist Corps
CARR Arthur MM Cpl 5109 2nd Lancashire Fusiliers
CARR Charles MM Cpl 291620 Northumberland Fusiliers
CARR Charles MM Cpl 47355 20 Light TM Bty RFA
CARR Daniel "MM,MID" Sjt 3225 1/10th Liverpool Regt
CARR E. MM Pte 20422 East Lancashire Regt
CARR Edward MM L/Cpl 3325 1/5th South Lancashire Regt
CARR Edwin MM Pte 15731 7th Northamptonshire Regt KIA 24.1.17.
CARR Ernest MM Pte 38545 RAMC
CARR Ernest Frederick MM Spr 254896 Royal Engineers
CARR Fred "MM,MID" Gnr 52019 A/256 Bde RFA Died 30.7.18.
CARR Frederick G. MM Pte 2159 Middlesex Regt
CARR Frederick G. MM Pte M2/200532 Army Service Corps
CARR Frederick J. MM 2nd Cpl 470466 Royal Engineers
CARR George MM Cpl 86891 Royal Engineers
CARR George MM Cpl 23124 Machine Gun Corps
CARR George S. MM Sjt S/9933 2nd Seaforth Highlanders
CARR Harold A.P. MM Pte 260606 1/1st City of London Yeo
CARR Harry MM L/Cpl 39442 4th Yorkshire Light Infantry
CARR Harry MM Pte 6444 1st Shropshire Light Infantry
CARR Herbert MM Pte 36959 1/5th West Yorkshire Regt
CARR Hugh MM Spr 151388 253 Tunnelling Coy Royal Engineers KIA 19.12.17.
CARR J. MM Pte 17528 1st Royal Dublin Fusiliers
CARR J.M. MM L/Cpl P/1627 Military Foot Police
CARR James MM Sjt 44401 Machine Gun Corps
CARR James MM Pte 14020 Yorkshire Regt
CARR James MM Pte 4/9440 Durham Light Infantry
CARR James MM Sjt 327152 1/9th Durham Light Infantry
CARR John MM Cpl 8453 10th Royal Warwickshire Regt

CARR John MM Sjt L/8908 1st East Kent Regt
CARR John MM Pte 30507 7th Border Regt
CARR John MM Sjt 240569 1/5th South Lancashire Regt DOW 22.10.18.
CARR John MM Dvr 23147 15 Bde RFA
CARR John MM Dvr 96744 B/230 Bde RFA
CARR John MM Pte 19467 Durham Light Infantry
CARR John W. MM Cpl 22218 12/13th Northumberland Fusiliers
CARR Michael MM Pte 10621 1st King's Own Scottish Borderers DOW 14.4.18.
CARR Norman MM Gnr 72027 RGA
CARR Peter MM Cpl 9841 1st Border Regt
CARR Philip "DCM,MM" CSM 11977 7th East Yorkshire Regt KIA 27.8.18.
CARR Robert MM L/Cpl 55036 21st Manchester Regt
CARR Robert MM Cpl 106963 41st Bn Machine Gun Corps
CARR Robert MM Gnr 10494 A/159 Bde RFA
CARR Samuel MM Pte 24748 23rd Middlesex Regt
CARR Samuel MM Cpl 14727 9th Norfolk Regt
CARR Septimus H. "DCM,MM" CSM 10560 12/13th Northumberland Fusiliers
CARR Stanley MM Pte 21993 10th York & Lancaster Regt
CARR Thomas MM L/Cpl 23/976 Northumberland Fusiliers
CARR Thomas MM Pte 33829 Machine Gun Corps
CARR Thomas Alexander MM Cpl 7377 Northumberland Fusiliers DOW 19.10.18.
CARR Thomas W. MM Cpl 200473 5th Liverpool Regt
CARR W. MM L/Cpl 20635 Royal Scots
CARR Wilfred J. MM Cpl 111637 10th Bn Tank Corps
CARR William MM Sjt 51649 Royal Fusiliers
CARR William MM Gnr 84685 HQ 11 Bde RFA
CARR William MM L/Cpl 28/231 Northumberland Fusiliers
CARR William A. MM+Bar Pte G/874 7th Royal Sussex Regt
CARR William F. MM Pte 18025 1st Coldstream Guards
CARR William H. MM Pte 25180 2nd Suffolk Regt
CARRACK Charles MM Cpl 13539 10th West Riding Regt
CARRADICE George MM L/Cpl 240846 1/5th Royal Lancaster Regt
CARRADICE Thomas MM Gnr 120778 106 Bde RFA
CARRADUS Walter MM Pte 35992 17th Lancashire Fusiliers
CARRATT Anthony MM Pte 16758 6th Lincolnshire Regt
CARRICK Charles MM L/Cpl 72398 Machine Gun Corps
CARRICK Edward MM Pte 201442 1/5th Durham Light Infantry
CARRICK John MM L/Cpl R/4287 13th King's Royal Rifle Corps
CARRICK John S. MM Gnr 7588 RFA
CARRICK Richard MM Pte 8294 8th Lincolnshire Regt
CARRICK Walter MM Cpl 18/464 18th Durham Light Infantry KIA 28.6.17.
CARRIE Charles MM Cpl 16561 4th Royal Fusiliers
CARRIGAN James MM Pte 17882 10th Durham Light Infantry KIA 17.10.17.
CARRIISON Herbert MM Spr 1992 Royal Engineers
CARRINGTON Francis R. MM Sjt 13376 6th Northamptonshire Regt
CARRINGTON Harold V. MM Pte 472019 RAMC
CARRINGTON Horace MM Pte 49245 RAMC
CARRINGTON James W. "MM,MSM" L/Cpl 391446 9th London Regt
CARRINGTON John William MM Sjt 51678 17th Royal Fusiliers
CARRINGTON Peter W. MM Sjt S/24604 5 Div Train Army Service Corps
CARRINGTON Stanley Francis MM Sjt 25531 22nd Manchester Regt KIA 4.10.17.
CARRINGTON Sydney S. MM L/Cpl 251054 3rd London Regt
CARRINGTON Walter MM Sjt 19478 8th Bedfordshire Regt
CARRINGTON William B. MM Cpl 236915 475 Fd Coy Royal Engineers
CARRINGTON William C. MM Sjt 559 RGA
CARROLL A.S. MM CSM 201114 5/6th Scottish Rifles
CARROLL Alfred MM Pte 10942 5th Royal Berkshire Regt
CARROLL Arthur A. "MM,MID" Cpl 68782 9 Bde RFA
CARROLL Edwin MM+Bar Sjt G/7810 11th Royal Fusiliers
CARROLL Frank MM L/Cpl 49380 1st Cheshire Regt
CARROLL George MM Pte 268388 Liverpool Regt
CARROLL Harry MM Pte 240290 1/5th North Lancashire Regt
CARROLL Henry J. MM Sjt 105915 RFA
CARROLL Herbert MM Cpl 377086 10th Manchester Regt
CARROLL J.J. MM+Bar Pte 350402 5th Manchester Regt
CARROLL James MM Pte 5/5487 Leinster Regt
CARROLL James MM Pte 3483 1st Irish Guards Died 15.12.16.
CARROLL James W. MM Pte 12492 2nd West Riding Regt
CARROLL John MM Sjt 8249 Royal Dublin Fusiliers
CARROLL John MM Pte 63856 RAMC
CARROLL John MM Pte 4009 1st Irish Guards
CARROLL John MM Cpl 7486 1st West Yorkshire Regt KIA 18.9.16.
CARROLL John C. MM Spr 252706 Royal Engineers
CARROLL Joseph MM Dvr 69739 130 Bty 40 Bde RFA
CARROLL Joseph MM Sjt 15840 289 Siege Bty RGA
CARROLL Joseph MM Pte 13416 2nd West Riding Regt DOW 8.5.18.
CARROLL Matt MM Pte 11049 2nd Royal Irish Rifles
CARROLL Michael MM Pte 9808 1st Royal Dublin Fusiliers
CARROLL Myles MM Pte 3/5113 2nd Royal Munster Fusiliers
CARROLL Oswald MM Pte 18/1186 18th Durham Light Infantry
CARROLL Patrick MM Cpl 19392 Royal Dublin Fusiliers
CARROLL Philip MM Sjt 8272 2nd South Wales Borderers KIA 28.9.18.
CARROLL R. MM Pte 280240 Highland Light Infantry
CARROLL Raymond MM Sjt 14/528 14th Royal Warwickshire Regt
CARROLL Richard MM Sjt 592737 18th London Regt
CARROLL Stanley MM Cpl 463088 Royal Engineers
CARROLL Stephen J. MM+Bar L/Sjt 370419 8th London Regt
CARROLL Thomas MM Pte 5/6026 2nd Royal Munster Fusiliers
CARROLL Thomas MM Cpl 12838 8th Yorkshire Regt
CARROLL Thomas MM Bdr 73019 40 Bde RFA
CARROLL Thomas MM L/Cpl 146006 155 Fd Coy Royal Engineers
CARROLL Timothy MM Spr 96278 282 Fd Coy Royal Engineers
CARROLL William MM Pte 21293 1st West Yorkshire Regt
CARROLL William MM Cpl 2834 7th Leinster Regt
CARROLL William G. "MM,MID" Sjt 282 RAMC
CARROLL William T. MM L/Sjt 91189 Durham Light Infantry
CARROTT George William MM Pte 27015 Lincolnshire Regt
CARRUTHERS Albert E. MM Pte 51323 11th Royal Scots
CARRUTHERS Alfred James MM Pte 11215 23rd Royal Fusiliers DOW 8.10.18.
CARRUTHERS Catherine M. MM Staff Nurse F TFNS
CARRUTHERS David J. MM Cpl 28664 2nd Royal Scots Fusiliers
CARRUTHERS Frank MM Pte 510743 2/14th London Regt
CARRUTHERS James MM Sjt 202651 5th Liverpool Regt
CARRUTHERS John MM Spr 362994 Att 68 Bde RGA Sig Sect Royal Engineers
CARRUTHERS John MM Cpl S/3417 Arg & Suth Highlanders
CARRUTHERS Matthew MM Sjt 275358 1/7th Arg & Suth Highlanders
CARRUTHERS Robert MM Cpl 200371 1/4th Royal Lancaster Regt
CARRUTHERS Robert MM Cpl 2255 1/5th Border Regt
CARRUTHERS Robert MM Cpl 23776 7 Fd Amb RAMC KIA 23.8.18.
CARRUTHERS Robert MM+Bar Sjt 715145 D/210 Bde RFA
CARRUTHERS William MM Pte 17762 1st Somerset Light Infantry
CARSE Derwent Albert "MC,MM(98019 Sjt)" 2Lt A/153 Bde RFA
CARSLAKE Percy MM Pte 10237 9th West Yorkshire Regt
CARSLAKE Thomas Henry MM Dvr 101993 A/160 Bde RFA
CARSON Andrew MM Pte 18/1644 Royal Irish Rifles
CARSON Charles H. MM Sjt S/1783 Rifle Brigade
CARSON Charles James MM Sjt 52040 8th Lincolnshire Regt
CARSON John MM Pte 47557 Machine Gun Corps
CARSON John MM Cpl 470287 526 Fd Coy Royal Engineers DOW 4.7.18.
CARSON Joseph "DCM,MM" Sjt 240655 1/5th South Lancashire Regt
CARSON Joseph MM L/Cpl 3/6173 1st Dorsetshire Regt
CARSON Robert James MM+Bar L/Cpl 10/14186 10th Royal Irish Rifles
CARSON Thomas MM Gnr 29786 RFA
CARSON William MM Pte S/11495 6th Cameron Highlanders DOW 10.6.18.
CARSON William MM Pte 14524 9th Royal Inniskilling Fusiliers
CARSTAIRS George MM Pte 290392 1/7th Royal Highlanders
CARSTAIRS Horace MM Bdr 960016 RFA
CARSTAIRS James G. MM Pte 375408 8th London Regt
CARSTAIRS James L. MM Bdr L/38091 RFA
CART Thomas MM+Bar Pte 11341 1st Coldstream Guards
CARTER A. MM Dvr 82927 RFA
CARTER A.H. MM Cpl 40544 Lancashire Fusiliers
CARTER Abraham MM Pte 21193 3rd Grenadier Guards DOW 16.10.18.
CARTER Albert MM L/Cpl 1357 2nd Manchester Regt
CARTER Albert MM Sjt 18639 Middlesex Regt
CARTER Albert MM L/Cpl 20906 23rd Royal Fusiliers KIA 25.3.18.
CARTER Albert E. MM Pte M2/156088 Army Service Corps
CARTER Albert Edward MM Cpl 547 MGC(Heavy Branch)

CARTER Albert P. MM Sjt 235021 Royal Welsh Fusiliers
CARTER Alexander MM Pte 295395 Somerset Light Infantry
CARTER Alfred MM Pte 25147 1st Royal West Surrey Regt
CARTER Alfred MM Pte 27961 10th Worcestershire Regt KIA 22.3.18.
CARTER Ambrose Archibald MM Pte M2/055308 Att 7 Fd Amb RAMC Army Service Corps
CARTER Arthur MM L/Cpl 20306 2nd Yorkshire Regt
CARTER Arthur MM Pte 200215 1/4th Royal Berkshire Regt
CARTER Arthur A. MM Spr 480667 82 Fd Coy Royal Engineers
CARTER Arthur G. MM Pte 20449 1st West Yorkshire Regt
CARTER Arthur Thomas MM Sjt 61073 40 Bde RFA
CARTER Benjamin MM Pte 9484 South Staffordshire Regt
CARTER Bertie C. MM Pte 12058 9th Essex Regt
CARTER C. MM Sjt 19215 1st Essex Regt
CARTER Charles MM Pte 17867 Machine Gun Corps
CARTER Charles B. MM Sjt 15115 7th Oxf & Bucks Light Infantry
CARTER Charles Frederick MM Pte 37134 2nd Yorkshire Light Infantry KIA 30.8.18.
CARTER Charles Henry MM Pte 45561 RAMC
CARTER Charles Louis MM Cpl 27453 Somerset Light Infantry
CARTER Charles S. MM Pte 4642 19th London Regt
CARTER Christopher MM Bdr 80373 101 Bde HQ RFA
CARTER Daniel MM Dvr 83928 RFA
CARTER Ebenezer S. MM Gnr 165860 RGA
CARTER Eddie MM Cpl 371108 68 Siege Bty RGA
CARTER Edward MM L/Cpl 97459 47th Bn Machine Gun Corps
CARTER Edward Ernest MM Pte 201737 10th Essex Regt
CARTER Eli MM Cpl 14331 7th Wiltshire Regt
CARTER Ernest MM Cpl 21720 2nd Grenadier Guards
CARTER Ernest MM Sjt 65550 62nd Bn Machine Gun Corps
CARTER Ernest Lionel MM Sjt 925 10th Royal Fusiliers
CARTER F. MM Pte 512394 3 Fd Amb RAMC
CARTER Francis James MM Sjt 11043 Grenadier Guards
CARTER Frank MM Gnr 138464 RFA
CARTER Frank L. MM Pte 16973 6th South Wales Borderers
CARTER Frederick "MM,MID" L/Cpl G/4710 8th East Surrey Regt
CARTER Frederick MM L/Cpl 16015 5 Coy Machine Gun Corps DOW 13.11.16.
CARTER Frederick MM L/Cpl 40010 Leicestershire Regt
CARTER Frederick Arthur MM Cpl 68071 1 Bde RFA
CARTER Frederick C. MM L/Cpl 202721 1st Royal West Surrey Regt
CARTER Frederick C. MM Pte 15875 7th Oxf & Bucks Light Infantry
CARTER Frederick C. MM Sjt 14464 Coldstream Guards
CARTER Frederick F. MM Pte 236316 8th West Yorkshire Regt
CARTER George MM Cpl 46191 4th Worcestershire Regt
CARTER George MM Pte 252423 3rd London Regt KIA 7.10.18.
CARTER George MM Cpl 201199 1/8th Worcestershire Regt
CARTER George MM L/Cpl P/260 1st Rifle Brigade KIA 1.9.18.
CARTER George MM Sjt 14139 7th North Lancashire Regt
CARTER George "MM+Bar,MID" Sjt 38203 27 Bde RFA
CARTER George MM Pte 32931 RAMC
CARTER George MM Sjt 86032 RGA
CARTER George H. MM Spr 25455 2 Sig Troop Royal Engineers
CARTER George R. MM Pte 18634 7th Wiltshire Regt
CARTER H. MM+Bar L/Cpl 405267 RAMC
CARTER H.W. MM Pte 238072 15th Yorkshire Light Infantry
CARTER Harold C. MM Sjt 3363 Machine Gun Corps
CARTER Harold J. MM Pte 10347 2nd Gloucestershire Regt
CARTER Harold Joseph "MM,VM(Rm)" Cpl 260743 1/1st 1st County of London Yeomanry (Middlesex Hussars)
CARTER Harold Y. MM Pte 32513 5th Oxf & Bucks Light Infantry
CARTER Harry MM Sjt 200040 1/4th Lincolnshire Regt
CARTER Harry MM Sjt 2229 1/4th Lincolnshire Regt
CARTER Harry Victor "MM,CG(B)" L/Cpl 10203 1st South Lancashire Regt
CARTER Henry MM Sjt 7217 1st Wiltshire Regt
CARTER Henry MM Sjt 15362 7th East Yorkshire Regt DOW 31.7.17.
CARTER Henry Richard MM Pte 25183 Royal Warwickshire Regt
CARTER Henry W. MM L/Cpl 2367 1/2nd London Regt
CARTER Herbert "DCM,MM" Sjt 897257 34th London Regt
CARTER Herbert MM Sjt 19670 Machine Gun Corps
CARTER Herbert MM Pte 14403 1st Lincolnshire Regt
CARTER Herbert Reginald MM Sjt 20484 D/48 Bde RFA
CARTER Herbert W. MM Pte 35761 8 Fd Amb RAMC
CARTER Horace Claude MM Gnr 45943 X/19 Med TM Bty RGA
CARTER J. MM Pte 267665 Royal Highlanders
CARTER J.H. MM Sjt 570 RFA
CARTER J.H. MM Cpl M1/06633 Army Service Corps
CARTER James MM Sjt 58715 C/84 Bde RFA
CARTER James MM+Bar Bdr 66229 286 Bde RFA
CARTER James MM Pte 13030 10th Lancashire Fusiliers
CARTER James MM Pte 18931 6th East Lancashire Regt
CARTER James Talbot MM Gnr 662 A/236 Bde RFA
CARTER John MM Sjt 21/554 21st West Yorkshire Regt
CARTER John MM Pte G/25634 11th Royal West Surrey Regt
CARTER John MM Pte 40493 RAMC
CARTER John MM Spr 93826 Royal Engineers
CARTER John MM Pte 28098 1st Grenadier Guards
CARTER John MM L/Cpl 39332 Royal Berkshire Regt
CARTER John MM Pte 8337 1st Royal Dublin Fusiliers
CARTER John MM Bdr 930848 RFA
CARTER John MM L/Sjt 2229 1/9th Durham Light Infantry KIA 15.6.16.
CARTER John MM Pte 9266 Scottish Rifles
CARTER John MM Gnr 36296 RFA
CARTER John Elias MM Pte 2234 6th Lincolnshire Regt Died 11.3.19.
CARTER John W. "MM,MID" Pte 9603 Coldstream Guards
CARTER John W. MM Gnr 765622 RFA
CARTER Joseph MM Spr 43743 12 Fd Coy Royal Engineers
CARTER Joseph MM Pte 10938 15th Hussars KIA 25.11.17.
CARTER Joseph MM Sjt 2666 11th Royal Fusiliers KIA 26.9.16.
CARTER Joseph MM Pte 240184 Lancashire Fusiliers
CARTER Joseph MM L/Cpl 15862 12th Durham Light Infantry
CARTER Leonard MM Sjt 8241 1st Suffolk Regt
CARTER Leonard J. MM Sjt 20012 Machine Gun Corps
CARTER Leslie Raymond MM Sjt 9626 B/71 Bde RFA
CARTER Maurice MM Pte 3892 1/1st Cambridgeshire Regt
CARTER Only E. MM Cpl 71810 4th Royal Fusiliers
CARTER Percy John MM L/Cpl 11900 Scots Guards
CARTER Percy W. MM S/Sjt 1401 1/3(South Midland)Fd Amb RAMC Died 8.11.18.
CARTER Philip E. MM L/Cpl 266228 18th Liverpool Regt
CARTER Ralph MM Sjt 38403 7th York & Lancaster Regt
CARTER Reginald MM Bdr L/5761 A/162 Bde RFA
CARTER Reuben MM Gnr L/3212 RFA
CARTER Richard MM Sjt 965019 RFA
CARTER Richard MM Pte 22446 RAMC
CARTER Robert MM Dvr 75213 23 Bty 40 Bde RFA DOW 13.5.18.
CARTER Robert MM Pte 44940 12/13th Northumberland Fusiliers KIA 26.4.18.
CARTER Robert George Woor MM Cpl 65284 126 Fd Coy Royal Engineers
CARTER Robert John MM Sjt 26874 122 Heavy Bty RGA
CARTER Ronald E. MM Cpl 5625 RGA
CARTER Samuel MM Sjt 313252 2/1(North Midland)Hy Bty RGA
CARTER Stafford Thomas MM Sjt 58899 2 Bde RFA
CARTER Stanley MM+Bar Cpl 45929 3rd Bn 76 Coy Machine Gun Corps
CARTER Theophilus MM Bdsm 1427 1/4th Oxf & Bucks Light Infantry
CARTER Thomas MM Pte 41365 Essex Regt
CARTER Thomas MM Pte 53339 1st Lancashire Fusiliers
CARTER Thomas MM+Bar Pte 510 2nd Manchester Regt
CARTER Thomas MM Pte 306511 Lancashire Fusiliers
CARTER Thomas MM L/Cpl 1633 1/4th Leicestershire Regt
CARTER Thomas MM Pte 6/540 3rd Rifle Brigade
CARTER Thomas W. MM+Bar Sjt 9260 2nd Coldstream Guards
CARTER Tom MM Cpl T4/253780 62 Div Train Army Service Corps
CARTER William MM Pte 261001 13th West Riding Regt
CARTER William MM Dvr T4/143156 Att 108 Coy Labour Corps Army Service Corps
CARTER William MM Pte 19904 8th Royal Highlanders
CARTER William MM Sjt 19539 13th Liverpool Regt DOW 19.7.16.
CARTER William MM L/Sjt 240737 1st Royal West Kent Regt
CARTER William MM L/Sjt 980 1/7th Worcestershire Regt
CARTER William MM Pte 13324 9th West Riding Regt
CARTER William MM Cpl 200093 Leicestershire Regt
CARTER William MM Gnr 153910 RGA
CARTER William MM Pte 201238 8th Manchester Regt Died 2.11.18.
CARTER William MM L/Cpl 39243 225 Coy Machine Gun Corps
CARTER William F. MM Pte 119562 Machine Gun Corps
CARTER William H. MM Sjt 13280 11th West Yorkshire Regt
CARTER William H. MM Pte 11848 6th Shropshire Light Infantry
CARTER William J. MM Pte 31350 2nd Bedfordshire Regt
CARTER William James MM+Bar Cpl 84649 2nd Bn Machine Gun Corps KIA 1.10.18.

CARTER William R. MM Pte 8111 2nd Bn Oxf & Bucks Light Infantry
CARTER William T. MM Cpl 28032 Wiltshire Regt
CARTER William Thomas "MC,MM(2613 Sjt 1st E Surrey)" T/2Lt 7th Bedfordshire Regt
CARTER Willie MM Pte 307627 7th West Riding Regt
CARTLAND James W. MM Pte 203772 1/4th Royal Berkshire Regt
CARTLEDGE Arthur MM Pte 26663 5th West Riding Regt
CARTLEDGE Harold MM L/Cpl 4753 Notts & Derby Regt
CARTLEDGE Reginald Arthur MM L/Cpl 320 1/1st HAC(Inf)
CARTLEDGE Robert MM Pte 241047 2/5th York & Lancaster Regt
CARTLEDGE William MM Cpl 25219 1st Northumberland Fusiliers
CARTLIDGE Absolam MM L/Sjt 29653 13th Yorkshire Regt
CARTLIDGE Joseph MM 2nd Cpl 492294 Royal Engineers
CARTLIDGE Peter MM L/Cpl 16417 9th Royal Fusiliers DOW 11.8.17.
CARTLIDGE Samuel MM Sjt 17810 1st Notts & Derby Regt
CARTMAN Fred MM L/Cpl 28172 West Yorkshire Regt
CARTMEL Alfred Edward MM Sjt 105084 1/1st Hertfordshire Yeomanry
CARTMEL Norman MM L/Cpl 86346 29th Bn Machine Gun Corps
CARTMELL Harold J. MM L/Sjt 393750 16th London Regt
CARTMELL Thomas MM Pte 306311 8th Liverpool Regt
CARTMELL William MM Pte 34926 Liverpool Regt
CARTNER William M. MM Pte 30387 2nd Grenadier Guards
CARTON Hugh MM Sjt 3132 1st Irish Guards KIA 15.9.16.
CARTON James MM Pte 1949 1/4th Royal Lancaster Regt DOW 10.1.17.
CARTON Joseph MM L/Cpl 40029 2nd Royal Irish Rifles KIA 23.11.17.
CARTWRIGHT A. MM Pte 302775 2nd Royal Scots
CARTWRIGHT A.E. MM L/Cpl 25688 East Surrey Regt
CARTWRIGHT Alfred MM Sjt 23732 Middlesex Regt
CARTWRIGHT Bert MM L/Sjt 38969 9th Northumberland Fusiliers
CARTWRIGHT Charles MM 2nd Cpl 79909 170 Tunnelling Coy Royal Engineers
CARTWRIGHT Charles Robinson MM L/Cpl 702 10th Lincolnshire Regt KIA 16.4.18.
CARTWRIGHT Donald M. MM Pte 14355 11th West Yorkshire Regt
CARTWRIGHT Edward MM Sjt 240541 1/5th South Lancaster Regt
CARTWRIGHT F. MM CoH 4389 2nd GMGR
CARTWRIGHT Francis G. MM Cpl 58532 RGA
CARTWRIGHT Frank "MM,MID" Cpl 10526 Royal Engineers
CARTWRIGHT Fred MM Pte 305937 West Riding Regt
CARTWRIGHT Frederick MM L/Sjt 265952 1/1st Bucks Bn Oxf & Bucks Light Infantry
CARTWRIGHT Frederick G. MM Sjt 201041 Royal Welsh Fusiliers
CARTWRIGHT Frederick J. MM Pte 13790 9th North Lancashire Regt
CARTWRIGHT George MM Cpl 42430 RAMC
CARTWRIGHT George Henry MM L/Cpl 12629 South Staffordshire Regt
CARTWRIGHT Henry MM Sjt 105202 Royal Engineers
CARTWRIGHT Herbert MM Sjt 46730 D/108 Bde RFA DOW 15.7.17.
CARTWRIGHT James MM BQMS 60159 198 Siege Bty RGA
CARTWRIGHT James MM Pte S/9202 Rifle Brigade
CARTWRIGHT John MM Pte 36925 2/4th North Lancashire Regt KIA 28.9.18.
CARTWRIGHT John MM SSM 5153 5th Lancers
CARTWRIGHT John A. MM Pte 419382 RAMC
CARTWRIGHT John Henry MM L/Cpl 506587 Inland Water Transport Royal Engineers
CARTWRIGHT John Maurice MM Dvr 78276 B/312 Bde RFA KIA 20.7.18.
CARTWRIGHT Joseph MM Spr 171997 4 Div Sig Coy Royal Engineers
CARTWRIGHT Leonard MM Pte 18408 1st Shropshire Light Infantry KIA 21.3.18.
CARTWRIGHT Moses MM Cpl 4433 RFA
CARTWRIGHT Oliver F. MM Pte 12497 8th North Staffordshire Regt
CARTWRIGHT Percy MM Pte 38350 54 Fd Amb RAMC
CARTWRIGHT Percy MM Dvr L/29323 A/168 Bde RFA
CARTWRIGHT Richard William "DCM,MM" CSM 8/13584 8th South Staffordshire Regt
CARTWRIGHT Stanley MM Cpl 365 RFA
CARTWRIGHT Thomas Hopper MM Pte 11599 20th Northumberland Fusiliers
CARTWRIGHT Thomas J. MM Pte 2039 West Riding Regt
CARTWRIGHT Thomas William MM Sjt 1435 1/4th York & Lancaster Regt
CARTWRIGHT Thomas William MM Cpl 7177 Machine Gun Corps
CARTWRIGHT Walter MM Pte 240334 1/5th North Lancashire Regt
CARTWRIGHT William MM Sjt 337662 120 Siege Bty RGA
CARTWRIGHT William MM Dvr 91357 A/75 Bde RFA
CARTWRIGHT William E. MM QMS 25329 RFA
CARTWRIGHT William E. MM Pte 142438 1st Bn Machine Gun Corps
CARTWRIGHT William H. MM Pnr 130425 Royal Engineers
CARTY Henry Owen MM Gnr Saddler 81069 D/69 Bde RFA
CARTY John MM Pte 16772 Liverpool Regt
CARVELL Albert C. MM Sjt 22827 1st Northamptonshire Regt
CARVELL John E. MM Dvr 71651 Guards Div Sig Coy Royal Engineers
CARVELL Robert MM Bdr 4620 C/153 Bde RFA KIA 11.7.17.
CARVELL Robert S. MM Cpl 6699 7th Hussars
CARVELL William MM L/Cpl 10734 5th Oxf & Bucks Light Infantry
CARVER Arthur "DCM,MM" Pte 21280 8th Border Regt
CARVER Charles MM Pte 17615 Yorkshire Light Infantry
CARVER Charles "MM,MC(G)" Sjt 4887 12th Arg & Suth Highlanders
CARVER Ernest H. MM Pte G/4536 8th Royal Sussex Regt
CARVER Frank MM Pte 16386 6th Lincolnshire Regt
CARVER Joseph E. MM L/Cpl 13373 Dorsetshire Regt
CARVER Percy MM Sjt 684323 22nd London Regt
CARVER Richard G. MM Pte 53026 26th Royal Fusiliers
CARVER William MM Gnr 61534 148 Siege Bty RGA
CARY Thomas MM Pte 38211 12th Gloucestershire Regt
CASBOLT Thomas Edward MM Sjt 54509 109 Railway Constr Coy Royal Engineers
CASBOURNE Oscar W. MM Cpl 275629 1/6th Essex Regt
CASE Albert J. MM L/Cpl A/202725 13th King's Royal Rifle Corps
CASE Cyril J. MM Spr 2119 Royal Engineers
CASE Lawrence MM Dvr 220483 RFA
CASE William MM Pte 20308 8th Royal Lancaster Regt
CASELEY Arthur Cecil James MM Sjt 5562 19 Fd Amb RAMC
CASELTON Thomas George "DCM,MM" CSM G/1940 7th East Kent Regt
CASELTON Tom MM L/Cpl T/21285 Att 9 Fd Amb RAMC Army Service Corps
CASEMORE Rowland Sydney MM Sjt 9103 1st West Yorkshire Regt KIA 21.3.18.
CASEWELL William MM+Bar Pte 8650 RAMC
CASEY Alfred T. MM Dvr 31171 RFA
CASEY Christopher MM Gnr 707420 RFA
CASEY Edward MM Pte 139 Cheshire Regt
CASEY Gregory MM Pte 12120 3rd Worcestershire Regt
CASEY Hugh MM BSM 14840 161 Siege Bty RGA
CASEY J. MM Sjt 28881 RFA
CASEY John MM Pte 25109 10th Royal Welsh Fusiliers
CASEY John MM Pte 40794 18th Lancashire Fusiliers
CASEY John P. MM 2nd Cpl 400123 126 Fd Coy Royal Engineers
CASEY John R. MM L/Cpl 25651 Machine Gun Corps
CASEY Michael MM Bdr 70284 11 Bde RFA
CASEY Patrick MM+Bar Pte 5/15424 5th South Wales Borderers
CASEY Patrick MM Sjt 13945 1st Grenadier Guards
CASEY T. MM Cpl 46068 8th West Yorkshire Regt
CASEY Thomas Robert MM L/Cpl 9835 Devonshire Regt
CASEY Walter John MM CSM 3079 Northumberland Fusiliers
CASEY William MM L/Cpl 15399 1 Special Coy Middlesex Regt
CASEY William "MM,MID" Pte 2753 1st Gloucestershire Regt
CASEY William M. MM Sjt 1779 1st Manchester Regt
CASEY William S. MM L/Cpl 13706 7th Duke of Cornwall's LI
CASH Edwin MM Dvr 58165 12 Bde RFA
CASH Ernest MM Cpl 9487 1st South Staffordshire Regt KIA 1.7.16.
CASH Harry MM Pte 1668 1/1st Cambridgeshire Regt KIA 26.7.17.
CASH Henry MM Pte 2343 6th Connaught Rangers
CASH Thomas MM+Bar Pte R/13821 King's Royal Rifle Corps
CASH William MM Pte 12561 1st Worcestershire Regt
CASH William Henry MM Cpl 84152 A/124 Bde RFA
CASH William Joseph MM Gnr 85103 23 Bty 40 Bde RFA
CASHEL James MM Pte 43539 2nd Royal Dublin Fusiliers
CASHER Benjamin MM Pte 51038 7th Worcestershire Regt
CASHMAN George Albert MM Dvr 10439 4 Div Ammn Col RFA
CASHMAN John P. MM Dvr 54281 RFA
CASHMORE Edgar E. MM Pte 235662 1/1st Gloucestershire Yeomanry
CASHMORE George MM Sjt 266361 2/7th Royal Warwickshire Regt DOW 2.4.18.
CASHMORE John McDonald MM Cpl S/4416 9th Royal Highlanders
CASHMORE Lawrence W. MM Sjt 810246 RFA

CASHMORE W. MM Sjt Shoeing Smith 58639 RFA
CASKIE James MM Cpl 23692 Machine Gun Corps
CASKIE William MM Pte 8931 1/8th Scottish Rifles KIA 19.4.17.
CASLAW John McC. MM L/Sjt 27032 24th London Regt
CASLEY William MM L/Cpl 24883 Duke of Cornwall's LI
CASPER Leonard MM Cpl 5909 2nd Royal Scots Fusiliers KIA 9.4.18.
CASS Albert MM BSM 48701 D/84 Bde RFA
CASS Frank MM Pte 3/8952 11th West Yorkshire Regt DOW 22.9.17.
CASS George A. MM L/Cpl L/14752 4th Middlesex Regt
CASS John Alexander MM+Bar Pte 22353 7th Royal Fusiliers DOW 30.8.18.
CASS William MM L/Cpl M2/191429 59 Div MT Coy Army Service Corps
CASSARLEY Vincent S. MM Pte 240344 West Yorkshire Regt
CASSELL John MM Pte 20654 22 Fd Amb RAMC
CASSELLS Archibald MM Pte 18426 12th Highland Light Infantry
CASSELS James MM Cpl 33622 12th Highland Light Infantry
CASSELS William MM Pte 43244 9th Scottish Rifles KIA 12.10.17.
CASSERLEY Andrew MM Spr 359771 19 Div Sig Coy Royal Engineers
CASSIDY Cyril MM Pte 10866 2/1st HAC(Inf)
CASSIDY Daniel MM Pte 4207 2nd Royal Irish Regt
CASSIDY F. MM Pte 508270 1st(London)Fd Amb RAMC
CASSIDY F. MM Pte 25659 Royal Dublin Fusiliers
CASSIDY George MM Pte 13501 20th Manchester Regt
CASSIDY Henry MM Pte 3330 22nd London Regt
CASSIDY J. MM L/Cpl 241205 7th Royal Highlanders
CASSIDY James MM Pte 11648 6th Royal Inniskilling Fusiliers
CASSIDY James MM Pte 5827 2nd Royal West Surrey Regt
CASSIDY John MM Pte 4685 2nd Leinster Regt
CASSIDY John MM Cpl 4790 1/4th Royal Highlanders KIA 3.9.16.
CASSIDY John MM 2nd Cpl 79678 Royal Engineers
CASSIDY John MM Pte 19225 6th South Wales Borderers
CASSIDY Martin MM Cpl 17463 Machine Gun Corps
CASSIDY Michael MM Pte 377065 Labour Corps
CASSIDY Patrick MM Pte 290204 8th Scottish Rifles
CASSIDY Peter MM Pte 20593 Machine Gun Corps
CASSIDY Robert MM L/Cpl 13186 8th Northumberland Fusiliers KIA 19.7.18.
CASSIDY William J. MM Pte 103532 10th Notts & Derby Regt
CASSIDY William J. MM Pte 9245 8/10th Gordon Highlanders
CASSIE Adam MM Pnr 130159 Royal Engineers
CASSIN Michael H. MM Cpl 42758 74 Fd Coy Royal Engineers
CASSINELLI Thomas MM Cpl 35327 Durham Light Infantry
CASSON Charles R. MM L/Cpl STK/642 10th Royal Fusiliers
CASSON Edward MM L/Cpl 101392 Royal Engineers
CASSON Ernest MM Pte R/14941 13th King's Royal Rifle Corps
CASSON George William MM Cpl 8057 11th Royal Fusiliers KIA 26.9.16.
CASSON Henry MM Cpl 9325 1st Essex Regt KIA 31.7.18.
CASSON James "MM,MC(G)" Pte 9/14430 9th East Lancashire Regt
CASSON James MM Bdr 93672 18 Div Ammn Col RFA
CASSON John R. MM Bdr 35177 RGA
CASSON Joseph MM Sjt 6350 2nd Worcestershire Regt
CAST John W. MM Pte 4550 Army Cyclist Corps
CASTEL William MM Pte 3278 20th London Regt
CASTELLANO Walter W. MM Sjt 40417 RGA
CASTELOW Fred MM Pte 28 RAMC
CASTLE Albert MM Pte 20397 Army Cyclist Corps
CASTLE Albert E. "DCM,MM" Sjt 676434 A/285 Bde RFA
CASTLE Albert Walter MM Dvr 20926 4 Div Ammn Col RFA
CASTLE Alfred James MM Sjt 333885 2nd Highland Light Infantry
CASTLE Arthur John MM Cpl 19190 Yorkshire Regt
CASTLE Charles F. MM Sjt 12737 5th Lancers
CASTLE Charles P. MM L/Cpl 40091 11th Royal West Surrey Regt
CASTLE Edmund MM L/Cpl G/5385 8th East Surrey Regt
CASTLE Edward MM Cpl 518900 559 Army Tps Coy Royal Engineers
CASTLE Edwin MM Sjt 1806 8th Royal Sussex Regt
CASTLE Franklin MM+Bar Pte 242034 5th West Riding Regt
CASTLE Harold F. MM L/Cpl 85940 Royal Engineers
CASTLE Harry MM Pte A/200259 12th King's Royal Rifle Corps KIA 2.4.18.
CASTLE Henry MM Dvr 87502 33 Bde RFA
CASTLE Herbert MM Pte 6737 9th East Surrey Regt
CASTLE Horace "DCM,MM" Bdr 58546 13 Bty 17 Bde RFA
CASTLE Horace MM Bdr 58546 45 Bde RFA
CASTLE J. MM Bdr 166111 RGA
CASTLE Joseph MM Cpl 1174 1/4th London Regt
CASTLE Percy A. MM L/Cpl 282564 1st Highland Light Infantry
CASTLE Percy W. MM Spr 71583 Royal Engineers
CASTLE S. MM L/Cpl 10568 Royal Warwickshire Regt
CASTLE Sidney T. MM Pte 20856 East Surrey Regt
CASTLE William MM CQMS 20040 9th West Yorkshire Regt
CASTLE William MM Dvr 925793 RFA
CASTLE William MM Sjt 91209 Labour Corps att RE
CASTLE William E.G. "DCM,MM" L/Cpl 235257 1/1st Gloucestershire Yeomanry
CASTLE William S. MM L/Sjt 202970 5th Royal Sussex Regt
CASTLEDINE George MM Pte R/20468 King's Royal Rifle Corps
CASTLEDINE George W. MM Sjt 12022 7th York & Lancaster Regt
CASTLEDINE John MM Sjt 31214 RGA
CASTLER F.R. MM Cpl 9069 4th King's Royal Rifle Corps
CASTLES Patrick MM Pte G/5734 13th Royal Fusiliers KIA 10.4.17.
CASTLING Frank MM Sjt 27/144 12/13th Northumberland Fusiliers
CASWELL Charles MM Bdr 56429 15 Bde RFA
CASWELL Jack Reading MM L/Sjt 55 10th Royal Warwickshire Regt DOW 15.5.18.
CASWELL Wilfred MM Pte 11720 6th Shropshire Light Infantry
CATCHPOLE Alfred George MM Sjt 5420 2nd Royal Sussex Regt KIA 9.9.16.
CATCHPOLE Charles Edward MM Sjt 14243 7th Suffolk Regt KIA 12.10.16.
CATCHPOLE Conrad MM Pte 14646 10th Essex Regt KIA 11.8.17.
CATCHPOLE Frank MM Bdr 124807 504 Bty 65 Bde RFA
CATCHPOLE Frederick MM Pte 8751 2nd Royal Berkshire Regt Died 18.11.18.
CATCHPOLE Harry MM Pte 240840 1/5th Lincolnshire Regt
CATCHPOLE Percy Reuben MM+Bar L/Sjt 20807 2nd York & Lancaster Regt KIA 24.9.18.
CATCHPOLE William B.G. MM Sjt 52888 Middlesex Regt
CATER Herbert H. MM Sjt 265215 8th Royal West Kent Regt
CATER William Frederick MM Pte 29210 2nd Suffolk Regt
CATER William H. MM Sjt 6500 Devonshire Regt
CATERER Charles E. MM Pte 17582 Middlesex Regt
CATERER William John MM Pte 71168 1st Devonshire Regt
CATHCART Frederick John MM Sjt 945223 58 Div Ammn Col RFA
CATHCART James A.C. MM Gnr 110861 RGA
CATHCART William MM Pte 14197 10th Royal Irish Rifles
CATHCART William MM Pte 5494 Royal Warwickshire Regt
CATHERALL John MM Cpl M2/204965 Army Service Corps
CATHERCOLE Joseph MM L/Cpl 10107 East Yorkshire Regt
CATHERWOOD Harry MM Pte 7031 8th Hussars
CATHEY James MM Pte 7937 Northumberland Fusiliers
CATHRO Albert MM L/Cpl 238127 9th Scottish Rifles KIA 25.10.18.
CATHRO Thomas MM Pte 2956 1/5th Royal Highlanders
CATLEY Alfred C. MM Bdr 120834 D/174 Bde RFA
CATLEY Cyril Kitching MM CQMS 619 23rd Royal Fusiliers
CATLEY James S. MM Sjt 200280 4th Gloucestershire Regt
CATLIN Edwin MM Cpl 13654 East Surrey Regt
CATLIN Harold MM Pnr 78295 Royal Engineers
CATLING Alfred G. MM+Bar Pte 18584 2nd Royal Irish Regt
CATLING Edward MM Sjt 9454 2nd Yorkshire Regt
CATLING George W. MM Pte 16359 8th Bedfordshire Regt
CATLING Robert David MM Pte 10210 1st Northamptonshire Regt
CATLOW Fred MM Pte 17484 8th East Lancashire Regt
CATLOW Thomas MM Pte 17475 9th East Lancashire Regt
CATNACH John James MM Sjt 15865 Durham Light Infantry
CATNER Albert Archer MM L/Cpl 701758 1/23rd London Regt
CATO Bert MM Pte 33024 Leicestershire Regt
CATO Herbert MM Pte 241183 Leicestershire Regt
CATON Alfred J. MM Pte 24787 Royal Lancaster Regt
CATON George "MM+Bar,MID" Cpl 1710 1/4th Yorkshire Light Infantry
CATON Tom MM Pte 18079 6th Yorkshire Light Infantry
CATON William MM Cpl 266956 West Riding Regt
CATT Edward MM Pte 18496 Wiltshire Regt
CATT Harold MM Sjt 14374 4th Bedfordshire Regt
CATTANACH Gordon MM Cpl 85642 2 Div Ammn Col RFA
CATTANEO Victor G. MM Pte 300030 7th Essex Regt
CATTANEO William E. MM L/Cpl 260557 1/1st County of London Yeomanry
CATTELL Joseph A. MM L/Cpl DM2/134722 Army Service Corps
CATTELL Walter W. MM Pte 265657 1/1st Bucks Bn Oxf & Bucks Light Infantry
CATTERALL A. MM Pte 53015 Liverpool Regt
CATTERALL George H. MM Gnr 8499 D/170 Bde RFA

CATTERALL John W. MM Sjt 15325 8th Royal Lancaster Regt
CATTERALL Robert MM Pte 202051 South Lancashire Regt
CATTERALL Samuel MM Cpl 18260 8th Border Regt DOW 8.8.17.
CATTERICK Frank S. MM Bdr 32766 RFA
CATTERMOLE Albert H. MM Sjt 18089 9th Cheshire Regt
CATTERMOLE John MM Dvr 755946 A/251 Bde RFA
CATTERMOLE William H. MM Pte 10158 RAMC
CATTERMOLE William John MM L/Cpl 75751 Signal Service Royal Engineers
CATTLE Albert MM Sjt 69427 RGA
CATTLE Arthur MM+Bar Sjt 279004 170 Siege Bty RGA
CATTLE John MM Dvr 198495 71 Bde RFA
CATTLE Joseph MM Pte 200645 1/5th East Lancashire Regt
CATTLE William MM L/Sjt 6/627 1st King's Royal Rifle Corps
CATTLIN James Albert MM Cpl 9336 8th Royal Fusiliers DOW 24.6.17.
CATTO James MM Pte 266514 1/4th Gordon Highlanders
CATTON Sidney MM Pte G8/5404 8th East Surrey Regt KIA 1.10.16.
CATTON Thomas W. MM Cpl 40195 61 Fd Coy Royal Engineers
CAUDLE Arthur H. MM Pte 306560 1/8th Royal Warwickshire Regt
CAUDLE Herbert MM Cpl 240200 1/5th Gloucestershire Regt
CAUDRON Gaston A. MM Pte 308747 4th Bn Tank Corps
CAUGHEY John William MM Sjt 240704 1/5th Seaforth Highlanders
CAUGHEY Joseph MM Cpl 16331 11th Royal Irish Rifles
CAUGHLIN Thomas L. MM Sjt 370168 1/8th London Regt
CAUL Joseph R. MM Pte 18383 South Lancashire Regt
CAULFIELD James MM Pte 265171 West Riding Regt
CAULFIELD Michael MM Cpl 7043 1st Irish Guards
CAULFIELD Thomas MM Pte 267472 1st Northumberland Fusiliers
CAULKIN John MM Sjt 2398 1/5th North Staffordshire Regt
CAULTON Charles MM L/Sjt 14990 1st Coldstream Guards
CAUNT A.B. "MM,MID" Sjt 14594 Notts & Derby Regt
CAUNT Alfred James MM Pte 12726 6th Royal Berkshire Regt
CAUNT Ben "DCM,MM" Pte 13791 1st Notts & Derby Regt KIA 31.7.17.
CAUNT George William Henry MM Sjt 301808 14th Bn Tank Corps
CAUNT Samuel MM+Bar Sjt 16024 2nd Royal Fusiliers
CAUNT William H. MM Pte 117171 Machine Gun Corps
CAUNTER James H. MM Pte 235157 1/5th Leicestershire Regt
CAUSER James H. MM Pte 241012 York & Lancaster Regt
CAUSEY Herbert B. MM L/Cpl 72211 1st Liverpool Regt
CAUSTON Alan H. MM Sjt 350967 7th London Regt
CAUSTON Leonard MM Sjt 6102 1st Norfolk Regt
CAUTLEY Laurence MM Sjt 12363 8th Yorkshire Regt Died 29.10.18.
CAUWOOD Robert MM Dvr 770455 63 Div Ammn Col RFA
CAUWOOD Sydney MM+Bar Pte 9222 2nd West Yorkshire Regt KIA 28.3.18.
CAUWOOD Thomas MM Gnr 765578 B/315 Bde RFA
CAVALIER Cecil F. MM Pte 1618 1/7th Middlesex Regt att MGC
CAVALIER Lawrence E. MM L/Bdr 105343 216 Siege Bty RGA
CAVAN John MM Pte 19/684 Royal Irish Rifles
CAVANAGH Charles MM CSM 8808 2nd Gordon Highlanders
CAVANAGH James MM Gnr 15049 D/72 Bde RFA
CAVANAGH James Joseph MM Pte 3/7184 1st Dorsetshire Regt KIA 1.7.16.
CAVANAGH Joseph MM Cpl 43836 Royal Engineers
CAVANAGH Michael Joseph MM Dvr 104038 B/177 Bde RFA
CAVANAGH Moyra MM Miss F SJAB(VAD)
CAVANNA Peter MM Gnr 31179 RFA
CAVE Barney MM Pte 18080 6th Yorkshire Light Infantry
CAVE Charles Ormond MM L/Cpl 298 London Cyclist Coy Army Cyclist Corps
CAVE Gilbert MM Gnr 22440 RGA
CAVE Joseph MM Sjt 11769 2nd Royal Scots Fusiliers
CAVE Leonard S. MM Sjt DM2/164387 Army Service Corps
CAVE Robert MM Pte 15092 6th Northamptonshire Regt DOW 5.4.18.
CAVE Robert MM L/Cpl 16847 Suffolk Regt
CAVE Sydney Frank "MM,MID" Cpl 1940 1/1st London Regt
CAVE W.T. MM Pte 7691 Royal West Kent Regt
CAVE William Edward MM Sjt 20288 12/13th Northumberland Fusiliers KIA 25.4.18.
CAVE William James MM Gnr 123172 RGA
CAVE William James King MM Sjt 42311 23 Bde RFA
CAVEILL William Henry MM Pte 66016 Cheshire Regt
CAVELL Clifford W. MM Sjt 11417 2/4th Hampshire Regt
CAVEN Robert H. MM L/Cpl 40944 108 Fd Amb RAMC
CAVENEY James MM Pte 4/23125 5th Royal Inniskilling Fusiliers
CAVENEY James MM Sjt 290269 1/7th Cheshire Regt
CAVERHILL John MM Pte 200152 4th King's Own Scottish Borderers
CAVES Fred MM Cpl 267415 7th Liverpool Regt
CAVES Frederick T. MM Pnr 78265 Royal Engineers
CAVES Frederick William MM Pte 22804 2nd Bedfordshire Regt
CAVEY John George "DCM,MM" CSM 7603 1st Cheshire Regt
CAVILL Ernest H. MM+Bar Pte 22677 8th East Surrey Regt
CAVILL Leopold MM Sjt 30049 5 Bde RFA
CAWDREY Christopher MM Pte 28445 West Yorkshire Regt
CAWKILL Sydney C. MM Pte 50045 16th King's Royal Rifle Corps
CAWKWELL Alfred MM Pte 44286 26 Coy Machine Gun Corps KIA 12.10.17.
CAWKWELL Arthur MM Pte 17878 2nd Yorkshire Regt DOW 3.9.18.
CAWKWELL Arthur A. MM Pte 132987 62nd Bn Machine Gun Corps
CAWKWELL Harold MM Cpl 710702 RFA
CAWLEY Herbert MM Sjt 2984 5th Lancashire Fusiliers
CAWLEY John MM Pte 3659 2nd Irish Guards KIA 27.11.17.
CAWLEY John Wandrum "MC,MM(1541 CQMS),MMV(It)" Capt 1/4th Royal Berkshire Regt
CAWOOD Owen Baldwin MM 2nd Cpl 83648 219 Fd Coy Royal Engineers KIA 1.7.17.
CAWSON David MM Pte 3090 Royal West Surrey Regt
CAWSTON Alfred Frederick MM Sjt 43894 73 Bty 5 Bde RFA KIA 5.9.16.
CAWTE George H. MM+Bar Pte 202475 2/4th Hampshire Regt
CAWTE William G. MM+Bar L/Cpl 18051 Devonshire Regt
CAWTHAN Claude MM Pte 117196 62nd Bn Machine Gun Corps
CAWTHERAY George MM Sjt 200986 Seaforth Highlanders
CAWTHORN Herbert MM+Bar 2nd Cpl 86036 Royal Engineers
CAWTHORN John L. MM L/Cpl 33118 6th Durham Light Infantry
CAWTHORNE Albert MM L/Cpl 4604 Machine Gun Corps
CAWTHORNE Ernest MM L/Cpl 17/27846 Notts & Derby Regt
CAWTHORNE Joseph MM Pte 18173 Durham Light Infantry
CAWTHORNE Lewis "DCM,MM" Sjt 8/4267 8th Northumberland Fusiliers
CAWTHRA James M. MM(3808 W Yorks)+Bar L/Cpl 477979 Royal Engineers
CAWTHRAY George MM Gnr 100401 17 Hy Bty RGA
CAYGILL Cecil W. "DCM,MM" Pte 326326 1/9th Durham Light Infantry
CAYGILL Charles MM Dvr 19686 C/59 Bde RFA
CAYGILL George MM Sjt 292150 133 Heavy Bty RGA
CAYGILL Richard MM Sjt 235473 9th Yorkshire Regt
CAYLESS Arthur W. MM Gnr 223104 RFA
CAYTON Thomas MM+Bar L/Cpl 12154 10th North Lancashire Regt
CAYZER Robert MM 2nd Cpl 35234 5 Fd Coy Royal Engineers
CECIL Charles MM Gnr 57510 C/86 Bde RFA
CEDARGREEN Edward Albert MM Gnr L/6300 RFA
CENEY Joseph MM Pte 241249 1/6th South Staffordshire Regt
CHACKSFIELD Cyril MM Pte 68322 4th Bn Machine Gun Corps
CHADBOURNE Douglas H. MM Gnr 86851 RFA
CHADBURN William MM Pte 40747 Leicestershire Regt
CHADDERTON Ernest MM Pte 268541 Liverpool Regt
CHADDERTON Frederick J. MM Sjt 43856 10th Notts & Derby Regt
CHADDERTON Hirst MM Pte 350680 1/9th Manchester Regt
CHADDERTON Walter Parry MM Pte 351932 1/9th Manchester Regt
CHADDERTON William MM L/Cpl 56075 13th Liverpool Regt
CHADFIELD Harry MM L/Bdr 96429 A/70 Bde RFA
CHADWICK Albert MM Pte 58677 Machine Gun Corps
CHADWICK Albert MM Cpl 200968 2/4th East Lancashire Regt KIA 21.3.18.
CHADWICK Alexander MM Pte 201620 5th Manchester Regt
CHADWICK Alfred MM Sjt 241974 2/5th York & Lancaster Regt
CHADWICK Alfred "DCM,MM" Sjt 10888 1/7th West Riding Regt
CHADWICK Arthur MM Sjt Z/418 3rd Rifle Brigade
CHADWICK Arthur MM Pte 21871 2nd Border Regt
CHADWICK Arthur MM Cpl 86514 A/87 Bde RFA
CHADWICK Edgar MM Pte 37461 East Lancashire Regt
CHADWICK Edmund MM Pte 8644 Machine Gun Corps
CHADWICK Edward MM Pte 3489 South Lancashire Regt
CHADWICK Ellis MM Sjt 241416 6th Lancashire Fusiliers
CHADWICK Fred MM L/Cpl 34928 Lancashire Fusiliers
CHADWICK Frederick MM Pte 17859 Leicestershire Regt
CHADWICK George Henry MM Pte 5512 1/5th West Yorkshire Regt KIA 9.10.17.
CHADWICK Herbert MM Pte 200720 2nd Suffolk Regt
CHADWICK Herbert MM L/Cpl 290818 7th Cheshire Regt
CHADWICK J. MM Pte 201946 Royal Warwickshire Regt

CHADWICK J.W. MM Gnr 805098 A/231 Bde RFA
CHADWICK James MM Sjt 200970 2/5th Lancashire Fusiliers KIA 20.10.18.
CHADWICK James MM Pte 23820 11th Manchester Regt KIA 21.3.18.
CHADWICK John MM L/Cpl 139260 Royal Engineers
CHADWICK Joseph MM L/Sjt 280962 Lancashire Fusiliers
CHADWICK Samuel B. MM Pte 403500 2 Fd Amb RAMC
CHADWICK Thomas MM Pte 79911 4th Royal Fusiliers
CHADWICK Thomas MM Pte 351960 10th Manchester Regt
CHADWICK Thomas MM Gnr 30287 RFA
CHADWICK Thomas MM L/Sjt 13620 9th Border Regt
CHADWICK Thomas A. MM Sjt 1730 1/4th Royal Lancaster Regt
CHADWICK Wallace MM Sjt 1730 1/4th Royal Lancaster Regt
CHADWICK Walter MM Pte 101779 RAMC
CHADWICK William MM Pte 34920 Labour Corps Died 26.7.18.
CHAFFE Clarence MM Cpl 59836 RGA
CHAFFE Reginald R. MM Sjt 78595 RGA
CHAFFER Joseph H. MM Pte 460 4th Bn GMGR
CHAFFER Richard F. MM Sjt 44131 Royal Engineers
CHAFFER William MM Sjt 97908 330 Siege Bty RGA
CHAFFEY Wilfred John MM Cpl 230196 1/1st Dorset Yeomanry KIA 21.11.17.
CHAINEY Arthur Benjamin MM Pte 544 8th Royal Fusiliers DOW 15.7.16.
CHAINEY Thomas W. MM Pte M2/133872 Army Service Corps
CHALCROFT Charles MM Sjt 6819 Machine Gun Corps
CHALDERS John W. MM L/Cpl 21522 7th Border Regt
CHALK Arthur MM CSM 513 1/8th Royal Warwickshire Regt KIA 27.8.17.
CHALK Edward G. MM Pte R/33825 King's Royal Rifle Corps
CHALK F. MM Pte 352070 London Regt
CHALK Frank R. MM Gnr 34748 5 Bde RFA
CHALK George MM Sjt 8276 1st Lincolnshire Regt
CHALK James MM Sjt 203375 11th Suffolk Regt
CHALK Jesse MM Pte 10663 Royal Berkshire Regt
CHALKE Frederick George MM Pte 31212 RAMC
CHALKLEY Arthur MM 2nd Cpl 312120 Royal Engineers
CHALKLEY Frederick Arthur MM Pte 36283 6th Royal Berkshire Regt
CHALKLEY Herbert MM Pte 266246 1/1st Hertfordshire Regt
CHALKLEY Leonard R. MM+Bar Sjt 265272 1/1st Hertfordshire Regt
CHALKLEY R. MM Cpl G/950 Royal West Surrey Regt
CHALLANS Frank B. MM Pte 13/50 East Yorkshire Regt
CHALLENDER George E. MM Pte 116967 37th Bn Machine Gun Corps
CHALLENOR Aaron MM Pte 339346 63 Fd Amb RAMC
CHALLENOR Herbert MM Sjt 33324 RFA
CHALLINOR Harold F. MM L/Cpl 3466 North Staffordshire Regt
CHALLIS Albert W. MM Gnr 149094 RFA
CHALLIS Albert William MM Cpl 27392 16th Notts & Derby Regt
CHALLIS Arthur MM L/Cpl 421440 2/10th London Regt KIA 21.3.18.
CHALLIS Arthur S. MM Bdr 625525 HAC(Arty)
CHALLIS Douglas J. MM Pte 37492 12th East Surrey Regt
CHALLIS Frederick E. MM Pte 3563 1/18th London Regt
CHALLIS H.M. MM Sjt 630359 2/20th London Regt
CHALLIS Joseph Alfred MM L/Sjt 22783 3rd Grenadier Guards Died 2.11.18.
CHALLIS William MM Bdr 3453 RFA
CHALLIS William H. MM L/Cpl 514288 14th London Regt
CHALLONER Edwin MM L/Cpl 63629 101 Fd Coy Royal Engineers
CHALLONER James Archibald MM Sjt 8885 1st Leicestershire Regt
CHALLONER John MM Bdr 308206 1/2nd(Lancashire)Heavy Bty RGA
CHALLONER John C. MM Pte 16350 5th Shropshire Light Infantry
CHALMER W.S. MM Cpl 316481 13th Royal Highlanders
CHALMERS Alexander MM L/Cpl 8562 2nd Gordon Highlanders KIA 27.10.18.
CHALMERS Andrew MM Pte S/20527 5th Cameron Highlanders
CHALMERS Andrew MM Pte 1858 1/9th Arg & Suth Highlanders
CHALMERS Andrew MM Cpl 276479 1/7th Arg & Suth Highlanders KIA 21.3.18.
CHALMERS David MM Pte 12624 Seaforth Highlanders
CHALMERS E. MM Sjt 312388 3 Div Sig Coy Royal Engineers
CHALMERS Edmund MM Pte 18554 Scottish Rifles
CHALMERS Edward MM Sjt 668 2nd Gordon Highlanders
CHALMERS George MM Pte 38214 Royal Scots
CHALMERS George MM Cpl L/7174 Y/7 Med TM Bty RFA
CHALMERS George B. MM 2nd Cpl 422163 Royal Engineers
CHALMERS George R. MM Pte 41711 1st Royal Scots Fusiliers
CHALMERS Hugh MM Gnr 10343 D/157 Bde RFA DOW 29.3.18.
CHALMERS Hugh B. MM Pte 14184 11th West Yorkshire Regt
CHALMERS J.R. MM Sjt 40619 Gordon Highlanders
CHALMERS James MM Pte M2/053834 Army Service Corps
CHALMERS John MM Pte 225130 5th Cameron Highlanders
CHALMERS John Cyril MM CSM 2050 1/4th Cameron Highlanders KIA 15.10.16.
CHALMERS John J. MM Pte G/42762 17th Royal Fusiliers
CHALMERS John Wisley "MC,DCM,MM" CSM 265154 1/7th Gordon Highlanders
CHALMERS John Young MM Pte 278681 1/7th Arg & Suth Highlanders
CHALMERS Robert MM Pte 201680 Gordon Highlanders
CHALMERS William MM Gnr 636056 RFA
CHALMERS William "MM,MSM" Dvr 645697 A/235 Bde RFA
CHALMERS William J. MM L/Sjt 202395 Scottish Rifles
CHAM Cyril E. MM L/Cpl 26178 1st East Surrey Regt
CHAMBERLAIN Arthur W. MM L/Cpl 47805 21st Bn Machine Gun Corps
CHAMBERLAIN Charles MM+Bar BSM 40915 C/310 Bde RFA
CHAMBERLAIN Charles W. MM CSM 19724 17th Lancashire Fusiliers
CHAMBERLAIN Elijah MM Pte 3094 1/7th West Riding Regt
CHAMBERLAIN Francis R. MM Sjt 7221 Coldstream Guards
CHAMBERLAIN Frank MM Pte 34644 1st East Surrey Regt
CHAMBERLAIN George MM Pte 19093 8th Lincolnshire Regt Died 29.11.18.
CHAMBERLAIN Henry John MM Sjt 49711 RFA
CHAMBERLAIN Herbert MM L/Cpl 43585 Norfolk Regt
CHAMBERLAIN Herbert John MM Pte 200548 1/5th Bedfordshire Regt
CHAMBERLAIN Hugh S. MM Pte 4742 1/1st HAC(Inf)
CHAMBERLAIN James MM Cpl 11388 12th Manchester Regt
CHAMBERLAIN James MM+Bar Gnr 89329 B/48 Bde RFA
CHAMBERLAIN John T. MM Pte M2/081008 Army Service Corps
CHAMBERLAIN Joseph MM Sjt 200969 5th South Staffordshire Regt
CHAMBERLAIN Kenneth Fitzrafe MM Pte C/7306 King's Royal Rifle Corps
CHAMBERLAIN Richard MM L/Cpl 12199 8th Yorkshire Regt
CHAMBERLAIN Valentine N. MM Pte 531936 15th London Regt
CHAMBERLAIN William MM Pte 17506 8th North Staffordshire Regt
CHAMBERLAIN William George MM Pte 36157 Machine Gun Corps
CHAMBERLAIN William John MM Cpl S/9292 1st Rifle Brigade KIA 8.8.16.
CHAMBERLAIN William R. MM Cpl 4881 2nd Dragoon Guards
CHAMBERS Albert C.V. MM Sjt 20750 Machine Gun Corps
CHAMBERS Albert S. MM Pte 24110 2nd Royal Dublin Fusiliers
CHAMBERS Alfred John MM Pte 7763 96 Coy Machine Gun Corps
CHAMBERS Arthur "MM+Bar,MSM" Sjt 41660 11 Div Sig Coy Royal Engineers KIA 2.9.18.
CHAMBERS Arthur MM L/Cpl 147457 30th Bn Machine Gun Corps
CHAMBERS Arthur Edward James MM Sjt 202306 4th Royal Welsh Fusiliers
CHAMBERS Edgar MM Pte 8560 1st West Yorkshire Regt
CHAMBERS Edward MM Bdr 67592 13 Siege Bty RGA
CHAMBERS Ernest G. MM Pte 21206 1st Grenadier Guards
CHAMBERS Frank MM Pte 17591 3rd Bn Machine Gun Corps
CHAMBERS Frederick MM Sjt 680612 1/22nd London Regt
CHAMBERS George MM Cpl 19801 1st Notts & Derby Regt
CHAMBERS George MM L/Cpl 325850 Durham Light Infantry
CHAMBERS George Thomas MM L/Cpl 2641 13th Royal Sussex Regt
CHAMBERS Gordon MM L/Cpl 1707 1/1st South Notts Hussars Yeo Died 27.5.18.
CHAMBERS Harold Frederick MM L/Cpl 4928 6th Royal West Kent Regt KIA 14.10.17.
CHAMBERS Harry E. MM L/Cpl 95186 Royal Engineers
CHAMBERS Herbert Elijah MM Cpl 26385 2 Fd Amb RAMC
CHAMBERS J. MM Pte 307891 1st Lancashire Fusiliers
CHAMBERS James D. MM Cpl 24091 1/5th Lancashire Fusiliers
CHAMBERS John R. MM Sjt 2188 Northumberland Fusiliers
CHAMBERS Joseph MM 2nd Cpl 480537 466 Fd Coy Royal Engineers
CHAMBERS Joseph W. MM L/Cpl 330677 6th Liverpool Regt
CHAMBERS Peter MM Spr 147557 176 Tunnelling Coy Royal Engineers
CHAMBERS Robert MM Cpl 12471 1/1st Hertfordshire Regt
CHAMBERS Robert G. MM L/Cpl R/32603 King's Royal Rifle Corps

CHAMBERS Robert H. MM+Bar Cpl 53040 5 Fd Coy Royal Engineers
CHAMBERS T. MM Gnr 29159 RGA
CHAMBERS Thomas MM Sjt 21474 1/7th Liverpool Regt
CHAMBERS Thomas MM Pte 41256 9th Royal Irish Fusiliers
CHAMBERS Thomas MM Gnr 5696 RGA
CHAMBERS W.M. MM Pte S/26024 Rifle Brigade
CHAMBERS Warren MM L/Cpl 11182 2nd Royal Welsh Fusiliers
CHAMBERS Wilfred E. MM Sjt 14476 8th Suffolk Regt
CHAMBERS William MM Sjt 11044 26 Fd Coy Royal Engineers
CHAMBERS William MM Pte 1351 8/9th Royal Irish Rifles KIA 21.3.18.
CHAMBERS William MM L/Cpl 27716 124 Coy Machine Gun Corps
CHAMBERS William B. MM Cpl 4023 Royal Lancaster Regt
CHAMBERS William H. MM+Bar Sjt 9895 2nd South Wales Borderers
CHAMINGS Reginald Gordon MM Pte 201129 Oxf & Bucks Light Infantry
CHAMP Albert MM Pte 32772 6th Oxf & Bucks Light Infantry
CHAMP William MM CQMS 250356 Manchester Regt
CHAMPION Alan Coultra MM L/Cpl STK928 10th Royal Fusiliers
CHAMPION Alfred Dudderidge MM Pte 22410 2nd Suffolk Regt KIA 28.3.18.
CHAMPION Arthur James MM Cpl 2084 1/1st Oxfordshire Yeomanry
CHAMPION George Ernest MM L/Cpl 203196 1st London Regt DOW 25.8.18.
CHAMPION George Frederick MM Sjt 4239 1st Royal Welsh Fusiliers DOW 3.9.16.
CHAMPION Nathaniel "DCM+Bar,MM" L/Sjt B/203252 13th Rifle Brigade
CHAMPS Charles A. MM Sjt 168920 C/190 Bde RFA
CHANCE Thomas "MM,MID" Sjt 11141 2nd Worcestershire Regt
CHANCELLOR Frank MM Pte 203362 4th Worcestershire Regt
CHANDLER Albert J. MM L/Cpl 62513 5th West Yorkshire Regt
CHANDLER Alfred MM Cpl 15198 7th Bedfordshire Regt KIA 24.4.18.
CHANDLER Arthur H. MM Pte M2/267747 Army Service Corps
CHANDLER Bertie Frederick Thomas MM Pte 24995 1st Hampshire Regt KIA 29.10.18.
CHANDLER E. MM Pte 36243 6th London Regt
CHANDLER Edward MM Pte 37219 11th Royal West Surrey Regt
CHANDLER Ernest George MM Gnr 29441 D/181 Bde RFA
CHANDLER Frederick MM Pte 15802 22th Royal Sussex Regt DOW 7.12.17.
CHANDLER Frederick W. MM Pte 2724 1/1st Cambridgeshire Regt
CHANDLER G.H. MM Pte 552419 London Regt
CHANDLER George W. MM Sjt 2331 1/5th Gloucestershire Regt
CHANDLER Harry Cecil MM Pte G/11218 11th Royal West Surrey Regt
CHANDLER Isaiah MM Pte 63625 Machine Gun Corps
CHANDLER J.J. "DCM,MM,MID" Sjt 201450 1st Bedfordshire Regt
CHANDLER Leslie W. MM Sjt 292 6th Royal West Kent Regt
CHANDLER Lewis MM L/Cpl 200049 1st Bn Tank Corps KIA 8.10.18.
CHANDLER Philip A.R. MM Pte 10980 1st Notts & Derby Regt
CHANDLER Samuel MM Spr 1174 Royal Engineers
CHANDLER Stanley MM+Bar Pte 13844 12th Gloucestershire Regt
CHANDLER Thomas MM Pte 2464 Army Cyclist Corps
CHANDLER Thomas MM Sjt 13852 6th Royal Irish Fusiliers
CHANDLER Thomas A. MM Cpl 152732 239 Army Tps Coy Royal Engineers
CHANDLER W.P. MM Gnr 38101 Machine Gun Corps
CHANDLER William MM Pte 65447 104 Fd Amb RAMC KIA 4.10.18.
CHANDLER William George MM Cpl 94983 35 Bty 22 Bde RFA
CHANDLER William J. MM Pte 12489 Gloucestershire Regt
CHANDLER William Joseph MM Cpl 240670 1/5th Gloucestershire Regt DOW 17.8.17.
CHANDLESS Charles Leslie "MM,MSM" CQMS 5387 2nd Royal Lancaster Regt
CHANDLEY George MM Sjt 11373 16th Lancashire Fusiliers
CHANEY Edward MM Pte 7592 RAMC
CHANEY Robert Frederick MM+Bar Sjt 3/7613 7th East Surrey Regt KIA 8.7.17.
CHANNEL William F. MM Gnr 51352 RGA
CHANNING Edward MM Sjt 12792 6th Somerset Light Infantry
CHANNING Walter MM Sjt 240598 Royal Warwickshire Regt
CHANNINGS Charles W. MM Pte 52938 4th Worcestershire Regt
CHANNON Cecil W.S. MM Cpl 64629 24 Bde RFA
CHANNON Frederick MM Pte 265777 6th Gloucestershire Regt
CHANNON Leonard MM Cpl S/12629 Rifle Brigade
CHANT George MM Pte 3971 1st Dragoon Guards
CHANT Howard F. MM Sjt 58019 23 Hy Bty RGA
CHANT Tom G. MM L/Cpl 42707 76 Fd Coy Royal Engineers
CHANT William MM Cpl 19426 13th Gloucestershire Regt
CHANTER Frank "MM,MID" Gnr 960633 175 Bde RFA
CHANTER Stanley H. MM Gnr 68342 86 Siege Bty RGA
CHANTERY John MM L/Sjt 200651 2/5th Manchester Regt KIA 9.10.17.
CHANTLER Arthur W. MM Cpl 2051 1/21st London Regt
CHANTLER William Henry Edward MM Pte 47067 1st Lancashire Fusiliers
CHANTRELL Charles MM Pte 14531 6th Northamptonshire Regt
CHANTRELL George Rutley "MM,MC(G)" Cpl 77810 39 Bty 19 Bde RFA
CHANTRILL Harold MM Cpl 1898 1(North Midland)Fd Amb RAMC
CHAPEL David MM Pte 53102 RAMC
CHAPELHOW George MM Cpl 21/1336 21st Northumberland Fusiliers KIA 1.7.16.
CHAPLIN Alfred William MM L/Cpl 8889 1st Royal Inniskilling Fusiliers KIA 9.8.16.
CHAPLIN Arthur MM L/Bdr 65435 RFA
CHAPLIN Arthur "MM,MID" Sjt 2032 1/7th West Yorkshire Regt
CHAPLIN Arthur H. MM L/Cpl 12867 2nd Worcestershire Regt
CHAPLIN C. MM Cpl 34805 1st Essex Regt
CHAPLIN George MM+Bar L/Cpl 681779 1/22nd London Regt
CHAPLIN Harold MM Pte 10583 2nd West Riding Regt
CHAPLIN Harold W. "DCM,MM+Bar" Sjt 19608 16th Royal Welsh Fusiliers
CHAPLIN Henry J.G. MM Pte 31650 77 Fd Amb RAMC
CHAPLIN Herbert H. MM Pte R/8741 King's Royal Rifle Corps
CHAPLIN Horace Herbert MM Pte 41366 10th Essex Regt
CHAPLIN Horace Owen Avondale MM Sjt 26816 33 Div Ammn Col RFA
CHAPLIN Jack W. MM Pte 78483 4th Royal Fusiliers
CHAPLIN James Henry MM+Bar Pte 200684 1/4th Suffolk Regt
CHAPLIN John A. MM Pte 14815 8th Norfolk Regt
CHAPLIN Joseph MM Dvr 22921 A/82 Bde RFA
CHAPLIN Joseph W. MM Cpl 7082 1st Dorsetshire Regt
CHAPLIN Leonard Ernest MM L/Sjt 14574 10th Essex Regt
CHAPLIN Percy MM Cpl B/2822 Rifle Brigade
CHAPLIN Robert William MM Sjt 6235 2/4th Gloucestershire Regt KIA 19.7.16.
CHAPLIN Sidney Charles MM Pte 202931 East Surrey Regt
CHAPLIN Walter MM L/Cpl 2760 16th Middlesex Regt
CHAPLIN Walter Henry MM L/Cpl 13975 6th Wiltshire Regt KIA 10.4.18.
CHAPMAN A. MM+Bar Pte 16308 1st Northamptonshire Regt
CHAPMAN Albert MM Spr 146040 179 Tunnelling Coy Royal Engineers
CHAPMAN Albert MM Cpl 19652 9th Welsh Regt DOW 8.11.18.
CHAPMAN Albert John MM Bdr NA/46218 33 Siege Bty RGA
CHAPMAN Alfred MM L/Sjt 350220 7th London Regt KIA 8.8.18.
CHAPMAN Alfred H. MM+Bar Sjt 17091 8th Somerset Light Infantry
CHAPMAN Alfred James Thomas MM+Bar CQMS 9027 King's Royal Rifle Corps
CHAPMAN Alfred W. MM Pte 17406 East Surrey Regt
CHAPMAN Archibald MM Pte 3562 11th Royal Scots
CHAPMAN Arthur MM Cpl Wheeler 775909 C/310 Bde RFA
CHAPMAN Arthur MM Sjt 19671 Machine Gun Corps
CHAPMAN Arthur MM Sjt 98578 Royal Engineers
CHAPMAN Arthur E. MM Dvr 820520 46 Div Ammn Col RFA
CHAPMAN Arthur E. "MM,MSM" Sjt 44719 17 Div Sig Coy Royal Engineers
CHAPMAN Arthur J. MM Spr 63349 Royal Engineers
CHAPMAN Aubrey MM Dvr M2/167605 Army Service Corps
CHAPMAN Benjamin MM Pte 40012 Leicestershire Regt
CHAPMAN Benjamin William MM Pte 680291 1/22nd London Regt
CHAPMAN Charles J. MM Pte 12335 1 Special Coy King's Royal Rifle Corps
CHAPMAN Charles R. MM L/Cpl 17059 7th Northamptonshire Regt
CHAPMAN Cyril MM Gnr 29130 RGA
CHAPMAN Daniel W. MM Sjt 8711 2nd Grenadier Guards
CHAPMAN David MM L/Cpl 139737 4th Bn Machine Gun Corps KIA 19.10.18.
CHAPMAN David Scott MM+Bar Sjt 1703 1/4th Yorkshire Regt
CHAPMAN David Sidney MM Bdr 68407 174 Bde RFA
CHAPMAN Douglas E.M. MM Pte 202746 4th Hampshire Regt
CHAPMAN E.A. MM Dvr 29817 RFA

CHAPMAN E.H. MM Sjt 4992 Rifle Brigade
CHAPMAN Edward MM L/Cpl 9709 1st Essex Regt
CHAPMAN Ernest MM Sjt 291918 132 Hy Bty RGA
CHAPMAN Ernest G. MM Pte 22145 1st Shropshire Light Infantry
CHAPMAN F. MM Pte 8203 2nd Essex Regt
CHAPMAN F.G.K. MM Pte 240368 1/5th Suffolk Regt
CHAPMAN Francis W. MM Pte 275002 23rd London Regt
CHAPMAN Frank MM Pte 266188 2nd Bedfordshire Regt KIA 4.11.18.
CHAPMAN Frank MM Pte 21503 Leicestershire Regt
CHAPMAN Frank Harvey MM L/Cpl 2195 1/1st London Regt KIA 15.9.16.
CHAPMAN Fred MM L/Cpl 12237 Devonshire Regt
CHAPMAN Fred MM Pte 16746 8th West Riding Regt
CHAPMAN Fred MM L/Cpl 1854 1/1st Leicestershire Yeomanry
CHAPMAN Fred MM Sjt 478021 460 Fd Coy Royal Engineers
CHAPMAN Fred MM 2nd Cpl 444510 Royal Engineers
CHAPMAN Frederick C. MM Bdr 53598 RFA
CHAPMAN Frederick C. MM+Bar Sjt 50179 RFA
CHAPMAN Frederick E. MM Dvr 945320 58 Div Ammn Col RFA
CHAPMAN Frederick G. MM Pte 10067 5th Northamptonshire Regt
CHAPMAN George MM CSM 16186 18th Lancashire Fusiliers
CHAPMAN George MM Sjt 35132 RFA
CHAPMAN George MM Sjt 50183 RFA
CHAPMAN George MM L/Cpl 105499 Machine Gun Corps
CHAPMAN George MM Cpl 323 MGC(Motors)
CHAPMAN George MM L/Cpl 12638 6th Oxf & Bucks Light Infantry
CHAPMAN George MM Cpl 64047 RAMC
CHAPMAN George B. MM Pte 52650 1/5th Cheshire Regt
CHAPMAN George Henry MM Sjt 3/7034 12th East Yorkshire Regt
CHAPMAN H. MM L/Cpl S/13155 Seaforth Highlanders
CHAPMAN Harold MM+Bar L/Cpl 2177 1/5th Liverpool Regt
CHAPMAN Harold MM+Bar Sjt 11/105 11th East Yorkshire Regt KIA 20.7.16.
CHAPMAN Harold E. MM Sjt 151280 104th Bn Machine Gun Corps
CHAPMAN Harry MM Pte 281922 4th Royal Fusiliers
CHAPMAN Harry MM Gnr L/42835 RFA
CHAPMAN Harry MM Pte 12795 1st Grenadier Guards
CHAPMAN Harry A. MM Pte 682088 22nd London Regt
CHAPMAN Harry W. MM Pte 307876 West Riding Regt
CHAPMAN Henry Francis MM Gnr L/5755 RFA
CHAPMAN Ivor Richard MM Pte 30211 East Lancashire Regt
CHAPMAN Jack MM Pte 28823 Notts & Derby Regt
CHAPMAN James MM Sjt 70174 A/106 Bde RFA
CHAPMAN James MM Pte 375055 10th Manchester Regt
CHAPMAN James MM Sjt 265063 West Riding Regt
CHAPMAN James MM Pte 385533 106 Coy Labour Corps
CHAPMAN James MM Bdr 3558 RFA
CHAPMAN James MM Sjt 7280 Norfolk Regt
CHAPMAN James MM Cpl 23381 2nd Border Regt KIA 26.10.17.
CHAPMAN James Edwin MM L/Sjt 17292 7th Norfolk Regt KIA 12.10.16.
CHAPMAN James Hutchinson MM L/Cpl 4141 54 Coy Machine Gun Corps DOW 22.10.17.
CHAPMAN James L. "DCM,MM" L/Cpl 11170 8th Lincolnshire Regt
CHAPMAN John MM RSM 14734 9th Norfolk Regt KIA 14.10.18.
CHAPMAN John MM Pte 18585 2nd Royal Irish Regt
CHAPMAN John MM Cpl 15255 17th Highland Light Infantry
CHAPMAN John MM Bdr 66588 A/104 Bde RFA
CHAPMAN John MM Dvr 15150 37 Bde RFA
CHAPMAN John G. MM Cpl 23773 5th West Riding Regt
CHAPMAN John L. MM L/Cpl 492165 46 Div Sig Coy Royal Engineers
CHAPMAN John T. MM Cpl 9122 RFA
CHAPMAN John W. MM L/Cpl 9958 2nd Royal West Surrey Regt
CHAPMAN Joseph MM Pte 53999 9th Royal Welsh Fusiliers KIA 10.6.18.
CHAPMAN L.A. MM Gnr 2232 RFA
CHAPMAN Leonard David MM Pte 14108 8th Royal Berkshire Regt
CHAPMAN Leonard J. MM Pte 15021 7th Royal Berkshire Regt
CHAPMAN Mark MM Cpl 14686 6th Northamptonshire Regt
CHAPMAN Percy MM Sjt 8359 1st East Yorkshire Regt KIA 22.3.18.
CHAPMAN Reginald MM Gnr 806111 RFA
CHAPMAN Reginald Percy MM Pte 38471 1st Essex Regt
CHAPMAN Richard F.J. MM+Bar Sjt 3663 62nd Bn Machine Gun Corps
CHAPMAN Robert MM Pte G/19913 2nd Royal Sussex Regt
CHAPMAN Robert MM Gnr 54869 RFA
CHAPMAN S. MM Cpl 265015 Liverpool Regt
CHAPMAN Samuel MM+Bar Sjt 31850 B/76 Bde RFA
CHAPMAN Samuel E. MM Sjt 17829 1st Scottish Rifles
CHAPMAN Sidney MM L/Cpl 43629 6th Northamptonshire Regt
CHAPMAN Sidney W. MM Pte 12/2157 1st York & Lancaster Regt KIA 11.10.16.
CHAPMAN Stanley P. MM Pte 740285 25th London Regt
CHAPMAN Thomas MM+Bar Cpl 1888 2(Northumbrian)Fd Amb RAMC
CHAPMAN Thomas MM Sjt 8504 2nd Durham Light Infantry
CHAPMAN Thomas E. MM Sjt 552038 Royal Engineers
CHAPMAN Thomas G. MM Cpl S/43160 2nd Arg & Suth Highlanders
CHAPMAN Thomas G. MM Bdr L/26791 RFA
CHAPMAN Thomas H. MM Pte 9262 21 Fd Amb RAMC
CHAPMAN Thomas J. MM Sjt 9548 10th Duke of Cornwall's LI
CHAPMAN Walter MM Cpl 265517 1/7th Liverpool Regt
CHAPMAN Walter Charles "MM,MID" Bdr 53051 A/95 Bde RFA
CHAPMAN William MM Cpl 412093 409 Fd Coy Royal Engineers
CHAPMAN William MM Cpl 84067 D/95 Bde RFA
CHAPMAN William MM Sjt 325157 1/9th Durham Light Infantry
CHAPMAN William Henry MM Cpl 391961 2/9th London Regt KIA 27.9.17.
CHAPMAN William T. MM+Bar Sjt 720662 24th London Regt
CHAPMAN William T. MM Pte 47450 36 Fd Amb RAMC
CHAPPELL Albert MM Pte 29281 Highland Light Infantry
CHAPPELL Allen Cecil MM Sjt 9254 7th Suffolk Regt
CHAPPELL Arthur W. MM Sjt 34243 8th North Lancashire Regt
CHAPPELL Bernard MM Gnr L/26649 D/50 Bde RFA
CHAPPELL Charles Humphrey MM L/Cpl 265879 8th Gloucestershire Regt Died 18.4.18.
CHAPPELL Claude J. MM Sjt 26239 7th South Staffordshire Regt
CHAPPELL Ernest "DCM,MM" Sjt 7141 89 Coy Machine Gun Corps
CHAPPELL Ernest H. MM Sjt 634921 20th London Regt
CHAPPELL Harry MM Pte 19102 8th South Wales Borderers
CHAPPELL Henry S. MM Pte 37098 9th South Lancashire Regt
CHAPPELL Leonard MM Pte 23478 4th Bedfordshire Regt
CHAPPELL Olave Peter MM Pte 14728 4th Bedfordshire Regt
CHAPPELL Thomas MM Pte 16011 East Surrey Regt
CHAPPELL W.J. MM Pte 33120 16th Highland Light Infantry
CHAPPELLS Albert MM Pte 43671 2nd Manchester Regt
CHAPPIN Henry MM Cpl 203193 11th Notts & Derby Regt
CHAPPLE Herbert MM Bdr 13100 2 Div Ammn Col RFA
CHAPPLE Philip MM Pte 44223 RAMC
CHAPPLE Phoebe MM Doctor F RAMC
CHAPPLE Thomas J. MM Sjt 200092 1/4th Royal Lancaster Regt
CHAPPLE William MM L/Sjt 2261 Manchester Regt
CHARD Edward MM Pte 9113 4th Worcestershire Regt Died 30.12.17.
CHARD Ernest Victor Frederick MM Pte 488 7th East Surrey Regt
CHARD J. MM Pte 3204 1/4th Gloucestershire Regt
CHARD William MM Pte 6005 2nd Scots Guards
CHARGE Robert Richard MM+Bar L/Sjt 201151 5th Bedfordshire Regt DOW 17.11.17.
CHARITY Walter William MM Pte R/9726 King's Royal Rifle Corps
CHARLES Fred MM Gnr 175539 RGA
CHARLES J. MM Pte 337605 RAMC
CHARLES Joseph Henry Brown MM L/Cpl 22616 7th Northamptonshire Regt
CHARLES Percy D. "DCM,MM" L/Cpl 300184 1/5th London Regt
CHARLES Thomas W. MM Cpl 27179 Shropshire Light Infantry
CHARLES William MM Cpl 164 1/1(East Riding)Fd Coy Royal Engineers
CHARLESON Henry "MM,CdeG(F)" L/Cpl 15296 13th Royal Scots
CHARLESWORTH Alexander MM Sjt 10/1201 10th East Yorkshire Regt
CHARLESWORTH C. MM Pte 405300 2/3rd(West Riding)Fd Amb RAMC
CHARLESWORTH George MM Dvr 104370 228 Fd Coy Royal Engineers
CHARLESWORTH Gordon MM Dvr 776598 A/310 Bde RFA
CHARLESWORTH Joseph MM Bugler 11222 6th Yorkshire Light Infantry
CHARLESWORTH Joseph MM 2nd Cpl 98466 74 Fd Coy Royal Engineers
CHARLESWORTH Teddy MM Gnr L/18895 RFA
CHARLETON William MM Cpl 55445 9th Northumberland Fusiliers
CHARLEY Daniel W. "MM,MID" Pte 14572 8th Royal Berkshire Regt
CHARLTON Alexander MM L/Cpl 19597 10th Northumberland Fusiliers KIA 25.9.16.
CHARLTON Alfred MM+Bar Pte 25966 19 Fd Amb RAMC
CHARLTON Andrew MM Sjt 393 19th Durham Light Infantry
CHARLTON Edward MM Pte 270537 11th Royal Scots

CHARLTON Edward MM Pte 17458 14th Durham Light Infantry
CHARLTON Gardiner J. MM Pte 42588 5th South Staffordshire Regt
CHARLTON George MM 2nd Cpl 211600 XI Corps Heavy Arty Sig Sect Royal Engineers
CHARLTON George B. "MM,MSM" L/Cpl MS/4572 Att 221 Siege Bty RGA Army Service Corps
CHARLTON H. MM L/Cpl 325391 Durham Light Infantry
CHARLTON James MM Pnr 147441 Royal Engineers
CHARLTON John MM Bdr 21626 RFA KIA 14.8.17
CHARLTON John W. MM+Bar Sjt 35521 Northumberland Fusiliers
CHARLTON Joseph D. MM Pte 3/10367 West Yorkshire Regt
CHARLTON Joseph Henry MM Cpl 39037 32 Coy Machine Gun Corps
CHARLTON Matthew MM Dvr 85842 8 Bty 13 Bde RFA
CHARLTON Matthew MM+Bar L/Cpl 9991 2nd Coldstream Guards
CHARLTON Percy F.T. MM Pte 61698 17th Royal Fusiliers
CHARLTON Robert MM Cpl 249436 38 Div Sig Coy Royal Engineers
CHARLTON Thomas MM+Bar Cpl 205042 2/4th Hampshire Regt DOW 4.11.18.
CHARLTON William MM Sjt 709 RFA
CHARLTON William MM Pte 242826 1/6th West Yorkshire Regt
CHARLTON William George MM Sjt 203054 8th Scottish Rifles
CHARLTON William Martin MM L/Cpl T/23120 12 Army Aux Horse Coy Army Service Corps
CHARMAN Allen MM Sjt M2/176677 Army Service Corps
CHARMAN Arthur Edward "MC,DCM,MM,CdeG" CSM 650382 1/21st London Regt
CHARMAN George MM L/Cpl 29758 Royal Engineers
CHARMAN Harold James MM Dvr 17354 D/108 Bde RFA
CHARMAN Leonard MM Sjt 811007 D/50 Bde RFA
CHARMAN Sydney A. "MM,MID" Sjt 42697 RGA
CHARMAN William G. MM L/Bdr 169079 110 Bty 24 Bde RFA
CHARMAN William T. MM Sjt 260055 8th Royal Sussex Regt
CHARNICK Thomas MM Cpl 11630 2nd Royal Berkshire Regt
CHARNLEY J. MM+Bar L/Cpl 34207 RAMC
CHARNLEY John MM L/Cpl 5053 1st Lancashire Fusiliers
CHARNLEY Robert F. MM Pte 3275 1st Welsh Guards
CHARNLEY Thomas MM Pte 74024 Notts & Derby Regt
CHARNOCK Albert Edward "MM,MSM" Sjt Wheeler 614142 2/1st(Warwick)Bty RHA
CHARNOCK Harry P.F. MM L/Cpl 2969 2nd Dragoon Guards
CHARNOCK Roger MM L/Cpl 38669 Northumberland Fusiliers
CHARNOCK Sydney MM Bdr 73115 Y/1 Med TM Bty RFA
CHARNOCK Thomas MM Pte 47502 23rd Northumberland Fusiliers
CHARNOCK William A. MM L/Cpl 35158 5th West Riding Regt
CHARPY George MM L/Cpl 15789 Devonshire Regt
CHARSLEY Alexander J. MM Sjt 24407 Machine Gun Corps
CHART Harry B. MM Pte 303156 5th London Regt
CHARTERS Andrew MM Pte 28596 6th King's Own Scottish Borderers
CHARTERS Herbert C. MM L/Cpl 7337 2nd Royal Fusiliers
CHARVILLE William J. MM Cpl 266106 1/1st Hertfordshire Regt
CHASE Alfred Walter "DCM,MM" Sjt 7953 2nd Scots Guards
CHASE Frederick MM Pte 7/10832 7th Lincolnshire Regt
CHASE Heber Lawson MM Pte 508479 RAMC
CHASE James MM L/Cpl 411 7th East Surrey Regt
CHASTEAUNEUF William Alfred MM Gnr 970254 D/63 Bde RFA
CHATBURN Edward MM L/Cpl 242199 2/5th East Lancashire Regt
CHATBURN James E. MM Pte 20407 Lancashire Fusiliers
CHATE William L. MM Sjt 013072 Army Ordnance Corps
CHATER Hugh Clement MM Gnr 53773 RGA
CHATFIELD Albert J. MM Gnr 62886 RGA
CHATFIELD F.J. MM Cpl 241811 Royal Warwickshire Regt
CHATFIELD Frederick L. MM Pte M2/102849 Army Service Corps
CHATFIELD George Patrick MM Sjt L/10258 1st Royal West Surrey Regt KIA 25.9.17.
CHATFIELD William A. MM Sjt 34690 24 Siege Bty RGA
CHATLEY Arthur A. MM Sjt 292797 RGA
CHATTAWAY Sydney A. MM Cpl 637 Machine Gun Corps
CHATTEN William H. MM Sjt 70589 135 Bty 32 Bde RFA
CHATTERLEY Walter MM Sjt 846 Royal Warwickshire Regt
CHATTERTON Albert MM Cpl 24071 8th North Staffordshire Regt
CHATTERTON Horace MM Pte 13/950 13th East Yorkshire Regt
CHATTERTON James MM+Bar L/Cpl 240197 1/6th Notts & Derby Regt
CHATTERTON Joseph "MM,MID" Sjt 5443 12th Manchester Regt
CHATTERTON Matthew MM Cpl 42416 RAMC
CHATTERTON Thomas Herbert MM Sjt 240536 5th Yorkshire Light Infantry
CHATTERTON Vernon MM Pte 47613 2/4th Yorkshire Light Infantry
CHATTERTON William MM Pte 147289 Machine Gun Corps
CHATTINGTON Thomas Henry MM Sjt 16470 6th South Wales Borderers KIA 21.8.18.
CHATWIN Ernest MM Cpl 10501 1st South Staffordshire Regt KIA 1.7.16.
CHATWIN John MM Spr 32709 25 Div Sig Coy Royal Engineers
CHAVE Cecil MM Pte 2713 1/8th Middlesex Regt DOW 18.8.17.
CHAWNER James R. MM Bdr Sig 73850 187 Siege Bty RGA
CHAWNER John W. MM Sjt L/29050 D/152 Bde RFA
CHAYTOR Joseph MM Pte 6624 2nd West Riding Regt KIA 3.5.17.
CHAYTOR Robert G. MM Cpl 166146 150 Siege Bty RGA
CHAZUEL W.S. MM Pnr 22119 3 Div Sig Coy Royal Engineers
CHEADLE John MM Sjt 17681 8th Royal Lancaster Regt
CHEADLE John F. MM Sjt 60 1/6th South Staffordshire Regt
CHEAL Arthur W. MM Sjt 30880 RAMC
CHEAL Druce E. MM Spr 540745 Royal Engineers
CHEALE Percy MM Cpl 11234 7 Fd Coy Royal Engineers
CHEAPE William E. MM L/Cpl 240546 2/8th Middlesex Regt
CHEARY Edwin MM L/Cpl 20502 2nd York & Lancaster Regt KIA 18.3.17.
CHEBSEY Henry MM Pte 200393 1/4th Shropshire Light Infantry
CHECKLAND H. MM Pte 242182 Border Regt
CHECKLEY Arthur A. MM Pte 16024 11th Notts & Derby Regt
CHECKLEY Herbert "MM,MID" Sjt 1370 West Yorkshire Regt
CHECKLEY Joseph W. MM BSM 785262 C/150 Bde RFA
CHEEK Edward C. MM+Bar Pte 4176 15th Hampshire Regt
CHEEK Frederick John MM Sjt 29537 V/15 TM Bty RGA DOW 10.4.17.
CHEERS Charles MM Pte 30154 2nd Welsh Regt
CHEESE Alfred William MM Sjt 16670 C/110 Bde RFA
CHEESE James H. MM Sjt 1482 1/2nd London Regt
CHEESEMAN Alfred MM L/Bdr 166142 RGA
CHEESEMAN Cecil Nelson MM Pte 1550 7th Royal West Kent Regt
CHEESEMAN Edward T. "DCM,MM" Pte 32203 1st Gloucestershire Regt
CHEESEMAN Francis W. MM Pte 51248 1st Cheshire Regt
CHEESEMAN Frederick G. MM Cpl 702061 23rd London Regt
CHEESEMAN Harry MM Sjt 36125 RGA
CHEESEMAN Horace MM Pte L/9713 2nd Royal West Kent Regt
CHEESEMAN Percival MM Pte 267115 6th Gloucestershire Regt
CHEESMAN Alfred J. MM 2nd Cpl 536197 492 Fd Coy Royal Engineers
CHEESMAN David MM L/Cpl 2235 8th Royal Sussex Regt
CHEESMAN F. MM Cpl 19590 1st Dragoon Guards
CHEESMAN J. MM Cpl 6814 Royal Sussex Regt
CHEESMAN Leslie MM Gnr 781093 RFA
CHEESWRIGHT Walter W.G. MM Cpl 2212 2nd London Regt
CHEETHAM Arthur C. MM Spr 46435 18 Div Sig Coy Royal Engineers
CHEETHAM Cecil L. MM Sjt 42661 8th North Staffordshire Regt
CHEETHAM Frank MM Pte 204393 Bedfordshire Regt
CHEETHAM Frederick MM L/Cpl 267053 Liverpool Regt
CHEETHAM John MM Pte 16805 10th North Lancashire Regt
CHEETHAM John MM Gnr 99749 RFA
CHEETHAM John Robert MM L/Cpl 13/178 13th York & Lancaster Regt
CHEETHAM Maurice H. MM Pte 32017 RAMC
CHEFFEY Arthur S. MM Pte 42304 Yorkshire Regt
CHEGWIN William MM Spr 78296 223 Fd Coy Royal Engineers
CHELL Albert MM L/Cpl 240619 Notts & Derby Regt
CHELL Herbert MM Sjt 16927 Lincolnshire Regt
CHELLEW Thomas John MM Sjt M2/054790 Army Service Corps
CHELMINSKI Harry MM Pte G/49298 24th Royal Fusiliers
CHENERY H. MM Pte 28888 Royal Fusiliers
CHENERY Montague B. MM Pte 337661 87 Fd Amb RAMC
CHENERY William Thomas MM Gnr 168439 B/186 Bde RFA
CHENEY Archibald Arthur MM BQMS 24284 RGA
CHENEY Clarence W. MM+Bar Sjt 201726 1st Royal Berkshire Regt
CHENEY Cuthbert S. MM Pte 66447 RAMC
CHENEY John MM Sjt 5390 8th East Surrey Regt
CHENEY William MM Cpl 11642 9th West Riding Regt
CHENNELL Arthur V. MM Gnr 39894 RFA
CHENNELL Bertie MM L/Cpl 48462 24th Royal Fusiliers Died 27.3.18.
CHERRETT Herbert George MM Sjt 7096 2nd Hampshire Regt
CHERRETT John David MM Pte 14614 11th Hampshire Regt
CHERRETT Norman A. MM Pte 131668 46th Royal Fusiliers
CHERRIE John MM Sjt 412374 Royal Engineers

CHERRIMAN Ernest H. "DCM,MM+Bar" Sjt 6525 8th Royal West Kent Regt
CHERRISON George Alfred MM Sjt 202599 Royal West Kent Regt
CHERRY Archibald Francis MM Cpl 38680 D/82 Bde RFA KIA 3.11.18.
CHERRY Edwin MM Sjt 9156 1st Liverpool Regt
CHERRY Frank Herbert MM Pte 203172 1st Dorsetshire Regt DOW 14.6.18.
CHERRY George MM Gnr 65926 40 Bde RFA
CHERRY Herbert MM Gnr 26176 RGA
CHERRY Hugh MM Pte 22539 1st Royal Irish Fusiliers
CHERRY John W. "DCM,MM" Sjt 1523 1/3rd(Northumbrian)Fd Amb RAMC
CHERRY Leonard MM Pte 2208 1/1st Hertfordshire Regt
CHERRY Reginald MM Dvr 27422 B/46 Bde RFA
CHERRY Richard T. MM Gnr 40173 RGA
CHERRY Sidney T. MM Sjt 82081 135 Bty 32 Bde RFA
CHERRY Walter MM Pte 28558 Oxf & Bucks Light Infantry
CHERRYMAN William J. MM Sjt 810428 RFA
CHESELDINE John MM+Bar Sjt 46313 Royal Engineers
CHESHER Arthur MM Bdr 947626 X/56 Med TM Bty RFA
CHESHER Charles W.F. "DCM,MM" Sjt 1271 1(East Anglian)Fd Coy Royal Engineers
CHESHER William MM Gnr 17448 C/87 Bde RFA
CHESHIRE Arthur MM Pte 10853 Coldstream Guards
CHESHIRE Charles Edward MM Sjt 270743 10th East Kent Regt
CHESHIRE Ernest MM Cpl 97949 RFA DOW 20.4.18.
CHESHIRE Fred MM+Bar Cpl 89437 Royal Engineers
CHESHIRE Geoffrey MM Pte 16590 10th Essex Regt
CHESHIRE J. MM L/Cpl 14972 Cheshire Regt
CHESMER W. MM Gnr 150376 RFA
CHESNEY David MM Sjt S/17708 5th Cameron Highlanders KIA 25.10.18.
CHESNEY Harry MM Pte M/205904 Army Service Corps
CHESNEY James Robert Henry MM Sjt 2046 19th Middlesex Regt KIA 3.10.18.
CHESNEY William S. "MM,MID" Pte 14764 6/7th Royal Scots Fusiliers
CHESSELL Harry MM Spr 63826 Royal Engineers
CHESSON Thomas W. MM Sjt 655 6th Royal West Kent Regt
CHESSUM Walter G. MM Pte 10807 6th Yorkshire Regt
CHESTER Albert MM Bdr 3238 B/121 Bde RFA
CHESTER Alfred MM Pte 43506 12th Royal Scots
CHESTER Arthur "MM,MID" Sjt 12/453 East Yorkshire Regt
CHESTER Charles MM Sjt 18936 14th Northumberland Fusiliers
CHESTER David MM Pte 14294 6th Lincolnshire Regt
CHESTER Ernest MM Cpl 14375 6th Northamptonshire Regt
CHESTER Frederick MM Pte 2040 1/4th Gloucestershire Regt
CHESTER George H. MM Cpl 11552 4th Shropshire Light Infantry
CHESTER Henry T. MM Pte 7557 21st London Regt
CHESTER John MM L/Cpl 18949 Machine Gun Corps
CHESTER Percy Edward MM Pte 2658 12th Middlesex Regt
CHESTER Thomas MM L/Cpl 200239 1/4th Royal Lancaster Regt
CHESTER William MM+Bar Dvr 179266 53 Bty 2 Bde RFA
CHESTERMAN John R. MM BQMS 27541 RGA
CHESTERMAN Robert MM Sjt 281192 RGA
CHESTERS Alfred "DCM,MM" Cpl 20822 11th Royal Lancaster Regt
CHESTERS David MM Pte 82315 7 Coy Machine Gun Corps
CHESTERTON George H. MM+Bar Pte 8846 2nd Worcestershire Regt
CHESTERTON John MM Pte 18481 6th Yorkshire Regt
CHESTNEY George H. MM+Bar Sjt 463167 50 Div Sig Coy Royal Engineers
CHESTNEY William T. MM L/Cpl L/13215 16th Lancers
CHESTNUT Joseph MM+Bar Cpl 57523 4th Liverpool Regt
CHESTON Harry L. MM Sjt 14019 12th Gloucestershire Regt
CHESWORTH Peter MM Sjt 341258 RAMC
CHESWORTH William MM Pte 11477 4th Royal Fusiliers KIA 9.5.17.
CHETLAND Henry MM L/Cpl 28558 15th Hampshire Regt KIA 16.10.18.
CHETLAND John MM Cpl 350268 7th London Regt
CHETWYND Tom MM Cpl 96841 Royal Engineers
CHEVIS Henry "MM,MID" CSM 9975 2nd King's Royal Rifle Corps
CHEW A.E. "DCM,MM" Cpl 37493 308 TM Bty RFA
CHEW Reginald MM Sjt 241856 6th West Yorkshire Regt
CHEW William MM Pte 23882 Machine Gun Corps
CHEW William E. MM Dvr 8783 RFA
CHEYNE Alexander MM Pte 32300 9th Highland Light Infantry
CHEYNE John D. MM+Bar Sjt 17374 8th South Wales Borderers
CHEYNE William MM Cpl 406481 Royal Engineers
CHEYNE William T. MM L/Cpl 201415 1/4th Gordon Highlanders
CHICK Ernest H.L. MM L/Cpl 31832 Wiltshire Regt
CHICK Reginald H. MM Spr 19252 92 Fd Coy Royal Engineers
CHICKEN Ernest William "MC,DCM,MM(12027 DLI)" T/2Lt 1st Border Regt
CHIDGEY Arthur James "MM,CdeG" Pte 27115 6th King's Own Scottish Borderers
CHIDGEY Ernest "DCM,MM,MIDx2" CSM 23115 35 Div Sig Coy Royal Engineers
CHIDGEY Ernest J. MM Pte 242264 5th Gloucestershire Regt
CHIDGEY Harry MM Sjt 78138 RGA
CHIDGEY Ronald J. MM Pte 115587 49th Bn Machine Gun Corps
CHIDGEY William W. "DCM,MM" Sjt 3/8106 6th Dorsetshire Regt
CHIDLER Ernest MM Pte 722721 24tth London Regt
CHIFFINCE George MM+Bar L/Cpl 88521 142 Fd Amb RAMC
CHIGNALL Horace Victor MM L/Cpl 26956 15th Hampshire Regt
CHILCOTT A.E. MM Sjt S/4093 Rifle Brigade
CHILCOTT Albert "DCM,MM" Cpl 18138 2nd Royal Scots Fusiliers
CHILCOTT Alfred S. MM Pte 44080 9th Welsh Regt
CHILCOTT Charles William MM L/Cpl L/5717 1st Royal Fusiliers
CHILCOTT George MM Pte 29764 1st Wiltshire Regt KIA 13.9.18.
CHILCOTT Thomas MM L/Cpl 546043 509 Fd Coy Royal Engineers
CHILCOTT William H. MM Pte 278115 1st Essex Regt
CHILD A.E. MM L/Cpl G/6696 1st East Kent Regt
CHILD Albert MM Gnr 74879 36 Bde RFA
CHILD Alfred J. MM Spr 277482 Royal Engineers
CHILD Arthur MM Sjt L/9073 A/150 Bde RFA
CHILD Benjamin MM S/Sjt 61618 RAMC
CHILD Charles A. MM L/Cpl 29756 3 Div Sig Coy Royal Engineers
CHILD Charles R. MM Pte 78007 16 Fd Amb RAMC
CHILD Edgar B. "DCM,MM" BSM 37731 16 Army Bde A Bty RHA
CHILD Frank MM Sjt 200485 1/4th Royal Berkshire Regt KIA 4.10.17.
CHILD Fred MM Pte 358794 10th Liverpool Regt KIA 10.4.18.
CHILD Harold MM Pte 15/195 15th West Yorkshire Regt
CHILD Harold S. "DCM,MM" L/Cpl 38523 15/17th West Yorkshire Regt
CHILD Henry W. MM Pte M2/018951 Army Service Corps
CHILD Joseph Arthur MM L/Cpl 266131 2/7th West Yorkshire Regt KIA 27.3.18.
CHILD Robert H. MM L/Cpl 21157 6th Border Regt
CHILD Ronald R. MM 2nd Cpl 42843 Royal Engineers
CHILD Samuel MM Pte 9475 2nd Yorkshire Light Infantry
CHILD Thomas MM Sjt 7794 1st West Yorkshire Regt
CHILD Walter MM Sjt 44584 12th Manchester Regt
CHILD Walter MM Pte 83617 108 Coy Machine Gun Corps
CHILD William MM Sjt 8122 2nd Lincolnshire Regt
CHILDS Alfred MM Sjt 895072 A/275 Bde RFA
CHILDS Archibald R. MM L/Cpl 6766 HAC(Inf)
CHILDS Arthur MM Dvr 89021 RFA
CHILDS Arthur F. MM Pte 119049 1st Bn Machine Gun Corps
CHILDS Ernest MM L/Cpl 60424 11 Div Sig Coy Royal Engineers
CHILDS F.J. MM Sjt 9413 11th Hussars
CHILDS F.R. MM L/Cpl 12334 2/4th Hampshire Regt
CHILDS Frederick MM Pte 15126 5th Shropshire Light Infantry
CHILDS Frederick A. MM Bdr 66988 6 Div Ammn Col RFA
CHILDS Frederick C. MM Sjt SE/15677 Army Veterinary Corps
CHILDS Harry MM Cpl 14997 Machine Gun Corps
CHILDS Harry MM Pte 16000 11th Notts & Derby Regt
CHILDS Henry MM Cpl 18795 1st Royal Inniskilling Fusiliers KIA 28.2.17.
CHILDS Maurice G. MM Spr 59153 Royal Engineers
CHILDS N. MM Pte 24874 Shropshire Light Infantry
CHILDS Raymond Victor MM Pte 34177 20 Coy Machine Gun Corps KIA 23.3.18.
CHILDS Robert MM+Bar Pte 9244 1st Border Regt
CHILDS Samuel MM L/Cpl 265330 1/6th Gordon Highlanders
CHILDS Sidney H. MM Pte 235004 Liverpool Regt
CHILDS Sidney J. MM L/Cpl 89026 8th Middlesex Regt
CHILDS Sydney MM Pte 12956 Northamptonshire Regt
CHILDS Walter E. MM Dvr 234378 Y/28 Med TM Bty RFA
CHILDS Walter James MM Cpl Wheeler 760425 A/317 Bde RFA DOW 1.11.17.
CHILDS William Charles MM Pte 14431 3rd Coldstream Guards KIA 30.7.17.
CHILDS William Henry MM Gnr 86286 D/46 Bde RFA KIA 23.9.16.
CHILLERY James MM Pte 242131 7th Royal West Kent Regt
CHILLINGWORTH Frederick C. MM Sjt 267673 D/255 Bde RFA
CHILLINGWORTH John P. MM Sjt 621 RFA

CHILLMAN Edward MM L/Cpl C/3593 17th King's Royal Rifle Corps
CHILMAID Fred MM Cpl 105132 283 Siege Bty RGA
CHILMAN Arthur Livingstone MM Private S/93 1st Royal West Surrey Regt DOW 27.9.17.
CHILMAN Thomas MM Cpl 320835 6th London Regt
CHILTON Alfred William MM Spr 97965 1 Fd Sqn Royal Engineers
CHILTON Arthur MM Pte 18972 1st Notts & Derby Regt KIA 7.7.16.
CHILTON Charles Henry MM Bdr 61289 88 Siege Bty RGA
CHILTON E. MM Spr 269627 Royal Engineers
CHILTON Harold MM Pte 42310 RAMC
CHILTON Harold MM+Bar Sjt 23818 9th North Lancashire Regt
CHILTON James T. MM Cpl 20091 Oxf & Bucks Light Infantry
CHILTON John MM L/Cpl 8691 2nd Seaforth Highlanders KIA 1.7.16.
CHILTON Samuel MM Sjt 592793 18th London Regt
CHILTON Tom MM L/Sjt 201125 1/4th West Riding Regt
CHILTON William B. MM Dvr 810011 AQ/232 Bde RFA
CHILVERS Ernest Bertrand MM Pte 6826 1/5th West Riding Regt
CHILVERS Frederick William Rodwell MM L/Cpl 16395 5 Fd Coy Royal Engineers
CHILVERS John MM Sjt 61236 130 Coy Machine Gun Corps
CHILVERS Percy Robert MM L/Cpl 41845 9th Essex Regt
CHINCHEN Albert G.S. MM Bdr 334088 RGA
CHINCHEN William J. MM Sjt 166062 87 Siege Bty RGA
CHINERY Albert G.E. MM Gnr Sig 123046 504 Bty 65 Bde RFA
CHINERY Frank MM Pte 82638 2nd London Regt
CHINERY Jack F.G. MM Spr 344852 Royal Engineers
CHINN Edward MM+Bar Pte 34566 9th York & Lancaster Regt
CHINNERY Amos J. MM Pte 13549 10th Essex Regt
CHINNOCK John H. MM Pte 22243 East Surrey Regt
CHIPCHASE D. MM L/Cpl 5900 13th Northumberland Fusiliers
CHIPPENDALE Lawson MM Sjt 5001 10th Northumberland Fusiliers
CHIPPENDALE Thomas MM Dvr 8546 RFA
CHIPPENDALE William MM L/Cpl C/311 1st King's Royal Rifle Corps
CHIPPS Charles MM L/Bdr 11782 B/107 Bde RFA
CHIRGWIN Frederick MM Pte 26741 Shropshire Light Infantry
CHIRRAY George MM Cpl 15398 13th Royal Scots
CHISHOLM Alexander MM Pte 30570 2nd Royal Dublin Fusiliers
CHISHOLM Charles Henry Shortt MM L/Cpl 159452 'M' Special Coy Royal Engineers
CHISHOLM Duncan MM Pte 40871 Cameron Highlanders
CHISHOLM Edward A. "MM,MSM" CQMS 76151 IV Corps Sig Coy Royal Engineers
CHISHOLM James MM Pte 53948 Manchester Regt
CHISHOLM James M. MM Sjt 34202 RAMC
CHISHOLM John Alexander MM+Bar Pte 126767 10th Cameron Highlanders
CHISHOLM John W. "DCM,MM" L/Cpl 9248 2nd Coldstream Guards
CHISHOLM Maire Lambert Chisholm Gooden MM Miss F BRCS
CHISHOLM Peter MM Cpl 265511 6th Seaforth Highlanders DOW 22.7.18.
CHISHOLM William MM Cpl 265938 Seaforth Highlanders
CHISHOLM William D. MM Cpl 18294 9th Scottish Rifles
CHISLETT Fred MM Cpl 7351 1st Somerset Light Infantry KIA 24.3.18.
CHISNALL Alliston W. MM Pte 24762 Lancashire Fusiliers
CHISNALL Harold "DCM,MM" Sjt 1619 1/9th Liverpool Regt
CHISNALL Robert Harold MM Sjt 38460 781 Coy Labour Corps
CHITTEL James W. MM Cpl 11994 King's Royal Rifle Corps
CHITTENDEN Walter R. MM Sjt 3477 9th Royal Sussex Regt
CHITTOCK Mabel MM Assistant Matron F SJAB
CHITTY Frank MM+Bar Sjt 32712 8th East Surrey Regt
CHITTY Frederick G. MM Spr 1405 Royal Engineers
CHITTY William MM Cpl 59648 11 Bde RFA
CHIVAS Alexander B. MM Cpl 26303 13th Royal Scots
CHIVERALL Albert E. MM Pte 8227 1st Norfolk Regt
CHIVERS Albert MM Pte 24053 Grenadier Guards
CHIVERS Charles E. MM Bdr 56216 26 Bde RFA
CHIVERS Charles J. MM+Bar Sjt 43595 Northamptonshire Regt
CHIVERS Ernest J. MM L/Sjt 345 Rifle Brigade
CHIVERS Frank MM Pte 8551 East Kent Regt
CHIVERS Fred MM L/Cpl 203817 1st Royal Warwickshire Regt KIA 19.9.18.
CHIVERS John MM Cpl 7373 3rd Middlesex Regt
CHIVERS John Aubrey Tilley MM Pte 651185 1/21st London Regt
CHIVERTON Charles MM+Bar Sjt 34272 2 Siege Bty RGA
CHIVERTON Robert James "MM,MSM" CSM M/19903 1 Cav Div Supply Col Army Service Corps
CHOAT Stanley John MM Cpl 43637 82 Fd Coy Royal Engineers KIA 20.9.17.
CHONEY Albert MM Sjt S/505 2nd Royal West Surrey Regt KIA 26.10.17.
CHONEY Ernest J. MM L/Sjt 10451 1st Royal West Surrey Regt
CHOPPEN Sidney MM Sjt 87478 110 Bty 24 Bde RFA
CHOPPING Newman MM L/Cpl 233464 74 Div Sig Coy Royal Engineers
CHORLTON James MM Pte 25441 North Lancashire Regt
CHORLTON Robert MM Sjt 14490 9th North Lancashire Regt
CHOWLES William G. MM Pnr 161681 Royal Engineers
CHRISMAS George E. MM Pte 252390 3rd London Regt
CHRISP Thomas MM Sjt 1946 1/8th Durham Light Infantry KIA 22.6.17.
CHRISP W.G. MM Sjt 18852 D/11 Bde RFA
CHRISTALL Walter E. MM Pte 78832 16 Fd Amb RAMC
CHRISTIAN Arthur Robert MM Pte 18364 7th Royal West Kent Regt KIA 3.5.17.
CHRISTIAN Clifford P. MM Sjt 826 1/21st London Regt
CHRISTIAN George MM Pte 36407 1/5th East Lancashire Regt
CHRISTIAN James E. MM+Bar Pte 244415 Cheshire Regt
CHRISTIAN John MM Pte 230366 1/2nd London Regt
CHRISTIAN Thomas MM L/Cpl 20014 1st Royal Dublin Fusiliers DOW 18.9.18.
CHRISTIE Charles MM Sjt 23719 152 Coy Machine Gun Corps KIA 23.4.17.
CHRISTIE Fred MM L/Cpl 290203 1/7th Gordon Highlanders
CHRISTIE G. MM Cpl 43388 Gordon Highlanders
CHRISTIE George "DCM,MM" Sjt S/43340 1st Gordon Highlanders
CHRISTIE Hugh MM Sjt 43448 2nd Royal Irish Rifles
CHRISTIE Huntly MM Pte 1879 6th Dragoon Guards
CHRISTIE James "MM+Bar,MID" Pte 9986 2nd Gordon Highlanders
CHRISTIE James MM Sjt 9479 2nd Gordon Highlanders
CHRISTIE James MM Dvr 715882 RFA
CHRISTIE John MM Pte 291053 Gordon Highlanders
CHRISTIE John MM Pte 1694 9th Lancers
CHRISTIE John "MM,MID" Sjt 10586 Cheshire Regt
CHRISTIE John MM L/Cpl 240656 Gordon Highlanders
CHRISTIE John A. MM Sjt 4088 RFA
CHRISTIE John Edward MM Sjt 5642 Northumberland Fusiliers
CHRISTIE Percy W. MM Spr 88984 Guards Div Sig Coy Royal Engineers
CHRISTIE Robert MM+Bar Pte 4498 12th Arg & Suth Highlanders
CHRISTIE Robert MM Cpl 33115 RAMC
CHRISTIE Thomas MM Pte 142115 9th Bn Machine Gun Corps
CHRISTIE William MM Spr 424082 50 Div Sig Coy Royal Engineers
CHRISTIE William "MM,MID" L/Cpl 17442 11th Hussars
CHRISTIE William MM Cpl S/4571 9th Royal Highlanders
CHRISTIE William F. MM L/Cpl 23266 Royal Engineers
CHRISTIE William J. MM L/Cpl 11647 15th Royal Irish Rifles
CHRISTINE Andrew MM+Bar Spr 284189 35 Lt Rly Op Coy Royal Engineers
CHRISTISON William MM Pte 4351 9th Royal Highlanders
CHRISTMAS Ernest V. MM Sjt 718005 23rd London Regt
CHRISTMAS George MM Sjt 7132 89 Coy Machine Gun Corps KIA 20.10.16.
CHRISTMAS Henry Charles MM Pte 7081 1/7th London Regt KIA 30.4.17.
CHRISTMAS Walter H. MM+Bar Sjt 23/624 Northumberland Fusiliers
CHRISTOPHER Alfred J. MM L/Cpl 512403 122 Fd Coy Royal Engineers
CHRISTOPHER Edwin MM Sjt 44833 241 Coy Machine Gun Corps
CHRISTOPHER Ernest MM Pte 27333 7th Border Regt
CHRISTOPHER H. MM Pte 202768 1st Royal West Kent Regt
CHRISTOPHER John Andrew MM Sjt 6762 1st Lincolnshire Regt
CHRISTOPHER S. MM Cpl 75264 37 Bty 27 Bde RFA
CHRISTOPHER Victor MM Pte 18218 7th South Lancashire Regt
CHRISTY Peter MM Pnr 51376 14 Div Sig Coy Royal Engineers
CHUBB Jonathan MM Cpl 514949 Royal Engineers
CHUDLEIGH Jack Eustace MM Pte 7206 1/14th London Regt DOW 19.9.16.
CHUDLEIGH Richard H. MM Sjt 17327 14th Welsh Regt
CHUNN Albert Sidney MM Pte 552582 2/16th London Regt
CHURCH A.W. MM Pte 320231 London Regt
CHURCH Albert "MM,MID" Cpl 1107 Royal Engineers
CHURCH Albert V. MM Pte M2/203986 Army Service Corps
CHURCH Arthur C. MM Pte 13528 8th Suffolk Regt
CHURCH Arthur G. MM Gnr 147615 RGA
CHURCH Benjamin MM Sjt MS/3789 Army Service Corps

CHURCH Bertram MM Sjt 6551 1st Northamptonshire Regt
CHURCH George MM Pte 12200 12th East Surrey Regt
CHURCH George W. MM Cpl 61526 153 Fd Coy Royal Engineers
CHURCH Harry MM Sjt 31425 RFA
CHURCH Harry MM L/Sjt 205306 7th Middlesex Regt
CHURCH Herbert W. MM Cpl 8091 1st Royal West Surrey Regt
CHURCH Horace G. "DCM,MM" Sjt 511934 1/14th London Regt
CHURCH John Reginald MM Cpl 24421 1st Royal West Surrey Regt DOW 22.5.17.
CHURCH Robert Thomas MM Pte 23020 2nd Royal Scots Fusiliers KIA 9.9.16.
CHURCH Thomas Owen MM L/Cpl 116 1/15th London Regt
CHURCH W. MM Pte 437253 RAMC
CHURCH William MM Pte 14315 10th Essex Regt KIA 26.4.18.
CHURCH William MM Pte 8787 1st Shropshire Light Infantry
CHURCH William MM Pte S/12759 Rifle Brigade
CHURCH William A. MM Dvr 97635 RFA
CHURCH William C. MM+Bar Sjt 1269 1/6th London Regt
CHURCH William C. MM Sjt 79644 MGC(Motors)
CHURCH William R. MM+Bar L/Cpl 17572 2nd Bedfordshire Regt
CHURCHER Frederick MM Sjt 8988 1st East Surrey Regt
CHURCHER Henry Thomas MM CSM 201109 2/4th Hampshire Regt DOW 19.9.18.
CHURCHILL Arthur Charles Northover MM Spr 558703 56 Div Sig Coy Royal Engineers
CHURCHILL Charles Henry MM Gnr 6281 RFA
CHURCHILL Edward MM Spr 49521 92 Fd Coy Royal Engineers
CHURCHILL George MM Pte G/25354 7th Royal West Surrey Regt KIA 4.9.18.
CHURCHILL Harry C. MM Spr 516017 16 AA Searchlight Section Royal Engineers
CHURCHILL T.H. MM Cpl 12160 7th Yorkshire Light Infantry
CHURCHILL Thomas MM Dvr 48171 C/103 Bde RFA
CHURCHLEY Alfred C. MM Pte 43425 2nd Worcestershire Regt
CHURCHLEY Arthur Charles MM Sjt 19628 35 Bde RFA
CHURCHMAN Ernest G. MM L/Cpl 66254 Royal Engineers
CHURCHMAN George R. MM Pte 33708 Royal Lancaster Regt
CHURCHMAN James MM Pte Sig 25060 3rd Grenadier Guards
CHURCHMAN John MM Pte 325921 1/1st Cambridgeshire Regt
CHURCHMAN William MM Dvr L/46907 L Bty RHA
CHURCHMAN William Baker "DCM,MM,MID,CdeG(F)" Sjt 550419 2/3rd(London)Fd Coy Royal Engineers
CHURCHUS Cecil MM Pte 5059 3rd Rifle Brigade
CHURCHWARD Thomas MM Spr 96110 575 Works Coy Royal Engineers
CHURCHYARD Albert MM Pte 202684 1st London Regt
CHURCHYARD Fred MM Sjt 5380 11th Hussars
CHURCHYARD Harold MM Pte 29408 2nd Grenadier Guards
CHURMS Edward Ernest Parry MM Pte 50749 10th Cheshire Regt
CHURMS Harry MM Cpl 685021 RFA
CHURNSIDE Edward MM Spr 96996 Royal Engineers
CHUTER A. MM Sjt 1248 4th Hussars
CHUTER Eric T.O. MM L/Cpl G/5234 13th Royal Fusiliers
CLABBON Frederick W. MM Gnr Sig 940582 D/280 Bde RFA
CLABBURN William MM Pte 251052 1/6th Arg & Suth Highlanders
CLACEY George R. MM Pte 39078 1st Royal Berkshire Regt
CLACK David MM Sjt 1949 1/6th Welsh Regt
CLACK Edward MM L/Cpl 9459 1st Wiltshire Regt
CLACK George MM Pte 43312 1st Leicestershire Regt
CLACK Harold G. MM CSM 12348 11th Hampshire Regt
CLACK Ronald Raymond Percival MM Bdr 94072 B/62 Bde RFA
CLACKEN Christopher MM Pte 7954 Irish Guards
CLACY Ernest Edward MM Cpl 72577 1/6th West Yorkshire Regt KIA 11.10.18.
CLADINGBOEL Sydney MM Pte 21716 14th Royal Welsh Fusiliers
CLADINGBOWL Robert Carl MM L/Cpl 182 Lincolnshire Regt
CLAGUE Robert MM L/Cpl 7065 Gordon Highlanders
CLAIR Michael Joseph MM+Bar Sjt 6373 2nd Royal Munster Fusiliers
CLAIR William MM+Bar Cpl 18192 Durham Light Infantry
CLAISEN Leslie T. MM Sjt 560325 47 Div Sig Coy Royal Engineers
CLAMMER Ronald C. "DCM,MM" Sjt 280605 3rd London Regt
CLAMP Arthur MM Pte 201557 Notts & Derby Regt
CLAMP Edward MM Pte 80919 Notts & Derby Regt
CLAMP Edwin MM Cpl 201080 5th Notts & Derby Regt
CLAMP Ernest MM CQMS 42224 73 Fd Coy Royal Engineers
CLAMP James "DCM,MM" Cpl 555168 1/16th London Regt
CLAMP Thomas MM Pte 44772 5th York & Lancaster Regt
CLAMP Thomas "MM,MID" Sjt 36446 17th Bn Machine Gun Corps
CLAMPETT Eric MM L/Cpl 41154 Northumberland Fusiliers

CLANCEY Thomas D MM+Bar Pte 2763 1st Welsh Guards
CLANCY Harold MM L/Bdr 56714 B/112 Bde RFA
CLANCY J. MM Sjt 52294 18th Gloucestershire Regt
CLANCY John W. MM L/Sjt H/71683 North Irish Horse
CLANCY Michael "DCM,MM" Sjt 6366 1st North Lancashire Regt
CLANCY Michael MM Pte 21627 6th Yorkshire Light Infantry
CLANCY Patrick "MM,MSM" CSM 781662 29th London Regt
CLANCY Reginald MM Pte 207935 10th Royal West Surrey Regt
CLAPHAM Albart W. MM Pte 43417 2nd Lincolnshire Regt
CLAPHAM Arthur Edward MM Pte 5627 1/16th London Regt
CLAPHAM Christopher MM Sjt 11101 8th West Riding Regt
CLAPHAM Frederick Thomas MM Pte 2181 1/5th Leicestershire Regt KIA 1.8.17.
CLAPHAM Robert MM Pte 41971 12th Manchester Regt
CLAPHAM Thomas A. MM Pte 1168 Lincolnshire Regt
CLAPHAM William MM Pte 11942 2nd Highland Light Infantry KIA 1.10.18.
CLAPP Edward MM 2nd Cpl 153806 Royal Engineers
CLAPP Rowland E. MM Pte 5358 10th Royal Warwickshire Regt
CLAPP Walter C. MM Pte 30251 1st Royal West Surrey Regt
CLAPP William MM Pte 35764 15 Fd Amb RAMC DOW 29.6.18.
CLAPP William F. MM Sjt 43147 75 Fd Coy Royal Engineers
CLAPPERTON Alexander MM Gnr 63427 RGA
CLAPSHAW George MM Sjt 8948 1st East Surrey Regt
CLAPSON Edward MM Pte 3784 1st Rifle Brigade
CLAPTON George MM Gnr 786544 RFA
CLAPTON George MM Cpl M2/100391 Att 449 Siege Bty RGA Army Service Corps
CLAPTON William MM L/Cpl 11938 8th Gloucestershire Regt
CLAPTON William E. MM Sjt 1206 Army Cyclist Corps
CLARE Alfred E. MM Sjt T2/SR/03588 16 Div Ammn Train HT Army Service Corps
CLARE Charles A. MM Pte 24853 Norfolk Regt att MGC.
CLARE Charles F. MM Pte 43591 Norfolk Regt
CLARE E. MM Pte 6427 2nd East Lancashire Regt
CLARE Edwin "DCM,MM" L/Sjt 40135 1/8th Liverpool Regt KIA 29.8.18.
CLARE Ernest MM Pte 21644 Manchester Regt
CLARE Fred MM Pte 81090 RAMC
CLARE Harry MM Gnr 21345 29 Bty 42 Bde RFA
CLARE Henry L. MM CSM 38666 Lancashire Fusiliers
CLARE Horace H. MM Pte 200562 1/4th Royal Berkshire Regt
CLARE J.F.T. MM Gnr 76796 34 Bde RFA
CLARE James MM+Bar Cpl 301048 1/7th Arg & Suth Highlanders
CLARE James Thomas MM L/Cpl 13974 Royal Lancaster Regt
CLARE Leonard MM Spr 45766 Royal Engineers
CLARE Samuel MM Cpl 14174 34 Bde RFA
CLARE Stanley A. MM Pte 13903 8th Suffolk Regt
CLARE Stephen MM L/Cpl 7692 Wiltshire Regt
CLARE William Edward MM Pte 2348 1/4th South Lancashire Regt
CLARENCE Daniel "MM,MID" Sjt 1039 4th Northumberland Fusiliers DOW 13.11.16.
CLARETT George P. MM Pte 495479 RAMC
CLAREY John George MM Pte 250415 20th Durham Light Infantry
CLARIDGE Charlie J. MM Pte 8421 1st Gloucestershire Regt
CLARIDGE Edwin J. MM Sjt 28938 8th Royal Lancaster Regt
CLARIDGE Frederick W. MM Cpl 20671 7th York & Lancaster Regt
CLARIDGE Harold J. MM Sjt 63987 27 Bde RFA
CLARK A. "MM,MID" Cpl 10037 1st Royal Scots
CLARK Albert MM Gnr 1382 RFA
CLARK Albert E. MM+Bar L/Cpl 14849 7th Somerset Light Infantry
CLARK Albert Edward MM L/Cpl 2513 1/16th London Regt KIA 28.3.18.
CLARK Albert F. MM Pte 2732 1/9th Durham Light Infantry
CLARK Albert H. MM L/Cpl 33949 1/5th Royal Warwickshire Regt
CLARK Albert W. MM Pte G/79212 9th Royal Fusiliers
CLARK Alex MM L/Sjt 200286 Gordon Highlanders
CLARK Alexander MM L/Cpl 63679 Royal Engineers
CLARK Alexander MM Pte 23563 2nd Highland Light Infantry KIA 25.3.18.
CLARK Alexander MM L/Sjt 10260 1st Seaforth Highlanders
CLARK Alfred MM Cpl 15683 2nd Coldstream Guards
CLARK Alfred MM Sjt 7547 11th Royal Fusiliers
CLARK Alfred MM Gnr 81116 RGA
CLARK Andrew MM Sjt T/31352 Att 19 Fd Amb RAMC Army Service Corps att RAMC
CLARK Andrew MM Cpl 7817 Arg & Suth Highlanders
CLARK Archibald E. MM Sjt 7272 Machine Gun Corps
CLARK Arthur MM L/Cpl 25966 10th West Riding Regt KIA 26.8.18.
CLARK Arthur MM Bdr 311370 RGA

CLARK Arthur MM+Bar Sjt 2190 1/4th East Yorkshire Regt
CLARK Arthur MM Pte G/1975 7th East Kent Regt DOW 21.11.17.
CLARK Arthur MM Gnr L/13972 RFA
CLARK Benjamin MM Pte 50731 Liverpool Regt
CLARK Cecil MM Cpl 94082 V/12 Heavy TM Bty RFA DOW 5.7.17.
CLARK Charles MM Bdr 63968 5 Bde RFA
CLARK Charles MM L/Cpl 17029 Machine Gun Corps
CLARK Charles MM Pte 9087 1st Hampshire Regt
CLARK Charles MM Cpl 357 509 Fd Coy Royal Engineers Died 24.12.16.
CLARK Charles MM Pte G/15385 Middlesex Regt
CLARK Charles MM Cpl 13254 2nd Highland Light Infantry
CLARK Charles MM Sjt 5903 18th Bn Machine Gun Corps
CLARK Charles B. MM L/Cpl 241145 5th Royal Sussex Regt
CLARK Charles C. MM L/Cpl 201584 Royal West Surrey Regt
CLARK Charles Ernest MM Sjt 372869 8th London Regt KIA 22.3.18.
CLARK Charles H. MM Bdr 50167 A/88 Bde RFA
CLARK Charles John "MM,CdeG(F)" Pte 42447 Essex Regt
CLARK Charles R. MM Sjt 3/5968 1st Dorsetshire Regt
CLARK Charles W. MM L/Cpl 34129 5th Gloucestershire Regt
CLARK Charles William MM L/Sjt 18062 1st Grenadier Guards KIA 20.11.17.
CLARK Cyril J. MM 2nd Cpl 43213 Royal Engineers
CLARK David MM+Bar Bdr 47695 RFA
CLARK David B. MM L/Cpl 33058 9th Yorkshire Regt
CLARK David B. MM Sjt T4/241613 779 Coy 16 AHT Army Service Corps
CLARK David Robertson MM L/Cpl S/8320 1/7th Royal Highlanders
CLARK Donald MM Sjt 365287 RGA
CLARK Douglas MM Sjt M2/133255 Army Service Corps
CLARK E. MM Pte 240950 4th Leicestershire Regt
CLARK E.J. MM Sjt SE/17644 Army Veterinary Corps
CLARK Edgar Leonard William MM L/Sjt 15677 9th Essex Regt
CLARK Edward W. MM Sjt 72055 RFA
CLARK Ernest MM Cpl 1776 4th Middlesex Regt
CLARK Ernest MM+Bar Cpl 7332 23rd Royal Fusiliers
CLARK Ernest MM Pte 67547 15th Cheshire Regt
CLARK Ernest MM Spr 43806 Royal Engineers
CLARK Ernest MM Pte 64729 RAMC
CLARK Ernest H. MM Pte 13690 10th Essex Regt
CLARK F.A. MM Cpl 287 16th Royal Warwickshire Regt
CLARK F.G. MM Pte 439199 RAMC
CLARK Frank MM Cpl Fitter 775205 310 Bde RFA DOW 11.5.17.
CLARK Frank MM Pte 24170 5th Yorkshire Light Infantry
CLARK Frank MM+Bar Pte 15831 6th Lincolnshire Regt
CLARK Frank Edward MM Cpl 8470 1st Royal West Surrey Regt
CLARK Frank G. MM Cpl 151898 33rd Bn Machine Gun Corps
CLARK Frank M. MM Pte 29005 RAMC
CLARK Frank W. MM Pte 202461 2/4th Hampshire Regt
CLARK Frederick MM BSM 49440 C/240 Bde RFA
CLARK Frederick C. MM+Bar Pte 15625 1 Special Coy Middlesex Regt
CLARK Frederick C. MM L/Cpl 1246 1/21st London Regt
CLARK George MM Pte 13257 2nd Worcestershire Regt
CLARK George MM Pte 25096 12th Hampshire Regt
CLARK George MM Sjt 64665 3rd Bn Machine Gun Corps
CLARK George MM Pte 200307 1/5th Highland Light Infantry
CLARK George MM Pte S/9905 14th Arg & Suth Highlanders
CLARK George MM Pte 682467 22nd London Regt
CLARK George MM Sjt 13866 24 Heavy Bty RGA
CLARK George MM Pte 16968 2nd Hampshire Regt
CLARK George "MM,MID" CSM 1215 2nd Royal Warwickshire Regt
CLARK George Edward MM L/Cpl 200783 Northumberland Fusiliers
CLARK George H. MM L/Bdr 79379 D/82 Bde RFA
CLARK George P. MM Pte 43724 Yorkshire Light Infantry
CLARK George William MM Cpl 73146 21 Div Sig Coy Royal Engineers
CLARK Gilbert MM Bdr 7460 B/102 Bde RFA
CLARK Harold MM BSM 146365 RGA
CLARK Harold B. MM Sjt 294347 RGA
CLARK Harold G. MM Gnr 136425 RGA
CLARK Harold John MM Pte 326525 1/1st Cambridgeshire Regt KIA 26.9.17.
CLARK Harold Thomas MM Pte 20933 Shropshire Light Infantry
CLARK Harold W. MM Gnr 168054 RGA
CLARK Harry MM L/Cpl G/19234 10th Royal West Kent Regt
CLARK Harry MM Sjt 72567 Machine Gun Corps
CLARK Harry MM L/Cpl 10165 5th Oxf & Bucks Light Infantry
CLARK Henry MM Cpl 682 13th East Yorkshire Regt
CLARK Henry MM Cpl L/12363 1st Royal Fusiliers
CLARK Henry J. MM Pte 279108 3rd London Regt
CLARK Henry J. MM Cpl 265885 Gordon Highlanders
CLARK Henry R. MM Cpl S/11719 1/7th Gordon Highlanders
CLARK Henry R. MM Pte 2790 1/22nd London Regt KIA 13.2.18.
CLARK Herbert MM Sjt 84331 150 Siege Bty RGA
CLARK Herbert W. MM Pte 48111 11th Royal Fusiliers
CLARK Horace MM Pte 200763 4th Yorkshire Light Infantry
CLARK Hubert John Hall MM Cpl 201785 2/5th Royal Warwickshire Regt
CLARK Hugh O. MM Cpl 350124 17th Royal Scots
CLARK J. MM L/Cpl 240430 1/5th Suffolk Regt
CLARK J. MM Cpl 86503 176 Tunnelling Coy Royal Engineers
CLARK J. MM+Bar Sjt 40695 Royal Engineers
CLARK J. MM Gnr 3209 RGA
CLARK J.G. MM+Bar Pte 41035 1/7th Arg & Suth Highlanders
CLARK J.S. MM Air Mech 1 1305 Royal Flying Corps
CLARK James MM Dvr T2/018160 Army Service Corps
CLARK James MM Sjt 6970 1st Scots Guards
CLARK James MM Sjt 10170 Northumberland Fusiliers
CLARK James MM Spr 71327 Royal Engineers
CLARK James MM Dvr 68668 46 Bty 39 Bde RFA
CLARK James MM Gnr Shoeing Smith 99070 RFA
CLARK James "MM+Bar,MID" Sjt 10535 Durham Light Infantry
CLARK James MM Cpl Sig 82278 255 Siege Bty RGA
CLARK James A. MM 2nd Cpl 207452 63 Div Sig Coy Royal Engineers
CLARK James A. MM Sjt 13154 Border Regt
CLARK James E. MM L/Cpl 16526 Machine Gun Corps
CLARK James Samuel MM L/Cpl 27/110 27th Northumberland Fusiliers KIA 1.7.16.
CLARK James W. MM L/Cpl 8549 1st West Yorkshire Regt
CLARK James William MM Pte 24251 7th York & Lancaster Regt KIA 21.3.18.
CLARK Joel MM Pte 21894 2/4th Royal West Surrey Regt KIA 29.7.18.
CLARK John MM Pte 10645 17th Royal Scots
CLARK John MM Cpl 114282 30th Bn Machine Gun Corps
CLARK John MM Pte 15979 1 Special Coy Middlesex Regt
CLARK John MM Cpl 559 D/119 Bde RFA
CLARK John MM Pte 888 1st Gordon Highlanders KIA 11.10.18.
CLARK John MM Gnr 52053 35 Bde RFA
CLARK John MM Pte 26/850 Northumberland Fusiliers
CLARK John MM Pte 524 8th Royal Fusiliers
CLARK John MM Pte 202073 1/1st Bucks Bn Oxf & Bucks Light Infantry
CLARK John MM L/Cpl 200125 1/1st London Regt
CLARK John C. MM Pte 67277 1st London Regt
CLARK John Charles MM Pte 1662 23rd Middlesex Regt
CLARK John E. MM Pte 48046 23rd Royal Fusiliers
CLARK John G. MM Gnr 751634 RFA
CLARK John G. MM Cpl 63093 RGA
CLARK John George MM Pte PS/7028 23rd Royal Fusiliers DOW 3.5.18.
CLARK John Graham MM L/Cpl 15/204 15th West Yorkshire Regt
CLARK John Robertson MM Sjr 400730 55 Div Sig Coy Royal Engineers DOW 29.4.18.
CLARK John T. MM Pte 241938 5th East Lancashire Regt
CLARK John W. MM Pte 1289 West Yorkshire Regt
CLARK John William MM Pte 95993 18 Squadron MGC (Cavalry)
CLARK John William MM L/Cpl 6674 11th Notts & Derby Regt KIA 23.10.18.
CLARK Joseph MM Sjt 9775 6th Yorkshire Light Infantry KIA 19.8.16.
CLARK Joseph MM Pte 49967 1st Royal Irish Fusiliers
CLARK Joseph MM Pte 18369 Royal Dublin Fusiliers
CLARK Joseph MM L/Cpl 21811 Machine Gun Corps
CLARK Joseph MM+Bar Pte 20959 13th Durham Light Infantry
CLARK Joseph MM Pte 14703 1st Bedfordshire Regt
CLARK Joseph Sydney MM Sjt 44551 12 Siege Bty RGA
CLARK Leslie M. MM Dvr 109961 37 Div Ammn Col RFA
CLARK Neil "MC,MM(7024 CQMS)" Lt 5/6th Scottish Rifles
CLARK Oliver MM Spr 459825 Royal Engineers
CLARK Percy J. MM Sjt 231805 2nd London Regt
CLARK Peter MM L/Sjt 310251 1/7th Gordon Highlanders
CLARK Peter MM Pte 202021 1st Royal Scots Fusiliers
CLARK Peter MM Cpl 63763 D/95 Bde RFA
CLARK Phillip Arthur Robert MM L/Cpl 17161 13th Essex Regt
CLARK R. MM Dvr 309 RFA
CLARK R.A. MM Cpl 781664 RFA

CLARK Reginald MM L/Cpl 84459 203 Fd Coy Royal Engineers KIA 7.6.18.
CLARK Richard MM Pte 14411 1st Royal Highlanders KIA 7.5.18.
CLARK Robert MM Sjt 275841 5/6th Royal Scots
CLARK Robert MM Pte 9009 1/7th Gordon Highlanders
CLARK Robert "DCM,MM+2 Bars" Sjt 13461 7th Lincolnshire Regt
CLARK Robert MM Gnr 1303 C/261 Bde RFA
CLARK Robert MM Sjt 52995 D/342 Bde RFA
CLARK Robert MM Pte 27413 7/8th King's Own Scottish Borderers
CLARK Robert Batson MM Sjt 16558 1st East Yorkshire Regt KIA 1.7.17.
CLARK Robert C. "DCM,MM+Bar" Sjt 100507 33 Div Sig Coy Royal Engineers
CLARK Robert I. MM Gnr Fitter 146670 RGA
CLARK Robert Wilfred MM Gnr 761420 RFA
CLARK Samuel MM Pte 300628 Arg & Suth Highlanders
CLARK Sidney "DCM,MM" Sjt 13234 12 Fd Coy Royal Engineers
CLARK Sidney MM Gnr 68512 174 Siege Bty RGA
CLARK Sidney A. MM L/Sjt 21176 Royal Fusiliers
CLARK Sidney H. MM Pte 17063 Royal Berkshire Regt
CLARK Sidney James MM L/Cpl 101887 92 Fd Coy Royal Engineers
CLARK Sidney Robert MM Sjt 326858 1/1st Cambridgeshire Regt
CLARK Simon MM Pte 39640 Northumberland Fusiliers
CLARK Stanley MM Pte 1144 2nd Arg & Suth Highlanders
CLARK Stanley MM Pte 101134 142 Fd Amb RAMC
CLARK Sydney MM Pte 19/245 Northumberland Fusiliers
CLARK Thomas MM Pte 270719 1/1st Northumberland Yeo
CLARK Thomas MM Dvr 25662 8 Sig Troop Royal Engineers
CLARK Thomas MM L/Cpl 24350 12th Northumberland Fusiliers
CLARK Thomas MM Gnr 775327 RFA
CLARK Thomas Frederick MM Pte 21364 10th Yorkshire Light Infantry KIA 16.10.17.
CLARK Thomas William MM Pte 270578 2nd Royal Scots KIA 4.5.18
CLARK Vernon Louis Augustus MM Gnr 96967 281 Siege Bty RGA
CLARK W. MM Sjt 386196 1 Fd Amb RAMC
CLARK W. MM L/Cpl 571007 London Regt
CLARK W.J. MM Staff SM S/21343 Army Service Corps
CLARK Walter MM L/Cpl M2/139072 Army Service Corps
CLARK Wilfred A. MM Pte 147997 32nd Bn Machine Gun Corps
CLARK William MM Pte 26790 Cameron Highlanders
CLARK William MM Cpl 53852 70 Siege Bty RGA
CLARK William MM Cpl 307605 1/8th Notts & Derby Regt
CLARK William MM L/Cpl 251596 1/6th Arg & Suth Highlanders
CLARK William MM Sjt 6728 1st Dorsetshire Regt
CLARK William MM L/Cpl 7102 21 Div Cyclist Coy Army Cyclist Corps
CLARK William MM Pte 70 Royal Fusiliers
CLARK William MM Bdr 965079 RFA
CLARK William MM Gnr 781434 Y/49 Med TM Bty RFA
CLARK William MM Cpl 4427 8th Northumberland Fusiliers
CLARK William MM Pte 300292 1/8th Arg & Suth Highlanders
CLARK William A. MM Sjt M2/051075 Army Service Corps
CLARK William Alfred MM Dvr 22304 C/93 Bde RFA
CLARK William Arthur MM Cpl 355 4th Middlesex Regt
CLARK William G. MM Pnr 259218 Royal Engineers
CLARK William George Ryland MM L/Cpl 550607 520 Fd Coy Royal Engineers
CLARK William R. MM Bdr 944535 RFA
CLARK William S. MM+Bar Pte 1569 1/18th London Regt
CLARK William W. MM QMS 869 3 Squadron Royal Flying Corps
CLARK Wilson MM Pte 29278 Highland Light Infantry
CLARK Zadok C. MM Sjt 27274 6 Div Sig Coy Royal Engineers
CLARKE A. MM Cpl 49872 1st Essex Regt
CLARKE A. MM Gnr 2548 RFA
CLARKE A.E. MM L/Cpl 15130 Manchester Regt
CLARKE Alan G.H. MM L/Cpl 41483 Royal Irish Fusiliers
CLARKE Albert MM Pte 49604 9th Royal Fusiliers KIA 30.11.17.
CLARKE Albert MM Cpl 71046 9th Notts & Derby Regt
CLARKE Albert MM Gnr 830519 D/187 Bde RFA
CLARKE Albert MM Pte B/201085 Rifle Brigade DOW 28.10.18.
CLARKE Albert MM Pte 15167 12th West Yorkshire Regt
CLARKE Albert MM Sjt 51087 73 Bty 5 Bde RFA
CLARKE Albert E. MM Spr 259297 Royal Engineers
CLARKE Albert W.A. MM Pte 5938 8th Royal West Surrey Regt
CLARKE Alexander MM Pte 32474 17th Notts & Derby Regt
CLARKE Alfred MM Sjt 10881 6th York & Lancaster Regt
CLARKE Alfred MM Pte 11020 5th Royal Berkshire Regt KIA 27.6.17.
CLARKE Alfred MM Bdr 760241 C/72 Bde RFA
CLARKE Alfred E. MM Pte 15052 2nd Suffolk Regt
CLARKE Alfred F. MM Pte 5518 12th Lancers
CLARKE Alfred G. MM Gnr 71011 41 Bde RFA
CLARKE Alfred Z. MM Cpl 11493 3rd Worcestershire Regt
CLARKE Algeson C.B. "MM,MID" Sjt 18113 9th Cheshire Regt
CLARKE Arthur MM Pte 242357 8th Worcestershire Regt
CLARKE Arthur MM Pte G/4312 8th Royal Sussex Regt
CLARKE Arthur J. MM Pte 24654 Royal Fusiliers
CLARKE Arthur W. MM Sjt 294882 RGA
CLARKE Benjamin MM Pte 240254 North Staffordshire Regt
CLARKE Bernard MM Bdr 4145 D/15 Bde RFA
CLARKE Bernard MM Pte 57824 15th Cheshire Regt KIA 28.3.18.
CLARKE Bertie MM L/Cpl M2/149262 884 MT Coy Army Service Corps
CLARKE Bertie V. MM Pte 10/19590 Northumberland Fusiliers
CLARKE C. MM Pte 1473 23rd Royal Fusiliers
CLARKE C.F. MM Pte 9909 Essex Regt
CLARKE C.M.S. MM Pte 350467 RAMC
CLARKE Cecil MM Pte 28413 Notts & Derby Regt
CLARKE Cecil Andrews MM Sjt 898 Middlesex Regt KIA 24.4.17.
CLARKE Charles MM Cpl 100075 26 Fd Coy Royal Engineers
CLARKE Charles MM Sjt M2/051908 Army Service Corps
CLARKE Charles MM Pte 202987 1st Gloucestershire Regt
CLARKE Charles MM Cpl 14620 9th Norfolk Regt KIA 15.9.16.
CLARKE Charles MM Pte 56348 9th Royal Welsh Fusiliers
CLARKE Charles Alfred MM L/Bdr 965678 RFA
CLARKE Charles Augustus MM Cpl 188 10th East Yorkshire Regt
CLARKE Charles E. MM+Bar Cpl 51489 RGA
CLARKE Charles F. MM L/Bdr 138931 283 Siege Bty RGA
CLARKE Charles F. MM CSM 7977 1st Norfolk Regt
CLARKE Charles H. MM Pte 5914 20th London Regt
CLARKE Charles H. MM L/Cpl 14744 7th Bedfordshire Regt
CLARKE Charles H. MM Sjt 57436 44 Bde RFA
CLARKE Charles Joseph MM L/Cpl 12552 1st Dorsetshire Regt KIA 1.7.16.
CLARKE Charles V. MM Pte 322803 11th London Regt
CLARKE Charles W. "DCM,MM" Sjt 6014 1st Scots Guards
CLARKE Charles S. MM Cpl 14652 7th Bedfordshire Regt
CLARKE Daniel William MM Bdr 27472 130 Bty 40 Bde RFA
CLARKE David MM L/Cpl 14077 9th Royal Irish Fusiliers
CLARKE E. MM Pte 320087 2/1st(Highland)Fd Amb RAMC
CLARKE Edward "MM,DM(B)" CSM S/7613 23rd Middlesex Regt
CLARKE Edward MM Pte 15541 10th Yorkshire Regt
CLARKE Edward MM L/Cpl 251244 1/5th Essex Regt
CLARKE Edward MM Pte 24124 15th Notts & Derby Regt KIA 25.8.17.
CLARKE Edward MM Sjt 8533 7th Border Regt KIA 26.8.18.
CLARKE Edward F. MM Pte 9945 2nd Shropshire Light Infantry
CLARKE Edward T. MM 2nd Cpl 522502 Royal Engineers
CLARKE Eldred MM Pte 17241 Grenadier Guards
CLARKE Ernest W. MM Cpl 43468 Suffolk Regt
CLARKE F. MM Sjt 6806 1st Dorsetshire Regt
CLARKE F. MM Cpl 19334 8th Yorkshire Light Infantry
CLARKE Francis MM L/Bdr 124837 328 Siege Bty RGA
CLARKE Francis "MM,MMV(lt)" 2nd Cpl 482072 Royal Engineers
CLARKE Francis E. MM L/Bdr 95875 RFA
CLARKE Francis F. MM Pte C/760 16th King's Royal Rifle Corps
CLARKE Francis G. MM Pte 60224 Royal Fusiliers
CLARKE Frank MM Sjt 11270 4th Yorkshire Light Infantry
CLARKE Frank MM+Bar L/Sjt 12862 1st Norfolk Regt
CLARKE Frank A. MM Pte 14213 1/1st Cambridgeshire Regt
CLARKE Fred MM Sjt 200254 Shropshire Light Infantry
CLARKE Fred MM Pte 2329 1/7th Liverpool Regt
CLARKE Frederick MM L/Bdr 930750 B/291 Bde RFA
CLARKE Frederick MM Pte 12511 7th Norfolk Regt
CLARKE Frederick MM Sjt 16568 7th Norfolk Regt KIA 12.10.16.
CLARKE Frederick MM Cpl R/7097 King's Royal Rifle Corps
CLARKE Frederick MM Cpl 355551 25th Royal Welsh Fusiliers
CLARKE Frederick C. MM Sjt 16072 11th Worcestershire Regt
CLARKE Frederick H. MM Cpl 48693 7th North Staffordshire Regt
CLARKE Frederick John MM Pte G/10832 11th Royal West Surrey Regt KIA 28.8.18.
CLARKE Frederick T. MM L/Cpl 5/5085 4th King's Royal Rifle Corps
CLARKE Frederick W.H. MM L/Cpl 479751 Royal Engineers
CLARKE G. MM Pte 1493 Royal Warwickshire Regt
CLARKE G.T. MM Dvr M2/226055 .K' Siege Park Army Service Corps
CLARKE George MM Sjt 350163 1(East Lancs)Fd Amb RAMC
CLARKE George MM Gnr 181096 A/285 Bde RFA

CLARKE George MM Cpl 13489 8th Yorkshire Regt
CLARKE George MM Sjt 8/16551 8th South Wales Borderers
CLARKE George MM Pte 9976 2nd East Lancashire Regt
CLARKE George MM Gnr 227122 RFA
CLARKE George "DCM,MM" Cpl 55606 Y/3 Medium TM Bty RGA
CLARKE George "DCM,MM" Spr 34882 Royal Engineers
CLARKE George MM(941 Cpl 1/4th Yorks)+Bar Sjt 23522 Machine Gun Corps
CLARKE George MM Dvr 11330 14 Bde RHA Died 22.6.17.
CLARKE George MM Gnr 112651 RGA
CLARKE George MM Pte 31293 53 Coy Labour Corps
CLARKE George MM Sjt 19772 2nd Dragoon Guards
CLARKE George Arthur MM Pte 24225 1st South Staffordshire Regt DOW 19.10.17.
CLARKE George B. MM Pte 201064 1/4th Norfolk Regt
CLARKE George C. MM+Bar Bdr 619 1/10(West Riding)Bty RFA
CLARKE George C. MM Pte 7624 North Staffordshire Regt
CLARKE George H. MM L/Cpl WR/27445 334 Rly Const Coy Royal Engineers
CLARKE George Herbert MM Pte 241483 13th Royal Sussex Regt Died 18.1.19.
CLARKE George John MM L/Cpl 43335 Middlesex Regt
CLARKE George Murray MM Sjt 955 16th Middlesex Regt KIA 1.7.16.
CLARKE George R. MM Pte 326056 1/1st Cambridgeshire Regt
CLARKE George R. MM Pte 40289 Scottish Rifles
CLARKE George W. MM Sjt G/18409 6th Royal West Kent Regt
CLARKE H. MM Pte 40618 1/1st Hertfordshire Regt
CLARKE H. MM Sjt 20812 York & Lancaster Regt
CLARKE Harold MM Sjt 203006 Yorkshire Light Infantry
CLARKE Harold MM Pte 52562 11th Cheshire Regt
CLARKE Harold MM Sjt 12238 RFA
CLARKE Harold H.G. MM+Bar Sjt 50513 24th Royal Fusiliers
CLARKE Harry MM Gnr 2501 1 Motorised Bde 11 Bty MGC(Motors)
CLARKE Harry MM L/Sjt 241188 6th Royal Warwickshire Regt
CLARKE Harry MM Pte 62969 5th Yorkshire Light Infantry
CLARKE Harry Albert MM Sjt 15703 7th Bedfordshire Regt KIA 3.5.17.
CLARKE Harry Hamilton MM Sjt 470410 12th London Regt KIA 7.9.18.
CLARKE Harry W. MM Gnr 82973 RFA
CLARKE Henry MM CSM 12398 7th Yorkshire Regt
CLARKE Henry MM Pte 201857 2/7th Worcestershire Regt DOW 24.8.17.
CLARKE Henry MM L/Cpl 17984 8th Northumberland Fusiliers
CLARKE Henry MM Sjt Shoeing Smith 52701 39 Bde RFA
CLARKE Henry C. MM Pte 16117 Royal Sussex Regt
CLARKE Henry Edgar MM L/Cpl 36036 237 Coy Machine Gun Corps
CLARKE Herbert MM+Bar Pte S/7048 7th Seaforth Highlanders
CLARKE Herbert G. MM Pte 301733 5th London Regt
CLARKE Herbert V. MM Pte 801 17th Royal Fusiliers
CLARKE Horace MM Pte 73280 RAMC
CLARKE Horace W. MM 2nd Cpl 312639 Royal Engineers
CLARKE Isaac MM Sjt L/17630 A/170 Bde RFA
CLARKE James MM Pte 63779 8th West Yorkshire Regt
CLARKE James MM Cpl 105919 Machine Gun Corps
CLARKE James MM Sjt 2066 7th Royal Irish Regt KIA 19.9.18.
CLARKE James MM Pte 40357 Lancashire Fusiliers
CLARKE James "DCM,MM" CSM 265159 1/6th Cheshire Regt
CLARKE James MM Sjt 1078 1st Gordon Highlanders
CLARKE James MM Cpl 331191 Liverpool Regt
CLARKE James MM L/Cpl 36309 RAMC
CLARKE James D. MM Pte 635031 20th London Regt
CLARKE James E.F. MM Pte 291804 1/7th Gordon Highlanders
CLARKE James Edward MM Cpl 3608 51 Coy Machine Gun Corps
CLARKE James H. MM Dvr T4/044015 29 Div Train Army Service Corps
CLARKE James H. MM Cpl 2514 South Lancashire Regt
CLARKE James R. MM L/Cpl S/24657 13th Rifle Brigade
CLARKE James W. MM Sjt 240343 5th Lincolnshire Regt
CLARKE Joe MM L/Cpl 40527 RAMC
CLARKE John MM Dvr 73461 5 Div Sig Coy Royal Engineers
CLARKE John MM+Bar Pte 10508 2nd Scottish Rifles
CLARKE John MM Pte 1968 1/4th South Lancashire Regt DOW 29.8.17.
CLARKE John MM Pte 12266 1st Royal Inniskilling Fusiliers KIA 30.11.17.
CLARKE John MM Cpl 16222 Royal Inniskilling Fusiliers
CLARKE John MM Gnr 52389 130 Heavy Bty RGA

CLARKE John A. MM L/Bdr 154863 RGA
CLARKE John C. MM L/Cpl 62689 9th Yorkshire Light Infantry
CLARKE John E. MM Pte 251309 1/6th Manchester Regt
CLARKE John H. MM Bdr 34398 RFA
CLARKE John James "MM,MSM" Sjt 58245 92 Fd Amb RAMC
CLARKE John Joseph MM+Bar Bdr 72718 A/47 Bde RFA KIA 3.5.17.
CLARKE John R. MM+Bar Sjt 42788 Royal Engineers
CLARKE John R. MM Pnr 253936 Royal Engineers
CLARKE John William MM Pte 3/7273 1st Norfolk Regt
CLARKE Jonas MM Pte 17690 1/4th York & Lancaster Regt KIA 13.10.18.
CLARKE Joseph MM Sjt 17444 11th Royal Irish Rifles
CLARKE Joseph MM Sjt 5164 2nd Royal Irish Rifles
CLARKE Joseph MM Pnr 147219 Royal Engineers
CLARKE Joseph MM Sjt 86788 Royal Engineers
CLARKE Joseph MM Pte 2172 1/4th South Lancashire Regt
CLARKE Joseph W. "MM,MSM" CSM 266539 2/7th Notts & Derby Regt
CLARKE Joseph William MM Pte 57164 58th Bn Machine Gun Corps KIA 28.8.18.
CLARKE Lawrence MM Cpl 4981 2nd Royal Irish Rifles KIA 24.3.18.
CLARKE Leslie W. MM Sjt 14894 8th Suffolk Regt att 1/1st Cambs Regt.
CLARKE Marshall Robert MM Pte M2/098018 Att 22 Div Ammn Col RFA Army Service Corps
CLARKE Oliver MM Bdr 79905 D/46 Bde RFA
CLARKE Oliver MM Sjt 5810 1st Notts & Derby Regt
CLARKE Oliver C. MM Spr 96548 Royal Engineers
CLARKE Percy MM Pte 3/7474 2nd Bedfordshire Regt
CLARKE Percy H. MM Pte 46452 37 Fd Amb RAMC
CLARKE Percy John MM L/Cpl B/200425 13th Rifle Brigade
CLARKE Philip MM Pte R/11273 King's Royal Rifle Corps
CLARKE Ralph MM L/Cpl 17951 1st Worcestershire Regt
CLARKE Raymond MM Sjt 22428 2 Fd Coy Royal Engineers
CLARKE Reginald MM Cpl 38405 Royal Warwickshire Regt
CLARKE Richard MM Gnr 96585 A/83 Bde RFA
CLARKE Robert MM Pte 8928 2nd Royal Berkshire Regt
CLARKE Robert "DCM,MM" Cpl 9/17614 9th Royal Inniskilling Fusiliers
CLARKE Robert L. MM L/Cpl 38069 1st East Surrey Regt
CLARKE Robert W. MM Pte 15389 2nd Leinster Regt
CLARKE Robert W. MM Pte 16658 8th Lincolnshire Regt
CLARKE Romaine MM 2nd Cpl 85385 Royal Engineers
CLARKE S. MM Pte 341493 RAMC
CLARKE Samuel G. MM Cpl 652916 21st London Regt
CLARKE Samuel James MM L/Cpl 41206 RAMC
CLARKE Sidney MM Spr 23847 5 Sig Troop Royal Engineers
CLARKE Sidney F. MM Pte 17869 6th Wiltshire Regt
CLARKE Sidney H. MM Pte 12336 7th Suffolk Regt
CLARKE Sidney J. MM Pte 200133 North Staffordshire Regt
CLARKE Sidney L. MM Pte 112399 3rd Light Bn Tank Corps
CLARKE Stanley MM Cpl 266261 Royal Welsh Fusiliers
CLARKE Stanley MM Sjt 400153 Royal Engineers
CLARKE Stephen MM Pte 86062 Machine Gun Corps
CLARKE Stephen Isaac MM Cpl 30196 68 Bty 14 Bde RFA
CLARKE Thomas MM Pte 56077 13th Liverpool Regt
CLARKE Thomas MM Cpl 19399 1st Royal Inniskilling Fusiliers
CLARKE Thomas MM Pte 45659 Royal Welsh Fusiliers
CLARKE Thomas MM Pte 16491 2nd Royal Irish Regt
CLARKE Thomas MM Pte 74646 6th Durham Light Infantry
CLARKE Thomas MM Pte 27399 1/7th Notts & Derby Regt
CLARKE Thomas MM Pte 12276 12th East Surrey Regt
CLARKE Thomas MM Pte 33363 6th Oxf & Bucks Light Infantry
CLARKE Thomas MM Pte 40730 2nd Suffolk Regt KIA 30.8.18.
CLARKE Thomas MM Gnr 76244 D/123 Bde RFA KIA 15.9.18.
CLARKE Thomas Albert MM 2nd Cpl 22761 10 Rail Op Depot Royal Engineers
CLARKE Thomas E. MM L/Cpl 28308 4th Bn Machine Gun Corps
CLARKE Thomas Henry MM Pte 10880 11th Royal West Kent Regt KIA 20.9.17.
CLARKE Thomas W. MM Gnr 27395 RFA
CLARKE Wallace Edwin MM L/Cpl 12806 Notts & Derby Regt
CLARKE Walter MM Pte 35702 Manchester Regt
CLARKE Walter MM Sjt A/4 King's Royal Rifle Corps
CLARKE Walter "DCM,MM" Sjt Wheeler 27415 B/46 Bde RFA
CLARKE Walter C. MM Pte 267891 1/7th Liverpool Regt KIA 20.9.17.
CLARKE Walter E. MM Pte 241214 Seaforth Highlanders
CLARKE Walter T. MM+Bar Pte 43600 2nd Suffolk Regt

CLARKE William MM L/Cpl 201988 4th North Staffordshire Regt
CLARKE William MM Sjt 2624 9th East Surrey Regt
CLARKE William "MM,MID" Spr 50337 Royal Engineers
CLARKE William MM L/Cpl 302290 1/9th Royal Scots
CLARKE William MM Pte 77885 10th Royal Fusiliers DOW 9.10.18.
CLARKE William MM Cpl 200332 13th Liverpool Regt KIA 27.9.18.
CLARKE William MM Cpl 64521 36 Div Sig Coy Royal Engineers
CLARKE William "DCM,MM+Bar" Sjt 360 4th Middlesex Regt
CLARKE William MM Pte 2612 1/4th South Lancashire Regt
CLARKE William MM L/Cpl 24937 22nd Manchester Regt
CLARKE William MM Pte 20337 1st Bedfordshire Regt
CLARKE William MM+Bar Cpl 16176 A/93 Bde RFA
CLARKE William MM Pte 18970 2nd Coldstream Guards
CLARKE William MM Cpl M2/032583 Army Service Corps
CLARKE William A. MM Pte 115440 Machine Gun Corps
CLARKE William A.C. MM Pte STK/5829 Royal Fusiliers
CLARKE William E. MM Pte 233175 2nd London Regt
CLARKE William Edward MM Cpl 51704 5th Liverpool Regt
CLARKE William George MM Pte 16535 7th Bedfordshire Regt KIA 1.7.16.
CLARKE William H. MM Pte 11457 Royal West Surrey Regt
CLARKE William H. MM Cpl 250056 Royal Engineers
CLARKE William Henry "DCM,MM" Pte 14472 2nd Grenadier Guards
CLARKE William Henry MM Cpl 60003 24 Div Sig Coy Royal Engineers
CLARKE William J. MM Cpl 328001 7th West Riding Regt
CLARKE William J.E. MM Sjt 53722 RFA
CLARKE William T. MM L/Cpl 250254 3rd London Regt
CLARKE William Thomas MM L/Cpl 70544 Royal Engineers
CLARKE William V. MM Pte 434053 RAMC
CLARKE Windsor MM L/Cpl 20031 11th South Wales Borderers
CLARKIN Michael MM Pte 2129 7th Leinster Regt
CLARKSON Arthur MM Bdr 31745 44 Bde RFA
CLARKSON Arthur R. MM Dvr 925611 RFA
CLARKSON Charles MM+Bar Pte 60221 33rd Bn Machine Gun Corps
CLARKSON Frederick "DCM,MM+Bar" Sjt 47082 18 Div Sig Coy Royal Engineers
CLARKSON George H. "DCM,MM" Cpl 312768 30 Div Sig Coy Royal Engineers
CLARKSON George William MM Bdr 307247 RGA
CLARKSON Harold MM Pte 52226 Liverpool Regt
CLARKSON Harry MM Sjt 775088 A/63 Bde RFA
CLARKSON James MM Pte 17542 4th Grenadier Guards DOW 18.7.16.
CLARKSON James C. MM Pte 11325 Machine Gun Corps
CLARKSON James W. MM Pte 15960 7th South Lancashire Regt
CLARKSON John MM L/Cpl 16369 9th North Staffordshire Regt KIA 21.3.18.
CLARKSON John "DCM,MM" Sjt 7422 1st Leicestershire Regt
CLARKSON John MM Pte 1402 11th East Yorkshire Regt
CLARKSON Leonard Charles MM Gnr Sig 160045 319 Siege Bty RGA
CLARKSON Philip MM Bdr 50858 B/58 Bde RFA
CLARKSON Thomas "MM,MID" CQMS 3/4453 York & Lancaster Regt
CLARKSON William H. MM L/Cpl 200414 1/4th North Lancashire Regt
CLARKSON William Henry MM Pte 14/20 14th York & Lancaster Regt DOW 4.7.16.
CLARSON Fred MM Dvr 5714 RFA
CLARVIS Clarence MM Cpl 240825 1st Lincolnshire Regt
CLARY Samuel Arthur MM Pte G/5434 12th Middlesex Regt DOW 25.10.17.
CLASPER Joseph MM Sjt 16980 12th Durham Light Infantry KIA 15.10.17.
CLATWORTHY Benjamin MM Cpl 164702 5 Fd Svy Bn Royal Engineers
CLATWORTHY Harry S. MM L/Bdr 111936 238 Siege Bty RGA
CLATWORTHY Stanley G. MM Sjt 36561 1st East Surrey Regt
CLAUGHTON Walter MM Gnr 197053 54 Bty 39 Bde RFA
CLAXTON Colin "DCM,MM" L/Sjt 305193 1/8th Notts & Derby Regt
CLAXTON John MM Cpl 25133 7th Royal Irish Regt
CLAXTON William MM Cpl 14034 3rd Coldstream Guards KIA 13.4.18.
CLAY Albert V. MM Sjt 10020 6th Lincolnshire Regt
CLAY Cecil Alfred MM Pte 241268 Worcestershire Regt
CLAY Frank MM Pte 46818 10th King's Own Scottish Borderers
CLAY Frank MM L/Cpl 26811 9th Devonshire Regt KIA 26.10.17.
CLAY George MM Pte 4737 2nd Notts & Derby Regt
CLAY George MM L/Cpl 25108 North Lancashire Regt
CLAY Godfrey MM Pte 350511 Manchester Regt
CLAY Harry "DCM,MM(613 Cpl S Notts Huss)" Sjt 164489 100th Bn Machine Gun Corps
CLAY Henry S. MM Cpl 325790 1/9th Durham Light Infantry
CLAY John MM Sjt 60548 2nd Manchester Regt DOW 8.11.18.
CLAY John MM Pte 20805 2nd Grenadier Guards
CLAY Joseph H. MM Pte 26010 Shropshire Light Infantry
CLAY William MM Spr 25958 54 Fd Coy Royal Engineers
CLAY William John MM L/Sjt 3/7462 8th Devonshire Regt
CLAY William Walter MM Pte 7311 1st Leicestershire Regt
CLAYDEN Leonard MM Cpl 43637 2nd Suffolk Regt
CLAYDON Albert B. MM Sjt 9556 2nd West Yorkshire Regt
CLAYDON Frederick W. MM Gnr L/38160 RFA
CLAYDON Horace MM L/Cpl 266360 1/1st Hertfordshire Regt DOW 3.11.17.
CLAYDON James MM Cpl 201803 1/5th Suffolk Regt
CLAYDON Joseph Stanley MM L/Cpl 326290 1/1st Cambridgeshire Regt KIA 15.11.17.
CLAYDON Sidney Charles MM L/Cpl 10674 1st East Lancashire Regt
CLAYDON Walter L. "DCM,MM" L/Cpl 15318 Royal West Surrey Regt
CLAYDON William A. MM Sjt 1407 1/7th London Regt
CLAYDON William R. MM Spr 29409 Royal Engineers
CLAYPOLE Edwin MM Pte 145521 1/1st Northamptonshire Yeomanry
CLAYS Edward MM Cpl 83559 30 Div Sig Coy Royal Engineers
CLAYSON Alfred E. MM L/Cpl 76288 1st London Regt
CLAYSON Christopher L. MM Pte 57816 1/6th Cheshire Regt
CLAYTON A.E. MM Pte 354348 London Regt
CLAYTON Abraham MM Cpl 37334 23rd Northumberland Fusiliers
CLAYTON Albert MM Cpl 13611 10th Scottish Rifles
CLAYTON Albert MM L/Cpl 139251 Machine Gun Corps
CLAYTON Albert E. MM Cpl 19919 Machine Gun Corps
CLAYTON Alfred MM Pte 33736 1st North Lancashire Regt
CLAYTON Alfred C. MM Sjt 796449 A/312 Bde RFA
CLAYTON Arthur MM Pte 8788 Coldstream Guards
CLAYTON Charles MM Pte 21282 Grenadier Guards
CLAYTON Charles MM L/Cpl 277277 6th Manchester Regt
CLAYTON Charles Bramley MM Pte 8510 2nd Lincolnshire Regt
CLAYTON Clifford MM L/Cpl 76820 RAMC
CLAYTON Ellis MM Pte 12897 Durham Light Infantry
CLAYTON Ernest E. MM Cpl Fitter 148133 49 Bty 40 Bde RFA
CLAYTON Frank MM L/Sjt 200646 1/4th Shropshire Light Infantry
CLAYTON Frank MM Sjt 263035 4th West Riding Regt
CLAYTON George MM L/Cpl 12208 6th South Lancashire Regt
CLAYTON George E. MM Pte 210 15th West Yorkshire Regt
CLAYTON Gilbert MM Pte 41579 West Yorkshire Regt
CLAYTON Harry MM L/Cpl 26681 15th Notts & Derby Regt
CLAYTON Harry MM Dvr 13879 16 Div Ammn Col RFA
CLAYTON Henry MM Gnr 108615 402 Bty 14 Bde RFA
CLAYTON Henry MM Gnr W/5606 B/120 Bde RFA
CLAYTON Horace R. MM Pte 5197 Royal Sussex Regt
CLAYTON J. MM Pte 390553 3 Fd Amb RAMC
CLAYTON J. MM Dvr 810512 RFA
CLAYTON James "DCM,MM+Bar" Sjt 168578 A/76 Bde RFA
CLAYTON James E. MM Pte 200586 Leicestershire Regt
CLAYTON John MM Pte 242290 2/5th North Lancashire Regt KIA 26.10.17.
CLAYTON John Edward MM L/Cpl 6358 52 Coy Machine Gun Corps DOW 6.1.18.
CLAYTON John Henry MM Pte 62599 92 Fd Amb RAMC KIA 30.9.18.
CLAYTON John W. MM Pte 7535 Middlesex Regt
CLAYTON John W. MM+Bar Sjt 89949 C/94 Bde RFA
CLAYTON Joseph G. MM Bdr 95296 RFA
CLAYTON Norris W. MM L/Cpl 34186 Middlesex Regt
CLAYTON Percy R. MM Pte 301803 1/8th Durham Light Infantry
CLAYTON Reginald A. MM Pte 3000 12th Middlesex Regt
CLAYTON Richard MM Cpl 34391 195 Coy Machine Gun Corps
CLAYTON Robert J. MM+Bar Sjt 21622 B/285 Bde RFA
CLAYTON Robert William MM L/Cpl 371357 2/8th London Regt KIA 30.10.17.
CLAYTON S. MM Pte 4635 20th Royal Fusiliers
CLAYTON Sydney MM Pte 46694 Machine Gun Corps
CLAYTON Thomas MM Bdr 66322 157 Siege Bty RGA KIA 9.4.18.
CLAYTON Thomas MM Cpl 43112 Att 1st Irish Guards RAMC
CLAYTON Thomas Cuerdon MM Gnr 155600 237 Siege Bty RGA KIA 9.4.18.

CLAYTON Tom MM+Bar L/Bdr 16929 A/82 Bde RFA
CLAYTON William MM Pte 16383 4th Grenadier Guards
CLAYTON William MM Sjt 3835 1st Leicestershire Regt
CLAYTON William MM Gnr 24505 6 Div Ammn Col RFA
CLAYTON William E. "DCM,MM" Cpl 30730 116 Heavy Bty RGA
CLAYTON William Henry MM Cpl R/3595 13th King's Royal Rifle Corps KIA 12.9.18.
CLAZEY Joseph MM Cpl 205687 5th Yorkshire Light Infantry
CLEAL Arthur Leonard MM Dvr L/36359 D/231 Bde RFA
CLEAL Ernest MM Pte 277582 1/6th Essex Regt
CLEAL Samuel Arthur MM Cpl 497477 3rd(Home Counties)Fd Amb RAMC
CLEALL Bertie L. MM Pte B/201404 1st Rifle Brigade
CLEAR Harold MM Pte 307882 Lancashire Fusiliers
CLEAR James J. MM L/Sjt 204418 Liverpool Regt
CLEARIE Robert MM Spr 86509 Royal Engineers
CLEARY Edward MM Pte 11872 6th Royal Inniskilling Fusiliers
CLEARY James MM Pte 1579 Irish Guards Died 28.7.17.
CLEARY John MM Pnr 161671 17 Div Sig Coy Royal Engineers DOW 4.11.17.
CLEARY John MM Spr 442590 Royal Engineers
CLEARY Patrick MM L/Sjt 15334 South Wales Borderers
CLEARY Victor MM Pte 25136 Royal Irish Regt
CLEARY William MM Pte 5581 Royal Irish Regt
CLEARY William P. MM Pte 20103 1st Royal Dublin Fusiliers
CLEAVELEY James Alfred MM Sjt 2064 1/17th London Regt
CLEAVER Charles W. MM+Bar BQMS 89621 D/106 Bde RFA
CLEAVER Ernest Alfred MM Pnr 146224 4 Special Bn Royal Engineers
CLEAVER Ernest C. MM Pte 533478 15th London Regt
CLEAVER Frank MM Cpl 242267 5th Gloucestershire Regt
CLEAVER Harry L. MM Cpl 44248 12th Suffolk Regt
CLEAVER J. MM Pte 1595 RAMC
CLEAVER Thomas MM Pte R/2193 King's Royal Rifle Corps
CLEAVER William MM Pte 6047 1st Manchester Regt
CLEAVER William H. MM Dvr 50177 RFA
CLEE Stanley C. MM Pte 19703 Shropshire Light Infantry
CLEE Thomas MM Sjt 34226 58 Coy Labour Corps
CLEE William MM+Bar Cpl 203696 5th Gloucestershire Regt
CLEECE Ellis MM Pte 18236 1st North Lancashire Regt
CLEETON George MM Gnr 51492 RGA
CLEEVE Albert H. MM Sjt SE223 Army Veterinary Corps
CLEEVE Fred MM 2nd Cpl 26491 26 Fd Coy Royal Engineers
CLEEVE George W. MM Pte 15198 Hampshire Regt
CLEGG Abraham Pickwell MM L/Cpl 388444 2/2(Northumbrian)Fd Amb RAMC
CLEGG Alfred J. MM Sjt 6014 Machine Gun Corps
CLEGG Benjamin MM Pte 105607 56 Fd Amb RAMC
CLEGG Bertram MM Pte 203774 Lancashire Fusiliers
CLEGG Edward MM Dvr 137125 50 Div Ammn Col RFA
CLEGG Ernest MM Cpl 72011 RFA
CLEGG Frank Moore MM Cpl 17474 3rd Coldstream Guards
CLEGG Gilbert MM Pte 339132 RAMC
CLEGG Harry MM Pte 20573 3rd Grenadier Guards
CLEGG Herbert MM Sjt 13903 1/4th Royal Lancaster Regt
CLEGG J. MM L/Cpl Unknown North Lancashire Regt
CLEGG James William MM Gnr 92846 183 Siege Bty RGA
CLEGG John W. MM Pte S/5583 Rifle Brigade
CLEGG Joseph MM L/Cpl 5408 8th Royal West Surrey Regt
CLEGG Norman MM Pte 60534 1st Cheshire Regt
CLEGG Percival C. MM Pnr 255142 Royal Engineers
CLEGG Percy MM Dvr 114585 RFA
CLEGG Richard William MM Cpl 821005 298 Bde RFA
CLEGG S. MM L/Sjt 10239 18th Manchester Regt
CLEGG William MM+Bar Sjt 91967 Tank Corps
CLEGG Willie MM Pte 72250 10th Notts & Derby Regt
CLEGG Wilson MM L/Cpl 26003 Machine Gun Corps
CLEGHORN H.J. MM Bdr 750177 RFA
CLEGHORN John W. MM Pte 89171 Machine Gun Corps
CLELAND James MM L/Sjt S/41538 7th Seaforth Highlanders
CLELAND James MM L/Cpl 412327 Royal Engineers
CLELLAND Fred MM Pte 50616 15th Suffolk Regt
CLELLAND James MM Cpl 17966 6th King's Own Scottish Borderers
CLELLAND Peter MM Cpl 81217 206 Fd Coy Royal Engineers
CLELLAND William MM Pte 17021 10th Scottish Rifles
CLELLAND William "MM,MSM" Sjt 345399 153 Siege Bty RGA
CLEM John MM Sjt 7675 2nd Worcestershire Regt
CLEMENS Henry MM Pte 534388 RAMC
CLEMENT Abraham E. MM Gnr 740551 B/266 Bde RFA
CLEMENT David MM L/Cpl STK1970 Royal Fusiliers
CLEMENT Frederick MM Cpl 29017 Royal Engineers
CLEMENT Frederick T. MM Sjt 1843 North Staffordshire Regt
CLEMENT George MM Cpl 112245 Royal Engineers
CLEMENT Horace MM Spr 25904 Royal Engineers
CLEMENTS Albert Edward "DCM,MM" Sjt 92659 5th Bn Tank Corps DOW 4.10.18.
CLEMENTS Alexander MM Pte 19731 RAMC
CLEMENTS Alfred W. MM Pte 326920 1/1st Cambridgeshire Regt
CLEMENTS Arthur S. MM Pte A/203188 King's Royal Rifle Corps
CLEMENTS C.H. MM Cpl 38105 Machine Gun Corps
CLEMENTS Charles Walter MM Cpl 9983 6th East Kent Regt
CLEMENTS Edward C. MM Pte S/14363 Rifle Brigade
CLEMENTS Edwin MM Pte 66500 2nd Durham Light Infantry
CLEMENTS Ernest MM Gnr 4552 RFA
CLEMENTS Francis W. MM CSM 877 1st Lancashire Fusiliers
CLEMENTS Frank MM Spr 71509 Royal Engineers
CLEMENTS Frank W. MM Pte 594165 18th London Regt
CLEMENTS Frederick "MM,MM(F)" Sjt L/8212 2nd Royal Sussex Regt
CLEMENTS Frederick MM Sjt 147627 Royal Engineers
CLEMENTS Frederick W. MM Pte 242335 York & Lancaster Regt
CLEMENTS George MM Sjt 12380 7th Wiltshire Regt
CLEMENTS George MM+Bar Sjt 4277 1/1st Hertfordshire Regt
CLEMENTS George MM Sjt 30605 RGA
CLEMENTS George E. MM Sjt 325875 1/1st Cambridgeshire Regt
CLEMENTS Harry MM Pte 12026 Leicestershire Regt
CLEMENTS James MM Pte 315092 9th Scottish Rifles
CLEMENTS James Henry MM Pte M2/074079 Att 97 Fd Amb RAMC Army Service Corps
CLEMENTS John MM Sjt G/262 10th Royal West Surrey Regt KIA 22.9.17.
CLEMENTS John MM L/Cpl R/13519 King's Royal Rifle Corps
CLEMENTS John MM+Bar Spr 312469 Royal Engineers
CLEMENTS John William MM Dvr 14417 115 Heavy Bty RGA RGA
CLEMENTS L.D.J. "DCM,MM" Sjt 776389 D/310 Bde RFA
CLEMENTS R.W. MM L/Cpl 2087 1/5th Border Regt
CLEMENTS Richard MM Pte 10083 5th Northamptonshire Regt
CLEMENTS Stuart O. "DCM,MM" Sjt 4395 95 Fd Coy Royal Engineers
CLEMENTS Thomas MM Cpl 17151 9th Royal Irish Fusiliers KIA 22.11.17.
CLEMENTS W. MM L/Sjt 41605 8th Royal Berkshire Regt
CLEMENTS W.G. MM L/Cpl 200286 1/4th Oxf & Bucks Light Infantry
CLEMENTS W.V. MM L/Cpl 6014 2nd Dragoon Guards
CLEMENTS Wilfred A. MM Sjt 15111 RFA
CLEMENTS William MM Pte 69254 6th Royal West Surrey Regt
CLEMENTS William Charles Thomas MM Bdr 27328 B/46 Bde RFA
CLEMENTS William G. MM Pte 4/6944 4th Bedfordshire Regt
CLEMENTS William H.J. MM Sjt 11880 Royal Engineers
CLEMENTS William Thomas MM Pte 14627 1st Essex Regt DOW 10.10.18.
CLEMENTSON Arthur "DCM,MM" Cpl 19484 1/4th Royal Lancaster Regt
CLEMINSON Frank MM Sjt 18293 Machine Gun Corps
CLEMINSON Joseph W. MM Pte 12529 Yorkshire Regt
CLEMMEY Sidney J. MM Gnr Sig L/35082 D/83 Bde RFA
CLEMMIT Arthur MM Gnr 71557 RFA
CLEMPSON David MM Pte 240151 1/6th South Staffordshire Regt
CLEMSON Albert MM Pte 17151 2nd Oxf & Bucks Light Infantry DOW 25.8.18.
CLENNELL Hugh MM Pte 35898 9th Yorkshire Regt
CLENNELL James W. MM Sjt 24302 Machine Gun Corps
CLENNEN Owen Thomas MM Cpl 30248 8th Somerset Light Infantry KIA 31.7.17.
CLEPHANE Hunter MM Pte 43681 Royal Scots
CLEUGH Thomas MM Pte 386337 1 Fd Amb RAMC
CLEVELEY Alfred MM Sjt 9627 1st South Staffordshire Regt KIA 12.5.17.
CLEVELEY Cecil Claud MM Gnr 144970 244 Siege Bty RGA
CLEVERLEY Charles MM Pte 50228 Royal Irish Fusiliers att 12th Royal Irish Rifles.
CLEVERLEY Frank MM Pte 186 10th Royal Warwickshire Regt KIA 23.8.18.
CLEVERLEY George D. MM Cpl 42421 Royal Engineers
CLEVERLEY Thomas MM L/Cpl R/16661 King's Royal Rifle Corps
CLEVERLY Norman MM Pte 49939 Royal Welsh Fusiliers
CLEVETT Albert Ernest MM L/Cpl 10479 Royal Sussex Regt
CLEWER Herbert James MM Sjt 43030 76 Fd Coy Royal Engineers

CLEWES Charles T.M. MM Cpl 152600 Royal Engineers
CLEWES Robert MM Pte 2648 1/8th Durham Light Infantry
CLEWES Thomas MM Sjt 47676 20th Hussars
CLEWLEY Alfred J. MM Pte 725672 24th London Regt
CLEWLEY James MM Pte 8487 10th Worcestershire Regt KIA 25.3.18.
CLEWLEY William MM Spr 97432 156 Fd Coy Royal Engineers KIA 9.9.16.
CLEWLOW Herbert Edwin MM Pte 63336 2/4th Yorkshire Light Infantry
CLEWLOW Joseph MM L/Cpl 235409 7th Lincolnshire Regt KIA 26.8.18.
CLEWS Chris MM Bdr 60260 A/268 Bde RFA
CLEWS Horace MM Cpl 265609 Royal Warwickshire Regt
CLIFF Albert MM Sjt 5096 1st Lincolnshire Regt
CLIFF Arthur MM Pte 29806 North Staffordshire Regt
CLIFF Arthur E. MM L/Bdr 62671 RHA
CLIFF Howard Stephen MM Sjt 459473 RAMC
CLIFF James MM Pte 1605 6th Connaught Rangers KIA 21.3.18.
CLIFF John W. MM Sjt 81988 5th Notts & Derby Regt
CLIFF Norman Down MM Pte 22360 1st Grenadier Guards
CLIFF Oswald "DCM,MM" Pte 28090 2nd Yorkshire Light Infantry
CLIFF William MM Pte 31164 RAMC
CLIFFE Arthur MM Spr 158616 257 Tunnelling Coy Royal Engineers
CLIFFE Charles MM Pte 242283 1/5th Yorkshire Light Infantry
CLIFFE Leigh MM Dvr T4/109728 19 Auxiliary Horse Coy Army Service Corps
CLIFFE Stanley MM Sjt M2/051926 Army Service Corps
CLIFFE Thomas Edward MM Pte 301115 2nd Manchester Regt KIA 4.11.18.
CLIFFORD Albert E. MM Cpl 291489 RGA
CLIFFORD Alfred MM Sjt 16718 12th Bn Machine Gun Corps
CLIFFORD Alfred George "MC,MM(5588 Sjt 11th Hussars)" 2Lt 8th Lincolnshire Regt
CLIFFORD Arthur Edward "DCM,MM+Bar" Cpl 9815 1st Leicestershire Regt
CLIFFORD Charles MM L/Cpl 13570 10th North Lancashire Regt KIA 28.4.17.
CLIFFORD Charles MM Gnr 955528 A/236 Bde RFA
CLIFFORD David MM Pte S/2322 1st Seaforth Highlanders
CLIFFORD Eustace George MM Sjt 200195 1/5th Bedfordshire Regt
CLIFFORD Francis T. "DCM,MM" Sjt 49440 94 Fd Coy Royal Engineers
CLIFFORD Frederick MM Pte S/978 Royal Fusiliers
CLIFFORD Frederick MM Pte 293611 Middlesex Regt
CLIFFORD Harry L. MM Cpl 142759 Machine Gun Corps
CLIFFORD Henry C. MM Gnr 837069 RFA
CLIFFORD John MM Sjt 20359 9th Northumberland Fusiliers AKA John Shaw.DOW 16.4.18.
CLIFFORD John C. MM Pte 43608 13th Middlesex Regt
CLIFFORD Joseph MM L/Bdr 216768 65 Bde RFA
CLIFFORD Thomas Edwin MM Pte 15943 2nd Coldstream Guards KIA 27.8.18.
CLIFFORD Timothy MM Sjt 89332 B/74 Bde RFA
CLIFFORD William MM Cpl 7108 1st Somerset Light Infantry
CLIFT Arthur E. MM Gnr 42534 D/190 Bde RFA
CLIFT Fred G. MM Gnr 810289 RFA
CLIFT George H. MM L/Cpl 242358 8th Worcestershire Regt
CLIFT Thomas MM Cpl 22555 10th Northumberland Fusiliers
CLIFT W.A. MM Bdr 87340 RFA
CLIFTON Albert MM Pte 15301 10th York & Lancaster Regt
CLIFTON Alec MM Pte 47223 RAMC
CLIFTON Alfred MM Pte 9178 1st Royal West Kent Regt
CLIFTON Arthur MM Pte 9830 1st Dorsetshire Regt
CLIFTON David MM Pte 47274 10th Northumberland Fusiliers
CLIFTON F. MM Pte 17896 Gloucestershire Regt
CLIFTON Gilbert MM Pte 24688 6th Royal West Kent Regt DOW 3.12.17.
CLIFTON Harold MM Cpl 33798 Bedfordshire Regt
CLIFTON James MM Pte 22922 1st Bedfordshire Regt
CLIFTON Robert MM Pte 14444 8th Royal Dublin Fusiliers
CLIFTON William MM Pte 3/7301 1st Dorsetshire Regt
CLIFTON William MM Pte 291054 1/8th Scottish Rifles
CLIFTON William Cottam MM Pte 24587 Dorsetshire Regt
CLIFTON Willie MM L/Cpl 28444 2nd Royal Dublin Fusiliers
CLIMIE James A. MM Pte 203198 1/7th Gordon Highlanders
CLINCH Frederick T. MM Bdr 84325 RFA
CLINCH W. MM L/Cpl 6815 Royal Sussex Regt
CLINES William MM Pte 34370 York & Lancaster Regt
CLINK John MM L/Cpl 290675 Royal Highlanders
CLINTON Christopher H. MM Cpl 1828 RAMC
CLINTON Edmund MM Dvr 117181 E/1 TM Bde RFA
CLINTON George MM L/Cpl 11383 Liverpool Regt
CLINTON Herbert MM Sjt L/14939 32 Div Ammn Col RFA
CLINTON Hugh MM Pte 27426 Royal Inniskilling Fusiliers
CLINTON Patrick MM Pte 4436 Leinster Regt
CLINTON Thomas MM+Bar Cpl S/5665 Gordon Highlanders
CLINTON William J.S. MM Sjt 2806 South Staffordshire Regt
CLIPSON Fred MM L/Cpl 464 10th East Yorkshire Regt
CLIPSON Frederick William MM Pte 72015 133 Fd Amb RAMC
CLIPSTON Frederick C. MM Pte 37466 Royal Berkshire Regt
CLISBY William Philip MM Gnr 86268 200 Siege Bty RGA KIA 2.7.18.
CLISSOLD Frederick MM Gnr 188645 126 Bty 29 Bde RFA
CLISSOLD George E. MM Pte 26204 7th South Wales Borderers
CLIST Wiliam G. MM L/Cpl 254239 Royal Engineers
CLITHEROE Henry MM L/Sjt 14465 6th East Yorkshire Regt
CLITHEROE J.F. MM Pte 40498 Lincolnshire Regt
CLITHEROE P. MM Cpl 8063 Machine Gun Corps
CLIVE Thomas MM Pte 276911 1/7th Arg & Suth Highlanders
CLIXBY Ernest MM Sjt 13393 Leicestershire Regt
CLOAD Harry MM Gnr 66144 125 Heavy Bty RGA Died 21.4.18.
CLODE Thomas B. MM Pte 8872 2nd Welsh Regt
CLOHESY M. MM Pte 4346 Northumberland Fusiliers
CLORLEY William Richard Griffiths MM Pte 10820 Shropshire Light Infantry
CLOSE Ernest MM L/Sjt R/3708 King's Royal Rifle Corps
CLOSE George MM Cpl T/15048 Att 14 Fd Amb RAMC Army Service Corps
CLOSE Gordon MM Pte 241334 1st Royal Lancaster Regt
CLOSE Hugh Henry MM L/Cpl 9486 8th Royal Inniskilling Fusiliers
CLOSE John G.D. MM L/Bdr 57193 120 Heavy Bty RGA
CLOSE John W. MM Sjt 695 1/5th Durham Light Infantry
CLOSE John W. MM Sjt T4/252530 62 Div Train Army Service Corps
CLOSE Joseph MM Pte H/71273 North Irish Horse
CLOSE Stephen MM Cpl 42157 5th Yorkshire Light Infantry
CLOSE Thomas MM L/Cpl 242296 Gordon Highlanders
CLOTHIER William MM Pte 18283 6th Duke of Cornwall's LI
CLOUDE Reginald "MM,MID" Pte M2/022049 Att 2 Fd Amb RAMC Army Service Corps
CLOUGH Arthur MM Pnr 39560 Royal Engineers
CLOUGH Arthur MM L/Sjt 2106 1st Royal Lancaster Regt
CLOUGH Cecil MM L/Cpl PS/7492 17th Royal Fusiliers
CLOUGH Frederick MM Pte 240449 1/6th Notts & Derby Regt
CLOUGH Frederick MM Pte 38102 RAMC
CLOUGH John MM+Bar Pte 386299 RAMC
CLOUGH John MM Pte 10063 12/13th Northumberland Fusiliers
CLOUGH John W. "MM,MSM" Sjt 7962 2nd Yorkshire Regt
CLOUGH Leonard MM L/Cpl 30854 94 Coy Machine Gun Corps
CLOUGH Philip R. MM L/Cpl 511574 14th London Regt
CLOUGH Reginald C. MM L/Cpl 444490 Royal Engineers
CLOUGH Robert MM Pte 31099 24th Manchester Regt
CLOUGH Samuel MM Spr 188755 Royal Engineers
CLOUGH Thomas MM CQMS 201103 5th Lancashire Fusiliers
CLOUGH W. MM+Bar Bdr 51540 41 Bde RFA
CLOUGH William MM Sjt 102748 179 Tunnelling Coy Royal Engineers
CLOUGH William MM L/Bdr 86296 A/59 Bde RFA
CLOUGH William MM Pte 10544 RAMC
CLOUGH William Edward MM Gnr 14304 109 Heavy Bty RGA
CLOUGHERTY Mark MM Pte 352247 Royal Scots
CLOUGHTON Henry MM Pte B/203088 9th Rifle Brigade
CLOUSTON James "DSO,MM(712 Bdr)" T/2Lt B/107 Bde RFA
CLOUSTON William B. MM+Bar Cpl 65716 RAMC
CLOUTING Charles H. MM Cpl 3/10127 9th Suffolk Regt
CLOW Amos William MM Pte 34572 1/1st Cambridgeshire Regt
CLOW Ernest Alfred MM Pte 203262 9th Devonshire Regt DOW 10.10.17.
CLOWE David MM Cpl 250418 5/6th Royal Scots
CLOWES Arthur MM L/Sjt 25266 3rd Grenadier Guards
CLOWES Arthur MM Bdr 112223 41 Div Ammn Col RFA
CLOWES Fred MM Cpl 85801 6th Durham Light Infantry
CLOWES Herbert A. MM L/Bdr 183700 129 Heavy Bty RGA
CLOWES Samuel MM Pte 46805 2nd South Staffordshire Regt
CLOWES William Dexter MM Pte 20045 9th Notts & Derby Regt KIA 4.11.18.
CLUBB John Alexander "MM,MIDx2,CG(F)" Sjt S4/237336 Army Service Corps att 2/2nd(West Riding)Fd Amb RAMC

CLUBB Robert MM Pte 20470 10th South Wales Borderers
CLUCAS Albert H. MM Pte 8975 2nd East Yorkshire Regt
CLUCAS Ralph MM+Bar L/Cpl 8953 2nd Scots Guards
CLUER Charles Percy MM Cpl 357735 Liverpool Regt
CLUER Jesse Moore MM Gnr 14865 D/70 Bde RFA KIA 13.4.17.
CLUES Geoffrey MM Pte 331561 Liverpool Regt
CLUETT Charles R. MM Cpl 25805 6 Div Sig Coy Royal Engineers
CLUGSTON William MM Pte M2/187217 719 Coy Army Service Corps
CLULEY George William "MM,CG(It)" CSM 7884 2nd Border Regt
CLUNAS James F. MM 2nd Cpl 207422 Royal Engineers
CLUNESS Alexander MM L/Cpl S/43374 Gordon Highlanders
CLUNESS Andrew T. MM L/Cpl 20376 Machine Gun Corps
CLUNEY John William "MM,CG(B)" Sjt 70231 Notts & Derby Regt
CLUNIE Alexander MM L/Cpl 27605 1/8th West Yorkshire Regt KIA 15.9.18.
CLUNIE Andrew MM Sjt 18567 9th Bn Machine Gun Corps KIA 21.3.18.
CLURG William MM Sjt 8253 2nd Scots Guards
CLUSKY John T. MM Pte 252438 Manchester Regt
CLUTTERBUCK Ernest MM Pte 235292 Gloucestershire Regt
CLUTTERBUCK Harold S.F. MM Pte 19766 26th Royal Fusiliers
CLUTTON Thomas Henry MM Sjt 375154 1/10th Manchester Regt KIA 31.8.18.
CLUTTON William MM Spr 92563 Royal Engineers
CLYDE John W. MM Pte S/10626 5th Cameron Highlanders
CLYNE James MM L/Cpl 240690 1/5th Gordon Highlanders KIA 17.5.17.
COAD Alfred MM Pte 38112 RAMC
COAD Reginald Henry MM Sjt 6398 6 Fd Amb RAMC
COADY Joseph MM L/Cpl 10701 2nd Royal Irish Regt KIA 21.3.18.
COADY Joseph H. MM Pte 40049 Royal Irish Rifles
COAKER William H. MM Pte 574028 17th London Regt
COAKES Robert C. "DCM,MM" Pte 250752 3rd London Regt
COAN James MM Spr 139290 Royal Engineers
COAN Thomas MM Sjt 354034 RAMC
COARD Isaac MM L/Cpl 8395 Irish Guards
COATES Alexander MM Pte 3/8233 2nd Northumberland Fusiliers
COATES Alfred MM Gnr 193689 C/51 Bde RFA
COATES Charles MM Gnr 85219 127 Bty 29 Bde RFA
COATES Charles "MM,MSM,CdeG(F)" Sjt L/5391 8th Royal Sussex Regt
COATES Charles T. MM Cpl 2144 1/4th London Regt
COATES Douglas A. MM Pte 1374 1/6th Royal Warwickshire Regt
COATES Edgar MM Gnr 771916 B/250 Bde RFA
COATES Edward MM Pte 201581 Seaforth Highlanders
COATES Ernest MM L/Cpl 31072 2nd South Lancashire Regt
COATES Ernest MM Pte R/1348 King's Royal Rifle Corps
COATES Fred MM Sjt 35266 Machine Gun Corps
COATES George MM L/Cpl 50163 15th Cheshire Regt
COATES George E. MM Pte 235290 13th Liverpool Regt
COATES George William MM L/Cpl 283836 4th London Regt
COATES Harry MM 2nd Cpl 192159 1 Div Sig Coy Royal Engineers
COATES Harry "DCM,MM" CSM 17551 9th Yorkshire Light Infantry
COATES Harry Gordon MM Pte 70955 165 Coy Machine Gun Corps
COATES Herbert "MM,MSM" Sjt 15918 10th Northumberland Fusiliers
COATES Herbert Wright MM L/Cpl 107658 9 Foreway Coy Royal Engineers
COATES Horace Albert MM Gnr Sig 61516 61 Siege Bty RGA
COATES James C. MM Sjt 42484 Royal Engineers
COATES James Henry Robert Horobin MM Cpl 3565 9th North Lancashire Regt
COATES John MM Cpl 7625 1st Leicestershire Regt
COATES John B. MM Sjt 241788 Liverpool Regt
COATES Joseph T. MM Pte 28282 1st Hampshire Regt
COATES Leonard MM Pte 16174 York & Lancaster Regt
COATES R.W. MM Pte 401494 RAMC
COATES Robert MM Pte 12419 Royal Sussex Regt
COATES Robert G. MM+Bar Sjt 46082 Royal Engineers
COATES Stephen G. MM L/Cpl 280840 4th London Regt
COATES Thomas MM L/Cpl 23501 Machine Gun Corps
COATES Thomas MM Pte 51367 1/4th Cheshire Regt
COATES Thomas M. MM L/Cpl 5173 Yorkshire Regt
COATES Walter MM Pte 20706 2nd Royal Warwickshire Regt
COATES William MM Pte 18/1706 Durham Light Infantry
COATES William MM Pte 47132 2nd Manchester Regt
COATES William MM L/Cpl 21040 Liverpool Regt
COATES William H. MM+Bar L/Cpl 13223 2nd Coldstream Guards
COATS Archibald MM Spr 43864 Royal Engineers

COATS Neil "DCM,MM" L/Sjt 10671 7th Seaforth Highlanders
COATSWORTH Albert MM L/Cpl 13307 8th East Yorkshire Regt
COATSWORTH Ernest William MM Pte 388420 2/2nd(Northumbrian)Fd Amb RAMC
COBB Albert E. MM CSM 8955 1st Dorsetshire Regt
COBB C. MM Cpl 7705 1st Rifle Brigade
COBB Frederick W. MM Pte 26797 1st Dorsetshire Regt
COBB John MM L/Cpl 325709 1/9th Durham Light Infantry
COBB John Joseph MM L/Cpl DM2/208887 Att 218 Siege Bty RGA Army Service Corps
COBB S. MM Pte 3/1540 1st Essex Regt
COBB W.F.S. MM Pte 57975 3rd Royal Fusiliers
COBB William G. MM Pte 25747 1st Dorsetshire Regt
COBBAN George MM+Bar Gnr 22912 B/82 Bde RFA
COBBETT Arthur E. MM Pte 3796 2nd Rifle Brigade
COBBETT Reginald MM Sjt 11066 Royal West Surrey Regt
COBBIN Peter MM Pte 9296 11th Suffolk Regt
COBBOLD Edward V. MM Pte 4972 8th East Surrey Regt
COBBOLD Ernest "DCM,MM" Cpl 242075 2/5th Gloucestershire Regt
COBBOLD Ernest Albert "MC,MM(13792 L/Cpl 11th Essex)" 2Lt 1/4th Royal Berkshire Regt
COBBOLD Herbert Alfred Harold MM Pte 29266 10th North Lancashire Regt
COBBY Edward MM Spr 94642 Royal Engineers
COBLEY George H. MM Sjt 678 Cheshire Regt
COBLEY Walter F. MM Spr 25471 2 Div Sig Coy Royal Engineers
COBLEY William MM Sjt 83918 RFA
COBNER Thomas MM Sjt 39008 Labour Corps
COBURN Alfred MM Pte M2/047468 Att 1 Div Sig Coy RE Army Service Corps
COCHRANE Alfred MM Sjt 93280 20th Durham Light Infantry
COCHRANE Archibald MM Cpl 38821 5/6th Royal Scots
COCHRANE Archibald F.F. MM L/Cpl 8915 Gordon Highlanders
COCHRANE George MM Pte 4033 X Corps Cyclist Bn Army Cyclist Corps
COCHRANE George MM L/Cpl 6364 East Kent Regt KIA 19.9.17.
COCHRANE Harry MM Pte 33847 South Wales Borderers
COCHRANE Henry Kirkwood MM L/Cpl 110677 Machine Gun Corps
COCHRANE James MM L/Cpl 3/2515 7th Royal Highlanders
COCHRANE James MM+Bar L/Sjt 1079 23rd Royal Fusiliers
COCHRANE John MM+Bar CSM 14712 8th Royal Lancaster Regt
COCHRANE John Jr. MM Cpl 25069 2/5th West Riding Regt
COCHRANE Joseph Swinton MM Cpl 10025 10th Arg & Suth Highlanders DOW 14.10.16.
COCHRANE Samuel MM L/Bdr 35852 RGA
COCHRANE Thomas MM Pte 220044 RAMC
COCHRANE Tom MM SM Mechanic M/23028 15 Div Train Army Service Corps
COCHRANE Walter MM Cpl 8044 9th Gordon Highlanders
COCHRANE William MM Sjt 10504 1st Royal Scots
COCHRANE William MM Pte 6528 2nd Gordon Highlanders
COCK Allen B. MM Sjt 510463 1/14th London Regt
COCK Charles MM L/Cpl 82186 194 Coy Machine Gun Corps
COCK John G. MM L/Sjt F/1418 16th Middlesex Regt
COCK Thomas MM Pte 29/488 Northumberland Fusiliers
COCKADAY Frederick W. MM L/Sjt 12990 9th Norfolk Regt
COCKAYNE Benjamin MM Gnr 781213 RFA
COCKAYNE Herbert MM Pte 241003 Lincolnshire Regt
COCKAYNE Thomas MM Sjt 11267 16th Lancashire Fusiliers
COCKAYNE William H. MM Cpl 331163 Liverpool Regt
COCKBILL Andrew MM Pte 39470 South Wales Borderers
COCKBILL Thomas W. MM 2nd Cpl 45436 Royal Engineers
COCKBURN Adam MM L/Cpl 20531 2nd Royal Scots KIA 14.7.16.
COCKBURN Alexander MM Sjt 38379 Northumberland Fusiliers
COCKBURN John MM Pte 73998 RAMC
COCKBURN Leonard D. MM Cpl 142880 Royal Engineers
COCKBURN Robert MM Dvr 144917 RFA
COCKBURNE W.S. MM Gnr 273 RGA
COCKCROFT Frank MM Cpl 15282 Manchester Regt
COCKCROFT Harold J. MM Gnr 1106 RFA
COCKCROFT William MM Pte 11080 2nd Arg & Suth Highlanders
COCKELL Edmund James Harry MM Bdr 32686 B/186 Bde RFA
COCKELL Edward John MM L/Cpl 241388 2nd Middlesex Regt KIA 1.4.18.
COCKER Arthur MM Pte 58067 24th Royal Welsh Fusiliers
COCKER Clement MM Pte 200469 1/4th Northumberland Fusiliers
COCKER John R. MM Cpl R/23931 King's Royal Rifle Corps
COCKER Joseph MM Dvr 800371 RFA

COCKER Leonard MM Pte 14849 33rd Bn Machine Gun Corps DOW 6.10.18.
COCKER Stanley MM Pte 240815 1/5th Seaforth Highlanders
COCKER William MM Gnr 161991 124 Heavy Bty RGA
COCKERHAM Charles MM Cpl R/13690 1st King's Royal Rifle Corps
COCKERHAM R. MM Pte 403642 2 Fd Amb RAMC
COCKERILL Basil MM+Bar Pte 266273 2/4th West Riding Regt
COCKERILL Francis H. MM Pte 40085 York & Lancaster Regt
COCKERILL John T. MM Sjt PW/5170 Middlesex Regt
COCKERILL Marshall Ingram MM 2nd Cpl 151598 170 Tunnelling Coy Royal Engineers
COCKERILL Thomas William MM Pte 58383 2/4th York & Lancaster Regt
COCKERILL William MM Pte 240491 1/5th Yorkshire Regt KIA 19.7.17.
COCKERTON Arthur MM Cpl 85983 155 Siege Bty RGA
COCKERTON Frank MM Pte 17201 Suffolk Regt
COCKETT Horace Edward MM+Bar Pte 1017 11th Royal Sussex Regt KIA 3.4.18.
COCKFIELD Matthew MM Cpl 14164 10th Scottish Rifles
COCKHILL Ernest MM L/Cpl 6/1106 13th King's Royal Rifle Corps DOW 5.8.18.
COCKILL Frank Rowland MM Spr 131213 233 Fd Coy Royal Engineers
COCKIN Edwin Gee MM Spr 526172 203 Fd Coy Royal Engineers
COCKING Albert J. MM Cpl 950916 A/18 Bde RFA
COCKING Frank MM Sjt 21915 RGA
COCKING James H. MM Pte 53240 9th Yorkshire Light Infantry
COCKING John R. MM Cpl 721126 24th London Regt
COCKING Percy MM L/Cpl 18045 6th King's Own Scottish Borderers
COCKLE Albert G.C. MM Pte 12752 6th Shropshire Light Infantry
COCKLE Thomas G. MM Spr 500389 Royal Engineers
COCKLEY John MM Pte 57519 2nd King's Royal Rifle Corps
COCKMAN Henry J. MM Sjt 2824 12th Lancers
COCKMAN Richard MM L/Cpl 265264 1/1st Hertfordshire Regt KIA 26.4.18.
COCKMAN William MM L/Cpl P/5820 1 Traffic Control Coy Military Foot Police
COCKRAM Charles MM Cpl 16012 9th Devonshire Regt
COCKRAM George MM Pte 7235 Coldstream Guards
COCKRAM Robert Saunders MM BQMS 96 RFA
COCKRAM Sidney MM L/Sjt 8241 2nd Northamptonshire Regt
COCKRAM William Wilfred "MM,MSM" Sjt 7374 2nd Devonshire Regt
COCKRAN William MM Pte Shoeing Smith 21002 15th Hussars
COCKREAN John MM 2nd Cpl 17017 9 Fd Coy Royal Engineers
COCKRELL Herbert E. MM Bdr 50464 7 Bde H Bty RHA
COCKROFT Sam MM Cpl 29674 2nd West Riding Regt KIA 30.8.18.
COCKS Edward MM Pte 11664 Royal Berkshire Regt
COCKS George A. MM Sjt 6451 RAMC
COCKS Henry "DCM,MM" Sjt 3775 52 Coy Machine Gun Corps
COCKSEDGE Frank Allen "MC,MM(8711 Sjt)" 2Lt 1st Norfolk Regt
COCKSEDGE Harry Edward MM Gnr 50621 D/121 Bde RFA DOW 15.9.18.
COCKSEY Joseph MM Pte 29886 2nd Manchester Regt KIA 2.10.18.
COCKSHOOT George MM L/Cpl 27222 2nd South Lancashire Regt KIA 25.9.18.
COCKSHOTT Harry S. MM Gnr 123243 RGA
COCKTON William MM Pte 240697 Border Regt
CODLING Gordon MM Sjt 355675 10th Liverpool Regt
CODLING Henry Walter MM Sjt 26279 173 Bde RFA
CODLING Mark MM Pte 14917 7th Dragoon Guards
CODLING Mark MM Gnr 21419 RFA
CODY G.J.V. MM Sjt 9937 Royal Highlanders
COE Albert MM L/Bdr 45905 RGA
COE Archibald Edward MM 2nd Cpl 12340 Survey Section Royal Engineers
COE Arthur Sydney MM CSM 7595 XVII Corps Cyclist Bn Army Cyclist Corps
COE Arthur William Evans MM S/Sjt Armt 605 Army Ordnance Corps
COE Charles Joseph MM Cpl 70854 16 Coy Machine Gun Corps
COE Edward MM Sjt 13933 11 Siege Bty RGA
COE Frank W. MM Sjt G/14671 2nd Royal Sussex Regt
COE Harold MM Cpl 242075 South Staffordshire Regt
COE Harry Everard MM Pte 200960 4th Lincolnshire Regt
COE James MM L/Sjt 46543 Northumberland Fusiliers
COE James Cecil MM Gnr 26302 90 Heavy Bty RGA
COE Reginald H. MM Pte 2693 1/24th London Regt
COE Sidney A. MM Pte 326624 Cambridgeshire Regt
COE Sidney M. MM Spr 85093 Royal Engineers
COE William G. MM Pte 14036 Northamptonshire Regt
COEN Timothy MM Pte 27995 6th Royal Dublin Fusiliers
COFFEY Frederick C. MM Sjt 10224 Royal Berkshire Regt
COFFEY Herbert MM Sjt 675336 RFA
COFFEY John MM Pte 17642 8th Yorkshire Light Infantry
COFFEY Philip F. MM Pte 689 11 Fd Amb RAMC
COFFEY Wilfred MM Sjt 276245 1/7th Manchester Regt
COFIELD Thomas H. MM Pte 44992 8th Royal Berkshire Regt
COGAN Aloysius MM L/Cpl 113063 Royal Engineers
COGAN John Thomas MM Pte 17010 12th Yorkshire Light Infantry KIA 30.9.18.
COGAN Leonard G. MM Pte 20444 East Surrey Regt
COGDELL Arthur MM Pte 2363 7th Royal West Kent Regt KIA 1.7.16.
COGGAN Fred MM Sjt 96437 RFA
COGGAN Frederick W. MM L/Cpl 108565 Royal Engineers
COGGER Frank C. MM Pte 111640 4th Bn Tank Corps
COGGER Oliver "DCM,MM" Sjt 720978 1/24th London Regt
COGGIN Joe MM Pte 267787 West Yorkshire Regt
COGGIN John Millington MM Pte 201172 1/4th York & Lancaster Regt
COGGINS Charles MM L/Cpl 10629 6th Somerset Light Infantry
COGGINS Henry A. MM Pte 14344 6th Wiltshire Regt
COGGON George MM Pte 52151 8th Rifle Brigade
COGGON Horace MM Pte 19161 West Yorkshire Regt
COGGRAVE Arthur MM Bdr 139166 'M' AA Bty RGA
COGGRAVE Arthur E. MM Pte M2/120553 Army Service Corps
COGGS George J. MM Pte 202126 7th Worcestershire Regt
COGHILL David MM L/Cpl 4379 Seaforth Highlanders
COGHILL Donald MM L/Cpl 40669 Seaforth Highlanders
COGHILL William MM Pte 3973 Yorkshire Regt
COGHLAN Michael MM Cpl 12925 East Surrey Regt
COGILL Jack MM Pte 104184 54 Fd Amb RAMC
COGLEY John "DCM,MM" Cpl 4616 2nd Royal Irish Regt
COGMAN Joseph Benjamin MM L/Cpl 14812 9th Norfolk Regt
COGSWELL Harry Frederick MM Spr 98107 1 Field Squadron Royal Engineers
COHEN Aaron MM Pte 283082 4th London Regt
COHEN David MM Pte 265697 1/6th Welsh Regt KIA 27.5.17.
COHEN Emanuel MM Pte 323563 6th London Regt
COHEN Jack MM Pte 233048 1/2nd London Regt KIA 27.8.18.
COHEN Morris MM Pte 267670 Oxf & Bucks Light Infantry
COHEN Moss MM Sjt 9666 2nd Durham Light Infantry KIA 24.9.18.
COHEN Philip MM Sjt 120669 'Q' Special Coy Royal Engineers
COHEN Philip MM Gnr 348234 RGA
COHEN Reuben MM L/Cpl R/32264 King's Royal Rifle Corps
COHEN S. MM AM2 44750 Royal Flying Corps att RGA.
COHEN Samuel MM Dvr 37722 RFA
COKE Andrew MM Gnr 109324 7 Div Ammn Col RFA
COKE Stanley V. MM Cpl 205348 4th York & Lancaster Regt
COLBECK Henry MM Gnr 58823 69 Siege Bty RGA
COLBECK Robert MM Sjt 101064 Royal Engineers
COLBERT Charles Thomas MM Pte 17113 1/1st Hertfordshire Regt DOW 9.12.18.
COLBINSON William MM Sjt 17393 110 Hy Bty RGA
COLBORNE William R. MM Sjt 12926 1st Dorsetshire Regt
COLBOURNE Ernest C. MM L/Cpl 25489 Wiltshire Regt
COLBRAN George T. MM Pte G/18790 7th Royal West Kent Regt
COLBRAN Lionel H. "DCM,MM" CQMS M2/079630 'C' Siege Park Army Service Corps
COLBURN Arthur N. MM Pte 3933 Royal Warwickshire Regt
COLBURN Henry A. MM Sjt 235223 1/1st Gloucestershire Yeomanry
COLCLOUGH Cecil H. MM Sjt 610143 1/19th London Regt
COLCLOUGH Edwin MM Sjt 49680 6th West Riding Regt
COLCLOUGH Edwin MM Bdr 805481 C/231 Bde RFA
COLCLOUGH Frederick MM Gnr 805100 2 Bde RFA
COLCLOUGH George W.G. MM Sjt B203266 Rifle Brigade
COLCLOUGH T. "DCM,MM,MID" Sjt 101154 Royal Engineers
COLDHAM Jack MM Cpl 103415 81 Fd Coy Royal Engineers KIA 9.6.18.
COLDICOTT Cecil MM+Bar Cpl 294899 RGA
COLDICOTT William H. MM L/Cpl 201361 15th Royal Warwickshire Regt
COLDMAN Edwin MM+Bar Sjt 31371 3 Fd Sqn Royal Engineers

COLDRIDGE George Henry MM Cpl 77513 RFA
COLDWELL Bertram MM Sjt 200203 4th York & Lancaster Regt
COLDWELL Edgar MM Pte 34412 York & Lancaster Regt
COLDWELL Frank MM Pte 47167 13th Rifle Brigade
COLDWELL Herbert MM Gnr 175901 126 Siege Bty RGA
COLDWELL Herbert MM L/Sjt 12/2360 8th Yorkshire Light Infantry
COLE A. MM Cpl 200985 5th West Yorkshire Regt
COLE A.E. MM Pte G/93832 2nd London Regt
COLE Albert MM RQMS 7314 1st Scottish Rifles
COLE Albert E. MM Pte 82256 23rd Royal Fusiliers
COLE Albert G. MM L/Cpl 492139 46 Div Sig Coy Royal Engineers
COLE Albert W. MM Sjt WR/254534 120 Rly Const Coy Royal Engineers
COLE Alfred H. MM Spr 17642 Royal Engineers
COLE Alfred J. MM Pte 25687 2nd Grenadier Guards
COLE Alfred Joseph MM Pte 8006 10th Royal Warwickshire Regt KIA 30.7.16.
COLE Archibald J. MM Pte 7895 1st Dorsetshire Regt
COLE Arthur MM L/Cpl 17701 6th Wiltshire Regt
COLE Arthur MM Cpl 22046 South Staffordshire Regt
COLE Arthur MM L/Cpl 34940 Royal Engineers
COLE Benjamin MM+Bar L/Cpl 202769 2nd Royal Scots Fusiliers
COLE Benjamin W. MM Pte 995 2nd Leinster Regt
COLE Bertram Arnold MM Dvr 33782 105 Bty 22 Bde RFA
COLE Charles MM Cpl K/934 Royal Fusiliers
COLE Charles MM Pte 329147 1/1st Cambridgeshire Regt
COLE Charles E. MM Drummer 720143 1/24th London Regt
COLE Charles R. MM Pte 510858 Labour Corps
COLE Edward J. MM Cpl 8978 4th Royal Fusiliers
COLE Ernest F. MM Sjt 14/41674 Royal Irish Rifles
COLE F.A. MM Pte 392743 13th London Regt
COLE Frank MM Pte 14793 1st Hampshire Regt
COLE Frederick MM Pte 19032 Hampshire Regt
COLE Frederick MM Pte 19561 11th Notts & Derby Regt
COLE Frederick MM Pte 16110 East Surrey Regt
COLE Frederick E. MM CSM 15797 6th Dorsetshire Regt
COLE Frederick George MM+Bar L/Sjt 4166 18th Bn Machine Gun Corps
COLE Frederick H. MM+Bar Sjt 79629 B/122 Bde RFA
COLE George MM Pte 203253 2nd Wiltshire Regt
COLE George MM Cpl 1703 1/2(South Midland)Fd Amb RAMC
COLE George Edward MM Cpl 17671 8th Gloucestershire Regt Died 10.4.18.
COLE George W. MM Cpl 12548 III Corps Sig Coy Royal Engineers
COLE Gilbert MM L/Cpl 7430 1st Gloucestershire Regt
COLE Harold MM Pte 28233 2nd Grenadier Guards
COLE Harold MM+Bar Sjt 5198 8th Royal West Surrey Regt KIA 11.10.18.
COLE Harry MM+Bar Bdr 36612 38 Div Ammn Col RFA
COLE Harry E. MM Cpl 29819 1st Wiltshire Regt
COLE Harry L. MM Sjt 10975 1st South Wales Borderers
COLE Henry E. MM Pte 4063 RAMC
COLE Henry William MM Pte 24652 2nd Grenadier Guards
COLE James Christopher MM Pte 13572 2nd Coldstream Guards
COLE James Edwin MM L/Cpl 76464 GHQ BEF Cable Section Royal Engineers
COLE John MM Pte G/38703 7th Royal West Kent Regt
COLE John MM Cpl 169 24th Royal Fusiliers
COLE John MM Pte 63532 10th Royal Fusiliers
COLE John MM Sjt 30954 RGA
COLE John MM Pte 228680 1st London Regt
COLE John R. MM Pte 82345 46th Bn Machine Gun Corps
COLE Michael Alexander MM Sjt 6169 2nd Irish Guards
COLE Norbert MM Pte 242301 2/5th East Lancashire Regt
COLE Norman C. MM Pte 267416 West Riding Regt
COLE Ralph MM Pte 235235 5th East Lancashire Regt
COLE Reginald H. MM Cpl 5058 9th Lancers
COLE Richard MM Pte L/11260 Royal West Surrey Regt
COLE Richard James MM Pte 49606 32nd Royal Fusiliers
COLE Robert MM Pte 267438 1/6th Gloucestershire Regt
COLE Robert A.V. MM Pte 39828 1/5th Gloucestershire Regt
COLE Sam MM Pte 10580 York & Lancaster Regt
COLE Sidney George MM Pte 21436 10th Royal West Surrey Regt KIA 26.3.18.
COLE Simeon MM Pte 172 York & Lancaster Regt
COLE Thomas H. MM Pte 203344 2nd Durham Light Infantry
COLE W.H. MM Gnr 3827 RFA
COLE Walter S. MM Pte 18105 Royal West Kent Regt
COLE William MM Pte 267278 18th Gloucestershire Regt
COLE William MM Pte 10152 1st Scots Guards
COLE William Charles MM L/Cpl 28263 1st Shropshire Light Infantry
COLE William E. MM L/Cpl 5849 Royal West Surrey Regt
COLE William G. MM Spr 165973 AK Cable Section Royal Engineers
COLE William R. MM L/Cpl 55385 Machine Gun Corps
COLEBOURN Arthur MM Sjt T4/043376 Army Service Corps
COLEBY William Summerson MM Pte 12555 9th Yorkshire Regt
COLECLIFFE James MM Sjt 350023 RAMC
COLEMAN A. MM Pte 1987 1/22nd London Regt
COLEMAN Albert MM Pte 653286 21st London Regt
COLEMAN Albert MM+Bar Sjt 7091 16th Manchester Regt
COLEMAN Albert E. MM Gnr 3283 RFA
COLEMAN Albert Victor MM Pte 67664 3rd London Regt Died 7.10.18.
COLEMAN Alfred H. MM+Bar Sjt 61042 9th Royal Fusiliers
COLEMAN Arthur "DCM+Bar,MM" Sjt G/1201 7th Royal West Kent Regt
COLEMAN Arthur Charles "DCM,MM,MSM" Pte 1898 7th East Kent Regt
COLEMAN Charles MM Pte 27116 Royal Fusiliers
COLEMAN Charles W. MM Cpl M1/6559 Army Service Corps
COLEMAN Cyril MM Cpl S/6280 Rifle Brigade
COLEMAN Edward MM Pte 27923 2nd Manchester Regt
COLEMAN Ernest Frederick MM Cpl 10548 1st Notts & Derby Regt
COLEMAN F. MM Pte 375356 London Regt
COLEMAN Frank MM Sjt C/12050 King's Royal Rifle Corps
COLEMAN Fred MM Gnr 1350 RFA
COLEMAN Frederick MM L/Cpl 491358 13th London Regt
COLEMAN George MM Cpl B/2890 9th Rifle Brigade
COLEMAN George F. MM Cpl 233640 4th London Regt
COLEMAN George J. MM Cpl 690019 4 Bde RFA
COLEMAN Gerald Cecil MM Cpl 322716 2/6th London Regt att KRRC.KIA 18.9.18.
COLEMAN Harry "DCM,MM" Sjt 241643 Gloucestershire Regt
COLEMAN Jack S. MM+Bar 2nd Cpl 49674 Royal Engineers
COLEMAN James "DCM,MM" L/Cpl 24375 Guards Div Sig Coy Royal Engineers
COLEMAN John MM Pte 67104 2nd London Regt
COLEMAN John MM Pte 9/33532 Cheshire Regt
COLEMAN John MM L/Cpl 1118 King Edward's Horse
COLEMAN John E. MM Sjt 340734 RGA
COLEMAN Leonard MM Pte 31901 1st Devonshire Regt
COLEMAN Montague "DCM,MM" Sjt 26394 91 Fd Coy Royal Engineers
COLEMAN Norman H. MM Sjt 29431 19th Bn Machine Gun Corps
COLEMAN P. MM Sjt 1639 RFA
COLEMAN P.E. MM Cpl 14238 11th Essex Regt
COLEMAN P.E. MM Cpl 1155 Royal Flying Corps
COLEMAN Patrick MM Pte 25786 1st Shropshire Light Infantry
COLEMAN Percy MM Cpl 200643 1/4th Seaforth Highlanders
COLEMAN Percy W. MM Pte 26472 Hampshire Regt
COLEMAN Peter MM L/Cpl 8082 2nd Royal Irish Rifles
COLEMAN Raymond Noel MM Pte 203141 2nd Royal Berkshire Regt KIA 16.8.17.
COLEMAN Robert MM Pte 278771 Arg & Suth Highlanders
COLEMAN Thomas MM L/Cpl 31906 York & Lancaster Regt
COLEMAN Thomas "DCM,MM" CSM 275428 1/7th Durham Light Infantry KIA 11.4.18.
COLEMAN Thomas MM L/Cpl 1/13093 1st South Wales Borderers DOW 4.12.16.
COLEMAN Thomas MM Sjt 7730 95 Coy Machine Gun Corps KIA 6.11.17.
COLEMAN Thomas MM Sjt 19922 10th Royal West Kent Regt
COLEMAN Thomas MM Gnr L/39009 RFA DOW 23.3.18.
COLEMAN Thomas G. MM Bdr 107507 RGA
COLEMAN Thomas H.C. MM+Bar Sjt 240596 1/8th Worcestershire Regt
COLEMAN Thomas R. MM Gnr 70643 RGA
COLEMAN Timothy J.G. MM Pte F/904 13th Middlesex Regt
COLEMAN Walter S. MM Pte 633012 20th London Regt
COLEMAN William MM Pte 35428 1st Yorkshire Light Infantry
COLEMAN William "DCM,MM,MSM" CSM 13055 9th Yorkshire Regt
COLEMAN William MM Cpl 4947 62 Coy Machine Gun Corps KIA 13.7.16.
COLEMAN William MM Gnr 26884 C/83 Bde RFA
COLEMAN William C. MM Sjt 6297 1st Wiltshire Regt
COLEMAN William E. MM Pte 48098 130 Fd Amb RAMC
COLEMAN William E. MM Cpl 34887 Leicestershire Regt
COLEMAN William G. MM Sjt 1312 1/4th Suffolk Regt

COLEMAN William J. MM Cpl 700411 1/23rd London Regt
COLEMAN William T. MM Pte 572862 17th London Regt
COLENUTT Thomas H. MM Dvr 851250 C/110 Bde RFA
COLENUTT William G. MM Sjt 50256 54th Bn Machine Gun Corps
COLER Ernest H. MM L/Cpl 702336 21st London Regt
COLER Henry MM Pte 1457 1/1st Cambridgeshire Regt
COLER Thomas MM Sjt 7890 282 Army Troops Coy Royal Engineers DOW 30.6.18.
COLERIDGE John William MM L/Cpl 11798 2nd Yorkshire Light Infantry KIA 6.2.18.
COLERIDGE Reginald MM Sjt 457013 24 Fd Amb RAMC
COLES Albert MM Pte 23436 16th Welsh Regt
COLES Alec MM Pte 31952 1st Bedfordshire Regt
COLES Alexander MM Pte 380196 15th Hampshire Regt
COLES Alfred Thomas "MM,MID" Sjt 1497 Gloucestershire Regt
COLES Arthur H. MM Pte 1722 27 Fd Amb RAMC
COLES Caleb William MM+Bar L/Cpl 19367 Royal Engineers
COLES Carl F. MM+Bar Sjt 48438 9 Div Sig Coy Royal Engineers
COLES Charles MM Pte 225488 1/1st Monmouthshire Regt
COLES Charles F. MM Sjt 56091 25 Bde RFA
COLES Charlie MM Cpl 71124 B/161 Bde RFA DOW 14.7.18.
COLES Edgar MM Pte 5799 6th Royal West Kent Regt
COLES Edward E. MM Pte 10192 2nd Royal Berkshire Regt
COLES Ernest MM Pte 9273 2nd Devonshire Regt
COLES Frank MM Cpl H/285171 1/1st Oxfordshire Yeomanry
COLES Frederick MM Sjt 2626 8 Railway Coy Royal Engineers
COLES Frederick MM Sjt 7197 1st West Yorkshire Regt
COLES George MM Cpl 13765 54 Fd Coy Royal Engineers
COLES George MM Pte 18963 13th Welsh Regt
COLES George "DCM,MM" Pte 3839 7th Dragoon Guards
COLES George MM Pte 2454 1st Gloucestershire Regt
COLES H. MM Pte 21552 Royal Warwickshire Regt
COLES H.V. MM Pte 28681 1st Hampshire Regt
COLES Harry MM Pte 1475 16th Royal Warwickshire Regt
COLES Herbert E. MM Cpl 1821 B/119 Bde RFA
COLES Herbert E. "DCM,MM" Sjt 16651 1st Grenadier Guards
COLES J. MM Pte 43305 West Yorkshire Regt
COLES James MM Pte 40788 5th Leicestershire Regt
COLES Joseph H. MM Cpl Fitter 31798 37 Bde RFA
COLES Josiah MM Cpl 947 1/5th Border Regt KIA 23.4.17.
COLES Leonard MM Pte 74099 138 Fd Amb RAMC
COLES Percy Henry MM Pte 2348 1/7th London Regt KIA 17.4.18.
COLES Samuel MM Pte 14746 1st Dorsetshire Regt KIA 11.1.17.
COLES Samuel H. MM Pte 40827 Worcestershire Regt
COLES Sidney Fisher MM L/Cpl 8853 2nd Lincolnshire Regt
COLES Thomas MM Cpl 42040 Lancashire Fusiliers
COLES Walter MM Pte 718094 23rd London Regt
COLES Walter Harold MM Bdr 70035 55 Bty 33 Bde RFA
COLES William MM Pte 38781 5th Gloucestershire Regt
COLES William MM Sjt 5255 2nd Devonshire Regt
COLES William MM L/Cpl 10354 2nd Seaforth Highlanders
COLES William A. MM Trumpeter 915039 14 Bde RFA
COLES William Ernest MM Pte 41814 2nd Worcestershire Regt
COLES William F. MM Gnr 63641 AQ/180 Bde RFA
COLES William Henry MM Pte 8663 4th Grenadier Guards
COLES William Price Vivian MM Sjt 1991 1/7th London Regt KIA 7.10.16.
COLESHILL William L. MM L/Cpl 89441 Machine Gun Corps
COLESHILL William T. MM Pte M2/102446 62 Div Train Army Service Corps
COLEY Frederick MM Pte 57156 Welsh Regt
COLEY John George MM L/Cpl 16805 2nd Northamptonshire Regt KIA 27.5.18.
COLEY Samuel MM Pte 4976 Leicestershire Regt
COLFAR Thomas MM Cpl 48194 Royal Engineers
COLGAN Alexander MM Sjt Piper 3283 12th Royal Scots
COLGAN George MM Pte 8271 1st Royal Inniskilling Fusiliers
COLGAN James MM Pte 10816 9th Scottish Rifles
COLGAN John MM Pte 1987 1/9th Durham Light Infantry KIA 15.9.17.
COLGAN Matthew MM Sjt 37541 30 Siege Bty RGA
COLGAN Patrick MM Cpl 5331 Leinster Regt
COLGATE Roger Edward MM Sjt 14914 2nd Grenadier Guards KIA 18.11.16.
COLHOUN A.R. MM Staff Nurse F QAIMNS
COLHOUN Martin MM Sjt 30575 RAMC
COLIN C.F. MM F/Sjt 4248 Royal Flying Corps
COLING Arthur MM Cpl 11322 Y/19 Medium TM Bty RFA KIA 7.11.18.
COLK Charles J. MM Pte 29663 1st Royal West Kent Regt

COLLAR T. MM L/Cpl 15273 Northamptonshire Regt
COLLARD Albert Ernest MM Pte 27660 15th Royal Warwickshire Regt
COLLARD Ernest MM Cpl S/16545 Rifle Brigade
COLLARD George MM+Bar Sjt 240241 Somerset Light Infantry
COLLARD George B. MM+Bar Bdr 77708 C/124 Bde RFA
COLLARD Stanley MM Pte 202966 Suffolk Regt
COLLARD William H. MM Pte S/4120 13th Rifle Brigade
COLLEDGE Albert MM Pte 201923 Notts & Derby Regt
COLLEDGE Edward MM L/Cpl 9/16039 9th Leicestershire Regt KIA 3.5.17.
COLLEDGE Samuel MM L/Sjt 25900 Notts & Derby Regt
COLLEDGE Thompson MM Pte 18179 6th Yorkshire Regt
COLLEGE Robson MM Pte 12785 8th Yorkshire Regt KIA 29.10.18.
COLLEGE Thomas G. MM L/Cpl 11411 7th Yorkshire Regt
COLLEPY Henry M. MM Pte 24323 8th West Yorkshire Regt
COLLETT A.E.F. MM L/Cpl T/2/12465 Army Service Corps
COLLETT Albert MM L/Cpl 486051 465 Fd Coy Royal Engineers
COLLETT Albert S. MM Pte 8939 1/4th Suffolk Regt
COLLETT Basil Arthur MM Sjt 49275 161 Coy Machine Gun Corps
COLLETT C.I. MM F/Sjt 413 Royal Flying Corps
COLLETT Frederick MM L/Cpl 17029 6th Oxf & Bucks Light Infantry
COLLETT Hammond A. MM Gnr 42708 RFA
COLLETT Harry E. MM Cpl 10024 1st Royal West Kent Regt
COLLETT Henry MM Pnr 261081 Royal Engineers
COLLETT Herbert J. MM Pte 285811 1/1st Oxfordshire Yeomanry
COLLETT James Blackwell MM L/Cpl 558208 29 Div Sig Coy Royal Engineers
COLLETT John William Henry MM Pte 21876 4th Grenadier Guards
COLLETT Rodney W. MM Sjt 300223 5th Liverpool Regt
COLLETT Sidney H. MM L/Cpl 474725 Royal Engineers
COLLETT William Edwin MM Bdr 48324 C/82 Bde RFA KIA 27.10.17.
COLLETT William F. MM Dvr 41073 109 Bty 281 Bde RFA
COLLETT William John MM Spr 75796 13 Div Sig Coy Royal Engineers
COLLEY Alick H. MM Sjt 39131 1st South Wales Borderers
COLLEY Harry MM 2nd Cpl 360434 17 Div Sig Coy Royal Engineers
COLLEY Isaac E. MM Sjt 1786 Royal Horse Guards
COLLEY James MM+Bar L/Cpl 240449 1/5th Lincolnshire Regt KIA 2.11.17.
COLLEY John Thomas MM Cpl L/6984 6th East Kent Regt KIA 10.5.17.
COLLEY Philip MM Pte 14132 11th West Yorkshire Regt
COLLEY R. MM Pte 36880 1/6th Essex Regt
COLLEY William MM Pte S/8555 1st East Kent Regt
COLLICK John Henry MM Gnr 64172 94 Siege Bty Royal Artillery DOW 18.11.16.
COLLIE Alexander MM Pte 16715 2nd Scots Guards
COLLIE James MM Cpl 201482 9th Northumberland Fusiliers
COLLIE James MM Sjt 265002 1/6th Gordon Highlanders
COLLIE William MM Pte 40478 2nd Arg & Suth Highlanders
COLLIER Albert MM Sjt 240381 1/5th North Lancashire Regt
COLLIER Alf Ellis MM L/Cpl 235806 4th York & Lancaster Regt
COLLIER Arthur MM Pte 15938 11th Manchester Regt
COLLIER Augustine A. MM Pte G/3523 9th Royal Sussex Regt
COLLIER David John MM L/Cpl 24238 16th Welsh Regt
COLLIER F. MM Sjt 7895 1st Wiltshire Regt
COLLIER Fletcher MM Pte 325143 8th West Yorkshire Regt
COLLIER Frank "DCM,MM" L/Sjt 265423 1/6th Cheshire Regt
COLLIER Frederick MM Cpl L/9485 B/149 Bde RFA
COLLIER Frederick T. MM L/Cpl 22325 Labour Corps
COLLIER G.(or J.) MM L/Cpl P1680 Military Foot Police
COLLIER George MM Dvr 761382 RFA
COLLIER George E. MM Pte 12664 9th Cheshire Regt
COLLIER George H. MM L/Cpl 240863 Devonshire Regt
COLLIER Gilbert MM L/Cpl 290711 Gordon Highlanders
COLLIER H. MM Sjt 1752 Oxf & Bucks Light Infantry
COLLIER Harry J. MM L/Cpl 201945 Notts & Derby Regt
COLLIER Horace D. MM Sjt 266084 7th Royal Warwickshire Regt
COLLIER John MM Pte S/7112 1st Gordon Highlanders
COLLIER John MM Pte 33509 9th Cheshire Regt DOW 23.8.18.
COLLIER John MM Pte 23934 1st Grenadier Guards
COLLIER John Albert MM Pte 2653 1/6th London Regt
COLLIER John Edwin MM 2nd Cpl 443909 66 Div Sig Coy Royal Engineers
COLLIER John Frank MM Spr 46478 3 Div Sig Coy Royal Engineers KIA 18.4.18.

COLLIER Reginald Jack MM Cpl 201116 1/4th Oxf & Bucks Light Infantry
COLLIER Robert MM Pte 5452 2nd Royal Dublin Fusiliers
COLLIER Sydney Clarence MM L/Cpl 392030 2/9th London Regt KIA 27.9.17.
COLLIER T. MM Pte 242070 Worcestershire Regt
COLLIER Thomas MM Pte 15617 Coldstream Guards
COLLIER Thomas MM Pte 4493 Manchester Regt
COLLIER Thomas Wilson MM Pte 16271 13th Royal Scots DOW 22.9.18.
COLLIER Tom MM L/Cpl 18568 2nd Grenadier Guards
COLLIER William MM Pte 51587 RAMC
COLLIER William C. MM Sjt 332170 Highland Light Infantry
COLLIER William G. MM Pte 13268 Royal West Surrey Regt
COLLIGAN John MM Pte 20844 11th Royal Scots
COLLIN Andrew M. MM Pte S/10316 8/10th Gordon Highlanders
COLLIN Henry MM Pnr 57379 73 Fd Coy Royal Engineers
COLLIN John L. MM Pte 300209 7th Liverpool Regt
COLLINGBORN Edward Arthur MM Cpl 96211 17 Squadron MGC(Cavalry)
COLLINGE Harold MM Pte 276047 1/7th Manchester Regt
COLLINGE James MM Gnr 116098 RFA
COLLINGRIDGE Alf W. MM Sjt 614126 1st(Warwickshire)Bty RHA
COLLINGS Albert MM L/Bdr 41027 71 Bty 36 Bde RFA
COLLINGS Alfred E. MM Pte 30008 12th East Surrey Regt
COLLINGS Arthur MM Pte 9696 1st Duke of Cornwall's LI
COLLINGS Frank MM Pte R/10408 11th King's Royal Rifle Corps
COLLINGS Franklin Thomas MM Sjt 11053 1st Scots Guards
COLLINGS John MM+Bar 2nd Cpl 29346 Royal Engineers
COLLINGS John MM Pte K/276 22nd Royal Fusiliers
COLLINGS Leonard MM L/Cpl 21859 6th Liverpool Regt
COLLINGTON Herbert "MM,CG(F)" Sjt 37166 116 Heavy Bty RGA
COLLINGWOOD C.W. MM Spr 147618 250 Tunnelling Coy Royal Engineers
COLLINGWOOD Frederick A. MM Sjt 81614 137 Coy Labour Corps
COLLINGWOOD George MM Pte 320612 21st London Regt
COLLINGWOOD John Robert MM L/Cpl 52337 75 Fd Coy Royal Engineers
COLLINGWOOD Philip "DCM,MM" Sjt 41369 18th Bn Machine Gun Corps DOW 2.9.18.
COLLINGWOOD Thomas MM Pte 40355 Northumberland Fusiliers
COLLINGWOOD Thomas D. "MM,MID" Sjt 101177 Royal Engineers
COLLINGWOOD Thomas Frederick MM Sjt 6913 7th Dragoon Guards
COLLINS A.E. MM Sjt 22005 Royal Welsh Fusiliers
COLLINS Albert MM Pte 25576 1st Royal West Surrey Regt
COLLINS Albert MM Cpl M1/08627 Army Service Corps
COLLINS Albert MM L/Cpl 2262 1st Lancashire Fusiliers
COLLINS Albert E. MM Cpl 163888 D/47 Bde RFA
COLLINS Albert E. MM L/Cpl 42297 Yorkshire Regt
COLLINS Albert E. MM Pte 6748 Royal Welsh Fusiliers
COLLINS Albert J. MM Cpl 94228 12th Liverpool Regt
COLLINS Alfred MM Pte 9841 4th Royal Fusiliers
COLLINS Alfred MM Pte 52916 Middlesex Regt
COLLINS Alfred Charles MM Dvr 112671 D/52 Bde RFA
COLLINS Andrew MM Pte 30570 2nd Highland Light Infantry
COLLINS Archibald F. MM Cpl 28699 Machine Gun Corps
COLLINS Arthur MM Bdr 750651 B/315 Bde RFA
COLLINS Arthur E. MM Bdr 38518 3 Siege Bty RGA
COLLINS Arthur E. MM Pte 15258 16th Highland Light Infantry
COLLINS Arthur John MM L/Cpl 200546 East Surrey Regt
COLLINS Arthur R. MM L/Sjt 2486 8th Royal Fusiliers
COLLINS C. MM RSM 723342 24th London Regt
COLLINS C.A. MM Cpl 205988 Yeomanry
COLLINS Cecil MM Sjt 25949 9th Yorkshire Regt
COLLINS Cecil E. MM L/Cpl 28756 2nd Northumberland Fusiliers
COLLINS Charles MM L/Cpl 9615 2nd Royal Berkshire Regt
COLLINS Charles MM CSM 250073 Manchester Regt
COLLINS Charles A. MM Cpl 71550 47th Bn Machine Gun Corps
COLLINS Charles Edward MM Sjt 59747 17th Royal Welsh Fusiliers DOW 24.12.18. Real name Coutart de Butts Taylor.
COLLINS Charles Frederick MM Pte 1899 1/4th London Regt KIA 9.4.17.
COLLINS Charles Thomas MM Cpl 6691 12th Middlesex Regt KIA 3.5.17.
COLLINS Charles William MM Pte 7026 IX Corps Cyclist Bn Army Cyclist Corps KIA 5.10.18.
COLLINS Clarence A.V. MM Sjt 302074 5th London Regt
COLLINS Clifford MM Dvr 12232 88 Bde RFA DOW 31.1.17.
COLLINS David MM Pte 26380 38th Bn Machine Gun Corps
COLLINS Dennis MM Bdr 69706 126 Bty 29 Bde RFA KIA 14.5.17.
COLLINS Donald A. MM Pte 28340 Northumberland Fusiliers
COLLINS E. MM L/Sjt 29786 2nd South Lancashire Regt
COLLINS E.C. MM Pte 10064? Grenadier Guards
COLLINS Edward MM Sjt 31850 Essex Regt
COLLINS Edward MM Dvr 51382 D/47 Bde RFA
COLLINS Ernest MM Pte 18143 1st Grenadier Guards
COLLINS Ernest D. MM Pte 106906 RAMC
COLLINS Ernest J. MM Pte 8250 1st Duke of Cornwall's LI
COLLINS Ernest W. MM L/Cpl L/10596 6th Royal West Surrey Regt
COLLINS F.G. MM Pte DM2/195396 Army Service Corps
COLLINS Francis MM Sjt S/10765 2nd Seaforth Highlanders
COLLINS Francis MM Pte 2608 19th Manchester Regt KIA 23.4.17.
COLLINS Francis John Sjt 124423 11th Labour Bn Royal Engineers
COLLINS Frank MM L/Cpl 11670 2nd Royal Berkshire Regt KIA 2.12.17.
COLLINS Frank Ewart MM Sjt 680134 1/22nd London Regt
COLLINS Frank V. MM Pte 14462 2nd Royal Fusiliers
COLLINS Frank William MM L/Cpl 20747 47 Coy Machine Gun Corps
COLLINS Fred MM Cpl 3071 2nd Royal Sussex Regt
COLLINS Frederick MM Sjt 7602 1st Middlesex Regt KIA 15.7.16.
COLLINS Frederick J. MM Cpl 11810 4th King's Royal Rifle Corps
COLLINS G. MM Pte M2/080108 Army Service Corps
COLLINS G. MM Pte 11876 Middlesex Regt
COLLINS George MM Pte 26580 Manchester Regt
COLLINS George MM Gnr 64167 X/47 Med TM Bty RGA
COLLINS George MM Sjt 678 8th Royal Highlanders KIA 3.5.17.
COLLINS George MM Bdr 23206 RFA
COLLINS George MM L/Cpl 10966 5th Oxf & Bucks Light Infantry
COLLINS George Henry MM Pte 5626 69 Coy Machine Gun Corps KIA 29.9.17.
COLLINS George John MM Sjt 10192 6th Somerset Light Infantry KIA 27.8.16.
COLLINS George T. MM Pte 38679 4th Gloucestershire Regt
COLLINS Harold J. MM+Bar Sjt 240078 Worcestershire Regt
COLLINS Harold S.G. MM Dvr T1/2494 12 Div Train Army Service Corps
COLLINS Harry E. MM Pte 26535 Hampshire Regt
COLLINS Harry T. MM Pte 31988 South Lancashire Regt
COLLINS Henry MM Pte 6590 11th Northumberland Fusiliers
COLLINS Henry Richard "DCM,MM" Cpl 8595 2nd Devonshire Regt KIA 4.9.17.
COLLINS Henry Richard MM Cpl 8595 2nd Devonshire Regt KIA 4.9.17.
COLLINS Herbert E. MM CSM G/3084 8th Royal West Surrey Regt
COLLINS Herbert Stanley MM Bdr 925535 RFA
COLLINS Horace H. MM L/Cpl G/17393 7th East Kent Regt
COLLINS J.E. MM Dvr 631991 RFA
COLLINS J.H. MM Pte 10226 2nd Oxf & Bucks Light Infantry
COLLINS James MM Pte 33592 7th Wiltshire Regt
COLLINS James MM Pte 44055 23rd London Regt
COLLINS James "DCM+Bar,MM+Bar" Cpl 267438 1/6th Seaforth Highlanders
COLLINS James MM Sjt 8519 1st Rifle Brigade
COLLINS James MM Pte 2374 Royal Irish Rifles
COLLINS James B.A. MM Pte 275486 Durham Light Infantry
COLLINS James C. MM Pte 42936 15th Hampshire Regt
COLLINS James H. MM Pte 129402 46th Royal Fusiliers
COLLINS James Robert MM Pte G/4723 8th East Surrey Regt KIA 1.7.16.
COLLINS John MM Sjt 1098 Royal Engineers
COLLINS John MM Pte 767 8th Royal Fusiliers KIA 7.10.16.
COLLINS John MM+Bar Cpl 241831 1/5th South Staffordshire Regt
COLLINS John MM Pte 9749 1st Devonshire Regt
COLLINS John Francis MM L/Cpl 241380 2/5th North Lancashire Regt
COLLINS John George MM Sjt 974 1/8th Notts & Derby Regt
COLLINS John William MM Cpl 350954 1/8th Manchester Regt
COLLINS Joseph MM Sjt 8558 1st Royal Inniskilling Fusiliers
COLLINS Joseph MM Pte 21418 Machine Gun Corps DOW 26.3.17.
COLLINS Joseph Henry MM L/Cpl 27496 15th Hampshire Regt
COLLINS Julius John MM Sjt 12469 4th Middlesex Regt
COLLINS L.C. MM L/Cpl 133018 45th Royal Fusiliers
COLLINS Lawrence G. MM Pte 1421 1/9th London Regt
COLLINS Lionel Richard MM Pte G/10538 11th Royal West Kent Regt

COLLINS Matthew A. MM L/Cpl 33394 6th King's Own Scottish Borderers
COLLINS Michael MM Spr 197969 170 Tunnelling Coy Royal Engineers
COLLINS Michael MM L/Sjt 11099 1st Irish Guards
COLLINS Patrick MM Dvr 1578 B/70 Bde RFA
COLLINS Percy Horace MM+Bar Cpl(MCDR) 54388 21 Div Sig Coy Royal Engineers
COLLINS Peter MM Pte 112 26th Northumberland Fusiliers
COLLINS Peter MM Pte 3746 8th Hussars att Cav Corps Sig Sqn.
COLLINS Peter "MM,MID" Sjt 23216 10th Duke of Cornwall's LI
COLLINS Phillips MM Pte 19596 10th Northumberland Fusiliers KIA 25.9.16.
COLLINS Richard MM Dvr L/7802 RFA
COLLINS Richard MM Pte 390 20th Northumberland Fusiliers
COLLINS Richard MM L/Cpl 12906 12th East Surrey Regt
COLLINS Robert MM L/Cpl 3/7934 1st Norfolk Regt DOW 3.6.17.
COLLINS S. MM Cpl 200106 1st Bn Tank Corps
COLLINS Stanley MM Sjt 89304 9 Div Ammn Col RFA
COLLINS Stephen John MM Sjt 457015 26 Fd Amb RAMC
COLLINS Stephen W. MM Sjt 68877 'A' Bty RHA
COLLINS Thomas MM Spr 201307 Royal Engineers
COLLINS Thomas MM Sjt 16385 18th Lancashire Fusiliers
COLLINS Thomas C. MM S/Sjt Farrier 32722 3 Bde RHA
COLLINS Thomas C.A. MM Pte 200329 Dorsetshire Regt
COLLINS Thomas E. MM Sjt 421061 RAMC
COLLINS Thomas H. MM Gnr 26193 RFA
COLLINS Thomas H. MM Cpl S/14216 Rifle Brigade
COLLINS Thomas J.F. MM Pte 123944 42nd Bn Machine Gun Corps
COLLINS Tom W. MM Pte 26454 4th Hampshire Regt
COLLINS Victor Charles MM Gnr L/20178 D/162 Bde RFA
COLLINS Wilfred S. MM 2nd Cpl 552303 Royal Engineers
COLLINS William MM Pte 36512 4th Yorkshire Light Infantry
COLLINS William MM L/Cpl 1535 23rd Royal Fusiliers
COLLINS William MM Sjt 2609 9th East Surrey Regt
COLLINS William MM Cpl 12301 6th Liverpool Regt
COLLINS William MM L/Cpl 107587 429 Fd Coy Royal Engineers
COLLINS William MM Dvr 1177 RFA
COLLINS William MM Sjt 48071 43 Bde RFA
COLLINS William MM Dvr 17090 B/86 Bde RFA
COLLINS William MM+Bar Sjt 2028 Middlesex Regt
COLLINS William H. MM Pte 39898 1st Wiltshire Regt
COLLINS William Henry MM Cpl 29442 B/181 Bde RFA
COLLINS William J. "MM,MID" Sjt 7345 RAMC
COLLINS William T. MM Sjt 8337 North Staffordshire Regt
COLLINS Williams MM Pte 75621 RAMC
COLLINSON Albert E. MM L/Cpl 202019 West Yorkshire Regt
COLLINSON David MM L/Cpl 8997 2nd Manchester Regt
COLLINSON Edgar MM Pte 12/830 12th East Yorkshire Regt
COLLINSON Frank L. MM L/Cpl 40196 Royal Engineers
COLLINSON Frederick George MM Pte 15908 9th Yorkshire Regt KIA 7.6.17.
COLLINSON George MM Pte 30940 Lancashire Fusiliers
COLLINSON James MM Pte 632585 2/20th London Regt KIA 29.11.17.
COLLINSON John MM Pte 266112 8th West Yorkshire Regt
COLLINSON John T. MM Pte 18730 1st Coldstream Guards
COLLINSON Joseph H. MM+2 Bars Sjt 19788 9th Yorkshire Regt
COLLINSON Joseph Willans MM Cpl 15/217 9th West Yorkshire Regt KIA 5.11.18.
COLLINSON Lionel MM Cpl 570265 1/17th London Regt KIA 24.3.18.
COLLINSON Richard MM Pte 10160 1st Yorkshire Light Infantry DOW 9.3.17.
COLLINSON Robert MM Pte 18181 1st Northumberland Fusiliers
COLLINSON Robert E. MM L/Cpl 26529 9th Yorkshire Light Infantry
COLLINSON Thomas L. MM Pte 232567 2nd London Regt
COLLINSON Walter MM L/Sjt 13388 Coldstream Guards
COLLINSON William MM L/Cpl 23806 2nd Manchester Regt
COLLINSON William E. MM Sjt 21711 7th Bn Machine Gun Corps
COLLINSON William H. MM Pte 23238 Hampshire Regt
COLLIS C.W. MM L/Cpl P/4809 Military Mounted Police
COLLIS Edwin A. MM Spr 64982 17 Div Sig Coy Royal Engineers
COLLIS Frank MM Pte 28945 2nd West Riding Regt
COLLIS Frederick George "DCM,MM+Bar" CSM 18024 Hampshire Regt
COLLIS George A. MM L/Cpl 65693 13th Royal Fusiliers
COLLIS George Alfred MM Dvr 38771 C/71 Bde RFA KIA 29.8.18.
COLLIS Roy N. MM Sjt 528553 Royal Engineers
COLLIS William MM+Bar Sjt L/8929 8th Royal West Surrey Regt KIA 26.3.18.
COLLIS William H. MM Gnr 168055 RGA
COLLIS William Henry MM Sjt 46576 101 Fd Coy Royal Engineers
COLLISHAW Arthur MM Bdr 58283 61 Siege Bty RGA
COLLISHAW Ernest Edward MM+Bar Pte 26166 18th Lancashire Fusiliers DOW 17.10.18.
COLLISON Archibald E. MM L/Cpl 8328 2nd Coldstream Guards
COLLISON George S. MM+Bar Spr 500248 Royal Engineers
COLLISON Harry MM Pte 23147 11th East Lancashire Regt
COLLISON William MM L/Cpl 159285 Royal Engineers
COLLISON William Ernest MM Pte 1629 1/24th London Regt KIA 14.9.17.
COLLMAN Ernest MM L/Cpl 240755 1/5th Devonshire Regt
COLLOFF Charles MM Sjt SE/9158 Army Veterinary Corps
COLLOP Henry MM L/Cpl 41287 15th Royal Irish Rifles
COLLS Charles H. MM Cpl 3696 Northumberland Fusiliers
COLLUM Archibald MM Pte 242976 1/5th South Lancashire Regt KIA 20.6.17.
COLLUM John MM Pte 15528 17th Lancashire Fusiliers
COLLYER Alfred MM Sjt 15711 Royal Scots Fusiliers
COLLYER Archibald W. MM Gnr 245356 290 Bde RFA
COLLYER Charles T. MM Dvr 198497 RFA
COLLYER John MM Sjt 20059 94 Siege Bty RGA
COLLYER Lewis W. MM L/Cpl 322070 6th London Regt
COLLYER Reuben H. MM Spr 24750 Royal Engineers
COLLYER Rudolph F. MM L/Bdr 229545 130 Bty 40 Bde RFA
COLLYER Stanley MM Pte 472037 12th London Regt
COLLYER William F. MM Pte 6326 3rd Rifle Brigade
COLMAN Andrew MM Cpl 275203 2nd Royal Scots
COLMAN Arthur MM Cpl 320203 12th Norfolk Regt
COLMAN Frank H. MM Cpl 23960 10th Duke of Cornwall's LI
COLMAN George MM L/Cpl 267455 8th West Yorkshire Regt
COLMAN James MM Gnr 19404 A/112 Bde RFA
COLMAN John "DCM,MM" Sjt 74828 55th Bn Machine Gun Corps
COLMAN Joseph MM Sjt 276342 7th Durham Light Infantry
COLMAN Michael MM+Bar Sjt S/3302 8th Seaforth Highlanders
COLMAN Richard G. MM Pte 267066 1/6th Cheshire Regt
COLNET John MM L/Bdr 5530 RFA
COLSON John Percy "MC,MM(7802 Sjt 4th Huss),MID" Lt 2nd West Riding Regt
COLSON Stephen MM Dvr 95912 RFA
COLSTON Albert MM Gnr 321486 46 Siege Bty RGA
COLT John W. MM Pte 41083 Rifle Brigade
COLTART John MM Sjt 3395 Royal Highlanders
COLTER Cecil MM L/Cpl Z/281 Rifle Brigade
COLTHART John MM Pte 301644 11th Arg & Suth Highlanders
COLTHART Thomas MM Pte S/10009 2nd Gordon Highlanders KIA 4.10.17.
COLTMAN Robert "MM,MID" Trumpeter 751224 D/250 Bde RFA Died 15.2.19.
COLTMAN Robert MM Pte 22/363 Durham Light Infantry
COLTMAN William H. MM Bdr 97952 A/48 Bde RFA
COLTMAN William Harold "VC,DCM+Bar,MM+Bar,MID,CG(F)" L/Cpl 241028 1/6th North Staffordshire Regt
COLTON Archie W. MM Pte 306000 1/8th Notts & Derby Regt
COLTON Charles Henry MM L/Cpl 4/6929 2nd West Yorkshire Regt KIA 29.5.18.
COLTON Edward MM Pte 7385 1st Cheshire Regt
COLTON Frank MM Cpl 476081 Royal Engineers
COLTON Frederick Joseph "MC,MM" CSM 7143 2nd Royal Scots
COLTON Herbert MM Gnr 701854 330 Bde RFA
COLTON Reuben J. MM Pnr 281750 Royal Engineers
COLTON Woodbine C. "MM,MSM" L/Cpl 92348 9th Bn Tank Corps
COLVILL W.W. MM 2nd Cpl 23768 Royal Engineers
COLVILLE Alexander MM L/Cpl 240686 1/5th Royal Scots Fusiliers DOW 21.9.18.
COLVILLE Ivor M. MM Pte 31661 1st Duke of Cornwall's LI
COLVILLE James MM Pte 17900 Machine Gun Corps
COLVILLE T. MM Pte 201644 7th Royal West Surrey Regt
COLVILLE William H. "MM,MSM" Sjt 14810 5 Fd Amb RAMC
COLVIN Alfred E. MM Pte 2161 1/4th London Regt
COLVIN Archibald L. MM Cpl 41007 Highland Light Infantry
COLWELL Edgar MM+Bar Bdr 374415 122 Siege Bty RGA
COLWELL Harry MM L/Cpl 16543 Welsh Regt
COLWELL Henry MM Pte 467 18th Durham Light Infantry
COLWELL John MM Pte 13522 2nd Royal Fusiliers
COLWELL Percy John MM Pte 48355 54th Bn 162 Coy Machine Gun Corps
COLYER George MM+Bar Pte 9991 1st Border Regt KIA 20.11.17.

COLYER William MM Pte 23070 Liverpool Regt
COMBE E.J. MM L/Cpl 10769 East Surrey Regt
COMBE James MM Sjt 1112 1st Arg & Suth Highlanders
COMBE William MM Pte 66128 4th Bn Machine Gun Corps
COMBER Thomas E. MM L/Cpl 52059 MGC(Cavalry)
COMBER William G. MM Sjt 11447 King's Royal Rifle Corps
COMBERBACH John William MM Bdr 92220 A/115 Bde RFA
COMBIE William MM Pte 8127 2nd Cameron Highlanders
COMBLEY Albert MM Pte 493217 9th London Regt
COMER Charles Herbert Elford "MM,MID" Sjt 17329 B/88 Bde RFA
COMERGORD Michael MM Pte 41242 King's Own Scottish Borderers
COMERY W.H. MM Cpl 3192 1/5th Notts & Derby Regt
COMESKY James MM L/Sjt 6277 Irish Guards
COMISH J. MM Pte 6622 10 Fd Amb RAMC
COMLEY Reginald Cyrus MM Pte 41481 1st South Staffordshire Regt
COMMER George H. MM Sjt 34267 7 Bde RHA
COMMON John MM Pte 64837 9th Yorkshire Light Infantry
COMMON Richard MM L/Cpl 25879 2nd Scottish Rifles KIA 25.3.18.
COMPSON Stanley Henry MM Pte 19059 10th Royal West Kent Regt KIA 23.3.18.
COMPTON Arthur MM Tpr 4411 2nd GMGR
COMPTON Charles F. MM Pte 20631 Wiltshire Regt
COMPTON Claude MM Pte 5895 Notts & Derby Regt
COMPTON E. MM Pte 31957 North Lancashire Regt
COMPTON Ernest A. MM+Bar L/Cpl 20586 Worcestershire Regt
COMPTON Francis John MM Pte 16011 5th Northamptonshire Regt
COMPTON Frederick MM Cpl 9127 1st Cheshire Regt
COMPTON Guy "DCM,MM" Sjt 658 11th Royal Sussex Regt KIA 27.7.17.
COMPTON Harry MM Cpl 220746 8th Royal Berkshire Regt
COMPTON James MM Sjt 3122 Middlesex Regt
COMPTON James W. MM Pte DM2/223914 Army Service Corps
COMPTON John MM Pte 88251 62nd Bn Machine Gun Corps
COMPTON John P. MM Sjt 5859 Middlesex Regt
COMPTON John W. MM Pte 63414 2nd West Yorkshire Regt
CONACHER Arthur S. MM Pte 203933 7th Middlesex Regt
CONBOY Herbert P. MM Bdr 187131 RFA
CONDELL Robert MM Pte 7781 2nd Royal Irish Regt
CONDER C. MM Sjt 202888 1st Essex Regt
CONDIE George MM Pte 290367 Royal Highlanders
CONDIE John MM Pte 5674 Gordon Highlanders
CONDLIFFE Ephraim MM L/Bdr 293554 136 Hy Bty RGA
CONDLIFFE William H. MM Pte 12515 8th North Staffordshire Regt
CONDON Charles Albert MM Pte 70928 111 Fd Amb RAMC
CONDON Christopher MM Sjt 6107 2nd Royal Irish Regt
CONDON George W. MM Sjt 373861 8th London Regt
CONDON John MM Pte 18250 15th Royal Scots KIA 9.4.17.
CONDON Michael "DCM,MM" Pte 355651 25th Royal Welsh Fusiliers
CONDON Patrick MM Pte 682249 22nd London Regt
CONDON Patrick MM Cpl 4/7181 Royal Munster Fusiliers
CONDON Richard MM Pte 266356 5th Gloucestershire Regt
CONDON Robert J. MM Gnr 45234 RFA
CONDON Thomas MM L/Cpl 64401 62nd Bn Machine Gun Corps KIA 14.9.18.
CONDON Thomas James MM Pte 4580 2nd Lincolnshire Regt
CONDREY Thomas Benjamin MM Cpl 6634 8th East Kent Regt
CONDRON Michael MM Pte 3956 1st Royal Irish Rifles KIA 2.12.17.
CONDRON Patrick MM Pte 49838 73 Fd Amb RAMC
CONDRY Frank Harry MM Cpl 200225 1/5th Royal Warwickshire Regt
CONE John W. MM L/Cpl 63171 3rd Royal Fusiliers
CONELY Arthur J. MM+Bar Sjt 9987 2nd Worcestershire Regt
CONEY Edward MM Pte 40568 2nd Worcestershire Regt
CONEY George MM Pte 6884 1st Royal Warwickshire Regt
CONEYWORTH William R. MM Cpl 632492 244 Div Emp Coy Labour Corps
CONGRAVE Sidney H. MM Dvr 38752 A/177 Bde RFA
CONKEY James MM Pte 17633 Northumberland Fusiliers
CONKIE George MM L/Cpl 94371 5th Liverpool Regt
CONLEY John MM Sjt 17334 12th Royal Scots
CONLEY Martin MM Gnr 71357 36 Bde RFA
CONLEY Peter MM Pte 6537 2nd Royal Irish Regt
CONLEY William MM Pte 30246 Yorkshire Regt
CONLIN William MM Pte 237612 Durham Light Infantry
CONLON Henry P. MM Pte 266958 1/7th West Yorkshire Regt
CONN Charles MM Sjt 82190 Royal Engineers
CONN Joseph P. MM Pte 73817 RAMC
CONN Robert MM Cpl 24957 11th Manchester Regt
CONN William MM Pte 240339 1/5th Royal Scots Fusiliers
CONNAH Arthur R. MM L/Cpl 202995 1st East Yorkshire Regt
CONNALLY Thomas MM Pte 72910 41st Bn Machine Gun Corps
CONNAUGHTON John MM Gnr 43236 RGA
CONNELL Alexander MM L/Cpl 30137 1st Scottish Rifles
CONNELL Arthur G. MM Sjt 42466 Guards Div Sig Coy Royal Engineers
CONNELL Edward MM Pte 369895 Labour Corps
CONNELL F. "DCM,MM" Sjt 2262 2nd Royal Highlanders
CONNELL Harry MM Cpl 23257 9th Yorkshire Regt
CONNELL James MM Pte 20957 9th Scottish Rifles
CONNELL James MM L/Cpl 5488 6th Dragoon Guards
CONNELL James MM Spr 107418 Guards Div Sig Coy Royal Engineers
CONNELL James MM L/Cpl 703280 23rd London Regt
CONNELL James MM CSM S/1008 7th Royal West Surrey Regt
CONNELL James MM L/Sjt 703 2nd Middlesex Regt KIA 31.7.17.
CONNELL John MM Pte 275570 1/7th Arg & Suth Highlanders
CONNELL Laurence MM Sjt 20012 1st Royal Dublin Fusiliers KIA 5.10.18.
CONNELL Matthew "MM,MC(G)" Sjt 11976 6/7th Royal Scots Fusiliers
CONNELL Peter MM Cpl 200837 1/5th Liverpool Regt
CONNELL R. "MM,MID" L/Cpl 1324 2nd Royal Warwickshire Regt
CONNELL Richard C. MM Sjt 9307 2nd Northamptonshire Regt
CONNELL Thomas MM Sjt 1123 58 Siege Bty RGA
CONNELL Thomas MM Pte 13921 Army Cyclist Corps
CONNELL Thomas B. MM L/Sjt 240728 1/6th Highland Light Infantry
CONNELL Thomas J. MM Sjt 14977 13th Royal Scots
CONNELL Tom MM Pte 12745 2nd Coldstream Guards
CONNELLY Andrew MM Pte S/25515 1/6th Seaforth Highlanders
CONNELLY Arthur Frederick MM Sjt 71261 34 Coy Machine Gun Corps
CONNELLY Charles MM L/Cpl 40327 Royal Engineers
CONNELLY Frederick MM L/Cpl 95079 13th Liverpool Regt
CONNELLY George MM+Bar Pte 721745 1/24th London Regt
CONNELLY Henry MM Sjt 10659 1st Royal Irish Rifles
CONNELLY James MM L/Cpl 46207 1/8th Scottish Rifles
CONNELLY James MM Sjt 151 1/3rd Monmouthshire Regt
CONNELLY James MM Sjt 10716 10th Arg & Suth Highlanders KIA 6.1.18.
CONNELLY John MM Pte 5930 Scottish Rifles
CONNELLY John David MM Pte 4/8618 2nd Arg & Suth Highlanders
CONNELLY John J. MM Cpl 423117 10th London Regt
CONNELLY Michael MM Gnr 282738 RGA
CONNELLY Michael MM Pte 3697 RAMC
CONNELLY Patrick MM Pte 19875 Royal Scots Fusiliers KIA 26.10.18.
CONNER Frederick MM Cpl 20087 Durham Light Infantry
CONNER James "MM,MID" Cpl 84756 340 Bty 44 Bde RFA
CONNER John MM Pte 1392 18th Hussars
CONNER John MM Pte 18151 Royal Scots Fusiliers
CONNER Joseph MM Pte 512 Northumberland Fusiliers
CONNER William MM Sjt 17335 Royal Scots
CONNETT John Wilson MM L/Cpl 19493 5th Dorsetshire Regt
CONNIFF Thomas MM Cpl 20810 6th Bn Machine Gun Corps
CONNIS David MM Pte 10912 2nd Leinster Regt
CONNOCHIE William MM+Bar Pte 16637 1/6th Royal Highlanders
CONNOCK Frederick MM Cpl 9213 2nd Gloucestershire Regt
CONNOLLY David MM L/Cpl 71603 1st North Irish Horse
CONNOLLY Dennis MM Pte 32422 2nd South Lancashire Regt
CONNOLLY Edward MM Pte 30170 1st Royal Dublin Fusiliers
CONNOLLY Francis E.G. MM Spr 322132 62 Div Sig Coy Royal Engineers
CONNOLLY Frank MM Pte 61961 RAMC
CONNOLLY Frank MM Gnr 711766 RFA
CONNOLLY Henry MM Pte 15/12678 Royal Irish Rifles
CONNOLLY Henry MM Pte 27226 1st Scottish Rifles
CONNOLLY J. MM Pte 38045 RAMC
CONNOLLY James Henry MM L/Cpl F/875 17th Middlesex Regt KIA 8.8.16.
CONNOLLY James Patrick MM Pte 200930 1/5th Durham Light Infantry KIA 15.6.18.
CONNOLLY John E. "MM,MSM" Spr 441908 66 Div Sig Coy Royal Engineers
CONNOLLY John Edward MM Sjt 1386 26th Northumberland Fusiliers
CONNOLLY John Joseph MM L/Sjt 3227 7th Leinster Regt

CONNOLLY Joseph MM Pte 240996 1/5th East Lancashire Regt
CONNOLLY Patrick MM Pte 10237 2nd Royal Dublin Fusiliers
CONNOLLY Sidney Charles Patrick MM Sjt 7383 8th Bn Machine Gun Corps KIA 24.4.18.
CONNOLLY Thomas MM Dvr 108789 C/76 Bde RFA
CONNOLLY Thomas MM Cpl 445464 Labour Corps
CONNOLLY Thomas MM Pte M1/07562 5 Mot Amb Convoy Army Service Corps
CONNOLLY Thomas B. MM Pte 388395 2(Northumbrian)Fd Amb RAMC
CONNOLLY W. MM Cpl 421168 RAMC
CONNOLLY William MM Pte 21423 17th Royal Scots
CONNOLLY William E. MM Cpl 4669 RFA
CONNOLLY William P. "DCM,MM" Gnr 685161 RFA
CONNON Alexander MM Spr 254820 50 Div Sig Coy Royal Engineers
CONNOR Alfred MM Pte 40639 Royal Inniskilling Fusiliers
CONNOR Angus MM Sjt 3924 1st Scots Guards KIA 21.8.18.
CONNOR Arthur MM Pte 18111 Royal Inniskilling Fusiliers
CONNOR Charles MM Pte M2/132247 Army Service Corps
CONNOR Charles MM Pte 325145 1/9th Arg & Suth Highlanders
CONNOR Charles MM Sjt 45811 35 Siege Bty RGA
CONNOR Charles E. MM Cpl 27179 Royal Welsh Fusiliers
CONNOR Edward MM Gnr 26706 RFA
CONNOR Edward MM Pte 14608 East Surrey Regt
CONNOR Edward Charles George MM Pte 2761 1/15th London Regt
CONNOR Fred MM Cpl 328082 1/1st Cambridgeshire Regt
CONNOR George MM Pte 1150 11th Manchester Regt
CONNOR George MM Cpl 47438 62 Siege Bty RGA
CONNOR George MM Sjt 3515 1st Irish Guards
CONNOR Harold "MM,MID" Bdr 8054 RFA
CONNOR James MM Cpl 305285 7th Highland Light Infantry
CONNOR James MM L/Cpl 200941 Manchester Regt
CONNOR John MM Spr 79845 185 Tunnelling Coy Royal Engineers
CONNOR John MM BSM 60880 226 Siege Bty RGA
CONNOR John MM Pte 7118 4th King's Royal Rifle Corps
CONNOR John MM Cpl 22923 Z Bty RHA
CONNOR John MM Pte 10399 6th East Yorkshire Regt
CONNOR Michael MM Pte 16327 2nd Royal Irish Regt
CONNOR Norman MM+Bar Sjt 2997 17th Highland Light Infantry KIA 4.9.17.
CONNOR P. MM Pte 10498 Irish Guards
CONNOR Patrick MM CSM 47655 13th Royal Inniskilling Fusiliers
CONNOR Patrick MM Pte 3558 2nd Connaught Rangers
CONNOR Patrick MM Pte 24/295 22nd Northumberland Fusiliers Died 21.3.18.
CONNOR Patrick MM Pte 30642 Liverpool Regt
CONNOR Percy C. MM Pte G/19511 2nd Middlesex Regt
CONNOR Phenix MM Pte 354448 1/3rd(East Lancashire)Fd Amb RAMC
CONNOR Richard MM Pte 307574 Lancashire Fusiliers
CONNOR Robert "DCM,MM,MID" Sjt 7844 2nd Highland Light Infantry
CONNOR Sidney MM Cpl 43447 Royal Engineers
CONNOR T. MM Bdr 45585 L(AA)Bty RGA
CONNOR Thomas P. MM L/Cpl 39615 West Yorkshire Regt
CONNOR William MM Pte 26640 17th Lancashire Fusiliers
CONNOR William James MM Pte 5/4963 8th King's Royal Rifle Corps
CONNORS Howell MM Cpl 17226 14th Welsh Regt
CONNORS Michael MM L/Cpl 11034 Royal Irish Regt
CONOLLY John MM S/Sjt Farrier 16276 12 Bde RFA
CONQUEST Thomas Howe MM Pte 16289 9th Devonshire Regt KIA 7.10.18.
CONROY A. MM Sjt 34173 York & Lancaster Regt
CONROY Christopher MM Cpl 124124 32nd Bn Machine Gun Corps
CONROY Edwin "DCM,MM" Pte 241662 1/5th Lincolnshire Regt
CONROY Frank MM Sjt 79856 175 Tunnelling Coy Royal Engineers
CONROY James MM Pte 12564 12th Northumberland Fusiliers
CONROY John MM Cpl 42064 1st South Wales Borderers
CONROY John M. MM Cpl T/32683 Army Service Corps
CONROY Joseph MM Sjt 9463 2nd North Lancashire Regt
CONROY Michael MM L/Cpl 9014 Irish Guards
CONROY Patrick MM Pte 30520 1st Royal Dublin Fusiliers
CONROY Thomas MM Cpl 9200 4th Liverpool Regt
CONROY Thomas MM Pte 202120 1/4th West Riding Regt KIA 27.6.17.
CONROY William MM Cpl 28351 206 Coy Machine Gun Corps
CONRY Richard E. MM Pte 275724 7th Manchester Regt

CONSON Francis M. MM CQMS 4156 1st King's Royal Rifle Corps
CONSTABLE Arthur A. MM Sjt 925539 A/290 Bde RFA
CONSTABLE Bertie J. MM Pte 1674 Worcestershire Regt
CONSTABLE George "MM,MSM" Pte 16244 4 Fd Amb RAMC
CONSTABLE Herbert MM Sjt 53958 RGA
CONSTABLE Richard Archibald MM 2nd Cpl 107318 40 Div Sig Coy Royal Engineers
CONSTABLE Silas MM Pte 7980 2nd Worcestershire Regt
CONSTABLE Thomas Henry "MC,MM(16370 CSM)" 2Lt North Lancashire Regt
CONSTABLE William A.C. MM Gnr 65991 RGA
CONSTABLE William E. "MM,MID" Sjt 61278 Royal Engineers
CONSTANT Albert Edward MM Pte 16091 10th Welsh Regt
CONSTANTINE Albert MM+Bar Pte 15952 13th Durham Light Infantry KIA 10.10.18.
CONSTANTINE Fred MM Pte 36213 Leicestershire Regt
CONSTANTINE Harold MM Pte 242211 1/5th Yorkshire Light Infantry
CONSTANTINE Sydney MM Spr 175407 257 Tunnelling Coy Royal Engineers
CONSTANTINE Tom MM Cpl 266961 2nd West Riding Regt KIA 20.10.18.
CONSTERDINE Ernest MM Pte 15975 Notts & Derby Regt
CONVERY Joseph MM Gnr 54959 'N' Bty RHA KIA 10.8.18.
CONWAY Christopher D. MM Pte 84877 4th Liverpool Regt
CONWAY Dennis MM Gnr 13435 RGA
CONWAY Francis MM Gnr 43568 RFA
CONWAY George MM L/Bdr 73303 41 Bty 42 Bde RFA
CONWAY George J. MM Sjt 22968 Border Regt
CONWAY Harry "DCM,MM" Sjt 10409 1st Wiltshire Regt
CONWAY Horace F. MM BSM 772 RFA
CONWAY James MM L/Cpl 8678 Machine Gun Corps
CONWAY James MM Pte 9978 1st Royal Inniskilling Fusiliers
CONWAY James MM+Bar L/Cpl 9729 2nd Royal Irish Regt
CONWAY John MM Bdr 166087 149 Siege Bty RGA DOW 23.9.17.
CONWAY John I. MM Cpl 55929 Machine Gun Corps
CONWAY John MacFadzean MM Pte 12680 8th Royal Irish Rifles KIA 2.7.16.
CONWAY John Vincent MM Pte 356693 10th Liverpool Regt
CONWAY Maurice MM CSM 200235 Worcestershire Regt
CONWAY Michael MM Sjt 10086 1st Royal Irish Fusiliers KIA 23.11.17.
CONWAY Patrick MM Pte 16507 2nd Royal Irish Regt
CONWAY Peter MM Pte 73535 2nd Durham Light Infantry
CONWAY Peter MM Pte 41096 1/6th Royal Highlanders
CONWAY Richard MM Pte 4569 1st Lancashire Fusiliers
CONWAY Robert MM Pte 34610 East Lancashire Regt
CONWAY Thomas MM Pte 32514 Welsh Regt
CONWAY Thomas MM CSM 21671 6th York & Lancaster Regt KIA 11.10.18.
CONWAY William Edward MM Sjt 5341 RAMC
COOGAN Harry MM Pte 17857 5th Manchester Regt
COOK A. MM Pte 2798 10th Essex Regt
COOK A. MM L/Cpl 14005 10th Essex Regt
COOK A.H. "DCM,MM+Bar" BSM 31138 113 Hy Bty RGA
COOK Albert MM BSM 352031 RGA
COOK Albert MM Bdr 78826 RFA
COOK Albert A. MM Dvr 147546 RFA
COOK Albert E. MM Pte 3041 32nd Bn Machine Gun Corps
COOK Albert E. MM Pte 92275 5th Bn Tank Corps
COOK Albert James MM Cpl 780367 B/246 Bde RFA
COOK Alexander D. MM Pte 202097 1st Northumberland Fusiliers
COOK Alfred MM Cpl 29632 15th Hussars
COOK Alfred MM L/Cpl 41738 4 Sqn MGC(Cavalry)
COOK Alfred E. MM+Bar Pte 873 6th Royal West Kent Regt
COOK Alfred F. MM Pte 8838 2nd Suffolk Regt
COOK Alfred J.H. MM Spr 1694 2 Div Sig Coy Royal Engineers
COOK Alfred John MM Sjt 45040 81 Fd Coy Royal Engineers
COOK Archibald MM 2nd Cpl 86533 176 Tunnelling Coy Royal Engineers
COOK Archibald MM Pte S/41168 7th Gordon Highlanders
COOK Archibald MM Pte 41105 Seaforth Highlanders
COOK Archibald MM L/Cpl 2328 1st Royal Highlanders
COOK Arthur MM L/Cpl 12646 26 Fd Coy Royal Engineers
COOK Arthur MM Gnr 297029 RGA
COOK Arthur H. "DCM,MM" CSM 9090 1st Somerset Light Infantry
COOK Arthur Harry "MM,MID" L/Sjt 19467 3rd Grenadier Guards KIA 12.7.16.
COOK Arthur Thomas MM Sjt 13675 6th Duke of Cornwall's LI Real name Seal.DOW 6.10.16.

COOK Bert MM Cpl 115920 48th Bn Machine Gun Corps
COOK Bertie MM Pte 1263 1/6th West Yorkshire Regt
COOK Bertie C. MM Gnr 280511 RGA
COOK Bertram MM Pte 200344 1/4th Royal Sussex Regt
COOK C.W. MM Cpl 7128 RGA
COOK Charles MM Cpl 6218 7th Hussars
COOK Charles MM L/Cpl 240750 1/5th Gloucestershire Regt
COOK Charles H. MM Gnr 955607 RFA
COOK Charles W. MM Sjt 560219 Royal Engineers
COOK Charles W. MM+Bar Pte 21487 10th Royal West Surrey Regt
COOK Charles W. MM 2nd Cpl 35881 Royal Engineers
COOK David MM+Bar Sjt 17054 3rd Worcestershire Regt DOW 12.4.18.
COOK Donald George MM Pte 70403 2nd Notts & Derby Regt KIA 9.7.18.
COOK Edgar MM L/Cpl 86297 171 Tunnelling Coy Royal Engineers DOW 29.10.17.
COOK Edward MM Sjt 66042 A/52 Bde RFA
COOK Edward MM L/Cpl 9207 HAC
COOK Edward C. MM Pnr 548961 Royal Engineers
COOK Edward J. MM Cpl 3323 12th Royal Fusiliers
COOK Ernest MM Pte 27127 Leicestershire Regt
COOK Ernest George MM Pte 25789 Lancashire Fusiliers
COOK Ernest Richard MM L/Sjt 1341 1/7th Northumberland Fusiliers DOW 29.7.17.
COOK Ernest William MM Pte 250101 1/5th Essex Regt
COOK F.W. MM Pte G/12814 7th East Kent Regt
COOK Francis MM Pte DM2/130085 Att 60 Fd Amb RAMC Army Service Corps
COOK Francis J.L. MM Bdr 50598 18 Bde RFA
COOK Frank MM Spr 82552 38 Div Sig Coy Royal Engineers
COOK Frank MM Pte 21104 Royal Fusiliers
COOK Frank H. MM Pte 36126 South Wales Borderers
COOK Fred MM Sjt 7506 5th Royal Berkshire Regt
COOK Frederick MM Sjt L/32939 C/177 Bde RFA
COOK Frederick C. MM Pte 11740 2nd Coldstream Guards
COOK Frederick Charles MM Cpl 86056 39 Div Ammn Col RFA
COOK Frederick Ernest MM Spr 63241 152 Fd Coy Royal Engineers KIA 15.11.16.
COOK Frederick J. MM Sjt 81891 RGA
COOK Frederick James MM Sjt 1487 1/6th London Regt
COOK Frederick W. MM Sjt 630629 20th London Regt
COOK George MM Sjt 96397 B/79 Bde RFA
COOK George MM Pte 321954 6th London Regt
COOK George MM Pte 306451 1/8th Notts & Derby Regt
COOK George MM+Bar L/Cpl 16721 Notts & Derby Regt
COOK George C. MM Pte 566484 Labour Corps
COOK George H. MM Pte 49002 1/1st Hertfordshire Regt
COOK George Henderson MM Pte 28717 10th Royal Warwickshire Regt KIA 19.4.18.
COOK George W. MM Pte 37288 Northumberland Fusiliers
COOK George William MM Sjt 72264 134 Fd Amb RAMC
COOK Gilbert MM L/Cpl 17729 9th Suffolk Regt
COOK H. MM L/Cpl 29422 15th Hussars
COOK Harry MM Pte 32908 12th Gloucestershire Regt
COOK Harry MM L/Cpl 57404 23rd Bn Machine Gun Corps
COOK Harry MM Pte 54665 48th Bn Machine Gun Corps
COOK Henry "DCM,MM" Sjt 9287 12th Highland Light Infantry
COOK Henry E. MM Spr 32833 Royal Engineers
COOK Henry George MM Pte 66620 99 Fd Amb. RAMC
COOK Henry J.A. MM Pte 41288 Royal Irish Rifles
COOK Herbert MM Cpl 755567 RFA
COOK Herbert MM Pte 1828 1/4th Yorkshire Regt DOW 15.1.17.
COOK Herbert F.A. MM Pte 28804 Royal Warwickshire Regt
COOK J. MM Pte G/77546 2nd Royal Fusiliers
COOK J. MM Sjt 19549 9th Royal Inniskilling Fusiliers
COOK J. MM Pte 270666 11th Royal Scots
COOK J. MM Pte 13761 RAMC
COOK Jack MM Sjt 102739 170 Tunnelling Coy Royal Engineers
COOK James MM Spr(MCDR) 362382 Att 76 Bde RGA Royal Engineers
COOK James MM Sjt S/2190 10th Arg & Suth Highlanders
COOK James MM Gnr 107506 RGA
COOK James A. MM Sjt 300555 1/8th Durham Light Infantry
COOK James A. MM Pte 353260 7th London Regt
COOK James A. MM L/Cpl 40843 South Staffordshire Regt
COOK James H. MM+Bar L/Cpl 4120 2nd Hampshire Regt
COOK John MM Pte 22226 8th Hussars
COOK John C. MM Pte G/11564 Royal West Surrey Regt
COOK John H. MM Cpl 74468 Royal Engineers
COOK John L. MM Pte G/95828 2nd London Regt
COOK John Richard MM+Bar Pte 101565 RAMC Att ShropsLI.
COOK John S. MM Gnr 70308 RFA
COOK John T. MM Cpl 238015 1st South Staffordshire Regt
COOK John T. MM Sjt 200820 South Staffordshire Regt
COOK John W. MM L/Cpl 200057 6th Notts & Derby Regt
COOK John W.D. MM Pte 47788 Northumberland Fusiliers
COOK Joseph MM Pte S/4384 1/5th Gordon Highlanders KIA 8.7.18.
COOK Joseph MM Pte 18654 Durham Light Infantry
COOK Joseph MM Pte 28852 Highland Light Infantry
COOK Joseph MM Dvr T/22034 Army Service Corps
COOK Joseph MM Pte 7268 2nd Royal Scots Fusiliers
COOK Leonard "DCM,MM+Bar,MID,CdeG(F)" SM 48551 7 Bde H Bty RHA
COOK Leslie H. MM Pte 241691 5th West Riding Regt
COOK Lionel George MM Sjt 80333 1/1st Essex Yeomanry
COOK Morgan T. MM Pte 6170 7th Dragoon Guards
COOK N.G.S. MM Sjt 21876 1st Wiltshire Regt
COOK Norman R. MM Pte 508259 RAMC
COOK Percy MM Pte 142818 1st Bn Machine Gun Corps
COOK Percy E. MM Sjt 14927 9th Norfolk Regt
COOK Phillip Howard MM L/Cpl 15257 17th Liverpool Regt KIA 30.7.16.
COOK Reginald "DCM,MM" S/Sjt 508344 RAMC
COOK Richard William MM Sjt 14329 Machine Gun Corps
COOK Robert MM Sjt 67312 RHA
COOK Simon H. MM Cpl 15664 6th Yorkshire Regt
COOK Sydney MM L/Cpl 9/14046 Leicestershire Regt
COOK Sydney W. MM Pte M2/105187 Army Service Corps
COOK T. MM Cpl 50682 9 Bde 28 Bde RFA
COOK Thomas MM Sjt 200834 1st London Regt
COOK Thomas MM Pte 26132 253 Coy Machine Gun Corps
COOK Thomas MM Pte 9211 Royal Fusiliers DOW 4.11.16.
COOK Thomas MM L/Cpl 371682 8th London Regt
COOK Thomas MM L/Cpl 46319 Welsh Regt
COOK Thomas "MM+2 Bars,CG(F)" Pte 18/238 18th Durham Light Infantry
COOK Thomas A. MM+Bar Pte 51472 2nd Lincolnshire Regt
COOK Thomas E. MM Cpl 151195 Royal Engineers
COOK Thomas M. MM Pte M2/119995 Army Service Corps
COOK Walter Bertram MM Cpl R/10222 King's Royal Rifle Corps
COOK William MM Pte 45039 1st Royal Inniskilling Fusiliers
COOK William MM L/Cpl 350850 6th Durham Light Infantry
COOK William MM Cpl 8283 1st Devonshire Regt
COOK William MM Pte 51369 16th Cheshire Regt
COOK William MM Pte 202648 1st London Regt
COOK William MM Pte 251682 3rd London Regt
COOK William MM Cpl 855 Northumberland Fusiliers KIA 8.8.18.
COOK William MM L/Sjt 25882 Shropshire Light Infantry
COOK William MM+Bar Cpl 10233 4th Worcestershire Regt
COOK William D. MM Sjt 8843 2nd Oxf & Bucks Light Infantry
COOK William Frank MM L/Cpl 42895 2nd South Staffordshire Regt
COOK William Frederick MM Pte 8510 1st East Kent Regt
COOK William H. MM Pte 15022 8th Border Regt
COOK William H. MM Spr 50280 21 Div Sig Coy Royal Engineers KIA 19.7.17
COOK William H. MM Sjt 31462 RGA
COOK William J. MM L/Cpl 74064 RAMC
COOK William R. "MM,MID" CQMS 9666 2nd South Wales Borderers
COOK William Walter MM Cpl 24283 10th Royal West Kent Regt
COOKE Albert MM Pte 11905 15th Royal Irish Rifles
COOKE Albert H. MM L/Cpl 39340 2/4th Yorkshire Light Infantry
COOKE Alex MM Pte 27878 Royal Inniskilling Fusiliers
COOKE Alfred MM L/Cpl 230204 10th Shropshire Light Infantry KIA 23.9.18.
COOKE Alfred S. MM Gnr 845266 RFA
COOKE Arthur E. MM Pte 511988 14th London Regt
COOKE Arthur Thomas MM L/Cpl 10058 11th Royal Warwickshire Regt KIA 14.11.16.
COOKE Charles "MM,MID" Pte 15411 9th Norfolk Regt
COOKE Charlie MM Bdr 96486 RFA
COOKE Courtney R. MM Gnr 40246 Tank Corps
COOKE David MM Pte 204541 Hampshire Regt
COOKE Edward MM L/Cpl 41637 1st King's Own Scottish Borderers
COOKE Ernest MM L/Cpl 242222 Yorkshire Light Infantry
COOKE Ernest MM Dvr 88238 RHA
COOKE Ernest A. MM Pte 28603 18th Hussars
COOKE Ernest G. MM Dvr 1594 RFA

COOKE Ernest V. MM Spr 74899 Royal Engineers
COOKE F.A. MM Pte 21349 Shropshire Light Infantry
COOKE Frank H. MM Pte 233132 London Regt
COOKE Fred MM Pte 77433 2nd Durham Light Infantry
COOKE Frederick W. MM Sjt TT/090 Army Veterinary Corps
COOKE Frederick W. MM L/Cpl 149073 Royal Engineers
COOKE George MM Cpl 3927 32nd Bn Machine Gun Corps
COOKE George Arthur MM Sjt 17530 7th Leicestershire Regt
COOKE George H. MM Cpl 15563 4th Coldstream Guards
COOKE George Henry MM L/Cpl 42706 North Staffordshire Regt
COOKE George S. MM Dmr 251723 3rd London Regt
COOKE H. MM Pte 376349 Manchester Regt
COOKE Harold MM Pte 66601 99 Fd Amb RAMC
COOKE Herbert MM Pte 267279 1/6th West Riding Regt
COOKE John Alfred MM Pte 32135 8th York & Lancaster Regt
COOKE Laurence C. MM Pte 29770 Worcestershire Regt
COOKE Levi MM Pte 12598 4th Royal Fusiliers
COOKE Norman MM L/Sjt 28441 7th Shropshire Light Infantry
COOKE Norman MM Pte 6458 Rifle Brigade
COOKE Percival George MM L/Cpl 18608 5th Oxf & Bucks Light Infantry
COOKE Reginald "DCM,MM+Bar" Sjt 5749 9th Rifle Brigade
COOKE Reginald MM Gnr 160212 A/14 Bde RFA
COOKE Robert MM Cpl 29554 6th Royal Warwickshire Regt
COOKE Robert MM L/Cpl 15423 10th Royal Inniskilling Fusiliers KIA 1.7.16.
COOKE Robert H.C. "DCM,MM" Sjt 200161 1/5th Liverpool Regt
COOKE Stanley MM Sjt 15664 1st Grenadier Guards
COOKE Thomas MM+Bar Cpl 34061 7th York & Lancaster Regt
COOKE Thomas MM Bdr 107386 RFA
COOKE Thomas MM Sjt 60790 29 Bde RFA
COOKE William MM Pte 41264 109 Fd Amb RAMC
COOKE William Edward MM Sjt 2646 1/4th Royal Berkshire Regt
COOKE William F. MM Cpl 40035 Northamptonshire Regt
COOKE William H. MM+Bar L/Cpl 27880 Royal Inniskilling Fusiliers
COOKMAN Albert V. MM Pte 200929 4th Yorkshire Light Infantry
COOKMAN Walter Arthur Victor MM Bdr 358526 352 Siege Bty RGA
COOKSEY Alfred P. MM L/Cpl 698208 22nd London Regt
COOKSEY Charles Henry MM Pte 202500 1/8th Worcestershire Regt
COOKSEY Ernest Henry "MM,CdiG)" Pte 36796 1/4th Royal Berkshire Regt
COOKSEY William MM Cpl 60235 RFA
COOKSEY William J. MM Pte 53768 Welsh Regt
COOKSLEY Frederick MM Pte 13086 7th South Lancashire Regt
COOKSON Herbert MM Pte 29781 4th South Lancashire Regt
COOKSON J.E. MM Sjt 200643 North Lancashire Regt
COOKSON John MM Gnr 28255 RFA
COOKSON John R. MM Bdr L/678 73 Bty 5 Bde RFA
COOKSON Robert MM Cpl 1334 1st Lancashire Fusiliers
COOKSON Thomas MM Spr 207491 Royal Engineers
COOKSON Walter Stanley MM Spr 554415 510 Fd Coy Royal Engineers
COOLE John T. MM Pte 63579 11 Fd Amb RAMC
COOLE Stanley MM Sjt 276782 140 Hy Bty RGA
COOLEY Albert MM Sjt 6822 2nd Oxf & Bucks Light Infantry
COOLEY Charles Edward MM Pte 242929 1/5th North Lancashire Regt
COOLEY Frank H. MM Pte 322802 6th London Regt
COOLEY John MM Pte 18079 1/4th Royal Lancaster Regt KIA 20.9.17.
COOLEY Joshua J. MM Sjt 6079 5 Fd Amb RAMC
COOLEY William A. MM L/Cpl 14768 10th Royal Fusiliers
COOLING Charles Frederick MM Gnr 800299 B/230 Bde RFA
COOLING Frank MM Spr 30898 3 Div Sig Coy Royal Engineers
COOLING Lewis MM Pte R/9078 13th King's Royal Rifle Corps
COOLING Stanley MM Dvr 780728 B/75 Bde RFA
COOLMAN Cyril MM Dvr 616521 20 Bde RHA
COOMBE James H. MM Cpl 322110 RGA
COOMBE Joseph C. MM Gnr 624370 HAC
COOMBER Alfred MM L/Cpl 569 8th Royal Fusiliers
COOMBER Arthur MM Sjt 716 7th East Surrey Regt
COOMBER Douglas G. MM Pte 104301 101 Fd Amb RAMC
COOMBER George MM Sjt 281164 RGA
COOMBER Herbert E. "DCM,MM" Pnr 316399 57 Div Sig Coy Royal Engineers
COOMBER William Divall "MM,MID" Sjt 1515 7th Royal West Kent Regt KIA 13.7.16.
COOMBES Albert MM Pte 7200 1st Coldstream Guards
COOMBES Alfred L. MM Drummer 10703 1st Middlesex Regt
COOMBES Arthur C. MM Sjt 10982 5th Oxf & Bucks Light Infantry
COOMBES C.H. MM Pte 241295 Cheshire Regt att MGC.
COOMBES E. MM Cpl 2556 South Lancashire Regt
COOMBES E.H. MM L/Sjt 17564 1st Dorsetshire Regt
COOMBES George MM CSM 29114 Royal Inniskilling Fusiliers
COOMBES George H. MM Bdr 19205 RFA
COOMBES James MM Sjt 12720 4th Worcestershire Regt
COOMBES James MM Pte 10212 Devonshire Regt
COOMBES John U. MM Pte 265157 1/8th Notts & Derby Regt
COOMBES Joseph MM Cpl 19323 Machine Gun Corps
COOMBES Percy G. MM Pte 10836 2nd Hampshire Regt
COOMBES Rowland MM Cpl 6/17499 South Wales Borderers
COOMBES Terence MM L/Cpl 40763 12th Middlesex Regt KIA 18.10.17.
COOMBES Walter MM Cpl 955365 A/236 Bde RFA
COOMBES William MM Pte 9460 1st Somerset Light Infantry
COOMBES William MM Pte 341603 RAMC
COOMBES William R. MM Pte G7/183 (sic) 7th East Surrey Regt
COOMBS Albert MM Sjt 472081 12th London Regt
COOMBS Alfred A. MM Gnr 68658 71 Bty 36 Bde RFA
COOMBS Bertram J. MM Pte 26170 Grenadier Guards
COOMBS Charles MM Cpl 125832 X/35 Med TM Bty RFA
COOMBS Francis John MM Sjt 2055 3rd Hussars
COOMBS Frank T. MM Pte 7539 2nd Wiltshire Regt
COOMBS Frederick J. MM Pte 36380 7th Wiltshire Regt
COOMBS Harry D. MM Gnr L/36223 RFA
COOMBS Harry J. MM L/Cpl 200651 Gloucestershire Regt
COOMBS Henry G. MM Sjt 201251 Somerset Light Infantry
COOMBS John MM L/Cpl PS/1558 16th Middlesex Regt
COOMBS John T. MM Pte 12217 9th Durham Light Infantry
COOMBS Stephen MM Pte 25925 Machine Gun Corps
COOMBS William MM Pte 16399 Hampshire Regt
COOMBS William MM Pte 63740 9th Yorkshire Light Infantry
COOMBS William MM Cpl 37217 RFA
COOMBS William H. MM Pte 80763 1(North Midland)Fd Amb RAMC
COOMBS William W. MM Cpl 17053 20th Manchester Regt
COOMES Frank C. MM Pte 16224 East Surrey Regt
COOMES G. MM Cpl 67135 126 Fd Coy Royal Engineers
COONAN Thomas MM Pte 18123 3rd Grenadier Guards KIA 7.5.18.
COONEY Jeremiah MM Pte 9916 2nd Leinster Regt
COONEY M. MM L/Cpl 11216 West Riding Regt
COONEY Michael MM Pte 26734 Royal Dublin Fusiliers
COOPE Thomas "MM,MID" Sjt 308007 314 Road Constr Coy Royal Engineers
COOPER A.S. MM Pte 310046 RAMC
COOPER Albert MM Sjt 20059 D/256 Bde RFA
COOPER Albert MM Pte 42082 8th Manchester Regt
COOPER Albert MM Pte 17684 2nd South Lancashire Regt
COOPER Albert "DCM,MM+Bar" CSM 22355 2nd South Wales Borderers
COOPER Albert C. MM Cpl 11123 5th Royal Berkshire Regt
COOPER Albert E. MM Pte 242310 5th Lincolnshire Regt
COOPER Alexander MM Cpl 53602 1st Royal Scots Fusiliers
COOPER Alfred MM Sjt 241776 1/4th Leicestershire Regt DOW 6.10.18.
COOPER Alfred MM Gnr 16136 C/83 Bde RFA
COOPER Alfred G. MM Pte 14338 7th Wiltshire Regt
COOPER Alfred G. MM Sjt 201228 1/4th Oxf & Bucks Light Infantry
COOPER Alfred J. MM+Bar Pte 6792 10th Royal West Surrey Regt
COOPER Alfred O. MM L/Cpl 880060 34th London Regt
COOPER Alfred T. MM Cpl 15032 1st Dorsetshire Regt
COOPER Alfred W. MM Pnr 186096 Royal Engineers
COOPER Allan M. MM Sjt 23905 5th Cameron Highlanders
COOPER Andrew MM Dvr 631579 255 Bde RFA
COOPER Anthony MM Cpl 6964 1st North Staffordshire Regt DOW 21.3.18.
COOPER Archibald MM L/Sjt 218 7th Royal Sussex Regt
COOPER Arthur A. MM Pte 20896 Royal Warwickshire Regt
COOPER Arthur B. MM Sjt 46078 2nd Notts & Derby Regt
COOPER Arthur E. MM Pte 20098 1st Shropshire Light Infantry
COOPER Arthur E. MM L/Cpl 51223 Welsh Regt
COOPER Arthur W. MM Pte G/8939 13th Royal Fusiliers
COOPER Benjamin MM Pte 1/11112 1st South Wales Borderers
COOPER Bert MM Pte M2/097847 Army Service Corps
COOPER C.B. MM Cpl 39390 106 Bde RFA
COOPER Cecil A. MM Pte 80401 RAMC
COOPER Charles MM Pte 23898 2nd York & Lancaster Regt
COOPER Charles MM Sjt Farrier 925636 B/290 Bde RFA

COOPER Charles C. MM Spr 34885 Royal Engineers
COOPER Charles Cecil MM Pte 40627 4th Bedfordshire Regt KIA 22.12.17.
COOPER Charles E. MM Cpl 35087 68 Fd Coy Royal Engineers
COOPER Charles Edward MM Pte 15036 15th Hampshire Regt KIA 1.7.18.
COOPER Charles Frost MM L/Cpl 200644 1/4th Royal Lancaster Regt
COOPER Charles Henry "MM,MSM" 2nd Cpl 43553 Royal Engineers
COOPER Charles J. MM Pte 103431 253 Coy Machine Gun Corps
COOPER Charles J.H. MM Sjt 59108 105 Fd Coy Royal Engineers
COOPER Charles N. MM Cpl 265497 5th Gloucestershire Regt
COOPER Charles Thorpe MM Sjt 46559 122 Coy Machine Gun Corps KIA 21.9.17.
COOPER Charles W. MM L/Cpl 38639 5th Royal Berkshire Regt
COOPER Charles W. MM Sjt 915265 D/251 Bde RFA
COOPER Charley MM QMS 1403 Royal Engineers
COOPER Claude Huntley MM Sjt 723 9th Royal Fusiliers Died(drowned)17.1.18.
COOPER Edward MM Sjt 12837 4th Worcestershire Regt DOW 11.1.18.
COOPER Edward G. MM Sjt 36266 RGA
COOPER Edward N. MM Pte 307035 Royal Warwickshire Regt
COOPER Edward R. MM+Bar Sjt M1/07776 1 Base MT Depot. Army Service Corps
COOPER Edward W. MM Gnr 122254 RGA
COOPER Ellis MM L/Cpl 9914 2nd East Lancashire Regt
COOPER Ernest MM Sjt 3/6869 7th East Yorkshire Regt
COOPER Ernest MM Pte 36214 5th Leicestershire Regt
COOPER Ernest MM Pte 591304 18th London Regt
COOPER Ernest MM L/Cpl 5574 Middlesex Regt
COOPER Ernest MM Pte 59589 16th Notts & Derby Regt DOW 9.1.17.
COOPER Ernest D. MM Pte 28540 1st East Surrey Regt
COOPER Ernest E. MM Sjt 28962 41st Bn Machine Gun Corps
COOPER Ernest Gilbert MM Pte 376457 2nd Royal Scots DOW 23.5.18.
COOPER Ernest H. MM Pte 11200 11th Hampshire Regt
COOPER Ernest H. MM Gnr L/26079 RFA
COOPER F. MM Cpl 76509 14th Bn Tank Corps
COOPER Francis G. MM Pte 652402 21st London Regt
COOPER Francis J. MM Pte 8055 8th West Yorkshire Regt
COOPER Francis S. MM Sjt 14614 Yorkshire Regt
COOPER Francis W. MM Cpl 170267 89 Fd Coy Royal Engineers
COOPER Frank MM Pte 21950 Grenadier Guards
COOPER Frank MM Sjt 35505 22nd Northumberland Fusiliers KIA 11.9.17.
COOPER Frank G. MM Gnr 138528 RGA
COOPER Frank P. MM Gnr 302040 Tank Corps
COOPER Frank W. MM Sjt 554071 511 Fd Coy Royal Engineers
COOPER Fred W. MM Pte 202749 4th Hampshire Regt
COOPER Frederick MM Dvr 50166 RFA
COOPER Frederick Alfred MM Pte 5095 13th Royal Sussex Regt
COOPER Frederick O. MM+Bar Sjt 701438 23rd London Regt
COOPER Frederick William Harvey MM L/Sjt G/8072 Royal West Kent Regt KIA 9.3.18.
COOPER Geoffrey J. MM L/Cpl 90307 5th Liverpool Regt
COOPER Geoffrey S. MM Pte 24936 11th Hussars
COOPER George MM S/Sjt Armourer T/767 Army Ordnance Corps
COOPER George MM L/Cpl 61033 8th West Yorkshire Regt
COOPER George MM Cpl 266822 1/6th Gordon Highlanders
COOPER George MM Pte 14561 Labour Corps
COOPER George MM Pte 242009 East Lancashire Regt
COOPER George MM Pte 20355 9th Worcestershire Regt
COOPER George MM Cpl 48187 RFA
COOPER George A. MM Pte 1399 Durham Light Infantry
COOPER George Augustus MM Pte 6156 1st Royal West Surrey Regt Died 7.11.18.
COOPER George E. MM Dvr 181066 RFA
COOPER George E. MM L/Cpl 42694 Highland Light Infantry
COOPER George R. MM+Bar Sjt 24466 121 Heavy Bty RGA
COOPER George R.J. MM Pte 265160 9th Middlesex Regt
COOPER George W. MM L/Cpl R/15223 King's Royal Rifle Corps
COOPER George W. MM Pte 108386 25th Liverpool Regt
COOPER George W. MM Bdr 772022 D/250 Bde RFA
COOPER George William MM Pte 47878 37 Fd Amb RAMC Died 4.10.16.
COOPER H.W. MM Sjt 321521 1/1st Northumberland Yeo
COOPER Harold MM Pte 242513 1st Royal Warwickshire Regt
COOPER Harold MM Sjt 325639 1/1st Cambridgeshire Regt
COOPER Harold C. MM Pte 1995 1/9th Liverpool Regt
COOPER Harold E. MM Pte 49009 2nd Devonshire Regt
COOPER Harry MM Pte 9971 25th Bn Machine Gun Corps
COOPER Harry MM Cpl 8993 1st Devonshire Regt
COOPER Harry G. MM Pte 202619 Seaforth Highlanders
COOPER Henry MM L/Cpl 54220 Durham Light Infantry
COOPER Henry E. "MM,MID" CSM 5082 Royal Engineers
COOPER Herbert MM Cpl 294699 RGA
COOPER Herbert J. MM Cpl 22775 5 Fd Coy Royal Engineers
COOPER Herbert W. MM Pte 2332 11th Manchester Regt
COOPER Horace MM Sjt 9/26643 9th Royal Lancaster Regt
COOPER Howard MM Pte 200884 5th Notts & Derby Regt
COOPER Hubert MM Pte 12057 1/5th Royal Welsh Fusiliers
COOPER Isaac J. MM Cpl 82681 RFA
COOPER Israel MM Bdr 40497 2 Bde RFA
COOPER J. MM Pte 240235 Middlesex Regt
COOPER J. MM Pte 5494 10th Lancashire Fusiliers
COOPER James MM Pte 29756 10th Shropshire Light Infantry
COOPER James "DCM,MM" Pte 18799 1st Border Regt
COOPER James MM Spr 79353 Royal Engineers
COOPER James MM Sjt M/31319 59 Div MT Coy Army Service Corps
COOPER James MM Dvr 21066 8 Bde RFA
COOPER James MM Sjt 24962 RGA
COOPER James A. MM Pte 3/12165 9th Durham Light Infantry
COOPER James D. MM Dmr 250629 3rd London Regt
COOPER James Ernest MM Pte 18143 9th Scottish Rifles KIA 14.2.17.
COOPER James N. MM L/Cpl 31105 1st King's Own Scottish Borderers
COOPER James R. MM Sjt S4/056806 Army Service Corps
COOPER John MM Pte 47108 110 Fd Amb RAMC
COOPER John MM Pte 8794 2nd Lincolnshire Regt KIA 12.4.18.
COOPER John MM Gnr 776708 RFA
COOPER John MM Sjt 175541 175 Tunnelling Coy Royal Engineers
COOPER John MM Pte 8682 1st Coldstream Guards
COOPER John MM Sjt C/9198 King's Royal Rifle Corps
COOPER John MM Pte 61603 RAMC
COOPER John MM Bdr 15539 RGA
COOPER John MM Sjt 1354 Royal Engineers
COOPER John MM Dvr 420051 Royal Engineers
COOPER John A. MM Gnr 677099 RFA
COOPER John Charles MM L/Cpl 9/14904 7th Lincolnshire Regt KIA 3.11.16.
COOPER John E.T. MM Cpl 21148 9th Lancashire Fusiliers
COOPER John H. MM L/Cpl 9831 12th Manchester Regt
COOPER John H. MM Pte 240790 1/5th Devonshire Regt
COOPER John Joseph MM Sjt 250499 1/6th Durham Light Infantry
COOPER John R. MM Cpl 42511 2nd South Staffordshire Regt
COOPER John R. MM Pte 22/949 Durham Light Infantry
COOPER John W. "MM,MID" Cpl 60955 RFA
COOPER John W. MM Gnr 3812 RFA
COOPER John William MM Pte 42858 5th Yorkshire Light Infantry KIA 27.3.18.
COOPER John William MM Pte 1512 1/7th West Yorkshire Regt DOW 27.9.16.
COOPER Joseph MM Sjt 5/53956 South Wales Borderers
COOPER Joseph MM Sjt 137869 Royal Engineers
COOPER Joseph G. MM Gnr 801484 RFA
COOPER Joseph K. MM Cpl 11204 RFA
COOPER Joseph R. MM Cpl 18649 1st Suffolk Regt
COOPER Joseph W. "DCM,MM" Cpl 10347 13th Middlesex Regt
COOPER Lancelot G. MM Pte 20489 South Staffordshire Regt
COOPER Leonard MM Pte 70797 9th Notts & Derby Regt
COOPER Leslie MM L/Cpl 481 Royal Fusiliers
COOPER Lindsay MM Pte M2/131616 Army Service Corps att 87 Fd Amb RAMC.
COOPER Maurice F. MM Pte 80759 RAMC
COOPER Michael MM Pte 6/2273 6th Royal Irish Regt DOW 14.8.17.
COOPER Owen MM Pte 23509 1/5th York & Lancaster Regt
COOPER Percy MM Dvr 83609 RFA
COOPER Percy O. MM Pte 306355 7th Royal Warwickshire Regt
COOPER Reginald H. MM Cpl 45845 18 Div Sig Coy Royal Engineers
COOPER Reginald Joseph MM L/Cpl 403564 1/2nd(West Riding)Fd Amb RAMC KIA 28.4.18.
COOPER Richard MM Sjt 33424 8th Devonshire Regt
COOPER Richard MM Pte 437470 1st(South Midland)Fd Amb RAMC

COOPER Robert MM Pte 20423 2nd York & Lancaster Regt KIA 21.3.18.
COOPER Robert MM+Bar Sjt 12359 1st East Lancashire Regt
COOPER Robert MM CSM 4944 Hampshire Regt
COOPER Robert William MM Pnr 123746 9 Light Rly Foreway Coy Royal Engineers
COOPER Robert William MM Pte 51679 Notts & Derby Regt
COOPER Samuel MM Pte 41978 3rd Worcestershire Regt DOW 12.11.18.
COOPER Samuel MM Gnr Sig 103822 76 Siege Bty RGA
COOPER Sidney MM Pte 14557 Machine Gun Corps
COOPER Sidney Arthur MM Sjt 34442 1st Wiltshire Regt
COOPER Stanley MM Pte 45554 37 Fd Amb RAMC
COOPER Sylvanus MM Pte 17515 19th Lancashire Fusiliers
COOPER T.W. MM Pte 630739 London Regt
COOPER Thomas MM Cpl 18642 9th Royal Inniskilling Fusiliers
COOPER Thomas MM Pte 235677 2nd East Lancashire Regt
COOPER Thomas MM L/Cpl 2604 York & Lancaster Regt
COOPER Thomas MM Pte 8781 1st Liverpool Regt
COOPER Thomas MM L/Cpl 10574 2nd Worcestershire Regt
COOPER Thomas MM Cpl 12114 12th Hampshire Regt
COOPER Thomas MM Cpl 305296 1/8th Liverpool Regt KIA 20.9.17.
COOPER Thomas A. MM Pte B/23161 26th Royal Fusiliers
COOPER Thomas Benjamin "MC+Bar,MM(1031 Sjt 20th Lond),MID" Capt 1/4th London Regt
COOPER Thomas C.L. MM Pte 107292 33rd Bn Machine Gun Corps
COOPER Thomas R. MM Sjt 652527 21st London Regt
COOPER Tom MM Sjt 39102 32 Coy Machine Gun Corps
COOPER Victor J. MM Spr 254299 Royal Engineers
COOPER Victor Stanley MM Gnr 17533 B/177 Bde RFA
COOPER Wallace C. "MM,MID" Sjt 43491 Royal Engineers
COOPER Walter J. MM L/Cpl 16663 Lincolnshire Regt
COOPER Walter John MM 2nd Cpl 65613 105 Fd Coy Royal Engineers
COOPER Wilfred T. MM Pte 86280 10th Royal Fusiliers
COOPER William MM Pte 12232 10th Worcestershire Regt KIA 10.4.18.
COOPER William MM Pte 38361 12th Northumberland Fusiliers KIA 13.4.17.
COOPER William MM Sjt 306515 West Riding Regt
COOPER William MM+Bar Pte 18245 9th Norfolk Regt
COOPER William MM Pte 351605 1/9th Royal Scots KIA 20.9.17.
COOPER William MM Pte 14554 7th Shropshire Light Infantry
COOPER William A. MM L/Cpl 4537 Royal West Surrey Regt
COOPER William A. MM Cpl 283818 2nd London Regt
COOPER William A.R. MM Pte M2/1329 4 Div Train Army Service Corps
COOPER William C. MM Pte 21006 1st Dorsetshire Regt
COOPER William Clifford MM Sjt 303008 2/7th West Yorkshire Regt
COOPER William H. MM Cpl 439905 Royal Engineers
COOPER William Henry MM Bdr 41917 24 Bty 38 Bde RFA KIA 28.7.17.
COOPER William J. MM L/Cpl 15087 1st Royal Fusiliers
COOPER William James MM L/Cpl 17421 6th Northamptonshire Regt DOW 14.7.16.
COOPER William John MM Sjt 14145 11th Royal Fusiliers KIA 7.8.18.
COOPER William Salisbury "DCM,MM" Sjt 19583 4th Grenadier Guards Died 14.5.18.
COOPER William T.F. MM Sjt 12516 2nd West Riding Regt
COOPEY Albert MM Sjt 240080 1/5th Gloucestershire Regt KIA 15.6.18.
COOPLAND Arthur MM Pte 1608 West Yorkshire Regt
COOPS John S. MM Sjt 25213 South Wales Borderers
COOTES Frederick MM Pte 29695 Bedfordshire Regt
COPE Albert MM Cpl 10676 6th Leicestershire Regt
COPE Benjamin MM Sjt 9624 1st Northamptonshire Regt
COPE Benjamin Joseph Thomas MM Cpl 1642 14th Royal Warwickshire Regt
COPE Bertie MM Sjt 204828 8th Somerset Light Infantry KIA 25.8.18.
COPE C.S. MM Pte 65202 10th Royal Fusiliers
COPE Cecil MM Dvr 60983 154 Fd Coy Royal Engineers
COPE Charles MM Cpl WR/125166 10 Rly Const Coy Royal Engineers
COPE Charles MM Pte 265982 Cheshire Regt
COPE Charles Edward MM Cpl 243108 7th Norfolk Regt DOW 22.10.18.
COPE Charles K. "MM,MID" BSM 710009 B/211 Bde RFA
COPE Cheverton Stanley MM L/Cpl 2814 Notts & Derby Regt
COPE Edwin John MM L/Cpl 491289 13th London Regt DOW 11.10.18.
COPE Frederick MM L/Cpl 200372 1/4th Royal Welsh Fusiliers
COPE Harry MM Cpl 3167 1/7th Worcestershire Regt
COPE Harry MM L/Cpl 26603 Shropshire Light Infantry
COPE John MM+Bar Sjt 18644 1st King's Own Scottish Borderers
COPE John Henry MM L/Cpl 32618 Leicestershire Regt
COPE John William MM Pte 10977 2nd Royal Fusiliers
COPE Robert MM Pte 52034 West Yorkshire Regt
COPE Walter MM Cpl 15702 2nd Royal Scots Fusiliers
COPELAND Frederick C. MM Sjt 371149 164 Siege Bty RGA
COPELAND George MM Pte M2/021105 Army Service Corps
COPELAND George MM Pte 5691 Royal Munster Fusiliers
COPELAND Herbert MM Sjt 12151 11th West Yorkshire Regt
COPELAND James A. MM Pte 291245 1/7th Cheshire Regt
COPELAND John MM Pte 25830 Scottish Rifles
COPELAND William MM Pte 3627 Highland Light Infantry
COPELAND William Hudson MM Dvr 760594 317 Bde RFA
COPEMAN Frederick MM L/Cpl 263009 6th West Riding Regt
COPEMAN Frederick MM Cpl 97648 47 Bty 41 Bde RFA
COPESTAKE Arthur MM Sjt 113325 RGA
COPESTAKE Henry MM Pte 1806 2nd Lincolnshire Regt Died 12.10.18.
COPESTAKE Samuel MM Sjt 2667 1/5th North Staffordshire Regt
COPLAND James MM Cpl 33598 13th East Lancashire Regt
COPLEY Arthur MM Pte 52204 Liverpool Regt
COPLEY Cecil A. MM Cpl 15935 Machine Gun Corps
COPLEY Clarence MM Pnr 107141 229 Fd Coy Royal Engineers KIA 24.11.17.
COPLEY E. MM Pte 4676 London Regt
COPLEY George MM Pte 307870 West Riding Regt
COPLEY George F. MM L/Cpl 38192 9th Yorkshire Regt
COPLEY George W. MM Sjt 70819 10th Notts & Derby Regt
COPLEY Joseph W. MM Sjt 35508 C/108 Bde RFA
COPOC Hugh MM Pte 12378 Liverpool Regt
COPP Reginald John MM Cpl 71453 Machine Gun Corps
COPPACK Arthur MM L/Cpl 350018 9th Liverpool Regt
COPPARD Ernest F. MM L/Cpl 510616 14th London Regt
COPPARD George A. MM Cpl 19012 Machine Gun Corps
COPPARD Robert MM Pte 2971 1st Royal West Kent Regt
COPPELL Thomas J. MM Sjt C/3265 King's Royal Rifle Corps
COPPER George W. MM Pte 14613 1st East Surrey Regt
COPPER Henry V. MM Sjt 14430 Hampshire Regt
COPPIN Arthur MM+Bar Sjt 240098 Lincolnshire Regt
COPPIN Charles George MM Pte 372835 8th London Regt KIA 23.3.18.
COPPING Arthur Milton MM L/Sjt 1325 12th London Regt KIA 18.9.16.
COPPING Henry Ezekiel MM Gnr Shoeing Smith 107905 D/119 Bde RFA
COPPINGER Herbert Charles MM Pte 49536 160 Coy Machine Gun Corps
COPPLESTONE E.F. MM Pnr 233479 Signal Service Royal Engineers
COPPOCK Albert E. MM+Bar L/Cpl 809 17th Royal Fusiliers
COPPOCK Arthur MM Sjt 1811 1/1st Oxfordshire Yeomanry
COPPOCK Evan MM Cpl 235260 South Staffordshire Regt
COPPOCK James MM Sjt 7438 1st Northamptonshire Regt
COPPS George A. MM+Bar Sjt 721073 1/24th London Regt
COPSEY Archibald MM Bdr 45538 RFA
COPSEY Wallace MM Sjt 200325 2nd Bn Tank Corps
COQUARD Henry MM L/Cpl 9679 11th Lancashire Fusiliers
CORAM William MM Pte 1894 1/6th North Staffordshire Regt Died 29.10.18.
CORAN Wilfred J. MM Pte 29806 8th Somerset Light Infantry
CORBETT Albert MM Pte 11119 1/4th Gordon Highlanders
CORBETT Alexander MM L/Cpl 10447 1st Gordon Highlanders
CORBETT Archibald MM Pte 240244 Worcestershire Regt
CORBETT Charles "DCM,MM" L/Cpl 10248 11th Royal Scots
CORBETT Charles W. MM Bdr 5252 RFA
CORBETT Edward C. MM CQMS 2221 1/8th Worcestershire Regt
CORBETT Ernest J.F. MM L/Cpl 9837 2nd Royal Sussex Regt
CORBETT George Ingle MM L/Sjt 15231 10th Royal Warwickshire Regt
CORBETT Harold MM+Bar L/Cpl 241908 2/4th York & Lancaster Regt
CORBETT Harry MM Pte 6/17433 6th South Wales Borderers
CORBETT John MM Sjt 43988 2nd Essex Regt

CORBETT John "DCM,MM" Sjt 4/8376 10th Arg & Suth Highlanders
CORBETT John Benjamin MM Sjt 8121 1st Worcestershire Regt
CORBETT Joseph Henry MM 2nd Cpl 507 528 Fd Coy Royal Engineers DOW 7.8.16.
CORBETT Robert K. MM Pte 8271 6th Dragoon Guards
CORBETT Robert W. MM+Bar Sjt 10977 6th Yorkshire Regt
CORBETT William MM Gnr 760756 RFA
CORBETT William MM Pte 15424 Shropshire Light Infantry
CORBETT William H. "MM,MID" RQMS 2403 1st Coldstream Guards
CORBETT William J. "DCM,MM" Sjt 9795 1st Gloucestershire Regt
CORBIN Arthur MM Pte 17607 6th Royal West Kent Regt KIA 21.9.18.
CORBIN Thomas F. MM Pte 022010 Army Ordnance Corps
CORBISHLEY John MM Sjt 31658 RAMC
CORBISHLEY Thomas MM Pte M2/097930 153 Siege Bty RGA Army Service Corps Died 2.11.18.
CORBY Ernest C. MM Pte 49276 Machine Gun Corps
CORBY James MM Gnr 92352 Tank Corps
CORBYN William G. MM Pte 5577 13th Hussars
CORCORAN John MM Pte 54430 2nd Welsh Regt
CORCORAN John MM Pte 2175 4th Grenadier Guards
CORCORAN Martin MM Pte 251954 1/6th Arg & Suth Highlanders
CORCORAN Michael MM Pte 43333 16th Middlesex Regt KIA 31.5.17.
CORCORAN Patrick MM Pte 591521 1/18th London Regt
CORCORAN Patrick MM Cpl 1/10993 1st South Wales Borderers
CORCORAN Thomas MM Gnr W/2507 38 TM Bty RFA
CORCORAN William MM Pte 9/5466 Royal Munster Fusiliers
CORCORAN William MM Spr 79690 Royal Engineers
CORDELL Ernest Walter MM Cpl 5391 8th East Surrey Regt KIA 21.1.18.
CORDELL John C. MM Sjt 4/7325 1st Bedfordshire Regt
CORDEN Alfred MM Sjt 57506 26th Royal Welsh Fusiliers
CORDER Charles MM Cpl M2/130550 402 Coy Army Service Corps
CORDING Charles A. MM Gnr 32198 40 Bde RFA
CORDING Henry "MM,MID" Sjt 12497 2nd Middlesex Regt DOW 17.7.16.
CORDING Lewis Edmund "MC,MM(9944 Sjt),MID" 2Lt 1st Rifle Brigade
CORDINGLEY Albert Richard MM Sjt 10705 1st Royal Lancaster Regt
CORDINGLEY Arthur MM Pte 200447 West Riding Regt
CORDINGLEY Dennis MM Gnr 156109 261 Siege Bty RGA
CORDINGLEY Thomas MM Pte 10741 6th Royal West Kent Regt
CORDIS Stanley Victor "MM,MID,OStG(R)" Sjt 45068 1/1st Surrey Yeomanry
CORDNER Henry MM L/Bdr 24711 135 Bty 32 Bde RFA
CORDUKES David S. MM Pte 62844 92 Fd Amb RAMC
CORDWELL Harry MM Sjt 20471 2nd Border Regt
CORDY Frederick J. MM Cpl 19567 7th Norfolk Regt
CORFE Samuel MM Pte 345282 24th Royal Welsh Fusiliers DOW 11.9.18.
CORFIELD Harold MM Gnr 85564 RFA
CORK Robert J. MM Pte 17435 2nd Coldstream Guards
CORK William MM Sjt 9181 32nd Bn Machine Gun Corps Died 31.10.18.
CORK William MM Pte Y/570 13th King's Royal Rifle Corps "KIA 2.11.18,"
CORK William H. MM Pte 40511 17th Royal Scots
CORKE Cecil Arthur MM L/Cpl 1249 1/5th West Yorkshire Regt
CORKE George MM Dvr 238458 C/232 Bde RFA
CORKE Percy MM 2nd Cpl 550369 Royal Engineers
CORKER Fred MM Pte 14830 1st Cheshire Regt
CORKER William Appleton MM Spr 127635 'F' Corps Sig Coy Royal Engineers
CORKETT James MM Pte 17674 2nd Bedfordshire Regt
CORKHILL Frederick "MM,MSM" Cpl CMT/2217 1 Div MT Coy Army Service Corps
CORKHILL William G. MM Sjt 14870 2nd Yorkshire Regt
CORKILL Norman L. MM Sjt 241259 2/6th Liverpool Regt
CORKILL Thomas S. MM Sjt 685756 B/277 Bde RFA KIA 5.4.18.
CORKILL Wilfred MM L/Cpl 22968 10th Royal West Surrey Regt
CORKIN Elsdon "MM,MM(F)" Pte 265906 1/6th Northumberland Fusiliers Died 27.5.18.
CORKIN Thomas MM L/Cpl 30740 Durham Light Infantry
CORKISH Ernest "MM,CG(B)" Sjt 72174 RGA
CORKISH Sidney MM Dvr 80961 D/64 Bde RFA
CORLESS A. MM Pte 29803 South Lancashire Regt
CORLESS J. MM Cpl 330498 Liverpool Regt
CORLESS John MM Sjt 18739 12 Coy Machine Gun Corps DOW 15.5.17.
CORLESS Joseph MM Cpl 12937 11th Liverpool Regt KIA 21.3.18.
CORLESS Robert E. MM Sjt 756058 A/251 Bde RFA
CORLETT Alfred J. MM Spr 282329 Royal Engineers
CORLETT Edward MM Cpl 51810 13th Liverpool Regt KIA 30.4.18.
CORLETT George MM Pte 316236 137 Fd Amb RAMC
CORLETT William John MM Sjt 7804 2nd Scots Guards
CORLEY Harry C. MM Cpl 470901 12th London Regt
CORLEY James Alma "MC,MM(50868 Sjt MGC)" 2Lt 2nd att 12th Manchester Regt
CORLISS John MM Pte 7109 2nd Irish Guards
CORMACK Alexander MM L/Cpl 240619 Seaforth Highlanders
CORMACK Andrew MM Sjt 3882 10th Highland Light Infantry
CORMACK George "DCM,MM" Sjt 265820 Seaforth Highlanders
CORMACK George MM Pte 2898 Seaforth Highlanders
CORMACK George MM Pte 40140 Seaforth Highlanders
CORMACK George E. MM Sjt 13868 King's Royal Rifle Corps
CORMACK George S. MM Spr 406271 58 Div Sig Coy Royal Engineers
CORMACK James J. MM L/Cpl 402814 Royal Engineers
CORMACK Robert MM+Bar Pte 43322 8th Royal Highlanders
CORMACK William MM Pte 2340 7th Seaforth Highlanders DOW 24.9.17.
CORMACK William G. MM Spr 849 Royal Engineers
CORMACK William James MM L/Sjt 12181 5th Cameron Highlanders
CORMODE William MM Pte 337255 RAMC
CORNALL Frederick H. MM Pte 22449 14 Fd Amb RAMC
CORNALL Harry MM Sjt 3059 1/8th Liverpool Regt KIA 20.11.17.
CORNELIUS Harry Arthur MM Pte 472987 2/12th London Regt KIA 24.4.18.
CORNELIUS Herbert P. MM+Bar Cpl 17718 1st Somerset Light Infantry
CORNELIUS Joseph H. MM Pte 4016 1st Welsh Guards
CORNELIUS W. MM Cpl 76728 121 Bty 27 Bde RFA
CORNELL Albert E. MM Pte 352958 7th London Regt
CORNELL Arthur William MM Pte 16514 1st Suffolk Regt
CORNELL C. MM Pte 242021 Border Regt
CORNELL Charles W.J. MM Pte 78069 10th Royal Fusiliers
CORNELL Leslie E. MM Spr 1669 405 Fd Coy Royal Engineers
CORNELL William MM Pte 10769 East Kent Regt
CORNER Arthur MM Spr 98035 155 Fd Coy Royal Engineers
CORNER Christopher G. MM Sjt 235566 1/1st Herefordshire Regt
CORNER Robert S. MM Cpl 6471 17 Fd Amb RAMC
CORNES Charles Henry MM Gnr 71380 A/82 Bde RFA
CORNEY Edward C. MM CSM 31275 4th Hampshire Regt
CORNEY Herbert MM Pte 570830 17th London Regt
CORNEY Owen MM Cpl 66855 138 Fd Amb RAMC
CORNEY William MM L/Cpl 16277 York & Lancaster Regt
CORNFIELD Hugh MM L/Cpl 19905 Worcestershire Regt
CORNFIELD Joseph MM Sjt 7758 1st Royal West Surrey Regt
CORNFORD Andrew A. MM Sjt 16934 42nd Bn Machine Gun Corps
CORNFORD Frank MM Sjt 70363 24 Bde RFA
CORNFORD George T. MM Pte 376983 10th Manchester Regt
CORNFORTH George W. MM Bdr 47983 RFA
CORNICK Arthur G. MM Sjt 29068 RGA
CORNISH Albert MM Pte 19338 Suffolk Regt
CORNISH Arthur MM Pte 633749 20th London Regt
CORNISH Charles MM Pte 15982 2nd Oxf & Bucks Light Infantry
CORNISH Charles F. MM Cpl 265479 1/6th Gloucestershire Regt
CORNISH Emanuel Lames MM Pte 49721 18th Welsh Regt KIA 13.4.18.
CORNISH Ernest MM Pte 14488 13th Royal Welsh Fusiliers KIA 22.4.18.
CORNISH Frank MM Pte 45095 Royal Irish Rifles
CORNISH Frank C. MM Sjt 46228 RAMC
CORNISH Frederick C. MM Pte G/4284 2nd Royal Sussex Regt
CORNISH Henry M. MM Cpl 15017 9th Norfolk Regt
CORNISH John Albert MM L/Cpl 6025 23rd Royal Fusiliers KIA 6.3.18.
CORNISH John L. MM Gnr 371035 RGA
CORNISH Samuel A. MM+Bar CSM R/5092 13th King's Royal Rifle Corps
CORNISH William B. MM Pte 62338 9th Royal Fusiliers
CORNS William G. MM Pte 31245 South Lancashire Regt
CORNTHWAITE T. MM Pte 52868 Durham Light Infantry
CORNWALL Albert MM Bdr 59780 41 Bde RFA
CORNWALL Albert H. MM+Bar Sjt 44803 Royal Engineers

CORNWALL Edward "DCM,MM" Sjt 200288 1/5th Liverpool Regt KIA 9.4.18.
CORNWALL Frank MM L/Bdr 13133 C/293 Bde RFA
CORNWALL Peter MM Cpl 330142 8th Royal Scots KIA 21.3.18.
CORNWALLIS Richard H. MM Pte A/203758 18th King's Royal Rifle Corps
CORNWELL Albert A. MM L/Cpl 151287 104th Bn Machine Gun Corps
CORNWELL Alfred MM+Bar Cpl S/20910 1st Rifle Brigade
CORNWELL Cecil Edward MM+Bar L/Cpl 13521 2nd Suffolk Regt KIA 8.10.18.
CORNWELL Enoch MM Sjt 138155 Royal Engineers
CORNWELL Harry "DCM,MM" Sjt 15105 8th Somerset Light Infantry
CORNWELL Horace MM L/Sjt 31803 47th Bn Machine Gun Corps
CORNWELL Percy W. MM Cpl 266197 7th Royal Sussex Regt
CORPE Thomas MM Pte 24184 Notts & Derby Regt
CORPES Robert L. MM Sjt 554088 511 Fd Coy Royal Engineers
CORPS Alfred J. MM Pte 7880 1st Duke of Cornwall's LI
CORPS John Thomas MM Pte 25151 1st Royal Irish Fusiliers KIA 24.8.18.
CORRELL John S. MM+Bar CSM 19856 10th Royal West Kent Regt
CORRIGAN Andrew MM Pte 1739 6th Connaught Rangers
CORRIGAN Bernard MM Pte 4099 1/5th South Lancashire Regt DOW 4.12.17.
CORRIGAN Charles MM Bdr 29607 2 Siege Bty RGA
CORRIGAN Dominick MM L/Cpl 291031 8th Scottish Rifles
CORRIGAN James MM Cpl 6696 1st Cameron Highlanders
CORRIGAN John MM L/Cpl 4042 Royal Irish Regt
CORRIGAN John P. MM Pte 74998 12/13th Northumberland Fusiliers
CORRIGAN P. MM Sjt 49848 23rd Lancashire Fusiliers
CORRY William MM Cpl 8252 29th Bn Machine Gun Corps DOW 29.9.18.
CORSIE John MM Pte 41682 15th Highland Light Infantry KIA 2.10.18.
CORSON A.L. MM Sjt 97613 Royal Flying Corps
CORSON Alexander MM L/Cpl 17718 1st King's Own Scottish Borderers
CORSON J.R. MM Pte 57197 11th Lancashire Fusiliers
CORSON John MM L/Cpl 198214 Royal Engineers
CORSTORPHINE John MM+Bar Cpl 4044 Machine Gun Corps
CORT Fred MM Cpl 16598 19 Coy Machine Gun Corps
CORY John Henry MM L/Cpl P/4609 Military Mounted Police Died 15.2.19.
COSANS William MM Pte 28295 Highland Light Infantry
COSBY S. MM Pte 29306 9th Essex Regt
COSENS Charles Harold MM S/Sjt Farrier 16863 RFA
COSFORD Frederick E.H. MM+Bar L/Cpl 1010 1st Welsh Guards
COSGROVE C.W. MM Air Mech 1 8857 Royal Flying Corps
COSGROVE Claude E. MM Sjt 49357 5 Bde RFA
COSGROVE Frank J. MM Pte 8420 2nd Cameron Highlanders
COSGROVE Henry MM Spr 551824 29 Light Rly Op Coy Royal Engineers
COSGROVE James Henry MM Pte 17161 8th South Lancashire Regt KIA 22.3.18.
COSGROVE John MM Sjt 10807 1st Scottish Rifles
COSGROVE Joseph MM Sjt 34979 1st North Lancashire Regt
COSGROVE William MM Pte 37301 2nd Welsh Regt
COSGROVE William MM+Bar Pte 40299 7/8th Royal Inniskilling Fusiliers
COSHAM Harry E. MM Pte 823 7th Royal Sussex Regt
COSHAM Henry J.V. MM L/Sjt R/3062 King's Royal Rifle Corps
COSNETT John J. "DCM,MM" Sjt 43427 105 Bty 22 Bde RFA
COSS Barrett MM Gnr 736136 RFA
COSSON William F. MM L/Cpl 10008 Middlesex Regt
COSSTICK William T. MM Pte 2872 Royal Sussex Regt
COSSUM Francis H. MM Cpl 69638 6th Bn Tank Corps
COSTA Dominic MM Pte 266029 1/7th Liverpool Regt KIA 14.4.18.
COSTA George T. MM Pte 25470 6th Northamptonshire Regt
COSTA Russell F. MM Cpl 92575 9th Bn Tank Corps
COSTALL George MM Cpl 8458 Royal Welsh Fusiliers
COSTAR John H. MM L/Cpl 494808 Royal Engineers
COSTELLO Arthur MM Sjt 56353 83 Bty 11 Bde RFA
COSTELLO Arthur MM L/Cpl 52545 Cheshire Regt
COSTELLO Daniel MM Pte 27116 1st Royal Scots Fusiliers
COSTELLO James W. "DCM,MM" Pte 10173 2nd Yorkshire Regt
COSTELLO John MM Pte 16676 8th West Riding Regt
COSTELLO Michael MM Dvr 36552 28 Bde RFA
COSTELLO Patrick MM Pte 9917 2nd Devonshire Regt KIA 24.4.18.
COSTELLO Robert MM Pte 5717 2nd Royal Irish Rifles DOW 14.1.18.
COSTELLO Thomas MM Sjt 9349 2nd Royal Scots KIA 26.9.17.
COSTELLO William MM Pte 3582 5th Connaught Rangers
COSTELLO William MM Sjt 4077 2nd Leinster Regt
COSTELLOE Patrick MM Pte R/15209 King's Royal Rifle Corps
COSTER Arthur MM Spr 500566 Royal Engineers
COSTER F.A. MM Pte 51350 Liverpool Regt
COSTER George Thomas MM Sjt 22381 A/124 Bde RFA Died 11.11.18.
COSTER Henry James MM 2nd Cpl 536172 Royal Engineers
COSTER William MM Dvr 606283 RHA
COSTIGAN C.M. MM Pte 449020 10 Fd Amb RAMC
COSTIGAN James MM Pte 18623 Royal Irish Fusiliers
COSTILLOW Edward MM Dvr 75583 72 Bde RFA DOW 17.10.18.
COSTIN Joseph MM L/Sjt 1929 1/1st Monmouthshire Regt
COTCHER Robert MM Sjt 73745 A/28 Bde RFA
COTE Alfred E. MM Sjt 20108 10th Hampshire Regt
COTE C. MM Pte 326256 1/1st Cambridgeshire Regt
COTE James MM Pte 49738 52nd Bn Machine Gun Corps DOW 20.9.18.
COTE John George MM Pte 1978 1/1st Cambridgeshire Regt KIA 22.8.18.
COTGRAVE George MM L/Cpl 6839 2nd Northumberland Fusiliers
COTGROVE W.T. MM Dvr 930096 RFA
COTIER Arthur Henry MM Gnr 58204 A/126 Bde RFA KIA 25.8.18.
COTON Arthur MM+Bar Pte 21392 2nd Grenadier Guards
COTON Fred MM Sjt 57386 A/82 Bde RFA
COTT Henry J. MM Sjt 2105 1/4th London Regt KIA 9.9.16.
COTT Joseph Albert MM Sjt 14104 Royal Lancaster Regt
COTTAGE Christopher MM Cpl 574063 17th London Regt
COTTAGE Frederick J. MM CSM 13282 2nd Suffolk Regt
COTTAM Eric MM Pte 203457 Lancashire Fusiliers
COTTAM George W. MM Sjt 31940 8 Div Ammn Col. RGA
COTTAM J. MM Pte 202424 1/4th South Lancashire Regt
COTTAM John H. MM Pte M2/131802 Army Service Corps
COTTAM Joseph T. "DCM,MM" Spr 428610 123 Fd Coy Royal Engineers
COTTAM Leonard MM Cpl 355946 10th Liverpool Regt
COTTEE Sydney H. MM Pte R/10698 King's Royal Rifle Corps
COTTENDEN George J. MM Cpl 203212 2/4th Royal West Kent Regt
COTTER Denis MM Bdr 23273 RGA
COTTER James MM Pte 1/9653 2nd Royal Munster Fusiliers
COTTER Timothy MM Cpl 4732 2nd Royal Munster Fusiliers att 5 Conn Rgrs.
COTTERELL F.W. MM Sjt 686838 RFA
COTTERELL Francis Arthur MM Pte 235702 1/1st Herefordshire Regt
COTTERELL Joseph MM L/Cpl 8129 2nd Royal Berkshire Regt
COTTERELL Oswald A.J. MM Pte 39678 Worcestershire Regt
COTTERHILL William L. MM L/Cpl 16198 MGC(Motors)
COTTERILL Albert MM Sjt 2/10205 2nd South Wales Borderers
COTTERILL E.W. MM Sjt 12718 8 Bde RFA
COTTERILL Ernest MM Shoeing Smith 3349 1/1st Worcestershire Yeomanry
COTTERILL Francis A. MM Sjt 17209 9th Gloucestershire Regt
COTTERILL George B. MM Sjt 308256 5 Supply Coy Tank Corps
COTTERILL John MM Pte 10170 2nd Worcestershire Regt
COTTERILL Lawrence MM Cpl 83058 Royal Engineers
COTTEY Fred MM Pte 43862 8th Yorkshire Light Infantry
COTTIER Arthur MM Pte 269748 1/7th Liverpool Regt
COTTINGHAM Cyril MM+Bar L/Cpl 39791 Royal West Surrey Regt
COTTINGHAM Isaac MM Cpl 95396 C/106 Bde RFA KIA 16.7.17.
COTTINGHAM William MM Pte 8/10730 2nd Lincolnshire Regt
COTTIS Albert Edward MM Dvr 926 A/281 Bde RFA KIA 12.4.18.
COTTLE H.W. MM Dvr 338 RGA
COTTLE Henry E. MM Drummer 1667 Gloucestershire Regt
COTTLE Robert C. MM Sjt 68962 81 Bty 5 Bde RFA
COTTLE William MM Pte 242089 1st Worcestershire Regt
COTTOM Thomas "DCM,MM" Sjt 6001 1st East Lancashire Regt
COTTON Albert B. MM Pte 11044 11th Hampshire Regt
COTTON Alfred A. MM Pte G/18577 2nd Royal Sussex Regt
COTTON Alfred A. MM Pte 1264 12th East Yorkshire Regt
COTTON Alfred S. MM Sjt M2/104279 Army Service Corps
COTTON Archibald "MM,MID" Sjt 49309 Royal Engineers
COTTON Arthur MM Pte 7083 1st Royal Berkshire Regt
COTTON Arthur Owin MM Pte 493856 1/13th London Regt
COTTON C. MM Sjt 22676 RGA
COTTON Charles H. MM Pte 7158 8th Devonshire Regt

COTTON Elijah MM Pte 28688 Royal Welsh Fusiliers
COTTON Fred MM Sjt 38611 2nd Yorkshire Light Infantry
COTTON Frederick MM Pte M2/182972 Army Service Corps
COTTON George MM Pte 7172 4th Bedfordshire Regt
COTTON George J.F. MM L/Cpl T4/240432 Army Service Corps
COTTON George Sidney MM Cpl G/979 1st East Kent Regt
COTTON Herbert P. MM Cpl 20258 L Corps Sig Coy Royal Engineers
COTTON Joseph MM Pte 41801 1st Royal Scots Fusiliers
COTTON Leonard Elvin MM Spr 43033 75 Fd Coy Royal Engineers DOW 12.9.18.
COTTON P. MM Sjt 17492 Essex Regt
COTTON Richard MM L/Cpl 551347 1/16th London Regt
COTTON Richard C. "DCM,MM" L/Cpl S/9725 8th Seaforth Highlanders
COTTON Sydney A. MM Pte M2/052750 Army Service Corps
COTTON Thomas A. MM Sjt 4842 2 Fd Svy Coy Royal Engineers
COTTON Thomas W. MM Cpl 136 6th Dragoons
COTTON William Alfred MM L/Cpl 15720 7th Northamptonshire Regt
COTTON William C. MM Pte 145530 1/1st Northamptonshire Yeomanry
COTTON William Robert MM L/Cpl 2727 7th East Kent Regt
COTTRELL Bernard E. MM Sjt 14179 11th Royal Welsh Fusiliers
COTTRELL Bert MM Dvr 1202 B/122 Bde RFA
COTTRELL John H. MM Pte 40172 Welsh Regt
COTTRELL John T. MM Dvr 207981 RFA
COTTRELL Samuel MM Dvr T3/024997 Army Service Corps
COTTRILL Herbert MM Cpl 82068 25th Bn 195 Coy Machine Gun Corps
COTTRILL Nephi MM Pte 240500 5th Notts & Derby Regt
COTTRILL William MM Gnr 135047 RFA
COTZIAS J. MM Pte 85621 29th Durham Light Infantry
COUBROUGH George MM+Bar CSM 332142 1/9th Highland Light Infantry
COUBROUGH Harry H. MM Cpl 8578 2nd East Lancashire Regt
COUCH Harold MM L/Cpl 439920 42 Div Sig Coy Royal Engineers KIA 23.10.18.
COUCH James "DCM,MM" Sjt 6305 2nd King's Royal Rifle Corps
COUCH Oscar P. MM+Bar L/Sjt 34 15th Royal Warwickshire Regt
COUCH William J. MM Pte 202155 1/4th Royal Berkshire Regt
COUCHMAN John T. MM Cpl 52254 4th London Regt
COUCIL W.H. MM Pte 18661 Border Regt
COUGHLAN Daniel MM L/Cpl 47102 15th Lancashire Fusiliers
COUGHLAN J.T. MM Sjt 2512 Royal Highlanders
COUGHLAN John MM Pte 55357 15th North Lancashire Regt
COUGHLAN Michael MM Pte S/1819 Arg & Suth Highlanders
COUGHLAN Timothy M. MM Pte 3521 Leinster Regt
COUGHLAN William MM Sjt 6060 1 Siege Coy R Anglesey RE
COUGHLIN Cornelius MM L/Cpl 330205 1/9th Highland Light Infantry
COUGHLIN William John MM Pte 306417 Royal Warwickshire Regt
COULES Robert Arthur "MM,MID" S/Sjt Fitter 89833 RFA
COULING Arthur MM Sjt 25309 366 Siege Bty RGA
COULING William MM Bdr 35671 115 Heavy Bty RGA
COULING William T. MM Pte 68713 Royal West Surrey Regt
COULL Donald MM Sjt 406214 Royal Engineers
COULL Peter MM Pte 2700 Seaforth Highlanders
COULL William MM+Bar Pte 202323 Scottish Rifles
COULSON Albert MM Sjt 18397 7th Leicestershire Regt KIA 27.5.18.
COULSON Albert E. MM Pte 15680 6th Lincolnshire Regt
COULSON Albert W. MM Cpl 260089 8th Gloucestershire Regt
COULSON Alfred MM Pte 2594 Northumberland Fusiliers
COULSON Arthur MM Sjt 854 18th Northumberland Fusiliers KIA 27.3.18.
COULSON Arthur MM Sjt T/17102 5 Reserve Park Army Service Corps
COULSON Bernard S. MM Pte 6035 York & Lancaster Regt
COULSON Ceceil MM Gnr 34642 28 Bde RFA
COULSON David MM Dvr 771580 D/251 Bde RFA
COULSON Edward MM Cpl 19427 Northumberland Fusiliers
COULSON Fred MM Pte 10327 Army Cyclist Corps
COULSON George H. MM L/Cpl 13705 6th Lincolnshire Regt
COULSON George William MM Sjt 1254 18th Middlesex Regt
COULSON Hardy H. MM Pte 104476 99 Fd Amb RAMC
COULSON Herbert MM Cpl 15596 Suffolk Regt
COULSON James MM Gnr 55245 29 Bty 42 Bde RFA
COULSON Matthew MM Pte 13437 Northumberland Fusiliers
COULSON Percy W. MM+Bar Cpl 22958 Machine Gun Corps
COULSON Reginald MM Sjt 17822 3 Div Sig Coy Royal Engineers
COULSON Sidney MM Sjt S/459 Rifle Brigade
COULSON Thomas Edwin MM Pte 200442 1/4th Yorkshire Regt
COULTARD Thomas S. MM L/Cpl 16056 Leicestershire Regt
COULTAS Benjamin George MM Gnr 95449 'G' Bn Tank Corps
COULTAS David MM Pte 308113 Liverpool Regt
COULTER Andrew MM Cpl 12479 1st Royal Scots Fusiliers KIA 30.12.16.
COULTER Isaac MM Pte 9357 1st Scots Guards DOW 25.3.18.
COULTER James MM Cpl 204347 Seaforth Highlanders
COULTER Joseph MM Pte 41530 9th Royal Irish Fusiliers KIA 7.10.18.
COULTER William Robert MM Spr 64369 150 Fd Coy Royal Engineers
COULTHARD Robert L. MM Sjt 104516 228 Fd Coy Royal Engineers
COULTHURST Richard MM Cpl 60155 Royal Welsh Fusiliers
COULTON Edward "DCM,MM" L/Cpl 22054 3rd Grenadier Guards DOW 4.11.18.
COULTON G. MM L/Cpl P2106 Military Mounted Police
COULTON George MM Cpl 18667 5th Royal Berkshire Regt
COULTON Henry L. MM L/Cpl M/353967 51 Div MT Coy Army Service Corps
COULTON William MM Gnr 44185 2 Div Ammn Col RFA
COUMBE James T. MM Gnr 192265 RFA
COUNCILL Arthur MM Pte 295388 12th Somerset Light Infantry
COUNDLEY Alfred MM L/Cpl 23298 1st Hampshire Regt
COUNSELL Evan James MM Gnr W/1203 B/119 Bde RFA
COUNSELL Frederick C. MM Sjt 2413 1/4th Gloucestershire Regt
COUNSELLOR Thomas Bell Small MM Sjt 1137 1/9th Durham Light Infantry Died 8.12.18.
COUNSELLOR William MM Sjt M2/054437 Army Service Corps
COUNTER John Henry MM Pte 11754 1st Devonshire Regt KIA 6.11.17.
COUNTY Sidney W. MM Pte 201544 6th East Kent Regt
COUPE Frederick MM Pte 200682 1/4th North Lancashire Regt
COUPE Robert MM Gnr 695072 RFA
COUPE Thomas MM Cpl 18098 5th Border Regt
COUPE William MM Pte 204054 1st Liverpool Regt
COUPER Henry William MM Sjt 550047 1/16th London Regt DOW 11.6.17.
COUPER J. MM+Bar Sjt 402 RFA
COUPLAND Alfred MM Gnr Sig 224946 A/256 Bde RFA
COUPLAND George B. MM Pte 5176 7th Royal West Surrey Regt
COUPLAND Henry F. MM Cpl 5604 Machine Gun Corps
COUPLAND John W. MM Pte 19890 Machine Gun Corps
COUPLAND Richard A. MM Sjt 9635 1st Coldstream Guards
COURAGE Henry G. MM 2nd Cpl 193115 Royal Engineers
COURAGE Percival MM Cpl 230178 1/1st Dorset Yeomanry
COURSE Philip MM Pte 8/19891 2nd Royal Dublin Fusiliers DOW 12.8.17.
COURSH Walter MM Bdr 48444 RGA
COURT Ernest J. MM Pnr 161174 Royal Engineers
COURT George E. MM Pte 12743 6th Royal Berkshire Regt
COURT Henry MM L/Cpl A/1762 9th King's Royal Rifle Corps
COURT Herbert J. MM Pte 15424 Royal West Kent Regt
COURT J.H. MM Dvr 3253 39 Bde RFA
COURT John L. "DCM,MM+Bar,MID" L/Cpl 2190 Middlesex Regt
COURT Sidney J. MM Pte 25483 12th East Surrey Regt
COURT Thomas J. MM Cpl 298008 4th London Regt
COURT Wilfred MM Pte 2791 1/5th Yorkshire Regt
COURT William MM Sjt 386774 Royal Engineers
COURTIS Elsie Agnes MM Miss F First Aid Nursing Yeomanry
COURTIS William F. MM Cpl 329137 RGA
COURTNELL George MM Pte G/30000 4th Royal Fusiliers
COURTNEY Ernest MM Sjt 9353 2nd Royal Welsh Fusiliers KIA 26.9.17.
COURTNEY Henry MM Gnr Sig 247749 C/310 Bde RFA
COURTNEY James MM Pte 6593 2nd Irish Guards
COURTNEY John MM CQMS 8/10424 8th South Staffordshire Regt
COURTNEY Norman "DCM,MM" Pte 10091 9th Devonshire Regt
COURTNEY Thomas MM Pte 43023 2nd Royal Irish Rifles KIA 23.11.17.
COURTNEY William R. MM Sjt 14319 1st Royal Irish Rifles
COUSENS Frederick Richard MM Pte 6154 9th Royal Fusiliers KIA 30.11.17.
COUSER Thomas MM Sjt 38244 A/124 Bde RFA
COUSIN Matthew MM Pte M2/132126 Army Service Corps
COUSINS Andrew MM L/Cpl 6044 1st Irish Guards
COUSINS Ernest MM Spr 26070 Royal Engineers

COUSINS Ernest James MM+2 Bars Cpl G/2826 12th Middlesex Regt
COUSINS Frederick MM L/Cpl 29078 8th Somerset Light Infantry KIA 25.5.18.
COUSINS Frederick MM Pte 26997 12th East Surrey Regt
COUSINS George MM Sjt 8614 1st Rifle Brigade
COUSINS George MM Spr 42558 Royal Engineers
COUSINS Gilbert MM Pte 6085 8 Fd Amb RAMC
COUSINS James MM Sjt 39250 1/6th Gloucestershire Regt
COUSINS John J. MM Cpl 15558 7th Bedfordshire Regt
COUSINS Mark "MM,Oleo(B)" Sjt 1501 1/5th Lincolnshire Regt
COUSINS Reginald MM L/Cpl 2866 Army Cyclist Corps
COUSINS Walter J. MM L/Cpl S/14206 13th Rifle Brigade
COUSINS William MM Sjt 14253 12th Royal Irish Rifles
COUSINS William MM Pte 10489 5th Royal Berkshire Regt
COUSINS William George MM Cpl 2162 Middlesex Regt
COUTHARD William C. MM Gnr L/17861 RFA
COUTTS David MM Pte 28456 12th East Surrey Regt
COUTTS David D. MM Cpl 91645 Royal Engineers
COUTTS David T. MM Pte 12 1st Arg & Suth Highlanders
COUTTS Herbert F. MM Pte 24718 2nd Grenadier Guards
COUTTS James MM Pte 14464 9th West Riding Regt KIA 7.7.16.
COUTTS James MM L/Sjt 2755 1/7th Gordon Highlanders
COUTTS James MM+Bar Sjt 330515 8th Royal Scots
COUTTS James M. MM L/Cpl 21970 Cameron Highlanders
COUTTS John "MM,MSM" Sjt 4506 C/157 Bde RFA DOW 20.12.17.
COUTTS John MM Pte 267978 8th Royal Highlanders KIA 19.7.18.
COUTTS John W. MM Dvr 42433 15 Bde RFA
COUTTS William MM Spr 154945 Royal Engineers
COUTTS William "MM,MID" Sjt 418063 52 Div Sig Coy Royal Engineers
COUTTS William MM Sjt 2231 1/14th London Regt
COUZENS Frank E. MM Pte 17901 2nd Coldstream Guards
COUZENS George H. MM L/Cpl M1/6157 8 Div Train Army Service Corps
COUZENS Persemmon A. MM Pte P4250 Rifle Brigade
COVALL Christopher Monson "MM,MID" Gnr 85495 A/60 Bde RFA
COVE Benjamin MM Sjt 825370 C/240 Bde RFA
COVELL Ernest MM L/Cpl 326499 1/1st Cambridgeshire Regt
COVELL Samuel Hill MM Sjt 15223 8th Royal Lancaster Regt KIA 16.8.16.
COVELL William E. MM Sjt 376945 10th Manchester Regt
COVENEY Alfred "MM,MID" Spr 17661 Royal Engineers
COVENTRY Charles MM Bdr 59381 8 Bde RFA
COVENTRY Edward MM L/Cpl 230112 1/2nd London Regt
COVENTRY Herbert MM Pte 3838 1/9th London Regt
COVENTRY Leonard Ernest MM L/Cpl R/11119 13th King's Royal Rifle Corps
COVERDALE Charles Harry "VC,MM" Sjt 4926 11th Manchester Regt
COVERDALE H. MM Sjt 4469 Lancers
COVERDALE Robert MM Sjt 3293 18th Lancashire Fusiliers
COVERLEY John E. MM Pte 65361 Machine Gun Corps
COVERLEY Joseph MM Cpl G/93269 24th Royal Fusiliers
COVEY Arthur S. MM Pte 20476 7th Royal Sussex Regt
COVILL Albert MM Pte 3/7582 2nd Suffolk Regt KIA 16.8.16.
COVUS Arthur T. MM Pte 32405 7th Wiltshire Regt
COWAN Alexander MM CSM 201242 1/5th Arg & Suth Highlanders
COWAN Alexander MM Pte 9254 1st Royal Highlanders
COWAN Andrew MM(MGC)+Bar L/Cpl 18529 5th Cameron Highlanders
COWAN Archibald MM Cpl 650396 C/78 Bde RFA
COWAN Charles MM Sjt 77635 139 Siege Bty RGA
COWAN Christopher "MM,MID" Sjt B/176 Rifle Brigade
COWAN Duncan S. MM Sjt 265850 1/6th Cheshire Regt
COWAN Frank MM Pte 29978 Liverpool Regt
COWAN George MM Cpl 326279 RGA
COWAN George MM Pte 30835 46th Bn Machine Gun Corps
COWAN James MM Cpl 65057 105 Fd Coy Royal Engineers
COWAN James MM Sjt 315260 Royal Highlanders Died 25.10.18.
COWAN James MM Sjt 22049 20th Liverpool Regt
COWAN James MM+Bar L/Cpl 949 1st Arg & Suth Highlanders
COWAN James A. "MM,MID" L/Cpl 7571 1/4th Royal Scots Fusiliers KIA 20.9.18.
COWAN James Mitchell MM L/Cpl 10949 2nd Scots Guards
COWAN James Robert MM Pte 69328 1/2nd London Regt
COWAN John MM L/Cpl 331950 9th Highland Light Infantry
COWAN John MM Pte 71908 135 Fd Amb RAMC
COWAN John MM Pte 128114 Machine Gun Corps
COWAN Malachi MM Bdr 987 B/109 Bde RFA
COWAN Robert H. MM Sjt 275822 Arg & Suth Highlanders
COWAN Samuel N. "MM,MID" Sjt 490870 13th London Regt
COWAN Sidney MM Pte 40148 Seaforth Highlanders
COWAN Sinclair Williamson MM Pte 790 4th Bn GMGR DOW 30.3.18.
COWAN Thomas MM Pte 47903 1/4th Royal Scots Died 26.10.18.
COWAN Thomas MM Bdr L/12604 RFA
COWAN Thomas MM Sjt 9085 10th Scottish Rifles
COWAN Walter MM Sjt 9993 1st King's Own Scottish Borderers
COWAN William MM Pte 275904 5/6th Royal Scots
COWAN William MM Pte 18995 1/4th Royal Scots
COWAN William MM Cpl 93574 C/46 Bde RFA
COWAN William K. MM Pte 331777 9th Highland Light Infantry
COWANS Cyril A. "DCM,MM" Sjt 23/822 Northumberland Fusiliers
COWANS Thomas William MM Gnr 113351 84 HAG RGA KIA 19.9.17.
COWANS William W. MM+Bar Sjt 386013 RAMC
COWARD Albert MM L/Cpl 242864 1/5th North Lancashire Regt
COWARD Arthur J. MM L/Cpl 6330 Royal West Kent Regt
COWARD Francis MM Pte 1742 1st Royal Lancaster Regt DOW 9.10.17.
COWARD Frederick Stanley MM Pte 356959 10th Liverpool Regt
COWARD George A. MM Pte 12543 5th Dorsetshire Regt
COWARD Henley C. MM Bdr 33269 11 Siege Bty RGA
COWARD Hugh M. MM Gnr Sig 109357 218 Siege Bty RGA
COWARD John "MM,MID" Sjt 2014 1/4th Royal Lancaster Regt
COWARD Joseph MM Cpl 12859 1st North Lancashire Regt
COWARD William H. MM Pte 24790 3rd Grenadier Guards
COWBURN Frank MM Pte 99190 6th Durham Light Infantry
COWDREY Basil S. MM Pte 200874 Royal West Surrey Regt
COWDREY Bruce S.H. MM Cpl 20792 15? Fd Coy Royal Engineers
COWDREY Ernest MM Sjt 59958 24 Bde RFA
COWDREY John MM Sjt 21320 1st Northumberland Fusiliers
COWE Andrew MM Pte 9814 2nd Gordon Highlanders
COWE George Young "MM,MID" Pte S/6779 2nd Gordon Highlanders KIA 1.7.16.
COWE Henry MM Pte 16472 13th Royal Scots
COWE John H. MM Pte 9628 1st Coldstream Guards
COWE Thomas MM Pte 19179 6/7th Royal Scots Fusiliers KIA 24.3.18.
COWE W. "MM,MID" Pte S/2938 9th Gordon Highlanders
COWELL Alec MM Pte 34721 4th West Riding Regt
COWELL Bob MM Pte B200532 10th Rifle Brigade
COWELL Frank Edward MM Gnr 170483 A/14 Bde RFA
COWELL George "MM,MID" Cpl 47460 93 Bty 18 Bde RFA
COWELL Herbert MM Spr 94190 IX Corps HAG Sig Sect Royal Engineers
COWELL Herbert MM Pte 242479 2/6th Lancashire Fusiliers
COWELL J. "DCM,MM(21018 Cpl 12 Fd Coy RE)+Bar" Sjt 78171 20 Squadron Royal Flying Corps
COWELL Joseph MM Pte 243453 1st Royal Lancaster Regt
COWELL Joseph Charles MM Pte 384605 19 Empl Coy Labour Corps
COWELL Richard MM Sjt 12787 7th York & Lancaster Regt KIA 18.10.16.
COWELL William J. MM Gnr 57436 RFA
COWEN Charles MM Pte 13641 Yorkshire Light Infantry
COWEN Charles H. MM Pte 14000 East Lancashire Regt
COWEN Joseph St.Clair MM+Bar Sjt 18753 1st Bn Machine Gun Corps KIA 29.9.18.
COWEN William MM Sjt 202267 2nd York & Lancaster Regt
COWEN William MM L/Cpl 240847 Border Regt
COWEY Joseph MM Pte 18/1627 Northumberland Fusiliers
COWGILL James MM Pte M2/021264 29 Div Train Army Service Corps
COWGILL John MM Dvr 4199 A/61 Bde RFA KIA 20.8.16.
COWGILL Robert MM Sjt 60783 RGA
COWGILL Tom W. MM Spr 253871 Royal Engineers
COWHAM George H. MM Gnr L/42636 RFA
COWICK William MM Pte 7690 East Yorkshire Regt
COWIE Alexander MM Pte 200419 Gordon Highlanders
COWIE Charles MM Pte 7304 9th Seaforth Highlanders
COWIE Donald MM L/Cpl 5111 1/10th Liverpool Regt DOW 30.11.16.
COWIE Frank MM Sjt 43294 1st Gordon Highlanders
COWIE Frank MM L/Cpl 240317 Seaforth Highlanders
COWIE Frank MM Dvr 663154 RFA
COWIE George MM Pte 242218 Gordon Highlanders
COWIE George MM L/Bdr 62502 2 Bde RFA
COWIE George MM Cpl 18435 Machine Gun Corps
COWIE George MM Gnr 4412 RFA

COWIE James MM Sjt 8531 2nd Royal Munster Fusiliers
COWIE James Alexander MM Sjt 106444 Royal Engineers
COWIE James B. MM L/Bdr 217977 C/76 Bde RFA
COWIE John MM Cpl 305260 2nd Highland Light Infantry
COWIE John MM Cpl 303313 2/1st(Highland)Fd Amb RAMC
COWIE John MM Cpl 265907 1/7th Gordon Highlanders
COWIE John MM L/Cpl S/2171 Arg & Suth Highlanders
COWIE John L. MM Sjt 220755 8th Royal Berkshire Regt
COWIE Peter MM+Bar Pte 15941 2nd Coldstream Guards
COWIE Thomas MM Cpl T3/030213 204 Coy Army Service Corps
COWIE Walter C. MM L/Cpl 43405 1st Gordon Highlanders
COWIE Walter J. MM Pte 266405 7th Gordon Highlanders
COWIE William MM L/Cpl 186359 'N' Special Coy Royal Engineers
COWIE William MM L/Cpl 32269 6th King's Own Scottish Borderers
COWIE William MM Sjt 25732 11th Durham Light Infantry
COWIN John Alfred MM Pte 30060 8th Royal Lancaster Regt KIA 13.4.18.
COWIN John James MM Pte 4346 12th Manchester Regt KIA 8.9.17.
COWIN Richard H. MM Pte 305379 Liverpool Regt
COWING George MM Cpl M2/181892 Army Service Corps
COWL Alfred George MM Pte 24102 14th Gloucestershire Regt
COWLAND G.A. MM Sjt 225485 London Regt
COWLARD William MM L/Cpl 2117 13th Royal West Surrey Regt
COWLE Albert MM Cpl 201498 1/5th Liverpool Regt KIA 9.4.18.
COWLES Frederick W. MM L/Sjt 240601 1/5th Devonshire Regt
COWLES John MM Sjt 9834 South Staffordshire Regt
COWLES Robert F. MM+2 Bars CSM 230691 2/2nd London Regt
COWLES William Arthur Gordon MM Pte 439522 2/3rd(South Midland)Fd Amb RAMC KIA 12.4.18.
COWLEY Archie L. MM L/Sjt 17268 2nd Northamptonshire Regt
COWLEY Charles MM Sjt 229691 13th Royal Fusiliers
COWLEY Eric MM Cpl 325332 1/1st Worcestershire Yeomanry
COWLEY Ernest A. MM Gnr 36161 RFA
COWLEY George MM Pte 24248 Yorkshire Regt
COWLEY James H. MM L/Cpl 302183 Manchester Regt
COWLEY John A. MM Cpl 52945 15 Bde RFA
COWLEY Joseph MM Cpl 92313 6th Bn Tank Corps
COWLEY Joseph MM L/Cpl 304138 5th London Regt
COWLEY Thomas John MM Gnr Sig 100856 52 Bty 15 Bde RFA
COWLEY Thomas Justin "DCM,MM" Bdr 19460 B/86 Bde RFA
COWLEY William A. MM L/Cpl 30095 2nd Welsh Regt
COWLEY William J. MM Sjt 318039 5th London Regt
COWLEY William M. MM Dvr 463055 Royal Engineers
COWLING Alfred G. MM Sjt 10237 9th West Yorkshire Regt
COWLING Arthur MM Sjt 203352 5th Notts & Derby Regt
COWLING Frederick George MM Sjt 825144 C/155 Bde RFA
COWLING George F. MM Sjt 12735 7th Bedfordshire Regt
COWLING Joseph R. MM S/Sjt 16190 12 Static Hosp RAMC
COWLING Thomas MM Gnr 681286 RFA
COWLING Walter H. MM Gnr W/3256 C/121 Bde RFA
COWLING William MM L/Cpl 28575 3rd Grenadier Guards
COWLING William MM+Bar Sjt 23127 69 Coy Machine Gun Corps KIA 27.9.17.
COWLISHAW George D. MM Cpl 120610 'C' Special Coy Royal Engineers
COWNDEN George MM Sjt T4/239964 60 Div Train Army Service Corps
COWNIE Stanley "DCM+Bar,MM" CSM 31424 13th Royal Scots
COWPER Charles F. "MM,MID" L/Sjt 11376 5th Shropshire Light Infantry
COWPER Keith T. MM Bdr 293527 136 Hy Bty RGA
COWSILL Frank A. MM Gnr 851246 RFA
COWSTICK Herbert O. "DCM,MM" L/Cpl 9555 2nd Royal West Surrey Regt
COWTON Harry MM Cpl 16352 2nd Yorkshire Regt
COX A. MM L/Cpl P2202 Military Foot Police
COX Albert MM Cpl 22369 2nd Highland Light Infantry
COX Albert MM Pte 50586 1/4th Cheshire Regt Died 27.11.18.
COX Albert MM Dvr 4520 RFA
COX Albert MM+Bar Sjt 9376 5th Royal Berkshire Regt
COX Albert MM+Bar Cpl 10869 1st Leicestershire Regt
COX Albert C. MM Sjt 10554 1st Hampshire Regt
COX Albert E. MM Pte 12310 9th Scottish Rifles
COX Albert F. MM Cpl 240832 5th West Riding Regt
COX Albert J. MM Dmr 2158 3rd Royal Warwickshire Regt
COX Albert J.M. MM Gnr 58974 RFA
COX Albert L. MM Sjt 13959 1st Grenadier Guards
COX Alfred "DCM,MM" Sjt 16153 Northamptonshire Regt
COX Arthur MM Cpl 201937 1/4th Suffolk Regt

COX Arthur MM Gnr 91017 RFA
COX Arthur MM Sjt 73008 Notts & Derby Regt
COX Arthur MM L/Sjt 10099 6th York & Lancaster Regt
COX Arthur MM L/Cpl 18743 Royal Berkshire Regt
COX Arthur MM Gnr 57143 5 Bde RFA
COX Arthur MM Sjt 47988 B/107 Bde RFA DOW 29.7.17.
COX Arthur MM Pte 17797 Royal West Kent Regt
COX Arthur C. MM Pte 90140 25th Bn Machine Gun Corps
COX Arthur Charles "MM,MBC(Rm)" Pte G/4852 2nd Royal Sussex Regt
COX Arthur Joseph MM Pte M2/133611 Att 55 Fd Amb RAMC Army Service Corps
COX Arthur Ravenhall MM Pte 39068 12th Gloucestershire Regt
COX Arthur W. MM Pte 24515 Royal Welsh Fusiliers
COX Bernard MM Pte 34244 4th North Lancashire Regt
COX Bernard K. MM S/Sjt M2/180873 30 Mot Amb Convoy Army Service Corps
COX Charles MM Pte 6146 1st Royal Berkshire Regt
COX Charles MM Sjt 2678 1/5th West Riding Regt KIA 5.8.16.
COX Charles MM Gnr 32600 192 Hy Bty RGA
COX Charles Alfred "DCM,MM" Sjt 49735 93 Fd Coy Royal Engineers DOW 3.11.18.
COX Charles E. MM Bdr 70203 72 Bty 38 Bde RFA
COX Charles Frederick MM Sjt 8/16122 8th South Wales Borderers DOW 19.9.18.
COX Charles George MM Gnr 19654 A/80 Bde RFA
COX Charles H. MM Sjt 265547 11th Somerset Light Infantry
COX Charles W. MM Sjt 64815 Labour Corps
COX Clifford S. MM Pte 71849 RAMC
COX Edward MM Pte 16803 Machine Gun Corps
COX Edward "DCM,MM,MID,MMV(It)" CQMS L/9326 2nd Royal West Surrey Regt
COX Edward MM L/Cpl 66313 23 Div Sig Coy Royal Engineers
COX Edward H. MM Pte 14319 Suffolk Regt
COX Ernest MM L/Cpl 4332 Royal West Surrey Regt
COX Ernest MM Sjt 90001 RAMC
COX Ernest R. MM Pte G/18572 2nd Royal Sussex Regt
COX Ernest W. MM Cpl 37257 Royal Fusiliers
COX Ernest William MM Pte 41076 8th Suffolk Regt
COX Francis J.H. MM Pte 31045 RAMC
COX Frank MM Pte 16716 6th Royal Berkshire Regt
COX Fred Paling MM Dvr 311273 152 Heavy Bty RGA Died 3.8.18.
COX Frederick MM Pte 200624 11th Bn Royal Scots
COX Frederick J. "MM,MSM,MID" Sjt 7509 Att HQ 8 Div Army Ordnance Corps
COX Frederick John "DCM,MM,MID" RQMS 3/7755 7th Somerset Light Infantry
COX Frederick R. MM Sjt 52262 42 Bde RFA
COX Frederick Thomas MM L/Cpl 35155 3rd Worcestershire Regt DOW 12.8.17.
COX Frederick W. MM Pte F/2803 23rd Middlesex Regt
COX Frederick Wilfred MM Pte 33455 6th Oxf & Bucks Light Infantry
COX G. MM L/Cpl 18025 13th Essex Regt
COX George MM L/Cpl 298006 1/8th Arg & Suth Highlanders KIA 31.7.18.
COX George MM Pte 6878 2nd Suffolk Regt
COX George MM Pte 20923 Machine Gun Corps
COX George MM Pte 10232 1st Middlesex Regt
COX George C. MM Spr 558407 56 Div Sig Coy Royal Engineers
COX George Herbert MM Pte L/11359 2nd Royal West Surrey Regt DOW 28.10.17.
COX George William MM Bdr 72471 183 Siege Bty RGA
COX George William MM Sjt 5306 3rd Dragoon Guards DOW 8.4.18.
COX Graeme V. MM Bdr 42773 RGA
COX Harold MM Sjt 266334 1/7th Liverpool Regt KIA 11.4.18.
COX Harry MM Sjt 326381 1/1st Cambridgeshire Regt
COX Hartley MM Pte 36801 5th East Lancashire Regt
COX Henry MM+Bar Sjt 5725 Machine Gun Corps
COX Henry E.M. MM L/Cpl S/7466 Middlesex Regt
COX Henry Thomas MM Sjt 531321 15th London Regt DOW 21.9.18.
COX Herbert MM Pte 241509 1/5th York & Lancaster Regt KIA 3.5.18.
COX Herbert MM Pte 1691 1/17th London Regt KIA 1.10.16.
COX Herbert Henry MM Pte 43058 6th Northamptonshire Regt KIA 5.4.18.
COX Horace Sidney MM Dvr 69965 120 Bty 27 Bde RFA
COX Hubert "MM,MID" CSM 12049 283 Army Tps Coy Royal Engineers

COX Irving Hepplewhite MM Pte 20386 6/7th Royal Scots Fusiliers
COX J. MM Pte 435334 RAMC
COX James "MM,MID" Cpl 13981 5th Royal Inniskilling Fusiliers
COX James L. MM Pte 310252 7th Gordon Highlanders
COX John MM Pte 306824 Royal Warwickshire Regt
COX John MM Pte 17807 Worcestershire Regt
COX John MM Pte 13475 2nd Grenadier Guards
COX John F. MM Cpl 33580 Yorkshire Regt
COX John W. MM Sjt 37330 366 Bty RFA
COX Joseph "MM,CG(B)" Sjt 44262 12th North Staffordshire Regt
COX Joseph MM Pte 241184 11th Notts & Derby Regt
COX Joseph MM Spr 86534 173 Tunnelling Coy Royal Engineers
COX Joseph MM Pte Z/1006 Rifle Brigade
COX Joseph MM L/Cpl 43040 Manchester Regt
COX Leslie MM Pte 200598 1/5th Royal Warwickshire Regt
COX Lionel Claude MM Sjt 500149 61 Div Sig Coy Royal Engineers
COX Noel MM+Bar Pte 241162 Lincolnshire Regt
COX Norman R. MM Spr 23256 Royal Engineers
COX Percival H. MM Pte 2886 1/21st London Regt
COX Percy MM L/Cpl 355400 25th Royal Welsh Fusiliers
COX Percy MM Pte 241857 5th West Riding Regt
COX Percy MM Bdr 118862 RFA
COX Percy Herbert MM Sjt 8953 2nd Devonshire Regt
COX Percy Stephen MM Gnr 89264 251 Siege Bty RGA
COX Percy V. MM Pte 40309 6th Royal Warwickshire Regt
COX Philip Henry MM Pte 534056 4th(London)Fd Amb. RAMC KIA 6.4.18.
COX R.E. MM Sjt 503 Royal Sussex Regt
COX Reginald MM Sjt 220270 5th Royal Berkshire Regt
COX Reginald A. MM Pte 12662 5th Lancers
COX Richard MM Dvr L/23691 RFA
COX Robert B. MM Pte 3288 1/8th Worcestershire Regt
COX Robert H. MM L/Bdr 44485 RFA
COX Samuel MM Pte 68807 1st Devonshire Regt
COX Sidney MM Pte 4/7036 1st Bedfordshire Regt
COX Sidney C. MM Pte 718286 23rd London Regt
COX Stanley J. MM L/Cpl G/24625 23rd Royal Fusiliers
COX Stephen John MM Cpl 5191 Leinster Regt
COX T. MM Pte 205109 ?Yeomanry
COX Thomas MM Gnr 251574 RFA
COX Thomas MM Sjt 6233 2 Fd Amb RAMC
COX Thomas MM Pte 202711 5th Liverpool Regt KIA 30.7.17.
COX Thomas A. MM L/Cpl 42787 6th Leicestershire Regt
COX Thomas D. MM Pte C/7863 King's Royal Rifle Corps
COX W. MM Pte 534200 RAMC
COX Walter "MM,MID" Cpl (MCDR) 75349 16 Div Sig Coy Royal Engineers
COX Walter MM Pte 20344 6th Leicestershire Regt KIA 26.3.18.
COX Walter Alexander MM Sjt 325434 1/1st Cambridgeshire Regt
COX Walter Edward MM Pte 56798 2/5th Lancashire Fusiliers
COX Walter Edward H. MM L/Bdr 39342 D/59 Bde RFA
COX Walter Jonas MM Cpl 49468 160 Coy Machine Gun Corps
COX Walter William MM Sjt 9136 B/245 Bde RFA DOW 20.5.18.
COX William MM Gnr 79331 RFA
COX William MM Sjt 7906 14th Royal Welsh Fusiliers
COX William MM Pte 70568 RAMC
COX William MM Gnr 4431 RFA
COX William Alec MM Sjt 56213 D/79 Bde RFA
COX William G. MM Dvr 16298 A/251 Bde RFA
COX William H. MM Pte 21303 Gloucestershire Regt
COX William Henry MM Pte 12075 South Staffordshire Regt
COX William J. MM L/Cpl 240640 1/5th Devonshire Regt
COX William L. MM Gnr 1697 316 Bde RFA
COX William R. MM Pte 200886 4th Bn Tank Corps
COX William S. MM Pte 2012 RAMC
COXALL A. MM Sjt 45845 1st Bedfordshire Regt
COXALL Walter Edmond MM Pte 11937 8th East Kent Regt
COXE Walter T. MM Pte G/46657 24th Royal Fusiliers
COXHEAD Francis J. MM+Bar Pte 22278 5th Royal Berkshire Regt
COXHEAD Joseph Allan MM Pte 20780 11th Liverpool Regt
COXHEAD Oscar J. MM Pte 32732 11 Fd Amb RAMC
COXON John W. MM Sjt 28/295 19th Northumberland Fusiliers
COXON Joseph MM Pte 16657 10th Durham Light Infantry
COXON William MM Cpl 16763 6th Yorkshire Regt
COXWELL Richard S. MM Sjt 21508 1st Somerset Light Infantry
COY George William MM Pte 53405 Notts & Derby Regt Died 2.5.18.
COY Thomas MM Pte MS/1256 Army Service Corps att RAMC
COYLE Albert V. MM Gnr 68058 44 Bde RFA
COYLE Edward MM Pte 11339 9th Scottish Rifles
COYLE James MM CQMS 9696 2nd Arg & Suth Highlanders
COYLE John MM Pte 28620 1st Border Regt
COYLE John MM Sjt S/1593 10th Arg & Suth Highlanders
COYLE John MM Gnr 92722 A/78 Bde RFA
COYLE Michael MM Spr 93877 41 Div Sig Coy Royal Engineers
COYLE Michael MM L/Cpl 325232 1/9th Arg & Suth Highlanders
COYLE Peter MM Sjt 12615 2nd Highland Light Infantry DOW 7.4.18.
COYLE Walter MM L/Cpl 3786 5th Lancers
COYNE Ernest MM Sjt 10798 1st Scottish Rifles KIA 20.7.16.
COYNE Francis MM L/Cpl 3146 1st Irish Guards
COYNE James MM Pte 90238 18 Fd Amb RAMC
COYNE James MM Pte 9272 4th Liverpool Regt
COYNE James Hollinhead MM Gnr 14015 D/180 Bde RFA
COYNE Joseph Peter MM Spr 108788 157 Fd Coy Royal Engineers
COYNE Patrick MM L/Cpl 4100 6th Connaught Rangers
COYNE Philip MM Cpl 397376 Royal Engineers
COZENS Albert Abernethy MM Sjt 1344 11th Middlesex Regt KIA 10.10.16.
COZENS Charles MM Pte 28/704 Northumberland Fusiliers att MGC.
COZENS Frederick "DCM,MM" Sjt G/8181 11th Royal West Kent Regt
COZENS Herbert W. MM Pte 554870 16th London Regt
CRABB Bertie MM Pnr 58622 Royal Engineers
CRABB Edwin J. "DCM,MM" CQMS 8403 7th Border Regt
CRABB George W. MM Cpl 350888 7th London Regt
CRABB Harold W. MM Pte A/204101 13th King's Royal Rifle Corps
CRABB James MM Sjt 201319 1/4th Gordon Highlanders
CRABB William C. MM Pte 19388 5th Dorsetshire Regt
CRABB William R. MM Trooper 2482 Royal Horse Guards
CRABBE Joseph MM Pte 41394 2nd Manchester Regt
CRABTREE Albert MM Sjt 202257 2/4th West Riding Regt
CRABTREE Alfred MM Pte 27003 1st Royal Berkshire Regt KIA 24.8.18.
CRABTREE Arthur MM Pte M2/265978 Army Service Corps
CRABTREE Charlie MM Pte 241781 6th West Riding Regt
CRABTREE George MM Bdr L/17717 A/170 Bde RFA
CRABTREE George W. MM Pte 102969 15 Fd Amb RAMC
CRABTREE Harrie MM Pte 10202 Royal Fusiliers
CRABTREE Horace MM CQMS 5559 Scots Guards
CRABTREE John MM Dvr 70737 A/91 Bde RFA
CRABTREE John W. MM Pte 13957 11th West Yorkshire Regt
CRABTREE Luther MM L/Cpl 269421 2/7th Liverpool Regt
CRABTREE Percy MM L/Cpl 24799 11th East Lancashire Regt
CRABTREE Sam M. MM Sjt 5453 10th Lancashire Fusiliers
CRABTREE Thomas MM Cpl 15530 Machine Gun Corps
CRABTREE Walter MM Sjt 40468 RAMC
CRABTREE William H. MM+Bar Pte 35407 4th West Riding Regt
CRABTREE William Thomas MM L/Cpl 19145 2/6th Lancashire Fusiliers
CRACK Charles MM Pte 326474 1/1st Cambridgeshire Regt
CRACK George E. MM L/Cpl 49917 Royal Engineers
CRACKLOW Daniel MM L/Cpl M2/120102 Army Service Corps
CRACKNELL Arthur T. MM Sjt 200551 Suffolk Regt
CRACKNELL Charles T. MM Cpl 13291 13th King's Royal Rifle Corps
CRACKNELL Charles W. MM Sjt 6866 25th Royal Fusiliers Died 21.5.18.
CRACKNELL George F. MM Dvr 3434 RFA
CRACKNELL Horace H. MM Pte 16220 1st Gloucestershire Regt
CRACKNELL Walter W. MM L/Cpl 33709 Border Regt
CRADDOCK Charles MM Cpl 265120 Y/4 Med TM Bty RFA
CRADDOCK Charles Thomas MM Sjt 17778 7th South Staffordshire Regt KIA 6.5.18.
CRADDOCK Edward Arthur MM Sjt 72277 134 Fd Amb RAMC
CRADDOCK Harry "DCM,MM" Sjt 16194 13th Durham Light Infantry DOW 20.9.17.
CRADDOCK Henry Harold MM Cpl 240513 1/5th Duke of Cornwall's LI KIA 17.4.18.
CRADDOCK J.W. MM Gnr 278233 RGA
CRADDOCK John W. MM L/Cpl 62708 7th West Yorkshire Regt
CRADDOCK Thomas MM L/Cpl 10610 9th Yorkshire Regt KIA 7.10.16.
CRAFT A.G. MM Pte 49617 Royal Fusiliers
CRAFT G. MM Sjt 250383 London Regt
CRAFT L.G. "DCM,MM" L/Sjt 495422 2/2(Home Counties)Fd Amb RAMC
CRAFT Stanley A. MM Bdr 890054 RFA
CRAGG A. MM Pte 265268 Notts & Derby Regt

CRAGG Dick MM Pte 3453 Suffolk Regt
CRAGG George MM Sjt 13366 Machine Gun Corps
CRAGG Henry MM Pte 38050 77 Fd Amb RAMC
CRAGG John W. MM Pte 202430 4th York & Lancaster Regt
CRAGG Leonard MM Sjt 12004 2nd Scots Guards
CRAGG Stanley MM Pte 9375 Army Cyclist Corps
CRAGG Thomas MM Pte 240242 5th Yorkshire Light Infantry
CRAGGS Harold MM Dvr 800367 B/230 Bde RFA
CRAGIE Robert MM Pte 27/151 2nd Northumberland Fusiliers
CRAGO Samuel MM L/Cpl 151653 Royal Engineers
CRAIB George Oliphant MM Pte 303421 89 Fd Amb RAMC
CRAIB John Alexander "MM,MID" Sjt 1779 RAMC
CRAIB Robert L. MM Pte M2/147814 Army Service Corps
CRAIG Adam H. MM Pte S/18578 7th Cameron Highlanders
CRAIG Andrew MM Sjt 10747 2nd Royal Scots
CRAIG Charles MM Gnr 756 RFA
CRAIG Charles T. MM SM Mech M2/106462 4 Army Tps MT Coy Army Service Corps
CRAIG Clement S. MM Sjt 34776 505 Bty 65 Bde RFA
CRAIG David MM Pte 561 2nd Gordon Highlanders
CRAIG Ernest G. MM Pte 78038 10th Royal Fusiliers
CRAIG Frank MM Pte 39222 Highland Light Infantry
CRAIG Frederick A. MM Pte 18/729 Northumberland Fusiliers
CRAIG Frederick G. "MM,MIDx2,CG(It)" Sjt 23441 2 Div Sig Coy Royal Engineers
CRAIG George MM Sjt 400100 400 Fd Coy Royal Engineers
CRAIG George MM Gnr 50786 B/124 Bde RFA
CRAIG George MM Pte 335844 8th Royal Scots
CRAIG George MM Cpl 23438 Royal Irish Fusiliers
CRAIG George MM Sjt 8973 1st Royal Irish Fusiliers KIA 11.5.17.
CRAIG George MM Gnr 97116 RFA
CRAIG George MM Pte 242177 1/5th Northumberland Fusiliers DOW 7.6.18.
CRAIG Hugh MM Sjt 10025 1st Seaforth Highlanders
CRAIG Hugh MM Pte 32976 Royal Scots
CRAIG J. MM Sjt 27163 13th West Riding Regt
CRAIG James MM Sjt S/4371 4/5th Royal Highlanders
CRAIG James MM Sjt 18557 Manchester Regt
CRAIG John MM Spr 32832 Cav Corps Cable Sect Royal Engineers
CRAIG John MM L/Sjt S/3149 Gordon Highlanders
CRAIG John MM Sjt 3437 1/6th Arg & Suth Highlanders DOW 23.5.17.
CRAIG John MM Pte 16139 Machine Gun Corps
CRAIG John MM Sjt 33757 RAMC
CRAIG John MM Pte 275567 1/7th Arg & Suth Highlanders
CRAIG John F. MM Sjt 29459 RGA
CRAIG John Findlay Black MM Bdr 269 D/50 Bde RFA
CRAIG John K. MM Pte 24188 Royal West Surrey Regt
CRAIG John K. MM+Bar Sjt 38108 18th Lancashire Fusiliers
CRAIG John L. MM Pte 42329 1/5th King's Own Scottish Borderers
CRAIG John William "DCM,MM" Sjt 2042 Durham Light Infantry
CRAIG P. MM Air Mech 1 32925 Royal Flying Corps
CRAIG Percival J.A. MM Cpl 337046 RGA
CRAIG Peter "DCM,MM" Sjt S/6212 8th Royal Highlanders
CRAIG Richard MM L/Cpl S/21184 1st Cameron Highlanders
CRAIG Robert MM L/Cpl 400195 Royal Engineers
CRAIG Robert "DCM,MM,CdeG" CSM 9826 6th King's Own Scottish Borderers
CRAIG Robert MM Cpl 20101 Machine Gun Corps
CRAIG Robert MM L/Cpl 41157 RAMC
CRAIG Robert MM CSM S/3280 Gordon Highlanders
CRAIG Samuel MM Cpl 17/458 Royal Irish Rifles
CRAIG Theodore W. MM Pte 200204 Gordon Highlanders
CRAIG Thomas MM Pte 40764 10th Highland Light Infantry
CRAIG William MM Pte 3281 6th Royal Inniskilling Fusiliers
CRAIG William MM Gnr 90 RGA
CRAIG William Dawson MM Sjt 203564 1/7th Durham Light Infantry
CRAIGHEAD Christopher Steward MM Sjt 14701 23rd Middlesex Regt Died 28.1.18.
CRAIGIE B. MM Cpl 18/135 Northumberland Fusiliers
CRAIGIE David MM Pte 8722 2nd Seaforth Highlanders
CRAIGIE James MM+Bar L/Cpl 16219 1/6th Seaforth Highlanders
CRAIGIE William P. MM Cpl 01396 5th Devonshire Regt
CRAIK Alexander MM Pte 18823 6th Royal West Surrey Regt
CRAIK Alexander MM Pte 16545 Royal Highlanders
CRAIK Alexander J. MM Pte 17162 Gordon Highlanders
CRAIK John MM Dvr 103769 14 Div Ammn Col RFA
CRAIK John J. MM Sjt 406465 51 Div Sig Coy Royal Engineers
CRAIK Nicholas "DCM,MM+Bar" BQMS 89950 A/50 Bde RFA
CRAIN Andrew MM Gnr 99371 133 Heavy Bty RGA
CRAINE John P MM Bdr 22283 1 Siege Bty RGA
CRAKE William MM L/Cpl 13883 Yorkshire Regt
CRAKER Charles W. MM L/Cpl 265658 West Yorkshire Regt
CRAKER George MM Pte 11603 11th Hampshire Regt
CRAKER William MM Pte 201219 7th Royal West Surrey Regt
CRAMB Duncan John MM Cpl 293574 2/10th Middlesex Regt KIA 12.3.18.
CRAMB John James MM Pte 18783 32nd Royal Fusiliers
CRAMOND Griffith MM Sjt 635417 RFA KIA 5.4.18.
CRAMOND James T. MM C/Sjt 9703 2nd Highland Light Infantry
CRAMP Albert R. MM Pte 18184 Royal Sussex Regt
CRAMP Arthur L. MM Cpl 94818 RGA
CRAMP Edmund MM Pte S/20627 13th Rifle Brigade
CRAMP George MM Cpl 905423 X/57 Med TM Bty RFA
CRAMP William A. MM Pte 31192 1st East Lancashire Regt
CRAMPIN Albert MM Sjt 223233 226 Empl Coy Labour Corps
CRAMPTON Charles Sydenham "MM,MID" Sjt 17153 King's Own Scottish Borderers
CRAMPTON James William MM Pte S/7128 2nd Rifle Brigade
CRAMPTON John MM Cpl 22593 Machine Gun Corps
CRAMPTON John Morley MM Pte 17390 1st King's Own Scottish Borderers DOW 1.12.17.
CRAMPTON Morris MM Pte 306012 1/7th West Riding Regt DOW 26.11.17.
CRANBROOK James MM Tpr 5445 3rd Bn GMGR
CRANDLEY Frederick G. MM Cpl 73522 15th Notts & Derby Regt
CRANE Albert MM Gnr L/46256 RFA
CRANE Albert J.W. MM Pte 51643 MGC(Cavalry)
CRANE Arthur MM Sjt 59155 44 Bde RFA
CRANE Charles MM Sjt R/15984 13th King's Royal Rifle Corps
CRANE Ernest MM L/Sjt 717 22nd Royal Fusiliers KIA 29.4.17.
CRANE Francis W.M. MM+Bar Sjt 356178 14th Liverpool Regt
CRANE Harry MM Cpl 90014 Labour Corps
CRANE Henry T. MM Pte 265983 1/1st Hertfordshire Regt
CRANE James C. MM Cpl 29997 7th Royal West Surrey Regt
CRANE John MM Spr 259307 9 Div Sig Coy Royal Engineers att RFA.
CRANE Percy C. MM+Bar Pte 72607 Machine Gun Corps
CRANE Percy D. MM Bdr 106358 RGA
CRANE Peter MM Cpl 302909 Royal Scots
CRANE Peter MM Pte 70314 32nd Bn Machine Gun Corps
CRANE Stanley MM Pte 10562 1st Middlesex Regt Died 14.12.17.
CRANE Thomas MM Pte 9614 Manchester Regt
CRANE Thomas E. "DCM,MM" CSM S/7196 13th Rifle Brigade
CRANE Thomas Henry MM CSM T4/243182 59 Div Train Army Service Corps
CRANE Walter Lawrence MM L/Cpl 41056 1/8th Middlesex Regt
CRANE William "MM,MID" SSM 4062 3rd Dragoon Guards
CRANER Thomas MM+Bar L/Cpl 15010 1st Coldstream Guards
CRANER Walter L. MM+Bar Sjt 30587 Gloucestershire Regt
CRANER William MM Cpl 242235 1/4th Gloucestershire Regt KIA 15.10.18.
CRANHAM Henry MM Bdr 37406 RFA
CRANK Thomas MM Pte 7481 Machine Gun Corps KIA 15.4.18.
CRANK William MM Spr 102834 172 Tunnelling Coy Royal Engineers
CRANKSHAW David MM Pte 14070 7th East Lancashire Regt
CRANMER Charles MM Pte 825 Durham Light Infantry
CRANMER George R. MM Sjt 1718 6th Royal Warwickshire Regt
CRANNAGE Wallace George MM L/Cpl 305473 1/8th Royal Warwickshire Regt
CRANNESS Frederick MM Sjt 14425 11th Essex Regt
CRANNEY Patrick MM L/Cpl 203582 1/9th Durham Light Infantry
CRANNEY William MM L/Cpl 18803 19th Durham Light Infantry KIA 1.10.18.
CRANNEY William James Victor MM Sjt 34998 84 Bty 11 Bde RFA
CRANSTON George MM Cpl 17748 Machine Gun Corps
CRANSTON Matthew MM Sjt 3814 Gordon Highlanders
CRANSTONE Stanley Gadenne MM Cpl 69035 35 Div Sig Coy Royal Engineers
CRANSTOUN David Tweedie MM Pte 83957 18 Fd Amb RAMC
CRANSWICK Wilfred MM+Bar Cpl 175448 1/1st Yorkshire Dragoons Yeo
CRAPPER Charles MM Sjt 34959 RAMC Died 26.4.18.
CRASK Veisey C. MM Pte 13901 8th Suffolk Regt
CRASKE Clifford W. MM Sjt 95316 70 Fd Coy Royal Engineers
CRASS Joseph MM Pte 325055 1/9th Durham Light Infantry
CRASTON George Vernon MM L/Cpl S/27464 13th Rifle Brigade DOW 16.5.18.
CRATCHLEY Arthur MM Spr 492078 46 Div Sig Coy Royal Engineers DOW 10.5.18.

CRATE Arthur C. MM L/Sjt 630986 20th London Regt
CRATE Harry MM Bdr 35225 116 Heavy Bty RGA
CRATE Robert MM Pte 11331 1st Royal Scots Fusiliers
CRATES Thomas MM Pte 11590 Coldstream Guards
CRATHERN Arthur E. MM Sjt 11145 1st Middlesex Regt
CRAVEN Alexander MM L/Cpl 276151 11th Manchester Regt
CRAVEN Alfred G. MM Pte 9818 King's Own Scottish Borderers
CRAVEN Arthur MM Cpl 15665 7/8th Royal Irish Fusiliers
CRAVEN Arthur E. MM Pte 63251 RAMC
CRAVEN George MM L/Cpl 9432 Coldstream Guards
CRAVEN Harry MM Sjt 82541 64 Bty 5 Bde RFA
CRAVEN Herbert P. MM Gnr 631719 D/117 Bde RFA
CRAVEN J. MM L/Cpl 43276 Royal Irish Fusiliers
CRAVEN Joseph MM Pte 49864 11th Cheshire Regt
CRAVEN Thomas MM Bdr 14160 2 Div Ammn Col RFA
CRAVEN Walter MM Gnr 66678 RFA
CRAWFORD A. MM Pte 10348 Scottish Rifles
CRAWFORD Alexander MM L/Cpl 6124 Royal Irish Fusiliers
CRAWFORD Alfred MM L/Cpl 24166 Worcestershire Regt att MGC
CRAWFORD Andrew MM Dvr 17920 25 Div Sig Coy Royal Engineers Died 9.11.18.
CRAWFORD Andrew MM L/Sjt 278589 1/9th Arg & Suth Highlanders
CRAWFORD Andrew M. MM L/Cpl 2472 1/4th Gordon Highlanders
CRAWFORD Charles MM Sjt 7362 Border Regt
CRAWFORD Charles R. MM+Bar L/Cpl 49606 Royal Engineers
CRAWFORD Charles W. MM Pte 84805 Machine Gun Corps
CRAWFORD David MM L/Cpl S/20268 1st Cameron Highlanders KIA 4.11.18.
CRAWFORD David MM Spr 197929 Royal Engineers
CRAWFORD David A. MM L/Cpl 33292 13th East Lancashire Regt
CRAWFORD Duncan MM Cpl 44483 1st Bn Machine Gun Corps
CRAWFORD Ernest MM Sjt 23072 31 Heavy Bty RGA
CRAWFORD F. MM Pte 305062 1/3rd(Highland)Fd Amb RAMC
CRAWFORD Felix Oliver MM Sjt 21529 10th Royal West Surrey Regt
CRAWFORD Francis C.H. MM Pte 8783 7th East Surrey Regt
CRAWFORD George MM Pte 516218 14th London Regt
CRAWFORD Gregor MM Sjt 325370 1/9th Arg & Suth Highlanders
CRAWFORD Herbert MM Gnr 188724 C/124 Bde RFA
CRAWFORD Herbert Edward MM Sjt T4/036308 27 Reserve Park Army Service Corps
CRAWFORD Hugh MM Sjt 50887 1 Squadron MGC(Cavalry) KIA 4.4.18.
CRAWFORD James MM Pte 1799 North Lancashire Regt
CRAWFORD James MM L/Cpl 131352 234 Fd Coy Royal Engineers
CRAWFORD James MM Cpl 879 Arg & Suth Highlanders
CRAWFORD James MM Dvr 650138 RFA
CRAWFORD John MM Sjt 22937 50th Bn Machine Gun Corps
CRAWFORD John MM Pte S/7949 2nd Seaforth Highlanders
CRAWFORD John MM Pte 35436 5/6th Scottish Rifles
CRAWFORD John MM Pte 1147 16th Middlesex Regt
CRAWFORD John MM Pte 15119 16th Highland Light Infantry KIA 18.11.16.
CRAWFORD John MM Dvr T/4/040650 Army Service Corps
CRAWFORD John MM Gnr 492 C/315 Bde RFA KIA 4.10.17.
CRAWFORD John MM Pte 9424 2nd Arg & Suth Highlanders
CRAWFORD John Frederick MM Sjt 61271 RFA
CRAWFORD Johnstone MM Sjt 132661 Royal Engineers
CRAWFORD Leonard MM Pte 43599 5th South Staffordshire Regt
CRAWFORD Leonard MM Gnr 705857 RFA
CRAWFORD Leonard G. "DCM,MM+Bar" Sjt 10502 2nd Highland Light Infantry
CRAWFORD Reginald H. MM L/Cpl 31826 5 Fd Amb RAMC
CRAWFORD Reuben "MM,MID" Bdr 4172 12 Bde RFA
CRAWFORD Robert MM Bdr 37037 RFA
CRAWFORD Robert MM Pte 17819 1st Royal Highlanders DOW 24.9.18.
CRAWFORD Robert Leonard MM Cpl 40428 70 Fd Coy Royal Engineers
CRAWFORD Samuel MM L/Sjt 16365 Royal Inniskilling Fusiliers
CRAWFORD Sydney MM Cpl 16891 Liverpool Regt
CRAWFORD Thomas MM L/Cpl 15544 9th Royal Dublin Fusiliers
CRAWFORD Thomas MM L/Cpl 27233 Border Regt
CRAWFORD Thomas A. MM Dvr 404112 106 Fd Coy Royal Engineers
CRAWFORD Thomas L. MM L/Cpl 267465 1/6th Seaforth Highlanders
CRAWFORD W. MM Sjt 20948 RGA
CRAWFORD William MM Pte 53606 1st Royal Scots Fusiliers
CRAWFORD William MM+Bar Pte 8909 1st South Staffordshire Regt
CRAWFORD William MM Sjt 9942 2nd Seaforth Highlanders
CRAWLEY Alfred J. MM Pte 45463 16th Lancashire Fusiliers KIA 23.8.18.
CRAWLEY Ernest William MM L/Cpl 44438 20th Manchester Regt
CRAWLEY F.T. MM Sjt 43174 10th Essex Regt
CRAWLEY George F. MM L/Cpl 630313 20th London Regt
CRAWLEY George H. MM Pte 704065 2/23rd London Regt
CRAWLEY Herbert Francis MM L/Cpl 552137 2/16th London Regt DOW 19.5.17.
CRAWLEY Joseph MM Pte 3142 1/9th Durham Light Infantry Died 14.2.17.
CRAWLEY Michael J. MM Pte 14551 1/1st Berkshire Yeomanry
CRAWLEY Ultimus George MM Pte 9829 6th Oxf & Bucks Light Infantry KIA 20.9.17.
CRAWLEY Walter MM Sjt 25679 B/177 Bde RFA
CRAWLEY William MM Pte 17422 Bedfordshire Regt
CRAWLEY William MM+Bar Sjt 17030 Royal Berkshire Regt
CRAWSHAW Clayton MM Sjt 265270 West Riding Regt
CRAWSHAW Edward "DCM,MM" Sjt L/389 C/148 Bde RFA
CRAWSHAW Ephraim MM Pte 12570 7th Royal Lancaster Regt
CRAWSHAW Frank MM L/Cpl 16276 7th East Yorkshire Regt
CRAWSHAW George MM Sjt 23588 Machine Gun Corps
CRAWSHAW George A. MM Bdr 34838 RFA
CRAWSHAW James "MM,MID" Pte 16044 5th Shropshire Light Infantry DOW 31.8.16.
CRAWSHAW Richard L. MM Pte 67466 1/5th Devonshire Regt
CRAWSHAW Smith MM Gnr 108279 RGA
CRAWSHAW Stanley MM Cpl 201480 Tank Corps
CRAY George MM Sjt 46164 A/46 Bde RFA
CRAY James MM L/Cpl 16061 9th Royal Fusiliers KIA 29.8.18.
CRAYSTON Matthew MM+Bar Sjt 15091 8th Border Regt
CRAZE John MM Sjt 94807 C/46 Bde RFA DOW 12.7.17.
CRAZE Joseph Martin MM Pte 459278 25 Fd Amb RAMC
CREALY Christopher Patrick MM Sjt 6889 2nd Royal Dublin Fusiliers
CREAN Charles MM Sjt 17742 Cheshire Regt
CREAN James MM Pte 14539 2nd Welsh Regt
CREASER Albert "MM,MID" Bdr 49911 'O' Bty RHA
CREASER David T. MM Pte 1362 West Yorkshire Regt
CREASER Fred MM Cpl 2205 Yorkshire Regt
CREASEY Arthur MM Cpl 19400 1st Essex Regt KIA 12.10.16.
CREASEY F.W.J. MM Cpl G/1459 7th East Kent Regt
CREASEY Henry P. MM Pte M2/082625 Army Service Corps
CREASEY John W. MM Pte 40798 8th Lincolnshire Regt
CREASEY Tom MM Cpl 2184 29 Bde RFA
CREASEY Walter MM L/Cpl 26996 12th East Surrey Regt
CREASEY Walter MM Pte 23123 Lincolnshire Regt
CREASEY William A. MM Pte 26847 Lincolnshire Regt
CREASY Frederick H. MM Pte 47387 RAMC
CREBBIN James Henry MM Pte 4153 1st Welsh Guards KIA 7.9.18.
CREBBIN Walter J. MM Gnr 77117 RGA
CREBER Richard William MM Pte 21662 9th Devonshire Regt KIA 26.10.17.
CRECRAFT Leonard MM Pte 2295 RAMC
CREDLAND Clark MM L/Cpl 14369 4th Dragoon Guards
CREDLAND William MM Sjt 39141 53 Coy Machine Gun Corps
CREE John Edgar MM Sjt 26674 Notts & Derby Regt
CREE John W. MM+Bar Spr 48806 23 Div Sig Coy Royal Engineers
CREECH Bertie MM Pte 25727 Somerset Light Infantry
CREED James "DCM,MM(201256 Manch Regt)" Sjt 205676 1st Wiltshire Regt
CREED James G.A. MM Pte 8673 8th East Surrey Regt
CREEDON John MM+Bar Sjt 16650 9th Bn Machine Gun Corps
CREEDON Patrick MM Pte 7054 1st Royal Munster Fusiliers
CREEDY Frederick W. MM 2nd Cpl 508155 Royal Engineers
CREEK Arthur E. MM Sjt 52353 RFA
CREEK Charles P. MM 2nd Cpl 1518 2/1(W Riding)Fd Coy Royal Engineers
CREEK Joseph MM L/Sjt 200846 1/5th Highland Light Infantry
CREER Alfred G. "DCM,MM" Sjt 64679 110 Bty 24 Bde RFA
CREER Stanley "MM,MID" Bdr 485 MGC(Heavy Branch)
CREES George C. MM+Bar Sjt 80027 1/1st Essex Yeomanry.
CREES Herbert MM Cpl 53829 Royal Engineers
CREESE John MM L/Cpl 18132 2nd Coldstream Guards
CREEVY William MM Sjt 147898 255 Tunnelling Coy Royal Engineers
CREFFIELD Thomas MM Pte 9270 2nd Royal Berkshire Regt
CREIGHTON Arthur F. MM Pte 74780 RAMC

CREIGHTON Bertram Buxton MM Pte 302825 10th Bn Tank Corps
CREIGHTON Charles MM Pte 12/6051 6th Lancashire Fusiliers
CREIGHTON Henry MM Gnr 42338 42 Bty 2 Bde RFA KIA 23.4.17.
CREIGHTON James T. MM Pte 45177 South Wales Borderers
CREIGHTON Thomas O. MM Dvr 64562 24 Bde RFA
CREITH Denis MM Pte M2/074211 Army Service Corps
CREKE John William Wakefield MM Pte 86651 21st Bn Machine Gun Corps
CRELLEY George MM Pte 24192 1/4th Yorkshire Light Infantry
CREMER A.H. MM+Bar Cpl G/7649 7th East Kent Regt
CRERAR Ernest MM Gnr 786312 B/312 Bde RFA
CRERAR Peter MM Cpl 201208 1/4th Royal Scots
CRERAR Willie MM Sjt 24601 1/6th West Riding Regt
CRESDEE Henry MM Pte 15773 15th Hampshire Regt
CRESSEL George E. MM L/Bdr 97550 B/123 Bde RFA
CRESSEY Robert MM Sjt 357 11th East Yorkshire Regt
CRESSWELL Albert MM Pte 26515 West Riding Regt
CRESSWELL Charles MM+Bar Cpl 67991 Royal Engineers
CRESSWELL Colin MM Dvr 97394 D/50 Bde RFA
CRESSWELL Harry MM Pte 25301 Notts & Derby Regt
CRESSWELL S.C. MM Cpl 46334 RGA
CRESSWELL Sidney MM CQMS 200841 5th South Staffordshire Regt
CRESSWELL William H. MM Sjt 9447 2nd York & Lancaster Regt
CRESWELL F. MM Sjt 377273 Manchester Regt
CRESWELL William MM Pte 21775 9th Notts & Derby Regt
CRESWICK Benjamin F. MM L/Cpl Y/112 3rd King's Royal Rifle Corps
CRESWICK William MM Sjt 776830 C/245 Bde RFA DOW 8.3.18.
CREW Albert Edward MM Sjt 10273 6th Somerset Light Infantry
CREW Daniel MM Pte 13957 2nd Lincolnshire Regt KIA 19.11.17.
CREW John MM Bdr 18708 C/86 Bde RFA
CREW Thomas MM Dvr 88664 22 Bde RFA
CREW William MM Pte 105545 13th Liverpool Regt
CREW William MM Sjt 27452 29 Bde RFA
CREWDSON Dorothea Mary Lynette MM Miss F BRCS(VAD)
CREWE Clifford MM Pte 26751 10th Royal Warwickshire Regt
CREWE George Charles "MM,MID" Cpl 38505 A/315 Bde RFA DOW 13.4.18.
CREWE George H. MM Pte 331076 Royal Scots
CREWE Hedley MM Pte 240528 Royal Welsh Fusiliers
CREWE William Ewart MM+Bar Sjt A/157 King's Royal Rifle Corps
CREWS Hubert Squires MM L/Cpl 2311 1/6th London Regt KIA 7.6.17.
CREWS William J. MM L/Sjt 18260 Machine Gun Corps
CRIBB Edwin MM L/Cpl 18811 2nd Dorsetshire Regt
CRIBB Herbert S. MM Pte 47406 Northumberland Fusiliers
CRIBBIN John H. MM Sjt 24498 20th Liverpool Regt
CRIBBIN William MM Bdr 91861 RFA
CRICH Adam MM L/Cpl 26148 Notts & Derby Regt
CRICHTON Alfred W. MM Pte G9855 Royal West Surrey Regt
CRICHTON Charles MM+Bar CSM 201017 8th Royal Lancaster Regt
CRICHTON Daniel MM L/Cpl 11864 9th Royal Irish Fusiliers
CRICHTON Donald MM L/Cpl 30504 1/4th King's Own Scottish Borderers
CRICHTON George Johnston MM Sjt 511063 2/14th London Regt
CRICHTON James MM Pte 41152 9th Scottish Rifles KIA 21.3.18.
CRICHTON James MM Pte 23908 5th Cameron Highlanders
CRICHTON Norman D. MM Sjt 9224 17th Manchester Regt
CRICHTON Thomas MM Sjt 50927 91 Fd Coy Royal Engineers
CRICK Amos MM Pte 10241 Royal Irish Regt
CRICK Ernest MM Sjt 24028 RGA
CRICK Frank F. MM L/Cpl 12560 9th Essex Regt
CRICK Frederick MM+Bar Pte 14818 1st Grenadier Guards
CRICK George Albert. MM L/Cpl 1072 8th East Surrey Regt KIA 12.10.17.
CRICK George William MM Cpl 102337 15th Bn Machine Gun Corps
CRICK Herbert J. MM L/Cpl 12145 7th Suffolk Regt
CRICKETT Maurice E. MM Gnr 970925 RFA
CRICKMORE John J. MM Pte 13904 8th Suffolk Regt
CRIDDLE Frederick MM Pte 21985 Royal Berkshire Regt
CRIDDLE Henry MM Dvr 13699 16 Bty 41 Bde RFA KIA 28.8.18.
CRIDDLE Sidney MM Bdr 84409 C/286 Bde RFA
CRIDLAN Evelyn M. MM Miss F First Aid Nursing Yeomanry
CRIDLAND George MM S/Sjt 97084 11th Bn Tank Corps
CRIDLAND William MM Pte 240190 Somerset Light Infantry
CRIGGIE James MM L/Cpl 11140 12th Royal Scots DOW 20.9.17.
CRIGHTON Harry MM 2nd Cpl 65408 122 Fd Coy Royal Engineers
CRIGHTON James W. MM Sjt 202278 1/4th Cheshire Regt
CRILLEY John MM+Bar Pte B/6860 1st Scottish Rifles
CRILLY Francis MM L/Cpl 16972 2nd South Lancashire Regt DOW 27.3.18.
CRILLY John MM Pte 14090 9th Royal Irish Fusiliers
CRILLY Michael MM L/Cpl 166834 73 Fd Coy Royal Engineers
CRIMES Henry MM Gnr 42919 127 Bty 29 Bde RFA
CRIMES Wilfred MM Pte 12853 11th Manchester Regt
CRIMMINS John MM Pte 32289 East Surrey Regt
CRIMMINS Patrick MM Pte 18385 1st Royal Irish Fusiliers KIA 24.8.18.
CRINIGAN John W. MM+Bar Sjt 38449 15th Lancashire Fusiliers
CRIPPS Alfred G. "DCM,MM,MID" Sjt 2245 23 Fd Amb RAMC
CRIPPS Edward G. MM Pte G/22501 26th Royal Fusiliers
CRIPPS Ernest G. MM Pte 143094 4th Bn Machine Gun Corps
CRIPPS Frank T. MM Pte 265473 1/1st Bucks Bn Oxf & Bucks Light Infantry
CRIPPS Frederick MM L/Cpl 18150 Bedfordshire Regt
CRIPPS George H. MM L/Cpl B/21165 2nd Highland Light Infantry
CRIPPS Herbert John "MM,CdiG(It)" Cpl 203850 1/4th Royal Berkshire Regt
CRIPPS James A. MM Pte M2/100273 Army Service Corps
CRIPPS Leonard G. MM Sjt 9821 1st Royal West Surrey Regt
CRIPPS Percy J. MM Pte 372983 8th London Regt
CRIPPS Richard W. MM 2nd Cpl 33865 Royal Engineers
CRIPPS Sidney MM Pte 10376 5th Royal Berkshire Regt
CRIPPS Thomas MM Gnr 30762 5 Bde RFA
CRIPPS William G.Y. MM Cpl 810063 RFA
CRIPSEY Arthur William MM Gnr 765466 2 Bde RFA
CRISFIELD William Thomas MM Pte 1228 23rd Northumberland Fusiliers
CRISFORD John R. "DCM,MM" Sjt 350196 1/7th London Regt
CRISP A. MM Sjt 1994 2nd Royal Highlanders
CRISP Albert E. MM Sjt 22138 1st Royal Warwickshire Regt
CRISP Alfred Leslie MM Cpl 18496 7th Norfolk Regt KIA 10.8.18.
CRISP Ambrose MM Cpl 99377 Royal Engineers
CRISP Arthur E. MM L/Cpl 5199 8th East Surrey Regt
CRISP Christopher MM L/Cpl 41745 8th Lincolnshire Regt
CRISP Ernest MM L/Cpl 9322 1st Royal Berkshire Regt
CRISP Frederick MM L/Cpl 235014 2nd Lincolnshire Regt
CRISP Frederick William "MM,MSM,MID" Sjt Drummer 4811 2nd Royal Warwickshire Regt
CRISP George MM Pte 9120 4th Worcestershire Regt
CRISP George Henry MM+Bar Cpl 64349 150 Fd Coy Royal Engineers
CRISP Harold John Francis MM L/Cpl 9289 1/5th London Regt
CRISP Harry MM Pte 8738 2nd Leicestershire Regt
CRISP Howard V. MM Pnr 199063 Royal Engineers
CRISP James Jarvis MM Sjt 64348 150 Fd Coy Royal Engineers
CRISP John C.H. MM Pte 468 10th Lincolnshire Regt
CRISP John Thomas MM Cpl 1569 190 Bde RFA
CRISP Leonard Short MM L/Sjt 11908 1st Scots Guards
CRISP Leslie MM Gnr 90703 228 Siege Bty RGA
CRISP William "MM,MID" Pte 2/10465 2nd South Wales Borderers
CRISPIN Ernest J. MM+Bar Sjt 240113 1/5th Devonshire Regt
CRISPIN Frederick A. MM Pte 457400 RAMC
CRISPIN Lewis "DCM,MM" Sjt 8826 2nd Devonshire Regt
CRIST Charles MM Pte 3766 Royal West Surrey Regt
CRISTOE William C. MM Sjt 69731 39 Bde RFA
CRITCHELL George W. MM Pte 633179 20th London Regt
CRITCHETT Frederick J. MM Cpl 46937 11th Northumberland Fusiliers
CRITCHLEY Arthur MM Pte 265325 1/7th Liverpool Regt
CRITCHLEY Edward MM Sjt 485 14th York & Lancaster Regt
CRITCHLEY Frank MM Pte 25357 10th Manchester Regt
CRITCHLEY Fred A. MM Sjt 64542 37 Div Sig Coy Royal Engineers
CRITCHLEY Frederick D. MM Spr 183791 461 Fd Coy Royal Engineers
CRITCHLEY George Frederick Andrew "MM,MSM" CSM 6793 48th Bn Machine Gun Corps
CRITCHLEY Harry MM Pte 265315 9th West Riding Regt
CRITCHLEY James MM Cpl 5072 A/121 Bde RFA
CRITCHLEY James MM Sjt 6340 Royal Engineers
CRITCHLEY John MM Sjt 11020 Liverpool Regt
CRITCHLEY John W. MM Cpl 4654 RFA
CRITCHLEY John William MM Sjt 241042 1/5th South Lancashire Regt
CRITCHLEY Joseph MM Pte 48962 17th Lancashire Fusiliers
CRITCHLEY Richard H. MM Cpl(MCDR) 29706 Royal Engineers
CRITCHLEY Robert MM Sjt 3716 A/122 Bde RFA

CRITCHLEY Robert Henry MM Pte 201049 2/4th North Lancashire Regt DOW 17.11.17.
CRITCHLOW James T. MM Pte 11579 9th North Staffordshire Regt
CRITCHLOW William H.C. MM L/Cpl 9943 1st Cheshire Regt
CRITCHLOW William Henry MM Dvr 48423 19 Div Sig Coy Royal Engineers
CRITTENDEN William G. MM Pte 7939 King's Royal Rifle Corps
CROAD Alfred J. MM Gnr 966653 RFA
CROAD Henry T. MM Pte 682291 22nd London Regt
CROAL Patrick MM Cpl 465 1/5th Highland Light Infantry KIA 8.11.17.
CROASDALE Harry MM Bdr 701294 B/330 Bde RFA
CROCKER Albert Ernest MM Pte 27795 King's Own Scottish Borderers
CROCKER Frank A. MM Pte 1289 1/5th London Regt
CROCKER Fred Ernest MM Dvr 20859 RFA
CROCKER G. MM Cpl 459018 RAMC
CROCKER Lewis F. MM Pte 235160 5th Leicestershire Regt
CROCKER William G. MM L/Cpl 470688 12th London Regt
CROCKETT Charles King MM Gnr 699 C/256 Bde RFA
CROCKETT George MM Pte 21971 Cameron Highlanders
CROCKETT John MM RQMS 6894 1st Wiltshire Regt
CROCKETT S.W. MM Bdr 970256 RFA
CROCKFORD Albert H.J. MM Cpl 304921 5th London Regt
CROCKFORD George W. MM Pte 201705 Royal Berkshire Regt
CROCKFORD John MM L/Cpl 10001 6th Somerset Light Infantry
CROCKFORD Leonard S. MM Sjt 36801 RGA
CROCKHAM Walter MM L/Cpl 203387 4th Yorkshire Light Infantry
CROCOMBE Austin H. MM Pte 55910 14th Welsh Regt
CROCOMBE Frederick H. MM Cpl 1113 Royal Engineers
CROFT Alfred MM Pte 277206 Manchester Regt
CROFT Christopher MM+Bar Sjt 45539 C/104 Bde RFA
CROFT Frederick H. MM Pte 11721 7th Duke of Cornwall's LI
CROFT George William "MM,CG(F)" Pte 318 15th Durham Light Infantry KIA 3.5.17.
CROFT Herbert MM Dvr 687302 RFA
CROFT James MM Pte 8525 2nd Yorkshire Regt
CROFT P. MM Cpl 200260 Royal Scots
CROFT Thomas MM Sjt 11679 1st Liverpool Regt
CROFT Thomas MM Pte 27218 6th Northamptonshire Regt
CROFT Thomas A. MM Cpl A/1639 1st King's Royal Rifle Corps
CROFT William MM Gnr 79677 RFA
CROFT William John MM Pte 9428 1st East Kent Regt KIA 14.4.18.
CROFTS Benjamin Philip MM L/Cpl 118654 7th Labour Bn Royal Engineers
CROFTS Herbert MM Pte 202671 Royal Highlanders
CROFTS Hermon E. MM+Bar Sjt 405160 RAMC
CROFTS James MM Cpl 240121 Royal Welsh Fusiliers
CROFTS Norman Herbert MM Sjt 810561 RFA
CROFTS Robert H. MM Pte 21839 8th York & Lancaster Regt
CROFTS T. MM L/Cpl P2105 Military Mounted Police
CROFTS Thomas MM Sjt 13989 1st Lincolnshire Regt KIA 7.9.18.
CROGHAN William "MM,MIDx2" Sjt 69997 D/76 Bde RFA
CROLL Edgar MM Cpl 2006 1/7th Notts & Derby Regt
CROLL Lindsay S. MM Sjt 9925 1/5th Seaforth Highlanders
CROLL Samuel A. MM+Bar Cpl 54951 RFA
CROLL Walter MM Pte 200315 1/4th Royal Highlanders
CROLLA Charles Joseph MM Pte 32342 Manchester Regt
CROMACK Walter Benjamin MM Sjt 56581 19 Div Sig Coy Royal Engineers
CROMARTY Alexander MM Cpl 66147 51st Bn Machine Gun Corps
CROMBIE Arthur MM Pte 16300 West Riding Regt
CROMBIE David MM Cpl 32738 66 Coy Machine Gun Corps
CROMBIE Edward MM Cpl 8157 1st Northumberland Fusiliers KIA 5.7.17.
CROMBIE Ernest A. MM Gnr 751638 A/93 Bde RFA
CROMBIE James MM Pte 295208 12th Royal Scots Fusiliers
CROMBIE James G. MM Pte 241336 8th Middlesex Regt
CROMBIE Leonard MM Dvr 1150 B/121 Bde RFA
CROME Frederick Arthur MM Sjt 61940 RFA
CROME James MM Dvr 15073 4 Div Ammn Col RFA
CROMER Harry MM+Bar L/Sjt 19192 13th Liverpool Regt
CROMIE Samuel MM Cpl 73765 Royal Engineers
CROMIE Thomas C. MM Pte 95248 3rd Bn Tank Corps
CROMPTON Albert Allen MM Pte 73176 Notts & Derby Regt
CROMPTON Albert Edward MM L/Cpl 430287 504 Fd Coy Royal Engineers
CROMPTON James MM Cpl 43828 5/6th Royal Scots
CROMPTON John MM Sjt 10736 1st North Lancashire Regt
CROMPTON John B. MM L/Cpl 7613 Royal Fusiliers
CROMPTON Joseph MM Pte 15164 24th Manchester Regt
CROMPTON Joseph MM Cpl 14605 2nd Suffolk Regt DOW 2.10.18.
CROMPTON Joseph A. MM Pte 243522 North Lancashire Regt
CROMPTON Peter MM L/Cpl 20392 4th Grenadier Guards
CROMPTON Philip MM Pte 9089 1st Hampshire Regt
CROMPTON Richard "DCM,MM" Sjt 23823 11th Manchester Regt
CROMPTON Stanley MM+Bar L/Cpl 16529 6th King's Own Scottish Borderers
CROMPTON Stanley MM Sjt 6855 16th Manchester Regt
CROMPTON Walter MM Pte 41521 1/3rd(Highland)Fd Amb RAMC
CROMPTON William MM Pte 84 GMGR
CROMPTON William T. MM Sjt 241101 Royal Lancaster Regt
CRONE Joseph MM Pte 9/14332 Royal Irish Rifles
CRONE Joseph Hunter MM Pte 25171 8th Border Regt DOW 21.4.18.
CRONE Robert MM Sjt 8157 1st Border Regt KIA 14.4.17.
CRONIN Alfred MM L/Cpl 392416 9th London Regt
CRONIN Arthur J. MM Cpl 76490 140 Siege Bty RGA
CRONIN Daniel MM L/Cpl 77480 Tank Corps
CRONIN Daniel "MM,MID" Pte 11492 3rd Grenadier Guards
CRONIN Daniel MM L/Cpl 6234 57 Fd Amb RAMC
CRONIN James MM Sjt 12712 4th Middlesex Regt
CRONIN John MM L/Cpl 6509 2nd Irish Guards
CRONIN John B. MM Sjt 533599 6th London Regt
CRONIN Peter MM Pte M2/115347 Army Service Corps
CRONIN W. MM Sjt W/2192 D/119 Bde RFA
CRONK Sidney "MM,MSM" CQMS 8129 1st Royal West Kent Regt
CROOK Alfred MM Sjt 205088 Lancashire Fusiliers
CROOK Alfred MM Cpl SE/2750 Army Veterinary Corps
CROOK Alfred Valentine MM Sjt 46854 Machine Gun Corps
CROOK Benjamin MM Pte 300700 1/8th Arg & Suth Highlanders
CROOK Clarence MM Cpl 265239 West Riding Regt
CROOK Edward MM Pte 722872 24th London Regt
CROOK Frank MM Sjt 240145 8th Middlesex Regt
CROOK Fred MM Gnr 57518 41 Bde RFA
CROOK Frederick E. MM L/Cpl 1603 1/1st Buckinghamshire Yeo
CROOK George MM Cpl 98268 3rd Bn Machine Gun Corps
CROOK George F. MM L/Sjt S/16030 Rifle Brigade
CROOK Harold MM Sjt 240394 Liverpool Regt
CROOK Harry MM Gnr 156302 238 Siege Bty RGA
CROOK Henry J. MM L/Sjt 2022 10th Royal Fusiliers
CROOK Herbert MM L/Cpl 16945 15th Hussars
CROOK Herbert MM Pte 357 9th Lancashire Fusiliers KIA 30.10.17.
CROOK Horace G. MM Pte 252685 11th Essex Regt
CROOK Jack MM Sjt 7457 11th Lancashire Fusiliers
CROOK James MM Pte 13385 10th Scottish Rifles
CROOK Reginald MM Pte 2524 1/6th West Riding Regt
CROOK William MM L/Sjt 203882 20th Durham Light Infantry
CROOK William MM Pte 59860 24th Royal Welsh Fusiliers
CROOK William MM Cpl 200509 1/4th Cheshire Regt
CROOK William MM Cpl 10941 8/10th Gordon Highlanders
CROOK William MM Cpl C/194 16th King's Royal Rifle Corps KIA 24.9.17.
CROOK William MM Cpl L/3201 D/149 Bde RFA Died 1.6.17.
CROOK William Augustus MM Gnr 83786 A/47 Bde RFA KIA 10.4.17.
CROOK William G. MM Gnr 71184 24 Bde RFA
CROOK William S. MM Pte 33615 Border Regt
CROOKE George MM L/Cpl 208919 74 Div Sig Coy Royal Engineers
CROOKES Edward MM L/Cpl 15521 Coldstream Guards
CROOKES James MM Cpl 40632 RGA
CROOKES Redfern Bateman MM Sjt 3883 Machine Gun Corps
CROOKS Albert MM Pte 261043 13th West Riding Regt
CROOKS Alfonso MM Pte 201203 Leicestershire Regt
CROOKS Henry Robert MM Pnr 283739 23 Light Rly Coy Royal Engineers
CROOKS James E. MM+Bar 2nd Cpl 482103 49 Div Sig Coy Royal Engineers
CROOKS James H. MM Cpl 10/992 East Yorkshire Regt
CROOKS John R. MM L/Cpl 243267 1st Lancashire Fusiliers
CROOKS Joseph MM Pte 22968 1/4th Yorkshire Light Infantry
CROOKS Thomas MM L/Cpl 72379 7th Royal West Surrey Regt
CROOKSTON Alexander MM Sjt 45730 RAMC
CROOKSTON James MM Spr 86381 Royal Engineers
CROOME Jessie Hedley "DCM,MM" Cpl 13064 IV Corps Cyclist Bn Army Cyclist Corps
CROOME William H.J. MM Pte 45043 1st Royal Inniskilling Fusiliers
CROPLEY Thomas MM Cpl 17931 9th Cheshire Regt

CROPLEY William H. MM Pte 36223 Royal Fusiliers
CROPLEY William Joseph MM Bdr 651456 RFA
CROPPER James MM Sjt 1554 1/6th Cheshire Regt
CROPPER Joseph "DCM,MM" CSM 238203 2/7th West Yorkshire Regt
CROPPER Robert H. MM Pte 61958 16th Cheshire Regt
CROSBIE Adam MM L/Cpl 45878 2nd Royal Scots
CROSBIE John A.M. MM Pte 32835 Royal Lancaster Regt
CROSBIE Robert MM S/Sjt Armourer T/1098 Army Ordnance Corps
CROSBY Arthur E. MM L/Bdr 151698 17 Div Ammn Col RFA
CROSBY Basil MM+Bar Sjt 200423 1/5th Liverpool Regt
CROSBY Frank MM Cpl M2/051525 Army Service Corps
CROSBY John MM Pte W/934 1st Cheshire Regt
CROSBY John MM Gnr 54590 RFA
CROSBY John M. MM Cpl 253845 4 Div Sig Coy Royal Engineers
CROSBY Joseph MM Pte 450068 Labour Corps
CROSBY Robert H. MM+Bar L/Cpl 240608 Border Regt
CROSBY Thomas MM Sjt 1087 1/22nd London Regt
CROSBY Thomas MM Sjt 17504 8th North Lancashire Regt KIA 4.9.17.
CROSBY Thomas MM Pte 15590 9th Royal Dublin Fusiliers
CROSBY William Edward MM CSM 73 1/6th Hampshire Regt Retrospective MM Mesopotamia.Died 1.9.16.
CROSER Thomas W. MM Sjt 16234 8th East Yorkshire Regt
CROSIER J.W. MM Sjt Farrier 36189 14 Bde RFA
CROSLAND Ernest MM Gnr L/29363 B/168 Bde RFA
CROSLAND Frederick MM Pte 37609 23 Fd Amb RAMC
CROSLAND George H. MM Sjt 203771 RFA
CROSLAND Reginald J.E. MM Pte 4709 3 Fd Amb RAMC
CROSLAND William D. MM+Bar Pte 240433 1/5th West Riding Regt
CROSS Ackrier MM L/Bdr 116509 RFA
CROSS Albert MM Pte 59207 10th West Yorkshire Regt
CROSS Albert Edward MM Dve 70912 35 Bde RFA KIA 18.10.17.
CROSS Albert G. MM Pte 12857 Northamptonshire Regt
CROSS Albert J. MM+Bar Sjt 265316 1/2nd Monmouthshire Regt
CROSS Alfred S. MM Pte 110795 Machine Gun Corps
CROSS Amos MM Cpl 15307 1 Special Coy Middlesex Regt
CROSS Arthur MM Pte 33423 1/5th Border Regt KIA 30.9.18.
CROSS Arthur MM Bdr 955364 A/236 Bde RFA
CROSS Arthur H. MM Dvr 44115 A/152 Bde RFA
CROSS Arthur Henry "VC,MM" Cpl 62990 40th Bn Machine Gun Corps
CROSS Arthur J. MM Sjt 69409 194 Siege Bty RGA
CROSS Cecil MM Cpl 235231 8th Worcestershire Regt
CROSS Cecil H. MM Sjt 8469 1st Norfolk Regt
CROSS Charles MM Sjt 9342 RGA
CROSS Christopher John MM Pte 43031 Bedfordshire Regt
CROSS Claud G. MM Cpl 325320 1/1st Cambridgeshire Regt
CROSS Cyril MM L/Cpl 255 9th Royal Fusiliers
CROSS Ernest "DCM,MM+Bar,MID,CG(F)" CSM 11775 15th Hampshire Regt
CROSS Eugene MM Pte 364291 RAMC
CROSS F.R. MM Pte 233152 London Regt
CROSS F.T. MM Sjt 24248 Cheshire Regt
CROSS Frank MM L/Cpl 18511 9th Royal Warwickshire Regt
CROSS Frank William L. "DCM,MM" Pte 40458 75 Fd Amb RAMC
CROSS Frederick J. MM+Bar Sjt 030824 81 Ammn Section Army Ordnance Corps
CROSS George MM Sjt 103756 2nd Notts & Derby Regt
CROSS Gilbert Rhodes "MC,MM" RSM 200026 1/5th Liverpool Regt
CROSS Harold C. MM Pte 302826 11th Bn Tank Corps
CROSS Harry James MM Sjt 14140 16th Highland Light Infantry
CROSS Henry E. MM Pte 265296 Oxf & Bucks Light Infantry
CROSS Henry J. MM Bdr 90541 RFA
CROSS James MM SQMS 235009 1/1st Gloucestershire Yeomanry
CROSS James MM+Bar L/Cpl 100459 33 Div Sig Coy Royal Engineers
CROSS John MM Pte 242303 1st East Lancashire Regt
CROSS John MM Sjt 9339 1st East Kent Regt
CROSS John MM Spr 148318 1 Div Sig Coy Royal Engineers
CROSS John A. "DCM,MM" Bdr 203495 D/83 Bde RFA
CROSS John Choulditch MM Pte B/200397 11th Rifle Brigade KIA 1.4.18.
CROSS John Robert MM L/Cpl 82534 12th Bn Machine Gun Corps
CROSS John Young MM Pte 203083 1/5th Royal Warwickshire Regt
CROSS Joseph MM L/Cpl 476479 Royal Engineers
CROSS Joseph A. MM Pte 204745 Royal West Kent Regt
CROSS Leonard E. MM L/Sjt 25521 Machine Gun Corps
CROSS Mark MM+Bar Sjt 12017 Northumberland Fusiliers
CROSS Matthew MM Gnr 37135 RFA
CROSS Norman Harold MM Pte S/35329 1/17th London Regt DOW 3.9.18.
CROSS Percival Sydney MM Pte 66014 75 Fd Amb RAMC
CROSS Percy MM Sjt 11131 38th Bn Machine Gun Corps
CROSS Percy MM Spr 14790 Royal Engineers
CROSS Phillip MM Sjt 4380 RGA
CROSS Samuel MM L/Sjt 307880 West Riding Regt
CROSS Samuel L. MM Pte 40210 West Yorkshire Regt
CROSS Sidney G. MM Bdr 86807 B/95 Bde RFA
CROSS Stanley MM Pte 24497 3rd Grenadier Guards
CROSS Stanley MM Cpl 2054 12th Royal Irish Rifles
CROSS Thomas MM+Bar Pte 238003 1/4th Royal Lancaster Regt
CROSS Thomas MM L/Cpl 24277 North Lancashire Regt
CROSS Thomas G. MM Sjt G/18484 3rd Royal Fusiliers
CROSS Tudor MM Pte 54500 Royal Welsh Fusiliers
CROSS W.G. MM Cpl 51644 Machine Gun Corps
CROSS Walter MM CQMS 1262 1/5th Cheshire Regt
CROSS Walter MM Sjt 21746 South Lancashire Regt
CROSS William MM Sjt 19012 RGA
CROSS William A. MM Cpl 1311 2nd Royal Welsh Fusiliers
CROSS William F. MM Sjt 67063 30 Bde RFA
CROSSAN Hugh MM L/Cpl 8299 11th Hussars
CROSSBY Leonard Godfrey MM Bdr 353508 RGA
CROSSDALE George MM Pte 24218 2nd South Wales Borderers KIA 11.4.18.
CROSSIN Robert G. MM Pte 14794 6/7th Royal Scots Fusiliers
CROSSKEY Charles P. MM Sjt 61524 RAMC
CROSSLAND Albert MM Pte 42070 South Wales Borderers
CROSSLAND Jack MM L/Cpl 263053 2/5th Yorkshire Light Infantry KIA 27.11.17.
CROSSLAND James MM Pte 17/515 West Yorkshire Regt
CROSSLAND James H. MM Pte 17497 8th Yorkshire Light Infantry
CROSSLAND John MM Pte 275794 5/6th Royal Scots
CROSSLAND Sidney MM Sjt 200405 1/4th York & Lancaster Regt
CROSSLEY Edward Charles MM Cpl 546579 512 Fd Coy Royal Engineers KIA 14.10.18.
CROSSLEY Eleazer MM Pte 12063 6th York & Lancaster Regt
CROSSLEY Frank MM Gnr Sig 159997 55 Bty 33 Bde RFA
CROSSLEY Fred MM Pte 17211 Yorkshire Light Infantry
CROSSLEY George W. MM Pte 38553 RAMC
CROSSLEY H. MM Pte 52281 Cheshire Regt
CROSSLEY James MM Dvr L/28113 B/168 Bde RFA
CROSSLEY James A. MM Pte 202081 Lancashire Fusiliers
CROSSLEY James H. MM+Bar Cpl 59215 70 Bty 34 Bde RFA
CROSSLEY John MM Pte 12580 16th Lancashire Fusiliers
CROSSLEY John MM BSM 112750 255 Siege Bty RGA
CROSSLEY John W. MM Sjt 50 1/4th West Riding Regt
CROSSLEY Leonard W. MM Pte 133650 Machine Gun Corps
CROSSLEY Robert MM Gnr 66495 RFA
CROSSLEY Sam MM Pte B/20290 Royal Fusiliers
CROSSLEY Samuel MM Sjt 21352 22nd Manchester Regt
CROSSLEY Thomas MM Pte 52869 13th Durham Light Infantry
CROSSLEY Wilfred MM Pte 285219 13th Welsh Regt
CROSSLEY William MM L/Cpl 201229 4th North Lancashire Regt
CROSSLEY William MM Cpl 45187 K Bty RHA
CROSSLEY William MM+Bar Pte 7285 66 Fd Amb RAMC
CROSSLEY William Enoch "MC,MM(13033 Pte)" T/2Lt North Lancashire Regt
CROSSLEY William George MM Pte 3066 1/15th London Regt
CROSSTHWAITE Daniel MM Pte 26731 Hampshire Regt
CROSSWELL Henry MM L/Cpl 18519 Royal Fusiliers
CROSTHWAITE Frederick MM Spr 34503 Royal Engineers
CROSTHWAITE Walter MM+Bar Sjt 682358 22nd London Regt
CROSTON Matthew MM L/Cpl 7275 Coldstream Guards
CROSTON R. MM Spr 610333 55 Fd Coy Royal Engineers
CROTHERS Henry MM Pte 76141 Notts & Derby Regt
CROTHERS Thomas MM L/Cpl 17510 14th Royal Irish Rifles
CROUCH Alfred MM L/Cpl G/7728 10th Royal West Surrey Regt Died 24.12.17.
CROUCH Arthur MM Pte 63373 Machine Gun Corps
CROUCH Arthur Edmund MM Pte 302522 19th Durham Light Infantry
CROUCH Ernest L. MM Dvr T4/238601 Army Service Corps
CROUCH Frank W. MM Spr 85850 Royal Engineers
CROUCH Frederick George MM Pte G/4209 13th Royal Fusiliers KIA 14.11.16.
CROUCH George MM Pte 49334 RAMC
CROUCH George H. MM Pte 30183 East Lancashire Regt
CROUCH John H. MM Pte 202892 5/6th Scottish Rifles

CROUCH Walter MM Pte R/33160 King's Royal Rifle Corps
CROUCHEN George Edmund MM L/Cpl 66791 110 Coy Machine Gun Corps KIA 11.10.17.
CROUCHER Charles MM+Bar Pte 18307 2nd Royal Irish Regt
CROUCHER Edwin MM Pte 205017 15th Hampshire Regt
CROUCHER Frank H. MM 2nd Cpl 30440 Royal Engineers
CROUCHER Richard "MM,CG(It)" Sjt 11034 1st Grenadier Guards
CROUCHER Walter H. MM Sjt 67283 3 Bde RHA
CROUCHER William H. MM Cpl 18241 59 Fd Coy Royal Engineers
CROUCHMAN Albert MM Dvr 546415 Royal Engineers
CROUDACE H. MM Pte 1136 17th Royal Fusiliers
CROUGHAN James MM Pte 28931 1st King's Own Scottish Borderers
CROW Alfred C. MM Dvr L/46695 D/250 Bde RFA
CROW Arthur M. MM+Bar Pte 610576 1/19th London Regt
CROW E. MM Pte 242227 1/8th Notts & Derby Regt
CROW Ernest MM Pte 240870 1/5th Leicestershire Regt DOW 5.6.18.
CROW Francis MM Bdr 750208 RFA
CROW Frederick J. MM Pte 25458 Suffolk Regt
CROW George Edward MM Pte 9808 2nd Lincolnshire Regt
CROW George H. MM L/Cpl M2/052308 Army Service Corps
CROW James E.G. "DCM,MM" Cpl 62836 D/110 Bde RFA
CROW Robert W. MM 2nd Cpl 27211 1 Cav Div Sig Sqn Royal Engineers
CROW Sidney C. MM Pte 325019 8th Royal Warwickshire Regt
CROW William F. MM Sjt 352596 RAMC
CROWCROFT Albert W. MM Pte 20058 280 Coy Machine Gun Corps
CROWCROFT Tom R. MM Pte 240328 1/5th Yorkshire Light Infantry
CROWDER Francis A. MM Cpl 42694 17th Liverpool Regt
CROWDER George W. MM L/Cpl 14018 8th Leicestershire Regt
CROWDER Thomas MM Gnr 70021 23 Siege Bty RGA KIA 14.11.16.
CROWDER William MM Sjt 24222 46th Bn Machine Gun Corps
CROWE Edward MM L/Cpl 14335 10th Royal Irish Rifles
CROWE Francis D. MM Pte 372343 8th London Regt
CROWE George MM Pte 86481 46th Bn Machine Gun Corps
CROWE George MM Bdr 785043 RFA
CROWE Gordon Thomas MM Sjt 895077 V/55 Heavy TM Bty RFA
CROWE Harry MM L/Cpl 18065 2nd Coldstream Guards
CROWE Herbert Charles "MM,MID" Sjt 3129 4th Rifle Brigade
CROWE James Alexander MM Sjt 21/1161 12th Northumberland Fusiliers DOW 28.8.18.
CROWE John MM Sjt 755269 A/251 Bde RFA
CROWE John MM Pte 20175 Royal Inniskilling Fusiliers
CROWE John C. MM Sjt 5621 Royal Irish Regt
CROWE Joseph G. MM Gnr 19385 RFA
CROWE Randall MM L/Cpl 301085 1/8th Arg & Suth Highlanders
CROWE Robert J. MM Pte 9819 Wiltshire Regt
CROWE Thomas MM Pte 13128 2nd Suffolk Regt
CROWE Victor George Hanley MM Pte 1358 12th Middlesex Regt Died 22.2.18.
CROWE Walter Nigel MM Sjt M2/223118 Army Service Corps att 180 Siege Bty RGA
CROWE Walter Stanley MM Gnr L/24802 150 Bde RFA
CROWE William MM L/Cpl 16229 5/6th Scottish Rifles
CROWE William MM Pte 4565 1/8th Liverpool Regt
CROWE William W. MM Cpl 99462 RFA
CROWHURST Arthur E.J. MM Sjt 37765 'U' Bty RHA
CROWHURST Charles William Thomas MM Pte 279087 3rd London Regt
CROWHURST Ernest "MM,MSM" Sjt 275001 15 Siege Bty RGA
CROWHURST George MM Sjt 1142 Army Cyclist Corps
CROWHURST John MM Sjt S/6618 8th Royal West Surrey Regt KIA 21.8.16.
CROWHURST Leslie MM Pte 205833 Royal West Kent Regt
CROWL William C. MM Cpl 66171 B/124 Bde RFA
CROWLE David MM L/Cpl 23405 Duke of Cornwall's LI
CROWLEY Duncan MM Spr 440160 Royal Engineers
CROWLEY Henry Stephen MM Pte G/2669 12th Middlesex Regt KIA 15.3.17.
CROWLEY John MM Cpl 18336 2nd Royal Irish Regt
CROWLEY Michael MM Cpl 18623 55 Fd Coy Royal Engineers
CROWLEY William MM Pte 15794 1st Royal Dublin Fusiliers KIA 29.3.18.
CROWLEY William MM Cpl WR/251861 6 Rly Op Coy Royal Engineers
CROWLIE Cecil H. "DCM,MM,MID" Cpl 94805 D/51 Bde RFA
CROWSON Charles Frederick MM Sjt 16372 13th York & Lancaster Regt DOW 28.3.18.
CROWSTON E. "DCM,MM" Sjt 64290 108 Siege Bty RGA
CROWTHER Alexander W. MM Pte 5313 14 Fd Amb. RAMC
CROWTHER Alfred E. MM+Bar Pte 13723 8th Gloucestershire Regt
CROWTHER Bert MM 2nd Cpl 147246 Royal Engineers
CROWTHER Clarence MM L/Cpl 265649 2/5th West Yorkshire Regt
CROWTHER Edward MM+Bar Pte 3466 Durham Light Infantry
CROWTHER Ernest MM Gnr 120852 RFA
CROWTHER Fred MM Pte 306861 2/7th West Riding Regt
CROWTHER Frederick MM Pte 21152 Royal West Surrey Regt
CROWTHER Frederick William MM Gnr Sig 142970 237 Siege Bty RGA
CROWTHER George L. MM Pte F/1475 Middlesex Regt
CROWTHER Harold MM Pte 14523 8th Devonshire Regt KIA 1.7.16.
CROWTHER John C. MM Pte 251602 Manchester Regt
CROWTHER Joseph MM Cpl 36065 RAMC
CROWTHER Lewis MM Pte 22644 Manchester Regt
CROWTHER Orlando MM Pte 53420 9th Yorkshire Light Infantry
CROWTHER Thomas MM Gnr 165297 238 Siege Bty RGA
CROWTHER William MM Bdr L/34215 RFA
CROWTHER William MM Dvr 229297 D/18 Bde RFA
CROXFORD Bert MM CQMS 741231 10th London Regt
CROXFORD Frank MM CQMS 16375 8th Bedfordshire Regt
CROXFORD J.W. MM Sjt 47293 20th Hussars
CROXFORD William Charles MM Pte 47472 9th Welsh Regt KIA 15.10.18.
CROXON Alfred Samuel MM Pte 241328 1st Middlesex Regt
CROXON Charles R. MM Sjt 63906 116 Bty 26 Bde RFA
CROXON F. MM Cpl W/2037 B/119 Bde RFA
CROXON L.A. MM Bdr 285182 24 Heavy Bty RGA
CROXON William MM Gnr 59607 RGA
CROXSON John E. MM Gnr 275316 RGA
CROYDON Edward MM Sjt 478128 456 Fd Coy Royal Engineers
CROYDON Fred MM Cpl 9254 2nd Devonshire Regt
CROYDON Walter George MM L/Cpl 723057 1/24th London Regt DOW 7.4.18.
CROZIER Bertram MM Bdr 36211 27 Siege Bty RGA
CROZIER Frank D. MM+Bar Cpl SPT/390 23rd Royal Fusiliers
CROZIER Henry C. MM+Bar L/Cpl L/12633 5th Lancers
CROZIER Henry Cyril MM Sjt 12/628 12th York & Lancaster Regt KIA 1.7.16.
CROZIER James MM Cpl 200074 1/5th King's Own Scottish Borderers
CROZIER James MM Cpl 325505 1/9th Durham Light Infantry
CROZIER John J. MM Sjt 7165 Royal Irish Rifles
CROZIER John J. MM Pte 3273 Northumberland Fusiliers
CROZIER John T. MM Pte 2109 Northumberland Fusiliers
CRUDDACE Harry MM+Bar Sjt 250391 Durham Light Infantry
CRUDDACE Robert MM Pte 386350 1/1st(Northumbrian)Fd Amb RAMC
CRUDDEN Peter MM+Bar Cpl 10834 1st Royal Dublin Fusiliers
CRUDEN Alexander MM Sjt 6341 8/10th Gordon Highlanders
CRUDGINGTON George Henry MM L/Cpl 350387 7th London Regt DOW 1.5.18.
CRUICKSHANK George J. MM Spr 402116 Royal Engineers
CRUICKSHANK George N. MM Sjt 240477 1/5th Cheshire Regt
CRUICKSHANK Gordon "MM+2 Bars,CG(F)" Pte 301239 89 Fd Amb RAMC
CRUICKSHANK James MM Cpl 49493 12 Bde RFA
CRUICKSHANK John MM+Bar Sjt 7239 C/70 Bde RFA
CRUICKSHANK John G. MM Pte S/23567 1/6th Gordon Highlanders
CRUICKSHANK William MM Sjt 290537 Gordon Highlanders
CRUICKSHANK William D. MM Sjt 265029 Gordon Highlanders
CRUICKSHANKS A. MM Sjt 266146 6th Royal Highlanders
CRUICKSHANKS Alexander MM Cpl 18710 1st King's Own Scottish Borderers
CRUICKSHANKS Arthur MM L/Cpl 788 4th GMGR
CRUICKSHANKS George Brown MM+Bar Sjt 200015 4/5th Royal Highlanders KIA 2.11.17.
CRUICKSHANKS James MM Pte 6887 2nd Royal Scots
CRUICKSHANKS John MM Sjt S/43243 2nd Seaforth Highlanders
CRUICKSHANKS Robert MM L/Cpl 13094 2nd Scottish Rifles
CRUIKSHANK Alexander F. "MM,CG(F)" Pte 40943 King's Own Scottish Borderers
CRUICKSHANKS Thomas MM Pte 11701 7th Yorkshire Regt
CRUM Thomas J. MM+Bar Sjt 18281 5th South Wales Borderers
CRUM William MM Sjt 41205 5/6th Scottish Rifles
CRUMB John Thomas MM L/Cpl 648 1st Welsh Guards DOW 6.9.17.

CRUMMACK E.S. MM Cpl 54152 Royal Engineers
CRUMMACK Fred MM L/Cpl 36615 7th Shropshire Light Infantry
CRUMP Charles MM Sjt 240497 1/6th Royal Warwickshire Regt
CRUMP Charles H. MM Pte 11780 38 Fd Amb RAMC
CRUMP Charles T. MM Pte 471827 12th London Regt
CRUMP Cyril E. "MM,MID" Bdr 91693 RFA
CRUMP Harry MM Gnr 19047 D/124 Bde RFA
CRUMP Henry MM Sjt 29122 113 Heavy Bty RGA
CRUMP John William MM Pte 12094 4th Worcestershire Regt KIA 16.8.17.
CRUMP Robert MM Sjt 9343 1st Royal Irish Regt
CRUMP Seymour H. MM Gnr 57374 RGA
CRUMP Sydney MM Pte 265304 Northumberland Fusiliers
CRUMP W.J. MM Cpl 58164 37 Bde RFA
CRUMP William MM Pte 23309 Oxf & Bucks Light Infantry
CRUMP William H. MM Cpl 22987 8th Royal Lancaster Regt
CRUMPLER George C. MM Pte 24268 Royal West Surrey Regt
CRUMPLIN Frank MM Pte 44297 2nd Worcestershire Regt
CRUMPLIN William "DCM,MM+Bar" Sjt 1685 7th Royal West Surrey Regt
CRUMPTON Frederick W. MM Sjt 200782 1st Norfolk Regt
CRUSE Ernest MM Gnr 675232 RFA
CRUSE George MM S/Sjt Farrier 519 5th Dragoon Guards
CRUTCH Albert F. MM Pte 44594 8th Royal Berkshire Regt
CRUTCHINGTON George MM Dvr 687045 RFA
CRUTCHLEY John George MM L/Cpl 31225 Worcestershire Regt
CRUTCHLEY Sydney C. MM L/Cpl 8232 6th Royal Irish Rifles
CRUTHERS John MM Pte 3187 1/8th Durham Light Infantry
CRUTTENDEN Harry Edwin MM Pte 67503 2/2nd London Regt
CRUWYS Lawrence E. MM Sjt 300368 5th London Regt
CRYDERMAN Norman W. MM Pte M2/153002 Army Service Corps
CRYER Frederick MM Sjt 265626 1/6th West Riding Regt
CRYLE Robert MM Pte 1708 22nd Northumberland Fusiliers KIA 1.7.16.
CRYMBLE Arthur MM Sjt 306144 8th West Yorkshire Regt
CRYSTAL John "DCM,MM" Sjt 83035 202 Fd Coy Royal Engineers
CRYSTAL Thomas Mostyn MM Dvr T/182 Army Service Corps
CRYSTALL Henry Albert MM Bdr 955545 B/236 Bde RFA
CUBBERLEY Thomas MM Pte 11120 2nd Worcestershire Regt DOW 21.9.16.
CUBBON Thomas E. MM Pte 42424 RAMC
CUBITT Charles MM Pte 6731 13th Hussars
CUDE Gordon W. MM Cpl 43606 1/7th Middlesex Regt
CUDE Robert MM+Bar Pte 2192 7th East Kent Regt
CUDWORTH George A. MM Sjt 417022 1 Fd Amb RAMC
CUFF Frederick W. MM Sjt 75279 1/1st Derbyshire Yeomanry
CUFF John "MM,MSM,MID" Sjt 225571 1/1st Monmouthshire Regt
CUFFE Benjamin MM Sjt 2141 1/4th Northumberland Fusiliers KIA 15.9.16.
CUFFE John MM Pte 34580 York & Lancaster Regt
CUGLEY George H. MM Bdr 41538 RFA
CULBERT Samuel MM Pte 11324 9th Royal Inniskilling Fusiliers
CULF Harold MM Gnr 45513 14 Heavy Bty RGA
CULHAM Alfred MM Spr 69904 18 Div Sig Coy Royal Engineers
CULHANE Edward MM Sjt 14984 RGA
CULL Edgar G. MM Pte 242194 8th Worcestershire Regt
CULL Sidney MM Pte 60980 7th Royal Fusiliers
CULL Thomas MM Pte 17271 3rd Bn Machine Gun Corps
CULLEN Arthur MM Sjt 3383 2nd Royal Irish Rifles
CULLEN Arthur Lionel MM L/Cpl 32051 2nd South Lancashire Regt KIA 14.4.18.
CULLEN Aubrey Neville "MM,MID" L/Cpl L/8407 1st East Kent Regt KIA 30.3.17.
CULLEN Cecil J. MM Gnr 91402 RFA
CULLEN Charles C. MM Pnr 83166 Royal Engineers
CULLEN Edward J. MM+Bar Cpl 11913 RGA
CULLEN Fergus McLean MM L/Cpl 25578 7/8th King's Own Scottish Borderers
CULLEN Francis MM Cpl 48012 13th Royal Inniskilling Fusiliers
CULLEN Francis Charles William MM Gnr 2167 241 Bde RFA
CULLEN Hugh MM Sjt 30009 51 Coy Labour Corps
CULLEN J. MM Sjt 19427 355 Siege Bty RGA
CULLEN James MM Pte 1228 7th Royal Irish Rifles
CULLEN James MM Pte 44330 134 Fd Amb RAMC
CULLEN James Cochrane Stevenson MM Cpl 751218 243 Bde RFA
CULLEN James W. MM Sjt 512109 1/18th London Regt
CULLEN Jasper Frederick Stephen MM Sjt 1688 8th East Surrey Regt DOW 23.8.18.
CULLEN John MM Pte 332186 1/6th Liverpool Regt
CULLEN John "MM,MID" Sjt 45988 Royal Engineers
CULLEN John Charles MM SSM 4087 6th Dragoon Guards
CULLEN Joseph MM Cpl 43589 Royal Inniskilling Fusiliers
CULLEN Martin MM Pte 43524 1st Royal Dublin Fusiliers
CULLEN Martin MM Pte 15132 13th Royal Scots
CULLEN Michael MM Pte R/12806 King's Royal Rifle Corps
CULLEN Michael MM Pte 29201 Royal Welsh Fusiliers
CULLEN Patrick MM Gnr 59646 96 Siege Bty RGA
CULLEN Peter MM Cpl 25159 2nd South Wales Borderers
CULLEN Thomas MM Cpl 35162 2nd Highland Light Infantry KIA 26.3.18.
CULLEN William MM Pte 243091 1st Royal Lancaster Regt
CULLEN William L. MM L/Cpl 29373 8th East Surrey Regt
CULLETON Patrick MM L/Cpl 16491 Welsh Regt
CULLEY Alfred MM Pte 19384 7th Norfolk Regt
CULLEY Alfred MM Pte 307180 1/8th West Yorkshire Regt
CULLEY Frederick MM Pte 16642 Royal Berkshire Regt
CULLEY George MM Pte 420012 1/10th London Regt
CULLEY Horace C. MM Cpl R/16801 2nd King's Royal Rifle Corps
CULLEY Samuel MM Bdr 65501 X/34 Med TM Bty RGA DOW 16.6.17.
CULLIGAN John H. MM Pte 44356 RAMC
CULLINANE Timothy MM Pte 43873 2nd Royal Inniskilling Fusiliers
CULLING Ernest F. MM Spr 520106 565 Army Tps Coy Royal Engineers
CULLING Herbert MM Pte 24447 1st Royal West Surrey Regt
CULLIP William H. MM Pte 461043 26 Fd Amb RAMC
CULLIS C.J. MM Pte 14959 South Staffordshire Regt
CULLITON Francis MM Bdsm 9593 2nd West Riding Regt
CULLUM Harry J. MM Sjt S/7303 Army Ordnance Corps
CULLUM Henry Richard MM Pte 242506 South Staffordshire Regt
CULLUM Stanley John "MM,MID" Sjt 46750 2 Bde RFA
CULLUM William MM Pte 306334 5th Bn Tank Corps DOW 7.10.18.
CULLUMBINE Alfred "MM,MSM" Sjt 23658 "49th Bn,148 Coy" Machine Gun Corps
CULLY Albert E. MM Pte 89842 Machine Gun Corps
CULLY Lewis Frank Warner MM Sjt 3341 HAC(Inf)
CULLY Robert MM Sjt 55934 B/104 Bde RFA
CULLY William J. MM Cpl 19608 Machine Gun Corps
CULNANE John MM Pte M/2/055497 2(West Riding)Fd Amb Army Service Corps
CULNANE Richard P. MM Pte MS/1650 HQ 3 Div Army Service Corps
CULPECK Philip MM Gnr 95629 D/83 Bde RFA
CULPIN Alfred H. MM Pte 241307 Leicestershire Regt
CULPIN Edgar MM Sjt 241248 6th Leicestershire Regt
CULPIN Joseph MM Pte 201924 Leicestershire Regt
CULROSS Robert E. MM Sjt M2/048890 Att 8 Fd Amb Army Service Corps
CULVER Joseph George MM Sjt 13845 10th Essex Regt
CULVER Leonard Alfred James MM Cpl 17344 X/38 TM Bty RFA KIA 30.5.17.
CULVERHOUSE Joab MM Cpl 12328 A/156 Bde RFA
CULVERHOUSE Thomas H. MM Pte 21796 8th Duke of Cornwall's LI
CULVERHOUSE Thomas William MM L/Cpl 8564 2nd Royal Irish Regt KIA 16.8.17.
CULVERWELL Henry William MM Bdr 78422 252 Siege Bty RGA KIA 29.5.18.
CULVERWELL Robert A. MM Cpl 62537 Royal Engineers
CULYER Harry C. MM Sjt 32486 D(AA)Bty RGA
CUMBER Henry B. MM 2nd Cpl 244865 1 Fd Svy Coy Royal Engineers
CUMBER John Edward "DCM,MM,CG(B)" Spr 558164 29 Div Sig Coy Royal Engineers
CUMBERBIRCH Ernest MM Sjt 3526 2nd Lancashire Fusiliers
CUMBERLAND Albert H. "DCM,MM" CSM 8773 2nd Royal Welsh Fusiliers
CUMBERLAND Alexander MM L/Cpl 14123 Highland Light Infantry
CUMBERLAND Ernest E. MM Cpl 61688 7th Royal Fusiliers
CUMBERLAND F. MM Sjt (Pioneer) 10767 2nd Durham Light Infantry
CUMBERLAND James MM Cpl 12692 15th Royal Irish Rifles
CUMBERLAND John Henry MM Sjt 10423 39 Bde RFA
CUMBERPATCH John Henry MM L/Cpl 9821 Lincolnshire Regt
CUMBERS James B. MM Pte 4101 17th Lancers
CUMBLEY Alfred Charles MM 2nd Cpl 25249 54 Fd Coy Royal Engineers
CUMES Alfred MM Gnr 89186 Guards Div Ammn Col RFA
CUMING Walter MM Pnr 358744 36 Div Sig Coy Royal Engineers

CUMMING Albert MM Pte 18763 10th Scottish Rifles
CUMMING George MM L/Sjt 11268 Gordon Highlanders
CUMMING James MM+2 Bars Sjt 631404 D/255 Bde RFA
CUMMING James MM Pte 3038 8th Seaforth Highlanders
CUMMING John A. MM L/Cpl 120798 73 Fd Coy Royal Engineers
CUMMING John J. MM Cpl 66152 Machine Gun Corps
CUMMING Peter R. MM Pte 41793 12th Royal Scots Fusiliers
CUMMING Samuel Burgess MM BSM 12817 2/1(Lancashire)Hy Bty RGA
CUMMINGS A. MM L/Cpl 41805 5 Sqn Machine Gun Corps
CUMMINGS Alexander MM Spr 504327 Royal Engineers
CUMMINGS Alexander MM CQMS 20541 Machine Gun Corps
CUMMINGS Frank MM Sjt 1308 Royal Engineers
CUMMINGS George S. MM Pte 3/8826 7th Yorkshire Regt
CUMMINGS George W. MM Pte 27181 2nd Oxf & Bucks Light Infantry
CUMMINGS Harold W. MM L/Cpl 9287 South Staffordshire Regt
CUMMINGS James MM Sjt 3/6724 2nd Gordon Highlanders
CUMMINGS James MM Pte 49873 7th Liverpool Regt
CUMMINGS James M. MM Spr 193278 258 Tunnelling Coy Royal Engineers
CUMMINGS John MM Pte S/17615 1/8th Arg & Suth Highlanders
CUMMINGS John H. MM L/Cpl 1938 1st Welsh Guards
CUMMINGS Richard MM Sjt 25516 B/61 Bde RFA
CUMMINGS Thomas MM L/Cpl 20/613 20th Durham Light Infantry KIA 28.4.18.
CUMMINGS Walter MM Pte 80216 14th Royal Welsh Fusiliers
CUMMINGS William MM Sjt 300080 1/8th Arg & Suth Highlanders
CUMMINGS William MM Sjt 3/6482 Arg & Suth Highlanders
CUMMINGS William MM Bdr 32508 B/86 Bde RFA
CUMMINS Albert MM Sjt 15052 Northumberland Fusiliers
CUMMINS Frederick G. MM L/Cpl 12492 4th Middlesex Regt
CUMMINS Joseph MM Bdr 29847 RGA
CUMMINS Lawrence MM L/Cpl 243172 North Lancashire Regt
CUMMINS Patrick MM Pte 25455 1st Royal Dublin Fusiliers
CUMMINS William MM Pte 2088 1st Royal Dublin Fusiliers
CUND Frederick MM Pte 201775 1/4th Royal Berkshire Regt
CUNDALL Benjamin MM Sjt 48132 36 Bde RFA
CUNDALL Elias Thomas MM Pte 9986 Machine Gun Corps
CUNDALL Reginald MM Cpl 98539 95 Fd Coy Royal Engineers
CUNDICK Horace William MM L/Cpl 202996 4th Dorsetshire Regt
CUNDIFF James Frederick MM Pte 275795 5/6th Royal Scots KIA 12.9.17.
CUNDY Bertie MM Pte 12801 9th Essex Regt DOW 5.7.16.
CUNDY John Thomas MM Sjt 15534 Lincolnshire Regt
CUNDY Lot MM Pte 38557 Lancashire Fusiliers
CUNLIFFE Brian MM Pte M2/115765 13 Lt Armd Mot Bty Army Service Corps
CUNLIFFE Edward L. MM Pte 341506 65 Fd Amb RAMC
CUNLIFFE Ellis MM L/Cpl 3377 1/8th West Yorkshire Regt
CUNLIFFE Frank MM L/Cpl 305406 8th Bn Tank Corps KIA 29.9.18.
CUNLIFFE Harold MM L/Cpl 14757 12th Liverpool Regt
CUNLIFFE Hugh MM Pte 68490 RAMC
CUNLIFFE James A. MM Pte 33892 1st Border Regt
CUNLIFFE Lewis MM+Bar Pte 202640 4th North Lancashire Regt
CUNLIFFE Nolan MM Dvr 4345 RFA
CUNLIFFE Sydney MM Sjt 36922 Machine Gun Corps
CUNLIFFE Thomas MM Pte 18231 Lincolnshire Regt
CUNLIFFE William MM Pte 14889 9th North Lancashire Regt
CUNLIFFE William MM Pte 36326 7th East Yorkshire Regt
CUNLIFFE William E. MM Pte 17666 8th East Lancashire Regt
CUNNAH Joseph MM Dvr T4/109298 38 Div Train Army Service Corps
CUNNANE John MM Pte 9343 1st Irish Guards
CUNNIFF John MM Bdsm 4649 Liverpool Regt
CUNNIFFE James MM L/Cpl 44998 2nd Lincolnshire Regt
CUNNING Thomas MM L/Cpl 288 Royal Irish Rifles
CUNNINGHAM Alexander MM Sjt 110096 227 Siege Bty RGA
CUNNINGHAM Alexander Nicol MM Pte 45725 RAMC
CUNNINGHAM Alexander Pinman MM Pte 16069 12th Royal Scots DOW 19.9.18.
CUNNINGHAM Anthony MM L/Cpl 9721 Royal Irish Regt
CUNNINGHAM Arthur MM+Bar Bdr 45600 94 Siege Bty RGA
CUNNINGHAM David MM Pte 32378 2nd Royal Scots Fusiliers
CUNNINGHAM David MM CSM 11554 2nd Notts & Derby Regt
CUNNINGHAM David MM L/Cpl 42125 3rd Hussars
CUNNINGHAM Denis MM Pte 16940 North Lancashire Regt
CUNNINGHAM Edward Samuel MM Bdr 600 41 Bde RFA
CUNNINGHAM F. MM Pte 341650 RAMC
CUNNINGHAM Frederick MM Gnr 755819 RFA
CUNNINGHAM George MM Gnr 66582 9 Bde RFA
CUNNINGHAM George MM+Bar Sjt 11177 1st Scottish Rifles
CUNNINGHAM Henry MM L/Cpl 201934 West Riding Regt
CUNNINGHAM Herbert W. MM Cpl 42315 Royal Engineers
CUNNINGHAM Hunter MM Cpl 23106 1st Scottish Rifles
CUNNINGHAM J. MM Sjt 6473 Hussars
CUNNINGHAM James MM Spr 404239 Royal Engineers
CUNNINGHAM James MM Sjt 20911 Royal Irish Fusiliers
CUNNINGHAM James MM Pte M2/020367 att 95 Fd Amb RAMC Army Service Corps
CUNNINGHAM James MM Pte 201165 1/4th Royal Scots Fusiliers DOW 29.11.17.
CUNNINGHAM James MM Sjt 265955 Royal Highlanders
CUNNINGHAM James McFarlane MM L/Cpl 315276 13th Royal Highlanders
CUNNINGHAM John MM+Bar Sjt 57119 5th Manchester Regt
CUNNINGHAM John "MM+Bar,MID" Sjt 196 10/11th Highland Light Infantry DOW 28.12.16.
CUNNINGHAM John MM L/Cpl 31043 Royal Welsh Fusiliers
CUNNINGHAM John MM L/Cpl 12050 10th Durham Light Infantry
CUNNINGHAM John MM Cpl S/9567 Gordon Highlanders
CUNNINGHAM John MM Pte 14078 South Wales Borderers
CUNNINGHAM John A. MM Spr 548829 87 Fd Coy Royal Engineers
CUNNINGHAM John H. MM Pte 28013 Royal Lancaster Regt
CUNNINGHAM Joseph Moloney MM Sjt 56616 17 Div Sig Coy Royal Engineers
CUNNINGHAM Patrick MM Sjt 273142 5/6th Royal Scots
CUNNINGHAM Peter A. MM Cpl 308605 3 Supply Coy Tank Corps
CUNNINGHAM Richard MM Pte 8263 2nd Yorkshire Regt
CUNNINGHAM Robert MM Spr WR/284188 239 Lt Rly Fwd Coy Royal Engineers
CUNNINGHAM Robert MM Pte 8860 1/8th Arg & Suth Highlanders KIA 15.5.17.
CUNNINGHAM Robert S. MM+Bar Pte 48721 RAMC
CUNNINGHAM Thomas MM Sjt 54364 1st Liverpool Regt
CUNNINGHAM Thomas MM Pte 12824 East Surrey Regt
CUNNINGHAM William MM Sjt 251020 1/6th Arg & Suth Highlanders
CUNNINGHAM William MM L/Cpl 310063 7th Gordon Highlanders
CUNNINGHAM William MM Pte 10940 6th Border Regt
CUNNINGHAM William MM Pte 11392 1st King's Own Scottish Borderers KIA 13.5.18.
CUNNINGTON Charles MM Sjt 49257 23rd Royal Fusiliers
CUNNINGTON Frank W. MM Spr 25500 Royal Engineers
CUNNINGTON Harry MM RSM 17223 245 Bde RFA
CUNNINGTON William MM Pte 268479 1/7th Royal Warwickshire Regt
CUNNINGTON William H. MM Pte 242486 7th Royal Warwickshire Regt
CUPIT Edgar MM Spr 121581 185 Tunnelling Coy Royal Engineers
CUPITT John MM Pte 10693 1st Middlesex Regt
CUPITT Thomas MM Bdr 48603 255 Siege Bty RGA
CUPITT William MM L/Cpl 3721 1/5th North Lancashire Regt
CUPPLES John Munro MM Pte 17189 10/11th Highland Light Infantry Died 6.3.18.
CURD Esli J. MM Cpl C/6413 King's Royal Rifle Corps
CURD George William MM Pte 23235 8th East Surrey Regt
CURD Oswald Vivian MM Drummer 220445 1st East Yorkshire Regt KIA 16.4.18.
CURD Sydney Percy MM L/Cpl S/9623 1st East Kent Regt KIA 5.12.17.
CURD William J. MM Pte 300014 7th Royal Warwickshire Regt
CURETON Reginald H. MM Sjt CMT/2192 4 Div MT Coy Army Service Corps
CURL Thomas Henry MM Pte G/6242 13th Royal Fusiliers KIA 25.4.17.
CURLE Charles MM Shoeing Smith L/7648 B/160 Bde RFA KIA 25.3.18.
CURLE John J. MM Cpl 494175 Royal Engineers
CURLEY Charles MM L/Cpl 21260 8th Middlesex Regt
CURLEY Frederick MM Pte 203182 1/4th Leicestershire Regt KIA 29.9.18.
CURLEY Michael MM Pte 11321 1st Irish Guards
CURLEY Robert MM Cpl 15112 12th Royal Scots
CURLEY Walter H. MM Pte 20495 Somerset Light Infantry
CURLING John MM Cpl G/13003 7th East Kent Regt
CURLING William James MM Cpl 256 9th Royal Fusiliers KIA 7.10.16.
CURME Walter T. "MM,MID" Cpl 200197 Gloucestershire Regt

CURME William Henry Gibbs MM L/Bdr Sig 159634 298 Siege Bty RGA
CURNOCK Bernard MM Pte 306294 1/8th West Yorkshire Regt KIA 7.11.18.
CURPHEY Alfred H. MM Pte 17066 Machine Gun Corps
CURPHEY Hugh MM Cpl 51547 Machine Gun Corps
CURR Leonard Edgar MM Cpl 40107 63 Fd Coy Royal Engineers
CURRALL G.H. MM Chief Master Mechanic 2679 Royal Air Force
CURRAN J. MM Sjt 22503 Lancashire Fusiliers
CURRAN James MM Cpl 19231 Royal Inniskilling Fusiliers
CURRAN James MM+Bar Pte 29130 Royal Welsh Fusiliers
CURRAN James P. MM Pte 8106 1st Cameron Highlanders
CURRAN John MM Sjt 7545 18th Highland Light Infantry
CURRAN John MM Dvr 836784 RFA
CURRAN John MM Sjt 20531 9th Bn Machine Gun Corps
CURRAN John MM Sjt 5993 10th Royal Highlanders
CURRAN John "DCM,MM" Sjt 38544 19th & 9th Manchester Regt
CURRAN Joseph MM Pte 46714 1st Liverpool Regt
CURRAN Joseph "DCM,MM+Bar,MID" Pte 9266 2nd Royal Scots
CURRAN Patrick MM L/Cpl 40549 Royal Dublin Fusiliers
CURRAN Richard MM Pte 2778 6th Connaught Rangers
CURRAN Stanley Arthur MM Pte 45602 15th Hampshire Regt KIA 4.9.18.
CURRAN William MM Sjt 1602 2nd Royal Scots
CURRAN William "MM,MID" Cpl 882 1/5th King's Own Scottish Borderers
CURRAN William MM Sjt 18528 Machine Gun Corps
CURRELL Bertram MM Pte 56072 13th Royal Welsh Fusiliers
CURRELL Henry Albert MM Pte 23670 4th Bedfordshire Regt Died 7.11.18.
CURRELL Herbert MM L/Cpl 4119 1/1st Hertfordshire Regt KIA 7.1.17.
CURRELL James Richard MM Pte 2588 1/5th West Yorkshire Regt DOW 10.7.17.
CURRELL John Thomas MM Pte 9783 1st West Yorkshire Regt KIA 25.9.16.
CURRELL Reginald E.J. MM Sjt 1811 26 Fd Amb RAMC
CURRELL Walter MM+Bar Pte 3/4548 10th York & Lancaster Regt
CURREN John MM Gnr 29782 6 Div Ammn Col. RFA
CURREY Ernest Learmouth MM Pte 27279 8th Yorkshire Regt
CURRIE Adam MM Pte 53603 1st Royal Scots Fusiliers DOW 2.9.18.
CURRIE Alexander MM Pte 1250 20th Northumberland Fusiliers
CURRIE Andrew MM Sjt 13039 6th Royal Dublin Fusiliers
CURRIE Archibald MM Sjt 15763 11th Royal Scots
CURRIE Christopher MM L/Cpl 110014 10th Bn Tank Corps KIA 21.8.18.
CURRIE Donald M. MM L/Cpl 418035 74 Div Sig Sqn Royal Engineers
CURRIE James MM Pte 124815 Machine Gun Corps
CURRIE James Blair "DCM,MM" L/Sjt A/7672 2nd Scottish Rifles
CURRIE James E.T. MM Sjt 1806 Royal Engineers
CURRIE James G. MM Pte 318125 2 Fd Amb RAMC
CURRIE John MM Pte 16211 6th Cameron Highlanders
CURRIE John MM Sjt 17630 1/1st Hertfordshire Regt
CURRIE John MM Drummer 304 18th West Yorkshire Regt
CURRIE John MM Sjt 37856 D/86 Bde RFA KIA 24.9.18.
CURRIE John MM Cpl 17771 6th King's Own Scottish Borderers Died 10.11.17.
CURRIE John MM Pte 1178 2nd Royal Highlanders
CURRIE Mark H. MM Pte 49779 12th Royal Scots
CURRIE Peter MM Sjt 52062 RFA
CURRIE Peter "MM,MID" Sjt 11223 2nd Royal Scots KIA 12.4.18.
CURRIE Robert MM Pte 40210 King's Own Scottish Borderers
CURRIE Thomas MM Pte 22429 15th Highland Light Infantry
CURRY Albert MM Pte 235274 1st Lancashire Fusiliers
CURRY Albert MM Dvr 76041 40 Bde RFA
CURRY Brian MM Pte 202260 Northumberland Fusiliers
CURRY Frank MM L/Cpl 240339 5th Gloucestershire Regt
CURRY Frederick MM 2nd Cpl 470386 Royal Engineers
CURRY George Hodgson MM Spr 47262 25 Div Sig Coy Royal Engineers
CURRY James MM CSM 13858 10th Scottish Rifles
CURRY John MM Sjt 6195 7th East Yorkshire Regt KIA 4.9.18.
CURRY John L. MM Pte 512001 14th London Regt
CURRY Joseph MM Pte 305868 8th West Yorkshire Regt
CURRY Patrick MM Pte 4837 1/7th Liverpool Regt
CURRY Robert MM Cpl 66845 RGA
CURRY Robert MM Sjt 1305 GMGR
CURRY W. MM Pte 93274 20th Durham Light Infantry
CURRY Wilfred Edwin MM L/Sjt 26041 Worcestershire Regt
CURRY William MM Pte 2/2494 2nd Royal Inniskilling Fusiliers
CURRY William MM Pte 1217 18th Durham Light Infantry
CURSON Harry G. MM Pte 14920 9th Norfolk Regt
CURSON James R. MM Cpl 28132 2 Siege Bty Royal Artillery
CURSON Thomas William MM Spr 482108 Royal Engineers
CURSON William MM Sjt 10548 1st Middlesex Regt
CURTICE Joseph MM Pte 202756 7th Royal West Surrey Regt
CURTIN Edmund MM Gnr 89889 296 Siege Bty RGA DOW 27.4.18.
CURTIN Jeremiah "DCM,MM" Sjt 3507 1st Irish Guards
CURTIN John MM L/Cpl 6682 2nd Royal Munster Fusiliers KIA 4.10.18.
CURTIN Owen MM Pte 7883 Royal Munster Fusiliers
CURTIN Patrick MM Pte 30283 15 Fd Amb RAMC KIA 4.10.17.
CURTIS A.M. MM Sjt 19393 North Staffordshire Regt
CURTIS Albert MM Pte 36090 Yorkshire Light Infantry
CURTIS Alexander MM Pte 111739 5th Bn Tank Corps
CURTIS Alexander E.V.T. MM Bdr 207789 B/232 Bde RFA
CURTIS Arthur J. MM Pte 15714 8th Lincolnshire Regt
CURTIS Arthur W. MM Cpl 21419 2 Div Sig Coy Royal Engineers
CURTIS Benjamin A. MM Pte 16590 1st Norfolk Regt
CURTIS C.W. MM Pte 201917 1/4th Royal Berkshire Regt
CURTIS Charles MM CSM 337 7th East Surrey Regt
CURTIS Charles MM Pte 242584 6th Royal Warwickshire Regt
CURTIS Charles A. MM Sjt 80078 1/1st Essex Yeomanry
CURTIS Cyril L. MM Gnr 284611 RGA
CURTIS Denis F. MM Gnr 249224 RFA
CURTIS Dennis MM Dvr 75990 RFA
CURTIS Edward George MM Gnr 160324 331 Siege Bty RGA DOW 8.11.17.
CURTIS Edward S. MM Pte 204262 6th Wiltshire Regt
CURTIS Edwin "MM,CG(F)" Pte 30356 41st Bn Machine Gun Corps
CURTIS Ernest MM Pte 44825 Royal Irish Rifles
CURTIS Ernest MM L/Cpl 2599 8th Hussars
CURTIS Ernest H. MM L/Cpl 2225 16th Middlesex Regt
CURTIS Frederick MM Sjt G/1580 11th Royal Fusiliers
CURTIS Frederick G. MM Pte 37106 8 Fd Amb RAMC
CURTIS Frederick John MM 2nd Cpl 239621 Railway Operating Division Royal Engineers
CURTIS George MM Pte 37230 Royal Berkshire Regt
CURTIS George F. "MM,MIDx2" Sjt 2283 1/1st Hertfordshire Regt
CURTIS Gilbert H. MM Sjt 682161 22nd London Regt
CURTIS Harry MM Sjt 300466 1/8th Arg & Suth Highlanders
CURTIS Henry MM Pte 9531 5/6th Scottish Rifles
CURTIS Henry J. MM Pte 4222 3rd Hussars
CURTIS J.W. MM Sjt 40627 Essex Regt
CURTIS J.W. MM Sjt 52556 2nd Manchester Regt
CURTIS James Henry "MM,MID" Pte 11947 2nd Notts & Derby Regt
CURTIS James William MM Sjt 200288 1/1st London Regt
CURTIS John "MM,MC(G)" Sjt T1/SR/912 573 Coy Army Service Corps
CURTIS John MM Sjt S/1161 13th Rifle Brigade
CURTIS Joseph F. MM Sjt 24195 1st South Staffordshire Regt
CURTIS Leslie MM Dvr 915736 D/223 Bde RFA
CURTIS R.H. MM Pte 392067 9th London Regt
CURTIS Reginald MM Sjt 40942 Royal Inniskilling Fusiliers
CURTIS Richard MM L/Cpl 41622 South Staffordshire Regt
CURTIS Robert "MM,Medaille Militaire(F)" Cpl 18753 14th Northumberland Fusiliers KIA 27.5.18.
CURTIS Ronald Eric William MM Gnr 202630 158 Bde(RFA) 2/1st(Berkshire)Bty(RHA) RHA
CURTIS T. MM Sjt 21168 Dragoon Guards
CURTIS Thomas MM Dvr 765510 RFA
CURTIS Thomas MM L/Cpl 16636 8th Leicestershire Regt Died 14.11.18.
CURTIS Thomas MM Sjt 43657 RFA
CURTIS Thomas Raymond MM L/Cpl 200740 2/4th Lincolnshire Regt
CURTIS W.G. MM Pte 12487 Royal Warwickshire Regt
CURTIS Walter MM+Bar Pte 14758 1/6th Welsh Regt
CURTIS Walter E. MM Pte 4474 7th Royal West Surrey Regt
CURTIS William MM Sjt 58074 1st Middlesex Regt
CURTIS William MM Pte S/37663 13th Rifle Brigade KIA 4.11.18.
CURTIS William H. MM Cpl 16314 1st Hampshire Regt
CURTIS William J. "MM,MID" L/Cpl 9699 King's Royal Rifle Corps
CURTIS William J. MM Spr 500294 Royal Engineers
CURTIS William John MM+Bar Sjt 112222 'H' Special Coy Royal Engineers DOW 7.6.18.
CURWEN A. MM Pte 612487 London Regt
CURWEN P. MM Pte 13413 East Lancashire Regt

CURWEN Robert MM Pte 2063 1/6th Liverpool Regt DOW 8.8.16.
CURWEN Thomas H. MM Sjt 3487 Liverpool Regt
CURWEN Tom MM Cpl 17296 19th Liverpool Regt KIA 30.7.16.
CURZON Andrew MM Pte 241004 6th Highland Light Infantry
CUSACK Bernard Stephen MM Sjt 20479 184 Siege Bty RGA
CUSACK J. MM L/Cpl D/3508 1st Dragoons
CUSACK William MM Sjt 6353 Notts & Derby Regt
CUSHING Frederick MM Pte 702902 23rd London Regt
CUSHION Albert E. MM Pte 201301 2/4th Royal West Surrey Regt
CUSHION Robert F. MM Sjt 18481 6th King's Own Scottish Borderers
CUSHLEY Charles T. MM Cpl 8000 Lincolnshire Regt
CUSHNIE J. MM Pte 5335 Liverpool Regt
CUSHNIE William MM Pte 40647 13th Royal Highlanders
CUSICK Thomas MM Sjt Farrier 15272 A/110 Bde RFA
CUSICK Vincent Ambrose MM Sjt 32810 12th Royal Scots
CUSKERN Francis MM L/Sjt 40148 6th York & Lancaster Regt
CUSMANO Antonio MM+Bar Dvr L/14305 RFA
CUSS F.H. MM L/Cpl 552729 509 Fd Coy Royal Engineers
CUSS James W. MM CQMS 2878 Gloucestershire Regt
CUSSANS Arthur James MM Cpl T/28800 5 Div Train Army Service Corps
CUSSENS Terrence "DCM,MM" Sjt Farrier T/20789 Att HQ 7 Div Army Service Corps
CUSSONS Ernest MM Pte 11664 10th West Yorkshire Regt
CUST James W. MM L/Cpl 3717 West Yorkshire Regt
CUSTANCE Arthur W. MM Gnr 40561 7 Siege Bty RGA
CUTCHEE Herbert MM Sjt 69405 RGA
CUTCLIFFE Ernest William MM Pte 41656 Manchester Regt DOW 18.6.18.
CUTCLIFFE Samuel W. MM Cpl 15980 8th Duke of Cornwall's LI
CUTHBERT Arthur MM Pte 6603 2nd Suffolk Regt
CUTHBERT Charles "MM,MID" Cpl 42116 Royal Engineers
CUTHBERT Fred MM Pte 7816 Duke of Cornwall's LI
CUTHBERT Frederick MM Sjt 24380 276 Siege Bty RGA KIA 30.10.18.
CUTHBERT Galanthe Mildred MM Sub-Section Leader F BRCS
CUTHBERT George W.B. MM Pte 40672 4th Hampshire Regt
CUTHBERT Gilbert MM Cpl 137700 237 Fd Coy Royal Engineers
CUTHBERT James MM Pte 341529 64 Fd Amb RAMC
CUTHBERT Peter MM Pte 39578 Royal Scots
CUTHBERT Thomas MM Spr 75970 18 Div Sig Coy Royal Engineers
CUTHBERTSON Gilbert Percival MM Gnr 70258 142 Heavy Bty RGA DOW 4.11.17.
CUTHBERTSON Gordon MM Cpl 62840 D/110 Bde RFA
CUTHBERTSON James MM Pte 241967 1/5th Seaforth Highlanders
CUTHBERTSON John MM Cpl 2703 2nd Royal Scots
CUTHBERTSON John Allan MM Cpl M2/221933 Army Service Corps att 238 Siege Bty RGA
CUTHBERTSON William MM Sjt 7188 Northumberland Fusiliers
CUTHBERTSON William "DCM,MM" L/Cpl 20842 9th Cheshire Regt KIA 24.3.18.
CUTHILL Robert MM Pte 23057 Scottish Rifles
CUTHILL William MM L/Cpl 14830 2nd Scots Guards
CUTLER Frank B. MM Pte 266058 1/1st Bucks Bn Oxf & Bucks Light Infantry
CUTLER Frederick MM Pte 27886 1st Dorsetshire Regt
CUTLER G.E. MM Pte 27510 Border Regt
CUTLER Harold S. MM Pte 39326 8th Royal Berkshire Regt
CUTLER Joseph MM Pte R/1841 16th King's Royal Rifle Corps
CUTLER Joseph William MM Cpl 241363 2/5th York & Lancaster Regt
CUTLER Leonard MM Pte 74743 101 Fd Amb RAMC Died 26.10.18.
CUTLER Samuel MM+Bar Sjt 31899 36 Bde RFA
CUTLER Sidney MM L/Cpl 720667 2/24th London Regt
CUTLER William MM Bdr 53752 141 Heavy Bty RGA
CUTLER William James MM Bdr 162003 119 Bty 27 Bde RFA
CUTMORE Charles MM Pte 12145 7th Norfolk Regt
CUTT John MM Sjt 112227 Royal Engineers
CUTTANCE Ely MM Pte 11547 7th Duke of Cornwall's LI
CUTTELL Willis MM Pte 46982 South Wales Borderers
CUTTER Charles MM Cpl 9780 1st Royal West Kent Regt
CUTTER James MM L/Cpl 8539 1st Norfolk Regt
CUTTING Robert MM Pte 532737 1/15th London Regt
CUTTING Thomas R. MM+Bar Cpl 536567 5 Fd Amb RAMC
CUTTING William MM Dvr 13449 45 Bde RFA
CUTTING William James MM Cpl L/20732 X/33 Med TM Bty RFA
CUTTLE Gilbert MM Pte 4601 2/4th Gloucestershire Regt Died 3.12.17.
CUTTS Alfred H. MM Sjt 36449 RAMC
CUTTS Arthur Wilson "MM,MM(F)" Pte 26642 1st York & Lancaster Regt
CUTTS Charles MM Gnr 207573 170 Siege Bty RGA
CUTTS Charles MM Gnr L/31864 X/38 Med TM Bty RFA KIA 6.7.18.
CUTTS Edward Thomas MM Pte 531332 1/15th London Regt
CUTTS Ernest D. MM Pte 26192 Norfolk Regt
CUTTS Frederick MM Pte 242019 5th Gloucestershire Regt
CUTTS George MM Gnr 27446 D/232 Bde RFA
CUTTS Herbert Henry MM Pte 21445 2nd York & Lancaster Regt
CUTTS John Joseph MM+Bar CSM 8667 2nd Lincolnshire Regt
CUTTS Joseph "MM+Bar,MID" Sjt 8936 2nd York & Lancaster Regt KIA 25.4.17.
CUTTS Robert MM Cpl 16859 7 Fd Coy Royal Engineers
CUTTS William E. MM Pte 4065 16th Lancers

D

DABB Charles W.S. MM Cpl M2/153868 Army Service Corps
DABLES George MM Dvr 59311 5 Bde RFA
DABORN Albert F. MM L/Cpl M2/149056 Army Service Corps
DABSON Bernard MM Pte 3268 Royal Sussex Regt
DACE Sidney A. MM+Bar Sjt 15176 8th Norfolk Regt
DACEY James MM Sjt 19253 Machine Gun Corps
DACK Frederick Hooton David MM Sjt 17257 7th Norfolk Regt
DACK Horace MM Sjt 10908 10th West Yorkshire Regt
DADDE L. MM Cpl 71583 RGA
DADE Albert E. MM L/Cpl 8132 2nd Royal West Kent Regt
DADSON Robert Clifford MM Pte 10708 10th Royal West Kent Regt
DADSWELL Reginald MM Sjt 55270 A Bty RHA
DADY George MM Cpl 19609 7th Norfolk Regt
DADY Joseph F. MM Pte M/36059 Army Service Corps att RAMC
DADY M.K. MM Pte 32894 Royal Warwickshire Regt
DAFFERN William MM Pte 52463 5th Lancashire Fusiliers
DAFFURN Victor MM Pte 43817 9th Royal Inniskilling Fusiliers
DAFFURN William MM Spr 63074 Royal Engineers
DAFT Arthur G. MM Bdr 121030 RFA
DAFT Clifford MM Pte 203297 5th West Riding Regt
DAGG George MM Cpl 42459 33rd Bn Machine Gun Corps
DAGG John T. MM Pte 40973 5th West Yorkshire Regt
DAGG N.V. MM Pte 352673 Royal Scots
DAGG Patrick MM Cpl 18621 8th Royal Dublin Fusiliers
DAGG Thomas Albert MM Sjt 71700 188 Siege Bty RGA KIA 1.10.17.
DAGGATT Walter MM Cpl 444212 Royal Engineers
DAGGER James H. MM Pte 201784 Royal Lancaster Regt
DAGGER Richard MM Pte 94496 Liverpool Regt
DAGGER Richard F. MM Pte 59305 12 Fd Amb RAMC
DAGGER Walter MM Pte 48130 Welsh Regt
DAGGETT William MM Sjt 1765 1/4th Yorkshire Regt
DAGLEAS John Archibald MM Gnr 951329 D/92 Bde RFA
DAGLEY Frederick H. MM Sjt 200624 1st London Regt
DAGLISH Arthur MM L/Cpl 200327 Tank Corps
DAGLISH Ralph MM Pte 17535 11th Durham Light Infantry
DAGLISH Robert MM Pte 18240 Durham Light Infantry
DAGNAN William J. MM Cpl 3058 5th Dragoon Guards
DAGNELL William MM L/Cpl 93796 Royal Engineers
DAGOSTENO Anthony MM Pte 48384 22nd Manchester Regt
DAHN John MM+Bar Pte 92397 Tank Corps
DAILY Charles J.E. MM Cpl 55162 23rd Bn Machine Gun Corps
DAINES Alfred J. MM Dvr 498344 476 Fd Coy Royal Engineers
DAINES William MM Bdr 103212 RFA
DAINES William James John MM Spr 85553 34 Div Sig Coy Royal Engineers
DAINS Frank MM Sjt R/7551 1st King's Royal Rifle Corps
DAINTREE Thomas MM Pte 43182 Royal Dublin Fusiliers
DAINTY Edward MM Cpl 13472 10th Lancashire Fusiliers DOW 28.4.18.
DAINTY John MM Cpl 681894 1/22nd London Regt
DAINTY Walter MM Pte 6660 7th South Staffordshire Regt
DAINTY William John MM L/Cpl R/12765 2nd King's Royal Rifle Corps KIA 30.3.18.
DAISLEY Albert Edward "MM,MID" Sjt L/12808 4th Middlesex Regt
DAKERS John M.C. MM Sjt Farrier 645640 A/256 Bde RFA
DAKERS William MM Sjt 23389 Highland Light Infantry
DAKIN Albert James MM Bdr 15279 RFA
DAKIN Bert MM Pte 491186 2nd(North Midland)Fd Amb RAMC
DAKIN Ernest MM L/Cpl 2887 Cheshire Regt

DAKIN George MM Pte 202586 Royal Berkshire Regt
DAKIN George William "MM,MBC(Rm)" CSM 570 1/6th Notts & Derby Regt
DAKIN Henry MM L/Cpl 203335 1/5th Notts & Derby Regt
DAKIN J. MM Pte 41764 1st Essex Regt
DAKIN James MM Cpl 43276 10th West Yorkshire Regt
DAKIN John MM Pte 26304 7th Shropshire Light Infantry DOW 28.3.18.
DAKIN Percy Godfrey MM Cpl 13999 8th Leicestershire Regt KIA 25.9.16.
DAKIN Richard "MM,MID" Pte 269 2nd Manchester Regt KIA 10.8.18.
DAKIN Samuel MM Pte 24493 RAMC
DAKIN Sydney MM Cpl 201402 4th Yorkshire Light Infantry
DALBY Harry MM Pte 17603 8th Devonshire Regt KIA 6.9.16.
DALBY Henry MM L/Cpl 6/1532 6th West Yorkshire Regt
DALBY Henry MM+Bar L/Sjt 19459 Notts & Derby Regt
DALBY J. MM L/Cpl 390559 3(Northumbrian)Fd Amb RAMC
DALBY John MM Sjt 106047 Royal Engineers
DALBY Walter David MM Bdr 84317 B/98 Bde RFA Died 4.7.18.
DALBY William "DCM,MM" Sjt 9/16057 7th Leicestershire Regt
DALDRY William J. MM Pte 41428 Gordon Highlanders
DALE A. MM Pte 31174 Devonshire Regt
DALE Alfred May MM Pte 3695 RAMC
DALE Arnold MM L/Cpl 631 12th York & Lancaster Regt
DALE Arthur MM+Bar Sjt Z/922 2nd Rifle Brigade KIA 25.9.17.
DALE Arthur MM Spr 48076 Royal Engineers
DALE Bertram MM Bdr 27041 118 Heavy Bty RGA
DALE Charles William MM Pte Y/26 13th King's Royal Rifle Corps DOW 14.7.16.
DALE Daniel MM BSM 56011 A/190 Bde RFA
DALE Edward MM Dvr 24996 C/112 Bde RFA
DALE Edwin MM Pte 241045 5th West Riding Regt
DALE Edwin "MM,MID" Sjt 71775 RFA
DALE Fred "MM,MID" Pte 12600 Royal Welsh Fusiliers
DALE Frederick MM Pte 139659 49th Bn Machine Gun Corps
DALE Frederick William MM Gnr Sig 43814 86 Bde RFA DOW 5.4.18.
DALE George E. MM Pte 31705 Royal Welsh Fusiliers
DALE Guy B. MM Gnr 151698 173 Siege Bty RGA
DALE Harold MM Pte 32594 2nd Manchester Regt
DALE Herbert MM CSM 7458 1st East Yorkshire Regt KIA 14.7.16.
DALE James W. MM L/Cpl 20849 14th Royal Welsh Fusiliers
DALE John MM S/Sjt 354054 2/3rd(East Lancashire)Fd Amb RAMC
DALE John Henry MM CSM 14407 10th Royal Irish Rifles KIA 21.3.18.
DALE John W. MM Bdr 114683 RFA
DALE Joseph MM L/Cpl 9563 11th Middlesex Regt
DALE Matthew MM L/Cpl 18384 Manchester Regt
DALE Percy MM Cpl 96701 323 Siege Bty RGA
DALE Richard MM Pte 202644 8th Worcestershire Regt
DALE Richard MM Bdr 103015 175 Siege Bty RGA
DALE Robert MM Pte 73270 15th Durham Light Infantry DOW 27.4.18.
DALE Robert W. MM L/Sjt 12178 11th Hampshire Regt
DALE Roland MM Bdr 103412 RGA
DALE Roland MM L/Cpl R/3420 13th King's Royal Rifle Corps
DALE Sidney E. MM+Bar CQMS STK/1517 23rd Royal Fusiliers
DALE Thomas MM Bdr 38252 17 Siege Bty RGA
DALE Victor R. MM Sjt 290431 1/7th Cheshire Regt
DALE Walter MM Gnr 24415 2 Siege Bty RGA
DALE William MM Sjt 240396 1/5th Royal Sussex Regt
DALES Jack "DCM,MM" Cpl 8891 1st South Staffordshire Regt
DALEY Albert Edward MM Sjt 12/7213 2nd Notts & Derby Regt
DALEY Harold MM L/Cpl 40155 Seaforth Highlanders
DALEY J. MM Pte 40352 Royal Inniskilling Fusiliers
DALEY James MM Pte 6411 2nd Durham Light Infantry
DALEY John MM+Bar Gnr 43007 70 Bty 34 Bde RFA
DALEY John MM Gnr 29277 D/91 Bde RFA Died 30.11.17.
DALEY John W. MM L/Cpl 22102 1st Yorkshire Light Infantry
DALEY Thomas MM Sjt 10606 11th Notts & Derby Regt
DALEY Thomas MM(323837 6th Lond)+Bar Pte 130074 45th Royal Fusiliers
DALEY William MM Sjt 200768 1/4th Yorkshire Light Infantry
DALEY William MM L/Cpl 306649 Lancashire Fusiliers
DALEY William H. MM Spr 560070 47 Div Sig Coy Royal Engineers
DALEY William Joseph MM+Bar Sjt 303461 1/7th Manchester Regt KIA 20.10.18.
DALGARNO John MM Sjt 204593 6th Dorsetshire Regt
DALGETTY William MM L/Cpl 240228 1/5th Royal Highlanders

DALGLEISH James MM Pte S/4868 11th Arg & Suth Highlanders
DALGLEISH John W. MM Pte 15897 2nd Scots Guards
DALGLEISH Joseph H. MM Sjt 290823 RGA
DALGLEISH Ronald MM Spr 423965 32 Div Sig Coy Royal Engineers
DALGLEISH William McC. MM Cpl S/11770 5th Cameron Highlanders
DALKIN James MM Pte 12412 King's Royal Rifle Corps
DALKIN Joseph W. MM L/Cpl C/12917 King's Royal Rifle Corps
DALL Robert MM Pte 29767 2nd Highland Light Infantry
DALL William MM Pte 16351 Royal Highlanders
DALLAS William MM Spr 400416 70 Fd Coy Royal Engineers
DALLENGER William Elma MM Sjt 546474 512 Fd Coy Royal Engineers
DALLEY Ernest S. MM Pte 70146 RAMC
DALLEY George MM Pte 8072 19th Hussars
DALLEY Robert S. MM Bdr 113841 RFA
DALLIMORE Albert V. MM Sjt 58202 14th Royal Welsh Fusiliers
DALLIMORE Horace MM Bdr L/37837 RFA
DALLIMORE William A. MM L/Sjt 267611 1/2nd Monmouthshire Regt
DALLING Frank MM Pte 26667 1st Grenadier Guards
DALLMAN Albert "MM,MID" Sjt 31324 RGA
DALLOW George MM Sjt 4483 RFA
DALMAS Julian MM Sjt M2/073346 Army Service Corps
DALRYMPLE Arthur MM Pte 295818 12th Royal Scots Fusiliers
DALRYMPLE John MM Cpl 309049 RGA
DALRYMPLE John MM Sjt 57372 6th Liverpool Regt DOW 17.9.18.
DALRYMPLE Peter MM Bdr 1554 MGC(Motors)
DALRYMPLE Robert MM Pte 2515 1/9th Highland Light Infantry KIA 15.7.16.
DALTON Albert MM Sjt 16995 6th North Lancashire Regt
DALTON Alfred MM L/Cpl 22511 East Surrey Regt
DALTON Benjamin MM Sjt 1016 13th East Yorkshire Regt
DALTON David MM Cpl 602013 18 Bde RHA
DALTON Edmund MM Pte 43119 Royal Irish Fusiliers
DALTON Edward MM Sjt 31818 2nd Northumberland Fusiliers
DALTON Ernest MM Pte 33457 4th Worcestershire Regt
DALTON Ernest MM Bdr 685422 RFA
DALTON George MM Cpl 10842 2nd York & Lancaster Regt
DALTON George Fox MM L/Cpl 53299 15th Durham Light Infantry KIA 31.3.18.
DALTON Gilbert MM Pte 57971 West Yorkshire Regt
DALTON Henry J. MM Sjt 3015 3rd Rifle Brigade
DALTON Herbert MM L/Cpl 128130 Machine Gun Corps
DALTON Martin "DCM,MM" Sjt 34424 9th York & Lancaster Regt
DALTON Patrick MM Sjt 8577 2nd Royal Irish Regt
DALTON Percy MM Sjt 202056 7th Worcestershire Regt
DALTON Roy L. "DCM,MM" Cpl 28104 2nd Hampshire Regt
DALTON Stanley MM Cpl 72330 Machine Gun Corps
DALTON Sydney MM Sjt Farrier 755050 RFA
DALTON William MM L/Cpl 9975 1st Royal Irish Regt
DALTON William MM Sjt 12274 West Yorkshire Regt
DALTON William Leonard "MM,MID" Cpl 3894 10th Royal West Surrey Regt
DALTREY George Hewitt "DCM,MM" L/Cpl 558088 29 Div Sig Coy Royal Engineers
DALTREY Reuben MM Sjt 860 56 Div Sig Coy Royal Engineers
DALWOOD Harry MM Sjt 536234 RAMC
DALY A.A. MM Pte 251383 3rd London Regt
DALY Alfred E. MM Pte 5526 2/4th Royal West Surrey Regt
DALY Charles MM Sjt 290151 1/8th Scottish Rifles
DALY Daniel Patrick J. MM Gnr 39088 A/98 Bde RFA
DALY David MM Gnr 68034 251 Bde RFA DOW 14.8.18.
DALY Denis MM Gnr Shoeing Smith 365106 RGA
DALY G. MM Pte 41669 8th North Staffordshire Regt
DALY H.A. MM Pte 302241 RAMC
DALY James MM Pte 6523 2nd Irish Guards DOW 30.3.18.
DALY James MM Pte 51035 1/6th Cheshire Regt KIA 15.6.18.
DALY John MM L/Cpl 4529 1st Irish Guards
DALY John MM Gnr 40646 11 Siege Bty RGA
DALY John MM Sjt 9381 1st North Staffordshire Regt
DALY John MM Pte 17036 1st Scottish Rifles
DALY John MM+Bar Bdr 11927 RGA
DALY Joseph MM Bdr 710610 RFA
DALY Martin MM Pte 9705 1st Connaught Rangers
DALY Michael "MM,MID" Sjt 12764 Royal Irish Fusiliers
DALY Peter MM Pte 14173 10th Scottish Rifles KIA 29.6.17.
DALY Peter MM+2 Bars Pte 11669 2nd Royal Dublin Fusiliers
DALZELL Frederick P. MM Cpl 22033 32nd Royal Fusiliers

DALZELL Samuel MM Pte 17558 15th Royal Irish Rifles
DALZIEL James "DCM,MM" Cpl 3/7544 8th Seaforth Highlanders
DALZIEL John MM Sjt 240277 King's Own Scottish Borderers
DALZIEL William MM Sjt 3/7895 7th Seaforth Highlanders
DALZIEL William Garriock MM Pte 375584 8th London Regt DOW 4.11.18.
DAMANT Herbert Geoffrey MM Cpl 15004 8th Suffolk Regt KIA 1.7.16.
DAMARELL George MM Pte 27120 7th Somerset Light Infantry
DAMME Rudolph MM Pte 42044 West Yorkshire Regt
DAMMS George H. MM Sjt 43313 10th West Yorkshire Regt
DAMMS T.E. "MM,MSM" CQMS 18524 Royal Engineers
DAMON Lewis R. MM Pte 3460 4th Dorsetshire Regt
DAMON William Henry MM Bdr 334519 RGA
DAMSELL Gilbert Frank MM Pte 30552 1st Worcestershire Regt DOW 21.12.17.
DANAGHER M. "DCM,MM" Sjt 2262 7th Leinster Regt
DANBURY William H. MM L/Cpl 8396 King's Royal Rifle Corps
DANBY Herbert Caple MM+Bar Spr 489939 46 Div Sig Coy Royal Engineers DOW 9.10.18.
DANBY Richard W. MM 2nd Cpl 62956 Signal Service Royal Engineers
DANCE Albert H. MM Gnr 39572 RGA
DANCE Arthur G. MM L/Cpl 11715 Royal Berkshire Regt
DANCE Frederick C. MM Cpl 15894 Dorsetshire Regt
DANCE Henry J. MM Sjt 1598 14th Royal Warwickshire Regt
DANCE Thomas W.E. MM Cpl S/33578 17th London Regt
DANCER Albert E. MM+Bar L/Cpl 206157 7th Royal West Surrey Regt
DANCER Thomas H.W. MM L/Cpl 6109 10th Royal Fusiliers
DANCY Thomas A. MM L/Cpl 18588 Dorsetshire Regt
DAND Thomas H. MM Pte 3565 8th North Staffordshire Regt
DANDO Fred MM Dvr 86323 A/86 Bde RFA
DANDO Frederick MM Pte 38627 RAMC
DANDO Herbert Henry MM Sjt 49329 RAMC
DANDO Wilfred S. MM Sjt 203250 1st Gloucestershire Regt
DANDY Ernest MM Cpl 16356 Manchester Regt
DANDY Herbert MM CSM 9642 1st Royal Welsh Fusiliers KIA 3.9.16.
DANE Gerald MM L/Cpl 16413 7th Somerset Light Infantry
DANFORTH Freeman MM Cpl 300090 20th Durham Light Infantry
DANGER John MM Gnr 1394 RFA
DANGERFIELD Alfred "MM,MID" Pte 15824 10th Worcestershire Regt
DANGERFIELD Joseph MM CSM 1056 1/6th South Staffordshire Regt
DANIEL Felix MM L/Cpl 11142 8th Hussars
DANIEL Harry MM Bdr 129385 A/165 Bde RFA
DANIEL J. MM Sjt 375085 Essex Regt
DANIEL Nelson MM Pte 2622 7th East Kent Regt
DANIEL Reginald MM S/Sjt Mechanic 76500 17th Armoured Car Bn Tank Corps
DANIEL T. MM Pte 205630 Royal Fusiliers
DANIEL Thomas MM Sjt 17055 8th South Lancashire Regt
DANIELL Edwin MM Sjt 3327 2/4th Royal Berkshire Regt
DANIELL Frank MM Pte 25805 Scottish Rifles
DANIELLS John MM Dvr 39879 RFA
DANIELS Arthur MM Sjt 401039 RAMC
DANIELS Arthur MM Pte 33306 1/5th Leicestershire Regt
DANIELS Arthur MM Pte 202236 South Lancashire Regt
DANIELS Charles MM Cpl 18327 Royal Welsh Fusiliers
DANIELS Charles MM Sjt 8077 2nd Suffolk Regt
DANIELS Ernest MM Cpl 200228 Notts & Derby Regt
DANIELS F.W. MM L/Cpl 1162 7th East Kent Regt
DANIELS Fred MM Pte 37710 RAMC
DANIELS Geoffrey MM Pte 306382 Liverpool Regt
DANIELS George MM L/Bdr 930098 D/79 Bde RFA
DANIELS George MM Bdr 875444 B/272 Bde RFA
DANIELS George MM Pte 14341 8th Royal Lancaster Regt
DANIELS Gilbert MM+Bar L/Cpl 13294 1/4th Oxf & Bucks Light Infantry
DANIELS Howard Baker MM Sjt 7151 261 Siege Bty RGA KIA 23.8.17.
DANIELS J. MM Pte 401346 RAMC
DANIELS James W. MM Sjt TT03221 Army Veterinary Corps
DANIELS John MM Cpl 91350 153 Coy Labour Corps
DANIELS John MM Cpl 1210 RFA
DANIELS John MM Cpl 1701 East Surrey Regt
DANIELS Joseph "DCM,MM" Pte 15198 23rd Middlesex Regt
DANIELS Joseph John MM CQMS 8665 1st Norfolk Regt KIA 9.5.17.
DANIELS Leslie M. MM Pte 23008 Royal Fusiliers
DANIELS R. MM Gnr 923 RGA
DANIELS Thomas A. MM Sjt 1573 1st Welsh Guards
DANIELS Walter MM L/Cpl 33144 Royal Engineers
DANIELS Wilfred J. MM Pte 18555 2nd Wiltshire Regt
DANIELS William MM Cpl 43838 86 Fd Coy Royal Engineers
DANIELS William MM Pte 65868 RAMC
DANIELS William C. MM Pte 72169 RAMC
DANIELS William G. MM 2nd Cpl 121085 Royal Engineers
DANIELS William George MM Pte G3505 3/4th Royal West Surrey Regt KIA 4.10.17.
DANIELS William H. MM Bdr 78694 RFA
DANIELS William J. MM Sjt 17065 20th Manchester Regt
DANIELS William Victor MM L/Cpl 6534 2nd Royal West Surrey Regt KIA 25.10.17.
DANKS Benjamin MM Dvr 10009 D/285 Bde RFA KIA 9.4.18.
DANKS Ernest G. MM Pte 10921 5th Oxf & Bucks Light Infantry
DANKS Joseph Thomas MM Pte 9571 2nd South Staffordshire Regt
DANKS William MM Cpl 117181 261 Siege Bty RGA
DANN Arthur MM Pte 266197 Gloucestershire Regt
DANN Ben MM Cpl 250142 5th Essex Regt
DANN Edwin C. MM Sjt 592774 18th London Regt
DANN Ewart J. MM Pte 651253 21st London Regt
DANN Frank "MM,MID" CQMS 24 1/22nd London Regt
DANN Frederick L. MM Sjt 265674 7th Royal West Kent Regt
DANN Harry MM Sjt 1378 Royal Highlanders
DANN Nelson MM Pte 1955 8th Royal Sussex Regt
DANN Percy E. MM L/Cpl 16988 Suffolk Regt
DANNAHY Henry James MM Spr 62172 12 Div Sig Coy Royal Engineers
DANNATT Arthur "MC,MM(48229 Cpl 14 Bde RHA),MID" 2Lt D/291 Bde RFA
DANSKIN James MM Pte 19706 10th Northumberland Fusiliers KIA 25.9.16.
DANSON Alexander MM L/Sjt 12784 10th North Lancashire Regt DOW 30.9.17.
DANSON Alfred MM Sjt 39419 47th Bn Machine Gun Corps
DANSON John T. MM L/Cpl 19387 2nd Coldstream Guards
DANSON William MM L/Cpl 201712 Royal Lancaster Regt
DARBROUGH Fred MM Pte 18933 2nd West Yorkshire Regt
DARBY Alfred MM Sjt 200992 1/7th Worcestershire Regt
DARBY Charles H. MM Dvr 39393 RFA
DARBY Ernest MM Pte 101910 29th Durham Light Infantry
DARBY Frank MM Cpl 486706 470 Fd Coy Royal Engineers
DARBY Frederick MM Pte 241945 Seaforth Highlanders
DARBY George Athelstone MM Bdr 624957 B/126 Bde RFA
DARBY Harold MM Pte 390882 1/9th London Regt
DARBY Harrison MM Pte 203842 South Lancashire Regt
DARBY John MM Pte 10530 Leicestershire Regt
DARBY Joseph MM Pte 16227 Yorkshire Light Infantry
DARBY Major MM Pte 16/1939 14th Royal Warwickshire Regt
DARBY Stanley James MM L/Cpl 265746 1st Bedfordshire Regt KIA 23.8.18
DARBY William MM Cpl 242476 9th Royal Warwickshire Regt
DARBY William J. MM Pte 202486 York & Lancaster Regt
DARBYSHIRE Charles MM Pte 94531 Liverpool Regt
DARBYSHIRE John MM Spr 362836 Royal Engineers
DARBYSHIRE John MM L/Cpl 101879 Royal Engineers
DARBYSHIRE Joseph William MM Pte 43764 4th North Staffordshire Regt
DARBYSHIRE Robert MM Gnr 11933 23 Bty 40 Bde RFA
DARCEY Lawrence MM L/Bdr 223721 RFA
DARCH Sidney T. MM Pte 25455 Gloucestershire Regt
DARCH William T. MM Cpl DM2/130010 51 Div Train Army Service Corps
DARCY F. MM Pte 3725 7th Royal Sussex Regt
DARCY Patrick MM+Bar Bdr 122207 D/84 Bde RFA
D'Arcy James MM Dvr T/973 Army Service Corps
D'Ardenne Percy Louis MM+Bar Sjt M2/050107 Army Service Corps att RAMC
DARE Henry T.A. MM Pte 61803 13th Royal Fusiliers
DARE Joseph H. MM Cpl 19176 15 Fd Coy Royal Engineers
DARE Sydney MM Bdr 955529 RFA
DARE William MM Pte 453120 11th London Regt
DARE William H. "MM,MSM" Cpl 14537 3 Fd Sqn Royal Engineers
DARGAVEL Robert MM Pte 260634 7th Border Regt
DARGO William C. MM Cpl 11659 2nd Highland Light Infantry
DARK Charles W. MM Gnr 112711 402 Bty 14 Bde RFA
DARK George W. MM Sjt CMT/60 4 Div MT Coy Army Service Corps

DARK John "MM,MID" Pte 7187 1st Royal Warwickshire Regt
DARK W.T. MM Cpl 66923 140 Fd Amb RAMC
DARKE Charles MM Pte 20592 8th Devonshire Regt KIA 4.10.17.
DARKE Frank MM L/Bdr 687374 RFA
DARKE S.G. MM SM 335 Royal Flying Corps
DARKENS Wilfred J. MM Pte 4729 8th East Surrey Regt
DARKES Edward MM Cpl 39312 5th Royal Berkshire Regt
DARKIN Bernard MM Pte 20316 12th Liverpool Regt
DARLEY Arnold William MM Sjt 11250 10th West Yorkshire Regt
DARLEY Frank "MM,MSM" Sjt 240203 1/5th Lincolnshire Regt
DARLEY Frank MM Pte 39183 2nd Yorkshire Light Infantry
DARLEY Robert MM CSM L/6078 2nd Royal West Kent Regt Died 27.10.16.
DARLEY William MM Sjt 358054 T(AA)Bty RGA
DARLING Alfred MM Pte 40316 2nd Northamptonshire Regt
DARLING Alfred MM Spr 59267 Royal Engineers
DARLING Arthur Edward MM L/Cpl 236967 249 Fd Coy Royal Engineers
DARLING Charles "MM,MID" Spr 20198 Royal Engineers
DARLING George MM Sjt 960755 B/310 Bde RFA
DARLING James MM L/Cpl 14519 13th Yorkshire Regt
DARLING Robert MM Cpl 56200 RGA
DARLING Robert MM Pte 19179 Royal Scots
DARLING Thomas MM Pte 27237 8th Royal Lancaster Regt KIA 23.8.18.
DARLING William MM Pte A/203516 13th King's Royal Rifle Corps
DARLING William MM Pte 213 2nd Arg & Suth Highlanders KIA 17.4.18.
DARLINGTON George MM Dvr 57036 B/112 Bde RFA
DARLINGTON George MM Pte 12901 4th Grenadier Guards KIA 12.4.18.
DARLINGTON Henry MM Pte 203653 5th West Riding Regt
DARLINGTON John Richard MM Pte 58787 8th West Yorkshire Regt
DARLINGTON John William MM Sjt 18518 13 Static Hosp RAMC
DARLINGTON Joseph MM Pte 82611 31st Bn Machine Gun Corps
DARLINGTON Ralph MM Gnr 695624 RFA
DARLINGTON Robert MM Cpl 2115 1/5th Liverpool Regt KIA 24.7.17.
DARLINGTON Tom "MC,MM(18125 Sjt Manch Regt)" T/2Lt 11th Royal West Surrey Regt KIA 1.10.18.
DARLOW Harold W. MM Pnr 165896 Royal Engineers
DARMODY Joseph Francis MM Cpl 532701 15th London Regt DOW 2.9.18.
DARNELL Harold MM Sjt 263106 17th Royal Sussex Regt
DARRAGH John MM L/Cpl 1202 Army Cyclist Corps
DARRELL Harry MM+Bar L/Cpl 837 2nd Yorkshire Light Infantry
DARRELL John Mark MM+Bar Pte 4/9081 20th Durham Light Infantry DOW 16.9.17.
DARRINGTON Ernest MM Cpl 17585 10th Essex Regt
DARROCH Duncan Gilbert MM Pte 15919 17th Liverpool Regt
DARROCH John MM Pte 315844 13th Royal Highlanders
DARROCH John C. MM Pte 3885 Liverpool Regt
DARROCK Archibald M. MM Sjt 62644 Royal Engineers
DARROLL William H. MM Pte 13426 Notts & Derby Regt
DART John MM L/Cpl P1299 Military Foot Police
DARVELL Arthur MM Pte 26266 5th Oxf & Bucks Light Infantry KIA 23.3.18.
DARVELL George MM L/Cpl 570400 1/17th London Regt
DARVILL William G. MM L/Cpl C/7265 King's Royal Rifle Corps
DARVILLE Thomas Newman MM Gnr 16204 D/93 Bde RFA KIA 29.5.16.
DARWELL Roger MM L/Bdr 293458 136 Hy Bty RGA AKA 9518 J Robinson Lanc Fus.
DARWEN W. "MM,MID" L/Cpl 12680 North Lancashire Regt
DARWENT Charles J. MM Pte 3/25969 South Wales Borderers
DARWIN Dennis MM Spr 139299 183 Tunnelling Coy Royal Engineers
DARWIN Philip E. MM Pte 412376 10th London Regt
DARWIN Thomas MM Gnr 80449 RFA
DARWOOD James "DCM,MM" Sjt 8087 2nd Worcestershire Regt
DASCOMBE Beatrice MM Staff Nurse F QAIMNS
DASH Edward W. MM Sjt 240624 1/8th Worcestershire Regt
DATSON Sidney MM Pte M2/077302 Army Service Corps
DAUGHTRY John MM Pte G2424 8th Royal Sussex Regt KIA 1.10.16.
DAULTRY Joseph MM Bdr 87931 RGA
DAUNCEY Edward James MM L/Sjt 224587 251 Coy Labour Corps
DAUNCEY Frederick MM Pte 19964 5th Dorsetshire Regt
DAUNCEY William H. MM Pte 242547 5th Gloucestershire Regt

DAUNT William MM L/Cpl 9289 2nd East Lancashire Regt
DAVENPORT Arthur MM Pte 305121 Lancashire Fusiliers
DAVENPORT Charles MM Sjt 235661 Yorkshire Light Infantry
DAVENPORT Charles Ernest MM Pte 32152 8th East Lancashire Regt
DAVENPORT Charles Sidney MM Gnr 108806 HQ 95 Bde RFA
DAVENPORT Christopher MM Pte 45598 15th Cheshire Regt KIA 20.4.18.
DAVENPORT David MM Pte C/6582 King's Royal Rifle Corps
DAVENPORT F.H. MM Sjt 44311 Manchester Regt
DAVENPORT Fred MM Pte 31157 4th Bedfordshire Regt DOW 26.4.17.
DAVENPORT George MM Sjt 240236 1/6th Notts & Derby Regt
DAVENPORT George A. MM Pte 279263 3rd London Regt
DAVENPORT Harold M. MM Pte 40971 2/7th Royal Warwickshire Regt
DAVENPORT Henry J. MM Spr 252716 Royal Engineers
DAVENPORT Howard MM Pte 243973 13th Yorkshire Regt
DAVENPORT James MM Pte C/126 16th King's Royal Rifle Corps
DAVENPORT James MM Sjt 14/544 14th Royal Warwickshire Regt
DAVENPORT Nathan S. MM Pte 84686 Machine Gun Corps
DAVENPORT R. "MM,MID" Cpl 9272 1st Liverpool Regt
DAVENPORT Robert MM Gnr 48257 RGA
DAVENPORT Thomas MM Pte 240966 4th North Lancashire Regt
DAVENPORT Thomas MM Pte R/16503 King's Royal Rifle Corps
DAVENPORT William Harvey MM Sjt 281383 1/7th Lancashire Fusiliers DOW 1.4.18.
DAVEY Albert MM Sjt 2566 1/7th Durham Light Infantry KIA 14.11.16.
DAVEY Albert Edward MM Bdr 6651 89 Siege Bty RGA
DAVEY Alfred E. MM Pte 2404 RAMC
DAVEY Arthur MM Pte 3699 1/5th Yorkshire Light Infantry
DAVEY Arthur H. MM L/Cpl 1189 Royal Sussex Regt
DAVEY Edward MM Sjt 17641 East Surrey Regt
DAVEY Edward MM Pte 10703 Royal West Surrey Regt
DAVEY Edward Robert Huntley MM Pte F/386 19th Middlesex Regt
DAVEY Francis R. MM Pte 531201 15th London Regt
DAVEY Francis W.H. MM S/Sjt Farrier 4290 15th Hussars
DAVEY Frederick MM Pte 25303 East Surrey Regt
DAVEY George A. MM L/Cpl 16740 1st Suffolk Regt
DAVEY Harold MM L/Cpl 253704 Royal Engineers
DAVEY Harold E. MM Sjt 2774 17th Lancers
DAVEY Herbert MM Cpl B/203348 13th Rifle Brigade
DAVEY James MM L/Cpl 14597 7th Border Regt
DAVEY John T. MM Dvr 36854 29 Bde RFA
DAVEY John William MM Pte 26753 46 Coy Machine Gun Corps
DAVEY Joseph Charles Jesse MM Sjt 26914 15th Hampshire Regt Died 2.10.18.
DAVEY Lawrence MM Cpl 4390 2nd Dragoons
DAVEY Leonard S. MM Sjt Fitter 676614 RFA
DAVEY Percy D. MM Spr 144586 Royal Engineers
DAVEY Reginald MM Cpl 8192 1st Shropshire Light Infantry
DAVEY Reginald J. MM Sjt 329125 RGA
DAVEY S.E. MM Cpl 13093 West Yorkshire Regt
DAVEY Samuel F. MM Sjt 242561 6th Liverpool Regt
DAVEY Thomas "MM,CG(F)" Pte 19743 9th Welsh Regt
DAVEY Thomas MM Pte 4204 2nd Rifle Brigade
DAVEY Victor A. MM Pte 203689 6th Royal West Surrey Regt
DAVEY W. MM Pte 722327 London Regt
DAVEY Walter J. MM Bdr 68277 HQ 11 Bde RFA
DAVEY Wilfred L. MM Cpl 1406 2nd Rifle Brigade
DAVEY William MM+Bar Cpl 15769 9th Norfolk Regt
DAVEY William MM Pte 3855 2/4th Gloucestershire Regt
DAVEY William MM Sjt 69232 39 Bde RFA
DAVEY William A. MM Pte 9948 6th Lincolnshire Regt
DAVEY William C. MM Pte 32279 1/1st Hertfordshire Regt
DAVEY William Henry MM Cpl 351054 1/7th London Regt
DAVEY William J. MM Gnr 32508 RGA
DAVID Alexander Fleming MM Cpl 16822 6th Cameron Highlanders
DAVID Daniel MM Cpl 348322 172 Siege Bty RGA
DAVID Hadyn MM L/Cpl 17896 Welsh Regt
DAVID Herbert MM Sjt 881 18 Fd Amb RAMC
DAVID Robert MM L/Cpl 34210 2nd South Lancashire Regt
DAVIDGE Edmund J. MM SSM 45185 4th Hussars
DAVIDSON A. MM Pte 266952 4th Gordon Highlanders
DAVIDSON A. MM Pte 200111 Royal Scots Fusiliers
DAVIDSON Adam MM Sjt 15744 Durham Light Infantry
DAVIDSON Albert MM Pte 10407 1st King's Own Scottish Borderers
DAVIDSON Alexander MM L/Cpl 93765 32 Div Sig Coy Royal Engineers

DAVIDSON Alexander MM Cpl 109371 B/159 Bde RFA
DAVIDSON Alexander MM Bdr 51785 RGA
DAVIDSON Alexander Hutton MM Sjt 24541 RGA
DAVIDSON Andrew S. MM Pte 46221 5/6th Scottish Rifles
DAVIDSON Angus "DCM,MM" Cpl S/21968 5th Cameron Highlanders
DAVIDSON Archibald MM L/Cpl 34814 North Staffordshire Regt
DAVIDSON Bruce MM Bdr 837141 RFA
DAVIDSON Charles MM Pte 265903 1st Gordon Highlanders
DAVIDSON Charles J. MM Pte 11916 15th Royal Irish Rifles
DAVIDSON David "DCM,MM+Bar" Sjt 8535 7th Seaforth Highlanders
DAVIDSON David MM Pte 11852 1st Royal Scots Fusiliers Died 18.9.18.
DAVIDSON David J. MM CSM 333 6th Royal West Kent Regt
DAVIDSON Donald MM Pte 6254 1st Lincolnshire Regt KIA 23.10.18.
DAVIDSON Duncan MM Sjt 240658 1/5th Seaforth Highlanders
DAVIDSON Edward MM Pte 1748 1/6th Arg & Suth Highlanders
DAVIDSON Edward J. MM Cpl 450604 11th London Regt
DAVIDSON Ernest J. MM Cpl 562211 Royal Engineers
DAVIDSON Francis W. MM Sjt Fitter 89640 RFA
DAVIDSON Frank MM Pte 9466 Cheshire Regt
DAVIDSON Frank A. MM Sjt 420 2nd Gordon Highlanders
DAVIDSON George MM Pte S/41309 1/6th Seaforth Highlanders
DAVIDSON George MM L/Cpl 265776 Gordon Highlanders
DAVIDSON Harry MM Bdr 99953 RGA
DAVIDSON James MM Pte 32631 1st Cameron Highlanders
DAVIDSON James MM Gnr 125850 RFA
DAVIDSON James MM Sjt 137566 179 Tunnelling Coy Royal Engineers
DAVIDSON James MM+Bar Pte S/32631 1st Cameron Highlanders
DAVIDSON James MM Pte 1052 Highland Light Infantry
DAVIDSON James MM Pte 14689 16th Royal Scots KIA 9.4.17.
DAVIDSON James A. MM Cpl 44822 Royal Engineers
DAVIDSON John MM Cpl S/4458 1/5th Royal Highlanders
DAVIDSON John MM Pte 30244 2nd Royal Scots
DAVIDSON John "MM,MSM" CQMS S/3373 7th Seaforth Highlanders
DAVIDSON John MM Pte 5132 2nd Lancashire Fusiliers
DAVIDSON John MM Sjt 5363 10th Lancashire Fusiliers
DAVIDSON John MM Sjt 240096 5/6th Scottish Rifles
DAVIDSON John MM Cpl 200877 1/5th Highland Light Infantry
DAVIDSON John S. MM Sjt 29256 Machine Gun Corps
DAVIDSON John T. MM Sjt 365003 RGA
DAVIDSON Joseph "MM,CG(F)" Cpl 4109 9th Royal Highlanders
DAVIDSON Joshua MM Pte S/9704 Arg & Suth Highlanders
DAVIDSON Margaret MM Miss F BRSC(VAD)
DAVIDSON Martin MM Pte 7731 Northumberland Fusiliers
DAVIDSON Matthew MM+Bar Sjt 137537 252 Tunnelling Coy Royal Engineers
DAVIDSON Neil MM L/Cpl 275879 Arg & Suth Highlanders
DAVIDSON Patrick MM Pte 41302 Royal Inniskilling Fusiliers
DAVIDSON R. MM Gnr 3187 RGA
DAVIDSON Richard MM Pte 40005 2nd Royal Scots Fusiliers
DAVIDSON Robert MM Bdr 630235 C/255 Bde RFA
DAVIDSON Robert MM+Bar Pte 3106 Royal Highlanders
DAVIDSON Robert MM Pte 325464 1/9th Royal Highland Light Infantry
DAVIDSON Robert MM+Bar Sjt 201027 Gordon Highlanders
DAVIDSON Robert M. MM Cpl 250810 5/6th Royal Scots
DAVIDSON Robert S. MM L/Cpl 510789 14th London Regt
DAVIDSON Samuel MM Pte 18181 Grenadier Guards
DAVIDSON Thomas MM Dvr 169224 A/231 Bde RFA
DAVIDSON Thomas MM Spr 457241 Royal Engineers
DAVIDSON Thomas MM Pte 12323 6/7th Royal Scots Fusiliers
DAVIDSON Tom MM L/Cpl 45347 18th Durham Light Infantry
DAVIDSON Victor "MM+Bar,MM(F)" Sjt 9316 11th Royal Welsh Fusiliers
DAVIDSON Walter MM Sjt 12822 2nd Worcestershire Regt
DAVIDSON William MM+Bar L/Cpl 290317 1st Gordon Highlanders
DAVIDSON William MM Sjt 20513 26 Coy Machine Gun Corps
DAVIDSON William MM L/Cpl 29/79 Northumberland Fusiliers
DAVIDSON William MM L/Cpl 265062 1/6th Gordon Highlanders
DAVIDSON William MM Pte 99922 Machine Gun Corps
DAVIDSON William MM Pte 3505 12th Royal Scots
DAVIDSON William S. MM Gnr 650780 RFA
DAVIE Andrew MM Sjt Fitter 2144 RFA
DAVIE David MM L/Cpl 291006 1/7th Royal Highlanders
DAVIE Duncan McKellar MM Sjt 200280 5/6th Scottish Rifles DOW 27.5.18.
DAVIE Edwin G. MM Dvr 45683 Royal Engineers
DAVIE Frank MM Cpl 296 11th East Yorkshire Regt DOW 2.6.17.
DAVIE Henry Shorr MM Cpl 56209 XX Cable Section Royal Engineers
DAVIE Isaac MM L/Cpl 5908 Gordon Highlanders
DAVIE J.C. MM Sjt 2049 1st Royal Highlanders
DAVIE Robert MM Pte 6289 2nd Gordon Highlanders
DAVIE Robert MM Sjt 19860 Royal Scots
DAVIE Stewart MM Sjt 29694 41st Bn Machine Gun Corps
DAVIE William MM Sjt S/2738 2nd Arg & Suth Highlanders KIA 18.8.16.
DAVIE William Taylor MM L/Cpl 40224 1/7th Royal Highlanders
DAVIES Albert MM Pte 11036 1/4th Shropshire Light Infantry
DAVIES Albert MM Pte 517 2nd Lancashire Fusiliers
DAVIES Albert A. MM L/Cpl 13373 South Wales Borderers
DAVIES Albert E. MM Cpl 5/14186 5th South Wales Borderers
DAVIES Albert E. MM Pte 15401 Royal Irish Fusiliers
DAVIES Albert H. MM+Bar Sjt L/17199 RFA
DAVIES Albert Henry MM Gnr 150442 32 Siege Bty RGA
DAVIES Albert J. MM Sjt 604017 RHA
DAVIES Alexander MM+Bar Pte 265404 Liverpool Regt
DAVIES Alfred MM Cpl 26114 1/4th Royal Lancaster Regt
DAVIES Alfred E. MM L/Sjt 19639 East Yorkshire Regt
DAVIES Alfred J. MM Cpl 242491 23rd Middlesex Regt
DAVIES Alfred J. MM L/Cpl Y/1834 1st King's Royal Rifle Corps
DAVIES Alfred W. MM Pte 235911 1/1st Herefordshire Regt
DAVIES Allan MM+Bar 2nd Cpl 93672 41 Div Sig Coy Royal Engineers
DAVIES Andrew MM Cpl 35791 RAMC
DAVIES Arthur MM Spr 93792 41 Div Sig Coy Royal Engineers
DAVIES Arthur MM Cpl 23732 1st Worcestershire Regt KIA 24.3.18.
DAVIES Arthur MM Cpl 46990 2/1st(Highland)Fd Amb RAMC
DAVIES Arthur MM L/Cpl 9704 11th Lancashire Fusiliers KIA 29.9.16.
DAVIES Arthur Edward MM L/Cpl 1861 23rd Royal Fusiliers KIA 3.5.17.
DAVIES Arthur G. MM Pte 200746 1/4th Shropshire Light Infantry
DAVIES Arthur John MM L/Cpl 25931 Welsh Regt
DAVIES B. MM Pte 10341 South Lancashire Regt
DAVIES B.Harold MM Spr 25792 Royal Engineers
DAVIES Benjamin MM Dvr 80460 B/92 Bde RFA
DAVIES Benjamin MM+Bar Cpl R/9813 King's Royal Rifle Corps
DAVIES C. MM CSM 200843 1st London Regt
DAVIES C. MM Pte 2896 13th Royal Sussex Regt
DAVIES Caradoc MM Pte 2885 1st Welsh Guards
DAVIES Caradog MM Pte 202672 1st Northamptonshire Regt DOW 31.10.18.
DAVIES Cecil MM L/Cpl 2266 1/21st London Regt
DAVIES Cedric MM Pte 21684 Cheshire Regt
DAVIES Charles Alfred MM L/Cpl 7174 25th Bn Machine Gun Corps
DAVIES Charles F. MM+Bar Cpl 30061 7th Worcestershire Regt
DAVIES Charles J.H. MM Sjt 57841 RAMC
DAVIES Charles R. MM Cpl 735049 RFA
DAVIES Charles W. MM Pte 27725 11th Border Regt
DAVIES Clifford MM L/Cpl 48005 42nd Bn Machine Gun Corps
DAVIES D.R. MM Air Mech 2 86151 Royal Air Force
DAVIES Daniel MM Bdr 81479 C/88 Bde RFA
DAVIES Daniel Newring MM Pte 91673 15th Durham Light Infantry DOW 6.10.18.
DAVIES David MM Pte 33344 1st South Wales Borderers
DAVIES David MM Pte 14634 7/8th King's Own Scottish Borderers
DAVIES David MM+Bar Cpl 18121 1st Royal Welsh Fusiliers KIA 9.10.17.
DAVIES David MM Gnr 11310 C/104 Bde RFA
DAVIES David "DCM,MM" Pte 54601 15th Welsh Regt
DAVIES David MM Spr 147634 Royal Engineers
DAVIES David MM Gnr 276270 RGA
DAVIES David MM Pte 37567 9th Welsh Regt
DAVIES David H. MM Cpl 9147 2nd Royal Welsh Fusiliers
DAVIES David Hopkin MM Cpl 19164 Royal Welsh Fusiliers
DAVIES David J. MM Sjt 20527 15th Welsh Regt
DAVIES David J. MM Pte 22966 Royal Lancaster Regt
DAVIES David J. MM Pte 88924 4 Fd Amb RAMC
DAVIES David J. MM L/Cpl 200467 5th Welsh Regt
DAVIES David James MM Spr 96013 222 Fd Coy Royal Engineers
DAVIES David John "MM,MID" Cpl 5417 1st Royal Welsh Fusiliers
DAVIES David M. MM Cpl 30231 East Lancashire Regt
DAVIES Edgar MM L/Cpl 49311 Royal Engineers
DAVIES Edward MM L/Cpl 14011 16th Cheshire Regt
DAVIES Edward MM+Bar Sjt 11450 1st South Wales Borderers

DAVIES Edward MM L/Cpl 235118 Royal Welsh Fusiliers
DAVIES Edward H. "MM,MID" Sjt 18391 RGA
DAVIES Edward J. MM L/Bdr 1732 RFA
DAVIES Edward J. MM+Bar L/Bdr 675391 RFA
DAVIES Edward M. MM Pte 58054 RAMC
DAVIES Edward S. MM L/Cpl 2169 1st Welsh Guards
DAVIES Edwin MM L/Bdr 74238 B/110 Bde RFA
DAVIES Edwin MM Pte 376013 Manchester Regt
DAVIES Edwin James MM L/Sjt 20157 5th Shropshire Light Infantry DOW 19.9.16.
DAVIES Enoch MM L/Cpl 6/17152 6th South Wales Borderers
DAVIES Epworth W. MM Cpl 112903 RGA
DAVIES Ernest John MM Sjt 528536 8 Div Sig Coy Royal Engineers KIA 16.8.17.
DAVIES Ernest John Howell MM Gnr 64777 121 Siege Bty RGA
DAVIES Evan MM Sjt 28346 C/91 Bde RFA
DAVIES Evan Lloyd MM L/Cpl 2439 1/4th Royal Berkshire Regt DOW 5.11.18.
DAVIES Evan M. MM Pte 211847 Labour Corps
DAVIES Evan William MM Bdr 31145 B/177 Bde RFA
DAVIES Faulkner Rowland MM Sjt 550275 1/16th London Regt
DAVIES Francis Gerald MM+Bar Cpl 604087 58 Div TM Bty RHA
DAVIES Frank MM Dvr 88990 RFA
DAVIES Frank MM L/Bdr 33001 RGA
DAVIES Frank MM Pte 19693 Manchester Regt
DAVIES Frank MM Sjt 54182 Royal Welsh Fusiliers
DAVIES Frank MM L/Cpl 17059 Suffolk Regt
DAVIES Frank E. MM Pte R/37196 King's Royal Rifle Corps
DAVIES Frederick MM Dvr 73368 135 Bty 32 Bde RFA
DAVIES Frederick MM Cpl 384532 1 Siege Coy R Monmouth RE
DAVIES Frederick MM L/Cpl 200293 1/5th North Staffordshire Regt
DAVIES Frederick MM Pte 38799 South Wales Borderers
DAVIES Frederick MM Sjt 39300 Royal Berkshire Regt
DAVIES Frederick MM Pte 6146 10th Rifle Brigade
DAVIES Frederick H. MM Pte 265277 6th Gloucestershire Regt
DAVIES Frederick J. MM Gnr 40660 RGA
DAVIES Frederick M. MM CQMS 3511 2/1st HAC (Inf)
DAVIES Frederick S. MM Spr 426148 419 Fd Coy Royal Engineers
DAVIES G. MM L/Cpl 11607 Shropshire Light Infantry
DAVIES G. MM Pte 69151 9th Royal Fusiliers
DAVIES G. MM Pte 26865 Hampshire Regt
DAVIES George MM L/Cpl 13/1058 6th York & Lancaster Regt
DAVIES George MM 2nd Cpl 86283 Royal Engineers
DAVIES George MM L/Cpl 12165 6th Shropshire Light Infantry
DAVIES George MM Pte G/3465 7th Royal West Surrey Regt KIA 4.4.18.
DAVIES George MM Pte 41157 Northumberland Fusiliers
DAVIES George A. MM Pte 6045 2nd Coldstream Guards
DAVIES George Cyril MM Cpl 1062 9th Lancers
DAVIES George E. MM Dvr 85814 RFA
DAVIES George Henry MM Pte 8836 2nd South Staffordshire Regt Died 1.10.17.
DAVIES George Herbert MM Cpl 172 14 Fd Amb RAMC
DAVIES George M. MM Gnr 163816 RFA
DAVIES George M. MM Gnr 371366 RGA
DAVIES George T. MM Sjt 35907 1/4th Shropshire Light Infantry
DAVIES George Thomas "MM,MID" Sjt 2398 1/5th Royal Sussex Regt
DAVIES Gwilym MM Dvr W/4767 A/230 Bde RFA
DAVIES H. MM Pte 10484 North Lancashire Regt
DAVIES H. MM L/Cpl 10711 Royal Welsh Fusiliers
DAVIES Hadyn MM Cpl 40685 Welsh Regt
DAVIES Handel MM Pte 44108 Welsh Regt
DAVIES Harold MM Pte 26524 4th West Riding Regt
DAVIES Harold MM Pte 35140 9th Welsh Regt
DAVIES Harold MM Gnr 68281 RGA
DAVIES Harry MM Sjt 75135 B/84 Bde RFA
DAVIES Harry MM Bdr 785656 RFA
DAVIES Harry MM Pte 27331 Liverpool Regt
DAVIES Harry MM Pte 23268 1st Cheshire Regt KIA 23.10.18.
DAVIES Henry MM Cpl 13569 Welsh Regt
DAVIES Henry MM Gnr 5395 RFA
DAVIES Henry Claude MM Dvr L/4936 A/289 Bde RFA
DAVIES Henry John MM Sjt T4/240523 Army Service Corps
DAVIES Henry Victor MM Gnr 83775 220 Siege Bty RGA
DAVIES Henry William MM Sjt 624861 HAC att 19 Bde RHA.
DAVIES Henry William MM Sjt 625861 Att 19 Bde RHA HAC (Arty)
DAVIES Herbert MM Pte 12611 10th Devonshire Regt
DAVIES Herbert MM Cpl 8813 2nd South Lancashire Regt
DAVIES Herbert MM L/Bdr 59420 H Bty RHA
DAVIES Herbert MM Cpl 11497 1st Worcestershire Regt
DAVIES Herbert E. MM Sjt 32337 Yorkshire Light Infantry
DAVIES Howard MM L/Cpl 21460 Welsh Regt
DAVIES Howell John MM Pte 14222 9th Royal Welsh Fusiliers DOW 4.10.18.
DAVIES Hubert MM Sjt 21506 Royal Lancaster Regt
DAVIES Hugh MM Gnr 66104 RFA
DAVIES Hugh N.C. MM+Bar Cpl G/3856 12th & 29th Royal Fusiliers
DAVIES Hugh Richard MM Pte 1069 15th Royal Warwickshire Regt Died 18.9.16.
DAVIES Humphrey MM Cpl 39171 Royal Welsh Fusiliers
DAVIES Humphrey Richard MM Gnr 60432 279 Siege Bty RGA
DAVIES Isaac MM L/Cpl 26541 1st Welsh Regt
DAVIES J. MM Pte 281252 Lancashire Fusiliers
DAVIES J. MM Pte 26745 1st Shropshire Light Infantry
DAVIES J. MM Pte 293526 Labour Corps
DAVIES J.E. MM Pte 339359 63 Fd Amb RAMC
DAVIES J.H. MM+Bar Sjt 7915 Royal Engineers
DAVIES J.H. MM Sjt 720154 London Regt
DAVIES James MM Dvr 51422 94 Bty 18 Bde RFA
DAVIES James MM Cpl 246829 Royal Engineers
DAVIES James MM Pte 19391 11th Highland Light Infantry DOW 24.4.18.
DAVIES James "MM,MID,CdG(B)" Sjt 482 Military Mounted Police
DAVIES James MM Gnr 70025 RFA
DAVIES James MM Dvr 42378 D/44 Bde RFA
DAVIES James MM+Bar Cpl 33291 1st Border Regt
DAVIES James E. MM L/Cpl 851 2nd Welsh Regt
DAVIES James H. MM Cpl 20003 9th West Yorkshire Regt
DAVIES James H. MM Gnr 153535 RGA
DAVIES James Herbert MM Bdr 32925 B/189 Bde RFA DOW 29.10.18.
DAVIES James Thomas MM Pte 4020 1st Welsh Guards DOW 7.11.18.
DAVIES Jeremiah J. MM L/Cpl 22732 15th Welsh Regt
DAVIES Jeremiah Jones MM Pte 22732 15th Welsh Regt
DAVIES Joe MM Pte 49513 19th Lancashire Fusiliers
DAVIES John MM Pte 39030 77 Fd Amb RAMC
DAVIES John MM Pte 13222 14th Royal Welsh Fusiliers
DAVIES John MM Cpl 15755 1st Worcestershire Regt
DAVIES John MM Bdr 22762 RFA
DAVIES John MM Spr 306941 Rly Ops Div Royal Engineers
DAVIES John MM L/Bdr 30734 RGA
DAVIES John MM+Bar Pte 8806 2nd Welsh Regt
DAVIES John MM L/Cpl 200246 2/5th North Staffordshire Regt Died 13.7.18.
DAVIES John MM Sjt 12953 Scots Guards
DAVIES John MM Sjt 4461 1/4th Royal Welsh Fusiliers
DAVIES John MM Sjt 8829 2nd Welsh Regt KIA 22.8.16.
DAVIES John MM Pte 56658 RAMC
DAVIES John MM Pte 18081 5th South Wales Borderers
DAVIES John MM Sjt 8292 1st South Staffordshire Regt
DAVIES John MM Pte 3317 11th Manchester Regt
DAVIES John MM Pte 358565 Liverpool Regt
DAVIES John MM+Bar Sjt 275151 1/7th Arg & Suth Highlanders
DAVIES John MM Dvr T3/023107 Army Service Corps att RAMC
DAVIES John MM Cpl S/5839 Rifle Brigade
DAVIES John MM Pte 7324 1st Shropshire Light Infantry
DAVIES John E. MM L/Cpl 356105 Liverpool Regt
DAVIES John E. "DCM,MM" Sjt 46707 35 Fd Amb RAMC
DAVIES John E. MM Sjt 79686 RGA
DAVIES John E. MM Sjt 200770 Welsh Regt
DAVIES John Evans MM Sjt 86205 Royal Engineers
DAVIES John F. MM 2nd Cpl 83143 Royal Engineers
DAVIES John F. MM Sjt 132668 RGA
DAVIES John H. MM Pte 15171 10th Royal Welsh Fusiliers
DAVIES John Henry MM Pte 29167 14th Highland Light Infantry
DAVIES John R. "DCM,MM" Sjt 62808 21st Bn Machine Gun Corps
DAVIES John R. MM Sjt 62808 Machine Gun Corps
DAVIES John S. MM Pte 260244 5th Gloucestershire Regt
DAVIES John S. MM 2nd Cpl 50755 Royal Engineers
DAVIES John T. MM L/Cpl 19002 Welsh Regt
DAVIES John W. MM Cpl 15108 9th Suffolk Regt
DAVIES Johnny C. MM Pte 14895 11th Welsh Regt DOW 25.9.18.
DAVIES Joseph MM Dvr 16067 177 Bde RFA
DAVIES Joseph "MC,MM(1811 Cpl)" 2Lt Royal Warwickshire Regt
DAVIES Joseph H. MM L/Cpl STK/64 10th Royal Fusiliers
DAVIES Joseph James "MC,MM(17713 L/Cpl 6th Wilts)" 2Lt 8th att 10th Royal Warwickshire Regt

DAVIES Joseph T. MM L/Cpl WR/285216 Railway Troops Royal Engineers
DAVIES Joshua James MM Cpl 41531 52 Fd Amb RAMC
DAVIES Kenyon MM L/Bdr 42116 116 Bty 26 Bde RFA
DAVIES Lawrence MM Pte CMT/3681 7 Div Train Army Service Corps
DAVIES Leonard A. MM Cpl 25666 1st Bn Machine Gun Corps
DAVIES Levi MM Cpl 26138 Welsh Regt
DAVIES Lewis Henry MM 2nd Cpl 32398 101 Fd Coy Royal Engineers
DAVIES Meirion MM Spr 153804 Royal Engineers
DAVIES Morgan MM Pte 34281 2nd Welsh Regt
DAVIES Moses MM L/Cpl 46604 Welsh Regt
DAVIES P.O. MM Pte 40189 RAMC
DAVIES P.S. MM BSM 52113 C/181 Bde RFA
DAVIES Percy MM Pte 48336 RAMC
DAVIES Ralph H. MM Pte 151330 104th Bn Machine Gun Corps
DAVIES Randell MM Pte M2/079311 Army Service Corps
DAVIES Reggie MM L/Cpl 216 1st Welsh Guards
DAVIES Reginald MM Pte 263024 1st Duke of Cornwall's LI
DAVIES Reginald W. MM Pte 19999 East Lancashire Regt
DAVIES Reuben "DCM,MM" Sjt 22035 1st North Lancashire Regt
DAVIES Reuben "MM,MID" Sjt T2/017662 Army Service Corps
DAVIES Rhys T. MM Pte 320556 24th Welsh Regt
DAVIES Richard "MM,CG(B)" Pte 32562 11th East Lancashire Regt
DAVIES Richard MM Pte 205537 2nd Essex Regt
DAVIES Richard MM Sjt 35664 RAMC
DAVIES Richard MM Pte M/324687 Army Service Corps
DAVIES Richard MM L/Cpl 18166 6th Shropshire Light Infantry KIA 26.3.18.
DAVIES Richard Edward MM Spr 64807 17 Div Sig Coy Royal Engineers
DAVIES Richard J. MM Sjt 18537 Royal Welsh Fusiliers
DAVIES Richard John MM L/Cpl 20501 15th Welsh Regt
DAVIES Robert MM Sjt 65807 200th Bn Machine Gun Corps
DAVIES Robert E. MM Pte 79363 142 Fd Amb RAMC
DAVIES Robert H. MM Sjt 50573 1st Cheshire Regt
DAVIES Robert W. MM Pte 10017 Machine Gun Corps
DAVIES Roger Evan MM Pte 202616 1/4th Royal Welsh Fusiliers
DAVIES Rupert J. MM Gnr 167286 326 Siege Bty RGA
DAVIES S. MM Pte 337250 RAMC
DAVIES Samuel MM Pte 200231 1/4th Shropshire Light Infantry
DAVIES Samuel MM Dvr 190737 RFA
DAVIES Samuel MM+Bar Sjt 244202 1/5th Cheshire Regt
DAVIES Samuel MM L/Cpl 202616 18th Highland Light Infantry
DAVIES Samuel MM L/Sjt R9310 King's Royal Rifle Corps
DAVIES Samuel MM Sjt 12799 9th York & Lancaster Regt
DAVIES Sidney G. MM Sjt 10758 1st Royal Welsh Fusiliers
DAVIES Sidney Victor MM Pte R/900 11th King's Royal Rifle Corps DOW 17.9.16.
DAVIES Sims MM L/Cpl 19726 17th Royal Welsh Fusiliers Died 1.9.18.
DAVIES Stanley MM Pte 61408 12th Manchester Regt
DAVIES Stanley MM Sjt 200389 1/4th Royal Welsh Fusiliers
DAVIES Stanley MM Pte 1489 1/1st Monmouthshire Regt
DAVIES T. MM Pte 133167 45th Royal Fusiliers
DAVIES T. MM Pte 40401 York & Lancaster Regt
DAVIES T.E. MM Pte 56659 RAMC
DAVIES T.G. MM Cpl 116887 Machine Gun Corps
DAVIES T.J. MM Sjt 33782 45 Fd Amb RAMC
DAVIES T.V. MM Pte 13148 1st Essex Regt
DAVIES Thomas MM Cpl 7767 Machine Gun Corps
DAVIES Thomas MM Pte 131846 63rd Bn Machine Gun Corps
DAVIES Thomas MM Cpl 25424 Royal Welsh Fusiliers
DAVIES Thomas MM Cpl 75018 Att Cdn Corps Sig Coy Royal Engineers
DAVIES Thomas MM 2nd Cpl 192447 Royal Engineers
DAVIES Thomas "DCM,MM" Sjt 200052 1/4th Royal Welsh Fusiliers
DAVIES Thomas MM Spr 43219 15 Div Sig Coy Royal Engineers
DAVIES Thomas MM Pte 304148 1/5th London Regt KIA 28.3.18.
DAVIES Thomas "MM,MID" CSM 8940 32nd Royal Fusiliers
DAVIES Thomas MM Cpl 11541 16th Lancashire Fusiliers
DAVIES Thomas Edward MM Sjt 15107 2nd Yorkshire Light Infantry KIA 3.10.18.
DAVIES Thomas H. MM Pte 17263 Royal Welsh Fusiliers
DAVIES Thomas H. MM Sjt 1144 1/6th Liverpool Regt
DAVIES Thomas H. MM Pte 315648 Royal Welsh Fusiliers
DAVIES Thomas J. MM L/Cpl 169515 Royal Engineers
DAVIES Thomas J. "DCM,MM" Pte 54631 15th Welsh Regt
DAVIES Thomas James MM Bdr 19317 108 Heavy Bty RGA
DAVIES Thomas R. MM Dvr 247561 B/251 Bde RFA
DAVIES Tommy MM Cpl 33811 1st Royal Warwickshire Regt
DAVIES Victor "MM,MID" Bdr 58166 9 Bde RFA
DAVIES W. MM L/Sjt 49816 84 Coy Labour Corps
DAVIES W. MM Pte 13101 13th Liverpool Regt
DAVIES W. MM Pte 29774 North Lancashire Regt
DAVIES W. MM Pte 266407 Royal Warwickshire Regt
DAVIES Walter MM L/Cpl 25898 17th Royal Welsh Fusiliers
DAVIES Walter Henry MM Cpl 1568 1/8th Liverpool Regt KIA 19.8.16.
DAVIES Walter S. MM Sjt 14546 RFA
DAVIES Wilfred MM Pte 11862 6th Shropshire Light Infantry
DAVIES Wilfred George MM Bdr 57566 12 Bde RFA
DAVIES Wilfred L. MM Pte 3081 23rd London Regt
DAVIES William MM+Bar Sjt 11946 9th Royal Welsh Fusiliers
DAVIES William MM Sjt 40324 Lancashire Fusiliers
DAVIES William MM Pte 10027 8th South Staffordshire Regt
DAVIES William MM L/Cpl 19393 13th Royal Welsh Fusiliers
DAVIES William MM Pte 10569 12/13th Northumberland Fusiliers
DAVIES William MM Pte 20119 Royal Scots
DAVIES William MM Sjt 240661 2/5th West Riding Regt KIA 26.3.18.
DAVIES William MM Pnr 107439 Royal Engineers
DAVIES William MM Dvr L/18682 35 Bty 22 Bde RFA
DAVIES William MM Bdr 1485 RFA
DAVIES William MM Cpl 6/16925 6th South Wales Borderers
DAVIES William MM Sjt 17780 Grenadier Guards
DAVIES William MM Pte 265370 Royal Welsh Fusiliers
DAVIES William MM Cpl 16332 7th Shropshire Light Infantry
DAVIES William MM Pte 5540 2nd Royal Welsh Fusiliers KIA 27.5.17.
DAVIES William MM L/Cpl 11680 5th Shropshire Light Infantry
DAVIES William MM Pte 16591 22nd Manchester Regt
DAVIES William Alfred MM L/Cpl 41549 3 Squadron MGC(Cavalry)
DAVIES William D. MM Pte S/3804 13th Rifle Brigade
DAVIES William E. MM Sjt 40404 4th York & Lancaster Regt
DAVIES William E. MM Pte 73019 15th Welsh Regt
DAVIES William Edmund MM Pte 48933 45 Fd Amb RAMC DOW 6.9.17.
DAVIES William F. MM Pte 54062 Welsh Regt
DAVIES William H. MM Pte M2/119685 566 MT Coy Army Service Corps
DAVIES William H. MM+Bar Pte 11397 1st Royal Welsh Fusiliers
DAVIES William H. MM Pte 39578 2nd South Wales Borderers KIA 28.1.17.
DAVIES William H. MM Pte 14171 7th Royal Berkshire Regt
DAVIES William J. MM Pte 29785 10th Shropshire Light Infantry
DAVIES William J. MM Pte 77659 1/3rd(Highland)Fd Amb RAMC
DAVIES William J. MM L/Cpl 14531 8th South Lancashire Regt
DAVIES William J. MM Dvr L/1435 C/23 Bde RFA
DAVIES William R. MM L/Sjt 43151 56th Bn Machine Gun Corps
DAVIES William R. MM Pte 241030 Welsh Regt
DAVIES William R. MM Pte 320384 24th Welsh Regt
DAVIES William R. MM Sjt 5317 1/4th Royal Welsh Fusiliers
DAVIES William S. MM Sjt 15321 Machine Gun Corps
DAVIES William T. MM Cpl 17818 Royal Welsh Fusiliers
DAVILL Henry MM L/Cpl 30318 9th Yorkshire Light Infantry DOW 14.11.18.
DAVIN Joseph MM Cpl 303290 1/9th Arg & Suth Highlanders
DAVIS A. MM Pte 131084 46th Royal Fusiliers
DAVIS A.E. MM Gnr 72960 RHA
DAVIS Albert MM Pte 8553 2nd Gloucestershire Regt
DAVIS Albert "MM,MSM" CSM 7887 2nd Worcestershire Regt
DAVIS Albert MM Sjt 7916 11th Royal Warwickshire Regt
DAVIS Albert E. MM Gnr 65150 156 Hy Bty RGA
DAVIS Albert G. MM Gnr 1474 RFA
DAVIS Albert H. MM Sjt 917 19 Fd Amb RAMC
DAVIS Albert Thomas MM Cpl 21192 141 Coy Machine Gun Corps KIA 30.10.16.
DAVIS Alfred MM Pte 10738 9th Essex Regt KIA 29.1.18.
DAVIS Alfred J. MM Cpl 67089 RFA
DAVIS Alfred W. MM Pte 43232 Royal Dublin Fusiliers
DAVIS Archibald H. MM Pte 7901 21 Fd Amb RAMC
DAVIS Arthur Edward MM L/Cpl R/14222 2nd King's Royal Rifle Corps DOW 23.7.16.
DAVIS Arthur Stuart MM Cpl F/1812 23rd Middlesex Regt
DAVIS Arthur W. MM Cpl 62542 40 Div Ammn Col RFA
DAVIS Benjamin "DCM,MM" Sjt L/8505 1st Royal West Kent Regt
DAVIS Bernard MM Pte 204859 Lancashire Fusiliers
DAVIS C.T. MM Pte 291005 Middlesex Regt

DAVIS Cecil Harry MM Pte S/43036 8th South Staffordshire Regt DOW 13.10.17.
DAVIS Cecil Tudor MM+Bar Sjt 283 17th Royal Fusiliers
DAVIS Charles MM L/Bdr 82010 RFA
DAVIS Charles MM Pte 315374 9th Royal Sussex Regt
DAVIS Charles MM Sjt 18282 20 Fd Coy Royal Engineers
DAVIS Charles E. MM Cpl 11280 6th Dorsetshire Regt
DAVIS Charles F. MM Sjt 3748 2nd Highland Light Infantry
DAVIS Charles Frederick MM Cpl M2/053961 49 Div Train Army Service Corps att RAMC
DAVIS Charles J. MM Cpl 56697 RFA
DAVIS Charles John MM Pte 19596 7th Shropshire Light Infantry Died 7.11.18.
DAVIS Cyril Leo MM Pte 439332 3(South Midland)Fd Amb RAMC
DAVIS D.E. MM Cpl 280922 London Regt
DAVIS Daniel MM Pte 6659 RAMC
DAVIS E. MM+Bar Pte 47173 RAMC
DAVIS Edward J. MM L/Cpl 25083 Royal Berkshire Regt
DAVIS Edward John MM Pte 10179 1st Gloucestershire Regt KIA 24.9.18.
DAVIS Edward John MM Dvr 21429 RFA
DAVIS Edwin Albert MM L/Cpl 27976 RAMC
DAVIS Ernest MM Pte 41523 RAMC
DAVIS Ernest Alfred MM Pte 18448 15th Hampshire Regt DOW 9.8.19.
DAVIS Ernest F. "MM,MID" L/Cpl 7893 4th King's Royal Rifle Corps
DAVIS Ernest J. MM CSM 240599 1/8th Worcestershire Regt
DAVIS F.A. MM Pte 512339 2 Fd Amb RAMC
DAVIS Francis Wood MM Pte 27357 2nd Royal Dublin Fusiliers KIA 21.3.18.
DAVIS Frank MM Cpl 39317 81 Bde RFA
DAVIS Fred MM Sjt 6630 7th East Yorkshire Regt KIA 11.10.18.
DAVIS Fred MM Sjt 200779 Lancashire Fusiliers
DAVIS Frederick MM Pte 202427 Middlesex Regt
DAVIS Frederick MM Pte 2159 1/24th London Regt
DAVIS Frederick MM L/Cpl 15106 8th Somerset Light Infantry
DAVIS Frederick MM Sjt 269649 Royal Engineers
DAVIS Frederick MM Gnr 53505 3 Bde RHA
DAVIS Frederick A. MM Sjt 265612 6th Gloucestershire Regt
DAVIS Frederick C. MM Cpl 532524 Royal Engineers
DAVIS Frederick Edward William MM Sjt 22160 93 Bde RFA DOW 26.9.18.
DAVIS Frederick W. MM Pte 1606 1st Gloucestershire Regt
DAVIS G. MM L/Cpl 6446 10th Hussars
DAVIS G. MM Pte 435194 1 Fd Amb RAMC
DAVIS G.W. MM S/Sjt Mech M/21095 Army Service Corps
DAVIS G.W. MM+Bar L/Cpl 6/261 2nd Rifle Brigade
DAVIS George MM Gnr 52189 RGA
DAVIS George MM Pte 8783 South Staffordshire Regt
DAVIS George MM Spr 253475 'F' Corps Sig Coy Royal Engineers
DAVIS George MM Sjt 7214 2nd Royal Irish Rifles KIA 7.7.16.
DAVIS George MM Pte 14986 8th Somerset Light Infantry DOW 24.4.17.
DAVIS George MM Cpl 20275 Machine Gun Corps
DAVIS George MM Sjt 39779 Worcestershire Regt
DAVIS George A.E. MM Pte 44399 2nd King's Royal Rifle Corps
DAVIS George E. MM Cpl 19276 9th Royal Sussex Regt
DAVIS George E. MM Pte 27343 Wiltshire Regt
DAVIS George H. MM Pte 133854 Machine Gun Corps
DAVIS George J. MM Cpl 30471 4th North Lancashire Regt
DAVIS H.L. MM L/Bdr 75705 129 Bty 42 Bde RFA
DAVIS H.W. MM Cpl 2672 Royal Warwickshire Regt
DAVIS H.W. MM Sjt 6494 London Regt
DAVIS Harold J. MM Gnr 830201 RFA
DAVIS Harry MM Pte 40128 2nd Royal Scots Fusiliers
DAVIS Harry MM Bdr 164920 157 Siege Bty RGA
DAVIS Harry MM L/Bdr 46255 29 Bde RFA
DAVIS Harry MM Dvr 610173 RHA
DAVIS Harry MM Sjt 1049 15th Royal Warwickshire Regt Died 20.5.19.
DAVIS Harry MM S/Sjt Saddler 13702 48 Bty 36 Bde RFA
DAVIS Harry MM CSM 11918 West Yorkshire Regt
DAVIS Henry MM Cpl 8153 9th Royal Fusiliers
DAVIS Henry MM Sjt 5569 1st Gloucestershire Regt
DAVIS Henry G. MM Sjt 275 1(Home Counties)Fd Coy Royal Engineers
DAVIS Henry J. MM+Bar Sjt 7404 1st Dorsetshire Regt
DAVIS Henry Mark MM Pte 51685 18th Welsh Regt KIA 13.4.18.
DAVIS Herbert Chope MM L/Cpl 110622 21 Squadron MGC(Cavalry) Died 28.10.18.
DAVIS Herbert J. MM Sjt 67102 C/123 Bde RFA
DAVIS Howard W. MM Sjt 5026 RFA
DAVIS Isaac "MM,MID" Sjt M2/135918 565 MT Coy Army Service Corps
DAVIS J. MM Pte 376315 Manchester Regt
DAVIS J. MM Pte 19955 Machine Gun Corps
DAVIS J.S. MM Pte 43934 10th Essex Regt
DAVIS Jack L. MM S/Sjt Armourer T/1194 Army Ordnance Corps
DAVIS James "MM,MID" Sjt 13390 10th West Riding Regt DOW 8.6.17.
DAVIS James MM Sjt S/1189 Rifle Brigade
DAVIS James C. "DCM,MM+Bar" CSM 200898 2/4th York & Lancaster Regt
DAVIS James H. MM Cpl 14112 1st Royal Berkshire Regt
DAVIS James W. MM Pte 71754 Machine Gun Corps
DAVIS James William MM Pte 1886 7th East Kent Regt
DAVIS John MM L/Cpl 30791 Royal Inniskilling Fusiliers
DAVIS John MM Bdr 61208 RFA
DAVIS John MM Pte 15944 Royal Irish Fusiliers
DAVIS John MM L/Cpl 14423 6th Royal Inniskilling Fusiliers
DAVIS John "DCM,MM+Bar,MID" Sjt 63537 15 Div Sig Coy Royal Engineers
DAVIS John MM L/Cpl 13588 10th West Riding Regt
DAVIS John MM Sjt 1728 1/7th Worcestershire Regt
DAVIS John MM Cpl 241215 1/8th West Yorkshire Regt
DAVIS John MM Sjt 8643 9th Essex Regt KIA 30.11.17.
DAVIS John Albert MM Sjt 4793 1st Royal Warwickshire Regt KIA 11.10.16.
DAVIS John T. MM L/Bdr 209244 21 Bty 2 Bde RFA
DAVIS Joseph C. MM Pte R/37896 King's Royal Rifle Corps
DAVIS Lawrence MM Cpl 173614 RGA
DAVIS Mary Ellen MM Sister F QAIMNS
DAVIS Norman Charles MM Sjt 28034 Royal Welsh Fusiliers
DAVIS Oswald H. MM Cpl 148768 Royal Engineers
DAVIS P. MM Sjt SR/3187 RGA
DAVIS Parks MM Cpl 58821 12th Bn Machine Gun Corps
DAVIS Patrick MM Bdr 69441 27 Bde RFA
DAVIS R. MM Sjt 11481 1st Highland Light Infantry
DAVIS Reginald MM Pte 50820 Manchester Regt
DAVIS Richard P. MM Spr 559902 Royal Engineers
DAVIS Robert MM L/Cpl 40808 1st Worcestershire Regt
DAVIS Robert MM L/Cpl 2753 2nd Rifle Brigade KIA 31.3.18.
DAVIS Samuel George MM L/Sjt F/295 16th Middlesex Regt
DAVIS Samuel J. "MM,MIDx2" Sjt 86119 170 Tunnelling Coy Royal Engineers
DAVIS Stanley Thomas MM Cpl 43013 1st Essex Regt
DAVIS Stephen MM L/Cpl 137783 237 Fd Coy Royal Engineers
DAVIS Stephen C. MM Pte DM2/118446 Army Service Corps
DAVIS Sydney MM Dvr 177390 RFA
DAVIS Sydney H. MM Gnr 136130 326 Siege Bty RGA
DAVIS Thomas MM Pte 28294 2nd Grenadier Guards
DAVIS Thomas MM Pte 10501 Royal West Surrey Regt
DAVIS Thomas MM Pte 17273 7th South Staffordshire Regt
DAVIS Thomas "MM,MID" Sjt 16/653 Royal Irish Rifles
DAVIS Thomas F. MM Sjt 12631 6th Royal Berkshire Regt
DAVIS Thomas James "MM,MSM,MID,CG(F)" Sjt 8357 2nd Coldstream Guards
DAVIS Thomas William MM Gnr 138330 B/74 Bde RFA Died 5.11.17.
DAVIS Valentine MM Cpl 2019 Royal West Surrey Regt
DAVIS Victor W.S. MM Sjt 63527 RFA
DAVIS W. MM Pte 40419 Lincolnshire Regt
DAVIS W.E. MM Pte 202713 6th London Regt
DAVIS Wallace A. MM+Bar Cpl 241626 Gloucestershire Regt
DAVIS Walter MM Sjt 10741 4th Royal Fusiliers
DAVIS Walter Edward "DCM,MM+Bar,MM(F)" CSM 9194 1st Lincolnshire Regt
DAVIS Walter Edwin MM Pte 203506 2/7th Worcestershire Regt
DAVIS Walter G. MM Pte 241694 Royal Warwickshire Regt
DAVIS Walter George MM Cpl 1943 2/5th Gloucestershire Regt KIA 19.8.16.
DAVIS Walter H. "MM,MID" Sjt 11218 4th Middlesex Regt
DAVIS Walter J. MM L/Sjt 552517 16th London Regt
DAVIS Walter J.H. MM Cpl 34193 153 Heavy Bty RGA
DAVIS Walter M. MM Sjt 6/641 Rifle Brigade
DAVIS Walter Stacey MM CSM L/8385 2nd East Kent Regt Died 29.1.17.
DAVIS Walter T. MM Pte 51167 7th Manchester Regt
DAVIS William MM Pte 50016 5/6th Royal Scots
DAVIS William MM Pte 20574 6th Dorsetshire Regt KIA 11.10.18.
DAVIS William MM Spr 94557 172 Tunnelling Coy Royal Engineers

DAVIS William MM Pte 265937 Gloucestershire Regt
DAVIS William MM+Bar BSM 45901 D/94 Bde RFA
DAVIS William MM Pte 18408 7th Border Regt
DAVIS William C. MM Pte 31223 RAMC
DAVIS William E. MM L/Cpl 532646 15th London Regt
DAVIS William F. MM Sjt 5981 2nd Worcestershire Regt
DAVIS William Frank MM Pte 608180 18th London Regt att 15th Royal Irish Rifles.KIA 20.10.18.
DAVIS William H. MM Sjt 676558 RFA
DAVIS William H. MM Sjt S/6293 Rifle Brigade
DAVIS William H. MM Bdr 55457 RFA
DAVIS William J. MM Bdr 11862 RFA
DAVIS William John "DCM,MM" Cpl 32518 7 Bty MGC (Motors)
DAVIS William McL. MM Pte 28940 6th King's Own Scottish Borderers
DAVIS or DAVIES Richard "DCM,MM" Sjt 35664 RAMC
DAVISON Andrew MM L/Cpl 21/927 22nd Northumberland Fusiliers
DAVISON Anthony MM Sjt 75548 MGC(Heavy Branch)
DAVISON Archibald MM L/Cpl 270159 1/1st Northumberland Yeo
DAVISON Armine MM Cpl 12345 11th Notts & Derby Regt KIA 15.6.18.
DAVISON Benjamin MM L/Cpl 325294 1/9th Durham Light Infantry
DAVISON Charles MM Pte 10972 Durham Light Infantry
DAVISON Charles MM Sjt 15306 23 Heavy Bty RGA
DAVISON Edward MM Gnr 141744 302 Siege Bty RGA
DAVISON Eugene Victor "MM+Bar,MID" Sjt 27556 D/103 Bde RFA
DAVISON Frederick William MM L/Cpl 19678 26th Royal Fusiliers
DAVISON George F. MM+Bar L/Cpl 87528 Royal Engineers
DAVISON Henry "MC,MM" RSM 6047 Scots Guards
DAVISON Herbert MM Pte 19754 9th Yorkshire Light Infantry
DAVISON James MM Cpl 14563 2nd Northumberland Fusiliers KIA 4.11.18.
DAVISON James Alexander MM Sjt L/31205 155 Bde RFA
DAVISON James Arthur MM+Bar Bdr 26365 114 Bty 25 Bde RFA
DAVISON James H. MM Pte 304928 17th Armoured Car Bn Tank Corps
DAVISON John "DCM,MM" CSM 33591 1/4th York & Lancaster Regt
DAVISON John MM Cpl 13420 6th Dorsetshire Regt
DAVISON John MM Pte 388562 87 Fd Amb RAMC
DAVISON Leslie MM L/Sjt G/52016 2nd Royal Fusiliers
DAVISON Michael MM Pte 200169 Northumberland Fusiliers
DAVISON Raymond MM L/Sjt 1106 23rd Northumberland Fusiliers
DAVISON Richard MM Dvr CHT/1086 Army Service Corps
DAVISON Robert MM Pte 37122 15/17th West Yorkshire Regt
DAVISON Thomas "MM,MID" Pte 18559 2nd West Riding Regt
DAVISON Thomas L. MM Pte 201851 Royal West Surrey Regt
DAVISON Walter Ernest MM L/Cpl 98878 Machine Gun Corps
DAVISON Walter H. MM Sjt 64305 108 Coy Labour Corps
DAVISON William MM Pte 18241 6th Yorkshire Regt
DAVITT Thomas MM Pte 513917 Labour Corps
DAVY David MM Spr 259311 63 Div Sig Coy Royal Engineers
DAVY John Amstrong MM Cpl 8968 1st King's Royal Rifle Corps KIA 29.9.18.
DAVY John E. MM Cpl 476330 458 Fd Coy Royal Engineers
DAVY Norman MM Spr 145100 Royal Engineers
DAW Clement MM Pte 25417 12th East Surrey Regt
DAW Herbert "MM,MID" Cpl 21445 Signal Service Royal Engineers
DAW Walter MM Cpl 356850 1/10th Liverpool Regt
DAWBER James MM Sjt 8168 1st North Lancashire Regt
DAWBORN Edward George MM Pte 58011 18th Liverpool Regt
DAWE Ernest R. MM Cpl F/2180 23rd Middlesex Regt
DAWE John MM Cpl 12271 12th East Surrey Regt AKA Leonard Baker.
DAWE Joseph H. MM Gnr 1617 23 Bty 40 Bde RFA
DAWE Leonard "DCM,MM" Sjt 43358 D/112 Bde RFA
DAWE Robert Edward MM Dvr M1/08546 Att 8(Cav)Fd Amb RAMC Army Service Corps
DAWE William H. MM Gnr 785857 B/312 Bde RFA
DAWES A. MM Gnr 68853 RFA
DAWES Benjamin MM L/Cpl 96914 Royal Engineers
DAWES Charles MM+Bar Dvr 82732 B/123 Bde RFA
DAWES Charles J. MM Pte 202330 Royal Sussex Regt
DAWES Clement MM L/Sjt 16935 Machine Gun Corps
DAWES Elijah MM Pte 44220 South Wales Borderers
DAWES Ernest MM Pte 46682 4th York & Lancaster Regt
DAWES Francis A. MM Pte 53583 18th Gloucestershire Regt
DAWES Frederick "MM,MSM" Cpl M2/104544 Army Service Corps att III Corps HAG.
DAWES George Henry MM CSM 1495 1/6th Royal Warwickshire Regt KIA 19.8.16.
DAWES Henry MM L/Cpl 240332 1/5th Leicestershire Regt
DAWES Hubert James MM L/Cpl 20234 26th Royal Fusiliers KIA 8.5.18.
DAWES L. MM Pte 51473 Lincolnshire Regt
DAWES Ralph O. MM Cpl 16170 7th Norfolk Regt
DAWES Richard MM Bdr 137258 410 Bty 96 Bde RFA
DAWES S. MM Pte 1790 Notts & Derby Regt
DAWKINS Albert MM Pte 14325 1st Dorsetshire Regt
DAWKINS Alec J. MM L/Cpl 705176 23rd London Regt
DAWKINS Alfred Edgar MM Sjt 15418 RFA
DAWS James Evelyn Granville MM Sjt B/2384 8th Rifle Brigade DOW 25.8.17.
DAWSON Albert MM Spr 448421 Royal Engineers
DAWSON Alexander MM L/Cpl 46512 207 Coy Machine Gun Corps
DAWSON Alexander MM Pte 351626 11th Royal Scots KIA 26.6.18.
DAWSON Alexander MM Sjt 201673 1/4th Seaforth Highlanders
DAWSON Alfred MM Bdr Sig 55821 57 Siege Bty RGA
DAWSON Alfred Edward MM Pte M2/116640 Army Service Corps att 75 Fd Amb RAMC
DAWSON Andrew MM Pte 352579 1/9th Royal Scots
DAWSON Andrew B. MM Gnr 45064 A/88 Bde RFA
DAWSON Anthony MM L/Cpl 15331 80 Group HQ Labour Corps
DAWSON Arthur MM Pte 46064 11th South Lancashire Regt
DAWSON Arthur MM Spr 310795 ? Div Sig Coy Royal Engineers
DAWSON Arthur MM Pte 303993 21st Manchester Regt
DAWSON Arthur "MM,MID" Sjt 86218 Royal Engineers
DAWSON Arthur J. MM Pte 403295 2 Fd Amb RAMC
DAWSON Bertie MM Sjt 28275 9th Yorkshire Regt
DAWSON Charles MM Sjt 13132 34th Bn Machine Gun Corps
DAWSON David MM L/Cpl 547769 Royal Engineers
DAWSON David H. MM CSM 15616 12th West Yorkshire Regt
DAWSON Donald MM L/Cpl 290577 4th Gordon Highlanders KIA 13.4.18.
DAWSON Edwin MM Sjt 63132 5th Yorkshire Light Infantry
DAWSON Erin S. MM L/Cpl 3154 1/21st London Regt
DAWSON Ernest MM Sjt 1654 3rd Rifle Brigade DOW 25.8.17.
DAWSON F.F. MM Air Mech 2 44243 Royal Flying Corps
DAWSON Francis G.C. "DCM,MM" Gnr 102005 12 Siege Bty RGA
DAWSON Frank MM Sjt 12888 1/4th Royal Lancaster Regt
DAWSON Frank "MM,CG(B)" Pte 133 12th Yorkshire Light Infantry
DAWSON Frank MM Pte 4795 2nd Leinster Regt DOW 10.6.16.
DAWSON Frank A. MM Sjt 37636 RFA
DAWSON Fraser MM L/Cpl S/40638 2nd Seaforth Highlanders
DAWSON Fred MM Cpl 769775 28th London Regt
DAWSON Frederick MM L/Cpl 57280 106 Fd Coy Royal Engineers
DAWSON Frederick Charles MM Pte 800777 1/6th London Regt att 2nd R Fus.
DAWSON Frederick F. MM Cpl 17901 10th Royal Fusiliers
DAWSON George MM Pte 41407 1st Duke of Cornwall's LI
DAWSON George MM Cpl 129 11th East Yorkshire Regt
DAWSON George W. MM L/Cpl 316355 36th Northumberland Fusiliers
DAWSON H. MM Sjt 13546 10th Essex Regt
DAWSON H.W. MM Gnr 93234 RGA
DAWSON Harold MM Pte 17948 6th Lincolnshire Regt
DAWSON Harry MM Sjt 200046 1/5th Liverpool Regt
DAWSON Harry "DCM,MM" Sjt 482141 62 Div Sig Coy Royal Engineers
DAWSON Henry MM Pte R/3379 King's Royal Rifle Corps
DAWSON Henry MM Gnr 608313 RHA
DAWSON Henry MM Gnr 641 12 Bty MGC(Motors)
DAWSON Horace B. MM Pte 203647 4th West Riding Regt
DAWSON Hubert MM Pte 10110 5th Connaught Rangers
DAWSON J.S. MM Pte G/59646 17th Royal Fusiliers
DAWSON Jack MM Cpl 41658 RFA
DAWSON James MM Sjt 50540 10th Royal Scots
DAWSON James MM Pte 9723 1/7th Royal Highlanders
DAWSON James MM Dvr 660236 RFA
DAWSON James Howard MM Sjt 49784 RFA
DAWSON John MM L/Cpl 19361 1st North Lancashire Regt
DAWSON John MM Pte 1788 1st Royal Lancaster Regt
DAWSON John MM L/Cpl 240072 1/5th Yorkshire Regt KIA 27.5.18.
DAWSON John MM L/Cpl 14069 2nd South Lancashire Regt
DAWSON John MM Pte 23402 4th Grenadier Guards
DAWSON John D. MM Pte 12271 Coldstream Guards
DAWSON John F. MM Sjt 223161 135 Bty 32 Bde RFA
DAWSON John G. MM Pte 126 2 Fd Amb RAMC
DAWSON John Henry MM Dvr 188998 326 Bde RFA
DAWSON John Henry MM Pte 240625 2/5th West Yorkshire Regt KIA 23.5.18.

DAWSON John S. MM Sjt 241258 Royal Lancaster Regt
DAWSON John Taylor "MM,MSM" Sjt 128034 256 Siege Bty RGA
DAWSON John W. MM L/Cpl 15939 Northumberland Fusiliers
DAWSON Nelson G. MM Pte G/2138 8th Royal Sussex Regt
DAWSON Peter MM Pte 96482 1st Liverpool Regt
DAWSON Richard MM L/Cpl 16071 18th Lancashire Fusiliers KIA 22.10.17.
DAWSON Robert "MM,MID" Sjt 240505 1/5th Northumberland Fusiliers
DAWSON Robert MM+Bar Sjt 14202 2nd Arg & Suth Highlanders
DAWSON Robert Edward MM Sjt 11368 34 Div Ammn Col RFA
DAWSON Samuel Percy MM Pte 6368 16th Manchester Regt
DAWSON Sidney MM Pte 21963 1/5th Leicestershire Regt KIA 24.9.18.
DAWSON Stanley MM Spr 448950 Royal Engineers
DAWSON Thomas "DCM,MM,MSM,MID" CSM 12728 9th Cheshire Regt
DAWSON Thomas MM L/Cpl 21358 10th Durham Light Infantry
DAWSON Thomas MM Sjt 6471 8th Royal Lancaster Regt DOW 8.5.18.
DAWSON Thomas B. MM Sjt 14643 4th Coldstream Guards
DAWSON Thomas J. MM Dvr 297084 RGA
DAWSON Thomas W. MM+Bar Sjt 19699 3 Siege Bty RGA
DAWSON Vincent L. MM Pte 537095 15th London Regt
DAWSON W. MM Pte 7266 2nd King's Own Scottish Borderers
DAWSON W. MM Pte 10/1014 East Yorkshire Regt
DAWSON W.E. MM Cpl 55094 Yeomanry
DAWSON W.H. MM Bdr 39740 RGA
DAWSON Willard R. MM Dvr L/9153 RFA
DAWSON William MM Gnr 59496 278 Siege Bty RGA
DAWSON William MM Sjt 12543 11th Royal Scots
DAWSON William MM Gnr 630554 C/250 RFA
DAWSON William MM Sjt 17229 6th South Wales Borderers
DAWSON William MM Pte 242661 1/5th Yorkshire Light Infantry
DAWSON William MM Pte 35912 1st North Lancashire Regt
DAWSON William MM Sjt 8424 12th Lancashire Fusiliers
DAWSON William G. MM Pte 512408 RAMC
DAWSON William Henry George MM Cpl 202602 2/4th Royal West Kent Regt KIA 24.12.17.
DAWSON William James MM L/Cpl 241202 13th Liverpool Regt KIA 8.10.18.
DAWSON William Joseph MM+Bar Cpl 47659 HQRA 29 Div RFA
DAWSON William Oliver MM Cpl 44849 92 Coy Machine Gun Corps
DAY A. MM Pte 354372 3 Fd Amb RAMC
DAY A. MM Pte 225116 Royal Fusiliers
DAY Albert E. MM Pte 11615 Royal Fusiliers
DAY Albert J. MM Sjt 2234 1/1st Hertfordshire Regt
DAY Albert V. MM Pte 200193 1st Bn Tank Corps
DAY Alfred MM Gnr 75794 D/58 Bde RFA
DAY Alfred G. MM Pte R/16056 King's Royal Rifle Corps
DAY Alfred H. MM Pte 201980 2/5th West Yorkshire Regt
DAY Allan James MM Cpl 78410 B/119 Bde RFA Died 22.10.18.
DAY Archibald MM L/Cpl 21325 1st Northumberland Fusiliers
DAY Arthur MM Sjt 18711 2nd Grenadier Guards
DAY Arthur MM Pte 16220 Norfolk Regt
DAY Arthur MM Gnr 45892 327 Siege Bty RGA
DAY Arthur S. MM Pte 30246 Suffolk Regt
DAY Bertie Thomas MM L/Cpl 76449 Tank Corps
DAY C. MM Pte G/13945 Middlesex Regt
DAY Charles MM Sjt 24801 115 Hy Bty RGA
DAY Charles MM Pte 245235 2nd London Regt
DAY Charles G. MM Pte 243274 Royal West Surrey Regt
DAY Charles T.G. MM Pte 16555 King's Royal Rifle Corps
DAY E. MM+Bar Sjt 31799 10th Essex Regt
DAY Ernest C. MM Cpl 506052 504 Fd Coy Royal Engineers
DAY Ernest J. MM Cpl 87251 40 Bde RFA
DAY Frank L. MM Sjt 32130 31 Heavy Bty RGA
DAY Frank Robert MM Gnr L/6138 D/156 Bde RFA
DAY Fred MM Cpl 524402 483 Fd Coy Royal Engineers
DAY Frederick MM Pte CMT/2556 3 Div Train Army Service Corps
DAY Frederick A. MM Cpl 22386 1 Fd Sqn Royal Engineers
DAY Frederick T. MM L/Cpl 24389 1st Northamptonshire Regt
DAY G.A. "MM,MID" Sjt 529 Military Mounted Police
DAY George MM L/Cpl 479 24th Royal Fusiliers DOW 17.12.17.
DAY George Alfred MM Cpl F/2253 23rd Middlesex Regt
DAY George Robert MM Sjt 13424 Lincolnshire Regt
DAY Haldane H. MM Pte G/6583 11th Royal Fusiliers
DAY Harry C. MM Pte M/271407 59 Div MT Coy Army Service Corps
DAY Henry Mountain MM L/Sjt 10633 2nd Scots Guards KIA 24.8.18.

DAY Herbert MM Pte 32054 South Lancashire Regt
DAY Horace Victor MM Gnr 18075 D/73 Bde RFA
DAY J. MM Pte 22682 Royal Fusiliers
DAY James MM Pte 15560 6th Yorkshire Regt
DAY James E. MM Cpl 81677 26th Royal Fusiliers
DAY James M. MM Cpl 74045 RFA
DAY John "MC,MM(10398 CQMS)" 2Lt 2nd Royal Scots
DAY John MM Cpl 3218 12th Middlesex Regt
DAY John "MM,MID" L/Cpl 26857 Royal Scots
DAY John A. MM L/Cpl 700385 1/23rd London Regt
DAY John A. MM Sjt 200415 1/4th Gordon Highlanders
DAY John Henry James MM Pte 202706 2/1st London Regt KIA 21.9.17.
DAY John T. MM Pte 242142 Yorkshire Light Infantry
DAY John W. MM Sjt 62874 32 Bde RFA
DAY Joseph MM Pte 12545 2nd King's Royal Rifle Corps
DAY Joseph MM Dvr T2/015607 Army Service Corps
DAY Joseph T. MM Cpl 7678 1st Royal Berkshire Regt
DAY Lawrence MM Pte 15004 Royal Munster Fusiliers
DAY Lewis E. MM+Bar Pte 10387 5th Dorsetshire Regt
DAY Marcus Percy "MM,MID" Sjt 67713 Royal Engineers
DAY Maurice MM L/Cpl 50354 11th Royal Fusiliers KIA 7.8.18.
DAY Maurice James MM L/Bdr 296218 152 Heavy Bty RGA
DAY Owen Samuel MM Sjt 7953 16th Cheshire Regt KIA 9.9.17.
DAY Percy MM Bdr 776064 C/245 Bde RFA DOW 10.10.17.
DAY Percy Albert MM Spr 126580 16 Div Sig Coy Royal Engineers
DAY Percy C. MM Pte G/14678 2nd Royal Sussex Regt
DAY Phillip MM Pte 593846 18th London Regt
DAY Reginald G. MM Pte 320609 15th Suffolk Regt
DAY Richard D. MM Cpl 203429 Middlesex Regt
DAY Robert MM Sjt 9311 7th Suffolk Regt
DAY Robert V. MM Pte 8978 2nd Suffolk Regt
DAY Sidney MM Dvr 135761 104 Bde RFA
DAY Sidney J. MM L/Cpl 27218 13th West Riding Regt
DAY Sidney W. MM L/Cpl 20169 2nd Suffolk Regt
DAY Stanley E. MM Pte 16930 Northamptonshire Regt
DAY Stanley George MM Cpl 121780 40th Bn Machine Gun Corps
DAY Thomas MM Gnr L/17425 C/83 Bde RFA
DAY Thomas Frederick MM Pte 21190 2nd Hampshire Regt DOW 27.1.18.
DAY Victor H. MM Sjt DM2/189055 Army Service Corps
DAY Walter MM Pte 204272 1/8th Worcestershire Regt
DAY Wilfred Thomas "MM,CG(B)" Sjt 570 132 Heavy Bty RGA
DAY William MM Cpl 9970 1/6th Lancashire Fusiliers
DAY William MM Pte 11432 2nd Royal Scots
DAY William MM L/Sjt 9993 2nd Essex Regt
DAY William MM Cpl 429 22nd Northumberland Fusiliers
DAY William A. MM L/Cpl 8548 East Lancashire Regt
DAY William Frederick MM Cpl 198892 2 Div Sig Coy Royal Engineers
DAY William G. MM Cpl 40207 2(Reserve)Bde W Bty RGA
DAY William George MM Pte 11732 2nd Worcestershire Regt KIA 15.7.16.
DAY William H. MM Pte 3367 12th Middlesex Regt
DAY William H. MM Pte 84081 Machine Gun Corps
DAY William H. MM Pte 266499 Seaforth Highlanders
DAY William J. MM+Bar Sjt 220314 1st Royal Berkshire Regt
DAYBLE Percy C. MM+Bar Gnr 318185 RGA
DAYKIN J. MM Pte 204568 Northumberland Fusiliers
DAYKINS John Brunton "VC,MM" Sjt 205353 2/4th York & Lancaster Regt
DAYMENT W.J. MM Pte 457517 2/3rd(West Riding)Fd Amb RAMC
DAYNES C. MM Pte 200952 Lancashire Fusiliers
DAYSH Charles MM L/Cpl 28918 Middlesex Regt
DAYUS Llewellyn C. MM Sjt 6435 Dorsetshire Regt
DAZLEY Charles Edward MM Pte 267484 1/6th Northumberland Fusiliers Died 27.5.18.
DAZLEY George MM Cpl 20/407 Durham Light Infantry
DE ABAITUA John B. MM Gnr 161433 RFA
DE ATH Edward A. MM L/Sjt 33143 9th Devonshire Regt
DE BANK Percival R. MM Pte 24684 2nd Oxf & Bucks Light Infantry
DE BEAU Maurice Lee MM Bdr 37230 RGA
DE BOLLA Joseph A. "MM,MSM" Cpl 632322 2/20th London Regt
DE BURGH Ulick A.E.H.d'E. MM Bdr 56957 RGA
DE CARTERET Percy E. MM Cpl 89302 C/53 Bde RFA
DE COURCY William MM L/Sjt G/11151 11th Royal West Surrey Regt KIA 1.8.17.
DE CUNHA Edward MM Pte 200896 5/6th Scottish Rifles
DE GRUCHY Francis P. MM Sjt 282245 RGA
DE GRUCHY Herbert MM L/Cpl 200847 1/4th Royal Berkshire Regt

DE GRUCHY W.P. MM Pte 29968 2nd Hampshire Regt
DE GUERIN Minnie Maude MM Sister F QAIMNS
DE LA COUR Walter Philip MM Dvr 35018 129 Bty 42 Bde RFA
DE LUSIGNAN Guy MM Cpl 45275 2nd Essex Regt
DE MELLIOM S.L. MM L/Bdr 57312 RHA
DE MONCHO Alfonso Joaquin Vicente MM Spr 1267 47 Div Sig Coy Royal Engineers
DE RUE Arthur C. MM Cpl 10341 2nd Yorkshire Regt
DE RYCK Charles MM L/Cpl 8360 Royal West Surrey Regt
DE SAINTE CROIX Sidney Alfred "DCM,MM" Sjt 10234 11th Royal Warwickshire Regt
DE SOUZA C.W.L. MM Pte 512520 3rd(London)Fd Amb RAMC
DE T'SERCLAES Elsie Blackall MM The Baroness F BRCS
DE WOOLF F. MM L/Cpl 738061 24th London Regt
DEA Patrick MM Bdr 40747 RGA
DEACON Charles MM Gnr 97175 296 Siege Bty RGA
DEACON Charles Edward MM Bdr 35797 B/181 Bde RFA
DEACON Charles Ernest MM Sjt 11405 47 Bty 41 Bde RFA
DEACON Charles H. MM L/Cpl 25724 15th Royal Warwickshire Regt
DEACON Cyril Hugh MM CSM 2583 1/14th London Regt
DEACON George MM Pte 29465 7th Bedfordshire Regt
DEACON George John Outlaw MM Pte 23458 8th Royal West Kent Regt KIA 9.9.17.
DEACON Herbert L. MM Sjt 235439 1st Worcestershire Regt
DEACON John MM Spr 121905 185 Tunnelling Coy Royal Engineers
DEACON Samuel T. MM Cpl 1995 RAMC
DEACON William MM L/Cpl 45425 Rifle Brigade att 5th London Regt
DEACON William Albert MM Sjt 1622 16th Lancers
DEACONS John MM Pte S/4774 11th Arg & Suth Highlanders
DEACY Ernest E. MM Gnr 52715 85 Bty 11 Bde RFA
DEADFIELD Francis W. MM Pte 42271 Middlesex Regt
DEADMAN Arthur J. MM+Bar L/Cpl 283154 4th London Regt
DEADMAN Cecil MM Cpl 65412 4th Royal Fusiliers
DEADMAN James MM Pte 11039 8th Royal West Surrey Regt
DEADMAN Thomas MM+Bar Cpl 37640 Machine Gun Corps
DEADMAN William MM Pte 17243 1st Somerset Light Infantry
DEAHL Norman V. MM L/Cpl 67169 Machine Gun Corps
DEAKIN Albert William Victor MM Pte 33035 East Yorkshire Regt
DEAKIN Archibald MM L/Sjt 71095 Notts & Derby Regt
DEAKIN Arthur MM L/Cpl 13/248 13th York & Lancaster Regt
DEAKIN Bernard MM L/Cpl S/2032 Rifle Brigade
DEAKIN Clement MM Pte 10440 Liverpool Regt
DEAKIN Frank MM Pte 10290 4th Worcestershire Regt
DEAKIN George MM+Bar Pte 13755 15th Lancashire Fusiliers
DEAKIN James E. MM L/Cpl 45450 1/1st Surrey Yeomanry
DEAKIN John Ernest MM L/Cpl 14978 7th Shropshire Light Infantry
DEAKIN John T. MM L/Cpl 12797 1st Worcestershire Regt
DEAKIN John W. MM Gnr 313334 136 Heavy Bty RGA
DEAKIN R.E. MM Sjt Mechanic 15824 Royal Air Force
DEAKIN Thomas MM Trumpeter 608163 20 Bde RHA
DEAKIN William MM Pte 11293 7th North Staffordshire Regt
DEAKIN Willis MM Sjt 17853 1st Northumberland Fusiliers
DEAKINS William MM Dvr 13238 A/76 Bde RFA KIA 20.6.18.
DEAL Evered A. MM 2nd Cpl 198162 Royal Engineers
DEAL George MM Spr 101563 Royal Engineers
DEAL Herbert E. MM Pte 36628 7th Wiltshire Regt
DEAL Percy R. MM Cpl 62737 RFA
DEALEY William Rupert MM L/Cpl 551267 1/16th London Regt DOW 5.11.18.
DEALING Ernest Francis "MC,MM(5884 CQMS 2nd Bn),MIDx2" 2Lt 9th Royal Welsh Fusiliers
DEAMER James MM Cpl 251239 2/3rd London Regt KIA 26.10.17.
DEAMER Josiah MM Cpl 522002 483 Fd Coy Royal Engineers
DEAMER William MM Bdr 3527 D/64 Bde RFA
DEAN A. MM Cpl 2903 Tank Corps
DEAN A.C. "DCM,MM" Sjt 43658 Manchester Regt
DEAN Albert E. MM Gnr 44814 RFA
DEAN Albert J. MM Sjt R/34846 16th King's Royal Rifle Corps
DEAN Albert L. MM Pte 1823 RAMC
DEAN Alfred MM L/Sjt 21282 Northumberland Fusiliers
DEAN Alfred Edwin MM L/Bdr 39730 A/107 Bde RFA
DEAN Alfred T. MM Sjt 10246 15th Lancashire Fusiliers
DEAN Arthur D. MM Sjt 9992 2nd East Lancashire Regt
DEAN Charles F. MM Pte 41638 2nd Northamptonshire Regt
DEAN Charlie MM Pte 22192 1st Dorsetshire Regt
DEAN Clifford MM Pte 6421 2nd Royal West Surrey Regt
DEAN Cyril S. MM L/Cpl C/1197 16th King's Royal Rifle Corps

DEAN Dennis MM Pte 26160 Machine Gun Corps
DEAN Edward MM Sjt 21008 18th Bn Machine Gun Corps
DEAN Frank MM Sjt 12391 8th West Riding Regt
DEAN Frank MM Air Mech 2 28666 Royal Flying Corps
DEAN Fred MM Pte 6658 1st Dorsetshire Regt
DEAN Fred MM Cpl 12749 10th West Yorkshire Regt
DEAN Frederick MM Pte 244772 4/5th North Lancashire Regt
DEAN Frederick John MM L/Cpl 17187 4th Grenadier Guards KIA 22.4.18.
DEAN George MM Cpl 45637 8th Royal Berkshire Regt
DEAN George A. MM 2nd Cpl 013577 Army Ordnance Corps
DEAN George Henry MM Bdr 35616 D/107 Bde RFA KIA 4.9.16.
DEAN George W. MM Pte G/92310 3rd London Regt
DEAN H. MM Pte 242542 Royal Warwickshire Regt
DEAN Harold MM Sjt 200619 Tank Corps
DEAN Harry MM L/Cpl 531814 98 Fd Coy Royal Engineers
DEAN Herbert MM+Bar Bdr 73987 43 Bde RFA
DEAN J. MM Unknown 201781 Liverpool Regt
DEAN J.E. MM Pte M2/021316 Army Service Corps
DEAN James MM Pte 235140 Liverpool Regt
DEAN John MM Pte 35448 Manchester Regt
DEAN John O. MM L/Cpl 21027 Durham Light Infantry
DEAN John Samuel MM Sjt 200875 1/5th Liverpool Regt DOW 7.11.18.
DEAN Joseph MM Sjt 5594 10th Northumberland Fusiliers
DEAN Joseph MM Pte 18016 Royal West Kent Regt
DEAN Joseph MM Pte 266668 Liverpool Regt
DEAN Joseph H. MM L/Cpl 11432 Machine Gun Corps
DEAN Leonard MM L/Cpl 78313 Royal Engineers
DEAN Noah MM Sjt 10733 1st East Lancashire Regt
DEAN Norman MM Cpl 1219 B/122 Bde RFA
DEAN R.H. MM L/Cpl 19317 Grenadier Guards
DEAN Robert MM Pte 8199 13th Middlesex Regt
DEAN Robert MM Spr 146048 509 Fd Coy Royal Engineers
DEAN Robert MM+Bar Pte 265756 6th Seaforth Highlanders
DEAN Robert J. MM Pte 37231 Royal Berkshire Regt
DEAN Samuel MM Gnr 97759 153 Bde RFA
DEAN Sidney J. MM Dvr 832148 D/11 Bde RFA
DEAN Stanley Irwin MM Pte 512229 RAMC
DEAN Stephen Edward MM Cpl STK/657 10th Royal Fusiliers
DEAN Sydney H. MM Pte 242360 4th Worcestershire Regt
DEAN Thomas "DCM,MM" Cpl 91513 4 Special Bn Royal Engineers
DEAN Thomas MM Sjt 2956 2/7th West Yorkshire Regt
DEAN Thomas Albert MM Sjt 250917 Manchester Regt
DEAN Thomas H. MM Sjt 382340 77 Siege Bty RGA
DEAN Walter MM Pte 29878 South Lancashire Regt
DEAN Walter MM Cpl 14135 7th Bedfordshire Regt
DEAN Wilfred S. MM Pte 47814 Notts & Derby Regt
DEAN Wilfrid MM L/Cpl 37266 East Lancashire Regt
DEAN William MM Pte 9658 4th Suffolk Regt
DEAN William MM Cpl 12357 8th Northumberland Fusiliers
DEAN William "MM,MID" Sjt 1653 4th Liverpool Regt
DEAN William E. MM Sjt 103451 2nd Notts & Derby Regt
DEAN William Henry MM Pte 22246 Worcestershire Regt
DEAN William J. MM Dvr 42647 RFA
DEAN-CORKE Frederick S. MM Pte 6980 Royal West Kent Regt
DEANE Anthony MM CSM 376823 10th Royal Scots
DEANE Edward D. MM L/Cpl 10282 10tth Hampshire Regt
DEANE Edwin MM Sjt SE/3329 Army Veterinary Corps
DEANE H.R. MM+Bar Air Mech 1 7773 Royal Flying Corps
DEANS Charles MM Gnr 630211 A/286 Bde RFA
DEANS George MM L/Cpl 20744 10th Scottish Rifles
DEANS James MM Sjt 201034 Royal Scots Fusiliers
DEANS John Kirkwood MM Pte 16004 17th Highland Light Infantry att MGC.
DEANS Robert W. MM Pte 200117 1/4th King's Own Scottish Borderers
DEANS William MM Pte 55050 21st Manchester Regt
DEANUS William MM Pte 200430 1/1st London Regt
DEAR Charles G. MM L/Cpl R/39655 13th King's Royal Rifle Corps
DEAR Frank MM Bdr 284966 RGA
DEAR Lawrence A. MM Pte 20821 King's Own Scottish Borderers
DEAR William C. MM Sjt 200433 1/7th Middlesex Regt
DEARDEN Ernest MM L/Cpl C/550 16th King's Royal Rifle Corps
DEARDEN Fred "MC,MM(19734 Cpl Manch Regt)" T/2Lt 1/6th Cheshire Regt
DEARDEN Joseph MM Pte C/544 16th King's Royal Rifle Corps
DEARDEN Robert Arthur MM Pte 276842 15th Manchester Regt
DEARDEN Sam MM Spr 211213 Third Army Sig Coy Royal Engineers

DEARDEN Willie MM Pte 48660 10th South Wales Borderers
DEARING Charles MM Cpl 300335 5th London Regt DOW 16.4.18.
DEARING Charles Leonard "MM,CG(B)" Cpl 805 11th East Yorkshire Regt
DEARLING Horace Charles MM Cpl 2924 12th Lancers
DEARMAN Thomas MM Pte 7477 Machine Gun Corps
DEARMAN William J. MM L/Cpl B/3470 Rifle Brigade
DEARN Benjamin MM CSM 275334 1/7th Arg & Suth Highlanders
DEARN George MM Pte 2013 1/5th Cheshire Regt
DEARNLEY Arthur "DCM,MM" Sjt 107988 122 Siege Bty RGA
DEARNLEY James A. MM Sjt 45042 34 Bde RFA
DEARY James Arthur "MM,CG(F)" Cpl 947 11th East Yorkshire Regt
DEARY John MM Spr 198199 Royal Engineers
DEARY John Bertie MM Pte 22262 9th Norfolk Regt
DEAS Alexander MM Cpl M2/193450 406 Coy Army Service Corps
DEAS Allan Miller MM L/Cpl 11923 8th Gloucestershire Regt KIA 31.7.16.
DEAS James MM Pte 39581 Royal Scots
DEAS James "DCM,MM" Cpl S/15696 1st Bn Cameron Highlanders
DEAS John MM Pte 34730 6th York & Lancaster Regt KIA 1.10.18.
DEAS William R.F. MM Pte 241211 1/7th Royal Highlanders
DEASON Henry R. MM Pte 76841 2nd Bn Tank Corps
DEASON Percy R. "MM,MID" Pte M2/120789 Army Service Corps
DEATH Charles E. MM Gnr 31493 RGA
DEATH Edward MM Sjt 1641 Royal Engineers
DEATH Ernest MM Sjt 2716 Royal Fusiliers
DEATH Frederick MM Cpl 91573 Royal Engineers
DEATH Henry W.T. "MM,MID" Pte 3/9216 2nd Suffolk Regt
DEATH Robert Arthur "MM,MSM,MID" Staff SM S/19274 Army Service Corps
DEATH Robert H. MM BQMS L/31659 C/119 Bde RFA
DEATH William Ben "MM,MID" Sjt 807 560 Coy Royal Engineers
DEAVES Arthur MM Pte R/6293 12th King's Royal Rifle Corps KIA 2.12.17.
DEAVES Arthur W. MM Spr 14192 1 Fd Sqn Royal Engineers
DEAVILLE Arthur MM Pte 6235 16th Manchester Regt DOW 3.8.17.
DEAVIN John MM Bdr 35672 41 Siege Bty RGA
DEBMAN Samuel MM SQMS 56774 MGC(Cavalry)
DEBNEY Jonah MM Cpl 13/244 York & Lancaster Regt
DEBOI Clarence MM Pte 3848 11th Middlesex Regt KIA 20.11.17.
DEBOO Jack MM Pte 41673 7th Worcestershire Regt
DEBUSE Edward MM Pte 354770 7th London Regt
DECKER John MM Pte 18/751 Royal Irish Rifles
DECORT Albert MM Cpl 63102 Machine Gun Corps
DEDMAN Walter J. MM Bdr 340263 RGA
DEDMAN William George MM Sjt 57438 17 Bty 41 Bde RFA
DEDMEN David MM L/Cpl 203435 Oxf & Bucks Light Infantry
DEE Silas "DCM,MM" Cpl 21814 1st Cheshire Regt
DEE Thomas H. MM L/Cpl 591485 1/18th London Regt
DEE4R Harry MM Pte 46241 37 Fd Amb RAMC
DEED Joseph MM Gnr 163274 RFA
DEEDMAN Frederick MM Sjt 8538 9th Lancers
DEEGAN Thomas MM L/Cpl 18870 14th Liverpool Regt
DEEGAN William MM Bdr 13810 10 Siege Bty RGA KIA 6.5.17.
DEEKS John MM Pte 38971 Lincolnshire Regt
DEEKS John A.J. MM+Bar Cpl 22479 Notts & Derby Regt
DEELEY Arthur MM Pte 13157 6th Oxf & Bucks Light Infantry
DEELEY Benjamin MM Sjt 290123 Labour Corps
DEELEY George S. MM+Bar Cpl 200496 1/5th Royal Warwickshire Regt
DEEM Stephen MM Sjt 102446 217 Siege Bty RGA
DEEMING Richard MM L/Cpl 9158 Royal Warwickshire Regt
DEEMING William MM L/Cpl 2355 1st Royal Warwickshire Regt
DEEPROSE Arthur J. MM+Bar Pte 40204 1/4th Cheshire Regt
DEEPROSE Victor Edwin Thomas MM L/Cpl 12300 11th Royal Sussex Regt
DEERE H.C. MM Pte 536329 RAMC
DEERING Francis MM Sjt 66087 10th Royal Scots
DEES Albert E. MM Cpl(MCDR) 211061 34 Div Sig Coy Royal Engineers
DEFFEE Edward MM Pte 8652 2nd Royal Berkshire Regt
DEFLEY Joseph "DCM,MM" CSM 8403 1st South Staffordshire Regt
DEFTY Robert "MM+Bar,CG(It)" Cpl 45880 12th Durham Light Infantry
DEFTY William MM Cpl 48982 285 Siege Bty RGA
DEGAVINO Ernest MM L/Cpl 7734 1st Royal West Kent Regt
DEGG George MM Sjt 240987 North Staffordshire Regt
DEGG Percy MM Cpl 138692 6th Bn Machine Gun Corps
DEGMAN James F. MM Dvr 94946 C/250 Bde RFA
DEGNAN Leslie A. MM Pte 3768 16th Lancers
DEGNAN Thomas MM Pte 201751 Royal Scots Fusiliers
DEGNAN William MM L/Cpl 7391 1st Shropshire Light Infantry
DEGNIN John MM Pte 29246 2nd Royal Inniskilling Fusiliers
DEGOMME Alfred MM Cpl 11324 12th Royal Fusiliers
DEGVILLE Harry MM L/Cpl 9445 2nd South Staffordshire Regt
DEIGHTON Charles Thomas MM Bdr 73799 137 Siege Bty RGA
DEIGHTON Douglas MM L/Sjt 10833 South Staffordshire Regt
DEIGHTON George H. MM Cpl 312023 RGA
DEIGHTON Henry Edward Ernest MM Dvr 26395 D/161 Bde RFA
DEIGHTON John R. MM Gnr 80851 RFA
DEIGHTON John W. MM Pte 35707 York & Lancaster Regt
DEIGHTON N. MM Gnr 780438 RFA
DEIGNAN Patrick MM Pte 266708 5th Seaforth Highlanders KIA 28.7.18.
DELACOURT James B. MM Bdr 125849 RFA
DELAHAYE Sydney P. MM Gnr 1304 RGA
DELAHUNTY James MM Pte B/2036 11th Rifle Brigade
DELAMARE William G. MM S/Sjt 12264 9 Fd Amb RAMC
DELAMERE Peter J. MM Pte 18339 8th Northamptonshire Regt
DELANEY Brinley John MM Sjt 200454 Welsh Regt
DELANEY Daniel MM Pte G/2416 12th Middlesex Regt
DELANEY Edward MM Cpl 18574 2nd Royal Irish Regt
DELANEY George Sidney "MM,MID" Cpl 16306 2nd South Staffordshire Regt
DELANEY Herbert MM L/Cpl 20460 3 Siege Bty RGA
DELANEY Jeremiah MM Pte 1431 23rd Royal Fusiliers KIA 27.7.16.
DELANEY John MM Pte 200050 2nd North Lancashire Regt
DELANEY John MM Pte 34582 York & Lancaster Regt
DELANEY John MM Cpl 7874 2nd Royal Dublin Fusiliers
DELANEY Joseph MM Pte 6123 RAMC
DELANEY Patrick "DCM,MM" CSM 9364 1st Royal Dublin Fusiliers
DELANEY Patrick MM Cpl 8714 Leinster Regt
DELANEY Paul Leo MM Sjt 47250 26th Royal Welsh Fusiliers
DELANEY Robert W. MM Sjt 10881 6th Royal West Kent Regt
DELANEY William MM Cpl 10999 2nd Royal Irish Regt Died 20.11.17.
DELF Alexander Robert MM Gnr 131764 D/69 Bde RFA KIA 13.10.18.
DELITTLE William D. MM Dvr 12322 RFA
DELL George Abel MM L/Cpl 201168 8th Royal Berkshire Regt KIA 20.9.18.
DELL Thomas MM Pte 39865 8th Worcestershire Regt
DELLENTY Osmond G. MM Pte 16587 Machine Gun Corps
DELLER William E. MM Pte 48010 3rd Rifle Brigade
DELLISTON George MM Sjt 43171 1st Leicestershire Regt
DELLOW Edward "MM,MID" Dvr L/10182 RFA
DELLOW Frederick MM Dvr 102758 49 Bty 40 Bde RFA KIA 16.9.18.
DELMAR John A. MM Drummer 8587 2nd South Staffordshire Regt
DELMAS Lester Louis MM+Bar Sjt 331604 1/9th Liverpool Regt KIA 28.8.18.
DELURY C. MM Sjt 7603 1st Royal Irish Rifles
DELURY Walter Sidney MM Pte 6957 6th Lincolnshire Regt
DELVES Charles H. MM Cpl 70750 42 Bde RFA
DELVES George F. MM+Bar Sjt L/6255 2nd Royal Sussex Regt
DELVES Harold MM Pte 301076 Arg & Suth Highlanders
DEMAINE Arthur MM Pte 106159 Notts & Derby Regt
DEMAINE William MM Sjt 15/1789 15/17th West Yorkshire Regt
DEMAY Ralph "MM,MSM" Sjt 47245 25 Div Sig Coy Royal Engineers
DEMELLWEEK John H. MM Pte 331281 Liverpool Regt
DEMNEY James E. MM Pte 2611 Durham Light Infantry
DEMOL John H. MM Cpl 56481 Royal Engineers
DEMPSEY Augustine MM Spr 313150 25 Div Sig Coy Royal Engineers
DEMPSEY Charles MM L/Cpl 1490 2nd Manchester Regt KIA 1.10.18.
DEMPSEY Ellis MM Bdr 705945 RFA
DEMPSEY Francis MM Sjt 67951 145 Army Troops Coy Royal Engineers
DEMPSEY George MM Pte 325394 1/9th Durham Light Infantry
DEMPSEY James MM L/Cpl 3010 5th Lancers
DEMPSEY John MM Pte 14814 York & Lancaster Regt
DEMPSEY John MM Sjt 21293 Royal Air Force
DEMPSEY John Pat MM Gnr 158520 RFA
DEMPSEY Michael MM Cpl 23/36 19th Durham Light Infantry
DEMPSEY Patrick MM Pte 8938 Royal Irish Regt
DEMPSEY Patrick MM Pte 7659 2nd South Lancashire Regt
DEMPSEY William Matthew MM Sjt 12377 5th Royal Berkshire Regt

DEMPSTER Alfred C. MM Pte 10/14357 10th Royal Irish Rifles
DEMPSTER Andrew MM Dvr 60980 81 Fd Coy Royal Engineers
DEMPSTER Benjamin MM Pte 4604 RAMC
DEMPSTER D. MM Pte 9748 2nd Seaforth Highlanders
DEMPSTER George MM Dvr 7461 B/83 Bde RFA
DEMPSTER John MM Cpl 202245 7th Royal Highlanders KIA 24.7.18.
DEMPSTER John MM Pte 4606 58th Bn Machine Gun Corps DOW 7.7.16.
DEMPSTER John R. MM Pte 85867 56th Bn Machine Gun Corps
DEMPSTER Robert MM Pte 35647 9th York & Lancaster Regt
DEMPSTER Robert MM Cpl 220057 V/10 Hy TM Bty RGA
DEMPSTER Robert MM Dvr 646136 RFA
DEMPSTER Thomas J. MM Cpl 40962 RAMC
DENANCE William MM Pte 93200 19 Fd Amb RAMC
DENBIGH John A. MM Sjt 14954 12th West Yorkshire Regt
DENBIGH Percy "MM,MIDx2" Sjt 773 West Yorkshire Regt
DENCH Charlie MM Gnr 16123 C/71 Bde RFA
DENCH Edward MM L/Cpl 29476 3rd Grenadier Guards
DENCH George MM Pte 72513 59th Bn Machine Gun Corps
DENDY Edward J. MM L/Cpl 50 7th Royal Sussex Regt
DENGATE Charles H. MM Sjt 295675 7th Royal Fusiliers
DENHAM Albert Seagar MM CQMS 8890 1st Royal Berkshire Regt
DENHAM Alfred S. MM Sjt 7525 Middlesex Regt
DENHAM Arthur MM Pte 203650 1/5th West Riding Regt
DENHAM Paul A. MM Sjt S/25840 Rifle Brigade
DENHOLM George MM Cpl 325028 8th Royal Scots
DENHOLM George MM Spr 107727 'Z' Special Coy Royal Engineers
DENHOLM George MM Gnr 7618 RFA
DENHOLM Robert B. MM Pte 325181 1/8th Royal Scots
DENHOLM Thomas MM L/Cpl 351365 9th Royal Scots
DENISON Ernest MM Cpl 265815 West Yorkshire Regt
DENISON Thomas William MM L/Cpl C/12823 21st King's Royal Rifle Corps KIA 7.10.16.
DENISSIEFF Sergei Sergeivitch MM+Bar Sjt 17430 3rd Lincolnshire Regt
DENLEY Thomas MM L/Sjt 201008 4th Gloucestershire Regt
DENLEY Thomas George MM Bde 24996 420 Bty 6 Bde RFA
DENLY Roland S. MM Pte 381931 25th Liverpool Regt
DENMAN Douglas F. MM Cpl M2/121874 Army Service Corps
DENMAN Frederick MM Pte 35430 RAMC
DENMAN George MM Pte 15573 1st Somerset Light Infantry KIA 28.3.18.
DENMAN Harry MM Pte 5509 2nd Leinster Regt
DENMAN John A. MM Pte A/200519 11th King's Royal Rifle Corps
DENMARK Harry MM Gnr 26029 31 Heavy Bty RGA
DENMARK James MM Cpl 79088 Royal Engineers
DENN Andrew "MM+Bar,MID" L/Sjt 1999 1st Irish Guards
DENNAIRD George "MM,MID" Pte 15831 12th Royal Scots
DENNANT George W. MM Pte 473050 88 Fd Amb RAMC
DENNEHY Timothy "MM,MID" L/Cpl 9503 1st Royal Munster Fusiliers
DENNER Reginald G. MM+Bar L/Cpl 3/7848 1st Dorsetshire Regt
DENNESS William A. MM+Bar Pte L/15186 4th Royal Fusiliers
DENNETT A. MM Sjt 279476 24th Royal Fusiliers
DENNETT Ernest MM Cpl 14021 Lincolnshire Regt
DENNETT Frederick J. MM L/Sjt 10330 5th Dorsetshire Regt
DENNETT Gordon Clarke Compton MM Pte 271029 10th East Kent Regt KIA 21.9.18.
DENNETT Maurice S.S. MM Cpl 9705 Royal Sussex Regt
DENNETT Peter MM Sjt 2369 1/5th South Lancashire Regt
DENNETT Walter MM Pte 72003 Machine Gun Corps
DENNEY Worner E. MM CSM 29223 1st Somerset Light Infantry
DENNING Charles William "MM,MID" Sjt 1740 1/20th London Regt
DENNING Ernest MM Pte 9957 1st Worcestershire Regt
DENNING Harold MM Sjt 1469 Army Cyclist Corps
DENNING Silas A. MM Spr 482085 Royal Engineers
DENNING Victor MM Pte 12810 1st Worcestershire Regt KIA 31.7.17.
DENNING William G. MM Pte 74296 RAMC
DENNINGTON Albert MM Pte 4425 2nd Rifle Brigade
DENNINGTON Alfred Frederick MM Pte 12322 12th East Surrey Regt
DENNINGTON Edward MM Dvr L/39736 D/144 Bde RFA
DENNIS Albert A. MM Cpl M2/134048 272 MT Coy Army Service Corps
DENNIS Albert G. MM Pte 59185 14th Leicestershire Regt
DENNIS Albert H. MM Sjt 3647 2nd King's Royal Rifle Corps
DENNIS Alfred E. MM Pte 31924 1/5th York & Lancaster Regt
DENNIS Alfred Ernest MM Gnr 109640 RGA
DENNIS Arthur MM Sjt 825082 C/240 Bde RFA
DENNIS Arthur MM Cpl 200052 1/5th Bedfordshire Regt
DENNIS Arthur J. MM S/Sjt Armourer 1238 Army Ordnance Corps att RGA.
DENNIS Arthur R. MM+Bar Spr 87475 Royal Engineers
DENNIS Duncan H. MM Pte 4831 2nd Leinster Regt
DENNIS Edward MM Cpl 4149 Rifle Brigade
DENNIS Edward F. MM Pte 1774 RAMC
DENNIS Edwin Gabriel MM Pte 240845 1st Devonshire Regt DOW 22.10.18.
DENNIS Ernest W. MM Pte 6/3194 6th Royal Irish Regt
DENNIS Frank MM Gnr 49757 RGA
DENNIS Frederick H. MM Pte 16505 9th Royal Fusiliers
DENNIS George Robert MM Pte 330768 1/1st Cambridgeshire Regt KIA 26.9.17.
DENNIS H.G. "MM,MID" Cpl 1123 23rd Royal Fusiliers
DENNIS Harold C. MM Pte 307089 13th Bn Tank Corps
DENNIS Harry MM Sjt 33078 37 Div Ammn Col RFA
DENNIS James H. MM Cpl 327 11th Middlesex Regt
DENNIS John MM Cpl 12858 2nd King's Royal Rifle Corps
DENNIS John MM Sjt 3470 13th Rifle Brigade
DENNIS John MM Cpl 307583 Royal Engineers
DENNIS John MM Pnr 193031 4 Special Coy Royal Engineers
DENNIS John MM Pte 40221 6th Leicestershire Regt KIA 25.8.18.
DENNIS Norman MM Pte 200172 West Riding Regt
DENNIS Robert MM L/Cpl 478421 Royal Engineers
DENNIS Stephen S. MM Pte 19527 Durham Light Infantry
DENNIS Thomas Kirk MM Sjt 16224 6th Leicestershire Regt KIA 25.3.18.
DENNIS William H.W. MM CSM 240957 5th West Riding Regt
DENNISON Arthur MM Pte 26598 12th Royal Scots
DENNISON B. MM Bdr 58016 7 Bde RHA
DENNISON Barney MM Sjt M2/152693 Army Service Corps
DENNISON Charles Goultbey MM Pte 17307 7th Bedfordshire Regt
DENNISON Harry MM Pte 267498 1/6th West Riding Regt
DENNISON John R. MM Cpl 7114 Army Cyclist Corps
DENNISON John R. MM Pte 72489 Liverpool Regt
DENNISON Reginald Sydney MM Pte 240595 2/5th Royal Lancaster Regt att 170 Bde LTM Bty.
DENNISON Rupert MM L/Cpl 4430 15th Hussars
DENNISON Thomas MM Pte 21611 4th Grenadier Guards
DENNISON William MM+Bar Pte 11111 10th West Riding Regt
DENNISON Willie MM Gnr 785708 RFA
DENNISTOUN Thomas MM Sjt 30465 13th Royal Scots KIA 1.8.17.
DENNY Charles W. MM Cpl 340787 RGA
DENNY Charles William MM Sjt 9520 9th Essex Regt KIA 22.8.18.
DENNY John William MM Sjt L/10902 D/148 Bde RFA
DENNY Spencer W. MM Pte 200514 1/4th Essex Regt
DENNY Thomas David William MM Sjt 8703 2nd Gloucestershire Regt Died 6.3.19.
DENNY William MM Sjt 6812 1st East Kent Regt
DENNY Willie Walter MM L/Cpl 26607 14th Hampshire Regt KIA 25.3.18.
DENOON David MM Pte S/40914 1/4th Gordon Highlanders Died 2.6.19.
DENSHAM Edgar W. MM Pte 155159 23rd Bn Machine Gun Corps
DENSHAM John Humphrey "MC,MM(1626 Surrey Yeo)" 2Lt 4th Royal West Kent Regt
DENSLEY Albert MM L/Cpl 266228 6th Gloucestershire Regt
DENSON George MM Cpl 354219 74 Div Sig Coy Royal Engineers
DENSON Richard MM Spr 198049 250 Tunnelling Coy Royal Engineers
DENT Albert MM L/Cpl 8517 8th Royal West Kent Regt
DENT Albert Hudson MM Pte 306807 8th Bn Tank Corps Died 30.8.18.
DENT Alexander G. MM Cpl 24807 Royal Engineers
DENT Alfred John MM Pte 17056 1st Coldstream Guards KIA 4.11.18.
DENT E. MM Sjt 2621 Army Service Corps
DENT Edmund MM Dvr 117274 RFA
DENT F. "MM,MSM" L/Cpl 405019 1/3rd(West Riding)Fd Amb RAMC
DENT Fred MM L/Bdr 141392 RGA
DENT Frederick MM Sjt Z/437 10th Rifle Brigade
DENT Frederick MM Pte 29759 Yorkshire Light Infantry
DENT George MM Cpl 38225 RAMC
DENT J. MM Cpl 43447 9th Essex Regt
DENT J.W. MM L/Cpl P/5963 Military Mounted Police
DENT James MM Sjt 3/8916 2nd Yorkshire Regt Died 6.10.18.

DENT John MM Pte 64565 12/13th Northumberland Fusiliers
DENT Robert MM Pte 275060 2nd Arg & Suth Highlanders
DENT Robert B. MM L/Cpl 17813 2nd Coldstream Guards
DENTITH Arthur MM Pte 43715 6th Northamptonshire Regt
DENTON Albert MM Gnr 20099 RGA
DENTON Alfred Bertie MM Pte 205355 2/4th York & Lancaster Regt
DENTON Fred MM Pte 20943 7th Northamptonshire Regt DOW 30.5.17.
DENTON Frederick J. "MM,MID" Cpl 12517 9th Essex Regt
DENTON Frederick Walter MM Cpl 895 1/1st London Regt
DENTON George MM Pte 3238 1/6th Northumberland Fusiliers DOW 13.4.18.
DENTON Harold MM Sjt 17534 Northamptonshire Regt
DENTON James Holroyd MM Gnr 167184 258 Siege Bty RGA
DENTON John C. MM Sjt 21278 Suffolk Regt
DENTON Joseph MM Sjt 1852 D/83 Bde RFA KIA 21.3.18.
DENTON Joseph E. MM L/Sjt 1048 1/1st Bedfordshire Yeomanry
DENTON Oscar MM Pte 151332 104th Bn Machine Gun Corps
DENTON Reginald E. MM Cpl 200791 2/4th Royal Berkshire Regt
DENTON Thomas A. MM Pte 268909 West Riding Regt
DENTON Victor Richard MM L/Cpl 15091 2nd Royal Munster Fusiliers
DENTON Walter MM Pte 9961 5th Northamptonshire Regt
DENTON William G. MM Pte 13835 7th Royal Berkshire Regt
DENTON William Watson MM Sjt 270122 10th East Kent Regt
DENTON-COX Frederick MM Sjt 9828 Machine Gun Corps
DENWOOD Thomas MM Bdr 715260 RFA
DENYER Benjamin Thomas MM Cpl 570522 1/17th London Regt
DENYER Frederick MM Sjt 49285 104 Bde RFA
DENYER Frederick John MM Sjt 41576 3 Squadron MGC(Cavalry)
DENYER George MM Pte 203232 1st London Regt
DENYER James MM Sjt SE/1728 Army Veterinary Corps
DENYER Percival Henry MM L/Sjt 2788 1/1st Cambridgeshire Regt
DENYER William John MM Pte M2/050069 Att 148 Fd Amb RAMC Army Service Corps
DEPLEDGE Thomas MM Bdr 20921 C/34 Bde RFA
DEPPER Edward E. "DCM,MM" Sjt 3331 7th Rifle Brigade
DERBY Batty MM Spr 32944 Royal Engineers
DERBY George E. MM Sjt 9595 7th Dragoon Guards
DERBYSHIRE Henry Colin MM Cpl 201380 1st Northumberland Fusiliers Died 21.3.18.
DERBYSHIRE John S. MM Gnr 191942 RFA
DERBYSHIRE John William MM L/Cpl R/13279 9th King's Royal Rifle Corps
DERBYSHIRE Lawrence MM L/Cpl 11789 19th Manchester Regt
DERBYSHIRE Thomas MM Pte 16041 Manchester Regt
DERHAM George MM Sjt 52566 Liverpool Regt
DERRETT Frederick "DCM,MM" Pte 6872 8th Royal Scots Fusiliers
DERRICK Arthur MM L/Cpl 305985 2nd Lancashire Fusiliers
DERRICK Harry S. MM Sjt 240859 1/5th Gloucestershire Regt
DERRICK Henry Albert MM Pte 13375 1st Worcestershire Regt
DERRICK William MM Gnr 107883 RGA
DERRIG Thomas H. MM Pte 301447 Manchester Regt
DERRINGTON Albert MM Pte Z/696 Rifle Brigade
DERRY Augustus MM Gnr 203467 B/286 Bde RFA
DERRY John O. MM Pte 18/1231 14th Northumberland Fusiliers
DESBOROUGH George "DCM,MM" Sjt 6425 1st East Yorkshire Regt KIA 4.10.17.
DESBOROUGH Percy Cluer MM Gnr 151922 434 Siege Bty RGA
DESBOROUGH Reginald MM Cpl 10745 3rd Hussars KIA 23.3.18.
DESMOND Cornelius MM Pte 13373 2nd Devonshire Regt
DESMOND Joseph Patrick MM L/Cpl 638 1st Royal Munster Fusiliers
DESMOND Patrick R. MM Spr 494859 Royal Engineers
DESOER E. MM Dvr W/2216 RFA
DESSAULT Barnaby MM L/Sjt 15994 9th West Riding Regt
DETHERIDGE Percival Arthur Charles MM Pnr 447133 17 Div Sig Coy Royal Engineers Died 18.9.18.
DEVANEY Harry MM Pte 16939 8th Royal Lancaster Regt KIA 23.8.18.
DEVANEY J. MM Pte 29683 North Lancashire Regt
DEVANEY Patrick MM Pte 11165 7th Yorkshire Regt
DEVANEY Richard MM Pte 62823 14 Fd Amb RAMC
DEVANNEY Francis MM Pte 11626 8th West Riding Regt
DEVANNEY James MM Pte 903 25th Northumberland Fusiliers
DEVANNEY Thomas MM Pte 341482 2 Fd Amb RAMC
DEVANY John William MM 2nd Cpl 192471 1 Special Coy Royal Engineers
DEVENHILL Charles MM Pte 61112 68 Fd Amb RAMC
DEVENISH James MM Pte 241912 North Lancashire Regt
DEVENNEY Denis MM L/Cpl 10200 Irish Guards
DEVENY John MM Cpl 14407 10th Cheshire Regt
DEVER J.W. MM Pte 47852 RAMC
DEVERALL Edgar MM CQMS 2458 1/8th Notts & Derby Regt
DEVERELL Albert Edward MM Pte 2178 XIII Corps Cyclist Bn Army Cyclist Corps
DEVEREUX Edward MM Sjt 8806 Durham Light Infantry
DEVEREUX Frank S. MM Sjt 13103 9th Gloucestershire Regt
DEVEREUX Henry MM+Bar L/Cpl 40144 63 Fd Coy Royal Engineers
DEVEREUX James MM Sjt 848 6th Connaught Rangers
DEVEREUX William C.A. MM Cpl 65325 RFA
DEVERILL Harry MM Cpl 15462 1st Duke of Cornwall's LI KIA 4.10.17.
DEVERILL William John MM Spr 70536 Second Army Sig Coy Royal Engineers
DEVERS John MM Pte 27 10th Highland Light Infantry
DEVEY George MM Cpl 18167 4th Grenadier Guards
DEVILLE Harry MM Pte 13735 Royal Welsh Fusiliers
DEVINE Allan MM Pte S/7642 Royal Highlanders
DEVINE Daniel MM Pte 3032 9th Seaforth Highlanders
DEVINE Francis MM Pte 9771 2nd Highland Light Infantry
DEVINE Harry MM Pte 40618 12th Middlesex Regt
DEVINE Hugh MM Dvr 21384 B/78 Bde RFA
DEVINE James MM Pte 7958 1st Irish Guards
DEVINE John MM L/Cpl 5912 1st Scottish Rifles KIA 20.7.16.
DEVINE Patrick MM Cpl 12687 1st Royal Dublin Fusiliers
DEVINE Patrick MM Pte 240568 6th Highland Light Infantry
DEVINE Patrick MM Dvr 53736 36 Bde RFA
DEVINE Peter MM Pte 2085 1/9th Highland Light Infantry
DEVINE Thomas MM L/Cpl 9380 10th Arg & Suth Highlanders KIA 2.10.18.
DEVINE Thomas MM Pte 386199 1/1(Northumbrian)Fd Amb RAMC Died 18.10.18.
DEVINE William MM+Bar Sjt 765415 RFA
DEVINE William Anthony MM Cpl 4021 Machine Gun Corps
DEVINS John MM Sjt 3104 1st Irish Guards
DEVIS Arthur Stanley MM Cpl 20338 36 Coy Machine Gun Corps KIA 29.9.18.
DEVITT Arthur James MM Pte 10192 Arg & Suth Highlanders AKA George Howard.
DEVITT Charles MM Cpl 285018 RGA
DEVITT Edward MM Gnr 94267 D/82 Bde RFA KIA 28.5.17.
DEVITT Harry MM L/Cpl 10601 9th Royal Fusiliers
DEVITT John MM L/Sjt 302099 1/8th Durham Light Infantry
DEVITT S. MM Dvr 880 RFA
DEVITT William H. MM Pte 25570 1st Royal Dublin Fusiliers
DEVLIN Alexander M. MM Sjt 52618 RAMC
DEVLIN Archibald Gordon MM L/Cpl 28549 2nd King's Own Scottish Borderers
DEVLIN Christopher MM Pte 268506 Royal Highlanders
DEVLIN James MM L/Cpl 4021 5th Lancers
DEVLIN James MM Dvr 7725 RFA
DEVLIN John MM Gnr 7033 D/177 Bde RFA
DEVLIN Michael MM Pte S/3317 2nd Arg & Suth Highlanders DOW 4.10.18.
DEVLIN Patrick MM Pte 2272 6th Connaught Rangers
DEVLIN Peter Aloysius MM 2nd Cpl 64704 Guards Div Sig Coy Royal Engineers
DEVLIN Roderick MM Pte 9238 Coldstream Guards
DEVLIN Thomas MM L/Cpl 22358 1st Royal Dublin Fusiliers
DEVLIN Thomas "MM,MC(G)" Pte 10154 1st Royal Scots
DEVLIN William MM Dvr 37251 24 Bde RFA
DEVON William MM Pte 40157 1/6th Seaforth Highlanders
DEVONISH William MM Sjt 2646 9th Essex Regt KIA 5.4.18.
DEVONPORT James MM Sjt 266400 7th Royal Warwickshire Regt
DEVONSHIRE Edward MM Sjt 491746 13th London Regt
DEVONSHIRE George MM Pte 1955 1st Royal Warwickshire Regt
DEW Albert A. MM Sjt 573054 17th London Regt
DEW Alfred "MM,MID" Cpl 9215 ? Hussars
DEW Arthur Wiliam MM Pte 30493 2nd Grenadier Guards
DEW Bertie MM Pte 31791 15th Hampshire Regt
DEW Frank G. "MM,MID" Sjt 922 1/21st London Regt
DEW George R. MM Pte 700931 1/23rd London Regt
DEW James MM Sjt 308252 4 Tank Bde 6 Supply Coy Tank Corps
DEW Thomas Henry MM Pte 30015 2/4th Dorsetshire Regt
DEWAR Alexander "MM,MID" Sjt 2134 1st Royal Highlanders
DEWAR Alexander Dick MM Pte 68537 58 Coy Machine Gun Corps
DEWAR Frederick William MM Sjt 71945 3 Bde RHA

DEWAR James MM Pte 203649 1/4th West Riding Regt KIA 27.6.17.
DEWAR James D. MM L/Cpl 34393 1/4th Royal Scots
DEWAR James Rodger MM Pte S/9875 8th Royal Highlanders KIA 12.10.17.
DEWAR John R. MM L/Cpl 242192 5th Royal Lancaster Regt
DEWAR William N.W. MM Sjt 43949 Machine Gun Corps
DEWAR William R. MM+Bar Sjt 960018 RFA
DEWE William George "MM,MID" L/Cpl 15638 6th Royal Berkshire Regt KIA 7.5.17.
DEWELL Ernest MM Pte 5207 8th East Surrey Regt
DEWELL Frederick MM Pte 826 7th Royal Sussex Regt
DEWEY Frank MM L/Cpl 7864 1st Royal West Surrey Regt
DEWEY Walter James MM Pte 41338 4th Royal Fusiliers
DEWHIRST Irvine MM L/Cpl 34405 5th West Riding Regt
DEWHURST Edward MM L/Cpl 275785 Royal Scots
DEWHURST George MM L/Cpl 16651 Machine Gun Corps
DEWHURST George MM Pte 26268 4th Liverpool Regt KIA 29.9.18.
DEWHURST Gilbert MM Pte 31516 27 Fd Amb RAMC
DEWHURST Henry MM Pte 19228 9th North Lancashire Regt DOW 23.4.18.
DEWHURST Nellie MM Miss F VAD att FANY
DEWHURST Robert MM Sjt R/7593 King's Royal Rifle Corps
DEWHURST Tom "MM,MSM" Cpl S4/064619 37 Railhead Supply Det Army Service Corps
DEWHURST Walter MM Cpl 265831 Liverpool Regt
DEWICK Harry B. MM L/Cpl 15821 1st Grenadier Guards
DEWICK William Henry MM L/Bdr Sig 98182 133 Heavy Bty RGA
DEWING William MM Sjt 4683 Royal West Kent Regt
DEWIS Horace MM Cpl 14752 10th West Riding Regt
DEWS George MM Cpl 267744 Royal Warwickshire Regt
DEWSNUP Frank MM Pte 30275 Border Regt
DEXTER Walter James MM Pte 7730 1/6th Northumberland Fusiliers Died 22.4.18.
DEY Alexander MM Pte 200732 1/4th Gordon Highlanders
DEY Alexander MM Sjt 29402 6th King's Own Scottish Borderers
DEY John MM Pte 550 1st Gordon Highlanders
DIACK Charles C. "DCM,MM" Sjt 32284 6th King's Own Scottish Borderers
DIAMOND Abraham S. MM Dvr 625862 HAC(Artillery)
DIAMOND James "DCM+Bar,MM+Bar" Sjt 330271 1/9th Highland Light Infantry
DIAMOND James A. MM Pte 856 23rd Royal Fusiliers
DIAMOND Peter MM Spr 148577 Royal Engineers
DIAMOND Samuel MM Gnr 690128 D/102 Bde RFA
DIAPER John B. "MM,MID" Sjt 9543 XIII Corps Cyclist Bn Army Cyclist Corps
DIAS George G. MM+Bar Pte 129662 Machine Gun Corps
DIBB Donald MM Cpl 1242 West Yorkshire Regt
DIBB William MM L/Cpl 860943 33rd London Regt
DIBBEN Arthur Francis MM Pte A/1896 King's Royal Rifle Corps
DIBBEN Leonard "MM,MSM,CG(B)" Sjt 49398 19 Div Sig Co Royal Engineers
DIBBLE Bertie MM Cpl CMT/1892 3 Advance Park Army Service Corps
DIBBLE Edwin G. MM Sjt 11232 15th Hussars
DIBBLE Samuel MM Cpl 79623 Royal Engineers
DIBBLE William Robert MM Pte 1672 13th East Surrey Regt KIA 26.3.18.
DIBBO Edward MM Pte 279 RAMC
DIBBS William H.R. MM Cpl G/29951 7th Royal West Kent Regt
DIBLEY Frederick Abel MM Pte 248020 1/5th Durham Light Infantry
DIBLEY George E. MM Pte 4963 8th Royal West Surrey Regt
DIBLEY Stanley Charles MM Sjt 18354 1st North Lancashire Regt
DICK Alexander MM Sjt 37493 Machine Gun Corps
DICK Alexander MM Pte 1004 Arg & Suth Highlanders
DICK Allen D. MM Dvr T4/040675 Army Service Corps
DICK Charles MM L/Cpl 41280 Royal Engineers
DICK G.S. MM L/Cpl 6531 5/6th Scottish Rifles
DICK George MM Sjt 14054 9th Royal Inniskilling Fusiliers Died 23.4.18.
DICK George Henry MM Bdr 48193 A/103 Bde RFA DOW 23.4.17.
DICK Ingram "MM,CG(B)" L/Cpl 20441 9th Royal Irish Fusiliers
DICK J. MM L/Cpl 38492 2nd Essex Regt
DICK J. MM L/Cpl G/42361 23rd London Regt
DICK James MM+Bar Sjt 39352 5/6th Royal Scots
DICK James MM Bdr 56908 C/103 Bde RFA DOW 5.6.17.Served as James RICHARD
DICK James MM Sjt 82 1/9th Durham Light Infantry DOW 28.10.17.
DICK John MM Cpl 49472 11th Royal Scots
DICK John MM Gnr Sig 109961 155 Siege Bty RGA
DICK John MM Sjt 241096 Liverpool Regt
DICK Joseph "MM,MSM" Cpl 812 Att 2OBLI RAMC
DICK Joseph MM Pte 2143 12th Liverpool Regt
DICK L. MM Pte 27032 Durham Light Infantry
DICK Quinton W.A. MM Pte 3628 9th Royal Sussex Regt
DICK R.M. "MM,MID" Sjt 29703 39 Bde RFA
DICK Robert MM 2nd Cpl 418052 52 Div Sig Coy Royal Engineers
DICK Thomas MM Sjt 375060 Royal Scots
DICK Walter MM Cpl 27504 RFA
DICK William MM Sjt MS/925 Army Service Corps
DICK William MM Pte 20738 Royal Highlanders
DICK William MM Cpl 33988 North Lancashire Regt
DICK William MM Cpl S/4351 9th Seaforth Highlanders
DICK William MM Cpl S/5351 9th Royal Highlanders DOW 2.11.18.
DICK William MM L/Cpl 8065 Seaforth Highlanders
DICKEN Samuel Edward MM Pte 20843 Leicestershire Regt
DICKENS Albert Edward MM+Bar Cpl 14695 8th Royal Lancaster Regt
DICKENS G. MM Pte 608037 London Regt
DICKENS G.C. MM Pte MS/933 Army Service Corps att RAMC.
DICKENS George MM Gnr 42961 A/84 Bde RFA
DICKENS George MM Pte 58081 4th York & Lancaster Regt
DICKENS George MM Pte 17324 2nd Northamptonshire Regt KIA 16.8.17.
DICKENS George A. MM 2nd Cpl 248247 Royal Engineers
DICKENS George R. MM Pte 15210 6th Lincolnshire Regt
DICKENS George R. MM L/Cpl 2662 1/7th London Regt
DICKENS Harry MM L/Cpl 22185 5th West Yorkshire Regt
DICKENS Herbert MM Sjt 47574 D/173 Bde RFA
DICKENS William MM Pte 266352 1/1st Bucks Bn Oxf & Bucks Light Infantry
DICKENSON Charles William MM Dvr M1/07861 Army Service Corps
DICKENSON George Ernest MM Cpl 47395 Y/9 Med TM Bty RGA KIA 1.7.17.
DICKENSON Henry MM Pte 30287 4th Bedfordshire Regt
DICKENSON James MM Cpl 9081 Army Cyclist Corps
DICKENSON James A. MM Pte 26437 Lancashire Fusiliers
DICKENSON John MM Pte 28755 Grenadier Guards
DICKENSON Joseph Albert MM CQMS 305509 2/8th Lancashire Fusiliers
DICKENSON Samuel MM Dvr 64250 15 Bde RFA
DICKENSON Sydney MM L/Cpl 6735 Manchester Regt
DICKENSON Thomas Fred MM Bdr 34800 RFA
DICKENSON Thomas Reginald MM Pte 25536 Scottish Rifles
DICKENSON William MM Pte 31512 South Lancashire Regt
DICKENSON William MM+Bar L/Cpl 18/729 18th Durham Light Infantry
DICKER Frederick MM L/Cpl 590474 1/18th London Regt
DICKER Richard "DCM,MM" Cpl 34062 1 Div Sig Coy Royal Engineers
DICKERSON Alfred E. MM Pte 251265 4th London Regt
DICKERSON Charles MM Pte DM2/097181 HQ 59 Div Army Service Corps
DICKERSON Ernest MM Cpl 200512 1/4th Norfolk Regt
DICKERSON George Bagshaw MM Sjt 7013 1st Norfolk Regt
DICKERSON Harry MM Spr 512674 218 Fd Coy Royal Engineers
DICKERSON John MM Bdr 80415 B/75 Bde RFA
DICKERSON Jonas W. MM Cpl 2828 12th Middlesex Regt
DICKERSON Thomas W. MM L/Cpl 14942 Royal Sussex Regt
DICKERSON W. MM Pte 203173 11th Essex Regt
DICKERSON William MM Pte 202798 8th Lincolnshire Regt
DICKESON Frederick R. MM Pte 538067 RAMC
DICKESON Henry MM Pte 568 28th Northumberland Fusiliers
DICKIE C. "MM,MID" Sjt 2275 1/5th Gordon Highlanders
DICKIE David MM 2nd Cpl 192444 Royal Engineers
DICKIE Edward D. MM Pte 40845 King's Own Scottish Borderers
DICKIE J. MM Pte 51389 2nd Royal Scots
DICKIE John MM L/Cpl 17474 10th Arg & Suth Highlanders KIA 12.10.17.
DICKIE Robert B. MM+Bar Cpl 198149 Royal Engineers
DICKINGS Alfred MM+Bar Sjt 12552 7th Lincolnshire Regt
DICKINS Charles MM Sjt 630570 20th London Regt
DICKINSON A. MM Pte 401391 RAMC
DICKINSON A.J. MM Pte 9222 1st Leicestershire Regt
DICKINSON Albert MM Pte 3849 1/8th Durham Light Infantry
DICKINSON Alec MM L/Bdr 162473 RGA
DICKINSON Alexander MM Pte 307088 9th West Riding Regt DOW 13.10.18.

DICKINSON Alfred MM Pte 266684 West Yorkshire Regt
DICKINSON Allan L. MM Spr 305188 218 Fd Coy Royal Engineers
DICKINSON Arthur MM CSM 200971 2/4th York & Lancaster Regt
DICKINSON Arthur MM CQMS 3/2131 6th Yorkshire Light Infantry KIA 8.5.17.
DICKINSON Arthur MM Pte 26254 1st West Yorkshire Regt
DICKINSON Bernard S. MM Cpl 26811 6th Northamptonshire Regt
DICKINSON Edward "DCM,MM" CSM 3880 18th Bn 53 Coy Machine Gun Corps
DICKINSON Ernest Cook MM Gnr 20489 D/91 Bde RFA
DICKINSON Frank MM Pte 266478 1/7th West Riding Regt DOW 13.4.18.
DICKINSON Frederick MM Sjt 20190 12th Liverpool Regt
DICKINSON George MM Sjt 112232 11th Bn Tank Corps
DICKINSON George MM Cpl 77542 RGA
DICKINSON George MM Sjt 192 25th Northumberland Fusiliers
DICKINSON George MM L/Cpl 15473 8th Royal Lancaster Regt DOW 20.7.17.
DICKINSON George MM Sjt 105143 229 Fd Coy Royal Engineers
DICKINSON George Brow MM Cpl 37701 Att 1KRRC RAMC KIA 17.2.17.
DICKINSON George H. MM Pte 84370 50th Bn Machine Gun Corps
DICKINSON George Hardie MM Pte 16/901 1st West Yorkshire Regt KIA 17.9.18.
DICKINSON George R. MM Pte 295055 Manchester Regt
DICKINSON H. "DCM,MM" Sjt 202739 Royal Lancaster Regt
DICKINSON Harold R. MM Gnr 64517 RFA
DICKINSON Henry MM Pte 13/255 4th York & Lancaster Regt
DICKINSON Henry MM L/Cpl 17303 Durham Light Infantry
DICKINSON Henry James MM+Bar Sjt 1544 2nd Lincolnshire Regt KIA 1.12.17.
DICKINSON Herbert MM Sjt 12008 718 Coy Labour Corps
DICKINSON Herbert MM Cpl 20946 Notts & Derby Regt
DICKINSON Hilda May MM Miss F First Aid Nursing Yeomanry
DICKINSON Jacob MM Sjt 260474 7th Border Regt
DICKINSON James MM Pte 393 Northumberland Fusiliers
DICKINSON James G. MM Sjt 270248 1/1st Northumberland Yeo
DICKINSON John MM Bdr 755828 RFA
DICKINSON John Henry Joseph MM Pte 202550 10th Lincolnshire Regt
DICKINSON Joseph MM Pte 201073 Manchester Regt
DICKINSON Louis Harold MM Cpl 241424 1/5th Royal Lancaster Regt KIA 30.11.17.
DICKINSON Mark MM L/Cpl 3767 11th Manchester Regt
DICKINSON Oswald E. MM Sjt 2300 Royal Engineers
DICKINSON Peter MM Pte 6214 Northumberland Fusiliers
DICKINSON Ralph Moffett MM Gnr 755829 2(Northumbrian)Bde RFA
DICKINSON Richard MM Pte 95471 14 Fd Amb RAMC
DICKINSON Robert MM Sjt 301908 13th Bn Tank Corps
DICKINSON Robert MM 2nd Cpl 48069 14 Div Sig Coy Royal Engineers
DICKINSON Robert MM Pte 12012 6th Bedfordshire Regt
DICKINSON Robert MM CSM 240803 2/5th East Lancashire Regt KIA 31.3.18.
DICKINSON Samuel MM Pte 201486 Yorkshire Regt
DICKINSON Sidney MM L/Sjt 200301 1/4th Royal Lancaster Regt
DICKINSON T.B. MM Pte 2320 8th Durham Light Infantry
DICKINSON Thomas MM Gnr 80616 X/6 Med TM Bty RFA
DICKINSON Thomas E. MM Pte 18489 9th West Yorkshire Regt
DICKINSON Walter MM L/Cpl 253904 Royal Engineers
DICKINSON William MM Pte 202854 5th Yorkshire Light Infantry
DICKMAN Robert "MM,MdH(F)" Pte 116599 29th Bn Machine Gun Corps
DICKS Frederick Richard John MM Drummer 7554 1/23rd London Regt DOW 4.7.17.
DICKS Frederick W. MM Pte 16914 Northamptonshire Regt
DICKS Herbert Francis MM Pte 25850 Bedfordshire Regt
DICKSON Adam MM Gnr 206815 83 Bty 11 Bde RFA
DICKSON Adam Ernest MM L/Cpl 315092 RAMC att Glasgow Yeomanry.
DICKSON Alexander MM Pte 22949 1/4th King's Own Scottish Borderers
DICKSON Alexander Graham MM Pte 11785 2nd Devonshire Regt
DICKSON Andrew Dias MM Pte S/9197 Royal Highlanders
DICKSON Arthur E. MM Bdr 16929 26 Bde RFA
DICKSON David MM Pte 88132 18th Liverpool Regt
DICKSON David MM+Bar L/Cpl S/11042 Cameron Highlanders
DICKSON David MM Pte M2/019811 Army Service Corps
DICKSON Edward MM Pte L/7167 2nd Royal West Kent Regt
DICKSON G. MM Pte 81323 RAMC
DICKSON George "MM,MID" Pte 280768 Highland Light Infantry
DICKSON George MM Sjt 10385 Seaforth Highlanders
DICKSON Gilbert MM Dvr L/35124 RFA
DICKSON Henry MM Sjt 16312 12th East Surrey Regt
DICKSON James MM Pte 27922 12th Royal Scots
DICKSON James MM Pte 201229 7th Seaforth Highlanders
DICKSON James "MM,MSM" S/Sjt Armt 535 8 Ord Mob Workshop Army Ordnance Corps
DICKSON James MM L/Cpl 3183 1/6th Arg & Suth Highlanders
DICKSON James MM Sjt 5869 2nd Coldstream Guards
DICKSON James MM Pte 240795 King's Own Scottish Borderers
DICKSON James L. MM Pte 91643 5th Bn Tank Corps
DICKSON James Seaton MM Pte 12291 2nd Scots Guards
DICKSON John "MM+Bar,MID" Sjt 251252 1/6th Arg & Suth Highlanders
DICKSON John MM Pte 51269 2nd Royal Scots
DICKSON John "DCM,MM" L/Sjt 13779 9th Royal Inniskilling Fusiliers
DICKSON John MM Gnr 3547 RFA
DICKSON John MM Pte 6550 2nd Royal Irish Rifles
DICKSON John H. MM Sjt 315389 5th London Regt
DICKSON Lionel MM Sjt 163 MGC(Heavy Branch)
DICKSON M. MM L/Cpl 290072 Gordon Highlanders
DICKSON Robert MM Sjt 23446 409 Bty 96 Bde RFA
DICKSON Robert "MM,MID" Sjt 11900 3rd Grenadier Guards
DICKSON Samuel MM Pte 33155 1st Royal Warwickshire Regt
DICKSON Stella MM Miss F BRSC(VAD)
DICKSON William MM L/Cpl 492039 46 Div Sig Coy Royal Engineers
DICKSON William MM Sjt 13259 11th Border Regt
DICKSON William MM L/Sjt 15973 17th Highland Light Infantry
DICKSON William MM Bdr 6825 A/159 Bde RFA
DICKSON William MM CQMS 10432 Seaforth Highlanders
DICKSON William Dumbrick MM Cpl 570733 1/17th London Regt
DIDDAMS John William MM BQMS 96181 A/91 Bde RFA
DIDSBURY Albert MM Pte 17833 1st North Lancashire Regt
DIDSBURY William MM+Bar L/Cpl 31639 2nd South Lancashire Regt
DIDYMUS Alfred L. MM Pte 66953 138 Fd Amb RAMC
DIEGAN William C. MM L/Cpl 15569 Middlesex Regt
DIEGUTIS Alexander MM Pte G/50167 24th Royal Fusiliers
DIER Frank John MM Pte 270082 10th East Kent Regt KIA 21.9.18.
DIFFIN Thomas A. MM L/Cpl 37079 Royal Berkshire Regt
DIFFLEY J. MM Cpl P2014 Military Foot Police
DIFFORD George Frederick MM Pte 700281 1/23rd London Regt
DIFFORD Victor H. MM Gnr 68014 5 Bde RFA
DIGANCE Harry MM Pte 201090 4th Hampshire Regt
DIGARD Eugene MM Sjt 07432 Army Ordnance Corps
DIGBY Arthur J.S. MM Gnr 57465 B/150 Bde RFA
DIGBY Ernest Frank MM Sjt 85302 36th Northumberland Fusiliers
DIGBY Harold E. MM L/Cpl 14602 9th Norfolk Regt
DIGBY Harry MM Dvr 75763 37 Div Ammn Col RFA
DIGBY Harry MM Cpl 12000 9th Essex Regt KIA 3.7.16.
DIGBY Herbert MM Gnr L/39835 RFA
DIGGETT Howard MM Gnr 80515 RFA Died 27.11.18.
DIGGINS G.L. MM Gnr 63805 15 Bde RFA
DIGGINS Leonard Arthur MM Cpl 29846 11 Bty 1 Bde RFA
DIGGINS Richard H. MM Sjt G/9672 Royal West Surrey Regt
DIGGLE Elijah MM Sjt 407 1/5th Leicestershire Regt
DIGGLE George MM Gnr 82928 RFA
DIGGLE George MM Cpl 24338 151 Coy Machine Gun Corps
DIGGLE Joseph MM Cpl 30232 9th North Lancashire Regt KIA 27.4.18.
DIGGLE Joseph MM+Bar Pte 20429 17th Lancashire Fusiliers DOW 1.11.18.
DIGGLE Nathan MM Sjt 999 2nd Lancashire Fusiliers
DIGGLE Robert MM L/Cpl 4660 12th Manchester Regt
DIGGLE T.G. MM Dvr 1907 RFA
DIGGLES H. MM Gnr 2240 RFA
DIGGORY George E. MM Pte R/6019 King's Royal Rifle Corps
DIGHT Percy "DCM,MM+Bar,MIDx2" Sjt 63498 130 Bty 40 Bde RFA
DIGHT William F. MM Pte 7436 1st Dorsetshire Regt
DIGHTAM Frederick Percy Charles MM L/Cpl 115089 61st Bn Machine Gun Corps
DIGHTON Frederick William MM Pte 43038 1st Bedfordshire Regt
DIGHTON William MM Pte 23260 4th Grenadier Guards
DIGNALL Thomas MM Pte S/11812 1st Cameron Highlanders
DIGNAM Abraham MM 2nd Cpl 440261 Royal Engineers
DIGWEED Reginald MM Cpl 200534 2/4th Hampshire Regt DOW 14.9.18.

DILKES Ernest William MM Sjt 9241 1st Notts & Derby Regt
DILKES Thomas MM Gnr 114890 RGA
DILKS Harry MM Pte 21881 Yorkshire Light Infantry
DILKS Henry H. MM Pte 6529 2nd Royal West Surrey Regt
DILLEY Ernest MM L/Cpl 203948 Royal West Kent Regt
DILLEY William J. MM Pte 354342 19th London Regt
DILLEY William R. MM Sjt 47189 20 Div Sig Coy Royal Engineers
DILLING Frederick G. MM L/Cpl 10085 1st Royal Berkshire Regt
DILLIWAY Albert MM Gnr 9059 C/87 Bde RFA
DILLON David MM Pnr 130268 Royal Engineers
DILLON Edward Joseph MM Cpl 512139 RAMC
DILLON Ernest Arthur MM Cpl 143070 Special Bde Royal Engineers
DILLON Hugh MM Sjt 37191 RFA
DILLON James MM Dvr 631592 C/113 Bde RFA
DILLON James MM Pte 15493 7/8th King's Own Scottish Borderers
DILLON John T. MM Pte S/31642 13th Rifle Brigade
DILLON Michael MM Sjt 307426 2nd Bn Tank Corps
DILLON Richard H. "MM,MID" Gnr 75999 RHA
DILLON Samuel G. MM Pte 292616 1/6th Royal Highlanders
DILLON Thomas MM L/Cpl 23351 West Yorkshire Regt
DILLON Thomas MM Sjt 12319 7th Somerset Light Infantry
DILLOWAY Walter MM L/Cpl SPTS/3812 23rd Royal Fusiliers
DILWORTH James MM Pte 2457 1/7th Liverpool Regt
DILWORTH John MM Pte 9231 2nd Lincolnshire Regt
DIMENT Albert J. MM Pte 15631 Dorsetshire Regt
DIMES Alfred J. MM Pte 203073 10th Essex Regt
DIMMICK Albert G. MM L/Cpl 7585 Royal West Kent Regt
DIMMOCK Albert V. MM Spr 284569 21 Div Sig Coy Royal Engineers
DIMMOCK Arthur J. MM+Bar Cpl 300459 16th Royal Warwickshire Regt
DIMMOCK John MM Pte 202338 Lancashire Fusiliers
DIMMOCK Walter MM Sjt L/12037 4th Royal Fusiliers
DIMON Harold Vincent William MM Bdr 930673 A/291 Bde RFA
DIMOND Joseph MM Pte 42434 RAMC
DINE Bertie MM Cpl 42540 D/15 Bde RFA
DINEEN William MM Dvr 12027 124 Bty 28 Bde RFA
DINES Sidney MM Sjt 16175 2nd Bedfordshire Regt
DINES Sidney J. MM L/Cpl 8565 1st Royal Berkshire Regt
DINES Walter MM Dvr 68602 RFA
DINES William MM Cpl 7764 2nd Yorkshire Light Infantry
DINGLE Albert W. MM Cpl 11076 4th Royal Fusiliers
DINGLE George L. MM Pte 81753 137 Coy Labour Corps
DINGLE Harry MM Spr 255003 Royal Engineers
DINGLE Harry R.T. MM Gnr 110483 RGA
DINGLEY Albert E. MM Cpl 810191 A/232 Bde RFA
DINGLEY Arthur E. MM Sjt 33267 2nd Middlesex Regt
DINGLEY Edmund MM Pte 101720 29th Durham Light Infantry
DINGLEY Edward MM Pte 80808 RAMC
DINGLEY John MM 2nd Cpl 552183 Royal Engineers
DINGSDALE Ernest MM Bdr 51784 RGA
DINGWALL Andrew B. MM+Bar Sjt 47816 Royal Engineers
DINGWALL Ronald MM+Bar Pte S/40676 Seaforth Highlanders
DINGWALL Thomas C. MM Sjt 200446 5/6th Scottish Rifles
DINGWALL William MM Cpl 265707 1/6th Seaforth Highlanders
DINGWALL William MM Cpl 42464 10/11th Highland Light Infantry DOW 31.8.17.
DINGWELL Adam MM Pte 205524 22nd Northumberland Fusiliers
DINNADGE Horace MM Dvr 156690 88 Bty 14 Bde RFA
DINNAGE Frederick J. "DCM,MM" Sjt 84559 21st Bn Machine Gun Corps
DINNAGE William MM Cpl 938 7th Royal Sussex Regt
DINNES George H. MM L/Cpl T4/241532 51 Div Train Army Service Corps
DINNIE William MM Pte 22829 Seaforth Highlanders
DINNING Frederick MM Pte 43467 Durham Light Infantry
DINNING John MM Sjt 113472 'E' Special Coy Royal Engineers
DINSDALE Albert MM Gnr Shoeing Smith 795766 49 Div Ammn Col RFA
DINSDALE Edwin MM L/Cpl 200032 5th Durham Light Infantry
DINSDALE George MM Pte 307475 1/7th West Yorkshire Regt
DINSDALE John MM L/Cpl 23018 21st Lancers
DINSDALE Robert MM Sjt 65893 RAMC
DINSDALE Walter MM Pte 23883 East Lancashire Regt
DINSDALE William C. MM L/Cpl R/22347 King's Royal Rifle Corps
DINSDALE William Henry "DCM,MM+Bar,CG(B)" Cpl C/6255 18th King's Royal Rifle Corps
DINSLEY Arthur John MM Pte 250163 1/6th Durham Light Infantry
DINSLEY James MM Pte 302273 1/8th Durham Light Infantry KIA 12.4.18.
DINWOODIE James MM Cpl 28796 East Surrey Regt
DINWOODIE John MM+Bar Sjt 40319 1st Bn Tank Corps
DION Jack MM Pte 12341 5th Northamptonshire Regt KIA 27.3.18.
DIPLOCK Horace Reginald MM Sjt 9685 8th Royal Sussex Regt KIA 9.8.17.
DIPPIE Thomas MM L/Cpl 200009 1/4th Royal Highlanders
DIPPLE Thomas W. MM L/Cpl 10168 1st East Yorkshire Regt
DIPROSE Ernest Frederick MM L/Cpl 700085 1/23rd London Regt
DIPROSE George MM L/Cpl 23228 142 Coy Machine Gun Corps
DIPROSE Harold F. MM Cpl 47938 16th Lancashire Fusiliers
DISBURY Alfred MM Sjt 202990 Oxf & Bucks Light Infantry
DISBURY George MM Pte 202187 1/4th Royal Berkshire Regt
DISCOMBE George MM Sjt 257348 1st Devonshire Regt
DISLEY Henry MM Pte 29957 1st Cheshire Regt
DISNEY Charles MM Cpl 56439 86 Fd Coy Royal Engineers
DISS Anthony C. MM Pte 302309 Manchester Regt
DITCHBURN George E. MM Cpl 13784 XIV Corps Cyclist Bn Army Cyclist Corps
DITCHBURN Robert MM Pte 743 20th Northumberland Fusiliers
DITCHBURN Thomas MM Pte 16716 2nd King's Own Scottish Borderers
DITCHFIELD John MM Pte 12700 Machine Gun Corps
DITTON Richard MM Spr 86726 Royal Engineers
DIVE Clifton E. MM Pte 74191 RAMC
DIVEN P. MM Pte 29771 1st Royal Inniskilling Fusiliers
DIVER Thomas MM L/Cpl 15459 2nd Royal Inniskilling Fusiliers KIA 29.9.18.
DIVERS Alfred MM Pte 9488 4th Middlesex Regt
DIVVER Bernard MM Bdr 66377 A/107 Bde RFA
DIX Albert Walter MM Pte 205735 3/4th Royal West Surrey Regt
DIX Archie V. MM Pte 7839 2nd Bedfordshire Regt
DIX Edward MM Pte 5944 Shropshire Light Infantry
DIX Edward MM Sjt 201779 Royal Berkshire Regt
DIX Frederick Arthur Herbert "MM,MID" Sjt 681 12th Royal Fusiliers
DIX Herbert George MM L/Cpl 22974 3rd Grenadier Guards
DIX Jack W.H. MM Cpl 12052 3 Div Ammn Col RFA
DIX Joseph MM Pte R/8947 12th King's Royal Rifle Corps
DIX Milson MM Pte 20237 10th Worcestershire Regt KIA 22.3.18.
DIX Thomas C. MM L/Cpl G/14526 2nd Royal Sussex Regt
DIX William MM Pte 24495 Machine Gun Corps
DIX William I.E. MM Gnr 26753 RGA
DIXEY Albert Edward MM Gnr 755370 B/251 Bde RFA
DIXON A.W. MM Pte 370334 London Regt
DIXON Albert MM Gnr 159858 70 Siege Bty RGA
DIXON Albert MM+Bar Cpl 20350 Manchester Regt
DIXON Albert E. MM CQMS 381 1/24th London Regt
DIXON Andrew MM Sjt 39487 125 Coy Machine Gun Corps DOW 18.12.17.
DIXON Archibald MM Pte 40031 11th Royal West Surrey Regt KIA 29.9.18.
DIXON Archie MM Pte 14401 8th Yorkshire Light Infantry
DIXON Charles A. MM Sjt 24007 Yorkshire Light Infantry
DIXON Charles B. MM Pte 5198 1st Coldstream Guards
DIXON Charles H. MM Pte M/37351 Army Service Corps
DIXON Charles R. MM Sjt 370617 8th London Regt
DIXON Edward MM Sjt 240295 1/5th Border Regt
DIXON F.J. MM Sjt TR/13/25586 Trg Res Bn
DIXON Francis W. MM Pte 2552 West Yorkshire Regt
DIXON Frank H. MM Pte 25168 Liverpool Regt
DIXON Fred J. MM Spr 463089 50 Div Sig Coy Royal Engineers
DIXON Frederick MM Pte 7013 1/6th South Staffordshire Regt
DIXON Frederick MM Pte H/35682 1/1st Northumberland Yeo
DIXON Frederick MM Bdr 165875 RGA
DIXON Frederick C. MM L/Bdr 201474 RFA
DIXON Frederick W. MM Pte 7003 HAC
DIXON George MM Sjt 265426 1/6th Seaforth Highlanders
DIXON George A. MM L/Cpl H/270073 1/1st Northumberland Yeo
DIXON George H. MM Sjt 285002 1/1st Bucks Bn Oxf & Bucks Light Infantry
DIXON George W. MM Sjt 13148 9th Northumberland Fusiliers
DIXON H.W. MM Bdr 687129 RFA
DIXON Harold MM L/Cpl C/573 16th King's Royal Rifle Corps
DIXON Harold MM Pte 50169 RAMC
DIXON Harry J. MM Gnr 172365 RHA
DIXON Henry MM L/Cpl 11531 1st Liverpool Regt
DIXON Henry MM Sjt 200780 1/4th Leicestershire Regt
DIXON Henry MM Sjt 14984 9th North Lancashire Regt
DIXON Herbert MM Dvr L/19562 RFA
DIXON Horace MM Sjt 12454 11th Hampshire Regt
DIXON J.R. MM Sjt P/5287 Military Mounted Police

DIXON James MM Pte 84233 11th Royal Fusiliers
DIXON James MM L/Cpl 18880 6th Somerset Light Infantry
DIXON James "MM,MID" Pte 2201 1/1 Warwickshire Yeomanry
DIXON James MM Gnr 37059 RFA
DIXON James MM Cpl 696103 A/285 Bde RFA
DIXON James MM Dvr 18925 B/103 Bde RFA
DIXON John MM Cpl 357929 Liverpool Regt
DIXON John "DCM,MM" CSM 19102 2/5th Lancashire Fusiliers KIA 4.7.18.
DIXON John MM Dvr 53567 Royal Engineers
DIXON John "MM,MID" Cpl 1659 1/6th Durham Light Infantry
DIXON John MM Pte 7501 2nd Coldstream Guards
DIXON John MM Cpl 246 10th East Yorkshire Regt
DIXON John MM Spr 121515 Royal Engineers
DIXON John MM Pte 201468 Durham Light Infantry
DIXON John MM CQMS 7860 2nd South Lancashire Regt
DIXON John MM Sjt 8903 1st Royal Irish Fusiliers
DIXON John Bailey MM Pte 39756 9th Yorkshire Light Infantry KIA 27.5.18.
DIXON John E. MM Dvr 90871 Royal Engineers
DIXON John J. MM Pte 44238 6th Cheshire Regt
DIXON John J. MM Cpl 241997 South Lancashire Regt
DIXON John J. MM Pte 19601 Northumberland Fusiliers
DIXON John Ralph MM Pte 24230 1st Northumberland Fusiliers KIA 23.8.18.
DIXON John Wilkinson MM Pte 48377 1st North Staffordshire Regt KIA 15.10.18.
DIXON Joseph MM Sjt 5905 1st Northumberland Fusiliers
DIXON Joseph MM Dvr 34403 RFA
DIXON Joseph MM Pte 74599 7th Royal Fusiliers
DIXON Joseph Isaac MM Pte 40527 7th Bedfordshire Regt
DIXON Lawrence MM L/Cpl 482125 Royal Engineers
DIXON Leonard MM Pte 12446 Royal Highlanders
DIXON Morgan "DCM,MM,MID" L/Cpl 14467 7th Shropshire Light Infantry
DIXON Oliver J. MM L/Cpl 8433 32nd Bn Machine Gun Corps
DIXON Percy E. MM Pnr 146878 Royal Engineers
DIXON Percy Henry MM Sjt 532 RFA
DIXON Robert MM Pte 9100 2nd Border Regt
DIXON Robert MM Pte 11325 2nd Scots Guards
DIXON Robert MM Pte 20/929 Durham Light Infantry
DIXON Robert MM Cpl 200215 Lancashire Fusiliers
DIXON Robert Sydney MM Pte 20584 2/5th Royal Lancaster Regt
DIXON Robert W. MM Pte 8972 14 Fd Amb RAMC
DIXON Robert William MM Cpl 27627 26th Royal Fusiliers KIA 5.9.18.
DIXON Sidney Albert MM Pte 34837 7th Royal Warwickshire Regt
DIXON Thomas MM Pte 241420 9th Royal Lancaster Regt
DIXON Thomas MM Cpl 7333 A/160 Bde RFA DOW 2.8.18.
DIXON Thomas E. MM L/Cpl S/6243 10th Arg & Suth Highlanders
DIXON Thomas E. MM Pte 16818 Suffolk Regt
DIXON Thomas Richard MM Pte 200854 Cheshire Regt
DIXON Thomas Sidney MM Sjt 290716 RGA
DIXON Thomas W. MM Pte 38958 Yorkshire Regt
DIXON Victor MM L/Cpl 256086 West Riding Regt
DIXON Victor T. MM L/Sjt 12398 1st Duke of Cornwall's LI
DIXON William MM Sjt 1734 129 Fd Amb RAMC
DIXON William MM Cpl 333855 9th Highland Light Infantry KIA 15.4.18.
DIXON William MM Cpl 15751 Durham Light Infantry
DIXON William MM Spr 846 Royal Engineers
DIXON William MM L/Cpl 20/1619 20th Northumberland Fusiliers KIA 1.7.16.
DIXON William A. "MM,MSM" Sjt 10904 25 Army Troops Coy Royal Engineers
DIXON William Albert MM Pte 372617 8th London Regt DOW 15.5.18.
DIXON William E. MM Pte 36035 Yorkshire Light Infantry
DIXON William T. MM Pte 242152 North Staffordshire Regt
D'Lewis Ernest W. MM Sjt P/850 Rifle Brigade
DOAR William "MM,MID" Cpl 189786 Railway Operating Division Royal Engineers
DOAR William H. MM 2nd Cpl 112837 172 Tunnelling Coy Royal Engineers
DOBB Arthur Harold MM Bdr L/23983 B/165 Bde RFA
DOBBIE David "DCM,MM+Bar" Sjt 20437 5/6th Royal Scots KIA 11.8.18.
DOBBIE John MM+Bar L/Cpl 200846 5/6th Scottish Rifles
DOBBIE John MM Pte 12931 2nd Scots Guards
DOBBIN Charles MM Pte 11740 11th Royal Scots
DOBBIN Robert MM Pte 1618 15th Royal Irish Rifles
DOBBIN Samuel MM Pte 7600 IX Corps Cyclist Bn Army Cyclist Corps
DOBBIN William "MM+Bar,CG(F)" Pte 352321 1/9th Royal Scots
DOBBING William "DCM,MM+Bar" CSM 49137 17th Liverpool Regt
DOBBINS James Henry MM Gnr 760366 3(Northumbrian)Bde RFA
DOBBINS John R. MM Spr 32351 Royal Engineers
DOBBINS William MM Pte 43117 Royal Irish Fusiliers
DOBBINSON Sydney W. MM Pte 19320 Royal Berkshire Regt
DOBBS Arnold MM Cpl H/1030 15th Hussars
DOBBS C. MM Pte 16168 10th Essex Regt
DOBBS Daisy Ellen MM Staff Nurse F TFNS
DOBBS Ernest MM L/Cpl 11/491 East Yorkshire Regt
DOBBS Fred MM Cpl 27370 Royal Lancaster Regt
DOBBS Harry MM Pte 11682 1st Coldstream Guards
DOBBS J.B. MM Sjt 1391 Northumberland Fusiliers
DOBBS James Appleyard MM Pte 10/507 10th East Yorkshire Regt KIA 2.8.18.
DOBBS John MM Pte 13753 4th Royal Fusiliers
DOBBS John Ernest Robinson MM Pte M2/133676 Army Service Corps
DOBBS Thomas H. MM Pte 19515 Durham Light Infantry
DOBBS William J. MM Pte 28554 Gloucestershire Regt
DOBBYN William MM Sjt M2/053265 Army Service Corps
DOBELL Alfred S. "DCM,MM" Cpl 575 MGC(Motors)
DOBIE Frederick Andrew MM Pte 10496 2nd Wiltshire Regt KIA 21.3.18.
DOBIE Sidney H. MM L/Cpl 13204 4th Middlesex Regt
DOBIE William B. MM L/Cpl M2/181058 Army Service Corps
DOBING Charles MM Cpl 191230 'M' AA Bty RGA
DOBINSON Arthur E. MM L/Cpl 63333 5th Bn Machine Gun Corps
DOBINSON Percy E. MM Pte 34998 25th Royal Welsh Fusiliers
DOBLE Alfred W.H. MM+Bar Cpl 8730 2nd Royal Berkshire Regt
DOBSON A. MM Sjt 35184 Northumberland Fusiliers
DOBSON Albert E. MM Bdr 15025 44 Bde RFA
DOBSON Arthur MM Gnr Sig 35672 A/108 Bde RFA
DOBSON Charles MM Pte 33892 9th York & Lancaster Regt
DOBSON Edwin MM Cpl Wheeler 608383 RHA
DOBSON Ernest MM Sjt 325119 1/9th Durham Light Infantry
DOBSON Francis MM L/Cpl 46301 9th Yorkshire Light Infantry
DOBSON Frank MM Pte 2454 10th Arg & Suth Highlanders
DOBSON Frederick MM L/Cpl 12363 6th Duke of Cornwall's LI
DOBSON Frederick James MM S/Sjt Armt 846 Army Ordnance Corps
DOBSON Frederick Robert MM Dvr 96488 47 Bde RFA DOW 11.4.18.
DOBSON George MM Pte 50609 8th West Yorkshire Regt
DOBSON George MM Cpl 9940 1st West Yorkshire Regt att 16 TM Bty. KIA 16.6.17.
DOBSON George B. MM Pte 240159 5th West Riding Regt
DOBSON George F. MM+Bar Cpl 10760 2nd York & Lancaster Regt
DOBSON Heath MM Pte 16101 8th Yorkshire Regt
DOBSON Henry MM Gnr Sig 31235 B/84 Bde RFA
DOBSON Herbert MM L/Sjt 2746 1/5th Royal Lancaster Regt KIA 9.8.16.
DOBSON James W. MM Cpl 104398 228 Fd Coy Royal Engineers
DOBSON John MM Sjt 200404 4th King's Own Scottish Borderers
DOBSON John E. MM Cpl 35389 RFA
DOBSON John P. "DCM+2 Bars,MM" CSM 8992 9th York & Lancaster Regt
DOBSON John R. MM Pte 260118 2nd Yorkshire Regt
DOBSON John R. MM S/Sjt Mechanic 76165 13th Bn Tank Corps
DOBSON Joseph MM Pte 12281 10th West Riding Regt DOW 21.9.17.
DOBSON Newton MM Pte 20437 10th West Riding Regt
DOBSON Oswald MM Pte 1917 7th Royal Munster Fusiliers
DOBSON Robert MM Bdr 42429 87 Bty 2 Bde RFA
DOBSON Thomas Clark MM Bdr 51981 130 Heavy Bty RGA
DOBSON Thomas George MM Sjt 3 1/4th Leicestershire Regt
DOBSON Walter "MM,MID" CSM 13610 1st Grenadier Guards
DOBSON Walter MM Pte 29043 8th East Yorkshire Regt
DOBSON William MM L/Cpl 65460 126 Fd Coy Royal Engineers KIA 22.3.18.
DOBSON William MM Pte 59113 Welsh Regt
DOBSON William "MM,MSM" Pte 12982 6/7th Royal Scots Fusiliers
DOBSON William "MM+Bar,MID" Sjt 200025 1/5th Durham Light Infantry
DOBSON William Arthur MM Sjt 9494 1st Essex Regt DOW 20.10.16.
DOBSON William H. MM Cpl 14565 13th West Riding Regt

DOCCHAR John MM Dvr 12214 RFA
DOCHAR Thomas H. MM Cpl 19248 2nd Lincolnshire Regt
DOCHERTY Anthony MM Pte 12418 9th Scottish Rifles
DOCHERTY Cecil Oswald MM Sjt 90743 B/285 Bde RFA
DOCHERTY Francis MM Pte 10756 2nd West Riding Regt
DOCHERTY George MM Pte 5752 1st Irish Guards
DOCHERTY J. MM Spr 459387 447 Fd Coy Royal Engineers
DOCHERTY J. MM Cpl 18370 2nd Royal Dublin Fusiliers
DOCHERTY James MM Cpl S/2553 2nd Seaforth Highlanders
DOCHERTY James MM Pte 45327 15th Highland Light Infantry DOW 29.5.18.
DOCHERTY James "DCM,MM" Sjt 8566 1st Royal Highlanders KIA 3.9.16.
DOCHERTY James MM Pte 423 10th Arg & Suth Highlanders KIA 12.10.17.
DOCHERTY John MM Pte 43506 9th Scottish Rifles
DOCHERTY John James MM Pte 41274 1/28th London Regt DOW 8.11.18.
DOCHERTY John James MM Pte 41274 Rifle Brigade att 1/28th London Regt
DOCHERTY Joseph MM Pte 7575 5th Connaught Rangers
DOCHERTY P. "DCM,MM" RSM 200629 5/6th Scottish Rifles
DOCHERTY Patrick MM Dvr 631614 RFA
DOCHERTY Peter MM+2 Bars Sjt 751082 A/250 Bde RFA
DOCHERTY Robert MM Sjt 79729 258 Tunnelling Coy Royal Engineers DOW 22.7.16.
DOCHERTY Thomas William Coupland MM Gnr 756176 A/251 Bde RFA Died 11.11.18.
DOCK John J. MM L/Cpl 322233 6th London Regt
DOCK William MM Cpl 30/131 25th Northumberland Fusiliers KIA 26.4.18.
DOCKA John MM Pte 36762 7th Norfolk Regt
DOCKERILL A. MM Gnr 46036 K Bty RHA
DOCKERILL Herbert MM Pte 17851 1st East Surrey Regt
DOCKERILL Leslie T. MM+Bar Cpl 21070 1st East Kent Regt
DOCKERILL Sydney C. "DCM+Bar,MM" CSM 325485 1/1st Cambridgeshire Regt
DOCKERY John Carter MM L/Sjt 40223 12th Highland Light Infantry
DOCKING Robert J. MM Pte 20151 4th Grenadier Guards
DOCURA William MM L/Cpl 43343 4th Bedfordshire Regt
DOD Alfred William MM Cpl G/6646 11th Royal West Surrey Regt DOW 4.8.18.
DODD Albert E. MM L/Cpl 36984 North Lancashire Regt
DODD Arthur Walter "MM+Bar,CG(B)" Sjt 558223 29 Div Sig Coy Royal Engineers Died 15.1.19.
DODD Christopher MM Sjt 28834 9th Norfolk Regt
DODD Frank MM Sjt 35521 RAMC
DODD Frederick MM Pte 2277 1st Royal Warwickshire Regt
DODD George "DCM,MM" Sjt 11916 9th South Staffordshire Regt
DODD George Baker MM Cpl 357745 Att 81 Bde RGA Royal Engineers DOW 20.9.18.
DODD Harold "MM+Bar,MID" Sjt 7563 1st Leicestershire Regt
DODD Harry MM Gnr 55351 RFA
DODD Harry S. MM Pte 26673 6th Liverpool Regt
DODD Henry MM L/Cpl 49482 11th Cheshire Regt KIA 13.8.17.
DODD Henry E. MM+Bar Sjt 241084 Liverpool Regt
DODD James Eden MM L/Cpl 50933 91 Fd Coy Royal Engineers
DODD James H. MM Gnr 32083 MGC(Heavy Branch)
DODD John MM L/Cpl 23400 16th Royal Welsh Fusiliers
DODD John MM Gnr 48999 RGA
DODD John MM L/Cpl 102292 177 Tunnelling Coy Royal Engineers
DODD John Walter MM Pte 14719 13th Cheshire Regt
DODD Joseph A. MM Pte 32213 4th West Riding Regt
DODD Nicolas MM Cpl 5596 Manchester Regt
DODD Richard H. MM Pte 27742 Royal Lancaster Regt
DODD Samuel MM Gnr 148363 RGA
DODD Thomas MM Pte 8190 2nd South Lancashire Regt KIA 3.7.16.
DODD Thomas H. MM Spr 49213 Royal Engineers
DODD Thomas Ismay MM Pte 10786 Seaforth Highlanders
DODD Thomas J. MM Pte 9231 2nd Royal Welsh Fusiliers
DODD Walter MM Bdr 36670 RFA
DODD William MM Pte 45029 15th Cheshire Regt KIA 1.11.17.
DODD William G. MM Spr 154166 Royal Engineers
DODD William Henry MM Dvr 19868 115 Bty 25 Bde RFA KIA 23.10.16.
DODD William Robert MM Sjt 2102 1/4th York & Lancaster Regt KIA 3.7.16.
DODDINGTON Thomas MM Pte 11225 7th East Kent Regt
DODDS Albert MM Sjt 17657 14th Northumberland Fusiliers
DODDS Andrew MM Cpl 25525 C/71 Bde RFA
DODDS Arnold Boyd MM L/Cpl 243233 1/4th Yorkshire Regt
DODDS Charles MM Pte 242897 1/6th West Yorkshire Regt
DODDS Daniel MM Pte 266194 1/7th Scottish Rifles
DODDS Edward MM Pte 133258 46th Royal Fusiliers
DODDS Edward MM+Bar Cpl 22/325 Durham Light Infantry
DODDS George Brown MM Bdr 6932 152 Heavy Bty RGA
DODDS Harry MM Pte 32715 6th Bn Machine Gun Corps
DODDS Henry K. MM+Bar Pte 40324 6th Royal Highlanders
DODDS J. "DCM,MM" Sjt 275111 1/4th Royal Scots
DODDS J.R. MM Pte 3031 Durham Light Infantry
DODDS James MM Cpl 257446 Durham Light Infantry
DODDS James MM L/Cpl 12559 2nd Royal Scots Fusiliers
DODDS James Beveridge MM Pte 19825 10th Northumberland Fusiliers KIA 4.10.16.
DODDS John MM Cpl 53363 12th Bn Machine Gun Corps
DODDS John "DCM,MM+Bar" L/Sjt 801 4th Bn GMGR
DODDS John "DCM,MM" CSM 275100 1/7th Arg & Suth Highlanders
DODDS John A. MM L/Cpl 1185 Royal Engineers
DODDS John T. MM Pte 17905 13th Durham Light Infantry
DODDS Joseph MM Pnr 129126 Royal Engineers
DODDS R. MM Pte 14188 5th Border Regt
DODDS Robert Norman "MC,DCM,MM(1934 Sjt)" T/2Lt 50 Div Sig Coy Royal Engineers
DODDS Thomas MM Sjt 1608 1/9th Durham Light Infantry
DODDS Thomas MM Cpl 35149 Highland Light Infantry
DODDS William MM L/Cpl 17976 10th Durham Light Infantry
DODDS William MM L/Cpl 10616 Seaforth Highlanders
DODDS William Beattie MM Cpl Shoeing Smith 751517 48 Bty 36 Bde RFA
DODGE Harry MM Sjt 8899 1st Dorsetshire Regt
DODGE Herbert MM+2 Bars Sjt 9923 2nd Notts & Derby Regt
DODGE Thomas MM Gnr 111065 'Z' Bty RHA
DODGE Walter Robert MM Pte 17337 20th Manchester Regt KIA 2.10.17.
DODGSON Frank MM Pte 242057 10th West Riding Regt
DODGSON John G.T. MM L/Cpl 23560 Machine Gun Corps
DODGSON Norman MM Gnr 105949 RGA
DODGSON Thomas "DCM,MM" CSM 8090 1/7th West Riding Regt
DODGSON William MM Sjt 27651 13th Yorkshire Regt
DODKIN Harold MM Pte 3438 1/8th Middlesex Regt
DODKINS James W. MM Cpl 14285 2nd Royal Fusiliers
DODMAN Thomas Edward MM Sjt 10783 1st King's Royal Rifle Corps KIA 10.3.17.
DODRIDGE Joseph T MM Pte 33277 Machine Gun Corps
DODS George A. MM L/Sjt 14415 1st Scots Guards
DODSLEY Ernest MM Pte 18681 Notts & Derby Regt
DODSON Arthur MM Sjt 83667 259 Siege Bty RGA
DODSON Charles MM Pte 13/263 13th York & Lancaster Regt KIA 17.7.16.
DODSON Francis Percy MM Pte 200477 Shropshire Light Infantry
DODSON Frederick F. MM Cpl 9901 2nd Royal Welsh Fusiliers
DODSON Henry MM Cpl 7750 2nd Oxf & Bucks Light Infantry
DODSON Henry "MM,MSM,CG(B)" Sjt 25980 156 Siege Bty RGA
DODSWORTH Harry M. MM Sjt 17466 Yorkshire Light Infantry
DODWELL Thomas MM L/Cpl 15199 9th Royal Inniskilling Fusiliers KIA 30.9.18.
DODWELL William F. "MM,MID" Sjt 19746 RAMC
DODWORTH George Thompson MM L/Cpl 38437 1st Northumberland Fusiliers KIA 27.9.18.
DODWORTH Gerald E. MM L/Cpl 12/637 2nd York & Lancaster Regt
DOE Charles A. MM Pte 15050 3rd Royal Fusiliers
DOE Charles F. MM CQMS 6537 2nd Coldstream Guards
DOE Charlie MM Pte 200982 2/5th West Yorkshire Regt
DOE Edward MM Cpl 67983 421 Bty RFA
DOE George D. MM L/Cpl 74413 Royal Engineers
DOE George E. MM Pte 21076 1st Royal West Kent Regt
DOE Leonard S. MM Gnr 74643 43 Bde RFA
DOE Percy William MM Sjt 1967 1/4th Lincolnshire Regt Died 23.1.19.
DOE William MM Cpl 54247 130 Heavy Bty RGA
DOE William V. MM Gnr 69737 Tank Corps
DOEL B.F.E. MM Bdr 72298 RFA
DOEL Ernest James "MM,MID" Sjt 7556 2nd Coldstream Guards
DOEL Leonard MM Sjt 9927 1st Wiltshire Regt DOW 10.9.16.
DOGAN John MM L/Cpl 11205 2nd Royal Welsh Fusiliers
DOGAN William MM Sjt 5275 2nd Royal Welsh Fusiliers
DOGGART Hugh MM L/Cpl 13/3914 13th Royal Irish Rifles KIA 16.8.17.

DOGGETT Albert Edward MM Cpl M2/054596 Army Service Corps att 50 Fd Amb RAMC.DOW 28.8.18.
DOGGETT J.D. MM Cpl 24571 Shropshire Light Infantry
DOGGETT Leopold MM Pte 9162 Machine Gun Corps
DOGGETT Thomas R. MM S/Sjt Fitter 148739 RGA
DOGHERTY Henry B. MM Pte 16439 15th Royal Irish Rifles
DOHENY Daniel MM Pte 9774 Royal Irish Regt
DOHERTY Arthur MM Spr 71026 Royal Engineers
DOHERTY Bernard MM L/Sjt E/1421 17th Royal Fusiliers
DOHERTY Charles MM L/Cpl 11271 Irish Guards
DOHERTY David MM Pte 1313 20th Manchester Regt
DOHERTY Frank MM L/Cpl 20320 2nd Royal Munster Fusiliers KIA 18.10.18.
DOHERTY Herbert MM Pte 45038 RAMC
DOHERTY James MM Pte 203195 6th Cameron Highlanders
DOHERTY James MM Pte 21217 8th Royal Irish Fusiliers KIA 7.9.16.
DOHERTY John MM L/Cpl 22427 2/5th Royal Lancaster Regt
DOHERTY John MM Sjt 5758 2nd Royal Inniskilling Fusiliers
DOHERTY Martin MM Pte 680855 1/22nd London Regt
DOHERTY Patrick MM Pte 4648 7/8th Royal Inniskilling Fusiliers KIA 21.3.18.
DOHERTY Peter MM Pte 37672 Machine Gun Corps
DOHERTY Peter MM Sjt 371043 17th London Regt
DOHERTY Philip MM Pte 28516 Royal Inniskilling Fusiliers
DOHERTY Terence MM Pte 27069 9th Royal Dublin Fusiliers KIA 17.8.17.
DOIDGE Percy J. MM Pte 459431 RAMC
DOIG Andrew Cochrane MM Gnr 6819 22 Bty 130 Bde RFA
DOIG David MM Gnr Sig 663088 A/250 Bde RFA
DOIG George Shepherd "DCM,MM" Cpl S/8866 8th Royal Highlanders
DOIG John MM Gnr 93237 RGA
DOLAN Aloysius Francis MM Sjt 200593 4/5th Royal Highlanders KIA 1.8.18.
DOLAN George MM Gnr 152137 119 Bde RFA
DOLAN Hugh MM Dvr 20063 87 Bty 2 Bde RFA
DOLAN J. MM Sjt 241298 Royal Lancaster Regt
DOLAN James MM Sjt 3/9065 8th Yorkshire Regt
DOLAN James MM Dvr 136613 108 Bty 23 Bde RFA
DOLAN John MM Pte 242130 10th Lancashire Fusiliers KIA 25.8.18.
DOLAN John J. MM Pte 17289 6th Royal Inniskilling Fusiliers
DOLAN Joseph MM Pte 203432 Lancashire Fusiliers
DOLAN Michael MM L/Cpl 9846 1st Connaught Rangers
DOLAN Oliver "DCM,MM+Bar" Sjt 341263 64 Fd Amb RAMC
DOLAND Frederick M. MM Dvr 14946 4 Div Sig Coy Royal Engineers
DOLBEAR Sydney W. MM 2nd Cpl 22622 1 Div Sig Coy Royal Engineers
DOLBEY Harry MM+Bar Cpl 253958 Signal Service Royal Engineers
DOLBY Donald T. MM Spr 45325 20 Div Sig Coy Royal Engineers
DOLBY George H. MM Pte 269827 Notts & Derby Regt
DOLBY Harry MM Gnr 86583 94 Siege Bty RGA
DOLBY Hudson "MM,MID" Sjt 476294 Royal Engineers
DOLBY Hugh MM Pte 63491 Machine Gun Corps
DOLBY Sydney MM Pte 22298 8th East Surrey Regt
DOLDING Charles MM Cpl 59251 Royal Engineers
DOLEMAN Charles H. MM Sjt 9699 11tth Lancashire Fusiliers
DOLITTLE J.H. "DCM,MM" Sjt 2761 Royal Flying Corps
DOLLAN James MM Pte 331771 9th Highland Light Infantry KIA 9.1.18.
DOLLAR William G. MM L/Cpl 9376 Irish Guards
DOLLERY Robert MM Pte 250074 3rd London Regt
DOLLEY Thomas W. MM Gnr 69619 Tank Corps
DOLLIN Frederick MM L/Cpl 240457 1/5th Devonshire Regt
DOLLIN Henry MM L/Cpl 5756 13th Royal Fusiliers
DOLLING Henry James MM Pte 66974 140 Fd Amb RAMC
DOLMAN Ernest MM Pte 9937 1st North Staffordshire Regt
DOLMAN George MM Pte G/20078 2nd Royal Sussex Regt
DOLMAN John Francis Hunt MM Pte 18221 2nd Coldstream Guards
DOLMAN Percy MM+Bar Sjt 10402 1st Gordon Highlanders KIA 1.10.18.
DOLMAN Richard MM Sjt 34300 7th Somerset Light Infantry
DOLPHIN John MM L/Sjt R/4084 13th King's Royal Rifle Corps DOW 26.8.18.
DOLPHIN Joseph Horner MM Pte 16855 10th Yorkshire Light Infantry
DOLPHIN Thomas "DCM,MM" Sjt 785383 C/150 Bde RFA
DOLTON Alfred MM Cpl 260357 Liverpool Regt
DOLTON Frank MM Pte 25616 8th Lincolnshire Regt
DOMINY George MM Pte 557216 16th London Regt
DOMMETT William John MM Pte 20994 2nd Devonshire Regt
DON Alexander James MM Bdr L/19161 D/52 Bde RFA KIA 16.5.17.
DON Peter Jack MM Pte 2028 Royal Highlanders
DONACHIE H. MM Pte 53556 Highland Light Infantry
DONACHIE Thomas MM Pte 26981 2nd King's Own Scottish Borderers
DONACHIE or DONOCHIE Christopher MM Pte 9117 1st Connaught Rangers
DONAGHER John MM Cpl 16404 18th Lancashire Fusiliers
DONAGHER or DANAGHER Michael MM Sjt 2262 7th Leinster Regt
DONAGHUE Walter C. MM Sjt 496121 Royal Engineers
DONAGHY David MM Pte 15475 Royal Inniskilling Fusiliers
DONAGHY Edward William MM Gnr 124480 49 Heavy Bde RGA
DONAGHY Henry MM Cpl 25268 Royal Inniskilling Fusiliers
DONAL Richard MM Pte 16800 18th Liverpool Regt
DONALD Alfred D. MM Cpl 533270 15th London Regt
DONALD Andrew MM+Bar CSM 1293 1st Gordon Highlanders
DONALD Archibald MM Sjt 6957 14th Highland Light Infantry
DONALD George MM Spr 406382 Royal Engineers
DONALD George "DCM,MM+Bar" Cpl 53028 1st Liverpool Regt
DONALD J. MM Pte 316248 RAMC
DONALD James MM L/Cpl 202483 Gordon Highlanders
DONALD John MM Sjt 14678 9th Royal Inniskilling Fusiliers
DONALD John MM L/Cpl 266571 6th Gordon Highlanders KIA 11.4.18.
DONALD John "MM,MID" CSM 23192 6 Div Sig Coy Royal Engineers
DONALD John C. MM Spr 16050 Royal Engineers
DONALD John D. MM L/Cpl 15669 8th Shropshire Light Infantry
DONALD John G. MM CSM 60166 2nd West Yorkshire Regt
DONALD John G. MM Pte S/25769 2nd Seaforth Highlanders
DONALD John McL. MM+Bar Sjt 57417 RAMC
DONALD Matthew MM Pte 20477 7th Royal Sussex Regt
DONALD Peter MM Pte 202377 5/6th Scottish Rifles
DONALD Robert MM L/Sjt 242076 Gordon Highlanders
DONALD Somerville MM Dvr T4/057270 Army Service Corps att 135 Fd Amb RAMC
DONALD T. MM L/Cpl 303124 2 Fd Amb RAMC
DONALD Thomas N. MM Pte 331035 Highland Light Infantry
DONALDSON Alexander MM+Bar CSM 14636 11th West Yorkshire Regt
DONALDSON Archibald A. MM Sjt 125614 C/255 Bde RFA
DONALDSON Charles H. MM Cpl 27087 VII Corps Sig Coy Royal Engineers
DONALDSON David MM Bdr 127991 263 Siege Bty RGA
DONALDSON David A. MM Pte 36793 Gloucestershire Regt
DONALDSON Edwin MM Pte 92557 1/7th Middlesex Regt
DONALDSON Evan A. MM Pte 14018 1/6th Gordon Highlanders KIA 9.4.18.
DONALDSON Fleming MM Pte 275577 1/7th Arg & Suth Highlanders
DONALDSON Gordon MM Pte 25222 12th East Surrey Regt DOW 2.10.18.
DONALDSON Harry MM Pte 5399 1/7th Royal Highlanders
DONALDSON Harry MM Pte 201795 Seaforth Highlanders
DONALDSON James MM Sjt 7268 8th East Lancashire Regt
DONALDSON James MM Sjt 71005 Royal Engineers
DONALDSON John J. "DCM,MM" Sjt 9944 7/8th Royal Irish Fusiliers
DONALDSON Joseph MM CSM S/3808 Gordon Highlanders
DONALDSON Launcelot MM Pte 1786 MGC(Heavy Branch)
DONALDSON Peter G. MM L/Cpl 2126 1/9th Highland Light Infantry KIA 1.11.16.
DONALDSON Robert MM Cpl M2/051407 Army Service Corps
DONALDSON Robert MM Pte 46138 Royal Scots
DONALDSON Thomas MM Pte 300573 Liverpool Regt
DONALDSON Thomas E. MM Sjt 12311 Machine Gun Corps
DONALDSON Walter S. "MM,MID" Sjt 16658 RGA
DONALDSON William MM CSM 48219 52nd Bn Machine Gun Corps
DONALDSON William MM L/Cpl 240529 1/5th South Lancashire Regt
DONALDSON William MM L/Sjt 40522 Royal Scots
DONALDSON William MM Pte 291010 Gordon Highlanders
DONATI Alexander C. MM Dvr 64959 87 Bty 2 Bde RFA

DONBAVAND Albert E. MM Pte 26364 Shropshire Light Infantry
DONBAVAND Edward MM Pte 240623 2/5th West Riding Regt
DONBAVAND Horace MM Bdr 735655 RFA
DONCASTER Frederick MM+Bar L/Cpl R/33810 King's Royal Rifle Corps
DONE John MM Pte 13384 10th Cheshire Regt
DONEGAN Alexander MM Cpl 8900 7th Cameron Highlanders KIA 20.8.17.
DONEGAN James MM Gnr 137791 RFA
DONELLY James MM+Bar Spr 86489 176 Tunnelling Coy Royal Engineers
DONEY William J. MM Pte 252195 2/3rd London Regt KIA 26.10.17.
DONFIELD John "DCM,MM" Cpl 10414 1st Royal Dublin Fusiliers
DONHOU E.J. "DCM,MM" Sjt 63285 Royal Engineers
DONINGER Joseph Henry MM Pte 250190 11th Royal Scots KIA 29.9.18.
DONKER Alfred MM Pte 43938 18th King's Royal Rifle Corps KIA 1.11.18.
DONKERSLEY William MM L/Cpl R/25074 9th King's Royal Rifle Corps DOW 21.3.18.
DONKIN Arthur MM Sjt 11582 29 Div Ammn Col RFA
DONKIN Arthur S. MM L/Cpl 34410 5th West Riding Regt
DONKIN Dixon MM Dvr 209289 Royal Engineers
DONKIN Ernest MM Pte 787 20th Durham Light Infantry
DONLEVY Joseph MM Pte 16369 9th Scottish Rifles
DONLEY Walter MM Pte 40508 10th Arg & Suth Highlanders
DONN Benjamin MM Pte 3044 1/5th Seaforth Highlanders KIA 14.5.17.
DONNACHIE Cumming MM Sjt 21432 Wiltshire Regt
DONNAN John MM Pte 203205 Durham Light Infantry
DONNAN Robert W. "DCM,MM" Gnr 31206 B/102 Bde RFA
DONNELAN John MM L/Sjt 8064 1st Connaught Rangers
DONNELL S. MM Cpl 15476 Royal Inniskilling Fusiliers
DONNELL Samuel MM Pte 11064 Royal Inniskilling Fusiliers
DONNELLY Albert "MM,MSM" S/Sjt 41162 110 Fd Amb RAMC
DONNELLY Andrew MM Pte 27585 Royal Scots
DONNELLY Charles MM Gnr 61088 250 Siege Bty RGA
DONNELLY Edward MM Pte 63490 RAMC
DONNELLY George MM Sjt 2438 1/5th Liverpool Regt
DONNELLY James MM L/Cpl 29216 6th Royal Inniskilling Fusiliers
DONNELLY James MM Cpl DM2/170330 Army Service Corps
DONNELLY James "MC,DCM+Bar,MM,CG(B)" CSM 13769 10th Durham Light Infantry
DONNELLY James "MM,MID" Pte 1397 12th Lancers
DONNELLY James MM L/Cpl 11718 Royal Scots
DONNELLY James Philip MM Cpl 17469 1st East Yorkshire Regt KIA 25.9.16.
DONNELLY John MM Sjt 277632 15th Durham Light Infantry
DONNELLY John MM Pte S/5707 1st Royal Highlanders
DONNELLY John MM CQMS 2922 1st Irish Guards
DONNELLY John MM Pte 3108 14 Fd Amb RAMC
DONNELLY John H. MM Pte 359387 Liverpool Regt
DONNELLY John J. MM Pte 28280 9th Royal Inniskilling Fusiliers
DONNELLY Leonard Herbert MM Pte 15486 Shropshire Light Infantry
DONNELLY Matthew P. MM Pte 23064 Scottish Rifles
DONNELLY Michael MM Pte 12109 13th Liverpool Regt
DONNELLY Patrick MM Sjt 5582 Royal Engineers
DONNELLY Patrick James MM Spr 56449 AK Cable Section Royal Engineers DOW 11.7.16.
DONNELLY Peter MM Sjt 2178 8/10th Gordon Highlanders KIA 1.8.17.
DONNELLY W. MM Cpl 13208 King's Own Scottish Borderers
DONNELLY William MM Cpl 715416 RFA
DONNISON Sidney V. MM Spr 563061 18 AA Coy Royal Engineers
DONOGHUE Benjamin MM Pte 5097 16th King's Royal Rifle Corps
DONOGHUE Charles MM Cpl 12018 Leicestershire Regt
DONOGHUE Daniel MM+Bar Pte S/10441 Rifle Brigade
DONOGHUE James MM Pte 17679 Devonshire Regt
DONOGHUE Jeremiah J. MM L/Cpl 3/5188 2nd Duke of Cornwall's LI
DONOGHUE John MM Sjt 7403 2nd Middlesex Regt
DONOGHUE John MM Pte 5/6753 Royal Munster Fusiliers
DONOGHUE John J. MM Gnr 21731 6 Siege Bty RGA
DONOGHUE Martin William MM Gnr Sig 68179 147 Siege Bty RGA
DONOGHUE Matthew MM L/Cpl 7608 2nd Leinster Regt KIA 20.11.17.
DONOGHUE Patrick MM L/Cpl T2/026004 Army Service Corps
DONOGHUE Peter MM Pte 20673 Machine Gun Corps
DONOHOE John MM Pte 11242 1st Royal Irish Fusiliers
DONOHOE Joseph MM Pte 17634 13th Northumberland Fusiliers KIA 16.6.17.
DONOHOE Patrick MM CSM 3056 1st Irish Guards KIA 30.3.18.
DONOHOE Thomas MM Gnr 43916 RGA
DONOHOE Thomas MM L/Sjt 3476 7th Leinster Regt DOW 8.2.17.
DONOHOE Thomas MM Pte 19582 Royal Dublin Fusiliers
DONOUGHUE Alfred MM Cpl 72525 Royal Fusiliers
DONOVAN Albert George MM Pte 20251 1st Somerset Light Infantry Died 1.11.18.
DONOVAN Andrew MM Pte 4455 2nd Leinster Regt
DONOVAN Arthur MM L/Cpl 7712 4th Middlesex Regt
DONOVAN George A. MM Sjt G/1422 7th Royal West Surrey Regt
DONOVAN George Henry MM+Bar Gnr 925060 A/280 & A/190 Bdes RFA
DONOVAN James MM Bdr 18158 35 Heavy Bty RGA Died 6.10.18.
DONOVAN James MM Gnr 83177 RFA
DONOVAN John MM Pte 9931 2nd Royal Munster Fusiliers
DONOVAN John MM+Bar Pte 14494 8th Royal Berkshire Regt
DONOVAN John MM Sjt 38577 32 Siege Bty RGA
DONOVAN John MM+Bar Sjt 203884 Lancashire Fusiliers
DONOVAN Michael MM L/Cpl 5328 Royal Irish Regt
DONOVAN Mike MM Cpl 1130 6th Royal West Kent Regt
DONOVAN Paul MM Pte A/203338 16th King's Royal Rifle Corps
DONOVAN Percival MM CSM 1293 21st London Regt
DONOVAN Stephen MM Pte 130641 46th Royal Fusiliers
DONOVAN William "MM,MID" Pte 19191 Welsh Regt
DONOVAN William MM Sjt 40238 Royal West Surrey Regt
DONSON H. MM Pte 16485 2nd Grenadier Guards
DOODNEY George H. MM Sjt 18901 Machine Gun Corps
DOODSON Albert E. MM Cpl 120648 'Q' Special Coy Royal Engineers
DOODY Charles MM Pte 242670 1/6th Royal Warwickshire Regt KIA 14.5.17.
DOODY Fred MM+Bar Pte 25510 9th Notts & Derby Regt
DOODY Frederick W.A. MM Sjt 113486 Royal Engineers
DOODY George MM Sjt 28803 Highland Light Infantry
DOODY Leonard MM Pte 39413 140 Fd Amb RAMC Died 24.3.18.
DOODY Patrick MM Pte 43076 1st Royal Dublin Fusiliers KIA 21.1.17.
DOODY William MM Pte 19037 1st Shropshire Light Infantry
DOOKS Harold MM Gnr 203773 B/123 Bde RFA
DOOKS Henry MM Pte 42474 2nd West Yorkshire Regt
DOOL James MM Cpl 7915 2nd Arg & Suth Highlanders
DOOLAN James MM+Bar Pte 2786 1st Irish Guards
DOOLAN Joseph MM Dvr 775451 C/310 Bde RFA
DOOLAN Michael MM Pte 4522 2nd Royal Irish Regt Died 26.4.17.
DOOLAN Paul MM Sjt 2867 1st Irish Guards
DOOLE Raymond E. MM Pte 19578 Royal West Kent Regt
DOOLE William MM CQMS T/21577 5 Div Train Army Service Corps
DOOLEY Edward Thomas   See 23712 Edward THOMAS.
DOOLEY James MM Dvr 68255 C/232 Bde RFA
DOOLEY John MM.MID Sjt 8/3601 8th Royal Munster Fusiliers
DOOLEY Joseph MM Sjt 15504 East Surrey Regt
DOOLEY Martin MM Pte 42204 RAMC
DOOLEY Michael MM Gnr 48129 262 Siege Bty RGA
DOOLEY Timothy MM Dvr 29198 84 Bty 11 Bde RFA
DOOLEY Valentine MM Cpl 36496 228 Coy Machine Gun Corps DOW 24.7.17.
DOOLEY Walter MM Pte 63981 13th Yorkshire Regt
DOONAN Fred J. MM L/Cpl 14594 Royal Inniskilling Fusiliers
DOONAN Thomas J. MM Pte 592051 18th London Regt
DOONER William MM+2 Bars Pte 22043 1st North Lancashire Regt
DOONEY Edward MM L/Cpl 8046 1st Irish Guards KIA 30.3.18.
DOORBAR Arthur MM Gnr 185713 C/223 Bde RFA
DOORIS William MM Cpl 25589 RFA
DOOTSON George MM Gnr 16073 C/23 Bde RFA
DOPSON Percy A. MM Gnr 43412 RFA
DOPSON Valentine T. MM Pte 203451 4th West Riding Regt
DORAN H. MM Air Mech 1 5720 Royal Flying Corps
DORAN James MM Dvr Sig 250427 14 Bde 401 Bty RHA
DORAN James MM+Bar Gnr 64961 33 Bde RFA
DORAN John MM Pte F/706 16th Middlesex Regt
DORAN John MM Cpl 79939 Royal Engineers
DORAN John H. MM Pte 240745 Border Regt
DORAN Michael MM Cpl 10919 1st King's Own Scottish Borderers
DORAN Patrick MM Cpl 19335 12th Liverpool Regt
DORAN Peter MM Pte 19792 Royal Inniskilling Fusiliers
DORAN Thomas MM Spr 420391 497 Fd Coy Royal Engineers
DORAN Thomas MM Pte S/4106 1st Royal Munster Fusiliers
DORAN Thomas A. MM Cpl 14981 8th East Lancashire Regt

DORAN William MM Cpl 960612 C/104 Bde RFA
DORAN William "DCM+Bar,MM" RSM 45028 139 Hy Bty RGA
DORAN William MM Sjt 4242 1/1st HAC(Inf)
DORE Arthur J. MM Sjt 3089 Royal Berkshire Regt
DORE J.G. MM Sjt 14547 2nd Grenadier Guards
DORE John MM Sjt 9282 1st Bn Machine Gun Corps
DORE Joseph MM Spr 65075 130 Fd Coy Royal Engineers
DORÉ Daniel MM Pte 45479 21st Bn Machine Gun Corps KIA 23.10.18.
DOREE Arthur "MM,MID" Sjt 188 11 Fd Coy Royal Engineers
DORGAN John W. MM Sjt 1251 1/7th Northumberland Fusiliers
DORLING Frederick Walter "MM,MSM,MID" Staff QMS S/19715 1 Div ASC HQ Army Service Corps
DORLING Victor MM Dvr 20117 D/162 Bde RFA
DORLING Walter S. MM Pte 23558 Norfolk Regt
DORMAN Alexander A. MM L/Cpl 11861 4th King's Royal Rifle Corps
DORMAN Christian C. MM Cpl R/183 King's Royal Rifle Corps
DORMAN Reginald P. MM L/Cpl 51196 MGC(Cavalry)
DORMAND Albert C. MM+Bar Cpl 550817 16th London Regt
DORMAND Ernest H. MM Pte 591815 18th London Regt
DORMER Charles R. MM L/Cpl 362914 5 Fd Svy Bn Royal Engineers
DORMER Fred MM L/Cpl 7471 2nd Oxf & Bucks Light Infantry
DORMER James MM L/Cpl S/26575 11th Rifle Brigade KIA 1.4.18.
DORNAN Charles MM Pte 7908 2nd Highland Light Infantry
DORNAN John MM Spr 155817 Royal Engineers
DORNAN Thomas MM L/Cpl 3/6795 2nd Gordon Highlanders DOW 3.4.17.
DORNION William J. MM Pte 5983 Seaforth Highlanders
DORR Frank MM Pte 17618 Northamptonshire Regt
DORR William E. "DCM,MM" 2nd Cpl 67149 126 Fd Coy Royal Engineers
DORRAN Thomas MM Sjt L/9756 RFA
DORRELL Francis James MM Sjt 50185 158 Coy Machine Gun Corps KIA 9.3.18.
DORRIL Leonard W. MM Pte 202033 Worcestershire Regt
DORRILL Albert Reginald "MM,MC(G)" Cpl 13883 7th Oxf & Bucks Light Infantry
DORRILL James MM L/Cpl 2160 1/9th London Regt
DORRINGTON David H.L. "MM(87288,12th Middx)+Bar" Pte 82866 2nd London Regt
DORRINGTON Ernest MM Pte 1665 1/1st Essex Yeomanry
DORRINGTON George MM Pte 813 5th Lancers
DORRINGTON Percival R. MM Pte 512080 3 Fd Amb RAMC
DORRINGTON Peter MM Pte 7689 11th Arg & Suth Highlanders
DORRINGTON Thomas MM Pte 354509 2/3(East Lancs)Fd Amb RAMC
DORRINGTON Thomas MM Sjt 17927 13th Gloucestershire Regt KIA 30.3.18.
DORROFIELD William George MM Cpl R/33836 13th King's Royal Rifle Corps DOW 4.11.18.
DORSETT Maurice MM Sjt 7948 2nd Oxf & Bucks Light Infantry
DORWARD William MM 2nd Cpl 88815 Royal Engineers
DOSSETT Halbert Edwin MM Pte 61649 23rd Royal Fusiliers DOW 1.9.18.
DOSWELL Frank MM Cpl 6652 2nd Royal West Surrey Regt
DOSWELL John MM Dvr 10729 B/148 Bde RFA
DOSWELL Thomas MM Cpl 33145 Border Regt
DOUBLE Charles A. MM Cpl 56324 RFA
DOUBLE Frederick William MM Gnr 58957 49 Siege Bty RGA
DOUBLE George W. MM Sjt 5999 2nd Suffolk Regt
DOUBLE Percy C. MM L/Cpl 13098 8th Royal Berkshire Regt
DOUBLEDAY John MM Pte 202411 2/6th Royal Warwickshire Regt KIA 24.10.18.
DOUCH Ernest J. MM Pte 512107 3 Fd Amb RAMC
DOUDS Harry MM Cpl 29958 11th Royal Scots DOW 4.10.18.
DOUDS James MM Cpl 241141 1/5th King's Own Scottish Borderers
DOUEL Edward Slowley MM Pte 235065 14th Royal Welsh Fusiliers
DOUGAL Joseph William MM Dvr 733 3(Northumbrian)Bde RFA
DOUGALL William MM Spr 397858 Royal Engineers
DOUGALL William MM Pte S/8612 1st Gordon Highlanders
DOUGAN David "DCM,MM+Bar" Sjt S/9966 5th Cameron Highlanders
DOUGAN J. MM Pte 372221 293 Army Emp Coy Labour Corps
DOUGAN Joseph MM Pte 7233 1st Royal Irish Fusiliers
DOUGAN Patrick MM Sjt 9498 Royal Irish Fusiliers
DOUGAN Robert MM Cpl 241271 1/5th Royal Scots Fusiliers
DOUGAN William MM Cpl 36722 11th Royal Scots

DOUGHERTY Edward MM Bdr 701260 RFA
DOUGHERTY George MM Sjt 1395 1st Gordon Highlanders
DOUGHERTY Henry MM 2nd Cpl 8876 21 Div Sig Coy Royal Engineers
DOUGHERTY James George MM L/Cpl 2744 2nd Royal Scots KIA 13.11.16.
DOUGHERTY John MM L/Cpl 14/410 2nd York & Lancaster Regt DOW 8.10.18.
DOUGHTY Alfred MM L/Cpl 12918 9th Yorkshire Regt
DOUGHTY Archibald G. MM L/Cpl 262926 8th Middlesex Regt
DOUGHTY Cecil R. MM L/Sjt 505236 18th London Regt
DOUGHTY Edward MM Pte 204978 4th Royal Welsh Fusiliers KIA 14.4.18.
DOUGHTY George E. MM Pte 14078 10th Scottish Rifles
DOUGHTY George R. MM Cpl 22998 Machine Gun Corps
DOUGHTY Horace MM L/Cpl 241470 1/5th Lincolnshire Regt
DOUGHTY James Clarence MM Pte 240958 Cheshire Regt
DOUGHTY John MM Cpl 149259 A/255 Bde RFA
DOUGHTY Lancelot W. MM Cpl 55194 33 Fd Amb RAMC
DOUGHTY Matthew MM Cpl 18893 11th Durham Light Infantry
DOUGHTY Robert MM Bdr 65263 'H' Bty RHA
DOUGHTY William MM Pte 23955 RAMC
DOUGHTY William MM Pte 332 20 Fd Amb. RAMC
DOUGHTY William T. MM Sjt 771787 A/251 Bde RFA
DOUGILL Thirkell MM Dvr 131639 235 Army Troops Coy Royal Engineers
DOUGLAS A. MM Pte 536439 RAMC
DOUGLAS A. MM L/Cpl 290360 Gordon Highlanders
DOUGLAS Alexander MM Sjt 40496 6th King's Own Scottish Borderers
DOUGLAS Alfred MM Pte 19668 2/4th Royal Berkshire Regt
DOUGLAS Alfred William MM Pte 1582 7th Royal West Surrey Regt DOW 3.9.16.
DOUGLAS Archibald Stair Montague MM Pte 68807 Att RFA RAMC
DOUGLAS Charles H. MM 2nd Cpl 91699 Royal Engineers
DOUGLAS Cyril MM Sjt 18143 B/119 Bde RFA
DOUGLAS Donald MM Pte 20264 9th Suffolk Regt
DOUGLAS Dugald MM Pte S/11222 5th Cameron Highlanders KIA 21.9.17.
DOUGLAS Duncan MM L/Sjt 13865 15th Highland Light Infantry KIA 19.4.17.
DOUGLAS Duncan MM Pte 14631 13th Royal Scots
DOUGLAS Edward MM Pte 48666 RAMC
DOUGLAS Ferdinand MM Pte 20408 Army Cyclist Corps
DOUGLAS Frederick William Charles "MM,CG(B)" Sjt 54077 15/17th West Yorkshire Regt
DOUGLAS George M. MM Pte 490293 1/13th London Regt
DOUGLAS George T. MM Cpl 200022 1/4th Oxf & Bucks Light Infantry
DOUGLAS H. MM Cpl 7743 East Yorkshire Regt
DOUGLAS Hugh MM Dvr 267573 457 Fd Coy Royal Engineers
DOUGLAS Hugh A. MM Sjt 446011 439 Fd Coy Royal Engineers
DOUGLAS J. MM Pte 290055 1st Northumberland Fusiliers
DOUGLAS James MM Pte S/26866 1/6th Seaforth Highlanders
DOUGLAS James MM Cpl 295625 12th Royal Scots Fusiliers
DOUGLAS James MM L/Cpl 26679 Machine Gun Corps
DOUGLAS James MM Sjt 8591 5th Cameron Highlanders KIA 18.7.18.
DOUGLAS James MM L/Cpl 14962 12th Highland Light Infantry
DOUGLAS James M. MM L/Cpl S/13133 Gordon Highlanders
DOUGLAS John MM Pte 4098 1/9th Highland Light Infantry KIA 27.5.17.
DOUGLAS John MM Dvr 750797 A/50 Bde RFA
DOUGLAS John MM Gnr 119241 RGA
DOUGLAS John R. MM Spr 154429 92 Fd Coy Royal Engineers
DOUGLAS John R. MM Pte 241402 8th Yorkshire Regt
DOUGLAS Joseph MM L/Cpl 23987 Machine Gun Corps
DOUGLAS Patrick MM Pte 2753 1st Royal Highlanders KIA 18.4.18.
DOUGLAS Peter MM Pte 425696 10th London Regt
DOUGLAS Peter James MM+Bar Cpl 9871 10th Royal West Kent Regt
DOUGLAS Pryce W. MM L/Cpl G/10734 Royal West Surrey Regt
DOUGLAS Richard MM Sjt 8521 6th Cameron Highlanders
DOUGLAS Robert MM Cpl 45612 8th Royal Berkshire Regt KIA 8.11.18.
DOUGLAS Robert MM Pte 11013 2nd Arg & Suth Highlanders KIA 20.9.18.
DOUGLAS Robert MM CSM 8889 1st Gordon Highlanders
DOUGLAS Stewart MM CSM 242273 8/10th Gordon Highlanders
DOUGLAS Thomas MM Pte 240253 5th Border Regt

DOUGLAS Thomas MM Sjt 308109 Lancashire Heavy Bty RGA
DOUGLAS Thomas H. MM Pte 330599 8th Royal Scots
DOUGLAS William MM Pte 19589 1st Cheshire Regt
DOUGLAS William MM Pte 75725 24th Royal Fusiliers
DOUGLAS William MM Pte S/21178 1/4th Gordon Highlanders
DOUGLAS William MM Gnr Sig 62370 112 Hy Bty RGA
DOUGLAS William MM Spr 414777 Royal Engineers
DOUGLAS William MM Gnr 120240 RFA
DOUGLAS William MM Sjt 2592 1/9th Highland Light Infantry
DOUGLAS William MM Gnr 159290 RFA
DOUGLAS William Henry MM Spr 139191 175 Tunnelling Coy Royal Engineers
DOUGLASS Edward J. MM L/Cpl 75054 12th Bn Tank Corps
DOUGLASS Edward R. MM Pnr 259599 Royal Engineers
DOULIN Ernest MM Pte 9684 2nd Oxf & Bucks Light Infantry
DOULT William Harry MM L/Cpl 1431 1/22nd London Regt
DOULTON Ernest James MM Sjt 30952 RAMC
DOURIS John MM Pte 21807 Seaforth Highlanders
DOUSE Charles MM Sjt 473010 RAMC
DOUSON Arthur MM Pte 28235 2/4th Hampshire Regt
DOUST Frank MM Sjt 23131 4 Div Sig Coy Royal Engineers
DOUST Leonard Arthur MM Dvr 156799 38 Div Ammn Col RFA
DOUST Leonard James MM Gnr 314266 Warwickshire Heavt Bty RGA
DOUTHART John MM L/Cpl 19137 1st Royal Inniskilling Fusiliers
DOUTHWAITE James W. MM Bdr 67521 RFA
DOUTHWAITE Thomas MM Sjt 251660 1/5th Manchester Regt
DOVASTON Samuel MM Spr 186814 Royal Engineers
DOVE Albert MM Pte 7889 GMGR
DOVE Bertie MM Pte 452721 11th London Regt
DOVE Edward MM L/Cpl 39615 1st Essex Regt
DOVE Ernest MM Cpl 29439 RGA
DOVE Frank Sydney MM Pte 91658 'E' Bn Tank Corps
DOVE Frederick A. MM Sjt 283288 4th London Regt
DOVE George Albert MM L/Cpl 2078 1/4th Yorkshire Regt
DOVE Jack MM L/Cpl 25451 12th East Surrey Regt
DOVE James MM Pte 71550 175 Coy Labour Corps
DOVE Joseph A. MM Pte 322834 6th London Regt
DOVE Sydney G. MM Bdr 58243 RGA
DOVE Thomas William MM Spr 98358 A/48 Bde RFA
DOVE William MM+Bar L/Cpl 9620 12th West Yorkshire Regt
DOVER Alexander MM Pte 332481 Highland Light Infantry
DOVER Daniel MM L/Cpl 22495 7/8th King's Own Scottish Borderers KIA 27.12.17.
DOVER Frederick W. MM Sjt 22998 RFA
DOVER George G. MM+Bar L/Sjt 40449 10th South Wales Borderers
DOVER Henry Charles MM Bdr 23481 A/95 Bde RFA
DOVER Herbert MM Pte 10/290 10th East Yorkshire Regt
DOVER John MM Pte 275380 3rd London Regt
DOVER Thomas MM Sjt 1336 1/7th Northumberland Fusiliers
DOVEY Arthur MM+2 Bars Sjt 4543 1st Essex Regt KIA 1.2.18.
DOVEY Frederick Arthur MM Spr 560530 2 Div Sig Coy Royal Engineers KIA 22.10.18.
DOVEY Richard MM L/Cpl 57278 32nd Bn Machine Gun Corps
DOVEY Thomas MM Mech S/Sjt 14782 Royal Engineers
DOW D. MM Sjt 5606 Royal Warwickshire Regt
DOW Frank Ernest MM Sjt S/2701 12th Rifle Brigade
DOW George C. MM Spr 418116 Royal Engineers
DOW Harold George MM Spr 70121 GHQ Sig Coy Royal Engineers
DOW Henry John MM Gnr 54362 Y/7 Med TM Bty RGA
DOW James MM Pte 49868 23rd Lancashire Fusiliers
DOW James T.W. MM Pte 34707 York & Lancaster Regt
DOW Lawrence MM Cpl 2357 1st Gordon Highlanders
DOW William MM Cpl 636409 C/256 Bde RFA
DOW William Y. "DCM,MM" Cpl 412653 409 Fd Coy Royal Engineers
DOWBEKIN Thomas MM Cpl 242139 North Lancashire Regt
DOWD James MM Sjt 7094 1st Lincolnshire Regt
DOWD Thomas MM Pte 5/14562 5th South Wales Borderers
DOWDALL John R.W. MM Pte 75682 Tank Corps
DOWDELL Charles A. MM Pte 11444 4th Middlesex Regt
DOWDELL Earl Sidney MM Sjt 118944 147 Siege Bty RGA
DOWDEN George E. MM Gnr 810721 RFA
DOWDING Walter MM Pnr 309735 Royal Engineers
DOWDING William MM Sjt 3/11639 11th Durham Light Infantry
DOWDS Daniel MM Sjt 16620 33rd Bn Machine Gun Corps
DOWE Jonathan MM Spr 285666 218 Fd Coy Royal Engineers
DOWE Percy A. MM Sjt 9452 Suffolk Regt
DOWELL Frederick R. MM Sjt 63101 RGA
DOWEN Albert MM L/Sjt S/1924 Rifle Brigade
DOWERS Frederick C. MM Gnr 25519 D/277 Bde RFA
DOWERS Thomas MM Spr 67742 Royal Engineers
DOWEY Edward MM Cpl 6143 D/251 Bde RFA
DOWEY Martin John MM Pte 241623 8th Yorkshire Regt
DOWIE J. MM Pte 44119 4th Hampshire Regt
DOWIE James MM Pte 7193 1/4th Yorkshire Light Infantry
DOWIE Joseph George MM Pte 19871 11th Northumberland Fusiliers KIA 12.6.16.
DOWIE Robert MM Pte S/13696 8th Royal Highlanders KIA 3.5.17.
DOWIE Robert MM Pte 16299 8th Yorkshire Regt
DOWIE William MM L/Cpl 39382 Royal Scots
DOWLAND Henry C. MM Pte 25554 1st Hampshire Regt
DOWLE Albert E. MM Spr 518541 468 Fd Coy Royal Engineers
DOWLE Frederick MM Cpl 231254 2nd London Regt
DOWLE John "DCM,MM+Bar" Sjt 18997 10th Gloucestershire Regt
DOWLER Sydney MM Bdr 8495 RFA
DOWLER W. MM Sjt 9 Royal Engineers
DOWLING Albert E. MM L/Cpl 6179 2nd Yorkshire Light Infantry
DOWLING Arthur MM Pte 76368 6th Durham Light Infantry
DOWLING Edward MM L/Cpl 10553 7th Leinster Regt KIA 31.7.17.
DOWLING J.T. MM Sjt 42211 48 Bty 36 Bde RFA
DOWLING James MM Sjt 38997 RGA
DOWLING James J. MM L/Cpl G/18438 11th Royal West Surrey Regt
DOWLING Richard "MM,MID" Sjt 3566 1 Fd Squadron Royal Engineers
DOWLING William Henry MM Air Mech 1 7748 Royal Flying Corps
DOWLMAN George William MM Sjt 134309 B/170 Bde RFA
DOWN Albert E. MM Pte 12038 2nd Hampshire Regt
DOWN Frederick MM Pte G/10447 10th Royal West Kent Regt KIA 15.9.16.
DOWN Frederick Henry MM Cpl 2220 2/3(South Midland)Fd Amb RAMC
DOWN Gilbert J. MM Pte 19281 Dorsetshire Regt
DOWN Harold E. MM+Bar Cpl 955321 RFA
DOWN Percy MM L/Bdr 184420 RFA
DOWN William Henry MM Pte 64406 213 Coy Machine Gun Corps
DOWNARD Augustus MM Cpl 20710 47th Bn Machine Gun Corps
DOWNEND Leonard MM Bdr 785900 RFA
DOWNER George MM Sjt 90151 41st Bn Machine Gun Corps
DOWNER George William Frederick Henry MM Sjt 39677 14 AA Sect(att) RHA att 14(AA)Section RGA
DOWNER Stephen MM Cpl 47345 94 Fd Coy Royal Engineers
DOWNER Thomas MM Spr 146033 70 Fd Coy Royal Engineers
DOWNER William H. MM+Bar Sjt 23398 C/107 Bde RFA
DOWNES Alfred MM Pte 42076 9th Royal Inniskilling Fusiliers
DOWNES Bert "MM,MSM" Bdr 865213 RFA
DOWNES David A. MM Pte 1260 1/17th London Regt
DOWNES Ernest MM Gnr 1057 MGC(Motors)
DOWNES Frank MM Sjt R/5985 King's Royal Rifle Corps
DOWNES George W. MM Cpl 325045 1/1st Cambridgeshire Regt
DOWNES Harry MM Pte 841 10th Lincolnshire Regt DOW 10.5.17.
DOWNES James MM Dvr 76398 RFA
DOWNES John E. MM L/Cpl 49295 Liverpool Regt
DOWNES Lawrence MM Cpl 48262 Rifle Brigade
DOWNES Thomas MM L/Cpl G1011 Royal West Surrey Regt
DOWNES Thomas MM Pnr 25746 6th Leicestershire Regt KIA 30.10.17.
DOWNES Thomas Herbert MM Cpl 17098 Machine Gun Corps
DOWNES Thomas J. MM Sjt 27310 Royal Engineers
DOWNES Thomas O. MM Pte 14619 5th Dorsetshire Regt
DOWNES William MM Pte 240705 6th North Staffordshire Regt
DOWNES William MM Pte 20848 2nd Grenadier Guards
DOWNES William MM 2nd Cpl 548494 510 Fd Coy Royal Engineers
DOWNES William S. MM Sjt 106088 Royal Engineers
DOWNEY Albert H. MM Pte 10052 8th Devonshire Regt
DOWNEY Arthur MM Pte 33888 1st Border Regt
DOWNEY Bertram MM Pte 44668 South Wales Borderers
DOWNEY James MM Sjt 58613 Machine Gun Corps
DOWNEY John MM Pte 19708 Northumberland Fusiliers
DOWNEY John MM Pte 4653 7th Royal Irish Rifles
DOWNEY John MM Pte 487 RAMC
DOWNEY John F. MM Pte 30618 Yorkshire Regt
DOWNEY Patrick MM 2nd Cpl 1096 1/2(North Midland)Fd Coy Royal Engineers KIA 17.9.16.
DOWNEY Richard MM Sjt 693 3rd Rifle Brigade
DOWNEY Robert MM Gnr 43988 68 Siege Bty RGA
DOWNEY Timothy MM L/Cpl 19325 Machine Gun Corps

DOWNEY William MM Pte 11699 2nd Royal Irish Regt
DOWNEY William MM Bdr 99864 RFA
DOWNIE Alexander MM Bdr 84585 RFA
DOWNIE Archibald MM L/Cpl S/16134 5th Cameron Highlanders
DOWNIE Daniel MM L/Cpl 3209 Machine Gun Corps
DOWNIE David MM Sjt 7674 1st Royal Scots Fusiliers DOW 11.4.17.
DOWNIE George MM Pte 34456 194 Coy Machine Gun Corps
DOWNIE James MM Sjt 375067 2nd Royal Scots
DOWNIE James W. MM Sjt 792 11th East Yorkshire Regt
DOWNIE James W. MM Sjt 13181 8th Border Regt
DOWNIE John Clements MM Pte 42637 8th Yorkshire Regt
DOWNIE Robert MM Cpl 305236 12th Bn Tank Corps
DOWNIE W. MM Sjt 275179 1/7th Arg & Suth Highlanders
DOWNIE William MM Cpl 171 A/161 Bde RFA
DOWNIE William Gibson MM Pte 7277 1st Scots Guards
DOWNING Albert MM Pte 24088 C Bn MGC(Heavy Branch)
DOWNING Alexander MM Pte 354 12th York & Lancaster Regt
DOWNING Frank H. MM Spr 140006 67 Fd Coy Royal Engineers
DOWNING Frederick E. MM Sjt 41906 Royal Engineers
DOWNING Frederick John MM Pte M2/116229 305 Coy Army Service Corps
DOWNING George H. MM Cpl 13050 1/4th Yorkshire Light Infantry
DOWNING George H. MM Dvr 810014 RFA
DOWNING Hubert MM Cpl 25123 1st Shropshire Light Infantry
DOWNING J.A. MM Pte 12258 4th Worcestershire Regt
DOWNING James T. MM Pte 3185 23rd Royal Fusiliers
DOWNING Joseph "MM,MID" Cpl 770 37 Siege Bty RGA
DOWNING Ralph MM Cpl 5108 1/5th North Staffordshire Regt
DOWNING W.T. "DCM,MM" Sjt 54977 A/282 Bde RFA
DOWNING William E. MM L/Bdr Sig 850523 215 Bde RFA
DOWNS Albert H. MM Pte 13948 10th West Yorkshire Regt
DOWNS Arthur H. MM Sjt 19588 Manchester Regt
DOWNS Charles MM Pte M2/055195 Army Service Corps
DOWNS Edward MM Pte 10019 1st East Kent Regt
DOWNS Fred "DCM,MM" Sjt 23743 55th Bn Machine Gun Corps DOW 26.6.18.
DOWNS G.H. MM Pte 351963 London Regt
DOWNS George MM Pte 11/715 11th East Yorkshire Regt KIA 23.4.18.
DOWNS George G. MM Pte 203436 4th York & Lancaster Regt
DOWNS Herbert MM Pte 43224 RAMC
DOWNS Herbert MM L/Cpl 6733 Machine Gun Corps
DOWNS Israel MM Pte 22507 15th Royal Welsh Fusiliers DOW 13.5.16.
DOWNS Joe MM Sjt 315313 23rd Cheshire Regt
DOWNS John MM Sjt G/21380 7th Royal West Kent Regt
DOWNS John Whittingham MM L/Cpl 2194 RAMC
DOWNS Robert MM+Bar Pte 240294 1/5th Leicestershire Regt
DOWNS Sam MM BSM L/39056 B/230 Bde RFA
DOWNS Samuel MM.MID CSM 3164 11th Royal Warwickshire Regt
DOWNS Thomas MM Sjt 5902 13th Manchester Regt
DOWNS Thomas C. MM L/Cpl 270047 1/1st Northumberland Yeo
DOWNS Walter MM Pte 18155 1st Grenadier Guards
DOWNS Walter MM Pte 275141 1/7th Manchester Regt
DOWNWARD Arthur J. MM+Bar Sjt 738018 24th London Regt
DOWNWARD Fred MM Pte 7938 Royal Fusiliers
DOWSE Edmund "MM,MSM" Sjt 11008 East Kent Regt
DOWSE Frederick G. MM Pte 32228 Gloucestershire Regt
DOWSE George MM Gnr 38746 Tank Corps
DOWSE James MM Pte 17996 Welsh Regt
DOWSETT Ernest Arthur MM L/Cpl A/200102 17th King's Royal Rifle Corps DOW 2.8.18.
DOWSETT George F. MM Sjt 12125 6th Duke of Cornwall's LI
DOWSETT Henry J. "MM,MID" Sjt 100511 33 Div Sig Coy Royal Engineers
DOWSETT Henry R. MM Pte 14832 5th Dorsetshire Regt
DOWSETT James MM Pte 69606 Tank Corps
DOWSETT John MM Pte 10610 HAC
DOWSETT William J. MM Sjt 680220 1/22nd London Regt
DOWSING Ernest MM Pte 645 6th Royal West Kent Regt
DOWSON Alfred E. MM L/Cpl 12858 Suffolk Regt
DOWSON Harry MM Pte 11994 9th West Yorkshire Regt
DOWSON Sydney MM Dvr 96083 RFA
DOWTHWAITE John Henry MM Cpl 27649 6th Border Regt
DOY Colin T. MM L/Cpl 22 VI Corps Cyclist Bn Army Cyclist Corps
DOY Ernest "DCM,MM+Bar" Pte 14971 8th Suffolk Regt
DOY William MM Pte 43693 11th Essex Regt
DOYDGE William MM Pte 201080 Gloucestershire Regt
DOYLE Albert MM Pte 9618 11th Leicestershire Regt

DOYLE Andrew MM Pte 18823 12th Highland Light Infantry KIA 25.4.17.
DOYLE Andrew MM Pte 3377 Machine Gun Corps
DOYLE Arthur John MM Pnr 549758 56 Div Sig Coy Royal Engineers
DOYLE Christopher MM Sjt 19412 Royal Dublin Fusiliers
DOYLE Finn MM Pte 4870 1/19th London Regt
DOYLE Francis "DCM,MM" Cpl 13845 10th North Lancashire Regt
DOYLE Francis W. MM Pte 1068 4th GMGR
DOYLE George MM Pte 8/4246 8th Royal Munster Fusiliers
DOYLE George P. MM Gnr 13570 RFA
DOYLE H. MM Pte 32872 2nd West Riding Regt
DOYLE Henry MM Gnr 100170 RFA
DOYLE Hugh MM Sjt 18506 Machine Gun Corps
DOYLE James MM Pte 30818 2nd Royal Dublin Fusiliers
DOYLE James MM L/Sjt 33148 11th Border Regt DOW 30.9.17.
DOYLE James MM Gnr 663022 RFA
DOYLE James MM Gnt 105314 RGA
DOYLE John MM Pte 3/3123 7th Yorkshire Light Infantry
DOYLE John MM BQMS 30924 RGA
DOYLE John MM Sjt 5921 Army Veterinary Corps
DOYLE John MM Sjt 342300 1/5th Gordon Highlanders
DOYLE John MM Cpl 230335 2nd London Regt
DOYLE Lawrence MM Pte 4434 7th Royal Irish Regt
DOYLE Martin "VC,MM" CSM 10864 1st Royal Munster Fusiliers
DOYLE Michael MM Gnr 49380 11 Bde RFA
DOYLE Michael MM Gnr 4240 D/250 Bde RFA
DOYLE Michael "MM,MSM" Pte 1748 18 Fd Amb RAMC Died 21.3.18.
DOYLE Michael MM Gnr 280718 RGA
DOYLE Michael MM Pte 16894 Royal Scots
DOYLE Michael MM Sjt 14346 8th North Lancashire Regt
DOYLE Nicholas MM Pte 9834 2nd East Lancashire Regt KIA 7.7.16.
DOYLE Patrick MM Pte 64888 7 Fd Amb RAMC
DOYLE Patrick MM Sjt 4/3459 7th Leinster Regt DOW 17.8.17.
DOYLE Patrick W. MM Pte 16298 8th East Lancashire Regt
DOYLE Peter MM+Bar L/Cpl 45288 88 Coy & 29th Bn Machine Gun Corps
DOYLE Peter Joseph MM Cpl 250071 Royal Engineers att 48 Heavy Artillery Group.
DOYLE Philip MM Pte 4998 1st Royal Dublin Fusiliers KIA 4.9.18.
DOYLE Robert C. MM Cpl 6927 HAC
DOYLE Thomas MM 2nd Cpl 458759 62 Div Sig Coy Royal Engineers
DOYLE Thomas MM Cpl 31346 1st Royal Dublin Fusiliers
DOYLE Walter MM Pte 242674 1/5th Royal Lancaster Regt
DOYLE William MM Gnr 84641 RFA
DOYLE William MM Pte 7558 1st Royal Inniskilling Fusiliers
DOYLE William MM+Bar L/Cpl 19551 13th Liverpool Regt
DRABBLE Albert MM Cpl 6980 16th Manchester Regt
DRABBLE Arthur M. MM+Bar Pte 31502 8th Lincolnshire Regt
DRABBLE Frank MM Cpl 240501 Notts & Derby Regt
DRABBLE Harold MM Pte 38968 South Staffordshire Regt
DRABBLE James MM Pte 6210 1st Royal Lancaster Regt
DRABBLE T. MM Pte 240951 Notts & Derby Regt
DRACUP Charlie MM Pte 300380 13th Bn Tank Corps
DRACUP John MM L/Sjt 2623 1/6th West Yorkshire Regt
DRAFFIN Alfred MM Pte 1704 3(Northumbrian)Fd Amb RAMC
DRAGE Arthur William MM L/Cpl 1210 1/8th Middlesex Regt KIA 26.9.18.
DRAGE Cyril Neal MM Pte 25149 6th Northamptonshire Regt
DRAGE Edgar J. MM Pte 8762 RAMC
DRAGE Ernest MM Pte 47893 2nd Notts & Derby Regt KIA 14.4.18.
DRAGE Frank MM Pte 2323 1/1st Cambridgeshire Regt
DRAGE Gilbert A.T. MM Bdr 4538 RFA
DRAGE Harry MM Sjt 18805 5th Yorkshire Light Infantry
DRAGE Oscar S. MM L/Bdr 102541 RGA
DRAGE Thomas Henry MM Cpl 328007 1/8th Lancashire Fusiliers KIA 27.9.18.
DRAGE Walter MM Sjt 56459 37 Div Sig Coy Royal Engineers
DRAGE William R. MM L/Cpl 17109 7th Northamptonshire Regt
DRAIN Joseph McK. MM Sjt 303265 1/8th Arg & Suth Highlanders
DRAKE Alan MM Spr 20153 54 Fd Coy Royal Engineers
DRAKE Alfred MM Gnr L/42101 D/290 Bde RFA
DRAKE Ben MM Pte 205420 5th West Riding Regt
DRAKE C. MM Pte 253472 London Regt
DRAKE Edgar MM Gnr 60141 28 Bde RFA
DRAKE Edward MM Sjt 61466 Royal Fusiliers
DRAKE Francis J. MM Cpl 47832 19th Welsh Regt

DRAKE Frederick W. MM CSM 38786 1st East Surrey Regt
DRAKE George MM L/Cpl 30168 17th Royal Sussex Regt
DRAKE George MM L/Sjt 15292 10th Essex Regt
DRAKE George MM Gnr 29918 D/178 Bde RFA AKA William George Whyatt.
DRAKE George MM Cpl 1726 2nd Manchester Regt
DRAKE Henry E. "DCM,MM" CSM 9963 7th Royal West Surrey Regt
DRAKE John R. MM Pte 1319 8th Royal West Kent Regt
DRAKE John William Mendelssohn MM Sjt 68535 122 Siege Bty RGA
DRAKE Joseph MM Dvr 785527 RFA
DRAKE Joseph W. MM Spr 238861 Royal Engineers
DRAKE Leonard MM Spr 105223 229 Fd Coy Royal Engineers
DRAKE Robert "MM,MSM,MID" Cpl 12988 9th West Riding Regt
DRAKE Robert S. MM Pte 125190 35th Bn Machine Gun Corps
DRAKE Roland "MM+Bar,MID" Bdr 26206 C/79 Bde RFA
DRAKE Sydney MM Pte 16678 8th West Riding Regt
DRAKE Thomas MM L/Cpl 10314 2nd Royal Dublin Fusiliers
DRAKE Thomas MM Sjt 10807 6th Dorsetshire Regt KIA 26.8.18.
DRAKE Thomas P. MM Pte 9728 1st Royal Lancaster Regt
DRAKE William George MM Pte 331275 1/8th Hampshire Regt
DRAKE William H. MM Pte 58951 1/5th West Yorkshire Regt
DRANE Stanley MM Pte M2/021560 Army Service Corps att 'T' Corps Sig Coy RE.
DRANSFIELD Allen MM Pte 20487 Manchester Regt
DRANSFIELD George MM Sjt 202990 9th West Riding Regt KIA 12.10.18.
DRANT Joseph MM L/Cpl 23552 Labour Corps
DRAPER Albert MM Pte 5299 8th East Kent Regt
DRAPER Albert E. MM Pte 204540 Worcestershire Regt
DRAPER Arthur MM Pte 50998 Liverpool Regt
DRAPER David A. MM Pte 33561 2nd Bedfordshire Regt
DRAPER Edward MM Pte 302691 11th Bn Royal Scots KIA 24.10.18.
DRAPER Ellis MM Pte 241470 1/5th North Lancashire Regt
DRAPER Ernest MM Sjt 16092 1 Div Sig Coy Royal Engineers
DRAPER Frank MM Pte 260141 1/8th Notts & Derby Regt
DRAPER Franklin N. MM L/Sjt 241596 1/5th West Riding Regt
DRAPER Frederick James MM L/Cpl 24232 8th Devonshire Regt
DRAPER Gilbert MM Dmr 202604 East Lancashire Regt
DRAPER Henry MM Dvr 102362 X/12 Med TM Bty RFA
DRAPER Henry Robert MM Sjt 12013 1st South Staffordshire Regt DOW 12.4.17.
DRAPER John H. MM L/Cpl 10976 8th Northumberland Fusiliers
DRAPER John H.W. MM Cpl 241394 12th East Surrey Regt
DRAPER M.R. MM Pte 81198 Att RGA RAMC
DRAPER Robert MM Pte 20164 6th Shropshire Light Infantry
DRAPER Sidney J. MM+Bar Pte 18411 Royal West Kent Regt
DRAPER Thomas William MM Pte 15110 6th Lincolnshire Regt
DRAPER Walter F. MM Cpl G/128056 11th Royal Fusiliers
DRAPER William H. MM L/Sjt 300153 7th Essex Regt
DRAPKIN Isidore Abraham MM Cpl 49739 32nd Royal Fusiliers
DRASDO Rudolph H. MM L/Cpl 266840 Royal Engineers
DRAWWATER William MM L/Cpl 11395 9th Royal Fusiliers
DRAY Alfred "DCM,MM" Sjt 606 17th Royal Fusiliers
DRAYCOTT Benjamin MM Pte 3730 2/8th West Yorkshire Regt KIA 7.4.17.
DRAYCOTT George MM L/Cpl 282422 62 Div Sig Coy Royal Engineers
DRAYCOTT George H. MM L/Sjt 29182 1st East Lancashire Regt
DRAYSON Samuel MM Pte 139292 Machine Gun Corps
DRAYTON Percy T. MM Sjt Farrier 88570 B/108 Bde RFA
DRAYTON William MM Pte 45104 5th Royal Berkshire Regt
DRENNEN Alexander MM Pte 324 1st Royal Highlanders
DRESS Frank MM Cpl 17743 2 Fd Amb RAMC
DRESSER Harold "MM+Bar,MMV(It)" L/Sjt 18609 8th Yorkshire Regt
DRESSER Harry Richard MM Pte 22159 2nd Middlesex Regt DOW 2.5.18.
DRESSER Leonard MM Pte 260275 Liverpool Regt
DRESSER Thomas Kennard MM Sjt 68296 20th Bn Machine Gun Corps
DREVER Colin McDonald "MM,MID" Sjt 10631 5th Cameron Highlanders
DREVER Fred Athol "MM,CG(B)" Pte 29556 2nd South Lancashire Regt
DREVER John William Cooper MM Pte 304423 13th Bn Tank Corps
DREW Albert E. MM Pte 1927 1/8th Worcestershire Regt
DREW Albert William MM Gnr 68013 9 Siege Bty RGA

DREW Edward George MM Pte 9323 1st Scots Guards
DREW Edward George MM Spr 61804 78 Fd Coy Royal Engineers
DREW Edward John "DCM,MM" Pte 9382 2nd East Yorkshire Regt
DREW Ernest MM L/Sjt 6550 205 Coy Machine Gun Corps KIA 11.10.17.
DREW Frank MM Pte 30326 1st Grenadier Guards
DREW George MM Pte 203140 9th Devonshire Regt KIA 8.10.17.
DREW George W. MM Bdr 111171 RFA
DREW Henry James MM Pte 201443 1/4th Gloucestershire Regt
DREW Henry James MM Pte 370747 2/8th London Regt DOW 6.1.18.
DREW John MM L/Cpl 10154 2nd Scottish Rifles
DREW John Shaw MM L/Cpl 1114 1/6th Royal Highlanders KIA 31.7.17.
DREW Robert MM Pte 6094 11th Northumberland Fusiliers
DREW Robert MM L/Cpl 43114 1st Lincolnshire Regt
DREW Thomas Albert MM Cpl 35202 RGA DOW 30.3.18.
DREW W. MM Pte 183822 37th Bn Machine Gun Corps
DREW William H. MM Pte 10813 1st Worcestershire Regt
DREW William Henry MM Pte 9440 1st Gloucestershire Regt KIA 9.9.16.
DREWE William MM CSM 630770 1/20th London Regt
DREWERY John MM Pte 40128 1st Northumberland Fusiliers
DREWERY John MM Pte 37570 Notts & Derby Regt
DREWETT Charles W. MM Spr 94299 1 Div Sig Coy Royal Engineers
DREWETT Edward J. MM Spr 506463 Royal Engineers
DREWETT Francis MM L/Cpl 19310 Royal Fusiliers
DREWETT J.J. MM Cpl 71588 25 Bde RFA
DREWETT Richard MM L/Cpl 5/18965 5th South Wales Borderers KIA 7.7.16.
DREWETT William R. MM CSM 1187 1/22nd London Regt
DREWEY Herbert W. MM L/Cpl G/1792 1/4th Royal Sussex Regt
DREWITT Percy MM L/Cpl 24247 139 Coy Machine Gun Corps
DREWRY Stanley MM Gnr 318961 1 Hy Bty RGA
DRIFFIELD Tom MM Sjt 71343 150 Coy Machine Gun Corps
DRING Arthur MM+Bar Cpl 201683 4th North Lancashire Regt
DRING George MM Pte 17691 9th Yorkshire Regt DOW 8.6.17
DRING Smith W. MM Cpl 60141 19th Bn Machine Gun Corps
DRINKALL Arnold MM Pte 40013 Lincolnshire Regt
DRINKWATER Arthur F. MM Pte 8944 RAMC
DRINKWATER George R. MM Pte 10723 Leinster Regt
DRINKWATER Harry MM Pte 3338 2nd Manchester Regt
DRINKWATER Harry MM L/Cpl 305360 1/8th Lancashire Fusiliers
DRINKWATER Harry MM Pte 281125 2/7th Lancashire Fusiliers DOW 25.3.18.
DRINKWATER Henry MM Bdr 44162 C/302 Bde RFA
DRINKWATER Jim MM Cpl 204390 12th East Surrey Regt
DRINKWATER Julian Henry MM Pte 14515 18th Hussars
DRINKWATER Percy MM Pte 11183 2nd Grenadier Guards Died 23.3.19.
DRINKWATER Thomas F. MM Pte 202694 Royal Berkshire Regt
DRISCOLL David T. MM L/Cpl G/2921 12th Middlesex Regt
DRISCOLL John MM Pte 230139 1/2nd London Regt
DRISCOLL Richard MM CSM 14061 1st Bedfordshire Regt
DRISCOLL Thomas MM Pte 7750 Irish Guards
DRIVER A. MM Gnr 2966 RFA
DRIVER Albert MM Sjt 68766 B/108 Bde RFA KIA 9.7.16.
DRIVER Charles MM Cpl 242097 2/5th Gloucestershire Regt KIA 7.4.17.
DRIVER Ernest MM Sjt 10622 1st King's Royal Rifle Corps
DRIVER Fred MM Sjt B/724 8th Rifle Brigade KIA 26.7.16.
DRIVER George MM Sjt 15696 1st Grenadier Guards
DRIVER George A. MM Sjt 16671 1st Coldstream Guards
DRIVER George H. MM Drummer 11297 2nd Worcestershire Regt
DRIVER Harry MM L/Cpl 267198 4th West Riding Regt
DRIVER Harry MM CQMS 46188 62nd Bn Machine Gun Corps
DRIVER Herbert W. MM Pte 14425 Suffolk Regt
DRIVER Hugh MM Gnr 71701 RGA
DRIVER John MM Cpl 70024 B/106 Bde RFA
DRIVER Joseph MM Pte 18905 East Yorkshire Regt
DRIVER Percy MM+Bar Pte 18950 Machine Gun Corps
DRIVER Robert MM CSM 200579 East Lancashire Regt
DRIVER Robert MM Sjt 17941 East Lancashire Regt
DRIVER Sharples Parkinson MM+Bar Pte 22134 6th King's Own Scottish Borderers KIA 3.5.17.
DRIVER Thomas MM Sjt 27012 11th Cheshire Regt
DRIVER William MM Pte 28971 1st Essex Regt
DRON Albert MM Pte 17307 Liverpool Regt
DRONFIELD Eric MM Pte 22120 Scottish Rifles

DRONFIELD Frank "DCM,MM" Sjt W/3350 505 Bty 65 Bde RFA
DRONFIELD Philiip MM L/Bdr L/5146 C/173 Bde RFA
DROUYN Frank T. MM(4094 7th R Irish Rif)+Bar Cpl 29970 2nd Hampshire Regt
DROY Horace D. MM Pte 245579 2nd London Regt
DRUGGITT William MM Sjt 6294 2nd Yorkshire Light Infantry KIA 14.4.17.
DRUMM Stephen J. MM Pte 421362 RAMC
DRUMMOND Alexander MM Cpl 266199 1/7th Royal Highlanders
DRUMMOND Alexander MM L/Cpl 12614 Scots Guards
DRUMMOND Andrew MM Spr 76306 F Corps Sig Coy Royal Engineers
DRUMMOND Charles H. MM CSM 293038 1/6th Royal Highlanders
DRUMMOND David MM L/Cpl 46045 91 Fd Amb RAMC
DRUMMOND Eric Russell MM Gnr 930787 A/291 Bde RFA
DRUMMOND George MM Pte 302808 1/9th Arg & Suth Highlanders
DRUMMOND Henry MM Pte 11968 10th Durham Light Infantry
DRUMMOND Hugh MM Cpl 295070 12th Royal Scots Fusiliers
DRUMMOND J. MM Pte 81510 4 Fd Amb RAMC
DRUMMOND John MM Pte 200844 1/5th Highland Light Infantry
DRUMMOND John MM Sjt 7834 2nd Scots Guards KIA 15.9.16.
DRUMMOND John R. MM Pte 139760 Machine Gun Corps
DRUMMOND Robert MM Pte 25917 Royal Scots
DRUMMOND Walter T. MM Pte 4445 9th Seaforth Highlanders
DRUMMOND William MM Pte M2/147714 Army Service Corps att RE.
DRUMMOND William MM Pte 307875 Liverpool Regt
DRUMMOND William James MM L/Cpl 16615 Scots Guards
DRURY Albert Edward MM CSM F/339 17th Middlesex Regt DOW 15.11.16.
DRURY Alfred MM L/Cpl 1523 Royal Sussex Regt
DRURY Alfred MM+Bar L/Cpl 2348 Royal Highlanders
DRURY Charles T. MM Pte M2/200306 Army Service Corps
DRURY Daniel H. MM Pte 84943 200th Bn Machine Gun Corps
DRURY Ernest MM L/Sjt 4577 Middlesex Regt
DRURY Ernest MM Sjt R/15465 1st King's Royal Rifle Corps KIA 17.2.17.
DRURY George MM Pte M2/055035 15 Div Train Army Service Corps
DRURY Gordon E. MM Drummer 1513 1/13th London Regt
DRURY Harry MM L/Bdr 83987 251 Siege Bty RGA
DRURY James E. MM Sjt 22731 Border Regt
DRURY Joe H. MM Gnr 311164 RGA
DRURY John MM Sjt 5640 1st Coldstream Guards
DRURY John MM Sjt 11820 2nd Notts & Derby Regt
DRURY John A. MM Pte 3540 24th Royal Fusiliers
DRURY John W. MM Pte 266664 6th Liverpool Regt
DRURY John William MM Pte 30474 8th Yorkshire Regt
DRURY Percy C. MM L/Bdr 194616 36 Bty 33 Bde RFA
DRURY Reginald C. MM L/Cpl 6322 Machine Gun Corps
DRURY Thomas MM Sjt 46586 35 Fd Amb RAMC
DRYBURGH Robert MM Pte 43011 1st Scottish Rifles
DRYDEN Andrew MM Pte 46482 'C' Bn Tank Corps
DRYDEN Edward MM Pte 21146 8th Yorkshire Regt
DRYDEN George MM L/Cpl 4497 Northumberland Fusiliers
DRYDEN John MM Pte 11069 6th Yorkshire Regt
DRYDEN John MM Dvr 7395 160 Bde RFA
DRYDEN Thomas MM Pte 22125 18th Highland Light Infantry KIA 22.3.18.
DRYSDALE Angus MM L/Cpl 10254 8/10th Gordon Highlanders
DRYSDALE David MM Pte 13180 Scots Guards
DRYSDALE J.D. MM Sjt 35419 268 Bty 366 Bde RFA
DRYSDALE James MM Pte 8213 2nd Highland Light Infantry
DRYSDALE Peter MM Sjt 267938 1/6th Royal Highlanders
DRYSDALE Thomas MM Pte S/23859 1/5th Arg & Suth Highlanders
DRYSDALE Ward MM L/Cpl 418552 Royal Engineers
DUBBER Charles MM Gnr 45811 RFA
DUCK George MM Pte 23077 6th Yorkshire Regt
DUCK Harry MM Sjt 2435 7th London Regt
DUCK Horace MM Cpl 423326 10th London Regt
DUCK Ralph L. MM Pte 511619 14th London Regt
DUCK Walter Knaggs MM Pte 100016 4th Royal Fusiliers Died 4.11.18.
DUCKENFIELD William MM+Bar Sjt 127580 56 Div Sig Coy Royal Engineers
DUCKER Allan MM Cpl 240765 Norfolk Regt
DUCKER Derrick MM Dvr T4/041244 Army Service Corps
DUCKER Reginald Harry Ernest MM Bugler 301180 1/5th London Regt
DUCKERING Thomas C. MM CSM 200999 5th Notts & Derby Regt

DUCKETT George MM Bdr 87357 RGA
DUCKETT James MM Spr 75988 19 Div Sig Coy Royal Engineers
DUCKETT John MM Pte 9011 2nd Royal Welsh Fusiliers
DUCKETT John MM 2nd Cpl 28565 Royal Engineers
DUCKETT William MM Sjt 41866 61 Fd Coy Royal Engineers
DUCKETT William H. MM Pte 50097 2nd Royal Scots Fusiliers
DUCKHAM Bernard MM Pte 35181 Machine Gun Corps
DUCKHOUSE John MM Cpl 26967 15th Notts & Derby Regt
DUCKMAN Henry William MM Pte 1073 1/22nd London Regt KIA 7.6.17.
DUCKWORTH Benjamin MM Pte 44882 Lincolnshire Regt
DUCKWORTH Frederick MM Cpl 9983 2nd Royal Lancaster Regt
DUCKWORTH George MM Sjt 7394 Machine Gun Corps
DUCKWORTH John MM Dvr 24635 150 Bde RFA
DUCKWORTH John MM Pte 40455 Liverpool Regt
DUCKWORTH John Roberts MM L/Cpl 67100 96 Fd Amb. RAMC
DUCKWORTH Lambert MM L/Bdr 181196 228 Siege Bty RGA Died 25.10.18.
DUCKWORTH Thomas MM L/Cpl 75053 12/13th Northumberland Fusiliers
DUCKWORTH Tom MM Pte M/336706 1015 Coy Army Service Corps
DUCKWORTH William MM Pte 241714 West Yorkshire Regt
DUDDELL Harry L. MM Pte 30054 3rd Grenadier Guards
DUDDRIDGE Louis MM L/Cpl 498212 Royal Engineers
DUDDRIDGE Samuel Mark MM Sjt W/341 13th Cheshire Regt KIA 7.8.17.
DUDDS James P. MM Pte 48656 RAMC
DUDDY Joseph MM Sjt 31760 169 Coy Machine Gun Corps
DUDDY Joseph Lewis MM L/Cpl 17551 2nd Grenadier Guards KIA 20.10.18.
DUDGEON Alexander A. MM+Bar Sjt 139414 252 Tunnelling Coy Royal Engineers
DUDGEON Alexander P. MM Pte 538188 6 Fd Amb RAMC
DUDGEON Edward C. "DCM,MM" Sjt 57808 36 Div Sig Coy Royal Engineers
DUDGEON Frank Earl MM+Bar Pte 204275 9th Norfolk Regt
DUDGEON William MM Cpl 11730 2nd Highland Light Infantry
DUDGEON William MM L/Cpl 332082 9th Highland Light Infantry DOW 21.11.18.
DUDLEY Albert MM Pte 8849 19 Fd Amb RAMC
DUDLEY Alfred William MM Sjt 8977 1st West Riding Regt
DUDLEY Ernest MM Sjt 1009 2nd Yorkshire Light Infantry
DUDLEY Frank MM L/Cpl 205421 6th Dorsetshire Regt
DUDLEY Frederick W. MM Pte 201478 1/6th Seaforth Highlanders
DUDLEY George MM L/Cpl 12118 9th North Staffordshire Regt
DUDLEY Sidney Smith MM SQMS 4957 5th Dragoon Guards
DUDLEY Walter W. MM Cpl 113958 100 Siege Bty RGA
DUDLEY William MM Pte B/203092 9th Rifle Brigade
DUDLEY William H. MM L/Cpl 20150 Middlesex Regt
DUDMAN Ernest MM L/Cpl 601 7th Royal Sussex Regt KIA 27.9.18.
DUDMAN George W. MM Sjt 3089 Royal Sussex Regt
DUERDEN Edward Francis MM Pte 241284 7th Liverpool Regt DOW 1.10.18.
DUERDEN Ernest MM Pte 14211 4th Coldstream Guards
DUERDEN Frederick MM Dvr 680915 B/286 Bde RFA
DUERDEN George MM Pte 65359 2nd Welsh Regt
DUERDEN George MM S/Sjt 17663 RAMC
DUERS Fergus MM L/Cpl 11/16412 11th Border Regt DOW 24.4.18.
DUFF Andrew MM Sjt 17143 1/7th Royal Highlanders
DUFF David MM Pte S/14312 1st Royal Highlanders
DUFF George MM Pte 8607 1st Cameron Highlanders
DUFF George MM Sjt 41516 Y/14 Med TM Bty RFA
DUFF Henry MM Pte 3210 Machine Gun Corps
DUFF Hugh MM Bdr 119690 RFA
DUFF John MM L/Cpl 3003 1st Irish Guards
DUFF William MM Pte S/8187 1/6th Seaforth Highlanders KIA 27.8.18.
DUFF William B. MM Cpl 75954 Imperial Sig Coy Royal Engineers
DUFF William George "MM,MID,MM(B)" Cpl L/5995 1st East Kent Regt DOW 6.12.7.
DUFFEE James Thomas MM Pte 15317 8th Royal Lancaster Regt
DUFFELL Albert MM Pte 5858 9th Lancers
DUFFELL Harry "DCM,MM" L/Cpl 18562 2nd Royal Irish Regt KIA 21.8.18.
DUFFELL Harry J. MM Pte 26307 Middlesex Regt
DUFFELL James MM Gnr 45471 41 Siege Bty RGA
DUFFETT Claude Joyce MM Sjt 250584 2/3rd London Regt
DUFFETT Frederick John MM Bdr 32717 RGA
DUFFETT John Frederick Bates MM Pte 493605 RAMC

DUFFEW Francis William Richard MM Pte 7819 3rd Dragoon Guards
DUFFEY James MM Gnr 44958 7 Div Ammn Col RFA
DUFFIE Patrick MM Pte 13248 1st Scottish Rifles
DUFFIE William MM Gnr 109392 RFA
DUFFIELD Gavin MM Cpl 8744 1st Royal Scots Fusiliers
DUFFIELD George W. MM Cpl 8970 1st Norfolk Regt
DUFFIELD Harry MM Pte 30152 Royal Inniskilling Fusiliers
DUFFIELD Richard MM Pte 24315 Grenadier Guards
DUFFILL Harold MM Sjt 47742 Royal Engineers
DUFFILL William Henry MM Pte 202603 Manchester Regt
DUFFIN Claude MM Cpl 203758 2/5th Lancashire Fusiliers DOW 8.9.18.
DUFFIN Norman MM Pte M2/049518 GHQ BEF Reserve MT Coy Army Service Corps
DUFFIN Robert MM+Bar Cpl 76167 2 Bde MGC(Heavy Branch)
DUFFIN William Harvey MM Sjt 42654 74 Fd Coy Royal Engineers
DUFFUS Charles MM+Bar Bdr 7801 D/88 Bde RFA KIA 21.3.18.
DUFFUS James S. MM Pte S/40109 2nd Gordon Highlanders
DUFFUS Norman W. MM Pte 242077 Gordon Highlanders
DUFFY Andrew "MM,MID" L/Cpl 20436 13th Northumberland Fusiliers
DUFFY Charles MM L/Cpl 4525 7th Royal Irish Rifles
DUFFY Charles MM Cpl 10318 2nd Scottish Rifles
DUFFY Edward MM Pte 3125 Royal Scots
DUFFY Edward MM Pte 335512 Royal Scots
DUFFY Edward MM Sjt 19515 13th Liverpool Regt
DUFFY Francis MM Pte 5/12566 5th Royal Inniskilling Fusiliers
DUFFY Francis J. MM L/Cpl 19039 13th Liverpool Regt
DUFFY George MM Cpl 463100 50 Div Sig Coy Royal Engineers
DUFFY Hugh MM Bdr 98417 306 Siege Bty RGA
DUFFY James MM Pte 21076 22nd Manchester Regt
DUFFY James MM Pte 2979 1st North Lancashire Regt
DUFFY James MM Gnr 44436 16 Siege Bty RGA
DUFFY James MM Sjt 2397 1/8th Liverpool Regt
DUFFY James H. MM Pte 17333 Machine Gun Corps
DUFFY John MM Sjt 20588 213 Siege Bty RGA
DUFFY John "MM,MID" 2nd Cpl 444058 42 Div Sig Coy Royal Engineers
DUFFY John "DCM,MM" L/Cpl 260109 1/5th Seaforth Highlanders
DUFFY John MM Sjt 6436 RFA
DUFFY John Albert MM L/Cpl 11959 8th Yorkshire Regt KIA 29.10.18.
DUFFY Joseph MM Cpl 357815 Att 113 Bde RFA Royal Engineers
DUFFY Joseph MM Pte 42548 Highland Light Infantry
DUFFY Lewis MM Pte 65183 5th Yorkshire Light Infantry
DUFFY Michael MM Spr 36587 Royal Engineers
DUFFY Owen MM Gnr L/11455 RFA
DUFFY Patrick MM Pte 27205 6th Royal Inniskilling Fusiliers
DUFFY Patrick MM Sjt 8778 2nd Royal Irish Rifles
DUFFY Peter MM Sjt 3/9369 10th West Yorkshire Regt DOW 6.7.16.
DUFFY Philip MM Sjt 29170 Highland Light Infantry
DUFFY Robert MM Pte 2694 Royal Highlanders
DUFFY Samuel Charles Rhodes MM Pte 1520 1/6th Liverpool Regt
DUFFY Thomas MM Pte 33355 1/5th Royal Warwickshire Regt
DUFFY Thomas MM CSM 2/6838 5th Connaught Rangers
DUFFY Thomas MM Bdr 751559 B/250 Bde RFA
DUFFY Thomas MM Pte 3/8875 8th Yorkshire Regt KIA 11.7.16.
DUFFY W.R. MM L/Cpl 26517 Gloucestershire Regt
DUFFY William MM L/Cpl 290309 1/7th Royal Highlanders KIA 31.7.17.
DUFFY William MM Sjt 7191 14th Royal Irish Rifles
DUFFY William J. MM Pte 4985 2nd Leinster Regt
DUFOUR Alexander MM L/Cpl 115186 4th Labour Bn Royal Engineers
DUFOUR William Edward MM Pte 44829 16th Royal Welsh Fusiliers
DUFTY Henry MM Sjt 202042 5th Gloucestershire Regt
DUGAN Charles MM L/Cpl 3/7169 Devonshire Regt
DUGAN Cyril MM Pte 20394 Hampshire Regt
DUGAN D. MM Pte 20142 Royal Inniskilling Fusiliers
DUGAN Frederick W. MM Gnr 645240 RFA
DUGAN Gordon Montague Pears MM Sjt 19112 15th Hampshire Regt
DUGAN Thomas MM Dvr 63467 RFA
DUGARD Joseph William MM Pte 241645 1/5th Lincolnshire Regt
DUGDALE Alfred J. MM Cpl 532291 490 Fd Coy Royal Engineers
DUGDALE Daniel MM L/Sjt 41581 1st West Yorkshire Regt
DUGDALE F. MM Pte 251196 Manchester Regt
DUGDALE Hartley MM Sjt 25807 9th Yorkshire Light Infantry
DUGDALE Herbert MM CQMS 11329 1 Fd Svy Bn Royal Engineers
DUGDALE James "DCM,MM" Sjt 21629 North Lancashire Regt
DUGDALE John MM L/Sjt 22/1191 22nd Northumberland Fusiliers KIA 5.6.17.
DUGDALE Richard MM L/Cpl 33981 18th Lancashire Fusiliers
DUGDALE Richard MM L/Cpl 10923 8th Border Regt
DUGDALE Robert MM Pte 63808 3(Highland)Fd Amb RAMC
DUGGAN Arthur Vincent MM+Bar Pte 4913 1/6th Northumberland Fusiliers
DUGGAN Edward MM Pte 4/7326 2nd Royal Munster Fusiliers
DUGGAN Herbert MM 2nd Cpl 86904 Royal Engineers
DUGGAN James MM L/Cpl 34156 1st Essex Regt
DUGGAN James MM Bdr 1490 3(Northumbrian)Bde RFA
DUGGAN John MM 2nd Cpl 56195 Royal Engineers
DUGGAN Michael MM Cpl 7221 109 Siege Bty RGA KIA 22.6.16.
DUGGAN Michael MM Sjt 895 D/150 Bde RFA
DUGGAN Thomas MM Pte 10629 1st East Lancashire Regt
DUGGIN Walter MM Pte 7824 9th Royal Fusiliers
DUGGIN William MM Sjt M/28895 1 Div Train Army Service Corps
DUGGINS Albert Henry "MM,MID" Sjt 830055 C/241 Bde RFA DOW 12.10.17.
DUGGINS Cyril James MM Cpl G/2611 8th Royal West Surrey Regt
DUGGINS Ernest MM Pte 53902 15/17th West Yorkshire Regt
DUGGLEBY Bernard MM Sjt 209 530 Fd Coy Royal Engineers
DUGMORE Henry MM Pte A/1598 King's Royal Rifle Corps
DUGUID Adam MM L/Cpl 200678 1/4th Gordon Highlanders
DUGUID Clarence Donald MM Sjt 1034 1/17th London Regt KIA 18.9.18.
DUGUID James MM Gnr L/21464 RFA
DUGUID John M. MM Pte 32654 12th Royal Scots Fusiliers
DUKE Charles MM Bdr 44905 38 Bde RFA
DUKE Charles H. MM Sjt 171654 Royal Engineers
DUKE Frederick R. MM Gnr 681733 70 Bty 34 Bde RFA
DUKE James MM Pte 32161 1/5th York & Lancaster Regt
DUKE James Henry Guy MM L/Sjt 145 13th Royal Sussex Regt
DUKE Larret MM L/Cpl 482442 Royal Engineers
DUKE Oriel St A. MM+Bar L/Cpl STK/1857 Royal Fusiliers
DUKE Ramsay MM Pte 444 17th Royal Fusiliers
DUKE Robert MM L/Cpl 8890 2nd Duke of Cornwall's LI
DUKE Thomas MM Dvr T/28880 5 Div Train Army Service Corps
DUKE Tom K. "DCM,MM" Bdr 86928 D/62 Bde RFA
DUKE Walter MM Pte 337317 RAMC
DUKE Walter J. MM Dvr 69050 C/104 Bde RFA
DUKE William MM Sjt 21355 C/46 Bde RFA
DUKE William H. MM L/Cpl 983 Royal Engineers
DUKES Alexander J. MM Sjt R/25195 King's Royal Rifle Corps
DULEY Arnold MM L/Cpl 17583 7th Somerset Light Infantry KIA 14.3.18.
DULEY James Francis "DCM,MM" Cpl 51306 364 Bty RFA DOW 5.10.17.
DULHANTY Frederick "DCM,MM" Cpl 280352 1/7th Lancashire Fusiliers
DULLAM Robert W. MM CSM 345491 16th Devonshire Regt
DULLEA John MM L/Cpl 49405 19 Div Sig Coy Royal Engineers Died 6.10.18.
DULLER Charles H. MM Pte 10502 4th Royal Fusiliers
DUMALINE Leslie W. MM Pte 40938 1st Norfolk Regt
DUMAYNE John A. MM Spr 546738 9 Fd Coy Royal Engineers
DUMBELL Alfred MM Pte 200272 South Lancashire Regt
DUMBELL Harold MM Cpl 93802 Royal Engineers
DUMBELL John C. MM Cpl 49157 Royal Engineers
DUMBELTON Harry George MM Pte G10/4553 8th East Surrey Regt KIA 12.10.17.
DUMBLING John R. MM Pte 64583 RAMC
DUMBRILL Charles Henry MM Pte S/25676 1st Rifle Brigade
DUMMER William C. MM 2nd Cpl 51929 Royal Engineers
DUMMETT Edward Charles MM Gnr 135559 X/24 Med TM Bty RFA Died 25.7.18.
DUMMIGAN William MM Pte 241249 Royal Scots Fusiliers
DUMPER Herbert MM L/Sjt 11053 11th Hampshire Regt
DUMSDAY Charles MM Pte 902 9 Fd Amb RAMC
DUNAWAY William H. MM Sjt 14163 Hampshire Regt
DUNBAR Anthony MM Pte 23/1404 11th Northumberland Fusiliers KIA 27.10.18.
DUNBAR James "MM,MID" Sjt 10084 1st Gordon Highlanders
DUNBAR John MM Sjt 265897 1/5th Seaforth Highlanders
DUNBAR Samuel MM Cpl 37736 Lancashire Fusiliers
DUNBAR William MM L/Cpl S/21459 Rifle Brigade
DUNBAR William MM Dvr T4/237100 51 Div Train Army Service Corps
DUNBAR William MM Spr 76736 'OO' Cable Section Royal Engineers

DUNBEBIN Walworth MM Pte 15795 10th Cheshire Regt
DUNCALF James MM Sjt 44076 12th North Staffordshire Regt
DUNCAN A. MM Sjt 27737 King's Own Scottish Borderers
DUNCAN Alexander MM L/Cpl 3165 6th Dragoon Guards
DUNCAN Alexander MM L/Cpl 3/5867 1st Gordon Highlanders
DUNCAN Andrew MM+Bar Pte S/2277 8/10th Gordon Highlanders
DUNCAN Arthur MM Pte 56102 55 Fd Amb RAMC
DUNCAN Charles MM Pte 240459 1st Royal Highlanders
DUNCAN Charles J. MM BQMS 18094 RGA
DUNCAN Daniel MM Pte 13876 2nd Royal Scots Died 19.4.17.
DUNCAN Douglas MM Sjt 8983 1st Scottish Rifles
DUNCAN Edward C. MM L/Cpl 240892 1/5th Seaforth Highlanders
DUNCAN Frank MM Pte 1709 9th Royal Highlanders
DUNCAN Frank Leitch MM Pte 48919 156 Coy Machine Gun Corps
DUNCAN Frederick "DCM,MM" Cpl 50726 75 Fd Coy Royal Engineers
DUNCAN G. MM Bdr 21511 RFA
DUNCAN George MM Pte 305238 1st Bn Tank Corps
DUNCAN George A. MM Pte 108447 11th Notts & Derby Regt
DUNCAN George T. MM Sjt 14899 31 Heavy Bty RGA
DUNCAN Harry MM Pte B/2421 Rifle Brigade
DUNCAN Henry MM Pte S/22644 10th Arg & Suth Highlanders
DUNCAN Henry G. MM RSM 62625 9th Yorkshire Light Infantry
DUNCAN Henry G. "DCM,MM" RSM 62625 9th Yorkshire Light Infantry
DUNCAN J. MM Pte 32130 Tank Corps
DUNCAN J. MM L/Bdr 23646 RFA
DUNCAN James MM Pte 5/12467 5th Royal Inniskilling Fusiliers
DUNCAN James MM L/Cpl 41455 Royal Scots Fusiliers
DUNCAN James MM Pte 201742 1/4th Gordon Highlanders
DUNCAN James MM L/Cpl 95079 Tank Corps
DUNCAN James MM Pte 10065 2nd Gordon Highlanders
DUNCAN James MM Sjt 78163 143 Siege Bty RGA DOW 23.9.18.
DUNCAN James MM Gnr 110605 RGA
DUNCAN James A. MM Cpl 11798 Royal Highlanders
DUNCAN James B. MM Pte S/27517 7th Seaforth Highlanders
DUNCAN John MM Pte 23031 9th Scottish Rifles
DUNCAN John MM Sjt 93106 12th Bn Tank Corps
DUNCAN John MM L/Cpl 3110 1/6th Gordon Highlanders
DUNCAN John MM Dvr 631076 RFA
DUNCAN John A. MM Sjt 200256 1/4th Royal Berkshire Regt
DUNCAN John A. MM Pte 31/56 Northumberland Fusiliers
DUNCAN John William MM Dvr 27511 C/52 Bde RFA KIA 11.8.18.
DUNCAN L. MM Bdr 2221 RGA
DUNCAN Neil MM Pte S/43411 1/4th Gordon Highlanders
DUNCAN Norman MM Pte 47372 MGC(Cavalry)
DUNCAN Peter MM L/Sjt 1053 1/6th Gordon Highlanders
DUNCAN Richard MM Pte 201007 4th Cheshire Regt
DUNCAN Robert MM Gnr 165635 B/70 Bde RFA
DUNCAN Robert MM Cpl 13243 6th Cameron Highlanders
DUNCAN Robert G. MM Cpl 73094 Notts & Derby Regt
DUNCAN Robert P. MM Dvr T1/SR/965 Army Service Corps att RAMC
DUNCAN T.H. MM Gnr 608379 RFA
DUNCAN Thomas MM Sjt 337701 RGA
DUNCAN Thomas MM Pte 7398 91 Coy Machine Gun Corps KIA 1.9.16.
DUNCAN William MM Pte 10029 5/6th Royal Scots
DUNCAN William MM Pte 330376 8th Royal Scots
DUNCAN William MM L/Cpl 265302 Royal Highlanders
DUNCAN William MM Sjt 16621 32nd Bn Machine Gun Corps
DUNCAN William MM Pte 1793 2nd Royal Highlanders
DUNCAN William MM Sjt 5775 1st Leicestershire Regt
DUNCAN William MM Sjt 48253 52nd Bn Machine Gun Corps
DUNCAN William A. MM+Bar L/Cpl 15395 2nd Scots Guards
DUNCAN William B. MM Pte 250330 Royal Scots
DUNCAN William B. MM Sjt 1576 Royal Highlanders
DUNCAN William O. MM L/Cpl T4/241810 Army Service Corps
DUNCAN William T.A. MM Pte S/24114 7th Seaforth Highlanders
DUNCANSON Alexander MM Cpl 275164 1/7th Arg & Suth Highlanders
DUNCANSON F. MM Pte S/12973 Royal Highlanders
DUNCANSON J. MM Pte 3563 16th Highland Light Infantry
DUNCANSON Robert MM Spr 50073 Royal Engineers
DUNCOMBE Alfred John William MM L/Cpl 33795 8th Bedfordshire Regt KIA 19.4.17.
DUNCOMBE L.G. MM Pte 26949 9th Essex Regt
DUNDAS Frederick MM Spr 21499 1 Fd Coy Royal Engineers
DUNDAS John J. MM+Bar Cpl 51286 2nd Royal Scots Fusiliers
DUNDERDALE William MM Sjt 49569 RAMC
DUNDON Patrick MM Pte 6712 Royal Munster Fusiliers
DUNDON William MM Cpl 30409 Royal Warwickshire Regt Died 3.11.18.
DUNFORD Arthur MM+Bar L/Bdr 25270 119 Hy Bty RGA
DUNFORD Ernest E. MM Pte 39129 Welsh Regt
DUNFORD Frank Aubrey MM Cpl 124934 286 Siege Bty RGA
DUNFORD Frederick "MM,MID" Spr 25416 12 Fd Coy Royal Engineers
DUNFORD Frederick J.L. MM Pte 32322 5th Devonshire Regt
DUNFORD John J. MM Sjt 11624 4th Liverpool Regt
DUNFORD Richard E. MM Dvr 150094 505 Bty 65 Bde RFA
DUNGEY Sidney Albert MM Sjt 42920 Machine Gun Corps
DUNGWORTH Charles H. MM Sjt 16847 9th York & Lancaster Regt
DUNGWORTH Colin MM Pte 201702 York & Lancaster Regt
DUNGWORTH L. MM Cpl 75106 1/1st Derbyshire Yeomanry
DUNGWORTH William MM Pte 35875 5th Yorkshire Light Infantry
DUNHAM Christopher George MM Spr 524578 105 Fd Coy Royal Engineers
DUNHAM Frank MM Cpl Sig 800669 D/230 Bde RFA
DUNHAM Henry William MM Sjt 23698 Royal Scots
DUNHAM James Kingston MM Gnr L/23989 D/170 Bde RFA
DUNHILL James Willie MM Pte 266793 1st West Yorkshire Regt
DUNHILL John Joseph Moore MM Pte 21927 8th York & Lancaster Regt
DUNK Albert MM L/Cpl 7648 2nd Royal Sussex Regt
DUNK Archibald E. MM Pte 8618 2nd Royal Sussex Regt
DUNK Arthur MM Sjt 478265 Royal Engineers
DUNK Herbert Walter MM Pte 2516 1/5th London Regt
DUNK John W.H. MM Pte 16755 Royal Sussex Regt
DUNKERLEY Fred MM Dvr 16809 C/23 Bde RFA
DUNKERLEY J. MM Sjt P/5265 Military Mounted Police
DUNKERTON John MM Bdr 32819 2 Div Ammn Col RFA
DUNKERTON William MM L/Cpl G/30949 17th Royal Sussex Regt
DUNKEY Benjamin MM L/Cpl 51874 MGC(Cavalry)
DUNKIN Edwin MM Pte 205604 1st Essex Regt
DUNKINSON George MM Pte 6495 9th Lancashire Fusiliers
DUNKINSON Joseph MM Dvr 12143 B/88 Bde RFA
DUNKLEY Albert E. MM Gnr 26443 RFA
DUNKLEY Arthur J. MM L/Cpl 522065 483 Fd Coy Royal Engineers
DUNKLEY Arthur W. MM Sjt 30437 1/1st Bedfordshire Yeomanry
DUNKLEY Frank MM Pte 10888 Royal Welsh Fusiliers
DUNKLEY Harry J. MM Pte 30895 1/1st Bedfordshire Yeomanry
DUNKLEY Horace MM Pte 205420 6th Royal West Surrey Regt
DUNKLEY Samuel MM Gnr 59915 118 Siege Bty RGA
DUNKLEY Scott W. MM L/Sjt 11126 2nd Oxf & Bucks Light Infantry
DUNKLEY Wilfred MM Cpl 20360 XV Corps Cyclist Bn Army Cyclist Corps
DUNKLEY William MM L/Cpl 201597 2/4th Oxf & Bucks Light Infantry
DUNKLING George MM L/Cpl S/28440 Rifle Brigade
DUNLAVY John MM Pte 3144 1/6th Northumberland Fusiliers KIA 23.3.18.
DUNLOP Archibald MM L/Cpl 295545 12th Royal Scots Fusiliers
DUNLOP Charles MM Cpl 53432 19th Bn Machine Gun Corps
DUNLOP David MM L/Cpl 5495 1st Royal Irish Rifles
DUNLOP David B. MM L/Cpl 41575 Gordon Highlanders
DUNLOP Duncan MM Pte S/14478 5th Cameron Highlanders
DUNLOP Edgar Arthur MM Bdr 123276 RFA
DUNLOP George MM Sjt M2/079623 Army Service Corps
DUNLOP George "MM,MSM,MID" Sjt 13311 15 Fd Amb RAMC
DUNLOP George MM Cpl 39953 2 Bde RFA
DUNLOP Hugh MM Sjt 295095 12th Royal Scots Fusiliers KIA 30.9.18.
DUNLOP James MM Pte 235126 1/6th Seaforth Highlanders
DUNLOP John MM Pte 12465 12th Middlesex Regt DOW 6.5.17.
DUNLOP John MM Pte 316420 RAMC
DUNLOP Ross Munn MM Pte S/31471 5th Cameron Highlanders
DUNLOP Stanley MM Pte M2/077515 Att 43 Fd Amb RAMC Army Service Corps KIA 24.3.18.
DUNLOP W. MM Sjt 43629 RFA
DUNLOP William MM Pte 28831 1st King's Own Scottish Borderers
DUNLOP William C. MM L/Sjt 350523 1/9th Royal Scots
DUNLOP William H. MM Sjt L/12326 RFA
DUNLOP William J. MM L/Bdr 352407 154 Hy Bty RGA
DUNMOW James MM Sjt 265038 1/9th Middlesex Regt
DUNMOW P.W. MM L/Bdr 70581 RFA
DUNMOW Sidney James MM L/Cpl 2389 1/17th London Regt
DUNN A. MM L/Sjt S/10439 Arg & Suth Highlanders
DUNN Albert MM Gnr 180930 RHA
DUNN Albert "MM,MSM" Cpl S/7253 2nd Royal Fusiliers

DUNN Albert MM+Bar Pte 74004 2nd Devonshire Regt
DUNN Alfred Edward MM Sjt 6658 RHA
DUNN Arthur MM+Bar Sjt 684282 22nd London Regt
DUNN Arthur Horace MM Pte 553 14th York & Lancaster Regt
DUNN Cecil F. MM Gnr 198749 B/251 Bde RFA
DUNN Charles MM CSM 9451 5/6th Royal Scots
DUNN Charles MM Cpl 241284 Gordon Highlanders
DUNN Clifford MM Sjt 751214 D/250 Bde RFA
DUNN David MM Pte 12737 15th Royal Irish Rifles
DUNN Edmund V. MM L/Cpl 40688 Northumberland Fusiliers
DUNN Edward MM Bdr 4384 RFA
DUNN Edward MM Pte 302099 Manchester Regt
DUNN Ernest William "MM,MID" Cpl 658 230 Bde RFA
DUNN F. "MM,MID" Bdr 10 RFA
DUNN Fred MM Pte 11840 6th Shropshire Light Infantry
DUNN Frederick MM L/Bdr 134572 C/87 Bde RFA
DUNN Frederick E. MM BQMS L/9030 B/150 Bde RFA
DUNN Frederick S. MM Pte M1/07473 Army Service Corps
DUNN George MM Sjt 33854 A/181 Bde RFA
DUNN George MM Sjt 13445 Royal Inniskilling Fusiliers KIA 9.10.17.
DUNN George MM Cpl 18057 Yorkshire Regt
DUNN George William MM Sjt 12138 3rd Grenadier Guards DOW 18.9.16.
DUNN Harry MM Spr 131450 59 Fd Coy Royal Engineers
DUNN Henry MM Pte 28132 Royal Dublin Fusiliers
DUNN Henry MM Spr 45148 Royal Engineers
DUNN Henry MM Pte 200979 1/5th North Staffordshire Regt KIA 20.5.18.
DUNN J. MM Air Mech 2 17942 Royal Flying Corps
DUNN James MM Pte 8087 11th Royal Warwickshire Regt
DUNN John MM Cpl 106524 Royal Engineers KIA 20.9.18.
DUNN John MM Cpl B/411 Rifle Brigade DOW 1.2.18.
DUNN John MM Sjt 11/891 11th East Yorkshire Regt
DUNN John Edward MM Pte 17143 2nd Notts & Derby Regt
DUNN John Edward MM Cpl 18488 8th East Lancashire Regt
DUNN John William MM L/Cpl 330526 15th Notts & Derby Regt
DUNN Joseph MM Pte R/14307 2nd King's Royal Rifle Corps DOW 11.3.17.
DUNN Leonard MM Sjt 44522 140 Coy Machine Gun Corps
DUNN Leonard MM CQMS 1035 1st Royal Highlanders
DUNN Lionel H.H. MM CQMS 569 1/3rd Monmouthshire Regt
DUNN M. MM L/Cpl 6452 Royal Warwickshire Regt
DUNN Michael MM L/Cpl 18109 11th Notts & Derby Regt
DUNN Patrick MM Pte 13258 Royal Irish Fusiliers
DUNN Peter MM Pte 382639 Labour Corps
DUNN Richard MM Sjt 16967 1st Bn Machine Gun Corps DOW 26.10.18.
DUNN Richard MM Spr 432059 Royal Engineers
DUNN Robert MM Pte 16006 12th Royal Scots
DUNN Robert MM+Bar Pte 4328 1/5th Gordon Highlanders
DUNN Robert J. MM Pte 8771 1st Royal Inniskilling Fusiliers
DUNN Samuel Leonard MM Sjt 18025 11th Cheshire Regt KIA 2.8.17.
DUNN Stanley E. MM Sjt 391889 9th London Regt
DUNN Thomas MM Spr 79776 185 Tunnelling Coy Royal Engineers
DUNN Thomas "DCM,MM" L/Cpl 10388 12th Royal Scots
DUNN Thomas MM Sjt 396 20th Northumberland Fusiliers
DUNN Thomas MM Pte 17401 6th Seaforth Highlanders DOW 31.8.18.
DUNN Thomas A.P. MM Cpl 136420 RGA
DUNN Thomas James Johnson MM+Bar Pte 12707 1st Royal West Surrey Regt KIA 13.4.18.
DUNN W. MM Bdr 490 C/285 Bde RFA
DUNN W. MM Pte 241007 5th Border Regt
DUNN W.A.H. MM Cpl 270227 10th East Kent Regt
DUNN William MM Sjt 72823 50th Bn Machine Gun Corps
DUNN William MM Pte 280958 2nd Lancashire Fusiliers
DUNN William MM Cpl 12734 15th Royal Irish Rifles
DUNN William MM L/Sjt S/5008 18 Ordnance Ammn Section Army Ordnance Corps
DUNN William MM Sjt 12832 2nd Worcestershire Regt KIA 31.10.16.
DUNN William MM Pte 8714 1st Liverpool Regt
DUNN William MM Pte 12319 9th North Staffordshire Regt
DUNN William MM Pte 34903 Royal Scots Fusiliers
DUNN William J. "DCM,MM" Sjt 700698 1/23rd London Regt
DUNNACHIE Robert John MM Sjt 121012 A/110 Bde RFA
DUNNE Daniel MM Pte 4488 1st Irish Guards
DUNNE George MM L/Cpl 41887 Middlesex Regt

DUNNE James "MM,MSM" Sjt 21125 55th Bn Machine Gun Corps
DUNNE John MM L/Cpl 4659 1st Irish Guards
DUNNE John MM Pte 21859 2nd Royal Dublin Fusiliers KIA 21.3.18.
DUNNE Patrick MM Spr 18919 Fifth Army Sig Coy Royal Engineers KIA 9.7.17.
DUNNE Robert MM CSM 7038 Royal Irish Fusiliers
DUNNE Thomas J. MM Pte 27468 Royal Inniskilling Fusiliers
DUNNETT John MM L/Cpl 15481 Royal West Surrey Regt
DUNNETT John MM Gnr 86958 151 Siege Bty RGA
DUNNETT Sinclair MM+Bar Cpl 42633 Highland Light Infantry
DUNNETT William Ernest MM Pte 92 1/9th London Regt
DUNNING Charles MM Cpl 5/18091 5th South Wales Borderers
DUNNING George MM CQMS 12011 16th Lancashire Fusiliers
DUNNING George MM Pte 12626 8th East Kent Regt
DUNNING Harnott R. MM Pte 57810 24th Royal Welsh Fusiliers
DUNNING John MM L/Cpl 103875 155 Fd Coy Royal Engineers
DUNNING Jonathan MM Cpl 23748 Durham Light Infantry
DUNNINGHAM John MM Pte 5979 9th Royal Sussex Regt
DUNPHY Edward MM Cpl 293128 1st Middlesex Regt KIA 24.10.18.
DUNSDON Ernest Y. MM Pte M2/149484 Army Service Corps
DUNSE James MM Pte 43010 Royal Scots
DUNSFORD Reginald MM L/Cpl 43752 Royal Inniskilling Fusiliers
DUNSFORD W.E.L. MM Pte 14045 12th Gloucestershire Regt
DUNSHEATH Nathaniel MM Pte 8307 2nd Arg & Suth Highlanders
DUNSIRE David MM Sjt 20140 Machine Gun Corps
DUNSMORE James A. MM Sjt 2116 10th Arg & Suth Highlanders
DUNSMORE James S. MM L/Cpl S/5548 Gordon Highlanders
DUNSTAN Edwin Charles Frank "MM,MID" Sjt 35147 RFA
DUNSTAN William Henry MM L/Cpl 132365 251 Tunnelling Coy Royal Engineers
DUNSTER Albert MM Sjt 45099 228 Coy Machine Gun Corps DOW 13.4.18.
DUNSTER Herbert MM Pte 1828 1/21st London Regt
DUNSTER Walter MM Sjt 1807 1/22nd London Regt
DUNSTONE Charles MM Pte 14990 2nd Scots Guards
DUNSTONE Edward James MM Sjt 470831 2/12th London Regt
DUNSTONE George H. MM(58261 RAMC)+Bar Spr 310230 Royal Engineers
DUNTON Frederick MM Pte 8572 2nd Bedfordshire Regt
DUNWELL Albert MM Pte 300135 2/7th Royal Warwickshire Regt
DUPREY Ernest MM Cpl 47486 13th Royal Inniskilling Fusiliers
DUPREY John MM L/Sjt 35 24th Northumberland Fusiliers
DURAND Robert MM Sjt 344306 RGA
DURANT Alfred MM Pte 370367 8th London Regt
DURANT William MM L/Cpl 7400 Coldstream Guards
DURBIN Frederick MM Sjt 14049 8th Shropshire Light Infantry
DURBIN Reginald E. MM Bdr 49013 U Bty RHA
DURBIN Robert H. MM Pte 9012 RAMC
DURBIN William Edward MM L/Cpl 16642 1st Border Regt KIA 15.10.18.
DURBRIDGE Alfred J. MM Spr 253806 Royal Engineers att RFA
DURBRIDGE W. MM Dvr 120790 RFA
DURBRIDGE William Edwin MM Cpl 738029 1/24th London Regt
DURDEN Albert W. MM Pte 9942 2nd Devonshire Regt
DURDEN Henry George Charles MM L/Cpl 274 6th Royal West Kent Regt
DURHAM Albert MM Pte 9560 2nd Bedfordshire Regt
DURHAM Edward Henry MM Sjt 48506 3 Bde RHA
DURHAM George MM Sjt 291351 Royal Highlanders
DURHAM Makin Bell MM Pte 35016 22nd Northumberland Fusiliers
DURHAM S. MM L/Sjt 2629 Rifle Brigade
DURHAM Thomas MM L/Cpl 14476 2nd South Lancashire Regt
DURHAM Walter MM Sjt 200345 1/4th Yorkshire Regt
DURHAM William MM Cpl 41004 MGC(Cavalry)
DURIE A. MM Cpl 12927 Royal Highlanders
DURKAN J. MM Sjt P1851 Military Foot Police
DURKIN John MM Pte 4944 2nd Irish Guards
DURKIN John T. MM Pte 60177 19th Royal Welsh Fusiliers
DURKING Jack MM Pte 67593 Royal West Surrey Regt
DURLING Joseph MM Pte 12715 7th Royal West Surrey Regt
DURLING William J. MM L/Cpl G/10276 9th Royal Sussex Regt
DURN Edgar MM Cpl M2/079270 Army Service Corps
DURNAN John Walter James MM L/Cpl 240372 1/5th York & Lancaster Regt
DURNELL Arthur MM Pte 23797 9th Gloucestershire Regt
DURNEN H. MM Cpl 53062 Guards Div Sig Coy Royal Engineers
DURNFORD Arthur Albert MM Gnr 10459 RFA
DURNFORD Philip S. MM 2nd Cpl 198198 5 Div Sig Coy Royal Engineers

DURNIN James MM Cpl 35143 RGA
DURNO William MM L/Cpl 408286 248 Fd Coy Royal Engineers
DURR Thomas Francis MM Sjt 26956 Royal Dublin Fusiliers
DURRAD William H. MM Pte 535544 15th London Regt
DURRAND Robert MM Pte 241857 Seaforth Highlanders
DURRANT Alfred Ernest MM L/Cpl 3338 1/4th Royal Sussex Regt KIA 4.9.18.
DURRANT Benjamin J. MM Pte 33255 4th Bn Machine Gun Corps
DURRANT Charles T. MM Cpl 6519 10th Royal West Surrey Regt
DURRANT Clements J. MM Gnr 111694 238 Siege Bty RGA
DURRANT Ernest MM Cpl 305404 1/8th West Yorkshire Regt KIA 28.7.18.
DURRANT Ernest G. MM Gnr 114022 RFA
DURRANT F. MM Sjt 130038 45th Royal Fusiliers
DURRANT Frederick Albert MM Dvr L/22301 RFA
DURRANT Frederick W. "MM,MSM" Sjt 34793 B/177 Bde RFA
DURRANT Henry MM Pte 29299 10th Essex Regt KIA 21.9.18.
DURRANT Herbert MM Cpl 19686 9th Bn Machine Gun Corps
DURRANT James W. MM+Bar L/Sjt 5/4453 King's Royal Rifle Corps
DURRANT Samuel MM L/Cpl 40103 Worcestershire Regt
DURRANT Sydney MM Pte 3943 1st Rifle Brigade
DURSLEY Joseph H. MM+Bar Spr 2640 48 Div Sig Coy Royal Engineers
DURSTON Frederick MM Sjt 7479 1st Somerset Light Infantry
DURSTON George MM Pte 265338 11th Somerset Light Infantry
DURSTON William J.C. MM Pte 23014 2nd Royal Fusiliers
DURWARD James MM Pnr 360623 35 Div Sig Coy Royal Engineers
DUTCH Joseph H. MM Pte 18792 8th Somerset Light Infantry
DUTFIELD Albert E. MM Sjt 115430 RGA
DUTFIELD George Robert MM+Bar Sjt 7362 2nd Scots Guards Died 18.3.19.
DUTHART Andrew MM Pte 302941 Royal Scots
DUTHIE Alexander MM Pte 2389 1/9th Highland Light Infantry DOW 15.10.18.
DUTHIE David MM Pte 11322 Scots Guards
DUTHIE Edward A. MM Sjt 201523 1/4th Gordon Highlanders
DUTHIE Frederick Watson MM Pnr 165585 47 Div Sig Coy Royal Engineers
DUTHIE Richard S. MM Sjt 240676 2nd Gordon Highlanders
DUTHOIT Edward MM Pte DM2/168792 Army Service Corps
DUTTON Albert MM Pte 60451 Royal Welsh Fusiliers
DUTTON Frank MM Sjt 41527 RAMC
DUTTON Frank W. MM L/Cpl 1438 1/5th Cheshire Regt
DUTTON Fred MM Sjt 14439 1/4th Cheshire Regt
DUTTON Frederick MM Pte 12770 1st Middlesex Regt
DUTTON George MM Pte 251489 Manchester Regt
DUTTON Harold MM Pte 241898 East Lancashire Regt
DUTTON Harry William MM+Bar Sjt 66354 100 Fd Amb RAMC
DUTTON Herbert MM Dvr 12562 89 Bde RFA Died 11.11.18.
DUTTON James MM Sjt 17423 33 Bde RFA
DUTTON Joe MM Cpl 266325 2/7th West Yorkshire Regt
DUTTON John A. MM Pte 415162 9th London Regt
DUTTON John F. MM Bdr 34581 RGA
DUTTON John W. MM Bdr 297226 156 Hy Bty RGA
DUTTON Joseph A. "MM,MID" Sjt 8591 2nd Royal Inniskilling Fusiliers
DUTTON Thomas W. MM L/Bdr 64717 A/112 Bde RFA
DUTTON Walter MM Dvr 430019 426 Fd Coy Royal Engineers
DUVAN F. MM Cpl 7863 15th Hampshire Regt
DUX Roy MM Sjt 14076 9th North Lancashire Regt KIA 10.4.18.
DUXBURY Andrew MM Cpl 15820 11th Manchester Regt
DUXBURY Arthur MM L/Sjt 201976 2/7th Lancashire Fusiliers DOW 23.3.18.
DUXBURY George H. MM Sjt 71659 162 Siege Bty RGA
DUXBURY Robert MM Pte 67479 1/5th Devonshire Regt
DUXBURY Thomas MM Gnr L/8580 RFA
DUXBURY Thomas MM L/Cpl 42691 Machine Gun Corps
DUXBURY William MM Sjt 710334 RFA
D'VAUSE Reginald MM Cpl 350682 7th London Regt
DWAN George C. MM Cpl 5805 Royal West Surrey Regt
DWAN Thomas MM Sjt 12060 East Surrey Regt
DWANE John MM Gnr Sig 80380 113 Siege Bty RGA
DWYER Bernard MM Pte 1061 2nd Irish Guards
DWYER E. MM BQMS 2921 RFA
DWYER John MM Pte 9060 2nd Royal Welsh Fusiliers
DWYER John MM Gnr 205612 Tank Corps
DWYER Joseph MM Pte 16917 6th Border Regt
DWYER Thomas "MM,MID" Sjt 6667 2nd Royal Irish Regt
DWYER Thomas MM Sjt 2117 1/4th South Lancashire Regt KIA 12.8.16.
DYALL Kenneth Arthur MM Pte 9026 2/1st HAC
DYAS John MM Cpl 9338 1st South Staffordshire Regt
DYBALL Herbert G. MM Sjt 201251 RFA
DYBALL Stanley J.C. MM Sjt CMT/3478 Army Service Corps
DYBELL Charles William MM Cpl 15263 11th Royal Sussex Regt
DYCHE Henry MM Pte 48696 Liverpool Regt
DYDE Percy Samuel MM L/Cpl S/23143 1st Rifle Brigade KIA 31.8.18.
DYE Albert MM Pte 142545 62nd Bn Machine Gun Corps
DYE Alfred MM L/Cpl 95125 13th Liverpool Regt
DYE Charles Frederick MM Gnr 24503 3 Siege Bty RGA
DYE Edward MM L/Cpl 1533 2nd Highland Light Infantry
DYE Harry John MM Pte 23043 Royal Welsh Fusiliers
DYE Henry T. MM L/Cpl 23254 Royal Engineers
DYE John C. MM Pte 240304 4th York & Lancaster Regt
DYE Robert MM Pte 267994 1/6th Royal Highlanders KIA 21.3.18.
DYE Sidney Fulcher MM Pte 28116 8th East Surrey Regt KIA 5.4.18.
DYE William MM Sjt 340019 RGA
DYE William J. MM 2nd Cpl 546391 Royal Engineers
DYER Albert Enos MM+2 Bars Sjt 48248 A/70 Bde RFA Died 17.2.19.
DYER Albert Henry MM CQMS 200469 4th Gloucestershire Regt
DYER Alfred MM Pte 26485 Gloucestershire Regt
DYER Arthur Reginald MM Gnr L/32215 D/175 Bde RFA
DYER Cecil R. MM C/Sjt 19112 8th Royal West Kent Regt
DYER David M. MM Pte 320270 1/15th London Regt
DYER Donald MM Pte 41307 6th Northamptonshire Regt
DYER Ernest W. MM CSM 10625 1st Hampshire Regt
DYER Frederick "MM,MID" Pte 14938 10th Hampshire Regt
DYER Frederick Alfred J. MM+Bar Cpl 60932 A/112 Bde RFA
DYER George MM Pte 33036 8th Leicestershire Regt
DYER George Henry MM L/Cpl 380930 1st Liverpool Regt KIA 29.9.18.
DYER Harold MM Gnr 213480 46 Bde RFA
DYER Harold Charles Ireland MM Sjt 8503 1st Scottish Rifles DOW 29.10.16.
DYER Henry S. MM 2nd Cpl 26716 3 Div Sig Coy Royal Engineers
DYER Herbert E. MM Sjt 15280 3 Fd Sqn Royal Engineers
DYER James MM Spr 58500 Royal Engineers
DYER James MM Sjt 36626 5th Bn Machine Gun Corps
DYER John MM Pte 17317 13th Durham Light Infantry
DYER John J. MM L/Cpl G/58869 10th Royal Fusiliers
DYER John T. MM L/Cpl 200507 1/4th Oxf & Bucks Light Infantry
DYER John T. MM Pte 38733 Manchester Regt
DYER John W. MM Pte 652374 21st London Regt
DYER Percy Thomas MM Sjt 660 1/5th London Regt
DYER Samuel MM+Bar Sjt 19477 4th Worcestershire Regt KIA 23.4.17.
DYER Samuel A. MM Cpl 390357 9th London Regt
DYER Sidney MM CSM 7025 11th Notts & Derby Regt
DYER Silas Daniel MM Pte 19882 1st Somerset Light Infantry
DYER Stanley A. MM Sjt 33680 RAMC
DYER Thomas Henry MM Sjt 55804 113 Railway Operating Coy Royal Engineers
DYER Thomas James MM Pte 17735 14th Welsh Regt KIA 22.10.16.
DYER W.J. MM Pte 27827 2nd Essex Regt
DYER Walter MM Spr 312591 Guards Div Sig Coy Royal Engineers
DYER Wilfred H. MM Sjt 40254 1 Tank Fd Coy Tank Corps
DYER William MM L/Cpl 200786 Shropshire Light Infantry
DYER William H. MM Pte 14787 7th Bedfordshire Regt
DYER William J. MM Pte DM2/207349 Army Service Corps
DYER William J.W. MM Gnr 66296 RGA
DYER William Joseph "MM,MSM" Cpl 4690 2nd Royal Welsh Fusiliers
DYKE Albert E. MM L/Cpl 265539 1/2nd Monmouthshire Regt
DYKE Frank George MM L/Sjt 5808 9th East Surrey Regt
DYKE John H. MM+Bar L/Cpl 137618 172 Tunnelling Coy Royal Engineers
DYKE William Thomas MM Sjt 9260 1st Shropshire Light Infantry
DYKE William W. MM Pte 34749 York & Lancaster Regt
DYKER Charles MM L/Cpl 40064 Gordon Highlanders
DYKER George MM L/Cpl 266470 2nd Gordon Highlanders KIA 26.10.17.
DYKES Abraham MM Sjt 14929 8th South Lancashire Regt
DYKES Arthur MM Cpl 33205 10th West Yorkshire Regt
DYKES Charles Peter MM Pte 50575 1st Cheshire Regt KIA 6.6.18.
DYKES Frank MM L/Cpl 40784 North Staffordshire Regt
DYKES Frederick C. "MM,MID" Sjt 1293 Yorkshire Regt

DYKES Harry MM Cpl 32891 1/6th Lancashire Fusiliers
DYKES Harry MM L/Cpl 19175 East Kent Regt
DYKES John W. MM Cpl 9502 RAMC
DYKES W.A. MM Pte 472329 London Regt
DYKES William "DCM,MM" Sjt 6063 2nd Dragoons
DYMENT Frederick MM Cpl L/42484 178 Bde HQ RFA
DYMOCK Frank MM Cpl 15091 10th North Lancashire Regt KIA 26.9.17.
DYMOCK George T. MM 2nd Cpl 94254 Royal Engineers
DYMOCK Mungo MM L/Cpl 350130 9th Royal Scots
DYMOND Albert G. MM Gnr 58722 RFA
DYMOND Percy Edward MM Spr 19888 Royal Engineers
DYMOND Robert MM Pte 15494 10th Royal Inniskilling Fusiliers
DYMOND William Henry MM Pte 457472 RAMC
DYNE H. MM Pte 8449 2nd Essex Regt
DYSON Alan MM Pte 8366 Northumberland Fusiliers
DYSON Albert MM Pte 14229 13th York & Lancaster Regt KIA 12.4.18.
DYSON Albert Edward MM Pte 17883 9th Yorkshire Regt
DYSON Arthur MM L/Cpl 22793 10th West Riding Regt KIA 17.10.17.
DYSON Ben S. MM Sjt 241704 5th West Riding Regt
DYSON Colin MM L/Sjt 856 Army Cyclist Corps
DYSON Frank MM Pte 23624 2/7th West Riding Regt
DYSON Frank MM L/Bdr 131302 41 Siege Bty RGA
DYSON Fred MM Sjt L/25742 B/168 Bde RFA
DYSON Harold MM Pte 307193 8th Lancashire Fusiliers
DYSON Harold MM Cpl 16799 2nd King's Own Scottish Borderers
DYSON Harry MM Pte 32123 8th York & Lancaster Regt
DYSON Henry Reuben MM Sjt R/518 9th King's Royal Rifle Corps
DYSON Herbert MM Sjt 18/261 18th West Yorkshire Regt KIA 1.7.16.
DYSON Jack MM Pte 47682 Notts & Derby Regt
DYSON James Beverley MM Pte 18221 18th Durham Light Infantry KIA 18.5.17.
DYSON John MM Pte 60690 14th Royal Welsh Fusiliers
DYSON Joseph MM Cpl 8464 1st Yorkshire Light Infantry
DYSON Joseph MM Gnr 70035 Y/1 Med TM Bty RFA KIA 31.10.16.
DYSON Julius MM Pte 305769 1/7th West Riding Regt
DYSON Norman MM Pte 19561 2nd Royal Scots Fusiliers
DYSON R. MM Pte 14937 7th Royal Lancaster Regt
DYSON Robert MM Sjt 36499 RAMC
DYSON Thomas MM Sjt 200180 Royal Warwickshire Regt
DYSON Walter MM Pte 28197 West Yorkshire Regt
DYSON William MM Sjt L/25516 A/152 Bde RFA
DYSON William MM Pte 30729 46 Fd Amb RAMC Died 30.5.17.
DYSON Willie MM Cpl 83393 63rd Bn Machine Gun Corps
DYSTER Charles MM Spr 63425 Royal Engineers

E

EABORN Harold J. MM L/Cpl 19208 1st Coldstream Guards
EACHUS Harry MM L/Cpl 305529 1/8th Lancashire Fusiliers
EACUPS Frederick Albert MM Pte 17938 Gloucestershire Regt
EAD Albert J.L. MM Pte 9267 HAC
EADE Arthur MM Pte 20308 Machine Gun Corps
EADE Edward MM+Bar Sjt 98191 156 Fd Coy Royal Engineers
EADE Frederick G. "MM,MID" Sjt 4931 3rd Rifle Brigade
EADE George MM L/Cpl 1777 3rd Rifle Brigade DOW 29.8.16.
EADE Henry MM 2nd Cpl 134023 152 Fd Coy Royal Engineers
EADE John MM Bdr 201834 RFA
EADE Sidney Percival MM Gnr 156395 268 Siege Bty RGA
EADE William MM Cpl 37412 'Q' Bty RHA
EADE William John MM Pte 1180 7th Royal Sussex Regt KIA 20.5.18.
EADES John "DCM,MM+Bar,MID" Sjt 13002 1st South Staffordshire Regt
EADES William D. MM L/Cpl 197249 Royal Engineers
EADIE J. MM Pte 13842 Scots Guards
EADIE James MM L/Cpl 201380 Highland Light Infantry
EADIE Jesse David MM Gnr 72597 D/88 Bde RFA
EADIE Joseph MM Pte 9993 2nd Welsh Regt
EADY Charles B. MM Pre 19924 Hampshire Regt
EADY Levi MM Cpl 15515 109 Heavy Bty RGA
EAGELTON Frederick W.G. MM Pte 393734 9th London Regt
EAGER Edward MM Sjt 9444 2nd Royal Irish Regt
EAGER James C. MM L/Cpl P/880 Military Mounted Police
EAGER Ward MM Sjt 129899 Special Brigade Royal Engineers

EAGIN Archibald Edgar MM Pte 53953 1/8th West Yorkshire Regt KIA 27.9.18.
EAGLAND Jack MM Pte 306146 West Riding Regt
EAGLE Edward MM Pte 202868 Worcestershire Regt
EAGLE Henry MM Sjt 19882 6th Dragoon Guards
EAGLE Herbert C. MM+Bar Sjt 10736 1st Worcestershire Regt
EAGLE James MM Cpl G/6608 11th Royal Fusiliers
EAGLE John MM Gnr 138917 RFA
EAGLE Oliver MM Bdr 80516 RFA
EAGLES Albert E. MM Pte 235667 1/1st Gloucestershire Yeomanry
EAGLESFIELD William James "MM,MSM" L/Cpl 1257 1/6th Liverpool Regt Died 15.11.18.
EAGLESHAM Allan MM Pte 2732 Yorkshire Regt
EAGLESHAM Frank MM Pte S/18303 5th Cameron Highlanders
EAGLESHAM Malcolm "MM+Bar,MID" CSM S/2626 8th Seaforth Highlanders
EAGLESHAM Todd MM Sjt 13403 10th Scottish Rifles KIA 28.3.18.
EAGLESON John MM L/Cpl 50087 9th Cheshire Regt
EAGLESTONE Alfred William MM Pte S/31675 13th Rifle Brigade
EAGLESTONE Arthur Elsden "MM,MSM" Spr 66109 19 Div Sig Coy Royal Engineers
EAGLETON Arthur John MM Pte 19393 8th Royal West Kent Regt DOW 22.1.18.
EAGLING Harry W. MM L/Cpl 241771 4th Yorkshire Light Infantry
EAGLING William E. MM Sjt 5269 2/1st HAC (Inf)
EAKERS Harry MM Pte 102063 Machine Gun Corps
EAKIN Wilfred MM Pte 27479 16th Notts & Derby Regt DOW 13.11.16.
EALES John H. "MM+Bar,MID" Sjt 41661 Royal Engineers
EALHAM Stuart G. MM Bdr 169454 C/174 Bde RFA
EALING Sydney MM+Bar Pte 9858 Seaforth Highlanders
EAMER Albert MM L/Cpl 31491 9th Devonshire Regt
EAMES Arthur L. MM Pte 33072 Border Regt
EAMES John J. MM Sjt 630957 20th London Regt
EAMES Sidney T. MM Sjt 17078 7th Shropshire Light Infantry
EAMES Walter MM Dvr 77124 RFA
EAMES William MM Cpl 34651 Royal Warwickshire Regt
EAMES William MM L/Cpl 14246 Royal Inniskilling Fusiliers
EARDLEY Alfred E. MM Cpl 27404 Machine Gun Corps
EAREY John W. MM Spr 550893 Royal Engineers
EAREY Walter MM Sjt 200660 1/4th Essex Regt
EARING Walter MM Pte 31175 1st Devonshire Regt DOW 23.10.18.
EARL Augustus James MM Cpl 84108 RFA
EARL Charles MM Pte 12466 7th Norfolk Regt
EARL Cyril MM Sjt 65938 RAMC
EARL Edward W. MM Pte 64319 108 Coy Labour Corps
EARL Frank Oliver MM Sjt 240858 Suffolk Regt
EARL Frederick MM L/Cpl 9822 1st East Kent Regt
EARL Frederick S. MM Pte 48049 11th Northumberland Fusiliers
EARL George MM+Bar Pte 635154 20th London Regt
EARL Henry J. MM L/Sjt 1664 2nd Royal Fusiliers
EARL Herbert A. MM Pte F/218 16th Middlesex Regt
EARL Herbert G. MM Cpl 15114 Royal Engineers
EARL John MM Pte 7034 Coldstream Guards
EARL John Douglas MM Pte 53653 164 Coy Machine Gun Corps
EARL Percy MM Sjt 845 RAMC
EARL Robert MM Cpl 201025 8th West Yorkshire Regt
EARL Robert MM L/Bdr 41408 RFA
EARL William MM Pte G/5836 13th Royal Fusiliers
EARL William MM Pte 200351 1/5th Highland Light Infantry
EARLE Douglas MM Pte 11604 13th King's Royal Rifle Corps
EARLE George A. MM Pte 78221 9th Notts & Derby Regt
EARLE James MM Cpl Z/333 2nd Rifle Brigade
EARLES Charles H. MM Dvr 770891 C/123 Bde RFA
EARLES Thomas MM Sjt 5934 61 Siege Bty RGA
EARLEY Frederick C. MM L/Cpl 356223 2nd Hampshire Regt
EARLEY John A. MM Pte 202433 2/4th Hampshire Regt
EARLEY William MM Pte 28180 East Yorkshire Regt
EARLY William J. MM Sjt 330253 Hampshire Regt
EARNSCLIFFE Victor A. "MM,MID" Sjt 240593 1/5th Seaforth Highlanders
EARNSHAW Fred MM Pte 43452 1/5th Royal Scots Fusiliers KIA 1.10.18.
EARNSHAW G. MM Pte 202226 Yorkshire Light Infantry
EARNSHAW Herbert MM Pte 8183 4 Fd Amb RAMC
EARNSHAW J. MM Cpl P2387 Military Foot Police
EARNSHAW Samuel "MM,MID" Bdr 43865 RGA
EARP Joseph James MM Cpl 54882 127 Bty 29 Bde RFA
EARP William F. MM Cpl 9616 2nd Royal Welsh Fusiliers
EARRIDGE Harold A. MM Sjt 9302 2nd Worcestershire Regt

EARWAKER William MM CQMS 11795 6th Dorsetshire Regt
EASBY Thomas L. MM L/Cpl 285174 1/1st Oxfordshire Yeomanry
EASDALE David MM Cpl 9050 Arg & Suth Highlanders
EASDALE Frank MM L/Cpl 1363 1st Royal Highlanders
EASDEN Herbert MM L/Cpl 8897 2nd Oxf & Bucks Light Infantry
EASEBY Norah MM Sister F QAIMNS
EASEY Thomas MM Pte 12611 9th Suffolk Regt
EASINGWOOD James H. MM Cpl 106963 Royal Engineers
EASON Charlie MM Pte 21425 1st West Yorkshire Regt
EASON Frederick Arthur MM Sjt 8092 Machine Gun Corps
EASON James Edward "MM,CG(F)" CSM 11041 3rd Grenadier Guards
EASON Richard MM+Bar Sjt 148 Royal Engineers
EASSOM William MM Pte 17477 6th Northamptonshire Regt
EAST Alfred MM Pte 48150 Royal Fusiliers
EAST Frank MM Dvr 134215 A/186 Bde RFA
EAST Frederick MM Dvr 69153 1 Div Ammn Col RFA
EAST Frederick J. MM Pte 240490 1/5th Suffolk Regt
EAST George T. MM Cpl Sig 45966 C/87 Bde RFA
EAST James MM Pte S/32160 Rifle Brigade
EAST John MM Sjt 12646 6th Oxf & Bucks Light Infantry
EAST John H. MM L/Cpl 1384 8th Royal West Kent Regt
EAST Oliver John "MM,MdH(F)" Sjt 1794 510 Fd Coy Royal Engineers
EAST Sidney W. MM Pte 9775 RAMC
EAST Victor V. MM Pte 17470 Oxf & Bucks Light Infantry
EAST William MM Staff SM 1st Cl T/13366 Army Service Corps
EASTBURN James A. MM L/Cpl 2715 West Yorkshire Regt
EASTER Charles E. MM L/Cpl 4919 19th Hussars
EASTER James MM Pte 18950 2nd Yorkshire Light Infantry
EASTER Percy C. MM Pte 132556 Machine Gun Corps
EASTER William M. MM Pte 203611 1st London Regt
EASTERBROOK George E. MM Pte 10452 1st East Lancashire Regt
EASTERBROOK Harold MM Pte 16938 1st Devonshire Regt
EASTERBROOK Henry MM Spr 107355 Royal Engineers
EASTERBY Miles T. MM L/Cpl 53869 10th Lancashire Fusiliers
EASTERLING John MM Cpl 62546 Royal Engineers
EASTES Arthur C. MM Spr 26177 3 Div Sig Coy Royal Engineers
EASTGATE Stanley MM Pte 22382 2/4th West Riding Regt
EASTHAM Frederick MM Sjt 34256 18th Lancashire Fusiliers DOW 17.4.18.
EASTHAM Frederick MM Pte 306054 Liverpool Regt
EASTHAM Richard MM Sjt 31667 44 Fd Amb RAMC KIA 19.8.16.
EASTHILL Cecil F. MM Cpl 590142 1/18th London Regt
EASTHOPE John MM Pte 114103 17th Liverpool Regt
EASTICK Arthur John MM Sjt 9889 13th King's Royal Rifle Corps
EASTICK Ernest Edgar MM Pte 235473 1st Northumberland Fusiliers KIA 23.8.18.
EASTMAN William MM Pte 8679 8th East Surrey Regt KIA 3.5.17.
EASTMENT Christopher MM Pte S/4772 13th Rifle Brigade
EASTMENT Henry J. MM Sjt 44201 RGA
EASTO Eric C. MM Pte 69315 2nd London Regt
EASTON Albert MM Pte 9977 10th Royal West Surrey Regt
EASTON Alexander MM L/Cpl 242305 Gordon Highlanders
EASTON Charles MM L/Sjt 240121 Gordon Highlanders
EASTON Edgar F. MM L/Cpl 242786 10th Royal West Surrey Regt
EASTON Frederick MM Spr 136336 179 Tunnelling Coy Royal Engineers
EASTON G. MM Sjt 10932 2nd Highland Light Infantry
EASTON George T. MM L/Cpl 406109 Royal Engineers
EASTON Henry MM Pte 20866 IX Corps Cyclist Bn Army Cyclist Corps
EASTON Joseph MM Pte 21/998 Northumberland Fusiliers
EASTON Leonard G. MM Sjt 265812 1/1st Hertfordshire Regt
EASTON Leonard John MM L/Cpl 17661 1st Coldstream Guards
EASTON Raymond MM Cpl M2/045637 Army Service Corps
EASTON Robert MM L/Cpl 23742 8th Worcestershire Regt
EASTON Smith MM Pte 241094 Royal Highlanders
EASTON Thomas Isaac MM Cpl 100939 67 Fd Coy Royal Engineers
EASTON William K. MM Pte 22765 11th Royal Scots
EASTTY Charles MM 2nd Cpl 85864 Royal Engineers
EASTWOOD Albert MM+Bar Cpl 7672 15th Lancashire Fusiliers KIA 30.9.18.
EASTWOOD Albert MM Cpl 350303 1/9th Manchester Regt
EASTWOOD Charles MM L/Cpl 16515 128 Coy Machine Gun Corps
EASTWOOD Frank MM Pte 2277 1/5th Leicestershire Regt KIA 27.12.17.
EASTWOOD Frank A. MM 2nd Cpl 95484 Royal Engineers
EASTWOOD Fred MM Sjt 346456 40 Coy Labour Corps
EASTWOOD Frederick MM Cpl 300991 7th Manchester Regt
EASTWOOD George Harry MM Pte 28341 6th York & Lancaster Regt KIA 1.10.18.
EASTWOOD Harry Ross MM Sjt 240719 2/5th West Riding Regt KIA 25.8.18.
EASTWOOD Herbert James "MM,CG(F)" Pte 31875 12th Hampshire Regt
EASTWOOD James MM Pte 22283 Lancashire Fusiliers
EASTWOOD Joseph "MM,MID" Cpl 11635 1st Liverpool Regt
EASTWOOD Mark MM Gnr 221318 B/330 Bde RFA
EASTWOOD Robert MM Pte 32584 7th Royal Lancaster Regt
EASTWOOD Thomas MM Spr 522202 Royal Engineers
EASTWOOD Thomas MM Bdr 1258 RFA
EASTWOOD William MM Pte 30600 East Lancashire Regt
EASTWOOD William J. MM L/Cpl 681047 1/22nd London Regt
EASY A. MM Pte 23871 Suffolk Regt
EATHERBY H. MM Pte DM2/166071 Army Service Corps
EATHERINGTON Arthur MM Dvr 13794 1 Div Ammn Col RFA
EATOCK James MM CQMS 358 1/5th North Lancashire Regt KIA 30.11.17.
EATON A. MM Cpl 1797 York & Lancaster Regt
EATON Alfred E. MM Dvr 164997 RFA
EATON David A. MM Sjt 53008 48th Bn Machine Gun Corps
EATON Edward MM Sjt 305527 8th Bn Tank Corps
EATON Frank MM Pte 10998 Royal Sussex Regt
EATON G. MM Pte 129120 45th Royal Fusiliers
EATON George Thomas "MM,MM(F)" Sjt 33387 78 Coy Machine Gun Corps
EATON Harry MM L/Cpl 201755 1/5th North Staffordshire Regt KIA 12.6.17.
EATON Herbert MM Pte 350877 Manchester Regt
EATON Jack MM Sjt 27545 31st Bn Machine Gun Corps
EATON James A. MM Cpl 6511 1st Notts & Derby Regt
EATON John "DCM,MM" Sjt 43162 12th Royal Irish Rifles
EATON John MM Cpl 43162 Royal Irish Rifles
EATON John D. MM Sjt WR/252810 295 Rly Const Coy Royal Engineers
EATON Joseph H. MM Pte 166204 1st Bn Machine Gun Corps
EATON Leonard MM Gnr 4637 RFA
EATON Percy MM Pte 1921 2nd Royal Munster Fusiliers DOW 8.11.18.
EATON Robert Charles George MM Gnr 955376 B/236 Bde RFA
EATON Thomas MM Pte 23290 15th Royal Warwickshire Regt
EATON Walter MM Pte 43037 1st Worcestershire Regt
EATON William Bert MM Pte 46259 23rd Northumberland Fusiliers KIA 24.8.18.
EATOUGH Andrew MM Bdr 66715 2 Div Ammn Col RGA KIA 28.8.18.
EATOUGH James MM Pte 8087 1st East Lancashire Regt
EATOUGH John MM Pte 2401 2/5th Lancashire Fusiliers KIA 9.7.17.
EATWELL George James "MM,MMV(It)" Cpl 11243 6th Royal Berkshire Regt
EATWELL Sydney MM Pte 15163 10th Yorkshire Light Infantry KIA 1.7.16.
EAVES Arthur MM Spr 432041 55 Div Sig Coy Royal Engineers
EAVES George A. MM Pte 18748 Hampshire Regt
EAVES Thomas MM Sjt 3/9686 12th Suffolk Regt KIA 12.10.17.
EAVES William Albert MM Sjt M2/055172 272 MT Coy Army Service Corps
EAYRS Warren MM Pte 109988 184 Coy Labour Corps
EBBATSON Amos MM+Bar Cpl 482176 62 Div Sig Coy Royal Engineers
EBBETTS Roland F. MM Cpl 776 1/5th London Regt
EBBITT Joseph MM Sjt 15797 2nd Royal Dublin Fusiliers KIA 28.3.18.
EBBS John William MM Pte 203254 2/5th Royal Warwickshire Regt
EBBS William MM Pte 373116 8th London Regt
EBDON John C. MM Pte 57072 Welsh Regt
EBLING Jim B. MM Sjt 57326 16th Manchester Regt
EBSWORTH Alfred Fielding MM Cpl 75348 3rd Bn Tank Corps
ECCLES George MM Pte 21214 13th Yorkshire Regt
ECCLES Harry MM Sjt 14315 7/8th King's Own Scottish Borderers KIA 9.4.17.
ECCLES Henry MM Cpl 5247 10th Lancashire Fusiliers
ECCLES Herbert MM Cpl 313098 RGA
ECCLES Isaac J. MM Sjt 1452 1/1st Westmorland & Cumberland Yeomanry

ECCLES James C. MM Pte 352353 Manchester Regt
ECCLES John MM L/Cpl 6795 12th Middlesex Regt KIA 3.5.17.
ECCLES John MM Pte 228323 4th London Regt
ECCLES John MM L/Cpl 9206 15th Royal Irish Rifles
ECCLES John MM Gnr 17317 1 Siege Bty RGA
ECCLES John T. MM Spr 47862 Royal Engineers
ECCLES Josiah MM Bdr 58813 RGA
ECCLES Percy MM Bdr 61421 352 Siege Bty RGA
ECCLES Thomas MM Pte M2/155957 Army Service Corps
ECCLES Thomas MM Pte 23324 West Yorkshire Regt
ECCLES Tom MM L/Cpl 241351 1/4th Royal Lancaster Regt DOW 26.6.18.
ECCLES William "DCM,MM+Bar,MID" L/Sjt 12137 1st Coldstream Guards
ECCLESHALL Charles MM L/Sjt 15574 2nd Grenadier Guards
ECCLESHELL Charles W. MM Pte 97110 11th Bn Tank Corps
ECCLESTON Joseph MM Pte 29051 18th Lancashire Fusiliers
ECCLESTON Thomas Frederick MM Gnr 2337 B/242 Bde RFA Died 17.11.18.
ECKERS Stanley MM Cpl 977 10th Hussars
ECKERSLEY Charles MM Pte 58375 17th Liverpool Regt
ECKERSLEY Harry MM Sjt 200038 South Lancashire Regt
ECKERSLEY James "MC,MM(240418 Sjt 2/5th Bn)" 2Lt 2/4th North Lancashire Regt
ECKERSLEY Walter MM Sjt 204724 25th Liverpool Regt
ECKERSLEY William Henry MM L/Cpl 10976 7th Yorkshire Light Infantry KIA 2.4.18.
ECKETT Elizabeth Jane MM Staff Nurse F TFNS
ECKETT George MM Pte 560 6th Royal West Kent Regt
ECKLES Charles William MM Pte 241056 1/5th Lincolnshire Regt
ECKLEY Harry S. MM Spr 198148 Royal Engineers
ECKMAN Frederick R. MM Pte S/9482 13th Rifle Brigade
ECOB Edward MM Pte 58115 9th Cheshire Regt Died 7.11.18.
ECOTT Herbert E. MM Pte 323302 18th London Regt
EDBROOK Alfred C. MM Pte A/205482 13th King's Royal Rifle Corps
EDDEN Alexander G. MM SSM 110505 MGC(Cavalry)
EDDEVANE Harold MM Pte 55835 Northumberland Fusiliers
EDDIE Charles G. MM L/Cpl 3490 Gordon Highlanders
EDDIE John MM Gnr 91184 275 Siege Bty RGA
EDDINGTON George W. MM Sjt 958 Royal Flying Corps
EDDINGTON Harry MM Trumpeter 881 4(West Riding)Bty RFA
EDDLESTON Joseph MM Sjt 22410 South Lancashire Regt
EDDLESTON William MM Pte 16910 2nd Manchester Regt DOW 4.11.18.
EDDOLLS Edward R. MM L/Cpl 2428 1/6th Gloucestershire Regt
EDDOLLS William A. MM Cpl 265972 1/6th Gloucestershire Regt KIA 9.10.17.
EDDOWES Harry MM Pte 18031 12th Highland Light Infantry
EDDY Cyril J. MM Spr 86857 Royal Engineers
EDDY Frank MM Pte 52840 7th Lancashire Fusiliers
EDDY Richard MM Pte 345266 5th Devonshire Regt
EDE Archibald John MM Pte 262987 1/7th Middlesex Regt
EDE Daniel MM Pte 251067 1/6th Durham Light Infantry
EDE Norman MM Pte R/15882 King's Royal Rifle Corps
EDE William MM Pte 60695 23rd Middlesex Regt DOW 5.11.18.
EDE William MM Pte 22297 Duke of Cornwall's LI
EDE William Allen MM Sjt 9733 22 Bde RFA
EDEN Bernard L. MM Pte 17644 Gloucestershire Regt
EDEN Charles MM Cpl 39688 15th Lancashire Fusiliers
EDEN Edward MM Sjt 652053 21st London Regt
EDEN Edward J. MM Sjt 88019 D/123 Bde RFA
EDEN George MM Bdr 810117 RFA
EDEN George MM L/Cpl 8620 1st Lincolnshire Regt
EDEN James E.J. MM Pte 11931 King's Royal Rifle Corps
EDEN Joseh B.F. MM Pte 62567 Welsh Regt
EDEN Robert Henry MM+Bar L/Sjt 43346 9th Royal Irish Fusiliers
EDENS Fred H. MM Cpl 46135 11th Hussars
EDEVANE Robert MM Pte 16266 8th Shropshire Light Infantry
EDEY Albert Edwin MM L/Bdr 102710 302 Siege Bty RGA
EDGAR A.R. MM Pte G/11160 Royal West Kent Regt
EDGAR Abraham MM Pte 266516 11th Royal Scots Fusiliers
EDGAR Albert C. MM L/Cpl 40407 Gordon Highlanders
EDGAR Alexander MM Sjt 14/7172 16th Royal Irish Rifles
EDGAR Alfred J. MM Pte 36502 1/4th Shropshire Light Infantry
EDGAR David "DCM,MM" Sjt 50345 32 Bty 33 Bde RFA
EDGAR Douglas "MM,VM(Rm)" Pte 24105 12th Lancashire Fusiliers DOW 22.4.18.
EDGAR Fergus MM Pte 7733 1/6th Northumberland Fusiliers KIA 27.3.18.
EDGAR Henry MM L/Cpl 3048 1/6th Royal Highlanders
EDGAR Hugh "DCM+Bar,MM+Bar" Sjt 45550 25 Div Sig Coy Royal Engineers
EDGAR James MM L/Cpl 17/1782 Royal Irish Rifles
EDGAR James MM L/Cpl 9302 Coldstream Guards
EDGAR James MM Spr 63061 Royal Engineers
EDGAR James Albert MM+Bar Pte R/14003 King's Royal Rifle Corps
EDGAR John MM L/Cpl 17562 1/6th Seaforth Highlanders KIA 25.10.18.
EDGAR John MM Pte 26247 15th Highland Light Infantry KIA 29.8.18.
EDGAR John James MM Cpl 13270 1st Cheshire Regt
EDGAR John W. MM Bdr 7536 112 Heavy Bty RGA
EDGAR Sam MM Gnr 75513 30 Bde RFA
EDGAR Thomas MM Pte 26395 2nd Royal Scots
EDGAR Thomas MM Pte 24719 Northumberland Fusiliers
EDGAR William K. MM Sjt Farrier 655189 B/158 Bde RFA
EDGAR William T. MM Pte 1826 Royal Lancaster Regt
EDGE Charles E. MM Cpl 8196 1st Royal Welsh Fusiliers
EDGE Charles E. MM Pte 5017 9 Fd Amb RAMC
EDGE Frank MM Spr 198216 Royal Engineers
EDGE Harold MM Sjt 26376 17th Royal Welsh Fusiliers
EDGE Harry MM Pte 14092 5th Leicestershire Regt
EDGE Herbert MM Bdr 67112 144 Siege Bty RGA
EDGE James MM Pte 41478 Cameron Highlanders
EDGE John MM CSM 39204 Royal Welsh Fusiliers
EDGE John A. MM Pte 01891 Army Ordnance Corps
EDGE Percy O. MM Sjt 22 16th Royal Warwickshire Regt
EDGE Ralph Ernest MM Pte 30156 1st East Lancashire Regt DOW 27.10.18.
EDGE Richard MM Pte 19094 Cheshire Regt
EDGE Samuel MM Cpl 57047 14th Royal Welsh Fusiliers KIA 6.11.18.
EDGE Squire H. MM L/Cpl 15948 1st Coldstream Guards
EDGE Thomas MM Cpl 68661 40 Bde RFA
EDGE W. MM Sjt 37804 Highland Light Infantry
EDGE William MM Gnr 155181 D/317 Bde RFA KIA 9.11.17.
EDGECOMBE Horace H. MM Cpl S/17084 Arg & Suth Highlanders
EDGECOMBE John Harold MM Spr 100569 33 Div Sig Coy Royal Engineers
EDGECOMBE Samuel J. MM Pte 13825 4th Coldstream Guards
EDGECOMBE William MM Pte R/7261 King's Royal Rifle Corps
EDGELER Henry MM Sjt 772 6th Royal West Surrey Regt
EDGELL J. MM Pte 403424 RAMC
EDGERTON Ernest MM Pte 201278 Lancashire Fusiliers
EDGERTON Harry (Horace) MM Dvr 795964 B/223 Bde RFA
EDGERTON Robert F. MM Pte S/18002 Rifle Brigade
EDGINGTON Alfred MM+Bar Cpl 683431 1/22nd London Regt
EDGINGTON Harry J. MM L/Cpl 535854 54 Div Sig Coy Royal Engineers
EDGINGTON John MM Cpl 8190 11th Royal Warwickshire Regt
EDGINGTON William A. MM Sjt 12747 Oxf & Bucks Light Infantry
EDGLEY Ernest Edwin "MC,MM(2169 Pte 1/16th London Regt)" Capt RFA
EDGLEY Thomas Samuel MM Cpl 8574 1st Essex Regt
EDGSON Ernest Victor MM Cpl Wheeler 945914 B/291 Bde RFA
EDGSON John Henry MM Sjt R/6948 9th King's Royal Rifle Corps Died 21.3.18.
EDGWORTH William MM Cpl 200094 8th Gloucestershire Regt
EDINBOROUGH Stephen Thomas MM Pte 495390 RAMC
EDINGTON Arthur MM Pte 2822 1/5th London Regt
EDIS Frederick Leslie MM Pte 14771 12th Liverpool Regt DOW 22.11.17.
EDISS Edward MM Gnr 161760 RFA
EDKINS Charles MM+Bar Pte 16501 4th Worcestershire Regt KIA 13.3.18.
EDKINS Ernest MM Gnr 188646 112 Bty 24 Bde RFA
EDKINS William Alfred Joseph MM Cpl 7137 21st Lancers att XIV Corps Cav Regt.
EDLINGTON John Holmes MM L/Cpl 12818 2nd Coldstream Guards KIA 27.8.18.
EDMANS Joseph MM Pte 9779 5th Royal Berkshire Regt DOW 5.4.18.
EDMED Claud V. MM Pte 6755 7th Dragoon Guards
EDMETT Fred MM Pte 16870 13 Coy Machine Gun Corps DOW 13.9.16.
EDMISTON John MM CQMS 124 5/6th Scottish Rifles
EDMISTON Robert W. MM Cpl 200186 5/6th Scottish Rifles
EDMOND Albert E. MM Sjt 5171 RFA

EDMOND Alex MM Dvr 645805 RFA
EDMONDS A. MM Pte 8098 Machine Gun Corps
EDMONDS Alfred B. MM Sjt 387726 6 Siege Coy Royal Engineers
EDMONDS Andrew MM L/Cpl 275410 Durham Light Infantry
EDMONDS Bernard D. MM L/Cpl 1641 1/22nd London Regt
EDMONDS Frederick MM Pte 36644 1/4th Royal Berkshire Regt
EDMONDS Frederick G. MM Pte 309298 17th Armoured Car Bn Tank Corps
EDMONDS George MM Spr 153684 Royal Engineers
EDMONDS George MM 2nd Cpl 474381 529 Fd Coy Royal Engineers
EDMONDS George MM Pte 7804 RAMC
EDMONDS George W. MM Pte 2674 1/18th London Regt
EDMONDS John MM Sjt 16089 100 Bty 31 Bde RFA
EDMONDS John S. "DCM+Bar,MM" CSM G/5989 13th Royal Fusiliers
EDMONDS Joseph MM Sjt 10596 7th Somerset Light Infantry
EDMONDS Joseph Henry MM Pte 15151 14th Royal Warwickshire Regt DOW 8.1.18.
EDMONDSON Arthur C. MM Sjt 906 Royal Engineers
EDMONDSON Ralph Benford MM Spr 538621 2 Div Sig Coy Royal Engineers
EDMONDSON Samuel MM L/Cpl 28636 Machine Gun Corps
EDMONDSON Thomas H. MM Sjt 13700 10th West Riding Regt
EDMONDSTONE William S. MM L/Cpl 351031 Royal Scots
EDMONSON Thomas MM Pte 29738 2nd Northumberland Fusiliers
EDMONSTON Frederick Thomas MM Pte 32082 RAMC
EDMUNDS Arthur F. MM Sjt 10521 8th Devonshire Regt
EDMUNDS Charles MM Pte 3929 21st Manchester Regt
EDMUNDS Edward MM Pte 326184 11th Essex Regt DOW 15.10.18.
EDMUNDS Frank MM Pte 241943 7th Lancashire Fusiliers
EDMUNDS Frederick MM Bdr 104525 D/174 Bde RFA
EDMUNDS Frederick MM Sjt 15023 7th South Wales Borderers
EDMUNDS George MM Gnr 74556 RFA
EDMUNDS H.H. MM Air Mech 2 49424 Royal Flying Corps
EDMUNDS J.H.E. MM Pte 43444 16 Fd Amb RAMC
EDMUNDS James "DCM,MM,MID" Sjt 34502 112 Bde RFA
EDMUNDS Leslie W. MM Pte 125036 Machine Gun Corps
EDMUNDS Reginald L. MM Gnr 150506 RFA
EDMUNDS Tom MM L/Cpl 21200 South Wales Borderers
EDMUNDS Walter F. MM Sjt 9878 2nd Royal Lancaster Regt
EDMUNDSON Charles MM Sjt 19092 13th Liverpool Regt
EDMUNDSON Fred MM Cpl 200536 9th Durham Light Infantry
EDMUNDSON Norman MM Dvr 760302 C/250 Bde RFA
EDMUNDSON William MM Cpl 56823 2nd Welsh Regt KIA 20.8.18.
EDNEY Henry MM Pte 29124 23rd London Regt
EDROFF Alfred MM Dvr 60377 RFA
EDSALL George MM Cpl 83616 RFA
EDSER George MM Sjt 2757 23rd Middlesex Regt
EDWARDS A.F. MM Cpl 19525 1st Essex Regt
EDWARDS A.R. MM Sjt 2126 Royal Flying Corps
EDWARDS Albert MM Pte 26022 17th Royal Welsh Fusiliers
EDWARDS Albert "MM+Bar,CG(It)" Pte 240800 9th York & Lancaster Regt
EDWARDS Albert E. MM Pte 11724 7th Duke of Cornwall's LI
EDWARDS Albert E. MM L/Cpl 30546 Liverpool Regt
EDWARDS Alfred MM Pte 16666 2nd South Wales Borderers
EDWARDS Alfred MM Pte 28389 1st Royal Lancaster Regt
EDWARDS Alfred MM Pte 19173 22 Coy Machine Gun Corps DOW 19.7.16.
EDWARDS Alfred E. MM Gnr 116189 RGA
EDWARDS Alfred Edward "MC,MM" CSM 200481 2/4th North Lancashire Regt
EDWARDS Alfred G. MM Pte 54290 Durham Light Infantry
EDWARDS Alfred H. MM Pte 1773 4th GMGR
EDWARDS Alfred O. "MM,MSM" Sjt STK/389 10th Royal Fusiliers
EDWARDS Amos Frederick George MM Gnr 39363 D/79 Bde RFA
EDWARDS Andrew MM Dvr T3/024076 Army Service Corps att RAMC.
EDWARDS Arthur MM L/Cpl 47152 1st Royal Inniskilling Fusiliers
EDWARDS Arthur MM Pte M2/120429 16 Motor Amb Convoy Army Service Corps
EDWARDS Arthur MM Cpl 3479 1/5th Liverpool Regt KIA 8.8.16.
EDWARDS Arthur MM Pte 3/8141 1st Norfolk Regt
EDWARDS Arthur MM Cpl 22737 1/5th Welsh Regt att 114 TM Bty.
EDWARDS Arthur MM Sjt 11497 11th Hampshire Regt
EDWARDS Arthur MM Bdr 64876 112 Bty 24 Bde RFA KIA 25.3.18.
EDWARDS Arthur G. MM Sjt 17465 Machine Gun Corps
EDWARDS Arthur George MM L/Cpl 12895 6th Royal Berkshire Regt DOW 21.2.17.
EDWARDS Arthur Henry MM L/Cpl 8/13519 8th South Staffordshire Regt
EDWARDS Arthur Lord MM Pte 36492 8th Leicestershire Regt KIA 27.5.18.
EDWARDS Arthur W. MM Cpl T4/243457 Army Service Corps
EDWARDS Arthur W.H. MM Sjt 5614 RFA
EDWARDS Benjamin MM Spr 479769 Royal Engineers
EDWARDS Bertram MM Pte 65309 RAMC
EDWARDS C.McD. MM+Bar Sjt 16037 1st Coldstream Guards
EDWARDS Cecil MM Pte 16706 Royal Welsh Fusiliers
EDWARDS Charles MM L/Cpl 10416 5th Royal Berkshire Regt
EDWARDS Charles MM Sjt 476404 Royal Engineers
EDWARDS Charles MM Pte M2/074192 Army Service Corps att RAMC.
EDWARDS Charles Gordon MM Spr 43683 7 Div Sig Coy Royal Engineers
EDWARDS Charles Henry MM Gnr 65797 89 Siege Bty RGA
EDWARDS Charles J. MM Pte 67313 5th Devonshire Regt
EDWARDS Charles J. MM Sjt 29500 5 Siege Bty RGA
EDWARDS Claud MM L/Cpl 200290 2/1st London Regt
EDWARDS Cyril MM L/Cpl 23721 10th Royal West Kent Regt
EDWARDS David MM Sjt 11178 1st South Wales Borderers
EDWARDS David MM L/Cpl 352390 9th Royal Scots Died 30.12.18.
EDWARDS David Edward MM Gnr 30054 B/48 Bde RFA
EDWARDS E. MM Bdr 2893 RFA
EDWARDS Edward MM Cpl 39085 65 Bde Ammn Col RFA
EDWARDS Edward MM Pte 345501 24th Royal Welsh Fusiliers
EDWARDS Edward MM Pte 345502 24th Royal Welsh Fusiliers
EDWARDS Edward MM Pte 12197 7th Royal Berkshire Regt
EDWARDS Edward MM Sjt 23704 16th Welsh Regt
EDWARDS Edward MM Pte 24070 Welsh Regt
EDWARDS Edward H. MM Pte G7/195 7th East Surrey Regt
EDWARDS Edward T. MM Sjt 39757 5th Gloucestershire Regt
EDWARDS Edwin MM Cpl 64606 2nd Welsh Regt
EDWARDS Edwin MM Gnr 700119 RFA
EDWARDS Edwin MM L/Cpl 2904 Royal Sussex Regt
EDWARDS Eric William "MM,MID" Cpl 1245 1/1st North Somerset Yeomanry
EDWARDS Ernest MM Sjt 265480 1/7th Liverpool Regt
EDWARDS Ernest Arthur MM Sjt 35746 8th York & Lancaster Regt
EDWARDS Ernest K. MM Cpl 57962 RAMC
EDWARDS Esau "MC+Bar,DCM,MM(7401 Sjt 91 Coy)" T/2Lt 8th Bn Machine Gun Corps
EDWARDS Francis J. MM Cpl 74444 17 Div Sig Coy Royal Engineers
EDWARDS Frank MM Cpl 91197 Durham Light Infantry
EDWARDS Frank MM+Bar L/Cpl A/3528 King's Royal Rifle Corps
EDWARDS Frank "MM,MID" Sjt S/2783 8th Seaforth Highlanders
EDWARDS Fred MM L/Cpl 265695 1/6th West Riding Regt
EDWARDS Frederick MM Sjt 31391 19th Welsh Regt
EDWARDS Frederick "DCM,MM" Pte 66044 206 Coy Machine Gun Corps
EDWARDS Frederick MM Pte 9065 2nd Devonshire Regt
EDWARDS Frederick C. MM Sjt 26553 Royal Engineers
EDWARDS Frederick Edward MM 2nd Cpl 130744 1 Special Coy Royal Engineers
EDWARDS Frederick G. MM Pte 155730 61st Bn Machine Gun Corps
EDWARDS Frederick Henry "MM,MSM" Sjt 260060 6th South Staffordshire Regt
EDWARDS Frederick J. MM L/Cpl 75075 4th Bn Tank Corps
EDWARDS Frederick J. MM Pte 5428 12th Lancers
EDWARDS Frederick J. MM Sjt 297 RFA
EDWARDS Frederick T. MM Pte 240320 1/6th Liverpool Regt
EDWARDS Frederick W. MM Pte 10231 2nd East Surrey Regt
EDWARDS G.D. MM Gnr 881874 D/18 Bde RFA
EDWARDS G.F. MM CSM L/17012 20th Royal Fusiliers
EDWARDS George MM Pte 54224 Durham Light Infantry
EDWARDS George MM Sjt 350425 7th London Regt DOW 31.8.18.
EDWARDS George MM Cpl 12241 6th Shropshire Light Infantry
EDWARDS George MM L/Cpl 25294 1st Cheshire Regt
EDWARDS George MM Pte 41642 RAMC
EDWARDS George MM Cpl 12120 6th Wiltshire Regt KIA 10.10.17.
EDWARDS George Roland MM Pte 19568 7th South Staffordshire Regt KIA 19.11.17.
EDWARDS George T. MM Cpl 21403 Border Regt
EDWARDS Gilbert John MM Gnr Sig 301973 156 Siege Bty RGA
EDWARDS Gilbert W. MM L/Cpl 20596 South Staffordshire Regt att RN Div.
EDWARDS H.F. MM L/Cpl 202244 1/4th Royal Berkshire Regt

EDWARDS Harold MM L/Cpl 8904 2nd Gloucestershire Regt
EDWARDS Harold MM Sjt 138646 RGA
EDWARDS Harold MM Sjt 204937 15th Hampshire Regt
EDWARDS Harry MM Gnr Sig 224969 16 Bty 32 Bde RFA
EDWARDS Henry MM Cpl 275717 1/6th Essex Regt
EDWARDS Henry B. MM Cpl 40139 King's Own Scottish Borderers
EDWARDS Henry C. MM Pte 372114 8th London Regt
EDWARDS Henry G. MM Pte 611918 19th London Regt
EDWARDS Henry J. MM Cpl 200061 Tank Corps
EDWARDS Henry S. MM Pte 40261 Lincolnshire Regt
EDWARDS Herbert MM Pte 376983 10th Royal Scots
EDWARDS Herbert "DCM,MM" Sjt 350244 7th London Regt
EDWARDS Herbert MM L/Cpl 242588 1/5th North Lancashire Regt
EDWARDS Herbert MM Pte 40992 South Wales Borderers
EDWARDS Herbert H. MM Pte G/12688 Royal Fusiliers
EDWARDS Herbert John MM Cpl 33606 130 Bty 40 Bde RFA
EDWARDS Horace MM Gnr 796529 62 Div Ammn Col RFA
EDWARDS Horace MM+Bar Pte 24179 4th Middlesex Regt
EDWARDS James MM Cpl 27891 RAMC
EDWARDS James MM Sjt 1241 23rd Northumberland Fusiliers
EDWARDS James Bruce MM Sjt 12314 9th Essex Regt
EDWARDS James Charles MM Pte 373921 8th London Regt
EDWARDS James J. MM Pte 241789 2nd London Regt
EDWARDS John MM Gnr 8465 RFA
EDWARDS John MM Pte 6600 9th Yorkshire Light Infantry KIA 15.8.18.
EDWARDS John MM Cpl 19764 6th South Wales Borderers
EDWARDS John MM Spr 250087 Signal Service Royal Engineers
EDWARDS John MM Bdr 715288 210 Bde RFA KIA 24.4.18.
EDWARDS John MM Dvr 104977 12 Div Ammn Col RFA
EDWARDS John MM Cpl 39079 RFA
EDWARDS John MM Pte 25862 13th East Surrey Regt
EDWARDS John MM Sjt 291328 703 Labour Coy Labour Corps
EDWARDS John MM Sjt 1853 1/6th Seaforth Highlanders
EDWARDS John MM L/Cpl 16370 9th North Staffordshire Regt
EDWARDS John MM Spr 24138 56 Coy Royal Engineers
EDWARDS John MM CQMS 75180 Royal Engineers
EDWARDS John MM Pte 13202 23rd Royal Fusiliers
EDWARDS John Alfred MM Dvr 51426 79 Fd Coy Royal Engineers
EDWARDS John E. MM Cpl 4105 2nd Lancashire Fusiliers
EDWARDS John G. MM Pte 43066 1st Bn Machine Gun Corps
EDWARDS John H. MM Pte 46998 17th Lancashire Fusiliers
EDWARDS John H. MM Sjt 265342 1/7th Liverpool Regt
EDWARDS John Henry MM+Bar Cpl 130030 45th Royal Fusiliers
EDWARDS John Marshall MM+Bar Cpl 2881 1/21st London Regt
EDWARDS John R. MM Bdr 42551 12 Hy Bty RGA
EDWARDS John Robert MM+Bar L/Sjt 14058 Royal Inniskilling Fusiliers
EDWARDS John S. MM Sjt 240637 1/5th South Lancashire Regt
EDWARDS John T. MM Pnr 128959 Royal Engineers
EDWARDS John William MM Cpl 11391 9th West Riding Regt
EDWARDS Joseph MM L/Bdr 161636 185 Siege Bty RGA
EDWARDS Joseph MM Gnr 69365 39 Bde RFA
EDWARDS Joseph Edward MM Pte 4453 1/6th Northumberland Fusiliers KIA 27.5.18.
EDWARDS Joseph William MM Pte 204403 1/4th York & Lancaster Regt
EDWARDS Laurence MM Pte 536787 15th London Regt
EDWARDS Leonard Nelson MM Spr 504576 503 Fd Coy Royal Engineers KIA 1.11.17.
EDWARDS Lewis MM Gnr 112978 B/178 Bde RFA
EDWARDS Llewellyn A. MM Cpl 310151 1/1(Welsh)Hy Bty RGA
EDWARDS Lloyd MM L/Cpl 16758 14th Royal Welsh Fusiliers
EDWARDS Llwellyn MM Pte 2333 1st Welsh Guards
EDWARDS Norman E. MM Pte 403533 2/2nd(West Riding)Fd Amb RAMC
EDWARDS Norman Souter MM Bdr 61903 111 Siege Bty RGA
EDWARDS Percy MM Pte 11894 1st South Wales Borderers
EDWARDS Percy J. MM Pte 40321 Leicestershire Regt
EDWARDS Phillip MM Sjt 20430 6th York & Lancaster Regt
EDWARDS R. MM Gnr 110344 RFA
EDWARDS Reg W. MM Pte 39552 South Wales Borderers
EDWARDS Reginald Watkin MM Bdr 15544 A/74 Bde RFA KIA 30.10.17.
EDWARDS Reynold MM Sjt 338391 RGA
EDWARDS Robert MM Pte 276856 Manchester Regt
EDWARDS Robert MM Pte 31303 12th Liverpool Regt KIA 16.8.17.
EDWARDS Robert MM Pte 325312 1/9th Durham Light Infantry
EDWARDS Robert MM Pte 31568 Liverpool Regt
EDWARDS Robert H. MM Sjt 6702 11th Notts & Derby Regt KIA 11.10.18.
EDWARDS Sam MM Pte 24217 8th Royal Lancaster Regt
EDWARDS Samuel John MM Bdr 13102 11 Div Ammn Col RFA
EDWARDS Sidney "MM,CdiG(It)" Pte 5492 1st Royal Welsh Fusiliers
EDWARDS Sidney MM L/Cpl 10328 7th Shropshire Light Infantry
EDWARDS Stanley W. MM Pte 65841 10th Royal Fusiliers
EDWARDS Thomas MM Sjt 45914 301 Siege Bty RGA
EDWARDS Thomas MM Pte 55469 10th Northumberland Fusiliers DOW 17.7.18.
EDWARDS Thomas MM L/Cpl 24388 4 Div Sig Coy Royal Engineers
EDWARDS Thomas MM Pte 45846 107 Coy Machine Gun Corps
EDWARDS Thomas MM Pte 42597 RAMC
EDWARDS Thomas MM Dvr L/15188 C/162 Bde RFA
EDWARDS Thomas MM Pte 24744 Notts & Derby Regt
EDWARDS Thomas F. MM Pte 65144 13th Royal Fusiliers
EDWARDS Thomas G. MM Spr 43662 Royal Engineers
EDWARDS Thomas G. MM Sjt 200749 Royal Welsh Fusiliers
EDWARDS Thomas H. MM Pte 52912 10th Lancashire Fusiliers
EDWARDS Thomas H. MM Sjt 13836 RFA
EDWARDS Thomas J. MM Sjt 36643 77 Fd Coy Royal Engineers
EDWARDS Thomas M. MM Gnr 51743 RGA
EDWARDS Thomas V. MM Pte 365905 Liverpool Regt
EDWARDS Trevor MM Gnr 77286 Tank Corps
EDWARDS Victor M. MM Pte 40055 8th Somerset Light Infantry
EDWARDS W. MM Pte 339226 RAMC
EDWARDS W.F. MM Pte 9069 1st Royal Scots Fusiliers
EDWARDS W.R. MM L/Cpl 2904 Royal Fusiliers
EDWARDS Walter MM Pte 103251 50th Bn Machine Gun Corps
EDWARDS Walter MM 2nd Cpl 22621 Royal Engineers
EDWARDS Walter MM Dvr 5609 RFA
EDWARDS Walter MM Cpl 21362 Machine Gun Corps
EDWARDS Walter Stannard MM Cpl C/1266 16th King's Royal Rifle Corps DOW 12.1.18.
EDWARDS Wilfred C. MM Cpl 200592 3rd Light Bn Tank Corps
EDWARDS William MM Pte 9557 1st Lincolnshire Regt
EDWARDS William MM Sjt 9469 2nd Essex Regt KIA 10.10.17.
EDWARDS William MM Cpl 276446 1/7th Arg & Suth Highlanders
EDWARDS William MM Pte 12735 South Staffordshire Regt KIA 21.9.18.
EDWARDS William MM Pte 40255 Leicestershire Regt
EDWARDS William MM Pte 4419 1st Royal Welsh Fusiliers
EDWARDS William MM Pte 5804 1/7th London Regt KIA 3.12.17.
EDWARDS William MM Gnr 188849 27 Siege Bty RGA
EDWARDS William MM Bdr 38898 118 Heavy Bty RGA
EDWARDS William A. MM+Bar Cpl 99948 C/293 Bde RFA
EDWARDS William Albert MM Pte 923 11th East Yorkshire Regt DOW 7.9.16.
EDWARDS William Ambrose MM Sjt 8512 1st East Kent Regt
EDWARDS William C. MM Pte 27872 Hampshire Regt
EDWARDS William D. MM Pte 61254 Royal West Surrey Regt
EDWARDS William D. MM L/Cpl S/2557 12th Rifle Brigade
EDWARDS William E. MM L/Cpl 680907 1/22nd London Regt
EDWARDS William E. MM Pte 29979 7th South Lancashire Regt KIA 31.7.17
EDWARDS William H. MM Pte 26628 10tth Welsh Regt
EDWARDS William H. MM Sjt 39139 South Wales Borderers
EDWARDS William H. MM L/Cpl 10173 Royal Irish Regt
EDWARDS William H. MM L/Sjt 14500 4th Royal Fusiliers
EDWARDS William H. MM Pte 6945 5th Shropshire Light Infantry
EDWARDS William J. MM Gnr 97969 D/49 Bde RFA
EDWARDS William R. MM L/Cpl 26565 15th Welsh Regt
EDWARDS William S. MM Bdr 78317 RGA
EDWARDS William Stephen MM L/Cpl 10940 5th Dorsetshire Regt
EDWICKER Arthur MM Pnr 128814 Royal Engineers
EDWORTHY George MM Pte M2/184131 Army Service Corps
EDWORTHY Sidney MM Sjt M2/181599 Army Service Corps
EELES Frank MM Sjt 200740 Yorkshire Regt
EELES Richard MM Pte 6209 1st Hampshire Regt
EELS Percy MM Pte 530872 1/15th London Regt
EELY Harry W. MM Cpl L/10420 4th Royal Fusiliers
EGAN Charles MM Sjt 13986 4th Middlesex Regt
EGAN Edgar MM Pte 26506 Middlesex Regt
EGAN Edward MM Pte 63844 13th Yorkshire Regt
EGAN Francis MM+Bar Sjt 9771 2nd Royal Dublin Fusiliers
EGAN Frederick C. MM L/Cpl 1865 4th Bn GMGR
EGAN George Herbert MM Cpl MS/1891 406 MT Coy Army Service Corps

EGAN James E. MM Sjt 33387 1/6th Royal Warwickshire Regt
EGAN John "DCM,MM" Sjt 10398 1st Worcestershire Regt
EGAN Michael MM+Bar Sjt 9250 2nd Yorkshire Regt
EGAN Michael MM Sjt 267272 West Riding Regt
EGAN Michael J. MM CQMS 6853 2nd Royal Munster Fusiliers
EGAN Patrick MM+Bar L/Sgt 10012 2nd Leinster Regt
EGAN Peter MM Pte 15523 1/4th King's Own Scottish Borderers
EGAN Robert Victor Vincent MM S/Sjt 16979 5 Fd Amb RAMC KIA 6.10.18.
EGAN Samuel E. MM Sjt 55908 RFA
EGAN Timothy J. MM Pte 102389 1st Notts & Derby Regt
EGAN William MM Pte 8361 6th Royal West Surrey Regt
EGGAR William H. MM Pte 8256 11th Royal Warwickshire Regt
EGGETT George H. MM Sjt 50531 310 Bde RFA
EGGIE Edward MM Pte 13709 1st Scots Guards DOW 17.5.18.
EGGINGTON Ralph MM Pte 242278 1/5th Royal Warwickshire Regt
EGGINS Sydney Ephraim MM Bdr 86671 A/72 Bde RFA
EGGINTON Arthur MM Cpl 15416 9th North Staffordshire Regt
EGGINTON Henry MM Pte 5628 2nd King's Royal Rifle Corps
EGGINTON Joseph C. MM L/Cpl 12277 4th Worcestershire Regt
EGGITT John W. MM L/Bdr 701840 B/330 Bde RFA
EGGLESTON James W. MM L/Cpl 40407 9th York & Lancaster Regt
EGGLESTON Percy MM Sjt T/1176 50 Div Train 3 Coy Army Service Corps
EGGLESTON Stephen "MM,MSM" Sjt 11822 4th Middlesex Regt
EGGLETON Albert G. MM+Bar Sjt 14523 11th West Yorkshire Regt
EGGLETON Frank H. MM Sjt 3 3rd Hussars
EGGLETON Henry MM Pte 26636 1st Grenadier Guards Died 5.11.18.
EGLETON Ernest E. "MM,MID" Bdr 28905 B/149 Bde RFA
EGLINGTON Edward J. MM Bdr 12741 110 Heavy Bty RGA
EGLINGTON Herbert MM L/Cpl 18785 1st Grenadier Guards
EGLINGTON Joseph J. MM+Bar Sjt 10640 1st Royal Dublin Fusiliers
EGLINGTON Walter MM Pte 918 IV Corps Cyclist Bn Army Cyclist Corps
EGLINTON Claude MM L/Cpl 240981 2/5th West Riding Regt KIA 27.11.17.
EGLINTON John MM Pte 46349 11th South Lancashire Regt
EGRE Percy A. MM L/Cpl 122703 Machine Gun Corps
EIDMANS Henry P. MM Cpl 76492 Tank Corps
EISELE Sidney P. MM Pte 19785 Machine Gun Corps
EKE Charles MM Pte 40247 Bedfordshire Regt
EKE Walter E. MM L/Cpl 21116 Border Regt
ELAM George MM Pte R/32712 King's Royal Rifle Corps
ELAND John MM Sjt L/5689 HQ 155 Bde RFA DOW 23.11.16.
ELAND Thorp MM Bdr 12184 RFA
ELAND Wallace Henry MM L/Cpl 29505 1/4th East Yorkshire Regt Died 7.8.18.
ELBORN Edwin W. MM Pte 3/8936 1st Suffolk Regt
ELCOAT Arthur MM Bdr 750207 250 Bde RFA
ELCOCK Albert E. MM Sjt 200517 3rd Worcestershire Regt
ELCOCK George H. MM Sjt 306378 1/8th Royal Warwickshire Regt
ELCOCK Roland Edward "VC,MM" Cpl 271410 11th Royal Scots
ELCOCK William MM Gnr 830101 111 Bty 24 Bde RFA DOW 20.9.18.
ELCOCKS Frank L. MM Gnr L/33409 RFA
ELCOMBE John George MM Cpl 2391 London Regt
ELCOMBE William V. MM Sjt 18602 Q Coy Royal Engineers
ELDER David MM L/Cpl 203025 Seaforth Highlanders
ELDER James MM Cpl 635695 B/256 Bde RFA
ELDER John MM Sjt 5727 11th Royal Scots Fusiliers
ELDER John MM Sjt 3747 1/5th Seaforth Highlanders
ELDER Orr MM Cpl 7648 2nd Cameron Highlanders
ELDER Peter MM Gnr 96402 A/81 Bde RFA
ELDER Thomas E. MM Pte 46849 2nd Worcestershire Regt
ELDERFIELD Leonard "DCM,MM" Sjt R/11709 9th King's Royal Rifle Corps
ELDERKIN Maxwell "DCM,MM" CSM L/8667 1st Royal West Surrey Regt KIA 12.4.18.
ELDRED Cecil W. MM Sjt 53062 RFA
ELDRED Henry MM Pte 13924 9th Royal Fusiliers
ELDRED James MM Pte 242984 8th Royal Warwickshire Regt
ELDRETT Ernest F. MM Bdr 9252 RFA
ELDRETT Henry MM Gnr 98645 C/106 Bde RFA
ELDRIDGE Albert J.S. MM Sjt 64084 4 Div Ammn Col RFA
ELDRIDGE Edwin George MM Pte 9979 6th East Kent Regt
ELDRIDGE Frank MM Sjt 235829 2nd Lancashire Fusiliers
ELDRIDGE Harold A. MM Pte M2/103842 Army Service Corps
ELDRIDGE Harold J. MM Cpl 235930 4th York & Lancaster Regt
ELDRIDGE Henry C. MM Cpl 49906 RFA
ELDRIDGE Phillip A. MM Dvr 1206 RFA
ELDRIDGE Wallace A. MM Pte 14150 8th Royal Berkshire Regt
ELDRIDGE William G. MM+Bar S/Sjt 30210 RAMC
ELDRIDGE William T. MM Cpl 76335 128 Coy Labour Corps
ELDRINGTON George MM+Bar Sjt 63409 U Bty RHA
ELEY Albert E. MM Gnr 47480 24 Bde RFA
ELEY Albert W. MM L/Cpl 15255 8th Royal Berkshire Regt
ELEY George MM L/Cpl 9138 2nd Bedfordshire Regt DOW 9.4.18.
ELEY H. MM Dvr 73695 128 Bty 29 Bde RFA
ELEY S.William MM Sjt 3/11984 10th West Riding Regt
ELEY Stanley A. MM L/Cpl 153503 Machine Gun Corps
ELEY William MM L/Cpl 35950 Notts & Derby Regt
ELEY William N. MM Bdr 41931 RGA
ELFMAN Max MM L/Cpl J/1449 38th Royal Fusiliers
ELIAS Edmund MM L/Cpl 31444 Welsh Regt
ELIAS Henry MM Pte 53373 12th Royal Scots
ELIAS James MM L/Cpl 53716 Royal Welsh Fusiliers
ELIFFE Frank MM Sjt 113361 Royal Engineers
ELKERTON James MM Pte 11662 6th Oxf & Bucks Light Infantry DOW 15.9.17.
ELKES George MM Cpl 34360 58 Coy Labour Corps
ELKINGTON Arthur Charles MM L/Cpl 13865 10th West Riding Regt KIA 19.9.17.
ELKINGTON Ernest W. MM Pte 393322 9th London Regt
ELKINGTON Roland G. MM Sjt R/811 King's Royal Rifle Corps
ELKINS James MM Cpl 372660 8th London Regt
ELKINS Leonard MM Pte 20730 9th North Lancashire Regt
ELKINS Percy S. MM L/Cpl 265226 1/1st Hertfordshire Regt
ELKINS William George MM Pte 65630 104 Fd Amb RAMC KIA 4.10.18.
ELKINS William George MM Bdr Sig 30472 78 Siege Bty RGA
ELKS James MM L/Cpl 241715 5th Royal Warwickshire Regt
ELL George J. MM+Bar Sjt 51571 27 Bde RFA
ELLABY Joseph D. MM Spr 187131 3 Fd Svy Coy Royal Engineers
ELLACOTT George T. MM Sjt 36120 11th Leicestershire Regt
ELLAM Archibald MM Pte 28173 1st Bedfordshire Regt
ELLAM George N.B. MM Cpl 15024 7th Leicestershire Regt
ELLAMES Thomas MM Pte 202153 5th Lancashire Fusiliers
ELLAMS James MM Pte 291239 1/7th Cheshire Regt
ELLAMS Thomas MM Pte 56426 14th Royal Welsh Fusiliers
ELLARD Harold James "MC,MM(966 L/Sjt 10th Bn)" T/2Lt 9th Royal Fusiliers
ELLAWAY Albert MM Pte 20488 Northamptonshire Regt
ELLAWAY Joseph MM Sjt 6/14526 6th South Wales Borderers
ELLAWAY Leslie G. MM Pte 41539 8th Royal Warwickshire Regt
ELLEL Harry MM Pnr 427936 57 Div Sig Coy Royal Engineers
ELLEMAN Charles MM Cpl 9226 3rd Worcestershire Regt KIA 27.5.18.
ELLEN Albert Hedley MM Pte 8800 8th East Kent Regt
ELLEN Herbert Frederick "MM,CG(B)" Sjt 558235 56 Div Sig Coy Royal Engineers
ELLENDER Reginald Alfred MM Pte 495231 2/2nd(Home Counties)Fd Amb RAMC Died 2.7.18.
ELLERAY Ernest MM Pte 45473 13th Rifle Brigade
ELLERBECK William John Henry MM Gnr L/13203 B/162 Bde RFA
ELLERBY James William "MM+Bar,MID" Sjt 12525 1st Lincolnshire Regt
ELLERBY Percy MM Cpl 38382 1st Northumberland Fusiliers Died 28.3.18.
ELLERINGTON Sydney MM Sjt 1329 1/4th East Yorkshire Regt
ELLERSHAW Albert Edward MM CSM 21391 22nd Manchester Regt
ELLERTON Thomas William MM Pte M2/073969 Army Service Corps att 104 Fd Amb RAMC
ELLERY Arthur John MM Pte 21348 Duke of Cornwall's LI
ELLERY Charles F. MM Pte 514802 14th London Regt
ELLERY Harry J. MM Cpl 22383 Royal Fusiliers
ELLERY Reginald MM Gnr 87684 C/51 Bde RFA
ELLETT Robert G. MM Sjt L/33663 55 Div Ammn Col RFA
ELLICOCK Charles MM Cpl 26221 9th Cheshire Regt
ELLIFF Arthur MM Cpl 96169 B/153 Bde RFA
ELLINGFORD Albert E. MM Bdr 74191 28 Bde RFA
ELLINGHAM James MM L/Cpl 215 Highland Light Infantry
ELLINOR Charles T. MM Gnr 81961 B/240 Bde RFA
ELLINS John E. MM Cpl 13836 8th Gloucestershire Regt
ELLINTHORPE R. MM Sjt 2267 West Riding Regt
ELLIOT Claude W. MM Sjt 514668 14th London Regt
ELLIOT Fred MM Gnr 152061 C/156 Bde RFA Died 14.11.18.

ELLIOT Hugh MM L/Cpl 126709 1/1st Lovat's Scouts Yeomanry
ELLIOT John "DCM,MM" Sjt 48265 21 Div Sig Coy Royal Engineers
ELLIOT Robert "DCM,MM" Sjt 307116 2/7th Royal Warwickshire Regt
ELLIOT William MM Cpl 267231 2/7th Royal Warwickshire Regt
ELLIOT William MM Pte S/40678 8th Seaforth Highlanders KIA 28.7.17.
ELLIOT William MM Pte 57784 18th Liverpool Regt KIA 22.9.17.
ELLIOTT Alexander MM Pte M2/102218 109 Fd Amb RAMC Army Service Corps
ELLIOTT Alfred MM Sjt 24830 14th Gloucestershire Regt
ELLIOTT Alfred MM Pte 25102 12th Hampshire Regt
ELLIOTT Alfred MM Gnr 102489 RGA
ELLIOTT Andrew MM Sjt L/13414 30 Div Ammn Col RFA
ELLIOTT Archie W. MM Gnr 184947 31 Hy Bty RGA
ELLIOTT Arthur E. MM Pte 737 Royal West Surrey Regt
ELLIOTT Arthur M. MM Pte 14654 2nd Scots Guards
ELLIOTT Benjamin MM Pte 19296 10th Northumberland Fusiliers
ELLIOTT Charles MM Pte 204988 Royal West Surrey Regt
ELLIOTT Charles Alfred MM Pte 4974 7th Royal West Kent Regt KIA 13.12.17.
ELLIOTT Charles C. MM Sjt 97464 RFA
ELLIOTT Charles F. MM L/Cpl 291044 Northumberland Fusiliers
ELLIOTT Christopher MM Spr 121805 Royal Engineers
ELLIOTT Clarence C.E. MM Dvr 72954 RFA
ELLIOTT Clarence W. MM L/Cpl 16177 6th Dragoons
ELLIOTT Daniel MM L/Cpl R/13122 13th King's Royal Rifle Corps KIA 5.10.17.
ELLIOTT David William MM Cpl 305183 2/8th West Yorkshire Regt
ELLIOTT Donald MM L/Cpl 12964 1st Scots Guards
ELLIOTT E. MM Cpl 43548 Essex Regt
ELLIOTT E.W. MM L/Cpl 305179 Liverpool Regt
ELLIOTT Edward H. MM Sjt 50302 Royal Engineers
ELLIOTT Ernest MM Pte 8198 9th Yorkshire Light Infantry
ELLIOTT Ernest MM Pte 6769 1st East Kent Regt
ELLIOTT Ernest MM Pte B/203507 Rifle Brigade
ELLIOTT Ernest J. MM Pte 17543 5th Northamptonshire Regt
ELLIOTT Ernest Stanley Luther MM Pte M2/054530 Army Service Corps att 57 Fd Amb RAMC.
ELLIOTT Frank MM Sjt 23024 15th Cheshire Regt
ELLIOTT Frank MM L/Cpl 241006 Gloucestershire Regt
ELLIOTT Frank J. MM Gnr 16678 RHA
ELLIOTT Fred MM Pte R/8830 King's Royal Rifle Corps
ELLIOTT Frederick MM Cpl 33043 54 Fd Coy Royal Engineers DOW 13.1.17.
ELLIOTT Frederick M. MM Pte 1876 141 Fd Amb RAMC
ELLIOTT George MM Cpl 780207 X/40 Med TM Bty RFA
ELLIOTT George MM Pte S/3053 Gordon Highlanders
ELLIOTT George A. MM 2nd Cpl 24477 Royal Engineers
ELLIOTT George A. "DCM,MM" L/Bdr 293180 138 Hy Bty RGA
ELLIOTT George Ernest MM Cpl T3/024173 Army Service Corps
ELLIOTT George G. MM Sjt 476425 Royal Engineers
ELLIOTT George M. MM Sjt 22368 1st Liverpool Regt
ELLIOTT George Needham MM Sjt 305374 West Yorkshire Regt
ELLIOTT Harold MM Pte 6227 12th Middlesex Regt
ELLIOTT Henry MM Pte 6257 Army Cyclist Corps
ELLIOTT Howitt M. MM Pte 37215 Machine Gun Corps
ELLIOTT James MM Pte 34069 13th Yorkshire Regt
ELLIOTT James MM Gnr 5686 Antrim Bde RGA
ELLIOTT James "MM,MID" Sjt 5755 23rd Bn Machine Gun Corps
ELLIOTT James MM Pte 14154 9th Royal Irish Fusiliers
ELLIOTT James A. MM L/Cpl 26861 23 Fd Coy Royal Engineers
ELLIOTT James V. MM Sjt 6894 7th Dragoon Guards
ELLIOTT John MM CSM 307967 7th West Riding Regt
ELLIOTT John MM L/Cpl 12217 5th Northamptonshire Regt
ELLIOTT John MM Pte 72891 Machine Gun Corps
ELLIOTT John MM Pte R/14292 9th King's Royal Rifle Corps
ELLIOTT John MM Pte 15803 10th Arg & Suth Highlanders
ELLIOTT John MM Pte 3659 7th Rifle Brigade KIA 21.3.18.
ELLIOTT John MM L/Sjt R/8016 King's Royal Rifle Corps
ELLIOTT John H. MM Sjt 1931 1/7th West Yorkshire Regt
ELLIOTT John J.S. MM+Bar CSM 34578 4th West Riding Regt
ELLIOTT John William MM Dvr 9742 A/71 Bde RFA
ELLIOTT Joseph MM Pte 240799 1/5th Border Regt
ELLIOTT Joseph Railton MM Pte 11/17541 8th Border Regt KIA 12.8.17.
ELLIOTT Lewis MM Cpl 538246 28 Div Sig Coy Royal Engineers
ELLIOTT Matthew MM Cpl 225198 10th Cameron Highlanders
ELLIOTT Michael MM Pnr 360608 35 Div Sig Coy Royal Engineers
ELLIOTT Owen R. MM Pte 13162 Yorkshire Light Infantry

ELLIOTT Percival H. MM Cpl 103528 48th Bn Machine Gun Corps
ELLIOTT R.H. MM Bdr 15684 RGA
ELLIOTT Reginald MM Cpl 33689 North Lancashire Regt
ELLIOTT Reuben MM Pte 19128 North Staffordshire Regt
ELLIOTT Reuben L. MM Cpl 1597 9th East Surrey Regt
ELLIOTT Richard MM Gnr 160194 122 Heavy Bty RGA
ELLIOTT Robert MM Pte 57970 141 Fd Amb RAMC
ELLIOTT Robert D. MM+Bar Sjt D/2893 2nd Dragoon Guards
ELLIOTT Robert W. "DCM,MM" Sjt 241052 2/8th Worcestershire Regt
ELLIOTT Seth MM Pte 8309 2nd Royal Welsh Fusiliers DOW 18.9.16.
ELLIOTT Solomon MM Pte 61884 Royal Fusiliers
ELLIOTT Stephen James "MM,MID" Sjt 4908 1st Essex Regt
ELLIOTT Thomas MM Sjt 1760 1st Dragoons
ELLIOTT Thomas G. MM L/Cpl 18091 9th Leicestershire Regt att ASC.
ELLIOTT Thomas William MM Sjt 93460 17th Royal Fusiliers DOW 9.11.18.
ELLIOTT Thomas William MM Pte 95468 15th Durham Light Infantry KIA 24.10.18.
ELLIOTT Tom MM Cpl 5809 8th Middlesex Regt
ELLIOTT Tom MM Bdr 780901 A/311 Bde RFA
ELLIOTT Vincent Kenneth MM Pte 10344 1st Royal West Kent Regt DOW 30.6.18.
ELLIOTT W.J. MM Pte 459029 RAMC
ELLIOTT Walter MM L/Cpl 227013 Royal Berkshire Regt
ELLIOTT Walter MM Pte 1145 RAMC
ELLIOTT William MM L/Cpl 27067 2nd Grenadier Guards
ELLIOTT William MM Pte 31812 11th Royal Scots Fusiliers
ELLIOTT William MM Pte 3188 1/5th Durham Light Infantry
ELLIOTT William MM Pte 1430 RAMC
ELLIOTT William MM+2 Bars Sjt 25790 110 Heavy Bty RGA
ELLIOTT William MM Bdr 100714 115 Hy Bty RGA
ELLIOTT William MM L/Cpl 17308 11th Royal Inniskilling Fusiliers
ELLIOTT William MM Pte 41333 Leicestershire Regt
ELLIOTT William H. "MM,MID" L/Cpl 11542 6th Somerset Light Infantry
ELLIOTT William H. MM L/Cpl S/3571 Rifle Brigade
ELLIOTT William H.H. MM Pte 21163 23rd Royal Fusiliers
ELLIOTT William W. MM Bdr 200662 520 Siege Bty RGA
ELLIS A. MM L/Cpl 191540 Royal Engineers
ELLIS Albert E. MM Cpl 92860 180 Siege Bty RGA
ELLIS Albert E. MM Pte 33046 RAMC
ELLIS Alfred H. MM+Bar Pte A/79 9th King's Royal Rifle Corps
ELLIS Alfred Henry MM L/Cpl 7323 1st South Wales Borderers DOW 2.12.17.
ELLIS Alfred J. MM Pte 33168 Middlesex Regt
ELLIS Arthur MM Pte 48966 20th Manchester Regt
ELLIS Arthur MM Sjt 89717 139 Fd Amb RAMC
ELLIS Arthur MM 2nd Cpl 1391 Royal Engineers
ELLIS Arthur MM L/Cpl 16494 8th East Yorkshire Regt
ELLIS Arthur MM Pnr WR/27 315 Rly Const Coy Royal Engineers
ELLIS Arthur MM Sjt 40115 York & Lancaster Regt
ELLIS Arthur Wilfred MM Cpl 21788 Machine Gun Corps
ELLIS Bernard MM 2nd Cpl 478112 Royal Engineers
ELLIS C. "DCM,MM" Cpl 35371 2nd Essex Regt
ELLIS Cecil MM Bdr 121321 RFA
ELLIS Charles MM Pnr 254707 Royal Engineers
ELLIS Charles A. MM Gnr 231291 B/78 Bde RFA
ELLIS Charles H. MM Pte 202066 5th West Riding Regt
ELLIS Charles S. MM Sjt 56151 Machine Gun Corps
ELLIS Charles V. MM Dvr 114742 RFA
ELLIS Clement T. MM Spr 44309 74 Fd Coy Royal Engineers
ELLIS Coulson Sidney MM Sjt 136066 183 Tunneling Coy Royal Engineers DOW 25.10.18.
ELLIS David MM Pte 8327 1st North Staffordshire Regt
ELLIS David William MM Sjt 1678 2/2 (West Riding) Fd Coy Royal Engineers Died 8.1.19.
ELLIS Edward "MM,MID" CSM 22201 16th Royal Welsh Fusiliers
ELLIS Edward MM Sjt 20059 9th Yorkshire Light Infantry KIA 1.7.16.
ELLIS Edward R. MM Gnr 109513 152 Hy Bty RGA
ELLIS Edwin D. MM Pte 202065 5th West Riding Regt
ELLIS Ernest MM Pte 24012 10th Yorkshire Light Infantry
ELLIS Ernest MM Pte 6945 1st Notts & Derby Regt
ELLIS Ernest E. MM+Bar Sjt 321784 6th London Regt
ELLIS Ernest Gordon MM Cpl G/1821 7th Royal West Surrey Regt KIA 8.11.16.
ELLIS Ernest Matthew MM Pte 241356 1/6th West Yorkshire Regt
ELLIS Eustace MM Sjt 18883 10th Scottish Rifles

ELLIS Ewart MM Pte 103653 106 Fd Amb RAMC
ELLIS F.J. MM S/Sjt 459017 RAMC
ELLIS Francis MM Gnr 174361 262 Siege Bty RGA
ELLIS Francis Edward MM Gnr 825595 B/240 Bde RFA
ELLIS Frank MM Sjt 202327 1st King's Own Scottish Borderers
ELLIS Frank MM Sjt 170 1 (Home Counties) Fd Coy Royal Engineers
ELLIS Fred MM Gnr 38638 20 Hy Bty RGA
ELLIS Fred W.T. MM Pte 25496 7th Wiltshire Regt
ELLIS Frederick MM Pte S/1549 21st Royal Fusiliers
ELLIS Frederick B. MM Cpl 12936 5th Northamptonshire Regt
ELLIS Frederick C.H. MM Pte 65683 Machine Gun Corps
ELLIS Frederick G. MM Air Mech 2 2911 Royal Flying Corps
ELLIS Frederick George MM Bdr 510443 2/2nd(London)Fd Amb RAMC
ELLIS Frederick Thomas "MM,MID" Cpl Wheeler 9782 17 Div Ammn Col RFA
ELLIS George MM Pte 235621 1/4th Gordon Highlanders
ELLIS George MM L/Sjt 200798 Royal Welsh Fusiliers
ELLIS George MM L/Cpl 17779 1st Royal Berkshire Regt
ELLIS George MM Sjt 302 13th Cheshire Regt Died 2.10.18.
ELLIS George Frederick MM Pte 9391 8th Norfolk Regt
ELLIS George P. MM Sjt 56079 Machine Gun Corps
ELLIS George W. MM Sjt 39961 1st Wiltshire Regt
ELLIS Gordon MM Gnr 46186 33 Siege Bty RGA
ELLIS H.E. MM L/Cpl 700940 23rd London Regt
ELLIS H.E. MM Pte 48879 Royal Welsh Fusiliers
ELLIS Harold Ernest MM Pte 20260 11 Fd Amb RAMC
ELLIS Harry "MM,MSM" CQMS 6773 25th Bn Machine Gun Corps
ELLIS Harry MM L/Cpl 250764 Durham Light Infantry
ELLIS Harry "DCM,MM+Bar" Sjt 482140 62 Div Sig Coy Royal Engineers
ELLIS Harry J. "MM,MID" Cpl MS/998 3 Advance Park Army Service Corps
ELLIS Henry A. MM Sjt 11969 King's Royal Rifle Corps
ELLIS Henry Barrowcliff MM Pte 18431 Royal West Kent Regt
ELLIS Henry H. MM L/Cpl 200738 1/7th Middlesex Regt
ELLIS James MM L/Cpl 23063 8th Royal Dublin Fusiliers
ELLIS James MM Sjt 855 5th Connaught Rangers
ELLIS James MM Pte 14380 5th South Lancashire Regt
ELLIS John MM Pte 200757 2/4th Hampshire Regt
ELLIS John MM Sjt 207482 63 Div Sig Coy Royal Engineers
ELLIS John MM Pte 19631 Royal Lancaster Regt
ELLIS John "DCM,MM" Sjt 9637 1st Liverpool Regt
ELLIS John MM Pte 21008 South Lancashire Regt
ELLIS John "MM,CG(F)" Sjt 357 12th Yorkshire Light Infantry
ELLIS John MM Pte 86440 Notts & Derby Regt
ELLIS John MM Sjt 10/243 East Yorkshire Regt
ELLIS John Arnott MM L/Cpl 201437 1/4th West Riding Regt KIA 13.4.18.
ELLIS John S. MM Spr 112715 185 Tunnelling Coy Royal Engineers
ELLIS John Thomas "MM,CG(F),MM(F)" Sjt 53077 Royal Engineers
ELLIS John W. MM Cpl WR/22159 311 Rly Const Coy Royal Engineers
ELLIS John W. MM Pte 14005 8th York & Lancaster Regt
ELLIS Joseph MM Pte 2533 1st Welsh Guards
ELLIS Joseph James Saunders MM Pte 12845 1st Dorsetshire Regt KIA 3.10.18.
ELLIS Leonard T. MM Sjt 44272 74 Fd Coy Royal Engineers
ELLIS Levi MM Sjt S/9329 Rifle Brigade
ELLIS Oscar MM Sjt 105859 200 Siege Bty RGA
ELLIS P. MM Sjt 11718 1st Worcestershire Regt
ELLIS Percy MM Pte 944 6th Royal West Kent Regt
ELLIS Reginald Victor MM Pte 24389 East Surrey Regt
ELLIS Robert MM Pte 241371 9th Scottish Rifles DOW 24.10.18.
ELLIS Robert MM Pte 10529 Yorkshire Light Infantry
ELLIS Robert MM Pte 40900 4th Hampshire Regt
ELLIS Roderic MM Sjt 479348 143 Coy Labour Corps
ELLIS Rylands MM Pte A/3589 King's Royal Rifle Corps
ELLIS S. MM L/Sjt 2426 Royal Fusiliers
ELLIS Sam MM Cpl 100022 6th Notts & Derby Regt
ELLIS Sidney "MM,MID" CQMS A/509 7th King's Royal Rifle Corps KIA 15.10.17.
ELLIS T.F. MM Pte G/25331 1st East Kent Regt
ELLIS Thomas MM Cpl 19712 7th Shropshire Light Infantry
ELLIS Tom MM L/Cpl 9904 1st York & Lancaster Regt
ELLIS Tom S. MM L/Cpl 224973 Labour Corps
ELLIS Victor F. MM Pte 201175 Royal West Surrey Regt
ELLIS Walter MM Pnr 307243 Royal Engineers
ELLIS Walter MM Cpl M2/100431 272 MT Coy Army Service Corps
ELLIS William MM Pte 41533 52 Fd Amb RAMC
ELLIS William MM Pte 10675 2nd King's Royal Rifle Corps DOW 1.7.16.
ELLIS William MM Cpl 15760 55 Fd Coy Royal Engineers
ELLIS William MM Pte 25078 2/5th West Riding Regt KIA 27.11.17.
ELLIS William MM Cpl 8421 1st Royal Welsh Fusiliers
ELLIS William "DCM+Bar,MM+Bar" Sjt 19066 11th Notts & Derby Regt
ELLIS William "DCM,MM" CSM 650433 1/21st London Regt
ELLIS William MM Sjt 2249 1/5th West Riding Regt
ELLIS William MM Pte 58411 12th Cheshire Regt
ELLIS William MM Cpl 300172 1/8th Arg & Suth Highlanders
ELLIS William David MM Cpl 552 1/2 Bty 1/4(Midland)Bde RFA
ELLIS William David MM Bdr 292435 133 Heavy Bty RGA
ELLIS Willie MM Dvr 786012 RFA
ELLISON Archie MM Pte 241841 1st East Lancashire Regt
ELLISON Cecil Monro MM Cpl 472276 2/12th London Regt
ELLISON Charles MM Pte 18972 12th Royal Irish Rifles DOW 21.8.18.
ELLISON Charles F. MM Cpl 164558 6th Bn Machine Gun Corps
ELLISON Frank MM Dvr 114037 C/48 Bde RFA
ELLISON Frank MM Pte 9299 West Yorkshire Regt
ELLISON George Alfred MM Bdr 70769 41 Bde RFA
ELLISON Harold MM Cpl 27076 North Lancashire Regt
ELLISON Harry MM Cpl 63034 25 Bde RFA
ELLISON James MM(39159 Lab C)+Bar Cpl 33103 13th East Lancashire Regt
ELLISON John MM Sjt 73548 16th Royal Welsh Fusiliers
ELLISON John MM Sjt 12539 Yorkshire Light Infantry
ELLISON John Percy MM Sjt 43690 D/115 Bde RFA
ELLISON Joseph MM 2nd Cpl 102255 177 Tunnelling Coy Royal Engineers
ELLISON Richard MM Pte 32673 Durham Light Infantry
ELLISON Thomas MM Sjt 200938 2/4th North Lancashire Regt
ELLISON Thomas F.E. MM Pte 306244 9th Bn Tank Corps
ELLISON Wilfred MM Pte 356307 2/10th Liverpool Regt
ELLISON William S. MM Pte 33286 15th Royal Welsh Fusiliers
ELLISS F.H. MM L/Cpl 573 7th East Kent Regt
ELLISTON Arthur J. MM Cpl 55592 Machine Gun Corps
ELLISTON John R. MM+Bar Sjt 16917 Suffolk Regt
ELLMER Arthur MM Cpl 17170 10th Northumberland Fusiliers
ELLOR Squire MM Sjt 39621 42nd Bn Machine Gun Corps
ELLOTT Ambrose Harry Frederick MM Sjt L/11684 A/165 Bde RFA
ELLTHORN Richard MM Pte M2/052781 Army Service Corps
ELLWOOD Edwin MM+Bar Bdr 348088 RGA
ELLWOOD Ernest W. MM Spr 311943 Royal Engineers
ELLWOOD F.C. MM Pte 536105 5 Fd Amb RAMC
ELLWOOD John MM Pte 6998 2nd Bedfordshire Regt
ELLWOOD John H. MM L/Cpl 4824 13th Middlesex Regt
ELLWOOD Mark MM Gnr 99560 RHA
ELLWOOD Samuel MM Gnr Fitter 92326 268 Siege Bty RGA
ELLWOOD Thomas MM Pte M2/150172 Army Service Corps att 148(RN)Fd Amb
ELLWOOD William MM L/Cpl 19445 11th Border Regt
ELLWOOD William D. MM Cpl 15129 8th Border Regt
ELMER Archibald T. MM Sjt 88719 4th Royal Fusiliers
ELMER Archie Ernest MM Pte 16016 8th Suffolk Regt
ELMER W.J. MM L/Bdr 93290 RFA
ELMES Philip Charles MM Cpl C/936 16th King's Royal Rifle Corps KIA 3.11.16.
ELMORE John MM Pte 590423 1/18th London Regt
ELMS Charles John Richard "MM,MSM" CSM 16310 232 Army Troops Coy Royal Engineers
ELMS Francis R. MM+Bar Sjt 225777 1/1st Monmouthshire Regt
ELMS Frank Charles MM Cpl 20426 10th Yorkshire Regt
ELMS Harry MM+Bar Sjt 5052 24th Royal Fusiliers
ELMS John Pierce MM Sjt 6452 1st Middlesex Regt
ELMS Walter F. MM Pte 34056 RAMC
ELMSLIE Dudley R. MM L/Cpl S/8452 Rifle Brigade
ELMSLIE P.B. "DCM,MM+Bar" Sjt 301288 2/1 (Highland) Fd Amb RAMC
ELMY Claude F. MM Bdr 776401 RFA
ELMY Frederick W. MM Bdr 52074 RGA
ELPHICK Edward MM Pte 34523 9th North Lancashire Regt Died 12.7.18.
ELPHICK James MM L/Sjt G/7660 7th Royal Sussex Regt
ELPHICK William MM L/Cpl 990 Royal Sussex Regt
ELRICK George M. MM Pte 290212 1/7th Gordon Highlanders
ELRICK John S.C.P. MM L/Sjt S/18927 2nd Gordon Highlanders
ELRICK Wilfred MM L/Cpl 22828 1st Coldstream Guards KIA 4.11.18.

ELSCEY George MM+Bar L/Cpl 9082 1st Norfolk Regt
ELSDEN Ernest MM Pte 1634 8th East Surrey Regt
ELSDON Albert Victor MM Sjt 13044 25th Royal Fusiliers
ELSDON John MM+Bar Cpl 17154 6th South Wales Borderers
ELSDON William MM Spr 22443 Royal Engineers
ELSE Edgar MM Pte 12231 6th Bedfordshire Regt
ELSE Edward MM Sjt 11480 1st Notts & Derby Regt KIA 27.4.17.
ELSE Elijah MM L/Cpl 9727 2nd York & Lancaster Regt
ELSE George MM Pte 6646 24 Coy Machine Gun Corps DOW 25.11.17.
ELSE H. MM Air Mech 1 87595 Royal Flying Corps
ELSE Thomas MM Pte R/4781 13th King's Royal Rifle Corps
ELSE William S.B. MM Pte 241612 Notts & Derby Regt
ELSEY Albert J. MM Sjt L/12260 13th Royal Fusiliers
ELSEY Frederick MM Pte 29011 2nd Royal Dublin Fusiliers
ELSEY George Henry MM Pte 29773 Middlesex Regt
ELSEY John M. MM L/Cpl G/1423 7th Royal West Surrey Regt
ELSEY Percy George "MM,MSM" Sjt 1791 HQ First Army RAMC
ELSEY Thomas MM L/Cpl 265246 1st East Kent Regt
ELSEY William George MM Pte 374254 1/17th London Regt KIA 12.5.18.
ELSMORE Maurice E. MM Pte 82788 2nd London Regt
ELSMORE Percy Stafford MM Sjt 511209 2/14th London Regt
ELSMORE Wilson Hugh "MM,VM(Rm)" Sjt 88352 58th Bn Machine Gun Corps
ELSON Arthur MM Dvr 45277 A/190 Bde RFA
ELSON Arthur MM Pte 1712 7th East Kent Regt
ELSON Arthur Llewellyn MM Sjt 13436 A/64 Bde RFA KIA 18.7.17.
ELSON Edward J. MM Pnr 311532 Royal Engineers att RGA.
ELSON Fred MM L/Cpl 8191 2nd Royal Welsh Fusiliers
ELSON Frederick MM Sjt 4709 8th East Kent Regt
ELSON Frederick J. MM Cpl 13131 6th Northamptonshire Regt
ELSON George Henry MM+Bar L/Cpl 26285 Notts & Derby Regt Died 8.12.18.
ELSON Harold MM Pte 202864 Leicestershire Regt
ELSON Henry Joseph William MM Gnr 111710 B/102 Bde RFA
ELSON Herbert MM Pte 22322 Royal West Surrey Regt
ELSON Jabez MM Pte 50299 15th Cheshire Regt
ELSON John MM+Bar Cpl SPTS/2586 24th Royal Fusiliers
ELSON Oliver Francis MM L/Cpl 28327 1st Royal Warwickshire Regt
ELSON Reginald Frank MM Bdr 88954 RFA
ELSON William C. MM Sjt 58253 16th Royal Welsh Fusiliers
ELSON William R. MM Pte 452192 11th London Regt
ELSTON George MM Pte 20122 10th Notts & Derby Regt
ELSTON John MM L/Cpl 4914 IX Corps Cyclist Bn Army Cyclist Corps
ELSTON John L. MM Pte 146 11th East Yorkshire Regt
ELSTONE John Harold "MC,MM(C/3436 L/Cpl KRRC)" T/2Lt 10th Essex Regt
ELSWORTH Albert MM Sjt 200797 2/4th York & Lancaster Regt
ELSWORTH Charles MM Cpl 266407 2/7th West Yorkshire Regt KIA 22.11.17.
ELSWORTH Clarence MM Bdr 58218 110 Siege Bty RGA
ELSWORTH Cyril MM Sjt 12670 1st Dorsetshire Regt
ELSWORTH Horace MM Pte 7345 16th Manchester Regt KIA 25.4.18.
ELTON Albert MM Pte 63249 32nd Bn Machine Gun Corps
ELTON E.J. "DCM,MM" Sjt 1429 22 Squadron Royal Flying Corps
ELTON Percy MM Pte 1558 1/3 (Northumbrian) Fd Amb RAMC
ELTON Percy Maurice MM Sjt 49000 89 Fd Coy Royal Engineers
ELVEY Frederick William MM Spr 548105 510 Fd Coy Royal Engineers
ELVIDGE Charles H. MM Sjt 23686 5th Bn Machine Gun Corps
ELVIN Thomas MM Sjt R/13926 12th King's Royal Rifle Corps
ELVIN Walter MM Pte 40851 South Wales Borderers
ELWELL Alfred J.R. MM Cpl 232497 2nd London Regt
ELWELL Daniel MM Sjt 9817 South Staffordshire Regt
ELWELL George MM Pte 19587 Machine Gun Corps
ELWELL Joseph MM Sjt 42404 9th Scottish Rifles
ELWELL T. MM Sjt 47612 10th Essex Regt
ELWES Winifred Millicent MM Miss F VAD att FANY
ELWIN Frederick George MM Pte 202087 1/4th Northumberland Fusiliers
ELWORTHY Ernest MM Pnr 38698 Somerset Light Infantry
ELY Alfred E. MM Pte 14177 Essex Regt
ELY Frank F. MM CQMS 29307 59 Fd Coy Royal Engineers
ELY Frederick J. MM+Bar Pte S/28935 13th Rifle Brigade
ELY James MM L/Cpl 79038 Royal Engineers
ELY John M. MM Gnr Sig 283356 109 Siege Bty RGA

EMANS Walter MM Gnr 37833 2 Siege Bty RGA
EMANS William Edward MM Sjt 12775 7th Duke of Cornwall's LI KIA 2.4.18.
EMANUEL Joseph MM L/Cpl 1802 1st Welsh Guards
EMBEARY William J. MM L/Cpl 7390 1st Devonshire Regt
EMBERSON Frank E. MM Pte M2/267697 Army Service Corps
EMBERSON W.A. MM Pte 10769 9th Essex Regt
EMBLETON Jacob E. MM Sjt 10277 14th Northumberland Fusiliers
EMBLETON Robert William MM Pte 16/1092 1/4th Northumberland Fusiliers KIA 23.3.18.
EMBURY William Hartley Wroe MM Bdr 56673 B/70 Bde RFA KIA 21.3.18.
EMDEN Philip MM Dvr 76585 RFA
EMERSON Charles A.V. MM Pte 65497 103 Fd Amb RAMC
EMERSON Fred MM+Bar Cpl 7291 11th Royal Fusiliers DOW 19.11.17.
EMERSON J.W. MM+Bar Pte 22911 Lincolnshire Regt
EMERSON John MM Pte 95994 17 Squadron MGC(Cavalry)
EMERSON John Harold MM Cpl 36501 Leicestershire Regt
EMERSON Joseph A. MM L/Cpl G/1999 1/4th Royal Sussex Regt
EMERSON Percy MM Gnr 37187 RGA
EMERSON Robert H. MM Cpl 63703 1st Bn Machine Gun Corps
EMERSON Wilfred MM L/Cpl 41103 Highland Light Infantry
EMERSON William MM Pte 28838 8th Royal Lancaster Regt
EMERSON William Robert MM Pte 201266 1/4th Suffolk Regt KIA 23.3.18.
EMERTON Harold MM Cpl 4838 Army Cyclist Corps
EMERTON Ronald MM Sjt 687198 RFA
EMERY Charles Thomas MM+2 Bars Cpl G/3410 7th Royal Sussex Regt
EMERY Charles W. MM 2nd Cpl 18482 3 Fd Sqn Royal Engineers
EMERY Edward MM Cpl 117705 2nd Gloucestershire Regt
EMERY Edward MM Sjt 30981 RFA
EMERY Ernest Edgar MM L/Cpl P5829 1 Traffic Control Coy Military Foot Police
EMERY Frederick MM Pte 15645 11th West Yorkshire Regt
EMERY Frederick G. MM Cpl 10581 13th Middlesex Regt
EMERY Frederick W. MM Spr 96597 Royal Engineers
EMERY George P. MM Bdr 33372 115 Heavy Bty RGA
EMERY James T. MM Pte 9065 RAMC
EMERY John MM Pte G/48830 26th Royal Fusiliers
EMERY John MM Pte 16883 Yorkshire Light Infantry
EMERY Oscar MM Pte 3/7163 4th Bedfordshire Regt
EMERY Ronald John MM Bdr 67605 18 Bde RFA
EMERY Stephen MM Pte 13509 Royal Welsh Fusiliers
EMERY Sydney James MM Bdr 67604 18 Bde RFA
EMERY William MM Sjt 200124 Shropshire Light Infantry
EMERY William MM Cpl 3/10375 9th South Staffordshire Regt
EMERY William MM Pte 1043 21st Northumberland Fusiliers
EMERY William J. MM Pte 720733 1/24th London Regt
EMINSON Thomas L. MM Sjt 143020 Royal Engineers
EMLER Harry Joseph MM L/Cpl 2692 1/15th London Regt
EMLER Henry Ernest MM Sjt 296720 712 Coy Labour Corps
EMMENS Walter "DCM,MM" Pte 19901 15th Cheshire Regt
EMMERSON Edward MM Sjt 300720 Durham Light Infantry
EMMERSON George T. MM Cpl 487975 Royal Engineers
EMMERSON James William MM Pte 32203 27 Fd Amb RAMC Died 28.7.18.
EMMERSON John MM Pte 19/1075 19th Northumberland Fusiliers
EMMERSON John MM Spr 182967 218 Fd Coy Royal Engineers
EMMERSON John J. MM Pte 12237 7th Norfolk Regt
EMMERSON Wilfred MM Bdr 66302 28 Bde RFA
EMMETT George MM Pte 17/682 West Yorkshire Regt
EMMETT George B. MM Cpl 241541 1/5th Leicestershire Regt
EMMETT Harry MM Pte 1966 West Yorkshire Regt
EMMETT James MM Pte 107519 180 Coy Labour Corps
EMMETT James MM Pte 306839 8th Lancashire Fusiliers
EMMETT James H. MM Pte 118029 2nd Notts & Derby Regt
EMMETT John MM L/Cpl 39715 Machine Gun Corps
EMMETT Norman MM Pte 267501 West Riding Regt
EMMETT Richard MM Pte 352357 7th London Regt KIA 20.4.18.
EMMETT Robert MM Pte 242874 1/4th West Riding Regt
EMMETT Stephen MM+Bar Cpl 18/383 8th West Yorkshire Regt
EMMETT Thomas MM 2nd Cpl 22275 4 Sig Troop Royal Engineers
EMMETT Walter MM L/Cpl 72723 2nd Yorkshire Light Infantry
EMMETT Walter MM Pte 67430 21st Bn Machine Gun Corps
EMMETT William Richard "DCM,MM,MIDx2" BSM 910 D/153 Bde RFA
EMMINGHAM Harry MM L/Cpl 201816 2nd Lincolnshire Regt
EMMITT G. MM Air Mech 1 9521 Royal Air Force

EMMOTT Gilbert MM Cpl 2372 1/6th West Yorkshire Regt KIA 9.10.17.
EMMOTT Harold MM Bdr 786143 RFA
EMMOTT John MM Pte 235052 2/5th East Lancashire Regt DOW 26.5.18.
EMMOTT Rennie MM L/Cpl 10050 Coldstream Guards KIA 31.7.17.
EMMOTT William MM Cpl 265883 1/6th West Riding Regt
EMMS Fred MM Sjt 15760 1/8th West Yorkshire Regt KIA 27.9.18.
EMMS Henry G. "DCM,MM" Sjt 4821 2nd York & Lancaster Regt
EMMS John Henry MM Bdr 85731 C/62 Bde RFA
EMMS Richard MM Dvr 138149 RFA
EMMS Thomas MM Pte 59620 8th West Yorkshire Regt
EMMS William MM Pte 305464 1/7th West Riding Regt
EMPSON Henry W. MM L/Cpl 15901 Middlesex Regt
EMSLEY Frederick M. MM L/Cpl 2726 8th Royal Sussex Regt
EMSLEY Joseph MM CSM 5841 1st West Yorkshire Regt
EMSLEY Richard MM+Bar Pte 3340 13th Royal Sussex Regt
EMSLIE Edward MM L/Cpl 263 12th East Yorkshire Regt
EMSLIE Frank MM Pte 3385 Gordon Highlanders
EMSLIE George M. MM Gnr 645806 RFA
EMSLIE Peter MM Pte 3132 1/7th Gordon Highlanders DOW 5.9.17.
EMSLIE Theodore Douglas MM Pte S/22758 2nd Arg & Suth Highlanders
ENDERSBY Edward J. MM Sjt M2/121887 Army Service Corps
ENDICOTT Ernest MM Sjt 56697 128 Bty 29 Bde RFA DOW 28.9.18.
ENGLAND Albert V. MM Pte 38905 2nd Suffolk Regt
ENGLAND Archer MM Cpl 11/368 11th East Yorkshire Regt
ENGLAND Basil MM Pte 18775 9th West Yorkshire Regt
ENGLAND Bertie MM Sjt 95432 9th Royal Fusiliers
ENGLAND Earle W. MM Cpl 66709 4th Bn Machine Gun Corps
ENGLAND Edgar MM Dvr 93499 RFA
ENGLAND Enos "DCM,MM" CSM 9421 6th Dorsetshire Regt KIA 24.8.18.
ENGLAND Harry MM S/Sjt S2/016542 11 Div Train Army Service Corps
ENGLAND Horace MM L/Cpl 34406 7th Leicestershire Regt
ENGLAND Jim MM Pte 10945 1st Grenadier Guards
ENGLAND John MM Pte 15429 8th Royal Berkshire Regt
ENGLAND Leonard T. MM Pte M2/177525 Army Service Corps
ENGLAND Reginald T. "DCM,MM" Sjt 17988 1st Royal Warwickshire Regt
ENGLAND Ronald Arthur MM Pte 27259 3rd Grenadier Guards
ENGLAND Sidney MM Cpl 230093 1/2nd London Regt
ENGLAND W.P.J. MM+Bar Cpl 73532 RFA
ENGLAND Walter MM Pte 9361 1st Bedfordshire Regt
ENGLAND William MM L/Cpl 38431 1/5th Northumberland Fusiliers
ENGLAND William C. MM Sjt 830 17th Royal Fusiliers
ENGLAND William Upton MM Gnr 44813 16 Heavy Bty RGA
ENGLEFIELD John MM Sjt 103133 32 Div Sig Coy Royal Engineers
ENGLISH Albert "MM+Bar,MID" Sjt 267183 Gloucestershire Regt
ENGLISH Albert E. MM Pte 1953 RAMC
ENGLISH Andrew MM Cpl 2286 1/7th Northumberland Fusiliers
ENGLISH Bernard Francis MM Cpl 16839 7th South Lancashire Regt DOW 30.4.18.
ENGLISH Charles R. MM+Bar Gnr 94005 C/76 Bde RFA
ENGLISH Ernest H. MM Cpl 772 13th East Yorkshire Regt
ENGLISH Francis W. MM Pte 22370 11th Hussars
ENGLISH Frederick MM Pte 26368 2nd Grenadier Guards
ENGLISH H.E. MM Pte 512541 3rd(London)Fd Amb RAMC
ENGLISH John MM Pte 11050 Royal Irish Regt
ENGLISH John K. MM Bdr 663014 RFA
ENGLISH Joseph MM Pnr 255039 Royal Engineers
ENGLISH Patrick MM Pte 6260 2nd Royal Irish Regt
ENGLISH Philip S. MM L/Cpl 25542 10th Hussars
ENGLISH R.T. MM Sjt 9927 10th East Kent Regt
ENGLISH Stanley MM L/Sjt 11858 1st Irish Guards
ENGLISH Sydney Charles "MM,MSM" BSM 34707 382 Bty 44 Bde RFA
ENGLISH Thomas MM Cpl 80584 RFA
ENGLISH Thomas H. MM Cpl 1420 25th Northumberland Fusiliers
ENGLISH Walter John MM L/Sjt 10383 6th Somerset Light Infantry KIA 18.8.16.
ENGLISH William MM L/Cpl 9427 South Lancashire Regt
ENGLISH William MM Pte 9136 1st Leinster Regt
ENGLISH William G. MM Dvr 182258 RFA
ENNALS Alexander H. MM Gnr 340213 RGA
ENNALS Spencer MM Pte S/25491 2nd Arg & Suth Highlanders

ENNION John Richard "MM,MID" Sjt 2056 1/4th Suffolk Regt KIA 20.7.16.
ENNIS John MM Pte 14691 8th Royal Dublin Fusiliers
ENNIS John MM+Bar Cpl 200146 1/6th West Riding Regt
ENNIS William MM Sjt 10568 9th West Riding Regt
ENNOS James C. MM L/Cpl 12125 6th Dorsetshire Regt
ENO Henry MM Pte 201496 2/4th Somerset Light Infantry DOW 29.11.17.
ENOCH Alfred W.G. MM L/Cpl 2528 1/5th Gloucestershire Regt KIA 21.7.16.
ENOCH Arthur R. MM Spr 47743 49 Div Sig Coy Royal Engineers
ENOCH James C. MM L/Cpl 21825 Royal Berkshire Regt
ENOCK Harold G.H. MM Pte 34604 RAMC
ENRIGHT John MM Pte S/9302 Seaforth Highlanders
ENRIGHT Timothy MM Pte 1/9403 1st Leinster Regt
ENSBY Alfred MM Sjt 265156 1/1st Hertfordshire Regt
ENSELL Edwin MM L/Cpl 18/1378 10th Northumberland Fusiliers
ENSOR Bernard Walter MM L/Cpl 203053 Gloucestershire Regt
ENSOR Richard MM Sjt 16294 6th Leicestershire Regt DOW 28.10.18.
ENSTONE Arthur MM Sjt 3530 Oxf & Bucks Light Infantry
ENTICOTT John H. "DCM,MM+Bar" Pte 18764 5th Oxf & Bucks Light Infantry
ENTWHISTLE T. MM Sjt 8 North Lancashire Regt
ENTWISTLE Alexander MM Sjt 24931 7th Bn Machine Gun Corps
ENTWISTLE Fred MM Sjt 123782 331 Siege Bty RGA
ENTWISTLE Frederick MM Pte 29253 RAMC
ENTWISTLE James A. MM Cpl 50192 Royal Engineers
ENTWISTLE James V. MM L/Cpl 22964 North Lancashire Regt
ENTWISTLE John Thompson MM Pte 331175 2/9th Liverpool Regt
ENTWISTLE Norman MM L/Cpl 17/8543 17th Manchester Regt
ENTWISTLE Samuel MM Pte 16197 9th North Lancashire Regt
ENTWISTLE Samuel MM Cpl 200434 East Lancashire Regt
ENTWISTLE Thomas MM Sjt 201207 Lancashire Fusiliers
ENTWISTLE William MM Cpl 203425 5th East Lancashire Regt
ENVILL Arthur MM Pte S/34792 3rd Rifle Brigade
EPPS Frank MM Sjt 48430 RFA
EPPS Reginald H. MM Gnr 1236 RGA
EPSLEY Grigg Francis MM+2 Bars Sjt 9309 5th Royal Berkshire Regt KIA 5.4.18.
EPTON William MM L/Cpl 46287 Royal Engineers
ERENTZ Patrick Gustavus MM Pte 19551 26th Royal Fusiliers
ERICKSON Aage MM Pte 204252 1st East Kent Regt
ERICKSON John Gottfried "MM,MID,CG(F)" Cpl Fitter 29015 A/93 Bde RFA KIA 9.4.17.
ERICSON Eric Charles MM Sjt 6392 9th East Surrey Regt KIA 18.9.18.
ERITH Herbert H. MM Cpl 26995 15th Hampshire Regt
ERNEST Charles G. MM Gnr L/45748 B/330 Bde RFA
ERRINGTON John MM Pte 51801 5th Yorkshire Light Infantry
ERRINGTON Matthew MM Bdr 760486 A/317 Bde RFA DOW 17.10.17.
ERRINGTON Thomas MM Pte 3322 2/22nd London Regt
ERRINGTON William Thomas Davies MM L/Cpl 58445 2/4th York & Lancaster Regt KIA 4.11.18.
ERSKINE Alexander MM Dvr 52489 157 Fd Coy Royal Engineers
ERSKINE Henry MM Pte 9140 2nd Bedfordshire Regt
ERSKINE James MM L/Cpl G/21521 7th Royal West Kent Regt
ERSKINE James MM Dvr 21600 Cav Corps Cable Sect Royal Engineers
ERSKINE W. MM Pte 6008 Machine Gun Corps
ERSKINE Walter MM Pte 350550 1/7th Royal Highlanders
ERSKINE Walter MM Pte R/37898 13th King's Royal Rifle Corps
ERSKINE William MM Pte 81242 75 Fd Amb RAMC
ERSSER Alfred William MM Gnr 15180 RFA
ERVIN James MM Cpl 229431 Royal Fusiliers
ERVINE Alexander Glendenning "MM,MSM" RQMS 14538 Royal Irish Rifles
ERVINE Andrew MM Pte 364683 145 Coy Labour Corps
ERWIN Robert J. MM Pte 10521 Irish Guards
ESBERGER George MM Gnr 77410 170 Bde RFA
ESCOLME James L. MM Gnr 114718 RGA
ESCOTT William Charles MM Pte 242708 1/4th Yorkshire Light Infantry KIA 28.4.18.
ESCREET Frank Henry MM Cpl 30984 East Yorkshire Regt
ESGROVE Samuel A. MM Pte S/30598 Rifle Brigade
ESHELBY John MM Gnr 776518 RFA
ESKDALE Thomas E. MM Pte 60471 14th Royal Welsh Fusiliers
ESLER James MM Sjt T3/030882 255(HT)Coy Army Service Corps
ESLICK James H. MM Sjt Farrier 40296 33 Bde RFA

ESNEY Patrick MM CSM 208 2nd Royal Munster Fusiliers
ESPENER Frederick MM Spr 252704 Second Army Sig Coy Royal Engineers
ESPIE Robert MM L/Cpl 325847 1/9th Arg & Suth Highlanders
ESPIE Thomas W. MM Pte 26043 Scottish Rifles
ESPIN Frederick MM Pte 14686 1st Lincolnshire Regt
ESPLEY George MM Spr 96953 175 Tunnelling Coy Royal Engineers
ESPLEY Samuel MM Bdr 21431 B/78 Bde RFA KIA 5.10.17.
ESS Charles MM Pte 3/8410 2nd Suffolk Regt KIA 8.10.18.
ESSERY Albert Edward MM Sjt 15307 8th Leicestershire Regt KIA 1.10.17.
ESSERY Arthur L. MM Sjt 45050 RFA
ESSERY James F. MM Cpl 202150 5th Devonshire Regt
ESSEX Edward MM Pte 10649 4th Dragoon Guards
ESSEX George E. MM+Bar L/Sjt 457355 RAMC
ESSEX Henry A. MM Sjt 931126 C/291 Bde RFA
ESSEX Horace A. MM Sjt 12175 11th Hampshire Regt
ESSEX Joseph J. MM L/Cpl 139190 30th Bn Machine Gun Corps
ESSEX William MM+Bar Sjt 3526 1st Royal Fusiliers
ESSLEMONT Andrew MM+Bar Sjt 290239 1/7th Gordon Highlanders
ESSLEMONT James MM Cpl 29891 Royal Scots
ESSLEMONT John J.A. MM Cpl S/8347 Gordon Highlanders
ESSON Frederick R. MM Cpl 4841 Army Cyclist Corps
ESSON Richard MM Sjt 365022 RGA
ESTELL Thomas MM Cpl 53238 RAMC
ESTELL William MM Sjt 37235 Northumberland Fusiliers
ESTHER James E. MM Cpl 750962 A/315 Bde RFA
ESTRIDGE Harry MM Pte 16822 32nd Bn Machine Gun Corps
ETCHELLS George Henry MM Pte 18846 10th Cheshire Regt KIA 7.6.17.
ETCHELLS Harry MM Pte 55333 14th Royal Welsh Fusiliers
ETCHELLS John Arthur MM Pte 242184 1/5th Border Regt
ETCHER H. MM Pte 4445 2nd Notts & Derby Regt Died 8.10.18.
ETHEARSON John MM Cpl 227 Seaforth Highlanders
ETHERIDGE Albert William MM Pte 10050 10th Royal West Kent Regt
ETHERIDGE Charles W. MM Pte 1329 6th Royal West Surrey Regt
ETHERIDGE Edward T. MM Pte 147968 47th Bn Machine Gun Corps
ETHERIDGE Eli MM Gnr 8455 RFA
ETHERIDGE George MM Dvr 59942 RFA
ETHERIDGE George MM Dvr 95444 RFA
ETHERIDGE George MM Gnr 77704 146 Siege Bty RGA
ETHERIDGE George William MM L/Cpl 326691 1/1st Cambridgeshire Regt DOW 8.10.17.
ETHERIDGE Hugh Dimsdale "MC,MM+Bar(1462 Pte)" T/2Lt 17th Royal Fusiliers
ETHERIDGE Lewis R. MM Gnr 783 RGA
ETHERIDGE Richard MM Dvr 199585 92 Fd Coy Royal Engineers
ETHERIDGE William J. MM Sjt 1827 24 Fd Amb RAMC
ETHERINGTON Arthur MM L/Cpl 6712 1st Middlesex Regt
ETHERINGTON Charles MM Sjt 3587 1st Rifle Brigade
ETHERINGTON Ernest E. MM+Bar Sjt G/1746 8th Royal Sussex Regt
ETHERINGTON Henry H. MM Cpl Fitter 32652 RFA
ETHERINGTON J. MM L/Cpl G/18885 Royal West Kent Regt
ETHERINGTON Sidney MM Pte 203361 1st East Surrey Regt
ETHERINGTON Walter MM Cpl 28010 6th Lancashire Fusiliers KIA 10.10.18.
ETHERINGTON William MM Gnr 9027 RFA
ETTE Fred M. MM Pte 3/10481 Northamptonshire Regt
ETTERSHANK R.G. MM Cpl 19145 Essex Regt
ETTRIDGE Edward A. MM Bdsm 6002 2nd Yorkshire Regt
ETTRIDGE Frank B.R. MM Sjt 890 7th Royal Sussex Regt
ETTY Robert MM L/Cpl 471052 526 Fd Coy Royal Engineers
ETWELL Edward J. MM L/Cpl 22955 17 Fd Coy Royal Engineers
EUNSON Robert Harvey MM Sjt 406125 Royal Engineers
EUSTACE Harry E.T. MM Pnr 24455 56 Fd Coy Royal Engineers
EUSTACE Thomas MM Pte 65994 RAMC
EUSTIS Thomas Ivor MM L/Cpl 46144 17th Royal Welsh Fusiliers
EUSTON Alfred J. MM L/Cpl 3670 Machine Gun Corps
EVA William H. MM Pte 16482 9th Scottish Rifles
EVANS A.G. MM Pte 27739 1/5th Border Regt
EVANS A.R. MM Pte G/21064 Royal West Kent Regt
EVANS Albert MM Pte 241360 Notts & Derby Regt
EVANS Albert MM Pte 2300 1/5th North Staffordshire Regt
EVANS Albert MM Cpl 27600 Royal Scots
EVANS Albert MM Sjt 61272 14 Bde RFA
EVANS Albert Charles MM Sjt 830133 A/241 Bde RFA Died 26.11.18.
EVANS Albert George MM Pte 49201 10th Cheshire Regt DOW 16.4.18.
EVANS Albert J. MM+Bar Sjt 6/13670 6th South Wales Borderers
EVANS Albert P. MM Cpl 1018 2nd Welsh Regt
EVANS Albert Pryse MM Pte 78181 16th Royal Welsh Fusiliers KIA 4.11.18.
EVANS Alexander H. MM L/Sjt PS/2347 16th Middlesex Regt
EVANS Alfred William "MM+Bar,CG(B)" CSM 70473 41st Bn Machine Gun Corps
EVANS Allan Edgar MM Gnr 686518 RFA
EVANS Andrew MM Sjt 200338 1/4th Royal Berkshire Regt
EVANS Andrew "DCM,MM+Bar" Cpl 10995 X/11 Med TM Bty RFA
EVANS Archibald MM Pte 32536 1st Gloucestershire Regt
EVANS Arthur MM L/Cpl 34010 South Lancashire Regt
EVANS Arthur H. MM CSM 251211 296 Rly Const Coy Royal Engineers
EVANS Arthur James MM Sjt 764 7th Royal Sussex Regt KIA 7.7.16.
EVANS Arthur T. MM Pte M2/020970 Army Service Corps
EVANS Benjamin MM Pte 265452 1/6th Welsh Regt
EVANS C.H.H. MM L/Cpl 33569 Oxf & Bucks Light Infantry
EVANS Charles MM Pte 30602 Worcestershire Regt
EVANS Charles MM Pte 11795 8th South Staffordshire Regt
EVANS Charles C. MM Pte 15127 7th South Wales Borderers
EVANS Charles C. MM Cpl S/27442 13th Rifle Brigade
EVANS Charles Thomas MM+Bar Cpl(MCDR) 28142 1 Div Sig Coy Royal Engineers
EVANS Charles W. MM Pte 50237 4th Liverpool Regt
EVANS Charles William MM Sjt 8356 C/148 Bde RFA
EVANS Claude P. MM Pte 5166 12th Royal Fusiliers
EVANS Clifford C. MM Bdr 43588 RGA
EVANS D.J. MM Pte 42049 Royal Welsh Fusiliers
EVANS Dan T. MM Pte 7744 1st Duke of Cornwall's LI
EVANS Daniel MM Pte 54305 Royal Welsh Fusiliers
EVANS Daniel R. MM L/Cpl 24617 4th Hussars
EVANS David MM Pte 55454 16th Royal Welsh Fusiliers
EVANS David MM Pte 1591 1/3rd Monmouthshire Regt
EVANS David MM Gnr 1256 X/47 Med TM Bty RGA Died 18.9.16.
EVANS David MM L/Cpl 276073 Arg & Suth Highlanders
EVANS David Elias MM Pte 14075 1st South Staffordshire Regt DOW 26.4.18.
EVANS David J. MM Pte 13308 Royal Welsh Fusiliers
EVANS David J. MM Dvr 229967 RFA
EVANS David J. MM L/Sjt 14922 8th South Lancashire Regt
EVANS David J. MM Pte 38944 Welsh Regt
EVANS David J. MM Pte 1360 1st Welsh Guards
EVANS David L. MM+Bar Cpl 440561 Royal Engineers
EVANS David Thomas MM L/Cpl 12166 1st Gloucestershire Regt KIA 20.8.16.
EVANS Dewi A. MM Cpl 20662 Welsh Regt
EVANS E. MM Pte 334020 Royal Welsh Fusiliers
EVANS Ebenezer MM Dvr W/211 D/119 Bde RFA
EVANS Edgar H.M. MM Sjt 07673 Army Ordnance Corps
EVANS Edward MM Pte 1316 64 Fd Amb RAMC
EVANS Edward MM Sjt 25751 B/173 Bde RFA
EVANS Edward MM Pte 201490 Shropshire Light Infantry
EVANS Edward MM Gnr 29517 RFA
EVANS Edward MM L/Cpl 18546 6th Oxf & Bucks Light Infantry KIA 20.9.17.
EVANS Edward MM Gne 155751 112 Siege Bty RGA
EVANS Edward Daniel MM Pte 27797 11th Royal Warwickshire Regt
EVANS Edward Idris MM Sjt 49945 9th Royal Welsh Fusiliers
EVANS Edwin John MM Pte 24621 5th Dorsetshire Regt
EVANS Eli MM Pte 24706 37th Bn Machine Gun Corps
EVANS Ernest MM Pte 200760 Royal Scots
EVANS Ernest MM L/Cpl 241135 York & Lancaster Regt
EVANS Ernest E. MM Pte 2168 1st King's Royal Rifle Corps
EVANS Ernest J. MM Gnr 96444 D/83 Bde RFA
EVANS Ernest W. MM Sjt 2257 2nd Dragoon Guards
EVANS Evan MM Sjt 48066 130 Fd Amb RAMC
EVANS Evan MM CSM 18902 13th Royal Welsh Fusiliers
EVANS Evan MM L/Cpl 3419 1/8th London Regt DOW 24.9.16.
EVANS Evan Pierce MM L/Cpl 159513 'O' Special Coy Royal Engineers DOW 9.9.17.
EVANS F.C. MM Sjt 8155 2nd East Kent Regt
EVANS Francis MM Pte 200990 1/4th Cheshire Regt DOW 16.10.18.

EVANS Francis E. MM+Bar Pte 8870 2nd Wiltshire Regt
EVANS Francis J. MM Cpl 82579 1st South Wales Borderers
EVANS Frank MM Sjt 19110 20th Manchester Regt
EVANS Frank Harry Butroyd MM+Bar Pte A/1907 16th King's Royal Rifle Corps Died 19.11.18.
EVANS Frank Thomas MM Sjt 31051 2nd Royal Welsh Fusiliers
EVANS Frank W. MM Pte 2498 8th Royal Sussex Regt
EVANS Fred MM Pte 47334 7th Lancashire Fusiliers
EVANS Fred MM Pte 200421 Tank Corps
EVANS Fred P. MM Sjt 50874 Machine Gun Corps
EVANS Frederick MM L/Cpl 21561 10th Royal West Surrey Regt
EVANS Frederick MM Pte M2/077699 Army Service Corps
EVANS Frederick MM Sjt 6647 Machine Gun Corps
EVANS Frederick A. MM Gnr 116475 RGA
EVANS Frederick H. MM Cpl 368036 7th London Regt
EVANS Frederick H. MM Pte 2271 1/18th London Regt
EVANS Frederick Henry MM Pte 9644 2nd Royal Welsh Fusiliers DOW 26.7.17.
EVANS Frederick J. MM Sjt 452456 30 Div Sig Coy Royal Engineers
EVANS Frederick L. MM Pte STK674 10th Royal Fusiliers
EVANS G. "MM,CdiG(It)" Pte 201753 1/4th Royal Berkshire Regt
EVANS George "DCM,MM" Sjt 2155 B/148 Bde RFA
EVANS George MM Sjt 2293 Royal Inniskilling Fusiliers
EVANS George MM Pte 27010 1st Royal Lancaster Regt KIA 5.12.17.
EVANS George MM Pte 241755 13th Welsh Regt
EVANS George MM Pte 45091 Lancashire Fusiliers
EVANS George MM Sjt 53590 Welsh Regt
EVANS George MM Sjt 4504 2nd Lancashire Fusiliers KIA 1.7.16.
EVANS George MM Pte 2121 1/4th Gloucestershire Regt
EVANS George MM Dvr L/43300 C/187 Bde RFA
EVANS George MM+Bar Bdr 106211 RGA
EVANS George F. MM Pte 29015 Oxf & Bucks Light Infantry
EVANS George H. MM L/Sjt 2036 West Yorkshire Regt
EVANS George P. MM+Bar Sjt 5779 1 Siege Coy R Monmouth RE
EVANS George William MM Pte 305103 15th Bn Tank Corps
EVANS Gomer W. MM Dvr 3374 RFA
EVANS H. "MM,MID" Cpl 435358 RAMC
EVANS Harold MM Pte 1750 2nd Lancashire Fusiliers
EVANS Harold James MM Sjt 238144 2nd Lincolnshire Regt DOW 3.11.18.
EVANS Harold S.W. MM L/Cpl 236085 1/1st Herefordshire Regt
EVANS Harold Samuel MM Pte 203336 Royal Welsh Fusiliers
EVANS Harold Victor "DCM,MM" Sjt 40619 12th West Yorkshire Regt KIA 20.11.17.
EVANS Harry MM Sjt M2/049777 180 Coy Army Service Corps
EVANS Harry MM Sjt M2/099416 Army Service Corps
EVANS Harry MM Pte M2/168152 283 MT Coy Army Service Corps
EVANS Harry MM L/Bdr 831353 A/223 Bde RFA
EVANS Harry MM Cpl 21514 South Wales Borderers
EVANS Harry MM Cpl 1570 1/6th Welsh Regt
EVANS Harry MM Sjt 296971 155 Hy Bty RGA
EVANS Harry MM L/Sjt 19111 Manchester Regt
EVANS Harry Allan MM Cpl 11693 1st Worcestershire Regt KIA 28.3.18.
EVANS Harry E.V. MM Pte 241808 1/6th Liverpool Regt
EVANS Harry M. MM Pte 240860 Welsh Regt
EVANS Harry R. MM Pte 11855 1st King's Royal Rifle Corps
EVANS Henry MM L/Sjt 267294 Gloucestershire Regt
EVANS Henry H. MM Pte 68148 RAMC
EVANS Henry J. MM Pte 282021 4th London Regt
EVANS Henry Joseph MM L/Cpl 24737 42 Labour Coy Labour Corps
EVANS Herbert "MM,OLeo(B)" Sjt L/10688 170 Bde RFA
EVANS Herbert MM Cpl 15875 11th Worcestershire Regt DOW 4.12.17.
EVANS Herbert A. MM Spr 538100 30 Div Sig Coy Royal Engineers
EVANS Horace Hughes MM Sjt 740751 D/123 Bde RFA DOW 22.5.18.
EVANS Horatio Ellis MM Pte 21069 10th South Wales Borderers KIA 17.9.18.
EVANS Hugh J. MM Sjt 44218 Manchester Regt
EVANS Hugh William MM Cpl 276334 Essex Regt
EVANS Idris MM L/Cpl 20333 11th Essex Regt KIA 9.11.16.
EVANS Isaac MM Pnr 210782 8 Div Sig Coy Royal Engineers DOW 29.3.18.
EVANS Isiah MM Gnr 606194 RHA
EVANS J. MM L/Cpl 240466 South Lancashire Regt
EVANS J.F. MM Cpl 20749 1st Essex Regt
EVANS Jack MM Cpl 9170 2nd Royal Munster Fusiliers
EVANS Jack MM L/Cpl 242222 6th King's Own Scottish Borderers KIA 25.4.18.
EVANS Jacob MM Spr 454462 Royal Engineers
EVANS James MM Bdr 371290 RGA
EVANS James MM Pte 946 7th Royal Sussex Regt
EVANS James MM+Bar Gnr 6079 RFA
EVANS James Edward "MM,MSM,MID" RQMS 7877 2nd Worcestershire Regt
EVANS James F. MM Cpl 328 RAMC
EVANS James Havard MM Pte 503 15th Royal Warwickshire Regt DOW 11.9.16.
EVANS John MM Bdr 30211 92 Bty 17 Bde RFA
EVANS John MM 2nd Cpl 87774 Royal Engineers
EVANS John MM Cpl 13485 9th Royal Welsh Fusiliers KIA 29.4.18.
EVANS John MM L/Bdr 9690 B/149 Bde RFA
EVANS John MM Pte 16644 1/5th Border Regt
EVANS John MM Sjt 25826 15th Lancashire Fusiliers KIA 30.9.18.
EVANS John MM Sjt 3589 RFA
EVANS John MM Pte 2275 1st Royal Lancaster Regt
EVANS John MM Sjt 10535 6th East Yorkshire Regt
EVANS John MM L/Cpl 41733 RAMC
EVANS John MM Gnr 188027 158 Bde(RFA) 2/1st(Berkshire)Bty(RHA) RHA
EVANS John MM L/Cpl 23156 2nd South Wales Borderers DOW 5.2.18.
EVANS John H. MM Pte 48348 RAMC
EVANS John Henry MM Sjt 40 231 Bde RFA
EVANS John Henry MM L/Cpl 3519 Liverpool Regt
EVANS John L. MM Sjt 310041 1/1(Welsh)Hy Bty RGA
EVANS John Lewis MM L/Cpl 158188 256 Tunnelling Coy Royal Engineers
EVANS John Owen "MM,MID" Spr 23287 Royal Engineers
EVANS John S. MM Sjt 19508 10th North Lancashire Regt
EVANS John Thomas "MM,MID" Sjt 12965 8th Yorkshire Light Infantry
EVANS John W. MM Spr 139257 Royal Engineers
EVANS Jonathan H. MM Pte 16546 Shropshire Light Infantry
EVANS Joseph MM SQMS L/12887 12th Lancers
EVANS Joseph MM Gnr 45242 RFA
EVANS Joseph MM Pte 3975 1/7th Worcestershire Regt
EVANS Joseph MM+Bar L/Sjt 14681 6th Northamptonshire Regt
EVANS Joseph MM L/Cpl 15830 7th South Lancashire Regt
EVANS Joseph P. MM+Bar Sjt 42503 1 Div Sig Coy Royal Engineers
EVANS Joseph R. MM Pte 423 1st Welsh Guards
EVANS Joseph Stanley MM Cpl 240352 15th Notts & Derby Regt
EVANS Joshua MM Pte 241205 2/6th South Staffordshire Regt KIA 21.3.18.
EVANS Lewis P. "DCM,MM" Cpl 5118 A/112 Bde RFA
EVANS Mabel Louise MM Sister F TFNS
EVANS Maurice S. MM L/Cpl 78456 Royal Engineers
EVANS Norman S. MM Pte 45745 RAMC
EVANS Oswald "MM,MSM" Spr 265596 22 Light Railway Train Crew Coy Royal Engineers
EVANS Owen MM Pte 31786 18th Welsh Regt
EVANS Owen MM Pnr 44132 10th South Wales Borderers DOW 30.4.18.
EVANS Percy MM Sjt 10678 2nd Royal Irish Fusiliers
EVANS Percy C.A. MM Cpl 3/38 Wiltshire Regt
EVANS Percy Makdwyn MM+Bar Dvr 1649 B/121 Bde RFA
EVANS Philip J. MM Dvr 64877 15 Bde RFA
EVANS Phillip F. MM L/Sjt 20040 10th South Wales Borderers
EVANS Reginald C. MM Gnr 199319 RFA
EVANS Reginald E. MM Cpl 73259 17th Royal Welsh Fusiliers
EVANS Richard MM Cpl 7695 1st East Surrey Regt
EVANS Richard MM L/Cpl 107168 40 Div Sig Coy Royal Engineers KIA 13.4.18.
EVANS Richard MM Cpl 10009 Liverpool Regt
EVANS Richard A. MM L/Cpl 22399 Royal West Surrey Regt
EVANS Richard P. MM Gnr 1832 RFA
EVANS Richard Stuart "MM,MID" Sjt 74748 MGC(Heavy Branch)
EVANS Robert David MM Pte 372011 1/8th London Regt DOW 23.3.18.
EVANS Robert E. MM Cpl 17326 19th Liverpool Regt
EVANS Robert George MM Sjt 17245 4th Liverpool Regt DOW 24.10.18.
EVANS Robert M. MM Cpl 242507 5th East Lancashire Regt
EVANS Robert O. MM Sjt 57293 Welsh Regt
EVANS Robert T. MM Sjt 9935 L Corps Sig Coy Royal Engineers
EVANS Robert W. MM+Bar L/Cpl 48547 Liverpool Regt

EVANS Samuel MM Sjt 14116 6th Leicestershire Regt
EVANS Samuel MM L/Cpl 106754 40 Div Sig Coy Royal Engineers
EVANS Samuel MM Sjt 18569 Royal Welsh Fusiliers
EVANS Samuel MM Pte 2705 Gloucestershire Regt
EVANS Samuel MM Dvr 75209 30 Bde RFA
EVANS Samuel E. MM Pte 6239 XV Corps Cyclist Bn Army Cyclist Corps
EVANS Samuel V. MM Cpl 32285 East Surrey Regt
EVANS Stanley Edwin MM Sjt 10675 2nd Worcestershire Regt
EVANS Stephen MM Cpl 139139 Royal Engineers
EVANS Sydney C. MM Spr 134287 23 Fd Coy Royal Engineers
EVANS Sydney Francis MM Sjt 13189 4th Royal Fusiliers DOW 23.9.18.
EVANS Sydney R.H. MM L/Cpl 10470 15th Hussars
EVANS T.J. MM Sjt W/936 256 Bde RFA
EVANS Thomas MM Pte 323963 6th London Regt
EVANS Thomas MM Pte 2130 4th Middlesex Regt
EVANS Thomas "DCM,MM" Gnr 22828 40 Bty 14 Bde RFA
EVANS Thomas MM Pte 3999 12th Durham Light Infantry KIA 11.7.17.
EVANS Thomas MM Pte 10653 Royal Welsh Fusiliers
EVANS Thomas MM Pte 24184 Machine Gun Corps
EVANS Thomas MM Sjt 9366 2nd Royal Welsh Fusiliers
EVANS Thomas MM Pte B/1486 Rifle Brigade
EVANS Thomas MM Pte 2851 1st Welsh Guards DOW 5.9.17.
EVANS Thomas MM Pte 6869 1st Cheshire Regt
EVANS Thomas Alexander Matthews MM Sjt 8163 2nd Scots Guards
EVANS Thomas C. MM Sjt 38637 49 Fd Amb RAMC
EVANS Thomas H. MM Pte 8773 Irish Guards
EVANS Thomas R. MM Pte 30646 4th Somerset Light Infantry
EVANS Thomas Richard MM L/Cpl 20815 9th Royal Welsh Fusiliers KIA 20.9.17.
EVANS Thomas W. MM L/Cpl 4614 2nd Border Regt
EVANS Thomas Young MM Pte 4250 1/3rd London Regt KIA 13.9.16.
EVANS W. MM Pte 237093 1/1st Herefordshire Regt
EVANS W. MM Sjt 245676 Manchester Regt
EVANS W.A. MM Pnr 206656 Royal Engineers
EVANS Walter MM Cpl 67561 B/190 Bde RFA
EVANS Walter MM Sjt S/13085 Rifle Brigade
EVANS Walter Hambrook MM Pte 200852 2/4th Lincolnshire Regt
EVANS Walter Richard MM L/Cpl 27617 1st Royal Welsh Fusiliers
EVANS Wilfred MM Sjt 15163 Royal Lancaster Regt
EVANS Wilfred MM CSM 7734 7th Shropshire Light Infantry
EVANS Wilfred Emlyn MM Cpl Shoeing Smith 735542 A/37 Bde RFA
EVANS William MM Pte 5731 4th Middlesex Regt
EVANS William MM Pte 14758 3rd Royal Fusiliers
EVANS William MM 2nd Cpl 192271 1 Fd Svy Bn Royal Engineers
EVANS William MM Sjt 11993 Middlesex Regt
EVANS William MM Pte 19858 4th Bn Machine Gun Corps
EVANS William MM Dvr 40307 21 Bde RFA
EVANS William "DCM,MM,MID" L/Cpl 13183 2nd Royal Welsh Fusiliers
EVANS William MM Pte S/9486 Gordon Highlanders
EVANS William MM Farrier S/Sjt 14386 37 Bde RFA
EVANS William MM Pte 1298 1/8th Middlesex Regt Died 26.6.16.
EVANS William MM Sjt 24107 2nd Lancashire Fusiliers
EVANS William MM Gnr 110594 RFA
EVANS William MM Sjt 10431 2nd Royal Warwickshire Regt
EVANS William C. MM Sjt 14972 8th East Lancashire Regt
EVANS William D. MM L/Cpl 6894 2nd Middlesex Regt
EVANS William David MM L/Sjt 16530 10th Cheshire Regt
EVANS William E. MM Pte DM2/190922 335 Coy Army Service Corps
EVANS William E. MM Pte 307089 Royal Warwickshire Regt
EVANS William E. MM Spr 62969 Royal Engineers
EVANS William E. MM+Bar Pte 307089 2/8th Royal Warwickshire Regt
EVANS William F. MM Pte B/2157 Rifle Brigade
EVANS William G. MM Cpl 51717 11th Royal Scots
EVANS William G. MM Sjt 5104 Machine Gun Corps
EVANS William George MM Sjt 120671 Special Brigade Royal Engineers
EVANS William H. MM Pte S/17675 1st Rifle Brigade
EVANS William H. MM Pte 14528 14th Welsh Regt
EVANS William H. MM Sjt 12612 5th Royal Berkshire Regt
EVANS William H. MM Pte 20153 Welsh Regt
EVANS William J. MM Pte 48112 RAMC
EVANS William John MM Dvr 29875 C/91 Bde RFA KIA 6.6.17.
EVANS William M. MM L/Cpl 144924 50th Bn Machine Gun Corps
EVANS William O. MM L/Sjt 5519 1/4th Royal Welsh Fusiliers
EVANS William Pearce MM Cpl 29008 8 Div Sig Coy Royal Engineers Died 31.7.20.
EVANSON Ernest MM RQMS 300931 1/5th London Regt
EVANSON George MM L/Cpl 86057 88 Coy Machine Gun Corps
EVANSON Thomas MM Pte 243216 Cheshire Regt
EVASON Arthur MM+Bar Sjt 15877 7th York & Lancaster Regt
EVASON Joseph MM 2nd Cpl 60203 106 Fd Coy Royal Engineers
EVE Albert Henry MM Pte 293593 3 Labour Coy Labour Corps
EVE Douglas H. MM L/Cpl 391986 9th London Regt
EVELEIGH Sidney MM L/Cpl 552703 1/16th London Regt
EVELY Arthur Lewis "MM,MID" Bdr 52575 16 Bde A Bty RHA
EVENDEN Arthur MM Cpl M2/114108 Army Service Corps
EVENDEN Edward F. MM Pte 19585 East Surrey Regt
EVENDEN Frank "DCM,MM" Pte G/1406 2nd Royal Sussex Regt
EVENDEN George W. MM Sjt 24411 Royal West Surrey Regt
EVENDEN William Henry MM Dvr 60894 79 Fd Coy Royal Engineers
EVENISS Edward H. MM L/Cpl 44001 Royal Fusiliers
EVERALL Herbert "MM,MID" Pre 65867 RAMC
EVERARD Bert MM Pte 42023 1/1st Hertfordshire Regt
EVERARD Herbert MM+Bar Sjt 240320 6th Royal Warwickshire Regt
EVERARD J.W. MM Pte 322502 London Regt
EVERED Arthur John MM Sjt 2064 1/4th Suffolk Regt
EVERED Percy H. MM Sjt 230601 2nd London Regt
EVERED William MM Sjt 3614 47th Bn Machine Gun Corps
EVEREST Albert John MM Pte 201075 Royal West Kent Regt
EVEREST Alfred G. MM CSM L/11384 Royal Fusiliers
EVEREST Frederick C. MM Pte 60735 7th Royal West Surrey Regt
EVEREST Victor George MM Pte 24345 8th Royal West Surrey Regt KIA 21.3.18.
EVERETT Albert B. MM Sjt 296 1/4th Suffolk Regt
EVERETT Albert Matthew MM Gnr 52715 RGA
EVERETT Alfred E. MM Pte 4151 1/24th London Regt
EVERETT Charles Edward MM L/Sjt S/26077 9th Rifle Brigade
EVERETT Frederick George MM Pte 15861 9th Norfolk Regt KIA 12.10.16.
EVERETT George MM Pte 202664 1st London Regt
EVERETT George A. MM L/Cpl 722937 24th London Regt
EVERETT George H. MM Sjt 26447 1st Norfolk Regt
EVERETT Harold MM Sjt 45062 1/1st Surrey Yeomanry
EVERETT Harry MM+Bar Cpl 12190 7th Suffolk Regt
EVERETT Horace MM L/Cpl M1/07250 44 Mot Amb Convoy Army Service Corps
EVERETT Joseph MM Pte 38603 1st Hampshire Regt
EVERETT Percy MM Sjt 16952 7th Norfolk Regt
EVERETT Ralph MM Pte 35995 7th Wiltshire Regt
EVERETT Richard Connell MM Sjt 72075 40 Bde RFA
EVERETT Samuel J. MM Sjt L/30427 36 Div Ammn Col RFA
EVERETT Stephen H. MM Pte 22771 1st Coldstream Guards
EVERIESS Frank MM Pte 7805 2nd Hampshire Regt
EVERISS Charles William MM Sjt 12140 4th Worcestershire Regt KIA 30.11.16.
EVERIST Clarence S. MM+Bar Sjt 18971 12th Bn Machine Gun Corps
EVERITT Albert MM Pte 45592 2nd Suffolk Regt
EVERITT Arthur J. MM Bdr 65198 RFA
EVERITT Frederick "MM+Bar,MID" Sjt 12050 1 Div Sig Coy Royal Engineers
EVERITT Harry MM L/Cpl 15505 1st Norfolk Regt
EVERITT John T. MM Dvr 158347 RFA
EVERITT Thomas MM L/Cpl 36375 13th York & Lancaster Regt DOW 30.9.18.
EVERITT William MM Pte 8527 2nd Northamptonshire Regt
EVERRETT Walter E. MM Pte 201059 Suffolk Regt
EVERS Owen MM Pte 405470 2/3rd(West Riding)Fd Amb RAMC
EVERS Richard MM Pte 34594 Worcestershire Regt
EVERSFIELD John MM Cpl 201117 8th Royal West Kent Regt
EVERSON Arthur George MM Sjt 2899 1/4th Suffolk Regt KIA 23.4.17.
EVERSON Ralph MM Pte 16156 6th Yorkshire Regt
EVERSON Richard "DCM,MM" Sjt 13806 10th West Riding Regt KIA 27.10.18.
EVERTON A. MM Sjt 31637 85 Bty 11 Bde RFA
EVERTON Abraham MM CSM 13757 7th Lincolnshire Regt
EVERY William Henry MM Bdr 1688 47 Siege Bty RGA KIA 2.9.16.
EVES Alfred Edward MM Bdr 22734 D/156 Bde RFA Died 12.6.18.

EVES Arthur W. MM Pte 390502 1/9th London Regt
EVES John MM Sjt 9038 1st Royal Irish Fusiliers
EVES Joseph P. MM Dvr 91366 81 Fd Coy Royal Engineers
EVES Richard MM Sjt L/6569 2nd Royal West Kent Regt
EVIS Bertie MM L/Cpl 16123 8th Somerset Light Infantry
EVISON Jack "DCM,MM" Sjt 25781 17th Royal Welsh Fusiliers
EVISON James R. MM Pte 39281 Royal Welsh Fusiliers
EVISON Sidney MM Pte 60595 23rd Lancashire Fusiliers
EVITTA Thomas MM Gnr 55652 56 Siege Bty RGA
EWAN Robert MM Sjt 2015 Gordon Highlanders
EWART Frank MM Cpl(MCDR) 28729 Royal Engineers
EWART George B. MM Pte 139501 Machine Gun Corps
EWART Joseph MM Pte 12761 11/13th Royal Irish Rifles
EWART Robert MM L/Cpl S/6268 8th Seaforth Highlanders
EWART Walter D. MM Pte S/2402 9th Seaforth Highlanders
EWBANK John MM+Bar L/Cpl 201557 2/5th West Yorkshire Regt
EWBANK Joseph Tate MM L/Cpl 27927 39th Bn Machine Gun Corps
EWBANK Spencer MM L/Cpl 52235 Middlesex Regt
EWELL R.C. MM Sjt 17673 Grenadier Guards
EWEN Charles MM Bdr 38092 RFA
EWEN Samuel MM Pte S/17304 7th Gordon Highlanders
EWEN Sidney Walter MM Pnr 130050 4 Special Coy Royal Engineers
EWEN Victor MM Pte 53354 10th Royal Fusiliers
EWENMECKLIN Frank MM Pte 17360 5th Northamptonshire Regt
EWENS Allan "DCM,MM(439,4th Hussars),MID" Sjt 31177 2nd Devonshire Regt
EWING A. MM Pte 40165 14th Arg & Suth Highlanders
EWING A. MM L/Cpl 859 Seaforth Highlanders
EWING Alfred MM Sjt R/1310 12th King's Royal Rifle Corps
EWING Alfred Peter MM Cpl 511666 2/14th London Regt
EWING Douglas James MM L/Cpl S/6281 8th Royal Highlanders Died 24.6.18.
EWING John Adams MM Sjt 14540 14th Royal Irish Rifles
EWING Robert MM Pte 2444 1/7th Royal Highlanders
EWING Wilfred Max MM L/Sjt R/7729 12th King's Royal Rifle Corps DOW 1.12.17.
EWING William "MM,MID" Pte 14687 12th Royal Scots
EWINGTON Charles H. MM Sjt L/11330 7th Middlesex Regt
EWINGTON George Ernest MM Dvr 85813 A/63 Bde RFA
EWINS Vincent Bryan MM Pte 302300 2/5th London Regt KIA 20.9.17.
EWLES Lewis MM Pte 16881 Norfolk Regt
EXALL Bert MM Sjt 10461 C/175 Bde RFA
EXCELL Frederick W. MM Pte 16498 Bedfordshire Regt
EXELBY Thomas MM Pte 201234 7th West Yorkshire Regt
EXELL Frank (Francis George?) MM Pte 529 6th Royal West Kent Regt KIA 4.5.17.
EXELL Walter MM Pte 23691 8th Royal Berkshire Regt
EXELL William MM L/Cpl 240127 1/5th Gloucestershire Regt KIA 10.4.18.
EXETER Arthur Thomas "MM+2 Bars,MID" Cpl R/23990 18th King's Royal Rifle Corps DOW 22.10 18.
EXLEY Alfred MM Pte DM2/155125 Army Service Corps att 'P' AA Bty RGA
EXLEY Charles H. MM Pte 242098 Royal Warwickshire Regt
EXLEY Herbert MM L/Cpl 2206 1/7th West Yorkshire Regt KIA 14.7.16.
EXLEY Norman C. MM Sjt DM2/154374 Army Service Corps
EXON William S. MM Pte 242215 York & Lancaster Regt
EXTALL George A. MM Pte R/7050 King's Royal Rifle Corps
EXTEN Charles MM Gnr 935848 B/82 Bde RFA
EXTENCE Edwin G. MM Sjt C/9613 20th King's Royal Rifle Corps KIA 15.6.17.
EYDEN Edward L. MM Pte 723147 24th London Regt
EYEVAL William MM L/Cpl 241353 1/4th Seaforth Highlanders
EYKELBOSCH Sidney W. MM Gnr 105315 RGA
EYLES Charles MM Sjt 67553 57th Bn Machine Gun Corps
EYLES Charles P. MM Pte 58056 Devonshire Regt
EYLES Frederick MM Pte 9604 2nd Bedfordshire Regt
EYLES George M. MM Spr 478725 18 Div Sig Coy Royal Engineers
EYLES William MM Pte 10632 4th Middlesex Regt
EYNSTONE William MM Sjt 12466 9th South Staffordshire Regt
EYRE Arthur H. MM Pte 17528 11th Notts & Derby Regt
EYRE Edwin MM Sjt 17617 20th Manchester Regt KIA 3.9.16.
EYRE Edwin MM Sjt 3/26957 South Wales Borderers
EYRE George Robert MM L/Cpl 23638 2nd Grenadier Guards
EYRE James MM Pte 2935 2nd Cheshire Regt
EYRE John W. "DCM,MM" Cpl 11527 1/4th York & Lancaster Regt
EYRE Richard MM Sjt 14/879 2nd York & Lancaster Regt
EYRES Gerald MM+Bar Pte 36761 1st Cheshire Regt
EYRES Henry James "MM,MID" Pte 26798 1st Dorsetshire Regt
EYRES Walter MM Pnr 237346 35 Div Sig Coy Royal Engineers
EYTON Ernest H. MM Pte 1381 9th Royal Fusiliers
EZZARD William MM+Bar Sjt 277538 RGA

F

FABIAN Charles MM L/Cpl 11915 Middlesex Regt
FABIAN Cyril Eric MM Sjt 260310 1/1st City of London Yeo
FABLING Katherine MM Miss F BRSC(VAD)
FACE Frank Leslie MM Cpl 106604 Special Bde Royal Engineers
FACER Frank MM Pte 11769 7th Lincolnshire Regt
FACER H.H. MM Spr 236670 Royal Engineers
FACER William MM Pte 27504 2nd Northamptonshire Regt
FACER William J. MM Pte 8659 9th Suffolk Regt
FACEY Frederick MM Cpl 18246 North Staffordshire Regt
FACEY George F. MM Gnr 68288 44 Bde RFA
FACEY John Henry MM Pte 72393 Cheshire Regt
FADDY Ralph MM Pte 33268 North Staffordshire Regt
FAGAN Bernard MM Pte 13368 2nd Notts & Derby Regt
FAGAN Howard Alexander "MM,MID" Sjt 1474 1/16th London Regt DOW 21.7.16.
FAGAN James MM Pte 73402 42nd Bn Machine Gun Corps
FAGAN John MM L/Cpl 34093 16th Royal Scots KIA 22.10.17.
FAGAN Patrick MM Sjt 9612 Royal Irish Regt
FAGAN Patrick MM Pte 5737 1st Lancashire Fusiliers
FAGAN Thomas J. MM Sjt 78797 Royal Engineers
FAGENCE Harry MM L/Cpl 292688 2nd Middlesex Regt
FAGG G.E. MM Pte 28523 East Surrey Regt
FAGG John MM Sjt 6638 1st East Yorkshire Regt
FAGG Robert Archibald MM Pte G/10569 10th Royal Fusiliers
FAGGETTER George Thomas MM Pte 10880 2nd Middlesex Regt
FAGHY Martin MM Sjt 20775 8th Northumberland Fusiliers
FAHEY Patrick MM Pte G/12097 19th Middlesex Regt
FAHEY William J. MM L/Cpl 954 22nd Royal Fusiliers
FAHIE Charles T. MM Pte M2/147697 Army Service Corps
FAHY Martin MM Sjt 203210 1/5th Lancashire Fusiliers
FAHY William John MM Sjt 10157 2nd Royal Irish Regt KIA 3.9.16.
FAICHEN Thomas MM Dvr 414088 410 Fd Coy Royal Engineers
FAICHEN William MM Pte 10575 1st Royal Scots
FAID James MM Gnr 37415 RFA
FAIERS George MM Cpl 9876 Machine Gun Corps
FAIL Henry "MM,MSM" CQMS 10772 11th Northumberland Fusiliers
FAIL William MM Cpl 20881 11 Div Ammn Col RFA
FAINT Robert James MM Cpl 340176 319 Siege Bty RGA KIA 23.4.18.
FAIR Albert MM Dvr 64790 84 Bty 11 Bde RFA
FAIR William MM Pte 1334 2nd Royal Warwickshire Regt
FAIRBAIRN Charles Stanley "MM,MID" Cpl 66441 3 Bde RHA
FAIRBAIRN D. MM Pte 235364 1/4th Seaforth Highlanders
FAIRBAIRN George W. MM Sjt 242182 Northumberland Fusiliers
FAIRBAIRN Henry MM L/Sjt 1395 1st Northumberland Fusiliers
FAIRBAIRN J. MM+Bar Cpl 10664 1/5th West Riding Regt
FAIRBAIRN James MM Pte 29551 East Yorkshire Regt
FAIRBAIRN James MM L/Cpl 33799 RAMC
FAIRBAIRN John MM Pte 15344 13th Royal Scots
FAIRBAIRN Peter MM Pte 352405 1/9th Royal Scots KIA 1.8.17.
FAIRBAIRN Thomas MM L/Cpl 201199 King's Own Scottish Borderers
FAIRBAIRN Thomas "MM,MID" Cpl 8317 2nd Durham Light Infantry
FAIRBAIRN W.A. "MM,MID" Sjt M1/07870 Army Service Corps
FAIRBAIRN Walter "DCM,MM" Cpl 89391 A/50 Bde RFA
FAIRBANK Frank Ernest MM Sjt 2044 1/6th West Yorkshire Regt
FAIRBANKS Ernest MM Pte 311 1st Welsh Guards
FAIRBANKS William H. MM Pte 12425 9th Cheshire Regt
FAIRBROTHER Bertram MM Pte 2547 XIX Corps Cyclist Bn Army Cyclist Corps
FAIRBROTHER Edward T. MM Pte 65884 RAMC
FAIRBROTHER Ernest MM+Bar Pte 6552 7th Royal West Kent Regt
FAIRBROTHER Frank MM Gnr 138845 RFA
FAIRBROTHER Harry MM Dvr 95025 24 Div Ammn Col RFA
FAIRBROTHER Jesse MM L/Cpl 291391 Cheshire Regt
FAIRBROTHER John MM Sjt 14954 6/7th Royal Scots Fusiliers
FAIRBROTHER John MM Pte 22489 Machine Gun Corps
FAIRBURN Frederick MM Pte 202385 2/4th Yorkshire Light Infantry

FAIRCLOUGH Albert MM Sjt 21441 2nd Highland Light Infantry
FAIRCLOUGH Alfred MM Pte 41422 5th Lancashire Fusiliers
FAIRCLOUGH Arthur MM L/Sjt 31373 6th York & Lancaster Regt
FAIRCLOUGH Fred MM Sjt 34484 C/181 Bde RFA KIA 2.12.17.
FAIRCLOUGH Frederick I. MM L/Cpl 18597 Liverpool Regt
FAIRCLOUGH George MM Gnr 132809 161 Siege Bty RGA KIA 13.5.17.
FAIRCLOUGH Horace Chadwick MM Pte 49272 13th Cheshire Regt
FAIRCLOUGH John MM Cpl 243015 1/4th South Lancashire Regt
FAIRCLOUGH Josiah MM L/Cpl 42301 11th Suffolk Regt
FAIRCLOUGH Richard MM Pte 204079 6th Liverpool Regt
FAIRCLOUGH Thomas MM Cpl 20639 9th Scottish Rifles
FAIRCLOUGH Thomas MM Dvr 686655 RFA
FAIRCLOUGH William MM L/Cpl 2220 1/6th Liverpool Regt
FAIRCLOUGH William MM Pte 77032 69 Fd Amb RAMC
FAIRES Thomas Albert MM Sjt 1606 3rd Dragoon Guards
FAIREY Arthur MM+Bar Sjt 8108 1st East Yorkshire Regt
FAIREY George E.C. MM Pte 28274 6th Northamptonshire Regt
FAIREY Henry William MM CSM 279336 10th Royal Fusiliers
FAIRFIELD William E.H.C. MM Pte 6331 5(Cav)Fd Amb RAMC
FAIRFULL Robert MM Pte 57531 19th Liverpool Regt KIA 22.3.18.
FAIRGRIEVE John MM L/Cpl 82024 Machine Gun Corps
FAIRGRIEVE Robert MM Pte S/8742 9th Gordon Highlanders
FAIRGRIEVE Thomas MM Cpl 39355 5 Siege Bty RGA
FAIRHALL Frederick J. MM Sjt 51057 124 Siege Bty RGA
FAIRHEAD Arthur MM Cpl 60987 7th Royal West Surrey Regt
FAIRHEAD Ernest John MM Pte 43841 114 Coy Machine Gun Corps KIA 27.10.17.
FAIRHEAD Frederick Samuel MM Pte 202961 1st East Yorkshire Regt
FAIRHOLM Joseph "MM,CG(F)" Cpl 1670 Northumberland Fusiliers
FAIRHURST Alexander "MM,MID" L/Cpl S/3265 8th Royal Highlanders
FAIRHURST Arthur MM Spr 51041 Signal Service Royal Engineers
FAIRHURST Harry MM Spr 37812 2 Div Sig Coy Royal Engineers
FAIRHURST Henry MM Sjt 18687 1st North Lancashire Regt DOW 28.9.16.
FAIRHURST John "MM,MID" Sjt 42523 Royal Engineers
FAIRHURST Thomas MM Pte 3011 2nd Northumberland Fusiliers
FAIRHURST Thomas MM Pte 11460 Liverpool Regt
FAIRHURST William MM Cpl 438637 430 Fd Coy Royal Engineers
FAIRHURST William MM Sjt 40590 21st Manchester Regt
FAIRHURST William "DCM,MM,Oleo(B)" CSM 14842 13th Liverpool Regt
FAIRLAMB Nicholas MM Cpl 1900 1/5th Durham Light Infantry
FAIRLESS Robert MM+Bar Pte 20331 55 Fd Amb RAMC
FAIRLESS Thomas Charles MM Sjt 2464 1/5th Durham Light Infantry
FAIRLESS William W. "DCM+Bar,MM" Sjt 457142 446 Fd Coy Royal Engineers
FAIRLEY Charles MM Pte 39568 8th West Yorkshire Regt
FAIRLEY Charles MM Pte 20930 1st Coldstream Guards
FAIRLEY David MM Pte 4161 9th Royal Highlanders
FAIRLEY James MM Pte 4230 Machine Gun Corps
FAIRLEY Matthew MM Spr 459215 Royal Engineers
FAIRLEY Patrick MM Pte 10004 1st Royal Scots Fusiliers
FAIRLEY Thomas MM Dvr 59439 69 Bty 31 Bde RFA
FAIRLEY William MM Pte 278813 Arg & Suth Highlanders
FAIRLEY William MM Pte 350858 9th Royal Scots DOW 5.4.18.
FAIRLEY William T. MM Sjt 31344 RAMC
FAIRLIE Alexander MM Pte 235705 Gordon Highlanders
FAIRLIE Peter MM Gnr Sig 635363 A/256 Bde RFA
FAIRLIE Robert MM Pte 251284 1/6th Arg & Suth Highlanders
FAIRLIE William MM Pte 8085 Arg & Suth Highlanders
FAIRMAN Bernard Wake "MM,MID" Sjt 1794 1/4th Oxf & Bucks Light Infantry
FAIRMAN Bertie H. MM Gnr Sig 880839 A/271 Bde RFA
FAIRMAN Charles D. MM Pte 353552 7th London Regt
FAIRMAN Edward MM Pte 281212 1/7th Highland Light Infantry
FAIRMAN Harry MM Sjt 702577 23rd London Regt
FAIRNINGTON Henry Nichol Wood MM L/Cpl 325090 9th Durham Light Infantry
FAIRWEATHER Alfred G. MM Spr 544035 50 Div Sig Coy Royal Engineers
FAIRWEATHER Archibald MM Pte 4002 1/1st Cambridgeshire Regt DOW 3.9.17.
FAIRWEATHER Edmund MM Sjt 635427 RFA
FAIRWEATHER Ernest William MM Pte 268187 4/5th Royal Highlanders KIA 1.4.18.
FAIRWEATHER Frederick MM L/Cpl 19122 11th Essex Regt KIA 2.6.18.
FAIRWEATHER Harold MM Pte S/1739 3rd Rifle Brigade
FAIRWEATHER John MM Pte 7065 8th Lincolnshire Regt KIA 3.11.18.
FAIRWEATHER John MM Sjt 9951 11th Royal Scots DOW 14.4.17.
FAIRWEATHER John H.G. MM Pte G/6790 12th Middlesex Regt
FAIRWEATHER Norman MM Sjt 8778 4th Bn Machine Gun Corps
FAIRWEATHER William MM Pte 145028 29th Bn Machine Gun Corps
FAIRWEATHER William MM Cpl 1365 Notts & Derby Regt
FAIRWEATHER William MM Pte 4358 13th Royal Fusiliers
FAIRWEATHER William L. MM Spr 37231 Royal Engineers
FAIRY G. MM Pte 42075 1st Essex Regt
FAITHFUL Louis MM Pte 653389 21st London Regt
FAITHFUL William H. MM L/Cpl 4358 13th Royal Fusiliers
FAITHORN Percy H. MM Tpr 170 1st Household Bn
FAITHORNE Richard E. MM CQMS 6111 1st Norfolk Regt
FAKE Albert "DCM,MM" CSM S/823 13th Royal Fusiliers
FALCKE David MM Pte 15751 Scots Guards
FALCONER Charles MM Sjt 64532 1st Bn Machine Gun Corps
FALCONER George MM Sjt 6135 D/251 Bde RFA
FALCONER Gregor (or George) MM Pte 265357 Seaforth Highlanders
FALCONER Ion S. "DCM,MM" Cpl 20166 2/5th West Yorkshire Regt
FALCONER J. MM Pte S/8155 Seaforth Highlanders
FALCONER James MM L/Cpl 278468 1/7th Arg & Suth Highlanders
FALCONER John R. MM L/Cpl 15146 13th Royal Scots
FALCONER John W. MM Pte 306971 8th Lancashire Fusiliers
FALCONER Mark S. MM Pte 201318 1/4th King's Own Scottish Borderers
FALCONER Robert MM Cpl 8403 2nd King's Own Scottish Borderers
FALCONER Robert MM Sjt 201643 1/5th Royal Warwickshire Regt
FALCONER Robert D. MM L/Cpl 41520 Scottish Rifles
FALCONER William E. MM Pte 24753 1/5th Seaforth Highlanders
FALCONER William G. MM Pte 3253 1/9th Highland Light Infantry
FALDER Charles E. MM+Bar L/Cpl 11617 2/4th Hampshire Regt
FALK Walter MM Bdr 12553 RFA
FALKINGHAM Hartley "DCM,MM" L/Sjt 265294 2/4th West Riding Regt
FALKINGHAM Herbert MM Dvr T4/252477 62 Div Train Army Service Corps
FALLAN Frank MM Pte M2/118675 Army Service Corps
FALLICK Gerald F. MM Bdr 855120 220 Bde RFA
FALLIS John "MM+Bar,MID" Sjt 20291 50 Siege Bty RGA
FALLIS William J. MM Sjt 4121 400 Bty 14 Bde RFA
FALLON Ernest MM Sjt 158261 257 Tunnelling Coy Royal Engineers
FALLON Henry MM+Bar Pte 3531 2nd Notts & Derby Regt
FALLON J.W. MM Pte 241034 North Lancashire Regt
FALLON James MM Sjt 20102 1st Royal Dublin Fusiliers
FALLON James MM Pte S/2095 Rifle Brigade
FALLON John MM Cpl 3330 2nd Notts & Derby Regt
FALLON John MM Pte 41441 1st West Yorkshire Regt
FALLON Michael J. MM Sjt 17335 1st Royal Irish Fusiliers
FALLON Patrick MM Sjt 16803 Royal Inniskilling Fusiliers
FALLON Patrick MM Pte 11355 2nd Scottish Rifles KIA 23.10.16.
FALLON Thomas MM Pte S/449 Rifle Brigade
FALLON Walter R. MM Cpl 12260 10th West Yorkshire Regt
FALLON William MM L/Cpl 1190 2nd Royal Highlanders
FALLOWFIELD Richard MM Sjt 55285 36 Fd Amb RAMC KIA 28.5.18.
FALLOWS William MM L/Cpl 241587 Lancashire Fusiliers
FALLS Andrew MM Cpl 350271 7th Royal Highlanders
FALLSHAW George MM Pte G/2763 3rd Royal Fusiliers
FALSHAW John MM Pte 266117 1/6th West Riding Regt
FANCETT Henry Fawcett MM L/Cpl 15809 2nd Essex Regt
FANE Bernard MM Pte 201233 1/5th Liverpool Regt
FANE Herbert MM Sjt 14980 Royal Lancaster Regt
FANNAN Edward L. MM Pte 2150 1/5th Northumberland Fusiliers
FANNER Frank H. MM Pte 37546 12th East Surrey Regt
FANNING Andrew MM Spr 15076 11Fd Coy Royal Engineers
FANNING Harry MM Cpl 23098 Scottish Rifles
FANNING Thomas MM Bdr L/41291 RFA
FANTHAM H. MM Cpl 19161 200th Bn Machine Gun Corps
FANTON Harry MM Cpl 311885 Royal Engineers
FARAGHER John Robert MM Cpl 8821 11th Lancashire Fusiliers
FARAGHER William MM L/Sjt 4348 12th Manchester Regt KIA 7.7.16.
FARBRIDGE Thomas W. MM Pte 386128 RAMC
FARDELL Bertie MM+Bar Sjt 63445 4th Royal Fusiliers
FARDEN Thomas MM Pte 27692 1st Northamptonshire Regt KIA 23.10.18.

FARDOE Herbert MM Sjt 12231 11th Liverpool Regt KIA 15.9.16.
FARDOE Thomas A. MM Pte 202449 4th South Lancashire Regt
FARDON William MM Sjt 24402 48th Bn Machine Gun Corps
FAREHAM Frank MM Pte 202405 York & Lancaster Regt
FAREHAM William MM Sjt 17636 251 Siege Bty RGA
FARENDEN Arthur MM Pte 254514 2nd London Regt
FARGE Francis MM Sjt 27079 28 Bde RFA
FARINO Thomas MM Pte G/20497 6th Royal West Kent Regt
FARISH Fleming MM Sjt 102709 Royal Engineers
FARLEY Albert C. MM Sjt 92981 Tank Corps
FARLEY Alfred W. MM Pte G/15906 2nd Royal Sussex Regt
FARLEY Bertram MM 2nd Cpl 553917 Royal Engineers
FARLEY Dennis MM Gnr 71062 RFA
FARLEY Edwin F. MM L/Cpl 9777 Coldstream Guards
FARLEY Frederick MM L/Cpl 8552 1st Worcestershire Regt
FARLEY George C. MM Dvr T4/065596 32 Div Train Army Service Corps
FARLEY George Edward MM Gnr 78751 179 Siege Bty RGA
FARLEY Henry MM Pte 3491 9th Royal Fusiliers
FARLEY James MM L/Cpl 201152 6th East Lancashire Regt
FARLEY James MM Pte 265445 Liverpool Regt
FARLEY John A. MM Spr 44523 Royal Engineers
FARLEY Joseph MM Cpl 206418 85 Coy Labour Corps
FARLEY Leonard MM Sjt 493390 3/1st(Home Counties)Fd Amb RAMC
FARLEY Patrick MM Pte 9794 1st Irish Guards
FARLEY Walter Thomas MM Sjt Fitter 285430 RGA
FARLEY William MM Pte M2/136297 Army Service Corps
FARLEY William Arthur MM Sjt 4725 13th Royal Fusiliers DOW 13.10.18.
FARMAN Edgar Edward MM Pte 37724 2/7th Royal Warwickshire Regt att 4th Bn MGC.
FARMBROUGH Joseph F. MM Cpl 69326 Royal Engineers
FARMER Alfred A. "MM,MID" Sjt 7864 19th Hussars
FARMER Alfred H. MM Cpl 21882 Royal West Surrey Regt
FARMER Charles H. MM Cpl 35279 RFA
FARMER Ernest E. MM Pte 2396 7th Royal West Kent Regt
FARMER Francis H. MM Cpl 200868 South Staffordshire Regt
FARMER Frederick J. MM Pte 2738 1/7th Royal Warwickshire Regt
FARMER Frederick W. MM Pte 7234 1st Cheshire Regt
FARMER George MM L/Cpl G/1960 8th Royal Sussex Regt
FARMER H.T. MM+Bar Pte 25191 7th East Kent Regt
FARMER Harold N. MM Air Mech 2 7911 Royal Flying Corps
FARMER Harry "MM,MID" Cpl S/3620 12th Rifle Brigade
FARMER Isaac Henry MM Cpl 1883 2nd Royal Sussex Regt DOW 24.10.18.
FARMER J. "DCM,MM" Sjt 19520 1st Essex Regt
FARMER James MM Cpl 17649 12/13th Northumberland Fusiliers
FARMER James MM L/Bdr 308143 RGA
FARMER John MM Pte 4558 Gordon Highlanders
FARMER John W. MM Sjt 43697 Machine Gun Corps
FARMER Joseph MM Pte 9313 17th Manchester Regt
FARMER Richard E. MM L/Sjt 700070 1/23rd London Regt
FARMER Sidney H. MM Sjt 235967 1/1st Herefordshire Regt
FARMER Sidney L. MM Spr 522845 414 Fd Coy Royal Engineers
FARMER Thomas MM Gnr 51787 RGA
FARMER William E. MM+Bar Pte 15982 Middlesex Regt
FARMER William Henry MM Sjt 6163 RFA
FARMERY Albert MM Sjt 46550 B/165 Bde RFA
FARMERY Frank MM L/Cpl 16180 7th Lincolnshire Regt
FARMERY John William MM Pte 9860 2nd Gordon Highlanders
FARMILOE John P. MM+Bar Cpl 10016 1st & 8th Gloucestershire Regt
FARNAN David MM Pte 53352 RAMC
FARNATH Harry MM+Bar Pte 26804 16th Notts & Derby Regt
FARNDALE George J. MM Sjt G/1445 7th Royal Sussex Regt
FARNDALE Herbert MM Pte 36143 10th Yorkshire Regt
FARNDELL William A. MM Gnr 53324 RFA
FARNDEN William MM Pte 13132 King's Royal Rifle Corps
FARNDON Joseph MM Gnr 840657 D/307 Bde RFA
FARNELL Albert MM Spr 74858 Royal Engineers
FARNELL Fred MM Cpl 15937 17th Highland Light Infantry
FARNELL William Robert MM Pte 34823 1/7th West Riding Regt
FARNFIELD Arthur F. MM 2nd Cpl 23900 5 Fd Coy Royal Engineers
FARNFIELD Charles W. MM Pte 24646 2nd Grenadier Guards
FARNFIELD Reginald D. MM L/Cpl O/61 Rifle Brigade
FARNSWORTH Christopher MM Pte 4689 Notts & Derby Regt
FARNUM James Thomas MM Sjt S/21446 1st Cameron Highlanders
FARNWORTH Augustine MM Cpl 24087 North Lancashire Regt
FARNWORTH H. MM Gnr 2927 RFA
FARNWORTH James MM Dvr L/229 D/158(How)Bde RFA
FARNWORTH John MM Pte 19654 13th Liverpool Regt
FARNWORTH Joseph MM Bdr L/13677 466 Bty 65 Bde RFA
FARNWORTH Robert MM Cpl 2087 9th North Lancashire Regt
FARNWORTH Thomas MM Pte 240412 1/4th North Lancashire Regt DOW 14.5.18.
FARNWORTH Walter MM L/Bdr 8555 RFA
FARNWORTH William MM Pte 18860 Manchester Regt
FARNWORTH William Henry MM Pte 23835 Machine Gun Corps
FARQUETT Reginald S.C. MM L/Cpl M2/106500 Army Service Corps
FARQUHAR Alexander MM Pte S/31964 5th Cameron Highlanders
FARQUHAR Alexander MM+Bar Pte 11464 2nd Highland Light Infantry
FARQUHAR Alexander Sinclair MM Pte 12589 7th Norfolk Regt KIA 30.11.17.
FARQUHAR Charles MM Pte 301533 1 Fd Amb RAMC
FARQUHAR Daniel Easton MM Cpl 34792 Essex Regt
FARQUHAR James MM L/Cpl 240259 1/4th Gordon Highlanders
FARQUHAR James MM Pte 1042 12th Royal Irish Rifles
FARQUHAR William MM Sjt 6823 2nd King's Own Scottish Borderers KIA 13.12.16.
FARQUHARSON Charles MM L/Cpl 412122 409 Fd Coy Royal Engineers
FARQUHARSON Charles F. MM Cpl STK/398 10th Royal Fusiliers
FARQUHARSON George D. MM Cpl 200266 1/4th Gordon Highlanders
FARQUHARSON J. MM Cpl 23125 Machine Gun Corps
FARQUHARSON James Moir MM Sjt 53762 228 Coy Machine Gun Corps
FARQUHARSON T.D. MM Pte 4055 1/4th Gordon Highlanders KIA 22.12.16.
FARQUHARSON W. "MM,MSM" L/Cpl 207573 63 Div Sig Coy Royal Engineers
FARR Albert MM Pte 9543 1st Hampshire Regt KIA 1.7.16.
FARR Alfred W. MM Cpl 27517 Hampshire Regt
FARR Arthur MM Gnr 39276 RFA
FARR George H.K. MM Cpl 28061 15th Hampshire Regt
FARR Harry MM Sjt 11761 2nd King's Own Scottish Borderers
FARR Jack S. MM L/Cpl 203908 1/4th Oxf & Bucks Light Infantry
FARR Robert MM Pte 29623 9th Royal Inniskilling Fusiliers
FARR Robert W. MM Cpl 200544 1/5th Arg & Suth Highlanders
FARR William Hopkin MM Sjt 5242 Royal Welsh Fusiliers
FARR William J. "MM,MSM" Sjt 69997 135 Army Tps Coy Royal Engineers
FARR William James MM Air Mech 1 7966 19 Balloon Coy Royal Flying Corps KIA 26.10.18.
FARRAGE William MM Cpl 2507 1/9th Durham Light Infantry
FARRALL A.H. MM Dvr 2690 RFA
FARRALL John MM Gnr 37597 RFA
FARRAND Fred MM Bdr 64650 122 Siege Bty RGA
FARRAND Walter MM Pte 250611 Manchester Regt att Lancs Fus.
FARRANT William MM Pte G/1965 8th Royal Sussex Regt
FARRAR Charles Ernest MM Gnr 960512 A/187 Bde RFA DOW 3.8.17.
FARRAR Frederick MM Sjt 52709 10th Royal Fusiliers
FARRAR George MM Pte 1079 4th Bn GMGR
FARRAR Hanson MM Pte 49023 7th Norfolk Regt KIA 18.10.18.
FARRAR Harry MM Cpl 200231 Yorkshire Light Infantry
FARRAR Sam MM Sjt 4807 252 Coy Machine Gun Corps
FARRAR Thomas MM Sjt 266105 Liverpool Regt
FARRELL Andrew MM L/Cpl 8526 2nd Royal Irish Rifles
FARRELL Christopher MM Pte 31842 RAMC
FARRELL Francis MM Sjt 6698 2nd Irish Guards DOW 19.4.18.
FARRELL George MM L/Sjt 10527 2nd King's Royal Rifle Corps
FARRELL Henry MM Pte 365075 7th London Regt
FARRELL Isaac MM Pte 240653 1/5th King's Own Scottish Borderers
FARRELL John MM Pte 377912 6th Manchester Regt
FARRELL John MM Gnr 75262 37 Bty 27 Bde RFA
FARRELL John MM Pte 2264 7th Leinster Regt
FARRELL Joseph MM Pte 7763 RAMC
FARRELL Joseph MM Pte 9199 2nd Cameron Highlanders
FARRELL Joseph MM Gnr Sig 100873 3 Bty 45 Bde RFA
FARRELL Joseph A. MM Pte 240392 East Lancashire Regt
FARRELL Michael MM Cpl 787 18th Northumberland Fusiliers
FARRELL Michael MM Bdr 91169 RFA
FARRELL Patrick MM L/Cpl 8870 1st Royal Inniskilling Fusiliers
FARRELL Patrick "MM,CG(F)" Pte 32580 13th East Lancashire Regt
FARRELL Patrick J. MM Sjt 4587 16th Lancers

FARRELL Peter MM Pte 5494 Leinster Regt
FARRELL Robert P. MM L/Cpl 214030 5th West Riding Regt
FARRELL Thomas MM Pte 49554 1st Royal Inniskilling Fusiliers
FARRELL Thomas MM Gnr 25207 6 Siege Bty RGA
FARRELL William MM+Bar Bdr 48382 RGA
FARRELLY Francis MM L/Sjt 5256 Leinster Regt
FARRELLY George MM Pte 11833 2nd Royal Irish Regt
FARRELLY George MM CSM 12815 8th Yorkshire Regt
FARRELLY Thomas MM Sjt 49064 RGA
FARRELLY Thomas MM Spr 46027 17 Div Sig Coy Royal Engineers
FARREN Noel S. MM Sjt 25859 10th Royal West Surrey Regt
FARREN Patrick MM Pte 31093 5/6th Royal Scots
FARRER Alexander McGregor MM Sjt 22445 7 Fd Coy Royal Engineers DOW 25.3.18.
FARRER Atheling MM Pte C/12555 21st King's Royal Rifle Corps DOW 10.10.16.
FARRER Walter MM L/Bdr 770621 D/95 Bde RFA
FARRIER William MM Sjt G/13562 7th East Kent Regt
FARRIES George MM Sjt S/6734 Seaforth Highlanders
FARRIMOND George MM Pte 341734 RAMC
FARRINGDON W.C. "DCM,MM" Sjt 37683 A/80 Bde RFA
FARRINGTON Bertie Edward MM Pte 29883 9th Norfolk Regt KIA 15.4.18.
FARRINGTON Frank MM Pte 16869 6th Border Regt
FARRINGTON George MM Cpl 19550 2/6th North Staffordshire Regt
FARRINGTON George MM Pte 17448 1st Shropshire Light Infantry
FARRINGTON Harold MM Pte 352882 Manchester Regt
FARRINGTON Herbert MM Sjt 13905 11th Cheshire Regt KIA 22.3.18.
FARRINGTON James MM L/Sjt 16020 9th North Lancashire Regt
FARRINGTON John MM+Bar Cpl 265637 1/7th Liverpool Regt
FARRINGTON Percy MM Pte 203223 2/7th Lancashire Fusiliers
FARRINGTON Thomas MM L/Cpl 326287 1/1st Cambridgeshire Regt
FARRINGTON William MM Sjt 16475 10th North Lancashire Regt
FARRISH Austin MM Pte 49730 21st Manchester Regt
FARROW Albert MM Pte 3371 3 Fd Amb RAMC
FARROW Albert MM Pte 586 6th Royal West Kent Regt
FARROW Arthur William MM Pte 60566 Royal Fusiliers
FARROW B. MM Pte S/43584 1/6th Royal Highlanders
FARROW Frank MM Sjt 7783 1st North Staffordshire Regt
FARROW Frank E. MM Pte 60547 23rd Middlesex Regt
FARROW Herbert B. MM Gnr L/35993 RFA
FARROW Reuben MM Cpl 325386 1/9th Durham Light Infantry
FARROW William MM L/Cpl 36518 Leicestershire Regt
FARROW William J. MM Gnr 49826 RGA
FARROW William James MM Pte 241337 Suffolk Regt
FARTHING Alfred Charles MM Sjt 20844 1st Leicestershire Regt
FARTHING George MM Dvr 457240 446 Fd Coy Royal Engineers KIA 3.1.18.
FARTHING Sidney Silvester George "MM,MSM" Sjt Farrier 78990 465 Bty 65 Bde RFA
FASHAM Alfred MM L/Cpl 17504 3rd Grenadier Guards
FASKEN John MM Sjt 303412 RAMC
FAST Thomas Montague MM+Bar Sjt S/10289 8th Royal Highlanders
FATHERS Frank MM+Bar L/Bdr 37868 RFA
FATHERS George H. MM Dvr 926233 D/290 Bde RFA
FAUCHEUX Antony R. MM Pte 698157 22nd London Regt
FAUD David James MM Sjt 52977 2nd Royal Scots Fusiliers
FAULCONBRIDGE Arthur MM Pte 71870 Notts & Derby Regt
FAULDER Arthur MM+Bar Sjt 7175 1st Bedfordshire Regt
FAULDER Evelyn MM Miss F First Aid Nursing Yeomanry
FAULDER F. MM Sjt 7003 1st Bedfordshire Regt
FAULDS George MM 2nd Cpl 112459 86 Fd Coy Royal Engineers
FAULDS H. MM Dvr 6762 RFA
FAULDS William MM Pte 358066 Liverpool Regt
FAULKES Bert MM Pte 12757 8th Leicestershire Regt
FAULKES Harry MM Cpl 2578 1/5th West Riding Regt
FAULKES J.H. MM Cpl 16265 Leicestershire Regt
FAULKNALL Walter F. MM Spr 207532 Signal Service Royal Engineers
FAULKNER Aileen Maude MM Miss F First Aid Nursing Yeomanry
FAULKNER Benjamin MM Pte 30007 2nd Royal Warwickshire Regt
FAULKNER Benjamin MM Pte 15224 Royal Sussex Regt
FAULKNER Charles MM Pte 131472 15th Bn Machine Gun Corps
FAULKNER Crampton MM Gnr 334674 328 Siege Bty RGA
FAULKNER E. MM Dvr L/2734 30 Div Ammn Col RFA
FAULKNER Edward MM Dvr 179096 37 Div Ammn Col RFA
FAULKNER Edward MM Cpl 6531 1st Liverpool Regt
FAULKNER Frederick MM Sjt 5771 1st Gloucestershire Regt
FAULKNER Frederick MM+Bar L/Sjt 26971 15th Hampshire Regt
FAULKNER George MM Sjt 38226 16th Lancashire Fusiliers
FAULKNER George MM Sjt 38746 'A' Bty RHA
FAULKNER George MM Pte 24943 Machine Gun Corps
FAULKNER Gordon S. MM L/Cpl B200440 10th Rifle Brigade
FAULKNER Harry "DCM,MM" Sjt 240126 1/8th Worcestershire Regt
FAULKNER James MM Pte 39601 Machine Gun Corps
FAULKNER John MM L/Sjt R/3533 King's Royal Rifle Corps
FAULKNER Thomas C. MM+Bar L/Cpl 56872 14th Royal Welsh Fusiliers
FAULKNER Thomas William MM L/Cpl 10338 Machine Gun Corps
FAULKNER William MM Sjt 7838 2nd Royal West Kent Regt
FAULKNER William MM Pte 16302 12th Cheshire Regt
FAULKS Albert Edward MM L/Sjt 7022 2nd South Staffordshire Regt
FAULTLESS Samuel MM Sjt 9071 2nd Worcestershire Regt
FAUTLEY Herbert Richard "DCM,MM" BSM 9280 D/189 Bde RFA
FAUTLEY Samuel MM Pte 4234 1st Dragoons
FAUVEL Lionel Georges MM Sjt 2484 1/1st Yorkshire Dragoons Yeo
FAUX Christopher Youraba MM L/Cpl K/720 Royal Fusiliers
FAVELL Frank T. MM Pte M2/152802 402 MT Coy Army Service Corps
FAVELL Harry "DCM,MM" CSM 680156 1/22nd London Regt KIA 2.9.18.
FAVELL J. MM Pte 14237 7th Bedfordshire Regt
FAWCETT Albert MM L/Cpl 2183 1/7th West Yorkshire Regt
FAWCETT Albert E. MM Pte M2/114179 Army Service Corps
FAWCETT Albert H. MM Sjt 39435 1st Manchester Regt
FAWCETT Benjamin MM L/Cpl 146320 Royal Engineers
FAWCETT Edward MM Pte 268237 West Riding Regt
FAWCETT Frank MM Cpl Sig 58895 120 Siege Bty RGA
FAWCETT Frederick James "MM,CG(B)" Sjt 16995 54 Fd Coy Royal Engineers
FAWCETT George MM Pte 201213 13th Liverpool Regt
FAWCETT George Henry MM Cpl 17840 Machine Gun Corps
FAWCETT George W. "MM,MID" Spr 160892 Royal Engineers
FAWCETT Henry MM Gnr 73825 38 Bde RFA
FAWCETT Herbert MM Pte 235031 West Yorkshire Regt
FAWCETT Horace MM L/Cpl 478159 456 Fd Coy Royal Engineers KIA 25.4.18.
FAWCETT John Percy MM Dvr 761430 C/110 Bde RFA
FAWCETT Joseph MM Sjt 4166 1st Irish Guards
FAWCETT Joseph S. MM Pte 307871 West Riding Regt
FAWCETT Richard MM Pte 30555 Durham Light Infantry
FAWCETT Thomas H. MM Pte 241326 5/6th Scottish Rifles
FAWCETT Thomas William MM Sjt 800250 B/230 Bde RFA
FAWCETT William MM Sjt 887 1st Dragoon Guards
FAWCUS John MM Sjt 95108 4th London Regt
FAWDON Thomas F. MM Sjt 15470 1st South Wales Borderers
FAWKES Frank MM Cpl 18648 9th Royal Inniskilling Fusiliers KIA 15.10.18.
FAWL Frank MM Spr 25210 Royal Engineers
FAWNS William MM L/Cpl 57620 2nd Highland Light Infantry
FAWSON Alfred Leonard MM L/Sjt 52386 15th Royal Irish Rifles KIA 22.10.18.
FAY Louis MM Pte 15005 Royal Munster Fusiliers
FAY Michael "MM,MID" Pte 4424 1st Lancashire Fusiliers
FAY Philip MM L/Cpl Z1650 9th Rifle Brigade KIA 4.4.18.
FAY Thomas MM Pte 5937 Royal Irish Rifles
FAYERS Alfred L. MM Cpl 3672 Machine Gun Corps
FAYERS Charles MM Cpl 200882 Cheshire Regt
FAYERS Sidney MM L/Cpl 703309 1/23rd London Regt KIA 25.3.18.
FAYERS Stanley F. MM CSM 12958 2nd Suffolk Regt
FAYLE Charles W. MM Pte 8828 Machine Gun Corps
FAZACKERLEY Albert Edward MM Pte 18/17052 18th Liverpool Regt KIA 9.4.17.
FAZACKERLY Edward MM Gnr 85278 127 Heavy Bty RGA
FAZACKERLY William J. MM Cpl 305533 Royal Warwickshire Regt
FEAKIN Ronald MM Pte 242079 King's Own Scottish Borderers
FEAR Clarence G. MM Sjt 8165 Royal West Surrey Regt
FEAR Edward G. MM Sjt 45071 25 Bde RFA
FEAR Ernest "MM,MID" Cpl 20921 57 Fd Coy Royal Engineers
FEAR Henry MM Spr 139283 Royal Engineers
FEARBY James O. "MM,MID" Spr 563 Royal Engineers
FEARN Charles H. MM Bdr 676179 B/296 Bde RFA
FEARN Frederick J. MM+Bar Dvr 930595 RFA
FEARN Horace E. MM L/Cpl 60347 15th Notts & Derby Regt
FEARN James H. MM+Bar Pte 39833 1st Royal West Surrey Regt
FEARN John MM Sjt 14222 24th Manchester Regt

FEARN Matthew MM Pte 57142 6th Manchester Regt
FEARN Sidney James MM Pte 437062 2(South Midland)Fd Amb RAMC
FEARN W.H. "MM,MID" Sjt 200010 5th West Yorkshire Regt
FEARN Walter "MM+Bar,MID" Sjt 49451 95 Fd Coy Royal Engineers
FEARNE William Edward MM Pte 18944 1st Royal Irish Fusiliers
FEARNETT Thomas MM Pte 54453 Royal Welsh Fusiliers
FEARNLEY Albert MM CSM 9/11134 9th Cheshire Regt
FEARNLEY E. MM Pte 11963 South Staffordshire Regt
FEARNLEY H. MM Sjt 201031 Royal Lancaster Regt
FEARNLEY James MM Pte 92745 10th Bn Tank Corps
FEARNLEY James Herbert MM Pte 18352 1st North Lancashire Regt KIA 14.11.17.
FEARNLEY Joseph MM Pte 57642 25th Liverpool Regt
FEARNLEY Leonard MM Pte 632895 1/20th London Regt
FEARNLEY William MM L/Cpl 47423 Manchester Regt
FEARON Edward G. MM Bdr 105037 X/9 Med TM Bty RFA
FEARON J.T. MM Sjt 8054 1st Essex Regt
FEARON John MM Dvr 82317 RFA
FEARON Michael J. MM Pte 131829 46th Royal Fusiliers
FEARRIA Herbert "MM,MID" 2nd Cpl 26820 152 Fd Coy Royal Engineers
FEASEY Arthur George MM Spr 127603 2 Div Sig Coy Royal Engineers DOW 30.5.17.
FEASEY John W. MM Pte 1582 142 Fd Amb RAMC
FEAST Alfred R. MM L/Cpl 10562 1st Notts & Derby Regt
FEAST William MM+Bar Cpl 7564 1st Royal West Kent Regt
FEATCH John MM L/Cpl 40083 Gordon Highlanders
FEATHER Eddie MM Pte 267128 2/4th West Riding Regt
FEATHER Eric MM Pte 307357 5th London Regt
FEATHER Ernest MM Sjt 19976 12th Highland Light Infantry
FEATHER George MM L/Cpl 15169 9th West Riding Regt DOW 20.9.18.
FEATHER Lewis MM L/Cpl 12123 10th West Riding Regt
FEATHER Tom MM Pte 14165 2/5th West Riding Regt DOW 24.7.18.
FEATHERSTON George MM Spr 202029 10 Railway Coy Royal Engineers
FEATHERSTON William S. MM 2nd Cpl 357434 Signal Service Royal Engineers
FEATHERSTONE Arthur MM L/Cpl 18866 Manchester Regt
FEATHERSTONE F. MM L/Cpl 201713 Lincolnshire Regt
FEATHERSTONE William MM Cpl 373288 8th London Regt
FEATHERSTONE William MM Sjt 240228 East Surrey Regt
FEATONBY Peter MM Pte 3122 1/8th Durham Light Infantry
FEAVEARYEAR Frederick W. MM Pte 250881 1/3rd London Regt
FEAVER Alfred Henry MM Sjt 6301 1st Hampshire Regt DOW 3.9.18.
FEAVER Francis H. MM Cpl 41250 Royal Engineers
FEAVER Stewart Samuel MM Cpl 9609 6th East Kent Regt
FEAVER Thomas MM Pte 6954 14th Hussars
FEAVER William G. MM L/Sjt 634492 20th London Regt
FEAVER William R. "DCM,MM" CSM 3099 23rd Middlesex Regt
FEAVIOUR Fred MM L/Cpl 37424 Royal Berkshire Regt
FEBERS Oliver MM Cpl 271512 Royal Scots
FEBTON George MM Pte 21312 1st Worcestershire Regt
FEE George S. MM Pte 13786 1st East Surrey Regt
FEE John MM Cpl(MCDR) 54430 14 Div Sig Coy Royal Engineers
FEELEY George MM Gnr 29627 26 Bde RFA
FEELEY Patrick F. MM L/Cpl 315229 5th London Regt
FEELY John MM Pte 2782 1st Welsh Guards
FEELY John H. MM Pte 54552 RAMC
FEENEY Frederick MM Dvr 23187 RFA
FEENEY Herbert MM Sjt 566 1st Northumberland Fusiliers
FEENEY John MM Pte 120 6th Royal Munster Fusiliers
FEENEY John MM Pte 4570 Lancashire Fusiliers
FEENEY Myles MM Dvr 650779 376 Bty 169 Bde RFA
FEENEY Thomas MM L/Cpl 4619 6th Connaught Rangers KIA 21.3.18.
FEENEY Vincent MM Pte 43648 Durham Light Infantry
FEERICK Thomas MM Pte 200241 Lancashire Fusiliers
FEERY Edward MM Sjt 9039 2nd East Lancashire Regt
FEESEY Richard W. MM Sjt 530449 15th London Regt
FEGAN Horace L.F. "MM,MID" Sjt 17119 7 Div Sig Coy Royal Engineers
FEGAN John MM Cpl 21059 9th Royal Irish Fusiliers
FEGAN John Adam "MM,MID" CQMS 12411 12th Royal Scots
FEHRENBACH Joseph A. MM Sjt 785062 RFA
FEIGHERY Gerald MM Pte 47030 1/8th Notts & Derby Regt
FEIGHERY William "DCM,MM" Sjt 2372 1st Irish Guards
FEILDING Dorothie Mary Evelyn MM Lady F Monro Motor Ambulance
FEIST John MM Sjt 676 Royal West Surrey Regt
FELCE Charles "DCM,MM" Cpl 20/1038 Northumberland Fusiliers
FELCE Horace MM Pte 9741 1st Northamptonshire Regt
FELD Reuben MM L/Cpl S/7234 Rifle Brigade
FELDON Albert MM Gnr 46651 RFA
FELDWICK Wilfred Ewart MM Cpl 838 13 Bty MGC(Motors)
FELGATE Arthur O. "MM,MID" Spr 21769 55 Fd Coy Royal Engineers
FELGATE William G. MM Pte 6321 5th Dragoon Guards
FELL Arthur MM Cpl 18296 Machine Gun Corps
FELL Fred MM Pte 306956 Royal Warwickshire Regt
FELL George Henry MM Pte 31522 56 Fd Amb RAMC
FELL James "DCM,MM" Pte 12519 1/7th Border Regt
FELL John MM Cpl 57619 RFA
FELL L.S. MM Cpl 200766 York & Lancaster Regt
FELL Samuel MM+Bar Sjt 112873 175 Tunnelling Coy Royal Engineers
FELL Stanley L. MM L/Cpl 15372 12/13th Northumberland Fusiliers
FELL William "MM,MID" L/Cpl 200 1/4th York & Lancaster Regt
FELL William S. MM+2 Bars L/Sjt 241013 1/5th Border Regt
FELLOWES Daniel MM Pte 15411 4th Liverpool Regt
FELLOWES Ernest A. MM Pte 263072 1st Gordon Highlanders
FELLOWS Alfred MM Gnr 811015 62 Div HQRA RFA
FELLOWS Arthur MM Pte 16176 2nd South Staffordshire Regt KIA 12.12.17.
FELLOWS Arthur E. "DCM+Bar,MM" L/Sjt G/24566 10th Royal Fusiliers
FELLOWS Arthur J. MM+Bar Gnr 78037 72 Bde RFA
FELLOWS Charles H. MM L/Cpl 19218 1st Northumberland Fusiliers
FELLOWS Edgar William MM Pte 11972 6th Duke of Cornwall's LI
FELLOWS Enos MM+Bar Cpl 3/7650 Yorkshire Regt
FELLOWS George F. MM Cpl 83893 RFA
FELLOWS Harry MM 2nd Cpl 193135 Royal Engineers
FELLOWS Joseph MM L/Cpl 13271 1/8th Worcestershire Regt KIA 23.10.18.
FELLOWS Joseph Thomas MM Cpl 17106 6th South Wales Borderers Died 31.10.18.
FELLOWS Richard MM Gnr 13383 286 Bde RFA
FELLOWS Richard "DCM,MM" Sjt 9988 2nd York & Lancaster Regt
FELLOWS William MM Pte 15941 South Staffordshire Regt
FELLOWS William R. MM Pte 9986 6th Lincolnshire Regt
FELLS Hayden C. MM Cpl 4172 Machine Gun Corps
FELLS Isidore MM Pte 23782 10th Duke of Cornwall's LI
FELLS William MM Dvr L/1625 26 Bty 17 Bde RFA
FELLS William MM Cpl 8083 1st Lancashire Fusiliers KIA 12.8.18.
FELSTEAD Frederick Joseph MM Bdr 30150 D/173 Bde RFA
FELSTEAD Henry Edmond MM Pte 2178 4 Fd Amb RAMC
FELSTEAD William MM L/Cpl 25310 12th East Surrey Regt
FELTHAM Albert C. "MM,MSM" Sjt 6792 1st Wiltshire Regt
FELTHAM Frank MM Pte 25947 Shropshire Light Infantry
FELTHAM Harold L. MM+Bar Cpl 500239 48 Div Sig Coy Royal Engineers
FELTHAM William J. MM Sjt 2819 17th Lancers
FELTHOUSE Arthur J. MM Gnr 97915 RGA
FELTON Charles MM Dvr 67503 5 Bde Ammn Col RFA
FELTON James E. MM CSM 12693 7th South Lancashire Regt
FELTON John MM Pte 20/1284 20th Northumberland Fusiliers
FELTON Thomas MM Sjt 12546 5th Royal Berkshire Regt
FELTON Thomas Vivian MM Spr 218864 Railway Operating Division Royal Engineers
FELTON W. MM L/Cpl 16888 Royal Dublin Fusiliers
FENDER Charles William Morris MM Gnr 775175 B/310 Bde RFA
FENDER George C. MM Pte 30414 Highland Light Infantry
FENELON Alfred MM Sjt 200401 1/5th Liverpool Regt
FENEMORE Harold G. MM Sjt 14940 Machine Gun Corps
FENEMORE John MM Sjt 8764 64 Coy Machine Gun Corps KIA 15.7.16.
FENLON Arthur James MM Pte 10745 10th Royal West Kent Regt DOW 1.10.18.
FENLON John MM Sjt Farrier 24888 RFA
FENLON T. MM Sjt 933 Military Foot Police
FENN Alfred MM Spr 248615 Royal Engineers att 104 Bde RFA Sig Section
FENN H. MM Gnr 45219 RGA
FENN Herbert MM Sjt 3609 Bedfordshire Regt att MGC.
FENN Horace MM Cpl 40130 2nd Royal Scots Fusiliers
FENN John A. MM Cpl 202755 9th Norfolk Regt

FENNA Arthur MM Sjt 350113 RAMC
FENNEL Tom MM Cpl 21362 1st Royal Lancaster Regt
FENNELL Arthur MM Cpl 17537 19th Lancashire Fusiliers
FENNELL Joseph MM+Bar L/Cpl 242439 9th Yorkshire Light Infantry
FENNELL Thomas MM L/Cpl 9712 1st Royal Irish Regt
FENNELL William MM Pte 13160 9th Gloucestershire Regt
FENNER Ernest A. MM Gnr 37157 RGA
FENNER Frank MM Gnr 65423 3 Bde RHA
FENNER Frederick H. MM Cpl 52146 7th Lincolnshire Regt
FENNER Harry Sidney MM Sjt Sig 340022 RGA
FENNER Sidney MM Pte 12975 6th Royal Berkshire Regt
FENNER William MM Farrier Sjt 35383 7 Bde RHA
FENNESSY James MM Sjt 51922 RGA
FENNIMORE Frank H. MM Spr 46848 Royal Engineers
FENNY Arthur MM Sjt 19/140 19th Durham Light Infantry
FENNY Frank MM Gnr 78656 B/83 Bde RFA
FENSOM James MM Pte 9241 7th Royal West Surrey Regt
FENSOM Thomas C. MM Pte 18854 12th Notts & Derby Regt
FENSOME Frederick MM Pte 20192 10 Fd Amb RAMC DOW 1.7.16.
FENSOME Sidney MM Sjt 14471 6th Royal West Surrey Regt
FENTEM Frank MM L/Cpl 202075 Tank Corps
FENTIE Francis W. MM Sjt 240919 Gordon Highlanders
FENTIMAN Henry John Norman MM Pte 320363 1/3rd(Highland)Fd Amb RAMC
FENTON Albert MM Gnr Sig 198833 B/75 Bde RFA
FENTON Arthur MM Bdr 77072 B/58 Bd4e RFA
FENTON Edward Vincent MM Pte 18873 1st Grenadier Guards KIA 21.10.17.
FENTON Harry MM Dvr 116580 RFA
FENTON Henry J. MM Cpl A/205490 13th King's Royal Rifle Corps
FENTON Herbert "DCM,MM" RSM 265102 1/7th West Yorkshire Regt KIA 16.4.18.
FENTON Herbert MM+Bar CSM 8464 10th Royal Warwickshire Regt
FENTON James MM Sjt 34409 9th Bn Machine Gun Corps
FENTON James MM Pte 41870 Northumberland Fusiliers
FENTON John MM Pte 528035 14th London Regt
FENTON Martin MM Pte 11835 2nd Scots Guards
FENTON StanleyW. MM Bdr 84367 RFA
FENTON Stuart MM L/Cpl 24474 Machine Gun Corps
FENTON Sydney "DCM,MM" Sjt 8520 5/6th Royal Scots KIA 4.4.18.
FENTON Timothy "DCM,MM+Bar,MMV(It)" Pte 19802 2nd Border Regt
FENTON W. MM L/Cpl 75086 Machine Gun Corps
FENTON William MM Cpl 175253 1/1st Yorkshire Dragoons Yeo
FENTON William MM Pte 25582 7/8th Royal Inniskilling Fusiliers KIA 16.8.17.
FENTON William B. MM Pte M2/174864 Army Service Corps
FENTON William P. MM Pte 164569 6th Bn Machine Gun Corps
FENWICK Albert V. MM L/Cpl 1617 1/8th London Regt
FENWICK Andrew MM Sjt 315770 Royal Highlanders
FENWICK Arthur MM Dvr 199220 7 Pontoon Park Royal Engineers
FENWICK Bertram MM Pte 20/76 Durham Light Infantry
FENWICK E. MM Cpl 42502 Northumberland Fusiliers
FENWICK Edward MM L/Cpl 24239 8th Northumberland Fusiliers
FENWICK Edward MM Pte 240286 5th Yorkshire Light Infantry DOW 12.9.18.
FENWICK James MM Cpl 242221 2nd Northumberland Fusiliers
FENWICK John MM L/Cpl 348022 9th Durham Light Infantry
FENWICK Jonathan MM Pte 59303 13th Welsh Regt DOW 19.9.18.
FENWICK Matthew MM Bdr 72577 46 Bde RFA
FENWICK Michael MM L/Cpl 276245 9th Durham Light Infantry
FENWICK Robert MM Spr 102231 258 Tunnelling Coy Royal Engineers
FENWICK Robert MM L/Cpl 16066 10th Scottish Rifles KIA 15.9.16.
FENWICK Tom MM Sjt 308394 4 Tank Bde 6 Supply Coy Tank Corps
FENWICK W.J. MM Sjt 8/4622 Northumberland Fusiliers
FENWICK William MM Cpl 19090 6th King's Own Scottish Borderers KIA 20.9.17.
FENWICK William MM Pte 5306 11th East Yorkshire Regt KIA 24.3.18.
FENWICK William A. MM Pte 41782 Lincolnshire Regt
FEREDAY Thomas MM Pte 39213 5th Bn Machine Gun Corps
FEREDAY Walter D. MM Cpl 51060 RGA
FERGUS Donald G. MM Pte 331062 9th Highland Light Infantry
FERGUS Thomas MM Spr 76732 Royal Engineers
FERGUS William MM Pte M2/099698 Army Service Corps

FERGUSON Alexander MM Pte 24296 1/6th Seaforth Highlanders
FERGUSON Alexander MM L/Cpl 10728 7th Seaforth Highlanders KIA 12.10.17.
FERGUSON Alexander MM Pte 514063 14th London Regt
FERGUSON Alexander MM Pte 265371 Royal Highlanders
FERGUSON Alexander Courtland MM+Bar Sjt 90956 D/311 Bde RFA
FERGUSON Alexander O. MM Sjt 378028 Manchester Regt
FERGUSON Alfred MM Cpl 2107 1/5th West Riding Regt KIA 3.9.16.
FERGUSON Andrew MM Sjt 420081 406 Fd Coy Royal Engineers
FERGUSON Archibald MM Pte 17645 6th Somerset Light Infantry KIA 16.9.16.
FERGUSON Charles MM Sjt 8135 1st East Surrey Regt
FERGUSON Charles MM Pte 15/12780 Royal Irish Rifles
FERGUSON Charles D. MM Sjt 1974 RAMC
FERGUSON Charles D. "DCM,MM" L/Cpl 29748 1st Border Regt
FERGUSON Charles D. MM Pte 12642 Manchester Regt
FERGUSON Charles E. MM Pte 129776 46th Royal Fusiliers
FERGUSON Charles H. MM Cpl 284335 RGA
FERGUSON Daniel MM Pte 44056 142 Coy Machine Gun Corps
FERGUSON Daniel MM Pte 5369 Highland Light Infantry
FERGUSON David MM Sjt 6802 RFA
FERGUSON David MM Pte 241764 8th Scottish Rifles
FERGUSON David MM Pte 276561 Arg & Suth Highlanders
FERGUSON David MM Pte 29388 7th East Yorkshire Regt
FERGUSON Duncan MM Cpl 17983 12th Highland Light Infantry
FERGUSON Duncan C. MM Cpl 142800 Royal Engineers
FERGUSON Edward MM L/Sjt 8492 Coldstream Guards
FERGUSON Edward Thornton MM Cpl 64183 Y/2 Medium TM Bty RGA KIA 22.9.18.
FERGUSON George MM Pte 21/1269 Northumberland Fusiliers
FERGUSON George A. MM Sjt 10345 Notts & Derby Regt
FERGUSON George Ernest MM Cpl 161601 50 Div Sig Coy Royal Engineers
FERGUSON George Webster "MC,MM+Bar(2243 Sjt)" 2Lt 1st Royal Highlanders
FERGUSON Hampton MM Pte 30597 King's Own Scottish Borderers
FERGUSON Henry MM Pte 15/14600 15th Royal Irish Rifles
FERGUSON Herbert MM Pte 5622 8th Border Regt
FERGUSON Hugh MM Sjt 18145 56 Fd Coy Royal Engineers
FERGUSON Hugh MM Pte 81204 RAMC
FERGUSON Hugh C. MM Pte S/6321 11th Arg & Suth Highlanders
FERGUSON J. MM Sjt 738064 24th London Regt
FERGUSON J. MM L/Bdr 151594 35 Bty 22 Bde RFA
FERGUSON J.L. MM L/Cpl 40526 Royal Scots
FERGUSON James MM Gnr Sig 760531 3 Bty 2/3rd(Northumbrian)Bde RFA
FERGUSON James MM Pte 41679 Scottish Rifles
FERGUSON James MM Pte S/27524 5th Cameron Highlanders
FERGUSON James MM Sjt 276099 Royal Scots
FERGUSON James MM Cpl 73848 42nd Bn Machine Gun Corps KIA 27.9.18.
FERGUSON James MM+Bar Sjt 8738 2nd Manchester Regt
FERGUSON James MM Pte 20/765 Northumberland Fusiliers
FERGUSON James MM L/Cpl 28654 2nd King's Own Scottish Borderers
FERGUSON James C. MM Cpl 42958 5/6th Royal Scots
FERGUSON James C. MM L/Cpl 200243 1/4th Gordon Highlanders
FERGUSON James S. MM Pte 7969 10th Arg & Suth Highlanders
FERGUSON John MM Cpl 18/85 1st Royal Irish Rifles
FERGUSON John MM Pte 315612 13th Royal Highlanders KIA 8.11.18.
FERGUSON John MM Spr 132718 172 Tunnelling Coy Royal Engineers
FERGUSON John MM Cpl M/205378 Army Service Corps
FERGUSON John MM L/Cpl 331470 9th Highland Light Infantry
FERGUSON John MM L/Cpl 41384 Seaforth Highlanders
FERGUSON John MM Pte 275267 1/7th Arg & Suth Highlanders
FERGUSON John "DCM,MM" Pte 8634 2nd Scots Guards
FERGUSON John "MM,MID" Sjt 36791 25 Bde RFA
FERGUSON John MM Sjt 21347 Machine Gun Corps
FERGUSON John D. MM Pte 82433 Machine Gun Corps
FERGUSON Joseph MM Pte 2241 1/5th Border Regt KIA 12.4.17.
FERGUSON Peter MM+Bar Pte 53617 1st Royal Scots Fusiliers KIA 27.9.18.
FERGUSON Robert MM L/Sjt D/6528 2nd Dragoons
FERGUSON Robert MM Pte 23016 5th Yorkshire Light Infantry
FERGUSON Robert MM Sjt 14188 9th Royal Irish Fusiliers

FERGUSON Robert "DCM,MM+Bar" CSM 9782 1/4th & 2nd Arg & Suth Highlanders
FERGUSON Robert MM Gnr 24142 51 Siege Bty RGA
FERGUSON Robert MM L/Cpl 39518 1/4th Royal Scots
FERGUSON Robert MM Cpl 250950 5/6th Royal Scots
FERGUSON Robert MM Pte M2/136330 Army Service Corps
FERGUSON Robert J. MM Pte 22994 Royal Irish Fusiliers
FERGUSON Robert Wilson MM Sjt 82524 9th Bn Machine Gun Corps KIA 20.10.18.
FERGUSON Thomas MM Sjt M2/047151 Army Service Corps
FERGUSON Thomas MM Pte 4485 Gordon Highlanders
FERGUSON Thomas MM Pte G/69332 2nd London Regt
FERGUSON Thomas Edward MM Pte 17794 9th Yorkshire Regt DOW 1.10.17.
FERGUSON Walter MM Pte 10362 Cameron Highlanders
FERGUSON William MM Pte 23774 Highland Light Infantry
FERGUSON William MM+Bar Pte 27869 Royal Inniskilling Fusiliers
FERGUSON William MM L/Cpl 37833 Royal Engineers
FERGUSON William Allan MM Pte 22518 5th Cameron Highlanders KIA 7.8.18.
FERGUSON William G. MM Pte 270865 Royal Scots
FERGUSON William McW. MM Pte 511501 14th London Regt
FERGUSSON Peter MM Gnr 84167 B/78 Bde RFA DOW 16.1.17.
FERIGAN Joseph E. MM 2nd Cpl 344926 Royal Engineers
FERN Harry MM L/Cpl 43036 11th Royal Inniskilling Fusiliers KIA 20.11.17.
FERN Henry MM Pte 90247 13 Fd Amb RAMC
FERN John MM Sjt 56732 74th Bn Machine Gun Corps
FERN William MM Sjt 239872 Railway Ops Div Royal Engineers
FERN Wilmot MM Spr 197765 185 Tunnelling Coy Royal Engineers
FERNE Percy O. MM Pte 345031 6th London Regt
FERNEE Harry "DCM,MM" Sjt 2532 1/8th London Regt
FERNEYHOUGH William MM Pte 15792 17th Lancashire Fusiliers
FERNIE Colin MM Pte 335768 Royal Scots
FERNIE David MM Pte 1122 1st Royal Highlanders
FERNIE Henry A. MM Gnr 155989 133 Heavy Bty RGA
FERNIE Thomas "DCM,MM" Cpl 50102 23 Div Sig Coy Royal Engineers
FERNIHOUGH Norman Theodore MM Pte 67360 15th Cheshire Regt DOW 4.10.18.
FERNS John R. MM Cpl 43527 Gordon Highlanders
FERNSIDE Daniel MM Pte 241660 North Lancashire Regt
FERRALL Robert MM Sjt 79092 Royal Engineers
FERRARI H. "MM,MID" L/Cpl 107397 Royal Engineers
FERRARO Alfred Joseph MM Bdr Sig 1180 B/78 Bde RFA
FERRELL William MM Pte 3766 2nd Rifle Brigade
FERRER Ernest MM Gnr W/5318 122 Bde RFA
FERRI Ronald Gale MM Pte 11383 2nd East Surrey Regt
FERRIDGE Edward V. "MM,MIDx2" CSM 11937 30 Div Sig Coy Royal Engineers
FERRIE T. MM+Bar L/Cpl 14481 10th Essex Regt
FERRIER Albert E. MM Sjt 3352 Royal Engineers
FERRIER Alexander "MM,MID" Pte 2095 1/5th Royal Highlanders
FERRIER David MM Gnr 656205 RFA
FERRIER Robert MM Cpl 23211 12th Royal Scots
FERRIER Thomas MM Sjt S/22582 1/6th Gordon Highlanders
FERRIER William B. MM Sjt CMT/2001 403 Coy Army Service Corps
FERRIMAN Archibald MM Pte 12812 2nd Oxf & Bucks Light Infantry
FERRIN Albert M. MM Cpl 253864 Royal Engineers
FERRINGTON Thomas MM Pte 27090 6th Shropshire Light Infantry KIA 1.4.18.
FERRIS Basil Lomas MM Pte 1762 1/7th London Regt KIA 24.12.16.
FERRIS Ernest Hugh MM Cpl 199037 Royal Engineers
FERRIS James MM Dvr 961327 RFA
FERRIS James MM Pte 12022 8th Gloucestershire Regt
FERRIS Patrick MM Bdr 60233 52 Bty 15 Bde RFA DOW 7.10.18.
FERRIS Samuel MM L/Cpl 14/17616 14th Royal Irish Rifles KIA 9.10.16.
FERRIS Samuel Charles MM Spr 98034 153 Fd Coy Royal Engineers
FERRIS William MM L/Cpl 1120 16 Fd Amb RAMC
FERRIS William Reginald MM+Bar Sjt 82567 123 Fd Coy Royal Engineers Died 4.11.18.
FERRISEY Frank MM Cpl 9113 2nd Welsh Regt
FERROL William MM Pte 9112 2nd King's Own Scottish Borderers
FERRY Francis William Henry MM Pte 15357 Hampshire Regt
FERRY George MM Cpl 935057 RFA
FERRY George Walter MM Gnr 21094 A/75 Bde RFA KIA 7.9.17.

FERRY William G. MM Dvr 21328 RFA
FETHNEY Charles MM Cpl 53602 Durham Light Infantry
FETTERER Philip John "MC,MM,MID" CSM 7479 Royal Fusiliers
FETTES Bernard George "MM,MSM" Sjt 83265 39th Bn Machine Gun Corps
FETTES James MM Pnr 406350 Royal Engineers
FEVER Frederick MM Pte 21077 Royal West Kent Regt
FEW Arthur L. MM Cpl 66917 Royal Engineers
FEWELL Charles William MM Sjt 9285 148 Coy Machine Gun Corps KIA 8.1.18.
FEWINGS Alfred W. MM Spr 510214 12 Div Sig Coy Royal Engineers
FEWINGS Charles MM Pte 29266 245 Coy Machine Gun Corps KIA 26.3.18.
FEWINGS William Edward MM Pte 40690 18th Welsh Regt KIA 24.3.18.
FEWSON Sidney MM Pte 10897 1st King's Royal Rifle Corps
FEWSTER Arthur Leslie MM Pte 394649 9th att 15th London Regt KIA 2.9.18.
FFITCH Maurice MM Pte 27222 Somerset Light Infantry
FIANDER George E.R.S. MM Cpl 305567 20th Bn Tank Corps
FIANDER Wilfred MM L/Cpl 50229 Cheshire Regt
FICKLING Bertie John MM Sjt 12911 8th Norfolk Regt KIA 8.8.18.
FICKLING Percy A. MM Sjt 472120 12th London Regt
FIDDES Alonzo F. "DCM,MM,MSM" L/Sjt 275258 1/6th Essex Regt
FIDDES Andrew MM Cpl S/4330 7th Seaforth Highlanders
FIDDES William MM Pte 277153 1/7th Arg & Suth Highlanders
FIDDESS Joseph MM Pte S/2535 Rifle Brigade
FIDLER Alfred D. MM Pte 39727 14 Fd Amb RAMC
FIDLER Arthur MM L/Cpl 10740 2nd King's Own Scottish Borderers
FIDLER Geoffrey MM Sjt 17725 19th Lancashire Fusiliers
FIDLER Herbert S. MM Bdr 8888 RFA
FIDLER J. MM L/Cpl P5243 Military Mounted Police
FIDLER John MM Pte 29713 2nd East Lancashire Regt KIA 20.11.17.
FIDLER Thomas MM Pte 70589 2nd Notts & Derby Regt
FIDLER William MM Cpl 275173 1/7th Manchester Regt
FIDLER William C. MM Pte 149654 12th Bn Machine Gun Corps
FIDLIN Frank MM Pte 17053 Liverpool Regt
FIDO Theodore F. MM Cpl Z/172 2nd Rifle Brigade
FIEGEHEN Augustus L. MM Sjt 5766 Machine Gun Corps
FIELD Albert E. MM Pte 5217 7th Royal West Kent Regt
FIELD Albert Harry MM Pte M2/120386 Army Service Corps att 62 Div Sig Coy RE.
FIELD Albert J.V. MM Pte 7240 7th Dragoon Guards
FIELD Alfred James MM Pte 16124 12th Royal Sussex Regt
FIELD Arthur MM Pte G/24327 7th Royal West Kent Regt
FIELD Arthur R. MM Pte 201034 7th Middlesex Regt
FIELD Bertie MM S/Sjt 4539 Army Ordnance Corps
FIELD Charles F. MM Pte 37520 RAMC
FIELD Charles M. MM L/Cpl 65316 32nd Bn Machine Gun Corps
FIELD Charles Robert MM L/Cpl 14215 11th Essex Regt KIA 22.4.17.
FIELD David MM CSM 267126 1/7th Royal Warwickshire Regt Died 8.8.18.
FIELD David MM CSM 267126 1/7th Royal Warwickshire Regt Died 8.8.18
FIELD E.W. MM Sjt 30 Lincolnshire Regt
FIELD Edmund MM Pte 267849 1/6th West Riding Regt
FIELD Edward W. MM Pte 4901 7th Dragoon Guards
FIELD Ernest MM Sjt 202095 260 Railway Coy Royal Engineers
FIELD Frank Victor MM L/Cpl 22503 7th Royal West Surrey Regt
FIELD Frederick "DCM,MM" Sjt 20281 2nd Worcestershire Regt
FIELD Frederick MM Pte 572876 17th London Regt
FIELD Frederick C. MM Sjt 44612 43 Bde RFA
FIELD Frederick Cecil MM Gnr 930718 291 Bde RFA
FIELD Frederick G. MM L/Cpl 31804 1st East Surrey Regt
FIELD Frederick H. MM Pte 201195 Bedfordshire Regt
FIELD George MM 2nd Cpl 532316 490 Fd Coy Royal Engineers
FIELD George MM L/Cpl 18210 2nd Suffolk Regt
FIELD George Arthur MM Gnr 93293 11 Div Ammn Col RFA
FIELD George Edward MM L/Cpl 24693 49th Bn Machine Gun Corps KIA 5.7.18.
FIELD Harry MM L/Cpl 204573 2nd West Riding Regt KIA 15.4.18.
FIELD Henry MM Pte 15489 6th Royal West Surrey Regt
FIELD Herbert S. MM Pte 31115 Royal West Kent Regt
FIELD Horace MM Pte 46427 6th York & Lancaster Regt
FIELD James "DCM,MM" CSM 9217 1st East Yorkshire Regt
FIELD James Herbert MM Cpl 251345 3rd London Regt KIA 29.10.18.
FIELD James T. MM Pte 31151 1st Royal West Kent Regt

FIELD John MM Pte 30097 4th Worcestershire Regt
FIELD John MM Pte 18787 5th Oxf & Bucks Light Infantry
FIELD John A. MM 2nd Cpl 40361 Royal Engineers
FIELD John W. MM Cpl 200158 1/5th Highland Light Infantry KIA 1.12.17.
FIELD John W. MM L/Cpl 2639 Yorkshire Light Infantry
FIELD Joseph MM Pte 6961 20th Hussars
FIELD Joseph E. MM Pte 9908 6th Lincolnshire Regt
FIELD Leonard MM Cpl 476432 Royal Engineers
FIELD Oliver F. MM Spr 158190 Royal Engineers
FIELD Percy MM Sjt 33 1/6th West Riding Regt
FIELD Reginald MM L/Sjt 240219 1/5th West Riding Regt
FIELD Sidney MM Pnr 360055 21 Div Sig Coy Royal Engineers
FIELD Sydney MM Pte 19/885 Northumberland Fusiliers
FIELD W. MM Pte 15400 Lincolnshire Regt
FIELD Walter MM Cpl 13160 11th West Yorkshire Regt
FIELD Walter H. MM Sjt 305882 1/8th Notts & Derby Regt
FIELD William C. MM Sjt 59509 B/83 Bde RFA
FIELD William J. MM Dvr 218532 RFA
FIELDEN Clement John MM Cpl 456016 2 Fd Amb RAMC
FIELDEN John MM Pte 202631 East Lancashire Regt
FIELDEN John Ewart MM Pte 46461 17th Manchester Regt
FIELDER Arthur MM Pte 7522 1st Rifle Brigade
FIELDER Douglas MM Pte 61974 RAMC
FIELDER Frederick G. MM Pte G/2144 8th Royal Sussex Regt
FIELDER George MM Sjt 9558 2nd Royal West Surrey Regt
FIELDER Harry MM Gnr 81176 B/75 Bde RFA
FIELDER Henry A. MM Pte 757 Army Cyclist Corps
FIELDER Horace E. MM+Bar L/Cpl 29772 Hampshire Regt
FIELDER Leonard G. MM 2nd Cpl 249734 15 Div Sig Coy Royal Engineers
FIELDER Thomas MM Spr 285212 218 Fd Coy Royal Engineers
FIELDHOUSE Frank MM Cpl 66094 10th Royal Scots
FIELDING Alfred MM+Bar Cpl 83269 200 Fd Coy Royal Engineers
FIELDING Arthur MM Cpl 35889 17th Lancashire Fusiliers
FIELDING Arthur MM Pte 129410 21st Bn Machine Gun Corps KIA 13.9.18.
FIELDING George E. MM+Bar Cpl 5907 East Lancashire Regt
FIELDING Herbert MM Dvr 201855 RFA
FIELDING J. MM Pte 39719 RAMC
FIELDING James MM Pte 30040 1st Duke of Cornwall's LI
FIELDING John MM Pte 25133 RAMC
FIELDING John Archibald MM Sjt 6330 10th West Yorkshire Regt
FIELDING Joseph MM+Bar Cpl 444566 42 Div Sig Coy Royal Engineers KIA 19.4.18.
FIELDING Joshua MM Pte 72851 15th Welsh Regt KIA 8.10.18.
FIELDING Mason MM Pte M2/105746 Army Service Corps
FIELDING Robert MM Pte 14261 7th Royal Lancaster Regt
FIELDING William Ernest MM Cpl Z/379 3rd Rifle Brigade DOW 13.10.16.
FIELDS Alfred MM Spr 6804 2 Siege Coy R Anglesey RE
FIELDS Fred "MM,MID" Sjt 27625 RFA
FIELDS Herbert N. MM Pte 51996 Liverpool Regt
FIELDS James MM Sjt 72935 24 Bde RFA
FIELDS John I. MM Pte 241837 9th Scottish Rifles
FIELDS Leonard MM Pte 26011 9th Yorkshire Light Infantry
FIELDUS Oscar MM L/Cpl 2181 7th Royal West Surrey Regt
FIFE Daniel MM+Bar Cpl 300946 1/8th Durham Light Infantry
FIFE John MM Pte 1595 1/7th Northumberland Fusiliers KIA 27.10.17.
FIFIELD Edward "DCM,MM" Sjt 66791 84 Bty RFA
FIFIELD Frank R. MM Sjt 44 7th East Surrey Regt
FIFIELD Guy MM Pte 35861 14th Royal Warwickshire Regt
FIFORD Charles MM L/Cpl 17773 2nd Hampshire Regt
FIGGINS William G. MM 2nd Cpl 63842 103 Fd Coy Royal Engineers
FIGGIS John Benjamin MM Pte 20345 3rd Grenadier Guards KIA 13.8.18.
FIGGURES Douglas Lionel MM Cpl 55484 C/46 Bde RFA DOW 15.10.18.
FILBY James MM Gnr 77465 8th Bn Tank Corps KIA 9.8.18.
FILCE Harry MM Pte 31091 5th Royal Inniskilling Fusiliers
FILDES Fred "DCM,MM" Cpl 33857 1st Border Regt
FILDES Harry MM Pte 4648 1/10th Liverpool Regt
FILE Charles E. MM Pte 2039 1/4th Seaforth Highlanders
FILER Reginald A. MM L/Cpl 1606 3rd(Northumbrian)Fd Amb RAMC
FILES Charles Henry MM Pte 16674 1st Grenadier Guards
FILKINS Charles Henry MM Cpl 12785 7th Northamptonshire Regt KIA 18.8.16.
FILKINS James W. MM Sjt 2298 1st Middlesex Regt
FILKINS Joseph MM Cpl 78723 RGA
FILLARY Joseph MM Cpl 123940 A/83 Bde RFA
FILLINGHAM John MM Pte 30085 1st Border Regt
FILLINGHAM Thomas MM L/Cpl 240281 1/5th South Lancashire Regt DOW 8.8.17.
FILLINGHAM William MM Pte 6620 Royal Fusiliers
FILLIS William MM Pte 24265 10th Royal Inniskilling Fusiliers KIA 21.3.18.
FILMORE Arthur F. MM Pte 37660 8th Royal Berkshire Regt
FILSELL Arthur MM Pte 58293 2nd Northamptonshire Regt
FINAGAN John "DCM,MM" CSM 19372 32nd Bn Machine Gun Corps
FINAL William MM Pte 11547 24th Royal Fusiliers
FINBOW Alfred E. MM Sjt 2244 1/16th London Regt
FINBOW Frederick MM Pte M2/176607 604 Coy Army Service Corps
FINCH Albert MM Pte 15946 1st North Lancashire Regt KIA 12.11.17.
FINCH Albert R. MM Pte 47206 7th Lancashire Fusiliers
FINCH Alfred E. MM L/Cpl 12/25547 12th Notts & Derby Regt KIA 1.9.17.
FINCH Alfred Lion MM Bdr 22761 122 Heavy Bty RGA KIA 19.8.17.
FINCH Archibald J. MM Sjt 3047 8th Hussars
FINCH Arthur F. MM Cpl M1/6427 Army Service Corps att 25 Fd Amb RAMC.
FINCH Cecil MM Pte 26422 Oxf & Bucks Light Infantry
FINCH Charles MM CSM 5428 8th East Surrey Regt
FINCH Charles W. MM Pte 30059 Norfolk Regt
FINCH Colin "MC,DCM,MM" RSM 265297 1/6th Northumberland Fusiliers
FINCH Daniel MM Pte 12833 2nd South Lancashire Regt KIA 1.8.17.
FINCH Edward H. MM Pte 80169 1/1st Essex Yeomanry
FINCH F. "MM,MSM" Cpl 1653 B/121 Bde RFA
FINCH Francis Leonard MM Gnr 885217 RFA
FINCH Frank MM CSM 240017 1/5th Gloucestershire Regt
FINCH Frank MM Pte 415015 9th London Regt
FINCH Frederick George "DCM,MM" Sjt 40653 C/122 Bde RFA
FINCH George MM Pte 2813 12th Middlesex Regt KIA 26.9.16.
FINCH George MM Bdr Sig 27548 56 Siege Bty RGA
FINCH Harry "DCM,MM" Sjt 59173 78 Fd Coy Royal Engineers
FINCH Henry MM Cpl 22519 RFA
FINCH Henry J. MM Pte 201728 Oxf & Bucks Light Infantry
FINCH James MM Pte 117366 5 Fd Amb RAMC
FINCH James J.G. MM Pte 8960 2nd Royal Sussex Regt
FINCH James John Arthur MM Sjt 57575 51 Bty 39 Bde RFA KIA 28.9.17.
FINCH John William MM L/Cpl 419552 136 Labour Coy Labour Corps
FINCH R.A. MM Pte 337527 RAMC
FINCH Ralph MM Pte 54633 RAMC
FINCH Robert C. MM Pte M2/078136 47 Div Train Army Service Corps att 5(London)Fd Amb RAMC.
FINCH Thomas MM Gnr 604133 RHA
FINCH Thomas MM Pte 34965 Labour Corps
FINCH Thomas H. MM Pte 17338 7th South Staffordshire Regt
FINCH Thomas Walter MM Sjt 518586 Royal Engineers
FINCH Walter L. MM Pte 37489 Royal Berkshire Regt
FINCH William H. MM L/Cpl 19017 Grenadier Guards
FINCH Willie "DCM,MM,MID" Sjt 8244 2nd Hampshire Regt
FINCHAM Cecil William MM Pte B/707 7th Rifle Brigade
FINCHAM Geoffrey MM Dvr 775729 RFA
FINCHAM Harry "MM,MID" Spr 1681 1/2(Home Counties)Fd Coy Royal Engineers
FINCHAM John "DCM,MM,MID" L/Cpl 16318 2nd Grenadier Guards
FINDING Clifford MM Pte 15038 7th Bedfordshire Regt
FINDLAY Adam MM Cpl 82647 Royal Engineers
FINDLAY Adam "DCM,MM" Sjt S/11585 Gordon Highlanders
FINDLAY Alexander MM L/Cpl 93761 41 Div Sig Coy Royal Engineers
FINDLAY Alexander MM L/Sjt 29109 6th King's Own Scottish Borderers DOW 17.9.18.
FINDLAY Angus MM L/Cpl 36718 101 Fd Coy Royal Engineers
FINDLAY David MM Pte 12505 2nd Scots Guards
FINDLAY George MM Sjt 47293 13th Royal Inniskilling Fusiliers
FINDLAY George MM Gnr 98 RFA
FINDLAY George W. MM Pte 4331 Seaforth Highlanders
FINDLAY Henry MM Dvr 10386 64 Bde RFA
FINDLAY James MM L/Cpl S/1570 1st Gordon Highlanders DOW 25.6.17.

FINDLAY John MM Sjt Wheeler 645191 RFA
FINDLAY John MM Cpl 76312 III Corps Heavy Artillery Sig Section Royal Engineers
FINDLAY John MM Gnr 96609 RFA
FINDLAY Robert MM Cpl 310264 Arg & Suth Highlanders
FINDLAY T. MM Pte 16165 East Surrey Regt
FINDLAY William MM L/Cpl 41132 2nd Royal Scots Fusiliers
FINDLOW Frederick L. MM L/Cpl 48768 131 Fd Amb RAMC
FINDLOW Henry M. MM Pte 552769 16th London Regt
FINDON Edward MM Pte 20677 Royal Irish Fusiliers
FINEGAN Patrick MM Pte 16484 Machine Gun Corps
FINEGAN William MM L/Cpl 95106 13th Liverpool Regt
FINERTY James MM L/Cpl 18472 Royal Dublin Fusiliers
FINGLAND Alexander MM Cpl 204631 6th Wiltshire Regt
FINGLAND Robert MM Cpl 62396 36th Northumberland Fusiliers
FINIGAN John C. MM Pte 7265 Cavalry Fd Amb RAMC
FINLAN Joseph "MM,MSM" Sjt 7952 2nd South Staffordshire Regt
FINLAY Alfred Edward MM Cpl 10099 1st Royal Dublin Fusiliers
FINLAY Daniel MM Sjt 9455 1st King's Own Scottish Borderers
FINLAY George W. MM Sjt S/3935 9th Gordon Highlanders
FINLAY Henry MM Pte 41016 Cameron Highlanders
FINLAY Hugh MM Pte 11699 7/8th Royal Inniskilling Fusiliers
FINLAY James MM Cpl 3/7242 Arg & Suth Highlanders
FINLAY John MM L/Cpl 173 12th Royal Irish Rifles
FINLAY Joseph MM Cpl 81040 Royal Engineers
FINLAY Peter Tom MM Pte 260324 1/1st County of London Yeomanry
FINLAY Samuel MM Pte 17/490 Royal Irish Rifles
FINLAY Thomas MM Pte 15517 10th Royal Inniskilling Fusiliers KIA 26.6.17.
FINLAY William "MM,MID" L/Sjt 11664 15th Royal Irish Rifles
FINLAY William MM Pte 20194 Royal Irish Fusiliers
FINLAYSON Alexander MM Cpl 271445 12th Royal Scots
FINLAYSON David T. MM Pte 32853 1st Royal Scots Fusiliers
FINLAYSON Duncan Alexander "MC,MM(1144 Sjt)" T/2Lt 81 Fd Coy Royal Engineers
FINLAYSON Hector MM Sjt 200306 1/4th Seaforth Highlanders
FINLAYSON James "DCM,MM,MID" Pte 5912 2nd Scots Guards
FINLAYSON John W. MM Cpl 107235 Machine Gun Corps
FINLAYSON Malcolm MM Bdr 676608 RFA
FINLAYSON Robert MM Bdr 34187 128 Bde RFA
FINLAYSON Robert A. "DCM,MM" L/Cpl 11290 11th Royal West Surrey Regt
FINLAYSON Thomas MM Pte 14853 16th Highland Light Infantry
FINLEY James MM Gnr 79387 RFA
FINN Aiden MM Spr 421019 34 Div Sig Coy Royal Engineers
FINN Albert MM Sjt 652554 21st London Regt
FINN Francis MM Pte 14701 5th Yorkshire Light Infantry
FINN Frank B. MM Cpl 630790 1/20th London Regt
FINN J. MM Sjt 8050 9th Essex Regt
FINN J.A. MM Pte 34413 Essex Regt
FINN James MM Pte 307887 Liverpool Regt
FINN James "DCM,MM" Sjt 64791 15 Bty 36 Bde RFA
FINN James F. MM Bdr 37968 RGA
FINN John MM Pte 3670 5th Connaught Rangers
FINN Joseph MM Cpl 7227 RAMC
FINN Pat MM Sjt 362372 RGA
FINN Patrick "DCM,MM+Bar" CSM 250449 1/6th Durham Light Infantry KIA 27.5.18.
FINN Patrick MM Bdr Sig 3408 22 Heavy Artillery Group HQ RGA
FINN William MM CQMS 282506 1/7th Lancashire Fusiliers
FINNAN Joseph MM Gnr 636202 42 Bde RFA
FINNEMORE Albert Charles Ward MM Pte 13207 3rd Coldstream Guards DOW 5.12.17.
FINNERAN Thomas MM Sjt 24/264 Northumberland Fusiliers
FINNERON Patrick MM Pnr 93680 41 Div Sig Coy Royal Engineers
FINNERTY James MM Sjt 240278 South Lancashire Regt
FINNERTY John MM Sjt 147170 'D' Special Coy Royal Engineers
FINNERTY John MM Pte 10219 1st Liverpool Regt KIA 30.11.17.
FINNERTY Thomas MM Cpl 200143 1/4th North Lancashire Regt AKA Thomas Healy.
FINNEY Ernest George "MM,MID" Pte 1787 3/4th(London)Fd Amb RAMC
FINNEY Herbert MM L/Cpl 52593 Liverpool Regt
FINNEY J. MM Cpl Fitter L/3063 C/152 Bde RFA
FINNEY Robert MM Sjt 8275 9th Worcestershire Regt
FINNEY Thomas MM Pte 19540 12th Notts & Derby Regt
FINNEY William MM Cpl 8600 A/150 Bde RFA
FINNEY William MM Spr 474513 Royal Engineers
FINNIE Alexander MM Pte 265452 1/6th Gordon Highlanders
FINNIE John Redican MM Cpl 29250 1st Royal Dublin Fusiliers KIA 14.10.18.
FINNIE Thomas MM Pte 9053 2nd Royal Scots
FINNIGAN John MM Cpl S/4041 13th Rifle Brigade
FINNIGAN John MM Pte 295417 12th Royal Scots Fusiliers
FINNIGAN John H. MM S/Sjt Armourer T/774 Army Ordnance Corps
FINNIMORE Robert MM Sjt 10281 15th Lancashire Fusiliers
FINNIS Alfred William MM Pte 8500 1st East Kent Regt
FINNIS Arthur A. MM Gnr 751 RFA
FINNIS Charles MM Pte 18484 8th East Surrey Regt DOW 6.10.16.
FINNISS Ernest A. MM Cpl 14830 86 Bty 32 Bde RFA
FINNISS James MM Sjt R/19250 King's Royal Rifle Corps
FIRBY William W. MM Sjt 19832 1st East Yorkshire Regt
FIRKINS Frederick MM Pte 453 1st Rifle Brigade
FIRMAN Arthur MM Spr 95072 Royal Engineers
FIRMAN Henry MM Sjt 836367 242 Bde RFA
FIRMAN W. MM Dvr 2550 D/74 Bde RFA
FIRMINGER Thomas MM Pte 700143 1/23rd London Regt
FIRSTBROOK Ernest Albert MM Pte 2941 24th Royal Fusiliers KIA 13.11.16.
FIRSTBROOK George H. MM L/Cpl 15235 11th Welsh Regt
FIRTH Albert W. MM Bdr 795655 62 Div Ammn Col RFA
FIRTH Arthur MM Sjt L/25425 A/168 Bde RFA
FIRTH Arthur MM Pte 38668 2nd York & Lancaster Regt
FIRTH Benjamin James MM Gnr 66759 78 Siege Bty RGA
FIRTH Charles Edward MM Sjt 203042 1/5th Durham Light Infantry
FIRTH Clement MM Pte 201535 1/4th West Riding Regt
FIRTH Edgar MM Cpl 59965 3rd Bn Machine Gun Corps
FIRTH Ernest MM Cpl 786598 RFA
FIRTH Ernest MM CQMS 240012 5th Yorkshire Light Infantry DOW 11.11.18.
FIRTH Frank MM Pte 45673 2nd York & Lancaster Regt
FIRTH Fred MM Gnr 176369 163 Siege Bty RGA
FIRTH George MM Spr 476737 Royal Engineers
FIRTH George MM Pnr 477191 Royal Engineers
FIRTH George Yewdall MM Dvr 9722 RFA
FIRTH Harry MM Gnr 45382 A/178 Bde RFA
FIRTH Harry MM Pte 267405 West Riding Regt
FIRTH Harry L. MM L/Cpl 15/330 West Yorkshire Regt
FIRTH Herbert MM Cpl 3341 Royal Sussex Regt
FIRTH Hubert B. MM Cpl L/34185 RFA
FIRTH Irwin MM Bdr 26552 C/83 Bde RFA
FIRTH James S. MM Pte 300121 1st West Yorkshire Regt
FIRTH John MM Pte 76297 4th Bn Tank Corps
FIRTH John MM Sjt 10061 11th East Lancashire Regt KIA 12.9.18.
FIRTH John H. "DCM,MM" Sjt 107000 40 Div Sig Coy Royal Engineers
FIRTH John R. MM Sjt M2/191227 Army Service Corps
FIRTH John R. MM Pte 16205 Notts & Derby Regt
FIRTH John W. MM Bdr 785865 RFA
FIRTH Joseph P. MM+Bar Bdr 1117 6(West Riding)Bty RFA
FIRTH Leonard MM Pte 41867 2nd York & Lancaster Regt
FIRTH Percy MM Pte 242821 West Riding Regt
FIRTH Stanley MM Pte 42252 10th Worcestershire Regt
FIRTH Stanley MM+Bar Sjt 786261 312 Bde RFA
FIRTH Walter "MM,MID" Spr 9179 15 Fd Coy Royal Engineers
FIRTH William E. MM Pte 7488 Northumberland Fusiliers
FISH Ernest G. MM Pte 3444 1/4th Leicestershire Regt
FISH Fred MM Bdr 275639 RGA
FISH Frederick W. "MM,MID" Sjt 14424 9th Norfolk Regt
FISH Herbert MM Cpl 8451 2nd Coldstream Guards KIA 2.10.16.
FISH Herbert MM Pte 13953 9th Lancashire Fusiliers
FISH James MM L/Cpl 266171 1/6th Cheshire Regt
FISH John W. MM L/Cpl 423484 10th London Regt
FISH Percy Valentine MM CSM 201403 2/4th York & Lancaster Regt KIA 22.7.18.
FISH Thomas G. MM Pte 25865 10th Royal West Surrey Regt
FISH William MM 2nd Cpl 60128 97 Fd Coy Royal Engineers
FISH William G. MM Sjt 47213 RFA
FISHBURN James MM L/Cpl 34588 9th York & Lancaster Regt KIA 22.9.17.
FISHENDEN George L. MM Pte 9373 6th Royal West Kent Regt
FISHENDEN Herbert E. MM+Bar Pte 307 Royal Sussex Regt
FISHENDEN Richard Albert MM Pte 46699 2nd Suffolk Regt
FISHER A. MM Pte 17048 1/4th Royal Berkshire Regt
FISHER A. MM+Bar Cpl 377006 10th Manchester Regt
FISHER A.W. MM Cpl 270087 Yeomanry
FISHER Albert E. MM Pte 229607 1st London Regt
FISHER Alfred MM Pte 78463 7th Royal West Surrey Regt
FISHER Amos MM Pte 22813 4th Worcestershire Regt

FISHER Arthur "MM,CG(F)" Cpl 27563 RAMC
FISHER Arthur MM L/Cpl 13/1269 13th East Yorkshire Regt
FISHER Arthur MM CSM 9391 1st Notts & Derby Regt
FISHER Arthur I. MM Gnr 785432 RFA
FISHER Arthur Jack "MM,MID" Pte 2401 Army Cyclist Corps
FISHER Arthur William MM Sjt G/2331 6th East Kent Regt
FISHER Barnard MM Bdr 68889 RHA
FISHER Charles John "DCM,MM" L/Cpl 16416 1st Royal Berkshire Regt DOW 28.7.18.
FISHER Charles Michael MM Gnr 129666 85 Bty 11 Bde RFA
FISHER Cyril Arthur MM Pte 19283 2nd South Wales Borderers Served as David John Wallace. KIA 1.7.16.
FISHER David MM Sjt 17636 Royal Irish Rifles
FISHER Dennis G. MM Pte 62078 15/17th West Yorkshire Regt
FISHER Edward A. MM Sjt 20352 RGA
FISHER Ernest MM Cpl 23001 1/6th Liverpool Regt DOW 9.9.18.
FISHER Ernest MM Cpl 4179 23rd Royal Fusiliers
FISHER Ernest Edgar MM Cpl 240632 Duke of Cornwall's LI
FISHER F. MM Sjt 8247 East Lancashire Regt
FISHER Francis N. MM Pte 243677 9th Cheshire Regt
FISHER Frederick MM Cpl 201834 2/4th Oxf & Bucks Light Infantry
FISHER Frederick C. MM Pte M2/187650 Army Service Corps
FISHER George MM Cpl 18/825 12th Royal Irish Rifles
FISHER George E. MM L/Bdr 98631 319 Siege Bty RGA
FISHER George E. MM Bdr 805251 RFA
FISHER George Herbert MM L/Cpl 123 1/1(West Riding)Fd Amb RAMC
FISHER George Patrick "DCM,MM,MID" Sjt 57031 38 Bde & 34 Bty 238 Bde RFA
FISHER George R. MM Pte 43278 West Yorkshire Regt
FISHER George W.H. MM Cpl 504579 503 Fd Coy Royal Engineers
FISHER George William MM Sjt 11024 11th Royal West Surrey Regt DOW 25.10.18.
FISHER Harold MM Cpl 831944 RFA
FISHER Harold MM Cpl 275834 Manchester Regt
FISHER Harry MM L/Cpl 26/905 9th Northumberland Fusiliers Died 11.4.18.
FISHER Harry MM Pnr 490257 Royal Engineers
FISHER Harry MM S/Sjt 50236 RAMC
FISHER Harry J. "MM,MSM" Gnr 73988 202 Siege Bty RGA
FISHER Hector F. MM L/Cpl 352619 Manchester Regt
FISHER Herbert MM+Bar Bdsm 5662 1st Royal Inniskilling Fusiliers
FISHER Herman B. MM Pte 305283 West Riding Regt
FISHER Horace MM Sjt 10/445 1/4th East Yorkshire Regt KIA 27.5.18.
FISHER Horace MM Pte 6177 Lancashire Fusiliers
FISHER Horace C. MM Cpl 33410 2nd Yorkshire Regt
FISHER Hubert John MM Sjt 268147 2/7th Royal Warwickshire Regt KIA 14.4.8.
FISHER J.W. MM Pte 40592 Essex Regt
FISHER James MM+Bar L/Cpl 17518 2nd Royal Scots Fusiliers
FISHER James MM L/Cpl 9946 1st Leicestershire Regt
FISHER James MM L/Cpl 18332 16th Lancashire Fusiliers
FISHER James "DCM+Bar,MM(14017 Manch Regt)" CSM 50183 1/5th Lancashire Fusiliers
FISHER James MM Pte 33209 Worcestershire Regt
FISHER James Herbert "MM,MMV(It)" L/Cpl 16197 11th West Yorkshire Regt
FISHER James Robert MM Pte S/18167 5th Cameron Highlanders DOW 15.10.18.
FISHER James W. MM Pte 13/956 East Yorkshire Regt
FISHER James W. MM L/Cpl 6907 2nd Dragoon Guards
FISHER James William Henry MM Cpl M2/054885 Army Service Corps
FISHER John MM Sjt 11336 2nd Royal Welsh Fusiliers
FISHER John MM Cpl 242115 5th South Lancashire Regt
FISHER John MM L/Sjt 30656 11th Cheshire Regt
FISHER John MM L/Cpl 11191 1st Welsh Regt
FISHER John H. MM Sjt 370061 8th London Regt
FISHER John R. MM Pte S/6977 Rifle Brigade
FISHER John William MM Sjt 7385 RFA
FISHER Joseph MM Sjt 8251 2nd Connaught Rangers
FISHER L. MM Pte 228112 Royal Fusiliers
FISHER Leonard MM Pte 21195 9th Yorkshire Light Infantry KIA 22.3.18.
FISHER Leslie H. MM Bdr 147103 154 Hy Bty RGA
FISHER Mark "DCM,MM+Bar" Sjt 22248 2nd Manchester Regt
FISHER Norman MM Spr 66171 Royal Engineers
FISHER Obadiah MM Gnr 150938 170 Siege Bty RGA
FISHER Philip John MM Sjt 1553 1/5th Cheshire Regt
FISHER R.R. MM Pte 51532 Imperial Camel Corps
FISHER Reginald J. MM Sjt 39097 7th Royal West Surrey Regt
FISHER Rigg MM Dvr 796216 X/62 Med TM Bty RFA
FISHER Robert MM Pte 291654 5/6th Scottish Rifles
FISHER Sidney MM Sjt 41299 9 Bde RFA
FISHER Stanley MM L/Sjt 267465 6th West Riding Regt
FISHER Sydney MM+Bar L/Cpl 41246 Machine Gun Corps
FISHER T.F. MM Dvr 2728 D/47 Bde RFA
FISHER Thomas MM Sjt 200069 1/5th Durham Light Infantry
FISHER Thomas MM L/Cpl 18669 Hampshire Regt
FISHER Thomas C. MM Pte 20804 Lancashire Fusiliers
FISHER Thomas H. MM+Bar Pte 203338 Worcestershire Regt
FISHER Thomas Henry MM Sjt 10790 Leinster Regt
FISHER Thomas W.R. MM Bdr 127231 RGA
FISHER Tom MM Pte 29/291 20th Northumberland Fusiliers
FISHER Victor MM Pte 45935 Lancashire Fusiliers
FISHER Walter MM L/Cpl 400261 400 Fd Coy Royal Engineers
FISHER Walter E. MM Sjt 148 16th Royal Warwickshire Regt
FISHER Walter George MM Sjt 9041 10th Royal West Kent Regt KIA 31.7.17.
FISHER Walter L. MM Bdr 82120 B/62 Bde RFA
FISHER Wilfred MM Pte 14621 12th Notts & Derby Regt KIA 21.3.18.
FISHER William MM Pte 82444 11th Royal Fusiliers
FISHER William MM CSM 1064 Army Cyclist Corps
FISHER William MM Sjt 19450 Machine Gun Corps
FISHER William MM L/Cpl 96141 17 Squadron MGC (Cavalry)
FISHER William MM L/Cpl 2297 1/1st Monmouthshire Regt
FISHER William MM L/Cpl 10463 9th West Yorkshire Regt
FISHER William MM Cpl 4686 RFA
FISHER William MM L/Cpl 240792 1/5th Royal Lancaster Regt KIA 30.11.17.
FISHER William MM Dvr 83465 23 Bty 40 Bde RFA
FISHER William Arthur MM 2nd Cpl 181071 Railway Ops Div Royal Engineers
FISHER William Ernest MM Pte M1/08602 21 Div Train Army Service Corps
FISHER William Francis MM L/Cpl 40169 Worcestershire Regt
FISHER William G. MM L/Cpl 290516 Royal Highlanders
FISHER William George MM Sjt 14064 71 Bde HQ RFA
FISHER William H. MM+Bar Pte 56221 1 Fd Amb RAMC
FISHER William James MM L/Cpl 13766 7th Suffolk Regt DOW 9.5.17.
FISHER Wolf MM L/Cpl 7957 1st Middlesex Regt
FISHLOCK Aynsley C. MM L/Cpl 1621 King Edward's Horse
FISHWICK John J. MM Sjt 73519 76 Fd Amb RAMC
FISHWICK Joshua "DCM,MM" Sjt 6581 2nd Dragoon Guards
FISHWICK Peter MM Cpl 18361 7th Border Regt
FISHWICK William MM Pte 2264 North Staffordshire Regt
FISK Alfred W. MM+Bar Sjt STK/1259 10th Royal Fusiliers
FISK C.F. MM Air Mech 2 43975 Royal Air Force
FISK Edward MM Cpl 3996 2nd Rifle Brigade
FISK Frederick MM L/Sjt 35881 51 Fd Amb RAMC
FISK Henry J. MM Cpl M2/101605 Army Service Corps
FISK William MM Pte 20294 18 Fd Amb RAMC KIA 21.3.18.
FISKEN Thomas MM L/Cpl 75631 Royal Engineers
FISKEN Thomas "MM,CG(F)" Cpl 30523 11th Scottish Rifles
FITALL James MM Sjt 12991 5th Dorsetshire Regt KIA 5.10.17.
FITCH A. MM Cpl 41803 RFA
FITCH Christopher Bertram MM Cpl 15697 7th Northamptonshire Regt DOW 12.7.16.
FITCH F. MM Dvr 3538 15 Bde RFA
FITCH George MM Bdr 114944 RFA
FITCH James B. MM L/Cpl 235131 Lincolnshire Regt
FITCH John P. MM L/Sjt 2283 1/9th London Regt
FITCH Louis Clifford MM Sjt S/4390 Rifle Brigade KIA 28.7.16.
FITCH Sidney Arthur "DCM,MM,MID" Sjt 33542 30 Fd Amb RAMC
FITCH Stanley George MM Pte 12744 2nd Grenadier Guards
FITCHETT Frank MM Sjt 37299 B/104 Bde RFA
FITCHETT John MM Pte 203591 10th Royal West Surrey Regt
FITCHIE Ernest MM Gnr 676671 D/275 Bde RFA
FITSALL Edward G. MM+Bar Sjt 6026 19th Hussars
FITT Patrick A. MM Pte 26908 1st Royal Irish Fusiliers
FITT Percy MM Pte 12955 Royal Berkshire Regt
FITTALL George Henry Barham MM Pte 2438 7th Royal West Kent Regt
FITTER Henry MM Sjt 10998 2nd Durham Light Infantry
FITTES Alfred MM Sjt 17711 13th Durham Light Infantry
FITTIN William "DCM,MM" CSM 230062 1/2nd London Regt
FITTON Abraham MM Pte 6766 11th Lancashire Fusiliers

FITTON Albert Lees MM Gnr Sig 131077 379 Siege Bty RGA att 10 Div Sig Coy RE
FITTON Frederick MM Pte C/712 16th King's Royal Rifle Corps
FITTON Herbert MM+Bar Pte 266656 Gordon Highlanders
FITTON John MM Pte 10155 33rd Bn Machine Gun Corps
FITTON John William MM L/Cpl 170 24th Royal Fusiliers KIA 1.10.18.
FITTON Stanley MM L/Cpl 221230 A/112 Bde RFA
FITTON Tom MM Pte 11543 16th Manchester Regt KIA 21.3.18.
FITTON Tom MM Sjt 310661 1/1st Warwickshire Yeomanry
FITTON William MM L/Cpl 3065 Northumberland Fusiliers
FITTON William MM Sjt 3061 Liverpool Regt Killed 19.8.18.
FITTON William H. MM L/Cpl 16546 Lancashire Fusiliers
FITTS Michael MM Pte 204981 2nd London Regt
FITZGERALD Alf R. MM Cpl 651361 21st London Regt
FITZGERALD Arthur MM Sjt 7030 1st Coldstream Guards KIA 9.10.17.
FITZGERALD Charles MM Bdr 11077 RFA
FITZGERALD Dennis MM L/Cpl 2776 Middlesex Regt
FITZGERALD Edward MM Pte 2164 1st Welsh Guards KIA 27.9.18.
FITZGERALD Ernest MM Pte 3215 16th Lancers
FITZGERALD Frank MM Gnr 46029 36 Bty 33 Bde RFA KIA 28.3.18.
FITZGERALD George Henry MM L/Sjt 18196 7th Bedfordshire Regt
FITZGERALD Hazelwood B. MM Cpl 700369 1/23rd London Regt
FITZGERALD Henry MM Pte 54696 RAMC
FITZGERALD Herbert William MM Sjt 240115 North Staffordshire Regt
FITZGERALD James MM Gnr 37241 RGA
FITZGERALD John MM Pte 17237 Machine Gun Corps
FITZGERALD John J. MM Pte 17367 7th Royal Berkshire Regt
FITZGERALD Leonard MM Dvr 44055 A/175 Bde RFA
FITZGERALD M. MM Pte 10094 1st Essex Regt
FITZGERALD Malcolm Charles "MC,MM(1718 L/Cpl 1/1st Surrey Yeo)" T/2Lt 2/10th Royal Scots
FITZGERALD Michael MM+Bar L/Cpl 4993 1st Irish Guards
FITZGERALD Percy "MM,CG(B)" Sjt 98680 Royal Engineers
FITZGERALD Richard MM Pte 13514 9th Lancashire Fusiliers
FITZGERALD Thomas MM Cpl 9938 1st Welsh Regt
FITZGERALD Thomas MM L/Cpl 43293 Bedfordshire Regt
FITZGERALD Thomas MM Pte 7520 1st Scots Guards
FITZGERALD Thomas E. MM Dvr 62847 RFA
FITZGERALD Thomas P. MM Sjt 19313 Machine Gun Corps
FITZGERALD Walter MM Sjt 19282 Lincolnshire Regt
FITZGERALD Walter MM Bdr 32348 RFA
FITZGERALD William Patrick MM Sjt 20434 Welsh Regt
FITZGERALD William Patrick Gerald MM Pte 1313 1st King Edward's Horse
FITZGIBBON Gerald John MM Sjt 8/4854 8th Royal Munster Fusiliers KIA 20.11.17.
FITZGIBBON James MM Bdr 82063 RFA
FITZGIBBON John "DCM,MM" CSM 8031 1st East Surrey Regt
FITZHARRIS George MM Pte 5311 RAMC att 39 Bde RFA.KIA 28.5.17.
FITZHUGH E. MM Pte 204260 1/1st Hertfordshire Regt
FITZHUGH William MM Cpl 17036 6th Northamptonshire Regt
FITZHUGH William MM Pte 31041 1/1st City of London Yeo
FITZJOHN Ernest Arthur MM Pte 25290 9th East Surrey Regt DOW 17.10.18.
FITZJOHN William MM Sjt 10436 1st Notts & Derby Regt
FITZMAURICE Thomas MM Pte M2/021505 Army Service Corps att 55 Fd Amb RAMC.
FITZMAURICE William H. "MM,CG(B)" L/Cpl 7301 2nd Leinster Regt
FITZPATRICK Edward MM Pte 201039 Lancashire Fusiliers
FITZPATRICK Edward C. MM Gnr 371 RFA
FITZPATRICK Frank MM+Bar L/Cpl 201377 2/5th Lancashire Fusiliers KIA 20.10.18.
FITZPATRICK Frederick MM 2nd Cpl 444140 66 Div Sig Coy Royal Engineers
FITZPATRICK Hugh MM Pte 333170 Highland Light Infantry
FITZPATRICK James "DCM,MM,MID" Sjt 432322 55 Div Sig Coy Royal Engineers
FITZPATRICK James MM Sjt 73337 382 Bty 44 Bde RFA KIA 20.9.18.
FITZPATRICK James D. "MM,MID" Sjt 700433 RFA
FITZPATRICK John MM L/Cpl 11825 2nd King's Own Scottish Borderers
FITZPATRICK John W. MM 2nd Cpl 157 Royal Engineers
FITZPATRICK Patrick MM Pte 5/19495 5th Royal Inniskilling Fusiliers
FITZPATRICK Peter MM Gnr 77377 37 Bty 27 Bde RFA
FITZPATRICK Peter MM Pte 537 13th Cheshire Regt
FITZPATRICK Thomas MM Sjt 18170 Durham Light Infantry
FITZPATRICK William H. MM Pte 23493 East Lancashire Regt
FITZSIMMONS Edward MM Pte 308881 2/8th Liverpool Regt
FITZSIMMONS James MM L/Cpl 9082 1st Scots Guards
FITZSIMMONS John MM Pte 58780 RAMC
FITZSIMMONS Leo MM Pte 12514 2nd South Lancashire Regt KIA 3.9.16.
FITZSIMONS James MM Sjt 17787 Machine Gun Corps
FITZSIMONS James MM Sjt 14609 14th Royal Irish Rifles
FITZSIMONS William MM Pte 200558 5th Cameron Highlanders
FIVEASH Harry G. MM Sjt 536120 5 Fd Amb RAMC
FLACK Alfred E. MM Dvr 110169 D/83 Bde RFA
FLACK Charles S. MM Sjt 10004 3rd Worcestershire Regt
FLACK Eustace MM Bdr 81007 RGA
FLACK Frederick John MM Pte R38188 7th King's Royal Rifle Corps DOW 16.9.17.
FLACK George MM L/Cpl 26146 17th Welsh Regt DOW 27.4.17.
FLACK Leonard MM Sjt 15929 8th Bedfordshire Regt
FLACK Leonard W. MM Pte 43946 18th King's Royal Rifle Corps
FLACK Thomas MM CQMS 46537 Northumberland Fusiliers
FLACK Walter MM Sjt 8517 37th Bn Machine Gun Corps
FLACK William R. MM Pte 16255 1/8th Hampshire Regt
FLACK William W. MM L/Cpl 15120 6th Royal West Kent Regt
FLAHERTY Edmund MM Pte 29820 10th Shropshire Light Infantry
FLAHERTY James MM Pte R/15106 13th King's Royal Rifle Corps
FLAHERTY John MM L/Sjt 6768 1st Irish Guards
FLAHERTY John MM Sjt 43355 RGA
FLAHERTY John W. MM Cpl 4355 C/104 Bde RFA
FLAHERTY Joseph MM Pte 7410 North Staffordshire Regt
FLAHERTY Patrick MM Pte 3/5703 5th Connaught Rangers
FLAHERTY Stephen MM Gnr 155047 C/148 Bde RFA
FLAHERTY William MM Pte 22457 Manchester Regt
FLAHERTY William F. MM Pte 98999 1st Royal Fusiliers
FLAIN William MM Pte 23653 Royal Scots
FLAMANK William D. MM Pte 10657 RAMC
FLANAGAN Denis MM Spr 89551 128 Fd Coy Royal Engineers
FLANAGAN Henry MM Pte 15864 South Lancashire Regt
FLANAGAN James MM Gnr W/2713 RFA
FLANAGAN James P. MM Pte 11156 Cheshire Regt
FLANAGAN Joe MM Sjt 34584 RFA
FLANAGAN John L. "MM,MSM" Sjt 74667 93 Bty 280 Bde RFA
FLANAGAN John W. MM Pte 33478 Royal Welsh Fusiliers
FLANAGAN Lawrence MM Pte 3207 1/15th London Regt DOW 22.9.16.
FLANAGAN Martin "DCM,MM" L/Cpl 11712 1st Irish Guards
FLANAGAN Michael MM Pte 43073 16th Manchester Regt
FLANAGAN Peter MM Pte 3/5231 1st Leinster Regt
FLANAGAN Stephen "DCM,MM" Sjt 14775 6th Northamptonshire Regt
FLANAGAN T. MM Sjt 63975 RGA
FLANAGAN Thomas MM Sjt 21043 North Lancashire Regt
FLANAGAN William MM Pte 57591 1 Fd Amb RAMC
FLANAGAN William MM Sjt S/1983 Rifle Brigade
FLANDERS Albert J.P. MM Bdr 340065 166 Siege Bty RGA
FLANNAGAN Bernard MM Pte 12362 11th Royal Scots Fusiliers
FLANNERY John MM Cpl 6033 1st West Yorkshire Regt
FLANNIGAN Frank MM Pte 40736 5/6th Royal Scots
FLANNIGAN James MM Pte 55314 18th Highland Light Infantry
FLANNIGAN Joseph MM Spr 86491 176 Tunnelling Coy Royal Engineers
FLANNIGAN Thomas MM+Bar Bdr L/201 C/64 Bde RFA KIA 11.12.17.
FLANNIGAN William MM Pte 300572 1/7th Royal Scots
FLATHER H. MM Air Mech 3 99481 Royal Air Force
FLATHER Herbert MM Pte 32149 5th Gloucestershire Regt
FLATHER John Noel MM CSM 1002 1/4th West Riding Regt
FLATLEY Samuel MM Pte 44140 12th North Staffordshire Regt
FLATOW Frederick W. MM Cpl 41725 11th East Yorkshire Regt
FLATT Edward N. MM Pte 9279 1st Middlesex Regt
FLATT George MM Gnr 78509 RFA
FLATT George MM Pte 267536 West Riding Regt
FLATT George MM Pte 7670 1st Middlesex Regt
FLATT Henry W. MM Sjt 1663 Royal Engineers
FLAVELL James William MM Pte 10020 1/5th South Staffordshire Regt KIA 12.10.18.
FLAVELL Tom MM Sjt 81983 305 Siege Bty RGA
FLAVILL Harry MM Cpl 401129 Manchester Regt
FLAVIN John MM+Bar Sjt 9445 Machine Gun Corps

FLAWN Wilfred G. MM Pte 473756 London Regt
FLAWS Leslie R. MM Cpl (MCDR) 444211 Royal Engineers
FLAXMAN Alfred George MM Gnr 16581 125 Bty 29 Bde RFA
FLAYE William F. MM Sjt L/31754 RFA
FLEAR Albert MM Sjt 47403 RAMC
FLECK Andrew K. MM L/Sjt 14677 16th Highland Light Infantry KIA 1.7.16.
FLECK Bertram MM Dvr 845442 242 Bde RFA DOW 23.10.18.
FLECK Thomas MM Pte 74105 1st Bn Machine Gun Corps
FLECKNEY Alfred John MM L/Cpl 29824 7th Bedfordshire Regt
FLECKNEY William F. MM Cpl 23141 5 Div Sig Coy Royal Engineers
FLECKNOE Guy A. MM Cpl M2/047800 48 Div Train Army Service Corps
FLEET George MM Cpl M1/5416 8 Div Advanced Park Army Service Corps
FLEET Henry A. MM Sjt 250059 1st London Regt
FLEET Henry O. MM L/Bdr 174376 224 Siege Bty RGA
FLEET Robert H. MM Pte 28474 20th Hussars
FLEET Thomas MM Sjt 100107 MGC(Cavalry)
FLEETING John MM Pte 1253 2nd Arg & Suth Highlanders
FLEETWOOD Arthur C. MM Sjt 13592 8th Duke of Cornwall's LI
FLEETWOOD John MM BSM 7495 109 Heavy Bty RGA
FLEMING Albert R.G. MM Pte 7979 Machine Gun Corps
FLEMING Alexander MM Pte 4026 1/6th Seaforth Highlanders
FLEMING Archie MM Pte 32628 2nd Highland Light Infantry
FLEMING Charles "MM,MID" Gnr 281661 24 Hy Bty RGA
FLEMING Charles MM L/Sjt 375276 2nd Royal Scots
FLEMING Ernest W. MM Pte 8561 2nd Devonshire Regt
FLEMING Frank MM Pte 1717 1/14th London Regt
FLEMING Frank MM L/Cpl 497 4th Bn GMGR
FLEMING George MM Pte 10573 Royal Irish Regt
FLEMING George MM Cpl 21 1/5th South Staffordshire Regt DOW 22.3.17.
FLEMING George MM Pte 11429 2nd Royal Scots Fusiliers
FLEMING George T. MM Dvr 761005 RFA
FLEMING Harold Osborne MM Pte 8564 1st Somerset Light Infantry KIA 8.8.16.
FLEMING Henry MM Sjt 19488 12th Royal Irish Rifles
FLEMING Hugh MM L/Cpl 266726 Railway Ops Division Royal Engineers
FLEMING J. MM Pte 241479 2nd East Lancashire Regt
FLEMING James MM Pte 3363 Arg & Suth Highlanders
FLEMING James MM+Bar Sjt 7317 RFA
FLEMING John MM Cpl S/15011 7th Royal Highlanders
FLEMING John MM L/Cpl 76563 Machine Gun Corps
FLEMING John MM Pte 40925 Royal Scots
FLEMING John MM Spr 79987 Royal Engineers
FLEMING John "DCM,MM" L/Cpl 22939 1st Grenadier Guards
FLEMING John MM Cpl 805427 C/231 Bde RFA
FLEMING John MM Pte 12357 7th North Lancashire Regt
FLEMING John MM Pte 17717 Machine Gun Corps
FLEMING John L. MM Pte 238 Army Cyclist Corps
FLEMING Norman MM+Bar Sjt 166019 11 Div Sig Coy Royal Engineers
FLEMING Peter "DCM,MM" Sjt 5074 1st Cameron Highlanders
FLEMING Robert MM Cpl 63556 RGA
FLEMING Robert MM Sjt S/9533 14th Arg & Suth Highlanders
FLEMING Robert MM Sjt 48134 68 Bty 14 Bde RFA
FLEMING Robert Govan Richmond MM Pte 202909 2/4th Oxf & Bucks Light Infantry
FLEMING Robert Smith Ritchie MM Sjt 11855 38th Bn Machine Gun Corps Died 4.11.18.
FLEMING Thomas MM CQMS 48154 Machine Gun Corps
FLEMING Walter G.C. MM Sjt M1/08466 701 Coy Army Service Corps
FLEMING William MM Gnr 7225 C/75 Bde RFA
FLEMING William MM Cpl 15518 Royal Inniskilling Fusiliers
FLEMING William MM Pte TT/03457 Army Veterinary Corps
FLEMING William G. MM Cpl 201647 Gloucestershire Regt
FLEMING William Roughead MM L/Cpl 265372 10th Scottish Rifles
FLETCHER Albert MM Dvr 486381 468 Fd Coy Royal Engineers
FLETCHER Albert MM Pte 22313 1/4th Northamptonshire Regt
FLETCHER Albert B. MM L/Cpl M2/053240 48 Div Train Army Service Corps
FLETCHER Albert E. MM Cpl 2958 North Staffordshire Regt
FLETCHER Alfred MM Gnr 93508 48 Bty 36 Bde RFA
FLETCHER Angus MM Pte 29764 Royal Scots
FLETCHER Arthur E. MM L/Bdr 147039 RGA
FLETCHER Arthur Frederick MM Pte 12553 5th Northamptonshire Regt
FLETCHER Ben MM Pte 20105 2nd Bedfordshire Regt
FLETCHER Benjamin MM Spr 132592 184 Tunnelling Coy Royal Engineers
FLETCHER Bernard MM Pte 41888 11th East Yorkshire Regt KIA 16.8.18.
FLETCHER Bertram Ernest MM Cpl 3/8950 Suffolk Regt
FLETCHER Charles MM Pte 94990 9th Bn Tank Corps
FLETCHER Charles Alexander MM Sjt 12891 6th Shropshire Light Infantry
FLETCHER Charles Henry MM L/Bdr 618100 20 Bde Hampshire Bty RHA
FLETCHER Charles J. MM Pte 15638 9th Welsh Regt
FLETCHER Charles L. MM Spr 28360 Royal Engineers
FLETCHER Charles S. MM Pte 266957 5th West Riding Regt
FLETCHER David MM Cpl 109984 10th Bn Tank Corps
FLETCHER Edmund MM Cpl Wheeler 705198 C/210 Bde RFA DOW 2.11.18.
FLETCHER Edward C. MM Sjt 8083 1st Wiltshire Regt
FLETCHER Ernest MM Pte 90693 Machine Gun Corps
FLETCHER Ernest MM Cpl 10973 1st Notts & Derby Regt
FLETCHER Ernest A. MM Spr 281731 Signal Service Royal Engineers
FLETCHER F. MM L/Cpl 630439 London Regt
FLETCHER Frank MM Pte 38929 Lincolnshire Regt
FLETCHER Frederick MM L/Cpl 15646 9th Norfolk Regt
FLETCHER Frederick MM+Bar Sjt 3/11220 9th West Riding Regt KIA 27.8.18.
FLETCHER George E. MM L/Cpl 42145 8th East Surrey Regt
FLETCHER George Herbert MM Spr 28441 Royal Engineers
FLETCHER H. MM Gnr L/8576 RFA
FLETCHER Harold MM Pte 243404 1/5th North Lancashire Regt KIA 2.9.18.
FLETCHER Harry MM L/Cpl 54172 20th Manchester Regt
FLETCHER Harry MM Gnr 26673 RFA
FLETCHER Harry MM Pte 240504 Notts & Derby Regt
FLETCHER Henry MM L/Cpl 5788 Machine Gun Corps
FLETCHER Henry MM Dvr 72983 125 Bty 29 Bde RFA
FLETCHER Henry William MM Bdr L/26901 C/210 Bde RFA DOW 13.4.18.
FLETCHER Herbert MM Pte 200044 1/4th Shropshire Light Infantry
FLETCHER Herbert A. MM Gnr 825 119 Heavy Bty RGA
FLETCHER Horace MM Pte 8347 1st Leicestershire Regt
FLETCHER Isaac Dixon MM Gnr 135498 41 Siege Bty RGA
FLETCHER James MM Cpl 16/1387 10th Northumberland Fusiliers
FLETCHER James MM L/Cpl 5101 1st Duke of Cornwall's LI
FLETCHER James MM Pte 41267 2nd Royal Scots Fusiliers KIA 25.10.18.
FLETCHER James MM Pte 16193 2nd Grenadier Guards
FLETCHER James MM Gnr 155041 91 Siege Bty RGA
FLETCHER James MM L/Cpl 51188 11th Royal Scots Fusiliers
FLETCHER James A. MM L/Cpl SPTS/4777 Royal Fusiliers
FLETCHER James T. "DCM,MM,MID" Spr 27323 1 Div Sig Coy Royal Engineers
FLETCHER John MM Pte 27404 Oxf & Bucks Light Infantry
FLETCHER John MM Pte 14156 10th North Lancashire Regt
FLETCHER John MM Pte 22481 Lancashire Fusiliers
FLETCHER John C. MM Cpl 88075 46th Bn Machine Gun Corps
FLETCHER John E. MM Pte 47398 MGC(Cavalry)
FLETCHER John F. MM Pte 53958 11th Royal Scots Fusiliers
FLETCHER John G. MM L/Cpl 6145 Royal West Surrey Regt
FLETCHER John H. MM Sjt 24529 321 Siege Bty RGA
FLETCHER John Henry MM Sjt 14/1291 14th York & Lancaster Regt
FLETCHER John R. MM Pte 718291 23rd London Regt
FLETCHER John Thomas "DCM,MM+Bar" CSM 240349 2/5th Yorkshire Light Infantry KIA 2.6.18.
FLETCHER John W. MM Sjt 200120 1/5th Notts & Derby Regt
FLETCHER John William MM L/Cpl 201887 1/4th Lincolnshire Regt
FLETCHER Joseph MM Pte 24102 North Staffordshire Regt
FLETCHER Joseph MM Pte 45566 Royal Welsh Fusiliers
FLETCHER Joseph Edwin MM Pte 202982 9th West Riding Regt DOW 20.9.18.
FLETCHER Kenneth MM Gnr 156401 C/50 Bde RFA
FLETCHER Lambert MM Pte 2537 Lancashire Fusiliers
FLETCHER Leonard "MC+Bar,MM(1065 Pte)" T/2Lt 9th Northumberland Fusiliers
FLETCHER Levi MM Pte 18374 7th South Staffordshire Regt
FLETCHER Lionel "DCM,MM" Sjt 241156 2/5th Gloucestershire Regt

FLETCHER Murdoch McKay MM Pte 3171 1/8th Arg & Suth Highlanders
FLETCHER Oswald E. MM Sjt 66222 RGA
FLETCHER Raymond MM Dvr 796227 RFA
FLETCHER Richard MM Spr 62104 103 Fd Coy Royal Engineers
FLETCHER Richard MM+Bar Sjt 108616 233 Fd Coy Royal Engineers
FLETCHER Richard A. MM+Bar Gnr 73780 14 Bde RFA
FLETCHER Samuel J. "DCM,MM" L/Cpl R/1294 12th King's Royal Rifle Corps
FLETCHER Sidney MM Pte 8120 11th Royal Fusiliers
FLETCHER Sidney George MM Pte 8307 7th East Surrey Regt KIA 20.11.17.
FLETCHER Stanley MM L/Cpl 19246 1/5th Border Regt
FLETCHER Stephen A. MM Pte 8420 1st Dragoons
FLETCHER Stephenson MM L/Cpl 532585 1/15th London Regt
FLETCHER Sydney MM Pte 67183 47 Fd Amb RAMC
FLETCHER Thomas MM Sjt 246345 5 Fd Svy Bn Royal Engineers
FLETCHER Thomas MM Pte S/4779 Royal Highlanders
FLETCHER Thomas MM Spr 46960 21 Div Sig Coy Royal Engineers
FLETCHER Thomas MM Pte 27486 Welsh Regt
FLETCHER Thomas MM Pte 24432 Durham Light Infantry
FLETCHER Thomas Alfred MM Pte 12037 2nd Royal Berkshire Regt DOW 2.3.18.
FLETCHER Thomas Edward "MC,DCM,MM" CSM 6403 2nd Border Regt
FLETCHER Thomas Fairbrother MM Pte DM2/138216 Army Service Corps att 275 Siege Bty RGA
FLETCHER Thomas Robert MM Pte 474681 12th London Regt
FLETCHER Tom MM Pte R/8496 King's Royal Rifle Corps
FLETCHER Tom MM Sjt 9179 Coldstream Guards
FLETCHER Tom MM Pte 202118 Lancashire Fusiliers
FLETCHER W. MM Pte 55258 Royal Fusiliers
FLETCHER Walter MM Sjt 10612 Notts & Derby Regt att Indian Army
FLETCHER Walter Charles MM L/Cpl 72436 22nd Royal Fusiliers
FLETCHER Walter S. MM Pte 59604 1/6th Manchester Regt
FLETCHER Wilfred T. MM Cpl 549761 56 Div Sig Coy Royal Engineers
FLETCHER William MM Dvr 21134 D/51 Bde RFA
FLETCHER William MM Pte 200289 1/4th East Yorkshire Regt DOW 30.3.18.
FLETCHER William "MM,MID" Sjt 8480 2nd Northamptonshire Regt
FLETCHER William MM Sjt 1763 6th Dragoons
FLETCHER William MM Gnr 58131 37 Bde RFA
FLETCHER William MM L/Cpl 9271 2nd South Staffordshire Regt
FLETCHER William MM Pte 1288 Coldstream Guards
FLETCHER William MM Pte B/201449 1/28th London Regt
FLETCHER William "MM,MC(G)" Pte 9/14423 9th East Lancashire Regt
FLETCHER William MM+Bar Sjt 659 1st Middlesex Regt
FLETCHER William MM Sjt 14/12061 West Yorkshire Regt
FLETCHER William C. MM Cpl 240310 1/5th Gloucestershire Regt
FLETCHER William C. MM Gnr 21601 25 Bde RFA
FLETCHER William J. MM Pte 72310 1st London Regt
FLETCHER William J. MM Gnr 318093 RGA
FLETCHER William T. MM Cpl 74293 2 Bde RFA
FLETT Alexander MM Pte 265691 Gordon Highlanders
FLETT John MM 2nd Cpl 65615 126 Fd Coy Royal Engineers
FLETT William A. MM Pte 266229 1/4th Seaforth Highlanders
FLEWITT Thomas Arthur MM Pte 31900 2nd South Lancashire Regt KIA 21.8.18.
FLEXON Albert MM Cpl 131009 6th Bn Machine Gun Corps
FLEXON John MM Pte 68250 RAMC
FLICKER James MM Pte S/10099 9th Rifle Brigade KIA 24.3.18.
FLIGHT Alfred MM Sjt 13706 8th Gloucestershire Regt
FLIGHT Arthur Benjamin MM L/Cpl 471469 12th London Regt
FLIGHT Frank Cooke "MM+Bar,CG(F),MM(F)" Spr 182255 Royal Engineers
FLIGHT Peter Thomas MM Pte G/5575 6th East Kent Regt KIA 30.11.17.
FLINDERS Edding MM Sjt 3939 3rd Hussars
FLING Alexander J. MM L/Bdr Sig 956131 A/187 Bde RFA
FLINGO Stephen MM Gnr 52367 RFA
FLINT Andrew H. MM Pte 339207 RAMC
FLINT Arthur John MM Sjt 56568 B/186 Bde RFA DOW 5.6.18.
FLINT Charles A.I. MM L/Cpl 241763 Leicestershire Regt
FLINT Douglas William MM Bdr 2574 RFA
FLINT Dyson MM L/Cpl 43635 15th Royal Scots KIA 26.8.17.
FLINT Frederick MM Cpl 20087 1st Royal West Kent Regt KIA 29.8.18.
FLINT Frederick MM Cpl G/1862 16th Royal Sussex Regt
FLINT George MM Sjt 266475 Royal Warwickshire Regt
FLINT Harry MM Pte 9563 2nd West Yorkshire Regt
FLINT J.W.W.J. MM L/Sjt 12370 1st Essex Regt
FLINT James F. MM Pte 3594 1/9th Highland Light Infantry
FLINT James William MM Pte 20291 9th Yorkshire Regt
FLINT Samuel MM L/Cpl 20547 10th Notts & Derby Regt
FLINT Stanley MM Pte 21886 17th Royal Welsh Fusiliers
FLINTHAM John MM Sjt 14/1551 2/4th York & Lancaster Regt
FLINTHAM John William MM L/Cpl 25145 6th Northamptonshire Regt
FLINTOFT Henry MM L/Cpl 201880 Royal Warwickshire Regt
FLINTOFT Joseph B. MM Cpl 1245 Yorkshire Regt
FLITCROFT James MM Pte 26055 5th Royal Lancaster Regt
FLITCROFT Sam "DCM,MM" Sjt 200055 1/4th West Riding Regt
FLOCKHART Charles G. "DCM,MM" Cpl S/2026 10th Arg & Suth Highlanders
FLOCKHART Robert MM Pte 152932 1/1st Berkshire Yeomanry
FLOCKHART Valentine MM Sjt 17898 6th Wiltshire Regt
FLOCKTON William Edwin MM Spr 48135 11 Div Sig Coy Royal Engineers
FLOOD Alfred MM Dvr 60553 127 Bty 29 Bde RFA
FLOOD Charles Henry MM+Bar Cpl 325569 1/1st Cambridgeshire Regt
FLOOD Edward MM Pte S/25153 6th Royal Highlanders
FLOOD Edwin G. MM Pte 23634 21st Manchester Regt
FLOOD Harry MM+Bar Sjt 325590 1/1st Cambridgeshire Regt
FLOOD James MM Pte 5229 2nd Leinster Regt
FLOOD Joseph MM Pte 10386 Leinster Regt
FLOOD Noel Cooper MM Cpl 92549 83 Bde RFA
FLOOD Patrick MM Pte 25295 Royal Inniskilling Fusiliers
FLOOD Patrick MM Pte 25295 Royal Inniskilling Fusiliers
FLOOD Walter MM Pte 15302 9th Welsh Regt
FLOOD William MM Spr 509310 Inland Water Transport Royal Engineers
FLOOD William MM Sjt 58589 14 Bde D Bty RHA
FLOOD William H. MM Pte 240998 1/5th Devonshire Regt
FLOOK Ernest Alfred MM Gnr 112933 14 Bde C Bty RHA
FLOOK Henry MM Pte 242449 Hampshire Regt
FLOOK Henry E. MM Sjt 10179 1st Royal Scots
FLORANDINE John MM Cpl 350533 1/5th Manchester Regt
FLORENCE Alexander G. MM Sjt 4415 C/157 Bde RFA
FLORENCE Arthur MM Pte 101733 29th Durham Light Infantry
FLORENCE Walter B. MM Pte 242162 8th Worcestershire Regt
FLORENTINE Vincent MM Pte 32230 12th Gloucestershire Regt
FLOWER Ernest MM Cpl L/5664 5th Lancers
FLOWER Henry W. MM(2nd OBLI)+Bar Sjt 54031 2nd King's Royal Rifle Corps
FLOWER John W. MM Pte 32763 RAMC
FLOWER Leonard MM Sjt 1432 Gloucestershire Regt
FLOWER Sidney Arthur MM Gnr 87717 D/124 Bde RFA
FLOWER Thomas MM L/Cpl 3442 21st Lancers
FLOWER Wilfred MM L/Cpl 235035 8th Somerset Light Infantry
FLOWERS Arthur MM Pte 36680 Worcestershire Regt
FLOWERS Charles MM L/Cpl 7339 East Kent Regt
FLOWERS Edwin Frank MM Pte 6775 1/5th West Riding Regt
FLOWERS Henry E. MM Sjt 12063 6th Dorsetshire Regt
FLOWERS John MM+Bar Spr 198847 2 Div Sig Coy Royal Engineers
FLOWERS John MM L/Cpl 14770 12th West Yorkshire Regt
FLOWERS Norman MM Pte 37318 Northumberland Fusiliers
FLOWERS Thomas MM Sjt 16843 11th Notts & Derby Regt
FLOWERS Wilfred S. MM Cpl 38220 Gloucestershire Regt
FLOWERS William Henry MM Gnr 84845 220 Siege Bty RGA
FLOYD Albert MM Pte 5427 East Surrey Regt
FLOYD F.J. MM Bdr W/2844 RFA
FLOYD Francis H. MM Sjt 100284 226 Fd Coy Royal Engineers
FLOYD Frederick MM L/Cpl 18317 Welsh Regt
FLOYD Harry MM Cpl 13603 3rd Royal Fusiliers
FLOYD Haydon S. MM L/Cpl 393238 9th London Regt
FLUCK George W. MM Bdr 39112 305 Siege Bty RGA
FLUKE George William MM Cpl 2404 1/4th Lincolnshire Regt
FLUX Harry MM Pte 242444 Lancashire Fusiliers
FLYNN Arthur MM Pte 11275 6th Duke of Cornwall's LI
FLYNN Barry MM Sjt 200654 2/1st London Regt
FLYNN Bernard MM Cpl 6328 7/8th Royal Irish Fusiliers
FLYNN Bernard J. MM Cpl 84632 Machine Gun Corps
FLYNN Christopher J. MM Sjt 371391 8th London Regt

FLYNN Daniel MM Pte 202860 16th Royal Welsh Fusiliers
FLYNN Ernest MM Sjt 7140 1st East Surrey Regt KIA 20.5.18.
FLYNN Hugh MM Pte 3859 Royal Scots
FLYNN James MM Cpl 81944 193 Siege Bty RGA
FLYNN James MM Pte 10224 1st Leinster Regt
FLYNN James MM Gnr 38220 RGA
FLYNN James MM Pte 27612 7/8th Royal Inniskilling Fusiliers
FLYNN James MM Pte 89068 RAMC
FLYNN James G. MM Pte 40497 Scottish Rifles
FLYNN James J. MM Cpl 19790 10th Northumberland Fusiliers
FLYNN Jeremiah MM Sjt 5797 Irish Guards
FLYNN John MM Pte 72182 Machine Gun Corps
FLYNN John MM Gnr 73358 15 Bde RFA
FLYNN John MM Pte 285207 Seaforth Highlanders
FLYNN John MM Bdr 650199 RFA
FLYNN John E. MM Pte 236976 1st Northumberland Fusiliers
FLYNN John W. MM L/Cpl 502249 Royal Engineers
FLYNN Michael MM Pte 10689 6th Leicestershire Regt
FLYNN Patrick MM Pte 3624 6th Connaught Rangers KIA 21.3.18.
FLYNN Peter MM Sjt 28237 Royal Scots Fusiliers
FLYNN Thomas MM Pte G/113 2nd Royal Munster Fusiliers KIA 12.10.18.
FLYNN William MM L/Cpl 200656 1/4th Royal Scots Fusiliers
FLYNN William MM Sjt 8365 1st Royal Munster Fusiliers
FLYNN William Norman MM L/Cpl 20825 1st Royal Dublin Fusiliers KIA 18.8.17.
FOADEN John H. MM L/Cpl 1621 1/5th London Regt
FOAKES H.W. MM Pte G4925 13th Royal Fusiliers
FOALE John C. MM Pte 20153 Devonshire Regt
FODDEN Aaron MM L/Cpl 325863 1/9th Durham Light Infantry
FODDY James MM Pte 53158 Liverpool Regt
FODEN Arthur F. MM L/Cpl 2757 1/10th Liverpool Regt
FODEN E. MM Cpl 2447 Machine Gun Corps
FOGARTY John MM L/Cpl 19384 21st Manchester Regt KIA 4.10.17.
FOGARTY Joseph MM Bdr 31923 111 Heavy Bty RGA
FOGARTY Thomas MM Cpl 34485 Machine Gun Corps
FOGARTY William MM Pte 240947 1/5th North Lancashire Regt
FOGARTY William J. MM Sjt 47962 295 Siege Bty RGA
FOGDEN George MM+Bar Cpl B/1196 Rifle Brigade
FOGELL Cecil MM Pte 25058 19th Lancashire Fusiliers
FOGG Edward MM Pte 4775 Royal Highlanders
FOGG Harry MM Gnr L/9980 RFA
FOGG William F. MM Sjt 41005 MGC (Cavalry)
FOGGO Harry MM Pte 16813 4th Liverpool Regt
FOGGO Thomas R. MM Pte 16814 6th Liverpool Regt
FOGGON J. MM Pte DM2/154115 Army Service Corps
FOGWILL J.L. MM Pte 241046 1/5th Devonshire Regt
FOLDS Cyril E. MM Pte 531580 15th London Regt
FOLEY C.A. MM Pte G/11896 7th East Kent Regt
FOLEY Cornelius MM Pnr 192497 Royal Engineers
FOLEY Cornelius MM Pte 6221 2nd Royal Munster Fusiliers
FOLEY Daniel MM CSM 31763 4th King's Own Scottish Borderers
FOLEY Edward MM Pte 5874 6th Dragoons
FOLEY F. "DCM,MM" L/Cpl 62011 RAMC
FOLEY George MM Pte 265378 1/6th Cheshire Regt
FOLEY Gladys Connie MM Sister F QAIMNS
FOLEY Henry MM Cpl 10060 1st Border Regt
FOLEY Henry Edward MM Cpl G/5983 13th Royal Fusiliers KIA 15.11.16.
FOLEY James "DCM,MM+Bar" Sjt 65638 106 Fd Coy Royal Engineers
FOLEY James MM Pte 40297 Royal Dublin Fusiliers
FOLEY John MM+Bar Sjt 7369 1st Shropshire Light Infantry att 1/1st Herefordsire Regt.
FOLEY John MM Pnr 428850 Royal Engineers
FOLEY Michael MM Pte 10251 2nd Royal Munster Fusiliers
FOLEY Richard MM Dvr 27620 RFA
FOLEY William MM CQMS 6570 2nd Royal Munster Fusiliers
FOLKARD William H. MM Dvr T3/024099 Army Service Corps att RAMC.
FOLKE Lynford William MM Pte 24301 1st Grenadier Guards
FOLKES Robert J. MM Pte 14599 4th Middlesex Regt
FOLKES William John MM Pte 49878 1st Essex Regt
FOLLETT Arthur V. MM L/Cpl 15582 17th Highland Light Infantry
FOLLETT Henry F. MM L/Cpl 45545 Lancashire Fusiliers
FOLLETT Joseph MM 2nd Cpl 546623 509 Fd Coy Royal Engineers
FOLLETT Rowland MM Cpl 268107 7th Royal Warwickshire Regt
FOLLEY William Henry MM Cpl 71655 135 Fd Amb RAMC
FOLLOWS William MM Pte 12596 8th North Staffordshire Regt
FOLWELL Albert MM+Bar Sjt 16998 1st Bn Machine Gun Corps
FOLWELL Harold MM Pte 49251 37 Fd Amb RAMC
FOLWELL James MM L/Cpl 11419 Leicestershire Regt
FOLWELL Percy MM Pte 10896 1st Leicestershire Regt
FONE Sydney MM Pte 45588 1/1st Surrey Yeomanry
FONE Thomas Henry MM Dvr 31078 C/177 Bde RFA
FONTAINE Alan MM Pte 12501 4th Dragoon Guards
FOOKES Arthur W. MM Sjt 96824 213 Siege Bty RGA
FOOKS Frank MM Sjt 5741 5th Lancers
FOOKS Richard Henry MM Gnr 41477 22 Heavy Bty RGA
FOORD Francis A. MM Pte 24707 Royal West Surrey Regt
FOORD N. MM Pte 534100 RAMC
FOORD Sydney MM Sjt 19607 RFA
FOOT Alfred Victor MM Dvr T3/029069 32 Div Train Army Service Corps
FOOT Cecil G. MM Pte 12260 11th Hampshire Regt
FOOT Charles MM+Bar Sjt 14484 8th South Lancashire Regt
FOOT John A. MM Pte 115607 2nd County of London Yeomanry
FOOT Joseph E. MM Sjt F/545 16th Middlesex Regt
FOOTE Alfred William MM Sjt P785 16th Rifle Brigade DOW 4.10.17.
FOOTE Bernard John MM Bdr 86633 D/62 Bde RFA
FOOTE Charles MM+Bar L/Cpl 680793 1/22nd London Regt
FOOTE Ernest MM Pte 21430 South Wales Borderers
FOOTE George MM Sjt 6550 1st Royal Highlanders
FORAN Thomas MM Cpl 10350 1st Royal West Kent Regt
FORBES Alexander MM Sjt 12714 Seaforth Highlanders
FORBES Alexander MM L/Cpl 200143 1/4th Gordon Highlanders
FORBES Alexander W. "DCM,MM" Sjt S/6948 Gordon Highlanders
FORBES Allan MM Gnr 167171 C/59 Bde RFA
FORBES Andrew MM Pte 26921 Royal Inniskilling Fusiliers
FORBES Angus M. MM Sjt 204310 1/5th Seaforth Highlanders
FORBES Archibald MM Pte 267819 6th Royal Highlanders KIA 10.4.18.
FORBES Arthur K. MM+Bar Sjt 301130 87 Fd Amb RAMC
FORBES Charles MM Pte 266173 1/1st Hertfordshire Regt
FORBES Donald MM Bdr Sig 1581 A/58 Bde RFA
FORBES Frederick MM L/Cpl R/16451 King's Royal Rifle Corps
FORBES Frederick J. MM Cpl 89278 75 Fd Coy Royal Engineers
FORBES George MM Pte 23769 1st Royal Scots Fusiliers
FORBES George MM Pte 8915 1st Royal Munster Fusiliers
FORBES George Anderson MM Pte 41219 2nd Royal Scots Fusiliers KIA 5.10.18.
FORBES Gordon MM Pte 20/145 20th Durham Light Infantry
FORBES Harry MM Cpl B/457 7th Rifle Brigade DOW 18.10.17.
FORBES Harry J. MM L/Sjt 1486 1/7th Middlesex Regt
FORBES Hugh MM Sjt 137565 179 Tunnelling Coy Royal Engineers
FORBES J. MM Pte 386538 RAMC
FORBES James MM CQMS 200159 1/4th Seaforth Highlanders
FORBES James MM Cpl 1390 16th Highland Light Infantry KIA 2.12.17.
FORBES James MM Pte 202675 Royal Highlanders
FORBES James Shiels MM Pte 13591 1st Scots Guards
FORBES John MM Pte 32010 20th Durham Light Infantry
FORBES John MM Sjt 635702 B/2556 Bde RFA DOW 2.4.17.
FORBES John "DCM,MM,MID" CSM 265502 1/6th Gordon Highlanders
FORBES John MM Pte 7767 RAMC
FORBES John D. MM CSM 256767 Railway Operating Division Royal Engineers
FORBES John E. MM CQMS 3383 16th Highland Light Infantry
FORBES Lachlan MM Cpl 365357 RGA
FORBES Lancelot D. MM L/Cpl S/20523 1/4th Gordon Highlanders
FORBES Peter MM Gnr 109015 RFA
FORBES Robert MM Spr 41614 Royal Engineers
FORBES Ronald MM CQMS 2202 1/4th London Regt
FORBES Stephen "DCM+Bar,MM+2 Bars,MMV(lt)" Sjt 34895 9th & 13th York & Lancaster Regt
FORBES Thomas MM Pte 327171 9th Durham Light Infantry
FORBES Thomas MM Pte 3183 Durham Light Infantry
FORBES William MM Cpl S/17062 1/4th Seaforth Highlanders
FORBES William MM Sjt 406010 Royal Engineers
FORBES William S. MM Sjt 510969 14th London Regt
FORD A. MM Sjt 24493 Royal Inniskilling Fusiliers
FORD A.J. "MM,MID" L/Cpl 15391 9th Essex Regt
FORD Albert MM Sjt 62989 119 Bty 27 Bde RFA DOW 8.10.18.
FORD Albert MM Pte 8959 1st East Lancashire Regt
FORD Albert MM Pte R/9365 King's Royal Rifle Corps
FORD Albert E. MM Sjt 2051 Royal Engineers
FORD Albert H.E. MM Pte 27213 Royal Welsh Fusiliers

FORD Alexander MM 2nd Cpl 617401 Royal Engineers
FORD Alexander MM L/Bdr 122235 D/110 Bde RFA
FORD Alfred Bennett MM L/Cpl 210507 6 Lt Rly Op Coy Royal Engineers
FORD Alfred Feltham Nepean MM Bdr 84500 126 Bde RFA
FORD Alfred R. MM Pte 44360 2nd Worcestershire Regt
FORD Alfred Samuel MM Pte 3101 13th Royal Sussex Regt KIA 30.6.16.
FORD Amos P. MM Pte 19805 4th South Wales Borderers
FORD Arthur MM Pte 3007 10th Essex Regt
FORD Arthur MM Pte 10078 2nd East Surrey Regt
FORD Arthur Harold MM L/Cpl 46945 1st Northumberland Fusiliers DOW 23.8.18.
FORD Arthur J. MM L/Cpl 16068 1st Devonshire Regt
FORD Arthur J.E. MM Pte 102497 Notts & Derby Regt
FORD C.F. MM F/Sjt 4248 Royal Flying Corps
FORD Charles MM L/Cpl 2958 24th Royal Fusiliers KIA 31.7.16.
FORD Charles "MM,VM(Rm)" CSM 16520 8th South Wales Borderers
FORD Daniel MM Sjt 41706 West Yorkshire Regt
FORD David MM Sjt 1066 MGC (Motors)
FORD Edward G. MM Cpl 4872 13th Middlesex Regt
FORD Ernest MM Pte 860524 33rd London Regt
FORD Ernest MM Gnr 116617 RFA
FORD Ernest B. MM Pte 265476 8th Somerset Light Infantry
FORD Ernest Edward MM Pte C/12778 18th King's Royal Rifle Corps KIA 31.7.17.
FORD Francis R. MM Dvr Wheeler 146146 RFA
FORD Frank Edward MM L/Cpl 22545 9th East Surrey Regt KIA 16.10.18.
FORD Frederick MM Cpl 8327 South Staffordshire Regt
FORD George MM L/Cpl 20778 Royal Warwickshire Regt
FORD Harold Douglas MM Gnr 938 47 Siege Bty RGA DOW 5.11.16.
FORD Harry MM Pte 8580 ? Lancers
FORD Henry E. MM Sjt 15268 9th South Staffordshire Regt
FORD Herbert MM L/Bdr 74205 114 Siege Bty RGA
FORD Herbert "MM,MSM" Sjt 17298 Machine Gun Corps
FORD Herbert John MM Cpl 15841 2nd Royal Dublin Fusiliers DOW 26.10.18.
FORD Herbert Morgan MM Cpl 79536 77 Bde RFA
FORD Horace N. MM L/Cpl 27149 Royal Engineers
FORD James MM Sjt 375366 10th Manchester Regt
FORD James MM Pte 16662 Lincolnshire Regt
FORD James B. MM Cpl 56499 RFA
FORD John MM Sjt 21317 15th Lancashire Fusiliers
FORD John MM Cpl S/7685 8th Royal Highlanders
FORD John G. MM Pte 202075 1st Royal Scots Fusiliers
FORD John M. MM Spr 178987 106 Fd Coy Royal Engineers
FORD Joseph A. MM Sjt 15522 5th Northamptonshire Regt
FORD Joseph A. MM Pte 38872 4th Liverpool Regt
FORD Michael MM L/Cpl 13390 Yorkshire Regt
FORD Percy MM Pte 13761 6th Somerset Light Infantry
FORD Percy H. MM Sjt 43820 6 Bty 40 Bde RFA
FORD Percy S. MM L/Cpl 21738 Royal West Surrey Regt
FORD Reginald Harry "DCM,MM" Sjt 201919 1/5th Notts & Derby Regt KIA 24.9.18.
FORD Reginald Richard MM 2nd Cpl 19883 'Z' Special Coy Royal Engineers KIA 3.4.17.
FORD Reginald W. MM L/Cpl 45617 15th Hampshire Regt
FORD Richard MM Sjt 309144 1 Heavy Bty RGA
FORD Robert MM Pte 2943 King's Royal Rifle Corps
FORD Robert E. MM Gnr 73783 RGA
FORD Sidney Clarence "DCM,MM+Bar" Bdr 944 280 Bde RFA
FORD Stanley MM Pte 1115 King Edward's Horse
FORD Thomas MM Pte 15086 1st Scots Guards KIA 15.10.18.
FORD Thomas MM Pte 3/3364 6th York & Lancaster Regt
FORD Victor R. MM Pte 42296 2/4th Hampshire Regt
FORD Walter W. MM Dvr 122167 RFA
FORD William MM Sjt 65140 1st Northumberland Fusiliers Died 23.8.18.
FORD William MM CQMS 200028 South Lancashire Regt
FORD William Gordon MM Sjt 201645 Royal West Surrey Regt
FORD William J. MM Pte 66189 RAMC
FORDE James MM Pte 54816 75 Fd Amb RAMC
FORDE John MM Pte 4370 1st Royal Munster Fusiliers Died 27.1.18.
FORDE Joseph MM Sjt 11037 1st Royal Irish Fusiliers
FORDER Edgar C. MM Sjt 9850 9th Lancers
FORDHAM Arthur MM Cpl 5510 2nd Suffolk Regt
FORDHAM Frederick Charles "MM,MSM" Cpl 64338 108 Coy Labour Corps
FORDHAM Maurice William MM Pte 55245 16th Welsh Regt
FORDHAM William G. MM Cpl 18097 RGA
FORDY Robert MM Cpl 9142 1st Northumberland Fusiliers KIA 15.6.18.
FORDYCE Alexander Hendry MM L/Cpl 292868 7th Royal Highlanders KIA 26.3.18.
FORDYCE George N. MM Cpl 125672 85 Bty 11 Bde RFA
FORDYCE Robert H. MM Spr 206279 Royal Engineers
FORDYCE William MM L/Cpl 265164 1/6th Gordon Highlanders
FOREMAN Albert P. MM Pte 4073 12th Royal Fusiliers
FOREMAN David MM Sjt 39908 RAMC
FOREMAN Edgar J. MM+Bar L/Cpl 36637 Lancashire Fusiliers
FOREMAN Ernest MM Sjt 19970 Machine Gun Corps
FOREMAN Ernest MM+Bar Gnr 776840 RFA
FOREMAN Frederick W. MM Bdr 42550 24 Bde RFA
FOREMAN George H. MM Cpl 457298 Royal Engineers
FOREMAN Henry George MM L/Cpl 102459 170 Tunnelling Coy Royal Engineers
FOREMAN Herbert MM L/Cpl 36929 Machine Gun Corps
FOREMAN James MM Gnr 4742 C/160 Bde RFA
FOREMAN John MM Pte 40529 17th Royal Scots DOW 6.8.18.
FOREMAN John MM Cpl 45498 Machine Gun Corps
FOREMAN Robert W. MM Pte 23559 Machine Gun Corps
FOREMAN Thomas MM Cpl 34625 46 Fd Amb RAMC DOW 26.5.17.
FOREMAN William MM Pte 678297 21st London Regt
FOREMAN William MM Dvr 49589 B/153 Bde RFA DOW 17.4.18.
FOREMAN William G. MM Bdr 29010 RFA
FORESTER Edward MM Pte 30654 9th Cheshire Regt
FORGAN John MM Pte 20324 Arg & Suth Highlanders
FORGIE Alexander G. MM L/Cpl 351098 9th Royal Scots
FORINGO Joseph MM+Bar Cpl 6133 18th King's Royal Rifle Corps
FORKER William G. MM Sjt S/5025 11th Arg & Suth Highlanders KIA 13.8.16.
FORKNALL John MM Gnr 242067 D/77 Bde RFA
FORMAN Sam MM Pte B/188 Rifle Brigade
FORMBY William A. MM Pte 204254 5th Liverpool Regt
FORMSTONE Joseph MM Gnr 735382 RFA
FORREST Alexander MM Pte 24952 Royal Scots
FORREST Alexander "DCM,MM" Sjt 57000 68 Bty 14 Bde RFA
FORREST Andrew B. MM Pte 40899 17th Highland Light Infantry
FORREST Clifford MM Dvr 101620 C/103 Bde RFA
FORREST Edward MM Cpl 4013 10th Lancashire Fusiliers
FORREST Ernest MM Cpl 156554 5 Special Bn Royal Engineers
FORREST Francis MM Cpl 40607 2nd Royal Scots Fusiliers KIA 21.3.18.
FORREST Frederick MM Pte 42052 1/5th Seaforth Highlanders
FORREST George MM Gnr 346697 RGA
FORREST George MM Sjt T/232893 Army Service Corps
FORREST James MM Spr 170933 Royal Engineers
FORREST James "MM,MSM" Sjt 14794 12th Royal Scots
FORREST John MM Pte 301417 Manchester Regt
FORREST John MM Spr 76472 Guards Div Sig Coy Royal Engineers
FORREST John H. MM Pte 131007 9th Bn Machine Gun Corps
FORREST John W. MM Pte 951 Durham Light Infantry
FORREST Norman MM Dvr 765580 2/1(Northumbrian)Bde RFA
FORREST Peter MM L/Cpl 200132 1/4th Royal Scots
FORREST Robert MM+Bar Cpl 15115 King's Own Scottish Borderers
FORREST Robert MM Pte 372955 8th London Regt
FORREST Stephen MM Pte 265656 Northumberland Fusiliers
FORREST Thomas Curry MM L/Cpl C1465 17th King's Royal Rifle Corps DOW 20.9.17.
FORRESTER Arthur A. MM Sjt 15452 4th Worcestershire Regt
FORRESTER Arthur W. MM L/Cpl 10558 8th Devonshire Regt
FORRESTER Charles MM Pte 21089 7th Yorkshire Regt
FORRESTER David MM L/Cpl 275803 1/7th Arg & Suth Highlanders
FORRESTER Edward MM L/Cpl 15109 3rd Coldstream Guards
FORRESTER Frank MM Pte 14809 1st Hampshire Regt
FORRESTER H. MM Pte 242669 North Staffordshire Regt
FORRESTER Hugh MM L/Cpl S/16439 6th Cameron Highlanders KIA 24.4.17.
FORRESTER John MM Sjt 20080 6th King's Own Scottish Borderers DOW 2.10.18.
FORRESTER John F. "MM,MSM" Cpl 7018 1st Gordon Highlanders
FORRESTER Thomas William MM Pte 24697 2nd Lancashire Fusiliers

FORRESTER W. MM Pte 241776 North Staffordshire Regt
FORRESTER Wilfred MM Pte 57572 1st Lancashire Fusiliers
FORRESTER William MM Sjt 33295 33rd Bn 19 Coy Machine Gun Corps
FORSBURY William MM L/Cpl 13563 8th South Staffordshire Regt
FORSCUTT H.A. MM Pte 21092 10th East Kent Regt
FORSDICK William A. MM Spr 518974 81 Fd Coy Royal Engineers
FORSE Lilian Audrey MM Miss F VAD
FORSHAW E.H. MM Cpl 54985 C Bty RHA
FORSHAW Edward MM L/Cpl 18581 3rd Worcestershire Regt
FORSHAW John MM Sjt 428460 Royal Engineers
FORSHAW John MM Sjt 6851 2 Siege Coy R Anglesey RE
FORSHAW Joseph MM Sjt 685171 B/290 Bde RFA
FORSHAW Nathan MM+Bar Sjt 70968 165 Coy Machine Gun Corps
FORSHAW William MM Dvr 697010 RFA
FORSTER Arthur MM Sjt 57746 Liverpool Regt
FORSTER D. MM Pte 10651 Northumberland Fusiliers
FORSTER Daniel MM Pte 13409 10th Scottish Rifles
FORSTER David MM Pte 200037 1/4th Northumberland Fusiliers
FORSTER Frederick MM Gnr 47570 Y/37 Med TM Bty RGA
FORSTER George MM L/Cpl 20/13 Durham Light Infantry
FORSTER Harold MM Sjt 705289 210 Bde RFA
FORSTER Harry H. MM L/Cpl 66178 Machine Gun Corps
FORSTER Herbert MM Sjt 42610 13th Liverpool Regt KIA 8.10.18.
FORSTER James MM Sjt 337130 RGA
FORSTER John MM Pte 58954 Machine Gun Corps
FORSTER John James MM Sjt 27804 18th Welsh Regt KIA 9.4.18.
FORSTER John Philip William MM Sjt 61787 154 Fd Coy Royal Engineers
FORSTER Joseph D. MM Gnr 1371 RFA
FORSTER Robert MM Gnr 149002 123 Bty 28 Bde RFA
FORSTER Robert MM L/Cpl 13264 Coldstream Guards
FORSTER Robert D. MM L/Cpl 37737 Yorkshire Light Infantry
FORSTER Rowland "DCM,MM,MID" CSM 1898 1/5th Yorkshire Regt
FORSTER Stanley "MM,MID" Sjt 10390 Manchester Regt
FORSTER Thomas MM Pte 31/100 Northumberland Fusiliers
FORSYTH Albert Laurie MM Cpl 350123 1/9th Royal Scots KIA 23.4.17.
FORSYTH Alexander MM L/Cpl 265354 1/6th Seaforth Highlanders
FORSYTH Alexander MM Cpl M2/118620 Army Service Corps
FORSYTH Alfred C. MM Pte 31229 RAMC
FORSYTH Andrew MM+Bar Cpl 363120 RFA
FORSYTH Cyril Alexander MM Sjt 17626 20th Manchester Regt
FORSYTH David MM+Bar Sjt S/3878 8th Royal Highlanders
FORSYTH Francis MM L/Sjt 201428 Yorkshire Regt
FORSYTH George MM Sjt 200027 5th Cameron Highlanders
FORSYTH James MM Cpl 18054 2nd King's Own Scottish Borderers
FORSYTH James MM Sjt 695 2nd Royal Highlanders
FORSYTH James MM L/Cpl 43231 1/4th Cameron Highlanders
FORSYTH Ludlow MM Sjt 2554 RFA
FORSYTH Richard MM Gnr 43870 3 Siege Bty RGA
FORSYTH Robert MM L/Cpl 50319 1/1st Lanarkshire Yeomanry att 7 Coy Imperial Camel Corps.
FORSYTH Robert MM Pte 1430 Northumberland Fusiliers
FORSYTH Robert MM Pte 41226 South Wales Borderers
FORSYTH Robert Wood MM Pte 351500 1/9th Royal Scots
FORSYTH Rowallan MM Sjt 6143 41 Div Ammn Col RFA
FORSYTH Stephen H. MM Spr 46084 Royal Engineers
FORSYTH Thomas MM Cpl 98179 Machine Gun Corps
FORSYTH William MM Sjt G895 Royal West Surrey Regt
FORSYTH William D. MM Spr 140024 Royal Engineers
FORSYTHE David John MM L/Cpl 17619 12th Royal Irish Rifles
FORSYTHE James MM Sjt 1953 7th Leinster Regt
FORSYTHE Peter A. MM Pte 12795 6th Shropshire Light Infantry
FORSYTHE Samuel MM Sjt 26908 1st Royal Inniskilling Fusiliers
FORT Robert MM Pte 95017 15th Durham Light Infantry
FORTH Tom MM L/Cpl 48617 13th Rifle Brigade
FORTNUM Ernest MM Pte 240783 5th Leicestershire Regt
FORTUNE Andrew MM Pte 325952 1/9th Durham Light Infantry
FORTUNE Francis W. MM Pte 71580 Royal Fusiliers
FORTUNE James M. MM L/Bdr 307044 RGA
FORTUNE John MM Pte 138313 3rd Bn Machine Gun Corps
FORTUNE John Glover MM Gnr Sig 930456 HQ 281 Bde RFA
FORTUNE Thomas MM Pte 200695 D Bn Tank Corps
FORTUNE William H. MM Sjt 306902 2 Supply Coy Tank Corps
FORTUNE William N. MM Sjt 200101 1/5th Liverpool Regt
FORWOOD George E. "DCM,MM" Sjt 8712 1st Scottish Rifles
FOSBROOKE Charles MM Pte 52521 Cheshire Regt

FOSKETT Arthur W. MM Pte R/28389 King's Royal Rifle Corps
FOSKETT Harry MM L/Cpl 60112 Royal Fusiliers
FOSKETT Henry J. MM BQMS 52588 RGA
FOSKETT John H. MM Sjt 1747 Royal Fusiliers
FOSKETT Sydney S. MM Gnr 59434 110 Siege Bty RGA
FOSS Francis MM Pte 337107 RAMC
FOSSEY Cecil H. "DCM,MM" L/Cpl 1015 15th Hussars
FOSSEY Charles MM Pte 11757 8th East Surrey Regt
FOSSEY George MM Cpl 8424 1st East Surrey Regt
FOSSEY George Robert MM L/Sjt 13168 XVII Corps Cyclist Bn Army Cyclist Corps
FOSSEY Victor MM S/Sjt Fitter 10263 RGA
FOSSITT Arthur W. MM L/Cpl 33919 Royal Berkshire Regt
FOSTER A. MM Pte 265454 Northumberland Fusiliers
FOSTER Albert MM Pte C/664 4th King's Royal Rifle Corps
FOSTER Albert E. MM Sjt 9240 1st Yorkshire Light Infantry
FOSTER Albert George MM Pte 40649 Middlesex Regt
FOSTER Albert J. MM Sjt 64135 25 Bde RFA
FOSTER Alfred MM L/Cpl 12332 Oxf & Bucks Light Infantry
FOSTER Alfred MM Pte 7096 1st North Staffordshire Regt
FOSTER Alfred MM Pte 7017 2nd Suffolk Regt
FOSTER Alfred George MM Sjt 57676 38 Bde RFA DOW 13.4.18.
FOSTER Arthur MM Pte 11604 10th West Riding Regt
FOSTER Arthur MM Cpl 16999 2nd Bn Machine Gun Corps
FOSTER Arthur MM L/Cpl 33344 1/4th York & Lancaster Regt KIA 26.4.18.
FOSTER Arthur MM L/Sjt 10419 1st Leicestershire Regt
FOSTER Arthur MM Spr 74116 Signal Service Royal Engineers
FOSTER Bertram C. "DCM,MM" Sjt 42817 19 Div Sig Coy Royal Engineers
FOSTER C. MM Pte 238055 1st Leicestershire Regt
FOSTER C.G. MM Cpl 18/956 Durham Light Infantry
FOSTER Caleb Henry MM Sjt SE/11441 Army Veterinary Corps att 45 Bde RFA
FOSTER Carl Laurence MM Cpl 44561 RFA
FOSTER Cecil MM Pte G/4481 Royal Sussex Regt
FOSTER Charles "DCM,MM" Sjt 9207 6th Northamptonshire Regt
FOSTER Charles Joseph Henry MM Spr 100333 33 Div Sig Coy Royal Engineers
FOSTER Charles O. MM Sjt 10431 HAC
FOSTER Charles W. "MM,MID" Sjt 44666 Royal Engineers
FOSTER Charles William MM Cpl 1514 B/250 Bde RFA
FOSTER Charley B. "DCM,MM,MID" Sjt 2000 9th East Surrey Regt
FOSTER Christopher C. MM Pte 353351 7th London Regt
FOSTER Christopher John MM Gnr 85673 RFA
FOSTER David MM Cpl 24/1391 Northumberland Fusiliers
FOSTER Donald G. MM Pte G/25485 2nd Royal Fusiliers
FOSTER Dorothy Penrose MM Sister F TFNS
FOSTER Edgar MM Sjt 9443 B/354 Bde RFA
FOSTER Edward MM Sjt 43153 2nd Royal Scots
FOSTER Edward MM Pte 341207 RAMC
FOSTER Edward MM Sjt 44461 Royal Engineers
FOSTER Edward MM Spr 104153 227 Fd Coy Royal Engineers
FOSTER Edward MM Gnr 777007 RFA
FOSTER Edwin MM Pte 52468 Middlesex Regt
FOSTER Edwin W. MM L/Cpl 50749 1st Royal Berkshire Regt
FOSTER Ernest MM Pte 52219 Machine Gun Corps
FOSTER Ernest J. MM Sjt 8211 2nd Devonshire Regt
FOSTER Ernest W. MM Pte 16015 1st Hampshire Regt
FOSTER Eugene O. MM Sjt 30893 RGA
FOSTER Ewart F. MM Pte 44692 12th North Staffordshire Regt
FOSTER Francis MM Pte 30061 3rd Grenadier Guards
FOSTER Frank MM Gnr 240644 RFA
FOSTER Frank S.L. MM Pte 10031 2nd Gordon Highlanders
FOSTER Frederick MM Cpl 25042 1st Liverpool Regt DOW 31.7.16.
FOSTER Frederick MM Pte 30990 East Yorkshire Regt
FOSTER Frederick MM Cpl 14175 9th Royal Irish Fusiliers KIA 1.7.16.
FOSTER Frederick G. MM Spr 24892 1 Div Sig Coy Royal Engineers
FOSTER Frederick W. MM L/Sjt 3782 North Staffordshire Regt
FOSTER Frederick W. MM Dvr 4974 RFA
FOSTER G.S. MM Sjt 24341 Machine Gun Corps
FOSTER G.W. MM Sjt 668 East Yorkshire Regt
FOSTER George MM Pte 13/957 East Yorkshire Regt
FOSTER George MM Sjt Wheeler 102 48 Div Ammn Col RFA
FOSTER George MM Pte 26408 4th Grenadier Guards
FOSTER George MM Cpl 306427 Royal Warwickshire Regt
FOSTER George A. MM L/Cpl G/11154 10th Royal West Kent Regt

FOSTER George Arthur MM Pte 203513 1/4th West Riding Regt Died 29.11.18.
FOSTER George C. MM L/Sjt 12898 8th South Staffordshire Regt
FOSTER George E. MM Cpl 109584 RFA
FOSTER George Edward MM Cpl 17988 Machine Gun Corps
FOSTER George H. MM Cpl 20580 8th Border Regt
FOSTER Graham Edwin MM L/Cpl 301666 2/5th London Regt KIA 20.9.17.
FOSTER Harold L. MM Pte 19255 RAMC
FOSTER Harry MM Pte 13246 Leicestershire Regt
FOSTER Harry W.K. MM Pte 254686 4th London Regt
FOSTER Henry MM L/Cpl 84995 4th Liverpool Regt
FOSTER Henry C. MM L/Cpl M2/099927 Army Service Corps
FOSTER Herbert MM Pte 203588 South Staffordshire Regt
FOSTER Herbert "MM,MID" Pte 1633 15th London Regt
FOSTER Herbert Sidney MM Pte 72622 102 Fd Amb RAMC
FOSTER Herbert William MM Sjt 16129 2nd South Staffordshire Regt DOW 17.9.16.
FOSTER Jack MM Cpl 801228 A/295 Bde RFA
FOSTER Jack MM Cpl 6988 16th Manchester Regt
FOSTER Jack Walker MM L/Cpl W/1146 13th Cheshire Regt
FOSTER James H. MM Pte 46587 Northumberland Fusiliers
FOSTER James Sherwood MM L/Cpl 65601 Notts & Derby Regt
FOSTER Jesse W.S. MM Sjt 3062 9th Royal Sussex Regt
FOSTER John MM Sjt 56320 D/256 Bde RFA
FOSTER John MM Pte 35022 RAMC
FOSTER John G. MM Pte 267497 1st Northumberland Fusiliers
FOSTER John G. MM Sjt 240731 Yorkshire Light Infantry
FOSTER John L. MM+Bar L/Cpl 335367 5/6th Royal Scots
FOSTER John L. MM 2nd Cpl 556529 468 Fd Coy Royal Engineers
FOSTER John L. MM Pte 47136 9th Royal Irish Fusiliers
FOSTER John Mathie MM Cpl 250439 1/6th Manchester Regt
FOSTER John Stephen MM Cpl 1985 1/1st London Regt DOW 21.9.16.
FOSTER John Thomas MM Cpl 29358 7 Siege Bty RGA
FOSTER John W. "DCM,MM" BSM 755005 A/251 Bde RFA
FOSTER John William MM Bdr 18614 D/94 Bde RFA
FOSTER Joseph MM Pte S/5535 12th Rifle Brigade
FOSTER Kenneth MM L/Cpl 290268 7th Royal Highlanders
FOSTER Langford MM Pte 22229 Northumberland Fusiliers
FOSTER Lewis Bertram "MM,MSM,MID" Sjt 38053 RFA
FOSTER Lewthwaite MM Sjt 45595 197 Coy Machine Gun Corps KIA 12.10.17.
FOSTER Oliver MM Pte 365085 7th London Regt
FOSTER Owen MM Pte 30253 Welsh Regt
FOSTER Percy MM Sjt 242562 North Lancashire Regt
FOSTER Percy MM Pte PW/3024 18th Middlesex Regt
FOSTER Percy MM Pte 15408 Royal Sussex Regt
FOSTER Reginald A. MM Sjt 9606 2nd Bedfordshire Regt
FOSTER Rennie James MM Cpl 1799 1/6th West Yorkshire Regt
FOSTER Richard MM+Bar Pte 16223 Royal Dublin Fusiliers
FOSTER Richard MM Pte 23109 Royal West Surrey Regt
FOSTER Robert MM L/Cpl 699 2nd Royal Munster Fusiliers
FOSTER Robert MM Sjt 201020 1st West Yorkshire Regt DOW 24.9.18.
FOSTER Robert H. "DCM,MM" Sjt 61886 91 Fd Amb RAMC
FOSTER Samuel Edward MM L/Cpl P2718 First Army HQ Military Foot Police
FOSTER Squire MM L/Sjt 16530 9th North Lancashire Regt
FOSTER Sydney MM Sjt 25845 10th Royal West Surrey Regt
FOSTER Thomas MM Sjt 7825 C Mountain Bty RGA
FOSTER Thomas MM Cpl 9721 2nd Worcestershire Regt
FOSTER Thomas MM Pte 350633 19th Durham Light Infantry
FOSTER Thomas MM Pte 331739 1st Liverpool Regt
FOSTER Thomas MM Pte 202934 1/4th Seaforth Highlanders DOW 31.3.18.
FOSTER Thomas MM Sjt S/6628 9th Royal Highlanders
FOSTER Thomas MM Pte 22494 Bedfordshire Regt
FOSTER Thomas MM Sjt 305195 1/8th Liverpool Regt
FOSTER Thomas MM Pte 18434 6th East Yorkshire Regt
FOSTER Thomas MM Pte 326376 Arg & Suth Highlanders
FOSTER Thomas W. MM Spr 132852 179 Tunnelling Coy Royal Engineers
FOSTER Thomas William MM Cpl 241962 Leicestershire Regt
FOSTER Tom MM L/Cpl 28498 Royal Engineers
FOSTER Walter MM L/Cpl C/12806 King's Royal Rifle Corps att RE.
FOSTER William MM Pte G/12855 11th Royal West Surrey Regt
FOSTER William MM Pte M2/078298 Army Service Corps att RAMC.
FOSTER William MM Cpl 266238 1/8th Notts & Derby Regt
FOSTER William MM Pte 40819 1st Royal Dublin Fusiliers
FOSTER William MM Sjt 200971 RGA
FOSTER William MM Cpl 43810 Arg & Suth Highlanders
FOSTER William MM Sjt 305479 West Riding Regt
FOSTER William MM Pte 50146 North Staffordshire Regt
FOSTER William MM Pte 50146 North Staffordshire Regt
FOSTER William MM Pte 14281 4th Liverpool Regt KIA 11.4.18.
FOSTER William MM Bdr 72521 RFA
FOSTER William A. MM Bdr 54052 RGA
FOSTER William J. "DCM,MM" L/Cpl S/6448 1st Rifle Brigade
FOSTER William Mellor MM L/Cpl 69809 136 Fd Amb RAMC Died 2.1.19.
FOSTER William Thomas MM L/Sjt 18441 16th Royal Warwickshire Regt
FOSTER William Varley MM Pte 200858 West Yorkshire Regt
FOSTON Horace J. MM L/Sjt 37358 Royal Berkshire Regt
FOTHERBY Harry "MM,MSM,MID" Sjt 9343 2nd Yorkshire Regt
FOTHERGILL Francis MM L/Cpl S/17302 4th Gordon Highlanders
FOTHERGILL Harry MM Sjt 12/20 1st Yorkshire Light Infantry
FOTHERGILL Oliver MM Pte 14616 Labour Corps
FOTHERGILL Robert W. "DCM,MM" Cpl 99296 5th Liverpool Regt
FOTHERGILL Thomas S. MM L/Cpl 40218 20th Manchester Regt
FOTHERGILL Walter A. MM L/Cpl 36411 East Yorkshire Regt
FOTHERINGHAM Alexander MM Pte 260024 1/6th Gordon Highlanders
FOTHERINGHAM Alexander MM+Bar Pte 10749 1st Royal Scots Fusiliers DOW 13.4.18.
FOTHERINGHAM Frank MM+2 Bars Sjt 444216 Royal Engineers
FOTHERINGHAM William MM Dvr 181 A/50 Bde RFA
FOULDING Fred MM+Bar Sjt R/897 11th King's Royal Rifle Corps DOW 30.11.17.
FOULDS Donald MM Sjt 241840 2/5th East Lancashire Regt
FOULDS Harry MM 2nd Cpl 476686 455 Fd Coy Royal Engineers
FOULDS Herbert MM Pte 84353 Machine Gun Corps
FOULDS Robert MM Pte 29164 Royal Welsh Fusiliers
FOULDS Walter MM L/Cpl 28839 8th Royal Lancaster Regt DOW 28.9.18.
FOULDS William "DCM,MM" L/Cpl 200800 2/4th West Riding Regt
FOULGER Francis MM Pte 23443 Lancashire Fusiliers
FOULGER Harry E. MM Pte 21945 Machine Gun Corps
FOULGER Harry Richard MM Pte G/57553 26th Royal Fusiliers KIA 25.10.18.
FOULGER Walter J. MM Pte 23069 7th Border Regt
FOULIS Andrew MM Pte 41653 1/7th West Yorkshire Regt
FOULKES Arthur MM Gnr 165584 RFA
FOULKES David Richard MM Pte 40508 12th Manchester Regt
FOULKES Edward "DCM,MM" L/Cpl 79118 36th Northumberland Fusiliers
FOULKES Evan L. MM Gnr 47295 RGA
FOULKES Frederick MM Spr 136053 Royal Engineers
FOULKES George MM Pte 330684 1st Liverpool Regt KIA 21.3.18.
FOULKES John MM L/Sjt 83904 31st Bn Machine Gun Corps
FOULKES Llewellyn MM Pte 26432 14th Royal Welsh Fusiliers
FOULKES Thomas MM Spr 86571 179 Tunnelling Coy Royal Engineers
FOULKES Thomas "MM,CG(B)" Cpl 39379 34 Coy Machine Gun Corps
FOULSHAM Herbert John MM Cpl 875538 B/272 Bde RFA
FOULSHAM Neil MM Pte M2/033453 Army Service Corps att RAMC.
FOULSTONE William MM Cpl 240658 2/5th Yorkshire Light Infantry KIA 27.11.17.
FOUNDLING Fred MM Pte 9625 South Staffordshire Regt
FOUNDLING William MM L/Cpl 47560 13th Royal Inniskilling Fusiliers
FOUNTAIN Alfred G. MM Sjt 265135 1/1st Bucks Bn Oxf & Bucks Light Infantry
FOUNTAIN William MM Pte S/24436 Rifle Brigade
FOUNTAINE Frederick P. MM Gnr 81435 RGA
FOURACRE George MM 2nd Cpl 508430 Royal Engineers
FOURT Francis MM L/Cpl 305457 8th Royal Warwickshire Regt
FOVARGUE A. MM+Bar Pte 23120 2nd Lincolnshire Regt
FOVARGUE Frank C. MM L/Cpl 34054 3 Div Sig Coy Royal Engineers
FOVARGUE John Thomas MM Pte 8/13786 2/5th Lincolnshire Regt DOW 31.8.18.
FOWDEN John MM Pte S/6553 9th Rifle Brigade
FOWDEN William H. "MM,MID" Sjt 8476 11th Lancashire Fusiliers
FOWELL Daniel MM Gnr 30976 75 Bde RFA
FOWELL Stephen H. MM L/Bdr 705997 B/104 Bde RFA

FOWERS John H. MM Dvr 810668 D/232 Bde RFA
FOWKES Francis S. MM Pte 441 Royal West Surrey Regt
FOWKES William MM Pte 25375 16th Notts & Derby Regt KIA 25.7.17.
FOWLE Louis Victor Alfred MM L/Cpl 1220 1/5th London Regt
FOWLER Albert MM Pte 133064 36th Bn Machine Gun Corps
FOWLER Alfred MM Sjt 13030 7th South Lancashire Regt
FOWLER Arthur J. "MM,MID" Sjt L/4098 9th Lancers
FOWLER Ben MM Gnr 29263 B/168 Bde RFA
FOWLER Bernard W. MM Pte 12998 3rd Worcestershire Regt
FOWLER Charles MM Pte 290931 1/4th Gordon Highlanders
FOWLER Charles "DCM,MM" Cpl 2909 13th Royal Sussex Regt
FOWLER Charles H. MM Cpl 74076 42 Bde RFA
FOWLER Christopher MM L/Cpl 14830 1st Middlesex Regt
FOWLER David MM Gnr 87508 RFA
FOWLER Edward MM Pte 17492 7th Royal Berkshire Regt
FOWLER Edward MM+Bar 2nd Cpl 9309 59 Fd Coy Royal Engineers
FOWLER Ernest MM Pte 200255 4th North Lancashire Regt
FOWLER Ernest H. MM Cpl 15668 8th Gloucestershire Regt
FOWLER F.T. MM Air Mech 1 7770 Royal Flying Corps
FOWLER Frank MM BSM 24814 81 Bty 5 Bde RFA
FOWLER Frank MM Sjt 48472 87 Fd Coy Royal Engineers
FOWLER Frank E. MM+Bar Spr 498495 Royal Engineers
FOWLER Fred MM Spr 201558 Royal Engineers
FOWLER Fred MM Cpl 295290 12th Somerset Light Infantry
FOWLER George MM Sjt 11860 2/4th Oxf & Bucks Light Infantry KIA 12.9.18.
FOWLER George MM Gnr 73984 D/235 Bde RFA KIA 27.3.18.
FOWLER George B. MM Sjt 15038 6th King's Own Scottish Borderers
FOWLER George E. MM Sjt 530772 1/15th London Regt
FOWLER George H. MM Pte 17144 20th Hussars
FOWLER George W. MM L/Cpl 165249 1/1st North Somerset Yeomanry
FOWLER Harry MM L/Cpl 38342 Yorkshire Light Infantry
FOWLER Henry E. "MM,MID" Gnr 528 RFA
FOWLER Horace J. MM Sjt 39409 329 Siege Bty RGA
FOWLER James MM+Bar L/Sjt 8888 2nd East Lancashire Regt
FOWLER James William MM Pte 21585 14th Gloucestershire Regt KIA 3.6.17.
FOWLER John MM Cpl 9607 RAMC
FOWLER John MM Pte 6921 11th East Yorkshire Regt KIA 27.3.18.
FOWLER John A. MM L/Cpl 8773 2nd Devonshire Regt
FOWLER John James MM Pte 6791 12th Middlesex Regt KIA 3.5.17.
FOWLER John S. MM Bdr 82875 RFA
FOWLER Jonathan MM Gnr 795482 A/190 Bde RFA
FOWLER Joseph W. MM L/Cpl P/1336 13th Rifle Brigade
FOWLER Norman E. MM Spr 131147 233 Fd Coy Royal Engineers
FOWLER Percy MM 2nd Cpl 522092 483 Fd Coy Royal Engineers
FOWLER Percy MM Spr 522883 Royal Engineers
FOWLER R. "MM,MID" Pte 4173 1st Border Regt
FOWLER Richard MM Pte 292230 1/7th Gordon Highlanders
FOWLER Richard MM CSM 13352 10th North Lancashire Regt KIA 22.3.18.
FOWLER Richard G. MM L/Cpl 11562 4th King's Royal Rifle Corps
FOWLER Robert MM CSM 245620 12th Manchester Regt
FOWLER Samuel James Robert MM Pte 92203 RAMC
FOWLER Sidney MM Sjt 18422 11th Worcestershire Regt
FOWLER T. MM Pte 25306 Liverpool Regt
FOWLER T.W. MM Cpl 235001 Gloucestershire Regt
FOWLER Thomas MM L/Cpl 21934 2nd Hampshire Regt
FOWLER Thomas P. MM Sjt 40166 RAMC
FOWLER Thornton MM L/Cpl 260661 1/1st 1st County of London Yeomanry (Middlesex Hussars)
FOWLER W. MM Sjt 201184 1st London Regt
FOWLER W.J. MM Sjt 19825 2nd Dragoon Guards
FOWLER Walter D. MM Pte 48707 Liverpool Regt
FOWLER William MM Bdr 3486 C/62 Bde RFA
FOWLER William MM Sjt 200189 7th Seaforth Highlanders
FOWLER William MM L/Sjt 201363 5th South Staffordshire Regt
FOWLER William MM Cpl 266414 1/1st Hertfordshire Regt
FOWLER William MM Sjt 240246 1/8th Middlesex Regt
FOWLER William MM Gnr 117779 B/181 Bde RFA
FOWLER William MM Cpl S/4074 13th Rifle Brigade
FOWLER William H.T. MM Cpl 12985 VIII Corps Cyclist Bn Army Cyclist Corps
FOWLER William Henry MM Sjt 333 1/4th Yorkshire Regt
FOWLER William Millward MM Pte 12150 11th Lancashire Fusiliers
FOWLES William MM L/Bdr 68933 123 Siege Bty RGA
FOWLIE Peter G. MM Pte 202442 5th Royal Scots Fusiliers
FOWLIS William MM Pte 13469 1st Scots Guards
FOX Albert MM Pte 263016 5th West Riding Regt
FOX Albert MM Pte 99494 Liverpool Regt
FOX Albert E. MM(15761 Gren Gds)+Bar Sjt 113 4th Bn GMGR
FOX Albert Henry MM Sjt 35 6th East Kent Regt
FOX Albert Victor MM Pte 8308 2nd York & Lancaster Regt
FOX Albert Victor MM L/Cpl 5343 Royal Warwickshire Regt
FOX Alexander MM Pte 14021 4th Hampshire Regt
FOX Alfred MM L/Cpl 25359 2nd Durham Light Infantry
FOX Alfred H. MM Sjt 354246 RAMC
FOX Allan MM Pte 16370 9th Norfolk Regt KIA 21.3.18.
FOX Andrew John MM Pte 947 9th Durham Light Infantry
FOX Anthony MM Pte 6626 Irish Guards
FOX Archibald A. MM Sjt 2105 16th Middlesex Regt
FOX Archibald W. MM Gnr 235133 B/155 Bde RFA
FOX Arthur MM Pte 8094 2nd Worcestershire Regt att 100 Light TM Bty.
FOX Arthur MM Sjt 281312 2/5th Lancashire Fusiliers
FOX Arthur MM Sjt 796343 RFA
FOX Arthur Bennett "MM,MID" Sjt 19597 C/68 Bde RFA
FOX Arthur F. MM Cpl 20031 2nd Royal Munster Fusiliers
FOX Arthur Frederick MM Cpl 120604 'M' Special Coy Royal Engineers
FOX Aubrey MM Pte 12901 6th Bedfordshire Regt KIA 9.7.16.
FOX Benjamin R. MM Pte 8806 1st Duke of Cornwall's LI
FOX Bernard MM L/Sjt 60081 9th Middlesex Regt
FOX Bernard MM Cpl 710191 RFA
FOX Cecil MM Cpl 13027 Leicestershire Regt
FOX Charles Edward MM CSM 1028 3rd Coldstream Guards DOW 12.3.18.
FOX Charles H. MM Cpl 10294 Leicestershire Regt
FOX Charles Percy MM Sjt M2/119422 564 Coy Army Service Corps
FOX Charles W. MM Sjt 12993 6th Oxf & Bucks Light Infantry
FOX Clarence H. MM Cpl 2260 North Staffordshire Regt
FOX Cornelius MM Pte 9851 1st Royal Dublin Fusiliers att MGC.
FOX David W. MM Spr 172362 33 Div Sig Coy Royal Engineers
FOX Edward MM Pte 10068 23 Fd Amb RAMC
FOX Edwin Willis Jim MM L/Sjt 15712 1st Royal Dublin Fusiliers KIA 11.5.18.
FOX Enock MM Pte 13/303 York & Lancaster Regt
FOX Ernest MM Sjt 9391 1st Bedfordshire Regt
FOX Ernest MM Cpl 200235 2/5th Lancashire Fusiliers
FOX Ernest S. MM L/Cpl 14371 7th Wiltshire Regt
FOX Ernest W. MM Pte 82267 Machine Gun Corps
FOX F.W. MM Cpl 495309 RAMC
FOX Francis MM Pte 8743 1st Highland Light Infantry
FOX Francis MM Cpl 16381 8th East Lancashire Regt
FOX Frederick MM Sjt M/31604 2 Cav Div Train Army Service Corps
FOX Frederick MM+Bar Pte G3/10077 7th East Surrey Regt
FOX Frederick J. MM Sig 880467 A/271 Bde RFA
FOX Frederick V. MM+Bar Pte 14506 4th Yorkshire Light Infantry
FOX Frederick W. MM Pte 838 Royal Fusiliers
FOX George MM L/Cpl 11645 23rd Middlesex Regt
FOX George MM Pte 140874 104th Bn Machine Gun Corps
FOX George "MM,MID" Cpl 8692 2nd West Riding Regt
FOX Harold T. MM+Bar Sjt 755167 RFA
FOX Harry MM Pte 306781 West Riding Regt
FOX Henry MM Pte 32538 1/5th South Lancashire Regt DOW 26.10.18.
FOX Henry MM Sjt 23564 63rd Bn Machine Gun Corps
FOX Henry B. MM L/Cpl 51258 Liverpool Regt
FOX Herbert Gerrard MM Sjt 25381 B/74 Bde RFA
FOX Herbert V. MM Pte 3/6889 1st Norfolk Regt
FOX Isaac Sowter MM Pte 39330 4th South Staffordshire Regt KIA 10.4.18.
FOX J. "MM,MID" Sjt 3925 3rd Coldstream Guards
FOX James MM Pte 16041 1st Coldstream Guards
FOX James MM Pte 393811 2nd Shropshire Light Infantry
FOX James MM Spr 132084 250 Tunnelling Coy Royal Engineers
FOX James MM Sjt 201652 Gloucestershire Regt
FOX James MM Sjt 14872 26 Fd Coy Royal Engineers Died 21.10.18.
FOX James MM Pte 12730 2nd Scottish Rifles
FOX James H. MM Sjt 26209 1st Lancashire Fusiliers
FOX James W. MM Spr 112689 Royal Engineers
FOX John MM Pte 13256 1st Bedfordshire Regt
FOX John MM Pte 26503 1st Royal Dublin Fusiliers
FOX John MM Gnr 521 MGC (Motors)

FOX John MM Sjt 3412 1/3rd London Regt
FOX John MM L/Cpl 23565 Machine Gun Corps
FOX Marcus MM Pte 200793 1/4th Lincolnshire Regt
FOX Michael MM Pte 267626 7th Liverpool Regt
FOX Morley "DCM,MM" L/Cpl 65 Volunteer Maxim Gun Coy Machine Gun Corps
FOX Percy MM Sjt 241146 5th Yorkshire Light Infantry KIA 2.9.18.
FOX Richard MM Cpl 2930 2nd Royal Scots
FOX Sidney MM Spr 148745 77 Airline Section Royal Engineers
FOX Sidney MM Pte 34063 Yorkshire Light Infantry
FOX Thomas MM Pte 69215 92 Fd Amb RAMC
FOX Thomas MM Pte 17893 20th Manchester Regt
FOX Thomas William MM Cpl 15822 9th West Riding Regt
FOX Tom MM Pte C/12354 King's Royal Rifle Corps
FOX Victor Henry MM Gnr 22611 C/82 Bde RFA
FOX Walter "MM,MID" Cpl M2/073398 336 Coy Army Service Corps
FOX Wilfred MM L/Cpl 2041 Notts & Derby Regt
FOX William MM Pte 72406 7th Royal West Surrey Regt
FOX William MM Pte 7551 RAMC
FOX William MM Cpl R/2479 4th King's Royal Rifle Corps KIA 7.11.18.
FOX William MM Sjt 476426 Royal Engineers
FOX William MM 2nd Cpl 412100 409 Fd Coy Royal Engineers
FOX William A. MM BQMS 715003 D/211 Bde RFA
FOX William G. MM Cpl 20580 6th York & Lancaster Regt
FOX William H. MM Pte 12096 2nd Wiltshire Regt
FOX William Henry MM Pte 250129 1/6th Manchester Regt KIA 7.1.18.
FOX William R. MM Sjt 17262 Yorkshire Light Infantry
FOX William S. MM Sjt 6740 2 Siege Coy R Anglesey RE
FOXALL Alfred T. MM Cpl 371955 8th London Regt
FOXALL George MM Sjt 240175 6th Royal Warwickshire Regt
FOXALL John MM Gnr 12382 107 Bty 23 Bde RFA
FOXALL Samuel MM Sjt 4509 Army Cyclist Corps
FOXCROFT Herbert Astley Gersham MM Cpl(MCDR) 73163 2 Div Sig Coy Royal Engineers
FOXCROFT Robert MM Sjt L/9531 409 TM Bty RFA
FOXFORD Alfred E. MM+Bar Bdr 76535 RGA
FOXLEY Thomas "MM,MSM,MID" CQMS 14209 11 Fd Coy Royal Engineers
FOXLEY Thomas J. MM Sjt 48338 RFA
FOXON George MM Sjt 10856 1/10th Liverpool Regt
FOXON Jesse MM Pte 1219 6 Div Cyclist Coy Army Cyclist Corps
FOXON Thomas MM Cpl 11364 1st Royal Warwickshire Regt
FOXWELL Sidney J. MM Gnr 110233 RGA
FOY Alfred R. MM Sjt 65728 102 Fd Amb RAMC
FOY George Collin MM+Bar Pte 327328 10th Arg & Suth Highlanders
FOY Henry MM Pte 203585 2/4th East Lancashire Regt KIA 9.10.17.
FOY John MM L/Cpl 39879 1st Wiltshire Regt
FOY John MM Pte 37448 Labour Corps
FOY William MM Cpl 40001 10th Arg & Suth Highlanders
FOZARD Ernest MM Pte 202654 3/1st London Regt
FOZARD Harry MM Pte 268208 West Yorkshire Regt
FOZZARD George MM Pte 267689 Seaforth Highlanders
FRADGLEY Arthur Cecil MM Pte 200236 13th Liverpool Regt
FRADGLEY William MM Gnr 770421 63 Div Ammn Col RFA
FRADLEY Frederick C. MM Sjt 4274 2nd Royal Fusiliers
FRADLEY Robert MM Sjt 11005 1st Scottish Rifles Died 28.2.18.
FRADLEY Thomas G. MM Pte 300347 1/1st Staffordshire Yeomanry
FRADRICK Charles MM Gnr 36350 RFA
FRAIN James MM Sjt 268855 1/7th West Yorkshire Regt
FRAME Andrew MM L/Cpl 38450 Yorkshire Light Infantry
FRAME Donald MM L/Cpl 335816 Royal Scots
FRAME George MM Pte 4668 11th Arg & Suth Highlanders
FRAME George K. MM+Bar CSM 18775 26 Fd Coy Royal Engineers
FRAME John T. MM Spr 412110 409 Fd Coy Royal Engineers
FRAME Joseph MM L/Bdr 54945 104 Bty 22 Bde RFA
FRAME Robert MM Cpl 48888 Royal Engineers
FRAME Robert MM Cpl 99567 19th Bn Machine Gun Corps
FRAME Robert D. MM Pte 15583 2nd Highland Light Infantry KIA 30.9.18.
FRAME Thomas A. MM Pte 266638 Royal Welsh Fusiliers
FRAME William MM Sjt 240227 1/6th Highland Light Infantry
FRAME William MM Sjt 9937 1st Notts & Derby Regt
FRAMP Ernest Alfred MM Sjt 233605 2/1st London Regt
FRAMPTON Ernest MM Pte 27705 2/4th Hampshire Regt
FRAMPTON George MM L/Cpl M2/019509 Army Service Corps att RGA
FRAMPTON George L. MM Cpl 519436 559 Army Troops Coy Royal Engineers
FRAMPTON William A. MM Sjt 50495 182 Siege Bty RGA
FRAMPTON William G. MM Sjt 71735 64 Bty 5 Bde RFA
FRANCE Albert MM Pte 23837 Royal Irish Fusiliers
FRANCE Arthur MM Cpl 21787 11th Notts & Derby Regt
FRANCE Harry MM Sjt 32153 5th Royal Berkshire Regt KIA 5.4.18.
FRANCE Harry MM Cpl 9727 Machine Gun Corps
FRANCE James MM Sjt 265235 1/6th Northumberland Fusiliers KIA 10.4.18.
FRANCE L. MM L/Cpl 5649 West Riding Regt
FRANCE Leonard MM Pte 51531 1st Cheshire Regt KIA 27.9.18.
FRANCE Thomas MM Pte 32660 2/5th Royal Lancaster Regt
FRANCE Thomas MM Dvr 785338 RFA
FRANCE Victor W. MM Sjt 470095 12th London Regt
FRANCE W. MM Pte P/316 Military Foot Police
FRANCE Walter MM Cpl L/25619? C/187 Bde RFA
FRANCE Walter "DCM,MM" Sjt G/12873 1st East Kent Regt
FRANCE William MM Pte 105266 62nd Bn Machine Gun Corps DOW 5.11.18.
FRANCEIS Sydney H. MM Sjt 279886 RGA
FRANCETTI George MM Pte R/7787 1st King's Royal Rifle Corps KIA 3.2.17.
FRANCIS A. MM Pte 60559 RAMC
FRANCIS Ainslie Norman "MC,MM(17102 Cpl MGC)" 2Lt 1st Lancashire Fusiliers DOW 30.4.18.
FRANCIS Albert MM Pte L/10694 11th Royal West Kent Regt
FRANCIS Albert MM+Bar Sjt 9166 7th East Surrey Regt
FRANCIS Albert MM Pte 87752 10th Royal Fusiliers
FRANCIS Albert MM 2nd Cpl 137803 Royal Engineers
FRANCIS Albert E. MM Pte 200077 1/4th Royal Sussex Regt
FRANCIS Albert W. MM Pte 89667 105 Fd Amb RAMC
FRANCIS Alfred G. MM 2nd Cpl 47875 14 Div Sig Coy Royal Engineers
FRANCIS Charles MM Sjt 1638 1/7th Notts & Derby Regt
FRANCIS Charles Eric MM L/Cpl 71816 135 Fd Amb RAMC
FRANCIS Charles F. MM Pte 202066 Suffolk Regt
FRANCIS Charles John MM+Bar Sjt 23807 A/110 Bde RFA
FRANCIS Cyril MM Pte M/317344 954 Coy Army Service Corps
FRANCIS Douglas Ernest MM Sjt 113559 'B' Special Coy Royal Engineers
FRANCIS Edward MM Gnr 51956 130 Heavy Bty RGA
FRANCIS Edward MM Pte 13784 3rd Middlesex Regt
FRANCIS Edwin John MM Pte 433106 RAMC
FRANCIS Ernest C. MM Gnr 103203 RGA
FRANCIS Ernest T. MM L/Sjt G/11308 2nd Royal West Kent Regt
FRANCIS F.W. MM Sjt 15510 10th Essex Regt
FRANCIS Francis MM Cpl 550252 1/16th London Regt
FRANCIS Frank Warner MM Sjt 925119 C/280 Bde RFA
FRANCIS Frederick MM Cpl 8294 1st Gloucestershire Regt
FRANCIS Frederick G. MM Bdr L/19390 RFA
FRANCIS Frederick J. MM Pte 12868 6th Bedfordshire Regt
FRANCIS Frederick Thomas MM Dvr 835893 RFA
FRANCIS George MM Sjt 29540 17th Royal Scots
FRANCIS George MM L/Cpl 95416 1st Middlesex Regt
FRANCIS George MM Pte 4179 6th Royal West Surrey Regt
FRANCIS George MM Cpl 14982 Middlesex Regt
FRANCIS George MM Pte 18434 11th Royal West Kent Regt KIA 20.9.17.
FRANCIS George E. MM Pte 60553 1st Cheshire Regt
FRANCIS George Hillier "MM,MSM" Sjt 504003 Royal Engineers
FRANCIS George V.R. MM Cpl M1/06231 First Army MT Coy Army Service Corps
FRANCIS H. MM Air Mech 2 56157 Royal Air Force
FRANCIS H.W. MM L/Cpl 651747 London Regt
FRANCIS Harold Victor MM L/Cpl 20291 9th Royal Fusiliers KIA 21.9.18.
FRANCIS Herbert F. MM Sjt 79587 MGC(Motors)
FRANCIS Herbert James MM Sjt 10/23054 1/7th Border Regt DOW 12.7.16.
FRANCIS J. MM Pte 355246 Royal Welsh Fusiliers
FRANCIS J. MM Dvr 2732 RFA
FRANCIS J.W. MM Pte 34137 1st Essex Regt
FRANCIS James MM Pte 58092 4th York & Lancaster Regt
FRANCIS James F. MM Dvr L/41747 RFA
FRANCIS John H.S. "DCM,MM" CSM 5657 2nd King's Royal Rifle Corps
FRANCIS John M. MM Sjt 2657 Yorkshire Regt
FRANCIS John W. "DCM,MM" Sjt H/7494 15th Hussars
FRANCIS Joseph MM L/Sjt 40976 17th Lancashire Fusiliers

FRANCIS Joseph MM Pte 15621 2nd Scots Guards
FRANCIS Kirby E. MM Sjt 292735 137 Hy Bty RGA
FRANCIS Lloyd MM Pte 352401 2(East Lancs)Fd Amb RAMC
FRANCIS Reginald MM Cpl 28669 25 Army Tps Coy (sic) Royal Engineers
FRANCIS Richard G. MM Sjt 590848 1/18th London Regt
FRANCIS Richard Llewellyn MM+Bar Sjt 30631 7th Border Regt
FRANCIS Robert Frederick MM Pte R/25270 17th King's Royal Rifle Corps DOW 19.4.18.
FRANCIS S.V. MM Pte 24032 7th Royal West Surrey Regt
FRANCIS Thomas H. MM Pte 69659 RAMC
FRANCIS Walter MM L/Sjt 6101 5th Royal Berkshire Regt KIA 11.3.17.
FRANCIS Walter Leonard MM Sjt 8421 2nd Royal Irish Regt
FRANCIS William MM Pte 413 9th Royal Fusiliers
FRANCIS William MM Dvr 102152 35 Div Ammn Col RFA
FRANCIS William MM Pte 45583 RAMC
FRANCIS William F. MM Pte 41858 1/1st Hertfordshire Regt
FRANCIS William G. MM Pte 59840 9th Welsh Regt
FRANCIS William H. "DCM,MM" Pte 574057 1/17th London Regt
FRANCIS William H. MM Sjt 8168 1st Dorsetshire Regt
FRANCIS William L.M. MM Pte 91686 Tank Corps
FRANCIS William Leslie MM Pte 76732 38 Fd Amb RAMC
FRANCIS William S. MM Bdr 3105 RFA
FRANCKE Frederick W.G. MM CSM 99190 10th Royal Fusiliers
FRANCKLOW Reginald G. MM L/Cpl 1636 Oxf & Bucks Light Infantry
FRANCOMBE Ivan Lionel MM Gnr Sig 117213 166 Siege Bty RGA
FRANCOMBE Roy F. MM Pte 38091 MGC(Heavy Branch)
FRANK Davenay MM Pte S/8163 10th Arg & Suth Highlanders att 47 TM Bty.DOW 12.7.16.
FRANK Frederick MM Pte 70982 RAMC
FRANK Thomas S. MM+Bar Pte 22602 5th West Riding Regt
FRANKCOM Sidney MM Sjt 11066 Somerset Light Infantry
FRANKCOMBE Charles MM Gnr 38894 Tank Corps
FRANKISH Arthur MM Pte S/28656 Rifle Brigade
FRANKLAND Harry MM S/Sjt Armourer T/895 Army Ordnance Corps
FRANKLAND John MM Sjt 2663 6th North Lancashire Regt
FRANKLAND Mark MM Cpl 13107 11th West Yorkshire Regt
FRANKLAND Richard MM Dvr 37328 RFA
FRANKLAND Thomas MM Pte 14982 East Yorkshire Regt
FRANKLAND William Hope MM Sjt 69865 135 Coy Royal Engineers
FRANKLIN Albert C. MM Pte 111827 10th Bn Tank Corps
FRANKLIN Alfred MM Dvr 3212 63 Bde RFA
FRANKLIN Alfred MM Pte 15514 2nd Bedfordshire Regt Died 31.10.18.
FRANKLIN Archibald J. MM Pte 48919 2nd South Wales Borderers
FRANKLIN Arthur MM Pte 49642 1st Royal Inniskilling Fusiliers
FRANKLIN Arthur T. MM Pte 15298 7th Bedfordshire Regt
FRANKLIN Arthur Walter MM Sjt 60277 93 Fd Amb RAMC DOW 22.4.18.
FRANKLIN Benjamin MM Pte 202029 Leicestershire Regt
FRANKLIN Bernard W. MM Sjt STK/1285 10th Royal Fusiliers
FRANKLIN Bert MM Pte 45111 5th Royal Berkshire Regt
FRANKLIN Cecil MM Cpl 7572 Royal Fusiliers
FRANKLIN Charles MM Cpl 15851 3 Div Sig Coy Royal Engineers
FRANKLIN Charles J. MM L/Cpl 23864 1st Norfolk Regt
FRANKLIN Charles S. MM Sjt 34187 57 Siege Bty RGA
FRANKLIN Cyril MM L/Cpl 50226 16th Royal Warwickshire Regt
FRANKLIN Elwyn G. MM+Bar Sjt A/200876 13th King's Royal Rifle Corps
FRANKLIN Ernest MM Pte R/13698 King's Royal Rifle Corps
FRANKLIN Ernest MM Sjt 545576 38 Sanitary Sect RAMC
FRANKLIN Frederick MM Sjt 13878 7 Pontoon Park Royal Engineers
FRANKLIN George MM L/Cpl 46566 North Staffordshire Regt
FRANKLIN George MM CSM 7456 1st Royal West Kent Regt
FRANKLIN George MM Pte 17442 1st Royal Welsh Fusiliers
FRANKLIN Harry MM Pte 4/7146 1st Bedfordshire Regt
FRANKLIN Herbert G. MM Pte 12397 7th Wiltshire Regt
FRANKLIN Hubert Ernest MM L/Cpl 11242 8th Gloucestershire Regt KIA 3.7.16.
FRANKLIN James MM Gnr L/39919 HQ 112 Bde RFA
FRANKLIN Joseph MM L/Cpl 2330 1/1st Cambridgeshire Regt
FRANKLIN Reginald MM Dvr 297086 RGA
FRANKLIN Thomas MM 2nd Cpl 139318 181 Tunnelling Coy Royal Engineers
FRANKLIN Thomas MM Sjt 49159 D/58 Bde RFA
FRANKLIN William MM Bdr 93980 A/64 Bde RFA

FRANKLIN William MM Pte 38648 RAMC
FRANKLIN William John "MM,MSM" Cpl 1373 5 Fd Amb RAMC
FRANKS Albert E. MM Gnr 30197 RGA
FRANKS Albert Hector MM Pte 570747 1/17th London Regt
FRANKS Andrew MM Pte 13855 8th York & Lancaster Regt
FRANKS Arthur MM Gnr 93059 C/113 Bde RFA
FRANKS Arthur James MM Pte 5568 8th East Kent Regt DOW 13.6.17.
FRANKS Charles MM Pte 938 1st Royal Warwickshire Regt
FRANKS George "DCM,MM+Bar" L/Sjt 10460 2nd York & Lancaster Regt KIA 12.5.17.
FRANKS Robert MM Gnr 5259 T Bty RHA
FRANKS Thomas E. MM Cpl G/17539 2nd Royal Sussex Regt
FRANKS Walter "MM,CG(F)" 2nd Cpl 65704 131 Fd Coy Royal Engineers
FRANKUM Albert A. MM L/Cpl 96187 222 Fd Coy Royal Engineers
FRANKUM T. MM Pte 40917 South Staffordshire Regt
FRAPE Laurence MM Sjt 46545 Royal Engineers
FRARY Ernest MM Pte 505299 18th King's Royal Rifle Corps
FRARY George Edward Singleton MM Pte 202122 1/4th Lincolnshire Regt
FRARY Herbert MM Pte 242102 Royal West Surrey Regt
FRASER A. MM Pte 36426 15th Highland Light Infantry
FRASER A.F. MM Sjt 78140 Royal Flying Corps
FRASER Alexander MM Pte M2/048112 9 Div MT Coy Army Service Corps
FRASER Alexander MM Sjt 223203 10th Cameron Highlanders
FRASER Alexander MM Pte S/43702 5th Cameron Highlanders
FRASER Alexander MM Sjt 9949 5th Cameron Highlanders
FRASER Alexander MM L/Cpl 292189 1/7th Royal Scots
FRASER Alexander MM Sjt 16597 11th Royal Scots
FRASER Alexander MM Pte 41090 Gordon Highlanders
FRASER Alexander MM Pte 38561 8th Yorkshire Light Infantry
FRASER Alexander MM Sjt 56684 Machine Gun Corps
FRASER Alexander MM CQMS 2168 9th Seaforth Highlanders
FRASER Alexander C. MM Pte 41118 5/6th Royal Scots
FRASER Alexander Edward MM Sjt 266144 1/6th Seaforth Highlanders DOW 27.3.18.
FRASER Alister MM L/Cpl S/4119 8th Royal Highlanders
FRASER Allan MM+Bar L/Sjt 1789 19th Middlesex Regt
FRASER Andrew MM Sjt 13667 15th Highland Light Infantry
FRASER Andrew MM L/Cpl 10067 1st Royal Scots
FRASER Andrew H. "MM,MIDx2" CSM 9294 2nd Seaforth Highlanders
FRASER Archibald MM Pte 13316 15th Highland Light Infantry KIA 5.12.17.
FRASER Arthur MM Pte 266711 1/6th Seaforth Highlanders
FRASER Campbell N. MM Pte 15581 17th Highland Light Infantry
FRASER Charles "MC,DCM,MM" CSM 437 2nd Arg & Suth Highlanders
FRASER Charles MM Sjt S/2398 10th Arg & Suth Highlanders
FRASER David MM L/Cpl 241334 Seaforth Highlanders
FRASER Donald MM Cpl 241958 1/5th Seaforth Highlanders
FRASER Donald MM Sjt M2/048901 326 Coy (8 MAC) Army Service Corps
FRASER Donald MM Sjt 125069 10th Cameron Highlanders
FRASER Donald MM CSM 8196 1st Seaforth Highlanders
FRASER Edward J. MM Pte 22528 Royal West Surrey Regt
FRASER Francis MM Pte 55805 Machine Gun Corps
FRASER Francis W. MM Sjt 1215 2nd Gordon Highlanders
FRASER Frank B. MM Pte S/43248 Gordon Highlanders
FRASER Frank Manson MM Sjt 32644 19th Bn Machine Gun Corps KIA 30.5.18.
FRASER Fred MM L/Cpl 125469 1st Lovat's Scouts Yeomanry
FRASER Frederick MM Pte 64442 RAMC
FRASER G. MM Pte 337056 RAMC
FRASER George MM Gnr 22137 B/82 Bde RFA
FRASER George MM+2 Bars Pte M2/050512 Army Service Corps
FRASER George MM Pte 9920 2nd Worcestershire Regt
FRASER George R. MM L/Cpl 31581 2nd Royal Scots KIA 2.9.18.
FRASER Hector MM Pte 8423 5th Cameron Highlanders
FRASER Hugh MM Sjt 459 1/5th Seaforth Highlanders
FRASER Hugh MM Cpl 20373 Machine Gun Corps KIA 19.8.16.
FRASER Hugh J. MM Cpl 200219 1/4th Seaforth Highlanders DOW 15.10.18.
FRASER J.S. MM Pte 303276 RAMC
FRASER J.S. MM+Bar Pte 277609 1/7th Arg & Suth Highlanders
FRASER James MM Pte 17824 1st Highland Light Infantry
FRASER James MM Pte 25208 Seaforth Highlanders
FRASER James MM Pte 10071 Royal Irish Fusiliers

FRASER James MM Bdr 166140 RFA
FRASER James A. MM Cpl 21001 28 Bde RFA
FRASER James C. MM L/Sjt 12782 4th Coldstream Guards
FRASER James P. MM Pte 19564 Gordon Highlanders
FRASER John MM Sjt 305006 RAMC
FRASER John MM Pte 73928 RAMC
FRASER John "MM,MID" Pte 13027 12th Royal Scots
FRASER John MM+Bar Cpl 41539 RAMC
FRASER John J. MM Sjt 335742 1/8th Royal Scots
FRASER Leon A. MM Dvr 213291 B/119 Bde RFA
FRASER Leonard MM Pte 8530 1st Cheshire Regt
FRASER Matthew MM Cpl 25924 35th Bn Machine Gun Corps
FRASER Murdo MM Spr 1269 1/2nd(South Midland)Fd Coy Royal Engineers
FRASER Oswald MM+Bar Pte 34254 1/5th York & Lancaster Regt KIA 29.4.18.
FRASER Peter MM Pte 11671 2nd Royal Scots
FRASER Robinson MM Pte 28946 8th Royal Lancaster Regt
FRASER Ronald MM Dvr 96940 RFA
FRASER Ronald Mackintosh MM Gnr 176261 31 Bty 35 Bde RFA
FRASER Samuel MM Pte 37660 7th Norfolk Regt
FRASER Simon MM Sjt 36631 48th Bn Machine Gun Corps
FRASER Stephen R. MM Pte 5722 2/1st HAC (Inf)
FRASER Thomas MM L/Cpl 285421 1/6th Seaforth Highlanders
FRASER Thomas MM Pte 30105 Machine Gun Corps
FRASER William MM Sjt 2667 1/5th West Riding Regt DOW 8.9.16.
FRASER William MM Gnr 346679 RGA
FRASER William "DCM+Bar,MM+Bar" Sjt 29955 1st Liverpool Regt
FRASER William MM CSM 11777 4th Liverpool Regt
FRASER William MM Pte 7263 Royal Fusiliers
FRASER William "MM,MLaS(Pan)" CQMS 10310 2nd Seaforth Highlanders
FRASER William MM L/Cpl S/40484 10th Cameron Highlanders
FRASER William MM Pte 200146 Seaforth Highlanders
FRASER William MM Sjt 265703 Seaforth Highlanders
FRASER William MM Sjt 200208 Seaforth Highlanders
FRASER William J. MM Sjt S/1689 9th Seaforth Highlanders
FRASER William John MM Dvr 38810 A/83 Bde RFA DOW 19.9.18.
FRASER William Kenyon MM Sjt 8132 2nd Arg & Suth Highlanders
FRASER William McL. MM Sjt 42506 A/99 Bde RFA
FRASER William Murdoch MM Sjt 51459 2nd Royal Scots DOW 24.9.18.
FRATER Robert MM Pte 34268 2nd Royal Scots
FRAWLEY J. MM Cpl 7256 1st Royal Munster Fusiliers
FRAWLEY James MM L/Sjt 265005 Royal Lancaster Regt
FRAWLEY John Charles MM Pte 11186 17th Manchester Regt
FRAY David MM Cpl 86016 A/26 Bde RFA
FRAY Ernest MM Pte 28083 RAMC
FRAY Owen Francis MM Pte 99394 1/5th Liverpool Regt DOW 29.9.18.
FRAY William A. MM Cpl 29150 2nd Royal Dublin Fusiliers
FRAYNE Thomas MM Pte 122086 Machine Gun Corps
FRAZER A. MM L/Cpl 18581 Manchester Regt
FRAZER Alexander Stewart MM Bdr 600 1 Bty 1/3rd(Highland)Howitzer Bde RFA
FRAZER Alfred William MM L/Cpl 18/489 18th Durham Light Infantry
FRAZER George H. MM Sjt 37526 RAMC
FRAZER John MM Pte 16384 11th Border Regt
FREAIL Charles W. MM Cpl 66267 141 Siege Bty RGA
FREAR Arthur MM Pte 241842 Royal Lancaster Regt
FREARSON William MM Pte 15190 Yorkshire Regt
FREDERICK Camille MM Pte 26994 16th Royal Welsh Fusiliers
FREDERICKS Charles MM+Bar Cpl 32595 23 Siege Bty RGA
FREDERICKS John MM Gnr 24832 RFA
FREDMAN Harry MM Cpl 56523 42 Bty 2 Bde RFA
FREDRICKSON Ernest MM+Bar Cpl 265253 6th West Riding Regt
FREE Benjamin MM Pte 77558 14th Royal Welsh Fusiliers
FREE George Thomas Owen MM Pte 15665 Gloucestershire Regt
FREE Michael William MM Cpl 10525 1st Essex Regt
FREEBAIRN Allan MM Pte 15088 1st Devonshire Regt
FREEBURY Frederick MM Sjt 7801 5th Wiltshire Regt
FREEDMAN Isaac MM Pte 71854 Notts & Derby Regt
FREEDMAN Myer MM Pte 13105 10th West Riding Regt KIA 19.9.16.
FREEDMAN Sam MM Pte 306837 8th West Yorkshire Regt
FREELAND Edward MM Dvr 56061 B/285 Bde RFA
FREELAND George MM Sjt 43740 16th Royal Scots
FREELAND George A. MM Pte 110685 MGC (Cavalry)
FREELAND John MM L/Cpl 21486 11th Royal Scots KIA 24.3.18.
FREELAND William MM+Bar L/Cpl 561 6th Royal West Surrey Regt

FREEMAN Albert "MM,MID." Sjt 46887 RAMC
FREEMAN Alfred B. MM Cpl 122675 RGA
FREEMAN Alfred H. MM Pte 241655 Worcestershire Regt
FREEMAN Alfred H. MM Spr 19268 7 Fd Coy Royal Engineers
FREEMAN Archibald W. "MM,MID" Sjt 240583 1/5th Suffolk Regt
FREEMAN Archie MM L/Cpl 24275 South Wales Borderers
FREEMAN Arthur E. MM Sjt 38476 162 Siege Bty RGA
FREEMAN Arthur J. MM Pte 17537 6th Northamptonshire Regt
FREEMAN Charles MM L/Cpl 23261 26th Royal Fusiliers KIA 12.6.17.
FREEMAN Charles A. MM Sjt 20887 15th Welsh Regt
FREEMAN Charles J. MM Spr 270292 Royal Engineers
FREEMAN Charles L. MM L/Cpl 33080 1st Hampshire Regt
FREEMAN Charles P. MM Pte 242272 5th York & Lancaster Regt
FREEMAN Edward MM Sjt 29067 8th Royal Lancaster Regt
FREEMAN Edward H. MM Pte 242683 East Lancashire Regt
FREEMAN Ernest MM Cpl R/5057 12th King's Royal Rifle Corps
FREEMAN Ernest MM Pte 266423 1/6th Seaforth Highlanders
FREEMAN Frank E. MM Pte 200768 1/5th Royal Warwickshire Regt
FREEMAN Frederick G. MM Spr 17053 2 Fd Coy Royal Engineers
FREEMAN Frederick G. MM Cpl 85959 155 Siege Bty RGA Redhill.
FREEMAN Frederick Richard MM Spr 251740 5 Div Sig Coy Royal Engineers DOW 5.8.18.
FREEMAN G. MM L/Cpl 1832 York & Lancaster Regt
FREEMAN George MM Pte 26539 1st Gloucestershire Regt
FREEMAN George MM Pte 39317 1/4th Royal Scots
FREEMAN George MM Bdr 38100 267 Siege Bty RGA
FREEMAN George David MM Pte 576202 17th London Regt
FREEMAN H. MM Pte 11478 1st East Surrey Regt
FREEMAN H. MM Pte 29769 Worcestershire Regt
FREEMAN H. MM Dvr 49479 94 Bty 18 Bde RFA
FREEMAN Harold George MM L/Cpl 73773 59th Bn Machine Gun Corps
FREEMAN Harry William MM Pte 41894 2nd Royal Irish Rifles KIA 24.3.18.
FREEMAN Herbert A. MM Spr 85245 Royal Engineers
FREEMAN Herbert Edgar MM L/Cpl 2491 1/6th London Regt
FREEMAN Horace A. MM Pte 30186 Labour Corps
FREEMAN J.E. MM Spr 139188 185 Tunnelling Coy Royal Engineers
FREEMAN J.W. MM Sjt P436 Military Foot Police
FREEMAN James MM Pte 31113 8th East Surrey Regt
FREEMAN James MM Sjt 200302 1/4th Shropshire Light Infantry KIA 30.12.17.
FREEMAN James MM L/Cpl 200877 1/4th Royal Berkshire Regt
FREEMAN James R. MM Spr 556573 4 Div Sig Coy Royal Engineers
FREEMAN James Slater MM L/Sjt 648 17th Northumberland Fusiliers
FREEMAN John MM Sjt 13968 Northamptonshire Regt
FREEMAN John MM Pte 8065 6th Yorkshire Regt
FREEMAN John MM Pte 202171 King's Royal Rifle Corps att 2/12th London Regt.
FREEMAN John A. MM Sjt T/21001 Army Service Corps
FREEMAN John C. MM Pte 860521 33rd London Regt
FREEMAN Jonathon MM Cpl 5775 Royal West Surrey Regt
FREEMAN Joseph MM Pte 12212 2nd South Lancashire Regt KIA 3.9.16.
FREEMAN Joseph F. MM Gnr 62794 RGA
FREEMAN Joseph H. MM Cpl 51540 RAMC
FREEMAN Joseph J. MM Sjt 8828 1st South Wales Borderers
FREEMAN Laurence G. MM+Bar Pte 14466 2nd & 1st Scots Guards
FREEMAN Patrick MM L/Cpl 9223 2nd Royal Dublin Fusiliers
FREEMAN Patrick MM Pte 5970 2nd Royal Munster Fusiliers
FREEMAN Reuben Victor Job MM Sjt 102564 174 Tunnelling Coy Royal Engineers
FREEMAN Richard MM Pte 31206 1/5th King's Own Scottish Borderers
FREEMAN Robert MM Pte 350250 1(East Lancs)Fd Amb RAMC
FREEMAN Samuel MM Sjt 20939 1st Yorkshire Light Infantry
FREEMAN Samuel MM Pte 242445 North Staffordshire Regt
FREEMAN Stanley "MM,MID" Sjt 965361 D/236 Bde RFA
FREEMAN Walter MM Pte 8145 2nd Scots Guards
FREEMAN Walter MM+Bar Pte 11014 1st Notts & Derby Regt
FREEMAN Walter MM Pte 31614 Duke of Cornwall's LI
FREEMAN Walter E. "DCM,MM" Sjt 5571 1st Norfolk Regt
FREEMAN Walter H. MM Sjt 452143 Royal Engineers
FREEMAN William MM Sjt 53326 11 Bde RFA

FREEMAN William MM Pte 201960 1st King's Own Scottish Borderers
FREEMAN William MM Cpl 5838 6th Dragoons
FREEMAN William MM Pte 37599 Lancashire Fusiliers
FREEMAN William C.H. MM L/Cpl 7731 9th Lancers
FREEMAN William H. MM L/Cpl 13073 IV Corps Cyclist Bn Army Cyclist Corps
FREEMAN William N.H. MM L/Cpl 2301 47 Div Sig Coy Royal Engineers
FREEMANTLE W.C.E. MM Bdr 71105 42 Bde RFA
FREEMONT Lawrence T. MM Pte 532027 15th London Regt
FREENEY James MM Pte 1124 Royal Irish Rifles
FREER Albert MM Pte 88280 7th Liverpool Regt
FREER Arthur MM Sjt 26274 Notts & Derby Regt
FREER Edward MM Pte 12151 7th East Yorkshire Regt
FREER Frank Richard "MM,MID" Pte 4409 7th Rifle Brigade
FREER George R. MM Pte M2/101129 Army Service Corps
FREER John MM Pte 18875 1st Leicestershire Regt
FREER Robert MM CSM 29918 8th Bedfordshire Regt
FREER Samuel E. MM Pte 15448 13th Liverpool Regt
FREER Walter B. MM Pte 532465 15th London Regt
FREESTONE Alfred G. MM Sjt 75897 Royal Engineers
FREESTONE Edmund "MM,MID" Cpl 20600 Cheshire Regt
FREESTONE George MM Pte 16805 7th Norfolk Regt
FREESTONE Gerrard MM Gnr 109077 267 Siege Bty RGA KIA 24.7.18.
FREESTONE Walter MM L/Cpl 17836 Northamptonshire Regt
FREETH Thomas B. MM Pte 19297 Machine Gun Corps
FREEZER Alexander R. MM Sjt 267201 Gloucestershire Regt
FREKE Roland MM Sjt 533905 2 Fd Svy Bn Royal Engineers
FRENCH Albert MM Pte 17348 6th Bedfordshire Regt
FRENCH Albert Frederick MM Pte 31561 1st Wiltshire Regt
FRENCH Arthur MM Cpl 3494 8th Royal West Kent Regt
FRENCH Arthur Ernest MM Pte 59180 6 Fd Amb RAMC
FRENCH Arthur G. MM Pte 37084 8th Royal West Surrey Regt
FRENCH Arthur H. MM Cpl R/11017 13th King's Royal Rifle Corps
FRENCH Arthur H. MM+Bar Pte 63899 4th Yorkshire Light Infantry
FRENCH Arthur Leslie MM Dvr M/271221 Army Service Corps att RAMC
FRENCH Christopher MM L/Cpl 19602 Wiltshire Regt
FRENCH David "DCM,MM" CSM 9207 2nd Bedfordshire Regt
FRENCH Ellis V. MM Dvr 234398 RFA
FRENCH Ernest W. MM Spr 254918 5 Div Sig Coy Royal Engineers
FRENCH Ernest W. MM L/Cpl 9291 19th Hussars
FRENCH Fred MM Gnr 776719 B/312 Bde RFA
FRENCH Frederick MM L/Cpl 240409 1/5th Lincolnshire Regt
FRENCH Frederick W. MM Pte 60912 1st Bn Machine Gun Corps
FRENCH George E. MM Pte 202411 Leicestershire Regt
FRENCH H.A. MM L/Cpl 459302 RAMC
FRENCH Harold MM Cpl 7412 1st Leicestershire Regt
FRENCH Harold J. MM L/Cpl 240311 Devonshire Regt
FRENCH Harry MM L/Cpl 34007 2 Div Sig Coy Royal Engineers
FRENCH Harry MM Pte 267981 West Riding Regt
FRENCH Henry MM Pte 13237 1st Scots Guards
FRENCH John MM Pte 15057 15th Royal Warwickshire Regt KIA 26.10.17.
FRENCH John MM Sjt 7741 6th King's Own Scottish Borderers DOW 31.1.18.
FRENCH John B. MM Pte G/57557 26th Royal Fusiliers
FRENCH John Thomas "MC,MM(144962 Sjt)" T/2Lt 178 Tunnelling Coy Royal Engineers
FRENCH Joseph "DCM,MM" CSM R/4184 12th King's Royal Rifle Corps
FRENCH L. MM Pte 45132 16th London Regt
FRENCH Percy W. MM L/Cpl 265328 Royal Warwickshire Regt
FRENCH Robert MM Sjt 13580 12th Royal Scots KIA 22.10.17.
FRENCH Robert W. MM Pte 22804 Northumberland Fusiliers
FRENCH Ronald P. MM Sjt 38262 14th Royal Warwickshire Regt
FRENCH Rupert MM Sjt T3/024937 Army Service Corps
FRENCH Samuel Thomas MM Gnr 86707 193 Heavy Bty RGA
FRENCH Sidney J. MM Spr 203311 Royal Engineers
FRENCH Thomas MM Pte 1816 RAMC
FRENCH Thomas Christopher MM Pte 4225 1/7th Durham Light Infantry KIA 10.4.18.
FRENCH Thomas William MM Gnr 7777 B/160 Bde RFA DOW 11.10.18.
FRENCH Walter MM Pte 15983 11th Royal Scots
FRENCH William MM L/Cpl 20783 6th Oxf & Bucks Light Infantry KIA 20.9.17.
FRENCH William MM Cpl 51306 25 Div Sig Coy Royal Engineers
FRENCH William MM Cpl 3582 1st Rifle Brigade
FRENCH William A. MM Pte 200398 1/4th Gordon Highlanders
FRENCH William Henry MM Cpl 232066 1/2nd London Regt DOW 28.2.18.
FRENCH William J. MM Pte 55209 Machine Gun Corps
FRENKENBERG Gerald MM Sjt 16073 Royal Engineers
FRENTZEL Walter Nicholas MM Cpl 301519 5th London Regt Died 9.11.18.
FRESHER Isaac MM Pte 201823 Suffolk Regt
FRESHFIELD Katherine Margaret MM Miss F VAD
FRESHNEY Sidney MM Pte 204459 West Riding Regt
FRESHWATER Ernest MM Pte 241735 2/4th West Riding Regt
FRESHWATER George MM Sjt 9878 2nd Bedfordshire Regt DOW 8.7.16.
FRESHWATER George MM Pte C/9305 20th King's Royal Rifle Corps DOW 3.1.17.
FRESHWATER Harold Ernest MM Pte 534218 2/4th(London)Fd Amb RAMC
FRESHWATER John J. "MM,MID" L/Cpl 78323 Royal Engineers
FRESHWATER John T. MM Pte 225682 4th London Regt
FRETER Charles MM L/Cpl 3042 1/1st HAC (Inf)
FRETTINGHAM Harry MM Cpl 5143 VI Corps Cyclist Bn Army Cyclist Corps
FRETWELL Hubert MM Pte 24300 2nd York & Lancaster Regt
FRETWELL James MM Pte 29077 2nd Bedfordshire Regt
FREW James MM Pte 351288 Royal Scots
FREW William MM Sjt 147584 254 Tunnelling Coy Royal Engineers
FREW William MM L/Cpl 2466 1/6th Royal Highlanders
FREWER Horace A. MM Pte 2696 8th Royal West Kent Regt
FREWIN Archibald Henry "MM,MID" Pnr 69007 35 Div Sig Coy Royal Engineers
FREY William Joseph Alois MM Cpl 1851 1/18th London Regt
FRICKER Leonard J. MM Sjt 200136 1/4th Wiltshire Regt
FRIDAY Cecil St.C. MM Cpl 28177 1st Somerset Light Infantry
FRIDAY Percy J. MM Pte 10515 1st East Surrey Regt
FRIDD George MM Sjt 66632 37 Bde RFA
FRIEL Hugh "DCM,MM" L/Sjt 278859 1/7th Arg & Suth Highlanders
FRIEL James "DCM,MM" Cpl S/21422 5th Cameron Highlanders
FRIEND Albert MM Pte 678078 21st London Regt
FRIEND Douglas R. MM Cpl 567 16th Royal Warwickshire Regt
FRIEND Ernest Alfred "MM,MM(P)" Spr 237725 Royal Engineers
FRIEND Frederick Harold MM Bdr 329206 RGA
FRIEND Harold Edward MM L/Cpl 1770 24th London Regt
FRIEND Harry MM Cpl 70855 111 Bty 24 Bde RFA
FRIEND Harry MM L/Cpl 307980 15th Bn Tank Corps
FRIEND Harry MM L/Cpl 548681 513 Fd Coy Royal Engineers
FRIEND Herbert J. MM CSM 9970 2nd Yorkshire Regt
FRIEND Reginald E.H. MM Sjt 22651 Hampshire Regt
FRIEND T.J. MM Pte 3681 7th East Kent Regt
FRIEND William MM Pte 18235 2nd Suffolk Regt
FRIER Edward MM Pte 17466 Machine Gun Corps
FRIGHT Stanley J. MM Sjt 87885 252 Siege Bty RGA
FRIPP Joseph MM Sjt M2/050401 Army Service Corps
FRIPP Thomas G. MM Bdr 60632 5 Bty 45 Bde RFA
FRIPP William Henry MM+Bar Sjt 83935 B/48 Bde & C/315 Bde RFA
FRISBY Ernest F.C. MM L/Cpl 268955 11th Notts & Derby Regt
FRISTON William E. MM Sjt 290828 RGA
FRITH A. MM Bdr 780208 RFA
FRITH Ernest MM L/Cpl 13788 13th Cheshire Regt
FRITH Frederick Vernon MM Sjt 13869 11th Border Regt
FRITH Harry MM Sjt 2437 5th Lancers
FRITH Herbert MM Cpl 2112 24th Royal Fusiliers
FRITH J. MM Sjt 227073 1st Royal Berkshire Regt
FRITH Joseph W. MM L/Cpl G/11223 Royal West Kent Regt
FRITH Lionel MM Gnr Sig 177499 C/282 Bde RFA
FRITH Robert W. "MM+Bar,MID" Sjt 97984 B/48 Bde RFA
FRITZ Walter R. MM Sjt 43082 Northamptonshire Regt
FRIZZELL Frederick J. MM L/Cpl 26018 Durham Light Infantry
FROBISHER Herbert MM Sjt 14987 6th Yorkshire Regt
FRODSHAM John MM Pte 20089 11th South Lancashire Regt KIA 23.3.18.
FROGGARTT Joseph H. MM Pte R/10859 King's Royal Rifle Corps
FROGGATT Bernard MM Pte 34873 York & Lancaster Regt
FROGGATT Cecil MM Pte 24406 2nd Royal Fusiliers
FROGGATT Jesse MM BSM 45518 25 Div Ammn Col RFA
FROOD Arthur T. MM Gnr 651759 RFA
FROOD Charles Frederick MM Sjt S/1186 12th Rifle Brigade
FROOD Charles Trefusis MM Pte 6246 16th Manchester Regt
FROOM F. MM Cpl 17518 Royal Flying Corps

FROOM Sidney H. MM Cpl 6689 1st Dragoon Guards
FROSDICK Albert W. MM Sjt 65324 104 Fd Amb RAMC
FROST Alfred E. MM Pte PS/10013 1st Royal Fusiliers
FROST Alfred W.G. "DCM,MM" Sjt 393276 9th & 1/16th London Regt
FROST Archibald T.E. MM Pte 200206 1/4th Leicestershire Regt
FROST Bertie MM L/Cpl 13317 8th Norfolk Regt
FROST Charles MM Cpl 240211 1/5th York & Lancaster Regt
FROST Charles MM Pte 17256 1st Leicestershire Regt
FROST Charles MM Pte 15525 1st Gloucestershire Regt DOW 27.9.18.
FROST Charles H. MM Sjt 10052 Royal West Kent Regt
FROST D. MM Pte 43844 1st Hertfordshire Regt
FROST Edward W. MM Cpl M2/019861 Army Service Corps
FROST Enoch MM Pte 11069 9th West Riding Regt
FROST Ernest MM L/Sjt 12882 2nd Grenadier Guards
FROST Ernest A. MM Sjt Farrier 805082 A/230 Bde RFA
FROST Ernest D. MM Pte 139628 49th Bn Machine Gun Corps
FROST F. MM Pte 242455 West Riding Regt
FROST Frederick MM L/Cpl 22971 Northamptonshire Regt
FROST Frederick H. MM Pte 8723 2nd Suffolk Regt
FROST George MM Cpl 37076 5 Div Ammn Col RFA
FROST George MM Spr 560522 Royal Engineers
FROST George MM Sjt L/12217 4th Royal Fusiliers
FROST George C. MM Pte 37879 6th East Yorkshire Regt
FROST George E. MM BSM 24562 153 Heavy Bty RGA
FROST Harold MM Pte 305097 West Riding Regt
FROST Harry MM Bdr 27327 76 Siege Bty RGA
FROST J. MM L/Cpl 8444 North Staffordshire Regt
FROST Jack MM Bdr 43702 56 Bty 34 Bde RFA
FROST James MM L/Cpl R/1744 10th King's Royal Rifle Corps KIA 9.5.17.
FROST John J.H. MM Spr 23924 11 Fd Coy Royal Engineers
FROST John Thomas MM Pte 33236 Leicestershire Regt
FROST John W. MM Sjt 15119 Machine Gun Corps
FROST Malcolm S. MM Pte 15359 1st Hampshire Regt
FROST Richard J. MM Sjt 380933 Hampshire Regt
FROST Samuel MM Pte 15782 Royal Welsh Fusiliers
FROST Thomas MM Pte 18010 2nd York & Lancaster Regt
FROST Thomas MM Gnr 48196 RFA
FROST W.H. MM Pte 34173 2nd Lancashire Fusiliers
FROST Walter MM Sjt 266608 7th Royal Warwickshire Regt
FROST Walter Edward "MM,CG(F)" Cpl 85020 Royal Engineers
FROST William MM Sjt 280534 4th London Regt
FROST William MM Gnr L/21937 RFA
FROST William MM Pte 8952 2nd Northamptonshire Regt
FROST William A. MM L/Cpl 52510 1st West Yorkshire Regt
FROST William Albert "MM,MID" L/Sjt 296592 1/5th Royal West Surrey Regt
FROST William E. MM Pte 3305 1/17th London Regt
FROST William Edward MM Sjt 8654 1st Lincolnshire Regt
FROST William J. MM Cpl 2783 15th Hussars
FROSTICK Alfred MM Pte 203952 4th London Regt
FROSTICK Raymond MM+Bar Sjt C/7009 18th King's Royal Rifle Corps
FROUD George K. MM Pte 510072 RAMC
FROUD Thomas B. MM BQMS 49623 26 Bde RFA
FROUD William J. MM Pte 266604 Liverpool Regt
FROUDE Stanley MM Bdr 40763 60 Siege Bty RGA
FROUDE Victor C.D. "DCM,MM" CSM 1893 1st Lancashire Fusiliers
FROW Harry MM Bdr 106923 RFA
FROW Walter MM Pte 240696 Lincolnshire Regt
FROWLEY Charles MM Pte 10571 7th East Surrey Regt KIA 3.10.16.
FRUEN Edward Thomas MM Pte 23427 1/6th North Staffordshire Regt KIA 26.3.18.
FRY Albert "DCM,MM" Cpl 113153 5 Special Bn Royal Engineers
FRY Albert J. MM L/Cpl 40309 10th South Wales Borderers
FRY Alfred J.R. MM Pte 132630 Machine Gun Corps
FRY Alfred Wyndham MM Pte 15494 8th Somerset Light Infantry
FRY Chares W. MM Pte 4287 2nd Rifle Brigade
FRY Charles MM Gnr 11136 RFA
FRY Edwin MM Pte 26452 2/4th Hampshire Regt
FRY Eric Rosewarne MM Sjt 207416 63 Div HQ Staff Royal Engineers
FRY F.H. MM Sjt 390016 3(Northumbrian)Fd Amb RAMC
FRY Frederick Walter "MC,MM(2352 Pte 1/5th Gloucs)" 2Lt 2/8th Worcestershire Regt
FRY George MM Cpl 348093 RGA
FRY George A. MM Pte 19405 1st Bn Machine Gun Corps
FRY George E. MM Pte 91676 5th Bn Tank Corps
FRY George S. MM Spr 85039 Royal Engineers
FRY James MM Gnr 931022 RFA
FRY Jesse MM L/Cpl 4448 6th Royal West Surrey Regt
FRY John MM Sjt 20588 Machine Gun Corps
FRY John T. MM Pte 2524 Gloucestershire Regt
FRY Joseph W. "MM,MSM" Pte 32016 47 Fd Amb RAMC
FRY Percy MM L/Cpl 13524 1st Bedfordshire Regt
FRY Reginald MM Spr 19144 20 Fd Coy Royal Engineers
FRY Thomas MM Sjt 18957 15 Div Ammn Col RFA
FRY Thomas John MM Sjt 1413 1/8th London Regt DOW 25.10.16.
FRY Thomas P. MM Cpl 1709 1/21st London Regt
FRY Walter William MM Cpl A/173 7th King's Royal Rifle Corps DOW 28.8.17.
FRY William MM 2nd Cpl 23598 150 Fd Coy Royal Engineers
FRY William MM Dvr T/22478 1 Div Train Army Service Corps
FRY William MM Cpl 4975 3rd Middlesex Regt
FRY William MM Pte 12372 Coldstream Guards
FRY William Arthur MM L/Cpl 51541 74 Fd Amb. RAMC
FRY William Henry MM Pte 32650 Wiltshire Regt
FRY Worthy MM Pte 7719 1st Devonshire Regt DOW 20.4.18.
FRYATT Charles H. MM Dvr 29517 RFA
FRYATT Sidney MM Pte 200250 1/4th Suffolk Regt
FRYER A.H. MM Pte 15533 8th Somerset Light Infantry
FRYER Arthur K. MM 2nd Cpl 44269 Royal Engineers
FRYER Edward MM Bdr 10192 D/75 Bde RFA KIA 22.10.16.
FRYER Ernest MM Cpl 268080 1/7th West Yorkshire Regt
FRYER Ernest Gladstone MM L/Cpl 66493 RAMC
FRYER George MM Bdr 117332 C/50 Bde RFA DOW 22.10.18.
FRYER George E. MM Pte 13130 1st Grenadier Guards
FRYER Harry MM Pte 401450 8 Fd Amb RAMC
FRYER John MM Sjt 204940 2nd Middlesex Regt
FRYER John Lockwood MM Bdr 94797 291 Siege Bty RGA KIA 13.4.18.
FRYER John T. MM Pte 5161 1st Royal West Kent Regt
FRYER Joseph W. MM+Bar CSM 7211 Royal Fusiliers
FRYER Reginald John MM L/Cpl R/735 King's Royal Rifle Corps
FRYER Robert "MM,MSM" Cpl 254984 Signal Service Royal Engineers
FRYER Sam MM Cpl 13739 8th Norfolk Regt
FRYER Thomas H. MM Gnr 40929 40 Bde RFA
FRYER William "DCM,MM" Pnr 94180 156 Fd Coy Royal Engineers KIA 27.3.18.
FRYER William MM Dvr 88837 40 Bde RFA
FRYER William Henry MM Sjt 96200 222 Fd Coy Royal Engineers
FRYER William James MM+Bar Pte 421062 3(North Midland)Fd Amb RAMC
FRYETT John MM Sjt 12390 7th Duke of Cornwall's LI
FRYETT John George MM L/Cpl 51542 Middlesex Regt
FUARY Andrew "MM,MID" Pte 21118 1/7th Royal Scots
FUDGE Bertram J. MM Cpl 72301 12 Bde RFA
FUDGE Harold MM Pnr 197174 Royal Engineers
FUDGE John William MM Pte 25992 1st Cheshire Regt KIA 5.9.16.
FUDGE Percy J. MM Pte 323543 6th London Regt
FUDGE Stanley Alfred MM Sjt 10089 8th Royal Berkshire Regt DOW 28.7.16.
FUDGE William MM Pte 201044 1st Gloucestershire Regt
FUGETT Reginald G. MM Pte 42293 2nd Hampshire Regt
FUGGLE Ernest "DCM,MM" CSM 18969 Machine Gun Corps
FUGGLE Osman Louis MM Bdr 7439 7 Siege Bty RGA DOW 7.6.17
FUGUEL Albert MM Sjt 403420 2(West Riding)Fd Amb RAMC
FULBECK James MM Pte 19611 10th Northumberland Fusiliers
FULBRIG Thomas John MM Pte 8987 1st Royal Inniskilling Fusiliers KIA 1.7.16.
FULCHER Horace George MM Sjt 34876 28 Siege Bty RGA
FULFORD George F. MM Dvr 96209 C/256 Bde RFA
FULFORD George L. MM Pnr 77529 Royal Engineers
FULFORD William MM Cpl 33273 28 Bde RFA
FULL Arthur Robert MM Pte M2/153780 Army Service Corps
FULLAGAR Arthur Edward MM Pte 127164 25th Bn Machine Gun Corps
FULLARD William H. MM Pte 50105 9th Cheshire Regt
FULLARTON Andrew MM Spr 93027 Royal Engineers
FULLBROOK Arthur MM L/Sjt 24506 8th Royal Berkshire Regt
FULLBROOK Frederick MM+Bar Cpl 40651 12th Middlesex Regt
FULLBROOK John MM Pte S/24672 7th Rifle Brigade KIA 23.3.18.
FULLER Albert MM Sjt 1062 4th Gordon Highlanders
FULLER Albert MM L/Cpl 2192 8th Royal Sussex Regt
FULLER Albert MM L/Cpl 99399 4th Royal Fusiliers
FULLER Albert E. MM Pte A/205495 13th King's Royal Rifle Corps

FULLER Alfred MM Sjt 800605 26th Royal Fusiliers att Royal Fusiliers
FULLER Alfred J. MM Dvr T/36900 Army Service Corps
FULLER Archie William MM Pte 240127 Norfolk Regt
FULLER Bert H. MM Sjt 200682 1/4th Royal Berkshire Regt
FULLER C. MM Pte 23652 10th Essex Regt
FULLER Charles MM Sjt 5786 9th Royal Sussex Regt
FULLER Charles E. MM L/Cpl 7051 7th London Regt
FULLER Christopher A. MM Sjt 22284 Suffolk Regt
FULLER Claude D. MM Cpl 769793 28th London Regt
FULLER Edward James "MC,MM(29898 Bdr),MID" 2Lt RGA Died 28.7.19.
FULLER Edwin William "MC,MM(34563 L/Cpl)" T/2Lt 4th King's Royal Rifle Corps
FULLER Ernest MM L/Cpl 13343 4th Hussars
FULLER Ernest MM Pte 3214 8th East Kent Regt
FULLER F. MM Pte 10190 Royal Sussex Regt
FULLER F. MM Sjt 29426 41 Bde RFA
FULLER Frank A.O. "MM,MSM" Pte 63780 107 Coy Labour Corps
FULLER Frederick MM Cpl 14691 9th Norfolk Regt
FULLER Frederick MM Cpl G/52059 24th Royal Fusiliers
FULLER George MM Pte 26188 4th Grenadier Guards
FULLER George MM Pte 15333 7th Bedfordshire Regt
FULLER George F. MM Pte 12090 5th Northamptonshire Regt
FULLER George F. MM Sjt 1481 16th Lancers
FULLER Henry O. MM Pte 738178 24th London Regt
FULLER Henry W. MM Sjt 23498 21 Div Amn Col RFA
FULLER Herbert MM Pte M2/201203 Army Service Corps
FULLER Herbert A. MM Gnr 50205 RFA
FULLER James MM L/Cpl 9343 9th East Surrey Regt KIA 27.3.18.
FULLER Joseph MM Pte G/17860 12th Royal Fusiliers
FULLER Louis MM Pte 8145 2nd Royal Sussex Regt
FULLER Montague Charles MM Pte G/9619 4th Royal Fusiliers
FULLER Percy MM Gnr 1729 36 Bty 33 Bde RFA KIA 21.7.17.
FULLER Richard MM Pte S/30938 16th Rifle Brigade
FULLER Sidney Alfred MM Cpl 13012 1st Middlesex Regt KIA 15.7.16.
FULLER Stanley Howard MM S/Sjt Art 630 Army Ordnance Corps Died 23.1.17.
FULLER Stephen MM Gnr 14557 159 Bde RFA
FULLER W. MM L/Cpl 28288 1st Essex Regt
FULLER Walter G. MM Pte 307291 2nd Hampshire Regt
FULLER Wells MM Pte 13264 Machine Gun Corps
FULLER William MM Pte 54953 11th Manchester Regt
FULLER William MM Pte 125897 32nd Bn Machine Gun Corps
FULLER William "MM,MID" Pte 537 6th Royal West Kent Regt
FULLER William C. MM Sjt 12558 23rd Bn Machine Gun Corps
FULLER William Edward "MM,MID" Sjt 7809 2nd Gordon Highlanders KIA 4.10.17
FULLERTON Alfred MM Pte 1448 6th East Kent Regt
FULLERTON Charles MM Cpl 11874 6th Royal Inniskilling Fusiliers
FULLERTON John MM L/Cpl 9504 2nd Royal Dublin Fusiliers DOW 28.10.16.
FULLILOVE Charles E. MM Pte 13188 1st Dorsetshire Regt
FULLILOVE Reginald J. MM Bdr 79001 RFA
FULLJAMES Leslie John MM+Bar Pte 47455 36 att 37 Fd Amb RAMC KIA 1.7.18.
FULLMAN George Edmund "MC,MM(42010 Sjt)" Lt RFA
FULLWOOD Howard MM Bdr 205 MGC(Motors)
FULLWOOD John W. MM Spr 37853 Cav Corps Sig Sqn Royal Engineers
FULTON Alexander MM Sjt 36491 15th Highland Light Infantry
FULTON Andrew MM Pte 202053 1/4th Gordon Highlanders
FULTON David MM Sjt 420083 406 Fd Coy Royal Engineers
FULTON Graeme W. MM Pte 266337 Seaforth Highlanders
FULTON James "DCM,MM" Sjt 22531 31st Bn Machine Gun Corps
FULTON John MM Pte S/15102 1st Royal Highlanders
FULTON John MM L/Cpl S/15513 7th Cameron Highlanders
FULTON John MM Cpl 137463 RGA
FULTON R. MM L/Cpl S/13448 Seaforth Highlanders
FULTON Robert MM Cpl 96741 D/148 Bde RFA DOW 2.5.18.
FULTON Robert MM 2nd Cpl 121910 Royal Engineers
FULTON Samuel MM Pte 201207 Cheshire Regt
FULTON William MM L/Cpl 275717 1/7th Arg & Suth Highlanders
FULTON William MM Pte 50246 1/4th Royal Scots Fusiliers
FUNK George MM Pte 22941 11th Royal West Surrey Regt
FUNKIE Robert D. MM Pte 19494 Royal Highlanders
FUNNELL Albert E. MM Dvr T1/4136 Army Service Corps
FUNNELL Ernest F. MM Cpl 19050 Machine Gun Corps
FUNNELL Frederick MM Tptr 900440 RFA
FUNNELL George T. MM+Bar Sjt 9789 1st Royal Berkshire Regt
FUNNELL James R.C. MM L/Cpl R/19174 King's Royal Rifle Corps
FUNNELL John George MM Trumpeter 2069 2nd Dragoons KIA 23.3.18.
FUNNELL Robert William MM Gnr 387 2 Bty MGC(Motors)
FUNNELL Samuel MM Pte 201055 2nd Royal West Surrey Regt
FURBER Albert MM L/Cpl 13734 9th Welsh Regt
FURBER George MM Sjt 32741 Lincolnshire Regt
FURBER Jonathan B. MM Pte 27383 Royal Berkshire Regt
FURBER Thomas MM Pte 200585 Shropshire Light Infantry
FUREY Daniel Albert MM Pte M2/175493 Army Service Corps
FUREY James MM Pte 202525 2nd Arg & Suth Highlanders
FUREY Michael MM Pte 242893 1/6th Liverpool Regt
FURLONG Frederick J. MM Gnr 27297 RGA
FURLONG John MM Pte 4522 1/10th Liverpool Regt
FURLONG Martin MM Pte 10358 Irish Guards
FURLONG Richard J. MM Pte 35228 RAMC att RFA
FURLONG Walter MM Pte 18528 Welsh Regt
FURMINGER Arthur MM L/Cpl 2248 8th Royal Sussex Regt
FURMINGER William MM S/Sjt 31672 RAMC
FURMSTON William R. MM L/Cpl 266655 2nd Bedfordshire Regt
FURNE James A. MM Cpl 422479 10th London Regt
FURNEAUX Alfred F. MM Cpl 24242 Royal Fusiliers
FURNEAUX Leonard MM Pte 241155 5th Devonshire Regt KIA 30.9.18.
FURNEAUX Samuel Richard "MM,MSM" Sjt 42818 81 Fd Coy Royal Engineers
FURNELL Albert MM Cpl 11250 6th Wiltshire Regt
FURNELL Louis N. MM Gnr 93245 RGA
FURNESS Arthur MM L/Cpl 108956 157 Fd Coy Royal Engineers
FURNESS Edward MM L/Cpl 21568 Grenadier Guards
FURNESS Fred MM RQMS 201134 2/4th West Riding Regt
FURNESS James Walter MM L/Cpl 8331 Royal Irish Regt
FURNESS Oliver MM Pte 18154 10th South Lancashire Regt
FURNESS Wilkinson MM Pte 37562 Northumberland Fusiliers
FURNEVAL H. MM Pte 14478 10th Yorkshire Regt
FURNEY Robert MM Pte 45790 Royal Welsh Fusiliers
FURNISS George S. "MM,MSM" Cpl(Eng Clk) 42083 12 Div Sig Coy Royal Engineers
FURNISS George Walter MM Sjt 33048 29 Fd Amb RAMC
FURNISS J. MM Pte M2/098663 Army Service Corps
FURNIVAL Joseph MM Bdr 77798 24 Bty 38 Bde RFA DOW 26.9.16.
FURNIVAL Lionel MM Bdr 1422 HQ 235 Bde RFA
FURR Arthur F. MM Sjt 10497 13th Royal Fusiliers
FURR Charles MM Pte 19157 2nd Bedfordshire Regt
FURRIE Bernard MM L/Cpl 14792 3rd Hussars
FURRIE George S. MM Spr 418024 52 Div Sig Coy Royal Engineers
FURSDON Frederick J. "DCM,MM" BSM 19829 274 Siege Bty RGA
FURSDON Harold MM Gnr 135468 RFA
FURSE Frederick C.C. MM Pte 972 9th East Surrey Regt
FURSMAN T.C. MM Pte 457090 RAMC
FURSSE Albert MM Sjt 550119 1/16th London Regt
FURST Robert M. MM Sjt 266640 11th Royal Scots Fusiliers
FURZE Albert Edward MM L/Cpl 46532 South Staffordshire Regt
FURZER Robert MM Spr 558018 Royal Engineers
FURZER Samuel MM CQMS 8222 2nd Border Regt
FURZER Sydney MM Pte 7693 3rd Rifle Brigade
FUSSELL Charles Henry MM Pte 6648 1st Somerset Light Infantry
FUSSELL Percy W. MM Pte 4570 1/8th Liverpool Regt Died 25.10.19.
FUSSEY Leonard MM Sjt 11/994 11th East Yorkshire Regt KIA 28.7.18.
FUTER Thomas March MM CSM 692 11th Middlesex Regt
FUTERS Stephen R. MM Pte 200832 Northumberland Fusiliers
FUZZENS Frederick I. "MM+Bar,MID" Sjt 24549 4 Div Sig Coy Royal Engineers
FUZZENS Henry S. MM Pte 9665 2nd Oxf & Bucks Light Infantry
FYFE Alexander MM Pnr 45498 14 Div Sig Coy Royal Engineers KIA 4.4.18.
FYFE David James MM Pte 202011 15th Highland Light Infantry
FYFE John MM Gnr 118796 B/51 Bde RFA
FYFE John J.M. MM Pte 11024 Seaforth Highlanders
FYFE Norman McD. MM Pte S/17756 6th Royal Highlanders
FYLAN Thomas MM Cpl 99669 1 Water Boring Section Royal Engineers
FYLES William A.P. MM Cpl 74431 Royal Engineers
FYMAN Archie MM Sjt 41610 Northumberland Fusiliers
FYNN Daniel "DCM,MM+Bar" Sjt 18817 2nd Bedfordshire Regt

FYNN Leonard James MM Pte 9178 2nd Bedfordshire Regt KIA 30.7.16.
FYSH George MM Pte 10529 6th Yorkshire Regt
FYSON John MM Pte 15626 8th Bedfordshire Regt
FYTCHE Charles L. MM Pnr 312873 Royal Engineers att RFA.
FYVIE George M. MM Sjt 200188 1/4th Gordon Highlanders

G

GABB Albert J. MM Cpl 203296 R Warw Royal Warwickshire Regt
GABB Thomas MM CSM 3050 1/4th Gloucs Gloucestershire Regt
GABBE E. MM Pte 14757 Royal Dublin Fusiliers
GABBEDEY Edward MM L/Cpl 546040 Royal Engineers
GABBUTT Frederick Ernest Bremner MM Sjt 700526 330 Bde RFA
GABRIEL Richard MM Sjt 432011 Royal Engineers
GABY Henry W. MM Pte 2095 2nd Lancashire Fusiliers
GACHET William MM Sjt 39196 RFA
GADBURY Sidney Frederick MM+Bar Pte 240300 1/8th Middlesex Regt
GADD Albert MM+Bar Pte 51157 1/6th Cheshire Regt
GADD Arthur William MM Pte 10469 2nd Wiltshire Regt
GADD Charles J. MM Pte 351262 7th London Regt
GADD Edwin J. MM Sjt 28977 55 Bty 33 Bde RFA
GADD Frederick H. MM Cpl 119419 267 Siege Bty RGA
GADD William D. MM L/Sjt 8767 Middlesex Regt
GADD William George MM Sjt 56430 227 Fd Coy Royal Engineers
GADSBY James MM Pte 71574 Machine Gun Corps
GADSBY Samuel MM Cpl 56728 1/8th Notts & Derby Regt
GADSBY Walter Ernest MM Pte 17906 2nd Bedfordshire Regt
GAFFEE Harry MM L/Cpl 202084 2nd Oxf & Bucks Light Infantry
GAFFING Daniel MM Sjt 18357 1/7th Border Regt KIA 23.4.17.
GAFFNEY Douglas MM Cpl 177970 79 Fd Coy Royal Engineers
GAFFNEY John MM Pte 10097 Cheshire Regt
GAFFNEY John James "DCM,MM+Bar" Sjt 200167 1st & 1/5th Liverpool Regt
GAFFNEY Michael MM Pte 44672 RAMC
GAFFNEY Michael MM Sjt 26965 Royal Dublin Fusiliers
GAFFNEY Patrick MM Pte 21221 7th Gloucestershire Regt
GAFFNEY Patrick MM Sjt 8624 1st Liverpool Regt
GAFFNEY Wallace H. "DCM,MM" Sjt 28883 30 Div Sig Coy Royal Engineers
GAFNEY Alfred MM Sjt 1298 7th East Kent Regt
GAGE Frederick G. MM L/Cpl 38502 7th Norfolk Regt
GAGE Frederick T. MM Dvr 87219 A/84 Bde RFA
GAGE Harry MM Cpl 1976 1/1st Cambridgeshire Regt
GAGE Wakter Frederick William MM L/Sjt 14671 12th Gloucestershire Regt
GAGE Walter MM Cpl 39444 3 Div Ammn Col RFA
GAGE Wilfred T. MM Pte 4239 Yorkshire Regt
GAGEBY William MM Spr 57442 150 Fd Coy Royal Engineers
GAGG Archibald MM L/Cpl 236996 1/1st Herefordshire Regt
GAGIN Thomas MM Pte 24683 Royal Welsh Fusiliers
GAHAGAN F. MM Pte 46613 2nd Essex Regt
GAHAN John MM Sjt 690045 RFA
GAHAN Patrick MM CSM 8405 1at North Lancashire Regt KIA 25.11.16.
GAIGER Harry MM Pte 1951 8 Fd Amb RAMC
GAIN Albert MM Cpl 28335 27 Siege Bty RGA
GAINES Sydney MM Sjt 776116 D/245 Bde RFA
GAINES W. MM+Bar Sjt 265176 1/1st Hertfordshire Regt
GAINES Walter MM CQMS 3/2637 8th Yorkshire Light Infantry
GAINEY Joseph MM Sjt 16501 23rd Middlesex Regt
GAINEY Morris MM Pte 8798 2nd Royal Scots
GAIR Ernest MM Sjt 37176 2nd Northumberland Fusiliers
GAIR James H. MM Sjt 465725 44 AA Section Royal Engineers
GAIR Thomas MM Pte 15329 Northumberland Fusiliers
GAITCH William MM Pte 7768 1st Dorsetshire Regt
GAITLEY Patrick MM Pte 9543 2nd East Lancashire Regt
GALBRAITH David MM Spr 159421 Royal Engineers
GALBRAITH Duncan MM Sjt 84 1/8th Arg & Suth Highlanders
GALBRAITH Hugh Harris MM Pte 28211 1st Royal Scots Fusiliers Died 5.5.17.
GALBRAITH James MM Pte 17286 11th Royal Scots Fusiliers
GALBRAITH James McInnes MM L/Sjt 265583 7th Scottish Rifles
GALBRAITH John MM L/Sjt 8743 2nd Irish Guards
GALE Archibald M. MM Dvr 11610 RFA
GALE Basil Richard MM Spr 84464 203 Fd Coy Royal Engineers KIA 7.6.18.
GALE Bruce Arthur MM Pte 28387 4th Grenadier Guards DOW 13.4.18.
GALE Charles Francis MM Pte 27015 1st Royal Berkshire Regt
GALE Ernest MM Gnr 111792 RGA
GALE Francis James MM Sjt 10422 240 Siege Bty RGA
GALE Frederick J. MM Cpl 33910 RAMC
GALE George H. MM Pte 72886 32nd Bn Machine Gun Corps
GALE Harold MM Sjt 316060 1/1(East Anglia)Hy Bty RGA
GALE Henry MM Cpl 23116 19th Welsh Regt
GALE Henry John Elliott "MC,MM(113366 Sjt)" T/2Lt 1 Special Coy Royal Engineers KIA 8.6.18.
GALE Howard B. MM Pte 108589 Machine Gun Corps
GALE Hubert E. MM Spr 74549 Royal Engineers
GALE J.C. MM Pte 17963 Yorkshire Regt
GALE Oliver MM Pte 592990 2/18th London Regt
GALE Richard J. MM Pte 20680 13th Royal Scots
GALE William MM Pte 241145 1/5th Devonshire Regt
GALE William A. MM L/Cpl 250077 3rd London Regt
GALE William C. MM Cpl 3376 RFA
GALE William H. MM Sjt 62690 Royal Engineers
GALE William Julien MM Sjt 13121 8th Norfolk Regt Died 3.11.18.
GALEN James Joseph MM Sjt 531949 1/15th London Regt
GALER Arthur MM Pte M2/120836 622 Coy Army Service Corps
GALER Frederick J. MM Cpl 23697 RFA
GALES Joseph M. MM Pte 22134 10th West Yorkshire Regt Died 1920.
GALEY Leonard MM Pte 10308 7th East Yorkshire Regt
GALL George Lowe MM Sjt 300724 2nd Arg & Suth Highlanders att RE
GALL Gilbert MM Pte 15062 1st Cameron Highlanders
GALLACHER Charles MM Pte 8982 5/6th Royal Scots
GALLACHER Charles MM Cpl M2/103592 340 Coy Army Service Corps
GALLACHER Edward MM Pte 30190 5/6th Royal Scots KIA 4.4.18.
GALLACHER John MM Cpl 8487 15th Highland Light Infantry
GALLACHER John MM+Bar Sjt 241419 5/6th Scottish Rifles
GALLACHER John MM Dvr 46786 D/98 Bde RFA
GALLACHER Patrick MM Pte 241876 1/7th Gordon Highlanders
GALLACHER Patrick MM Dvr 24977 11 Fd Coy Royal Engineers
GALLACHER Thomas MM Pte 10509 31st Bn Machine Gun Corps
GALLAGHER Charles Michael MM Pnr 221692 58 Div Sig Coy Royal Engineers
GALLAGHER Edward MM L/Sjt 78274 15th Notts & Derby Regt
GALLAGHER Francis J. MM Sjt 11227 RGA
GALLAGHER Frank MM Bdr 96820 RFA
GALLAGHER G. MM Cpl 17445 9th South Lancashire Regt
GALLAGHER George "DCM,MM" Sjt 5691 16 Fd Amb RAMC
GALLAGHER Isaac MM Dvr L/8724 30 Div Ammn Col RFA
GALLAGHER J. MM Pte 11742 Royal Inniskilling Fusiliers
GALLAGHER J. MM L/Cpl 86598 Royal Engineers
GALLAGHER James "MM,MID" Sjt 4495 Lancashire Fusiliers
GALLAGHER James MM Sjt 4452 12th Arg & Suth Highlanders
GALLAGHER James MM Gnr 76455 B/61 Bde RFA
GALLAGHER James MM Pte 59309 52nd Bn Machine Gun Corps
GALLAGHER James MM Cpl 1/8242 1st Royal Munster Fusiliers
GALLAGHER John MM Spr 87800 Royal Engineers
GALLAGHER John MM Pte 71164 14th Bn Machine Gun Corps
GALLAGHER John MM Dvr 91346 RFA DOW 13.4.17.
GALLAGHER John MM Sjt 10180 Cheshire Regt
GALLAGHER John MM L/Cpl 15531 Royal Inniskilling Fusiliers
GALLAGHER John C. MM Sjt 77570 RFA
GALLAGHER John George MM Pte 25336 2/7th West Riding Regt
GALLAGHER John H. MM Pte 3405 1st Dragoons
GALLAGHER John W. MM Pte 301100 RAMC
GALLAGHER John W. MM Pte 35082 Northumberland Fusiliers
GALLAGHER Joseph MM Pte 9536 1st Royal Dublin Fusiliers
GALLAGHER Joseph MM Pte 4047 6th Connaught Rangers
GALLAGHER Joseph V. MM Sjt 492326 Royal Engineers
GALLAGHER Joseph W. MM Pte 61631 RAMC
GALLAGHER Martin MM Cpl 73409 56 Coy Machine Gun Corps KIA 24.9.17.
GALLAGHER Patrick MM Pte 48149 13th Royal Inniskilling Fusiliers
GALLAGHER Patrick MM Pte 14301 10th Yorkshire Regt
GALLAGHER Patrick MM Cpl 3/7319 8th East Yorkshire Regt
GALLAGHER Terence MM Spr 145214 212 Fd Coy Royal Engineers
GALLAGHER Thomas MM Sjt 9787 4th Worcestershire Regt
GALLAGHER Thomas MM Pte 26696 Royal Inniskilling Fusiliers
GALLAGHER Thomas MM Pte 28295 15/17th West Yorkshire Regt
GALLAGHER William MM Bdr 11556 B/160 Bde RFA

GALLAGHER William MM Gnr 81411 RFA
GALLAGHER William J. MM Pte 72248 134 Fd Amb RAMC
GALLAHER William "DCM,MM" Sjt 44098 17th Bn Machine Gun Corps
GALLANT Noel E. MM Sjt 530435 1/15th London Regt
GALLANT Percy MM Cpl 10232 10th Royal West Surrey Regt
GALLERY Joseph "MM,MID" Spr 20510 1 Div Sig Coy Royal Engineers
GALLEWSKI Myer MM L/Cpl 64548 100 Fd Amb RAMC DOW 19.2.17.
GALLEY Ernest MM Pte 325979 1/9th Durham Light Infantry
GALLEY Frederick William MM Pte 29376 10th Essex Regt
GALLEY George MM Sjt 40030 11th Essex Regt KIA 22.3.18.
GALLEY George MM Pte 351190 9th Manchester Regt
GALLEY James MM Pte 3685 11th Manchester Regt KIA 16.8.17.
GALLEY Percy "DCM,MM" Sjt 10638 6th York & Lancaster Regt
GALLEY Peter Herbert MM Pte 27141 Grenadier Guards
GALLEY Thomas E. MM Pte 5717 2nd Worcestershire Regt
GALLEY William MM Sjt 19041 Durham Light Infantry
GALLEY William Drabble MM L/Sjt 200311 1/4th York & Lancaster Regt
GALLEY William James MM Pte F/2771 23rd Middlesex Regt
GALLIE George MM Pte 202213 Scottish Rifles
GALLIERS Richard Henry MM Sjt 30130 124 Coy Machine Gun Corps
GALLIFORD Herbert MM Dvr T4/210581 515 Coy Army Service Corps
GALLILAND John Barton MM CQMS 3/10325 7th Norfolk Regt
GALLIMORE Frederick MM Spr 70185 Signal Section Royal Engineers
GALLIMORE Job "DCM,MM" L/Cpl 8336 1st North Staffordshire Regt
GALLIMORE William MM Pte 350067 9th Liverpool Regt
GALLIVAN James MM Bdr 276913 RGA
GALLIVAN Michael J. MM Cpl 8040 Royal Munster Fusiliers
GALLON James MM Gnr 43558 RGA
GALLOP Bertie W. MM Pte 205459 Royal West Surrey Regt
GALLOP James MM Sjt 2082 RGA
GALLOP William MM Sjt 30714 33 Bde RFA
GALLOW George MM L/Cpl 72171 Machine Gun Corps
GALLOWAY Charles MM L/Cpl 10217 8th Seaforth Highlanders KIA 20.8.17.
GALLOWAY Fred MM Pte 2357 1/5th York & Lancaster Regt
GALLOWAY G.H. MM+Bar Sjt G/11537 1st East Kent Regt
GALLOWAY George MM Sjt 11229 8th Royal Lancaster Regt
GALLOWAY George MM Piper 1543 1/7th Royal Highlanders
GALLOWAY James MM Pte 201879 West Riding Regt
GALLOWAY James MM Cpl 38847 Royal Scots
GALLOWAY James MM Dvr 88574 RHA
GALLOWAY James Melville MM Sjt 530098 2/15th London Regt
GALLOWAY John MM Pte 16589 Seaforth Highlanders
GALLOWAY John R. MM CQMS 19495 13th Liverpool Regt
GALLOWAY P. MM Pte 251103 1/6th Arg & Suth Highlanders
GALLOWAY Robert MM Cpl 104992 41st Bn Machine Gun Corps
GALLOWAY Robert "MM,MSM." Sjt 10418 1st King's Own Scottish Borderers
GALLOWAY Robert Gardiner MM Sjt 768 4 Bty MGC(Motors) KIA 30.12.17.
GALLOWAY Thomas MM L/Cpl 8721 2nd Royal Irish Rifles
GALLOWAY Walter MM Cpl 61146 29 Bde RFA
GALLOWAY William MM Pte 241180 1/5th Royal Scots Fusiliers
GALLOWAY William MM Cpl 25720 Machine Gun Corps
GALLOWAY William MM Gnr 143370 D/83 Bde RFA
GALLOWAY William MM Cpl 113236 Royal Engineers
GALLYER Thomas A. MM Pte 39244 8th East Surrey Regt
GALPIN Albert MM Spr 14251 4 Div Sig Coy Royal Engineers
GALPIN C.T. MM Cpl 10591 Royal Flying Corps
GALPIN Herbert J. MM L/Cpl 13734 5th Dorsetshire Regt
GALPIN Richard MM Spr 16193 5 Fd Coy Royal Engineers
GALPIN William MM Pte 37803 17th Welsh Regt
GALSWORTHY William MM Dvr 12634 D/86 Bde RFA
GALT Daniel "DCM,MM" Pte S/18846 6th Cameron Highlanders DOW 17.7.17.
GALTON Edward S. MM Cpl 16798 1st Dorsetshire Regt
GALTON J.A. MM Pte 59698 Northumberland Fusiliers
GALVIN Daniel MM Gnr 67606 RFA
GALVIN Henry W. MM Sjt L/1887 C/174 Bde RFA
GALVIN Nellie MM Sister F QAIMNS
GALVIN Patrick MM Pte 19730 6th Royal Dublin Fusiliers KIA 17.10.18.
GALWAY William James MM Pte 8/12805 Royal Irish Rifles
GALYER Charles W. MM Sjt 9125 East Yorkshire Regt
GAMACK George MM Pte 891 10th Arg & Suth Highlanders
GAMAGE A. MM Bdr 36003 RFA
GAMBELL Herbert David MM Pte 6063 1st East Kent Regt
GAMBIER Charles Edward MM Pte 201268 1/1st London Regt
GAMBLE Arthur MM Pte M2/136537 Army Service Corps att RGA
GAMBLE Bernard MM Cpl 8409 37th Bn Machine Gun Corps
GAMBLE Frank L. MM L/Bdr 800818 C/295 Bde RFA
GAMBLE Frederick MM Gnr Fitter 820156 RFA
GAMBLE James MM Pte 13528 Yorkshire Light Infantry
GAMBLE John M. MM+Bar Pte 19/443 Royal Irish Rifles
GAMBLE John William MM Sjt 25951 8th Yorkshire Regt
GAMBLE Percy MM Gnr 72071 RFA
GAMBLE Thomas MM Pte 6770 2nd Royal Irish Rifles
GAMBLE Walter David "DCM,MM" Sjt 67778 19 Div Sig Coy Royal Engineers
GAMBLE William MM Pte 10803 Leicestershire Regt
GAMBLE William MM L/Cpl 2266 1/4th Leicestershire Regt KIA 7.12.16.
GAMBLES Robert MM L/Cpl 40152 West Yorkshire Regt
GAMBLIN Charles MM Dvr 105790 RFA
GAMBLING William MM Sjt C/9508 20th King's Royal Rifle Corps KIA 16.10.17.
GAMBRILL William Frederick MM Sjt 13317 2nd Grenadier Guards
GAME Ambrose Edward MM L/Cpl 8915 7th East Surrey Regt DOW 12.8.16.
GAME H. MM 2nd Cpl 42987 Royal Engineers
GAME Joseph G. MM+Bar Cpl 16933 2/4th Yorkshire Light Infantry
GAMLEN James Arthur MM Dvr 492146 46 Div Sig Coy Royal Engineers
GAMMIE Alexander MM Sjt 2500 Royal Highlanders
GAMMIE William C. MM L/Cpl 265339 1/6th Gordon Highlanders
GAMMON Jack MM Sjt F/1262 16th Middlesex Regt
GAMMON John Henry Samuel MM Pte 6192 12th Middlesex Regt KIA 24.8.18.
GAMMON Percy F. MM L/Cpl 9549 1st Northamptonshire Regt
GAMMON Richard MM Pte P/678 Rifle Brigade
GAMMOND Tom A. MM Cpl 275201 1/7th Manchester Regt
GAMMONS Charles Craddock MM+Bar Sjt 12523 5th Northamptonshire Regt
GAMMONS Clarence MM Pte 66669 Royal Fusiliers
GAMMONS Herbert John MM L/Cpl 14805 7th Bedfordshire Regt KIA 10.8.17.
GANDELL William Ernest MM Pte 2327 1/8th London Regt
GANDER Albert Ernest MM Sjt 391038 1/9th London Regt
GANDER Frank L. MM Pte 201155 1/4th Dorsetshire Regt
GANDERTON James MM Pte 16015 2nd South Lancashire Regt KIA 2.8.17.
GANDY Christopher James MM Cpl 724050 2/24th London Regt
GANDY Henry MM Pte 241944 2/4th South Lancashire Regt
GANDY Leonard MM Pte 17539 5th Northamptonshire Regt
GANDY Thomas Moreton MM L/Cpl 20920 22nd Manchester Regt KIA 14.3.17.
GANE Harold MM Bdr 125022 285 Siege Bty RGA
GANLY Francis MM Sjt 29565 102 Siege Bty RGA
GANNICOTT W. MM Cpl 335 Royal Guernsey LI
GANNON Charles MM SSM T/20387 2 Div Train Army Service Corps
GANNON Frank MM Pte 850 2nd Lancashire Fusiliers
GANNON Harold MM L/Cpl 415087 2/1st(North Midland)Mounted Bde Fd Amb RAMC
GANNON Hugh G. MM Spr 83464 Royal Engineers
GANNON James Joseph MM Sjt 200319 1/5th Royal Warwickshire Regt
GANNON John MM Pte 8/4616 8th Northumberland Fusiliers
GANNON John MM Pte 7435 1st North Staffordshire Regt KIA 11.2.17.
GANNON Patrick MM Gnr 73957 B/275 Bde RFA KIA 18.4.18.
GANNON Patrick MM Pte 330209 8th Royal Scots KIA 4.12.17.
GANNON Peter MM Pte 11864 6th Royal Dublin Fusiliers
GANNON Thomas P.T. MM Bdr Sig 715233 420 Bty RFA
GANT Arthur MM Sjt 132902 Royal Engineers
GANT Frank MM Cpl 29111 4th Bn Machine Gun Corps KIA 14.5.18.
GANT Frederick A. MM Pte 300609 5th London Regt
GANT Henry T. MM Pte 2825 Lincolnshire Yeomanry
GANT Herbert G. MM Sjt 500367 61 Div Sig Coy Royal Engineers
GANTER Percy MM Cpl L/19032 A/187 Bde RFA
GAPPER John MM Cpl 265102 2/5th Gloucestershire Regt
GAPPER John H. MM Pte M2/046563 177 Coy Army Service Corps

GAPPER Richard L. MM Sjt 49716 85 Coy Machine Gun Corps
GAPPER William MM Dvr 37032 RFA
GARAHY Edward MM Gnr 74673 199 Siege Bty RGA
GARBETT Alfred MM Cpl 13167 1/6th South Staffordshire Regt
GARBETT Frank "MM,MID" L/Cpl 18280 Royal Engineers
GARBETT George MM Spr 106741 Royal Engineers
GARBETT John Richard MM+Bar Sjt 36787 61st Bn Machine Gun Corps KIA 12.4.18.
GARBETT S. MM L/Sjt 241783 West Yorkshire Regt
GARBUTT Charles Standish MM L/Cpl 12/923 12th York & Lancaster Regt
GARBUTT Harry MM L/Cpl 98725 Royal Engineers
GARBUTT James W. MM Pte 241707 5th West Riding Regt
GARBUTT Oswald J. MM Sjt 9372 Yorkshire Regt
GARBUTT Robert MM Sjt 30131 Durham Light Infantry
GARBUTT Thomas MM Pte 3758 2nd Rifle Brigade
GARBUTT William Herbert MM Gnr 28420 A/93 Bde RFA
GARD Frederick A. MM Pte 30961 1st Royal West Kent Regt
GARDEN Alexander MM Sjt S/40133 1st Cameron Highlanders
GARDEN Alexander MM Cpl 200560 3rd Bn Tank Corps
GARDEN John MM Cpl 400670 105 Fd Coy Royal Engineers
GARDEN John MM L/Bdr 63738 RGA
GARDENER George MM Sjt 1997 1/9th Durham Light Infantry
GARDENER Leslie. MM Pte 88299 RAMC
GARDINER Alfred Ernest MM Sjt 280102 1/4th London Regt Died 20.5.17.
GARDINER Arthur W. MM Dvr 52673 RFA
GARDINER Bertie MM L/Cpl 178984 207 Fd Coy Royal Engineers
GARDINER Charles MM Sjt 94352 4th Liverpool Regt
GARDINER Charles MM Sjt 30660 Notts & Derby Regt
GARDINER Charles James MM Sjt 56231 RHA
GARDINER Edwin MM L/Cpl 17118 Royal Fusiliers
GARDINER Edwin James MM Pte 206732 2/4th Royal West Surrey Regt KIA 1.8.18.
GARDINER George MM+2 Bars Cpl 200821 Seaforth Highlanders
GARDINER Harry MM Sjt 112233 Royal Engineers
GARDINER J.H. MM Cpl 634889 20th London Regt
GARDINER James MM+Bar Pte 40234 Royal Scots
GARDINER James B. "DCM,MM" Sjt 504325 503 Fd Coy Royal Engineers
GARDINER John MM Pte 3708 9th Lancashire Fusiliers
GARDINER John G. "DCM,MM" Sjt 202664 1/4th Seaforth Highlanders
GARDINER Maurice MM Spr 457462 449 Fd Coy Royal Engineers
GARDINER Percy John MM Pte 5946 2nd Royal Sussex Regt KIA 9.9.16
GARDINER Peter W. MM+Bar Sjt 3899 1/7th Royal Highlanders
GARDINER Ralph "DCM,MM" Spr 103826 8 Div Sig Coy Royal Engineers
GARDINER Reginald Frank MM Pte 2416 1/4th Gloucestershire Regt
GARDINER Robert MM Pte 40190 1/8th Arg & Suth Highlanders
GARDINER Robert MM L/Cpl 921 1st Royal Highlanders
GARDINER Robert H. MM Pte 1519 Royal Irish Rifles
GARDINER Sidney James MM Spr 87495 39 Div Sig Coy Royal Engineers
GARDINER Thomas H. MM Sjt Sig 450235 1/11th London Regt
GARDINER William MM Pte 2723 7th East Kent Regt
GARDINER William MM Sjt 202134 5/6th Scottish Rifles KIA 8.5.18.
GARDINER William MM Sjt 9188 2nd Royal West Surrey Regt
GARDINER William A. MM Sjt 18315 Royal Inniskilling Fusiliers
GARDINER William C. MM Cpl 834 1st Welsh Guards
GARDINER William Charles MM L/Sjt 320649 15th Suffolk Regt
GARDINER William L. MM Dvr 246722 C/165 Bde RFA
GARDINER William Thomas MM Pte 12047 Leicestershire Regt
GARDINER William W.G. MM Pte 7130 1st Hampshire Regt
GARDNER Alan E. MM L/Cpl 307885 8th Royal Warwickshire Regt
GARDNER Albert MM Pte 3540 North Staffordshire Regt
GARDNER Albert MM Gnr 60285 56 Div Ammn Col RFA
GARDNER Albert E. MM Sjt 19857 4th Hampshire Regt
GARDNER Albert H. MM Gnr 233461 RFA
GARDNER Alexander MM Pte 34828 North Staffordshire Regt
GARDNER Archibald MM Pte 1593 23rd Royal Fusiliers
GARDNER Archie MM Pte 15716 2nd Scots Guards KIA 12.10.17.
GARDNER Arthur MM Sjt 39058 1st South Wales Borderers
GARDNER Arthur MM+Bar Sjt 13115 6th Northamptonshire Regt
GARDNER Arthur Henry MM Pte 37396 Essex Regt
GARDNER Arthur J. "DCM,MM+Bar,MID" Sjt 18682 10th Worcestershire Regt
GARDNER Charles MM+Bar Sjt 10600 11th Royal West Kent Regt
GARDNER Charles MM Sjt 13800 Machine Gun Corps
GARDNER Charles H. MM Sjt 2664 West Riding Regt
GARDNER Charles R. MM Spr 63067 Royal Engineers
GARDNER Charles William Edward MM Pte 295141 12th Somerset Light Infantry
GARDNER David MM Sjt S/7016 Royal Highlanders
GARDNER David B. MM L/Cpl 350424 Royal Scots
GARDNER Edmund MM Pte 3382 Worcestershire Regt
GARDNER Edward W. MM 2nd Cpl 193191 51 Div Sig Coy Royal Engineers
GARDNER Fred MM+Bar Sjt 43400 152 Fd Coy Royal Engineers
GARDNER Frederick MM Sjt 4700 22 Fd Amb RAMC
GARDNER Frederick MM Pte 20854 22nd Manchester Regt DOW 26.10.16.
GARDNER Frederick MM L/Cpl 14419 Welsh Regt
GARDNER Frederick Henry MM Sjt 24401 Machine Gun Corps
GARDNER George MM Pte 41781 Royal Scots
GARDNER George MM Sjt 9737 1st South Staffordshire Regt
GARDNER George Frederick MM Pte 202406 12th Royal Sussex Regt
GARDNER George Thomas MM Pte 146011 1/1st Northamptonshire Yeomanry
GARDNER Gilbert Charles MM Pte 72519 RAMC
GARDNER Gilbert S. MM Cpl 240946 Gloucestershire Regt
GARDNER Harold John MM Cpl G/6666 Royal Fusiliers
GARDNER Harry MM Pte 241899 2/5th Gloucestershire Regt KIA 2.12.17.
GARDNER Harry Victor MM Pte 6722 2/4th Oxf & Bucks Light Infantry KIA 14.3.17.
GARDNER Henry MM Sjt M2/098578 Army Service Corps
GARDNER Henry James MM Pte 11985 2nd Irish Guards
GARDNER Henry W. MM Sjt 45859 33 Fd Amb RAMC
GARDNER Herbert MM L/Cpl 320212 16th Royal Sussex Regt DOW 3.10.18.
GARDNER Herbert MM Sjt 46808 41 Bde RFA
GARDNER Herbert "DCM,MM" Pte 15770 2nd Grenadier Guards
GARDNER Herbert MM Pte 3322 9th Royal Sussex Regt
GARDNER Herbert S. MM L/Cpl 1338 17th Royal Fusiliers
GARDNER J. MM Pte 6854 7th East Lancashire Regt
GARDNER James MM Cpl 19217 16th Royal Scots KIA 21.3.18.
GARDNER James MM Pte 238004 Leicestershire Regt
GARDNER James MM Sjt 3202 3rd Dragoon Guards
GARDNER James MM Pte 23793 2nd West Riding Regt
GARDNER James R. MM L/Cpl 267401 Northumberland Fusiliers
GARDNER John MM Pte 9284 5th Royal Berkshire Regt
GARDNER John MM Sjt 1120 A/256 Bde RFA KIA 21.3.18.
GARDNER John E. MM Sjt 77426 Tank Corps
GARDNER John Evans MM Bdr 73943 28 Bde RFA
GARDNER John H. MM Sjt 2763 12th Lancers
GARDNER John Henry MM+Bar L/Cpl 200135 1/1st London Regt
GARDNER Joseph MM+Bar Sjt 265364 2/7th Royal Warwickshire Regt
GARDNER Joseph MM Pte 21320 7th Gordon Highlanders
GARDNER Joseph Samuel MM Pte 16710 11th Notts & Derby Regt
GARDNER Osmond MM Gnr 121186 RGA
GARDNER Percy W. MM L/Cpl 536399 5 Fd Amb RAMC
GARDNER Reginald MM L/Sjt 35990 4th Oxf & Bucks Light Infantry
GARDNER Robert MM L/Cpl 332343 Highland Light Infantry
GARDNER Robert MM Sjt 128660 232 Siege Bty RGA
GARDNER Robert MM L/Cpl 1028 2nd Manchester Regt
GARDNER Robert MM L/Cpl 12939 7th South Lancashire Regt
GARDNER Robert MM L/Cpl 16816 7th Cameron Highlanders
GARDNER Robert J. MM Cpl S/23520 13th Rifle Brigade
GARDNER Roderick B.McDonald MM Gnr 159255 254 Siege Bty RGA
GARDNER Samuel MM Sjt M2/101076 50 Div Train Army Service Corps
GARDNER Thomas MM Pte 110247 1st Bn Tank Corps
GARDNER Thomas MM Cpl 67866 62nd Bn Machine Gun Corps
GARDNER Thomas "DCM,MM" Sjt 8264 12th Highland Light Infantry
GARDNER Thomas MM Dvr 136727 157 Fd Coy Royal Engineers
GARDNER Thomas H. MM Cpl 27499 Worcestershire Regt
GARDNER Tom MM L/Cpl 89180 Machine Gun Corps
GARDNER W. MM Pte 205726 East Yorkshire Regt
GARDNER W.R. MM Sjt 1728 RFA
GARDNER Walter H. MM Gnr 159486 235 Siege Bty RGA
GARDNER Walter P. MM Sjt 59085 23 Bde RFA
GARDNER William MM Pte 25841 1st South Wales Borderers
GARDNER William MM L/Cpl 11301 Royal Welsh Fusiliers

GARDNER William MM Pte 276059 Arg & Suth Highlanders
GARDNER William MM Sjt 15241 8th Royal Lancaster Regt DOW 8.2.17.
GARDNER William C. MM Spr 109155 Royal Engineers
GARDNER William Henry MM+Bar Pte 7541 8th East Surrey Regt
GARE Vernon MM Sjt 1549 1/1st Oxfordshire Yeomanry KIA 24.5.17.
GARFAT Tom K. MM Sjt 28437 Lancashire Fusiliers
GARFIELD Frank MM Pte 73060 11th Notts & Derby Regt KIA 5.10.18.
GARFITT George W. MM Cpl 31209 Machine Gun Corps
GARFITT William MM Pte Shoeing Smith SE/13666 Army Veterinary Corps
GARFOOT John Charles MM Pte 9344 Lincolnshire Regt
GARIOCH John G.G. MM L/Bdr 45308 RGA
GARLAND A. MM Pte 11622 South Wales Borderers
GARLAND Charles Henry MM Pte 1229 16th Royal Warwickshire Regt
GARLAND Ernest MM Pte 56511 18th King's Royal Rifle Corps
GARLAND Frank G. MM Sjt 74505 16 Bty 41 Bde RFA
GARLAND Harold MM Pte 295247 12th Somerset Light Infantry
GARLAND Isaac Stewart MM Cpl 4739 65 Bde RFA
GARLAND Jack MM L/Cpl 10612 1st Lincolnshire Regt
GARLAND James MM CQMS S/13510 7th Cameron Highlanders
GARLAND John MM L/Cpl 20529 1st Royal Irish Fusiliers KIA 21.3.18.
GARLAND John Joseph MM L/Bdr 30035 B/156 Bde RFA
GARLAND John W. MM Spr 552823 218 Fd Coy Royal Engineers
GARLAND Peter MM Pte 1627 1/5th Liverpool Regt Died 4.5.18.
GARLAND Philip Albert MM Bdr 46318 113 TM Bty RGA
GARLAND Thomas E. MM+Bar Sjt 435013 RAMC
GARLAND Walter MM L/Cpl 134425 227 Fd Coy Royal Engineers
GARLAND William MM L/Cpl 12134 7th Somerset Light Infantry
GARLICK Albert MM Sjt 240528 7th Lancashire Fusiliers
GARLICK Arthur J. MM Pte 71091 Notts & Derby Regt
GARLICK Charles MM Pnr 311852 Royal Engineers
GARLICK Cyril G. MM L/Cpl 477028 Royal Engineers
GARLICK Ernest L.W. MM L/Cpl 15182 9th Royal Lancaster Regt
GARLICK George MM L/Sjt 11670 4th Grenadier Guards
GARLICK James MM Pte 10441 5th Royal Berkshire Regt
GARLICK James MM L/Cpl 3031 West Riding Regt
GARLICK Thomas MM Bdr 12643 B/58 Bde RFA
GARLICK Thomas MM Sjt 21327 1st Lancashire Fusiliers
GARLICK William MM Cpl S/40183 7th Seaforth Highlanders
GARLINGE William James MM Pte G/5196 8th East Kent Regt DOW 17.7.16.
GARMAN Victor MM Pte 1322 22nd Royal Fusiliers DOW 24.11.16.
GARMENT Thomas MM L/Sjt 13292 1/1st Hertfordshire Regt
GARMSTON George MM Cpl 16146 Shropshire Light Infantry
GARMSTON James H. MM Gnr Shoeing Smith 37826 RFA
GARNER Allen MM Cpl Shoeing Smith 90590 B/48 Bde RFA
GARNER Archie MM Cpl T/36884 Army Service Corps
GARNER Charles P. MM Sjt 1882 1/1st Leicestershire Yeomanry
GARNER Charles R. "DCM,MM+Bar" Sjt 32790 8 Div Sig Coy Royal Engineers
GARNER Francis H.J. MM L/Cpl 75155 17th Royal Fusiliers
GARNER Fred MM Sjt 20324 Royal Welsh Fusiliers
GARNER Frederick C. MM Spr 32798 Royal Engineers
GARNER George MM Pte T4/107763 Army Service Corps
GARNER George MM Pte 35383 8th Yorkshire Light Infantry
GARNER George H. MM L/Cpl 12964 6th Bedfordshire Regt
GARNER H. MM Pte 41903 Lancashire Fusiliers
GARNER Harold MM Gnr 92661 RFA
GARNER Herbert MM Pte 13698 Lancashire Fusiliers
GARNER Hugh E. MM Sjt 69426 RFA
GARNER James MM Spr 96763 EE Cable Section Royal Engineers
GARNER John MM 2nd Cpl 21396 Royal Engineers
GARNER John A. MM Cpl 65894 8 Bde RFA
GARNER John E. MM Pte 30331 5th Royal Inniskilling Fusiliers
GARNER John F. MM Pte 16613 6th Yorkshire Regt
GARNER Leonard MM CQMS 280648 7th Lancashire Fusiliers
GARNER Samuel "MM,MM(F)" Sjt 44604 B/116 Bde RFA
GARNER Stephen MM L/Sjt 8397 2nd Welsh Regt
GARNER Sydney Allen MM Cpl 85402 32 Labour Group Labour Corps
GARNER Thomas MM Pte 2649 East Surrey Regt
GARNER Thomas Clive MM Pte 17727 6th Wiltshire Regt
GARNER Thomas Montague MM Sjt 240480 1/6th South Staffordshire Regt KIA 21.8.18.
GARNER Walter MM Bdr 81236 RFA
GARNER Walter J. MM L/Cpl 3072 1/15th London Regt
GARNER William MM Spr 44421 Royal Engineers
GARNER William H. MM Pte 16888 Shropshire Light Infantry
GARNER William J. MM+Bar Pte 16358 2nd Royal Irish Regt
GARNETT Albert Henry MM Pte 86488 237 Coy Machine Gun Corps
GARNETT Clifford MM Cpl R/11671 9th King's Royal Rifle Corps KIA 18.8.17.
GARNETT Edwin Baron MM Cpl 27519 RFA
GARNETT Ernest MM Pte 11926 7th Yorkshire Light Infantry
GARNETT Fred MM L/Cpl 556523 16th London Regt
GARNETT Frederick George MM Gnr Sig 10897 D/255 Bde RFA
GARNETT Harry MM Pte 44313 1/9th Durham Light Infantry
GARNETT Joseph J. MM Pte 39446 West Yorkshire Regt
GARNETT R.J. MM Pte 85406 Labour Corps
GARNETT Richard H. MM Sjt 32129 17th Lancashire Fusiliers
GARNETT T.H. MM Sjt 266926 West Riding Regt
GARNETT Wilfred MM Pte 3850 1st Welsh Guards
GARNETT William MM Sjt 17320 17 Fd Amb RAMC
GARNETT William MM Pte M2/152958 Army Service Corps att 494 Siege Bty RGA.
GARNETT William T. MM L/Cpl 377999 2/10th Manchester Regt
GARNHAM George MM Sjt 1069 1/17th London Regt
GARNHAM Harry MM CSM 8314 1/6th North Staffordshire Regt DOW 5.10.18
GARNHAM James W. MM L/Cpl 720292 1/24th London Regt
GARNHAM Philip MM Pte 241940 North Staffordshire Regt
GARNHAM Robert W. MM Sjt 42426 Lincolnshire Regt
GARNIER Armand MM Gnr 91295 25 Bde RFA
GARNIER Bernard D. MM Cpl 54250 Royal Engineers
GARRAHY James Thomas MM+Bar Cpl 145887 106 Fd Coy Royal Engineers
GARRARD John MM Sjt 473307 9th London Regt
GARRARD John MM Pte 12168 Coldstream Guards
GARRARD John MM Pte 12484 3rd Coldstream Guards KIA 15.9.16.
GARRARD R. MM L/Cpl 451438 Labour Corps
GARRATT Albert MM Gnr 96175 51 Bde RFA
GARRATT Arthur R. MM Pte 275839 1/6th Essex Regt
GARRATT Bernard MM Dvr 776937 A/245 Bde RFA
GARRATT Bertie MM L/Cpl 15375 9th York & Lancaster Regt KIA 7.6.17.
GARRATT Ernest Vernon MM Pte 316 23rd Royal Fusiliers
GARRATT Frederick MM Cpl 570353 1/17th London Regt
GARRATT George MM Pte 44826 5th Royal Berkshire Regt
GARRATT George Frederick MM Pte 307644 1/8th Notts & Derby Regt DOW 29.4.18.
GARRATT Harry MM Pte 10590 9th Royal Warwickshire Regt
GARRATT Herbert Bates MM Pte 242376 1/5th Leicestershire Regt
GARRATT Sidney MM+Bar L/Bdr 179611 A/15 Bde RFA
GARRATT Thomas MM Sjt 18018 D/84 Bde RFA
GARRATT Walter MM Cpl 12784 6th Oxf & Bucks Light Infantry
GARRAWAY Charles William MM Sjt 388109 2/2nd(Northumbrian)Fd Amb RAMC
GARRAWAY Ernest MM Sjt 1691 1/4th Gloucestershire Regt KIA 23.7.16.
GARRETT Alfred MM Sjt 42390 94 Bty 18 Bde RFA DOW 26.9.18.
GARRETT Arthur Cyril MM Pte 201222 1/5th Bedfordshire Regt "KIA 27.7.17,"
GARRETT C.H. MM Pte 242166 Worcestershire Regt
GARRETT C.R. MM Cpl 461344 RAMC
GARRETT E. MM Staff Nurse F QAIMNS
GARRETT Edward MM Pte 5239 Leinster Regt
GARRETT Ellis J. MM Sjt 200150 Royal Berkshire Regt
GARRETT Ernest William MM L/Cpl 25486 5th Dorsetshire Regt KIA 3.11.17.
GARRETT Frank R. MM L/Cpl 2973 Oxf & Bucks Light Infantry
GARRETT H.S. "MM,MID" Sjt 200724 1/4th Oxf & Bucks Light Infantry
GARRETT Hubert G. MM L/Cpl 391990 9th London Regt
GARRETT J.T.H. MM Pte 1756 1/18th London Regt
GARRETT James MM Sjt 17452 Welsh Regt
GARRETT Norman MM Pte 24392 13th Liverpool Regt
GARRETT Walter MM Pte 557 RAMC att 1st Hampshire Regt.KIA 4.10.17.
GARRETT William H. MM Gnr 111489 RGA
GARRICK Hugh MM L/Cpl 240787 Seaforth Highlanders
GARRIGAN Bernard MM L/Cpl 4341 2nd Royal Welsh Fusiliers
GARRIGAN Michael MM Pte 14715 6/7th Royal Scots Fusiliers
GARRINGTON William MM L/Cpl 16364 3rd Worcestershire Regt

GARRIOCH Bertram W. MM Cpl M2/152841 Army Service Corps
GARRITY Ernest George MM Sjt 540932 490 Fd Coy Royal Engineers
GARRITY John MM Cpl 3846 Liverpool Regt
GARRITY Michael MM Cpl 325224 9th Durham Light Infantry
GARRITY Patrick MM Cpl 240471 2nd Yorkshire Light Infantry
GARROD Henry MM Pte 103407 10th Notts & Derby Regt
GARROD Herbert MM Pte 14163 8th Suffolk Regt KIA 19.5.17.
GARROD Russell W. MM Pte 43663 2nd Suffolk Regt
GARROD Walter Frederick MM CSM 16354 8th Bedfordshire Regt
GARROD William George MM Sjt 321931 1/6th London Regt
GARROOD Harry J. MM Sjt 208945 74 Div Sig Coy Royal Engineers
GARRY George MM Sjt 34637 RAMC
GARRY J.W. MM Dvr 265376 RFA
GARRY Patrick MM Pte 4339 10th Lancashire Fusiliers
GARRY Thomas MM Pte 350458 Royal Scots
GARRY Thomas MM Pte 12/376 13th York & Lancaster Regt
GARSIDE Alfred B. MM Pte 202634 York & Lancaster Regt
GARSIDE Arthur MM Dvr L/34631 505 Bty 65 Bde RFA
GARSIDE Arthur MM Pte 11010 8th West Riding Regt KIA 26.4.17.
GARSIDE Charles MM Pte S/9777 Gordon Highlanders
GARSIDE Frank MM Spr 59338 Royal Engineers
GARSIDE Frederick H. MM Spr 476436 Royal Engineers
GARSIDE George F. MM Cpl 18/158 8th West Yorkshire Regt
GARSIDE Harold MM Pte 351864 9th Manchester Regt
GARSIDE Harold MM L/Sjt 14/148 14th York & Lancaster Regt
GARSIDE Harold M. MM Spr 242625 70 Fd Coy Royal Engineers
GARSIDE Joe MM Pte 23889 West Riding Regt
GARSIDE John MM+Bar Sjt 240847 West Riding Regt
GARSIDE John Herbert MM Cpl 28243 38 CCS RAMC Died 14.7.18.
GARSIDE Leonard MM Pte 39585 Yorkshire Light Infantry
GARSIDE Robert Ollerenshaw MM Cpl 106098 Royal Engineers
GARSIDE Samuel MM Pte 14018 12th Cheshire Regt
GARSTANG Reginald Thomas MM Gnr 197361 C/223 Bde RFA
GARTH John MM Sjt 19866 Scottish Rifles
GARTLAND Henry MM+Bar L/Cpl 250131 13th Durham Light Infantry KIA 5.10.18.
GARTON Alfred G.H. MM Cpl 15414 Royal Sussex Regt
GARTON James William MM L/Cpl 235319 12th Yorkshire Light Infantry
GARTON Leonard MM Sjt 200936 Notts & Derby Regt
GARTSHORE James MM Cpl 303324 Arg & Suth Highlanders
GARVEY Arthur MM Sjt 14921 10th Yorkshire Regt KIA 6.11.17.
GARVEY Charles G. MM Cpl 15946 Durham Light Infantry
GARVEY James MM Cpl 59403 40 Div Ammn Col RFA
GARVEY John Thomas MM L/Cpl 201272 2/4th South Lancashire Regt DOW 31.5.18.
GARVEY Michael MM Pte 85293 125 Coy Machine Gun Corps
GARVEY Patrick I. MM Pte H/625 8th Hussars
GARVEY Robert MM Sjt 31712 Wireless Sig Coy Royal Engineers
GARVEY Robert MM Cpl 7828 1st Scottish Rifles
GARVEY Thomas MM Spr 79792 185 Tunnelling Coy Royal Engineers
GARVEY W.G. MM Pte 8308 1st Scottish Rifles
GARVEY William MM Pte 29893 11th Manchester Regt
GARVIN A. MM Pte 12340 12th Manchester Regt
GARVIN George MM Pte 15538 10th Royal Inniskilling Fusiliers
GARVIN John MM Pte 38306 Gloucestershire Regt
GARWOOD G. MM Pte 23909 Essex Regt
GARWOOD George H. MM Sjt 11912 1st Worcestershire Regt
GARWOOD Hugh L. MM Bdr 81325 RFA
GARWOOD Sidney W. MM Pte M2/018801 Army Service Corps att RE
GASCOIGNE Alec MM Pte 116970 10th Notts & Derby Regt
GASCOIGNE Alfred G. MM L/Cpl 13910 Rifle Brigade
GASCOIGNE Frank MM L/Cpl 1846 1/6th Liverpool Regt
GASCOIGNE Jonathan MM L/Cpl 2373 Northumberland Fusiliers
GASCOIGNE W. MM L/Cpl P2535 Military Mounted Police
GASCOYNE Arthur MM Pte 14/44694 Royal Irish Rifles
GASCOYNE Joseph MM Pte 17550 York & Lancaster Regt
GASH Arthur MM Pte 250444 Durham Light Infantry
GASH William MM Pte 45600 58 Coy Machine Gun Corps
GASKARTH John "DCM,MM,MID" Sjt 56152 72 Fd Coy Royal Engineers
GASKELL George D. MM Cpl 12376 Machine Gun Corps
GASKELL John MM Sjt 8722 11th East Lancashire Regt
GASKELL John MM Pte 21397 9th Lancashire Fusiliers
GASKELL Peter MM Pte 14145 13th Liverpool Regt
GASKELL Sydney MM Sjt 8231 Lancashire Fusiliers
GASKELL Thomas MM Gnr 64873 RFA
GASKELL William MM Pte 35000 9th Manchester Regt
GASKIN Claude MM L/Cpl 16233 1st Grenadier Guards KIA 30.3.18.
GASKIN John MM Pte 8695 Royal Irish Rifles
GASKIN Leonard MM Sjt R/4407 13th King's Royal Rifle Corps
GASKING E.A. MM Pte 9461 East Kent Regt
GASKINS John William MM Bdr 66961 C/78 Bde RFA KIA 26.2.17.
GASS James C. MM Pte 235131 Northumberland Fusiliers
GASS John MM Cpl 12932 Gordon Highlanders
GASS Joseph E. "DCM,MM+Bar" Sjt 47750 25 Div Sig Coy Royal Engineers
GASS Robert Henry MM Cpl 14386 54 Fd Coy Royal Engineers
GASS Thomas MM Sjt 59599 2nd Royal Scots
GASSER Frederick MM Gnr 851190 215 Bde RFA
GASSON Arthur C. MM Bdr 65584 RFA
GASSON George B. MM Gnr 935508 RFA
GASSON Hubert MM Cpl 534044 Royal Engineers
GASSTON Francis Strong MM Sjt 323040 1/7th Durham Light Infantry
GAST George C. MM Bdr 26679 RGA
GAST James E. MM Gnr 34295 RGA
GASTALL Arthur MM Sjt 200060 16th Lancashire Fusiliers
GASTALL Harry MM Pte 34349 2nd South Lancashire Regt DOW 2.10.18.
GASTEEN Frederick E. MM Sjt 27317 1st Royal Dublin Fusiliers
GASTON Charles H. MM Pte 2664 1/5th Royal Sussex Regt
GATE Thompson MM L/Cpl 43485 Suffolk Regt
GATEHOUSE Samuel MM L/Cpl 8236 7th Yorkshire Regt
GATELEY Frederick MM L/Cpl 307160 Royal Warwickshire Regt
GATENBY John MM Spr 207572 Royal Engineers
GATENBY William A. MM Pte 2485 1/5th West Yorkshire Regt
GATER Ernest MM Spr 550292 Royal Engineers
GATER John T. MM Sjt 242360 North Staffordshire Regt
GATER Robert W. MM Cpl 935 9th Royal Fusiliers
GATES Alfred MM Pte 823 9th East Surrey Regt
GATES Arthur Cyril MM Pte 251716 3rd London Regt KIA 7.10.18.
GATES Bertram MM Cpl 45727 42nd Bn Machine Gun Corps
GATES Charles W. MM Gnr 50904 RGA
GATES Edward Daniel MM Pte 8325 2nd Coldstream Guards KIA 27.5.18.
GATES Fred MM Sjt 16972 6th Northamptonshire Regt
GATES Frederick Cuthbert MM Pte 52334 2nd Royal Fusiliers
GATES George F.W. "MM,MID" Cpl 70505 N Corps Sig Coy Royal Engineers
GATES George S. MM Sjt 10986 2nd Royal Irish Regt DOW 1.10.18.
GATES Harry MM Sjt 19441 9 Fd Amb RAMC
GATES Harry MM Gnr L/8290 152 Bde RFA
GATES James MM Dvr 39177 D/36 Bde RFA
GATES John MM Sjt 1354 15th Royal Warwickshire Regt
GATES Richard MM Dvr 52161 154 Fd Coy Royal Engineers
GATES Robert Victor "DCM,MM" CSM 97618 156 Fd Coy Royal Engineers
GATES Septimus MM Pte 8755 2nd South Lancashire Regt
GATES Sidney T. MM Cpl 55871 Machine Gun Corps
GATES Sydney F. MM L/Cpl 231739 2nd London Regt
GATES Thomas E. MM L/Cpl 326124 1/1st Cambridgeshire Regt
GATES Walter J. "DCM,MM" Cpl 71219 88 Bty 15 Bde RFA
GATES William MM Sjt 1489 1/5th Royal Sussex Regt
GATES William George MM Sjt 58350 Y/2 Med TM Bty RFA
GATES William R. "MM,MSM" 2nd Cpl 251608 X Corps Sig Coy Royal Engineers
GATES William Roberts MM Pte 318163 5th London Regt
GATHERCOLE Charles MM L/Sjt 5439 8th East Surrey Regt
GATHERN Sydney A.E. MM Sjt 7014 Gloucestershire Regt
GATHIER René MM Gnr 54462 RFA
GATLAND Arthur F. MM Bdr 16560 108 Heavy Bty RGA
GATLAND Reginald E. MM+Bar Sjt 120571 Royal Engineers
GATLEY Frank MM Pte 17624 1st Border Regt
GATLEY Fred MM L/Cpl 308099 8th Liverpool Regt
GATLIFFE Adam C. MM Sjt 2137 1/5th Cheshire Regt
GATTING Charles A. MM Sjt 370073 8th London Regt
GATWARD Albert Leslie MM Pte 29390 East Lancashire Regt
GATWARD Arthur R. MM Cpl 510103 RAMC
GATWARD Frederick James MM Cpl 1548 1/1st Cambridgeshire Regt DOW 25.4.18.
GAUCHWIN Malachy MM Pte 21151 5th South Lancashire Regt
GAUCKWIN John MM L/Cpl 17024 2/4th South Lancashire Regt DOW 29.8.18.

GAUD Edwin Henry "MC,MM(3863 Cpl)" 2Lt 2/1st HAC(Inf)
GAUDERN Albert MM Pte 17755 7th Leicestershire Regt
GAUGHRAN Christopher MM Sjt 28857 RGA
GAUGHRAN Patrick J. MM Pte 31288 Liverpool Regt
GAUKROGER J.L. MM Pte 68631 RAMC
GAUL Ernest Frank MM Cpl 16593 7th Norfolk Regt
GAULD Alexander MM Sjt 200354 Gordon Highlanders
GAULD Alexander MM Pte 241585 1/4th Gordon Highlanders KIA 25.3.18.
GAULD Charles MM Pte 301225 RAMC
GAULD James MM Pte 49450 74 Fd Amb RAMC DOW 22.10.18.
GAULD John MM Pte 265573 1/6th Gordon Highlanders
GAULT James MM Pte 10436 Irish Guards
GAULT John D. MM Pte 43697 Durham Light Infantry
GAUNT Alfred A. MM Cpl 801408 D/295 Bde RFA
GAUNT Irwin MM Pte 306810 8th West Yorkshire Regt
GAUNT James Halliday MM Gnr 167794 C/62 Bde RFA
GAUNT Ralph MM Dvr 70621 27 Bty 32 Bde RFA
GAUTON Harry MM Pte 240178 York & Lancaster Regt
GAUTON Reginald MM Sjt 112183 'A' Special Coy Royal Engineers
GAVAGHAN John MM Pte 21973 King's Own Scottish Borderers
GAVAGHAN Thomas MM Pte 16462 Machine Gun Corps
GAVIN Alexander MM Sjt 254 Royal Engineers
GAVIN Augustine J. MM Pte 41783 Lancashire Fusiliers
GAVIN Crichton S. MM Pte 10754 2/1st HAC (Inf)
GAVIN Daniel H. MM Bdr 76039 42 Bde RFA
GAVIN James MM+2 Bars Pte 9738 South Staffordshire Regt
GAVIN James G. MM Pte 84522 42nd Bn Machine Gun Corps
GAViN John MM Pte 1201 XIV Corps Cyclist Bn Army Cyclist Corps
GAVIN Robert MM Pte 27648 1/5th Highland Light Infantry
GAVIN Robert K. MM L/Cpl 203755 1/6th Gordon Highlanders
GAVIN Thomas MM Pte 7520 1st Scottish Rifles
GAVIN Thomas A. MM Pte 20 1st East Kent Regt
GAVIN Thomas G. MM Dvr 925543 280 Bde RFA
GAVIN Tim MM Pte 111044 44th(Garr) Royal Fusiliers
GAVINS Fred MM Pte 41373 8th Northumberland Fusiliers
GAVINS Jim MM Sjt 2929 2/7th West Yorkshire Regt
GAWLER George Harry MM Cpl 65169 107 Fd Coy Royal Engineers
GAWLER William J. MM L/Sjt 11074 1st South Wales Borderers
GAWN Edwin MM Pte 10161 17th Lancers
GAWTHORPE Harold MM Dvr 35619 RFA
GAWTHROP Sidney MM Pte A/200576 King's Royal Rifle Corps
GAY Alfred John Noel MM Pte 240335 1/5th Norfolk Regt
GAY Arthur J. MM Dvr 87210 RFA
GAY George Alfred MM Pte 353965 2/7th London Regt KIA 20.9.17.
GAY George F. MM L/Cpl 700141 1/23rd London Regt
GAY Henry D. MM Sjt 512515 14th London Regt
GAY Joseph MM Pte 5500 5th Royal Irish Regt
GAYLARD Frank MM Pte 6266 1st Scots Guards
GAYLARD Tom MM Pte 3778 5th Dragoon Guards
GAYLER Alec V. MM Sjt 34351 2nd Middlesex Regt
GAYLER Frank C. MM Pte 14595 8th Yorkshire Light Infantry
GAYLOR William MM Pte 200645 1/4th Essex Regt
GAYNOR James MM L/Cpl 5354 Leinster Regt
GAYNOR John James MM L/Cpl 12265 15th Royal Irish Rifles
GAYNOR W. MM Sjt 1502 West Riding Regt
GAYTER Alfred MM Cpl L/9463 Y/30 Med TM Bty RFA
GAYTON Harry Bird MM Pte 6172 7th Royal West Kent Regt DOW 18.12.17.
GAYWOOD Walter MM Pte 200543 1/5th Royal Warwickshire Regt
GAZE Harry S. MM L/Cpl S/199 13th Rifle Brigade
GAZE John William MM Sjt 11785 8th Leicestershire Regt
GAZE Thomas H. MM+Bar Sjt 427930 57 Div Sig Coy Royal Engineers
GAZELEY George MM Sjt 8081 1st Bedfordshire Regt
GEACH William Arthur MM Cpl 15203 8th Somerset Light Infantry KIA 28.4.17.
GEAIRNS Alex J.E. MM L/Sjt 403576 RAMC
GEALE Henry MM Pte 931 11th Middlesex Regt
GEALER Sidney John MM L/Cpl 57320 Machine Gun Corps
GEAR Arthur MM Pte 9475 1st East Yorkshire Regt KIA 9.4.17.
GEAR Harold J. MM Pte 21113 Machine Gun Corps
GEAR Henry MM L/Cpl 49469 19th Lancashire Fusiliers DOW 6.11.18.
GEARD Samuel MM Cpl 10270 2nd Leinster Regt
GEARING Arthur J. MM Sjt 265663 7th Royal West Kent Regt
GEARING Charles W. MM Pte 10818 2/1st HAC (Inf)
GEARING David J. MM Pte 33749 Royal Berkshire Regt
GEARLE HenryC. MM Sjt 1854 1/4th London Regt

GEARON Daniel J. MM Cpl 31549 RFA
GEARY Edward G. MM Spr 71698 Royal Engineers
GEARY Frederick H. MM Spr 44590 Signal Service Royal Engineers
GEARY Herbert John MM Cpl 21116 Machine Gun Corps
GEARY John MM Pte 26/919 Northumberland Fusiliers
GEARY Joseph MM Cpl 238009 6th Yorkshire Light Infantry
GEARY Oliver MM Pte C/729 16th King's Royal Rifle Corps
GEARY Richard J. "DCM,MM" Sjt 11089 1st South Wales Borderers
GEARY W. MM Pte 6221 12th Middlesex Regt
GEARY Wilfred MM Pte 28121 8th East Surrey Regt
GEARY William MM L/Cpl 15227 8th Yorkshire Light Infantry
GEAUGHEN Daniel MM Pte S/7636 2nd Arg & Suth Highlanders
GEBBETT Andrew MM Dvr 46474 282 Bde RFA Died 25.9.17.
GEBBETT Frederick Graham MM L/Cpl 71175 2nd Bn Machine Gun Corps
GEBBIE John MM Cpl S/2155 7th Seaforth Highlanders KIA 12.10.17.
GECHIE George G. MM Sjt 12819 Seaforth Highlanders
GEDDES David MM L/Cpl 267335 Seaforth Highlanders
GEDDES James MM Sjt 64193 3rd Bn Machine Gun Corps
GEDDES James MM L/Cpl 17646 1st Scottish Rifles
GEDDES John William MM Sjt L/12481 V/34 Hy TM Bty RFA KIA 12.12.16.
GEDDES Robert MM Pte 30272 1st King's Own Scottish Borderers DOW 23.10.18.
GEDDES Robert MM L/Cpl 17577 1st Royal Dublin Fusiliers
GEDDES William MM Pte 32430 16th Highland Light Infantry
GEDDES William F. MM L/Cpl 40095 Royal Scots
GEDEN Arthur MM Pte 12164 6th Oxf & Bucks Light Infantry
GEDGE Arthur W. MM Cpl 43734 2nd Suffolk Regt
GEDNEY George MM Pte 18745 8th Lincolnshire Regt
GEDNEY Hubert Chaston MM Sjt 15142 9th Suffolk Regt Died 26.3.18.
GEDNEY James MM Sjt 15121 45 Bde RFA
GEE A.W. MM Cpl G/14608 7th East Kent Regt
GEE A.W. MM Cpl 88166 Royal Flying Corps
GEE Albert Edward MM Sjt 776117 RFA
GEE Arnold MM Gnr 775984 B/245 Bde RFA
GEE Arthur MM Pte M2/116744 50 Div Train Army Service Corps
GEE Charles MM Pte 28404 9th Cheshire Regt
GEE Charles MM+Bar Cpl 700337 RFA
GEE Fred MM L/Cpl 11674 9th Cheshire Regt
GEE Harold MM Sjt 47304 A/178 Bde RFA
GEE Harry MM Pte 22571 9th Notts & Derby Regt
GEE Henry MM Pte 15661 Coldstream Guards
GEE John MM L/Cpl 40208 1st Royal Dublin Fusiliers
GEE John B. MM Pte 17120 1st King's Own Scottish Borderers
GEE John Henry MM Cpl 8037 12th Lancashire Fusiliers KIA 14.9.16.
GEE Oliver Francis MM Gnr 71144 272 Siege Bty RGA
GEE Robert MM Pte 39849 77 Fd Amb RAMC
GEE Walter T. MM Bdr 36673 RFA
GEE William MM Pte 15018 Cheshire Regt
GEE William MM Pte 7099 1st Leicestershire Regt
GEE William MM+Bar Cpl 29528 1st Royal West Surrey Regt
GEE William MM Sjt T/33648 7 Div Train Army Service Corps
GEEHAN John "DCM,MM" Pte 83 5th Connaught Rangers
GEEN William MM Spr 146554 250 Tunnelling Coy Royal Engineers
GEER Stanley W. MM Pte 554578 16th London Regt
GEERE Henry T. MM Cpl 45720 Royal Engineers
GEEVES Herbert MM Pte 27584 Notts & Derby Regt
GEEVES William MM Pte 21059 12th Lancashire Fusiliers
GEGG Cecil G. MM Gnr 107735 RGA
GEGG Ivan Frederick MM Pte 241682 5th Gloucestershire Regt
GEGGIE Robert MM Pte 38954 9th Yorkshire Regt
GELDARD Charles W. MM Sjt 27733 C/50 Bde RFA
GELDARD William MM Sjt 119915 230 Siege Bty RGA
GELDERT Sidney MM Pte 12/111 5th York & Lancaster Regt
GELDERT Thomas William MM Pte 260356 1st Border Regt KIA 22.10.18.
GELL Francis Cyril MM Sjt 1661 Notts & Derby Regt
GELL John Thomas MM Pte 12474 Yorkshire Regt
GELLATLY Edward P. MM Pte 60691 Machine Gun Corps
GELLATLY George MM Sjt 315010 13th Royal Highlanders
GELLATLY Thomas B. MM Pte 22837 Seaforth Highlanders
GELLER Henry MM Pte R/19027 King's Royal Rifle Corps
GELLEY William MM Pte 203442 West Yorkshire Regt
GELLING James MM L/Cpl 18411 11th East Lancashire Regt KIA 18.10.18.

GELLING John Stephen MM L/Cpl 69882 138 Army Troops Coy Royal Engineers
GELLING William E. MM L/Cpl 250086 F Corps Sig Coy Royal Engineers
GELLING William Henry MM Pte 260155 8th Border Regt
GELSON John R. MM Pte 201252 15th Durham Light Infantry
GEMMELL Andrew MM Pte S/22115 1st Cameron Highlanders
GEMMELL D. MM Cpl 125116 Yeomanry
GEMMELL George MM+Bar Cpl 10852 6th Border Regt
GEMMELL Hugh MM Pte 252388 1/6th Arg & Suth Highlanders
GEMMELL James MM Pte 14113 Seaforth Highlanders
GEMMELL James B. MM Sjt 316469 47 Fd Amb RAMC
GEMMELL Norman Lewthwaite MM Pte 36365 10th East Yorkshire Regt
GEMMELL Peter Scott MM Gnr 804 11 Bty MGC(Motors) KIA 29.9.18.
GEMMELL Robert MM Pte 285390 Seaforth Highlanders
GEMMELL Thomas MM Pte 266165 Scottish Rifles
GEMMILL John MM Spr 248192 Royal Engineers
GENNIS James R. MM Sjt 139168 Royal Engineers
GENSAVAGE Matthew MM Spr 482034 Royal Engineers
GENT Benjamin MM Sjt 112774 Royal Engineers
GENT Charles MM Pte 184 1/4th North Lancashire Regt
GENT F.W. MM L/Cpl P5050 Military Foot Police
GENT Frank MM Pte 2504 15th Hussars
GENT Frederick MM Pte 4948 1/4th North Lancashire Regt KIA 28.6.16.
GENT Frederick G. MM L/Sjt 181 Royal Fusiliers
GENT George MM Pte 21188 Northumberland Fusiliers
GENT Harry MM Pte 47312 Northumberland Fusiliers
GENT John E. MM Pte 87497 13th Liverpool Regt
GENT Robert "DCM,MM" Sjt 9322 1st Dorsetshire Regt
GENTLE Alfred E. MM Cpl 85154 Royal Engineers
GENTLE Edwin MM Cpl 30014 RGA
GENTLE Frederick MM Sjt 68352 180 Siege Bty RGA
GENTLE John E. MM Pte 290253 Royal Welsh Fusiliers
GENTLE Oliver MM Cpl R/13923 King's Royal Rifle Corps
GENTLE Oswald MM Sjt 10190 1st Bn Bedfordshire Regt KIA 4.10.17.
GENTLE William MM L/Cpl 13200 RAMC att 11 Fd Coy RE.KIA 14.4.18.
GENTLEMAN James W. MM+Bar Sjt 266954 6th Seaforth Highlanders
GENTRY Alfred MM Bdr 59025 RFA
GENTRY Edwin Q. MM Spr 2023 Royal Engineers
GENTRY Frederick MM Pte R/4535 13th King's Royal Rifle Corps KIA 28.4.18.
GENTRY George James MM Pte 1418 11 Fd Amb RAMC DOW 20.5.18.
GENTRY John W. MM Bdr 152052 RFA
GENTRY Percy MM Pte 12400 9th Essex Regt
GENTRY Wesney MM Pte 42285 2nd Lincolnshire Regt
GENTRY William G. MM Sjt 12087 5th Northamptonshire Regt
GEOGHEGAN William MM Gnr 88469 RFA
GEORGE Albert Jacob MM Pte 17644 6 Royal Berkshire Regt KIA 12.10.17.
GEORGE Albert Laurence Cyril "MM,MMV(It)" Sjt 70045 27 Bde RFA
GEORGE Alexander MM Pte 81630 RAMC
GEORGE Alexander MM+Bar Sjt 30454 1/7th Gordon Highlanders
GEORGE Alexander MM Pte 608573 18th London Regt
GEORGE Alfred W. MM Gnr Sig 178448 D/255 Bde RFA
GEORGE Amos MM L/Cpl 268519 1/7th Royal Warwickshire Regt
GEORGE Arthur Henry MM Cpl 5058 1/10th Liverpool Regt KIA 22.11.16.
GEORGE Bartholomew MM Gnr 34124 RFA
GEORGE Cecil N. MM Pte 8016 Highland Light Infantry
GEORGE Clifford Henry MM Gnr 152794 200 Siege Bty RGA
GEORGE David A. MM L/Cpl M2/098119 Army Service Corps
GEORGE David Victor MM Pte 81G/ 10th Royal West Surrey Regt KIA 7.6.17.
GEORGE Edgar MM Sjt 242061 Worcestershire Regt
GEORGE Edward MM L/Cpl 10209 6th Somerset Light Infantry KIA 18.8.16.
GEORGE Enos J. "MM,MID" CSM 11747 6th Oxf & Bucks Light Infantry
GEORGE Ezekiel R. MM Pte 103061 Machine Gun Corps
GEORGE Francis MM Sjt G1146 7th East Kent Regt
GEORGE Frederick Henry MM Sjt 60856 Machine Gun Corps
GEORGE George MM Pte 13331 Northamptonshire Regt
GEORGE Gordon MM Sjt 9633 1st Lincolnshire Regt
GEORGE Harry MM Pte 435096 56 Fd Amb RAMC
GEORGE Henry MM Bdr 19127 RFA
GEORGE Henry Peat MM Bdr 760098 C/155 Bde RFA KIA 29.8.18.
GEORGE Herbert MM Pte M2/120030 Army Service Corps
GEORGE Herbert Frederick MM CQMS 200187 1st London Regt
GEORGE J. MM Pte 15047 Border Regt
GEORGE J.C. MM Pte 23005 Worcestershire Regt
GEORGE John MM Cpl 5226 3rd Rifle Brigade
GEORGE John MM Pte 25419 12th East Surrey Regt KIA 25.3.18.
GEORGE John Ieuan MM Sjt 34526 11th East Lancashire Regt KIA 14.7.18.
GEORGE Joseph C. MM Cpl 019329 Army Ordnance Corps
GEORGE Leonard MM Pte 48113 20th Northumberland Fusiliers
GEORGE Louis Kocher "MM,MSM" Sjt 103661 D/86 Bde RFA
GEORGE Nathaniel MM Pte 18348 10th Yorkshire Regt KIA 11.4.17.
GEORGE Oliver J. MM Cpl 242660 12th East Surrey Regt
GEORGE Richard MM Pte 41119 Manchester Regt
GEORGE Robert MM Pte 275103 1/7th Arg & Suth Highlanders KIA 12.10.18
GEORGE Thomas MM Sig 608052 20 Bde RHA
GEORGE Thomas MM Sjt 56598 9 Div Sig Coy Royal Engineers
GEORGE Walter MM Sjt 235543 1st Leicestershire Regt KIA 23.10.18.
GEORGE Walter R. MM Pte 681977 22nd London Regt
GEORGE Wilfred E. "MM,MSM" S/Sjt 266 20 Fd Amb RAMC
GEORGE William "MM,MID" CSM 5325 21st Bn Machine Gun Corps
GEORGE William MM Sjt 51178 86 Coy Labour Corps
GEORGE William MM Sjt 11204 4th King's Royal Rifle Corps Died 27.11.16.
GEORGE William MM Pte 41328 RAMC
GEORGE William MM Pte 8/25650 South Wales Borderers
GEORGE William MM Pte 6656 Machine Gun Corps
GEORGE William E. MM Pte 147092 3rd Bn Machine Gun Corps
GEORGE William H. MM Spr 74867 Royal Engineers
GEORGE William Isaac MM Bdr 837 D/121 Bde RFA
GERAGHTY Michael MM Pte 129728 18th Bn Machine Gun Corps
GERAGHTY Patrick MM Pte 7361 RAMC
GERAGHTY Thomas MM Cpl 68193 RAMC
GERARD Clyde Robertson MM Bdr 79506 D/282 Bde RFA DOW 2.8.17.
GERARD Joseph William MM Bdr 7637 18 Div Ammn Col RFA
GERARD W. MM Cpl S/8520 Gordon Highlanders
GERAUGHTY John MM Pte 5198 Northumberland Fusiliers
GERDES Edwin A. MM+Bar Pte 25004 Durham Light Infantry
GERHARDI Victor MM Pte 20589 1 Special Coy Middlesex Regt
GERITY John "MM,MM(F)" Sjt 6960 1st North Staffordshire Regt
GERITY William MM L/Cpl 13761 2nd Scots Guards
GERMAN Frederick J. MM Pte 202820 Essex Regt
GERMAN John MM L/Cpl 241633 5th North Lancashire Regt
GERMAN Joseph MM Gnr 1829 1 Motorised Bde 11 Bty MGC(Motors)
GERMANEY Percy MM Gnr 152639 C/50 Bde RFA
GERMANEY William Thomas MM Cpl 75930 137 Fd Amb RAMC
GERRARD Christopher MM Pte 85697 166 Coy Machine Gun Corps
GERRARD Frederick B. MM L/Bdr 149519 RFA
GERRARD George MM L/Sjt 242198 1/5th Gordon Highlanders
GERRARD Henry MM L/Cpl 14823 12th Liverpool Regt
GERRARD Henry MM L/Bdr 76856 RGA
GERRARD J. MM Pte 341646 RAMC
GERRARD James "DCM,MM" Pte 12177 9th Cheshire Regt
GERRARD James A. MM Sjt 65676 10th Lancashire Fusiliers
GERRARD Oliver Charles MM L/Sjt 2561 2nd Rifle Brigade KIA 23.10.17.
GERRARD Thomas MM+Bar Sjt 280262 1/7th Lancashire Fusiliers
GERRARD William MM Spr 79833 Royal Engineers
GERRIE Robert MM L/Cpl 12402 Gordon Highlanders
GERRISH Henry Q. MM Pte S/1064 Royal Fusiliers
GERRISH Walter H. MM Pte 225812 1st London Regt
GERRISH William MM Bdr 32580 RGA
GERRY Arthur R. MM Gnr 137388 266 Siege Bty RGA
GERRY S. MM Pte 54174 12th Durham Light Infantry
GERRY Thomas MM L/Cpl A/203505 1st King's Royal Rifle Corps
GESSEY Frank MM L/Cpl 392990 1/9th London Regt
GETGOOD Thomas MM Sjt 9/18996 Royal Irish Rifles
GETHING David A. MM Pte 32779 2nd South Lancashire Regt
GETHING Henry MM Dvr 971160 C/189 Bde RFA

GETHING John Thomas MM Pte 34033 1/1st Bucks Bn Oxf & Bucks Light Infantry
GETHING Samuel MM Pte 14729 Machine Gun Corps
GETHING William H. MM Gnr 198962 B/312 Bde RFA
GETHINS Peter "DCM,MM+Bar" Pte 3158 1/4th Royal Highlanders
GETTINGS John W. MM L/Cpl 24/330 Northumberland Fusiliers
GETTINGS Robert MM Pte 388397 2(Northumbrian)Fd Amb RAMC
GETTY Andrew Semple MM Pte 357758 2/10th Liverpool Regt
GETWOOD William MM Pte 316357 2 Fd Amb RAMC
GEYELIN Sidney MM Sjt 201131 F(AA)Bty RGA
GEYER Ernest W. MM Pte S/13038 6th Cameron Highlanders
GHILONI Ralph MM Pte 301682 Durham Light Infantry
GIBB Alexander MM Cpl 200767 1/4th King's Own Scottish Borderers
GIBB Andrew C. MM Pte 50894 MGC(Cavalry)
GIBB Cecil Harry MM S/Sjt 538 RAMC
GIBB David MM Sjt M2/201029 Y Siege Park Army Service Corps
GIBB David MM Spr 71928 Royal Engineers
GIBB Francis MM Pte 200660 1/4th Gordon Highlanders
GIBB G. MM Pte 21180 Leicestershire Regt
GIBB George W. MM Cpl 81111 Royal Engineers
GIBB J.A. MM Sjt 147671 A/291 Bde RFA
GIBB John MM Gnr 7020 D/75 Bde RFA
GIBB John MM Pte 12719 2nd Scottish Rifles
GIBB Joseph MM Sjt 240046 Royal Highlanders
GIBB Robert M. MM Gnr 110727 1 Hy Bty RGA
GIBB Thomas MM Pte 7125 West Riding Regt
GIBB William MM Sjt 14896 12th Royal Scots
GIBB William D. MM S/Sjt 980 RAMC
GIBBARD Robert MM Pte 242804 Royal West Surrey Regt
GIBBENS Arthur B. MM+Bar Pte 40132 6th Royal West Surrey Regt
GIBBENS Edward MM Pte 7661 Royal West Surrey Regt
GIBBENS Ernest MM Pte 22398 Hampshire Regt
GIBBENS Walter MM+Bar Sjt 37338 29 Bde RFA
GIBBENS William MM Sjt 1922 13th Middlesex Regt
GIBBERD Edward MM Gnr 39347 RFA
GIBBIN John MM Sjt 11305 6th South Wales Borderers
GIBBINGS James William Charles MM Pte 17682 1st Somerset Light Infantry
GIBBINS Charles Henry MM Sjt 720286 2/24th London Regt Died 8.12.17.
GIBBINS Ernest MM Pte 11077 1st Royal West Kent Regt DOW 11.4.17.
GIBBINS Frederick William MM Pte 7/4112 7th Royal Irish Rifles
GIBBINS G. MM Pte 22182 Northumberland Fusiliers
GIBBINS John MM Cpl 19532 RFA
GIBBINS Mellis Joseph William MM Sjt 43424 79 Fd Coy Royal Engineers KIA 21.3.18.
GIBBINS Thomas MM Gnr 765378 RFA
GIBBINS Thomas MM L/Cpl 11349 6th South Lancashire Regt
GIBBINS Valentine G. MM Dvr 27812 RFA
GIBBLING Charles E. MM Cpl 1413 1/12th London Regt
GIBBON Albert Jacob MM Sjt 14081 14th Hampshire Regt KIA 9.10.16.
GIBBON George William MM Sjt 250051 1/6th Manchester Regt
GIBBON Henry C. MM Pte 348122 6th London Regt
GIBBON John D. "DCM,MM" Sjt 240679 1/5th & 4/5th Welsh Regt
GIBBON John S. MM Bdr 81473 RFA
GIBBON Richard "DCM,MM" Pte 24307 24/27th & 8th Northumberland Fusiliers
GIBBON Robert MM Dvr 760403 RFA
GIBBON Robert "DCM,MM" Cpl 155753 182 Tunnelling Coy Royal Engineers
GIBBONS Albert MM Pte 12986 6th Northamptonshire Regt
GIBBONS Albert E. MM L/Cpl 10231 6th Lincolnshire Regt
GIBBONS Albert John MM Dvr 87198 A/64 Bde RFA
GIBBONS Alfred MM Pte 3/8423 1st West Yorkshire Regt KIA 24.9.17.
GIBBONS Arthur MM L/Cpl 19192 Machine Gun Corps
GIBBONS Arthur MM Cpl 291833 2/10th Middlesex Regt
GIBBONS Arthur E. MM Pte 201698 1st London Regt
GIBBONS Charles G. MM Dvr 53383 RFA
GIBBONS Charles Samuel MM Pte 8335 12th Royal Scots Fusiliers KIA 24.7.18.
GIBBONS Edward MM Pte 10824 2nd Durham Light Infantry
GIBBONS Edward MM Pte 17897 10th Cheshire Regt
GIBBONS Frederick MM Pte DM2/189663 Army Service Corps
GIBBONS Frederick J. MM Pte 62116 RAMC
GIBBONS George MM Pte 94298 RAMC
GIBBONS Herbert George MM Pte 46974 Machine Gun Corps
GIBBONS Herbert S. MM Dvr 42127 RFA
GIBBONS Isaac MM Pnr 289086 18 Div Sig Coy Royal Engineers
GIBBONS Jack MM L/Bdr 78278 RFA
GIBBONS John MM Gnr 19713 RGA
GIBBONS John S. "MM,MID" Cpl 960318 RFA
GIBBONS Joseph Harold "MM,CG(F)" Pte 10474 11th Essex Regt
GIBBONS Ralph A. MM Spr 253126 Royal Engineers
GIBBONS Sidney MM Cpl 590183 1/18th London Regt
GIBBONS Sidney Richard MM Cpl 30667 4th South Staffordshire Regt
GIBBONS Thomas MM Pte 53593 8th Middlesex Regt
GIBBONS Thomas MM Pte 9448 Durham Light Infantry
GIBBONS Timothy MM Sjt 13360 8th Norfolk Regt KIA 19.7.16.
GIBBONS Walter MM Pte 35560 2/4th York & Lancaster Regt
GIBBONS William E. MM Sjt 630440 1/20th London Regt
GIBBS A. MM L/Sjt 201887 1st East Surrey Regt
GIBBS Albert MM Spr 63108 Royal Engineers
GIBBS Albert MM Sjt 7527 2nd South Staffordshire Regt
GIBBS Albert MM Dvr T3/024013 Army Service Corps
GIBBS Albert Henry MM Dvr A/1021 7th King's Royal Rifle Corps DOW 29.4.17.
GIBBS Alfred MM Pte 43553 9th Essex Regt KIA 4.4.18.
GIBBS Alfred MM Pte 13394 Lancashire Fusiliers
GIBBS Arthur E.E. MM Bdr 36832 RFA
GIBBS Bernard Stanley MM Pte 345160 16th Devonshire Regt "KIA 3.12.17,"
GIBBS Bertie MM Pte 7274 Coldstream Guards
GIBBS C. MM Pte S/1308 Rifle Brigade
GIBBS Cecil Horace MM L/Cpl 28616 10th Essex Regt
GIBBS Charles MM Cpl 84816 Royal Engineers
GIBBS Charles C. MM Pte 2561 1/1st Warwickshire Yeomanry
GIBBS Charles Edward MM L/Cpl 22838 1st Border Regt KIA 19.5.17.
GIBBS Charles J. MM Cpl 281965 4th London Regt
GIBBS Charles R. MM Pte 30183 RAMC
GIBBS David MM L/Cpl 15751 R Cable Section Royal Engineers
GIBBS Edward A.J. MM Pte 13455 Royal West Surrey Regt
GIBBS Ernest George MM Sjt 32 1st Welsh Guards DOW 30.6.16.
GIBBS Francis Edgar MM Pte 2302 23rd Middlesex Regt KIA 25.6.17.
GIBBS Frank MM 2nd Cpl 30479 226 Fd Coy Royal Engineers
GIBBS Frank MM Sjt 83474 RFA
GIBBS Frank E. MM Sjt 16772 Machine Gun Corps
GIBBS Frederick MM Sjt 33654 C/187 Bde RFA
GIBBS Frederick J. MM L/Cpl 22237 7th Wiltshire Regt
GIBBS George MM+Bar Sjt 6235 1st South Wales Borderers
GIBBS George MM Cpl 10070 5th Wiltshire Regt
GIBBS George MM Sjt 8759 1/5th South Staffordshire Regt
GIBBS George A. MM L/Cpl 21170 2nd Grenadier Guards
GIBBS George Walter MM Pte 1885 12th Royal Sussex Regt
GIBBS George William MM Gnr 925976 Y/56 Med TM Bty RFA
GIBBS Gerald George Albert MM Spr 207840 63 Div Royal Engineers
GIBBS Henry MM Sjt 534036 RAMC
GIBBS Henry J.S. MM Pte 35496 RAMC
GIBBS James R. MM Dvr 44047 Royal Engineers
GIBBS John MM Cpl 48561 13th Royal Inniskilling Fusiliers
GIBBS Joseph MM Pte 12786 1 Special Coy King's Royal Rifle Corps
GIBBS Joseph "DCM,MM,MMV(It)" Pte 364 8th York & Lancaster Regt
GIBBS Leonard MM Bdr 26386 4 Siege Bty RGA
GIBBS Norman H. MM Bdr 118868 354 Siege Bty RGA
GIBBS Owen Arthur MM Cpl 49274 17 Div Sig Coy Royal Engineers KIA 19.11.17.
GIBBS Robert MM Pte 200211 Gloucestershire Regt
GIBBS Rupert J. MM Pte 2313 9th East Surrey Regt
GIBBS Russell A. MM Pte 32315 30 Fd Amb RAMC
GIBBS Stanley MM Gnr 87553 D/64 Bde RFA KIA 5.8.17.
GIBBS Thomas MM L/Cpl 5449 Leinster Regt
GIBBS Thomas MM Gnr 6932 25 Bde RFA
GIBBS Thomas H. MM Dvr 496732 Royal Engineers
GIBBS Thomas M. MM L/Cpl 371397 8th London Regt
GIBBS Tom MM Pte 2144 1st Welsh Guards DOW 28.3.18.
GIBBS Walter B. MM L/Cpl 21178 47th Bn Machine Gun Corps
GIBBS Walter D. MM Sjt 5268 6 Div Sig Coy Royal Engineers
GIBBS WalterJ. MM CQMS 250013 3rd London Regt
GIBBS William MM Sjt 127482 5 Fd Svy Bn Royal Engineers
GIBBS William MM Pte 202639 2/5th West Riding Regt KIA 27.11.17.

GIBBS William F. MM+Bar Pte 15328 2nd Hampshire Regt
GIBBS William Thomas MM Cpl 83971 403 Bty RFA KIA 27.10.18.
GIBLETT Thomas H. "DCM,MM" Sjt 249524 41 Div Sig Coy Royal Engineers
GIBLIN Albert MM Cpl 2163 Manchester Regt
GIBLIN Stephen MM Cpl 32030 14th Northumberland Fusiliers
GIBNEY Robert C. MM Cpl 60738 1st Middlesex Regt
GIBSON A. MM Pte B/201647 Rifle Brigade
GIBSON Adam MM Pte S/3837 8th Royal Highlanders
GIBSON Albert E. MM Cpl 250306 Royal Engineers
GIBSON Alexander MM Bdr 620392 B/223 Bde RFA
GIBSON Alexander MM Pte 70952 165 Coy Machine Gun Corps
GIBSON Alfred MM Sjt 528054 14th London Regt
GIBSON Andrew MM Pte 5344 Highland Light Infantry
GIBSON Andrew D. MM Pte 42692 5/6th Scottish Rifles
GIBSON Arthur MM Sjt 6/416 10th King's Royal Rifle Corps KIA 2.12.17.
GIBSON Arthur MM Cpl 43544 96 Fd Coy Royal Engineers
GIBSON Arthur MM L/Cpl 5509 13th Royal Sussex Regt DOW 4.8.17.
GIBSON Bertram W. MM L/Cpl 67761 62nd Bn Machine Gun Corps
GIBSON C. MM Bdr 549 RFA
GIBSON Cecil Herbert MM 2nd Cpl 50957 83 Fd Coy Royal Engineers
GIBSON Charles Edmund MM Cpl 27674 C/186 Bde RFA DOW 26.9.17.
GIBSON Charles T. MM Sjt M2/104574 Army Service Corps
GIBSON Douglas W. MM Spr 139850 Royal Engineers
GIBSON Edward MM Pte 17370 8th East Lancashire Regt
GIBSON Edwin R. MM L/Cpl 6339 4th Middlesex Regt
GIBSON Ernest MM Sjt 156307 Royal Engineers
GIBSON Ernest George MM Cpl 43669 13th Royal Irish Rifles KIA 11.4.18.
GIBSON Fred Harold MM Pte 37341 20th Northumberland Fusiliers "KIA 9.4.17,"
GIBSON Frederick Thomas MM Cpl 42580 73 Fd Coy Royal Engineers KIA 25.6.17.
GIBSON Frederick W. MM L/Cpl 2822 1/18th London Regt
GIBSON Gavin MM L/Cpl 412632 409 Fd Coy Royal Engineers
GIBSON George MM Pte 303320 Arg & Suth Highlanders
GIBSON George "DCM,MM,CG(F)" Cpl 16531 1st Royal Dublin Fusiliers
GIBSON George Leonard MM Dvr 1615 14 Bde RFA
GIBSON George Victor MM Spr 48526 89 Fd Coy Royal Engineers
GIBSON George W. MM L/Cpl 16653 1st Grenadier Guards
GIBSON Harold MM Spr 82344 350 Elect & Mech Coy Royal Engineers
GIBSON Harold G. MM Sjt 488366 469 Fd Coy Royal Engineers
GIBSON Harry MM Sjt 76289 255 Siege Bty RGA
GIBSON Harry MM+Bar Pte 266321 8th West Yorkshire Regt
GIBSON Herbert MM Pte 1614 1/1st(Northumbrian)Fd Amb RAMC
GIBSON Herbert A. MM L/Cpl G/7307 24th Royal Fusiliers
GIBSON Hugh MM Gnr 51516 35 Bde RFA
GIBSON James MM Pte 94 2nd Royal Highlanders DOW 19.11.18.
GIBSON James MM Cpl 240943 Gordon Highlanders
GIBSON James MM 2nd Cpl 57984 36 Div Sig Coy Royal Engineers
GIBSON James MM+Bar Sjt 497261 2/3rd(Wessex)Fd Amb RAMC
GIBSON James MM Cpl R/12890 16th King's Royal Rifle Corps KIA 2.12.17.
GIBSON James Arthur Frederick MM Pte 6440 1st Royal Warwickshire Regt
GIBSON James M. MM Pte 2109 Royal Highlanders
GIBSON John MM Pte 30330 16th Highland Light Infantry
GIBSON John MM Dvr 135009 505 Bty 65 Bde RFA
GIBSON John MM Dvr 17406 5 Bty 45 Bde RFA
GIBSON John MM Pte 132155 Machine Gun Corps
GIBSON John MM Sjt 49936 RFA
GIBSON John MM CSM 16/521 Royal Irish Rifles
GIBSON John MM Pte S/13001 Arg & Suth Highlanders
GIBSON John MM Gnr 640198 RFA
GIBSON John MM Pte 34787 York & Lancaster Regt
GIBSON John E. MM Dvr 457199 Royal Engineers
GIBSON John M. MM Cpl 9479 Royal Engineers
GIBSON Joseph P. MM Pte S/15857 14th Arg & Suth Highlanders
GIBSON Leonard G. MM L/Cpl 80169 Royal Engineers
GIBSON Leslie Albert George MM Pte 29100 8th Somerset Light Infantry KIA 18.9.18.
GIBSON Margaret Annabella Campbell MM Unit Administrator F QMWAAC
GIBSON Noel MM Spr 63573 Royal Engineers
GIBSON Percy Montague "MC,MM(3756 L/Cpl)" 2Lt Middlesex Regt DOW 6.9.18.
GIBSON Richard MM Pte 100653 72 Fd Amb RAMC
GIBSON Robert MM L/Cpl 44810 7th Lincolnshire Regt
GIBSON Robert MM L/Cpl 3206 8th Royal Highlanders
GIBSON Robert MM Pte E/11962 2nd Royal Fusiliers
GIBSON Robert MM Pte 13994 Yorkshire Regt
GIBSON Robert C. MM Pte 14415 2nd Hampshire Regt
GIBSON Robert Henry MM Sjt 503 1st Royal Warwickshire Regt KIA 11.5.18.
GIBSON Samuel MM Dvr 46511 B/104 Bde RFA
GIBSON Samuel MM Pte 42219 4th Yorkshire Light Infantry
GIBSON Samuel MM Pte 106031 Machine Gun Corps
GIBSON Samuel O. MM Pte 241230 Seaforth Highlanders
GIBSON Stephen MM Pte 23/849 Northumberland Fusiliers
GIBSON Stephen MM Pte 276 18th Durham Light Infantry
GIBSON Thomas MM Sjt 352132 Durham Light Infantry
GIBSON Thomas MM Pte 56042 Notts & Derby Regt
GIBSON Thomas MM Pte S/6767 Rifle Brigade
GIBSON Thomas MM Sjt 4483 18th Highland Light Infantry
GIBSON Thomas "MM,MSM" Sjt 8123 A/152 Bde RFA
GIBSON Thomas H. MM Pte 78920 RAMC
GIBSON W. MM Cpl 31334 2nd Essex Regt
GIBSON W. MM Cpl 116 RFA
GIBSON W.I. MM Spr 139315 171 Tunnelling Coy Royal Engineers
GIBSON Walter B. MM+Bar Spr 406100 Royal Engineers
GIBSON Walter Clement MM Pte M2/080208 Army Service Corps
GIBSON Walter John MM L/Cpl 49749 24th Royal Fusiliers Died 7.5.17.
GIBSON William MM Cpl 4021 2nd Manchester Regt
GIBSON William MM Cpl 295157 12th Royal Scots Fusiliers
GIBSON William "MM,MID" Cpl S/3072 Gordon Highlanders
GIBSON William MM Cpl 292678 781 Coy Labour Corps
GIBSON William MM Spr 323927 Royal Engineers
GIBSON William MM Sjt 20049 Northumberland Fusiliers
GIBSON William MM+Bar Spr 64549 19 Light Railway(Train Crew)Coy Royal Engineers
GIBSON William MM Sjt 665 Durham Light Infantry
GIBSON William MM Sjt 5683 1st Scots Guards
GIBSON William E. MM Pte 46376 1st Rifle Brigade
GIBSON William E. MM Sjt 13768 10th West Riding Regt
GIBSON William Henry MM+Bar Gnr 89885 250 Siege Bty RGA
GIBSON William J. MM+Bar Sjt 14425 13th Royal Fusiliers
GIBSON William J. MM Gnr 68388 RHA
GIBSON William J. MM+Bar L/Cpl 45404 108 Fd Amb RAMC
GIBSON William R. MM Sjt 307230 15th Bn Tank Corps
GIDDINGS C. MM Bdr 12650 RFA
GIDDINGS Charles MM Pte 4327 Royal Fusiliers
GIDDINGS Frank MM Sjt 12872 2nd Royal Berkshire Regt KIA 2.12.17.
GIDDINGS Fred E. MM Sjt 99834 149 Siege Bty RGA
GIDDINGS George MM L/Cpl 631687 20th London Regt
GIDDINGS Harold Fred MM L/Cpl 7597 2nd Wiltshire Regt KIA 5.11.18.
GIDDINGS Henry MM Pte 13260 10th Gloucestershire Regt
GIDDINGS Horace J. MM Pte 4021 Royal West Surrey Regt
GIDDINGS Richard MM L/Cpl 39062 7th Royal West Surrey Regt
GIDDINGS Robert MM L/Cpl 306839 Royal Warwickshire Regt
GIDDINGS William MM Sjt 6549 4th Middlesex Regt
GIDDINGS William MM Pte 40264 2nd Lincolnshire Regt KIA 22.3.18.
GIDLEY W. MM T/Sjt R/1011 Army Veterinary Corps
GIDMAN William MM L/Cpl 20554 15th Welsh Regt
GIFF Thomas H. MM Pte 59136 138 Fd Amb RAMC
GIFFARD Edward P. MM Pte 4237 Royal Irish Rifles
GIFFEN Albert B. MM Pte 278860 1/7th Arg & Suth Highlanders
GIFFEN George MM Pte 266914 Middlesex Regt
GIFFORD Edwin MM Bdr 40975 24 Bde RFA
GIFFORD George MM Cpl 32898 RGA
GIFFORD Herbert MM Pte A/204131 13th King's Royal Rifle Corps
GIFFORD John MM Pte 55543 Royal Welsh Fusiliers
GIFFORD John Alexander MM Dvr 98353 14 Div Ammn Col RFA
GIFKINS George E. MM Cpl 16802 1 Fd Sqn Royal Engineers
GIGG Frederick W. MM L/Cpl R/16832 King's Royal Rifle Corps
GIGGAL Arthur J. "MM,MIDx2" Armt S/Sjt 676 Army Ordnance Corps att RGA.
GIGGS James MM Dvr 45972 2 Div Ammn Col RFA
GIGNER John MM Cpl 65432 104 Fd Amb RAMC
GILBANK Edward MM Sjt 12282 6th Shropshire Light Infantry DOW 4.9.16.

GILBARD Evelyn MM CQMS 4169 2nd West Riding Regt
GILBERT Albert MM L/Cpl 240870 8th Royal Warwickshire Regt
GILBERT Albert A. MM L/Cpl 14030 2nd Middlesex Regt
GILBERT Alexander MM L/Cpl 1629 Army Cyclist Corps
GILBERT Alfred MM Sjt 13239 6th Northamptonshire Regt KIA 18.9.18.
GILBERT Alfred MM Sjt 150574 119 Railway Coy Royal Engineers
GILBERT Alfred William MM Sjt 141061 D/315 Bde RFA KIA 21.3.18.
GILBERT Daniel MM Pte 26382 Shropshire Light Infantry
GILBERT E. MM L/Bdr Sig 56951 121 Hy Bty RGA
GILBERT Edwin MM L/Sjt 26151 Notts & Derby Regt
GILBERT Frank Rettie MM Sjt 20118 Machine Gun Corps
GILBERT Frederick W. MM Dvr 53224 B/95 Bde RFA Died 22.11.18.
GILBERT George MM Pte C/6373 18th King's Royal Rifle Corps KIA 16.5.18.
GILBERT George H. MM Sjt 50680 5 Bde RFA
GILBERT George J. MM Pte 10095 5th Northamptonshire Regt
GILBERT Harold MM L/Sjt 1876 1st Welsh Guards
GILBERT Harry MM Pte 32809 99 Fd Amb RAMC
GILBERT Harry MM Dvr 34191 RFA
GILBERT Harry T. MM L/Cpl 10546 2/1st HAC(Inf)
GILBERT Henry MM Sjt 43662 120 Heavy Bty RGA
GILBERT Henry H. MM Sjt 200059 2nd Yorkshire Light Infantry
GILBERT Herbert MM Cpl 35343 RFA
GILBERT James MM Pte A/202619 King's Royal Rifle Corps att MGC.
GILBERT James MM Sjt 9879 1st Royal West Kent Regt
GILBERT James J. MM S/Sjt Fitter 16710 RGA
GILBERT John MM Gnr 765702 102 Bde RFA
GILBERT John MM Sjt 34833 Labour Corps
GILBERT John D. MM S/Sjt 1323 RAMC
GILBERT John H. MM Pte 9924 1st Royal Scots Fusiliers
GILBERT John Lawrence MM Cpl Fitter 915442 223 Bde RFA
GILBERT Joseph MM L/Cpl Z/2478 Rifle Brigade
GILBERT Joseph James MM Sjt 2885 1/24th London Regt
GILBERT Joseph Noel MM Cpl 3/25818 1st South Wales Borderers
GILBERT Louisa Mary MM Staff Nurse F QAIMNS
GILBERT Matthew MM L/Cpl 1576 1/1st Cambridgeshire Regt
GILBERT Richard MM Pte 8784 1st Royal Irish Fusiliers
GILBERT Robert MM Spr 44373 4 Well Boring Section Royal Engineers
GILBERT W MM Pte 6184 1st Dragoon Guards
GILBERT William MM Cpl 241259 South Staffordshire Regt
GILBERT William MM Gnr 1190 4 Div Ammn Col RFA
GILBERT William A. MM CQMS 200772 4th Leicestershire Regt
GILBERT William C. MM Pte 42132 1st Gordon Highlanders
GILBERT William H. MM CSM 9169 1st Royal Scots Fusiliers
GILBERT William H. MM Sjt 239 26th Northumberland Fusiliers
GILBERT William M. MM+Bar L/Cpl 44093 1st Royal Berkshire Regt
GILBERT Young MM Sjt Piper 16084 17th Highland Light Infantry
GILBERTSON Archibald R. MM Pte 7932 21 Fd Amb RAMC
GILBERTSON James MM Gnr 96785 RFA
GILBERTSON Robert "DCM,MM" CSM 14542 9th North Lancashire Regt
GILBEY Harold MM Pte 11747 9th West Riding Regt
GILBRIDE Bernard MM Sjt 486102 465 Fd Coy Royal Engineers
GILBRIDE Martin MM L/Cpl 356639 Liverpool Regt
GILCHRIST Alexander R. MM L/Cpl 38528 Royal Scots
GILCHRIST Colin C. MM Dvr 77205 RFA
GILCHRIST Hugh MM Cpl 330988 1/9th Highland Light Infantry
GILCHRIST James MM Sjt 22159 Machine Gun Corps
GILCHRIST John MM Pte 38410 Yorkshire Light Infantry
GILCHRIST Richard MM Sjt 17706 12th Royal Irish Rifles
GILCHRIST William "DCM,MM" Pte 9431 2nd Gordon Highlanders
GILCHRIST William "MM,MSM" Spr 76170 IV Corps Sig Coy Royal Engineers
GILCHRIST William MM+Bar L/Cpl 200282 5/6th Scottish Rifles
GILCHRIST William R. MM Cpl 49452 10th Royal Scots
GILDER Ernest MM Sjt 23386 4th North Staffordshire Regt
GILDER Frederick C. MM L/Cpl 75919 2nd Bn Tank Corps
GILDER G.C. "DCM,MM" Sjt 27246 1st Essex Regt
GILDER Sidney MM Pnr 254907 31 Div Sig Coy Royal Engineers
GILDER Sidney E. MM Pte 30800 1/1st Bedfordshire Yeomanry
GILDER William MM Cpl 1468 RFA
GILDERSLEEVE Victor MM Pte 26979 13th Royal Welsh Fusiliers
GILDING James MM Sjt 6376 1st Norfolk Regt
GILES Albert A. MM CQMS 15060 Middlesex Regt
GILES Albert A. MM Sjt 2250 1/20th London Regt
GILES Albert Charles MM Cpl 40907 11 Div Sig Coy Royal Engineers
GILES Cecil MM Pte 70484 1/1st Berkshire Yeomanry
GILES Ernest MM Pte 2202 3rd Rifle Brigade
GILES Ernest George MM Sjt 5/8433 2nd Worcestershire Regt
GILES Frederick C. MM Sjt 1542 1/4th Royal Berkshire Regt
GILES Harold MM L/Sjt 703073 23rd London Regt
GILES James MM Pte 12582 Gordon Highlanders
GILES James MM Sjt 12269 8th East Surrey Regt KIA 31.3.18.
GILES James Charles MM Sjt 1039 Royal Sussex Regt
GILES Job H. MM Gnr 47468 18 Siege Bty RGA
GILES John MM CSM 19206 57 Fd Coy Royal Engineers
GILES Robert G. MM Sjt 19596 C/161 Bde RFA
GILES Sydney G. MM Pte 31866 Somerset Light Infantry
GILES Thomas W. MM Sjt 6863 King's Royal Rifle Corps
GILES Walter Bernard Frank MM L/Cpl 322267 2/6th London Regt KIA 4.4.18.
GILES William Henry MM Cpl 7774 1st Gloucestershire Regt DOW 25.9.18.
GILFILLAN Daniel MM L/Cpl 14206 Arg & Suth Highlanders
GILFILLAN J. MM Cpl 40590 Cameron Highlanders
GILFORD Dennis MM Pte 201156 Royal Berkshire Regt
GILFORD Walter MM Pte 68801 106 Fd Amb RAMC
GILHAM Edward Percy MM Spr 541070 155 Fd Coy Royal Engineers
GILHAM George W. MM Cpl 203754 1st London Regt
GILHAM William Frenk MM Sjt 3982 26 Heavy Bty RGA
GILHESPY Glenville MM+Bar Pte 18850 Royal West Surrey Regt
GILHOLME Henry MM Sjt 844 1/4th Northumberland Fusiliers
GILHOOLEY John MM L/Sjt 21090 1st Northumberland Fusiliers KIA 28.3.18.
GILHOOLY John MM Pte 7361 1st Scottish Rifles KIA 29.10.16.
GILKES Herbert W. MM Pte R24216 King's Royal Rifle Corps
GILKES Joseph MM Pte 28144 Royal Warwickshire Regt
GILKS Joseph MM Pte 3549 Royal Warwickshire Regt
GILKS William MM Pte 18165 1st Royal Warwickshire Regt
GILL Albert MM Pte 15744 8th Yorkshire Regt
GILL Albert MM Gnr 55563 27 Siege Bty RGA
GILL Alfred MM L/Cpl 28816 2nd Royal Dublin Fusiliers DOW 7.10.18.
GILL Arthur MM Bdr L/12384 RFA
GILL Arthur MM Bdr 775077 3 Bty 124 Bde RFA Died 26.8.18.
GILL Arthur MM Pte 10494 Cheshire Regt
GILL Arthur MM BSM 761392 317 Bde RFA
GILL Charles MM Cpl L/15821 RFA
GILL Charles Dale "MM,VM(Rm)" Pte 37138 9th South Lancashire Regt
GILL Charles Percival MM Cpl 459246 2/2nd(Wessex)Fd Amb RAMC
GILL Charles Samuel MM+Bar L/Cpl 240913 5th Lincolnshire Regt DOW 15.10.18.
GILL Edgar N. MM Gnr 82745 B/84 Bde RFA
GILL Edward C. MM Air Mech 1 4708 Royal Flying Corps
GILL Ernest MM Cpl 36692 10th East Yorkshire Regt
GILL Ernest "DCM,MM" Cpl 325637 1/9th Durham Light Infantry
GILL Ernest MM Pte 510694 1/14th London Regt KIA 29.8.18.
GILL Fred MM Gnr 41191 D/104 Bde RFA KIA 6.8.16.
GILL George F. MM Pte 3035 8th Royal West Surrey Regt
GILL George N. MM Sjt 240569 6th South Staffordshire Regt
GILL Henry H. MM Bdr L/14076 RFA
GILL Henry J. MM Slt 20403 South Wales Borderers
GILL Henry P. MM L/Cpl 40890 Royal Dublin Fusiliers
GILL Herbert MM Pte 137348 9th Bn Machine Gun Corps
GILL Herbert Frank "MC,MM(2704 Pte 1/20th Lond)" 2Lt Royal Engineers
GILL Herbert James MM Sjt 14860 8th Devonshire Regt
GILL Herbert V. MM Pte 2092 1/7th London Regt
GILL Hugh MM Pte 6007 1st Arg & Suth Highlanders
GILL James MM Gnr 65210 RFA
GILL John MM+Bar CSM 65155 1st Northumberland Fusiliers
GILL John MM Sjt 6782 2nd Royal Welsh Fusiliers
GILL John MM L/Cpl 457032 Royal Engineers
GILL John MM Pte 23187 Lancashire Fusiliers
GILL John MM Cpl 2/9153 2nd Royal Munster Fusiliers
GILL Joseph B. MM Pte 30510 15th Highland Light Infantry
GILL Michael J. MM Pte 28377 South Lancashire Regt
GILL Norman MM Cpl 145458 129 Fd Coy Royal Engineers
GILL Norman MM Pte 5218 1st London Regt
GILL Norman MM Dvr 127755 B/87 Bde RFA
GILL Percy MM Sjt 1320 RAMC

GILL Percy MM Pte 240626 South Lancashire Regt
GILL Robert H. MM Sjt A/3060 9th King's Royal Rifle Corps
GILL Rowland "MC,MM(31822 Pte RAMC)" 2Lt Liverpool Regt KIA 19.4.18.
GILL Sidney MM L/Cpl 325513 1/1st Cambridgeshire Regt KIA 26.9.17.
GILL Sydney M. MM L/Cpl 8789 1st South Staffordshire Regt
GILL Thomas MM L/Cpl 40531 1/9th Durham Light Infantry
GILL Thomas MM L/Cpl 7390 2nd Seaforth Highlanders
GILL Thomas MM L/Cpl 330686 9th Liverpool Regt DOW 1.9.18.
GILL Tom MM Gnr 20157 C/123 Bde RFA
GILL Valentine MM Sjt 2782 2nd Northumberland Fusiliers
GILL Victor MM Sjt 201664 2nd London Regt
GILL Wilfred MM Pte 1750 1/6th Welsh Regt
GILL William MM L/Cpl 34421 2nd South Lancashire Regt
GILL William MM Sjt 36707 169 Siege Bty RGA
GILL William MM Pte 51188 13th Liverpool Regt KIA 24.10.18.
GILL William MM Sjt 147518 Royal Engineers
GILL William MM Pte 18219 12th Durham Light Infantry Died 12.10.18.
GILL William MM Gnr 74020 126 Siege Bty RGA KIA 21.3.18.
GILL William E. MM Dvr 136902 RFA
GILL William H. MM Pte 201328 4th Yorkshire Light Infantry
GILLAM Charles MM Sjt 43386 RFA
GILLAM William H. MM Sjt 1764 Leicestershire Regt
GILLAN Albert MM L/Cpl S/23010 7th Royal Highlanders
GILLAN James MM Pte 20407 Yorkshire Regt
GILLAN Thomas MM Sjt 9458 2nd Royal Irish Fusiliers
GILLAN W.G. MM Pte 10884 Highland Light Infantry
GILLAN William MM Cpl 290097 1/8th Scottish Rifles
GILLAN William MM Pte 16136 Arg & Suth Highlanders
GILLANDERS James Gray MM L/Cpl 3669 1/1st HAC(Inf)
GILLANDERS Kennett MM Cpl 15506 Royal Engineers
GILLANDERS Robert MM Pte 1552 Royal Highlanders
GILLANDERS Robert MM Pte 16105 9th Royal Irish Fusiliers
GILLARD Edgar E. MM Pte 202018 4th Somerset Light Infantry
GILLARD Ernest F. MM Sjt 650998 21st London Regt
GILLARD John James MM L/Cpl 37685 9th Bn Machine Gun Corps DOW 16.4.18.
GILLBE Edward Walter MM Sjt 10338 2nd Royal Welsh Fusiliers
GILLEARD Henry Douglas MM+Bar Cpl L/32442 Y/32 Med TM Bty RFA
GILLEECE Patrick MM Sjt Farrier 57216 23 Bde RFA
GILLEN Charles J. MM L/Cpl 1/10902 Connaught Rangers
GILLEN Hugh MM Pte 202015 1/6th Arg & Suth Highlanders
GILLENDER Frederick MM Dvr 53904 22 Bde RFA
GILLENEY Samuel MM+Bar Cpl 308110 RGA DOW 4.4.18.
GILLES Camille MM Pte 21833 Royal Irish Fusiliers
GILLESPIE Charles MM Sjt 5679 9th Scottish Rifles
GILLESPIE Dougald MM Pte 4752 2nd Highland Light Infantry KIA 23.8.18.
GILLESPIE Ephraim MM Pte 14/50 14th York & Lancaster Regt
GILLESPIE Finlay MM Sjt 40684 11th Royal Scots KIA 13.4.18.
GILLESPIE Hector MM Pte 15234 9th Yorkshire Regt
GILLESPIE Hugh MM Pte 201350 1/5th Arg & Suth Highlanders
GILLESPIE John MM L/Bdr 640219 RFA
GILLESPIE John MM 2nd Cpl 418100 Royal Engineers
GILLESPIE Robert S. MM+Bar S/Sjt 40988 RAMC
GILLESPIE Theodore MM Sjt 301009 89 Fd Amb RAMC
GILLESPIE W. MM Pte 200851 Scottish Rifles
GILLESPIE William MM L/Cpl 13259 9th Northumberland Fusiliers KIA 22.3.18.
GILLESPIE William A. MM Sjt 64892 17th Worcestershire Regt
GILLETT Aleck W. MM Pnr 100419 33 Div Sig Coy Royal Engineers
GILLETT Alexander MM Pte 10566 1st Liverpool Regt
GILLETT Sidney W. MM L/Cpl 9854 11th Welsh Regt
GILLETT Walter MM L/Cpl 19955 Royal Engineers
GILLETT William MM Cpl 29786 8th Somerset Light Infantry
GILLETT William MM Sjt 15887 RGA
GILLHAM Albert J.W. MM Spr 534623 466 Fd Coy Royal Engineers
GILLHAM George MM Spr 127529 25 Div Sig Coy Royal Engineers
GILLHAM John MM Cpl 506480 Royal Engineers
GILLHAM Richard MM Sjt 14696 11th Royal Welsh Fusiliers
GILLIBRAND George MM Pte 242790 East Lancashire Regt
GILLIBRAND Horace MM Pte 260357 7th Border Regt
GILLIBRAND Thomas MM Cpl 201196 2/4th North Lancashire Regt
GILLIE Charles L. MM+Bar Cpl 76667 3rd(Light)Bn Tank Corps
GILLIES Alexander MM Spr 198878 256 Tunnelling Coy Royal Engineers
GILLIES Alexander MM Pte 225266 10th Cameron Highlanders
GILLIES Daniel MM Cpl 656282 D/275 Bde RFA
GILLIES David F. MM Pte S/4302 Arg & Suth Highlanders
GILLIES Donald MM Pte 2520 1/8th Arg & Suth Highlanders
GILLIES Dougal MM Pte 8553 2nd Highland Light Infantry
GILLIES Harry J. MM L/Cpl 241962 8th Gloucestershire Regt
GILLIES James MM Sjt 43306 81 Fd Coy Royal Engineers
GILLIES James C. MM Sjt 45733 112 Bde RFA
GILLIES John MM Pte S/7129 9th Seaforth Highlanders
GILLIES Lindsay "DCM,MM" Sjt 38657 99 Fd Amb RAMC
GILLIES Thomas MM Pte 300828 Arg & Suth Highlanders
GILLIES Thomas MM Sjt 306068 RGA
GILLIES Thomas John MM Gnr 61000 C/76 Bde RFA DOW 10.11.17.
GILLIES Walter Neil MM Pte 40448 5th Cameron Highlanders KIA 19.7.18.
GILLIES William MM Pte 300819 1/8th Arg & Suth Highlanders KIA 26.4.18.
GILLIGAN Frank MM Cpl 73835 42nd Bn Machine Gun Corps
GILLIGAN James MM Pte 18495 Royal Irish Regt
GILLIGHAN Patrick MM Pte 2443 2nd Manchester Regt
GILLILAND John Lurburam MM Sjt 9261 2nd Devonshire Regt KIA 1.7.16.
GILLILAND Thomas J. MM Pte 290184 Welsh Regt
GILLILAND William MM Dvr 57905 Royal Engineers
GILLIN William MM Cpl 2199 1/6th Northumberland Fusiliers
GILLINGHAM Allen MM Sjt 3479 9th Lancers
GILLINGHAM Herbert G. MM Cpl 203150 1/4th Hampshire Regt
GILLINGHAM Joseph Gordon Stuart MM Gnr 206299 W Bty RHA
GILLINGHAM William Albert MM Sjt 7469 2nd Royal Berkshire Regt KIA 27.4.18.
GILLINGHAM William George MM Cpl 21502 88 Coy Machine Gun Corps KIA 20.11.16.
GILLINGHAM William H. MM Sjt 14444 11th Suffolk Regt
GILLINGS Arthur MM Pte 220257 East Yorkshire Regt
GILLINGS Benjamin MM Sjt 325013 Durham Light Infantry
GILLINGS C. MM Cpl 40118 York & Lancaster Regt
GILLINGS Robert W. MM Pte 11000 6th Yorkshire Regt
GILLINGS Walter MM L/Cpl 59972 32nd Bn Machine Gun Corps
GILLINGWATER Edward H. MM Bdr 68225 12 Bde RFA
GILLINS James MM Dvr 27740 C/50 Bde RFA
GILLIONS Walter MM Pte 65845 Royal Fusiliers
GILLIVER Albert MM Spr 312859 6 Div Sig Coy Royal Engineers
GILLIVER Albert MM Sjt 12755 Liverpool Regt
GILLMAN Harold MM Cpl 90948 Royal Engineers
GILLMAN Harold Edward MM Cpl 83714 C/48 Bde RFA
GILLMAN Herbert MM Sjt 7322 1st Gloucestershire Regt
GILLMAN W.C. "DCM,MM+Bar" Pte 41145 2nd Royal Irish Rifles
GILLMORE William MM Pte C/6477 King's Royal Rifle Corps
GILLON John McL. MM Pte S/8487 2nd Arg & Suth Highlanders KIA 21.3.18.
GILLON Partick MM Pte 10491 2nd Scottish Rifles DOW 30.7.17.
GILLOTT Herbert J. MM Sjt 75053 1/1st Derbyshire Yeomanry
GILLOTT William H. MM Pte 2275 2nd York & Lancaster Regt
GILLULEY James MM Pte 71783 11th Notts & Derby Regt KIA 7.10.18.
GILMAN Frank John MM L/Cpl 201465 1/4th Gordon Highlanders
GILMAN George MM Sjt 1337 1st Lancashire Fusiliers KIA 1.7.16.
GILMAN Sydney MM L/Cp 240594 2/6th Notts & Derby Regt KIA 21.3.18.
GILMARTIN Michael MM Sjt 2359 1/7th Liverpool Regt
GILMARTIN Peter MM Pte 40472 1st Northumberland Fusiliers
GILMER David W. MM Dvr 70962 40 Bde RFA
GILMORE Alexander MM L/Cpl 20733 10th York & Lancaster Regt
GILMORE Edgar Frederick MM Gnr 26261 Y/18 Med TM Bty RFA DOW 5.9.18.
GILMORE George H. MM Pte 29727 9th Yorkshire Regt
GILMORE Harry MM L/Cpl 14/14705 Royal Irish Rifles
GILMORE John William MM Sjt 58426 57 Bde RFA
GILMORE Roger MM Pte 52054 2nd Manchester Regt
GILMORE Thomas MM Sjt 3234 11th Royal Irish Rifles
GILMORE William "DCM,MM" Sjt 26/934 26th Northumberland Fusiliers
GILMOUR David MM Pte 43324 8th Royal Highlanders KIA 19.7.18.
GILMOUR Edgar H. MM Pte 82751 25th Liverpool Regt
GILMOUR John MM Spr 412494 409 Fd Coy Royal Engineers
GILMOUR John MM L/Cpl 65589 127 Fd Coy Royal Engineers
GILMOUR John H. MM Sjt 337852 RGA
GILMOUR Thomas MM+Bar Sjt 290334 1/8th Scottish Rifles
GILMOUR William MM Sjt 265356 1/6th Royal Highlanders
GILPIN George MM L/Cpl 50403 RAMC

GILROY James MM Pte 28674 Welsh Regt
GILROY James MM L/Cpl 4078 9th Seaforth Highlanders
GILROY James McF. MM Pte 1139 1st Gordon Highlanders
GILROY John MM Bdr 760913 RFA
GILROY John MM Pte 10251 6th King's Own Scottish Borderers
GILROY John MM L/Cpl 64805 100 Fd Amb RAMC
GILROY Joseph MM L/Cpl 5278 1st Royal Munster Fusiliers
GILROY Michael MM Sjt 5876 2nd Leinster Regt
GILSON Frederick J. MM L/Cpl 10688 2/1st HAC(Inf)
GILSON Harry William MM+Bar L/Cpl 10035 1st North Staffordshire Regt KIA 1.12.17.
GILSON Percy G. MM BQMS 33637 42 Bde RFA
GILSON Richard MM Pte 320327 2/6th London Regt KIA 10.9.18.
GILTRAP Thomas Arthur MM Sjt 11494 Liverpool Regt
GILZEAN Thomas MM L/Sjt 290227 9th Royal Highlanders
GIMBERT Harold J. MM Pte 10996 8th East Surrey Regt
GIMSON Stanley George MM Cpl 149 22nd Royal Fusiliers
GINGELL Alfred Henry MM Pte G/14750 6th East Kent Regt
GINGELL Herbert MM Cpl 71148 15 Bde RFA
GINGELL William G. MM Sjt 9646 3rd Coldstream Guards
GINGELL William J. MM Cpl 266892 Gloucestershire Regt
GINGELL William John MM Pte 5285 2nd Coldstream Guards
GINGER Herbert MM Pte 36265 10th Notts & Derby Regt
GINKS Alec Saville MM Pte 38024 2/10th London Regt KIA 7.9.18.
GINNETT Harold Joseph MM L/Cpl 242530 1/6th North Staffordshire Regt
GIPP Frederick MM Sjt 22251 Suffolk Regt
GIPSON Edward G. MM Sjt M2/104088 F Ammn Park Army Service Corps
GIPSON James W. MM Cpl G/60498 9th Royal Fusiliers
GIPSON John MM Pte 14116 1st Grenadier Guards
GIRDLER Arthur MM+Bar Sjt 1205 7th Royal West Surrey Regt
GIRDLER Cecil MM Sjt S/1587 10th Rifle Brigade
GIRDLESTONE Albert Edward James MM Pte 10835 2nd Bedfordshire Regt KIA 5.1.18.
GIRDLESTONE W. MM Cpl 1356 Northumberland Fusiliers
GIRLING Arthur MM Pte 92623 8th Middlesex Regt
GIRLING Edward Joseph "MM,MID" Sjt 58534 A/14 Bde RFA KIA 16.9.17.
GIRLING Edwin Percy MM+Bar Pte 8905 1st Leicestershire Regt
GIRLING H.W. MM Cpl 322223 London Regt
GIRLING Henry MM QMS Farrier 20412 44 Bde RFA
GIRLING John Frederick MM L/Cpl M/321725 51 Div Train Army Service Corps
GIRLING Percy W. MM Cpl S/5880 Royal West Surrey Regt
GIRVAN David MM L/Cpl 8/12272 Royal Irish Rifles
GIRVAN George B. MM Sjt 51985 13th Liverpool Regt
GIRVAN John McA. MM Cpl 1970 Arg & Suth Highlanders
GIRVIN Samuel K. MM Sjt 15/11665 Royal Irish Rifles
GISBORNE Albert Maurice MM Sjt 241362 1/8th Worcestershire Regt KIA 5.10.18.
GISBORNE Claude MM Gnr 89965 RFA
GISBY Edward MM+Bar Pte 10085 1st Border Regt AKA ROBERTS.
GISBY Sydney H. MM Spr 142257 62 Div Sig Coy Royal Engineers
GISBY Vernon Frederick MM+Bar Gnr 960046 C/235 Bde RFA KIA 2.9.18.
GISSANE John MM Cpl 422142 10th London Regt
GISSING Edward MM Cpl 45229 Royal Engineers
GITTENS Evelyn "DCM,MM" Sjt M2/050304 Army Service Corps att 16 Siege Bty RGA.
GITTENS Robert Henry MM Sjt 18869 Machine Gun Corps
GITTINGS James MM Pte 26777 3 Coy Machine Gun Corps
GITTINS Albert MM Pte 242561 Yorkshire Light Infantry
GITTINS George MM Pte 10477 1st Royal Welsh Fusiliers KIA 20.7.16.
GITTINS James B. MM Pte 58314 7th Bn Machine Gun Corps
GITTINS Robert MM L/Cpl 9153 1st Scots Guards
GIVEN Alfred E. MM Cpl 60679 7th Royal West Surrey Regt
GIVEN Maurice MM Cpl 266478 2/7th Notts & Derby Regt Died 17.5.18.
GIVERNS Thomas William MM Pte 5605 18th Northumberland Fusiliers
GLADDERS Thomas MM L/Cpl 17220 6th York & Lancaster Regt
GLADDING Reginald Thomas MM Pte 202912 Northamptonshire Regt
GLADDIS Harry MM L/Bdr 115489 RFA
GLADDISH William W. MM L/Sjt 241990 6th South Staffordshire Regt
GLADDISS Percy George MM Spr 65933 12 Div Sig Coy Royal Engineers
GLADDY Felix MM Gnr 107390 296 Siege Bty RGA
GLADING Arthur MM Pte 26376 2/4th West Riding Regt
GLADMAN Leslie MM Pte S/4729 13th Rifle Brigade
GLADMAN P.G.A.G. MM CSM 40687 14th Welsh Regt
GLADSTONE Thomas MM L/Cpl 869 2nd Arg & Suth Highlanders
GLADWELL Daniel MM Cpl 17080 HQ/113 Bde RFA
GLADWELL John E. MM Pte 204835 15th Hampshire Regt
GLADWELL Thomas MM Cpl 79068 36th Northumberland Fusiliers
GLADWIN Charles Dent "DCM,MM(20288,9YorksR)" L/Cpl 63056 2nd West Yorkshire Regt
GLADWIN Charlie MM Pte 240388 5th Yorkshire Light Infantry
GLADWIN Ernest P. MM Pte M2/050549 Army Service Corps
GLADWIN Herbert Frank MM Pte 235720 1/1st Herefordshire Regt
GLADWIN William MM Pte 52049 2nd Yorkshire Light Infantry
GLADWIN William MM Pte 320726 12th Norfolk Regt
GLADWISH George MM Sjt 93887 12 Div Ammn Col RFA
GLAISTER Jacob "DCM,MM" Gnr 32242 D Coy MGC(Hy Sect)
GLAISTER John Norman MM Pte 16365 11th Border Regt KIA 4.7.17.
GLAIZER Percy MM Sjt 48567 RFA
GLANCEY Mark MM Dvr 7357 A/160 Bde RFA Died 19.2.19.
GLANCEY Thomas MM L/Cpl 302866 1/9th Arg & Suth Highlanders
GLANCY Michael MM Cpl 9650 2nd Leinster Regt att 17 Bde MG Coy.
GLANFIELD Albert MM Sjt 29578 D/330 Bde RFA
GLANFIELD Thomas Alfred MM Sjt 293739 141 Heavy Bty RGA
GLANVILL Frederick MM L/Cpl S/3185 Rifle Brigade
GLANVILLE Frederick George MM Pte 13270 10th Devonshire Regt
GLANVILLE Joshua MM Pte 40529 Durham Light Infantry
GLANVILLE Samuel MM Pte 2547 7th Leinster Regt
GLANVILLE Walter F. MM BQMS 28342 RGA
GLASGOW Alexander MM Pte 40385 Royal Scots
GLASGOW James Wood MM Pte 278981 10th Arg & Suth Highlanders DOW 11.8.18.
GLASPER Charles W. MM Cpl 20173 Yorkshire Regt
GLASS Albert E. MM Dvr 947529 312 Bde RFA
GLASS Benjamin MM Sjt 1451 Gordon Highlanders
GLASS Edgar G.W. MM Sjt 127 4th Bn GMGR
GLASS George A. MM Pnr 130749 Royal Engineers
GLASS George W. MM L/Bdr 70372 46 Bty 39 Bde RFA
GLASS Harold MM Sjt 326501 1/1st Cambridgeshire Regt
GLASS J.G. MM Air Mech 2 98930 Royal Flying Corps
GLASS John William MM Sjt 70702 44 Bde RFA
GLASS Joseph MM Pte 18143 Welsh Regt
GLASS Norman MM Pte 322056 1 Fd Amb RAMC
GLASS William MM Pte 26337 2/5th West Riding Regt KIA 5.11.18.
GLASS William Alfred MM Tpr 1455 Household Bn
GLASSBROOK Roger MM L/Bdr 95717 323 Siege Bty RGA
GLASSEY Francis MM Pte 230514 10th Shropshire Light Infantry
GLASSON Arthur James MM Gnr Fitter 47201 379 Bty 109 Bde RFA
GLASSON Frederick George MM Pte 241259 1/5th Border Regt
GLATHORN George F. MM Pte 71562 10th Notts & Derby Regt
GLAVEY Michael MM Staff SM S/18242 GHQ Troops Army Service Corps
GLAYSHER Alfred MM Sjt 309305 14th Bn Tank Corps
GLAYSHER William Frank MM Gnr Fitter 47232 RFA KIA 9.4.18.
GLAZE Albert MM Sjt 201348 Royal West Surrey Regt
GLAZE George MM Pte 101731 RAMC
GLAZE William MM Pte 261012 18th Gloucestershire Regt
GLAZEBROOK Ernest J. MM L/Cpl 98550 Machine Gun Corps
GLAZEBROOK Frederick T. MM Sjt 60068 RFA
GLEADEN William MM Cpl 235396 6th Leicestershire Regt
GLEADHALL John G. MM Pte 16849 York & Lancaster Regt
GLEADHILL Walter "DCM,MM" L/Cpl 12608 7th East Yorkshire Regt
GLEASE William MM Pte 37581 1st North Lancashire Regt
GLEAVE Edward MM Pte 337532 RAMC
GLEAVE Harry MM Cpl 32533 Cheshire Regt
GLEAVE Leigh MM Pte R/19741 16th King's Royal Rifle Corps KIA 10.1.18.
GLEAVE William MM Sjt 7374 16th Manchester Regt
GLEAVES L.C. MM Air Mech 2 49624 Royal Air Force
GLEDHILL Charles MM+Bar Pte 7350 1st Coldstream Guards
GLEDHILL Edward MM Sjt 240717 1/5th York & Lancaster Regt
GLEDHILL Fred MM Sjt 23 West Riding Regt
GLEDHILL James MM Cpl 202206 2/5th West Riding Regt
GLEDHILL Joseph MM Pte 13239 16th Lancashire Fusiliers
GLEDHILL Raymond MM Cpl 200127 West Riding Regt
GLEDHILL Thomas MM Pte 11052 2nd Highland Light Infantry
GLEDHILL W.J. MM Pte 240874 York & Lancaster Regt

GLEDHILL Walter MM+Bar Sjt 5339 10th Lancashire Fusiliers
GLEED Harold MM BQMS 947660 282 Bde Ammn Col RFA
GLEED William E. MM Pte 58290 1 Special Coy King's Royal Rifle Corps
GLEESON Henry J. MM Spr 132987 Royal Engineers
GLEESON Horace MM Pte 9037 2nd South Staffordshire Regt
GLEESON Richard MM Cpl 11481 1st Royal Dublin Fusiliers KIA 4.9.18.
GLEN Barclay MM Pte 15729 1st Scots Guards
GLEN Charles MM+Bar Pte 8730 2nd Royal Scots DOW 27.5.18.
GLEN Daniel MM+Bar Cpl S/10599 7th Cameron Highlanders
GLEN David MM Sjt 16611 13th Royal Scots KIA 9.4.17.
GLEN James MM Cpl 957 6th Royal West Kent Regt
GLEN Michael MM Pte 23272 26 Coy Machine Gun Corps
GLEN Reginald S. MM Sjt 65130 6th Yorkshire Regt
GLEN Robert MM Pte S/43223 8th Royal Highlanders
GLEN Walter C. MM Bdr 40577 RFA
GLEN William MM Pte 1894 8th Seaforth Highlanders
GLEN William MM Cpl 21610 Machine Gun Corps
GLEN William MM Cpl 5814 RAMC
GLENCROSS Andrew MM Sjt 12441 Royal Highlanders KIA 18.4.18.
GLENCROSS John MM Sjt 290095 1/8th Scottish Rifles
GLENCROSS John MM Sjt 60199 54 Bty 39 Bde RFA Died 2.10.16.
GLENDAY Francis MM Pte 118512 1st Bn Machine Gun Corps
GLENDENNING James MM Pte 28999 2nd Grenadier Guards
GLENDINING W.H. MM Sjt H/71157 North Irish Horse
GLENDINNING John MM Cpl 33101 7th Wiltshire Regt
GLENDINNING William MM Pte 514563 14th London Regt
GLENISTER Frank MM Pte 55074 4th Hampshire Regt
GLENISTER H. MM Pte 1264 Royal Sussex Regt
GLENISTER Leslie A. MM Sjt CMT/3586 Army Service Corps
GLENISTER William H. MM CQMS 8188 1st Royal Berkshire Regt
GLENN George MM+Bar Pte 17069 Machine Gun Corps
GLENN William T. MM Pte 202776 5/6th Scottish Rifles
GLENNAN John Willie MM Sjt 3/3706 6th York & Lancaster Regt
GLENNIE Alexander MM Pte 40172 Gordon Highlanders KIA 25.8.18.
GLENNIE William MM L/Cpl 2727 17th Highland Light Infantry
GLENNIE William Alexander MM Pte S/5908 1st Cameron Highlanders
GLENNON John "DCM,MM" Pte 26243 1/6th Cheshire Regt
GLENNY Thomas MM Cpl 59448 61 Div Sig Coy Royal Engineers
GLENTON George MM Pte 148285 23rd Bn Machine Gun Corps
GLENTON James Reginald MM S/Sjt 390057 3rd(Northumbrian)Fd Amb RAMC
GLENTON John William MM L/Cpl 1767 1/4th Yorkshire Regt KIA 26.3.18.
GLENWOOD G. MM Pte 54922 Royal Fusiliers
GLEW Harry MM BQMS 47989 RFA
GLEW Tom MM Pte C/12341 12th King's Royal Rifle Corps KIA 2.4.18.
GLIDDON Norman MM 2nd Cpl 47316 94 Fd Coy Royal Engineers
GLIDLE George MM 2nd Cpl 43071 121 Fd Coy Royal Engineers
GLINTERNICK Solomon MM Pte 6437 Manchester Regt
GLINWOOD George F. "DCM,MM" L/Sjt 54922 11th Royal Fusiliers
GLOSSOP George Edward MM Pte M2/054000 Army Service Corps att 23 Fd Amb RAMC.
GLOSSOP John David MM Bdr 27797 K Bty RHA
GLOSSOP John Henry MM Gnr 74032 RFA
GLOSTER Thomas Richard MM Cpl 1969 1/7th Middlesex Regt
GLOVER Albert E. MM Pte 41939 13th Liverpool Regt
GLOVER Archibald Norman MM L/Cpl P/800 Military Mounted Police
GLOVER Arthur E. MM Pte 266698 1/1st Hertfordshire Regt
GLOVER Charles H. MM Bdr 1350 RFA
GLOVER Christopher MM L/Cpl 25442 Leicestershire Regt
GLOVER Edwin MM+Bar Dvr 430270 446 Fd Coy Royal Engineers
GLOVER Frank MM Sjt 50906 Middlesex Regt
GLOVER Frank MM Pte 57521 26th Royal Welsh Fusiliers
GLOVER George MM Pte 44420 RAMC
GLOVER George MM Pte 1374 2nd Royal Warwickshire Regt
GLOVER George F. MM Gnr 141122 RGA
GLOVER GeorgeW. MM Cpl 558381 29 Div Sig Coy Royal Engineers
GLOVER Harold Jenkins MM Cpl 72951 30th Bn Machine Gun Corps KIA 21.3.18.
GLOVER Harry MM Pte DM2/207016 44 Mot Amb Convoy Army Service Corps
GLOVER Henry P. MM Pte 20388 1st Dorsetshire Regt
GLOVER Henry Thomas MM Cpl 20860 Gloucestershire Regt
GLOVER Howard Rigby MM L/Sjt R/4022 13th King's Royal Rifle Corps DOW 12.3.18.
GLOVER James MM Sjt 200160 1/5th Highland Light Infantry
GLOVER James A. MM L/Cpl 53079 3rd Worcestershire Regt
GLOVER John MM Sjt 200986 1/5th Manchester Regt KIA 2.9.18.
GLOVER John MM L/Cpl 30226 North Lancashire Regt
GLOVER John MM Cpl 242 15th Royal Warwickshire Regt
GLOVER Joseph MM L/Sjt 240787 4th South Lancashire Regt
GLOVER Joseph B. MM Sjt 52445 15 Bde RFA
GLOVER Percy MM Sjt 46058 Machine Gun Corps
GLOVER Reginald MM Pte 240622 1st Leicestershire Regt
GLOVER Reuben MM+Bar L/Cpl 28/534 Northumberland Fusiliers
GLOVER Samuel H. MM Sjt 200167 South Lancashire Regt
GLOVER Thomas MM L/Cpl 265634 12th North Lancashire Regt
GLOVER Thomas "MM,CG(F)" Sjt 9142 2nd Cheshire Regt
GLOVER Thomas MM+Bar Sjt 112491 RGA
GLOVER William MM Bdr 926004 X/56 Med TM Bty RFA
GLOVER William MM Sjt 29741 North Lancashire Regt
GLOVER William MM Pte 5407 12th Royal Fusiliers
GLOVER William MM L/Cpl 14653 10th Royal Irish Rifles
GLOVER William John MM Sjt 1523 1/7th Notts & Derby Regt KIA 1.7.16.
GLOYNE Francis E. MM+Bar Sjt 240149 Liverpool Regt
GLUCKSTEIN Cyril Samuel MM Pte 41542 52 Fd Amb RAMC KIA 6.8.16.
GLUE William MM Bdr 62536 143 Siege Bty RGA
GLYDE George Samuel MM Pte 305543 5th Bn Tank Corps KIA 3.10.18.
GLYNN Charles MM L/Cpl 8259 2nd Royal Dublin Fusiliers
GLYNN John L. MM Pte 281262 1/7th Lancashire Fusiliers
GLYNN Martin "DCM,MM" Pte 2393 1st Manchester Regt
GLYNN Michael MM Dvr 39100 11 Bde RFA
GLYNN Thomas MM Pte 40366 Royal Inniskilling Fusiliers
GLYNN Thomas J. MM Pte 84064 Machine Gun Corps
GLYNN Thomas P. MM+Bar Cpl 23253 1st Royal Dublin Fusiliers
GLYNN William MM Spr 41183 Royal Engineers
GLYNN William "DCM,MM+Bar" Sjt 9025 2nd Manchester Regt
GOACHER Francis Sydney MM Pte 24472 1st Royal West Surrey Regt KIA 21.9.18.
GOACHER Raymond P. MM Pte L/12184 2nd Royal Sussex Regt
GOAN Bernard MM Pte S/2620 9th Seaforth Highlanders
GOATCHER George MM Sjt 5515 6th Dragoon Guards
GOATCHER William MM L/Sjt 202449 Royal West Surrey Regt
GOATER Charles H. MM CQMS 19259 1st Devonshire Regt
GOATER Sidney H. MM Pte 323065 6th London Regt
GOBBA Matthew Joseph MM Sjt 67719 Royal Engineers
GOBBI Francis Julio MM Gnr 197097 D/275 Bde RFA
GOBEY Frederick G. MM Dvr 62232 1 Div Ammn Col RFA
GOBLE Arthur MM Pte 232432 2nd London Regt
GOBLE Ernest MM Sjt 55103 43 Bde RFA
GOBLE Ernest G. MM L/Sjt 1341 Royal Sussex Regt
GOBLE Frank E. MM Sjt 99009 13th Royal Fusiliers
GOBLE George T. MM Pte 300 7 Fd Amb RAMC
GOBLE George W. MM Pte 202920 6th Royal West Kent Regt
GOBLE Harry H. MM Pte 19234 Hampshire Regt
GOCH John F. MM Sjt 376953 Labour Corps
GODART Arthur W. MM Pte 42940 76 Fd Amb RAMC
GODBEER James MM Pte 14292 5th South Lancashire Regt
GODBER William MM Pte 242359 10th Notts & Derby Regt
GODBERT Robert MM+Bar Cpl 12700 6th King's Own Scottish Borderers
GODBOLD Charles MM Pte 39342 17th Royal Scots DOW 9.10.18.
GODBOLD George F. MM Pte 17067 Suffolk Regt
GODBOLD Henry MM Pte 24439 13th Cheshire Regt KIA 10.8.17.
GODBOLD Herbert "DCM,MM" Sjt 52222 2nd Lincolnshire Regt
GODBOLD J. MM Pte 508360 RAMC
GODBOLD William P. MM L/Cpl 62825 Machine Gun Corps
GODBY Arthur MM Pte R/13899 King's Royal Rifle Corps
GODDARD A. MM L/Cpl 461233 RAMC
GODDARD Albert J. MM Pte 205555 15th Hampshire Regt
GODDARD Albert V. MM Cpl 900904 HQ 99 Bde RFA
GODDARD Archie MM Pte 26393 1st Norfolk Regt
GODDARD Arthur MM Sjt 168977 Royal Engineers
GODDARD Arthur E. MM L/Cpl 544 7th East Surrey Regt
GODDARD Arthur H. MM Pte 1781 RAMC
GODDARD Charles MM Pte 201373 Hampshire Regt
GODDARD Charles R. MM Cpl 70014 Royal Engineers
GODDARD Frank MM Sjt 13545 2nd Coldstream Guards
GODDARD Frederick MM Pte 15304 1st Hampshire Regt

GODDARD Frederick G. MM Cpl 14049 15th Hussars
GODDARD Frederick J. MM Pte 31135 1st Royal West Kent Regt
GODDARD George MM Pte 241607 2/5th Hampshire Regt KIA 20.11.17.
GODDARD George MM Spr 601966 Royal Engineers
GODDARD George Alfred MM Sjt 11132 1st Notts & Derby Regt
GODDARD Henry C. MM L/Cpl 10502 5th Royal Berkshire Regt
GODDARD Henry Charles "DCM,MM,MM(F)" CSM R/4808 13th King's Royal Rifle Corps
GODDARD Herbert MM Pte 2604 7th East Kent Regt
GODDARD Isaac MM Cpl 19287 13th Liverpool Regt
GODDARD James MM Cpl 478091 90 Coy Labour Corps
GODDARD John H. MM Pte 2238 8th Royal Sussex Regt
GODDARD Percy W. MM Sjt G5517 13th Royal Fusiliers
GODDARD Robert W. MM+Bar Sjt 3499 1/5th Seaforth Highlanders
GODDARD Thomas William MM Sjt 72867 71 Coy Machine Gun Corps
GODDARD Victor James MM L/Cpl 3/6462 6th Duke of Cornwall's LI KIA 4.9.16.
GODDARD Walter MM+Bar Cpl 69305 36 Bde RFA
GODDARD Walter MM Gnr 27714 Y/36 Med TM Bty RFA KIA 20.11.17.
GODDARD William MM Sjt 158 1/6th Notts & Derby Regt KIA 1.7.16.
GODDARD William A. "DCM,MM(19849 Pte Welsh Regt)" Sjt 26000 19th Bn Machine Gun Corps
GODDARD William G. MM Pte B/200627 Rifle Brigade
GODDARD William Rogers MM Spr 62023 6 Div Sig Coy Royal Engineers
GODDEN Albert MM Pte 13650 East Kent Regt
GODDEN Arthur MM Pte 19789 Hussars
GODDEN Arthur T. MM Spr 103170 Royal Engineers
GODDEN Charles MM Pte 14315 1st Royal Dublin Fusiliers
GODDEN Edward W. MM L/Cpl 10323 Royal West Surrey Regt
GODDEN Fred R. MM Pte 38951 1st Duke of Cornwall's LI
GODDEN Frederick W. MM CSM L/7407 2nd Royal West Kent Regt
GODDEN Stanley F. MM Bdr 40857 RGA
GODDIN Daniel MM Sjt SPTS/3953 17th Royal Fusiliers
GODDIN John G. MM Pte 10642 Royal West Kent Regt
GODDING Edward MM Sjt 7459 3rd Coldstream Guards
GODFREY A.D. MM Sjt 10020 Leicestershire Regt
GODFREY Alfred MM Pte 40133 8th York & Lancaster Regt
GODFREY Alfred MM Pte 19256 1st Northamptonshire Regt
GODFREY C. MM Pte 17587 11th Essex Regt
GODFREY Charles MM Sjt 12904 7th Northamptonshire Regt
GODFREY Charles M. MM Dvr 47140 51 Bty 39 Bde RFA
GODFREY Edgar S. MM Pte 260694 1/1st 1st County of London Yeomanry (Middlesex Hussars)
GODFREY Edward MM Pte 17269 Royal Inniskilling Fusiliers
GODFREY Frederick MM Pte 14/377 5th York & Lancaster Regt
GODFREY Frederick MM CSM 10889 5th Oxf & Bucks Light Infantry KIA 15.9.16.
GODFREY Frederick Arthur "DCM+Bar,MM" Sjt 9083 1st Royal Munster Fusiliers DOW 2.10.18.
GODFREY Harry MM L/Cpl 27541 7th Royal Warwickshire Regt
GODFREY Henry J. MM Pte 52612 37th Bn Machine Gun Corps
GODFREY Herbert MM Sjt 105355 Royal Engineers
GODFREY Herbert Samuel MM Cpl 5799 Royal Munster Fusiliers
GODFREY Jack A. MM Cpl 550198 517 Fd Coy Royal Engineers
GODFREY Lemuel MM Cpl 36711 49th Bn Machine Gun Corps
GODFREY R. MM Pte 303199 Arg & Suth Highlanders
GODFREY Reginald Bertram MM Gnr 102475 P Bty RHA
GODFREY Sidney A. MM Pte 23184 Wiltshire Regt
GODFREY Valentine MM Pte 18463 1st King's Own Scottish Borderers
GODFREY Walter MM Cpl 36903 Royal Berkshire Regt
GODFREY Walter Ernest MM L/Cpl 255289 Fifth Army HQ Sig Coy Royal Engineers
GODFREY Walter Ernest "DCM,MM" Pte 13247 2nd Grenadier Guards
GODFREY William MM Pte 26226 2/4th Yorkshire Light Infantry
GODFREY William Harry MM Pte 1414 Royal Warwickshire Regt att MGC.KIA 29.5.18.
GODFREY William Henry MM Sjt 492524 13th London Regt
GODFREY William Henry James MM Gnr 46006 C/189 Bde RFA DOW 6.11.17.
GODKIN Arthur MM L/Cpl 204545 1st Essex Regt
GODLEY John MM Cpl 1210 West Riding Regt
GODLEY John T. MM Pte 3702 Royal West Surrey Regt
GODLEY Sidney Frank MM Sjt 6421 RFA
GODLEY William MM Pte 10240 2nd York & Lancaster Regt
GODMAN Arthur W. MM Sjt 721334 2/24th London Regt
GODMAN Wilfred MM Pte 12704 7th East Yorkshire Regt
GODSALL Horace J. MM Sjt 44859 12th North Staffordshire Regt
GODSALL Sidney Herbert MM Pte 19575 1st Bedfordshire Regt
GODSMAN William MM Pte 266093 1/6th Gordon Highlanders
GODSMARK Percy MM Cpl 9535 1/5th London Regt
GODSMARK Ronald MM Sjt 30166 18th Hussars
GODSON Henry MM Pte B/1589 7th Rifle Brigade KIA 26.8.17.
GODSON Herbert MM L/Cpl 530 4th Bn GMGR
GODWIN Alfred C. MM Pnr 309033 Royal Engineers
GODWIN Frank E. MM L/Cpl 25566 2nd Worcestershire Regt
GODWIN Frederick C.J. MM Sjt 306273 Liverpool Regt
GODWIN Frederick W.B. MM Pte 665 1/1st Wiltshire Yeomanry
GODWIN George E. MM Sjt 300131 1/6th West Riding Regt KIA 11.10.18.
GODWIN Henry A. MM Pte 1556 1/1st Berkshire Yeomanry
GODWIN Herbert C. MM Pte 54972 2nd Hampshire Regt
GODWIN John MM L/Cpl 8546 1st South Wales Borderers
GODWIN John MM Spr 44744 Royal Engineers
GODWIN John Emmanuel MM Pte 203615 1/4th Oxf & Bucks Light Infantry
GODWIN Richard MM Pte R/35209 13th King's Royal Rifle Corps
GODWIN William "DCM,MM" CSM 21541 57th Bn Machine Gun Corps
GODWIN William G.T. MM Pte 241951 1/6th Royal Warwickshire Regt
GODWIN William T. MM Gnr 93417 17 Bty 41 Bde RFA
GODWYN James A. "DCM,MM" Spr 1545 2(London)Fd Coy Royal Engineers
GOFF Frederick T. MM L/Cpl 291544 1/1st Hertfordshire Regt
GOFF Harold T. MM Pte 14303 11th Hampshire Regt
GOFF Hugh MM Sjt 205342 7th Royal West Kent Regt
GOFF Thomas MM Pte 2579 7th Leinster Regt
GOFF William J. MM Pte 79436 9th Royal Fusiliers
GOFFE C.R. MM Sjt 77335 Royal Flying Corps
GOFFEE Frank MM Sjt 2887 11th Northumberland Fusiliers
GOFFIN William MM+Bar Sjt 352212 1/9th Durham Light Infantry
GOGGIN William MM Cpl 265792 Liverpool Regt
GOLBEY George MM Sjt 14510 6th Northamptonshire Regt KIA 27.9.16.
GOLBOURNE Samuel John MM Pte Z/1635 Rifle Brigade
GOLD Arthur "DCM,MM" L/Cpl 98373 1/6th London Regt
GOLD Charles MM Cpl 50811 57 Bde RFA
GOLD Cyril MM Pte S/5793 1st Rifle Brigade DOW 22.7.17.
GOLD David MM Cpl 59261 RGA
GOLD Frederick James MM L/Cpl 534050 4(London)Fd Amb RAMC
GOLD Richard MM L/Cpl 2607 Royal Warwickshire Regt
GOLD Robert K. MM Sjt 63414 F(AA)Bty RGA
GOLD William J. MM Bdr 78107 RFA
GOLDBERG Sidney MM Pte G/21511 7th Royal West Kent Regt
GOLDBURN Jacob MM Pte 8135 Northumberland Fusiliers
GOLDEN Arthur Wilfred "DCM,MM" Sjt SD/1766 11th Royal Sussex Regt DOW 24.4.18.
GOLDEN Charles E. MM Pte 65300 RAMC
GOLDEN Frank MM Sjt 18280 140 Fd Amb RAMC
GOLDEN John MM+Bar Pte 29581 RAMC
GOLDER Josiah MM Pte 55183 Machine Gun Corps
GOLDFARB Cecil MM Pte G/25211 7th East Kent Regt DOW 1.10.18.
GOLDIE Alexander M. MM Pte 330855 9th Highland Light Infantry
GOLDIE Charles MM CSM 11360 1st Worcestershire Regt DOW 26.9.16.
GOLDIE Francis H. MM Cpl Sig 697479 C/276 Bde RFA
GOLDIE George H. MM Pte 18622 Royal Highlanders
GOLDIE James Hutchison MM Sjt 13477 1st Scots Guards
GOLDIE John MM Pte 2953 1/4th Gordon Highlanders
GOLDIE Robert MM Pte 33503 1/5th Royal Scots Fusiliers
GOLDIE William MM L/Cpl 18380 Royal West Kent Regt
GOLDIE William H. MM Pte 12894 11th Royal Scots DOW 5.5.18.
GOLDING Albert G. MM Spr 37051 11 Div Sig Coy Royal Engineers
GOLDING Alfred Samuel MM 2nd Cpl 100019 226 Fd Coy Royal Engineers
GOLDING Clement MM Cpl 4537 1st Hampshire Regt
GOLDING E. MM Cpl 1328 Military Foot Police
GOLDING Edwin G. MM L/Cpl 102905 Machine Gun Corps
GOLDING Ernest MM L/Cpl 8243 Royal Irish Regt
GOLDING Frederick Hope MM Gnr 18008 27 Siege Bty RGA Died 20.2.20.

GOLDING Frederick Walter MM Cpl 44781 352 E&M Coy Royal Engineers DOW 10.8.18.
GOLDING George MM Sjt 266285 West Riding Regt
GOLDING George MM Pte 13908 6th Northamptonshire Regt KIA 10.11.16.
GOLDING Harold C. MM L/Cpl 506471 504 Fd Coy Royal Engineers
GOLDING John S. MM Pte 1296 East Surrey Regt
GOLDING Joseph MM Pte 5486 5th Shropshire Light Infantry KIA 24.8.16.
GOLDING Sidney MM Pte 47854 RAMC
GOLDING W.C. MM Sjt 14771 1st Bn Grenadier Guards
GOLDING William MM Pte 74100 1st Bn Machine Gun Corps
GOLDRICK Edward MM Pte 243048 5th Royal Lancaster Regt
GOLDS Albert MM Pte 6977 Royal Sussex Regt
GOLDS John MM Pte 17717 1st Royal Fusiliers
GOLDS John Richard MM Cpl 12689 6th Dragoon Guards
GOLDS Thomas MM Pte 3581 Royal Sussex Regt
GOLDS Walter A. MM Sjt 280465 18 Siege Bty RGA
GOLDS Walter B. MM Sjt 9958 2nd Royal Sussex Regt
GOLDSBOROUGH Arthur MM+Bar Sjt 2873 1/5th West Riding Regt
GOLDSBOROUGH J. MM L/Cpl 30339 1st Royal Dublin Fusiliers
GOLDSBOROUGH Walter MM Pte 25955 West Yorkshire Regt
GOLDSBY Clement MM Cpl 73208 5 Bde RFA
GOLDSBY Herbert Roye MM Sjt 12854 9th Royal Welsh Fusiliers KIA 27.6.16.
GOLDSBY Richard MM Pte 8359 8th Yorkshire Light Infantry KIA 23.1.17.
GOLDSMITH Bernard A. MM Sjt 2544 1/21st London Regt
GOLDSMITH Bert MM Dvr 66708 11 Bde RFA
GOLDSMITH Frank MM Sjt 34671 109 Heavy Bty RGA
GOLDSMITH George C. MM L/Sjt 17114 West Yorkshire Regt
GOLDSMITH James MM Pte 3117 Royal Sussex Regt
GOLDSMITH Joseph T. MM Dvr 120517 RFA
GOLDSMITH Percy C. MM Pte 3676 Seaforth Highlanders
GOLDSMITH Thomas F. MM Pte 203420 1st London Regt att MGC.
GOLDSMITH Thomas George MM Pte 13505 XVIII Corps Cyclist Bn Army Cyclist Corps
GOLDSON William S. MM Sjt 14422 Labour Corps
GOLDSTEIN Abraham MM Pte 422404 2/10th London Regt KIA 22.9.18.
GOLDSTONE Alfred J. MM Cpl R/2847 King's Royal Rifle Corps
GOLDSTONE Leonard MM Pte 69387 9th Royal Fusiliers KIA 21.9.18.
GOLDSTONE Leonard MM Pte 44748 12th Royal Irish Rifles KIA 21.3.18.
GOLDSTRAW Harry MM Pte 16200 1/5th Leicestershire Regt KIA 28.6.17.
GOLDSTRAW John A. MM Pte 29408 4th North Lancashire Regt
GOLDSTRAW Thomas MM 2nd Cpl 45197 Royal Engineers
GOLDSWAIN John MM L/Cpl 1908 1/1st Bucks Oxf & Bucks Light Infantry
GOLDTHORP Harry MM Pte 33434 West Yorkshire Regt
GOLDTHORPE Forshaw MM Cpl 38878 Northumberland Fusiliers
GOLDTHORPE Henry MM L/Cpl 38453 15th Highland Light Infantry
GOLDTHORPE James MM Sjt SB/107 6th Royal West Surrey Regt
GOLDTHORPE Lewis MM Pte 7380 10th Worcestershire Regt KIA 13.7.17.
GOLDTHORPE W.G. MM Pte 200631 1/5th Arg & Suth Highlanders
GOLIGHTLY Harold MM L/Cpl 250360 1/6th Durham Light Infantry DOW 19.11.17.
GOLLAND Arthur William MM Cpl 352747 7th London Regt "KIA 26.7.18,"
GOLLANDS John MM L/Cpl 325465 1/1st Cambridgeshire Regt
GOLLAR William D. MM Pte 200681 1/4th Essex Regt
GOLLEDGE R. MM Cpl 38050 10th Essex Regt
GOLLEDGE Richard MM Sjt 21586 Welsh Regt
GOLLEDGE Stanley Vyvyan MM Cpl 25990 10th West Riding Regt
GOLLER John Thomas MM Cpl 61706 17th Royal Fusiliers
GOLLICHER John MM Pte 3771 1/5th York & Lancaster Regt
GOLLICK Sam MM Sjt 3/3091 6th Yorkshire Light Infantry KIA 24.4.18.
GOLLOP Arthur MM Pte 41400 1st Duke of Cornwall's LI KIA 23.10.18.
GOLLOP Arthur MM L/Cpl 1761 2nd Northumberland Fusiliers
GOLLOP Ralph Gilbert MM Cpl 3/6513 1st Dorsetshire Regt
GOLSBY Walter MM Pte 235149 13th Liverpool Regt
GOLSON William A. MM Pte 3219 Machine Gun Corps
GOLTON Leonard W. MM Pte 305098 5th London Regt
GOMERSALL Edward MM Bdr 49417 A/56 Bde RFA
GOMERSALL William H. "DCM,MM" Pte 6435 57 Coy Machine Gun Corps
GOMERY Charles MM Dvr 79494 A/147 Bde RFA
GOMM Frederick MM Pte 29572 15th Cheshire Regt KIA 24.3.18.
GOMM Henry MM Gnr 59211 X/11 Med TM Bty RFA
GOMM W.J. MM Gnr 57028 RGA
GOMMO Edwin MM Pte 26081 2/5th Gloucestershire Regt
GOOCH Arthur V. MM Pte 32708 5th South Lancashire Regt
GOOCH Bertie MM S/Sjt 46292 100 Fd Amb RAMC
GOOCH Frederick George MM Sjt 31500 76 Fd Amb RAMC
GOOCH Frederick John MM L/Cpl 9910 2nd Essex Regt DOW 14.4.17.
GOOCH Harry MM Pte 3162 3rd Dragoon Guards
GOOCH Harry MM Sjt 17863 Suffolk Regt
GOOCH William MM Sjt 49475 1st Royal Inniskilling Fusiliers
GOOCH William MM 2nd Cpl 137785 237 Fd Coy Royal Engineers
GOOD Ben A. MM Cpl 8567 1st Scottish Rifles
GOOD Cuthbert MM Sjt 17520 48 Fd Amb RAMC
GOOD Ernest W. MM Pte 1658 East Surrey Regt
GOOD George MM Pte 52266 107 Fd Amb RAMC
GOOD Ralph MM Pte 36630 1st Gloucestershire Regt
GOOD Sydney H. "DCM+Bar,MM" Sjt 926310 290 Bde RFA
GOOD W.L. MM Spr 18461 5 Fd Coy Royal Engineers
GOOD William Cunningham MM L/Cpl 88417 19th Bn Machine Gun Corps
GOODA Charles MM Gnr 60343 8 Bde RFA
GOODACRE Herbert Edgar MM Sjt 67333 97 Fd Amb RAMC
GOODACRE William G. MM L/Cpl S/10303 Rifle Brigade
GOODALL Andrew MM Pte 202077 1/4th Royal Highlanders
GOODALL Arthur MM Pte 267197 8th West Yorkshire Regt
GOODALL Arthur MM Pte 300560 1/5th London Regt
GOODALL Charles H. MM Spr 249622 Royal Engineers
GOODALL Charlie Vernon MM Bdr 285767 254 Siege Bty RGA KIA 21.4.18.
GOODALL David "MM,MID" Sjt 20/9 20th Northumberland Fusiliers
GOODALL Ernest MM Gnr 69178 315 Siege Bty RGA
GOODALL Ernest G. MM L/Cpl M2/079250 Army Service Corps
GOODALL Frank E.J. MM Sjt 28183 1st Somerset Light Infantry
GOODALL Frederick H. MM Gnr 60194 1 Div Ammn Col. RFA
GOODALL George MM Pte 202501 1/4th Gordon Highlanders DOW 6.8.18.
GOODALL Harry H. MM Cpl M2/182345 Army Service Corps
GOODALL Holmes MM Cpl 23836 Machine Gun Corps
GOODALL Jeremiah MM L/Cpl 19892 South Staffordshire Regt
GOODALL Joseph "DCM,MM" Sjt 70718 54 Coy Machine Gun Corps
GOODALL Robert J. MM Pte G/12142 6th Royal West Kent Regt
GOODALL Samuel Henry MM Sjt WR/27474 HQ BEF Royal Engineers
GOODALL Thomas Brooker MM+Bar Sjt 8066 1st East Kent Regt
GOODAYLE Charles J. MM Gnr Fitter 281803 285 Siege Bty RGA
GOODBODY Albert MM Pte F/635 16th Middlesex Regt att RE.
GOODBRAND Harry MM Cpl 20629 22nd Manchester Regt KIA 14.3.17.
GOODCHILD Edwin MM Sjt 20043 8th Royal Berkshire Regt
GOODCHILD Herbert A. MM Cpl 44041 A/175 Bde RFA
GOODCHILD John H. MM Pte 31967 3rd Grenadier Guards
GOODCHILD Leopold MM Pte 2452 24th Royal Fusiliers
GOODCHILD Reginald G. MM Pte 551204 16th London Regt
GOODCHILD Robert Charles MM L/Sjt 3/9619 7th Suffolk Regt
GOODCHILD Walter William MM Sjt 9820 64 Coy Machine Gun Corps
GOODCHILD William C. MM Dvr 76959 RHA
GOODCHILD William G. MM Pte 204767 15th Hampshire Regt
GOODE A. MM Bdr 14605 RFA
GOODE Albert E. MM Cpl 40535 1st Royal Dublin Fusiliers
GOODE Charles Edward MM Cpl 55644 198 Coy Machine Gun Corps
GOODE Harry MM Cpl 8773 3rd Rifle Brigade
GOODE Herbert MM Sjt 10387 1st Royal Irish Fusiliers
GOODE Horace B. MM Sjt 10100 2nd Yorkshire Light Infantry
GOODE Jack MM Pte 268601 1/7th Royal Warwickshire Regt
GOODE Joseph Edward MM Sjt 320718 1/6th London Regt
GOODE Lemuel J. "DCM,MM" Sjt 19281 33rd Bn Machine Gun Corps
GOODE Lewis MM Pte 419149 RAMC
GOODE Sidney A. MM Sjt 113449 Royal Engineers
GOODE Sydney Maurice MM Cpl 241288 2/5th Gloucestershire Regt DOW 14.4.17.
GOODE Thomas Edward MM CQMS 265309 1/7th Royal Warwickshire Regt

GOODE Tom MM CSM 200371 1/4th Northamptonshire Regt
GOODE Walter MM Pte 20229 4th Worcestershire Regt
GOODE William MM CSM 6170 1st Rifle Brigade
GOODE William MM L/Cpl 20245 Leicestershire Regt
GOODEN William H. MM Sjt 318080 RGA
GOODENOUGH Ernest MM Gnr 25565 RGA
GOODENOUGH John MM L/Cpl 200115 1/4th Royal Berkshire Regt
GOODENOUGH Leonard Tom MM Sjt 1547 1/4th Royal Berkshire Regt
GOODENOUGH William MM Sjt 352133 'S' AA Bty RGA
GOODENS Alfred MM Pte 200362 1/4th East Yorkshire Regt
GOODERHAM Arthur MM Pte 41088 Suffolk Regt
GOODERHAM Philip Robert MM Cpl 13342 8th Norfolk Regt
GOODERIDGE Dennis J. MM Cpl 34325 North Lancashire Regt
GOODERIDGE Walter "DCM,MM" Cpl 6621 2nd York & Lancaster Regt
GOODEVE George MM L/Cpl 256 East Riding Fortress Coy Royal Engineers
GOODEY Alfred G. MM 2nd Cpl 59482 Royal Engineers
GOODFELLOW Andrew MM Pte 18327 12th Highland Light Infantry
GOODFELLOW Charles Irvine MM SQMS 7029 5th Lancers
GOODFELLOW Harold MM Pte 19130 11th Suffolk Regt
GOODFELLOW Harry MM Pte 200955 4th Yorkshire Light Infantry
GOODFELLOW Henry MM Sjt 1244 23rd Royal Fusiliers KIA 1.8.16.
GOODFELLOW John MM Sjt 280570 1/7th Highland Light Infantry
GOODFELLOW John M. MM Sjt 14898 Coldstream Guards
GOODFELLOW John McConnachie MM Spr 242124 63 Fd Coy Royal Engineers
GOODFELLOW Robert A. MM Pte 28033 11th Liverpool Regt
GOODFIELD Charles Chester MM Sjt 16640 4th Royal Fusiliers KIA 27.9.18.
GOODGAME George W. MM Spr 221796 18 Div Sig Coy Royal Engineers
GOODGE Frederick MM Pte 1676 27 Fd Amb RAMC
GOODGER Ernest MM Cpl M2/134515 51 Div Train Army Service Corps
GOODGER Frederick H. MM Pte 59081 13th Rifle Brigade
GOODGER Samuel William MM Dvr 25013 29 Bde RFA
GOODHAND Walter MM Dvr 64053 119 Bty 27 Bde RFA
GOODHEART Oswald Frank MM Sjt 5491 16th Lancers
GOODHEW Arthur MM Pte 1424 RAMC
GOODHEW Charles H. MM Pte 51099 7th Lincolnshire Regt
GOODHIND William MM Sjt 6006 1st Somerset Light Infantry
GOODIER Edwin MM Pte 200377 North Lancashire Regt
GOODIER Frederick MM Dvr 14540 D/157 Bde RFA
GOODIER Thomas MM Pte 17050 South Lancashire Regt
GOODING Adolphus MM Pte 202049 4th Somerset Light Infantry
GOODING Alonzo T. MM CSM 9833 5th Dorsetshire Regt
GOODING Donald MM Sjt 3003 1/15th London Regt KIA 7.10.16.
GOODING Fred MM L/Sjt B/200441 10th Rifle Brigade KIA 30.11.17.
GOODING Louis Frederick MM Pte 130795 45th Royal Fusiliers
GOODING Roy V.G. MM Sjt 19574 Machine Gun Corps
GOODING Walter Hubert Peters MM L/Cpl 32933 1st Essex Regt KIA 30.11.17.
GOODINSON Thomas Henry MM Pte 40766 1/5th North Staffordshire Regt KIA 17.4.1`8.
GOODISON George MM+Bar Bdr 71397 41 Bde RFA
GOODISON John Henry MM Pte G/9851 11th Royal West Kent Regt
GOODLAKE Arthur MM Pte 60209 Royal Fusiliers
GOODLIFF Albert "DCM,MM+Bar" Pte 17442 7th & 2nd Bedfordshire Regt
GOODLIFF George Jenkins MM Sjt 79708 Machine Gun Corps
GOODLIFFE John C. MM Sjt 175349 1/1st Yorkshire Dragoons Yeo
GOODMAN Archibald Neville MM Sjt 229690 1st London Regt
GOODMAN Arthur MM Cpl H/3551 7th Hussars
GOODMAN Cyril MM Cpl 9075 3rd Worcestershire Regt
GOODMAN Edward MM Sjt 350667 7th London Regt
GOODMAN Edwin MM Pte 12379 7th Wiltshire Regt
GOODMAN Edwin M. MM Pte M2/152909 659 Coy Army Service Corps
GOODMAN F.A. MM SSM 91 1/1st North Somerset Yeo
GOODMAN Fred MM Pte 266931 Oxf & Bucks Light Infantry
GOODMAN Frederick William MM Pte 5200 2nd Coldstream Guards
GOODMAN George A. MM Pte 72837 2nd Notts & Derby Regt
GOODMAN Joseph MM Cpl 10/437 10th East Yorkshire Regt
GOODMAN Mathew MM Pte 7193 21st Royal Fusiliers
GOODMAN Robert MM Pte 18/953 Northumberland Fusiliers
GOODMAN Roland Henry MM Sjt 2285 Leicestershire Regt
GOODMAN Sam MM Sjt 20100 Yorkshire Light Infantry
GOODMAN Thomas H.F. MM Pte 9/13770 6th Lincolnshire Regt
GOODMAN Thomas J. MM Sjt 550161 Royal Engineers
GOODMAN Wallace MM Sjt 19195 9th York & Lancaster Regt
GOODMAN Walter Edward MM Pte 15662 11th Hampshire Regt KIA 24.3.18.
GOODMAN William MM L/Sjt 12214 7th Norfolk Regt KIA 16.10.16.
GOODMAN William Henry MM Sjt 6/16401 6th South Wales Borderers DOW 15.6.16.
GOODMAN William Humphrey MM L/Cpl S/27090 13th Rifle Brigade KIA 2.8.17.
GOODMAN William R. MM Cpl 935109 RFA
GOODRAM Gilbert MM Pte 17603 4th North Lancashire Regt
GOODRAM William MM Pte 36729 1/4th North Lancashire Regt KIA 1.10.18.
GOODRICH Alfred J. MM Spr 96225 Royal Engineers
GOODRIDGE Charles W. MM Spr 510074 Royal Engineers
GOODRIDGE Frank Eli MM L/Cpl 10302 Machine Gun Corps
GOODRIDGE H. MM Pte 4985 London Regt
GOODRUM Frank Henry MM Spr 150367 Railways Op Div Royal Engineers
GOODRUM Harry L. MM Cpl 64897 17th Worcestershire Regt
GOODRUM Thomas E. MM Spr 480632 460 Fd Coy Royal Engineers
GOODSHIP Abel Andrew MM Cpl 18361 Royal Welsh Fusiliers
GOODSHIP William C. MM L/Cpl 24202 South Wales Borderers
GOODSHIP William R. MM L/Cpl 84949 Royal Engineers
GOODSIR Thomas B. MM+Bar Cpl 482135 62 Div Sig Coy Royal Engineers
GOODSIR William Michie MM Pte 24546 51st Bn Machine Gun Corps DOW 25.10.18.
GOODSMAN John MM Gnr 42494 RGA
GOODSON Frank MM Sjt 42837 32nd Bn Machine Gun Corps
GOODWAY Charles "DCM,MM" Sjt 17544 8th Gloucestershire Regt
GOODWILL John MM L/Cpl 8555 9th Northumberland Fusiliers
GOODWILL John W. MM Gnr 89517 RGA
GOODWILL William MM Pte 43221 6th Royal Inniskilling Fusiliers
GOODWIN Alfred MM Pte 241914 Yorkshire Light Infantry
GOODWIN Arthur Benjamin MM+Bar Sjt 293046 138 Heavy Bty RGA
GOODWIN Arthur Cecil MM Pte 102037 1(London)(Cav)Fd Amb RAMC
GOODWIN Bertram L. MM Cpl 25304 17th Royal Welsh Fusiliers
GOODWIN Charles MM Pte 16430 8th Yorkshire Light Infantry
GOODWIN Charles J.H. MM Pte 291178 North Lancashire Regt
GOODWIN David W. MM Cpl 22320 South Lancashire Regt
GOODWIN E.F. MM L/Cpl P/5817 Military Mounted Police
GOODWIN Edward MM Sjt 290863 126 Hy Bty RGA
GOODWIN Edwin MM Pte 242159 Royal Lancaster Regt
GOODWIN Francis J. MM Pte 51846 1 Fd Amb RAMC
GOODWIN Fred MM Bdr 706212 RFA
GOODWIN Frederick MM Bdr 901203 RFA
GOODWIN Frederick MM Pte 14027 6th Duke of Cornwall's LI KIA 25.4.18.
GOODWIN Frederick MM L/Cpl 2034 2nd Royal Fusiliers DOW 28.11.17.
GOODWIN George H. MM L/Cpl 25296 North Lancashire Regt
GOODWIN George Herbert MM Pte 260350 Liverpool Regt
GOODWIN George William MM L/Cpl 6266 Royal West Surrey Regt
GOODWIN GeorgeA. MM Sjt 31760 45 Bde RFA
GOODWIN Henry George MM+Bar Cpl 23765 10th Essex Regt
GOODWIN Hugh MM Gnr L/18471 A/151 Bde RFA
GOODWIN James Henry MM Pte 45127 15th Cheshire Regt
GOODWIN James R. MM Pte 27978 13th Liverpool Regt
GOODWIN James Richard MM Pte 2408 1/13th London Regt DOW 31.12.17.
GOODWIN John MM Cpl 132424 25th Bn Machine Gun Corps
GOODWIN John MM+Bar Cpl 241453 York & Lancaster Regt
GOODWIN John MM Gnr 48562 RGA
GOODWIN John W. "DCM,MM+Bar" Sjt 47257 25 Div Sig Coy Royal Engineers
GOODWIN Leslie MM Sjt 1079 13th Cheshire Regt
GOODWIN Percy MM Sjt 3420 13th Rifle Brigade
GOODWIN R. MM+2 Bars Sjt S/12042 Gordon Highlanders
GOODWIN Reginald MM Pte 203618 North Staffordshire Regt
GOODWIN Richard MM Pte 41272 Royal Irish Rifles
GOODWIN Stanley MM L/Cpl 15185 7th Bedfordshire Regt KIA 24.4.18.
GOODWIN Thomas D. MM Cpl 266501 1/7th Royal Highlanders
GOODWIN Walter Edward MM Pte 10292 6th Leicestershire Regt

GOODWIN Wilfred Jesse MM Spr 430258 55 Div Sig Coy Royal Engineers
GOODWIN William MM Sjt 82630 40 Bty 25 Bde RFA
GOODWIN William MM Gnr 60771 RGA
GOODWIN William MM+Bar Gnr 93860 RFA
GOODWIN William G. MM Pte 240904 8th Royal West Kent Regt
GOODY Albert MM Dvr 41025 D/153 Bde RFA
GOODY Walter "MC,MM,OLeo(B)" RSM 9691 Suffolk Regt
GOODYEAR William MM Sjt 8553 2nd Devonshire Regt
GOODYER Arthur MM Gnr 11453 HQ 20 Bde RFA
GOODYER Leonard MM+Bar Pte 7231 7th Royal Sussex Regt
GOOLD Marshall N. MM Pte M2/055174 Army Service Corps
GOOSE George MM L/Cpl 13/393 13th York & Lancaster Regt KIA 30.9.18.
GOOSEY William Herbert MM Sjt 200358 1/4th Northamptonshire Regt
GORAM Charles MM Pte 42946 Machine Gun Corps
GORBEY Robert MM Pte 6970 2nd Irish Guards
GORDGE Robert Edgar MM L/Cpl 142530 'BP' Cable Section Royal Engineers
GORDON Adam "DCM,MM" Sjt 235991 9th West Yorkshire Regt
GORDON Adam MM Dvr 6276 RFA
GORDON Alexander MM Pte 201407 1/4th Gordon Highlanders
GORDON Alexander "MC+Bar,DCM,MM(8012 L/Cpl Scots Gds)" Capt 2nd Royal Scots
GORDON Alexander MM L/Cpl 265426 1/6th Gordon Highlanders
GORDON Alexander McKenzie MM Pte 3093 1/5th Royal Scots
GORDON Alexander P. MM Sjt 345674 14th Royal Highlanders
GORDON Alfred G. MM Pte 62943 Machine Gun Corps
GORDON Allan L. MM+Bar Pte 291071 2nd Gordon Highlanders
GORDON Archibald MM Spr 79853 Royal Engineers
GORDON Arthur C. MM Gnr 67771 121 Bty 27 Bde RFA
GORDON C. MM Sjt 311845 Signal Service Royal Engineers
GORDON C. MM Pte J/951 38th Royal Fusiliers
GORDON Charles MM L/Cpl 19394 Manchester Regt
GORDON Charles B. MM Pte 16754 12th Gloucestershire Regt
GORDON Clifford MM Spr 831 Royal Engineers
GORDON David MM Cpl 18380 12th Highland Light Infantry
GORDON Douglas Arthur MM Bdr 171226 157 Siege Bty RGA
GORDON Ernest J. MM Pte 352899 19th London Regt
GORDON Ernest W. "DCM,MM+Bar" Pte 872 1st Welsh Guards
GORDON F.E.P. MM Cpl 11104 Durham Light Infantry
GORDON Frederick H. MM Pte G/11000 2nd Royal Sussex Regt
GORDON George MM Sjt 37749 RAMC
GORDON George MM Pte 33 2nd Gordon Highlanders att MGC
GORDON George MM L/Cpl 8992 Arg & Suth Highlanders
GORDON George MM Pte 9457 1/5th London Regt
GORDON George T. MM Sjt 202826 1/4th Gordon Highlanders
GORDON Gerald MM Dvr L/46306 B/190 Bde RFA
GORDON H.W. MM L/Cpl 241330 Gordon Highlanders
GORDON Isaac MM+Bar Pte 9468 1st Cameron Highlanders
GORDON James MM Spr 101939 90 Fd Coy Royal Engineers
GORDON James J. MM Cpl 161947 Royal Engineers
GORDON James R. MM Pte 6352 1/4th Gordon Highlanders
GORDON John MM Cpl 240951 8th Royal Highlanders
GORDON John MM Sjt 86506 Royal Engineers
GORDON John MM Bdr 307374 2/1(Lowland)Hy Bty RGA
GORDON John MM L/Cpl 240344 1/5th Seaforth Highlanders
GORDON John MM Pte 9207 1st Gordon Highlanders
GORDON John MM Sjt 5274 1 Siege Coy Royal Anglesey Royal Engineers
GORDON John MM L/Cpl 151636 Tunneling Coy Royal Engineers
GORDON John MM Pte 9464 2nd Royal Scots
GORDON John MM Pte S/8990 2nd Gordon Highlanders
GORDON John MM Pte 43311 1/9th Royal Scots
GORDON John MM Pte 201432 Royal Highlanders
GORDON John D. MM Pte 5991 2nd Manchester Regt
GORDON John G. MM Pte 8200 6th Yorkshire Regt
GORDON John H. MM Sjt 22574 North Staffordshire Regt
GORDON Joseph MM L/Cpl 23174 3 Div Sig Coy Royal Engineers
GORDON Patrick MM Pte 66435 62nd Bn Machine Gun Corps
GORDON Peter MM Dvr 876576 107 Bty 23 Bde RFA
GORDON Peter MM Pte 33096 2nd Royal Scots
GORDON Peter R. MM CSM 203376 Royal Highlanders
GORDON Robert MM Dvr 630035 A/225 Bde RFA
GORDON Robert MM Cpl 58801 67 Siege Bty RGA
GORDON Robert MM Gnr 27989 RFA
GORDON Robert MM+2 Bars Sjt 13053 10th Durham Light Infantry
GORDON Robert D. MM Pte 114066 17th Liverpool Regt
GORDON Stuart B. MM Sjt 303482 5th London Regt
GORDON Thomas Alexander MM Cpl 16/701 16th Northumberland Fusiliers KIA 1.2.18.
GORDON Thomas E. MM Sjt 931349 337 Bde RFA
GORDON Walter V. MM Cpl 46787 110 Fd Amb RAMC
GORDON William MM+Bar CSM 16972 1st Royal Scots Fusiliers
GORDON William MM L/Cpl 2384 1/7th Gordon Highlanders
GORDON William MM L/Sjt 2339 Notts & Derby Regt
GORDON William MM Pte 10576 1st Scottish Rifles DOW 30.7.18.
GORDON William MM Pte 3/10694 2nd Durham Light Infantry
GORDON William MM L/Cpl 14185 2nd Devonshire Regt
GORDON William MM+Bar Cpl 9838 Gordon Highlanders
GORDON William MM Sjt 6011 9th Manchester Regt KIA 8.10.18.
GORDON-BROWN Evelyn MM Miss F First Aid Nursing Yeomanry
GORE Arthur MM Cpl Fitter 11273 C/78 Bde RFA
GORE Arthur F. MM BQMS 925221 A/280 Bde RFA
GORE C. MM Cpl 265207 Liverpool Regt
GORE Ernest MM L/Cpl 10874 Wiltshire Regt
GORE George MM Sjt 9569 2nd Royal Welsh Fusiliers
GORE George James MM L/Cpl 161163 First Army HQ Sig Coy Royal Engineers
GORE James MM Pte 42527 26th Royal Welsh Fusiliers
GORE James George MM Sjt 39625 RAMC
GORE Job MM Pte 39190 66 Labour Coy Labour Corps
GORE Joe MM Cpl 71230 10th Notts & Derby Regt
GORE John Thomas "MC,DCM,MM(1775 Sjt)" Capt 23rd Royal Fusiliers
GORE Leslie Frank MM Sjt 558103 56 Div Sig Coy Royal Engineers
GORE Thomas MM Sjt 1353 1st Lancashire Fusiliers
GORE William MM Bdr 115123 RGA
GORE William Frederick MM Pte 1287 South Irish Horse KIA 27.9.18.
GOREE John C. MM Pte 228610 4th London Regt
GOREY J. MM Cpl 21010 Machine Gun Corps
GORF Francis W. MM+Bar Pte 202419 5th Leicestershire Regt
GORFIN Joseph E. MM Sjt 3/4649 1st Devonshire Regt
GORFIN William MM Bdr 78382 RGA
GORHAM Frederick H. MM L/Sjt 240411 1/5th Suffolk Regt
GORING Frederick Alfred MM Sjt 320873 1/6th London Regt
GORING George Thomas MM Cpl M2/047757 272 MT Coy Army Service Corps
GORING Thomas Roberts MM Sjt 44748 'U' AA Bty RGA
GORLEY Charles MM Sjt 112267 Royal Engineers
GORMALLY Michael MM Gnr 116672 RFA
GORMAN Arthur MM Dvr 39559 42 Bde RFA
GORMAN David William MM L/Cpl 250166 1/6th Manchester Regt
GORMAN Edward "DCM,MM+Bar" Sjt M2/120585 Army Service Corps att 11 Fd Amb RAMC
GORMAN Frederick MM Spr 550429 520 Fd Coy Royal Engineers
GORMAN Frederick MM Pte 350549 1/9th Manchester Regt
GORMAN Frederick C. MM Sjt M1/07581 5 Motor Amb Convoy Army Service Corps
GORMAN George W. MM Pte 20572 East Yorkshire Regt
GORMAN J. MM Pte 390051 RAMC
GORMAN James MM Pte 3928 Leinster Regt
GORMAN James H. MM L/Sjt 4033 Gordon Highlanders
GORMAN James V. MM Sjt 9317 13th Yorkshire Regt
GORMAN John MM Sjt 79013 A/58 Bde RFA
GORMAN John MM+Bar L/Sjt 2568 2nd Royal Munster Fusiliers
GORMAN Matthew MM Pte 20938 Royal Irish Fusiliers
GORMAN Pat MM Pte S/7600 9th Rifle Brigade KIA 24.3.18.
GORMAN Patrick MM Pte 11642 2nd Royal Dublin Fusiliers
GORMAN Samuel MM Pte 28006 1st Scottish Rifles
GORMAN Thomas MM Sjt 13649 RFA
GORMAN William MM Sjt 241171 South Lancashire Regt
GORMAN William H. MM Pte 200748 Devonshire Regt
GORMLAY James MM Pte 22156 12th Durham Light Infantry DOW 18.7.16.
GORMLEY Edward MM Pte 12380 1st Gordon Highlanders
GORMLEY Henry MM Pte 405941 13th Liverpool Regt
GORMLEY James MM RSM 7796 2/4th York & Lancaster Regt
GORMLEY Joseph MM L/Cpl 43770 Machine Gun Corps
GORMLEY Peter J. MM Sjt 64514 42 Bde RFA
GORRIE Angus MM Pte 11021 5th Cameron Highlanders
GORRIE Angus MM+Bar Sjt 305181 2/1(Highland)Fd Amb RAMC
GORRINGE George Edward MM L/Sjt 240614 1/5th Lincolnshire Regt
GORRY Joseph "MM,CG(B)" L/Sjt 24825 8/9th Royal Dublin Fusiliers
GORRY Joseph MM Pte 10789 12th Liverpool Regt KIA 16.9.16.
GORSE Edwn MM Pte 201548 5th East Lancashire Regt

GORSE Thomas J. MM Dvr 710516 RFA
GORST Frederick MM Pte 13047 5th Dorsetshire Regt
GORST Harold MM Bdr L/10667 C/79 Bde RFA
GORSUCH Douglas MM Spr 322403 Royal Engineers
GORTON Edward MM Pte 200281 2nd East Lancashire Regt
GORTON Edward G. MM Pte S/29920 Rifle Brigade
GORTON Francis MM L/Cpl 9462 5th Wiltshire Regt
GORTON Francis Pope MM Pte 86145 54 Coy Machine Gun Corps
GORTON Frederick MM L/Cpl 200756 1/4th North Lancashire Regt
GORTON George A. MM Pte 355220 1/10th Liverpool Regt
GORTON George B. MM L/Cpl 17064 8th East Lancashire Regt
GORTON Harry S. MM Sjt 240146 6th North Staffordshire Regt
GORWOOD Frank MM+Bar Pte 8790 2nd Gloucestershire Regt
GORWYN Herbert L. MM L/Cpl 61125 Machine Gun Corps
GOSDEN Alfred MM Sjt 22475 6th East Kent Regt DOW 8.9.18.
GOSDEN Ernest T. MM Pte 304497 15th Bn Tank Corps
GOSDEN Frederick MM Pte 14173 6th Dragoons
GOSDEN John H. MM Pte 500257 6 Fd Amb RAMC
GOSDEN Montague MM Pte 512746 1/14th London Regt att MGC.
GOSHAWK Ronald R. MM Cpl 23713 Suffolk Regt
GOSLIN Frederick S. "MM,MSM" Sjt 961448 C/237 Bde RFA
GOSLIN Thomas Claude MM L/Cpl 497029 82 Fd Amb RAMC
GOSLING Alfred MM Pte 10629 2nd Hampshire Regt
GOSLING Alfred Harry MM Pte 18491 8th Royal Berkshire Regt
GOSLING Frederick MM Bdr 30885 RGA
GOSLING Frederick J. MM Sjt 329554 187 Siege Bty RGA
GOSLING George MM Cpl 79965 173 Tunnelling Coy Royal Engineers
GOSLING James MM Pte 32634 Hampshire Regt
GOSLING Leslie MM Sjt 4942 4th Dragoon Guards
GOSLING Percy S. MM Cpl 108135 Machine Gun Corps
GOSLING Stanley Charles MM Pte 200953 5th Tank Corps DOW 16.4.18.
GOSLING Walter Henry MM Sjt 18298 20 Coy Machine Gun Corps
GOSLING William Robert MM Sjt R/4498 13th King's Royal Rifle Corps KIA 21.3.18.
GOSNELL Albert Edward MM Sjt 558245 56 Div Sig Coy Royal Engineers
GOSNEY Frederick MM Pte 19235 Hampshire Regt
GOSNEY Harry MM Pte R/32056 2nd King's Royal Rifle Corps
GOSNEY Harry George MM Cpl 61875 81 Fd Coy Royal Engineers
GOSNEY William E. MM Sjt 14291 12th Gloucestershire Regt
GOSS Francis A. MM Sjt 992 1st East Surrey Regt
GOSS Harry H. MM L/Cpl 7879 2nd Oxf & Bucks Light Infantry
GOSS John P. MM Pte 200212 4th Hampshire Regt
GOSS Stanley Earl MM Pte 13015 VI Corps Cyclist Bn Army Cyclist Corps
GOSS Sydney A. MM Spr 64952 18 Div Sig Coy Royal Engineers
GOSS William MM Pte 12860 7th Bedfordshire Regt
GOSSMAN Alexander MM S/Sjt Fitter 88952 RFA
GOSSMAN Thomas MM Cpl S/41666 6th Royal Highlanders
GOSTLING Edward MM Pte 72884 Royal Welsh Fusiliers
GOSTLING Frank A. MM Sjt 47764 V Bty RHA
GOSTLING L. MM Pte 17776 10th Essex Regt
GOSWELL Alfred W. MM Sjt 6305 RAMC
GOSWELL Edwin MM Bdr 61002 RFA
GOTH William MM Cpl 19383 6th South Wales Borderers
GOTHARD Douglas S. MM L/Cpl 151414 104th Bn Machine Gun Corps
GOTHARD Harry MM Dvr T/4/055538 Army Service Corps att 1st Rifle Brigade
GOTT Arthur MM Pte 205 RAMC
GOTT George MM Pte 24723 7th Yorkshire Regt
GOTT George MM Pte 200966 Lincolnshire Regt
GOTTS William H. MM Pte 31557 RAMC
GOUCHER Tom E. MM Pte 25213 Notts & Derby Regt
GOUDE Frank MM Sjt 9652 2nd Scottish Rifles DOW 26.3.18.
GOUDIE James MM L/Cpl S/12406 Cameron Highlanders
GOUDIE William MM Cpl M2/052166 282 Coy Army Service Corps
GOUGH Albert MM Pte 65948 25th Bn Machine Gun Corps
GOUGH Albert F. MM L/Cpl 17633 5 Fd Coy Royal Engineers
GOUGH Archibald Frank MM Gnr 950242 B/235 Bde RFA
GOUGH Edward Joseph MM Sjt G/50256 2nd Royal Fusiliers
GOUGH Ernest S. MM Bdr Sig 99012 41 Siege Bty RGA
GOUGH Frank MM Pte 51962 8th Lincolnshire Regt
GOUGH Frank MM Cpl 12656 6th Royal Berkshire Regt KIA 30.9.16.
GOUGH Frank R. MM L/Cpl 266566 1/1st Hertfordshire Regt
GOUGH Frederick MM Pte 18266 Machine Gun Corps
GOUGH Frederick MM Sjt 20886 145 Coy Machine Gun Corps
GOUGH Frederick C. MM Pte 13690 Army Cyclist Corps
GOUGH Frederick H. MM Pte 63431 67 Fd Amb RAMC
GOUGH George E. MM Pte 14622 7th Bedfordshire Regt
GOUGH Harold T. MM Sjt 305385 1/8th West Yorkshire Regt
GOUGH Harry W. "MM,MID" Pte 10721 5th Shropshire Light Infantry
GOUGH Henry MM Gnr 831425 311 Bde RFA
GOUGH Henry M. MM Cpl 506554 504 Fd Coy Royal Engineers
GOUGH Herbert MM L/Bdr 736130 D/157 Bde RFA
GOUGH Horace MM Pte 17358 9th Manchester Regt
GOUGH Jack Thomas MM Pte M2/192060 Army Service Corps
GOUGH James MM L/Bdr 99988 RGA
GOUGH John MM Gnr 745175 97 Bty 104 Bde RFA
GOUGH John MM L/Sjt 420 1st Welsh Guards
GOUGH John Joseph MM Spr 98416 223 Fd Coy Royal Engineers
GOUGH John R. MM Gnr 766 RGA
GOUGH Leonard MM Sjt 15899 9th South Staffordshire Regt
GOUGH Richard MM Spr 19352 21 Div Sig Coy Royal Engineers
GOUGH Richard Allison MM L/Sjt 265588 1/1st Hertfordshire Regt
GOUGH Thomas MM Cpl 19719 Dorsetshire Regt
GOUGH W. MM Pte 240444 Notts & Derby Regt
GOUGH Walter MM Pte 306873 West Yorkshire Regt
GOUGH Walter MM Pte 201163 4th Worcestershire Regt KIA 30.9.18.
GOUGH William MM Pte 43554 5th Royal Berkshire Regt
GOUGH William MM Pte 15439 7th South Lancashire Regt
GOUK George MM Pte 240240 1/5th Royal Highlanders
GOULD Albert MM Pnr 100448 33 Div Sig Coy Royal Engineers
GOULD Allan R. MM L/Sjt 201071 2nd Durham Light Infantry
GOULD Arthur H. MM L/Cpl 427124 10th London Regt
GOULD Charles MM Pte 66539 RAMC
GOULD Charles MM Pte 4974 1st Lancashire Fusiliers
GOULD Charles MM Sjt 11197 1st Grenadier Guards
GOULD Edward MM Pte 15556 13th Northumberland Fusiliers DOW 1.10.16.
GOULD Edward MM Pte 1164 11th East Yorkshire Regt KIA 12.4.18.
GOULD Fred MM Spr 43749 Royal Engineers
GOULD Fred MM L/Cpl 12821 9th Essex Regt DOW 11.5.17.
GOULD George MM Sjt 23253 1st Royal West Kent Regt
GOULD George MM Sjt 4/8988 2nd Arg & Suth Highlanders DOW 23.9.18.
GOULD George H. MM Pte 307376 Notts & Derby Regt
GOULD George Herbert MM Sjt 27678 B/95 Bde RFA KIA 24.10.18.
GOULD Harold MM Sjt 1048 Military Foot Police
GOULD Harry MM Bdr 635023 RFA
GOULD Harry S.S. "DCM,MM+Bar" CSM 4874 8th East Surrey Regt
GOULD Henry E. MM Sjt 95599 Royal Engineers
GOULD Horace C. MM Pte 23761 7th Royal West Surrey Regt
GOULD James MM Spr 148129 21 Div Sig Coy Royal Engineers
GOULD John E. MM+Bar Sjt 40134 1st South Staffordshire Regt
GOULD John H.A. MM Pte 12499 6th Shropshire Light Infantry
GOULD John Hunter MM L/Cpl 18539 8th Devonshire Regt
GOULD Reuben J. MM Dvr 30319 30 Div Ammn Col RFA
GOULD Robert MM Sjt 84808 Royal Engineers
GOULD Samuel MM 2nd Cpl 69015 35 Div Sig Coy Royal Engineers KIA 19.10.17.
GOULD Sydney J. MM Cpl 43709 16th Bn Machine Gun Corps
GOULD Thomas B. MM Pte G/95213 3rd London Regt
GOULD Thomas H. MM Spr 172355 21 Div Sig Coy Royal Engineers
GOULD Walter MM L/Cpl 9/12857 7th Leicestershire Regt DOW 28.4.18.
GOULD Watkin MM Cpl 241600 Welsh Regt
GOULD William MM Bdr 950239 233 Bde RFA
GOULD William MM Cpl 251577 7 Div Sig Coy Royal Engineers
GOULD William E. MM Gnr 1424 RFA
GOULD William Edward MM Sjt F/1691 Middlesex Regt
GOULD William George MM Pte 13822 10th Devonshire Regt KIA 25.4.17.
GOULD William H. MM Gnr 329945 RGA
GOULD William J. MM Sjt 345150 16th Devonshire Regt
GOULD William J. MM Gnr 292566 RGA
GOULDEN George MM CSM 15128 8th Yorkshire Light Infantry KIA 27.9.17.
GOULDEN Richard E MM CSM 13447 10th Gloucestershire Regt att Royal West Kent Regt.
GOULDING Arthur Abraham MM+Bar L/Sjt 26167 16th & 15th Notts & Derby Regt
GOULDING Bartholomew MM Cpl 2037 16 Fd Amb RAMC
GOULDING David MM Pte 65370 Machine Gun Corps
GOULDING Ernest MM L/Cpl 11034 7th Lincolnshire Regt

GOULDING Herbert Tom MM Sjt 22259 RGA
GOULDING Michael MM L/Cpl 18944 9th Royal Dublin Fusiliers DOW 17.8.17.
GOULDING Patrick MM L/Cpl 12314 7th North Lancashire Regt KIA 15.6.17.
GOULDING William James MM Bdr 83595 51 TM Bty RFA KIA 10.3.17.
GOULDS R.S. MM Bdr 41467 27 Bde RFA
GOULDTHORPE Oliver "DCM,MM" L/Sjt 240664 Lincolnshire Regt
GOULSBRA William T. MM Cpl 40052 6th Lincolnshire Regt
GOULT Percy Joseph MM Sjt 438 2/1st HAC(Inf)
GOULT William G. MM+Bar Bdr 186876 B/156 Bde RFA
GOUNDRY R. MM Pte 19612 West Yorkshire Regt
GOURLAY Arthur MM Pnr 75326 Royal Engineers
GOURLAY David MM Sjt 242306 Gordon Highlanders
GOURLAY James MM Sjt S/4872 8th Royal Highlanders
GOURLAY James MM Pte 2469 Royal Highlanders
GOURLAY James MM Pte 17082 2nd Royal Scots Fusiliers DOW 16.6.17.
GOURLAY John Robertson MM Sjt 350109 1/9th A Coy Royal Scots DOW 20.9.17.
GOURLAY William MM Sjt 66101 10th Royal Scots
GOURLAY William MM Pte 9788 3rd Dragoon Guards
GOURLEY Cyril Edward "VC,MM" Sjt 681886 D/276 Bde RFA
GOURLEY Robert MM Pte 29358 Yorkshire Regt
GOURLEY Straghan MM Pte 14390 Northumberland Fusiliers
GOVAN James Henry "DCM,MM" Pte 12175 1st Scots Guards
GOVAN William MM Pte 13883 King's Own Scottish Borderers
GOVERD Reginald C. MM Cpl 35795 14 Bde RFA
GOVIER John MM Pte 38072 Lancashire Fusiliers
GOW Alexander P. MM+Bar Sjt S/5375 1/7th Royal Highlanders
GOW David MM Sjt 55829 D/18 Bde RFA
GOW Edward MM Bdr 651227 C/315 Bde RFA
GOW J. MM Sjt 200251 Royal Highlanders
GOW John MM Sjt 225277 5th Cameron Highlanders
GOW John B. MM 2nd Cpl 43594 Royal Engineers
GOW William MM Sjt 61709 Machine Gun Corps
GOW William Oliphant MM Cpl T4/110868 8 Railhead Supply Depot Army Service Corps
GOWAN Francis MM Pte 8229 2nd Irish Guards
GOWAN William R. MM+Bar Sjt 54731 42 Bde RFA
GOWANLOCK Walter MM Pte 265463 1/8th Scottish Rifles KIA 29.7.18.
GOWANS Harry MM Bdr 635041 D/82 Bde RFA DOW 18.9.18.
GOWANS Reginald MM+Bar Sjt 4051 54 Coy Machine Gun Corps DOW 11.12.17.
GOWARD Alfred J. MM Cpl 10862 Royal Fusiliers
GOWARD Hilling MM Sjt G/2430 8th Royal Sussex Regt
GOWARD John J. MM Gnr 19941 RFA
GOWARD Robert MM L/Cpl 13846 1st Yorkshire Light Infantry
GOWARD William MM+2 Bars Sjt 77447 3rd Light Bn Tank Corps
GOWDEY Lawrence Cragg MM L/Cpl 75282 Royal Engineers
GOWDIE John F. MM Sjt 303059 Royal Scots
GOWDY John MM Spr 64511 36 Div Sig Coy Royal Engineers
GOWDY Joseph "MM,MSM" C/Sjt 17744 2nd Royal Irish Rifles
GOWDY R. MM L/Cpl 17739 12th Royal Irish Rifles
GOWDY William J. MM+Bar 2nd Cpl 57607 121 Fd Coy Royal Engineers
GOWEN William J. MM Pte 40746 Middlesex Regt
GOWER Albert MM Pte 61752 23rd Royal Fusiliers
GOWER Alfred MM L/Cpl 2104 2nd Middlesex Regt
GOWER Ernest James MM Pte 40187 3rd Worcestershire Regt
GOWER Francis C. MM Sjt 92467 Tank Corps
GOWER Henry W. MM Pte 700846 23rd London Regt
GOWER Herbert MM Cpl 81080 RFA
GOWER James MM Pte 424407 10th London Regt
GOWER Sydney J. MM L/Cpl 13818 Royal Engineers
GOWER Thomas Henry MM Sjt 305674 2/8th West Yorkshire Regt DOW 23.11.17.
GOWER William C. MM Pte 57865 5th Lancashire Fusiliers
GOWER William R. MM Pte 265376 1/6th Welsh Regt
GOWERS Alfred MM Bdr 96357 156 Siege Bty RGA
GOWERS Arthur Edward MM Pte S/15174 3rd Rifle Brigade
GOWERS Cyril MM Sjt 9158 A/71 Bde RFA
GOWERS George Thomas MM Pte 25525 2nd Northamptonshire Regt
GOWERS Henry MM Pte 8828 3rd Royal Fusiliers
GOWING Ernest MM Cpl 85556 Royal Engineers
GOWING William S. MM Cpl SP/3081 24th Royal Fusiliers
GOWLAND Charles MM L/Cpl 16491 13th Durham Light Infantry
GOWLAND John MM Cpl 90243 23rd Bn Machine Gun Corps
GOWLAND Percy G. MM L/Cpl 10522 2nd East Lancashire Regt
GOWLAND Thomas MM L/Cpl 201056 8th Yorkshire Light Infantry
GOWLAND Thomas F. MM Pte 15336 Durham Light Infantry
GOWLAND Thomas R. MM Pte 2326 Northumberland Fusiliers
GOWLING James H. MM Pte 37971 1st Worcestershire Regt
GOWRIE James Simpson MM Pte 11232 1st Scots Guards
GOY A. MM Sjt 43657 16th London Regt
GOY Horace William MM L/Cpl 80390 Royal Engineers Died 28.11.18.
GRABHAM Arthur C. MM L/Sjt 14532 10th Devonshire Regt
GRABHAM Horace Meynel MM Pte 41250 21 Squadron MGC(Cavalry)
GRACE A. MM Sjt 12/1012 Yorkshire Light Infantry
GRACE Albert George Ernest MM L/Cpl 62954 Machine Gun Corps KIA 18.12.17.
GRACE Charles W. MM Cpl 265156 Oxf & Bucks Light Infantry
GRACE Frederick MM Pte 66485 10th Royal Fusiliers
GRACE George F. MM Pte 769803 28th London Regt
GRACE Henry MM Gnr 194628 235 Siege Bty RGA
GRACE Herbert James MM Pte 43092 Northamptonshire Regt
GRACE Hugh MM Pte 3872 Oxf & Bucks Light Infantry
GRACE Isaac MM Pte 67315 97 Fd Amb RAMC
GRACE Lawrence MM Pte 9692 1st Royal Dublin Fusiliers
GRACE Michael MM L/Cpl 22079 Royal West Surrey Regt
GRACE Thomas MM Pte 39887 6th Leicestershire Regt
GRACEY James MM Gnr 23024 RGA
GRACEY John MM Cpl 21290 1st North Lancashire Regt
GRACIE Alexander Porteous "MM,MID" CSM 510213 2/14th London Regt
GRACIE David MM Pte 33500 5th West Riding Regt
GRACIE Robert MM+Bar Sjt 300303 1/8th Arg & Suth Highlanders
GRACIE William MM L/Cpl 16795 1st King's Own Scottish Borderers
GRACIE William MM+Bar L/Bdr 751294 D/250 Bde RFA
GRADDAGE C.H. MM Sjt 3068 5 Div Ammn Col RFA
GRADDEN Edward MM L/Cpl 254941 Royal Engineers
GRADWELL Charles E. MM Bdrd 163052 RGA
GRADWELL John MM Cpl 200661 10th North Lancashire Regt
GRADWELL Thomas MM Pte 129300 Machine Gun Corps
GRADY James MM Sjt 2/5848 2nd Royal Munster Fusiliers
GRADY John MM L/Cpl 278509 1/7th Arg & Suth Highlanders DOW 10.9.17.
GRADY Peter MM Pte 43601 133 Fd Amb RAMC
GRADY Richard MM CQMS 3972 1st Irish Guards DOW 18.9.16.
GRADY William MM L/Sjt 977 8th Royal Munster Fusiliers
GRAFF Phillip E. MM Sjt 34136 South Lancashire Regt
GRAFFHAM George MM Pte M2/162192 Army Service Corps
GRAFFHAM Robert MM L/Cpl G/3645 1st Royal West Surrey Regt KIA 15.7.16.
GRAFTON Alfred MM Pte 66717 Royal Fusiliers
GRAHAM A. MM Pte 16842 West Riding Regt
GRAHAM A. MM Sjt 6349 Gordon Highlanders
GRAHAM Albert MM Gnr 44354 100 Siege Bty RGA
GRAHAM Alex MM Dvr 663092 256 Bde RFA
GRAHAM Alex MM Sjt 9713 2nd Royal Inniskilling Fusiliers
GRAHAM Alex MM Pte 17081 Arg & Suth Highlanders
GRAHAM Alexander MM Spr 197917 Royal Engineers
GRAHAM Alexander Goodwin MM Sjt 267726 1/6th Seaforth Highlanders
GRAHAM Alfred "MM,MIDx2" CQMS MS/2362 305 MT Coy Army Service Corps
GRAHAM Alfred MM Sjt 1948 1/5th Cheshire Regt
GRAHAM Alfred E.W. MM+Bar Pte 204866 1st Northamptonshire Regt
GRAHAM Allen MM Pte 828 GMGR
GRAHAM Andrew MM Pte 3/7380 1st Seaforth Highlanders
GRAHAM Andrew "MM,DM(B)" Pte 3657 15 Fd Amb. RAMC att 122 Bty RFA
GRAHAM Andrew Archibald MM Pte 265230 5/6th Scottish Rifles
GRAHAM Angus MM L/Cpl 200169 5/6th Scottish Rifles
GRAHAM Arthur MM Pte 240665 1/5th King's Own Scottish Borderers KIA 31.10.18.
GRAHAM Arthur D. MM L/Cpl 203285 7th Seaforth Highlanders
GRAHAM Charles MM Cpl 241344 1/6th Royal Highlanders KIA 28.7.18.
GRAHAM Charles "DCM,MM" SQMS L/12579 5th Lancers
GRAHAM Charles MM Pte M/366614 Army Service Corps
GRAHAM Colin MM Pte 30128 Royal Scots
GRAHAM Daniel MM Cpl 205003 7th Seaforth Highlanders

GRAHAM Daniel J. MM Cpl 28910 2nd Northumberland Fusiliers
GRAHAM David MM Pte 241756 8th Seaforth Highlanders
GRAHAM David MM Cpl 335 C/106 Bde RFA KIA 16.8.16.
GRAHAM David MM Pte 21614 Durham Light Infantry
GRAHAM Duncan MM Pte 278484 1/7th Arg & Suth Highlanders DOW 2.9.18.
GRAHAM Edward MM Sjt 191613 RGA
GRAHAM Ernest MM Pte 17570 8th Border Regt KIA 10.4.18.
GRAHAM Ernest MM Sjt 965729 RFA
GRAHAM Francis Joseph MM L/Cpl 26/928 26th Northumberland Fusiliers KIA 17.3.16.
GRAHAM Frank MM Cpl 240082 5/6th Scottish Rifles
GRAHAM Frank Harold MM Pte 24534 3rd Grenadier Guards
GRAHAM Frank Lancelot MM Dvr 88781 84 Bty 11 Bde RFA
GRAHAM Fred MM L/Cpl 13043 Coldstream Guards
GRAHAM Fred C. MM Pte 129680 Machine Gun Corps
GRAHAM Frederick MM Sjt 248045 1/9th Durham Light Infantry
GRAHAM George MM Sjt 200282 Durham Light Infantry
GRAHAM George MM Pte 202649 5/6th Scottish Rifles KIA 17.4.18.
GRAHAM George MM Pte 34499 2nd South Lancashire Regt
GRAHAM George MM+Bar Pte 7772 1st Scottish Rifles
GRAHAM George MM Pte 17355 8th Royal Berkshire Regt KIA 27.4.18.
GRAHAM George MM Pte 19258 14th Liverpool Regt
GRAHAM George MM Pte S/15820 10th Arg & Suth Highlanders
GRAHAM George MM Pte 9548 2nd Arg & Suth Highlanders
GRAHAM George B. MM Pte 242080 Gordon Highlanders
GRAHAM George John MM+Bar L/Cpl STK/985 10th Royal Fusiliers
GRAHAM George W. MM Pte 21937 17th Royal Scots
GRAHAM George William MM Pte 4352 13th Middlesex Regt KIA 20.9.17.
GRAHAM H. MM Pte 386057 RAMC
GRAHAM Harold E. MM L/Cpl 30052 1st Duke of Cornwall's LI
GRAHAM Harry Albert MM CSM 3200 1/12th London Regt
GRAHAM Henry MM Pte 18244 5th Connaught Rangers
GRAHAM Herbert E MM Cpl 311707 Royal Engineers
GRAHAM Hirst MM Pte 240310 2/5th West Riding Regt DOW 16.3.18.
GRAHAM Hugh MM Gnr 144867 154 Siege Bty RGA
GRAHAM Isaac "DCM,MM" Cpl 37143 11th Northumberland Fusiliers
GRAHAM J.C. MM Cpl 39515 10th Essex Regt
GRAHAM James MM L/Cpl 273088 11th Royal Scots
GRAHAM James MM L/Cpl 55060 21st Manchester Regt
GRAHAM James MM Spr 197390 Royal Engineers
GRAHAM James MM Pte 40513 Royal Scots Fusiliers
GRAHAM James MM Cpl M2/182246 Army Service Corps
GRAHAM James MM L/Cpl 240160 5/6th Scottish Rifles KIA 6.11.18.
GRAHAM James MM Pte 322083 2/2nd(North Midland)Fd Amb RAMC KIA 21.3.18.
GRAHAM James MM Pte 6180 16th Lancers
GRAHAM James MM L/Cpl 8796 2nd Royal Irish Rifles KIA 22.10.18.
GRAHAM James MM L/Sjt 9711 2nd Dragoons
GRAHAM James "MC,MM(925243 Bdr)" Lt C/303 Bde RFA
GRAHAM James MM Sjt 36219 RFA
GRAHAM James Barclay MM L/Cpl 19312 2nd Royal Scots Fusiliers
GRAHAM James Coxon MM L/Sjt 16595 10th East Yorkshire Regt KIA 28.6.18.
GRAHAM James G. MM Pte 35033 5th Yorkshire Light Infantry
GRAHAM James P. MM Pte 201733 13th Liverpool Regt
GRAHAM James W. MM+Bar Pte S/23028 5th Cameron Highlanders
GRAHAM James W.H. MM Cpl 41589 6th King's Own Scottish Borderers
GRAHAM John MM Pte 11538 2nd Durham Light Infantry
GRAHAM John MM Cpl 11897 11th Royal Scots DOW 18.10.18.
GRAHAM John MM L/Cpl 267828 6th West Riding Regt
GRAHAM John "MM,MSM" Sjt 53437 RAMC
GRAHAM John MM Gnr 172693 37 Bty 27 Bde RFA KIA 6.11.18.
GRAHAM John MM L/Bdr 130332 87 Siege Bty RGA
GRAHAM John MM Pte 26465 2nd Wiltshire Regt KIA 20.10.18.
GRAHAM John MM Pte 36148 12th Highland Light Infantry KIA 25.3.18.
GRAHAM John MM Pte 982 Northumberland Fusiliers
GRAHAM John MM Sjt 9423 2nd Coldstream Guards
GRAHAM John MM Pte 4966 1/5th Liverpool Regt
GRAHAM John MM L/Cpl 14233 9th Royal Irish Fusiliers
GRAHAM John MM L/Cpl 266090 1/6th Gordon Highlanders
GRAHAM John MM Pte 10557 1st Dragoon Guards
GRAHAM John Aitken MM+Bar Gnr 945 C/82 Bde RFA DOW 7.8.17.
GRAHAM John B. MM Sjt 265381 7th Scottish Rifles
GRAHAM John G. MM Bdr 39075 RFA
GRAHAM John George MM Cpl 108921 185 Tunnelling Coy Royal Engineers
GRAHAM John R. MM L/Cpl 412334 409 Fd Coy Royal Engineers
GRAHAM John R. MM L/Cpl 20231 9th Royal Inniskilling Fusiliers
GRAHAM Joseph MM Spr 89514 34 Div Sig Coy Royal Engineers
GRAHAM Joseph MM Dvr 67268 112 Bde RFA
GRAHAM Joseph MM L/Cpl 2831 15th Royal Irish Rifles KIA 21.3.18.
GRAHAM Nicholas MM Pte 202500 Durham Light Infantry
GRAHAM Peter MM Pte 14/726 9th York & Lancaster Regt
GRAHAM Reginald MM Sjt 238002 East Lancashire Regt
GRAHAM Reginald Oswald Horace MM Bdr 34803 35 Heavy Bty RGA
GRAHAM Richard "MM+Bar,CG(B)" Sjt 27911 1st Border Regt
GRAHAM Richard J. MM Gnr 200562 RFA
GRAHAM Robert MM Gnr 218033 A/119 Bde RFA
GRAHAM Robert MM Cpl 22313 Cameron Highlanders
GRAHAM Robert MM CSM 200304 East Lancashire Regt
GRAHAM Robert MM Sjt 79834 RFA
GRAHAM Robert F. MM Sjt 14455 8th Border Regt
GRAHAM Robert Smith MM Bdr 23801 C/110 Bde RFA
GRAHAM Ronald MM BSM 19950 A/153 Bde RFA
GRAHAM Samuel MM Cpl 1453 8th Hussars
GRAHAM Samuel MM+Bar Pte 11218 1st Cameron Highlanders
GRAHAM T.W. MM Cpl 20406 7th Border Regt
GRAHAM Thomas MM Pte 7987 1st Scottish Rifles
GRAHAM Thomas MM Sjt 240938 1/5th Royal Scots Fusiliers
GRAHAM Thomas MM Pte 39487 Highland Light Infantry
GRAHAM Thomas MM L/Sjt 17053 Hampshire Regt
GRAHAM Thomas MM Sjt 106317 'D' Special Coy Royal Engineers
GRAHAM Thomas MM Pte 242409 Northumberland Fusiliers
GRAHAM Thomas MM Pte 23558 Border Regt
GRAHAM Thomas Hubert Gordon MM L/Cpl 13782 11th Border Regt
GRAHAM Thomas W. MM Pte 32878 4th York & Lancaster Regt
GRAHAM Thomas Wilfred MM Pte 1608 1/5th Durham Light Infantry
GRAHAM Thomas William MM Spr 93786 41 Div Sig Coy Royal Engineers
GRAHAM Wallace J. MM Cpl 454184 Royal Engineers
GRAHAM William MM Gnr Sig 186185 3 Siege Bty RGA
GRAHAM William MM Sjt 12003 101 Siege Bty RGA
GRAHAM William MM Gnr 97255 RFA
GRAHAM William MM Spr 151966 Royal Engineers
GRAHAM William MM+Bar Sjt 18193 Machine Gun Corps
GRAHAM William MM Sjt 35360 8 Div Ammn Col RGA
GRAHAM William "DCM,MM,CdeG" Sjt 29353 1st King's Own Scottish Borderers
GRAHAM William MM Pte 18926 Royal Irish Fusiliers
GRAHAME Arnold MM Pte 364374 RAMC
GRAIN George W. MM Sjt 318050 5th London Regt
GRAIN Thomas MM BQMS 295133 129 Hy Bty RGA
GRAIN Thomas MM Sjt 37509 RGA
GRAINGER Charles MM L/Cpl 515 Middlesex Regt
GRAINGER Clarence MM L/Cpl 265588 1/6th West Riding Regt
GRAINGER Cyril MM Sjt 1729 1/8th Notts & Derby Regt
GRAINGER Edward MM Sjt 8833 Coldstream Guards
GRAINGER Ernest G. MM Gnr 81023 RFA
GRAINGER Fred MM Gnr 99759 121 Bty 27 Bde RFA
GRAINGER George MM Pte 10713 1st Royal Berkshire Regt DOW 7.3.18.
GRAINGER George MM Spr 6595 69 Fd Coy Royal Engineers KIA 13.10.16.
GRAINGER Gordon S. MM Pte 76811 1st Royal Fusiliers
GRAINGER Herbert MM Gnr 388209 2nd(Northumbrian)Fd Amb RAMC
GRAINGER James MM Pte 9016 7th Lincolnshire Regt
GRAINGER Percy T. MM Pte 302894 5th London Regt
GRAINGER Richard "DCM,MM" BSM 19484 90 Heavy Bty RGA
GRAINGER Samuel MM Pte 31907 1/5th York & Lancaster Regt DOW 23.4.18.
GRAINGER Thomas MM Pte 28938 24th Royal Welsh Fusiliers
GRAINGER William MM Pte 71423 6th Notts & Derby Regt
GRAINGER William A. MM Dvr T3/026897 Army Service Corps

GRALEY Joseph MM Pte 306341 8th Bn Tank Corps
GRANADOS Francisco A. MM BQMS 10019 RFA
GRAND Arthur J.A. MM Sjt 300024 1st Notts & Derby Regt
GRAND William George "DCM,MM" Sjt 18170 1st Northamptonshire Regt
GRANDISON William MM Spr 51080 9 Div Sig Coy Royal Engineers
GRANDY Francis H. MM CSM 13169 4 Fd Svy Bn Royal Engineers
GRANEY John MM+Bar Sjt 632492 20th London Regt
GRANGE George W. MM Gnr 113530 RGA
GRANGE Harry MM Pte 307079 1/7th West Riding Regt
GRANGE Marshall MM Pte 31838 2nd Lancashire Fusiliers
GRANGE Robert MM Sjt 57811 36 Div Sig Coy Royal Engineers
GRANGE William J. MM Pte 201217 Essex Regt
GRANGER Frank MM L/Cpl 46665 Northumberland Fusiliers
GRANGER Frederick MM L/Cpl 207822 10th Royal West Surrey Regt
GRANGER Harold Reginald MM L/Cpl 43670 6th Northamptonshire Regt
GRANGER Sydney B. MM Dvr 960455 RFA
GRANGER Thomas H. MM Cpl 15000 2nd Devonshire Regt
GRANSHAW Charles MM Spr 47376 Royal Engineers
GRANT Albert V. MM Cpl 31032 50 Siege Bty RGA
GRANT Alexander MM L/Cpl 266488 6/7th Gordon Highlanders
GRANT Alexander MM Gnr 650990 371 Bty 169 Bde RFA
GRANT Alexander MM Cpl 133877 21 Div Arty HQ RFA
GRANT Alexander MM Pte 268024 Royal Highlanders
GRANT Alexander "DCM,MM+Bar" L/Cpl S/3670 11th Arg & Suth Highlanders
GRANT Alister MM Pte 25214 5/6th Royal Scots
GRANT Andrew MM Pte 202837 Gordon Highlanders
GRANT Bernor F. MM L/Cpl 10109 1st Royal Berkshire Regt
GRANT Charles MM L/Sjt 265246 6/7th Gordon Highlanders
GRANT Charles MM Sjt 19628 24th Royal Fusiliers
GRANT Charles F. MM Pte 12928 20th Durham Light Infantry
GRANT David MM Sjt 55288 15th Welsh Regt
GRANT Donald MM Dvr 23259 D/102 Bde RFA Died 26.10.18.
GRANT Donald K. MM Gnr 200655 RFA
GRANT Duncan MM Pte 22938 Seaforth Highlanders
GRANT Edgar MM Sjt 10647 5th Oxf & Bucks Light Infantry
GRANT Edward MM Sjt 104380 228 Fd Coy Royal Engineers
GRANT Eugene MM Cpl 357953 5 Fd Svy Bn Royal Engineers
GRANT Evan MM L/Cpl 5189 1st Cameron Highlanders
GRANT Evan G. MM Pte S/2389 12th Rifle Brigade
GRANT Francis MM Pte 36221 Leicestershire Regt
GRANT Francis MM Pte 26891 2nd Royal Scots KIA 27.9.18.
GRANT Frank MM Pte 16449 Scots Guards
GRANT Fred MM Spr 13079 15 Fd Coy Royal Engineers KIA 20.7.16.
GRANT Frederick MM Gnr 38862 RFA
GRANT Frederick Arthur MM+Bar L/Sjt 512173 2/14th London Regt
GRANT Frederick James MM Pte 2777 1/8th London Regt
GRANT George MM Sjt 63672 27 Bty 32 Bde RFA
GRANT George MM Pte 28779 16th Highland Light Infantry
GRANT George MM Pte 1017 1/4th Seaforth Highlanders KIA 21.3.18.
GRANT George Edward MM Sjt 6891 2nd Bedfordshire Regt
GRANT George H. MM Sjt 230550 1/2nd London Regt
GRANT George Henry MM Sjt 3/1145 11th Essex Regt
GRANT George J. MM Pte 48267 52nd Bn Machine Gun Corps
GRANT George J. MM Sjt 280153 1/4th London Regt
GRANT George W. MM Pte 34188 12/13th Northumberland Fusiliers
GRANT Harold E. MM Pte 18209 6th Yorkshire Light Infantry
GRANT Henry E. MM Cpl S/7110 8th Royal West Surrey Regt
GRANT Henry E. MM Spr 482445 Royal Engineers
GRANT Henry George MM Pte 570753 1/17th London Regt
GRANT Herbert C. MM Cpl 676107 12 Bde RFA
GRANT Jack MM Pte 305888 1/8th West Yorkshire Regt
GRANT James MM Pte 45434 15th Highland Light Infantry
GRANT James MM Sjt 201062 5th Cameron Highlanders
GRANT James MM Pte 268021 1/6th Royal Highlanders
GRANT James MM+Bar L/Cpl 13643 Scots Guards
GRANT James MM Pte S/8698 2nd Gordon Highlanders
GRANT James MM Pte 4246 9th Royal Highlanders KIA 13.11.17.
GRANT James MM Sjt 23265 Machine Gun Corps
GRANT James A. MM Pte 265533 Seaforth Highlanders
GRANT James D. MM Gnr Sig 365295 109 Siege Bty RGA
GRANT James G. MM L/Cpl 15133 Hampshire Regt
GRANT James Herbert MM Cpl 6051 Royal Fusiliers
GRANT James T. MM L/Cpl 75396 4th London Regt
GRANT John MM Dvr 7811 RFA
GRANT John MM Pte 291378 Gordon Highlanders
GRANT John "DCM,MM" Sjt 8/15143 8th Border Regt KIA 13.4.16.
GRANT John MM L/Sjt 265499 Seaforth Highlanders
GRANT John D. MM Pte 17419 Machine Gun Corps
GRANT John H. MM Cpl 725111 RFA
GRANT John McL. MM Pte 1518 RAMC
GRANT Keith MM Sjt 38501 B/98 Bde RFA
GRANT Leslie Ian MM Cpl 87506 Royal Engineers
GRANT M. MM CSM 9260 Seaforth Highlanders
GRANT Neil MM Pte 11343 11th Arg & Suth Highlanders KIA 20.4.18.
GRANT Nevill MM+Bar L/Cpl 207267 Guards Div Sig Coy Royal Engineers
GRANT Peter MM Pte 40593 Cameron Highlanders
GRANT Richard MM Pte 24780 4th Worcestershire Regt
GRANT Robert MM Pte M2/078344 Army Service Corps
GRANT Robert MM Pte 40796 Gordon Highlanders
GRANT Robert MM Pte 325058 1/8th Royal Scots
GRANT Robert MM Gnr L/21460 RFA
GRANT Robert MM L/Cpl 1609 1/10th Gordon Highlanders
GRANT Stephen J. MM Pte 86805 Middlesex Regt
GRANT Thomas Joseph MM Cpl 675093 RFA
GRANT Thomas M. MM Cpl 51800 Royal Scots
GRANT Walter MM Cpl 99017 15th Durham Light Infantry
GRANT Walter MM Pte 8/5056 Northumberland Fusiliers
GRANT Walter H.E. MM Dvr 59473 23 Bde RFA
GRANT Walter Harry MM Sjt 9535 2nd South Staffordshire Regt Died 10.11.18.
GRANT William MM Pte 315333 13th Royal Highlanders
GRANT William MM Pte 388339 2nd(Northumbrian)Fd Amb RAMC
GRANT William MM Pte 1145 18th Durham Light Infantry KIA 10.7.18.
GRANT William "DCM,MM" Sjt 13334 3rd Grenadier Guards
GRANT William MM Cpl 69013 37 Bde RFA
GRANT William MM Sjt 1960 Cameron Highlanders
GRANT William MM L/Cpl 4332 1/4th Gordon Highlanders
GRANT William MM L/Sjt 474 2nd Gordon Highlanders
GRANT William MM Pte 202859 5/6th Scottish Rifles
GRANT William MM Pte 11590 12th King's Royal Rifle Corps KIA 30.8.18.
GRANT William A. MM Sjt 579 Seaforth Highlanders
GRANT William G. MM Pte 1794 1/2nd London Regt
GRANT William J. "DCM,MM" Sjt 20372 1st Bn Machine Gun Corps
GRANT William James MM Pte 5402 7th Royal Irish Regt KIA 25.3.18.
GRANT Willie P. MM Sjt 81463 RGA
GRANTHAM "Albert H," MM Cpl 2622 1 Div Sig Coy Royal Engineers
GRANTHAM Arthur MM Sjt 93795 RFA
GRANTHAM David R. MM Sjt 29202 17th Liverpool Regt
GRANTHAM Harold MM Sjt 22596 55th Bn Machine Gun Corps
GRANTHAM Harry MM L/Cpl 82621 32nd Bn Machine Gun Corps
GRANTHAM Herbert MM L/Bdr 36261 179 Siege Bty RGA
GRANVILLE Frank MM Cpl 80352 A/190 Bde RFA
GRAPE Harold Sydney MM Sjt G/48507 9th Royal Fusiliers KIA 21.9.18.
GRASBY Hugh MM Cpl (MCDR) 74572 Royal Engineers
GRASBY John W. MM Pte 3429 West Yorkshire Regt
GRASBY Lawrence MM Pte 2921 1/4th East Yorkshire Regt
GRASS Charles MM Sjt 36186 35th Bn Machine Gun Corps
GRASSBY Oliver MM L/Cpl 30871 7th East Yorkshire Regt KIA 11.10.18.
GRATE Wilfred MM Pte 392464 9th London Regt
GRATION George H. MM Pte 14247 Notts & Derby Regt
GRATRIX John MM Pte 1255 1/6th Cheshire Regt KIA 31.7.17.
GRATTON Albert MM Cpl 55391 11 HAG HQ RGA KIA 20.11.17.
GRATTON James MM S/Sjt 45 RAMC
GRATTON James E. MM Cpl 240805 6th Notts & Derby Regt
GRATTON Matthew W. MM Bdr 83728 RFA
GRATWICK Sidney MM Pte 232 7th Royal Sussex Regt
GRAUBNER Henry MM Sjt 10698 5th Oxf & Bucks Light Infantry
GRAVELING Reginald MM Pte 18567 1st Lincolnshire Regt KIA 23.10.18.
GRAVELINS. Louis Herbert MM Cpl 90157 196 Siege Bty RGA
GRAVER Henry George MM Pte 43630 8th Norfolk Regt
GRAVER J.J. MM Sjt 283621 RGA
GRAVES Charles Stanley MM Pte 202518 1/5th Liverpool Regt KIA 15.10.18.
GRAVES Edward MM Pte 31739 Machine Gun Corps

GRAVES Frederick G. MM Bdr 22218 RGA
GRAVES George MM Pte 242065 5th Yorkshire Light Infantry
GRAVES Ivor L. MM L/Cpl 203291 4th Yorkshire Light Infantry
GRAVES N. MM Pte 10195 Royal Fusiliers
GRAVES Thomas MM Pte 201535 9th Highland Light Infantry KIA 13.4.18.
GRAVES William MM(12709 Rif Bde)+Bar Pte 27717 7th Shropshire Light Infantry
GRAVESTOCK Walter MM 2nd Cpl 60098 37 Div Sig Coy Royal Engineers
GRAY A. MM Sjt SE/12767 Army Veterinary Corps
GRAY Adam MM Sjt 14432 25 Labour Coy Labour Corps
GRAY Albert E. MM Gnr 92062 RFA
GRAY Albert Edward MM Sjt 12920 Hampshire Regt
GRAY Alexander MM Pte S/6408 9th Gordon Highlanders
GRAY Alexander MM Cpl 69124 RFA
GRAY Alexander MM L/Cpl 2867 1/4th Royal Lancaster Regt
GRAY Alexander MM 2nd Cpl 400020 Royal Engineers
GRAY Alexander B. MM Gnr 170177 C/110 Bde RFA
GRAY Alexander F. MM L/Cpl 241348 Hampshire Regt
GRAY Alfred MM Pte 1119 1/5th York & Lancaster Regt
GRAY Alfred Henry MM Pte M/281244 att 51 Fd Amb RAMC Army Service Corps
GRAY Alfred S. MM Cpl 1803 1/21st London Regt
GRAY Andrew MM Sjt 35243 15th Highland Light Infantry
GRAY Archibald MM 2nd Cpl 151615 170 Tunnelling Coy Royal Engineers
GRAY Arthur MM Spr 47738 Royal Engineers
GRAY Arthur MM Pte 301633 5th London Regt KIA 10.8.18.
GRAY Arthur G.P. MM Gnr 785862 RFA
GRAY Arthur S. "MM,MID" RSM 11063 Signal Service Royal Engineers
GRAY Attiwell John MM Pte M2/034982 273 Coy Army Service Corps
GRAY Barrington MM Sjt 330461 1/8th Hampshire Regt
GRAY Beresford John MM Sjt 8015 1st Gloucestershire Regt KIA 8.9.16.
GRAY Charles MM Pte 266216 6/7th Gordon Highlanders
GRAY Charles MM L/Cpl 241996 Gordon Highlanders
GRAY Charles MM Pte S/1818 Arg & Suth Highlanders
GRAY Charles Caswell MM L/Cpl 200677 1/4th Oxf & Bucks Light Infantry DOW 24.6.18.
GRAY Charles Edward MM Sjt 11932 11th Royal Fusiliers
GRAY Charles H. MM Cpl 97390 126 Fd Coy Royal Engineers
GRAY Charles James MM Gnr 23808 X/25 Med TM Bty RFA
GRAY Clifford S. MM Pte 242914 Royal Warwickshire Regt
GRAY Cyril MM Spr 221836 23 Div Sig Coy Royal Engineers
GRAY Dan MM L/Cpl 325501 1/1st Cambridgeshire Regt
GRAY Daniel MM Pte S/12067 1st Gordon Highlanders
GRAY Daniel MM L/Bdr 92710 HQ 59 Bde RFA
GRAY David MM L/Cpl 240079 1/5th Seaforth Highlanders
GRAY David MM Sjt 14840 12th Liverpool Regt
GRAY Donald MM L/Sjt 13201 Norfolk Regt
GRAY Edgar MM Pte 12039 7th Norfolk Regt
GRAY Edward MM Sjt 48171 Welsh Regt
GRAY Edward J. MM Bdr 12045 7 Siege Bty RGA
GRAY Edwin MM+Bar CSM 12887 8th Royal Berkshire Regt
GRAY Eric MM Pte 567297 65 Coy Labour Corps
GRAY Ernest MM Pte 6576 1/4th York & Lancaster Regt KIA 2.5.17.
GRAY Ernest MM Pte 41647 Northumberland Fusiliers
GRAY Evan Richard MM Sjt 67205 D/110 Bde RFA
GRAY F. MM Bdr 79392 RFA
GRAY F.J. MM L/Cpl P1438 Military Foot Police
GRAY Francis MM L/Cpl 18729 Royal Irish Fusiliers
GRAY Frank "MC,MM(2574 Sjt)" 2Lt 1/15th London Regt
GRAY Frank MM Pte 200762 5th Royal Warwickshire Regt
GRAY Frederick MM Pte 51812 5th Yorkshire Light Infantry
GRAY Frederick MM Pte 634 5th Dragoon Guards
GRAY Frederick G. MM Sjt 52967 57 Bde RFA
GRAY Frederick J. MM Cpl 5187 2nd Wiltshire Regt
GRAY George MM Pte 325291 1/5th Durham Light Infantry
GRAY George MM Cpl 5701 RFA
GRAY George MM Sjt 20513 1/6th Cheshire Regt
GRAY George MM CSM 240331 4th York & Lancaster Regt
GRAY George MM Dvr 890055 RFA
GRAY George "DCM,MM+Bar" CQMS 6373 1st Dorsetshire Regt
GRAY George R. MM L/Cpl G/8924 Royal West Kent Regt
GRAY George Thomas MM Cpl 35432 2nd Essex Regt
GRAY George W. MM Cpl G/6004 2nd Royal Sussex Regt
GRAY H. MM L/Sjt 295354 12th Royal Scots Fusiliers

GRAY Harold Bertram MM Cpl 840974 D/306 Bde RFA
GRAY Harry M. MM Sjt 20183 25th Bn Machine Gun Corps
GRAY Henry MM Sjt 3580 11th Royal Scots KIA 9.4.17.
GRAY Henry Alfred MM L/Cpl R/6726 7th King's Royal Rifle Corps
GRAY Henry H. MM Pte 73111 Durham Light Infantry
GRAY Herbert MM Cpl 101079 Royal Engineers
GRAY Hubert MM Pte 2694 1st Gloucestershire Regt
GRAY Hubert Ernest MM Pte 18180 1st Bedfordshire Regt KIA 27.9.18
GRAY James MM Pte 10004 10th Royal West Kent Regt
GRAY James MM L/Cpl 29954 9th Royal Inniskilling Fusiliers
GRAY James MM+Bar Cpl 37281 Northumberland Fusiliers
GRAY James MM+Bar Sjt 23391 15th Durham Light Infantry KIA 24.10.18.
GRAY James "MM+Bar,CG(F)" Cpl 630251 255 Bde RFA
GRAY James MM+Bar Pte 26554 Scottish Rifles
GRAY James B. "MM,MID" Sjt 9347 2nd Seaforth Highlanders
GRAY James S. MM Pte 241992 Gordon Highlanders
GRAY James W. MM Sjt 806 XIV Corps Cyclist Bn Army Cyclist Corps
GRAY John MM Pte 11155 1st Scots Guards
GRAY John MM Sjt S/5290 1st Royal Highlanders
GRAY John MM Cpl L/3793 11 Div Ammn Col RFA
GRAY John MM Gnr 4371 157 Bde RFA
GRAY John MM Gnr 68841 RFA
GRAY John MM Pte 9/14736 Royal Irish Rifles
GRAY John MM Cpl 24/761 Northumberland Fusiliers
GRAY John MM+Bar Sjt 21/782 Northumberland Fusiliers
GRAY John MM Cpl 47834 35 Bty 22 Bde RFA KIA 2.10.17.
GRAY John MM Pte 43285 9th Scottish Rifles DOW 14.4.17.
GRAY John MM+Bar Pte 290318 Gordon Highlanders
GRAY John MM Dvr 133643 B/46 Bde RFA
GRAY John A. MM Sjt 291204 1/7th Gordon Highlanders
GRAY John N. MM L/Cpl 40403 8th North Staffordshire Regt
GRAY John R. MM Bdr 63308 RFA
GRAY Joseph MM Pte 10268 2nd Royal Irish Fusiliers
GRAY Joseph MM Bdr 45867 18 Bde RFA
GRAY Maxwell MM Sjt 200503 6th King's Own Scottish Borderers
GRAY Norman MM L/Cpl S/6385 Gordon Highlanders
GRAY Percival W. MM Pte 390472 1/9th London Regt
GRAY Percy MM Sjt 22381 Royal Inniskilling Fusiliers
GRAY Percy MM Pte 40286 King's Own Scottish Borderers
GRAY Peter MM Pte 21207 Durham Light Infantry
GRAY Reginald V.F. MM Cpl Fitter 43479 5 Bde RFA
GRAY Richard J. MM Sjt 456 1/4th Yorkshire Regt
GRAY Robert MM Pte 14245 2nd Royal Dublin Fusiliers
GRAY Robert MM Sjt 8487 11th Highland Light Infantry
GRAY Robert MM Sjt 266547 1st Gordon Highlanders KIA 27.9.18.
GRAY Robert MM Pte 49736 157 Coy Machine Gun Corps
GRAY Robert MM+Bar Cpl 19286 6th East Yorkshire Regt
GRAY Robert E. MM Pte H/270808 1/1st Northumberland Yeo
GRAY Robert John MM L/Cpl 14663 10th Royal Irish Rifles
GRAY Robert S. MM Pte 55602 Northumberland Fusiliers
GRAY Samuel G. MM Cpl 9894 1st Royal West Kent Regt
GRAY Stanley C. MM Gnr 101464 RGA
GRAY Stanley V. MM Dvr 889555 D/168 Bde RFA
GRAY Sydney E. MM+Bar Cpl 40016 Norfolk Regt
GRAY Thomas MM Pte 200435 1/4th Royal Scots
GRAY Thomas MM Cpl 63307 C/113 Bde RFA
GRAY Thomas MM Pte 14005 13th Liverpool Regt
GRAY Thomas MM 2nd Cpl 1173 2(London)Fd Coy Royal Engineers
GRAY Thomas H. MM Gnr 34529 RFA
GRAY Thomas R. MM Pte 12087 Manchester Regt
GRAY Thomas Robert MM Pte 5979 Northumberland Fusiliers
GRAY Tom MM Pte 45591 RAMC
GRAY W. MM L/Cpl 321622 London Regt
GRAY W.W. MM Dvr 109901 C/190 Bde RFA
GRAY Walter MM Gnr 116894 D/286 Bde RFA
GRAY Walter Charles MM L/Sjt 27936 2nd Royal Welsh Fusiliers KIA 4.11.18.
GRAY Walter J. MM Sjt 696279 57 TM Bty RFA
GRAY William MM Pte S/17715 1st Gordon Highlanders
GRAY William MM Pte 38052 5/6th Royal Scots
GRAY William MM Pte 16877 2nd Hampshire Regt DOW 24.11.17.
GRAY William MM Sjt 11157 6/7th Royal Scots Fusiliers
GRAY William MM Cpl 17285 Machine Gun Corps
GRAY William MM Cpl 29672 Royal Engineers
GRAY William MM Cpl 138360 18th Bn Machine Gun Corps
GRAY William MM Pte 22007 1st Royal Irish Rifles KIA 2.10.18.

GRAY William MM Gnr 47769 16 Hy Bty RGA
GRAY William MM Sjt 14937 8th East Lancashire Regt
GRAY William MM Gnr 651978 C/74 Bde RFA KIA 25.12.17.
GRAY William Alfred MM Pte 573800 17th London Regt
GRAY William Ernest MM Pte 43359 Bedfordshire Regt
GRAY William George MM Gnr 95687 221 TM Bty RFA KIA 15.10.17.
GRAY William J. MM Pte 14503 Dorsetshire Regt
GRAYDON Fred MM Pte 64135 111 Fd Amb RAMC
GRAYSON A. MM Pte 16/107 8th West Yorkshire Regt
GRAYSON Frank MM Sjt 91932 9th Bn Tank Corps
GRAYSON John MM Pte 201434 West Yorkshire Regt
GRAYSON Joseph MM L/Cpl 43060 14th Durham Light Infantry Died 5.7.17.
GRAYSON Samuel MM Sjt 300108 15/17th West Yorkshire Regt
GRAYSON Thomas H. MM L/Cpl 20055 3rd Grenadier Guards
GRAYSON Thomas H. MM Gnr 58209 RGA
GRAYSTONE Herbert MM Pte 10/633 10th East Yorkshire Regt
GRAZIER John H. MM L/Cpl 47874 Royal Fusiliers
GREANEY Bernard Joseph MM+Bar Pte 52312 15th Royal Irish Rifles
GREANEY James H. MM L/Cpl 683100 London Regt
GREANY Michael J. MM+Bar CSM 3847 1st Irish Guards
GREANY Percy Marks MM Sjt 24938 17th Liverpool Regt DOW 7.12.18
GREARSON Herbert C. MM Cpl 9787 5th Wiltshire Regt
GREASBY Sidney MM L/Cpl 203228 Yorkshire Light Infantry
GREASER Milvia MM Pte 41160 Yorkshire Light Infantry
GREASLEY Arthur E. MM Gnr 112421 71 Hy Bty RGA
GREATBANKS George Henry MM Pte 11215 Manchester Regt
GREATBANKS Sidney MM Cpl 21861 Liverpool Regt
GREATBANKS William B. MM Gnr 55151 RFA
GREATHEAD Alfred MM L/Cpl 17104 12th Gloucestershire Regt
GREATHOLDER George MM Cpl 24233 2nd South Wales Borderers
GREATOREX A.J. MM Air Mech 2 7500 Royal Flying Corps
GREATOREX Richard MM Sjt 6537 Border Regt
GREATOREX Thomas MM L/Cpl 44385 59 Coy Machine Gun Corps
GREATREX George MM Spr 450506 att 81 Bde RGA Royal Engineers DOW 17.9.18.
GREATREX Richard George MM Sjt 2919 South Staffordshire Regt
GREATWICH Sydney MM CQMS 13186 6th Shropshire Light Infantry
GREAVES Alfred MM Sjt 3789 Machine Gun Corps
GREAVES Arthur H. MM Pte Z/547 Rifle Brigade
GREAVES Charles "MM,MID" Cpl 9503 1st Liverpool Regt KIA 15.11.16.
GREAVES Charles E. MM CQMS 200047 2/5th West Yorkshire Regt
GREAVES Ernest MM L/Cpl 128727 Royal Engineers
GREAVES Ernest MM Sjt 1986 1/4th York & Lancaster Regt
GREAVES Ernest G. MM Cpl 41751 2nd Yorkshire Regt
GREAVES Fred MM Cpl 8230 11th Lancashire Fusiliers
GREAVES Frederick MM Cpl 250078 Signal Service Royal Engineers
GREAVES Frederick Henry MM Pte 50053 9th Cheshire Regt
GREAVES Gaions MM Pte 44327 5th Royal Berkshire Regt
GREAVES George MM Pte 22320 Notts & Derby Regt
GREAVES George Frederick MM Pte 15516 East Surrey Regt
GREAVES Gordon Stewart MM Gnr 167178 222 Siege Bty RGA
GREAVES Harold MM L/Cpl 201726 5th York & Lancaster Regt
GREAVES James MM Pte 13328 9th South Lancashire Regt
GREAVES John MM Sjt 23824 55th Bn Machine Gun Corps DOW 10.8.18.
GREAVES John R. MM+Bar Sjt 12886 5th West Riding Regt
GREAVES John W. MM L/Cpl A/2737 King's Royal Rifle Corps
GREAVES Joseph MM Sjt 8893 1st Royal Inniskilling Fusiliers
GREAVES Norman MM Bdr 65466 RFA
GREAVES Robert "MM,MM(F)" Cpl 3203 1/5th Liverpool Regt KIA 9.4.18.
GREAVES Thomas MM Pte 11238 9th Cheshire Regt
GREAVES W. MM Pte 7113 Manchester Regt
GREAVES William MM Pte 9172 1st Cheshire Regt
GREAVETT Francis William MM Pte 18576 10th West Yorkshire Regt
GREBBELL Edwin MM Sjt 102209 RFA
GREEDY Benjamin MM Pte 241281 Somerset Light Infantry
GREEN A. MM Pte 403640 2/2nd(West Riding)Fd Amb RAMC
GREEN A. "DCM,MM" Sjt 390188 RAMC
GREEN Albert MM+Bar L/Cpl 33752 1st East Surrey Regt

GREEN Albert MM Pte 31561 RAMC
GREEN Albert MM Pte L/13804 4th Royal Fusiliers KIA 8.6.17.
GREEN Albert MM Pte L/12044 4th Royal Fusiliers
GREEN Albert E. MM L/Cpl 43122 139 Fd Amb RAMC
GREEN Albert Henry MM L/Cpl 66691 22 Div Sig Coy Royal Engineers
GREEN Alfred MM Cpl 46123 94 Fd Coy Royal Engineers
GREEN Alfred MM Cpl 285192 1/6th Gloucestershire Regt Died 9.10.17.
GREEN Alfred MM L/Cpl 18434 Royal Engineers
GREEN Alfred MM L/Cpl 10494 6th Bedfordshire Regt
GREEN Alfred E. MM Gnr 64176 RFA
GREEN Alfred Ernest "DCM+Bar,MM" Sjt 42951 81 Fd Coy Royal Engineers
GREEN Alfred F. MM Dvr T4/251769 Army Service Corps
GREEN Alfred F. MM Pte 2858 1st Irish Guards
GREEN Alfred J. MM(73513 RFA)+Bar 2nd Cpl 253855 Royal Engineers
GREEN Alfred J. MM Bdr 68041 12 Bde RFA
GREEN Alfred Louis MM Pte 15198 9th Notts & Derby Regt DOW 5.10.17.
GREEN Algernon F.D. MM Bdr 101358 RGA
GREEN Allan McI. MM L/Cpl 241186 Gloucestershire Regt
GREEN Arthur MM Sjt C/109 16th King's Royal Rifle Corps
GREEN Arthur MM Dvr 82639 RFA
GREEN Arthur "MM+Bar,MSM" Sjt 96455 X/38 Med TM Bty RFA
GREEN Arthur Charles MM Pte 72117 133 Fd Amb RAMC
GREEN Arthur Edward MM Pte 33100 10th Yorkshire Regt
GREEN Arthur Edward MM L/Cpl 17/1080 West Yorkshire Regt
GREEN Arthur W. MM CQMS 36268 275 Coy Machine Gun Corps
GREEN Bertie J.C. MM Pte 147646 37th Bn Machine Gun Corps
GREEN C. MM Pte 266124 West Yorkshire Regt
GREEN Cecil G. MM Sjt 17179 8th Bedfordshire Regt
GREEN Cecil L. MM Pte 1869 16th Middlesex Regt
GREEN Cecil Lindsay MM Gnr L/13800 258 Bde RFA
GREEN Charles MM Cpl 4488 Highland Light Infantry
GREEN Charles E. MM(19137 Norf)+Bar Pte 3904 8th Royal Irish Regt
GREEN Charles Henry MM L/Cpl 19546 1st Coldstream Guards
GREEN Charles W. MM Sjt 19131 Machine Gun Corps
GREEN Charles Wesley MM Gnr 167770 182 Siege Bty RGA
GREEN Christopher MM Sjt 250264 1/5th Essex Regt
GREEN Christopher MM Dvr 56897 RFA
GREEN Clifford MM Pte 18115 8th Royal Lancaster Regt KIA 26.7.18.
GREEN Douglas MM Gnr L/10130 RFA
GREEN Ebenezer MM Pte 20906 10th Royal Warwickshire Regt
GREEN Edmond MM Pte 8/1669 8th Royal Munster Fusiliers
GREEN Edward MM L/Cpl R/11719 King's Royal Rifle Corps
GREEN Edward MM Spr 74149 'SV' Cable Section Royal Engineers
GREEN Edward MM Bdr 671 RHA
GREEN Edward MM L/Cpl 8/43104 8th South Staffordshire Regt
GREEN Edward A. MM Sjt 36061 3 Siege Bty RGA
GREEN Edward G. MM Bdr 186961 RGA
GREEN Edward J. MM Cpl 198907 Royal Engineers
GREEN Edward William "MM,MID,CG(B)" Sjt 281783 RGA
GREEN Edwin James MM Bdr L/17742 A/170 Bde RFA KIA 20.12.16.
GREEN Eric J. MM L/Cpl 62503 5th West Yorkshire Regt
GREEN Ernest MM Gnr 32777 RGA
GREEN Ernest MM L/Sjt 25662 East Surrey Regt
GREEN Ernest MM Spr 106720 Royal Engineers
GREEN Ernest MM Pte 18527 Royal Warwickshire Regt
GREEN Ernest MM Spr 548468 130 Fd Coy Royal Engineers
GREEN Ernest A. MM Gnr 128806 RHA
GREEN Ernest Alfred MM Sjt 15/399 15th West Yorkshire Regt
GREEN Ernest R. MM Sjt L/12430 Middlesex Regt
GREEN Ernest T. MM L/Cpl 1254 17th Royal Fusiliers
GREEN Ewart MM Pte 316717 36th Northumberland Fusiliers
GREEN F. MM Dvr L/28097 RFA
GREEN Francis MM Pte 3911 1/7th Durham Light Infantry
GREEN Frank MM+Bar Pte 305986 1/8th Notts & Derby Regt
GREEN Frank MM Pte 8315 12 CCS RAMC
GREEN Frank MM L/Cpl 140808 Royal Engineers
GREEN Frank MM Pte 18591 Manchester Regt
GREEN Frank "MM,DM(B)" Cpl 201073 2/8th Worcestershire Regt
GREEN Frank B. MM L/Sjt 307768 Liverpool Regt
GREEN Frank W. MM+Bar Bdr 35930 RGA
GREEN Fred MM Pte 29615 East Lancashire Regt
GREEN Frederick MM L/Cpl 19031 3 Pontoon Park Royal Engineers

GREEN Frederick MM Pte 25633 Welsh Regt
GREEN Frederick MM+Bar Sjt R/14350 King's Royal Rifle Corps
GREEN Frederick MM Sjt 6771 Machine Gun Corps
GREEN Frederick E. MM L/Cpl T/23596 Army Service Corps
GREEN Frederick G. MM Sjt 13788 4th Middlesex Regt
GREEN Frederick J. MM Pte H/285673 1/1st Oxfordshire Yeomanry
GREEN Frederick W. MM Pte 203006 Middlesex Regt
GREEN G.H. MM Gnr 1596 RFA
GREEN G.W. MM Sjt 207979 11th Royal West Surrey Regt
GREEN George MM Dvr 99824 71 Bty 36 Bde RFA
GREEN George MM Cpl 19455 RGA
GREEN George MM Gnr 108043 RFA
GREEN George MM Pte 29888 8th Norfolk Regt
GREEN George MM Pte 235253 West Riding Regt
GREEN George MM Pte 425178 Labour Corps
GREEN George "DCM,MM" BSM 275925 201 Siege Bty RGA
GREEN George MM Pte 5338 22nd London Regt
GREEN George MM Pte 260019 Liverpool Regt
GREEN George E. MM Sjt 57148 1st Worcestershire Regt
GREEN George E. MM L/Cpl 40582 Leicestershire Regt
GREEN George H MM Pte 345047 6th London Regt
GREEN George H. MM Pte 36361 2nd Yorkshire Regt
GREEN George Henry MM Cpl 9034 1st East Surrey Regt
GREEN George Henry MM Pte 11332 1st Shropshire Light Infantry
GREEN George Thomas MM Pte R/6329 7th King's Royal Rifle Corps
GREEN George W. MM Sjt 10472 Coldstream Guards
GREEN George W.E. MM L/Cpl 10314 VIII Corps Cyclist Bn Army Cyclist Corps
GREEN George William MM Pte 70449 Notts & Derby Regt
GREEN Gordon MM Pte Stk414 10th Royal Fusiliers
GREEN H. MM Pte 49095 8th Lancashire Fusiliers
GREEN H. MM Sjt 53382 Highland Light Infantry
GREEN H.G. MM Sjt 1496 RFA
GREEN Harold MM Cpl 16296 Liverpool Regt
GREEN Harold Arthur MM Cpl 26918 15th Hampshire Regt
GREEN Harry MM Pte 243439 5th Lancashire Fusiliers
GREEN Harry MM Pte 24271 1/4th Royal Lancaster Regt
GREEN Harry MM Gnr 52106 A/116 Bde RFA
GREEN Harry MM L/Sjt 203777 1/4th York & Lancaster Regt
GREEN Harry MM Pte 87412 198 Coy Machine Gun Corps
GREEN Harry MM Pte 3/8294 1st West Yorkshire Regt
GREEN Harry MM Sjt R/7730 King's Royal Rifle Corps
GREEN Harry MM Sjt 13266 9th South Staffordshire Regt
GREEN Harry G. MM L/Cpl 30217 Somerset Light Infantry
GREEN Henry MM Cpl 50881 Royal Engineers
GREEN Henry MM Sjt 241313 1/5th South Lancashire Regt DOW 21.9.17.
GREEN Henry MM Cpl 78835 81 Bty 5 Bde RFA
GREEN Henry MM Pte 37073 Yorkshire Light Infantry
GREEN Henry MM Cpl 21219 22nd Manchester Regt
GREEN Henry MM Sjt 7203 2nd King's Royal Rifle Corps
GREEN Henry MM Pte 6424 1st Dorsetshire Regt
GREEN Henry MM Pte 232712 2nd London Regt
GREEN Henry MM L/Cpl 12740 East Kent Regt
GREEN Henry A. MM Pte 123912 Machine Gun Corps
GREEN Henry William MM Pte 38544 Royal Berkshire Regt
GREEN Herbert MM Pte DM2/097015 Army Service Corps
GREEN Herbert R. MM Sjt 2162 6th London Regt
GREEN Herbert T. MM Pte S/20251 Rifle Brigade
GREEN Herbert William MM Sjt 12116 2nd Scots Guards KIA 12.10.17.
GREEN Horace MM Pte 9/14615 Leicestershire Regt
GREEN Horace MM Pte 15703 2nd B Coy Worcestershire Regt KIA 3.11.16.
GREEN Horace C. MM L/Cpl 5616 Machine Gun Corps
GREEN Horace T. MM Pte 34484 York & Lancaster Regt
GREEN Hubert C. MM Pte 63501 16th Lancashire Fusiliers
GREEN Hubert W. MM Pte 19271 7th Shropshire Light Infantry
GREEN Irvine MM Pte 202309 4th Lincolnshire Regt DOW 21.4.18.
GREEN J. MM Dvr 76937 RFA
GREEN James MM Cpl 8776 2nd Leinster Regt
GREEN James MM Sjt 8921 6th Lancashire Fusiliers
GREEN James MM Gnr 202094 115 Hy Bty RGA
GREEN James MM Sjt 64976 11 Bde RFA
GREEN James MM Spr 480641 460 Fd Coy Royal Engineers
GREEN James MM Pte 303087 Royal Scots
GREEN James MM Pte 16285 2nd South Staffordshire Regt
GREEN James MM Cpl 10127 2nd East Lancashire Regt
GREEN James MM Pte 40673 Royal Scots Fusiliers
GREEN James C. MM Sjt 9075 1st Oxf & Bucks Light Infantry
GREEN James C. MM 2nd Cpl 522031 Royal Engineers
GREEN James Frederick MM Sjt 9106 2nd Lincolnshire Regt
GREEN James R. MM Pte 421347 10th London Regt
GREEN James W. MM Sjt 67668 24th Bn Machine Gun Corps
GREEN Jamrs David MM Dvr 800191 A/230 Bde RFA
GREEN John MM+Bar CSM 8719 1st Royal Irish Rifles
GREEN John MM Sjt 21128 4th Bn Machine Gun Corps
GREEN John MM Sjt 79615 176 Tunnelling Coy Royal Engineers
GREEN John MM Gnr 65331 115 Hy Bty RGA
GREEN John MM Cpl 56850 RFA
GREEN John MM Sjt 18561 1st Shropshire Light Infantry
GREEN John MM L/Cpl 8602 2nd Royal Welsh Fusiliers
GREEN John MM Sjt 19396 Manchester Regt
GREEN John MM+Bar Bdr L/16194 D/251 Bde RFA Died 1.10.18.
GREEN John Arthur MM+Bar 2nd Cpl 156063 179 Tunnelling Coy Royal Engineers
GREEN John C. MM Cpl 8612 2nd Northamptonshire Regt
GREEN John E. "DCM,MM+Bar" L/Cpl 34256 8th York & Lancaster Regt att 70 Light TM Bty
GREEN John George MM Pte 16431 Durham Light Infantry
GREEN John Henry MM Pte A/3199 8th King's Royal Rifle Corps DOW 23.8.17.
GREEN John James MM Sjt 155891 Tunnelling Coy Royal Engineers
GREEN John S. MM Cpl 19951 Cheshire Regt
GREEN John T. MM Pte 241725 South Staffordshire Regt
GREEN John Thomas MM Gnr 65405 3 Bde RHA
GREEN John V. MM Sjt 36505 RAMC
GREEN John W. MM Pte 3450 HAC
GREEN John W. MM Sjt 7243 2nd Yorkshire Light Infantry
GREEN John William "DCM,MM" Sjt 375395 1/7th Manchester Regt KIA 21.8.18.
GREEN Joseph MM Pte 19959 1/5th East Lancashire Regt
GREEN Joseph N. MM Cpl 22/248 Durham Light Infantry
GREEN Joseph Peter MM Cpl 465037 4 Fd Amb RAMC KIA 27.9.18.
GREEN Leonard MM Cpl G/42340 13th Royal Fusiliers KIA 24.10.18.
GREEN Leslie MM+Bar Sjt 19122 7th Royal West Kent Regt
GREEN Luther MM Pte 12376 7th Leicestershire Regt KIA 19.4.18.
GREEN M.E. MM L/Cpl 3529 8th East Kent Regt
GREEN Mark MM Pte 240269 1/6th North Staffordshire Regt
GREEN Matthew MM Pte G/11961 16th Royal Sussex Regt
GREEN Maurice E. MM L/Sjt 720982 1/24th London Regt
GREEN Michael MM L/Bdr 776462 RFA
GREEN Michael MM Pte 28739 Royal Dublin Fusiliers
GREEN Norman Walker MM Pte 105765 22 Fd Amb RAMC
GREEN Patrick MM Bdr 76700 RGA
GREEN Patrick MM Pte 23438 Royal Dublin Fusiliers
GREEN Percy MM Cpl 80087 1/1st Essex Yeomanry
GREEN Percy MM+Bar L/Cpl 893 3rd Rifle Brigade
GREEN Percy Douglas MM Gnr 194830 'Q' Bty RHA
GREEN Percy Henry MM Gnr 85742 23 Siege Bty RGA
GREEN Philip MM L/Cpl 84753 207 Fd Coy Royal Engineers
GREEN R.S. MM Pte 42817 2nd Essex Regt
GREEN Ralph MM L/Cpl 78023 10th Royal Fusiliers
GREEN Reginald MM L/Bdr 228647 D/75 Bde RFA
GREEN Reginald A. MM L/Cpl 394310 16th London Regt
GREEN Richard MM Spr 132574 184 Tunnelling Coy Royal Engineers
GREEN Richard H. MM Sjt 293502 223 Siege Bty RGA
GREEN Robert MM Cpl S/40121 1st Cameron Highlanders
GREEN Robert MM L/Cpl E/848 17th Royal Fusiliers KIA 24.2.17.
GREEN Robert MM Cpl 11197 9th Royal Inniskilling Fusiliers
GREEN Robert MM Gnr 115412 D/1 Bde RFA
GREEN Robert MM L/Cpl 8172 1st West Yorkshire Regt
GREEN Robert MM+Bar Cpl 31746 Northumberland Fusiliers
GREEN Robert MM Pte 14952 12th Royal Sussex Regt
GREEN Robert Charles MM Pte 200735 Norfolk Regt
GREEN Robert M. MM S/Sjt Mechanician 75149 Tank Corps
GREEN Robert P. MM Bdr Sig 625866 HAC(Arty) att 309 Siege Bty RGA
GREEN Sam MM Cpl 241662 1/5th South Lancashire Regt Died 11.11.18.
GREEN Samuel MM Pte 3/7029 1st Norfolk Regt
GREEN Sidney J. MM Dvr 162878 D/246 Bde RFA
GREEN Stanley MM Pnr 551842 Royal Engineers
GREEN Stanley MM Gnr 65713 RGA
GREEN Stanley Robert Martin MM Pte 22298 8th York & Lancaster Regt

GREEN Sydney F. MM L/Cpl 528447 Royal Engineers
GREEN T. MM L/Cpl P4491 Military Foot Police
GREEN T. "MM,MID" Dvr 99939 42 Bde RFA
GREEN Thomas MM Sjt 493 1/6th South Staffordshire Regt DOW 3.7.16.
GREEN Thomas MM Pte 15525 1st Coldstream Guards
GREEN Thomas MM L/Cpl T4/035713 6 Reserve Park Army Service Corps
GREEN Thomas MM Sjt 18644 RGA
GREEN Thomas MM Spr 6503 London Electrical Engineers Royal Engineers
GREEN Thomas MM Pte R/10845 King's Royal Rifle Corps
GREEN Thomas A. MM Pte 235283 Lincolnshire Regt
GREEN Thomas J. MM Pte 60684 1st Middlesex Regt
GREEN Thomas J. MM Dvr 745725 RFA
GREEN Thomas W. MM L/Cpl 4847 Machine Gun Corps
GREEN Thomas William MM Pte 37824 2nd Bedfordshire Regt KIA 21.9.18.
GREEN Tom MM Pte 15585 4th Coldstream Guards Died 7.11.18.
GREEN Tom "DCM,MM+Bar" CSM 44495 6th South Wales Borderers
GREEN W. MM Pte 8261 Machine Gun Corps
GREEN W. MM Pte 75027 Machine Gun Corps
GREEN W. MM Pte 337665 RAMC
GREEN Walter MM+Bar Pte 14810 8th Suffolk Regt
GREEN Walter MM Pte DM2/130337 Army Service Corps att RGA
GREEN Walter D. MM L/Cpl 519 GMGR
GREEN Walter W. MM Gnr 625476 HAC
GREEN Wilfred MM L/Cpl 8590 4th King's Royal Rifle Corps
GREEN Wiliam R. MM Pte 1859 RAMC
GREEN William MM Pte 22890 6th Northamptonshire Regt
GREEN William MM Pte 11748 9th Royal Fusiliers DOW 21.9.18.
GREEN William MM Cpl 75059 190 Siege Bty RGA
GREEN William MM Pte 7731 1st North Staffordshire Regt
GREEN William MM Pte 3187 3rd Rifle Brigade
GREEN William MM Cpl 19406 1st Duke of Cornwall's LI
GREEN William MM Cpl 130026 45th Royal Fusiliers
GREEN William "DCM,MM+Bar" Sjt 8021 13th Royal Fusiliers
GREEN William MM Cpl 26022 8th Royal Inniskilling Fusiliers KIA 15.7.16.
GREEN William MM L/Sjt 14963 7th Lincolnshire Regt DOW 9.3.17.
GREEN William MM Sjt T4/248048 Army Service Corps
GREEN William MM Pte 15551 10th Worcestershire Regt Died 7.11.18.
GREEN William E. MM Pte 201375 Yorkshire Light Infantry
GREEN William F. MM Pte 55155 Machine Gun Corps
GREEN William Frederick MM Pte 6/1164 7th King's Royal Rifle Corps KIA 22.12.17.
GREEN William George MM Gnr 98209 C/331 Bde RFA KIA 30.3.18.
GREEN William H. MM Pte 15101 4th Royal Fusiliers
GREEN William H. MM Cpl 20482 Northamptonshire Regt
GREEN William Henry MM L/Sjt 22462 23rd Manchester Regt KIA 24.4.18.
GREEN William Henry MM Pte 18709 2nd Coldstream Guards
GREEN William Henry MM+Bar Cpl 8596 West Yorkshire Regt
GREEN William J. MM Pte 24926 6th Lancashire Fusiliers
GREEN William J. MM Cpl 749 1st Rifle Brigade
GREEN William J. MM Cpl 202431 South Wales Borderers
GREEN William James MM Pte 203979 6th Bedfordshire Regt
GREEN William L. MM Pte G/47617 10th Royal Fusiliers
GREEN William Leslie "MC,MM(1212 Sjt)" 2Lt 1/8th Notts & Derby Regt
GREEN William Marshall MM Sjt M2/022126 Army Service Corps
GREEN William S. MM Pte 200625 1st London Regt
GREEN Willie S. MM.MID Cpl 70648 29 Bde RFA
GREENACRE George Alfred MM Pte 8813 Norfolk Regt
GREENALL Frederick MM Pte 29229 Manchester Regt
GREENALL George MM L/Cpl 16985 11th Cheshire Regt KIA 20.4.18.
GREENALL Harry MM Pte 44114 8th Worcestershire Regt
GREENAN Lawrence MM Pte S/4249 2nd Arg & Suth Highlanders
GREENAN William "MM,MID" Pte 4248 Arg & Suth Highlanders
GREENAWAY Arthur R. MM L/Cpl 630931 20th London Regt
GREENAWAY Frederick MM Sjt 61937 23rd Royal Fusiliers
GREENAWAY George MM Pte L/8416 1st Royal Fusiliers
GREENAWAY Harry Lewis MM Pte 4376 2/1st HAC(Inf) DOW 9.8.18.
GREENAWAY J.A. MM L/Cpl 204297 1st Somerset Light Infantry
GREENAWAY James MM Pte 26030 1st North Lancashire Regt DOW 18.9.18.

GREENBANK Harry MM Pte 241471 1st Royal Lancaster Regt KIA 25.10.18
GREENBANK William MM Pte 28835 1st East Lancashire Regt
GREENBERRY Henry MM Pte 71788 Machine Gun Corps
GREENBURG Joe MM Sjt 11286 1st Notts & Derby Regt
GREENBURY William Purvis MM Pte 67611 1st Notts & Derby Regt
GREENE Daniel "DCM,MM" Pte 10/19847 10th Northumberland Fusiliers KIA 4.8.16.
GREENE Francis N. MM Pte 300504 1/5th London Regt
GREENE John MM Pte 2298 RAMC
GREENE Lawrence M. MM Pte 7032 2nd Irish Guards
GREENER Charles Edward MM Pte 75712 23rd Royal Fusiliers DOW 9.10.18.
GREENER William MM Pte 43637 19th Durham Light Infantry
GREENFIELD Arthur MM L/Cpl 9176 1st Royal Fusiliers KIA 7.6.17.
GREENFIELD Bertram MM L/Bdr 960935 RFA
GREENFIELD Charles MM Pte 20856 Machine Gun Corps
GREENFIELD Charles Rowland MM Spr 64998 19 Div Sig Coy Royal Engineers
GREENFIELD George M. MM Pte 43789 2nd Yorkshire Light Infantry
GREENFIELD Harry MM L/Cpl G/4184 7th Royal West Surrey Regt "KIA 1.7.16,"
GREENFIELD Henry J. MM Pte 16299 1st Coldstream Guards
GREENFIELD Joseph MM Pte 3659 2nd Royal Inniskilling Fusiliers
GREENFIELD Percy MM Cpl 300395 5th London Regt
GREENFIELD Richard MM L/Sjt 9571 Royal West Surrey Regt
GREENFIELD Robert Spence "MM,DM(B)" Pte 41307 108 Fd Amb RAMC
GREENGRASS Daniel MM L/Cpl 1286 7th Royal West Kent Regt
GREENHALF Walter George MM L/Cpl 12191 2nd Grenadier Guards
GREENHALGH Alfred MM Sjt 3948 RFA
GREENHALGH Arthur MM L/Cpl 241800 East Lancashire Regt
GREENHALGH F. MM Gnr 172737 RFA
GREENHALGH Frank H. MM Sjt 19528 13th Liverpool Regt
GREENHALGH Frederick MM Pte C/180 16th King's Royal Rifle Corps
GREENHALGH George MM Spr 362085 Signal Service Royal Engineers
GREENHALGH Harold MM L/Cpl 2260 8th Royal Lancaster Regt
GREENHALGH Harold MM Pte 35440 2nd Lancashire Fusiliers
GREENHALGH Harry MM Dvr T3/030465 211 Coy Army Service Corps
GREENHALGH James MM L/Cpl 243435 North Lancashire Regt
GREENHALGH John MM Gnr 3941 B/165 Bde RFA DOW 28.9.17.
GREENHALGH Joseph MM Pte 242311 2/5th North Lancashire Regt
GREENHALGH Percy MM Gnr 38683 RGA
GREENHALGH Richard MM L/Cpl 142952 Machine Gun Corps
GREENHALGH Thomas MM Pte 36973 North Lancashire Regt
GREENHALGH William MM Pte 21587 21st Manchester Regt DOW 26.10.17.
GREENHAM Alfred W. MM Cpl 334411 353 Siege Bty RGA
GREENHAM Ernest MM Pte 350509 3(Northumbrian)Fd Amb RAMC
GREENHAM Frederick Bernard MM L/Cpl 25468 1st Gloucestershire Regt
GREENHAM Henry MM Pte 34568 2nd Welsh Regt KIA 4.10.18.
GREENHILL Andrew MM Pte 45865 RAMC
GREENHILL William Thomas MM Pnr 161461 18 Div Sig Coy Royal Engineers
GREENHOW Harry MM Cpl L/16410 C/149 Bde RFA
GREENHOW Harry MM L/Cpl 79705 10th West Yorkshire Regt
GREENING Charles MM Bdr 18017 4 Siege Bty RGA
GREENING Charles T. MM Sjt 171682 Royal Engineers
GREENING Frank MM Sjt 83677 A/46 Bde RFA
GREENING Frank V. MM Pte 762737 28th London Regt
GREENLAND Albert Victor MM Cpl 18849 1st Wiltshire Regt DOW 23.10.18.
GREENLAND Frederick W. MM Cpl 6651 East Surrey Regt
GREENLAND George B. MM Gnr 935277 RFA
GREENLAND Harry D. MM Sjt 24002 Middlesex Regt
GREENLAND John H. "DCM,MM+Bar" Sjt 909 RAMC
GREENLAW George MM Pte 40265 Royal Highlanders
GREENLAW John MM Pte 10595 1/5th Durham Light Infantry
GREENLEES Alfred MM Pte S/8653 1st Gordon Highlanders KIA 17.6.17.
GREENOUGH Ernest MM Cpl 15227 1/4th Royal Lancaster Regt
GREENOUGH Horace MM Cpl 32583 North Staffordshire Regt

GREENOUGH James MM L/Cpl 18309 1/5th Border Regt
GREENOUGH Philip William MM Pte 57822 2/8th Worcestershire Regt
GREENOUGH Reginald G. MM Spr 95586 Royal Engineers
GREENOUGH Robert MM Pte 6501 1st Shropshire Light Infantry KIA 18.4.17.
GREENSHIELDS James MM Pte 38548 5/6th Scottish Rifles
GREENSHIELDS Thomas MM CQMS 275019 1/7th Arg & Suth Highlanders Died 21.2.19.
GREENSILL Bernard MM Dvr 5972 RFA
GREENSLADE Charles "DCM,MM" Sjt 33172 2nd Devonshire Regt
GREENSLADE Charles MM Pte 512402 RAMC
GREENSLADE Daniel MM Pte 6795 2nd Devonshire Regt
GREENSLADE John M. MM Pte 74820 13th Royal Fusiliers
GREENSLADE Thomas A. MM Pte 1792 1/2nd Monmouthshire Regt
GREENSLADE Thomas H. MM L/Cpl 14168 Machine Gun Corps
GREENSLADE Wilfred MM Cpl 320357 1/6th London Regt
GREENSLADE William H. MM Cpl 46803 Royal Engineers
GREENSMITH Edward MM Pte 241683 2/4th York & Lancaster Regt
GREENWAY George A. MM 2nd Cpl 47278 Royal Engineers
GREENWAY John "DCM,MM" CSM 40828 8th North Staffordshire Regt
GREENWAY Sidney MM L/Cpl 51067 MGC(Cavalry)
GREENWAY Stanley MM Cpl 41714 8th Royal Lancaster Regt
GREENWELL Alexander MM Sjt 15653 East Yorkshire Regt
GREENWELL Joseph MM Sjt 325144 9th Durham Light Infantry
GREENWELL Richard MM Bdr 751514 B/250 Bde RFA
GREENWOOD Albert MM Pte 244939 1/5th North Lancashire Regt
GREENWOOD Albert MM Pte 60979 RAMC
GREENWOOD Ambrose MM Pte 45231 92 Fd Amb RAMC
GREENWOOD Andrew R. MM Sjt 5062 East Lancashire Regt
GREENWOOD Charles MM+Bar L/Sjt 11579 Grenadier Guards KIA 22.3.18.
GREENWOOD Charles MM Pnr 98753 Royal Engineers
GREENWOOD Charles D. MM Spr 311603 32 Div Sig Coy Royal Engineers
GREENWOOD Charles William MM Bdr 825669 87 Bty 2 Bde RFA
GREENWOOD Clarence MM Sjt 204102 2/5th Lancashire Fusiliers
GREENWOOD Edward Charles MM+Bar Pte 10527 6th Royal West Kent Regt KIA 9.4.18.
GREENWOOD Ernest MM Sjt 200977 4th West Riding Regt
GREENWOOD Francis Leonard MM Sjt L/28975 D/150 Bde RFA KIA 5.4.18.
GREENWOOD Frank MM Cpl 10506 2nd Royal Scots Fusiliers
GREENWOOD Frank H. MM Sjt 40314 Tank Corps
GREENWOOD Fred MM Pte 21623 Border Regt
GREENWOOD Fred MM Spt 101805 Royal Engineers
GREENWOOD Fred "DCM,MM+Bar" Pte S/11400 1st Rifle Brigade
GREENWOOD Fred MM L/Cpl 24522 10th West Riding Regt
GREENWOOD Frederick W. MM Pte 9919 1/2nd(Highland)Fd Amb RAMC
GREENWOOD George MM Pte 325168 1/1st Cambridgeshire Regt
GREENWOOD George MM Sjt 60770 9th Northumberland Fusiliers
GREENWOOD George MM L/Cpl 11190 2nd Worcestershire Regt KIA 15.7.16.
GREENWOOD George MM+Bar Dvr 755076 C/251 Bde RFA
GREENWOOD George MM Sjt 260695 Gordon Highlanders
GREENWOOD George William MM Sjt 14108 24th Manchester Regt
GREENWOOD H. MM Gnr 2928 RFA
GREENWOOD Haigh MM+Bar L/Cpl 201484 2/4th West Riding Regt
GREENWOOD Harold MM L/Sjt 201630 4th West Riding Regt
GREENWOOD Harold MM Cpl 29662 Norfolk Regt
GREENWOOD Harold E. MM Dvr 776093 RFA
GREENWOOD Harold P. MM Cpl 3/3531 8th York & Lancaster Regt
GREENWOOD Harry MM Sjt 241046 9th West Yorkshire Regt
GREENWOOD Harry MM Sjt 3403 16th Lancashire Fusiliers
GREENWOOD Harry MM Dvr 710313 RFA
GREENWOOD Harry MM+Bar Cpl 201215 1/4th Seaforth Highlanders DOW 24.3.18.
GREENWOOD Henry W.V. MM Pte 77711 13th Royal Fusiliers
GREENWOOD Jack MM L/Cpl 94255 13th Liverpool Regt
GREENWOOD James Lindsay MM Sjt 8396 1st Royal Lancaster Regt KIA 22.10.16.
GREENWOOD James William MM Pte R/13002 King's Royal Rifle Corps
GREENWOOD John "DCM,MM" Sjt M2/020766 Army Service Corps
GREENWOOD John "DCM,MM+Bar" Cpl 250310 1/6th Durham Light Infantry att 151 LTM Bty
GREENWOOD John Edwin MM Cpl 40997 9 Fd Amb RAMC KIA 16.8.17.
GREENWOOD John R. MM Pte 283617 4th London Regt
GREENWOOD John S. MM L/Cpl 11806 1st East Surrey Regt
GREENWOOD John W. MM Cpl 28792 1/6th Highland Light Infantry KIA 27.8.18.
GREENWOOD John W. MM Pte 16972 8th East Lancashire Regt
GREENWOOD Joseph MM Dvr 62738 RFA
GREENWOOD Lawrence MM L/Cpl 67621 9th Yorkshire Light Infantry
GREENWOOD Leonard MM Pte 306774 8th West Yorkshire Regt
GREENWOOD Norman MM Spr 51023 30 Div Sig Coy Royal Engineers
GREENWOOD Percival MM Sjt 18/906 18th West Yorkshire Regt DOW 5.5.17.
GREENWOOD Percy H. MM S/Sjt 806 RAMC
GREENWOOD Richard MM Sjt S/11775 1st Gordon Highlanders
GREENWOOD Robert MM Sjt 4180 12th Manchester Regt
GREENWOOD Robert MM L/Cpl 17604 10th North Lancashire Regt Died 13.7.18.
GREENWOOD Samuel MM Cpl 26224 15th Lancashire Fusiliers KIA 30.9.18.
GREENWOOD Samuel MM Cpl 1232 21st Manchester Regt KIA 11.10.18.
GREENWOOD Sydney MM Pte 26940 10th Lancashire Fusiliers KIA 18.9.18.
GREENWOOD Thomas MM Pte 41748 5th Lancashire Fusiliers
GREENWOOD Thomas MM Pte 201715 1/4th Cheshire Regt
GREENWOOD Thomas MM Sjt 2923 1/8th Liverpool Regt
GREENWOOD Thomas MM Pte 241406 Lancashire Fusiliers
GREENWOOD Thomas MM Cpl 12/6837 12th Royal Irish Rifles
GREENWOOD W.C. MM Sjt L/228 B/159 Bde RFA
GREENWOOD Wilfred MM Gnr 66834 RGA
GREENWOOD Wilfred MM Gnr 102985 RGA
GREENWOOD William MM L/Bdr 58435 B/48 Bde RFA
GREENWOOD William MM Pte 4274 1/6th West Yorkshire Regt
GREENWOOD William MM+2 Bars L/Cpl 49144 4th Royal Fusiliers
GREENWOOD William A. MM Gnr 476 RGA
GREENWOOD William C. MM Sjt 32126 RGA
GREENWOOD William F. MM Dvr 52693 RFA
GREENWOOD William H. MM Bdr 11046 RFA
GREENWOOD William J. MM Sjt Farrier 100360 D/168 Bde RFA
GREER A. MM+Bar Pte 277007 7th Manchester Regt
GREER David S. MM Sjt 202676 Royal Highlanders
GREER James MM Sjt 19446 Machine Gun Corps
GREER John MM Pte 51427 12th Royal Scots
GREER John MM Pte 33294 8th York & Lancaster Regt
GREER Thomas MM Cpl 17137 189 Coy Machine Gun Corps DOW 19.12.17.
GREER William MM L/Cpl 335840 1/8th Royal Scots KIA 11.4.18.
GREEST William MM Bdr 47851 RFA
GREGG Henry MM Dvr 21406 RFA
GREGG John MM Pte Z/2511 Rifle Brigade
GREGG John W. MM+2 Bars Cpl 21152 8th Yorkshire Light Infantry
GREGG Joseph MM+Bar Sjt 13287 10th North Lancashire Regt
GREGG Nathan MM Cpl 8/15142 8th Border Regt
GREGG William "VC,DCM,MM" Sjt S/6522 13th Rifle Brigade
GREGG William MM Sjt 300325 1/5th Durham Light Infantry
GREGG Winter T. MM Pte 87 1st Royal Guernsey LI
GREGOR Frederick MM 2nd Cpl 75890 16 Div Sig Coy Royal Engineers
GREGOR William MM L/Cpl 45740 80 Fd Coy Royal Engineers
GREGORY A.E. MM Sjt P1156 Military Mounted Police
GREGORY Albert MM Gnr 806587 408 Bty 96 Bde RFA
GREGORY Alfred Edward MM Pte 36834 9th Cheshire Regt KIA 12.4.18.
GREGORY Anthony MM L/Cpl PW/1022 18th Middlesex Regt
GREGORY Arthur William MM Cpl 9055 2nd Hampshire Regt
GREGORY Benjamin MM Cpl 276028 1/7th Manchester Regt
GREGORY Charles MM Pte 1774 1/12th London Regt
GREGORY Charles H. MM L/Cpl 43064 Royal Inniskilling Fusiliers
GREGORY Cornelius "DCM,MM" CSM 164 2nd Lancashire Fusiliers
GREGORY Dick MM Sjt 165234 101st Bn Machine Gun Corps
GREGORY Edmund Oates MM Pte DM2/224394 42 Div Train Army Service Corps
GREGORY Edward MM+Bar L/Cpl 25498 Gloucestershire Regt
GREGORY Ernest MM Pte 405152 RAMC

GREGORY Ernest "MM,CG(F)" Sjt M2/021058 Army Service Corps att 1/2nd(Highland)Fd Amb RAMC.
GREGORY Ernest "DCM,MM" Pte S/9909 Rifle Brigade
GREGORY F.A. MM Cpl 20575 10 Fd Amb RAMC
GREGORY Francis Arthur MM Pte 70878 16 Coy Machine Gun Corps
GREGORY Frank MM Pnr 443926 Royal Engineers
GREGORY Frank MM Pte 20457 Royal Fusiliers
GREGORY Frank MM Pte 31712 North Lancashire Regt
GREGORY Frederick MM+Bar Pte 240464 1/5th North Lancashire Regt
GREGORY Frederick William MM Cpl 18267 7th Bn Machine Gun Corps
GREGORY George MM Sjt 482349 62 Div Sig Coy Royal Engineers
GREGORY George MM Pte 26135 Devonshire Regt
GREGORY George F. MM Cpl 30741 East Surrey Regt
GREGORY George Stanley "DCM,MM" CSM 2099 1/1st Hertfordshire Regt
GREGORY Harry MM Spr 5473 42 Army Troops Coy Royal Engineers
GREGORY Harry MM Pte 39516 42nd Bn Machine Gun Corps
GREGORY Harry F. MM CSM 235509 8th Yorkshire Regt
GREGORY Harry William George "MM,MSM,MID" Sjt 10831 22 CCS RAMC
GREGORY Henry James MM Pnr 127602 2 Div Sig Coy Royal Engineers
GREGORY Herbert MM Pte 85744 Machine Gun Corps
GREGORY James MM L/Cpl 10991 4th Hussars DOW 10.4.18.
GREGORY James MM Gnr 68006 128 Heavy Bty RGA
GREGORY James MM+Bar Pte 21904 8th Royal Lancaster Regt KIA 23.8.18.
GREGORY John MM Sjt 280056 1st Hampshire Regt
GREGORY John MM Cpl 13439 6th Northamptonshire Regt
GREGORY Laurie L. MM Gnr 103250 RFA
GREGORY Leopold Richard MM Pte 1865 12th Middlesex Regt KIA 26.9.16.
GREGORY Lily Anne MM Miss F VAD
GREGORY Richard MM Gnr 118021 A/102 Bde RFA DOW 30.9.17.
GREGORY Samson MM Pte 32364 6th Somerset Light Infantry
GREGORY Samuel MM L/Cpl 25048 Royal Welsh Fusiliers
GREGORY Sidney David MM Bdr 925239 280 Bde RFA
GREGORY Stanley E.H. MM Pte 28060 4th North Lancashire Regt
GREGORY Thomas MM Pte 40660 76 Fd Amb RAMC
GREGORY Thomas MM Sjt L/16204 A/150 Bde RFA DOW 25.10.16.
GREGORY Thomas MM Dvr 67163 15 Div Ammn Col RFA
GREGORY Thomas W. MM Spr 83483 Royal Engineers
GREGORY Walter R. MM L/Cpl 34984 1/5th Border Regt
GREGORY William MM Pte 33391 2nd Hampshire Regt
GREGORY William MM Pte 203287 2nd Wiltshire Regt
GREGORY William MM Pte 698 5th Royal Irish Regt
GREGORY William MM Gnr 52883 128 Hy Bty RGA
GREGORY William MM Sjt 16703 70 Bde Ammn Col RFA
GREGORY William Henry MM Pte 240381 Royal Warwickshire Regt
GREGORY William Henry MM Pte 277365 2/7th Manchester Regt KIA 21.3.18.
GREGORY Wright MM Sjt 99548 D/117 Bde RFA
GREGSON Arthur MM Pte 23838 North Lancashire Regt
GREGSON George MM Sjt 240398 East Lancashire Regt
GREGSON George M. MM Pte 40359 27 Fd Amb RAMC
GREGSON Harry MM Gnr 2291 A/311 Bde RFA
GREGSON John MM Pte 203522 North Lancashire Regt
GREGSON John G. MM Gnr 96178 D/251 Bde RFA
GREGSON John Matthew MM Pte 35711 17th Lancashire Fusiliers
GREGSON John W. MM Pte 204046 Lancashire Fusiliers
GREGSON Joseph "MM,MSM" 2nd Cpl 69945 138 Army Troops Coy Royal Engineers
GREGSON Thomas MM Pte 59379 4th Liverpool Regt KIA 20.11.17.
GREGSON Thomas Henry MM Sjt 202229 2/4th South Lancashire Regt
GREGSON W. MM Sjt 405380 2/3rd(West Riding)Fd Amb RAMC
GREGSON Walter MM Cpl (MCDR) 444246 Royal Engineers
GREIG Alexander MM Pte 325340 12th Royal Scots
GREIG Alexander MM Pte 62827 32nd Bn Machine Gun Corps
GREIG Alfred "DCM,MM+2 Bars,OLeo(B)" Sjt 291290 1/7th Royal Highlanders
GREIG Charles MM Pte 33037 2nd King's Own Scottish Borderers
GREIG Duncan MM Dvr 92914 RFA
GREIG Frederick MM Gnr 326130 1/1st(Clyde)Hy Bty RGA
GREIG Gavin MM Sjt 1596 1st(Highland)Fd Amb RAMC
GREIG George MM L/Cpl 6809 Royal Highlanders
GREIG George F. MM Cpl 1138 Royal Engineers
GREIG Herbert Edward MM Pte 368084 7th London Regt KIA 8.9.18.
GREIG John MM Pte 29398 East Yorkshire Regt
GREIG Melville MM 2nd Cpl 79374 205 Fd Coy Royal Engineers KIA 20.10.18.
GREIG Melville Logan MM Pnr 25116 1 Div Sig Coy Royal Engineers DOW 26.9.16.
GREIG R. MM Sjt A/156 King's Royal Rifle Corps
GREIG Robert MM Cpl 3/7224 Gordon Highlanders
GREIG Robert A. MM Pte 18249 Royal Highlanders
GREIG Thomas MM Sjt 376190 2nd Royal Scots
GREIG Thomas MM L/Cpl S/13714 2nd Gordon Highlanders
GREIG Thomas Paterson MM L/Cpl 530827 15th London Regt
GREIG William MM L/Cpl 291017 Royal Highlanders
GREIG William MM Pte 290347 1/7th Gordon Highlanders
GREIG William MM L/Cpl 20800 2nd Royal Scots
GREIG William J. MM L/Cpl 44410 Royal Engineers
GREIG William Thomas MM BSM 36064 RFA
GRENDON Henry William MM L/Cpl STK/696 10th Royal Fusiliers
GRENDON William J. MM Cpl 240271 1/6th Royal Warwickshire Regt
GRENFELL James Anthony MM Sjt 22485 10th Duke of Cornwall's LI
GRENFELL Richard "DCM,MM" BQMS 952 A/122 Bde RFA
GRENNEN John MM Pte 68265 RAMC
GRENYER William D. MM L/Cpl 1691 Royal Sussex Regt
GRESHAM Cecil P. MM L/Cpl Pnr 25474 1 Div Sig Coy Royal Engineers
GRESHAM Fred MM L/Bdr 382371 77 Siege Bty RGA
GRESHAM Frederick Njilima MM Pte 90624 5th Bn Machine Gun Corps
GRESTY Fletcher Lea MM Cpl 356429 10th Liverpool Regt
GRETTON Henry MM Sjt 26915 15th Notts & Derby Regt
GREVATT William MM Gnr 76150 127 Bty 29 Bde RFA
GREW Harry MM Pte 16460 9th North Lancashire Regt
GREW Henry MM Sjt 8/12188 8th South Staffordshire Regt
GREWCOCK Arthur MM Pte 22386 Labour Corps
GREY Charles E. MM+Bar Spr 207566 63 Div Sig Coy Royal Engineers
GREY Charles P. MM Pte 46428 17th Lancashire Fusiliers
GREY Ernest MM L/Cpl A/200001 King's Royal Rifle Corps
GREY John Alfred MM Spr 179148 Royal Engineers
GREY John G. MM Bdr 72731 RFA
GREY Sydney V. MM Pte M2/182231 Army Service Corps
GREY Thomas MM L/Cpl 9500 Royal Fusiliers
GREY William G. "DCM,MM" Sjt 43893 18 Div Sig Coy Royal Engineers
GREYSON Ernest MM Pte 14986 7th Dragoon Guards
GRIBBEN Patrick MM Pte 20941 Royal Irish Fusiliers
GRIBBLE Charles MM Sjt R/17233 13th King's Royal Rifle Corps DOW 10.1.18.
GRIBBLE Charles "MM,MSM,MID" CSM 103162 32 Div Sig Coy Royal Engineers
GRIBBLE Wallace Charles MM Spr 2949 520 Fd Coy Royal Engineers DOW 22.8.18.
GRICE Arthur Leslie MM Sjt 9946 6th Somerset Light Infantry
GRICE Charles MM Pte 32508 1/6th Cheshire Regt
GRICE Edwin MM L/Cpl 8596 2nd Royal Warwickshire Regt
GRICE Herbert MM Cpl 37887 Royal Berkshire Regt
GRICE Herbert J. "MM,MIDx2" Sjt 13051 2 Fd Sqn Royal Engineers
GRICE John Henry MM Pte 202645 2/5th Lancashire Fusiliers
GRICE Stephen MM Pte 7773 2nd Lincolnshire Regt
GRICE Thomas MM Cpl 50693 Machine Gun Corps(Cav)
GRIDLEY Alfred J. MM Cpl G4687 13th Royal Fusiliers
GRIEF Walter H. MM Dvr 135765 15 Bty 36 Bde RFA
GRIER Andrew MM Pte S/3139 7th Seaforth Highlanders
GRIER Henry MM Pte 4/8516 Durham Light Infantry
GRIER John MM Pte 2355 1/8th Arg & Suth Highlanders
GRIERSON Charles MM Cpl 250611 5/6th Royal Scots
GRIERSON David MM L/Cpl S/296(0?)7 8th Royal Highlanders KIA 14.7.16.
GRIERSON Henry R. MM Pte 301630 1/7th Royal Scots
GRIERSON Joseph MM Pte 30808 RAMC
GRIERSON Joseph MM Pte 283371 4th London Regt
GRIERSON Robert MM Sjt 14064 7th Cameron Highlanders
GRIERSON Robert William MM Cpl 380282 24 Labour Coy Labour Corps
GRIERSON Walter MM Pte 30536 15th Highland Light Infantry

GRIEVE A. MM+Bar Sjt 251597 Royal Engineers
GRIEVE Alexander MM Sjt 28610 2nd King's Own Scottish Borderers
GRIEVE Andrew MM Pte S/19995 6th Royal Highlanders
GRIEVE Andrew MM Gnr 116680 270 Siege Bty RGA
GRIEVE D. MM Pte 6826 King's Own Scottish Borderers
GRIEVE David MM Pte S/40077 1st Royal Highlanders
GRIEVE George MM Pte S/17768 8th Royal Highlanders
GRIEVE George L. "DCM,MM" Sjt 5060 1/14th London Regt
GRIEVE Harry MM L/Cpl 830 4th Bn GMGR
GRIEVE J. MM Gnr 841 RFA
GRIEVE John 2nd Cpl 89994 Royal Engineers
GRIEVE John MM Pte 5626 Royal Warwickshire Regt
GRIEVE John C. MM L/Cpl 250497 5/6th Royal Scots
GRIEVE John G. MM L/Cpl 21049 2nd Dragoon Guards
GRIEVE William MM Pte 4199 Gordon Highlanders
GRIEVE William Porter MM L/Cpl 1635 89 Fd Amb RAMC
GRIEVSON Sydney J. MM L/Cpl R/9805 King's Royal Rifle Corps
GRIFFEN Albert MM Sjt 400057 400 Fd Coy Royal Engineers
GRIFFEN James MM Cpl 238019 9th Scottish Rifles
GRIFFEN James MM Pte 42578 2nd Bedfordshire Regt DOW 5.11.18.
GRIFFEN Leonard Lionel MM L/Cpl 18524 1st Wiltshire Regt KIA 12.4.18.
GRIFFEN Peter MM L/Cpl S/2311 10th Arg & Suth Highlanders
GRIFFEN Thomas "DCM,MM" L/Cpl 30576 King's Own Scottish Borderers
GRIFFEN William MM Spr 251710 Royal Engineers
GRIFFEY Frederick B. MM Gnr 837094 RFA
GRIFFIN A.E. MM Pte 772 Yeomanry
GRIFFIN Alfred MM Sjt 1056 4th Dragoon Guards
GRIFFIN Anthony "DCM,MM" CSM 4637 39th Bn Machine Gun Corps
GRIFFIN Archibald MM Pte 38763 11th Northumberland Fusiliers DOW 21.4.18.
GRIFFIN Arthur E.C. MM L/Cpl 11221 6th Somerset Light Infantry
GRIFFIN Arthur J. MM Sjt 51846 D/286 Bde RFA
GRIFFIN Arthur William MM Sjt R/4003 12th King's Royal Rifle Corps DOW 28.2.17.
GRIFFIN Bertie MM Sjt 3491 17th Bn Machine Gun Corps
GRIFFIN Christopher G. MM Pte 354403 7th London Regt
GRIFFIN Cyril MM Pte 14583 9th East Lancashire Regt
GRIFFIN Daniel MM Pte 12610 1st Scots Guards
GRIFFIN Edward MM Sjt 785 Royal Fusiliers
GRIFFIN Edward MM Gnr Fitter 82696 RFA
GRIFFIN Edward F. MM Pte 1387 1/7th London Regt
GRIFFIN Ellis Arthur MM+Bar Cpl 95856 95 Fd Coy Royal Engineers
GRIFFIN Eric MM Pte 57445 Machine Gun Corps
GRIFFIN Ernest MM Pte M2/035213 335 Coy Army Service Corps
GRIFFIN Frank MM+Bar Sjt 9/13675 5th South Wales Borderers
GRIFFIN Frederick MM Pte 6697 Royal Sussex Regt
GRIFFIN George MM L/Cpl 8918 1st Scottish Rifles
GRIFFIN George MM Pte 40628 Essex Regt
GRIFFIN George MM Pte 2302 4th Rifle Brigade
GRIFFIN George J. MM Sjt 23304 1st Grenadier Guards
GRIFFIN Guy Featherstone MM L/Cpl 290487 12th Middlesex Regt
GRIFFIN Harry MM 2nd Cpl 24064 11 Fd Coy Royal Engineers
GRIFFIN Harry MM L/Cpl 19348 6th Shropshire Light Infantry
GRIFFIN Harry W. "DCM,MM+Bar" Sjt 4764 8th East Surrey Regt
GRIFFIN Henry MM QMS Farrier 25 RFA
GRIFFIN Henry H. MM Sjt 71191 2nd Bn Machine Gun Corps
GRIFFIN Herbert H. MM Pte 52656 RAMC
GRIFFIN James MM Pte 2234 2nd Northumberland Fusiliers
GRIFFIN James MM Cpl 2690 1/9th Liverpool Regt
GRIFFIN James Peddie MM Sjt 40860 D/242 Bde RFA DOW 6.11.18.
GRIFFIN John MM Sjt 7695 Irish Guards
GRIFFIN John MM Pte 5294 Lancashire Fusiliers
GRIFFIN John William MM Dvr 1588 381 Bty 158 Bde RFA "Died 30.7.18."
GRIFFIN Joseph MM Pte 240764 4th Yorkshire Light Infantry
GRIFFIN Joseph MM L/Cpl 8639 Royal Dublin Fusiliers
GRIFFIN Joseph MM Gnr 71191 24 Bde RFA
GRIFFIN Leonard Richard MM Sjt 178 1/4th Oxf & Bucks Light Infantry
GRIFFIN Matthew MM L/Cpl 3/6367 East Yorkshire Regt
GRIFFIN Patrick MM L/Cpl 41297 Notts & Derby Regt
GRIFFIN Patrick John MM 2nd Cpl 20709 15 Fd Coy Royal Engineers KIA 7.7.17.
GRIFFIN Reginald MM Cpl 87923 RFA
GRIFFIN Thomas MM Pte 295366 12th Royal Scots Fusiliers
GRIFFIN Thomas MM L/Cpl 13277 Welsh Regt
GRIFFIN Thomas MM Sjt 7898 1st East Yorkshire Regt
GRIFFIN Wallace MM Sjt 241667 Royal Warwickshire Regt
GRIFFIN William MM Cpl 19347 7th Shropshire Light Infantry
GRIFFIN William MM Pte 13568 6th Lincolnshire Regt
GRIFFIN William H. MM Sjt 200241 Royal Highlanders
GRIFFIN William H. MM Sjt 240198 1/8th Worcestershire Regt
GRIFFIN William M. MM Gnr 147137 194 Siege Bty RGA
GRIFFITH Benjamin MM Bdr 54584 D/84 Bde RFA
GRIFFITH Charles Paul MM Pte M2/131231 22 Tpt Repair Pk Army Service Corps
GRIFFITHS Albert MM L/Cpl 18402 Coldstream Guards
GRIFFITHS Albert Edward MM L/Cpl 26801 2nd South Wales Borderers KIA 21.11.17.
GRIFFITHS Alfred MM Gnr 72340 D/47 Bde RFA
GRIFFITHS Alfred C. MM+Bar L/Cpl 3177 1/8th London Regt
GRIFFITHS Alfred J. MM Gnr 624747 att 309 Siege Bty RGA HAC(Arty)
GRIFFITHS Archibald MM Pte 58292 13th Welsh Regt
GRIFFITHS Arthur MM Bdr Sig 730417 267 Bde RFA
GRIFFITHS Bernard L. MM CQMS 82057 226 Fd Coy Royal Engineers
GRIFFITHS C. MM Sjt 265114 Monmouthshire Regt
GRIFFITHS Charles MM Pte 300557 1st Essex Regt KIA 23.8.18.
GRIFFITHS Charles MM Dvr 87135 A/71 Bde RFA
GRIFFITHS Charles A. MM Pte 241085 2/8th Worcestershire Regt
GRIFFITHS Daniel MM Gnr 24481 D/75 Bde RFA
GRIFFITHS David MM L/Cpl D/12233 2nd Dragoons
GRIFFITHS David MM Pte 61479 Machine Gun Corps
GRIFFITHS David MM Pte 21703 9th Royal Inniskilling Fusiliers
GRIFFITHS David MM Pte 9461 2nd Royal Irish Rifles
GRIFFITHS David MM Cpl 282634 194 Siege Bty RGA DOW 8.9.18.
GRIFFITHS David MM Pte 200946 1/4th Royal Welsh Fusiliers
GRIFFITHS David MM Pte 9745 Royal Fusiliers
GRIFFITHS David MM Sjt 28212 Royal Scots Fusiliers
GRIFFITHS David T. MM L/Cpl 43398 RAMC
GRIFFITHS Edward MM Pte 240202 1/5th South Lancashire Regt
GRIFFITHS Edward MM Pte 240086 Royal Welsh Fusiliers
GRIFFITHS Edward MM Gnr 112475 127 Bty 29 Bde RFA
GRIFFITHS Edward J. MM Cpl 83746 B/47 Bde RFA
GRIFFITHS Edwin MM L/Cpl M2/046065 Army Service Corps att RFA
GRIFFITHS Elias MM Cpl 9927 1st York & Lancaster Regt
GRIFFITHS Elihu MM Spr 112547 Royal Engineers
GRIFFITHS Evan MM Pte 64097 72 Coy Machine Gun Corps
GRIFFITHS Evan F. MM Gnr 294541 RGA
GRIFFITHS Evan James MM Pte 12259 1st Grenadier Guards
GRIFFITHS Evan Thomas MM Pte 19232 16th Royal Welsh Fusiliers KIA 24.8.18.
GRIFFITHS Frank MM Sjt 820058 46 Div Ammn Col RFA
GRIFFITHS Frank MM SQMS 6174 18th Hussars
GRIFFITHS Frank MM Pte 2015 1/4th Cheshire Regt
GRIFFITHS Frank G. MM Pte 236418 1/1st Herefordshire Regt
GRIFFITHS Frederick J. MM Pte 236640 1/1st Herefordshire Regt
GRIFFITHS George MM Sjt 345256 24th Royal Welsh Fusiliers
GRIFFITHS George MM Gnr 84022 A/306 Bde RFA DOW 19.4.18.
GRIFFITHS George H. MM Cpl 200992 1/5th Liverpool Regt
GRIFFITHS George H. MM Spr 42106 Royal Engineers
GRIFFITHS George L. "DCM,MM" Sjt 70497 42nd Bn Machine Gun Corps
GRIFFITHS Gwilym MM Pte 16440 Welsh Regt
GRIFFITHS Gwynne G.W. MM Sjt 225322 1/1st Monmouthshire Regt
GRIFFITHS Henry MM L/Cpl 34654 1st Royal Welsh Fusiliers
GRIFFITHS Henry MM Cpl 10726 7th South Wales Borderers
GRIFFITHS Henry B. MM Pte 90561 22 Fd Amb RAMC
GRIFFITHS Henry T. MM Cpl 3961 13th Middlesex Regt
GRIFFITHS Henry T. MM Cpl 720543 1/24th London Regt
GRIFFITHS Ivor J. MM Pte 265580 1/2nd Monmouthshire Regt
GRIFFITHS J.W. MM Pte 734 15th Hussars
GRIFFITHS James MM Pte 240522 1/5th South Lancashire Regt
GRIFFITHS James MM Gnr 212847 D/295 Bde RFA
GRIFFITHS James MM Pte 9849 1st Grenadier Guards
GRIFFITHS James MM Pte 12553 1st Worcestershire Regt
GRIFFITHS James Charles MM Pte 16699 2nd South Staffordshire Regt KIA 28.7.16.
GRIFFITHS James William MM Cpl 26181 18th Welsh Regt KIA 24.3.18.

GRIFFITHS John MM Gnr 686208 C/175 Bde RFA
GRIFFITHS John MM Pte 1680 Monmouthshire Regt
GRIFFITHS John MM Pte C/198 16th King's Royal Rifle Corps
GRIFFITHS John MM Sjt 15260 11th Welsh Regt
GRIFFITHS John MM L/Cpl 14693 11th Royal Welsh Fusiliers
GRIFFITHS John MM Pte 265687 Gloucestershire Regt
GRIFFITHS John MM Gnr 18173 RFA
GRIFFITHS John E. MM Cpl 300283 13th Bn Tank Corps
GRIFFITHS John H. MM L/Cpl 108540 233 Fd Coy Royal Engineers
GRIFFITHS John H. MM Sjt 14893 7th Yorkshire Regt
GRIFFITHS John W. MM Sjt 10740 1st Royal Welsh Fusiliers
GRIFFITHS Joseph MM L/Cpl 16427 4th Worcestershire Regt
GRIFFITHS Joseph S. MM L/Cpl 16011 7th Leicestershire Regt
GRIFFITHS Kenneth MM Gnr 112678 RGA
GRIFFITHS Morgan MM Sjt 30578 RAMC
GRIFFITHS Percy Albert MM Sjt 4860 5th Connaught Rangers
GRIFFITHS R. MM Sjt 594 RFA
GRIFFITHS Reginald MM Pte 22133 Middlesex Regt
GRIFFITHS Richard MM L/Cpl 1370 1/6th Liverpool Regt
GRIFFITHS Richard J. MM Pte 46794 1st South Wales Borderers
GRIFFITHS Richard Joseph MM Pte 40661 4th Worcestershire Regt KIA 20.11.17.
GRIFFITHS Robert MM Sjt 16308 South Lancashire Regt
GRIFFITHS Samuel H. MM Cpl 56527 RFA
GRIFFITHS Thomas MM Cpl 35805 North Staffordshire Regt
GRIFFITHS Thomas MM Sjt 56748 Machine Gun Corps
GRIFFITHS Thomas MM Pte 2759 1st Welsh Guards KIA 10.3.18.
GRIFFITHS Thomas David Edgar "MM,MID,VM(Rm)" Cpl 98695 D/57 Bde RFA
GRIFFITHS Thomas E. MM Cpl 96981 Royal Engineers
GRIFFITHS Thomas T. MM Pte 48694 10 Fd Amb RAMC
GRIFFITHS W.E. MM Pte 23014 Lancashire Fusiliers
GRIFFITHS William MM Cpl 6838 Northumberland Fusiliers
GRIFFITHS William MM L/Cpl 202829 Oxf & Bucks Light Infantry
GRIFFITHS William MM Sjt 21707 2nd South Wales Borderers
GRIFFITHS William MM L/Cpl 16884 6th South Wales Borderers
GRIFFITHS William MM Sjt 29619 RGA
GRIFFITHS William MM Cpl 58148 118 Bty 130 Bde RFA
GRIFFITHS William MM Pnr 225169 Royal Engineers
GRIFFITHS William B. MM Cpl 40615 1/5th Lincolnshire Regt
GRIFFITHS William E. MM Pte 8608 2nd Worcestershire Regt
GRIFFITHS William George "DCM,MM+Bar" Sjt 330557 9th Liverpool Regt KIA 28.8.18.
GRIFFITHS William H. MM Pte 3/8303 2nd Yorkshire Regt
GRIFFITHS William H. MM Dvr 53564 212 Fd Coy Royal Engineers
GRIFFITHS William H. MM Sjt 20206 15th Welsh Regt
GRIFFITHS William H. MM Pte 302582 1/6th Manchester Regt
GRIFFITHS William H. MM Pte 15809 4th Worcestershire Regt
GRIFFITHS William J. MM Pte 306526 5th Lancashire Fusiliers
GRIFFITHS William J. MM Sjt 202931 South Lancashire Regt
GRIFFITHS William T. MM+Bar Pte 23034 Royal Welsh Fusiliers
GRIGG Arthur R. MM Cpl 386858 Royal Engineers
GRIGG James C. MM Gnr 128258 235 Siege Bty RGA
GRIGG William H. "DCM,MM" Sjt 20020 Sig Service Royal Engineers
GRIGGS Bart MM L/Cpl 5386 23rd Middlesex Regt
GRIGGS Ernest MM L/Cpl 7407 Machine Gun Corps
GRIGGS Frank J. MM Dvr 34260 RFA
GRIGGS Frederick MM Sjt 13664 West Riding Regt
GRIGGS Frederick John MM Bdr 68608 12 Siege Bty RGA
GRIGGS Frederick John MM Pte 89197 2nd Middlesex Regt Died 6.11.18.
GRIGGS Frederick Leslie MM Pte 18684 1st Devonshire Regt DOW 8.11.18.
GRIGGS Henry J. MM Pte 7637 Royal West Surrey Regt
GRIGGS Percy W. "DCM,MM" CQMS 8586 1st East Yorkshire Regt
GRIGGS Robert MM Pte 11293 7th Duke of Cornwall's LI KIA 30.11.17.
GRIGGS Thomas William MM Pnr 361821 Royal Engineers
GRIGGS William MM Gnr L/31031 A/177 Bde RFA KIA 1.8.18.
GRIGOR Gordon MM Pte 2307 Seaforth Highlanders
GRIGSBY Philip E. MM Gnr 106543 A/26 Bde RFA
GRIMBLEY Ernest MM Dvr 72831 RFA
GRIME Charles MM Sjt 22399 North Lancashire Regt
GRIME Henry MM Pte 240690 1/5th North Lancashire Regt
GRIME Richard MM Pte 240812 2/5th East Lancashire Regt
GRIME William MM Pte 26962 2/5th Royal Lancaster Regt
GRIMES Arnold J. MM L/Cpl 200520 1st Royal Warwickshire Regt
GRIMES Bennett MM L/Cpl 18952 Machine Gun Corps
GRIMES Edward MM Pte S/2187 9th Seaforth Highlanders
GRIMES Frederick MM Sjt 48541 Royal Fusiliers
GRIMES James MM L/Cpl 15650 9th Norfolk Regt
GRIMES Stanley A. MM L/Cpl 52008 RAMC
GRIMES Thomas MM L/Cpl 7973 2nd Welsh Regt
GRIMES Thomas F. MM Pte 25774 1/6th Cheshire Regt
GRIMES William MM Sjt 11242 2nd King's Own Scottish Borderers
GRIMLEY Daniel MM Pte 76738 1 Tank Fd Coy Tank Corps
GRIMLEY William E. MM L/Cpl 12076 6th Dorsetshire Regt
GRIMLEY William J. MM Gnr 199017 29 Bty 42 Bde RFA
GRIMMER Arthur MM Sjt 7224 1st Norfolk Regt
GRIMMER George MM Cpl 14482 9th Norfolk Regt KIA 4.12.17.
GRIMMER John C. MM Pte 17035 2nd Coldstream Guards
GRIMMETT Henry MM Pte 242253 7th Gloucestershire Regt att Royal West Kent Regt.
GRIMMITT Albert H. MM Cpl 58330 142 Fd Amb RAMC
GRIMMOND James MM Bdr 347492 223 Siege Bty RGA
GRIMSEY George A. MM L/Cpl 4389 Rifle Brigade
GRIMSEY Leonard MM L/Cpl S/1491 Rifle Brigade
GRIMSEY Robert F. MM L/Cpl 721615 1/24th London Regt
GRIMSHAW Arthur MM Sjt 242507 4/5th North Lancashire Regt
GRIMSHAW Francis E. MM Pte 203004 Middlesex Regt
GRIMSHAW Fred MM Pte 21457 Border Regt
GRIMSHAW Frederick MM Sjt 6564 5th Oxf & Bucks Light Infantry
GRIMSHAW George E. MM 2nd Cpl 551985 Royal Engineers att RFA.
GRIMSHAW Harry MM Pte 5897 1st Royal Lancaster Regt
GRIMSHAW James MM Pte 12804 7th East Lancashire Regt
GRIMSHAW John MM Sjt 16671 Lancashire Fusiliers
GRIMSHAW Jonathan MM Sjt 229715 Royal Engineers
GRIMSHAW Joseph H. MM Pte 200731 1/4th Royal Scots
GRIMSHAW Laurence E. MM L/Cpl 112573 216 Siege Bty RGA
GRIMSHAW T. MM Sjt 49229 Cheshire Regt
GRIMSHAW Thomas MM L/Cpl 241573 East Lancashire Regt
GRIMSHAW William MM Pte M2/167031 56 Div Train Army Service Corps
GRIMSHAW Wright MM Pte 36526 Royal Fusiliers
GRIMSTEAD A. MM Cpl 414327 Manchester Regt
GRIMSTEAD E.F. MM Sjt 200140 Royal Sussex Regt
GRIMSTER Jesse MM L/Cpl S/18359 2nd Rifle Brigade
GRIMSTER William MM Pte 27169 6th Oxf & Bucks Light Infantry
GRIMSTON John MM Cpl 2389 1/4th London Regt
GRIMWADE Albert E. MM L/Cpl 56874 14th Royal Welsh Fusiliers
GRIMWADE Herbert William "MM+Bar,MdH(F)" Pte 46774 10th King's Own Scottish Borderers
GRIMWADE Mark MM Pte 41600 Royal Fusiliers
GRIMWOOD Albert Edward MM L/Cpl 12950 2nd Suffolk Regt DOW 4.7.18.
GRIMWOOD Alfred H. MM Sjt 40219 2nd Royal West Surrey Regt
GRIMWOOD Frank MM Sjt 20126 2nd Royal Munster Fusiliers
GRIMWOOD George MM L/Cpl S/23429 16th Rifle Brigade
GRIMWOOD Thomas MM Sjt 246850 21 Bty 2 Bde RFA
GRIMWOOD Walter J. MM Gnr 153611 RGA
GRINDLE Thomas MM Pte 40962 2nd South Wales Borderers KIA 23.10.18.
GRINDLE William G. MM Cpl 106545 Royal Engineers
GRINDLEY Frederick C. MM L/Cpl 95067 Liverpool Regt
GRINDLEY George MM Sjt 37791 26th Royal Welsh Fusiliers
GRINDLEY Herbert MM Pte 24467 3rd Grenadier Guards
GRINDROD Arthur MM Gnr 681340 RFA
GRINDROD C.T. MM Gnr 106923 238 Siege Bty RGA
GRINDROD Edward MM CQMS 1289 Royal Lancaster Regt
GRINDROD John MM(25238 N Lancs)+Bar L/Sjt 28995 9th East Surrey Regt
GRINDROD John T. MM Pte 242149 Border Regt
GRINDROD Joseph MM Sjt 305556 1/8th Lancashire Fusiliers
GRINDROD Wilfred MM L/Sjt PS/9067 Royal Fusiliers
GRINNELL Albert MM Pte 240736 2/8th Worcestershire Regt
GRINNELL Samuel MM L/Cpl 134953 Royal Engineers
GRINSTED Herbert J. MM Cpl 39733 RGA
GRINTER Thomas W. MM Pte 307520 Royal Warwickshire Regt
GRINYER William Richard MM Sjt 41178 1 Squadron Machine Gun Corps(Cav)
GRISDALE Gordon MM Sjt 43047 2nd Manchester Regt
GRIST Charles MM Gnr 116023 RGA
GRIST Ernest MM Cpl 355882 1/10th Liverpool Regt
GRIST George MM Pte 799 6th Royal West Surrey Regt
GRIST Stephen W. MM Spr 62692 Royal Engineers
GRISTON Philip A. MM+Bar Pte 17333 7th Royal Sussex Regt
GRITTON Harry MM Pte 12876 1st Coldstream Guards
GRIVOEL Arthur Ernest MM Pte 16808 7th South Lancashire Regt KIA 8.11.16.

GRIZZELL Richard MM L/Cpl 911 1st Dragoons KIA 25.6.16.
GROAT Isaac MM Pte 20562 13th Royal Scots KIA 31.7.17.
GROAT James "MM,MID" Sjt 9741 2nd Royal Scots
GROCOTT John MM+Bar Sjt 40062 South Staffordshire Regt
GROCOTT Joseph Norman MM L/Cpl 17637 20th Manchester Regt
GROCOTT Oliver S. MM Gnr 805610 D/231 Bde RFA
GRODEN John MM L/Cpl 32391 2nd Royal Scots Fusiliers
GRODNER Alfred MM Pte 17489 6th Duke of Cornwall's LI
GROGAN Edwin MM Pte 309 2nd Notts & Derby Regt
GROGAN James E. MM L/Cpl Z/2796 13th Rifle Brigade
GROGAN Rowland MM Sjt 55416 D/83 Bde RFA
GROGAN Thomas "MM,MID" Sjt 14993 12th West Yorkshire Regt
GROGNET Charles MM Cpl 241173 1/5th North Lancashire Regt
GROHMAN Augustus MM Sjt 703327 23rd London Regt
GROOM Ambrose E. MM Sjt 14492 1st Coldstream Guards
GROOM Charles MM CSM 21714 Durham Light Infantry
GROOM Fred MM Sjt 96977 184 Tunnelling Coy Royal Engineers
GROOM George W. "MM,MID" Dvr 41835 14 Bde RFA
GROOM John W. MM Pte 18236 Suffolk Regt
GROOM Joseph MM Pte 5519 Middlesex Regt
GROOM Sidney MM Pte 17935 8th Bedfordshire Regt
GROOM Thomas MM Pte 332081 9th Liverpool Regt
GROOM Walter P. MM L/Cpl 6982 3rd Dragoon Guards
GROOM William MM Pte 41364 Royal Irish Rifles
GROOM William A. MM Pte 2634 1/1st Hertfordshire Regt
GROOME Albert Frank MM Pte G/16427 9th Royal Sussex Regt
GROOMS Alfred Herbert MM Sjt 201348 2/4th Leicestershire Regt KIA 24.3.18.
GROSCH Albert Edward MM L/Cpl 7940 1st Duke of Cornwall's LI DOW 7.2.17.
GROSE William R. MM Cpl 45616 Devonshire Regt
GROSSART George MM Pte 29778 RAMC
GROSSART William MM Gnr 192985 RFA
GROSSE George J. MM Sjt 24734 3 Fd Amb RAMC
GROSSMITH Leslie MM L/Cpl G/6571 8th East Surrey Regt KIA 1.7.16.
GROSVENOR-SMYTH Cecil MM L/Cpl 62922 1/6th West Yorkshire Regt
GROUNDS James H. MM Pte 17334 Royal Welsh Fusiliers
GROUT Henry MM Sjt 8981 2nd Rifle Brigade
GROUT James H. MM L/Cpl 39362 Royal Berkshire Regt
GROUT William MM Sjt 17988 Royal Engineers
GROVE A.C. MM Pte 240723 15th Suffolk Regt
GROVE Edwin G. MM Bdr 34595 115 Hy Bty RGA
GROVE F. MM Gnr 55302 RHA
GROVE Frank H. MM Pte 15275 North Staffordshire Regt
GROVE George MM Gnr 76647 23 Bde RFA
GROVE Harry MM CQMS 22115 6th Royal West Surrey Regt
GROVE John C. MM Spr 534568 Royal Engineers
GROVE Maurice Buller MM Gnr 15278 D/70 Bde RFA KIA 9.4.17.
GROVE T. MM Pte 55730 Machine Gun Corps
GROVE William James MM Pte 10233 10th Royal West Surrey Regt
GROVER Arthur Harry MM L/Cpl 6033 1st North Staffordshire Regt
GROVER Charles W.H. MM L/Cpl G/9533 Royal West Kent Regt
GROVER Frederick MM L/Cpl 201511 2/4th Royal Berkshire Regt DOW 3.4.18.
GROVER George H. MM Pte 206755 2/4th Royal West Surrey Regt KIA 27.12.17.
GROVER Walter E. MM Pte 17582 Royal Sussex Regt
GROVER Walts John MM Gnr 12555 RFA
GROVES Albert MM L/Cpl 13096 2nd Yorkshire Light Infantry KIA 19.8.18.
GROVES Alfred Ernest MM Sjt G/1899 8th Royal West Surrey Regt DOW 2.8.17.
GROVES Alfred Henry MM Pte R/39191 13th King's Royal Rifle Corps KIA 4.11.18.
GROVES Alfred J. MM Pte 7468 5th Dragoon Guards
GROVES Alfred L. MM+Bar Pte 1282 7th Royal Sussex Regt
GROVES Alfred Thomas MM L/Cpl 12264 3rd Coldstream Guards
GROVES Archibald John Joseph MM Bdr 146184 B/310 Bde RFA
GROVES Arthur MM Pte 3287 8th Royal West Surrey Regt
GROVES Arthur MM Bdr 68748 32 Bde RFA
GROVES Cecil A. MM Pte 525897 14th London Regt
GROVES Charles MM L/Cpl 300977 1/1st Staffordshire Yeomanry
GROVES Edward MM C/Sjt 4902 1st Royal Scots Fusiliers
GROVES Frank MM Pte 203018 South Lancashire Regt
GROVES Fred MM Pte 26 Army Cyclist Corps
GROVES George A. MM Pte 42441 RAMC
GROVES Harold William MM L/Sjt 20132 2/5th Gloucestershire Regt KIA 11.8.18.
GROVES Harry MM Gnr 59565 RHA
GROVES Harry MM Pte 9384 1st Scots Guards KIA 27.11.17.
GROVES Harry C. MM Pnr 165469 Royal Engineers att RFA
GROVES James MM Spr 156441 176 Tunnelling Coy Royal Engineers
GROVES John MM Pte 14620 4th Coldstream Guards
GROVES Thomas MM L/Cpl 5428 Royal West Surrey Regt
GROVES W.F. MM Sjt 26083 Hampshire Regt
GROVES William MM Pte 14020 9th Notts & Derby Regt
GROVES William "MM,MID" Sjt 7127 2nd Royal Warwickshire Regt
GROWCOTT L. MM Cpl 8/12406 South Staffordshire Regt
GROWCOTT T. MM Cpl 268204 Cheshire Regt
GRUBB Edward MM L/Cpl 32120 1/5th Bedfordshire Regt
GRUBB Frederick MM Pte 301250 1/8th Arg & Suth Highlanders
GRUBB James MM Pte 202737 Seaforth Highlanders
GRUBB John MM Pte 43005 Highland Light Infantry
GRUBB Robert B. MM Sjt 250553 Royal Scots
GRUBB Walter MM Cpl 18325 15th Hampshire Regt
GRUBB William MM Spr 1720 Royal Engineers
GRUBB William S. MM Pte 320164 12th Norfolk Regt
GRUDGINGS Joseph H. MM Gnr Sig 127310 A/241 Bde RFA
GRUGEL John MM Cpl 306039 Liverpool Regt
GRUMMETT William MM Sjt 82364 RFA
GRUMMITT Richard MM Dvr 95822 B/70 Bde RFA
GRUNCELL Ernest Joseph MM Cpl 67963 131 Fd Coy Royal Engineers
GRUNDELL John William MM Pte 8692 2nd East Yorkshire Regt
GRUNDY A.S. MM Sjt 201328 2/4th Hampshire Regt
GRUNDY Alfred MM Sjt 240017 1/5th North Lancashire Regt
GRUNDY David V. MM L/Cpl 203493 8th Seaforth Highlanders
GRUNDY Frank MM L/Sjt 14060 24th Manchester Regt
GRUNDY Fred MM Sjt 10405 2nd Notts & Derby Regt KIA 29.9.16.
GRUNDY Frederick MM Sjt 63102 15th Lancashire Fusiliers
GRUNDY George MM Sjt 240853 1/5th East Lancashire Regt KIA 6.11.18.
GRUNDY Harry MM Sjt C/541 16th King's Royal Rifle Corps
GRUNDY Harry Theodore MM Sjt 12417 10th Gloucestershire Regt KIA 23.7.16.
GRUNDY Henry T. MM Pte 2291 1/8th Worcestershire Regt
GRUNDY J.W. MM Pte 26803 Hampshire Regt
GRUNDY James MM Pte 201557 Lancashire Fusiliers
GRUNDY William "DCM,MM" L/Cpl 21682 20th Lancashire Fusiliers Died 26.1.18.
GRUNDY William MM Sjt 132657 254 Tunnelling Coy Royal Engineers
GRUNDY William MM L/Sjt 7883 1st Royal Scots Fusiliers
GRUNDY William M. MM Sjt 320742 6th London Regt
GRUNEWALD Henry MM L/Cpl 307774 15th Bn Tank Corps
GRUNSELL George Henry MM Gnr 44269 12 Siege Bty RGA
GUBBINS Jesse "MM,OStG(R)" Sjt 9699 7th Oxf & Bucks Light Infantry Died 29.10.18.
GUDGE Henry MM Pte L/16639 7th Royal Fusiliers KIA 3.12.17.
GUDGE Lawrence Lionel MM Pte 3656 Liverpool Regt
GUDGEON P.E. MM AM1 7546 Royal Flying Corps
GUDGEON Thomas W. MM Gnr 11539 RFA
GUDGER W. "MM,MID" Bdr 1573 RFA
GUDGIN Frederick Charles MM+Bar Pnr 127751 Royal Engineers att 119 Bde RFA
GUDGIN Harold Walter MM Cpl 2481 Yorkshire Light Infantry
GUDGIN Herbert Thomas MM Cpl 39712 28 Bde RFA
GUERINS Albert J. MM Sjt 63865 RAMC
GUESS Walter MM Pte 16589 Bedfordshire Regt
GUEST Alfred E. MM+Bar Dvr 38264 RFA
GUEST Arthur MM+Bar Pte 23509 20th & 17th Lancashire Fusiliers
GUEST Augustus MM Pte 42351 2nd Yorkshire Regt DOW 2.11.18.
GUEST Charles MM Sjt 240381 1/8th Worcestershire Regt
GUEST Clarence MM Pte 53584 9th Yorkshire Regt
GUEST Donald Rupert MM Gnr Fitter 57773 C/153 Bde RFA DOW 23.10.18.
GUEST Herbert MM L/Cpl 1266 1st Royal Warwickshire Regt
GUEST Isaac MM Pte 57158 2nd Royal Welsh Fusiliers KIA 21.6.18.
GUEST John MM Gnr L/8812 A/150 Bde RFA
GUEST John D. MM QMS Armourer 898 Army Ordnance Corps
GUEST John T. MM Pte 48716 Liverpool Regt
GUEST Joseph E. MM Pte 9721 7th South Staffordshire Regt
GUEST Lawrence B. MM Sjt G/938 12th Middlesex Regt
GUEST Norman MM L/Cpl 20232 12th Liverpool Regt
GUEST Reuben Clarke MM Pte 241714 2/5th York & Lancaster Regt KIA 27.11.17.

GUEST Robert MM Pte 70613 Notts & Derby Regt
GUEST Sidney MM Sjt 836320 B/311 Bty RFA
GUEST Thomas F. MM Sjt 12/721 12th East Yorkshire Regt
GUEST Tom MM Pte 242272 Royal Scots Fusiliers
GUEST William MM Pte 202236 7th Royal Warwickshire Regt
GUEST William MM Spr 32816 5 Div Sig Coy Royal Engineers
GUEST William MM Cpl 30086 16th Royal Warwickshire Regt Died 26.8.17.
GUEST William MM Pte 28037 York & Lancaster Regt
GUGGENHEIM Edgar C. MM L/Cpl 20391 1st Dorsetshire Regt
GUIEL Herbert J. MM Pte 17829 Royal Sussex Regt
GUILD David MM Sjt 20417 1st Bn Machine Gun Corps
GUILDFORD George H. MM L/Cpl 185 11th Royal Sussex Regt
GUILDFORD Harold J. MM L/Cpl 38086 7th Royal Warwickshire Regt
GUILE Ernest Henry MM Spr 538572 'L' Corps Sig Coy Royal Engineers
GUILE John MM Pte 47715 15th Lancashire Fusiliers
GUILFORD William H. MM Pte 45084 Machine Gun Corps(Heavy Branch)
GUILMARTIN Daniel John MM+Bar Cpl 42665 86 Bty 32 Bde RFA DOW 31.8.18.
GUINANE Thomas MM Sjt 19342 1st Royal Dublin Fusiliers
GUISE Arthur Leonard "DCM,MM" L/Cpl 4060 9th Royal Fusiliers KIA 21.10.17.
GUISE Charles MM Sjt 8821 2nd Worcestershire Regt
GUISE Hugh B. MM Gnr 4995 C/121 Bde RFA
GUISE Thomas H. MM Cpl 33496 1/1st Bucks Bn Oxf & Bucks Light Infantry
GUISE William F. MM Cpl 266452 1/1st Bucks Bn Oxf & Bucks Light Infantry
GUITE Thomas MM Cpl 3/1123 2nd Yorkshire Light Infantry
GUIVER Charles B. MM Dvr 17051 A/174 Bde RFA
GUIVER Henry Sidney "MC,MM(52850 Sjt RHA)" 2Lt 139 Bde RFA
GUIVER Leonard MM Sjt Farrier 39779 RFA
GUKENBIEHL Albert MM Pte 46897 18th Lancashire Fusiliers DOW 19.6.18.
GULBRANDSEN Oscar A. MM Pte Z/613 3rd Rifle Brigade
GULLEFER George MM L/Cpl 6/47 9th Rifle Brigade
GULLEN George MM+Bar Pte 19313 1/7th Arg & Suth Highlanders
GULLEN James B.W. MM Pte G/22317 Royal Fusiliers
GULLEY James Arthur MM Dvr 780385 B/246 Bde RFA
GULLICK Cecil J. MM L/Cpl 322136 18th London Regt
GULLICK Fred G. MM Cpl 348210 96 Siege Bty RGA
GULLIVER Alfred W. MM Sjt 128373 238 Siege Bty RGA
GULLIVER Frederick James MM L/Cpl 25525 Royal Warwickshire Regt
GULLIVER Sidney H. MM Pte A/202658 9th King's Royal Rifle Corps
GULLY A.F. MM L/Cpl 391115 London Regt
GULLY Charles William Gordon MM Bdr 76843 45 Bde RFA
GULLY James MM+Bar Sjt 242 Machine Gun Corps(Heavy Branch)
GULLY Patrick MM Cpl T/33458 Army Service Corps
GULVIN James MM Pte 5464 Leinster Regt
GUMBRILL Lawrence A. MM Pte L/9902 2nd Royal Sussex Regt
GUMERSELL Arthur MM Pte 36493 Manchester Regt
GUMM Albert E. MM Spr 27135 Royal Engineers
GUMM George MM L/Cpl 6679 1st Wiltshire Regt
GUMMER Tom MM Sjt 240797 2/5th York & Lancaster Regt
GUMMERY Edward MM L/Cpl 13801 35th Bn Machine Gun Corps
GUNDLACH Robert T. "MM,MID" L/Cpl G/639 7th East Kent Regt
GUNDRY Joseph "DCM,MM" Pte 273099 1/9th Durham Light Infantry
GUNDRY W. MM Cpl 3721 Royal Flying Corps
GUNN Albert MM Pte 47093 4th York & Lancaster Regt
GUNN Alfred MM L/Cpl 412321 Royal Engineers
GUNN Basil MM Sjt 6922 Machine Gun Corps
GUNN Bertie W. "MM+Bar,MID" Sjt 65457 RAMC
GUNN D. "DCM,MM" Sjt 23300 Machine Gun Corps
GUNN David W. MM Cpl 8942 1/7th Arg & Suth Highlanders
GUNN Donald MM Cpl 4076 1st Royal Scots
GUNN George MM Pte S/4668 9th Seaforth Highlanders
GUNN George MM Pte 240752 1/5th Seaforth Highlanders
GUNN George MM Sjt 240520 1/5th Seaforth Highlanders
GUNN George R. MM Cpl 31234 RFA
GUNN George Robertson Lawson MM Sjt 31132 58th Bn Machine Gun Corps
GUNN James MM Sjt 250808 13th Royal Scots
GUNN James "MM,MIDx2" L/Cpl 9796 1st Royal Inniskilling Fusiliers
GUNN John A. MM L/Cpl 240783 Seaforth Highlanders
GUNN John W. MM Sjt 4940 9th Bn Machine Gun Corps
GUNN Murdo M. MM Pnr 196013 Royal Engineers
GUNN Percy MM Gnr 13162 110 Bty 24 Bde RFA
GUNN Ralph MM Pte 200019 1/4th Royal Scots
GUNN Stanley MM Cpl 39196 2nd Yorkshire Light Infantry
GUNN Walter H. MM Pte 265674 1/1st Hertfordshire Regt
GUNN William MM Pte 265654 Gordon Highlanders
GUNNELL Arthur O. MM Pte 235262 16th Royal Warwickshire Regt
GUNNELL Frank C. MM Pte R/9510 King's Royal Rifle Corps
GUNNELL Frederick Charles MM Sjt 9143 1st Royal Munster Fusiliers
GUNNER George W. MM Cpl 14343 8th Royal Berkshire Regt
GUNNER John George MM Pte 85423 119 Coy Machine Gun Corps DOW 27.11.17.
GUNNER Reginald L. MM Cpl 202427 1st London Regt
GUNNER Walter MM Pte 51568 Royal Fusiliers
GUNNER William MM Gnr 74566 28 Bty 9 Bde RFA
GUNNILL H.F. MM Cpl 24360 RFA
GUNNING John G. MM Dvr 57543 RFA
GUNNING Michael MM L/Sjt 3477 Irish Guards
GUNNING William MM Pte 9345 16th Highland Light Infantry
GUNSON Frederick C. MM L/Cpl E/353 Royal Fusiliers
GUNSON William MM+Bar Pte 203090 1/4th Essex Regt
GUNSTEAD Thomas MM Dvr 20603 RFA
GUNSTON Harry W. MM L/Cpl 1085 16th Lancers
GUNSTONE Cecil H. MM Sjt 10311 Wiltshire Regt
GUNTER Frederick J. MM Cpl 300223 13th Bn Tank Corps
GUNTER John MM Cpl 2247 1st Royal Warwickshire Regt
GUNTER Thomas James MM Spr 500559 50 Div Sig Coy Royal Engineers
GUNTER Thomas James MM Gnr 57177 120 Heavy Bty RGA Died 21.2.17.
GUNTHER Heinrich H. MM Sjt 1454 Royal Engineers
GUNTHORPE Galby MM L/Cpl 45834 5th Royal Berkshire Regt
GUNTON Archibald Henry Philip "DCM,MM,MID,CG(F)" Sjt 85109 34 Div Sig Coy Royal Engineers
GUNTON John K. MM Sjt 320264 12th Norfolk Regt
GUNTON Percy MM Cpl 8852 2nd Suffolk Regt
GUNTON Richard Jenkinson MM L/Cpl 16148 1st South Staffordshire Regt
GUNTRIP Ernest Albert MM Pte 1982 1/5th Royal Warwickshire Regt
GUPPY Arthur MM Pte 10680 5th Dorsetshire Regt
GUPPY Ivor MM Pte 30242 52 Fd Amb RAMC
GURDLER Albert MM L/Cpl 5759 7th Leinster Regt KIA 22.3.18.
GURL Jesse N. MM L/Cpl 200819 Oxf & Bucks Light Infantry
GURNELL Tom E. MM Spr WR/267599 Transp Svce Royal Engineers
GURNETT Frank MM Pte 77451 2nd Durham Light Infantry
GURNEY Albert Cecil MM Cpl 69923 53 Bty 2 Bde RFA KIA 29.7.18.
GURNEY Arthur "DCM,MM+Bar" L/Cpl 15364 2nd Bedfordshire Regt
GURNEY Bert Arthur MM Cpl 7584 2nd Royal Berkshire Regt KIA 28.10.16.
GURNEY Charles Walter MM Pte 4224 1st North Lancashire Regt
GURNEY Douglas C. MM Sjt 33269 1st Border Regt
GURNEY Frederick C. MM Sjt A/3666 King's Royal Rifle Corps
GURNEY George MM Cpl 9297 2nd Bedfordshire Regt KIA 22.3.18.
GURNEY George J. MM Cpl 4568 9th Lancers
GURNEY Mark MM Pte 67233 2nd London Regt
GURNEY Richard Edward MM 2nd Cpl 25402 423 Fd Coy Royal Engineers
GURNEY Stanley MM CSM 74013 Notts & Derby Regt
GURNEY William A. MM Cpl 240931 1/8th Middlesex Regt
GURNEY William George "MM,MdH(F)" Pte 45064 82 Coy Machine Gun Corps
GURNEY William J. MM Pte 205966 1/1st Buckinghamshire Yeomanry
GURR A. MM Cpl 900342 220 Bde RFA
GURR Arthur "DCM,MM" Bdr 3368 443 Bty RFA
GURR Frederick William MM+Bar Cpl 251551 2/3rd London Regt
GURR John F. MM L/Cpl 18497 8th Royal Berkshire Regt
GURR Thomas F. MM Sjt 96505 RFA
GURRY Albert MM Pte G/11224 2nd Royal Sussex Regt
GURRY Albert C. MM Pte 543511 4 Fd Amb RAMC
GUSH Archibald W. MM+Bar 2nd Cpl 66338 23 Div Sig Coy Royal Engineers
GUSH Edward E. MM L/Cpl 1254 1/21st London Regt
GUSHLOW Robert MM Pte G/15982 11th Royal Fusiliers

GUSTERSON Thomas MM Pte 12396 Duke of Cornwall's LI
GUSTHART Norman MM Pte 20178 1st Coldstream Guards
GUTHRIE Alexander MM Pte 30/113 Northumberland Fusiliers
GUTHRIE Alexander MM Sjt 290540 1/7th Royal Highlanders KIA 26.3.18.
GUTHRIE Charles Stewart MM L/Cpl 17908 20th Manchester Regt
GUTHRIE Francis F. MM+Bar Pte S/11239 1st Gordon Highlanders
GUTHRIE George MM Cpl 11950 11th Royal Scots
GUTHRIE George MM Sjt 3183 Royal Highlanders
GUTHRIE George H. MM Sjt 265556 7th West Yorkshire Regt
GUTHRIE Harry Sydney MM L/Cpl 17/26327 17th Manchester Regt KIA 11.10.16.
GUTHRIE Joseph MM Sjt 49237 162 Coy Machine Gun Corps
GUTHRIE Richard MM Cpl 265428 1/6th Cheshire Regt
GUTHRIE Thomas MM Pte 11366 2nd Scots Guards
GUTHRIE William MM Pte 64650 RAMC
GUTHRIE William MM Pte 32209 44 Fd Amb RAMC
GUTTERIDGE Arthur MM Pte 202273 Oxf & Bucks Light Infantry
GUTTERIDGE Bertie MM Dvr 79137 A/76 Bde RFA
GUTTERIDGE Charles William George MM Gnr 64556 RGA
GUTTERIDGE Edward Newton MM Sjt 950975 A/18 Bde RFA
GUTTERIDGE Frederick John MM Cpl 32191 1/1st Hertfordshire Regt
GUTTERIDGE George S. MM Cpl 33408 41 Bde RFA
GUTTERIDGE Harold F. MM L/Cpl A/202649 King's Royal Rifle Corps
GUTTERIDGE Levi W. MM L/Cpl 3069 2nd East Surrey Regt
GUTTRIDGE Albert E. MM Bdr 889553 RFA
GUTTRIDGE Albert J. MM L/Cpl 17437 Royal Berkshire Regt
GUTTRIDGE Richard MM L/Cpl 2691 13th Royal Sussex Regt DOW 24.2.18.
GUTTRIDGE William Henry MM Cpl 5349 10th Lancashire Fusiliers KIA 2.8.18.
GUY Alfred "MM,MSM" Sjt 29196 A/14 Bde RFA
GUY Alfred "DCM,MM" Cpl 17048 2 Fd Sqn Royal Engineers
GUY Arthur H. MM Cpl 16951 17th Bn Machine Gun Corps
GUY Arthur S. MM L/Cpl 20071 6th Dorsetshire Regt
GUY Benjamin MM L/Sjt 12214 1st Coldstream Guards
GUY Clifford MM Sjt 546514 Royal Engineers
GUY Cyril R. MM Pte 266142 Oxf & Bucks Light Infantry
GUY Daniel MM Pte 46195 2nd York & Lancaster Regt
GUY Edward C. MM+Bar Sjt 19 22nd Royal Fusiliers
GUY Edwin S.G. MM Gnr 334497 123 Siege Bty RGA
GUY Elijah MM Sjt 43719 West Yorkshire Regt
GUY Ernest MM Cpl 22690 1st Hampshire Regt Died 24.10.18.
GUY Harold MM L/Cpl 320464 16th Royal Sussex Regt
GUY Henry MM Pte 14827 Yorkshire Regt
GUY Isaac MM Cpl 13/1479 4th York & Lancaster Regt
GUY James F.J. MM Pte 235354 1st Notts & Derby Regt
GUY John W. MM L/Sjt 11/15285 1st Border Regt
GUY Thomas MM L/Cpl 12827 1st Dragoons
GUY Tom "MM,MID" Cpl 474200 529 Fd Coy Royal Engineers
GUY Walter MM L/Sjt 11672 1st Notts & Derby Regt
GUY William MM CoH 5536 3rd Bn GMGR
GUY William Eltringham MM L/Cpl 1729 1/9th Durham Light Infantry Died 14.6.17.
GUYATT Frederick C. MM Pte 55842 Machine Gun Corps
GUYATT George "MC,MM(691 Pte)" 2Lt 9th Royal Fusiliers
GUYMER Bertie James "DCM,MM+Bar" Sjt 3/8038 9th Norfolk Regt
GUYMER Joseph MM Pte 11601 2nd Royal Sussex Regt Died 13.10.18
GWATKIN Charles F. MM Spr 510513 Royal Engineers
GWILLIM Edwin W. MM Pte 25869 6th Lancashire Fusiliers
GWILLIM John MM 2nd Cpl 198929 Royal Engineers
GWILT Edward MM Cpl 79269 185 Tunnelling Coy Royal Engineers
GWILT George T. MM Sjt 5862 14 Fd Amb RAMC
GWINNELL Clarence George MM Sjt 49355 Royal Engineers
GWINNUTT James MM Cpl 240740 Lancashire Fusiliers
GWYN Claude V. MM Pte 12088 6th Somerset Light Infantry
GWYN Douglas P. MM Sjt C/6053 King's Royal Rifle Corps
GWYN George MM L/Cpl 16991 Royal Welsh Fusiliers
GWYNN William MM Pte M/33663 Army Service Corps
GWYNNE Griffith D. MM Sjt 53607 2nd Welsh Regt
GWYTHER Alfred MM L/Cpl 267409 Royal Warwickshire Regt
GYDE George B. MM Sjt 55455 123 Siege Bty RGA
GYTE Arthur MM Sjt 26222 1st Notts & Derby Regt
GYTON Stanley H. "MM,MID" Cpl 558406 Royal Engineers

H

HAACKE Ernest Charles MM L/Cpl 2486 1/6th London Regt KIA 8.10.16.
HAAGMANN Eleazer MM Pte 372754 8th London Regt
HABEN Albert H. MM L/Cpl R/27545 1st King's Royal Rifle Corps
HABERFIELD Harold MM L/Cpl 38620 1st Lancashire Fusiliers
HABERGHAM George E. MM Pte 35457 2nd Yorkshire Regt
HABGOOD A. MM Pte 201812 Royal West Surrey Regt
HABGOOD Alfred C. MM Sjt 21457 Machine Gun Corps
HABGOOD Bert C. MM Pte 6026 1st Dragoon Guards
HABGOOD Frank MM Pte 235447 9th York & Lancaster Regt
HACK Alfred James MM Pte 28269 2/6th Royal Warwickshire Regt
HACK Frederick MM Pte 17667 Hampshire Regt
HACK H.J. MM Cpl 1756 1/1st Leicestershire Yeomanry
HACKER Herbert P. MM Dvr 496560 476 Fd Coy Royal Engineers
HACKETT Charles A. MM+Bar 2nd Cpl 49612 Royal Engineers
HACKETT David Frederick Mackness MM CQMS 7033 1st Leicestershire Regt KIA 22.8.18.
HACKETT Dudley MM Gnr 57534 RGA
HACKETT Edmund MM Pte 167 4th Bn GMGR
HACKETT F.W. MM CSM 8620 11th Royal Warwickshire Regt
HACKETT Frederick C. MM Pte S/30363 Rifle Brigade
HACKETT Jabez MM Pte 17340 1st Royal Warwickshire Regt
HACKETT James MM L/Cpl 1840 1/21st London Regt
HACKETT James MM Sjt 8348 2nd Royal Berkshire Regt
HACKETT James MM Pte 2051 RAMC att 1st Royal West Surrey Regt.KIA 23.4.17.
HACKETT James Bernard MM Sjt 11006 Notts & Derby Regt
HACKETT John MM Pte 15988 10th North Lancashire Regt
HACKETT John H. MM+Bar L/Cpl 19381 4th Worcestershire Regt
HACKETT John R. MM+Bar Sjt 21297 18th Lancashire Fusiliers
HACKETT Sidney MM Pte 292396 8/10th Gordon Highlanders
HACKETT Stephen L. MM Cpl 22491 130 Fd Coy Royal Engineers
HACKETT W.J. MM Spr 358820 1 Div Sig Coy Royal Engineers
HACKETT Wilford MM Pte 6495 Manchester Regt
HACKFORD William A. MM Pte 2168 1/5th Gloucestershire Regt
HACKING Abraham Thomas MM Cpl(MCDR) 73410 50 Div Sig Coy Royal Engineers
HACKING George Samuel MM L/Sjt 10797 8th Cheshire Regt
HACKING Thomas MM L/Cpl 71738 137 Fd Amb RAMC
HACKING Thomas MM Dvr 8641 RFA
HACKING William MM Bdr L/24398 D/165 Bde RFA
HACKITT John "DCM+Bar,MM" L/Cpl 11/1456 East Yorkshire Regt
HACKLETT Tom MM L/Cpl 241763 Worcestershire Regt
HACKMAN Charles W. MM Pte 40673 1/1st Cambridgeshire Regt
HACKNEY Edgar MM Pte 18092 7th Northamptonshire Regt
HACKNEY Ernest MM Pte 65877 30th Bn Machine Gun Corps
HACKNEY George MM Pte 200584 10th Manchester Regt
HACKNEY Joseph W. MM Gnr 42691 RFA
HACKNEY Thomas W. MM Pte 25281 Cheshire Regt
HACKWOOD Cecil F. MM Pte 35013 8th Royal Berkshire Regt
HACQUOIL James MM Cpl 40777 9th Essex Regt DOW 11.8.18
HADAWAY Edward MM Sjt 61850 127 Bty 29 Bde RFA
HADCOCK Richard A. MM Pte 18279 6th Yorkshire Regt
HADCROFT Albert MM Pte 19722 2nd Coldstream Guards Died 31.10.18.
HADDEN George A. MM 2nd Cpl 406331 Royal Engineers
HADDEN James MM Pte 266168 7th Seaforth Highlanders DOW 1.10.18.
HADDEN William A. MM Sjt 60781 RAMC
HADDOCK John R. MM Dvr 131145 233 Fd Coy Royal Engineers
HADDOCK William MM Pte 8126 11th Royal Fusiliers
HADDON Frederick J. MM Pte 307082 7th West Riding Regt
HADDON John "MM,MSM" CQMS 5417 1st Northumberland Fusiliers
HADDOW Archibald MM+Bar Pte 488 12 Fd Amb RAMC
HADDOW Archibald MM Gnr 104319 B/94 Bde RFA
HADEN J. MM L/Cpl 3210 Royal Warwickshire Regt
HADEN J. MM Sjt 7131 1st Royal Scots Fusiliers
HADEN William MM Sjt 201259 2nd Worcestershire Regt
HADERER Percy T.S. MM Sjt 511 15th Royal Warwickshire Regt
HADFIELD Albert MM Pte 4676 22 Fd Amb RAMC KIA 4.10.17.
HADFIELD Austin MM Sjt 275218 Manchester Regt
HADFIELD Edwin MM L/Cpl 6863 1/4th East Yorkshire Regt
HADFIELD Ernest G. MM Sjt 250483 Manchester Regt
HADFIELD Frank MM Pte 34429 58 Coy Labour Corps
HADFIELD George MM Pte 31662 16th Royal Welsh Fusiliers
HADFIELD George W. MM Cpl L/23990 D/165 Bde RFA

HADFIELD Harold MM Cpl 681727 RFA
HADFIELD Harry MM Pte 37413 Machine Gun Corps
HADFIELD James A. MM Cpl G/48926 11th Royal Fusiliers
HADFIELD Joseph L. MM Sjt 100837 RGA
HADFIELD Leonard MM L/Cpl 13526 7th East Lancashire Regt
HADFIELD Leonard Harry "MM,MID" Cpl 823 1/2nd Hampshire Army Troops Coy Royal Engineers
HADFIELD Robert MM Sjt 60504 48th Bn Machine Gun Corps
HADFIELD Sam MM Sjt 240853 Notts & Derby Regt
HADFIELD Samuel MM Pte 48685 12th Manchester Regt
HADFIELD Thomas MM Pte 26971 North Lancashire Regt
HADFIELD Tom MM L/Cpl 34703 Cheshire Regt
HADFIELD Walter MM Sjt 19581 20th Lancashire Fusiliers
HADLEY Bernard MM Cpl 98092 54 Fd Coy Royal Engineers
HADLEY Cornelius MM Pte S/1561 Rifle Brigade
HADLEY George MM L/Bdr Sig 800569 435 Bty RFA
HADLEY Hubert E. MM Sjt 24441 Worcestershire Regt
HADLEY John MM Cpl 57581 RGA
HADLEY Thomas MM Pte 241700 2/4th York & Lancaster Regt
HADLEY Walter Hammond MM Cpl 20295 9th Royal Sussex Regt KIA 4.11.18.
HADLEY William MM L/Cpl 7836 2nd Worcestershire Regt
HADLEY William James MM L/Cpl 29841 2/7th Royal Warwickshire Regt DOW 11.11.18.
HADLEY William Percy MM Gnr Sig 84429 213 Siege Bty RGA
HADLINGTON Ernest A. MM L/Bdr 113800 RGA
HADLINGTON John Thomas MM Gnr 111499 102 Bde RFA
HADLOW Edward W. MM Sjt 76099 Tank Corps
HADLOW Herbert J. MM L/Sjt 630720 20th London Regt
HADLOW John Thomas "MM,GMV(S)" L/Cpl 2773 RAMC
HADNUM Joseph G. MM Pte 20763 1/5th Arg & Suth Highlanders
HADSLEY Henry H. MM Pte 40133 6th Royal West Surrey Regt
HADWEN Charles Eugene MM Sjt 2588 24th Royal Fusiliers KIA 12.9.18.
HAFFENDEN William E. MM+Bar Cpl 532186 Royal Engineers
HAFFNER George C.A. MM CQMS 240393 East Lancashire Regt
HAGAN John Michael MM Bdr 28721 173 Bde RFA
HAGAN Leonard MM Cpl 301001 1/5th Liverpool Regt
HAGERTY J. MM Cpl 26267 Royal Inniskilling Fusiliers
HAGGAR William Muston MM L/Cpl 23224 2/6th Worcestershire Regt KIA 21.3.18.
HAGGART Andrew M. MM 2nd Cpl 146308 'Q' Special Coy Royal Engineers
HAGGART Archibald "MM,CG(F)" Pte 23703 Machine Gun Corps
HAGGART Robert MM Spr 79698 Royal Engineers
HAGGAS Edgar MM Pte 203728 West Riding Regt
HAGGAS William MM L/Cpl 202682 2nd Highland Light Infantry
HAGGER Harry MM Pte 8967 2nd West Riding Regt AKA Harry WEAKE
HAGGER William MM+Bar Sjt R/22200 King's Royal Rifle Corps
HAGGER William George MM Sjt 49738 B/102 Bde RFA KIA 15.6.18.
HAGGER William H. MM Pte S/1316 12th Rifle Brigade
HAGGERTY Cornelius MM Pte S/19434 1st Gordon Highlanders
HAGGERTY John MM Pte 19339 Machine Gun Corps
HAGGIS Charles L. MM L/Cpl 500323 Royal Engineers
HAGUE Charles MM+Bar Pte 8/11632 8th Lincolnshire Regt DOW 7.5.17.
HAGUE Clement MM Gnr 121815 RFA
HAGUE Frank MM CSM 1098 6th Cheshire Regt
HAGUE Harold G. MM Sjt 92634 175 Bde RFA
HAGUE Horace MM Gnr 831649 RFA
HAGUE J.L. MM L/Cpl 3918 York & Lancaster Regt
HAGUE James MM Pte 405169 1(West Riding)Fd Amb RAMC
HAGUE John MM Gnr 70193 20 Div Ammn Col RFA
HAGUE John George MM L/Cpl 88025 33 Coy Machine Gun Corps
HAGUE Joseph MM Pte S/13903 1st Gordon Highlanders KIA 11.4.17.
HAGUE Percy S. MM Sjt 531706 15th London Regt
HAGUE Samuel "DCM,MM" Sjt 43740 1st Notts & Derby Regt
HAGUE William H. MM 2nd Cpl 86251 Royal Engineers
HAGUES Charles MM Cpl 305006 1/8th Notts & Derby Regt
HAGUES Harry MM Pte 2734 Notts & Derby Regt Awarded for 'Easter Rising'.
HAHN G.H. MM Drummer 18/737 West Yorkshire Regt
HAIG Adam MM Sjt 2168 Machine Gun Corps
HAIG Alexander Weir MM Sjt 8742 1st Cameron Highlanders KIA 17.10.18.
HAIG Charles MM Sjt 351110 1/9th Royal Scots
HAIG Peter MM Pte 310357 1/7th Gordon Highlanders KIA 4.12.17.

HAIGH Arthur MM+Bar Sjt 202122 2/4th West Riding Regt KIA 29.9.18.
HAIGH Charles Thomas MM Sjt 8879 2nd West Yorkshire Regt KIA 16.8.17.
HAIGH Ernest MM+2 Bars Pte G/93193 Royal Fusiliers
HAIGH Fenwick MM Pte 50624 1/8th Lancashire Fusiliers
HAIGH George MM Spr 1650 Royal Engineers
HAIGH George MM Sjt 282774 RGA
HAIGH George A. MM Pte 306026 2/4th West Riding Regt
HAIGH H. MM Pte 1320 West Riding Regt
HAIGH Harry MM L/Cpl 7084 62nd Bn Machine Gun Corps
HAIGH Harry MM L/Sjt 1927 West Yorkshire Regt
HAIGH Herbert "DCM,MM" CSM 200135 1/4th West Riding Regt
HAIGH James Herbert MM Cpl 240135 1/5th West Riding Regt
HAIGH John B. MM Spr 169567 228 Fd Coy Royal Engineers
HAIGH Kenneth C. MM Pte 403575 2(West Riding)Fd Amb RAMC
HAIGH Walter MM Pte 235832 2/4th Yorkshire Light Infantry
HAIGH William MM Pte 48379 West Yorkshire Regt
HAIGH William N. MM Pte 27859 5th York & Lancaster Regt
HAIGHTON Thomas MM Pte 21980 3rd Coldstream Guards
HAIL George MM 2nd Cpl 71000 'AU' Cable Section Royal Engineers
HAIL Joseph MM L/Cpl 30701 Worcestershire Regt
HAIL William MM Pte 241529 1/5th Border Regt
HAILE F. MM Sjt 15770 10th Gloucestershire Regt
HAILEY Ernest A. MM Sjt 10772 7th Shropshire Light Infantry
HAILEY George F. MM Pte 38181 8th East Surrey Regt
HAILEY Maurice MM Sjt 395038 2(N Midland)Fd Amb RAMC
HAILEY William MM Cpl 31088 South Lancashire Regt
HAILLEY C.C. MM Cpl 315282 13th Royal Highlanders
HAILS Frederick MM Pte 7779 12th Northumberland Fusiliers
HAILSTONE Ernest Henry MM Pnr 147217 5 Special Bn Royal Engineers DOW 1.10.16.
HAILSTONE Frederick MM Pte 1229 1/1st Cambridgeshire Regt
HAILSTONE William MM L/Cpl 3/8185 1/5th Suffolk Regt
HAILSTONES Thomas MM+Bar Pte S/4333 9th Royal Highlanders
HAILWOOD Thomas MM Pte 306848 2nd Lancashire Fusiliers
HAIN Edwin W. MM Spr 223088 Royal Engineers
HAIN Harry MM Spr 151324 253 Tunnelling Coy Royal Engineers
HAINE David MM L/Cpl 26806 1st Dorsetshire Regt
HAINE Frederick MM Pte 24404 7th Yorkshire Light Infantry att MGC.
HAINES Albert E. MM Pte 201285 Royal Berkshire Regt
HAINES Albert Henry MM Spr 103175 32 Div Sig Coy Royal Engineers
HAINES Albert J. MM L/Cpl 25257 Duke of Cornwall's LI
HAINES Bertie F. MM Bdr 124062 57 Bty 45 Bde RFA
HAINES Charles Herbert MM Pte 31298 12th York & Lancaster Regt
HAINES Cyril Arthur MM Spr 108243 'F' Corps Sig Coy Royal Engineers
HAINES Eric MM Bdr 371347 2/2nd Pembroke Hy Bty RGA
HAINES Ernest MM Dvr T4/144213 Army Service Corps
HAINES Farnham A.S. MM Pte 288011 Gloucestershire Regt
HAINES Francis G. MM Pte 437509 RAMC
HAINES Frank McL. MM BQMS 935016 D/282 Bde RFA
HAINES Frederick "MM,MID" Sjt B/1221 Rifle Brigade
HAINES Frederick C. MM L/Cpl 8003 2nd Royal Berkshire Regt
HAINES Harry MM Gnr 16165 D/113 Bde RFA
HAINES James MM L/Cpl 8728 1st Duke of Cornwall's LI KIA 20.8.17.
HAINES James MM Gnr 94742 A/285 Bde RFA
HAINEY William MM Dvr 12600 B/87 Bde RFA
HAINGE Albert "DCM+Bar,MM" Cpl 7860 1st Royal Berkshire Regt
HAINING James MM Pte 35616 York & Lancaster Regt
HAINING Thomas MM L/Cpl 4489 9th Seaforth Highlanders Died 18.1.18.
HAINING William MM Pte 39506 York & Lancaster Regt
HAINSWORTH Albert MM Pte 240174 West Yorkshire Regt
HAINSWORTH Charles Alfred Sears MM Cpl 14872 8th Border Regt
HAINSWORTH Lawrence MM Pte 306659 West Riding Regt
HAINSWORTH William MM+Bar Cpl 11165 2nd West Riding Regt
HAIR Alfred MM Pte 268513 Royal Warwickshire Regt
HAIR George MM Sjt 55293 B/331 Bde RFA
HAIRE Samuel MM L/Cpl 3622 1st Royal Inniskilling Fusiliers
HAIST R. MM Pte 16546 10th Essex Regt
HAITH Joe C. MM Sjt 776040 B/245 Bde RFA
HAITHWAITE William L. MM Cpl 72345 Royal Engineers
HAIZELDEN Stanley MM Pte 14569 3rd Grenadier Guards
HAKE William Channon Skinner MM L/Cpl 43445 78 Fd Coy Royal Engineers

HAKES William E. MM Sjt 935074 A/282 Bde RFA
HALBARD Rupert MM Pte 10147 Northamptonshire Regt
HALCOMB(E) Charles F. MM+Bar Pte S/12643 2nd Rifle Brigade KIA 27.4.18.
HALDANE Alexander MM Pte 275371 5/6th Royal Scots
HALDANE George "MM,CG(F)" Pte 9678 10th Arg & Suth Highlanders DOW 19.10.18.
HALDANE Gilbert MM Pte 10837 2nd Arg & Suth Highlanders
HALDENBY James M. MM Pte 7489 Northumberland Fusiliers
HALE Albert MM Pte 62242 9th Manchester Regt
HALE B.G. MM Pte 24233 10th East Kent Regt
HALE Charles MM Gnr 52316 47 Siege Bty RGA
HALE Edward MM Sjt 9317 2nd Bedfordshire Regt
HALE Edward William MM Dvr 83706 2 Div Ammn Col RFA
HALE Ernest MM Cpl 3184 1/6th South Staffordshire Regt
HALE Fernley George MM Pte 241029 1/5th Devonshire Regt
HALE Fred MM Pte 13075 7th Shropshire Light Infantry
HALE Frederick MM Bdr 104242 RGA
HALE Frederick G. MM Sjt 200130 8th Royal Berkshire Regt
HALE George MM L/Cpl 12522 9th Devonshire Regt
HALE George Alfred Joseph MM Dvr 1036 6 Div CRE Staff Royal Engineers
HALE George H. MM Dvr 85678 Royal Engineers
HALE Gilbert MM Pte 35274 14th Welsh Regt KIA 10.7.16.
HALE Henry G. MM CQMS 200009 1/1st London Regt
HALE Henry G. MM Pte 551749 16th London Regt
HALE Henry J. MM Cpl 888 1st Dragoon Guards
HALE Henry T. MM Sjt 240635 6th Royal Warwickshire Regt
HALE James MM CQMS 720114 1/24th London Regt
HALE John MM Sjt 265769 1/2nd Monmouthshire Regt
HALE John MM L/Cpl 27222 1st King's Own Scottish Borderers
HALE John MM Sjt 5179 RGA
HALE John C. MM Pte M1/7588 5 Mot Amb Convoy Army Service Corps
HALE Peter Charles MM Pte 10120 4th Liverpool Regt
HALE R. MM L/Cpl R/9968 King's Royal Rifle Corps
HALE Richard MM Bdr 675845 RFA
HALE Samuel MM Pte 15432 2nd South Staffordshire Regt
HALE William MM Sjt 13622 B/76 Bde RFA KIA 22.10.17.
HALES Albert Edward MM Gnr 170024 D/165 Bde RFA
HALES Arthur MM Gnr 30431 A/74 Bde RFA
HALES Arthur C. MM Pte 4862 15th London Regt
HALES Casper H. MM L/Cpl 1673 1/21st London Regt
HALES Charles MM+Bar Sjt 73672 18th Bn Machine Gun Corps
HALES Charles E. MM Pte 19110 Grenadier Guards
HALES Henry A. MM Sjt 142267 19th Bn Machine Gun Corps
HALES John MM Pte 44468 South Wales Borderers
HALES Saul George MM Pte 634306 2/20th London Regt
HALES Sydney M. MM Sjt 14030 6th Northamptonshire Regt
HALES William MM Cpl 12315 7th Norfolk Regt
HALES William MM Sjt 62110 Machine Gun Corps
HALES William "DCM,MSM,MM,MID" SM 2978 208 Army Troops Coy Royal Engineers
HALES William E MM Pte 11371 Oxf & Bucks Light Infantry
HALEWOOD David H. MM L/Cpl 40363 2nd South Lancashire Regt
HALEWOOD Frank MM Sjt 182779 57 Fd Coy Royal Engineers
HALEY Arthur R. MM L/Cpl 41179 1st Royal Lancaster Regt
HALEY Ernest C. MM Sjt 8716 1st Duke of Cornwall's LI
HALEY Frank MM Cpl 37371 63 Coy Labour Corps
HALEY Fred MM Sjt 200072 1/4th Oxf & Bucks Light Infantry
HALEY Frederick MM Pte 2845 2nd Royal Fusiliers
HALEY Henry N. MM Cpl 970283 21 Bty 8 Bde RFA
HALEY Len W. MM Gnr 780619 C/255 Bde RFA
HALEY Samuel MM Sjt 26/963 26th Northumberland Fusiliers KIA 6.5.17.
HALEY Thomas B. MM+Bar Pte 401024 RAMC
HALEY William W. MM L/Cpl 62773 91 Fd Amb RAMC
HALFACRE Charles Richard MM Pte M2/049655 131 MT Coy Army Service Corps
HALFACRE WilliamR. MM Sjt 26 1/9th London Regt
HALFHIDE Charles H. MM Pte 57548 7th Manchester Regt
HALFORD Alfred John MM Cpl 106556 1 Special Coy Royal Engineers DOW 22.5.16.
HALFORD Arthur E.H. MM Cpl 12112 6th Shropshire Light Infantry
HALFORD Edgar T. MM Pte 104589 175 Coy Labour Corps
HALFORD Enoch MM Pte 33496 Durham Light Infantry
HALFORD F. MM Pte 22121 9th Notts & Derby Regt
HALFORD James MM Sjt 8344 1st Leicestershire Regt KIA 23.10.18.
HALFORD Raymond Walter MM Pte 204073 2nd Worcestershire Regt
HALFORD Rupert MM+Bar Sjt 22391 Liverpool Regt
HALFPENNY Albert MM Pte 200286 1/5th Bedfordshire Regt
HALFPENNY J. MM Cpl 7/1252 Royal Irish Rifles
HALIFAX Herbert Emerson Will MM Pte M2/267649 Army Service Corps att 'M' AA Bty RGA.
HALIFAX Thomas W. MM Bdr 99154 RFA
HALKET J. MM L/Cpl 70620 4 Fd Amb RAMC
HALKET James John MM+Bar Sjt 231080 2/2nd London Regt
HALKSWORTH Frederick C. MM Bdr 116635 RFA
HALL A. MM Sjt 73851 RFA
HALL Albert MM Pte 10456 1/4th Oxf & Bucks Light Infantry
HALL Albert MM Pte 34202 Machine Gun Corps
HALL Albert E. MM Spr 78195 VII Corps Sig Coy Royal Engineers
HALL Albert E. MM Gnr 102491 RGA
HALL Albert E. MM Sjt 31721 North Lancashire Regt
HALL Albert E. MM Pte 202324 Suffolk Regt
HALL Albert J. MM L/Cpl 80523 1/1st Essex Yeomanry
HALL Albert L. MM Cpl 351177 2nd Manchester Regt
HALL Albert V. MM L/Cpl 44761 2/7th Manchester Regt
HALL Alexander L.R. MM Pte 1588 9th Seaforth Highlanders
HALL Alfred MM Cpl 68449 Machine Gun Corps
HALL Alfred MM Pte 37016 55 Fd Amb RAMC
HALL Alfred MM Sjt 50446 Royal Engineers
HALL Alfred "DCM,MM" Sjt 16211 36 Bde RFA
HALL Alfred E. MM Pte 48672 1st Northamptonshire Regt
HALL Alfred Ernest MM Cpl 57558 16th Lancashire Fusiliers KIA 4.11.18.
HALL Alfred George MM Sjt 19180 2nd Bedfordshire Regt KIA 18.9.18.
HALL Algernon Edward Charles MM Pte 202655 1/4th Seaforth Highlanders KIA 13.10.18.
HALL Amos MM Pte 43743 9th Royal Inniskilling Fusiliers
HALL Andrew MM Pte 18/767 18th West Yorkshire Regt
HALL Arnold H. MM Sjt 16453 Machine Gun Corps
HALL Arthur MM Pte M2/079275 Army Service Corps
HALL Arthur MM Pte 28061 1st North Staffordshire Regt
HALL Arthur G. MM L/Cpl 16723 2nd Grenadier Guards
HALL Arthur James MM Pte G/17168 Royal West Kent Regt
HALL Arthur Morris MM Cpl 26487 Machine Gun Corps
HALL Augustus MM L/Cpl 250774 Royal Engineers
HALL Benjamin MM Pte 54382 10th Notts & Derby Regt
HALL Benjamin MM Pte 7474 1st East Yorkshire Regt KIA 16.4.18.
HALL Bertram MM Pte 102952 Machine Gun Corps
HALL Cecil Adrian MM Pte 22504 1st Royal West Surrey Regt DOW 29.5.18.
HALL Charles MM Spr 198234 Royal Engineers
HALL Charles MM Pte S/13166 Rifle Brigade
HALL Charles MM L/Cpl 22236 1st Wiltshire Regt KIA 24.3.18.
HALL Charles C. MM Sjt 550751 1/16th London Regt
HALL Charles Harold "MM,MSM,MID" CQMS 9044 2nd South Lancashire Regt
HALL Charles J. MM Sjt 14989 Royal West Surrey Regt
HALL Charles R. MM 2nd Cpl 267343 Royal Engineers
HALL Charles W. MM Pnr 23251 17 Fd Coy Royal Engineers
HALL Christopher Sinclair MM Pte 5272 8th East Kent Regt
HALL Cornelius P. MM Pte 5/247 Rifle Brigade
HALL Cuthbert "DCM,MM" Sjt 40013 64 Fd Coy Royal Engineers DOW 25.4.18.
HALL David MM Spr 139031 Royal Engineers
HALL David MM Pte 11503 8th Cheshire Regt
HALL David MM Pte 17/1417 West Yorkshire Regt
HALL David MM L/Cpl 2350 6th Royal Lancaster Regt
HALL E. MM Sjt 60434 RFA
HALL Edward J. MM Cpl 2806 1st Life Guards
HALL Edward K. MM Cpl 42323 119 Bty 27 Bde RFA
HALL Edward L. MM Pte 13570 8th Royal Berkshire Regt
HALL Edward T. MM Cpl 9277 Royal West Kent Regt
HALL Edwin Denison MM Pte 15638 11th Northumberland Fusiliers
HALL Ernest MM Pte 3/10845 7th Norfolk Regt
HALL Ernest MM Sjt 197248 Royal Engineers
HALL Ernest E.J. MM L/Sjt 203050 8th Gloucestershire Regt
HALL Ernest G. MM Pte 33843 North Lancashire Regt
HALL Ernest H. MM Bdr 23944 111 Heavy Bty RGA
HALL F.G. MM+Bar Sjt Y/84 13th King's Royal Rifle Corps
HALL Frank MM Pte 241886 Leicestershire Regt
HALL Frank MM Gnr L/24888 RFA
HALL Frank MM Pte M2/150482 Army Service Corps att 'S' AA Bty RGA

HALL Fred MM Pte 242440 Northumberland Fusiliers
HALL Frederick MM Sjt 73 1/6th London Regt
HALL Frederick "DCM,MM,MID" Sjt 1081 2nd Lancashire Fusiliers
HALL Frederick MM Pte 18026 Royal West Kent Regt
HALL Frederick George MM Pte 29651 Hampshire Regt DOW 14.9.18.
HALL Frederick George MM Sjt 1440 1/6th London Regt KIA 15.9.16.
HALL Frederick R. MM Sjt 44726 31 Siege Bty RGA
HALL Frederick R. MM Pte 17844 6th Liverpool Regt
HALL Frederick R. MM Sjt Pnr 7853 2nd Royal Fusiliers
HALL Frederick William MM Cpl 40241 Y/12 Med TM Bty RGA "KIA 16.9.17."
HALL G. MM Dvr 6901 RFA
HALL George MM Pnr 128945 Royal Engineers
HALL George MM Cpl 201201 Gloucestershire Regt
HALL George MM Dvr 17234 Machine Gun Corps
HALL George MM+Bar Pte 28080 11th Liverpool Regt
HALL George MM Dvr 604237 RHA
HALL George A. MM Sjt 43490 C/251 Bde RFA
HALL George Albert "MM,MSM" Sjt 25175 6th Dorsetshire Regt
HALL George Arthur MM Pte 11357 2nd Arg & Suth Highlanders
HALL George C.L. MM Cpl 305539 8th Royal Warwickshire Regt
HALL George D. MM Sjt 490011 469 Fd Coy Royal Engineers
HALL George Henry "MM,CG(B)" Sjt 27701 12th Suffolk Regt
HALL George W. MM Cpl 17449 10th Yorkshire Regt
HALL Gilbert M. MM Pte 22217 Royal Warwickshire Regt
HALL Gilbert Vincent MM Bdr W/3851 RFA
HALL Gilby MM Sjt 9338 9th Lancashire Fusiliers
HALL Harold MM Sjt 1810 Royal Engineers
HALL Harold MM Gnr 191275 'M'(AA)Bty RGA
HALL Harry MM Pte 29160 24th Royal Welsh Fusiliers
HALL Harry MM Sjt 200502 10th Notts & Derby Regt
HALL Harry MM Spr 57818 Royal Engineers
HALL Harry MM Pte G/9615 11th Royal West Kent Regt
HALL Harry MM Sjt 7472 2nd Northamptonshire Regt
HALL Harry Charles "MM,MID" 2nd Cpl 70201 'E' Corps Sig Coy Royal Engineers
HALL Harry S. MM Sjt 198197 'E' Corps Sig Coy Royal Engineers
HALL Henry MM Cpl 94821 Royal Engineers
HALL Henry MM Pte 25748 North Lancashire Regt
HALL Henry MM Pte 235572 4th West Riding Regt
HALL Henry MM Sjt 14112 6th King's Own Scottish Borderers
HALL Henry MM Pte G/21048 Royal West Kent Regt
HALL Henry MM Pte 202152 1/5th Lancashire Fusiliers Died 17.11.18.
HALL Henry MM Pte 40594 9th York & Lancaster Regt
HALL Henry G. MM L/Cpl 24028 2 Div Sig Coy Royal Engineers KIA 26.9.17.
HALL Henry Herbert MM S/Sjt Fitter 86722 A/175 Bde RFA
HALL Henry Lewis MM Sjt B/4889 11th King's Royal Rifle Corps KIA 30.11.17.
HALL Henry T. MM Sjt 9756 2nd Duke of Cornwall's LI
HALL Henry W. MM Pte 420488 1/10th London Regt
HALL Herbert MM Pte 4977 8th Royal West Surrey Regt
HALL Herbert MM Pte 54383 10th Notts & Derby Regt
HALL Herbert MM Sjt 21589 4th Grenadier Guards
HALL Herbert H. MM Spr 255006 Royal Engineers
HALL Herbert William MM Pte 82826 29th Bn Machine Gun Corps
HALL Horace MM Sjt 18240 1st Royal Scots Fusiliers
HALL Horace MM Pte 158865 31st Bn Machine Gun Corps
HALL Isaac MM CSM 344 1/8th Durham Light Infantry
HALL Isaac D. MM Bdr 103284 RGA
HALL J. MM Spr 821610 179 Tunnelling Coy Royal Engineers
HALL J. MM Pte 77371 10th Bn Tank Corps
HALL J.A. MM Shoeing Smith 692 RFA
HALL James "DCM,MM" Pte 63318 2nd West Yorkshire Regt
HALL James MM Pte 24632 5th Royal Lancaster Regt
HALL James MM Cpl 440215 431 Fd Coy Royal Engineers
HALL James MM+Bar Cpl 45602 38 Fd Amb RAMC
HALL James MM Pte 18/871 8th Royal Irish Rifles
HALL James MM 2nd Cpl 402444 404 Fd Coy Royal Engineers
HALL James MM Sjt 202371 6th Leicestershire Regt KIA 23.10.18.
HALL James MM Pte 240507 Royal Lancaster Regt
HALL James MM Pte 194441 Labour Corps
HALL James MM Pte 16847 Yorkshire Light Infantry
HALL James MM Pte 13485 11th Durham Light Infantry
HALL James A. MM L/Cpl 23960 1/5th Royal Warwickshire Regt
HALL James G. MM Pte 5/5021 13th King's Royal Rifle Corps
HALL James H. MM Cpl 60976 12/13th Northumberland Fusiliers
HALL James Henry William MM+Bar Cpl S/9204 7th Seaforth Highlanders KIA 3.5.17.
HALL James R. MM Gnr 275156 RGA
HALL James Thomas MM Sjt 837052 78 Bde RFA
HALL John MM L/Cpl 11907 9th North Staffordshire Regt
HALL John MM L/Cpl 15806 6th Northamptonshire Regt KIA 29.9.18.
HALL John MM L/Cpl 8914 1st Royal Lancaster Regt
HALL John MM L/Sjt 12539 1st Bedfordshire Regt
HALL John MM Pte 13/407 13th York & Lancaster Regt
HALL John MM Cpl 21658 Z/5 Med TM Bty RFA KIA 4.6.16.
HALL John MM Pte 6172 1/5th Royal Highlanders
HALL John MM L/Cpl S/14476 10th Arg & Suth Highlanders
HALL John MM Sjt 86881 62 Bde RFA
HALL John MM Pte 301014 1/8th Durham Light Infantry
HALL John William MM L/Cpl 66735 153 Siege Bty RGA
HALL John Albert MM L/Cpl 372661 8th London Regt
HALL John Alfred MM Pte 25061 19th Lancashire Fusiliers KIA 25.4.18.
HALL John E. "MM,MID" Gnr 49384 RGA
HALL John Edward MM Bdr 112378 216 Siege Bty RGA
HALL John George MM Gnr 32947 B/177 Bde RFA
HALL John Henry MM Pte 13046 8th Norfolk Regt KIA 21.3.18.
HALL John Radcliffe MM Bdr L/13393 C/250 Bde RFA
HALL John Richard MM Pte 13045 7th Duke of Cornwall's LI DOW 5.6.16.
HALL John T. MM Pte 82348 Machine Gun Corps
HALL John Thomas MM Pte 13755 10th West Riding Regt KIA 23.5.17
HALL John W. MM Gnr 1467 9(West Riding)Bty RFA
HALL John W. MM L/Sjt 1652 1/5th Lincolnshire Regt
HALL John W.C. MM Dvr 64224 RFA
HALL John William MM Sjt 280792 30 Siege Bty RGA Died 7.11.18.
HALL Jonathan MM Gnr 136096 76 Bde RFA
HALL Joseph MM Pte 49724 75 Fd Amb RAMC DOW 2.5.18.
HALL Joseph MM Pte S/6708 2nd Royal West Surrey Regt KIA 14.3.17.
HALL Joseph H. MM Pte 22162 17th Royal Scots
HALL Joseph S. MM Spr 85197 Royal Engineers
HALL Joseph W. MM+Bar L/Cpl 38696 20th Durham Light Infantry
HALL Leonard MM Pte 44234 2nd South Wales Borderers
HALL Leonard MM Pte 3264 Gloucestershire Regt
HALL Leonard Thomas MM Spr 89576 144 Army Troops Coy Royal Engineers
HALL Louis MM Pte 46575 4th North Staffordshire Regt
HALL Luke H. MM L/Cpl 6065 Machine Gun Corps
HALL Mark William MM L/Cpl 3115 1/15th London Regt
HALL Maurice MM Pte 11461 4th Worcestershire Regt
HALL Michael MM Pte 72392 Machine Gun Corps
HALL Michael MM L/Cpl 1752 Royal Engineers
HALL N.M. MM Pte 39505 RAMC
HALL Noah A. MM Pte 267950 West Yorkshire Regt
HALL Percy MM+Bar Cpl 14627 1/4th & 8th Suffolk Regt
HALL Percy J. MM Sjt 33142 Liverpool Regt
HALL R. MM Cpl 351933 Manchester Regt
HALL Reginald S. MM Pte 510410 2 Fd Amb RAMC
HALL Richard MM Sjt 2358 1/5th Durham Light Infantry
HALL Richard B. MM Pte 335 4th Middlesex Regt
HALL Robert MM L/Cpl 49707 5th West Riding Regt
HALL Robert MM Pte 3443 Coldstream Guards
HALL Robert MM Pte 304851 5th Bn Tank Corps
HALL Robert "MM,MID" Pte 1426 1/5th Royal Welsh Fusiliers KIA 7.11.17.
HALL Robert MM Sjt 41001 RAMC
HALL Robert Charles MM Pte 45975 123 Coy Machine Gun Corps KIA 26.9.17.
HALL Robert J. MM Gnr 322813 155 Siege Bty RGA
HALL Robert Lawton "DCM,MM" Sjt 2680 1/6th Cheshire Regt
HALL Robert W. "DCM,MM" CSM 240407 1/5th York & Lancaster Regt
HALL Samuel MM Pte 14109 24th Manchester Regt
HALL Samuel B. MM Sjt 33530 8th East Surrey Regt
HALL Sidney G. MM Pte 39033 2/4th Hampshire Regt
HALL Stanley E. MM Spr 463052 50 Div Sig Coy Royal Engineers
HALL Stanley G. MM Sjt 106322 Royal Engineers
HALL Sydney Owen MM Pte M/401947 Army Service Corps att 231 Fd Amb RAMC
HALL T. MM Pte 11018 Royal Warwickshire Regt
HALL Thomas MM Cpl 8131 Worcestershire Regt
HALL Thomas MM Pte 11512 South Staffordshire Regt att RE.

HALL Thomas "MM,MID" Sjt 9819 2nd Worcestershire Regt
HALL Thomas MM Pte 38619 20th Northumberland Fusiliers KIA 9.4.17.
HALL Thomas MM L/Sjt S/2518 Gordon Highlanders
HALL Thomas MM Pte 4536 2nd Royal Irish Rifles
HALL Thomas MM Pte 204425 Lancashire Fusiliers
HALL Thomas E. MM Pte 9077 2nd Yorkshire Regt
HALL Thomas G. MM Sjt 6405 2nd Royal Welsh Fusiliers
HALL Thomas J. MM Cpl 21426 Durham Light Infantry
HALL Thomas M. MM Pte 34801 Northumberland Fusiliers
HALL Thomas V. MM Cpl 285022 7th Gordon Highlanders
HALL Thomas W. MM Gnr 74345 51 Bde RFA
HALL Thomas W. MM Pte 24073 15th Notts & Derby Regt
HALL Thomas W. MM Sjt 930168 RFA
HALL Tom MM L/Cpl 200527 1/4th York & Lancaster Regt
HALL Victor C. MM Cpl 720501 1/24th London Regt
HALL Victor S. MM L/Cpl 138805 50th Bn Machine Gun Corps
HALL Walter MM L/Cpl 302793 13th Durham Light Infantry
HALL Walter "MM,CG(B)" Sjt 10/847 10th East Yorkshire Regt
HALL Walter MM Cpl 98847 Machine Gun Corps
HALL William MM Pte 18567 9th Northumberland Fusiliers
HALL William MM Pte 63543 75 Fd Amb RAMC
HALL William MM Gnr 25434 3 Siege Bty RGA
HALL William MM Cpl 23080 Yorkshire Light Infantry
HALL William MM Sjt 170191 RFA
HALL William MM Pte 147771 29th Bn Machine Gun Corps
HALL William MM Sjt 20960 20th Middlesex Regt
HALL William MM Sjt 680215 A/286 Bde RFA
HALL William "MM+Bar,CG(B)" CSM 17279 12th East Surrey Regt
HALL William MM Pte 35383 14th Royal Welsh Fusiliers
HALL William MM L/Sjt 13103 10th Lancashire Fusiliers
HALL William MM Pte 20029 1st King's Own Scottish Borderers att Yorkshire Light Infantry
HALL William MM Spr 282431 18 Div Sig Coy Royal Engineers
HALL William MM Pte 24699 Dorsetshire Regt
HALL William G. MM L/Cpl 27182 8th East Surrey Regt
HALL William George MM Pte 28633 15th Royal Warwickshire Regt KIA 26.10.17.
HALL William Harold MM Cpl 308132 15th Bn Tank Corps
HALL William Henry "MM,CG(F)" Pte 23691 1st East Yorkshire Regt
HALL William J. MM Pte 375551 2/8th London Regt
HALL William J. MM Pte 18504 13 Fd Amb RAMC
HALL William M. MM Pte 41179 Northumberland Fusiliers
HALL William R. MM Sjt 8594 2nd Royal Inniskilling Fusiliers
HALL William T. MM Pte M1/08606 Army Service Corps att RAMC
HALL William W.C. MM Cpl 4976 14 Fd Amb RAMC
HALLADAY Lawrence A. MM L/Cpl 1713 2nd Royal Warwickshire Regt
HALLAHAN Patrick MM Cpl 14075 Royal Engineers
HALLAM George MM Pte 9697 2nd Notts & Derby Regt
HALLAM Henry MM Pte 1389 Army Cyclist Corps
HALLAM John MM Sjt 13/1092 13th East Yorkshire Regt KIA 13.11.16.
HALLAM John S. "DCM,MM+Bar" CSM C/424 16th King's Royal Rifle Corps
HALLAM Joseph S. MM Cpl 19156 12/13th Northumberland Fusiliers
HALLAM Percy MM Pte 37338 Welsh Regt
HALLAM Robert MM+Bar Sjt T/20690 Army Service Corps att 6 Cav Fd Amb RAMC
HALLAM Sidney MM Pte 16683 8th East Lancashire Regt DOW 23.11.16.
HALLAM William P. MM L/Cpl 15347 9th Northumberland Fusiliers
HALLAS Gilbert MM Pte 306297 2/8th West Yorkshire Regt
HALLAS Walter MM Pnr 341041 'L' Corps Sig Coy Royal Engineers
HALLATT Edmund MM+Bar Sjt 112899 183 Tunnelling Coy Royal Engineers
HALLAWAY Maurice T. MM Pte 534043 RAMC
HALLAWAY S.W. "DCM,MM" Sjt P/3 Military Foot Police
HALLERON John MM Pte 7737 2nd York & Lancaster Regt
HALLETT Albert S. MM Pte 20038 Royal Fusiliers
HALLETT Archibald A. MM Pte 41074 1st Dorsetshire Regt
HALLETT Charles MM Spr 48463 Royal Engineers
HALLETT Charles G. MM Cpl 304655 20th Bn Tank Corps
HALLETT Edward J. MM Bdr 783 RGA
HALLETT Ellis MM Pte 241130 1/5th Lincolnshire Regt
HALLETT Hubert C. "MM,MID" Sjt 954 19 Fd Amb RAMC
HALLETT James H.A. MM Spr 103274 32 Div Sig Coy Royal Engineers
HALLETT Patrick MM Pte 608341 18th London Regt
HALLETT Walter MM Sjt 8095 9th South Staffordshire Regt DOW 10.7.17.
HALLETT William H. MM Pte 43083 15th Royal Irish Rifles
HALLEY William MM Cpl 161606 50 Div Sig Coy Royal Engineers
HALLEY William "MM,MID" Pte 2485 Royal Highlanders
HALLEY William B. MM Pte 38166 RAMC
HALLIDAY Archie MM Pte 315119 13th Royal Highlanders
HALLIDAY Brian Joseph "MC,MM(12475 Sjt 7th Bn)" 2Lt 1/4th Lincolnshire Regt
HALLIDAY Cecil A. MM Pte 13898 East Kent Regt
HALLIDAY E. MM Sjt 58475 RFA
HALLIDAY Gilbert M. MM Gnr 136522 RFA
HALLIDAY John MM Pte 41824 2nd Highland Light Infantry
HALLIDAY John MM Gnr 59437 110 Siege Bty RGA
HALLIDAY John MM L/Sjt 11366 6/7th Royal Scots Fusiliers
HALLIDAY John William "DCM,MM" CSM 14148 10th North Lancashire Regt KIA 22.3.18.
HALLIDAY Robert MM Sjt 173429 150 Siege Bty RGA
HALLIDAY Samuel MM Bdr 750157 RFA
HALLIDAY Stephen MM+Bar Gnr 18228 B/93 Bde RFA KIA 8.10.17.
HALLIGAN Charles C. MM Gnr 925390 HQ 280 Bde RFA
HALLIGAN Thomas MM+Bar Pte 18125 2nd Leinster Regt
HALLIGAN William J. MM Sjt 69837 117 Bty 26 Bde RFA
HALLINAN Albert MM Cpl 4349 D/74 Bde RFA
HALLINAN Denis "DCM,MM" Sjt 11348 6th Dorsetshire Regt
HALLING John Samuel MM Sjt 200569 1/5th South Staffordshire Regt KIA 29.8.17.
HALLIWELL Albert MM Sjt 47966 113 Fd Amb RAMC
HALLIWELL Arthur MM Pte 10368 RAMC
HALLIWELL Arthur MM Cpl 5836 RFA
HALLIWELL Frederick Bertram "MM,MID" Sjt 43387 RGA
HALLIWELL Frederick James MM L/Cpl 16337 8th York & Lancaster Regt
HALLIWELL George MM Pte 15631 2nd Manchester Regt DOW 14.4.17.
HALLIWELL George MM Pte 38837 1st South Wales Borderers
HALLIWELL George MM L/Cpl 78928 Royal Engineers
HALLIWELL James MM+Bar Pte 300291 8th Manchester Regt
HALLIWELL James MM Dvr 79650 RFA
HALLIWELL James MM+Bar L/Cpl 240971 5th West Riding Regt
HALLIWELL Joseph MM Gnr 74235 C/122 Bde RFA
HALLIWELL Joseph Henry MM Sjt 1431 D/18 Bde RFA
HALLIWELL Maurice E. "MM,MID" Cpl S/7277 Rifle Brigade
HALLIWELL Percy MM Sjt 4980 Lancashire Fusiliers
HALLIWELL Richard MM Sjt 4921 Royal Lancaster Regt
HALLIWELL Thomas Mitchell MM Gnr 676321 55 Div Ammn Col RFA
HALLIWELL Walter MM Sjt 710194 RFA
HALLIWELL William MM Cpl 19391 Royal Lancaster Regt
HALLIWELL William "DCM,MM" Cpl 13460 10th North Lancashire Regt
HALLORAN Edward MM Pte 24424 5th Oxf & Bucks Light Infantry KIA 3.5.17.
HALLORAN L. MM Sjt 705325 RFA
HALLOWELL Morris Lambert MM+Bar Pte 19911 26th Royal Fusiliers KIA 20.9.17.
HALLPORT Cresswell MM Pte M2/182288 Army Service Corps att RAMC
HALLS Alfred G.T. MM Pte 29679 1st Bedfordshire Regt
HALLS Edmund MM Pte 12852 Essex Regt
HALLS George H. MM Sjt 312113 Royal Engineers att RFA.
HALLS George R. MM Pte 351335 1/7th London Regt
HALLS Henry MM Pte 6456 1/24th London Regt
HALLS J.A. MM+Bar Pte 18001 1st Grenadier Guards
HALLS Percy W. MM Sjt 37324 RFA
HALLS Thomas G. MM Bdr 52309 37 Bde RFA
HALLSTEAD James MM Pte 60175 5/6th Royal Scots
HALLSWORTH Harry MM Bdr 33374 RFA
HALLUM Thomas MM Cpl 200176 1/5th South Staffordshire Regt
HALLWELL Edward MM Sjt 830614 2 Bde RFA
HALLWOOD Reginald MM Sjt 14977 12th Liverpool Regt
HALLWORTH William MM L/Cpl 25106 2nd Grenadier Guards
HALLWORTH William H. MM Pte 50287 6th Manchester Regt
HALLYBURTON John MM Spr 46096 Royal Engineers
HALPERN Jack "MM,MID" Bdr 75629 RFA att 15 Div Sig Coy RE
HALPIN Charles MM Cpl Z/1259 11th Rifle Brigade KIA 3.12.17.
HALPIN James "MM,MID" Sjt 4/9725 Durham Light Infantry
HALPIN John MM Pte 26586 Royal Inniskilling Fusiliers
HALPIN Michael MM Pte 4441 2nd Leinster Regt KIA 20.10.18.

HALPIN Thomas "DCM,MM" Cpl 92639 19 Div Sig Coy Royal Engineers DOW 7.6.18.
HALSALL George MM Pte 27633 4th Liverpool Regt
HALSALL James MM Sjt 201277 North Lancashire Regt
HALSALL John MM 2nd Cpl 428351 423 Fd Coy Royal Engineers
HALSALL Thomas H. MM L/Sjt 9336 1st Coldstream Guards
HALSALL Walter MM Pte 16403 11th Border Regt
HALSALL Walter MM L/Cpl 360449 30 Div Sig Coy Royal Engineers
HALSALL Wilfred MM Cpl 7313 Royal Fusiliers
HALSE Charles Henry MM L/Cpl 500318 61 Div Sig Coy Royal Engineers
HALSE George Frederick MM L/Cpl T/15273 21st Middlesex Regt
HALSE Gilbert MM Spr 463237 50 Div Sig Coy Royal Engineers Died 22.8.18.
HALSE William MM CSM 240139 5th West Riding Regt
HALSEY Charles W. MM Pte 15054 10th Essex Regt
HALSEY George MM Pte 16261 7th Bedfordshire Regt
HALSEY Reginald Charles MM Sjt 15610 2nd Bedfordshire Regt KIA 24.10.18.
HALSEY William Henry MM Sjt 138755 279 Rly Constr Coy Royal Engineers
HALSTEAD George W. MM F/Sjt 856 Royal Flying Corps
HALSTEAD Henry MM Pte 1343 Royal Fusiliers
HALSTEAD Herbert MM Dvr 140976 72 Bty 38 Bde RFA
HALSTEAD Joseph MM Dvr W/4019 122 Bde RFA
HALSTEAD T. MM L/Cpl 240368 West Riding Regt
HALTON Ernest MM Dvr 1440 A/245 Bde RFA
HALTON James A. MM 2nd Cpl 104365 228 Fd Coy Royal Engineers
HALTON James E. MM L/Bdr 293481 136 Hy Bty RGA
HALTON Thomas MM Pte 2002 RAMC
HALTON Thomas MM 2nd Cpl 550757 520 Fd Coy Royal Engineers
HALYAR G. MM L/Cpl 17561 Machine Gun Corps
HALYAR P.E. MM L/Cpl C/7081 King's Royal Rifle Corps
HAM Arthur G. "DCM,MM" L/Sjt 1663 1st Welsh Guards
HAM John MM Sjt M2/201177 363 MT Coy Army Service Corps
HAM W.L. MM Pte 1276 Yeomanry
HAMAR Edgar MM Pte 10786 7th Shropshire Light Infantry
HAMBLETON Albert MM Pte 8186 Coldstream Guards DOW 21.2.17.
HAMBLETON Arthur C. MM Gnr 201487 RFA
HAMBLETON Frederick MM Pte 41981 West Yorkshire Regt
HAMBLETON John H. MM Bdr 130019 C/62 Bde RFA
HAMBLETON Noah MM L/Cpl 8325 2nd South Staffordshire Regt
HAMBLETON Thomas MM Sjt 12179 6th Shropshire Light Infantry
HAMBLEY Francis MM Gnr 70672 113 Hy Bty RGA
HAMBLIN Joseph MM Sjt 21/1049 9th Northumberland Fusiliers
HAMBLIN William MM Spr 175609 184 Tunnelling Coy Royal Engineers
HAMBLING Charles MM Pte 8495 1st West Yorkshire Regt
HAMBLING Herbert M.H. MM L/Cpl 235327 1/1st Gloucestershire Yeomanry
HAMBLY Stanley MM L/Cpl 23693 Duke of Cornwall's LI
HAMBRIDGE Walter MM L/Cpl G/15328 Royal West Surrey Regt
HAMBROOK Douglas V. MM Pte 1641 RAMC
HAMER Charles D. MM Cpl 75517 16th Bn Tank Corps
HAMER David MM Gnr 290346 RGA
HAMER Fred MM Sjt 375360 1/5th Manchester Regt
HAMER Harry Plant MM Pte M2/053967 Army Service Corps att 28 Fd Amb RAMC.
HAMER James Edward MM L/Cpl 307405 2/6th Notts & Derby Regt KIA 21.3.18.
HAMER James G. MM Sjt 399 RFA
HAMER Joseph Robert MM Pte 55278 Machine Gun Corps
HAMER Josiah MM Gnr 71797 24 Hy Bty RGA
HAMER Thomas H. "MM,MID" Sjt 46986 Royal Engineers
HAMER William MM Cpl 243476 1/5th North Lancashire Regt
HAMER William H. MM Pte 19040 13th Liverpool Regt
HAMES Cecil B. MM Pte 19867 Somerset Light Infantry
HAMIL Edward MM L/Cpl 267137 Northumberland Fusiliers
HAMILL Charles William MM Gnr 7756 40 Div Ammn Col RFA DOW 9.10.18.
HAMILL Herbert MM Cpl 8792 4th Hussars
HAMILL John MM Cpl 20020 Royal Dublin Fusiliers
HAMILL Joseph MM Pte 325075 9th Durham Light Infantry
HAMILL Robert J. MM+Bar CoH 1176 Household Bn
HAMILL Thomas H. MM Spr 97703 Royal Engineers
HAMILL Thomas James MM 2nd Cpl 57631 150 Fd Coy Royal Engineers
HAMILTON Albert MM Spr 463218 50 Div Sig Coy Royal Engineers
HAMILTON Alex MM Cpl 661043 57 Div Ammn Col RFA
HAMILTON Alexander MM Pte 64877 RAMC
HAMILTON Alexander MM F/Sgt 820 Royal Flying Corps
HAMILTON Alexander MM Sjt 350022 1st(East Lancashire)Fd Amb RAMC
HAMILTON Alexander MM Pte 107596 Machine Gun Corps
HAMILTON Alfred MM Cpl 201481 1/5th Arg & Suth Highlanders DOW 14.11.17.
HAMILTON Andrew MM Gnr 656268 RFA
HAMILTON Arthur Sidney MM Sjt 2020 1/1st City of London Yeo
HAMILTON Bradshaw O. MM Pte 31514 Liverpool Regt
HAMILTON Charlie MM L/Cpl 13064 55 Coy Machine Gun Corps KIA 19.10.17.
HAMILTON Claude G. MM L/Cpl 1127 12th Middlesex Regt
HAMILTON Claude N. MM Bdr 353719 RGA
HAMILTON Daniel MM Pte 250797 2nd Royal Scots
HAMILTON Daniel MM Pte 26376 8th Hussars
HAMILTON David MM Pte 4676 1st Royal Highlanders KIA 28.5.18.
HAMILTON David MM Pte 6401 5/6th Scottish Rifles
HAMILTON David "DCM,MM" CSM 10391 1st King's Own Scottish Borderers KIA 30.11.17.
HAMILTON Edward MM Dvr 90989 106 Fd Coy Royal Engineers
HAMILTON Edward MM Spr 198113 Royal Engineers
HAMILTON George B. MM Sjt 511991 14th London Regt
HAMILTON George Lewis MM L/Cpl 18380 20th Manchester Regt DOW 27.10.16.
HAMILTON Harold MM Pte 19472 6/7th Royal Scots Fusiliers
HAMILTON Henry D. MM Dvr M2/080387 Army Service Corps
HAMILTON J. MM L/Cpl 240321 Highland Light Infantry
HAMILTON James MM Dvr 6353 RFA
HAMILTON James MM Pte S/4680 7th Seaforth Highlanders
HAMILTON James MM Pte 28943 6th King's Own Scottish Borderers
HAMILTON James MM Pte 927 1st Arg & Suth Highlanders
HAMILTON James MM Cpl 7367 2nd Seaforth Highlanders KIA 2.11.18.
HAMILTON James MM Pte 43533 Gordon Highlanders
HAMILTON James MM Pte 25906 Lancashire Fusiliers
HAMILTON James "DCM,MM" Sjt 17011 8th York & Lancaster Regt
HAMILTON James MM Pte 12996 7th Shropshire Light Infantry
HAMILTON James MM L/Cpl 463027 50 Div Sig Coy Royal Engineers
HAMILTON James MM Pte 17559 Gordon Highlanders
HAMILTON James Campbell MM Cpl 49772 Royal Engineers
HAMILTON James Joseph MM L/Cpl 64445 150 Fd Coy Royal Engineers
HAMILTON John MM Dvr 631481 D/255 Bde RFA
HAMILTON John MM L/Cpl 241165 1/5th King's Own Scottish Borderers
HAMILTON John MM Pte 14282 9th Royal Irish Fusiliers KIA 16.8.17.
HAMILTON John MM Spr 40055 Royal Engineers
HAMILTON John MM Pte 26424 11th Royal Scots KIA 9.4.17.
HAMILTON John MM L/Cpl 43544 18th Highland Light Infantry
HAMILTON John MM Sjt 1099 10th Arg & Suth Highlanders DOW 30.3.18.
HAMILTON John MM Sjt 5975 Machine Gun Corps
HAMILTON John MM Pte 201146 1/4th Seaforth Highlanders
HAMILTON John Campbell MM Cpl 93681 41 Div Sig Coy Royal Engineers
HAMILTON John Carson MM 2nd Cpl 57453 121 Fd Coy Royal Engineers
HAMILTON John T. MM Pte 31103 Notts & Derby Regt
HAMILTON John W. MM L/Cpl 27342 Durham Light Infantry
HAMILTON Joseph MM Sjt 14140 7th King's Own Scottish Borderers
HAMILTON Malcolm John MM Pte 517340 1/14th London Regt
HAMILTON Nathaniel MM Pte 8/14834 Royal Irish Rifles
HAMILTON Oliver MM+2 Bars Sjt 431933 Royal Engineers
HAMILTON Patrick MM Cpl 11291 1st Royal Dublin Fusiliers
HAMILTON Robert MM Pte 16218 1st Shropshire Light Infantry
HAMILTON Robert "DCM,MM" CSM 15572 9th Royal Inniskilling Fusiliers KIA 23.3.18.
HAMILTON Thomas MM Pte 26288 5th Royal Inniskilling Fusiliers
HAMILTON Thomas MM Pte 30367 9th Scottish Rifles
HAMILTON Thomas H. MM Cpl 1438 Durham Light Infantry
HAMILTON Victor MM Cpl 32524 69 Siege Bty RGA
HAMILTON W. MM L/Bdr 175639 A/251 Bde RFA
HAMILTON Wallace MM Cpl 32698 Signals Service Royal Engineers

HAMILTON William MM+Bar Sjt 251512 5/6th Royal Scots
HAMILTON William MM L/Cpl S/9628 Seaforth Highlanders
HAMILTON William MM Cpl 47317 RAMC
HAMILTON William MM L/Cpl 17102 Royal Scots
HAMILTON William MM Pte 4217 Seaforth Highlanders
HAMILTON William D. MM L/Sjt 17962 9th Royal Inniskilling Fusiliers
HAMILTON William G. MM+Bar Sjt 205688 5th Yorkshire Light Infantry
HAMILTON William Geddes MM L/Cpl 514089 1/14th London Regt
HAMLETT Albert MM Pte 11798 7th Shropshire Light Infantry
HAMLETT Fred MM Pte 39504 2nd South Wales Borderers
HAMLETT John Edward MM+Bar L/Cpl 26155 13th & 10th Cheshire Regt
HAMLETT Walter J. MM Spr 495276 50 Div Sig Coy Royal Engineers
HAMLIN Frank MM Pte 66607 101 Fd Amb RAMC
HAMLIN W. MM Bdr 110161 RFA
HAMM Alfred MM Gnr 28404 112 Heavy Bty RGA
HAMMACOTT Wilfred MM+Bar Pte 29681 Wiltshire Regt
HAMMER Leonard S. MM L/Cpl 66426 100 Fd Amb RAMC
HAMMERSLEY William MM L/Cpl 13243 Leicestershire Regt
HAMMERTON Fred MM Pte 12154 2nd Hampshire Regt
HAMMERTON Herbert MM CSM 9815 2nd Royal West Surrey Regt
HAMMERTON James MM BSM 5581 39 Div Ammn Col RFA
HAMMERTON Percy W. MM Pte 203903 4th York & Lancaster Regt
HAMMETT Albert T. MM S/Sjt Farrier 70925 136 Hy Bty RGA
HAMMETT Harold J. MM L/Cpl 9683 1st Middlesex Regt
HAMMETT Henry Alexander MM Dvr 107401 70 Bde RFA
HAMMETT Walter MM Sjt 11101 26 Fd Coy Royal Engineers
HAMMETT William MM Gnr 3291 RFA
HAMMOND A. MM Cpl 12884 12th Royal Fusiliers
HAMMOND Albert E. MM Pte 27248 9th East Surrey Regt
HAMMOND Ambrose MM L/Cpl 24406 37th Bn Machine Gun Corps
HAMMOND Arthur G. MM Pte 54122 20th Manchester Regt
HAMMOND Aubrey F. MM Sjt 14696 12th Gloucestershire Regt
HAMMOND Cecil A. MM Spr 23743 Royal Engineers
HAMMOND Charles MM Sjt G/3258 6th East Kent Regt KIA 5.4.18.
HAMMOND David MM+Bar Cpl 3335 Yorkshire Regt
HAMMOND E. MM Sjt 1272 RFA
HAMMOND Edward C. MM Dvr 1402 Royal Engineers
HAMMOND Ernest MM Sjt 39376 Royal Berkshire Regt
HAMMOND Frederick Rupert MM Sjt 86759 Signal Service Royal Engineers
HAMMOND Frederick William MM Pte 2239 7th Royal West Kent Regt
HAMMOND G. MM Sjt P/713 Military Mounted Police
HAMMOND George MM Sjt 9338 12th East Surrey Regt KIA 4.9.18.
HAMMOND George C. MM Sjt G/2219 8th Royal Sussex Regt
HAMMOND George Donaldson MM Bdr 7356 376 Bty 169 Bde RFA
HAMMOND Harry MM Pte 13052 7th East Kent Regt
HAMMOND Harry MM Sjt 16650 Royal Engineers
HAMMOND Henry S. MM Cpl 41413 Royal Engineers
HAMMOND Hubert MM Sjt 905143 B/82 Bde RFA
HAMMOND Hugh MM Gnr 625461 HAC(Artillery)
HAMMOND Irvin P. MM Pte 34779 10th East Yorkshire Regt
HAMMOND James MM Cpl 143064 'H' Special Coy Royal Engineers KIA 21.3.18.
HAMMOND James MM Cpl 619 1st Arg & Suth Highlanders
HAMMOND James Alfred MM Sjt L/10143 1st Royal West Surrey Regt KIA 24.8.16.
HAMMOND James H. "DCM,MM" Sjt 44237 74 Fd Coy Royal Engineers
HAMMOND John MM Pte 15554 9th West Yorkshire Regt
HAMMOND John J. MM L/Cpl 92366 7 Pontoon Park Royal Engineers
HAMMOND John W.G. MM CSM 5656 1st Royal Berkshire Regt
HAMMOND Joseph MM Pte 39820 3rd Worcestershire Regt KIA 10.4.18.
HAMMOND Joseph Laurence MM Pte 204295 1/6th Durham Light Infantry DOW 17.1.19.
HAMMOND Josiah MM+Bar Pte 1392 1st Welsh Guards KIA 6.11.18.
HAMMOND Kenneth MM Cpl 32950 7th Norfolk Regt
HAMMOND Leonard R. MM Pte 17754 2nd Coldstream Guards
HAMMOND Oswald MM+Bar L/Sjt 13646 8th Norfolk Regt
HAMMOND Richard G. MM Pte 59579 Northumberland Fusiliers
HAMMOND Richard J. MM Pte G/33093 Middlesex Regt
HAMMOND S. MM Cpl 25493 2nd Welsh Regt

HAMMOND Sidney MM Cpl 266832 Royal Warwickshire Regt
HAMMOND Stephen MM L/Sjt 325545 9th Durham Light Infantry
HAMMOND Sydney A. MM Sjt 300556 1/5th London Regt
HAMMOND Thomas S. "MM+Bar,MSM" CSM 18067 13th Durham Light Infantry
HAMMOND Tom William MM Cpl 58655 95 Fd Coy Royal Engineers KIA 22.12.16.
HAMMOND Walter MM Pte 27962 16th Lancashire Fusiliers DOW 1.3.18.
HAMMOND Walter MM Pte 14237 East Surrey Regt
HAMMOND Walter MM Pte 18312 7th Leicestershire Regt KIA 14.7.16.
HAMMOND Walter G. MM Sjt PS/8808 24th Royal Fusiliers
HAMMOND Walter Sidney MM L/Cpl 7493 5th Royal Berkshire Regt KIA 27.4.17.
HAMMOND William MM Cpl C/8064 18th King's Royal Rifle Corps KIA 7.6.17.
HAMMOND William MM+Bar CSM 30400 2nd Manchester Regt
HAMMOND William H. MM Cpl 15673 7th Northamptonshire Regt
HAMMOND William J. MM Pte 60723 Royal Fusiliers
HAMMOND William Thomas MM Pte M2/203719 406 MT Coy Army Service Corps
HAMP Alfred Clifford MM Cpl R/13197 9th King's Royal Rifle Corps KIA 24.8.16.
HAMP Wilfrid Ernest "DCM,MM" CSM 240440 1/5th Lincolnshire Regt KIA 26.6.17.
HAMPER Arthur William MM Sjt 95304 A/62 Bde RFA
HAMPER Thomas MM Cpl 374084 RGA
HAMPS Joseph F. MM Sjt 325758 11th Suffolk Regt
HAMPSHIRE Wilfred MM Dvr 74042 26 Bde RFA
HAMPSHIRE William MM L/Cpl 24169 9th Notts & Derby Regt
HAMPSON Albert MM L/Cpl 36931 Machine Gun Corps
HAMPSON Arthur MM Sjt 1696 12th Middlesex Regt
HAMPSON Arthur MM Pte 3999 13th Middlesex Regt
HAMPSON Edward MM Pte 14428 13th Liverpool Regt
HAMPSON Frederick T. MM Sjt 158073 257 Tunnelling Coy Royal Engineers
HAMPSON George MM Pte 260120 10th South Wales Borderers
HAMPSON George "MM,CG(F)" L/Cpl 15205 1/5th King's Own Scottish Borderers
HAMPSON Harry MM Cpl 201554 4th Yorkshire Light Infantry
HAMPSON Harry "MM,MID" Sjt 13379 55 Fd Coy Royal Engineers
HAMPSON Henry MM Pte 20305 13th Liverpool Regt
HAMPSON John MM Sjt 710402 211 Bde RFA
HAMPSON Joseph Bell MM Pte 30127 11th Border Regt DOW 28.11.17.
HAMPSON Ronald MM Pte 201995 1/4th South Lancashire Regt
HAMPSON William MM Sjt 14296 12th West Yorkshire Regt
HAMPSON William R. MM L/Cpl 20701 18 Fd Amb RAMC
HAMPSON Wright MM Pte 41405 Lancashire Fusiliers
HAMPTON Arthur MM Pte 60567 1st Cheshire Regt
HAMPTON Charles MM L/Cpl 3185 Durham Light Infantry
HAMPTON Colin McK. MM Sjt 2338 MGC(Motors)
HAMPTON E. MM Sjt Farrier 31310 RFA
HAMPTON Edward E. MM Pte G/8388 2nd Royal Fusiliers
HAMPTON Ernest MM Sjt 280350 1/7th Lancashire Fusiliers
HAMPTON Henry A. "DCM,MM,MID" Sjt 24115 2nd South Wales Borderers
HAMPTON James MM 2nd Cpl 81385 Royal Engineers
HAMPTON James Oswald MM L/Cpl 19793 16th Royal Scots KIA 9.4.17.
HAMPTON Kenneth V. MM Pte 60519 9th Royal Welsh Fusiliers
HAMPTON Richard Quale MM Cpl 28226 Hampshire Regt
HAMPTON Robert MM L/Cpl 142341 18th Bn Machine Gun Corps
HAMPTON Walter J. MM L/Cpl 20060 1/4th Wiltshire Regt
HAMPTON William J. MM Pte 202769 4th Hampshire Regt
HAMS C. MM L/Cpl 15508 3rd Grenadier Guards
HAMSHAW Alfred John MM L/Cpl 230072 1/2nd London Regt
HAMSHAW Henry William MM Sjt 9764 4th Worcestershire Regt KIA 22.10.16.
HAMSHAW John MM Sjt 15807 West Riding Regt
HAMSHERE John MM Pte 16011 1st Coldstream Guards
HAMSHERE John Henry MM Cpl 21680 Royal Engineers
HAMSTEAD James H. MM Pte A/205504 13th King's Royal Rifle Corps
HAMSTEAD William MM Bdr 59805 20 Bty 9 Bde RFA
HANAFIN Jeremiah MM Pte 9/446 9th Royal Munster Fusiliers
HANAWAY John MM Spr 30449 Royal Engineers
HANBURY B. MM+Bar L/Cpl 700433 London Regt
HANBURY Evan Hugh MM L/Cpl M2/153348 Army Service Corps

HANBURY John Humphrey "DCM,MM,CG(B)" L/Cpl PS/2620 16th Middlesex Regt
HANBY George MM Dvr L/12180 C/161 Bde RFA
HANBY Joseph MM Cpl 51726 11th Royal Scots KIA 5.8.18.
HANBY William Alphonsus MM Cpl 48560 'Z' Special Coy Royal Engineers DOW 6.4.17.
HANCE Charles MM Dvr 47326 RFA
HANCE Ernest Richard MM L/Cpl 45490 2 Coy Machine Gun Corps
HANCE William H. MM Sjt 8445 1st Shropshire Light Infantry
HANCHARD Albert H. MM Bdr 29668 RFA
HANCOCK A. MM Pte 43268 Middlesex Regt
HANCOCK Albert MM 2nd Cpl 16175 57 Fd Coy Royal Engineers
HANCOCK Albert MM Pte 375353 Manchester Regt
HANCOCK Andrew MM Sjt 14127 9th York & Lancaster Regt
HANCOCK Arthur MM Cpl 9869 Royal Berkshire Regt
HANCOCK Charles E. MM Pte 200821 Norfolk Regt
HANCOCK Charles Robert MM Sjt 1559 4th(London)Fd Amb RAMC DOW 8.4.18.
HANCOCK Christopher Henry MM Cpl G/69778 1/22nd London Regt KIA 11.1.18.
HANCOCK Claude MM L/Cpl 240289 1/6th Notts & Derby Regt
HANCOCK Daniel MM Pte 4599 Seaforth Highlanders
HANCOCK David MM+Bar Pte 33658 South Wales Borderers
HANCOCK Frank MM Pte 28992 2nd Leicestershire Regt
HANCOCK Gilbert MM Cpl 10414 1st King's Royal Rifle Corps
HANCOCK Herbert MM Pte 251446 Manchester Regt
HANCOCK Herbert R. MM Gnr 9745 35 Bde RFA
HANCOCK Jack A. MM Sjt 71702 4th Royal Fusiliers
HANCOCK John MM Spr 89743 135 Army Tps Coy Royal Engineers
HANCOCK John MM Sjt 9323 1st Duke of Cornwall's LI
HANCOCK John MM Dvr 29953 18 Div Ammn Col RFA
HANCOCK Jonas MM Pte 285264 1/1st Oxfordshire Yeomanry
HANCOCK Joseph MM L/Cpl S/2035 13th Rifle Brigade
HANCOCK Joseph MM L/Cpl 56484 RAMC
HANCOCK Joseph MM Bdr 35800 RGA
HANCOCK Reginald MM Sjt 85798 6th Durham Light Infantry
HANCOCK Sidney F. MM Pte 15347 1st Gloucestershire Regt
HANCOCK Walter Henry MM Pte 204618 11th Notts & Derby Regt KIA 5.10.18.
HANCOCK Wilfred Gordon MM Sjt 10694 5th Oxf & Bucks Light Infantry
HANCOCK William "MM,MID" BSM 47198 20 Bty 9 Bde RFA
HANCOCK William J. MM Pte 9337 Coldstream Guards
HANCOCKS Albert L. MM L/Cpl 19116 10th Royal Warwickshire Regt
HANCOCKS Harold MM Cpl 14067 7th Oxf & Bucks Light Infantry
HANCOCKS Herbert F. MM Cpl 1342 1/7th Northumberland Fusiliers
HANCOCKS P.W. "MM,MID" L/Sjt 2682 Royal Warwickshire Regt
HANCOX Thomas MM Gnr 142072 RGA
HAND Arthur E. MM CQMS 9529 1st North Staffordshire Regt
HAND Bernard MM Pte M2/073450 Army Service Corps
HAND Ernest G. MM Pte 2118 1/1st Lincolnshire Yeomanry
HAND Frederick C. MM Cpl 65791 RFA
HAND George MM Sjt 238128 2nd Lincolnshire Regt
HAND George W. MM Gnr 45623 114 Bty 25 Bde RFA
HAND Harry Howard MM Pte 510237 2/2nd(London)Fd Amb RAMC
HAND John MM Gnr 44948 13 Bde RFA
HAND John MM Sjt 241353 1/5th South Lancashire Regt KIA 1.12.17.
HAND Joseph J. MM Pte 40223 North Staffordshire Regt
HAND Percy MM Sjt 17335 Machine Gun Corps
HAND Walter MM Pte 27038 1st Royal Warwickshire Regt KIA 3.5.17.
HAND William G. MM Sjt 9722 1st Dorsetshire Regt
HAND William G. MM Pte 74050 Devonshire Regt
HANDEL Albert E. MM L/Sjt 12704 2nd Royal Warwickshire Regt
HANDFORD Albert MM Pte 28885 1st East Lancashire Regt
HANDFORD D.T. MM Pte S/3074 12th Rifle Brigade
HANDFORD Samuel MM Pte 2078 1/5th Notts & Derby Regt KIA 13.3.17.
HANDFORTH James "MM,MSM" Cpl 76697 2nd Bn Tank Corps
HANDLEY Arthur MM Sjt 204675 1st Shropshire Light Infantry
HANDLEY Cecil MM L/Cpl 44895 Royal Engineers
HANDLEY Charles E. MM Cpl M2/054996 'C' Siege Park Army Service Corps
HANDLEY Ernest MM Pte 73027 Notts & Derby Regt
HANDLEY Fred Coulam MM Sjt 22619 1/5th Notts & Derby Regt Died 16.10.18.
HANDLEY Frederick J. MM Cpl 77076 RGA
HANDLEY Harry S. MM Pte 15184 Northumberland Fusiliers
HANDLEY Jack MM Pte S/21054 1/6th Royal Highlanders
HANDLEY James MM Cpl 18994 1st King's Own Scottish Borderers
HANDLEY James H. MM Pte 377466 10th Manchester Regt
HANDLEY John Gregory MM Pte 29771 13th Yorkshire Regt
HANDLEY Walter A. MM Pte 698088 22nd London Regt
HANDLEY William A. MM Gnr 293695 248 Siege Bty RGA
HANDOVER Bernard MM Bdr 293266 140 Heavy Bty RGA
HANDS Albert Gadsall MM Pte 30266 Dorsetshire Regt
HANDS Charles H. MM Sjt 26087 4th Worcestershire Regt
HANDS Ernest L. MM L/Cpl 5115 11th Royal Warwickshire Regt
HANDS Ernest MM Pte 3438 1/8th London Regt
HANDS Frank B. MM Pte 65201 RAMC
HANDS J. MM Cpl 12184 1st Worcestershire Regt
HANDS John B. MM Bdr 835358 RFA
HANDS Robert MM Sjt 11804 RFA
HANDS Thomas Philip MM Sjt 2789 1/6th Royal Warwickshire Regt KIA 1.7.16.
HANDS Thomas William MM Pte 33769 5th Royal Berkshire Regt KIA 22.9.18.
HANDS Wilfred C. "DCM,MM" Cpl 2349 1/18th London Regt
HANDS William Henry MM Sjt 14542 11th West Yorkshire Regt DOW 12.5.17.
HANDS William T. MM Gnr 836555 RFA
HANDSCOMB Walter MM Pte 201290 1/4th Suffolk Regt
HANDSLEY Will MM+Bar Sjt 6125 6th Lincolnshire Regt
HANDY Albert C. MM L/Cpl 27586 Suffolk Regt
HANDY Alexander Kingstone MM Cpl L/3293 151 Bde RFA
HANDY Edward William MM L/Cpl 52737 13th Royal Fusiliers KIA 4.9.18.
HANDY Walter James MM Cpl 17120 6th Somerset Light Infantry
HANDYSIDE William MM Spr 24598 Royal Engineers
HANES Charles W. "DCM,MM" CSM 4803 12th Manchester Regt
HANES Herbert Frank MM Pte 22373 4th Grenadier Guards
HANEY James MM Pte 46155 3rd Worcestershire Regt DOW 27.9.18.
HANFORD Arthur MM Pte 9392 8th King's Royal Rifle Corps KIA 19.8.17.
HANFORD Thomas MM Pte 13791 1st South Wales Borderers KIA 8.9.16.
HANHAM Frederick MM Pte 10768 5th Dorsetshire Regt
HANKEY Herbert Edward MM Sjt 677035 B/275 Bde RFA KIA 18.4.18.
HANKEY William MM Pte 2661 12th Liverpool Regt KIA 20.11.17.
HANKIN Courtney MM Pte M2/119799 Army Service Corps att 15 Fd Amb RAMC
HANKIN Richard MM Pte 266156 Liverpool Regt
HANKIN Septimus E. MM Cpl 202190 18th Liverpool Regt
HANKIN William George MM Pte 19023 Machine Gun Corps
HANKINS Arthur C. MM Pte R/33394 King's Royal Rifle Corps
HANKINS Edward Augustus MM CQMS 6527 Scots Guards
HANKINS Ernest C. MM CSM 373431 17th London Regt
HANKINS George E. MM Sjt 4425 Royal Warwickshire Regt
HANKINS Herbert MM Sjt 95566 C/74 Bty RFA KIA 2.3.17.
HANKINS Joseph MM Bdr 891216 B/270 Bde RFA
HANKINS William J. MM Pte 26166 Shropshire Light Infantry
HANKINSON Gilbert MM 2nd Cpl 46186 80 Fd Coy Royal Engineers
HANKINSON James MM Sjt 685246 RFA
HANKINSON Philip MM Cpl Wheeler 680735 RFA
HANKINSON William MM Pte 17431 2nd Grenadier Guards
HANKS George W. MM Pte L/10686 2nd Middlesex Regt
HANKS John C.E. MM Pte S/13779 Rifle Brigade
HANKS Joseph L. "MM,MSM,MID" Sjt 43810 17 Div Sig Coy Royal Engineers
HANKS Reginald William MM Pte 439517 3rd(South Midland)Fd Amb RAMC
HANLEY Harry MM Pte 20300 13th Liverpool Regt
HANLEY Matthew MM Pte 3244 1/8th Durham Light Infantry
HANLEY Patrick MM Pte 97867 Machine Gun Corps
HANLEY Peter MM+Bar L/Cpl 12968 2nd Royal Dublin Fusiliers
HANLEY Vincent MM Dvr 676201 RFA
HANLIN Thomas MM Cpl 267242 7th Royal Warwickshire Regt
HANLON Andrew MM Spr 156500 250 Tunnelling Coy Royal Engineers
HANLON Edward MM Pte 201226 5/6th Scottish Rifles
HANLON Hardy MM Pte 26625 7th East Kent Regt
HANLON John MM Pte 251478 Royal Scots
HANLON John MM Pte 14244 8th Yorkshire Regt

HANLON Joseph MM+Bar Pte 1688 12th Lancers
HANLON P. MM Sjt 130319 46th Royal Fusiliers
HANLON Patrick MM Pte 27757 Royal Dublin Fusiliers
HANLON Peter "MM,CG(F)" Sjt 7475 2nd Leinster Regt
HANLON Peter MM Cpl 13011 94 Siege Bty RGA
HANLON T. MM Cpl 10868 RFA
HANLON Thomas MM Pnr 143037 Royal Engineers
HANLON William MM Cpl 98018 109 Heavy Bty RGA
HANLON William MM Pte 6632 2nd Irish Guards
HANLON William MM Pte 4222 Leinster Regt
HANMER Edward Henry John "MC,MM(56279 Cpl)" T/Lt 2 Div Sig Coy Royal Engineers
HANN A.J. MM Pte 206153 6th East Kent Regt
HANN Ernest E. MM Sjt G/2121 8th Royal Sussex Regt
HANN Frederick MM Cpl 61909 Z/12 Med TM Bty RGA
HANN Jonathan MM Pte 19/623 Northumberland Fusiliers
HANN Michael MM Pte 2686 1/9th Durham Light Infantry KIA 21.7.18.
HANN Thomas MM Gnr 34120 RFA
HANN Thomas O. MM Cpl 15 1/6th Durham Light Infantry
HANN William Hart MM Sjt 454021 556 Army Troops Coy Royal Engineers
HANNA Charles H. MM L/Cpl 530712 1/15th London Regt
HANNA Francis MM Pte 24558 6th Royal Inniskilling Fusiliers DOW 3.10.18.
HANNA Frederick George MM Pte S/11570 6th Cameron Highlanders KIA 31.7.17.
HANNA George William MM Sjt 4764 2nd West Riding Regt
HANNA John MM Pte 278865 1/7th Arg & Suth Highlanders KIA 17.4.17.
HANNA John "MM,MSM,MID" CSM 7746 2nd Royal Inniskilling Fusiliers
HANNA Joseph MM Gnr 681010 C/78 Bde RFA
HANNA Robert C. MM BSM 34337 B/183 Bde RFA
HANNA William MM Pte 200880 1/4th Royal Lancaster Regt
HANNA William J. MM Pte 2387 1/7th Liverpool Regt
HANNAFORD John Parker MM Pte 15493 2nd Devonshire Regt KIA 16.9.16.
HANNAFORD Richard.William MM Gnr 1832 138 Heavy Bty RGA
HANNAFORD William H. "DCM,MM" Sjt PW/3263 19th Middlesex Regt
HANNAH Alexander MM Sjt 43009 6th King's Own Scottish Borderers DOW 19.12.17.
HANNAH Andrew MM L/Cpl 3490 6 Coy Labour Corps
HANNAH Charles MM Cpl 200932 2nd Royal Scots Fusiliers KIA 13.10.18.
HANNAH Duncan MM Spr 75537 Royal Engineers
HANNAH James MM L/Cpl 20/485 20th Durham Light Infantry KIA 25.3.18.
HANNAH John MM Cpl 307125 7th Royal Warwickshire Regt
HANNAH John MM L/Cpl 11924 38th Bn Machine Gun Corps
HANNAH Richard MM Cpl 42514 Machine Gun Corps
HANNAH Richard MM L/Cpl 76186 Notts & Derby Regt
HANNAH Samuel MM Pte 7874 1st Cameron Highlanders
HANNAH Samuel MM Pte 10196 RAMC
HANNAH Thomas MM L/Cpl 41865 Royal Engineers
HANNAH Walter B. "DCM,MM" L/Sjt 240443 1/6th Liverpool Regt
HANNAM George MM Pte 28447 15/17th West Yorkshire Regt
HANNAM Walter MM Sjt 205860 10th Royal West Surrey Regt
HANNAN Henry MM Pte 203564 2nd Yorkshire Light Infantry
HANNANT Ernest Francis MM Pte 9263 10th Royal West Kent Regt
HANNAS John MM Cpl A/1349 King's Royal Rifle Corps
HANNAT Sidney MM L/Cpl 19215 Suffolk Regt
HANNAWIN Hugh MM Sjt 10147 5th Connaught Rangers
HANNEN Robert MM Dmr 1486 1/6th Royal Highlanders
HANNEY Michael MM Pte 39161 Lancashire Fusiliers
HANNIGAN James MM L/Cpl 25766 Liverpool Regt
HANNIGAN James H. MM Gnr 78228 RFA
HANNIGAN Peter "DCM,MM" CSM 290048 1/8th Scottish Rifles
HANNIGAN Richard Robert MM Cpl 34671 43 Fd Amb RAMC
HANNIGHAN Frank MM Cpl 36386 51st Bn Machine Gun Corps
HANNINGTON William MM Gnr 119639 260 Siege Bty RGA
HANNIS George Henry MM Sjt 9444 6th Oxf & Bucks Light Infantry
HANNIS J. MM Pte 24710 Royal West Kent Regt
HANNON Henry MM L/Cpl 23889 9 Fd Coy Royal Engineers
HANNON Jeremiah MM Sjt 27411 37 Siege Bty RGA
HANNON John MM L/Cpl 5004 1st Irish Guards
HANNON John MM Pte 10421 1st Royal Munster Fusiliers KIA 22.3.18.
HANNON John MM Pte 32505 York & Lancaster Regt
HANNON Luke Patrick MM Pte 10449 2nd Irish Guards
HANNON Patrick MM Pte 7850 Royal Munster Fusiliers
HANNS James MM Pte 8452 1/4th Royal Scots Fusiliers
HANRAHAN Joseph MM Pte 5/6608 2nd Royal Munster Fusiliers
HANRAHAN Michael MM Sjt 7575 1st Royal Irish Regt
HANRATTY William "MM,MID" Pte 14013 7th King's Own Scottish Borderers
HANSCOMBE Bert MM Sjt 828 7th East Surrey Regt
HANSELL Fred M. MM+Bar Cpl 1766 Durham Light Infantry
HANSELL Isaac Henry MM Sjt S/4096 13th Rifle Brigade KIA 10.7.16.
HANSELL Louis John MM Cpl 67308 3 Bde RHA
HANSEN James Edgar MM Gnr 36136 14 Siege Bty RGA KIA 23.5.17.
HANSER Ernest G. MM+Bar Cpl 3217 16th Lancers
HANSFORD Albert S. MM+Bar Pte 266544 1/1st Hertfordshire Regt
HANSFORD Edwin George MM Spr 546857 516 Fd Coy Royal Engineers
HANSFORD George H. MM Cpl 16519 10th West Riding Regt
HANSFORD Percy Edgar MM Bdr 340105 RGA
HANSFORD William H. MM L/Cpl 84388 Royal Engineers
HANSLIP Nelson S. MM+Bar Cpl 290553 1/7th Gordon Highlanders
HANSON Albert MM Sjt 76162 10th Bn Tank Corps
HANSON Arthur Cornelius MM Sjt 69572 91 Fd Coy Royal Engineers
HANSON Arthur D. MM Pte 356660 Hampshire Regt
HANSON Ernest MM Cpl 63531 13th Yorkshire Regt
HANSON Frederick MM Pte 14321 6th East Yorkshire Regt
HANSON Frederick W. MM L/Cpl 4970 10th Royal Warwickshire Regt
HANSON George MM Spr 66452 Royal Engineers
HANSON George H. MM Pte 242240 1/5th Lincolnshire Regt
HANSON Harry MM L/Cpl 201148 West Riding Regt
HANSON Harry E. MM Pte 37094 Gloucestershire Regt
HANSON James Henry MM Cpl 14/14853 Royal Irish Rifles
HANSON James Wood MM Pte 20790 8th East Lancashire Regt KIA 31.5.17.
HANSON John MM CSM 12149 7th East Yorkshire Regt
HANSON Joseph E. MM Pte 36346 11th East Lancashire Regt
HANSON Leonard MM Gnr 93692 RGA
HANSON Norman MM Sjt 18/1170 12th West Yorkshire Regt DOW 12.10.18.
HANSON Robert MM Pte 202059 6th West Yorkshire Regt
HANSON Thomas MM Pte 203730 9th West Riding Regt
HANSON Thomas Reginald MM L/Cpl 14/380 14th Royal Warwickshire Regt KIA 23.7.16.
HANSON William MM L/Cpl S/6080 1st Royal Highlanders
HANSON William MM L/Cpl 41618 1st Essex Regt
HANSON William MM Pte B/1510 Rifle Brigade
HANSON William MM Sjt 36349 10th East Yorkshire Regt
HANSTOCK James MM Sjt T4/250911 62 Div Train Army Service Corps
HANT Cyril MM Pte 2384 10th West Yorkshire Regt KIA 25.8.18.
HANWELL Herman MM L/Cpl C/12805 King's Royal Rifle Corps
HAPPELL James MM L/Sjt 17758 12th Highland Light Infantry KIA 13.8.16.
HARAM Albert E. MM CQMS 19/432 19th Northumberland Fusiliers
HARAN John MM Cpl 12/608 12th East Yorkshire Regt
HARBERT Robert T.M. MM Pte 201370 1/4th Royal Scots
HARBINSON James "DCM,MM,CG(B)" Sjt 19551 12th Royal Irish Rifles
HARBINSON Robert MM Pte 19117 Royal Inniskilling Fusiliers
HARBIRD Frederick John "MM,MdH(F)" Bdsm 7681 1st York & Lancaster Regt
HARBOD Bert W. MM L/Cpl 1583 1/4th Oxf & Bucks Light Infantry
HARBORNE Alfred MM Pte 200922 Royal Warwickshire Regt
HARBORNE George MM+Bar Pte 13523 9th Royal Inniskilling Fusiliers KIA 21.3.18.
HARBOTTLE Moses MM Pte 9428 21 Fd Amb RAMC
HARBOUR James B. MM Cpl 93151 2nd Durham Light Infantry
HARBOUR Joseph MM+Bar Pte 96410 1/5th Liverpool Regt
HARBOUR Stanley A. MM Pte 55939 Labour Corps
HARBOURNE Arthur MM Pte M2/201055 Army Service Corps
HARBRIDGE Edward J. MM Cpl 260006 5th Royal Lancaster Regt
HARBRIDGE Ernest MM Pte 204366 East Surrey Regt
HARBRON Albert MM 2nd Cpl 50260 87 Fd Coy Royal Engineers
HARBRON George Henry MM L/Cpl 240268 Lincolnshire Regt
HARBY John MM Pte 21508 2nd Notts & Derby Regt
HARCOMBE Albert John MM Pte 242103 1/5th South Lancashire Regt

HARCOMBE J.D. MM Sjt 11919 6th Somerset Light Infantry
HARCOURT Ebenezer James MM Pte 22079 Yorkshire Light Infantry
HARCOURT James MM L/Sjt 14002 1st Grenadier Guards
HARCUS Alexander MM Gnr 630252 A/255 Bde RFA
HARD Bertie C. MM L/Cpl 18268 Machine Gun Corps
HARD George Gilbert MM Sjt 260819 340 Rd Constr Coy Royal Engineers
HARD Solomon H. MM Pte 240203 West Yorkshire Regt
HARDACRE Albert MM Pte 24913 134 Fd Amb RAMC
HARDACRE George MM Pte 19528 Coldstream Guards
HARDACRE L. MM Cpl 59566 RGA
HARDACRE Leonard MM Sjt 781651 C/246 Bde RFA KIA 29.5.18.
HARDACRE William MM Pte 243561 4/5th North Lancashire Regt
HARDAGE Herbert Charles "MM,MID" Sjt 61393 2 Bde RFA
HARDAKER Charles MM L/Cpl 38671 10th South Wales Borderers
HARDCASTLE Bertram F. MM Sjt 250973 3rd London Regt Att KAR.
HARDCASTLE Clifford MM+Bar Pte 267320 7th West Riding Regt
HARDCASTLE Frederick MM Pte 32417 2/4th West Riding Regt
HARDCASTLE George Edwin MM L/Cpl 15158 Yorkshire Regt
HARDCASTLE Harry MM L/Cpl 97874 Notts & Derby Regt
HARDCASTLE Stanley MM Gnr 710356 RFA
HARDCASTLE Thomas MM Cpl 14/519 9th York & Lancaster Regt
HARDCASTLE Thomas Edward MM Sjt 2147 1/5th Yorkshire Regt
HARDCASTLE Thomas W. MM Pte 2211 1/5th Northumberland Fusiliers
HARDCASTLE W.C. "MM,CG" L/Cpl 18303 13th Essex Regt
HARDCASTLE William MM Cpl 1422 Army Cyclist Corps
HARDEN James MM Sjt 610286 1/19th London Regt DOW 12.12.17.
HARDICK William J. MM+Bar Sjt 57665 RFA
HARDICRE Frederick MM Pte 3786 11th Manchester Regt
HARDIE Ernest C. MM Pte 18101 1/5th Border Regt
HARDIE Frederick MM Pte 7697 East Kent Regt
HARDIE James MM Sjt M2/021867 44 Mot Amb Convoy Army Service Corps
HARDIE James MM Spr 249116 350 Elec & Mech Coy Royal Engineers
HARDIE James MM Pte 1626 1/9th Highland Light Infantry
HARDIE James MM+Bar Pte 265453 1/6th Seaforth Highlanders
HARDIE James Leslie MM Pte 315627 13th Royal Highlanders
HARDIE John MM Sjt 10048 1st Gordon Highlanders
HARDIE John Alexander MM Pte 202599 1/4th Seaforth Highlanders DOW 3.9.17.
HARDIE Richard MM Pte S/24127 7th Seaforth Highlanders
HARDIE Rodney James MM Pte 10916 2nd East Lancashire Regt
HARDIE Thomas MM Pte 15559 Scots Guards
HARDIE Walter R. MM Cpl 303422 1/8th Arg & Suth Highlanders
HARDIKER James MM Pte B/203281 13th Rifle Brigade
HARDIMAN E.G. MM+Bar Pte 15610 7th Royal West Surrey Regt.
HARDIMAN Robert G. "MM,MID" L/Sjt 4177 Machine Gun Corps
HARDIMAN William MM Sjt 52605 135 Hy Bty RGA
HARDIMAN William G. MM Pte 292642 1/7th Middlesex Regt
HARDING A. MM L/Cpl G/40039 11th Royal West Surrey Regt
HARDING Albert MM Pte 67860 7th Royal Fusiliers
HARDING Albert Arthur MM Pte 7146 1st Lincolnshire Regt
HARDING Alfred MM Sjt 9434 2nd East Surrey Regt
HARDING Alfred J. MM Sjt 10077 1st East Surrey Regt
HARDING Allan N. MM Pte 56575 16th King's Royal Rifle Corps
HARDING Arthur MM Pte 19319 5th Dorsetshire Regt
HARDING Aubrey J. MM L/Cpl 65937 Royal Engineers
HARDING Charles C. MM Spr 492420 Royal Engineers
HARDING Charles R. MM Dvr 4882 RFA
HARDING Clanmorris W. MM Pte 62352 Royal Fusiliers
HARDING Claude MM Sjt 265395 1/6th West Riding Regt KIA 12.4.18.
HARDING Clifford V. MM Pte 76013 Tank Corps
HARDING Edgar "MM+Bar,CG(F)" Gnr 9775 B/73 Bde RFA
HARDING Edward MM L/Bdr 107877 RFA
HARDING Edward MM Spr 155132 Royal Engineers
HARDING Francis G. MM Pte 18836 2nd Bedfordshire Regt
HARDING Frank "MC,MM(8809 Sjt R Lanc Regt),CG(F)" T/2Lt 11th East Lancashire Regt
HARDING Frank MM Spr 218488 260 Railway Coy Royal Engineers
HARDING Frank MM Pte 76227 1/4th London Regt KIA 2.11.18.
HARDING Frank R. MM SSM H/71109 North Irish Horse
HARDING Frederick MM Sjt 24301 277 Bde RFA
HARDING Frederick E. MM Pte 6338 15th Hampshire Regt
HARDING Frederick H. MM Pte 275016 3rd London Regt
HARDING Frederick J. MM Pte 14464 13th Royal Welsh Fusiliers
HARDING G. MM Pte 592505 London Regt
HARDING George MM Cpl M/205238 GHQ Reserve MT Coy Army Service Corps
HARDING George MM Bdr 806667 B/250 Bde RFA
HARDING George MM L/Cpl 38827 14th Durham Light Infantry KIA 4.10.17.
HARDING George A. MM Pte 9873 2nd Bedfordshire Regt
HARDING Harold MM Pte 5/4864 18th King's Royal Rifle Corps KIA 13.6.17.
HARDING Horace Gwynn MM Dvr 810760 A/232 Bde RFA DOW 15.9.17.
HARDING Horatio Henry MM Cpl 98123 Royal Engineers
HARDING Hubert J. MM Pte 39891 RAMC
HARDING J. MM Sjt 5225 4th Dragoon Guards att MMP.
HARDING James A. MM Spr 63043 38 Div Sig Coy Royal Engineers
HARDING John MM Cpl 19888 11th Northumberland Fusiliers
HARDING John MM Sjt 23/312 23rd Northumberland Fusiliers
HARDING John MM Pte 40195 Welsh Regt
HARDING John MM Pte 14196 10th Notts & Derby Regt
HARDING John Harold MM+Bar L/Cpl G/981 1st Royal West Surrey Regt KIA 24.4.17.
HARDING Maurice MM L/Cpl 7651 1st Royal Berkshire Regt
HARDING N.B. MM Gnr 30998 RFA
HARDING Percy MM L/Cpl 504158 500 Fd Coy Royal Engineers
HARDING Percy Charles MM Gnr 925061 280 Bde RFA
HARDING R. MM Pte 23647 Royal Welsh Fusiliers
HARDING Richard MM Pte 33662 23rd Middlesex Regt
HARDING Robert E. MM Pte 7585 Royal Fusiliers
HARDING Samuel Collis MM L/Sjt 2653 1/4th Leicestershire Regt KIA 22.8.17.
HARDING Samuel Ernest MM Pte DM2/228357 Army Service Corps att RAMC
HARDING Samuel J. MM L/Sjt 3182 9th Royal Sussex Regt
HARDING Sydney L. MM Sjt 1368 1/1st North Somerset Yeomanry
HARDING Thomas MM Sjt 95225 3rd London Regt
HARDING Thomas MM+Bar Sjt 470043 528 Fd Coy Royal Engineers
HARDING Thomas A. MM L/Bdr 44102 RGA
HARDING Thomas D. MM Spr 558485 58 Div Sig Coy Royal Engineers
HARDING Thomas H. MM Bdr 57830 RFA
HARDING V. MM Pte 265803 Liverpool Regt
HARDING Victor E. MM L/Cpl 28872 1/5th Royal Warwickshire Regt
HARDING Wilfred J. MM 2nd Cpl 25739 Royal Engineers
HARDING William MM Cpl 675618 B/285 Bde RFA KIA 9.4.18.
HARDING William MM Pte 12093 19th Manchester Regt
HARDING William George MM Pte 21915 14th Gloucestershire Regt
HARDING William Oliver MM Gnr 98013 B/48 Bde RFA
HARDINGE William MM Dvr 36827 RFA
HARDINGHAM Albert Ernest MM L/Cpl 41274 2nd Essex Regt
HARDISTY Edgar MM RQMS 417 1/4th Yorkshire Regt
HARDISTY George MM 2nd Cpl 86492 Royal Engineers
HARDISTY Henry MM CSM 129908 45th Royal Fusiliers
HARDISTY James MM Sjt 14787 13th Yorkshire Regt KIA 29.4.18.
HARDISTY Joshua MM Cpl 16258 11th Border Regt KIA 18.11.16.
HARDISTY Percy MM Cpl 134 1st Seaforth Highlanders
HARDMAN Arthur MM Bdr 25035 RFA
HARDMAN Arthur MM CQMS 240796 2/6th Lancashire Fusiliers
HARDMAN Arthur R. MM L/Cpl 67593 15th Cheshire Regt
HARDMAN Benjamin Packer MM Sjt L/22567 166 Bde RFA
HARDMAN George MM Pte 241722 East Lancashire Regt
HARDMAN George E. MM Pte 46382 1st South Wales Borderers
HARDMAN Harold MM Gnr 706147 C/250 Bde RFA
HARDMAN Harold MM Pte 34679 1st East Surrey Regt KIA 20.10.18.
HARDMAN John MM Gnr 78185 D/71 Bde RFA
HARDMAN Joseph MM L/Bdr 112831 49 Bty 40 Bde RFA
HARDMAN Joseph MM Cpl 28904 Highland Light Infantry
HARDMAN Richard MM Pte 12895 7th Royal Lancaster Regt
HARDMAN Richard MM Pte 17618 9th North Lancashire Regt
HARDMAN Robert "DCM+Bar,MM" CSM 41172 9th Northumberland Fusiliers
HARDMAN Stanley MM Bdr 292262 RGA
HARDMAN Thomas P. MM Cpl 9262 2nd Royal Scots Fusiliers DOW 4.5.16.
HARDMAN William H. MM Pte 12369 Lancashire Fusiliers
HARDS William MM Pte 33312 1/5th Royal Warwickshire Regt

HARDSTAFF Thomas MM Cpl 122526 Machine Gun Corps
HARDWELL Reginald G. MM Gnr 239595 D/290 Bde RFA
HARDWICK Albert C. MM Pte 612695 19th London Regt
HARDWICK Charles B. MM Sjt 14022 35 Bde RFA
HARDWICK George MM Pte 29520 6th Liverpool Regt
HARDWICK Harry MM+Bar L/Cpl 16089 Coldstream Guards
HARDWICK James Walter MM Sjt 775247 150 Bde Ammn Col RFA
HARDWICK Joe MM Sjt 18534 6th York & Lancaster Regt DOW 27.4.18.
HARDWICK O. MM Spr 71618 Royal Engineers
HARDWICK Reginald J. MM Pte 32245 Lancashire Fusiliers
HARDWICK Reginald L.A. MM Sjt 1663 Royal Warwickshire Regt
HARDWICK Thomas MM Sjt 203423 1/5th South Staffordshire Regt KIA 10.8.18.
HARDWICK Walter H. MM L/Cpl 76389 128 Coy Labour Corps
HARDWICK William Joseph MM Pte 58093 Cheshire Regt
HARDWIDGE Charles H. MM Pte 81825 32nd Bn Machine Gun Corps
HARDY Albert E. MM Sjt 43789 Royal Engineers
HARDY Albert John MM Bdr 86688 Y/29 Med TM Bty RFA
HARDY Albert N. MM Pte M2/034460 Army Service Corps
HARDY Amyas L. MM Pte SS/954 3 Cav Div Supply Column Army Service Corps
HARDY Arthur MM Cpl 30943 East Yorkshire Regt
HARDY Arthur MM Cpl 2430 1/5th Notts & Derby Regt
HARDY Arthur MM+Bar Sjt 47292 504 Bty 65 Bde RFA KIA 5.12.17.
HARDY Arthur J. MM Cpl 387 RGA
HARDY Charles MM Sjt 203406 5th Notts & Derby Regt
HARDY Charles MM Sjt 5938 7th Suffolk Regt
HARDY Charles H. MM Pnr 129860 Royal Engineers
HARDY David MM Pte 63690 1/6th West Yorkshire Regt DOW 3.11.18.
HARDY David MM Pte 77800 15th Durham Light Infantry
HARDY Edward "DCM,MM" Sjt 8414 6th Bn Machine Gun Corps
HARDY Edward MM L/Bdr 45393 HQ/102 Bde RFA
HARDY Edwin "MM,MSM,MID." Sjt 17379 6 Fd Amb RAMC
HARDY Ernest MM Cpl 130512 359 Siege Bty RGA
HARDY Ernest A. MM Pte 13513 Army Cyclist Corps
HARDY Francis MM Pte 5698 2nd Royal Dublin Fusiliers
HARDY Fred MM Cpl 241306 1/5th North Lancashire Regt DOW 13.9.18.
HARDY Frederick MM L/Cpl 2273 1/4th Suffolk Regt
HARDY Frederick Henry MM Spr 77850 'BL' Cable Section Royal Engineers
HARDY George MM Sjt 457166 446 Fd Coy Royal Engineers
HARDY George MM L/Cpl 23224 North Staffordshire Regt
HARDY George MM Pte 40016 1st Northumberland Fusiliers DOW 21.9.18.
HARDY George MM Pte 25755 Hampshire Regt
HARDY George MM Pte 1421 1/5th Notts & Derby Regt
HARDY Harry MM Spr 40919 69 Fd Coy Royal Engineers
HARDY Herbert MM Gnr 42632 9 Bde RFA
HARDY Herbert E. MM Sjt 52295 RAMC
HARDY Horace MM Pte 51202 Machine Gun Corps(Cavalry)
HARDY J. MM Pte 200412 Northumberland Fusiliers
HARDY Jack MM+Bar Sjt 18618 Devonshire Regt
HARDY James MM L/Cpl 325498 1/9th Durham Light Infantry
HARDY John MM Dvr 71781 RFA
HARDY John MM Pte 17/300 Royal Irish Rifles
HARDY John MM Pte 70414 Machine Gun Corps
HARDY John C. MM L/Cpl M2/104030 Army Service Corps
HARDY John Thomas MM Pte 20/139 20th Durham Light Infantry KIA 1.10.16.
HARDY Joseph MM Pte 16634 9th Scottish Rifles
HARDY L.J.A. MM Pte 38765 17th London Regt
HARDY Reuben MM L/Bdr 58928 C/123 Bde RFA
HARDY Richard MM L/Sjt 22716 13th Royal Welsh Fusiliers
HARDY Richard S. "DCM,MM+Bar" Cpl 14284 1st Dorsetshire Regt
HARDY Thomas MM Pte 27558 15th Royal Warwickshire Regt
HARDY Thomas MM Pte 1274 2nd Lincolnshire Regt DOW 17.4.18.
HARDY W. MM Pte 417491 1st(North Midland)Fd Amb RAMC
HARDY W. "MM,MID" Sjt 8243 1st Essex Regt
HARDY W. MM Pte 40058 Manchester Regt
HARDY Walter MM Bdr 127368 156 Siege Bty RGA
HARDY Walter MM Cpl 41462 2nd Manchester Regt
HARDY Walter Charles MM Pte 28465 6th East Yorkshire Regt
HARDY Walter P. MM L/Cpl 68631 115 Coy Labour Corps
HARDY Watts Chadderton MM Pte 29827 2nd Manchester Regt
HARDY William MM Cpl 610901 2/19th London Regt
HARDY William MM Gnr 11174 B/152 Bde RFA
HARDY William H. MM Cpl 9949 Labour Corps
HARDY William J. MM Sjt 209 1/2nd London Regt
HARE Alfred E. MM Pte 43344 Manchester Regt
HARE Arthur MM Sjt 22745 23rd Manchester Regt KIA 23.7.16.
HARE Clement J. MM Pte 13042 2nd Bedfordshire Regt
HARE Frederick J. MM Sjt 28513 4th South Staffordshire Regt
HARE Harry J. MM CSM 44341 9th Essex Regt
HARE Herbert Arthur MM Pte 30203 6/7th Royal Scots Fusiliers
HARE Richard R. MM CSM 11518 1st Liverpool Regt
HARE V. MM Sjt 770 Military Mounted Police
HARE Walter MM Pte 18716 1st Bedfordshire Regt
HARE William G. MM Sjt 101020 188 Siege Bty RGA
HARE William Harold MM Cpl 45901 20th Durham Light Infantry
HARES Thomas MM Pte 1452 19th Welsh Regt
HARESNAPE William Townley MM Pte 31708 8th Devonshire Regt DOW 1.11.18.
HARFIELD James MM 2nd Cpl 65363 106 Fd Coy Royal Engineers
HARFIELD John MM Pte 33955 Royal Warwickshire Regt
HARFORD John A. MM Pte G40067 Royal West Surrey Regt
HARFORD Walter J. "MM,MID" CoH 2502 2nd Life Guards
HARGOOD Arthur MM Pte 72411 103 Fd Amb RAMC
HARGRAVES Thornton MM Sjt 24103 7th West Riding Regt
HARGREAVES Albert MM Pte 28686 1/4th Royal Lancaster Regt
HARGREAVES D.E. MM Pte 241376 East Lancashire Regt
HARGREAVES Ernest MM L/Cpl 17650 Royal Scots
HARGREAVES Frank MM Pte 20008 34 Coy Labour Corps
HARGREAVES George E. MM Pte 266715 Liverpool Regt
HARGREAVES George E. MM 2nd Cpl 312741 Royal Engineers
HARGREAVES J. MM L/Cpl 46063 Royal Engineers
HARGREAVES Jack MM Pte 243893 1/5th North Lancashire Regt KIA 1.10.18.
HARGREAVES James MM Pte 5652 1st East Lancashire Regt
HARGREAVES James Ernest MM Pte 67025 96 Fd Amb RAMC
HARGREAVES James H. MM L/Cpl 305316 1/8th Lancashire Fusiliers
HARGREAVES Joe MM Gnr 72683 RFA
HARGREAVES John MM Dvr 57053 D/112 Bde RFA
HARGREAVES John A. MM Pte 40686 1/1st Hertfordshire Regt
HARGREAVES John Charles MM Pte 3/940 2nd Yorkshire Light Infantry KIA 18.11.16.
HARGREAVES John W. MM Pte 240642 Royal Lancaster Regt
HARGREAVES Joseph MM Pte 11714 Coldstream Guards
HARGREAVES Joshua MM Cpl Fitter 776145 245 Bde RFA
HARGREAVES Robert MM+Bar Bdr 705470 RFA
HARGREAVES Samuel "DCM,MM,MID" L/Cpl 13384 7th & 7/8th King's Own Scottish Borderers
HARGREAVES Sydney MM Pte 3053 2/5th Lancashire Fusiliers
HARGREAVES T. MM Cpl 145513 1/1st Northamptonshire Yeomanry
HARGREAVES Thomas "MM,MID" Cpl 2079 1/5th East Lancashire Regt
HARGREAVES W. MM Air Mech 1 40277 Royal Flying Corps
HARGREAVES Walter "MM,MSM" Sjt 240053 1/5th East Lancashire Regt
HARGREAVES William MM Bdr 75137 RFA
HARGREAVES William A. MM Pte 282470 Lancashire Fusiliers
HARKER Albert MM Sjt 760747 RFA
HARKER Charles MM Pte 1424 17th West Yorkshire Regt
HARKER Frederick T. MM Pte M2/050841 Army Service Corps
HARKER George MM Gnr 65993 RGA
HARKER George MM Pte 3/9298 Durham Light Infantry
HARKER Harry MM Pte 99256 6th Durham Light Infantry
HARKER James MM+Bar Spr 40492 Royal Engineers
HARKER Richard MM Cpl 240261 1/5th Border Regt
HARKER Simon John MM Pte 33195 15th Royal Warwickshire Regt
HARKER William E. MM Spr 74995 21 Div Sig Coy Royal Engineers
HARKER William H. MM Sjt 755356 B/251 Bde RFA
HARKER William Mitchell MM Sjt 703669 23rd London Regt
HARKES George MM Cpl 54670 251 Siege Bty RGA KIA 14.4.18.
HARKIN James MM L/Cpl 200989 1/4th East Lancashire Regt
HARKINS James John MM L/Cpl 291173 11th Northumberland Fusiliers KIA 15.6.18.
HARKNESS David MM Dvr 111235 C/223 Bde RFA
HARKNESS George MM Sjt 715221 210 Bde RFA
HARKNESS George K. MM Sjt 512270 RAMC
HARKNESS Robert "MM,MSM" Sjt 13626 9th Royal Inniskilling Fusiliers
HARKNESS Thomas M. MM Cpl 40510 9th Scottish Rifles
HARLAND Thomas MM Pte 306188 2/8th West Yorkshire Regt
HARLAND Tom MM Cpl 13275 6th Yorkshire Regt

HARLAND William MM L/Cpl 38490 9th Yorkshire Regt
HARLE G.D. MM Cpl S/11192 Rifle Brigade
HARLE Norman MM Pte 202590 Gordon Highlanders
HARLE Sidney James MM Pte 202531 1st Dorsetshire Regt
HARLE Thomas MM Pte 17032 13th Durham Light Infantry
HARLE Thomas William MM Dvr 1229 RFA
HARLEY Alexander MM Pte 40191 1st Royal Highlanders DOW 20.9.18.
HARLEY Andrew MM Pte 23131 14th London Regt
HARLEY Arthur Percy Cutts MM L/Cpl 128964 4 Special Coy Royal Engineers DOW 27.4.18.
HARLEY Charles "MM,MM(F)" Pte 14567 8th Royal Scots Fusiliers
HARLEY Ernest A. MM Sjt 27741 23rd Bn Machine Gun Corps
HARLEY Ernest F.B. MM Pte C/862 King's Royal Rifle Corps
HARLEY George A. MM 2nd Cpl 95852 89 Fd Coy Royal Engineers
HARLEY John A. MM BSM 348073 RGA
HARLEY Reuben MM Sjt 20457 1 Siege Bty RGA
HARLEY Richard MM Cpl 14433 11th Suffolk Regt KIA 9.4.17.
HARLEY Sidney MM Bdr 77083 RGA
HARLEY William MM Cpl Z/779 1st Rifle Brigade KIA 23.10.16.
HARLING Arthur MM Sjt 200123 2/5th Lancashire Fusiliers DOW 21.9.18.
HARLING Bertram MM Pte 15465 9th Yorkshire Regt
HARLING Charles H. MM Sjt 13613 1/7th Worcestershire Regt
HARLING Ernest MM Bdr W/2068 RFA
HARLING John Thomas MM Pte 6750 16th Manchester Regt KIA 1.7.16.
HARLING Walter William MM Pte 4830 16 Fd Amb RAMC
HARLOCK Thomas MM Pte 20054 6th Northamptonshire Regt
HARLOW Eric H. MM L/Cpl 17388 10th Notts & Derby Regt
HARLOW Joseph MM Sjt 1525 MGC (Motors)
HARLOWE John MM Sjt 14819 2nd Royal Fusiliers
HARMAN Albert Edward MM Dvr 651935 A/330 Bde RFA
HARMAN Arthur W. MM Spr 20010 11 Fd Coy Royal Engineers
HARMAN Charles MM Cpl 77248 RHA
HARMAN Charles MM Sjt 200263 1/4th Royal Berkshire Regt
HARMAN Edward MM Pte 402 7th Royal Sussex Regt
HARMAN Edward E. MM Cpl 77995 97 Bty 147 Bde RFA
HARMAN Frederick MM Pte 1346 1/17th London Regt
HARMAN George MM Pte G/13047 7th East Kent Regt
HARMAN George William MM L/Sjt 7855 East Kent Regt
HARMAN John G. MM Pte 39569 4th Gloucestershire Regt
HARMAN John W. MM Pte 12803 7th Norfolk Regt
HARMAN Leonard W. MM Pte 8989 1st Royal Berkshire Regt
HARMAN Richard Charles MM+Bar Sjt 8713 2nd Lincolnshire Regt
HARMAN Walter C. MM Pte 17835 11th Somerset Light Infantry
HARMAN William E. MM Bdr 32019 14 Bde RFA
HARMAN William F. MM Cpl 199027 Tunnelling Coy Royal Engineers
HARMER Albert MM+Bar Sjt 48474 88 Bty 14 Bde RFA KIA 26.3.18.
HARMER Cecil Claude MM Cpl 89111 C/66 Bde RFA
HARMER Charles MM Pte 122385 6th Bn Machine Gun Corps
HARMER Daniel MM Pte 31615 44 Fd Amb RAMC
HARMER Edward Gordon MM Sjt 1408 1/22nd London Regt KIA 7.6.17.
HARMER Francis Guy MM Sjt 2435 1/24th London Regt
HARMER Frank O. MM L/Cpl 242547 1st Lancashire Fusiliers
HARMER John W. MM Pte 10696 10th Royal West Surrey Regt
HARMER John W. MM Pte 32552 15th Lancashire Fusiliers
HARMER John William MM Bdr 374056 69 Siege Bty RGA
HARMER Thomas MM L/Cpl 17257 Machine Gun Corps
HARMER W.J. MM Cpl 43003 Essex Regt
HARMER Walter J. MM Cpl 11751 6th Duke of Cornwall's LI
HARMES Harry MM Cpl 5720 Royal West Surrey Regt
HARMON James MM Pte 2341 16th Middlesex Regt DOW 29.4.17.
HARMSWORTH John James MM Cpl L/6506 1st Royal West Surrey Regt KIA 15.7.16.
HARMSWORTH William Frederick MM Sjt 95205 D/62 Bde RFA
HARN Herbert MM+Bar Sjt 18225 4th Liverpool Regt
HARN R. MM Pte 7874 11th Royal Fusiliers
HARNESS John MM+Bar Pte 17379 Durham Light Infantry
HARNETT Leo MM Pte 12067 1st Devonshire Regt
HARNEY John F. MM+Bar Sjt 29825 1st North Lancashire Regt
HARNEY Thomas Joseph MM Pte 20086 1st West Yorkshire Regt KIA 25.9.16.
HAROLD Alexander MM Dvr 53976 3 Pontoon Park Royal Engineers
HAROLD Patrick MM Sjt T/25127 Army Service Corps Died 3.11.18.
HARPER Albert MM Cpl 108509 Royal Engineers
HARPER Albert E. MM L/Sjt 21568 23rd Middlesex Regt
HARPER Albert G. MM L/Cpl 4518 Royal Warwickshire Regt
HARPER Albert H. MM Cpl 112264 Royal Engineers
HARPER Archie MM Pte 15469 9th Gloucestershire Regt
HARPER Bert MM Pte 10250 1st Shropshire Light Infantry
HARPER C.H. MM L/Bdr Sig 21273 49 Siege Bty RGA
HARPER Charles MM Pte 49449 Liverpool Regt
HARPER David MM Pte 265101 1/6th Gordon Highlanders
HARPER Dennis John MM Gnr 177804 C/317 Bde RFA
HARPER E. MM Cpl 5303 Royal Flying Corps
HARPER Edward C. MM Sjt 519739 18th London Regt
HARPER Edwin Frederick MM Cpl 51069 Machine Gun Corps(Cavalry)
HARPER Eric MM Pte 241567 6th North Staffordshire Regt
HARPER Ernest MM Sjt 31406 8th Devonshire Regt
HARPER Ernest MM Pte 40045 7th Leicestershire Regt KIA 10.10.17.
HARPER F.A. MM Pte 9434 1st Essex Regt
HARPER F.J. MM L/Cpl 235872 1/1st Herefordshire Regt
HARPER F.R. MM Pte 26403 2nd Bedfordshire Regt
HARPER Frank MM L/Sjt 45949 Durham Light Infantry
HARPER Frederick MM Spr 44778 93 Fd Coy Royal Engineers
HARPER Frederick MM Pte 29660 21st Manchester Regt
HARPER George Henry James MM Sjt 35807 RGA
HARPER Harold MM Pte 13319 2nd Worcestershire Regt
HARPER Harry MM BSM 47244 D/77 Bde RFA
HARPER Henry G. MM Pte 48675 5th Royal Berkshire Regt
HARPER J.L. MM L/Cpl P/255 Military Mounted Police
HARPER James E. MM Sjt 307340 Tank Corps
HARPER James Henry MM L/Cpl 26968 10th Duke of Cornwall's LI KIA 25.3.18.
HARPER John MM Pte 20878 12th Royal Scots
HARPER John MM+Bar L/Cpl 2329 1/5th Durham Light Infantry
HARPER John MM Sjt 14388 8th Royal Scots Fusiliers
HARPER John MM+Bar Sjt L/16131 C/165 Bde RFA
HARPER John T. MM Pnr 98665 Royal Engineers
HARPER Joseph A. MM Pte 84307 37th Bn Machine Gun Corps
HARPER Joseph R. MM Pte 100982 37 Fd Amb RAMC
HARPER Matthew Thomas MM Sjt 16575 13th Royal Irish Rifles KIA 23.11.17.
HARPER Philip MM Dvr 39994 RFA
HARPER Robert MM L/Cpl 2957 Seaforth Highlanders
HARPER Robert MM L/Cpl 35509 Northumberland Fusiliers
HARPER Samuel Henry MM Sjt 45835 56th Bn Machine Gun Corps
HARPER Samuel J. MM Sjt 14340 9th Devonshire Regt
HARPER Stephen "MM,MID" Pte 805 Royal Warwickshire Regt
HARPER Thomas MM Sjt 9929 2nd North Staffordshire Regt
HARPER Thomas MM Bdr 39025 6 Bty 40 Bde RFA KIA 9.10.17.
HARPER Thomas MM Pte 15480 7/8th King's Own Scottish Borderers
HARPER Thomas MM Pte 29777 14th Worcestershire Regt
HARPER Thomas R. MM Bdr 840700 RFA
HARPER William MM Pte 25972 10th West Riding Regt
HARPER William MM Spr 84683 Royal Engineers
HARPER William Henry MM Sjt 235448 1/1st Herefordshire Regt
HARPER William J. MM Pte 16460 9th Gloucestershire Regt
HARPER William J. MM L/Sjt 470685 12th London Regt
HARPER William Thomas MM Gnr L/13631 RFA
HARPER William Thomas MM Sjt 1967 1/3rd London Regt KIA 11.4.17.
HARPER Willis H. MM Cpl 265873 7th Middlesex Regt
HARPER Wilson MM Sjt 13260 9th West Riding Regt
HARPHAM Harold F. MM Sjt 202126 Notts & Derby Regt
HARPHAM John MM Pte 14267 Yorkshire Light Infantry
HARPHAM Marcus MM Bdr 83341 RFA
HARPIN Sam William Capel MM Sjt 105001 230 Army Troops Coy Royal Engineers
HARPLE Frank MM Pte 1935 9 Fd Amb RAMC
HARRADINE Joseph C. MM Pte 45772 RAMC
HARRADINE William MM Pte 26188 2nd Welsh Regt
HARRAWAY Albert Edward MM Gnr 31597 RFA
HARRELL George MM Pte 9597 2nd Royal Fusiliers
HARRIES David MM Spr 49843 Royal Engineers
HARRIES John MM+Bar Sjt 275952 RGA
HARRIES William A. MM+Bar Pte 1972 1st Welsh Guards
HARRIGAN James MM Pte 8104 1st East Kent Regt
HARRILD Horton John MM Pte 6/9793 Rifle Brigade
HARRIMAN Arthur MM Spr 89824 78 Fd Coy Royal Engineers KIA 16.10.17.
HARRIMAN Harold MM Pte 10116 9th Royal Fusiliers DOW 14.8.16.

HARRINGTON A.W. MM+Bar Sjt 8523 1st Essex Regt
HARRINGTON Albert J. MM Cpl 9748 2nd Worcestershire Regt
HARRINGTON Charles MM Pte 17175 1st Suffolk Regt
HARRINGTON Clifford MM L/Cpl 12/943 4th York & Lancaster Regt
HARRINGTON Cornelius MM Gnr 29494 RFA
HARRINGTON Frank MM+Bar Sjt 13168 2nd Middlesex Regt
HARRINGTON Frederick J. MM Bdr 38691 RFA
HARRINGTON George William MM Sjt 95512 15th Bn Tank Corps
HARRINGTON Herbert J. MM CoH 1643 Household Bn
HARRINGTON Hugh V. MM Pte 692 Royal Fusiliers
HARRINGTON James Aloysius MM Spr 27168 33 Div Sig Coy Royal Engineers
HARRINGTON Jeremiah MM Pte 7715 2nd Durham Light Infantry
HARRINGTON John George MM Gnr 65343 RFA
HARRINGTON Michael MM Pte 19062 Royal Dublin Fusiliers
HARRINGTON Richard MM Pte 594343 18th London Regt
HARRINGTON Sydney MM L/Cpl 718311 23rd London Regt
HARRINGTON Thomas MM Pte 21398 22nd Manchester Regt
HARRINGTON Timothy W. MM Pte 721164 24th London Regt att MGC.
HARRINGTON William MM Bdr 54305 RGA
HARRINGTON William MM Pte 10447 6th Royal West Kent Regt
HARRINGTON William Maurice "MC,MM(13121 L/Sjt)" 2Lt 18th King's Royal Rifle Corps
HARRIS A.J. MM Sjt L/9771 1st East Kent Regt
HARRIS A.J. MM Pte 43195 Essex Regt
HARRIS Albert MM Cpl 8093 1st Devonshire Regt DOW 28.9.16.
HARRIS Albert C. MM Cpl 13393 7th Wiltshire Regt
HARRIS Albert C. MM Sjt 18975 10th Worcestershire Regt
HARRIS Albert E. "MM,MSM" WO2(Sub-Conductor) 01929 Army Ordnance Corps
HARRIS Albert F. MM Cpl 23688 3rd Royal Fusiliers
HARRIS Albert Thomas MM Sjt G/6011 13th Royal Fusiliers KIA 4.10.17.
HARRIS Alexander MM Cpl 350392 1/7th Royal Highlanders
HARRIS Alfred MM Cpl P/228 Rifle Brigade
HARRIS Alfred MM Pte 4762 Notts & Derby Regt
HARRIS Alfred E. MM Cpl 45559 5th Lancashire Fusiliers
HARRIS Alfred Edward MM Sjt 624210 HAC(Artillery) att A/2 Bde RHA
HARRIS Alfred H. MM Pte 8598 74 Fd Amb RAMC
HARRIS Alfred John MM Sjt 200465 Tank Corps
HARRIS Allan MM Cpl 306567 Royal Warwickshire Regt
HARRIS Arthur MM Bdr 27804 RFA
HARRIS Arthur MM Pte 14021 7/8th King's Own Scottish Borderers
HARRIS Arthur MM Gnr 159770 250 Bde RFA
HARRIS Arthur MM Cpl 650 2nd Royal Highlanders
HARRIS Arthur MM Sjt 26470 RGA
HARRIS Arthur C.M. MM Pte 9486 1st Devonshire Regt
HARRIS Arthur George MM L/Sjt 4445 3rd Coldstream Guards
HARRIS Arthur H. MM Sjt S/18410 13th Rifle Brigade
HARRIS Arthur J. MM Pte S/390 8th Royal Sussex Regt
HARRIS Arthur Robert MM Pte 3527 1/7th Royal Warwickshire Regt
HARRIS Arthur Victor MM Pte C/1401 16th King's Royal Rifle Corps KIA 2.12.17.
HARRIS Arthur W. MM Cpl 186951 RGA
HARRIS Benjamin MM Pte 18759 Grenadier Guards
HARRIS Bert MM Pte 23441 11th Worcestershire Regt
HARRIS Brindley MM Pte 26204 5th West Riding Regt
HARRIS Charles MM Pte 36645 9th Northumberland Fusiliers KIA 31.10.18.
HARRIS Charles MM Cpl 305749 1/7th West Riding Regt Died 22.11.18.
HARRIS Charles MM Pte 24205 33rd Bn Machine Gun Corps
HARRIS Charles MM Sjt 29734 RGA
HARRIS Charles "MM,MID" Cpl 10337 1st Royal West Kent Regt
HARRIS Charles MM Spr 40209 14 Div Sig Coy Royal Engineers
HARRIS Charles MM+Bar Sjt 300391 13th Bn Tank Corps
HARRIS Charles Frederick MM Sjt 1139 1/5th Gloucestershire Regt KIA 16.8.16.
HARRIS Charles J. MM Sjt 191649 RGA
HARRIS D. MM Sjt 1098 Royal Lancaster Regt
HARRIS D. MM Cpl 253428 London Regt
HARRIS D.S. MM Pte 7301 RAMC
HARRIS David MM Pte 18839 1st Grenadier Guards
HARRIS David MM Pte 320185 1/6th London Regt
HARRIS David A. MM Pte 305162 1/3rd(Highland)Fd Amb RAMC
HARRIS David P. MM Pte 275227 3rd London Regt
HARRIS David William MM Spr 51184 Royal Engineers
HARRIS E.C. MM Pte 39386 8th Royal Berkshire Regt
HARRIS Edward MM Cpl 966 Army Cyclist Corps
HARRIS Edward H. MM Dvr 165230 C/50 Bde RFA
HARRIS Edwin J. MM Pte 220481 2nd Royal Berkshire Regt
HARRIS Emris MM Pte 22333 11th Royal Lancaster Regt KIA 28.3.18.
HARRIS Ernest MM Sjt 27018 15th Hampshire Regt
HARRIS Ernest MM Pte 8428 95 Coy Machine Gun Corps KIA 3.10.17.
HARRIS Ernest MM Pte 26632 7th East Kent Regt
HARRIS Ernest MM Sjt 83372 Machine Gun Corps
HARRIS Ernest "DCM,MM,MID" Sjt 7601 1st & 2nd Royal Berkshire Regt KIA 3.8.16.
HARRIS Ernest B. MM L/Cpl 94256 30th Bn Machine Gun Corps
HARRIS Ernest R. MM Cpl 11102 Machine Gun Corps
HARRIS F. MM Sjt 457004 RAMC
HARRIS F. MM Pte 15573 South Staffordshire Regt
HARRIS Francis Hugh "MM+Bar,MID" Cpl 14752 D/71 Bde RFA
HARRIS Frank MM L/Cpl 27525 10th Essex Regt KIA 8.8.18.
HARRIS Frank MM Pte 26895 7th Shropshire Light Infantry
HARRIS Frank MM Bdr 34960 'C' Bty RHA
HARRIS Frank MM Pnr 40072 Royal Engineers
HARRIS Frank MM Gnr 109887 RGA
HARRIS Frederick MM Pte 37194 7th Norfolk Regt
HARRIS Frederick MM Pte 11799 10th West Riding Regt KIA 27.10.18.
HARRIS Frederick Edward MM Sjt 27710 4th Bn Machine Gun Corps DOW 10.6.18.
HARRIS Frederick G. MM Pte 66323 RAMC
HARRIS Frederick J. MM Cpl 10033 Middlesex Regt
HARRIS Frederick Leslie MM Gnr 188488 B/157 Bde RFA
HARRIS Frederick W.T. MM Sjt 101552 Royal Engineers
HARRIS G.R. MM Pte 200257 South Staffordshire Regt
HARRIS George MM Spr 91130 25 Div Sig Coy Royal Engineers
HARRIS George MM Pte 34679 7th Wiltshire Regt DOW 21.10.18.
HARRIS George MM Pte 18478 1st King's Own Scottish Borderers
HARRIS George MM L/Sjt 201552 1/4th Oxf & Bucks Light Infantry
HARRIS George MM Gnr 161979 RFA
HARRIS George MM+Bar Pte 11246 2nd Royal Scots
HARRIS George MM Sjt 19/1833 24th Northumberland Fusiliers
HARRIS George MM Pte 34773 8th South Wales Borderers
HARRIS George MM Cpl T4/243733 Army Service Corps
HARRIS George MM Dvr 930179 A/281 Bde RFA
HARRIS George B. MM Pte 405309 RAMC
HARRIS George E. MM Pte 5824 6th Royal West Kent Regt
HARRIS George Edward "MM,CG(B)" Pte 71959 Machine Gun Corps
HARRIS George F. MM Pte 38161 RAMC
HARRIS George Henry MM Pte 30173 1st Liverpool Regt KIA 29.9.18.
HARRIS George Hugh MM Sjt L/6327 RFA
HARRIS George W. "MM,MIDx2" Pte 13598 Northumberland Fusiliers
HARRIS George W. MM+Bar Sjt 33549 RFA
HARRIS Graham Crosskey MM Cpl 320024 16th Royal Sussex Regt
HARRIS Harold MM Cpl 11604 16th Lancashire Fusiliers DOW 3.4.18.
HARRIS Harold MM Dvr 13281 RFA
HARRIS Harold A. MM Pte 129879 19th Bn Machine Gun Corps
HARRIS Harry MM Pte 41573 6th North Staffordshire Regt
HARRIS Harry MM Pte 6992 1st East Surrey Regt
HARRIS Harry Frank Beaconsfield MM CQMS 43219 15th Royal Irish Rifles
HARRIS Heber Clarke MM Sjt Mech 307171 3 Tank Supply Coy Tank Corps
HARRIS Henry MM Pte 252219 1st Essex Regt
HARRIS Henry MM Sjt 12/24439 1st South Wales Borderers DOW 21.6.18.
HARRIS Henry MM Sjt 226176 332 Rd Constr Coy Royal Engineers
HARRIS Henry MM Pte C/4378 King's Royal Rifle Corps
HARRIS Henry J. MM Sjt 29673 RFA
HARRIS Henry P. MM Cpl 29437 31 Heavy Bty RGA
HARRIS Herbert A. MM Sjt 200631 1/4th Oxf & Bucks Light Infantry
HARRIS Herbert E. MM Sjt 348316 138 Siege Bty RGA
HARRIS Herbert George MM Sjt 472284 2/12th London Regt KIA 24.4.18.
HARRIS Herbert J. MM Sjt 61051 RAMC
HARRIS Herbert S. MM Pte 348012 8th Manchester Regt
HARRIS Hubert C. MM L/Cpl 200519 1/4th Oxf & Bucks Light Infantry

HARRIS Hugh "MM,MIDx2" CSM 11572 9th Royal Inniskilling Fusiliers
HARRIS Jack MM Pte 13083 6th Dorsetshire Regt
HARRIS James MM Pte 202870 6th King's Own Scottish Borderers
HARRIS James MM L/Cpl 492 1st Welsh Guards
HARRIS James MM Sjt 2176 1/5th Royal Highlanders DOW 9.1.17.
HARRIS James MM+Bar L/Cpl 29590 Middlesex Regt
HARRIS James MM Pte 8/43117 8th South Staffordshire Regt
HARRIS James MM Pte 20/1068 20th Durham Light Infantry
HARRIS James MM Pte 352053 7th London Regt KIA 14.4.18.
HARRIS James B. MM Pte 202452 15th Suffolk Regt
HARRIS James E. MM Sjt 9509 Gloucestershire Regt
HARRIS James H. MM Gnr 30021 RFA
HARRIS James J. MM L/Cpl 8092 1st Royal West Kent Regt
HARRIS James Richard MM Gnr L/21309 RFA
HARRIS James T. MM Pnr 52614 Royal Engineers
HARRIS John MM Pte 10719 10th Gloucestershire Regt KIA 7.8.16.
HARRIS John MM+Bar Sjt 16037 1st Royal Berkshire Regt att MGC
HARRIS John MM Sjt 58307 25th King's Royal Rifle Corps
HARRIS John MM Dvr 154501 RFA
HARRIS John A. MM L/Cpl 1513 2nd Royal Warwickshire Regt
HARRIS John B. MM Cpl 14053 2nd Scots Guards
HARRIS John Burns MM Spr 146030 228 Fd Coy Royal Engineers
HARRIS John Edwin MM L/Cpl 9873 1st Shropshire Light Infantry KIA 7.7.17.
HARRIS John F. MM Pte 325229 1/1st Cambridgeshire Regt
HARRIS John F. MM Cpl 77902 RGA
HARRIS John H. MM Pte 2945 Army Cyclist Corps
HARRIS Joseph MM Sjt 4/7086 2nd Bedfordshire Regt
HARRIS Joseph MM L/Cpl 200017 5th Lincolnshire Regt
HARRIS Joseph MM Sjt 9462 11th Worcestershire Regt
HARRIS Leonard MM Cpl 510321 Royal Engineers
HARRIS Lewin MM L/Cpl 381933 25th Liverpool Regt
HARRIS Lewis MM Pte S/7392 Rifle Brigade
HARRIS Maurice MM Pte 31241 RAMC
HARRIS Norman Bradford MM Sjt 1594 18th Royal Fusiliers
HARRIS Oswald MM Pte 42563 2nd Worcestershire Regt
HARRIS P.G. MM Pte 495483 RAMC
HARRIS Percival F. MM Bde 49292 RFA
HARRIS Percy MM Gnr 950666 B/251 Bde RFA
HARRIS Percy MM Sjt 9430 8th Devonshire Regt DOW 17.11.17.
HARRIS R.S. MM Sjt 7/11735 7th Lincolnshire Regt
HARRIS Reginald A. MM Pte 11334 1/4th Royal Welsh Fusiliers
HARRIS Richard MM Gnr 1345 RGA
HARRIS S. MM L/Cpl 613597 19th London Regt
HARRIS Samuel MM Sjt 45422 87 Fd Coy Royal Engineers
HARRIS Sidney MM Gnr 109762 B/10 Bde RFA DOW 25.3.18.
HARRIS Sidney J. MM L/Cpl 235456 1/1st Gloucestershire Yeomanry
HARRIS Stanley G. MM Pte 34076 1st Middlesex Regt
HARRIS Sydney MM Spr 56531 Royal Engineers
HARRIS Sydney C.G. MM Pnr 282391 34 Div Sig Coy Royal Engineers
HARRIS Sydney James MM+Bar Pte 25466 2nd Bedfordshire Regt DOW 28.10.18.
HARRIS Thomas "MM,MdH(F)" Pte 18985 2nd Cheshire Regt
HARRIS Thomas MM L/Sjt 830 9th East Surrey Regt KIA 17.4.17.
HARRIS Thomas MM L/Sjt 6135 1st Irish Guards
HARRIS Thomas MM Pte 66541 RAMC
HARRIS Thomas MM Cpl 29642 Machine Gun Corps
HARRIS Thomas James "VC,MM" Sjt 358 6th Royal West Kent Regt
HARRIS Thomas P. MM L/Cpl 18829 Royal West Kent Regt
HARRIS Thomas W.A. MM L/Cpl 44016 4th Royal Berkshire Regt
HARRIS W.O. MM+Bar Cpl 3245 East Kent Regt
HARRIS Walter MM Sjt 48951 25 Siege Bty RGA
HARRIS Walter MM L/Sjt 200428 1/4th Lincolnshire Regt
HARRIS Walter S. MM Pte 240648 5th Duke of Cornwall's LI
HARRIS William MM Pte 88017 RAMC
HARRIS William MM Gnr 105527 RFA
HARRIS William MM Cpl 2/9125 2nd South Wales Borderers KIA 1.7.16.
HARRIS William MM L/Cpl 265591 1/7th Royal Warwickshire Regt
HARRIS William MM Cpl 202196 1/5th Yorkshire Light Infantry DOW 27.8.18.
HARRIS William MM L/Cpl P6361 Military Mounted Police
HARRIS William MM Cpl 565092 16th London Regt
HARRIS William "DCM,MM" Sjt 70331 98 Coy Machine Gun Corps
HARRIS William MM+Bar L/Sjt 5667 1st Leicestershire Regt
HARRIS William MM Cpl 200071 1/4th Gloucestershire Regt
HARRIS William MM Pte 48222 130 Fd Amb RAMC
HARRIS William MM Pte 204051 1st London Regt
HARRIS William Albert MM Gnr 66764 78 Siege Bty RGA
HARRIS William Albert MM Cpl 240860 Worcestershire Regt
HARRIS William C. MM Cpl 63965 13th Yorkshire Regt
HARRIS William D. MM CSM 17573 Hampshire Regt
HARRIS William Edward MM+Bar Cpl 650328 1/21st London Regt KIA 1.9.18.
HARRIS William F. MM Pte 2822 1/9th Highland Light Infantry
HARRIS William H. MM Pte 321976 6th London Regt
HARRIS William H. "DCM,MM" Sjt 1131 2nd Royal Warwickshire Regt
HARRIS William H. MM Pte 31242 RAMC
HARRIS William Harold MM Pte 1986 1/15th London Regt
HARRIS William J. MM Cpl 15329 54 Fd Coy Royal Engineers
HARRIS William L. "DCM,MM+Bar" Sjt G/3710 1st Royal West Surrey Regt
HARRIS William N. MM Sjt 22237 23 Fd Coy Royal Engineers
HARRIS William R. MM Pte 19834 Cheshire Regt
HARRIS William S. MM Spr 500474 48 Div Sig Coy Royal Engineers
HARRIS William W. "MM,MID" Sjt 42694 Royal Engineers
HARRISON A. MM Pnr 106975 Royal Engineers
HARRISON A. MM L/Cpl 9569 South Staffordshire Regt
HARRISON A. MM Dmr 7477 Middlesex Regt
HARRISON A. MM Gnr S/7255 RGA
HARRISON Albert MM Pte 15464 1/5th South Lancashire Regt KIA 11.4.18.
HARRISON Alfred MM L/Cpl 3059 North Staffordshire Regt
HARRISON Alfred H. MM Cpl 203090 5th Gloucestershire Regt
HARRISON Alfred W. MM L/Bdr 151503 49 Siege Bty RGA
HARRISON Alfred W. "DCM,MM" CSM 8655 2nd West Riding Regt
HARRISON Arthur MM Pte 38954 8th Lincolnshire Regt
HARRISON Arthur MM Pte 40941 Leicestershire Regt
HARRISON Arthur MM Pte 9437 2nd Notts & Derby Regt
HARRISON Arthur MM L/Cpl 3/11640 15th Durham Light Infantry
HARRISON Arthur MM Pte 29706 East Lancashire Regt
HARRISON Arthur MM Pte 24657 13th Yorkshire Regt KIA 23.11.17.
HARRISON Arthur MM Pte 11/1299 11th East Yorkshire Regt
HARRISON Arthur J. MM L/Cpl 34913 Yorkshire Light Infantry
HARRISON Austin MM Pte 202489 5th Lancashire Fusiliers
HARRISON B. MM Air Mech 2 10720 Royal Flying Corps
HARRISON Bert MM Pte 26361 Cameron Highlanders
HARRISON Charles MM Gnr 172679 A/54 Bde RFA
HARRISON Charles MM Pte 17403 12th Durham Light Infantry
HARRISON Charles George MM Sjt 8402 1st Dorsetshire Regt
HARRISON Charles R. MM Pte 28209 20th Hussars
HARRISON Charles V. MM L/Cpl 41633 1st South Staffordshire Regt
HARRISON Charles W. MM Pte 437115 RAMC
HARRISON Chris MM Bdr 776679 310 Bde RFA
HARRISON Clarence MM Pte 10322 8th East Surrey Regt
HARRISON Clarence James MM Pte 56180 Machine Gun Corps(Cavalry)
HARRISON Claude MM Pte 205022 6th Royal West Surrey Regt KIA 19.9.18.
HARRISON Daniel MM Sjt 10206 2nd Scottish Rifles KIA 16.8.17.
HARRISON E. MM L/Cpl 2339 1/5th North Lancashire Regt
HARRISON Edgar B. MM Pte 12/284 12th East Yorkshire Regt
HARRISON Edward MM Bdr 80621 142 Siege Bty RGA
HARRISON Edward MM+Bar Bdr 39897 RFA
HARRISON Edward MM Sjt 15080 9th South Staffordshire Regt KIA 27.8.17.
HARRISON Edward Billington MM Pte 302379 1/8th Manchester Regt KIA 30.8.18.
HARRISON Edwin B. MM Sjt 9125 2nd Royal Berkshire Regt
HARRISON Ernest MM Cpl 10959 7th East Yorkshire Regt KIA 27.8.18.
HARRISON Ernest C. MM Pte 34563 5th West Riding Regt
HARRISON Ernest Edward MM Sjt 200244 1/4th Lincolnshire Regt
HARRISON Ernest Frederick MM Pte 10660 2nd South Wales Borderers
HARRISON Ernest George MM Sjt 18523 Scottish Rifles
HARRISON Ernest R. MM Cpl 47638 RAMC
HARRISON Frank MM Sjt 338059 94 Siege Bty RGA
HARRISON Fred MM Pte 242249 5th Royal Lancaster Regt
HARRISON Fred MM Cpl 11/463 11th East Yorkshire Regt DOW 21.8.18.
HARRISON Fred MM Gnr 781747 C/246 Bde RFA
HARRISON Frederick MM L/Cpl 202484 Gordon Highlanders

HARRISON Frederick "MM,MID" Pte 21153 10th Worcestershire Regt
HARRISON Frederick MM Pte 200604 1/7th Worcestershire Regt
HARRISON Frederick B. MM L/Cpl 2995 22nd London Regt
HARRISON Frederick G. MM Pte 52611 Durham Light Infantry
HARRISON Frederick J. MM Gnr 25035 4 Siege Bty RGA
HARRISON Frederick James MM Sjt 50780 109 Bty 281 Bde RFA KIA 28.3.18.
HARRISON Frederick W. "DCM,MM" Sjt 202180 2/5th Lancashire Fusiliers
HARRISON Frederick. MM Sjt 265188 Notts & Derby Regt
HARRISON George MM Bdr 72396 166 Siege Bty RGA
HARRISON George MM Cpl 34296 RGA
HARRISON George "MM,MID" Cpl 28895 RFA
HARRISON George MM Pte 281185 Lancashire Fusiliers
HARRISON George MM Pte 3358 West Riding Regt
HARRISON George MM L/Cpl 1393 RAMC
HARRISON George MM Pte 1783 Royal Warwickshire Regt
HARRISON George MM Pte 18000 Royal Lancaster Regt
HARRISON George MM L/Cpl 10222 6th Somerset Light Infantry
HARRISON George MM Cpl 23438 34 Div Ammn Col RFA
HARRISON George B. MM+Bar Sjt 249500 9 Div Sig Coy RE
HARRISON George E. MM Bdr 96233 RFA
HARRISON George Robson MM Pte 25892 10th Royal Warwickshire Regt DOW 14.8.18.
HARRISON George V. MM Pte 60747 12th Bn Machine Gun Corps
HARRISON George W. MM Pte 37916 RAMC
HARRISON H. MM Pte 613090 London Regt
HARRISON Harold "DCM,MM+Bar" Sjt 300448 1/8th Manchester Regt
HARRISON Harold MM Sjt 203 Royal Engineers
HARRISON Harold MM Sjt 1481 9th Royal Fusiliers
HARRISON Harry MM Gnr 761257 RFA
HARRISON Henry MM L/Cpl 8068 11th Royal Warwickshire Regt
HARRISON Henry MM Sjt 776671 RFA
HARRISON Henry Gibson MM Pte 20163 12th Durham Light Infantry KIA 27.10.18.
HARRISON Herbert E. MM Pte 241269 Liverpool Regt
HARRISON Herbert E. MM Cpl 17650 12th Highland Light Infantry
HARRISON Herbert G. MM Sjt 19706 4th Hampshire Regt
HARRISON J. MM Pte 23053 Notts & Derby Regt
HARRISON J. MM CQMS 8495 1st Scottish Rifles
HARRISON James MM Spr 197531 Royal Engineers
HARRISON James MM Pte 632338 229 Empl Coy Labour Corps
HARRISON James MM Cpl 74202 RAMC
HARRISON James MM Cpl 40847 D Bty 1 TM Bde RFA
HARRISON James B. MM Pte 41657 1st Royal Irish Fusiliers
HARRISON James P. MM Cpl 65597 103 Fd Amb RAMC
HARRISON James P. MM Pte 52486 7th Lincolnshire Regt
HARRISON James William MM BSM 795810 2nd(West Riding)Bde RFA
HARRISON James William MM Bdr 765432 RFA
HARRISON John MM Pte G/14716 6th East Kent Regt
HARRISON John MM Cpl 68510 27 Bde RFA
HARRISON John MM Pte 7611 1st Cheshire Regt
HARRISON John MM L/Sjt 19137 15th Cheshire Regt KIA 27.2.18.
HARRISON John MM Spr 82106 Royal Engineers
HARRISON John MM L/Cpl 19793 19th Liverpool Regt KIA 21.7.17.
HARRISON John MM Pte 11652 9th West Riding Regt
HARRISON John MM Sjt 9102 2nd Notts & Derby Regt KIA 3.7.17.
HARRISON John "MC,MM" T/2Lt 1st Royal Warwickshire Regt
HARRISON John MM L/Cpl 22902 King's Own Scottish Borderers
HARRISON John A. MM Pte 19/1306 19th Northumberland Fusiliers
HARRISON John A. MM Cpl 7152 3rd Rifle Brigade
HARRISON John Darwin "MC,MM(41103 Cpl 14th Bn)" 2Lt 12th Royal Irish Rifles
HARRISON John George MM Cpl 9194 1st Northumberland Fusiliers
HARRISON John J. MM Pte 39497 8th West Yorkshire Regt
HARRISON John Leonard MM Dvr 755302 A/257 Bde RFA
HARRISON John M. MM L/Cpl 6407 1st Liverpool Regt
HARRISON John R. MM+Bar Cpl 23531 Machine Gun Corps
HARRISON John T. MM+Bar Pte 203132 5th Yorkshire Light Infantry
HARRISON John W. MM+Bar Sjt 35187 21st Bn Machine Gun Corps
HARRISON John W.G. MM Cpl 50601 RGA
HARRISON Joseph MM L/Cpl 201087 South Staffordshire Regt
HARRISON Joseph Butcher MM Gnr 1366 RFA
HARRISON Joseph Thomas MM Pte 12047 6th Royal Berkshire Regt
HARRISON Joshua MM Cpl 294782 146 Heavy Bty RGA KIA 5.6.17.
HARRISON Lawrence MM Pte 27797 13th Liverpool Regt
HARRISON Leonard MM Pte M2/133162 Army Service Corps att RFA
HARRISON Miles James MM Pte 573791 1/17th London Regt
HARRISON Ninian MM Sjt 51521 Machine Gun Corps(Cavalry)
HARRISON Norman MM Cpl 22/1206 Northumberland Fusiliers
HARRISON Norman MM+Bar Pte 305135 15th Bn Tank Corps
HARRISON Paul A. MM Cpl 54285 Royal Engineers
HARRISON Percy MM Bdr 697293 D/150 Bde RFA
HARRISON Percy F.G. MM Bdr 126173 RGA
HARRISON Peter MM+Bar Pte 341628 1/3rd(West Lancashire)Fd Amb RAMC
HARRISON Peter MM Pte 331313 1/9th Liverpool Regt
HARRISON Ralph Cowburn MM Cpl 200794 2/5th Manchester Regt
HARRISON Reginald MM+Bar Bdr 92787 48 Bty 36 Bde RFA
HARRISON Reginald MM Sjt 13738 Machine Gun Corps
HARRISON Reginald MM Sjt R/4780 13th King's Royal Rifle Corps
HARRISON Richard MM Pte 21540 9th Yorkshire Light Infantry
HARRISON Richard MM Cpl 221511 'R' Corps Sig Coy Royal Engineers
HARRISON Richard MM Pte 24178 10th West Riding Regt
HARRISON Richard MM Pte 265115 Northumberland Fusiliers
HARRISON Richard Henry MM+Bar Cpl 17644 3rd London Regt
HARRISON Robert MM L/Cpl 12388 2nd Notts & Derby Regt
HARRISON Robert MM Pnr 199062 Royal Engineers
HARRISON Robert E. MM L/Cpl 205506 8th West Yorkshire Regt
HARRISON Robert McP. MM Spr 120956 Royal Engineers
HARRISON S. MM Cpl 201268 Gloucestershire Regt
HARRISON Samuel "DCM,MM+Bar" CSM 15/16546 15th Royal Irish Rifles
HARRISON Samuel E. MM Pte 14784 1st Border Regt
HARRISON Samuel T. MM Pte 24982 3rd Grenadier Guards
HARRISON Sidney MM Cpl 46553 15th Durham Light Infantry DOW 26.10.18.
HARRISON Sidney MM Sjt 685098 RFA Died 5.11.18.
HARRISON Stephen David MM Pte 230242 2nd London Regt DOW 29.8.17.
HARRISON Sydney MM Sjt 13396 Leicestershire Regt
HARRISON T. MM Pte 40175 South Staffordshire Regt
HARRISON T. MM Pte 13528 North Lancashire Regt
HARRISON T.J. MM Dvr 750364 RFA
HARRISON Thomas "DCM,MM" Sjt 7533 2nd Yorkshire Regt
HARRISON Thomas MM Cpl 335817 Royal Scots
HARRISON Thomas "MM,MID" Pte M2/131524 Army Service Corps
HARRISON Thomas MM Pte 40774 4th Cheshire Regt
HARRISON Thomas "DCM,MM" CSM 14421 8th Royal Lancaster Regt
HARRISON Thomas "MM,MID" Gnr 94420 RFA
HARRISON Thomas MM Pte 13021 2nd King's Own Scottish Borderers
HARRISON Thomas H. MM Pte 66947 43 Coy Machine Gun Corps
HARRISON Thomas Henry MM Pte 41280 18th West Yorkshire Regt KIA 3.5.17.
HARRISON Thomas James MM Pte 13/17838 13th Royal Irish Rifles KIA 1.7.16.
HARRISON Thomas W. MM Pte 10234 2nd East Lancashire Regt
HARRISON Tom MM L/Cpl 32768 20th Durham Light Infantry
HARRISON Victor J.G. MM Sjt A/2938 King's Royal Rifle Corps
HARRISON W. MM Pte 268039 Cheshire Regt
HARRISON Walter MM Pte 63020 5th West Yorkshire Regt
HARRISON Walter MM Pte 26743 2nd West Riding Regt
HARRISON Walter MM Pte 63716 9th Yorkshire Light Infantry
HARRISON Walter MM Cpl 73757 28 Bde RFA
HARRISON Walter Henry MM Pte 28045 3rd Grenadier Guards
HARRISON Walter R. MM Pte 31550 RAMC
HARRISON Walter Thomas MM Pte 73214 21st Bn Machine Gun Corps
HARRISON Walter William MM+Bar Sjt 9993 Machine Gun Corps
HARRISON Wilfred John Martin MM Cpl 95862 156 Fd Coy Royal Engineers
HARRISON William MM Spr 440021 Royal Engineers
HARRISON William MM Sjt 775335 245 Bde RFA
HARRISON William MM Pte 242089 South Lancashire Regt
HARRISON William MM Pte 20495 Grenadier Guards
HARRISON William A. MM Pte 204188 3rd London Regt
HARRISON William George MM Pte 2906 4th Yorkshire Regt

HARRISON William H. MM L/Cpl 8858 1st Coldstream Guards
HARRISON William Henry MM L/Cpl 24839 9th Yorkshire Light Infantry
HARRISON William Henry "MM,MID" Bdr 1266 RFA
HARRISON Wilmot MM L/Sjt 15035 9th North Staffordshire Regt
HARRISS Charles H. MM+Bar Sjt 3196 Royal Engineers
HARROCKS Charles E. "DCM,MM+Bar" Sjt 371540 1/8th London Regt
HARROD Edward MM 2nd Cpl 25911 3 Fd Sqn Royal Engineers
HARROD Frederick MM Spr 65355 106 Fd Coy Royal Engineers
HARROD James T. MM+Bar Cpl 558065 Royal Engineers
HARROD Percy MM Sjt 924 1st Royal Warwickshire Regt
HARROD Stephen MM Gnr 316411 RGA
HARROLD George MM L/Cpl 16085 11th Worcestershire Regt
HARROLD Sidney H. MM L/Cpl 390921 9th London Regt
HARROLD Thomas MM Sjt 14746 31st Bn Machine Gun Corps
HARROLD Walter Phillips Gordon MM L/Sjt 2698 13th Royal Sussex Regt KIA 3.9.16.
HARROP Albert MM+Bar Sjt 55779 4th York & Lancaster Regt
HARROP Albert R. MM Sjt 21733 RAMC
HARROP Ben E. MM Cpl R/13481 King's Royal Rifle Corps
HARROP Ernest MM Gnr 203528 57 Bty 45 Bde RFA
HARROP Harold MM Pte 35526 11th Lancashire Fusiliers
HARROP Isaac MM Gnr 706363 RFA
HARROP Stanley MM Pte 153557 37th Bn Machine Gun Corps
HARROP W. MM Pnr 49486 Royal Engineers
HARROP William MM L/Cpl 346093 239 Div Emp Coy Labour Corps
HARROTT Herbert MM L/Cpl 13833 7th Yorkshire Light Infantry KIA 2.4.18.
HARROW Frank MM Pte 2668 1st Royal Highlanders
HARROW Walter F. MM L/Cpl 33955 Middlesex Regt
HARROWELL Ernest C. MM Sjt 815170 RFA
HARROWER Andrew MM L/Cpl 290699 1/7th Royal Highlanders
HARROWER George MM Pte 40538 1/8th Arg & Suth Highlanders DOW 26.12.17.
HARROWER James MM Sjt M2/105368 Army Service Corps
HARROWER Matthew MM Pte 250626 5/6th Royal Scots KIA 28.8.18.
HARROWER Robert J.D. MM Sjt 9239 8/10th Gordon Highlanders
HARROWING Thomas C. MM Cpl 511815 14th London Regt
HARRY David MM Pte 13606 Welsh Regt
HARRY Edwin R. MM Pte 381385 1st Liverpool Regt
HARRY James MM Pte 25336 Royal Lancaster Regt
HARRY Robert Henry Clifford MM Sjt 240086 1/8th Middlesex Regt
HARRY William A. MM L/Cpl 536311 RAMC
HARRY William H. MM Pte 17126 2nd Royal Berkshire Regt
HARSANT John H. MM Dvr 50882 RFA
HARSENT George MM Pte 96348 3rd Royal Fusiliers
HARSTON John C. MM Cpl 27287 11th East Lancashire Regt
HART Albert MM Pte 240089 1/5th Norfolk Regt
HART Albert MM Cpl 25909 2nd Lancashire Fusiliers
HART Albert MM Gnr 901478 RFA
HART Albert G. MM Sjt 322532 6th London Regt
HART Alec MM L/Cpl 267772 7th West Yorkshire Regt
HART Alfred MM Sjt 255959 Royal Engineers
HART Alfred John MM Pte 203484 2/4th West Riding Regt
HART Amos MM Pte 57115 Machine Gun Corps DOW 27.8.18.
HART Andrew "MM,MID" Sjt 15278 6/7th Royal Scots Fusiliers
HART Andrew MM Dvr 37858 RFA
HART Arthur J. MM Sjt 265036 1/1st Buckinghamshire Bn Oxf & Bucks Light Infantry
HART Benjamin James MM Sjt 31215 Labour Corps
HART Cecil H. MM Pte 1443 1/24th London Regt
HART Charles A. MM L/Cpl 19896 1/1st Hertfordshire Regt
HART Charles H. MM SM 18717 11 CCS RAMC
HART Charles Henry MM Cpl 40933 C/34 Bde RFA DOW 23.10.18.
HART Charles Reginald MM L/Cpl 9539 1st Northamptonshire Regt
HART Colin MM Pte 19671 Army Cyclist Corps
HART Cornelius MM Dvr 72240 A/83 Bde RFA Died 7.11.18.
HART David J. MM+Bar Cpl 70807 Royal Engineers
HART Edward MM Spr 70358 III Corps Sig Coy Royal Engineers
HART Edward MM Cpl 7566 2nd Durham Light Infantry
HART Ernest MM Pte 540 10th Lincolnshire Regt
HART Ernest A. MM Cpl 14301 1st Royal Fusiliers
HART F.J. MM Sjt 10352 1st Royal West Kent Regt
HART Frederick MM Cpl 5185 12th Royal Fusiliers
HART Frederick MM Pte 3322 1/1st Hertfordshire Regt
HART Frederick MM Pnr 237912 Royal Engineers
HART George "DCM,MM,DM(B)" Sjt 389 6th Royal West Surrey Regt
HART George MM Pte 352571 1/7th Royal Scots
HART George MM L/Cpl 1942 23rd Middlesex Regt
HART George M. MM Pte 275511 26th Durham Light Infantry
HART Guy Richard Gregor "MM,MID" Sjt 8470 19th Hussars
HART H. MM Cpl 70070 Yeomanry
HART Harry MM Pte 13679 11th Royal West Surrey Regt
HART Harry MM Pte 241295 2/8th Middlesex Regt
HART Harry MM Cpl 14772 5 Fd Coy Royal Engineers
HART Harry MM Cpl 25875 Machine Gun Corps
HART Harry A. MM Pte 200313 1/4th Suffolk Regt
HART Henry Edward MM Sjt 345502 RGA
HART Herbert MM Cpl 200873 1/4th Royal Berkshire Regt
HART Herbert E. MM Cpl 60470 9th Royal Fusiliers
HART Hezekiah MM Pte 19031 9th Yorkshire Light Infantry
HART J. MM Pte 12168 West Yorkshire Regt
HART James Walter MM Pte 27436 14th Royal Welsh Fusiliers
HART John MM Sjt L/11434 13th Middlesex Regt
HART John MM Pte 24324 2nd Dorsetshire Regt Died 4.11.18.
HART John MM L/Cpl 2340 1/5th Royal Sussex Regt
HART John D. MM Cpl 56708 RAMC
HART Joseph MM L/Cpl 25978 Scottish Rifles
HART Leonard MM Pte 54405 7th West Yorkshire Regt
HART Michael MM 2nd Cpl 86709 Royal Engineers
HART Milton MM Pte 201869 Worcestershire Regt
HART Montague MM L/Sjt 240315 Liverpool Regt
HART Oliver F. MM Dvr 11588 RFA
HART Peter MM L/Cpl 11496 Border Regt
HART Richard S. MM Pte 3111 8th East Kent Regt
HART Robert MM Sjt 113510 Royal Engineers
HART Robert William MM Gnr 915429 RFA
HART Sidney MM Pte 15850 1st Gloucestershire Regt
HART Sidney G. MM Cpl 15893 HQ 65 Bde RFA
HART Stanley MM L/Cpl 2118 1/6th London Regt
HART Sydney James MM Cpl 27094 40 Siege Bty RGA
HART Thomas MM Pte 13402 10th North Lancashire Regt
HART Victor MM Pnr 26255 Royal Engineers
HART Victor MM Cpl 294789 RGA
HART Walter "MC+Bar,MM(4727 Cpl)" T/2Lt 24th Royal Fusiliers
HART Walter Y. MM Bdr 715815 A/71 Bde RFA
HART William MM Pte 19975 1/4th Gordon Highlanders DOW 15.10.18.
HART William MM Gnr 78560 RHA
HART William MM Pte 20951 Durham Light Infantry
HART William H. MM L/Cpl 281822 4th London Regt
HART William T. MM Pte 9861 11th Lancashire Fusiliers
HARTE Edward MM Pte 17088 6 Coy Machine Gun Corps
HARTE Edward MM Gnr 54631 25 Siege Bty RGA KIA 5.2.17.
HARTE John MM Pte 15589 2nd Royal Inniskilling Fusiliers DOW 22.3.18.
HARTE William Taylor MM Pte 3/12005 9th Royal Dublin Fusiliers KIA 21.8.16.
HARTELL Ralph MM Sjt 1523 2/5th Gloucestershire Regt
HARTERY Robert W. MM L/Cpl 19823 Machine Gun Corps
HARTGA Sidney MM Pte 29122 1st Grenadier Guards
HARTIGAN John MM Sjt 5181 1/6th Lancashire Fusiliers
HARTILL Albert James MM Cpl 155835 177 Tunnelling Coy Royal Engineers
HARTILL Frederick MM Pte 10699 Leicestershire Regt
HARTILL Robert MM L/Sjt 14144 17th Lancashire Fusiliers
HARTINGTON George O. MM Pte 19357 1st East Lancashire Regt
HARTLAND William MM Pte 16616 11th Worcestershire Regt
HARTLE Albert D. MM Pte 13412 King Edward's Horse
HARTLE George MM Pte 203690 1/7th Worcestershire Regt
HARTLESS George MM Pte 1366 2nd South Lancashire Regt
HARTLEY Albert Eastwood MM Gnr W/1568 C/122 Bde RFA
HARTLEY Alfred MM Pte 266149 Liverpool Regt
HARTLEY Arthur MM Pte 6430 East Lancashire Regt
HARTLEY Charles T. MM Pte 7491 2 Fd Amb RAMC
HARTLEY Charles William MM Sjt 1959 21st Lancers
HARTLEY Clement MM Spr 443976 4 Fd Svy Bn Royal Engineers
HARTLEY Clough MM Gnr 114983 RFA
HARTLEY E. MM Cpl 1368 2/5th Lancashire Fusiliers
HARTLEY Edward MM Bdr 706388 RFA
HARTLEY Ernest MM Sjt 9460 1st Royal Irish Regt
HARTLEY France MM Pte 241978 5th West Riding Regt
HARTLEY Frank MM L/Cpl 429936 57 Div Sig Coy Royal Engineers DOW 26.5.18.
HARTLEY Fred MM Pte 50827 Machine Gun Corps
HARTLEY Fred MM L/Cpl 243113 1/5th Royal Lancaster Regt KIA 30.11.17.

HARTLEY Fred Mosley MM+Bar L/Cpl 103961 18 Div Sig Coy Royal Engineers
HARTLEY Frederick MM Sjt 25888 155 Heavy Bty RGA
HARTLEY George MM Pte 8128 11th Royal Warwickshire Regt KIA 24.9.17.
HARTLEY George MM Pte 14162 10th North Lancashire Regt
HARTLEY Harry MM Pte 51190 5th Liverpool Regt
HARTLEY Harry "DCM,MM" Sjt 15149 10th Royal Welsh Fusiliers
HARTLEY Henry MM Sjt 2332 1/6th West Riding Regt
HARTLEY Henry MM Gnr 1930 C/276 RFA
HARTLEY Herbert MM L/Cpl 3/2830 2nd York & Lancaster Regt
HARTLEY Irvin MM Pte 143310 Machine Gun Corps
HARTLEY Jack MM Cpl 75234 2nd Bn Tank Corps Died 15.2.19.
HARTLEY James MM Sjt 200346 1/4th North Lancashire Regt
HARTLEY James William MM Pte 29655 East Lancashire Regt
HARTLEY James William MM Pte 15621 11th Essex Regt
HARTLEY John MM Cpl 8683 RFA
HARTLEY John MM L/Sjt 16/901 16th Royal Warwickshire Regt
HARTLEY John MM L/Cpl 46597 Northumberland Fusiliers
HARTLEY Lawrence MM L/Cpl 268276 West Riding Regt
HARTLEY Luther MM L/Cpl 37466 Rifle Brigade
HARTLEY Matthew "MM,MID" L/Cpl 20768 4th Grenadier Guards
HARTLEY Reginald MM Gnr 750480 250 Bde RFA
HARTLEY Robert H. MM L/Cpl 2211 1/6th Liverpool Regt
HARTLEY Ronald "DCM,MM" L/Sjt 12800 9th West Riding Regt
HARTLEY Rowland MM L/Sjt 357489 1/10th Liverpool Regt
HARTLEY Thomas B. "DCM,MM" Spr 432237 Royal Engineers
HARTLEY Tom MM Pte C/66 16th King's Royal Rifle Corps
HARTLEY William MM Gnr 161292 2 Siege Bty RGA
HARTLEY William MM Pte 240200 East Lancashire Regt att MGC
HARTLEY William Guest MM Pte 4952 1/1st HAC(Infantry) KIA 8.8.18.
HARTLEY William H. MM Cpl 235332 Lancashire Fusiliers
HARTNELL Henry James MM Sjt 557 18th Lancashire Fusiliers KIA 31.10.18.
HARTNETT Timothy MM Pte 306537 2/8th Liverpool Regt KIA 2.11.17.
HARTNEY Arthur MM Sjt 18778 18th Bn Machine Gun Corps
HARTNUP John Rowland MM L/Cpl G/5907 8th Royal West Surrey Regt DOW 20.8.16.
HARTOP Ben MM Pte 35599 1st Essex Regt DOW 11.9.18.
HARTOPP Frederick Arthur MM Gnr 151885 217 Siege Bty RGA
HARTRUP Charles W. MM Pte 30402 RAMC
HARTS Victor MM Pte 630937 1/20th London Regt DOW 6.12.17.
HARTSHORN Frank MM Pte 241135 Middlesex Regt
HARTSHORN James H. MM Pte 4259 Notts & Derby Regt
HARTSHORNE Christopher MM L/Cpl 13893 2nd Grenadier Guards
HARTSHORNE Ernest MM Pte 70976 Notts & Derby Regt
HARTSHORNE George E. MM Cpl R/11288 2nd King's Royal Rifle Corps
HARTSHORNE Joseph MM Pte 203156 6th Lincolnshire Regt
HARTSILVER Cyril D. MM Gnr 53479 RFA
HARTSON Arthur MM Sjt 200674 Yorkshire Regt
HARTUNG Charles Stanley MM Sjt 7919 6th Lincolnshire Regt
HARTUP Henry H. MM Pte 202067 Suffolk Regt
HARTUP Robert MM Pte 21155 2nd Bedfordshire Regt KIA 3.7.18.
HARTWELL Albert MM L/Bdr 70161 RGA
HARTWELL Francis J. MM Pte 37850 52 Fd Amb RAMC
HARTWELL Oliver MM Pte 72773 132 Fd Amb RAMC
HARVATT James W. MM Pte 10084 Army Cyclist Corps
HARVEY A. MM Pte 43474 Norfolk Regt
HARVEY Abraham MM 2nd Cpl 197413 Royal Engineers
HARVEY Albert George Gordon "DCM,MM" Sjt 44786 323 Siege Bty RGA
HARVEY Albert Victor MM+Bar Bdr 94078 18 Div Ammn Col RFA
HARVEY Alexander MM Pte 240467 6/7th Royal Scots Fusiliers
HARVEY Alfred MM Sjt 204772 15th Hampshire Regt
HARVEY Alfred W. MM Sjt 13937 15 Fd Coy Royal Engineers
HARVEY Archibald Edward MM Pte 11841 2nd Wiltshire Regt KIA 21.3.18.
HARVEY Arthur MM+Bar Pte 1711 1st & 2nd Royal Highlanders
HARVEY Arthur "DCM,MM" CSM 7885 2nd West Riding Regt
HARVEY Arthur MM L/Cpl S/13124 Rifle Brigade
HARVEY Ashton Ellis MM L/Sjt 16/144 West Yorkshire Regt KIA 22.3.18.
HARVEY Bernard MM Pte 405195 98 Fd Amb RAMC DOW 2.10.18.
HARVEY Bernard MM Pte 13304 7th York & Lancaster Regt DOW 25.3.18.
HARVEY C. MM Sjt 75901 Machine Gun Corps
HARVEY Cecil Alan MM Pte 86813 48th Bn Machine Gun Corps
HARVEY Charles MM Pte 320657 15th Suffolk Regt
HARVEY Clifford MM L/Cpl 200542 Notts & Derby Regt
HARVEY Cyril J. MM Pte 9588 2/1st HAC (Inf)
HARVEY Edwin E. MM Gnr 249562 B/155 Bde RFA
HARVEY Edwin Granville MM L/Cpl 14925 1st Bedfordshire Regt KIA 24.7.16.
HARVEY Ernest MM Pte 36946 RAMC
HARVEY Francis G. MM Pte 27948 Worcestershire Regt
HARVEY Frank MM Pte 1678 XIII Corps Cyclist Bn Army Cyclist Corps
HARVEY Frank MM Pte 136665 29th Bn Machine Gun Corps
HARVEY Fred MM Pte 40786 North Staffordshire Regt
HARVEY Fred MM Cpl 293120 7th Cheshire Regt
HARVEY Frederick MM Pte 4190 Leicestershire Regt
HARVEY Geoffrey W. MM Pte G/17576 2nd Royal Sussex Regt
HARVEY George MM Pte 495439 2 Fd Amb RAMC
HARVEY George MM+Bar Pte 18898 1st South Wales Borderers
HARVEY George MM Bdr 1318 RGA
HARVEY George MM+2 Bars Pte C/6663 13th King's Royal Rifle Corps
HARVEY George E. MM Pte 321612 6th London Regt
HARVEY George E. MM Pte 1833 North Staffordshire Regt
HARVEY George M. MM Gnr 95111 RFA
HARVEY George R. MM Gnr 59375 RGA
HARVEY George W. MM CSM 59657 67 Fd Coy Royal Engineers
HARVEY George W. MM Sjt 5951 1st Devonshire Regt
HARVEY Harold "MM,CG(F)" Pte 44448 12th North Staffordshire Regt
HARVEY Harry MM Spr 478588 225 Fd Coy Royal Engineers
HARVEY Harry MM Pte 41550 9th Essex Regt
HARVEY Harry MM L/Cpl 15121 7/8th King's Own Scottish Borderers
HARVEY Harry E. "DCM,MM" L/Cpl 73175 17th & 18th Royal Fusiliers
HARVEY Harry Frederick George MM Cpl 558122 56 Div Sig Coy Royal Engineers
HARVEY Harry Henry MM AC1 143510 Royal Air Force
HARVEY Henry MM Gnr 16997 5 Siege Bty RGA
HARVEY Henry Valentine MM Bdr 43685 D/175 Bde RFA KIA 1.11.18.
HARVEY Herbert G. MM Bdr 68755 41 Bde RFA
HARVEY James MM Pte 20474 12 Fd Amb RAMC
HARVEY James MM Sjt 186858 RGA
HARVEY James MM Sjt 12/17844 12th Royal Irish Rifles KIA 1.7.16.
HARVEY James Bell MM Pte 318096 1/2nd(Lowland)Fd Amb RAMC
HARVEY James H. MM Pte 28657 Notts & Derby Regt
HARVEY John MM L/Cpl 17499 6th Bedfordshire Regt
HARVEY John MM Pte 41390 1/7th Royal Highlanders
HARVEY John MM L/Cpl 502139 Inland Water Transport Div Royal Engineers
HARVEY John MM Pte 301405 1/7th Arg & Suth Highlanders DOW 29.3.18.
HARVEY John MM Pte 32490 10/11th Highland Light Infantry
HARVEY John J.S. MM Cpl 31928 Notts & Derby Regt
HARVEY John R.R. MM Spr 148507 Royal Engineers
HARVEY Joseph MM L/Sjt 4120 Royal Welsh Fusiliers
HARVEY Joseph MM Sjt 63512 95 Fd Amb RAMC DOW 3.11.16.
HARVEY Josiah G. MM+Bar Pte 15008 2nd Worcestershire Regt
HARVEY Lawrence MM+Bar BSM 755003 65 Bde RFA
HARVEY Leonard G. MM Pte 251266 Essex Regt
HARVEY Michael H. MM Cpl 63039 RFA
HARVEY Percy MM L/Sjt 401090 RAMC
HARVEY Percy F.W. MM Pte 14743 Welsh Regt
HARVEY Peter MM Pte 21120 Royal Irish Fusiliers
HARVEY Peter J. MM Sjt 20024 8 Siege Bty RGA
HARVEY Raymond King MM Sjt 17998 RGA
HARVEY Reginald MM Spr 558036 29 Div Sig Coy Royal Engineers
HARVEY Richard MM L/Cpl 305074 8th Notts & Derby Regt
HARVEY Richard MM Cpl 74058 1st Bn Machine Gun Corps
HARVEY Rowan MM L/Cpl 350504 12th Highland Light Infantry
HARVEY S. MM Sjt 7346 Royal Warwickshire Regt
HARVEY Samuel George MM Pte 13598 North Staffordshire Regt
HARVEY Thomas MM Sjt 305989 8th Royal Warwickshire Regt
HARVEY Thomas MM Pte 2559 1st Lancashire Fusiliers
HARVEY Victor MM Pte 3/8202 2nd Devonshire Regt
HARVEY William MM Cpl 69198 Labour Corps
HARVEY William MM L/Cpl 12/17789 12th Royal Irish Rifles
HARVEY William MM Pte 43435 Gordon Highlanders

HARVEY William Alfred MM Pte M/285519 Army Service Corps att 'O' AA Bty RGA.
HARVEY William Henry MM Cpl 91269 RFA KIA 23.10.18.
HARVEY William Horace MM Pte 8747 1st Norfolk Regt KIA 21.8.18.
HARVEY William J. "DCM,MM" L/Cpl 3/7901 1st Norfolk Regt
HARVEY William R.J. MM Sjt 9635 23rd Royal Fusiliers
HARVEY William Willis MM Pte 14863 2nd Bedfordshire Regt KIA 21.9.18.
HARVIE Charles W.M. MM Sjt 262979 Middlesex Regt
HARVIE David MM Pte 6195 1st Scots Guards
HARVIE James MM Pte S/41060 1/4th Seaforth Highlanders
HARVIE John MM Cpl 4/9742 Arg & Suth Highlanders
HARWIN Herbert S. MM Gnr 20103 7 Siege Bty RGA
HARWOOD Albert Frederick MM Sjt 33694 RGA
HARWOOD Andrew MM Sjt L/8491 RFA
HARWOOD Arthur MM Sjt 277 6th East Kent Regt
HARWOOD Arthur E. MM Sjt 200133 1/5th Liverpool Regt
HARWOOD Arthur J. MM Pte 16722 11th Worcestershire Regt
HARWOOD Cecil W. MM L/Cpl G/50734 26th Royal Fusiliers
HARWOOD Charles MM Cpl 200679 1/4th Lincolnshire Regt
HARWOOD Frank MM Pte 21091 22nd Manchester Regt
HARWOOD Frederick MM Pte 13598 2nd Middlesex Regt
HARWOOD G. "DCM,MM" Sjt 33416 59th Bn Machine Gun Corps
HARWOOD George L. "DCM,MM" Sjt 20637 2nd York & Lancaster Regt
HARWOOD George S. MM Gnr 760401 C/317 Bde RFA
HARWOOD Harold C. MM Pte 78086 9th Bn Tank Corps
HARWOOD Harry "MM,CG(F)" Pte 32780 66 Coy Machine Gun Corps
HARWOOD Herbert MM Pte 45729 12/13th Northumberland Fusiliers DOW 2.11.18.
HARWOOD James MM Pte 12919 2nd King's Royal Rifle Corps
HARWOOD James MM L/Sjt 200236 1/4th Royal Sussex Regt KIA 25.9.18.
HARWOOD John W. MM Sjt 3183 10th Hussars
HARWOOD Percy MM Pte 242889 1/5th South Lancashire Regt
HARWOOD Sidney MM Pte 9004 Scots Guards
HARWOOD Stanley MM Bdr 720297 RFA
HARWOOD Sylvester G. MM Cpl 33915 16th Royal Warwickshire Regt
HARWOOD T. MM Gnr 69846 23 Bde RFA
HARWOOD William MM Sjt 49049 B/67 Bde RFA KIA 31.8.16.
HARWOOD William R. MM Dvr 316065 136 Hy Bty RGA
HARWOOD William T. MM Pte 39768 RAMC
HARYOTT J.A.H. MM Cpl 607 Royal Engineers
HASELDINE William N. "DCM,MM" Sjt 32220 28 Fd Amb RAMC
HASELDON Frederick C. MM Sjt 36542 RFA
HASKAYNE Frank MM+Bar Cpl 13174 13th Liverpool Regt
HASKELL L.V. MM Cpl 8693 2nd East Kent Regt
HASKELL Reginald W. MM Pte 16434 5th Dorsetshire Regt
HASKELL William MM Pte 10221 5th Dorsetshire Regt
HASKETT Albert George MM Pte 33475 2nd Wiltshire Regt KIA 6.11.18.
HASKEY Joseph Herbert Bonnington MM L/Cpl 58668 8th West Yorkshire Regt
HASKEY Thomas W. MM Gnr 72355 44 Bde RFA
HASKINS Ernest Percy MM Cpl 34125 2/4th Oxf & Bucks Light Infantry KIA 16.4.18.
HASKINS George MM Pte 28688 North Lancashire Regt
HASKINS George MM Gnr 826210 RFA
HASLAM Arnold MM Pte R/3196 King's Royal Rifle Corps
HASLAM Arthur MM L/Cpl 241064 2/5th North Lancashire Regt
HASLAM Arthur MM Spr 7859 Royal Engineers
HASLAM Clifford MM L/Cpl 7688 23rd Royal Fusiliers KIA 29.4.17.
HASLAM Frank S. MM Pte 18/16818 18th Liverpool Regt
HASLAM Fred MM Dvr L/9921 149 Bde RFA
HASLAM Frederick MM Pte S/7049 1st Rifle Brigade
HASLAM Frederick MM Sjt 3884 Machine Gun Corps
HASLAM Harry MM Bdr 12828 A/162 Bde RFA
HASLAM Herbert MM Pte 103741 1(Cav)Fd Amb RAMC
HASLAM James MM L/Cpl 4098 6th North Lancashire Regt Died 16.11.18.
HASLAM James F. "DCM,MM" CSM 8615 11th Lancashire Fusiliers
HASLAM John MM Pte 13524 2nd Grenadier Guards
HASLAM Robert MM Gnr L/2812 RFA
HASLAM Samuel MM Pte 15238 Manchester Regt
HASLAM Walter MM Gnr 785507 RFA
HASLAM William MM L/Cpl R4418 13th King's Royal Rifle Corps
HASLEDEN William MM Sjt 91799 C/160 Bde RFA KIA 7.10.18.
HASLEGRAVE Herbert Victor Wilson MM Pte 2014 16th Middlesex Regt KIA 15.9.16.
HASLER James W. MM Pte 7592 11th Royal Fusiliers
HASLER John Kenneth MM Pte 51159 1st Liverpool Regt
HASNIP Harry MM+Bar Sjt 1974 2/2nd(West Riding)Fd Coy Royal Engineers
HASSALL Frank MM Pte 25268 7th Shropshire Light Infantry
HASSALL Richard MM Gnr 80573 C/54 Bde RFA
HASSAN Matthew MM L/Cpl 19095 Royal Inniskilling Fusiliers
HASSAN Victor MM Cpl 721450 2/24th London Regt
HASSARD Alex MM Pte 29729 2nd Royal Inniskilling Fusiliers
HASSELL Charles MM Cpl 5267 5th Royal Irish Regt
HASSEY David MM Sjt 25802 284 Siege Bty RGA
HASTIE James MM Dvr 976 83 Bty 11 Bde RFA
HASTIE William "MM,MID" Cpl 9972 1st Royal Scots
HASTILOW Ernest MM Pte 36146 21 Fd Amb RAMC
HASTINGS Alfred MM L/Cpl 32253 2/5th Notts & Derby Regt DOW 11.4.18.
HASTINGS Alfred Phillip MM Pte 5891 3rd Coldstream Guards
HASTINGS Andrew MM Pte 49308 1st Rifle Brigade
HASTINGS Frank S. MM Bdr 51226 RGA
HASTINGS Frederick MM Sjt 25258 286 Siege Bty RGA
HASTINGS George MM Pte 7577 2nd Gordon Highlanders
HASTINGS Harold MM L/Cpl 8239 9th East Surrey Regt
HASTINGS John MM Pte 11462 2nd Hampshire Regt KIA 2.10.18
HASTON Alexander MM Pte 54426 2nd Highland Light Infantry
HASTON Herbert MM Pte 23527 North Lancashire Regt
HASTON James MM Spr 93524 219 Fd Coy Royal Engineers
HASTON William MM Pte 42476 9th Scottish Rifles
HASTWELL Allan L. MM L/Cpl 241688 5th Royal Lancaster Regt
HASTY Anthony MM Sjt 240938 2/5th East Lancashire Regt
HASWELL G.B. MM Pte 32784 Royal Scots
HATCH Alfred George MM Pte M2/022025 Army Service Corps att 1 Fd Amb RAMC
HATCH Benjamin MM Dvr 23963 30 Bde RFA
HATCH Edward Francis MM Dvr 865441 D/293 Bde RFA
HATCH Francis MM Pte R/17187 13th King's Royal Rifle Corps
HATCH John MM Cpl 253417 1 Water Boring Section Royal Engineers
HATCHARD Alfred MM Pte 8303 1st South Wales Borderers
HATCHER Archibald S. MM Gnr 1991 MGC(Motors)
HATCHER Bert Harry MM Pte 2546 82 Fd Amb RAMC
HATCHER Bertram A. MM L/Cpl R/41025 1st King's Royal Rifle Corps
HATCHER Edwin P. MM Cpl 39695 RGA
HATCHER Ernest H. MM Pte 12560 1 Special Coy King's Royal Rifle Corps
HATCHER Herbert William MM Sjt 75590 'D' Bn Machine Gun Corps(Heavy Branch) Died 5.10.18.
HATCHER Reginald P. MM Cpl 352549 77 Siege Bty RGA
HATCHER Robert S. MM Pte 31512 Hampshire Regt
HATCHETT Harry MM Pte 203099 2nd Oxf & Bucks Light Infantry
HATCHLEY George W.M. MM Sjt 6605 Royal West Kent Regt
HATELEY David Charles MM Pte 8796 South Staffordshire Regt
HATFIELD Herbert MM Sjt 13/437 13th York & Lancaster Regt
HATFIELD Percy "MM,MID" Sjt 78727 'Y' Corps Sig Coy Royal Engineers
HATHAWAY Albert MM Pte 40194 21st Manchester Regt
HATHAWAY Albert Edward MM Cpl 21431 Welsh Regt
HATHAWAY Harold MM L/Cpl 9737 2nd Coldstream Guards KIA 16.9.16.
HATHAWAY Henry R. MM Cpl 508232 RAMC
HATHAWAY John C. MM Pte 41647 Suffolk Regt
HATHAWAY Joseph MM Sjt S/9833 13th Rifle Brigade
HATHAWAY Mark MM Pte M2/184237 Army Service Corps att RAMC
HATHERALL Henry T. MM L/Cpl 1233 1/2nd Monmouthshire Regt
HATHERELL Benjamin R. "MM,MID" Gnr 40159 Machine Gun Corps
HATHERELL Clifford MM Sjt 11050 9th South Staffordshire Regt
HATHERLEY George MM Pte 8821 South Staffordshire Regt
HATHERLEY Nathaniel MM Pte 132539 25th Bn Machine Gun Corps
HATHERLY Francis A.J. MM Pnr 25564 Royal Engineers
HATHERTON James MM Cpl 10499 1st South Wales Borderers
HATHWAY Frederick James MM Pte M2/176108 Army Service Corps
HATLEY Frederick John MM+Bar L/Cpl 560228 47 Div Sig Coy Royal Engineers
HATSWELL Robert T. MM Sjt 251278 3rd London Regt

HATT George A. MM L/Cpl 235907 West Yorkshire Regt
HATT Thomas MM Pte 203736 Oxf & Bucks Light Infantry
HATT Thomas Edgar MM Cpl 590293 1/18th London Regt KIA 21.3.18.
HATTEN Christopher Geoffrey MM L/Sjt 13727 4th Grenadier Guards KIA 6.1.18.
HATTERSLEY James William MM Cpl 795487 62 Div Ammn Col RFA
HATTERSLEY Joseph MM Pte 1529 RAMC
HATTERSLEY William MM Sjt 19259 10th York & Lancaster Regt KIA 15.11.16.
HATTERSLEY William Charles MM Cpl 1579 A/133 Bde RFA
HATTIE John MM Dvr 656004 D/77 Bde RFA
HATTLE William MM Pte 1398 24/27th Northumberland Fusiliers
HATTON Albert MM Dvr 8853 RFA
HATTON Arthur MM L/Cpl 57682 13th Liverpool Regt
HATTON Charles MM Spr 253709 Royal Engineers
HATTON Edmund MM Pte 50767 6th Liverpool Regt
HATTON F. MM L/Sjt 200468 Yorkshire Light Infantry
HATTON George MM Pte 53449 Liverpool Regt
HATTON George L. MM Pte 534724 15th London Regt
HATTON George William MM Gnr 4562 B/153 Bde RFA KIA 28.8.17.
HATTON H. MM Pte 2432 York & Lancaster Regt
HATTON Herbert MM Pte 17541 Royal Sussex Regt
HATTON Jabez MM Bdr 99657 RFA
HATTON James MM Pte 38476 Welsh Regt
HATTON James MM Pte 32731 7th South Staffordshire Regt
HATTON James F. MM Pte 201334 1/4th Cheshire Regt
HATTON John MM L/Cpl 1833 Yorkshire Light Infantry
HATTON S. MM Sjt 200920 South Staffordshire Regt
HATTON Thomas MM Pte 38155 RAMC
HATTON Thomas MM Cpl 72280 C/82 Bde RFA
HATTON Victor L. MM L/Cpl 16526 2 Fd Coy Royal Engineers
HATTON Walter MM Sjt 201428 South Lancashire Regt
HATTON William MM L/Cpl 54409 1st West Yorkshire Regt DOW 15.9.18.
HATTON William MM+Bar Sjt 1486 7th Royal West Surrey Regt
HATTON William C. MM Spr 207584 63 Div Sig Coy Royal Engineers
HATTON William M. MM Pte 42487 9th Scottish Rifles
HAUGH John Gavin MM Pte 53912 27 Fd Amb RAMC KIA 3.5.17.
HAUGH Patrick J. MM Sjt 5203 5th Connaught Rangers
HAUGH Robert S. MM Sjt 300278 6th Liverpool Regt
HAUGHAN J.T. MM Pte 64406 RAMC
HAUGHEY John MM Sjt 156380 285 Army Tps Coy Royal Engineers
HAUGHNEY James MM Pte 6908 8th Hussars
HAVELL Charles W. MM L/Cpl 16608 Machine Gun Corps
HAVELOCK John Alan MM L/Cpl 18/646 18th Northumberland Fusiliers KIA 17.4.18.
HAVEN John MM Pte 12108 2nd Yorkshire Light Infantry
HAVERCROFT Fred MM RQMS 969 1/5th Lincolnshire Regt
HAVERCROFT Walter MM Pte 270063 Royal Scots
HAVERS Alfred MM+Bar Gnr 128581 RFA
HAVERS Harry Arthur MM Sjt 13290 8th Norfolk Regt
HAVERS John W. MM Cpl 61183 17th Indian Div MG Bn Machine Gun Corps
HAVERSON Frank MM Pte 300624 1/1st Staffordshire Yeomanry
HAVILL Sidney J. MM Pte 2391 1st Lancashire Fusiliers
HAVILLE Ernest MM Sjt 90558 RFA
HAVRON George MM Dvr 35383 C/94 Bde RFA Died 28.10.18.
HAVVOCK George MM Gnr 1313 D/124 Bde RFA
HAW Harold MM Pte 49515 8th West Yorkshire Regt
HAWBROOK Arthur MM+Bar Pte 20458 10th Notts & Derby Regt
HAWDON Percy C.W. MM Pte 6675 12th (or 5th) Lancers
HAWDON Richard M. MM Spr 165008 Royal Engineers
HAWE Albert MM Spr 254779 9 Div Sig Coy Royal Engineers
HAWE Samuel MM Cpl 81583 126 Fd Coy Royal Engineers
HAWES Andrew J. MM Dvr 53018 RFA
HAWES Ernest MM Pte 5227 Coldstream Guards
HAWES George MM Pte 252771 3rd London Regt
HAWES Harry MM Pte 331144 1/8th Hampshire Regt KIA 2.11.17.
HAWES James MM Pte 30295 6th Northamptonshire Regt
HAWES John MM Gnr L/25902 B/236 Bde RFA
HAWES Robert MM L/Cpl G/2166 9th Royal Fusiliers
HAWES Rowland MM L/Cpl 285366 1/1st Oxfordshire Yeomanry
HAWES William J. MM Pte 201603 7th Suffolk Regt
HAWES William James MM L/Cpl 41617 1st Essex Regt KIA 30.11.17.

HAWGOOD Arthur Ashley MM Pte 200366 'B' Bn Tank Corps
HAWKE Reginald MM Cpl 266872 264 Railway Coy Royal Engineers
HAWKE Robert MM L/Cpl 16758 8th Somerset Light Infantry
HAWKE Sydney Frederick MM Cpl 33369 2nd Hampshire Regt KIA 31.5.18.
HAWKEN James N. MM+Bar Pte 510220 RAMC
HAWKEN Richard Charles MM Cpl 491865 1/13th London Regt KIA 14.8.18.
HAWKEN Richard W. MM L/Cpl 285243 1/1st Oxfordshire Yeomanry
HAWKER Arthur T. MM Pte 201451 1/5th Liverpool Regt
HAWKER Frank MM Sjt 10510 RFA
HAWKER Frederick W. MM Cpl 34441 41 Siege Bty RGA
HAWKER George Stanley MM Pte 14315 Gloucestershire Regt
HAWKER Heber MM Pte 10819 1st Devonshire Regt
HAWKER James MM Sjt 6053 1st Middlesex Regt
HAWKER James MM Spr 104941 171 Tunnelling Coy Royal Engineers
HAWKER William James Edwin MM Cpl M2/054673 Army Service Corps att 1/3rd(Highland)Fd Amb RAMC
HAWKES Alfred D. MM Sjt 11397 2nd Highland Light Infantry
HAWKES Arthur John MM Cpl 70182 'L' Corps Sig Coy Royal Engineers
HAWKES Arthur R. MM L/Cpl 2790 1/17th London Regt
HAWKES Edward C. MM Pte 45812 1/1st Surrey Yeomanry
HAWKES Edward Charles Stanley Leight MM Gnr 17387 C/112 Bde
HAWKES Ernest MM Pte 7923 2nd Oxf & Bucks Light Infantry DOW 26.11.16.
HAWKES Francis "MM,MIDx2" Bdr 16263 29 Bde RFA
HAWKES Frank H. MM Cpl 4684 1st Royal West Kent Regt
HAWKES Frederick S. MM Pte 11205 8th Royal Berkshire Regt
HAWKES George MM L/Cpl 72345 59 Coy Machine Gun Corps
HAWKES James "MM,MSM" Cpl 20847 Machine Gun Corps
HAWKES James Ernest MM Gnr 699 35 Bde RFA
HAWKES John H. MM Pte 49592 RAMC
HAWKES T.G.H. MM Sjt 19965 RFA
HAWKESWORTH Sidney MM L/Bdr L/4568 B/110 Bde RFA
HAWKESWORTH T.W. MM Pte 1557 Leicestershire Regt
HAWKETT Henry MM Cpl 2499 Royal Sussex Regt
HAWKETTS William H. MM L/Sjt 13350 Army Cyclist Corps
HAWKIN Walter Ernest MM Gnr 203670 C/331 Bde RFA
HAWKING Richard E. MM Sjt 203127 6th Bedfordshire Regt
HAWKINS A. MM Cpl 53738 Machine Gun Corps
HAWKINS A.J. MM Pte 19579 6th Royal West Kent Regt
HAWKINS Albert "MM,MID" Pte 8878 1st Oxf & Bucks Light Infantry
HAWKINS Alfred MM+Bar Pte 26175 Shropshire Light Infantry
HAWKINS Arthur MM L/Cpl 267581 1/7th West Yorkshire Regt
HAWKINS Arthur MM Spr WR/267604 Railway Troops Royal Engineers
HAWKINS Arthur MM Pte 200737 Gloucestershire Regt
HAWKINS Arthur MM Sjt 58323 32 Bde RFA
HAWKINS Bert MM Pte 4718 Machine Gun Corps
HAWKINS Bert MM Cpl 55423 RFA
HAWKINS Charles A. MM Spr 79500 Royal Engineers
HAWKINS Charles Frederick MM Cpl 764096 28th London Regt
HAWKINS Charles G. MM Sjt G/53950 1/19th London Regt
HAWKINS Charles H. MM Sjt 10185 Leicestershire Regt
HAWKINS Charles R. MM Pte 13321 5th Dorsetshire Regt
HAWKINS Dent MM L/Sjt 13463 9th West Riding Regt
HAWKINS E.W. MM Sjt 46910 Machine Gun Corps
HAWKINS Edward T. MM Pte 238233 6th West Yorkshire Regt
HAWKINS Edwin Ernest "DCM,MM" L/Cpl 30262 1st Somerset Light Infantry
HAWKINS Elijah MM Pte 40519 4th Middlesex Regt
HAWKINS Frank MM Sjt 320087 1/6th London Regt
HAWKINS Frank V. MM Pte 201638 East Yorkshire Regt
HAWKINS Frank W. MM Pte 2877 3rd Dragoon Guards
HAWKINS Frederick MM Cpl 40632 West Yorkshire Regt
HAWKINS George E. MM Sjt 767 18th Durham Light Infantry
HAWKINS George Frederick "MM,MID" Pte 9958 2nd Royal Fusiliers KIA 1.7.16.
HAWKINS George James MM Pte 26715 10th Essex Regt DOW 18.10.16.
HAWKINS George W. MM Sjt 913 10th Hussars
HAWKINS Harry MM Gnr 61299 57 Siege Bty RGA DOW 5.12.17.
HAWKINS Harry MM Pte 413 12th Lancers
HAWKINS Harry B. MM Cpl 498331 Royal Engineers
HAWKINS Henry MM Pte 45847 164 Coy Machine Gun Corps
HAWKINS Herbert C.J. MM Sjt 471108 12th London Regt
HAWKINS Howell MM Pte 45208 2nd Worcestershire Regt

HAWKINS James MM Pte 53667 RAMC
HAWKINS James Robert MM Sjt 24243 135 Siege Bty RGA DOW 4.4.17
HAWKINS John MM Bdr 31376 RFA
HAWKINS Joseph MM Pte 7381 1st Somerset Light Infantry
HAWKINS Joseph MM Sjt 22718 RFA
HAWKINS Lawrence Henry "MM,CG(F)" Sjt 9495 2nd East Surrey Regt
HAWKINS Leonard W. "DCM,MM,MID" BSM 51052 24 Bde RFA
HAWKINS Leonard Wells Herbert MM Pte 3057 1/4th Oxf & Bucks Light Infantry
HAWKINS Oliver MM+Bar Pte 235158 1st North Lancashire Regt
HAWKINS Oliver J. MM Sjt 24170 Machine Gun Corps
HAWKINS P. MM Pte 15201 Yeomanry
HAWKINS Percy Edward MM Cpl 5269 6th East Kent Regt
HAWKINS Percy J. MM+Bar L/Cpl G/264 6th Royal West Surrey Regt
HAWKINS Robert MM L/Cpl 95068 13th Liverpool Regt
HAWKINS S.W. MM Pte 451886 London Regt
HAWKINS Thomas "MC,DCM,MM(10343 Sjt 1st S Staffs)" T/2Lt 16th Manchester Regt
HAWKINS Thomas H. MM L/Cpl H/8342 3rd Hussars
HAWKINS Thomas W. MM Pte M2/191235 63 Div Train Army Service Corps
HAWKINS Victor Henry MM L/Cpl 39821 3rd Worcestershire Regt KIA 28.4.18.
HAWKINS William MM Pte 10411 5th Dorsetshire Regt
HAWKINS William MM Pte 17185 5th Dorsetshire Regt
HAWKINS William MM Sjt 46209 Royal Air Force
HAWKINS William MM Sjt 12289 15th Royal Irish Rifles KIA 1.7.16.
HAWKINS William MM Sjt 67228 73 Bty 5 Bde RFA
HAWKINS William MM Pte 20439 CHECK (SITE U/S) Manchester Regt DOW 30.6.18.
HAWKINS William J. MM CSM 700745 1/23rd London Regt
HAWKINS Winnieford Muriel MM Sister F TFNS
HAWKSBEE John MM+Bar Bdr L/30599 RFA
HAWKSBY David C. MM Pte 14092 Gordon Highlanders
HAWKSBY John E. MM 2nd Cpl 61632 54 Fd Coy Royal Engineers
HAWKSBY Tom MM Gnr 81087 323 Bty RFA DOW 8.6.18.
HAWKSEY Edward MM Pte 332062 Liverpool Regt
HAWKSEY James MM Sjt 32865 1st Royal Lancaster Regt
HAWKSLEY Frank MM L/Cpl 82025 Royal Engineers
HAWKSLEY Oliver MM Pte G/461 Royal Fusiliers
HAWKSWORTH Frederick MM Pte 107683 10th Notts & Derby Regt
HAWKSWORTH Harry C. MM Cpl 482521 Royal Engineers
HAWKSWORTH Herbert MM L/Sjt 15983 Coldstream Guards
HAWKSWORTH Lawrence MM Pte 121 7 Fd Amb RAMC
HAWKSWORTH Louis H. MM+Bar Pte 202616 4th Liverpool Regt
HAWKSWORTH William MM Pte M2/188785 'Y' Siege Park Army Service Corps
HAWKYARD Clement MM Pte 1581 Yorkshire Light Infantry
HAWLEY Frank MM Spr 478522 Royal Engineers
HAWLEY Frank MM Pte 9263 22 Fd Amb RAMC
HAWORTH Albert MM Cpl 2512 1/4th Royal Lancaster Regt
HAWORTH E. MM Pte 235203 Lancashire Fusiliers
HAWORTH Fred MM Gnr 146158 245 Siege Bty RGA
HAWORTH Fred MM Gnr 150857 267 Siege Bty RGA Died 8.7.18.
HAWORTH Frederick T. MM L/Cpl 27058 Lancashire Fusiliers
HAWORTH Harry MM Sjt 10777 18th Manchester Regt
HAWORTH James Boothman MM Pte 4947 24th Royal Fusiliers
HAWORTH Sydney S. MM Pte 8955 1st Coldstream Guards
HAWORTH William MM Pte 28849 Royal Lancaster Regt
HAWORTH William Edgar MM Sjt 56067 C/102 Bde RFA
HAWSON William H. MM Spr 156064 182 Tunnelling Coy Royal Engineers
HAWTHORN Charles "MC,DCM,MM(44013 Cpl)" 2Lt 6th King's Own Scottish Borderers
HAWTHORN John W. MM Pte 3/10181 2nd Durham Light Infantry
HAWTHORN Thomas MM Cpl 259440 Royal Engineers
HAWTHORN William MM Pte 10535 5th London Regt
HAWTHORN William MM Gnr 91561 143 Siege Bty RGA DOW 25.9.18.
HAWTHORNE J. MM Pte 7739 Irish Guards
HAWTHORNE Sidney Edwin MM Sjt 19469 4th Worcestershire Regt
HAWTHORNE Walter MM Cpl 60149 101 Coy Labour Corps
HAWTHORNE Wilfred L. MM Pte 149598 19th Bn Machine Gun Corps
HAWTIN George R. MM Sjt 70254 355 Siege Bty RGA
HAWTIN William H.G. MM Sjt 14430 Essex Regt
HAXELL Frederick J. MM CSM 350255 7th London Regt
HAXTON Alexander MM Pte 1844 Royal Highlanders
HAXTON Colin MM Pte 331614 9th Highland Light Infantry
HAXTON Wilfred MM+Bar L/Cpl 204072 12th East Surrey Regt
HAY Albert A. MM Pte S/24239 1st Royal Highlanders
HAY Andrew MM Pte 40546 16th Highland Light Infantry
HAY Baird MM Sjt 235186 Scottish Rifles
HAY Cecil Richard MM L/Cpl 7823 2nd Scots Guards
HAY Charles A. MM Cpl 3004 1/1st Duke of Lancaster's Own Yeo
HAY George MM L/Cpl 1130 1/6th Gordon Highlanders
HAY George MM+Bar Pte 20/801 9th Northumberland Fusiliers DOW 17.4.18.
HAY George E. MM L/Cpl 204785 15th Hampshire Regt
HAY Harry MM L/Cpl 301342 RAMC
HAY Henry MM Pte 40791 1/4th Gordon Highlanders
HAY J. MM Pte 11288 Yorkshire Regt
HAY J.McD. "DCM+Bar,MM+Bar" CSM 200545 5/6th Scottish Rifles
HAY James MM Pte 235408 7th Middlesex Regt
HAY James D. MM Sjt 232902 2nd London Regt
HAY James Robert MM Pte 6069 8th Seaforth Highlanders
HAY Jenkins MM Pte 9561 1st Gordon Highlanders
HAY John MM L/Cpl 351001 5/6th Royal Scots
HAY John MM Sjt 402264 Royal Engineers
HAY John R. MM Pnr 197171 Royal Engineers
HAY John R. MM Sjt 106606 Royal Engineers
HAY John S.S. MM Pte 1911 RAMC
HAY John Walter MM Pte 243155 6th East Kent Regt
HAY Joseph N. "MM,MID" Sjt 20/176 Northumberland Fusiliers
HAY Leslie H. MM Sjt 625624 HAC(Artillery) att 309 Siege Bty RGA
HAY Peter "MM,MID" Sjt 275715 Railway Operating Division Royal Engineers
HAY Robert MM Pte 37323 Northumberland Fusiliers
HAY Robert A.T.D. MM Pte 114157 30th Bn Machine Gun Corps
HAY Thomas MM Pte 15381 12th Durham Light Infantry KIA 27.10.18.
HAY Thomas A. MM Cpl M2/079743 Army Service Corps
HAY William MM Cpl 108517 Royal Engineers
HAY William MM Pte 6374 9th Gordon Highlanders DOW 6.6.18.
HAY William G. MM Sjt 34745 York & Lancaster Regt
HAYBALL Frederick MM L/Cpl 1755 1/6th Gloucestershire Regt Died 13.7.16.
HAYBYRNE Francis MM Sjt 5562 4th Rifle Brigade Died 16.9.16
HAYCOCK George MM L/Cpl 20965 1st Worcestershire Regt
HAYCOCK Harry G. MM Sjt 282324 16 Hy Bty RGA
HAYCOCK James Edwin MM Pte 15783 2nd Coldstream Guards
HAYCOCK Lewis MM Pte 1751 1/7th Worcestershire Regt
HAYCOCK Samuel "DCM,MM" Pte 12791 4th Grenadier Guards
HAYCOCK Stanley H. MM Sjt 1781 1/15th London Regt
HAYCOCK Thomas H. MM Pte 36411 Yorkshire Light Infantry
HAYCOX Ernest B. MM Cpl L/11184 B/83 Bde RFA
HAYCRAFT G.M. MM Air Mech 1 11843 Royal Air Force
HAYDEN Albert L. MM Cpl 9161 1st Royal Berkshire Regt
HAYDEN Augustus MM Sjt 18344 17 Fd Amb RAMC
HAYDEN Clarence MM L/Cpl 242550 Gloucestershire Regt
HAYDEN Edward MM Spr 148786 Royal Engineers
HAYDEN Ernest J. MM L/Cpl 15008 12th Middlesex Regt
HAYDEN Frederick H. MM L/Cpl L/12807 1st Royal Fusiliers
HAYDEN George MM Spr 424151 74 Div Sig Coy Royal Engineers
HAYDEN George William "MM+Bar,MMV(lt)" Sjt G/12393 11th Royal West Kent Regt
HAYDEN Henry MM CSM 202567 Royal Warwickshire Regt
HAYDEN J.G. MM+Bar L/Cpl 357863 Royal Engineers
HAYDEN M. MM Pte G/11125 10th Royal Fusiliers
HAYDEN William J. "DCM,MM" CSM 5924 1/4th Hampshire Regt
HAYDOCK Amos MM Sjt 200003 5th East Lancashire Regt
HAYDOCK Charles MM Pte 242989 1/5th North Lancashire Regt KIA 27.7.17.
HAYDOCK James Herbert MM Bdr L/16509 B/149 Bde RFA
HAYDOCK John K. MM Cpl 696681 RFA
HAYDOCK William MM L/Cpl 14527 6th Lancashire Fusiliers
HAYDON Archie MM Pnr 225029 4 Special Coy Royal Engineers
HAYDON Arthur Ellis MM Sjt R/7434 12th King's Royal Rifle Corps
HAYDON Frank R. MM Sjt 201252 4th Royal Berkshire Regt
HAYDON James H. MM Bdr 46510 RFA
HAYDON Walter MM L/Cpl 15281 11th Welsh Regt
HAYEMES William J. MM L/Cpl 720212 1/24th London Regt
HAYERS Rupert Shepherd MM Cpl 3395 Oxf & Bucks Light Infantry
HAYES Alexander R. MM L/Cpl 17225 Grenadier Guards
HAYES Alfred MM Pte 8908 1st Royal Inniskilling Fusiliers
HAYES Arthur MM L/Cpl 17590 Liverpool Regt
HAYES Arthur MM L/Cpl 21141 Middlesex Regt

HAYES Charles MM L/Cpl 5893 4th Dragoon Guards
HAYES Charles MM Gnr 2499 RFA
HAYES Charles H.J. MM Pte 69392 9th Royal Fusiliers
HAYES Charles William MM Gnr 72227 183 Siege Bty RGA
HAYES Christopher G. MM Cpl L/11827 3rd Middlesex Regt
HAYES Cyril Joseph Harold MM L/Bdr 23388 190 Bde RFA
HAYES Denis MM Bdr 30375 RFA
HAYES Ernest MM L/Cpl 29299 7th Duke of Cornwall's LI
HAYES Ernest MM+2 Bars Cpl 203928 2nd Yorkshire Light Infantry
HAYES Francis L. MM Cpl 16040 6th Leicestershire Regt
HAYES Fred MM Gnr 3115 D/148 Bde RFA KIA 25.4.18.
HAYES George MM Pte 19149 1st Leicestershire Regt
HAYES George MM Pte 20/513 20th Durham Light Infantry KIA 23.3.18.
HAYES George T. MM Dvr 62323 RFA
HAYES H.J. MM Air Mech 1 9236 Royal Flying Corps
HAYES Harold H. MM Sjt 351 MGC(Motors)
HAYES Harold James MM Pnr 103104 32 Div Sig Coy Royal Engineers
HAYES Harry MM L/Cpl 3/7414 2nd Bedfordshire Regt DOW 13.10.16.
HAYES Harry Joseph MM Dvr 39743 77 Bde RFA
HAYES Henry MM Cpl 276210 109 Heavy Bty RGA
HAYES Henry Edward MM Cpl 87157 77 Siege Bty RGA KIA 3.5.18.
HAYES Herbert MM Sjt 36167 178 Siege Bty RGA DOW 7.7.17.
HAYES Herbert MM S/Sjt Mechanic 205021 4th Bn Tank Corps
HAYES Herbert MM Cpl 201210 1/5th Manchester Regt
HAYES Herbert J. MM Pte 2473 1/8th London Regt
HAYES J. MM CQMS 71 7th Royal Sussex Regt
HAYES James MM Pte 241945 2/4th South Lancashire Regt
HAYES James MM+Bar Cpl 56132 X/37 Med TM Bty RFA DOW 13.11.18.
HAYES James MM Pte 5/5463 2nd Royal Munster Fusiliers DOW 30.8.16.
HAYES James MM Sjt 19737 Royal Welsh Fusiliers
HAYES James A. MM L/Cpl 96711 Royal Engineers
HAYES James E. "DCM,MM" L/Cpl 307245 8th Liverpool Regt
HAYES James J. MM L/Sjt 370411 1/8th London Regt
HAYES James T. MM Pte 141845 Machine Gun Corps
HAYES John MM Pte 18482 2nd Royal Irish Regt
HAYES John MM Cpl 6931 1st Wiltshire Regt
HAYES John MM L/Cpl 304070 5th London Regt
HAYES John Ernest MM Pte 82756 49 Coy Machine Gun Corps KIA 21.3.18.
HAYES John Hardwick MM Gnr 129110 D/48 Bde RFA
HAYES John J. MM L/Cpl 16802 1st Notts & Derby Regt
HAYES John T. MM+Bar Pte 21/1602 Northumberland Fusiliers
HAYES Joseph MM Spr 41419 Royal Engineers
HAYES Joseph R. MM Pte 10135 10th Manchester Regt
HAYES Peter MM Pte 2671 1/6th North Staffordshire Regt
HAYES Richard MM Sjt 29109 2nd Cheshire Regt
HAYES Robert "MM,MID" Pte 5780 1st Royal Dublin Fusiliers
HAYES Samuel MM Pte 9201 11th Royal Warwickshire Regt
HAYES Stanley F. "MM,MSM" 2nd Cpl 56218 16 Div Sig Coy Royal Engineers
HAYES Thomas MM Pte 6532 7th Shropshire Light Infantry
HAYES Thomas MM L/Cpl 201941 6th East Lancashire Regt
HAYES Thomas J.E. MM Sjt 67602 Royal Engineers
HAYES Thomas M. MM Gnr 77704 RFA
HAYES Thomas Senior MM Cpl 3271 1/4th York & Lancaster Regt
HAYES Tom MM L/Cpl 12583 West Riding Regt
HAYES Walter George "MM,MSM" Sjt 37221 RGA
HAYES William MM Pte 356851 10th Liverpool Regt
HAYES William MM Spr 57812 36 Div Sig Coy Royal Engineers
HAYES William MM Dvr 94451 RFA
HAYES William MM Pte 17675 South Lancashire Regt
HAYES William Albert MM Sjt 23242 47th Bn Machine Gun Corps
HAYES William Austin MM Sjt 200511 2/5th North Staffordshire Regt KIA 21.3.18.
HAYES William John MM Gnr 35894 RFA
HAYES William T.J. MM Dvr 177236 'N' Bty RHA
HAYFORD Edward J. MM Pte 49220 38 Fd Amb RAMC
HAYHO James Henry MM Cpl 950340 X/47 Med TM Bty RFA
HAYHOW Cyril MM Pte 72039 3rd Bn Machine Gun Corps
HAYHOW Joseph MM+Bar Sjt C/4719 13th King's Royal Rifle Corps
HAYHOW William MM Sjt 914 1st King Edward's Horse
HAYHURST Arthur MM Pte 315020 16th Royal Sussex Regt
HAYHURST Frank MM Pte 276486 7th Manchester Regt
HAYHURST John D. MM Cpl 14765 8th Border Regt
HAYLER Frederick MM Sjt 5111 Machine Gun Corps
HAYLER John MM BSM 61780 C/177 Bde RFA
HAYLES George William MM Gnr L/6336 RFA
HAYLES Leonard MM 2nd Cpl 552751 456 Fd Coy Royal Engineers
HAYLLAR William MM Pte 200467 1/5th Bedfordshire Regt
HAYLOCK Frederick J. MM Pte 49221 RAMC
HAYLOCK George MM Pte 242583 1/7th West Yorkshire Regt
HAYLOCK George MM Gnr 85584 460 Bty 15 Bde RFA
HAYLOCK John O. MM L/Cpl 9899 1/5th London Regt
HAYLOCK Thomas H. MM Sjt 1900 1st Welsh Guards
HAYLOR George C. MM Gnr 54208 25 Bde RFA
HAYMAN Arthur S. MM Pte STK/1684 Royal Fusiliers
HAYMAN Frederick Matthew MM Cpl 22489 C/162 Bde RFA
HAYMAN John T. MM Cpl 9677 2nd Scottish Rifles
HAYMAN William L. MM Spr 540986 153 Fd Coy Royal Engineers
HAYNE Herbert G. MM Pte 31143 51 Fd Amb RAMC
HAYNE William B. MM L/Cpl 390083 1/9th London Regt
HAYNES Albert E. MM Sjt 280472 1/4th London Regt
HAYNES Arthur MM L/Cpl 230536 2/2nd London Regt
HAYNES Arthur MM Pte 2926 1/5th Liverpool Regt
HAYNES Charles MM Pte 16232 Northamptonshire Regt
HAYNES Charles E. MM Pte 5531 Coldstream Guards
HAYNES Charles W. MM L/Cpl 19376 Gloucestershire Regt
HAYNES Cyril "DCM,MM,MID" Sjt 61245 25 Bde RFA
HAYNES E.W. "DCM,MM,MID" Cpl 51657 5 Bde RHA
HAYNES Egerton Joseph MM Cpl 61515 70 Fd Coy Royal Engineers
HAYNES Ernest MM+Bar Pte 46783 RAMC
HAYNES Ernest R. MM L/Cpl 25707 9th West Riding Regt
HAYNES Ernest W. MM L/Cpl 22184 2nd Grenadier Guards
HAYNES Francis J. MM Gnr 33968 RFA
HAYNES Frederick MM Cpl 36478 East Yorkshire Regt
HAYNES Frederick George MM Gnr 71016 71 Heavy Bty RGA
HAYNES George E. MM Cpl 3/3029 6th York & Lancaster Regt
HAYNES George Ernest MM Pte 2937 1/18th London Regt
HAYNES George F. MM Sjt 70049 RFA
HAYNES Harold H. MM Pte 277 17 Fd Amb RAMC
HAYNES Harry MM Pte 40931 South Staffordshire Regt
HAYNES Harry MM Pte 11025 1st South Staffordshire Regt
HAYNES Harry MM Sjt 2379 West Yorkshire Regt
HAYNES Harry MM Cpl 810120 A/232 Bde RFA
HAYNES Herbert MM Sjt 9250 2nd Leicestershire Regt
HAYNES James MM Cpl 51025 RHA
HAYNES James W. MM 2nd Cpl 83226 Royal Engineers
HAYNES John MM Pte 295077 Manchester Regt
HAYNES John G. MM Pte 1805 Oxf & Bucks Light Infantry
HAYNES John William MM Pte 30209 14th Royal Warwickshire Regt KIA 14.4.18.
HAYNES Lawrence MM S/Sjt Armourer T/804 Army Ordnance Corps
HAYNES Leonard MM Pte 49036 1st Northamptonshire Regt
HAYNES Neville J. MM Sjt 6843 19th Hussars
HAYNES Randolph B. MM+2 Bars Sjt 242599 5th Leicestershire Regt
HAYNES Reginald H. MM Cpl G/9780 6th Royal West Kent Regt
HAYNES Samuel MM Pte 17918 20th Manchester Regt DOW 12.7.16.
HAYNES Samuel MM Cpl 41749 2nd South Wales Borderers
HAYNES Shirley E. MM Cpl 10212 Labour Corps
HAYNES W. MM L/Cpl H/41210 1/1st Leicestershire Yeomanry
HAYNES William MM Pte 201394 Notts & Derby Regt
HAYNES William MM Sjt 40547 Royal Scots
HAYNES William J.K. MM Pte 16572 11th Notts & Derby Regt
HAYNES William Leonard MM Spr 387957 6 Siege Coy Royal Monmouthshire Royal Engineers Died 31.10.18.
HAYNS Lancelot R. MM Spr 492103 46 Div Sig Coy Royal Engineers
HAYS Albert E.J. MM Dvr 62219 D/236 Bde RFA
HAYS George MM+Bar Cpl 73112 18 Div Ammn Col RFA
HAYSHAM Ernest MM Pte 240775 1/5th Somerset Light Infantry KIA 22.11.17.
HAYSMAN Lawrence Frederick MM Pte 7557 22nd London Regt
HAYSOM Albert J. MM Gnr 127 RGA
HAYSTON William MM L/Cpl 2719 Gordon Highlanders
HAYTER Albert MM Spr 510304 Royal Engineers
HAYTER Albert H. MM Cpl 203046 1st London Regt
HAYTER George MM Pte 8296 1st West Yorkshire Regt
HAYTER H. MM Pte 32302 1st Gloucestershire Regt
HAYTER Herbert E. MM Pte 20770 1st Essex Regt
HAYTER John W. MM Pte 5302 1/2nd(Highland)Fd Amb RAMC
HAYTER Joseph B. MM Pte 3600 Royal Sussex Regt

HAYTER Sydney MM Cpl S/2696 12th Rifle Brigade DOW 21.9.16.
HAYTER Thomas MM Sjt 21769 16th Royal Welsh Fusiliers
HAYTON Arnold MM Pte 18091 2nd Border Regt
HAYTON Ernest MM Cpl 13445 4th Coldstream Guards
HAYTON Ernest W. MM Gnr 69629 Tank Corps
HAYTON Herbert W. MM Pnr 325692 62 Div Sig Coy Royal Engineers
HAYTON Sydney MM L/Sjt 10706 Machine Gun Corps
HAYWARD Albert MM Pte 17981 7th Shropshire Light Infantry
HAYWARD Albert MM Sjt 3/1974 2nd Yorkshire Light Infantry
HAYWARD Arthur MM Cpl 6335 2nd Lincolnshire Regt
HAYWARD Arthur C. MM Pte 405133 RAMC
HAYWARD Basil C. MM Cpl 329002 1/1st Cambridgeshire Regt
HAYWARD Charles R. MM+Bar Sjt 370772 1/8th London Regt
HAYWARD Edward MM+Bar Sjt 18608 21st Manchester Regt
HAYWARD Edward Elias MM Sjt 20679 RGA
HAYWARD Ernest Albert MM Pte 24298 8th Gloucestershire Regt DOW 20.9.17.
HAYWARD Ernest J. MM Sjt 27864 1st Wiltshire Regt
HAYWARD Ernest James MM 2nd Cpl 805 Royal Engineers
HAYWARD Ernest W. "DCM,MM" Cpl 553 Machine Gun Corps(Heavy Branch)
HAYWARD F.E.G. MM Cpl 2969 2/2nd London Regt
HAYWARD Frank MM Pte 240639 1/5th Suffolk Regt
HAYWARD Frank T. MM Pte M1/5481 7 Div Train Army Service Corps
HAYWARD Frederick H. MM Sjt 10701 King's Royal Rifle Corps
HAYWARD Frederick J. MM Cpl 13699 8th Gloucestershire Regt
HAYWARD Frederick O. "DCM,MM" CSM 12988 6th Shropshire Light Infantry
HAYWARD George MM Pte 9428 2nd Royal Warwickshire Regt
HAYWARD George MM Pte 16441 3rd Coldstream Guards
HAYWARD George MM Sjt 14/1133 14th York & Lancaster Regt
HAYWARD George Arthur MM Pte 31619 1(Cav)Fd Amb RAMC Died 26.10.18.
HAYWARD George L. MM Cpl 5560 3rd Bn GMGR
HAYWARD H.E. MM Sjt 17894 RFA
HAYWARD Harold MM Pte M/2/133526 46 Div Ammn Supply Park Army Service Corps
HAYWARD Harry G. MM Sjt 240533 1/4th Gloucestershire Regt
HAYWARD Henry Cecil MM Sjt S/3012 11th Rifle Brigade KIA 4.4.17.
HAYWARD John MM Sjt 21775 Machine Gun Corps
HAYWARD Joseph Henry Allen MM Sjt 56467 16 Div Sig Coy Royal Engineers
HAYWARD Samuel Graham MM Pte 16017 9th North Lancashire Regt DOW 27.4.18.
HAYWARD Sidney A.J. MM Pte 20020 Machine Gun Corps
HAYWARD T.R. MM Sjt 38271 RGA
HAYWARD Thomas MM Pte 12/395 2nd Yorkshire Light Infantry KIA 7.9.18.
HAYWARD Thomas L. MM Sjt WR/251462 278 Rly Const Coy Royal Engineers
HAYWARD Walter George MM Cpl Z/2723 13th Rifle Brigade
HAYWARD Walter John MM Sjt 580 8th Rifle Brigade DOW 26.8.16.
HAYWARD William MM Pte 6517 Middlesex Regt
HAYWARD William MM Sjt 99976 38th Bn Machine Gun Corps KIA 9.11.18.
HAYWARD William MM L/Cpl 23046 Gloucestershire Regt
HAYWARD William F. MM Bdr 53511 'C' Bty RHA
HAYWARD William Glenfred MM Pte 10045 2nd South Staffordshire Regt KIA 30.11.17.
HAYWARD William H. MM Pte 141 7th Royal Sussex Regt
HAYWARD William Herbert MM L/Cpl 2799 Royal Warwickshire Regt
HAYWARD William J. MM Cpl 9537 1st Somerset Light Infantry
HAYWOOD Albert William MM L/Sjt 9/14225 Leicestershire Regt
HAYWOOD Alfred MM Pte 21035 Worcestershire Regt
HAYWOOD Charles MM Pte 38176 Worcestershire Regt
HAYWOOD E.L. MM 2nd Cpl 549871 56 Div Sig Coy Royal Engineers
HAYWOOD Frederick Allen Victor MM L/Cpl 46707 Machine Gun Corps
HAYWOOD George MM Cpl 24110 18th Lancashire Fusiliers
HAYWOOD Harold MM Pte 241352 5th West Riding Regt
HAYWOOD Harry MM L/Cpl 40633 8th West Yorkshire Regt
HAYWOOD James MM Pte 19606 9th Worcestershire Regt
HAYWOOD John MM L/Cpl 44228 75 Fd Coy Royal Engineers
HAYWOOD John MM Cpl 18736 11th Notts & Derby Regt
HAYWOOD John Thomas MM Pte 19699 2nd Notts & Derby Regt
HAYWOOD Percy Charles MM Pnr 225030 4 Special Coy Royal Engineers
HAYWOOD Richard A. MM Cpl 7163 2nd East Yorkshire Regt
HAYWOOD William Alfred MM Pte M/281394 Army Service Corps att 'G'(AA)Bty RGA.
HAZEL Roger MM Sjt 12053 9th Cheshire Regt
HAZEL William MM Gnr 52031 36 Siege Bty RGA DOW 22.5.17.
HAZELDEN Frederick MM Pte 325041 8th Royal Warwickshire Regt
HAZELGROVE Frank MM Cpl 4555 2nd GMGR
HAZELHURST Ernest MM Bdr 102634 RGA
HAZELHURST John MM Pte 13767 7/8th King's Own Scottish Borderers KIA 6.6.18.
HAZELL Albert M. MM Sjt 16243 RGA
HAZELL Arnold D. MM Pte 201394 Yorkshire Light Infantry
HAZELL F. MM+Bar Pte 6663 2nd Essex Regt
HAZELL Frederick William MM Sjt L/13566 11th Royal Fusiliers KIA 10.8.17.
HAZELL George MM Pte 3573 7th Royal Lancaster Regt
HAZELL George A. MM Bdr 961036 RFA
HAZELL Herbert Joseph MM Cpl 21495 11th Royal West Surrey Regt
HAZELL John MM Sjt M2/174809 406 MT Coy Army Service Corps
HAZELL Oscar Reginald MM Sjt 43012 11th Suffolk Regt KIA 19.4.18.
HAZELL Sidney G. MM+Bar Pte G/7337 2nd London Regt
HAZELL Walter MM L/Cpl 9865 1st Royal Warwickshire Regt
HAZELTINE Walter C.E. MM L/Cpl 10084 4th Hussars
HAZELTON Fred MM Pte 1669 1/4th Suffolk Regt
HAZELTON Frederick W. MM Sjt 143781 41st Bn Machine Gun Corps
HAZELTON William J. MM Pte 8889 Suffolk Regt
HAZELWOOD Arthur MM Pte 326288 1/1st Cambridgeshire Regt KIA 28.4.18.
HAZLE Robert MM+Bar Sjt 242879 5th West Riding Regt
HAZLEHURST David T. MM Sjt 9092 2nd York & Lancaster Regt
HAZLETON Charles L. MM Pte 1251 16th Royal Warwickshire Regt
HAZLETON William MM Pte 754 8th Royal Fusiliers
HAZLETT Francis Henry MM Sjt 86 8(London)Howitzer Bde RFA
HAZLETT George MM Dvr 59746 RFA
HAZLETT William MM Pte 266709 7th Scottish Rifles
HAZLEWOOD Alfred W. MM L/Cpl 721092 24th London Regt
HAZLEWOOD Ben MM Sjt 13334 Hampshire Regt
HAZLEWOOD Eddie Jabez "DCM,MM" Cpl 14821 8th Suffolk Regt
HAZLEWOOD Stanley MM Gnr 41070 112 Heavy Bty RGA
HAZLEWOOD Thomas MM Cpl 5025 18th Hussars
HAZLEWOOD W. MM L/Cpl 12199 Suffolk Regt
HAZZARD Reuben MM Cpl 6662 Royal Berkshire Regt
HAZZARD Sidney MM+Bar Pte 37101 1st Royal West Surrey Regt
HEAD Albert MM Pte 4166 12th East Surrey Regt
HEAD Albert W. MM Bdr 46807 39 Bde RFA
HEAD Arthur MM Sjt 46081 36 Bde RFA DOW 6.9.18.
HEAD Arthur J. MM Pte 59972 7th Royal West Surrey Regt
HEAD Charles A. MM Pte S/26621 2nd Rifle Brigade
HEAD Ernest F. MM Pte 268341 Royal Warwickshire Regt
HEAD Frederick G. MM+Bar Cpl 2357 1/17th London Regt
HEAD Frederick J. MM CQMS G/71985 7th Royal Fusiliers
HEAD George MM Bdr 149079 C/256 Bde RFA
HEAD George MM Pte 260234 10th Duke of Cornwall's LI
HEAD George MM Sjt 30758 RGA
HEAD George T. MM+Bar Sjt 47277 19 Div Sig Coy Royal Engineers
HEAD H.E. MM Pte 34262 York & Lancaster Regt
HEAD Henry MM L/Cpl 3/2317 8th Yorkshire Light Infantry
HEAD Richard MM+Bar Cpl 14624 22 Bde RFA
HEAD William MM Gnr 90085 D/312 Bde RFA
HEAD William J. MM Sjt L/29856 D/178 Bde RFA
HEADFORD James MM Spr 127929 21 Div Sig Coy Royal Engineers
HEADLAND Albert E. MM Pte 15434 Middlesex Regt
HEADLONG Tom MM Cpl 10582 C/78 Bde RFA
HEADS Alexander MM Spr 93527 219 Fd Coy Royal Engineers
HEADWORTH Henry MM Sjt 28063 4th North Staffordshire Regt
HEAFIELD William MM Pte 15367 9th York & Lancaster Regt
HEAL Abraham Louis James MM CSM 30670 8th Devonshire Regt
HEAL Frank MM Pte 9909 6th Somerset Light Infantry KIA 16.9.16.
HEAL Frederick MM+Bar Pte 9912 6th Somerset Light Infantry
HEAL George MM Dvr 17295 'O' Bty RHA
HEAL John W.D. MM Sjt 28/596 Northumberland Fusiliers
HEAL Thomas MM Sjt 12792 Machine Gun Corps
HEAL William Reginald MM Sjt 616277 RHA att 158 Bde RFA.

HEALD Harry MM Dvr 780913 B/256 Bde RFA
HEALD Harry MM Pte 265221 Royal Warwickshire Regt
HEALD Harry MM L/Cpl 76285 Tank Corps
HEALD James MM Sjt 48443 32 Siege Bty RGA
HEALD James W. MM Spr 212883 70 Fd Coy Royal Engineers
HEALD Joe MM Pte 201974 4th Yorkshire Light Infantry
HEALD Robert MM Gnr 710664 RFA
HEALD Thomas MM Pte 3524 16th Lancashire Fusiliers
HEALEY Alfred MM Gnr Sig 29033 D/152 Bde RFA
HEALEY Alfred T. MM Pte 30106 5th West Riding Regt
HEALEY Edward MM Cpl 36614 Machine Gun Corps
HEALEY Ernest MM L/Cpl 9937 2nd Worcestershire Regt
HEALEY Harry MM Sjt 20226 9th Manchester Regt
HEALEY Horace MM+Bar Cpl 240132 2nd West Yorkshire Regt
HEALEY John MM Pte S/20039 7th Cameron Highlanders
HEALEY John Haydon MM Pte 102086 15th Notts & Derby Regt KIA 17.7.18.
HEALEY Joseph H. MM Pte 22780 Yorkshire Light Infantry
HEALEY O.D. MM Pte 11345 5th Yorkshire Light Infantry
HEALEY William MM Pte 3591 6th Dragoons
HEALEY William MM Dvr 37522 RFA
HEALING Vernon MM Pte 17741 1/4th Wiltshire Regt
HEALY Declan MM Bdr 15108 31 Heavy Bty RGA
HEALY Frank MM Cpl 15006 7/8th King's Own Scottish Borderers
HEALY James MM Pte 21423 Lancashire Fusiliers
HEALY John MM Pte 6864 2nd Royal Welsh Fusiliers
HEALY John W. MM L/Sjt 203602 Manchester Regt
HEALY Lawrence MM Cpl 61190 Northumberland Fusiliers
HEALY Michael "DCM,MM+Bar" Sjt 5130 2nd Royal Munster Fusiliers DOW 2.3.17.
HEALY Patrick MM Pte 772 9th Royal Munster Fusiliers
HEALY Thomas MM+Bar Cpl 200158 4/5th Royal Highlanders KIA 27.5.18.
HEALY Thomas MM Sjt S/4598 9th Seaforth Highlanders
HEALY Timothy MM Cpl 17780 RGA
HEALY William MM Cpl 34554 9th Scottish Rifles
HEALY William MM Pte 17902 Machine Gun Corps
HEALY William MM Sjt 6029 37th Bn Machine Gun Corps
HEANEY Adam MM L/Cpl 20882 Army Cyclist Corps
HEANEY Bernard MM Cpl 111224 237 Lt Rly Fwd Coy Royal Engineers
HEANEY Daniel MM Sjt 17286 Machine Gun Corps
HEANEY James MM L/Cpl 8572 Irish Guards
HEANEY John MM Pte 27664 1st Royal Irish Fusiliers
HEANEY T.J. MM L/Cpl 25676 Royal Inniskilling Fusiliers
HEAP Arthur MM Sjt 11978 16th Lancashire Fusiliers
HEAP Charles H. MM Sjt 32948 10th West Yorkshire Regt
HEAP Fred MM Sjt 352224 2(East Lancashire)Fd Amb RAMC
HEAP Henry MM L/Cpl 312414 Signal Service Royal Engineers att 150 Bde RFA.
HEAP James MM Pte 20183 2nd Grenadier Guards
HEAP Thomas MM L/Sjt 17252 2nd Coldstream Guards
HEAP William MM Pte 51826 Liverpool Regt
HEAPHY Patrick MM L/Cpl 25679 Machine Gun Corps
HEAPS Fred B. MM Cpl C/12624 18th King's Royal Rifle Corps
HEAPS John MM Sjt 200057 1/4th North Lancashire Regt KIA 30.11.17.
HEAPS Tom MM Pte 201197 4th Yorkshire Light Infantry
HEARD Albert MM Sjt 10768 2nd Hampshire Regt DOW 25.3.18.
HEARD Albert Edward "MM,MID" Sjt 3335 Machine Gun Corps
HEARD Albert H. MM Cpl M2/082035 360 Coy Army Service Corps
HEARD Arthur MM Pte 241863 2/6th West Yorkshire Regt
HEARD Horace E. MM Pte 681492 1/22nd London Regt
HEARD James MM Pte 295566 12th Somerset Light Infantry
HEARD John MM Cpl 57500 D/310 Bde RFA
HEARD Reuben W. MM Sjt 450924 11th London Regt
HEARD Wilfred MM Spr 459537 447 Fd Coy Royal Engineers Died 11.10.18.
HEARD William MM Bdr 14862 RFA
HEARD William Charles MM L/Cpl 28751 Duke of Cornwall's LI
HEARD William E. MM Pte 63347 Machine Gun Corps
HEARD William H. MM Gnr 123023 RFA
HEARDLEY George "DCM,MM" Pte 280993 1/7th Lancashire Fusiliers DOW 27.9.18.
HEARN Albert MM L/Cpl 22772 Grenadier Guards
HEARN Arthur MM Cpl 200569 Seaforth Highlanders
HEARN Benjamin MM Pte G/4153 9th Royal Sussex Regt
HEARN Charles MM CSM 10372 3rd Grenadier Guards KIA 14.9.16.
HEARN Edwin R. MM Spr 510307 Royal Engineers
HEARN Jack F. "DCM,MM" Sjt 422540 2/10th London Regt
HEARN James H. MM Pte 42194 9th Scottish Rifles
HEARN James William MM+Bar Sjt 17638 1st Royal Berkshire Regt KIA 17.5.18.
HEARN John MM Gnr 68840 RHA
HEARN Percy MM Cpl 9777 1st Northamptonshire Regt
HEARN Samuel MM Pte 307543 10th Bn Tank Corps
HEARN Stanley W. MM Pte 533774 15th London Regt
HEARN Thomas A. MM Pte 9944 1st Royal Berkshire Regt
HEARN W.H. MM Air Mech 1 402998 Royal Air Force
HEARN William Henry "MC,MM,MID" RQMS 2911 3rd Rifle Brigade
HEARNE Huntley H. MM Cpl 1920 17th Royal Fusiliers
HEARNE J. MM Cpl P/2503 Military Foot Police
HEARNE James MM Pte 10440 Cheshire Regt
HEARNE Joseph MM Sjt Farrier 616329 158 Bde RHA
HEARNE William MM+Bar Sjt 37010 62 Div Sig Coy Royal Engineers
HEARNSHAW Herbert MM Cpl 47217 17th Liverpool Regt
HEARSEY Ashton C. MM Gnr 78353 Tank Corps
HEARSEY William Edward MM L/Cpl 266592 1/6th Gloucestershire Regt KIA 9.8.18.
HEARSON H.R. MM Bdr 29800 RGA
HEASMAN Horace MM L/Cpl 240772 1/5th Royal Sussex Regt
HEASMAN William MM Spr 32846 Guards Div Sig Coy Royal Engineers
HEASMAN William B. MM Sjt 722859 24th London Regt
HEASTER Herbert A. MM L/Cpl 200153 1/4th Essex Regt
HEATH Albert MM Sjt 54822 22 Heavy Bty RGA
HEATH Albert Ernest MM Pte 81875 122 Coy Machine Gun Corps
HEATH Albert James "MM,MID" Spr 95876 204 Fd Coy Royal Engineers
HEATH Alfred T. MM+Bar L/Cpl 700129 1/23rd London Regt
HEATH Charles MM Dvr 107227 RFA
HEATH Charles MM Spr 179486 21 Div Sig Coy Royal Engineers
HEATH Charles MM Pte 240458 1/5th Devonshire Regt
HEATH Charles MM Dvr 745267 RFA
HEATH Ernest John MM Sjt 940057 D/281 Bde RFA KIA 8.12.17.
HEATH Frank MM Pte 19463 11th Notts & Derby Regt
HEATH Frank E. MM Cpl 65068 126 Siege Bty RGA
HEATH Fred MM+Bar Sjt 275254 1/7th Manchester Regt DOW 24.4.18.
HEATH Frederick C. MM Sjt 17220 56 Fd Coy Royal Engineers
HEATH George MM L/Cpl 240798 North Staffordshire Regt
HEATH George MM L/Cpl 12479 11th Hampshire Regt
HEATH George MM Pte 72047 112 Fd Amb RAMC
HEATH George H. MM Dvr L/32235 D/235 Bde RFA
HEATH Harry MM Gnr 795541 RFA
HEATH Herbert MM Sjt 241944 1st Cheshire Regt
HEATH Herbert MM Pte 47431 RAMC
HEATH John MM Pte 18237 East Yorkshire Regt
HEATH John H. MM Sjt 23085 Duke of Cornwall's LI
HEATH John Joseph "MC,DCM,MM" CSM 527 2nd Royal Warwickshire Regt
HEATH John William MM Sjt 9728 5th Shropshire Light Infantry DOW 5.11.17.
HEATH Oliver MM Pte 43351 10th Royal Warwickshire Regt
HEATH Percy MM Pte 37698 9th Yorkshire Light Infantry KIA 25.4.17.
HEATH Percy Thomas MM L/Cpl 7/17896 7th South Wales Borderers KIA 5.5.18.
HEATH Richard S. MM+Bar Cpl 241638 1/6th Royal Warwickshire Regt
HEATH Samuel P. MM Sjt 30408 1st Devonshire Regt
HEATH Stanley George MM L/Cpl 29660 15th Hampshire Regt KIA 20.9.17.
HEATH Thomas Henry MM L/Cpl 103283 32 Div Sig Coy Royal Engineers
HEATH Thomas Joseph MM Pte 71715 2nd Royal Fusiliers
HEATH W.H. MM Pte 31990 Essex Regt
HEATH William MM Pte 382780 113 Coy Labour Corps
HEATH William Charles MM Pte 9557 2nd Hampshire Regt KIA 17.10.16.
HEATH William H. MM Pte 80445 RAMC
HEATH William R. MM+Bar Cpl 39676 4th Worcestershire Regt
HEATH William S. MM Dmr 1193 1/8th Notts & Derby Regt
HEATHCOCK Harold MM Sjt 9154 2nd Duke of Cornwall's LI
HEATHCOTE Charles MM L/Cpl 59648 10th Notts & Derby Regt
HEATHCOTE Charles MM Pte 123763 Machine Gun Corps
HEATHCOTE Charles MM L/Cpl 17783 6th York & Lancaster Regt
HEATHCOTE Edmund MM Sjt 15047 13th Cheshire Regt

HEATHCOTE Frank MM Cpl 18918 18th Liverpool Regt
HEATHCOTE Harry MM Sjt 1107 A/190 Bde RFA
HEATHCOTE John M. MM L/Cpl R/10514 King's Royal Rifle Corps
HEATHCOTE Joseph MM+Bar Sjt 5304 10th Lancashire Fusiliers
HEATHCOTE Joseph J. MM Pte 11268 2nd Notts & Derby Regt
HEATHCOTE Sidney MM Dvr 61241 42 Bde RFA
HEATHCOTE Walter MM L/Sjt 23391 4th(ER) North Staffordshire Regt
HEATHER Alfred W. MM L/Cpl 6014 6th Dragoons
HEATHER Frederick William MM L/Cpl 10210 3rd Hussars
HEATHER H.B. MM Bdr 75391 38 Bde RFA
HEATHER Norman MM Sjt 2372 RAMC
HEATHER Richard MM Spr 152278 Royal Engineers
HEATHERILL Archibald MM Sjt 422019 416 Fd Coy Royal Engineers KIA 14.8.17.
HEATHERINGTON Colin MM Pte 251528 5/6th Royal Scots
HEATHFIELD Stephen MM Sjt M2/074782 39 Div MT Coy Army Service Corps Died 3.11.18.
HEATHFIELD Stephen MM Pte 8836 1st East Kent Regt
HEATHFIELD William MM L/Cpl 194 11th Royal Sussex Regt
HEATLEY Edward MM L/Sjt 240308 Liverpool Regt
HEATLEY Robert W. MM Bdr 49359 24 Bde RFA
HEATLEY Thomas MM Gnr 751034 250 Bde RFA
HEATON Anthony "DCM,MM" BSM 51308 B/187 Bde RFA
HEATON Edward MM Dvr 30470 41 Bde RFA
HEATON Elias MM Bdr 34506 RFA
HEATON Ernest Arthur MM L/Sjt 12388 2nd Scots Guards
HEATON George Stanley MM Pte 42474 11th Essex Regt DOW 29.10.18.
HEATON Harold MM Cpl 4798 9th Royal Fusiliers KIA 8.8.18.
HEATON Harold MM Pte 18/558 18th West Yorkshire Regt
HEATON Harry MM L/Sjt 201217 2/4th West Riding Regt
HEATON J. MM+Bar Sjt 710239 B/211 Bde RFA
HEATON James MM Cpl 240204 1/5th North Lancashire Regt
HEATON James P. MM Gnr Sig 926284 D/290 Bde RFA
HEATON John MM Cpl 201043 1/5th Royal Warwickshire Regt
HEATON John Thomas MM Sjt 426255 422 Fd Coy Royal Engineers
HEATON Leeman MM Pte MS/1133 Army Service Corps att RE.
HEATON Raymond Moorhouse MM Dvr 786216 RFA
HEATON Robert L. MM Bdr 56803 102 Bde RFA
HEATON Samuel MM Sjt 242570 4/5th North Lancashire Regt
HEATON Sydney MM Sjt 2124 1/5th Royal Lancaster Regt
HEATON Thomas MM L/Cpl 306568 West Riding Regt
HEATON Thomas H. MM Gnr 69204 RGA
HEATON Walter MM Bdr 26250 C/70 Bde RFA DOW 17.8.16.
HEAVEN Victor MM Cpl R/33992 16th King's Royal Rifle Corps
HEAVENS Wilfred MM Pte 43508 1st Royal Inniskilling Fusiliers
HEAVER Edward MM L/Sjt 12237 8th York & Lancaster Regt
HEAVER William MM Pte 18661 8th Royal Berkshire Regt
HEAVEY Martin T. MM L/Cpl 23919 Notts & Derby Regt
HEAVICAN Viscount MM Bdr 48671 RGA
HEAVYSIDE Thomas MM Pte 241166 5th Royal Lancaster Regt
HEAWOOD Sidney MM Pte 201589 Leicestershire Regt
HEAYNES H. MM Cpl 202636 Worcestershire Regt
HEBBERD Reginald Clifford MM Sjt 4786 1/4th London Regt KIA 1.7.16.
HEBBLETHWAITE George MM Pte 62719 9th Yorkshire Light Infantry
HEBBLETHWAITE John MM Sjt 785284 RFA
HEBBLEWHITE Edward MM Pte 1810 1/7th Royal Warwickshire Regt KIA 14.7.16.
HEBBLEWHITE Walter MM Dvr 790107 RFA
HEBBURN Charles H. MM Cpl SR/2472 11th Royal Fusiliers
HEBDEN Charles MM+Bar Pte 12653 1/1st Hertfordshire Regt
HEBDEN Edwin MM Pte 38778 Northumberland Fusiliers
HEBDON Bernard MM+Bar Sjt 10445 Royal Fusiliers
HEBDON Wilfred MM Pte 36438 8th Northumberland Fusiliers
HEBNER Ian Donald Munro MM Pnr 113949 13 Cav Bde Sig Troop Royal Engineers
HEBRON Robert MM Pte 33687 Northumberland Fusiliers
HEBRON Thomas MM Pte 4/7930 West Yorkshire Regt
HECKRATH Walter Edward MM Pte R/6568 King's Royal Rifle Corps
HECTOR John MM Cpl 77829 Royal Engineers
HEDDITCH Clarence James MM Sjt 30883 7th Royal West Surrey Regt
HEDGE John W. MM+Bar Sjt 73925 C/312 Bde RFA
HEDGE Thomas John MM Cpl 19078 2nd Bedfordshire Regt KIA 21.8.18.

HEDGECOCK Hubert F. MM Cpl G/17938 11th Royal Fusiliers
HEDGECOCK Wiliiam Tebbutt MM Bdr 33448 158 Siege Bty RGA DOW 30.4.17.
HEDGECOX Alfred MM Bdr 39413 A/102 Bde RFA Died 10.3.18.
HEDGELEY Sidney MM L/Cpl 7247 1st Norfolk Regt DOW 8.7.17.
HEDGER Frank MM Pte 2827 2/4th London Regt
HEDGER Harry MM L/Cpl 8676 2nd Royal West Surrey Regt
HEDGER Thomas MM L/Cpl 85815 212 Fd Coy Royal Engineers
HEDGER Thomas J. MM Pte 19368 Hampshire Regt
HEDGES Bernard MM Pte 17143 7th Somerset Light Infantry
HEDGES Bertie Charles MM Sjt 616288 RHA
HEDGES Christopher C.T. MM Sjt 6214 RGA
HEDGES Edward Robert MM L/Cpl 26811 1/5th Royal Lancaster Regt Died 29.10.17.
HEDGES Fred MM Pte S/4725 13th Rifle Brigade
HEDGES Frederick MM Sjt 240058 1/8th Middlesex Regt
HEDGES James MM Sjt 851476 RFA
HEDGES Jesse MM Pte 306616 8th Royal Warwickshire Regt
HEDGES John MM Pte 57825 36 Fd Amb RAMC
HEDGES Reginald C. MM Pte 50284 8th Bn Machine Gun Corps
HEDGES William MM Sjt 52554 'L' Bty RHA
HEDGMAN Walter William MM Pte 47146 1/5th York & Lancaster Regt
HEDINGHAM Frank MM+Bar Bdr 81623 41 Bty 42 Bde RFA
HEDLEY Frederick Aubrey "MM(16387,178 Bde RFA)+Bar" Cpl 253119 40 Div Sig Coy Royal Engineers
HEDLEY John MM Spr 266346 Royal Engineers
HEDLEY Robert MM Spr 158624 179 Tunnelling Coy Royal Engineers
HEDLEY Robert MM CSM 15339 10th Royal Welsh Fusiliers
HEDLEY Robert MM Pte 79055 12th Durham Light Infantry
HEDLEY Robert MM Pte 16121 Durham Light Infantry
HEDLEY Thomas N. MM Sjt H/271004 1/1st Northumberland Yeomanry
HEDLEY William MM Sjt 1182 1/1(Northumbrian)Fd Coy Royal Engineers
HEDLEY William "DCM,MM" Sjt 15674 8th Somerset Light Infantry
HEELEY Charles MM Sjt 11540 3rd Worcestershire Regt
HEELEY Harry MM Pte 23388 6th North Lancashire Regt
HEELEY Phillip MM Pte 65185 5th Yorkshire Light Infantry
HEELEY William MM Cpl 265193 4th Liverpool Regt
HEENEY Nicholas MM L/Cpl 23928 1st Royal Dublin Fusiliers
HEENIGAN Thomas MM Pte 1780 2nd South Lancashire Regt
HEEPS Jack MM Pte M2/048916 Army Service Corps att RAMC
HEFFEL Alfred MM Bdr 11575 6 Div Ammn Col RFA
HEFFER Frederick MM Pte 231154 2nd London Regt
HEFFER Randall MM Spr 221625 55 Div Sig Coy Royal Engineers
HEFFERNAN Edward MM Pte 8/3690 8th Royal Munster Fusiliers
HEFFORD James MM Pte 307119 West Riding Regt
HEGAN Phillip MM Pte 10975 6th Border Regt
HEGARTY John MM Pte 51539 1st Cheshire Regt
HEGARTY John MM Pte 17165 8th Royal Inniskilling Fusiliers KIA 28.2.17.
HEGARTY Michael MM Cpl 31007 RGA
HEGARTY Richard MM Pte 205531 4th West Riding Regt
HEGARTY Richard MM Sjt 11789 7th South Lancashire Regt KIA 22.7.16.
HEGARTY Thomas MM Sjt 43931 RAMC
HEGARTY William MM Gnr L/3405 RFA
HEGGARTY Henry MM Gnr 91350 A/54 Bde RFA
HEGGIE Hugh G. MM Cpl S/18871 Cameron Highlanders
HEGGIE W. MM F/Sjt 3574 Royal Flying Corps
HEIGHLEY Sydney Victor MM Pte 18/16240 18th Liverpool Regt
HEIGHTON Alfred MM Pte 12177 20th Hussars
HEIGHTON Leonard R. MM Pte 255380 1/1st Leicestershire Yeo
HEILBRON Victor Israel MM Gnr 78800 B/15 Bde RHA DOW 27.4.17.
HEINSON F.E. MM Pte 34922 1st Essex Regt
HEINZ Francis Ernest MM Cpl 68628 43 Bde RFA
HEISE Albert William MM Cpl 3186 11th Royal Sussex Regt KIA 27.4.18.
HEITMAN Henry Alfred MM Bdr 82437 D/38 Bde RFA DOW 5.8.17.
HEKE Arthur H. "DCM,MM" Cpl 41803 A/69 Bde RFA
HELCOOP Edward MM Pte 53301 17th Royal Fusiliers
HELINGOE John MM Pte 21858 23rd Manchester Regt
HELLEWELL Albert MM Dvr Fitter 147472 C/317 Bde RFA
HELLEWELL George W. MM Dvr 785365 C/232 Bde RFA
HELLIAR Kenneth MM L/Cpl 355364 1/10th Liverpool Regt KIA 9.4.18.
HELLIER Percival H. MM Pte 128381 Machine Gun Corps

HELLIER William MM Sjt 54212 'E' Corps Sig Coy Royal Engineers
HELLINGS Sidney P. MM L/Cpl 372698 8th London Regt
HELLIWELL Benjamin MM Pte 200536 West Riding Regt
HELLIWELL Clement MM Pte 240214 West Riding Regt
HELLIWELL Douglas MM Sjt 240309 Notts & Derby Regt
HELLIWELL Ernest MM Gnr 112395 RGA
HELLIWELL George MM Pte 2766 1st Rifle Brigade
HELLIWELL H.R. MM L/Cpl 26255 West Yorkshire Regt
HELLIWELL Harold Naylor MM Pte 30212 4/5th North Lancashire Regt
HELLIWELL Herbert M. MM Dvr 312636 RGA
HELLIWELL James S. MM Gnr 66031 146 Siege Bty RGA
HELLIWELL Luther MM Pte 86005 3rd Bn Machine Gun Corps
HELLYER William James MM 2nd Cpl 41270 Royal Engineers
HELM George Dodd MM Pte 34717 11th Lancashire Fusiliers
HELM William MM Sjt 19123 9th North Lancashire Regt
HELME Harold MM Pte 201418 Royal Lancaster Regt
HELMER Bertie MM Sjt 113039 Royal Engineers
HELPS Albert "MM,MIDx2" Pnr Sjt 186 2nd Coldstream Guards
HELPS Arthur Stafford MM Pte 43612 18th London att 13th Royal Irish Rifles
HELSBY Enos MM Pte 200958 1/4th South Lancashire Regt
HELSBY Joseph MM+Bar Cpl 47427 Manchester Regt
HELSHAM George D. MM Pte 307424 5th London Regt
HELSTRIP John MM Dvr 19790 D/155 Bde RFA
HEMBOROUGH James MM Sjt 7732 10th Devonshire Regt DOW 11.2.17.
HEMINGWAY Arthur MM Pte 41555 West Yorkshire Regt
HEMINGWAY Norman MM Bdr 70419 RGA
HEMLIN Thomas H. MM L/Cpl 19413 8th Royal Lancaster Regt
HEMM Arthur MM+Bar Sjt 6154 11th Royal Scots Fusiliers
HEMMAWAY John W. MM Pte G/12860 Royal West Surrey Regt
HEMMETT Alfred J. MM Cpl 8779 2nd South Lancashire Regt
HEMMING Albert E. MM L/Cpl 664 1st Royal Warwickshire Regt
HEMMING Alfred Francis MM Pte 23862 3rd Grenadier Guards
HEMMING Anthony "MM,MID" Pte 1836 RAMC
HEMMING Arthur MM Sjt 6111 1st Worcestershire Regt
HEMMING E. MM Sjt 72 Royal Warwickshire Regt
HEMMING Ernest MM Cpl 24397 3 Div Sig Coy Royal Engineers
HEMMING Frederick T. MM Sjt 32257 6th York & Lancaster Regt
HEMMING Joseph Charles MM Pte 8505 2nd Coldstream Guards KIA 9.10.17.
HEMMING Raymond C. MM Gnr 66641 RFA
HEMMING W. MM L/Cpl 1194 Worcestershire Regt
HEMMING W.T. MM Pte 57364 RAMC
HEMMINGFIELD S. MM Sjt 80867 19th Durham Light Infantry
HEMMINGS Albert MM Dvr 38539 RHA
HEMMINGS Albert H. MM Spr 189925 Royal Engineers
HEMMINGS Bertie MM L/Cpl 200653 1/4th Leicestershire Regt
HEMMINGS Charles MM Sjt 7087 1st East Surrey Regt
HEMMINGS Fred MM Pte 45344 Yorkshire Light Infantry
HEMMINGS Frederick MM Dvr 84506 41 Bty 42 Bde RFA
HEMMINGS Ivor MM Cpl 21423 1st South Wales Borderers
HEMMINGS John H. MM L/Cpl 16506 Gloucestershire Regt
HEMMINGS Lancelot MM Pte 13275 10th Gloucestershire Regt
HEMMINGS William Richard MM CQMS 9252 1st Scottish Rifles KIA 1.7.16.
HEMMINGTON Frank "DCM,MM" L/Cpl 2825 23rd Royal Fusiliers
HEMPSALL George MM Sjt 77634 RGA
HEMPSALL Robert MM Pte 28317 6th Lincolnshire Regt
HEMS John MM Sjt 942 1st Royal Warwickshire Regt
HEMS William Thomas MM Gnr 123768 282 Siege Bty RGA DOW 28.9.17.
HEMSLEY Alfred William MM Cpl 14292 72 Bde RFA
HEMSLEY Charles MM Sjt M/321602 'Y' Siege Park Army Service Corps
HEMSLEY Charles Phillip "MM,MSM" Sjt 52984 321 Siege Bty RGA
HEMSLEY Edward MM Gnr 38085 A/94 Bde RFA
HEMSLEY G. MM 2nd Cpl 25915 Royal Engineers
HEMSLEY Harold MM+Bar Pte L/9919 2nd Royal Sussex Regt
HEMSLEY Harry MM L/Cpl 2209 1/6th North Staffordshire Regt
HEMSLEY Horace MM L/Cpl 88 IX Corps Cyclist Bn Army Cyclist Corps
HEMSLEY John William MM Pte 30990 8th Bn Machine Gun Corps
HEMSLEY Joseph Arthur MM Sjt 942 A/245 Bde RFA
HEMSLEY Norman H. MM Sjt 100957 169 Siege Bty RGA
HEMSLEY Spencer Harold MM Cpl 202190 2nd Royal Sussex Regt DOW 28.9.18.
HEMSLEY William H. MM Pte B/200688 13th Rifle Brigade
HEMSON William "MM,MID" L/Cpl 1450 4th Rifle Brigade

HENBEST James MM L/Cpl 6957 1st Hampshire Regt KIA 24.10.16.
HENDER William C. MM Sjt 19297 RFA
HENDERSON A. MM+Bar Pte 265324 1/6th Royal Highlanders
HENDERSON A.S. MM S/Sjt 524 Army Veterinary Corps
HENDERSON Alexander MM L/Cpl 153342 14 Div Sig Coy Royal Engineers
HENDERSON Alexander MM Pte 13215 1/7th Gordon Highlanders KIA 26.3.18.
HENDERSON Alexander MM Sjt 79057 Royal Engineers DOW 15.4.17.
HENDERSON Alexander MM L/Sjt 200471 1/4th Gordon Highlanders
HENDERSON Alfred V. MM Cpl 24664 RAMC
HENDERSON Andrew MM Sjt 650238 169 Bde RFA
HENDERSON Andrew Beaton MM Pte 2365 2nd Royal Scots KIA 26.9.17.
HENDERSON Angus MM Pte 22213 10th Arg & Suth Highlanders
HENDERSON Angus MM+Bar L/Cpl A/7051 2nd & 1st Royal Scots Fusiliers
HENDERSON Archibald Cameron MM Pte R/17631 King's Royal Rifle Corps
HENDERSON Bertram MM Sjt R/2516 King's Royal Rifle Corps
HENDERSON Charles MM Sjt 95263 434 Siege Bty RGA
HENDERSON Charles MM Dvr 635160 256 Bde RFA
HENDERSON Charles MM Pte 4333 18th Highland Light Infantry
HENDERSON David MM Pte 252430 1/6th Arg & Suth Highlanders
HENDERSON David MM Pte 32784 16th Royal Warwickshire Regt
HENDERSON David MM Pte 2146 1/7th Arg & Suth Highlanders
HENDERSON David F. MM Pte 3587 11th Royal Scots
HENDERSON Donald "MM,MID" Cpl S/4423 9th Seaforth Highlanders
HENDERSON Edwin W. MM Sjt 23956 Machine Gun Corps
HENDERSON Ernest H. MM Sjt 67430 113 Coy Labour Corps
HENDERSON Francis MM Cpl 57306 106 Fd Coy Royal Engineers
HENDERSON Frank MM Cpl 645601 RFA
HENDERSON George MM Pte 8648 7/8th King's Own Scottish Borderers KIA 31.7.17.
HENDERSON George MM L/Cpl 22608 1/5th Seaforth Highlanders
HENDERSON George MM Sjt 1825 Northumberland Fusiliers
HENDERSON George MM Sjt S/6414 9th Gordon Highlanders
HENDERSON George MM Gnr 70421 69 Div Ammn Col RFA Died 25.10.18.
HENDERSON Gordon "MC,MM(2016 Cpl 1/21st London)" 2Lt 21st Middlesex
HENDERSON Gregor MM Sjt 344315 RGA
HENDERSON Harold MM Pte 12682 4th West Riding Regt
HENDERSON Harry "MM+Bar,MSM" Dvr 64956 52 Bty 15 Bde RFA
HENDERSON Henry MM+Bar Gnr 180424 499 Siege Bty RGA
HENDERSON Henry MM Pte 292469 Royal Highlanders
HENDERSON Isaiah MM L/Cpl 45096 15th Highland Light Infantry
HENDERSON J. MM Pte 21074 Royal Irish Fusiliers
HENDERSON James MM Sjt 330600 9th Highland Light Infantry
HENDERSON James MM Sjt TT/02981 Army Veterinary Corps
HENDERSON James MM Cpl 42908 41st Bn Machine Gun Corps
HENDERSON James MM Pte 19697 1/4th Royal Scots Fusiliers
HENDERSON James MM Pte 48399 North Staffordshire Regt
HENDERSON James MM Sjt 590627 1/18th London Regt
HENDERSON James MM Pte 22595 Highland Light Infantry
HENDERSON James MM Dvr 701024 49 Bty 40 Bde RFA DOW 8.5.18.
HENDERSON James W. MM Gnr 346183 RGA
HENDERSON James William MM Pnr 147254 Royal Engineers
HENDERSON John MM Pte 24563 10th West Riding Regt
HENDERSON John MM Pte 357477 Liverpool Regt
HENDERSON John "DCM,MM" Sjt 8480 1st Cameron Highlanders
HENDERSON John MM Sjt 8502 2nd Royal Scots
HENDERSON John MM Pte 2880 1st Northumberland Fusiliers
HENDERSON John "MM,MID" Sjt 3/6217 Arg & Suth Highlanders
HENDERSON John MM Pte 78255 11th Northumberland Fusiliers
HENDERSON John MM Pte 27785 King's Own Scottish Borderers
HENDERSON John MM Pte 8505 2nd Scots Guards
HENDERSON John MM Dvr 77371 RFA
HENDERSON John MM Pte S/29089 Rifle Brigade
HENDERSON John Alexander MM Pte 7510 11th Northumberland Fusiliers
HENDERSON John Davidson MM Dvr 81383 Guards Div Ammn Col RFA
HENDERSON John E. "MM,MID" Cpl 51927 RFA
HENDERSON John H.D. MM Cpl 39762 RAMC

HENDERSON John James MM Pte 17024 13th Durham Light Infantry KIA 21.9.17.
HENDERSON John P.. MM 2nd Cpl 19428 Royal Engineers
HENDERSON Luke MM L/Cpl 93804 Royal Engineers
HENDERSON Mark MM Sjt 19203 203 Siege Bty RGA
HENDERSON Martin MM SM 12947 RAMC
HENDERSON Matthew MM Sjt S/40429 1/8th Royal Highlanders
HENDERSON Matthew McLaren MM Gnr 120560 2 Siege Bty RGA
HENDERSON Peter MM Cpl 132134 250 Tunnelling Coy Royal Engineers
HENDERSON Peter Aitken MM Pte 44307 213 Coy Machine Gun Corps
HENDERSON Robert MM Sjt 10411 1st Scots Guards
HENDERSON Robert MM L/Cpl 268737 8th Royal Highlanders
HENDERSON Robert MM+Bar Pte 3170 1/7th Royal Highlanders
HENDERSON Robert MM Gnr 55311 130 Heavy Bty RGA
HENDERSON Robert MM Cpl 200332 1/4th Royal Scots KIA 27.9.18.
HENDERSON Robert MM Cpl 830 1st Gordon Highlanders
HENDERSON Robert MM Cpl 528 C/86 Bde RFA DOW 9.9.17.
HENDERSON Robert Walton MM Pte 54578 2 Fd Amb RAMC
HENDERSON Roxby MM Sjt 16115 8th Somerset Light Infantry
HENDERSON Septimus K. MM Pte 202152 12th Royal Scots Fusiliers
HENDERSON Thomas MM L/Cpl 325178 1/5th Durham Light Infantry
HENDERSON Thomas "MM,MID" Pte 3984 RAMC
HENDERSON Thomas MM Spr 463204 50 Div Sig Coy Royal Engineers DOW 13.4.18.
HENDERSON Thomas MM Spr 2989 Royal Engineers
HENDERSON Thomas MM Sjt 122422 174 Siege Bty RGA KIA 25.9.18.
HENDERSON Thomas MM Pte 697 King Edward's Horse
HENDERSON Thomas Henry MM Gnr 141546 49 Siege Bty RGA KIA 9.7.18.
HENDERSON William MM Cpl 22840 B/82 Bde RFA
HENDERSON William MM Cpl 41278 Scottish Rifles
HENDERSON William MM Sjt 2147 1/4th Royal Highlanders
HENDERSON William MM Pte 11976 15th Royal Irish Rifles
HENDERSON William MM Pnr 343535 Royal Engineers
HENDERSON William MM L/Cpl 200202 1/4th Seaforth Highlanders
HENDERSON William C. MM Cpl 241609 8th Worcestershire Regt
HENDERSON William John MM Dvr 13289 35 Div Ammn Col RFA
HENDERSON William S. "MM,MID" L/Sjt 58068 7th Liverpool Regt
HENDEY H.S. MM Sjt 200711 Worcestershire Regt
HENDLE George W. MM Pte 2491 2nd Rifle Brigade
HENDLEY Arthur MM Pte 9032 2nd Worcestershire Regt
HENDLEY Frederick A. MM L/Cpl L/9003 2nd Royal Sussex Regt
HENDLEY George E. MM Sjt 13736 B/74 Bde RFA
HENDLEY Peter James Ransford MM Pte 18591 7th South Staffordshire Regt KIA 19.8.17.
HENDON George A. MM Sjt 78311 Tank Corps
HENDREN John MM L/Cpl 240493 1/5th Royal Scots Fusiliers
HENDREY Francis James Gardiner "DCM,MM" Sjt 56272 Royal Engineers
HENDRICK James Joseph MM Sjt 15655 60 Siege Bty RGA
HENDRICKSON Isaac MM Dvr 680936 A/286 Bde RFA
HENDRIE James MM Pte 302010 5/6th Royal Scots
HENDRIE James MM Sjt 3/7068 1st Gordon Highlanders
HENDRIE Robert MM+Bar Sjt 22940 33rd Bn Machine Gun Corps Died 9.9.18.
HENDRIE William MM Pte 129962 Machine Gun Corps
HENDRY Alexander MM Pte 275133 1/7th Arg & Suth Highlanders
HENDRY Bertram MM Pte 1778 1/9th Highland Light Infantry
HENDRY Daniel MM Pte 51047 1st Royal Scots Fusiliers
HENDRY Duncan W. MM Cpl 42515 Northumberland Fusiliers
HENDRY Frederick J. MM Spr 310873 Royal Engineers
HENDRY George MM+Bar Sjt 630327 B/255 Bde RFA KIA 29.7.18.
HENDRY Henry O. MM L/Cpl 2886 1/7th London Regt
HENDRY James MM Sjt 200345 1/4th Seaforth Highlanders
HENDRY James MM Sjt 43413 5/6th Scottish Rifles
HENDRY John MM L/Cpl 350599 18th Highland Light Infantry
HENDRY John "DCM,MM" Cpl 275723 1/7th Arg & Suth Highlanders
HENDRY Peter MM Pte 28453 6th King's Own Scottish Borderers
HENDRY Peter MM Cpl S/3050 2nd Arg & Suth Highlanders
HENDRY Robert MM Spr 86180 Royal Engineers
HENDRY Thomas MM Pte 40812 Gordon Highlanders
HENDRY Victor Albert MM Pte 1365 Army Cyclist Corps
HENDRY William MM Cpl 307130 2/7th Royal Warwickshire Regt
HENDRY William MM Pte 350 7th Royal Sussex Regt KIA 2.11.16.
HENDRY William MM Sjt 37435 Northumberland Fusiliers
HENDRY William MM Sjt 9449 1st Gordon Highlanders
HENDRY William MM Pte 17804 8th Yorkshire Regt
HENDRY William Hugh MM Pte 204773 15th Hampshire Regt
HENDY Alfred "MM,MID" L/Cpl 19238 2nd Wiltshire Regt
HENDY Ernest MM Pte 21411 Somerset Light Infantry
HENDY Gilbert John MM Pte 28670 18th Welsh Regt KIA 13.4.18.
HENDY Thomas MM Pte 6644 1/28th London Regt
HENERY John MM Dvr 84971 50 Bde RFA
HENIGAN Bartholomew MM Sjt 658148 RFA
HENINGTON Sidney C. MM L/Cpl 550282 Royal Engineers
HENKEN Albert William MM Gnr 120224 297 Siege Bty RGA
HENKER Alfred MM Gnr 5027 23 Heavy Bty RGA
HENLEY Arthur MM Pte 28880 Shropshire Light Infantry att 1/1st Herefordshire Regt
HENLEY Clifford MM Pte 202046 2/4th West Riding Regt
HENLEY George W. MM Pte G/62757 Royal Fusiliers
HENLEY Henry Thomas MM Sjt 7/6558 Royal Irish Rifles KIA 8.3.17.
HENLEY Joseph MM Sjt 306367 1/8th Notts & Derby Regt
HENLEY Leopold G. MM L/Sjt 10898 Royal West Surrey Regt
HENLEY Leslie W. MM L/Cpl 12809 5th Dragoon Guards
HENLEY William "DCM,MM" Cpl G/60813 24th Royal Fusiliers
HENN Norman Conrad George MM Gnr 831058 RFA
HENNEDY Robert J. MM Cpl 66948 33rd Bn Machine Gun Corps
HENNEFER William MM Pte 29569 4th North Lancashire Regt
HENNESSEY Herbert MM Pte 5213 Liverpool Regt
HENNESSEY James "DCM,MM" Pte 293143 1/7th Royal Highlanders
HENNESSEY Thomas MM Pte 16159 1st Cameron Highlanders
HENNESSY Herbert William MM Sjt 1233 22nd Royal Fusiliers KIA 17.2.17.
HENNESSY James MM Pte 1040 Army Cyclist Corps
HENNESSY Patrick MM Sjt 5617 8th Somerset Light Infantry KIA 1.7.16.
HENNESSY Richard MM Pte 4810 Leinster Regt
HENNESSY Timothy MM Pte 8316 1st Royal Munster Fusiliers
HENNESSY William MM Pte 2989 1/5th Northumberland Fusiliers DOW 16.11.16.
HENNEY James MM Dvr 24091 13 Bty 17 Bde RFA
HENNIG Sydney W. MM Cpl 01332 Army Ordnance Corps
HENNIKER George W. MM L/Bdr 62025 3 Siege Bty RGA
HENNING Matthew MM Pte 7/25367 7th Royal Irish Regt
HENRETTY John MM Pte 33706 6th York & Lancaster Regt
HENRI Paul MM Pte 241676 Liverpool Regt
HENRICK Ernest A. "DCM,MM" CQMS 720625 1/24th London Regt
HENRY Alfred MM L/Cpl 204754 1/5th York & Lancaster Regt DOW 11.3.18.
HENRY Edward. MM Cpl 27346 13th West Riding Regt
HENRY Edward. MM Sjt 240863 1/5th South Lancashire Regt
HENRY George Adams MM L/Sjt 41401 9th Royal Irish Fusiliers DOW 26.3.18.
HENRY George M. "DCM,MM+Bar,MID" Sjt 17833 12th Highland Light Infantry
HENRY Hugh MM L/Sjt 350927 7th London Regt
HENRY James MM Pte 32948 67 Coy Machine Gun Corps
HENRY James MM Pte 17621 1st Coldstream Guards
HENRY James MM+Bar L/Cpl 31380 1st Royal Welsh Fusiliers KIA 3.5.18.
HENRY John MM+Bar Sjt 476433 461 Fd Coy Royal Engineers
HENRY John MM Cpl 1454 1st Gordon Highlanders
HENRY John MM Sjt 39131 Machine Gun Corps
HENRY John Cody MM Spr 252894 'L' Corps Sig Coy Royal Engineers
HENRY Joseph C. MM Gnr 34546 RFA
HENRY Percival MM L/Cpl 40519 1/9th Durham Light Infantry
HENRY Richard MM Gnr 27084 RGA
HENRY Robert MM L/Cpl 20185 11th Durham Light Infantry
HENRY Thomas B. MM Spr 520205 565 Army Tps Coy Royal Engineers
HENRY W. MM Pte 1708 1/7th Notts & Derby Regt
HENRY Walter MM Dvr T2/015618 577 Aux Horse Tpt Coy Army Service Corps
HENRY William MM Sjt 95502 11th Bn Tank Corps
HENRY William MM Sjt 240837 Lancashire Fusiliers
HENRY William MM Sjt 8843 2nd Worcestershire Regt
HENRY William MM Pte 12895 Royal Irish Rifles
HENRY William MM L/Cpl S/10434 1st Cameron Highlanders
HENRYS William MM Cpl 81759 42nd Bn Machine Gun Corps

HENSBY Charles H. MM+2 Bars 2nd Cpl 66799 25 Div Sig Coy Royal Engineers
HENSBY Robert MM Cpl 241935 8th West Yorkshire Regt
HENSBY Thomas Edgar MM Pte 20435 XVIII Corps Cyclist Bn Army Cyclist Corps
HENSHALL Jonathan MM+Bar Sjt 25114 B/64 Bde RFA
HENSHALL William MM Cpl 432030 55 Div Sig Coy Royal Engineers
HENSHAW Andrew MM Pte 31248 17th Notts & Derby Regt DOW 21.9.17.
HENSHAW John MM Sjt 256694 Liverpool Regt
HENSON Charles T.S. MM Pte 91045 1st Notts & Derby Regt
HENSON Ernest Edward MM Pte 33155 2nd Devonshire Regt
HENSON George MM Pte 50426 RAMC
HENSON Harold Easter "MC,MM(2371 Sgt 1/4th Yorks LI)" T/2Lt 63rd Bn Machine Gun Corps
HENSON Harold W.J. MM CQMS 851 1st Royal Warwickshire Regt
HENSON Henry MM L/Cpl S/25474 1st Rifle Brigade
HENSON Henry Thomas "MM,MSM" Cpl 47880 Royal Engineers
HENSON J.W. MM Sjt C/225 16th King's Royal Rifle Corps
HENSON William H. MM Pte 14620 Leicestershire Regt
HENSTRIDGE Albert E. MM L/Cpl 20542 13th Liverpool Regt
HENSTRIDGE Cecil MM Pte 320647 15th Suffolk Regt
HENTHORNE Harry MM Spr 81930 97 Fd Coy Royal Engineers KIA 2.10.17.
HENTON Ernest H. MM Dvr T4/237672 Army Service Corps
HENTY Frederick F. MM Pte 76392 Notts & Derby Regt
HENTY James MM Cpl 10060 2nd Royal Sussex Regt
HENTY Thomas A. MM Pte 52063 1st West Yorkshire Regt
HENWOOD Arthur MM Gnr 646 (690055) RFA DOW 22.8.18.
HENWOOD Francis J. MM Sjt 1978 25 Fd Amb RAMC
HENWOOD Thomas MM Gnr 155676 RFA
HEPBURN Alexander P. MM+Bar Pte G/87687 4th Royal Fusiliers
HEPBURN Andrew MM Pnr 48019 15 Div Sig Coy Royal Engineers KIA 4.4.18.
HEPBURN Charles MM Sjt 3354 6th Dragoon Guards
HEPBURN D.P. MM Air Mech 2 19723 Royal Flying Corps
HEPBURN James MM Pte 202184 1/6th Royal Highlanders
HEPBURN James MM Pte 4/4300 Arg & Suth Highlanders
HEPBURN James B. MM L/Cpl D/8021 2nd Dragoons
HEPBURN Thomas MM Pte 10681 2nd Gordon Highlanders
HEPDEN Amos MM Sjt 265145 1/6th Gloucestershire Regt
HEPPEL George E. MM Sjt 9082 1st Border Regt
HEPPELL Arthur MM Spr 552875 Royal Engineers
HEPPELL John G. MM Cpl 558078 56 Div Sig Coy Royal Engineers
HEPPELL John W. MM Sjt 25453 2nd West Riding Regt
HEPPELL Sydney MM Cpl 46885 RFA
HEPPELL W.J. MM Pte 14375 Bedfordshire Regt
HEPPENSTALL George MM+Bar Cpl 240470 1/5th York & Lancaster Regt KIA 15.4.18.
HEPPENSTALL Harry MM Pte 17465 1st East Yorkshire Regt KIA 21.11.16.
HEPPENSTALL Silas MM L/Cpl 305423 West Riding Regt
HEPPER Richard G. MM Pte 35819 9th York & Lancaster Regt
HEPPLE Elsdon MM Sjt 72533 41 Bde RFA
HEPPLE John MM Gnr 376115 RGA
HEPPLE Thomas MM Pte 20/1626 Northumberland Fusiliers
HEPPLESTON Charles MM Gnr 19671 RFA
HEPPLESTON Clifford MM Dvr 796563 311 Bde RFA
HEPPLEWHITE William MM Gnr 18875 RFA
HEPTINSTALL Ernest MM L/Cpl 242310 1/5th Yorkshire Light Infantry att 148 Lt TM Bty
HEPTINSTALL Henry MM Pte 15321 9th Yorkshire Regt
HEPTINSTALL John Willie MM L/Bdr 62884 121 Bde RFA Died 24.6.18.
HEPTONSTALL Briscoe MM L/Cpl 240391 1/5th York & Lancaster Regt
HEPWOOD Albert MM Pte 1766 2/7th Worcestershire Regt
HEPWORTH Alfred E. MM Sjt 1798 1/1st Oxfordshire Yeomanry
HEPWORTH Harold MM Cpl 83697 210 Fd Coy Royal Engineers
HEPWORTH John Samuel MM Sjt 2631 1/6th West Riding Regt KIA 22.9.16.
HEPWORTH John William MM L/Cpl 11872 10th Durham Light Infantry KIA 24.8.17.
HEPWORTH Thomas "MM,MID" Sjt 240763 5th West Riding Regt
HEPWORTH Thomas MM Pte 11771 2nd Durham Light Infantry KIA 17.10.18.
HEPWORTH William H. MM Bdr 795717 RFA
HERALD Patrick MM Sjt 28042 9th Royal Inniskilling Fusiliers
HERBENER Frederick MM Gnr 358600 RGA

HERBERT Arthur MM Pte 266461 Oxf & Bucks Light Infantry
HERBERT Arthur A. MM Pte CMT/791 3 Div Train Army Service Corps
HERBERT Charles MM Sjt 7941 Gloucestershire Regt
HERBERT Edward MM L/Sjt S/11699 10th Rifle Brigade
HERBERT Ernest W. MM Pte 30919 8th Somerset Light Infantry
HERBERT Frank Harold MM Pte 225280 1/1st Monmouthshire Regt
HERBERT George MM Pte 60728 14th Welsh Regt
HERBERT Gilbert A. MM Cpl 41728 1st Royal Berkshire Regt
HERBERT Henry MM Pte 7435 1st Royal West Kent Regt
HERBERT Henry W. MM Gnr 48450 RFA
HERBERT James MM Cpl 331757 9th Highland Light Infantry
HERBERT John MM Bdr 115337 72 Bty 38 Bde RFA KIA 30.10.17.
HERBERT John Henry MM Cpl Sig 22565 A/82 Bde RFA
HERBERT John J. MM Sjt 19005 1st Royal Dublin Fusiliers
HERBERT John William MM Cpl 354179 3(East Lancashire)Fd Amb RAMC
HERBERT Julia Ashbourne MM Sister F TFNS
HERBERT L.A. MM Sjt 2866 Royal Flying Corps
HERBERT Osbert "DCM,MM" Pte 19321 1st & 6th Northamptonshire Regt
HERBERT P.J. MM L/Cpl 207211 6 Sig Tp Royal Engineers
HERBERT Ray MM Dvr 84507 15 Div Ammn Col RFA
HERBERT Reginald G. MM CQMS 240028 2/4th Royal West Surrey Regt
HERBERT Sydney Kingham MM Pte 536407 5 Fd Amb RAMC
HERBERT Thomas O. MM Pte 200969 1/4th Cheshire Regt
HERBERT Walter MM Sjt 2536 1/4th Leicestershire Regt
HERBERT William MM Pte 5750 1st Gloucestershire Regt
HERBERT William S. MM Cpl 768 23rd Middlesex Regt
HERCHER Philip MM Spr 408277 Royal Engineers
HERD Alfred S. MM Bdr 840862 RFA
HERD Edward MM+Bar Pte 4239 1/7th Liverpool Regt
HERD Ernest William MM Pte M2/132560 Army Service Corps att 54 Fd Amb RAMC.KIA 24.9.18.
HERD Henry MM Sjt 139324 183 Tunnelling Coy Royal Engineers
HERD William MM Sjt 345375 14th Royal Highlanders
HERD William MM L/Sjt 240549 1/5th King's Own Scottish Borderers
HERD William MM Pte 3/2858 1/5th Royal Highlanders
HERD William B. MM Spr 422562 218 Fd Coy Royal Engineers
HERDMAN Francis MM Sjt 2805 1/14th London Regt
HERDMAN William MM Sjt 2152 1/9th Durham Light Infantry
HEREFORD John MM Pte 610918 19th London Regt
HERITAGE Frank MM Bdr 374136 RGA
HERITAGE Jack MM Sjt 52885 66 Siege Bty RGA KIA 21.4.18.
HERITAGE Sidney MM Pte 15964 6th East Yorkshire Regt
HERIVAL William Peter MM Gnr 89285 A/53 Bde RFA
HERLIHY M.J.I. MM Pte 722078 London Regt
HERLIHY Michael P. MM Gnr 940398 RFA
HERMAN Carl MM Cpl 10/429 10th East Yorkshire Regt
HERMAN Charles MM Cpl 14571 Machine Gun Corps
HERMAN Leslie Charles MM Pte 48565 5th Royal Berkshire Regt
HERMAN Walter R. MM L/Cpl 20058 Royal Berkshire Regt
HERMANN Edgar MM Sjt 1029 10th East Yorkshire Regt DOW 17.11.16.
HERMISTON Richard N. MM CQMS 9933 1st Northumberland Fusiliers
HERMITAGE Edward MM Pte 16429 Royal Sussex Regt
HERMON Francis W. MM Cpl 10499 5th Royal Berkshire Regt
HERMON Reginald MM Pte 21688 1st Coldstream Guards
HERMON Thomas William MM L/Cpl 2315 1/4th Oxf & Bucks Light Infantry DOW 24.8.16.
HERN Charles William MM Cpl 20071 6th Royal Berkshire Regt
HERNBERG David MM L/Cpl 570828 London Regt
HERNIMAN Francis H. MM Sjt 825119 C/312 Bde RFA
HERNIMAN George MM Pte 30262 1st Devonshire Regt
HERNIMAN Harry MM Spr 212165 513 Fd Coy Royal Engineers
HEROD William MM Pte 12387 Leicestershire Regt
HERON Albert G. MM Sjt 16685 Machine Gun Corps
HERON F. MM L/Cpl 200184 Yorkshire Regt
HERON Frank MM Pte 12678 2nd West Riding Regt
HERON George MM Sjt 293292 1/7th Royal Highlanders
HERON James F. MM Pte 200751 1/4th King's Own Scottish Borderers
HERON Thomas MM Dvr 77190 'A' Bty RHA
HERON Thomas MM Pte 300509 1/8th Durham Light Infantry
HERON Thomas A. MM Gnr 97300 RGA
HERON William MM Pte 2009 Northumberland Fusiliers
HERRICK Alfred V.E. MM+Bar Dvr 147213 RFA

HERRIDGE Albert E. MM Sjt 25470 11th Oxf & Bucks Light Infantry
HERRIDGE Sydney J. MM Pte 12105 Machine Gun Corps
HERRIES Thomas MM Pte 19167 Durham Light Infantry
HERRING Alfred MM L/Bdr 52606 17 Hy Bty RGA Died 17.2.19.
HERRING Arthur James Mead MM Pte M2/022237 Army Service Corps att RAMC
HERRING Cecil MM+Bar L/Cpl 17003 5th Shropshire Light Infantry
HERRING George W. MM+Bar Gnr L/12452 RFA
HERRING Henry MM Pte 2927 12th Middlesex Regt
HERRING John MM Gnr 38695 D/83 Bty RFA
HERRING Matthew R. MM Pte 7180 1st Bedfordshire Regt
HERRING Maurice H. MM Sjt 200222 1/4th Suffolk Regt
HERRINGTON George MM L/Sjt 5/8264 6th Royal Irish Rifles
HERRINGTON Henry MM L/Sjt 8233 1st Hampshire Regt
HERRINGTON Henry "MM,MSM" CSM 47943 70 Fd Coy Royal Engineers
HERRINGTON John "MC,MM(18642 L/Sjt)" 2Lt 9th South Staffordshire Regt
HERRINGTON William G. MM Pte 35250 Royal Fusiliers
HERRIOTT Henry G. MM Pte 20488 Hampshire Regt
HERRON John MM Pte 23998 9th Manchester Regt
HERRON Matthew MM Cpl 325251 Durham Light Infantry
HERRON William MM Sjt 57814 36 Div Sig Coy Royal Engineers
HERSEY Alfred J. MM Sjt 20282 Royal Sussex Regt
HERSEY James MM Pte 424770 1/10th London Regt
HERSEY John MM Sjt 6014 A/190 Bde RFA
HERTWICK John F. MM Pte 36518 Lancashire Fusiliers
HERWIN Ernest MM L/Cpl 12708 47th Bn Machine Gun Corps
HERYET Robert MM Pte 4104 1/20th London Regt
HESELTINE Charles S. MM Cpl 253749 Royal Engineers
HESELTINE Jeffrey MM Pte 35524 Cheshire Regt
HESELTINE Leonard MM Pte 240937 2/6th West Yorkshire Regt
HESELTINE Thomas Arnold MM Pte 37076 9th Yorkshire Light Infantry Died 12.11.18.
HESFORD E. MM Pte 53281 4th Middlesex Regt
HESKETH Donald MM Pte M/321094 50 Aux Bus Coy Army Service Corps
HESKETH John MM Cpl 28966 Manchester Regt
HESKETH Thomas MM Pte 308185 8th Liverpool Regt
HESKETH Thomas Percival MM Gnr 188299 462 Bty RFA KIA 21.3.18.
HESKETH William MM Pte A/2434 King's Royal Rifle Corps
HESLEWOOD Alfred MM Pte 652308 21st London Regt
HESLEWOOD Herbert MM Gnr 1206 1/2(West Riding)Bde RFA
HESLOP George MM Pte 41239 Royal Scots Fusiliers
HESLOP George Henry MM Gnr 765565 RFA
HESLOP Herbert MM Pte 3451 Northumberland Fusiliers
HESLOP Joseph T. MM Sjt 22/100 Northumberland Fusiliers
HESLOP Robert MM Pte 285008 Gordon Highlanders
HESLOP William B. MM Pte 235728 4th West Riding Regt
HESLOP William R. MM Pte 203692 Manchester Regt
HESLOP William W.A. MM Spr 107399 Royal Engineers
HESP James MM Gnr 19246 HQ 2 Siege Bde RGA
HESSION Austin MM Pte 9344 Royal Dublin Fusiliers
HESSLEWOOD John William MM Pte 1622 1/4th Yorkshire Regt
HESTER George MM Pte 200267 Royal Berkshire Regt
HESTER James MM Pte 14254 East Surrey Regt
HESTER Percy MM Pte 2248 Gloucestershire Regt
HESTER Robert MM Pte 9270 6th Royal West Kent Regt
HESTER William MM Bdr 126743 'W' Bty RHA
HESTER William Henry MM L/Cpl 19606 5th Royal Berkshire Regt
HESTON John MM L/Cpl 66810 10th Royal Fusiliers
HETHERINGTON Arthur E. MM Gnr 156086 342 Siege Bty RGA
HETHERINGTON Ernest MM L/Cpl 24632 Durham Light Infantry
HETHERINGTON Harry MM Sjt 53 1/1st(West Riding)Fd Coy Royal Engineers DOW 9.8.16.
HETHERINGTON Hugh MM Sjt 9662 13th Durham Light Infantry
HETHERINGTON Hugh MM Sjt 13659 Royal Inniskilling Fusiliers
HETHERINGTON James MM Cpl 14782 8th Border Regt
HETHERINGTON John "DCM,MM" Sjt 42297 9th Scottish Rifles
HETHERINGTON Joseph MM Pte 70413 151 Coy Machine Gun Corps
HETHERINGTON Percy MM Bdr 750566 RFA
HETHERRINGTON William MM Sjt 241291 5th Royal Lancaster Regt
HEUGH James MM Sjt 335166 11th Royal Scots
HEWARD Albert E. MM Spr 477025 Royal Engineers
HEWARTSON George MM L/Cpl 200434 1/4th Royal Lancaster Regt
HEWER Albert MM Pte 30859 19th Welsh Regt
HEWERDINE A.H. MM Pte 241192 5th Leicestershire Regt
HEWERDINE William A. MM Cpl 27155 8th East Surrey Regt
HEWERTSON Herbert MM L/Cpl 240644 5th Royal Lancaster Regt
HEWETT Alexander MM L/Cpl F/1138 16th Middlesex Regt att MGC
HEWETT Frederick MM Pte 206216 8th East Surrey Regt
HEWETT George "MM,CG(F)" Pte 203096 11th Essex Regt KIA 2.6.18.
HEWETT George MM Sjt 44091 115 Bty 25 Bde RFA KIA 1.7.16.
HEWETT George MM L/Bdr 15977 59 Siege Bty RGA
HEWETT Henry William Douglas MM Cpl 42587 15 Bde RFA
HEWETT Sidney MM Cpl 86373 170 Bde RFA
HEWETT Sidney F. MM Pte 684333 22nd London Regt
HEWETT William C.H. MM Cpl 203636 7th East Kent Regt
HEWGILL George MM Sjt 28122 9th Yorkshire Regt
HEWICK William H. MM Cpl 9859 1st East Yorkshire Regt
HEWINS Albert J. MM Cpl R/9175 13th King's Royal Rifle Corps
HEWINS Edward MM Cpl 56730 Northumberland Fusiliers
HEWINS George MM Pte 12570 8th Lincolnshire Regt
HEWIS Joseph H. MM Pte 34960 Manchester Regt
HEWISON Thomas W. MM Cpl 14312 Yorkshire Regt
HEWITSON Arthur MM L/Cpl C/12716 King's Royal Rifle Corps
HEWITSON Fenwick MM Pte 14977 7th Yorkshire Regt KIA 12.5.17.
HEWITSON Harry MM Pte 638 16th West Yorkshire Regt
HEWITSON James MM Pte 27828 9th North Lancashire Regt KIA 25.4.18.
HEWITSON William E. MM Pte 300284 18th Liverpool Regt
HEWITT A.H. MM Cpl 9301 Gloucestershire Regt
HEWITT Albert E. MM L/Cpl 200494 1/4th North Lancashire Regt
HEWITT Albert Edward MM Cpl 220014 1/4th East Yorkshire Regt Died 10.10.18.
HEWITT Alfred MM Sjt 29056 15 Bde RFA
HEWITT Arthur MM L/Cpl S/27094 13th Rifle Brigade
HEWITT Ben MM Pte 32114 Gloucestershire Regt att Royal West Kent Regt.
HEWITT Bertram W. "MM,MID" Pte MS/318 Army Service Corps att 52 Fd Amb RAMC.
HEWITT Cecil G. MM Sjt 240474 1/5th Cheshire Regt
HEWITT Charles MM Cpl 352863 8th Manchester Regt
HEWITT Charles A. MM Cpl 241940 Notts & Derby Regt
HEWITT Clement Temple MM+Bar Cpl 66653 228 Coy & 39th Bn Machine Gun Corps
HEWITT Edward "MM,MID" Sjt 34641 RFA
HEWITT Ernest Edward MM Pte 200979 20th Durham Light Infantry
HEWITT Ernest John MM Sjt 58663 B/72 Bde RFA
HEWITT Frederick MM Pte 201446 10th Durham Light Infantry
HEWITT George MM Sjt 6657 Border Regt
HEWITT George MM Cpl 15294 B/157 Bde RFA
HEWITT George MM Sjt R/12279 King's Royal Rifle Corps
HEWITT George MM Sjt 95555 Royal Engineers
HEWITT George Edward MM L/Cpl 204505 13th Durham Light Infantry KIA 5.10.18.
HEWITT Harry MM Pte 27630 2/4th Hampshire Regt KIA 28.8.18.
HEWITT Howard J. MM Pte 32157 Gloucestershire Regt
HEWITT Isaac MM Sjt 488121 Royal Engineers
HEWITT Jack MM Sjt R/35278 2nd King's Royal Rifle Corps
HEWITT John MM Spr 167542 103 Fd Coy Royal Engineers
HEWITT John MM Pte 204765 13th Liverpool Regt
HEWITT John "MM,MM(F)" Pte 14889 9th Royal Lancaster Regt
HEWITT John "MM,MID" L/Cpl 8326 1st Leicestershire Regt
HEWITT John MM Spr 63624 Royal Engineers
HEWITT John MM Sjt 1367 1/8th Liverpool Regt
HEWITT John MM Sjt 8130 11th Royal Warwickshire Regt
HEWITT John Bruce Cuthbert "MM,MID" Cpl 90418 RFA
HEWITT Joseph MM Pte 201511 Manchester Regt
HEWITT Joseph MM Pte M2/116541 Army Service Corps att RAMC.
HEWITT Joseph R. MM Pte 27974 1st Cheshire Regt
HEWITT Leonard MM Pte 21560 16th Notts & Derby Regt KIA 31.3.18.
HEWITT Percy Richard MM Pte 126402 Machine Gun Corps KIA 16.6.18.
HEWITT Peter MM Sjt 14842 West Riding Regt
HEWITT Richard MM Dvr L/28159 73 Bty 5 Bde RFA
HEWITT Robert E. MM Sjt 1814 1/3rd London Regt
HEWITT Sam MM Pte 241227 2/5th York & Lancaster Regt
HEWITT Sydney MM Gnr 34680 115 Heavy Bty RGA
HEWITT Thomas C. MM Pte 18856 12th Liverpool Regt
HEWITT Thomas W. MM L/Cpl M2/175722 Army Service Corps
HEWITT W. MM AM2 47936 Royal Flying Corps
HEWITT Walter H. MM Cpl 840930 D/307 Bde RFA
HEWITT William MM Dvr 75676 B/58 Bde RFA
HEWITT William MM Gnr 750787 RFA

HEWITT William MM L/Cpl 28895 Border Regt
HEWITT William MM Sjt 5853 Machine Gun Corps
HEWITT William MM Pte 5226 2nd Leinster Regt KIA 4.9.18.
HEWITT William Barrett MM Pte 11394 11th King's Royal Rifle Corps DOW 20.9.17.
HEWITT William H. MM Gnr 785448 150 Bde RFA
HEWITT William L. MM L/Sjt 12141 4th Leicestershire Regt
HEWITT William M. "DCM,MM" CSM G/2776 7th Royal Fusiliers
HEWITT William R. MM Pte 325697 1/9th Durham Light Infantry
HEWITT William V. MM L/Cpl 240093 Lincolnshire Regt
HEWKIN John Cecil MM SM A/407031 Exp Force Canteen Army Service Corps
HEWLETT Arthur Gilbert MM L/Cpl 203 'D' Bn Machine Gun Corps(Heavy Branch)
HEWLING Arthur MM Sjt 16/1746 16th Royal Warwickshire Regt
HEWSON Albert MM Sjt 200630 West Yorkshire Regt
HEWSON Albert E. MM Pte 570925 1/17th London Regt
HEWSON Charles MM L/Sjt 39745 5th Gloucestershire Regt
HEWSON Henry MM Pte 71954 RAMC
HEWSON Henry MM Cpl 8943 2nd Shropshire Light Infantry
HEWSON John MM Pte W/206 13th Cheshire Regt
HEWSON Thomas MM Cpl 12834 1st Dragoons
HEWSON William Steel MM S/Sjt 390216 1/3(Northumbrian)Fd Amb RAMC
HEXT Alfred MM Dvr 27792 51 Bde RFA
HEXT Jethro MM Pte 11722 7th Yorkshire Regt
HEXT Phillip MM Pte 13247 9th Royal Welsh Fusiliers
HEXT Sidney MM Pte 29754 1st Somerset Light Infantry
HEXTALL Cyril J. MM Sjt 22639 Machine Gun Corps
HEY Arthur MM L/Cpl 267177 2/4th West Riding Regt "KIA 20.7.18,"
HEY George Alfred MM Cpl 15766 1st Essex Regt KIA 27.11.17.
HEY Herbert MM Sjt 201000 4th West Riding Regt
HEY Herbert MM Pte 23411 20th Durham Light Infantry
HEY John R. "DCM,MM" Sjt 312088 39 Div Sig Coy Royal Engineers att RFA.
HEY Thomas V.H. MM Pte 8296 Border Regt
HEY Walter MM Pte 242871 West Riding Regt
HEYBOURNE Edward MM Sjt 23760 5th Royal Berkshire Regt
HEYDENRYCH George E. MM L/Cpl 14318 Machine Gun Corps
HEYDON Frederick L. MM+2 Bars Cpl 6707 9th Royal Fusiliers
HEYES Frank MM Pte 300044 7th Liverpool Regt
HEYES Frederick MM Pte 16245 7th South Lancashire Regt
HEYES George MM Cpl 280967 2/4th London Regt
HEYES Harry MM Sjt 265501 Cheshire Regt
HEYES Henry MM Pte 341619 1/3rd(West Lancashire)Fd Amb RAMC
HEYES Jesse MM L/Cpl 203625 North Lancashire Regt KIA 3.9.18.
HEYHOE John James MM Sjt 34269 2 Siege Bty RGA
HEYMAN Frederick A. MM Gnr 85252 RFA
HEYS Richard MM Pte 152049 42nd Bn Machine Gun Corps
HEYWARD Harry MM Sjt 240100 Devonshire Regt
HEYWARD Henry Thomas MM Pte 17727 8th Devonshire Regt DOW 7.10.17.
HEYWOOD Albert H. MM+Bar 2nd Cpl 34405 82 Fd Coy Royal Engineers
HEYWOOD Brook MM Cpl 41187 11th West Yorkshire Regt
HEYWOOD Charles "MM,MSM" Sjt 2968 11th South Lancashire Regt
HEYWOOD Ellis MM Sjt 113391 Royal Engineers
HEYWOOD H. MM Pte 337728 RAMC
HEYWOOD J. MM Sjt 9330 South Staffordshire Regt
HEYWOOD John MM Pte 200208 1/5th Lancashire Fusiliers
HEYWOOD John MM Pte 11243 6th Border Regt
HEYWOOD John W. MM CQMS 1089 1/4th North Lancashire Regt
HEYWOOD Percy MM Sjt 74612 A/173 Bde RFA
HEYWOOD Sam MM+Bar Cpl 39279 Machine Gun Corps
HEYWORTH Barker MM Pte 30437 20th Lancashire Fusiliers
HEYWORTH James MM Pte M2/187274 594 Coy Army Service Corps
HIBBARD Bert MM Pte 17477 7th Somerset Light Infantry
HIBBARD Clifford J. MM+Bar Cpl 766476 17th & 28th London Regt
HIBBARD Walter Henry MM Sjt 8796 2nd Lincolnshire Regt
HIBBART Frederick C. MM L/Cpl 611127 1/19th London Regt
HIBBERD A.P. MM Bdr 16234 RFA
HIBBERD George MM Cpl 8174 1st Gloucestershire Regt KIA 26.8.16.
HIBBERD Harry E. MM Pte S/14215 Rifle Brigade
HIBBERD Oliver MM Spr 2581 1/1(Home Counties)Fd Coy Royal Engineers
HIBBERD William Thomas MM Pte 22329 2nd Wiltshire Regt DOW 16.6.18.

HIBBERT Alfred MM Pte 11250 8th Royal Lancaster Regt
HIBBERT Cyril J.G. MM Pte 326264 9th Essex Regt
HIBBERT Edward MM Sjt 36506 RFA
HIBBERT James Frederick MM+Bar Gnr 292208 125 & 23 Heavy Bty RGA KIA 28.3.18.
HIBBERT John MM Sjt 6473 1st Royal Scots Fusiliers
HIBBERT Percy MM Gnr 13685 3 Siege Bty RGA
HIBBERT Thomas MM L/Bdr 29639 D/74 Bde RFA
HIBBERT Walter MM+Bar Cpl 17293 42 Bty 2 Bde RFA
HIBBERT William H. MM Pte 5466 Machine Gun Corps
HIBBIN Albert Victor MM Pte 15325 6th Royal West Kent Regt DOW 2.12.17.
HIBBINS Arthur MM Bdr 880050 RFA
HIBBIT William Thomas MM L/Sjt 17330 8th Bedfordshire Regt DOW 28.4.17.
HIBBITT Amos W. MM Pte 20346 9th Leicestershire Regt
HIBBS Edward Emanuel MM Dvr 19796 B/307 Bde RFA
HIBBS Gilbert MM Pte 655 1st Royal Warwickshire Regt
HIBBS Henry George MM Pte 270665 10th East Kent Regt
HIBBS Norman MM Sjt 23789 18th Liverpool Regt
HICK Jefferson MM L/Cpl 22874 30th Bn Machine Gun Corps
HICKEN Daniel MM Pte 10845 7th South Staffordshire Regt
HICKEN John MM Pte 57584 12th Suffolk Regt
HICKEY Christopher T. MM Sjt 23198 Machine Gun Corps
HICKEY George F. MM Pte 16895 2nd Grenadier Guards
HICKEY Henry MM Bdr 25115 RFA
HICKEY James MM Pte 5573 1st Royal Dublin Fusiliers
HICKEY James MM Cpl 11382 Machine Gun Corps
HICKEY John James MM+Bar Bdr 73391 2 Bde RFA
HICKEY Patrick MM Pte 1718 6th Royal Irish Regt
HICKEY Thomas MM Cpl 1581 7th Leinster Regt
HICKEY Thomas MM L/Cpl 8890 2nd Lincolnshire Regt KIA 23.10.16.
HICKEY William J. MM Sjt 6401 X Corps Cyclist Bn Army Cyclist Corps
HICKEY William M. MM Pte 75561 24th Royal Fusiliers
HICKFORD W. MM Pte 240924 Suffolk Regt
HICKIN Archibald P. MM Pte 15776 Leicestershire Regt
HICKIN Thomas W. MM Pte DM2/209873 406 MT Coy Army Service Corps
HICKINBOTHAM Charles MM Sjt 17362 19th Lancashire Fusiliers
HICKINBOTHAM J.W. MM Pte 101193 RAMC
HICKING Reggie MM Cpl 22137 9th Yorkshire Light Infantry
HICKINSON Fred MM Sjt 41240 11th West Yorkshire Regt
HICKLING Albert MM Pte 240094 1/5th Leicestershire Regt
HICKLING Arthur MM Cpl 8949 1st Scottish Rifles
HICKLING Edward MM Pte 38666 RAMC
HICKLING Evan J. MM Sjt 57187 41 Bde RFA
HICKLING Herbert "DCM,MM+Bar" Cpl 26553 2nd South Staffordshire Regt
HICKLING Joseph MM Cpl 27307 Notts & Derby Regt
HICKMAN Arthur MM Gnr 76365 RFA
HICKMAN Arthur MM Gnr 90785 X/11 Med TM Bty RFA
HICKMAN Arthur C. MM L/Sjt 20798 Border Regt
HICKMAN Bert MM Pte 3066 Machine Gun Corps
HICKMAN Edward Harold "MM,MM(F)" Cpl 1373 47 Div Ammn Col RFA
HICKMAN F. MM Sjt 437412 RAMC
HICKMAN Francis MM Cpl 740699 A/104 Bde RFA
HICKMAN Frank Henry Charles MM Sjt 2117 1/9th London Regt KIA 1.7.16.
HICKMAN George MM Sjt 9268 5th Oxf & Bucks Light Infantry
HICKMAN George H. MM Cpl 81661 Machine Gun Corps
HICKMAN Henry MM L/Cpl 1817 1/8th Notts & Derby Regt
HICKMAN Henry C. MM Dvr L/38184 RFA
HICKMAN James C. MM L/Cpl 265013 Royal Warwickshire Regt
HICKMAN John E. MM L/Sjt 21162 Grenadier Guards
HICKMAN John W. MM Pte 10915 7th South Staffordshire Regt
HICKMAN Joseph J. "DCM+2 Bars,MM+Bar" L/Sjt F/3055 "17th,21st & 2nd" Middlesex Regt
HICKMAN Samuel D. MM Pte 307207 13th Bn Tank Corps
HICKMAN Walter MM Pte 14606 24th Manchester Regt
HICKMAN William George MM Pte 34147 6th West Riding Regt
HICKOX Walter MM Pte 28294 Essex Regt
HICKS A.P. MM Cpl 246936 1 Fd Svy Bn Royal Engineers
HICKS Albert MM Sjt 78067 D/119 Bde RFA
HICKS Alfred MM+Bar Sjt 76596 B/291 Bde RFA
HICKS Alfred T. MM Spr 49041 Royal Engineers
HICKS Arthur MM L/Cpl 744 1st Welsh Guards
HICKS Arthur MM Cpl Shoeing Smith 69902 14 Bde RFA

HICKS Bertram Betteridge MM Pte M/321544 Army Service Corps
HICKS Cecil Lewis MM Gnr 134051 B/150 Bde RFA
HICKS Charles J. MM Sjt 562115 Searchlight Section Royal Engineers
HICKS Cyril MM Pte M2/117120 39 Ammn Sub-Park Army Service Corps
HICKS F. MM Pte 143971 Machine Gun Corps
HICKS Francis A. MM L/Cpl 2072 Oxf & Bucks Light Infantry
HICKS Francis W.M. MM Bdr 69298 11 Bde RFA
HICKS Frank MM Pte 97658 207 Coy Machine Gun Corps
HICKS Frank MM CQMS 4802 Labour Corps
HICKS Frederick MM Pte 31413 25th Bn Machine Gun Corps
HICKS Frederick Charles MM Pte G/87564 13th Royal Fusiliers KIA 24.10.18.
HICKS George MM L/Sjt 17901 1st East Surrey Regt
HICKS Gordon Bert MM Sjt 11538 A/15 Bde RFA
HICKS Harold D. MM Cpl 553991 16th London Regt
HICKS Henry MM Pte 1651 8th East Surrey Regt
HICKS Henry MM Pte 23040 South Staffordshire Regt
HICKS Horace Edwin MM Pte 531664 1/15th London Regt
HICKS James MM Pte 11943 6th Shropshire Light Infantry
HICKS John MM Pte 285989 1/1st Oxfordshire Yeomanry
HICKS John A. MM Pte 36556 8th Worcestershire Regt
HICKS John W. MM Cpl 6444 Machine Gun Corps
HICKS Joseph C. MM Pte 24501 Gloucestershire Regt
HICKS Reuben E. MM Pte 18300 Royal West Kent Regt
HICKS Sidney Charles MM Pte 11964 6th Dorsetshire Regt KIA 30.3.18.
HICKS Sidney W. MM Pte 5858 Machine Gun Corps
HICKS Thomas MM Cpl M2/119604 Army Service Corps att 'K' AA Bty RGA
HICKS Thomas W. MM Dvr 16539 7 Fd Coy Royal Engineers
HICKS W. MM Cpl 2066 West Riding Regt
HICKS W.T. MM Sjt 15556 3rd Grenadier Guards
HICKS William MM Pte 8987 1st Oxf & Bucks Light Infantry Died 18.6.16.
HICKS William MM Pte 302554 Manchester Regt
HICKSON Bert MM Sjt 660 Royal Engineers
HICKSON George MM Pte 21/94 1st West Yorkshire Regt
HICKSON Ireton MM Sjt 269205 1/1st Hertfordshire Regt
HICKSON John Walter MM L/Cpl 8584 2nd Lincolnshire Regt
HICKSON Leonard MM Pte DM2/228566 Army Service Corps att 91 Fd Amb RAMC
HICKSON Robert MM Pte 19644 Durham Light Infantry
HICKSON William MM Sjt 135507 A/187 Bde RFA
HICKS-USSHER Wallis Edward MM Pte 1828 1/13th London Regt
HICKTON George Henry MM+Bar Cpl L/7836 C/152 Bde RFA
HICKTON John T. MM Pte 10011 10th Royal West Kent Regt
HIDER Harry "MM+Bar,MID" Sjt 43640 Royal Engineers
HIDER Henry W. MM L/Cpl 198120 Royal Engineers
HIDON Walter "MM,MID" Sjt 17836 Yorkshire Light Infantry
HIELD Eustace John MM Pte 403508 2/1(West Riding)Fd Amb RAMC DOW 7.11.18.
HIERONS Roy Leonard MM Pte G/5696 7th East Kent Regt
HIETT Edwin R.L. MM Pte 12475 7th Wiltshire Regt
HIGBEE Frederick MM BSM 55536 D/160 Bde RFA
HIGDON Charles E. MM Cpl 42734 RFA
HIGGIN Richard Thomas "MM,MID" Cpl CMT/2985 Army Service Corps
HIGGIN Robert MM Bdr 625 C/64 Bde RFA Died 18.10.17.
HIGGINBOTHAM Harold MM Gnr 62461 Y/35 Med TM Bty RGA
HIGGINBOTTOM Charles MM Sjt 9/12478 9th Cheshire Regt
HIGGINBOTTOM Ernest MM Pte 50378 9th Liverpool Regt
HIGGINBOTTOM John George "MM+Bar,MID" Sjt 43233 Royal Engineers
HIGGINS Albert MM Dvr 135877 RFA
HIGGINS Albert E. MM Pte 41150 4th Worcestershire Regt
HIGGINS Alexander MM Cpl 79263 2nd Durham Light Infantry
HIGGINS Arthur MM Pte 40563 Essex Regt
HIGGINS Charles MM Cpl 24716 14 Siege Bty RGA DOW 23.5.17.
HIGGINS Charles MM Pte 300456 1/7th Royal Scots
HIGGINS Charles MM Sjt 23835 Duke of Cornwall's LI
HIGGINS Charles MM Pte 4206 1st East Kent Regt
HIGGINS Charles MM Sjt 15228 6th Yorkshire Regt KIA 25.9.17.
HIGGINS Charles F. MM Cpl 552848 16th London Regt
HIGGINS Charles G. MM Pte 3623 4th Rifle Brigade
HIGGINS Daniel MM Pte 38237 2nd Yorkshire Regt
HIGGINS Edward J. MM Pte 25267 15th Welsh Regt
HIGGINS Ernest E. MM Cpl 201205 4th Hampshire Regt

HIGGINS Frederick Henry MM L/Cpl 10084 5th Dorsetshire Regt KIA 1.10.18.
HIGGINS George MM Sjt 9263 2nd Worcestershire Regt DOW 15.10.17.
HIGGINS George MM L/Cpl 12425 2nd King's Own Scottish Borderers
HIGGINS H.F. MM Bdr 68689 RFA
HIGGINS Harold MM L/Cpl 25343 17th Welsh Regt KIA 25.11.17.
HIGGINS Harold MM L/Cpl 21525 4th Grenadier Guards KIA 25.9.16.
HIGGINS Harry MM Sjt 15282 2nd Bedfordshire Regt
HIGGINS Herbert "DCM,MM+Bar" Sjt 1226 2nd Royal Irish Rifles
HIGGINS Herbert Sidney MM Sjt 23315 Royal Engineers
HIGGINS J.T. MM 2nd Cpl 26422 15 Fd Coy Royal Engineers
HIGGINS James MM Sjt S/6735 1/5th Royal Highlanders
HIGGINS James MM Pte 16653 Royal Irish Fusiliers
HIGGINS James MM Cpl 200300 1/4th Royal Scots Fusiliers
HIGGINS James MM Pte 580 17 Fd Amb RAMC
HIGGINS James MM Pte 20422 11th Royal Scots DOW 12.5.17.
HIGGINS James MM Pte 2825 East Kent Regt
HIGGINS John MM Cpl 29527 7th Royal Warwickshire Regt
HIGGINS John MM Dvr 66662 B/104 Bde RFA
HIGGINS John MM Cpl M1/08821 Army Service Corps
HIGGINS John MM Cpl 41595 King's Own Scottish Borderers
HIGGINS John "DCM,MM" Sjt 11588 4th Grenadier Guards
HIGGINS John MM Pte 29097 Highland Light Infantry
HIGGINS John MM Gnr 95453 'G' Bn Tank Corps
HIGGINS John L. MM Pte 18185 Devonshire Regt
HIGGINS John L. MM Sjt 16517 Machine Gun Corps
HIGGINS Joseph MM Pte 242000 East Lancashire Regt
HIGGINS Leonard MM L/Cpl 40195 1st Cameron Highlanders
HIGGINS Michael "MM,MID" L/Cpl 7749 2nd Royal Munster Fusiliers
HIGGINS Michael MM L/Cpl 7493 2nd Irish Guards KIA 15.9.16.
HIGGINS Oban Douglas MM L/Sjt B/203208 13th Rifle Brigade KIA 12.9.18.
HIGGINS Patrick "DCM,MM+Bar,MID" Cpl A/7311 2nd Highland Light Infantry
HIGGINS Percy J. MM Pte 40600 York & Lancaster Regt
HIGGINS Peter MM Sjt 291156 Northumberland Fusiliers
HIGGINS Robert MM+Bar Pte 8598 4th Liverpool Regt
HIGGINS Samuel MM L/Cpl 19202 9th York & Lancaster Regt KIA 31.10.18.
HIGGINS Thomas Charles MM Sjt 12942 1st Scots Guards
HIGGINS Walter MM L/Cpl 39802 5th South Wales Borderers
HIGGINS William MM Pte 265168 7th Liverpool Regt Died 15.10.18.
HIGGINS William MM L/Sjt 6159 1st West Yorkshire Regt
HIGGINS William George MM Dvr 250018 Signal Service Royal Engineers
HIGGINS William H. MM S/Sjt Fitter 148927 RGA
HIGGINS William John MM Pte 10122 5th Dorsetshire Regt
HIGGINSON Harold MM Sjt 58842 41 Bde RFA
HIGGINSON Harry MM Cpl 145535 1/1st Northamptonshire Yeomanry
HIGGINSON James MM Sjt 294523 145 Hy Bty RGA
HIGGINSON John MM Pte 37389 Labour Corps
HIGGINSON Percy MM+Bar Sjt 41546 52 Fd Amb RAMC
HIGGINSON Percy W.H. MM Pte 8741 Coldstream Guards
HIGGINSON Robert MM+Bar Sjt 9188 1st Liverpool Regt
HIGGINSON Samuel MM Pte 245252 2nd Manchester Regt
HIGGINSON Vincent J. MM Bdr 835517 RFA
HIGGINSON William MM Sjt 681839 466 Bty 65 Bde RFA
HIGGINSON William J.S. MM L/Cpl 266908 Gloucestershire Regt
HIGGON John MM Sjt 19438 Royal Welsh Fusiliers
HIGGS Albert MM Pte 12009 7th York & Lancaster Regt KIA 6.4.18.
HIGGS Alfred A.H. MM Pte 35742 Royal Fusiliers
HIGGS Arthur MM Pte M2/052601 Army Service Corps
HIGGS Charles MM Sjt 26503 7th Royal Irish Regt
HIGGS Charles Ethelbert MM L/Cpl 20730 Bedfordshire Regt
HIGGS Edward Henry MM Sjt 548140 510 Fd Coy Royal Engineers
HIGGS Edward J. MM Sjt 3027 Royal Warwickshire Regt
HIGGS Francis Edward "MM,MID" Gnr 1417 C/230 Bde RFA
HIGGS G.F. MM Sjt 6508 4th Hussars
HIGGS George H. MM L/Cpl 36687 Royal Engineers
HIGGS R.C. MM Sjt 6/400 Rifle Brigade
HIGGS Sidney W. MM Cpl 86851 326 Siege Bty RGA
HIGGS Stanley G. MM Spr 103158 32 Div Sig Coy Royal Engineers
HIGGS Thomas G. MM Pte G/20784 26th Royal Fusiliers
HIGGS W. MM Sjt 338 Royal Warwickshire Regt
HIGGS Walter MM+Bar Cpl 830065 408 Bty 96 Bde RFA

HIGGS Walter G. MM Gnr 291938 132 Heavy Bty RGA
HIGGS William R. MM+Bar Sjt 6195 2nd Royal Scots Fusiliers
HIGGS William T. MM Pte 37001 2nd South Staffordshire Regt
HIGGS Woodford A. MM Pte M2/153346 33 Div Train Army Service Corps
HIGH Charles Arthur MM Pte 17341 7th Norfolk Regt
HIGH Henry MM Cpl 44439 Royal Engineers
HIGH Richard MM L/Cpl 22656 East Surrey Regt
HIGH Sydney Bernard MM Sjt 797 RFA
HIGH William MM Pte 2004 1/5th Royal Highlanders
HIGHAM Ambrose MM Pte 28117 2nd Wiltshire Regt
HIGHAM John MM Spr 282235 Royal Engineers
HIGHAM John H. MM Sjt 62344 RAMC
HIGHAM John William MM L/Cpl R/14355 13th King's Royal Rifle Corps
HIGHAM Joseph MM Sjt 200653 1/5th Liverpool Regt
HIGHAM Walter MM Pte 28740 2nd Manchester Regt
HIGHAM William MM L/Cpl 20476 2nd Grenadier Guards
HIGHAM William N. MM Pte 201123 Cheshire Regt
HIGHCOCK Ernest MM Pte 341097 1/3(West Lancashire)Fd Amb RAMC
HIGHET Alexander G. "MM,MID" Sjt 76242 4 Sig Constr Coy Royal Engineers
HIGHFIELD Frank L. MM Cpl 45864 Royal Engineers
HIGHFIELD Howard MM Pte 202894 1st London Regt
HIGHGATE Edwin "DCM,MM+2 Bars" L/Cpl G/3833 7th Royal Sussex Regt
HIGHMAN Alfred John "MM,MSM" Cpl 5043 2nd Royal Irish Rifles
HIGHMORE Alfred E. "DCM+Bar,MM+Bar" Pte M2/053918 Army Service Corps att 1/2(Highland)Fd Amb RAMC
HIGHMORE Robert Leonard MM Sjt 50415 Royal Engineers
HIGHO Thomas William MM Cpl 11466 11th Hampshire Regt KIA 9.9.16.
HIGHTON Charles "MM,CG(B)" Sjt 13/1164 11th East Yorkshire Regt
HIGHTON Harold MM Pte 13906 1st East Kent Regt KIA 18.9.18.
HIGNEY James "MM,MID" L/Cpl 1945 1st King's Royal Rifle Corps
HIGSON James MM Gnr 176126 258 Siege Bty RGA
HIGSON John H. MM L/Cpl 30302 Border Regt
HIGSON John Richard MM Bdr 18730 D/23 Bde RFA
HIGSON Paul MM Pte 70387 166 Coy Machine Gun Corps
HIGSON Peter MM Sjt 16947 1st North Lancashire Regt KIA 30.9.18.
HILBERT Hedley MM Pte 3/748 2nd Yorkshire Light Infantry
HILBOURNE G.F. "DCM,MM" L/Cpl 29231 8th East Surrey Regt
HILBURY F. MM Pte 200760 Essex Regt
HILDER Harry MM Pte 4767 8th East Surrey Regt KIA 3.5.17
HILDERSLEY Alexander MM L/Cpl 17875 14th Royal Irish Rifles KIA 1.7.16.
HILDERSLEY Frank MM Pte 11261 Seaforth Highlanders
HILDITCH W. MM Pte 376173 Manchester Regt
HILDRED H.N. MM Pnr 259602 Royal Engineers
HILDRETH Mark Summersgill MM Pte 1399 1/5th Yorkshire Regt DOW 3.8.18.
HILDRICK Stanley MM Sjt 44212 11 Bde RFA
HILDYARD Ernest I. MM Sub-Conductor 6764 Army Ordnance Corps
HILES Albert E. MM Pte 474411 12th London Regt
HILES Ernest L. MM L/Cpl 50305 Royal Engineers
HILES Harold Corney MM Bdr 1634 1(South Midland)Bde RFA
HILES John H.A. MM Sjt 695069 22nd London Regt
HILEY Ernest J. MM Pte 43908 18th King's Royal Rifle Corps
HILKER G.L. MM Cpl 214339 Royal Engineers
HILL A. MM CSM M2/222790 954 Coy Army Service Corps
HILL A.B. MM L/Cpl 79724 13th Royal Fusiliers
HILL Aaron MM Bdr L/3238 B/255 Bde RFA
HILL Albert MM Cpl 12144 7th East Yorkshire Regt
HILL Albert MM CSM 12998 9th Notts & Derby Regt
HILL Albert MM L/Cpl 2611 Lincolnshire Regt
HILL Albert MM Pte 42538 26th Royal Fusiliers KIA 22.6.17.
HILL Albert MM Cpl 591762 18th London Regt
HILL Albert MM L/Sjt 20761 Manchester Regt
HILL Albert A. MM L/Cpl 20713 1st Somerset Light Infantry
HILL Albert E. MM Cpl 17 Army Veterinary Corps
HILL Albert Edward "MM,MMV(It)" Sjt 290152 8th Devonshire Regt
HILL Albert Edward MM Pte 49253 45 Fd Amb RAMC
HILL Albert S. MM Sjt 703555 23rd London Regt
HILL Albyn MM L/Cpl 16822 York & Lancaster Regt
HILL Alex MM Pte 34714 219 Coy Machine Gun Corps
HILL Alexander MM Pte 289844 700 Coy Labour Corps
HILL Alexander B. MM Pte 332326 4th Liverpool Regt
HILL Alfred MM L/Cpl 32231 1/5th Bedfordshire Regt
HILL Alfred MM CSM 7453 2nd Lancashire Fusiliers KIA 12.10.16.
HILL Alfred MM Pte 8942 2nd Suffolk Regt DOW 18.8.16.
HILL Alfred MM Pte 1496 Yorkshire Regt
HILL Alfred Charles MM Pte 240658 1/8th Worcestershire Regt
HILL Alfred F. MM Pte R/38553 King's Royal Rifle Corps
HILL Alfred R. MM Pte R/34410 2nd King's Royal Rifle Corps
HILL Allan MM Sjt 205896 6th Northamptonshire Regt
HILL Archibald Leonard MM Pte 472331 12th London Regt
HILL Arnold Victor MM Bdr 88031 RHA
HILL Arthur MM Gnr 72859 23 Div Ammn Col RFA
HILL Arthur MM Pte 8811 2nd Welsh Regt
HILL Arthur MM Pnr 452436 19 Div Sig Coy Royal Engineers
HILL Arthur MM L/Cpl 22953 Machine Gun Corps
HILL Arthur MM Pte 10272 6th Yorkshire Light Infantry DOW 15.9.16.
HILL Arthur MM L/Cpl 14631 6th Northamptonshire Regt
HILL Arthur MM Pte 17/612 11th West Yorkshire Regt DOW 21.9.17.
HILL Arthur A. MM Spr 89811 Royal Engineers
HILL Arthur C. MM Sjt 36959 RAMC
HILL Arthur Johnson MM Pte 17180 14th York & Lancaster Regt DOW 15.3.17.
HILL Arthur S. MM Pte 3683 1st Welsh Guards
HILL Arthur W. MM Spr 207585 Royal Engineers
HILL Arthur William MM Pte 43274 55 Coy Machine Gun Corps KIA 1.3.17.
HILL C. MM L/Cpl 442143 RAMC
HILL Cecil Thomas MM Pte 20403 3rd Grenadier Guards
HILL Charles MM Cpl 7746 2nd Essex
HILL Charles "DCM,MM" Sjt 200282 1/5th South Staffordshire Regt
HILL Charles MM Pte 40680 8th North Staffordshire Regt
HILL Charles MM Sjt 4342 19th Bn Machine Gun Corps KIA 26.3.18.
HILL Charles MM Sjt 63831 RFA
HILL Charles A. MM Sjt 46290 RAMC
HILL Charles F.S. MM Pte 49689 2nd Bedfordshire Regt
HILL Charles Finlay MM Pte 22227 62 Coy Machine Gun Corps KIA 27.9.16.
HILL Charles H. MM Pte 53083 Royal Fusiliers
HILL Charles H.G. MM Cpl 2128 5th Lancers
HILL Charles L. MM L/Cpl 53131 1st Royal Scots Fusiliers
HILL Charles W. MM Pte 3892 1st Northumberland Fusiliers
HILL Christopher MM Cpl 200896 1/7th Worcestershire Regt
HILL Clarence MM Dvr 63991 5 Div Ammn Col RFA
HILL Clifford MM Pte 10107 8th Suffolk Regt
HILL David "MM,MID" Pte 9101 2nd Royal Scots
HILL David MM L/Cpl 43739 Royal Scots
HILL David L. MM Cpl 282645 90 Siege Bty RGA
HILL E. MM Gnr 2173 RFA
HILL E.A. MM Cpl 17750 Wiltshire Regt
HILL Edgar J. MM Pte 698083 22nd London Regt
HILL Edmund Leonard MM Pte 17203 9th Essex Regt KIA 7.4.18.
HILL Edward MM Cpl 18547 15th Hampshire Regt DOW 5.10.16.
HILL Edward MM Sjt 241458 2/5th North Lancashire Regt KIA 26.10.17.
HILL Edwin Arthur Knight MM Gnr 132288 250 Siege Bty RGA
HILL Edwin Charles MM Sjt 10818 16th Manchester Regt KIA 14.10.16.
HILL Eric B. MM Pte 107114 Machine Gun Corps
HILL Ernest MM Pte 3120 11th Manchester Regt
HILL Ernest MM Cpl 32813 Lincolnshire Regt
HILL Ernest G. MM Sjt 153193 291 Siege Bty RGA
HILL Ernest G.C. MM L/Cpl 17731 6th Wiltshire Regt
HILL Ernest W. MM Sjt 90958 99 Fd Amb RAMC
HILL Francis L. "DCM,MM" Pte M2/047351 59 Div Train Army Service Corps
HILL Francis O. MM CQMS R/5522 13th King's Royal Rifle Corps
HILL Frank MM L/Bdr 322168 93 Siege Bty RGA
HILL Frank C. "DCM,MM" Sjt 36577 8th East Surrey Regt
HILL Fred MM Pte 241115 1/5th Devonshire Regt
HILL Fred MM Pte 11229 4th King's Royal Rifle Corps
HILL Fred MM Pte 13031 7th Royal Lancaster Regt
HILL Fred MM Cpl 10862 8th Devonshire Regt KIA 20.7.26.
HILL Fred MM Pte 202461 7th Lincolnshire Regt
HILL Frederick MM L/Cpl 13615 2nd Middlesex Regt
HILL Frederick MM L/Cpl 9142 2nd South Staffordshire Regt
HILL Frederick MM Pte 200858 1/4th Yorkshire Light Infantry KIA 26.4.19.
HILL Frederick MM 2nd Cpl 2632 Royal Engineers
HILL Frederick MM L/Cpl R/3431 13th King's Royal Rifle Corps

HILL Frederick MM Bdr 89352 B/47 Bde RFA
HILL Frederick G. MM Gnr 155862 RFA
HILL Frederick R. MM Sjt 46033 'Q' Bty RHA
HILL Frederick T. MM Sjt 720857 1/24th London Regt
HILL Frederick W. "MM,CG(B)" Cpl 10588 6th King's Own Scottish Borderers
HILL G.M. MM Pte R/6008 King's Royal Rifle Corps
HILL G.W. MM Pte 267934 Notts & Derby Regt
HILL George MM Pte 21706 9th Leicestershire Regt
HILL George MM Gnr 362804 354 Siege Bty RGA
HILL George MM L/Cpl 18187 5th South Wales Borderers
HILL George MM Pte 19077 Somerset Light Infantry
HILL George MM L/Cpl 9821 Worcestershire Regt
HILL George C. "DCM,MM" Sjt 49308 87 Fd Coy Royal Engineers
HILL George Edward MM Pte 16227 Machine Gun Corps
HILL George Ernest MM+Bar Sjt 15207 RFA
HILL George H. MM Pte 46599 Northumberland Fusiliers
HILL George Henry MM+Bar L/Cpl F/2236 23rd Middlesex Regt KIA 18.10.18.
HILL George Richard MM Sjt 9881 2nd Yorkshire Regt
HILL George W. MM Cpl Fitter 960536 7(London)Bde RFA
HILL H. MM L/Cpl 403549 RAMC
HILL Henry MM Spr 436085 Royal Engineers
HILL Henry MM L/Bdr 21093 RFA
HILL Henry MM Pte 11/375 11th East Yorkshire Regt KIA 8.8.18.
HILL Henry MM Pte 13353 IX Corps Cyclist Bn Army Cyclist Corps
HILL Henry P. MM Pte 6638 2nd South Staffordshire Regt
HILL Henry T. MM Cpl 300023 Notts & Derby Regt
HILL Herbert MM Spr 42059 Royal Engineers
HILL Herbert MM Sjt 10196 1st Bedfordshire Regt
HILL Herbert J. MM Pte 31910 8th Somerset Light Infantry
HILL Horace MM Cpl 504477 Railway Op Div Royal Engineers
HILL Howard MM Pte M1/08339 Army Service Corps
HILL Howard George MM Cpl 3133 1/23rd London Regt
HILL Howard M. MM L/Cpl 19843 2nd Worcestershire Regt
HILL Hugh MM Pte 11517 Royal Warwickshire Regt
HILL J. MM L/Cpl 538042 6 Fd Amb RAMC
HILL J.E.C. MM Spr 265034 Notts & Derby Regt
HILL James MM Pte 31615 2nd South Staffordshire Regt
HILL James MM+Bar Pte 16050 12th Royal Scots
HILL James MM Sjt 200984 2/5th Royal Warwickshire Regt
HILL James "DCM,MM" Sjt 18428 88 Coy Machine Gun Corps
HILL James MM Pte 20975 South Wales Borderers
HILL James D. MM+2 Bars Cpl 68868 D/250 Bde RFA
HILL James F. MM Bdr L/36318 RFA
HILL James Henry MM Pte 241094 2/4th South Lancashire Regt DOW 6.10.18.
HILL James W.H. MM Spr 19233 Royal Engineers
HILL James William "MM,CG(F)" Cpl 36807 RFA
HILL Jesse MM Pte 44589 Northumberland Fusiliers
HILL Jesse MM Pte 16267 9th York & Lancaster Regt
HILL Job MM Pte 23844 9th Notts & Derby Regt
HILL John MM Pte 352841 12th Royal Scots
HILL John MM Pte 57723 4th York & Lancaster Regt
HILL John MM L/Cpl R/3867 13th King's Royal Rifle Corps
HILL John MM Pte 3716 1st Dragoon Guards
HILL John MM Pte 10704 1st Seaforth Highlanders
HILL John MM Pte 34426 5th West Riding Regt
HILL John MM Cpl 23969 16th Welsh Regt
HILL John MM 2nd Cpl 155938 181 Tunnelling Coy Royal Engineers
HILL John MM Pte 47837 Northumberland Fusiliers
HILL John MM L/Cpl 10872 8th Yorkshire Regt KIA 21.10.17.
HILL John MM Pte R/4644 13th King's Royal Rifle Corps
HILL John Ernest MM Pte 12102 North Lancashire Regt
HILL John F. MM Sjt 19783 13th Liverpool Regt
HILL John George MM Gnr 33294 121 Heavy Bty RGA
HILL John Harold MM Sjt 9049 1st Lincolnshire Regt
HILL John Henry MM Pte 350285 1/5th Highland Light Infantry
HILL John R. MM Sjt 13849 11th Border Regt
HILL John R.F. MM Sjt M/270774 Army Service Corps
HILL John S. MM L/Cpl M2/103251 Army Service Corps
HILL John W. MM Pte R/8405 King's Royal Rifle Corps
HILL John W. MM Pnr 83323 Royal Engineers
HILL Joseph MM L/Cpl 2630 6th Royal Irish Regt
HILL Joseph MM Spr 81173 Royal Engineers
HILL Joseph MM Pte 702 Northumberland Fusiliers
HILL Joseph MM+Bar L/Cpl 70205 Royal Welsh Fusiliers
HILL Joseph "DCM,MM" Cpl 89597 103 Fd Coy Royal Engineers
HILL Joseph MM Cpl 13332 8th Yorkshire Regt
HILL Joseph Walter MM Sjt 1036 Royal Engineers
HILL Joseph William MM Dvr 831378 C/311 Bde RFA
HILL Jubilee MM Cpl 8819 2nd Royal Welsh Fusiliers
HILL L.C. MM L/Cpl 75877 Machine Gun Corps
HILL Levi MM Pte 57717 4th York & Lancaster Regt
HILL Morris MM+Bar Pte 30041 6th Somerset Light Infantry DOW 18.12.17.
HILL Percy MM L/Cpl 92840 1st Middlesex Regt
HILL Percy MM Gnr 6456 13 Siege Bty RGA KIA 17.9.16.
HILL Percy MM L/Cpl 23338 9th Royal Welsh Fusiliers
HILL Ralph G. MM Cpl S4/070797 Army Service Corps
HILL Ralph Victor Eugene MM Pte 11198 7th Somerset Light Infantry
HILL Raymond MM L/Cpl 39468 34 Coy Machine Gun Corps
HILL Richard MM Gnr 108974 RGA
HILL Richard F. MM Spr 63181 Royal Engineers
HILL Richard G. MM Cpl 75116 74 Div Sig Coy Royal Engineers
HILL Richard George MM Pte M2/031524 Army Service Corps att 'B' AA Bty RGA
HILL Robert McL. MM Cpl 95534 5th Bn Tank Corps
HILL Rowland Miles MM Sjt 15203 2nd Grenadier Guards
HILL Sam MM L/Cpl 21597 7th East Lancashire Regt KIA 10.12.17.
HILL Samson Gideon MM Pte 21199 4th Worcestershire Regt KIA 14.10.18.
HILL Samuel MM Pte 10597 2nd West Riding Regt
HILL Samuel MM Pte 14322 7th Cameron Highlanders
HILL Samuel "MM,MSM" Sjt 14206 24th Manchester Regt
HILL Sidney MM Pte 22592 13th Royal Welsh Fusiliers
HILL Silas MM Bdr 88543 RFA
HILL Sydney W. MM L/Cpl 28680 Machine Gun Corps
HILL Thomas MM Dvr 242724 134 Bty 32 Bde RFA
HILL Thomas "MM,MID" Sjt 5653 9th Manchester Regt
HILL Thomas MM L/Cpl 99613 Middlesex Regt
HILL Thomas MM L/Cpl 241423 1/6th Liverpool Regt DOW 30.11.17.
HILL Thomas MM Sjt 27394 3 Div Ammn Col RFA
HILL Thomas Alfred MM Sjt 5001 2nd Royal Fusiliers
HILL Thomas E. MM Dvr 45725 'G' Bty RHA
HILL Thomas Harold MM Sjt 19063 179 Bde RFA
HILL Thomas Henry MM Bdr 53332 27 Siege Bty RGA
HILL Thomas W. MM Gnr 312420 RGA
HILL Victor Gordon MM Spr 182818 12 Div Sig Coy Royal Engineers KIA 14.5.18.
HILL W. MM Pte M2/229335 352 Coy Army Service Corps
HILL W. MM Pte 9147 2nd East Yorkshire Regt
HILL W.J. MM L/Sjt 9731 2nd Bedfordshire Regt
HILL W.S. MM+Bar Bdr W/1756 A/121 Bde RFA
HILL Walter MM 2nd Cpl 311066 Royal Engineers
HILL Walter Bridges Arthur MM Sjt 194655 3 Fd Svy Bn Royal Engineers
HILL Wilfred MM Pte 241528 2nd London Regt
HILL William MM Pte 307762 8th Royal Warwickshire Regt
HILL William "DCM,MM" CSM 8647 12th East Surrey Regt
HILL William MM+Bar L/Cpl 34468 2nd Royal Scots DOW 28.9.18.
HILL William "DCM,MM" Cpl 240101 5/6th Scottish Rifles DOW 23.10.18.
HILL William MM Pte 18458 10th Worcestershire Regt
HILL William MM Pte 1682 1/4th Yorkshire Regt
HILL William MM Pte S/12799 Rifle Brigade
HILL William MM Pte 10761 2nd Oxf & Bucks Light Infantry
HILL William MM+Bar Gnr 24100 97 Bty 147 Bde RFA
HILL William A. "MM,MSM" 2nd Cpl 92679 138 Army Troops Coy Royal Engineers
HILL William C. MM Sjt 8876 B/72 Bde RFA
HILL William F.L. MM+Bar CQMS 268692 1/5th Royal Highlanders
HILL William Harry MM Gnr 87732 D/153 Bde RFA
HILL William Henry MM Dvr 92134 B/88 Bde RFA
HILL William Henry MM Spr 94297 Royal Engineers
HILL William J. MM Pte 242021 Liverpool Regt
HILL William J. MM Pte 232711 2nd London Regt
HILL William John "DCM,MM" Cpl 47245 15 Bde RFA
HILL William Quintus Ewart MM L/Cpl 14/16595 14th Royal Irish Rifles KIA 16.8.17.
HILL William S. MM CSM M/27836 5 Ammn Park Army Service Corps
HILLABY Harold MM Pte 350479 1(East Lancs)Fd Amb RAMC
HILLABY Samuel MM Spr 472123 479 Fd Coy Royal Engineers
HILLAM Albert MM L/Sjt 32919 2nd Lincolnshire Regt
HILLAM Louis MM Pte 3/11090 7th Northamptonshire Regt KIA 9.6.17.
HILLARD John William MM Pte M/283275 Army Service Corps

HILLBECK Alfred MM Dvr 2555 D/251 Bde RFA KIA 18.4.18.
HILLBECK James MM Cpl 84028 Royal Engineers
HILLER Louis MM Pte 35341 Yorkshire Light Infantry
HILLERBY John MM L/Cpl 403567 RAMC
HILLIAM John MM Pte 16726 Machine Gun Corps
HILLIAM Joseph H. MM Pte 405451 3(West Riding)Fd Amb RAMC
HILLIAR Joseph MM L/Cpl 2180 RAMC
HILLIARD Frederick Herbert MM Pte 22435 1st Wiltshire Regt DOW 1.9.18.
HILLIARD John H. MM Pte 46905 18th Lancashire Fusiliers
HILLIARD William MM Sjt 325416 1/1st Cambridgeshire Regt
HILLIER Albert J. MM L/Bdr 179659 268 Siege Bty RGA
HILLIER George MM Sjt 10461 1st Royal Berkshire Regt KIA 20.4.17.
HILLIER George A. MM Sjt 69632 38 Bde RFA
HILLIER George A. MM Pte 13390 4th Coldstream Guards
HILLIER Harry Arthur MM Gnr 9497 A/71 Bde RFA
HILLIER John Robert MM Pte 202848 2/4th Hampshire Regt
HILLIER Robert MM Sjt 241887 Northumberland Fusiliers
HILLIER William Henry MM+Bar CSM 14173 8th Somerset Light Infantry Died 24.10.18.
HILLIKER William MM Bdr 39893 1 Siege Bty RGA
HILLING James A. MM L/Cpl 370437 1/8th London Regt
HILLING W.R. MM Sjt P/1526 Military Foot Police
HILLIS Joseph MM Spr 44155 Royal Engineers
HILLMAN Albert "MM,MC(G)" Pte 32403 12th Hampshire Regt
HILLMAN Alfred J. MM Pte 62621 6th West Yorkshire Regt
HILLMAN Frank MM+Bar L/Cpl 476264 Royal Engineers
HILLMAN Fred W. MM Cpl 31782 Cheshire Regt
HILLMAN Herbert R.N. MM Pte 320244 16th Royal Sussex Regt
HILLMAN Robert G. MM Pte 40775 2/5th Lancashire Fusiliers
HILLMAN William H. MM L/Cpl 65386 Royal Fusiliers
HILLOCK Edward MM L/Sjt 6471 2nd Irish Guards
HILLS Charles MM L/Cpl R/15982 King's Royal Rifle Corps
HILLS Charles B. MM Pte 28318 Border Regt
HILLS Edgar MM Gnr 85806 A/64 Bde RFA
HILLS Ernest Archer MM Pte 36020 11th South Wales Borderers KIA 3.8.17.
HILLS Ernest Sidney MM Pte 6483 Royal West Surrey Regt
HILLS Fred MM Sjt 9407 1st East Kent Regt
HILLS Frederick G. MM Pnr 12697 6th Dorsetshire Regt
HILLS Frederick H. MM+Bar Cpl 720858 1/24th London Regt
HILLS Frederick W. MM Gnr 1328 RFA
HILLS George MM Pte 8937 2nd Bedfordshire Regt DOW 12.11.17.
HILLS H.W. MM Cpl 17759 Royal Air Force
HILLS Harry MM Pte G/6539 2nd Royal Sussex Regt
HILLS Henry T. MM Sjt 350074 1/9th Royal Scots
HILLS Herbert W. MM Spr 2900 2/3(London)Fd Coy Royal Engineers
HILLS J.H. MM+2 Bars L/Cpl 10758 1st Royal Scots Fusiliers
HILLS James MM Pte 21/654 Northumberland Fusiliers
HILLS James MM Gnr 152803 RFA
HILLS Jesse MM Pte 18876 76 Coy Machine Gun Corps DOW 4.5.18.
HILLS Joseph MM Cpl 750429 250 Bde RFA
HILLS Joseph John MM Spr 161741 'BT' Cable Section Royal Engineers
HILLS Leslie G. MM L/Cpl 1343 1/21st London Regt
HILLS Maurice G. MM Cpl 40276 Royal Engineers
HILLS Owen MM L/Bdr 71566 RGA
HILLS Reginald M. MM Cpl 24265 Royal Fusiliers att RE.
HILLS Samuel MM L/Cpl 4238 3rd Rifle Brigade
HILLS Thomas MM Sjt 17169 100 Coy Machine Gun Corps
HILLS Thomas William MM Pte 74197 113 Fd Amb RAMC DOW 16.9.16.
HILLS William MM Pte 203755 1/4th Seaforth Highlanders
HILLS William Alfred MM Cpl S/3971 13th Rifle Brigade KIA 23.4.17.
HILLS William G. MM Cpl 7626 6th East Kent Regt
HILLSON Edward J. MM Cpl 89503 Machine Gun Corps
HILLYARD A.H. MM Sjt 16298 Essex Regt
HILLYARD William "DCM+Bar,MM" CSM 242031 6th King's Own Scottish Borderers KIA 22.10.18.
HILLYER Harvey F. MM L/Cpl R/35725 1st King's Royal Rifle Corps
HILSON George H. MM+Bar Sjt 98924 50th Bn Machine Gun Corps
HILSTON James MM Pte 70922 201 Coy Machine Gun Corps
HILTON Alexander Charles MM Pte M1/08039 21 Div Train Army Service Corps
HILTON Alfred MM L/Cpl 2043 1/9th Liverpool Regt KIA 31.7.17.
HILTON Charles H. MM Bdr 820087 RFA
HILTON Daniel MM Gnr 69907 2 Bde RFA
HILTON F.H. MM S/Sjt Fitter 607 RFA
HILTON Frank MM Pte 7322 11th Royal Fusiliers
HILTON George "DCM,MM" Sjt 10160 5th Cameron Highlanders
HILTON Harold MM Pte 63803 RAMC
HILTON Harry MM L/Cpl A/545 8th King's Royal Rifle Corps
HILTON Henry MM Bdr 46728 RFA
HILTON J. MM Pte M2/275370 Army Service Corps
HILTON James MM Pte 204757 1st London Regt
HILTON John MM Gnr 206831 57 Bty 45 Bde RFA
HILTON John MM Pte 11853 6th Border Regt
HILTON John MM BQMS 281693 RGA
HILTON John MM Cpl 115598 Royal Engineers
HILTON John Christopher MM L/Cpl 25854 Notts & Derby Regt
HILTON Matthew MM Pte 26311 Cameron Highlanders
HILTON Norman Percy MM Bdr 735919 X/74 Med TM Bty RFA
HILTON R. MM L/Cpl 250232 Durham Light Infantry
HILTON Reginald MM Pte 27309 2nd Border Regt
HILTON Robert MM Cpl 15233 1st Lancashire Fusiliers
HILTON Robert E. MM Cpl 12594 16th Lancashire Fusiliers
HILTON Thomas MM Pte 47696 Royal Fusiliers
HILTON Thomas MM Sjt 4190 RFA
HILTON Wilfred MM Cpl 76420 'B' Bn Tank Corps Died 8.11.17.
HILTON William F. MM Sjt 208058 249 Fd Coy Royal Engineers
HIMMEL Harold MM Sjt 56169 Northumberland Fusiliers
HIMSON Stanley V. MM Pte 13882 8th Suffolk Regt
HIMSWORTH Sydney MM Pte 47052 9th West Yorkshire Regt
HINCHAN Joseph MM Pte 23063 2nd Yorkshire Light Infantry
HINCHCLIFF Clifford MM Pte 41339 1st Royal Lancaster Regt
HINCHCLIFF G. MM Spr 475934 50 Div Sig Coy Royal Engineers
HINCHCLIFF Hervey MM Cpl 42996 5th Yorkshire Light Infantry
HINCHCLIFFE Fred MM L/Sjt 48626 12th Liverpool Regt KIA 30.11.17.
HINCHCLIFFE Mark MM Sjt 15077 93 Siege Bty RGA
HINCHLIFF John T. MM Sjt 241214 5th West Riding Regt
HINCHLIFFE Arthur MM L/Cpl 72691 69 Coy Machine Gun Corps DOW 30.9.17.
HINCHLIFFE B. MM Pte 203315 West Riding Regt
HINCHLIFFE Charles Ernest MM Sjt 11286 West Riding Regt KIA 20.7.18.
HINCHLIFFE Frank MM Pte 241325 1/5th West Riding Regt
HINCHLIFFE Herman MM L/Cpl 11546 1st Coldstream Guards
HINCHLIFFE James "MM,MSM,MID" Sjt M2/102123 Army Service Corps
HINCHLIFFE Thomas MM Gnr 159933 462 Bty RFA
HINCHLIFFE Thomas I. MM Pte 594 RAMC
HINCHLY Victor Charles Louis MM Sjt 16407 5th Shropshire Light Infantry
HINCKLEY Albert E. MM Cpl 10166 Royal Welsh Fusiliers
HINCKLEY P. MM Bdr 76844 139 Hy Bty RGA
HINCKLIEFF Alexander MM Pte 38494 8th West Yorkshire Regt
HINCKS Sam MM Pte 201992 Leicestershire Regt
HIND Charles H. MM Sjt 47305 89 Fd Coy Royal Engineers
HIND Fred MM Sjt 201233 4th North Lancashire Regt
HIND John F. "DCM,MM" Sjt 403243 1/2(West Riding)Fd Amb RAMC
HIND Joseph MM Pte 200968 West Riding Regt
HIND Neville MM Pte 38485 Lancashire Fusiliers
HIND Robert L. MM Pte 242476 5th Lincolnshire Regt
HIND Steve MM Pte 240996 1/6th Lancashire Fusiliers
HIND Thomas MM Pte 19655 24 Coy Machine Gun Corps
HIND Walter MM Sjt 4986 2nd West Yorkshire Regt
HINDE Robert MM Sjt 1136 1st Manchester Regt
HINDE Robert F. MM L/Cpl 201720 Royal Lancaster Regt
HINDE William T. MM Bdr 16187 37 Bde RFA
HINDER George MM L/Cpl R/4467 13th King's Royal Rifle Corps KIA 28.2.17.
HINDER John MM Sjt 16575 19 Coy Machine Gun Corps DOW 1.11.16.Real Name HILL.
HINDES Alfred George MM L/Cpl 172053 40 Div Sig Coy Royal Engineers
HINDLE Arthur MM Cpl 26630 62nd Bn Machine Gun Corps
HINDLE Charles MM Sjt 82246 A/46 Bde RFA
HINDLE Fred MM L/Sjt 320216 24th Welsh Regt
HINDLE Henry Bury MM CQMS 14683 8th Royal Lancaster Regt
HINDLE James W. MM Dvr 75802 24 Bde RFA
HINDLE John MM Sjt 16088 8th Royal Lancaster Regt
HINDLE John H. MM Pte 81526 RAMC
HINDLE Joseph MM Cpl 696090 RFA
HINDLE Raymond S. MM Sjt 40681 A/190 Bde RFA
HINDLE Walter MM Pte 201480 North Lancashire Regt

HINDLEY Jess MM Pte 8067 2nd Worcestershire Regt
HINDLEY Lawrence MM L/Cpl 20372 11th Essex Regt KIA 15.10.16.
HINDLEY Samuel MM Sjt 27038 13th Liverpool Regt
HINDLEY Sidney MM Spr 480589 32 Div Sig Coy Royal Engineers
HINDLEY William MM Sjt 21676 1st Grenadier Guards
HINDLEY William MM L/Cpl 11091 1st Royal Lancaster Regt
HINDMARCH Ernest MM L/Cpl 325673 1/9th Durham Light Infantry DOW 29.4.18.
HINDMARCH Joseph M. MM Pte 57357 RAMC
HINDMARCH Norman MM L/Sjt 2407 1/5th Northumberland Fusiliers
HINDMARSH George MM Pte 22/749 Northumberland Fusiliers
HINDMARSH Matthew MM+2 Bars Cpl 761034 A/317 Bde RFA
HINDMOOR William MM L/Cpl 113581 258 Coy Machine Gun Corps
HINDREY A.E. MM Pte 12376 7th Norfolk Regt
HINDRY Herbert Charles MM Sjt 13542 8th Norfolk Regt
HINDS George F. MM Sjt 22565 RGA
HINDS Louis MM Pte 41110 8th Royal Lancaster Regt
HINDS Robert MM Pte 28/32 Northumberland Fusiliers
HINDS William G. MM CQMS 200117 1/4th Royal Lancaster Regt
HINDSON William MM Pte 65327 1st Northumberland Fusiliers
HINE Edmund J. MM Pte 18029 11th Cheshire Regt
HINE George F. MM Sjt 201628 Essex Regt
HINE Herbert Josiah MM CSM 12112 Royal Berkshire Regt KIA 25.8.28.
HINE Reginald MM L/Cpl 13067 8th Royal Berkshire Regt
HINE Thomas MM Gnr Fitter 151495 49 Siege Bty RGA
HINES Benjamin MM Pte 63690 105 Fd Amb RAMC
HINES Horace MM+Bar Cpl 241489 1/5th York & Lancaster Regt
HINES William MM Sjt 11740 1st Border Regt
HINES William MM Pte 14655 8th Suffolk Regt
HINES William MM Cpl 265803 1/1st Buckinghamshire Bn Oxf & Bucks Light Infantry
HINETT Aubrey MM L/Cpl 16283 11th Notts & Derby Regt
HINETT George W. MM L/Cpl 30867 14th Worcestershire Regt
HINGLEY Charles R. MM Gnr 1968 MGC(Motors)
HINGLEY Frederick A. MM Sjt 52346 Machine Gun Corps(Cavalry)
HINGLEY Walter MM Pte 3972 RAMC
HINKLER Frederick MM Pte 24193 9th York & Lancaster Regt
HINKLEY Alfred Thomas MM L/Sjt 11709 9th Notts & Derby Regt DOW 5.10.17.
HINKLEY Henry MM+Bar Sjt 2606 9th Notts & Derby Regt
HINKLEY S.H. MM Cpl 8599 2nd East Kent Regt
HINKLEY William F. MM Sjt 5461 8th East Surrey Regt
HINKS Edwin A. MM Pte 301517 14th Bn Tank Corps
HINLEY Gerald "MM,MID" Pte 2018 1/16th London Regt
HINMAN Frederick George MM L/Cpl 105200 229 Fd Coy Royal Engineers
HINSHAW William MM Pte S/2551 1st Gordon Highlanders KIA 18.7.16.
HINSLEY Clifford Smith MM Dvr 1402 2(West Riding)Bty RFA
HINSLEY Edward MM Dvr 810197 RFA
HINSLEY Harry MM Sjt 21128 22nd Manchester Regt
HINSLEY James Walter MM Gnr 87727 C/76 Bde RFA
HINTON Alexander F. MM Pte 24516 Machine Gun Corps
HINTON Alfred MM+Bar Pte 40942 Manchester Regt
HINTON Arthur J. MM Pte 95615 173 Coy Labour Corps
HINTON Charles MM Sjt 53548 2nd Welsh Regt KIA 31.10.18.
HINTON Frank J. MM Cpl 115310 RGA
HINTON Frederick MM Sjt 6414 1st Scots Guards
HINTON Frederick J. MM Pte 11568 8th Gloucestershire Regt
HINTON Harry MM Cpl 82205 177 Siege Bty RGA DOW 14.10.17.
HINTON J. MM Pte 13949 1st South Staffordshire Regt
HINTON James Edward Lewis MM Sjt 10130 5th Oxf & Bucks Light Infantry KIA 3.5.17.
HINTON JamesM. MM L/Sjt 9842 2/1st HAC(Inf)
HINTON Martin MM L/Cpl 17621 2nd Royal Scots Fusiliers
HINTON Percy Herbert MM Pte 271039 10th East Kent Regt
HINTON William Richard MM Cpl 3427 2/4th Oxf & Bucks Light Infantry KIA 10.9.17.
HINVEST John H. MM Cpl 5966 1st Dragoon Guards att 1st Life Guards
HINWOOD Neville MM Cpl 548240 510 Fd Coy Royal Engineers
HINXMAN Albert William MM Cpl M1/08942 5 Lt Armd Car Patrol Army Service Corps
HIOM Ernest W. MM Pte 203453 1st London Regt
HIPKIN Albert Preston MM Sjt 241759 1/5th York & Lancaster Regt DOW 30.10.17.
HIPKISS John W. MM Pte 202049 2nd Worcestershire Regt
HIPKISS William E. MM S/Sjt Fitter 128151 115 Siege Bty RGA
HIPPISLEY Albert MM Pte 14543 12th Somerset Light Infantry
HIPPISLEY David MM Pte 26222 Norfolk Regt
HIPPMAN W.F. MM Cpl 15874 Royal Fusiliers
HIPPS James MM Cpl 305958 8th West Yorkshire Regt
HIPWOOD Joseph MM Sjt 201066 2/4th West Riding Regt
HIPWOOD Wilfred MM Gnr 326553 160 Siege Bty RGA Died 2.9.18.
HIRCOCK Frank MM Gnr 146582 D/1 TM Bde RFA
HIRD Benjamin T. MM Pnr 99253 Royal Engineers
HIRD George MM Cpl 36442 Lancashire Fusiliers
HIRD Henry MM Pte 242959 5th Yorkshire Light Infantry
HIRD James "DCM,MM,MIDx2" Sjt L/38423 C/186 Bde RFA
HIRD John MM Pte 203589 East Lancashire Regt
HIRD John MM Pte 200148 Royal Highlanders
HIRD John William MM L/Cpl 241394 1/6th West Yorkshire Regt
HIRD Joseph MM L/Cpl 13548 8th Border Regt KIA 27.8.18.
HIRD Robert MM Pte 11301 2nd West Riding Regt
HIRD Samuel MM Pte 266948 2/5th West Riding Regt KIA 29.3.18.
HIRON George MM L/Cpl 38303 Worcestershire Regt
HIRON Joseph Alfred MM L/Cpl 439349 2/3(South Midland)Fd Amb RAMC
HIRONS Leonard MM Pte 7228 1st Leicestershire Regt
HIRONS William Frank MM L/Cpl 23150 7th Northamptonshire Regt KIA 28.3.18.
HIRSCHFiELD Frederick "DCM,MM,MIDx2" CQMS 10415 4th Worcestershire Regt
HIRSCHKOP Charles S. MM Spr 254601 Signal Service Royal Engineers
HIRST Aaron MM Cpl 404 12th Yorkshire Light Infantry
HIRST Albert E. MM Pte 41540 Leicestershire Regt
HIRST Archie MM Pte 59890 10th Royal West Surrey Regt
HIRST Arthur MM Pte 39440 8th West Yorkshire Regt
HIRST Charles MM Dvr 50636 RFA
HIRST Clifford MM L/Cpl 265062 West Yorkshire Regt
HIRST Edward Thomas MM L/Cpl 43258 15th Royal Irish Rifles KIA 21.3.18.
HIRST Edwin "DCM,MM+Bar" Sjt 401178 1 Fd Amb RAMC
HIRST Elliot MM Cpl 24565 9th West Riding Regt
HIRST Epaphias MM Sjt 18 C/48 Bde RFA
HIRST Ernest MM L/Cpl 26261 2nd Lancashire Fusiliers
HIRST Frank MM Pte 33258 8th Royal Warwickshire Regt
HIRST George MM Pte C/774 16th King's Royal Rifle Corps
HIRST Harold A. MM Spr 471709 29 Div Sig Coy Royal Engineers
HIRST Henry MM Sjt 307747 1/7th West Riding Regt KIA 29.4.18.
HIRST James "MM,MID" Sjt 1184 1/20th London Regt KIA 14.9.18.
HIRST James MM Pte 306561 2/8th C Coy West Yorkshire Regt KIA 27.11.17.
HIRST John Henry William MM Sjt 43537 16 Heavy Bty RGA KIA 11.9.18.
HIRST John William MM+Bar Bdr 64438 A/153 Bde RFA KIA 5.12.17.
HIRST Joseph MM Bdr 161152 315 Bde RFA
HIRST Nelson MM Pte 22162 King's Own Scottish Borderers
HIRST Thomas MM Sjt 17312 10th Yorkshire Regt
HIRST Thomas MM Pte 201804 1st Bn Tank Corps
HIRST Thomas MM L/Cpl 4/8001 West Yorkshire Regt
HIRST William MM.MID Sjt 240131 1/5th York & Lancaster Regt
HIRST William MM Sjt 21/383 West Yorkshire Regt
HIRST William MM Pte 11413 1st Liverpool Regt
HIRST William MM Pte 242520 1/6th West Yorkshire Regt
HIRST Willie R. MM Pte 267516 West Riding Regt
HISCOCK Charles H. MM Pte 29542 1st Grenadier Guards
HISCOCK George William "MM,MC(G)" L/Cpl 9151 7th Royal Berkshire Regt
HISCOCK Herbert J. MM Sjt 43476 31 Siege Bty RGA
HISCOCK Herbert Sidney MM Gnr 27430 122 Heavy Bty RGA
HISCOCK Wilfred Henry MM Sjt 44759 RFA
HISCOCKS Percy C. MM Cpl 530301 1/15th London Regt
HISCOKE Charles MM Sjt 9613 Royal Fusiliers
HISCOX Thomas MM Pte 23148 South Wales Borderers
HISCUTT Reginald Frank MM L/Sjt 10334 2nd Wiltshire Regt
HISKETT Frank MM Cpl 100412 33 Div Sig Coy Royal Engineers
HISLOP Adam MM+Bar Cpl 8920 2nd Cameron Highlanders
HISLOP Bertram T. MM Cpl 4561 6th Dragoon Guards
HISLOP James MM Sjt S/5176 1st Royal Highlanders
HISLOP John MM+Bar Cpl 43841 16th Royal Scots KIA 16.4.18.
HISLOP John W. MM Cpl 200848 5/6th Scottish Rifles
HISLOP Samuel MM Sjt 18228 Royal Inniskilling Fusiliers
HISLOP William MM Sjt S/40111 1st Cameron Highlanders

HISLOP William L. MM Pte 35040 RAMC
HISLOP William McCosh MM Cpl 365091 7th London Regt DOW 6.10.18.
HISSEY John "MM,MID" Pte 168 1st Royal West Kent Regt
HISTEAD Arthur "MM+Bar,MID" Cpl 10563 5th Royal Berkshire Regt
HISTED Cyril MM Sjt 568355 30 Div Sig Coy Royal Engineers
HISTED W.C. MM Pte 8498 6th East Kent Regt
HITCHCOCK Albert Victor Baker "MM,MID" Sjt 950297 235 Bde RFA
HITCHCOCK Harold J. MM Pte 41544 55 Fd Amb RAMC
HITCHCOCK Harris Henson "MM,MID" Sjt 590501 1/18th London Regt
HITCHCOCK Henry J. MM Cpl 89602 62nd Bn Machine Gun Corps
HITCHCOCK Nigel A. MM Cpl 38961 1st Duke of Cornwall's LI
HITCHCOCK R. MM L/Cpl 200286 Liverpool Regt
HITCHCOCK Ralph Wightwick MM Pte 2707 1/18th London Regt
HITCHCOCK William MM L/Cpl 11404 Leicestershire Regt
HITCHCOCK William Alfred MM L/Cpl 16713 9th Devonshire Regt KIA 25.10.18.
HITCHCOX Ernest J. MM Pte 59592 Royal Fusiliers
HITCHEN Alfred MM Pte 15987 9th Yorkshire Regt
HITCHEN Harry MM Pte 12845 10th Cheshire Regt
HITCHEN Thomas MM Cpl 65192 106 Fd Coy Royal Engineers
HITCHENS Henry T. MM Spr 518404 98 Fd Coy Royal Engineers
HITCHENS Joseph MM Pte 18391 5th South Wales Borderers
HITCHIN Charles H.B. MM Dvr 831 RFA
HITCHIN Harold Everett "DSO,MC,MM+Bar(19625 Sjt)" 2Lt 18th Durham Light Infantry
HITCHINS C.G. MM Pte 102189 Labour Corps
HITCHINS Henry G. MM L/Cpl R/3121 King's Royal Rifle Corps
HITCHINSON Percy MM Pte 266791 14th Liverpool Regt
HITCHINSON William MM Bdr 37782 B/77 Bde RFA DOW 5.4.18.
HITCHMAN Albert MM Cpl 3320 2/5th Gloucestershire Regt
HITCHMAN Arthur MM Sjt 240920 2/5th Gloucestershire Regt
HITCHMAN Fred MM Sjt 1038 1/7th West Riding Regt KIA 10.8.17.
HITCHMAN John MM L/Cpl 19018 9th Worcestershire Regt
HITCHMAN Robert MM Pte 10989 1/4th Oxf & Bucks Light Infantry
HITCHOCK Alfred MM Sjt 305158 2/7th West Riding Regt
HITCHON George MM Pte 119334 Machine Gun Corps
HITCHON Hubert MM Cpl 56790 RFA
HITCHON John MM L/Cpl 202606 Lancashire Fusiliers
HITTER O.D. MM Sjt 14598 10th Essex Regt
HIVEY George MM Gnr 636705 D/256 Bde RFA
HIX Joe G. MM Cpl 200164 1st Bn Tank Corps
HIX John MM Pte 7838 5th Dragoon Guards
HIXON Harry Herbert MM Cpl 200315 2/4th Hampshire Regt
HIXON Thomas C. MM L/Cpl 27757 Royal Fusiliers
HOAD Edward MM Pte 200365 1/4th Royal Sussex Regt
HOAD Frederick Thomas MM Spr 534248 491 Fd Coy Royal Engineers KIA 24.7.18.
HOAD Stanley MM Sjt 320034 16th Royal Sussex Regt
HOADLEY Victor Sidney MM Cpl 301251 1/5th London Regt
HOAR Albert B. MM Pte 20697 Cheshire Regt
HOAR Francis MM Cpl 30736 2nd Welsh Regt
HOAR Ralph R. MM+Bar Cpl 16957 1st Bedfordshire Regt
HOAR William MM Sjt M2/079807 Army Service Corps
HOAR William MM Pte 43341 1st Royal Irish Fusiliers
HOARD Clifford John Allen MM Pte 17952 5th Shropshire Light Infantry DOW 27.4.17.
HOARE Albert V. MM Pte 202524 1st London Regt
HOARE Arthur Charles MM Pte 25207 12th East Surrey Regt
HOARE Bernard MM Gnr 65223 8 Bde RFA
HOARE Charles MM Sjt 508589 470 Fd Coy Royal Engineers
HOARE Francis MM Pte 266540 14th Liverpool Regt
HOARE Frank J. MM L/Cpl 20986 Grenadier Guards
HOARE Frederick MM Pte 90092 RAMC
HOARE Frederick H.W. MM Cpl 265948 1/6th Welsh Regt
HOARE Frederick W. MM Gnr 36710 36 Bde RFA
HOARE George MM Pte 35512 18th Lancashire Fusiliers
HOARE George E. MM Pte 20153 South Staffordshire Regt
HOARE George F. MM Pte 26133 Liverpool Regt
HOARE George R. MM Dvr 33671 RFA
HOARE Henry G. "MM,MSM" Sjt 56208 15 Div Sig Coy Royal Engineers
HOARE Herbert S. MM Spr 1862 Royal Engineers
HOARE James MM Pte 8731 7th East Surrey Regt KIA 20.11.17.
HOARE Levi MM Pte 16670 Coldstream Guards
HOARE Percival H. MM Sjt 120045 284 Siege Bty RGA
HOARE Rodney George MM L/Cpl P12146 Military Mounted Police
HOARE Sidney MM L/Cpl 2969 12th Middlesex Regt
HOARE W.J. MM Pte 8293 2nd East Kent Regt
HOARE Walter O. MM Sjt 513493 14th London Regt
HOARE Wilfred B. MM Pte 457453 56 Fd Amb RAMC
HOATH Alfred MM+Bar Pte 21238 2nd Hampshire Regt
HOATH Clarence MM Pte 42850 11th Suffolk Regt
HOATSON William MM Sjt 18297 King's Own Scottish Borderers
HOBAN William Leo MM Pte 31164 1st Royal West Kent Regt
HOBART Percy J. MM Pte 11471 11th Hampshire Regt
HOBBS Albert MM Sjt 26217 RFA
HOBBS Albert Thomas MM Sjt 7053 2nd Wiltshire Regt
HOBBS Alex MM Cpl 76797 36 Bde RFA
HOBBS Alexander E. MM Cpl R/21498 1st King's Royal Rifle Corps
HOBBS Alfred E. MM L/Cpl 613537 19th London Regt
HOBBS Arnold William MM Cpl 1628 18th Royal Fusiliers KIA 9.4.17.
HOBBS Edward Alfred MM Bdr L/11771 156 Bde RFA
HOBBS Francis W. MM+Bar L/Cpl 241233 Notts & Derby Regt
HOBBS Francis W.J. MM Gnr 82756 RFA
HOBBS Frank MM Spr 75642 Royal Engineers
HOBBS George MM Bdr 25456 5 Siege Bty RGA
HOBBS George H. MM Spr 446107 'F' Corps Sig Coy Royal Engineers
HOBBS George W. "DCM,MM" Sjt 242501 1/5th Gloucestershire Regt
HOBBS George William MM Pte 16724 7th Oxf & Bucks Light Infantry Died 12.10.18.
HOBBS H. MM L/Cpl 17898 10th Essex Regt
HOBBS Harry J. MM Bdr 41019 40 Bde RFA
HOBBS Henry G. MM Pte G/4507 13th Royal Fusiliers
HOBBS John MM+2 Bars Pte G/2565 Middlesex Regt
HOBBS John H. "DCM,MM" Sjt 265954 1/1st Hertfordshire Regt
HOBBS Joseph Henry MM L/Cpl 134777 'Z' Special Coy Royal Engineers
HOBBS Moreton "DCM,MM" CSM 8258 2nd Devonshire Regt
HOBBS Percy William MM L/Cpl 115145 Machine Gun Corps
HOBBS Richard G. MM Pte 2868 8th Royal West Surrey Regt
HOBBS Richard W. MM Pte 22973 13th Royal Welsh Fusiliers Died 28.2.19.
HOBBS Samuel MM Gnr 54628 16 Heavy Bty RGA
HOBBS Sidney J. MM Cpl 334072 RGA
HOBBS Thomas Henry Charles MM L/Sjt 16565 8th Royal Fusiliers
HOBBS Walter Luigi MM Sjt 40474 Royal Engineers
HOBBS William MM Pte G/13045 1st East Kent Regt
HOBBS William N. MM+Bar Sjt 201785 Oxf & Bucks Light Infantry
HOBBS William P. MM L/Cpl 26463 Hampshire Regt
HOBBY Grenville Howard MM Cpl 2106 Monmouthshire Regt KIA 20.10.18.
HOBDAY Joseph MM Dvr 925844 A/280 Bde RFA
HOBDAY Leonard C.H. MM L/Bdr 625486 A/2 Bde HAC(Artillery)
HOBDAY William A. MM Sjt 64545 15 Bde RFA
HOBDAY William N. MM Pte 21835 RAMC
HOBDELL Frederick J. MM Dvr 128823 RHA
HOBDEN Arthur F. MM+Bar Cpl 8786 East Surrey Regt
HOBDEN Frederick C. MM Pte 723480 24th London Regt
HOBDEN George F. MM Pte 47269 Lancashire Fusiliers
HOBGEN Gravatt Bundell MM Bdr 943 5 Bty 281 Bde RFA KIA 20.9.16.
HOBIN David MM Pte 9233 1st South Staffordshire Regt
HOBIN Patrick MM Pte 300288 1/8th Durham Light Infantry
HOBKIRK Thomas S. MM Gnr 750078 RFA
HOBLEY Leonard T. MM CQMS 10741 1st Scottish Rifles
HOBSON Albert MM Bdr 25399 A/75 Bde RFA
HOBSON Arthur E. MM Pte 38562 Northumberland Fusiliers
HOBSON Arthur G. MM L/Cpl 9325 1st North Staffordshire Regt
HOBSON Bertie MM Sjt 1516 19th Durham Light Infantry
HOBSON Edwin MM Pte 3201 11th Manchester Regt
HOBSON Ernest MM L/Cpl 305228 West Riding Regt
HOBSON Ernest MM Pte 42049 9th Yorkshire Regt KIA 3.10.18.
HOBSON Ernest MM Pte 9136 1st York & Lancaster Regt
HOBSON Frank MM Pte 4/8680 1st West Yorkshire Regt
HOBSON George MM+Bar Sjt 265517 1/6th Cheshire Regt
HOBSON George Henry MM Pte 66010 190 Coy Machine Gun Corps
HOBSON George William "MM,MID" L/Sjt 386 Lincolnshire Regt
HOBSON Harold MM L/Cpl 15114 24th Manchester Regt
HOBSON Harold A. MM Cpl 203021 5th York & Lancaster Regt
HOBSON Harry MM L/Cpl 18189 11th Notts & Derby Regt
HOBSON Harry William MM Sjt 240236 1/5th Seaforth Highlanders KIA 14.3.18.
HOBSON Herbert MM Pte 32171 27 Fd Amb RAMC

HOBSON Hubert MM Sjt 200844 2/5th Royal Warwickshire Regt
HOBSON James MM Pte R/40903 4th King's Royal Rifle Corps
HOBSON James MM L/Cpl R/14290 13th King's Royal Rifle Corps
HOBSON John MM+Bar Pte 18819 Northumberland Fusiliers
HOBSON John A. MM Pte 203744 West Yorkshire Regt
HOBSON John Thomas MM Sjt 9250 17th Manchester Regt KIA 1.7.16.
HOBSON Samuel G. MM CQMS 1743 2nd Northumberland Fusiliers
HOBSON Thomas H. MM Pte 55621 RAMC
HOBSON Walter MM Sjt 61976 110 Siege Bty RGA
HOBSON Webster MM Pte 41590 West Yorkshire Regt
HOBSON William A. MM Dvr 46620 RFA
HOBSON William T. MM Cpl 50457 Royal Engineers
HOCKADAY Ralph G. MM Pte 266444 2/6th Devonshire Regt
HOCKENHULL Leonard "DCM,MM+Bar" Sjt 7943 1st Shropshire Light Infantry
HOCKEY Hubert Thomas MM Sjt 498083 Royal Engineers
HOCKHEIMER Reginald MM Pte 4567 RAMC
HOCKIN Frederick G. MM Pte 439488 RAMC
HOCKING Arthur MM Spr 223512 23 Fd Coy Royal Engineers
HOCKING Arthur W. MM Sjt 358030 RGA
HOCKING Charles MM Pte 25612 Royal Fusiliers
HOCKING Edwin C. MM Pte 235357 1st Notts & Derby Regt
HOCKING Frank J. MM Pte 4923 2/22nd London Regt
HOCKING George MM Cpl 45602 Devonshire Regt
HOCKING H. MM Sjt 356 RGA
HOCKING Harold "MM(15925,7th Dorset)+Bar" Pte 8439 Devonshire Regt
HOCKING Percy F. "DCM,MM" CSM 589076 1/17th London Regt
HOCKING Walter MM Pte 25388 14th Royal Warwickshire Regt
HOCKINGS George A. MM Pte 88393 Liverpool Regt
HOCKLEY Albert MM Sjt SE/3587 Army Veterinary Corps
HOCKLEY Charles MM L/Cpl 4373 6th Royal West Surrey Regt
HOCKLEY Charles E. MM Dvr T/29046 Army Service Corps att 9 Fd Amb RAMC
HOCKLEY Charles W. MM L/Cpl WR/20081 301 Rd Const Coy Royal Engineers
HOCKLEY Clement B. MM Bdr 49398 9 Bde RFA
HOCKLEY Daniel MM Pte 250905 1/5th Essex Regt
HOCKLEY George MM L/Cpl 3976 Royal West Surrey Regt
HOCKLEY Henry J. MM Pte 531585 15th London Regt
HOCKLEY Peter MM Gnr 17665 D/18 Bde RFA KIA 8.5.17.
HOCKLEY Samson MM L/Cpl 26108 1st South Wales Borderers KIA 1.9.18.
HOCKLEY Sidney H. MM Sjt 50559 'A' Cable Section Royal Engineers
HOCKNALL C.A. MM Pte 1573 Lincolnshire Regt
HOCKNEY Thomas B. MM L/Cpl S/3010 Rifle Brigade
HODDER Albert E. MM Sjt 89344 144 Army Tps Coy Royal Engineers
HODDER Albert James MM Sjt 121067 Royal Engineers
HODDER Alfred MM Pte 15568 Middlesex Regt
HODDER George MM Cpl 18643 D/87 Bde RFA
HODDINOTT Alfred V. MM L/Cpl 21531 7th Royal West Kent Regt
HODDINOTT Ralph MM Sjt 285223 1/1st Oxfordshire Yeomanry
HODDINOTT Thomas MM Pte 67389 15th Cheshire Regt
HODGE Albert MM Pte 39664 12th Royal Scots KIA 25.4.18.
HODGE Alexander MM Sjt 95087 9th Bn Tank Corps
HODGE Alexander MM Pte 29470 17 Fd Amb RAMC DOW 3.4.18.
HODGE Alfred W. MM Pte 66115 10th Royal Scots
HODGE Cecil J. MM Pte 7539 Scots Guards
HODGE Charles MM L/Sjt 240917 1/5th Devonshire Regt
HODGE George MM Sjt 13/815 East Yorkshire Regt
HODGE George Francis MM Sjt 3335 1st Royal West Surrey Regt KIA 13.4.18.
HODGE Harry MM Spr 83716 Royal Engineers
HODGE Harry J. MM Sjt 778018 1/28th London Regt
HODGE Herbert William MM Cpl 98162 HQ 11 Div RFA
HODGE Isaac W. MM Spr 498098 Royal Engineers
HODGE John MM Gnr 44770 RFA
HODGE John Arthur MM Spr 244933 19 Div Sig Coy Royal Engineers
HODGE John James MM Sjt 137635 179 Tunnelling Coy Royal Engineers
HODGE Robert MM+Bar Cpl 265676 Liverpool Regt
HODGE Robert MM Gnr 114313 RGA
HODGE Robert W. MM Sjt 9152 1st Dorsetshire Regt
HODGE William MM L/Sjt 14593 2nd Scots Guards
HODGE William MM Pte 24568 1st Royal Lancaster Regt
HODGE William A. MM Gnr 141976 RGA

HODGEN John MM Pte 47489 2nd Royal Irish Rifles
HODGERS Nicholas MM Bdr 49553 226 Siege Bty RGA DOW 3.1.18.
HODGERT William MM Pte 21337 22nd Manchester Regt
HODGES Alexander MM Pte R/14351 2nd King's Royal Rifle Corps
HODGES Alfred Ernest MM Cpl R/13226 9th King's Royal Rifle Corps DOW 22.10.17.
HODGES Archie MM Gnr 46492 RFA
HODGES Cecil F. MM Pte 45912 8th Royal Berkshire Regt
HODGES Charles MM L/Cpl 101430 Royal Engineers
HODGES Charles H. MM Pte 8998 1st Royal Warwickshire Regt
HODGES Charles Henry MM Sjt 21737 2nd Welsh Regt
HODGES Edward MM Pte 20/582 Durham Light Infantry
HODGES Edward Ernest "MM,CG(F)" Pte 40966 Essex Regt
HODGES Francis MM L/Sjt 18311 8th Worcestershire Regt
HODGES Fred MM Gnr 62860 RFA
HODGES Frederick A. MM S/Sjt 65863 RAMC
HODGES Frederick W. MM L/Cpl 204787 15th Hampshire Regt
HODGES G.A. "DCM,MM" RSM 8910 1st Essex Regt
HODGES George MM Sjt 225149 1/3rd Monmouthshire Regt
HODGES Harold MM L/Cpl 504529 503 Fd Coy Royal Engineers
HODGES Herbert "MM,MID" L/Cpl 25827 Gloucestershire Regt
HODGES Herbert Henry MM Pte 265194 2/7th Notts & Derby Regt DOW 11.4.18.
HODGES Hugh MM Pte 1823 9th Royal Irish Rifles DOW 23.11.18.
HODGES Hugh W. MM Sjt 302727 5th London Regt
HODGES James T. MM Cpl 203706 Gloucestershire Regt
HODGES John MM Cpl 18194 Machine Gun Corps
HODGES Percy H. MM Pte 76834 RAMC
HODGES Ralph MM Pte 44167 Welsh Regt
HODGES Samuel MM L/Cpl 267043 2/6th West Riding Regt
HODGES Thomas MM+Bar Sjt 21454 15th Highland Light Infantry
HODGES Thomas H. MM L/Sjt 6581 4th Middlesex Regt
HODGES W.G. MM AM1 8361 Royal Flying Corps
HODGES William MM Gnr L/19998 61 Bde RFA
HODGES William J. MM Sjt 7922 1st Royal Berkshire Regt
HODGES William J. MM Pte 8685 1st Somerset Light Infantry
HODGES William James MM Pte 14706 1st South Wales Borderers KIA 20.7.18.
HODGETT Daniel MM L/Cpl 28183 1st Liverpool Regt
HODGETTS Arthur E. MM+Bar Sjt 40644 8th Worcestershire Regt
HODGETTS Arthur T. MM Sjt 78161 RFA
HODGETTS Frederick MM L/Cpl 12338 6th Royal Berkshire Regt
HODGETTS Frederick S. MM Sjt 5227 RGA
HODGETTS Harry Owen MM Pte 16406 Coldstream Guards
HODGETTS James MM 2nd Cpl 278257 Royal Engineers
HODGETTS Thomas H. MM Pte R/8908 King's Royal Rifle Corps
HODGIN John MM Pnr 443928 42 Div Sig Coy Royal Engineers
HODGKIN Charles MM+Bar Sjt 864 Army Cyclist Corps
HODGKINS E. MM Sjt 65050 Royal Engineers
HODGKINS Frederick MM Cpl 7292 2nd Middlesex Regt KIA 20.11.17.
HODGKINS Thomas MM Cpl 281734 4th London Regt
HODGKINS Walter MM Pte 16909 Liverpool Regt
HODGKINS Walter C. MM Sjt 207286 3rd Worcestershire Regt
HODGKINS William G. MM Pte A1867 King's Royal Rifle Corps
HODGKINSON Albert MM Pte 6258 2nd Notts & Derby Regt KIA 19.9.18.
HODGKINSON Archibald MM Pte 10180 2nd Notts & Derby Regt
HODGKINSON E.W.G. MM Pte 161 1/5th London Regt
HODGKINSON Frank MM Pte 71108 61 Coy Machine Gun Corps
HODGKINSON George Edward August MM Gnr 153409 222 Siege Bty RGA
HODGKINSON George Herbert MM Gnr 53021 9 TM Bty RGA DOW 26.6.17.
HODGKINSON H. MM Spr 50100 2 Div Sig Coy Royal Engineers
HODGKINSON J.H. MM L/Cpl T4/109731 Army Service Corps
HODGKINSON James W. MM Pte 4988 2nd Lancashire Fusiliers
HODGKINSON John MM Pte 23382 11th Notts & Derby Regt KIA 5.10.18.
HODGKINSON Joseph MM Bdr 57600 RGA
HODGKINSON Peter MM L/Bdr 690402 RFA
HODGKINSON Reginald MM Cpl 1618 1/7th West Riding Regt
HODGKINSON Robert MM Spr 432352 Royal Engineers
HODGKINSON Thomas MM Pte 352760 5/6th Royal Scots
HODGKINSON Thomas MM Gnr 88459 RHA
HODGKINSON Timothy MM L/Cpl 5826 Lancashire Fusiliers
HODGKINSON William MM Sjt 28378 19th Bn Machine Gun Corps
HODGKINSON William MM S/Sjt Armourer T/1458 Army Ordnance Corps

HODGKINSON William MM Pte 70618 2nd Notts & Derby Regt KIA 23.3.18.
HODGKISS Bert MM Pte 33792 2nd Yorkshire Regt
HODGKISS Charles B. MM L/Cpl 22289 17th Lancashire Fusiliers
HODGKISS David E.E. MM 2nd Cpl 312362 Signal Service Royal Engineers
HODGKISS Joseph Arthur MM Cpl 35451 B/94 Bde RFA DOW 6.10.17.
HODGKISS Thomas MM Bdr 44119 RFA
HODGSON A. MM Sjt 1485 West Riding Regt
HODGSON A. MM Pte 53355 Cheshire Regt
HODGSON Albert MM Gnr 676710 RFA
HODGSON Albert J. MM Pte C/316 16th King's Royal Rifle Corps
HODGSON Alfred MM Sjt 201550 4th York & Lancaster Regt
HODGSON Alfred Ernest MM Pte 358351 1/10th Liverpool Regt
HODGSON Algernon Percy MM L/Cpl 30125 22nd Durham Light Infantry DOW 21.7.17.
HODGSON Allan MM L/Cpl 22374 2nd Grenadier Guards
HODGSON Arthur MM Pte 15911 2nd Scots Guards Died 22.11.18.
HODGSON Arthur MM 2nd Cpl 81494 Royal Engineers
HODGSON Benjamin MM Pte 21955 RAMC
HODGSON Clifford H. MM L/Cpl 6649 2/1st HAC(Infantry)
HODGSON Francis MM Pte 77444 133 Fd Amb RAMC
HODGSON Frederick MM Gnr L/7709 RFA
HODGSON Frederick P. MM Pte 18269 12th Liverpool Regt
HODGSON George MM Gnr Shoeing Smith 1954 RFA
HODGSON George MM Pte 27/1555 Northumberland Fusiliers
HODGSON George Herbert "MC,MM(1418 Pte),MID" 2Lt 1/6th West Yorkshire Regt
HODGSON Harold MM Dvr 925812 A/290 Bde RFA
HODGSON Henry H. MM Pte S/11019 Royal Highlanders
HODGSON Herbert MM Gnr 111139 RFA
HODGSON Herbert MM Pte 49352 10th West Yorkshire Regt
HODGSON Isaac MM Sjt 30215 Border Regt
HODGSON J.T. MM Cpl 9509 9th Scottish Rifles
HODGSON James MM Pte 7074 2nd Yorkshire Regt
HODGSON James T. MM Pte 10774 2nd Yorkshire Regt
HODGSON James W. MM Pte 93663 5th Notts & Derby Regt
HODGSON John MM Sjt 292532 705 Coy Labour Corps
HODGSON John MM Pte 156095 50th Bn Machine Gun Corps
HODGSON John MM Pte 11758 Machine Gun Corps
HODGSON John G. MM Pte 23968 RAMC
HODGSON John Henry MM Pte 21339 3rd Hussars KIA 30.4.18.
HODGSON John J. MM Cpl 44949 Royal Engineers
HODGSON John S. MM+Bar Cpl 18103 10th West Riding Regt
HODGSON John William MM Spr 79836 179 Tunnelling Cot Royal Engineers KIA 9.7.16.
HODGSON John William MM Sjt 14843 9th East Lancashire Regt
HODGSON Joseph MM Cpl 13989 7th North Lancashire Regt
HODGSON Joseph MM L/Sjt 1119 Durham Light Infantry
HODGSON Leslie MM Pte 201872 5th Yorkshire Regt DOW 11.4.18.
HODGSON Levi MM Spr 166868 478 Fd Coy Royal Engineers
HODGSON Lionel MM Pte 16491 9th Yorkshire Regt KIA 1.10.17.
HODGSON Martin MM Pte 49402 10th Cheshire Regt KIA 16.1.17.
HODGSON Percy MM L/Cpl 41865 16th Manchester Regt KIA 25.4.18.
HODGSON Robert W. MM Pte 306929 Lancashire Fusiliers
HODGSON Sam MM Pte 32515 8th North Staffordshire Regt DOW 6.10.17.
HODGSON Samuel MM Sjt 311951 Royal Engineers
HODGSON Samuel W. MM Pte M2/032329 Army Service Corps
HODGSON Thomas MM Pte 32388 6th Shropshire Light Infantry KIA 30.11.17.
HODGSON Thomas MM Sjt 2523 1/5th North Lancashire Regt
HODGSON Thomas MM Pte 2120 1/5th Royal Lancaster Regt
HODGSON Wilfred N. MM Pte 270160 9th West Yorkshire Regt
HODGSON William "MM,MID" Sjt 4068 1st Irish Guards
HODGSON William Edward MM Bdr 209 RGA
HODKIN Arthur MM Sjt 52468 13th Liverpool Regt
HODKINSON Alfred MM Pte 136296 1 Fd Amb RAMC
HODKINSON Arthur MM L/Cpl 266876 2/6th West Riding Regt
HODKINSON Arthur MM Sjt 4824 Lancashire Fusiliers
HODKINSON Arthur MM Pte 31051 South Lancashire Regt
HODKINSON Harold MM Sjt 15985 2nd Grenadier Guards
HODKINSON Richard MM Cpl 99745 Royal Engineers
HODKINSON Samuel MM L/Cpl 27005 7th Shropshire Light Infantry
HODSDON Henry W. MM Pte 474387 9th London Regt
HODSEN William E. MM Gnr Sig 141828 275 Siege Bty RGA
HODSON Charles MM Gnr 201279 Tank Corps

HODSON Charles H. MM Pte 3551 Royal West Surrey Regt
HODSON Frank MM Pte 39677 50th Bn Machine Gun Corps
HODSON Frank MM Pte 19044 7th Lincolnshire Regt
HODSON Frank MM Pte 72003 133 Fd Amb RAMC
HODSON Fred MM Cpl 14725 North Lancashire Regt
HODSON Fred MM Gnr 711671 C/178 Bde RFA
HODSON Geoffrey Henley "MM,MSM" Sjt 924 1/5th Royal Sussex Regt
HODSON George H. MM L/Cpl 3186 11th Manchester Regt
HODSON Gordon Victor MM Sjt 17154 54 Fd Coy Royal Engineers
HODSON Harry MM Pte 11351 Machine Gun Corps
HODSON Harry MM Cpl 96541 Royal Engineers
HODSON James MM L/Cpl 156354 Royal Engineers
HODSON Thomas MM Sjt 11412 7th Duke of Cornwall's LI KIA 22.3.18.
HODSON William MM Pte 133024 45th Royal Fusiliers
HODSON William MM Pte 27344 RAMC
HOEY Frederick H. MM Cpl 15845 Liverpool Regt
HOEY James MM Sjt 3875 2nd Leinster Regt
HOEY James MM L/Cpl 19593 Royal Dublin Fusiliers
HOEY Robert MM Pte 42247 1st Gordon Highlanders
HOEY Samuel MM Cpl 76218 Royal Engineers
HOFFMAN Frederick William MM Cpl 3/8686 9th Yorkshire Regt
HOFFMAN George A. MM Pte 26926 1st North Lancashire Regt
HOFFMAN Samuel MM Pte 42617 Royal Irish Rifles
HOFMAN William MM Cpl L/6517 1st Middlesex Regt KIA 27.2.18.
HOGAN Alfred MM Pte 17229 4th Bn Machine Gun Corps
HOGAN Dennis "DCM,MM" Sjt L/16879 20th Middlesex Regt
HOGAN Ernest J. MM Bdr 95346 B/63 Bde RFA
HOGAN Frank MM Cpl 26868 1st North Lancashire Regt
HOGAN George MM Cpl 341391 RAMC
HOGAN James MM L/Cpl 20514 'F' Cable Section Royal Engineers
HOGAN James MM L/Cpl 8210 2nd Royal Welsh Fusiliers
HOGAN John MM Sjt 16811 2nd Royal Dublin Fusiliers
HOGAN John J. MM Pte 28572 14th Royal Welsh Fusiliers
HOGAN Joseph MM Dvr 47683 29 Bde RFA
HOGAN Michael MM Pte 10299 12th King's Royal Rifle Corps DOW 3.5.17.
HOGAN Patrick MM Spr 157910 185 Tunnelling Coy Royal Engineers
HOGAN Peter MM Bdr 751297 250 Bde RFA DOW 26.10.17
HOGAN Robert MM Pte R/15950 King's Royal Rifle Corps
HOGAN Thomas MM Pte 4123 Leinster Regt
HOGAN William MM Pte 265354 1/7th Scottish Rifles
HOGAN William MM Bdr 41527 20 Siege Bty RGA
HOGAN William Thomas MM Dvr 830629 33 Bde RFA DOW 21.3.18.
HOGARTH Alexander MM Spr 46401 Royal Engineers
HOGARTH Anthony MM Pte 2922 1/6th Northumberland Fusiliers
HOGARTH John H. MM Pte 271091 1/1st Northumberland Yeo
HOGARTH Robert MM Sjt 19410 18th Liverpool Regt
HOGARTH W.R. MM Dvr 27697 RFA
HOGARTH William MM Pte 267201 Northumberland Fusiliers
HOGARTH William E. "MM,MID" Sjt 200204 1/4th Cheshire Regt
HOGBIN John H. MM Sjt 225866 10th Royal Fusiliers
HOGG Alan MM L/Cpl 552407 16th London Regt
HOGG Alfred MM Pte 79726 13th Royal Fusiliers
HOGG Arthur S. MM Sjt 8479 2nd King's Royal Rifle Corps
HOGG Charles M. MM Pte 41040 Gordon Highlanders
HOGG George MM Sjt 512 1st Gordon Highlanders
HOGG George Matthew MM L/Cpl 17274 11th Royal Inniskilling Fusiliers KIA 14.8.17.
HOGG Hector E. MM Sjt 34989 RAMC
HOGG Henry A. MM Pte M2/153345 Army Service Corps
HOGG Henry B. MM Sjt 6655 1st Royal Scots Fusiliers
HOGG Henry M. MM Cpl CMT/1364 Army Service Corps
HOGG I.S. MM Dvr 1567 RFA
HOGG James MM Pte 41046 17th Highland Light Infantry
HOGG James MM L/Sjt 12281 Royal Irish Fusiliers
HOGG James MM Pte 205069 2/4th Hampshire Regt KIA 6.11.18.
HOGG James MM Sjt 6794 1st King's Own Scottish Borderers KIA 2.10.16.
HOGG James MM+Bar Sjt S/10357 8th Royal Highlanders
HOGG James MM Pte 10563 2nd Scottish Rifles
HOGG John MM Dvr 412142 409 Fd Coy Royal Engineers
HOGG John MM+Bar Sjt 14551 1st Northumberland Fusiliers
HOGG John MM Cpl 24198 Royal Lancaster Regt
HOGG John "DCM,MM" Sjt S/9045 8th Seaforth Highlanders KIA 22.8.17.
HOGG John "MC,MM(7821 Sjt)" 2Lt 1st Cameron Highlanders

HOGG John E. MM Pte 1481 10th Highland Light Infantry
HOGG Patrick McH. MM Pte 145861 33rd Bn Machine Gun Corps
HOGG Ralph MM Pte 16929 2nd Royal Berkshire Regt
HOGG Richard MM Pte 241882 2/4th York & Lancaster Regt
HOGG Robert MM Pte 17296 2nd King's Own Scottish Borderers
HOGG Robert MM Spr 1317 Royal Engineers
HOGG Robert MM Pte 19803 16th Royal Scots KIA 14.4.18.
HOGG Robert MM Cpl 7334 RFA
HOGG Robert Telford MM Pte 13746 11th Border Regt KIA 2.12.17.
HOGG Samuel MM L/Cpl 15/9214 1st Royal Irish Rifles
HOGG Samuel A. MM Pte 55742 RAMC
HOGG Samuel F. MM L/Cpl 27105 Somerset Light Infantry
HOGG Thomas MM L/Cpl 315283 13th Royal Highlanders
HOGG Thomas MM L/Cpl 249166 Second Army Sig Coy Royal Engineers
HOGG Thomas "MM,MSM" Sjt 27800 62nd Bn Machine Gun Corps
HOGG Thomas MM Cpl 240384 1/5th King's Own Scottish Borderers
HOGG Thomas MM Cpl 43483 15th Royal Scots KIA 28.4.17.
HOGG Walter MM Pnr 259625 18 Div Sig Coy Royal Engineers
HOGG Walter R. MM Pte 16/343 17th Northumberland Fusiliers
HOGG William MM S/Sjt Saddler 15314 'W' Bty RHA
HOGG William "MM,MID" SCM 3026 1st Life Guards
HOGG William G. MM L/Bdr 608375 4 Bde RFA
HOGG William H. MM Sjt 19432 10/11th Highland Light Infantry Died 3.10.18.
HOGGARD Harry MM L/Cpl 23133 Machine Gun Corps
HOGGARD Ronald F. MM Pte 137380 29th Bn Machine Gun Corps
HOGGART H.G. MM Sjt 2944 Royal Air Force
HOGGE D.M. MM 2nd Cpl 602521 Royal Engineers
HOGGER Newton MM Pte M1/07708 Army Service Corps
HOGSFLESH William MM Pte 44120 Middlesex Regt
HOGWOOD Daniel MM Dvr 22712 156 Bde RFA
HOGWOOD Harry MM Drummer 1737 1/15th London Regt
HOHBACH Frank MM Pte 61710 Machine Gun Corps
HOILE Arthur James MM Pte 11055 Gordon Highlanders
HOITT Sidney MM Sjt 8616 2nd West Yorkshire Regt KIA 1.7.16.
HOLBECHE Edward MM Sjt 64947 RFA Died 6.11.18.
HOLBERRY Joseph MM+Bar Sjt 15269 8th Yorkshire Light Infantry
HOLBEVY George MM Pte 1948 1/8th Notts & Derby Regt
HOLBORN George "DCM,MM" Sjt 32160 15th Durham Light Infantry
HOLBORN Robert MM Cpl 325603 1/9th Durham Light Infantry
HOLBOROW Francis Reginald MM L/Cpl 300307 14th Arg & Suth Highlanders
HOLBOURN Frederick W. MM Pte 323801 6th London Regt
HOLBROOK Henry MM Pnr 254838 21 Div Sig Coy Royal Engineers
HOLBROOK Herbert MM Pte 832 1st Welsh Guards
HOLBROOK James MM L/Cpl 306367 2nd Bn Tank Corps
HOLBROOK Thomas MM Pte 16959 Yorkshire Regt
HOLBROW Thomas A. MM Sjt 56961 39 Bde RFA
HOLD Horace MM Gnr 63852 168 Siege Bty RGA
HOLDAWAY Ernest MM Sjt 10866 2nd Hampshire Regt
HOLDAWAY Leonard H. MM Cpl 19538 Hampshire Regt
HOLDCROFT Aaron MM Cpl 13627 8th South Staffordshire Regt
HOLDCROFT Hiram MM L/Cpl 29042 Royal Welsh Fusiliers
HOLDEN Alfred Watson MM Sjt 785390 RFA
HOLDEN Arthur MM Sjt 62750 287 Siege Bty RGA
HOLDEN Arthur H. MM Cpl 47596 RFA
HOLDEN Charles MM L/Cpl 34788 9th Royal Fusiliers KIA 14.8.18.
HOLDEN David MM Pte 9853 Machine Gun Corps
HOLDEN F. MM Pte 265184 Cheshire Regt att MGC.
HOLDEN Frank F. MM Pte 240836 1/5th Royal West Surrey Regt
HOLDEN Frederick MM Pte 5872 Rifle Brigade
HOLDEN G. MM Cpl 9541 2nd Essex Regt
HOLDEN George MM Bdr 56002 RFA
HOLDEN George Entwistle MM Sjt 28458 C/76 Bde RFA
HOLDEN H. MM L/Cpl 31209 1st Northamptonshire Regt
HOLDEN Harry MM Bdr 20774 111 Heavy Bty RGA
HOLDEN Harry MM+Bar Pte 350077 Manchester Regt
HOLDEN Henry E. MM Gnr 358238 RGA
HOLDEN J.E. MM Pte 352157 3(Northumbrian)Fd Amb RAMC
HOLDEN James MM Pte 20442 17th Lancashire Fusiliers
HOLDEN James MM Pte 10548 Coldstream Guards
HOLDEN James Arthur MM Pte S/30010 11th Rifle Brigade KIA 1.4.18.
HOLDEN James T. MM Sjt 24518 RFA
HOLDEN Jim MM Sjt 306271 West Riding Regt
HOLDEN John MM L/Cpl 14861 Lancashire Fusiliers

HOLDEN John Frederick MM CQMS 2341 8th Rifle Brigade KIA 15.9.16.
HOLDEN John W. MM Cpl 16178 18th Lancashire Fusiliers
HOLDEN Josiah MM L/Cpl 43693 Yorkshire Light Infantry
HOLDEN Lawrence MM Pte 202948 West Riding Regt
HOLDEN Lawrence MM Pte 42763 11th West Yorkshire Regt
HOLDEN Richard MM Pte 235155 Liverpool Regt
HOLDEN Richard MM L/Cpl 52912 Liverpool Regt
HOLDEN Samuel MM Cpl 243145 North Lancashire Regt
HOLDEN Thomas MM Pte 17344 3rd Coldstream Guards
HOLDEN Thomas MM Sjt 28804 Highland Light Infantry
HOLDEN Walsh H. MM Cpl 12326 7th East Lancashire Regt
HOLDEN Walter MM Pte 76127 135 Fd Amb RAMC
HOLDEN William MM Sjt 94743 Royal Engineers
HOLDEN William MM Pte 57403 44 Fd Amb RAMC
HOLDEN William MM Sjt 48850 87 Fd Coy Royal Engineers KIA 8.5.17.
HOLDEN William Henry MM Pte 18534 Royal Welsh Fusiliers
HOLDEN William Henry MM Pte 490212 1/13th London Regt
HOLDEN William Henry MM Pte 241030 2/5th East Lancashire Regt
Holden William Maurice "MC,MM(14788 Sjt 12th Liverpool Regt)" 2Lt Lanc Fus
HOLDER Arthur F. MM Cpl 201708 'R'(AA)Bty RGA
HOLDER Arthur H. MM Gnr 616309 RHA
HOLDER Bertie MM Pte 7953 2nd Royal Sussex Regt
HOLDER Charles George MM Pte 38551 2nd Royal Berkshire Regt KIA 11.6.18.
HOLDER Claud T. MM Pte 7101 1st Somerset Light Infantry
HOLDER Edward Ernest MM Bdr 122362 'J'(AA)Bty RGA
HOLDER Frederick MM Sjt 8487 1st Gloucestershire Regt
HOLDER Henry J. MM Sjt W/4699 D/122 Bde RFA
HOLDER William MM Sjt 30063 8th Somerset Light Infantry
HOLDER William R. MM Pte 203486 4th York & Lancaster Regt
HOLDERNESS Walter MM Pte 766567 21st Royal Fusiliers
HOLDFORTH Thomas B. MM Pte 240619 1/5th Royal West Surrey Regt
HOLDGATE Joe MM+Bar L/Cpl 10/15772 10th Cheshire Regt
HOLDHAM Albert George MM Pte M2/120388 33 Div Train Army Service Corps
HOLDING Thomas MM Pnr 198620 Railway Op Div Royal Engineers
HOLDING William J. MM L/Cpl 44176 21st Manchester Regt
HOLDMAN Frederick H. MM Sjt 8347 2nd Wiltshire Regt
HOLDOM George Alfred MM Pte 23449 4th Bedfordshire Regt
HOLDRIDGE Albert MM+Bar L/Cpl 36118 51 Fd Amb RAMC
HOLDROYD John Edward MM 2nd Cpl 104363 228 Fd Coy Royal Engineers
HOLDSWORTH Albert "MM,MID" Sjt 11843 Machine Gun Corps
HOLDSWORTH Douglas MM CSM G/10811 11th Royal West Surrey Regt
HOLDSWORTH Frank MM Pte 29366 8th West Yorkshire Regt
HOLDSWORTH Frederick Ernest MM L/Sjt 252298 1/5th West Riding Regt
HOLDSWORTH Harold E. MM Pte 56110 Northumberland Fusiliers
HOLDSWORTH Harry MM Sjt T4/250951 62 Div Train Army Service Corps
HOLDSWORTH Herbert MM Dvr 72634 14 Div Ammn Col RFA
HOLDSWORTH James A. MM Pte C/7551 King's Royal Rifle Corps
HOLDSWORTH James Harold MM Pte 75076 135 Fd Amb RAMC
HOLDSWORTH Walter MM Pte 39899 5th Leicestershire Regt
HOLDSWORTH Walter MM Sjt 10601 B/245 Bde RFA
HOLDSWORTH William MM Pte 269454 2/7th Liverpool Regt
HOLDSWORTH William Arthur MM+Bar Sjt 776852 B/251 Bde RFA KIA 13.11.17.
HOLDWAY Herbert J. MM Dvr 57494 RHA
HOLDWAY John A. MM Dvr 965044 RFA
HOLE E.J. MM Pte 722332 24th London Regt
HOLE Richard P. "MM,MSM" BQMS 19638 27 Siege Bty Royal Artillery
HOLE W.E. MM Sjt STK/433 10th Royal Fusiliers
HOLE William MM L/Cpl 13821 6th Northamptonshire Regt
HOLEY William MM Pte 14919 7th Dragoon Guards
HOLEYWELL Charles E. MM L/Sjt 26230 Notts & Derby Regt
HOLEYWELL Francis Cecil MM Sjt 19672 Machine Gun Corps
HOLFORD Frank MM Gnr Fitter 170637 121 Bty 27 Bde RFA
HOLFORD Frank MM L/Cpl 7454 Royal West Kent Regt
HOLFORD John Thomas MM Pte 54131 1/5th West Yorkshire Regt
HOLFORD Mornington MM+Bar Pte 28864 19th & 2nd Royal Welsh Fusiliers
HOLFORD Richard J. MM Pte 13634 10th Gloucestershire Regt

HOLGARTH G. MM Cpl 27248 5th Royal Lancaster Regt
HOLGATE Benjamin Rawson MM Gnr 77848 RGA
HOLGATE Charles Alfred MM Pte 24580 2nd Northamptonshire Regt KIA 27.5.18.
HOLGATE Frederick MM Sjt 14106 Middlesex Regt
HOLGATE Herbert MM Sjt Sig 870 1(West Riding)Bde RFA
HOLGATE Joseph W. MM Cpl 275684 Manchester Regt
HOLIDAY Charles MM Spr 14753 54 Fd Coy Royal Engineers
HOLIDAY Richard Alan MM Pnr 52772 12 Div Sig Coy Royal Engineers
HOLL Samuel H. MM Sjt 379 Military Mounted Police
HOLLAMBY Charles H. MM Sjt 47777 Royal Engineers
HOLLAND Abraham H. "DCM,MM" Sjt 785447 7 Bty 3 Bde RFA
HOLLAND Albert Edward MM Dvr 846205 61 Div Ammn Col RFA
HOLLAND Alfred MM Pte 9220 1st King's Royal Rifle Corps
HOLLAND Alfred "MM,CG(B)" L/Cpl 93974 41 Div Sig Coy Royal Engineers
HOLLAND Archibald MM Cpl 21945 Grenadier Guards
HOLLAND Arthur MM Cpl 241712 2/5th Royal Lancaster Regt KIA 28.9.18.
HOLLAND Arthur MM Pte 55024 2/4th Hampshire Regt KIA 30.9.18.
HOLLAND Arthur MM Pte 15306 Leinster Regt
HOLLAND Arthur J. MM Pte L/11670 4th Royal Fusiliers
HOLLAND Charles MM Pte 33193 1/4th Gloucestershire Regt
HOLLAND Charles William MM 2nd Cpl 46699 92 Fd Coy Royal Engineers
HOLLAND David "MM,MID" Spr 26514 Royal Engineers
HOLLAND Enoch MM L/Sjt 11872 16th Lancashire Fusiliers
HOLLAND Ernest MM Sjt 13865 24 Hy Bty RGA
HOLLAND Ernest MM Pte 302586 5th London Regt
HOLLAND Francis W. MM Cpl 58052 1/4th Cheshire Regt
HOLLAND Frank MM Pte 5736 17th Lancashire Fusiliers
HOLLAND Frank MM L/Cpl 301934 13th Bn Tank Corps
HOLLAND Frederick MM Pte 202125 2/4th Royal West Surrey Regt
HOLLAND Frederick A. MM Cpl 65821 RGA
HOLLAND George MM Pte 8983 2nd King's Royal Rifle Corps
HOLLAND George MM Sjt 265352 1/6th Cheshire Regt
HOLLAND George Alfred MM L/Cpl 7559 23rd London Regt
HOLLAND George Arthur MM Sjt 7584 10th Lincolnshire Regt DOW 25.11.16.
HOLLAND Gilbert MM Pte 033384 Army Ordnance Corps
HOLLAND Gordon M. MM Pte 50515 Royal Fusiliers
HOLLAND Harold E. MM+Bar Dvr 9988 D/70 Bde RFA KIA 2.9.18.
HOLLAND Harold Edward MM CQMS 8719 8th East Surrey Regt KIA 1.9.18.
HOLLAND Harrison MM Pte 8888 12th Lancashire Fusiliers
HOLLAND Harry MM Sjt 13766 RFA
HOLLAND Harry MM Spr 87774 Royal Engineers
HOLLAND Henry MM Pte 11566 7th East Yorkshire Regt
HOLLAND Herbert H. MM Sjt 51811 27 Bde RFA
HOLLAND Herbert Richard MM Gnr 69135 12 Bty 35 Bde RFA DOW 8.10.17.
HOLLAND Jack MM L/Cpl R/11938 2nd King's Royal Rifle Corps
HOLLAND James MM L/Sjt 307245 15th Lancashire Fusiliers
HOLLAND James MM L/Cpl 266768 Gordon Highlanders
HOLLAND James MM Sjt 13604 12th Cheshire Regt
HOLLAND Jesse MM Sjt 13071 6th Bedfordshire Regt
HOLLAND John MM Dvr 152547 C/83 Bde RFA
HOLLAND John MM Pte 358593 1/10th Liverpool Regt
HOLLAND John MM L/Cpl 23861 Royal Lancaster Regt
HOLLAND John MM Cpl 687304 RFA
HOLLAND John MM Pte 30491 Manchester Regt
HOLLAND John MM Pte 266592 1/1st Hertfordshire Regt DOW 1.6.18.
HOLLAND John F. MM Pte 2204 1/5th Cheshire Regt
HOLLAND John W. MM Dvr 3441 RFA
HOLLAND Jonathan MM Pte 6649 6th Lancashire Fusiliers
HOLLAND Joseph MM CSM 11915 16th Lancashire Fusiliers
HOLLAND Joseph G. MM Pte 2554 Army Cyclist Corps
HOLLAND Joseph R. MM Sjt 72633 D/153 Bde RFA
HOLLAND Leonard MM Cpl 352256 2/2(East Lancashire)Fd Amb RAMC
HOLLAND Percy S. MM Pte 6090 1/1st Hertfordshire Regt
HOLLAND Philip F. MM Pte 239545 1/1st Herefordshire Regt
HOLLAND Richard W. MM L/Cpl 247382 49 Div Sig Coy Royal Engineers
HOLLAND Robert MM CQMS 12583 10th Durham Light Infantry DOW 17.12.17.
HOLLAND Samuel MM Pte 265856 1/5th Cheshire Regt
HOLLAND Thomas MM Cpl 20306 15th Welsh Regt
HOLLAND Vernon MM Pte 308025 1st Liverpool Regt KIA 21.3.18.
HOLLAND Walter MM Cpl 3450 1/6th South Staffordshire Regt
HOLLAND William MM L/Cpl 241300 1/5th North Lancashire Regt KIA 30.11.17.
HOLLAND William D. MM Pte 43748 Suffolk Regt
HOLLAND William E. MM Pte 350669 Royal Scots
HOLLAND William Toft MM Pte 9869 18th Manchester Regt
HOLLANDS Arthur E. MM Pte 200869 1/4th Royal Sussex Regt
HOLLANDS Edward H. MM Sjt G/18445 10th Royal West Kent Regt
HOLLANDS Frederick MM+Bar Sjt 18441 10th Royal West Kent Regt
HOLLANDS Harold John MM Spr 46681 20 Div Sig Coy Royal Engineers
HOLLAS Tom Harry MM Dvr 154020 RFA
HOLLERAN Matthew MM L/Cpl 23443 6th Dorsetshire Regt
HOLLES Alfred Henry MM L/Cpl 502198 IWT Div Royal Engineers
HOLLEY Edward MM L/Sjt 7604 1st Somerset Light Infantry
HOLLEY Harry MM Pte 13111 7th Dragoon Guards
HOLLEY Herbert J. MM Sjt 22057 119 Heavy Bty RGA
HOLLEY John MM L/Cpl 17529 Machine Gun Corps
HOLLEY Raymond Alec MM Gnr 16364 B/73 Bde RFA
HOLLEY Stanley MM Sjt 67383 RFA
HOLLEY William MM Spr 556033 Royal Engineers
HOLLEYHEAD George MM Gnr 786570 RFA
HOLLICK Harry MM Gnr 314180 RGA
HOLLICK Louis H. MM Cpl 6559 8th Royal West Kent Regt
HOLLIDAY Albert J. MM Pte C/6393 2nd King's Royal Rifle Corps
HOLLIDAY C.H. MM Gnr 706898 B/232 Bde RFA
HOLLIDAY Charles MM Sjt 20737 Yorkshire Regt
HOLLIDAY Charles James MM L/Cpl 9245 2nd Royal Scots Fusiliers
HOLLIDAY George MM Gnr 3896 55 Bty 33 Bde RFA DOW 24.6.17.
HOLLIDAY George MM L/Cpl M2/103350 Army Service Corps
HOLLIDAY George W. MM L/Cpl 301773 5/6th Royal Scots
HOLLIDAY Harry M. MM Sjt 28488 Royal Welsh Fusiliers
HOLLIDAY Herbert MM Sjt 22797 51st Bn Machine Gun Corps
HOLLIDAY John A. MM Sjt 382378 RGA
HOLLIDAY Oscar A. MM Pte STK/121 Royal Fusiliers
HOLLIDAY R. MM Pte 201935 West Yorkshire Regt
HOLLIDAY Reginald MM Sjt 11629 Grenadier Guards
HOLLIDAY Walter MM Pte 30749 12th Gloucestershire Regt
HOLLIDAY William MM Sjt 282253 127 Siege Bty RGA
HOLLIDAY William Charles MM CSM 8632 1st Royal West Surrey Regt
HOLLIDAY William J. MM Pte M2/182196 Army Service Corps
HOLLIDGE Joseph S. MM Pte 320351 12th Norfolk Regt
HOLLIER Frank J. MM L/Cpl 5800 22 Fd Amb RAMC
HOLLIER Gilbert MM L/Cpl M/339982 Army Service Corps
HOLLIN W. MM Pte 9015 Royal Fusiliers
HOLLINDRAKE A. MM Pte 51631 6th Lancashire Fusiliers
HOLLINGDALE Albert E. "DCM,MM" Cpl 87188 D/59 Bde RFA
HOLLINGS Arthur MM Pte 36181 1st Welsh Regt
HOLLINGS Frederick MM Cpl 241152 8th West Yorkshire Regt
HOLLINGS George MM Pte 10047 2nd West Yorkshire Regt
HOLLINGS George MM Sjt 230732 2nd London Regt
HOLLINGS Isaac MM Pte 60 RAMC
HOLLINGSHEAD Ernest John MM Bdr 31214 C/177 Bde RFA
HOLLINGSWORTH Albert MM+Bar L/Cpl 20101 2nd & 6th Yorkshire Light Infantry DOW 13.9.18.
HOLLINGSWORTH Alfred C. MM BSM 52253 23 Bde RFA
HOLLINGSWORTH Henry A. MM L/Cpl 6208 4th Dragoon Guards
HOLLINGSWORTH James T. MM Sjt 3802 Machine Gun Corps
HOLLINGSWORTH Richard E. MM Cpl 240263 1/5th Leicestershire Regt
HOLLINGSWORTH Vivian "DCM,MM" Sjt 6/1024 King's Royal Rifle Corps
HOLLINGTON Charles MM Sjt 23245 32nd Bn Machine Gun Corps
HOLLINGTON Thomas W. MM L/Cpl 1633 1/17th London Regt
HOLLINGWORTH Arthur MM Gnr 62410 RFA
HOLLINGWORTH David MM Pte 142093 25th Bn Machine Gun Corps
HOLLINGWORTH Frank MM Pte 4360 8th London Regt
HOLLINGWORTH Harold MM L/Cpl 305187 1/5th West Riding Regt
HOLLINGWORTH James MM Pte 67107 RAMC
HOLLINGWORTH James MM Sjt 351254 2/9th Manchester Regt
HOLLINGWORTH Thomas A. MM Cpl 102637 1st Notts & Derby Regt
HOLLINRAKE George MM Pte 15571 8th Royal Lancaster Regt
HOLLINS Frank MM L/Cpl 14966 9th North Staffordshire Regt
HOLLINS G. MM Spr 446975 Royal Engineers

HOLLINSHEAD Frank MM Pte 240358 1/6th Notts & Derby Regt
HOLLINSHEAD John MM L/Cpl 2846 12th Royal Fusiliers
HOLLINSHEAD William MM Sjt 104475 228 Fd Coy Royal Engineers
HOLLIS Albert E. MM Cpl 142719 Royal Engineers
HOLLIS Frank H. MM Bdr 20078 RFA
HOLLIS Harold MM Pte 18926 Shropshire Light Infantry
HOLLIS Hugh MM Sjt 25036 Highland Light Infantry
HOLLIS John MM Sjt 57030 24th Royal Welsh Fusiliers
HOLLIS John MM Cpl M2/100641 Army Service Corps att 5 Australian Div Supply Column
HOLLIS John MM Pte 27350 Notts & Derby Regt
HOLLIS John W. MM Pte 276272 1st Essex Regt
HOLLIS Richard MM Cpl 22066 Machine Gun Corps
HOLLIS Robert S. MM Cpl 14011 Leicestershire Regt
HOLLIS Samuel MM Bdr 71363 RFA
HOLLIS Vigand MM Pte 15242 Leicestershire Regt
HOLLIS William MM+Bar Sjt 37635 2/4th Hampshire Regt
HOLLIS William MM Dvr 179857 19 Div Ammn Col RFA
HOLLIS William B. MM Pte 306170 Notts & Derby Regt
HOLLIS William H. MM Pte 44674 South Wales Borderers
HOLLISEY Stephen G. MM L/Cpl 2382 XIV Corps Cyclist Bn Army Cyclist Corps
HOLLISTER Henry MM Gnr 49206 18 Bde RFA
HOLLOBON Ernest F. "MM,MID" Sjt 25327 8 Siege Bty RGA
HOLLOBONE Frederick R. MM Pte 25820 4th Grenadier Guards
HOLLOBONE John MM Gnr 39148 RGA
HOLLOCKS Charles S. MM Pte 555390 16th London Regt
HOLLOM Albert MM Pte 82723 2nd London Regt
HOLLOWAY Albert H. MM Gnr 36280 RFA
HOLLOWAY Alec MM+Bar Sjt 12456 7th Wiltshire Regt
HOLLOWAY Alfred MM Pte 260322 Gloucestershire Regt
HOLLOWAY Arthur Frederick MM Pte 2/9240 2nd South Wales Borderers KIA 6.10.17.
HOLLOWAY Arthur J. MM Spr 86301 Royal Engineers
HOLLOWAY Frank MM Pte 17054 King's Royal Rifle Corps
HOLLOWAY Frank MM Sjt 240301 Royal Warwickshire Regt
HOLLOWAY Frederick MM Gnr 95449 A/64 Bde RFA
HOLLOWAY G.R. MM+Bar Sjt 8120 1st East Kent Regt
HOLLOWAY George A. MM Sjt 14934 7th Bedfordshire Regt
HOLLOWAY George Richard MM Dvr 120161 25 Div Ammn Col RFA
HOLLOWAY George William MM Dvr 429 48 Div Ammn Col RFA
HOLLOWAY Harry W. MM Cpl 52823 RFA
HOLLOWAY Henry A. MM Pte 7103 1st London Regt
HOLLOWAY Henry Francis "MC,MM(8984 Sjt 2nd Bn)" Capt 7th East Lancashire Regt KIA 11.4.18.
HOLLOWAY Henry J. MM CQMS 101 1/22nd London Regt
HOLLOWAY Jesse MM Pte 19080 Oxf & Bucks Light Infantry
HOLLOWAY John MM Pte 17113 Worcestershire Regt
HOLLOWAY John MM Gnr 96607 RFA
HOLLOWAY John W. MM Bdr 37094 41 Siege Bty RGA
HOLLOWAY Louis MM RSM 8113 2nd Wiltshire Regt
HOLLOWAY Percy George MM Cpl 200459 8th Royal Berkshire Regt DOW 7.9.18.
HOLLOWAY Reuben MM Pte 650074 1/21st London Regt
HOLLOWAY Robert Henry MM Pte 16439 14th Royal Warwickshire Regt
HOLLOWAY Samuel MM CSM 17435 1/6th South Staffordshire Regt KIA 3.10.18.
HOLLOWAY Seth "MM,CG(B)" Spr 106647 40 Div Sig Coy Royal Engineers
HOLLOWAY Stanley "DCM,MM" Sjt 1285 1/1st London Regt
HOLLOWAY Thomas Henry MM Spr 87401 39 Div Sig Coy Royal Engineers
HOLLOWAY Tom "DCM,MM" Sjt 200052 1/4th Royal Berkshire Regt
HOLLOWAY Walter C. MM Pte 4712 3 Fd Amb RAMC
HOLLOWAY William MM L/Sjt 3285 2nd Northumberland Fusiliers
HOLLOWAY William Alfred Howard MM Pte 81011 7th Dragoon Guards KIA 8.8.18.
HOLLOWFIELD Lewis MM Pte 13972 8th Shropshire Light Infantry
HOLLOWS Richard "MM+Bar,MM(F)" Sjt 18619 6th East Yorkshire Regt
HOLLWAY Jack E. MM Pte 129157 45th Royal Fusiliers
HOLLWEY William H. MM 2nd Cpl 494710 479 Fd Coy Royal Engineers
HOLLY William Herbert MM L/Cpl 19744 6th Dorsetshire Regt DOW 13.9.18.
HOLLYER C.W. MM Pte 30827 6th Royal Inniskilling Fusiliers
HOLLYER H.B. MM Sjt 41896 RAMC
HOLLYER Henry William Dennis MM Pte 3706 23rd Royal Fusiliers
HOLLYER Reginal J.G. MM Sjt M/31470 Army Service Corps
HOLLYHEAD George MM Pte 13018 10th Royal Warwickshire Regt KIA 21.5.17.
HOLLYHEAD J.J. MM Air Mech 2 45311 Royal Flying Corps
HOLLYHEAD James MM Pte 9289 2nd South Staffordshire Regt
HOLLYOAK Walter MM Cpl 2161 2/6th Royal Warwickshire Regt
HOLLYOAKE Albert Ernest MM L/Sjt 21015 2nd Oxf & Bucks Light Infantry
HOLLYOAKE Arthur G. MM Cpl 265119 1/1st Buckinghamshire Bn Oxf & Bucks Light Infantry
HOLLYWOOD Harold MM Pte 23435 11th Lancashire Fusiliers
HOLMAN Burton MM Pte DM2/166067 Army Service Corps att RE.
HOLMAN Charles Victor MM Pte 41946 1st Essex Regt
HOLMAN Ernest MM L/Sjt G/3115 6th East Kent Regt
HOLMAN Ernest Wilfred MM Sjt G/206 6th East Kent Regt KIA 7.10.16
HOLMAN Frederick MM 2nd Cpl 621 2/3(London)Fd Coy Royal Engineers
HOLMAN Henry MM Pte 280254 1/7th Lancashire Fusiliers
HOLMAN J.F. MM Pte 34130 Machine Gun Corps
HOLMAN Reginald Palmer "MM,CG(F)" Cpl 320176 12th Norfolk Regt
HOLMAN Richard MM L/Cpl 545 7th Royal Sussex Regt
HOLMAN Robert R. MM Cpl 56713 1 Div Ammn Col RFA
HOLMAN Sidney L. MM L/Cpl 24305 Royal West Surrey Regt
HOLMAN William J. MM Cpl 42145 RGA
HOLME Alfred MM Pte 11039 1st Grenadier Guards
HOLME Arnold MM Pte 540469 15th London Regt
HOLME George Henry "MM,MSM" Sjt 130 1st Welsh Guards
HOLMES Albert MM Pte 10249 1st Royal Inniskilling Fusiliers
HOLMES Albert Edward MM Cpl 12608 2nd Devonshire Regt KIA 27.3.17.
HOLMES Albert Stuart MM Sjt 11844 19th Manchester Regt
HOLMES Albert T. MM Cpl 64726 25 Bde RFA
HOLMES Alfred E. MM Pte 41 RAMC
HOLMES Alfred G. MM Sjt 202167 Royal Lancaster Regt
HOLMES Archie MM L/Cpl 19788 Machine Gun Corps
HOLMES Arnold MM Cpl 240503 1/5th Leicestershire Regt
HOLMES Arthur MM Gnr 45357 RFA
HOLMES Arthur "MM,CG(B)" 2nd Cpl 83901 211 Fd Coy Royal Engineers
HOLMES Arthur MM Pte 290885 1/4th Gordon Highlanders
HOLMES Arthur F. MM Spr 84558 Royal Engineers
HOLMES Arthur T. MM Pte 17475 8th Gloucestershire Regt
HOLMES Charles MM Pte 75995 135 Fd Amb RAMC
HOLMES Charles MM Pte 201133 1/8th Manchester Regt KIA 30.8.18.
HOLMES Charles MM L/Cpl 14686 17th Lancashire Fusiliers
HOLMES Charles MM Bdr 8987 RFA
HOLMES Charles MM Dmr 240592 South Staffordshire Regt
HOLMES Charles F. MM Dvr 50112 119 Bty 27 Bde RFA
HOLMES Christopher H. MM Pte 91404 9th Durham Light Infantry
HOLMES Christopher J. MM Pte 17722 Shropshire Light Infantry
HOLMES Clarence W. MM Pte 41497 18th Highland Light Infantry
HOLMES David T. "MM,MIDx2" Cpl 4823 15th Hussars
HOLMES Dennis "MM,MID" L/Cpl 17781 4th Worcestershire Regt
HOLMES Edgar Elijah MM L/Cpl 8466 12th Suffolk Regt DOW 26.9.17.
HOLMES Edward MM Pnr 528144 Royal Engineers
HOLMES Edward MM Pte 200938 1/5th Bedfordshire Regt KIA 2.11.17.
HOLMES Edward or Frederick MM Sjt 6087 5th Royal Berkshire Regt
HOLMES Ernest L. MM Pte 32225 RAMC KIA 17.4.18.
HOLMES Ernest Orde MM Pte 442 16th Middlesex Regt
HOLMES F. MM Bdr 776162 D/245 Bde RFA
HOLMES Francis Sloman MM Gnr 18292 71 Bde RFA
HOLMES Frank MM L/Cpl M/26972 1 Cav Div Supply Col Army Service Corps
HOLMES Frank H.W. MM Spr 482343 62 Div Sig Coy Royal Engineers
HOLMES Fred MM Sjt 267261 2/4th West Riding Regt
HOLMES Frederick MM Pte 20501 4th Coldstream Guards
HOLMES Frederick W. MM Pte 10668 2nd Grenadier Guards
HOLMES Frederick W. MM Cpl 135525 RFA
HOLMES G.F. MM Sjt 83764 257 Tunnelling Coy Royal Engineers
HOLMES George MM Pte 55217 18th Scottish Rifles
HOLMES George MM Sjt M2/116365 Army Service Corps
HOLMES George MM Pte 238058 1st Leicestershire Regt

HOLMES George MM CSM 200467 1/4th Royal Lancaster Regt
HOLMES George MM L/Cpl 27813 8th Royal Lancaster Regt KIA 23.3.18.
HOLMES George MM Cpl 884 1/1st South Notts Hussars Yeo
HOLMES George MM Pte 37946 Machine Gun Corps
HOLMES George A. MM Dvr 65495 4 Div Ammn Col RFA
HOLMES George Edward MM Spr 463144 50 Div Sig Coy Royal Engineers
HOLMES Harold MM Cpl 18975 Notts & Derby Regt
HOLMES Harold Ernest MM Spr 69070 35 Div Sig Coy Royal Engineers
HOLMES Harold H. MM Pte 41012 2/7th Royal Warwickshire Regt
HOLMES Harry MM Pte 55971 Welsh Regt
HOLMES Harry MM Pte 423019 10th London Regt
HOLMES Harry MM Cpl 5985 1st Royal Welsh Fusiliers
HOLMES Harry MM Spr 121669 Royal Engineers
HOLMES Harry MM Sjt 12269 10th West Riding Regt
HOLMES Hedley MM Sjt 15779 9th North Lancashire Regt
HOLMES Henry MM Sjt 680270 RFA
HOLMES Herbert MM Pte 12291 8th Yorkshire Light Infantry
HOLMES Herbert MM Gnr 19980 D/95 Bde RFA
HOLMES James MM Pte 205542 10th West Yorkshire Regt
HOLMES James MM Spr 254929 34 Div Sig Coy Royal Engineers
HOLMES James MM Cpl 20193 15th Durham Light Infantry
HOLMES James MM Cpl 57460 122 Fd Coy Royal Engineers
HOLMES James G. MM L/Sjt 2204 12th Middlesex Regt
HOLMES Jeremiah MM Cpl 12959 6th Royal Berkshire Regt
HOLMES John MM L/Cpl 9252 2nd North Lancashire Regt
HOLMES John MM L/Bdr 4779 C/34 Bde RFA
HOLMES John MM L/Cpl 140594 Royal Engineers
HOLMES John E. MM Pte 306948 Lancashire Fusiliers
HOLMES John G. MM Pte 41173 RAMC
HOLMES John H. MM Sjt 111750 Labour Corps
HOLMES John J. MM Cpl 631401 RFA
HOLMES John James MM Gnr 90937 D/82 Bde RFA
HOLMES John T. MM Sjt 36152 RAMC
HOLMES John Thomas MM Gnr 21342 C/113 Bde RFA
HOLMES John W. MM Pte 266752 1/6th Seaforth Highlanders KIA 23.9.17.
HOLMES John W. MM Spr 47733 92 Fd Coy Royal Engineers
HOLMES John William MM L/Cpl 10926 2/4th West Riding Regt KIA 20.7.18.
HOLMES Joseph MM Spr 142829 Royal Engineers
HOLMES Joseph MM L/Cpl 240391 Notts & Derby Regt
HOLMES Joseph MM Pte 17328 10th West Riding Regt
HOLMES Joseph John MM L/Cpl 183258 133 Army Troops Coy Royal Engineers
HOLMES L.J. "MM,MID" Dvr 139 Army Service Corps
HOLMES Leslie H. MM Pte 52978 4th Middlesex Regt
HOLMES Noel MM L/Cpl 266587 11th Somerset Light Infantry
HOLMES Norman MM L/Cpl 16246 6th Dragoons
HOLMES Osborne James MM Dvr 26582 D/59 Bde RFA
HOLMES Percy MM Pte 117247 5th Notts & Derby Regt
HOLMES Percy MM Cpl 17311 8th Royal Berkshire Regt
HOLMES Percy Stewart MM Pte 20712 9th Notts & Derby Regt
HOLMES Robert MM L/Sjt 20640 Durham Light Infantry
HOLMES Robert Ferguson MM Cpl 64795 86 Bty 32 Bde RFA DOW 8.10.17.
HOLMES Sam "MM,MID" Pte 8164 2nd West Yorkshire Regt
HOLMES Samuel MM Pte 3/9265 2nd Yorkshire Regt
HOLMES Stanley G. MM Pte M2/078930 Army Service Corps
HOLMES Sylvester MM Pte 16783 6th Royal Inniskilling Fusiliers
HOLMES Thomas MM Spr 82068 172 Tunnelling Coy Royal Engineers
HOLMES Thomas MM Sjt 22989 11 Fd Coy Royal Engineers
HOLMES Thomas MM Gnr 2268 X/36 Med TM Bty RFA KIA 26.9.18.
HOLMES Thomas MM Pte 53030 Royal Fusiliers
HOLMES Tom MM Gnr 165223 RFA
HOLMES W.J. MM Sjt 8088 York & Lancaster Regt
HOLMES W.N. MM Sjt 66635 Royal Flying Corps
HOLMES Walter MM+Bar Bdr 675441 RFA
HOLMES Walter MM Sjt 875287 D/95 Bde RFA
HOLMES Wilfred "DCM,MM,CG(B)" Cpl 27568 89 Fd Amb RAMC
HOLMES William MM Pte 205018 7th Seaforth Highlanders
HOLMES William MM Sjt 5433 2nd Royal Dublin Fusiliers
HOLMES William MM Cpl 254133 RFA
HOLMES William MM Sjt 2444 RGA
HOLMES William E. "DCM,MM,MID" Sjt 8232 1st Shropshire Light Infantry
HOLMES William E. MM Pte 4470 Machine Gun Corps
HOLMES William H. MM Cpl 98236 Machine Gun Corps
HOLMES William Henry MM Sjt 47620 282 Bde RFA
HOLMES William James A. MM Sjt 19053 Machine Gun Corps
HOLNESS Albert Thomas MM L/Sjt G8399 10th Royal West Kent Regt KIA 9.8.17.
HOLNESS Edmund MM Pte 1631 5(London)Fd Amb RAMC
HOLNESS Ernest MM+Bar Cpl 76476 4th Royal Fusiliers KIA 27.9.18.
HOLNESS Herbert MM+Bar Sjt 63881 D/95 Bde RFA KIA 25.10.17.
HOLNESS Walter W. MM Cpl 41689 RGA
HOLOHAN Michael MM Pte 5744 1st Leinster Regt
HOLROYD Albert MM Pte 5663 12th Manchester Regt
HOLROYD Andrew "MM,MID" Sjt 305362 West Riding Regt
HOLROYD George MM Sjt 62107 162 Siege Bty RGA
HOLROYD George MM Sjt 2346 Notts & Derby Regt
HOLROYD George Willie MM Pte 240855 5th West Riding Regt
HOLROYD William MM Gnr 680415 RFA
HOLROYDE Ben MM Pte 23901 5th West Riding Regt
HOLT Albert MM+Bar Sjt 202647 4th North Lancashire Regt
HOLT Albert MM Pte 36576 6th East Lancashire Regt
HOLT Arthur "DCM,MM" Cpl 20539 9th Devonshire Regt
HOLT B. MM Dvr 710164 37 Bty 27 Bde RFA
HOLT Carl Harold Manwell MM Pte 43250 11 Fd Amb RAMC DOW 16.5.18.
HOLT Edward J. MM Cpl 334378 RGA
HOLT Edwin MM L/Cpl 515157 14th London Regt
HOLT Frank MM Pte 1805 1/15th London Regt
HOLT George MM Pte 201007 5th Bn Tank Corps
HOLT George MM Pte 9764 1/4th Gordon Highlanders
HOLT George MM Pte 15437 9th Notts & Derby Regt
HOLT George H. MM L/Cpl 2108 1/4th West Riding Regt
HOLT George Thomas MM Sjt 241608 2/5th North Lancashire Regt
HOLT George W. MM Pte 281056 Lancashire Fusiliers
HOLT Harold Ainsworth "DCM,MM" Cpl 1683 6 Fd Amb RAMC DOW 13.3.17.
HOLT Herbert MM Pte 265532 2/7th Royal Warwickshire Regt DOW 8.12.17.
HOLT James MM Pte 64870 9th Yorkshire Light Infantry
HOLT James Clifford MM Pte T4/245898 66 Div Train Army Service Corps
HOLT James E. MM Pte 203387 Lancashire Fusiliers
HOLT James W. MM+Bar Pte 13696 6th Lincolnshire Regt
HOLT Jesse MM 2nd Cpl 61516 70 Fd Coy Royal Engineers
HOLT John MM Pte 202405 Lancashire Fusiliers
HOLT John Edward MM Pte 50841 10th Cheshire Regt
HOLT John L. MM Pte 45948 Durham Light Infantry
HOLT Joseph MM Cpl 235816 2nd East Lancashire Regt
HOLT Joseph MM Gnr 840651 D/306 Bde RFA
HOLT Joseph H. MM Pte 19943 Lancashire Fusiliers
HOLT Joseph Samuel MM 2nd Cpl 45773 97 Fd Coy Royal Engineers KIA 29.5.18.
HOLT L.E. MM L/Cpl P/6293 Military Mounted Police
HOLT Ralph MM Pte 25506 22nd Manchester Regt
HOLT Richard MM+Bar Sjt 67052 96 Fd Amb RAMC
HOLT Richard MM L/Cpl 1705 16th Royal Warwickshire Regt
HOLT Robert MM Gnr Sig 127218 109 Siege Bty RGA
HOLT Stephen MM Pte 13297 2nd Yorkshire Regt
HOLT W. MM Gnr W/2578 RFA
HOLT Walter James MM Cpl 127949 301 Siege Bty RGA
HOLT Wilfred MM Pte 200900 Lancashire Fusiliers
HOLT Wilfred MM Cpl 14656 Machine Gun Corps
HOLT William MM Pte 202427 Royal Warwickshire Regt
HOLT William MM Cpl 11414 1st Worcestershire Regt
HOLTHAM Percival H. MM L/Cpl 39858 Royal West Surrey Regt
HOLTHAM Richard MM L/Bdr 755773 D/251 Bde RFA
HOLTHAM William G. MM Spr 504243 Royal Engineers
HOLTON A.E. MM L/Cpl 20381 10th Essex Regt
HOLTON Albert MM L/Cpl 7525 7th Bedfordshire Regt
HOLTON Clarence L.H. MM L/Sjt 200105 1/7th Middlesex Regt
HOLTON Edgar John MM L/Cpl A/2797 2nd King's Royal Rifle Corps KIA 17.10.18.
HOLTON Henry MM Pte 35822 10 Fd Amb RAMC
HOLTON James "DCM,MM+Bar" Sjt 16814 7/8th Royal Irish Fusiliers DOW 26.8.17.
HOLTORP Paul S.V. MM Sjt 305442 5th London Regt
HOLWAY Stanley C. MM Gnr 959 RFA
HOLWAY William MM CQMS 8393 Royal West Kent Regt
HOLWEY W. MM L/Cpl 32749 16th Yorkshire Light Infantry
HOLWILL William H. MM Bdr 38622 RGA

HOLYOAK Charles H. MM Gnr Sig 841082 D/290 Bde RFA
HOLYOAKE George C. MM Cpl 85522 Royal Engineers
HOLYOAKE Noah MM L/Cpl 18242 Durham Light Infantry
HOLYOAKE Walter Herbert MM Pte 200610 8th Cheshire Regt
HOLYOAKE William MM Pte 7403 6th Leicestershire Regt DOW 9.10.18.
HOMAN George Harold MM Sjt 2012 1/4th Royal Berkshire Regt
HOMAN James MM Pte 200641 2/1st London Regt
HOMANS Arthur MM Pte 36178 North Lancashire Regt
HOMBURG William J. MM Gnr 950616 RFA
HOME Alexander MM Sjt 9448 10th Arg & Suth Highlanders
HOME J.G. MM Cpl 1835 Northumberland Fusiliers
HOME John "DCM,MM+Bar" CSM 5655 1st Dorsetshire Regt
HOME Samuel B. MM Gnr 168606 495 Siege Bty RGA
HOMER Edward L. "DCM,MM" CSM 11525 8th Yorkshire Regt
HOMER Fred MM Sjt 15731 Lancashire Fusiliers
HOMER Harold MM Pte 9717 1st Northumberland Fusiliers
HOMER Hope MM Sjt 16142 18 Coy Machine Gun Corps
HOMER Howard MM L/Cpl T4/036284 9 Aux HT Coy Army Service Corps
HOMER Joseph MM L/Cpl 205534 2nd Essex Regt
HOMER Samuel H. MM Pte 201594 1/8th Worcestershire Regt
HOMER Sidney H. "DCM,MM" Pte 6809 3rd Coldstream Guards
HOMER William MM Pte 20795 10th Worcestershire Regt
HOMERSHAM Donald Arthur MM Gnr 87989 Z/21 Med TM Bty RFA KIA 6.10.16.
HOMERSHAM Frank S. "DCM,MM+Bar" Sjt 45807 9th Royal Irish Fusiliers
HOMEWOOD Arthur MM Pte 19054 Machine Gun Corps
HOMEWOOD Ernest MM Pte 12292 Royal West Kent Regt
HOMEWOOD Harry MM L/Cpl 206110 3/4th Royal West Surrey Regt
HOMEWOOD William MM Sjt 940509 D/293 Bde RFA
HONAN Denis MM Pte 128767 91 Fd Amb RAMC
HONE Harry MM Pte 437239 2 Fd Amb RAMC
HONEY Edward "DCM,MM" Sjt 446012 89 Fd Amb RAMC
HONEY Edward E. MM Pte M2/180925 30 Mot Amb Convoy Army Service Corps
HONEY Frank MM Cpl 2768 Machine Gun Corps(Motors)
HONEY J.A. MM Cpl 493643 London Regt
HONEY James MM Pte 572739 17th London Regt
HONEY James MM Sjt S/323 2nd Royal West Surrey Regt
HONEYBALL P.A. MM Cpl 8859 Suffolk Regt
HONEYBALL Thomas Maurice MM Pte 81589 19 Coy Machine Gun Corps KIA 26.3.18.
HONEYBOURNE Arthur MM Sjt 944569 RFA
HONEYCHURCH Bertie MM L/Cpl 27359 Hampshire Regt
HONEYMAN Alexander MM L/Sjt 16131 Arg & Suth Highlanders
HONEYSETT David G. MM CSM 6426 Royal Sussex Regt
HONEYWILL George E. MM Pte 220099 23 Fd Amb RAMC
HONEYWOOD William John MM Sjt 15833 11th Suffolk Regt KIA 21.8.18.
HONHOLD Arthur Thomas MM Gnr 34491 28 Siege Bty RGA
HONHOLD Frederick Henry MM Pte 21569 26th Royal Fusiliers KIA 25.9.17.
HONIG Herbert G. MM Pte 350754 1/7th London Regt
HONIG William MM CSM 280671 2/4th London Regt
HONOUR Herbert MM Pte 43507 Lincolnshire Regt
HONOUR John MM Pte 6/9955 2nd Rifle Brigade
HONOUR Reginald Alexander MM Pte 18320 1st Coldstream Guards DOW 17.10.18.
HOOD Albert E. MM Gnr 82407 RFA
HOOD Alexander MM L/DSjt S/2644 1st Arg & Suth Highlanders
HOOD Arthur N. MM Sjt 3452 1/14th London Regt
HOOD Cyril W. "DCM,MM" Sjt 16113 7th Yorkshire Light Infantry
HOOD Daniel MM Dvr 63121 'A' Bty RHA
HOOD Edward T. MM L/Cpl L/10362 7th Royal West Kent Regt
HOOD Frederick W. MM Pte M2/177065 Army Service Corps att RGA.
HOOD George MM Pte 147550 32nd Bn Machine Gun Corps
HOOD George MM Gnr 86982 277 Siege Bty RGA
HOOD Harold MM Pte 9/15011 Leicestershire Regt
HOOD Harold MM 2nd Cpl 19786 9 Fd Coy Royal Engineers
HOOD Harry MM Cpl 13790 8th North Staffordshire Regt
HOOD James MM Pte 37229 1/8th Scottish Rifles
HOOD James MM L/Cpl 81312 206 Fd Coy Royal Engineers
HOOD James E. MM Cpl 351546 1/7th London Regt
HOOD John MM Sjt 16025 8th Somerset Light Infantry KIA 1.7.16.
HOOD John W. MM Sjt 4942 Machine Gun Corps
HOOD Robert MM Pte 16018 2nd Highland Light Infantry
HOOD Robert H. MM L/Cpl 16105 9th Cheshire Regt
HOOD Robert J. MM L/Cpl 17382 Northumberland Fusiliers
HOOD William MM Pte 7770 West Yorkshire Regt
HOOD William A. MM Pte G/48861 23rd Royal Fusiliers
HOOD William H.R. MM Cpl 661230 RFA
HOODLESS J.W. MM Pte 9513 75 Fd Amb RAMC
HOODLESS John G. MM Pte 6550 HAC
HOODLESS Percy W. MM L/Cpl 43673 1st Middlesex Regt
HOOF William MM Pte 38000 Labour Corps
HOOK Albert MM Sjt 27695 12th Suffolk Regt
HOOK Arthur MM Cpl 58104 63rd Bn Machine Gun Corps KIA 30.9.18.
HOOK Charles R. MM Spr 494747 103 Fd Coy Royal Engineers
HOOK Ernest MM Dvr T4/251001 Army Service Corps
HOOK Frank MM Pte 508373 1 Fd Amb RAMC
HOOK George MM Dvr 201425 B/47 Bde RFA Died 26.4.17.
HOOK George E. MM Pte 265237 West Riding Regt
HOOK George Raymond "MM,MID" Sjt L/36974 RFA
HOOK Henry MM L/Cpl 19590 3 Fd Squadron Royal Engineers
HOOK Henry C. MM CQMS 2451 7th Gloucestershire Regt
HOOK Henry J. MM+Bar Sjt 7837 1st Gloucestershire Regt
HOOK John T. MM L/Cpl G/9425 1st East Kent Regt
HOOK Sidney Richard MM+Bar Cpl 37794 RFA
HOOK Walter S. MM Pte 1766 10 Fd Amb RAMC
HOOK William MM Pte 18754 6th East Kent Regt
HOOK William "DCM,MM+Bar" Sjt 57693 29 Bty 42 Bde RFA KIA 27.8.18.
HOOK William C. MM L/Cpl 96811 Middlesex Regt
HOOK William J. MM Dvr T4/185019 Army Service Corps att 67 Fd Amb RAMC.
HOOKER Arthur Horace MM Pte 11859 2nd Notts & Derby Regt
HOOKER Arthur W. MM Pte 1415 10th Royal West Surrey Regt
HOOKER Edward MM Pte 58203 6th Northamptonshire Regt
HOOKER Harry Wright MM Sjt L/9177 2nd Royal West Surrey Regt DOW 9.8.16.
HOOKER Herbert James MM Sjt 67 6th Royal West Kent Regt KIA 14.10.17.
HOOKER John MM Pte 17991 Machine Gun Corps
HOOKER Mark MM Pte 10492 1st Royal West Surrey Regt
HOOKER P.F. MM Air Mech 1 4111 Royal Flying Corps
HOOKER Samuel MM Pte 41589 8th Yorkshire Regt
HOOKER William Henry "DCM,MM+Bar,CG(B)" Cpl G/9441 11th Royal West Kent Regt
HOOKEY N.H.J. MM Sjt 815 Military Mounted Police
HOOKHAM Ernest MM Sjt 1868 1/3rd Monmouthshire Regt
HOOKHAM Frederick A. MM Pte 203480 West Riding Regt
HOOKHAM Joseph H. MM Dvr 181917 32 Div Sig Coy Royal Engineers
HOOKINGS Ernest MM L/Cpl 36176 1/5th Somerset Light Infantry
HOOKINS Sidney MM Pte 201404 2/4th Oxf & Bucks Light Infantry DOW 14.4.18.
HOOKS J. MM L/Cpl P9998 Military Foot Police
HOOKWAY Sidney MM Gnr 11572 A/84 Bde RFA
HOOKWAY Sydney MM Air Mech 1 61856 Royal Flying Corps
HOOLE Harry MM Gnr 73442 RFA
HOOLE W.D. MM Gnr 26919 RGA
HOOLEY Harold MM Pte 377944 5th Manchester Regt
HOOLEY James A. MM Sjt 265180 1/6th Cheshire Regt
HOOLEY Richard MM L/Cpl 72748 24th Bn Machine Gun Corps
HOOLEY William MM+Bar Sjt 9278 1st Yorkshire Light Infantry DOW 2.11.18.
HOOPELL Benjamin H. MM L/Cpl 202323 Gloucestershire Regt
HOOPER Alexander MM Pte 15607 Hampshire Regt
HOOPER Alfred MM Pte 57550 37th Bn Machine Gun Corps
HOOPER Alfred C. MM Pte 241089 1/5th Devonshire Regt
HOOPER Alfred H.J. MM Pte 353883 7th London Regt
HOOPER Alfred R.C. MM CQMS 12632 9 Fd Coy Royal Engineers
HOOPER Arthur "DCM,MM" L/Cpl 6211 1st Coldstream Guards
HOOPER Arthur G. MM Pte 4761 3rd London Regt
HOOPER Arthur J. MM Sjt M2/033407 Army Service Corps
HOOPER Austin Edward MM L/Sjt 9245 2nd Coldstream Guards KIA 27.8.18.
HOOPER Cecil Charles MM Gnr 1113 71 Bde RFA
HOOPER Charles MM CQMS 5634 North Lancashire Regt
HOOPER Charles Harold MM Pte 331869 9th Liverpool Regt KIA 30.9.18.
HOOPER Daniel MM L/Cpl 42045 2nd Bedfordshire Regt
HOOPER Edmund MM Pte 17071 7th Duke of Cornwall's LI
HOOPER Edward MM Sjt 47871 A/124 Bde RFA Died 27.7.17.
HOOPER Edwin MM Pte 24294 1st Royal Dublin Fusiliers

HOOPER Frank A. MM Pte 74126 139 Fd Amb RAMC
HOOPER Frederick W. MM S/Sjt 60316 RAMC
HOOPER G.W. MM L/Cpl 1357 Royal Engineers
HOOPER Harold MM L/Cpl 240156 1/5th Duke of Cornwall's LI
HOOPER Harold MM Spr 508141 Royal Engineers
HOOPER Harry MM Pte 44763 8th Manchester Regt
HOOPER Horace C.M. MM Pte 37483 RAMC
HOOPER James MM Pte 240272 1st Somerset Light Infantry
HOOPER James MM Pte 9282 1st Somerset Light Infantry
HOOPER John F. MM Pte 20738 9th Devonshire Regt
HOOPER John H. MM Gnr 57822 RGA
HOOPER Joseph H. MM 2nd Cpl 130395 Royal Engineers
HOOPER Reginald MM L/Cpl 51072 Royal Engineers
HOOPER Richard MM L/Cpl 16905 7th East Lancashire Regt KIA 18.11.16.
HOOPER Sydney John MM L/Cpl 391837 2/9th London Regt KIA 23.9.17.
HOOPER Thomas MM Cpl 18116 10th North Lancashire Regt KIA 11.4.17.
HOOPER Thomas MM L/Cpl 13325 9th Royal Welsh Fusiliers KIA 3.7.16.
HOOPER Thomas H. MM Pte 10893 5th Royal Berkshire Regt
HOOPER William MM Pte 5421 1st Royal Welsh Fusiliers
HOOPER William MM Pte 512343 1/14th London Regt
HOOPER William Arthur MM Pte 392631 9th London Regt
HOOPER William Duncan Westly MM L/Sjt A/1560 3rd King's Royal Rifle Corps
HOOPER William E. MM Cpl 25604 4th Liverpool Regt
HOOPER William G. MM Pte 1065 1/6th Welsh Regt
HOOPER William George MM Bdr 845056 48 Div Ammn Col RFA
HOOPER William John MM Pte 14077 2nd South Lancashire Regt KIA 26.5.18.
HOOPS Douglas MM L/Cpl 6441 2nd Gordon Highlanders
HOOSON Henry B. MM Sjt 300554 5th London Regt
HOOSON James MM Pte 31238 Lancashire Fusiliers
HOOSON James MM Gnr 56344 RFA
HOOSON James B. MM Dvr 675436 RFA
HOOSON Robert MM L/Cpl 21160 2nd Bedfordshire Regt
HOOTON Arthur E. MM Bugler 10283 2nd Scottish Rifles
HOOTON James MM Cpl 28493 2nd Royal Dublin Fusiliers
HOOTON James MM L/Cpl 81620 200 Fd Coy Royal Engineers
HOOTUN Fred MM Pte 29220 1st East Lancashire Regt Died 4.10.17.
HOPCRAFT John "MM,MIDx2" Pte 12491 2nd Royal Fusiliers
HOPE Archibald MM Pte S/41025 Seaforth Highlanders
HOPE Edward William MM Cpl 11854 11th Royal Fusiliers KIA 10.8.17.
HOPE Frederick MM L/Cpl 570239 1/17th London Regt
HOPE George MM Pte A/7402 2nd Scottish Rifles
HOPE George MM Bdr 107288 RFA
HOPE George E. MM Pte 38940 Yorkshire Regt
HOPE George H. MM Pte M2/136559 Army Service Corps
HOPE Harold MM Pte 12540 8th East Kent Regt
HOPE Harry MM Pte 60832 RAMC
HOPE Herbert Henry MM Pte STK/1316 10th Royal Fusiliers
HOPE James MM Pte S/19565 1st Royal Highlanders
HOPE James MM L/Cpl 7850 1/7th Royal Highlanders
HOPE James MM Cpl 760135 RFA
HOPE John MM Pte 23679 1st King's Own Scottish Borderers KIA 16.8.17.
HOPE John MM Cpl 74593 Royal Engineers
HOPE John MM Sjt 14148 15th Durham Light Infantry
HOPE John Carlyle MM Sjt 111488 2nd Labour Bn Royal Engineers
HOPE John Kennedy MM L/Cpl 14/16600 14th Royal Irish Rifles
HOPE John Richardson MM Pte 18612 14th Durham Light Infantry KIA 18.9.16.
HOPE Joseph MM Sjt 265131 1/7th Royal Warwickshire Regt
HOPE Joseph Berry MM Sjt 86176 278 Railway Coy Royal Engineers
HOPE Joseph Lowrie MM Pte 22975 King's Own Scottish Borderers
HOPE Percy MM Cpl 42506 58th Bn Machine Gun Corps
HOPE Robert MM Gnr 117107 RFA
HOPE Robert MM Pte 113 23rd Royal Fusiliers DOW 28.3.18.
HOPE Robert B. MM Cpl 34141 Manchester Regt
HOPE Robinson N. MM Sjt 21760 Durham Light Infantry
HOPE Sidney MM Cpl 78773 RFA
HOPE Stanley MM Sjt 33013 Machine Gun Corps
HOPE Walter MM L/Cpl 721402 1/24th London Regt
HOPE William MM Gnr 150859 217 Siege Bty RGA
HOPE William S. MM Sjt 12023 2nd Grenadier Guards

HOPES Henry MM Cpl 201136 Gloucestershire Regt
HOPES Samuel MM Pte 21863 Royal Berkshire Regt
HOPGOOD Charles MM Cpl 200955 Royal Berkshire Regt
HOPGOOD John Stephen MM Cpl 17545 2nd. Hampshire Regt
HOPKIN Herbert MM Pte 65764 Machine Gun Corps
HOPKIN JohnT. MM Pte 2155 2nd York & Lancaster Regt
HOPKINS A.W. MM Pte 720260 London Regt
HOPKINS Alfred MM Pte 141782 Machine Gun Corps
HOPKINS Arthur MM Pte 15362 7th Royal Irish Fusiliers
HOPKINS Arthur T. MM Pte A/202314 13th King's Royal Rifle Corps
HOPKINS Charles James MM Pte 6130 1st Somerset Light Infantry KIA 25 10 17.
HOPKINS Edward Francis MM CQMS 2603 Gloucestershire Regt
HOPKINS Ernest MM Gnr 690398 RFA
HOPKINS Ernest A. MM Gnr 98177 RFA
HOPKINS Ernest W. MM+Bar Cpl 10517 6th Duke of Cornwall's LI
HOPKINS Frank MM 2nd Cpl 36956 134 Army Tps Coy Royal Engineers
HOPKINS Fred A. MM Pte 201383 1/4th Royal Berkshire Regt
HOPKINS Frederick MM Pte 491355 13th London Regt
HOPKINS George MM Dvr 78080 RFA
HOPKINS George L. MM Pte 491937 13th London Regt
HOPKINS George L. MM Pte 341136 RAMC
HOPKINS Gilbert H. MM Pte 8960 2nd Devonshire Regt
HOPKINS Harold MM Pte 702 23rd Royal Fusiliers KIA 13.11.16.
HOPKINS Harry MM Pte 21431 2nd Coldstream Guards
HOPKINS Harry MM Dvr 27793 9 Div Ammn Col RFA
HOPKINS Harry MM Pte 362 16th Royal Warwickshire Regt
HOPKINS Henry J. MM Pte 12922 1st East Surrey Regt
HOPKINS Hopkin MM Pte 18871 11th Welsh Regt
HOPKINS Horace MM Pte 27177 18th Liverpool Regt
HOPKINS J. MM Pte 24600 Yorkshire Light Infantry
HOPKINS James "MM,MID" Pte Z/1596 4th Rifle Brigade
HOPKINS James A. MM Pte 41576 Royal Fusiliers
HOPKINS James H. MM Pte 74080 RAMC
HOPKINS James R. MM L/Sjt 8208 Devonshire Regt
HOPKINS John MM Sjt 8368 2nd Royal Inniskilling Fusiliers
HOPKINS John M. MM Pte 16679 Shropshire Light Infantry
HOPKINS John S. MM Sjt 697377 B/181 Bde RFA
HOPKINS Michael MM Pte 13566 10th West Riding Regt
HOPKINS Oliver MM Pte 16336 11th Suffolk Regt KIA 9.4.17.
HOPKINS Percy MM Bugler 1561 1/21st London Regt
HOPKINS Richard H. MM Pte 139257 Machine Gun Corps
HOPKINS Robert MM L/Cpl 267467 1/6th Royal Highlanders DOW 4.8.18.
HOPKINS Robert "DCM,MM" CSM G/4821 8th East Surrey Regt
HOPKINS Robert N. MM L/Cpl 43114 Royal Irish Fusiliers
HOPKINS Russell John MM Sjt 1056 11th Royal Sussex Regt
HOPKINS Stanley J. MM Pte 8382 2nd Oxf & Bucks Light Infantry
HOPKINS Sydney B. MM Pte 16347 1st Royal Welsh Fusiliers
HOPKINS Thomas MM+Bar Sjt 96884 177 Tunnelling Coy Royal Engineers
HOPKINS Thomas Emanuel MM Sjt 364023 RAMC
HOPKINS Thomas G. "DCM,MM" Sjt 48124 RAMC
HOPKINS Thomas W. MM Dvr 163091 123 Fd Coy Royal Engineers
HOPKINS Walter MM 2nd Cpl 310983 Royal Engineers
HOPKINS William MM Cpl 55050 17 Hy Bty RGA
HOPKINS William MM Sjt 71 1/6th Notts & Derby Regt
HOPKINS William MM Pte 59634 RAMC
HOPKINS William Graham MM Pte 11469 9th Devonshire Regt KIA 22.4.17.
HOPKINS William J. MM Pte 72717 2nd Notts & Derby Regt
HOPKINS William James MM Pte 18643 10th Worcestershire Regt KIA 4.9.16.
HOPKINSON Alfred Holt MM Pte 46817 16th Manchester Regt KIA 21.3.18.
HOPKINSON Charles MM Cpl Fitter 765394 C/87 Bde RFA
HOPKINSON Ernest MM+Bar Pte 203320 York & Lancaster Regt
HOPKINSON Ernest MM L/Cpl 26950 4 Div Sig Coy Royal Engineers
HOPKINSON Frederick H. MM Pte M/321789 Army Service Corps att 242 Siege Bty RGA
HOPKINSON Horace MM L/Cpl 27213 Royal Engineers
HOPKINSON James MM Pte 8385 2nd Scots Guards
HOPKINSON James MM Pte 2531 1/4th East Yorkshire Regt
HOPKINSON James Edward MM L/Cpl 36564 11th East Lancashire Regt
HOPKINSON John MM Gnr Sig 146155 151 Hy Bty RGA
HOPKINSON John J. MM L/Cpl 202347 2/4th Hampshire Regt
HOPKINSON Joshua MM L/Cpl 160130 Royal Engineers

HOPKINSON Oswald MM Cpl 106628 Special Brigade Royal Engineers
HOPKINSON Percy Clement MM Gnr 100077 321 Siege Bty RGA KIA 3.9.18.
HOPLEY James "DCM,MM+Bar" Pte 10997 6th York & Lancaster Regt
HOPLEY William MM Pte 2492 1/9th Liverpool Regt
HOPPER Arthur H. MM Sjt 800431 C/230 Bde RFA
HOPPER Francis MM Pte S/11061 2nd Arg & Suth Highlanders
HOPPER Frank MM Sjt 22756 22nd Manchester Regt
HOPPER Fred "MM,MM(F)" Sjt 14057 Yorkshire Regt
HOPPER Frederick Henderson MM Sjt 26809 18 Div Ammn Col RFA
HOPPER George MM Sjt 761526 28th London Regt
HOPPER Henry W. MM Pte 5819 RAMC
HOPPER John G. MM Dvr 74428 24 Bde RFA
HOPPER Joseph MM Cpl 16300 Royal Inniskilling Fusiliers
HOPPER Mathew MM L/Cpl 200616 Northumberland Fusiliers
HOPPER Robert MM Pte 19/1359 Northumberland Fusiliers
HOPPER Robert Arthur MM Pte 37178 10th Yorkshire Light Infantry
HOPPER Thomas L. MM L/Cpl S/27652 Rifle Brigade
HOPPING Isaac A. MM L/Cpl 2185 16th Middlesex Regt
HOPPITT William H. MM Sjt 10526 2nd Border Regt
HOPPS Robert MM Pte 370 22nd Durham Light Infantry
HOPPS Robert W. MM Pte 551 Army Cyclist Corps
HOPSON Theodore MM Sjt 206799 6th Royal West Surrey Regt
HOPSON William MM Pte 39917 RAMC
HOPSON William H. MM+Bar L/Cpl 200379 1/4th Gloucestershire Regt
HOPTON Albert Edward MM L/Cpl 265907 1/6th Gloucestershire Regt DOW 21.11.17.
HOPTON David MM Pte 25081 Scottish Rifles
HOPTON Ernest MM Cpl 4988 Army Cyclist Corps
HOPWOOD Charles MM Sjt 5250 21st Manchester Regt KIA 2.4.17.
HOPWOOD Frederick William MM Sjt 6750 11th Royal West Kent Regt
HOPWOOD Gayland MM Gnr 15901 RFA
HOPWOOD Harry MM Sjt 14059 7th North Lancashire Regt KIA 23.7.16.
HOPWOOD Harry MM Gnr 76732 C/74 Bde RFA
HOPWOOD Joe MM Pte 241505 1st Royal Lancaster Regt
HOPWOOD John MM Pte 17488 Shropshire Light Infantry
HOPWOOD John Ivor MM Pte 73573 17th Royal Welsh Fusiliers KIA 4.11.18.
HOPWOOD Lawrence F. MM Pte 40318 2nd South Lancashire Regt
HOPWOOD Thomas MM Cpl 19031 RGA
HOPWOOD Thomas MM Pte 4084 11th Lancashire Fusiliers
HOPWOOD Thomas Frederick MM Pte 200310 1/5th Lancashire Fusiliers
HOPWOOD W.H. "MM,MID" QMS 10719 12 Fd Amb RAMC
HORAM Charles MM Pte 12820 10th North Lancashire Regt
HORAM William H. MM Bdr L/39217 RFA
HORAN Andrew MM Pte 29006 Machine Gun Corps
HORAN C. MM Pte 686117 22nd London Regt
HORAN Edmund MM Spr 448489 Royal Engineers
HORAN Harry MM Sjt 38935 24 Heavy Bty RGA
HORAN J. MM Pte M2/229884 Army Service Corps
HORAN James MM Pte 24384 Notts & Derby Regt
HORAN John MM Pte 4632 1st Irish Guards
HORAN John MM L/Cpl 9293 South Staffordshire Regt
HORAN John MM Sjt 240650 1/6th Liverpool Regt
HORAN John C. MM Pte S/30438 13th Rifle Brigade
HORAN Joseph MM Pte 53673 16 Coy Machine Gun Corps
HORAN William J. MM Sjt 37139 43 Bde RFA
HORBROUGH Robert Thomas MM Sjt 40782 7 Div Sig Coy Royal Engineers KIA 30.9.17.
HORBURY Ernest E. MM Gnr 16332 12 Bty 35 Bde RFA
HORDERN Joseph MM L/Sjt 7311 1st Shropshire Light Infantry KIA 10.10.16.
HORE William MM L/Cpl 33288 8th Devonshire Regt KIA 27.10.18.
HORFORD Thomas MM Sjt 6386 16th Manchester Regt
HORGAN Edward MM Bde 94520 B/187 Bde RFA
HORGAN Jeremiah MM Sjt 16656 Royal Irish Fusiliers
HORINE George H. MM Sjt 20591 6th Bn Machine Gun Corps
HORKAN Patrick MM Pte 30363 Worcestershire Regt
HORLER Frederick J. MM Cpl 29898 Wiltshire Regt
HORLER Robert J. MM Pte 16613 3rd Grenadier Guards
HORLEY Albert H. MM L/Cpl 25008 17 Fd Coy Royal Engineers
HORLEY William E. MM Pte 1975 1/7th London Regt
HORLOCK George MM Pte 44077 2nd Middlesex Regt DOW 15.10.18.
HORLOCK Joseph MM Gnr 61796 'U' Bty RHA
HORLOCK Thomas MM L/Sjt 19576 24 Coy Machine Gun Corps
HORN Alfred MM Pte 34455 York & Lancaster Regt
HORN C.H.E. MM L/Cpl 13754 10th Essex Regt
HORN Charles Louis MM L/Cpl 3323 1/5th Royal Highlanders
HORN Frank W. "MM,MID" Bdr 49450 RFA
HORN Frederick W. MM Cpl 1461 1/1st Cambridgeshire Regt
HORN George MM Cpl 26459 RFA
HORN H. MM L/Cpl 200429 Yorkshire Regt
HORN Harry MM CSM 625121 19th London Regt
HORN Robert H. MM Cpl 204474 11th Somerset Light Infantry
HORN Walter E. MM Pte 49646 Royal Fusiliers
HORN William MM Pte 17398 13th Durham Light Infantry
HORN William MM CQMS 275308 1/7th Arg & Suth Highlanders
HORN William H. MM L/Cpl 26882 1st Shropshire Light Infantry
HORN William H. MM Sjt 40036 RAMC
HORNAL George Wright MM Spr 76323 'CC' Cable Section Royal Engineers
HORNAL Walter James MM CSM 1523 1/12th London Regt KIA 9.9.16.
HORNALL James MM Pte 31260 2nd King's Own Scottish Borderers
HORNBUCKLE Frederick MM Pte 473373 53 Labour Coy Labour Corps
HORNBY Arthur Stanley MM Sjt L/15606 32 Div Ammn Col RFA
HORNBY G. MM+Bar L/Cpl 2340 Royal Engineers
HORNBY George MM Pte 2839 1/5th Yorkshire Regt Died 7.8.18.
HORNBY Herbert MM Cpl 13921 32 Div Ammn Col RFA
HORNBY James MM 2nd Cpl 81663 Royal Engineers
HORNBY John MM Pte 241158 2/4th South Lancashire Regt KIA 2.9.18.
HORNBY Joseph MM+Bar Sjt 266595 1st Notts & Derby Regt
HORNBY Percy H. MM L/Cpl 392213 9th London Regt
HORNBY Tom MM Sjt 13357 Northumberland Fusiliers
HORNBY Walter MM Cpl 3226 Machine Gun Corps
HORNBY William MM Sjt 12297 7th Yorkshire Regt
HORNE Abraham MM Pte 7910 11th Royal Warwickshire Regt
HORNE Albert E. MM Sjt 64351 RGA
HORNE Andrew Young MM Spr 418069 52 Div Sig Coy Royal Engineers
HORNE Arthur W. MM+Bar Sjt 1312 2nd Royal Sussex Regt
HORNE Augustus MM Pte 42657 Northumberland Fusiliers
HORNE Frederick John MM Sjt 19874 Machine Gun Corps
HORNE Harold MM Pte 24031 1/5th East Lancashire Regt
HORNE Harry MM L/Cpl 236 York & Lancaster Regt
HORNE Harry "MM,MID" Sjt 352088 1/2(East Lancashire)Fd Amb RAMC
HORNE James MM+Bar Pte 983 Middlesex Regt
HORNE John W. MM 2nd Cpl 44802 7 Div Sig Coy Royal Engineers
HORNE Jonathan MM Cpl 836562 RFA
HORNE Joseph MM L/Cpl 241402 1/6th North Staffordshire Regt KIA 28.9.18.
HORNE Joseph J. MM L/Cpl 17157 1st Royal Berkshire Regt
HORNE Norman G. MM L/Cpl 52319 15 Fd Amb RAMC
HORNE Patrick MM Pte 203505 2nd Seaforth Highlanders
HORNE Reginald MM Sjt 23443 8th Yorkshire Light Infantry
HORNE Reginald MM Pte 23405 Lancashire Fusiliers
HORNE Robert MM L/Cpl 8345 Royal Irish Regt
HORNE Robert MM Pte 32553 8th York & Lancaster Regt
HORNE Stephen James MM Pte 9060 2nd Worcestershire Regt KIA 4.12.17.
HORNE Thomas MM Gnr 84904 RFA
HORNE Thomas MM 2nd Cpl 141886 283 Army Troops Coy Royal Engineers
HORNE W.R.D. MM Cpl S/43170 2nd Gordon Highlanders
HORNE Walter Ernest MM Pte 19350 11th Essex Regt KIA 22.3.18.
HORNE Wilfred G. MM Pte 16399 5th Northamptonshire Regt
HORNE William J. MM Pte 8630 2nd Dragoon Guards
HORNER Alfred MM Cpl 26505 11th Notts & Derby Regt
HORNER Alfred MM Pte 242878 1/6th West Yorkshire Regt KIA 25.4.18.
HORNER Arthur Henry "MM,MSM" CQMS M/28901 4 Div Train Army Service Corps
HORNER Charles W. MM Cpl 205032 4th Hampshire Regt
HORNER Ernest M. "DCM,MM+Bar" Sjt 482005 3 Div Sig Coy Royal Engineers
HORNER George MM Pte 49260 1st Rifle Brigade
HORNER Harry MM Dvr 108421 111 Bty 24 Bde RFA

HORNER James MM Pte 15352 11th Notts & Derby Regt
HORNER James MM Pte 200615 1/4th Royal Scots Fusiliers
HORNER James F. "DCM,MM" Sjt 306966 8th West Yorkshire Regt
HORNER James H. MM Sjt 2393 Northumberland Fusiliers
HORNER Jim MM Pte 93097 2nd Durham Light Infantry
HORNER John Hedley MM Pte 13786 13th Royal Fusiliers
HORNER John Newsam MM Bdr 81738 D/46 Bde RFA
HORNER Luther MM Pte 16/694 16th West Yorkshire Regt
HORNER Ralph E. MM Cpl 9132 2nd Northamptonshire Regt
HORNER Robert MM L/Sjt 16166 3rd Coldstream Guards
HORNER Robert J. MM Pte 265029 4th Liverpool Regt
HORNER Roger MM Pte 202398 2/4th West Riding Regt
HORNER Samuel C. MM Bdr 129342 RFA
HORNER Thomas Metcalfe MM Pte 267054 2/6th West Riding Regt
HORNER William MM Sjt 1437 1/9th Highland Light Infantry
HORNER William MM Sjt 17/1192 17th West Yorkshire Regt
HORNETT Joseph MM L/Cpl 10753 2nd Royal Fusiliers
HORNIBROOK G. MM Gnr 1980 RFA
HORNIGOLD Walter MM Sjt 14266 Machine Gun Corps
HORNSBY Albert Edward MM Sjt 12836 6th Bedfordshire Regt
HORNSBY Alfred Francis MM Sjt 10108 8th Norfolk Regt
HORNSBY David R. MM Pte 47089 1/4th Northamptonshire Regt
HORNSBY Ernest R. MM 2nd Cpl M2/076546 Army Service Corps
HORNSBY Frank MM Cpl 62247 RFA
HORNSBY Frank E. MM Dvr 60094 Royal Engineers
HORNSBY Stanley J. MM Gnr 183273 B/82 Bde RFA
HORNSBY William MM L/Cpl 28755 Northumberland Fusiliers
HORNSEY Albert MM Spr 197365 Royal Engineers
HORNSEY Charles G. MM Cpl 92565 Tank Corps
HOROBIN Charles H. MM Cpl 42552 Worcestershire Regt
HORRIDGE John MM+Bar Sjt 27472 Machine Gun Corps
HORRIDGE John MM Pte 27355 19th Lancashire Fusiliers
HORRIDGE S. MM Gnr 1666 RFA
HORRIDGE William MM Sjt 5931 2nd South Lancashire Regt
HORRIGAN John MM Sjt 122336 'V' AA Bty RGA
HORROBIN John E. MM+Bar Pte 17016 6th South Wales Borderers
HORROCKS Adam Wilson MM Sjt 3950 3rd Coldstream Guards
HORROCKS Archibald MM Cpl 226289 311 Rly Constr Coy Royal Engineers
HORROCKS Edward MM Pte 3395 Machine Gun Corps
HORROCKS George Arthur MM Gnr 136391 42 Bty 2 Bde RFA KIA 30.11.17.
HORROCKS John MM Pte R/9278 13th King's Royal Rifle Corps
HORROCKS Joseph MM Pte 41663 RAMC
HORROCKS Thomas MM L/Cpl 5064 22 Fd Amb RAMC
HORROCKS William MM Pte 49728 75 Fd Amb RAMC
HORSBRUGH Richard MM Cpl 56691 25th King's Royal Rifle Corps
HORSBRUGH Robert K. MM Pte 351189 Royal Scots
HORSBURGH Frederick MM 2nd Cpl 503831 Signal Service Royal Engineers
HORSBURGH Hugh G. MM L/Cpl 202358 5/6th Scottish Rifles
HORSBURGH James MM L/Bdr Sig 630136 255 Bde RFA
HORSBURGH Leslie MM Pte 320053 3 Fd Amb RAMC
HORSCROFT Archibald MM Gnr 9732 B/71 Bde RFA
HORSCROFT Arthur MM L/Cpl 1659 2nd Royal Sussex Regt
HORSCROFT Harry MM L/Cpl 13482 2nd Middlesex Regt
HORSEFIELD Ernest MM Pte 49979 10th Cheshire Regt DOW 31.5.18.
HORSEWELL Frederick MM Pte 290180 Gloucestershire Regt
HORSEY Harold F. MM Sjt 230206 1/1st Dorset Yeomanry
HORSEY Reginald MM L/Cpl 295212 1/1st West Somerset Yeomanry
HORSFALL Arthur MM L/Cpl 74 2nd Lancashire Fusiliers
HORSFALL Harold MM Sjt 14532 8th Royal Lancaster Regt
HORSFALL Lawrence Joseph MM Pte 1663 3(Northumbrian)Fd Amb RAMC Died 23.9.18.
HORSFIELD Alfred "DCM,MM+Bar" Cpl 459142 447 Fd Coy Royal Engineers
HORSFIELD Ernest MM Sjt 250471 1/6th Durham Light Infantry
HORSFIELD Frederick M. MM S/Sjt 18409 13 Fd Amb RAMC
HORSFIELD George H. MM Sjt 200412 Yorkshire Light Infantry
HORSFIELD James "DCM,MM" Sjt 350239 1/9th Manchester Regt
HORSFIELD Richard MM+Bar Pte 34143 4th Liverpool Regt
HORSFIELD Thomas "MM,CG(F)" L/Cpl 33246 Leicestershire Regt
HORSFIELD William MM Gnr 780654 2/3(West Riding)Bde RFA
HORSFORD John T. MM L/Cpl 145380 1/1st Northamptonshire Yeomanry
HORSFORD Wilfred MM L/Cpl 32129 King's Royal Rifle Corps
HORSLEY Albert MM Pte 24819 Suffolk Regt
HORSLEY Archibald E. MM Sjt 513631 14th London Regt
HORSLEY George MM Sjt MS/3827 Army Service Corps
HORSLEY George A. MM Cpl 16926 1 Siege Bty RGA
HORSLEY John MM Pte 896 22nd Northumberland Fusiliers
HORSLEY Joshua MM Cpl 16237 Northumberland Fusiliers
HORSLEY Marmaduke "MM,MID" Cpl L/12147 16 Bty 41 Bde RFA
HORSLEY Thomas MM Sjt 57709 B/160 Bde RFA KIA 11.10.18.
HORSMAN Albert MM CoH 2315 1st Life Guards KIA 19.5.18.
HORSMAN George D. MM L/Cpl 91482 Tank Corps
HORSMAN John MM Pte S/28805 13th Rifle Brigade
HORSNELL Sidney MM+Bar Cpl 49299 75th Bn Machine Gun Corps
HORSPOOL Lewis MM Sjt 5931 Gloucestershire Regt
HORSWELL F.J. MM L/Cpl G7/70 East Surrey Regt
HORT Arthur T. "MM,MID" S/Sjt 17319 RAMC
HORTON Albert Edward MM Cpl 7902 1st Lincolnshire Regt
HORTON Arthur MM L/Cpl 6373 3rd Coldstream Guards
HORTON Arthur MM Pte 7475 1st Irish Guards
HORTON Arthur Ernest MM Pte M2/131214 HQ Third Army MT Coy Army Service Corps
HORTON Ernest MM Pte 23824 Oxf & Bucks Light Infantry
HORTON Ernest John MM L/Bdr 64753 92 HAG RGA
HORTON Fred MM L/Cpl 476847 455 Fd Coy Royal Engineers KIA 11.4.18.
HORTON Frederick I. MM Gnr 77852 'Q' Bty RHA
HORTON George MM Pte T4/247952 Army Service Corps
HORTON Harry MM Pte DM2/190928 Army Service Corps
HORTON Harry MM Pte 49980 10th Cheshire Regt KIA 23.3.18.
HORTON Henry J. MM Cpl 200269 1/4th Royal Sussex Regt
HORTON Herbert MM+Bar L/Sjt 14870 Royal Dublin Fusiliers
HORTON Herbert E. MM Pte 320 Royal Sussex Regt
HORTON John MM Cpl 488241 469 Fd Coy Royal Engineers
HORTON John "DCM,MM" RSM 5421 1st King's Royal Rifle Corps
HORTON John MM Gnr L/10844 D/150 Bde RFA DOW 11.4.17.
HORTON John MM Pte 3593 13th Royal Fusiliers
HORTON John James MM Cpl 9937 6th East Kent Regt
HORTON John T. MM Spr 96814 170 Tunnelling Coy Royal Engineers
HORTON John William MM Cpl 39645 15th Lancashire Fusiliers
HORTON John William MM Sjt 13968 8th York & Lancaster Regt KIA 7.6.17.
HORTON Joseph MM Pte 2517 2nd Manchester Regt
HORTON Leonard MM Cpl 67388 10 Bty 147 Bde RFA
HORTON Lewis "DCM,MM" Pte 17447 9th Yorkshire Regt
HORTON Neville A. MM Sjt Farrier 40063 RFA
HORTON Rawcliffe MM Sjt 306340 West Riding Regt
HORTON Stanley MM Pte 17382 Grenadier Guards
HORTON Thomas "DSO,MC,MM(31722 Cpl,12 Sge Bty),MID" Maj RGA
HORTON William MM Pte 63214 4th Bn Machine Gun Corps
HORTON William MM Pte 265494 7th Royal Warwickshire Regt
HORTON William MM Pte 19507 2nd South Wales Borderers
HORTON William H. MM Pte 241698 2nd Yorkshire Light Infantry
HORTON William Henry MM Pte 2399 1/7th Royal Warwickshire Regt KIA 14.7.16.
HORTON Willie MM Dvr L/18935 B/155 Bde RFA
HORWOOD Charles MM+Bar CSM 12572 6th Royal Berkshire Regt
HORWOOD Ernest MM L/Cpl 9872 Royal Berkshire Regt
HORWOOD Frederick W. MM Sjt 7270 7th Somerset Light Infantry
HORWOOD George MM Cpl 23416 Machine Gun Corps
HORWOOD Sidney MM Sjt 4766 16th Lancers
HOSBORNE J. "MM,MID" Sjt 608326 RHA
HOSE Arthur W. MM Pte 30425 5th Royal Inniskilling Fusiliers
HOSE John H. MM Spr 325511 Signal Service Royal Engineers
HOSFORD Joseph MM+Bar L/Cpl 8766 1st Royal Munster Fusiliers
HOSIE Alexander MM Pte 66420 Royal Fusiliers
HOSIE James MM Pte S/16701 1st Cameron Highlanders
HOSIE Walter MM Pte 28161 1st Royal Dublin Fusiliers
HOSIE William MM Sjt 331942 Highland Light Infantry
HOSIER Alfred "MM,CG(B),MID" Sjt 2284 2nd Northumberland Fusiliers
HOSIER Harry MM Sjt 200181 Royal Berkshire Regt
HOSKER John "DCM+Bar,MM" Sjt 11500 2nd East Lancashire Regt
HOSKIN Frederick Stanley MM L/Cpl 41158 1 Squadron Machine Gun Corps(Cavalry)
HOSKIN William MM Pte 91460 153 Coy Labour Corps
HOSKING Alfred G. MM Spr 457535 Royal Engineers
HOSKING Joseph K. MM L/Cpl 11333 Devonshire Regt
HOSKING Nicholas Sidney MM Spr 132256 251 Tunnelling Coy Royal Engineers
HOSKING Ralph V. MM Cpl 930868 464 Bty 179 Bde RFA

HOSKINS Alfred MM L/Sjt 19892 2nd Royal Welsh Fusiliers
HOSKINS Charles H. MM Pte 22273 7th Gloucestershire Regt
HOSKINS Edgar James MM Pte M2/135616 6 Motor Amb Convoy Army Service Corps
HOSKINS Victor MM Spr 159986 Royal Engineers
HOSKINS William MM CSM 6447 1st Suffolk Regt
HOSKINS William Henry MM Spr 74013 First Army Sig Coy Royal Engineers
HOSLER Thomas MM Pte 201396 Manchester Regt
HOSMER Frank S. MM Cpl 10822 1st Wiltshire Regt
HOSSACK Allan John MM Sjt 15227 8th Royal Lancaster Regt KIA 27.4.18.
HOSSACK John MM CSM 8989 2nd Seaforth Highlanders
HOSSACK William MM Sjt S/2149 9th Seaforth Highlanders
HOTCHIN John MM Pte 11778 8th Lincolnshire Regt
HOTCHKISS George "DCM,MM" Cpl S/41092 1/5th Seaforth Highlanders
HOTCHKISS Harold MM Gnr 881452 B/159 Bde RFA
HOTCHKISS Henry B. MM Pte 203317 South Lancashire Regt
HOTCHKISS John E. MM Sjt 11710 9th Cheshire Regt
HOTSON Arthur MM Pte 327647 1/1st Cambridgeshire Regt
HOTSON Campbell G. MM Sjt 17444 Suffolk Regt
HOUCHIN Harry MM Pte 13239 8th Lincolnshire Regt
HOUGH Arthur MM Sjt 469 'C' Bn Machine Gun Corps(Heavy Branch)
HOUGH Arthur MM Cpl 22011 11 Fd Coy Royal Engineers KIA 23.4.17.
HOUGH Bertram "MM,MSM" Sjt 310181 1/1st Warwickshire Yeomanry
HOUGH Daniel MM 2nd Cpl 269237 Royal Engineers
HOUGH Frederick J. MM Pte 320612 15th Suffolk Regt
HOUGH Harry MM Pte 200496 Yorkshire Light Infantry
HOUGH Harry MM Cpl L/3031 RFA
HOUGH Henry MM CQMS 6089 2nd Worcestershire Regt
HOUGH Isaac MM L/Cpl 13774 10th Cheshire Regt
HOUGH James H. MM Pte 243736 Liverpool Regt
HOUGH John J. MM Pte 206007 Royal West Surrey Regt
HOUGH Norman MM Pte 47018 RAMC
HOUGH Patrick MM Pte 10140 2nd Leinster Regt
HOUGH Thomas W. MM Pte 16403 12th Cheshire Regt
HOUGHTON Edgar S. MM Sjt 13883 8th Suffolk Regt
HOUGHTON Ernest MM Gnr 112388 RGA
HOUGHTON Francis Hugh MM L/Cpl 202710 1/4th Dorsetshire Regt
HOUGHTON Fred MM Sjt 165672 101st Bn Machine Gun Corps
HOUGHTON Frederick T. MM Spr 164603 Royal Engineers
HOUGHTON George MM Pte 39219 3rd Bn Machine Gun Corps
HOUGHTON Gilbert MM Pte DM2/155719 62 Div Train Army Service Corps
HOUGHTON Harold R. MM Pte 300858 5th London Regt
HOUGHTON Henry MM Sjt 1653 1/6th London Regt
HOUGHTON Herbert MM Cpl 240308 1/5th North Lancashire Regt KIA 30.11.17.
HOUGHTON James MM+Bar Pte 34129 RAMC
HOUGHTON James MM Sjt 201925 2/5th Manchester Regt
HOUGHTON James MM Gnr 681097 RFA
HOUGHTON James Harold MM Pte 41329 Manchester Regt
HOUGHTON John MM Pte 267539 7th Liverpool Regt
HOUGHTON John MM Pte 18620 21st Manchester Regt
HOUGHTON John B. MM L/Cpl 148464 Royal Engineers
HOUGHTON John Edward MM Gnr 45784 41 Siege Bty RGA
HOUGHTON John Thomas Stanley MM Pte 24845 13th Yorkshire Regt
HOUGHTON Percy MM Spr 202055 Royal Engineers
HOUGHTON Ralph MM Cpl 240814 1/5th South Lancashire Regt
HOUGHTON Richard MM Pte 20564 7th Dragoon Guards
HOUGHTON Robert MM Spr 42708 Royal Engineers
HOUGHTON Thomas MM Sjt 25178 1/8th Liverpool Regt
HOUGHTON Thomas MM L/Sjt 11211 2nd Royal Fusiliers
HOUGHTON Walter MM Pte 13638 1/8th Notts & Derby Regt
HOUGHTON Walter S. MM Pte 47859 6th Manchester Regt
HOUGHTON William MM Sjt 4570 D/75 Bde RFA
HOUGHTON William MM Sjt 95027 Liverpool Regt
HOUGHTON William MM Pte 49512 7th Liverpool Regt
HOUGHTON William H. MM Cpl 16210 6th Lincolnshire Regt
HOULDEN Alfred MM Sjt 776943 A/245 Bde RFA
HOULDEN Amos MM Sjt 12681 1st Northamptonshire Regt
HOULDEN Jesse MM Pte 53214 6th Bn Machine Gun Corps
HOULDEN Lewis MM L/Cpl 13929 8th West Riding Regt KIA 27.8.17.
HOULDEN William MM Bdr 14767 RFA
HOULDEN William John MM Bdr 17799 B/112 Bde RFA
HOULDER Howard F. MM Sjt 50228 RAMC
HOULDER John MM Pte S/7521 2nd Gordon Highlanders
HOULDER Percy MM Cpl 2412 24th Royal Fusiliers
HOULDER W. MM Cpl 20900 RFA
HOULDING Thomas Samuel MM Pte 35904 3rd Bn Machine Gun Corps
HOULDRIDGE Robert MM Gnr 106925 RFA
HOULDSWORTH Frank MM Pte 21682 Notts & Derby Regt
HOULKER George MM Sjt 113436 2 Special Coy Royal Engineers
HOULKER Harold MM Pte 17962 Machine Gun Corps
HOULTON David MM Pte 5419 3rd Dragoon Guards DOW 25.3.18.
HOULTON Walter MM Pte 6470 3rd Coldstream Guards
HOUNSELL Ernest MM Cpl 52196 Royal Engineers
HOUNSLOW Edith "MM,ARRC" Nurse F SJAB
HOUNSLOW George Horace MM Gnr 24461 3 Siege Bty RGA DOW 5.8.17.
HOUNSLOW Louis MM Pte 17765 Royal West Kent Regt
HOUNSOME William G. MM Sjt 11484 1st East Surrey Regt
HOURD Wilbert A. MM Pte M2/153316 Army Service Corps
HOUSBY Albert MM L/Cpl 8290 1st North Staffordshire Regt
HOUSDEN Charles G. MM L/Cpl 54762 15th Welsh Regt
HOUSDEN Harold S. MM Sjt 207407 63 Div Sig Coy Royal Engineers
HOUSE Albert E.R. MM SM 5 24 Fd Amb RAMC
HOUSE Alfred MM Pte 40010 2nd Royal Irish Rifles KIA 21.3.18.
HOUSE Arthur P. MM Pte 491976 13th London Regt
HOUSE Frederick W. MM Pte 66505 100 Fd Amb RAMC
HOUSE George H. MM Spr 500322 Royal Engineers
HOUSE John MM+Bar Sjt 28786 9th East Surrey Regt
HOUSE Percival T.W. MM Cpl 44385 Royal Engineers
HOUSE Robert MM Pte 57040 2nd Lancashire Fusiliers
HOUSE William Robert MM Pte 47307 1st Royal Irish Rifles
HOUSELEY Phillip Burton MM Pte 241770 9th Notts & Derby Regt
HOUSLEY Benjamin MM Spr 104470 98 Fd Coy Royal Engineers
HOUSLEY Frank MM Cpl 245473 21st Manchester Regt KIA 24.10.17.
HOUSLEY Thomas G. MM Pte 76174 Machine Gun Corps(Heavy Branch)
HOUSON L. MM Pte 24486 York & Lancaster Regt
HOUSTON Charles MM L/Cpl 200335 5/6th Scottish Rifles
HOUSTON Edward MM L/Cpl 11024 2nd Royal Scots DOW 19.4.17.
HOUSTON George MM Sjt 13580 6/7th Royal Scots Fusiliers
HOUSTON Hugh MM CSM 34795 8th York & Lancaster Regt
HOUSTON James MM Pte 295721 12th Royal Scots Fusiliers
HOUSTON James MM Gnr 93483 A/147 Bde RFA KIA 4.10.18.
HOUSTON James MM Cpl 302597 1/5th London Regt KIA 28.3.18.
HOUSTON James MM Cpl 54180 42 Siege Bty RGA
HOUSTON James W. MM Pte 10667 6th Bedfordshire Regt
HOUSTON John "MC,MM(4527 Pte)+Bar(331705 L/Sjt)" 2Lt 9th Highland Light Infantry
HOUSTON John MM Pte S/24061 8th Royal Highlanders
HOUSTON John MM L/Sjt 3239 1/4th Royal Highlanders
HOUSTON John MM+Bar Sjt 7574 2nd Royal Irish Rifles
HOUSTON Joseph B. MM Pte 42567 1st East Yorkshire Regt
HOUSTON Lennox James MM Pnr 121265 8 Div Sig Coy Royal Engineers KIA 16.8.17.
HOUSTON Nathaniel MM+Bar Cpl 43462 19th Durham Light Infantry
HOUSTON Robert MM L/Cpl 20187 4th Grenadier Guards
HOUSTON Robert MM Sjt 7254 Royal Irish Rifles
HOUSTON Roy MM Sjt 8155 1st Cameron Highlanders
HOUSTON Samuel MM Pte 23059 6th King's Own Scottish Borderers
HOUSTON Thomas MM+Bar Cpl 10892 2nd Highland Light Infantry KIA 24.3.18.
HOUSTON William MM Pte S/9357 8th Royal Highlanders KIA 12.10.17.
HOVELL Arthur MM L/Cpl 331320 Highland Light Infantry
HOVELL James MM L/Cpl 293052 Royal Highlanders
HOVELLS Henry MM Cpl 66379 3 Bde RHA
HOVERSTADT John MM Cpl 18117 Army Cyclist Corps
HOW Alexander Guthrie MM Pte 242747 1/6th West Yorkshire Regt
HOW Alfred MM Cpl 370 9th Royal Fusiliers
HOW Clarence George MM Bdr 9469 A/72 Bde RFA DOW 1.12.16.
HOW F.W. MM Sjt 27785 9th Essex Regt
HOW Percy MM Pte 16936 1st Bedfordshire Regt
HOW Thomas MM Sjt 700413 1/23rd London Regt

HOW William Charles MM Bdr 715795 RFA
HOW William G. MM Pte 5287 19th London Regt
HOWARD A.O. MM Pte 5296 3 CCS RAMC
HOWARD Albert MM Pte 13625 8th Yorkshire Light Infantry
HOWARD Albert MM Bdsm 10747 2nd Arg & Suth Highlanders
HOWARD Albert MM Sjt 775071 C/310 Bde RFA
HOWARD Albert MM S/Sjt 15351 Royal Engineers
HOWARD Albert John MM Pte 1236 1/1st Essex Yeomanry
HOWARD Alfred Joseph MM Sjt 46208 16 Heavy Bty RGA
HOWARD Alfred T. MM Gnr 61697 226 Siege Bty RGA
HOWARD Archibald Robert MM Sjt 9380 D/72 Bde RFA KIA 23.4.17.
HOWARD Bertie G. MM Sjt 47153 18th Hussars
HOWARD Bertram MM Pte 128228 63rd Bn Machine Gun Corps KIA 2.10.18.
HOWARD Charles MM Pte 42728 Worcestershire Regt
HOWARD Charles Stanley MM Spr 100499 Imperial Sig Coy Royal Engineers
HOWARD Edward MM Gnr 59665 RGA
HOWARD Edward A. MM Cpl 769827 5th London Regt
HOWARD Ernest MM Pte 20/681 Durham Light Infantry
HOWARD Ernest MM Cpl 307737 Lancashire Fusiliers
HOWARD Ernest Henry MM Sjt 300386 2/5th London Regt
HOWARD Ernest S. MM Cpl 8998 1st York & Lancaster Regt
HOWARD Ernest S. MM Dvr 12386 RFA
HOWARD Ernest W. MM Pte 40900 1st Northamptonshire Regt
HOWARD F. MM Gnr 11728 RFA
HOWARD Francis P. MM Pte 142099 62nd Bn Machine Gun Corps
HOWARD Frank MM L/Cpl 13221 16th Lancers
HOWARD Frank MM Cpl 5048 7th East Kent Regt
HOWARD Frank S. MM Cpl 681788 RFA
HOWARD Fred MM Pte 265314 Liverpool Regt
HOWARD Frederick MM Sjt 28361 Durham Light Infantry
HOWARD Frederick J. MM Bdr 75338 24 Bde RFA
HOWARD Frederick Jubilee "MM,MSM" Sjt 33956 RGA
HOWARD George MM Pte 35451 1st East Lancashire Regt
HOWARD George MM Cpl 695 XIII Corps Cyclist Bn Army Cyclist Corps
HOWARD George MM Pte 8209 Devonshire Regt
HOWARD George MM Sjt 1861 1/4th Suffolk Regt KIA 18.8.16.
HOWARD George B. MM CSM 570558 1/17th London Regt
HOWARD George Herbert MM Pte 43283 Essex Regt
HOWARD George James MM Gnr 46032 C/84 Bde RFA
HOWARD George P. MM Dvr 786324 B/312 Bde RFA
HOWARD George William MM Cpl 104515 228 Fd Coy Royal Engineers
HOWARD H.G. MM Sjt 12737 Royal Air Force
HOWARD Harry "MM,MID" Sjt 9088 1st East Kent Regt
HOWARD Harry MM L/Cpl 12490 1st Northamptonshire Regt
HOWARD Harry MM L/Cpl 40340 20th Manchester Regt KIA 9.8.18.
HOWARD James MM L/Cpl 266035 4th Liverpool Regt
HOWARD James MM Cpl 104434 Labour Corps
HOWARD James H. MM Sjt M2/099288 Army Service Corps
HOWARD James R. MM L/Cpl 66981 Machine Gun Corps
HOWARD James S. MM Gnr 67056 4 Bde RFA
HOWARD John MM Dvr L/26296 B/246 Bde RFA
HOWARD John MM Dvr 85215 33 Bty 33 Bde RFA
HOWARD John MM Cpl 45085 RAMC
HOWARD John MM+Bar Sjt 19382 12th Liverpool Regt
HOWARD John MM Sjt 10636 Royal Warwickshire Regt
HOWARD John H. MM Sjt 9299 Royal Scots
HOWARD John Hugh MM Pte 12806 7th` Norfolk Regt
HOWARD Joseph MM L/Cpl 30047 8th Yorkshire Light Infantry
HOWARD Leonard MM Pte 11522 4th Middlesex Regt
HOWARD Leonard MM Pte 1628 1/1st Essex Yeomanry
HOWARD Leonard Alfred MM Pte 201979 Oxf & Bucks Light Infantry
HOWARD Lewis William MM L/Cpl 25982 10th Royal West Kent Regt KIA 23.3.18.
HOWARD Martin William MM Cpl 34105 South Lancashire Regt
HOWARD Norman MM Pte 332783 1/7th Liverpool Regt KIA 20.9.17.
HOWARD P. MM Pte 21805 Essex Regt
HOWARD Percy R. MM Pte 35149 Royal Fusiliers
HOWARD Peter MM Gnr 16006 C/165 Bde RFA
HOWARD Reginald MM Dvr 109998 RFA
HOWARD Reginald W. MM Bdr 66677 5 Bde RFA
HOWARD Robert MM Cpl 43970 10th Essex
HOWARD Robert E. MM Pte 1221 16th Royal Warwickshire Regt
HOWARD Sydney MM Dvr 56157 RFA
HOWARD Sydney George MM Cpl 818 485 Fd Coy Royal Engineers
HOWARD Thomas MM Pte 265780 7th Liverpool Regt
HOWARD Thomas MM Gnr 781229 RFA
HOWARD Thomas M. MM Pte 351400 Manchester Regt
HOWARD Vincent MM Pte 7358 1st Scots Guards
HOWARD Walter John "DCM,MM(7808 1st Devons),MID" Sjt 93825 16th Royal Welsh Fusiliers
HOWARD Wilfred MM Sjt 93841 C/63 Bde RFA KIA 6.5.17.
HOWARD William MM Sjt 7159 1st Cheshire Regt
HOWARD William MM Cpl 11817 North Staffordshire Regt
HOWARD William MM S/Sjt 1168 RAMC
HOWARD William MM+Bar Sjt 20290 Northamptonshire Regt
HOWARD William MM Pte 241683 1/5th Lincolnshire Regt
HOWARD William G. MM L/Cpl 3459 Liverpool Regt
HOWARD William Henry MM Pte 95697 Tank Corps
HOWARD William Morgan MM Sjt 27749 A/51 Bde RFA DOW 25.10.16.
HOWARD William T. MM Sjt 11723 1/9th Liverpool Regt
HOWARD William T. MM Pte 1509 1/8th London Regt
HOWARTH Abraham MM Sjt 39497 56th Bn Machine Gun Corps
HOWARTH Alfred MM Pte 17598 North Lancashire Regt
HOWARTH Alfred E. MM Pte 203097 Dorsetshire Regt
HOWARTH Charles E. MM Sjt 48514 Manchester Regt
HOWARTH Charley MM Cpl 200247 2/5th Lancashire Fusiliers
HOWARTH Daniel MM L/Cpl 14439 7th Duke of Cornwall's LI
HOWARTH David MM Sjt 19921 Welsh Regt
HOWARTH Edward MM Sjt 14249 24th Manchester Regt
HOWARTH Frank MM Sjt 55841 11th Manchester Regt
HOWARTH Frank MM Pte 201687 West Riding Regt
HOWARTH Fred MM Pte 280988 10th Lancashire Fusiliers
HOWARTH George MM L/Cpl 242125 1st East Lancashire Regt
HOWARTH George Adam "MM,MM(F),MID" Sjt 9619 B/102 Bde RFA
HOWARTH George Henry MM Cpl 606 1/5th North Lancashire Regt KIA 20.9.17.
HOWARTH Harry MM Cpl 28249 2nd Lancashire Fusiliers
HOWARTH Henry MM Pte 18/411 West Yorkshire Regt
HOWARTH Henry MM Pte 88173 120 Coy Machine Gun Corps Died 19.9.18.
HOWARTH Herbert MM L/Cpl 201674 2/4th East Lancashire Regt
HOWARTH Horsfield MM Pte 241251 1st Lancashire Fusiliers
HOWARTH J. MM Sjt 18910 Manchester Regt
HOWARTH James MM Sjt 32913 7th Lincolnshire Regt
HOWARTH James "DCM,MM" Sjt 29649 17th Liverpool Regt
HOWARTH James MM Dvr 42391 RFA
HOWARTH Jesse MM Sjt 33072 RAMC
HOWARTH Joseph MM Gnr L/40535 RFA
HOWARTH Joseph MM Gnr 4910 10 Div Ammn Col RFA
HOWARTH Joseph MM Pte 46794 1st Border Regt
HOWARTH Lawrence P. MM Dvr 625303 HAC
HOWARTH Leslie P.D. MM Pte 10462 Coldstream Guards
HOWARTH Robert MM Pte 12688 17th Lancashire Fusiliers
HOWARTH Robert J. MM Cpl 42118 Lancashire Fusiliers
HOWARTH Samuel MM Gnr 74674 D/75 Bde RFA
HOWARTH Thomas MM Pte 15827 18th Lancashire Fusiliers
HOWARTH W. MM Pte 19375 East Lancashire Regt
HOWARTH William MM Spr 51213 106 Fd Coy Royal Engineers
HOWARTH William MM Sjt 305757 1/8th Liverpool Regt
HOWARTH William MM Sjt 25153 13th Liverpool Regt KIA 27.9.18.
HOWARTH William E. MM RSM 29585 11th East Lancashire Regt
HOWARTH William J. MM Cpl 81078 A/256 Bde RFA
HOWARTH Wright MM L/Bdr 710338 RFA
HOWATSON Kenneth MM Pte 331222 2/9th Liverpool Regt att 172 Light TM Bty
HOWCROFT Alfred MM Pte 30499 2nd Grenadier Guards
HOWCROFT Charles Edward MM Sjt 13013 2nd South Wales Borderers KIA 1.7.16.
HOWCROFT Frederick MM Pte 14308 10th Essex Regt
HOWDEN Robert Fairley MM Pte 27205 6th King's Own Scottish Borderers
HOWDEN Stephen Henry MM Bdr 800276 B/230 Bde RFA
HOWDLE William M. MM L/Cpl 45434 Royal Engineers
HOWE Alfred MM Pte 1407 1/8th Middlesex Regt
HOWE Alfred Arthur MM Sjt 9120 1st Royal Lancaster Regt KIA 3.7.16.
HOWE E. MM Pte 497539 2/3rd(Home Counties)Fd Amb RAMC
HOWE Edwin Walter "MM,MID" Sjt S4/060461 Army Service Corps
HOWE Ernest W. MM Pte 241687 5th Royal Warwickshire Regt
HOWE Frank S. MM L/Cpl 72818 7th Royal Fusiliers

HOWE Fred MM Gnr 34585 3 Div Ammn Col RFA
HOWE Frederick MM Pte 39087 Welsh Regt
HOWE Frederick G. MM Pte 1922 1/2nd London Regt
HOWE Frederick John MM Sjt 20965 2nd Border Regt KIA 26.10.17.
HOWE George MM Pte 18998 8th North Staffordshire Regt
HOWE George MM Cpl 36826 West Yorkshire Regt
HOWE George W. MM+Bar Spr 207549 63 Div Sig Coy Royal Engineers
HOWE George W.B. MM Pte 27783 Royal Lancaster Regt
HOWE Harold MM Pte 18646 2nd Royal Irish Regt
HOWE Harry MM Pte M2/034505 Army Service Corps
HOWE Henry MM Sjt 81635 Royal Fusiliers
HOWE Henry Arthur MM Dvr 102921 15 Div Ammn Col RFA
HOWE Herbert MM Dvr T3/024717 8 Div Train Army Service Corps
HOWE Herbert T. MM Cpl 51895 9th Cheshire Regt
HOWE James MM Pte 11791 Duke of Cornwall's LI
HOWE John MM Sjt 22065 17th Royal Scots
HOWE John MM+Bar Sjt 7292 8th Scottish Rifles
HOWE John MM Pte 302310 Manchester Regt
HOWE John W. MM Pte 325604 1/9th Durham Light Infantry
HOWE Joseph MM Sjt 16003 Royal Warwickshire Regt
HOWE Joseph E. MM Pte 91258 9th West Yorkshire Regt
HOWE Joseph Parker MM Cpl 2364 Yorkshire Regt
HOWE Robert "DCM,MM,MSM" CSM 5978 7th Duke of Cornwall's LI
HOWE T. MM Pte 15237 2nd Leinster Regt
HOWE Thomas William MM Pte 37633 2/4th York & Lancaster Regt KIA 2.9.28.
HOWE W. MM Bdr 775207 RFA
HOWE Walter MM Sjt 16418 Welsh Regt
HOWE Wilfred MM Pte 35187 Welsh Regt
HOWE William MM Spr 24182 3 Div Sig Coy Royal Engineers
HOWE William MM Pte 45964 Durham Light Infantry
HOWE William B. MM Pte 7318 Royal West Kent Regt
HOWE William F. MM Sjt 14783 7th Royal West Surrey Regt
HOWE William J. MM Sjt 8800 Royal Munster Fusiliers
HOWELL Albert V. MM Cpl 78881 1st Royal West Surrey Regt
HOWELL Alfred T. MM Cpl 16320 3rd Worcestershire Regt
HOWELL Arthur J. MM Pte 32358 York & Lancaster Regt
HOWELL Douglas Joseph MM Gnr 1479 30 Div Ammn Col RFA
HOWELL Edgar W. MM Sjt 165292 1/1st North Somerset Yeomanry
HOWELL Edward Charles "MM,MSM" Sjt M2/022131 638 Coy Army Service Corps
HOWELL Francis George MM Pte M2/113369 Army Service Corps att HAG RGA
HOWELL Francis J. MM L/Sjt 10996 5th Royal Berkshire Regt
HOWELL Frederick A. MM Cpl 2379 1/17th London Regt
HOWELL Frederick A. MM 2nd Cpl 9198 15 Fd Coy Royal Engineers
HOWELL George MM Sjt 13379 5th North Staffordshire Regt
HOWELL George F. MM Sjt SE/6704 Army Veterinary Corps
HOWELL Harry "DCM,MM,MM(F)" Pte 10683 7th Duke of Cornwall's LI
HOWELL Ivan MM Sjt 390856 1/9th London Regt
HOWELL John Seymour MM Pte 9058 1st Norfolk Regt
HOWELL John W. MM Sjt 17870 3rd Worcestershire Regt
HOWELL John Willie MM Pte 11472 6th Yorkshire Light Infantry DOW 20.5.17.
HOWELL Joseph MM Pte 31310 4th Liverpool Regt
HOWELL Samuel MM L/Cpl M2/166383 406 Coy Army Service Corps
HOWELL Sidney MM Pte F/499 Middlesex Regt
HOWELL Walter G. MM Cpl 59298 RGA
HOWELL William E. MM Bdr 675036 RFA
HOWELL William H. MM Pte 13091 1st Scots Guards
HOWELL William J. MM Cpl 794 26 Fd Amb RAMC
HOWELLS Albert MM L/Cpl 201168 Gloucestershire Regt
HOWELLS Benjamin MM Pte 11244 2nd Royal Welsh Fusiliers
HOWELLS Ebenezer G. MM Pte 36949 RAMC
HOWELLS Edward J. MM L/Cpl 23530 16th Royal Welsh Fusiliers
HOWELLS Frank J. MM L/Sjt 300640 2/5th London Regt
HOWELLS Frederick "MM,MSM" Sjt 22430 5 Siege Bty RGA
HOWELLS Gwilym MM Pte 769811 28th London Regt
HOWELLS Harry MM Spr 18135 106 Fd Coy Royal Engineers
HOWELLS Harry MM Pte 43101 Machine Gun Corps
HOWELLS Henry J. MM Pte 11741 8th Royal Welsh Fusiliers
HOWELLS John "MM,MID" Cpl 7343 16th Manchester Regt
HOWELLS John MM Pte 31131 South Wales Borderers
HOWELLS Joseph H. MM Sjt 22/354 Durham Light Infantry
HOWELLS Leslie "MM,MID" Sjt 203380 1/4th Oxf & Bucks Light Infantry
HOWELLS Thomas MM Dvr 97899 B/71 Bde RFA
HOWELLS Thomas MM Sjt 200685 1/7th Worcestershire Regt
HOWELLS Thomas J. MM Pte 201063 1st South Wales Borderers
HOWELLS W. MM Pte 5950 Royal Warwickshire Regt
HOWELLS William MM Pte 14152 2nd Devonshire Regt
HOWELLS William MM Pte 52605 Cheshire Regt
HOWELLS William J. MM Dvr W/5075 RFA
HOWES Albert Charles MM L/Cpl 231846 1/1st Dorset Yeomanry
HOWES Albert J. MM Cpl 241690 5th Yorkshire Light Infantry
HOWES E.C. MM Pte M2/152282 Army Service Corps
HOWES E.J. "MM,MID" Cpl 85147 34 Div Sig Coy Royal Engineers
HOWES Edward Victor "MM,MID,MM(F)" Staff SM S/18313 Army Service Corps
HOWES George Herbert MM Pte 33043 10th Yorkshire Regt
HOWES Harry Pollard MM Sjt 34873 122 Heavy Bty RGA DOW 2.5.17.
HOWES Henry Austin MM Sjt 9051 1st Leinster Regt
HOWES Henry Edward MM Cpl 7802 Royal West Kent Regt Died 18.1.21
HOWES John C. MM Pte 87885 Liverpool Regt
HOWES Lloyd Carnegie MM Bdr 781230 D/311 Bde RFA DOW 29.9.17.
HOWES R.V. MM Sjt 307698 Royal Warwickshire Regt
HOWES Sidney "DCM,MM" Sjt 282876 409 Siege Bty RGA
HOWES William MM Pte 9668 1st East Lancashire Regt
HOWES William H. MM Cpl 13643 8th Norfolk Regt
HOWES William S. MM Pte 43741 Suffolk Regt
HOWETT Edward G. MM Pte 361619 9th London Regt
HOWEY Andrew MM Cpl 21746 2nd Bn Machine Gun Corps
HOWEY James MM Cpl 337051 RGA
HOWICK Edwin MM Pte 4483 8th Royal West Surrey Regt
HOWIE Alexander MM Pte 9536 1st Gordon Highlanders
HOWIE George MM+Bar Sjt 265568 1/6th Royal Highlanders
HOWIE Henry MM Cpl 203837 1/4th Seaforth Highlanders
HOWIE Oliver "DCM,MM+Bar" CSM 14823 12th Royal Scots
HOWIE Robert Thorburn MM Cp[l 18225 Cameron Highlanders
HOWIE William MM+Bar Pte 18441 Machine Gun Corps
HOWISON James MM Cpl 30289 Scottish Rifles
HOWISON William MM Pte S/12148 Arg & Suth Highlanders
HOWITT Arthur MM Sjt 2938 Gloucestershire Regt
HOWITT Cecil MM L/Sjt 14032 17th Lancashire Fusiliers
HOWITT Jesse MM Pte 27620 Notts & Derby Regt
HOWITT Reginald MM L/Cpl 201354 1st Royal Scots Fusiliers
HOWKER William MM Pte 203551 1/4th West Riding Regt
HOWKINS Francis MM Pte 22732 XVII Corps Cyclist Bn Army Cyclist Corps
HOWKINS Percy William MM Bdr 47217 16 Heavy Bty RGA
HOWLAND Walter MM Pte 4487 West Yorkshire Regt
HOWLDEN C. "DCM,MM" Cpl 44593 21 Div Sig Coy Royal Engineers
HOWLE William H. MM Pte 200537 6th North Staffordshire Regt
HOWLETT Albert MM Pte 9031 2nd Northamptonshire Regt
HOWLETT Claude MM+Bar L/Cpl 9100 Royal West Surrey Regt
HOWLETT George F. MM Sjt 69720 6th Bn Tank Corps
HOWLETT Herbert F. MM+Bar Pte 1059 Royal West Surrey Regt
HOWLETT James MM L/Cpl 13/298 13th East Yorkshire Regt
HOWLETT James J. MM Sjt 5982 2nd Suffolk Regt
HOWLETT John E. MM Pte 13848 6th Northamptonshire Regt
HOWLETT Joseph MM Pte 16581 Suffolk Regt
HOWLETT Percy MM Pte 242522 7th Lincolnshire Regt
HOWLETT Robert William MM Pte 18982 2nd Royal Sussex Regt KIA 23.10.18.
HOWLETT S.E. MM Sjt 15790 8th West Riding Regt
HOWLETT Thomas W. MM Spr 84823 Royal Engineers
HOWLETT Trevelyan Benjamin MM Pte 17591 Suffolk Regt
HOWLEY Albert L. MM Sjt 32014 RFA
HOWLEY Edward MM Pte 15132 2nd Notts & Derby Regt
HOWLEY Edward MM Cpl 52827 A/106 Bde RFA
HOWLEY John MM Dvr T4/252753 Army Service Corps
HOWLEY John MM L/Sjt 19781 12th West Yorkshire Regt
HOWLEY Richard C. MM Cpl 935509 RFA
HOWORTH Frank Hamer MM Cpl M2/223174 Army Service Corps att XIII Corps HAG.KIA 6.10.18.
HOWORTH George Frankton Wix MM Cpl 3138 1/19th London Regt
HOWORTH James MM Pte T4/245899 66 Div Train Army Service Corps
HOWORTH John "DCM,MM" Sjt 31477 1st Northumberland Fusiliers

HOWSAM Wallace MM Dvr 26668 D/150 Bde RFA
HOWSE Charles Conway MM Dvr 825134 43 Bty 24 Bde RFA
HOWSE Herbert J. MM Sjt 200362 1/4th Oxf & Bucks Light Infantry
HOWSE John S. MM L/Cpl 650599 21st London Regt
HOWSE Sidney J. MM Cpl 19617 9th Scottish Rifles
HOWSON A.E. MM+Bar Sjt 41949 RAMC
HOWSON Arthur Balfour MM CSM 2644 Lincolnshire Regt
HOWSON Benjamin MM Dvr 13782 24 Bde RFA
HOWSON Douglas G.F. MM Pte 100151 1/1st Hampshire Yeomanry att HLI.
HOWSON Fred Henry MM Sjt 15655 9th Norfolk Regt DOW 19.9.16.
HOWSON George MM Pte 8621 Royal Fusiliers
HOWSON Joseph MM L/Sjt 15315 24th Manchester Regt
HOWSON O. MM Cpl 16495 10th York & Lancaster Regt
HOWSON Vincent O. MM L/Cpl 20791 Royal Warwickshire Regt
HOY Alexander MM Pte 3557 11th Royal Scots
HOY Archer Frederick MM Cpl 19509 Middlesex Regt
HOY Arthur MM Pte 200200 1/4th Essex Regt
HOY Charles MM Pte 15599 East Surrey Regt
HOY Charles W. MM Dvr 56330 B/110 Bde RFA
HOY Frank MM Sjt 283963 2nd London Regt
HOY Frederick George MM Cpl G/11750 10th Royal West Surrey Regt KIA 22.9.17.
HOY James MM Pte 9384 7th Suffolk Regt KIA 3.7.16.
HOY John Charles MM Pte 10023 151 Coy Machine Gun Corps
HOY Jonathan Reginald "MM,MM(F)" Cpl 65160 107 Fd Coy Royal Engineers
HOY Robert F. MM L/Cpl 2778 1/5th Liverpool Regt
HOY Walter MM Pte 18/782 12th Royal Irish Rifles
HOY William Henry MM Spr 62387 16 Div Sig Coy Royal Engineers
HOYE Charles R. MM Dvr 316614 8 Div Sig Coy Royal Engineers
HOYE Walter C. MM Sjt 58239 50th Bn Machine Gun Corps
HOYES Ernest MM L/Cpl 201840 2/4th Lincolnshire Regt
HOYES Francis Arthur MM Pte 40750 8th North Staffordshire Regt KIA 6.6.18.
HOYLAND John MM Spr 3373 1/2(West Riding)Fd Coy Royal Engineers
HOYLAND Lawrence MM Pte 405079 3(West Riding)Fd Amb RAMC
HOYLE Charles MM Pte 13906 4th Coldstream Guards
HOYLE Ernest MM Cpl 241886 Lancashire Fusiliers
HOYLE Ernest H. MM Sjt 200877 4th West Riding Regt
HOYLE Ernest W. MM L/Cpl 5310 8th Royal West Kent Regt
HOYLE John MM Pte 10/19716 10th Northumberland Fusiliers KIA 31.8.16.
HOYLE Joseph MM Pte 12581 Liverpool Regt
HOYLE M. MM Pte 305946 West Riding Regt
HOYLE R.A. MM Sjt 2869 2/5th Lancashire Fusiliers
HOYLE Thomas Robinson MM Pte 357034 1/10th Liverpool Regt
HOYLE W. MM Dvr 100867 RFA
HOYLE William MM+Bar L/Cpl 13615 10th West Riding Regt
HOYLE William H. MM Sjt 345498 16th Devonshire Regt
HOYLES Frank MM Gnr Fitter 697301 32 Bde RFA
HOYLES Frank MM Pte 13180 6th Northamptonshire Regt KIA 17.2.17.
HOYLES George Alfred Helleur MM Cpl 29984 2nd Hampshire Regt
HOYLES William MM Cpl S/3237 13th Rifle Brigade
HUBBALL George MM Cpl 202138 Cheshire Regt
HUBBALL Joseph MM Gnr 26920 D/87 Bde RFA
HUBBALL W.F. MM Cpl 40134 Worcestershire Regt
HUBBARD Albert D. MM Pte R3787 King's Royal Rifle Corps
HUBBARD Bertie MM Pte 18666 Leicestershire Regt
HUBBARD Charles MM L/Sjt 24562 Duke of Cornwall's LI
HUBBARD Charles MM Sjt 59816 8th West Yorkshire Regt
HUBBARD Charles F. MM L/Cpl 86115 Machine Gun Corps
HUBBARD Ernest MM Pte 8423 2nd Leicestershire Regt
HUBBARD George MM Cpl 571279 1/17th London Regt
HUBBARD H. MM Sjt 534233 RAMC
HUBBARD Harold MM Pte 32703 13th East Lancashire Regt Died 25.12.18.
HUBBARD James W. MM Sjt 14217 2nd Grenadier Guards
HUBBARD John MM Pte 1797 GMGR
HUBBARD John Willie MM Pte 422420 2/10th London Regt DOW 25.6.18.
HUBBARD Jonathan MM Pte 40247 1st Royal Dublin Fusiliers
HUBBARD Oscar J. MM Pte 593029 18th London Regt
HUBBARD Percy William MM Pte 2094 7th Royal Fusiliers KIA 6.6.18
HUBBARD Sidney MM Pte G/61710 17th Royal Fusiliers
HUBBARD Sidney "DCM,MM" Sjt 6616 61st Bn Machine Gun Corps

HUBBARD Thomas MM Bdr 200911 A(AA)Bty RGA
HUBBARD Thomas MM Sjt 5201 18th Lancashire Fusiliers
HUBBARD William MM Gnr 12838 42 Bde RFA
HUBBARD William MM Sjt 141742 RGA
HUBBARD William MM Bdr 58089 39 Bde RFA
HUBBARD William Henry "DCM,MM" Pte 19394 Machine Gun Corps
HUBBARDE Harold O. MM Sjt 14114 11th Welsh Regt
HUBBERSTEY Robert MM Sjt 1659 7th East Kent Regt
HUBBERT Henry J. MM Pte 200568 1st London Regt
HUBBLE Fred MM+Bar L/Cpl 1562 7th Royal West Kent Regt
HUBBLE Thomas Harry MM Sjt 3471 174 Bde RFA KIA 25.5.18.
HUBBLE Walter MM S/Sjt SS/1553 HQ ASC 7 Cav Bde Army Service Corps
HUBBLE Walter G. MM Pte 1590 20th London Regt
HUBBOCK Ernest MM Pte 201499 Royal Berkshire Regt
HUBLING John Alfred MM Pte 30904 RAMC
HUBY Albert MM CQMS 7936 2nd West Yorkshire Regt
HUCKER Frederick W. MM Pte 30815 Lancashire Fusiliers
HUCKER Victor W. MM Spr 499935 61 Div Sig Coy Royal Engineers
HUCKER Wilfred Thomas MM L/Cpl 3/6836 6th Somerset Light Infantry
HUCKERBY Frederick MM Cpl 240349 1/6th Notts & Derby Regt
HUCKERBY Henry MM Sjt 13015 9th Notts & Derby Regt
HUCKERBY James MM Pte C/7299 King's Royal Rifle Corps
HUCKERBY William H. MM Cpl H/285435 1/1st Oxfordshire Yeomanry
HUCKFIELD C.T. "DCM,MM" Sjt 44 Royal Warwickshire Regt
HUCKINS James H. MM Sjt 6395 1st Duke of Cornwall's LI
HUCKLESBY Charles W. MM L/Cpl 606 3rd Middlesex Regt
HUCKSON William F. MM Gnr 102038 RGA
HUCKSTEP George MM Dvr 805555 C/231 Bde RFA
HUCKSTEP William Herbert MM L/Cpl G/2810 7th East Kent Regt KIA 13.10.17.
HUCKSTEPP Arthur R. MM Pte 4061 21st London Regt
HUCKVALE Charles F. MM L/Cpl 26988 Royal Engineers
HUDD Albert A. MM Cpl 263156 Worcestershire Regt
HUDD John MM Pte 4643 2/4th Gloucestershire Regt
HUDD Walter MM Pte 439506 RAMC
HUDDART Solomon MM L/Cpl 14774 8th Border Regt
HUDDISON A.E. MM Pte 40872 Northamptonshire Regt
HUDDLESTONE Thomas William MM+Bar Sjt 240154 1/5th Lincolnshire Regt
HUDDY William MM Pte 201410 Duke of Cornwall's LI
HUDGELL John MM L/Sjt 11926 2nd Coldstream Guards
HUDGHTON Frederick MM Cpl 65109 106 Fd Coy Royal Engineers
HUDSON Alfred MM Pte 45772 15th Cheshire Regt KIA 29.9.18.
HUDSON Alfred MM Pte 11346 1/4th Oxf & Bucks Light Infantry
HUDSON Arthur MM Sjt 37009 Royal West Surrey Regt
HUDSON Arthur Charles MM Pte 203313 7th East Surrey Regt
HUDSON Benjamin MM Sjt 39965 13th York & Lancaster Regt
HUDSON Charles MM Cpl 40526 2nd South Wales Borderers KIA 11.4.18.
HUDSON Charles A. MM Pte 14233 9th West Riding Regt
HUDSON Charles E. MM L/Cpl M/298926 402 Coy Army Service Corps
HUDSON Charles H. MM Cpl 12366 Machine Gun Corps
HUDSON David C. MM Cpl 36404 Yorkshire Light Infantry
HUDSON Edward MM+Bar Pte 16267 11th Northumberland Fusiliers
HUDSON Edward G. "DCM,MM+Bar" Cpl G/63292 11th Royal Fusiliers
HUDSON Ernest MM L/Cpl 63786 Royal Engineers
HUDSON Ernest Archibald MM Pte 242239 Hampshire Regt
HUDSON Ernest W. "MM,MID" Pnr 130005 Royal Engineers
HUDSON Ernest William MM Pte 2598 7th East Kent Regt
HUDSON F.E. MM Cpl 2040 Royal Warwickshire Regt
HUDSON Frank MM Sjt 200499 2/5th Lancashire Fusiliers KIA 31.7.17.
HUDSON George MM L/Sjt 201704 1/4th York & Lancaster Regt KIA 26.4.18.
HUDSON George MM Pte 14804 24th Manchester Regt
HUDSON George "MM,MID" Sjt 1008 1/1st Lothian & Border Horse Yeo
HUDSON George MM L/Cpl 266402 6th Gloucestershire Regt
HUDSON George Edward MM Sjt 9809 1st Cheshire Regt
HUDSON Gordon R. MM Pte 12/50104 Royal Irish Rifles
HUDSON Harold MM Cpl 201906 4th York & Lancaster Regt
HUDSON Harold "MM,MID" Pte 7991 2nd Durham Light Infantry

HUDSON Harry MM Pte 16312 6th Leicestershire Regt KIA 25.8.18.
HUDSON Harry E. MM L/Cpl R/4236 13th King's Royal Rifle Corps
HUDSON Harry R. MM Pte 115974 1/1st County of London Yeomanry
HUDSON Henry MM L/Bdr 211450 B/45 Bde RFA
HUDSON Henry T. MM L/Cpl 558411 Royal Engineers
HUDSON Herbert MM Gnr 608277 C/223 Bde RFA
HUDSON Herbert MM Gnr 312208 RGA
HUDSON Herbert W. MM Bdr 876494 D/282 Bde RFA
HUDSON James MM Pte 25217 35th Bn Machine Gun Corps
HUDSON James MM Gnr 9059 RFA
HUDSON James MM Pte 41201 Essex Regt
HUDSON James MM Dvr 20047 C/92 Bde RFA
HUDSON James A. MM L/Cpl 240153 Lancashire Fusiliers
HUDSON James W. MM Sjt 37574 8th Northumberland Fusiliers
HUDSON John MM Sjt 3259 RFA
HUDSON John "MM,MSM" Sjt 19552 13th Liverpool Regt
HUDSON John MM L/Bdr 70343 B/83 Bde RFA
HUDSON John MM L/Cpl 325832 1/9th Durham Light Infantry
HUDSON John W. MM Pte 204672 9th West Riding Regt
HUDSON John W. MM Dvr 82485 RFA
HUDSON Jonas MM Sjt 240750 5th Royal Lancaster Regt
HUDSON Joseph MM Pte 30077 1st Duke of Cornwall's LI
HUDSON L. MM L/Cpl P/2198 Military Foot Police
HUDSON Leonard J. MM Pte 7615 5th Dragoon Guards
HUDSON Lionel MM Pte 25834 21st Manchester Regt
HUDSON Matthew Henry MM Pte 56111 1st Northumberland Fusiliers
HUDSON Matthias MM Sjt 51010 Royal Engineers
HUDSON Oliver MM Pte 104934 139 Fd Amb RAMC
HUDSON Percival MM Sjt 501291 Inland Water Transport Div Royal Engineers
HUDSON Robert MM Sjt 81987 D/148 Bde RFA
HUDSON Robert MM Cpl 40591 14th Arg & Suth Highlanders
HUDSON Roland H. MM Pte 33421 2nd Yorkshire Regt
HUDSON S. MM Pte 203335 South Staffordshire Regt
HUDSON Thomas MM Dvr 7792 34 Div Ammn Col RFA KIA 20.8.18.
HUDSON Thomas H. MM L/Cpl 21089 1st King's Own Scottish Borderers
HUDSON Tom MM Cpl 200463 5th West Yorkshire Regt
HUDSON Vivien Walter MM Sjt 9461 1st Shropshire Light Infantry
HUDSON Walter MM Pte 201299 1/7th Worcestershire Regt
HUDSON Walter James MM Pte 33047 1/5th Yorkshire Regt
HUDSON William MM L/Cpl 306068 2/8th West Yorkshire Regt KIA 19.1.18.
HUDSON William MM Pte 32821 Oxf & Bucks Light Infantry
HUDSON William MM Cpl 46595 Machine Gun Corps
HUDSON William MM Sjt 68117 37 Bde RFA
HUDSON William A. MM Sjt 459382 Royal Engineers
HUDSON William D. MM Sjt 10800 1st Royal Lancaster Regt
HUDSON William F. MM Gnr 810310 RFA
HUDSON William G. MM Cpl 16793 12th Gloucestershire Regt
HUDSON William H.B. MM Cpl 240967 5th Devonshire Regt
HUDSPETH Albert MM Pte 388367 2 Fd Amb RAMC
HUDSPETH Arthur MM Pte 15902 Northumberland Fusiliers att MGC
HUDSPITH J. MM Pte 241910 Northumberland Fusiliers
HUETT Sidney J. MM Bdr 122291 RFA
HUFFER Charles MM Pte 17355 2nd Grenadier Guards DOW 3.12.17.
HUFTON John Thomas MM Sjt 41415 21 Div Sig Coy Royal Engineers KIA 22.3.18.
HUGALL Albert Ernest MM Pte 45009 13th Royal Welsh Fusiliers KIA 22.4.18.
HUGGET Charles F. MM Gnr 119447 260 Siege Bty RGA
HUGGETT George E. MM Pte 8001 2nd Yorkshire Light Infantry
HUGGETT James MM L/Cpl 38154 RAMC
HUGGINS Arthur MM Sjt 11404 RGA
HUGGINS Arthur MM Pte 26093 7th Yorkshire Light Infantry KIA 30.11.17.
HUGGINS Edgar MM Sjt 2005 1/5th Durham Light Infantry
HUGGINS Jesse A. MM L/Cpl 6986 1st Norfolk Regt
HUGGINS John W. MM Sjt 201012 West Yorkshire Regt
HUGGINS Percy MM Pte 354224 7th London Regt DOW 31.8.18.
HUGGINS Thomas G. MM+Bar Sjt 8209 1st Royal Berkshire Regt
HUGGINS Thomas W. MM Pte 13069 Seaforth Highlanders
HUGGINS Wallace F. MM Spr 494639 Royal Engineers
HUGGON Thomas MM Cpl 20499 8th Royal Lancaster Regt DOW 25.3.18.

HUGGONSON William MM Cpl 51969 Liverpool Regt
HUGHAN William MM Pte 23069 1st Royal Scots Fusiliers
HUGHES A. MM+Bar Sjt 478483 459 Fd Coy Royal Engineers
HUGHES Albert MM Pte G/336 6th East Kent Regt DOW 4.8.16.
HUGHES Albert MM Sjt 35455 C/108 Bde RFA DOW 6.10.17.
HUGHES Albert MM Sjt 16/1156 16th Royal Warwickshire Regt KIA 6.10.17.
HUGHES Albert E. MM Pte 45641 15th Hampshire Regt
HUGHES Albert V. MM Pte 16/339 16th Royal Warwickshire Regt
HUGHES Alec Victor MM Gnr 169526 244 Siege Bty RGA
HUGHES Alfred MM Pte M2/175029 Army Service Corps
HUGHES Alfred H. "DCM,MM,MID" CSM 31 1st Manchester Regt
HUGHES Alfred J. MM Gnr Sig 138938 280 Siege Bty RGA
HUGHES Alfred W. MM Pte S/4537 13th Rifle Brigade
HUGHES Arthur MM Pte 41012 Northumberland Fusiliers
HUGHES Arthur MM Cpl 22419 Liverpool Regt
HUGHES Arthur MM Sjt 345157 24th Royal Welsh Fusiliers
HUGHES Arthur MM Bdr 695213 RFA
HUGHES Arthur MM Dvr 705274 RFA
HUGHES B. MM L/Cpl 267413 7th Liverpool Regt
HUGHES Bernard MM Pte 73466 152 Coy Machine Gun Corps
HUGHES Charles MM Gnr 78303 Tank Corps
HUGHES Charles MM L/Cpl 247894 Royal Engineers
HUGHES Charles A. MM Pte 10969 5th Shropshire Light Infantry
HUGHES Charles E. MM CSM 7719 2nd Hampshire Regt
HUGHES Charles G. MM Pte 271040 East Kent Regt
HUGHES Charles J. MM Pte 12/17902 12th Royal Irish Rifles
HUGHES Clement Graham MM 2nd Cpl 549958 Royal Engineers
HUGHES Cornelius B. MM Sjt 20014 South Wales Borderers
HUGHES Daniel MM Gnr 23662 9 Siege Bty RGA
HUGHES Daniel MM L/Cpl R/946 10th King's Royal Rifle Corps DOW 30.11.17.
HUGHES Daniel Herbert MM L/Cpl 9102 21st Royal Fusiliers
HUGHES David MM L/Cpl S/3907 11th Arg & Suth Highlanders
HUGHES David MM+Bar Pte 200408 9th Royal Welsh Fusiliers DOW 24.10.18.
HUGHES David MM Sjt 25394 Royal Welsh Fusiliers
HUGHES David MM Pte 15081 10th Royal Welsh Fusiliers
HUGHES David MM Gnr 46867 321 Siege Bty RGA KIA 8.8.17.
HUGHES David Henry "DCM,MM+Bar" Cpl 40733 12th Middlesex Regt KIA 9.4.18.
HUGHES David Hugh MM Cpl 21246 13th Royal Welsh Fusiliers KIA 22.4.18.
HUGHES David J. MM Pte 42772 Worcestershire Regt
HUGHES David Lewis MM Dvr 745274 26 Bty 17 Bde RFA DOW 29.10.18.
HUGHES E. MM Pte 200828 Liverpool Regt
HUGHES Edgar MM Cpl 12907 4th Royal Fusiliers KIA 20.11.17.
HUGHES Edgar R. MM Sjt 300449 1/5th London Regt
HUGHES Edward MM L/Cpl 15609 8th Royal Berkshire Regt KIA 1.3.18.
HUGHES Edward MM Cpl 17974 2nd Border Regt
HUGHES Edward MM Spr 55824 113 Railway Coy Royal Engineers
HUGHES Edward John "MC,MM(17266 Sjt)" 2Lt Liverpool Regt KIA 20.10.18.
HUGHES Edward John Terrance MM Sjt 32302 124 Bty 28 Bde RFA DOW 28.9.17.
HUGHES Edward P. MM Pte 308541 Liverpool Regt
HUGHES Elias P. MM Pte 25346 17th Royal Welsh Fusiliers
HUGHES Ellis B. MM Pte 48887 10th Lancashire Fusiliers
HUGHES Ellis Wynne MM Pte 290509 14th Royal Welsh Fusiliers
HUGHES Ernest F. "MM+Bar,MID" Sjt 530777 1/15th London Regt
HUGHES Ernest M. MM Sjt 610304 1/19th London Regt
HUGHES Evan MM Pte 7675 15 Fd Amb RAMC
HUGHES F. MM Pte 5845 2nd Royal Sussex Regt
HUGHES Frank MM Pte 241818 1/8th Worcestershire Regt KIA 5.10.18.
HUGHES Frank MM Sjt 32869 7 Div Sig Coy Royal Engineers
HUGHES Frank MM Dvr 78096 RFA
HUGHES Frank MM Gnr 30427 37 Bde RFA
HUGHES Frank MM Pte 16489 2nd Grenadier Guards
HUGHES Frank G. MM+Bar Pte 82476 11th Royal Fusiliers
HUGHES Fred MM L/Cpl 9663 2nd Seaforth Highlanders DOW 14.10.16.
HUGHES Frederick MM L/Cpl 8541 3rd Coldstream Guards
HUGHES Frederick T. MM L/Sjt 698047 22nd London Regt
HUGHES G. MM Gnr 85288 RGA
HUGHES George MM Pte 12/163 12th Yorkshire Light Infantry
HUGHES George MM Sjt L/18191 A/104 Bde RFA KIA 29.7.17.
HUGHES George MM Bde 112552 B/186 Bde RFA

HUGHES George MM L/Cpl 130754 Royal Engineers
HUGHES George MM Spr 139536 212 Fd Coy Royal Engineers
HUGHES George MM Pte 18233 9th Yorkshire Regt DOW 20.9.17.
HUGHES George E. MM Sjt 34680 RAMC
HUGHES George K. MM Bdr 37210 RGA
HUGHES George Reginald MM Cpl 11348 16th Lancashire Fusiliers
HUGHES George Richard MM Sjt A/782 8th King's Royal Rifle Corps
HUGHES George W. MM Cpl Y/530 13th King's Royal Rifle Corps
HUGHES George W. MM Sjt M2/081106 Army Service Corps
HUGHES Gerald Golding MM Sjt 12683 7th Norfolk Regt
HUGHES Gilbert Alfred MM L/Cpl 49694 2nd Bedfordshire Regt
HUGHES Harold MM L/Cpl 200156 1/5th South Staffordshire Regt
HUGHES Harry MM Sjt 94416 170 Tunnelling Coy Royal Engineers
HUGHES Harry MM L/Cpl 99690 200 Fd Coy Royal Engineers
HUGHES Harry MM Sjt 681410 D/232 Bde RFA
HUGHES Harry MM Sjt 24515 11th Cheshire Regt
HUGHES Harry MM Pte 13037 7th East Lancashire Regt
HUGHES Henry MM Pte 16966 Lincolnshire Regt
HUGHES Henry Edward MM Cpl 56188 18 Div Sig Coy Royal Engineers
HUGHES Henry William MM Sjt 7985 2nd Border Regt KIA 20.10.17.
HUGHES Herbert MM L/Cpl 127944 Royal Engineers
HUGHES Howard MM Pte 57033 RAMC
HUGHES Hugh MM Pte 39978 14th Royal Welsh Fusiliers
HUGHES Hugh MM Dvr 76506 RFA
HUGHES Idris R. MM Cpl B/19692 26th Royal Fusiliers
HUGHES J. MM Bdr L/19391 RFA
HUGHES J.H. MM Gnr 1456 B/240 RFA
HUGHES J.I. MM L/Cpl G/21034 Royal West Kent Regt
HUGHES James MM Cpl 345115 24th Royal Welsh Fusiliers
HUGHES James MM L/Cpl 15497 Liverpool Regt
HUGHES James MM Sjt 26040 Welsh Regt
HUGHES James MM Pte 43131 RAMC
HUGHES James MM Sjt 70727 26 Bde RFA
HUGHES James MM Pte 4614 Royal Welsh Fusiliers
HUGHES James "DCM,MM" Sjt 4517 9th Royal Irish Fusiliers KIA 29.3.18.
HUGHES James MM Sjt 8123 8th Royal Lancaster Regt
HUGHES James MM Sjt 2352 1st Lancashire Fusiliers
HUGHES James MM Pte 18191 9th Scottish Rifles
HUGHES James MM Pte 7915 22 Fd Amb RAMC
HUGHES James MM L/Cpl 57587 Liverpool Regt
HUGHES James MM Pte 2727 6th Connaught Rangers KIA 21.3.18.
HUGHES James Albert MM Cpl 14924 12th Liverpool Regt
HUGHES James Henry MM Cpl 74081 B/70 Bde RFA DOW 21.9.16.
HUGHES John MM+Bar L/Cpl 21822 5th South Wales Borderers
HUGHES John MM Pte 265458 Royal Welsh Fusiliers
HUGHES John MM Pte 34142 13th Welsh Regt
HUGHES John MM Pte 43144 16th Highland Light Infantry
HUGHES John MM Dvr 83466 219 Fd Coy Royal Engineers
HUGHES John MM L/Cpl 43686 16th Royal Welsh Fusiliers
HUGHES John MM Sjt 240170 South Lancashire Regt
HUGHES John MM Pte Z/2354 13th Rifle Brigade
HUGHES John MM Sjt 21346 South Wales Borderers
HUGHES John "DCM,MM" L/Cpl 11590 16th Royal Welsh Fusiliers
HUGHES John MM Sjt 19062 Durham Light Infantry
HUGHES John MM Wheeler QMS 64196 18 Bde RFA
HUGHES John MM Dvr 6620 RFA
HUGHES John MM Pte 265591 17th Royal Welsh Fusiliers KIA 31.8.18.
HUGHES John MM Sjt 995 2nd South Lancashire Regt Died 27.5.18.
HUGHES John MM Cpl 5949 Connaught Rangers
HUGHES John E. "MM,MSM" S/Sjt Fitter 58074 130 Heavy Bty RGA
HUGHES John F. MM Pte 28902 Royal Inniskilling Fusiliers
HUGHES John H. MM Sjt 6889 Middlesex Regt
HUGHES John H. MM+Bar L/Cpl 307924 8th Liverpool Regt
HUGHES John Henry MM Pte 56668 55 Fd Amb RAMC DOW 9.11.17.
HUGHES John J. MM Cpl 25592 4th South Wales Borderers
HUGHES John P. MM Bdr 100874 'R'(AA)Bty RGA
HUGHES John S. MM Pte 8010 6th Dragoon Guards
HUGHES Joseph MM Pte 48522 2nd Welsh Regt
HUGHES Joseph E. MM Cpl 240168 1/5th South Lancashire Regt
HUGHES Joseph Edward MM Cpl 52057 D/126 Bde RFA Died 2.12.18.
HUGHES Joseph H. MM CSM 2561 24th Royal Fusiliers
HUGHES Joseph Patrick MM Pte 13377 Yorkshire Regt
HUGHES Leonard MM Sjt 14890 12th Gloucestershire Regt
HUGHES Leonard A. MM Pte 21141 1st Grenadier Guards
HUGHES Llewellyn C. MM Pte 42084 RAMC
HUGHES Llewellyn S. MM Pte 90263 8th Bn Machine Gun Corps
HUGHES Louis MM Cpl 446316 439 Fd Coy Royal Engineers
HUGHES Matthew MM Sjt 240699 5th Royal Lancaster Regt
HUGHES Norman Walter MM Sjt 41538 17th Middlesex Regt KIA 3.1.18.
HUGHES Owen MM L/Cpl 26/959 Northumberland Fusiliers
HUGHES Patrick MM L/Cpl 6052 1/6th Seaforth Highlanders DOW 24.11.17.
HUGHES Patrick "DCM,MM" Bdr 52006 29 Bty 42 Bde RFA KIA 1.11.16.
HUGHES Percy MM Pte 240206 1/5th Somerset Light Infantry
HUGHES Percy MM Pte 15901 13th Royal Welsh Fusiliers
HUGHES R. MM Pte 30004 Scottish Rifles
HUGHES R.J. MM Bdr 52984 RFA
HUGHES Richard MM Pte 102190 Labour Corps
HUGHES Richard John William MM Pte 136833 9th Bn Machine Gun Corps DOW 9.10.18.
HUGHES Richard T. MM Pte 29129 7th Shropshire Light Infantry
HUGHES Robert MM Sjt 375387 Manchester Regt
HUGHES Robert E. MM Pte 13248 Coldstream Guards
HUGHES Robert J. MM L/Cpl 55362 2nd Welsh Regt
HUGHES Samuel MM L/Cpl 6934 25th Bn Machine Gun Corps KIA 9.10.18.
HUGHES Samuel Gordon MM Gnr 326347 2/2(Clyde)Coy RGA
HUGHES Sidney "MM,MID" Sjt 21951 Royal Engineers
HUGHES Stanley MM Spr 452186 Royal Engineers
HUGHES Sydney J.P. MM Cpl 24568 7th Royal West Surrey Regt
HUGHES T. MM Pte 201385 North Lancashire Regt
HUGHES T.C. MM Gnr 1297 RFA
HUGHES T.W. MM L/Sjt 16917 1st Grenadier Guards
HUGHES Thomas "MM,CG(B)" Cpl 345225 24th Royal Welsh Fusiliers
HUGHES Thomas MM Dvr 72587 43 Bde RFA
HUGHES Thomas MM Sjt 240109 Royal Welsh Fusiliers
HUGHES Thomas "DCM,MM" Pte 9836 2nd Royal Welsh Fusiliers KIA 23.4.17.
HUGHES Thomas MM Pte 74520 RAMC
HUGHES Thomas MM Pte 17290 9th South Lancashire Regt
HUGHES Thomas MM Bdr 685980 RFA
HUGHES Thomas MM Spr 120905 250 Tunnelling Coy Royal Engineers
HUGHES Thomas MM Pte 332581 9th Liverpool Regt
HUGHES Thomas E. MM Pte 292438 1st Gordon Highlanders
HUGHES Thomas Harry MM Pte 21672 2nd Coldstream Guards
HUGHES Thomas J. MM Pte 39232 Royal Welsh Fusiliers
HUGHES Tom A. MM Sjt 273 1st Welsh Guards
HUGHES W. MM Pnr WR/23681 319 Rly Const Coy Royal Engineers
HUGHES William MM Sjt 52 16th Royal Irish Rifles
HUGHES William MM L/Cpl 26774 Royal Inniskilling Fusiliers
HUGHES William MM Pte 11246 6th Shropshire Light Infantry
HUGHES William MM Gnr 181794 355 Siege Bty RGA
HUGHES William MM Cpl 1081 2nd Durham Light Infantry
HUGHES William MM Pte 42123 South Lancashire Regt
HUGHES William MM Sjt 511865 14th London Regt
HUGHES William MM Pte 22223 Welsh Regt
HUGHES William MM Pte 14309 13th Liverpool Regt
HUGHES William MM Pte 9/14379 9th East Lancashire Regt
HUGHES William MM L/Sjt 240175 1/4th South Lancashire Regt KIA 20.9.17.
HUGHES William E. MM Cpl 290031 14th Royal Welsh Fusiliers
HUGHES William H. MM Sjt 11384 16th Lancashire Fusiliers
HUGHES William H. MM Gnr 76548 RGA
HUGHES William J. MM Cpl 17635 16th Royal Welsh Fusiliers
HUGHES William J. MM Gnr 6004 RFA
HUGHES William James "MM,MID" Sjt 12371 11th Hampshire Regt
HUGHES William R. MM 2nd Cpl 248552 Signal Service Royal Engineers
HUGHES William R. MM Bdr 139280 RGA
HUGHES William Robert MM L/Cpl 9655 10th Cheshire Regt KIA 3.5.18.
HUGHES William V. MM Pte 37216 RAMC
HUGHESDON Reginald "DCM,MM" L/Cpl 4208 1/1st HAC(Inf)
HUGHESTON Peter MM Pte 9525 2nd Royal Irish Rifles
HUGHSON W. MM+Bar L/Cpl 2925 1/6th Royal Highlanders

HUGILL James MM L/Cpl 1889 Royal Horse Guards
HUGILL John MM Pte 1969 1/4th Yorkshire Regt
HUGO Ernest R. MM L/Cpl 69954 Tank Corps
HUIE James W. MM Pte 201493 Durham Light Infantry
HUIE Robert MM Pte 44316 165 Coy Machine Gun Corps
HUISH Arthur J. MM Sjt 205655 1st Wiltshire Regt
HUISH George W. MM Spr 246796 Royal Engineers
HUKINS Harold MM Pte M2/194877 Army Service Corps
HULAN John MM Pte 33071 1/5th Royal Warwickshire Regt
HULATT Edgar T. MM Pte 40430 6th Northamptonshire Regt
HULBERT Adolphus MM Spr 144932 251 Tunneling Coy Royal Engineers
HULBERT Edward J. MM Pte M2/098079 Army Service Corps att RAMC
HULBERT Frederick C. MM L/Cpl 33088 Border Regt
HULBERT Octavius MM Cpl 20847 South Wales Borderers
HULBERT Stanley MM L/Cpl 12944 16th Manchester Regt
HULBERT William MM Pte 21530 6th Duke of Cornwall's LI KIA 22.8.17.
HULETT Frederick W.J. MM Cpl 5521 Machine Gun Corps
HULFORD Douglas MM Pte STK/441 10th Royal Fusiliers
HULFORD Harry "DCM,MM,MID" Sjt 8576 Royal West Kent Regt
HULIN William John Lambert MM Gnr 291108 127 Heavy Bty RGA
HULKS Frederick Alfred MM Pte 290807 2nd Devonshire Regt
HULL Albert E. MM L/Cpl 2226 11th Royal Irish Rifles
HULL Albert Victor MM Spr 48026 Guards Div Sig Coy Royal Engineers
HULL Alfred J. MM Sjt 363008 7(Cav)Fd Amb RAMC
HULL Cyril B. MM Sjt 530704 15th London Regt
HULL Edward MM Pte 7177 Northumberland Fusiliers
HULL Erneat E. MM L/Cpl 23421 14th Royal Warwickshire Regt
HULL Ernest "MM,MID" Bdr 40279 RGA
HULL Frederick MM Pte 154623 14th Bn Machine Gun Corps
HULL George MM Pte 4445 10th Lancashire Fusiliers
HULL George H. MM Spr 49534 Royal Engineers
HULL H. MM Cpl 200378 Northamptonshire Regt
HULL Harold MM Pte 15790 10th Worcestershire Regt
HULL Harold E. MM Cpl 9380 1st East Yorkshire Regt
HULL Henry C. MM Sjt L/16166 1st Middlesex Regt
HULL Herbert MM+Bar Bdr 610310 RHA
HULL James E. MM L/Cpl 540478 15th London Regt
HULL John A. MM Pte 201932 North Lancashire Regt
HULL Joseph Arthur MM Pte 25594 1st South Wales Borderers KIA 4.6.18.
HULL Laurence MM Gnr 157674 C/223 Bde RFA
HULL Marshall W. MM+Bar L/Cpl 11935 Leicestershire Regt
HULL Richard MM Pte 331089 1/9th Liverpool Regt
HULL Thomas MM Cpl 46433 Northumberland Fusiliers
HULL Thomas MM Gnr 16655 D/48 Bde RFA
HULL Thomas MM Pte 266376 7th Liverpool Regt
HULL Thomas MM Spr 143347 Royal Engineers
HULL Thomas MM Pte 72852 Machine Gun Corps
HULL Walter MM Sjt 11445 6th Yorkshire Light Infantry
HULL William "MM,MSM,MIDx2" S/Sjt S/26825 1 Div Train Army Service Corps
HULL William MM Pte 9736 2nd South Lancashire Regt
HULLAH Irvin MM+Bar Sjt 62495 C/107 Bde RFA KIA 4.4.18.
HULLAH John T. MM Gnr 165811 C/235 Bde RFA
HULLAND Herbert G. MM Sjt 25488 Worcestershire Regt
HULLAND Reginald P. MM Cpl 2173 1/6th London Regt
HULLER John W. MM L/Cpl 28109 9th Yorkshire Regt
HULLEY Francis MM Cpl 202655 4th York & Lancaster Regt
HULLEY Frank MM Pte 290948 1/7th Cheshire Regt
HULLEY George Wiiiliam MM Pte 8981 2nd Lancashire Fusiliers DOW 30.6.17.
HULLOTT Frank MM CSM 7/5882 7th Lincolnshire Regt
HULME Benjamin "DCM,MM" Sjt 440220 431 Fd Coy Royal Engineers
HULME Bertram MM Pte 19281 11th Notts & Derby Regt
HULME James MM Sjt 8641 17th Manchester Regt
HULME James F. MM Spr 311520 XIII Corps Sig Coy Royal Engineers
HULME John "MM,MID" Sjt 3470 2nd South Lancashire Regt
HULME Joseph MM L/Cpl W/1036 13th Cheshire Regt
HULME Percy MM Gnr 49546 RGA
HULME Peter "MM,MID" RSM 240338 1/6th Royal Warwickshire Regt
HULME R. MM Pte 307277 Royal Warwickshire Regt
HULME Samuel MM Pte 376609 1/10th Manchester Regt
HULME Stanley H. MM Bdr 845256 RFA
HULME Thomas MM Pte 15532 8th Royal Lancaster Regt
HULME William MM Pte 26780 21st Manchester Regt KIA 11.5.17.
HULMES Joseph "DCM,MM" Sjt 14707 1st Grenadier Guards
HULSE Gerald MM Sjt 438351 430 Fd Coy Royal Engineers
HULSE Herbert MM Pte DM2/165724 Army Service Corps
HULSE James MM Pte 39445 Liverpool Regt
HULSTON Arthur W. MM Pte 33113 Leicestershire Regt
HULSTROM Walter Edward MM LCpl A/200824 18th King's Royal Rifle Corps
HUMAN Harry MM Cpl 13219 8th Lincolnshire Regt
HUMBLE John MM Spr 457467 209 Fd Coy Royal Engineers
HUMBLE John S. MM Pte 12996 King's Royal Rifle Corps
HUMBLES Ernest J. MM Pte 15111 2nd Bedfordshire Regt
HUME Alexander W. MM+Bar Sjt 3110 1/9th Royal Scots
HUME David D. MM Pte 29613 5/6th Royal Scots
HUME Frank MM Pte 11932 9th Yorkshire Light Infantry
HUME George Henderson MM Cpl 3444 V/61 Heavy TM Bty RFA
HUME James "DCM,MM" Sjt 18719 36th Bn Machine Gun Corps
HUME James M. MM Sjt 8344 King's Own Scottish Borderers
HUME John MM Pte S/9555 8th Royal Highlanders
HUME Robert "MM,MID" L/Cpl 63432 Royal Engineers
HUME Robert Charles Drummond MM Pte 331973 9th Highland Light Infantry KIA 6.11.18.
HUME William MM L/Cpl 19471 11th Border Regt
HUME William A. MM Pte 21472 1st Gordon Highlanders
HUMM T.H. MM Pte 7598 1st Suffolk Regt
HUMM William MM Pte 263188 4th Yorkshire Light Infantry
HUMPHERYES George Ernest "MM,MM(F)" Sjt L/21377 C/113 Bde RFA
HUMPHREY Adam MM Pte 7795 1st King's Own Scottish Borderers KIA 17.8.17.
HUMPHREY Albert MM Pte 36141 RAMC
HUMPHREY Bertie MM Pte 292760 1/7th Cheshire Regt
HUMPHREY Emlyn MM Pte 8796 13th Hussars
HUMPHREY Frank MM Pte 8346 IX Corps Cyclist Bn Army Cyclist Corps
HUMPHREY Frederick A.W. MM Pte S/35379 Rifle Brigade
HUMPHREY Frederick T. MM L/Cpl 16099 1st Grenadier Guards
HUMPHREY George MM L/Cpl 266686 2nd Bedfordshire Regt
HUMPHREY George MM L/Cpl 282263 4th London Regt
HUMPHREY George H. MM+Bar L/Cpl 12329 2nd Worcestershire Regt
HUMPHREY Harold MM L/Cpl 202522 7th East Yorkshire Regt
HUMPHREY Horace "MM,MSM" Pte 16109 8th Bedfordshire Regt
HUMPHREY James MM Cpl 8855 4th King's Royal Rifle Corps
HUMPHREY James MM Pte 11/1325 11th East Yorkshire Regt
HUMPHREY John "DCM,MM" Pte 14729 24th Manchester Regt
HUMPHREY John Charles MM Pte 5149 2/1st HAC(Infantry)
HUMPHREY Stanley "DCM,MM" L/Cpl 18925 55 Fd Coy Royal Engineers
HUMPHREY Thomas MM Cpl 65645 RAMC
HUMPHREY Walter MM Pte 232900 London Regt
HUMPHREY William MM Cpl 23431 118 Heavy Bty RGA
HUMPHREY William H. MM L/Cpl 42563 8th Yorkshire Regt
HUMPHREYS Albert MM Pte 9687 2nd South Staffordshire Regt KIA 17.2.17.
HUMPHREYS Albert M. MM Sjt 10523 31 Army Troops Coy Royal Engineers
HUMPHREYS Alfred John Oliver MM Sjt 29 1st Welsh Guards KIA 10.9.16.
HUMPHREYS Edward MM Pte 60493 RAMC
HUMPHREYS Eric William MM Gnr 120990 C/102 Bde RFA
HUMPHREYS F.T. MM Pte 17504 2nd Essex Regt
HUMPHREYS Frank MM Pte 205202 5th Yorkshire Light Infantry
HUMPHREYS Frank Leslie MM Cpl 240122 6th South Staffordshire Regt
HUMPHREYS H. MM Pte 39138 Royal Welsh Fusiliers
HUMPHREYS Harold "MM,MID" Pte 2098 South Lancashire Regt
HUMPHREYS Harry W. MM Pte 14372 6th Royal Dublin Fusiliers
HUMPHREYS Hugh MM Cpl 56500 16th Royal Welsh Fusiliers
HUMPHREYS John MM+Bar Cpl 17922 Royal Scots
HUMPHREYS John E. "DCM,MM" Sjt 805059 A/231 Bde RFA
HUMPHREYS John Henry MM Cpl 1080 RAMC
HUMPHREYS Percy MM Cpl 37527 HQ 66 Bde RFA
HUMPHREYS Phillip "DCM,MM+Bar" BSM 54871 C/122 Bde RFA
HUMPHREYS Robert MM Pte 40490 Royal Welsh Fusiliers
HUMPHREYS Robert John MM Sjt 15/12878 15th Royal Irish Rifles
HUMPHREYS Sydney MM L/Cpl 5550 1st Royal Welsh Fusiliers
HUMPHREYS Thomas MM Pte 241117 1/5th North Lancashire Regt
HUMPHREYS Walter Sydney MM Pte S/29067 3rd Rifle Brigade

HUMPHREYS Wilfred J. MM Sjt 79016 140 Siege Bty RGA
HUMPHREYS William "MM,MID" Pte 18794 2nd South Lancashire Regt
HUMPHREYS William MM Pte 11977 15th Royal Irish Rifles
HUMPHREYS William MM L/Cpl 315246 1st Royal Welsh Fusiliers
HUMPHREYS William Arthur MM+Bar Sjt 113143 Royal Engineers
HUMPHREYS William C.H. MM Pte 33532 12th East Surrey Regt
HUMPHREYS William H. MM Pte 11823 4th Dragoon Guards
HUMPHREYS William H. MM Sjt 7880 2nd Royal Welsh Fusiliers
HUMPHRIES Archer W. MM Gnr 569 RGA
HUMPHRIES Arthur MM Sjt 10665 6th Duke of Cornwall's LI
HUMPHRIES C.J. MM CSM 12560 5th Royal Berkshire Regt
HUMPHRIES Elizabeth Mountford MM Matron F TFNS
HUMPHRIES Ernest J. MM L/Cpl 316042 16th Cheshire Regt
HUMPHRIES George E. MM Pte 41390 1st Royal Dublin Fusiliers
HUMPHRIES George E. MM Spr 2125 Royal Engineers
HUMPHRIES Gilbert R. MM Pte 40239 Worcestershire Regt
HUMPHRIES Harry MM Pte 43597 15/17th West Yorkshire Regt
HUMPHRIES Henry J. MM L/Cpl 1813 1/18th London Regt
HUMPHRIES Herbert James MM Pte 13416 10th Gloucestershire Regt KIA 16.11.17.
HUMPHRIES Hugh M. MM Pte 37094 Royal Welsh Fusiliers
HUMPHRIES Humphrey "DCM,MM" Sjt 14721 116 Coy 39th Bn Machine Gun Corps
HUMPHRIES J. MM L/Cpl 26782 Hampshire Regt
HUMPHRIES Joseph MM Pte G/2590 12th Middlesex Regt
HUMPHRIES King Samuel MM Sjt 156409 258 Tunnelling Coy Royal Engineers
HUMPHRIES Noel MM Pte 36750 Cheshire Regt
HUMPHRIES Richard MM Pte 7826 2nd Highland Light Infantry
HUMPHRIES Sebert W.G. MM Pte 2840 Gloucestershire Regt
HUMPHRIES Sidney MM Pte 19245 1st South Staffordshire Regt
HUMPHRIES Stephen MM+Bar Sjt 11392 1st Worcestershire Regt
HUMPHRIES W. MM Pte 354279 RAMC
HUMPHRIES Walter MM L/Cpl 3/6952 1st Devonshire Regt
HUMPHRIES William MM Pte 42450 4th Worcestershire Regt
HUMPHRIES William MM Pte 27420 1/8th Middlesex Regt
HUMPHRIES William A. MM Pte 514682 Labour Corps
HUMPHRIES William Edward MM Pte M2/021834 18 Div Train Army Service Corps
HUMPHRYS Robert MM Pte 2260 1st Royal Irish Rifles
HUMPSTON(E) Jarvis MM Dvr 801502 B/295 Bde RFA KIA 18.9.17.
HUNN Frederick Edward MM Pte C/6956 18th King's Royal Rifle Corps
HUNN Reginald MM Pte R22156 King's Royal Rifle Corps
HUNNABALL Frank "DCM,MM" Sjt 19005 Machine Gun Corps
HUNNEYBELL Leonard MM+Bar Sjt 238141 2nd Worcestershire Regt
HUNNEYBELL William J. MM Pte 20516 Hampshire Regt
HUNNISETT William R. MM Sjt 330587 1/1st Cambridgeshire Regt
HUNSLEY Edgar MM L/Cpl 241818 5th Yorkshire Light Infantry
HUNSLEY Frank MM Pte 77255 2nd Durham Light Infantry
HUNSTON John MM Pte 275745 5/6th Royal Scots
HUNT A.G. MM Pte 201386 Royal West Kent Regt
HUNT Abel MM Sjt 7770 Devonshire Regt att Nigeria Regt WAFF.
HUNT Albert MM Pte 9668 2nd Royal Berkshire Regt
HUNT Albert J. MM Pte 18648 24th Welsh Regt
HUNT Albert S. MM Sjt 265872 Notts & Derby Regt
HUNT Albert Victor MM Pte 39748 77 Fd Amb RAMC KIA 21.3.18.
HUNT Alfred MM Sjt 835029 A/307 Bde RFA DOW 17.9.17.
HUNT Alfred C. MM Pte 154975 19th Bn Machine Gun Corps
HUNT Arthur MM Dvr 685911 C/293 Bde RFA
HUNT Arthur MM Pte 85666 29th Bn Machine Gun Corps
HUNT Arthur MM 2nd Cpl 23605 1 Fd Squadron Royal Engineers
HUNT Arthur MM Dvr 27254 D/173 Bde RFA
HUNT Arthur Elias William MM Pte 10842 2nd Essex Regt KIA 28.3.18.
HUNT Arthur K. MM Sjt STK/1018 10th Royal Fusiliers
HUNT C.V. MM Pte 19187 21 Fd Amb RAMC
HUNT Charles MM Sjt 710 9th Royal Sussex Regt
HUNT Charles MM Pte 50005 Middlesex Regt
HUNT Charles Edward "MM,MSM" Cpl 33235 229 Siege Bty RGA
HUNT Charles I. MM L/Cpl 511930 14th London Regt
HUNT Charles James MM Pte 10910 Leicestershire Regt
HUNT Charles William MM Cpl 67573 42 Bde RFA
HUNT Colin MM Pte 4520 Worcestershire Regt
HUNT Cyril Charles MM Pte 702338 23rd London Regt
HUNT Douglas L. MM Pte 538246 RAMC
HUNT Edwin MM Sjt 26030 1st Gloucestershire Regt KIA 15.9.18.
HUNT Ernest MM Sjt S/7107 1st Royal Highlanders
HUNT Ernest Albert MM Gnr 2633 Machine Gun Corps(Motors)
HUNT Ernest E. MM Sjt 67948 70 Fd Amb RAMC
HUNT F.J. MM Sjt 34481 RFA
HUNT Frank MM Pte 15316 1st Gloucestershire Regt KIA 17.11.17.
HUNT Fred MM Spr 23502 17 Fd Coy Royal Engineers
HUNT Fred MM Cpl 50527 1st Cheshire Regt
HUNT Frederick MM Pte 26346 1st Grenadier Guards
HUNT Frederick A. MM Sjt 201539 4th Yorkshire Light Infantry
HUNT Frederick W. MM Pte 16208 2nd Royal Irish Regt
HUNT George F. MM Pte 49828 Liverpool Regt
HUNT George J. MM Pte 95112 13th Liverpool Regt
HUNT Hans L.B. MM Cpl 10178 2nd Leinster Regt DOW 15.4.18.
HUNT Harold MM L/Cpl H/285285 1/1st Oxfordshire Yeomanry
HUNT Harry MM Sjt 877 RFA
HUNT Harry Percival "MM,MID" Sjt 49874 72 Fd Amb RAMC
HUNT Henry F.J. MM Pte S/17271 Rifle Brigade
HUNT Herbert E. MM Bdr 26205 RFA
HUNT J.J.G. MM Cpl 417041 1(North Midland)Fd Amb RAMC
HUNT James MM+Bar Sjt 240165 1/6th Royal Warwickshire Regt KIA 4.10.17.
HUNT James "DCM,MM,MID" Cpl 34902 2 Div Sig Coy Royal Engineers
HUNT James Alfred MM Cpl G/9344 6th Royal West Kent Regt
HUNT James William MM Pte G/6076 6th East Kent Regt KIA 3.7.16.
HUNT John MM L/Sjt 241922 2/4th South Lancashire Regt
HUNT John MM Pte 6229 RAMC
HUNT John MM Cpl 20794 18 Fd Amb RAMC
HUNT John MM Pte 245083 1/9th Durham Light Infantry
HUNT John J. MM L/Cpl 10848 Irish Guards
HUNT John Raymond MM Cpl 6761 2nd Gloucestershire Regt
HUNT John Robert MM Pte 21520 1st Lincolnshire Regt DOW 28.4.18.
HUNT John Samuel MM L/Cpl 13362 4th Coldstream Guards
HUNT John W. MM Cpl 14822 8th Suffolk Regt
HUNT John W. MM Pte 202547 Lancashire Fusiliers att MGC.
HUNT Joseph MM Pte 74755 109 Fd Amb RAMC
HUNT Joseph "MC,MM(41287 Cpl)" 2Lt RGA
HUNT Joseph MM Pte 16202 9th Scottish Rifles
HUNT Joseph W. MM Sjt 301945 Durham Light Infantry
HUNT Lionel MM Pte 31893 21st Northumberland Fusiliers KIA 10.9.17.
HUNT Louis Edwin MM L/Cpl 32705 5th Oxf & Bucks Light Infantry KIA 21.3.18.
HUNT Martin "MM,MMV(lt)" Sjt 79905 Royal Engineers
HUNT P.G. MM Cpl 240712 1/5th Royal West Surrey Regt
HUNT Percy C. MM Pte 131029 45th Royal Fusiliers
HUNT Peter MM L/Cpl 291168 1/7th Royal Highlanders
HUNT Raymond A.S. MM L/Cpl 381962 25th Liverpool Regt
HUNT Reuben MM Pte 5021 1st East Surrey Regt
HUNT Richard MM L/Cpl 42170 Yorkshire Light Infantry
HUNT Richard "MM,MSM" Bdr 32283 41 Siege Bty RGA
HUNT Richard M. MM Pte 320480 1/6th London Regt
HUNT S.A. MM Pnr 311588 Royal Engineers
HUNT Sidney Thomas MM Pte 40773 RAMC
HUNT Stanley C. MM Pte 201464 Tank Corps Died 30.11.18.
HUNT Thomas MM Sjt 16579 Machine Gun Corps
HUNT Thomas MM Spr 65025 105 Fd Coy Royal Engineers KIA 17.7.17.
HUNT Thomas H. MM Sjt 8640 1st Gordon Highlanders
HUNT Thomas Stephen MM Pte 51037 Cheshire Regt
HUNT Walter MM Pte 50125 8th Cheshire Regt
HUNT Walter F. MM Pte 202432 4th York & Lancaster Regt
HUNT William MM Sjt 11373 1st Notts & Derby Regt
HUNT William MM L/Cpl 4822 Royal Sussex Regt
HUNT William B. MM Pnr 255026 Royal Engineers
HUNT William B. MM Bdsm 70 9th Lancers
HUNT William C. MM L/Cpl 54756 Machine Gun Corps
HUNT William D. MM L/Cpl 266621 1st Scottish Rifles
HUNT William F.H. MM L/Cpl 200154 1/1st London Regt
HUNT William J. MM Sjt 95394 Tank Corps
HUNTBACH John MM Cpl 203421 1/6th South Staffordshire Regt
HUNTER Alan B. MM Pte M2/104991 Army Service Corps
HUNTER Alfred Graham MM Pte 35234 18th Bn Machine Gun Corps
HUNTER Andrew MM L/Cpl 275371 1/8th Arg & Suth Highlanders
HUNTER Andrew MM Pte 19276 2nd Yorkshire Regt
HUNTER Arthur MM Pte D/13531 2nd Dragoons
HUNTER Arthur MM Pte 201543 2nd Bn Tank Corps
HUNTER Arthur K. MM CSM 201006 2/4th York & Lancaster Regt

HUNTER Benjamin MM+Bar Cpl 201212 6th Bn Tank Corps
HUNTER Benjamin MM Cpl 15616 Royal Inniskilling Fusiliers
HUNTER Bertie MM Gnr 876073 C/275 Bde RFA
HUNTER Cecil H. MM Gnr 43641 D/76 Bde RFA
HUNTER Charles G. MM Cpl 201309 1/4th Gordon Highlanders
HUNTER Christopher MM Pte 292529 Gordon Highlanders
HUNTER David MM Sjt 86386 Royal Engineers
HUNTER David MM Pte 266877 1st Royal Highlanders Died 28.8.18.
HUNTER Edward MM Pte 52839 1st Royal Scots Fusiliers
HUNTER Edward MM Gnr Sig 242947 A/275 Bde RFA
HUNTER Edward MM Cpl 56781 Machine Gun Corps(Cavalry)
HUNTER Edward MM L/Cpl R/18395 King's Royal Rifle Corps
HUNTER Edward G. MM Pte 328414 1/1st Cambridgeshire Regt
HUNTER Ernest MM Pte S/12097 Royal Highlanders
HUNTER Ernest MM 2nd Cpl 484131 Royal Engineers
HUNTER F. MM Pte 276445 Arg & Suth Highlanders
HUNTER Francis R. MM Cpl 8643 Army Cyclist Corps
HUNTER Frank MM Cpl 74636 36 Bde RFA
HUNTER Fred MM Sjt 44017 7th Lincolnshire Regt
HUNTER Fred MM Cpl 19554 Cheshire Regt
HUNTER George MM Gnr 59007 RGA
HUNTER George MM Pte 8048 2nd South Staffordshire Regt
HUNTER George MM Pte 12155 7/8th King's Own Scottish Borderers
HUNTER George MM Sjt 1430 Durham Light Infantry
HUNTER George MM Cpl 11406 7th Duke of Cornwall's LI
HUNTER George MM Pte 7714 1st West Yorkshire Regt
HUNTER George MM Spr 412719 409 Fd Coy Royal Engineers
HUNTER George Miller MM Pte 9927 7th Royal West Kent Regt
HUNTER George S. MM Pte 283281 3rd London Regt
HUNTER George S. MM+Bar Sjt 7339 1st Royal Highlanders
HUNTER H. MM L/Cpl 235022 Northumberland Fusiliers
HUNTER Henry MM Pte 4123 Machine Gun Corps
HUNTER Hugh MM L/Cpl 10576 8/10th Gordon Highlanders
HUNTER Isaac MM L/Cpl 5556 8th Border Regt KIA 21.3.18.
HUNTER J. MM Pte S/41923 1/6th Royal Highlanders
HUNTER J. MM Spr 470458 Royal Engineers
HUNTER J.W. MM Gnr 771377 RFA
HUNTER James MM Cpl 12281 1/6th Highland Light Infantry
HUNTER James MM Sjt 290794 1/7th Royal Highlanders
HUNTER James MM Cpl 56632 37 Bde RFA
HUNTER James MM Bdr 53967 16 Siege Bty RGA
HUNTER James MM Pte 37970 15th Highland Light Infantry DOW 30.9.18.
HUNTER James MM Cpl 9212 2/2(Highland)Fd Coy Royal Engineers
HUNTER James MM Pte 20546 Gordon Highlanders
HUNTER James A. "DCM,MM" Sjt 19929 11th Royal Inniskilling Fusiliers
HUNTER James Boyd MM Pte 53552 Welsh Regt
HUNTER James J. MM Gnr 35761 RFA
HUNTER James W. MM Sjt 19/134 Northumberland Fusiliers
HUNTER Jim MM Pte 266170 1/7th West Yorkshire Regt
HUNTER John MM Sjt 457225 446 Fd Coy Royal Engineers
HUNTER John MM Cpl S/43700 5th Cameron Highlanders
HUNTER John MM Dvr 65482 D/106 Bde RFA
HUNTER John MM+Bar SM 17084 5 Fd Amb RAMC
HUNTER John MM Sjt 202460 Scottish Rifles
HUNTER John MM L/Cpl 12601 2nd Scottish Rifles
HUNTER John MM Sjt 325 Royal Irish Rifles
HUNTER John MM L/Cpl 251474 5/6th Royal Scots
HUNTER John MM Pte 26374 Royal Inniskilling Fusiliers
HUNTER John MM L/Cpl 31683 RAMC
HUNTER John MM Pte 245 23rd Northumberland Fusiliers
HUNTER John "MM,MID" Sjt 11130 2nd Durham Light Infantry
HUNTER John MM+Bar Pte 16803 1st Royal Scots Fusiliers
HUNTER John MM Cpl 412197 409 Fd Coy Royal Engineers
HUNTER John C. MM Pte 16360 17th Highland Light Infantry
HUNTER John C. MM Cpl S/2654 9th Seaforth Highlanders
HUNTER John George MM L/Cpl 42144 12th Manchester Regt KIA 18.10.18.
HUNTER John J. MM Pte 11183 King's Own Scottish Borderers
HUNTER John W.M. MM Cpl 650401 RFA
HUNTER Joseph Jenkins MM Sjt 13334 C/77 Bde RFA DOW 24.3.18.
HUNTER Lawies MM Pte 35055 2/5th Yorkshire Light Infantry
HUNTER Malcolm MM Cpl 7789 Arg & Suth Highlanders
HUNTER Matthew MM+Bar 2nd Cpl 95229 130 Fd Coy Royal Engineers
HUNTER Murray MM Sjt 305016 11 Fd Amb RAMC
HUNTER P. MM Pte 201163 1/4th Royal Scots
HUNTER Peter MM Sjt 12261 North Lancashire Regt
HUNTER Peter W. MM L/Cpl S/12450 5th Cameron Highlanders
HUNTER R.E. MM Sjt 113201 Royal Engineers
HUNTER Richard MM L/Cpl 8143 8th Seaforth Highlanders
HUNTER Robert "DCM,MM" Sjt 52693 128 Bty 29 Bde RFA
HUNTER Robert MM Sjt 200539 1/4th Seaforth Highlanders
HUNTER Robert MM Sjt 14652 11th Royal Scots KIA 7.6.17.
HUNTER Robert MM Sjt 82800 6th Bn Machine Gun Corps
HUNTER Robert MM Gnr 62756 191 Siege Bty RGA Died 12.12.18.
HUNTER Robert B. MM Pte 17115 Royal Scots
HUNTER Robert Wilkinson MM Spr 102699 171 Tunnelling Coy Royal Engineers
HUNTER Samuel MM Sjt 27413 9th Royal Inniskilling Fusiliers
HUNTER Samuel MM Sjt L/6894 C/159 Bde RFA
HUNTER Samuel MM Pte 50457 RAMC
HUNTER T.M. MM Cpl 65521 13 Bde RFA
HUNTER T.W. MM Pte 401401 RAMC
HUNTER Thomas "MM,MID" Pte 8150 2nd Scots Guards
HUNTER Thomas MM Pte 14904 2nd Royal Fusiliers
HUNTER Thomas "MM,MID" Sjt 2388 Notts & Derby Regt
HUNTER Thomas C. MM Pte 42963 Liverpool Regt
HUNTER Victor Gordon "MC,MM(2246 Sjt Northbd Fus)" T/2Lt Machine Gun Corps
HUNTER W.L. MM Pte 357782 Liverpool Regt
HUNTER Walter H. MM Cpl L/38505 39 Div Ammn Col RFA
HUNTER Walter R. MM Pte 241503 Royal Lancaster Regt
HUNTER William MM Pte 3575 Royal Highlanders
HUNTER William MM Pte 240285 5th Royal Lancaster Regt
HUNTER William MM L/Cpl 21251 6th Cameron Highlanders
HUNTER William MM 2nd Cpl 64043 Royal Engineers
HUNTER William MM Pte 17740 7/8th King's Own Scottish Borderers
HUNTER William Boyle MM Sjt 16539 10th Gloucestershire Regt DOW 1.8.16.
HUNTER William Crawford MM L/Cpl 230535 1/2nd London Regt
HUNTER William S. MM Sjt 780039 RFA
HUNTER William Stirling MM Sjt 11/13300 11th Border Regt KIA 1.7.16.
HUNTER William T. MM Pte 1915 1/5th Gordon Highlanders KIA 31.7.17.
HUNTINGTON Harold MM Pte 309251 Tank Corps
HUNTINGTON Reginald MM Sjt 8409 6th Lancashire Fusiliers
HUNTLEA Henry MM Sjt 30637 A/112 Bde RFA
HUNTLEY A.J. MM Sjt P/412 1 Traffic Control Coy Military Foot Police
HUNTLEY Ernest Edward MM L/Cpl 11031 3rd Grenadier Guards
HUNTLEY J. MM Cpl 45000 Royal Engineers
HUNTLEY James C. MM+Bar L/Cpl 353278 7th London Regt
HUNTLEY John Henry MM Gnr 87361 D/62 Bde RFA KIA 25.10.16.
HUNTLEY William J. MM Cpl 387152 1 Siege Coy R Monmouth RE
HUNTON John J. MM Sjt G/2455 8th Royal Sussex Regt
HUNTON Thomas "MM,MID" Cpl 9235 2nd Durham Light Infantry
HUNTRISS W. MM Pte 1780 1/5th Royal Lancaster Regt
HUNTROD William MM Gnr 27761 C/50 Bde RFA
HUPTON Frderick George MM Pte 16521 7th Norfolk Regt
HURCOMBE Harry MM Gnr 69682 78 Siege Bty RGA Died 27.8.17.
HURD Francis W. MM L/Sjt 5294 7th Border Regt
HURD George A. MM L/Cpl 6982 East Surrey Regt
HURD Henry MM Cpl 12172 4 Siege Bty RGA
HURD James MM+Bar L/Sjt 46711 4th York & Lancaster Regt
HURD John MM Cpl 63845 1/4th Cheshire Regt
HURD John P.G. MM Cpl 171928 11 Div Sig Coy Royal Engineers
HURD William MM Cpl 220446 1st East Yorkshire Regt KIA 24.8.18.
HURDMAN John Sanderson MM Pte 38406 2nd Durham Light Infantry DOW 22.3.18.
HURDUS John MM Dvr 188659 B/160 Bde RFA
HURFORD Albert MM(13092 W Yorks)+Bar Sjt 50884 1st East Yorkshire Regt KIA 24.10.18.
HURFORD Albert William MM Sjt 288012 2/6th Gloucestershire Regt
HURFORD Frank MM L/Sjt 21392 11th Hampshire Regt
HURFORD George MM Cpl 16028 Devonshire Regt
HURFORD James H. MM Gnr Sig 825974 A/240 Bde RFA
HURFORD Walter MM Cpl 230505 1/2nd London Regt
HURFORD Walter MM BSM 6539 463 Bty 179 Bde RFA
HURKETT Ernest MM Pte 1253 6th Leinster Regt
HURL Albert Edward MM Pte 85449 196 Coy Machine Gun Corps
HURLEY Archibald MM L/Sjt 12250 7th Somerset Light Infantry

HURLEY Arthur MM Pte 720 9th Royal Munster Fusiliers
HURLEY Edmund E. MM L/Cpl 43060 1st Worcestershire Regt
HURLEY Edwin MM+Bar Pte 50002 Manchester Regt
HURLEY Edwin MM Pte 16592 Welsh Regt
HURLEY Ernest MM L/Cpl 95411 Royal Engineers
HURLEY Gilbert H. MM Gnr 71099 D/255 Bde RFA
HURLEY James MM Bdr 371057 RGA
HURLEY James MM BQMS 49534 B/298 Bde RFA
HURLEY John "MM+Bar,MID,MdH(F)" Pte 1034 2nd Welsh Regt
HURLEY John MM Pte 43032 Machine Gun Corps
HURLEY Joseph MM Sjt 240065 East Lancashire Regt
HURLEY Lewis James MM Sjt 21674 Welsh Regt
HURLEY Michael MM Pte 10059 1st Irish Guards
HURLEY William MM Pte 25657 Machine Gun Corps
HURLL Walter G. MM Sjt 4711 1st Hampshire Regt
HURLSTON Frederick G. MM Cpl 840392 RFA
HURN Albert MM Pte 16235 Norfolk Regt
HURRAN George P. MM Cpl 7223 12th East Surrey Regt
HURRELL Charles MM Cpl 33460 Bedfordshire Regt
HURRELL Claud W. MM L/Cpl 12560 Machine Gun Corps
HURRELL Herbert W. MM Pte 9551 7th East Yorkshire Regt
HURRELL Samuel H. MM Sjt 18703 2nd Yorkshire Regt
HURRELL William MM Pte 13664 Royal Irish Fusiliers
HURREN Harry MM Bdr 35516 27 Siege Bty RGA
HURREN Hugh Maurice MM Sjt 1664 1/8th Royal Warwickshire Regt KIA 1.7.16.
HURRIE James MM Sjt 40208 Royal Scots Fusiliers
HURRING Charles MM Pte 73230 Notts & Derby Regt
HURRY Edward MM Dvr 84324 3 Div Ammn Col RFA
HURSEY Frederick MM Dvr 80151 92 Fd Coy Royal Engineers
HURSEY James MM L/Cpl 130416 46th Royal Fusiliers
HURST Alex A.J. MM Gnr 800568 C/230 Bde RFA
HURST Arthur MM L/Cpl 17177 Machine Gun Corps
HURST Arthur MM Cpl 49994 10th Essex Regt KIA 23.10.18.
HURST Arthur E. MM Sjt 4248 6th Royal West Surrey Regt
HURST Charles Harold MM L/Bdr 23512 X/34 Med TM Bty RFA
HURST Christopher MM 2nd Cpl 428355 423 Fd Coy Royal Engineers DOW 16.11.18.
HURST Edmund J. "DCM,MM" Sjt 45715 Royal Engineers
HURST Edward Robert MM Pte 18014 Machine Gun Corps
HURST Ernest MM Pte 43660 10th Lincolnshire Regt Died 26.8.17.
HURST Ernest W. MM Sjt 2262 46 Div Sig Coy Royal Engineers
HURST Frank MM Pte 12186 8th Seaforth Highlanders KIA 19.3.18.
HURST Frank M. MM Gnr 317232 RGA
HURST Frederick Roland MM Cpl 13346 D/17 Bde RFA
HURST George MM Sjt 28262 RFA
HURST George MM Sjt 10664 2nd Highland Light Infantry
HURST George H. MM Sjt 113262 'G' Special Coy Royal Engineers
HURST Harold MM Gnr 301950 13th Bn Tank Corps
HURST James J. MM L/Cpl 143334 17th Bn Machine Gun Corps
HURST John "DCM,MM" Cpl 2100 11th Royal Fusiliers
HURST John W. MM Pte 19988 Welsh Regt
HURST Leonard W. MM Gnr 249107 RFA
HURST Robert MM Pte 36940 10th North Lancashire Regt
HURST Robert Charles MM Sjt 590913 1/18th London Regt
HURST S. MM+Bar Sjt L/9298 1st Royal West Surrey Regt
HURST Thomas MM Pte 375246 1/10th Manchester Regt
HURST William "DCM,MM,CG(F)" Spr 107401 8 Div Sig Coy Royal Engineers
HURST William MM Dvr 57114 C/110 Bde RFA
HURST William MM Pte 8971 Royal Fusiliers
HURT Albert T. MM Bdr 65845 14 Bde RHA
HURT George MM Pte 49038 7th Leicestershire Regt
HURT George MM Dvr 99636 RFA
HURT Joseph Woodward MM Sjt 2800 1/7th Notts & Derby Regt KIA 1.7.16.
HURT Leonard MM Cpl 200294 1/4th Lincolnshire Regt
HURT Seth "DCM,MM" L/Cpl 12821 1/8th Notts & Derby Regt KIA 3.10.18.
HURTLEY Jack T. MM Pte 401344 1 Fd Amb RAMC
HURTLEY Tom MM Pte 203517 13th West Riding Regt
HURWORTH Harold MM Pte 21606 Durham Light Infantry
HUSBAND Albert Edward MM Dvr 104230 234 Fd Coy Royal Engineers
HUSBAND William T. MM Gnr 116856 RGA
HUSE Henry MM Gnr 68292 70 Bde RFA
HUSH Douglas S. MM Cpl 35726 11th Royal Scots
HUSK Charles L. MM Pte 283623 4th London Regt
HUSK Leonard MM Pte 2094 9th East Surrey Regt
HUSKINSON Edgar MM Pte 12908 9th Northumberland Fusiliers
HUSKINSON Royce MM Pte 6931 2/1st HAC (Inf)
HUSKISSON George MM L/Cpl 20310 6th Yorkshire Regt
HUSON Arthur MM Pte 2912 1/6th London Regt
HUSON John Middleton MM Gnr 80395 'S' AA Bty RGA
HUSSELBEE Benjamin MM Bdr 39495 57 Bty 45 Bde RFA
HUSSEY Albert E. MM Pte 45642 15th Hampshire Regt
HUSSEY Frank MM Pte 424385 Labour Corps
HUSSEY Frank MM Sjt 1753 8th Royal Warwickshire Regt KIA 4.10.17.
HUSSEY Hector MM Cpl 24891 10th Royal Welsh Fusiliers KIA 16.8.16.
HUSSEY Nathaniel John MM Pte 42037 2nd Worcestershire Regt
HUSSEY Peter MM L/Cpl 12877 6th Northamptonshire Regt
HUSSEY Stephen J. MM L/Cpl 552466 Royal Engineers
HUSSEY Thomas Patrick MM Pte 9399 2nd King's Royal Rifle Corps
HUSSEY William MM Pte 3/7171 6th Somerset Light Infantry
HUSSIES Lewis MM Pte 53379 12th Royal Scots
HUSTLER Edward MM Pnr 106934 70 Fd Coy Royal Engineers
HUSTLER Harold MM Gnr 1779 2(West Riding)Bde RFA
HUSTLER William MM Spr 34663 67 Fd Coy Royal Engineers Died 23.9.16.
HUSTWAITE John H. MM Cpl 36889 Yorkshire Light Infantry
HUTCHBY Joseph W. MM Pte 11985 7th East Yorkshire Regt
HUTCHENCE Fred Lovell MM Sjt 30145 196 Siege Bty RGA DOW 30.6.18.
HUTCHEON Alexander MM Spr 135567 10 Railway Coy Royal Engineers
HUTCHEON Alexander MM Cpl 84365 RFA
HUTCHESON John MM+2 Bars Cpl 13442 10th Scottish Rifles
HUTCHESON R.S. MM Pte 240345 Royal Highlanders
HUTCHIN Walter J. MM+Bar Pte 282737 4th London Regt
HUTCHINGS Alfred J. MM L/Cpl 67024 2nd London Regt
HUTCHINGS Arthur MM Pte 202101 4th Gloucestershire Regt
HUTCHINGS Charles Francis MM Sjt 291609 RGA Died 19.1.19.
HUTCHINGS Ernest B. MM Sjt 3262 1/9th London Regt
HUTCHINGS F. "MM,MID" CQMS 6667 3rd Coldstream Guards
HUTCHINGS George MM L/Cpl 650479 1/21st London Regt
HUTCHINGS George R.C. MM Spr 66304 Royal Engineers
HUTCHINGS George W. "DCM,MM" L/Sjt 200631 1/4th Royal Berkshire Regt
HUTCHINGS H.J. MM Pte 16479 Gloucestershire Regt
HUTCHINGS Harold MM Gnr 87254 52 Div Ammn Col RFA
HUTCHINGS Henry F. MM+Bar L/Sjt 1063 1st Welsh Guards
HUTCHINGS Henry James MM Cpl 391149 1/9th London Regt KIA 25.8.18.
HUTCHINGS Horace G. MM Pte 13/1275 13th East Yorkshire Regt
HUTCHINGS James MM Pte 16137 Royal Sussex Regt
HUTCHINGS James William Charles MM Pte 393723 8th London Regt
HUTCHINGS John MM Pte 15929 1st Coldstream Guards
HUTCHINGS John MM Pte 3/7594 1st Devonshire Regt DOW 12.9.16.
HUTCHINGS John MM+Bar Bdr 37096 RFA
HUTCHINGS John MM Pte 16964 7th Bedfordshire Regt
HUTCHINGS John M. MM L/Cpl 10425 1st South Wales Borderers
HUTCHINGS Percival R. MM L/Cpl 10354 Gordon Highlanders
HUTCHINGS Reginald MM Sjt 2523 Gloucestershire Regt
HUTCHINGS Samuel MM L/Cpl 1592 Welsh Regt
HUTCHINGS Walter W. MM Dvr 826173 A/170 Bde RFA
HUTCHINS A.E. MM Pte 40964 10th Essex Regt
HUTCHINS Alfred MM L/Cpl 1401 1st King Edward's Horse
HUTCHINS Arthur H. MM Pte 41420 1st Duke of Cornwall's LI
HUTCHINS Ernest MM Pte 375343 1/10th Manchester Regt KIA 20.10.18.
HUTCHINS George H. MM Pte 3/7668 2nd Bedfordshire Regt
HUTCHINS Henry J. MM Pte 861163 33rd London Regt
HUTCHINS John MM BQMS 44978 C/124 Bde RFA
HUTCHINS John MM L/Cpl 37553 2nd Royal Fusiliers
HUTCHINS Percy R. MM Cpl 1797 1/7th Middlesex Regt
HUTCHINS William George MM Pte S/9300 2nd Rifle Brigade KIA 25.8.16.
HUTCHINSON Andrew MM L/Cpl 60157 Machine Gun Corps
HUTCHINSON Archibald "MM,MID" Sjt 510020 RAMC
HUTCHINSON Arthur MM L/Cpl 200756 2/4th Yorkshire Light Infantry
HUTCHINSON Arthur MM Pte 30555 2nd Royal Inniskilling Fusiliers
HUTCHINSON Arthur G. MM L/Cpl 478417 Royal Engineers
HUTCHINSON Charles MM Pte M/288018 37 Mob Amb Col Army Service Corps

HUTCHINSON Cuthbert MM Gnr 45252 RFA
HUTCHINSON D.J. MM Gnr 45458 18 Bde RFA
HUTCHINSON David MM Gnr 307144 RGA
HUTCHINSON Edward MM Pte 7118 1st Leicestershire Regt
HUTCHINSON Ernest MM Pte 240955 1/6th Notts & Derby Regt
HUTCHINSON Ernest C.C. MM Cpl 255352 1/1st Leicestershire Yeo
HUTCHINSON Ernest W. MM Pte 205120 9th Northumberland Fusiliers
HUTCHINSON Ethel MM Staff Nurse F QAIMNS
HUTCHINSON Frank MM Pte 126836 Machine Gun Corps
HUTCHINSON George MM Pte 12822 Machine Gun Corps
HUTCHINSON George Poole MM Gnr 211852 C/103 Bde RFA
HUTCHINSON George Scotland MM Sjt 6989 2nd Coldstream Guards
HUTCHINSON George W. MM Pte 15219 South Lancashire Regt
HUTCHINSON Harry MM Sjt 13308 1/6th South Staffordshire Regt
HUTCHINSON Harry MM Cpl 15/490 15/17th West Yorkshire Regt
HUTCHINSON Herbert L. MM Pte 9263 Royal Fusiliers
HUTCHINSON James MM Cpl 751656 RFA
HUTCHINSON James MM Pte 20089 7th Northumberland Fusiliers
HUTCHINSON John MM Pnr 211492 5 Div Sig Coy Royal Engineers
HUTCHINSON John B. MM Pte 266045 1/7th Scottish Rifles
HUTCHINSON John G. MM L/Cpl 51560 Machine Gun Corps
HUTCHINSON John J. MM Sjt T/32848 3 Div Train Army Service Corps
HUTCHINSON John Oliver MM Sjt 116401 195 Coy Labour Corps KIA 20.5.18.
HUTCHINSON John R. MM Bdr 68518 5 Bde RFA
HUTCHINSON John W. MM Pte 352892 8th Manchester Regt
HUTCHINSON Joseph MM Pte 201163 4th Leicestershire Regt
HUTCHINSON Joseph MM Pte 4313 1st North Lancashire Regt
HUTCHINSON Joseph MM Pte 25812 16th Notts & Derby Regt
HUTCHINSON Joseph MM Pte 93810 4th Liverpool Regt KIA 11.10.18.
HUTCHINSON Leo R. MM L/Cpl 5464 15th London Regt
HUTCHINSON M.A. MM Pte 306274 West Yorkshire Regt
HUTCHINSON Norman Beaumont MM Pte 204069 West Riding Regt
HUTCHINSON Peter S. MM Gnr 105451 208 Siege Bty RGA
HUTCHINSON Ralph MM Pte R/16529 13th King's Royal Rifle Corps
HUTCHINSON Robert MM Pte 42158 1/5th Highland Light Infantry KIA 2.6.18.
HUTCHINSON Robert MM 2nd Cpl 40336 12 Div Sig Coy Royal Engineers
HUTCHINSON Robert L. MM Pte 200172 1st Bn Tank Corps
HUTCHINSON Robert S. MM Dvr 18718 38 Bde RFA
HUTCHINSON Samuel MM Pte 10365 2nd Royal Irish Rifles KIA 22.10.18.
HUTCHINSON Thomas MM Pte 7523 1st Scots Guards
HUTCHINSON Thomas John MM Dvr 6000 A/155 Bde RFA
HUTCHINSON Thomas S. MM L/Cpl 18/1567 18th Durham Light Infantry
HUTCHINSON W. MM Pte 18885 Durham Light Infantry
HUTCHINSON Walter MM Pte 32172 York & Lancaster Regt
HUTCHINSON William MM CQMS 73115 32nd Bn Machine Gun Corps
HUTCHINSON William MM Pte 13642 9th Royal Lancaster Regt
HUTCHINSON William MM Pte S/22666 7th Seaforth Highlanders
HUTCHINSON William MM Pte 24775 Durham Light Infantry
HUTCHINSON William MM Cpl 1500 West Yorkshire Regt
HUTCHINSON William MM Pte 37808 Yorkshire Light Infantry
HUTCHINSON William MM S/Sjt 12712 8 Fd Amb RAMC
HUTCHINSON Willie MM Pte 28905 West Yorkshire Regt
HUTCHISON David MM CSM 265140 7th Scottish Rifles
HUTCHISON James MM Pte 11274 Royal Highlanders
HUTCHISON James MM Pte 3260 Royal Highlanders
HUTCHISON James Sim MM Pte 4129 Highland Light Infantry
HUTCHISON John MM Pte 4252 Gordon Highlanders
HUTCHISON Matthew W. MM L/Cpl G/25367 1st East Kent Regt
HUTCHISON Thomas W. MM Pte 109754 12th Bn Tank Corps
HUTCHISON William "DCM,MM" Sjt 40762 2nd Seaforth Highlanders
HUTCHISON William "DCM,MM" Cpl S/7675 1st Royal Highlanders
HUTLEY Thomas MM Gnr 46604 26 Bde RFA
HUTSON Albert J. MM Pte 16373 1st Coldstream Guards
HUTSON Arthur MM Sjt 122423 245 Siege Bty RGA
HUTSON George H. MM Cpl 3480 1 Fd Amb RAMC
HUTSON Lochart W. MM L/Cpl 39604 Scottish Rifles
HUTSON Martin Luther MM L/Cpl 49853 9th Royal Fusiliers
HUTSON William MM Sjt 795205 RFA
HUTSON William A. MM Gnr Fitter 319482 329 Siege Bty RGA
HUTT A. MM Sjt 4643 38 Bde RFA
HUTT George E. MM Pte 4224 9th East Surrey Regt
HUTT George H. MM Sjt 11888 Royal Berkshire Regt
HUTT James MM Pte 1995 2nd Royal Highlanders
HUTT Victor G. MM Pte 71214 2nd Devonshire Regt
HUTT William James MM Sjt 65335 128 Fd Coy Royal Engineers
HUTTLESTONE William John MM Sjt 2392 A/82 Bde RFA
HUTTON A. "DCM,MM" L/Cpl 15347 2nd Durham Light Infantry
HUTTON Alexander McL. MM Pte 200174 1/4th Royal Scots
HUTTON Alfred MM+Bar Sjt 9779 9th Essex Regt
HUTTON Andrew Neilson MM Sjt 7821 Arg & Suth Highlanders
HUTTON Benjamin MM Sjt 11125 10th Duke of Cornwall's LI
HUTTON Charles Frederick MM+Bar Sjt 325036 9th Durham Light Infantry
HUTTON David "DCM+Bar,MM,MID" Sjt 3631 9th Royal Highlanders
HUTTON Ernest MM Pte 318164 2 Fd Amb RAMC
HUTTON Frank MM Gnr L/36742 RFA
HUTTON Henry MM Gnr 27070 31 Heavy Bty RGA
HUTTON Herbert MM Cpl 444551 2 Div Sig Coy Royal Engineers
HUTTON Horace MM Spr 478032 Royal Engineers
HUTTON James MM Pte 88395 27 Fd Amb RAMC
HUTTON James MM L/Cpl 12562 1/7th Arg & Suth Highlanders DOW 20.10.18.
HUTTON John MM L/Sjt 241190 1/5th Border Regt
HUTTON John MM Cpl 1322 Lincolnshire Regt
HUTTON John MM Sjt 90412 B/50 Bde RFA DOW 20.9.17.
HUTTON John Arthur MM Pte M/280708 Army Service Corps
HUTTON Ralph MM Pte 277288 1/7th Durham Light Infantry
HUTTON Richard MM Pte 1446 RAMC
HUTTON Robert MM L/Cpl 146004 129 Fd Coy Royal Engineers
HUTTON Robert MM Sjt 18932 Machine Gun Corps
HUTTON Thomas MM Pte 41364 4 Fd Amb RAMC
HUTTON Walter MM Cpl 482045 38 Div Sig Coy Royal Engineers
HUTTON Walter John MM Cpl 10978 3 Div Ammn Col RFA
HUTTON William J. MM Pte 41582 Yorkshire Regt
HUXLEY George L. MM+Bar L/Cpl 33747 12th East Surrey Regt
HUXLEY John MM L/Cpl 230463 10th Shropshire Light Infantry
HUXLEY William MM Pte 26403 South Lancashire Regt
HUXTABLE Edward J. MM Pte 345796 16th Devonshire Regt
HUXTABLE Harry MM L/Cpl 14475 8th South Lancashire Regt
HUXTABLE Percy J. MM Gnr 132761 130 Bty 40 Bde RFA
HUXTER Oliver MM Cpl 15845 7th Royal Berkshire Regt
HUYTON Albert J. MM Dvr 690181 D/290 Bde RFA
HUZZEY George V. MM Sjt 6355 3rd Worcestershire Regt
HYAM Herbert MM Sjt 240681 1/6th Liverpool Regt
HYAMS Fred MM Pte 41940 1st West Yorkshire Regt
HYAMS Henry C. MM Pte G/78566 9th Royal Fusiliers
HYAMS Roy MM Pte 5541 13th Royal Fusiliers
HYAMSON James MM+Bar Cpl 686141 RFA
HYATT Edward MM+Bar Pte 720244 1/24th London Regt
HYDE Arthur MM L/Cpl G/1889 7th East Kent Regt KIA 21.3.18.
HYDE Arthur MM Pte 27189 8th Royal Lancaster Regt
HYDE Austin O. MM Pte 242790 Liverpool Regt
HYDE Charles MM Pte 18551 16th Royal Welsh Fusiliers
HYDE Charles MM+Bar Sjt 14768 8th Border Regt
HYDE Charles E. MM Air Mech 1 1182 Royal Flying Corps
HYDE Charles M. MM Cpl 32963 13th East Lancashire Regt
HYDE Dan MM Pte 41605 Lancashire Fusiliers
HYDE David MM Gnr 238878 RFA
HYDE Ernest W. MM Bdr Sig 40999 41 Div Ammn Col RFA
HYDE Francis G. MM L/Cpl 356103 Hampshire Regt
HYDE Frank MM Cpl 32726 Royal Engineers
HYDE Frederick G. MM CQMS 16877 Suffolk Regt
HYDE George MM Dvr 52948 30 Bde RFA
HYDE George Arthur MM Pte 201899 1/5th South Staffordshire Regt KIA 3.10.18.
HYDE George H. MM Pte 35979 35 Fd Amb RAMC
HYDE Gilbert MM Bdr 44203 RFA
HYDE H.H. MM Sjt P10740 Military Mounted Police
HYDE Ham(Harry?) MM Pte 291834 Royal Welsh Fusiliers
HYDE Harold Edward MM Pte 3267(1?) 1/4th London Regt KIA 9.9.16.
HYDE Harry "DCM,MM+Bar" Cpl Z/2065 2nd Rifle Brigade
HYDE James MM+Bar Sjt 5627 12th Manchester Regt
HYDE James Bernard "MM+2 Bars,CG(B)" Sjt 45610 104 Fd Amb RAMC

HYDE John T. MM L/Cpl 97667 7 Pontoon Park Royal Engineers
HYDE John W. MM Pte 1914 1/8th Middlesex Regt
HYDE Joseph MM Pte 32878 Manchester Regt
HYDE Leonard MM L/Cpl 276171 1/7th Manchester Regt
HYDE Percy G. "DCM,MM" Sjt 10554 2nd Scottish Rifles
HYDE Reginald R. MM Sjt 3113 2/4th London Regt
HYDE Reuben MM Sjt 7933 2nd South Staffordshire Regt
HYDE Sydney MM Sjt 147273 Royal Engineers
HYDE Sydney Norman MM Pte 29859 11th Royal Warwickshire Regt
HYDE Thomas MM Sjt 986 2nd Royal Munster Fusiliers DOW 27.10.18.
HYDE Thomas "MM,MSM" Gnr 7473 HQRA V Corps RGA
HYDE William A. MM Pte G/19148 9th Royal Sussex Regt
HYDE William H. MM L/Cpl 8/14777 8th Border Regt
HYDER George A. MM Spr 107250 67 Fd Coy Royal Engineers
HYDER Harold Amos Standing MM Pte 350358 7th London Regt DOW 30.4.18.
HYDER William MM Pte 17409 1 Special Coy Middlesex Regt
HYDES Ernest Vivian MM Sjt 24224 Notts & Derby Regt
HYDES Frank MM Dvr L/23343 34 Div Ammn Col RFA
HYDES Walter MM Spr 3512 Royal Engineers
HYDON John E. "MM,MID" Pte 21451 5th Leicestershire Regt
HYDON Sydney MM Sjt 43843 86 Fd Coy Royal Engineers
HYETT Albert H. MM L/Cpl 236518 1/1st Herefordshire Regt
HYETT Albert H. MM Bdr 57990 RFA
HYLAND Anthony MM Cpl 18204 29th Bn Machine Gun Corps
HYLAND Edward MM L/Cpl 2184 1/9th Liverpool Regt KIA 12.8.16.
HYLAND George F. MM Sjt 930209 B/281 Bde RFA
HYLAND Henry MM Pte 10125 2nd Royal Irish Fusiliers
HYLAND John MM Cpl 4/5726 Connaught Rangers
HYLAND Patrick MM L/Cpl 9790 1st Royal Irish Rifles
HYLAND William H. MM Pte M2/052925 48 Div Train Army Service Corps
HYLANDS Howard T. MM CSM 8168 1st Royal West Kent Regt
HYMAN Arthur MM Pte 240758 Leicestershire Regt
HYMAS Arthur J. MM Gnr 202232 RFA
HYMERS William J. MM Pte 38465 1st Scottish Rifles
HYMNS Edward John MM Gnr 36160 A/190 Bde RFA DOW 11.4.18.
HYNARD George A. MM Pte 8128 1st Bedfordshire Regt
HYNCH Robert MM Sjt 9777 12th Arg & Suth Highlanders
HYND Henry G. MM Pte S/44792 1st Gordon Highlanders
HYNDMAN Ernest "DCM,MM" L/Sjt 14161 2nd East Lancashire Regt
HYNDS John "DCM,MM+Bar" L/Cpl 352379 1/9th Royal Scots
HYNES Albert MM Sjt 960315 RFA
HYNES Frederick MM Sjt 3275 4th Dragoon Guards
HYNES Henry MM Pte 240176 West Riding Regt
HYNES James MM Pte 11681 1st Irish Guards
HYNES John MM Pte 17065 2nd King's Own Scottish Borderers
HYNES Robert MM Pte 8416 1st Scottish Rifles
HYSLOP Andrew D. MM L/Cpl 295319 12th Royal Scots Fusiliers
HYSLOP Gavin J. MM Pte 3580 Army Cyclist Corps
HYSLOP George MM Spr 147647 Royal Engineers
HYSLOP Hugh MM Pte 40714 1/7th Gordon Highlanders
HYSLOP James MM Sjt 2459 14th London Regt KIA 5.11.18.
HYSLOP James MM Spr 37230 Royal Engineers
HYSLOP Maurice J.K.N. MM Bdr 69292 RGA
HYSON Henry MM Sjt 32782 1 Div Sig Coy Royal Engineers
HYSON William A. "MM,MSM,MID" Pte 8566 1st Shropshire Light Infantry
HYSTED Charles MM Pte L/9854 2nd Royal West Surrey Regt KIA 1.9.16.
HYTCH Charles E. MM Pte 40621 1st Leicestershire Regt

I

I'ANSON Alexander E. "DCM,MM" Sjt 39686 D/76 Bde RFA
I'ANSON Miles MM Sjt 75220 30 Bde RFA
IBBERSON G. MM L/Cpl 18608 Notts & Derby Regt
IBBETSON George H. MM+Bar L/Cpl 201477 1/4th Seaforth Highlanders
IBBETT Christie MM CQMS 530209 1/15th London Regt
IBBITSON George C. MM CSM 83763 210 Fd Coy Royal Engineers
IBBITSON GeorgeS. MM Sjt 266627 7th West Yorkshire Regt
IBBITSON John H. MM Pte 39331 West Yorkshire Regt
IBBITSON John W. MM L/Cpl 401205 RAMC
IBBOTSON Albert MM Pte S/9904 1st Royal Highlanders
IBBOTSON Charles MM Cpl 8391 2nd Royal Welsh Fusiliers KIA 28.11.17.
IBBOTSON Edward MM Sjt 74002 14 Bde RFA
IBBOTSON George Gilbert MM Pte 55689 3/1(East Lancashire)Fd Amb RAMC
IBBOTSON Henry MM Pte 12142 1st Coldstream Guards
IBBOTSON Henry MM L/Cpl 3636 1/4th York & Lancaster Regt KIA 3.5.17.
IBBOTSON Herbert J. MM Pte 15960 4th Coldstream Guards
IBBOTSON Percy MM+Bar Cpl 242859 5th West Riding Regt
IBBOTSON Robert MM Gnr 90922 151 Heavy Bty RGA
IBBOTSON Thomas E. MM Cpl 201844 4th York & Lancaster Regt
IBBOTSON Willie MM Pte 267732 West Yorkshire Regt
IDDESON Cecil C. MM Pte 62352 10th West Yorkshire Regt
IDDON George "MM,MID" Pte 12326 7th Border Regt
IDDON Wellington MM Pte 28925 9th East Surrey Regt
IDE Albert E. MM Sjt 12821 7 Div Ammn Col. RFA
IDE Ernest MM Spr 536311 86 Fd Coy Royal Engineers KIA 3.10.18.
IDELL John MM Gnr 166599 RGA
IFOULD Frank MM Pte 7770 2nd Hampshire Regt DOW 21.1.18.
IFOULD Fred MM Sjt 63132 D/155 Bde RFA KIA 23.10.17.
IGGLESDEN Sidney D. MM Cpl Sig 910525 220 Bde RFA
ILDERTON John R. MM Pte 3330 Durham Light Infantry
ILES George Robert MM+Bar Bdr L/33496 77 Bde RFA
ILES Henry E. MM Sjt 265754 Welsh Regt
ILES Jack C. MM Cpl 240192 1/5th Gloucestershire Regt
ILES James MM Sjt 3344 2nd Dragoon Guards KIA 22.3.18.
ILES Reginald H. MM L/Cpl 494402 Royal Engineers
ILES William G. MM Cpl 26862 RFA
ILEY Charles H. MM L/Cpl 15637 Royal Fusiliers
ILEY Reginald H. MM L/Cpl 49128 Royal Engineers
ILEY Robert William "MM,MID" L/Cpl C/12336 King's Royal Rifle Corps
ILIFFE Arthur MM L/Cpl 12794 9th Notts & Derby Regt
ILIFFE Charles L. MM Sjt 165808 87 Siege Bty RGA
ILIFFE George K. MM Spr 478505 49 Div Sig Coy Royal Engineers
ILIFFE Herbert W. MM Pte 45525 Durham Light Infantry
ILIFFE Horace MM Sjt 203186 Leicestershire Regt
ILIFFE John MM Sjt 200184 Notts & Derby Regt
ILLGER Frederick MM Sjt 204791 1/8th Notts & Derby Regt
ILLIDGE Arthur Ernest MM Sjt 1238 1/6th South Staffordshire Regt
ILLINGWORTH Alfred MM Sjt 201109 Gordon Highlanders
ILLINGWORTH Edwin MM BQMS 73732 D/11 Bde RFA
ILLINGWORTH F.W. MM Cpl 46750 RGA
ILLINGWORTH W. MM Gnr 2674 Machine Gun Corps
ILLINGWORTH William MM Pte 37396 Lancashire Fusiliers
ILLSLEY Albert MM Sjt 8339 1st Royal Berkshire Regt KIA 8.10.18.
ILLSLEY George MM Pte 18630 1st Royal Welsh Fusiliers KIA 27.8.16.
ILLSLEY Harry MM Pte 9301 2nd Royal Berkshire Regt
ILLSLEY Leonard MM Pte 19932 2nd Grenadier Guards
ILOTT George "DCM,MM" RSM 8253 1st Bedfordshire Regt
ILOTT Horace William MM Gnr 67158 111 Siege Bty RGA
ILOTT R. MM Pte 2745 1/1st Hertfordshire Regt
ILSLEY Henry MM Gnr 616302 RHA
ILSLEY William J. MM L/Cpl 21998 Grenadier Guards
IMBER Ernest A. MM Pte 303533 5th London Regt
IMBER Leonard Charles "MM,CG(F)" Gnr 128398 31 Div Ammn Col RFA
IMBER Richard MM Pte 1710 8th East Kent Regt
IMBER Sidney MM Sjt 9224 1st Somerset Light Infantry
IMESON Charles "DCM,MM" Pte 798 19th Durham Light Infantry
IMESON Fred MM Gnr 1502 RGA
IMESON John C.B. MM+Bar L/Bdr 35090 C/83 Bde RFA
IMISSON George "MC,DCM,MM,MID" T/RSM 200433 1/4th York & Lancaster Regt
IMLACH Henry Theodore MM Sjt 102 1/6th Liverpool Regt
IMLAH Lewis MM Cpl 266362 1/6th Gordon Highlanders Died 25.3.18.
IMMS Frederick MM L/Cpl 8211 2nd Oxf & Bucks Light Infantry
IMPETT Frederick MM Gnr 31243 RFA
IMPETT S.A. "MM+Bar,MSM." Sjt G/420 6th East Kent Regt
IMPEY Horace MM L/Cpl 25008 7th Suffolk Regt DOW 28.3.18.
IMPEY Samuel MM L/Sjt 15115 7th Bedfordshire Regt
IMRAY John MM Cpl 266954 1/6th Gordon Highlanders
IMRIE John MM L/Cpl 64125 RAMC
IMRIE William MM Pte 49338 5/6th Royal Scots
IMRIE William MM Cpl 43034 Highland Light Infantry
INCE Archie MM Pte 24994 Welsh Regt

INCE Arthur R. MM Sjt 7519 1st Suffolk Regt
INCE Ernest V. MM Cpl 16179 7th Royal Irish Regt
INCE John Pearson MM Pte 8157 1/4th Northumberland Fusiliers Died 10.4.18.
INCE Leonard MM L/Cpl 17751 6th Wiltshire Regt
INCE Octavius Cecil MM L/Cpl 17752 6th Wiltshire Regt
INCE William MM L/Sjt 200026 1/4th Cheshire Regt
INCE William MM Sjt 12021 7th South Lancashire Regt KIA 14.11.16.
INCH James MM L/Sjt 265220 1/6th Seaforth Highlanders
INCH William G. MM L/Cpl 240600 Duke of Cornwall's LI
INCHLEY Charles MM Pte 9065 2nd Wiltshire Regt
ING Ernest C. MM Pte M1/06957 4 Ammn Park Army Service Corps
INGALL F. MM Pte 2061 Lincolnshire Regt
INGAMELLS Archibald C. MM L/Cpl 1244 1/5th Lincolnshire Regt
INGAMELLS Charles F. MM Pte 35388 Yorkshire Light Infantry
INGER John Henry MM CSM 1874 1/6th North Staffordshire Regt KIA 6.6.17.
INGHAM Ernest MM Sjt 1259 1st Lancashire Fusiliers
INGHAM John MM Cpl 29773 2nd Northumberland Fusiliers
INGHAM John George MM Sjt 9736 1st Gloucestershire Regt
INGHAM Richard MM Pte 12480 2nd East Lancashire Regt
INGHAM Thomas W. MM Sjt 12271 Grenadier Guards
INGHAM William MM Pte 201050 2/4th North Lancashire Regt
INGLE Charles W. MM L/Cpl 423198 10th London Regt
INGLE Ernest MM Pte 201701 Suffolk Regt
INGLE F. MM Pte 43770 5th London Regt
INGLE Walter John MM Sjt 113648 21 Div Sig Coy Royal Engineers
INGLEBY Albert E. MM L/Cpl 46752 Northumberland Fusiliers
INGLEBY Arthur MM Sjt 200114 West Yorkshire Regt
INGLEBY John Heywood MM Pte 13992 9th Yorkshire Regt KIA 5.10.18.
INGLEBY Thomas MM Bdr 45030 RGA
INGLEDEW Charles J. MM Cpl 484159 Royal Engineers
INGLEDEW Ernest MM+Bar Sjt 43355 Royal Engineers
INGLEDEW George MM Sjt 1296 XV Corps Cyclist Bn Army Cyclist Corps
INGLES Arthur E. MM L/Cpl 15079 Royal West Kent Regt
INGLES John H. MM Pte 686127 22nd London Regt
INGLES Robert MM Sjt 660310 379 Bty RFA
INGLESANT Joseph MM Pte 29637 6th Royal Dublin Fusiliers
INGLETT Edward MM Cpl 60509 12 Div Sig Coy Royal Engineers
INGLEY James MM Pte 86285 74 Coy Machine Gun Corps
INGLIS Andrew MM Sjt 307153 1/8th West Yorkshire Regt KIA 4.1.18.
INGLIS Andrew MM Pte 12018 Royal Highlanders
INGLIS Andrew MM Pte S/15664 Cameron Highlanders
INGLIS David MM Bdr 306132 139 Hy Bty RGA
INGLIS George MM Pte 41675 18th Highland Light Infantry
INGLIS Gilbert MM Dvr 32293 D/92 Bde RFA
INGLIS Hugh MM Pte 14113 Scots Guards
INGLIS James MM Sjt 290797 11th Royal Highlanders
INGLIS John MM Spr 50108 Royal Engineers
INGLIS John F. MM Sjt 46724 3 Div Sig Coy Royal Engineers
INGLIS Jonathan MM Gnr 84868 RFA
INGLIS R. "DCM,MM" RSM S/8758 1/5th Gordon Highlanders
INGLIS Thomas MM Sjt 8883 2nd Highland Light Infantry
INGLIS William MM Bdr 1177 RFA
INGMAN George Richard MM Pte 12921 9th Royal Welsh Fusiliers
INGRAM Alexander Ian MM L/Sjt 11544 Scots Guards
INGRAM Aubrey Edward MM Pte 72502 15 Fd Amb RAMC
INGRAM Charles MM L/Cpl 13607 2nd Scots Guards
INGRAM Christopher MM L/Sjt 21085 14th Liverpool Regt
INGRAM E.H. MM+Bar Sjt 8806 Royal West Surrey Regt
INGRAM Edward MM Pte 17851 11th Royal Warwickshire Regt
INGRAM Frank Charles Ronald MM Pte M2/226032 Army Service Corps
INGRAM George MM Pte 8476 1st Lincolnshire Regt DOW 27.9.16.
INGRAM George A. MM Pte 265448 Gordon Highlanders
INGRAM George E. MM Cpl 240604 5th West Riding Regt
INGRAM Gilbert MM Pte 2136 1/7th Royal Warwickshire Regt
INGRAM Gordon Victor MM L/Cpl P3058 Military Mounted Police att HQ 63 Div
INGRAM Harold MM Sjt 8242 2nd Coldstream Guards DOW 27.9.18.
INGRAM Harry MM Sjt 56392 2nd King's Royal Rifle Corps
INGRAM J. "DCM,MM" S/Sjt 39213 77 Fd Amb RAMC
INGRAM James Douglas "MM,MSM" Sjt 56626 17 Bty 41 Bde RFA
INGRAM John "MM,MID" L/Sjt 7862 2nd Worcestershire Regt
INGRAM Joseph MM Pte 15294 1st Coldstream Guards DOW 15.5.18.
INGRAM Joseph MM L/Cpl 8756 1st Leicestershire Regt
INGRAM Owen William MM Gnr 1414 B/236 Bde RFA
INGRAM Robert Henry "MM,CG(B)" L/Cpl 61767 13th Royal Fusiliers
INGRAM Thomas P. MM Pte 024 1st Devonshire Regt
INGRAM Wallace MM L/Cpl 290251 1/7th Royal Welsh Fusiliers
INGRAM William "DCM,MM" Pte 20482 16th Cheshire Regt
INGRAM William MM Sjt 12075 2nd Middlesex Regt
INGRAM William Henry MM Pte 20973 10th Royal Warwickshire Regt KIA 6.9.18.
INGS Neville A. MM L/Cpl 28125 Duke of Cornwall's LI
INGS Robert MM+Bar Sjt 23123 8th Royal Lancaster Regt
INKPEN James T. MM Pte 76 Royal Sussex Regt
INKPEN W.G. MM Pte 16380 Middlesex Regt
INKSON Alfred MM Pte 265230 Seaforth Highlanders
INKSTER John MM L/Cpl 42815 1st Royal Inniskilling Fusiliers
INKSTER John James MM Bdr 56132 RGA
INMAN A. MM Pte 29271 10th Essex Regt
INMAN Ernest Edward MM Sjt 2093 1/5th York & Lancaster Regt DOW 8.12.16
INMAN Frank MM Pte 242243 15th Royal Warwickshire Regt
INMAN John MM Bdr 801103 B/295 Bde RFA
INMAN Joseph F. MM Pte 32474 1st Border Regt
INMAN Percy "DCM,MM" Sjt 210 1/5th York & Lancaster Regt
INMAN William MM Pte 203072 1/4th West Riding Regt KIA 11.4.18.
INMAN William MM Sjt 2208 1/4th Lincolnshire Regt KIA 1.7.17.
INNES Alexander MM Pte 265543 1/6th Gordon Highlanders
INNES Alexander Coutts MM Cpl 2949 Gordon Highlanders
INNES Alick MM Pte 200699 1/4th Gordon Highlanders KIA 25.3.18.
INNES Andrew MM Pte 7959 9th Scottish Rifles
INNES Andrew MM Pte 2355 1/5th Royal Highlanders
INNES Charles H. MM Pte 7757 2nd Scottish Rifles
INNES Gordon MM Sjt 200175 1/4th Gordon Highlanders
INNES Hector MM Cpl 10307 8th Seaforth Highlanders
INNES James MM Pte 9685 Scots Guards
INNES James MM 2nd Cpl 156422 184 Tunnelling Coy Royal Engineers
INNES James MM Pte 2234 1/6th Seaforth Highlanders
INNES John MM+Bar Cpl 254371 Signal Service Royal Engineers
INNES John "MM,MID" Cpl 9484 1st Gordon Highlanders
INNES John L. MM Sjt S/41386 1/7th Royal Highlanders
INNES John L. MM Pte S/11448 8th Royal Highlanders
INNES Reginald MM Dvr 54561 RFA
INNES Robert Barclay MM Sjt 3128 13th London Regt DOW 19.1.17.
INNES Thomas M. MM Cpl 265843 1/4th Gordon Highlanders
INNES Thomas Richmond MM Pte 31768 5th Cameron Highlanders
INNES William P. MM L/Cpl 265883 Seaforth Highlanders
INNESS Andrew MM Pte 325198 1/9th Durham Light Infantry KIA 12.9.18.
INNS Frank H. MM Spr 96639 Royal Engineers
INNS William MM Sjt 7579 6th Bedfordshire Regt
INSALL Thomas P. MM Pte 227030 1st Royal Berkshire Regt
INSCH James Gordon MM Pte 3072 Gordon Highlanders
INSCOE Henry MM L/Cpl 43278 8th Royal Berkshire Regt
INSKIP Walter George MM Sjt 89876 D/280 Bde RFA
INSKIPP Humphrey MM Pte 82331 RAMC DOW 21.8.16.
INSLEY Albert MM Pte 42783 2/7th Manchester Regt DOW 21.3.18.
INSLEY Frank A. MM Pte 18515 10th Worcestershire Regt
INSLEY Henry S. MM L/Sjt 2844 12th Middlesex Regt
INSOLL Robert MM Sjt 235182 1/1st Gloucestershire Yeomanry
INSTALL Frederick J.W. MM Pte 48183 Worcestershire Regt
INSTON John MM Spr 140256 105 Fd Coy Royal Engineers
INSTONE Francis C. MM Pte 132167 Machine Gun Corps
INSULL Arthur MM Pte R/12151 16th King's Royal Rifle Corps KIA 12.10.18.
INSULL John MM+Bar Sjt 305546 7th Royal Warwickshire Regt
INWOOD Henry James MM Trumpeter 47160 38 Bty RFA
INWOOD Tom MM Sjt 1550 2nd Rifle Brigade
INWOOD William Allan MM Bdr 91331 173 Bde RFA
IONS Harold MM Sjt 202990 1/5th Durham Light Infantry
IONS John MM Pte 204895 11th South Lancashire Regt
IORNS John E. MM L/Cpl 240953 Worcestershire Regt
IREDALE Edward Elisha MM CSM 1588 1/5th West Yorkshire Regt KIA 28.8.16.
IRELAND Alfred E. "MM,MSM" S/Sjt Mechanician CMT/2199 1 Cav Div Supply Column Army Service Corps
IRELAND Andrew MM Dvr 635892 D/256 Bde RFA
IRELAND David MM Pte 12976 1st Scots Guards
IRELAND David M. MM Pte 111481 6th(Light)Bn Tank Corps

IRELAND Edward MM Pte 737 16th Royal Irish Rifles
IRELAND Enoch MM Pte 36001 Welsh Regt
IRELAND Ernest William MM Pte 11678 8th Gloucestershire Regt
IRELAND Horace MM Gnr 124348 163 Siege Bty RGA KIA 17.9.18.
IRELAND James Henry Martin MM Sjt 112751 217 Siege Bty RGA KIA 9.4.18.
IRELAND Maxwell H. MM Pte 36370 RAMC
IRELAND Percy W. MM L/Cpl 240641 1/5th Gloucestershire Regt
IRELAND R.W. MM Pte 3928 9th Lancashire Fusiliers
IRELAND Robert MM Sjt 240534 1/5th King's Own Scottish Borderers
IRELAND Roger "MM+Bar,CG(F)" Sjt 240852 11th East Lancashire Regt
IRELAND Thomas MM Cpl 333056 Highland Light Infantry
IRELAND Thomas MM Pte 12826 7th North Lancashire Regt
IRELAND William MM Pte 24693 North Lancashire Regt
IRELAND William MM Pte 4174 1/4th Seaforth Highlanders DOW 1.8.18.
IRESON Edward J. "MM,MID" Cpl 32620 RAMC
IRESON Francis MM Sjt 3/10540 5th Northamptonshire Regt
IRESON Harold Dudley MM Pte 4224 7th Dragoon Guards DOW 14.4.18.
IRESON Henry MM Pte 228015 Royal Fusiliers
IRIS Ralph MM Cpl 12917 Army Cyclist Corps
IRISH Albert Edgar MM Sjt 9991 2nd Royal West Surrey Regt
IRISH Clifford G. MM Pte 30490 8th Devonshire Regt
IRISH Denman Augustus MM Cpl 3385 1/3rd London Regt DOW 9.5.17.AKA J.L.YOUNG.
IRISH Percival H. MM Bdr 121109 305 Siege Bty RGA
IRLAM Stanley Duncan MM L/Cpl 6762 16th Manchester Regt
IRLE Horace MM Sjt 34954 D/109 Bde RFA
IRONMONGER Bertie MM Cpl 31132 RGA
IRONMONGER George H. MM Pte 18350 1st Grenadier Guards
IRONMONGER Harold Edward. MM Sjt 1704 1/6th London Regt
IRONS Albert MM Cpl 394237 1/9th London Regt
IRONS Albert Henry MM Sjt 146403 RGA
IRONS Alfred W. MM Pte 66275 RAMC
IRONS Harry L. MM Sjt 329 1/3rd London Regt KIA 16.8.17.
IRONS Henry MM+Bar Cpl 935 X Corps Cyclist Bn Army Cyclist Corps
IRONS Jacob MM L/Cpl 10274 10th Royal Fusiliers
IRONS Robert H. MM L/Cpl 325611 7th London Regt
IRONS William MM Sjt 9120 6th Northamptonshire Regt
IRONS William W. MM Pte 9384 5th Wiltshire Regt
IRONSIDE John MM L/Cpl 39646 Lancashire Fusiliers
IRONSIDE Peter MM Bdr 650160 86 Bde RFA
IRONSIDE Robert S. MM Pte S/8613 Royal Highlanders
IRVINE Arthur Ernest Philpot MM Pte 14559 1st Royal West Surrey Regt KIA 14.4.18.
IRVINE Francis MM Pte 60150 Machine Gun Corps
IRVINE Frederick "DCM,MM" Pte G/48510 17th Royal Fusiliers
IRVINE George MM Pte 21473 1st Gordon Highlanders KIA 15.6.18.
IRVINE James MM Cpl 418030 9 Div Sig Coy Royal Engineers
IRVINE James MM Pte 39263 2nd Highland Light Infantry
IRVINE John MM Pte 9502 2nd Royal Scots Fusiliers
IRVINE John MM Cpl 2091 5/6th Scottish Rifles
IRVINE John MM Sjt 20783 9th Royal Inniskilling Fusiliers KIA 6.12.17.
IRVINE Robert MM Sjt 5934 Seaforth Highlanders
IRVINE Robert MM Cpl 646020 RFA
IRVINE Samuel MM Pte 23106 5th Highland Light Infantry
IRVINE T. MM L/Cpl 22622 Highland Light Infantry
IRVINE Thomas MM Sjt 41156 9th Scottish Rifles
IRVINE Thomas MM Pte 11884 Scots Guards
IRVINE William MM Pte S/12721 Cameron Highlanders Died 13.12.18.
IRVING Edward MM Pte 10414 5th Royal Berkshire Regt
IRVING Edward MM Pte 47112 Northumberland Fusiliers
IRVING George MM Sjt 18358 20th Manchester Regt KIA 1.7.16..
IRVING Henry MM Pte 13579 7th King's Own Scottish Borderers
IRVING John MM Sjt 201115 West Yorkshire Regt
IRVING John MM Pte 13231 11th Border Regt
IRVING John A. MM Pte 295681 12th Royal Scots Fusiliers
IRVING John N. MM Pte 13558 1st East Surrey Regt
IRVING Rowland MM L/Cpl 20185 2nd North Lancashire Regt
IRVING Thomas J.G. MM Pte S/10467 2nd Gordon Highlanders
IRVING William MM Cpl 470717 Royal Engineers
IRVING William F. MM Cpl 24546 Border Regt
IRVING William J. MM CQMS 1163 1/15th London Regt
IRWIN Albert MM Gnr 59579 RGA
IRWIN Andrew M. MM Cpl 22961 Durham Light Infantry or URWIN
IRWIN Francis G. MM Cpl 1306 Royal Engineers
IRWIN Fred MM Sjt 15631 Royal Inniskilling Fusiliers KIA 16.8.17.
IRWIN George MM Pte 53201 RAMC
IRWIN George MM+Bar L/Cpl 3383 1st Royal Irish Fusiliers Died 1.6.18.
IRWIN Henry "MC,MM(13699 Sjt 7th KSLI)" 2Lt 7th Shropshire Light Infantry
IRWIN Henry E. MM+Bar Sjt 101472 C/273 Bde RFA
IRWIN Herbert J. MM Pte 14/910 Royal Warwickshire Regt
IRWIN Horace Charles MM Cpl 2394 10th Arg & Suth Highlanders KIA 20.7.18.
IRWIN John MM Pte 40393 King's Own Scottish Borderers
IRWIN John W.F. MM Gnr 58718 23 Hy Bty RGA
IRWIN Robert MM L/Cpl 16898 Royal Inniskilling Fusiliers
IRWIN Robert MM Pte 9214 1st Royal Inniskilling Fusiliers KIA 1.7.16.
IRWIN Robert Samuel MM Sjt 15630 Royal Inniskilling Fusiliers
IRWIN Stanley MM Pte 251799 Manchester Regt
IRWIN Stewart MM Cpl 11931 7th Royal Irish Fusiliers KIA 5.9.16.
IRWIN Thomas MM Cpl S/8656 Royal Highlanders
IRWIN Thomas F.A. MM L/Cpl 29522 2nd Royal Dublin Fusiliers
IRWIN W.L. MM Pte 29258 Essex Regt
IRWIN Walter MM Pte 8973 2nd East Lancashire Regt Died 31.5.17.
IRWIN William L. MM Pte 536637 15th London Regt
ISAAC C. "MM,MSM" Sjt 650 Military Mounted Police
ISAAC Charles Christopher MM Pte 13866 10th Essex Regt KIA 30.6.16.
ISAAC Elias MM+Bar Sjt 26020 Welsh Regt
ISAAC F. MM Dvr 16493 33 Bde RFA
ISAAC George MM Pte 14778 7th Shropshire Light Infantry
ISAAC George Francis MM Pnr 151802 6 Div Sig Coy Royal Engineers
ISAAC John Goodall MM Pte 20021 43 Coy Machine Gun Corps KIA 19.8.16.
ISAAC Leonard B. MM Dvr 46679 RFA
ISAAC Thomas MM L/Cpl 240825 1/5th King's Own Scottish Borderers
ISAAC Thomas MM Pte S/11064 7th Cameron Highlanders
ISAAC Thomas E. MM Cpl SPTS/2970 24th Royal Fusiliers
ISAAC William Henry MM Sjt 765505 RFA
ISAACS William Thomas MM Cpl 830653 311 Bde RFA
ISAM Charles Arthur MM L/Cpl 88046 21st Bn Machine Gun Corps
ISARD Edward MM Pte 16763 9th Royal Sussex Regt
ISBELL Albert O. MM Sjt 320336 16th Royal Sussex Regt
ISBELL Ernest MM Pte 129531 Machine Gun Corps
ISBELL Henry MM Gnr 26231 Y/18 Med TM Bty RFA
ISBISTER Andrew MM L/Cpl 6932 2nd Scottish Rifles
ISETON Fred MM L/Cpl 459626 1/3(Northumbrian)Fd Coy Royal Engineers
ISGATE Walter J. MM Pte 37165 12th Gloucestershire Regt
ISHAM Ernest William "MM,MID,CG(B)" Cpl T4/084140 Army Service Corps
ISHAM James G. MM Pte 48653 5th Royal Berkshire Regt
ISHERWOOD Henry MM Pte 37586 2/4th North Lancashire Regt
ISHERWOOD Herbert MM Bdr 161078 B/317 Bde RFA
ISHERWOOD John MM Pte 13611 38th Bn Machine Gun Corps DOW 28.9.18.
ISHERWOOD John Arthur MM L/Cpl 8702 Scots Guards
ISHERWOOD John B. MM(10706 R Lanc)+Bar Spr 311149 3 Div Sig Coy Royal Engineers
ISHERWOOD Richard MM Sjt 426066 Royal Engineers
ISHERWOOD Vincent MM Pte 11069 East Lancashire Regt
ISITT Charles MM Pte B/200346 Rifle Brigade AKA Charles SMITH
ISLES A.E. MM Sjt 10597 Royal Air Force
ISLES Charles MM Sjt 98310 17th Bn Machine Gun Corps
ISLES John MM Pte 18929 4th North Lancashire Regt
ISLES Samuel MM Pte S/15995 Royal Highlanders
ISLEY Frederick James MM Pte 10308 2nd Essex Regt
ISMAY George MM Cpl 552087 16th London Regt
ISMAY Joseph MM Sjt 121614 Royal Engineers
ISMAY William T. MM L/Cpl 240890 1/5th Border Regt
ISON Arthur MM L/Cpl 55428 Machine Gun Corps
ISON Charles A. "DCM,MM+Bar" Sjt 64732 B/50 Bde RFA
ISON William MM L/Cpl B/200755 1st Rifle Brigade
ISTEAD E.J. MM L/Cpl G/6383 6th East Kent Regt
ISTED Samuel MM Pte 3788 Royal Sussex Regt
ISTED Thomas A. MM Cpl 67957 33 Bde RFA
ISWORTH Harold Cattle MM Sjt 31418 45 Bty 42 Bde RFA DOW 19.5.17.

ITTER Alfred E. "MM,MSM" Sjt 12483 5 Fd Amb RAMC
IVATT James MM Pte 242394 5th Lincolnshire Regt
IVE George "MM,MID" Gnr 94148 B/63 Bde RFA
IVE John F. MM Pte M2/049701 'E' Siege Park Army Service Corps
IVENS E.O. MM L/Cpl P8339 Military Mounted Police
IVERMEE Richard MM Pte 85963 29th Bn Machine Gun Corps
IVERSON Albert E. MM Pte 321002 6th London Regt
IVERSON Walter W. MM L/Cpl 14802 East Surrey Regt
IVES Alfred G. MM Cpl 472163 12th London Regt
IVES Charles Reuben MM Pte 201387 10th Royal West Kent Regt
IVES Edwin Isaac MM Sjt 370483 8th London Regt DOW 6.10.18.
IVES George A. MM Sjt 30214 East Lancashire Regt
IVES H.J. MM L/Cpl 21647 9th Essex Regt
IVES John MM Pte 29089 1st Middlesex Regt
IVES John MM+Bar Sjt 21407 2nd Notts & Derby Regt
IVES Reginald A. MM Pte 39429 RAMC
IVES S. MM Sjt 29032 27 Bde RFA
IVES Sidney MM CSM 1284 1/4th Suffolk Regt
IVES Thomas MM Spr 166970 63 Fd Coy Royal Engineers
IVES Thomas H. MM L/Cpl 26261 7th Royal Irish Regt
IVES William Edmund MM L/Cpl 590446 20th London Regt
IVES William H. MM Pte 65447 Royal Fusiliers att RE
IVESON Charles MM Cpl 3/9562 1st Northumberland Fusiliers
IVESON Frederick W. MM Spr 25381 Royal Engineers
IVESON Ingham MM L/Cpl 53747 1st Lancashire Fusiliers
IVESON Joseph MM Pte 21981 Royal Fusiliers
IVEY Henry G. MM Bdr 40873 RFA
IVEY Richard MM Sjt 64233 'E' Bty RHA
IVEY Stephen Oxnam MM L/Cpl 217650 82 Fd Coy Royal Engineers
IVILL John MM Dvr 177180 'B' Bty RHA
IVILL William MM L/Sjt 14655 2nd Grenadier Guards
IVIN Cedric MM Cpl 19984 4th Middlesex Regt KIA 13.8.18.
IVINS David J. MM Pte 13050 1st South Wales Borderers
IZATT Richard MM L/Cpl S/26870 14th Royal Highlanders KIA 23.10.18.
IZATT Robert MM+Bar L/Cpl 266418 2/8th West Yorkshire Regt
IZETT Ernest MM Pte 306864 8th West Yorkshire Regt
IZOD Albert MM Sjt 200395 1/7th Middlesex Regt
IZZARD Albert MM L/Cpl 4/7118 1st Bedfordshire Regt Died 30.1.19.
IZZARD William J. MM Pte 14365 Royal Sussex Regt

J

JACK Alexander MM L/Sjt 265177 Seaforth Highlanders
JACK Alexander B. MM Sjt 29344 2nd Royal Scots KIA 12.4.18.
JACK Andrew MM Cpl 2372 2nd Royal Scots
JACK Andrew MM+Bar CSM S/7979 Royal Highlanders
JACK Archibald G. "MM,MID" Cpl 1491 1/1st Lothian & Border Horse Yeo
JACK David MM Sjt 301347 1(Highland)Fd Amb RAMC
JACK James MM Cpl M2/032206 33 MT Coy Army Service Corps
JACK James MM+Bar Sjt 23192 2nd Royal Scots
JACK James MM Pte S/18278 5th Cameron Highlanders
JACK John MM Sjt 89169 134 Army Tps Coy Royal Engineers
JACK John MM Pte 15357 7th Cameron Highlanders
JACK John E. MM Cpl 308090 RGA
JACK John H. MM+Bar L/Sjt 332002 1/9th Highland Light Infantry
JACK Joseph MM Pte 41206 Seaforth Highlanders
JACK Leonard W. MM Pte L/11408 4th Middlesex Regt
JACK Peter MM Pte 276996 Arg & Suth Highlanders
JACK Robert MM Gnr 661226 C/250 Bde RFA
JACK Thomas MM Sjt 225344 10th Cameron Highlanders
JACK Thomas MM L/Sjt 281065 Highland Light Infantry
JACK Thomas MM L/Cpl 29474 King's Own Scottish Borderers
JACK William MM L/Cpl 43140 Highland Light Infantry
JACK William MM Sjt 37471 RFA
JACK William Anderson MM Pte 265437 1/5th Seaforth Highlanders Died 28.10.18.
JACKLIN Alfred MM Sjt 240667 5th Lincolnshire Regt
JACKLIN Frederick MM L/Cpl 88045 Royal Engineers
JACKMAN Charles MM Pte 25296 14th Gloucestershire Regt
JACKMAN Herbert MM Sjt 5244 8th East Surrey Regt
JACKMAN John M. MM Pte 306231 West Riding Regt
JACKMAN Osbert William MM Sjt 18617 Royal Berkshire Regt DOW 7.11.18.
JACKMAN Peter MM L/Cpl 3833 1st Northumberland Fusiliers

JACKMAN W. MM Pte 69566 RAMC
JACKS Thomas Edgar MM Cpl 33862 RGA
JACKSON A. MM L/Cpl 200637 York & Lancaster Regt
JACKSON Albert MM Pte 267937 5th Notts & Derby Regt
JACKSON Albert MM L/Cpl 16312 11th Notts & Derby Regt
JACKSON Albert MM Pte MS/2574 4 Div Train Army Service Corps
JACKSON Albert MM+Bar Sjt 21003 7th Royal West Kent Regt
JACKSON Albert MM Pte 267871 West Riding Regt
JACKSON Albert MM Pte 240954 Lancashire Fusiliers
JACKSON Albert Edward MM Pte 57267 1st West Yorkshire Regt KIA 17.9.18.
JACKSON Albert H. MM Bdr 54050 A/116 Bde RFA
JACKSON Albert H. "DCM,MM+Bar" 2nd Cpl 57821 36 Div Sig Coy Royal Engineers
JACKSON Albert H. MM Cpl 2540 12th Middlesex Regt
JACKSON Albert Henry MM Pte S/18115 1st Rifle Brigade KIA 13.10.17.
JACKSON Alexander MM Pte 204842 1/8th Notts & Derby Regt
JACKSON Alfred MM+Bar Cpl 15691 9th Bn Machine Gun Corps
JACKSON Alfred MM L/Cpl 575 GMGR
JACKSON Alfred "MM,MID" Sjt 71503 43 Bde RFA
JACKSON Alfred G. MM Pte 51156 Royal Fusiliers
JACKSON Alfred T. MM Sjt 8969 Suffolk Regt
JACKSON Allan MM Pte 403595 113 Coy Labour Corps
JACKSON Allan MM Dvr 154893 D/82 Bde RFA
JACKSON Andrew "MM,MID" Pte 12441 2nd Royal Scots Fusiliers
JACKSON Archibald L. MM Sjt 11877 9th Border Regt
JACKSON Arthur "MM,MID" Sjt 240289 1/5th Gloucestershire Regt
JACKSON Arthur MM L/Cpl 21/817 21st Northumberland Fusiliers
JACKSON Arthur MM+Bar L/Cpl 18516 Grenadier Guards
JACKSON Arthur Reginald MM Sjt 43023 RFA
JACKSON Austin Roy MM Pte B/450 Rifle Brigade
JACKSON B. MM Pte 303113 1/2nd(Highland)Fd Amb RAMC
JACKSON Barnard MM Sjt 46539 Northumberland Fusiliers
JACKSON Baron "MM,MSM" Pte M1/08997 Army Service Corps att 'G'(AA) Bty RGA
JACKSON Bertie MM Pte 8/12942 8th Leicestershire Regt KIA 25.9.16.
JACKSON Bertram J. MM Bugler 10428 5th Oxf & Bucks Light Infantry
JACKSON Castor MM Pte 36279 7th Leicestershire Regt KIA 27.5.18.
JACKSON Charles MM Sjt 44601 13th Durham Light Infantry
JACKSON Charles MM+Bar Pte 720735 24th London Regt KIA 22.8.18.
JACKSON Charles MM L/Cpl 39182 Yorkshire Regt
JACKSON Charles MM L/Cpl 12412 15th Notts & Derby Regt KIA 28.3.18.
JACKSON Charles Joseph MM Sjt 86259 Royal Engineers
JACKSON Clifford MM Pte M2/115095 Army Service Corps
JACKSON Clifford MM Sjt 686958 435 Bty 6 Bde RFA
JACKSON David MM CQMS 7611 7/8th King's Own Scottish Borderers
JACKSON David MM Gnr 39224 RFA
JACKSON E. MM Pte 9746 1st Essex Regt
JACKSON Edgar "DCM,MM" Cpl 1747 West Riding Regt
JACKSON Edgar MM Spr 146595 459 Fd Coy Royal Engineers
JACKSON Edgar Thomas MM L/Cpl 31868 63 Coy Machine Gun Corps
JACKSON Edward MM Pte 203822 Lancashire Fusiliers
JACKSON Edward MM Cpl 11164 B/152 Bde RFA
JACKSON Edward MM Cpl 11019 10th West Yorkshire Regt
JACKSON Edward MM L/Cpl 24174 Royal Irish Fusiliers
JACKSON Edward MM L/Cpl 276424 1/7th Manchester Regt DOW 27.3.18.
JACKSON Edward A. MM Pte 10901 6th Dragoons
JACKSON Edward W. MM Gnr 53472 RFA
JACKSON Edwin B. "MM,MID" Pte 14274 2nd Royal Fusiliers
JACKSON Eric Standish MM Sjt 2906 1/8th Durham Light Infantry
JACKSON Ernest "MM,MID" CSM 19/200 19th Durham Light Infantry
JACKSON Ernest MM L/Cpl 1629 9th Yorkshire Light Infantry KIA 7.11.18.
JACKSON Ernest C. MM Pte 61221 Welsh Regt
JACKSON Ernest Edward "MM,MID" Sjt 113655 GHQ BEF Sig Coy Royal Engineers
JACKSON Ernest T. MM L/Cpl 200438 1/4th South Lancashire Regt
JACKSON Evan MM L/Sjt 110534 1/1st Duke of Lancaster's Own Yeomanry
JACKSON F. MM Cpl 182 RFA

JACKSON F. MM Bdr 84551 RGA
JACKSON Francis MM L/Cpl 2251 1/6th Cheshire Regt
JACKSON Fred MM Cpl 200162 Royal Lancaster Regt
JACKSON Fred MM Pte 65439 Machine Gun Corps
JACKSON Frederick MM Pte M2/076128 Army Service Corps att RAMC
JACKSON Frederick MM Bdr 80437 RFA
JACKSON Frederick MM L/Cpl 39187 33 Coy Machine Gun Corps
JACKSON Frederick C. MM Cpl M2/104393 Army Service Corps
JACKSON Frederick G. MM Pte 11015 5th York & Lancaster Regt
JACKSON Frederick Herbert James MM Sjt F/807 16th Middlesex Regt
JACKSON Frederick J. "DCM,MM" Sjt 20247 49th Bn Machine Gun Corps
JACKSON Frederick O. MM L/Sjt 17895 Durham Light Infantry
JACKSON G.W. MM Pte 37455 4th Yorkshire Light Infantry
JACKSON G.W. MM Gnr 49925 45 Siege Bty RGA
JACKSON George MM Dvr 50770 Royal Engineers
JACKSON George MM Pte 23376 Bedfordshire Regt
JACKSON George MM Gnr 21604 A/47 Bde RFA
JACKSON George MM Pte 9250 2nd Notts & Derby Regt
JACKSON George MM Cpl 24251 59 Fd Coy Royal Engineers
JACKSON George MM Pte 11714 Royal Berkshire Regt
JACKSON George MM Cpl 15882 9th West Yorkshire Regt
JACKSON George MM Pte 15256 1/4th Northamptonshire Regt Died 15.10.18.
JACKSON George MM Pte 9043 1st South Staffordshire Regt
JACKSON George MM Cpl 16608 6th Royal Warwickshire Regt
JACKSON George MM Sjt C/12756 King's Royal Rifle Corps
JACKSON George Edward MM Pte 2344 1/5th York & Lancaster Regt
JACKSON George F. MM Gnr 1263 RFA
JACKSON George G. MM Sjt 771523 250 Bde RFA
JACKSON George H. MM Pte 14543 7th Yorkshire Regt
JACKSON George H. MM Pte 20268 2nd Notts & Derby Regt
JACKSON George H. MM Sjt 12297 8th Yorkshire Light Infantry
JACKSON George R. "MM+Bar,MSM" CSM 49045 103 Fd Coy Royal Engineers
JACKSON George V. MM Sjt 8365 7th Worcestershire Regt
JACKSON H. MM Gnr 13084 RHA
JACKSON H. MM Pte 337234 RAMC
JACKSON Harold MM Bdr 780109 B/246 Bde RFA
JACKSON Harold MM Pte 242141 15th Cheshire Regt DOW 7.4.18.
JACKSON Harold MM L/Cpl 13140 9th Royal Fusiliers
JACKSON Harry MM Pte 241833 5th Royal Lancaster Regt
JACKSON Harry MM Pte 241784 8th Lancashire Fusiliers
JACKSON Harry MM Pte 204146 1/4th Hampshire Regt
JACKSON Harry E. MM CSM 2961 Royal Engineers
JACKSON Harry M. MM L/Cpl S/3996 13th Rifle Brigade
JACKSON Henry MM Sjt 39106 560 Coy Labour Corps
JACKSON Henry A. MM Pte 325034 8th Lancashire Fusiliers
JACKSON Henry Charles MM Pte 1476 4th Bn GMGR
JACKSON Herbert MM Pte 20/184 Northumberland Fusiliers
JACKSON Herbert MM Cpl S/775 Rifle Brigade
JACKSON Herbert MM Pte 13612 Suffolk Regt
JACKSON Herbert MM Pte 240599 Yorkshire Light Infantry
JACKSON Herbert "MM,MID" Cpl 15/1321 15/17th West Yorkshire Regt
JACKSON Horace MM Pte 3706 Royal Lancaster Regt
JACKSON Horace H. MM L/Cpl 7774 2nd Oxf & Bucks Light Infantry
JACKSON Horace J. MM+Bar Spr 44384 Royal Engineers
JACKSON Horace Walter MM 2nd Cpl 198875 25 Div Sig Coy Royal Engineers
JACKSON Isaac MM Sjt 19/973 19th Northumberland Fusiliers
JACKSON J. MM Pte 242950 1/5th Yorkshire Light Infantry
JACKSON James MM Sjt 91970 15th Durham Light Infantry
JACKSON James MM Pte 295883 12th Royal Scots Fusiliers
JACKSON James MM+Bar Sjt 15634 1st Royal Inniskilling Fusiliers KIA 22.3.18.
JACKSON James MM RSM 16553 Royal Welsh Fusiliers
JACKSON James MM Gnr 28275 RFA
JACKSON James MM CSM 6699 Liverpool Regt
JACKSON James MM Pte 13914 2nd Dragoon Guards
JACKSON James MM+Bar Bdr 73261 41 Bde RFA
JACKSON James MM Pte 1517 2nd South Lancashire Regt
JACKSON James MM Pte 24789 13th Durham Light Infantry
JACKSON James MM Gnr 160061 68 Bty 14 Bde RFA
JACKSON James T. MM Pte 11586 7th East Yorkshire Regt
JACKSON James T. "MM,MID" L/Cpl 13592 7th Northamptonshire Regt
JACKSON Jesse Barker "MM,MID" Sjt 96230 20 Squadron Machine Gun Corps(Cavalry)
JACKSON Joe MM Sjt 19326 North Staffordshire Regt
JACKSON John MM L/Cpl 16400 6th Bn Machine Gun Corps
JACKSON John MM Cpl 15356 Machine Gun Corps
JACKSON John MM L/Cpl 12768 7th Cameron Highlanders
JACKSON John MM Pte 15689 3rd Coldstream Guards
JACKSON John MM Sjt 1034 1/6th Cheshire Regt KIA 13.11.16.
JACKSON John "MM,MID" Sjt R/226 King's Royal Rifle Corps
JACKSON John MM Cpl 9426 King's Royal Rifle Corps
JACKSON John A. "DCM,MM,MID" CSM 51321 98 Fd Coy Royal Engineers
JACKSON John Cyril MM Pte 27113 15th Hampshire Regt KIA 5.8.17.
JACKSON John G. MM Pte S/4375 13th Rifle Brigade
JACKSON John H. MM Dvr 95111 RFA
JACKSON John J. MM Sjt 35015 Border Regt
JACKSON John L. MM Pte 34747 4th North Lancashire Regt
JACKSON John Main MM Sjt M2/175804 Army Service Corps
JACKSON John W. MM Pte 1868 7th Royal West Surrey Regt
JACKSON John William MM Pte 31853 1st Duke of Cornwall's LI KIA 4.10.17.
JACKSON Jonathan MM Sjt 1996 1/2nd Monmouthshire Regt KIA 1.7.16.
JACKSON Joseph MM Pte 18303 1st East Lancashire Regt DOW 16.3.17.
JACKSON Joseph MM Pte 203077 19th Durham Light Infantry
JACKSON Joseph MM Cpl 13719 8th Lincolnshire Regt
JACKSON Joseph MM Cpl 46111 Royal Engineers
JACKSON Joseph MM Pte 16117 7th Border Regt
JACKSON Joseph C. MM Sjt 203536 1st Dorsetshire Regt
JACKSON Joseph E. MM Sjt 11663 2nd South Wales Borderers
JACKSON Joseph H. MM Pte 1973 1/4th Royal Lancaster Regt
JACKSON Joseph Henry MM Pte 16221 12th West Yorkshire Regt DOW 14.9.16.
JACKSON Joseph P. MM Cpl 35138 RFA
JACKSON Joshua MM Pte 13783 1/5th Border Regt
JACKSON Leonard MM Cpl 715644 RFA
JACKSON Leonard MM+Bar Sjt 4735 C/56 Bde RFA
JACKSON Matthew MM Pte 63679 9th Yorkshire Light Infantry
JACKSON Nicholas MM Pte 201195 5th East Lancashire Regt
JACKSON Oliver D. MM Cpl 53464 2nd Highland Light Infantry
JACKSON Percy MM Gnr 291183 127 Heavy Bty RGA
JACKSON Percy MM+Bar Sjt 14036 7th Norfolk Regt DOW 23.8.18.
JACKSON Percy William MM L/Sjt 2779 17th London Regt KIA 30.16.16.Served as PW TURNER.
JACKSON R. MM Cpl L/2693 RFA
JACKSON Ralph MM Sjt 750331 B/250 Bde RFA
JACKSON Richard MM L/Cpl 15931 Shropshire Light Infantry
JACKSON Richard C. MM Sjt 1628 1/5th Gloucestershire Regt
JACKSON Richard N. "MM,MID" Sjt 1367 1/5th Royal Lancaster Regt
JACKSON Richard Noble "MM,MID" Sjt 2710 1/4th Royal Lancaster Regt
JACKSON Richard W. MM Pte 20440 Liverpool Regt
JACKSON Robert MM Spr 159485 176 Tunnelling Coy Royal Engineers
JACKSON Robert "DCM,MM" L/Cpl 12/17939 12th Royal Irish Rifles
JACKSON Robert MM Dvr 680228 RFA
JACKSON Robert MM Cpl 19313 8th Yorkshire Regt KIA 22.9.17.
JACKSON Robert Crippin MM Spr 440350 Royal Engineers
JACKSON Robert James MM Pte 24201 1/4th Royal Lancaster Regt
JACKSON S.H. MM Pte 40970 Norfolk Regt
JACKSON Samuel MM L/Cpl 1868 Royal Engineers
JACKSON Samuel "MM(4174,12th Manch Regt)+Bar" Sjt 33302 6th Leicestershire Regt KIA 22.3.18.
JACKSON Samuel MM Sjt 3112 East Surrey Regt
JACKSON Samuel Harold MM Dvr 42841 B/152 Bde RFA
JACKSON Septimus MM L/Cpl 13977 12th Manchester Regt
JACKSON Sidney MM Sjt 240681 Lincolnshire Regt
JACKSON Sidney MM Sjt 36716 RGA
JACKSON Sidney MM Pte M2/021247 3 MT Coy Army Service Corps
JACKSON Stanley MM Cpl 345712 Royal Welsh Fusiliers
JACKSON Stanley MM Sjt 240484 1/5th Yorkshire Regt
JACKSON Stephen "DCM,MM" CSM 11990 1st South Staffordshire Regt KIA 26.10.17.
JACKSON Stephen MM L/Bdr 104024 302 Siege Bty RGA
JACKSON Sydney MM Cpl 200343 Shropshire Light Infantry

JACKSON Sydney R. MM Sjt G/36625 4th Royal Fusiliers
JACKSON Thomas MM L/Sjt A/3229 1st King's Royal Rifle Corps KIA 24.8.18.
JACKSON Thomas MM L/Cpl 200197 1/4th Royal Lancaster Regt KIA 20.11.17.
JACKSON Thomas MM Gnr L/12072 HQ 161 Bde RFA DOW 25.7.17.
JACKSON Thomas "MM,MID" Sjt 240092 Notts & Derby Regt
JACKSON Thomas MM Cpl 42146 West Yorkshire Regt
JACKSON Thomas MM Pte 38196 Northumberland Fusiliers
JACKSON Thomas MM Spr 127329 2 Light Railway Section Royal Engineers
JACKSON Thomas MM Pte 18315 Durham Light Infantry
JACKSON Thomas MM L/Sjt 11507 6th Border Regt
JACKSON Thomas MM Sjt 11508 6th Oxf & Bucks Light Infantry
JACKSON Thomas C. MM L/Bdr Sig 83296 C/51 Bde RFA
JACKSON Thomas E. MM Pte 268429 Liverpool Regt
JACKSON Thomas George MM L/Cpl 15889 9th Northumberland Fusiliers DOW 5.10.17.
JACKSON Thomas H. MM 2nd Cpl 459213 447 Fd Coy Royal Engineers
JACKSON Thomas P. MM Pte 24869 16th Royal Warwickshire Regt
JACKSON Thomas Richard MM+Bar Sjt 341318 87 Fd Amb RAMC KIA 4.4.18.
JACKSON Thomas W. MM Pte 27234 Labour Corps
JACKSON Thomas Wiliam MM Pte 11546 6th East Yorkshire Regt
JACKSON Tom MM Sjt 12664 Leicestershire Regt
JACKSON Vincent MM Sjt 57875 36 Div Sig Coy Royal Engineers
JACKSON W. MM Cpl 42524 RFA
JACKSON W.D. MM L/Cpl 1278 Military Foot Police
JACKSON W.D. MM Pte 12548 6th Shropshire Light Infantry
JACKSON Wallace H. "MM,MID" Sjt 522073 483 Fd Coy Royal Engineers
JACKSON Walter MM Pte 82159 1/9th Durham Light Infantry DOW 14.9.18.
JACKSON Walter S. MM Cpl 8313 1st East Yorkshire Regt
JACKSON Wilfred B. MM Pte C/1736 King's Royal Rifle Corps
JACKSON Wilfred H. MM Pnr 482130 62 Div Sig Coy Royal Engineers
JACKSON William MM Pte 78047 9th Durham Light Infantry
JACKSON William MM Pte 13/540 6th York & Lancaster Regt
JACKSON William MM Gnr 75837 C/159 Bde RFA DOW 28.9.18.
JACKSON William MM Pte 14716 1st Scots Guards
JACKSON William MM Cpl 6892 8th Somerset Light Infantry
JACKSON William MM Pte 251114 3rd London Regt
JACKSON William MM Pte 5459 11th Manchester Regt
JACKSON William MM Pte 37479 RAMC
JACKSON William MM Pte 2058 1/4th Northumberland Fusiliers KIA 1.11.16.
JACKSON William "MM,MID" Sjt 9342 Coldstream Guards
JACKSON William MM Pte 17154 2nd South Staffordshire Regt KIA 13.11.16.
JACKSON William MM Cpl 10936 2nd Wiltshire Regt
JACKSON William Edward MM+Bar Cpl 24227 4th York & Lancaster Regt
JACKSON William H. MM Sjt 266824 13th Liverpool Regt
JACKSON William H. MM Gnr 8598 RFA
JACKSON William J. MM Cpl 57466 41 Bde RFA
JACKSON William Leslie MM L/Cpl 31428 22nd Northumberland Fusiliers KIA 27.8.17.
JACOB Arthur A. MM Pte 3523 17th London Regt
JACOB Frank B. MM Pte M2/032359 Army Service Corps
JACOB Frederick MM Pte 9077 11th Royal Warwickshire Regt
JACOB G. MM L/Cpl 228791 Royal Fusiliers
JACOB George H. "MM,OStG(R)" Pte 18/782 18th Durham Light Infantry
JACOB Gwynne "DCM,MM+Bar" Sjt 10204 King's Royal Rifle Corps KIA 1.8.19.
JACOB Horace MM Sjt 41890 Machine Gun Corps
JACOB Michael Judah MM Pte 2622 82 Fd Amb RAMC
JACOB Philip Christopher MM Sjt B/203621 1st Rifle Brigade
JACOBS Albert MM L/Cpl 29681 2nd Grenadier Guards
JACOBS C.R. MM Pte 240874 Lincolnshire Regt
JACOBS Charles MM Gnr 91087 288 Siege Bty RGA
JACOBS George MM Sjt 44352 75 Fd Coy Royal Engineers
JACOBS Harold MM Gnr 222645 B/150 Bde RFA
JACOBS Henry J.C. MM Pte 6217 Machine Gun Corps
JACOBS J. MM F/Sjt 11219 Royal Air Force
JACOBS James MM Spr 45047 Royal Engineers
JACOBS Michael MM Pte 12051 6th Royal Berkshire Regt
JACOBS Sidney T. MM 2nd Cpl 24214 Royal Engineers
JACOBS Stanley F. MM Cpl 23388 33rd Bn Machine Gun Corps
JACOBS Walter "MM,MID" Sjt 200778 1/4th Northamptonshire Regt
JACOBS William MM Gnr 156972 RFA
JACOBS William MM Pte 781701 1st London Regt
JACQUES Daniel S. MM L/Sjt 73420 2nd Royal Welsh Fusiliers
JACQUES Edgar MM Cpl 18277 2/8th Notts & Derby Regt
JACQUES Frank MM Pte 12199 West Yorkshire Regt
JACQUES Joe MM Cpl 88407 Royal Engineers
JACQUES John MM Pte 281044 1st Lancashire Fusiliers
JACQUES John Sydney MM L/Cpl 204794 15th Hampshire Regt
JACQUES John T. MM Pte 40165 6th Lincolnshire Regt
JACQUES Joseph MM Pte 23722 South Wales Borderers
JACQUES R. MM Pte 18361 Yorkshire Regt
JACQUES Robert MM Gnr 110557 RFA
JACQUES William MM Cpl 705747 RFA
JACQUES William MM L/Cpl 20/186 20th Northumberland Fusiliers KIA 27.4.17.
JACQUES William MM L/Cpl 17471 Leicestershire Regt
JACQUEST Frederick MM Pte M1/08191 Army Service Corps
JAFFRAY Alexander M. MM Pte 1829 1/5th Gordon Highlanders KIA 25.7.16.
JAGGARD Charles MM L/Sjt 10697 2nd Royal Scots
JAGGARD James MM Sjt 9888 1st Bedfordshire Regt
JAGGER Ernest "DCM,MM,CG(F)" L/Cpl 241 'D' Bn Tank Corps
JAGGER George MM L/Cpl 200125 1/4th Yorkshire Light Infantry
JAGGER George H. MM L/Cpl 65352 Machine Gun Corps
JAGGER Harold H. "DCM,MM" L/Cpl 38596 20th Northumberland Fusiliers
JAGGER John J. "MM,MID" L/Cpl 4909 2nd Dragoon Guards
JAGGER Norman MM Bdr 108115 RGA
JAGGERS Ronald H. MM Cpl G/22089 26th Royal Fusiliers
JAGGERS Sydney H. MM Pte 4532 1st Royal West Surrey Regt
JAGGS George "DCM,MM,MID" CSM 14485 10th Essex Regt
JAGGS George E. MM Cpl 652 17th Royal Fusiliers
JAGO Charles Knight MM+Bar L/Cpl 167458 11 Fd Coy Royal Engineers
JAGO John G.G. MM L/Cpl 17660 Hampshire Regt
JAGO Philips J. MM Sjt 372974 8th London Regt
JAGO Richard Kingston MM Sjt 239 South Irish Horse
JAGO William H.E. MM Gnr 212489 RFA
JAGOE Allen Wilson "MC,MM(2878 L/Sjt R Fus)" T/2Lt Machine Gun Corps
JAKEMAN Frederick John "MM,MID" Spr 107372 4 Div Sig Coy Royal Engineers
JAKES Arthur MM Pte 66997 Royal Fusiliers
JAKES Percy John MM Cpl 13194 6th Northamptonshire Regt
JAKES William MM L/Cpl 18461 1st Bedfordshire Regt
JAKEWAY Leonard James MM Cpl 12438 58 Coy Machine Gun Corps KIA 24.4.18.
JAKINS John MM Pte 12985 7th Leicestershire Regt
JAMES A.C. MM L/Cpl 20014 7th East Kent Regt
JAMES A.M. MM Pte 21090 10th South Wales Borderers
JAMES Albert MM Pte 26537 8th Somerset Light Infantry
JAMES Albert E. MM L/Cpl 574021 17th London Regt
JAMES Albert E. MM Pte 18159 8th Royal Berkshire Regt
JAMES Albert Edward MM Cpl 830195 RFA
JAMES Alfred MM Sjt 10484 1st Worcestershire Regt
JAMES Alfred MM Sjt 756158 B/251 Bde RFA KIA 27.10.18.
JAMES Alfred MM Pte 13430 9th Welsh Regt
JAMES Alfred J. MM Gnr 58862 RFA
JAMES Algernon Willie MM+Bar Cpl 141715 91 Fd Coy Royal Engineers
JAMES Arthur MM CSM 201106 2/8th Worcestershire Regt att Middlesex Regt
JAMES Arthur MM L/Cpl 11087 5th Shropshire Light Infantry
JAMES Arthur Leonard MM Spr 216413 Royal Engineers
JAMES Arthur S. MM Pte 52628 18th Gloucestershire Regt
JAMES Arthur Wilfred Robert MM Gnr 831519 B/241 Bde RFA
JAMES Charles MM Pte 19906 Machine Gun Corps
JAMES Charles MM Pte 11064 8th Shropshire Light Infantry
JAMES Charles MM+Bar CSM 280489 1/4th London Regt
JAMES Charles A. MM Pte L/6222 12th Lancers
JAMES David MM L/Cpl 613 1st Welsh Guards KIA 16.9.16.
JAMES David C. MM Pte 12685 Arg & Suth Highlanders
JAMES David George MM Sjt S/3253 13th Rifle Brigade KIA 14.11.16.
JAMES David Henry MM Spr 45952 25 Div Sig Coy Royal Engineers KIA 25.7.17.
JAMES David J. MM Spr 448085 Royal Engineers

JAMES David John MM Sjt 33220 10th South Wales Borderers
JAMES David John "MM,CG(F)" L/Cpl 43035 75 Fd Amb RAMC
JAMES David Owen MM Sjt 33247 Welsh Regt
JAMES E. MM Cpl 36849 130 Coy Machine Gun Corps
JAMES Edward MM Pte 14811 2nd Grenadier Guards
JAMES Edward "MM,MID" Pte 3276 2nd Lancashire Fusiliers
JAMES Edward William MM Cpl T4/037135 19 Div Train Army Service Corps
JAMES Edwin MM Cpl 14221 6th Dragoons
JAMES Edwin MM Cpl 18400 5th South Wales Borderers
JAMES Edwin Valentine MM Pte S1691 12th Rifle Brigade
JAMES Essex MM Pte 14330 9th Welsh Regt
JAMES Francis A. MM Pte 239027 1/1st Herefordshire Regt att 1st Shropshire LI.
JAMES Frank MM Pte 31562 9th Royal Welsh Fusiliers
JAMES Frank MM Pte 10928 1st Coldstream Guards
JAMES Frank MM L/Bdr 77167 D/69 Bde RFA
JAMES Frank MM L/Cpl 253069 3rd London Regt
JAMES Frank Ernest MM Pte 12927 6th Oxf & Bucks Light Infantry
JAMES Frank L. MM Pte 45159 14th Royal Irish Rifles
JAMES Frank O. MM Pte 275786 5/6th Royal Scots
JAMES Fred MM Pte R/34250 12th King's Royal Rifle Corps KIA 2.4.18.
JAMES Frederick MM Spr 244924 1 Fd Svy Bn Royal Engineers
JAMES Frederick Albert MM+Bar L/Cpl 18094 13th Essex Regt
JAMES Frederick C. MM Pte 205031 15th Hampshire Regt
JAMES Frederick C. MM Pte 44885 14th Royal Irish Rifles
JAMES Frederick J. MM Sjt 14703 59 Fd Coy Royal Engineers
JAMES Frederick Thomas "DCM,MM" Sjt 10180 12th East Surrey Regt DOW 8.12.18.
JAMES George Henry MM Pte 16891 5th Royal Berkshire Regt
JAMES George J. MM Gnr L/32177 A/277 Bde RFA
JAMES George Joseph MM Bdr 66180 28 Bde RFA
JAMES George M. MM Pte 107638 32nd Bn Machine Gun Corps
JAMES Griffith MM Cpl 248607 Royal Engineers
JAMES H. MM Pte 536442 RAMC
JAMES Harold MM Pte 20960 Cheshire Regt
JAMES Harold V. "MM,MID" Pte 27852 9th Gloucestershire Regt
JAMES Harry MM Pte 11644 9th Gloucestershire Regt
JAMES Harry MM Sjt 45320 Machine Gun Corps
JAMES Harry MM Gnr 785776 232 Bde RFA KIA 27.4.17.
JAMES Harry C. MM Sjt 42983 231 Siege Bty RGA
JAMES Henry MM Cpl 25591 RFA
JAMES Henry MM SM 320 4 Squadron Royal Flying Corps
JAMES Henry C. MM Pte R/19400 King's Royal Rifle Corps
JAMES Henry E.A. MM Bdr 618127 RFA
JAMES J. "DCM,MM" Sjt 50611 24 Div Sig Coy Royal Engineers
JAMES Jack MM Pte STK/718 10th Royal Fusiliers DOW 17.4.17.
JAMES James MM L/Cpl 17700 Royal Welsh Fusiliers
JAMES James Oliver MM Bdr 72691 HQ 12 Bde RFA KIA 26.9.16.
JAMES James Thomas MM Cpl 19000 2nd Yorkshire Regt
JAMES John MM Cpl 20982 South Wales Borderers
JAMES John MM Gnr Sig 800388 C/286 Bde RFA
JAMES John MM Sjt 6258 1st North Staffordshire Regt
JAMES John MM Pte 11891 11th Royal Fusiliers
JAMES John A. MM Cpl 61360 12th Manchester Regt
JAMES John Emlyn "MM,MID" Cpl 235733 1/1st Herefordshire Regt
JAMES John Robert MM Bdr 78259 A/102 Bde RFA
JAMES John S. MM L/Bdr 32969 C/177 Bde RFA
JAMES John T. MM Spr 249997 Royal Engineers
JAMES John William MM Pte 43894 1st Royal Irish Rifles KIA 27.3.18.
JAMES Joseph MM Sjt 1056 1st Royal Lancaster Regt
JAMES Joseph W. MM Cpl 40620 4th Yorkshire Light Infantry
JAMES L.E. MM Sister F QAIMNS
JAMES Malcolm MM Pte 18470 2nd Royal Scots DOW 27.9.17.
JAMES Nicholas MM Pte 17618 Royal Welsh Fusiliers
JAMES R. MM Sjt Farrier W/2899 RFA
JAMES Reginald J. MM Gnr 24493 RGA
JAMES Reginald Wilfred MM Pte 27405 13th West Riding Regt
JAMES Reuben MM L/Cpl 17593 9th Suffolk Regt
JAMES Richard MM Pte 28012 15th Lancashire Fusiliers
JAMES Richard MM 2nd Cpl 63124 Royal Engineers
JAMES Robert MM Gnr W/4778 D/119 Bde RFA
JAMES Robert MM Cpl 200532 1/5th Durham Light Infantry KIA 12.4.18.
JAMES Robert F. MM Pte 333120 Highland Light Infantry
JAMES Robert W. MM Pte L/16791 12th Lancers
JAMES Robert William MM Pte 235312 Lancashire Fusiliers
JAMES Rowland Enoch MM L/Cpl 39572 2nd Royal Welsh Fusiliers
JAMES Sidney G. MM Dvr 102960 RFA
JAMES Sidney T. MM Pte 17971 8th Gloucestershire Regt
JAMES Sydney P. MM L/Cpl 25908 10th Royal West Surrey Regt
JAMES Thomas MM Sjt 650652 21st London Regt
JAMES Thomas MM Pte 54535 9th Welsh Regt
JAMES Thomas Cyril MM+Bar Sjt 71761 C/104 Bde RFA
JAMES Thomas E. "MM,MSM" Cpl 776418 D/310 Bde RFA
JAMES Thomas L. "MM,MID" Spr 29461 Cav Sig Sqn Royal Engineers
JAMES Thomas Victor MM Pte 2856 2nd Manchester Regt
JAMES Tom MM+Bar Sjt 240062 1/5th Border Regt
JAMES Walter MM+Bar Pte 48981 RAMC
JAMES Walter MM Pte 19956 6th South Wales Borderers
JAMES Walter H. MM Pte 57174 1/6th Manchester Regt
JAMES William MM Cpl 1894 2nd Welsh Regt
JAMES William MM Dvr 227051 A/123 Bde RFA
JAMES William MM Pte 59900 Royal Scots
JAMES William "DCM,MM" Pte 1728 8th East Surrey Regt KIA 4.4.18.
JAMES William MM Pte 30397 Welsh Regt
JAMES William David MM 2Lt 13th Royal Welsh Fusiliers KIA 8.10.18.
JAMES William H. MM L/Cpl 5464 12th East Surrey Regt
JAMES William J. MM 2nd Cpl 27123 Royal Engineers
JAMES William J. MM Cpl 6270 2nd Welsh Regt
JAMES William L. MM Pte 25710 10th Royal West Surrey Regt
JAMES William Maurice "MC,MM(2014 Cpl)" Capt 1/14th London Regt
JAMES William S.G. MM Pte 23188 Grenadier Guards
JAMES William T. MM Gnr 2250 RFA
JAMESON Frank MM Spr 66868 180 Tunnelling Coy Royal Engineers
JAMESON George MM L/Cpl 356621 2/4th Hampshire Regt
JAMESON George MM L/Cpl R/919 12th King's Royal Rifle Corps
JAMESON George "MM,MSM" Sjt 166797 295 Siege Bty RGA
JAMESON Harry MM Cpl 152229 Royal Engineers
JAMESON J. MM Pte 51993 West Yorkshire Regt
JAMESON John MM L/Cpl 15948 8th Royal Lancaster Regt
JAMESON John MM Cpl 22077 1st North Lancashire Regt
JAMESON John MM Pte S/17875 2nd Cameron Highlanders
JAMESON Phillips O. MM Pte 49762 Royal Fusiliers
JAMESON Robert MM Cpl 44030 Royal Engineers
JAMESON Robert MM Pte 202478 South Lancashire Regt
JAMESON William MM Gnr 146239 168 Siege Bty RGA DOW 18.10.18.
JAMFREY Fred "DCM,MM" Cpl 300438 1/8th Durham Light Infantry
JAMIE Montague MM L/Cpl 1141 4/5th Royal Highlanders DOW 1.8.17.
JAMIESON Adam MM Pte 9268 2nd Dragoons
JAMIESON Albert A. MM Pte M2/153481 Army Service Corps
JAMIESON Alexander MM Cpl 3/2670 Royal Highlanders
JAMIESON George MM Pte 9809 1st East Kent Regt
JAMIESON H. MM Pte 130423 46th Royal Fusiliers
JAMIESON James MM Pte 3529 76 Fd Amb RAMC
JAMIESON James MM Pte 7635 1st King's Own Scottish Borderers KIA 3.12.17.
JAMIESON James MM L/Cpl 290372 1/7th Gordon Highlanders
JAMIESON James MM Cpl 18343 12th Highland Light Infantry
JAMIESON James MM Pte 14777 7/8th King's Own Scottish Borderers
JAMIESON James D. MM Sjt 64769 RAMC
JAMIESON James Penney MM Pte 285067 10th Seaforth Highlanders
JAMIESON James R. "DCM,MM+Bar" CQMS 350425 1/9th Royal Scots
JAMIESON John MM Pte 251477 Royal Scots
JAMIESON Joseph MM Pte 300269 11th Manchester Regt
JAMIESON Matthew MM L/Cpl 315545 13th Royal Highlanders
JAMIESON Percy J.H. MM Cpl 43512 Royal Engineers
JAMIESON Robert MM Sjt 330827 1/9th Highland Light Infantry
JAMIESON Robert MM Pte 624 VII Corps Cyclist Bn Army Cyclist Corps
JAMIESON Robert MM S/Sjt Fitter 88359 2 Bde RHA
JAMIESON Robert Archer MM Gnr 961333 152 Bde RFA
JAMIESON Robert Beresford "MM,MSM" S/Sjt Mechanician MS/169 594 MT Coy Army Service Corps
JAMIESON Robert M. MM L/Cpl 47230 RAMC
JAMIESON Thomas MM Cpl 10255 1st Seaforth Highlanders
JAMIESON W. MM Sjt 7759 Royal Inniskilling Fusiliers
JAMIESON William MM Sjt 23941 RFA

JAMIESON William MM Pte S/16513 Arg & Suth Highlanders
JAMISON Thomas MM Sjt 71660 1st North Irish Horse
JANAWAY William H. MM Pte 653110 21st London Regt
JANE John A. MM L/Cpl 22230 1st Duke of Cornwall's LI
JANES Alfred MM Sjt 1561 1/5th Notts & Derby Regt
JANES Alfred J. MM+Bar Sjt 65632 126 Fd Coy Royal Engineers
JANES Charles MM Pte 79166 2nd Royal Fusiliers
JANES Frank MM Pte 40114 1st Bedfordshire Regt
JANES Fred Albert MM L/Cpl 42491 38th Bn Machine Gun Corps
JANES George MM Bdr 179712 B/286 Bde RFA
JANES Hawley Jack MM Pte 35579 5th Oxf & Bucks Light Infantry KIA 4.4.18.
JANES Horace MM Pte 10701 10th Royal West Kent Regt KIA 31.7.17.
JANES John MM Cpl 42231 76 Fd Amb RAMC KIA 28.5.18.
JANES Owen "DCM,MM,MID" Gnr 302079 E' Coy Tank Corps
JANES Silas MM Pte 122732 Machine Gun Corps
JANES Wallis C. MM L/Cpl 254292 2 Div Sig Coy Royal Engineers
JANSON Arthur MM Pte 17906 1st North Lancashire Regt KIA 10.7.18.
JAQUES Alfred "DCM,MM" L/Sjt 46027 12/13th Northumberland Fusiliers
JAQUES Richard A. MM Sjt 46690 RFA
JAQUES Thomas C. MM Pte 25174 10th West Riding Regt
JARDINE Alexander MM Sjt 10005 2nd Scottish Rifles KIA 23.10.16.
JARDINE Andrew MM L/Cpl 45523 Royal Engineers
JARDINE David William MM Gnr 11596 A/160 Bde RFA KIA 6.2.18.
JARDINE Frank MM L/Sjt S/10742 1st Royal Highlanders
JARDINE Frederick MM Pte 12447 6th Royal Inniskilling Fusiliers
JARDINE George Brown MM Pte 2564 1/5th Durham Light Infantry
JARDINE James MM Sjt 27731 17 Siege Bty RGA DOW 29.10.18.
JARDINE James R. MM Spr 63867 Royal Engineers
JARDINE John MM Pte 325554 Arg & Suth Highlanders
JARDINE John J. MM Sjt 240982 6th King's Own Scottish Borderers
JARDINE Marshall "DCM,MM" Sjt 60773 3rd Bn Machine Gun Corps
JARDINE T. MM Sjt 9964 Coldstream Guards
JARDINE William MM Gnr Fitter 655795 RFA
JARDINE William MM Pte 43785 2nd Royal Warwickshire Regt
JARDINE William MM L/Cpl 14220 10th Scottish Rifles DOW 19.8.17.
JARMAIN Walter Henry MM+Bar Pte 10138 1st Royal West Surrey Regt KIA 21.9.18.
JARMAN Alfred H. MM Gnr 36776 RFA
JARMAN Alfred J. MM Pte 18452 Royal West Kent Regt
JARMAN Charles MM L/Cpl 236251 1/1st Herefordshire Regt
JARMAN Frederick MM Gnr 9142 RFA
JARMAN Frederick W. MM Pte 251015 11th Essex Regt
JARMAN Henry L. MM+Bar L/Cpl 3163 1/24th London Regt
JARMAN James MM Pte G/66334 17th Royal Fusiliers
JARMAN John R. MM Gnr 74536 25 Bde RFA
JARMAN William MM Pte 68090 RAMC
JARMAN William Thomas MM Pte G/2822 6th East Kent Regt KIA 24.10.18.
JARRAM Bernard MM Sjt 31277 7th South Lancashire Regt att MGC.KIA 18.4.18.
JARRARD Cecil Herbert MM Pte 3/3586 1st Essex Regt KIA 12.10.16.
JARRARD George MM Pte 8937 1st Scots Guards
JARRATT Arthur MM Cpl 38692 Notts & Derby Regt
JARRATT Frank MM Sjt 240540 1/4th Yorkshire Regt
JARRATT S. MM Sjt 229515 26th Royal Fusiliers
JARRATT William MM Pte 8/14106 8th South Staffordshire Regt
JARRETT Ernest S. MM Gnr 207693 RFA
JARRETT John MM Pte 14969 Worcestershire Regt
JARRETT Joseph Churchill MM Cpl 13486 1st Bedfordshire Regt KIA 4.9.16.
JARRETT Percival Leonard MM Pte 493543 2/1(Home Counties)Fd Amb RAMC
JARRETT Thomas F. "MM,MID" Pte 5003 1st Royal West Kent Regt
JARRETT Walter MM L/Cpl 3430 6th East Kent Regt KIA 26.3.18.
JARRETT William MM Pte 48503 1st Devonshire Regt DOW 29.10.18.
JARROLD Percival John Joshua "DCM,MM" Sjt 6109 2nd Suffolk Regt
JARVIE Hugh MM Pte 265278 8th Scottish Rifles
JARVIE James MM Pte 41115 Seaforth Highlanders
JARVIE R. MM Pte 235810 York & Lancaster Regt
JARVIE William MM Pte S/25981 2nd Arg & Suth Highlanders
JARVIS Albert MM Bdr 16315 2/3rd SARB RGA
JARVIS Albert MM Cpl 116480 5 Labour Bn Royal Engineers
JARVIS Albert H. MM(2649 Pte 2nd London)+Bar Cpl 25834 Machine Gun Corps
JARVIS Alfred W. MM Sjt 267721 Royal Warwickshire Regt
JARVIS Andrew MM Pte 13810 Northumberland Fusiliers
JARVIS Archibald L. MM Pte 12045 7th Norfolk Regt
JARVIS Arthur L. MM Sjt 110183 1/1st Duke of Lancaster's Own Yeomanry
JARVIS Cecil E. "DCM,MM+Bar" Sjt 12856 2/4th Hampshire Regt
JARVIS Charles H. MM Sjt 5928 9th Royal Sussex Regt
JARVIS Edward MM Pte 18429 Northamptonshire Regt
JARVIS Emmanuel MM Pte 38826 2/4th Royal Berkshire Regt
JARVIS Ernest F. MM Pte C/7413 King's Royal Rifle Corps
JARVIS Ernest H. MM Gnr 216919 D/124 Bde RFA
JARVIS Frank MM L/Cpl 75954 Tank Corps
JARVIS Frederick C. MM Sjt 905 Royal Engineers
JARVIS Frederick George MM Cpl 2981 2nd Rifle Brigade KIA 26.6.16.
JARVIS Frederick J. MM Pte 26160 Devonshire Regt
JARVIS George MM Dvr 115040 RFA
JARVIS George Henry MM Pte 667 11 Fd Amb RAMC KIA 5.4.18.
JARVIS H.A.E. MM Cpl 52985 4th Middlesex Regt
JARVIS Harold MM+Bar Pte 251475 6th Manchester Regt
JARVIS Henry A. MM Sjt S/2672 Rifle Brigade
JARVIS Henry G. MM Pte 305827 1st Bn Tank Corps
JARVIS James MM Pte 202430 10th Essex Regt
JARVIS James W. MM Pte 13841 8th Norfolk Regt
JARVIS John H. MM Gnr 42911 188 Bde RFA
JARVIS Leonard MM L/Cpl 10/1191 11th East Yorkshire Regt DOW 13.7.18.
JARVIS Leonard MM+Bar Sjt 8628 2nd Worcestershire Regt KIA 24.6.18.
JARVIS Maurice MM+Bar Cpl 8281 2nd Border Regt
JARVIS Oswald V. MM Cpl 300472 5th London Regt
JARVIS Reginald Arthur "MM,CG(B)" Sjt 18582 York & Lancaster Regt
JARVIS Sydney MM Gnr 165812 76 Bde RFA
JARVIS Sydney F. MM Pte 39200 5th Gloucestershire Regt
JARVIS Thomas H. MM Pte 241090 1/5th Devonshire Regt
JARVIS Thomas H. MM Sjt 790 Lincolnshire Regt
JARVIS Thomas Sylvester MM L/Cpl 16983 2nd Scottish Rifles
JARVIS Victor E. MM L/Sjt 4388 2/1st HAC (Inf)
JARVIS Walter MM Pte 240117 6th Leicestershire Regt
JARVIS William MM Pte 20934 Manchester Regt
JARVIS William MM Pte 7969 1st East Kent Regt
JARVIS William MM Gnr 12523 RFA
JARVIS William Edward MM L/Cpl 16/51 16th Royal Warwickshire Regt Died 16.9.18.
JASPER Arthur W. MM S/Sjt 06183 Army Ordnance Corps
JASPER Leslie L. MM Spr 167868 Royal Engineers
JASPER Sampson Edward MM Pte 240332 1st Duke of Cornwall's LI KIA 30.8.18.
JASPER Sidney MM Pte 12793 1st Bedfordshire Regt
JASPER W. MM Dvr 61972 14 Bde RFA
JASPER William MM Cpl 3667 8th Royal West Kent Regt
JASPER William MM Sjt 11213 1st Scots Guards
JATER Albert MM Pte R/39336 13th King's Royal Rifle Corps
JAUNCEY William H. MM Sjt 82004 RGA
JAY Albert MM Cpl 22188 11th South Wales Borderers KIA 31.7.17.
JAY Archibald MM CQMS 305463 8th Royal Warwickshire Regt
JAY Arthur J. MM+Bar Sjt 15389 2nd Suffolk Regt
JAY George MM Cpl P416 Military Foot Police DOW 24.3.18.
JAY Joseph MM Bdr 73372 24 Bde RFA
JAY Percy G. "MM(13803,L/Cpl 10th Essex Regt)+Bar" Cpl 310821 4 Fd Svy Bn Royal Engineers
JAYCOCK Henry MM Pte 51912 1/5th Liverpool Regt
JAYE Thomas MM+Bar Sjt 13543 Durham Light Infantry
JAYES James MM Sjt 27329 Notts & Derby Regt
JAYNES Edward MM Cpl 26563 16th Notts & Derby Regt
JEACOCK Alexander William Arthur MM Sjt 242661 6th Royal Warwickshire Regt
JEACOCK Ernest E. MM L/Cpl 41052 Royal Irish Rifles
JEAL Roland J. MM Spr 495333 61 Div Sig Coy Royal Engineers
JEANES Ernest C. MM Pte 8587 6th Royal Irish Regt
JEANES Henry MM Pte 1708 1/5th Leicestershire Regt
JEANES Herbert W. MM SM Armourer T/264 Army Ordnance Corps
JEANES John Victor MM+Bar Sjt Sig 12813 2nd Grenadier Guards
JEANS Clement MM Gnr 1350 B/235 Bde RFA
JEANS George E. MM L/Bdr 35844 57 Siege Bty RGA
JEARY Arthur James MM Pte 53765 50th Bn Machine Gun Corps

JEARY Sydney V. MM Cpl 8337 15th Hussars
JEATER Henry William MM L/Cpl 552120 518 Fd Coy Royal Engineers
JEBB Henry MM Cpl 202035 Notts & Derby Regt
JEE Charles MM Sjt 78832 RFA
JEEVES Charles Anthony Victor MM L/Cpl 14391 Royal Dublin Fusiliers KIA 20.9.17.
JEEVES Charles Frederick MM Cpl 33034 2nd Bedfordshire Regt
JEEVES Frederick MM+Bar Cpl 38283 RFA
JEFCOAT Francis H. MM Pte 25098 5th West Riding Regt
JEFFCOAT Samuel MM Pte 29776 Yorkshire Regt
JEFFCOCK Clifford MM L/Cpl 307762 15th Bn Tank Corps KIA 27.9.18.
JEFFCOCK Walter W. MM Sjt 8610 RFA
JEFFCOTT Leonard James MM Sjt 43893 1st Royal Irish Rifles
JEFFCOTT Leslie Arthur MM Sjt 2297 46 Div Sig Coy Royal Engineers
JEFFEREY Henry Thomas MM Pte 203189 1/4th York & Lancaster Regt KIA 13.10.18.
JEFFERIES Albert MM L/Cpl 18907 1st Border Regt
JEFFERIES Albert E. MM Sjt 6934 2nd Wiltshire Regt
JEFFERIES Alfred E.T. MM L/Cpl 133181 36th Bn Machine Gun Corps
JEFFERIES Alfred W. MM Pte 3835 4th Dragoon Guards
JEFFERIES Cecil "DCM,MM" Cpl 522025 483 Fd Coy Royal Engineers
JEFFERIES Charles E. MM Pte 7452 2nd Wiltshire Regt
JEFFERIES Cornelius G. MM Cpl 10745 7th Wiltshire Regt
JEFFERIES Edward C.F. MM Sjt 55056 43 Bde RFA
JEFFERIES John MM Pte 78103 9th Bn Tank Corps
JEFFERIES Joseph MM Gnr 29907 91 Bde RFA
JEFFERIES Stanley MM Sjt 11267 11th Hampshire Regt
JEFFERIES W. MM Cpl 592413 18th London Regt
JEFFERIES William MM Pte 11254 6th Yorkshire Light Infantry
JEFFERIES William Thierry MM Sjt M2/193147 Army Service Corps
JEFFERIS Edward William MM Cpl 19955 30 Mot Amb Convoy RAMC
JEFFERIS William H. MM Pte 301410 6th Durham Light Infantry
JEFFERS James MM Sjt 11527 9th Scottish Rifles
JEFFERS James W. MM Pte 17712 Durham Light Infantry
JEFFERSON Arthur P. MM Pte 13928 8th East Yorkshire Regt
JEFFERSON Charles W. "DCM,MM" Cpl 718254 1/23rd London Regt
JEFFERSON Charles W. MM Cpl 17417 Durham Light Infantry
JEFFERSON F.J.H. MM Gnr L/22141 B/296 Bde RFA
JEFFERSON Geoffrey MM Pte 12043 Gordon Highlanders
JEFFERSON J.W. MM+Bar Sjt 9993 26 Fd Coy Royal Engineers
JEFFERSON James MM Pte 12515 8th West Riding Regt
JEFFERSON John MM+Bar Pte 22848 15th Durham Light Infantry KIA 4.10.17.
JEFFERSON John Drysdale "DCM,MM+Bar" Sjt 24346 Northumberland Fusiliers
JEFFERSON Joseph MM Sjt R/994 King's Royal Rifle Corps
JEFFERSON Robert MM Dvr 765610 RFA
JEFFERSON Samuel MM Cpl 36776 11th West Yorkshire Regt
JEFFERSON Thomas MM Gnr 710924 330 Bde RFA
JEFFERSON Thomas W. MM Pte 266003 Northumberland Fusiliers
JEFFERSON William MM Pte 11258 1st Cheshire Regt KIA 21.8.18.
JEFFERSON William MM Bdr 27443 8 Siege Bty RGA
JEFFERSON William Edward MM Bdr 46442 9 Siege Bty RGA
JEFFERY Albert MM Pte 20383 10th West Riding Regt
JEFFERY Ernest MM Gnr 68817 'C' Bty RHA
JEFFERY Fred MM Spr 257206 Royal Engineers
JEFFERY George Alfred MM L/Cpl 11/136 11th East Yorkshire Regt KIA 26.3.18.
JEFFERY Harold MM Pte 268078 1/8th West Yorkshire Regt
JEFFERY Harry G. MM Cpl 10282 RFA
JEFFERY Herbert MM Cpl 786041 312 Bde RFA
JEFFERY Horace John MM Sjt 7782 1st Royal West Kent Regt
JEFFERY Jack MM Cpl 701974 23rd London Regt
JEFFERY James P. MM L/Cpl 370407 1/8th London Regt
JEFFERY John MM L/Cpl 81129 Royal Engineers
JEFFERY John H. MM Bdr 845309 D/242 Bde RFA
JEFFERY John Henry MM Pte 59879 8th Northumberland Fusiliers
JEFFERY Sydney MM Pnr 316549 57 Div Sig Coy Royal Engineers
JEFFERY Thomas R. MM Pte 3878 Royal Sussex Regt
JEFFERY W.C. MM Cpl 70314 25 Bde RFA
JEFFERY Wallace MM Cpl 321927 6th London Regt
JEFFERY Walter MM Sjt 8111 6th Royal West Kent Regt
JEFFERYES Frederick MM Sjt 8874 2nd Worcestershire Regt

JEFFERYS Louis Thomas MM L/Cpl R/3396 12th King's Royal Rifle Corps KIA 18.9.16.
JEFFERYS Nathan MM Sjt 965 1st Lancashire Fusiliers
JEFFERYS Richard MM Bdr 14586 D/64 Bde RFA
JEFFORD J.W. MM Cpl 49124 RHA
JEFFREY Frederick MM Sjt 5402 Army Veterinary Corps
JEFFREY Frederick C. MM Pte 31554 2nd Bedfordshire Regt
JEFFREY Frederick J. MM Pnr 221769 Royal Engineers
JEFFREY G.A. MM Pte 24178 Duke of Cornwall's LI
JEFFREY George "MM,MID" Sjt 200216 1/4th King's Own Scottish Borderers
JEFFREY George "DCM+Bar,MM,CG(F)" CSM 4800 7th Seaforth Highlanders
JEFFREY John MM Sjt 700723 B/330 Bde RFA Died 19.4.18.
JEFFREY John F. "MM,MID" Cpl 508 Army Cyclist Corps
JEFFREY Joseph MM Pte 271444 12th Royal Scots
JEFFREY Robert MM Pte 15644 Royal Inniskilling Fusiliers
JEFFREY Robert MM L/Cpl 24486 154 Coy Machine Gun Corps DOW 23.11.17.
JEFFREY Thomas Henry MM Pte 20/981 20th Durham Light Infantry KIA 4.9.18.
JEFFREY Walter B. MM L/Sjt C/968 King's Royal Rifle Corps
JEFFREY Walter G. MM L/Cpl 277174 Manchester Regt
JEFFREY William "MM,MSM" Sjt TT0/3042 Army Veterinary Corps att C/317 Bde RFA
JEFFREYS Albert S. MM Pte 43845 King's Royal Rifle Corps att 13th London Regt
JEFFREYS Charles J. MM+Bar L/Cpl 12111 2nd Grenadier Guards
JEFFREYS Daniel "MM,MSM" S/Sjt 63912 91 Fd Amb RAMC
JEFFREYS G. MM Sjt 3/9429 Durham Light Infantry
JEFFREYS Walter H. MM Pte 59268 11th Royal Scots Fusiliers
JEFFRIE Peter MM L/Cpl S/6262 10th Arg & Suth Highlanders
JEFFRIES Alec J. MM Pte 8465 2nd Suffolk Regt
JEFFRIES Frederick S. "MM,MID" Sjt 27037 'K' Cable Section Royal Engineers
JEFFRIES George W. MM Sjt 9729 Royal West Surrey Regt
JEFFRIES Harold MM L/Cpl 261136 Royal Engineers
JEFFRIES Henry MM L/Cpl B/301445 Rifle Brigade
JEFFRIES Henry A. MM 2nd Cpl 560023 Royal Engineers
JEFFRIES Henry C. MM L/Cpl 17757 6th Wiltshire Regt
JEFFRIES James Joseph MM Gnr 75233 8 Bde RFA
JEFFRIES John MM Pte 25/302 Northumberland Fusiliers
JEFFRIES Louis F. MM Pte 133800 1st Royal Fusiliers
JEFFRIES Percy James "MM,MSM" 2nd Cpl 137865 Royal Engineers
JEFFRIES W. MM Pte 85745 6th Durham Light Infantry
JEFFRIES W. MM Pte 14308 Essex Regt
JEFFRIES William MM Pte 3633 1st Notts & Derby Regt
JEFFRIES William H. MM L/Bdr 39126 RGA
JEFFRYES Henry A. MM Sjt 373937 17th London Regt
JEFFS Alfred MM Pte 9324 Oxf & Bucks Light Infantry
JEFFS Charles James MM Pte G/9924 11th Royal West Kent Regt
JEFFS E.W.B. MM Sjt 137 Liverpool Regt
JEFFS George MM L/Sjt 27687 Lancashire Fusiliers
JEFFS Samuel MM Pte 17832 Royal West Kent Regt
JELDEN Robert Charles MM L/Cpl 1767 6th East Kent Regt
JELFS George W. MM L/Cpl 241538 2/8th Worcestershire Regt
JELFS Norman MM Spr 169725 Royal Engineers
JELLEY Albert F.P. MM+Bar Sjt 14264 RFA
JELLEY Sidney MM Cpl 1169 7th Royal West Surrey Regt KIA 23.8.18.
JELLEY Walter J. MM Pte 3666 18th London Regt att Royal Irish Rifles.
JELLY R. MM Pte 6551 York & Lancaster Regt
JELLYMAN John MM Sjt 56772 27 Bde RFA
JEMMETT Edward MM L/Cpl 6687 Rifle Brigade
JEMMETT William F. "MM,MID" L/Bdr 317100 1 Hy Bty RGA
JEMPSON Albert E. MM Spr 134811 Royal Engineers
JENKIN Arthur MM Pte 2244 1/24th London Regt KIA 15.9.16.
JENKIN Jack MM Pte 201693 Duke of Cornwall's LI
JENKING Eric Fleetwood MM 2nd Cpl 387308 6 Div Sig Coy Royal Engineers Died 3.11.18.
JENKINS A. MM Cpl 74142 Signal Service Royal Engineers
JENKINS Albert Edgar MM Pte 8813 2nd Royal Welsh Fusiliers KIA 23.4.17.
JENKINS Arnold A. MM Pte 16648 Welsh Regt
JENKINS Arthur MM L/Cpl 16592 Machine Gun Corps
JENKINS Arthur Joseph MM Gnr 2047 HQ 305 Bde RFA
JENKINS Benjamin David MM Pte 31227 1st Royal Welsh Fusiliers KIA 27.2.17.

JENKINS Charles MM Pte 19497 Dorsetshire Regt
JENKINS Charles MM Sjt 17858 5 Div Ammn Col RFA
JENKINS David E. MM Sjt 3587 119 Bde RFA
JENKINS David G. MM Sjt 337736 RGA
JENKINS David J. MM Pte 33697 Welsh Regt
JENKINS David Llewellyn MM Gnr 76574 40 Bde RFA
JENKINS Edmund G. "MM,MID" Bdr 16526 3 Bty 45 Bde RFA
JENKINS Edward MM Gnr 512 RFA
JENKINS F.J. MM Sjt L/9928 1st East Kent Regt
JENKINS F.J. MM Cpl 7959 Royal Flying Corps
JENKINS Frank Mason MM Sjt 12903 9th Royal Welsh Fusiliers DOW 8.5.18.
JENKINS Frederick MM Sjt 6393 Shropshire Light Infantry
JENKINS Frederick H. MM Cpl 30910 RFA
JENKINS Frederick Joseph MM Pte M2/135133 627 Coy Army Service Corps
JENKINS George MM Pte 23390 8th Gloucestershire Regt
JENKINS George W. MM L/Cpl 84847 Machine Gun Corps
JENKINS H. MM Gnr 11724 RFA
JENKINS Harold MM Sjt 23661 56 Fd Coy Royal Engineers DOW 26.4.17.
JENKINS Harry MM Pte 7075 76 Fd Amb RAMC
JENKINS Harry MM Spr 97926 Royal Engineers
JENKINS Henry MM L/Bdr 6407 99 Bty 20 Bde RFA
JENKINS Henry MM Cpl 19921 3rd Dragoon Guards
JENKINS Henry "MM,MID" Pte 15327 11th Welsh Regt
JENKINS Herbert Clement MM Cpl 20378 10th South Wales Borderers Died 12.3.19.
JENKINS Hugh F. MM Cpl 9805 1/7th Arg & Suth Highlanders
JENKINS Ivor MM L/Cpl 20871 Welsh Regt
JENKINS James MM Gnr Sig 92957 61 Siege Bty RGA
JENKINS James MM L/Cpl 8517 2nd Irish Guards
JENKINS James MM Cpl 606 1st Arg & Suth Highlanders
JENKINS James MM+Bar Sjt 276030 1/7th Arg & Suth Highlanders
JENKINS John MM L/Cpl 304685 15th Bn Tank Corps
JENKINS John "DCM,MM" Pte 16551 1st Grenadier Guards
JENKINS John MM Gnr 50545 26 Heavy Bty RGA
JENKINS John MM+Bar 2nd Cpl 62945 38 Div Sig Coy Royal Engineers
JENKINS John B. MM Pte 202695 15th Welsh Regt
JENKINS John G. MM L/Cpl 15007 Liverpool Regt
JENKINS John H. MM Pte 532704 15th London Regt
JENKINS Joseph MM Pte 95141 15th Durham Light Infantry
JENKINS Lewis E. MM Bdr 730438 RFA
JENKINS Norman Macdonald MM Cpl S/13679 1st Cameron Highlanders
JENKINS Owen G. MM Cpl 23563 16th Royal Welsh Fusiliers
JENKINS P.N. MM Sjt 701 London Regt
JENKINS Robert MM Pnr 129927 'G' Special Coy Royal Engineers
JENKINS Robert MM Cpl 241141 1/5th Welsh Regt
JENKINS S. MM Pte 3637 Seaforth Highlanders
JENKINS S.S. MM Sjt Saddler 17959 36 Bde RFA
JENKINS Samuel MM S/Sjt 95432 Royal Engineers
JENKINS Stephen J. MM Pte S/23979 8th Royal Highlanders
JENKINS Thomas Arthur MM Sjt 253057 Signal Service Royal Engineers
JENKINS Thomas Edmund MM Pte 9258 8th Gloucestershire Regt
JENKINS Walter MM Cpl 18329 5th Yorkshire Light Infantry
JENKINS William MM L/Sjt 11501 1st Irish Guards
JENKINS William MM Cpl 10153 2nd Leinster Regt
JENKINS William MM Pte 38297 9th Welsh Regt
JENKINS William MM Sjt 265071 1/2nd Monmouthshire Regt
JENKINS William MM Cpl 371183 RGA
JENKINS William A. MM Dvr 121074 RFA
JENKINS William Edward MM+Bar Sjt 463118 50 Div Sig Coy Royal Engineers
JENKINS William Edward MM L/Cpl 43388 1st Royal Inniskilling Fusiliers KIA 1.10.18.
JENKINS William G. MM+Bar Pte 13107 1st South Wales Borderers
JENKINS William H. MM Pte M2/116398 Army Service Corps
JENKINS William H. MM L/Bdr 56770 25 Bde RFA
JENKINS William J. MM Pte 202434 14th Welsh Regt
JENKINS William S. MM Pte 15620 2nd South Wales Borderers
JENKINS William S. MM Pte 77644 RAMC
JENKINS William W.B. MM Sjt MS/2604 Army Service Corps
JENKINSON Albert MM Sjt 99207 Royal Engineers
JENKINSON Arthur MM Gnr 50662 RGA
JENKINSON Arthur MM L/Cpl 21320 8th Royal Lancaster Regt
JENKINSON Fred S. "DCM,MM" Sjt 785321 C/232 Bde RFA
JENKINSON Frederick MM L/Sjt R/7056 13th King's Royal Rifle Corps
JENKINSON Henry MM Sjt 19043 14th Liverpool Regt
JENKINSON John H. MM Pte 405146 RAMC
JENKINSON John H. MM Pte 32108 RAMC
JENKINSON Matthew MM Cpl 44403 23rd Bn Machine Gun Corps
JENKINSON Percy MM L/Cpl 200743 1/4th York & Lancaster Regt
JENKINSON Robert A. MM Pte 19418 Manchester Regt
JENKINSON Samuel MM Pte 11/8157 11th Notts & Derby Regt
JENKINSON Samuel Arthur MM Pte 350147 1/1(East Lancashire)Fd Amb RAMC
JENKINSON Walter MM Cpl 204013 Lancashire Fusiliers
JENKINSON Walter Frederick MM Sjt 12308 C/189 Bty RFA KIA 17.7.17.
JENKINSON Walter Gyles MM+Bar L/Cpl 17862 7th Royal Sussex Regt
JENKINSON William MM Spr 477036 429 Fd Coy Royal Engineers
JENKINSON William MM Sjt 715072 210 Bde RFA
JENKS Bertie James MM L/Cpl 2935 1/4th Lincolnshire Regt
JENKS Edwin C. MM+Bar Pte 8207 1st Shropshire Light Infantry
JENKS Frank MM+Bar Pte 54408 25th Royal Welsh Fusiliers
JENKS Thomas MM Sjt 47075 16 Heavy Bty RGA
JENKYNS Eric C. MM Sjt 15/518 15th West Yorkshire Regt
JENNER Arthur E. MM L/Cpl 200696 7th Royal West Surrey Regt
JENNER Charles T. MM Sjt 472072 12th London Regt
JENNER Douglas Pratt MM Cpl G/1074 7th C Coy East Kent Regt KIA 18.9.18.
JENNER Edwin J. MM Sjt DM2/151467 Army Service Corps att RGA.
JENNER Ernest Stephen MM SQMS 6256 9th Lancers
JENNER George "DCM,MM" Cpl 657 6th Royal West Kent Regt
JENNER Henry J. MM Pte 202389 6th South Staffordshire Regt
JENNER James H. MM Pte 1813 1/8th London Regt
JENNER John "DCM,MM" CSM 10086 1st Border Regt
JENNER Robert Henry MM Cpl 106135 Y/4 Med TM Bty RFA
JENNER Samuel MM Dvr 915635 D/223 RFA
JENNER Stanley MM Sjt 275288 2/7th Manchester Regt
JENNEY Herbert MM Sjt 249513 9 Div Sig Coy Royal Engineers
JENNEY Tom Henry MM Pte 241015 1/5th Yorkshire Regt
JENNINGS Albert J. MM Cpl L/7519 2nd Royal Sussex Regt
JENNINGS Alby MM Pte 41263 2nd Royal Scots Fusiliers
JENNINGS Alfred Reginald MM+Bar Sjt 18926 1/5th Somerset Light Infantry Died 8.10.18.
JENNINGS Arthur E. MM+Bar Pte 613628 1/19th London Regt
JENNINGS Arthur P. MM Pte 144992 50th Bn Machine Gun Corps
JENNINGS Bernard C.G. MM L/Cpl 202664 West Riding Regt
JENNINGS Charles MM Sjt 53737 61st Bn Machine Gun Corps
JENNINGS Charles Edward MM L/Cpl 200862 5th Liverpool Regt
JENNINGS Edward MM Gnr Fitter 53129 RFA
JENNINGS Ewart Reginald MM Pte 15882 2nd Lincolnshire Regt
JENNINGS Francis MM L/Cpl 41338 9th Royal Irish Fusiliers
JENNINGS Frederick MM Pte 266576 6th Notts & Derby Regt
JENNINGS G. MM L/Cpl P5411 Military Mounted Police
JENNINGS George MM Pte 16571 1st Devonshire Regt
JENNINGS George MM L/Cpl 11271 8th Gloucestershire Regt
JENNINGS George Kickweed MM Cpl 17409 13th East Surrey Regt KIA 26.7.17.
JENNINGS Harold J. MM Cpl 74097 Royal Engineers
JENNINGS Harry MM Pte 59371 19th Liverpool Regt
JENNINGS Harry MM Pte 48390 131 Fd Amb RAMC
JENNINGS Henry MM Pte 235158 13th Liverpool Regt
JENNINGS Henry A. "DCM,MM" L/Bdr 68208 C/295 Bde RFA
JENNINGS Herbert MM L/Cpl 29210 Middlesex Regt
JENNINGS James MM Spr 136246 Royal Engineers
JENNINGS James "MM,MID" L/Cpl 3399 Machine Gun Corps
JENNINGS James MM L/Cpl 39607 125 Coy Machine Gun Corps KIA 6.9.17.
JENNINGS James MM Cpl 11270 8th West Riding Regt
JENNINGS James S. MM Cpl F/1620 16th Middlesex Regt
JENNINGS John MM Sjt 965991 D/44 Bde RFA
JENNINGS John MM+Bar Sjt 21041 22nd Manchester Regt
JENNINGS John MM L/Sjt 54 2nd Gordon Highlanders
JENNINGS Joseph MM+Bar Cpl 36891 RGA
JENNINGS Joseph MM+Bar Cpl 70310 1 Div Sig Coy Royal Engineers
JENNINGS Leonard H. MM+Bar Cpl 165 6th Royal West Kent Regt
JENNINGS Mabel MM Sister F TFNS
JENNINGS Michael MM Pte 200772 6th East Lancashire Regt
JENNINGS Owen Edward MM+Bar Pte 19429 5th Dorsetshire Regt
JENNINGS P. MM Cpl 202333 11th Suffolk Regt
JENNINGS Percy "DCM,MM" Sjt 2582 1/1st(Buckinghamshire)Bn Oxf & Bucks Light Infantry

JENNINGS Percy Charles MM+Bar Sjt 15221 RFA
JENNINGS Percy Sumners MM Cpl 300797 1/8th Arg & Suth Highlanders
JENNINGS Philip MM Pte 15114 25th Royal Fusiliers att MGC
JENNINGS Raymond MM Pte 240883 5th West Riding Regt
JENNINGS Richard MM Sjt 804 RAMC
JENNINGS Robert S.G. MM Sjt 645188 51 Div Ammn Col RFA
JENNINGS Sidney Seely MM Pte 48727 RAMC
JENNINGS Sydney Ernest MM Gnr 70539 RGA
JENNINGS Thomas MM Pte 237094 1/1st Herefordshire Regt
JENNINGS Thomas G. MM Pte 11842 2nd Highland Light Infantry
JENNINGS Walter E. MM Sjt 260259 Monmouthshire Regt att 6th South Wales Borderers
JENNINGS William MM Sjt 240045 1/8th Worcestershire Regt
JENNINGS William MM Dvr 700633 2 Div Ammn Col RFA
JENNINGS William MM Cpl 1163 1/1st Cambridgeshire Regt KIA 23.9.16.
JENNINGS William MM Cpl 403490 RAMC
JENNINGS William A. MM 2nd Cpl 181797 Royal Engineers
JENNINGS William David MM L/Cpl 1595 1/6th Welsh Regt KIA 20.7.16.
JENNINGS WilliamF. MM Cpl 20656 2 Fd Coy Royal Engineers
JENNIONS William H. MM Pte 276973 7th Manchester Regt
JENNISON George MM L/Cpl 40200 2nd South Wales Borderers
JENRICK G.W. "MM,MID" Pte 7655 1st East Kent Regt
JENSEN Norham "MM,MSM" Sjt 1442 50 Div Sig Coy Royal Engineers
JENSEN William MM L/Cpl 458769 50 Div Sig Coy Royal Engineers
JEPHGOTT Hugo B. MM L/Cpl 374448 8th London Regt
JEPSON Cecil MM Pte 3766 Notts & Derby Regt
JEPSON George MM Pte 15231 9th Notts & Derby Regt
JEPSON George E. MM Pte 42307 9th Scottish Rifles
JEPSON J. MM Pte 7952 2nd Essex Regt
JEPSON John H. MM Cpl 60366 48th Bn Machine Gun Corps
JEPSON Oscar MM Gnr Shoeing Smith 12569 RFA
JEPSON RobertS. MM Sjt 5973 1st East Lancashire Regt
JEPSON Stanley MM Pte 99560 6th Liverpool Regt
JEPSON William MM Pte 19686 2nd Coldstream Guards
JEPSON Willie MM Pte 252020 11th Manchester Regt
JEREMY David J. MM L/Cpl 200468 1/4th Welsh Regt
JERMY Cubitt E. MM Pte 5662 8th East Surrey Regt
JERMY George MM Gnr 751222 RFA
JERMY William J. "DCM,MM" Cpl 32033 9th Norfolk Regt
JEROMSON John Scott "MM,MID" Bde 7437 B/82 Bde RFA
JERRAM Edward C. MM L/Cpl 131715 46th Royal Fusiliers
JERRAM Herbert Harry MM L/Cpl 33372 2nd Hampshire Regt KIA 2.10.18.
JERRAM John MM Pnr 358037 37 Div Sig Coy Royal Engineers
JERRAM John Albert MM L/Cpl 98315 157 Fd Coy Royal Engineers
JERRARD Arthur Samuel MM Dvr 128274 A/70 Bde RFA
JERRED Arthur MM+Bar Sjt 5281 8 Fd Amb RAMC
JERROM Sydney G. MM Pte 45064 8th Royal Berkshire Regt
JERVIS Abraham James MM Pte 493720 2/1(Home Counties)Fd Amb RAMC
JERVIS Alfred S. MM Bdr 885186 RFA
JERVIS Herbert MM+Bar Sjt 492018 46 Div Sig Coy Royal Engineers
JERVIS William MM CSM 21258 Duke of Cornwall's LI
JESS John MM Pte 24561 Highland Light Infantry
JESSE Joseph H. MM Pte 235901 Lancashire Fusiliers
JESSOP Francis W. MM Pte 11862 20th Hussars
JESSOP Francis W. MM Pte 11862 20th Hussars
JESSOP George MM Sjt 11809 Royal Engineers
JESSOP Harry MM Pte 40347 5th Yorkshire Light Infantry
JESSOP James MM Dvr T3/027012 Army Service Corps
JESSOP Richard MM Dvr 63727 B/95 Bde RFA Died 27.5.18.
JESSOP Robert W. MM(C/12647 Cpl KRRC)+Bar Sjt 75500 2nd Bn Tank Corps
JESSOP Stanley MM L/Sjt 201219 1/4th West Riding Regt
JESSOP William MM+Bar Pte 16126 10th Northumberland Fusiliers
JESSUP Harry MM Sjt 8149 11th Royal Fusiliers
JESSUP J.T. MM Sjt 49110 C/79 Bde RFA
JESSUP Oliver Elijah MM L/Cpl 15403 9th Norfolk Regt KIA 21.3.18.
JESSUP William J. MM Gnr 31889 RGA
JESSUP William J. MM Pte 451126 1/11th London Regt
JESTER Arthur MM L/Cpl G/1857 8th Royal Sussex Regt
JETEN Stephen E. MM Cpl L/13259 4th Royal Fusiliers KIA 31.8.18.
JEVONS Henry MM L/Cpl 10209 3rd Coldstream Guards
JEVONS Thomas A. MM Gnr 167717 D/276 Bde RFA
JEVONS William MM CSM 7757 2nd South Staffordshire Regt
JEW George E. MM Pte 17001 10th Worcestershire Regt
JEWELL Arthur MM Cpl 34977 1st Northumberland Fusiliers
JEWELL Ernest P. MM Pte S/18462 Rifle Brigade
JEWELL Fred MM Pte 19035 Devonshire Regt
JEWELL George Fred MM Sjt 38210 Welsh Regt
JEWELL Oliver Wilson MM Bdr 755878 D/251 Bde RFA
JEWELL Percy R. MM Gnr 40132 279 Siege Bty RGA
JEWELL Samuel Herbert MM Gnr 51656 4 Div Ammn Col RGA
JEWELL Thomas H. MM Cpl 244718 4 Fd Svy Bn Royal Engineers
JEWELL William MM Gnr 29368 RFA
JEWESS J. MM Sjt 117 RGA
JEWISS Alfred MM L/Cpl 321651 6th London Regt
JEWISS Ernest H. MM+Bar L/Cpl G/79118 10th Royal Fusiliers
JEWITT Fred MM Sjt 35775 2nd Yorkshire Light Infantry
JEWITT Robert W. MM Sjt 382341 77 Siege Bty RGA
JEWKES Charles Henry MM Dvr 135305 B/114 Bde RFA
JEWKES Thomas MM Pte 21985 Northumberland Fusiliers
JEYNES Albert MM Bdr 27964 RFA
JEYNES Alfred MM Pte 72010 Machine Gun Corps
JEYNES Frederick W. MM Pte 6933 3rd Worcestershire Regt
JEYNES Herbert James MM Gnr 835259 B/242 Bde RFA
JEZARD George "MM,MID" Sjt 74125 286 Siege Bty RGA
JEZARD Samuel MM Sjt 24507 5 Div Sig Coy Royal Engineers
JIGGINS Alan J. MM Spr 90801 Royal Engineers
JIGGINS Percy W. MM Spr 127504 25 Div Sig Coy Royal Engineers
JILKS William MM Pte 20718 12th Gloucestershire Regt att 7th Royal West Kent Regt.
JINKS Cornelius MM L/Cpl 15255 7th Northamptonshire Regt
JINKS James MM Pte 40640 9th West Yorkshire Regt
JINKS James Albert MM Cpl 22216 311 Rly Const Coy Royal Engineers
JINKS John MM Gnr 224390 112 Bde RFA
JINKS Reginald Thomas MM Pte 27521 Royal Welsh Fusiliers
JOB Hugh MM Pte 40857 Royal Welsh Fusiliers
JOB Robert E. MM Sjt 371048 RGA
JOBBER Horace MM Cpl 26278 11th Lancashire Fusiliers KIA 27.5.18.
JOBBINS Arthur G. MM Pte 3243 1/1st City of London Yeomanry
JOBE John E. MM Sjt 15588 Middlesex Regt
JOBES John James MM Gnr 50015 50 Div Ammn Col RFA
JOBES William MM Pte 376439 Royal Scots
JOBLING Fred MM Pte 3/8091 2nd Yorkshire Regt KIA 8.5.18.
JOBLING Frederick William MM Gnr L/27674 A/161 Bde RFA KIA 8.8.17.
JOBLING George A. MM Gnr L/12205 RFA
JOBLING George G. MM Spr 457374 Royal Engineers
JOBLING Henry M. MM L/Cpl 59644 152 Fd Coy Royal Engineers
JOBLING James MM Pte 2022 1/4th Northumberland Fusiliers
JOBLING John "DCM,MM" Pte 12544 Coldstream Guards
JOBLINS John W. MM Pte 19/636 Durham Light Infantry
JOBSON John E. MM Cpl 19/688 19th Northumberland Fusiliers
JOBSON John William R. MM L/Cpl 15699 10th Northumberland Fusiliers
JOBSON Oswald MM L/Cpl 10382 XI Corps Cyclist Bn Army Cyclist Corps
JOBSON Robert MM Pte 10661 Northumberland Fusiliers
JOBSON Thomas Samuel MM Pte G/19679 21st Middlesex Regt DOW 1.3.18.
JOCEYLINN Patrick MM Pte 11156 1st Royal Dublin Fusiliers DOW 9.5.18.
JODRELL Joseph MM Pte 308009 West Riding Regt
JOEL H.McC. MM L/Cpl P4760 Military Mounted Police
JOEL Joseph H. MM Sjt 7510 8th Royal Fusiliers
JOHANNESSON Axel William MM Pte 4558 1/6th Gloucestershire Regt
JOHANSEN W.L. MM Sjt 10/1865 West Riding Regt
JOHN Albert MM Pte 141 1st Welsh Guards
JOHN Arthur E. MM Cpl 368026 2 Fd Amb RAMC
JOHN Benjamin "MM,MID" L/Sjt 17719 Grenadier Guards
JOHN David W. MM Pte 2680 2nd Lancashire Fusiliers
JOHN Emrys MM Pte 26752 15th Welsh Regt
JOHN George MM Gnr 117756 RFA
JOHN George Rees MM Sjt 200131 1/5th Liverpool Regt
JOHN John A. MM Cpl 2395 Royal Engineers
JOHN Llewellyn MM Pte 63410 Machine Gun Corps
JOHN Thomas MM Pte 22217 13th Welsh Regt KIA 8.10.18.
JOHN Thomas H. MM Cpl 44001 RGA
JOHN Thomas Henry MM Pte 19442 2nd Welsh Regt DOW 27.12.16.
JOHN William MM Dvr 42376 RFA

JOHN William L. MM Sjt 20229 Shropshire Light Infantry
JOHNCOCK Percy C. MM L/Cpl 267156 6th Notts & Derby Regt
JOHNCOCK William Frederick MM Spr 179527 490 Fd Coy Royal Engineers
JOHNCOX J. MM L/Cpl G2344 8th Royal Sussex Regt
JOHNS Alfred MM Spr 132332 251 Tunnelling Coy Royal Engineers
JOHNS Andrew MM L/Cpl 718119 23rd London Regt
JOHNS Benjamin MM Cpl 291106 RGA
JOHNS Cyril B. MM Pte 53202 4th Middlesex Regt
JOHNS David A. MM Pte 508052 1 Fd Amb RAMC
JOHNS Ernest E. MM Cpl 3/7166 Devonshire Regt
JOHNS Harry MM Pte 201050 1/5th Bedfordshire Regt KIA 27.7.17.
JOHNS J. MM Bdr 155065 RFA
JOHNS John C. MM Pte 236863 1/1st Herefordshire Regt
JOHNS Joseph "DCM,MM(682490 1/22nd London Regt)+Bar" Sjt 129110 46th Royal Fusiliers
JOHNS Leonard "MM,MC(G)" Sjt 11998 11th Welsh Regt
JOHNS Leonard D. MM L/Cpl C/111 16th King's Royal Rifle Corps
JOHNS Wilfred N. MM Sjt 63739 Royal Fusiliers
JOHNS William F. MM Pte 315728 5th Devonshire Regt
JOHNS William Henry MM Cpl 11532 8th King's Royal Rifle Corps DOW 15.10.17.
JOHNSON A. MM Pte 41973 West Yorkshire Regt
JOHNSON Aaron MM Sjt 18/1033 12/13th Northumberland Fusiliers
JOHNSON Albert MM Cpl 18520 East Kent Regt
JOHNSON Albert MM Sjt 11861 19th Manchester Regt
JOHNSON Albert MM Sjt 42242 6th South Wales Borderers
JOHNSON Albert MM Sjt 9771 3rd Rifle Brigade
JOHNSON Albert E. MM Gnr Sig 173527 C/124 Bde RFA
JOHNSON Albert E. "DCM,MM+Bar" Sjt G/2153 8th Royal West Surrey Regt
JOHNSON Albert E. MM Pte 19347 Yorkshire Regt
JOHNSON Albert E. "MM,MID" Spr 26963 Royal Engineers
JOHNSON Albert E. MM L/Sjt 1795 1st Welsh Guards
JOHNSON Albert E.C. MM Dvr T4/251813 Army Service Corps
JOHNSON Alexander MM Pte S/18339 Rifle Brigade
JOHNSON Alfred MM Pte M2/153657 Army Service Corps att RGA.
JOHNSON Alfred MM Cpl S/18430 9th Rifle Brigade
JOHNSON Alfred MM Cpl 710347 RFA
JOHNSON Alfred MM Sjt 8720 2nd Royal Berkshire Regt
JOHNSON Alfred MM Sjt 265240 1/6th Cheshire Regt
JOHNSON Alfred MM Gnr 26976 B/91 Bde RFA
JOHNSON Alfred Barham MM Pte 22435 1st Norfolk Regt KIA 28.6.18.
JOHNSON Alfred George MM Spr 548882 33 Div Sig Coy Royal Engineers DOW 24.10.18.
JOHNSON Alfred J. MM Cpl 23382 Welsh Regt
JOHNSON Alfred J. MM L/Cpl 63049 Machine Gun Corps
JOHNSON Alfred M. MM Pte 46939 6th Leicestershire Regt
JOHNSON Alfred William MM Pte 9542 1st Coldstream Guards KIA 8.11.18.
JOHNSON Andrew B. MM Sjt 2741 2nd Northumberland Fusiliers
JOHNSON Angus MM Pte 241300 1/5th Royal Scots Fusiliers
JOHNSON Arthur "MM,MID" Sjt 44761 58 Bty 35 Bde RFA
JOHNSON Arthur MM L/Cpl Y/1276 King's Royal Rifle Corps
JOHNSON Arthur MM Pte 203036 1/5th Royal Warwickshire Regt KIA 4.10.17.
JOHNSON Arthur MM L/Cpl 4/8325 West Yorkshire Regt
JOHNSON Arthur Edgar "DCM,MM" CSM 47721 Royal Engineers
JOHNSON Arthur Edwin MM L/Cpl 203966 20th Durham Light Infantry "KIA 23.3.18,"
JOHNSON Arthur George MM Sjt 940093 D/281 Bde RFA
JOHNSON Arthur H. MM Pte M1/5742 Army Service Corps
JOHNSON Arthur Lionel Coomber MM Bdr 139017 RGA
JOHNSON Arthur S. MM Cpl 240796 10th Notts & Derby Regt
JOHNSON Barnaby MM Pte 266431 Liverpool Regt
JOHNSON Benjamin MM Sjt 374526 RGA
JOHNSON Benjamin A. MM Pte 56484 13th King's Royal Rifle Corps
JOHNSON Benjamin Harold MM Pte 50006 Northamptonshire Regt
JOHNSON Bert W. MM L/Cpl 9800 7th South Staffordshire Regt
JOHNSON Bertram Foster MM L/Cpl 14511 7th Duke of Cornwall's LI
JOHNSON Cecil MM Pte 7688 20th Manchester Regt
JOHNSON Cecil Noble MM Sjt 702596 2/23rd London Regt KIA 30.3.18.
JOHNSON Charles MM Dvr 36143 8 Bde RFA
JOHNSON Charles MM Pte 36752 Royal Lancaster Regt
JOHNSON Charles MM Sjt 1420 1st Lancashire Fusiliers
JOHNSON Charles Borthwick MM Pte 22/430 22nd Northumberland Fusiliers KIA 1.7.16.
JOHNSON Charles E.S. MM Cpl 241039 King's Own Scottish Borderers
JOHNSON Charles Ernest MM CQMS 12773 8th Gloucestershire Regt
JOHNSON Charles H. MM Pte 15616 9th South Staffordshire Regt
JOHNSON Charles R. MM Gnr 706213 RFA
JOHNSON Charles Richard MM Pte C/3844 20th King's Royal Rifle Corps
JOHNSON Charles W. MM L/Cpl 484024 14 Div Sig Coy Royal Engineers
JOHNSON Christopher A. MM Cpl S/3981 13th Rifle Brigade
JOHNSON Claude MM L/Cpl 16/617 16th Royal Warwickshire Regt
JOHNSON Claude Douglas MM Sjt 67526 Machine Gun Corps
JOHNSON Claude R. MM Sjt 47146 RAMC
JOHNSON David MM+Bar L/Cpl 12633 6th Shropshire Light Infantry
JOHNSON David W. MM Cpl 59581 87 Siege Bty RGA
JOHNSON E. MM Sjt 200330 Yorkshire Regt
JOHNSON E. MM L/Cpl P1695 Military Foot Police
JOHNSON E. MM L/Cpl 13168 Coldstream Guards
JOHNSON Edmund MM Pte 26116 2nd Yorkshire Light Infantry
JOHNSON Edward MM Sjt 241319 1/4th Royal Lancaster Regt
JOHNSON Edward MM Pte 12944 13th Cheshire Regt
JOHNSON Edward MM Pte 3236 24th Royal Fusiliers
JOHNSON Edward "MM,CdeG" CQMS 6863 1st Bedfordshire Regt
JOHNSON Edward MM Cpl 18326 Machine Gun Corps
JOHNSON Edward MM Pte M2/139211 Army Service Corps att RAMC.
JOHNSON Edward Albert MM Cpl 293732 129 Heavy Bty RGA KIA 1.9.18.
JOHNSON Ernest MM Spr 153968 465 Fd Coy Royal Engineers
JOHNSON Ernest MM L/Bdr 755104 A/251 Bde RFA
JOHNSON Ernest MM Pte 200111 1/4th Yorkshire Light Infantry
JOHNSON Ernest MM Pte 44699 18th Gloucestershire Regt
JOHNSON Ernest MM Spr 73446 'BL' Cable Section Royal Engineers
JOHNSON Ernest MM L/Cpl 16707 Suffolk Regt
JOHNSON F. MM Sjt 5792 West Riding Regt
JOHNSON F. MM Pte 1708 London Regt
JOHNSON Francis A. MM L/Cpl 703320 23rd London Regt
JOHNSON Frank MM Spr 156787 20 Broad Gauge Op Coy Royal Engineers
JOHNSON Frank MM Cpl 241438 1/5th York & Lancaster Regt KIA 29.4.18.
JOHNSON Frank MM Dvr 86601 RFA
JOHNSON Frank C. MM S/Sjt Fitter 52142 RFA
JOHNSON Frank Neville MM Sjt 53016 32nd Royal Fusiliers DOW 22.6.17.
JOHNSON Frank W. "DCM,MM" Sjt 66535 21 Div Sig Coy Royal Engineers
JOHNSON Fred MM Pte 202264 9th Yorkshire Light Infantry
JOHNSON Fred MM Pte 13201 9th West Riding Regt KIA 17.9.17.
JOHNSON Fred MM Pte 25480 12th Durham Light Infantry KIA 14.5.17.
JOHNSON Fred MM Pte C/12918 21st King's Royal Rifle Corps
JOHNSON Fred R. MM Cpl 89293 RFA
JOHNSON Frederick MM Pte 16101 5th Shropshire Light Infantry
JOHNSON Frederick MM Pte 9097 7th East Yorkshire Regt
JOHNSON Frederick MM Cpl 9108 10th Royal West Kent Regt
JOHNSON Frederick MM Pte 684402 22nd London Regt
JOHNSON Frederick MM L/Cpl 246890 Royal Engineers
JOHNSON Frederick MM Pte 301017 Essex Regt
JOHNSON Frederick "MM,MID." Sjt 7321 2nd Notts & Derby Regt
JOHNSON Frederick MM Pte 18653 6th Yorkshire Light Infantry
JOHNSON Frederick Arthur MM Bdr 50515 77 Siege Bty RGA
JOHNSON Frederick Charles MM Pte 28424 8th Somerset Light Infantry DOW 29.10.18.
JOHNSON Frederick Charles MM Pte MS/249 Army Service Corps
JOHNSON Frederick E. MM Pte 34551 5/6th Scottish Rifles
JOHNSON Frederick J. MM Sjt 12937 7th Royal Berkshire Regt
JOHNSON Frederick Marshall MM Pte 1658 23rd Middlesex Regt
JOHNSON Frederick W. MM Spr 78475 Royal Engineers
JOHNSON G.E. MM CoH 3028 Life Guards
JOHNSON George MM Cpl 40902 1/7th Cheshire Regt
JOHNSON George MM Cpl 10913 1st Coldstream Guards
JOHNSON George MM Cpl 206024 1st Royal West Surrey Regt
JOHNSON George MM Bdr 67642 RFA
JOHNSON George MM Sjt 30228 Liverpool Regt
JOHNSON George MM Sjt 17628 Liverpool Regt

JOHNSON George MM L/Cpl 241742 West Riding Regt
JOHNSON George MM Bdr 29108 D/152 Bde RFA
JOHNSON George MM Sjt 27470 Border Regt
JOHNSON George MM Pte 11678 9th York & Lancaster Regt
JOHNSON George MM Gnr 5901 32 Bde RFA
JOHNSON George MM Spr 69627 85 Fd Coy Royal Engineers
JOHNSON George MM Pte 36413 RAMC
JOHNSON George MM Pte 22/568 Northumberland Fusiliers
JOHNSON George MM Pte 9281 3rd Royal Fusiliers
JOHNSON George MM Pte 20439 13th Liverpool Regt
JOHNSON George MM Pte 9205 1st Cameron Highlanders
JOHNSON George A. MM CSM 53371 12th Suffolk Regt
JOHNSON George Alfred MM Sjt R/7281 2nd King's Royal Rifle Corps DOW 29.9.16.
JOHNSON George Charles John MM Sjt 9118 2nd Royal Munster Fusiliers
JOHNSON George Frank MM Pte 93877 1/6th Notts & Derby Regt DOW 7.11.18.
JOHNSON George Frederick MM Sjt 785 Lincolnshire Regt
JOHNSON George Henry MM Pte 53192 4th Worcestershire Regt
JOHNSON George W. MM L/Cpl 11347 7th East Yorkshire Regt
JOHNSON H. MM Pte 49786 1st Essex Regt
JOHNSON H. MM Pte 4817 Royal Warwickshire Regt
JOHNSON H.H. MM CSM 10148 Machine Gun Corps
JOHNSON H.P. MM Pte 352994 Manchester Regt
JOHNSON Hance MM Pnr 165989 Guards Div Sig Coy Royal Engineers
JOHNSON Harold MM Pte 15667 10th North Lancashire Regt KIA 11.8.16.
JOHNSON Harold MM+Bar L/Cpl 18373 6th Leicestershire Regt
JOHNSON Harold E. MM Pte DM2/165334 Army Service Corps
JOHNSON Harold Frederick MM L/Bdr 18079 270 Bde RFA
JOHNSON Harold Reuben MM Sjt 650862 21st London Regt att 142 TM Bty.DOW 21.10.18.
JOHNSON Harry MM Pte 18964 9th West Yorkshire Regt
JOHNSON Harry MM Cpl 51613 16th Royal Welsh Fusiliers
JOHNSON Harry MM Cpl 835219 C/84 Bde RFA
JOHNSON Harry MM L/Cpl 20599 8th Border Regt
JOHNSON Harry Alfred MM Pte 87568 Machine Gun Corps
JOHNSON Harry H. "MM,MID" L/Sjt 466 1/1st Northamptonshire Yeomanry
JOHNSON Harry Lewis MM Pte 13225 XVII Corps Cyclist Bn Army Cyclist Corps
JOHNSON Henry MM Pte 242307 5th South Lancashire Regt
JOHNSON Henry MM Sjt 55657 Machine Gun Corps
JOHNSON Henry MM Pte 31116 8th East Surrey Regt KIA 22.3.18.
JOHNSON Henry MM Sjt Farrier 11401 39 Bde RFA
JOHNSON Henry C. "DCM,MM,MID" Sjt 86196 D/76 Bde RFA
JOHNSON Henry Ernest MM S/Sjt Fitter 52136 A/58 Bty RFA DOW 12.9.17.
JOHNSON Herbert MM Cpl 325180 9th Durham Light Infantry
JOHNSON Herbert MM Pte 401436 1/1(West Riding)Fd Amb RAMC DOW 23.3.18.
JOHNSON Herbert MM Sjt 5059 7th Dragoon Guards
JOHNSON Herbert H. MM+Bar Cpl 294894 147 Heavy Bty RGA
JOHNSON Herbert J. MM Cpl 48313 RGA
JOHNSON Herman MM Pte 304379 17th Armoured Car Bn Tank Corps
JOHNSON Horace MM Pte 2015 1/1st Cambridgeshire Regt
JOHNSON Horace MM Sjt 16583 2nd Royal Fusiliers
JOHNSON Hubert MM L/Bdr 9896 400 Bty 14 Bde RFA
JOHNSON Hugh MM L/Sjt 43122 Bedfordshire Regt
JOHNSON J. MM Pte 59588 5th West Yorkshire Regt
JOHNSON J. MM+Bar Gnr 365855 132 Hy Bty RGA
JOHNSON J. MM Cpl 240444 Gordon Highlanders
JOHNSON Jack MM+Bar Sjt 12614 2nd Royal Warwickshire Regt
JOHNSON James MM L/Cpl 1619 6th Connaught Rangers
JOHNSON James MM Sjt R/10785 2nd King's Royal Rifle Corps
JOHNSON James MM Sjt 345380 14th Royal Highlanders
JOHNSON James "DCM,MM,MID" Sjt 9054 2nd Cameron Highlanders
JOHNSON James "DCM,MM(31813 10th N Lancs)" Pte 29017 9th East Surrey Regt
JOHNSON James MM Gnr L/10985 A/148 Bde RFA KIA 1.7.17.
JOHNSON James MM Sjt 34824 RFA
JOHNSON James "MM,MID" Gnr 39852 RFA
JOHNSON James Daniel MM Sjt 330037 9th Liverpool Regt
JOHNSON James H. MM Sjt 780556 26th Royal Fusiliers
JOHNSON James Samuel "DCM,MM+Bar" Sjt 15962 7th Norfolk Regt KIA 14.10.17.
JOHNSON James W. MM Cpl 280301 1/4th London Regt
JOHNSON Jasper MM Pte 27263 2nd Hampshire Regt DOW 1.8.18.
JOHNSON John MM Pte 240841 1/5th Seaforth Highlanders
JOHNSON John MM L/Cpl 426184 419 Fd Coy Royal Engineers
JOHNSON John MM Pte 74707 210 Coy Machine Gun Corps
JOHNSON John MM L/Cpl 16485 8th East Yorkshire Regt KIA 30.9.16.
JOHNSON John MM Pte S/8853 8th Seaforth Highlanders DOW 17.10.16.
JOHNSON John MM Pte 28217 Royal Inniskilling Fusiliers
JOHNSON John MM Pte 21093 1/23rd London Regt
JOHNSON John MM Sjt 1304 3rd Dragoon Guards
JOHNSON John MM Sjt 10326 14th Northumberland Fusiliers
JOHNSON John E. MM Pte 33014 4th West Riding Regt
JOHNSON John G. MM L/Cpl 17632 Border Regt
JOHNSON John H. MM Cpl 53648 Durham Light Infantry
JOHNSON John Levi MM Sjt 4078 7th Royal West Kent Regt KIA 12.10.17.
JOHNSON John R. MM Cpl 148842 RFA
JOHNSON John Simm MM Pte 22493 North Lancashire Regt
JOHNSON John T. MM Pte 50749 6th West Yorkshire Regt
JOHNSON John T. MM Cpl 26988 Machine Gun Corps
JOHNSON John T. MM Pte 66279 Machine Gun Corps
JOHNSON John Thomas MM Pte 16000 8th Yorkshire Light Infantry DOW 6.6.17.
JOHNSON John Thomas MM+Bar Pte 20/190 11th Northumberland Fusiliers KIA 27.10.18.
JOHNSON John W. MM Pte 17162 6th York & Lancaster Regt
JOHNSON John William Arthur MM Dvr 23292 40 Bde RFA
JOHNSON Joseph MM L/Cpl 458771 Royal Engineers
JOHNSON Joseph MM Cpl 38460 131 Bty 19 Bde RFA
JOHNSON Joseph MM Pte 60242 62nd Bn Machine Gun Corps
JOHNSON Joseph MM+Bar Pte 13121 9th Notts & Derby Regt
JOHNSON Joseph MM+Bar Pte 22484 4th West Riding Regt
JOHNSON Joseph MM Cpl M2/021596 Army Service Corps att 95 Fd Amb RAMC
JOHNSON Joseph MM L/Cpl MT/2922 2 Ammn Park Army Service Corps
JOHNSON Joseph MM Cpl 314210 1/1(Warwick)Hy Bty RGA
JOHNSON Joseph F. MM Pte 24657 7th Seaforth Highlanders
JOHNSON Joseph L. MM Spr 510037 Royal Engineers
JOHNSON Joseph W. MM Pte 423352 10th London Regt
JOHNSON Joshua MM Cpl S/8398 1/5th Seaforth Highlanders
JOHNSON Laurence MM Pte 40716 Scottish Rifles
JOHNSON Leonard MM Pte 35923 Liverpool Regt
JOHNSON Marshall MM Sjt 250812 2/6th Manchester Regt
JOHNSON Matthew MM L/Cpl 60110 33rd Bn Machine Gun Corps
JOHNSON Maurice A. "MM,MID" Sjt 550569 1/16th London Regt
JOHNSON Moses MM Pte 281297 Lancashire Fusiliers
JOHNSON Norman B. MM L/Sjt S/3795 13th Rifle Brigade
JOHNSON Percy MM Pte 11812 East Surrey Regt
JOHNSON Percy MM Pte 3599 Liverpool Regt
JOHNSON Percy Salmon MM Sjt 15/1164 15/17th West Yorkshire Regt
JOHNSON Peter MM Dvr T/392389 Army Service Corps
JOHNSON Philip MM Pte 230819 1/1st Dorset Yeomanry
JOHNSON Philip D. MM Pte 17691 11th Notts & Derby Regt
JOHNSON R. MM AM1 8009 Royal Flying Corps
JOHNSON Ralph MM Pte 12720 8th North Staffordshire Regt
JOHNSON Ralph William MM Cpl 31315 41st Bn Machine Gun Corps
JOHNSON Raymund Edward MM+Bar Pte 419404 2 Fd Amb RAMC
JOHNSON Reuben MM Pte 17936 Royal Welsh Fusiliers
JOHNSON Reuben MM Pte 15497 6th Royal West Surrey Regt
JOHNSON Richard MM Pte 200804 1/4th Cheshire Regt
JOHNSON Richard MM Sjt 8370 5th Northamptonshire Regt
JOHNSON Richard MM Dvr 11472 RFA
JOHNSON Richard MM L/Sjt 1153 1st Manchester Regt
JOHNSON Richard Ernest MM Dvr 10161 251 Bde RFA
JOHNSON Richard H. MM Pte 240449 Royal Welsh Fusiliers
JOHNSON Richard Herbert MM 2nd Cpl 78476 25 Div Sig Coy Royal Engineers DOW 25.10.18.
JOHNSON Richard Llewelyn MM Gnr 75442 D/83 Bde RFA DOW 11.11.18.
JOHNSON Richard S. MM Sjt 250203 Manchester Regt
JOHNSON Robert MM Gnr 134857 RFA
JOHNSON Robert MM Sjt 12938 8th Royal Irish Rifles
JOHNSON Robert MM Bdr 1159 2/3(Northumbrian)Bde RFA

JOHNSON Robert MM L/Cpl 16098 11th Manchester Regt DOW 6.10.17.
JOHNSON Robert MM Pte 44418 Machine Gun Corps
JOHNSON Robert A. MM L/Cpl 570362 17th London Regt
JOHNSON Robert C. MM Sjt 241778 7th Lancashire Fusiliers
JOHNSON S. MM Cpl R/3099 2nd King's Royal Rifle Corps
JOHNSON Samuel MM L/Cpl 241278 Worcestershire Regt
JOHNSON Samuel MM Pte 42696 North Staffordshire Regt
JOHNSON Sarah Evelyn MM Staff Nurse F QAIMNS
JOHNSON Sidney MM L/Sjt 6165 7th Norfolk Regt
JOHNSON Sidney MM Pte 21697 6th York & Lancaster Regt
JOHNSON Sidney MM CSM 73301 15th Notts & Derby Regt
JOHNSON Sidney MM Pte 13900 East Kent Regt
JOHNSON Sidney MM CSM 109607 Royal Engineers
JOHNSON Sidney C. MM Pte 11956 1st Irish Guards
JOHNSON Sidney E. MM Pte 4660 8th London Regt
JOHNSON Sidney James MM Cpl 132169 251 Tunnelling Coy Royal Engineers
JOHNSON Stanley G. MM Cpl(MCDR) 172249 Royal Engineers
JOHNSON Stanley H. MM Cpl 510857 14th London Regt
JOHNSON Sydney H. MM L/Sjt 350176 9th Highland Light Infantry
JOHNSON Thomas MM Pte 35639 5th West Riding Regt
JOHNSON Thomas MM Pte 4051 North Staffordshire Regt
JOHNSON Thomas MM Pte 20382 Royal Welsh Fusiliers
JOHNSON Thomas MM Pte 42034 7th Norfolk Regt
JOHNSON Thomas MM L/Cpl 53035 Machine Gun Corps
JOHNSON Thomas MM Pte 7034 10th Lancashire Fusiliers
JOHNSON Thomas "DCM,MM" Pte S/3447 12th Rifle Brigade
JOHNSON Thomas "DCM,MM" Cpl 201525 North Staffordshire Regt
JOHNSON Thomas MM Pte 15729 1/4th Royal Lancaster Regt
JOHNSON Thomas MM Pte 291354 1/7th Cheshire Regt
JOHNSON Thomas MM Cpl 64333 RGA
JOHNSON Thomas A. MM Sjt 47061 15th Lancashire Fusiliers
JOHNSON Thomas Alfred MM Sjt 41670 76 Fd Amb RAMC DOW 4.5.17.
JOHNSON Thomas E. MM L/Cpl G/11459 Royal West Kent Regt
JOHNSON Thomas Edgar MM Pte 27292 1st Leicestershire Regt
JOHNSON Thomas F. MM Pte 1820 RAMC
JOHNSON Thomas Frederick "DCM,MM" Sjt 20999 22nd Manchester Regt
JOHNSON Thomas H. MM L/Cpl 13119 6th Dragoon Guards
JOHNSON Thomas H. MM Spr 442127 429 Fd Coy Royal Engineers
JOHNSON Thomas L. MM Sjt 14452 12th West Yorkshire Regt
JOHNSON Thomas Silvester MM L/Cpl 12971 4th(ER) South Staffordshire Regt DOW 24.4.18.
JOHNSON Thomas William MM Bdr 70444 215 Siege Bty RGA
JOHNSON Tom "MM,MID" Dvr 735 RFA
JOHNSON Tom MM BQMS 293 RFA
JOHNSON Tom MM Pte 14/468 9th York & Lancaster Regt
JOHNSON Tom MM Pte 34167 8th East Lancashire Regt
JOHNSON V.W. MM Dvr 74816 29 Bde RFA
JOHNSON Valentine MM Cpl 242250 1/5th North Lancashire Regt
JOHNSON Victor MM Dvr 81390 20 Div Ammn Col RFA
JOHNSON Victor MM Sjt G/116 6th Royal West Surrey Regt
JOHNSON W. MM Sjt 200185 South Lancashire Regt
JOHNSON W. "DCM,MM" Sjt 107394 8 Div Sig Coy Royal Engineers
JOHNSON W. MM Pte 419224 RAMC
JOHNSON W.T. MM Pte 1568 1st Welsh Guards
JOHNSON Walter MM Pte 40038 South Staffordshire Regt
JOHNSON Walter MM Sjt M2/050166 Army Service Corps
JOHNSON Walter MM Pte 306412 5th Royal Warwickshire Regt
JOHNSON Walter Edwin MM Spr 32925 2 Fd Coy Royal Engineers DOW 27.5.16.
JOHNSON Walter Henry Frank MM Sjt 62855 118 Siege Bty RGA
JOHNSON Walter Saweard MM Sjt 6949 2nd Royal Scots
JOHNSON Wilfred MM Bdr 21599 RFA
JOHNSON Wilfred "MM,MID" Sjt 22520 Machine Gun Corps
JOHNSON William MM Pte 47978 RAMC
JOHNSON William MM Pte 23530 16th Welsh Regt
JOHNSON William MM L/Cpl 182 4th Bn GMGR
JOHNSON William MM Spr 253476 'F' Corps Sig Coy Royal Engineers
JOHNSON William MM Sjt 203534 3rd Worcestershire Regt
JOHNSON William MM Pte 322664 6th London Regt
JOHNSON William MM Dvr 62268 RFA
JOHNSON William MM Gnr 187556 RGA
JOHNSON William MM Pte 13868 8th Bedfordshire Regt
JOHNSON William MM Pte R/8530 12th King's Royal Rifle Corps
JOHNSON William MM Gnr 110339 RFA
JOHNSON William "MM,MID" L/Cpl 7249 2nd Oxf & Bucks Light Infantry
JOHNSON William MM Pte 10277 5th Oxf & Bucks Light Infantry
JOHNSON William MM Pte 13666 10th West Riding Regt
JOHNSON William MM Bdr 64041 RGA
JOHNSON William MM Pte 22472 Manchester Regt
JOHNSON William MM Pte 240764 7th Lincolnshire Regt KIA 12.10.17.
JOHNSON William MM Pte 265962 7th Liverpool Regt KIA 9.4.18.
JOHNSON William MM Sjt 40510 20th Manchester Regt KIA 9.8.18.
JOHNSON William A. MM Sjt 850 North Staffordshire Regt
JOHNSON William Alfred MM Sjt 9680 A/71 Bde RFA
JOHNSON William E. MM Dvr 103297 RFA
JOHNSON William Foster MM Cpl 22194 12th West Yorkshire Regt KIA 19.5.18.
JOHNSON William Frank MM Pte 4215 Rifle Brigade
JOHNSON "William H," MM Pte 421178 10th London Regt
JOHNSON William H. MM Pte 53550 15th Cheshire Regt
JOHNSON William H. MM Pte 23459 16th Royal Warwickshire Regt
JOHNSON William Henry MM Bdr 761318 C/317 Bde RFA
JOHNSON William Henry "VC,MM,MM(F)" Sjt 306122 1/5th Notts & Derby Regt
JOHNSON William Henry MM Pte 32550 Notts & Derby Regt
JOHNSON William J. MM+Bar Pte 718123 23rd London Regt
JOHNSON William James "MM,MC(G)" L/Cpl 8492 10th Hampshire Regt
JOHNSON William L. MM Gnr 40813 RFA
JOHNSON Worthy George MM Sjt 8293 Worcestershire Regt
JOHNSTON Albert W. MM Pte 30/60 Northumberland Fusiliers
JOHNSTON Alex MM Pte 40880 Royal Irish Rifles
JOHNSTON Alexander MM Sjt 240042 1/7th Gordon Highlanders
JOHNSTON Alexander MM 2nd Cpl 770 401 Fd Coy Royal Engineers DOW 2.4.18.
JOHNSTON Andrew "MM,MIDx2" Pte 12565 9th Royal Warwickshire Regt Died 29.6.17.
JOHNSTON Andrew MM Pte 1709 Arg & Suth Highlanders
JOHNSTON Andrew Bernard MM Pte 41988 Machine Gun Corps(Cavalry)
JOHNSTON Angus McD. MM Pte 10051 1st King's Own Scottish Borderers
JOHNSTON Archibald C. MM Sjt 224458 Labour Corps
JOHNSTON Arthur W.H. MM Gnr 147273 RFA
JOHNSTON C. MM Pte 18326 East Surrey Regt
JOHNSTON Charles MM L/Cpl 3454 1/9th Royal Scots
JOHNSTON Charles Wright MM Sjt 14112 11th Royal Scots KIA 12.10.17.
JOHNSTON Christopher MM L/Cpl 325253 1/9th Durham Light Infantry
JOHNSTON Enoch MM Pte 8027 Royal Irish Rifles
JOHNSTON Francis MM Spr 157837 Royal Engineers
JOHNSTON Frank MM Spr 13569 153 Fd Coy Royal Engineers
JOHNSTON Frederick MM Sjt 11205 9th Royal Inniskilling Fusiliers
JOHNSTON Frederick MM Bdr 23271 A/104 Bde RFA KIA 31.7.17.
JOHNSTON Geoffrey MM L/Cpl 28983 6th Royal Inniskilling Fusiliers
JOHNSTON George MM Sjt 14991 15th Royal Irish Rifles
JOHNSTON George MM Sjt 15646 2nd Royal Inniskilling Fusiliers
JOHNSTON George MM Cpl 17975 12th Royal Irish Rifles
JOHNSTON George A. MM Pte 23224 RAMC
JOHNSTON George Dixon MM Pte 203544 1/4th Yorkshire Light Infantry
JOHNSTON Gertrude Francis MM Section Leader F BRCS
JOHNSTON Harry MM Sjt 19233 33 Coy Labour Corps
JOHNSTON J. MM+Bar Sjt 318033 2 Fd Amb RAMC
JOHNSTON J. MM Pte 1917 1/8th Middlesex Regt
JOHNSTON James MM Sjt 285422 1/1st Oxfordshire Yeomanry DOW 15.4.18.
JOHNSTON James MM Pte 345038 Manchester Regt
JOHNSTON James MM Sjt 346672 178 Siege Bty RGA
JOHNSTON James MM Sjt 275122 1/7th Arg & Suth Highlanders
JOHNSTON James MM Pte 350836 Royal Scots
JOHNSTON James C. MM Sjt 16668 13th Royal Scots
JOHNSTON James T. "MM,MID" Sjt 1690 18th Royal Fusiliers
JOHNSTON John MM+Bar CSM 275123 1st Arg & Suth Highlanders
JOHNSTON John MM Pte 88391 27 Fd Amb RAMC
JOHNSTON John MM Pte 51478 2nd Royal Scots
JOHNSTON John MM Pte 12945 5th Cameron Highlanders

JOHNSTON John "MM,MSM" Sjt 14525 16th Highland Light Infantry
JOHNSTON John MM Pte S/43046 1/6th Gordon Highlanders
JOHNSTON John MM Pte 40289 15th Highland Light Infantry KIA 15.7.17.
JOHNSTON John MM Pte 40820 1/7th Royal Highlanders KIA 15.4.18.
JOHNSTON John E.W. MM Cpl 43137 King's Own Scottish Borderers
JOHNSTON John W. MM Sjt 596 RAMC
JOHNSTON Joseph MM Pte 250750 5/6th Royal Scots
JOHNSTON Malcolm Victor MM Pte 52861 17 Squadron Machine Gun Corps(Cavalry)
JOHNSTON Robert MM Sjt 14358 9th Royal Irish Fusiliers
JOHNSTON Robert MM Pte 9905 Scots Guards
JOHNSTON Robert MM+Bar Sjt 12236 Highland Light Infantry
JOHNSTON Robert MM Pte 6700 1st Scottish Rifles
JOHNSTON Robert MM Pte 200041 1/4th Royal Highlanders
JOHNSTON Samuel MM Cpl 16245 Royal Inniskilling Fusiliers
JOHNSTON Samuel MM Gnr 100901 RFA
JOHNSTON Samuel J. MM+Bar Sjt 15006 14th Royal Irish Rifles
JOHNSTON Sydney MM Pte 40710 Manchester Regt
JOHNSTON Thomas MM Cpl 105927 9th Bn Machine Gun Corps
JOHNSTON Thomas MM Sjt 7400 1st Gordon Highlanders
JOHNSTON Thomas "DCM,MM" CSM 5593 5th Cameron Highlanders
JOHNSTON Thomas MM Sjt 39312 117 Bty 26 Bde RFA DOW 2.11.17.
JOHNSTON Thomas B. MM L/Cpl S/10840 1st Gordon Highlanders
JOHNSTON Thomas C. MM Cpl 40078 16th Highland Light Infantry
JOHNSTON W. MM Pte 1838 1st Royal Highlanders
JOHNSTON W. MM Pte S/17094 Arg & Suth Highlanders
JOHNSTON W. MM Sjt 40735 9th South Staffordshire Regt
JOHNSTON Walter MM Pte 13791 7th East Lancashire Regt
JOHNSTON William MM Pte 24934 Royal Inniskilling Fusiliers
JOHNSTON William MM Pte 8047 33 Fd Amb RAMC
JOHNSTON William MM Gnr 630912 C/72 Bde RFA
JOHNSTON William MM Pte S/21177 1st Cameron Highlanders KIA 18.11.16.
JOHNSTON William MM Pte 3/7003 1/5th Arg & Suth Highlanders
JOHNSTON William MM Pte 42936 5/6th Scottish Rifles
JOHNSTON William MM Sjt 22177 17th Lancashire Fusiliers KIA 23.10.17.
JOHNSTON William MM L/Cpl 325362 9th Durham Light Infantry
JOHNSTON William MM Pte 24789 Border Regt
JOHNSTON William A. MM Sjt G/63377 2nd Royal Fusiliers
JOHNSTON William F. MM Pte S/41116 7th Seaforth Highlanders
JOHNSTON William Irvine MM Sjt 16/1086 16th Royal Irish Rifles
JOHNSTON William J. MM Cpl H/71404 North Irish Horse
JOHNSTONE Alexander MM Pte 202257 Scottish Rifles
JOHNSTONE Alexander MM Dvr 80685 RFA
JOHNSTONE Alexander MM L/Cpl 14970 9th Royal Irish Rifles
JOHNSTONE Andrew "DCM,MM" Pte 330103 1/9th Highland Light Infantry
JOHNSTONE Bernard David "DCM,MM" Sjt 844 RAMC
JOHNSTONE C. MM Pte 4606 2nd GMGR
JOHNSTONE Charles D. MM Cpl M2/136343 11 Pontoon Park Army Service Corps
JOHNSTONE Clement G. MM Pte 203903 5/6th Scottish Rifles
JOHNSTONE David MM Sjt 76086 8 Div Sig Coy Royal Engineers
JOHNSTONE David McD. MM Pte 9417 Arg & Suth Highlanders
JOHNSTONE Edward MM Pnr 316580 Royal Engineers
JOHNSTONE F. MM Pte 27861 4th Yorkshire Light Infantry
JOHNSTONE Gavin MM Pte 241618 1/4th King's Own Scottish Borderers
JOHNSTONE George MM L/Cpl 7918 1/7th Arg & Suth Highlanders
JOHNSTONE Harold MM Pte 354182 44 Fd Amb RAMC
JOHNSTONE Harry MM L/Cpl 4026 4th Liverpool Regt
JOHNSTONE Hugh MM Pte 34306 2nd Royal Scots DOW 30.9.17.
JOHNSTONE James MM Sjt 9808 17th Highland Light Infantry
JOHNSTONE James MM Sjt 250751 5/6th Royal Scots
JOHNSTONE James MM Sjt 3415 Gordon Highlanders
JOHNSTONE James MM Pte 46017 Northumberland Fusiliers
JOHNSTONE John MM Sjt 235359 4th Yorkshire Light Infantry
JOHNSTONE John MM S/Sjt Fitter 326218 RGA
JOHNSTONE John MM Sjt 280419 1/7th Highland Light Infantry
JOHNSTONE John F. MM Cpl 95608 RGA
JOHNSTONE John William MM Spr 1940 50 Div Sig Coy Royal Engineers KIA 12.4.18.
JOHNSTONE Joseph MM Spr 86188 170 Tunnelling Coy Royal Engineers

JOHNSTONE Robert MM Cpl 4545 19th Bn Machine Gun Corps
JOHNSTONE Robert MM+Bar Pte 16278 12th Manchester Regt
JOHNSTONE Robert MM Pte 331676 1/9th Highland Light Infantry
JOHNSTONE Robert Edward "MM,CG(F)" Pte 8312 2/4th Hampshire Regt
JOHNSTONE Thomas MM L/Cpl 15597 8th Border Regt
JOHNSTONE Thomas MM Cpl 19282 5th Dorsetshire Regt KIA 16.8.17.
JOHNSTONE Thomas B. MM Sjt M2/073687 Army Service Corps
JOHNSTONE Thomas J. MM Spr 361274 2 Div Sig Coy Royal Engineers
JOHNSTONE Thomas J. MM Pte 32337 RAMC
JOHNSTONE Wiliam MM Pte S/14002 7th Cameron Highlanders
JOHNSTONE William MM Sjt 267176 6th Royal Highlanders
JOHNSTONE William MM Pte 379 2nd Gordon Highlanders
JOHNSTONE William MM Cpl 412108 Royal Engineers
JOHNSTONE William MM Dvr 80774 RFA
JOHNSTONE William MM Cpl 21285 2nd Royal Scots
JOHNSTONE William MM Pte S/40054 10th Arg & Suth Highlanders
JOHNSTONE William Bruce MM Pte 38489 1st Lancashire Fusiliers KIA 9.10.17.
JOHNSTONE William D. MM Sjt 11289 Cheshire Regt
JOHNSTONE William R. MM L/Cpl 200670 1/5th Arg & Suth Highlanders
JOINER Hector MM Sjt 45375 120 Heavy Bty RGA
JOINES Harry E. "MM,MID" Pte 532884 15th London Regt
JOINT Frederick W. MM Pte 8923 2nd Devonshire Regt
JOINT Richard MM Cpl 239156 Royal Engineers
JOISCE Phillip MM Pte 20/573 Northumberland Fusiliers
JOLL Jack MM+Bar Cpl 7780 11th Lancashire Fusiliers
JOLLANDS Robert MM Sjt 55278 111 Railway Coy Royal Engineers
JOLLEY Arthur MM Sjt 13178 5 Fd Amb RAMC
JOLLEY Bert MM Pte 1758 1/1st Cambridgeshire Regt
JOLLEY Edward MM Pte 2613 2nd Rifle Brigade
JOLLEY Harry MM Sjt 11478 7th Wiltshire Regt
JOLLEY Isaac MM Pte 68212 RAMC
JOLLEY James MM Sjt 376666 Manchester Regt
JOLLEY James G. "MM,MID" Sjt 93343 Royal Engineers
JOLLEY John H. MM Pte 25096 Durham Light Infantry
JOLLEY John Henry MM Pte 240495 5th Devonshire Regt
JOLLEY Joseph MM L/Sjt 8266 1st Scots Guards
JOLLEY W. MM Dvr 671619 A/325 Bde RFA
JOLLIFFE Charles Vear MM Sjt 7292 1st Wiltshire Regt
JOLLIFFE Cuthbert Lovell York MM Cpl 225103 1/1st Monmouthshire Regt
JOLLIFFE Richard Charles "MM,MID." Cpl 1330 1/13th London Regt
JOLLIFFE Thomas S. MM Cpl 2432 8th Royal West Surrey Regt
JOLLY Charles MM+Bar Sjt 42887 D/188 Bde RFA
JOLLY David MM Pte S/23004 1st Cameron Highlanders
JOLLY Ernest W. MM Pte 9445 2nd Suffolk Regt
JOLLY George L. MM Pte 76716 76 Fd Amb RAMC att 13th Cheshire Regt.
JOLLY James MM Pte 240477 1/5th Royal Highlanders
JOLLY Reginald MM Pte S/18103 Rifle Brigade
JOLLY William MM Cpl L/14844 20th Royal Fusiliers KIA 16.4.17.
JOLLY William MM Sjt 630001 255 Bde RFA
JOLLYE Sidney H. MM Sjt 42746 A/175 Bde RFA
JONAS James MM Gnr 190197 RFA
JONES A. MM Pte 3038 Royal Warwickshire Regt
JONES A. MM Pnr 357395 Royal Engineers
JONES A.E. MM Gnr 58843 RFA
JONES A.G. MM Sjt P/2335 Military Foot Police
JONES A.S. MM+Bar L/Cpl 29372 10th Essex Regt
JONES Adam MM Sjt 39233 Northumberland Fusiliers
JONES Albert MM L/Cpl 4578 Notts & Derby Regt
JONES Albert MM Pte 8571 1st South Staffordshire Regt
JONES Albert MM Pte 201961 1/4th South Lancashire Regt
JONES Albert MM Sjt 17772 6th South Lancashire Regt
JONES Albert MM Pte 11275 2nd Royal Welsh Fusiliers
JONES Albert MM L/Cpl 3875 Liverpool Regt
JONES Albert B. MM L/Cpl 146034 1/1st Northamptonshire Yeomanry
JONES Albert C.E. MM Bdr 54318 RHA
JONES Albert C.W. MM Gnr 352654 RGA
JONES Albert E. MM Cpl 19349 Machine Gun Corps
JONES Albert G. MM Pte 56483 16th Royal Welsh Fusiliers
JONES Albert G. MM 2nd Cpl 20099 9 Fd Coy Royal Engineers
JONES Albert John MM L/Cpl 1345 1/21st London Regt
JONES Albert Oliver MM Gnr Fitter 19285 C/95 Bde RFA

JONES Albert V.W. MM Spr 19840 Royal Engineers
JONES Albert Vincent MM Bdsm 10404 2nd Royal Welsh Fusiliers
JONES Albert William Charles MM L/Cpl 12319 5th Northumberland Fusiliers
JONES Alexander MM Pte 10414 12th Manchester Regt
JONES Alexander Francis MM Sjt 15128 1st Grenadier Guards KIA 12.9.16.
JONES Alfred MM Gnr 725449 RFA
JONES Alfred MM Sjt W/623 D/119 Bde RFA
JONES Alfred MM Sjt 41891 Machine Gun Corps
JONES Alfred MM Pte 16833 10th Notts & Derby Regt
JONES Alfred MM L/Sjt 200325 1/4th Royal Welsh Fusiliers
JONES Alfred MM L/Cpl 15804 1st Grenadier Guards
JONES Alfred MM Cpl 350 Royal Engineers
JONES Alfred MM Cpl 3322 1/10th Liverpool Regt
JONES Alfred MM Cpl 97190 RFA
JONES Alfred MM L/Cpl 17936 11th Cheshire Regt
JONES Alfred C. MM Pte 10277 7th East Kent Regt
JONES Alfred E. MM Sjt 24818 504 Bty 65 Bde RFA
JONES Alfred E. MM L/Cpl 60292 26th Royal Fusiliers
JONES Alfred E. MM+Bar Sjt 240154 6th South Staffordshire Regt
JONES Alfred J. MM L/Cpl 8660 Machine Gun Corps
JONES Alfred Lloyd MM Pte 20453 Machine Gun Corps KIA 20.4.18.
JONES Alfred T. MM Sjt 18915 1st East Surrey Regt
JONES Alfred V. MM+Bar Sjt 15949 4th Bedfordshire Regt
JONES Alfred W. MM Pte 7030 2/1st HAC (Inf)
JONES Allen MM Pte 15679 10th Worcestershire Regt
JONES Andrew MM Pte 468 1st Welsh Guards DOW 18.9.18.
JONES Archibald E. MM Pte 265794 1/6th Gordon Highlanders
JONES Arnold H. MM Pte 46387 4th North Staffordshire Regt
JONES Arthur MM Gnr 107480 66 Div Ammn Col RFA
JONES Arthur MM Bdr Sig 153813 'A' Bty RHA
JONES Arthur MM Sjt 128950 46th Royal Fusiliers
JONES Arthur MM Pte 680515 1/22nd London Regt
JONES Arthur MM+Bar Cpl 325854 1/9th Durham Light Infantry
JONES Arthur MM Gnr 87382 RGA
JONES Arthur MM Pte 7855 1st Hampshire Regt
JONES Arthur MM Pte 17545 2nd Grenadier Guards DOW 7.10.16.
JONES Arthur MM L/Cpl 19071 9th York & Lancaster Regt
JONES Arthur MM Pte 14979 10th Cheshire Regt
JONES Arthur MM L/Cpl 16578 6th Shropshire Light Infantry
JONES Arthur "MM,MID" Cpl MS/3614 Army Service Corps att 16 Fd Amb RAMC.
JONES Arthur MM Pte 20551 Northamptonshire Regt
JONES Arthur MM Cpl 200622 Royal Welsh Fusiliers
JONES Arthur MM Gnr 296442 RGA
JONES Arthur E. MM L/Cpl 76439 1/9th Durham Light Infantry
JONES Arthur G. MM Pte 200920 West Riding Regt
JONES Arthur H. MM Pte 28982 1/1st Herefordshire Regt
JONES Arthur H. MM Pte 92498 Tank Corps
JONES Arthur H. MM Sjt 57806 2nd Welsh Regt
JONES Arthur H. MM L/Bdr 47626 RFA
JONES Arthur H. MM Cpl 240341 1/5th East Lancashire Regt
JONES Arthur J. MM L/Sjt 14295 2nd South Lancashire Regt
JONES Arthur L. MM Pte 48795 RAMC
JONES Arthur Percy MM Spr 528087 54 Div Sig Coy Royal Engineers
JONES Arthur R. MM Pte 11992 Wiltshire Regt
JONES Arthur R. MM Pte 200594 1/4th Royal Welsh Fusiliers
JONES Arthur T. MM+Bar Sjt 12133 6th Oxf & Bucks Light Infantry
JONES Arthur T. MM Sjt 17285 6th South Wales Borderers
JONES B. "MM+Bar,MID" Sjt 341509 RAMC
JONES B.F. MM Pte 70389 Machine Gun Corps
JONES Benjamin MM Sjt 240620 2/6th South Staffordshire Regt
JONES Benjamin MM Pte 23034 4th Worcestershire Regt
JONES Benjamin MM Gnr 16886 B/70 Bde RFA
JONES Benjamin D. MM L/Bdr 141016 RGA
JONES Benjamin I. MM Spr 450351 103 Fd Coy Royal Engineers
JONES Bernard MM Cpl 6197 1st Royal West Surrey Regt KIA 14.4.18.
JONES Bertie MM L/Bdr L/4803 D/231 Bde RFA
JONES Bertie MM Dvr 38638 27 Bde RFA
JONES Bertram MM Sjt 17472 2nd London Regt
JONES Bertram J. MM Cpl 27265 9th East Surrey Regt
JONES C. MM L/Cpl 3127 Royal Warwickshire Regt
JONES C.E. MM Pnr 259173 Royal Engineers
JONES Caradoc R.W. MM Pte 490720 1/13th London Regt
JONES Cardigan P. MM S/Sjt SE/32310 Army Veterinary Corps
JONES Cecil MM L/Cpl 26369 7th Royal West Kent Regt

JONES Charles MM Cpl 19711 3 Siege Bty RGA
JONES Charles MM Pte 58149 6th East Kent Regt
JONES Charles MM+Bar Pte 300295 7th Liverpool Regt
JONES Charles MM L/Cpl 19357 Worcestershire Regt
JONES Charles MM Pte 200891 1/5th South Staffordshire Regt KIA 3.10.18.
JONES Charles MM Pte R/26474 13th King's Royal Rifle Corps
JONES Charles MM Pte 87114 2/7th Liverpool Regt DOW 31.10.18.
JONES Charles MM Cpl 28078 Welsh Regt
JONES Charles MM Pte 396517 Labour Corps
JONES Charles MM Sjt 3419 23rd Royal Fusiliers DOW 28.4.18.
JONES Charles "DCM,MM" Sjt 9200 2nd Royal Welsh Fusiliers
JONES Charles MM Sjt 15837 8th King's Own Scottish Borderers
JONES Charles MM Cpl 16087 Machine Gun Corps KIA 28.4.17.
JONES Charles MM Pte 97572 33rd Bn Machine Gun Corps
JONES Charles MM L/Cpl 16004 Royal Engineers
JONES Charles MM Gnr 13316 RFA
JONES Charles A. MM+Bar Pte M2/079260 Army Service Corps
JONES Charles E. MM L/Cpl 12190 6th Shropshire Light Infantry
JONES Charles E. "MM,MSM,MID" CSM 6535 3 Pontoon Park Royal Engineers
JONES Charles F. MM Sjt 531214 15th London Regt
JONES Charles H. MM Cpl 14538 8th Yorkshire Light Infantry
JONES Charles Henry Reginald MM 2nd Cpl 551040 Royal Engineers
JONES Charles J. MM L/Cpl 724017 24th London Regt
JONES Charles P. MM L/Cpl 1562 1/7th Middlesex Regt
JONES Charles V. MM Pte 9168 South Staffordshire Regt
JONES Charles W. MM+Bar L/Cpl 200513 1/4th Leicestershire Regt
JONES Charles W. MM Pte 4235 Rifle Brigade
JONES Colin G. MM L/Cpl 201909 5th North Staffordshire Regt
JONES D.J. MM Cpl Mechanic 22074 Royal Air Force
JONES Daniel MM Cpl 41628 2nd Royal Inniskilling Fusiliers
JONES Daniel MM Pte 704 2nd Yorkshire Light Infantry
JONES Daniel "MM,MID" Cpl 13933 B/61 Bde RFA
JONES Daniel Evan MM Pte 3015 1st Welsh Guards DOW 14.10.18.
JONES Darby MM Pte 24947 Machine Gun Corps
JONES David MM Pte 203701 9th Royal Welsh Fusiliers
JONES David MM Cpl 39247 4th North Staffordshire Regt
JONES David MM Dvr 707241 RFA
JONES David MM Pte 35645 Machine Gun Corps
JONES David MM Pte 16155 Welsh Regt
JONES David MM Pte 45365 1st Lancashire Fusiliers
JONES David MM Pte 21704 13th Welsh Regt
JONES David MM L/Cpl 62823 Royal Engineers
JONES David MM Pte 32495 Lancashire Fusiliers
JONES David MM Pte 241139 Royal Warwickshire Regt
JONES David MM Gnr 380 RGA
JONES David MM Pte 5297 22nd London Regt
JONES David MM Sjt 47974 RAMC
JONES David "DCM,MM" Sjt 25660 1st Bn Machine Gun Corps
JONES David MM Pte 267946 1/6th Cheshire Regt KIA 31.8.18.
JONES David MM Spr 132582 250 Tunnelling Coy Royal Engineers
JONES David MM Pte M2/121922 Army Service Corps
JONES David A. "DCM,MM+Bar" CSM 19864 Welsh Regt
JONES David F. MM Bdr 17826 RFA
JONES David J. MM Pnr 155374 Royal Engineers
JONES David J. "MM,MIDx2" Cpl 49287 RAMC
JONES David John MM Pte 15903 13th Royal Welsh Fusiliers KIA 19.9.18.
JONES David O. MM Cpl 27206 1st South Wales Borderers
JONES David Owen MM Pte 2251 1st Welsh Guards
JONES David Owen MM Bdr 23522 A/78 Bde RFA
JONES David Rhys MM Sjt 25046 17th Welsh Regt
JONES David Rice MM Pte 1523 1st Welsh Guards KIA 10.9.16.
JONES David T. MM Pte 18239 16th Royal Welsh Fusiliers
JONES David W. MM Pte 19614 Royal Welsh Fusiliers
JONES David W. MM Gnr 43840 RGA
JONES David W. MM Pte 91159 Machine Gun Corps
JONES David W.J. MM Pte 62367 2nd Manchester Regt
JONES David William MM Cpl 52475 95 Fd Coy Royal Engineers
JONES Dennis MM Cpl 9444 2nd Shropshire Light Infantry
JONES Donald A. MM 2nd Cpl 134856 Royal Engineers
JONES Douglas MM Pte 3806 1/5th Royal Highlanders
JONES E. MM Pte 265078 Notts & Derby Regt
JONES Edgar MM Pte 3792 1/1st Monmouthshire Regt
JONES Edgar MM L/Cpl 19438 Machine Gun Corps
JONES Edgar Alfred MM Pte 75531 77 Fd Amb RAMC
JONES Edward MM Pte 241134 6th Royal Warwickshire Regt

JONES Edward MM Pte 49096 72 Fd Amb RAMC
JONES Edward MM Cpl 265075 6th Royal Welsh Fusiliers
JONES Edward MM Cpl 16997 Coldstream Guards
JONES Edward MM Dvr 105474 106 Bty 22 Bde RFA
JONES Edward MM Sjt 137588 171 Tunnelling Coy Royal Engineers
JONES Edward MM Pte 2259 1st Manchester Regt
JONES Edward "DCM,MM" Sjt 13444 C/74 Bde RFA
JONES Edward MM Pte 17038 11th Durham Light Infantry
JONES Edward MM Bdr 117961 RFA
JONES Edward MM Spr 66763 Royal Engineers
JONES Edward A. MM Sjt 27047 Royal Welsh Fusiliers
JONES Edward A. MM Pte 241157 Gloucestershire Regt
JONES Edward Charles Stanley MM Cpl 9108 11th Royal Warwickshire Regt
JONES Edward D. MM+Bar Sjt 241929 Liverpool Regt
JONES Edward Ernest MM Gnr 61055 118 Bty 130 Bde RFA
JONES Edward Frank "DCM,MM+Bar" Sjt 9382 1st Royal Berkshire Regt DOW 8.10.18.
JONES Edward George MM L/Cpl 50089 9th Cheshire Regt
JONES Edward H. MM Cpl 16026 Royal Welsh Fusiliers
JONES Edward Henry MM Sjt 1034 1st King Edward's Horse DOW 28.12.18.
JONES Edward L. MM Pte 2627 1st Welsh Guards
JONES Edward L. MM Pte 19908 4th Liverpool Regt
JONES Edwin MM Dvr 12682 48 Bty 36 Bde RFA
JONES Edwin MM 2nd Cpl 75429 Royal Engineers
JONES Edwin MM Pte 4096 Royal Fusiliers
JONES Edwin MM Sjt L/3250 RFA
JONES Edwin MM Pte 15465 11th Notts & Derby Regt
JONES Elias "DCM,MM+Bar" Cpl 20589 14th Royal Welsh Fusiliers DOW 23.4.18.
JONES Elias MM Spr 140159 Royal Engineers
JONES Elisha Frank MM Cpl 10738 B/232 Bde RFA KIA 3.10.18.
JONES Ellis MM Pte 26097 Royal Welsh Fusiliers
JONES Emlyn MM+Bar L/Cpl 12433 1st Gordon Highlanders DOW 5.9.18.
JONES Emyr Griffith MM Pte 9728 Machine Gun Corps DOW 18.9.18.
JONES Ernest MM Dvr L/33311 RFA
JONES Ernest MM Pnr 444238 Royal Engineers
JONES Ernest MM Sjt 35448 Machine Gun Corps
JONES Ernest MM Pte 19522 20th Lancashire Fusiliers
JONES Ernest MM Sjt 13948 10th Yorkshire Regt KIA 5.10.17.
JONES Ernest MM Dvr 13706 2 Div Ammn Col
JONES Ernest MM Sjt 30174 8th Royal Lancaster Regt
JONES Ernest MM Pte 14277 24th Manchester Regt
JONES Ernest MM L/Cpl 2363 1/6th Welsh Regt KIA 10.12.16.
JONES Ernest MM Sjt 240098 Royal Warwickshire Regt
JONES Ernest MM Pte 54182 Durham Light Infantry
JONES Ernest A. MM Sjt 18253 Machine Gun Corps
JONES Ernest E. MM Pte 18/777 Northumberland Fusiliers
JONES Ernest Frederick MM Pte 13224 XVII Corps Cyclist Bn Army Cyclist Corps
JONES Ernest G. MM Pte 25929 Machine Gun Corps
JONES Ernest H. MM Cpl 241211 Worcestershire Regt
JONES Ernest Henry MM L/Cpl 10573 7th Duke of Cornwall's LI
JONES Ernest J. MM L/Cpl 21508 Royal Welsh Fusiliers
JONES Ernest R. MM Spr 207587 Royal Engineers
JONES Ernest T. MM Sjt 83822 340 Bty 44 Bde RFA
JONES Ernest V. MM Spr 145206 Royal Engineers
JONES Ernest W. MM Cpl 13784 7th Bedfordshire Regt
JONES Ernest William MM Spr 77587 4 Div Sig Coy Royal Engineers
JONES Ernest William MM Cpl 11333 2nd Royal Welsh Fusiliers Died 6.7.16.
JONES Evan MM Pte 9042 2nd Royal Welsh Fusiliers
JONES Evan "DCM,MM" Sjt 9614 1st Liverpool Regt
JONES Evan MM Sjt 1753 Liverpool Regt
JONES Evan Griffith MM Sjt 11209 2nd Royal Welsh Fusiliers Died 22.2.17.
JONES Evan J. MM Pte 68454 9th Royal Welsh Fusiliers
JONES Evan M. MM Pte 112335 Tank Corps
JONES F. MM Cpl 214425 'J' Special Coy Royal Engineers
JONES F. MM L/Cpl 23363 1st Royal Inniskilling Fusiliers
JONES F.G. MM Cpl 37841 Machine Gun Corps
JONES Francis MM Sjt 71979 D/112 Bde RFA
JONES Francis MM Pte 82103 26th Royal Fusiliers
JONES Francis MM Cpl 1680 1/6th South Staffordshire Regt
JONES Francis Harold MM Pte 20666 Welsh Regt
JONES Francis L. MM Pte 14/1230 14th Royal Warwickshire Regt
JONES Francis Leonard Clarence "MC,MM(16167 L/Cpl Gren Gds)" 2Lt 2nd Royal Welsh Fusiliers KIA 1.9.18.
JONES Francis Thomas MM Pte 13745 7th Shropshire Light Infantry KIA 18.8.16.
JONES Frank MM Cpl 22106 Lancashire Fusiliers
JONES Frank "DCM,MM" Sjt 51349 'T' Bty 14 Bde RHA
JONES Frank MM Gnr 166252 RGA
JONES Frank E. MM Sjt 46352 127 Bty 29 Bde RFA
JONES Frank G. MM Cpl 14774 8th Somerset Light Infantry
JONES Frank H. MM Pte 93876 Notts & Derby Regt
JONES Frank Heald MM+Bar Cpl M2/133598 2 Div Train Army Service Corps
JONES Frank L. MM Sjt 34806 Labour Corps
JONES Frank V. "MM,MIDx2" 2nd Cpl 27312 Royal Engineers
JONES Frank W. MM Pte 15560 9th Norfolk Regt
JONES Fred MM Pte 13352 1st Royal Lancaster Regt
JONES Frederick MM L/Cpl 36836 Machine Gun Corps
JONES Frederick MM Sjt 5561 10th Hussars
JONES Frederick MM Pte 12080 5th Northamptonshire Regt
JONES Frederick MM Cpl 7723 1st Northamptonshire Regt
JONES Frederick MM Pte 7083 2nd South Staffordshire Regt
JONES Frederick MM Pte 4500 23rd Royal Fusiliers KIA 31.12.17.
JONES Frederick MM Pte 21933 11th South Wales Borderers
JONES Frederick A. MM Bdr 47217 RFA
JONES Frederick B. MM L/Cpl 2181 6th Dragoon Guards
JONES Frederick C. MM Gnr 178507 232 Siege Bty RGA
JONES Frederick D. MM Pte 17867 18th Liverpool Regt
JONES Frederick D. MM Pte 5489 3rd Dragoon Guards
JONES Frederick George MM Pte 14/169 14th Royal Warwickshire Regt KIA 23.7.16.
JONES Frederick J. MM L/Cpl 9625 South Wales Borderers att RWF.
JONES Frederick J. MM Cpl 25287 92 Bty 17 Bde RFA
JONES Frederick J. MM L/Cpl 494491 Royal Engineers
JONES Frederick James MM L/Cpl 2904 1/21st London Regt KIA 26.10.17.
JONES Frederick Richard MM Pte 201316 2/7th Worcestershire Regt
JONES Frederick S. MM Pte 28038 Royal Lancaster Regt
JONES Frederick Samuel MM L/Cpl 21878 11th Royal Fusiliers DOW 24.10.17.
JONES Frederick T. MM L/Sjt 6763 3rd Middlesex Regt
JONES Frederick T. MM Pte 38378 Gloucestershire Regt
JONES Frederick Thomas MM Pte 18195 Army Cyclist Corps
JONES G.F. "MM,MID" Sjt 9743 1st Scottish Rifles
JONES G.H.L. MM Pte 13040 8th Royal Welsh Fusiliers
JONES George MM Pte 1736 Army Cyclist Corps
JONES George MM Pte 16022 8th York & Lancaster Regt
JONES George MM Pte 21006 6th Shropshire Light Infantry
JONES George MM Pte 11303 7th East Kent Regt
JONES George MM Pte 9175 19th Durham Light Infantry
JONES George MM Pte 75633 1/2(Highland)Fd Amb RAMC
JONES George MM Pte S/9710 4th Royal Fusiliers
JONES George MM Gnr L/39228 RFA
JONES George MM Pte 12953 12th East Surrey Regt
JONES George MM Pte 4820 1/4th Royal Welsh Fusiliers
JONES George MM Sjt 12129 7/8th King's Own Scottish Borderers
JONES George MM Pte 16357 7th Shropshire Light Infantry
JONES George MM Cpl 11089 1st King's Royal Rifle Corps
JONES George MM Sjt 47891 Royal Engineers
JONES George A. MM Pte 211 16th Royal Warwickshire Regt
JONES George A. MM+Bar Sjt 68087 RFA
JONES George Archibald MM Pte 40467 1/4th Leicestershire Regt DOW 8.10.18.
JONES George Boardman MM Cpl 2419 Middlesex Regt
JONES George C. MM+Bar Cpl 107776 41st Bn Machine Gun Corps
JONES George Duncan MM Sjt 24255 A/75 Bde RFA
JONES George E. MM+Bar Sjt 1312 XV Corps Cyclist Bn Army Cyclist Corps
JONES George E. MM Cpl 17059 Liverpool Regt
JONES George E. MM Pte A/598 King's Royal Rifle Corps
JONES George E. MM Sjt W/3532 B/50 Bde RFA
JONES George H. MM Pte 20501 Grenadier Guards
JONES George H. MM Pte 12763 9th York & Lancaster Regt
JONES George L. MM Pte 356116 Liverpool Regt
JONES George Owen "MM,CdiG(It)" Pte 241708 1/6th Royal Warwickshire Regt
JONES George Thomas MM Sjt 27444 12th Suffolk Regt

JONES George Victor MM Pte 9556 16th Lancashire Fusiliers KIA 23.8.18.
JONES George W. MM Sjt 8999 2nd Royal Welsh Fusiliers
JONES Gilbert Griffith MM L/Cpl 521939 201 Fd Coy Royal Engineers
JONES Gordon MM Pte 16985 1st Grenadier Guards DOW 12.10.17.
JONES Griffith J. MM Pte 49805 Royal Welsh Fusiliers
JONES Griffith Thomas MM Sjt 14729 11th Royal Welsh Fusiliers
JONES Griffith W. MM L/Cpl 276986 Arg & Suth Highlanders
JONES Gwendolyn Gerrish Peyton MM Miss F First Aid Nursing Yeomanry
JONES Gwilym MM L/Cpl 40295 14th Royal Welsh Fusiliers
JONES Gwilym MM Cpl 200239 15th Welsh Regt
JONES Gwilym J. MM Pte 17441 8th Seaforth Highlanders KIA 22.8.17.
JONES Gwilym Parry MM Sjt 22329 15th Royal Welsh Fusiliers
JONES H. MM Pte 4983 6th Royal West Surrey Regt
JONES H. MM Air Mech 1 38377 Royal Air Force
JONES Harold MM Pte 306100 7th West Riding Regt
JONES Harold MM Cpl 83055 Royal Engineers
JONES Harold MM L/Cp 52199 Liverpool Regt
JONES Harold MM Pte 16132 1st Grenadier Guards
JONES Harold "MM+Bar,MID" Dvr 66768 RFA
JONES Harold MM L/Cpl 242591 South Staffordshire Regt
JONES Harold J. MM Pte M2/156635 Army Service Corps
JONES Harry MM Pte 16596 5th Oxf & Bucks Light Infantry
JONES Harry MM Pte 15968 10th York & Lancaster Regt
JONES Harry MM L/Cpl 132023 254 Tunnelling Coy Royal Engineers
JONES Harry MM Sjt 10802 2nd Yorkshire Regt KIA 22.3.18.
JONES Harry MM Pte S/16294 Rifle Brigade
JONES Harry MM Cpl 03319 Army Ordnance Corps
JONES Harry MM Sjt 265672 1/6th Cheshire Regt
JONES Harry MM L/Cpl 21190 9th Essex Regt
JONES Harry D. MM BQMS 27258 RGA
JONES Harry E. MM Pnr 171794 Royal Engineers
JONES Harry T. MM+Bar L/Cpl 700189 1/23rd London Regt
JONES Henry MM Pte 31149 Machine Gun Corps
JONES Henry MM Bdr 70160 44 Bde RFA
JONES Henry MM Pte 20643 13th Liverpool Regt
JONES Henry MM Cpl 230836 10th Shropshire Light Infantry
JONES Henry MM Sjt 4454 6th Dragoons
JONES Henry MM Pte 29703 Lancashire Fusiliers
JONES Henry B. "DCM,MM+Bar" Sjt L/9238 1st & 2nd Royal West Surrey Regt
JONES Henry F. MM Gnr 676762 C/124 Bde RFA
JONES Henry G. MM Pte 267385 Gloucestershire Regt
JONES Henry J. "DCM,MM+Bar" CSM 3/8688 2nd Suffolk Regt
JONES Henry W. MM L/Cpl 90097 Machine Gun Corps
JONES Herbert MM Gnr 48379 81 Siege Bty RGA
JONES Herbert MM Pte 301455 8th Manchester Regt
JONES Herbert MM L/Sjt 281738 Lancashire Fusiliers
JONES Herbert "DCM,MM" Sjt 54137 198 Coy 66th Bn Machine Gun Corps
JONES Herbert E. MM Gnr 215317 C/83 Bde RFA
JONES Herbert Edward MM Pte 15966 18th Lancashire Fusiliers DOW 1.8.18.
JONES Herbert Henry MM Pte 474415 12th London Regt KIA 24.4.18.
JONES Herbert Kay MM Pte 84133 Machine Gun Corps
JONES Herbert O. MM Pte 345200 24th Royal Welsh Fusiliers
JONES Herbert Robert MM Gnr 362444 239 Siege Bty RGA DOW 16.5.18.
JONES Herbert W. MM Cpl 352603 7th London Regt
JONES Horace MM L/Sjt 16442 Royal Berkshire Regt
JONES Howard R. MM Sjt 14160 7th Northamptonshire Regt
JONES Howell G. MM Cpl 16082 13th Royal Welsh Fusiliers
JONES Hugh MM Pte 20700 14th Royal Welsh Fusiliers
JONES Hugh MM Pte 14860 11th Royal Welsh Fusiliers
JONES Hugh MM Pte 6675 2nd Royal Welsh Fusiliers
JONES Hugh MM Pte 21280 Royal Welsh Fusiliers
JONES Hugh J. MM Pte 203246 2nd Royal Welsh Fusiliers
JONES Hugh W. MM Pte 60772 14th Royal Welsh Fusiliers
JONES Humphrey A. MM Pte 18034 Royal Welsh Fusiliers
JONES I.W. "DCM,MM+Bar" Sjt W/305 RFA
JONES Isaac MM Pte 203987 4th Yorkshire Light Infantry
JONES Isaac MM Bdr L/24483 D/104 Bde RFA
JONES Isaac "DCM,MM" Pte 9650 1st & 4th Liverpool Regt
JONES Isaac MM Pte 26555 10th Shropshire Light Infantry
JONES Isaac MM Spr 56042 33 Div Sig Coy Royal Engineers
JONES Ivor MM Cpl 166 1st Welsh Guards
JONES J. MM Sjt 17074 Welsh Regt
JONES J. MM L/Cpl 31637 Machine Gun Corps
JONES J.E. MM Pte 51081 Middlesex Regt
JONES J.W.O. MM L/Cpl P/2899 Military Mounted Police
JONES Jack MM Dvr 706445 RFA
JONES James MM Pte 21866 1st Worcestershire Regt
JONES James MM Cpl 3/7312 2nd Arg & Suth Highlanders
JONES James MM Dvr 35910 98 Bty 1 Bde RFA
JONES James MM+Bar Pte 235425 16th Royal Welsh Fusiliers
JONES James MM Pte 201555 9th Bn Tank Corps
JONES James MM Pte 50092 Welsh Regt
JONES James MM+Bar Pte 35631 9th Yorkshire Light Infantry
JONES James MM Pte 16268 7th Shropshire Light Infantry KIA 3.5.17.
JONES James MM Sjt M2/103432 Army Service Corps
JONES James Aubrey MM Spr 104901 177 Tunnelling Coy Royal Engineers
JONES James C. MM L/Sjt 240747 1/8th Worcestershire Regt
JONES James Edward MM L/Cpl 22132 Liverpool Regt
JONES James Ira Thomas "MC,DFC+Bar,MM(6326 AM1),MID" T/Lt RFC/RAF
JONES James L. MM Bdr 681764 D/276 Bde RFA
JONES James R. MM Pte 21568 Machine Gun Corps KIA 9.4.17.
JONES James Robert MM Cpl 15231 8th Somerset Light Infantry
JONES James William MM Pte 16627 7th Shropshire Light Infantry
JONES Jasper MM Pte 56734 RAMC
JONES Jeremiah MM L/Cpl 54123 Royal Welsh Fusiliers
JONES Joel Arthur MM Cpl 8156 2nd Royal Irish Regt
JONES John MM Pte 33909 16th Royal Warwickshire Regt
JONES John MM Cpl 28807 16th Royal Welsh Fusiliers
JONES John MM Pte 9361 Cheshire Regt
JONES John MM Cpl 24703 Royal Welsh Fusiliers
JONES John MM Pte 240851 South Staffordshire Regt
JONES John MM Sjt 24905 Liverpool Regt
JONES John MM L/Cpl 325226 1/9th Durham Light Infantry
JONES John MM+Bar L/Cpl 15644 2nd Bedfordshire Regt
JONES John MM Pte 40040 2nd South Wales Borderers
JONES John MM 2nd Cpl 217423 427 Fd Coy Royal Engineers
JONES John MM Sjt 25897 23rd Cheshire Regt
JONES John MM Cpl 17902 11th Notts & Derby Regt
JONES John MM Sjt 290448 RGA
JONES John MM Cpl 57232 41 Bde RFA
JONES John MM Pte B/1519 Rifle Brigade
JONES John MM L/Cpl 75523 Royal Engineers
JONES John MM Pte 15641 8th Duke of Cornwall's LI
JONES John MM Cpl 7213 9th King's Royal Rifle Corps DOW 29.10.17.
JONES John MM Sjt 6374 2nd Dragoons
JONES John "MM,MSM,MID" CSM 2851 King's Royal Rifle Corps
JONES John MM Spr 6662 2 Siege Coy Royal Anglesey Royal Engineers
JONES John MM Sjt 2012 1/2nd Monmouthshire Regt
JONES John MM Sjt 3/9050 1st South Wales Borderers DOW 4.6.17.
JONES John MM Sjt 13526 1st Grenadier Guards
JONES John MM Spr 486205 Royal Engineers
JONES John MM Pte 1439 6th Dragoons
JONES John MM Pte 44835 Durham Light Infantry
JONES John MM+Bar Pte 15153 8th Border Regt KIA 19.4.18.
JONES John MM Cpl S/7108 2nd Rifle Brigade
JONES John MM Pte 19299 Shropshire Light Infantry
JONES John A. MM Cpl 331658 Liverpool Regt
JONES John B. MM Pte 68445 RAMC
JONES John Bagnall MM 2nd Cpl 65147 105 Fd Coy Royal Engineers KIA 11.4.18.
JONES John Beaconsfield MM Dvr T2/13685 8 Reserve Park Army Service Corps
JONES John C. MM Pte 242532 6th South Staffordshire Regt
JONES John C. "DCM,MM" SM 54 1 Aircraft Depot Royal Flying Corps
JONES John E. MM Pte 33899 1st Border Regt
JONES John E. MM Cpl 37174 Royal Welsh Fusiliers
JONES John E. MM Pte 28952 Welsh Regt
JONES John Edward MM Pte 307536 Royal Warwickshire Regt
JONES John Edward MM Pte 5475 1st Royal Welsh Fusiliers
JONES John Edward MM Pte 28198 1st Somerset Light Infantry DOW 1.9.18.
JONES John Evan MM Dvr 111270 38 Div Ammn Col RFA

JONES John Gabriel MM Pte 6834 13 Fd Amb. RAMC
JONES John Goronwy MM Pte 4068 1st Welsh Guards DOW 6.11.18.
JONES John H. MM Pte 25992 Welsh Regt
JONES John H. MM Sjt 69063 RAMC
JONES John Herbert MM Pte 16931 7th Leicestershire Regt KIA 14.7.16.
JONES John J. MM Cpl 113426 Royal Engineers Died 31.5.18.
JONES John James "DCM,MM" Sjt 64042 32nd Bn Machine Gun Corps
JONES John L. MM Dvr 604413 RHA
JONES John M. MM BSM 310006 1/1(Welsh)Hy Bty RGA
JONES John N. MM Pte 251551 Manchester Regt
JONES John O. MM Pte 54601 Royal Welsh Fusiliers
JONES John Owen MM Pte 26162 17th Royal Welsh Fusiliers
JONES John Owen MM Pte 54606 14th Welsh Regt
JONES John S. MM Spr 126410 2 Light Rly Coy Royal Engineers
JONES John T. MM Cpl T4/250028 Army Service Corps
JONES John T. MM Sjt 14647 10th Royal Welsh Fusiliers
JONES John T. MM Pte 13674 10th Yorkshire Regt
JONES John T. MM Sjt 17059 6th South Wales Borderers
JONES John T. MM Sjt 45250 Royal Engineers
JONES Joseph MM Pte 17886 6th Royal Inniskilling Fusiliers
JONES Joseph MM Pte 53473 1/8th Middlesex Regt DOW 31.8.18.
JONES Joseph MM Pte 52397 15th Royal Irish Rifles
JONES Joseph MM Dvr 676520 RFA
JONES Joseph MM Sjt 200885 Royal Welsh Fusiliers
JONES Joseph MM L/Cpl 14455 Royal Fusiliers
JONES Joseph H. MM L/Cpl 202753 Welsh Regt
JONES Joseph H. MM Pte 200708 4th Cheshire Regt
JONES Joseph J. MM Pte 511951 14th London Regt
JONES Joseph R.L. MM L/Cpl 267079 Liverpool Regt
JONES Joseph T. MM L/Cpl 13490 4th Liverpool Regt
JONES Joshua James MM Dvr 2351 D/121 Bde RFA
JONES L.E.P. MM Spr 21347 Cav Corps Wireless Sqn Royal Engineers
JONES Leicester MM Cpl 330776 1/7th Liverpool Regt
JONES Leonard MM Pte 235104 16th Lancashire Fusiliers
JONES Leonard MM Pte 17516 2nd South Staffordshire Regt KIA 23.8.17.
JONES Leonard G. MM Pte M2/193632 Army Service Corps
JONES Leonard H. MM Pte M2/181217 Army Service Corps
JONES Lewis MM Pte 54600 16th Royal Welsh Fusiliers
JONES Lewis MM Pte 45008 13th Durham Light Infantry
JONES Lewis MM Sjt 25977 Royal Welsh Fusiliers
JONES Lewis MM Sjt 18557 Welsh Regt att Australian Tunnelling Coy
JONES Lewis MM Pte 243657 North Lancashire Regt
JONES Lewis A. MM Pte 6851 1/4th Royal Welsh Fusiliers
JONES Lionel MM Pte 13572 8th Gloucestershire Regt
JONES Llewellyn MM L/Cpl 202827 16th Royal Welsh Fusiliers KIA 8.10.18.
JONES Llewellyn MM Gnr 50593 18 Bde RFA
JONES Llewellyn "MM,MIDx3" L/Cpl 7850 2nd Suffolk Regt
JONES Lord A.S. MM Pte 27363 RAMC
JONES Louis MM Sjt 551113 16th London Regt
JONES Louis MM Cpl 109866 Tank Corps
JONES M.A. MM L/Cpl 16981 Royal Inniskilling Fusiliers
JONES Malcolm W. MM L/Cpl S/30915 Rifle Brigade
JONES Martin J.E. MM Cpl 19788 10th Duke of Cornwall's LI
JONES Michael MM L/Cpl M1/07595 5 Mot Amb Convoy Army Service Corps
JONES Michael MM Sjt 94400 34 Div Sig Coy Royal Engineers
JONES Milroy MM Pte 26632 1st Scottish Rifles
JONES Morgan R. MM Pte 31604 1st East Lancashire Regt
JONES Moses "MM,MID" Pte 82 1st Welsh Guards
JONES Norman F. MM Sjt 285372 1/1st Oxfordshire Yeomanry
JONES Oliver MM Pte 45621 8th Devonshire Regt
JONES Oliver C. MM Spr 30158 Royal Engineers
JONES Oswald "DCM,MM" Cpl 22193 1st North Lancashire Regt
JONES Owen MM Cpl 102155 17th Bn Machine Gun Corps
JONES Owen MM CSM 7627 2nd North Lancashire Regt
JONES Owen MM Cpl 40940 10th Royal Welsh Fusiliers
JONES Owen MM Pte 252752 3rd London Regt
JONES Owen MM Pte 33079 Cheshire Regt
JONES Owen MM Pte D/7011 6th Dragoons
JONES Owen MM Sjt 568051 Royal Engineers
JONES Owen Morris MM Pte 203399 1/4th Royal Welsh Fusiliers KIA 6.4.18.
JONES Owen William MM Pte 381019 Liverpool Regt
JONES P. MM Cpl 14380 Devonshire Regt
JONES P. MM 2/Cpl 108008 RE
JONES P.H. MM Pte 7622 East Surrey Regt
JONES Patrick MM L/Cpl 8756 2nd Royal West Surrey Regt
JONES Percival James MM Pte 354225 7th London Regt DOW 28.3.18
JONES Percival V. MM Pte 1581 RAMC
JONES Percy MM Gnr 84400 RFA
JONES Percy E. MM Cpl 153 1st Welsh Guards
JONES Percy MacDonald MM Spr 75831 'F' Corps Sig Coy Royal Engineers
JONES Percy Pugh MM Pte C/865 16th King's Royal Rifle Corps DOW 20.5.17.
JONES Peter MM CQMS 8745 1st Liverpool Regt KIA 8.8.16.
JONES Pritchard MM L/Bdr 5510 RFA
JONES R.G. MM L/Cpl 355814 Liverpool Regt
JONES Raymond MM Cpl 56621 10th Welsh Regt KIA 2.8.17.
JONES Rees MM Pte 24086 12th South Wales Borderers
JONES Rees MM Dvr 4514 RFA
JONES Reginald MM Spr 549769 56 Div Sig Coy Royal Engineers
JONES Reginald MM Gnr 860856 RFA
JONES Reginald R. MM Pte C/6034 King's Royal Rifle Corps
JONES Reuben MM+Bar Sjt R/22441 13th King's Royal Rifle Corps
JONES Rhys E. MM L/Cpl 21449 Royal Welsh Fusiliers
JONES Richard MM Pte 17421 13th Royal Welsh Fusiliers
JONES Richard MM L/Cpl 143380 Royal Engineers
JONES Richard MM+Bar Cpl 15680 1st King's Own Scottish Borderers
JONES Richard MM Cpl 266296 Cheshire Regt
JONES Richard MM Spr 45337 Royal Engineers
JONES Richard MM Pte 11985 Leicestershire Regt
JONES Richard MM L/Cpl 2737 1/4th Royal Welsh Fusiliers
JONES Richard MM L/Cpl 202888 Royal Welsh Fusiliers
JONES Richard Henry MM Cpl 16129 2nd South Lancashire Regt KIA 6.11.16.
JONES Richard I. MM Cpl 26109 17th Royal Welsh Fusiliers
JONES Richard Lewis MM Pte 235064 1/4th Royal Lancaster Regt KIA 21.6.18.
JONES Richard N. MM Sjt M2/020051 Army Service Corps
JONES Richard W. MM+Bar Cpl 266978 Liverpool Regt
JONES Robert MM Spr 438055 Royal Engineers
JONES Robert MM Pte 28598 Welsh Regt
JONES Robert MM Pte 632339 229 Empl Coy Labour Corps
JONES Robert MM+Bar Pte 12328 1st Norfolk Regt
JONES Robert MM Sjt 43127 Gordon Highlanders
JONES Robert MM L/Cpl 20761 Royal Welsh Fusiliers
JONES Robert MM Sjt 6999 1/4th Royal Welsh Fusiliers KIA 7.6.17.
JONES Robert MM Pte 16/800 16th Royal Irish Rifles
JONES Robert Ellis MM Pte 10981 4th Grenadier Guards
JONES Robert G. MM L/Cpl 44432 Royal Engineers
JONES Robert H. "MM+Bar,MID" L/Sjt 23057 Liverpool Regt
JONES Robert J. MM Pte 25506 17th Royal Welsh Fusiliers
JONES Robert James MM 2nd Cpl 548844 1/2(London)Fd Coy Royal Engineers
JONES Robert O. MM Pte 380205 6th Liverpool Regt
JONES Robert Samuel MM Cpl 265293 Royal Welsh Fusiliers
JONES Robert Thomas MM Cpl 35500 37th Bn Machine Gun Corps
JONES Robert W. MM Pte 25472 Royal Welsh Fusiliers
JONES Rowland MM Bdr 284697 277 Siege Coy RGA
JONES Rowland W. MM Pte 265620 Royal Welsh Fusiliers
JONES Roy MM Cpl 106546 3rd Bn Machine Gun Corps DOW 28.9.18.
JONES S. MM Cpl 203991 4th Yorkshire Light Infantry
JONES Samuel MM L/Cpl 8427 1st Royal Lancaster Regt DOW 2.7.16.
JONES Samuel MM Pte T/33515 ASC "See 39820 John ROBERTS,Welsh Regt"
JONES Samuel MM Pte 20893 1st Gloucestershire Regt
JONES Samuel MM Dvr 25328 30 Bde RFA
JONES Samuel MM L/Cpl 16623 10th Welsh Regt
JONES Samuel MM Pte 10082 South Staffordshire Regt
JONES Samuel MM Sjt 53734 28 Bde RFA
JONES Samuel John MM Sjt 930216 B/281 Bde RFA
JONES Sidney MM Pte 62855 18th Lancashire Fusiliers
JONES Sidney MM Pte 16086 5th Royal Berkshire Regt
JONES Sidney J. MM Pte R/42309 13th King's Royal Rifle Corps
JONES Stanley MM Cpl 2165 6th Liverpool Regt DOW 20.10.16.
JONES Stephen William MM Sjt 19617 13th Gloucestershire Regt
JONES Stewart J.D. MM Pte 251434 1/6th Arg & Suth Highlanders
JONES Sydney MM Pte 12714 9th North Staffordshire Regt

JONES Sydney D. MM L/Cpl 11827 18th Hussars
JONES Sydney E. MM Sjt S/6228 10th Arg & Suth Highlanders
JONES Sydney Evan MM Sjt M2/139243 Army Service Corps
JONES Sylvanus H. MM Pte 25271 Royal Welsh Fusiliers
JONES T. MM Pte 240793 Worcestershire Regt
JONES T. MM Pte 341510 RAMC
JONES Thomas MM Pte 8844 2nd Shropshire Light Infantry
JONES Thomas MM L/Cpl 19980 Welsh Regt
JONES Thomas MM Pte 66838 RAMC
JONES Thomas MM Pte 25459 1st South Wales Borderers
JONES Thomas MM Cpl 55661 17 Fd Amb RAMC
JONES Thomas MM Pte 320869 24th Welsh Regt
JONES Thomas MM Pte 53296 3rd Bn Machine Gun Corps
JONES Thomas MM Pte 2091 7th Dragoon Guards
JONES Thomas MM Dvr 18653 A/282 Bde RFA
JONES Thomas "MM+Bar,MIDx2" Sjt 40145 Royal Engineers
JONES Thomas MM Pte 8585 1st Royal Irish Regt
JONES Thomas MM Sjt 7514 1st Duke of Cornwall's LI
JONES Thomas MM Pte 355867 25th Royal Welsh Fusiliers
JONES Thomas MM Pte 15012 Worcestershire Regt
JONES Thomas MM Pte 34906 Lancashire Fusiliers
JONES Thomas MM Pte 21612 11th South Lancashire Regt
JONES Thomas "DCM,MM" Sjt 95398 1st Liverpool Regt KIA 25.8.18.
JONES Thomas MM Sjt 1964 1/13th London Regt
JONES Thomas MM Cpl 6428 Royal Welsh Fusiliers
JONES Thomas MM Sjt 7320 Notts & Derby Regt
JONES Thomas MM+Bar Sjt 5975 Welsh Regt
JONES Thomas MM Sjt 20204 Durham Light Infantry
JONES Thomas MM Pte 4656 14th Liverpool Regt
JONES Thomas MM Cpl 770132 50 Div Ammn Col RFA
JONES Thomas MM Pte 1576 9th Welsh Regt
JONES Thomas MM Sjt 22649 Royal Lancaster Regt
JONES Thomas A. MM Pte 24330 2nd South Wales Borderers
JONES Thomas B. MM L/Cpl 48325 23rd Royal Fusiliers
JONES Thomas Charles MM Pte 21235 14th Royal Welsh Fusiliers KIA 10.7.16.
JONES Thomas E.J. MM Sjt 57960 12th Bn Machine Gun Corps
JONES Thomas Edward MM Pte 332105 9th Liverpool Regt DOW 3.10.18
JONES Thomas Edward MM Pte 34304 1/4th North Lancashire Regt KIA 9.4.18.
JONES Thomas George MM Cpl 36312 33 Div Sig Coy Royal Engineers
JONES Thomas H. MM Pte 166182 32nd Bn Machine Gun Corps
JONES Thomas Idwal MM Cpl 2271 1/18th London Regt KIA 31.8.18.
JONES Thomas J. MM Pte 20948 Royal Welsh Fusiliers
JONES Thomas J. MM Dvr WT/4/069655 Army Service Corps
JONES Thomas J. MM Pte 200073 1/4th Welsh Regt
JONES Thomas J. MM+Bar Cpl 48586 130 Fd Amb RAMC
JONES Thomas J. MM Spr 86351 Royal Engineers
JONES Thomas J. MM Pte R/12519 King's Royal Rifle Corps
JONES Thomas James "MM,MMV(It)" Sjt 15/519 2nd Royal Warwickshire Regt
JONES Thomas L. MM Pte 202464 Royal Welsh Fusiliers
JONES Thomas Lewis MM Cpl 235604 14th Royal Welsh Fusiliers
JONES Thomas Stephen MM L/Cpl 201176 2/4th Oxf & Bucks Light Infantry
JONES Thomas W. MM L/Sjt 17423 6th Northamptonshire Regt
JONES Thomas W. MM Pte 12414 6th Shropshire Light Infantry
JONES Thomas W.A. MM Sjt 9562 1st South Wales Borderers
JONES Thomas W.E. MM Pte 242438 Lancashire Fusiliers
JONES Thomas William MM L/Cpl 9815 1st North Staffordshire Regt KIA 21.3.18.
JONES Tom MM Pte 36662 1st Gloucestershire Regt
JONES Tom MM Pte 301510 8th Manchester Regt
JONES Tom MM Pte 19038 6th South Wales Borderers
JONES Tom MM L/Cpl 1320 1/3rd Monmouthshire Regt
JONES Tom Israel MM Pte 34724 6th Royal Warwickshire Regt
JONES Trevor MM+Bar Pte 13367 9th Royal Welsh Fusiliers KIA 31.7.17.
JONES Trevor G. MM Cpl 28325 Welsh Regt
JONES Trevor M. MM L/Cpl 2708 1st Welsh Guards
JONES Valentine H. MM Cpl 836346 RFA
JONES Victor D. MM S/Sjt 51480 RAMC
JONES Victor S. MM Pte 75871 1/1st Derbyshire Yeomanry
JONES W. MM Sjt 3/11967 West Riding Regt
JONES W. MM Pte 54314 Welsh Regt
JONES W.E. MM Pte 11717 Royal West Surrey Regt
JONES W.J. MM Sjt 139041 180 Tunnelling Coy Royal Engineers DOW 28.7.17.
JONES W.O. MM Pte 20731 10th Royal Welsh Fusiliers
JONES Wallace MM Pte 19475 2nd East Lancashire Regt KIA 22.5.18.
JONES Wallace E.F. MM Pte 15623 9th Royal Welsh Fusiliers
JONES Walter MM Pnr 151794 18 Div Sig Coy Royal Engineers
JONES Walter MM Spr 63003 38 Div Sig Coy Royal Engineers
JONES Walter R. MM Sjt 15138 9th North Lancashire Regt
JONES Walter Swinford MM Bdr 826132 281 Bde RFA Died 3.9.18.
JONES Walter T. MM Pte 36771 Machine Gun Corps
JONES Watkin MM Cpl 36820 Lancashire Fusiliers
JONES Wiilfred Grantley MM Pte 53028 19th Bn Machine Gun Corps
JONES William MM CQMS 4235 18th Bn Machine Gun Corps
JONES William MM L/Sjt 265203 1/2nd Monmouthshire Regt
JONES William MM Cpl 22916 Royal Dublin Fusiliers
JONES William MM Pte 24774 4th South Wales Borderers
JONES William MM Cpl 201407 Northamptonshire Regt
JONES William MM Pte 23242 Welsh Regt
JONES William MM Gnr 25737 RFA
JONES William MM Pte 14726 1st Grenadier Guards
JONES William MM+Bar Pte 53638 2nd Welsh Regt
JONES William MM Gnr 736176 36 Bde RFA
JONES William MM L/Cpl 18001 6th King's Own Scottish Borderers
JONES William MM Sjt 10672 13th Liverpool Regt
JONES William MM Sjt 240415 1/8th Middlesex Regt
JONES William MM Pte 70236 14th Royal Welsh Fusiliers
JONES William MM Pte 21296 10th South Wales Borderers
JONES William MM Pte 52031 6th Somerset Light Infantry
JONES William MM Bdr 84072 D/94 Bde RFA
JONES William MM Pte 38122 South Staffordshire Regt
JONES William MM Dvr 35096 RFA
JONES William MM Pte 55577 Royal Welsh Fusiliers
JONES William MM Pte 200374 1/4th Royal Welsh Fusiliers KIA 2.2.18.
JONES William MM L/Sjt 12895 9th North Lancashire Regt
JONES William MM Spr 139491 Royal Engineers
JONES William MM Sjt 36384 RAMC
JONES William MM Gnr L/2089 A/148 Bde RFA KIA 24.7.17.
JONES William MM Pte 1189 1st Welsh Guards KIA 10.9.16.
JONES William MM Bdr 50107 18 Bde RFA
JONES William MM Sjt 13993 5th South Wales Borderers
JONES William MM Pte L/12342 2nd Royal Fusiliers
JONES William MM Gnr 51696 RGA
JONES William MM Pte 3299 Manchester Regt
JONES William MM Pte 242638 Royal Warwickshire Regt
JONES William MM Bdr 65227 29 Bde RFA
JONES William MM Sjt 10328 Cheshire Regt
JONES William MM Dvr 25838 RFA
JONES William A. MM Sjt 37365 RFA
JONES William D. "DCM,MM" Pte 26595 Border Regt
JONES William D. MM Pte 21983 Welsh Regt
JONES William D. MM Pte 3558 1st Welsh Guards
JONES William David MM Sjt M2/054796 5 Bde Ammn Col Army Service Corps
JONES William E. MM Pte 17839 Shropshire Light Infantry
JONES William E. MM Pte R/6554 King's Royal Rifle Corps
JONES William E. "MM,MID" Spr 28402 Royal Engineers
JONES William E. MM Pte 5336 IX Corps Cyclist Bn Army Cyclist Corps
JONES William E. MM Sjt 18778 1st Royal Welsh Fusiliers
JONES William F. MM Pte G/24935 Middlesex Regt
JONES William G. "DCM,MM" Sjt 20549 14th Royal Welsh Fusiliers
JONES William G.H. MM Pte C/786 16th King's Royal Rifle Corps
JONES William H. MM Pte 23775 1st Royal Warwickshire Regt
JONES William H. MM QMS 39536 RAMC
JONES William H. MM L/Cpl 9953 Leicestershire Regt
JONES William H. MM Pte 48584 RAMC
JONES William H. MM Pte 570910 17th London Regt
JONES William H.S. MM L/Cpl 1610 1st Royal Warwickshire Regt
JONES William Henry MM Sjt 12746 16th Lancashire Fusiliers Died 3.11.18.
JONES William Henry MM Gnr 736026 RFA
JONES William J. MM 2nd Cpl 44773 92 Fd Coy Royal Engineers
JONES William J. MM Pte 3/8226 1st Devonshire Regt
JONES William J. MM Spr 357616 Signal Service Royal Engineers
JONES William J. MM Pte 350054 13th Liverpool Regt
JONES William J. MM Spr 137597 Royal Engineers
JONES William J. MM+Bar Pte 9176 2/1st HAC(Inf)

JONES William J. MM L/Cpl 423295 10th London Regt
JONES William L. MM Pte 11623 1st South Wales Borderers
JONES William M. MM+Bar L/Sjt 756 1st Welsh Guards
JONES William M. MM Pte 39695 2nd Royal Welsh Fusiliers
JONES William M. MM Sjt 47793 RAMC
JONES William M. MM Bdr 30453 8 Div Ammn Col RGA
JONES William Moses MM Pte 266194 1/6th Royal Welsh Fusiliers KIA 9.3.19.
JONES William R. MM Sjt 147764 255 Tunnelling Coy Royal Engineers
JONES William R. MM Pte DM2/163103 Army Service Corps
JONES William Richard MM Cpl 37463 5 Bde RFA
JONES William T. MM Pte 36869 1st Gloucestershire Regt
JONES William T. MM BQMS W/5256 38 Div Ammn Col RFA
JONES William T. MM Spr 108187 Royal Engineers
JONES William T. MM Sjt 15899 Royal Welsh Fusiliers
JONES William T. MM Pte 40083 Royal Welsh Fusiliers
JONES William Thomas MM Cpl 16614 13th Royal Welsh Fusiliers
JONES William V. MM Bdr 681745 RFA
JONES Willie MM Gnr 151876 217 Siege Bty RGA
JOPLING Robert MM Cpl 67009 Royal Engineers
JOPLING William MM L/Cpl 10502 2nd Durham Light Infantry
JOPSON George MM L/Cpl 26377 Machine Gun Corps
JOPSON William G. MM L/Cpl 13218 11th Border Regt
JORDAN Albert H. MM Cpl 14668 Royal Engineers
JORDAN Alfred MM Dvr T/364956 62 Div Train Army Service Corps
JORDAN Arthur MM Sjt 12957 Leicestershire Regt
JORDAN Arthur V. MM Pte 37251 South Staffordshire Regt
JORDAN Bert R. MM Pte 45344 15th Royal Irish Rifles
JORDAN Charles MM L/Cpl 2285 1/18th London Regt
JORDAN Charles MM Bdr 88643 AA Section RGA
JORDAN Charles MM Pte 714 6th East Kent Regt
JORDAN Charles Arthur MM Trumpeter 38938 RGA
JORDAN Charles J. MM Cpl 39091 South Wales Borderers
JORDAN Charles W. "MM,MID" Sjt 1851 Middlesex Regt
JORDAN Claude A. MM L/Cpl R/15141 King's Royal Rifle Corps
JORDAN Edwin MM L/Cpl 1373 Notts & Derby Regt
JORDAN Elles A.G. MM Cpl 250508 Essex Regt
JORDAN Ernest MM Sjt 8869 2nd Devonshire Regt
JORDAN Ernest G.R. MM Pte 24459 1st Gloucestershire Regt
JORDAN Ernest W.C. MM Pte 32037 6th Dorsetshire Regt
JORDAN F. MM Pte 680319 London Regt
JORDAN Frank T. MM L/Cpl 201052 Royal Warwickshire Regt
JORDAN Frederick "MM,CG(B)" Sjt 10256 1st East Yorkshire Regt
JORDAN Frederick G. MM Pte 7656 1/2nd(Highland)Fd Amb RAMC
JORDAN George H. MM Sjt 5469 RAMC att Yorkshire LI.
JORDAN George R. MM Pte 365260 12/13th Northumberland Fusiliers
JORDAN Guy MM+Bar Pte 15136 9th Suffolk Regt
JORDAN Harold MM Sjt 20216 8th Gloucestershire Regt
JORDAN Harry MM Cpl 15449 Royal Sussex Regt
JORDAN Harry MM Cpl 37065 RGA
JORDAN Harry Victor MM Sjt 13842 11th West Yorkshire Regt
JORDAN Henry MM Pte 51343 Royal Fusiliers
JORDAN Herbert F. MM L/Sjt 1677 4th GMGR
JORDAN James MM Spr 79118 Royal Engineers
JORDAN James B. MM Pte 34779 Royal Lancaster Regt
JORDAN James H. MM Pte 7536 1st Suffolk Regt
JORDAN John MM+Bar Cpl 27395 3rd Bn Machine Gun Corps
JORDAN John MM Pte 17375 8th East Lancashire Regt
JORDAN John Helmuth MM Pte 510291 RAMC
JORDAN John T. MM L/Cpl S/24308 Rifle Brigade
JORDAN Joseph MM Pte 300424 1/8th Arg & Suth Highlanders DOW 23.3.17.
JORDAN Joseph MM Pte 27/1418 Northumberland Fusiliers
JORDAN Joseph Henry MM L/Cpl 42087 56 Coy Machine Gun Corps
JORDAN Lawson MM Sjt L/24570 D/190 Bde RFA
JORDAN Leonard MM Cpl 15808 6th Leicestershire Regt
JORDAN Leonard MM Pte 90447 11 Fd Amb RAMC
JORDAN Lowry MM Pte 4034 2nd Rifle Brigade
JORDAN Melville MM Dmr 240062 1/5th Gloucestershire Regt
JORDAN Patrick MM Pte 303365 1/8th Arg & Suth Highlanders DOW 21.3.18.
JORDAN Percy MM Pte 63355 18th Bn Machine Gun Corps
JORDAN Percy MM Gnr 884584 RFA
JORDAN Thomas MM Spr 270363 Railways Div Royal Engineers
JORDAN Thomas MM Spr 82208 Royal Engineers
JORDAN Thomas MM+Bar Pte 11780 6th Shropshire Light Infantry
JORDAN Thomas MM Pte 633687 20th London Regt DOW 5.9.18.
JORDAN Thomas MM+Bar Spr 104514 228 Fd Coy Royal Engineers
JORDAN Thomas M. MM Cpl 87343 Royal Engineers
JORDAN Walter MM Gnr 134579 124 Bty 28 Bde RFA
JORDAN William MM L/Cpl 245324 2nd Manchester Regt
JORDAN William MM Sjt 10813 8th Devonshire Regt
JORDAN William "DCM+Bar,MM" Sjt 62146 19 Fd Amb RAMC
JORDAN William MM Pte 25306 10th Durham Light Infantry KIA 16.9.16.
JORDAN William MM Pte 6299 1st Dragoon Guards
JORDAN William MM Sjt 265306 1/6th Northumberland Fusiliers
JORDAN William MM Pte 12336 8th Royal Welsh Fusiliers
JORDAN William C. MM Cpl S/117 Rifle Brigade
JORDAN William H. "DCM,MM" Sjt 7012 1st Somerset Light Infantry
JORDISON Herbert "MM,MID" Sjt 13808 Northumberland Fusiliers
JORDON Albert MM Pte 14326 12th Gloucestershire Regt
JOSE Charles W. "MM,MID" L/Cpl 62831 Royal Engineers
JOSE William MM L/Cpl 144971 Royal Engineers
JOSEPH Alan Jephson MM Pte B/461 7th Rifle Brigade KIA 15.9.16.
JOSEPH Evan Victor "DCM,MM" Sjt 9189 1st Worcestershire Regt DOW 6.2.19.
JOSEPH Fred MM 2nd Cpl 6701 Royal Engineers
JOSEPH John MM Cpl 151167 268 Railway Coy Royal Engineers
JOSEPH Thomas H. MM Gnr 38860 RFA
JOSEPHS William J. MM Gnr 34382 4 Siege Bty RGA
JOSEPHSON Edmund George MM Pte 8247 5th Dragoon Guards DOW 3.3.19.
JOSEY Ernest Louis MM Dvr 60684 75 Fd Coy Royal Engineers
JOSEY James MM Sjt 240420 1/6th Highland Light Infantry
JOSHUA William MM L/Cpl 23183 1st Welsh Regt
JOSLAND Alfred E. MM Pte 11362 Royal Sussex Regt
JOSS Edward James MM Sjt S/5737 10th Royal Highlanders
JOSS James MM Pte S/6640 11th Arg & Suth Highlanders KIA 15.9.16.
JOST John MM Pte 241721 2/5th North Lancashire Regt
JOTHAM Harold MM L/Cpl 436181 Royal Engineers
JOUGHIN Alfred MM Pte 64087 5th Bn Machine Gun Corps
JOUGHIN John MM Pte 46735 RAMC
JOUGHIN Joseph MM Pte 241879 Liverpool Regt
JOUGUET Archibald James MM Sjt 7340 Northamptonshire Regt
JOULE George MM L/Cpl 11256 Cheshire Regt
JOURNEAUX Henry Francis MM Cpl 4133 7th Royal Irish Rifles
JOURNET Frederick A. MM L/Cpl 30077 9th Yorkshire Light Infantry
JOURNET Henry T. MM Sjt 18386 Norfolk Regt
JOUXSON Ernest Walter MM L/Cpl 10971 6th Somerset Light Infantry KIA 22.8.17.
JOW George F. MM Pte 17416 4th York & Lancaster Regt
JOW George R. MM+Bar Bdr 785747 RFA
JOWETT Ellis MM Pte 204369 Northumberland Fusiliers
JOWETT Harold F. MM Spr 28649 Royal Engineers
JOWETT Lewis MM Pte 19401 West Yorkshire Regt
JOWETT William H. MM Pte 21/983 21st West Yorkshire Regt
JOWITT Herbert MM Cpl B/203704 Rifle Brigade
JOWLE Robert MM L/Cpl 6636 16th Manchester Regt
JOWSEY Thomas MM L/Cpl 5222 9th Northumberland Fusiliers
JOY Amos MM Pte 16018 10th York & Lancaster Regt
JOY Charles V. MM L/Cpl 203954 Middlesex Regt
JOY Edmund J. MM+Bar Sjt 19002 Royal Berkshire Regt
JOY Frederick C. MM Pte 4436 4th Royal Berkshire Regt
JOY George Arthur MM L/Cpl 13832 2nd Middlesex Regt
JOY George H. MM Gnt 112799 RGA
JOY Henry G. MM Sjt 1878 1/22nd London Regt
JOY Isaac A. MM Cpl 9685 1st Royal Scots Fusiliers
JOY Oliver J. MM L/Cpl M2/074492 Army Service Corps
JOY Stanley T. MM Sjt 11023 7th Duke of Cornwall's LI
JOY Thomas G.L. MM+Bar L/Cpl 359734 2 Div Sig Coy Royal Engineers
JOY William MM L/Cpl 66510 62nd Bn Machine Gun Corps
JOYCE Alexander Hugh Sinclair MM Cpl 22101 7th Bedfordshire Regt DOW 20.8.18.
JOYCE Alfred MM Pte 420502 10th London Regt
JOYCE Alfred MM Pte 18421 7th South Staffordshire Regt
JOYCE Alfred MM Pte 10258 South Staffordshire Regt formerly Alfred Tuft.
JOYCE Alfred C. MM Pte 201066 Bedfordshire Regt
JOYCE Arthur MM Pte 12925 4th Grenadier Guards
JOYCE Arthur MM Pte 8896 2nd Lincolnshire Regt
JOYCE Cecil MM Pte 192 4th GMGR
JOYCE Ernest A. MM Pte 290480 9th Royal Sussex Regt
JOYCE Ernest S. MM L/Cpl L/8456 11th Royal West Surrey Regt
JOYCE Frederick E.T. MM Sjt 320032 1/1st Wiltshire Yeomanry

JOYCE George T. MM Pte 392532 9th London Regt
JOYCE Henry Charles MM L/Cpl C/7069 18th King's Royal Rifle Corps DOW 28.3.18.
JOYCE Herbert MM Pte 27192 Royal Dublin Fusiliers
JOYCE Herbert Thomas "MM,MSM" Sjt 281946 120 Siege Bty RGA
JOYCE James M. MM Cpl 46205 Royal Engineers
JOYCE John MM+Bar Cpl 45860 Royal Engineers
JOYCE John MM CSM 275281 7th Manchester Regt
JOYCE John MM Dvr 51715 'C' Bty RHA
JOYCE John MM Pte 295640 12th Royal Scots
JOYCE John Edward MM Pte 28312 15th West Yorkshire Regt KIA 27.3.18.
JOYCE John Henry MM Sjt 25090 1st Cheshire Regt
JOYCE John S. MM+Bar Cpl 60376 8th Bn Machine Gun Corps
JOYCE Norman MM L/Cpl 9956 1st Royal Inniskilling Fusiliers
JOYCE Patrick MM Cpl 3979 Connaught Rangers
JOYCE Patrick Francis MM Sjt 1767 1st Irish Guards
JOYCE Percy William MM Pte 6267 1st Royal West Surrey Regt KIA 13.4.18.
JOYCE Peter J. MM Spr 151972 Royal Engineers
JOYCE Thomas MM Sjt 1032 1/4th Yorkshire Regt
JOYCE Thomas S. MM Pte 201221 Cheshire Regt
JOYCE William C. MM Pte 24163 Suffolk Regt
JOYCE William H. MM Sjt 3278 2nd Rifle Brigade
JOYCE William P. MM Sjt 1415 1st Royal West Kent Regt
JOYES Frank MM+Bar Pte 25733 9th West Riding Regt
JOYNER Bertram C. MM Cpl 7263 RAMC att Coldstream Guards.
JOYNER Percy MM Sjt 19431 RGA
JOYNES Edward MM Cpl 268056 1/6th West Riding Regt KIA 29.4.18.
JOYNES G.A. MM Cpl 11113 Labour Corps
JOYNES William MM Pte 19498 2nd Northamptonshire Regt DOW 14.8.18.
JOYNSON George MM Sjt 17929 Royal Scots
JOYNSON William Alfred MM Pte 291062 1/7th Cheshire Regt KIA 23.7.18.
JOYNSON William James MM Cpl 34 10th Cheshire Regt KIA 28.5.18.
JOYNT James Roland MM Pte 6521 2nd Notts & Derby Regt KIA 16.10.16.
JUBB Albert MM Cpl 56884 8 Bde RFA
JUBB John MM Pte 202774 4th York & Lancaster Regt
JUBB John H. MM Pte 450705 1/11th London Regt
JUBB William MM Dvr 884 RFA
JUBB William MM Cpl 57014 95 Siege Bty RGA
JUBY Herbert James MM Sjt 21674 35 Coy Machine Gun Corps KIA 30.11.17.
JUDD Arthur MM Pte 186 4th Bn GMGR
JUDD Arthur W. MM S/Sjt 65429 RAMC
JUDD Ernest John MM Pte 3192 8th Royal West Kent Regt
JUDD Harry Herbert MM Sjt (ORS) 9147 1st Leicestershire Regt
JUDD Richard MM L/Cpl 19193 7th South Staffordshire Regt
JUDE Alfred G. MM Sjt 71826 18th Bn Machine Gun Corps
JUDE Andrew MM+Bar Pte 291877 Royal Highlanders
JUDEN Louis John MM Spr 166178 IV Corps HAG Sig Sect Royal Engineers
JUDGE Albert MM Sjt 200383 1/4th Northamptonshire Regt
JUDGE Arthur A. "MM,MSM" L/Cpl 89442 138 Army Troops Coy Royal Engineers
JUDGE Harry MM Gnr 40060 'Q' Bty RHA
JUDGE J. MM Cpl 204010 Middlesex Regt
JUDGE Richard MM L/Cpl 14571 1st Scots Guards
JUDGE Sydney R. MM Pte 105280 1/1st Herefordshire Yeomanry
JUDGE William J. MM Pte 15385 1st Royal West Kent Regt
JUDKINS Charles MM L/Cpl 11469 6th Wiltshire Regt DOW 21.4.18.
JUDKINS Walter MM Cpl 17074 6th South Wales Borderers
JUDSON Albert MM Gnr 751392 D/317 Bde RFA KIA 9.11.17.
JUDSON Brooks MM Pte 305703 8th Bn Tank Corps
JUDSON Charles Frederick MM Bdr 72049 126 Bty 29 Bde RFA KIA 22.7.17.
JUDSON Charles H. MM Cpl 19029 A/83 Bde RFA
JUDSON Edgar F. MM Pte 533192 15th London Regt
JUDSON Milton MM Sjt 15002 5th West Riding Regt
JUDSON William MM L/Cpl 13517 1st Grenadier Guards
JUETT William H. MM Sjt 10086 10th West Yorkshire Regt
JUGG George Henry MM Pte 1643 1/1st Cambridgeshire Regt KIA 24.9.16.
JUGGINS Arthur MM CQMS 15757 10th Worcestershire Regt
JUGGINS Thomas Henry James MM Cpl 13049 8th Gloucestershire Regt

JUKES Benjamin MM Pte M2/133649 Army Service Corps att RFA.
JUKES Edward MM Spr 32778 8 Div Sig Coy Royal Engineers
JUKES George William MM Cpl 73857 42nd Bn Machine Gun Corps DOW 27.9.18.
JUKES William MM Sjt R/3152 King's Royal Rifle Corps
JULIAN William MM Pte 9189 22 Fd Amb RAMC
JULIER H.T. MM CQMS 13655 10th Essex Regt
JULINGS Thomas G. MM Pte 202469 1/1st Cambridgeshire Regt
JULL Charles Henry MM Pte 51500 Royal Fusiliers
JULL Ernest MM Cpl 6396 1st Dragoons
JUNIPER Ernest MM Pte 12901 10th Essex Regt KIA 12.4.18.
JUNOR Alexander MM Pte 316104 1/3(Highland)Fd Amb RAMC
JUNOR D. MM Pte 202668 1/4th Gordon Highlanders
JUNOR George MM Pte 240568 1/4th Gordon Highlanders DOW 1.9.18.
JUPE A.H.C. MM L/Cpl P/837 Military Mounted Police
JUPP Arthur H. MM Spr 167925 Royal Engineers
JUPP Ernest J. MM Cpl 75914 Tank Corps
JUPP Ernest Stephen MM Pte 260084 Hampshire Regt
JUPP Frederick MM L/Sjt 9995 1st Royal West Kent Regt
JUPP Henry G. MM Sjt 10599 9 Fd Amb RAMC
JUPP John R. MM Pte 17471 1st Somerset Light Infantry
JUPP Thomas "DCM,MM" Sjt 23159 6 Div Sig Coy Royal Engineers
JUPP W.R. MM Sjt P1074 Military Foot Police
JURY Theodore MM Dvr 19862 A/277 Bde RFA
JUSON Frank MM Pte 21606 Machine Gun Corps
JUST John Edward MM Dvr 765573 RFA
JUSTICE Charles MM Pte 5266 7th East Kent Regt
JUSTICE Henry G. MM L/Cpl 1682 XIII Corps Cyclist Bn Army Cyclist Corps
JUSTICE Thomas MM Pte 8660 2nd Seaforth Highlanders KIA 1.7.16.
JUSTICE Walter MM Sjt 7145 1st Northamptonshire Regt
JUSTICE William Thomas MM Spr 166287 457 Fd Coy Royal Engineers
JUTSAM Gilbert MM Pte 16115 9th Devonshire Regt
JUTTING George Herbert MM Sjt 558060 29 Div Sig Coy Royal Engineers

K

KADWELL Albert T. MM Dvr T/33675 Army Service Corps att HQ 3 Inf Bde
KAIGH George H. MM Pte 307129 15th Bn Tank Corps
KAIL Alfred MM Pte 28016 10th Royal Warwickshire Regt
KAILL Albert MM+Bar Cpl 613604 1/19th London Regt
KAIN Henry MM L/Cpl 6751 9th Gordon Highlanders Died 13.5.18.
KALMER Robert MM Sjt 52789 'N' Bty RHA
KAMESTER Joseph MM Pte 18923 6th Royal West Kent Regt KIA 30.11.17.
KAMP Ernest B. MM Gnr 152910 259 Siege Bty RGA
KAMPFF Harold George MM Pte 529445 18th London Regt
KANDES Harry MM+Bar Spr 49677 23 Div Sig Coy Royal Engineers
KANE Edward MM Cpl 10460 2nd Scottish Rifles KIA 22.9.16.
KANE F. MM Pte 41688 Highland Light Infantry
KANE Francis MM Pte 22068 Machine Gun Corps
KANE Frederick G. MM L/Cpl 18435 8th Royal Berkshire Regt
KANE George MM Pte 26155 33rd Bn Machine Gun Corps
KANE Harry MM Pte 10039 Irish Guards
KANE Henry Ernest MM Pte 10998 1st Notts & Derby Regt DOW 5.10.16.
KANE Hugh "DCM,MM+Bar" Cpl 203285 1/4th West Riding Regt DOW 13.5.18.
KANE J. MM Pte 266046 Northumberland Fusiliers
KANE James MM Pte 20424 Royal Scots
KANE John MM Pte S/9274 Royal Highlanders
KANE John H. MM L/Cpl 11450 2nd Royal Scots
KANE Michael T. MM Pte 140717 Machine Gun Corps
KANE Robert "MM+Bar,CG(B)" Pte 3956 2nd Royal Inniskilling Fusiliers
KANE Robert "MM,MSM" Pte 351176 1/9th Manchester Regt
KANE Robert MM Pte 17544 Royal Inniskilling Fusiliers
KANE Samuel MM Pte 200159 1/5th Arg & Suth Highlanders
KANE Victor W. MM Pte 65648 6th Cheshire Regt
KANNON W. MM Pte 54050 22nd Manchester Regt
KARLE Frederick "MM,MSM" Pte 93302 156 Coy Labour Corps
KATER Robert MM S/Sjt Fitter 88146 9 Bde RFA
KATES Charles James MM Sjt 391669 9th London Regt

KATON Alfred MM Cpl 13313 Royal Engineers
KATTAN Henry A.V. MM Pte 370029 8th London Regt
KAUFMAN Henry MM Sjt 19963 20th Lancashire Fusiliers
KAVANAGH C. MM Sjt 160257 174 Coy Labour Corps
KAVANAGH George C. MM Pte M2/104931 Army Service Corps
KAVANAGH Henry MM Bdr 20135 RFA
KAVANAGH James MM Pte 5915 2nd Royal Irish Rifles KIA 7.9.18.
KAVANAGH James "MM,CG(It)" Pte 39548 8th Yorkshire Light Infantry
KAVANAGH John MM Dvr 1410 RFA
KAVANAGH Joseph MM Sjt 7277 2nd Leinster Regt
KAVANAGH Thomas MM Cpl 31928 8 Bde RFA
KAVANAGH William MM Pte 240205 1/5th South Lancashire Regt
KAY Alexander "MM,CG(F)" Pte 2220 1/7th Royal Scots
KAY Alfred MM Gnr 221439 RFA
KAY Alfred MM L/Cpl 306209 4th Bn Tank Corps
KAY Alfred MM+Bar Gnr 75078 A/94 Bde RFA
KAY Alfred Daniel MM 2nd Cpl 58742 11 Div Sig Coy Royal Engineers
KAY Charles MM Sjt 28400 22nd Manchester Regt
KAY David MM Cpl 645616 RFA
KAY David C. MM Pte M2/132732 Army Service Corps att RAMC
KAY Ernest MM Bdr 855 X/55 Med TM Bty RFA KIA 9.3.17.
KAY F. MM Pte 200860 East Lancashire Regt
KAY Fred MM L/Cpl 86331 237 Coy Machine Gun Corps
KAY George MM Pte 201860 East Lancashire Regt
KAY George MM Sjt 8568 2nd Royal Scots
KAY George P. MM Pte 16802 Border Regt
KAY Harry MM Sjt 2870 Manchester Regt
KAY Harry "DCM,MM" Sjt 241387 2nd North Lancashire Regt
KAY Hedley G. MM Cpl 265595 1/6th West Riding Regt
KAY Herbert MM Pte 42462 RAMC
KAY Jack S. MM Cpl Wheeler T/232 Army Service Corps
KAY James MM Sjt 132652 Royal Engineers
KAY James MM L/Cpl 15394 1/5th Border Regt DOW 24.8.18.
KAY James W. MM Pte 8779 2nd Manchester Regt
KAY John MM Sjt S/5475 7th Royal Highlanders
KAY John MM Sjt 1629 York & Lancaster Regt
KAY John MM Pte 30636 15th Cheshire Regt DOW 5.5.18.
KAY John MM Pte 19747 South Lancashire Regt
KAY John A. MM Pte 307357 West Riding Regt
KAY John B. MM Pte M2/048535 Army Service Corps
KAY John C. MM L/Cpl 63253 4th Yorkshire Light Infantry
KAY Joseph MM L/Cpl 402067 409 Fd Coy Royal Engineers
KAY Joseph MM Sjt 46364 90 Fd Coy Royal Engineers KIA 18.7.16.
KAY Joseph MM Pte 46837 10th South Wales Borderers
KAY Percy N. MM Spr 43489 Royal Engineers
KAY Peter MM Sjt R/9284 1st King's Royal Rifle Corps KIA 17.2.17.
KAY Robert MM Pte 235871 9th Northumberland Fusiliers
KAY Robert MM Pte 242292 North Lancashire Regt
KAY Robert MM Gnr 218104 RFA
KAY Robert G. MM Gnr 145426 133 Siege Bty RGA
KAY S. MM Pte 32343 RAMC
KAY Samuel MM Pte 3744 5th Lancashire Fusiliers
KAY Stanley J. MM+Bar Sjt 339198 RAMC
KAY Stephen MM Sjt 10737 4th West Riding Regt
KAY Thomas Henry MM Gnr 71453 5 Bde RFA
KAY Thomas Wilfred MM Tpr 135 Household Bn
KAY W. MM+Bar Pte 27875 North Lancashire Regt
KAY William MM Pte 73058 15th Welsh Regt
KAY William MM Pte 6951 1st Scots Guards
KAY William MM Sjt 293140 8th Cheshire Regt
KAY William MM Gnr 645994 RFA
KAY William Henry MM Cpl 10892 6th North Lancashire Regt
KAYE Albert MM Pte 22741 Machine Gun Corps
KAYE Albert MM Sjt 608316 18th London Regt
KAYE Ernest MM Pte 3291 West Riding Regt
KAYE George W. MM L/Cpl C/12330 King's Royal Rifle Corps
KAYE Harold MM+Bar Pte 28828 Leicestershire Regt
KAYE Horace Hilton "MC,MM(920 Cpl 16th Bn)" T/2Lt 14th Royal Warwickshire Regt
KAYE James H. MM Cpl 14090 11th West Yorkshire Regt
KAYE Stanley MM Gnr 221120 43 Bty 24 Bde RFA KIA 18.10.18.
KAYE William C. MM Pte 269938 Liverpool Regt
KAYLOR John MM Cpl 7545 XVII Corps Cyclist Bn Army Cyclist Corps
KEABLE James William MM Cpl 11/1348 7th East Yorkshire Regt DOW 5.11.18.
KEABLE John MM Pte 74426 66 Coy Machine Gun Corps
KEABLE William MM Cpl 8434 2nd Royal Welsh Fusiliers

KEAL George William MM Sjt 6385 3rd Coldstream Guards
KEALEY Harry MM Cpl 1699 1/8th Durham Light Infantry
KEALEY Samuel MM L/Cpl 15651 Royal Inniskilling Fusiliers
KEAM Herbert MM Cpl 14509 12th Cheshire Regt
KEAN Charles MM Pte 13618 2nd Royal Scots Fusiliers Died 30.7.16.
KEAN George H. MM Pte 241846 1/5th Border Regt
KEAN Henry Edward MM BSM 2153 27 Bty 32 Bde RFA
KEAN Richard J. MM Sjt 38342 78 Siege Bty RGA
KEAN Robert Irwin MM Pte M2/101595 32 Div Train Army Service Corps
KEANE Charles W. MM Dvr 253382 Royal Engineers
KEANE Henry Edward MM Pte 34153 RAMC
KEANE J. MM L/Cpl 350896 15th Yorkshire Light Infantry
KEANE John MM Pte 9/4612 1st Royal Munster Fusiliers KIA 9.9.16.
KEANE Joseph MM Cpl 277184 7th Manchester Regt
KEANE P. MM Pte 32880 Royal Scots Fusiliers
KEANE Patrick MM Pte 33931 9th Welsh Regt
KEANE Robert G. MM Sjt 562650 69 AA Section Royal Engineers
KEANE Thomas MM Pte 9308 1st Royal Munster Fusiliers
KEANE Thomas "MM,MID" Pte 8830 1st Royal Munster Fusiliers
KEANE Thomas MM L/Cpl 1115 4th Bn GMGR
KEANEY Edward MM Sjt 36729 185 Hy Bty RGA
KEANING John MM Pte 1483 2nd Gordon Highlanders
KEANY Patrick MM+Bar Sjt 11737 298 Siege Bty RGA
KEARFORD J. MM Pte 19970 Yorkshire Light Infantry
KEARLE William MM Pte 14121 8th Shropshire Light Infantry
KEARLEY John MM L/Cpl 202496 4th Hampshire Regt
KEARNE P.H. MM Pte 34076 North Lancashire Regt
KEARNEY Charles "DCM,MM" Sjt 26955 3 Div Sig Coy Royal Engineers
KEARNEY David John "MM,CdiG(It)" CQMS 53895 1st Royal Welsh Fusiliers
KEARNEY G.S. MM Gnr 75944 4 Bde RFA
KEARNEY Hugh MM Gnr 881838 RFA
KEARNEY James MM Cpl 2293 6th Connaught Rangers
KEARNEY John MM Pte 82380 20th Durham Light Infantry
KEARNEY Joseph MM Pte 10856 6th Royal Irish Rifles
KEARNEY Michael MM Pte 73147 48 Coy Machine Gun Corps
KEARNEY Norman William MM L/Cpl 9590 11th Middlesex Regt
KEARNEY Patrick MM Sjt 4957 1st Irish Guards KIA 30.11.17.
KEARNEY Robert J. MM L/Cpl 40440 Gordon Highlanders
KEARNEY William MM Pte 570858 1/17th London Regt
KEARNS Edward James MM Spr 312161 'T' Corps Sig Coy Royal Engineers
KEARNS John MM Sjt 10729 1st Royal Irish Fusiliers
KEARNS Joseph Patrick MM Sjt 2611 6th Connaught Rangers
KEARNS P. MM Pte 23678 Royal Dublin Fusiliers
KEARON Douglas G. MM Pte 23368 10th Royal West Surrey Regt
KEARON H. MM Pte 71983 V Corps Cyclist Bn North Irish Horse
KEARSEY William F. MM Gnr 815175 RFA
KEARSLEY Alfred MM Cpl 29506 4th North Lancashire Regt
KEARSLEY Edward MM+Bar Sjt 48748 2 Bde RFA
KEARTON Joseph B. MM Pte 205149 Northumberland Fusiliers
KEARY James MM Cpl 5436 RFA
KEAST Frederick MM Spr 147563 184 Tunnelling Coy Royal Engineers
KEATE Arnold Edward MM Pte 28598 3rd Grenadier Guards
KEATES Thomas MM Pte PW/1547 19th Middlesex Regt
KEATING Edward George Joseph MM 2nd Cpl 12842 5 Div Sog Coy Royal Engineers
KEATING M. MM Sjt 16356 2nd Royal Irish Regt
KEATING Nicholas MM Sjt 57407 104 Bty 22 Bde RFA
KEATING Timothy MM CQMS 11906 10th Durham Light Infantry KIA 9.4.17.
KEATING W. MM Cpl 240259 6th Highland Light Infantry
KEATING W. "MM,MID" Pte 3945 Lancashire Fusiliers
KEATING Walter MM Pte 18570 9th Cheshire Regt
KEATING William MM Pte 11144 Royal Irish Regt
KEATING William "DCM,MM" Sjt 5914 11th Lancashire Fusiliers
KEATINGS John MM Pte 9458 Royal Highlanders
KEATLEY Alfred MM Sjt 28907 East Yorkshire Regt
KEATLEY John Charles MM Cpl 268521 West Yorkshire Regt
KEATLEY Joseph MM Cpl 14124 8th South Staffordshire Regt KIA 12.1.17.
KEATS Alfred MM L/Cpl G/15632 7th East Kent Regt DOW 7.3.17.
KEATS Frank Alfred MM Pte 10664 9th Devonshire Regt KIA 26.10.17.
KEATS William MM L/Cpl R/42147 1st King's Royal Rifle Corps

KEATT Tom M. MM Sjt 321045 390 Siege Bty RGA
KEATY J. MM+Bar Pte 50215 104 Fd Amb RAMC
KEAY Ernest Albert MM+Bar Bdr 38692 D/82 Bde RFA
KEBBY Albert MM Sjt 20342 118 Heavy Bty RGA
KEDDIE Harold B. MM Pte 202370 Royal Highlanders
KEDDIE J. MM Air Mech 1 51542 Royal Air Force
KEDDIE Thomas MM Pte 3475 Royal Scots
KEDDY John G. MM Pte 20082 7th Border Regt
KEDGLEY Alfred Edmund MM Gnr 1066 C/83 Bde RFA KIA 17.10.18.
KEEBLE Alfred S. MM Cpl 235319 2nd South Staffordshire Regt
KEEBLE Alfred T. "DCM,MM" Sjt K/95 22nd Royal Fusiliers
KEEBLE Arthur "MM,MID" Gnr 21074 48 Heavy Bty RGA
KEEBLE Arthur William MM Sjt 13247 100 Coy Machine Gun Corps
KEEBLE Frederick William MM Sjt 14194 7th Suffolk Regt
KEEBLE J. MM Cpl 14168 1st Essex Regt
KEECH Aubrey Charles MM Pte 59447 6th Northamptonshire Regt
KEECH George E. MM+2 Bars Cpl 558453 Royal Engineers
KEECH John MM L/Cpl 53164 Royal Engineers
KEECH John H. MM Pte 15276 Leicestershire Regt
KEEFE Frederick MM CSM 698 4th Royal Fusiliers
KEEFE John MM Pte 19160 14th Liverpool Regt DOW 27 1 19.
KEEFE Patrick "MM,MIDx2" Sjt 8655 2nd Border Regt
KEEFFE Thomas W. MM Pte 241744 5th Royal Lancaster Regt
KEEFFE Thomas W. MM Pte 241744 5th Royal Lancaster Regt
KEEFFE or KEEFE James MM Pte 9524 2nd Royal Irish Fusiliers
KEEGAN James MM Sjt 200848 Manchester Regt
KEEGAN James MM BSM 65582 128 Bty 29 Bde RFA
KEEGAN Michael "MM,MID" SM 346 Royal Flying Corps
KEEGAN Patrick MM Pte 6417 2nd Royal Irish Regt
KEEGAN Patrick MM Gnr 27997 D/51 Bde RFA KIA 25.4.18.
KEEGAN Thomas MM Sjt 10880 1st Royal Dublin Fusiliers
KEEL Walter F. MM Cpl 44777 RGA
KEELE Frederick C. MM Sjt 10835 London Regt
KEELER Frederick W. MM Pte 45631 RAMC
KEELEY Andrew MM Pte 13440 Royal Irish Fusiliers
KEELEY Arthur J. MM Pte 701578 23rd London Regt
KEELEY Charles MM Pte 25685 12th Bn Machine Gun Corps
KEELEY Edward G. MM Sjt M2/031866 Army Service Corps
KEELEY Edwin Ernest MM Pte 3343 24th Royal Fusiliers
KEELEY Frank MM Pte 9861 1st Duke of Cornwall's LI
KEELEY Harry MM Sjt 20351 4thBn Machine Gun Corps DOW 29.3.18.
KEELEY William MM+Bar Sjt 9204 10th Royal Warwickshire Regt
KEELING Alfred MM Gnr 135062 505 Bty 65 Bde RFA
KEELING Charles MM Pte 29800 7tth South Staffordshire Regt
KEELING Frederick MM Pte 133775 57th Bn Machine Gun Corps
KEELING Frederick Hillersdon MM CSM 12347 6th Duke of Cornwall's LI KIA 18.8.16.
KEELING George MM L/Cpl 10225 Royal Irish Rifles
KEELING George W. MM Cpl 11888 8th West Riding Regt
KEELING H.B. MM Pte 5461 West Riding Regt
KEELING John MM Pte 13390 1st Royal Fusiliers
KEEN Albert Morris MM Sjt 22555 Machine Gun Corps
KEEN Arthur MM Cpl 31379 35 Siege Bty RGA DOW 31.3.17.
KEEN Charles A. MM Pte 41906 7th Norfolk Regt
KEEN Ernest MM Cpl 24447 2nd Royal Fusiliers KIA 13.4.18.
KEEN Francis Charles MM Gnr 103691 62 Bde RFA
KEEN Frank MM Cpl 12288 2nd Royal Fusiliers
KEEN Frederick N. MM L/Cpl Z/1280 Rifle Brigade
KEEN G.A. MM Pte 10420 1st East Kent Regt
KEEN George Henry Marriott MM Cpl 614060 1/1(Warwickshire)Bty RHA
KEEN Henry MM Gnr 63103 RGA
KEEN James MM Cpl SE/9073 53 Mobile Vet Sect Army Veterinary Corps
KEEN James W. MM Cpl 46793 Northumberland Fusiliers
KEEN JosephW. MM Sjt 590710 18th London Regt
KEEN Philip M. MM Cpl 625538 HAC
KEEN Reginald A. MM Cpl 18957 East Surrey Regt
KEEN Stanley MM 2nd Cpl 253866 Royal Engineers
KEEN Wiilfred MM L/Cpl 58777 8th West Yorkshire Regt
KEEN William MM Pte 74580 RAMC
KEENAGHAN James MM Pte 13362 10th North Lancashire Regt
KEENAN Daniel MM Dvr 93288 RFA
KEENAN Daniel MM Sjt 58163 RAMC
KEENAN Edward MM+Bar L/Sjt 10595 1st Irish Guards
KEENAN Henry "MM,MID" L/Cpl 12377 8th Cheshire Regt
KEENAN J. MM Pte 8752 Highland Light Infantry
KEENAN James MM Cpl M2/178178 Army Service Corps

KEENAN James MM Pte 200145 1/4th South Lancashire Regt
KEENAN James MM Gnr 232085 RFA
KEENAN James MM Sjt 78775 RFA
KEENAN John MM Pte 18491 Durham Light Infantry
KEENAN Joseph MM Cpl 3820 Leinster Regt
KEENAN Peter MM Pte 8228 1st Irish Guards
KEENAN Thomas MM Gnr Fitter 196089 RGA
KEENAN Thomas MM Pte 125 2nd Seaforth Highlanders
KEENAN William MM Sjt 3607 7 Coy Labour Corps
KEENAN William J. MM+Bar Sjt 40285 4th Worcestershire Regt
KEENE Albert Henry MM Cpl 11630 D/83 Bde RFA KIA 17.10.17.
KEENE Frederick C. MM Gnr 148369 D/168 Bde RFA
KEENE Frederick H. MM Sjt CMT/3003 Army Service Corps
KEENE Harold W. MM Spr 255011 48 Div Sig Coy Royal Engineers
KEENE Henry W. MM Cpl 102432 RGA
KEENE Robert MM Pte 36885 9th Yorkshire Light Infantry
KEENOR Edwin G. MM Pte 333 6th Royal West Surrey Regt
KEEP Arthur MM Cpl 703371 23rd London Regt
KEEP Joseph F. MM L/Cpl 12430 Seaforth Highlanders
KEEP Percy William MM Cpl 20346 4th Grenadier Guards KIA 29.3.18.
KEEP William MM Sjt 3742 Machine Gun Corps
KEEPING Benjamin R. MM Sjt 10946 2nd Royal Dublin Fusiliers
KEEPING Frederick A. MM Cpl 9497 2nd Royal Dublin Fusiliers
KEETCH Sidney MM L/Cpl 2526 1/3rd Monmouthshire Regt
KEFFORD Henry S. MM Cpl 200317 1/4th Essex Regt
KEGGIE John M. MM Pte 32898 Royal Scots Fusiliers
KEGGIN James H. MM Cpl 996 13th Cheshire Regt
KEGGIN William MM+Bar L/Cpl 28533 3rd Grenadier Guards
KEHOE Bernard MM Pte 266763 West Riding Regt
KEHOE Harold MM L/Cpl 23465 1st Lancashire Fusiliers DOW 29.12.17.
KEHOE Joseph MM Pte 69320 RAMC
KEHOE Luke MM Gnr 200749 11 Tank Labour Coy Tank Corps
KEHOE Martin MM Pte 266387 7th Liverpool Regt
KEIGHER John MM L/Cpl 19445 5th South Wales Borderers
KEIGHLEY Charlie MM Spr 354847 50 Div Sig Coy Royal Engineers
KEIGHLEY Edward MM Pte 280716 7th Lancashire Fusiliers
KEIGHLEY Fred MM Cpl 63721 101 Fd Coy Royal Engineers
KEIGHLEY Lawson MM Cpl 13438 11th West Yorkshire Regt
KEIGHLEY Mornington MM Gnr 710279 RFA
KEIGHLEY Snowden MM L/Cpl 18/203 West Yorkshire Regt KIA 12.4.18.
KEIGHT Joseph MM Cpl 16048 18th Lancashire Fusiliers
KEIGHTLEY Alfred H. "MM,MSM" Cpl 375555 1/10th Manchester Regt
KEIGHTLEY William H. MM Cpl 115798 Machine Gun Corps
KEILLER John B. MM Pte S/22946 Cameron Highlanders
KEILLOR William Smith MM Dvr T4/123849 Army Service Corps att 103 Fd Amb RAMC
KEILY Valentine MM Pte 5810 RAMC
KEIR Adam M. MM Cpl 100667 122 Fd Coy Royal Engineers
KEIR Falconer MM Gnr 110737 RFA
KEIR Henry S. MM Gnr Sig 650154 169 Bde RFA
KEIR John MM Gnr 166253 11 Siege Bty RGA
KEIR Norman MM Pte 330642 1/9th Highland Light Infantry
KEIR Peter MM Gnr 70276 RFA
KEIR William MM Spr 414193 Royal Engineers
KEIRBY W. MM Sjt 2202 RFA
KEIRNS Francis MM Pte 3223 Royal Irish Fusiliers
KEITCH Frederick G. MM Pte 145972 18th Bn Machine Gun Corps
KEITH Alexander MM+Bar Pte 77596 23rd Royal Fusiliers
KEITH Andrew MM Cpl 16653 12th Royal Irish Rifles
KEITH Charles MM Pte M2/049902 Army Service Corps att 1/3(West Lancashire)Fd Amb RAMC
KEITH D. MM Cpl 50960 Manchester Regt
KEITH George MM Bdr 44005 D/311 Bty RFA KIA 13.9.17.
KEITH Herbert Charles Bevan MM Pte 28486 12th East Surrey Regt
KEITH James S. MM Cpl (MCDR) 148083 Royal Engineers
KEITH John MM Pte 202659 1/5th Gordon Highlanders
KELHAM Frederick MM Pte 31965 2nd East Lancashire Regt
KELHAM Morel R. MM Dvr 42860 RFA
KELL Archibald MM Dvr 645019 51 Div Ammn Col RFA
KELLAWAY Sydney Clarence MM Cpl 108715 Y/16 Med TM Bty RFA
KELLAWAY William Albert MM Pte 64507 225 Coy Machine Gun Corps
KELLEHER Cornelius MM Pte 7571 1st Royal Munster Fusiliers
KELLEHER Denis MM Pte 7871 2nd Irish Guards
KELLEHER George MM Pte 7475 1st Royal Munster Fusiliers

315

KELLEHER William MM Pte 226822 Monmouthshire Regt
KELLER Albert E. MM L/Cpl T4/251745 Army Service Corps
KELLETT Albert MM Pte M2/134404 Army Service Corps
KELLETT Andrew MM Pte 200287 2/8th Liverpool Regt
KELLETT Arthur MM Gnr 47867 3 Bde RHA
KELLETT Jack MM L/Cpl 201751 1/4th Seaforth Highlanders
KELLETT John MM L/Cpl 11914 Northumberland Fusiliers
KELLETT John W. MM Pte 3950 Machine Gun Corps DOW 21.11.16.
KELLETT Joseph MM Pte M2/188431 'Y' Siege Park Army Service Corps
KELLETT W. MM Pte 403591 RAMC
KELLETT Walter MM Pte 13159 9th South Staffordshire Regt KIA 31.7.16.
KELLETT William MM Sjt 223562 Labour Corps
KELLEWAY Thomas MM Sjt 357712 3 Fd Svy Bn Royal Engineers
KELLEY James MM Cpl 241372 5th York & Lancaster Regt
KELLEY Roy R.V. MM Pte G/100064 11th Royal Fusiliers
KELLIE Arthur MM Sjt 1688 1/6th Cheshire Regt
KELLIE Douglas MM Gnr 1923 4 Bty Machine Gun Corps(Motors)
KELLINGHAM W. MM Spr 158196 257 Tunnelling Coy Royal Engineers
KELLOCK George D. MM Sjt 71480 29th Bn Machine Gun Corps
KELLOCK Stewart MM Pte 250885 1/6th Arg & Suth Highlanders
KELLOW John "MM,MID" Gnr 29027 RFA
KELLS Frederick George MM Sjt 44598 39 Bde RFA
KELLY Albert MM Gnr 785925 RFA
KELLY Albert H. MM Sjt 27298 91 Fd Amb RAMC
KELLY Alexander MM Pte 1815 1/5th Liverpool Regt
KELLY Alfred MM Pte 24847 59th Bn Machine Gun Corps
KELLY Alfred MM CSM 202702 4th North Lancashire Regt
KELLY Andrew MM Pte 132173 Machine Gun Corps
KELLY Andrew MM L/Sjt H/4268 8th Hussars
KELLY Arthur "DCM,MM" L/Cpl 235156 1st North Lancashire Regt
KELLY Bernard MM L/Sjt 265377 Royal Welsh Fusiliers
KELLY Burnam MM Sjt 9138 2nd South Wales Borderers
KELLY Campbell "MC,MM(34071 Sjt)" 2Lt RGA
KELLY Charles MM Pte 53148 4th Worcestershire Regt
KELLY Charles MM Sjt 200258 1/5th Arg & Suth Highlanders
KELLY Charles MM Cpl 119135 62nd Bn Machine Gun Corps
KELLY Charles W. MM Pte R/23936 King's Royal Rifle Corps
KELLY Christopher "MM,MID" Sjt 1110 4th Bn GMGR
KELLY Dan MM Bdr 56886 47 Siege Bty RGA
KELLY Daniel MM Cpl 2464 1/5th Northumberland Fusiliers DOW 29.6.16.
KELLY Daniel Patrick MM Pte 203443 Seaforth Highlanders
KELLY David MM Pte 9/928 15th Royal Irish Rifles
KELLY David MM Pte 5606 Royal Irish Rifles
KELLY Denzil Edward MM Bdr 187936 179 Bde RFA
KELLY Edward MM Pte 10600 2nd Gordon Highlanders
KELLY Edward "MM,MID" Dvr 50717 5 Pontoon Park Royal Engineers
KELLY Edward MM L/Cpl 11034 2nd Irish Guards KIA 12.4.18.
KELLY Edwin MM Pte 4645 2nd Border Regt KIA 4.10.17.
KELLY Edwin G. MM Pte 200692 Worcestershire Regt
KELLY Ernest MM Spr 100331 Royal Engineers
KELLY Ernest E. MM Cpl 26760 26 Heavy Bty RGA
KELLY F. MM Pte 327199 Durham Light Infantry
KELLY Francis MM Pte 241223 Royal Highlanders
KELLY Frank MM Spr 46744 21 Div Sig Coy Royal Engineers
KELLY Frederick MM Pte 3445 21st London Regt
KELLY Frederick M. MM Pte 64209 RAMC
KELLY Frederick S. MM+Bar Pte 200218 South Lancashire Regt
KELLY George MM 2nd Cpl 461086 Fifth Army Tramway Coy Royal Engineers
KELLY George E. MM Pte 305242 1/8th Liverpool Regt
KELLY George Henry MM Cpl 16483 2nd Bedfordshire Regt KIA 30.7.16.
KELLY George Wilson MM Pte S/13337 1/5th Gordon Highlanders KIA 28.7.18.
KELLY H. MM Bdr 35687 RFA
KELLY Harry MM Pte 305069 1/8th Lancashire Fusiliers
KELLY Harry MM Pte S/3500 9th Seaforth Highlanders
KELLY Henry MM RSM 6644 2nd Royal Irish Regt
KELLY Henry MM Sjt 6305 1st West Yorkshire Regt
KELLY Henry MM Gnr 78404 46 Siege Bty RGA
KELLY Henry T. MM+Bar Cpl 66882 34 Bde RFA
KELLY Hugh MM L/Cpl 43204 2nd Royal Scots Fusiliers
KELLY Hugh MM Pte 15995 1st Royal Irish Fusiliers
KELLY Hugh MM Pte 2595 7th Leinster Regt
KELLY J. MM Pte 14509 Border Regt
KELLY J.E. MM Pte 1794 Royal Warwickshire Regt
KELLY James MM L/Cpl 203527 1st Dorsetshire Regt
KELLY James MM Pte 9436 2nd Manchester Regt
KELLY James MM Pte 8925 2nd West Yorkshire Regt
KELLY James MM+Bar Pte 8660 1st Liverpool Regt
KELLY James MM Pte 9/240 9th Royal Irish Rifles
KELLY James MM+Bar Cpl 14900 East Yorkshire Regt
KELLY James MM Pte 18314 Royal Irish Fusiliers
KELLY James E. MM Pte 15/1300 16th Royal Warwickshire Regt
KELLY James P. MM L/Cpl 10780 Border Regt
KELLY John MM L/Cpl S/18641 7th Cameron Highlanders KIA 28.4.17.
KELLY John MM Sjt 200420 1/5th South Staffordshire Regt KIA 4.5.17.
KELLY John MM Pte 40494 Manchester Regt
KELLY John MM L/Cpl 201997 8th West Yorkshire Regt
KELLY John MM Pte 4/5830 2nd Royal Irish Regt
KELLY John MM Pte 15533 Royal Dublin Fusiliers
KELLY John MM Pte 7970 1st North Staffordshire Regt DOW 2.9.16.
KELLY John MM Pte 8653 1st East Lancashire Regt
KELLY John MM Pte 17578 9th Cheshire Regt
KELLY John MM L/Sjt 8962 13th Royal Fusiliers
KELLY John M. MM Pte 24146 Royal Fusiliers
KELLY John O. MM Pte 81864 75 Fd Amb RAMC
KELLY John Patrick MM Sjt 14653 Royal Dublin Fusiliers
KELLY John S. MM+Bar Sjt 88230 50th Bn Machine Gun Corps
KELLY John S. "DCM,MM" Sjt 242264 1/5th Seaforth Highlanders
KELLY John W. "DCM,MM" L/Sjt 67608 Machine Gun Corps
KELLY Joseph MM Pte G/2596 12th Middlesex Regt
KELLY Joseph MM Pte 40026 2nd South Wales Borderers
KELLY Joseph MM Sjt 356127 Liverpool Regt
KELLY Joseph MM Pte 9633 2nd Royal Fusiliers
KELLY Joseph MM Gnr 95759 'I' Bn Tank Corps KIA 29.8.18.
KELLY Joseph MM Pte 4590 1st Manchester Regt
KELLY Joseph C. MM Cpl 301414 8th Manchester Regt
KELLY Leonard MM L/Bdr 244981 128 Bty 29 Bde RFA
KELLY Martin MM L/Cpl 10187 Northumberland Fusiliers
KELLY Michael MM Pte 3169 1/7th Gordon Highlanders
KELLY Millward L. MM Pte 21536 7th Royal West Kent Regt
KELLY Owen MM Pte 8633 1st Leinster Regt
KELLY P. MM Pte 131858 46th Royal Fusiliers
KELLY Patrick MM Pte 6095 1st Royal Irish Fusiliers KIA 21.3.18.
KELLY Patrick MM Pte 8790 2nd Royal Dublin Fusiliers
KELLY Patrick J. MM L/Sjt 530274 15th London Regt
KELLY Paul MM Sjt 5608 RFA
KELLY Percy H. MM Pte 24312 Liverpool Regt
KELLY Peter MM Gnr 119506 RFA
KELLY R. MM Cpl 7283 Northumberland Fusiliers
KELLY Richard MM Sjt 36649 Liverpool Regt
KELLY Richard MM Pte 30614 1st East Surrey Regt
KELLY Stephen MM L/Cpl 4613 9th Royal Munster Fusiliers
KELLY Sydney C. MM 2nd Cpl 146008 Royal Engineers
KELLY T. MM Sjt 265271 West Yorkshire Regt
KELLY Thomas MM Sjt 13408 9th Royal Lancaster Regt
KELLY Thomas MM Pte 32340 1st North Lancashire Regt
KELLY Thomas MM Dvr 5653 B/88 Bde RFA
KELLY Thomas MM Pnr 309672 319 Rly Constr Coy Royal Engineers
KELLY Thomas MM Pte 202075 2/4th West Riding Regt
KELLY Thomas MM Gnr 32391 C/90 Bde RFA
KELLY Thomas MM Pte 57296 Machine Gun Corps
KELLY Thomas MM Dvr T3/022484 8 Div Train Army Service Corps
KELLY Thomas MM+Bar Sjt 8613 B/150 Bde RFA
KELLY Thomas MM Pte 53894 RAMC
KELLY Thomas Henry MM Pte 12270 2nd Welsh Regt DOW 27.7.16.
KELLY Thomas J. MM Pte 7195 1st Royal Munster Fusiliers
KELLY Thomas W. MM Cpl 240945 6th North Staffordshire Regt
KELLY Thomas W. MM Pte 32656 Yorkshire Light Infantry
KELLY Thomas W. MM Pte 140944 11th Bn Machine Gun Corps
KELLY W. MM Sjt 41070 Labour Corps
KELLY W. MM L/Cpl P900 Military Mounted Police
KELLY Walter MM Pte A/1545 18th King's Royal Rifle Corps
KELLY Walter "MM,MID" Sjt 96251 C/47 Bde RFA
KELLY Wilfred J. MM+Bar Sjt 593251 18th London Regt
KELLY William MM Pte 241205 2/5th South Lancashire Regt
KELLY William MM Pte 22055 7th Royal West Surrey Regt
KELLY William MM Pte 14393 9th Royal Irish Fusiliers

KELLY William MM Pte 8980 RAMC
KELLY William MM Cpl 5617 18th Highland Light Infantry
KELLY William MM Sjt 12746 15 Bde RFA
KELLY William MM Gnr 70195 B/106 Bde RFA
KELLY William MM Pte 19044 1st Royal Inniskilling Fusiliers
KELLY William MM Cpl 238045 5/6th Scottish Rifles KIA 25.10.18.
KELLY William MM Cpl 240237 Border Regt
KELLY William Edward MM Pte M2/131206 Army Service Corps att 73 Fd Amb RAMC
KELLY William F. MM Sjt 115876 250 Siege Bty RGA
KELLY William H. MM Pte 41934 11th Suffolk Regt
KELLY William J. MM Cpl 266875 Liverpool Regt
KELLY William John MM L/Cpl 8876 2nd South Wales Borderers KIA 23.4.17.
KELLY William R. MM Cpl 21016 Middlesex Regt
KELLYN Alfred "DCM,MM" Sjt 50329 9 Fd Coy Royal Engineers
KELMAN Albert G. MM Cpl 63067 RFA
KELMAN Alexander T. MM Pte 240759 2nd Gordon Highlanders
KELMAN Robert MM Bdr 630330 B/255 Bde RFA
KELMAN Robert MM Pte 201661 Gordon Highlanders
KELMAN Robert Taylor "MM,MID" L/Cpl 831 1st Dragoons
KELSALL James MM Pte 27766 Royal Lancaster Regt
KELSALL John E. MM L/Cpl 202654 Lancashire Fusiliers
KELSALL Percy MM Cpl 46343 4th North Staffordshire Regt KIA 29.9.18.
KELSEY Arthur R. MM Gnr 1073 7(West Riding)Bty RFA
KELSEY Benjamin R. MM Gnr Sig 265591 D/187 Bde RFA
KELSEY David MM Pte 45992 142 Fd Amb RAMC
KELSEY Edmund MM Gnr 95978 211 Siege Bty RGA DOW 31.10.18.
KELSEY Henry J.R. MM+Bar L/Cpl 1834 1/15th London Regt
KELSEY Richard Cecil MM Pte 5003 2nd Royal Sussex Regt KIA 24.9.18.
KELSEY Thomas G. MM Pte 593335 18th London Regt
KELSEY William T. "DCM,MM" Sjt 55981 D/38 Bde RFA
KELSO Frederick James MM Sjt 805 13th Royal Irish Rifles
KELSO Samuel MM+Bar Sjt 14365 16th Highland Light Infantry
KELSON Frederick Joseph "MM,CdG(F)" Spr 503793 48 Div Sig Coy Royal Engineers
KELTIE George MM L/Bdr 75441 12 Heavy Bty RGA
KELWAY Charles W.T. MM L/Cpl 19210 11th Royal West Kent Regt
KEMBER Arthur MM Pnr 51251 Royal Engineers
KEMBLE Henry MM Sjt 40129 2nd Bedfordshire Regt KIA 21.9.18.
KEMLO James W. MM L/Cpl 22361 Royal Engineers
KEMP A. MM L/Sjt 339160 RAMC
KEMP Albert MM Pte 6/213 3rd Rifle Brigade
KEMP Albioni MM Pte 29083 2nd Grenadier Guards
KEMP Alec E. MM Pte 14846 Machine Gun Corps
KEMP Alfred MM Pnr 198790 Royal Engineers
KEMP Archibald MM Pte 119513 Machine Gun Corps
KEMP Arthur MM Pte 781453 2nd London Regt
KEMP Arthur Charles MM Spr 95698 12 Div Sig Coy Royal Engineers KIA 12.3.17.
KEMP Arthur F. "MM,MSM,MID" Sjt 42821 78 Fd Coy Royal Engineers
KEMP Arthur James MM Pte 17846 9th Suffolk Regt KIA 16.9.16.
KEMP Arthur L. MM 2nd Cpl 85963 Royal Engineers
KEMP C.R. MM Sjt 267273 14th Gloucestershire Regt
KEMP Charles MM Sjt 8/176 6th Royal West Surrey Regt
KEMP Charles MM Bdr 10571 RFA
KEMP Charles MM Gnr 121277 D/82 Bde RFA
KEMP Charles A. MM Sjt 2863 55 Fd Coy Royal Engineers
KEMP Charles Albert MM Pte 1497 1/21st London Regt DOW 8.9.18.
KEMP Charles W. MM Sjt 200368 1/4th Gloucestershire Regt
KEMP Charles William MM L/Cpl 21175 4th Grenadier Guards KIA 13.4.18.
KEMP Daniel Arthur MM Pte G/10268 11th Royal West Kent Regt
KEMP Edgar MM Sjt 14615 Manchester Regt
KEMP Ernest E. MM Sjt 61141 A/190 Bde RFA
KEMP Frank George MM Cpl 801044 402 Bty 14 Bde RFA
KEMP Frank T. MM L/Cpl M2/176662 Army Service Corps
KEMP Frederick "DCM,MM" Sjt 39675 A/107 Bde RFA
KEMP Frederick MM Cpl 142540 RGA
KEMP Frederick E. "DCM(53/2 Bde),MM" Gnr 53343 B/189 Bde RFA
KEMP George Charles "DCM,MM" Sjt 200219 1/1st London Regt
KEMP George William MM+Bar Pte 43603 Northamptonshire Regt
KEMP Harry MM L/Sjt 9472 1st Coldstream Guards
KEMP Harry MM Pte 12308 Duke of Cornwall's LI

KEMP Harvey MM Pte 201387 Oxf & Bucks Light Infantry
KEMP Henry MM CQMS 42517 1st Royal Inniskilling Fusiliers
KEMP Herbert E. MM Gnr 147179 RGA
KEMP John MM Pte 12738 7th Bedfordshire Regt
KEMP John MM Pte 200 1st Arg & Suth Highlanders
KEMP John A. MM Pte 5991 2nd Highland Light Infantry
KEMP Joseph MM Pte 45955 1st Cheshire Regt
KEMP Joseph Charles MM Gnr 2499 C/150 Bde RFA Died 21.7.18.
KEMP P. MM Pte 205631 6th Royal Fusiliers
KEMP Philip J. MM L/Cpl 13397 4th Middlesex Regt
KEMP Robert MM+Bar Pte S/7791 2nd Gordon Highlanders
KEMP Robert A. MM Dvr 233270 RFA
KEMP Rowland MM Gnr 930234 281 Bde RFA
KEMP Roy P. MM Pte 29286 East Yorkshire Regt
KEMP Sidney C. MM Gnr 53858 RFA
KEMP Sidney James MM Spr 556195 521 Fd Coy Royal Engineers
KEMP Thomas Henry "DCM,MM" Cpl 27701 45 Bty 42 Bde RFA
KEMP Walter MM Bdr 174435 41 Div Ammn Col RFA
KEMP William MM Pte 571583 17th London Regt
KEMP William MM Pte 2358 10th Arg & Suth Highlanders
KEMP William MM Gnr 18922 15 Div Ammn Col RFA
KEMP William H. MM Dvr 9571 29 Bty 42 Bde RFA
KEMP William J. MM Pte 30164 South Wales Borderers
KEMPEN William MM Pte 12002 8th East Surrey Regt
KEMPLEN Henry W. MM Sjt 265118 9th Middlesex Regt
KEMPLEY Thomas MM Cpl G/2589 12th Middlesex Regt KIA 3.5.17.
KEMPNER David MM Gnr 39612 A/106 Bde RFA
KEMPS Charles Albert MM Cpl 79192 159 Heavy Bty RGA
KEMPSON George MM Pte 3/7489 2nd Bedfordshire Regt
KEMPSON George MM Sjt 11480 11th Hampshire Regt
KEMPSTER Arthur MM Sjt 64611 110 Bty 24 Bde RFA
KEMPSTER Benjamin MM Pte 331473 6th Liverpool Regt
KEMPSTER George MM Staff SM Class 1 T/19506 Army Service Corps
KEMPSTER Gerald MM Pte 301505 Durham Light Infantry
KEMPSTER Harry MM Pte 55259 Royal Welsh Fusiliers
KEMPSTER John T. MM Cpl 22/485 Northumberland Fusiliers
KEMPSTER William H. "DCM,MM" Sjt 64708 135 Bty 32 Bde RFA
KEMPTON Arthur Edward MM L/Cpl G/15633 7th East Kent Regt
KEMPTON Charles G. "MM,MID" CSM 6088 1st Border Regt
KENCH Harold Marshall MM Pte 80136 RAMC
KENCH William MM Sjt 304237 1/5th London Regt KIA 28.3.18.
KENDAL James MM Cpl 362359 RGA
KENDAL Seth MM Pte 200872 1/6th Arg & Suth Highlanders
KENDALL Charles MM Bdr 65662 114 Bty 25 Bde RFA DOW 5.11.18.
KENDALL Ernest E.H. MM Cpl 10775 2/1st HAC (Inf)
KENDALL G.H. "MM,MIDx2" Sjt 1962 35 Bde RFA
KENDALL George MM Spr 41456 Royal Engineers
KENDALL Henry T. "MM,MSM" Sjt 6689 1st King's Royal Rifle Corps
KENDALL Jeremiah MM L/Cpl 201244 1/9th Durham Light Infantry KIA 12.9.18.
KENDALL John MM L/Cpl 245044 1/8th Durham Light Infantry
KENDALL John L. MM Cpl 39627 42nd Bn Machine Gun Corps
KENDALL John W. MM Cpl 5121 Machine Gun Corps
KENDALL Joseph MM Sjt 201047 2/7th Worcestershire Regt
KENDALL Nathaniel MM Bdr 31139 74 Bde RFA
KENDALL Richard MM Sjt 16662 10th Welsh Regt
KENDALL Samuel MM Sjt 41938 17th Lancashire Fusiliers
KENDALL Thomas MM Pte 267019 2/5th Gloucestershire Regt
KENDALL Tom MM Cpl 10129 6th Leicestershire Regt
KENDALL William J. MM L/Cpl 48151 130 Fd Amb RAMC
KENDON Frederick MM L/Cpl 14251 6th Wiltshire Regt KIA 8.7.16.
KENDRICK Arthur MM Pte S1/1254 32 Div Train Army Service Corps
KENDRICK E.T. MM Cpl 604070 RHA
KENDRICK George MM Pte 137062 33rd Bn Machine Gun Corps
KENDRICK Harry MM Pte 267133 Northumberland Fusiliers
KENDRICK Maurice E. MM S/Sjt 421011 RAMC
KENDRICK Reginald MM Sjt 14686 9th Leicestershire Regt DOW 14.7.16.
KENDRICK Richard MM+Bar L/Cpl 8817 1st South Staffordshire Regt
KENEFICK Edward MM Pte 10107 2nd Royal Munster Fusiliers
KENEFICK Michael MM L/Cpl 11351 10th West Riding Regt
KENHAM William MM Sjt 14185 7th Shropshire Light Infantry
KENIRY John MM Sjt 2746 2nd Irish Guards KIA 27.11.17.
KENISTON Frederick C. MM Cpl 165958 1 Fd Svy Bn Royal Engineers
KENLOCK Albert E. MM Pte 12599 1st Grenadier Guards

KENNA Edward MM Pte 21076 2nd Royal Dublin Fusiliers
KENNA George MM Pte 23219 2nd Royal Dublin Fusiliers
KENNARD Albert MM Sjt 14986 D/70 Bde RFA KIA 24.4.17.
KENNARD Frank MM Bdr 47312 56 Bty 44 Bde RFA
KENNARD Leonard G. MM L/Cpl S/13589 Gordon Highlanders
KENNARD W.E. MM Sjt 3195 8th Royal West Surrey Regt
KENNARD William V. MM CSM 42505 14th Worcestershire Regt
KENNAWAY John MM L/Cpl 300395 10th Arg & Suth Highlanders
KENNEA Arthur MM+Bar L/Sjt 14347 7th Shropshire Light Infantry
KENNEALLY Thomas MM BSM 24724 83 Siege Bty RGA
KENNEDY Alexander MM Pte 254052 1/6th Arg & Suth Highlanders
KENNEDY Alexander MM Pte 8716 1st Royal Irish Rifles
KENNEDY Alexander C. MM L/Cpl 275260 1/7th Arg & Suth Highlanders
KENNEDY Allan MM Pte M2/050554 Army Service Corps
KENNEDY Angus MM Pte 41174 Highland Light Infantry
KENNEDY Archibald MM Dvr 133668 RFA
KENNEDY Archibald W.J. MM L/Cpl 18888 Machine Gun Corps
KENNEDY Arthur MM Pte 41265 108 Fd Amb RAMC
KENNEDY Charles MM Cpl 86441 176 Tunnelling Coy Royal Engineers
KENNEDY Charles MM L/Sjt 201517 1/4th Seaforth Highlanders
KENNEDY Charles MM Pte 267544 13th Liverpool Regt
KENNEDY Charles MM Pte 42357 RAMC
KENNEDY Clifford MM Pte 39356 8th West Yorkshire Regt
KENNEDY Daniel MM Pte 325468 1/6th Arg & Suth Highlanders
KENNEDY David MM Sjt 141687 326 Siege Bty RGA
KENNEDY Dominick MM Sjt 18324 2nd Royal Dublin Fusiliers KIA 16.8.17.
KENNEDY Donald Hall MM Sjt 14196 16th Highland Light Infantry KIA 18.11.16.
KENNEDY Edward MM+Bar Cpl 925 Northumberland Fusiliers
KENNEDY Francis George MM L/Cpl 16619 22nd Manchester Regt KIA 4.10.17.
KENNEDY Gabriel MM L/Cpl 22/713 1st Northumberland Fusiliers
KENNEDY George MM Pte 56666 Machine Gun Corps
KENNEDY George Thomson MM Cpl 2176 'C' Bn Machine Gun Corps(Heavy Branch)
KENNEDY H.J. MM Sjt 8218 1st Shropshire Light Infantry
KENNEDY Henry MM Spr 410286 Royal Engineers
KENNEDY Henry MM Pte 15026 Leinster Regt
KENNEDY J.L. MM Pte 276812 Arg & Suth Highlanders
KENNEDY James "MM,MID" CSM 40340 Royal Engineers
KENNEDY James MM Sjt 9010 1st Royal Irish Rifles
KENNEDY James MM Pte 31518 1st East Yorkshire Regt
KENNEDY James G. MM Sjt 331422 1/9th Highland Light Infantry
KENNEDY James Laing MM Pte 2245 Royal Fusiliers KIA 28.10.18.
KENNEDY Jeremiah MM+Bar L/Cpl 5/5797 2nd Royal Munster Fusiliers
KENNEDY John MM L/Cpl 20947 9th Royal Irish Fusiliers
KENNEDY John MM Sjt 8847 9th Scottish Rifles DOW 30.9.18.
KENNEDY John MM Pte 17/739 9th Royal Irish Rifles
KENNEDY John MM L/Cpl 10499 1st East Lancashire Regt
KENNEDY John MM Pte 17800 8th Yorkshire Regt
KENNEDY John MM Sjt 26450 South Lancashire Regt
KENNEDY John MM L/Cpl 242295 10th West Riding Regt KIA 26.8.18.
KENNEDY John Dunlop MM Cpl 80451 114 Bty 25 Bde RFA
KENNEDY John Thomas MM L/Cpl 27/1547 Northumberland Fusiliers
KENNEDY John W.L. MM Pte 82107 Royal Fusiliers
KENNEDY John William "MM,CG(F)" Cpl 44544 12th North Staffordshire Regt
KENNEDY Joseph MM Cpl 33047 275 Siege Bty RGA
KENNEDY Martin MM Pte 8702 2nd Irish Guards
KENNEDY Martin J. MM Pte 60479 RAMC
KENNEDY Patrick MM Pte 8/4857 8th Royal Munster Fusiliers
KENNEDY Patrick J. "MM,MIDx2" Pte 10826 6th Manchester Regt
KENNEDY Thomas MM Cpl 265447 West Riding Regt
KENNEDY Thomas MM+Bar Sjt 39343 2/4th Yorkshire Light Infantry
KENNEDY Thomas MM Pte 390156 RAMC
KENNEDY Thomas MM Gnr 770138 50 Div Ammn Col RFA
KENNEDY William MM Pte 355177 10th Highland Light Infantry
KENNEDY William MM Pte M2/102212 Army Service Corps
KENNEDY William MM L/Cpl 94438 13th Liverpool Regt
KENNEDY William MM L/Cpl 11008 2nd Irish Guards
KENNEDY William MM Pte 25891 1/5th Border Regt
KENNEDY William MM Sjt 30443 RGA
KENNEDY William MM Pte 40822 4/5th Royal Highlanders KIA 18.9.18.
KENNEDY William MM L/Sjt 7244 Irish Guards
KENNEDY William A. MM Sjt 202821 13th Royal Highlanders
KENNEDY William B. MM Pte 152060 42nd Bn Machine Gun Corps
KENNEFORD William MM Pte 14610 Royal Lancaster Regt
KENNELL William "DCM(Hertf Regt),MM" L/Cpl 17672 6th Bedfordshire DOW 15.7.18.
KENNERELL Sydney MM Cpl S/26835 3rd Rifle Brigade
KENNERLEY Frank R. MM Pte 106029 RAMC
KENNERLEY Harry MM Pte 38586 10th South Wales Borderers
KENNERLEY Joe MM Spr 438645 Royal Engineers
KENNERLEY Joseph MM Cpl 9749 1st South Staffordshire Regt
KENNERLEY Roscoe MM L/Cpl 132394 25th Bn Machine Gun Corps
KENNETT A.E. MM Pte 2152 8th East Kent Regt
KENNETT Archibald Stanley MM Bdr 30179 RGA
KENNETT Henry Thomas MM Sjt L/21132 B/167 Bde RFA
KENNETT John Lancelot MM Cpl 87360 Royal Engineers
KENNEY Albert E. MM Gnr 77445 9 Siege Bty RGA
KENNEY Charles MM Cpl 325146 Durham Light Infantry
KENNEY Edmund A. MM L/Cpl 32807 Royal Engineers
KENNICK John MM L/Cpl 18/100 18th Durham Light Infantry
KENNING Arthur MM Sjt 24289 19th Hampshire Regt
KENNING Frank H. MM+Bar Pte 18055 1st Coldstream Guards
KENNING Samuel J. "MM,MID" 2nd Cpl 59059 Royal Engineers
KENNING Walter MM Pte 16108 7th Yorkshire Regt
KENNINGS Robert MM Pte 682474 1/22nd London Regt DOW 23.8.18.
KENNINGTON Frederick James "MM,MID" CQMS 11016 1st South Wales Borderers
KENNY Albert MM Pte 39011 4th Hampshire Regt
KENNY Henry Charles MM Sjt 23715 D/282 Bde RFA
KENNY John MM L/Cpl 16443 7th East Lancashire Regt KIA 4.7.16.
KENNY Joseph MM Sjt S/6099 12th Middlesex Regt
KENNY Joseph MM Pte 39373 225 Coy Machine Gun Corps
KENNY Joseph MM Dvr 780122 RFA
KENNY Martin MM Pte 5939 1st Irish Guards
KENNY Maurice "MM,MID" Sjt 112 1st Irish Guards
KENNY Patrick MM Pte 9/4561 6th Royal Munster Fusiliers
KENNY Robert MM Sjt 5451 1st Lancashire Fusiliers DOW 2.12.17.
KENNY Stephen MM Pte 593721 448 Agric Coy Labour Corps
KENNY Thomas MM+Bar L/Cpl 308787 Liverpool Regt
KENNY Thomas MM+Bar L/Cpl 7598 1st North Staffordshire Regt
KENNY Thomas MM Bdr 89374 RGA
KENNY Thomas P. MM Sjt 8465 Irish Guards
KENNY William MM Sjt 7359 2nd Royal Dublin Fusiliers
KENNY William MM Sjt 29300 Royal Inniskilling Fusiliers
KENNY William MM Pte 13180 4th Liverpool Regt
KENNY William MM Pte 3953 7th Royal Lancaster Regt
KENRICK Cuthbert W. MM L/Cpl 26169 9th Yorkshire Light Infantry
KENRICK John M. MM Pte 30666 4th Liverpool Regt
KENT Allan R. MM Pte 22592 6th Royal West Surrey Regt
KENT Arthur H. MM Pte 631436 1/20th London Regt
KENT Bernard Edward MM L/Cpl 265908 1/1st Hertfordshire Regt DOW 29.3.18.
KENT C.F.G. MM+Bar Pte M2/118946 Army Service Corps
KENT Charles MM Spr 140893 Royal Engineers
KENT Charles R. "MM,MID" L/Cpl 14448 11th Scottish Rifles
KENT Charles W. MM L/Cpl 6014 Royal Sussex Regt
KENT Edgar J. "MM,MID" Pte 9077 2nd Northamptonshire Regt
KENT Edwin MM Sjt 1367 2nd Manchester Regt KIA 2.4.17.
KENT Ernest MM Dvr 72737 RFA
KENT Frank E. MM Cpl 5/4714 King's Royal Rifle Corps
KENT Frederick J. MM L/Cpl 29764 Royal Engineers
KENT G.H. "MM,MID" Pte 345419 Royal Welsh Fusiliers
KENT George MM Pte 9953 Coldstream Guards
KENT George E. MM L/Cpl 46322 Royal Engineers
KENT George Edmund MM Dvr 11822 B/156 Bde RFA
KENT George H. MM Sjt 16380 Royal Engineers
KENT George Vincent MM Sjt 21836 A/91 Bde RFA
KENT Gilbert MM Sjt 250645 1/6th Manchester Regt KIA 20.10.18.
KENT Harold MM Pte 44506 8th Lincolnshire Regt
KENT Harold A. MM Pte 60522 9th Royal Fusiliers
KENT Harold G. MM Cpl 201284 Bedfordshire Regt
KENT Harry E. MM Gnr 68608 D/123 Bde RFA
KENT Herbert MM Pte 32139 4th Bedfordshire Regt DOW 27.8.18.
KENT Herbert MM Pte 265874 1/1st Hertfordshire Regt DOW 30.8.18.
KENT Herbert G. MM Bdr 202650 RFA
KENT John MM Cpl 57439 24th Royal Fusiliers
KENT John MM Sjt 424980 36 Coy Labour Corps

KENT John E. MM Pte 59066 4th Liverpool Regt
KENT Joseph Albert MM Sjt 2404 1/24th London Regt
KENT Joseph W. MM Sjt 46319 Royal Engineers
KENT Neville MM Pte 43834 43 Coy Machine Gun Corps
KENT Rae MM Pte 2882 2nd Royal Fusiliers
KENT Reginald A. MM Pte 202440 2/4th Hampshire Regt
KENT Sidney Francis Reginald MM Pte 74102 1st Bn Machine Gun Corps
KENT Walter MM Cpl 5208 2nd Coldstream Guards
KENT William MM Cpl 27466 1st Shropshire Light Infantry
KENT William MM Sjt 200020 7th Norfolk Regt
KENT William MM Pte 29002 Bedfordshire Regt att 1/1st Hertfordshire Regt
KENT William MM Pte R/13649 10th King's Royal Rifle Corps KIA 5.2.17.
KENT William MM Sjt 17003 7/8th King's Own Scottish Borderers KIA 23.7.18.
KENT William A. MM Sjt 374 1st King Edward's Horse
KENT William A. MM Gnr 20693 Y/50 Med TM Bty RFA
KENT William J. MM L/Cpl 19019 3rd Grenadier Guards
KENT William J. MM L/Cpl 11128 5th Royal Berkshire Regt
KENTESBER William L. MM Pte 33038 4th Bedfordshire Regt
KENTON Alfred Edward MM 2nd Cpl 94235 49 Div Sig Coy Royal Engineers
KENTON George MM L/Cpl 21856 Hampshire Regt
KENWARD Albert Owen King MM Pnr 527944 319 Railway Constr Coy Royal Engineers
KENWARD E. MM Pte 70566 16th Royal Welsh Fusiliers
KENWARD Ernest S. MM Pte 3381 Royal Sussex Regt
KENWARD Thomas William Ernest "MM,MID" Cpl 12766 III Corps Sig Coy Royal Engineers
KENWARD Vernon W. MM+Bar Pte 28125 East Surrey Regt
KENWOOD George MM L/Cpl 5479 1st Duke of Cornwall's LI
KENWORTHY Charles MM Pte DM2/228062 Army Service Corps
KENWORTHY Francis H. MM Pte 36935 Durham Light Infantry
KENWORTHY H. MM Pte 268541 West Riding Regt
KENWORTHY James MM+Bar Pte 9995 2nd Manchester Regt
KENWORTHY John W. MM Pte 260093 Monmouthshire Regt att South Wales Borderers
KENWORTHY Thomas MM Sjt 45552 28 Div Ammn Col RFA
KENWORTHY William MM Sjt PW/1216 18th Middlesex Regt
KENYON Arthur MM Sjt 242548 West Riding Regt
KENYON Christopher MM Pte 27597 8th Royal Lancaster Regt
KENYON Emmanuel MM Gnr 112 48 Bde RFA
KENYON Frederick A. MM Pte 41769 East Yorkshire Regt
KENYON George MM L/Cpl 5347 4th Dragoon Guards
KENYON George MM L/Cpl 6346 2nd Oxf & Bucks Light Infantry
KENYON George MM Bdr 122066 RFA
KENYON Harry MM Pte 17449 12th East Surrey Regt
KENYON Harry MM Spr 51325 Royal Engineers
KENYON James R. MM L/Cpl 249764 12 Div Sig Coy Royal Engineers
KENYON John MM Cpl 24824 1/4th Royal Lancaster Regt DOW 8.6.18.
KENYON John MM+Bar L/Cpl G8/5038 8th East Surrey Regt
KENYON John MM Pte 10286 17th Manchester Regt
KENYON Patrick MM Pte 19221 Devonshire Regt
KENYON Richard Norman MM Gnr 1537 RFA
KENYON Robert MM L/Cpl 26291 Lancashire Fusiliers
KENYON Robert "MM,MID" Pte 13888 7/8th King's Own Scottish Borderers
KENYON Robert G. MM Bdr 8771 B/150 Bde RFA
KENYON Sam MM+Bar Sjt 81970 Royal Engineers
KENYON Seth MM Cpl 306156 7th West Riding Regt
KENYON Thomas MM L/Cpl 18012 Grenadier Guards
KENYON William "DCM,MM,CdiG(It)" Cpl 48634 21st Manchester Regt
KEOGAN Patrick MM L/Cpl 13983 Yorkshire Regt
KEOGH Arthur MM Dvr 23966 11 Fd Coy Royal Engineers
KEOGH Frank H. MM Cpl 201008 Leicestershire Regt
KEOGH John MM Sjt 40851 RGA
KEOGH John "MM,MID" Sjt 40552 Royal Scots
KEOGH Joseph W. MM L/Cpl 242777 5th West Riding Regt
KEOGH William MM Sjt 10143 1st Royal Irish Regt
KEOGH William Jesse MM Dmr 250846 3rd London Regt DOW 2.9.18.
KEOHANE Dennis MM Pte 16917 6th South Wales Borderers
KEOHANE James MM Sjt 112338 B/86 Bde RFA
KEOHANE Michael MM Gnr 78375 38 Bde RFA Died 30.1.19.
KEOUGH Francis MM Pte 9898 2nd Lancashire Fusiliers

KEOWN Francis J. "DCM,MM,MID" CSM 2807 1st Irish Guards
KEPPY Victor H. MM Pte 88053 RAMC
KERFOOT Benjamin MM Pte 17899 1st Border Regt
KERFOOT J. MM Cpl 60915 33rd London Regt
KERFOOT James MM Sjt 265773 1/5th Cheshire Regt
KERGAN John "MM+Bar,MMV(It)" Sjt 4796 Northumberland Fusiliers
KERLEY Alfred H. MM Cpl 202341 4th Royal Berkshire Regt
KERLEY Bertie J. MM+Bar 2nd Cpl 496852 Royal Engineers
KERLEY George MM L/Sjt 23183 1st Coldstream Guards
KERLEY Harry MM Sjt 49016 Royal Engineers
KERMAN Frank MM Pte G/8066 7th East Kent Regt DOW 7.8.18.
KERMODE William Frederick "DCM,MM" Cpl 13335 Coldstream Guards
KERNAGHAN Hugh MM Pte 5357 Royal Irish Rifles
KERNOHAN James MM Cpl 750310 RFA
KERNOTT Albert V. MM Cpl 9649 2nd East Surrey Regt
KERNOTT Harry W. "MM,MIDx2" Sjt 11986 2nd Royal Fusiliers
KERNS William MM L/Bdr 215140 C/110 Bde RFA
KERNS William Taylor MM C/Sjt 1975 2nd Lancashire Fusiliers Died 4.11.16.
KERR Allison MM+Bar Cpl 14961 12th Royal Scots DOW 22.10.17.
KERR Andrew Yuill MM Pte M2/021524 Army Service Corps att 141 Fd Amb RAMC.
KERR Archibald McNair MM Dvr T4/247029 Army Service Corps att 1/2(Lowland)Fd Amb RAMC.
KERR David MM 2nd Cpl 121926 180 Tunnelling Coy Royal Engineers
KERR David MM CSM 13457 King's Own Scottish Borderers
KERR Edward MM Sjt 19855 4(Cav)Fd Amb RAMC
KERR George MM Pte 295282 12th Royal Scots Fusiliers
KERR George MM Pte S/7031 1st Gordon Highlanders
KERR George MM Bugler 1616 1/9th Highland Light Infantry
KERR Harold MM+Bar Sjt 45671 80 Fd Coy Royal Engineers
KERR Henry MM Pte 240962 Royal Scots Fusiliers
KERR Henry MM Pte 275194 5/6th Royal Scots
KERR Henry R. MM Cpl L/44965 41 Div Ammn Col RFA
KERR Hugh R. MM L/Bdr 65134 RGA
KERR James MM Pte 20978 6th King's Own Scottish Borderers
KERR James MM Pte 55626 207 Coy Machine Gun Corps
KERR James MM Sjt 325061 5/6th Royal Scots
KERR James MM Pte 241584 1/4th King's Own Scottish Borderers
KERR James MM Pte 6471 1st Gordon Highlanders
KERR James MM Spr 132585 251 Tunnelling Coy Royal Engineers KIA 25.2.18.
KERR James MM Sjt 12687 55 Fd Coy Royal Engineers
KERR James MM Pte 43056 1/7th Royal Scots
KERR James MM L/Cpl 310052 1/7th Gordon Highlanders
KERR James MM Pte 40785 Highland Light Infantry
KERR James MM Pte 202541 2/6th Royal Warwickshire Regt
KERR James G. MM Sjt 15956 Liverpool Regt
KERR James W.E. MM Cpl 240307 1/5th King's Own Scottish Borderers
KERR John MM Pte 40599 15th Highland Light Infantry
KERR John MM Cpl 312130 RGA
KERR John A.P. MM Sjt 265642 1/6th Royal Highlanders
KERR John Dunlop MM 2nd Cpl 76333 'GQ' Cable Section Royal Engineers
KERR John McAllister MM Sjt 300601 6 Tank Carrier Coy Tank Corps
KERR John Pollock MM Spr 47267 25 Div Sig Coy Royal Engineers DOW 18.4.18.
KERR John W. MM L/Cpl 9795 4th Somerset Light Infantry
KERR Joseph MM Pte 45770 102 Coy Machine Gun Corps
KERR Joseph F. MM Gnr 198164 525 Siege Bty RGA
KERR P. MM Pte 41597 Highland Light Infantry
KERR Peter "MC,MM" CSM 21944 17th Royal Scots
KERR Robert MM Sjt 4203 Labour Corps
KERR Robert MM Gnr 80748 RFA
KERR Robert B. MM Pte 271321 17th Royal Scots
KERR Robert F. MM Pte 325309 Durham Light Infantry
KERR Robert Wyllie "MM,MID" L/Cpl 2617 52 Div Sig Coy Royal Engineers
KERR Thomas MM+Bar Cpl 17167 2nd Scots Guards
KERR Thomas D. MM Pte 201106 6th (Light) Bn Tank Corps
KERR Thomas Henry MM Sjt 17991 11/13th Royal Irish Rifles
KERR Thomas O. MM Cpl 16542 Durham Light Infantry
KERR Walter MM Pte 11385 8th Cheshire Regt
KERR Walter Matthew MM Sjt 42288 Machine Gun Corps
KERR William MM L/Cpl 295815 12th Royal Scots Fusiliers

KERR William MM S/Sjt Fitter 45429 101 Siege Bty RGA
KERR William MM Pte 21346 29th Bn Machine Gun Corps
KERR William MM Pte 10070 1st Royal Inniskilling Fusiliers
KERR William MM Cpl 112152 Royal Engineers
KERR William A. MM Cpl 769846 28th London Regt
KERR William L. MM Cpl 432071 Royal Engineers
KERRIDGE David MM L/Sjt 420177 1/10th London Regt KIA 10.12.17.
KERRIDGE George MM Sjt 201099 Suffolk Regt
KERRIDGE George H. MM Dvr 926265 D/290 Bde RFA
KERRIDGE James Walley MM Sjt 15362 21st Middlesex Regt DOW 31.3.18.
KERRIDGE Reuben B.J. "MM,MID" Cpl 13766 15 Fd Coy Royal Engineers
KERRIGAN Christopher MM Pte 44166 12th North Staffordshire Regt
KERRIGAN Francis Eugene MM CSM 5134 2nd Leinster Regt Died 25.8.16.
KERRIGAN James MM Pte 1184 South Lancashire Regt
KERRIGAN James MM+Bar Pte 29/201 Northumberland Fusiliers
KERRIGAN Joseph MM Pte 18932 Manchester Regt
KERRISON Reginald J. MM Cpl 75171 Machine Gun Corps
KERRY Arthur J. MM L/Cpl 722954 24th London Regt
KERRY Arthur J. MM Bdr 340591 RGA
KERRY Edward Buxton Campbell MM Sjt 470736 2/12th London Regt
KERRY George V. MM Sjt 3767 Notts & Derby Regt
KERRY James W. MM Pte 12/305 12th East Yorkshire Regt
KERRY John MM Pte 30593 6th Royal Inniskilling Fusiliers
KERRY John C. MM Gnr 93446 RGA
KERRY Luke MM L/Cpl 19528 1/5th Yorkshire Regt
KERRY Thomas MM Sjt 200973 20th Middlesex Regt Died 8.1.19.
KERRY William J. "DCM,MM" CSM G/61690 17th Royal Fusiliers
KERSEY Alfred John MM Gnr 14446 5 Div Ammn Col RFA
KERSEY Hammond MM Pte 65452 26th London Regt
KERSEY Reginald C. MM Pte 241214 6th North Staffordshire Regt
KERSEY Thomas Bolitho MM Pte 79193 RAMC
KERSHAW Arthur MM Pte 25975 East Yorkshire Regt
KERSHAW Arthur MM Pte 238024 West Riding Regt
KERSHAW Cornelius "DCM,MM" Sjt 13600 1st Coldstream Guards
KERSHAW Edwin MM Pte 3768 2nd Manchester Regt
KERSHAW Frank MM Pte 40198 Northumberland Fusiliers
KERSHAW George MM Dvr 74483 25 Bde RFA
KERSHAW James William MM Pte 12519 West Riding Regt
KERSHAW John MM Pte 25563 9th West Riding Regt
KERSHAW John H. MM Cpl 43122 Scottish Rifles
KERSHAW John K. MM Pte 266180 Liverpool Regt
KERSHAW Joseph W. MM Bdr 34480 RFA
KERSHAW R. MM Sjt 1404 38 Div Ammn Col RFA
KERSHAW R. MM Pte 242196 Royal Lancaster Regt
KERSHAW R.W. MM L/Cpl P13309 Military Mounted Police
KERSHAW Richard T. MM Pte 34322 17th Lancashire Fusiliers
KERSHAW T. MM Pte 49063 7th Norfolk Regt
KERSHAW William MM Pte 36738 1/5th Border Regt
KERSLAKE Frank A. MM Bdr 7874 A/152 Bde RFA
KERSLAKE Leonard MM L/Cpl 42101 4th Worcestershire Regt KIA 14.10.18.
KERSLAKE Lewis W. MM Pte 205898 1st Devonshire Regt
KERSLAKE William MM L/Cpl 9997 2nd East Surrey Regt
KERSLEY Thomas G. MM Pnr 253358 4 Div Sig Coy Royal Engineers
KERTON T.W. MM Pte 263186 4th York & Lancaster Regt
KERTON William J. MM Bdr 34343 116 Heavy Bde RGA
KERVILLE Albert E. MM Pte 202427 2/4th Hampshire Regt
KERWAN William MM Spr 15784 4 Div Sig Coy Royal Engineers
KERWIN George MM Sjt 102517 25th Bn Machine Gun Corps
KERWIN J. MM L/Cpl 6579 West Riding Regt
KESKEYS Thomas W. MM Cpl 23987 9 Fd Coy Royal Engineers
KESSELL Frank E. MM Sjt 197582 Royal Engineers
KESSON David Benzie MM Cpl 7175 2nd Scots Guards
KESTLE William MM Sjt 57116 102 Fd Coy Royal Engineers
KETCH Percy MM Pte 200570 1/5th Durham Light Infantry
KETCHEN James MM Pte 41530 2nd Royal Scots Fusiliers
KETCHLEY Frederick W. MM Sjt 11123 5th Dorsetshire Regt
KETLEY Albert Victor MM Pte 72447 7th Royal West Surrey Regt
KETLEY Charles Walter MM Cpl 42855 15 Div Sig Coy Royal Engineers KIA 11.4.17.
KETLEY Noel J. MM L/Cpl 25535 12th East Surrey Regt
KETLEY William MM Pte 40821 Middlesex Regt
KETT Albert "DCM,MM,MSM" CSM 15528 9th Norfolk Regt

KETT Albert James MM Cpl 40081 1st Norfolk Regt
KETT Robert MM Sjt 550037 1/16th London Regt
KETTLE Frederick MM Pte 235276 1/1st Herefordshire Regt
KETTLE G. MM L/Cpl 18610 11th Essex Regt
KETTLE Henry Arthur MM Pte 20860 Machine Gun Corps
KETTLE John MM Pte 12956 1st North Lancashire Regt KIA 18.4.18.
KETTLE William MM L/Cpl 433094 RAMC
KETTLEWELL Ernest MM+Bar Pte 21188 Lincolnshire Regt
KETTLEWELL Fred MM Pte 1897 Lincolnshire Regt
KETTLEWELL Frederick J. MM Cpl 12383 19th Manchester Regt
KETTLEWELL John MM Sjt Farrier 786045 RFA
KETTLEWELL John "DCM,MM" CSM 12854 9th West Riding Regt
KETTLEWELL John C. MM 2nd Cpl 108575 103 Fd Coy Royal Engineers
KETTLEY William "DCM,MM" CSM 23320 92 Coy 31st Bn Machine Gun Corps
KEVAN Ernest J. MM L/Cpl 29364 East Surrey Regt
KEVAN John "MM,CG(F)" Pte 240667 1/5th King's Own Scottish Borderers
KEVAN John "DCM,MM" L/Cpl S/9568 1/7th Gordon Highlanders
KEVELIGHAN William R. MM Cpl 265472 Liverpool Regt
KEVERN William H. MM Pte 18679 Royal West Kent Regt
KEVERNE Samuel J. MM Pte 27390 Wiltshire Regt
KEW Arthur MM L/Sjt 401234 RAMC
KEW Charles F. MM Gnr 947898 A/280 Bde RFA
KEW Dan "MC+Bar,DCM,MM(203021 L/Sjt R Berks)" 2Lt 1st Bedfordshire Regt att 1/1st Bn Hertfordshire Regt.
KEW George A. MM Pte 17342 6th South Wales Borderers
KEW John Richard MM Pte 36015 1/4th Yorkshire Light Infantry
KEWLEY Edward MM Pte 72939 Notts & Derby Regt
KEWLEY Frederick. "DCM,MM" Sjt 21042 22nd Manchester Regt
KEWLEY Joseph D. MM Pte 99917 51st Bn Machine Gun Corps
KEY Alfred R. MM Sjt 9346 1st South Wales Borderers
KEY Charles MM Pte 34488 5th West Riding Regt
KEY Charles Norman MM Spr 212069 216 Army Troops Coy Royal Engineers
KEY Frank MM L/Cpl L/9559 1st Royal Fusiliers
KEY George MM Pte 22531 2nd Highland Light Infantry
KEY John W. MM Sjt 6271 Royal Sussex Regt
KEY Walter O. MM Pte 2068 1/1st Glasgow Yeomanry
KEY William R. MM Sjt 52507 Machine Gun Corps
KEYLOCK William Thomas MM Pte 301455 13th Bn Tank Corps KIA 3.10.18.
KEYMER Frank William MM Pte 13086 1st Norfolk Regt
KEYNES George Robert MM Pte 8454 2nd Royal Irish Regt
KEYNORTH C. MM Pte 39935 6th Leicestershire Regt
KEYS Charles Jesse MM Pte M2/182212 Army Service Corps att 53 Fd Amb RAMC.DOW 22.8.18.
KEYS Ernest G. MM Pte 130214 Machine Gun Corps
KEYS Sidney MM Pte 35438 11th Notts & Derby Regt KIA 16.9.17.
KEYS Thomas MM Pte 11545 11th Royal Inniskilling Fusiliers
KEYSELL Harry MM L/Cpl 345555 24th Royal Welsh Fusiliers
KEYSER E. MM L/Cpl 3014 1/20th London Regt
KEYTE Caleb R. "DCM,MM" Sjt 33963 10th & 6th Duke of Cornwall's LI
KEYTE Ernest L. MM Dvr 9550 A/71 Bde RFA
KEYTE Joseph G. MM Sjt 14639 Grenadier Guards
KEYTE Wilson "MM,MC(G)" Pte 30818 11th Worcestershire Regt
KEYWORTH Arthur T. MM Cpl 1207 36th Northumberland Fusiliers
KEYWORTH Charles MM+Bar Pte 14056 10th King's Royal Rifle Corps KIA 20.11.17.
KEYWORTH Frederick Burgess MM+Bar Bdr 57499 122 Siege Bty RGA
KEYWORTH Frederick L. MM L/Cpl 78024 9th Bn Tank Corps
KEYWORTH William MM Cpl 197 529 Fd Coy Royal Engineers
KEYZOR Frank C. MM Pte 18587 1st Lincolnshire Regt DOW 24.10.18.
KIBBEY Albert Ernest MM Sjt 1142 Royal Engineers
KIBBEY George Heny MM L/Sjt 1973 Royal Sussex Regt
KIBBLE Alfred B. MM Pte 2245 12th Middlesex Regt
KIBBLE Richard MM Sjt 397158 2 Siege Coy R Mon RE Royal Engineers
KIBBLE T.W. MM L/Cpl G/7707 1st East Kent Regt
KIBBLE Thomas H. MM Pte 15677 6th Lincolnshire Regt
KIBBLE Thomas Nelson MM Gnr 293136 138 Heavy Bty RGA
KIBBLE W.J. MM Air Mech 2 67653 Royal Air Force
KIBBY Albert E. MM Pte 31208 4th Hampshire Regt
KIBBY Douglas MM Pte 301486 5th London Regt
KIDD Alexander Chisholm MM Gnr 76310 459 Bty 118 Bde RFA

KIDD Charles MM Cpl 46041 C/88 Bde RFA DOW 9.10.17.
KIDD David MM Spr WR/125035 279 Rly Const Coy Royal Engineers
KIDD David MM Pte 19978 Royal Highlanders
KIDD Edward MM Pte 6659 11th Royal Irish Rifles
KIDD Ernest MM Pte 2748 1/8th Middlesex Regt
KIDD Frank MM Pte 2247 1/5th Durham Light Infantry
KIDD Frederick James MM Cpl 821028 B/246 Bde RFA
KIDD George T. MM Cpl S/13295 Rifle Brigade
KIDD Henry MM Pte 23736 East Lancashire Regt
KIDD Herbert MM Spr 57581 150 Fd Coy Royal Engineers
KIDD Hugh George MM Cpl 10945 9th Essex Regt KIA 20.11.17.
KIDD James MM Cpl 6272 1st Dragoon Guards
KIDD John Crawford MM Sjt 1828 1/5th Liverpool Regt
KIDD John R. MM Gnr 26384 RFA
KIDD Robert MM Sjt 7753 2nd Seaforth Highlanders
KIDD Robert MM CSM 6573 8th King's Royal Rifle Corps DOW 21.3.18.
KIDD William MM Pte 18733 7th Yorkshire Regt
KIDDER James MM Pte 40092 20th Manchester Regt
KIDDLE Percy MM Sjt 235345 2nd South Staffordshire Regt
KIDDLE Reginald A. MM Pte 28517 15th Hampshire Regt
KIDDY John MM Pte 56674 RAMC
KIDGER Bertram William C. MM Cpl 33101 Devonshire Regt
KIDGER Ernest MM L/Cpl 71014 Notts & Derby Regt
KIDLEY Harry MM Sjt 388155 1 Siege Coy R Monmouth RE
KIDMAN Charles William MM Cpl 26725 14th Hampshire Regt
KIDMAN Walter J. MM L/Cpl M/272942 Army Service Corps att RFA.
KIDNER Dennis H. MM Sjt 43338 3rd Bn Machine Gun Corps
KIDSON George W. MM Pte 38026 9th Yorkshire Regt
KIDWELL John C. MM Cpl 46736 RFA
KIELTY John MM Dvr T4/061881 577 Aux Horse Tpt Coy Army Service Corps
KIERANS Terence MM Pte 9867 2nd Royal Irish Rifles
KIERNAN Michael MM Pte 24/278 24th Northumberland Fusiliers
KIERSEY Michael MM Sjt 1372 9th Royal Munster Fusiliers
KIERSTENSON Edward Ola Olin MM Pte 75889 2/2nd London Regt
KIFF John MM Pte 40765 Worcestershire Regt
KIGHTLEY Christopher F.W. "DCM,MM" Sjt 128715 Special Brigade Royal Engineers
KIGHTLEY W.C. MM Pte R/6322 18th King's Royal Rifle Corps
KILBEY William John MM Pte 14614 2nd Royal Sussex Regt
KILBRIDE J. MM Sjt 240231 Royal Lancaster Regt
KILBRIDE William H. MM Pte 72269 Machine Gun Corps
KILBURN Frederick C. MM Sjt 759 RFA
KILBURN George MM Sjt 775262 B/245 Bde RFA
KILBURN George MM Pte PS/7401 24th Royal Fusiliers
KILBURN John MM+Bar L/Cpl 265424 4th Liverpool Regt
KILBURN John W. MM Cpl 42286 10th West Yorkshire Regt
KILBURN Roger MM S/Sjt Mechanic 92069 9th Bn Tank Corps
KILBY George E. "MM,MID" Sjt 291320 128 Siege Bty RGA
KILDAY Michael G. MM Gnr Sig 201023 C/93 Bde RFA
KILFEDDAR Felix MM L/Cpl 24550 Royal Inniskilling Fusiliers
KILGALLON Francis MM Pte 33942 Middlesex Regt
KILGALLON Joseph MM Sjt 47172 Royal Engineers
KILGARIFF Michael MM Cpl R/12535 King's Royal Rifle Corps
KILGOUR A.S. MM Pte 722710 London Regt
KILGOUR Andrew MM L/Cpl 312850 6 Div Sig Coy Royal Engineers
KILGOUR Andrew B. MM Gnr Sig 366009 138 Siege Bty RGA
KILGOUR William MM L/Sjt 57319 5th Liverpool Regt
KILGOUR William "MM,MC(G)" Pte 33421 78 Coy Machine Gun Corps
KILKENNY Anthony MM Pte 5319 1st Irish Guards
KILKENNY Thomas MM Cpl 295471 12th Royal Scots Fusiliers
KILL Thomas W. MM Cpl 11198 1st Notts & Derby Regt
KILLAN Alfred MM Sjt 36049 RAMC
KILLEEN Albert C. MM L/Cpl 201 4th GMGR
KILLEEN John MM Pte 19879 2nd Royal Dublin Fusiliers
KILLEEN John MM Sjt 13869 13th Durham Light Infantry
KILLEEN John MM+Bar Cpl 55913 Machine Gun Corps
KILLEEN Patrick MM Pte 20840 10th Durham Light Infantry
KILLEEN Patrick MM Pte 11570 2nd Royal Dublin Fusiliers
KILLEEN Patrick MM Pte 6782 2nd Royal Irish Rifles
KILLEEN William MM+Bar Sjt 20800 33 DAC & B/250 Bde RFA
KILLEN Robert Charles MM L/Cpl 200308 1/5th Liverpool Regt DOW 21.11.17.
KILLEN Walter MM Sjt Farrier 9263 B/157 Bde RFA
KILLIAN Thomas MM Gnr 148330 RGA
KILLICK Edmund MM Sjt 240064 10th Royal West Surrey Regt
KILLICK Henry MM L/Cpl M2/077976 Army Service Corps
KILLICK Herbert Henry MM Spr 92957 Signal Service Royal Engineers
KILLICK Percy P. MM Spr 71045 2 Div Sig Coy Royal Engineers
KILLICK Thomas W. MM Sjt 47244 20th Hussars
KILLIKELLY Garrett "DCM,MM,MSM" Sjt 18311 2nd Leinster Regt
KILLIN William MM L/Sjt S/6379 8th Seaforth Highlanders
KILLINGBECK Jim MM Pte 62387 RAMC
KILLINGRAY C.H. MM Pte 14648 8th Norfolk Regt
KILLINGTON Herbert MM L/Sjt 15888 Grenadier Guards
KILLINGWORTH Harry MM Pte 27378 Durham Light Infantry
KILLIP George MM Pte 20/1440 Northumberland Fusiliers
KILMARTIN Frank MM Cpl 53561 2nd Welsh Regt
KILMINSTER John E. MM Drummer 265821 Gloucestershire Regt
KILMINSTER William Frank "MM,MID" Pte 8302 1st Duke of Cornwall's LI
KILMINSTER William John MM L/Cpl 200406 2nd Bn Tank Corps KIA 8.8.18.
KILNER Colin MM Cpl 622362 RHA
KILNER Thomas Richard Burgess MM Pte 6092 Royal Warwickshire Regt KIA 18.6.18
KILOH George MM Sjt 265773 Gordon Highlanders
KILPATRICK David MM Dvr 635629 B/256 Bde RFA
KILPATRICK George MM Pte 1970 West Riding Regt
KILPATRICK High(sic) MM Pte 285031 Seaforth Highlanders
KILPATRICK James MM Sjt 27101 Machine Gun Corps
KILPATRICK John MM L/Sjt 325018 1/6th Arg & Suth Highlanders
KILPATRICK John Rennie MM Pte 1494 RAMC
KILPATRICK Samuel MM Pte 4817 11th Arg & Suth Highlanders
KILPATRICK Thomas MM Pte 18572 5th Cameron Highlanders
KILROY Thomas MM Cpl 25160 7/8th Royal Inniskilling Fusiliers
KILSBY Alan MM Pte 37448 Royal Berkshire Regt
KILSBY William S. MM Pte 106290 RAMC
KILVINGTON Fred MM Pte 41947 Northumberland Fusiliers
KIMBER Alfred MM Pte 8755 1st Hampshire Regt
KIMBER Arthur F. MM Sjt 8166 2nd Royal Sussex Regt
KIMBER David MM Spr 100748 5 Fd Coy Royal Engineers
KIMBER Ernest H. MM Pte 322736 6th London Regt
KIMBER Henry MM Pte 5874 9th East Surrey Regt
KIMBER Henry George MM L/Cpl L/10740 2nd Royal West Surrey Regt KIA 26.10.17.
KIMBER Stanley MM Pte 36572 1st Gloucestershire Regt
KIMBER William H. MM Pte 24092 Machine Gun Corps
KIMBER William J. MM Cpl 40553 RGA
KIMBER William Joseph MM Spr 558260 69 Div Sig Coy Royal Engineers
KIMBERLEY Alfred MM Sjt 495380 2/1(Home Counties)Fd Amb RAMC
KIMBERLEY George MM Cpl 200602 1/4th Oxf & Bucks Light Infantry
KIMBERLEY George Augustus MM Spr 74066 VII Corps Sig Coy Royal Engineers
KIMBERLEY John Henry A. MM Gnr 44216 RFA
KIMBERLEY Joseph Lane MM Sjt 52617 120 Heavy Bty Royal Artillery DOW 13.5.17.
KIMBERLEY Thomas Berthram MM L/Cpl 6204 1/6th Royal Warwickshire Regt KIA 4.10.17.
KIMBERLEY Victor Henry Arthur MM Pte DM2/137823 Army Service Corps att 'P'(AA)Bty RGA
KIMBERLY John H. MM L/Sjt 242920 6th Royal Warwickshire Regt
KIMBLE Albert MM Pte 12743 6th Oxf & Bucks Light Infantry
KIME G.H.E. MM Pte 4679 1/1st HAC(Inf)
KIME George MM+Bar Sjt 18473 8th Yorkshire Light Infantry
KIMMET Peter MM Sjt 40298 1st Scottish Rifles
KIMMETT Edward MM+Bar Gnr 275363 264 Siege Bty RGA DOW 13.5.18.
KIMPTON Alfred H. MM Sjt 281077 60 Siege Bty RGA
KIMPTON E. MM+Bar Cpl 9044 B/72 Bde RFA
KIMPTON Edwin John MM Pte 15381 9th Essex Regt
KINCH Frank E.S. MM Cpl 291388 128 Hy Bty RGA
KINCH Frederick MM Pte 17890 20th Hussars
KINCHEN William A. MM Pte 17053 6th Oxf & Bucks Light Infantry
KIND William MM Cpl 11061 Leicestershire Regt
KINDELL Raymond H. MM Pte 531509 1/15th London Regt
KINDER Ben MM L/Cpl C/7404 13th King's Royal Rifle Corps
KINDER Edward M. MM Pte 46838 South Wales Borderers
KINDER Harold MM Pte 58195 54th Bn Machine Gun Corps
KINDER Leo MM Pte 6767 12th Manchester Regt
KINDER Thomas MM Sjt 28057 RFA
KINDLAN Michael MM Dvr 707142 RFA

KING A. MM Gnr 155056 RFA
KING A. MM Cpl 14961 Suffolk Regt
KING A.E. MM L/Cpl 200477 Oxf & Bucks Light Infantry
KING A.J. MM Pte 35183 14th Worcestershire Regt
KING A.J. MM Cpl 187041 RFA
KING A.J. MM Sjt 1109 London Regt
KING Albert MM Sjt 10193 4th Worcestershire Regt
KING Albert MM Cpl 7374 2nd King's Royal Rifle Corps
KING Albert MM Pte 1891? 1/5th Royal Sussex Regt
KING Albert A. MM Pte 7571 1st Norfolk Regt
KING Albert C. MM Pte 275926 1/6th Essex Regt
KING Albert H. MM Cpl 96890 Royal Engineers
KING Albert V. MM Spr 558161 56 Div Sig Coy Royal Engineers
KING Alexander MM Sjt 204301 7th Norfolk Regt
KING Alexander MM Pte 129546 Machine Gun Corps
KING Alexander MM L/Cpl 1641 7th Seaforth Highlanders
KING Alfred MM Cpl 208062 6th Royal West Surrey Regt
KING Alfred MM Gnr 322633 86 Siege Bty RGA
KING Alfred G. MM Pte 7801 10th Royal West Kent Regt
KING Allen MM Sjt 23257 353 Elect & Mech Coy Royal Engineers
KING Arthur MM Sjt M2/047484 Army Service Corps
KING Arthur MM Pte 8455 1st Bedfordshire Regt
KING Arthur MM Sjt 11495 5th Shropshire Light Infantry KIA 24.8.16.
KING Arthur MM Pte 201622 7th Royal West Kent Regt
KING Arthur MM Pte 241445 West Yorkshire Regt
KING Arthur MM Pte 39578 4th Gloucestershire Regt
KING Arthur D. MM Pte 44311 1st Yorkshire Light Infantry
KING Arthur F. MM Pte 6780 Leinster Regt
KING Arthur G.F. MM+Bar Cpl 18809 6 Div Sig Coy Royal Engineers
KING Arthur R. MM Dvr 960465 C/236 Bde RFA
KING Arthur William George MM Gnr 29332 28 Siege Bty RGA
KING Aubrey T. MM Sjt 14846 RFA
KING Benjamin MM Bdr 41860 RFA
KING Bernard MM Pte 13982 2nd Yorkshire Regt
KING Bernard George MM L/Bdr 292845 137 Heavy Bty RGA Died 6.11.18.
KING Bert "DCM,MM+Bar" Sjt 17934 10th Worcestershire Regt
KING Bert MM Pte 82054 RAMC
KING Bertie L. MM Pte 54252 1st Devonshire Regt
KING C. MM L/Bdr 41701 RGA
KING C.E. MM L/Cpl 11316 10th Royal West Surrey Regt
KING Cecil Charles MM 2nd Cpl 46630 98 Fd Coy Royal Engineers DOW 6.11.17.
KING Cecil F. MM Sjt 51437 Machine Gun Corps
KING Charles MM Pte 2795 2nd Rifle Brigade
KING Charles MM Pte 84254 141 Labour Coy Labour Corps
KING Charles A. MM Sjt 200162 Royal West Surrey Regt
KING Charles E. MM Sjt G/14790 4th Royal Fusiliers
KING Charles Frederick MM L/Cpl M2/151682 2 Motor Ambulance Group
KING Charles J. MM L/Cpl 20079 Royal Dublin Fusiliers
KING Charles S. MM CSM 14724 9th Norfolk Regt
KING Charles W. MM L/Cpl 9082 7th Suffolk Regt
KING Charles W.M. MM Sjt 13887 Arg & Suth Highlanders
KING Charles Walter MM Pte 2334 1 Fd Amb RAMC KIA 25.9.16.
KING Charles William MM Sjt 19364 460 Bty 15 Bde RFA
KING Daniel MM L/Sjt 1812 8th East Surrey Regt
KING David MM Pte 43205 2nd Royal Scots Fusiliers
KING David MM Pte 12260 Labour Corps
KING E. MM Pte 300019 RAMC
KING Edward MM Gnr 43349 RGA
KING Edward MM L/Cpl 558231 56 Div Sig Coy Royal Engineers
KING Edward E. MM Pte 265981 5th Gloucestershire Regt
KING Edward Thomas MM L/Cpl 326011 1/1st Cambridgeshire Regt
KING Edward W. MM Sjt 15488 Grenadier Guards
KING Edwin MM L/Cpl 2003 2nd Manchester Regt
KING Eric J. "MM,MID" Sjt 730 1/7th Middlesex Regt
KING Ernest MM Cpl 110877 88 Heavy Artillery Group RGA
KING Ernest MM Pte G/5930 11th Royal West Surrey Regt
KING Ernest Samuel George MM L/Cpl 18924 6th Royal West Kent Regt
KING Ernest W. MM Sjt 4591 8th Royal Lancaster Regt
KING F. MM Sjt 339197 RAMC
KING F.C. MM Air Mech 2 44350 Royal Flying Corps
KING F.W. MM L/Sjt 3759 ? Hussars
KING Francis MM L/Cpl 10610 South Wales Borderers
KING Francis C. MM Pte 72081 Notts & Derby Regt
KING Francis J. MM Pte 31045 8th Somerset Light Infantry
KING Francis J. MM Gnr 34222 2 Div Ammn Col RFA

KING Frank MM Gnr 97475 RFA
KING Fred MM Gnr 99573 RFA
KING Fred "DCM,MM" Sjt 18133 6th Yorkshire Light Infantry
KING Fred MM+Bar Cpl 9704 5th Gloucestershire Regt
KING Frederick MM Pte S/2775 12th Rifle Brigade
KING Frederick MM Sjt 13887 8th South Staffordshire Regt
KING Frederick MM Sjt 12272 RAMC
KING Frederick MM Sjt 55494 37 Siege Bty RGA
KING Frederick MM Pte 1601 18th Durham Light Infantry KIA 19.7.18.
KING Frederick George MM Sjt Farrier 26320 B/124 Bde RFA Died 6.11.18.
KING Frederick J. "DCM,MM" Sjt G/9448 10th Royal West Surrey Regt
KING Frederick W. MM L/Cpl 251234 3rd London Regt
KING Frederick W. MM Pte DM2/190174 Army Service Corps att RFA.
KING Frederick William MM Pte 70744 80 Fd Amb RAMC
KING Frederick William MM Cpl 5468 Machine Gun Corps
KING G. MM Pte 40922 Essex Regt
KING G. MM Pte 53444 Liverpool Regt
KING George MM Cpl 16752 18 Hy Bty RGA
KING George "MM,MSM" L/Cpl 82154 26th Royal Welsh Fusiliers
KING George MM Pte 24073 Gloucestershire Regt
KING George MM Sjt 9963 1st Essex Regt KIA 23.8.18.
KING George MM Sjt 99062 Royal Engineers
KING George "MM,MID" Pte 14229 7th Suffolk Regt
KING George MM Cpl 25255 RFA
KING George H. MM Bdr 73643 2 Bde RFA
KING George William MM Cpl 57971 36 Div Sig Coy Royal Engineers
KING Gerald "DCM,MM" Sjt 20654 8th Royal Inniskilling Fusiliers KIA 21.3.18.
KING Gladys Victoria MM Miss F BRCS(VAD)
KING Godfrey W. MM L/Cpl 200458 Oxf & Bucks Light Infantry
KING H.J. MM Pte 28073 Hampshire Regt
KING Harold MM Pte 316298 23rd Cheshire Regt
KING Harold "DCM,MM" CSM 8985 2nd West Yorkshire Regt
KING Harold MM Pte 7468 1/4th Royal Welsh Fusiliers
KING Harold Royce MM CSM 324 1/6th West Yorkshire Regt
KING Harry MM L/Cpl 124373 104th Bn Machine Gun Corps
KING Harry MM Sjt 10705 1st Scottish Rifles
KING Harry MM Cpl 374229 122 Siege Bty RGA KIA 27.9.18.
KING Harry Ebenezer "MM,MID" Sjt 52972 21 Div Sig Coy Royal Engineers
KING Harry H. MM Pte 6820 1st Norfolk Regt
KING Henry MM Pte 23439 11th Manchester Regt
KING Henry MM Pte 30936 1st King's Own Scottish Borderers
KING Henry MM Sjt 11892 4th Royal Fusiliers
KING Henry John MM Cpl 10583 B/58 Bde RFA
KING Henry S. MM Sjt 19710 RAMC
KING Henry T. MM Cpl 17837 1st Duke of Cornwall's LI
KING Herbert MM Cpl 30183 1st Royal Dublin Fusiliers
KING Herbert MM Sjt 56036 17 Bty 41 Bde RFA
KING Herbert C. MM Pte 12405 7th Wiltshire Regt
KING Herbert F. MM Pte 26588 3rd Bn Machine Gun Corps
KING Herbert H. MM Pte 4185 2nd Rifle Brigade
KING Herbert Reginald MM Sjt 52092 RHA
KING Horace MM L/Cpl 60442 7th West Yorkshire Regt
KING Horace MM Cpl 7192 Royal West Surrey Regt
KING Horace MM Gnr 2216 RFA
KING Hubert J. MM Cpl 149655 12th Bn Machine Gun Corps
KING Hubert R. "DCM,MM" Sjt 42414 1/1st Hertfordshire Regt
KING Hugh MM Pte 9543 Seaforth Highlanders
KING Hugh MM Pte 7628 Irish Guards
KING Hugh MM L/Cpl 3792 Gordon Highlanders
KING J. MM Spr 470859 Royal Engineers
KING James MM Pte 201909 5th Notts & Derby Regt
KING James MM Sjt 10548 2nd Border Regt
KING James "DCM,MM" Sjt 13329 RFA
KING James MM Gnr 97141 D/75 Bde RFA
KING James MM Pte 3558 1st Northumberland Fusiliers
KING James MM Cpl 253675 24 Div Sig Coy Royal Engineers DOW 7.11.18.
KING James B. MM Cpl 276775 Arg & Suth Highlanders
KING James E. MM Pte 81015 RAMC
KING James Percival MM Sjt 9277 1st Bedfordshire Regt
KING John MM Sjt 295042 12th Royal Scots Fusiliers
KING John MM Dvr 72252 49 Bty 40 Bde RFA
KING John MM Pte 326148 Royal Scots

KING John MM Sjt 5190 1st Lincolnshire Regt
KING John MM Gnr 4249 X/8 Med TM Bty RGA KIA 27.5.18.
KING John MM Gnr 139316 RFA
KING John C. MM Pte 1298 1/24th London Regt
KING John George MM Sjt 9596 Grenadier Guards
KING John H. MM Pte 14717 4th Middlesex Regt
KING Joseph MM L/Cpl 19454 14th Hampshire Regt KIA 31.3.18.
KING Joseph MM Pte 291831 1/7th Northumberland Fusiliers
KING Joseph MM L/Cpl 36227 Yorkshire Regt
KING Joseph MM Pte 301020 15th Durham Light Infantry KIA 18.9.18.
KING Joseph MM L/Sjt 11771 Coldstream Guards
KING Joseph MM Pte 9349 2nd Bedfordshire Regt
KING Joseph MM L/Cpl 432353 Royal Engineers
KING Joseph MM Bdr 33111 16 Div Ammn Col RFA
KING Joseph MM Sjt 266488 1/1st Hertfordshire Regt
KING Joseph W. MM Cpl 28205 8th Lincolnshire Regt
KING Leonard MM Pte 43460 Bedfordshire Regt
KING Leonard Ernest MM Sjt 1622 1/23rd London Regt
KING Louis A.N. MM L/Cpl 1229 Seaforth Highlanders
KING Louis Thomas Horace William MM Pte 41195 Worcestershire Regt DOW 19.4.18.
KING M. MM Gnr 651047 RFA
KING Malcolm P. MM Sjt 200364 1/4th Cameron Highlanders
KING Marshall MM Pte 68110 RAMC
KING Matthew MM Pte 250715 1/4th Royal Scots
KING Oscar MM Sjt 241402 9th Royal Lancaster Regt
KING Percy James Church MM Bdr 777 11(W Riding)Bty RFA KIA 24.10.17.
KING Peter MM Dvr T1/5350 Army Service Corps att 21 Fd Amb RAMC.
KING Philip MM Cpl 94061 168 Siege Bty RGA
KING R. MM Pte 16493 11th Essex Regt
KING Ralph MM Gnr 64526 23 Bty 40 Bde RFA
KING Reginald MM Pte 114761 109 Coy Machine Gun Corps
KING Reginald E. MM Spr 126614 Royal Engineers
KING Reuben MM Cpl 40125 24 Bde RFA
KING Richard H. MM Sjt 65402 121 Fd Coy Royal Engineers
KING Robert MM Sjt 39748 5th Gloucestershire Regt
KING Robert MM L/Cpl 295144 12th Royal Scots Fusiliers
KING Robert MM+Bar Sjt 99182 37th Bn Machine Gun Corps
KING Robert MM Pte 18028 12th Royal Irish Rifles
KING Robert Douglas MM Pte 633102 1/20th London Regt
KING Robert George MM Gnr 14805 D/70 Bde RFA KIA 13.4.17.
KING Robert H. MM Cpl 37846 Royal Engineers
KING Robert J. MM Sjt 1447 1/4th Royal Highlanders
KING Samuel MM Bdr 67648 A/282 Bde RFA
KING Samuel MM Gnr 5574 RFA
KING Samuel W. MM Pte 21905 3rd Rifle Brigade
KING Seth MM 2nd Cpl 482170 62 Div Sig Coy Royal Engineers
KING Sidney MM Cpl 1379 1/3rd London Regt
KING Sidney MM L/Cpl 10130 Royal Irish Regt
KING Sidney MM Pte 388348 2(Northumbrian)Fd Amb RAMC
KING Sidney Harry MM L/Cpl 53548 Durham Light Infantry
KING Stanley MM Sjt 1298 6th Royal West Surrey Regt
KING Stanley R. MM Dvr Fitter 154032 20 Bty 9 Bde RFA
KING Sydney MM Sjt 40503 Lincolnshire Regt
KING T.G. MM Pte 229536 Royal Fusiliers
KING Thomas MM Sjt 43277 6th Royal Inniskilling Fusiliers
KING Thomas A. MM RSM 315258 10th London Regt
KING Thomas Arthur MM Cpl M2/119169 12 Motor Ambulance Convoy Army Service Corps
KING Timothy MM Pte 3998 15 Fd Amb. RAMC
KING W. MM L/Cpl G/60865 24th Royal Fusiliers
KING W.S. MM Pte 17105 7th Wiltshire Regt
KING Walter MM Spr 62255 15 Div Sig Coy Royal Engineers DOW 12.4.17.
KING Walter MM Pte 40809 Lincolnshire Regt
KING Walter J. MM L/Cpl 5/4830 2nd King's Royal Rifle Corps
KING Walter James MM Sjt L/38057 RFA
KING Walter Thomas MM Sjt 37790 B/84 Bde RFA
KING Wilfred G.A. MM Sjt PW/175 18th Middlesex Regt
KING William MM Pte 126452 32nd Bn Machine Gun Corps
KING William MM Pte 11994 8th Lincolnshire Regt
KING William MM Pte 12599 2nd Scots Guards KIA 11.10.17.
KING William MM Sjt 41819 37th Bn Machine Gun Corps
KING William "MM,CG(F)" Cpl 295072 12th Royal Scots Fusiliers
KING William MM L/Cpl SPTS/1940 24th Royal Fusiliers KIA 1.10.18.
KING William A. MM+Bar Cpl 87280 Royal Engineers
KING William Albert MM Sjt 280308 1/4th London Regt KIA 16.8.17.
KING William Charles Thomson MM Sjt 67 1/21st London Regt
KING William F. MM Pte M2/168097 884 Coy Army Service Corps
KING William F. MM Cpl 558215 29 Div Sig Coy Royal Engineers
KING William G. MM Dvr 128237 B/181 Bde RFA
KING William G. MM Pte 17575 Royal Berkshire Regt
KING William George MM Pte 241065 5th Yorkshire Regt KIA 28.3.18.
KING William H. MM Cpl M2/138439 491 MT Coy Army Service Corps
KING William H. MM Sjt L/23086 RFA
KING William H. MM Gnr 374 RFA
KING William Henry "MM,CG(F)" CSM 7326 10th Hampshire Regt
KING William T. MM Pte 633311 20th London Regt
KING William T.C. MM Sjt 53531 Durham Light Infantry
KING William Walter MM L/Bdr 291540 RGA
KINGDOM Robert G. MM Gnr 208295 112 Bde RFA
KINGDON John MM Sjt 49756 RFA
KINGE Percy W. MM Sjt 45113 114 Bty 25 Bde RFA
KINGE William F.J. MM CSM 9504 1st Scottish Rifles
KINGHAM Ernest Frank MM Pte 15047 7th Bedfordshire Regt KIA 3.5.17.
KINGHAM Frank MM Cpl 25279 2nd Suffolk Regt
KINGHAM Philip Edward MM Cpl 2563 1/1st Hertfordshire Regt Died 19.5.18.
KINGHAM Sidney MM Sjt 201583 West Riding Regt
KINGHAM Sydney G. MM Sjt 593167 18th London Regt
KINGHAM W. MM Pte 201287 Bedfordshire Regt
KINGHAM William James MM Pte 1747 1/7th Middlesex Regt KIA 16.9.17.
KINGHORN John MM Pte 250489 5/6th Royal Scots
KINGHORN William Niblock MM Cpl 15078 10th Royal Irish Rifles KIA 7.6.17.
KINGSBURY George MM L/Cpl 22998 8th Border Regt DOW 3.5.18.
KINGSBURY Thomas MM L/Cpl B/1349 Rifle Brigade
KINGSBURY Wilson F. MM Cpl 309150 14th Bn Tank Corps
KINGSCOMBE Alfred MM L/Cpl 10913 2nd Devonshire Regt
KINGSFORD Walter MM+2 Bars Sjt G/616 6th East Kent Regt KIA 13.8.17.
KINGSHOTT Edmund G. MM Gnr 212917 D/48 Bde RFA
KINGSLAND Edgar T. MM Bdr 20734 111 Heavy Bty RGA
KINGSLEY Charles W. MM Sjt 35677 42 Bde RFA
KINGSLEY Frederick MM Pte 953 2nd Dragoons
KINGSLEY Frederick L. MM L/Cpl 4821 4th Middlesex Regt
KINGSLEY H. MM Spr 426038 Royal Engineers
KINGSMAN Sidney H. MM+Bar Cpl 7883 1st Bedfordshire Regt
KINGSMILL Sidney MM Pnr 255251 6 Div Sig Coy Royal Engineers
KINGSNORTH George S. MM Sjt 47320 RAMC
KINGSNORTH Harry MM Gnr 41573 1/1(North Midland)Bde RGA DOW 18.6.17.
KINGSNORTH S.H. MM L/Cpl 65067 Royal Fusiliers
KINGSNORTH William F. MM Cpl 376702 Labour Corps
KINGSTON A.R. MM Sjt 650389 21st London Regt
KINGSTON C. MM Pte 419378 RAMC
KINGSTON Joseph A. MM Sjt 281472 4th London Regt
KINGSTON Lloyd MM Pte 19188 Durham Light Infantry
KINGSTON Nigel F. MM Sjt 832001 C/306 Bde RFA
KINGSTON Oscar G. MM L/Cpl 11499 8th Gloucestershire Regt
KINGSTON Thomas MM L/Cpl 10471 2nd Worcestershire Regt
KINGSTON Tom MM Cpl 99601 151 Heavy Bty RGA
KINGSTON William MM Spr 548323 510 Fd Coy Royal Engineers
KINGSTON William A. MM Gnr 73880 11 Bde RFA
KINGSWELL Alfred H. MM Sjt 850668 215 Bde RFA
KINGTON W. "DCM,MM" Pte 13540 Essex Regt
KINGWELL Reginald J. MM Pte 241004 Devonshire Regt
KINLEY James "MM,MID" Sjt 440049 Royal Engineers
KINLEY Samuel MM Dvr L/1370 25 Div Ammn Col RFA
KINLEY William MM+Bar L/Cpl 20424 18 Fd Amb RAMC
KINLOCH Joseph L. MM Pte 41974 1/5th King's Own Scottish Borderers
KINLOCH Robert B. MM Pte 316442 1 Fd Amb RAMC
KINMAN William Norman MM+Bar Sjt 614376 1/1st(Warwickshire)Bty RHA
KINMOND James MM Cpl S/13129 2nd Gordon Highlanders
KINMOND N.D. "MM,MID" Pte 1565 RAMC
KINNAIRD James MM Pte M2/073154 Army Service Corps att 46 Fd Amb RAMC
KINNEAR Harry MM+Bar Pte M/331557 62 Div MT Coy Army Service Corps

KINNEAR Hugh MM L/Cpl 7541 Royal Irish Regt
KINNEAR James MM L/Cpl 43038 1/6th Highland Light Infantry
KINNEAR John MM Pte 479 1st Royal Highlanders
KINNEAR William MM Sjt 344010 RGA
KINNES William MM Dvr 120759 251 Bde RFA
KINNINMONTH David MM Sjt 344316 RGA
KINNIS Jack MM+Bar Cpl 75215 2nd Bn Tank Corps KIA 1.8.18.
KINNISON Robert MM Cpl 201545 Seaforth Highlanders
KINNLY J. MM Pte 15468 1st Scots Guards
KINSELLA Edward MM Sjt 36570 RFA
KINSELLA Hugh "DCM,MM+Bar,CG(F)" Sjt 303279 1/8th Arg & Suth Highlanders KIA 21.7.18.
KINSELLA J. MM Pte 350149 Manchester Regt
KINSELLA James MM Sjt 9891 1st Royal Dublin Fusiliers
KINSELLA Michael MM L/Cpl 45908 Machine Gun Corps
KINSEY Arthur MM Pte M2/187229 44 Mot Amb Convoy Army Service Corps
KINSEY Stanley F. MM Sjt 65822 7 Bde RHA
KINSLEY Harry MM Pte 300301 4th Liverpool Regt
KINSMAN Joseph H. MM L/Cpl 59616 7th West Yorkshire Regt
KINSMAN Thomas MM L/Cpl 277163 1/7th Arg & Suth Highlanders
KINSON George MM Pnr 360061 21 Div Sig Coy Royal Engineers
KIRBY Albert MM Pte Y/413 2nd King's Royal Rifle Corps
KIRBY Alfred MM Pte S/28079 Rifle Brigade
KIRBY Archibald MM Sjt 83678 RFA
KIRBY Arthur E. MM Sjt 1259 7th Dragoon Guards
KIRBY Arthur H.A. MM Pte 3/5079 1st East Yorkshire Regt
KIRBY Arthur W. MM Cpl 250836 3rd London Regt
KIRBY Charles Alfred MM Pte 36754 8th East Surrey Regt
KIRBY Colonel Charles Bernard MM Cpl 6385 RAMC att 1st Cheshire Regt.
KIRBY Edward Joseph MM Sjt 2578 8th Royal West Kent Regt
KIRBY Ernest A. "DCM,MM" Gnr L/29599 D/242 Bde RFA
KIRBY Fred MM Sjt 240067 Yorkshire Light Infantry
KIRBY Frederick MM Sjt L/44846 B/187 Bde RFA
KIRBY Frederick D. MM Pte 151 23rd Royal Fusiliers
KIRBY Frederick W. MM Spr 154970 23 Fd Coy Royal Engineers
KIRBY George MM Pte 33879 1st Middlesex Regt
KIRBY George Lawrenson MM Spr 241453 490 Fd Coy Royal Engineers
KIRBY George Leonard MM Pte 23087 10th Durham Light Infantry
KIRBY George T. MM Sjt 9154 2nd Scottish Rifles
KIRBY George W. MM Pte 49809 2nd West Riding Regt
KIRBY Harold MM Dvr T4/251759 Army Service Corps
KIRBY Herbert G. "DCM,MM" Sjt 325546 1/1st Cambridgeshire Regt
KIRBY Herbert J. MM Gnr 174454 321 Siege Bty RGA
KIRBY Isaac C. MM Pte 36007 Northumberland Fusiliers
KIRBY James MM Pte 21652 2nd East Lancashire Regt Died 26.4.19.
KIRBY John R. MM Gnr 218774 RFA
KIRBY John T.F. MM Pte 20894 Gloucestershire Regt
KIRBY Joshua Harry MM Sjt 22815 Machine Gun Corps
KIRBY Lawrence "MM,MID" SQMS 6954 5th Lancers
KIRBY Luke "MM,CG(F)" CSM 15670 2nd Royal Inniskilling Fusiliers
KIRBY Martin Henry MM Pte 325595 1/1st Cambridgeshire Regt Died 19.11.18.
KIRBY Oliver MM L/Cpl 197918 Royal Engineers
KIRBY Oswald H. MM CSM 40811 2nd Bedfordshire Regt
KIRBY Richard MM Dvr 114482 RFA
KIRBY Robert Gladstone MM Sjt 9517 2nd Bedfordshire Regt KIA 26.7.17.
KIRBY Stephen B. MM L/Cpl 22180 Oxf & Bucks Light Infantry
KIRBY Thomas MM Gnr 74681 147 Heavy Bty RGA
KIRBY Thomas Henry MM Bdr 676 C/119 Bde RFA KIA 5.8.17.
KIRBY Thomas R. MM Pte 20/386 Durham Light Infantry
KIRBY Tom MM Pte 12908 8th Yorkshire Light Infantry
KIRBY W. MM Pte 403134 2(West Riding)Fd Amb RAMC
KIRBY Walter E. MM L/Cpl 70591 1/1st Berkshire Yeomanry
KIRBY William E. MM L/Cpl 9248 2nd Devonshire Regt
KIRBY William G. MM Sjt 771607 A/251 Bde RFA
KIRBY William H. MM Cpl 306568 8th Royal Warwickshire Regt
KIRBY William J. MM+Bar Gnr 155007 355 Siege Bty RGA
KIRBY or KIRKBY Frank MM Spr 46182 Royal Engineers
KIRBYSON David MM Pte 38191 RAMC
KIRCHIN Albert Arthur MM Pte 9/15003 9th Leicestershire Regt DOW 27.9.16.
KIRK Arnold V. MM Gnr 296070 RGA
KIRK Charles MM Pte 235814 Lancashire Fusiliers
KIRK Charles A. MM Pte 200788 4th Leicestershire Regt
KIRK Denys MM Pte 44709 Manchester Regt

KIRK Douglas S MM+Bar Pte 268926 13th Liverpool Regt
KIRK Edmund W. MM Pte 18/531 18th Durham Light Infantry
KIRK Frederick MM Pte S/4417 13th Rifle Brigade
KIRK George MM Pte S/8795 Royal Highlanders
KIRK George A. MM Sjt 20/423 20th Northumberland Fusiliers
KIRK Harold MM Pte 265637 7th West Yorkshire Regt
KIRK Harold MM L/Cpl 6473 11th Northumberland Fusiliers KIA 27.5.18.
KIRK Harry "MM+Bar,MSM" CSM 201208 2/4th South Lancashire Regt
KIRK Henry MM Pte 16387 Middlesex Regt
KIRK J. MM Spr 93818 Royal Engineers
KIRK James MM Sjt 17280 Machine Gun Corps
KIRK James MM Pte 25776 Scottish Rifles
KIRK James H. MM Bdr 71460 49 Bty 40 Bde RFA
KIRK James H. "MM,MID" L/Cpl 15065 9th Leicestershire Regt
KIRK John MM Pte S/12990 2nd Gordon Highlanders
KIRK John MM Bdr 776421 RFA
KIRK John Henry MM Pte 6149 1st Leicestershire Regt KIA 21.7.18.
KIRK Lawrence MM L/Cpl 3000 1/7th West Yorkshire Regt DOW 21.7.16.
KIRK Leonard MM Sjt 72951 15th Notts & Derby Regt
KIRK Leonard F. MM CQMS 292862 7th Royal Highlanders
KIRK Lewis "MM,MSM" Sjt 69080 35 Div Sig Coy Royal Engineers
KIRK Nelson MM Pte 15310 2nd Lincolnshire Regt
KIRK Robert MM Pte 5346 Northumberland Fusiliers
KIRK Robert S. MM L/Cpl 15273 Leicestershire Regt
KIRK Sidney MM Pte 459 Lincolnshire Regt
KIRK Stanley R. MM L/Bdr 925784 B/290 Bde RFA
KIRK Thomas Stanley MM Cpl 290684 RGA
KIRK Walter MM L/Cpl 21054 2nd Notts & Derby Regt KIA 23.3.18.
KIRK Walter MM Cpl 21418 10th Duke of Cornwall's LI Died 9.6.18.
KIRK Walter MM Sjt 24119 9th Lancashire Fusiliers
KIRK William MM Gnr 184377 RFA
KIRK William H. MM Cpl 43287 15th Durham Light Infantry
KIRKBRIDE Benjamin E. MM Gnr 707152 B/331 Bde RFA
KIRKBRIDE Robert G. MM Pte 7320 Royal West Kent Regt
KIRKBY Alfred MM Pte 305301 9th Notts & Derby Regt
KIRKBY Ernest MM Sjt 200023 Lancashire Fusiliers
KIRKBY John T. MM L/Cpl 200968 1/4th East Yorkshire Regt
KIRKBY Richard MM RSM 240026 1/5th Royal Lancaster Regt
KIRKBY Stephen MM Pte 24762 West Riding Regt
KIRKBY Thomas MM Pte 243107 6th Royal Lancaster Regt
KIRKE Roy William "MC,MM(12392 Cpl 1st Bn),CG(F)" 2Lt 2nd Royal Fusiliers
KIRKHAM Adam D. MM Cpl 58180 RAMC
KIRKHAM Alfred MM Dvr 521658 Royal Engineers
KIRKHAM Bernard MM Sjt 241656 5th Yorkshire Light Infantry
KIRKHAM E.R. MM L/Cpl 50853 7 Fd Coy Royal Engineers
KIRKHAM John MM Pte 9549 2/5th Lancashire Fusiliers
KIRKHAM John R. MM Dvr 771885 63 Div Ammn Col RFA
KIRKHAM Joseph MM Pte 25232 25th Liverpool Regt
KIRKHAM Joseph MM Pte 2415 1/4th Royal Lancaster Regt
KIRKHAM Leo MM Cpl 352158 1/2(East Lancashire)Fd Amb RAMC
KIRKHAM Robert MM L/Cpl 14828 2nd Scots Guards
KIRKHAM Samuel MM L/Cpl 25779 8th Cheshire Regt Died 19.7.16.
KIRKHAM Stanley MM L/Cpl 142674 35 Div Sig Coy Royal Engineers
KIRKHAM Wilbraham MM Pte 6327 2nd Shropshire Light Infantry
KIRKLAND Charles H. MM Pte 24777 Yorkshire Light Infantry
KIRKLAND Clarence MM+Bar Sjt 16980 11th Notts & Derby Regt
KIRKLAND Frank MM Pte 36229 7th Leicestershire Regt
KIRKLAND Harold MM Cpl 62229 9th Royal Fusiliers
KIRKLAND Richard MM Pte 16472 5th Northamptonshire Regt
KIRKLAND Robert "DCM,MM" Sjt 275277 1/7th Arg & Suth Highlanders
KIRKLAND Thomas MM Pte 50947 Liverpool Regt
KIRKLAND William MM CSM 15834 Labour Corps
KIRKLEY Ralph MM Sjt 17227 8th East Lancashire Regt
KIRKMAN George MM L/Cpl 8569 Machine Gun Corps
KIRKMAN James MM Pte 29867 7th South Lancashire Regt KIA 25.9.17.
KIRKMAN John "DCM,MM,MM(F)" Cpl 24308 8th Royal Lancaster Regt
KIRKMAN Joseph Henry MM Spr 46206 21 Div Sig Coy Royal Engineers DOW 29.3.18.
KIRKMAN Percy D. MM Cpl 300264 1/1st Staffordshire Yeomanry
KIRKMAN Thomas MM Pnr 443929 42 Div Sig Coy Royal Engineers
KIRKMAN W. MM Sjt 305445 Liverpool Regt

KIRKMAN William MM L/Cpl 14830 South Lancashire Regt
KIRKMAN William "DCM,MM" L/Cpl 20376 9th Welsh Regt
KIRKPATRICK Alexander MM Pte 24938 6th King's Own Scottish Borderers
KIRKPATRICK Arthur J. MM Sjt 315263 13th Royal Highlanders
KIRKPATRICK Charles MM Pte 31088 Cameron Highlanders
KIRKPATRICK Frank MM Gnr 6559 121 Bty 27 Bde RFA
KIRKPATRICK James MM Pte 17838 6th Royal West Kent Regt
KIRKPATRICK James MM Cpl 1611 12th Royal Irish Rifles
KIRKPATRICK Robert MM Pte 7128 16th Manchester Regt
KIRKUM Henry J. MM Pte 6535 9th East Surrey Regt
KIRKUM James MM Sjt 49789 B/190 Bde RFA
KIRKUP George Robson MM+Bar Sjt 12133 RFA
KIRKUP James MM Pte 20/44 Durham Light Infantry
KIRKUP John MM Cpl 21908 13th Durham Light Infantry KIA 5.10.18.
KIRKUP Joseph MM Pte 13722 9th Yorkshire Regt
KIRKUP Samuel T. MM Sjt 270224 1/1st Northumberland Yeo
KIRKWOOD Alexander MM Sjt 137945 192 Siege Bty RGA
KIRKWOOD John MM L/Cpl 4941 Royal Highlanders
KIRKWOOD Robert MM Cpl 4/9138 Arg & Suth Highlanders
KIRKWOOD Stewart MM Pte 43489 1st Scottish Rifles
KIRKWOOD Thomas MM L/Cpl 14242 Machine Gun Corps
KIRKWOOD William MM Pte 42550 Machine Gun Corps
KIRKWOOD William MM Pte 56426 5/6th Scottish Rifles
KIRKWOOD William MM Cpl 33975 Machine Gun Corps
KIRLEY William H. MM Sjt 11992 2nd Worcestershire Regt
KIRRAGE Frederick George MM Pte G/11729 11th Royal West Kent Regt
KIRSOPP Albert MM Pte 4786 7th Seaforth Highlanders
KIRTON Alexander MM Gnr 630257 A/255 RFA
KIRTON Alfred Hall MM Gnr 630946 A/255 RFA
KIRTON Charles W. MM Cpl 306966 2/4th West Riding Regt
KIRTON John W. MM Pte 30788 12th Cheshire Regt
KIRTON Robert MM Sjt 15618 14th Durham Light Infantry KIA 18.9.16.
KIRTON Thomas MM L/Cpl 41751 1st South Staffordshire Regt
KIRVAN Stanley MM L/Cpl 17918 13th Essex Regt
KIRWAN John MM Pte 21294 1st Royal Dublin Fusiliers
KIRWEN James MM Pte 301332 1/8th Manchester Regt KIA 22.12.17.
KIRWIN Walter MM+Bar Sjt 49892 74 Fd Amb RAMC
KISBY Arthur Hill MM Sjt 35718 35 Coy Machine Gun Corps
KISBY Percy MM Pte 18036 Royal West Kent Regt
KISBY Thomas MM Pte 24980 12th
KISBY W.E. MM Cpl 15353 13th Royal Scots
KITCH Fred MM Sjt 6981 East Surrey Regt
KITCHEMAN Ernest MM 2nd Cpl 27214 85 Motor Airline Sect Royal Engineers
KITCHEN Albert Edward "MM,MSM,MID" Sjt 58003 RAMC
KITCHEN Alfred MM Cpl 3431 1/5th Liverpool Regt KIA 17.9.16.
KITCHEN Alfred R. MM L/Cpl 12653 East Surrey Regt
KITCHEN E. MM CQMS 1323 Royal Warwickshire Regt
KITCHEN Edward MM Pte 142701 49th Bn Machine Gun Corps
KITCHEN Frank MM Cpl 16529 8th West Riding Regt
KITCHEN George MM Pte 7939 1st Lincolnshire Regt
KITCHEN George E. MM Pte 32178 York & Lancaster Regt
KITCHEN John William MM Pte PW/4902 Middlesex Regt
KITCHEN Joseph MM Pte 279392 1/3rd London
KITCHEN Samuel R. MM Sjt 3/3065 1st York & Lancaster Regt
KITCHEN W. MM Pte 37054 South Lancashire Regt
KITCHEN Walter "MM,MdH(F)" Sjt 13534 9th Royal Lancaster Regt
KITCHEN William MM Pte 19426 21st Manchester Regt KIA 11.5.17.
KITCHENER Charles MM Pte M2/103311 Army Service Corps
KITCHENER George MM Pte 14677 5th South Wales Borderers
KITCHENER Herbert MM Spr 49661 96 Fd Coy Royal Engineers DOW 5.10.16.
KITCHER Frederick MM L/Cpl 4976 13th Hussars
KITCHER George MM Cpl 29825 Wiltshire Regt
KITCHER Roland G. MM Dvr 80735 RFA
KITCHING Charles H. MM Pte 12/650 11th East Yorkshire Regt
KITCHING Edward MM Cpl 6773 1st East Yorkshire Regt
KITCHING Edwin Victor MM Sjt 308552 1/5(Lancashire)Heavy Nty RGA Died 18.10.18.
KITCHING Harry MM Pte 200538 9th Durham Light Infantry
KITCHING Herbert MM L/Cpl 47468 4th Yorkshire Light Infantry
KITCHINGMAN Leonard Charles MM L/Cpl 8947 1st East Kent Regt
KITE John Frederick MM Sjt 16251 B/79 Bde RFA
KITE Joseph MM Bdr 630816 255 Bde RFA
KITE Thomas G. MM Pte B/200573 1st Rifle Brigade
KITE William R. MM Pte 270458 East Kent Regt
KITEBY William MM Pte 27809 Bedfordshire Regt
KITHER Harold George MM+Bar Cpl 252834 3rd London Regt KIA 28.8.18.
KITLEY Reginald Arthur "MM,MID" Pte 21260 Wiltshire Regt
KITLEY Thomas MM Pte 204610 Hampshire Regt
KITNEY Ralph Norman MM+Bar Sjt 540073 497 Fd Coy Royal Engineers
KITSON Frank MM Pte 93675 5th Notts & Derby Regt
KITSON George MM Pte 49847 12th Royal Scots Fusiliers
KITSON Herbert E. MM+Bar Spr 504768 18 Div Sig Coy Royal Engineers
KITSON James H. MM L/Cpl 325221 1/1st Cambridgeshire Regt
KITSON John Edward MM Gnr 31331 X/9 Med TM Bty RFA
KITSON Thomas R. MM L/Cpl 200703 West Yorkshire Regt
KITSON Walter Charlie MM L/Cpl 107322 231 Fd Coy Royal Engineers
KITT Edgar C. MM Pte 42100 1st Devonshire Regt
KITT Francis J. MM Gnr 50474 RGA
KITTLE Ernest E. MM L/Cpl 20287 Middlesex Regt
KITTLE John P. MM L/Cpl 43577 Northamptonshire Regt
KITTOW William J. MM Pte 23727 Devonshire Regt
KITTS Frederick MM Pte 17106 7th Wiltshire Regt
KIVELL Henry MM Pte 14494 1/6th Cheshire Regt KIA 15.9.18.
KLEIN William T. MM Cpl 24797 10th Royal Warwickshire Regt
KLIPPSTEIN C.E. MM Spr 103672 Royal Engineers
KNAGGS Frederick "DCM,MM" L/Cpl 18275 2nd Royal Scots Fusiliers DOW 12.4.18.
KNAGGS H. MM Sjt 401327 RAMC
KNAGGS Joseph MM Pte 28041 Royal Lancaster Regt
KNAGGS Robert W. MM Cpl 16117 9th Royal Irish Fusiliers
KNAGGS William R. MM Sjt 101171 RAMC
KNAPMAN Maurice W. MM Cpl 200479 1/7th Middlesex Regt
KNAPP Albert "DCM,MM(194 Coy)" Sjt 36494 23rd Bn Machine Gun Corps
KNAPP Frederick MM Pte 37147 RAMC
KNAPP George MM L/Cpl 3894 8th Northumberland Fusiliers
KNAPP Harry MM Gnr 113598 RFA
KNAPP Leonard MM Cpl 50874 C/86 Bde RFA
KNAPPER Harry MM Cpl 23415 46th Bn Machine Gun Corps DOW 6.7.18.
KNAPPETT Arthur E. MM Cpl STK/1427 10th Royal Fusiliers
KNAPPETT Charles Henry MM Sjt G/1480 6th East Kent Regt
KNAPPITT Roland P. MM Gnr 168387 A/77 Bde RFA
KNEALE Charles MM Sjt 12758 9th Royal Welsh Fusiliers
KNEALE George E. "MM,MID" Sjt 18812 12th Liverpool Regt
KNEALE Harold E. MM Pte 18765 12th Liverpool Regt
KNEALE John Henry MM Pte 241992 1/5th East Lancashire Regt
KNEALE William Edward MM Cpl 29825 2/7th Liverpool Regt
KNELL Alfred T. MM Pte 24311 1st Royal West Kent Regt
KNELL Frederick MM Pte 65623 RAMC
KNELLER Frederick C. MM Gnr 68664 90 Siege Bty RGA
KNELLER Peter MM Pte 8447 2nd Hampshire Regt
KNEVETT Alfred MM Cpl 7519 Royal West Kent Regt
KNEVITT C. MM AM 1st Class 105647 Royal Air Force
KNIBB William Benjamin MM L/Cpl 2017 1/8th London Regt
KNIBB William Thomas MM Pte 32550 11th Royal Warwickshire Regt
KNIBBS Albert E. MM Sjt 28184 1 Cav Div Sig Sqn Royal Engineers
KNIBBS Walter MM Sjt 61327 RFA
KNIGHT Albert MM Pte 24529 Royal Berkshire Regt
KNIGHT Albert E.J. "DCM,MM" Sjt 374413 163 Siege Bty RGA
KNIGHT Albert Edward MM Pte 11792 1st East Kent Regt KIA 2.8.18.
KNIGHT Albert H. MM Pte 51077 9 Sqn Machine Gun Corps(Cavalry)
KNIGHT Albert S. MM L/Cpl 9127 8th East Kent Regt KIA 4.8.17.
KNIGHT Alex MM Cpl 635137 RFA
KNIGHT Alexander MM Cpl 1396 Royal Engineers
KNIGHT Alexander MM Pte 353112 7th London Regt KIA 25.7.18.
KNIGHT Alexander MM L/Cpl 24902 4th South Wales Borderers
KNIGHT Alfred MM Pte 16982 2nd Bedfordshire Regt
KNIGHT Alfred MM L/Cpl 77892 10th Royal Fusiliers
KNIGHT Alfred C. MM Cpl 8835 2nd Royal Sussex Regt
KNIGHT Algernon P. MM Pte 11682 RAMC
KNIGHT Archibald MM Pte 20167 5th Dragoon Guards
KNIGHT Archibald J. MM Pte 74013 RAMC
KNIGHT Arthur MM Pte 22073 Gloucestershire Regt

KNIGHT Arthur MM Bdr 27670 RGA
KNIGHT Bertram MM Cpl G/23668 2nd Royal West Kent Regt
KNIGHT Cecil MM Sjt 145222 1/1st Northamptonshire Yeomanry
KNIGHT Cecil Murless "MM,MID" Sjt 21605 RFA
KNIGHT Charles MM Sjt 114200 16 Div Ammn Col RFA
KNIGHT Charles MM Sjt L/33408 B/175 Bde RFA
KNIGHT Charles F. MM Spr 95352 Royal Engineers
KNIGHT Charles James MM Sjt G/2319 6th East Kent Regt Died 2.12.17.
KNIGHT Charles John MM Sjt 30582 2nd Yorkshire Regt
KNIGHT Christopher J. MM Bdr 88195 RHA
KNIGHT Edgar L. MM Pte 16007 9th South Staffordshire Regt
KNIGHT Edward MM L/Sjt 15592 3rd Grenadier Guards
KNIGHT Edward M. MM Cpl 2005 1/1st Leicestershire Yeomanry
KNIGHT Edwin Clarence MM Dvr 705150 210 Bde RFA
KNIGHT Edwin E. MM Pte 18887 Machine Gun Corps
KNIGHT Ernest MM Pte R/9891 9th King's Royal Rifle Corps DOW 6.4.18.
KNIGHT Ernest MM Pte 2723 Royal Sussex Regt
KNIGHT Ernest Emmanuel MM Sjt 17541 6th Bedfordshire Regt
KNIGHT F. MM Pte 46828 Royal Welsh Fusiliers
KNIGHT Frank MM L/Cpl 242590 8th Worcestershire Regt
KNIGHT Frank MM Cpl 112138 5 Fd Svy Bn Royal Engineers
KNIGHT Frank N. MM Sjt 92419 2nd Bn Tank Corps
KNIGHT Frank R. MM Pte R/32126 King's Royal Rifle Corps
KNIGHT Fred MM Pte 8679 2nd Hampshire Regt
KNIGHT Frederick MM Cpl 9601 1st Royal West Surrey Regt
KNIGHT Frederick MM+Bar Pte M2/153406 Army Service Corps
KNIGHT Frederick John MM Sjt 19380 8th Suffolk Regt
KNIGHT Frederick R. MM Pte 62690 105 Coy Labour Corps
KNIGHT Frederick T. MM Bdr 50618 RGA
KNIGHT George MM L/Bdr 10143 2 Div Ammn Col RFA
KNIGHT George MM Pte 201283 Bedfordshire Regt
KNIGHT George MM Sjt 96830 Tunnelling Coy Royal Engineers
KNIGHT George MM+Bar Pte 7500 1st West Yorkshire Regt
KNIGHT George MM Dvr 19549 A/79 Bde RFA
KNIGHT George A.W. MM Pte 16533 1 Special Coy Middlesex Regt
KNIGHT George Edward MM Sjt M1/07599 5 Motor Ambulance Convoy Army Service Corps
KNIGHT George Edward MM Gnr 70650 D/286 Bde RFA DOW 9.4.18.
KNIGHT George H. MM Pte 3609 10th Hussars
KNIGHT George R. MM L/Cpl 36481 Royal Welsh Fusiliers
KNIGHT George William MM Pte 11790 1st King's Royal Rifle Corps KIA 27.7.16.
KNIGHT George William MM L/Cpl 205064 1st Royal West Surrey Regt KIA 21.9.18.
KNIGHT H. MM Gnr 1037 RGA
KNIGHT Harold MM L/Cpl 137 2(West Riding)Fd Amb RAMC
KNIGHT Harold Henry "MC,MM(10803 Cpl R Sussex)" 2Lt 5th Bedf
KNIGHT Harry MM L/Cpl 9465 19th Hussars
KNIGHT Henry MM 2nd Cpl 57165 Signal Service Royal Engineers
KNIGHT Henry C. MM Pte 15250 2nd Royal Fusiliers
KNIGHT Henry F. MM Cpl 245482 18 Div Sig Coy Royal Engineers
KNIGHT Henry L. MM Cpl 71177 RGA
KNIGHT Henry T. MM L/Cpl 3066 1/19th London Regt
KNIGHT Horace A.T. MM Sjt 41822 1/1st Cambridgeshire Regt
KNIGHT Horace G. MM Gnr 146655 RFA
KNIGHT James MM Pte 29465 2nd West Riding Regt DOW 13.10.17.
KNIGHT James MM Sjt 14645 13th East Surrey Regt
KNIGHT James MM Pte PW/2920 18th Middlesex Regt
KNIGHT John "MC,MM(19804 Sjt)" T/2Lt 41st Bn Machine Gun Corps
KNIGHT John MM Gnr 13147 A/232 Bde RFA
KNIGHT John Taylor MM Cpl 106227 Royal Engineers
KNIGHT John Thomas MM Sjt 3885 Machine Gun Corps
KNIGHT Joseph MM Gnr 79563 211 Siege Bty RGA
KNIGHT Joseph T. MM Cpl 500206 Royal Engineers
KNIGHT Metford Tom MM L/Cpl 2605 1/4th Gloucestershire Regt
KNIGHT Moses MM Pte 58509 RAMC
KNIGHT Norman George MM+Bar Cpl 531510 15th London Regt KIA 2.9.18.
KNIGHT Percy J. MM Pte M2/177869 Army Service Corps
KNIGHT Reginald W. MM Pte 3552 3rd Rifle Brigade
KNIGHT Richard MM L/Cpl 2947 13th Royal Sussex Regt
KNIGHT Robert MM Cpl 70924 111 Bty 24 Bde RFA
KNIGHT Robert M. MM Cpl 43743 16th London Regt
KNIGHT Roger MM Pte 17258 7th York & Lancaster Regt
KNIGHT Samuel MM L/Cpl 8055 2nd Worcestershire Regt
KNIGHT Stanley J. MM Pte 240869 1/5th Devonshire Regt
KNIGHT T.F. MM Pte 43570 Essex Regt
KNIGHT Thomas F.W. MM Pte 41439 12th Royal Irish Rifles
KNIGHT Thomas Trower MM Gnr 39869 83 Siege Bty RGA
KNIGHT Tom MM L/Cpl 87588 2nd Bn Machine Gun Corps
KNIGHT W. MM Air Mech 2 25674 Royal Flying Corps
KNIGHT William MM Spr 431 Royal Engineers
KNIGHT William MM L/Cpl 123458 Machine Gun Corps
KNIGHT William MM Pte 241907 Essex
KNIGHT William MM Cpl 17347 15th Hampshire Regt DOW 3.7.16.
KNIGHT William MM L/Cpl 22188 Machine Gun Corps
KNIGHT William E. MM Cpl PS/1905 16th Middlesex Regt
KNIGHT William Edward MM Pte 235382 9th York & Lancaster Regt Sentenced to death (commuted) for desertion Oct 1917.
KNIGHT William Henry MM Bdsm 8545 1st Leicestershire Regt
KNIGHTON Frederick MM Spr 99398 Royal Engineers
KNIGHTON George James MM Abdr 7561 130 Heavy Bty RGA
KNIGHTON Reginald F. MM Cpl 145144 1/1st Northamptonshire Yeomanry
KNIGHTON W.H. MM Spr 79838 176 Tunneling Coy Royal Engineers
KNIGHTON William MM Pte 2647 Lancashire Fusiliers
KNIGHTS Alfred Ernest "MC,MM(17122 Pte)" 2Lt Norfolk Regt
KNIGHTS Arthur MM Sjt 21657 RFA
KNIGHTS Daniel C. MM Sjt 23634 11th Suffolk Regt
KNIGHTS Herbert MM Bdr 70587 RGA
KNIGHTS Percy J. MM Pnr 30824 Royal Engineers
KNIGHTS Robert Edward Vallis MM Sjt 26 1/13th London Regt
KNIGHTS Thomas William George MM Pte 87766 11th Liverpool Regt
KNIGHTS Walter MM Pte 19387 7th Norfolk Regt KIA 14.10.17.
KNIGHTS Wilfred Henry Ethelbert MM L/Cpl 16776 Machine Gun Corps
KNILL Charles Henry MM Pte 266193 2nd Devonshire Regt
KNOCK George MM Pte 10618 4th Worcestershire Regt KIA 30.11.17.
KNOCKER Frank R. MM Pte 45626 RAMC
KNOPE Harry E. MM Pte 19491 7th Royal Sussex Regt
KNOPWOOD James MM L/Cpl 17/1721 1st West Yorkshire Regt
KNOTT Arthur J. MM Sjt 32725 35 Div Sig Coy Royal Engineers
KNOTT G.E. MM Pte 533625 London Regt
KNOTT James MM Sjt 19619 36 Bde RFA
KNOTT John "MM,MSM" Sjt 36000 D/11 Bde RFA
KNOTT John MM Pte 19810 1st Border Regt DOW 28.4.17.
KNOTT John H. MM Pte 22887 1st Coldstream Guards
KNOTT John J. MM Pte 1905 1/4th Northumberland Fusiliers
KNOTT John T. MM Pte 12410 2nd Worcestershire Regt
KNOTT John T. MM Pte 17175 2nd Hampshire Regt
KNOTT John Thomas MM L/Cpl 1552 (240175) 1/5th Leicestershire Regt KIA 21.11.17.
KNOTT William MM QMS Eng Clk 3039 Railways Section Royal Engineers
KNOWLER Arthur MM Sjt 9600 2nd Royal West Surrey Regt
KNOWLER Herbert Joseph MM 2nd Cpl 94173 3 Div Sig Coy Royal Engineers
KNOWLES Albert MM Pte 40622 21st Manchester Regt
KNOWLES Alfred MM Pte 14617 Worcestershire Regt
KNOWLES Alfred MM Pte 200085 1/5th Notts & Derby Regt DOW 21.9.18.
KNOWLES Alfred MM Cpl 482291 Royal Engineers
KNOWLES Alfred MM+Bar Sjt 21531 12th Manchester Regt
KNOWLES Alfred Edward MM Pnr 30893 4 Div Sig Coy Royal Engineers
KNOWLES Arthur MM L/Cpl 16205 39th Bn Machine Gun Corps
KNOWLES Arthur MM L/Cpl 13/1324 13th York & Lancaster Regt
KNOWLES Arthur MM Pte 241486 Notts & Derby Regt
KNOWLES Arthur F. MM Pte 201727 Royal Lancaster Regt
KNOWLES Arthur Robert MM Pte 473375 53 Labour Coy Labour Corps
KNOWLES Benjamin "MC,MM(389 Sjt KEH),MID,MB" Capt RAMC
KNOWLES Charles MM Sjt 34480 Yorkshire Light Infantry
KNOWLES Clarence MM Cpl 780248 B/246 Bde RFA
KNOWLES Edmund H. MM L/Cpl 552412 Royal Engineers
KNOWLES Emerson MM Pte M/304095 Army Service Corps
KNOWLES Ernest MM L/Cpl 482297 62 Div Sig Coy Royal Engineers
KNOWLES F.J. MM Air Mech 2 403944 Royal Flying Corps
KNOWLES Frank MM Pte 10486 14 Fd Amb RAMC
KNOWLES Fred MM L/Cpl 9566 1st Northamptonshire Regt
KNOWLES Frederick J.A. MM Sjt S/1118 2nd Royal Sussex Regt

KNOWLES Frederick William MM Gnr 93988 C/62 Bde RFA
KNOWLES Harry T. MM Pte 46438 17th Lancashire Fusiliers
KNOWLES Henry MM Cpl 2453 VIII Corps Cyclist Bn Army Cyclist Corps
KNOWLES Herbert R. MM Sjt 52176 12 Bde RFA
KNOWLES J. "MM,CG" L/Cpl 19343 10th Essex Regt
KNOWLES John MM Sjt 63076 RGA
KNOWLES John MM L/Cpl 11101 Royal Warwickshire Regt
KNOWLES John D. MM Pte 50502 16 Fd Amb RAMC
KNOWLES John Thomas MM L/Sjt 12139 1st East Lancashire Regt DOW 17.11.18.
KNOWLES Joseph MM Sjt 4901 2nd Notts & Derby Regt KIA 16.9.16.
KNOWLES Joseph MM Cpl 352570 Royal Scots
KNOWLES Leonard Alfred MM L/Cpl R/13622 13th King's Royal Rifle Corps KIA 4.11.18.
KNOWLES Percy MM L/Cpl 240935 Notts & Derby Regt
KNOWLES Reginald J. MM Pte 6687 East Surrey Regt
KNOWLES Richard MM Pte 3697 South Lancashire Regt
KNOWLES Robert MM Sjt 200895 1/4th North Lancashire Regt KIA 9.4.18.
KNOWLES Robert N. MM Sjt 17277 17 Fd Amb RAMC
KNOWLES Thomas MM Sjt 201783 West Riding Regt
KNOWLES Thomas MM L/Sjt 14040 2nd Scots Guards
KNOWLES Thomas MM Cpl 31428 2nd York & Lancaster Regt KIA 3.5.18.
KNOWLES Thomas W. MM L/Cpl 26920 8th East Surrey Regt
KNOWLES William MM Sjt 14505 2nd Grenadier Guards
KNOWLES William A. MM Sjt 307591 11th Tank Corps
KNOWLES William E. MM L/Cpl 315269 1/1st Westmorland & Cumberland Yeomanry
KNOWLES William H. MM L/Cpl T4/041525 32 Div Train. Army Service Corps
KNOWLES William Henry MM Dvr 950027 RFA
KNOWLSON Arthur MM Dvr 32663 'U' Bty RHA KIA 8.10.18.
KNOX Alexander MM Cpl 41625 5/6th Scottish Rifles
KNOX Alfred MM L/Cpl 315495 13th Royal Highlanders KIA 4.11.18.
KNOX Andrew MM Pte 12252 6/7th Royal Scots Fusiliers
KNOX Andrew MM Sjt 21745 Machine Gun Corps
KNOX David MM Gnr 84304 266 Siege Bty RGA
KNOX Edgar MM Pte 13123 2nd Dragoon Guards
KNOX Ernest MM L/Cpl 101287 Royal Engineers
KNOX Guy MM L/Cpl 15860 2nd Cameron Highlanders
KNOX Isaac MM Pte 4063 Gordon Highlanders
KNOX Lindsay MM Pte 275210 1/7th Arg & Suth Highlanders
KNOX R. MM Pte 1645 West Riding Regt
KNOX Robert MM Pte 11175 6th Leicestershire Regt KIA 17.7.16.
KNOX Robert MM L/Cpl 13412 9th Royal Lancaster Regt
KNOX Thomas MM Sjt 778 1st Northumberland Fusiliers att 9 Coy MGC
KNOX Walter Ernest MM L/Cpl 3750 16th London Regt
KNOX Walter Etheridge MM Pte 7955 Arg & Suth Highlanders
KNOX William Gordon MM L/Cpl 26303 9th Royal Inniskilling Fusiliers DOW 24.10.18.
KNOX William Robert MM Sjt 79870 Machine Gun Corps
KNUCKEY Reuben L. MM Pte 252975 3rd London Regt
KNUCKEY W.T. MM Sjt 27113 Duke of Cornwall's LI
KOHLER L.J. MM Pte 9064 1/8th Arg & Suth Highlanders
KOHLER Wolfe MM L/Cpl 74831 6th Durham Light Infantry
KOLLER Charles Frederick "MM,MSM" Sjt M2/078931 Army Service Corps
KOOL Cornelius MM L/Cpl 228463 1st London
KORDIK O. MM Air Mech 1 8875 Royal Air Force
KRAFT John Henry MM Cpl L/43525 Z/41 Med TM Bty RFA
KRAMER Frederick MM Dvr 947895 280 Bde RFA
KRAMER Gerald MM Cpl 2417 1/8th London
KRAMER Montague MM Pte 391176 16th London Regt
KREKEMYER William MM L/Cpl 90257 Royal Engineers
KREMER Isidore MM Pte 43194 1st Leicestershire Regt
KREMER Walter Ernest William MM Sjt 52977 D/59 Bde RFA
KROGH Henry C. MM L/Cpl 1377 King Edward's Horse
KRONENBERG Nathan MM Pte 1920 1/6th Welsh Regt
KRUSE Arthur William MM Cpl 98543 Machine Gun Corps
KUHLER Robert MM Gnr 119767 351 Siege Bty RGA DOW 16.10.17.
KUHN George C. MM Pte G/61200 24th Royal Fusiliers
KUHN John Hendrich MM Pte 22373 1st North Lancashire Regt
KUNZ Frederick H.C. MM Pte 41254 Suffolk Regt
KURTON Charles MM Pte 3/9102 1st Royal Berkshire Regt
KURTSHNER John MM Cpl 20436 Machine Gun Corps

KYLE James MM Dvr 59763 RFA
KYLE Robert MM L/Cpl 15/11996 15th Royal Irish Rifles
KYLES Alexander MM Pte 351524 9th Royal Scots
KYLES Henry MM Pte 16/1395 16th Northumberland Fusiliers
KYNASTON Alfred E. MM Cpl 10984 5th Shropshire Light Infantry
KYNASTON Edward MM Cpl 12214 Shropshire Light Infantry
KYNASTON Thomas Victor MM 2nd Cpl 663 518 Fd Coy Royal Engineers
KYNMAN Harold MM L/Cpl 242344 1/5th Yorkshire Light Infantry KIA 23.7.17.
KYNNERSLEY Frederick J. MM Sjt 49529 Liverpool Regt
KYNNERSLEY William J. MM Sjt 306436 7th Royal Warwickshire Regt
KYNOCK James MM Pte 3/1340 2nd Yorkshire Light Infantry
KYTE Herbert Charles MM Cpl 27394 92 Coy Machine Gun Corps
KYTE Jack MM Pte 7426 2nd Wiltshire Regt
KYTE Sidney H. MM Pte M2/182177 Army Service Corps
KYTE William MM Pte Y/250 2nd King's Royal Rifle Corps

L

LA HAYE George MM Cpl 201768 'G'(AA)Bty RGA
LA NAUZE Brazil W. MM Cpl 198926 Royal Engineers
LA ROCHE Frederick MM Pte 41528 9th Norfolk Regt
LABBETT Henry MM L/Cpl 15251 Leicestershire Regt
LABDON Charlie Alfred Richardson MM Gnr 34427 123 Heavy Bty RGA att 2 Fd Coy RE.DOW 15.2.17.
LABRAM Albert E. MM Pte 40561 Suffolk Regt
LACE Albert "DCM,MM" Cpl G/148 3rd Royal Fusiliers KIA 4.11.18.
LACE Charles MM Pte 3/6289 2nd Seaforth Highlanders
LACEY Arthur MM Pte 320 1st East Surrey Regt
LACEY Arthur MM Pte 57789 2nd Worcestershire Regt
LACEY Arthur Wisley George "MM,MID" Sjt 49728 93 Fd Coy Royal Engineers
LACEY Charles MM Pte 85646 13th Liverpool Regt KIA 22.9.18.
LACEY Charles William MM Pte 6488 1st Scots Guards
LACEY Edward MM Pte 270067 2nd Manchester Regt
LACEY Edward H. MM Cpl 21808 Somerset Light Infantry
LACEY F.H. MM L/Cpl 16447 2nd Grenadier Guards
LACEY Frederick MM Pte 24151 13th Liverpool Regt
LACEY James MM Cpl 8872 30th Bn Machine Gun Corps
LACEY James MM+Bar 2nd Cpl 312337 3 Div Sig Coy Royal Engineers
LACEY Joseph MM Pte 9264 1st Leicestershire Regt
LACEY Robert MM Bdr 107176 RFA
LACEY Robert H. MM Gnr 801750 A/256 Bde RFA
LACEY Rostron MM Cpl R/16600 13th King's Royal Rifle Corps DOW 10.1.18.
LACEY Walter MM Sjt 795531 63 Div Ammn Col RFA
LACEY William MM Pte 202697 2/4th Oxf & Bucks Light Infantry
LACEY William Edgar MM Pte 9815 Royal Berkshire Regt
LACEY William H. MM L/Cpl 2159 1/8th Notts & Derby Regt
LACEY William James MM Cpl 52586 'P' Bty RHA
LACK Bert MM Spr 84467 130 Fd Coy Royal Engineers KIA 27.5.18.
LACK Frederick MM Pte 204226 7th Somerset Light Infantry
LACK James MM Pte 3/9734 Northamptonshire Regt
LACK Reginald Walter "MM,MID" Cpl 22938 Royal Engineers KIA 29.9.16.
LACK Thomas MM L/Cpl 71122 3rd Royal Fusiliers
LACKEY James MM L/Cpl 18/533 18th Durham Light Infantry KIA 3.5.17.
LACKEY Thomas "DCM,MM" Pte 7152 2nd Lancashire Fusiliers
LACKFORD R. MM Pte M/371288 Army Service Corps
LACON George F. MM Cpl 3454 Rifle Brigade
LACY P. MM Pte 63049 Notts & Derby Regt
LACY R. "MM,MID" Sjt 22337 280 Army Tps Coy Royal Engineers
LADBROOK W. MM Pte A/3079 King's Royal Rifle Corps
LADD Edward James MM Bdr 95152 87 Bde RFA
LADD Frank MM Cpl 56796 'D' Bty RHA
LADDEN William W. MM Pte M1/6726 93 MT Coy Army Service Corps
LADE Henry J. MM Pte G/7739 8th Royal Sussex Regt
LADE Percy H. MM Pre 40300 Royal Engineers
LADE Thomas John MM Sjt 16162 6th Royal West Kent Regt "KIA 21.9.18."
LADELL Herbert Sizzey MM Gnr 78521 RFA
LADEN Owen MM Pte 59568 8th Northumberland Fusiliers

LADKIN Charles Gilbert MM Sjt T4/127932 106 Coy Army Service Corps
LADYMAN Daniel "MM,MM(F)" Bdr 54112 37 Siege Bty RGA
LAFFAN James MM Pte 12844 8th Yorkshire Light Infantry
LAFFERTY Hume "DCM,MM" Sjt 3245 45 Coy Machine Gun Corps
LAFLAIN George MM Sjt 9558 2nd Royal Scots
LAGDON William MM Bdr 43964 'J' Bty RHA KIA 27.10.16.
LAGER Harry MM Pte 49895 72 Fd Amb RAMC
LAGGETT John B. MM Sjt 524187 Royal Engineers
LAHMERS George MM Pte Z/1736 Rifle Brigade
LAIDLAW James MM Pte 682362 22nd London Regt
LAIDLAW James MM Pte S/16483 6th Cameron Highlanders KIA 24.8.16.
LAIDLAW John David "DCM,MM" Sjt 202004 5/6th Royal Scots
LAIDLAW John R. MM Bdr 650282 211 Bde RFA
LAIDLAW R. "MM,MID" Pte 7467 5th Dragoon Guards
LAIDLAW Reginald MM Spr 48180 Royal Engineers
LAIDLAW Robert MM Pte 3197 Arg & Suth Highlanders
LAIDLAW Thomas MM Pte 69619 17th Royal Fusiliers
LAIDLAW Thomas MM Gnr 128860 263 Siege Bty RGA
LAIDLAW Thomas Douglas MM L/Cpl S/14561 5th Cameron Highlanders
LAIDLAW William MM Cpl S/3092 10th Arg & Suth Highlanders KIA 12.6.17.
LAIDLAW William MM Cpl 23847 King's Own Scottish Borderers
LAIDLAW William MM Pte 13776 1st Scots Guards
LAIDLAW William MM L/Cpl 40757 12th Royal Scots KIA 21.10.18.
LAIDLAW William H. MM Pte 53512 RAMC
LAIDLER James MM Pte 203202 1/4th Northumberland Fusiliers Died 22.3.18.
LAIDLER Sidney James MM Sjt 10816 5th Royal Berkshire Regt
LAIDLER William MM+Bar L/Cpl 34968 9th Yorkshire Light Infantry
LAIDMAN J.O. MM Sjt 240494 1/5th Border Regt
LAINCHBURY William B. MM L/Sjt 2390 Oxf & Bucks Light Infantry
LAING Albert MM Sjt 37150 34 Fd Amb RAMC
LAING Andrew MM Pte M2/149934 Army Service Corps
LAING Bertie MM L/Sjt 275380 1/7th Arg & Suth Highlanders DOW 26.3.18.
LAING David MM Pte 41260 13th Royal Scots DOW 5.3.18.
LAING Edward MM Cpl 113607 GHQ BEF Carrier Pigeon Section Royal Engineers
LAING Frank "MM+Bar,CG(F)" Sjt 290636 1/7th Gordon Highlanders
LAING Fred MM+Bar L/Cpl 6942 Royal West Kent Regt
LAING George MM Cpl 265276 Seaforth Highlanders
LAING George Edgar MM+Bar Cpl 66255 40 Bde RFA
LAING George Morgan MM Pte 888 2 Coy Labour Corps
LAING Hugh MM Cpl 44467 Royal Engineers
LAING John MM L/Sjt 325090 1/8th Royal Scots
LAING Joseph MM Sjt 22/596 22nd Northumberland Fusiliers
LAING McGregor H. MM Dvr 73666 RFA
LAING Robert MM Pte 512358 77 Fd Amb RAMC
LAING Robert MM Pte 17440 6/7th Royal Scots Fusiliers
LAING Robert MM Pte 13431 Scots Guards
LAING Stanley MM L/Cpl 243775 6th Liverpool Regt
LAING Thomas MM Pte 63576 2nd West Yorkshire Regt
LAING W.C.A. MM Sjt 51292 RAMC
LAING William Harry MM Sjt 6346 8th Northumberland Fusiliers
LAING William W. MM L/Cpl 350228 1/9th Royal Scots
LAINSBURY Lawrence W. MM Pte 576251 17th London Regt
LAIRD Albert MM Pte S/10928 1st Rifle Brigade
LAIRD Alexander MM Sjt 9258 Royal Engineers
LAIRD Alexander MM Sjt 56405 25 Div Sig Coy Royal Engineers
LAIRD Alexander MM Pte 20206 153 Coy Machine Gun Corps KIA 30.7.16.
LAIRD Alexander MM L/Cpl 13504 12th Royal Scots
LAIRD Charles Balfour MM Sjt 650059 377 Bty RFA
LAIRD George MM L/Cpl 332619 2nd Highland Light Infantry
LAIRD John MM Pte 204542 1/6th Seaforth Highlanders
LAIRD John MM L/Bdr 109990 312 Siege Bty RGA
LAIRD John MM Sjt 10278 Royal Engineers
LAIRD Malcolm MM Pte 1503 1/7th Arg & Suth Highlanders DOW 17.4.17.
LAIRD Reginald MM Cpl 4912 HAC
LAIRD Robert MM L/Cpl 351065 1/9th Royal Scots
LAIRD Robert John MM L/Cpl 12/292 12th Royal Irish Rifles
LAIRD W. MM Cpl 265683 Gordon Highlanders
LAIRD William MM+Bar Sjt 14695 Royal Inniskilling Fusiliers
LAIRD William MM Sjt S/8330 8th Royal Highlanders
LAIRD Wilson MM 2nd Cpl 418226 21 Div Sig Coy Royal Engineers

LAISHLEY Arthur "DCM,MM" L/Cpl 268306 2/7th Royal Warwickshire Regt
LAISHLEY Frederick MM Sjt 2649 Army Cyclist Corps
LAISTER Alfred MM Cpl 37767 RFA
LAISTER William MM Gnr 246839 C/82 Bde RFA
LAIT Charles J. MM Pte 720537 24th London Regt
LAIT George S. MM Gnr 183489 RFA
LAIT Roland Alec MM Cpl 207057 11th Royal West Surrey Regt
LAITY Edward MM Pte 261178 8th Royal Warwickshire Regt
LAITY William MM Dvr 135523 B/47 Bde RFA
LAKE Albert MM 2nd Cpl 482271 62 Div Sig Coy Royal Engineers
LAKE Alec MM Sjt 290524 4th Middlesex Regt
LAKE Alfred H. MM Pte R/22737 King's Royal Rifle Corps
LAKE Arthur E. MM L/Cpl 154033 5 Fd Coy Royal Engineers
LAKE Arthur Norman MM Spr 85613 207 Fd Coy Royal Engineers KIA 19.1.17.
LAKE Charles David MM Sjt 1394 RFA
LAKE Cyril D. MM Gnr 138922 290 Siege Bty RGA
LAKE Cyril R. MM Pte 37116 Machine Gun Corps
LAKE Edward MM Pte 6850 Northumberland Fusiliers
LAKE Edward W. MM Cpl 76284 4th Bn Tank Corps
LAKE George MM Sjt 59 Northumberland Fusiliers
LAKE George MM Dvr 23428 'F' Bty RHA KIA 28.7.17.
LAKE George MM Pte G/2005 7th East Kent Regt KIA 3.10.16.
LAKE Herbert Henry MM Cpl 405088 3(West Riding)Fd Amb RAMC
LAKE James MM Pte 721744 24th London Regt KIA 18.9.18.
LAKE James MM Cpl 37881 RFA
LAKE John William MM L/Cpl 240217 Lincolnshire Regt
LAKE Percy J. MM Cpl 35202 North Lancashire Regt
LAKE Richard David MM Pte 24137 7th Norfolk Regt
LAKE Robert S. MM Spr 41972 Royal Engineers
LAKE Thomas Edward MM Spr 58265 79 Fd Coy Royal Engineers
LAKE Walter J. MM Pte 20615 Hampshire Regt
LAKE William MM Sjt 10440 5th Oxf & Bucks Light Infantry
LAKE William MM Pte M2/227093 Army Service Corps
LAKE William R. MM Gnr 29783 RFA
LAKELIN Harry "MM,MSM" Sjt 52992 39th Bn Machine Gun Corps
LAKER Edward MM Gnr Sig 245545 73 Bty 5 Bde RFA
LAKER Ernest G. MM Pte G/849 8th Royal Sussex Regt
LAKER Percy MM L/Cpl 7567 4th Hussars
LAKER William H. MM Cpl 7977 Machine Gun Corps
LAKEY Jack MM Cpl 84997 34 Div Sig Coy Royal Engineers
LAKIE David MM Sjt 10575 1st Scots Guards
LAKIN Albert Frederick Noah MM Pte 437086 1/2(South Midland)Fd Amb RAMC
LAKIN Arthur MM Spr 354872 18 Div Sig Coy Royal Engineers
LAKIN John MM Pte 291660 7th Gordon Highlanders
LAKIN John MM Pte 9603 7th South Staffordshire Regt
LAKIN Oliver James MM Pte 9721 2nd South Staffordshire Regt
LAKIN Percy MM Pte 17502 1/5th York & Lancaster Regt
LAKIN Samuel MM Pte 18811 1st Royal Warwickshire Regt
LAKIN William MM Pnr 25465 Royal Engineers
LAKIN William B. MM Cpl 164721 100th Bn Machine Gun Corps
LAKING George H. MM Cpl 51061 8th Worcestershire Regt
LALLEY James MM Sjt 68673 30 Bty 39 Bde RFA
LALLY James MM Sjt 13533 9th Royal Inniskilling Fusiliers
LALLY John MM Sjt 10256 1st Yorkshire Light Infantry
LALLY Peter MM Pte 18176 2nd Leinster Regt
LALOR Michael MM Pte 62507 RAMC
LAMB Alexander MM Pte S/41176 6th Gordon Highlanders
LAMB Arthur MM L/Sjt 1419 1/5th Cheshire Regt
LAMB Arthur J. MM CQMS 2215 4th Liverpool Regt
LAMB Augustus Charles MM Cpl 20928 Middlesex Regt
LAMB Charles F. MM L/Bdr 232509 RFA
LAMB Charles W. MM L/Cpl 200904 West Yorkshire Regt
LAMB Clarence MM Pte 266229 1/6th Cheshire Regt
LAMB Craigie MM L/Cpl 330221 1/8th Royal Scots
LAMB Edgar MM Sjt 52111 Lincolnshire Regt
LAMB Edmund MM(1496 Nbld Fus)+Bar Cpl 93096 24th Royal Fusiliers
LAMB Edward MM Cpl 5423 2nd Leinster Regt KIA 7.9.17.
LAMB Foster MM Gnr 760561 3 Div Amm Col RFA
LAMB Francis Osmond MM Sjt 15894 Durham Light Infantry
LAMB Frank MM Cpl 44216 Royal Engineers
LAMB Frank C. MM Gnr 208985 B/82 Bde RFA
LAMB Frederick MM Pte 331783 9th Liverpool Regt
LAMB Harry J. MM L/Sjt 15105 16th Highland Light Infantry
LAMB Herbert MM Pte 50613 Machine Gun Corps(Cavalry)
LAMB Isaac MM 2nd Cpl 79744 184 Tunnelling Coy Royal Engineers

LAMB J.W.R. MM Pte 301169 RAMC
LAMB James MM Sjt 2713 West Riding Regt
LAMB James "MC,MM(2025 L/Cpl)" T/2Lt 12th Highland Light Infantry
LAMB John MM Pte 14042 10th North Lancashire Regt
LAMB John MM Gnr 680313 RFA
LAMB John "DCM,MM" Pte 335053 1/8th Royal Scots
LAMB John MM Pte 14226 10th Scottish Rifles
LAMB John MM Cpl 64389 Y/19 Med TM Bty RFA DOW 8.11.18.
LAMB John D. MM Gnr 127857 RGA
LAMB Joseph MM Pte 201096 Highland Light Infantry
LAMB Octavius MM Bdr 67143 336 Siege Bty RGA
LAMB Percy MM Sjt 6117 8th Royal Fusiliers KIA 1.9.17.
LAMB Peter MM CSM 44531 12th Manchester Regt DOW 26.8.18.
LAMB Richard MM Pte 109510 4th Liverpool Regt
LAMB Richard MM Pte 51766 13th Liverpool Regt
LAMB Richard C. MM 2nd Cpl 552307 Royal Engineers
LAMB Robert MM Gnr 33151 D/70 Bde RFA
LAMB Robert E. MM Pte 15067 15th Durham Light Infantry
LAMB Samuel MM+Bar Pte 32606 Notts & Derby Regt
LAMB Thomas MM Pte 70942 50th Bn Machine Gun Corps
LAMB Thomas F. MM+Bar L/Sjt 11/720 11th East Yorkshire Regt
LAMB Thomas William MM Sjt 200698 1/4th Suffolk Regt
LAMB Vincent MM Sjt 20/1321 Northumberland Fusiliers
LAMB William MM+Bar Sjt 38094 7th Royal Warwickshire Regt
LAMB William MM Pte 10008 South Staffordshire Regt
LAMB William MM Bdr 59840 28 Bde RFA
LAMB William A. MM L/Cpl 34174 RAMC
LAMB William L. MM Pte S/25070 7th Seaforth Highlanders
LAMBDEN Robert E. MM+Bar Sjt 200663 8th Royal Berkshire Regt
LAMBE Richard MM L/Cpl 7363 11th Royal Fusiliers
LAMBE William "MM,MID" L/Cpl 8572 2nd Welsh Regt
LAMBERT A. MM Sjt 265668 6th West Riding Regt
LAMBERT Alma H. MM L/Sjt 8175 Coldstream Guards
LAMBERT Arthur MM Gnr 34428 49 Bty 40 Bde RFA KIA 28.9.18.
LAMBERT Arthur MM Cpl 12216 7th Suffolk Regt
LAMBERT B.G. MM Gnr 998 B/121 Bde RFA
LAMBERT Charles Graham MM Gnr 192452 B/174 Bde RFA KIA 12.11.17.
LAMBERT Charles W. MM L/Cpl 2354 East Surrey Regt
LAMBERT David MM Gnr 8765 HQ/155 Bde RFA
LAMBERT Edward MM Pte 12677 9th Cheshire Regt
LAMBERT Edward W. MM Pte 30816 East Surrey Regt
LAMBERT F.C. MM Pte L/17883 7th London Regt
LAMBERT Fred MM Sjt 19430 Manchester Regt
LAMBERT Frederick MM Pte G/1156 9th Royal Fusiliers
LAMBERT Frederick C. MM Cpl 201473 5th Notts & Derby Regt
LAMBERT Frederick G. MM Cpl 12730 1st Liverpool Regt
LAMBERT George MM Sjt 19424 4th Bedfordshire Regt
LAMBERT Gilbert A.G. MM Sjt 11167 6th Somerset Light Infantry
LAMBERT Harold A. MM Pte 28334 1st Royal Warwickshire Regt
LAMBERT Henry W. MM Pte 3065 1/21st London Regt
LAMBERT Herbert A. MM L/Sjt 275169 3rd London Regt
LAMBERT Horace J. MM L/Cpl 5667 Royal West Surrey Regt
LAMBERT John W. MM Spr 49683 Royal Engineers
LAMBERT Joseph "DCM,MM" Gnr 73735 83 Bty 11 Bde RFA KIA 7.8.16.
LAMBERT Joseph R. MM Pte 1394 4th Rifle Brigade
LAMBERT Joshua MM L/Cpl 154402 218 Fd Coy Royal Engineers
LAMBERT Matthew MM L/Cpl 3/2370 Yorkshire Light Infantry
LAMBERT Reginald C. MM Pte 5481 17th Lancers
LAMBERT Robert MM Cpl 2166 1/1st Cambridgeshire Regt DOW 26.9.17.
LAMBERT Robert P. MM Pte 803 Durham Light Infantry
LAMBERT Simeon Vickers MM Gnr 676709 275 Bde RFA
LAMBERT Thomas MM Sjt 193230 Royal Engineers
LAMBERT Thomas Frank MM Pte 15085 Dorsetshire Regt
LAMBERT William MM Sjt 1523 1/11st Leicestershire Yeomanry
LAMBERT William MM+Bar Sjt 14034 24th Manchester Regt
LAMBERT William MM L/Sjt 14845 Royal Irish Fusiliers
LAMBERT William F. MM Gnr 340131 RGA
LAMBERT William F. MM Cpl 015809 Army Ordnance Corps
LAMBERTGORWYN Hector B. MM 2nd Cpl 510406 Royal Engineers
LAMBERTH Bertie MM L/Cpl 2538 1/21st London Regt
LAMBERTON Henry E. MM L/Cpl 251638 Royal Engineers
LAMBIE David MM Sjt 16210 1st Royal Scots
LAMBIE Malcolm MM Pte S/10245 1st Gordon Highlanders KIA 18.6.17.
LAMBKIN George F. MM Cpl 51213 4th Liverpool Regt
LAMBLE Howard MM Gnr 43749 40 Bde RFA
LAMBLEY Joseph Thomas MM Sjt 19894 C/317 Bde RFA
LAMBLEY Percy MM Gnr 23105 RFA
LAMBLEY Thomas MM Sjt 15448 8th Somerset Light Infantry
LAMBORN Charles A. MM Cpl 60841 9th Welsh Regt
LAMBOURN James W. MM+Bar Sjt 200795 Royal Berkshire Regt
LAMBOURN William Edward MM L/Sjt 1691 3(South Midland)Fd Amb RAMC
LAMBOURNE William MM Pte 265498 1/1st(Bucks)Bn Oxf & Bucks Light Infantry
LAMBURNE Cecil MM L/Cpl 322829 London Regt
LAMERTON Arthur Reginald MM Pte 24380 6th Dorsetshire Regt DOW 29.10.18.
LAMERTON Bertram MM Bdr 99031 B/25 Bde RFA
LAMERTON William G. MM Cpl 280270 1/4th London Regt
LAMIE John MM Spr 86383 171 Tunnelling Coy Royal Engineers
LAMIN Harry MM Pte 241057 Northumberland Fusiliers
LAMING Albert H. MM Sjt 2853 1/8th London Regt
LAMING Charles MM L/Cpl 610994 19th London Regt
LAMING Christopher J. MM Pte 9992 2nd Royal Sussex Regt
LAMING George Edward MM Sjt 52341 48 Bty 36 Bde RFA Died 31.10.18.
LAMING George W. MM L/Cpl 14248 2nd Grenadier Guards
LAMKIN Leonard B. "DCM,MM" Pte 11412 1st Coldstream Guards
LAMKIN Victor MM Pte 350716 7th London Regt
LAMKIN William A. MM Cpl 370898 1/8th London Regt
LAMMIMAN Leonard "DCM,MM" Pte 390290 1/3(Northumbrian)Fd Amb RAMC
LAMMING Harry MM Sjt 34915 4 Siege Bty RGA
LAMMING John William MM Tpr 5639 3rd Bn GMGR
LAMOND A. MM Pte 352324 Royal Scots
LAMOND Daniel MM L/Cpl 19767 XVII Corps Cyclist Bn Army Cyclist Corps
LAMONT John MM Cpl 20223 Royal Munster Fusiliers
LAMONT Joseph MM Sjt 17827 12th Royal Fusiliers
LAMONT Peter MM Pte 20570 13th Royal Scots
LAMONT Samuel Scott MM Pte 332982 9th Highland Light Infantry
LAMONT Thomas R. MM Cpl(SS) 700547 RFA
LAMPARD Sidney MM Pte 5214 9th Northumberland Fusiliers DOW 11.4.18.
LAMPARD William J. MM Dvr 29425 C/91 Bde RFA
LAMPETT Ernest MM+Bar Pte 6345 11th Royal Warwickshire Regt
LAMPLOUGH John MM Pte 29110 Yorkshire Regt
LAMPON R.B. MM Sjt 41953 B/123 Bde RFA
LAMPORT Leonard MM Pte 41404 4th Worcestershire Regt KIA 14.10.18.
LANAGHAN John MM Pte 10720 11th Northumberland Fusiliers
LANATHEN Patrick MM Pte 19812 Royal Dublin Fusiliers
LANCASHIRE Thomas MM Cpl 3801 2nd Lancashire Fusiliers
LANCASHIRE William H. MM Pte 21003 Yorkshire Light Infantry
LANCASTER Alexander MM+Bar Sjt 3/7669 7th Bedfordshire Regt
LANCASTER Alfred MM L/Cpl 122 7th Dragoon Guards
LANCASTER Arnold Busk MM L/Sjt 3346 London Regt DOW 11.4.18.
LANCASTER Arthur MM RQMS 19215 6th York & Lancaster Regt
LANCASTER Arthur MM L/Cpl 53056 2nd Royal Fusiliers
LANCASTER Bernard MM Pte 3/8635 1st West Yorkshire Regt KIA 21.3.18.
LANCASTER Cecil MM Pte 653795 21st London Regt
LANCASTER Frank MM Pte 20048 Somerset Light Infantry
LANCASTER Frederick C. MM Sjt 202522 2/7th West Yorkshire Regt
LANCASTER George MM L/Sjt 15094 1st Grenadier Guards
LANCASTER George MM Sjt L/8967 Royal West Surrey Regt Died 13.10.18.
LANCASTER George MM Sjt 13694 South Staffordshire Regt
LANCASTER Gilbert MM L/Bdr 79144 RGA
LANCASTER Harry MM Pte 21024 1st Royal Lancaster Regt KIA 18.4.18.
LANCASTER Harry MM Sjt 4409 7th Royal Lancaster Regt DOW 3.4.18.
LANCASTER Henry MM Cpl 10059 1st North Lancashire Regt
LANCASTER Henry MM Pte 2298 1/4th West Riding Regt DOW 30.1.18.
LANCASTER Herbert MM Spr 238398 Royal Engineers
LANCASTER James MM Sjt 1984 1/4th North Lancashire Regt
LANCASTER James W. MM Pte C/7280 King's Royal Rifle Corps
LANCASTER John MM Gnr 78173 RHA
LANCASTER John W. MM Pte 308174 Liverpool Regt
LANCASTER Joseph MM Pte 200139 West Riding Regt

LANCASTER Thomas H. MM Cpl M2/102053 Army Service Corps
LANCE Alfred William "DCM,MM+Bar" L/Cpl 553070 1/16th London Regt
LANCELEY David MM L/Cpl 18071 12th Liverpool Regt
LANCELEY William C. MM CSM 265005 1/6th Gloucestershire Regt
LANCELOTTE Charles MM BSM 23396 337 Bde RFA
LANCETT William MM Pte 27827 1st Royal Warwickshire Regt
LAND Albert P. MM L/Cpl 6952 1st Norfolk Regt
LAND John Henry MM Sjt 471036 12th London Regt
LAND Reginald James "MM,MID" Bdr 10374 RFA
LAND William MM Pte 45796 2nd Notts & Derby Regt
LAND William MM Dvr 2655 RFA
LAND William MM Sjt 930490 RFA
LAND William Charles MM Gnr 875598 272 Bde RFA
LANDEG William MM Pte 2772 Welsh Regt
LANDELS Adam MM Sjt 9758 2nd Royal Scots
LANDELS Archibald MM Pte 13932 6th Yorkshire Light Infantry DOW 21.8.18.
LANDEN Archibald MM Cpl 204566 7th East Kent Regt
LANDEN Harold MM Pte 243063 Cheshire Regt
LANDER Francis MM Pte 87754 35th Bn Machine Gun Corps
LANDER H. MM Cpl 10361 Royal Irish Regt
LANDER William Edwin MM Sjt 17176 6th South Wales Borderers KIA 15.4.18.
LANDES Harry MM Bdr 131540 136 Hy Bty RGA
LANDON Harold W. MM Sjt 112186 'E' Special Coy Royal Engineers
LANDRAGIN Edward John MM Dvr T2/015804 Army Service Corps
LANDRETH Gilbert MM+2 Bars L/Cpl 325479 1/9th Durham Light Infantry
LANDY John MM Dvr 681499 D/286 Bde RFA
LANDYMORE Frederick MM Pte 68 7th East Surrey Regt KIA 20.11.17.
LANE A. MM Pte R/9636 16th King's Royal Rifle Corps
LANE Abraham MM Pte 15896 1st Hampshire Regt KIA 23.10.16.
LANE Abraham Edward MM+Bar Sjt 8222 2nd South Staffordshire Regt
LANE Albert MM Pte 11996 2nd King's Own Scottish Borderers
LANE Albert MM Sjt 15788 2 Siege Bty RGA
LANE Albert R. MM Pte 4237 1/8th London Regt
LANE Alfred MM Spr 175704 179 Tunnelling Coy Royal Engineers
LANE Alfred E. MM Cpl 868 Royal West Surrey Regt
LANE Alfred E. MM Pte 43148 Bedfordshire Regt
LANE Alfred Richard MM Pte 268074 2/7th Royal Warwickshire Regt
LANE Algernon Roland MM Spr 59547 154 Fd Coy Royal Engineers DOW 1.10.17.
LANE Amos M. MM Sjt 8551 1st Scottish Rifles
LANE Arthur MM Pte 240598 1st Middlesex Regt KIA 23.10.18.
LANE Cecil H. MM+Bar L/Cpl 10300 10th South Wales Borderers
LANE Charles MM L/Cpl 46792 17th Lancashire Fusiliers
LANE Charles MM Pte A/1212 2nd King's Royal Rifle Corps
LANE Charles MM Pte 10611 6th Bedfordshire Regt
LANE Charles Frederick MM Pte 233423 1/2nd London Regt KIA 16.8.17.
LANE Charles H. MM Cpl C/320 16th King's Royal Rifle Corps
LANE Charles J.V. MM Pte 722594 24th London Regt
LANE Charles R. MM Pte 94871 10th Bn Tank Corps
LANE Clifford MM L/Bdr 291298 RGA
LANE Cyril V. MM+Bar Cpl 79040 RFA
LANE Cyril W. MM Pte 718122 23rd London Regt
LANE Eric MM Pte 306798 1/8th Liverpool Regt
LANE Ernest MM Pte 5601 1/6th South Staffordshire Regt
LANE Ernest MM Sjt A/201281 13th King's Royal Rifle Corps
LANE Ernest J. MM Pte 33247 Machine Gun Corps
LANE Ernest L. MM Sjt 55539 138 Siege Bty RGA
LANE Evan R. MM Pte S/37393 Rifle Brigade att 2/17th London Regt.
LANE Fred MM Pte 30276 2nd North Lancashire Regt KIA 31.10.18.
LANE G. MM Pte 75073 Royal Fusiliers
LANE George MM Cpl 11677 6th Shropshire Light Infantry
LANE George "MM,MdH(F)" Pte 12243 3rd Oxf & Bucks Light Infantry
LANE George R. MM Pte 461333 3 Fd Amb RAMC
LANE George Robert "MM+Bar,MID" Sjt 12047 8th & 10th Yorkshire Regt
LANE Gerald MM Sjt 200617 1/4th Gloucestershire Regt
LANE Harold E. MM Pte 14556 10th Notts & Derby Regt
LANE Harry MM Pte S/6780 2nd Rifle Brigade KIA 28.8.18.
LANE Herbert MM Pte 32263 6th York & Lancaster Regt
LANE Herbert C. MM Pte 11194 2nd South Wales Borderers
LANE Horace MM Pnr 254393 37 Div Sig Coy Royal Engineers
LANE Isaiah MM Cpl 236448 1/1st Herefordshire Regt
LANE James MM Gnr 40608 40 Bde RFA
LANE James A. MM Pte 71527 15th Notts & Derby Regt
LANE James B. MM CSM 11251 5th Royal Berkshire Regt
LANE John MM Cpl 14016 1st South Wales Borderers
LANE John "DCM,MM+Bar" Pte 240275 1/5th North Lancashire Regt KIA 1.10.18.
LANE John MM Cpl 7254 1st East Surrey Regt KIA 18.7.17.
LANE John "MM,MID" Gnr 46144 33 Bde RFA
LANE John MM Pte 1737 1/5th North Lancashire Regt
LANE John MM Pte 9532 Machine Gun Corps
LANE John H. MM L/Cpl 235675 1/1st Gloucestershire Yeomanry
LANE John William MM Cpl 376470 1/10th Manchester Regt
LANE Joseph H. MM Pte 650219 1/21st London Regt
LANE Josiah N. MM QMS 3880 Royal Engineers
LANE Leonard Wilson MM Pte 14335 11th West Yorkshire Regt KIA 6.10.16.
LANE Norman W.. MM L/Cpl 43320 Lincolnshire Regt
LANE Philip Allan MM+2 Bars Cpl 110829 319 Siege Bty RGA
LANE Raymond MM Pte 19128 11th Hussars
LANE Reginald Surrey MM Sjt 65630 126 Fd Coy Royal Engineers
LANE Richard MM Sjt 16387 South Staffordshire Regt
LANE Richard Harold MM Cpl 242148 1/6th Royal Warwickshire Regt KIA 27.8.17.
LANE Robert MM Pte 14737 2nd Lincolnshire Regt
LANE Sidney MM+Bar Cpl 200615 1/4th Seaforth Highlanders
LANE Sidney Herbert MM Cpl 12893 Gloucestershire Regt
LANE Stanley Alfred MM Sjt 490543 1/13th London Regt
LANE Sydney MM Pte 06112 Army Ordnance Corps
LANE W. MM Pnr 214282 Royal Engineers
LANE W.M.H. "MM,MSM" Sjt 254111 Fifth Army Sig Coy Royal Engineers
LANE Walter MM Dvr 837075 C/232 Bde RFA
LANE William MM Pte 591771 18th London Regt
LANE William MM L/Cpl 70932 Notts & Derby Regt
LANE William MM Gnr 64388 RFA
LANE William Alfred MM Pte 10885 8th East Kent Regt
LANE William J. MM Pte 51365 Machine Gun Corps
LANES Frederick MM Pte 593504 18th London Regt
LANG Alfred MM Pte 265780 West Riding Regt
LANG Austin MM Sjt 15657 11th East Lancashire Regt KIA 2.7.16.
LANG Christian MM Dvr 947690 C/281 Bde RFA
LANG Ernest E. MM L/Cpl 2952 8th Royal West Surrey Regt
LANG Francis MM L/Cpl 27621 1st Duke of Cornwall's LI
LANG G.R.H. MM Cpl 14771 Yorkshire Regt
LANG George MM L/Cpl 49849 93 Fd Coy Royal Engineers KIA 14.10.18.
LANG Henry H. MM Pte 202577 8th Royal West Kent Regt
LANG Hugh MM Pte 330426 1/9th Highland Light Infantry
LANG James MM Pte S/12455 2nd Arg & Suth Highlanders
LANG John MM Gnr Sig 73151 121 Siege Bty RGA
LANG John MM L/Cpl 325736 1/9th Durham Light Infantry
LANG John MM Pte R/6032 8th King's Royal Rifle Corps DOW 14.9.16.
LANG John MM+Bar Sjt 325390 1/7th Arg & Suth Highlanders
LANG John F. MM Pte 10970 Wiltshire Regt
LANG Joseph J. MM Pte 23772 1/5th Devonshire Regt
LANG Robert MM Pte 119322 Machine Gun Corps
LANG Sydney Frank "MM,MSM,MIDx2" CQMS 1484 8 Div Cyclist Coy Army Cyclist Corps
LANG William MM Pte 326394 1/7th Arg & Suth Highlanders
LANG William MM Cpl 67760 15 Bde RFA
LANGAN Ambrose J. MM L/Cpl 3054 5th Lancers
LANGAN George MM Sjt 22773 2nd Yorkshire Light Infantry
LANGAN George H. MM Gnr 97089 RGA
LANGAN James MM Pte 31828 1/4th King's Own Scottish Borderers
LANGBRIDGE Sydney George MM Pte 31673 59 Coy Machine Gun Corps
LANGDALE Albert MM Bdr 26982 B/91 Bde RFA
LANGDALE George C. MM L/Cpl 27338 7th Northamptonshire Regt
LANGDEN Joseph MM Dvr 26385 35 Bde RFA
LANGDON Albert H. MM Pte 74399 RAMC
LANGDON Arthur J. MM Pte S/44201 7th Gordon Highlanders
LANGDON Frederick MM Pte 21815 15th Royal Welsh Fusiliers KIA 12.10.16.
LANGDON Frederick John MM Pte 240652 1/5th Duke of Cornwall's LI KIA 11.9.18.

LANGDON Thomas MM L/Cpl 4478 Machine Gun Corps
LANGDOWN Arthur E. MM Pte 17098 7th Wiltshire Regt
LANGDOWN George Leonard MM Pte T/201597 3/4th att 7th Royal West Surrey Regt DOW 27.10.18.
LANGFIELD Alexander MM Cpl M2/098831 Army Service Corps
LANGFIELD James MM Pte 376652 Manchester Regt
LANGFIELD Richard William MM Bdr 141608 287 Siege Bty RGA
LANGFORD Adam MM Pte 21768 4th Grenadier Guards KIA 13.4.18.
LANGFORD Alfred Aaron MM Bdr 11420 C/174 Bde RFA KIA 1.9.18.
LANGFORD Charles Frederick MM Sjt W/1406 D/122 Bde RFA
LANGFORD Edward MM Pte 75069 RAMC
LANGFORD Edwin H.A. MM Pte 13194 16th Lancers
LANGFORD Fred "DCM(1/4th Bn),MM" Sjt 7133 5th Shropshire Light Infantry
LANGFORD G. MM Pte 47802 1/4th Yorkshire Light Infantry
LANGFORD Harold Wilfred MM Sjt 200589 Worcestershire Regt
LANGFORD Henry MM CSM 1375 1/5th Durham Light Infantry
LANGFORD Herbert W. MM Pte 28187 5th Border Regt
LANGFORD John MM Cpl M2/104712 Army Service Corps
LANGFORD John MM L/Cpl 36172 Cheshire Regt
LANGFORD John MM Bdr 48134 RGA
LANGFORD Leonard MM Spr 26675 155 Fd Coy Royal Engineers
LANGFORD Robert H. "DCM,MM" Cpl 19772 9 Fd Coy Royal Engineers
LANGFORD Thomas "DCM,MM" Cpl 32628 14th Royal Warwickshire Regt
LANGFORD Thomas MM L/Cpl 86111 170 Tunnelling Coy Royal Engineers
LANGHAM Harold MM Cpl 14314 2nd Royal Fusiliers
LANGHAM Herbert G. MM Bdr 875396 RFA
LANGHAM Samuel MM Sjt 49202 109 Bty 281 Bde RFA
LANGHAM W. MM Gnr 127054 RFA
LANGHAM William Robert "MM,CG(F)" Pte 18260 Scottish Rifles
LANGHORNE Charles MM L/Cpl 83570 19 Coy Machine Gun Corps
LANGLEY A.E. MM Pte 29106 1st Essex Regt
LANGLEY Albert Harry MM Cpl 18602 13th Middlesex Regt KIA 4.11.18.
LANGLEY Amos MM Cpl 84216 37th Bn Machine Gun Corps
LANGLEY Arthur William MM Pte 25300 1st Royal West Surrey Regt KIA 21.9.18.
LANGLEY Charles E. MM Pte 5321 8th East Kent Regt
LANGLEY Charles Herbert "MM,MID" Sjt 1444 D/110 Bde RFA KIA 4.5.18.
LANGLEY Frances Edger MM Pte 10502 6th Somerset Light Infantry
LANGLEY Frank MM+Bar Pte 23294 Border Regt
LANGLEY Frederick C. MM Cpl 403297 2/3rd(West Riding)Fd Amb RAMC
LANGLEY Frederick W. MM L/Cpl 21343 Suffolk Regt
LANGLEY George Henry MM Pte 9528 11th Royal West Kent Regt
LANGLEY George Henry MM Sjt 64626 29 Bty 42 Bde RFA Died 25.4.18.
LANGLEY George William MM Pte 2050 1/4th Yorkshire Regt
LANGLEY Henry James MM L/Cpl 6219 12th Middlesex Regt KIA 3.5.17.
LANGLEY Herbert MM Pte 240733 1/5th South Lancashire Regt KIA 21.9.17.
LANGLEY James MM L/Cpl 12/432 2nd York & Lancaster Regt
LANGLEY John W. MM L/Cpl 332994 1st Liverpool Regt KIA 11.8.18.
LANGLEY L. MM Pte 51661 Lincolnshire Regt
LANGLEY Maurice MM Spr 210618 Royal Engineers
LANGLEY Richard A. MM Sjt 12517 East Surrey Regt
LANGLEY Richard H. MM Pte 11445 Royal Berkshire Regt
LANGLEY Robert K. MM Sjt 3644 12th Royal Scots
LANGLEY Samuel Edmond MM Spr 341086 58 Div Sig Coy Royal Engineers
LANGLEY Sidney MM Sjt 42013 27 Bde RFA
LANGLEY Thomas W. MM Pte 225713 Northamptonshire Regt
LANGLEY Victor C. MM Sjt 52285 4 Bde RFA
LANGLEY William L. MM Pte 13725 3rd Royal Fusiliers
LANGMAN William MM Cpl 82566 Royal Engineers
LANGRIDGE H.E. MM L/Cpl P/5366 1 Traffic Control Coy Military Foot Police
LANGRIDGE William MM Gnr 353473 RGA
LANGRILL John MM Sjt 3346 1st Irish Guards
LANGRISH Frank E. MM Sjt 282425 4th London Regt
LANGRISH James MM+Bar Gnr 293263 140 Heavy Bty RGA
LANGSDALE William Anthony "MM,MID." Sjt 19405 Royal Fusiliers KIA 22.3.18.
LANGSTAFF Frank MM Bdr 800147 A/230 Bde RFA
LANGSTAFF George W. MM Pte 33170 13th East Lancashire Regt
LANGSTON Arthur H. MM Spr 558091 56 Div Sig Coy Royal Engineers
LANGSTON Bert MM+Bar Cpl 265058 2nd Oxf & Bucks Light Infantry
LANGSTON Fritz A. MM Sjt 311 RFA
LANGSTON George MM Pte 13714 2/4th Hampshire Regt
LANGSTON John William MM L/Cpl 40330 1/1st City of London Yeo
LANGTHORNE John Henry MM Pte 16541 1st Coldstream Guards
LANGTON E. MM Cpl 43363 Royal Engineers
LANGTON Isaac MM Dvr 681500 RFA
LANGTON John H. MM Sjt 35142 RAMC
LANGTON John W. MM Pte 201129 6th Leicestershire Regt
LANGTON Wallace MM L/Cpl 5126 9th Lancers
LANGTON William MM Pte 20901 8th Border Regt
LANGTON William T.E. MM Sjt 9637 1st East Kent Regt
LANHAM Frederick C.J. MM Pte 325790 1/1st Cambridgeshire Regt
LANHAM Frederick P. MM Pte 461531 RAMC
LANHAM James William MM(9th Bn)+Bar Pte 12258 1st Essex Regt
LANHAM John MM Pte 10194 2nd Yorkshire Regt
LANHAM Walter "MM,MSM" Bdr 371217 114 Siege Bty RGA
LANHAM William MM Gnr 17964 108 Heavy Bty RGA
LANIGAN Daniel MM Pte 4123 2nd Lancashire Fusiliers
LANIGAN John MM Sjt 103 1st Royal Irish Rifles
LANK Ernest W. MM Cpl 251709 Royal Engineers
LANSBURY Ralph Henry MM Pte 472130 12th London Regt
LANSBURY Reginald Thomas "DCM,MM" CSM 8721 1st Bedfordshire Regt KIA 20.7.18.
LANSDELL Lewis Joseph MM Bdr 67078 144 Siege Bty RGA
LANSDOWN William Daniel MM Pte 48472 1/28th London Regt
LANSDOWNE Frederick MM Sjt 200183 4th Hampshire Regt
LANSLEY Frederick C. MM Sjt 4554 9th Lancers
LANSLEY Harold F. MM Cpl 251270 3rd London Regt
LANTY John Walter MM Pte 1267 2/2(Northumbrian)Fd Amb RAMC DOW 27.5.18.
LAPPAGE E. MM Sjt 9503 6th North Staffordshire Regt
LAPPIN Patrick MM Gnr 84175 RFA
LAPPING John MM Cpl 10493 York & Lancaster Regt KIA 22.4.17.
LAPSLEY Douglas MM Pte S/8766 Arg & Suth Highlanders
LAPTHORNE Richard MM Sjt 329237 159 Hy Bty RGA
LAPWORTH George R. MM Sjt 147333 238 Army Troops Coy Royal Engineers
LAPWORTH John C. MM Pte A/2805 King's Royal Rifle Corps
LAPWORTH Joseph T. MM Pte 38121 12th Gloucestershire Regt
LAPWORTH Thomas MM Sjt 5376 10th Royal Warwickshire Regt KIA 23.3.18.
LARBEY George MM Cpl 9977 2nd Royal Sussex Regt
LARCOMBE Albert MM Sjt 27183 18 Bde RFA
LARCOMBE Arthur Stanley MM Pte 26068 17th Welsh Regt KIA 25.11.17.
LARCOMBE Wilfred MM Pte 5342 Leinster Regt
LARDEN George MM Pte 2330 Middlesex Regt
LARDER Donald Alexander MM Sjt 60803 41 Bde RFA
LARDER Victor MM Sjt 61686 9 Bde RFA
LARDNER Ernest MM L/Cpl 76267 Machine Gun Corps(Heavy Branch)
LARGE Arthur MM(15530 Lincs Regt)+Bar L/Cpl 82215 26th Royal Welsh Fusiliers
LARGE Charles MM Spr 48146 3 Div Sig Coy Royal Engineers
LARGE Edwin MM Pte 240837 6th Notts & Derby Regt
LARGE Gilbert MM Pte 359104 10th Liverpool Regt
LARGE Henry G. MM Sjt 947684 56 Div Ammn Col RFA
LARGE Henry J. MM L/Cpl 240455 Royal Lancaster Regt
LARGE Herbert MM Cpl 10316 Coldstream Guards
LARGUE William E. MM Cpl 677 Northumberland Fusiliers
LARK George MM Pte 8112 1st Norfolk Regt
LARK Henry W. MM Cpl 15931 2nd Hampshire Regt
LARKE Herbert George MM Pte 16067 7th Yorkshire Regt
LARKIN Albert Jesse MM L/Cpl 45330 58 Coy Machine Gun Corps
LARKIN Alec Cecil MM Cpl 202198 Suffolk Regt
LARKIN Arthur MM Cpl 493397 2/2(Home Counties)Fd Amb RAMC
LARKIN James MM Pte 17113 7th North Lancashire Regt
LARKIN James E. MM L/Sjt 12233 1st Irish Guards
LARKIN John MM Pte 24991 6th Royal Dublin Fusiliers
LARKIN John E. MM Bdr 132121 RGA
LARKIN Michael MM Sjt 6229 6th Royal Irish Regt KIA 2.8.17.

LARKIN Robert G. "DCM,MM" Pte 4621 16th Lancers
LARKIN Samuel MM Sjt 3798 2nd Lancashire Fusiliers
LARKIN Samuel MM Pte 240212 1/5th Border Regt
LARKIN William MM Pte 8136 1st Scottish Rifles DOW 15.8.16.
LARKING Allan "MM,MID" Pte 9680 RAMC
LARKING Reginad P. MM Pte 10567 1st Royal West Kent Regt
LARKINS Frederick J. MM L/Cpl 703378 23rd London Regt
LARKINS Henry C. MM Sjt G/7730 Royal West Surrey Regt
LARKINS Herbert MM Cpl 24204 Royal West Surrey Regt
LARKINS Percy W. MM L/Cpl 205561 6th Lancashire Fusiliers
LARKMAN James MM Cpl Y/1472 1st King's Royal Rifle Corps KIA 20.4.16.
LARMAN Leonard Victor MM Dvr 945410 C/52 Bde RFA
LARMONT Thomas M. MM Spr 197559 Royal Engineers
LARMOUR Alexander MM Pte 11/16662 12th Royal Irish Rifles DOW 11.4.18.
LARMOUR John MM Gnr 46043 113 Heavy Bty RGA
LARNACH Henry MM Spr 107813 185 Tunnelling Coy Royal Engineers
LARNACH Thomas MM Cpl 19699 1st Royal Scots Fusiliers
LARNER Herbert Charles MM Pte 202537 1/4th Gloucestershire Regt KIA 9.10.17.
LARNER James MM Pte 10095 2 Fd Amb RAMC
LARNER Richard MM L/Cpl 463029 50 Div Sig Coy Royal Engineers
LARRETT Frank W. MM Dvr T4/250082 32 Div Train Army Service Corps
LARTER Ivan C. MM L/Cpl 267662 Royal Highlanders
LARUM George "DCM,MM" Sjt 12489 7th Yorkshire Regt
LARVIN Dennis MM Pte 14837 1st Worcestershire Regt KIA 7.8.16.
LARWOOD Ernest MM Sjt 45781 25th Royal Welsh Fusiliers KIA 8.9.18.
LASCELLES Kenneth W. MM Pte M2/132748 Army Service Corps att RAMC
LASEBY Henry MM Sjt 16347 2nd Northumberland Fusiliers
LASENBY Alexander MM+Bar Sjt 15124 1st Bedfordshire Regt
LASHBROOK Christopher E. MM Pte 23118 1st Duke of Cornwall's LI
LASKEY George MM Sjt 7713 8th Royal West Kent Regt KIA 16.10.18.
LASKEY William R. "DCM,MM" Pte 2139 1/9th Durham Light Infantry
LASSETTER Cecil F. MM L/Cpl 1535 Royal Sussex Regt
LAST Frederick MM Pte 80593 1/1st Essex Yeomanry
LAST Herbert MM Pte 15353 10th Worcestershire Regt KIA 19.1.18.
LAST James Thomas MM Pte 41394 13th Rifle Brigade DOW 14.11.18.
LAST John MM Sjt 98901 B/103 Bde RFA KIA 26.9.17.
LAST Joseph MM L/Cpl 13008 8th Suffolk Regt
LAST Stanley J. MM Pte 71526 Machine Gun Corps
LAST Thomas MM Sjt 13223 9th Suffolk Regt
LAST William MM Sjt 201405 Suffolk Regt
LAST William F. MM Pte 14590 8th Suffolk Regt
LATARCHE Charles A. MM Pte Z/1675 3rd Rifle Brigade
LATCHAM Albert E. MM 2nd Cpl 506481 504 Fd Coy Royal Engineers
LATCHAM Joseph MM L/Cpl S/8039 8th Royal Highlanders
LATHAM Albert E. MM L/Sjt 48347 15th Royal Warwickshire Regt
LATHAM Carl Stanley MM Sjt 3286 1/14th London Regt KIA 1.7.16.
LATHAM Donald P. MM Dvr 935511 RFA
LATHAM Edward MM L/Cpl 28271 South Lancashire Regt
LATHAM Edward Bryan MM Pte 9609 1/5th London Regt
LATHAM Edwin MM Pte 2553 1/4th North Lancashire Regt
LATHAM Fred MM Sjt 76641 Machine Gun Corps(Heavy Branch)
LATHAM Fred MM Pte 15952 11th Manchester Regt KIA 7.6.17.
LATHAM George MM Bdr 12246 39 Siege Bty RGA
LATHAM George G. MM Sjt 20248 Machine Gun Corps
LATHAM Henry MM Cpl 34168 Royal Warwickshire Regt
LATHAM Henry MM Pte 276648 Manchester Regt
LATHAM James MM Pte 300303 18th Liverpool Regt
LATHAM John MM Bdr 117958 RGA
LATHAM John MM Pte 1298 20 Fd Amb RAMC
LATHAM John Edward MM Sjt 78008 Labour Corps
LATHAM Robert MM Cpl 755 Army Veterinary Corps
LATHAM Stanley MM Dvr 105831 RFA
LATHAM William MM L/Cpl 207976 248 Fd Coy Royal Engineers
LATHAM William MM Pte 41267 11th Manchester Regt
LATHAM William MM L/Cpl 201219 1/5th North Staffordshire Regt
LATHWOOD Samuel J. "DCM,MM" Sjt 253433 2nd London Regt
LATIMER Alfred MM Sjt 97797 153 Bty RFA KIA 4.10.18.
LATIMER Edward J. MM+Bar Pte 140439 Machine Gun Corps
LATIMER Frank MM Sjt T4/243455 31 Div Train Army Service Corps
LATIMER Henry MM Cpl 24377 Y/18 Med TM Bty RFA
LATIMER Thomas L. MM L/Bdr 262932 303 Siege Bty RGA
LATTA William "DCM,MM,MID" L/Sjt 11372 3rd Grenadier Guards
LATTER Frederick "MM,CG(F)" Pte 10762 3rd Middlesex Regt
LATTER Horatio Nelson MM Sjt 41349 Royal Engineers
LATTER Sydney A. MM Cpl 591212 1/18th London Regt
LATTER Walter George MM Sjt G/4092 6th East Kent Regt
LATTIMER Frederick MM Pte 49654 Royal Fusiliers
LATTIMER Thomas Henry MM Pte 23626 13th Durham Light Infantry DOW 6.8.16.
LATTIMORE Joseph W. MM Pte 20462 1st Northamptonshire Regt
LATTIMORE Samuel "MM,MID." Sjt 12982 12th East Surrey Regt
LATTIMORE William Herbert MM Cpl 71887 Machine Gun Corps
LATTO Alexander MM Cpl 305066 8th West Yorkshire Regt
LAUCHLAND George MM Pte 252307 3rd London Regt
LAUDER Albert Alexander John MM Cpl S/2543 12th Rifle Brigade KIA 31.7.17.
LAUDER Alexander MM Sjt S/8389 2nd Gordon Highlanders
LAUDER Alexander D.H. MM Cpl 574 2nd Dragoons
LAUDER Alfred James "MM,CG(F)" Gnr 301078 3 Mountain Bty RGA
LAUDER George MM Pnr 503780 8 Div Sig Coy Royal Engineers
LAUDER James MM+Bar Pte 26161 3rd Hussars
LAUDER James MM Pte 326974 Arg & Suth Highlanders
LAUDER Joseph Beaumont MM Cpl 15769 15th Durham Light Infantry KIA 16.9.16.
LAUGHLAN James MM Pte 34764 York & Lancaster Regt
LAUGHLIN Ernest Albert MM Bdr 156695 A/48 Bde RFA
LAUGHLIN James MM Pte 71529 North Irish Horse
LAUGHLIN William MM Bdr 645017 RFA
LAUGHRAN C. MM Pte 17771 Yorkshire Regt
LAUGHTON Albert E. MM Pte 10626 2nd Scottish Rifles
LAUGHTON David J. MM L/Cpl 10835 Seaforth Highlanders
LAUGHTON Dorothy Ann MM Sister F TFNS
LAUGHTON Walter MM Sjt 1393 Royal Sussex Regt
LAUGHTON William MM(240053 N&D)+Bar L/Sjt 235577 1st Lincolnshire Regt
LAUNDER Archibald E.E. MM Pte 18546 Wiltshire Regt
LAUNDER F.P. MM Bdr 32387 5 Siege Bty RGA
LAUNDON Edward Ronald MM L/Cpl 200288 1/4th Northamptonshire Regt KIA 27.11.17.
LAURANTE George MM Cpl 556202 Royal Engineers
LAURENCE Charles MM Gnr L/9479 RFA
LAURIE Arthur MM Spr 40697 Royal Engineers
LAURIE Donald "MM,MID" L/Cpl 15735 6th Liverpool Regt
LAURIE Harry MM L/Bdr 50929 RGA
LAURIE James "MC,MM(9303 Sjt)" 2Lt 2nd Arg & Suth Highlanders
LAURIE John MM Sjt 4001 9th Seaforth Highlanders
LAURIE Michael MM L/Sjt 25503 Durham Light Infantry
LAVELL Hugh MM Pte 17447 11th Durham Light Infantry
LAVELLE Duncan MM L/Cpl 3520 1/6th Arg & Suth Highlanders KIA 28.9.18.
LAVELLE Edward "DCM,MM" Sjt 1483 2nd Manchester Regt
LAVELLE John MM Pte 6474 1st Irish Guards
LAVELLE Michael MM L/Cpl 43422 Royal Irish Fusiliers
LAVELLE Thomas MM Cpl 8651 2nd Worcestershire Regt
LAVEN John W. MM Cpl 61646 C/256 Bde RFA
LAVEN Michael "MM,CG(B)" Pte 33467 13th East Lancashire Regt
LAVENDER Alfred MM Cpl 8351 2nd North Staffordshire Regt
LAVENDER Horace MM L/Cpl 18531 1st Grenadier Guards
LAVENDER Joseph MM Gnr 676933 B/285 Bde RFA
LAVENDER Owen E. MM Pte 6996 2nd Suffolk Regt
LAVENDER Robert Daniel "DCM,MM" 2nd Cpl 87806 8 Railway Coy Royal Engineers
LAVENDER Robert H. MM Pte 203398 Yorkshire Light Infantry
LAVENDER Thomas MM L/Sjt 4645 5th Connaught Rangers
LAVENDER William MM Pte 242558 Worcestershire Regt
LAVENDER William MM Gnr 122288 D/103 Bde RFA
LAVERACK George MM Pte 15451 8th Somerset Light Infantry
LAVERACK Thomas Victor "MM,MSM" Sjt 9224 2nd West Riding Regt
LAVERACK Wilfred MM Pte 269234 5th West Riding Regt
LAVERANCE J. MM Pte 12510 6th King's Own Scottish Borderers
LAVERICK Hunter MM CSM 275397 1/7th Durham Light Infantry
LAVERICK John G. MM L/Cpl 20/1319 Northumberland Fusiliers
LAVERICK Walter F. MM Gnr 311067 RGA
LAVERICK William MM Pte 42772 North Staffordshire Regt
LAVERICK William MM L/Cpl 12398 10th Durham Light Infantry KIA

16.9.16.
LAVERTON Herbert M. MM+Bar L/Cpl 42440 7th Lincolnshire Regt
LAVERTY John MM Pte S/570 Rifle Brigade
LAVERTY John MM L/Cpl 11880 10th Durham Light Infantry
LAVERTY John MM L/Cpl 21495 7/8th Royal Irish Fusiliers KIA 20.11.17.
LAVERTY Samuel MM Cpl 19054 Royal Irish Rifles
LAVERY Andrew MM Pte 21200 Royal Irish Fusiliers
LAVERY Daniel MM Pte 19633 9th Northumberland Fusiliers KIA 22.6.17.
LAVERY John Patrick MM Sjt 12763 7/8th King's Own Scottish Borderers
LAVERY Mark "DCM,MM" Pte 10511 1st Royal Scots Fusiliers
LAVERY William MM Pte 17611 9th Royal Inniskilling Fusiliers
LAVILL John MM Pte 25543 Yorkshire Regt
LAVIN Martin MM Pte 9999 1st Cheshire Regt
LAVIN Thomas MM Pte 10634 Royal Irish Regt
LAVIN William J. MM Gnr 16613 RFA
LAVINGTON Frank MM SSM 427 1/1st North Somerset Yeo
LAVIS Fred MM L/Cpl 42259 2nd Suffolk Regt
LAW A.A.E. MM Cpl 16444 2nd South Staffordshire Regt
LAW Albert MM+Bar Pte 328133 1/1st Cambridgeshire Regt
LAW Alfred MM Pte 10423 18th Manchester Regt
LAW Arthur MM Pte 88389 RAMC
LAW Arthur MM Pte M2/104907 Army Service Corps
LAW Arthur H. MM Pte 242302 Worcestershire Regt
LAW Clifford MM Bdr 19407 C/160 Bde RFA Died 21.3.18.
LAW Edgar J. MM Pte 202848 Suffolk Regt
LAW Ernest MM Pte 202018 1/5th Royal Warwickshire Regt
LAW Ernest Godfrey MM Gnr 65362 29 Bty 42 Bde RFA
LAW Ernest Granville MM Cpl 58481 81 Fd Coy Royal Engineers
LAW George M. MM Pte 202099 Liverpool Regt
LAW Hugh MM Pte 27513 9th Royal Inniskilling Fusiliers DOW 24.3.18.
LAW J.B. MM Sjt 95384 Royal Engineers
LAW James MM L/Cpl 13509 Machine Gun Corps
LAW James MM Spr 251986 Royal Engineers
LAW Joseph MM L/Sjt 9308 Coldstream Guards
LAW Richard MM Sjt 240747 2/5th East Lancashire Regt
LAW Richard J. MM Sjt CMT/443 17 Div MT Coy Army Service Corps
LAW Richard J. MM Pte 35223 Royal Lancaster Regt
LAW Samuel MM L/Cpl 242288 1/5th Royal Lancaster Regt
LAW Sydney MM Cpl 7540 4th Hussars
LAW Thomas MM Pte 26129 1/6th West Riding Regt
LAW Thomas H. MM Sjt 201295 1/5th Bedfordshire Regt
LAW Walter A. MM Pte 13425 8th Yorkshire Light Infantry
LAW William MM Sjt M2/101551 'K' Siege Park Army Service Corps
LAW William MM Sjt 392919 16th London Regt
LAW William MM Pte 204407 10th Scottish Rifles
LAW William MM L/Cpl 2679 1/7th Worcestershire Regt
LAW William MM Pte 25977 Oxf & Bucks Light Infantry
LAW William Henry "MM,MSM" L/Cpl 72599 XI Corps Sig Coy Royal Engineers
LAWCOCK George MM L/Cpl 16340 8th York & Lancaster Regt
LAWER Alfred M. MM Spr 155158 Royal Engineers
LAWER C. MM Pte 240408 Duke of Cornwall's LI
LAWER Harry MM Pte 536 18th Durham Light Infantry
LAWER Harry MM+Bar Pte 15416 1st Coldstream Guards KIA 27.9.18.
LAWER Henry J. MM Spr 155296 Royal Engineers
LAWES Frederick W. "DCM,MM" Sjt 22630 11 Fd Coy Royal Engineers
LAWES George MM+Bar Cpl 63095 23rd Royal Fusiliers
LAWES Gilbert Bernard Aloysius MM Sjt 40575 2nd Lancashire Fusiliers
LAWES Lawrence J. MM L/Cpl 207832 10th Royal West Surrey Regt
LAWES W.M. MM Pte 388550 2 Fd Amb RAMC
LAWES William Frederick MM Pte 37535 55 Fd Amb RAMC
LAWFORD Harold MM+Bar Pte 2182 Middlesex Regt
LAWFORD John MM Sjt 240069 2/6th West Yorkshire Regt
LAWIE Alexander MM Sjt 773 1/7th Gordon Highlanders KIA 13.11.16.
LAWLER Andrew H. MM Sjt 2269 8th London Regt
LAWLER Archibald MM Pte 19287 1st Highland Light Infantry
LAWLER Dennis MM Cpl S/8427 13th Rifle Brigade
LAWLER J. MM Sjt 14111 2nd Royal Munster Fusiliers
LAWLER James MM L/Sjt 14897 15th Hussars
LAWLER John MM Sjt 909 1/5th North Lancashire Regt
LAWLER John MM Cpl 43497 Highland Light Infantry
LAWLER Reginald J. MM Sjt 12474 7th Suffolk Regt
LAWLER Samuel MM Sjt 13690 4th South Wales Borderers
LAWLER Terence "DCM,MM+Bar" Pte 43583 41st Bn Machine Gun Corps DOW 28.10.18.
LAWLER Thomas MM Pte 36194 4th Yorkshire Light Infantry
LAWLESS Edward "MM,MID" Sjt 9613 1st North Staffordshire Regt
LAWLESS George MM Pte 202149 8th Border Regt
LAWLESS Joseph MM Pte 8039 1st Royal Lancaster Regt
LAWLESS Matthew MM Pte 2741 2nd Royal Irish Fusiliers
LAWLESS Richard J. MM Dvr M/371822 Army Service Corps
LAWLESS William MM Sjt 492972 13th London Regt att KAR.
LAWLESS William MM+Bar Pte 25243 1st Royal Dublin Fusiliers
LAWLEY Herbert MM Pte 27614 8th Lincolnshire Regt
LAWLEY John MM Pte 11508 5th Shropshire Light Infantry KIA 3.5.17.
LAWLEY William Henry Frederick "MM,CG(B)" Sjt 21728 4th Worcestershire Regt
LAWLEY William T. MM Sjt 240 Royal Engineers
LAWLOR Fenton MM 2nd Cpl 16555 2 Fd Coy Royal Engineers
LAWLOR Patrick MM Sjt 7504 2nd Royal Dublin Fusiliers
LAWLOR Robert MM+Bar Cpl 457864 446 Fd Coy Royal Engineers DOW 7.11.18.
LAWMAN James T.W. MM Pte 201305 Bedfordshire Regt
LAWN Charles MM Pte 43656 1/6th(Ireland?) Norfolk Regt Died 1.2.17.
LAWN Geoffrey MM L/Cpl 202953 1/4th Yorkshire Regt DOW 30.3.18.
LAWN James E. MM Cpl 26458 12th Norfolk Regt
LAWRANCE Charles MM L/Cpl 203206 York & Lancaster Regt
LAWRANCE Charles H. MM L/Cpl 29054 5th Border Regt
LAWRANCE Frederick George MM CSM 16135 6 Div Sig Coy Royal Engineers
LAWRANCE William H. MM Pte 245018 2nd London Regt
LAWREEN John MM Pte SPTS/2413 24th Royal Fusiliers
LAWRENCE Albert Henry MM Cpl 10012 5th Northamptonshire Regt KIA 11.8.17.
LAWRENCE Albert J. MM Pte 20086 4th Coldstream Guards
LAWRENCE Albert Victor MM Bdr 62393 V/5 Heavy TM Bty RGA DOW 1.6.18.
LAWRENCE Alfred MM+Bar Bdr L/12560 RFA
LAWRENCE Andrew MM Pte 241161 Royal Scots Fusiliers
LAWRENCE Arthur MM Sjt 459 1st Northumberland Fusiliers
LAWRENCE Arthur Edwin MM Sjt 1964 A/79 Bde RFA DOW 11.9.18.
LAWRENCE Arthur S. MM Gnr 229796 B/178 Bde RFA
LAWRENCE Boyce H. MM Pte 90155 Machine Gun Corps
LAWRENCE C.H. MM Cpl 28748 41 Div Ammn Col RFA
LAWRENCE Charles MM Sjt 9876 1st Royal Irish Rifles
LAWRENCE Charles MM Sjt 610341 1/19th London Regt
LAWRENCE Charles Casio MM Pte B/2128 7th Rifle Brigade KIA 12.10.17.
LAWRENCE Charles E. MM L/Cpl 59338 13th Royal Fusiliers
LAWRENCE Cyril MM Pte G/87666 4th Royal Fusiliers
LAWRENCE David G. MM+Bar Pte 14668 5th South Wales Borderers
LAWRENCE E. "DCM,MM" Sjt P/8087 Military Mounted Police
LAWRENCE Ernest Ford MM Pte 43169 10th Essex Regt
LAWRENCE Francis A. MM Gnr 2210 RFA
LAWRENCE Frank MM Sjt 14228 3rd Grenadier Guards
LAWRENCE Frederick MM Pte C/3741 King's Royal Rifle Corps
LAWRENCE Frederick Charles MM Pte A/203302 13th King's Royal Rifle Corps
LAWRENCE Frederick Edwin MM Cpl 25107 6th Royal West Kent Regt
LAWRENCE Frederick J. MM Gnr 257 RFA
LAWRENCE Frederick R. MM Pte 24149 Royal West Surrey Regt
LAWRENCE G. MM Pte 42147 Labour Corps
LAWRENCE George "MM,MID" Sjt 22236 38 Coy Labour Corps
LAWRENCE George MM Pte 145447 50th Bn Machine Gun Corps
LAWRENCE George MM Pte 32721 13th East Lancashire Regt KIA 6.11.18.
LAWRENCE George MM+Bar Sjt 8110 C/82 Bde RFA
LAWRENCE Harold G. MM Pte 52271 Liverpool Regt
LAWRENCE Harry MM Cpl 141775 RGA
LAWRENCE Harry A. MM L/Bdr 97429 35 Siege Bty RGA
LAWRENCE Harry J. MM Pte 4758 7th Royal Sussex Regt
LAWRENCE Harry J. MM Pte 1369 Army Cyclist Corps
LAWRENCE Henry MM Pte 58100 4th Middlesex Regt
LAWRENCE Henry E. MM Sjt 966486 RFA

LAWRENCE Henry William MM Sjt 265241 1st East Kent Regt
LAWRENCE J.J. MM Pte 2267 Royal Fusiliers
LAWRENCE Jack MM Pte 37096 1/5th Bedfordshire Regt KIA 22.12.17.
LAWRENCE James MM Cpl 9181 1st Royal Fusiliers
LAWRENCE James A. MM L/Cpl 26997 2nd Grenadier Guards
LAWRENCE James F. MM Pte 4557 2nd Royal West Surrey Regt
LAWRENCE James T. MM Pte 1872 7th East Kent Regt
LAWRENCE James W. MM L/Cpl 14633 8th Yorkshire Light Infantry
LAWRENCE John MM Gnr 681381 A/286 Bde RFA
LAWRENCE John "MM,MID" Sjt 9508 RGA
LAWRENCE John MM Dvr 99728 RFA
LAWRENCE John S.D.J. MM Spr 37821 Royal Engineers
LAWRENCE Joseph MM Dvr L/5677 RFA
LAWRENCE Joseph MM Bdr 37358 RFA
LAWRENCE Joseph C. MM Pte 490601 13th London Regt
LAWRENCE Leonard MM Sjt 315016 RGA
LAWRENCE Moses MM Cpl 28067 11th East Yorkshire Regt KIA 12.4.18.
LAWRENCE Oswald MM Pte 53962 1st Royal Welsh Fusiliers DOW 1.10.16.
LAWRENCE Percy MM Pte S/10091 Rifle Brigade
LAWRENCE Peter MM Gnr 262131 C/285 Bde RFA
LAWRENCE R. MM Pte 18388 Border Regt
LAWRENCE Ralph MM Sjt 7 7th Royal Sussex Regt
LAWRENCE Raymond H. MM Pte MS/2668 7 Div Train Army Service Corps
LAWRENCE Richard MM Pte 2607 2nd Royal Munster Fusiliers
LAWRENCE Richard MM Gnr 796062 59 Div Ammn Col RFA
LAWRENCE Sidney Frank MM Gnr 23788 D/18 Bde RFA
LAWRENCE Sydney Jones MM Spr 311498 23 Div Sig Coy Royal Engineers KIA 15.6.18.
LAWRENCE Thomas MM Pte 275112 20th London Regt
LAWRENCE Thomas Hornby MM Pte 7727 2nd Yorkshire Regt KIA 29.9.18.
LAWRENCE V.C. MM Sjt 28339 10th Essex Regt
LAWRENCE W. MM Cpl 70963 D/117 Bde RFA
LAWRENCE Walter MM Pte 1893 1/4th London Regt
LAWRENCE Walter MM Pte 67351 5th Devonshire Regt
LAWRENCE Walter MM Gnr 93536 C/46 Bde RFA
LAWRENCE Walter G. MM Pte 10989 Grenadier Guards
LAWRENCE William MM 2nd Cpl 82717 Royal Engineers
LAWRENCE William MM Cpl 65806 154 Fd Coy Royal Engineers DOW 18.5.18.
LAWRENCE William MM Pnr 197101 1 Special Coy Royal Engineers KIA 9.4.18.
LAWRENCE William MM Pte 326323 1/1st Cambridgeshire Regt
LAWRENCE William J. MM Bdr 318599 RGA
LAWRENCE William Victor MM Pte 8632 1st East Yorkshire Regt
LAWRENCESON Harold MM Sjt 331551 9th Liverpool Regt
LAWRENSON Herbert E. MM Gnr 181115 RGA
LAWRENSON Walter MM Pte 3581 1/4th North Lancashire Regt KIA 30.11.17.
LAWRIE Andrew MM Sjt 29826 28 Siege Bty RGA
LAWRIE Francis MM Pte 9302 2nd Seaforth Highlanders
LAWRIE George H. MM Sjt S/4621 Seaforth Highlanders
LAWRIE John MM Cpl 207931 Royal Engineers
LAWRIE John "MM,MID,CG(F)" Sjt 3/7965 2nd Arg & Suth Highlanders
LAWRIE John MM Pte 350987 1/9th Royal Scots
LAWRIE Martin MM Pte 300733 1/7th Arg & Suth Highlanders
LAWRIE William MM 2nd Cpl 209692 2 Special Coy Royal Engineers
LAWRIE William MM L/Sjt S/3007 2nd Arg & Suth Highlanders
LAWRY Archie MM Cpl 13020 1st Dragoons
LAWRY J.T. MM Pte 40793 10th Essex Regt
LAWS Albert Edward MM Pte 325977 1/9th Durham Light Infantry
LAWS Albert H. MM BSM 32463 RFA
LAWS Charles MM Pte 5512 Northumberland Fusiliers
LAWS Edward Harrison MM L/Sjt 13498 1/5th Yorkshire Regt DOW 11.4.18.
LAWS Fred MM Dvr 180902 D/150 Bde RFA
LAWS Frederick MM L/Cpl 63891 213 Coy Machine Gun Corps
LAWS Herbert E. MM Pte M2/119926 Army Service Corps
LAWS John MM Pte 16863 7th Somerset Light Infantry
LAWS Ralph H. MM Spr 463097 Royal Engineers
LAWS Samuel Palmer MM Cpl 7649 B/160 Bde RFA
LAWS Wilfred MM L/Cpl 75141 RAMC
LAWS William Arthur MM Sjt 11234 2nd Notts & Derby Regt
LAWSON A. "DCM,MM" Sjt 290085 1st Gordon Highlanders

LAWSON Albert M. MM L/Cpl 2753 1/22nd London Regt
LAWSON Alexander MM Pte 200596 Tank Corps
LAWSON Alexander J. MM Bdr 365055 RGA
LAWSON Arthur MM Pte 25/1077 Northumberland Fusiliers
LAWSON Arthur MM Pte 7730 1st Duke of Cornwall's LI
LAWSON Arthur Edwin MM Spr 74330 Royal Engineers
LAWSON Cecil Thomas MM Pte STK/1038 10th Royal Fusiliers DOW 23.4.17.
LAWSON Charles MM Sjt 6409 10th Notts & Derby Regt KIA 18.9.18.
LAWSON David MM Pte 24075 19th Durham Light Infantry Died 31.10.18.
LAWSON Ernest MM Pte R/12889 King's Royal Rifle Corps
LAWSON Fred MM Sjt 52197 234 Siege Bty RGA
LAWSON Frederick A. MM Pte DM2/075794 Army Service Corps
LAWSON G. MM Pte 240497 1/5th Northumberland Fusiliers
LAWSON G.M. MM+Bar Cpl 303039 RAMC
LAWSON George MM+Bar L/Cpl 266089 1/7th Gordon Highlanders
LAWSON George MM Sjt 17560 7th Royal Berkshire Regt
LAWSON George Crawford MM+Bar L/Sjt 18/308 18th Durham Light Infantry
LAWSON James "MM+Bar,MID" Bdr 53128 11 Bde RFA
LAWSON James MM+Bar Pte 290625 Royal Highlanders
LAWSON James B. MM Sjt 402095 Royal Engineers
LAWSON Jess MM Pte 268523 1/6th West Riding Regt KIA 28.4.18.
LAWSON John MM Gnr 87239 RGA
LAWSON John MM Sjt 2257 1/14th London Regt
LAWSON John MM Dvr 46351 RFA
LAWSON John MM Bdr 56390 RFA
LAWSON John O. MM Bdr 111385 RFA
LAWSON John R. MM Pte 3409 3rd Royal Fusiliers
LAWSON Matthew MM Pte 18396 10th Scottish Rifles KIA 24.4.17.
LAWSON Percy Levy MM Pte 45050 9th Essex Regt
LAWSON Richard MM L/Sjt 25 1st Welsh Guards
LAWSON Robert MM 2nd Cpl 53047 Royal Engineers
LAWSON Robert MM Cpl 25966 East Yorkshire Regt
LAWSON Robert J. MM Cpl 56529 18th King's Royal Rifle Corps
LAWSON Robert P. "MM,MID" S/Sjt 88 RAMC
LAWSON Thomas E. MM L/Cpl 10182 1st Royal West Surrey Regt
LAWSON W. MM Pte 352589 RAMC
LAWSON Walter MM Spr 267334 Royal Engineers
LAWSON Wilfred L. MM L/Cpl 350922 1/9th Royal Scots
LAWSON William MM Cpl 1279 1st Royal Highlanders
LAWSON William MM Cpl 34870 2nd Royal Scots Fusiliers
LAWSON William MM Pte 22/1223 Northumberland Fusiliers
LAWSON William MM Gnr 951559 383 Bty 179 Bde RFA KIA 30.3.18.
LAWSON William G. MM Pte 357430 Liverpool Regt
LAWSON William McC. MM Sjt 229370 Royal Engineers
LAWTON Arthur MM Sjt 23318 Liverpool Regt
LAWTON Charles MM Sjt 16852 3rd Grenadier Guards
LAWTON Charles A. MM L/Cpl 11396 4th Middlesex Regt
LAWTON Clarence W. MM Pte 35795 4th North Staffordshire Regt
LAWTON Ernest MM Pte 65337 Northumberland Fusiliers
LAWTON Fred MM Cpl 117003 RFA
LAWTON George MM Pte 34448 14th Royal Warwickshire Regt
LAWTON Harry MM Sjt 4/9413 1st South Staffordshire Regt
LAWTON John MM Pnr 148434 3 Div Sig Coy Royal Engineers
LAWTON John Thomas MM Sjt 241365 5th North Lancashire Regt
LAWTON L. "MC,MM(16164 Pte),MID" T/2Lt 9th Yorkshire LI
LAWTON Lewis MM Gnr 68451 126 Siege Bty RGA
LAWTON William MM Cpl 1131 Z/55 Med TM Bty RFA DOW 10.1.17.
LAWTON William MM L/Cpl 304363 15th Bn Tank Corps
LAWTON William A. MM L/Cpl 40688 1st Bedfordshire Regt
LAWTON William T. MM Pte 201510 1/4th Cheshire Regt
LAWTY Alfred "MM,MID" Pte 10508 Durham Light Infantry
LAX Edmund MM Gnr 202866 RFA
LAX Francis C. MM L/Cpl 182112 Royal Engineers
LAX John B. MM Pte 232302 2nd London Regt
LAX Tom MM Pte 307108 8th West Yorkshire Regt
LAXTON Benjamin F. MM Pte 25151 1st Northamptonshire Regt
LAXTON Ernest MM Pte 27379 Royal Warwickshire Regt
LAXTON Ernest MM Sjt 7949 Leicestershire Regt
LAXTON Henry MM Bdr 9100 RFA
LAXTON Thomas Ivan MM Sjt 482310 62 Div Sig Coy Royal Engineers
LAY A. MM Cpl P/1262 Military Foot Police
LAY Charles MM Pte 19857 8th Bedfordshire Regt
LAY Frank MM Pte 31333 8th East Yorkshire Regt

LAY G. "DCM,MM" Sjt 3498 120 Bty 27 Bde RFA
LAY Henry "DCM,MM+Bar" CSM 9669 2nd Oxf & Bucks Light Infantry
LAY Henry J. MM Cpl 1201 1/21st London Regt
LAYBERRY G. MM Pte 4032 North Staffordshire Regt
LAYBOURN Robert MM Gnr 760085 RFA
LAYBOURN Stanley MM Dvr 95084 64 Bde RFA
LAYBOURNE William MM Sjt 4/8122 West Yorkshire Regt
LAYCOCK Augustus MM Sjt 8838 2nd Bedfordshire Regt KIA 29.6.16.
LAYCOCK Christopher MM Sjt 60780 Northumberland Fusiliers
LAYCOCK Colin MM Cpl 15546 9th York & Lancaster Regt
LAYCOCK Edward MM Pte 5561 2nd Scots Guards
LAYCOCK Frank MM Pte 12699 8th West Riding Regt
LAYCOCK Frederick M. MM L/Cpl 58293 16th Royal Welsh Fusiliers
LAYCOCK Frederick William MM Gnr 140566 A/76 Bde RFA Died 4.11.18.
LAYCOCK Hayden MM Sjt 300029 West Riding Regt
LAYCOCK Henry MM L/Cpl 78731 Tank Corps
LAYCOCK James MM Pte 41060 4th Worcestershire Regt
LAYCOCK Lewis MM Dvr 10054 7 Div Ammn Col RFA
LAYCOCK Percy MM Cpl Wheeler 35461 C/108 Bde RFA
LAYCOCK Thomas MM Pte 235139 1/4th Northumberland Fusiliers
LAYCOCK Thomas MM Cpl 63440 Royal Engineers
LAYCOCK Thomas E. MM Pte 11861 10th West Riding Regt
LAYCOCK William A. MM Sjt 16140 7 Div Sig Coy Royal Engineers
LAYDON John MM Sjt 3/10800 15th Durham Light Infantry
LAYDON Stewart T. MM Pte 3699 12th Lancers
LAYE Enos MM Pte 51865 13th Liverpool Regt
LAYEN William G. MM Pte 87268 13th Royal Fusiliers
LAYFIELD Robert MM Pte 18929 Machine Gun Corps
LAYFIELD Thomas MM Pte 2212 1/23rd London Regt
LAYFIELD William MM Pte 45460 7th Lincolnshire Regt
LAYLAND Thomas MM Pte 46555 10th Royal Fusiliers
LAYMAN Thomas Walter MM 2nd Cpl 52175 80 Fd Coy Royal Engineers
LAYT Clifford "MM+Bar,CG(It)" Pte 13427 11th West Yorkshire Regt KIA 24.6.18.
LAYTON Arthur Herbert MM Cpl 106891 40 Div Sig Coy Royal Engineers
LAYTON Bertram MM Pte 94582 1/5th Notts & Derby Regt
LAYTON Cecil MM Cpl G/2953 12th Middlesex Regt
LAYTON David L. MM Sjt 15/67 Royal Warwickshire Regt
LAYTON H.E. MM+Bar L/Sjt 10944 Essex Regt
LAYTON Jack MM Pte 325522 1/1st Cambridgeshire Regt
LAYTON James G. MM L/Sjt 3715 Royal West Surrey Regt
LAYTON John MM+Bar Spr 23971 2 Div Sig Coy Royal Engineers
LAYTON John William MM Cpl 58081 38 Bde RFA
LAYTON Percy MM Cpl 10119 1st Shropshire Light Infantry
LAYTON Robert MM Cpl 24286 10th Durham Light Infantry
LAYTON Tom MM L/Cpl 235974 9th West Yorkshire Regt
LAYTON William "DCM,MM" Pte 9044 1st Shropshire Light Infantry att HQ 18 Inf Bde.
LAYTON William J.H. MM Pte 295140 8th Manchester Regt
LAYZELL W.E. MM Sjt Mechanic 29263 Royal Air Force
LAZARUS Nathan MM Pte 37312 West Yorkshire Regt
LAZARUS Philip MM Pte 701905 23rd London Regt
LAZELL Godfrey MM Sjt 1828 4th Liverpool Regt
LAZENBY Foster Chaplin MM 2nd Cpl 98802 Royal Engineers
LAZENBY Fred MM Pte 35566 8th Yorkshire Light Infantry KIA 9.6.17.
LAZENBY W. MM L/Cpl P3494 Military Foot Police
LAZENBY William Arthur MM Pte 32914 11th East Yorkshire Regt DOW 13.7.18.
LAZINBY Walter MM Sjt 98936 RFA
LAZOREK William MM Cpl 67146 37 Bde RFA
LE BESQUE Theobald F.M. MM Pte 304295 15th Bn Tank Corps
LE BIHAN Edward T. MM Pte M2/200266 Army Service Corps
LE COCQ Edward T. MM Pte 52756 1st Northumberland Fusiliers
LE COMBER Joseph E. MM Pte 57351 17th London Regt
LE DUC Charles A. MM+Bar Gnr 93301 RFA
LE GRESLEY George MM Sjt 3347 Royal Engineers
LE GROS Paul MM L/Cpl 12123 8th Bedfordshire Regt
LE LIEVRE William MM Pte 21854 Royal Irish Fusiliers
LE MAITRE Clifford MM Pte 514 18th Lancashire Fusiliers
LE NOURY Henry G. MM Pte 26370 1st Wiltshire Regt
LE PAVOUX John MM L/Cpl 19833 Middlesex Regt
LE PETIT William MM Pte 31255 1st Royal West Kent Regt
LE ROY Joseph Peter MM Pte 54672 Machine Gun Corps KIA 30.11.17

LE TISSIER Clifford S. MM Gnr 831495 RFA
LE VEDERE Peter F. MM Pte 29941 RGA
LEA Alfred E. MM Pte 1269 Royal Warwickshire Regt
LEA Arthur MM S/Sjt Fitter 22809 197 Siege Bty RGA
LEA Conrad MM Sjt 610546 1/19th London Regt KIA 26.3.18.
LEA Edgar MM Sjt 31591 South Lancashire Regt
LEA Ernest W. MM Pte 200174 1/1st London Regt
LEA Frank MM L/Sjt 9039 2nd South Staffordshire Regt
LEA Frederick MM Bdr 71297 RFA
LEA George MM Cpl 9171 2nd Royal West Surrey Regt
LEA George Charles MM Cpl 9346 19th Bn Machine Gun Corps
LEA Harry MM+Bar Cpl 7946 2nd Royal Welsh Fusiliers
LEA James MM Sjt 33639 1st Cheshire Regt
LEA John MM Cpl 12523 5th Royal Inniskilling Fusiliers
LEA Paul "MM,MID" Pte 341462 64 Fd Amb RAMC
LEA Peter MM Pte 85550 3rd Bn Machine Gun Corps
LEA Richard MM Pte 12574 Coldstream Guards
LEA Solomon MM L/Cpl 6983 2/1(West Lancashire)Fd Coy Royal Engineers
LEA T.H. MM Air Mech 2 49338 Royal Flying Corps
LEA Thomas MM Sjt 10876 2nd Coldstream Guards
LEA W. MM Sjt P/978 Military Mounted Police
LEA William A. MM L/Cpl C/9261 20th King's Royal Rifle Corps
LEACH Albert MM Pte 3443 2/7th West Yorkshire Regt
LEACH Albert E. "DCM,MM" CSM 11783 2nd Grenadier Guards
LEACH Alfred John MM L/Cpl 63831 1/5th Devonshire Regt
LEACH Arthur MM Pte 46252 Welsh Regt
LEACH Benjamin MM Pte 101794 72 Fd Amb RAMC
LEACH Bert A. MM Pte 9162 1st Royal Munster Fusiliers
LEACH Challis MM Pte 354166 1/3(East Lancashire)Fd Amb RAMC
LEACH Charles E. MM Pte 36848 Gloucestershire Regt
LEACH Claude E. MM Sjt 26439 15th Notts & Derby Regt
LEACH E. MM Sjt 305070 West Riding Regt
LEACH Edward J. MM Gnr 318560 RGA
LEACH Ernest Victor MM+Bar Sjt 3772 10th Royal Warwickshire Regt
LEACH Frederick MM Sjt 240962 17th Lancashire Fusiliers
LEACH Frederick C. MM L/Bdr 65069 45 Bty 42 Bde RFA
LEACH Frederick William MM Cpl 18925 Army Cyclist Corps
LEACH G.H. MM Gnr 56156 22 Bde RFA
LEACH George MM Sjt 200491 North Lancashire Regt KIA 28.4.18.
LEACH George J. MM Cpl 511361 14th London Regt
LEACH George Scott MM Sjt 4023 13th Middlesex Regt KIA 15.4.17.
LEACH Harold A. MM Pte 242311 13th Liverpool Regt
LEACH Harry G. MM L/Cpl 52757 Durham Light Infantry
LEACH Irvine MM Gnr 338182 RGA
LEACH James H. MM Pte 34214 15th Cheshire Regt
LEACH James William MM Cpl 6/10061 6th Lincolnshire Regt KIA 27.11.16.
LEACH John MM Cpl 240526 5th Devonshire Regt
LEACH John MM Cpl 29523 Middlesex Regt
LEACH John MM Sjt 4424 14th Royal Warwickshire Regt
LEACH John MM Cpl 43150 Gordon Highlanders
LEACH John A. MM Cpl 40695 6th South Wales Borderers
LEACH John C. MM+Bar Pte 71622 Royal Fusiliers
LEACH John H. MM Cpl 43179 5th Bn Machine Gun Corps
LEACH John S. MM Pte 43457 Machine Gun Corps
LEACH Robert MM Pte 7259 11th Lancashire Fusiliers
LEACH Robert MM Gnr 163510 106 Siege Bty RGA
LEACH Robert George MM Cpl 36454 18th Bn Machine Gun Corps
LEACH Rowland MM Pte 145261 1/1st Northamptonshire Yeomanry
LEACH Stanley MM Pte 15659 9th Norfolk Regt
LEACH Stephen J. MM Pte 25204 11th Royal West Kent Regt
LEACH T. MM Sjt 16/53 19th Northumberland Fusiliers
LEACH Thomas MM Sjt C/494 16th King's Royal Rifle Corps
LEACH Thomas R. MM Spr 45995 Royal Engineers
LEACH William MM Sjt 12090 A/86 Bde RFA
LEACH William MM L/Cpl 61028 8th West Yorkshire Regt
LEACH William MM Cpl 575665 17th London Regt
LEACH William MM Sjt 2193 1/7th Notts & Derby Regt
LEACH Willie W. MM+2 Bars Sjt 15394 57 Fd Coy Royal Engineers
LEACHMAN Charles MM Cpl 240120 5th Lincolnshire Regt
LEADBEATER Daniels MM Sjt 265037 2/7th Notts & Derby Regt KIA 21.3.18.
LEADBEATER John Henry MM Pte 49572 17th Liverpool Regt DOW 30.4.18.
LEADBEATER Samuel MM Spr 360682 18 Div Sig Coy Royal Engineers
LEADBETTER Frederick MM+Bar Sjt 1654 7th Royal West Surrey Regt

LEADBETTER Robert MM Sjt 685500 RFA
LEADBETTER Thomas MM Cpl 650689 RFA
LEADBETTER Robert F. MM Spr 146248 89 Fd Coy Royal Engineers
LEADBITTER Thomas MM Cpl 325910 1/9th Durham Light Infantry
LEADER Edwin Charles MM Pte 321129 6th London Regt KIA 9.8.18.
LEADER George MM Pte 683397 1/22nd London Regt
LEADER Percy MM+Bar Pte 14791 8th Suffolk Regt
LEAF Arthur MM Pte 7624 Royal Fusiliers
LEAF Ernest MM Gnr 786049 A/880 Bde RFA DOW 18.7.17.
LEAGO Frank MM+Bar Sjt 31745 RGA
LEAH Albert MM L/Cpl 10176 1st Cheshire Regt
LEAH John MM L/Sjt 49821 Labour Corps
LEAH Joseph MM Pte 32326 Shropshire Light Infantry
LEAH Stephen MM Pte 556549 16th London Regt
LEAH Thomas N. "DCM,MM" Sjt 676565 D/275 Bde RFA
LEAHY Alexander T. MM Sjt S/5597 8th Seaforth Highlanders
LEAHY Frederick MM Pte 3161 1st King's Royal Rifle Corps DOW 15.4.17.
LEAHY Jeremiah MM Pte 42975 17th Royal Scots
LEAHY John MM Pte 4575 9th Royal Munster Fusiliers
LEAHY William MM Sjt 5379 1st Gloucestershire Regt
LEAK Edwin Owen MM Sjt M2/032040 604 MT Coy Army Service Corps KIA 29.10.17.
LEAK James MM Pte 11388 9th West Riding Regt DOW 10.12.18.
LEAK Robert MM L/Cpl 52141 7th Bn Machine Gun Corps
LEAKE Edward MM Sjt 1220 1st King Edward's Horse
LEAKE Frank Harper MM Pte 28179 Duke of Cornwall's LI
LEAKE Frederick C. MM Pte 12424 1st Shropshire Light Infantry
LEAKE George MM Cpl 26638 Notts & Derby Regt
LEAKE Hugh G. MM Pte 142500 62nd Bn Machine Gun Corps
LEAKE James R. MM L/Cpl 39596 West Yorkshire Regt
LEAKE John E. MM Cpl 236108 9th West Yorkshire Regt
LEAKE Samuel John MM Cpl 11378 6th Dorsetshire Regt
LEAKEY William J. MM Pte 52138 Rifle Brigade att 28th London Regt.
LEALMAN Francis MM Cpl 93569 16 Bty 41 Bde RFA
LEAMAN A.E. MM Pte 352253 London Regt
LEAMAN George H. MM CSM 7802 Coldstream Guards
LEAMAN James B. MM+Bar Sjt M2/204762 Army Service Corps
LEAMON Herbert J. MM Sjt 78993 1 Fd Svy Bn Royal Engineers
LEAR Charles MM Pte 11258 1st Devonshire Regt
LEAR King L. MM Pte 230353 1/1st Dorset Yeomanry
LEAR Mark D. MM Pte S/31978 13th Rifle Brigade
LEAR Robert Alfred MM Pte 11101 7th Gloucestershire Regt
LEAR Ronald John MM L/Cpl 22138 2nd Devonshire Regt KIA 27.5.18.
LEAR Samuel MM Pte 55843 RAMC
LEAR Victor MM Cpl 850158 408 Bty 96 Bde RFA
LEARMONTH L.A. MM Pte 1565 RAMC
LEARMOUTH Charles MM Sjt 10118 2nd Gordon Highlanders
LEARMOUTH Henry D. MM Pte 2176 1/7th Northumberland Fusiliers
LEARY Arthur L. MM Cpl 76372 211 Siege Bty RGA
LEARY Edward MM+Bar Cpl 13235 17th Lancers
LEARY Fred MM Pte 242197 Lincolnshire Regt
LEARY John MM Pte 8344 1st South Staffordshire Regt
LEARY John MM Pte 6143 Royal West Kent Regt
LEARY John Christopher "MM,MSM" 2nd Cpl 21587 42 Army Troops Coy Royal Engineers
LEARY John H. MM Sjt 591030 1/18th London Regt
LEARY Patrick MM Pte 7904 2nd Leinster Regt
LEARY William MM Cpl 350346 1/7th London Regt
LEASK Charles Y. MM Pte 13529 Arg & Suth Highlanders
LEASK James R.S. MM L/Bdr 87164 RGA
LEASON William E. MM Cpl 240408 1/6th South Staffordshire Regt
LEATHAM John MM Cpl 6177 1st Royal Irish Rifles
LEATHAM Tom MM Pte 3452 1/6th Royal Highlanders
LEATHEM John Edward MM Pte 20/1075 22nd Northumberland Fusiliers
LEATHEN Louis MM Pte 4886 9th Seaforth Highlanders
LEATHER Albert MM Gnr 73941 36 Bde RFA
LEATHER Albert MM Sjt 330325 1/7th Liverpool Regt
LEATHER James MM Gnr 56871 RFA
LEATHER R. MM Pte 17999 North Lancashire Regt
LEATHERBARROW John MM+Bar Cpl 266996 Liverpool Regt
LEATHERBARROW Joseph MM Dvr 560568 Royal Engineers
LEATHERLAND Ernest MM Sjt 43299 Lincolnshire Regt
LEATHERLAND Frank R. "MM,MID" Sjt 14625 6th Northamptonshire Regt
LEATHERLAND William T. "DCM,MM" Pte 21115 9th West Yorkshire Regt
LEATHLEY Norman MM Pte 200711 1/4th East Yorkshire Regt
LEATON Frederick MM Cpl 45973 A/306 Bde RFA KIA 30.11.17.
LEAVER Arthur E. MM Sjt A/1031 King's Royal Rifle Corps
LEAVER George H. MM Spr 263168 218 Fd Coy Royal Engineers
LEAVER Harry MM L/Cpl 201897 York & Lancaster Regt
LEAVER Herbert MM Sjt 93870 259 Coy Machine Gun Corps
LEAVEY Frederick Walter "MC,MM(49863 Sjt)" T/2Lt 56 Div Sig Coy Royal Engineers
LEAVEY Harry MM Cpl 15166 8th Devonshire Regt
LEAVIS Thomas MM Sjt 242485 1/5th North Lancashire Regt
LEBBON Edward A. MM L/Sjt 43255 Norfolk Regt
LEBEDEFF-LESSIN Michael A. MM Pnr 255130 Royal Engineers
LEBLANC Thomas L. MM Pte 27272 74 Fd Amb RAMC
LEBURN Leonard Edwin MM Pte 42447 9th Royal Irish Fusiliers
LECHMERE Bertie MM Sjt M2/020775 Army Service Corps
LECHMERE Thomas H. MM Pte 310773 Tank Corps
LECKEY John MM L/Sjt 17610 6th Royal Inniskilling Fusiliers
LECKEY William MM Pte 23304 9th Royal Inniskilling Fusiliers
LECKIE(or LEEKIE) Charles MM L/Cpl 73395 56 Coy Machine Gun Corps
LECOUNT J.C. MM L/Cpl P4839 Military Mounted Police
LECOUNT Louis MM Sjt 36860 342 Siege Bty RGA
LECROIR Charles MM Cpl 50912 RFA
LEDBETTER William MM Spr 87478 Royal Engineers
LEDDER Walter MM Pte 29332 West Yorkshire Regt
LEDDIE Michael MM Pte 30211 12th Royal Scots Fusiliers
LEDGER Alexander F. MM Pte 823 Northumberland Fusiliers
LEDGER Herbert MM Gnr 75045 Tank Corps
LEDGER John MM Pte A/202112 King's Royal Rifle Corps
LEDGER John William MM Pte 9697 2nd York & Lancaster Regt
LEDGER Matthew MM Sjt 50605 1st East Yorkshire Regt KIA 7.11.18.
LEDGER William H. MM Pte 263042 5th Yorkshire Light Infantry
LEDGERWOOD William MM L/Cpl 240439 Liverpool Regt
LEDINGHAM Alexander G. MM Pte 43668 9th Scottish Rifles
LEDINGHAM Archibald MM Spr 406058 51 Div Sig Coy Royal Engineers
LEDRAN Thomas C. MM Gnr 1449 RGA
LEDRAW George Edward MM Pte 10/7 7th East Yorkshire Regt
LEDSON Samuel MM Cpl 675195 275 Bde RFA
LEDWIDGE John J. "DCM,MM" Sjt 3130 1st Royal Irish Fusiliers
LEDWITH James MM Pte 7986 2nd Lincolnshire Regt
LEE A. MM Pnr 84510 Royal Engineers
LEE A.E. MM Bdr 201238 B/107 Bde RFA
LEE A.G. MM Pte 508196 RAMC
LEE A.W. MM L/Sjt 38635 Royal Berkshire Regt
LEE Albert "MM,MSM,MID" Sjt SR/120 7th Royal Sussex Regt
LEE Albert MM Sjt 14121 6th Lincolnshire Regt
LEE Albert "DCM,MM" L/Cpl 8533 7th & 2nd Leinster Regt KIA 25.8.18.
LEE Albert MM L/Cpl 2146 1/9th Liverpool Regt
LEE Albert Edward MM Spr 67767 'Q' Special Coy Royal Engineers
LEE Alfred MM Pte 63833 9th Yorkshire Light Infantry
LEE Alfred MM L/Cpl 13524 6th Northamptonshire Regt
LEE Alfred MM Pte 25110 5th West Riding Regt
LEE Alfred MM Pte 9038 9th East Surrey Regt
LEE Alfred MM Sjt 14784 10th Yorkshire Light Infantry
LEE Alfred Edward MM Cpl 32198 'A' Bn Tank Corps
LEE Alfred J. "DCM,MM" Sjt H/46306 15th Hussars
LEE Alfred J. MM Spr 359496 Guards Div Sig Coy Royal Engineers
LEE Amos MM Gnr 17772 D/108 Bde RFA
LEE Andrew MM Pte 17123 6th Yorkshire Regt KIA 27.8.17.
LEE Andrew MM Pte 28512 Manchester Regt
LEE Anthony C.J. MM Pte 21416 Royal West Surrey Regt
LEE Arthur MM Pte 24189 10th West Riding Regt
LEE Austin MM Pte 24246 61 Fd Amb RAMC
LEE Charles MM Sjt 5487 1/4th Royal Welsh Fusiliers
LEE Charles W. MM Pte 12034 7th Lincolnshire Regt
LEE Claude "MM,MID" Cpl 857 5(West Riding)Bty RFA
LEE Clifford MM Pte 1286 1/4th Yorkshire Regt
LEE Cline M. MM Gnr 19279 RGA
LEE David R. MM Cpl 14328 9th Devonshire Regt
LEE E. MM Cpl 87924 RHA
LEE Edgar J. MM Pte 5026 8th Royal West Surrey Regt
LEE Edward MM Pte 233468 2nd London Regt
LEE Edward G. MM Cpl 87332 Machine Gun Corps

LEE Ernest MM Cpl 240209 Norfolk Regt
LEE Ernest "DCM,MM" Sjt 29161 2nd Royal Welsh Fusiliers
LEE Ernest MM Sjt 147542 Royal Engineers
LEE Ernest MM Sjt 2923 West Riding Regt
LEE Frank A. MM+Bar Cpl 19781 Machine Gun Corps
LEE Fred MM Bdr 202346 Y/57 Med TM Bty RFA
LEE Fred MM Pte 200537 1/5th Manchester Regt DOW 22.8.18.
LEE Fred MM L/Sjt 2138 Notts & Derby Regt
LEE Frederick MM L/Cpl 1117 2nd Welsh Regt Died 12.3.18.
LEE Frederick MM L/Cpl 12051 6th Bedfordshire Regt
LEE Frederick H. MM Sjt 51827 RFA
LEE Frederick L. MM Sjt 265085 1/1st(Buckinghamshire)Bn Oxf & Bucks Light Infantry
LEE George MM Cpl 300408 8th Manchester Regt
LEE George MM Pte M2/175997 Army Service Corps
LEE George MM Cpl 200778 2/4th Yorkshire Light Infantry
LEE George MM Sjt 8356 2nd Royal Welsh Fusiliers
LEE George MM Sjt 57432 41 Bde RFA
LEE George MM Pte 7936 1st Royal Welsh Fusiliers
LEE George MM Pnr 197114 Special Brigade Royal Engineers
LEE George MM Gnr 17397 RGA
LEE George MM Pte 36297 34th Bn Machine Gun Corps
LEE George Audenby MM L/Cpl 104576 228 Fd Coy Royal Engineers KIA 26.3.18.
LEE George H. MM Pte 17734 Royal Welsh Fusiliers
LEE George H. MM Pnr 259274 Royal Engineers
LEE George John MM Sjt 6340 6th Border Regt
LEE George W. MM Sjt 17857 11th Somerset Light Infantry
LEE Gerald M. MM Sjt 301493 5th London Regt
LEE H.J. MM AM1 8601 Royal Flying Corps att RGA
LEE Harold MM Sjt 698 9th East Surrey Regt
LEE Harold S. MM+Bar Pte 592765 18th London Regt
LEE Harold V. MM L/Cpl 43256 Norfolk Regt
LEE Harry MM Pte 2197 1/6th Cheshire Regt
LEE Harry W. MM Cpl L/21631 B/317 Bde RFA
LEE Hector McLean MM L/Cpl S/8262 Arg & Suth Highlanders KIA 18.10.16.
LEE Henry MM Pte 268423 Liverpool Regt
LEE Henry W. MM Pnr 41437 11 Div Sig Coy Royal Engineers
LEE Herbert MM Pte 26401 8th Yorkshire Regt
LEE Herbert MM Sjt 63795 1st Royal West Surrey Regt KIA 13.4.18.
LEE Herbert Jacob MM+Bar L/Cpl 13289 5th Leicestershire Regt
LEE Horace MM Pte 50821 Highland Light Infantry
LEE Horace W. "MM,MSM" QMS 33148 8 Military Ambulance Convoy RAMC
LEE J. MM Gnr 931727 A/119 Bde RFA
LEE J.E. MM L/Cpl 200522 Manchester Regt
LEE Jack MM L/Bdr 36620 RGA
LEE James MM Gnr 193026 115 Hy Bty RGA
LEE James MM L/Cpl 55732 16th Royal Welsh Fusiliers
LEE James MM Cpl 22154 252 Coy Machine Gun Corps
LEE James MM Sjt 23758 57 Bde RFA
LEE James MM L/Sjt S/7759 8th Royal Highlanders
LEE James MM Pte 10111 1st Duke of Cornwall's LI
LEE James MM+Bar Pte 8307 22 Fd Amb RAMC
LEE James MM Spr 148234 52 Div Sig Coy Royal Engineers
LEE James A. MM Pte 22181 Notts & Derby Regt
LEE John MM L/Cpl 33294 8th Devonshire Regt
LEE John MM Pte 11672 1st South Wales Borderers
LEE John MM Pte 50270 15th Cheshire Regt
LEE John MM Pte 233122 2nd London Regt
LEE John MM Sjt 20206 Royal Engineers
LEE John D. MM Pte 1366 2nd Arg & Suth Highlanders
LEE John L. MM Pte 42962 4th Royal Fusiliers
LEE John M. MM Pte 633581 20th London Regt
LEE John Thomas MM Pte 25946 1st South Wales Borderers KIA 18.4.18.
LEE John W. MM Pte 9529 8th Lincolnshire Regt
LEE Joseph MM Cpl L/13475 23rd Royal Fusiliers
LEE Joseph MM(389 L/Cpl Northbld Fus)+Bar Sjt 46514 15th Durham Light Infantry
LEE Joseph MM L/Sjt 7917 2nd King's Own Scottish Borderers
LEE Joseph Frederick MM L/Cpl 10284 2nd Royal Lancaster Regt
LEE Leonard MM Sjt T/30255 5 Div Train Army Service Corps
LEE Oscar MM Pte 200488 West Riding Regt
LEE P. MM L/Cpl 30167 Yeomanry
LEE Percy MM Gnr 23449 2 Siege Bty RGA
LEE R.G. MM Pte R/5241 King's Royal Rifle Corps
LEE Reginald MM Pte 45845 13th Rifle Brigade
LEE Reginald J. MM Cpl 200575 West Yorkshire Regt
LEE Reuben Frederick Summers MM Dvr 61012 81 Fd Coy Royal Engineers
LEE Richard MM Pte 240333 1/5th Royal West Surrey Regt
LEE Richard MM Pte 3296 12th Middlesex Regt
LEE Richard MM Pte 49991 13th Cheshire Regt
LEE Richard MM Sjt 330047 1/7th Liverpool Regt
LEE Robert MM Sjt 10/1000 10th East Yorkshire Regt
LEE Robert MM Dvr 760465 A/317 Bde RFA
LEE Robert M. MM L/Bdr 38265 RGA
LEE Sydney N. MM Pte 40834 4th North Lancashire Regt
LEE Theodore J. MM Spr 311529 Royal Engineers att RFA
LEE Thomas MM Pte 27309 Duke of Cornwall's LI
LEE Thomas MM Sjt 2013 1/6th Welsh Regt
LEE Thomas E. "DCM,MM" Bdr 42451 23 Bde RFA
LEE Tom MM L/Cpl 26422 10th Royal Warwickshire Regt
LEE W.G.P. MM Sjt P/1326 Military Foot Police
LEE William MM Pte 30706 1st Border Regt
LEE William MM Pte 93985 16th Royal Welsh Fusiliers
LEE William MM Gnr 175 'D' Bn Machine Gun Corps(Heavy Branch)
LEE William MM Pte 280115 1/7th Highland Light Infantry
LEE William MM Cpl 240963 6th Liverpool Regt
LEE William MM L/Cpl 14641 7th Somerset Light Infantry
LEE William MM Pte 25689 Scottish Rifles
LEE William MM Pte 235017 Hampshire Regt
LEE William MM Spr 64905 104 Fd Coy Royal Engineers
LEE William H. MM Pte 17535 Royal Sussex Regt
LEE William J.J. MM Cpl 44098 76 Fd Coy Royal Engineers
LEE William T. MM Cpl 10531 1st East Surrey Regt
LEE Willie MM CQMS 6607 2nd Border Regt
LEEBURN William J. MM Sjt 10355 2nd Royal Inniskilling Fusiliers
LEECH Enoch MM+Bar Pte 235449 Lancashire Fusiliers
LEECH Ernest MM L/Cpl 12043 2nd Grenadier Guards KIA 27.8.18.
LEECH Harold C. MM Pnr WR/284527 234 Lt Rly Fwd Coy Royal Engineers
LEECH Joseph MM Bdr 152287 B/250 Bde RFA
LEECH Sidney MM Sjt 15630 Leicestershire Regt
LEECH W. MM Pte 200141 Yorkshire Regt
LEECH W.H.B. MM Pte G/13061 7th East Kent Regt
LEECH W.W. MM L/Cpl 73042 Notts & Derby Regt
LEECH William MM Sjt 20939 22nd Manchester Regt
LEEDER C. MM Pte 13367 1st East Surrey Regt
LEEDER James A. MM L/Cpl 54953 Royal Welsh Fusiliers
LEEDER Moses MM Pte 43257 1st Norfolk Regt
LEEDING G.O. MM Air Mech 2 22629 Royal Flying Corps
LEEDS George John MM L/Cpl 200774 Oxf & Bucks Light Infantry
LEEDS William A. MM Cpl 283 7th East Surrey Regt
LEEK Albert E. MM L/Cpl T4/240529 Army Service Corps
LEEK Alfred James MM Pte 26069 3rd Worcestershire Regt DOW 13.8.17.
LEEK Harris MM Pte 200091 1/4th Suffolk Regt
LEEKE J. MM Pte O/710 13th Rifle Brigade
LEEKE John MM CSM 7570 1st South Staffordshire Regt
LEEKS Hardy E. MM Pte 32057 Suffolk Regt
LEEMAN Ben MM Pte 31859 15th Notts & Derby Regt KIA 23.8.18.
LEEMBRUGGEN Clarence MM Cpl 508105 Royal Engineers
LEEMING Ernest MM Pte 51855 Lincolnshire Regt
LEEMING Harry MM Pte 16/744 1st West Yorkshire Regt
LEEMING John C. MM Cpl 8062 A/150 Bde RFA
LEEMING Joseph MM Pte 23437 Yorkshire Regt
LEEPER Frederick Caldwell Clement MM CSM 5586 13th Royal Fusiliers KIA 16.7.16.
LEES Alexander Robertson MM Sjt 1590 1/14th London Regt
LEES Andrew MM Cpl 315554 13th Royal Highlanders
LEES Arthur MM Sjt T3/023039 Army Service Corps
LEES Arthur J. MM Pte 27904 Notts & Derby Regt
LEES Bertie B. MM Pte 278705 1/7th Arg & Suth Highlanders
LEES Charles MM Cpl 202144 5/6th Scottish Rifles
LEES David MM Pte S/13014 Gordon Highlanders
LEES E.V. MM Sjt 203878 5th York & Lancaster Regt
LEES Ernest MM Dvr 56054 A/103 Bde RFA KIA 2.6.17.
LEES Harold Bernard MM Pte 9291 2nd Royal Welsh Fusiliers KIA 20.7.16.
LEES Herbert MM Sjt 14008 24th Manchester Regt
LEES James Carrington MM Cpl 10305 Manchester Regt
LEES James Pithie MM Cpl 330088 RAMC att Yorkshire Light Infantry
LEES James W. MM Sjt 28019 12th Royal Scots KIA 23.3.18.
LEES John MM Pte 37862 East Lancashire Regt
LEES John MM Sjt 1894 2nd Royal Highlanders
LEES John H. MM L/Cpl S/5579 12th Rifle Brigade

LEES Joseph MM Spr 104453 63 Fd Coy (sic) Royal Engineers
LEES Noah MM Pte 15198 6th Shropshire Light Infantry
LEES Norman M. MM Pte 305348 1/8th Notts & Derby Regt
LEES Peter H. MM Pte S/7497 9th Gordon Highlanders
LEES Robert MM L/Cpl 22632 Machine Gun Corps
LEES Samuel R. "DCM,MM" Sjt 375179 1/10th Manchester Regt
LEES Sidney MM Sjt 51160 'O' Bty RHA
LEES Thomas MM Sjt 17148 20th Manchester Regt
LEES Thomas MM L/Cpl 21172 2nd Bedfordshire Regt
LEES Tom MM Cpl 2372 1/5th Durham Light Infantry
LEES Walter H. MM Gnr 930542 2/2(London)Bde RFA
LEES William MM L/Cpl 26621 Notts & Derby Regt
LEES William MM Pte 128832 Machine Gun Corps
LEES William A. MM Sjt 18069 9th North Lancashire Regt
LEESON Fred MM Pte 14325 8th Border Regt
LEESON George MM Gnr 59449 141 Siege Bty RGA
LEESON Herbert J. MM Pte 8391 Machine Gun Corps
LEESON William MM Pte 201284 Arg & Suth Highlanders
LEESON William MM Sjt 6580 12th Lancashire Fusiliers
LEESON William Joel MM Gnr 12335 RFA
LEETCH Ernest Ashley MM Gnr L/25302 RFA Died 19.3.19.
LEETE Fred MM L/Cpl 38476 9th Yorkshire Regt
LEETLE M. MM Sjt 2594 Connaught Rangers
LEFEVRE Douglas MM Pte 301393 2/1st(Highland)Fd Amb RAMC
LEFFLY Leonard MM Pte 33688 15/17th West Yorkshire Regt KIA 24.3.18.
LEFTLY Edward W. MM Pte 9983 Wiltshire Regt
LEFTWICH W. MM Gnr 92094 'H' Bn Tank Corps DOW 26.4.18.
LEGAULT Emile MM Pte 4186 5th Liverpool Regt
LEGG George H. MM Sjt 16849 Machine Gun Corps
LEGG Harry MM+Bar Pte 67954 Royal Fusiliers
LEGG John MM Pte 22/114 9th Northumberland Fusiliers
LEGG John J. MM Pte 241788 Border Regt
LEGG Joseph W. MM Ndr 67914 'Q' Bty RHA
LEGG Laurence Stanley MM Sjt 18449 10th Essex Regt KIA 12.4.18.
LEGG Leonard MM Cpl 350512 1st Essex Regt
LEGG Robert MM L/Cpl 5619 18th Highland Light Infantry
LEGG William MM Dvr 52097 RFA
LEGG William MM Gnr 82188 RGA
LEGG William Henry MM Pte 8718 2nd Gloucestershire Regt KIA 1.9.18.
LEGGAT Graham MM Spr 406114 Royal Engineers
LEGGAT William D. MM Spr 402825 404 Fd Coy Royal Engineers
LEGGATE Alexander MM 2nd Cpl 412194 409 Fd Coy Royal Engineers
LEGGATE John MM Sjt 8805 11th Highland Light Infantry
LEGGATE Robert MM Pte 3840 8th Royal Highlanders
LEGGATE Robert MM Pte 4365 9th Royal Highlanders
LEGGATT Alexander B. MM Pte S/12757 1/7th Gordon Highlanders KIA 21.3.18.
LEGGATT Arthur MM Sjt SE/1641 Army Veterinary Corps
LEGGATT Thomas MM L/Cpl G/2836 8th Royal Sussex Regt
LEGGATT William MM Sjt 9789 8/10th Gordon Highlanders
LEGGE George MM Pte 10299 6th Dorsetshire Regt KIA 11.10.18.
LEGGE Harry J.V. MM Pte 14090 8th Shropshire Light Infantry
LEGGE Henry MM L/Sjt 29517 Yorkshire Regt
LEGGE Henry G. MM Pte 240551 1st Gordon Highlanders KIA 23.10.18.
LEGGE Robert N. MM Pte 142325 Machine Gun Corps
LEGGETT Alfred H. MM L/Cpl 16543 8th Lincolnshire Regt
LEGGETT Arthur MM Pte 300077 8th Durham Light Infantry
LEGGETT Charles MM Cpl M2/149825 Army Service Corps att 42 Siege Bty RGA
LEGGETT Cyril MM Pte 7930 1st Norfolk Regt
LEGGETT Frank R. MM Pte 147593 37th Bn Machine Gun Corps
LEGGETT Frederick Robert MM Cpl 201002 1/1st Cambridgeshire Regt Died 22.9.18.
LEGGETT George T. MM+2 Bars Sjt 58392 4th York & Lancaster Regt
LEGGETT John MM L/Cpl 20401 12th Gloucestershire Regt
LEGGETT Joseph Alfred MM Sjt 7719 7th Norfolk Regt KIA 30.11.17.
LEGGETT Martin MM Pte G/3956 3rd Royal Fusiliers
LEGGETT T. MM Pte 5041 2nd Royal Irish Rifles
LEGGETT Victor S. MM Pte 242487 West Riding Regt
LEGGETT William J. MM Pte 20359 Suffolk Regt
LEGGETT William J. MM+Bar L/Cpl 200299 1/4th Suffolk Regt
LEGGO Henry MM Cpl 59075 1 Bty RFA
LEGGOTT George Harold "MM,MSM" Sjt 44843 D/102 Bde RFA
LEGGOTT William Clement MM L/Cpl 57240 Welsh Regt
LEGH Harcourt E.A. MM L/Sjt 491481 1/13th London Regt
LEHAN William C. MM Pte 3962 15th London Regt
LEICESTER James MM L/Cpl 10308 2nd Seaforth Highlanders
LEIGH C. MM L/Cpl 13050 10th West Riding Regt
LEIGH Edgar H. MM Pte 73130 Notts & Derby Regt
LEIGH Ernest MM Sjt 8610 6th York & Lancaster Regt
LEIGH Ernest MM Cpl 275858 Manchester Regt
LEIGH Frank MM L/Cpl G/10515 7th Royal West Kent Regt
LEIGH Harry "MM,MID" Sjt M2/046677 Army Service Corps
LEIGH Herbert MM+Bar Sjt 240590 4th North Lancashire Regt
LEIGH James MM Pte 41759 RAMC
LEIGH John H. MM Cpl 341531 RAMC
LEIGH Mark J. MM Gnr 3194 RFA
LEIGH Robert MM Pte 243069 North Lancashire Regt
LEIGH Samuel "MM,MBC(Rm)" Pte 51840 13th Liverpool Regt
LEIGH Sidney F. MM+Bar L/Sjt 10064 Worcestershire Regt
LEIGH Tom MM Cpl 124309 RGA
LEIGH Walter MM Cpl 250487 20th Manchester Regt
LEIGH Walter "DCM,MM" Pte 13306 7th North Lancashire Regt
LEIGH William MM Dvr 18451 381 Bty RFA
LEIGH William A. MM Pte 241984 4th South Lancashire Regt
LEIGHFIELD William C. MM CSM 3/9140 2nd Wiltshire Regt
LEIGHTON Adam MM L/Cpl 22024 Royal Scots
LEIGHTON Albert MM Gnr 51018 RFA
LEIGHTON Alexander MM Gnr 41366 RGA
LEIGHTON Arthur MM L/Sjt 22888 1/4th Royal Scots
LEIGHTON Charles MM L/Cpl 20594 1st Royal Scots
LEIGHTON David MM+Bar Cpl S/10272 5th Cameron Highlanders
LEIGHTON David MM Bdr 371168 RGA
LEIGHTON Frank MM Sjt 11392 6th Dorsetshire Regt
LEIGHTON George MM L/Cpl 351069 Royal Scots
LEIGHTON James MM Sjt 24/630 Northumberland Fusiliers
LEIGHTON John R. MM Sjt 203301 20th Durham Light Infantry
LEIGHTON John S. MM Pte 238893 1/1st Herefordshire Regt att Shropshire Light Infantry
LEIGHTON John V. MM L/Sjt 61684 6th Yorkshire Regt
LEIGHTON Joshua MM Pte 265899 1/5th Cheshire Regt
LEIGHTON Noah MM Pte 242631 Yorkshire Light Infantry
LEIGHTON Oliver T. MM Pte 6019 9th Royal Sussex Regt
LEIGHTON Richard MM Pte 7893 1st North Staffordshire Regt
LEIGHTON Samuel "MM,MC(G)" Sjt 12864 8th Shropshire Light Infantry
LEIGHTON Thomas Henry MM Pte 10184 1st Coldstream Guards Died 23.8.18.
LEIGHTON Tom MM Cpl 38368 East Yorkshire Regt
LEIKIN Samuel MM Pte 85406 188 Coy Machine Gun Corps
LEIPER Frank "DCM,MM" Sjt 2797 17th Highland Light Infantry
LEIPER Robert "MM,MID" Cpl 60595 112 Bde RFA
LEIPER Walter MM Pte 55241 Highland Light Infantry
LEISHMAN Alexander MM Pte 21345 King's Own Scottish Borderers
LEITCH Alexander MM Cpl 265207 1/6th Gordon Highlanders
LEITCH Allan MM Spr 86801 Royal Engineers
LEITCH Angus MM Pte 738096 24th London Regt
LEITCH Angus MM L/Cpl 2595 Seaforth Highlanders
LEITCH George W. MM Spr 328829 Royal Engineers
LEITCH Herbert MM Cpl 38342 5 Div Ammn Col RFA
LEITCH James MM Pte S/17895 1/4th Gordon Highlanders
LEITCH James J. MM L/Cpl 345074 14th Royal Highlanders
LEITCH John MM Sjt 220326 5th Cameron Highlanders
LEITCH John MM Pte 59247 RAMC
LEITCH Lachlan MM Cpl 266065 1/7th Scottish Rifles
LEITCH Robert "MM,MID" Sjt 156419 184 Tunnelling Coy Royal Engineers
LEITCH Stanley Ridley MM L/Cpl 300314 1/7th Essex Regt
LEITH Alfred MM+Bar Sjt 23553 4 Div Sig Coy Royal Engineers
LEITH Edward MM Sjt SPTS/1257 17th Royal Fusiliers
LEITH Harry MM Sjt 3/6678 8/10th Gordon Highlanders
LEITH James MM Pte 10527 1st Gordon Highlanders
LEITH Robert MM Pte 14033 Gordon Highlanders
LEITH W.P. MM Pte 303132 2/1st(Highland)Fd Amb RAMC
LEIVERS Alfred Bruce MM CSM 9291 1st Notts & Derby Regt
LEMMINGS Alfred W. MM+Bar Sjt 200229 1/4th Oxf & Bucks Light Infantry
LEMON Albert Victor MM L/Cpl 205471 Royal West Surrey Regt
LEMON Charles MM Sjt 16820 Machine Gun Corps
LEMON John MM Pte M2/049808 Army Service Corps
LEMON Mark MM Pte 295475 1/4th London Regt
LEMON Robert MM Pte 11285 8th Devonshire Regt

LEMON Thomas MM Sjt 1349 11th Hussars
LEMON Thomas MM Spr 40079 8 Div Sig Coy Royal Engineers
LENG Amos MM Cpl 189447 HQ 88 Bde RFA
LENG Herbert "MM+Bar,MID" L/Sjt 702194 23rd London Regt
LENG Richard "DCM,MM" Sjt 241031 2nd Yorkshire Light Infantry DOW 8.11.18.
LENNARD Alfred MM Pte 388506 2/2(Northumbrian)Fd Amb RAMC
LENNARD John MM Pte 5657 1st Gordon Highlanders
LENNARD Michael "DCM,MM" L/Cpl 25/1070 25th Northumberland Fusiliers KIA 15.4.18.
LENNEY Michael MM Bdr 5516 RGA
LENNIE Alexander H. MM Sjt 418203 65 Div Sig Coy Royal Engineers
LENNIE Daniel "DCM,MM,MID" Cpl 50346 90 Fd Coy Royal Engineers
LENNIE Neil MM Bdr 93572 RFA
LENNIE Thomas MM Pte S/5193 7th Seaforth Highlanders
LENNON Adam MM Pte 11349 6/7th Royal Scots Fusiliers
LENNON Charles MM Cpl 3801 24th Royal Fusiliers
LENNON David MM Pte 6685 3rd Coldstream Guards
LENNON George MM Pte 108 11th Highland Light Infantry
LENNON Hugh MM Pte 6408 1st East Lancashire Regt
LENNON James MM Pte S/17721 1st Gordon Highlanders
LENNON John MM Pte 20532 Royal Dublin Fusiliers
LENNON Joseph "MC,DCM,MM(9820 Sjt 1st Bn)" 2Lt 2nd Royal Irish Fusiliers
LENNON Thomas MM Pte 4732 North Lancashire Regt
LENNOX Samuel MM Pte 40445 Royal Scots Fusiliers
LENNOX William MM Pte 9767 2nd Cameron Highlanders
LENNOX William R. MM Pte 71885 Machine Gun Corps
LENSLEY William MM L/Cpl 41540 Lincolnshire Regt
LENTELL Stanley V. MM Sjt 11710 2nd Coldstream Guards
LENTERN Charles MM Sjt 9018 Coldstream Guards
LENTON Harold Bertram MM Sjt 2235 16th Middlesex Regt KIA 30.10.17.
LENTON John H. MM CSM 27496 8th Royal Berkshire Regt
LENYGON Fred MM Sjt 293381 10th Middlesex Regt
LENZ John MM Spr 42944 Royal Engineers
LENZER Frank Charles MM Pnr 495868 6 Mounted Bde Sig Troop Royal Engineers Died 4.11.18.
LEONARD A. MM L/Cpl 240501 Lincolnshire Regt
LEONARD Alfred T. MM Pte 54258 Labour Corps
LEONARD Andrew MM Sjt 10248 2nd Royal Dublin Fusiliers
LEONARD Arthur "DCM,MM" Sjt 32963 119 Bty 27 Bde RFA
LEONARD Charles "DCM,MM,MID" Pte 49861 Machine Gun Corps
LEONARD D. MM L/Cpl 24448 Yorkshire Regt
LEONARD Edmund MM Sjt 24589 10th Cheshire Regt
LEONARD Edward MM Pte 23/461 12/13th Northumberland Fusiliers
LEONARD George MM Pte 1869 (200216) 9th Yorkshire Light Infantry KIA 25.4.18.
LEONARD Gilbert W. MM Pte 266390 Gloucestershire Regt
LEONARD James MM Pte 25241 10th Royal Dublin Fusiliers
LEONARD James MM+Bar Cpl 426 Royal Fusiliers
LEONARD James MM+Bar Sjt 13375 10th North Lancashire Regt
LEONARD John MM Pte 48891 11th Royal Fusiliers
LEONARD John MM Sjt 3150 9th Lancashire Fusiliers
LEONARD Martin MM L/Cpl 1070 23rd Northumberland Fusiliers
LEONARD Myles MM Pte 4339 Labour Corps
LEONARD Patrick "DCM,MM" Cpl 15231 32nd Bn Machine Gun Corps DOW 1.10.18.
LEONARD Patrick MM L/Cpl 14889 Royal Dublin Fusiliers
LEONARD Ralph E. MM Dvr 68322 42 Bde RFA
LEONARD Thomas MM Gnr 97741 163 Siege Bty RGA
LEONARDI James MM L/Cpl 19084 9th York & Lancaster Regt
LEPPARD Charles Harold "DCM,MM" L/Sjt SD/3861 7th Royal Sussex Regt
LEPPARD William H. MM 2nd Cpl 532605 497 Fd Coy Royal Engineers
LEPPINGTON James W. MM Gnr 686875 RFA
LEPTS Arthur M. MM Gnr 105276 21 Bty 27 Bde RFA
LEROY J. MM L/Cpl 307411 Liverpool Regt
LERPINIERE Arthur Charles H. MM Sjt 32943 RAMC
LERWELL Thomas MM Pte 15954 Welsh Regt
LESAGE Alfred MM Sjt Farrier 225579 120 Hy Bty RGA
LESLIE Alexander MM L/Bdr Sig 631527 255 Bde RFA
LESLIE Alexander G. MM Sjt T4/043479 51 Div Train Army Service Corps
LESLIE David MM Gnr 170213 A/14 Bde RFA
LESLIE Ernest C. MM Pte 8492 1st Border Regt

LESLIE Frederick E. MM L/Cpl 2931 1st Life Guards
LESLIE George MM Cpl 5385 6th Dragoon Guards
LESLIE George MM L/Sjt 569 5th Dragoon Guards
LESLIE Horace Leonard MM Pte 52999 4th Middlesex Regt
LESLIE James MM Pte 40024 1st Royal Dublin Fusiliers
LESLIE James MM Dvr 635671 256 Bde RFA
LESLIE James MM Bdr 5101 92 Bty 17 Bde RFA
LESLIE John MM Cpl 332069 Highland Light Infantry
LESLIE John MM Pte 4551 Machine Gun Corps
LESLIE John Marcus MM Sjt 702030 1/23rd London Regt
LESLIE Joseph H. MM Pte 3/12700 9th West Riding Regt
LESLIE Matthew Alexander MM Pte 19735 25th Bn Machine Gun Corps KIA 28.5.18.
LESLIE Peter MM+2 Bars Cpl 1186 6th Leinster Regt
LESLIE Peter R. MM 2nd Cpl 133463 128 Fd Coy Royal Engineers
LESLIE Robert MM Pte 4506 6th London Regt
LESLIE Ronald J.M. MM Cpl 43526 1st Royal Scots
LESLIE Thomas MM Pte 19620 2nd East Lancashire Regt
LESLIE William MM Pte 73581 RAMC
LESLIE William MM Cpl 750139 RFA
LESSIMORE Edward John MM Sjt 1052 1/4th Gloucestershire Regt
LESSLIE Wallace S. "MM,MID" Armt S/Sjt T/261 Army Ordnance Corps
LESTER Algernon H. MM L/Cpl 357736 Liverpool Regt
LESTER Arthur "DCM,MM+Bar" Sjt 25909 A/123 Bde RFA
LESTER Charles MM Sjt 63158 7 Bde RHA
LESTER George Raymond MM Pte M2/022059 Army Service Corps att 141 Fd Amb RAMC
LESTER Harold Ernest MM Pte 13112 8th South Staffordshire Regt DOW 13.5.17.
LESTER John MM Pte 201632 2/7th Worcestershire Regt
LESTER Richard MM Pte 111597 10th Bn Tank Corps
LESTER Wiliam H. MM Sjt 69990 RGA
LESTER William MM Bdr 57782 Z/24 Med TM Bty RGA
LESTER William E. MM Cpl 240095 1/5th Leicestershire Regt
LETCH Frank MM Gnr 14334 32 Bde RFA
LETCHFORD Sydney C. MM Pte 19906 RAMC
LETCHFORD Walter MM Pte S/36201 13th Rifle Brigade
LETHAM Frederick H. MM L/Cpl 47379 Machine Gun Corps(Cavalry)
LETHBRIDGE William Quantick MM Sjt 240568 1/5th Devonshire Regt
LETT Daniel MM BSM 950019 A/18 Bde RFA
LETT Stephen MM Pte 7889 1st Royal Dublin Fusiliers
LETTEN Edward H. MM Spr 28485 Royal Engineers
LETTERS Robert MM Pte 6359 12th Royal Irish Rifles
LETTIS George MM Pte 3213 2nd Royal Scots KIA 22.7.16.
LETTS Augustus MM+Bar Pte 8773 1st South Staffordshire Regt
LETTS Frank MM Pte S/43714 1/6th Royal Highlanders
LETTS John F. MM+Bar Pte 200921 4th Bn Tank Corps
LETTY William H. MM L/Cpl 48001 Rifle Brigade
LEUCHARS Alfred MM+Bar L/Cpl 240169 1/5th Royal Highlanders
LEUCHARS Andrew MM Cpl 268132 1/6th Royal Highlanders
LEVELL Leonard J. MM Pte 10563 2nd Wiltshire Regt
LEVELL Thomas C. MM L/Cpl 14740 9th Norfolk Regt
LEVER Arthur George MM Sjt 5310 5 Fd Amb RAMC KIA 19.2.17.
LEVER Harry MM Pte 27801 8th North Lancashire Regt
LEVER Robert MM L/Cpl 240945 1/5th North Lancashire Regt KIA 30.11.17.
LEVER Thomas MM Pte 9311 2nd Manchester Regt
LEVER Thomas MM Dvr 675294 RFA
LEVER Walter MM Pte 240115 1/5th East Lancashire Regt
LEVER William John MM Gnr 72042 35 Bde RFA
LEVERETT Albert MM Pte 7631 11th Royal Fusiliers
LEVERETT Benjamin E. MM+Bar Pte 17360 9th Norfolk Regt
LEVERETT George MM L/Sjt 11190 1st Notts & Derby Regt
LEVERICK Ernest G. MM Pte 722176 24th London Regt
LEVERIDGE Albert MM S/Sjt Farrier 225336 113 Heavy Bty RGA
LEVERITT Herbert MM L/Cpl 4322 23rd Royal Fusiliers
LEVERSUCH Albert Edward MM Pte 452100 1/22nd London Regt
LEVERTON Ben MM Pte M1/6387 Army Service Corps
LEVESLEY H.T. MM L/Cpl 2420 York & Lancaster Regt
LEVESLEY John Henry MM Sjt 200955 2/4th York & Lancaster Regt
LEVETT Alfred E. MM+Bar Pte 14349 2nd Royal Fusiliers
LEVETT George MM 2nd Cpl 14548 Royal Engineers
LEVETT Samuel MM Pte R/525 12th King's Royal Rifle Corps
LEVEY Frederick J. MM Pte 80178 1/1st Essex Yeomanry
LEVEY Otto Lemuel Herbert MM CSM 530583 1/15th London Regt
LEVI Abraham MM Sjt 47905 13th Royal Inniskilling Fusiliers

LEVI Samuel MM Pte 98373 206 Coy Machine Gun Corps KIA 26.10.17.
LEVICK William MM Gnr 294213 RGA
LEVIE Archibald MM Pte 14440 20th Middlesex Regt
LEVINSKY A. MM Pte 574075 London Regt
LEVITT Frank MM Pte 2580 1/1st Cambridgeshire Regt
LEVITT Frank S. MM Pte 61165 24th Royal Fusiliers
LEVITT George MM Dvr T/34088 Army Service Corps
LEVITT George MM Sjt G/8569 11th Royal West Kent Regt DOW 1.8.17.
LEVITT Joseph MM Cpl DM2/075418 Army Service Corps
LEVITT Walter MM L/Cpl 13/157 13th East Yorkshire Regt
LEVITT William A. MM Bdr 67900 RHA
LEVY Arthur T. MM Cpl 19803 8 Fd Amb RAMC
LEVY Emanuel MM Pte 573957 17th London Regt
LEVY Ernest F. MM Pte 28799 4th Hampshire Regt
LEVY Isaac MM+Bar Sjt 235629 5th West Riding Regt
LEVY Lazarus MM Pte 2667 2nd Manchester Regt
LEVY Samuel MM Pte 358452 10th Liverpool Regt
LEVY William Edward Harry MM Cpl 460 'D' Bn Machine Gun Corps(Heavy Branch)
LEWCOCK Herbert MM L/Cpl 5965 2nd Dragoond
LEWENDON Albert W. MM+2 Bars CSM 10896 5th Oxf & Bucks Light Infantry
LEWENDON Benjamin MM Pte 43551 8th Lincolnshire Regt
LEWENDON Clifford MM Bdr 11294 RFA
LEWENDON Cyril "MM,MID" Cpl 24304 15th Notts & Derby Regt
LEWENDON George MM Sjt P/868 Military Mounted Police
LEWER Ernest MM Pte 6400 1st Royal Fusiliers
LEWIN Albert MM Pte 339229 RAMC
LEWIN Albert MM Sjt 2576 4th Rifle Brigade
LEWIN Edward G. MM Pte G/164 6th Royal West Kent Regt
LEWIN Frederick MM+Bar L/Sjt 77956 10th Royal Fusiliers
LEWIN Frederick J. MM+Bar Pte 202760 2/4th York & Lancaster Regt
LEWIN George "MM,MSM" Sjt 265469 Z/32 Med TM Bty RFA
LEWIN Herbert MM L/Cpl 10094 1st Royal Berkshire Regt
LEWIN Herbert MM Sjt 240571 1/5th Lincolnshire Regt
LEWIN Horace MM Cpl 18411 7th Bedfordshire Regt KIA 1.7.16.
LEWIN John Henry MM 2nd Cpl 69954 156 Fd Coy Royal Engineers
LEWIN Robert E. MM Sjt 19278 10th Royal Warwickshire Regt
LEWIN William MM L/Cpl 30878 33rd Bn Machine Gun Corps
LEWINGTON Charles J. MM Pte 391369 15th London Regt
LEWINGTON Ernest T. MM Pte 33126 4th Hampshire Regt
LEWINGTON Herbert W. MM Sjt 76228 D/121 Bde RFA
LEWINS George MM Sjt 20885 11th Royal Inniskilling Fusiliers
LEWINS George MM Pte 333368 Highland Light Infantry
LEWINS Thomas MM+Bar Sjt 16788 7th Somerset Light Infantry
LEWINS William T. MM+Bar Pte 22046 12th Durham Light Infantry
LEWIS A.J. MM Cpl 8435 RFA
LEWIS Albert MM Sjt 632750 20th London Regt
LEWIS Albert Charles MM Gnr 68399 D/100 Bde RFA
LEWIS Albert E. MM L/Cpl G/14704 2nd Royal Sussex Regt
LEWIS Albert Edward MM Pte 2743 24th London Regt KIA 27.1.17.
LEWIS Albert George MM Bdr 36380 37 Heavy Artillery Group RGA
LEWIS Albert H. MM Sjt 81329 RGA
LEWIS Alfred Ernest "DCM,MM" Pte 22539 15th Royal Welsh Fusiliers
LEWIS Archibald MM+Bar Cpl 4177 RFA
LEWIS Arthur MM L/Cpl 45226 4th Worcestershire Regt
LEWIS Arthur MM Pte 74632 7th Royal Fusiliers
LEWIS Arthur MM Pte 24304 6th East Lancashire Regt
LEWIS Arthur J. MM Pte 536804 15th London Regt
LEWIS Arthur M. MM L/Cpl 591610 1/18th London Regt
LEWIS B.E.W. MM Sjt 439490 RAMC
LEWIS Benjamin "MM,MID" L/Cpl T4/041632 35 Div Train Army Service Corps
LEWIS Benjamin James MM Pte 16794 6th South Wales Borderers DOW 31.5.18.
LEWIS Charles "DCM,MM" Cpl 53839 Y/38 Med TM Bty RGA
LEWIS Charles MM L/Cpl 20578 1/8th West Yorkshire Regt KIA 1.9.18.
LEWIS Charles MM Pte 8877 3rd Rifle Brigade
LEWIS Charles E. MM Sjt 3832 Army Cyclist Corps
LEWIS Charles H. MM Cpl 37340 4th Worcestershire Regt
LEWIS Christopher T. MM Pte 20161 14th Royal Welsh Fusiliers
LEWIS Daniel MM Gnr 102730 RGA
LEWIS David MM Sjt 19083 6th York & Lancaster Regt
LEWIS David T. MM Pte 244878 North Lancashire Regt

LEWIS David T. MM Pte 277085 Manchester Regt
LEWIS David Thomas MM Sjt 91032 207 Coy Machine Gun Corps
LEWIS David W. MM Pte 99235 Machine Gun Corps
LEWIS David William MM Dvr 2827 D/64 Bde RFA DOW 28.10.17.
LEWIS E. MM L/Cpl P2410 Military Foot Police
LEWIS E.R. MM+Bar Pte 12317 1st Essex Regt
LEWIS Edward MM Cpl R/3888 13th King's Royal Rifle Corps
LEWIS Edward A. MM Pte 10719 6th Royal West Kent Regt
LEWIS Edward George MM Bdr 50129 57 Bde RFA
LEWIS Edward J. MM Pte 66674 140 Fd Amb RAMC
LEWIS Edwin R. MM Sjt 230559 10th Shropshire Light Infantry
LEWIS Egdar MM Pte 15843 10th Welsh Regt KIA 23.12.17.
LEWIS Eric MM Cpl 432072 Royal Engineers
LEWIS Ernest MM Pte 201236 6th Bn Tank Corps
LEWIS Ernest MM Pte 40032 South Lancashire Regt
LEWIS Ernest MM Pte 165882 1/1st North Somerset Yeomanry
LEWIS Ernest I. MM Sjt 67222 113 Coy Labour Corps
LEWIS Evan MM Sjt 38 1st Welsh Guards
LEWIS Evan MM Pte 25658 Welsh Regt
LEWIS Ewart MM Sjt 11125 23rd Middlesex Regt
LEWIS Ewart Edmund MM Sjt 91747 C/117 Bde RFA DOW 21.3.18.
LEWIS Francis A. MM Sjt 535 1/15th London Regt
LEWIS Frank MM L/Cpl 198865 Royal Engineers
LEWIS Frank MM Cpl 282156 Lancashire Fusiliers
LEWIS Frank MM Pte 3/5813 1st Cameron Highlanders
LEWIS Fred MM Pte 30152 Worcestershire Regt
LEWIS Frederick MM Bdr 761 129 Bty 42 Bde RFA DOW 24.10.18.
LEWIS Frederick "MM,CG(B)" L/Cpl 31403 11th East Lancashire Regt
LEWIS Frederick James MM Sjt 43518 15 Div Sig Coy Royal Engineers KIA 1.7.16.
LEWIS Frederick William MM Sjt 22934 RGA
LEWIS G. MM Sjt 7585 2nd South Staffordshire Regt
LEWIS George MM Pte 240206 Royal Welsh Fusiliers
LEWIS George "DCM,MM" Pte 25478 2nd Cheshire Regt
LEWIS George "MM,MID" Pte 9279 2nd Royal Welsh Fusiliers
LEWIS George MM+Bar Pte 6897 Middlesex Regt
LEWIS George MM Gnr 207213 RFA
LEWIS George MM Sjt 882 18th Middlesex Regt KIA 16.4.18.
LEWIS George C. MM Spr 138878 Royal Engineers
LEWIS George E. MM Cpl 47303 26th Royal Welsh Fusiliers
LEWIS George H. MM Cpl 830 2nd Royal Irish Regt
LEWIS George H. MM Cpl 80888 RFA
LEWIS George Martin MM Pte M2/134059 Army Service Corps att 11 Fd Amb RAMC
LEWIS George Richard MM Cpl 73268 Army Sig Coy(Mesopotamia) Royal Engineers
LEWIS Godfrey MM L/Cpl 38516 5th Gloucestershire Regt
LEWIS Graham MM Cpl 290213 8th Scottish Rifles
LEWIS Griffith MM Pte 14036 7th Shropshire Light Infantry
LEWIS Guy Mainwaring "MM,MID" Cpl 158502 A/152 Bde RFA
LEWIS Harold MM Pte 57898 Cheshire Regt
LEWIS Harold G. MM Pte 37595 9th South Lancashire Regt
LEWIS Harold J. "DCM,MM" CSM 53723 9th Welsh Regt
LEWIS Harold Nicholson MM L/Cpl 3347 Liverpool Regt KIA 18.10.17.
LEWIS Harold W.C. MM L/Cpl 102834 Machine Gun Corps
LEWIS Harry MM Cpl 52478 8th Lancashire Fusiliers
LEWIS Harry MM Pte 21533 South Wales Borderers
LEWIS Harry MM Sjt 92421 154 Coy Labour Corps
LEWIS Harry MM L/Cpl 34427 11th East Lancashire Regt
LEWIS Harry MM Sjt T2/14847 Army Service Corps
LEWIS Harry MM Cpl 80214 238 Siege Bty RGA
LEWIS Henry MM Cpl 53107 RGA
LEWIS Henry MM Pte R/15487 King's Royal Rifle Corps
LEWIS Henry T. MM Pte 71925 3rd Bn Machine Gun Corps
LEWIS Herbert MM Pte 12925 4th Worcestershire Regt
LEWIS Herbert Owen MM L/Cpl 1300 1/6th Liverpool Regt
LEWIS Irwin MM Pte 266112 1/2nd Monmouthshire Regt
LEWIS Ivor MM Pte 14787 5th South Wales Borderers DOW 3.6.17.
LEWIS Jack E. MM Cpl 4032 14th Liverpool Regt
LEWIS Jacob H. MM Sjt 47038 29 Bde RFA
LEWIS James MM Sjt 33463 11th Hampshire Regt
LEWIS James MM Spr 506391 504 Fd Coy Royal Engineers
LEWIS James MM Pte 51087 1st Royal Scots Fusiliers
LEWIS James MM L/Cpl 5592 Machine Gun Corps
LEWIS James MM Pte 14229 11th Royal Welsh Fusiliers
LEWIS James MM Cpl 754 RFA
LEWIS James MM Pte 25656 Welsh Regt
LEWIS James MM Pte 2661 1st Welsh Guards

LEWIS James MM Pte 40436 York & Lancaster Regt
LEWIS James E. MM Pte 290346 Royal Welsh Fusiliers
LEWIS James L. MM Pte 75497 10th Royal Welsh Fusiliers
LEWIS Jenkin MM Dvr 29023 RFA
LEWIS Joe Edward MM L/Cpl 242067 Worcestershire Regt
LEWIS John MM Pte 17350 14th Welsh Regt KIA 10.7.16.
LEWIS John MM Bdr 3637 C/286 Bde RFA
LEWIS John "MM,CG(B)" Pte 10/1306 10th East Yorkshire Regt
LEWIS John MM L/Cpl 10436 1st South Wales Borderers
LEWIS John MM Sjt 2203 East Surrey Regt
LEWIS John A. MM Pte 51672 6th Liverpool Regt
LEWIS John H. MM Sjt 17284 6th South Wales Borderers
LEWIS John J. MM Pnr 130362 Royal Engineers
LEWIS John T. MM Cpl 117734 Machine Gun Corps
LEWIS John W. MM Sjt 15125 19th Lancashire Fusiliers
LEWIS John W. MM L/Cpl 11834 6th Shropshire Light Infantry
LEWIS Joseph MM Cpl 62937 70 Bty 34 Bde RFA
LEWIS Joseph MM Sjt 13708 10th North Lancashire Regt
LEWIS Joshua MM Pte 202942 Manchester Regt
LEWIS Lemuel MM Pte 17246 6th South Wales Borderers KIA 10.10.16.
LEWIS Leonard MM Sjt 19231 Suffolk Regt att 1/1st Cambridgeshire Regt
LEWIS Leonard T. MM Sjt 7921 Machine Gun Corps
LEWIS Leonard W. MM Sjt G/8665 2nd Royal Sussex Regt
LEWIS Leslie N. MM+2 Bars Cpl 40483 Royal Engineers
LEWIS Lord MM Pte B/382283 Exp Force Canteen Army Service Corps
LEWIS Louis MM Pte 29271 Welsh Regt
LEWIS Maurice MM Sjt 48938 23rd Royal Fusiliers
LEWIS Michael MM Pte 10028 1st Irish Guards KIA 14.7.17.
LEWIS N. MM Gnr 119094 132 Hy Bty RGA
LEWIS P. MM Pte 33452 Worcestershire Regt
LEWIS Penry MM Gnr 229306 175 Bde RFA
LEWIS Percy MM L/Cpl 22455 Liverpool Regt
LEWIS Reginald MM Spr 451937 406 Fd Coy Royal Engineers
LEWIS Richard MM+Bar Sjt 275 23rd Royal Fusiliers
LEWIS Richard H. MM Cpl 108101 23 Fd Coy Royal Engineers
LEWIS Robert J. MM Sjt 13386 8th Shropshire Light Infantry
LEWIS Rowland Clifford MM Sjt 202842 2/4th Oxf & Bucks Light Infantry
LEWIS Samuel MM Sjt 22128 Machine Gun Corps
LEWIS Samuel MM Dvr 34739 RFA
LEWIS Samuel MM Pte 57936 Liverpool Regt
LEWIS Samuel H. "DCM,MM" Sjt 426525 Royal Engineers
LEWIS Sidney T.V. MM Sjt 31897 RFA
LEWIS Sidney Thomas MM L/Sjt 13886 4th Grenadier Guards KIA 26.11.17.
LEWIS Sidney W. MM L/Cpl 332673 9th Liverpool Regt
LEWIS Stanley J. "MM,MID" Sjt 71141 Royal Engineers
LEWIS Sydney MM Sjt 300416 5th London Regt
LEWIS Sydney MM Pte 34185 South Lancashire Regt
LEWIS T. "DCM,MM+Bar" Sjt 15003 8th South Lancashire Regt
LEWIS T.H. MM Dvr 25024 RFA
LEWIS T.J. MM Pte 55034 Royal Welsh Fusiliers att MGC
LEWIS T.J. MM Air Mech 2 8485 Royal Flying Corps
LEWIS Taliesin MM Pte 5067 2nd Royal Irish Rifles
LEWIS Thomas MM L/Cpl 28778 8th Somerset Light Infantry
LEWIS Thomas MM Pte 16903 11th Cheshire Regt Died 17.7.18.
LEWIS Thomas MM L/Cpl 9337 King's Royal Rifle Corps
LEWIS Thomas Henry "MM,MC(G)" L/Cpl 22682 11th Royal Welsh Fusiliers
LEWIS Thomas R. MM Pte 55263 Royal Welsh Fusiliers
LEWIS W.H. MM Sjt 139388 250 Tunnelling Coy Royal Engineers
LEWIS W.J. MM Pte 91272 RFA
LEWIS Wallace MM Sjt 7253 11th Notts & Derby Regt
LEWIS Walter MM+Bar Sjt 25161 110 Coy Machine Gun Corps DOW 26.3.18.
LEWIS Walter J. MM L/Cpl 22165 7th Gloucestershire Regt
LEWIS Warren A. MM Sjt 200282 1/4th Royal Welsh Fusiliers
LEWIS William MM Pte M2/073647 Army Service Corps
LEWIS William MM Spr 49965 218 Fd Coy Royal Engineers
LEWIS William MM L/Cpl 43318 7th Bedfordshire Regt KIA 10.8.17.
LEWIS William MM Pte 11215 1st South Wales Borderers
LEWIS William MM Sjt 403 17th Royal Fusiliers
LEWIS William MM Pte 17469 Shropshire Light Infantry
LEWIS William MM L/Cpl 30155 2nd Welsh Regt
LEWIS William MM Pte 48799 129 Fd Amb RAMC
LEWIS William MM Cpl 15061 12th Cheshire Regt
LEWIS William Charles "DCM,MM" CSM 12017 1st Wiltshire Regt
LEWIS William Henry MM Pte 14387 7th Shropshire Light Infantry
LEWIS William Henry MM+Bar L/Cpl 4353 9th Royal Welsh Fusiliers
LEWIS William J. MM Dvr 4702 RFA
LEWIS William J. MM Pte 3/18484 1st South Wales Borderers
LEWIS William J. MM Pte 529 1st Welsh Guards
LEWIS William John MM Cpl 14698 7th Shropshire Light Infantry KIA 28.3.18.
LEWIS William N. MM Sjt 22378 Machine Gun Corps
LEWIS William T. MM+Bar Sjt 83550 D/74 Bde RFA
LEWRY Arthur MM Cpl 16717 1st Royal West Kent Regt
LEWRY Herbert P. MM Sjt 11360 8th East Surrey Regt
LEWRY Wilfred MM Gnr 102800 35 Siege Bty RGA
LEWTAS George MM Gnr Fitter 32213 C/64 Bde RFA
LEWTHWAITE Emanuel MM Pte 202517 South Wales Borderers
LEWTHWAITE George MM Sjt 13220 11th Border Regt
LEWTHWAITE John W. MM Dvr 8343 RFA
LEWTHWAITE Thomas W. MM Pte 88825 7th Liverpool Regt
LEY Frederick MM Dvr 82645 RFA
LEY Thomas MM L/Sjt 40887 Royal Scots
LEY Walter F. MM Spr 349000 Royal Engineers
LEYBOURN Frederick Percy "MM,MID" Pte 17410 20th Manchester Regt KIA 1.11.18.
LEYBOURNE A.S. MM L/Cpl P5184 Military Foot Police
LEYBOURNE James MM Sjt 330022 Liverpool Regt
LEYDEN Duncan Paton MM Pte S/15298 Cameron Highlanders
LEYDEN John MM Pte R/16587 King's Royal Rifle Corps
LEYDEN Terence MM Dvr 50920 5 Pontoon Park Royal Engineers
LEYDON Gilbert J. MM Sjt 9826 1st Somerset Light Infantry
LEYLAND Charles MM Pte 42244 76 Fd Amb RAMC KIA 7.6.17.
LEYLAND James MM Cpl 21783 8th Royal Lancaster Regt
LEYLAND Peter MM Pte 42571 1st Lancashire Fusiliers
LEYLAND Robert MM Spr 91975 Royal Engineers
LEYLAND S.L. MM Air Mech 2 94425 Royal Flying Corps
LEYLAND Samuel MM Cpl 200202 1/5th Liverpool Regt
LEYLAND T. MM Air Mech 1 17116 Royal Flying Corps
LEYS James MM Pte 290485 Gordon Highlanders
LEYS John MM Pte 3015 1/4th Royal Highlanders
LEYS John H. MM Cpl 402381 404 Fd Coy Royal Engineers
LEYS Robert S. MM Dvr 631093 19 Bty 9 Bde RFA
LEYSHON Frederick Frank Herbert MM Gnr 110265 219 Siege Bty RGA DOW 5.8.17.
LEYTON Joseph MM Pte 69457 RAMC
LIBBEY Albert MM Pte 2649 1/4th Yorkshire Regt
LIBBY Charles "DCM,MM" Pte 23406 10th Duke of Cornwall's LI
LIBBY Frank Thomas MM Cpl 302391 5th London Regt DOW 19.4.18.
LIBERTON John MM Cpl 325239 1/8th Royal Scots
LICENCE Alfred MM Pte 11540 1st Notts & Derby Regt
LICENCE Herbert N. MM Pte 12546 7th Suffolk Regt
LICHFIELD William Henry MM CQMS 7458 2nd South Staffordshire Regt DOW 10.8.16.
LICKESS Harry MM Pte 403425 2 Fd Amb RAMC
LIDBURY John H. "MM,MSM" Cpl 4978 1st Royal West Kent Regt
LIDDELL Charles MM Gnr 715327 D/210 Bde RFA KIA 21.4.18.
LIDDELL Robert MM Pte 25/1056 Northumberland Fusiliers
LIDDELL Robert E. MM Spr 495234 Royal Engineers
LIDDELL Sydney MM Sjt 388039 2(West Riding)Fd Amb RAMC
LIDDELL Thomas MM Spr 400729 19 Div Sig Coy Royal Engineers
LIDDELL Thomas MM L/Cpl 20/448 Durham Light Infantry
LIDDELL Tom MM Sjt C/12394 18th King's Royal Rifle Corps DOW 28.3.18.
LIDDELL Walter MM L/Cpl 313154 Royal Engineers
LIDDELL William H. MM L/Cpl 32275 8th East Surrey Regt
LIDDERDALE William MM Pte 28301 1st North Lancashire Regt
LIDDIARD Charles J. MM Pte 698101 22nd London Regt
LIDDIARD Fred MM Pte 7650 9th Lancashire Fusiliers
LIDDIARD George MM+Bar Cpl 40997 40 Bde RFA
LIDDIARD George Andrew MM Sjt 511866 1/14th London Regt
LIDDIARD Jack MM Pte R/6018 King's Royal Rifle Corps
LIDDIARD John T. "MM,MSM" Sjt 208052 294 Fd Coy Royal Engineers
LIDDIARD Leslie E. MM Pte H/321567 1/1st Wiltshire Yeo
LIDDIARD Sydney G. MM L/Cpl 50704 11th Cameron Highlanders
LIDDIATT Arthur W. MM L/Cpl 22764 Royal Warwickshire Regt
LIDDICOAT James MM Cpl 23851 10th Duke of Cornwall's LI
LIDDICOAT William John MM Pte 24222 10th Duke of Cornwall's LI
LIDDLE Adam W. MM Pte 10129 1st King's Own Scottish Borderers
LIDDLE Alexander MM L/Cpl 40117 6th King's Own Scottish Borderers
LIDDLE Andrew B. MM Pte 276103 1/8th Arg & Suth Highlanders

LIDDLE George MM Pte 31437 6th King's Own Scottish Borderers
LIDDLE John MM+Bar Sjt 6314 17 Fd Amb RAMC
LIDDLE William MM Sjt 817 1/8th Durham Light Infantry
LIDGETT Archibald K. MM Pte M1/5001 Army Service Corps
LIDGETT Ernest M. MM Pte 255562 1/1st Leicestershire Yeo
LIDGETT Harry J. MM Pte DM2/221108 Army Service Corps
LIDGETT Lancelot MM L/Sjt 15946 3rd Coldstream Guards
LIDYARD Frank MM Sjt 240091 1/8th Middlesex Regt
LIEBERMANN Frederick W. MM Pte 148958 41st Bn Machine Gun Corps
LIEBERMANN W.J. MM CQMS 200009 Oxf & Bucks Light Infantry
LIEBRICK Albert MM CSM 5685 6th East Yorkshire Regt
LIFE William Edward MM L/Cpl 8133 10th Royal West Kent Regt
LIFFITON Harry MM L/Cpl 82795 2nd London Regt
LIGGETT James Alex MM Cpl 73796 25th Bn Machine Gun Corps
LIGHT Allen J. MM L/Cpl 6476 1st Hampshire Regt
LIGHT Daniel MM Sjt 66593 40 Bde RFA
LIGHT George MM Pte 5742 Royal Sussex Regt
LIGHT Herbert MM Gnr 77544 Y/47 Med TM Bty RFA
LIGHT Rowland "MM,MID" Sjt 200221 West Yorkshire Regt
LIGHT Vernon E. MM Pte 45068 8th Royal Berkshire Regt
LIGHT William MM L/Cpl 151869 33rd Bn Machine Gun Corps
LIGHTBODY Arthur B. MM Bdr 55786 39 Bde RFA
LIGHTBODY William MM Gnr 60832 197 Siege Bty RGA
LIGHTBOWN Joseph MM+Bar Sjt R/12970 1st King's Royal Rifle Corps
LIGHTENING Sydney MM Pte 11187 Royal Scots
LIGHTFOOT Arthur Sydney MM Pte 80 9th Royal Sussex Regt
LIGHTFOOT Charles MM L/Cpl 15302 Leicestershire Regt
LIGHTFOOT Harry MM Sjt 266959 1/7th West Yorkshire Regt KIA 3.5.18.
LIGHTFOOT Herbert MM Pte 13761 Yorkshire Regt KIA 21.10.17.
LIGHTFOOT John H. MM L/Cpl 5947 19th Hussars
LIGHTFOOT Roland MM+Bar Sjt 201150 1/4th Gloucestershire Regt
LIGHTNING Frank MM Pte G/11677 11th Royal West Surrey Regt KIA 4.7.18.
LIGHTON William Henry MM Pte 41329 Northumberland Fusiliers
LIHOU George C. MM L/Cpl 16327 6th South Wales Borderers
LILBURN Herbert P. MM RQMS 200019 1/4th Cheshire Regt
LILES J.B. MM Cpl 23193 11th Essex Regt
LILES John MM Pte 9760 2nd Lancashire Fusiliers
LILL Collin MM Cpl 282609 18th Lancashire Fusiliers
LILL Frederick A. MM Sjt G/3170 12th Middlesex Regt
LILL Hubert MM L/Cpl 16308 2nd York & Lancaster Regt KIA 22.4.17.
LILL Stephen P. MM Cpl 482537 Royal Engineers
LILL Tom MM Cpl 548628 513 Fd Coy Royal Engineers
LILLEY A.E. MM Pte 201729 Suffolk Regt
LILLEY Albert MM L/Cpl 546578 226 Fd Coy Royal Engineers
LILLEY Alfred MM L/Cpl 4182 Machine Gun Corps
LILLEY Arthur MM Sjt 8486 2nd Lincolnshire Regt
LILLEY Arthur E. MM Pte 79269 2nd Durham Light Infantry
LILLEY Charles MM Bdr 54071 18 Bde RFA
LILLEY Enoch "DCM,MM+Bar" Sjt R/4348 11th King's Royal Rifle Corps
LILLEY George MM Pte 203345 York & Lancaster Regt
LILLEY Gilbert MM L/Cpl 16255 12th West Yorkshire Regt
LILLEY Harry MM Sjt 326803 1/1st Cambridgeshire Regt
LILLEY Herbert S. MM Pte 37475 RAMC
LILLEY Herbert W.J. MM Spr 22052 1 Div Sig Coy Royal Engineers
LILLEY Robert MM Cpl 278608 1/7th Arg & Suth Highlanders
LILLEY Thomas MM Pte 17418 15th Royal Scots DOW 10.4.17.
LILLEY Walter MM L/Cpl 15726 2nd Grenadier Guards
LILLEY Wilfred MM+Bar L/Cpl 240317 1/5th Leicestershire Regt
LILLEY William MM CSM 32334 16th Yorkshire Light Infantry
LILLEY William MM Cpl 770141 50 Div Ammn Col RFA
LILLEY William Fred MM Sjt 2849 Lincolnshire Regt KIA 24.4.18.
LILLFORD William MM Gnr 133629 166 Siege Bty RGA
LILLICO John W. MM Gnr Saddler 7758 RFA
LILLICO Robert J. MM Pte 291713 Northumberland Fusiliers
LILLICRAP Alfred Bailey "MM,MSM,MID" CSM 2876 20 Fd Coy Royal Engineers
LILLIE Thomas MM Pte 19641 23rd Northumberland Fusiliers Died 21.3.18.
LILLIE Thomas Scott MM L/Cpl 330132 1/9th Highland Light Infantry
LILLINGTON Alfred H. MM Sjt R/4168 13th King's Royal Rifle Corps
LILLIS Robert Mervyn MM BSM 20067 28 Bty 9 Bde RFA
LILLIS William MM Pte 9057 2nd Royal Irish Regt
LILLY James MM Dvr 3975 D/83 Bde RFA

LIMB Frederick MM Pte 19891 Notts & Derby Regt
LIMB John Henry "MM,MMV(lt)" L/Cpl 59254 Liverpool Regt
LIMB John T. MM Pte 200504 West Riding Regt
LIMBACH Louis MM Pte 269204 7th West Riding Regt
LIMBERT Rowland MM Cpl 7905 1st Royal Berkshire Regt KIA 24.8.18.
LIMBRICK Mark MM Sjt 24019 RGA
LIMER John MM+Bar Pte 47639 RAMC
LIMERICK Fergus Henry MM Pte 203154 1/4th Yorkshire Regt
LIMMER Thomas William "MC,MM,MID" CSM 265413 1/6th West Riding Regt
LINATHAN Colin J. MM Sjt 15885 12th Notts & Derby Regt
LINAY Percy Herbert MM CSM 56059 52nd Bn Machine Gun Corps KIA 2.9.18.
LINCOLN Arthur H.J. MM+Bar Gnr 75290 Machine Gun Corps
LINCOLN Bertie MM L/Cpl 200498 1/4th Suffolk Regt
LINCOLN Charles F. MM Pte 15180 Machine Gun Corps
LINCOLN Henry MM Pte 267859 West Yorkshire Regt
LINCOLN Henry C. MM L/Bdr 97775 135 Bty 32 Bde RFA
LINCOLN Robert MM L/Cpl 57805 Liverpool Regt
LINCOLN William MM Gnr 68095 26 Bde RFA
LIND Robert Gordon Forbes MM L/Cpl 201058 1/4th Gordon Highlanders KIA 23.4.17.
LINDBERG Robert MM+Bar Pte 3392 1st Royal Irish Fusiliers
LINDEN Ed MM Gnr 645062 RFA
LINDEN William J. MM L/Cpl 11576 6th Border Regt
LINDER Frank G. MM Pte 15387 8th Suffolk Regt
LINDER Thomas T. MM Pte S/10055 1st Royal Highlanders
LINDIE James MM Pte 252226 1/7th Arg & Suth Highlanders
LINDLEY Albert Victor MM Pte 9834 2/1st HAC(Infantry) DOW 8.5.17.
LINDLEY Arthur MM Cpl 58518 47th Bn Machine Gun Corps
LINDLEY Charles MM Sjt 64608 RGA
LINDLEY Frank MM L/Cpl 50615 Cheshire Regt
LINDLEY George MM Gnr 99676 RFA
LINDLEY Herbert MM Gnr 73597 C/83 Bde RFA
LINDLEY Herbert MM Pte 1585 West Yorkshire Regt
LINDLEY John W. MM Pte 263004 5th Yorkshire Light Infantry
LINDOP Harold MM Sjt 16492 4th Royal Fusiliers KIA 18.9.18.
LINDOP Harry MM Pte 1210 Royal Fusiliers
LINDOP Robert MM Sjt 3902 Machine Gun Corps
LINDORES John Moyes "MM,MID" Sjt 7027 2nd Scots Guards
LINDSAY Alexander D. MM Sjt 540 1/6th Royal Highlanders
LINDSAY Alexander E. MM Pte 32833 RAMC att RFA
LINDSAY Arthur J. MM L/Cpl 398 6th Royal West Kent Regt
LINDSAY Harold "MM,MSM,MIDx3" Sjt 8527 Royal Lancaster Regt
LINDSAY Hugh MM Spr 249490 9 Div Sig Coy Royal Engineers
LINDSAY Ian W. MM Pte 28432 8th Somerset Light Infantry
LINDSAY James MM Pte 14043 1st Scots Guards KIA 15.10.18.
LINDSAY James MM Pte 39442 RAMC
LINDSAY James MM L/Cpl 2172 1 Coy Machine Gun Corps KIA 18.6.16.
LINDSAY James MM Cpl 24959 Royal Scots
LINDSAY James MM Pte 17483 1st King's Own Scottish Borderers
LINDSAY James MM Pte 64341 107 Coy Machine Gun Corps
LINDSAY James MM Pte 11142 9th Royal Highlanders
LINDSAY James B. MM Sjt 19631 10th Northumberland Fusiliers
LINDSAY James M. "MM,MID" Sjt 2543 Tank Corps
LINDSAY John MM Sjt 19/198 15th Royal Irish Rifles
LINDSAY John MM Dvr 18862 C/223 Bde RFA
LINDSAY John MM S/Sjt Farrier 29278 RFA
LINDSAY John Broome MM Cpl 15684 8th Royal Lancaster Regt
LINDSAY John S. "DCM,MM+Bar" Sjt 9418 X Corps Cyclist Bn Army Cyclist Corps
LINDSAY Joseph MM Cpl S/10052 1st Gordon Highlanders
LINDSAY Joseph MM L/Cpl S/1833 8/10th Gordon Highlanders
LINDSAY Joseph "MM,MID" Sjt 14229 10th Scottish Rifles
LINDSAY Robert Bruce MM 2nd Cpl 65278 106 Fd Coy Royal Engineers
LINDSAY The Hon Edward Reginald MM Gnr 163884 211 Siege Bty RGA
LINDSAY W.C. MM Air Mech 1 14115 Royal Flying Corps
LINDSAY Walter MM L/Cpl 266506 1/6th Royal Highlanders
LINDSAY Walter MM L/Cpl 3623 11th Arg & Suth Highlanders
LINDSAY Watson E. MM L/Cpl S/40387 Royal Highlanders
LINDSAY William MM Pte 14282 11th Royal Scots
LINDSAY William MM Bdr 655204 D/250 Bde RFA
LINDSAY William MM Pte 11/19601 11th Royal Irish Rifles
LINDSAY William Thomas "MM,MSM" Sjt 35903 47 Fd Amb RAMC
LINDSELL John W. MM Pte 268041 7th West Yorkshire Regt

LINDSELL Joseph MM+Bar CSM 308012 West Riding Regt
LINDSELL Leo MM Pte 683124 22nd London Regt
LINDSELL R. MM Pte 41770 Manchester Regt
LINDSEY Charles W. MM Sjt K/646 22nd Royal Fusiliers
LINDSEY Henry J. MM+Bar Sjt 23636 7th Yorkshire Light Infantry
LINDSEY John MM Pnr WR/283665 231 Lt Rly Op Coy Royal Engineers
LINDSEY John MM L/Cpl 12451 Royal Lancaster Regt
LINDSEY Leonard A. MM Pte 45633 RAMC
LINDSEY Walter MM Pte 202314 Lancashire Fusiliers
LINDSLEY James MM Pte 32/550 Northumberland Fusiliers att RE.
LINEGAR Charles "DCM,MM" L/Cpl 6811 1st Royal West Surrey Regt
LINEHAM R. MM Sjt 32312 RGA
LINEKER Tom MM Gnr 77779 RGA
LINES Aubrey MM Cpl 4377 2/1st HAC(Inf)
LINES Benjamin T MM Dvr 83537 200 Fd Coy Royal Engineers
LINES Charles MM Pte 2541 18th Hussars
LINES Frank H. MM Sjt 840012 D/241 Bde RFA
LINES Frederick MM Pte 200816 1/5th Liverpool Regt
LINES Frederick G. MM Pte 66624 99 Fd Amb RAMC
LINES John C. MM Pte 22457 20th Liverpool Regt DOW 29.10.16.
LINES John F. MM Pte 75110 RAMC
LINES Joseph MM Pnr 128680 Royal Engineers
LINES Walter H. "DCM,MM" Pte 12290 7th Norfolk Regt
LINES William MM Pte 28513 2nd Royal Dublin Fusiliers
LINES William MM Pte 14677 Northumberland Fusiliers
LINFOOT Ernest William MM Bdr 80640 275 Siege Bty RGA
LINFOOT Fred MM Sjt 7535 1st West Yorkshire Regt KIA 14.7.18.
LINFORD Albert MM Cpl 200817 North Lancashire Regt
LINFORD Alfred W. MM Sjt 20279 Royal Sussex Regt
LINFORD Joseph MM Pte 16/665 16th West Yorkshire Regt
LING Alfred J.E. MM Sjt 275702 1/6th Essex Regt
LING Frederick G. MM Pte 15935 9th Norfolk Regt
LING Frederick W. MM L/Cpl 312060 Royal Engineers
LING John W. MM Pte 238025 4th London Regt
LING Maurice MM L/Cpl M2/047041 Army Service Corps
LING Richard MM Cpl Wheeler 105838 D/71 Bde RFA
LING William S. MM Sjt 6338 Army Veterinary Corps
LINGARD Albert MM Pte 10720 1st Notts & Derby Regt
LINGARD Arthur MM Pte 63698 105 Fd Amb RAMC
LINGARD George E. MM Sjt 10758 Cheshire Regt
LINGE John MM Pte 518 1st Royal West Kent Regt KIA 12.3.17.
LINGE Robert E. MM L/Cpl 3513 1/1st Hertfordshire Regt
LINGLEY Sidney T. "MM+Bar,MID" Pte 11179 Scots Guards
LINGS George W. "DCM,MM" CSM 14994 8th Leicestershire Regt
LINGWOOD Charles MM Dvr L/7981 B/112 Bde RFA KIA 10.10.18.
LINGWOOD John A. MM Sjt 624219 HAC
LINGWOOD Joseph MM Sjt 9813 1st East Yorkshire Regt
LINIGHAN John MM Gnr 28045 B/50 Bde RFA
LINK Benjamin T. MM Pte 260092 Royal Sussex Regt
LINK Oliver MM Cpl 10467 9th West Riding Regt
LINKINS James MM Pte 471840 12th London Regt
LINKLATER James MM L/Cpl S/16335 5th Cameron Highlanders
LINKLATER Joseph George MM Cpl M2/048703 46 Div Train Army Service Corps
LINLEY Arthur MM Pte 72 RAMC
LINLEY James Walter MM Pte 44253 2nd Lincolnshire Regt
LINLEY William MM Cpl 260146 7th Gordon Highlanders
LINN Alexander MM Pte 200119 5/6th Scottish Rifles
LINN Edgar E. MM L/Cpl 17/998 1st West Yorkshire Regt
LINN James MM Sjt 33586 38 Bde RFA
LINNANE Joseph F. MM Sjt 4319 1st Irish Guards
LINNELL Arthur MM Sjt 200373 1/5th South Staffordshire Regt KIA 14.3.17.
LINNELL Harry C. MM CQMS 83928 19th Bn Machine Gun Corps
LINNELL Henry John MM Pte 3109 1/15th London Regt
LINNEY Herbert Wilfred Fullick MM+Bar Sjt 940056 D/280 Bde RFA
LINNINGTON H.W. MM Pte 54909 15th Hampshire Regt
LINSCOTT Charles William MM Pte 37546 RAMC
LINSCOTT Frederick C. MM+Bar Gnr 64927 RGA
LINSEAY Frederick C. MM Sjt 326134 1/1st Cambridgeshire Regt
LINSELL George MM Pte 41516 9th Royal Fusiliers KIA 22.10.18.
LINSEY Frederick James MM Cpl 201126 3/4th Royal West Surrey Regt
LINSLEY Bertie "DCM,MM" L/Cpl 25262 5th West Riding Regt
LINSLEY Thomas MM L/Cpl 301132 1/8th Durham Light Infantry att 151 TM Bty.
LINSLEY William MM+Bar Pte 16587 2nd Yorkshire Regt KIA 2.11.18.

LINTER George MM Sjt 157558 RGA
LINTERN Albert E. MM S/Sjt Farrier 34543 134 Bty 32 Bde RFA
LINTERN Frank MM Pte 459362 2 Fd Amb RAMC
LINTERN Henry E. MM Sjt 9550 5th Wiltshire Regt
LINTHWAITE James Ernest MM Sjt 4028 19th Hussars KIA 25.11.17.
LINTON Andrew MM S/Sjt 45908 RAMC
LINTON Charles MM Sjt 23655 Machine Gun Corps
LINTON Charles W. MM Cpl 39852 RFA
LINTON George B. MM Pte 4254 Northumberland Fusiliers
LINTON George Frederick MM Pte S/8689 9th Rifle Brigade KIA 22.8.17.
LINTON Harold MM L/Cpl 300874 1/8th Arg & Suth Highlanders
LINTON James MM Pte 31792 North Lancashire Regt
LINTON John MM Sjt 49330 Royal Engineers
LINTON Samuel "DCM,MM" Bdr 110751 RFA
LINTON Sidney MM Pte 61979 1st Northumberland Fusiliers
LINTON Thomas MM Cpl 99439 Royal Engineers
LINTOTT Austin W. MM Cpl 281242 2/4th London Regt
LINTOTT Richard MM Cpl 6812 9th Royal Sussex Regt
LINTOTT Walter C. MM 2nd Cpl 250509 Railway Troops Royal Engineers
LINTOTT William James MM L/Cpl 34167 RAMC
LIPMAN Alfred MM Pte 571245 17th London Regt
LIPMAN Joe MM Pte 11760 10th West Riding Regt
LIPP Robert MM Pte 201561 1/4th Gordon Highlanders KIA 23.11.17.
LIPPETT Edward MM Pte 6930 1st Somerset Light Infantry
LIPPETT Francis George MM Pte 208 GMGR
LIPPETT Victor C.H. MM L/Cpl 201796 4th Royal West Surrey Regt
LIPPIATT Charles E. MM Sjt 43325 Machine Gun Corps
LIPPIATT Ernest MM L/Cpl 345320 14th Royal Highlanders
LIPPIATT Frederick John Oliver MM Sjt 960265 C/236 Bde RFA DOW 7.4.18.
LIPSCOMBE Alfred MM Pte 13651 10th Essex Regt
LIPSCOMBE Bertram MM Pte 3/155 7th Wiltshire Regt
LIPSCOMBE George MM Pte 49331 161 Coy Machine Gun Corps
LIPSCOMBE Harold MM Pte M1/06721 93 MT Coy Army Service Corps
LIPSCOMBE Thomas A. MM Pte 36091 10th South Wales Borderers
LIPSCOMBE William E. MM Pte 25378 Middlesex Regt
LIPSETT J. MM Cpl Sig 22201 D/58 Bde RFA
LIPTROT John MM Pte 20920 Liverpool Regt
LIPYEART Frank MM Pte 25920 6th South Wales Borderers
LIPYEAT Thomas A. MM Sjt 9135 RFA
LIRON Henry C.T. MM Dvr 249284 52 Bty 15 Bde RFA
LISETT William B. MM Pte 350072 RAMC
LISHER Charles Alfred MM Pte 2137 13th Royal Sussex Regt KIA 8.3.18.
LISHMAN Alfred MM Gnr 128114 D/78 Bde RFA KIA 10.10.18.
LISHMAN Thomas "MM,MID" Sjt 592784 18th London Regt
LISHMAN Thomas B. MM Pte 30118 11th Border Regt
LISLE Albert MM Pte 34220 8th York & Lancaster Regt
LISLE Andrew "MM,MMV(lt)" Sjt 457373 2/1(Northumbrian)Fd Coy Royal Engineers
LISLE Henry MM Pte 308017 West Riding Regt
LISLE James MM Bdr 44536 RFA
LISLE John R. MM+Bar Sjt 29560 1st Northumberland Fusiliers
LISLE Stanley MM Gnr 37266 D/94 Bde RFA
LISNEY Maurice Charles MM L/Cpl 15171 2nd Scots Guards
LISNEY William MM Pte 22308 1st Gloucestershire Regt DOW 25.8.16.
LISON Arthur L. MM Sjt 382339 RGA
LISSEMORE Arthur James MM Bdsm 9467 2nd Royal Warwickshire Regt
LISSETER David W. MM Sjt 12979 5th Oxf & Bucks Light Infantry
LIST Clive Charles Arthur MM Dvr 22439 311 Bde RFA
LIST Fred MM+Bar L/Cpl 42290 12th Middlesex Regt
LISTER Adam Harkness MM S/Sjt Fitter 138893 251 Siege Bty RGA DOW 8.10.18.
LISTER Alfred MM Cpl 12985 11th West Yorkshire Regt
LISTER Alfred D.W. MM RQMS 1540 9th East Surrey Regt
LISTER Arthur MM Pte 12430 10th West Yorkshire Regt DOW 12.2.17.
LISTER Clifford MM Cpl 786380 C/232 Bde RFA
LISTER Cyril MM Gnr 148898 B/74 Bde RFA
LISTER Edward G. MM Sjt L/8132 7th Royal Sussex Regt
LISTER Ernest R. MM Spr 312344 Royal Engineers
LISTER Frank "DCM,MM" CSM 7244 1st King's Royal Rifle Corps

LISTER Frank H. MM Sjt 22059 'VV' Cable Section Royal Engineers
LISTER George F. MM Spr 498080 Royal Engineers
LISTER Harold MM L/Cpl 307287 West Riding Regt
LISTER Henry John MM Pte 20199 10th Royal Warwickshire Regt
LISTER Herbert MM Pte 49836 2/4th West Riding Regt
LISTER Herbert E. MM Pte Z/2330 Rifle Brigade
LISTER Hugh MM Pte 18686 Cameron Highlanders
LISTER Jack MM Gnr 86882 64 Bde RFA
LISTER Leonard MM Pte 241112 1/5th Suffolk Regt
LISTER Norman Armitage MM Pte 22579 165 Coy Machine Gun Corps KIA 7.8.16.
LISTER Richard MM Sjt 878 13th Cheshire Regt
LISTER Rudolph B. MM Pte 3405 1/1st Cambridgeshire Regt
LISTER Sam MM Sjt 16/1091 15/17th West Yorkshire Regt KIA 22.9.18.
LISTER Stephen MM Pte 13724 2nd South Wales Borderers DOW 3.2.18.
LISTER Thomas MM Cpl Saddler 46452 462 Bty RFA
LISTER Thomas H. MM Pte 24088 11th Manchester Regt
LISTER W.E. MM AM1 10220 Royal Flying Corps att RGA.
LISTON John MM Cpl 16175 17th Highland Light Infantry
LISTON Robert G. MM L/Cpl 19829 Royal Scots
LITCHFIELD Ben MM Cpl 6080 16th Northumberland Fusiliers
LITCHFIELD F.W. MM Cpl 84584 RFA
LITCHFIELD Harold MM Pte 3719 1/15th London Regt
LITCHFIELD Harry MM Sjt 200054 Yorkshire Light Infantry
LITCHFIELD Walter J. MM+Bar Sjt 265457 1/1st Hertfordshire Regt
LITHERLAND Harry MM Sjt 14473 Coldstream Guards
LITHGOW Francis MM Gnr 90795 C/102 Bde RFA KIA 6.7.17.
LITHGOW Joseph MM L/Cpl 10559 1/9th Royal Scots
LITTERICK Robert MM L/Sjt 290198 1/8th Scottish Rifles
LITTLE A.F. MM CSM 12885 10th Essex Regt
LITTLE Albert MM Pte 280533 1/7th Lancashire Fusiliers
LITTLE Alexander MM Pte 201189 2/4th South Lancashire Regt
LITTLE Alfred MM Pte 27964 Welsh Regt
LITTLE Andrew MM Sjt 16908 62nd Bn Machine Gun Corps
LITTLE Andrew MM Pte 6671 8/10th Gordon Highlanders
LITTLE Andrew MM Pte 5667 12th Arg & Suth Highlanders
LITTLE Benjamin MM CQMS 203298 1/4th West Riding Regt KIA 13.10.18.
LITTLE Charles T. MM Sjt 49490 RFA
LITTLE Daniel MM L/Cpl 13654 9th Royal Inniskilling Fusiliers
LITTLE David MM+Bar Pte 241668 1st King's Own Scottish Borderers
LITTLE Dixon MM L/Cpl 20586 22nd Manchester Regt
LITTLE Edward R. MM Sjt 18/315 18th Durham Light Infantry
LITTLE Elliot C. MM Pte 200791 1/4th King's Own Scottish Borderers
LITTLE Ernest Winn MM Sjt 94338 D/95 Bde RFA
LITTLE George MM Gnr 32531 Machine Gun Corps(Motors)
LITTLE George MM Sjt 12709 9th Gloucestershire Regt
LITTLE George D. MM L/Cpl 133338 46th Royal Fusiliers
LITTLE George G. MM Pte 38138 10th Royal Scots
LITTLE George R. MM Pte 55101 1/1st Lincolnshire Yeomanry
LITTLE Henry J. MM L/Cpl 3104 8th Royal West Surrey Regt
LITTLE Herbert MM Pte 14205 9th Yorkshire Regt KIA 7.6.17.
LITTLE James MM Pte 42817 1st Scottish Rifles
LITTLE James MM L/Cpl 332349 9th Highland Light Infantry
LITTLE James MM Pte S/3224 2nd Gordon Highlanders
LITTLE John MM Pte 8440 1/7th Royal Highlanders
LITTLE John MM Pte 19500 2nd York & Lancaster Regt
LITTLE John MM+Bar Pte 57987 23rd Royal Fusiliers
LITTLE John MM Gnr 69493 RGA
LITTLE John MM Gnr Fitter 156886 RFA
LITTLE John H. MM Dvr 26810 38 Bde RFA
LITTLE John H. MM L/Cpl 68452 Machine Gun Corps
LITTLE John T. MM Pte 721849 24th London Regt
LITTLE John William MM Pte 16242 4th Border Regt
LITTLE Robert MM Cpl 951593 D/157 Bde RFA
LITTLE Robert MM Pte 240601 1/6th South Staffordshire Regt
LITTLE Robert Anderson MM Pte 386544 1/1(Northumbrian)Fd Amb RAMC
LITTLE Sidney George MM Sjt 9574 12th Gloucestershire Regt KIA 28.6.18
LITTLE Thomas MM Pte 18410 7th Royal West Kent Regt DOW 28.8.18.
LITTLE Thomas "DCM,MM" Sjt 1065 1/5th Yorkshire Regt
LITTLE Thomas MM Pte 20603 4th Grenadier Guards
LITTLE Trevor Bartlett MM Cpl 69039 35 Div Sig Coy Royal Engineers
LITTLE W. MM Pte 14247 9th Royal Inniskilling Fusiliers
LITTLE William MM Bdr Sig 751249 D/250 Bde RFA
LITTLE William MM Cpl 267136 West Yorkshire Regt
LITTLE William MM Sjt R/5559 10th King's Royal Rifle Corps
LITTLE William MM L/Cpl 17481 11th Border Regt
LITTLE William H. MM Sjt 19414 15th Hampshire Regt
LITTLE William Henry "MM+Bar,MSM" BSM 5887 D/150 Bde RFA
LITTLE William J. MM Pte 41194 9th South Staffordshire Regt
LITTLE William P. MM Pte 266375 Royal Welsh Fusiliers
LITTLEBURY William C. MM Pte 45826 1st Royal Irish Fusiliers
LITTLECHILD Edward W. MM Cpl 41963 25 Bde RFA
LITTLECHILD Ernest MM Pte 14498 6th Bedfordshire Regt
LITTLECHILD M. MM Cpl 72099 RFA
LITTLEFAIR Herbert MM Pte 241788 5/6th Scottish Rifles KIA 22.9.18.
LITTLEFAIR Thomas MM Pte 1358 South Lancashire Regt
LITTLEFIELD Harry C.F. MM L/Cpl 23718 Royal Berkshire Regt
LITTLEHALES Charles MM Pte 2354 Gloucestershire Regt
LITTLEHALES Joseph Alfred MM Pte 325760 1/1st Worcestershire Yeomanry DOW 14.11.17.
LITTLEJOHN Cyril MM SM 422 2 Wing Royal Flying Corps
LITTLEJOHN David MM Sjt S/3445 8th Royal Highlanders KIA 3.5.17.
LITTLEJOHN Samuel H. MM Pte 74032 RAMC
LITTLEJOHNS Ernest MM Cpl 260096 7th Duke of Cornwall's LI
LITTLEJOHNS Walter Charles MM Spr 56686 15 Div Sig Coy Royal Engineers
LITTLEMORE John MM Pte 15905 1st Northamptonshire Regt
LITTLEPROUD Leonard MM Cpl 43658 8th Norfolk Regt
LITTLER Harry MM Dvr 4992 C/54 Bde RFA
LITTLER James MM Cpl 12751 1st North Staffordshire Regt KIA 21.3.18.
LITTLER Joseph MM Dvr 8646 RFA
LITTLEWOOD Albert MM Cpl 207993 11th Royal West Surrey Regt
LITTLEWOOD Charles MM Cpl 755042 RFA
LITTLEWOOD Christopher MM Cpl 55554 Y/21 Med TM Bty RGA
LITTLEWOOD Frank MM Sjt 68483 299 Siege Bty RGA
LITTLEWOOD Fred MM Pte 27955 2nd Yorkshire Light Infantry
LITTLEWOOD Joseph MM CSM 8784 2nd West Yorkshire Regt
LITTLEWOOD Kaye MM Sjt 25693 RFA
LITTLEWOOD Robert MM+Bar Sjt 200109 1/4th East Lancashire Regt
LITTLEWOOD Samuel MM CSM 200557 1/5th Notts & Derby Regt
LITTLEWOOD William MM Gnr 785386 RFA
LITTLEWOOD William MM+Bar Sjt 300920 12th Durham Light Infantry
LITTLEWOOD William Edward MM L/Cpl 15459 12th Royal Sussex Regt
LITTLEWOOD William H. MM Gnr 122497 140 Hy Bty RGA
LITTON Cyril George MM Dvr 15184 RFA
LITTS Peter M MM Pte S/6175 10th Arg & Suth Highlanders DOW 14.10.17.
LIVERMORE Harry MM+Bar L/Cpl 2579 2nd Rifle Brigade
LIVERMORE Thomas George MM Gnr L/22356 B/166 Bde RFA
LIVERMORE Wilfred William MM L/Cpl 60989 40th Bn Machine Gun Corps Died 24.5.18.
LIVERMORE William St.Lawrence MM Gnr Sig 150505 290 Siege Bty RGA Died 26.10.18.
LIVERSEDGE Frank MM Bdr 26923 A/94 Bde RFA KIA 25.9.17.
LIVERSEDGE John MM Sjt 3/12059 2nd West Riding Regt
LIVERSEDGE or LIVERSIDE Thomas MM Dvr L/26561 HQ 245 Bde RFA
LIVERSIDGE Alfred J. MM Cpl S/21774 13th Rifle Brigade
LIVERSKI A. MM Pte 99241 6th Durham Light Infantry
LIVESAY Alfred H. MM+Bar Sjt 23958 1st North Lancashire Regt
LIVESAY H. MM Pte 30304 North Lancashire Regt
LIVESAY J. MM Sjt 666 Military Mounted Police
LIVESAY John MM Pte 235016 Hampshire Regt
LIVESEY Christopher MM L/Cpl 241925 5th East Lancashire Regt
LIVESEY F. MM L/Cpl 380513 Liverpool Regt
LIVESEY George Howcroft MM Pte 18536 2nd Border Regt
LIVESEY Percy MM Sjt 24511 RFA
LIVESEY Peter MM Pte 267247 2/4th West Riding Regt
LIVESEY Peter MM Gnr 34644 RFA
LIVESEY Thomas MM Pte 88814 1/7th Liverpool Regt
LIVESEY William MM L/Cpl 1951 1/5th Royal Lancaster Regt
LIVESLEY A. MM Dvr 2639 RFA
LIVESLEY James L. MM Sjt 275326 Manchester Regt
LIVETT Benjamin Thomas MM Pte 11197 5th Royal Berkshire Regt
LIVINGS Frederick Louis "DCM,MM+Bar,CG(B)" Sjt 23186 9th Essex Regt

LIVINGS Horace R. "MM,MSM" L/Cpl 148635 170 Tunnelling Coy Royal Engineers
LIVINGS Robert MM Cpl 201060 2/5th Gloucestershire Regt
LIVINGSTONE Alfred MM Cpl 200334 Royal Highlanders
LIVINGSTONE Allan MM Sjt 7399 D/124 Bde RFA
LIVINGSTONE Andrew MM Cpl 301352 RAMC
LIVINGSTONE David Thomson "MC+Bar,MM(3545 L/Cpl)" 2Lt 1/9th Highland Light Infantry
LIVINGSTONE James MM Pte S/17092 1st Gordon Highlanders
LIVINGSTONE John MM Dvr 310 C/71 Bde RFA DOW 1.8.18.
LIVINGSTONE John MM L/Cpl 16730 Welsh Regt
LIVINGSTONE John MM Gnr 60612 37 Siege Bty RGA
LIVINGSTONE Stewart MM Pte 3910 Royal Highlanders
LIVINGSTONE William MM L/Cpl 53792 11th Royal Scots Fusiliers
LIVINGSTONE William MM Sjt 46610 77 Fd Coy Royal Engineers
LLEWELLYN Charles MM Pte 18207 11th Worcestershire Regt
LLEWELLYN E.F. MM Dvr 92590 RFA
LLEWELLYN Evan D. MM Cpl 203575 24th Welsh Regt
LLEWELLYN Evan D. MM Pte 15170 10th West Yorkshire Regt
LLEWELLYN George H. MM Cpl 4537 RFA
LLEWELLYN Henry J. MM Spr 500554 Royal Engineers
LLEWELLYN Herbert MM Cpl 201241 1/4th Gloucestershire Regt
LLEWELLYN Thomas MM+Bar Sjt 49063 14th Royal Welsh Fusiliers
LLEWELLYN Thomas Edward MM Sjt 44630 30 Bde RFA KIA 27.10.18.AKA FOSTER.
LLEWELLYN William MM Pte 40055 14th Royal Welsh Fusiliers
LLEWELLYN William MM Pte 42465 RAMC
LLEWELYN William E. MM Sjt 320527 24th Welsh Regt
LLEWELYN John MM L/Bdr 13 RFA
LLOYD Albert MM Pte 37532 RAMC
LLOYD Albert Seymour MM Gnr 15757 C/78 Bde RFA KIA 19.4.17.
LLOYD Albert V. MM L/Cpl 275240 1/6th Essex Regt
LLOYD Allan MM Pte 31068 2nd Royal Welsh Fusiliers KIA 26.9.17.
LLOYD Arthur MM Gnr 776873 245 Bde RFA
LLOYD Arthur J. MM Pte 10227 2nd West Riding Regt
LLOYD Arthur W. MM L/Cpl 1402 1/22nd London Regt
LLOYD Bertram MM Pte 030192 Army Ordnance Corps
LLOYD Charles MM L/Cpl 11192 Royal Welsh Fusiliers
LLOYD Charles Arthur MM Cpl 16514 2 Fd Coy Royal Engineers
LLOYD David MM L/Cpl 14887 11th Welsh Regt
LLOYD David John MM Cpl 9859 8th Royal Fusiliers
LLOYD E. MM L/Cpl 33372 Devonshire Regt
LLOYD Edward MM Pte 38886 Liverpool Regt
LLOYD Edward "DCM,MM" L/Cpl 8914 2nd Worcestershire Regt
LLOYD Edward MM Sjt 6532 1/4th Royal Welsh Fusiliers
LLOYD Edwin MM L/Cpl 245553 2 Fd Svy Bn Royal Engineers
LLOYD Ernest J. MM+Bar Sjt 45903 Durham Light Infantry
LLOYD Francis James MM Sjt 391012 9th London Regt
LLOYD Frank MM+Bar Sjt 8424 South Staffordshire Regt
LLOYD Frank MM+Bar Pte M2/050226 Army Service Corps
LLOYD Frank MM Pte 29778 North Lancashire Regt
LLOYD Fred MM Pte 202973 1/4th North Lancashire Regt DOW 14.6.18.
LLOYD Frederick Ralph MM L/Cpl 56559 18th Lancashire Fusiliers DOW 2.10.18.
LLOYD Frederick W. MM Gnr 119725 RGA
LLOYD Frederick William MM Pte 1674 1/17th London Regt
LLOYD George MM Pte 421466 RAMC
LLOYD George H. MM Pte 280189 Royal Welsh Fusiliers
LLOYD Giilbert H. MM Pte 5070 Royal Irish Rifles
LLOYD Gilbert MM L/Bdr 74197 B/113 Bde RFA
LLOYD Gwilym MM Sjt 19135 Royal Welsh Fusiliers
LLOYD Henry MM Cpl T4/069724 38 Div Train Army Service Corps Died 25.11.18.
LLOYD Henry Gordon MM Pte 48918 6th Northamptonshire Regt
LLOYD Hugh Bernard MM Pte 251677 1/6th Durham Light Infantry
LLOYD James MM Pte R/40523 13th King's Royal Rifle Corps
LLOYD James MM Bdr 66771 C/256 Bde RFA DOW 16.10.17.
LLOYD James A. MM Pte 9683 4th King's Royal Rifle Corps
LLOYD James Arthur MM Sjt 926484 A/290 Bde RFA
LLOYD James Rodger MM Pte 63452 Machine Gun Corps
LLOYD John MM Cpl 25164 14th Royal Welsh Fusiliers
LLOYD John MM Cpl 13205 2nd Worcestershire Regt
LLOYD John MM L/Cpl 2033 9th Gordon Highlanders
LLOYD John MM L/Cpl 1070 Royal Sussex Regt
LLOYD John Edward MM Spr 362082 Royal Engineers att 87 Bde RGA.
LLOYD John H. MM L/Cpl 19498 2nd Oxf & Bucks Light Infantry
LLOYD John N. MM Dvr 755154 C/251 Bde RFA
LLOYD Joseph MM Pte 202 1st Welsh Guards
LLOYD Joseph MM Pte 265890 Liverpool Regt
LLOYD Joseph MM Pte 10981 5th Shropshire Light Infantry
LLOYD Joseph P. MM Pte 37565 14th Royal Welsh Fusiliers
LLOYD Lionel V.L. MM L/Cpl 26031 1/4th Royal Berkshire Regt
LLOYD Norman MM+Bar Sjt 67877 24 Bde RFA
LLOYD Oswald Octavius MM Pte 764100 1/28th London Regt
LLOYD R. "MM,MID" Pte 11128 Shropshire Light Infantry
LLOYD Rees MM L/Cpl 46302 Welsh Regt
LLOYD Richard MM Pte 6446 5th Shropshire Light Infantry KIA 16.9.16.
LLOYD Richard Jones MM L/Cpl 75953 14th Royal Welsh Fusiliers
LLOYD Robert MM Dvr 25669 RFA
LLOYD Robert MM Pte 5077 16th Lancers
LLOYD Robert MM Pte 25327 Liverpool Regt
LLOYD Robert K. MM+Bar Pte 41664 2nd Yorkshire Regt
LLOYD Robert W. MM Sjt 13536 9th Royal Inniskilling Fusiliers
LLOYD Solomon MM Sjt 771078 RFA
LLOYD Stanley W. MM L/Cpl 796 Seaforth Highlanders
LLOYD T. MM Pte 5803 Liverpool Regt
LLOYD Thomas MM Pte 40789 22nd Manchester Regt
LLOYD Thomas L. MM Cpl 12079 7th Norfolk Regt
LLOYD Wallace E. "MM,MIDx2" Pte 1554 88 Fd Amb RAMC
LLOYD Walter MM Pte 17422 3rd Royal Fusiliers
LLOYD Walter H. MM Cpl 300826 1/7th Essex Regt
LLOYD William MM Dvr L/9176 RFA
LLOYD William MM+Bar Sjt 10198 1st Worcestershire Regt KIA 22.10.16.
LLOYD William MM Pte 241086 Welsh Regt
LLOYD William C. "DCM,MM" Cpl 320877 12th Norfolk Regt
LLOYD William George MM L/Cpl 22726 Worcestershire Regt
LLOYD William George MM Cpl 85313 288 Siege Bty RGA
LLOYD William J. MM Sjt 10182 8th King's Royal Rifle Corps
LLOYD William J. MM L/Cpl 2369 1st Gloucestershire Regt
LLOYD William T. MM Bdr 117117 RFA
LLOYD-BRYANT Reginald MM Sjt 49723 23rd Lancashire Fusiliers KIA 27.9.18.
LOACH Albert MM Pte 17913 7th South Staffordshire Regt
LOACH Frederick John MM+Bar Cpl 266417 Royal Warwickshire Regt
LOACH John T. MM Cpl 294962 RGA
LOACH William MM L/Sjt 27703 Notts & Derby Regt
LOADE William H. MM Gnr 835506 C/240 Bde RFA
LOADER Charles MM Sjt 570686 17th London Regt
LOADER Eli H. MM Pte 24943 2nd Hampshire Regt
LOADER Frederick Charles MM CSM M2/074990 7 Auxiliary Steam Coy Army Service Corps
LOADER Herbert MM Pte 24290 16th Welsh Regt
LOADER Sydney Thomas MM L/Cpl 703221 1/23rd London Regt KIA 7.6.17.
LOADER William MM Cpl 9880 5th Wiltshire Regt
LOADER William P. MM Pte M2/201500 Army Service Corps
LOADES Arthur MM Gnr 32393 'D' Bn Machine Gun Corps(Heavy Branch)
LOADES Ernest F. MM L/Cpl 22026 1 Signal Troop Royal Engineers
LOADS Edward Frank MM Sjt 5014 4th Dragoon Guards DOW 26.3.18.
LOAKES Frederick W. MM Sjt 65775 RAMC
LOAKMAN B.J.P. "MM,MSM" Sjt 7521 Army Ordnance Corps
LOAN Thomas MM+Bar Sjt 57364 RFA
LOASBY G.F. MM Sjt 14603 Norfolk Regt
LOBB H.G. MM Air Mech 2 10498 Royal Air Force
LOBB Loveridge MM Sjt 36388 Duke of Cornwall's LI
LOBB Nathaniel MM Sjt 5818 12 Fd Coy Royal Engineers
LOBBAN Alexander MM Sjt 18531 Gloucestershire Regt
LOBEL Frank MM L/Cpl 7568 Middlesex Regt
LOBER William MM Pte 8580 1st East Surrey Regt
LOBLEY Alfred MM Pte 15919 11th West Yorkshire Regt DOW 10.11.16.
LOBLEY Alfred MM Sjt 781842 2(West Riding)Bde RFA Died 26.7.18.
LOBLEY John MM Pte 24228 Royal Inniskilling Fusiliers
LOCHREY Daniel MM Pte 47522 RAMC
LOCHRIE Edward MM L/Sjt 14501 13th Royal Scots
LOCHRIN Owen MM Pte 276126 1/7th Arg & Suth Highlanders
LOCHTIE W.J. MM Pte S/12209 6th Royal Highlanders
LOCK Albert Victor MM Pte 35513 11th Lancashire Fusiliers
LOCK Alfred MM Pte 10577 1st Royal Dublin Fusiliers
LOCK Arthur H. MM Pte 2647 1/24th London Regt
LOCK Arthur S. MM Pte A/1019 18th King's Royal Rifle Corps

LOCK Charles MM Pte 232695 2nd London Regt KIA 15.6.17.
LOCK Charles MM Sjt 265413 1/2nd Monmouthshire Regt
LOCK Charles A. MM Sjt 388771 15 Fd Coy Royal Engineers
LOCK Charles Edward MM Gnr 78661 'H' Bn Tank Corps
LOCK Charles Ferris MM L/Cpl 320204 16th Royal Sussex Regt
LOCK Courtney Wilson "DCM,MM" Sjt 8827 2nd Devonshire Regt KIA 29.10.16.
LOCK Ernest MM Pte 8601 2nd Dorsetshire Regt
LOCK Ernest MM Cpl 8704 2nd Lincolnshire Regt
LOCK Ernest William MM Pte 10467 Machine Gun Corps
LOCK Francis MM Pte 202711 7th Royal West Kent Regt
LOCK Frank MM Dvr 59385 'L' Bty RHA
LOCK George H. MM Pte 3/7889 1st Norfolk Regt
LOCK George J. "MM,MID" Cpl 68335 23 Bde RFA
LOCK John MM L/Cpl 23113 2nd Wiltshire Regt
LOCK John MM+Bar Pte 16709 Devonshire Regt
LOCK Joseph MM Pte 10373 3 Fd Amb RAMC
LOCK Richard George MM Pte 30333 1st Devonshire Regt KIA 7.11.18.
LOCK Spencer MM Pte 56001 2nd Manchester Regt
LOCK Thomas "DCM,MM" CSM 280019 1/4th London Regt
LOCK William Ernest MM L/Cpl 558347 Royal Engineers
LOCK William Henry MM Pte 16268 1/5th Suffolk Regt
LOCKART Hugh MM Pte 3/29198 5th Royal Inniskilling Fusiliers
LOCKE Frank MM L/Sjt 19634 4th Grenadier Guards KIA 7.8.18.
LOCKE George MM Pte 8238 1st Leinster Regt
LOCKE John E. MM Sjt 134985 Royal Engineers
LOCKE Richard G.R. MM Pte 10669 11th Hussars
LOCKE Thomas MM Cpl 30779 C/74 Bde RFA DOW 30.8.18.
LOCKE William MM Pte 9578 4th Dragoon Guards
LOCKE William Grace MM Cpl S/11365 1st Rifle Brigade KIA 4.10.17.
LOCKER Albert C. MM L/Cpl 14/940 14th Royal Warwickshire Regt
LOCKETT Arthur MM Pte 2662 Royal Irish Rifles
LOCKETT Frank MM Sjt 80415 135 Coy Labour Corps
LOCKETT James MM Pte 305230 1/8th Lancashire Fusiliers
LOCKETT Percy MM Sjt 250177 Manchester Regt
LOCKETT Stanley MM L/Sjt 41707 Hampshire Regt
LOCKETT Thomas "DCM,MM" CSM 8912 1st South Staffordshire Regt
LOCKEY Ernest Hanson MM Sjt 201104 Royal Lancaster Regt
LOCKEY Henry MM Pte 30231 Durham Light Infantry
LOCKEY Henry James MM Spr 55841 269 Railway Coy Royal Engineers
LOCKEY John G. MM Sjt 38121 Northumberland Fusiliers
LOCKEY Thomas G. MM Cpl 19134 Durham Light Infantry
LOCKEY William MM Dvr 12534 RFA
LOCKHART David MM Pte S/42147 1/7th Gordon Highlanders
LOCKHART James MM Pte 51435 10th Manchester Regt
LOCKHART James MM Pte 23984 Royal Scots
LOCKHART Melville S. MM Pte 68816 RAMC
LOCKHART Robert MM Pte 266027 Gordon Highlanders
LOCKHART Thomas MM Pte S/17660 10th Arg & Suth Highlanders
LOCKHART William MM L/Cpl 202217 5/6th Scottish Rifles
LOCKHART William Ernest MM Pte 9597 1/5th London Regt
LOCKIE Frederick MM Pte 302228 1/8th Arg & Suth Highlanders
LOCKING Albert MM Pte 241956 2/5th West Riding Regt
LOCKINGTON James E. MM Pte 405039 3(West Riding)Fd Amb RAMC
LOCKLEY Arthur MM Sjt 68029 RGA
LOCKLEY Ernest MM Cpl 87699 Liverpool Regt
LOCKLEY John Thomas MM Pte 26141 Grenadier Guards
LOCKLEY Thomas MM Sjt 204180 8th Lancashire Fusiliers
LOCKLEY Walter "DCM+Bar,MM" CSM 55786 1st Notts & Derby Regt
LOCKRIDGE William MM+Bar Sjt 306483 8th West Yorkshire Regt
LOCKSMITH Fred MM Sjt 200525 1/4th Suffolk Regt
LOCKWOOD Albert MM Pte 46990 2nd South Staffordshire Regt
LOCKWOOD Arthur MM Pte 32641 2/4th West Riding Regt
LOCKWOOD Bernard MM L/Cpl 201457 4th York & Lancaster Regt
LOCKWOOD Charles Willis MM Pte 35451 Yorkshire Light Infantry
LOCKWOOD Fletcher MM Pte 203349 York & Lancaster Regt
LOCKWOOD Frederick MM Cpl 133 Royal Engineers
LOCKWOOD George Hope MM Gnr 141246 D/280 Bde RFA
LOCKWOOD H. MM L/Sjt R/11060 13th King's Royal Rifle Corps
LOCKWOOD Harold MM Sjt 8432 2nd West Riding Regt KIA 12.10.16.
LOCKWOOD Harold MM Pte 18840 12th West Yorkshire Regt KIA 17.8.16.
LOCKWOOD Harold MM Pte 15894 Machine Gun Corps
LOCKWOOD Harry MM Pte 41450 Northumberland Fusiliers
LOCKWOOD Henry Heeley MM L/Cpl 356397 1/10th Liverpool Regt
LOCKWOOD Herbert MM L/Cpl 241860 2/6th West Riding Regt
LOCKWOOD James MM Sjt 3151 8th East Kent Regt
LOCKWOOD Jimmey MM Pte 44513 8th Lincolnshire Regt
LOCKWOOD John William "MM,MID" Sjt 1116 10 Fd Amb RAMC
LOCKWOOD Joshua MM Pte 24043 South Wales Borderers
LOCKWOOD Lewis MM Pte 202759 West Yorkshire Regt
LOCKWOOD Mark MM Pte 238024 8th Yorkshire Light Infantry
LOCKWOOD Morgan MM Pte 29224 8th East Surrey Regt
LOCKWOOD Norman MM L/Cpl 12628 9th West Riding Regt
LOCKWOOD Philip J. MM Pte 4851 1/17th London Regt
LOCKWOOD Raymond MM Pte 12631 9th West Riding Regt
LOCKWOOD Tom MM Pte 36233 7th Leicestershire Regt
LOCKWOOD Tom MM L/Cpl 21388 York & Lancaster Regt
LOCKWOOD Walter MM L/Sjt 17506 King's Own Scottish Borderers
LOCKWOOD Wharton MM Dvr 796302 49 Div Ammn Col RFA
LOCKWOOD Willie MM Dvr T4/253666 62 Div Train Army Service Corps
LOCKYEAR Leonard MM 2nd Cpl 1359 1/1(South Midland)Fd Coy Royal Engineers
LOCKYER Alfred George MM L/Cpl S/3705 13th Rifle Brigade
LOCKYER Harold J. MM Pte 27772 Somerset Light Infantry
LOCKYER James MM Pte 19551 10th Northumberland Fusiliers att 176 Tunnelling Coy RE
LOCKYER Walter "MM,MID" RSM 4473 12th Lancers
LOCKYER William G. MM Pte 265993 2/10th Middlesex Regt
LOCOCK Arthur W. MM 2nd Cpl 94246 Royal Engineers
LOCOCK Henry C. MM Pte 51133 1/2nd(Highland)Fd Amb RAMC
LOCOCK William MM Pte G/12224 23rd Royal Fusiliers
LODDER Frederick MM Spr 29793 Signal Service Royal Engineers
LODER Charles R. MM Pte G/5931 3rd Royal Fusiliers
LODGE A.C. MM Pte 37122 Essex Regt
LODGE Arthur MM Cpl B/3174 Rifle Brigade
LODGE Benjamin MM L/Cpl 205617 9th Yorkshire Light Infantry
LODGE Charles D. MM Cpl 531195 15th London Regt
LODGE Ernest MM L/Cpl 516929 14th London Regt
LODGE Frederick MM Cpl 32719 8 Bde RFA
LODGE Frederick G. MM Cpl 439131 3(South Midland)Fd Amb RAMC
LODGE George A. MM Cpl 482190 62 Div Sig Coy Royal Engineers
LODGE James MM Sjt 71317 30 Bde RFA
LODGE James John MM Pte 21808 2nd Suffolk Regt
LODGE Joseph Edwin MM L/Cpl 148420 Imperial Sig Coy Royal Engineers
LODGE Luther MM Pte 241636 2/5th York & Lancaster Regt
LODGE Percy Frederick "MM,MSM" 2nd Cpl 41828 23 Div Sig Coy Royal Engineers
LOE Horace MM Sjt 59286 C/93 Bde RFA DOW 5.10.18.
LOE James MM Sjt 73935 116 Bty 26 Bde RFA
LOETSCHERT J.H. MM Spr 77972 Cav Corps Wireless Sqn Royal Engineers
LOFFHAGEN William Henry MM Gnr 926119 281 Bde RFA
LOFT Frederick W. MM Sjt 541551 Royal Engineers
LOFT George Ernest MM Sjt 27153 1st East Surrey Regt
LOFT Nicholas E. MM Sjt 6042 1st Royal West Kent Regt
LOFTHOUSE Henry MM Dvr 18019 171 Bde RFA
LOFTHOUSE James Walter MM Pnr 61970 Guards Div Sig Coy Royal Engineers KIA 22.10.18.
LOFTHOUSE John A. MM Pte 44518 Lincolnshire Regt
LOFTHOUSE Thomas MM Pte 200910 1/4th Royal Lancaster Regt KIA 9.4.18.
LOFTING John MM Sjt 51265 22 Bde RFA
LOFTS Ernest MM Pte 250273 1/5th Essex Regt
LOFTS Fred MM+Bar Sjt 8033 1st Lincolnshire Regt
LOFTS John F. MM Pte 6876 9th Lancers
LOFTS Leonard MM Pte 8677 1st Royal West Surrey Regt
LOFTUS John MM Dvr 59229 8 Bde RFA
LOFTUS John T. MM Sjt 266338 Royal Highlanders
LOFTUS Patrick J. MM L/Cpl H/73881 1/1st Northumberland Yeo
LOFTUS William MM Pte 266075 Cheshire Regt
LOFTUS William C. MM Cpl 16105 7th Liverpool Regt
LOFTY Percy A. MM Pte 12071 Middlesex Regt
LOGAN Andrew MM Pte 12649 5th Royal Inniskilling Fusiliers Died 19.10.17.
LOGAN Andrew Crindle MM Pte S/14862 2nd Arg & Suth Highlanders
LOGAN Bernard MM Pte 17962 Cameron Highlanders
LOGAN Daniel S. MM Sjt 705648 211 Bde RFA
LOGAN Frank MM Pte 40929 Gordon Highlanders

LOGAN George MM L/Cpl 3365 Gordon Highlanders
LOGAN James MM Gnr 751394 RFA
LOGAN James MM Pte 273062 Royal Scots
LOGAN John MM L/Sjt 200431 1/5th Highland Light Infantry
LOGAN John R. MM Pte 17502 1/1st Hertfordshire Regt
LOGAN John S. MM Pte 32232 2nd Lancashire Fusiliers
LOGAN Oliver MM Pte 5192 Gordon Highlanders
LOGAN Oliver P. MM Sjt S/4132 1st Royal Highlanders
LOGAN R. MM Pte 1569 Durham Light Infantry
LOGAN Thomas MM Pte S/43814 10th Arg & Suth Highlanders
LOGAN Thomas MM L/Sjt 325459 13th Royal Scots
LOGAN Thomas MM Pte 200555 1/5th Arg & Suth Highlanders
LOGAN Thomas Miller MM 2nd Cpl 100572 33 Div Sig Coy Royal Engineers
LOGAN Thomas W. MM Pte 3/9687 9th Northumberland Fusiliers
LOGAN Walter L. MM Sjt 345373 RGA
LOGAN William MM Pte 18263 1st Royal Scots Fusiliers
LOGAN William MM Bugler 1619 1/9th Highland Light Infantry
LOGAN William MM Pte 11482 Northumberland Fusiliers
LOGAN William MM Pte S/7308 8th Royal Highlanders KIA 12.10.17.
LOGAN William MM Dvr 44799 RFA
LOGAN William Alexander MM Pte 39420 1st Royal West Surrey Regt KIA 10.8.18.
LOGIE Herbert John "MM+Bar,CG(F)" Cpl 17260 D/152 Bde RFA
LOHFINK Daniel W. MM Pte 295680 11th Royal Fusiliers
LOHMANN Berkeley H. MM Pte 1502 1/20th London Regt
LOINES Benjamin MM L/Cpl 29053 9th East Surrey Regt
LOMAN Alick M. MM Sjt 7385 1st Devonshire Regt
LOMAS Alfred D. MM Sjt 30018 Labour Corps
LOMAS Arthur S. MM Sjt 2119 South Lancashire Regt
LOMAS Charles Albert MM Cpl 9904 2nd Worcestershire Regt KIA 15.4.18.
LOMAS Frederick MM Cpl 22903 13th Hussars
LOMAS Joseph MM Sjt 2168 9th Royal Fusiliers
LOMAS Joseph MM Pte 21684 4th Grenadier Guards
LOMAS Robert Graham MM L/Cpl 14/169 14th York & Lancaster Regt KIA 1.7.16.
LOMAS Roland J. MM+Bar Sjt 250751 111 Railway Coy Royal Engineers
LOMAS Walter MM Pte 242019 North Lancashire Regt
LOMAS William MM+Bar Cpl 40554 Norfolk Regt
LOMAS William MM Sjt 6176 Army Cyclist Corps
LOMAS William MM Pte 200322 Manchester Regt
LOMATH Thomas MM Pte 22343 23rd Bn Machine Gun Corps
LOMATH Tom MM CSM 218942 Royal Engineers
LOMAX Fred MM Gnr Sig 85447 237 Siege Bty RGA
LOMAX Herbert MM Cpl 381624 4th Liverpool Regt
LOMAX J. MM Sjt 354337 RAMC
LOMAX James Henry MM Pte 1739 2nd South Lancashire Regt
LOMAX John MM L/Cpl 11512 6th Wiltshire Regt
LOMAX Joseph Passey MM CQMS 3879 10th North Lancashire Regt KIA 7.10.17.
LOMAX Peter MM Spr 22131 3 Fd Sqn Royal Engineers
LOMAX Richard T. MM Pte 24612 South Wales Borderers
LOMBARDI George W. MM Pte 166124 7th Bn Machine Gun Corps
LONDON George R. MM L/Cpl 12721 6th Royal Berkshire Regt
LONDON James W. MM Sjt 37592 RGA
LONDON Sydney G. MM+Bar Sjt 21087 99 Siege Bty RGA
LONERGAN John J. MM+Bar CSM 20403 15th Hampshire Regt
LONERGAN V.J. MM Pte 19393 Gloucestershire Regt
LONG A.H. MM L/Cpl 43164 1/1st Hertfordshire Regt
LONG Albert MM Pte 10614 1st Royal Warwickshire Regt KIA 15.4.18.
LONG Albert MM+Bar Sjt 201063 West Yorkshire Regt
LONG Albert MM Pte P/917 Rifle Brigade
LONG Albert E. MM L/Cpl 29033 9th Royal Fusiliers
LONG Albert G. MM Pte 32111 Somerset Light Infantry
LONG Alfred MM Cpl 6777 Royal Engineers
LONG Alfred MM Sjt 20618 12th Durham Light Infantry KIA 18.5.17.
LONG Alfred John MM Cpl 8146 1st Essex Regt
LONG Alfred T. MM Pte 104 Royal Fusiliers
LONG Arthur MM Pte 9304 1st Royal Berkshire Regt
LONG C.L. MM Pte 25719 8th Suffolk Regt
LONG Charles MM Pte 16695 2nd Royal Scots Fusiliers
LONG Charles MM Gnr 58203 381 Bty 158 Bde RFA DOW 21.11.17.
LONG Charles MM Sjt 65054 12 Bde RFA
LONG Edward V. MM Pte 353917 7th London Regt
LONG Edwin MM Pte 8785 4th King's Royal Rifle Corps
LONG Eric D. MM Pte 3218 1/16th London Regt
LONG Ernest MM Cpl 240452 Royal Warwickshire Regt
LONG Ernest MM L/Cpl 26134 East Yorkshire Regt
LONG Ernest Harold "DCM,MM" L/Sjt 4765 10th Royal Warwickshire Regt KIA 31.5.18.
LONG Evan MM Sjt 86537 170 Tunnelling Coy Royal Engineers
LONG Frank MM Cpl 136334 X/37 Med TM Bty RFA
LONG Frederick MM Sjt 49982 Machine Gun Corps
LONG Frederick A. MM Pte Z/2784 13th Rifle Brigade
LONG Frederick J. MM Bdr 8445 RFA
LONG Geoffrey MM Pte 241049 Gloucestershire Regt
LONG George MM L/Cpl 6856 20th Middlesex Regt
LONG George MM Sjt 43319 46th Bn Machine Gun Corps
LONG George MM Pte 15703 Dorsetshire Regt
LONG George MM Spr 89931 78 Fd Coy Royal Engineers KIA 14.10.18.
LONG George Edwin MM+Bar Sjt 12338 7th Norfolk Regt
LONG George F. MM Cpl 235351 2nd South Staffordshire Regt
LONG George H. MM Sjt 38844 RAMC
LONG Gilbert Ashleigh MM Cpl 21119 22nd Manchester Regt
LONG Harold MM Sjt 8140 1st Suffolk Regt
LONG Harry MM Pte 23136 Royal Highlanders
LONG Henry MM CQMS 293129 1/7th Cheshire Regt
LONG Henry E. MM Gnr 625064 HAC att B/126 Bde RFA
LONG Herbert MM Cpl 2658 1/1st Cambridgeshire Regt
LONG Herbert Edwin MM Gnr 11159 114 Heavy Bty RGA
LONG Jack MM Pte 9377 2nd Coldstream Guards KIA 30.11.17.
LONG James MM Sjt 56349 36 Div Sig Coy Royal Engineers
LONG James Beer MM Pte 12881 9th Northumberland Fusiliers
LONG James J. MM Sjt 36202 RGA
LONG James William MM Pte 40282 8th Bedfordshire Regt
LONG Joe MM Pte 9181 2nd Gloucestershire Regt
LONG John MM Sjt 2134 18th Durham Light Infantry KIA 12.4.18.
LONG John MM Pte 241122 1/5th Yorkshire Regt
LONG John MM Pte 7804 Royal West Kent Regt
LONG John MM Sjt 43464 9th Royal Irish Fusiliers
LONG John MM Pte 90273 Labour Corps
LONG John A. MM Sjt L/14473 D/159 Bde RFA
LONG John A.W. MM Pte 53431 Lancashire Fusiliers
LONG John Henry MM Gnr 1699 2/1(West Riding)Bde RFA
LONG John Richard MM L/Cpl R/8729 1st King's Royal Rifle Corps DOW 29.4.17.
LONG Joseph MM Pte 9053 1st Somerset Light Infantry
LONG Joseph E. MM Dvr 945631 RFA
LONG Joseph W. MM Bdr 77310 RGA
LONG Percy G. MM Pte 3/8084 1st Norfolk Regt
LONG Percy W. MM Dvr 67528 RFA
LONG Reginald MM L/Cpl 233686 2nd London Regt
LONG Sidney Frederick MM Spr 558149 56 Div Sig Coy Royal Engineers
LONG Thomas MM Gnr 5179 D/186 Bde RFA
LONG Thomas G. MM Pte 23023 Yorkshire Light Infantry
LONG Thomas Henry MM Gnr 53995 B/93 Bde RFA
LONG Thomas W. MM L/Cpl 8332 East Surrey Regt
LONG Victor C. MM Pte 15348 2nd Scots Guards
LONG W. MM Pnr 192999 Royal Engineers
LONG Walter J. MM Cpl 9684 B/84 Bde RFA
LONG William MM Cpl 16340 9th Royal Inniskilling Fusiliers
LONG William MM Cpl 15640 10th Gloucestershire Regt
LONG William F. MM Cpl 12097 1st Middlesex Regt
LONG William Frank MM L/Cpl 24996 4th Grenadier Guards KIA 6.1.18.
LONG William H. MM Spr 20571 11 Fd Coy Royal Engineers
LONG William J.R. MM Sjt T4/058375 Army Service Corps
LONGBOTTOM Ernest MM Pte 63912 8th West Yorkshire Regt
LONGBOTTOM Ernest MM Cpl 72115 12 Bde RFA
LONGBOTTOM Ernest MM L/Cpl 10105 East Yorkshire Regt AKA CHETWYN
LONGBOTTOM Ernest MM Cpl 18/1587 11th West Yorkshire Regt
LONGCAKE Thomas MM Sjt 686754 D/312 Bde RFA
LONGDEN George MM Sjt 31383 East Yorkshire Regt
LONGDEN George MM Pte 240042 2/5th York & Lancaster Regt
LONGDEN James MM Pte 200967 York & Lancaster Regt
LONGDEN John MM Dvr T4/274895 Army Service Corps
LONGDEN John Arthur MM L/Cpl 11694 7th East Yorkshire Regt
LONGDEN William E. MM Spr 169204 81 Fd Coy Royal Engineers
LONGDON Albert E. MM Pte 60975 Notts & Derby Regt
LONGDON Frederick MM Pte 1784 1st Rifle Brigade
LONGFORD Arthur W. MM Pte 15452 2nd Gloucestershire Regt
LONGFORD C.H. MM Pte 266324 Liverpool Regt

LONGHORN Edward MM Sjt 235448 Lancashire Fusiliers
LONGHURST Charles MM Pte L/11326 1st Royal West Surrey Regt
LONGHURST Harry MM Pte 6740 11th Hussars
LONGHURST Herbert E. MM L/Cpl 137802 Royal Engineers
LONGHURST Horace MM Tpr 4646 2nd GMGR
LONGHURST James MM Pte 18070 25th Bn Machine Gun Corps Died 1.11.18.
LONGHURST John Frederick MM L/Cpl 41157 2nd Royal Irish Rifles
LONGHURST Oscar MM Sjt 49477 1st Royal Inniskilling Fusiliers
LONGHURST W.S.R. MM Sjt 12974 Royal Engineers
LONGLAND William MM Sjt 307686 Royal Warwickshire Regt
LONGLEY Albany "MM,MSM" Bdr 35599 A/38 Bde RFA
LONGLEY C.William MM Gnr 1613 RFA
LONGLEY Edwin Stanley "MM+Bar,MID" Sjt 46167 19 Siege Bty RGA
LONGLEY Oliver MM Cpl 40140 RFA
LONGMAN Albert J. MM Spr 24996 5 Div Sig Coy Royal Engineers
LONGMAN Sidney MM Pte 675044 21st London Regt
LONGMAN Stanley Frederick MM L/Cpl G/3401 6th Royal West Kent Regt
LONGMAN Stephen W.H. MM Sjt 3799 RGA Died 11.3.19.
LONGMAN Walter W. MM Sjt 202406 8th Royal Berkshire Regt
LONGMEAD Charles MM Gnr 99319 RFA
LONGMUIR Henry Ferguson MM Cpl 3401 1/24th London Regt DOW 15.1.17.
LONGMUIR William MM Pte S/17961 1st Royal Highlanders
LONGRIGG Joseph MM L/Sjt 23098 3rd Grenadier Guards
LONGRIGG Peter MM Spr 427985 Royal Engineers
LONGSON John MM Pte 375813 1/10th Manchester Regt
LONGSON Thomas MM Sjt 200320 21st Manchester Regt
LONGSON Wilfred Bernard MM Sjt 1464 Notts & Derby Regt
LONGSTAFF George MM Spr 102680 176 Tunnelling Coy Royal Engineers
LONGSTAFF George R. "DCM,MM" Sjt S/41542 7th Seaforth Highlanders
LONGSTAFF Harold MM Cpl 9587 5th Wiltshire Regt
LONGSTAFF John MM Cpl 47234 1st Royal Inniskilling Fusiliers
LONGSTAFF William E. MM Cpl 4870 2nd Northumberland Fusiliers
LONGTHORNE William G. MM Sjt 2731 1/1st Hertfordshire Regt
LONGTOFT Lewis MM Sjt 824 9th Lancers
LONGTON James MM L/Cpl 120930 79 Fd Coy Royal Engineers
LONGTON Joseph MM L/Cpl 15849 Liverpool Regt
LONGTON Norman MM Pte 34626 Cheshire Regt
LONGWORTH Charles MM+Bar Cpl 8041 1st Duke of Cornwall's LI
LONGWORTH Harry MM+Bar Pte 242768 5th East Lancashire Regt
LONGWORTH Peter MM Cpl 19766 1st Border Regt
LONGWORTH William MM Pte 17707 7th Shropshire Light Infantry KIA 24.3.18.
LONGWORTH William MM Pte 17765 8th North Lancashire Regt
LONIE Thomas MM Pte 14153 11th Royal Scots KIA 3.5.17.
LONON James MM Cpl 352300 7th London Regt
LONSDALE John MM Pte 5336 1st Royal West Kent Regt
LONSDALE Joseph R. MM Cpl 19/1350 19th Northumberland Fusiliers
LONSDALE Percival S. MM Pte 63753 33rd Bn Machine Gun Corps
LONSDALE Richard MM Cpl 56818 Machine Gun Corps(Cavalry)
LONSDALE William H. MM Dvr 49215 Royal Fusiliers
LONSDALE William L. MM Pte 41605 18th Liverpool Regt
LOOKER Frederick G. MM Pte G/10227 2nd Royal West Kent Regt
LOOKER Richard Henry MM Cpl 30360 1/1st Bedfordshire Yeomanry
LOOKER Sidney S. MM Pte S/10861 Rifle Brigade
LOOKER William MM Pte 10977 1st Middlesex Regt DOW 24.9.18.
LOOMES Albert A. MM Pte 242543 Leicestershire Regt
LOOMES Frederick "MM,MSM,MID" Cpl 6526 1st King's Royal Rifle Corps
LOONE Charles Benjamin MM Sjt 11590 4th Worcestershire Regt
LOONEY Cornelius MM Pte 4/6841 2nd Royal Munster Fusiliers
LOONEY Daniel MM Pte 3686 1st Irish Guards
LOONEY Percy MM L/Cpl 26042 Liverpool Regt
LOONEY Richard H. "MM,MSM" BQMS 90019 C/112 Bde RFA
LOORAN John MM Pte 3272 Irish Guards
LOOSEMORE Albert W. MM L/Cpl 510199 58 Div Sig Coy Royal Engineers
LORAM James MM+Bar Cpl 1659 RAMC att RFA
LORAM William Henry MM L/Sjt 8973 8th East Kent Regt
LORD Albert MM Spr 145222 80 Fd Coy Royal Engineers
LORD Albert MM Pte 28696 15/17th West Yorkshire Regt
LORD Albert C.J. MM Pte 21149 Royal Fusiliers

LORD Albert Edward MM Pte 16/280 West Yorkshire Regt DOW 29.4.18.
LORD Andrew MM Pte 11446 9th Lancers
LORD Benjamin Dawson MM Pte 9172 23rd Royal Fusiliers
LORD Bernard MM+Bar Cpl 240673 1/5th York & Lancaster Regt
LORD Ernest MM Gnr 14771 D/306 Bde RFA
LORD Frederick George MM L/Cpl STK/158 Royal Fusiliers
LORD Geoffrey MM Pte 202786 2/5th Lancashire Fusiliers KIA 22.3.18.
LORD George Norman "MM,MID" Cpl 24827 9th West Riding Regt
LORD Godfrey J. MM+Bar Sjt 13150 8th Bedfordshire Regt
LORD Harold Percy MM Sjt M2/151899 Army Service Corps att 20 Siege Bty RGA.
LORD Harry MM Pte 5179 10th Lancashire Fusiliers
LORD J. MM Pte 20625 18 Fd Amb RAMC
LORD James MM+Bar Sjt 14430 17th Lancashire Fusiliers
LORD James MM Dvr 32918 C/177 Bde RFA
LORD James MM Bdr 13672 RFA Died 4.11.18.
LORD James MM Cpl 840162 C/240 Bde RFA
LORD James E. MM Pte 266994 West Riding Regt
LORD James H. MM Sjt 266031 Liverpool Regt
LORD Jesse M. MM L/Cpl 81555 23rd Royal Fusiliers
LORD John MM Gnr L/343 RFA
LORD John MM Dvr 11811 6th East Lancashire Regt
LORD John H. MM Pte 26051 8th Royal Lancaster Regt
LORD John J. "MM,MID" Pte 4961 18th Hussars
LORD Jonathan MM Cpl 54596 28 Bde RFA
LORD William G. MM Bdr 89147 RFA
LORD William H. MM Pte 23803 Yorkshire Regt
LORD William Thomas "MC,MM(R/30902 Pte KRRC)" 2Lt 1st Royal Berkshire Regt
LORDAN Daniel MM Pte 52083 2/7th West Yorkshire Regt
LORDAN Denis MM Pte G/11019 2nd Royal Sussex Regt
LORE A. MM L/Cpl R/3645 King's Royal Rifle Corps
LORETTO Cecil R. MM Pte 62149 RAMC
LOREY James MM Sjt 8859 2nd Devonshire Regt
LORIMER John MM Bdr 116596 RGA
LORIMER John MM Sjt 290051 Gordon Highlanders
LORIMER William MM Cpl 9788 1st Gordon Highlanders
LORING Francis Henry MM Pte 2559 1/5th Yorkshire Light Infantry
LORING Leonard G. MM Bdr 955188 127 Bty 29 Bde RFA
LORRAINE Robert MM Pnr 424140 Royal Engineers
LORRAINE Sidney G. MM Pte 63631 13th Yorkshire Regt
LORRAINE William George MM Pte 242013 14th Gloucestershire Regt
LOSE Leonard Cory MM Sjt 200089 Tank Corps
LOSH Peter MM Pnr 204923 Lancashire Fusiliers
LOTE Horace MM L/Cpl 1074 Royal Engineers
LOTE James Thomas MM Sjt 5745 8th Gloucestershire Regt
LOTEN Arthur MM Pte 26849 14th Hampshire Regt KIA 1.8.17.
LOTHIAN John MM Pte 10515 1st Gordon Highlanders
LOTHIAN John B. MM Pte 267072 1/6th Royal Highlanders
LOTHIAN R. MM Pte 322887 London Regt
LOTHIAN Thomas MM Pte 273209 17th Royal Scots
LOTINGA Charles L. MM Bdr 61560 RFA
LOTT Charles MM Sjt 37963 RGA
LOTT Harry MM Pte 493242 13th London Regt
LOTT Percy H. MM Cpl 70366 RFA
LOTT Wallace W. MM Pte B/19549 26th Royal Fusiliers
LOUDEN Albert Edward MM Pte 45641 19th Royal Welsh Fusiliers
LOUDEN Alexander D. MM L/Cpl S/4600 Rifle Brigade
LOUDEN Samuel MM Pte 16/789 16th Royal Irish Rifles
LOUDON Andrew MM Sjt 18429 Machine Gun Corps
LOUDON James MM Pte 12981 11th Royal Scots KIA 12.4.17.
LOUDON Robert MM L/Cpl 332182 1/9th Highland Light Infantry
LOUDOUN James MM Bdr 656077 RFA
LOUDWELL Sidney William MM Pte G/2305 7th Royal West Kent Regt
LOUGH Arthur H. MM Gnr 626204 HAC(Artillery) att 109 Siege Bty RGA.
LOUGH Bartholomew MM Sjt 322969 168 Siege Bty RGA
LOUGH Frank MM L/Cpl 15172 10th Royal Irish Rifles
LOUGH William D. MM Cpl 510990 14th London Regt
LOUGHEED Walter E. MM Pte 53066 Machine Gun Corps
LOUGHENS Ernest MM Pte 1601 2nd Leinster Regt KIA 27.3.18.
LOUGHER Oswald MM Pte 11083 1st South Wales Borderers
LOUGHLIN Daniel "MM+Bar,CG(F)" Cpl 15876 9th&10th Royal Inniskilling Fusiliers
LOUGHLIN Hugh MM Bdr 685742 C/293 Bde RFA KIA 6.11.17.
LOUGHLIN John MM Pte G/11425 Middlesex Regt

LOUGHRAN Bernard MM Pte 24518 Royal Irish Fusiliers
LOUGHRAN Francis MM Pte 1798 2nd Royal Irish Regt
LOUGHRAN Francis MM Pte 3996 Connaught Rangers
LOUGHRAN Herbert MM Pte 38957 Northumberland Fusiliers
LOUGHRAN John H. MM Cpl 1573 2nd South Lancashire Regt
LOUGHTON William MM Pte 45258 RAMC
LOUND Edward Lawrence MM Sjt 10767 2nd Notts & Derby Regt
LOUNDES George Henry MM 2nd Cpl 75818 14 Div Sig Coy Royal Engineers
LOUNDS John H. MM Sjt 19954 South Staffordshire Regt
LOUNDS W. MM Sjt 51522 Yorkshire Light Infantry
LOUNT J. MM Pte 200681 Leicestershire Regt
LOURIE Edward John MM Pte 35562 25th Northumberland Fusiliers KIA 28.4.17.
LOUTH Alfred MM+Bar Gnr 13273 'O' Bty RHA
LOUTH Arthur MM Cpl 17356 Grenadier Guards
LOUTH William MM Cpl 241478 8th Lincolnshire Regt
LOUTITT William MM+Bar Pte 202649 1/4th Seaforth Highlanders
LOVATT George MM CSM 17335 10th Highland Light Infantry
LOVATT Herbert C. MM Pte 1244 GMGR
LOVATT Percy Clifford Finch MM Pte 32850 Notts & Derby Regt
LOVATT Robert MM Pte 39618 12th Royal Scots
LOVATT Thomas MM Sjt 19443 5th South Wales Borderers
LOVE Albert Victor MM L/Cpl 390086 1/3(Northumbrian)Fd Amb RAMC
LOVE Alexander MM Pte 275450 1/7th Arg & Suth Highlanders
LOVE Alfred MM Pte R/10545 9th King's Royal Rifle Corps
LOVE Alfred George "MM,MID" Gnr 85169 22 Bde RFA
LOVE Cyril Bertie MM Pte 2320 1/5th Leicestershire Regt
LOVE David MM+Bar Cpl 8887 1st Royal Irish Rifles
LOVE Duncan Cameron MM Pte 301606 1/8th Arg & Suth Highlanders
LOVE Ernest E. MM L/Cpl 13151 6th Northamptonshire Regt
LOVE H. MM Bdr 42836 RFA
LOVE Harold Charles MM Cpl 69274 35 Div Sig Coy Royal Engineers
LOVE Henry MM Pte G/38424 4th Royal Fusiliers
LOVE Henry John MM Cpl 10432 5th Royal Berkshire Regt
LOVE J.H. MM L/Cpl P/13658 Military Mounted Police
LOVE James W. MM Pte 682099 22nd London Regt
LOVE John Edward MM Gnr 2613 B/308 Bde RFA
LOVE Lewis Herbert MM L/Cpl 63283 90 Fd Coy Royal Engineers Died 23.3.18.
LOVE Matthew W. MM Sjt 24/1197 8th Northumberland Fusiliers
LOVE Patrick MM Sjt 9995 2nd Seaforth Highlanders
LOVE Percy MM Cpl 12018 6th Dorsetshire Regt
LOVE William MM Spr 100477 2 Div Sig Coy Royal Engineers
LOVEBOND Thomas E. MM Cpl 345415 24th Royal Welsh Fusiliers
LOVEDAY John MM L/Cpl 112313 Royal Engineers
LOVEDAY William G. MM Gnr L/39426 RFA
LOVEGROVE Ernest MM Sjt 205670 9th Essex Regt
LOVEGROVE John MM Cpl 7947 2nd Hampshire Regt
LOVEJOY F.A. MM Sjt P/646 Military Foot Police
LOVELAND Archibald MM Pte 37772 7th Royal West Surrey Regt KIA 28.4.18.
LOVELAND George William MM Sjt 10523 4th Middlesex Regt DOW 7.5.17.
LOVELESS George H. MM Bdr 73818 38 Bde RFA
LOVELESS Leonard C. MM+Bar Sjt 591481 1/18th London Regt
LOVELESS Walter Jeffrey MM Cpl 837076 RFA
LOVELL Arthur Edward MM Pte 15336 8th North Staffordshire Regt KIA 19.11.16.
LOVELL Bert MM L/Cpl 17522 Royal Sussex Regt
LOVELL Edward W. MM L/Cpl 16621 Royal West Kent Regt
LOVELL Frank W. MM Gnr 515 RGA
LOVELL George MM L/Cpl 9130 1st Leicestershire Regt KIA 15.9.16.
LOVELL Harry MM Sjt 62631 9th Yorkshire Light Infantry
LOVELL Hugh W. MM Sjt 925013 RFA
LOVELL James MM L/Cpl 220739 8th Royal Berkshire Regt
LOVELL John MM Bdr 18348 RFA
LOVELL Joseph W. MM L/Cpl 9250 2nd Northamptonshire Regt
LOVELL Owen MM Cpl 9303 2nd Northamptonshire Regt
LOVELL Reginald H. MM Gnr 120983 RFA
LOVELL Samuel MM Pte 9095 2nd Bedfordshire Regt DOW 23.8.18.
LOVELL Sidney MM Sjt 265712 1/1st Bucks Bn Oxf & Bucks Light Infantry
LOVELL Tom MM Pte 49659 Royal Fusiliers
LOVELL W.E. MM Pte S/11127 Rifle Brigade
LOVELL Wilfred Ernest MM Pte 72528 2/2(Northumbrian)Fd Amb RAMC
LOVELL William H. MM Sjt 1349 Royal Engineers
LOVELL William R. MM Cpl 11794 2 Fd Coy Royal Engineers
LOVELOCK Arthur MM Cpl 63353 Royal Engineers
LOVELOCK Henry H. MM Sjt 34267 282 Siege Bty RGA
LOVELOCK Henry William MM L/Cpl 2418 (350569) 1/7th London Regt KIA 7.10.16.
LOVELOCK James MM Cpl 6835 1st East Surrey Regt DOW 24.8.18.
LOVELOCK Reginald MM Bdr 40787 RGA
LOVERIDGE Henry N. MM Bdr 75091 RGA
LOVERIDGE Thomas Gill MM Sjt 295095 12th Somerset Light Infantry KIA 19.9.18.
LOVERING George MM Pte 260107 Duke of Cornwall's LI
LOVERING George E.R. MM Pte 202364 Royal West Surrey Regt
LOVERING Percival MM Pte 9593 1st Devonshire Regt KIA 13.9.16.
LOVERING W.H. MM Sjt L/11570 17th Royal Sussex Regt
LOVERSEED John MM L/Cpl 11926 2nd Notts & Derby Regt
LOVESEY C. MM Pte 21103 East Kent Regt
LOVESEY John Henry MM Cpl M2/156128 Army Service Corps att 2/1(Wessex)Fd Amb RAMC
LOVETT Clare MM L/Cpl STK/1886 10th Royal Fusiliers
LOVETT Frederick M. MM Pte 34041 Machine Gun Corps
LOVETT George H. MM Sjt 370142 1/8th London Regt
LOVETT Harold MM Pte 204456 7th South Staffordshire Regt
LOVETT Harry MM L/Cpl 81246 86 Coy Machine Gun Corps
LOVETT James H. MM Cpl 24549 Shropshire Light Infantry
LOVETT Joseph MM L/Cpl 15531 8th Royal Lancaster Regt
LOVETT Wallace MM Sjt 305290 8th Royal Warwickshire Regt
LOVETT William R. MM Pte 37 RAMC
LOVEWELL Charles E. MM Cpl 2089 1st Lancashire Fusiliers
LOVEWELL Charles James Albert MM L/Cpl 41146 1st Bedfordshire Regt
LOVICK Archibald MM Pte 2072 6th Royal West Surrey Regt
LOVIE George Skinner MM Pte M/205713 Army Service Corps att 1/1(East Lancashire)Fd Amb RAMC
LOW Alfred MM Cpl 25585 Seaforth Highlanders
LOW Cameron MM Pte 315895 13th Royal Highlanders
LOW George MM 2nd Cpl 402648 404 Fd Coy Royal Engineers
LOW George MM Bdr 71328 RFA
LOW George M. "MM+Bar,MID" Cpl 406027 Royal Engineers
LOW Henry MM Pte S/9641 Seaforth Highlanders
LOW James Cosmo "MM,MM(F)" CSM 1422 1/14th London Regt
LOW John MM Pte 54558 Machine Gun Corps
LOW John MM+Bar Pte 5880 8/10th Gordon Highlanders
LOW John Jackson "MC,MM(106266 Cpl)" 2Lt 'F' Special Coy Royal Engineers KIA 3.12.17.
LOW Peter MM Cpl 290110 1/7th Gordon Highlanders DOW 20.7.18.
LOW Robert MM Pte 9300 1st Scots Guards KIA 15.9.16.
LOW William Gordon MM Sjt 350359 1/9th Royal Scots KIA 24.5.17.
LOW William J. MM Pnr 309065 Royal Engineers
LOWANS James MM Pte 14/18108 14th Royal Irish Rifles
LOWBRIDGE William Henry MM Sjt 70954 17th Notts & Derby Regt KIA 13.10.17.
LOWCOCK Harold MM Sjt 72968 RFA
LOWDELL William James MM Pte 1514 1st Rifle Brigade KIA 2.9.28.
LOWDEN George MM L/Cpl 9075 2nd Lincolnshire Regt
LOWDEN George H. MM Pnr 32731 2 Div Sig Coy Royal Engineers
LOWDEN James R. MM Sjt 329196 RGA
LOWDEN William MM Cpl S/15944 8th Royal Highlanders
LOWDON Roger MM Pte 35124 1st East Yorkshire Regt
LOWE A. MM Bdr 707337 RFA
LOWE Albert MM Sjt 240239 1/5th North Lancashire Regt
LOWE Albert E. MM+Bar Pte 17540 1st Dorsetshire Regt
LOWE Albert E. MM Gnr 291465 RGA
LOWE Arthur MM CSM 3/6979 1st East Yorkshire Regt
LOWE Arthur H. MM Pte 202116 7th Middlesex Regt
LOWE B. MM Pte 266594 Seaforth Highlanders
LOWE Charles MM L/Cpl 15801 10th Gloucestershire Regt
LOWE Charles E. MM Sjt 1481 2/1(West Riding)Fd Coy Royal Engineers KIA 20.9.16.
LOWE Charles E. MM Pte 45595 2nd Durham Light Infantry
LOWE Charles Thomas MM Cpl 2301 'C' Bn Machine Gun Corps(Heavy Branch)
LOWE Charles William MM Pte 19828 7th Border Regt KIA 28.10.17.
LOWE Clifton A.B. MM+Bar Sjt 16071 Royal Engineers

LOWE Daniel MM Sjt 3734 1st Irish Guards
LOWE David MM Pte 1036 4/5th Royal Highlanders DOW 17.11.16.
LOWE David MM Pte 305141 RAMC
LOWE Edward Arthur Rowland MM Spr 69072 35 Div Sig Coy Royal Engineers
LOWE Frank MM Pte R/2181 12th King's Royal Rifle Corps
LOWE Frederick MM Cpl 15030 10th Cheshire Regt
LOWE Frederick H. MM Pte 435507 1 Fd Amb RAMC
LOWE George MM Sjt 8501 2nd Lancashire Fusiliers
LOWE George MM L/Cpl 120378 75th Bn Machine Gun Corps
LOWE George MM L/Cpl 1991 2nd Northumberland Fusiliers
LOWE George Cossar MM Pte 350572 Royal Scots Died 7.12.18.
LOWE George E.S. MM Cpl 21142 2nd York & Lancaster Regt
LOWE George H. MM Gnr 83929 RFA
LOWE H.W. MM Cpl 12517 HAC
LOWE Harold Scott MM+Bar Cpl 303197 1/5th London Regt KIA 5.4.18.
LOWE Harry "MM,MSM" Sjt 41638 Royal Engineers
LOWE Harry A. MM Spr 67695 Royal Engineers
LOWE Harry H. MM S/Sjt 932 Army Ordnance Corps
LOWE Harry L. MM Pte 201224 8th Yorkshire Light Infantry
LOWE Harry Mansfield MM L/Cpl 14133 11th Royal Scots DOW 10.4.17.
LOWE Henry MM Cpl 1839 23rd Middlesex Regt
LOWE Herbert MM Dvr 47055 RFA
LOWE Hereward Harry MM Dvr 686607 D/148 Bde RFA KIA 25.4.18.
LOWE Horace MM Bdr 29654 RFA
LOWE J. MM Sjt 43630 Scottish Rifles
LOWE J. MM+Bar Pte 24699 Grenadier Guards
LOWE J. MM Pte 421252 RAMC
LOWE James MM L/Cpl 8711 9th Worcestershire Regt
LOWE James E. MM Sjt 23587 49th Bn Machine Gun Corps
LOWE James J. MM Pte 7968 1st Shropshire Light Infantry
LOWE John MM Pte 14691 14th Durham Light Infantry KIA 3.12.17.
LOWE John MM Pte 12249 19th Durham Light Infantry
LOWE John T. MM L/Sjt 80970 1/1st Essex Yeomanry
LOWE Joseph MM Sjt 53868 RAMC KIA 26.3.18.
LOWE Katherine Robertson MM Staff Nurse F TFNS
LOWE Matthew MM Pte 19176 9th North Lancashire Regt
LOWE Percy "MM,CG(B)" Cpl 201185 2/4th North Lancashire Regt
LOWE R. MM L/Cpl 17311 South Lancashire Regt
LOWE Richard T. MM L/Cpl 16571 12th Notts & Derby Regt
LOWE S. MM L/Sjt 12674 Grenadier Guards
LOWE Samuel MM Pte 9987 South Staffordshire Regt
LOWE T.S. MM Pte 695023 London Regt
LOWE Thomas MM Pte 200617 1/5th Manchester Regt
LOWE Thomas MM Gnr 284132 155 Siege Bty RGA
LOWE Thomas MM Cpl 395561 9th London Regt
LOWE Thomas MM Pte 30530 16th Highland Light Infantry
LOWE Thomas MM Cpl 677081 RFA
LOWE Thomas W. MM Sjt 200344 1/4th Leicestershire Regt
LOWE Thomas William MM Cpl 2239 1/8th Notts & Derby Regt
LOWE W. MM Pte 202113 Manchester Regt
LOWE Walter Wilson MM Pte 241079 4th Leicestershire Regt
LOWE William MM Sjt 12955 7th York & Lancaster Regt
LOWE William MM Sjt 16148 18th Lancashire Fusiliers
LOWE William MM L/Cpl 10344 Leicestershire Regt
LOWE William Everett MM Cpl 471234 Royal Engineers
LOWE William James MM Pte B/200563 16th Rifle Brigade
LOWE William T. MM Pte 238181 4th West Riding Regt
LOWE Willie MM Pte 20534 Royal Welsh Fusiliers
LOWEN George Edward MM Pte 11/1244 11th East Yorkshire Regt DOW 24.3.18.
LOWENS Arthur T. MM Sjt R/5585 13th King's Royal Rifle Corps
LOWER Charles E. MM L/Cpl 9310 2nd East Yorkshire Regt
LOWER Richard J. MM Spr 2795 Royal Engineers
LOWER William MM L/Cpl 38837 9th Welsh Regt
LOWERSON Gilbert MM Pte 46748 2nd Durham Light Infantry
LOWERY Bernard MM L/Sjt 12802 2nd South Lancashire Regt KIA 14.6.17.
LOWERY D. "DCM,MM+Bar" L/Cpl 672 17th Royal Fusiliers
LOWERY John MM L/Cpl 15235 11th Durham Light Infantry
LOWERY Walter MM Bdr 5262 RFA
LOWERY William MM L/Cpl 29941 Liverpool Regt
LOWES Arthur MM Spr 9379 15 Fd Coy Royal Engineers KIA 27.5.18.
LOWES Nicholas MM Spr 463239 50 Div Sig Coy Royal Engineers
LOWES Robert J. MM Cpl 355451 1/10th Liverpool Regt
LOWES Thomas MM Pte 23/974 1st Northumberland Fusiliers
LOWES William MM Pte 4086 2nd Northumberland Fusiliers
LOWES William MM Pte 51774 15th Cheshire Regt
LOWES William J. MM Pte 72989 Durham Light Infantry
LOWIN Charles MM Cpl 53519 Machine Gun Corps
LOWIS Charles H. MM Spr 536168 Royal Engineers
LOWIS Frederick J. MM L/Sjt 390533 1/9th London Regt
LOWMAN A. MM Pte 34148 Hampshire Regt
LOWMAN Edward MM Sjt 70158 29 Div Sig Coy Royal Engineers
LOWMAN Russell William MM Pte 1976 1/16th London Regt
LOWNDES Charles MM Pte 201751 2nd King's Own Scottish Borderers
LOWNDES Daniel MM Cpl 14959 Leicestershire Regt
LOWNDES Patrick MM Pte 23641 Royal Dublin Fusiliers
LOWNDS John MM Gnr L/34223 155 Bde RFA
LOWNDS William MM Cpl 207816 Royal Engineers
LOWRIE Ralph MM Sjt 760061 C/242 Bde RFA
LOWRY Edward MM Pte M/379472 Army Service Corps
LOWRY George MM Pte 17/790 15th Royal Irish Rifles
LOWRY George J. MM Sjt 89488 RFA
LOWRY Henry MM L/Cpl 240997 Northumberland Fusiliers
LOWRY Robert MM Pte 28834 Durham Light Infantry
LOWRY Stephen "DCM,MM+Bar" Cpl 57994 36 Div Sig Coy Royal Engineers
LOWRY William MM L/Cpl 371219 8th London Regt
LOWSON Charles H. MM Cpl 14557 East Yorkshire Regt
LOWSON Robert MM Gnr 750807 C/315 Bde RFA
LOWSON William MM Pte 204559 Northumberland Fusiliers
LOWTH H. MM Pte 203188 West Riding Regt
LOWTHER A.C.M. MM Pte 33160 1st Essex Regt
LOWTHER Charles J. MM Spr 175571 Royal Engineers
LOWTHER G. MM Sjt 99672 RFA
LOWTHER George Norton "DCM,MM" Cpl 761201 RFA
LOWTHER Harry "DCM,MM" Sjt 21354 29th Bn Machine Gun Corps
LOWTHER John M. MM Dvr 7325 RFA
LOWTHER John William MM Pte 12033 13th Yorkshire Regt DOW 15.4.18.
LOWTHER Marcus A. MM L/Cpl 15705 10th Royal Inniskilling Fusiliers
LOWTHER Thomas MM Bdr 64586 RFA
LOWTHER Thomas H. MM Spr 182769 Royal Engineers
LOWTHER William MM Sjt 2360 1/5th York & Lancaster Regt
LOWTHORP Alfred T. "MM,MID" Pte 1867 1/24th London Regt
LOWTON John Frederick MM L/Cpl 11402 6th Wiltshire Regt KIA 23.3.18.
LOWTON Thomas MM Sjt 241379 5th South Lancashire Regt
LOXLEY John MM Pte 337 20 Fd Amb RAMC
LOXTON Frederick G. MM Sjt 3668 Royal Engineers
LOXTON W. MM Pte 14115 4th South Wales Borderers
LOYDELL Harry MM Pte 200538 1/4th Royal Lancaster Regt
LOYNES Walter MM Bdr 2609 Machine Gun Corps(Motors)
LOYNES William S. MM Bdr 338542 270 Siege Bty RGA
LUBY Thomas MM L/Sjt 5764 1st Irish Guards
LUCAS Albert MM Pte 21298 Machine Gun Corps
LUCAS Albert E. MM Cpl 77483 Tank Corps
LUCAS Albert Horace "DCM,MM" Cpl 8859 4 Fd Amb RAMC DOW 27.8.18.
LUCAS Albert Maxwell MM Pte 265077 Royal Warwickshire Regt
LUCAS Arthur MM Pte 46070 Durham Light Infantry
LUCAS Bertie MM Sjt 2363 Royal Warwickshire Regt
LUCAS C. MM Cpl 18007 13th Essex Regt
LUCAS Charles E. MM Pte 63472 2nd West Yorkshire Regt
LUCAS Charles James MM Pte 90291 151 Coy Labour Corps
LUCAS Charles William MM Sjt 55112 Railways Troops Royal Engineers
LUCAS E. MM Sjt 678 Military Mounted Police
LUCAS Ernest MM Pte A/1706 King's Royal Rifle Corps
LUCAS Frederick MM Pte 205117 7th Royal West Surrey Regt
LUCAS Frederick MM S/Sjt 572 Army Ordnance Corps att 66 Siege Bty RGA.DOW 23/24.7.16.
LUCAS Frederick MM Sjt 14313 71 Bty 36 Bde RFA KIA 24.10.17.
LUCAS Frederick MM Gnr 38849 RGA
LUCAS Frederick J. MM Pte G/21481 7th Royal West Kent Regt
LUCAS George MM Cpl 43251 13th West Riding Regt
LUCAS George MM Pte 49004 8th Devonshire Regt
LUCAS George MM Cpl 16800 1st Royal Irish Rifles KIA 2.10.18.
LUCAS George E. MM Gnr 43600 RFA
LUCAS Harold MM Pte 204266 6th Wiltshire Regt
LUCAS Harry "MM,MSM" Cpl(SS) L/33294 C/160 Bde RFA
LUCAS Henry MM Cpl 2664 12th Middlesex Regt

LUCAS Henry George MM Pte 684040 22nd London Regt KIA 30.8.18.
LUCAS Henry Joseph "MC,DCM,MM(6662 Sjt)" Capt 2nd Yorkshire Regt
LUCAS Herbert MM Sjt 9615 1st Royal Warwickshire Regt
LUCAS Herbert G. MM BQMS 39585 B/108 Bde RFA
LUCAS J. MM Pte 10292 South Lancashire Regt
LUCAS James William MM Pte 2209 7th Royal West Kent Regt
LUCAS John MM Pte 10/16686 10th Royal Irish Rifles
LUCAS Reginald G. MM L/Cpl 148375 Royal Engineers
LUCAS Robert "DCM,MM" CSM 14414 9th Royal Irish Fusiliers
LUCAS Thomas MM Pte 16046 13th Royal Sussex Regt KIA 21.3.18.
LUCAS Thomas G. MM Pte 1631 1st Welsh Guards
LUCAS Walter MM Drummer 8117 1st Royal Fusiliers
LUCAS Wilfred Edgar MM Sjt 11160 1st Worcestershire Regt
LUCAS William F. MM L/Cpl 11534 1st Border Regt
LUCAS William J. MM Cpol R/6149 King's Royal Rifle Corps
LUCAS William John MM Pte 84269 141 Coy Labour Corps
LUCAS William John MM Gnr 67115 111 Siege Bty RGA
LUCAS William Thomas MM Pte 2701 3rd Rifle Brigade
LUCAS William Thomas MM Pte 10618 6th Leicestershire Regt KIA 30.7.16.
LUCAS William Wentworth MM L/Cpl 9465 Machine Gun Corps
LUCCOCK George MM Sjt 14749 Machine Gun Corps
LUCE James MM 2nd Cpl 79144 185 Tunnelling Coy Royal Engineers
LUCE John A. MM L/Cpl 4152 Royal Irish Rifles
LUCHFORD A.T. MM Pte 1038 East Kent Regt
LUCK Albert MM+Bar Sjt 15644 7th Northamptonshire Regt
LUCK Charles Walter "MC,MM(32149 Sjt MGC)" T/2Lt 15th Bn Tank Corps
LUCK Joseph H. MM Pte 65863 13th Royal Fusiliers
LUCK Thomas A. MM Cpl 31388 28 Fd Amb RAMC
LUCK Walter MM L/Cpl 183 9th Royal Fusiliers
LUCK Wilfred H. MM Spr 142754 Royal Engineers
LUCK William A. "MM,MID" Pte 17879 1st Northamptonshire Regt
LUCK William Alfred MM L/Sjt 867 4th Bn GMGR
LUCKCUCK Henry B. MM Sjt 250783 2/3rd London Regt
LUCKETT Ernest George MM Pte 2099 7th Royal West Kent Regt
LUCKHURST Arthur MM Pte 18640 Northumberland Fusiliers
LUCKHURST William A. MM Gnr L/22238 C/93 Bde RFA
LUCKIN E.F. MM Sjt 12643 9th Essex Regt
LUCKIN John William MM Pte R/11819 King's Royal Rifle Corps
LUCKIN William A. MM Pte 11372 5th Royal Berkshire Regt
LUCY Albert Edward MM(A/60 Bde)+Bar(C/34 Bde) Dvr 98692 RFA
LUCY Joseph "MC,DCM,MM" CSM 19442 21st Manchester Regt
LUDBROOK Percy Archibald MM L/Cpl 444393 66 Div Sig Coy Royal Engineers KIA 20.10.18.
LUDDINGTON Arthur MM Pte 201184 1/4th Essex Regt
LUDGATE Joseph MM Pte 10790 8th Cheshire Regt
LUDLAM James MM Pte 201439 1/4th Leicestershire Regt
LUDLOW Ezra Stephen MM Dvr 140109 'A' Bty RHA DOW 8.4.18.
LUDLOW F. MM Cpl Mechanic 18387 Royal Air Force
LUDLOW Fred MM Pte 9523 2nd Bedfordshire Regt
LUDLOW James "MM,MID" Pte 20340 20 Fd Amb RAMC
LUDLOW Jesse MM Pte 7672 1st Worcestershire Regt KIA 15.11.16.
LUDLOW John MM Pte M2/187629 Army Service Corps
LUDLOW Rowland George MM(1/4th Bn)+Bar(6th Bn) L/Cpl 200767 Royal Berkshire Regt
LUDWIG Arthur R. MM Cpl P6133 Military Mounted Police
LUFF Edward H. MM Pte 9019 6th Royal West Kent Regt
LUFF Frederick MM Sjt 265576 West Yorkshire Regt
LUFF Harry "MM,MSM" SQMS 56772 'C' Squadron Machine Gun Corps(Cavalry)
LUFF Maurice MM Sjt G/886 9th Royal Sussex Regt
LUGG Edwin S. MM Cpl 24352 Worcestershire Regt
LUGG Harold MM L/Cpl 1673 1st Gloucestershire Regt
LUGG Walter W. MM Gnr 11297 RFA
LUGO Eric A. MM Pte 48176 12th East Surrey Regt
LUGTON George MM Gnr 45349 17 Siege Bty RGA
LUGTON James MM Sjt 16444 11th Royal Scots
LUGTON James MM Sjt 27/1064 Northumberland Fusiliers
LUHMANN Frederick Charles MM Bdr 41511 B/174 Bde RFA KIA 6.12.17.
LUKE Arthur MM Pte 33368 Devonshire Regt
LUKE Edwin MM Sjt 21440 Duke of Cornwall's LI
LUKE Frank MM Spr 139311 Royal Engineers
LUKE Frederick B. "MM,MID" Pte 18323 1 Fd Amb RAMC
LUKE John MM Pte 12643 1st Devonshire Regt
LUKE John "DCM,MM" Sjt 200354 Durham Light Infantry
LUKE John MM Pte 13193 6/7th Royal Scots Fusiliers
LUKE John MM L/Sjt 18215 6th Yorkshire Regt
LUKE Peter MM Pte 9291 Royal Highlanders
LUKE Ralph MM Pte 7791 Northumberland Fusiliers
LUKE Robert W. MM Sjt 25/1365 Northumberland Fusiliers
LUKE Sydney Thomas MM L/Cpl 62914 Machine Gun Corps
LUKE Thomas MM L/Cpl 905 Northumberland Fusiliers
LUKE William MM Pte 17054 Durham Light Infantry
LUKE William MM Dvr 610365 RFA
LUKER David J. MM+Bar Cpl 162 1st Welsh Guards
LUKER Jesse MM L/Sjt 12910 1st Grenadier Guards
LUKER John MM L/Cpl 2629 1/8th Royal Warwickshire Regt KIA 1.7.16.
LUKOSZEVIEZE Antanas MM Gnr 250523 B/51 Bde RFA
LULAND Charles E. MM Gnr 153880 RGA
LULHAM Frederick G. MM Pte 25968 4th Grenadier Guards
LUMB Arthur MM Pte 41830 10th West Yorkshire Regt
LUMB George MM Pte 18/353 18th West Yorkshire Regt
LUMB Harry D. MM Bdr 43119 RFA
LUMBER William MM Cpl 24177 2nd Royal Dublin Fusiliers
LUMBY Harry MM Gnr Sig 710442 D/250 Bde RFA
LUMGAIR Ernest G. MM Sjt 53548 RAMC
LUMKIN Arthur J. MM Gnr 85719 A/62 Bde RFA
LUMLEY George MM Pte 201544 1/8th West Yorkshire Regt KIA 2.9.18.
LUMLEY Harry MM Pnr 482088 49 Div Sig Coy Royal Engineers
LUMLEY Tom MM Pnr 406328 51 Div Sig Coy Royal Engineers
LUMLEY William MM Pte 201086 Yorkshire Regt
LUMSDALE John MM Pte 13598 2/5th Yorkshire Regt KIA 27.8.18.
LUMSDALE Joshua MM Pte 12275 10th Durham Light Infantry
LUMSDEN Alec Miller MM Sjt 650388 A/291 Bde RFA
LUMSDEN George MM Pte 88102 RAMC
LUMSDEN J. MM Pte 321442 London Regt
LUMSDEN James MM Sjt 292457 8th Royal Highlanders
LUMSDEN James L. MM Piper 1276 1/6th Seaforth Highlanders
LUMSDEN James R. MM Gnr 117872 244 Siege Bty RGA
LUMSDEN John MM CSM 125 1/7th Royal Highlanders DOW 3.7.16.
LUMSDEN Thomas MM Sjt 9858 1st Royal Highlanders
LUMSDON John MM Pte 25363 Royal Inniskilling Fusiliers
LUND Charles MM Bdr 681527 D/286 Bde RFA
LUND Harry MM Cpl 63825 D/11 Bde RFA DOW 28.12.17.
LUND John "DCM,MM+Bar" Sjt 12983 8th Yorkshire Light Infantry att 70 Lt TM Bty
LUND John W. MM L/Cpl 242623 6th West Riding Regt
LUND Morris MM Gnr 681034 A/286 Bde RFA
LUND Peter MM Cpl 202278 Liverpool Regt
LUND Tom MM Bdr 48958 RGA
LUNDBERG Frederick Martin MM L/Cpl 1893 1/8th Liverpool Regt
LUNDIE Henry MM Sjt 284907 236 Siege Bty RGA
LUNDIE Thomas MM Pte 334 16 Fd Amb RAMC
LUNDY Henly MM Pte 31888 7/8th King's Own Scottish Borderers
LUNDY Richard MM Pte 19129 13th Liverpool Regt
LUNGLEY A.J. MM Sjt 2407 Essex Regt
LUNGLEY Bertie G. MM Pte 27524 2nd Northamptonshire Regt
LUNGLEY H.C. MM Sig 880054 440 Bty 271 Bde RFA
LUNN Albert E. MM Pte R/39362 King's Royal Rifle Corps
LUNN Alexander MM Pte 14/13409 11th West Yorkshire Regt
LUNN Charles MM Pte 30068 1st Yorkshire Light Infantry
LUNN Ernest MM Pte 890 7th East Surrey Regt
LUNN George MM Pte 9832 South Staffordshire Regt
LUNN George Robert MM L/Cpl 241750 4th Lincolnshire Regt Died 11.12.17.
LUNN Herbert MM Sjt 64085 RGA
LUNN J. MM Gnr 2868 RFA
LUNN Walter MM Pte 28407 Royal Warwickshire Regt
LUNN William MM L/Sjt 2484 1/6th North Staffordshire Regt
LUNN William MM Dvr 35212 52 Bty 15 Bde RFA
LUNN William H. MM Cpl 7888 6th Yorkshire Regt
LUNNESS Walter MM Pte 27123 Yorkshire Regt
LUNNON Herbert MM Sjt 45640 8th Royal Berkshire Regt KIA 28.8.18.
LUNNY James MM Pte 15263 9th Royal Inniskilling Fusiliers
LUNT Ernest MM L/Cpl 265292 Royal Welsh Fusiliers
LUNT Thomas P. "MM,MID" Bdr 48671 26 Bde RFA
LUPSON Walter MM L/Cpl 2369 1/1st Cambridgeshire Regt
LUPTON Bert MM Pte 51189 2nd Royal Scots
LUPTON Frank MM Sjt 28936 D/236 Bde RFA

LUPTON Fred MM Cpl 202006 4th York & Lancaster Regt
LUPTON Richard MM Cpl 101942 19th Durham Light Infantry
LUPTON William MM Sjt 786046 D/312 Bde RFA
LUPTON William MM Pte 3897 9th Lancashire Fusiliers DOW 1.10.16
LURCOCK Arthur W. MM Pte 53463 RAMC
LUSBY Richard MM Cpl 73025 RGA
LUSCOMBE Albert V. MM CQMS 133402 Royal Engineers
LUSCOMBE Fernley R. MM L/Cpl 240436 5th Devonshire Regt
LUSCOMBE James MM L/Cpl 13526 3 Fd Sqn Royal Engineers
LUSCOMBE William Thomas Charles MM Pte 27169 15th Hampshire Regt DOW 11.8.17.
LUSH Allen MM L/Cpl 18303 15th Hampshire Regt KIA 4.9.18.
LUSH Frederick MM Cpl 8092 5th Dorsetshire Regt
LUSH Harold J. MM Pte 8361 Royal Irish Regt
LUSH Joseph Thomas MM Cpl 825534 RFA
LUSHER Samuel MM Pte 36760 East Yorkshire Regt
LUSTED George "MM,MID" Sjt 1647 1/5th Royal Sussex Regt
LUSTED Henry Amos MM Gnr 50277 C/187 Bde RFA
LUSTY Ernest MM Pte 11510 2nd Grenadier Guards
LUSTY Richard MM L/Cpl 12289 Royal Inniskilling Fusiliers
LUTMAN Herbert J. MM Pte 48668 Manchester Regt
LUTON John MM L/Sjt 354173 7th London Regt
LUTON William A. MM L/Cpl 201267 1st Somerset Light Infantry
LUTWICK Marie Dow MM Sister F QAIMNS
LUTZES Abraham MM Pte 56870 12 Fd Amb RAMC enlisted as Alfred FREEMAN
LUXFORD Edward MM Bdr 65732 99 Siege Bty RGA
LUXFORD Frederick Thomas MM Pte A/201403 8th King's Royal Rifle Corps KIA 4.12.17.
LUXFORD George H. MM Sjt 457112 497 Fd Coy Royal Engineers
LUXFORD George T. MM Pte 14099 8th Royal Berkshire Regt
LUXFORD Sidney A. MM Sjt 32370 115 Heavy Bty RGA
LUXFORD William MM L/Cpl 16794 11th Royal Sussex Regt
LUXFORD William MM Cpl 200225 'B' Bn Tank Corps KIA 23.11.17.
LUXTON Augustine MM Pte 204242 6th Wiltshire Regt
LUXTON Charles William MM Gnr 41480 297 Siege Bty RGA
LUXTON Thomas "MM,MSM" 2nd Cpl 20460 25 Army Troops Coy Royal Engineers
LYALL Alexander MM CSM 200011 1/5th Arg & Suth Highlanders
LYALL Christopher MM L/Sjt 8029 2nd Leinster Regt
LYALL David W MM Cpl 265169 1/6th Gordon Highlanders
LYALL George MM Cpl 96449 25 Div Sig Coy Royal Engineers
LYALL George MM L/Sjt 17613 2 Fd Coy Royal Engineers
LYALL John William "MM+Bar,MSM" Sjt 17892 9th Yorkshire Regt
LYALL William MM Pte 33016 Machine Gun Corps
LYALL William MM+Bar Pte 12594 Seaforth Highlanders
LYCETT William MM+Bar Sjt 32500 1st South Staffordshire Regt
LYDDIATT Archibald L. MM Pte 17632 13th Royal Fusiliers
LYDDON Alfred MM Gnr 290354 38 Hy Bty RGA
LYDIARD John Henry MM Gnr 1198 66 Siege Bty RGA
LYDIART Hugh E. MM Cpl 350378 2/7th London Regt
LYDIATE Francis MM Spr 48070 Royal Engineers
LYDON John MM Pte 3948 1st Irish Guards
LYDON Michael MM Cpl 13/714 6th East Yorkshire Regt KIA 13.3.18.
LYE William James MM L/Cpl 56808 81 Motor Airline Section Royal Engineers
LYFORD Edward A. MM Sjt 1668 2nd Lancashire Fusiliers
LYLE A. MM Sjt S/6125 Arg & Suth Highlanders
LYLE Alan John MM Spr 237347 62 Div Sig Coy Royal Engineers KIA 20.11.17.
LYLE Cuthbert P. MM Pte 328071 3 Fd Amb RAMC
LYLE Ernest Gordon MM Cpl S/12234 5th Cameron Highlanders
LYLE Henry MM Cpl 18410 Machine Gun Corps
LYLE John MM Sjt 2209 11/13th Royal Irish Rifles
LYLE John MM Pte 292305 1/7th Gordon Highlanders KIA 30.7.18.
LYLE William MM Bdr 5734 298 Siege Bty RGA
LYLE William MM CSM 17/1616 West Yorkshire Regt
LYLE William MM Pte 277628 Arg & Suth Highlanders
LYMAN James Jessie MM Pte 32723 2nd Oxf & Bucks Light Infantry KIA 11.9.18.
LYMBERY Frank MM Bdr 624272 HAC(Artillery)
LYMER Benjamin MM Pte 12134 Coldstream Guards
LYMER Frank MM Pte 4157 York & Lancaster Regt
LYMER George MM L/Cpl 11886 3rd Coldstream Guards
LYMN Frank MM Dvr 91254 66 Div Ammn Col RFA
LYNAM Edward MM Pte 26211 Royal Inniskilling Fusiliers
LYNAM Joseph Leo MM Cpl 37911 Lancashire Fusiliers
LYNAS R.H. MM CSM P/391 Military Foot Police

LYNCH Alfred MM Pte 243126 1st Norfolk Regt
LYNCH Charles MM Pte 7998 2nd Irish Guards att 7th Entrenching Bn
LYNCH Christopher MM L/Cpl 8542 2nd Royal Dublin Fusiliers
LYNCH Daniel MM Spr 144853 179 Tunnelling Coy Royal Engineers
LYNCH Daniel MM Pte 14283 East Surrey Regt
LYNCH Daniel MM Pte 40893 5th Cameron Highlanders KIA 18.9.17.
LYNCH Edward MM Pte 4772 6th Highland Light Infantry
LYNCH Edward "MM,MID" Pte 8117 2nd Royal Highlanders
LYNCH Ernest Michael MM Pnr 280067 332 Rail Constr Coy Royal Engineers
LYNCH Gerald MM+Bar Cpl 77716 311 Bde RFA
LYNCH James MM Gnr 45258 C/103 Bde RFA DOW 17.8.17.
LYNCH John MM Pte 28531 East Yorkshire Regt
LYNCH Martin MM Pte 23109 4th Grenadier Guards
LYNCH Patrick MM Sjt 12508 6th Royal Berkshire Regt KIA 19.7.16.
LYNCH Robert MM Sjt 14801 50 Bty 34 Bde RFA KIA 11.10.17.
LYNCH Robert Greenwood Kingston MM Spr 77585 Signal Service Royal Engineers
LYNCH Ronald MM L/Cpl 156334 258 Tunnelling Coy Royal Engineers
LYNCH Thomas MM Cpl 40001 South Staffordshire Regt
LYNCH Thomas "MC,DCM,MM(458 Sjt 1st Bn)" Capt 2nd Royal Warwickshire Regt
LYNCH Thomas MM Sjt 7834 2nd Oxf & Bucks Light Infantry
LYNCH Thomas MM Spr 89596 128 Fd Coy Royal Engineers
LYNCH William MM Dvr 756108 C/251 Bde RFA
LYNDON Herbert MM L/Cpl 53192 5th Liverpool Regt
LYNE Albert Charles MM Pte 514220 2/14th London Regt Died 31.10.18.
LYNE Dan MM Sjt 53312 12th Bn Machine Gun Corps
LYNE E.F. MM Spr 70863 Royal Engineers
LYNE Francis William George MM Sjt 2368 1/8th Middlesex Regt KIA 9.4.17.
LYNE Henry "DCM,MM,MID" Sjt 62984 38 Div Sig Coy Royal Engineers
LYNE Robert MM Cpl 951 Royal Engineers
LYNESS William MM Pte 51797 Royal Scots
LYNHAM Edward MM Cpl R/40039 13th King's Royal Rifle Corps Died 10.11.18.
LYNN Arthur MM Pte 20029 10th Hussars
LYNN Charles MM Sjt 301422 Tank Corps
LYNN Ernest MM Pte 18253 1st King's Own Scottish Borderers
LYNN Ernest MM Bde 73679 D/187 Bde RFA
LYNN F.E. MM Sjt 43957 RFA
LYNN Frederick J. MM Sjt 43652 'Q' Bty RHA
LYNN George "MM,MM(P)" Cpl P13 Military Mounted Police
LYNN Harry MM Sjt 276482 7th Manchester Regt
LYNN J. MM L/Sjt 38621 Northumberland Fusiliers
LYNN James MM Bdr 32072 12 Bde RFA
LYNN John "DCM,MM" RSM 308015 West Riding Regt
LYNN Sidney J. MM Pte 7609 2nd East Surrey Regt
LYNN Thomas MM Cpl 8715 2nd Highland Light Infantry
LYNN William J. MM Pte 15864 Royal Irish Fusiliers
LYON Albert Edward MM Pte B/200400 11th Rifle Brigade
LYON Charles MM L/Cpl 14406 1st Essex Regt KIA 12.10.16.
LYON Daniel MM Bdr 96621 169 Bde RFA
LYON George MM Pnr 359676 15 Div Sig Coy Royal Engineers
LYON James MM Pte 10261 6th Lincolnshire Regt
LYON John MM+Bar Sjt S/4094 11th Arg & Suth Highlanders
LYON John W. MM Dvr 686539 RFA
LYON Joseph "DCM,MM" Sjt 10371 2nd Grenadier Guards KIA 15.9.16.
LYON R. MM Sjt 200015 Highland Light Infantry
LYON Richard Mark MM Spr 72851 Second Army Sig Coy Royal Engineers
LYON Robert MM RSM 5357 15th Cheshire Regt
LYON William E. MM Pte 70037 Tank Corps
LYON William E. MM Cpl 10256 1st York & Lancaster Regt
LYON William G. MM Dvr 3452 RFA
LYONS Albert MM Pte 36628 South Lancashire Regt
LYONS Charles MM+Bar Pte S/9937 5th Cameron Highlanders
LYONS Charles MM Pte 276719 Manchester Regt
LYONS Frank MM Drummer 266258 2/4th West Riding Regt
LYONS G.J. MM Sjt 391367 London Regt
LYONS George H. MM Pte 58840 Machine Gun Corps
LYONS George Henry Penrose MM+Bar Pte 30161 1st Royal Warwickshire Regt

LYONS Henry MM Sjt 201566 2/5th West Yorkshire Regt KIA 20.7.18.
LYONS J. MM Sjt 17311 6th York & Lancaster Regt
LYONS John MM L/Cpl 62763 1/7th West Yorkshire Regt
LYONS John MM Pte 10874 2nd Royal Irish Regt
LYONS John MM Pte 240666 Border Regt
LYONS John MM L/Cpl 7320 Royal Irish Regt
LYONS Jonathan M. MM Pte 71777 11th Notts & Derby Regt KIA 5.10.18.
LYONS Martin MM Pte 3652 9th Lancashire Fusiliers AKA O'HANLON
LYONS Michael MM L/Cpl 8192 1st Leinster Regt
LYONS Morris J. MM Cpl 422461 10th London Regt
LYONS Patrick John MM Sjt 11328 Z/30 Med TM Bty RGA KIA 7.12.16.
LYONS Percy MM Sjt 9361 1st Royal Inniskilling Fusiliers
LYONS Thomas MM Sjt 7176 2nd King's Royal Rifle Corps
LYONS Thomas J. MM Snt 682128 22nd London Regt
LYONS William MM Pte 471103 12th London Regt
LYONS William Francis MM L/Cpl 49040 103 Fd Coy Royal Engineers DOW 21.2.17.
LYONS William J. MM Sjt 265095 Royal Warwickshire Regt
LYSAGHT Charles R. MM Pte 26920 Royal Dublin Fusiliers
LYTH Edward MM Spr 79929 176 Tunnelling Coy Royal Engineers
LYTH Frederick William MM Pte 32922 1/4th Royal Lancaster Regt
LYTH Henry MM L/Cpl 19/20 19th Durham Light Infantry KIA 25.8.17.
LYTHGOE Herbert MM Pte 53606 2nd Lancashire Fusiliers
LYTHGOE James MM Pte 265656 7th Liverpool Regt
LYTHGOE James MM Dvr 91754 19 Div Ammn Col RFA
LYTHGOE Richard MM Dvr 70336 RFA
LYTLE Edgar MM Pte 76066 Tank Corps
LYTTLE Robert S. MM S/Sjt Fitter 309204 RGA

M

MAACK John H. MM L/Cpl 390111 1/3(Northumbrian)Fd Amb RAMC Died 15.12.18.
MABBATT Clarence W. MM Pte M2/055323 Army Service Corps
MABBATT William MM Cpl 24305 1st Royal Lancaster Regt
MABBERLEY Frank MM L/Bdr 191658 45 AA Section RGA
MABBETT George James MM Pte 15925 10th Gloucestershire Regt
MABBETT Hubert MM Trumpeter 3273 4th Hussars
MABBITT Leslie MM Sjt 550069 1/16th London Regt
MABBOTT Dennis MM Cpl 13637 37th Bn Machine Gun Corps
MABBOTT Thomas MM Pte 40660 Lincolnshire Regt
MABBOTT William MM Gnr 22437 D/88 Bde RFA
MABBS Frederick S. MM Cpl 12512 7th Norfolk Regt
MABBUTT Albert MM Pte 10917 7th Shropshire Light Infantry KIA 27.3.18.
MABBUTT Clarence T. MM Cpl 16600 11th Suffolk Regt
MABBUTT E. MM Cpl Mechanic 8680 Royal Air Force
MABE Francis MM L/Cpl 591071 18th London Regt
MABER Mark MM Pte 2782 1/1st Berkshire Yeomanry
MABLESTON Leonard MM Dvr 800027 1(North Midland)Bde RFA
MABON John McC. MM Bdr 52004 RFA
MACADIE Stanley Claude "DCM,MM" Cpl 505223 18th King's Royal Rifle Corps
MacARTHUR George MM Sjt 339024 RAMC
MACARTHUR John MM L/Cpl 3/5675 2nd Gordon Highlanders
MACASKILL Duncan MM Spr 77149 17 Div Sig Coy Royal Engineers
MACAULAY Archibald MM L/Cpl 1961 Arg & Suth Highlanders
MACAULAY Edward MM L/Cpl 43465 5/6th Royal Scots
MACAULAY John MM Cpl 4115 Seaforth Highlanders
MACAULAY John Morrison MM Pte S/8983 8th Royal Highlanders KIA 12.10.17.
MACAULAY John William MM Cpl S/9947 Royal Highlanders
MACAULEY Bingham MM L/Cpl 35683 Cheshire Regt
MACAULEY David Mason "DCM+Bar,MM,CG(F)" Pte 14952 1st South Wales Borderers KIA 18.10.18.
MACAULEY Hugh MM L/Cpl S/3704 Gordon Highlanders
MACAULEY James MM Pte 50580 4th Liverpool Regt
MACBAIN Hugh MM Pte 8699 2nd Scots Guards
MACBAIN J. MM Pte 126763 Yeo
MACBEAN Alexander MM Pte 203428 5th Cameron Highlanders
MACBETH Edward MM Sjt 69667 149 Army Troops Coy Royal Engineers
MACBRYDE Hugh MM L/Bdr 159601 188 Siege Bty RGA
MACCABEE Sydney W. MM Pte 590246 1/18th London Regt
MACCALLUM Duncan L. MM Pte 300728 1/8th Arg & Suth Highlanders
MacCALLUM James MM Gnr 63579 RGA
MACCARTHY Geoffery MM Sjt 452417 42 Div Sig Coy Royal Engineers
MACCARTHY George Edward MM Sjt 5096 2nd Irish Guards
MACCOLL Duncan MM Cpl 16473 1st King's Own Scottish Borderers
MACCOMBIE Alexander "DCM,MM" Cpl 200345 1/4th Gordon Highlanders
MACCORQUODALE John MM Sjt 350035 Royal Scots
MACCOWAN Thomas E. "DCM(23rd Bn),MM" Sjt K/564 22nd Royal Fusiliers
MACDIARMID J. MM Sjt 57184 Royal Fusiliers
MACDIARMID P. MM Gnr 128804 RHA
MACDONALD Alexander MM Pte 51725 Royal Scots
MACDONALD Alexander MM Cpl 1917 2/2(Northumbrian)Fd Amb RAMC KIA 27.10.16.
MACDONALD Alexander MM Pte 43663 52 Fd Amb RAMC
MACDONALD Alexander MM Pte 267254 1/6th Seaforth Highlanders KIA 10.4.18.
MACDONALD Alexander A. MM+Bar L/Cpl G/8208 6th East Kent Regt
MACDONALD Andrew MM Pte 22298 Cameron Highlanders
MACDONALD Bernard J. MM Bdr 1182 RFA
MACDONALD C. MM Sjt S/40643 Seaforth Highlanders
MACDONALD Charles MM+Bar Sjt 200533 1/4th Seaforth Highlanders
MACDONALD Charles MM Sjt 750514 RFA
MACDONALD Colin MM Pte 7212 2nd Seaforth Highlanders
MACDONALD Colin A.C. MM Pte 40260 1/6th Royal Highlanders
MACDONALD D. MM Pte 39628 1st Essex Regt
MACDONALD D. MM L/Cpl S/40115 Cameron Highlanders att RE
MACDONALD Donald MM Pte 21431 2nd Cameron Highlanders
MACDONALD Donald MM L/Cpl 200254 1/4th Seaforth Highlanders
MACDONALD Donald MM L/Cpl 7093 5/6th Scottish Rifles
MACDONALD Donald MM Sjt 25948 Royal Scots
MACDONALD Donald MM L/Sjt 7872 2nd Scots Guards
MACDONALD Ewen MM L/Cpl 3/5238 5th Cameron Highlanders
MACDONALD Finlay MM L/Cpl 200265 1/4th Seaforth Highlanders
MACDONALD George MM Cpl 31717 16th Royal Welsh Fusiliers
MACDONALD George MM Pte 352252 1/2(East Lancashire)Fd Amb RAMC
MACDONALD George R. MM L/Sjt S/8436 9th Royal Highlanders
MACDONALD Harry MM Pte 202208 Lancashire Fusiliers
MACDONALD Herbert MM L/Cpl 18778 9th Yorkshire Light Infantry
MACDONALD Hugh "DCM,MM" CSM 8512 10/11th Highland Light Infantry
MACDONALD J. MM L/Cpl 9768 Seaforth Highlanders
MACDONALD James MM Cpl 13958 Army Cyclist Corps
MACDONALD James MM Pte 29127 6th King's Own Scottish Borderers
MACDONALD James A. MM Pte 203366 2nd Seaforth Highlanders
MACDONALD John MM L/Cpl S/43331 1st Cameron Highlanders
MACDONALD John MM Pte 301211 1/8th Arg & Suth Highlanders
MACDONALD John MM Pte 1569 1/3(Lowland)Fd Amb RAMC
MACDONALD John MM L/Cpl S/27648 2nd Cameron Highlanders
MACDONALD John MM Gnr 110736 RGA
MACDONALD John MM Sjt 8259 1st Highland Light Infantry
MACDONALD John Urquhart MM L/Cpl 26840 1st Cameron Highlanders
MACDONALD Joseph MM Cpl 240363 1/6th Highland Light Infantry
MACDONALD Kenneth MM Pte 241473 Seaforth Highlanders
MACDONALD Murdo MM+Bar Sjt 7342 2nd Seaforth Highlanders
MACDONALD R. MM Pte 14024 Gordon Highlanders
MACDONALD R. MM Pte 292371 Gordon Highlanders
MACDONALD Robert MM Pte 12230 1st Highland Light Infantry
MACDONALD Roderick A. MM BSM 365004 RGA
MACDONALD Ronald MM Pte 5156 5th Cameron Highlanders
MACDONALD Thomas MM Sjt 351151 1/9th Royal Scots
MACDONALD Thomas MM Pte 9714 1st Gordon Highlanders
MACDONALD Thomas MM Pte 1079 2nd Royal Warwickshire Regt
MACDONALD Thomas MM L/Cpl 275682 Royal Scots
MACDONALD Thomas MM Pte 16419 Hampshire Regt
MACDONALD Valentine MM Pte 301357 RAMC
MACDONALD William MM L/Cpl S/40136 1st Cameron Highlanders
MacDONALD William MM Sjt 2496 6th Dragoons
MACDONALD William MM L/Cpl 240094 Seaforth Highlanders

MACDONALD William MM Cpl 14607 Gordon Highlanders
MACDONALD William MM Pte 6244 Gordon Highlanders
MACDOUGALL Dugald MM L/Cpl 300525 1/9th Arg & Suth Highlanders
MACDOUGALL Frederick MM Bdr 650410 86 Bde RFA
MACDOUGALL William John "MC,MM+Bar(1458 CQMS)" 2Lt 7th Seaforth Highlanders
MACDOWELL Horace MM Pte 301996 1/9th Royal Scots
MACE Arthur MM L/Cpl M2/053232 Army Service Corps att 29 Fd Amb RAMC
MACE Frederick MM Sjt 13269 9th Norfolk Regt
MACE Gilbert MM Pte 8046 1st West Yorkshire Regt
MACE Harold MM L/Sjt 39963 15th Cheshire Regt
MACE Henry Charles MM Pte 15600 2nd Royal Berkshire Regt KIA 27.4.18.
MACE Herbert William MM Sjt 1179 RFA
MACE Hugh M. MM Sjt 16054 Royal Engineers
MACE Oswald MM Cpl 52802 16th Highland Light Infantry
MACEWAN Alexander MM Sjt 300616 1/8th Arg & Suth Highlanders
MACEWAN John MM Sjt S/40230 1st Cameron Highlanders Died 2.3.19.
MACEY Charles E. MM Sjt 2367 B/57 Bde RFA
MACEY Frederick William John MM Pte 285934 1/1st Oxfordshire Yeomanry KIA 1.7.17
MACEY James MM Sjt 5075 16th Royal Welsh Fusiliers
MACEY Richard MM Pte 3/8786 9th West Yorkshire Regt KIA 9.10.17.
MacFARLANE Alfred D. MM Bdr 116796 RGA
MACFARLANE Edward Allan MM L/Cpl 15037 16th Highland Light Infantry
MACFARLANE James MM Pte 12016 5th Royal Berkshire Regt
MACFARLANE James Thomas MM Pte 28561 3rd Worcestershire Regt
MacFARLANE John C. MM Pte 9649 Arg & Suth Highlanders
MACFARLANE Malcolm P.A. MM Gnr 242692 C/251 Bde RFA
MACFARLANE Robert H. MM+Bar Cpl 41551 8th Royal Highlanders
MACFARLANE Thomas C. MM Sjt 295589 12th Royal Scots Fusiliers
MACFARLANE Walter MM Pte 2952 1/9th Highland Light Infantry
MACFARLANE Walter W. MM L/Sjt 2166 1/18th London Regt
MACFARLANE William J. MM Sjt 19554 Royal Scots
MACFIE Robert Andrew Scott MM CQMS 3087 1/10th Liverpool Regt
MACGILLIVRAY Leonard MM L/Cpl S/13332 7th Cameron Highlanders
MACGILP Angus MM Cpl 50556 RGA
MacGOWAN Edward MM Cpl 3135 6th Dragoon Guards
MACGREGOR David L. MM Pte S/27762 5th Cameron Highlanders
MACGREGOR Frederick Malcolm "MC,MM(15748 CSM 17th HLI)" 2Lt 2nd Northamptonshire Regt
MACGREGOR George W. MM L/Cpl 107614 33rd Bn Machine Gun Corps
MACGREGOR Henry T. MM Sjt 3485 Royal Highlanders
MACGREGOR Hugh MM Sjt 1229 1/8th Arg & Suth Highlanders KIA 9.4.17.
MACGREGOR James MM Pte 73421 Machine Gun Corps
MacGREGOR John H. MM Pte 320420 1/6th London Regt
MACGREGOR Matthew MM Pte 43596 9th Scottish Rifles KIA 20.7.18.
MACGREGOR Norman MM+Bar Sjt S/5629 12th Arg & Suth Highlanders
MACGREGOR Peter MM Pte 20920 2nd Dragoons
MACHEN A. MM Pte 241092 Yorkshire Regt
MACHEN Walter MM+Bar Pte 202468 4th York & Lancaster Regt
MACHIN Edwin MM Sjt 9243 15th Royal Warwickshire Regt KIA 26.10.17.
MACHIN Ferdinand W. MM Pte 14329 1st Grenadier Guards
MACHIN James MM Gnr 294557 RGA
MACHIN Joe MM Cpl 242945 2/5th Yorkshire Light Infantry
MACHIN John E. MM Cpl 60977 12/13th Northumberland Fusiliers
MACHIN Stuart Edward MM Pte 439416 2/3(South Midland)Fd Amb RAMC
MACHRAY George MM Pte 138146 42nd Bn Machine Gun Corps
MACHRAY Robert MM Pte 41305 Seaforth Highlanders
MACINDOE Andrew MM Cpl 15015 18th Highland Light Infantry
MACINNES Daniel King MM Gnr 67437 RFA DOW 22.1.17.
MACINNES Donald MM Sjt 200244 5th Cameron Highlanders
MACINNES Gilbert MM+Bar Sjt 300886 1/8th Arg & Suth Highlanders

MACINNES John MM Pte S/16252 6th Cameron Highlanders
MACINTOSH Donald MM Pte 15720 17th Highland Light Infantry KIA 1.7.16.
MACINTOSH James MM Sjt 40116 Cameron Highlanders
MacINTOSH John MM Pte 300839 1/8th Arg & Suth Highlanders
MACINTOSH John A. MM Pte 51390 Machine Gun Corps
MACINTOSH Peter MM Sjt 630328 255 Bde RFA
MacINTOSH Peter W. MM Pte 252570 Arg & Suth Highlanders
MACINTOSH W.G. MM Sjt 25491 Cameron Highlanders
MACINTOSH William "DCM,MM" Cpl 512587 14th London Regt
MACINTYRE Donald MM+Bar Pte 315383 13th Royal Highlanders
MACINTYRE Donald George "MM,CG(B)" Cpl 93734 41 Div Sig Coy Royal Engineers
MACINTYRE Duncan MM Sjt 47411 Machine Gun Corps(Cavalry)
MACINTYRE Hugh McD. MM+Bar Sjt 48225 52nd Bn Machine Gun Corps
MACINTYRE James Alexander MM Sjt 418065 Royal Engineers
MACINTYRE Joseph MM Spr 231750 Royal Engineers
MACINTYRE Robert E. MM Cpl 510762 14th London Regt
MACISAAC Neil MM Pte 3/5582 Cameron Highlanders
MacIVER Murdo MM Sjt 3803 5th Cameron Highlanders
MACIVOR Charles M. MM+Bar L/Cpl 241719 7th Seaforth Highlanders
MacIVOR David Steele MM Cpl 18848 16th Royal Scots KIA 1.7.16.
MACK Alexander MM L/Cpl 24888 6th Northamptonshire Regt DOW 5.11.18.
MACK Arthur J. MM Pte 7125 1st Norfolk Regt
MACK Bertie Thomas MM Bdr L/26840 A/174 Bde RFA DOW 24.3.18.
MACK Cornelius "MM,MIDx2" Sjt 6907 2nd Welsh Regt
MACK Ernest Frank MM Pte G/8023 6th East Kent Regt KIA 17.7.17.
MACK James E. MM Sjt 14382 16th Highland Light Infantry DOW 15.4.17.
MACK James W. MM Pte 021178 Army Ordnance Corps
MACK John "MM,MID" S/Sjt 318003 2 Fd Amb RAMC
MACK John "MM,MID" Sjt 20317 7/8th King's Own Scottish Borderers DOW 30.7.18.
MACK Peter MM Pte 131675 46th Royal Fusiliers
MACK Richard Arthur MM L/Cpl 16531 7th Norfolk Regt DOW 7.10.18.
MACK Thomas MM Pte 46982 6th Leicestershire Regt KIA 27.5.18.
MACK William MM Pte 13539 East Surrey Regt
MACKAY Alexander MM Sjt 127151 6th Bn Machine Gun Corps
MACKAY Alexander "DCM,MM" Sjt 241020 1/5th Seaforth Highlanders
MACKAY Angus McL. MM Pte M2/082693 Army Service Corps
MACKAY Charles "DCM,MM" Sjt S/1962 7th Seaforth Highlanders
MACKAY Charles S. MM Sjt 42490 RAMC
MACKAY Donald MM Cpl 21465 2nd King's Own Scottish Borderers
MACKAY Donald MM Pte 9325 7th Seaforth Highlanders KIA 12.10.16.
MACKAY Donald MM Pte 3393 16th Highland Light Infantry
MACKAY Donald MM L/Sjt 267683 1/5th Seaforth Highlanders
MacKAY Duncan MM L/Cpl 240141 1/5th Seaforth Highlanders
MACKAY G. MM Pte 6200 Gordon Highlanders
MACKAY Gavin S. MM Dvr 22949 RFA
MACKAY George MM Cpl 250496 1/6th Durham Light Infantry
MACKAY George D. MM Dvr Sig 56688 19 Bty 9 Bde RFA
MACKAY James MM Pte 254016 1/6th Arg & Suth Highlanders
MACKAY James MM L/Cpl 23358 Machine Gun Corps KIA 1.11.18.
MACKAY James MM Pte 17414 Seaforth Highlanders
MACKAY John MM Bdr 24784 RFA
MACKAY John "MM,CG(F)" Cpl 240629 1/5th Seaforth Highlanders KIA 12.10.18.
MacKAY John MM Pte 292165 1/7th Gordon Highlanders
MACKAY John MM Cpl 7320 2nd Seaforth Highlanders
MACKAY John MM Pte 40037 Seaforth Highlanders
MacKAY John MM Pte 6309 Seaforth Highlanders
MACKAY John MM Spr 65900 Royal Engineers
MACKAY John P. "MM,MID" Cpl 85102 RFA
MACKAY John T. MM L/Cpl 51126 5th Royal Scots Fusiliers
MACKAY John W.L. MM Sjt 7180 Northumberland Fusiliers
MACKAY Kenneth MM+Bar Sjt 200298 5th Cameron Highlanders
MACKAY Murdo MM Pte 19061 Royal Scots
MACKAY Richard T. MM Pte 12144 5th Northamptonshire Regt
MACKAY Robert MM Pte 241421 6th Seaforth Highlanders
MACKAY Robert Cecil MM Pte 220601 1st Royal Berkshire Regt
MACKAY Thomas D. MM Pte 29506 King's Own Scottish Borderers
MACKAY W. "DCM,MM" Sjt S/15916 13th Arg & Suth Highlanders

MACKAY William MM Pte 25220 6th King's Own Scottish Borderers
MacKAY William MM L/Sjt 10391 Cameron Highlanders
MACKAY William MM Cpl 612 1/6th Seaforth Highlanders
MACKAY William MM Pte 242484 Gordon Highlanders
MACKEL Frederick MM Dvr 7630 RFA
MACKENZIE Albert MM Gnr 45699 13 Siege Bty RGA
MACKENZIE Albert John MM Pte 1369 1/13th London Regt
MACKENZIE Alexander MM Pte 301205 10th Arg & Suth Highlanders
MACKENZIE Alexander MM+Bar Sjt 25957 1/4th Cameron Highlanders
MACKENZIE Alexander J. MM Sjt G5770 13th Royal Fusiliers
MACKENZIE Alick MM Cpl 85171 206 Fd Coy Royal Engineers
MACKENZIE Angus MM L/Cpl 200245 1/4th Seaforth Highlanders
MACKENZIE Donald MM Cpl 200194 1/4th Seaforth Highlanders
MACKENZIE Duncan MM Sjt S/23999 1st Cameron Highlanders
MacKENZIE Duncan MM Sjt 130932 MGC(Cavalry)
MACKENZIE Edward MM Sjt 2950 Royal Fusiliers
MACKENZIE Ernest A. MM Cpl M2/082628 Army Service Corps
MACKENZIE Francis MM Pte S/40790 Gordon Highlanders KIA 21.10.18.
MACKENZIE Harry MM L/Cpl 16359 Yorkshire Regt
MACKENZIE Hugh MM Cpl 9396 1st Cameron Highlanders
MACKENZIE James MM Pte M2/134374 Army Service Corps
MACKENZIE James "DCM,MM" Sjt 49134 81 Fd Coy Royal Engineers KIA 9.6.18.
MACKENZIE James MM Pte 18352 Scottish Rifles KIA 3.5.17.
MACKENZIE James Melville MM Pte S/12141 9th Gordon Highlanders
MACKENZIE John MM Sjt 200173 1/4th Seaforth Highlanders
MACKENZIE John MM L/Bdr 346827 32 Siege Bty RGA
MACKENZIE John MM Pte 6361 8th Seaforth Highlanders
MACKENZIE John MM+Bar Sjt 265217 1/6th Seaforth Highlanders Died 25.3.18.
MACKENZIE John MM L/Cpl 201292 1/4th Seaforth Highlanders KIA 1.8.17.
MACKENZIE John MM Pte 350089 1/9th Royal Scots
MACKENZIE John R. MM S/Sjt 40829 51 Fd Amb RAMC
MACKENZIE Kenneth MM Sjt M2/051706 51 Div Train Army Service Corps
MACKENZIE Kenneth P. MM Bdr 143866 RFA
MACKENZIE Robert MM L/Cpl 154682 Royal Engineers
MACKENZIE Robert MM Pte 901 1/5th Seaforth Highlanders DOW 19.4.17.
MACKENZIE Roderick "DCM,MM" Sjt 82385 RGA
MACKENZIE Thomas MM Sjt 14245 East Surrey Regt
MACKENZIE Thomas G. MM 2nd Cpl 254113 Signal Service Royal Engineers
MACKENZIE W. MM Sjt 631 15th West Yorkshire Regt
MACKENZIE William John MM Pte 267387 Seaforth Highlanders
MACKENZIE William O. MM Pte 33596 1st King's Own Scottish Borderers
MACKERELL Walter "DCM,MM" CSM 129580 'P' Special Coy Royal Engineers
MACKERETH George MM Pte 201229 1/4th Royal Lancaster Regt
MACKERETH James MM Sjt 2224 Royal Lancaster Regt
MACKERETH John James MM Pte 4866 11th Lancashire Fusiliers
MACKEW Archie MM Sjt 14090 2nd Royal Dublin Fusiliers KIA 17.10.18.
MACKEY Donald MM Pte 241383 Leicestershire Regt
MACKEY George W. MM L/Cpl 373003 London Regt
MACKEY Hayden MM Pte 120083 36 Fd Amb RAMC
MACKEY John MM Pte S/4433 13th Rifle Brigade
MACKIE A. MM Pte 538532 6 Fd Amb RAMC
MACKIE Alex G. MM Pte 92903 RAMC
MACKIE Alexander MM Sjt 240474 1/6th Highland Light Infantry
MACKIE Andrew Mitchell MM Pte 305284 1/3(Highland)Fd Amb RAMC
MACKIE David MM+Bar L/Cpl 41993 2nd Royal Scots
MACKIE David Kerr MM Cpl 8627 Royal Engineers
MACKIE Frederick William MM Spr 49096 Royal Engineers
MACKIE James MM Cpl 31812 RAMC
MACKIE James MM Sjt 19451 Royal Scots Fusiliers
MACKIE John O. MM Sjt 4083 Machine Gun Corps
MACKIE Joseph MM Pte 42221 Highland Light Infantry
MACKIE Robert MM Gnr 196359 RFA
MACKIE Robert MM L/Cpl 203547 York & Lancaster Regt
MACKIE Thomas MM Sjt 7478 Royal Fusiliers
MACKIE Warner MM Cpl 143083 Royal Engineers
MACKIE William MM L/Cpl 676 XIX Corps Cyclist Bn Army Cyclist Corps
MACKIE William "DCM,MM" L/Cpl 265141 1/6th Gordon Highlanders
MACKIE William MM Sjt Farrier 645110 RFA
MACKIE William Hogg MM Pte 10159 Machine Gun Corps
MACKILLOP Hugh MM L/Cpl 16192 16th Highland Light Infantry
MACKINDER Joseph L. MM+Bar Pte 14257 2nd Suffolk Regt
MACKINLEY Charles W. MM Pte 13589 1st Dorsetshire Regt
MACKINNON D. MM Pte 125045 Yeo
MACKINNON Malcolm Angus MM Sjt S/78819 8/10th Gordon Highlanders
MACKINTOSH A. MM Pte 280623 London Regt
MACKINTOSH Duncan MM Sjt 23202 47th Bn Machine Gun Corps
MACKINTOSH Hugh MM Pte 203269 2nd Seaforth Highlanders
MACKINTOSH J.S. MM Pte S/43037 1st Cameron Highlanders
MACKINTOSH Walter H. MM Pte 30682 15th Notts & Derby Regt
MACKISON Thomas MM Pte S/10550 2nd Gordon Highlanders
MACKLAM Henry MM 2nd Cpl 269946 Royal Engineers
MACKLEN Douglas J. MM Spr 42859 Royal Engineers
MACKLEN Henry G. MM Pte 30823 Lancashire Fusiliers
MACKLIN William MM Sjt CMT/931 Army Service Corps
MACKNAY John MM Pte 14865 Yorkshire Regt
MACKRELL Albert Edward MM Sjt 22294 Machine Gun Corps
MACKRELL Douglas William MM Sjt 2651 1/1st HAC(Inf)
MACKRELL F.S. "DCM,MM" Air Mech 1 4917 Royal Flying Corps
MACKRELL Shaw MM L/Cpl 203121 5th West Riding Regt
MACKRELL William MM Pte 2891 8th Royal Highlanders
MACLACHLAN Alexander "DCM,MM" Pte 300739 1/7th Royal Scots
MACLACHLAN Robert MM Pte 15708 13th Royal Scots
MacLACHLAN William MM L/Cpl 23/44 Northumberland Fusiliers
MacLAREN Frederick MM Sjt 200294 6th Cameron Highlanders
MACLEAN Angus MM Cpl 13922 15th Highland Light Infantry
MACLEAN David MM Spr 45240 20 Div Sig Coy Royal Engineers
MACLEAN Donald MM L/Cpl 265290 Seaforth Highlanders
MACLEAN Duncan MM Cpl 333113 1/9th Highland Light Infantry
MACLEAN John MM Sjt 49649 74th Bn Machine Gun Corps
MACLEAN K. MM L/Cpl 315388 13th Royal Highlanders
MACLEAN Kenneth MM CSM 200267 1/4th Seaforth Highlanders
MACLELLAN J. MM Pte 12779 9th West Riding Regt
MACLENNAN Donald MM Pte 83187 RAMC
MACLENNAN Duncan Campbell "MC,MM(70027 Sjt)" 2Lt RFA
MACLENNAN Roderick MM L/Cpl 200252 1/4th Seaforth Highlanders
MACLEOD Alexander MM Sjt 143475 C/86 Bde RFA
MACLEOD Angus MM L/Cpl 7213 Seaforth Highlanders
MACLEOD Donald MM Pte 75081 13 Fd Amb RAMC
MACLEOD Donald "MM,MID" Sjt 6622 2nd Gordon Highlanders
MACLEOD Donald MM Sjt 3/5219 1st Cameron Highlanders KIA 3.9.16.
MACLEOD Donald MM Cpl 7823 14 Coy Labour Corps
MACLEOD Donald MM Sjt 5398 5th Cameron Highlanders KIA 12.10.17.
MACLEOD Donald A. MM Pte S/13552 1st Cameron Highlanders
MACLEOD Duncan MM Pte 514117 14th London Regt
MACLEOD Duncan MM Bdr 58986 RGA
MACLEOD J. MM Pte 8355 5th Cameron Highlanders
MACLEOD J. MM Sjt 241859 Seaforth Highlanders
MACLEOD J. MM L/Cpl 201128 Seaforth Highlanders
MACLEOD John MM+Bar Pte S/15565 6th Cameron Highlanders KIA 23.7.18.
MACLEOD K.M. MM Pte M2/187493 Army Service Corps
MACLEOD M. MM Gnr 600102 RFA
MACLEOD M. MM L/Cpl 9007 Seaforth Highlanders
MACLEOD M. MM L/Cpl 6938 Seaforth Highlanders
MACLEOD N. MM Cpl 3/5563 Cameron Highlanders
MACLEOD R. MM L/Sjt 200186 Seaforth Highlanders
MACLOUAD William J. MM Pte 9879 19th Hussars
MACLURE D. MM Pte 240402 Royal Scots Fusiliers
MACMAHON J.J. MM Cpl 29417 Middlesex Regt
MACMAHON William F. MM Spr 146566 184 Tunnelling Coy Royal Engineers
MACMASTER Lachlan MM L/Cpl 14398 Seaforth Highlanders
MACMILLAN A. MM L/Cpl M2/115265 Army Service Corps
MACMILLAN Duncan S. MM Pte S/23270 1/7th Arg & Suth Highlanders
MACMURCHIE John Stuart "DCM,MM+Bar,MID" Sjt 2301 1st Royal Highlanders KIA 3.5.17.
MACNAB John MM Sjt 1797 1/9th Highland Light Infantry
MACNAE John C. MM Pte 40946 1st Royal Scots Fusiliers DOW 3.5.17.
MACNAMARA John MM Pte 3/7645 East Yorkshire Regt

MACNAMARA Patrick MM Sjt 11397 6th Dorsetshire Regt
MACNAMARA Peebles A. MM Gnr 221261 RFA
MACNICOLL Herbert MM+Bar L/Cpl 241392 Liverpool Regt
MACPHEDRAN Donald MM Cpl 93113 Royal Engineers
MACPHEE Cecil MM Gnr 52106 RGA
MACPHEE Donald MM+Bar Sjt 42324 RFA
MACPHEE Hugh MM Sjt 13981 1st Scots Guards
MACPHERSON Donald "DCM,MM" Pte 8748 1st Gordon Highlanders
MACPHERSON Douglas MM L/Cpl 17228 1st Scots Guards
MACPHERSON James MM Pte 200140 1/4th Seaforth Highlanders KIA 21.3.18.
MACPHERSON James MM Pte M2/049704 Army Service Corps
MACPHERSON John MM Pte 5061 5th Cameron Highlanders
MACPHERSON John MM L/Sjt 200622 9th Seaforth Highlanders
MACPHERSON Murdo R.J. MM Pte 240112 Seaforth Highlanders
MACPHERSON Ronald MM Sjt 331391 9th Highland Light Infantry
MACPHERSON William S. MM Pte S/5183 Royal Highlanders
MACQUALTER William T. MM Sjt 15858 Royal Engineers
MACQUEEN George W. MM L/Cpl 10/7011 Northumberland Fusiliers
MACQUEEN William R. "DCM,MM" Sjt 29053 119 Coy Machine Gun Corps
MACRAE Alexander MM Sjt 418043 52 Div Sig Coy Royal Engineers
MACRAE Donald Cameron MM Pte 266662 1/6th Royal Highlanders
MACRAE Duncan MM Cpl 200801 Seaforth Highlanders
MACRAE Finlay MM Pte 223232 10th Cameron Highlanders
MACRAE Finlay MM+Bar Sjt 19308 16th Royal Scots KIA 26.8.18.
MACRAE George MM Bdr 366040 RGA
MACRAE John MM Sjt 367 1/6th Arg & Suth Highlanders
MACRAE William MM Sjt 14316 2nd Scots Guards
MACRANK Patrick MM Pte 1865 1/5th Arg & Suth Highlanders DOW 18.1.18.
MACREA John D. MM Cpl 267511 Seaforth Highlanders
MACREADIE William "MM,MSM" S/Sjt Farrier D/1875 3rd Dragoon Guards
MACRO John MM Pte 8193 129 Fd Amb RAMC
MACROW Frederick A. MM Pte 241810 2nd Northumberland Fusiliers
MACVICAR James F. MM Pte 202265 5/6th Scottish Rifles
MACWALTER J.R. "DCM,MM" Sjt 9682 1st East Kent Regt
MADDAMS John T. MM Bdr 67297 3 Bde RHA
MADDEN Albert MM Pte 40606 South Wales Borderers
MADDEN Andrew MM+Bar Pte 25710 Royal Dublin Fusiliers
MADDEN Bernard MM L/Sjt 330909 2/9th Liverpool Regt
MADDEN C. MM Sjt 330084 Liverpool Regt
MADDEN Charles Henry MM Pte 491803 1/13th London Regt KIA 3.10.18.
MADDEN Francis J. MM Pte 18652 Manchester Regt
MADDEN Hugh MM L/Cpl 267958 Cheshire Regt
MADDEN J. MM Gnr 2472 RFA
MADDEN James MM Sjt 55685 35 Bde RFA
MADDEN Joseph MM C/Sjt 7660 1st North Staffordshire Regt
MADDEN Joseph MM Pte 241031 2/5th South Lancashire Regt
MADDEN L.J. MM Sjt 835054 RFA
MADDEN Peter MM Pte 7075 Irish Guards
MADDEN Thomas MM Pte 54221 Royal Welsh Fusiliers
MADDEN Thomas MM Spr 103746 82 Fd Coy Royal Engineers
MADDICK T. MM Sjt 34633 4th Oxf & Bucks Light Infantry
MADDIGAN Andrew "DCM,MM" Pte 18224 11th West Yorkshire Regt
MADDISON Dennis Stanley MM Sjt 8722 12th East Surrey Regt KIA 21.9.17.
MADDISON Edward MM Sjt 3031 1/9th Durham Light Infantry
MADDISON George H.F. MM Spr 546697 Royal Engineers
MADDISON Herbert MM+Bar Cpl 7/12921 7th Lincolnshire Regt
MADDISON J.G. MM Sjt 14295 Yorkshire Regt
MADDISON John MM Sjt 48372 43 Bde RFA
MADDISON Joseph MM Cpl 15761 West Riding Regt
MADDISON Robert C. MM Dvr T4/057599 Army Service Corps
MADDOCK Ezra MM Gnr 610317 A/223 Bde RFA KIA 13.10.17.
MADDOCK Frederick E. MM Pte 718127 1/12th London Regt
MADDOCK George MM Pte 14123 Middlesex Regt
MADDOCK John MM Sjt 9833 1st North Staffordshire Regt
MADDOCK William MM Sjt 14/18301 14th Liverpool Regt
MADDOCKS Richard MM Pte 90895 Liverpool Regt
MADDOCKS Samuel J. MM Sjt 54219 63 Div Sig Coy Royal Engineers

MADDOCKS Thomas MM Pte 241455 Royal Warwickshire Regt
MADDOCKS Vincent D. MM Spr 229448 Royal Engineers
MADDOCKS William MM Dvr 168469 19 Div Ammn Col RFA
MADDOX Carr R.C. MM Dvr 750830 RFA
MADDOX Edward "DCM,MM" Sjt 201216 2/4th Yorkshire Light Infantry
MADDOX G. "MM,MSM" Sjt 29978 D/92 Bde RFA
MADDOX Harry MM Pte 352169 2 Fd Amb RAMC
MADDOX James Edward MM Sjt 10773 5th Shropshire Light Infantry
MADDRELL George MM Sjt 201076 Royal Lancaster Regt
MADELAINE Vernon F. MM Sjt 9913 1st Royal West Surrey Regt
MADELEY Archibald C. "MM,MID" L/Cpl 23843 3 Div Sig Coy Royal Engineers
MADELEY Frederick George MM L/Cpl 19176 4th Grenadier Guards
MADELEY Frederick J. MM Pte 45737 15th Cheshire Regt
MADELEY Herbert John MM Pte 202090 2/6th South Staffordshire Regt KIA 21.3.18.
MADELEY Wilfred MM L/Cpl 26586 10th Shropshire Light Infantry
MADELEY William MM Sjt 6893 2nd King's Royal Rifle Corps
MADGE Frederick MM Sjt 68253 RAMC
MADGE James Henry MM Cpl 252666 Signal Service Royal Engineers att 91 HAG RGA.
MADGE William George MM Sjt 4604 35 Bty 22 Bde RFA
MADGWICK A.E. MM+Bar L/Cpl 5638 Royal Sussex Regt
MADGWICK Frederick C. MM CQMS 773 23rd Royal Fusiliers
MADGWICK W. MM Pte 25033 16th Royal Warwickshire Regt
MADIGAN Frederick MM L/Cpl 47384 20th Hussars
MADIGAN Peter MM Pte 7411 Connaught Rangers
MADIGAN Richard MM Pte 7213 2nd West Yorkshire Regt DOW 30.5.17.
MADIN George MM Pte R/8744 2nd King's Royal Rifle Corps
MADIN George MM Sjt 96213 RFA
MADIN John W. MM L/Cpl S/40143 1st Cameron Highlanders
MADINE William J. MM Pte 23392 1/4th Royal Lancaster Regt
MADLEY William Charles MM Pte 493620 RAMC
MAEDER Frederick MM Pte 1733 1/17th London Regt KIA 16.9.17.
MAEER Tom MM Bdr 16417 RFA
MAGEE Bernard MM Gnr 26306 RGA
MAGEE Edward J. MM Sjt 45894 15th Durham Light Infantry
MAGEE George MM Pte 51292 86 Coy Labour Corps
MAGEE James MM L/Cpl 10333 2nd Royal Inniskilling Fusiliers KIA 1.4.17.
MAGEE Robert MM Pte 18/1520 18th Royal Irish Rifles
MAGEE Thomas MM Sjt 17497 19th Lancashire Fusiliers
MAGEE William MM Sjt 15/12054 15th Royal Irish Rifles
MAGEE William MM Pte 3269 Royal Inniskilling Fusiliers
MAGEE William George "MM,CG(B)" Pte 27808 1st Royal Inniskilling Fusiliers
MAGEEHAN Hugh MM Sjt 444161 Royal Engineers
MAGENNIS Hugh MM Pte 7/1640 Leinster Regt
MAGER Harold C. MM+Bar Sjt L/5157 B/173 Bde RFA
MAGGS George R. MM L/Cpl 18988 Royal Engineers
MAGGS Wallis E. MM Cpl 321094 6th London Regt
MAGGS William Charles MM Cpl 15301 15th Hampshire Regt DOW 2.9.18.
MAGILL James MM Cpl 5256 Royal Irish Rifles
MAGILL James MM Pte 1909 1st Dragoon Guards
MAGILL James Harrison MM Pte M2/226075 59 Div Train Army Service Corps
MAGILL Malcolm MM Pte 15845 Royal Inniskilling Fusiliers
MAGILL Samuel MM L/Cpl 1198 'S' Squadron South Irish Horse
MAGILL William Arthur MM Sjt 12/18394 12th Royal Irish Rifles KIA 1.7.16.
MAGILL William S. MM Cpl 75560 Royal Engineers
MAGINESS Albert Edward "MM,MID" CSM 16/183 16th Royal Irish Rifles
MAGNAN David MM Sjt S/368 12th Rifle Brigade
MAGNAY Joseph "DCM,MM" CSM 20079 43 Coy Machine Gun Corps
MAGNAY William "MM,MID" Cpl 750879 B/315 Bde RFA
MAGNER Herbert MM Pte 9981 2nd Dragoon Guards
MAGNESS George Henry MM Pte 42564 West Yorkshire Regt
MAGNESS Henry J. MM Pte 266688 Welsh Regt
MAGOOKIN David MM 2nd Cpl 57598 122 Fd Coy Royal Engineers
MAGOR Cecil MM Pte 85027 2/4th London Regt
MAGOWAN Andrew MM Cpl 18058 9th Royal Irish Fusiliers KIA 10.8.17.
MAGOWAN James MM Sjt 18425 13th Royal Irish Rifles

MAGOWAN Robert MM Dvr M2/100199 Army Service Corps
MAGOWAN William MM Pte 22379 Royal Inniskilling Fusiliers
MAGRATH John George "MC,MM(64553 Sjt RE)" T/2Lt 56th Bn MGC
MAGRAW James MM Pte 35417 2nd Manchester Regt
MAGSON Albert MM Cpl 352047 7th London Regt
MAGUIRE Charles MM Sjt 6681 12th East Surrey Regt KIA 15.9.16
MAGUIRE Cyril Clifford MM Bdr 9474 B/71 Bde RFA KIA 19.3.17.
MAGUIRE Edward MM Pte 40416 King's Own Scottish Borderers
MAGUIRE Edward MM Cpl 29347 RGA
MAGUIRE F. MM Dvr 37586 12 Bde RFA
MAGUIRE Francis MM Dvr 19689 RFA
MAGUIRE Frederick J. MM Sjt 48739 1 Div Ammn Col RFA
MAGUIRE George T. MM L/Cpl 307744 Liverpool Regt
MAGUIRE Henry MM Cpl S/2621 2nd Gordon Highlanders KIA 20.7.16.
MAGUIRE Herbert Joseph MM Sjt 34910 6 Coy Machine Gun Corps
MAGUIRE J. MM Pte 341448 RAMC
MAGUIRE James MM Pte 30376 4th Liverpool Regt
MAGUIRE James MM Sjt 22477 15th Highland Light Infantry
MAGUIRE James MM Pte 6648 2nd Irish Guards
MAGUIRE John MM Pte 26675 20th Lancashire Fusiliers
MAGUIRE John MM Cpl 275705 Manchester Regt
MAGUIRE John F. "MM,MSM" Sjt 8090 2nd West Yorkshire Regt
MAGUIRE John Nathaniel MM L/Cpl 50578 23rd Royal Fusiliers
MAGUIRE John P. MM Gnr 158875 RFA
MAGUIRE Joseph MM L/Cpl 2006 7th Royal Sussex Regt
MAGUIRE Patrick MM Pte 8751 2nd Royal Dublin Fusiliers
MAGUIRE Richard MM Pte 2284 Durham Light Infantry
MAGUIRE Thomas "MM,MSM" Sjt 892 1/5th North Staffordshire Regt
MAGUIRE Thomas MM L/Cpl 21220 Royal Irish Fusiliers
MAGUIRE Thomas MM Pte 9458 2nd Irish Guards
MAGUIRE Thomas MM Pte 15320 9th Cheshire Regt
MAGUIRE William A. MM Pte 28647 20th Hussars
MAGUIRE William J. MM Dvr 238966 RFA
MAHADY William MM Gnr 12504 7 Bde RHA
MAHAN Frederick MM Cpl 2230 1/7th Notts & Derby Regt KIA 1.7.16.
MAHER Edward J. MM+Bar Pte 30033 Border Regt
MAHER Edward Phillip MM Pte 13424 9th Welsh Regt
MAHER J. MM Pte 54225 Royal Welsh Fusiliers
MAHER James MM Gnr 47668 38 Bde RFA
MAHER John MM+Bar Sjt 18788 7th Border Regt KIA 25.8.18.
MAHER Martin MM Cpl 8/23023 8th Royal Dublin Fusiliers
MAHER Martin MM Pte 17191 1st Royal Dublin Fusiliers KIA 29.3.18.
MAHER P.J. MM L/Cpl 17298 2nd Royal Dublin Fusiliers
MAHERS James MM Sjt 283 RFA
MAHON Hugh MM CSM 10430 15th Lancashire Fusiliers
MAHON Patrick MM Cpl 9372 2nd Leinster Regt
MAHON Thomas MM Sjt 1852 1/8th Liverpool Regt
MAHONEY Charles "MM,MSM" Sjt 9360 Royal Fusiliers
MAHONEY George J. MM L/Cpl 350261 1 Fd Amb RAMC
MAHONEY Herbert James "MM,MID" Sjt 26713 RGA DOW 24.10.18.
MAHONEY James MM Pte 10286 Royal Berkshire Regt AKA L.W.PERRIS
MAHONEY James MM Pte 200452 Cheshire Regt
MAHONEY James G. MM Pte 8040 West Yorkshire Regt
MAHONEY John MM L/Cpl 11318 6th Duke of Cornwall's LI
MAHONEY Leonard J. MM Pte 11341 Royal West Surrey Regt
MAHONEY Patrick MM L/Cpl 22538 South Wales Borderers
MAHONEY Stanley MM L/Cpl 51186 2nd Border Regt
MAHONEY Thomas MM Dvr 30482 Gds Div Ammn Col RFA Died 24.11.18.
MAHONEY Thomas G. MM Pte 226277 1/1st Monmouthshire Regt
MAHONEY Timothy MM L/Cpl 31372 Machine Gun Corps
MAHONEY W. MM Pte 29125 2nd South Wales Borderers
MAHONEY William MM L/Cpl 2561 1/19th London Regt DOW 10.6.17.
MAHONY Joseph MM Sjt 11132 1st Royal Irish Fusiliers
MAHONY Kate MM Sister F QAIMNS
MAHY Eugene MM Gnr 89204 C/50 Bde RFA KIA 25.4.18.
MAIDEN Alfred Horace MM Pte 14710 6th Shropshire Light Infantry KIA 20.9.16.
MAIDEN Bertie MM Pte 99763 Machine Gun Corps
MAIDEN Gordon MM Gnr 2054 Machine Gun Corps(Motors)
MAIDEN James Thomas MM Cpl 14346 8th York & Lancaster Regt KIA 8.10.16.
MAIDEN Peter MM Pte 56441 16th Royal Welsh Fusiliers
MAIDEN Thomas MM Cpl 17210 6th South Wales Borderers
MAIDER Thomas M. MM Pte 44669 20th Durham Light Infantry
MAIDMENT Frederick MM Cpl 703161 23rd London Regt KIA 22.8.18.
MAIDMENT H. "MM,MID" CQMS 9009 2nd Bedfordshire Regt
MAIDMENT William MM Pte 648100 20th London Regt
MAIL Sidney MM Sjt 40918 Northumberland Fusiliers
MAILER Daniel MM Cpl 69260 28 Bde RFA
MAILER John McVie MM Cpl 67512 33 Bde RFA
MAILER Robert MM Pte 350348 1/7th Arg & Suth Highlanders
MAILES Allen MM L/Cpl 76354 Tank Corps
MAILES William MM Cpl 5046 8th East Surrey Regt
MAILING Clarence MM L/Cpl 13192 4th Bedfordshire Regt KIA 23.4.17.
MAILING Harry MM Gnr 915953 D/291 Bde RFA
MAILLARDET William MM Sjt 26857 RFA
MAIN Alex R. MM Dvr 645671 C/291 RFA
MAIN Daniel MM L/Cpl 41378 12th Royal Scots KIA 17.10.18.
MAIN David MM Cpl 265592 1/6th Gordon Highlanders
MAIN Henry MM Cpl 240504 5th Devonshire Regt KIA 13.9.18.
MAIN James MM+Bar Sjt 265495 1/6th Seaforth Highlanders
MAIN John MM Cpl 645603 RFA
MAIN John Alexander MM L/Cpl 266030 1/4th Seaforth Highlanders
MAIN Roland MM Spr 463119 25 Div Sig Coy Royal Engineers
MAIN William Edwards MM L/Cpl 200280 1/4th Gordon Highlanders
MAINDS David A. MM L/Cpl 6/17412 Royal Inniskilling Fusiliers
MAINE George MM Dvr 32549 21 Div Sig Coy Royal Engineers
MAINE Victor Henry MM Bdr L/38454 Z/41 Med TM Bty RFA
MAINEY Richard MM Sjt Z/1164 1st Rifle Brigade
MAINPRICE William R. MM Pte 354424 7th London Regt
MAINWARING Cyril J. MM+Bar L/Cpl 390577 1/9th London Regt
MAINWARING George MM L/Cpl PW/1785 19th Middlesex Regt
MAINWARING Henry Charles Samuel B MM Gnr 84837 327 Siege Bty RGA
MAINWARING Morgan "MM,MID" Pte 22177 1st South Wales Borderers
MAINWARING R.L. MM Sjt A/1104 1st King's Royal Rifle Corps
MAINWARING Samuel MM Sjt 2609 3rd Hussars
MAIR Alexander MM Pte 240895 Gordon Highlanders
MAIR Alexander MM CSM 7544 1/6th Seaforth Highlanders
MAIR Alexander MM Cpl 645672 255 Bde RFA
MAIR Charles D. MM Pte 41642 1/7th Royal Highlanders
MAIR Daniel MM Spr 148603 Royal Engineers
MAIR David MM Cpl 23945 5th Cameron Highlanders KIA 28.9.18.
MAIR Hugh MM Sjt 10252 5th Cameron Highlanders
MAIR James MM Spr 121916 Royal Engineers
MAIR James P. MM Cpl 22469 1/4th Gordon Highlanders
MAIR James R. MM Pte 18209 Gordon Highlanders
MAIR John MM Pte 2769 17th Royal Scots
MAIR John MM+Bar Cpl 8968 2nd Yorkshire Light Infantry
MAIR William MM CSM 295011 12th Royal Scots Fusiliers
MAIR William Harley MM Cpl 2772 1/14th London Regt
MAIRS Arthur J. MM Pte 108213 Machine Gun Corps
MAIRS Samuel MM Pte S/18559 1/7th Arg & Suth Highlanders KIA 22.4.18.
MAIS John MM L/Cpl 24465 Northumberland Fusiliers
MAISEY Alfred MM Pte 72084 11th Notts & Derby Regt
MAISEY Frank H. MM+Bar Sjt 83800 RFA
MAITLAND John MM Pte 10316 1st King's Own Scottish Borderers DOW 14.3.18.
MAITLAND Walter Clark MM L/Cpl M2/048721 1 Cav Div MT Coy Army Service Corps
MAITLAND William D. MM L/Sjt 6074 Arg & Suth Highlanders
MAJOR Arthur Leslie MM Cpl 31505 RGA
MAJOR Benjamin MM Pte 18202 9th West Yorkshire Regt
MAJOR Bertie E. MM Cpl MS/4279 Army Service Corps
MAJOR Charles W. MM Cpl 235243 2nd Yorkshire Light Infantry
MAJOR Frederick C. MM CSM T/16435 Army Service Corps
MAJOR Frederick H. "DCM,MM" Cpl 17773 23 Fd Coy Royal Engineers
MAJOR Frederick W. MM L/Cpl 20328 2nd Gloucestershire Regt
MAJOR George MM Cpl 20973 2nd Border Regt KIA 9.8.18.
MAJOR George H. MM Sjt 16552 Machine Gun Corps
MAJOR Harry Victor MM L/Cpl 35071 Royal Welsh Fusiliers
MAJOR J. MM Cpl 240769 Lincolnshire Regt
MAJOR James MM Pte 12002 10th Devonshire Regt
MAJOR John Henry MM L/Cpl R/5623 13th King's Royal Rifle Corps DOW 30.8.18.
MAJOR W.E. MM Pte 14730 King's Royal Rifle Corps

MAJOR William E. MM Pte 15377 Royal West Kent Regt
MAJOR William T. MM Cpl 34637 RGA
MAKEHAM Ernest Samuel MM Sjt 17508 12th Bn Machine Gun Corps KIA 26.5.18.
MAKEPEACE Alfred MM Pte 2326 1/5th Northumberland Fusiliers KIA 14.11.16.
MAKEPEACE Sidney R. MM Sjt 266393 2/7th Royal Warwickshire Regt
MAKEPEACE William G. MM Pte 656332 23rd London Regt
MAKER Norman F. MM L/Cpl 10132 8th Devonshire Regt
MAKIN J.W. MM Pte 2698 Machine Gun Corps
MAKIN John MM Cpl 14407 7th East Lancashire Regt
MAKIN John D. MM Sjt 64453 Labour Corps
MAKIN Thomas MM Sjt 20800 15th Welsh Regt
MAKINSON Harry MM Cpl 18869 9th Royal Irish Fusiliers DOW 11.4.18.
MAKINSON Henry MM Bdr 83838 'Q' Bty RHA
MALAM James MM Pte 16314 9th North Staffordshire Regt
MALARKIE James W. MM Pte 112296 14th Bn Tank Corps
MALATSKI Morris MM Pte 10877 8th West Riding Regt
MALBON Joseph MM L/Cpl 22452 North Staffordshire Regt
MALBY A.J. MM Sjt T2/017117 Army Service Corps
MALBY Herbert E. "DCM,MM" Sjt 5729 70 Coy 23rd Bn Machine Gun Corps
MALCOLM Alexander MM+Bar Sjt 290182 1/7th Gordon Highlanders
MALCOLM Alexander MM Gnr 175717 RFA
MALCOLM Andrew MM Pte 316640 13th Royal Highlanders
MALCOLM Archibald S. MM Gnr 640558 94 Bty 18 Bde RFA
MALCOLM George MM L/Cpl 51093 1st Royal Scots Fusiliers
MALCOLM J.A. MM L/Cpl 653 East Kent Regt
MALCOLM James MM Pte 12632 1/4th Seaforth Highlanders KIA 12.10.18.
MALCOLM John MM Pte 13566 15th Highland Light Infantry
MALCOLM John MM Sjt 22/1027 Northumberland Fusiliers
MALCOM A.H. MM Cpl 85339 RGA
MALCOM H.L. MM CQMS 129 Imperial Camel Corps
MALE Arthur "MM,MSM" S/Sjt 18903 2(Cav)Fd Amb RAMC
MALE Frederick George MM Bdr 14511 D/168 Bde RFA
MALE George E. MM Spt 542457 456 Fd Coy Royal Engineers
MALE Joseph MM Pte 15394 Lancashire Fusiliers
MALE Mortimer G. MM Pte 203148 1st Essex Regt
MALE Sidney MM L/Cpl 6965 6th Dragoons
MALER John William MM Gnr 926010 C/177 Bde RFA
MALES Alfred J.V. MM BQMS 56466 B/86 Bde RFA
MALES William Henry MM Pte 2776 1/6th London Regt DOW 22.9.16.
MALEY Patrick MM Pte 33067 1st Royal Warwickshire Regt
MALEY Thomas MM Sjt 200364 1/5th South Staffordshire Regt
MALHAM Arthur MM Gnr 776523 Y/62 Med TM Bty RFA
MALHAM George MM Pte 201932 5th Yorkshire Light Infantry
MALIA Joseph MM+Bar Sjt 1329 1/1(Northumbrian)Fd Amb RAMC
MALIN Morris MM Pte 44725 8th Royal Berkshire Regt
MALIN Reginald MM Pte 65640 11th Royal Fusiliers
MALIN Robert Edwin MM Gnr 915958 5 Div Ammn Col RFA
MALING Arthur Charles Frederick MM L/Cpl 16469 2 Fd Coy Royal Engineers
MALINS Leonard Edward MM+Bar Pte R/17168 King's Royal Rifle Corps
MALKIN Percy MM Pte 21879 6th Leicestershire Regt
MALKIN Thomas MM Pte 13/611 13th York & Lancaster Regt
MALKINSON Charles Herbert MM Sjt 2842 2/19th London Regt
MALLABONE William MM Gnr 62089 RFA
MALLARD Alexander John MM Sjt 17859 Hampshire Regt
MALLEA Patrick MM Pte MS/2753 2 Ammn Park Army Service Corps
MALLEN T.F. MM L/Cpl 63764 9th Yorkshire Light Infantry
MALLENBY R.T.   See 4373 John TODD
MALLETT Charles H. MM Sjt T2/13001 Army Service Corps
MALLETT Ernest W. MM Sjt 55111 40 Bty 25 Bde RFA
MALLETT G.H. MM+Bar Cpl 63894 11th Royal Fusiliers
MALLETT John Arnold MM Pte 15262 3rd Hussars
MALLETT Robert Henry MM Pte 10905 2nd Yorkshire Light Infantry Died 19.10.19.
MALLETT Walter MM Pte 18219 2nd Coldstream Guards
MALLETT William MM Sjt 530936 15th London Regt
MALLETT William MM Cpl 49049 Devonshire Regt
MALLETT William J.R. MM L/Sjt 12386 7th Suffolk Regt
MALLEY John MM Pte 201215 1/5th Highland Light Infantry
MALLEY Reginald MM Pte 1680 RAMC
MALLEY William MM Pte 200424 1/4th Royal Scots Fusiliers
MALLIN Frederick W. MM Sjt 20254 47 Coy RGA
MALLIN William "DCM,MM" Sjt 17628 2nd South Lancashire Regt KIA 1.9.18.
MALLINDER Harold MM Gnr 63730 RFA
MALLINSON Benjamin MM L/Sjt 12698 South Staffordshire Regt
MALLINSON Bernard MM 2nd Cpl 482409 62 Div Sig Coy Royal Engineers
MALLINSON Charles MM Pte 28851 8th Royal Lancaster Regt
MALLINSON Ernest MM Cpl 18892 A/155 Bde RFA KIA 3.10.18.
MALLINSON Frank MM Pte 20208 10th West Riding Regt
MALLINSON Frederick MM Pte 24690 11th Border Regt
MALLINSON James Henry P. MM Sjt 796431 311 Bde RFA
MALLINSON Joseph E. MM Pte 41287 Liverpool Regt
MALLINSON Samuel "DCM,MM" Sjt 37902 400 Bty 14 Bde RFA
MALLION Albert MM Pte 1179 1st Rifle Brigade DOW 9.8.16.
MALLISON Gilbert MM Sjt 795460 62 Div Ammn Col RFA
MALLOCH Frank W. MM Sjt 40452 King's Own Scottish Borderers
MALLON David MM Pte 43890 10th Highland Light Infantry
MALLON Edward J. MM CSM 51324 1st Royal Scots Fusiliers
MALLON Edwin H. MM Pte 18272 1st Royal Munster Fusiliers
MALLON James MM Pte 131587 18th Bn Machine Gun Corps
MALLON John MM L/Cpl S/6137 10th Arg & Suth Highlanders
MALLON John MM Pte 20711 12th Royal Scots
MALLON Lawrence MM+Bar L/Cpl 22461 1st Royal Dublin Fusiliers
MALLOWS Edward G. MM+2 Bars Sjt 16418 2 Div Sig Coy Royal Engineers
MALLOY Patrick MM Pte S/16514 5th Cameron Highlanders
MALONE Harold Stanley MM L/Cpl 200679 2/5th Lancashire Fusiliers DOW 30.4.18.
MALONE James MM L/Cpl 10356 12th East Surrey Regt
MALONE James "MM,MSM" Sjt 6800 2nd Royal Scots
MALONE James MM Pte 201363 Seaforth Highlanders
MALONE John "MM,MID" Sjt 250016 Durham Light Infantry
MALONE John MM Cpl 10404 1st Royal Irish Rifles
MALONE John T. MM Pte 49136 15th Lancashire Fusiliers
MALONE Patrick MM Pte 40004 Seaforth Highlanders
MALONE Patrick MM Pte 22354 Royal Dublin Fusiliers
MALONE Thomas A. MM Gnr 2975 RFA
MALONEY Alfred MM Cpl G/434 6th East Kent Regt KIA 7.6.17.
MALONEY Arthur MM Pte 25250 Cheshire Regt
MALONEY Charles MM Pte 76488 2nd Bn Tank Corps
MALONEY James MM Cpl 16551 32nd Bn Machine Gun Corps
MALONEY John MM BSM 23068 73 Bty 5 Bde RFA
MALONEY John MM Pte 19190 9th Essex Regt
MALONEY John MM L/Cpl 20897 2 Fd Coy Royal Engineers
MALONEY John MM Sjt 275503 5/6th Royal Scots
MALONEY Joseph MM Pte 32537 1/5th East Lancashire Regt KIA 24.9.18.
MALONEY Joseph MM Cpl 8207 Machine Gun Corps
MALONEY Joseph "MM,MID" Sjt 49900 RFA
MALONEY T. MM Sjt 4292 2nd Leinster Regt
MALONEY Thomas MM Pte 82497 11th Royal Fusiliers
MALPAS Archibald H. MM Cpl 345351 24th Royal Welsh Fusiliers
MALPAS Thomas MM Sjt 290064 Royal Highlanders
MALPASS Charles MM Sjt 1838 Durham Light Infantry
MALPASS J.T. MM L/Cpl P3749 Military Foot Police
MALSBURY Thomas Dennis MM Bdr 76259 RFA
MALSHER Levi MM Sjt 200187 1/4th Northamptonshire Regt
MALT Victor MM Cpl 11648 7th Shropshire Light Infantry KIA 21.8.18.
MALTBY Geoffrey MM Bdr 29185 A/86 Bde RFA
MALTBY George E. MM Pte 201935 5/6th Scottish Rifles KIA 24.10.18.
MALTBY George H. MM L/Bdr 133839 342 Siege Bty RGA
MALTBY Henry "DCM,MM" Sjt 72057 39th Bn Machine Gun Corps
MALTBY Herbert MM Cpl 32706 RFA
MALTBY Neville F. MM Gnr 945281 RFA
MALTBY Percy MM Pte 10654 6th Lincolnshire Regt
MALTMAN James MM Pte 252116 1/6th Arg & Suth Highlanders
MALTMAN John MM Pte 17840 1st Royal Scots Fusiliers
MALTMAN Stanley MM Pte 57810 Liverpool Regt
MALTON John MM Sjt 48413 83 Coy Machine Gun Corps
MALTON John S. MM Pte 241963 Lincolnshire Regt
MALTSON Thomas MM Pte 2947 10th Hussars
MALYAN Herbert R. MM Pte 103345 10th Notts & Derby Regt
MALYON Charles F. MM Spr 310232 Royal Engineers
MALYON George Thomas MM CQMS 8798 7th Northamptonshire Regt
MALYON Thomas MM Pte 69223 Royal Fusiliers

MANCEY Ernest G. MM L/Cpl 21907 Suffolk Regt
MANCEY Walter MM Pte 41846 RAMC
MANCHESTER Arthur MM Bdr 294622 RGA
MANCLARK William MM L/Cpl 8910 2nd Cameron Highlanders
MANDALL Charles A. MM Pte M/297084 Army Service Corps
MANDALL Henry MM Sjt 57477 Royal Engineers
MANDELKAN William MM Cpl 254301 14th Arg & Suth Highlanders
MANDER Robert MM Pte 9794 Royal Warwickshire Regt
MANDERS A. MM Gnr 1041 RGA
MANDERS George MM Gnr 58369 RGA
MANDERS George William MM Pte 16570 10th Hampshire Regt
MANDERS Jacob MM S/Sjt Fitter 165998 RGA
MANDERSON Edmund J. MM Sjt 5320 2nd Royal Irish Rifles
MANDEVILLE Joseph "DCM,MM" Sjt 10313 1st Cheshire Regt KIA 4.8.17.
MANDLEY Arthur MM Pte 31237 Northamptonshire Regt
MANDS Alexander MM Pte 200509 Royal Highlanders
MANEY John MM Sjt 375551 Labour Corps
MANFIELD Moses Philip MM L/Cpl 26486 2nd Welsh Regt KIA 15.9.18.
MANFORD William MM Pte 14962 7th Shropshire Light Infantry KIA 13.2.18.
MANGAN Charles MM Pte 93238 Machine Gun Corps
MANGAN James MM Pte 10794 4th Liverpool Regt
MANGAN Patrick J. "DCM,MM" CSM 16540 8th Royal Dublin Fusiliers
MANGER Arthur G. MM Pte 18868 1st Northamptonshire Regt
MANGER James MM Pte 43109 Manchester Regt
MANGHAM Luke MM L/Cpl 40063 Northamptonshire Regt
MANGLES Thomas Robson MM Gnr 18871 B/93 Bde RFA KIA 2.11.16.
MANHIRE John Richard MM Pte 200445 3rd Light Bn Tank Corps
MANHIRE Samuel H. MM Sjt 240096 5th Duke of Cornwall's LI
MANKELOW Edwin MM Cpl M2/046076 Army Service Corps
MANKELOW Walter MM Pte 656 6th Royal West Kent Regt KIA 7.10.16.
MANKLOW N.E. MM L/Cpl P/5376 1 Traffic Control Coy Military Foot Police
MANKTELOW Edgar "DCM,MM" Sjt S/4400 13th Rifle Brigade
MANKTELOW Ernest George MM Pte 17363 2nd Coldstream Guards KIA 27.8.18.
MANKTELOW George Thomas MM Cpl 2132 7th Royal West Kent Regt DOW 26.11.16.
MANLEY Christopher MM Pte 20728 1st Lancashire Fusiliers
MANLEY Frederick Charles "MM,MSM,CG(F)" Staff SM S/19420 Army Service Corps
MANLEY Harold MM Pte 16218 East Surrey Regt
MANLEY Harry MM+Bar Sjt 3337 9 Siege Bty RGA
MANLEY Herbert MM Sjt 11551 6th East Lancashire Regt KIA 9.3.17.
MANLEY Herbert Ernest W.J. MM Sjt 10908 8th Devonshire Regt
MANLEY Norman W. MM Gnr 41805 RFA
MANLEY Wallace G. MM Pte 8255 2nd Devonshire Regt
MANLEY William C. MM Sjt 13209 7th Royal Berkshire Regt
MANLOND Andrew MM Sjt 2011 1/5th Liverpool Regt
MANLOVE William MM Pte 13297 9th Notts & Derby Regt
MANLOW William John MM Bdr 46201 125 Bty 29 Bde RFA
MANLY Christopher MM BQMS 352357 293 Siege Bty RGA
MANN Alexander MM Sjt 9/15543 9th Royal Irish Rifles
MANN Alexander Nicol Johnson "MM,MC(G)" Pte 26961 8th Royal Scots Fusiliers
MANN Alfred A. MM+Bar Sjt 240375 Lincolnshire Regt
MANN Alfred H. MM Gnr 116254 RGA
MANN Andrew MM Cpl S/8794 Arg & Suth Highlanders
MANN Arthur Edward MM L/Cpl 201168 2/4th York & Lancaster Regt DOW 2.10.18.
MANN Arthur G. MM Spr 82417 130 Fd Coy Royal Engineers
MANN Cecil W. MM Pte 277790 2nd Manchester Regt
MANN Charles Henry MM Pte 328184 1/1st Cambridgeshire Regt KIA 25.3.18.
MANN Charles W. MM L/Cpl 13861 9th Suffolk Regt
MANN E. MM Pte 242615 Royal Lancaster Regt
MANN F.F. MM Pte 8992 Suffolk Regt
MANN Frederick Henry MM Cpl 65812 132 Fd Amb RAMC DOW 25.10.16.
MANN Frederick J. MM Pte 2200 8th Royal Sussex Regt
MANN Frederick W. MM Sjt 8339 1st Royal West Kent Regt
MANN George MM Pte 21351 9th Notts & Derby Regt
MANN George G. MM Pte 240159 1/5th Devonshire Regt

MANN George Henry MM Sjt 235374 2nd South Staffordshire Regt DOW 1.10.18.
MANN George L. MM L/Cpl G/11824 9th Royal Sussex Regt
MANN Harold B. MM L/Sjt STK/749 10th Royal Fusiliers
MANN Harold B. MM Cpl 12669 9th Essex Regt KIA 8.7.16.
MANN Harry MM Pte G/14631 3rd Royal Fusiliers
MANN Harry "DCM,MM" CQMS 8594 11th Suffolk Regt
MANN Herbert F. MM Cpl 18767 4th Royal Fusiliers
MANN Hubert MM Pte 40576 Northumberland Fusiliers
MANN Hubert F.J. MM Gnr 237075 RFA
MANN James MM BQMS 49765 B/91 Bde RFA
MANN James MM Pte 21813 1/6th Gordon Highlanders
MANN James Meikle MM Bdr 104486 RFA
MANN John MM Pte 15074 8th North Lancashire Regt KIA 10.10.16.
MANN John E. MM Spr 197307 Royal Engineers
MANN John W. MM L/Cpl 33727 6th York & Lancaster Regt
MANN John William T. "DCM,MM" Sjt 19223 9th York & Lancaster Regt
MANN Joseph MM Pte 32349 6th York & Lancaster Regt
MANN Joseph W. MM Pte 52370 7th Lancashire Fusiliers
MANN Mark Percy MM Pte G/14619 2nd Royal Sussex Regt KIA 24.9.18.
MANN Noel T. MM Pte 29548 1st Norfolk Regt
MANN Percy S. MM Pte 52119 1st Lincolnshire Regt
MANN Robert MM CSM 167 1/7th Middlesex Regt
MANN Stephen William MM Sjt 2530 2nd London Regt KIA 27.3.19.
MANN Thomas "MM,MID" Sjt 8094 1st Rifle Brigade
MANN Thomas MM Pte 17769 10th West Riding Regt
MANN Thomas C. MM L/Cpl 12182 8th Leicestershire Regt
MANN William H. MM Cpl 242677 East Surrey Regt
MANN William R. MM Dvr T1/580 Army Service Corps
MANN William Roderick Maurice MM L/Cpl 514521 1/14th London Regt
MANNERING Richard MM+Bar Pte 681499 22nd London Regt
MANNERINGS John A. MM Dvr T/21788 62 Div Train Army Service Corps
MANNERS Albert G. MM Cpl M2/116457 Army Service Corps
MANNERS Claude Edward MM Pte M2/194802 Army Service Corps
MANNERS Ernest MM Gnr 199480 A/18 Bde RFA
MANNERS John W. MM Sjt 29420 50 Coy Labour Corps
MANNING A. MM Gnr 75841 RFA
MANNING Albert MM Dvr 40317 63 Fd Coy Royal Engineers
MANNING Albert MM Pte 4898 1st East Surrey Regt
MANNING Albert T. MM Pte 145940 1/1st Northamptonshire Yeomanry
MANNING Alfred MM Cpl 28703 Essex Regt
MANNING Arthur MM Sjt 22163 Liverpool Regt
MANNING Arthur E. MM Pte 1816 1st Middlesex Regt
MANNING Arthur J. MM L/Cpl 52089 13th Rifle Brigade att 8th London Regt.
MANNING B. MM Gnr 1033 RFA
MANNING Daniel MM Sjt 99208 10th Royal Fusiliers
MANNING Edgar Oliver MM Pte 3219 6th Royal West Kent Regt
MANNING Ernest MM Pte 74179 RAMC
MANNING Ernest W. MM Pte 14107 8th Suffolk Regt
MANNING Frederick J. MM Pte 240235 1/5th Suffolk Regt
MANNING Frederick R. MM Bdr 618013 20 Bde RHA
MANNING George MM Sjt 8902 69 Coy Machine Gun Corps
MANNING George H. MM Sjt 44548 RFA
MANNING George J. MM Pte 683575 1/22nd London Regt
MANNING James J. MM Pte 12681 1st Irish Guards
MANNING John MM Gnr 73889 C/78 Bde RFA
MANNING Joseph MM Sjt 22748 Yorkshire Light Infantry
MANNING Leopold MM Dvr 31372 RFA
MANNING Lewis A. MM Dvr 46681 RFA
MANNING Percy D. MM Pte 302763 10th Bn Tank Corps
MANNING Reginald MM Pte 14526 9th Norfolk Regt
MANNING Richard MM Pte 9020 1st Royal Dublin Fusiliers
MANNING Robert J. MM Sjt DM2/118556 Army Service Corps
MANNING Ruben MM Pte 20054 12 Fd Amb RAMC
MANNING Samuel MM L/Cpl 29914 14th Royal Warwickshire Regt
MANNING Stanley MM Pte 202898 1st East Yorkshire Regt
MANNING William H. MM Spr 71605 Royal Engineers
MANNINGS Victor A. MM Bdr 13206 29 Div Ammn Col RFA
MANNION Charles MM Pte 20424 Grenadier Guards
MANNION Christopher MM Sjt 46609 59th Bn Machine Gun Corps KIA 21.3.18.
MANNION John MM Dvr L/8955 RFA
MANNION Michael MM Pte 44026 King's Own Scottish Borderers

MANNION Thomas MM Spr 51215 30 Div Sig Coy Royal Engineers KIA 21.3.18.
MANNIS George MM Sjt 19683 12th Royal Irish Rifles
MANNOOCH Frederick G. MM Pte 202875 2/4th Hampshire Regt
MANNOOCH John Thomas MM Pte 19728 2nd Royal Berkshire Regt KIA 1.8.17.
MANSBRIDGE Edward A. MM Pte 102423 10 Fd Amb RAMC
MANSBRIDGE James MM Pte 283218 1/3rd London Regt
MANSELL Alfred MM L/Sjt 9722 2nd Oxf & Bucks Light Infantry
MANSELL George MM Pte 12929 9th Notts & Derby Regt
MANSELL Harry MM Pte 15493 1st Grenadier Guards
MANSELL Harry MM Pte 10463 1st Border Regt
MANSELL Horace MM Pte 9591 2nd Lancashire Fusiliers
MANSELL Joseph MM Pte 9685 Worcestershire Regt
MANSELL Leonard Percy MM Pte 40102 1st South Staffordshire Regt
MANSELL Samuel MM Cpl 14392 2nd Middlesex Regt
MANSELL Timothy MM L/Sjt 64270 RAMC
MANSELL William MM Pte G/3383 12th Middlesex Regt KIA 5.8.17.
MANSELL William Henry MM Pte 29542 15th Cheshire Regt
MANSELL William James MM Pte 203214 4th Worcestershire Regt DOW 23.8.18.
MANSER Charles H. MM Pte 3/5793 Royal Munster Fusiliers
MANSER Frederick MM L/Cpl 2792 1/20th London Regt KIA 1.10.16.
MANSER Joe MM Farrier S/Sjt 4273 10th Hussars
MANSEY Henry MM Sjt 17835 Royal Fusiliers
MANSFIELD A.S. MM L/Cpl 14213 Essex Regt
MANSFIELD Albert "DCM,MM" Sjt 27223 1st Northamptonshire Regt
MANSFIELD Albert MM Sjt 9817 4th Middlesex Regt
MANSFIELD Arthur MM Pte 3922 7th Dragoon Guards
MANSFIELD Benjamin MM Pte 14/1466 1/5th York & Lancaster Regt
MANSFIELD Bertie MM Sjt 240112 1/4th Suffolk Regt
MANSFIELD C.H. "DCM,MM,MID" Sjt 75041 1/1st Derbyshire Yeomanry
MANSFIELD Charles MM Pte B/203462 10th Rifle Brigade KIA 21.11.17.
MANSFIELD E.G. MM Pnr 602427 Royal Engineers
MANSFIELD Ernest W.E. MM Sjt 229597 Royal Fusiliers
MANSFIELD Gladstone S. MM Pte 42599 4th North Staffordshire Regt
MANSFIELD James MM Dvr 78610 RFA
MANSFIELD James D. MM Pte S/4905 Rifle Brigade
MANSFIELD James W. MM Pte 21928 Duke of Cornwall's LI
MANSFIELD John Henry MM L/Cpl 10706 6th Yorkshire Regt
MANSFIELD Joseph MM Pte 75779 1/1st Derbyshire Yeomanry
MANSFIELD Robert MM Pte 32042 2nd Middlesex Regt
MANSFIELD Thomas MM 2nd Cpl 24173 1 Div Sig Coy Royal Engineers
MANSFIELD Thomas MM CQMS 14450 7th Wiltshire Regt
MANSFIELD Walter F. MM Pte 18009 26th Royal Fusiliers
MANSFIELD William E. MM Sjt 570204 1/17th London Regt
MANSFIELD William J. MM Bdr 14185 B/77 Bde RFA
MANSHIP George MM Dvr 18828 B/94 Bde RFA
MANSON Donald MM L/Cpl 40976 Highland Light Infantry
MANSON Francis McKenzie MM L/Cpl 36014 1/4th North Lancashire Regt KIA 22.10.18.
MANSON James MM Sjt 1205 1st Gordon Highlanders
MANSON James D. MM L/Cpl 300390 1/7th Royal Scots
MANSON James F. MM Pte 27270 16th Highland Light Infantry
MANSON Robert MM Bdr 202217 RFA
MANSON Sinclair MM L/Cpl 64363 68 Coy Machine Gun Corps
MANSON Thomas MM Cpl 240834 1/6th Highland Light Infantry
MANSON William A. MM L/Cpl S/14099 2nd Gordon Highlanders
MANSON William Andrew MM Cpl 436 1/7th Gordon Highlanders
MANSSUER Albert MM Pte 100187 RAMC
MANT John MM L/Cpl 5325 9th Royal Sussex Regt
MANT William G. MM Pte 5815 7th Royal West Surrey Regt
MANTERFIELD C. MM L/Cpl 235226 York & Lancaster Regt
MANTHORP Cyril "MM,MMV(lt)" Sjt 530147 1/15th London Regt
MANTLE Arthur MM Cpl 9290 1st. Royal Scots Fusiliers
MANTLE George MM Pte M2/130919 594 Coy Army Service Corps
MANTLE Herbert Richard MM+Bar Cpl 16709 1st Northumberland Fusiliers
MANTLE Horatio T. MM L/Cpl 9687 2nd Royal West Surrey Regt
MANTLE Richard MM Pte 24372 9th Yorkshire Regt
MANTLE Stephen "MM+Bar,MMV(lt)" Cpl 6893 1st South Staffordshire Regt
MANTLE William F. MM Cpl 31389 'O' Cable Section Royal Engineers
MANTON Alfred J. MM Gnr L/19210 RFA
MANTON Frank MM Pte 1260 1/5th Cheshire Regt DOW 11.9.16.
MANTON John MM L/Cpl 306167 1/7th West Riding Regt
MANUEL William MM Sjt 1050 1st Welsh Guards
MANVELL Ernest James MM Sjt 2519 8th Royal Sussex Regt KIA 23.3.18.
MANVILLE William MM L/Cpl 40631 9th York & Lancaster Regt KIA 21.9.17.
MANWARING Ralph C. MM Pte 5928 7th Dragoon Guards
MANZI Alfred P. MM Sjt 491575 1/13th London Regt
MANZI Andrew "DCM,MM" Sjt 1171 9th Royal Fusiliers
MANZIES A. MM Pte 430 Royal Highlanders
MAPLETHORPE Charles Henry William MM Sjt 923 1/13th London Regt KIA 29.8.18.
MAPLETHORPE Sidney MM Pte 60493 Machine Gun Corps
MAPLETHORPE William MM Bdr 84830 X/12 Med TM Bty RFA
MAPLETOFT William MM Sjt 24109 1/6th Notts & Derby Regt
MAPP William MM+Bar Pte 210916 2/7th & 10th Worcestershire Regt
MAPPLE Ernest Henry "MM,MSM" S/Sjt Mech M2/052846 3 Cav Div MT Coy Army Service Corps
MAPPLETHORPE Frank MM Pte 470088 1/12th London Regt
MAPSTON George T. "DCM,MM" L/Cpl 5569 8th East Surrey Regt
MAQUIRE J. MM Pte 4530 Royal Irish Rifles
MARAGHAN Francis B. MM Sjt 34863 RHA
MARAH Thomas "DCM,MM" Cpl 32611 59 Siege Bty RGA
MARCH Albert Prince Victor George "DCM,MM" L/Cpl 723000 1/24th London Regt KIA 29.8.18.
MARCH Alfred MM Pte 52308 2/7th West Yorkshire Regt
MARCH Alfred H. MM Spr 504502 Royal Engineers
MARCH Ernest MM Pte 203226 East Yorkshire Regt
MARCH Frederick MM Sjt 9812 2nd Yorkshire Regt
MARCH Gordon MM Pte 356908 10th Liverpool Regt
MARCH Henry J. MM Cpl L/42178 B/181 Bde RFA
MARCH John E. MM+2 Bars Sjt 325402 1/9th Durham Light Infantry
MARCH Martin Caleb MM Pte 16383 1st Worcestershire Regt KIA 31.7.17.
MARCH Richard MM Pte 30102 Border Regt
MARCH Thomas MM Gnr 86753 RFA
MARCH Thomas R. MM 2nd Cpl 16765 Royal Engineers
MARCH Wallace N. MM Sjt 19767 RGA
MARCH Walter Henry MM Pte 36066 Notts & Derby Regt
MARCHANT Alfred MM Pte 201943 4th Gloucestershire Regt
MARCHANT Charles R. MM L/Cpl 8903 7th Shropshire Light Infantry
MARCHANT E.J. MM Pte 242564 Worcestershire Regt
MARCHANT Frank MM Pte 18700 Devonshire Regt
MARCHANT Frederick MM Pte 22369 Welsh Regt
MARCHANT Frederick W. MM Pte 11406 1st Dorsetshire Regt
MARCHANT George MM Sjt 15176 6th Lincolnshire Regt
MARCHANT George F. "MM,MID" Dvr 63163 22 Bde RFA
MARCHANT Herbert MM Sjt 35001 9th Royal Fusiliers
MARCHANT Herbert Hartley "MM,MID" Sjt L/13085 B/156 Bde RFA
MARCHANT Jesse MM L/Cpl 9948 2nd Highland Light Infantry
MARCHANT Maurice W. MM L/Cpl 1595 7th Royal West Surrey Regt
MARCHANT Ronald Norman MM Sjt 493441 2/1(Home Counties)Fd Amb RAMC
MARCHANT Wilfred Bernard "DCM,MM" Sjt 200573 1/7th Worcestershire Regt
MARCHANT William G. "MM+Bar,MID" Sjt 7/28515 7th & 2nd Royal Dublin Fusiliers
MARCHANT William H. MM Spr 534194 218 Fd Coy Royal Engineers
MARCHANT William H. MM Pte 322035 6th London Regt
MARCHBANK James MM Pte 330096 1/8th Royal Scots
MARCHBANK John MM L/Cpl 330063 Liverpool Regt
MARCHBANK Robert MM L/Cpl 229467 Royal Fusiliers
MARCHBANK Robert Bruce MM L/Cpl 18175 12th Liverpool Regt DOW 19.8.17.
MARCHBANK Robert K. MM Sjt 40245 Royal Scots
MARCHETTI Sottero Mario MM Pte S/25215 9th Rifle Brigade KIA 3.5.17.
MARCHINGTON Benjamin MM Cpl 240699 2/5th Yorkshire Light Infantry DOW 4.1.18.
MARCHINGTON John H. MM Gnr 104585 RGA
MARDELL Edward S. MM L/Cpl 36398 Royal Berkshire Regt
MARDELL William MM Pte 630405 20th London Regt

MARDELL William Alfred MM Pte 266531 1/1st Hertfordshire Regt
MARDLE Frank MM Dvr 800506 C/230 Bde RFA
MARDLING Henry W. MM Sjt 7232 2nd Bedfordshire Regt
MARDON Henry Wallace MM Spr 510261 58 Div Sig Coy Royal Engineers KIA 25.10.17.
MARFLETT Harry MM Sjt 26495 2nd Highland Light Infantry
MARGERISON Harold MM Pnr 452100 Royal Engineers
MARGERSON Thomas MM Pte 30049 9th North Lancashire Regt KIA 22.3.18.
MARGETTS Arthur MM Pte 4262 Oxf & Bucks Light Infantry
MARGETTS George D. "MM,MSM" L/Cpl 681 3rd County of London Yeomanry
MARGETTS Leonard M. MM Pte 703385 23rd London Regt
MARGETTS Norman J. "MM,MID" Bdr 95931 RFA
MARGETTS William H. MM Pte 83203 Machine Gun Corps
MARGINSON Fred Sharp MM Spr 429756 55 Div Sig Coy Royal Engineers
MARGINSON James MM Gnr 71913 34 Bde RFA
MARGRAVE Percy MM L/Cpl 67349 RAMC
MARGREAVE J.W. MM L/Cpl 8608 King's Own Scottish Borderers
MARGRETT Charles W. MM Sjt 880 7th Seaforth Highlanders
MARGROVE Ernest MM Cpl 610556 1/19th London Regt
MARIE Frederick MM Dvr 39528 D/82 Bde RFA
MARIE William A. MM Pte S/10789 Rifle Brigade
MARIES Arthur G. MM L/Sjt 9061 1st Duke of Cornwall's LI
MARIS Horace MM Pte 405199 RAMC
MARJORAM George E. MM Pte 300850 Essex Regt
MARJORAM James E. MM L/Sjt 11728 1st Royal Berkshire Regt KIA 8.10.18.
MARJORAM William H. MM Gnr 59078 RGA
MARK John MM L/Sjt 4/8184 West Yorkshire Regt
MARK William MM Pte 19976 Royal Scots
MARK William J. MM Sjt 58310 9th Bn Machine Gun Corps
MARKER John MM Bdr 67484 RGA
MARKEY Frank Francis MM Dvr 53830 C/50 Bde RFA
MARKEY Thomas MM Pte 2130 10th Hussars
MARKHAM Alfred W. MM Pte 613819 19th London Regt
MARKHAM Charles A. MM Pte 8394 8th London Regt
MARKHAM Edward MM Sjt 15285 9th South Staffordshire Regt
MARKHAM Edwin Louis MM Pte 25381 1st York & Lancaster Regt
MARKHAM Fred MM Sjt 5197 18th Hussars
MARKHAM Harold Edgar MM Pte 10478 9th Essex Regt
MARKHAM Herbert MM Spr 546881 4 Div Sig Coy Royal Engineers
MARKHAM James MM Pte 4643 8th Royal Munster Fusiliers
MARKHAM Joseph Thomas MM Sjt 424 6th Royal West Kent Regt KIA 7.10.16.
MARKHAM Richard MM Pte 17608 1st Northamptonshire Regt KIA 21.7.18.
MARKHAM Robert MM L/Cpl 40914 West Yorkshire Regt
MARKHAM Roland Charles MM Pte 200228 1/4th Suffolk Regt
MARKHAM Thomas MM Cpl 25475 8th Lincolnshire Regt KIA 25.8.18.
MARKHAM Thomas MM+Bar Pte 6996 1st Northamptonshire Regt
MARKHAM Thomas B. MM Pte 12548 7th Yorkshire Light Infantry
MARKHAM Tom Sidney MM Pte 21059 1st Lincolnshire Regt
MARKHAM William MM Gnr 34427 84 Bde RFA
MARKILLIE Ernest MM Pte 48835 Royal Fusiliers
MARKIN Frank MM Cpl 14384 9th Welsh Regt DOW 28.7.16.
MARKINSON James Arthur MM Pte 29116 10th West Riding Regt
MARKINSON John "DCM,MM" Cpl 305208 8th West Yorkshire Regt
MARKLAND Herbert MM Cpl 19797 6th Border Regt
MARKLEW Frank MM Sjt 41109 1 Squadron Machine Gun Corps(Cavalry) DOW 23.3.18.
MARKS Albert T. MM Cpl 172200 Second Army Sig Coy Royal Engineers
MARKS Charles J. MM Pte 200582 1/4th Wiltshire Regt
MARKS Frank "DCM,MM" CSM 15261 3rd Grenadier Guards
MARKS George Graham MM Gnr 3021 RGA
MARKS Harvey MM Dvr 785579 A/312 Bde RFA
MARKS J.F. MM Cpl C/9857
MARKS John H. MM Sjt L/15338 2nd Middlesex Regt
MARKS Lionel Y. MM Pte 34141 15th Royal Warwickshire Regt
MARKS Moses "MM,MID" Sjt 5705 3rd Coldstream Guards
MARKS Moss Harris MM Sjt 21352 A/154 Bde RFA
MARKS Thomas MM L/Cpl 14116 2nd Royal Dublin Fusiliers
MARKS Thomas James Morris MM Sjt 8901 1st Wiltshire Regt
MARKS William Edwin "MC,MM(45691 Pte Devon Regt)" 2Lt 1/6th Gloucestershire Regt
MARKS William G. "MM,MID" Sjt 4/6663 Bedfordshire Regt
MARKS William J. MM Pte 69949 10th Royal West Surrey Regt
MARKS William J. MM Pte 320932 24th Welsh Regt
MARKWELL Frederick MM Pte G/21502 16th Royal Sussex Regt
MARKWICK Albert MM Pte G/11861 13th Royal Fusiliers KIA 23.4.17.
MARKWICK Fred MM Sjt 94235 221 Coy Machine Gun Corps
MARKWICK William Henry MM Pte 3544 6th Dragoons KIA 24.3.18.
MARKWORTH Walter L. MM Pte 6829 1st Royal West Surrey Regt
MARL James MM Gnr 171904 Y/19 Med TM Bty RFA
MARLAND George MM Pte 240286 Liverpool Regt
MARLAND James MM Pte PW/1498 19th Middlesex Regt KIA 20.9.17.
MARLAND James MM Pte 3226 2nd Manchester Regt
MARLAND John MM Pte 18990 Royal Lancaster Regt
MARLAND John MM Pte 37551 2nd Manchester Regt
MARLAND William MM L/Cpl 200848 1/5th Royal Lancaster Regt KIA 9.4.18
MARLBOROUGH Thomas A. "DCM,MM+Bar" Sjt 669 6 Fd Amb RAMC
MARLE H. MM Sjt 8638 Royal Welsh Fusiliers
MARLER Charles W. MM Gnr 67823 D/108 Bde RFA
MARLEY Bernard Leslie "MM,MID" Sjt 22314 Machine Gun Corps
MARLEY John G. MM Cpl 21436 8th Somerset Light Infantry
MARLEY William MM Sjt 57944 RAMC
MARLOR Garibaldi MM Pte 2185 West Riding Regt
MARLOR Stanley "MM,MSM" Sjt 13640 16th Lancashire Fusiliers
MARLOW Alfred MM Gnr 38421 'R' Bty RHA
MARLOW Charles MM Sjt 200559 Bedfordshire Regt
MARLOW Charles H. MM Pte 55088 22nd Manchester Regt
MARLOW Ernest M. MM L/Cpl 451204 11th London Regt
MARLOW Harold MM Pnr 479973 Royal Engineers
MARLOW John MM Bdr 106264 RFA
MARLOW William MM Pte 30127 Royal Warwickshire Regt
MARMONT George E. MM Pte 44952 2nd Lincolnshire Regt
MARNER John MM Pte 1108 3 Fd Amb RAMC DOW 19.10.17.
MARNEY Frederick MM Pte S/11438 11th Rifle Brigade
MARNEY George T.H. MM Cpl 5140 Royal Sussex Regt
MARNEY John MM Pte 12518 1/4th Royal Berkshire Regt
MARNOCK Farquharson MM Pte 4326 Gordon Highlanders
MARONEY William MM L/Cpl 8758 2nd West Yorkshire Regt
MAROTT Joseph T. MM Sjt 66062 RFA
MARPLES George MM Gnr 27555 D/94 Bde RFA
MARPLES John W. MM Cpl 18104 9th York & Lancaster Regt
MARPLES Norman "DCM,MM,CG(F)" Sjt 482134 62 Div Sig Coy Royal Engineers
MARQUIS William G. MM Sjt 11837 3rd Middlesex Regt
MARR Alexander MM Pte 35888 1st Royal Scots Fusiliers KIA 2.9.18.
MARR Alexander MM+Bar L/Cpl 201451 1/4th Gordon Highlanders
MARR Arthur MM Sjt 306500 8th Liverpool Regt
MARR Charles MM Pte 8977 54 Fd Amb RAMC
MARR Edward MM L/Cpl 37782 2nd Welsh Regt KIA 23.12.16.
MARR G.D. MM Sjt 1071 1/7th London Regt
MARR Henry MM Pte 290507 Gordon Highlanders
MARR James MM Sjt 2939 8th Royal Highlanders
MARR James MM Bdr 47964 X/24 Med TM Bty RGA KIA 31.5.17.
MARR John MM Sjt 86316 172 Tunnelling Coy Royal Engineers
MARR John MM L/Cpl 40098 1st Bn Tank Corps
MARR William MM Pte 41160 9th Scottish Rifles
MARRABLE Frederick G. "MM,MID" Sjt 1270 12 Fd Amb RAMC
MARREN Harold MM Bdr 805445 C/231 Bde RFA
MARRIAGE Victor W. MM L/Cpl 26250 Machine Gun Corps
MARRIAN Herbert L.L. MM Pte 19987 Royal Fusiliers
MARRINER Matthew MM Cpl 48284 Royal Engineers
MARRIOT Isaac P. MM Pte 43179 Northamptonshire Regt
MARRIOTT Charles G. MM Sjt 73407 A/51 Bde RFA
MARRIOTT Charles Kenneth "MM,MID" CQMS 13729 2nd Grenadier Guards
MARRIOTT Ernest MM+Bar Cpl 241408 5th West Yorkshire Regt
MARRIOTT Eustace Cameron MM Pte 129429 46th Royal Fusiliers
MARRIOTT Fred MM Pte 2584 1/5th Notts & Derby Regt KIA 22.10.17.
MARRIOTT George F. MM Pte 43594 6th South Staffordshire Regt
MARRIOTT Henry J. MM Sjt 421084 10th London Regt
MARRIOTT John MM Sjt 3/2820 Essex Regt
MARRIOTT John MM+Bar Dvr 186804 D/82 Bde RFA
MARRIOTT John MM Pte 28465 RAMC
MARRIOTT John MM Cpl 20052 Machine Gun Corps
MARRIOTT John E. MM Pte 57969 Middlesex Regt
MARRIOTT John G. MM Cpl 17577 5th Northamptonshire Regt
MARRIOTT John Henry MM Bdr 127458 RGA

MARRIOTT L. MM Sjt M1/6039 Army Service Corps
MARRIOTT Nathan MM Sjt 1574 12th London Regt
MARRIOTT Ralph MM Pte 50559 RAMC
MARRIOTT William MM Cpl 12984 48th Bn Machine Gun Corps
MARRIOTT William "MM,VM(Rm)" Spr 184971 432 Fd Coy Royal Engineers
MARRIOTT William Henry MM Pte 10053 8th Gloucestershire Regt Died 5.11.18.
MARRISON Thomas R. MM Pte 633140 20th London Regt
MARRITT Ernest William MM Gnr 43135 RFA
MARRITT Frederick Charles MM Cpl 320134 1/6th London Regt KIA 30.11.17.
MARRON James MM Pte 18211 2nd Leinster Regt
MARRON Michael MM Pte S/1747 12th Rifle Brigade
MARROWS Harry MM Spr 107665 209 Fd Coy Royal Engineers
MARRS John H. MM Sjt 266065 Royal Warwickshire Regt
MARSCH Archie MM Dvr 960312 A/251 RFA
MARSDEN Albert MM Pte 44771 41st Bn Machine Gun Corps
MARSDEN Arthur MM L/Sjt 45196 2nd Royal Berkshire Regt
MARSDEN Charles MM Pte 243294 4/5th North Lancashire Regt
MARSDEN Charles F. MM Pte 12702 10th West Riding Regt
MARSDEN Charles Willie MM L/Cpl 31224 8th York & Lancaster Regt
MARSDEN Edward MM Cpl 50939 RGA
MARSDEN Edwin MM Pte 10683 Manchester Regt
MARSDEN Ernest MM Gnr 103701 RGA
MARSDEN Ernest MM Pte 10/495 10th East Yorkshire Regt
MARSDEN Frank Audsley MM Sjt 18605 8th Yorkshire Light Infantry
MARSDEN Fred "DCM,MM" L/Cpl 19015 7th Yorkshire Regt KIA 18.9.17.
MARSDEN George "DCM,MM" Sjt 16453 11th Cheshire Regt
MARSDEN George MM Pte 9595 Royal Lancaster Regt
MARSDEN George MM L/Cpl 240052 Liverpool Regt
MARSDEN George W. MM Spr 442120 Royal Engineers
MARSDEN Harold MM Cpl 308339 Liverpool Regt
MARSDEN Harry MM Pte 23450 12th Royal Scots
MARSDEN Harry MM Pte 24923 Liverpool Regt
MARSDEN Herbert MM Sjt 201162 2/4th East Lancashire Regt
MARSDEN John MM Dvr 676137 B/285 Bde RFA
MARSDEN John "DCM,MM" CSM 13833 9th North Lancashire Regt
MARSDEN John MM Pte 240496 1/5th North Lancashire Regt
MARSDEN John T. MM Pte 235711 2nd East Lancashire Regt
MARSDEN John W. MM Pte 85107 Machine Gun Corps
MARSDEN Luke MM Pte 201633 1/4th Royal Lancaster Regt KIA 20.11.17.
MARSDEN Maurice MM 2nd Cpl 102754 179 Tunnelling Coy Royal Engineers
MARSDEN Percy MM Pte 131781 30th Bn Machine Gun Corps
MARSDEN Percy MM Gnr 93809 RFA
MARSDEN Peter MM L/Cpl 90892 1st Liverpool Regt
MARSDEN Robert MM Sjt 49578 81 Siege Bty RGA
MARSDEN Rowland MM Pte 12/443 12th York & Lancaster Regt
MARSDEN Samuel MM Pte 41135 11th West Yorkshire Regt KIA 20.9.17.
MARSDEN Thomas MM+Bar Pte R/8843 King's Royal Rifle Corps
MARSDEN Victor P. MM Sjt 472 8th East Surrey Regt
MARSDEN Walter MM L/Cpl 8755 2nd West Yorkshire Regt
MARSDEN William MM+Bar L/Cpl 31058 Durham Light Infantry
MARSDEN William MM Sjt 21674 177 Bde RFA
MARSDEN William MM Pte 15572 1/5th Lincolnshire Regt
MARSDEN William "MM,MC(G)" Pte 16285 12th Cheshire Regt
MARSDEN William Hardcastle MM Pte 403343 2/2nd(West Riding)Fd Amb RAMC
MARSDEN William Thomas MM Dvr 775441 B/310 Bde RFA
MARSDEN Willie MM Pte 241417 West Riding Regt
MARSDEN Willie B. MM Gnr Sig 118141 65 Siege Bty RGA
MARSH Albert MM Pte 332494 9th Liverpool Regt
MARSH Albert George MM Bdr 11600 D/83 Bde RFA DOW 23.3.18.
MARSH Alfred H. MM Sjt 1720 1/7th Durham Light Infantry
MARSH Alfred Henry MM Pte M2/223441 HQ X Corps MT Coy Army Service Corps
MARSH Bertie Frederick MM+Bar L/Cpl 66717 140 Fd Amb RAMC
MARSH Bridger "MM,MID" Bdr 83411 HQ 39 Bde RFA
MARSH Charles A. MM Pte 1871 8th East Kent Regt
MARSH Clarence "DCM,MM" Sjt 10594 1st Coldstream Guards
MARSH Edward MM Gnr 120572 RFA
MARSH Edwin D. MM Pte 495632 6th London Regt
MARSH Frank MM Pte 41069 Worcestershire Regt
MARSH Frank MM Sjt 200063 1/4th Gloucestershire Regt KIA 25.7.18
MARSH Frank MM Pte 14368 11th West Yorkshire Regt KIA 7.6.17.
MARSH Fred MM Pte R/19929 King's Royal Rifle Corps
MARSH George MM Pte 20914 Shropshire Light Infantry
MARSH George MM Sjt 49045 Lancashire Fusiliers
MARSH George MM Sjt 99759 C/50 Bde RFA
MARSH George MM Sjt 675405 RFA
MARSH George MM Pte 41142 4th Worcestershire Regt
MARSH George Henry MM Pte 61919 1/8th West Yorkshire Regt KIA 27.9.18.
MARSH George J. MM Sjt 350271 7th London Regt
MARSH George V.F. MM Pte M2/153797 Army Service Corps
MARSH George W. MM Bdr 8950 RFA
MARSH Giles W.F. MM Pte 2047 1/21st London Regt
MARSH Harry MM+Bar Sjt 23817 Machine Gun Corps
MARSH Harry W. MM L/Cpl 26889 Notts & Derby Regt
MARSH Henry MM L/Sjt 20356 4th Grenadier Guards KIA 13.4.18.
MARSH Henry MM Dvr 28024 'C' Bty RHA
MARSH Henry Herbert MM Sjt 36348 88 Bty 14 Bde RFA
MARSH Henry J. MM Sjt 9943 6th Dorsetshire Regt
MARSH Jacob MM Sjt 53138 RFA
MARSH James MM Spr 143468 94 Fd Coy Royal Engineers
MARSH James MM L/Cpl 5347 Leinster Regt
MARSH James MM Pte 32480 12th Middlesex Regt
MARSH James William MM CSM 18822 60th Bn Machine Gun Corps Died 7.10.18.
MARSH John MM Cpl 16429 138 Hy Bty RGA
MARSH John MM Pte 86017 29th Bn Machine Gun Corps
MARSH John MM Pte 38863 RAMC
MARSH John W. MM Pte 6732 6th East Kent Regt
MARSH Jolly MM L/Sjt 265510 Seaforth Highlanders
MARSH Joseph William MM L/Cpl 39573 2nd South Wales Borderers DOW 22.11.17.
MARSH Keith O. MM Cpl 70795 1 Bty 45 Bde RFA
MARSH Melville MM Pte 8641 11th Royal West Kent Regt DOW 16.6.17.
MARSH Norman MM+Bar Bdr 706160 B/255 Bde RFA
MARSH Norman E. MM Bdr 50405 RHA
MARSH Osborne George MM Sjt 11604 16th Manchester Regt KIA 31.7.17.
MARSH Reginald B. MM Sjt 620139 RFA
MARSH Robert E.S. MM Sjt 32472 121 Hy Bty RGA
MARSH Rowland J. MM Bdr 50974 RFA
MARSH Rowland Victor Parry MM Cpl S/1034 11th Rifle Brigade
MARSH S.A. MM Cpl 33035 15 Bde RFA
MARSH Stanley MM Pte 36325 Yorkshire Regt
MARSH Thomas MM L/Cpl 243192 North Lancashire Regt
MARSH Thomas MM Pnr 128560 Royal Engineers
MARSH Thomas MM Cpl 29647 East Lancashire Regt
MARSH Vincent J. MM Pte S/28274 Rifle Brigade
MARSH Walter MM Cpl 18158 East Lancashire Regt
MARSH William "MM,MSM" Sjt 78655 Royal Engineers att 90 HAG RGA.
MARSH William MM Pte 11/928 11th East Yorkshire Regt
MARSH William MM L/Cpl 25207 Machine Gun Corps
MARSH William MM L/Cpl 246779 Royal Engineers
MARSH William MM Pte 41771 11th Essex Regt KIA 12.10.18.
MARSH William MM Sjt 14200 11th Essex Regt KIA 22.3.18.
MARSH William MM Pte 41760 RAMC
MARSH William MM Gnr 40965 40 Bde RFA
MARSH William E. MM Sjt 520063 565 Army Troops Coy Royal Engineers
MARSHALL A. MM Pte 403468 RAMC
MARSHALL Alan S. MM Sjt 240519 1st Norfolk Regt
MARSHALL Albert MM Pte 10398 1st Notts & Derby Regt KIA 31.7.17.
MARSHALL Albert "MM,MID" Trumpeter 4220 19th Hussars
MARSHALL Albert E. MM Cpl 476248 Royal Engineers
MARSHALL Albert O. MM Gnr 155104 RFA
MARSHALL Albert R. MM L/Cpl 23516 8th Yorkshire Light Infantry
MARSHALL Albert W. MM Cpl 43546 2nd Royal Dublin Fusiliers
MARSHALL Alexander McA. MM L/Sjt 11932 Scottish Rifles
MARSHALL Alfred MM L/Cpl 7380 11th Royal Fusiliers KIA 6.8.18.
MARSHALL Alfred MM Pte 29674 15th Cheshire Regt DOW 2.11.17.
MARSHALL Alfred E. "MM,MSM" Sjt 392122 9th London Regt
MARSHALL Alfred S. MM Dvr 212930 RFA
MARSHALL Alick "MM,MID" L/Cpl 406358 Royal Engineers
MARSHALL Andrew MM Pte 13/6028 11th Royal Irish Rifles KIA 1.7.16.
MARSHALL Arthur MM Pte 20437 Grenadier Guards

MARSHALL Arthur MM Pte 157430 18th Bn Machine Gun Corps
MARSHALL Arthur MM Pte 71362 Notts & Derby Regt
MARSHALL Arthur MM Pte 47530 23rd Manchester Regt KIA 22.10.17.
MARSHALL Arthur E. MM Spr 84458 Royal Engineers
MARSHALL Arthur Frederick MM Pte 22154 12th Suffolk Regt KIA 9.1.18.
MARSHALL Arthur H. MM Sjt 37204 12th Somerset Light Infantry
MARSHALL Arthur T. MM Pte 3107 West Yorkshire Regt
MARSHALL Augustus MM+Bar CSM G/10137 10th Royal West Kent Regt
MARSHALL C. MM Pte 4061 Seaforth Highlanders
MARSHALL C.H. MM Sjt 37672 D/157 Bde RFA
MARSHALL Cecil MM+Bar Pte 4169 2nd Royal West Surrey Regt
MARSHALL Charles MM Pte 20372 2nd East Surrey Regt
MARSHALL Charles MM Gnr 67021 X/34 Med TM Bty RGA DOW 26.12.17
MARSHALL Charles A. MM Sjt G/18463 10th Royal West Kent Regt
MARSHALL Charles Edmund MM Pte 1635 9 Fd Amb RAMC
MARSHALL Charles Justice MM Pte 6845 7th East Yorkshire Regt
MARSHALL Charles Stuart "MC,MM(R/6196 Sjt)" T/2Lt 13th King's Royal Rifle Corps
MARSHALL Charlie MM Cpl 5113 5th Connaught Rangers KIA 10.10.18.
MARSHALL Clifford J. MM Sjt G/714 7th Royal Sussex Regt
MARSHALL Cyril MM Cpl 16884 6th Oxf & Bucks Light Infantry
MARSHALL Daniel MM Pte 2635 2nd Royal Highlanders KIA 22.4.16.
MARSHALL David MM Gnr 7558 RFA
MARSHALL Denis "DCM+Bar,MM,MID" BSM 52363 D/156 Bde RFA
MARSHALL Edward MM+Bar Pte B/203482 1st Rifle Brigade
MARSHALL Edward J. MM Pte 266814 1/1st Hertfordshire Regt
MARSHALL Ernest MM Pte 55573 11th Northumberland Fusiliers DOW 18.6.18.
MARSHALL Ernest MM Pte 12353 6th Royal Berkshire Regt
MARSHALL Ernest A. MM Pte 70078 11th Royal West Surrey Regt
MARSHALL Ernest A. MM Cpl 570495 1/17tth London Regt
MARSHALL Ernest H. MM L/Cpl 482148 Royal Engineers
MARSHALL Francis James MM Gnr 89178 172 Siege Bty RGA
MARSHALL Frank A. MM Cpl 32820 6 Div Sig Coy Royal Engineers
MARSHALL Frank E. MM Gnr 88303 RGA
MARSHALL Frank G. MM Pte 202964 1st London Regt
MARSHALL Fred "MM,MID" L/Cpl 1852 Yorkshire Light Infantry
MARSHALL Fred MM Pte 19086 9th York & Lancaster Regt
MARSHALL Frederick MM Bdr 56138 RGA
MARSHALL Frederick MM Pte R/17562 King's Royal Rifle Corps
MARSHALL Frederick C. MM Pte 235251 Gordon Highlanders
MARSHALL Frederick J. MM Pte 11350 4th Royal Fusiliers
MARSHALL George MM Pte 39434 16th Lancashire Fusiliers
MARSHALL George MM Pte 12615 9th Essex Regt
MARSHALL George MM Sjt A/2044 2nd King's Royal Rifle Corps
MARSHALL George MM Pte 3589 1/1st Cambridgeshire Regt
MARSHALL George MM Pte M2/105416 Army Service Corps
MARSHALL George Arthur MM Cpl 147047 'B' Special Coy Royal Engineers
MARSHALL George Edward MM Sjt 27553 6th Yorkshire Regt
MARSHALL George F. MM Bdr 39119 RGA
MARSHALL George H. MM Pte 200206 1/5th West Yorkshire Regt
MARSHALL George Harry MM Pte 49335 Machine Gun Corps
MARSHALL George J. MM Pte 470449 12th London Regt
MARSHALL Gilbert MM Bdr 112644 D/77 Bde RFA Died 2.9.18.
MARSHALL H. MM Pte 24403 West Riding Regt
MARSHALL H.J. MM+Bar Cpl 108568 233 Fd Coy Royal Engineers
MARSHALL Harold MM Pte C/8037 King's Royal Rifle Corps
MARSHALL Harry MM Spr 51617 24 Div Sig Coy Royal Engineers
MARSHALL Harry MM L/Cpl 306779 West Riding Regt
MARSHALL Harry E. MM Gnr 855 RFA
MARSHALL Herbert F.S. MM Sjt 43652 9th Bn Machine Gun Corps
MARSHALL Hewitt MM Pte 24218 5th Notts & Derby Regt
MARSHALL Horace MM Pte 45387 122 Coy Machine Gun Corps
MARSHALL Hubert C. MM Pte 11502 2nd West Riding Regt
MARSHALL J. MM L/Cpl 33571 Yorkshire Regt
MARSHALL J.W. MM Sjt 16095 9th West Yorkshire Regt
MARSHALL James MM Sjt 7576 31 Army Tps Coy Royal Engineers
MARSHALL James MM Sjt 275111 1/7th Arg & Suth Highlanders
MARSHALL James MM Pte R/10902 King's Royal Rifle Corps
MARSHALL James H. MM Sjt 1501 RFA
MARSHALL James Paton MM Sjt 49450 Royal Engineers
MARSHALL John MM Gnr 178162 291 Siege Bty RGA
MARSHALL John MM Pte 35765 2nd Highland Light Infantry
MARSHALL John MM Pte 24042 10th Lancashire Fusiliers
MARSHALL John J. MM Cpl 28728 8th Royal Berkshire Regt
MARSHALL John T. MM Pte 16325 Shropshire Light Infantry
MARSHALL John William MM Pte 18252 9th Royal Irish Fusiliers KIA 25.7.18.
MARSHALL Joseph MM CSM 23708 18th Welsh Regt
MARSHALL Joseph W. MM Bdr 785473 C/150 Bde RFA
MARSHALL Kenneth MM L/Cpl 553990 1/16th London Regt
MARSHALL Malcolm MM Cpl 21357 2nd Northumberland Fusiliers
MARSHALL Mary Devas MM Miss F First Aid Nursing Yeomanry
MARSHALL Maurice Edgar MM Pte 16/721 11th West Yorkshire Regt
MARSHALL P. MM Pte M/378618 Army Service Corps
MARSHALL P.H. MM Cpl 25076 Royal Flying Corps
MARSHALL Percy MM Pte 18668 Royal Berkshire Regt
MARSHALL Peter MM L/Sjt 40436 8th Royal Highlanders KIA 19.7.18.
MARSHALL Ralph A. MM Gnr 341066 RGA
MARSHALL Richard MM Pte 40341 1/7th Lancashire Fusiliers
MARSHALL Richard MM Cpl 66809 RFA
MARSHALL Robert MM Cpl 41114 Royal Scots Fusiliers
MARSHALL Robert MM Spr 64119 121 Fd Coy Royal Engineers
MARSHALL Robert "DCM,MM" Sjt 631561 B/255 Bde RFA
MARSHALL Robert MM Pte 29703 East Yorkshire Regt
MARSHALL Robert Douglas MM Pte 57882 15th Cheshire Regt KIA 28.2.18.
MARSHALL Samuel MM Gnr 76653 Tank Corps
MARSHALL Sidney MM Pte 41049 1st South Wales Borderers
MARSHALL Sydney A. MM Gnr 41122 8 Bde RFA
MARSHALL Thomas MM Gnr 68719 25 Bde RFA
MARSHALL Thomas MM Cpl 4344 1/6th Arg & Suth Highlanders
MARSHALL Thomas MM Pte 73082 164 Coy Machine Gun Corps
MARSHALL Thomas E. MM L/Cpl M2/077740 Army Service Corps
MARSHALL Tom R. MM Sjt 200693 West Yorkshire Regt
MARSHALL W.E. MM Pte 202518 York & Lancaster Regt
MARSHALL W.J. MM Pte 14449 2nd Grenadier Guards
MARSHALL Walter MM Pte 25892 Wiltshire Regt
MARSHALL Walter MM Pte 115 17th West Yorkshire Regt
MARSHALL Walter Ernest MM Cpl 14837 9th North Lancashire Regt
MARSHALL Walter John MM Pte 17558 2nd Coldstream Guards KIA 1.12.17.
MARSHALL Wilfred MM Gnr 141938 103 Siege Bty RGA
MARSHALL Wilfred O. MM Sjt L/13297 1st Middlesex Regt
MARSHALL William MM L/Cpl 201014 Notts & Derby Regt
MARSHALL William MM Bdr 26986 RFA
MARSHALL William MM Gnr 631436 RFA
MARSHALL William MM Sjt 43512 Highland Light Infantry
MARSHALL William MM Cpl 18851 3rd Hussars
MARSHALL William MM Pte 1650 Arg & Suth Highlanders
MARSHALL William MM Pte 29241 Royal Welsh Fusiliers
MARSHALL William A. MM L/Cpl 9703 2nd Royal Berkshire Regt
MARSHALL William A. MM Pte 266394 4th West Riding Regt
MARSHALL William A. MM Gnr 63126 RGA
MARSHALL William C.W. MM Cpl 7728 4th Hampshire Regt
MARSHALL William F. MM Pte 83339 RAMC
MARSHALL William J. MM Gnr 220427 C/78 Bde RFA
MARSHALL William M. MM Sjt 99771 RFA
MARSHALL William W. MM Pte 5489 Northumberland Fusiliers
MARSHALSEY William MM L/Cpl S/40520 Royal Highlanders
MARSHMAN Percy MM Dvr 113443 D/82 Bde RFA
MARSHMAN William J. MM Pte 16666 Northumberland Fusiliers
MARSKELL A.J. MM Cpl 750537 B/315 Bde RFA
MARSKELL George MM Pte PW/5064 Middlesex Regt
MARSLAND Herbert MM Spr 51941 Royal Engineers
MARSLAND John MM L/Bdr 47291 40 Div Ammn Col RFA
MARSLAND Thomas H. MM Gnr 680947 286 Bde RFA
MARSLAND William R. MM Sjt 247917 Royal Engineers
MARSLIN William MM CQMS 9401 1st Royal West Kent Regt
MARSON George MM Dvr 80527 20 Div Ammn Col RFA
MARSON George R. MM L/Cpl 351111 1/7th London Regt
MARSON William MM Gnr 42198 RFA
MARSTON Frederick G. MM Sjt 12964 2nd Royal Fusiliers
MARSTON Frederick L.B. MM Cpl 2994 18th London Regt
MARSTON John MM Pte 10143 1st Shropshire Light Infantry
MARSTON John L.I. MM Pte 63252 RAMC
MARSTON Joseph C. MM Sjt 265280 Royal Warwickshire Regt
MARSTON Norman MM Pte 23682 6th Royal West Surrey Regt
MARSTON Thomas MM+2 Bars Sjt 241289 5th Leicestershire Regt
MARSTON William MM Sjt 65938 18 Bde RFA

MARTEN Cyril E.H. MM+Bar Cpl 207578 63 Div Sig Coy Royal Engineers
MARTIN A.S. MM Spr 18332 Royal Engineers
MARTIN Albert MM Pte 43983 5th Royal Berkshire Regt
MARTIN Albert "MM,MID" Bdr 54848 44 Siege Bty RGA
MARTIN Albert MM Pte 18914 Royal West Surrey Regt
MARTIN Albert E. MM Sjt 9209 2nd Wiltshire Regt
MARTIN Albert William MM Gnr 94409 B/290 Bde RFA
MARTIN Alfred MM Sjt 11616 B/156 Bde RFA
MARTIN Alfred MM L/Cpl 304271 London Regt
MARTIN Alfred Edward MM Cpl 8029 Army Cyclist Corps
MARTIN Alfred J. MM Sjt 370151 1/8th London Regt
MARTIN Alfred W. MM Pte 77959 10th Royal Fusiliers
MARTIN Alfred W. MM Pte 13664 9th Worcestershire Regt
MARTIN Alfred W. MM Sjt 240380 1/5th Leicestershire Regt
MARTIN Alfred William MM Pte 13/43646 12th Royal Irish Rifles
MARTIN Allan W. MM Pte 47673 RAMC
MARTIN Anthony MM Dvr 103834 RFA
MARTIN Arthur E. MM+Bar L/Bdr 40293 RFA
MARTIN Arthur Theodore MM Sjt 18357 15th Hampshire Regt
MARTIN Arthur W. MM L/Cpl 11484 6th Wiltshire Regt
MARTIN Arthur William MM Sjt 9644 1st Scottish Rifles KIA 20.7.16.
MARTIN Augustus H. MM Pte 19096 8th Somerset Light Infantry
MARTIN Baron MM Pte L/14667 3rd Royal Fusiliers
MARTIN Bernard "MM,MID" Sjt 11763 5th Royal Irish Fusiliers
MARTIN Bertram Charles MM Cpl 10964 4th Royal Fusiliers KIA 13.4.17.
MARTIN C.S. "DCM,MM" Sjt A/2096 9th King's Royal Rifle Corps
MARTIN Cecil MM Cpl 37655 Yorkshire Light Infantry
MARTIN Charles MM L/Cpl P/4365 Rifle Brigade
MARTIN Charles MM L/Cpl 14493 King's Own Scottish Borderers
MARTIN Charles MM Pte 8817 1st Scots Guards
MARTIN Charles MM Pte 14892 1st Scots Guards
MARTIN Charles A. MM Cpl 439624 3rd(South Midland)Fd Amb RAMC
MARTIN Charles Amos MM Pte 9258 142 Fd Amb RAMC
MARTIN Charles E. MM Pte 1480 1/1st London Regt
MARTIN Charles Frederick Hunter MM Pte K/1551 22nd Royal Fusiliers
MARTIN Charles G. MM Sjt 12165 3rd Middlesex Regt
MARTIN Charles G. MM L/Cpl 18364 Royal Lancaster Regt
MARTIN Charles Horace Henry MM Pte 7570 6th Royal West Kent Regt KIA 30.6.18.
MARTIN Charles J. MM Pte S/8162 Seaforth Highlanders
MARTIN Charles T. MM L/Cpl S/3016 Rifle Brigade
MARTIN Claude MM+Bar Pte 201034 Suffolk Regt
MARTIN Cornelius MM Pte 358263 1/10th Liverpool Regt
MARTIN Cyril MM Sjt 10520 3rd Dragoon Guards
MARTIN Daniel MM CQMS 200105 1/4th Seaforth Highlanders
MARTIN Daniel W. MM Sjt 32498 45 Bde RFA
MARTIN David MM Sjt 30502 Scottish Rifles
MARTIN David "MM,MSM,MID" SM 252 Royal Flying Corps
MARTIN David MM Pte 34454 13th Manchester Regt
MARTIN David McA. MM Pte 40743 Arg & Suth Highlanders
MARTIN David Wallace MM Pte 5487 8th East Surrey Regt KIA 3.5.17.
MARTIN Denis "DCM,MM" Sjt 61429 12th Manchester Regt
MARTIN Dennis MM Pte 16658 Machine Gun Corps
MARTIN Donald MM Pte 17474 8 Coy Machine Gun Corps KIA 3.5.17.
MARTIN Donald R. MM Pte 1340 Royal Warwickshire Regt
MARTIN E. MM Sjt 1366 5th Yorkshire Light Infantry
MARTIN E. MM CQMS 473 1/6th North Staffordshire Regt
MARTIN Edgar MM Sjt 87820 RGA
MARTIN Edgar A.O. MM Sjt T4/251921 62 Div Train Army Service Corps
MARTIN Edgar Shemilt MM Pte 201973 2/5th North Staffordshire Regt DOW 21.8.18.
MARTIN Edgar T. "DCM,MM+Bar,MID" Sjt 58230 'H' & 'N' Btys RHA
MARTIN Edmund Clarence "DCM,MM" CSM 65658 126 Fd Coy Royal Engineers
MARTIN Edward MM L/Cpl 241548 1/6th West Yorkshire Regt DOW 7.10.17.
MARTIN Edward MM Sjt 14056 7th North Lancashire Regt
MARTIN Edward C. MM Pte M2/178387 Army Service Corps att RN Div
MARTIN Edwin MM Cpl 82298 15th Bn Machine Gun Corps
MARTIN Edwin MM Sjt L/13465 19th Middlesex Regt KIA 15.4.18.
MARTIN Edwin MM L/Cpl 21181 7th Royal West Surrey Regt KIA 28.8.18.

MARTIN Ernest V. MM+Bar Pte 52340 Royal Fusiliers
MARTIN Ernest W. MM BQMS L/1226 189 Bde RFA
MARTIN F. MM Cpl 38317 9th Northumberland Fusiliers
MARTIN F. MM L/Bdr L/39474 D/175 Bde RFA
MARTIN Frank MM Pte 7/4447 Royal Irish Rifles
MARTIN Frank MM Gnr 71572 137 Siege Bty RGA
MARTIN Frank W. MM Pte 9/26263 9th Royal Lancaster Regt
MARTIN Fred MM Sjt 31252 2nd Northamptonshire Regt
MARTIN Fred MM Pte 23284 7th East Lancashire Regt
MARTIN Frederick MM Spr 267490 Royal Engineers
MARTIN Frederick MM Spr 79246 Royal Engineers
MARTIN Frederick MM Spr 100470 33 Div Sig Coy Royal Engineers
MARTIN Frederick MM Gnr 83299 RGA
MARTIN Frederick A. MM Pte 200718 2/7th Middlesex Regt
MARTIN Frederick J. MM Cpl 22218 Dorsetshire Regt
MARTIN Frederick T. MM Pte 48158 130 Fd Amb RAMC
MARTIN Frederick William MM Sjt 930256 A/281 Bde RFA
MARTIN G. MM Cpl 10708 Duke of Cornwall's LI
MARTIN George MM Pte 22822 6th Royal West Surrey Regt
MARTIN George MM Pte 6600 6th East Kent Regt
MARTIN George MM Dvr 85215 RFA
MARTIN George MM Pte 43975 1/8th Middlesex Regt KIA 24.8.18.
MARTIN George MM Cpl 15103 11th Essex Regt DOW 19.9.18.
MARTIN George MM Pte S/16186 1st Royal Highlanders
MARTIN George MM Cpl T4/045136 Army Service Corps
MARTIN George MM Pte 5859 Worcestershire Regt
MARTIN George Charles MM Cpl M2/137489 654 MT Coy Army Service Corps
MARTIN George E. "DCM,MM" CSM 9242 6th Wiltshire Regt
MARTIN George H. MM CSM 40033 7th Northamptonshire Regt
MARTIN George H. MM Sjt 67543 12th Bn Machine Gun Corps
MARTIN George H. MM Sjt 50988 40 Bde RFA
MARTIN George W. MM Cpl 68644 40 Bde RFA
MARTIN Gerald MM Pte 1196 3rd Hussars
MARTIN Guy Stanislaus MM Spr 25002 5 Div Sig Coy Royal Engineers KIA 25.8.18.
MARTIN H.A. MM S/Sjt Farrier 4324 10th Hussars
MARTIN H.F. MM L/Cpl 44137 Devonshire Regt
MARTIN Harold MM Pte 22494 2nd Northumberland Fusiliers
MARTIN Harold MM L/Cpl 21270 10th Yorkshire Light Infantry KIA 17.9.16.
MARTIN Harold S. MM+Bar Cpl 18782 3 Div Sig Coy Royal Engineers
MARTIN Harry MM Sjt 7683 2nd Manchester Regt DOW 13.9.18.
MARTIN Harry MM Pte 28215 15th Hampshire Regt
MARTIN Harry MM Sjt 13651 35 Heavy Bty RGA
MARTIN Harry MM L/Cpl 1112 2nd Royal Warwickshire Regt
MARTIN Harry M. MM Sjt 22163 Royal Engineers
MARTIN Harry Phipp MM Pte 17409 Leicestershire Regt
MARTIN Hedley Roy MM Sjt 35313 14th Royal Warwickshire Regt
MARTIN Henry MM L/Cpl SD/4956 16th Royal Sussex Regt
MARTIN Henry MM Dvr 37607 43 Bde RFA
MARTIN Henry A. MM 2nd Cpl 543913 Royal Engineers
MARTIN Henry F. MM+Bar Cpl 15260 1st Hampshire Regt
MARTIN Henry G. MM Pte 377135 8th London Regt
MARTIN Henry J. MM L/Cpl R/3118 13th King's Royal Rifle Corps
MARTIN Herbert MM+Bar 2nd Cpl 170040 233 Fd Coy Royal Engineers
MARTIN Herbert E. MM Gnr 5079 RFA
MARTIN Herbert W. MM L/Cpl 48762 North Staffordshire Regt
MARTIN Herbert William MM Pte 8850 13th Middlesex Regt KIA 28.4.17.
MARTIN Horace MM L/Cpl 16/157 10th West Yorkshire Regt
MARTIN Hugh MM Pte 9236 1st Highland Light Infantry
MARTIN Hugh Mullins MM Pte 230129 1/1st Dorset Yeomanry
MARTIN J. MM Pte 6978 Irish Guards
MARTIN J.R. MM Pte 200176 Scottish Rifles
MARTIN J.S. MM Gnr 14037 RFA
MARTIN James MM L/Cpl 24475 Royal West Surrey Regt
MARTIN James MM Pte 15543 9th Royal Dublin Fusiliers
MARTIN James MM Sjt 37180 Northumberland Fusiliers
MARTIN James Charles MM L/Cpl 12848 9th Norfolk Regt KIA 21.3.18.
MARTIN James F. MM 2nd Cpl 66379 21 Div Sig Coy Royal Engineers
MARTIN Jesse MM Spr 194504 Royal Engineers
MARTIN John "MM,MID" Sjt 7616 1st Hampshire Regt
MARTIN John MM Pte DM2/129938 Army Service Corps att 155 SBAC RGA
MARTIN John MM Gnr 7980 RFA

MARTIN John MM Sjt 41453 10th Scottish Rifles
MARTIN John MM Cpl 446196 438 Fd Coy Royal Engineers
MARTIN John MM Pte 5531 Seaforth Highlanders
MARTIN John MM Spr 155855 251 Tunnelling Coy Royal Engineers DOW 10.4.18.
MARTIN John MM L/Cpl 325126 1/9th Durham Light Infantry KIA 24.5.18.
MARTIN John MM Pte 34900 Middlesex Regt
MARTIN John MM Pte 55596 RAMC
MARTIN John MM Sjt 49992 5 Pontoon Park Royal Engineers
MARTIN John A. MM Bdr 39675 8 Siege Bty RGA
MARTIN John T. MM Pte 3704 1 Fd Amb RAMC
MARTIN John T. MM Bdr 915456 RFA
MARTIN John W. MM Gnr 35601 A/123 Bde RFA
MARTIN John William MM Sjt T/26588 8 Reserve Park Army Service Corps
MARTIN Joseph MM L/Cpl 9249 1st Royal Irish Fusiliers
MARTIN Joseph MM Pte 27874 Labour Corps
MARTIN Joseph MM Pte 17624 1st Leicestershire Regt Died 3.11.18.
MARTIN Joseph MM Cpl 265791 1/6th Northumberland Fusiliers
MARTIN Joseph J. MM L/Cpl 29959 9th Yorkshire Light Infantry
MARTIN Julian T. MM Cpl 21944 7 Fd Coy Royal Engineers
MARTIN Leslie J. MM Cpl 64934 RFA
MARTIN Leslie R. MM Spr 282326 36 Div Sig Coy Royal Engineers
MARTIN Louis MM Pte 114184 17th Liverpool Regt
MARTIN Louis H. MM Pte 18084 5th Wiltshire Regt
MARTIN Mark MM Pte 28175 9th Yorkshire Regt DOW 17.10.18.
MARTIN Mathew MM Pte 11977 Liverpool Regt
MARTIN Nicholas MM Cpl 470384 Royal Engineers
MARTIN Patrick MM L/Cpl 250381 5/6th Royal Scots
MARTIN Percy William Henry MM Sjt 200167 1st Bn Tank Corps
MARTIN Rankin MM Sjt 282 22nd Royal Fusiliers Died 12.7.18.
MARTIN Reginald MM 2nd Cpl 134947 Royal Engineers
MARTIN Reginald MM Pte 530512 2/15th London Regt DOW 14.10.18.
MARTIN Reginald C. MM Bdr 69180 25 Bde RFA
MARTIN Reginald S.W. MM+Bar Sjt 32743 Lincolnshire Regt
MARTIN Richard MM Cpl 15149 1st Bedfordshire Regt
MARTIN Richard MM Gnr 163616 C/317 Bde RFA
MARTIN Richard MM Sjt 16165 Machine Gun Corps
MARTIN Richard L. MM Cpl G/18470 7th Royal West Kent Regt
MARTIN Robert MM L/Cpl 240266 1/5th King's Own Scottish Borderers
MARTIN Robert MM Pte G/19180 9th Royal Sussex Regt
MARTIN Robert MM L/Cpl 36043 Yorkshire Light Infantry
MARTIN Robert MM L/Cpl 275687 1/7th Arg & Suth Highlanders
MARTIN Robert "MM,MID" Sjt 17126 Machine Gun Corps
MARTIN Robert MM Sjt 2328 1/5th Royal Highlanders
MARTIN S. MM Pte G/27350 8th Middlesex Regt
MARTIN Sam MM Sjt 12759 7th B Coy Lincolnshire Regt KIA 28.8.17.
MARTIN Samuel MM Pte 275425 1/7th Arg & Suth Highlanders
MARTIN Samuel G. MM+2 Bars 2nd Cpl 56757 18 Div Sig Coy Royal Engineers
MARTIN Samuel Henry MM+Bar Sjt 12225 11th Royal Fusiliers KIA 23.3.18.
MARTIN Silas MM Dvr 95644 RFA
MARTIN Stanley MM Pte 106119 32nd Bn Machine Gun Corps
MARTIN Stanley MM Sjt 1440 1/7th Middlesex Regt
MARTIN Stanley MM Sjt 200620 1/4th Royal Berkshire Regt KIA 18.9.18.
MARTIN Stephen J. MM Sjt 33494 8th Somerset Light Infantry
MARTIN Sydney MM Pte S/19880 Rifle Brigade
MARTIN Sydney Arthur MM Cpl 14719 11th Essex Regt DOW 15.9.17.
MARTIN Sydney R. MM Pte MS/4281 Army Service Corps
MARTIN T. MM Pte 4548 London Regt
MARTIN T. MM Pte 17513 Gordon Highlanders
MARTIN T.H. MM Sjt 228 RGA
MARTIN Thomas MM Cpl 751253 D/250 Bde RFA
MARTIN Thomas MM+Bar Pte 82498 11th Royal Fusiliers
MARTIN Thomas MM L/Sjt 2402 1/8th Notts & Derby Regt
MARTIN Thomas MM L/Cpl 1277 1/5th Durham Light Infantry DOW 26.6.17.
MARTIN Thomas MM L/Cpl S/9300 Seaforth Highlanders
MARTIN Thomas MM Cpl 9715 B/71 Bde RFA
MARTIN Thomas James William MM Gnt Fitter 86694 25 Bde RFA
MARTIN Thompson MM L/Sjt 21047 13th Northumberland Fusiliers
MARTIN W. MM Dvr 4327 RFA
MARTIN Wallace MM+Bar Sjt 375337 10th Manchester Regt
MARTIN Walter MM Pte L/8782 1st East Kent Regt DOW 28.10.18.
MARTIN Walter "MM,MIDx2" Sjt 48712 96 Fd Coy Royal Engineers
MARTIN Walter MM Spr 2923 Royal Engineers
MARTIN Walter MM+Bar Cpl 4079 Machine Gun Corps
MARTIN Walter J. MM Pte 5956 10th Royal Warwickshire Regt
MARTIN Walter R. MM Sjt 23745 Royal Engineers
MARTIN William MM Gnr 65372 Z/6 Med TM Bty RGA
MARTIN William MM Pte 20462 15th Welsh Regt KIA 30.8.18.
MARTIN William MM+Bar Pte 348019 1/8th Manchester Regt
MARTIN William MM Sjt 305544 1/8th Notts & Derby Regt
MARTIN William MM+Bar Sjt 265466 1/6th Royal Highlanders
MARTIN William MM Cpl 241412 Notts & Derby Regt
MARTIN William MM Pte 31972 Royal Scots Fusiliers
MARTIN William "MM,MSM" BQMS 31242 229 Siege Bty RGA
MARTIN William MM Pte 229147 6th South Wales Borderers
MARTIN William A. MM Sjt 203104 2/4th Royal West Surrey Regt
MARTIN William D. MM Pte 18989 7th South Staffordshire Regt
MARTIN William E. MM L/Cpl 10147 9th Royal Sussex Regt
MARTIN William F. MM L/Sjt S/7797 4th Middlesex Regt
MARTIN William F. MM CSM M/31723 6 Div Train Army Service Corps
MARTIN William H. MM Pte 307628 1/8th Notts & Derby Regt
MARTIN William H. MM Dvr 13791 RFA
MARTIN William H. MM Cpl 8032 1st Gloucestershire Regt
MARTIN William H. MM Bdr 296 RGA
MARTIN William J. MM Pte 241072 1/5th Devonshire Regt
MARTIN William J. MM CQMS 8920 1st Royal Scots Fusiliers
MARTIN William J. MM Dvr 796893 63 Div Ammn Col RFA
MARTIN William John "DCM,MM" L/Sjt 13243 2nd Middlesex Regt att 1st Bn
MARTIN William John MM L/Cpl 18218 13th Royal Sussex Regt
MARTIN William John MM Pte 36031 2nd South Lancashire Regt KIA 3.4.18.
MARTIN William John Edward MM Pte 20348 3rd Grenadier Guards
MARTIN William Joseph "MM,CG(F)" L/Cpl 14969 8th Duke of Cornwall's LI
MARTIN William M. MM Cpl 14368 1/8th Arg & Suth Highlanders
MARTIN William Thomas MM L/Cpl 12391 6th Dorsetshire Regt
MARTIN William Thomas MM Pte M2/132476 699 MT Coy Army Service Corps
MARTINDALE Arthur Percy MM Sjt 590594 1/18th London Regt
MARTINDALE Fred MM Pte 1933 1st Royal Lancaster Regt
MARTINDALE Peter MM Cpl 11339 9th West Riding Regt
MARTINDALE Robert MM Cpl 5354 B/68 Bde RFA
MARTINDALE Thomas MM Pte 204458 5th Liverpool Regt
MARTINDALE William MM L/Bdr 48016 RFA
MARTINELLI John "MM,MID" Pte 5/4981 1st King's Royal Rifle Corps
MARTINSCROFT Samuel MM Pte 21210 Royal Lancaster Regt
MARTYN John N. MM Spr 63663 130 Fd Coy Royal Engineers
MARTYN William MM Sjt 54857 Royal Fusiliers
MARVEN Frank James MM 2nd Cpl 559439 29 Div Sig Coy Royal Engineers
MARVIN Alfred F. MM CSM 27582 Somerset Light Infantry
MARVIN Arthur MM 2nd Cpl 25933 Royal Engineers
MARWICK A. MM L/Sjt 115792 4th Bn Machine Gun Corps
MARWICK J. MM Pte 3/2139 Imperial Camel Corps
MARWICK Thomas MM Sjt 19/516 19th Northumberland Fusiliers
MARWICK William MM L/Cpl 22330 Cameron Highlanders
MARWOOD John MM Pte 18798 7th Yorkshire Regt
MARWOOD Vincent MM Bdr 30594 RFA
MARYGOLD Ernest J. MM Sjt 27938 2nd Notts & Derby Regt
MASCALL Edward C. MM Pte 21213 Machine Gun Corps
MASCALL George Samuel MM Gnr Fitter 17586 377 Bty RFA
MASE Reginald MM Cpl 59076 9th Northumberland Fusiliers
MASEY Arthur W. MM Cpl 59588 147 Army Tps Coy Royal Engineers
MASH George MM Pte P/914 Rifle Brigade
MASH George William MM Sjt MS/2808 1 Div Train Army Service Corps
MASH William John Rutland MM Cpl 530111 2/15th London Regt
MASHEDER Wiliam "DCM,MM" CSM 14770 Yorkshire Regt
MASHITER Joseph Wren MM L/Sjt 240389 1/5th Royal Lancaster Regt
MASKELL Alfred MM Pte 29944 Somerset Light Infantry
MASKELL Arthur MM Cpl 44273 Manchester Regt
MASKELL C.Harry MM Sjt 250399 Manchester Regt
MASKELL E. MM RSM 2587 6 Div Ammn Col RFA
MASKELL Edward Charles William MM Sjt 27910 143 Heavy Bty RGA

MASKELL George F. MM L/Cpl G/2067 8th Royal Sussex Regt
MASKELL James MM Dvr 13278 463 Bty 179 Bde RFA
MASKELL Sidney MM Pte 49439 Royal Fusiliers
MASKELL Thomas MM L/Cpl 200932 South Lancashire Regt
MASKELL Victor G. MM Sjt 3065 9th Royal Sussex Regt
MASKELL Walter C. MM Pte 28889 Royal Warwickshire Regt
MASKELL William Jethro "MM+Bar,MID,CG(F)" L/Sjt 9246 1st Northumberland Fusiliers
MASKERY William A. MM Sjt 486316 268 Fd Coy Royal Engineers
MASKILL Henry MM Sjt 240719 Yorkshire Light Infantry
MASKREY Ernest MM Gnr 800687 D/230 Bde RFA
MASKREY Herbert L. MM Sjt 15584 5 Div Sig Coy Royal Engineers
MASKREY Isaac Mart MM Bdr 5779 B/161 Bde RFA DOW 11.12.17.
MASKREY John W. MM Cpl 7719 15 Fd Amb RAMC
MASLIN Jesse MM+Bar 2nd Cpl 87537 Royal Engineers
MASON Albert MM L/Cpl 6785 1st Devonshire Regt
MASON Albert J. MM Cpl 2977 1/15th London Regt
MASON Albert J. MM Pte 4509 13th Middlesex Regt
MASON Alfred MM Pte 240118 6th South Staffordshire Regt
MASON Alfred MM Pte G/2177 12th Middlesex Regt KIA 3.5.17.
MASON Alfred MM L/Cpl 24263 South Wales Borderers
MASON Archibald Douglas MM Pte S/13260 6th Cameron Highlanders DOW 25.9.16.
MASON Arthur MM Pte 16817 9th Gloucestershire Regt
MASON Arthur Frederick MM Pte 461047 26 Fd Amb RAMC
MASON Bertie MM Pte 14091 Grenadier Guards
MASON Charles MM Sjt 23094 13th Liverpool Regt
MASON Charles MM Pte 20450 Royal Sussex Regt
MASON Charles MM L/Cpl 13622 102 Coy Machine Gun Corps
MASON Charles MM Pte D/20479 7th Dragoon Guards
MASON Charles MM Gnr 66892 RGA
MASON Charles F. MM Pte 4406 1st Border Regt
MASON E. MM Pte 322534 London Regt
MASON Edmund MM Pte 16270 Machine Gun Corps AKA Edmund Moore
MASON Edward MM Bdr 29870 B/92 Bde RFA
MASON Edwin "MM,MSM" Sjt 28880 DE/160 Bde RFA
MASON Edwin MM Sjt 427 15th Royal Warwickshire Regt
MASON Ernest MM L/Cpl 10214 8th King's Royal Rifle Corps
MASON Ernest E. MM Pte 2690 1/1st Cambridgeshire Regt
MASON Ernest Frank MM L/Sjt 8817 1st North Staffordshire Regt
MASON Ernest M. "DCM,MM+Bar" Sjt 6/1091 21st King's Royal Rifle Corps
MASON Francis MM+Bar Pte 11836 Arg & Suth Highlanders
MASON Frank MM Pte 60482 Machine Gun Corps
MASON Frank MM Pte 66166 80 Fd Amb RAMC
MASON Frank Edward MM Pte 19874 1st Lancashire Fusiliers
MASON Frederick MM Cpl 69213 35 Div Sig Coy Royal Engineers
MASON Frederick MM Pte 21083 6th Dragoons
MASON Frederick MM Pte 2244 Royal Sussex Regt
MASON Frederick MM+Bar Cpl 10019 1st South Staffordshire Regt
MASON Frederick C. MM Sjt 835109 C/240 Bde RFA
MASON Frederick Henry MM L/Cpl 9212 11th Royal Warwickshire Regt DOW 9.8.17.
MASON Frederick T. MM L/Bdr 80005 RGA
MASON Frederick W. MM+Bar Pte 302686 7th Essex Regt
MASON Gabriel MM Gnr Sig 183330 283 Siege Bty RGA
MASON George MM Pte 81900 137 Coy Labour Corps
MASON George MM L/Sjt 8037 1st Royal Lancaster Regt
MASON George MM Pte 307365 1/7th West Riding Regt KIA 14.12.17.
MASON George F. MM Sjt 230580 1/2nd London Regt
MASON George F. MM Sjt MS/2727 Army Service Corps att RAMC
MASON George H. MM Sjt 3010 Machine Gun Corps
MASON Harold MM Dvr 12669 19 Div Ammn Col RFA
MASON Harold MM L/Cpl 43536 Royal Engineers
MASON Harold MM Sjt 14330 8th South Lancashire Regt KIA 14.6.17.
MASON Harry MM Gnr 418 RGA
MASON Harry MM Pte 18/14 18th West Yorkshire Regt
MASON Harry G. MM BQMS 91409 RFA
MASON Harry Leslie MM Sjt 45208 2nd South Wales Borderers
MASON Henry MM S/Sjt 2204 1/1st Northumberland Yeo
MASON Henry MM Pte 13495 3rd Coldstream Guards DOW 17.1.18.
MASON Henry MM Pte 40054 1st South Staffordshire Regt KIA 26.10.17.
MASON Henry M. MM Pte 302152 Durham Light Infantry
MASON Herbert MM Spr 46391 Royal Engineers
MASON Herbert MM Pte M2/102479 Army Service Corps
MASON Horace MM Pte 241391 1/6th West Yorkshire Regt
MASON J. MM Pte 40645 21st Manchester Regt
MASON J. MM Cpl 13911 Royal Flying Corps
MASON James MM Pte 40409 4th Worcestershire Regt
MASON James MM+Bar L/Cpl 512753 14th London Regt
MASON James MM L/Cpl 10671 2nd Royal Irish Regt
MASON James MM Gnr 35358 RFA
MASON James Alfred MM Sjt 339149 3/2(West Lancashire)Fd Amb RAMC
MASON James H. MM Sjt 478127 Royal Engineers
MASON James P. MM Dvr 74156 37 Bde RFA
MASON James W. MM Pte 30444 Worcestershire Regt
MASON James Walter MM Bdr 8769 162 Siege Bty RGA
MASON John MM Cpl 148473 179 Tunnelling Coy Royal Engineers
MASON John MM L/Cpl 1642 8th Lincolnshire Regt
MASON John MM Gnr 23713 275 Siege Bty RGA
MASON John MM Cpl A/1783 King's Royal Rifle Corps
MASON John MM Sjt 11726 Royal Fusiliers
MASON John MM Sjt 14878 9th South Staffordshire Regt
MASON John E. MM Pte 356089 15th Hampshire Regt
MASON John H. "DCM,MM" Sjt 128675 232 Siege Bty RGA
MASON John Irving MM Pte 10062 1st Scots Guards
MASON John Rowland MM Dvr 33156 A/51 Bde RFA
MASON John Thomas MM Pte 17994 Machine Gun Corps
MASON John W.A. MM Dvr 87602 RFA
MASON Jonas MM L/Cpl 16680 9th North Lancashire Regt
MASON Joseph MM Spr 249264 Royal Engineers
MASON Joseph MM Cpl 8179 2nd Bedfordshire Regt
MASON Joseph Charles MM L/Cpl 8361 1st King's Royal Rifle Corps KIA 29.11.17.
MASON Joseph H. MM Pte G/23753 Middlesex Regt
MASON Joseph W. MM Pte 29764 North Lancashire Regt
MASON Josiah MM Sjt 7336 8th Suffolk Regt KIA 31.7.17.
MASON Leonard MM Sjt 241337 1/5th North Lancashire Regt
MASON Lionel "DCM,MM+2 Bars" Pte G/4269 7th East Kent Regt
MASON Lionel F. MM Sjt 33857 Liverpool Regt
MASON Louis MM+Bar CQMS 6065 2nd Royal Warwickshire Regt KIA 4.5.17.
MASON Oscar E.W. MM Pte 7890 1st Northamptonshire Regt
MASON Percy C. MM Pte 55577 9th Bn Machine Gun Corps
MASON R.J. "MM,MSM" Sjt 470848 1/12th London Regt
MASON Reginald E. MM+Bar CSM 14932 7th Duke of Cornwall's LI
MASON Richard MM Sjt 11243 1st Royal Irish Fusiliers KIA 16.8.16.
MASON Richard MM Sjt 265690 West Riding Regt
MASON Robert MM L/Cpl 331116 9th Highland Light Infantry
MASON Robert MM L/Cpl 2592 1/7th Northumberland Fusiliers
MASON Robert MM Pte 2136 1/9th Royal Scots
MASON Robert MM Pte 9909 1st Scots Guards
MASON Sydney MM Pte 15/622 15/17th West Yorkshire Regt
MASON T. MM Pte 2414 Royal Warwickshire Regt
MASON T.E. MM L/Cpl 11883 9th Border Regt
MASON Thomas MM L/Cpl 2494 2nd Irish Guards
MASON Thomas MM Sjt Farrier 44014 13 Bde RFA
MASON Thomas MM Cpl 350154 1/9th Royal Scots
MASON Thomas Bond MM Pte 5405 64 Coy Machine Gun Corps
MASON Thomas Claude "DCM,MM" Pte M2/130588 594 Coy Army Service Corps
MASON Thomas P. MM Pte 32983 13th East Lancashire Regt
MASON Walter MM Pte 4290 10th Lancashire Fusiliers
MASON Walter G. MM Pte 204807 15th Hampshire Regt
MASON Walter James Charles "MM,MID" Bdr L/10127 22 Bde RFA
MASON William MM Pte 8413 1st Gordon Highlanders
MASON William MM Pte 850 2nd Royal Irish Regt
MASON William MM Cpl 197522 Royal Engineers
MASON William MM Spr 308498 Royal Engineers
MASON William MM Sjt 15719 8th Royal Lancaster Regt KIA 17.6.18.
MASON William C. "DCM,MM,MID" RSM 11007 19th Durham Light Infantry
MASON William E. MM L/Cpl G/42550 13th Royal Fusiliers
MASON William E. MM Bdr L/22990 RFA
MASON William F. MM Cpl 13957 10th Essex Regt
MASON William George Trowbridge MM Sjt 1131 1/5th London Regt att MGC
MASON William H. MM Cpl G/1898 8th Royal Sussex Regt
MASON William H. MM Gnr 4290 RFA
MASON William J. MM Pte R/20419 King's Royal Rifle Corps
MASON William S. MM+Bar Pte 15684 7th Bedfordshire Regt
MASSER Walter MM Pte 11334 1st Coldstream Guards
MASSEY Albert G. MM Gnr L/7931 RFA

MASSEY Arthur H. MM Sjt 776313 D/330 Bde RFA
MASSEY Charles MM L/Cpl 28913 13th Royal Welsh Fusiliers
MASSEY Charles MM Pte 50879 1st East Yorkshire Regt
MASSEY Charles MM Dvr 13651 75 Bde RFA
MASSEY Charles MM Spr 100925 Royal Engineers
MASSEY Charles W. MM Pte 332589 1st Liverpool Regt
MASSEY Eli MM Pte 3770 11th Manchester Regt
MASSEY Ernest MM Bdr 53157 Y/34 Med TM Bty RGA
MASSEY F.R. MM Cpl 45642 RGA
MASSEY Frank MM Pte R/9311 King's Royal Rifle Corps
MASSEY Frederick MM Bdr 12507 D/86 Bde RFA KIA 3.7.16.
MASSEY George MM Pte 4927 Border Regt
MASSEY Harold MM+Bar L/Cpl 5485 12th Manchester Regt
MASSEY Harold MM Sjt 28228 RFA
MASSEY Henry MM Pte 13005 1st Coldstream Guards
MASSEY Herbert MM L/Cpl 82714 Royal Engineers
MASSEY James Arthur MM Pte 235437 2/7th Liverpool Regt KIA 27.9.18.
MASSEY John MM Sjt 55875 RFA
MASSEY John MM Pte 81934 Notts & Derby Regt
MASSEY John MM Sjt 8177 2nd South Staffordshire Regt KIA 7.9.16.
MASSEY John A. MM Pte 497 6th Royal West Surrey Regt
MASSEY John Thomas "MM,MM(F)" Pte 202133 2/4th West Riding Regt
MASSEY Raymond Francis MM Cpl M2/121038 Army Service Corps att 96 Siege Bty RGA
MASSEY Robert MM L/Bdr 42269 RFA
MASSEY Samuel MM Sjt 9222 1st Royal Irish Rifles
MASSEY Thomas MM Pte 19203 21st Manchester Regt KIA 1.7.16.
MASSEY Thomas MM Pte 12728 Devonshire Regt
MASSEY Tom MM+Bar Sjt 4681 1st Lancashire Fusiliers
MASSEY W. MM Pte 15633 8th South Lancashire Regt
MASSEY Walter MM Sjt 328065 8th Lancashire Fusiliers
MASSEY Watson MM Pte M2/264035 Army Service Corps
MASSEY William MM Pte DM2/169513 Army Service Corps
MASSHEDER John H. MM+Bar Pte 10504 2/4th West Riding Regt
MASSIE Edward John MM Sjt M2/073189 Army Service Corps att 58 Fd Amb RAMC
MASSINGHAM Charles MM Sjt 1390 1/4th Yorkshire Regt
MASSON Alexander MM Sjt 84302 RFA
MASSON George MM Cpl 4369 1/4th Gordon Highlanders
MASSON John MM Sjt 337 2nd Gordon Highlanders
MASSON Leslie MM Pte 33095 6th King's Own Scottish Borderers
MASSON Robert MM Pte 16038 2nd Scots Guards
MASSON William MM Pte 301258 89 Fd Amb RAMC DOW 6.10.17.
MASSON William P. MM Cpl 290647 1/7th Gordon Highlanders
MASTERMAN Charles William MM Sjt 28117 190 Siege Bty RGA KIA 14.8.17.
MASTERMAN G.H. "DCM,MM" Sjt 15175 1st Grenadier Guards
MASTERMAN Robert MM Pte 28010 2nd Grenadier Guards
MASTERS Charles MM Sjt 285072 217 Siege Bty RGA
MASTERS Charles G. MM Cpl 11364 2nd King's Royal Rifle Corps
MASTERS Charles Henry John MM Dvr 90670 C/50 Bde RFA Died 31.10.18.
MASTERS Charles T. MM L/Cpl 81583 24th Bn Machine Gun Corps
MASTERS Frank MM Pte 553135 16th London Regt
MASTERS Frederick MM Sjt 3745 13th Royal Sussex Regt
MASTERS Frederick C. MM Cpl 39911 1st Wiltshire Regt
MASTERS George T. MM Dvr 62266 RFA
MASTERS Godfrey MM Sjt 358063 RGA
MASTERS Herbert J. MM Dvr 64836 RFA
MASTERS Howard Norman MM L/Cpl Y/739 12th King's Royal Rifle Corps
MASTERS John "MM,MID" Pte 45453 RAMC
MASTERS John T. MM Pte 1754 2nd Rifle Brigade
MASTERS Montague H. MM Bdr 191445 'A'(AA)Bty RGA
MASTERS Percy MM Bdr 218627 D/306 Bde RFA
MASTERS Thomas Frederick MM Sjt 15496 9th Norfolk Regt KIA 15.9.16.
MASTERS Tom MM Pte 24335 1st Royal West Kent Regt
MASTERS William MM Pte 421041 38 Coy Labour Corps
MASTERS William Frederick MM Gnr 85731 124 Bty 28 Bde RFA
MASTERS William H. MM L/Cpl 17585 Royal Warwickshire Regt
MASTERS William T. MM Sjt 2798 1/9th London Regt
MASTERSON George MM Pte 8580 1st East Lancashire Regt
MASTERSON J. MM Cpl 29687 RFA
MASTERSON Vincent MM+Bar Pte 34706 York & Lancaster Regt
MASTERTON David MM Sjt 28954 Highland Light Infantry
MASTERTON George MM Sjt 6587 RFA
MASTERTON Henry MM Sjt 200689 1/5th Highland Light Infantry
MASTERTON Walter MM Pte 325607 Royal Scots
MASTIN Sidney MM Sjt 8406 1st Leicestershire Regt
MATCHAM Harold MM+Bar Sjt 204813 15th Hampshire Regt
MATCHET Albert MM Pte 25234 West Riding Regt
MATCHETT George MM Dvr 67580 128 Bty 29 Bde RFA
MATCHETT William MM+Bar Sjt 330409 1/9th Highland Light Infantry
MATE Henry T. MM Sjt 18031 5th Dorsetshire Regt
MATEAR Henry MM Pte 6939 2nd Irish Guards KIA 27.11.17.
MATES William MM Cpl 16923 1st East Yorkshire Regt KIA 9.4.17.
MATHER Adam MM L/Cpl 20735 1st Liverpool Regt
MATHER Arthur MM Pte 270753 10th East Kent Regt
MATHER Arthur MM Pte 15969 11th Notts & Derby Regt
MATHER Ernest MM Spr 21133 23 Fd Coy Royal Engineers
MATHER Frank MM L/Cpl R/1099 11th King's Royal Rifle Corps
MATHER Fred MM Sjt 32963 2nd Lincolnshire Regt DOW 20.9.18.
MATHER George MM Cpl 4474 2nd Lancashire Fusiliers
MATHER George MM L/Cpl 12035 16th Lancashire Fusiliers
MATHER Harold MM Sjt 37157 16th Royal Welsh Fusiliers
MATHER James MM Pte 125209 Machine Gun Corps
MATHER James "MM,MID" Sjt 19636 8th Royal Lancaster Regt
MATHER James MM Dvr 217799 RFA
MATHER James MM(16207 Pte 8th N Lancs)+Bar Spr 360024 25 Div Sig Coy Royal Engineers
MATHER John MM Cpl 46431 99 Siege Bty RGA
MATHER John MM Pte 41903 8th North Staffordshire Regt KIA 7.8.18.
MATHER Joseph MM L/Cpl 148022 32nd Bn Machine Gun Corps
MATHER Joseph MM Cpl 241405 2/5th North Lancashire Regt KIA 12.10.18.
MATHER L. MM Cpl 341058 RAMC
MATHER Raymond MM Cpl 45454 Royal Engineers
MATHER S. MM+Bar Cpl B/1113 Rifle Brigade
MATHER Walter MM+Bar Sjt 796450 62 Div Ammn Col RFA
MATHER William MM Gnr 16832 8 Siege Bty RGA
MATHER William MM Pte 35335 10th Northumberland Fusiliers KIA 29.10.18.
MATHER William E. MM Pte 7374 11th Royal Fusiliers
MATHERICK William H. MM Pte 102016 Machine Gun Corps
MATHERS Arthur MM+Bar L/Cpl 13184 10th Cheshire Regt
MATHERS Robert MM Sjt 241514 5/6th Scottish Rifles
MATHERS Walter Edward MM Pte 275920 1/6th Essex Regt
MATHERS William P.F. MM Bdr 107080 RGA
MATHESON David MM Pte 21615 6th Royal Inniskilling Fusiliers
MATHESON Donald MM Pte 40454 Seaforth Highlanders
MATHESON Frank E. MM Pte 537427 15th London Regt
MATHESON George MM Pte 240495 1/5th Seaforth Highlanders
MATHESON George MM Gnr 136655 202 Siege Bty RGA DOW 23.4.18.
MATHESON Hugh "DCM,MM" Sjt 202823 1/5th Seaforth Highlanders KIA 13.10.18.
MATHESON Hugh MM Pte 27425 King's Own Scottish Borderers
MATHESON Hugh B. MM Cpl 333060 Highland Light Infantry
MATHESON James MM L/Cpl 1719 1/6th Seaforth Highlanders
MATHESON James MM Sjt 4589 9th Seaforth Highlanders
MATHESON James R. MM Pte 43492 Gordon Highlanders
MATHESON James T. MM 2nd Cpl 26707 3 Fd Sqn Royal Engineers
MATHESON Munro MM Gnr 167257 88 Bty 14 Bde RFA
MATHESON Stewart Farquhar MM Cpl 67106 Royal Engineers
MATHEWS Charles E. MM Cpl 550190 1/16th London Regt
MATHEWS Patrick MM Pte 201544 4th West Riding Regt
MATHEWSON Alexander MM Pte 266381 Gordon Highlanders
MATHEWSON James MM Pte 315901 13th Royal Highlanders
MATHEWSON James W. MM Cpl L/4036 RFA
MATHEWSON John MM Gnr 96493 RFA
MATHIAS Sidney MM Pte 8115 1st North Staffordshire Regt
MATHIAS T.G. MM L/Cpl 19971 Welsh Regt
MATHIE Robert MM Pte 43463 1st Scottish Rifles KIA 21.9.18.
MATHIE Thomas L. MM Pte 5518 Royal Highlanders
MATHIESON Alexander MM Spr 96627 Royal Engineers
MATHIESON Alexander MM Pte 11325 1st Scottish Rifles
MATHIESON Harry MM Pte 14060 6th East Yorkshire Regt
MATHIESON Hugh MM Cpl 400523 400 Fd Coy Royal Engineers
MATHIESON James MM Pte 19868 Royal Scots
MATHIESON John MM Pte 16147 4th Bn Machine Gun Corps
MATHIESON John MM Pte 1037 Highland Light Infantry
MATHIESON John MM Dvr 92891 C/82 Bde RFA

MATHIESON Lindsay MM Pte S/40043 8th Royal Highlanders KIA 23.3.18.
MATHIESON Peter MM Pte 40861 King's Own Scottish Borderers
MATHIESON Roderick MM Cpl 16975 8th King's Own Scottish Borderers
MATHIESON Thomas MM Pte 267925 7th Royal Highlanders
MATHIESON Thomas Simpson Hugh MM+Bar L/Cpl 20/62 15th Durham Light Infantry DOW 24.10.18.
MATHIESON William MM Gnr Sig 104159 A/58 Bde RFA
MATIER Thomas MM+Bar Sjt 400 12th Royal Irish Rifles
MATKIN Ernest "MM,MID" Sjt 19729 Durham Light Infantry
MATKIN George Henry MM L/Cpl 22302 Leicestershire Regt
MATLEY William MM Pte 39652 42nd Bn Machine Gun Corps
MATLOCK Horace V. MM Pte 14013 Leicestershire Regt
MATON Alfred MM+Bar Pte 7219 1st Gloucestershire Regt
MATON Edward MM Cpl 86714 145 Labour Coy Labour Corps
MATON Eric W. MM Pte 320500 Welsh Regt
MATSON Harmon MM CSM 219150 7 Light Railway Operating Coy Royal Engineers
MATTEY John MM Sjt 75763 36 Bde RFA
MATTHEW James MM Pte 240237 1/5th Gordon Highlanders KIA 31.7.17.
MATTHEW John N. MM Pte 266285 10th Scottish Rifles
MATTHEWS A.E. MM Sjt 825807 RFA
MATTHEWS A.W. MM Sjt 459014 RAMC
MATTHEWS Abraham MM Pte 49720 2nd Royal Inniskilling Fusiliers KIA 15.10.18.
MATTHEWS Albert MM Sjt 44435 2nd South Wales Borderers
MATTHEWS Alfred C. MM Pte 17021 1st Bn Machine Gun Corps
MATTHEWS Angus B. MM Sjt 241168 5th Royal Lancaster Regt
MATTHEWS Arthur MM Pte 7127 78 Coy Machine Gun Corps
MATTHEWS Arthur MM L/Cpl 13079 9th Devonshire Regt KIA 1.7.16.
MATTHEWS Arthur C. MM Sjt 19927 Machine Gun Corps
MATTHEWS Arthur G.J. MM Cpl 29632 10th Royal West Surrey Regt
MATTHEWS Bennett MM Pte 290241 8th Royal Highlanders
MATTHEWS Bert MM Cpl 780958 RFA
MATTHEWS Bert MM(186 Bde)+Bar(160 Bde) Gnr Sig L/38213 RFA
MATTHEWS Bertie H. MM Cpl 140240 332 Siege Bty RGA
MATTHEWS Charles MM Pte 12792 8th North Staffordshire Regt KIA 8.6.17.
MATTHEWS Charles Samuel MM L/Cpl 13623 10th Essex Regt KIA 20.7.16.
MATTHEWS Charles W. MM Cpl 20372 7 Fd Coy Royal Engineers
MATTHEWS David John "MM,MID" Bdr 24272 D/75 Bde RFA
MATTHEWS E. MM Pte 16245 7th Border Regt
MATTHEWS E.C. MM CoH 2994 Household Bn
MATTHEWS Edward MM Dvr 775129 B/245 Bde RFA
MATTHEWS Edward MM Sjt 7161 1st North Staffordshire Regt KIA 29.8.18.
MATTHEWS Edward MM Pte 1458 1/6th Welsh Regt
MATTHEWS Edward MM Pte 6308 1st Northumberland Fusiliers
MATTHEWS Edward MM Pte 7176 5th Lancers
MATTHEWS Edwin Samuel MM Pte 1539 9th East Surrey Regt
MATTHEWS Ernest MM Bdr 63189 91 Siege Bty RGA
MATTHEWS Ernest MM CSM 8030 2nd Suffolk Regt DOW 2.10.18.
MATTHEWS Ernest MM Sjt 50385 'Z' Bty RHA
MATTHEWS Ernest W. MM L/Cpl 7365 1st Norfolk Regt
MATTHEWS Francis Bernard Thomas MM Pte 32635 1st South Staffordshire Regt
MATTHEWS Frank MM Pte 376317 8th Manchester Regt
MATTHEWS Frank William MM Pte 11248 1st Coldstream Guards DOW 21.8.18.
MATTHEWS Fred MM Cpl 11353 2nd West Riding Regt KIA 31.8.18.
MATTHEWS Fred MM L/Sjt G/1655 7th East Kent Regt KIA 13.7.16.
MATTHEWS Frederick MM Pte 50577 4th Middlesex Regt
MATTHEWS Frederick MM Cpl 48645 18 Bde RFA
MATTHEWS Frederick MM Sjt 279994 191 Siege Bty RGA
MATTHEWS Frederick C. MM L/Cpl 548192 Royal Engineers
MATTHEWS George MM Pte 39775 1st Wiltshire Regt
MATTHEWS George MM Sjt PW/340 18th Middlesex Regt
MATTHEWS George MM Bdr 64435 B/86 Bde RFA
MATTHEWS George E. MM+Bar Bdr 65767 11 Bde RFA
MATTHEWS George William MM Pte 33651 2nd Bedfordshire Regt
MATTHEWS H. MM Dmr 18209 Middlesex Regt
MATTHEWS Harold E. MM Pte 10011 4th Hussars
MATTHEWS Hendry J. MM Pte 263 1st Welsh Guards
MATTHEWS Henry MM Spr 8894 57 Fd Coy Royal Engineers
MATTHEWS Henry MM Bdr 53020 Y/50 Med TM Bty RGA KIA 30.9.17.
MATTHEWS Henry C. MM Pte 15886 10th Duke of Cornwall's LI
MATTHEWS Herbert J. MM Cpl 10506 5th Royal Berkshire Regt
MATTHEWS Herbert John MM Spr 217551 Signal Service Royal Engineers
MATTHEWS Herbert Thomas MM L/Cpl 5077 1st Royal Irish Rifles Died 12.11.16.
MATTHEWS James MM L/Bdr 21528 C/91 Bde RFA
MATTHEWS James MM L/Cpl 201436 1/4th Gordon Highlanders
MATTHEWS James A. MM Pte 4918 Middlesex Regt
MATTHEWS James C.F. MM+Bar Sjt 8786 2nd South Staffordshire Regt
MATTHEWS James E. MM L/Cpl 242470 5th Gloucestershire Regt
MATTHEWS James H. MM Sjt 28912 Machine Gun Corps
MATTHEWS James Percy "MM,MSM" CQMS 89516 145 Army Troops Coy Royal Engineers
MATTHEWS John MM Dvr 54908 117 Bty 26 Bde RFA
MATTHEWS John MM Bdr 771021 RFA
MATTHEWS John MM L/Cpl 45605 Devonshire Regt
MATTHEWS John MM Cpl 19483 11 Fd Coy Royal Engineers Died 4.10.17.
MATTHEWS John MM Cpl 265466 1/6th Gordon Highlanders DOW 23.5.18.
MATTHEWS John J. MM Cpl 70224 24 Bde RFA
MATTHEWS John P. "DCM,MM" Cpl 57322 9th Devonshire Regt
MATTHEWS John P. MM Pte 29895 Worcestershire Regt
MATTHEWS John Pavey MM Bdr 1005 4(Northumbrian)Bde RFA
MATTHEWS John T. MM BQMS 12681 504 Siege Bty RGA
MATTHEWS Joseph E. MM L/Cpl 38649 2nd York & Lancaster Regt
MATTHEWS Joseph Edward MM Pte 207289 3rd Worcestershire Regt DOW 24.10.18.
MATTHEWS Leslie Gerald MM Pte 41950 1st West Yorkshire Regt
MATTHEWS Lewis A. "DCM+Bar,MM,MID" CSM 9544 1st Gordon Highlanders
MATTHEWS Mark MM L/Cpl G/1848 8th Royal Sussex Regt
MATTHEWS Patrick MM L/Cpl 248189 32 Div Sig Coy Royal Engineers
MATTHEWS Percy "MM,CG(F)" L/Cpl 10566 Essex Regt att Int Corps
MATTHEWS Percy G. MM+Bar 2nd Cpl 532227 Royal Engineers
MATTHEWS R.W.C. MM L/Cpl 44987 1st King's Royal Rifle Corps
MATTHEWS Reginald D. MM Pte 35163 7th Royal Warwickshire Regt
MATTHEWS Richard David MM Pte 22139 13th Welsh Regt
MATTHEWS Richard L. MM Pte 240806 Duke of Cornwall's LI
MATTHEWS Robert MM Gnr 23550 109 Bty 281 Bde RFA KIA 19.1.17.
MATTHEWS Robert MM Pte 202383 1/4th Gloucestershire Regt
MATTHEWS Robert MM Pte 13001 20th King's Royal Rifle Corps KIA 27.2.18.
MATTHEWS Robert C. MM+Bar Pte 12676 7th Norfolk Regt
MATTHEWS Squire MM Pte 242628 West Riding Regt
MATTHEWS Stanley MM L/Cpl 1734 1/8th Notts & Derby Regt
MATTHEWS T. MM Pte 8602 South Wales Borderers
MATTHEWS Thomas MM Pte 12293 2nd Royal Fusiliers
MATTHEWS Thomas MM L/Cpl 16/799 16th Royal Irish Rifles
MATTHEWS Thomas "MM,MID" Sjt 9482 2nd York & Lancaster Regt
MATTHEWS Thomas MM L/Cpl 12296 2nd Royal Fusiliers
MATTHEWS Thomas E. MM Pte 2830 6th South Lancashire Regt
MATTHEWS Thomas Edward "MM,OStG(R)" Cpl 11600 10th Devonshire Regt
MATTHEWS Thomas Henry MM Cpl 457155 2/1(Wessex)Fd Amb RAMC
MATTHEWS Thomas P. MM Sjt DM2/189958 Army Service Corps
MATTHEWS Thomas Pat MM Sjt 49462 Liverpool Regt
MATTHEWS Walter MM CSM 61003 23rd Lancashire Fusiliers
MATTHEWS Walter MM Sjt 6725 13th Hussars
MATTHEWS Wilfred Raymond MM Cpl 161792 'BT' Cable Section Royal Engineers
MATTHEWS William MM Pte M2/188884 32 Div Train. Army Service Corps
MATTHEWS William MM Sjt 10182 2nd Royal Welsh Fusiliers
MATTHEWS William MM Spr 2252 Royal Engineers
MATTHEWS William MM Pte 10687 1st Welsh Regt
MATTHEWS William MM(10512 L/Cpl Worcs Regt)+Bar L/Cpl 198141 Royal Engineers
MATTHEWS William MM Pte 11942 6th Shropshire Light Infantry
MATTHEWS William C. MM Pte 4443 1/24th London Regt

MATTHEWS William C. MM Pte 17407 1st Coldstream Guards
MATTHEWS William Edward "MM,MSM" CQMS 19111 15th Hampshire Regt
MATTHEWS William George MM Gnr 326823 346 Siege Bty RGA
MATTHEWS William H. MM+Bar Pte 67550 1/5th Devonshire Regt
MATTHEWS William John "DCM,MM" Sjt 326837 Suffolk Regt
MATTHEWSON Henry Robson MM Pte 35534 21st Northumberland Fusiliers
MATTHEWSON William H. MM Pte 139303 Machine Gun Corps
MATTHEY Henry Edward MM L/Cpl 391152 9th London Regt
MATTHIAS Thomas MM Sjt G/5865 2nd Royal Sussex Regt KIA 24.9.18.
MATTICK Ivor MM Pte 205245 1st London Regt
MATTINGLEY Francis H.W. MM Pte 50405 Middlesex Regt
MATTINGLEY Sidney MM Cpl 43549 4th Yorkshire Light Infantry
MATTINSON James H. MM Sjt 2695 1/4th Oxf & Bucks Light Infantry
MATTISON Cuthbert MM Pte 678 23rd Northumberland Fusiliers
MATTOCKS Bertram MM Pte 201166 6th(Light) Bn Tank Corps
MATTOCKS James MM Dvr 34430 RFA
MATTON John MM Pte 21406 Shropshire Light Infantry
MATTOX Thomas W. MM Bdr 66779 84 Bty 11 Bde RFA
MATTRICK Arthur MM+Bar Sjt 38726 Northumberland Fusiliers
MATZ Bertram J. MM S/Sjt Fitter 88342 RFA
MAUCHLINE John MM Dvr 10779 62 Bty 3 Bde RFA
MAUD George R. MM Cpl 98473 223 Fd Coy Royal Engineers
MAUD Herbert H. MM Pte 7226 23rd Middlesex Regt
MAUDE Charles E. MM Cpl 37654 Yorkshire Light Infantry
MAUDE E. MM Sister F QAIMNS
MAUDE Ernest Edmund MM Pte 44199 8th Royal Irish Rifles KIA 22.6.17.
MAUDE George MM+Bar L/Cpl 265611 1/6th West Riding Regt KIA 1.11.18.
MAUDE George W. MM Dvr 457308 446 Fd Coy Royal Engineers DOW 2.1.18.
MAUDE Herbert MM Pte 307574 4th West Riding Regt
MAUDE Samuel MM Cpl 30646 East Lancashire Regt
MAUDLIN Norman MM Pte 18842 12th Durham Light Infantry
MAUGHAM Henry MM Pte 266 7th Royal Sussex Regt
MAUGHAN George MM L/Cpl 19/1315 19th Northumberland Fusiliers
MAUGHAN George G. MM Pte 34990 Yorkshire Light Infantry
MAUGHAN John MM L/Cpl Z/1715 13th Rifle Brigade
MAUGHAN John MM Spr 131345 234 Fd Coy Royal Engineers
MAUGHAN John MM L/Cpl 17252 9th Yorkshire Regt
MAUGHAN Thomas MM Cpl 6710 1st King's Royal Rifle Corps
MAUGHAN Thomas MM CSM 10130 7th East Yorkshire Regt
MAUGHAN William MM Pte 24796 Durham Light Infantry
MAUL John MM Pte 402 1/22nd London Regt
MAULE Harry MM L/Cpl 6492 5/6th Scottish Rifles
MAULE Henry J. "DCM,MM" Sjt 16023 49th Bn Machine Gun Corps
MAULKIN John Eli Salvador MM Sjt 5172 33rd Bn Machine Gun Corps
MAUND William MM Cpl 147241 4 Special Coy Royal Engineers
MAUNDER Frederick MM Pte 23290 2/5th Gloucestershire Regt DOW 30.4.18.
MAUNDER Frederick John MM Cpl 925067 A/280 Bde RFA
MAUNDER George MM Pte 2277 1/5th Cheshire Regt
MAUNDER Harold F. MM Pte 492245 13th London Regt
MAUNDER John MM Sjt 295183 12th Somerset Light Infantry
MAUNDER Sidney "MM,MIDx2" Gnr 89324 B/47 Bde RFA
MAUNDER William Charles "MC,MM(9415 Sjt)" 2Lt 2nd Devonshire Regt
MAUNDER William R. MM L/Cpl 29623 1st Somerset Light Infantry
MAUNDERS Robert C. MM Cpl 41377 RFA
MAURICE James MM Pte Y/673 King's Royal Rifle Corps
MAURY Phillip MM Sjt 1735 RAMC
MAVIN Thomas MM Gnr 59335 46 Siege Bty RGA
MAVIR Tom MM Cpl 1417 1/5th Border Regt
MAVITY Beresford W. MM Gnr 13066 B/57 Bde RFA
MAW George MM CSM 15639 Durham Light Infantry
MAW James V. MM Pte 2583 West Yorkshire Regt
MAW John MM Gnr 7470 A/160 Bde RFA
MAW Thomas Ancliffe MM Cpl 27344 1st Royal Lancaster Regt
MAWBEY Ernest MM L/Sjt 13725 2nd Grenadier Guards
MAWBY Alfred MM Sjt 60234 26th Royal Fusiliers
MAWBY Henry MM Pte 200142 1/5th Notts & Derby Regt
MAWDSLEY John MM CQMS 1148 1/9th Liverpool Regt
MAWDSLEY Thomas MM 2nd Cpl 46035 17 Div Sig Coy Royal Engineers

MAWER Alfred MM Pte 116441 10th Notts & Derby Regt
MAWER Matthew MM Sjt 241104 2/5th East Lancashire Regt
MAWER Peter MM L/Cpl 3073 Gordon Highlanders
MAWER William MM L/Sjt 330939 Liverpool Regt
MAWHINNEY Francis "MM,MSM" CSM 2735 1st Royal Inniskilling Fusiliers
MAWSON Ernest MM Pte 37844 Northumberland Fusiliers
MAWSON George MM L/Cpl 240616 1/5th Royal Lancaster Regt
MAWSON Harry MM Cpl 60476 88 Siege Bty RGA
MAWSON John W. MM Pte DM2/168763 Army Service Corps att RFA
MAWSTON John Thomas MM Sjt 7028 Machine Gun Corps
MAXEY Harry MM Cpl 12232 6th Lincolnshire Regt
MAXEY Kate MM Sister-in-Charge F TFNS
MAXFIELD Thomas Henry MM Cpl 33859 North Lancashire Regt
MAXFIELD Tom Martin MM Cpl 482124 Royal Engineers
MAXFIELD William MM Bdr 38012 6 Bty 40 Bde RFA
MAXIM Herbert F. MM 2nd Cpl WR/250750 111 Rly Coy Royal Engineers
MAXTED George Arthur "MM,MID" Sjt 28053 RGA DOW 28.9.17.
MAXTON Robert A. MM 2nd Cpl 40966 Royal Engineers
MAXWELL Bryce MM Pte 17/373 Royal Irish Rifles
MAXWELL David P. MM Sjt S/25532 7th Cameron Highlanders
MAXWELL G. MM Sjt 356694 Liverpool Regt
MAXWELL George MM Pte 6035 Highland Light Infantry
MAXWELL Gordon MM Cpl 220613 1st East Yorkshire Regt
MAXWELL Gordon W. MM L/Cpl 41264 Machine Gun Corps(Cavalry)
MAXWELL James MM Pte 15574 12th Royal Irish Rifles
MAXWELL James MM Pte 288003 Northumberland Fusiliers
MAXWELL James MM Cpl S/5032 11th Arg & Suth Highlanders
MAXWELL James MM L/Sjt 6696 1st King's Royal Rifle Corps
MAXWELL James Farrow MM Sjt 21634 12th Highland Light Infantry KIA 26.4.18.
MAXWELL John MM Cpl 43274 11th Royal Scots
MAXWELL John MM Sjt 2280 9th Highland Light Infantry KIA 11.12.16.
MAXWELL John MM L/Cpl 13386 3rd Coldstream Guards
MAXWELL Joseph MM Sjt 15677 17th Highland Light Infantry
MAXWELL Kirkpatrick MM Pte M2/047892 Army Service Corps att 111 Fd Amb RAMC
MAXWELL Patrick MM L/Cpl 11587 2nd King's Own Scottish Borderers
MAXWELL Thomas H. MM Bdr 19700 RGA
MAXWELL Walter MM Dvr L/17058 B/173 Bde RFA
MAXWELL William MM Pte 28526 1st King's Own Scottish Borderers
MAY Albert Edward MM Pte R/12129 King's Royal Rifle Corps
MAY Alfred E. MM Cpl 14443 7th Wiltshire Regt
MAY Arthur MM Pte 309106 17th Armoured Car Bn Tank Corps
MAY Arthur MM L/Cpl 1755 1st Northumberland Fusiliers
MAY Arthur W. MM Pte 24680 7th Royal Berkshire Regt
MAY Augustus A. MM Pte 288840 1/1st Worcestershire Yeomanry
MAY Austin William MM Pte 203383 1/4th Oxf & Bucks Light Infantry KIA 16.8.17.
MAY Charles Ernest MM Pte 19088 14th York & Lancaster Regt
MAY Cyril C. MM Gnr 78010 RGA
MAY Dan MM Cpl 3164 7th York & Lancaster Regt
MAY Dick MM Sjt 4128 7th Hussars att South Persia Rifles
MAY Edgar MM Pte 96049 7th Royal Fusiliers
MAY Ernest F. MM Bdr 51048 RFA
MAY Frank MM Pte 14920 2nd Royal Fusiliers
MAY Frederick MM Cpl 13039 8th Royal Berkshire Regt
MAY Frederick MM L/Cpl 41684 4 Squadron Machine Gun Corps(Cavalry)
MAY Frederick "DCM,MM" Sjt G/11571 1st Royal Fusiliers
MAY Frederick MM L/Cpl 41966 RAMC
MAY George MM Pte 48692 10th Royal Fusiliers
MAY George H. MM Pte 17950 1st King's Own Scottish Borderers
MAY H. MM Pte 200296 4th Hampshire Regt
MAY Harold V. "DCM,MM" Sjt 16662 63 Div Sig Coy Royal Engineers
MAY Harry E. MM Sjt S/41250 1st Gordon Highlanders
MAY Henry MM(3324 Gloucs Regt)+Bar L/Cpl 206118 2nd Devonshire Regt
MAY Henry Charles MM Pte 21503 14th Hampshire Regt KIA 2.8.17.
MAY Henry G.J. MM Drummer 1426 2/2nd London Regt
MAY Herbert MM Pte 29536 2/8th Royal Warwickshire Regt
MAY James S. MM+Bar Pte 2204 Gordon Highlanders

MAY James W. MM Sjt 23425 'R' Cable Section Royal Engineers
MAY John MM Dvr 760903 317 Bde RFA DOW 2.12.17.
MAY John MM Gnr 58443 RFA
MAY John Charles MM Sjt 2476 2/6th London Regt
MAY John H. MM Pte 146183 62nd Bn Machine Gun Corps
MAY John Paul "MC,MM(18196 Pte att 1st R Mun Fus)" 2Lt Royal Dublin Fusiliers
MAY Joseph W. MM Spr 457907 50 Div Sig Coy Royal Engineers
MAY Leonard MM Sjt 201516 1st London Regt
MAY Leonard C. MM Pte 2491 1/22nd London Regt
MAY Leonard H. MM Pte 13486 8th Royal Berkshire Regt
MAY Nathaniel MM L/Cpl 18453 12th Royal Irish Rifles
MAY Percy Y.P. "DCM,MM" CSM 204513 2nd York & Lancaster Regt
MAY Reginald MM Cpl 19787 Somerset Light Infantry
MAY Robert John MM L/Sjt 28027 Royal Welsh Fusiliers
MAY Thomas MM Pte 13426 9th Welsh Regt
MAY Thomas J. MM Pte 19854 Arg & Suth Highlanders
MAY Thomas R. MM+Bar Cpl 49703 RFA
MAY Victor MM Pte 24337 Royal West Kent Regt
MAY William MM L/Cpl 20305 61st Bn Machine Gun Corps KIA 22.3.18.
MAY William A. MM Sjt 201950 1st London Regt
MAY William A. "MM,MID" Pte 8219 East Kent Regt
MAY William C. MM Bdr 42015 RGA
MAY William Everett "MC,MM(365 Sjt)" 2Lt Middlesex Regt
MAYALL Harry MM Dvr 841127 D/70 Bde RFA
MAYALL William MM Pte 67720 1 Coy Machine Gun Corps
MAYBANK Joseph MM Sjt 266836 1/6th Cheshire Regt
MAYBERRY John MM Pte 38371 24th Northumberland Fusiliers DOW 9.4.17.
MAYBERRY William MM Pte 5285 59 Coy Machine Gun Corps KIA 30.11.17.
MAYBOUR Montague MM L/Cpl 21613 15th Hampshire Regt KIA 4.8.18.
MAYBURY Albert Arthur MM L/Cpl 13409 1/5th Leicestershire Regt
MAYBURY David MM L/Cpl 19326 Royal Inniskilling Fusiliers
MAYBURY Franklin MM Pte 18125 1st King's Own Scottish Borderers
MAYBURY Jeremiah MM Sjt 2600 2/5th Lancashire Fusiliers
MAYBURY Richard MM Pte 17203 6th South Wales Borderers
MAYBURY Thomas MM Gnr 180975 230 Siege Bty RGA
MAYCOCK Arnold MM Pte R/1736 12th King's Royal Rifle Corps
MAYCOCK Charles H. MM Sjt 64498 RAMC
MAYCOCK Edgar W. MM Pte 27099 1st Duke of Cornwall's LI
MAYCOCK Frederick MM Sjt 8865 2nd Northamptonshire Regt KIA 21.11.17.
MAYCOCK Harry MM Pte 57783 13th Yorkshire Regt
MAYCOCK Jack H. MM Sjt 240210 North Staffordshire Regt
MAYCOCK John Arthur MM Pte 19568 1/5th Royal Warwickshire Regt KIA 9.9.18.
MAYCOCK Stanley A. MM Pte M/33573 5 Div Train Army Service Corps
MAYCOCK Thomas MM+Bar Sjt 10514 5th Oxf & Bucks Light Infantry
MAYCOCK Thomas M. MM Pte 22141 Yorkshire Light Infantry
MAYELL Frederick MM Cpl 17572 19th Lancashire Fusiliers att RE.
MAYER Alfred N. MM Cpl 6206 10th Hussars
MAYER Ernest MM Pte G/5920 13th Royal Fusiliers
MAYER Gustave MM L/Cpl S/25859 1st Rifle Brigade
MAYER J. MM L/Cpl P/2445 Military Mounted Police
MAYER Peter MM Gnr 70842 43 Bde RFA
MAYER Tom B. "MM,MID" Pte 11001 Scots Guards
MAYERS Arthur MM Gnr 24990 RFA
MAYES Albert E. MM Dvr 90997 106 Fd Coy Royal Engineers
MAYES Alfred MM Spr 97609 218 Fd Coy Royal Engineers
MAYES Arthur E. MM Pte 373757 London Regt
MAYES Charles P. MM L/Cpl 333 7th Royal Sussex Regt
MAYES David MM Pte G/5265 8th East Surrey Regt
MAYES Fred MM Pte 42833 Durham Light Infantry
MAYES Horace G. MM Pte 10489 7th Bedfordshire Regt
MAYES James MM Pte 5977 11th Arg & Suth Highlanders
MAYES James MM Sjt 12669 7th Cameron Highlanders
MAYES John MM Gnr 40398 RGA
MAYES Robert W. MM Cpl 43333 1st Northamptonshire Regt
MAYES Sydney MM Pte 15910 6th Northamptonshire Regt
MAYES Thomas MM Pte 290633 8th Royal Highlanders
MAYES Thomas MM Pte 52634 Royal Welsh Fusiliers
MAYES William MM Gnr 26322 RFA
MAYFIELD Jim MM Pte 268888 Notts & Derby Regt
MAYGER W.M. MM Cpl 1649 Royal Flying Corps
MAYHEAD Victor Leslie MM L/Cpl 207836 10th Royal West Surrey Regt
MAYHEAD William MM Sjt 6839 10th Royal West Surrey Regt
MAYHEW George MM Pte M2/148407 Army Service Corps
MAYHEW Henry MM Cpl 13271 7th Royal West Surrey Regt
MAYHEW James S. MM Gnr 925512 RFA
MAYHEW John Danton MM Sjt 374104 163 Siege Bty RGA
MAYLE Herbert Charles MM Pte 20797 1/8th Royal Warwickshire Regt
MAYLE William MM Pte S/11593 2nd Rifle Brigade
MAYLED Jesse MM Cpl 242599 6th Lancashire Fusiliers
MAYLES Ralph "MM,MID" L/Cpl 3224 1st King's Royal Rifle Corps
MAYLETT George "DCM,MM" Sjt 12327 13th Liverpool Regt
MAYLETT Sidney P. MM Sjt 2231 Worcestershire Regt
MAYLOR John P.J. MM Pte 21959 Cheshire Regt
MAYLOR Joseph H. MM Pte 34541 Labour Corps
MAYLOR Robert George MM Sjt 28161 6th Shropshire Light Infantry
MAYMAN William A. MM S/Sjt 12618 4(Cav)Fd Amb RAMC
MAYNARD Albert MM Pte 3/7024 2nd Bedfordshire att 1/1st Hertfordshire Regt
MAYNARD C.H. MM+Bar Gnr 93077 RFA
MAYNARD George MM Pte 36485 3rd Worcestershire Regt
MAYNARD James MM Pte 13673 2nd Lincolnshire Regt
MAYNARD Sidney MM Cpl 22012 32nd Royal Fusiliers
MAYNE Alfred MM Sjt 250648 3rd London Regt
MAYNE Arthur MM L/Cpl 300458 18th Liverpool Regt
MAYNE George MM+Bar Sjt 17951 11 Coy 4th Bn Machine Gun Corps
MAYNE Lewis H. MM Pte 127015 Machine Gun Corps
MAYNE Patrick MM Gnr 139604 255 Siege Bty RGA
MAYNE Percy G. MM Pte C/7610 King's Royal Rifle Corps
MAYNEORD Sidney MM+Bar Pte 703089 23rd London Regt
MAYO Frederick W. MM L/Cpl 9059 2nd. Worcestershire Regt
MAYO Ivor MM Pte CMT/96 5 Ammn Park Army Service Corps
MAYOH Samuel MM Cpl 240848 1/5th Seaforth Highlanders
MAYOH William MM Pte 241910 East Lancashire Regt
MAYORS John MM+2 Bars L/Cpl 308388 8th Liverpool Regt
MAYRICK Cecil Jack MM Sjt 201265 Tank Corps
MAYS John Robert MM L/Cpl 17196 6th Royal Berkshire Regt
MAYS Thomas J. MM Spr 63690 Royal Engineers
MAYSON Mark "DCM,MM" Sjt 2071 5th Lancers KIA 9.8.18.
MAYSON Ralph H. MM Cpl 116052 RFA
MAYSTON Robert William "DCM,MM.CG(B)" CSM 25434 12th East Surrey Regt
MAZEY Jack MM+Bar Cpl 203843 8th Royal Berkshire Regt
MAZZEY C.H. MM Pte 3784 Dragoon Guards
McADAM Alfred MM Pte S/31864 5th Cameron Highlanders
McADAM David MM Sjt 250559 1/4th London Regt
McADAM John MM Pte 28968 Welsh Regt
McADAM Robert MM Sjt 251420 11th Royal Scots
McADAM William MM Pte 330647 Royal Scots
McALARNEY James MM Pte 200272 1/4th Royal Lancaster Regt KIA 9.4.18.
McALDEN David MM+Bar Gnr 31023 A/108 Bde RFA
McALEAVEY Patrick Bernard MM Pte 23551 1st Royal Irish Fusiliers KIA 11.7.17.
McALINDEN Joseph MM Pte 146656 62nd Bn Machine Gun Corps
McALLEN Charles F. MM L/Bdr L/29165 D/175 Bde RFA
McALLISTER Arthur MM Gnr 22872 RGA
McALLISTER Duncan MM L/Cpl 140224 Royal Engineers
McALLISTER J.McK. MM Sjt 650161 RFA
McALLISTER John MM L/Cpl 32681 16th Highland Light Infantry
McALLISTER John MM Pte 6896 23rd Middlesex Regt KIA 9.8.18.
McALLISTER John MM Cpl 18207 Machine Gun Corps
McALLISTER Patrick MM L/Cpl 278875 Arg & Suth Highlanders
McALLISTER Robert MM Pte S/6837 Royal Highlanders
McALLISTER Robert MM Spr 79091 Royal Engineers
McALLISTER Robert MM Sjt 242321 1/5th Gordon Highlanders DOW 8.5.18.
McALLISTER Ronald MM+Bar Cpl 12003 2nd Royal Berkshire Regt
McALLISTER Samuel MM L/Cpl 241077 1/6th Highland Light Infantry
McALLISTER Thomas MM CQMS S/11946 7th Cameron Highlanders
McALLISTER William MM Pte 908 GMGR
McALONEN James MM Dvr 70071 D/298 Bde RFA KIA 9.4.18.
McALPINE Alexander F. MM Sjt 17569 12th Highland Light Infantry
McALPINE Charles MM Spr 57988 36 Div Sig Coy Royal Engineers
McALPINE Donald L. MM Sjt 14530 15th Highland Light Infantry

McALPINE George MM Pte 7299 2/5th Royal Warwickshire Regt KIA 21.10.16.
McALPINE James M. MM Pte 60174 5/6th Royal Scots
McALPINE Robert MM Sjt 28064 1st Scottish Rifles
McALPINE William MM Cpl 25600 1st Bn Machine Gun Corps
McANARY James "MM,MIDx2" Pte 9197 1st Royal Inniskilling Fusiliers KIA 30.11.17.
McANDREW Bartholomew MM Pte 2220 West Yorkshire Regt KIA 3.6.18.
McANDREW Isaac MM Pte R/16595 12th King's Royal Rifle Corps
McANDREW William MM(1227 Pte Nbld Fus)+Bar L/Cpl 50638 1st East Yorkshire Regt
McANDREW William A. MM Pte 290399 Royal Highlanders
McARA Henry MM Cpl 950983 2/14(City of London)Bde RFA
McARA John MM Cpl(MCDR) 406409 51 Div Sig Coy Royal Engineers
McARA Peter S. MM Pte 19041 King's Own Scottish Borderers
McARDLE Alexander F. MM Sjt Fitter 751361 D/223 Bde RFA
McARDLE Edwin James MM Pte 47996 68 Fd Amb RAMC
McARDLE Francis MM Pte 10924 2nd Leinster Regt
McARDLE Francis MM Pte 200151 1/5th Liverpool Regt
McARDLE J.W. MM Pte 265446 Liverpool Regt
McARDLE John D. MM Pte 9617 2nd Lancashire Fusiliers
McARDLE Thomas "MM,MSM" Cpl 463022 50 Div Sig Coy Royal Engineers
McARTHUR Alexander George MM Bdr 62816 7 Bde RHA
McARTHUR David MM Cpl 6575 Lancashire Fusiliers
McARTHUR Frederick MM Cpl 201594 2/5th Liverpool Regt
McARTHUR George MM Cpl 19514 10/11th Highland Light Infantry KIA 28.4.17.
McARTHUR James MM Pte 18238 Machine Gun Corps
McARTHUR James MM+Bar Cpl 331734 1/9th Highland Light Infantry KIA 12.10.18.
McARTHUR Malcolm "DCM,MM" Sjt 1342 2nd Arg & Suth Highlanders KIA 7.3.17.
McARTHUR Neil MM Spr 357620 Royal Engineers
McARTHUR Peter "DCM+Bar,MM,MID" CSM 7804 8th Royal Highlanders
McARTHUR Robert MM Pte S/10191 7th Cameron Highlanders
McARTHUR William Hicks MM Gnr 222652 C/96 Bde RFA DOW 22.8.18.
McASLAN Robert MM Pte 280758 1/7th Highland Light Infantry
McATAMNEY William MM Pte 14159 9th Royal Inniskilling Fusiliers
McATEE Patrick MM Sjt 240493 1/5th King's Own Scottish Borderers KIA 31.10.18.
McATEER John MM Pte 13241 9th Royal Irish Rifles
McATEER John MM L/Cpl 10443 2nd Irish Guards KIA 13.4.18.
McATEER Samuel MM Pte 10092 1st Royal Scots
McATEER William J. MM Pte 44503 10th Royal Scots att 1st OBLI.
McAUGHTRY Lionel MM Pte 19/757 Northumberland Fusiliers
McAULEY Dennis MM L/Cpl 11581 2nd Highland Light Infantry
McAULEY J. MM Cpl 200581 Seaforth Highlanders
McAULEY Robert MM Spr 64528 36 Div Sig Coy Royal Engineers KIA 21.3.18.
McAULEY Robert MM Pte 21232 11th Highland Light Infantry
McAULEY Thomas MM Pte 315923 13th Royal Highlanders
McAULIFFE Daniel MM Cpl 38132 Welsh Regt
McAULIFFE Frederick Charles MM Spr 198124 Guards Div Sig Coy Royal Engineers KIA 27.8.18.
McAULIFFE John Arthur MM Cpl 93797 41 Div Sig Coy Royal Engineers
McAULIFFE Patrick MM Pte 7094 2nd Leinster Regt
McAUSLAN Alexander MM Sjt 106496 Royal Engineers
McAUSLAND George Lauder "MM,DM(B)" Pte 53722 73 Fd Amb RAMC
McAUSLANE George MM Gnr 229534 RFA
McAVAN Brian MM Sjt 12257 13th West Riding Regt KIA 3.5.17.
McAVOY James MM Pte 6038 Seaforth Highlanders
McAVOY Thomas E. MM Pte 202033 1/4th York & Lancaster Regt
McBAIN Alexander MM Pte 1188 1/4th Seaforth Highlanders
McBAIN Alexander MM Pte 15052 1st Scots Guards
McBAIN Angus MM Pte S/17595 Cameron Highlanders
McBAIN John MM Cpl 24499 51st Bn Machine Gun Corps
McBAIN Peter MM+Bar Pte S/17016 2nd Arg & Suth Highlanders
McBAIN William MM Pte 202749 1/4th Seaforth Highlanders
McBEAN Alexander W. MM Pte 88639 38 Fd Amb RAMC
McBEAN John Robert MM Pte 28228 9th Yorkshire Regt DOW 14.1.18.
McBEATH Alexander MM+Bar L/Cpl 9338 7th Seaforth Highlanders KIA 1.10.18.

McBEATH George A. MM L/Cpl S/6588 8th Seaforth Highlanders
McBEATH James MM L/Sjt 330547 1/9th Highland Light Infantry
McBEATH William MM CSM 3/8438 1/5th Seaforth Highlanders
McBETH Patrick MM Pte S/21501 1st Gordon Highlanders
McBEY Robert MM 2nd Cpl 192668 'G' Special Coy Royal Engineers
McBRATNEY William MM Pte 9876 1st Royal Irish Rifles
McBRAYNE John A. MM Sjt 300427 1/8th Arg & Suth Highlanders
McBRAYNE Neil MM L/Cpl 293162 8th Royal Highlanders
McBREARTY James MM Pte 352560 1/9th Royal Scots
McBREARTY Patrick MM Sjt 17910 12th Highland Light Infantry
McBRIDE Hugh MM L/Cpl 17059 16th Highland Light Infantry
McBRIDE James MM Sjt S/2058 7th Seaforth Highlanders KIA 14.7.16.
McBRIDE James MM Tpr 2983 2nd Life Guards
McBRIDE James MM Pte 21164 6th King's Own Scottish Borderers
McBRIDE John MM Pte 251545 1/6th Arg & Suth Highlanders
McBRIDE John "MM,MID" Cpl 6946 RFA
McBRIDE John "DCM,MM" Cpl 282547 17th Highland Light Infantry
McBRIDE John MM Pte 11616 6th Cameron Highlanders
McBRIDE Richard MM Pte 24571 16th Highland Light Infantry
McBRIDE Samuel MM Pte 482488 Labour Corps
McBRIDE Thomas MM Pte PW/443 18th Middlesex Regt
McBRIDE William MM L/Cpl 22935 Royal Irish Fusiliers
McBRIDE William MM L/Cpl 17325 West Yorkshire Regt
McBRIEN William "DCM,MM" Sjt 47384 34 Fd Amb RAMC
McBRIEN William J. MM Bdr 160779 RFA
McBRIER J. "DCM,MM" Sjt 18585 9th Bn Machine Gun Corps
McBRINE James MM Cpl 8478 1st Dragoon Guards
McBRINN Arthur MM+Bar Sjt 56204 18 Div Sig Coy Royal Engineers
McBURNIE Samuel MM L/Cpl 10123 1st King's Own Scottish Borderers DOW 8.6.18.
McBURNIE Spiers MM L/Cpl 10204 2nd Gordon Highlanders
McBURNIE William J. MM Cpl 51197 2nd Royal Scots
McCABE Charles MM Pte 325199 1/8th Royal Scots
McCABE Dennis MM Sjt SPTS/2966 24th Royal Fusiliers
McCABE H. MM Pte 538255 RAMC
McCABE Harry George MM Sjt 9346 3rd Coldstream Guards
McCABE Henry MM Pte 54646 RAMC
McCABE James MM Pte 6951 2nd Royal Scots Fusiliers KIA 1.7.16.
McCABE James MM Sjt T3/026513 Army Service Corps
McCABE James Bernard MM Pte 13240 4th Liverpool Regt KIA 11.4.18.
McCABE John MM Pte 40089 Royal Irish Rifles
McCABE Joseph MM Pte 5237 1st Irish Guards
McCABE Philip MM L/Sjt 290429 7th Royal Highlanders
McCABE Robert MM L/Sjt 2827 1st Irish Guards
McCABE Robert MM L/Cpl 12949 6/7th Royal Scots Fusiliers KIA 12.8.16.
McCABE William MM Pte 10791 6th Royal Irish Rifles
McCADDEN Daniel MM Pte 303341 Arg & Suth Highlanders
McCADDEN George William MM Sjt 267169 2/6th Gloucestershire Regt
McCAFFERTY Daniel MM Pte 241813 Gloucestershire Regt
McCAFFERTY John C. MM Sjt 3076 20th London Regt
McCAFFERY Edward "MM,MID" L/Cpl 76017 Royal Engineers
McCAFFERY John MM Pte 22785 Royal Irish Fusiliers
McCAFFREY David S. MM Sjt 48970 25th Royal Welsh Fusiliers
McCAFFREY Edward MM L/Sjt S/43162 8th Royal Highlanders
McCAFFREY John MM Pte 7866 1st Irish Guards
McCAFFREY Thomas "MM,MID" Sjt 6638 71 Bty 36 Bde RFA
McCAIG Angus MM+Bar Sjt S/2372 10th Arg & Suth Highlanders
McCAIG Joseph MM Pte 59721 11th Royal Scots Fusiliers
McCAIG Joseph MM L/Sjt 1438 1/9th Highland Light Infantry KIA 15.7.16.
McCALL John MM L/Cpl 32546 6th King's Own Scottish Borderers
McCALL John MM Sjt 38770 RAMC
McCALL John A. "MM,MID" Cpl 7257 2nd King's Royal Rifle Corps
McCALL Thomas MM L/Cpl 266202 1st Northumberland Fusiliers
McCALL William MM+2 Bars L/Cpl 20165 Royal Irish Fusiliers
McCALLAN Thomas H. MM L/Cpl 172510 16 Div Sig Coy Royal Engineers
McCALLUM Angus MM Pte 254012 Arg & Suth Highlanders
McCALLUM D. MM Bdr 2810 RGA
McCALLUM George MM Pte 200419 1/4th Royal Scots Fusiliers
McCALLUM George MM Sjt 22373 10th Highland Light Infantry
McCALLUM George R. MM Pte S/3749 11th Arg & Suth Highlanders
McCALLUM John MM+Bar L/Cpl 1616 7th Royal West Kent Regt KIA 12.4.18.

McCALLUM Joseph MM Bdr 39853 4 Siege Bty RGA
McCALLUM Robert MM Sjt Saddler 645037 RFA
McCALLUM Simon MM Cpl 14089 8th Yorkshire Regt
McCALLUM T.B. MM Pte 39442 19th Durham Light Infantry
McCALLUM Thomas MM Sjt T4/237101 51 Div Train Army Service Corps
McCALLUM W. MM Pte 11376 1st Royal Inniskilling Fusiliers
McCALMAN Godfrey MM Pte 4/9331 Arg & Suth Highlanders
McCAMLEY Joseph "MM,MSM" Sjt 9362 2nd Royal Irish Rifles
McCAMMOND George MM Dvr 1197 Royal Engineers
McCANCE William MM Sjt 577 11th Highland Light Infantry
McCANDLESS Robert J. MM L/Cpl 15434 Royal Irish Fusiliers
McCANN Edward MM L/Cpl 27437 King's Own Scottish Borderers
McCANN Francis "DCM,MM" Pte G/3874 6th Royal West Surrey Regt
McCANN Frank MM Cpl 41070 RAMC
McCANN George R. MM Pte 279026 1/7th Arg & Suth Highlanders
McCANN Henry "MM,MID" Pte 13497 12th Northumberland Fusiliers
McCANN Herbert H.E. MM Pte 202307 Border Regt
McCANN Hugh MM Pte 68092 RAMC
McCANN James MM Sjt 14457 5 Fd Amb RAMC
McCANN John MM Pte 16678 2nd Royal Scots Fusiliers
McCANN John MM Cpl 305168 Liverpool Regt
McCANN Joseph MM Pte 8890 2nd Royal Irish Rifles
McCANN Oliver MM L/Cpl 9667 Irish Guards
McCANN Patrick MM Pte 10449 1st Royal Irish Fusiliers
McCANN Patrick MM Bdr 27386 RFA
McCANN Patrick MM Pte 7909 2nd Royal Dublin Fusiliers
McCANN Patrick MM Bdr 97104 RFA
McCANN Percy J. MM 2nd Cpl 13294 2 Fd Coy Royal Engineers
McCANN Peter MM Pte 3234 19 Fd Amb RAMC
McCANN Thomas MM Pte 573709 London Regt
McCANNAH Joseph MM Sjt 24436 RFA
McCARLE John MM Pte 268126 Royal Highlanders
McCARLEY William MM Pte 41329 9th Royal Irish Fusiliers
McCARRICK Joseph MM Pte 18884 4th Grenadier Guards
McCARRICK Joseph MM Bdr 71910 34 Bde RFA
McCARROLL John MM Sjt 815177 D/250 Bde RFA
McCARROLL Robert H. MM Pte S/16372 1/5th Arg & Suth Highlanders
McCARROLL W. MM Pte 240940 Seaforth Highlanders
McCART Daniel MM Pte 10338 1st Scots Guards
McCART William MM Pte 19525 11th Highland Light Infantry
McCARTE Hugh MM Pte 73129 Machine Gun Corps
McCARTEN James MM L/Cpl 21563 1st Royal Dublin Fusiliers
McCARTEN John C. "DCM,MM" CSM 330526 Liverpool Regt
McCARTEN Patrick MM Pte 9262 Northumberland Fusiliers
McCARTH John MM Bdr 776686 C/312 Bde RFA
McCARTHY Arthur MM Pte 242241 North Staffordshire Regt
McCARTHY Cornelius "MM,MID" Sjt 67110 11 Bde RFA
McCARTHY Daniel MM Cpl 6341 Y/21 Med TM Bty RGA KIA 26.6.16.
McCARTHY Daniel MM Gnr 77560 D/231 Bde RFA
McCARTHY Daniel MM Sjt 16608 3 Bde RHA
McCARTHY Denis MM Cpl 62429 71 Bty 36 Bde RFA
McCARTHY Dennis MM Pte 251325 Manchester Regt
McCARTHY Edwin MM Pte 3152 2nd Leinster Regt
McCARTHY Francis J. MM Pte 129894 17th Bn Machine Gun Corps
McCARTHY Frank MM L/Cpl 11030 2nd Royal Irish Regt
McCARTHY Frederick MM+Bar Bdr 45353 RFA
McCARTHY George MM Cpl 11272 7th Duke of Cornwall's LI KIA 16.9.16.
McCARTHY Harry Edward MM Sjt 22311 D/190 Bde RFA
McCARTHY Hugh William MM Gnr 39401 A/180 Bde RFA
McCARTHY J.W. MM Sjt 200207 Essex Regt
McCARTHY Jack MM Pte 305657 1/8th Royal Warwickshire Regt
McCARTHY James MM Sjt 69329 2 Bde RFA
McCARTHY Jeremiah MM L/Cpl 9664 1st Welsh Regt
McCARTHY John MM Sjt 5979 6th Border Regt
McCARTHY John MM Sjt 5712 1st King's Royal Rifle Corps
McCARTHY John MM Pte 6676 Royal Munster Fusiliers
McCARTHY John MM Pte 15085 12th Durham Light Infantry KIA 7.10.16.
McCARTHY John MM L/Cpl L/12179 13th Royal Fusiliers KIA 28.4.17.
McCARTHY John MM Sjt 25989 7th Royal Irish Regt
McCARTHY John MM Cpl 43067 1st Royal Dublin Fusiliers
McCARTHY John MM Bdr 355 122 Bde RFA
McCARTHY John MM Pte DM2/112059 Army Service Corps
McCARTHY John J. MM Spr 74159 Royal Engineers

McCARTHY John P. MM Sjt 51682 RFA
McCARTHY Joseph MM Cpl 9911 2nd Border Regt
McCARTHY Michael MM Pte 5265 2nd Royal Munster Fusiliers
McCARTHY Michael Joseph MM Sjt 16762 1st Royal Dublin Fusiliers DOW 5.10.17.
McCARTHY Patrick MM Pte 15033 Leinster Regt
McCARTHY Patrick MM Pte 265437 Labour Corps
McCARTHY Patrick MM Pte 9754 2nd Irish Guards
McCARTHY Robert MM Sjt 6528 2nd Irish Guards KIA 15.9.16.
McCARTHY Stephen MM Sjt 332667 1/9th Liverpool Regt
McCARTHY Thomas MM Pte 8619 Royal Irish Rifles
McCARTHY Thomas MM Sjt 8657 2nd Leinster Regt KIA 31.7.17.
McCARTHY Thomas Joseph MM 2nd Cpl 25280 2 Fd Sqn Royal Engineers KIA 25.9.16.
McCARTHY Thomas W. MM Gnr 944587 D/210 Bde RFA
McCARTHY Timothy MM Pte 11319 2nd South Wales Borderers
McCARTHY Timothy MM L/Sjt 8348 6th Royal Irish Regt DOW 27.9.18.
McCARTHY Timothy "MM,MID" Pte 9631 2nd Leinster Regt
McCARTHY William C. MM Spr 470874 206 Fd Coy Royal Engineers
McCARTHY William G. MM Sjt 37993 115 Heavy Bty RGA
McCARTNEY Bernard MM Pte 14884 Yorkshire Regt
McCARTNEY Edward M. MM Cpl 30546 407 Bty 96 Bde RFA
McCARTNEY Ernest G. MM Cpl 1390 Y/21 Med TM Bty RGA
McCARTNEY George "DCM,MM,MC(G)" Sjt 12668 11th Scottish Rifles
McCARTNEY Henry MM Pte 17360 9th Royal Inniskilling Fusiliers KIA 29.3.18.
McCARTNEY James MM Cpl 2193 1/5th Durham Light Infantry
McCARTNEY James P. MM BSM 940008 D/280 Bde RFA
McCARTNEY Joseph MM Pte 316235 1/1(Lowland)Fd Amb RAMC
McCARTNEY Peter MM Pte 7028 1st Royal Scots Fusiliers
McCARTY James MM Pte 21611 12th Manchester Regt
McCARTY Thomas MM Sjt 19950 7th Border Regt
McCASKIE Thomas MM Cpl 50200 Liverpool Regt
McCASKILL Alastair MM Pte 300456 1/8th Arg & Suth Highlanders
McCASKILL Angus MM Cpl 14901 11th Royal Inniskilling Fusiliers KIA 1.7.16.
McCAUGHAN George MM L/Cpl 16692 1st Royal Irish Rifles KIA 4.9.18.
McCAUGHEY Jack MM Cpl 119404 RFA
McCAUGHY Patrick MM BSM 7531 65 Bty 28 Bde RFA
McCAUL Leopold William MM Cpl M2/054816 14 Bde RGA Ammn Col Army Service Corps
McCAULEY William MM Sjt 18856 8th Royal Dublin Fusiliers
McCAUSLAND Mark MM Sjt 675174 RFA
McCAVER Robert J. MM Sjt 17759 49th Bn Machine Gun Corps
McCHESNEY Samuel MM Pte 15354 9th Royal Irish Rifles
McCHYSTAL John "DCM,MM" Pte 21738 8th Royal Lancaster Regt
McCLAFFERTY Edward F. "MM,MSM" Sjt 53050 'AW' Cable Section Royal Engineers
McCLAFFERTY J. MM Dvr 325 RFA
McCLARNON Henry MM Pte 9133 1st Royal Irish Rifles
McCLARTY Frank "MM,CG(B)" Pte 18216 12th Royal Irish Rifles
McCLATCHEY Thomas MM Pte 15357 15th Royal Irish Rifles
McCLAY Thomas "DCM,MM" CSM 13603 9th Royal Inniskilling Fusiliers
McCLAY William MM Cpl 21202 1st Royal Inniskilling Fusiliers KIA 22.3.18.
McCLEAN D. MM Cpl 4265 12th Royal Irish Rifles
McCLEAN James P. MM Pte 602486 18th London Regt
McCLELLAN Charles MM CSM 240742 1/5th Border Regt
McCLELLAN Harry MM Sjt 350258 15th Highland Light Infantry
McCLELLAN S. "MM,MID" L/Cpl S/8035 Gordon Highlanders
McCLELLAND Frederick C. MM Sjt 32729 33 Div Sig Coy Royal Engineers
McCLELLAND George B. MM Pte 49741 9th Royal Irish Fusiliers
McCLELLAND James MM Pte 13288 6th Royal Inniskilling Fusiliers
McCLELLAND Thomas A. MM Pte 41307 Royal Irish Fusiliers
McCLELLAND William Henry MM Pte 357001 1/10th Liverpool Regt
McCLEMENTS Andrew MM Cpl 15637 9th Royal Irish Rifles
McCLEMENTS Lewis MM L/Cpl 204683 15th Hampshire Regt
McCLEW John W. MM 2nd Cpl 29365 XVII Corps HAG Sig Det Royal Engineers
McCLINTOCK James W. MM Pte 34759 5th West Riding Regt
McCLINTOCK Robert MM Sjt 14091 2nd Royal Inniskilling Fusiliers
McCLINTOCK Samuel MM Cpl 9/15368 9th Royal Irish Rifles
McCLINTOCK Thomas MM L/Cpl 17245 Royal Inniskilling Fusiliers
McCLORY Patrick MM Sjt 330327 1/8th Royal Scots

McCLOUD William MM Pte 11829 1st Liverpool Regt
McCLOY John MM Gnr 94630 RFA
McCLUCKIE William MM Cpl 3/3999 1st Royal Highlanders
McCLUMPHA Thomas MM Pte 175 20th Durham Light Infantry
McCLUMPHIE Charles MM L/Cpl 40127 Scottish Rifles
McCLUNEY Hugh MM Pte 22696 Royal Irish Fusiliers
McCLUNIE Robert S. MM Pte 30981 7/8th King's Own Scottish Borderers
McCLURE Andrew R. MM Pte 46866 Northumberland Fusiliers
McCLURE David MM+2 Bars Pte 15013 7/8th King's Own Scottish Borderers
McCLURE George MM Pte 15920 11th Northumberland Fusiliers
McCLURE James MM L/Sjt 13989 XVII Corps Cyclist Bn Army Cyclist Corps
McCLURE John MM Sjt 12337 8th Royal Irish Rifles
McCLURE Robert MM L/Cpl 2829 Northumberland Fusiliers
McCLURE Robert Calderwood MM Gnr 169828 B/102 Bde RFA
McCLURE Stewart MM Pte 202274 5/6th Scottish Rifles
McCLURE Thomas "DCM,MM" Sjt 21877 142 Siege Bty RGA
McCLURG Matthew MM L/Cpl 75237 2nd Bn Tank Corps
McCLURG Robert MM L/Cpl 856 16th Royal Irish Rifles
McCLUSKEY Francis John MM Sjt 15373 2nd Highland Light Infantry
McCLUSKEY James MM Pte 5784 6th King's Own Scottish Borderers KIA 25.4.18.
McCLUSKEY James Joseph Patrick MM L/Cpl 16867 12th Royal Scots
McCLUSKEY John MM Cpl 4762 Gordon Highlanders
McCLUSKIE John MM Pte 8419 2nd King's Own Scottish Borderers
McCLUSKIE R. MM Pte 17247 1st Royal Scots Fusiliers
McCLYMONT Daniel MM L/Sjt 17141 23rd Bn Machine Gun Corps
McCLYMONT James MM Gnr Fitter 148699 256 Siege Bty RGA
McCLYMONT Matthew MM Spr 93640 219 Fd Coy Royal Engineers
McCLYMONT Samuel MM Sjt 240462 1/5th Royal Scots Fusiliers
McCOEY Frank MM Pte 3540 6th Royal Irish Regt
McCOLE James MM Spr 121169 Royal Engineers
McCOLGAN James MM Gnr 24923 X/6 Med TM Bty RGA
McCOLL Alexander MM+Bar Cpl 44141 11 Bde RFA
McCOLL Alexander M. MM+Bar Sjt 19805 Machine Gun Corps
McCOLL Alfred MM Pte 44070 Yorkshire Light Infantry
McCOLL Duncan MM L/Cpl 300189 1/8th Arg & Suth Highlanders
McCOLL Duncan MM Pte M2/047893 621 Coy Army Service Corps
McCOLL James MM Sjt Piper 16062 10th Scottish Rifles
McCOLL John MM Sjt 104 1st East Surrey Regt
McCOLL John MM Pte 301329 1/8th Arg & Suth Highlanders
McCOLL John MM Gnr 54664 17 Heavy Bty RGA
McCOLL Joseph MM Cpl 45408 43 Bde RFA
McCOLL Peter MM Sjt 645029 RFA
McCOLM Samuel MM Sjt 6567 RFA
McCOMB William "MM,MID" Pipe Maj 15006 Highland Light Infantry
McCOMBE Charles A. MM+Bar L/Cpl 295519 12th Royal Scots Fusiliers
McCOMBE George MM Sjt 11155 6th King's Own Scottish Borderers
McCOMBIE Charles MM Pte 231031 2/2nd London Regt
McCOMBIE James M. MM Pte 303061 RAMC
McCONACHIE John MM Sjt 350349 1/9th Royal Scots
McCONDACHIE Henry MM Pte 23942 2nd Highland Light Infantry
McCONKEY Campbell MM Sjt 20444 Royal Irish Fusiliers
McCONNACHIE Alexander MM Cpl 200093 1/4th Gordon Highlanders
McCONNACHIE Henry MM Pte 265812 Gordon Highlanders
McCONNACHIE James E. MM Sjt 30450 7th Royal West Surrey Regt
McCONNACHIE Thomas H. MM L/Cpl 41177 Scottish Rifles
McCONNELL Edward MM Sjt 14801 Northumberland Fusiliers
McCONNELL George MM Spr 103086 121 Fd Coy Royal Engineers
McCONNELL Henry MM Cpl 13068 8th Royal Irish Rifles
McCONNELL Hugh MM Pte 1703 2 Fd Amb RAMC
McCONNELL James MM Pte 26986 2nd Highland Light Infantry
McCONNELL James MM Gnr 686 260 Bde RFA
McCONNELL James MM Pte DM2/172030 Army Service Corps
McCONNELL James MM CQMS 240013 Border Regt
McCONNELL John MM+Bar L/Cpl 21260 13th Liverpool Regt
McCONNELL John MM Pte 202288 1/4th Royal Highlanders
McCONNELL Joseph MM Cpl 2368 11th Lancashire Fusiliers KIA 1.5.18
McCONNELL Joseph MM Pte 14703 10th Royal Inniskilling Fusiliers KIA 7.12.17.
McCONNELL Robert J. MM L/Sjt 8662 1st Irish Guards
McCONNELL Robert Joseph MM Pte 6158 14th Royal Irish Rifles
McCONNELL Samuel MM L/Cpl 240152 5/6th Scottish Rifles
McCONNELL Samuel MM L/Cpl 15374 14th Royal Irish Rifles DOW 21.11.17.
McCONNELL Thomas MM Pte 29986 1st King's Own Scottish Borderers
McCONNELL Walter MM L/Cpl 6343 1st Irish Guards DOW 19.9.18.
McCONVILLE J. MM Pte 241936 Lancashire Fusiliers
McCORD John MM Sjt 375029 2nd Royal Scots
McCORD Thomas MM L/Sjt 41461 18th Highland Light Infantry KIA 30.9.18.
McCORKINDALE Charles MM Cpl 8123 18th Highland Light Infantry
McCORMAC A.G. MM Sjt 9798 King's Own Scottish Borderers att KAR.
McCORMACK Charles MM Sjt 10086 2nd East Surrey Regt
McCORMACK David MM Sjt 8961 1st Royal Munster Fusiliers DOW 24.4.17.
McCORMACK F.W. MM Sjt 90350 RFA
McCORMACK Frank MM Pte 18267 11th Scottish Rifles
McCORMACK George MM Pte 290514 Gordon Highlanders
McCORMACK H. MM Pte 34843 York & Lancaster Regt
McCORMACK Herbert MM L/Cpl 2759 Cheshire Regt
McCORMACK James MM Cpl 2300 2nd Leinster Regt
McCORMACK John J. MM Sjt 27020 10th Royal Dublin Fusiliers KIA 8.2.17.
McCORMACK Neil MM Dvr 45943 A/86 Bde RFA
McCORMACK Patrick MM Pte 9874 1st Connaught Rangers
McCORMACK Percy J. MM Cpl 1278 King Edward's Horse
McCORMACK Robert J. MM Gnr 46798 RFA
McCORMACK William MM Dvr 35774 2 Div Ammn Col RFA
McCORMACK William MM Pte 331006 Liverpool Regt
McCORMACK William MM+Bar Sjt 139247 252 Tunnelling Coy Royal Engineers
McCORMACK William J. MM L/Cpl 9/15377 9th Royal Irish Rifles
McCORMICK Albert J. MM Pte M2/053927 Army Service Corps
McCORMICK Charles MM Pte 20910 1st Royal Dublin Fusiliers
McCORMICK Charles MM Pte 10322 2nd Royal Sussex Regt
McCORMICK Charles MM L/Cpl 202126 Liverpool Regt
McCORMICK Daniel H. MM L/Cpl L/10184 7th Royal West Kent Regt
McCORMICK Edward MM Cpl 217296 RFA
McCORMICK Edward C. MM Bdr 73625 120 Bty 27 Bde RFA
McCORMICK James "MM,MSM" L/Cpl 24125 23 Fd Coy Royal Engineers
McCORMICK James MM Bdr 34791 RGA
McCORMICK James MM Pte 303337 Arg & Suth Highlanders
McCORMICK James MM Pte 300351 Manchester Regt
McCORMICK John MM Pte 24261 South Wales Borderers
McCORMICK Joseph MM Cpl 3764 9th Royal Highlanders
McCORMICK Robert J. MM Pte 14566 Royal Irish Fusiliers
McCORMICK Robert J. MM Pte 39218 Liverpool Regt
McCORMICK Thomas MM L/Cpl 9818 1st Royal Inniskilling Fusiliers
McCORMICK Thomas MM Pte 18205 1st Cameron Highlanders
McCORMICK William MM Pte 26599 7th Royal Irish Regt KIA 31.10.18.
McCORMICK William MM L/Sjt 200975 Seaforth Highlanders
McCORMICK William MM Pte 41075 109 Fd Amb RAMC KIA 16.8.17.
McCORMICK William J. MM Pte 7849 1st Dorsetshire Regt
McCORQUODALE James MM Dvr 80453 Royal Engineers
McCOUBREY Samuel James MM L/Cpl 14/16738 14th Royal Irish Rifles
McCOURT David MM Sjt 9405 1st Royal Irish Rifles
McCOURT Dixon MM+Bar Sjt 240841 5th Border Regt
McCOURT Edward MM L/Cpl 306240 West Yorkshire Regt
McCOURT James "MM,MID" Sjt 216 22nd Northumberland Fusiliers
McCOWAN James MM+Bar Pte 57532 26th Royal Welsh Fusiliers
McCOWAN William MM L/Sjt 266569 Royal Highlanders
McCOY Bernard MM Gnr 37385 A/78 Bde RFA
McCOY David MM Cpl 10523 Leicestershire Regt
McCOY Henry MM Sjt 48993 11th South Lancashire Regt
McCOY James MM Pte 302220 1/9th Durham Light Infantry
McCOY John MM Sjt 12720 4th Liverpool Regt
McCOY John MM Sjt 8872 1st East Lancashire Regt
McCOY John James MM L/Cpl 16982 11th Notts & Derby Regt
McCOY Lawrence "MM,MSM" Pte 242894 6th Royal Warwickshire Regt
McCOY William MM Pte 267137 Liverpool Regt
McCOY William J. MM Cpl 15178 25 Army Tps Coy Royal Engineers

McCOY William J. MM Pte 53353 RAMC
McCRACKEN Edward MM+Bar Cpl 1105 King Edward's Horse
McCRACKEN Harry MM Pte 355860 Liverpool Regt
McCRACKEN James MM Sjt 147900 Royal Engineers
McCRACKEN James MM Pte 40786 Highland Light Infantry
McCRACKEN Peter MM Cpl 98782 Machine Gun Corps
McCRACKEN Robert MM Pte 6285 6th Dragoons
McCRACKEN Thomas S.C. "DCM,MM" Sjt 448 6 Bty MGC(Motors)
McCRACKEN William MM L/Cpl 56447 52nd Bn Machine Gun Corps
McCRAE Alexander MM Pte 23132 11th Royal Scots
McCRAE John MM L/Cpl 43042 King's Own Scottish Borderers
McCRAE William M. MM Cpl 406129 51 Div Sig Coy Royal Engineers
McCRAITH Terence Patrick MM Pte 350099 1/7th London Regt
McCRAW John MM Cpl S/43192 7th Seaforth Highlanders
McCRAW William MM Pte 51226 1st Royal Scots Fusiliers
McCRAY John MM Sjt 7178 2nd Leinster Regt
McCREA Frank E. MM Sjt 700069 1/23rd London Regt
McCREA William MM L/Cpl 15383 10th Royal Irish Rifles
McCREADIE A. MM Pte 5556 10th Royal Highlanders
McCREADIE James MM Pte 28498 Scottish Rifles
McCREADIE James MM Pte 41281 Royal Highlanders
McCREADIE John MM Gnr 685406 B/277 Bde RFA
McCREADIE John "MM,MID" Sjt 8660 9th Scottish Rifles
McCREADIE Kennedy MM Pte 88387 RAMC
McCREADIE William MM Pte 4655 9th Bn Machine Gun Corps
McCREADY David MM Pte 26769 Royal Inniskilling Fusiliers
McCREADY Ernest MM Pte 21411 Royal Irish Fusiliers
McCREADY Thomas Roulstone Vaughan MM Cpl 307403 8th West Yorkshire Regt
McCREADY William MM L/Cpl 10399 1st Scots Guards
McCREANOR Hugh MM Cpl 27282 1st King's Own Scottish Borderers
McCREARY Matthew MM Pte 35467 RAMC
McCREATH John MM+2 Bars Sjt 42902 15 Div Sig Coy Royal Engineers KIA 24.4.17.
McCREDDIN T. "MM,MID" Spr 10420 55 Fd Coy Royal Engineers
McCREDIE Alexander MM Cpl 81156 95 Fd Coy Royal Engineers
McCREE Arthur MM Spr 492431 18 Div Sig Coy Royal Engineers
McCREEDY William MM Pte 136839 32nd Bn Machine Gun Corps KIA 9.11.18.
McCRINDLE Andrew MM Sjt 17978 1st Royal Scots Fusiliers
McCRON William "MM,CG(B)" Pte 29972 18th Highland Light Infantry
McCRONE Joseph MM Sjt 8871 1st Cheshire Regt
McCRORIE David MM Pte 240285 1/5th Royal Scots Fusiliers
McCRORY Thomas MM Pte 11448 9th Scottish Rifles
McCROW William John MM Cpl 29749 V/19 Heavy TM Bty RGA
McCRUDDEN Robert MM Spr 10363 18 Div Sig Coy Royal Engineers
McCRUM D. MM Gnr 14436 RGA
McCRUM Joseph MM Pte 13175 15th Royal Irish Rifles
McCUBBIN James MM L/Cpl 241188 1/5th King's Own Scottish Borderers
McCUBBREY William MM Cpl 49441 Royal Engineers
McCUDDEN Francis MM L/Cpl 14863 Royal Dublin Fusiliers
McCUDDEN James Thomas Byford "VC,DSO+Bar,MC+Bar,MM(892 F/Sjt)" Maj Att RFC General List Died 9.7.17.
McCUE Edward MM L/Cpl 18645 Royal Dublin Fusiliers
McCUE Henry MM Sjt S/9230 2nd Gordon Highlanders
McCUE John MM Sjt Farrier 44197 45 Bty 42 Bde RFA
McCULLAGH Edward MM Cpl 3224 1st Irish Guards
McCULLAGH George David MM Cpl 26447 2nd Royal Dublin Fusiliers KIA 28.3.18.
McCULLAGH Michael MM Sjt 9314 1st Royal Dublin Fusiliers
McCULLOCH Andrew A.S.B. MM Cpl 10304 13th Middlesex Regt
McCULLOCH David MM Sjt 5401 1st Scots Guards
McCULLOCH Donald MM+Bar Cpl 267271 Seaforth Highlanders
McCULLOCH Francis MM Pte 51489 Royal Scots
McCULLOCH H. MM Sjt 37090 171 Siege Bty RGA
McCULLOCH Henry J. MM Cpl 93373 219 Fd Coy Royal Engineers
McCULLOCH John MM Sjt 715006 RFA
McCULLOCH John MM L/Cpl 9807 Cameron Highlanders
McCULLOCH John MM Cpl 43621 2nd Royal Scots
McCULLOCH Robert MM Pte 4452 1st Royal Highlanders DOW 6.9.18.
McCULLOCH Robert MM L/Cpl 4457 3rd Dragoon Guards
McCULLOCH Robert B. MM Pte 310030 Gordon Highlanders
McCULLOCH Sid R. MM Sjt 1139 Middlesex Regt
McCULLOCH William MM L/Cpl 121908 250 Tunnelling Coy Royal Engineers
McCULLOCH William "DCM,MM+Bar,MID" Sjt 10218 1st Scots Guards
McCULLOCH William MM Pte 201113 Scottish Rifles
McCULLOCH William K. MM Pte S/12848 14th Arg & Suth Highlanders
McCULLOCH William O. MM Pte 27545 Royal Scots
McCULLOCK Alexander S.C. MM+Bar Cpl 93684 Royal Engineers
McCULLOCK Archibald MM Pte 41900 142 Coy Machine Gun Corps
McCULLOCK James MM Pte 28788 East Yorkshire Regt
McCULLOCK John MM Pte 43045 21 Fd Amb RAMC
McCULLOCK Robert MM Gnr 56990 28 Bty 9 Bde RFA
McCULLOGH Joseph J. MM Pte M2/105065 Army Service Corps
McCULLOUGH George MM L/Cpl 265769 1/6th Royal Highlanders
McCULLOUGH James MM Sjt 30080 16 Bde Ammn Col RHA
McCULLOUGH James "DCM,MM" Sjt 14555 9th Royal Irish Fusiliers
McCULLOUGH James F. MM L/Cpl 15/12388 15th Royal Irish Rifles
McCULLOUGH John MM Pte 408026 89 Fd Amb RAMC
McCULLOUGH William MM Pte 16709 10th Royal Irish Rifles
McCULLOUGH William MM Pte M2/131056 Att 250 Tunnelling Coy RE Army Service Corps
McCULLUM Sidney George MM L/Cpl 352108 7th London Regt
McCURLEY Roderick MM Cpl 20962 7/8th Royal Irish Fusiliers
McCURRIE Edward MM Sjt 96039 RFA
McCUSKER Frank "MM,MID" CSM 1910 1st Irish Guards
McCUTCHEON Alexander MM L/Cpl 16229 6/7th Royal Scots Fusiliers
McCUTCHEON Charles MM Pte 17083 1st Royal Scots Fusiliers KIA 14.7.16.
McCUTCHEON John MM Sjt 40727 Highland Light Infantry
McCUTCHEON John MM Pte 3988 2nd Highland Light Infantry
McCUTCHEON John MM Dvr 41579 130 Bde Ammn Col RFA
McCUTCHEON Samuel MM Bdr 760536 A/317 Bde RFA
McDADE James MM+Bar Sjt 8037 2nd Seaforth Highlanders
McDADE John MM Gnr 22753 RGA
McDADE Percival MM Pte 63675 RAMC
McDAID James MM Sjt 750 1st Arg & Suth Highlanders
McDAID James MM Spr 93117 Royal Engineers
McDAVID Frank Armstrong MM L/Cpl 547869 8th Mounted Bde Sig Troop Royal Engineers
McDAVITT John MM L/Cpl 19528 11th Highland Light Infantry
McDEAN Joseph MM Pte S/9705 7th Seaforth Highlanders
McDERMOTT Bernard MM Cpl 42964 2nd Yorkshire Light Infantry
McDERMOTT Charles J. MM L/Cpl 14493 10th York & Lancaster Regt
McDERMOTT Cornelius MM Cpl 9317 1st Leinster Regt
McDERMOTT Frederick J. "MM,MID" Sjt 56381 Machine Gun Corps
McDERMOTT Henry MM L/Cpl 2481 8th Royal West Surrey Regt
McDERMOTT Hubert MM Pte 97392 Notts & Derby Regt
McDERMOTT J. MM Cpl 341178 RAMC
McDERMOTT John MM L/Cpl 12/19644 12th Royal Irish Rifles
McDERMOTT John "MM,CG(B),MIDx3" Sjt 10317 1st King's Own Scottish Borderers
McDERMOTT John MM Pte 10411 Royal Irish Rifles
McDERMOTT John B. MM Pte 14399 6th Border Regt
McDERMOTT Joseph MM Pte 49531 1st Royal Inniskilling Fusiliers
McDERMOTT Joseph MM Pte 352005 6th Manchester Regt
McDERMOTT Matthew J. MM L/Cpl 371243 8th London Regt
McDERMOTT Michael MM Pte 3/8441 Royal Irish Rifles
McDERMOTT Samuel MM Pte 19190 21st Manchester Regt KIA 29.8.16.
McDERMOTT William "DCM,MM" Pte 4/6715 2nd Arg & Suth Highlanders
McDERMOTT William MM Pte 6/2502 6th Royal Irish Regt
McDIARMID A. MM Sjt Piper 330075 9th Highland Light Infantry
McDIARMID Alexander (Alick) MM+Bar L/Sjt S/16245 6th Cameron Highlanders KIA 24.4.17.
McDIARMID William MM 2nd Cpl 12547 Royal Engineers
McDILL "J.

J." MM Pte 2001 Royal Highlanders
McDINE George MM Pte 6242 69 Coy Machine Gun Corps
McDONAGH Edward MM Sjt 6787 Royal Engineers
McDONAGH James Thomas "MM,MSM,MID" Sjt 7724 3rd Coldstream Guards
McDONAGH John MM Pte 18917 5th Royal Irish Fusiliers
McDONALD Adam "DCM,MM" Cpl 16660 13th Royal Scots

McDONALD Adam MM Bdr 7723 65 Bde RFA KIA 23.5.18.
McDONALD Alexander MM Sjt G/59488 17th Royal Fusiliers
McDONALD Alexander MM+Bar Sjt 6765 1/4th Cameron Highlanders
McDONALD Alexander MM Pte 3/7744 Arg & Suth Highlanders
McDONALD Alexander MM Pte 240211 1/5th King's Own Scottish Borderers
McDONALD Alexander MM Pte 301867 14th Bn Tank Corps
McDONALD Alexander MM Cpl 80997 RFA
McDONALD Alexander MM L/Cpl 17814 Royal Scots
McDONALD Alexander MM Cpl 9593 7th Norfolk Regt
McDONALD Alexander MM Pte 266 2nd Gordon Highlanders
McDONALD Alexander MM Sjt 7690 2nd Scottish Rifles DOW 30.3.18.
McDONALD Alexander MM L/Sjt 14362 13th Royal Scots KIA 23.4.17.
McDONALD Alexander MM+Bar Bdr 651054 RFA
McDONALD Alexander MM Sjt 645185 51 Div Ammn Col RFA
McDONALD Alexander MM L/Sjt 6425 1/4th Gordon Highlanders
McDONALD Alexander MM Cpl 17540 8th Royal Highlanders KIA 19.7.18.
McDONALD Alexander J. MM L/Cpl 4804 XVII Corps Cyclist Bn Army Cyclist Corps
McDONALD Alexander R. MM Spr 406069 Royal Engineers
McDONALD Alfred Joseph MM L/Cpl 3380 7th Royal West Kent Regt
McDONALD Allan T. MM Sjt 1617 Royal Engineers
McDONALD Andrew MM Dvr 420304 406 Fd Coy Royal Engineers
McDONALD Andrew MM Sjt 6947 1st Shropshire Light Infantry
McDONALD Andrew MM L/Cpl 330174 1/8th Royal Scots
McDONALD Andrew MM Pte 2266 1/6th Seaforth Highlanders DOW 13.4.17.
McDONALD Angus MM Sjt 3/6233 7th Seaforth Highlanders
McDONALD Angus MM Spr 237357 Royal Engineers
McDONALD Angus MM Pte 3894 6th East Kent Regt
McDONALD Archibald MM Sjt 6145 2nd Arg & Suth Highlanders
McDONALD Arthur MM Pte S/2051 11th Rifle Brigade
McDONALD Bernard MM Cpl 330008 1/8th Royal Scots
McDONALD C. MM L/Cpl 9353 2nd Royal Dublin Fusiliers
McDONALD C. MM+Bar Gnr 76259 RFA
McDONALD Charles MM CQMS 265476 1/7th Gordon Highlanders
McDONALD Charles MM Pte M2/055055 Army Service Corps
McDONALD Charles MM+Bar Pte 11435 2nd Royal Scots Fusiliers
McDONALD Charles MM L/Cpl G/2252 8th Royal West Surrey Regt
McDONALD Colin L. MM Spr 51761 2 Div Sig Coy Royal Engineers
McDONALD David MM+Bar Sjt 266166 1/7th Gordon Highlanders
McDONALD David "DCM,MM" L/Cpl 1383 1/5th Gordon Highlanders
McDONALD David MM Cpl 146 B/73 Bde RFA DOW 29.8.16.
McDONALD David D. MM L/Cpl 45200 Royal Engineers
McDONALD Donald MM+Bar Sjt 13352 D/123 Bde RFA
McDONALD Donald MM Pte 19856 1st Royal Scots Fusiliers
McDONALD Donald MM Pte 4438 Seaforth Highlanders
McDONALD Edmund MM Pte S/40940 10th Arg & Suth Highlanders
McDONALD Francis MM Pte 15831 5th Royal Irish Fusiliers
McDONALD Francis MM Pte 200854 8th Royal Highlanders
McDONALD George MM L/Cpl 41733 Royal Scots
McDONALD George MM Pte 18997 12th Highland Light Infantry
McDONALD George MM Pte 49635 13th Welsh Regt
McDONALD George MM L/Cpl 8852 Arg & Suth Highlanders
McDONALD George G. MM L/Cpl 43697 10th Cameron Highlanders
McDONALD Hugh MM Sjt 3135 3 Fd Amb RAMC
McDONALD Hugh MM Gnr L/6816 RFA
McDONALD Hugh MM Pte 32451 12th Highland Light Infantry KIA 25.3.18.
McDONALD Hugh MM Cpl 14977 11th Scottish Rifles
McDONALD Huyton MM Pte 352012 1/9th Royal Scots
McDONALD J. MM Pte 240403 Northumberland Fusiliers
McDONALD J.C. MM Gnr 76259 RFA
McDONALD J.T. MM Pte 14018 7th North Staffordshire Regt
McDONALD James MM Pte 22156 1st Royal Irish Fusiliers
McDONALD James MM CQMS 39537 2nd Bn Machine Gun Corps
McDONALD James MM Cpl 10475 1st Border Regt
McDONALD James MM Sjt 200190 1/4th Seaforth Highlanders KIA 29.7.18.
McDONALD James MM L/Cpl 400014 Royal Engineers
McDONALD James "DCM,MM" L/Cpl 9358 1st East Lancashire Regt
McDONALD James MM Pte 6359 2nd Gordon Highlanders KIA 26.10.17.
McDONALD James MM Sjt 4386 1st Irish Guards
McDONALD James MM Cpl 275736 1st Arg & Suth Highlanders
McDONALD James H. MM Pte 9474 King's Own Scottish Borderers att Indian Army
McDONALD John MM Pte 240187 1/5th Royal Scots Fusiliers
McDONALD John MM Gnr 104134 C/187 Bde RFA
McDONALD John MM Sjt 2895 12th Royal Scots
McDONALD John MM Pte 9676 15th Royal Irish Rifles
McDONALD John MM Sjt 7960 7th Shropshire Light Infantry
McDONALD John MM Cpl 316685 13th Royal Highlanders
McDONALD John MM L/Bdr 110788 206 Siege Bty RGA
McDONALD John MM Cpl 201839 Seaforth Highlanders
McDONALD John MM Pte M2/077442 Army Service Corps
McDONALD John MM Cpl 4140 1st North Lancashire Regt
McDONALD John MM L/Cpl 27594 1/5th King's Own Scottish Borderers DOW 22.10.18.
McDONALD John MM+Bar Cpl 1292 2nd Arg & Suth Highlanders KIA 24.4.17.
McDONALD John MM Pte 267317 Seaforth Highlanders
McDONALD John MM Pte 288006 Seaforth Highlanders
McDONALD John MM Dmr 1003 1st Seaforth Highlanders
McDONALD John MM L/Cpl 265475 1/6th Seaforth Highlanders DOW 26.3.18.
McDONALD John MM Dvr 59113 8 Bde RFA
McDONALD John MM L/Cpl 20939 Royal Highlanders
McDONALD John MM Pte 12762 Seaforth Highlanders
McDONALD John A. MM L/Cpl 14925 16th Highland Light Infantry
McDONALD John A. MM L/Cpl 10282 1st Seaforth Highlanders
McDONALD John Alexander MM Pte 7207 14th Hussars
McDONALD John Christopher MM L/Cpl 10453 1st Notts & Derby Regt KIA 31.7.17.
McDONALD John Morris MM Dvr 7784 RFA
McDONALD John Munro MM+Bar L/Cpl 14247 5th Cameron Highlanders
McDONALD John W. MM Cpl 681352 1/22nd London Regt
McDONALD Joseph MM Sjt 11884 9th Border Regt
McDONALD Joseph MM Pte 15154 1st Scots Guards KIA 15.10.18.
McDONALD Lawrence MM Gnr Shoeing Smith 5975 155 Bde RFA
McDONALD Malcolm MM Pte 22198 16th Highland Light Infantry
McDONALD Neil MM Pte S/40092 2nd Seaforth Highlanders
McDONALD Neil MM+Bar Pte S/10392 1st Cameron Highlanders
McDONALD P. MM L/Cpl Z/846 Rifle Brigade
McDONALD Roderick MM Pte 4686 1st Scots Guards
McDONALD Roderick MM Pte 3580 3(Cav)Fd Amb RAMC
McDONALD Sidney MM Cpl 4209 3rd Rifle Brigade
McDONALD Simon MM Pte 13478 10th Scottish Rifles
McDONALD Stephen MM Pte 330344 1/9th Liverpool Regt Died 11.10.18.
McDONALD T. MM Sjt 265804 Seaforth Highlanders
McDONALD Thomas MM Pte 27766 9th Royal Inniskilling Fusiliers
McDONALD Thomas MM Sjt 238066 8th Seaforth Highlanders DOW 21.4.18.
McDONALD Thomas MM Cpl 46934 35th Bn Machine Gun Corps
McDONALD Thomas MM Pte 265899 Gordon Highlanders
McDONALD Thomas "DCM,MM" CSM 582 11th Manchester Regt
McDONALD Thomas MM Sjt Piper 1321 1/7th Royal Highlanders
McDONALD Thomas J. MM Sjt 2513 2nd Northumberland Fusiliers
McDONALD Thomas John Mays MM Cpl 510364 14th London Regt DOW 7.5.18.
McDONALD William MM L/Cpl 265063 1/6th Seaforth Highlanders KIA 28.7.18.
McDONALD William MM Spr 197764 Royal Engineers
McDONALD William A. MM Cpl 7678 2nd Yorkshire Regt
McDONALD William C. MM Pte S/21795 7th Seaforth Highlanders
McDONALD William H. MM Pte 147944 21st Bn Machine Gun Corps
McDONELL Angus MM Pte 126764 1st Lovat's Scouts Yeomanry KIA 3.11.18.
McDONNELL Albert M. MM+Bar Pte 32266 RAMC
McDONNELL Charles MM Pte 8773 Royal Irish Rifles
McDONNELL Harry A. MM Cpl 24926 Leicestershire Regt
McDONNELL Henry MM L/Cpl 19/1174 Durham Light Infantry
McDONNELL J. MM L/Cpl 4247 East Lancashire Regt
McDONNELL James A. MM Dvr 496486 Royal Engineers
McDONNELL John MM L/Sjt 7924 12th Manchester Regt
McDONNELL Joseph MM+Bar Cpl 19164 1st Royal Dublin Fusiliers
McDONNELL Joseph MM+Bar Bdr 825 RFA
McDONNELL Martin Joseph MM Cpl 7937 2nd Irish Guards DOW 24.1.17.
McDONNELL Nicholas MM Pte 16102 6 Fd Amb RAMC
McDONNELL Robert MM Cpl 27671 Durham Light Infantry

McDONOUGH James Giuseppe MM Pte M/316930 Army Service Corps att RGA
McDONOUGH Joachim MM Pte 5845 9th Royal Munster Fusiliers
McDONOUGH John MM Pte 16317 2nd Royal Irish Regt
McDONOUGH John MM Sjt 6906 10th Scottish Rifles
McDONOUGH Thomas MM L/Cpl 9526 1st Yorkshire Light Infantry
McDOUGALL Alexander MM Sjt T4/040985 Army Service Corps att 137 Fd Amb RAMC
McDOUGALL Alexander MM Pte 4/7629 2nd Arg & Suth Highlanders
McDOUGALL Angus MM Gnr 660670 179 Bty 383 Bde RFA KIA 30.2.18.
McDOUGALL Angus J. MM Pte 14267 Scots Guards
McDOUGALL Archibald MM Cpl 645256 RFA
McDOUGALL Charles "MM,CG(F)" Sjt 17656 31st Bn Machine Gun Corps
McDOUGALL David MM Sjt 91893 181 Tunnelling Coy Royal Engineers
McDOUGALL Duncan MM Pte 290685 8th Scottish Rifles
McDOUGALL James MM Sjt 201917 1/4th Seaforth Highlanders
McDOUGALL James MM Pte 265326 1/6th Royal Highlanders
McDOUGALL John MM Pte 202133 10th Arg & Suth Highlanders
McDOUGALL John MM L/Cpl S/16957 7th Cameron Highlanders KIA 16.7.16.
McDOUGALL John MM L/Cpl 2901 8th Seaforth Highlanders
McDOUGALL John McPhee MM Pte 332475 1/9th Highland Light Infantry
McDOUGALL Mungo MM Gnr 1462 3rd Bn MGC(Motors)
McDOUGALL Robert MM Cpl 198091 Royal Engineers
McDOUGALL Robert S. "DCM,MM,MID" Sjt 418022 52 Div Sig Coy Royal Engineers
McDOUGALL Roderick MM Sjt 40423 8/10th Gordon Highlanders KIA 22.8.17.
McDOUGALL Thomas MM Dvr 249573 51 Div Sig Coy Royal Engineers
McDOUGALL William MM Pte 266788 Scottish Rifles
McDOUGALL William MM Cpl 57277 9 Bty 41 Bde RFA
McDOUGALL William MM L/Cpl 19304 16th Royal Scots KIA 26.8.17.
McDOUGALL William MM Sjt 53496 32nd Bn Machine Gun Corps
McDOWALL Cyril James Lamport "MC,MM(741 Sjt 10th R Fus)" T/2Lt 7th South Lancashire Regt
McDOWALL David MM Sjt 290649 1/8th Scottish Rifles
McDOWALL James MM Pte 8518 10th Arg & Suth Highlanders
McDOWALL John MM L/Sjt 12915 1st Scots Guards
McDOWALL Robert MM Spr 53044 Royal Engineers
McDOWELL Albert MM+Bar Pte 2446 2nd Royal Inniskilling Fusiliers
McDOWELL Charles William MM Sjt 27253 60 Siege Bty RGA
McDOWELL George MM CQMS 8339 2nd King's Own Scottish Borderers
McDOWELL George MM Tpr(SS) 2713 2nd Life Guards
McDOWELL George H. MM Sjt 9676 11th Lancashire Fusiliers
McDOWELL James MM Sjt 15393 9th Royal Irish Rifles
McDOWELL William H. MM L/Cpl 1930 1/5th Royal Lancaster Regt
McDUNNA Herbert MM Cpl 13451 2nd South Lancashire Regt
McEACHAN Vincent MM L/Cpl 9381 2nd Arg & Suth Highlanders
McEACHERN Donald MM Gnr 97001 D/178 Bde RFA
McEACHERN Peter MM Cpl 43578 Gordon Highlanders
McELHATTON James W. MM Cpl 2586 5 CCS RAMC
McELHILL James MM Spr 121333 447 Fd Coy Royal Engineers Died 23.10.18.
McELHINNEY Robert MM+Bar Sjt 12924 Machine Gun Corps
McELHOLM Hugh MM L/Cpl 300487 1/7th Arg & Suth Highlanders
McELHONEY Patrick MM Pte 36594 RAMC
McELROY James MM Sjt 6255 2nd Manchester Regt DOW 11.8.18.
McELROY John T. MM Pte 6643 2nd Irish Guards
McELROY Patrick J. MM Gnr 112499 RGA
McELROY Raymond MM Pte 203019 2nd Border Regt
McELROY Thomas MM Pte 11119 Cameron Highlanders
McELWAINE James MM Pte 18308 Royal Irish Rifles
McELWEE Peter MM Pte 18900 14th Northumberland Fusiliers
McENTIVEY Henry MM Sjt 28061 244 Siege Bty RGA
McEUNE Christopher S. MM Pte 301293 10th Bn Tank Corps
McEVOY Andrew MM Sjt 17967 Royal Scots
McEVOY Daniel "DCM,MM" Cpl 2711 1st Lancashire Fusiliers
McEVOY Dennis MM Pte 26621 4th Grenadier Guards
McEVOY J. MM Pte 4815 Liverpool Regt
McEVOY James MM Dvr 127895 RFA
McEVOY John MM Pte 266745 14th Liverpool Regt
McEVOY Lawrence MM Pte 265487 4th Liverpool Regt
McEVOY Patrick MM Drummer 3584 2nd Royal Irish Regt
McEVOY Patrick W. MM CSM 5829 2nd Royal Munster Fusiliers
McEVOY Peter MM Gnr 1095 Machine Gun Corps(Motors)
McEVOY Thomas MM L/Sjt 3930 1st Irish Guards DOW 3.12.17.
McEVOY William MM Pte 2831 2nd Rifle Brigade
McEWAN A. MM Pte 200690 King's Own Scottish Borderers
McEWAN Alexander MM Cpl 709 1/3(Highland)How Bde RFA
McEWAN Bernard L. MM Pte 8966 2nd Dragoons
McEWAN Duncan MM L/Cpl 20753 2nd Royal Scots Fusiliers
McEWAN George MM Pte 12350 12th Royal Scots
McEWAN James MM Sjt 3993 1/8th Arg & Suth Highlanders KIA 23.7.18.
McEWAN James MM Pte 9409 Arg & Suth Highlanders
McEWAN John MM RQMS 240035 1/5th Seaforth Highlanders
McEWAN Neil MM Pte 42159 Royal Scots
McEWAN William MM Sjt 651045 RFA
McEWAN William MM Pte 276162 1/7th Arg & Suth Highlanders
McEWAN William MM Pte 26693 Scottish Rifles
McEWAN William C. MM Pte 331770 1/9th Highland Light Infantry KIA 12.10.18.
McEWEN Francis MM Spr 14452 427 Fd Coy Royal Engineers
McEWEN James` MM Pte 7838 21 Fd Amb RAMC
McEWEN Joseph MM Sjt 18431 48th Bn Machine Gun Corps
McEWEN Peter MM Pte 146 1st Royal Highlanders
McEWEN William MM L/Cpl S/40701 7th Seaforth Highlanders
McEWEN William MM Pte 241144 King's Own Scottish Borderers
McEWEN William T. MM Pte 681001 1/22nd London Regt
McEWING R. MM Pte 300420 Arg & Suth Highlanders
McFADDEN A. MM Pte 353000 Royal Scots
McFADDEN Andrew MM+Bar Pte 278747 1/7th Arg & Suth Highlanders
McFADDEN David MM L/Cpl 57653 121 Fd Coy Royal Engineers
McFADDEN James MM L/Cpl 13541 5th Dragoon Guards
McFADDEN Richard MM CSM F/162 17th Middlesex Regt DOW 23.10.16.
McFADYEN Adam MM Pte 202286 1st Scottish Rifles KIA 11.7.18.
McFADYEN Angus MM Pte S/4084 8th Royal Highlanders
McFADYEN Archibald MM Pte S/14258 10th Arg & Suth Highlanders DOW 17.5.17.
McFADYEN Charles MM Pte 325642 1/7th Arg & Suth Highlanders
McFADYEN Donald MM Cpl 200483 1/5th Arg & Suth Highlanders
McFADYEN John MM Cpl 13462 15th Highland Light Infantry KIA 3.7.16.
McFADYEN William MM Pte 50557 Machine Gun Corps
McFADYEN William MM Pte 40017 Royal Highlanders
McFADZEAN Allan MM Pte 241906 1/5th Royal Scots Fusiliers
McFALL Thomas MM Sjt 18279 12th Royal Irish Rifles
McFARLAND Alexander MM Spr 236947 Royal Engineers
McFARLAND Andrew MM Sjt 7674 1st Royal Irish Rifles
McFARLAND Edward James MM Pte 32820 16th Royal Warwickshire Regt KIA 19.10.18.
McFARLAND John James MM Pte 14097 6th Royal Inniskilling Fusiliers
McFARLAND Thomas "DCM,MM" Pte 300813 1/7th Arg & Suth Highlanders
McFARLAND William MM Cpl 495 4 Fd Amb RAMC
McFARLANE Albert MM Pte 41955 Royal Scots
McFARLANE Alex MM Pte G/7050 8th Royal Sussex Regt
McFARLANE Alexander S. MM Pte 125408 Lovat's Scouts Yeomanry
McFARLANE Alfred H.S. MM Cpl 2/10311 South Wales Borderers
McFARLANE Andrew MM L/Cpl S/9258 Royal Highlanders
McFARLANE Andrew MM Sjt 37906 7th Bn Machine Gun Corps
McFARLANE Archibald MM Sjt 33405 52 Bty 15 Bde RFA
McFARLANE Duncan MM L/Cpl 88771 Royal Engineers
McFARLANE G. MM Pte 11116 1st Scottish Rifles
McFARLANE J.G. MM L/Cpl 200942 Royal Highlanders
McFARLANE James MM Pte 50588 3 Fd Amb RAMC
McFARLANE James MM Pte S/43581 1/6th Royal Highlanders
McFARLANE James MM L/Sjt 4183 11th Arg & Suth Highlanders
McFARLANE John MM Cpl 10814 1st Royal Dublin Fusiliers DOW 8.7.16.Real name McELHAGGA.
McFARLANE John MM L/Cpl 43386 Scottish Rifles
McFARLANE John J.N. MM Pte 6432 5/6th Scottish Rifles
McFARLANE John R. MM Cpl 41768 9th Scottish Rifles
McFARLANE Murdo MM Cpl 3/7147 2nd Seaforth Highlanders
McFARLANE Percival C. MM L/Cpl 32354 RAMC
McFARLANE Peter MM Pnr 152610 19 Div Sig Coy Royal Engineers

McFARLANE R.W. MM Pte 63189 5th Yorkshire Light Infantry
McFARLANE Robert MM Pte 39695 Northumberland Fusiliers
McFARLANE Robert MM+Bar Sjt 882 2nd Arg & Suth Highlanders
McFARLANE Robert MM Sjt 6448 2nd Irish Guards
McFARLANE William MM L/Sjt 295200 12th Royal Scots Fusiliers
McFARLANE William MM Spr 423105 Royal Engineers
McFEAT J. MM L/Cpl 51811 Machine Gun Corps
McFEE James Kennedy MM Pte 74129 33rd Bn Machine Gun Corps
McFEE Robert MM L/Cpl 51125 1/14th London Regt
McFEETERS George Robert MM Cpl 57873 36 Div Sig Coy Royal Engineers
McFERRAN J. "MM,MSM" Sjt 18282 12th Royal Irish Rifles
McFERRAN Thomas MM Sjt 19624 Machine Gun Corps
McFETTERS John MM Cpl 19973 12th Royal Scots
McFIGGANS James MM Sjt 275737 1/7th Arg & Suth Highlanders
McGAHAN Thomas MM Bdr 363 RFA
McGAHAN William MM Sjt 458774 Royal Engineers
McGAHEY George MM Sjt 7069 2nd Royal Dublin Fusiliers
McGAHEY James MM Cpl 290139 701 Coy Labour Corps
McGAIR Robert James "DCM,MM+Bar,CG(F)" Cpl 24768 24th Royal Welsh Fusiliers
McGAIRY William L. MM Sjt 46982 RFA
McGANN Ernest MM Pte 41817 18th Scottish Rifles
McGANN Michael MM CSM 2315 1/5th South Lancashire Regt
McGANN Thomas MM Pte 22117 9th Royal Dublin Fusiliers
McGARR Thomas MM Pte 13738 9th North Lancashire Regt
McGARRAGAN F. "DCM,MM" Sjt 79984 174 Tunnelling Coy Royal Engineers
McGARRELL Daniel MM Sjt 242683 5th York & Lancaster Regt
McGARRELL John MM+Bar Sjt 311323 1(Nbrn)Heavy Bty RGA
McGARRELL William MM Pte 5709 2nd Royal Irish Rifles DOW 16.4.18.
McGARRIGLE John MM Cpl 19687 X Corps Cyclist Bn Army Cyclist Corps
McGARRITY James MM Pte S/41014 1/7th Arg & Suth Highlanders
McGARRY James MM Pte 267265 2/7th Royal Warwickshire Regt KIA 8.11.17.
McGARRY John MM Pte 16430 9th Scottish Rifles
McGARRY Joseph MM Pte 14787 Royal Inniskilling Fusiliers
McGARRY Patrick MM L/Cpl 470058 526 Fd Coy Royal Engineers
McGARRY T. MM Gnr 971457 D/233 Bde RFA
McGARVA Alexander MM L/Cpl 276598 Arg & Suth Highlanders
McGARVA Andrew MM Pte 44914 Durham Light Infantry
McGARVA James MM+Bar CSM 13729 15th Highland Light Infantry
McGARVA Robert MM Pte 17268 Highland Light Infantry
McGARVA Robert A. MM Sjt 240802 1/5th King's Own Scottish Borderers
McGARVA Scott MM Sjt 17142 Machine Gun Corps
McGARVA William MM Sjt 41129 6th King's Own Scottish Borderers
McGARVEY Michael MM Pte 34860 4th West Riding Regt
McGARVIE Robert T. MM Sjt 645618 RFA
McGAULEY John W. MM L/Cpl 28731 Welsh Regt
McGAURAN Patrick MM Sjt 9223 Connaught Rangers
McGAVIN James MM Cpl 103090 217 Army Tps Coy Royal Engineers
McGAW David MM CSM 43121 Royal Scots Fusiliers
McGAW James MM Cpl 3410 2nd Arg & Suth Highlanders KIA 24.10.18.
McGEACH R. MM Pte 12269 2nd Royal Irish Regt
McGEACHY C. MM Pte 30130 12th Royal Scots Fusiliers
McGEACHY Donald MM+Bar Cpl 58527 19 Div Sig Coy Royal Engineers
McGECHIAN Peter MM Pte 2946 1/7th Arg & Suth Highlanders Died 4.11.18.
McGEE John MM Cpl 44737 15 Div Ammn Col RFA
McGEE Peter MM Pte 28980 Royal Inniskilling Fusiliers
McGEE Robert MM Pte 43366 9th Scottish Rifles KIA 29.9.18.
McGEE Thomas MM L/Cpl 28845 2nd Northumberland Fusiliers
McGEE William MM+Bar L/Sjt 8992 RAMC
McGEE William MM CSM 200194 1/5th Durham Light Infantry
McGEE William Charles MM Pte 266550 Royal Warwickshire Regt
McGEEHAN Francis J. MM Gnr 40674 RFA
McGEEHIN James MM Pte 7517 1st Highland Light Infantry
McGEENEY Michael MM L/Cpl 18624 2nd Royal Dublin Fusiliers
McGEEVER Andrew MM Gnr 167882 D/104 Bde RFA
McGEEVER Thomas MM L/Cpl 37451 11th West Yorkshire Regt
McGERR John MM Pte 20263 9th Royal Inniskilling Fusiliers
McGHAN James MM Pte 3695 Gordon Highlanders
McGHEE Archibald MM Pte 115968 Labour Corps

McGHEE George D. MM L/Sjt 27391 Royal Warwickshire Regt
McGHEE Patrick MM Cpl 11900 2nd King's Own Scottish Borderers
McGHEE Peter MM Pnr 128013 Royal Engineers
McGHIE Andrew MM Pte S/14410 14th Arg & Suth Highlanders
McGHIE John MM L/Cpl 3578 1/4th Royal Scots
McGHIE Michael MM Pte S/8770 2nd Seaforth Highlanders DOW 6.1.18.
McGHIE Samuel George Copeland MM Sjt 12322 6/7th Royal Scots Fusiliers
McGIBBON George MM Sjt 315042 13th Royal Highlanders
McGIBBON James MM Pte 331456 1/6th Highland Light Infantry
McGIBBON Robert B. MM Sjt 23695 51st Bn Machine Gun Corps
McGIBNEY William MM Drummer 668 1st Arg & Suth Highlanders
McGILL Arthur MM Pte CMT/3614 Army Service Corps
McGILL Colin MM CSM 200187 1/4th Royal Scots Fusiliers
McGILL George MM L/Cpl 42464 1/5th King's Own Scottish Borderers
McGILL George MM Pte 43026 King's Own Scottish Borderers
McGILL Henry A. MM Sjt 70395 41 Bde RFA
McGILL James MM Pte 5747 1st Cameron Highlanders
McGILL James John MM L/Sjt 722175 2/24th London Regt
McGILL John MM Pte 22860 Royal Irish Fusiliers
McGILL John R.B. MM Bdr 146742 RGA
McGILL Thomas MM Sjt 10877 2nd Highland Light Infantry
McGILL Thomas MM Pte 73644 154 Coy Machine Gun Corps
McGILL William MM+Bar Sjt 15518 11th Northumberland Fusiliers
McGILL William MM L/Cpl 200912 Royal Lancaster Regt
McGILL William G. MM+Bar Cpl 43121 RFA
McGILLIVRAY Angus B. MM Sjt 240321 1/5th Gordon Highlanders
McGILLIVRAY D. MM Pte 5571 Gordon Highlanders
McGILLIVRAY James MM Pte 115519 Labour Corps
McGILLIVRAY James MM Pte 18625 19th Lancashire Fusiliers
McGILLIVRAY William Dow "MM,CG(B)" Sjt 5497 Machine Gun Corps
McGILP Donald H. MM Sjt S/16536 7th Cameron Highlanders
McGILP Harry MM Dvr 420344 406 Fd Coy Royal Engineers
McGILVRAY Donald MM Cpl 1908 1/6th Royal Highlanders
McGINLAY John MM Pte 17218 10/11th Highland Light Infantry KIA 28.4.17.
McGINLAY Thomas MM Pte 291546 1st Gordon Highlanders
McGINLEY David MM Gnr 34487 RGA
McGINLEY Patrick MM Gnr 37947 'G' Bty RHA
McGINLEY William MM Pte R/13850 13th King's Royal Rifle Corps
McGINN John MM Pte S/9145 1st Royal Highlanders
McGINN Patrick MM Pte 10003 12th Royal Scots KIA 25.4.18.
McGINN Thomas MM Pte 15013 1st Grenadier Guards DOW 13.9.16.
McGINNIE John MM L/Cpl 275860 5/6th Royal Scots
McGINNIS Charles MM Pte 5532 2nd Irish Guards DOW 13.10.17.
McGINNIS Molly MM Sister F SJAB
McGINTRY William MM+Bar Pte 43339 2nd Scottish Rifles
McGINTY Patrick MM Pte 3697 Connaught Rangers
McGIRE Bernard MM L/Sjt 6985 2nd Irish Guards
McGIVERIN William MM Pte 241549 1/5th King's Own Scottish Borderers
McGIVERING David MM Pte 15979 9th Cheshire Regt
McGIVERN John J. MM Cpl 33479 RAMC
McGIVNEY Thomas MM L/Cpl 17486 Royal Irish Fusiliers
McGLADE John MM Dvr 46770 D/51 Bde RFA
McGLONE Frank "DCM,MM" Pte S/2700 8th Seaforth Highlanders att 15 Div Sig Coy RE
McGLONE Robert MM Pte 20830 5/6th Royal Scots KIA 11.8.18.
McGLOUGHLIN William MM Pte 18048 Lancashire Fusiliers
McGLYNN John MM Pte 20009 2nd Royal Dublin Fusiliers KIA 3.5.17.
McGLYNN Thomas MM L/Cpl 40823 2nd Highland Light Infantry
McGLYNN Thomas MM Cpl 240201 East Lancashire Regt
McGLYNN Vincent MM Pte Z/1803 1st Rifle Brigade
McGOFF David MM Pte 8406 1st Gordon Highlanders
McGOLDRICK James MM Cpl 33012 8th York & Lancaster Regt
McGOLDRICK John MM Pte 23060 Royal Irish Fusiliers
McGONIGLE John MM Pte 7349 2nd Arg & Suth Highlanders
McGONIGLE Samuel MM L/Cpl 23644 Royal Inniskilling Fusiliers
McGORRIN Robert MM Dvr 79338 RFA
McGOUGAN John MM Sjt 300176 1/8th Arg & Suth Highlanders
McGOUGH Archibald MM Cpl 2069 8th Gordon Highlanders
McGOUGH James MM Sjt 6/10540 6th Royal Irish Rifles
McGOVERN Albert MM Cpl 42977 1st Royal Inniskilling Fusiliers
McGOVERN James MM Pte 22579 18th Lancashire Fusiliers
McGOVERN Patrick MM Cpl 240211 1/7th Royal Highlanders

McGOVERN Patrick MM Pte 9/4688 Royal Munster Fusiliers
McGOVERN Thomas MM Pte S/23439 7th Cameron Highlanders
McGOWAN Albert H. MM Sjt 43312 41 Bde RFA
McGOWAN Alfred W. MM Pte 10597 1st East Surrey Regt
McGOWAN Angus MM Pte 19157 Royal Inniskilling Fusiliers
McGOWAN Anthony MM Pte 235247 2/8th West Yorkshire Regt
McGOWAN Arthur MM Pte S/14218 1st Royal Highlanders
McGOWAN D. MM L/Cpl 400054 447 Fd Coy Royal Engineers
McGOWAN Daniel "DCM,MM+Bar" Sjt 14421 13th Royal Scots
McGOWAN Edward MM Pte 34565 East Lancashire Regt
McGOWAN Frank MM Pte 265225 4th Liverpool Regt
McGOWAN G. MM Bdr 16109 80 Bty 15 Bde RFA
McGOWAN Harry MM Pte 40563 9th Scottish Rifles KIA 21.3.18.
McGOWAN Harvey MM Sjt 786051 RFA
McGOWAN James "MM,CG(F)" Pte 200848 1/5th Arg & Suth Highlanders DOW 29 10 18.
McGOWAN James MM Sjt 16986 9th York & Lancaster Regt DOW 17.6.18.
McGOWAN James Alexander MM L/Cpl S/13888 7th Cameron Highlanders DOW 9.10.18.
McGOWAN James C. MM Dvr 771143 315 Bde RFA
McGOWAN John MM Pte 14715 16th Highland Light Infantry
McGOWAN John MM L/Cpl 322086 1/3rd(Highland)Fd Amb RAMC
McGOWAN John MM Pte 13522 7/8th King's Own Scottish Borderers
McGOWAN John Firth MM Pte 71981 113 Fd Amb RAMC
McGOWAN Patrick MM Sjt 7663 1st Scottish Rifles KIA 29.10.16.
McGOWAN Robert MM Cpl 7484 Seaforth Highlanders
McGOWAN Thomas MM Pte 5728 1st Irish Guards
McGOWAN William MM Pte 27724 Liverpool Regt
McGOWAN William MM Bdr 12827 RFA
McGOWAN William F. MM Sjt 51280 86 Coy Labour Corps
McGOWAN William M. MM Spr 402904 218 Fd Coy Royal Engineers
McGRAA John Thomas MM Bandsman 10085 3rd Royal Fusiliers KIA 4.10.18.
McGRADY Frank MM Pte 14528 11th West Yorkshire Regt
McGRADY John "MM,MID" Pte 7004 1st Gordon Highlanders
McGRADY Joseph MM L/Cpl 20016 Lancashire Fusiliers
McGRANE Michael MM Pte 8456 2nd Royal Dublin Fusiliers
McGRANN David MM Pte 7693 9th Royal Irish Fusiliers KIA 16.8.17.
McGRATH Annie Marie MM Staff Nurse F QAIMNS
McGRATH Arthur J. MM+Bar CSM 205909 6th Northamptonshire Regt
McGRATH Charles MM Cpl 10075 2nd East Surrey Regt
McGRATH Edward MM+Bar L/Cpl 103695 98 Fd Coy Royal Engineers KIA 16.6.17.
McGRATH Edward Albert MM Gnr 46618 40 Bde RFA
McGRATH Frank MM L/Cpl 28193 7/8th Royal Inniskilling Fusiliers
McGRATH James MM L/Cpl 23818 North Staffordshire Regt
McGRATH John MM Bdr 65641 93 Bty 18 Bde RFA
McGRATH Robert MM Sjt S/11951 7th Cameron Highlanders
McGRATH Thomas MM Pte S/17044 1st Cameron Highlanders
McGRATH Thomas MM L/Cpl 40624 9th York & Lancaster Regt KIA 30.9.17.
McGRATH William MM+2 Bars Pte 23133 12th Royal Scots
McGRAW Peter MM+Bar Pte 3725 11th Arg & Suth Highlanders
McGRAW Thomas "DCM,MM" Spr 147648 185 Tunnelling Coy Royal Engineers
McGREARY Richard MM Dvr 4377 D/75 Bde RFA
McGREAVY James MM Dvr 720382 66 Div Ammn Col RFA Died 13.11.18.
McGREEGHAN Hugh MM Pte 18291 12th Royal Irish Rifles
McGREGOR Adam MM+Bar L/Cpl 23055 Scottish Rifles
McGREGOR Alexander MM Pte 24430 1/7th Royal Highlanders
McGREGOR Alexander MM Pte 15451 1st Scots Guards
McGREGOR Alexander MM Pte 242319 1/5th Gordon Highlanders
McGREGOR Alexander MM Pte 10738 12th Royal Scots Fusiliers Died 17.8.19.
McGREGOR Alexander D. MM Pte 5/4225 King's Royal Rifle Corps
McGREGOR Archibald MM Cpl 17502 10th Yorkshire Regt
McGREGOR Charles MM Bdr 13598 D/180 Bde RFA KIA 3.8.17.
McGREGOR Charles C. MM Cpl C/9295 King's Royal Rifle Corps
McGREGOR Christopher MM Sjt S/26308 1st Cameron Highlanders
McGREGOR Daniel or Donald MM+Bar Sjt 300141 Arg & Suth Highlanders
McGREGOR Duncan MM Pte 1524 Royal Highlanders
McGREGOR Edward MM Sjt 331457 9th Highland Light Infantry
McGREGOR George MM Pte 267675 Royal Highlanders
McGREGOR J. MM+Bar L/Cpl 275614 Arg & Suth Highlanders
McGREGOR J.C. MM Sjt 206088 7th East Kent Regt
McGREGOR James MM BSM 881784 C/74 Bde RFA
McGREGOR James MM Sjt 316229 1 Fd Amb RAMC
McGREGOR James MM Cpl 51489 Cheshire Regt
McGREGOR James MM L/Cpl S/11338 8th Royal Highlanders KIA 3.5.17.
McGREGOR James W. MM Pte 27250 16th Highland Light Infantry
McGREGOR John MM Sjt 265437 11th Royal Scots Fusiliers
McGREGOR John MM Gnr 218192 B/50 Bde RFA
McGREGOR John MM Pte 352285 1/9th Royal Scots
McGREGOR John MM Pte 2130 8/10th Gordon Highlanders
McGREGOR John MM Pte 20476 West Yorkshire Regt
McGREGOR John Suttle MM L/Cpl 3348 1/9th Royal Scots
McGREGOR Percival MM Pte 280212 1/4th London Regt
McGREGOR Percy MM Cpl 27428 14th Royal Welsh Fusiliers
McGREGOR Percy MM 2nd Cpl 167285 'P' Special Coy Royal Engineers
McGREGOR Ralph MM Sjt 12623 1st Royal Inniskilling Fusiliers KIA 22.3.18.
McGREGOR Robert MM Pte 266462 1/6th Royal Highlanders
McGREGOR Robert MM Pte DM2/164086 Army Service Corps
McGREGOR W.M. MM Pte 301198 RAMC
McGREGOR William MM Sjt 14377 17th Lancashire Fusiliers
McGREGOR William MM Pte 202848 1/5th King's Own Scottish Borderers
McGREGOR William MM Pte 201163 Royal Highlanders
McGREGOR William MM Pte 375395 Royal Scots
McGREGOR William "MM,MID" L/Cpl 12348 1st Cameron Highlanders
McGRIGOR Robert Jnr MM Spr 232018 497 Fd Coy Royal Engineers
McGROARTY Daniel MM Cpl 8232 Arg & Suth Highlanders
McGROGAN Patrick MM Pte 22141 2nd Royal Dublin Fusiliers
McGRORY Alexander MM Pte 278846 1/7th Arg & Suth Highlanders
McGRORY William J. MM Bdr 43070 RFA
McGROTTY James MM Pte 14823 16th Highland Light Infantry
McGUCKIAN Johnstone "MM,MID" Sjt 111526 Royal Engineers
McGUCKIN Joseph MM L/Cpl 3/8228 Yorkshire Regt
McGUCKIN Robert MM Cpl 2982 2nd Leinster Regt
McGUFFIN Hugh MM Pte S/12032 Arg & Suth Highlanders
McGUGAN Charles MM Cpl 30966 6th Royal Inniskilling Fusiliers
McGUIGAN Daniel MM Cpl 7497 2nd Highland Light Infantry
McGUIGAN Henry MM+Bar Pte 3421 Leinster Regt
McGUIGAN J. MM Cpl 32129 RFA
McGUIGAN John MM Gnr Sig 250437 14 Bde 401 Bty RHA
McGUIGAN John A. MM Sjt 89044 Royal Engineers
McGUIGAN Michael MM Gnr Sig 771986 4(Northumbrian)How Bde RFA
McGUINESS Francis MM Dvr 22199 D/74 Bde RFA
McGUINESS John MM Pte 31167 1st Royal Inniskilling Fusiliers DOW 14.10.18.
McGUINESS Joseph MM L/Cpl SPTS/3550 24th Royal Fusiliers
McGUINESS Michael MM Pnr 129868 Royal Engineers
McGUINESS Robert MM L/Sjt 43384 5/6th Scottish Rifles
McGUINNESS Edward C. MM Spr 154710 Royal Engineers
McGUINNESS Francis MM Pte 266668 Scottish Rifles
McGUINNESS John MM Cpl 5590 5th Connaught Rangers
McGUINNESS John H. MM L/Cpl 21810 Liverpool Regt
McGUINNESS John J. MM Pte 17381 10th North Lancashire Regt
McGUINNESS Phillip MM Pte 49436 2nd Lincolnshire Regt
McGUINNESS Thomas MM Sjt 671358 D/77 Bde RFA
McGUINNESS Thomas MM Pte 15754 8th Border Regt
McGUINNESS W. MM Pte 2207 North Lancashire Regt
McGUINNESS Wilfred MM Cpl 22273 Northumberland Fusiliers
McGUIRE Alexander Thomas MM+Bar Cpl 49687 Royal Engineers
McGUIRE Alfred MM Sjt 7553 5 Div Sig Coy Royal Engineers
McGUIRE Conn MM L/Cpl 12764 5/6th Scottish Rifles
McGUIRE James MM Pte 56054 21st Northumberland Fusiliers
McGUIRE John MM Pte 51116 12th Royal Scots Fusiliers
McGUIRE John MM Pte 335140 1/8th Royal Scots
McGUIRE John MM Cpl 6817 1st Royal Scots Fusiliers
McGUIRE John MM Pte 421148 Labour Corps
McGUIRE John MM Pte 8769 2nd Highland Light Infantry
McGUIRE John MM Pte 13400 12th Royal Scots
McGUIRE Michael MM Gnr 5558 RGA
McGUIRE Patrick MM Dvr 96945 127 Bty 29 Bde RFA
McGUIRE Patrick MM Sjt 10655 2nd Seaforth Highlanders
McGUIRE Peter MM Cpl 45358 RHA
McGUIRE T. MM Pte 18230 2nd Royal Irish Regt

McGUIRE Thomas MM Pte 201914 1/5th Liverpool Regt
McGUIRE Thomas MM Sjt 17960 20 Fd Amb RAMC
McGUIRK Daniel MM Sjt 330158 9th Highland Light Infantry
McGUIRK Daniel MM L/Cpl 21338 Royal Dublin Fusiliers
McGUIRK John E. MM Dvr 616145 RHA
McGUNNIGLE Frank MM Pte 14426 13th Royal Scots
McGURK Charles MM Cpl 23331 50th Bn Machine Gun Corps
McGURK James "MM,MID" Pte 12635 2nd Durham Light Infantry
McGURRIN William MM L/Cpl 7053 2nd Irish Guards
McHAFFIE James MM BSM 316002 142 Heavy Bty RGA
McHALE Fabian MM Gnr 780673 B/72 Bde RFA DOW 18.10.18.
McHALE John MM+Bar Pte 16343 9th Scottish Rifles
McHALE Stephen MM L/Cpl 10171 Irish Guards
McHALLAM John MM L/Cpl 295382 12th Royal Scots Fusiliers
McHARDY Alexander MM Cpl 6867 B/106 Bde RFA
McHARDY Alexander MM Sjt 14057 1/7th Gordon Highlanders
McHARDY Frederick "DCM,MM" Sjt 202681 1/4th Gordon Highlanders
McHARDY James A. MM L/Cpl 40733 1st Gordon Highlanders
McHARDY John MM Pte 303152 1/8th Arg & Suth Highlanders KIA 13.5.17.
McHARDY Joseph "DCM,MM" Sjt 3/4083 8th Royal Highlanders
McHARDY William "DCM,MM" Sjt 6312 2nd Dragoons
McHARG Alexander MM Spr 282592 12 Div Sig Coy Royal Engineers
McHARG Hugh MM 2nd Cpl 81199 Royal Engineers
McHARG James MM Spr 307204 Royal Engineers
McHARRIE John MM L/Cpl 292364 Gordon Highlanders
McHARRIE Randolph D. MM L/Cpl 43356 2nd King's Own Scottish Borderers
McHATTIE Alexander MM Sjt 375005 2nd Royal Scots
McHATTIE James MM Gnr 117145 RGA
McHENRY Henry MM Sjt 770037 50 Div Ammn Col RFA
McHENRY John MM Pte 19541 11th Highland Light Infantry
McHOWAT Matthew MM Pte 19199 1/7th Arg & Suth Highlanders
McHUGH Daniel MM Pte 13696 4th Coldstream Guards
McHUGH Daniel MM Sjt 8593 1st West Riding Regt
McHUGH Frank MM Pte 1156 GMGR
McHUGH Frank MM Cpl 2909 4/5th Royal Highlanders KIA 28.7.18.
McHUGH Harold MM L/Cpl 13610 1st Bedfordshire Regt
McHUGH James MM Cpl 202658 Liverpool Regt
McHUGH James MM Pte M2/099818 Army Service Corps
McHUGH James MM Bdr 52626 RGA
McHUGH John A. MM Sjt 3808 2/7th West Yorkshire Regt
McHUGH Michael MM Pte 18662 Manchester Regt
McHUGH Myles MM CSM 295056 12th Manchester Regt
McHUGH Patrick MM Sjt 201012 West Riding Regt
McHUGH Patrick J. MM Bdr 39376 4 Siege Bty RGA
McHUGH Patrick S. "DCM,MM+Bar" CSM 275355 1/7th Manchester Regt
McHUGH Robert MM Spr 236938 Royal Engineers
McHUGH Robert MM Pte 15054 12th Cheshire Regt
McHUGH Samuel MM Pte 4636 13th Middlesex Regt
McHUGH Thomas MM Pte S/11621 South Staffordshire Regt
McHUTCHEON W. MM Pte 33807 Royal Warwickshire Regt
McILHERON Tom MM CQMS 200675 1/4th Royal Lancaster Regt
McILREE Matthew MM Pte 7315 Arg & Suth Highlanders
McILROY Henry E. MM Pte 90768 RAMC
McILROY James MM+Bar L/Cpl S/3817 11th Arg & Suth Highlanders KIA 10.7.17.
McILROY John MM Pte 53618 13 Fd Amb RAMC
McILROY John MM Pte 25510 9th Royal Inniskilling Fusiliers
McILROY Peter MM L/Cpl 6328 XV Corps Cyclist Bn Army Cyclist Corps
McILROY Philip MM Gnr 645129 RFA
McILROY Samuel MM Cpl 17641 Scottish Rifles
McILROY Thomas MM L/Cpl 19878 2nd Royal Inniskilling Fusiliers Died 21.3.18.
McILVEEN John MM+Bar Sjt 14/6755 14th Royal Irish Rifles
McILVENNY David "MM,CG(F)" Pte M2/288402 Army Service Corps att 1/3rd(S Midland)Fd Amb RAMC
McILVENNY James Green MM Pte 3/9060 1st Royal Irish Rifles
McILWAIN Bertram MM 2nd Cpl 131323 234 Fd Coy Royal Engineers
McILWAIN Thomas "DCM,MM" Sjt 18394 27 Coy Machine Gun Corps
McILWAINE James MM L/Cpl 16247 Royal Inniskilling Fusiliers
McILWAINE Samuel MM Spr 64050 122 Fd Coy Royal Engineers
McILWAINE Samuel MM L/Cpl 19/174 14th Royal Irish Rifles
McILWAINE William J. MM Pte 28486 2nd Hampshire Regt

McILWRAITH James MM Spr 8810 Royal Engineers
McILWRAITH Samuel "DCM,MM,MID" 2nd Cpl 57961 36 Div Sig Coy Royal Engineers
McILWRAITH Samuel MM Sjt 7337 Machine Gun Corps
McILWRATH James MM Cpl 9/13154 15th Royal Irish Rifles
McILWRATH William MM Pte 8848 2nd Royal Irish Rifles
McINDOE Jack MM L/Cpl 6874 East Yorkshire Regt
McINDOE John MM Bdr 631923 RFA
McINERNEY William MM Spr 156265 180 Tunnelling Coy Royal Engineers
McINESPIE Patrick MM Pte 18241 2nd Royal Dublin Fusiliers
McINNES Alexander MM Pte 40407 Royal Scots Fusiliers
McINNES Alfred MM Dvr 630729 29 Bde RFA
McINNES Angus MM L/Sjt 10495 5th Cameron Highlanders
McINNES Archibald S. MM L/Cpl 200708 5/6th Scottish Rifles
McINNES Colin "DCM,MM" L/Sjt 300376 1/8th Arg & Suth Highlanders
McINNES Hugh MM Dvr 73626 52 Bty 15 Bde RFA
McINNES Hugh MM Pte 1451 16th Highland Light Infantry
McINNES James MM Pte 202686 1/7th Arg & Suth Highlanders
McINNES John MM Pte 223230 10th Cameron Highlanders
McINNES John MM Pte 31004 119 Coy Machine Gun Corps
McINNES John M. MM Pte 39373 1 Fd Amb RAMC
McINNES Malcolm MM Gnr 31868 A/108 Bde RFA
McINNES Thomas MM Pte 1820 1/9th Highland Light Infantry
McINROY James MM Pte 265483 1/6th Royal Highlanders
McINTOSH Adam MM Sjt 240023 Seaforth Highlanders
McINTOSH Alex MM Gnr Sig 665647 129 Bty 42 Bde RFA
McINTOSH Alexander MM Sjt 290066 Gordon Highlanders
McINTOSH Alexander MM Gnr 125857 RFA
McINTOSH Alexander P. MM Cpl 106394 Royal Engineers
McINTOSH Angus MM Cpl 43076 2 Div Ammn Col RFA
McINTOSH Angus John Baxter MM Pte 32583 7th Royal Warwickshire Regt
McINTOSH Charles "MM,CG(F)" Cpl 266223 1/6th Seaforth Highlanders
McINTOSH Charles MM CQMS 747 1st Royal Warwickshire Regt
McINTOSH David MM Pte 6826 1st Scottish Rifles
McINTOSH David MM Dvr 25127 5 Div Sig Coy Royal Engineers
McINTOSH David MM Cpl 23256 154 Coy Machine Gun Corps
McINTOSH David Anderson MM Sjt 39115 138 Fd Amb RAMC
McINTOSH Donald MM Sjt 92607 5th Bn Tank Corps
McINTOSH Ernest Cameron MM Cpl 17313 11th Border Regt KIA 18.11.16.
McINTOSH Harold MM Pte 16266 1/5th Border Regt
McINTOSH Irvine "DCM+Bar,MM,MIDx2" Pte 604 10th Arg & Suth Highlanders
McINTOSH J. MM Pte 43511 Machine Gun Corps
McINTOSH James MM Sjt 15582 2nd West Yorkshire Regt KIA 24.7.17.
McINTOSH James MM Pte 301535 RAMC
McINTOSH James MM L/Cpl 402379 Royal Engineers
McINTOSH John MM Pte 18800 1st Royal Irish Fusiliers
McINTOSH John MM Gnr 93613 46 Bde RFA
McINTOSH John MM L/Cpl 7648 1st Gordon Highlanders
McINTOSH John T. MM Pte 38552 Yorkshire Light Infantry
McINTOSH Joseph MM Pte 9461 2nd Seaforth Highlanders DOW 2.7.16.
McINTOSH Peter MM Pte 37559 Highland Light Infantry
McINTOSH Robert MM Pte R/1627 King's Royal Rifle Corps
McINTOSH Robert MM Cpl 14440 13th Royal Scots KIA 1.8.17.
McINTOSH Samuel MM Pte 3/10569 2nd West Riding Regt KIA 1.7.16.
McINTOSH Thomas MM Gnr L/968 C/153 Bde RFA
McINTOSH William MM Pte D/17549 1st Lovat's Scouts Yeomanry
McINTOSH William MM Cpl 265468 Seaforth Highlanders
McINTOSH William A. MM Pte 17863 Grenadier Guards
McINTOSH William Alexander Hugh MM Pte 285482 1/1st Oxfordshire Yeomanry
McINTOSH William Campbell MM Pte 276914 1/7th Arg & Suth Highlanders KIA 19.5.18.
McINTYRE Alexander MM Dvr 17650 'P' Bty RHA
McINTYRE Andrew T. MM Pte 371164 8th London Regt
McINTYRE Charles C. MM Pte 5268 20th Royal Fusiliers
McINTYRE David MM Sjt 19702 2nd Royal Inniskilling Fusiliers
McINTYRE Donald MM Spr 93007 Royal Engineers
McINTYRE Donald MM 2nd Cpl 48109 Royal Engineers
McINTYRE Dugald MM Sjt 6694 Arg & Suth Highlanders
McINTYRE George MM+Bar Sjt 295024 12th Royal Scots Fusiliers
McINTYRE Hugh MM Pte 48441 5/6th Royal Scots

McINTYRE James MM(15858 R Innis Fus)+Bar Spr 359494 36 Div Sig Coy Royal Engineers
McINTYRE James MM Pte 30184 100 Coy Machine Gun Corps KIA 25.4.17.
McINTYRE James MM L/Cpl 40109 5/6th Scottish Rifles
McINTYRE James Y. MM Pte 240784 1/6th Highland Light Infantry
McINTYRE John MM+Bar Sjt 26592 1st Scottish Rifles
McINTYRE John MM Pte 300919 1/7th Arg & Suth Highlanders DOW 1.8.18.
McINTYRE John MM Pte 40753 14th Arg & Suth Highlanders
McINTYRE John "DCM,MM,MIDx2" Pte 7259 1/8th Highland Light Infantry
McINTYRE John "MM,MSM" Cpl S/3597 8th Royal Highlanders
McINTYRE John "MM,MID" Sjt 10147 2nd Royal Scots Fusiliers
McINTYRE John MM+Bar Sjt 10849 6th East Yorkshire Regt
McINTYRE John MM Pte 278667 1/7th Arg & Suth Highlanders
McINTYRE Robert MM Sjt 755812 RFA
McINTYRE Stewart MM Gnr 726 260 Bde RFA
McINTYRE William MM Pte 48226 13th Royal Inniskilling Fusiliers
McINTYRE William MM Pte M2/102930 340 Coy Army Service Corps
McINTYRE William H. MM+Bar Pte 23565 Northumberland Fusiliers
McINTYRE William L. MM Pte S/23623 1/7th Arg & Suth Highlanders
McISAAC Dugald MM Sjt 112203 Royal Engineers
McISAAC Gerge William MM L/Cpl 9397 Royal Highlanders
McIVER Alexander John MM Cpl 300595 1/1(Bute)Mountain Bty RGA
McIVER Donald MM+Bar CSM 10696 2nd Seaforth Highlanders
McIVER Ernest Albert MM Cpl T4/238248 Army Service Corps
McIVER Hugh "VC,MM+Bar" Pte 12311 2nd Royal Scots KIA 2.9.18.
McIVER John MM Pte S/12006 Arg & Suth Highlanders
McIVER Malcolm MM Pte 4413 1/6th Seaforth Highlanders KIA 10.4.18.
McIVER Richard MM Sjt 1706 9th West Yorkshire Regt KIA 27.8.17.
McIVER Sidney Ernest MM Pte 7788 6th Lincolnshire Regt
McIVOR John MM Sjt 412325 Royal Engineers
McIVOR Robert MM 2nd Cpl 249514 Royal Engineers
McJENNETT James Patrick MM Sjt 17047 232 Coy Machine Gun Corps
McKANE Archibald MM Spr 57834 36 Div Sig Coy Royal Engineers
McKANE James MM Sjt 43923 Durham Light Infantry
McKANE Joseph T. MM Cpl 87744 RFA
McKANNA Reginald MM+Bar Sjt STK/743 10th Royal Fusiliers
McKAY A. MM L/Cpl P3165 Military Foot Police
McKAY Albert J. MM Pte 11/879 11th East Yorkshire Regt
McKAY Alexander MM Dvr L/6575 A/139 Bde RFA
McKAY Alexander MM Pte S/9444 1st Gordon Highlanders
McKAY Alexander MM Pte S/7893 10th Arg & Suth Highlanders KIA 12.10.17.
McKAY Alexander C. MM Pnr 302133 63 Div Sig Coy Royal Engineers
McKAY Angus MM Pte 1517 1/9th Highland Light Infantry
McKAY Angus MM Pte 6125 2nd Gordon Highlanders
McKAY Angus I. MM Pte 81023 RAMC
McKAY Archibald MM Sjt 1448 1/5th Liverpool Regt
McKAY Archibald MM Sjt 45059 Royal Engineers
McKAY Archie MM L/Cpl 18/356 18th Royal Irish Rifles
McKAY Charles W. MM Cpl 129376 45th Royal Fusiliers
McKAY Donald MM+Bar Cpl 6945 1st Cameron Highlanders DOW 7.5.18.
McKAY Donald MM L/Cpl 20206 13th Royal Scots
McKAY Duncan MM L/Cpl 3476 Royal Highlanders att MGC.
McKAY Duncan MM+Bar Pte S/11139 7th Cameron Highlanders
McKAY Frank MM Pte S/10001 Royal Highlanders
McKAY Hugh MM Pte 306827 1/8th Royal Warwickshire Regt KIA 27.8.17.
McKAY Irvine MM L/Cpl 66475 Royal Engineers
McKAY J. MM Pte 240330 Seaforth Highlanders
McKAY James MM Sjt 400250 Royal Engineers
McKAY James MM Cpl 2523 2/5th Lancashire Fusiliers KIA 9.9.16.
McKAY James MM L/Sjt 3626 Army Cyclist Corps
McKAY John MM Pte 240110 1/5th Royal Scots Fusiliers
McKAY John MM Pte 1195 1/6th Gordon Highlanders
McKAY John MM Pte 18513 10/11th Highland Light Infantry KIA 31.7.17.
McKAY John MM Pte 5660 1st Gordon Highlanders
McKAY John S. MM Pte 271403 12th Royal Scots
McKAY Malcolm MM Pte 3/5394 5th Cameron Highlanders
McKAY Owen MM Dvr 6035 D/82 Bde RFA

McKAY P. MM Pte 330852 Liverpool Regt
McKAY R. MM Sjt 49473 Labour Corps
McKAY Robert MM Sjt S/6158 9th Seaforth Highlanders
McKAY Robert "MM,MID" Unknown 54753 RAMC
McKAY Robert MM Cpl 47707 Royal Scots Fusiliers
McKAY Samuel "MM,CG(F)" Sjt 355560 1/10th Liverpool Regt
McKAY Samuel MM Pte 31610 15th Highland Light Infantry KIA 27.11.17.
McKAY Thomas MM Pte 11509 2nd Royal Scots
McKAY William MM Pte 84441 32nd Bn Machine Gun Corps
McKAY William MM Pte 201596 Arg & Suth Highlanders
McKAY William MM Gnr 47900 22 Bde RFA
McKAY William MM Gnr 117089 RGA
McKAY William MM L/Bdr 54029 245 Siege Bty RGA
McKAY William MM Pte 41216 RAMC
McKAY William Boyne MM L/Sjt 265434 Seaforth Highlanders
McKAY William S. MM SQMS 2937 12th Lancers
McKEACHAN Alexander MM Pte 301425 1/7th Arg & Suth Highlanders
McKEAN John MM Cpl 161022 25 Div Sig Coy Royal Engineers
McKEARNEY John MM Sjt 67015 RFA
McKECHNIE Angus MM Pte 85269 1st Bn Machine Gun Corps DOW 19.10.18.
McKECHNIE Charles MM Pte 12305 100 Coy Machine Gun Corps
McKECHNIE David "MM,MSM" S/Sjt 35258 Staff ADMS 11 Div RAMC
McKECHNIE Donald MM L/Cpl 9819 Arg & Suth Highlanders
McKECHNIE Hector MM Pte 59979 2nd Royal Scots DOW 19.9.18.
McKECHNIE J. MM Pte 13185 Notts & Derby Regt
McKECHNIE James MM Pte 2289 1/8th Worcestershire Regt
McKECHNIE John MM Pte 203290 Scottish Rifles
McKEE David MM Sjt 49374 111 Bty 24 Bde RFA
McKEE James MM Spr 64431 150 Fd Coy Royal Engineers
McKEE James MM Pte 8332 2nd Highland Light Infantry DOW 10.12.17.
McKEE John MM Pte 250729 1/6th Arg & Suth Highlanders
McKEE John MM Pte 10/15426 15th Royal Irish Rifles
McKEE John MM Pte 11/6658 12th Royal Irish Rifles
McKEE Patrick MM Pte 20912 7/8th Royal Irish Fusiliers KIA 20.11.17.
McKEE Robert MM Cpl 3/16801 Royal Irish Rifles
McKEE Robert Henry MM Cpl 148533 183 Tunnelling Coy Royal Engineers
McKEE Samuel MM Pte 40205 10th South Wales Borderers
McKEE William Andrew MM Pte 23308 2nd Yorkshire Light Infantry KIA 2.12.17.
McKEEVER Samuel MM Sjt 18160 12th Royal Irish Rifles
McKEITH George MM Pte S/43103 Gordon Highlanders
McKELL William MM+Bar Pte 21510 1st Gordon Highlanders
McKELLAN Roderick MM Pte M2/153494 Army Service Corps
McKELLAR Archibald MM Dvr T4/260354 62 Div Train Army Service Corps
McKELLAR Donald A. MM Pte 285231 Royal Highlanders
McKELVEY Robert MM Cpl 265771 Royal Highlanders
McKENDRICK Gilbert MM Pte 41133 8th Royal Lancaster Regt
McKENDRICK John MM Pte 13077 12th Royal Scots
McKENDRICK John E. MM+Bar Spr 237567 Royal Engineers
McKENNA D.M. MM Sjt 21053 Machine Gun Corps
McKENNA Edward MM Pte G/68287 10th Royal Fusiliers
McKENNA Edward MM Cpl 17821 Cameron Highlanders
McKENNA George MM Cpl 40259 39 Bde RFA
McKENNA George P. MM L/Cpl 25439 9th Border Regt
McKENNA Herbert MM Spr 147675 Royal Engineers
McKENNA James MM Cpl 2968 7th Leinster Regt
McKENNA John Thomas MM Pte 1429 9th Durham Light Infantry
McKENNA Joseph MM L/Cpl 21909 Durham Light Infantry
McKENNA P. MM Pte 32473 1/4th South Lancashire Regt
McKENNA Peter MM Cpl 9156 1st Shropshire Light Infantry
McKENNA Thomas MM Pte 26/474 26th Northumberland Fusiliers KIA 8.4.16.
McKENNA William MM Pte 201428 5/6th Scottish Rifles KIA 23.10.18.
McKENZIE A.E. MM+Bar L/Cpl 19393 Royal Engineers
McKENZIE Alexander MM Pte 34020 2nd Royal Scots Fusiliers
McKENZIE Alexander MM L/Cpl 23251 154 Coy Machine Gun Corps
McKENZIE Alexander MM Sjt S/27417 Cameron Highlanders
McKENZIE Alexander D. MM Bdr 121785 RGA
McKENZIE Alexander Y. MM Pte 5961 2nd Dragoons
McKENZIE Angus MM Pte 131589 45th Royal Fusiliers

McKENZIE Archibald MM+Bar Pte S/3368 9th Seaforth Highlanders KIA 11.10.17.
McKENZIE Arthur MM L/Cpl 50619 Machine Gun Corps(Cavalry)
McKENZIE Charles D. MM Sjt L/38530 39 Div Ammn Col RFA
McKENZIE Christopher MM CSM S/5607 7th Seaforth Highlanders DOW 7.11.18.
McKENZIE D.P. MM Pte 13479 Seaforth Highlanders
McKENZIE Donald MM Pte 200060 1/4th Seaforth Highlanders
McKENZIE Donald "MM,MID" RQMS 200542 1/5th Arg & Suth Highlanders
McKENZIE Donald MM Sjt 492 Royal Engineers
McKENZIE Duncan MM Pte 3792 1/4th Seaforth Highlanders KIA 20.7.18.
McKENZIE Duncan MM Pte S/40716 6th Cameron Highlanders KIA 28.3.18.
McKENZIE Ewen MM Cpl 201880 1/4th Seaforth Highlanders KIA 9.4.18.
McKENZIE Farquhar MM Pte 200243 Seaforth Highlanders
McKENZIE Finlay MM Pte 372512 8th London Regt
McKENZIE George MM L/Bdr 630439 C/255 Bde RFA
McKENZIE George I. MM Cpl 660133 B/262 Bde RFA
McKENZIE George Murray MM Dvr 59347 RHA
McKENZIE H. MM Sjt 715043 RFA
McKENZIE Harry MM Pte 17971 Royal Scots
McKENZIE Harry MM Sjt 48332 97 Bty 147 Bde RFA
McKENZIE Henry MM Pte S/12689 Seaforth Highlanders
McKENZIE Henry John MM Cpl 142266 Royal Engineers
McKENZIE James MM L/Cpl 17357 9th Bn Machine Gun Corps
McKENZIE James MM Pte S/16466 1/5th Seaforth Highlanders
McKENZIE James MM Pte 43041 1st Royal Scots Fusiliers
McKENZIE James MM Pte M2/174905 32 Div Train. Army Service Corps
McKENZIE James MM Cpl 266296 Seaforth Highlanders
McKENZIE James MM Sjt 90136 RAMC
McKENZIE James Kerr MM Pte 14774 1st Scots Guards
McKENZIE John MM Pte 292005 1/8th Royal Highlanders
McKENZIE John MM Pte 200358 1/4th Seaforth Highlanders
McKENZIE John MM Spr 127256 8 Div Sig Coy Royal Engineers
McKENZIE John MM Cpl 202256 4th South Lancashire Regt
McKENZIE John MM Sjt 78686 RGA
McKENZIE John MM Pte 8441 Arg & Suth Highlanders
McKENZIE John Alexander MM Sjt 291246 3/10th Middlesex Regt
McKENZIE John Hendry MM Cpl 76405 'F' Corps Sig Coy Royal Engineers
McKENZIE John Hutchinson MM Pte 14356 10th Essex Regt KIA 8.3.17.
McKENZIE John Maxwell MM Pte 303175 1/8th Arg & Suth Highlanders KIA 20.11.17.
McKENZIE John R. MM Sjt 75669 Tank Corps
McKENZIE Kenneth MM+Bar Cpl 203211 1/7th Gordon Highlanders
McKENZIE Kenneth MM L/Cpl 10672 2nd Seaforth Highlanders
McKENZIE Malcolm MM L/Cpl 3/5190 6th Cameron Highlanders KIA 26.4.17.
McKENZIE Murdo MM Sjt 200251 1/4th Seaforth Highlanders
McKENZIE Patrick MM Pte 7173 RAMC
McKENZIE Peter MM Sjt 5071 Royal West Kent Regt
McKENZIE Peter J.McB. MM Drummer 712 2nd Seaforth Highlanders
McKENZIE Robert MM Pte 1487 9th Seaforth Highlanders
McKENZIE Robert MM Pte 1461 1/4th Seaforth Highlanders
McKENZIE Robert E. MM Dvr 630730 RFA
McKENZIE Robert M. MM L/Cpl 266646 11th Royal Scots Fusiliers
McKENZIE Robert W. "MM,MID" Spr 64871 30 Div Sig Coy Royal Engineers
McKENZIE Roderick MM Pte 250948 1/6th Arg & Suth Highlanders
McKENZIE Roderick MM 2nd Cpl 139365 Royal Engineers
McKENZIE Roderick MM Pte 23214 Seaforth Highlanders
McKENZIE Roderick MM L/Cpl 41534 1st Gordon Highlanders KIA 23.8.18.
McKENZIE Simon MM Sjt 202205 Seaforth Highlanders
McKENZIE Thomas MM Pte 265815 Seaforth Highlanders
McKENZIE Thomas D. MM Pte 93847 1 Fd Amb RAMC
McKENZIE Victor R. MM Cpl 1966 14 Lt Armd Car Bty MGC(Motors)
McKENZIE William MM Pte 291205 1/8th Scottish Rifles
McKENZIE William MM Cpl 220309 6th Cameron Highlanders
McKENZIE William "MM,MID" Pte 17378 2nd King's Own Scottish Borderers
McKENZIE William MM Spr 59234 Royal Engineers
McKENZIE William MM Sjt Piper 8248 1st King's Own Scottish Borderers
McKENZIE William MM Sjt 290292 1/8th Scottish Rifles
McKENZIE William MM L/Cpl 10166 1st Seaforth Highlanders
McKENZIE William F. MM CQMS 200001 1/4th Royal Highlanders
McKENZIE William J. MM Sjt 32807 15th Royal Warwickshire Regt
McKEON John MM Pte 6843 Shropshire Light Infantry
McKEOWN David MM Pnr 313086 Royal Engineers
McKEOWN Edward W. MM+Bar Pte 21257 6th Dragoons
McKEOWN George MM Cpl 27517 1st Royal Inniskilling Fusiliers
McKEOWN James MM Cpl 9604 1st Royal Irish Rifles
McKEOWN James W. MM Pte S/898 Rifle Brigade
McKEOWN John MM+Bar CSM 6/2487 6th Connaught Rangers
McKEOWN Michael MM Pte 124830 37th Bn Machine Gun Corps
McKEOWN Patrick "MM,MID" L/Cpl 13015 12th Royal Scots
McKEOWN Patrick MM+Bar L/Cpl 40842 51 Fd Amb RAMC
McKEOWN William MM Cpl 13610 9th Royal Inniskilling Fusiliers
McKEOWN William "DCM,MM" Sjt 51357 1st Royal Scots Fusiliers
McKERNAN Edward MM CSM 21108 7th Royal Inniskilling Fusiliers KIA 16.8.17.
McKERNAN John MM Cpl L/6696 2nd Royal Sussex Regt
McKERRELL Lyle Manus MM Pte 28089 15th Hampshire Regt
McKERRON William MM L/Cpl 200863 1/4th Gordon Highlanders
McKERROW Andrew MM Cpl 202670 2nd King's Own Scottish Borderers DOW 29.8.18.
McKERROW James MM Sjt S/21782 1st Gordon Highlanders
McKIBBIN Alexander MM+Bar Bdr L/6677 RFA
McKIBBIN Henry MM Pte 18063 4th Liverpool Regt
McKIBBIN Robert MM Pte 19/1300 19th Northumberland Fusiliers
McKIE David C. "MM,MID" Cpl 33564 15 Fd Coy Royal Engineers
McKIE George MM Sjt 10566 9th Northumberland Fusiliers
McKIE P. MM Sjt 331241 1/9th Highland Light Infantry
McKIE Thomas MM Pte 333003 Highland Light Infantry
McKIE William MM Sjt 23698 15th Welsh Regt
McKIERNAN Michael Vincent MM+Bar L/Sjt 7777 Irish Guards DOW 11.5.18
McKILLOP Frederick MM Pte 6532 1st Royal Berkshire Regt
McKILLOP James MM Pte 303235 Arg & Suth Highlanders
McKILLOP John S. MM Cpl 2360 5/6th Royal Scots
McKIM Henry M. MM Gnr 681458 88 Bde RFA
McKIM William "MM,MID" Sjt 323007 RAMC
McKIM William "MM,MIDx2" Bdr 82379 B/66 Bde RFA
McKIMMIE James "DCM,MM" Sjt 936 2nd Gordon Highlanders
McKIMMIE John MM Cpl 44982 Royal Engineers
McKINLAY Archibald MM L/Cpl 290855 Royal Highlanders
McKINLAY Daniel MM Pte 355036 15th Highland Light Infantry
McKINLAY George MM Pte 200416 1/4th Royal Scots Fusiliers KIA 2.10.18.
McKINLAY John MM Sjt 275680 1/7th Arg & Suth Highlanders
McKINLAY John MM Pte 6225 2nd Dragoons
McKINLAY Robert MM Pte 30325 16th Highland Light Infantry
McKINLAY Robert O. MM L/Cpl S/8981 Arg & Suth Highlanders
McKINLAY William MM Cpl 1924 Royal Engineers
McKINLEY George MM Cpl 40503 1/9th Arg & Suth Highlanders
McKINLEY John MM Pte 18297 13th Royal Scots
McKINLEY Joseph MM Sjt 13943 8th Royal Dublin Fusiliers KIA 29.4.16.
McKINLEY Samuel MM Pte 10444 King's Own Scottish Borderers
McKINLEY William MM Dvr 55630 15 Bty 36 Bde RFA
McKINLEY William "MM,MSM" Gnr 17363 RGA
McKINLEY William R. MM Sjt 1070 1/15th London Regt
McKINNELL Albert MM Pte 39098 Royal Scots
McKINNEY Isaac MM Pte 9230 Irish Guards
McKINNEY Robert MM L/Cpl 9661 1st Royal Inniskilling Fusiliers
McKINNIE William MM Pte 204345 Seaforth Highlanders
McKINNIE William MM Pte 3393 2 Fd Amb RAMC
McKINNON Alexander MM Cpl 645030 C/156 Bde RFA
McKINNON Angus MM Pte 303157 1/8th Arg & Suth Highlanders
McKINNON D. MM Gnr 655520 RFA
McKINNON David C. MM Pte 3546 Liverpool Regt
McKINNON Donald MM Pte 26781 Cameron Highlanders
McKINNON Donald MM Spr 223941 Royal Engineers
McKINNON Donald N. MM Cpl S/41671 1/4th Seaforth Highlanders
McKINNON J. MM L/Cpl S/17682 Cameron Highlanders
McKINNON John MM Cpl 9708 2nd Arg & Suth Highlanders
McKINNON John MM+Bar Cpl 40613 Highland Light Infantry
McKINNON John MM L/Cpl 93161 218 Fd Coy Royal Engineers KIA 3.11.18.
McKINNON John MM Pte 202678 Gordon Highlanders
McKINNON John A. MM Cpl 452043 Royal Engineers
McKINNON Joseph MM Pte 9020 2nd Durham Light Infantry
McKINNON Kenneth MM Pte 200553 7th Scottish Rifles

McKINNON Peter MM L/Cpl 5705 5th Cameron Highlanders KIA 14.6.18.
McKINNON R. MM L/Cpl S/8784 Arg & Suth Highlanders
McKINNON Roderick MM Sjt 265378 7th Royal Highlanders
McKINNON Thomas MM L/Cpl 94056 217 Army Tps Coy Royal Engineers
McKINNON William MM Sjt 663032 256 Bde RFA
McKINSTRAY James MM Pte 270336 Royal Scots
McKINVEN Robert MM Pte 59103 11th Royal Scots Fusiliers
McKISSACK John R. MM Pte 12709 1st Scots Guards
McKNIFF Joseph MM L/Cpl 16207 13 Coy Machine Gun Corps KIA 23.9.16.
McKNIGHT Alexander MM Sjt 330132 6th Liverpool Regt
McKNIGHT David MM Pte 40524 1st Scottish Rifles
McKNIGHT Henry MM Pte 2845 15th Royal Irish Rifles
McKNIGHT John MM Sjt 5340 3rd Dragoon Guards
McKNIGHT Samuel "MM,MID,CG(B)" RQMS 5330 5/6th Scottish Rifles
McKNIGHT Simon MM Gnr 122347 RFA
McKNIGHT Stephen MM Pte 8/3622 1st Royal Munster Fusiliers KIA 22.3.18.
McKNIGHT William MM Pte 15310 2nd Leinster Regt
McKNIGHT William J. MM L/Cpl 14/6520 14th Royal Irish Rifles
McKNIGHT William T. "MM,MID" L/Cpl 57774 121 Fd Coy Royal Engineers
McKONE Llewellyn MM Pte 200910 Middlesex Regt
McKRILL David F. "DCM,MM" CSM 13233 West Riding Regt
McLACHLAN Angus MM+Bar BSM 26434 RFA
McLACHLAN Duncan MM Spr 75208 Royal Engineers
McLACHLAN G. MM+Bar Pte 2209 2nd Royal Highlanders
McLACHLAN Hugh MM Pte 49845 12th Bn Machine Gun Corps
McLACHLAN Hugh Cameron MM Pte C/6147 King's Royal Rifle Corps
McLACHLAN John MM Gnr 5039 RGA
McLACHLAN John M. MM L/Cpl 93134 Royal Engineers
McLACHLAN Lachlan MM Cpl 202157 1st Royal Scots Fusiliers
McLACHLAN Robert MM+Bar Cpl 412079 409 Fd Coy Royal Engineers
McLAGGAN Thomas MM Sjt 350045 1/6th Royal Highlanders
McLARDY John MM Pte 41395 Scottish Rifles
McLAREN Alexander MM Sjt 275777 1/7th Arg & Suth Highlanders
McLAREN Alexander Low MM Sjt 503 21 Div Ammn Col RFA
McLAREN Alistair James MM Gnr 172445 B/119 Bde RFA
McLAREN Archibald MM Pte 292450 1/7th Gordon Highlanders
McLAREN Archibald MM Sjt 139214 179 Tunnelling Coy Royal Engineers
McLAREN Donald "MM,MID" Cpl 3164 Arg & Suth Highlanders att RE.
McLAREN Duncan MM L/Sjt S/5799 12th Arg & Suth Highlanders
McLAREN Duncan MM Pte 202672 Seaforth Highlanders
McLAREN Edward MM L/Cpl 23109 20th Liverpool Regt KIA 8.9.17.
McLAREN Francis H. MM Spr 71268 Royal Engineers
McLAREN George MM L/Cpl 265922 7th Royal Highlanders KIA 26.3.18.
McLAREN James MM Cpl 3856 8th Royal Highlanders
McLAREN James MM Cpl 47422 13th Royal Inniskilling Fusiliers
McLAREN James MM+Bar Pte 3818 2nd Dragoons
McLAREN John MM Dvr 631612 RFA
McLAREN John MM Pte 1199 1/6th Royal Highlanders
McLAREN John MM Pte 12900 10th Highland Light Infantry
McLAREN Joseph MM L/Cpl 101834 150 Fd Coy Royal Engineers
McLAREN Malcolm MM Pte 126664 Lovat's Scouts Yeomanry
McLAREN William James MM Pte 2232 1/12th London Regt DOW 14.4.17.
McLAREN William Ross MM L/Cpl 2718 1/6th Royal Highlanders
McLASKEY Thomas Henry Walter MM Sjt 511953 1/14th London Regt
McLAUCHLAN Daniel MM Pte 275311 1/7th Arg & Suth Highlanders
McLAUCHLAN J. MM Pte 53110 10th Royal Fusiliers
McLAUCHLAN John MM L/Sjt 3391 1/4th Royal Highlanders DOW 3.1.17.
McLAUCHLAN Martin A. MM Pte 350529 1/9th Royal Scots
McLAUGHLAN D. MM Sjt 301216 10th Arg & Suth Highlanders
McLAUGHLAN Harry MM Pte 202297 5/6th Scottish Rifles KIA 3.10.18.
McLAUGHLAN Hugh MM Pte 13034 15th Highland Light Infantry
McLAUGHLAN James MM Pte 29025 Highland Light Infantry
McLAUGHLAN John MM Sjt 15052 Royal Inniskilling Fusiliers
McLAUGHLAN Robert MM L/Cpl 412577 Royal Engineers
McLAUGHLIN Alfred J. MM Pte 47975 2nd Lancashire Fusiliers
McLAUGHLIN Daniel MM Cpl 86133 170 Tunnelling Coy Royal Engineers
McLAUGHLIN Henry "DCM,MM" L/Cpl 14224 2nd Royal Scots Fusiliers
McLAUGHLIN Hugh MM+Bar Sjt 661267 RFA
McLAUGHLIN James MM Gnr 663054 RFA
McLAUGHLIN John MM L/Cpl 42076 South Wales Borderers
McLAUGHLIN John MM Pte 6/11421 6th Royal Irish Rifles
McLAUGHLIN John P. MM Pte 20976 Royal Irish Fusiliers
McLAUGHLIN Joseph MM Sjt 30957 88 Siege Bty RGA KIA 27.4.18.
McLAUGHLIN Joseph MM Pte 15287 6/7th Royal Scots Fusiliers
McLAUGHLIN Joseph MM Pte 241095 Seaforth Highlanders
McLAUGHLIN Joseph J. MM Pte A/7853 2nd Highland Light Infantry
McLAUGHLIN Michael MM+Bar L/Cpl 17504 Royal Irish Fusiliers
McLAUGHLIN Rodger Francis MM+Bar Sjt S/8482 8th Royal Highlanders DOW 29.9.18.
McLAUGHLIN Stephen A. MM Pte 511472 14th London Regt
McLAURIN John MM Sjt 147103 Royal Engineers
McLAY David MM Pte 39655 Royal Scots
McLAY George MM Sjt 19059 16th Royal Scots KIA 22.10.17.
McLAY Richard MM Dvr 64724 376 Bty 169 Bde RFA
McLEAN Abraham MM Pte 34192 8th Northumberland Fusiliers DOW 15.2.18.
McLEAN Albert MM Pte 11472 1st Royal Irish Fusiliers KIA 21.3.18.
McLEAN Alexander MM Sjt 65498 A/123 Bde RFA
McLEAN Alexander MM Pte 28049 Machine Gun Corps
McLEAN Alexander MM Pte 9551 Seaforth Highlanders
McLEAN Allan S. MM Pte 235284 Gordon Highlanders
McLEAN Allen MM Dvr 6123 RFA
McLEAN Archibald MM L/Cpl 1080 2/3rd (London) Fd Coy Royal Engineers
McLEAN Archibald MM+Bar L/Cpl 202328 4/5th Royal Highlanders KIA 28.7.18.
McLEAN C. MM Cpl 275468 Arg & Suth Highlanders
McLEAN C.C. MM Cpl 200181 Highland Light Infantry
McLEAN Charles MM Spr 310759 46 Div Sig Coy Royal Engineers
McLEAN Charles "MC+Bar,MM(6053 CSM Cam H)" Capt 1st North Lancashire Regt
McLEAN Christina MM Staff Nurse F QAIMNS
McLEAN Donald MM Pte 12937 9th Scottish Rifles
McLEAN Donald MM Cpl 73403 56 Coy Machine Gun Corps
McLEAN Donald MM Gnr 133982 159 Bde RFA
McLEAN Donald MM Pte S/17840 5th Cameron Highlanders KIA 14.10.18.
McLEAN Donald MM L/Cpl 300171 10th Arg & Suth Highlanders
McLEAN Duncan "MM,MID" Pte 2155 1/4th Gordon Highlanders
McLEAN Edward MM Spr 420278 121 Fd Coy Royal Engineers
McLEAN Ernest MM L/Cpl 18635 155 Fd Coy Royal Engineers
McLEAN Frank W. "MM+Bar,CG(It)" Pte 18630 6th & 8th Yorkshire Regt
McLEAN G.H. MM 2nd Cpl 221567 Royal Engineers
McLEAN George MM Pte 139744 Machine Gun Corps
McLEAN George MM Pte S/14069 Cameron Highlanders
McLEAN George R. MM Cpl M2/051758 Army Service Corps
McLEAN Gordon MM Sjt 841152 A/70 Bde RFA
McLEAN Hugh MM Sjt 1568 Northumberland Fusiliers
McLEAN J. MM Dvr 39320 RFA
McLEAN J. MM Pte 2386 Arg & Suth Highlanders
McLEAN J. MM L/Cpl 268079 Royal Highlanders
McLEAN James MM L/Cpl 25903 1st Liverpool Regt KIA 24.3.18.
McLEAN James S. MM Sjt 17654 Scottish Rifles
McLEAN John MM Sjt 41988 7th Royal Highlanders
McLEAN John MM Sjt 13625 2 Div Sig Coy Royal Engineers
McLEAN John MM Sjt MS/1551 HQ III Corps Army Service Corps
McLEAN John MM Pte 18675 12th Highland Light Infantry
McLEAN John MM L/Cpl 9448 1st (Highland) Fd Coy Royal Engineers KIA 19.11.16.
McLEAN John MM Pte S/13466 7th Cameron Highlanders
McLEAN John C.M. MM Cpl S/41863 1/6th Royal Highlanders
McLEAN John G. MM L/Cpl 444505 Royal Engineers
McLEAN Joseph C. "DCM,MM" Sjt 10574 2nd Royal Scots Fusiliers
McLEAN Lachlan MM Pte 123630 61st Bn Machine Gun Corps
McLEAN Leslie G. MM Gnr 4239 157 Bde RFA
McLEAN Malcolm MM Sjt 1790 1/1st Glasgow Yeomanry
McLEAN Matthew MM Cpl 10423 1st Seaforth Highlanders
McLEAN McGregor MM Bdr 7040 RFA
McLEAN Murdo MM L/Sjt S/15952 1/6th Seaforth Highlanders
McLEAN Murdo A. MM Sjt 201779 Seaforth Highlanders
McLEAN Murdoch MM Pte 310268 Gordon Highlanders

McLEAN Neil MM L/Cpl 10779 1/6th Gordon Highlanders
McLEAN Neil MM L/Cpl M2/052233 Army Service Corps att RGA
McLEAN Peter "DCM,MM" L/Cpl 266946 Gordon Highlanders
McLEAN Peter C. MM Sjt S/10537 2nd Arg & Suth Highlanders
McLEAN R. MM Bdr 385 RGA
McLEAN R. MM Pte 20665 18 Fd Amb RAMC
McLEAN Robert MM Cpl 8464 Seaforth Highlanders
McLEAN Robert MM Pte 43044 RAMC
McLEAN Robert W. MM Pte 53660 RAMC
McLEAN Samuel Joseph MM L/Cpl 8056 1st North Staffordshire Regt Died 22.10.18.
McLEAN Thomas MM Pte 141199 51st Bn Machine Gun Corps
McLEAN Thomas MM Cpl 406103 Royal Engineers
McLEAN Thomas MM Pte 275935 1/7th Manchester Regt
McLEAN William MM Cpl 325238 1/8th Royal Scots
McLEAR James MM Pte Y/1396 12th King's Royal Rifle Corps
McLEAY E. MM Sjt 6004 Middlesex Regt
McLEAY George MM Sjt 10427 2nd Scottish Rifles
McLEISH Howard MM L/Cpl 4212 4/5th Royal Highlanders
McLEISH W.R. MM Pte 300037 Liverpool Regt
McLEISH William MM L/Cpl 266186 1/6th Royal Highlanders
McLELLAN Angus MM Sjt 4819 2nd Dragoons
McLELLAN Charles MM Piper S/5745 9th Seaforth Highlanders
McLELLAN Colin MM L/Sjt 12676 2nd Scots Guards
McLELLAN Donald MM Pte 31038 Highland Light Infantry
McLELLAN Donald MM Cpl 12312 100 Coy Machine Gun Corps KIA 3.11.16.
McLELLAN Donald MM Pte 8776 12th Highland Light Infantry
McLELLAN Frederick N. MM L/Cpl 41829 Royal Scots
McLELLAN Gilbert MM L/Cpl 353150 Highland Light Infantry
McLELLAN Hector MM Sjt 228343 26th Royal Fusiliers
McLELLAN James MM+2 Bars Pte 12460 10th Highland Light Infantry
McLELLAN James A. MM Pte 10094 1st Arg & Suth Highlanders
McLELLAN John MM L/Cpl 350180 1/9th Royal Scots
McLELLAN John MM Pte 5555 18th Highland Light Infantry
McLELLAN John MM Pte 1493 Arg & Suth Highlanders
McLELLAN John MM Pte S/10571 1st Gordon Highlanders KIA 20.3.18.
McLELLAN John MM Pte S/16086 7th Cameron Highlanders
McLELLAN Mungo MM Spr 420273 Royal Engineers
McLELLAN Robert MM Pte 26336 12th Royal Scots
McLELLAN Rowatt MM Cpl 5490 2nd Seaforth Highlanders KIA 12.6.18.
McLELLAND Alexander MM L/Cpl 8271 12th Arg & Suth Highlanders KIA 19.9.18.
McLELLAND William MM L/Cpl 16136 6/7th Royal Scots Fusiliers
McLEMAN David L. MM Sjt 42160 15/17th West Yorkshire Regt
McLENACHAN William MM Pte 21305 Cameron Highlanders
McLENAGHAN Cochrane MM+Bar Pte 13005 6/7th Royal Scots Fusiliers
McLENNAN Alexander MM Pte 200257 1/4th Seaforth Highlanders
McLENNAN Andrew S. MM L/Sjt 98151 46th Bn Machine Gun Corps
McLENNAN Donald MM Pte 350859 Royal Highlanders
McLENNAN George A. MM Pte 42504 RAMC
McLENNAN James MM Cpl 635877 B/256 Bde RFA
McLENNAN K. MM Pte 36662 Highland Light Infantry
McLENNAN Kenneth MM Cpl 34560 RAMC
McLENNAN Robert A. MM Sjt 350270 9th Royal Scots
McLENNAN T.C. "MM,MID" Pte 200879 Devonshire Regt
McLENNAN William MM L/Cpl 202153 2/5th Manchester Regt KIA 22.11.17.
McLENNAN William W. MM+Bar Pte 330412 1/8th Royal Scots
McLENNON William MM Gnr 17074 2 Siege Bty RGA
McLEOD A. MM Cpl 700 1st (Cheshire) Fd Coy Royal Engineers
McLEOD Albert C. MM Pte 250509 1/7th Royal Scots
McLEOD Alexander MM Pte 9061 2nd Highland Light Infantry
McLEOD Alexander MM Cpl 365625 RGA
McLEOD Alexander MM Dvr 93641 36 Bty 33 Bde RFA
McLEOD Angus MM Pte 3/5571 5th Cameron Highlanders
McLEOD D. MM Pte 303315 RAMC
McLEOD Daniel MM+Bar Sjt Piper 200029 1/4th Royal Highlanders
McLEOD David W. MM+Bar Sjt 632114 245 Coy Labour Corps
McLEOD Donald MM 2nd Cpl 159069 212 Fd Coy Royal Engineers
McLEOD Donald "DCM,MM" Sjt 8770 1/4th Seaforth Highlanders
McLEOD Duncan A. MM Pte 41664 2nd Royal Scots Fusiliers
McLEOD Farquhar MM Pte S/25212 Cameron Highlanders
McLEOD Frederick W. MM Pte 591275 1/18th London Regt
McLEOD George "DCM,MM" L/Sjt 7061 2nd Royal Irish Regt

McLEOD Harry B. MM Pte 20546 Arg & Suth Highlanders
McLEOD Hugh MM Dvr 6127 RFA
McLEOD J. MM Cpl 164767 100th Bn Machine Gun Corps
McLEOD J. MM Cpl 200169 Seaforth Highlanders
McLEOD J. MM Pte 302897 1/7th Royal Scots
McLEOD J. MM Pte 7391 Seaforth Highlanders
McLEOD J.G. MM+Bar Pte 240636 1/5th Seaforth Highlanders
McLEOD J.I. MM Dvr 110918 RFA
McLEOD James MM Pte 7000 2nd Arg & Suth Highlanders KIA 26.6.18.
McLEOD James MM Sjt 137538 Royal Engineers
McLEOD James MM Pte 235425 Yorkshire Light Infantry
McLEOD James H. MM L/Cpl 516 2nd Seaforth Highlanders Died 26.2.17.
McLEOD John MM Sjt 265306 1/7th Scottish Rifles
McLEOD John MM+Bar Pte 3082 2nd Gordon Highlanders KIA 12.7.18.
McLEOD John MM L/Cpl 3079 9th Gordon Highlanders DOW 17.4.18.
McLEOD M. MM Pte 300039 RAMC
McLEOD N. MM Pte 267006 1/6th Royal Highlanders
McLEOD N.H. MM Cpl 334261 Highland Light Infantry
McLEOD Norman MM Pte 200930 5/6th Scottish Rifles KIA 14.4.18.
McLEOD P.G.K. MM Pte 6600 RAMC
McLEOD R. MM L/Cpl 41034 Royal Scots Fusiliers
McLEOD R.R. MM L/Cpl 17311 Scottish Rifles
McLEOD Robert MM Sjt 2766 8th Seaforth Highlanders KIA 9.3.18.
McLEOD Stewart MM L/Cpl S/15826 1st Gordon Highlanders Died 30.10.18.
McLEOD W. MM L/Cpl 8470 South Lancashire Regt
McLEOD William MM Sjt 12048 Machine Gun Corps
McLEOD William MM Pte 200078 1/4th Seaforth Highlanders
McLERNON Francis MM L/Cpl 18524 2nd Royal Irish Regt
McLERNON Harold William MM Sjt 25059 25 Siege Bty RGA
McLEVIN James MM Bdr 96111 RGA
McLEVY James MM Pte 69267 17th Royal Fusiliers
McLINDEN Felix MM Pte 70969 55th Bn Machine Gun Corps
McLINDON Bernard MM Pte 2483 1/6th Durham Light Infantry
McLOONE John MM L/Cpl 1148 4th Bn GMGR
McLORIMAN Joseph "MM,MID" Sjt 12970 12th West Yorkshire Regt
McLOUGHLIN Benjamin MM Pte 203508 2/4th East Lancashire Regt KIA 10.10.17.
McLOUGHLIN Charles Edward MM+Bar Sjt 5313 1st Coldstream Guards
McLOUGHLIN Fred MM Pte 12766 2nd South Lancashire Regt KIA 16.6.17.
McLOUGHLIN Harold MM Cpl 3414 2nd South Lancashire Regt
McLOUGHLIN James "MM,MID" Pte 35444 East Lancashire Regt
McLOUGHLIN James MM Cpl 20368 Liverpool Regt
McLOUGHLIN John MM L/Cpl 11468 Royal Irish Fusiliers
McLOUGHLIN John D. MM Pte 359726 Liverpool Regt
McLOUGHLIN Marshall Neal MM Pte 300135 1/5th London Regt
McLOUGHLIN Michael Joseph MM Sjt 25245 2nd Royal Dublin Fusiliers
McLOUGHLIN Phillip MM Pte 25899 8th Royal Dublin Fusiliers
McLOUGHLIN Thomas MM CSM 6187 4th Liverpool Regt
McLYNN Thomas MM Pte 40314 20th Manchester Regt
McMACKEN John MM Gnr 51674 RHA
McMAHON Edward MM Sjt 12119 5th Royal Irish Fusiliers
McMAHON Frank MM Pte 25854 Scottish Rifles
McMAHON Hugh MM Pte 44547 164 Coy Machine Gun Corps
McMAHON James MM Pte 45891 15th Durham Light Infantry
McMAHON James MM L/Sjt 9037 5th Connaught Rangers
McMAHON James MM Pte 9564 Royal Highlanders
McMAHON James MM Pte 241790 1/6th Liverpool Regt
McMAHON John MM Cpl 2964 Royal Sussex Regt
McMAHON Marshall MM Pte 241197 Notts & Derby Regt
McMAHON Robert MM+Bar Sjt 6640 15 Fd Coy Royal Engineers
McMAHON Robert W. MM Pte 17941 Durham Light Infantry
McMAHON Terence MM L/Cpl 5407 8th Royal Munster Fusiliers
McMAHON Thomas MM Cpl 4170 9th Royal Highlanders
McMAHON Thomas "MM+Bar,MID" L/Cpl 21715 10th West Yorkshire Regt
McMAHON William MM Spr 17597 3 Fd Sqn Royal Engineers
McMANAMIN Frank MM Pte 3/8822 1st Dorsetshire Regt KIA 17.3.17.
McMANOMNY John MM Sjt 26916 38th Bn Machine Gun Corps
McMANUS Edward MM Sjt 6449 Army Cyclist Corps
McMANUS George MM Pte 151873 33rd Bn Machine Gun Corps
McMANUS James MM Cpl 202233 10th Royal Highlanders

McMANUS James MM Pte 39090 Northumberland Fusiliers
McMANUS James MM Sjt 1571 6th Connaught Rangers
McMANUS James MM L/Cpl 5216 2nd Leinster Regt DOW 4.6.18.
McMANUS John MM Pte 19870 1st Royal Dublin Fusiliers KIA 25.8.28.
McMANUS John MM Sjt 7699 21st Manchester Regt
McMANUS John "DCM,MM" Sjt 40313 1st Royal Dublin Fusiliers
McMANUS John Joseph MM Pte 6823 5/6th Scottish Rifles
McMANUS Joseph MM L/Cpl 34380 Machine Gun Corps
McMANUS Michael MM Pte 21352 36 Fd Amb RAMC
McMANUS Michael MM Pte 29526 East Yorkshire Regt
McMANUS Patrick MM Pte 16391 Middlesex Regt
McMANUS Thomas MM Cpl 1096 Lancashire Fusiliers
McMANUS Thomas MM L/Bdr L/883 160 Bde RFA
McMARTIN Valentine MM Pte 15/3407 15th Royal Irish Rifles
McMARTIN William MM Pte 6336 1/5th Arg & Suth Highlanders
McMASTER Alexander MM Cpl 41161 Royal Engineers
McMASTER Arthur MM Sjt 15311 9th Royal Irish Fusiliers Awarded for 'Easter Rising'.
McMASTER David MM Gnr 76408 Tank Corps
McMASTER John MM Cpl 18885 12th Highland Light Infantry KIA 27.3.18.
McMASTER Lendrick MM L/Cpl 1075 12th Arg & Suth Highlanders KIA 19.9.18.
McMASTER Wallace MM Cpl 7623 1st Shropshire Light Infantry KIA 20.4.17.
McMEEKAN James MM Pte 241040 1st Royal Scots Fusiliers
McMENEMY John MM Pte 333049 1/9th Highland Light Infantry
McMENENY Thomas MM Pte 242063 1/5th West Riding Regt
McMICHAEL David T. MM Gnr 227597 RFA
McMILLAN Alexander MM Pte 53 1st Arg & Suth Highlanders
McMILLAN Alexander MM Pte 276660 Royal Scots
McMILLAN Angus MM Pte 267142 1/7th Royal Highlanders KIA 24.7.18.
McMILLAN Archibald MM Sjt 9/14179 9th East Lancashire Regt
McMILLAN Arthur MM L/Cpl 242672 Liverpool Regt
McMILLAN Christopher MM Cpl Fitter 16202 141 Siege Bty RGA
McMILLAN Daniel MM Pte 51855 8th West Yorkshire Regt
McMILLAN David "DCM,MM" Sjt 11372 10th Scottish Rifles
McMILLAN George MM Pte 57409 8th Manchester Regt
McMILLAN George MM Sjt 25400 Royal Lancaster Regt
McMILLAN George MM L/Cpl 235634 Gordon Highlanders
McMILLAN Harry MM Pte 315 2nd Gordon Highlanders
McMILLAN James MM Pte 592394 1/18th London Regt DOW 5.12.17.
McMILLAN James "MM,MSM" Sjt 11145 1st Highland Light Infantry
McMILLAN James MM Pte 39301 30 Coy Machine Gun Corps
McMILLAN James MM Pte 20184 1st King's Own Scottish Borderers
McMILLAN John MM Pte S/11072 Arg & Suth Highlanders
McMILLAN John MM Spr 402779 Royal Engineers
McMILLAN Joseph MM Pte 18326 Arg & Suth Highlanders
McMILLAN Malcolm G. MM Sjt 10993 1st Scots Guards
McMILLAN Murdoch MM Pte 201938 1/4th Seaforth Highlanders
McMILLAN Norman MM Pte 316069 1(Lowland)Fd Amb RAMC
McMILLAN Peter MM Sjt 270403 1/1st Northumberland Yeo
McMILLAN Robert MM Pte S/20738 1/5th Arg & Suth Highlanders
McMILLAN Samuel MM+Bar Sjt 6923 1st Royal Irish Fusiliers
McMILLAN Thomas MM Pte 276438 Arg & Suth Highlanders
McMILLAN Thomas MM L/Sjt 330714 Highland Light Infantry
McMILLAN Thomas MM Bdr 3457 RFA
McMILLAN Waverley A. MM Gnr 7689 A/71 Bde RFA
McMILLAN William MM Pte 377 12th Royal Irish Rifles
McMILLAN William MM Cpl S/11904 5th Cameron Highlanders
McMILLAN William MM L/Cpl 443918 66 Div Sig Coy Royal Engineers
McMILLIN William MM L/Cpl 339344 RAMC
McMINN Andrew MM Pte 202391 1/8th Arg & Suth Highlanders
McMINN Duncan MM Pte 32160 18th Highland Light Infantry Died 6.11.18.
McMINN W. MM Pte 276438 King's Own Scottish Borderers
McMOIL John MM Sjt 47316 20th Hussars
McMONAGLE Thomas MM L/Cpl 41332 1/6th Royal Highlanders
McMONIES Donald MM Pte M2/051413 47 Div Train Army Service Corps
McMONNIES John MM Sjt 40612 15th Highland Light Infantry
McMORRAN Harold MM Pte 27468 2nd Northamptonshire Regt
McMORRAN John F. MM Pte 250221 5/6th Royal Scots KIA 2.10.18.
McMORRAN T. MM Pte 16543 13th Royal Scots

McMULLAN David MM+Bar Pte 8/13138 8th Royal Irish Rifles
McMULLAN James MM Pte 350475 18th Highland Light Infantry
McMULLAN John MM Pte 97926 Machine Gun Corps
McMULLAN Joseph MM Bdr 51891 RGA
McMULLAN Neil MM L/Cpl 225671 10th Cameron Highlanders
McMULLEN Alexander MM L/Cpl 14162 Royal Inniskilling Fusiliers
McMULLEN John Wilkie MM Sjt 122246 RGA
McMULLIN John MM Pte 14048 13th Liverpool Regt
McMULLIN Ralph MM Pte 45328 76 Coy Labour Corps
McMULLINS Arthur J. MM Sjt 8909 1st Scottish Rifles
McMURCHY John "DCM,MM" Sjt 300054 1/8th Arg & Suth Highlanders
McMURDO James MM L/Cpl 203362 9th Lancashire Fusiliers
McMURDO Robert MM Pte S/15437 6th Cameron Highlanders
McMURDO Thomas MM L/Cpl 159941 228 Fd Coy Royal Engineers
McMURDO William MM L/Sjt 9997 1st Border Regt
McMURRAY Ernest MM CQMS 375245 10th Manchester Regt
McMURRAY Isaac MM Bdr 32928 38 Bde RFA
McMURRAY Joseph MM Pte DM2/189902 Army Service Corps
McMURRAY William MM Sjt H/71279 North Irish Horse
McMURRAY William Weir "MM,MSM" Sjt 76152 IV Corps Sig Coy Royal Engineers
McMURTRIE James MM Pte 36093 2nd Yorkshire Regt
McMURTRIE John A. MM Cpl 320187 3 Fd Amb RAMC
McMURTRIE Thomas R. MM Gnr 170178 RGA
McMURTRY James MM Sjt 28939 RFA
McNAB Angus MM Pte 302903 Arg & Suth Highlanders
McNAB David MM L/Cpl R/37996 King's Royal Rifle Corps
McNAB George MM Pte 6957 1st Royal Irish Fusiliers
McNAB John MM Gnr 71266 56 Div Ammn Col RFA
McNAB Ronald MM Pte S/3862 8th Seaforth Highlanders
McNAB William "MM,MID" Sjt 19164 12th Highland Light Infantry
McNAB William MM Pte 32985 11th Royal Scots
McNABB John MM L/Sjt 4/8972 Arg & Suth Highlanders
McNABNEY John "DCM,MM+Bar,MID" Sjt 57836 36 Div Sig Coy Royal Engineers
McNAIR Allan G. MM Pte 15363 17th Highland Light Infantry
McNALLY George M. MM Gnr 78753 Tank Corps
McNALLY H. MM Pte 20966 10th Essex Regt
McNALLY Herbert C. MM Pte 25901 6th Lincolnshire Regt
McNALLY James Joseph MM Pte 4/8123 11th West Yorkshire Regt KIA 29.9.17.
McNALLY Joseph B. MM Pte 23981 Machine Gun Corps
McNALLY Patrick MM Cpl 7719 2nd Leinster Regt
McNALLY Peter MM Bdr 53994 'U' Bty RHA
McNALLY Thomas G. "DCM,MM" BQMS L/5579 B/155 Bde RFA
McNALLY William MM CSM 42668 9th Royal Inniskilling Fusiliers
McNALLY William "VC,MM+Bar" Sjt 13820 8th Yorkshire Regt
McNAMARA Felix MM Sjt 330023 1/8th Royal Scots KIA 11.4.18.
McNAMARA Frederick J. MM Pte 21924 Gloucestershire Regt att Royal West Kent Regt.
McNAMARA Hugh MM Pte 7052 2nd Highland Light Infantry
McNAMARA James MM Cpl 9064 1st Connaught Rangers
McNAMARA John MM Cpl 242869 Yorkshire Light Infantry
McNAMARA Michael "DCM,MM" Cpl 9432 2nd Leinster Regt
McNAMARA Peter MM Sjt 16350 6th East Lancashire Regt DOW 1.5.17.
McNAMARA Simon P. MM Cpl 33320 20th Manchester Regt
McNAMARA Thomas MM Dvr T/28501 81 Coy Army Service Corps
McNAMARA Thomas MM Pte 5828 Leinster Regt
McNAMARA William MM Pte 591527 18th London Regt
McNAMARA William MM Pte 8192 1st Royal Fusiliers
McNAMARA William MM+Bar Pte 376322 1/10th Manchester Regt
McNAMEE G.G.P. MM Pte 302764 Royal Scots
McNAMEE John F. MM Pte 13633 Royal Inniskilling Fusiliers
McNAMEE Michael MM Pte 25579 17th Royal Scots
McNAUGHT James MM Sjt 200992 1/5th Highland Light Infantry
McNAUGHT William MM Pte 281326 1/7th Highland Light Infantry
McNAUGHTON A.McDonald MM Sjt 315265 13th Royal Highlanders
McNAUGHTON Alexander W. MM+Bar Pte 43582 6th Royal Highlanders
McNAUGHTON Andrew "DCM,MM" Cpl 39918 D/15 Bde RFA
McNAUGHTON Arthur MM Pte 201371 Norfolk Regt
McNAUGHTON David MM Pte M2/049844 Army Service Corps att 113 Fd Amb RAMC
McNAUGHTON Finlay MM Pte 49477 RAMC
McNAUGHTON John MM Pte 20133 Machine Gun Corps
McNAUGHTON John MM Pte 13862 5th Cameron Highlanders KIA 14.10.18.

McNAUGHTON Robert MM Pte 31548 6th King's Own Scottish Borderers
McNAUGHTON Robert MM L/Cpl 1313 Royal Highlanders
McNAULTY A. MM CSM 601 West Riding Regt
McNAY Joseph MM Sjt 14732 Durham Light Infantry
McNAY Wilfred MM Sjt 306388 West Riding Regt
McNEAL Thomas MM Pte 19085 Durham Light Infantry
McNEE James MM Pte 24510 1/6th Royal Highlanders
McNEE Owen MM Cpl S/4460 9th Seaforth Highlanders
McNEELY Joseph MM Sjt 23998 1st Royal Dublin Fusiliers
McNEIL Albert V. MM Sjt 35601 8th Duke of Cornwall's LI
McNEIL Alexander MM Pte 13091 7th Cameron Highlanders
McNEIL F. MM Pte 17038 Machine Gun Corps
McNEIL G. MM Sjt 240612 Cheshire Regt
McNEIL Hector MM Sjt 251185 1/6th Arg & Suth Highlanders
McNEIL J. MM+Bar Pte 291244 1/7th Royal Highlanders
McNEIL James MM Cpl 76654 'OO' Cable Section Royal Engineers
McNEIL James MM+Bar Pte 31515 East Yorkshire Regt
McNEIL James S. MM Sjt R/23526 King's Royal Rifle Corps
McNEIL John MM Pte 316446 1/3rd (Lowland) Fd Amb RAMC
McNEIL John MM Sjt 144887 Royal Engineers
McNEIL P. MM Pte 240915 Northumberland Fusiliers
McNEIL Robert MM Pte 250671 1/6th Arg & Suth Highlanders
McNEIL William MM Gnr 81301 RFA
McNEILAGE Thaddeus MM L/Cpl 10625 2nd Arg & Suth Highlanders
McNEILL Alexander MM Pte S/40141 6th Cameron Highlanders
McNEILL Alexander MM Pte 19826 11th Highland Light Infantry
McNEILL Angus McColl MM Cpl 76238 Notts & Derby Regt
McNEILL Charles MM Bdr 31907 RGA
McNEILL Colin MM Sjt 33355 78 Coy Machine Gun Corps
McNEILL David MM L/Cpl 13957 1st Scots Guards
McNEILL David MM Sjt 44648 Machine Gun Corps
McNEILL David W. MM Pte 10619 7th Cameron Highlanders
McNEILL Duncan MM L/Sjt 300111 14th Arg & Suth Highlanders
McNEILL Forbes MM Pte 352460 Royal Scots
McNEILL James MM CQMS 265022 1/6th Royal Highlanders
McNEILL James MM Pte 70735 Machine Gun Corps
McNEILL John MM Gnr 145672 151 Hy Bty RGA
McNEILL Robert MM Pte 235990 4th York & Lancaster Regt
McNEILL Robert MM+Bar Sjt 8612 2nd Royal Inniskilling Fusiliers
McNEILL S. MM Pte 201075 Cheshire Regt
McNEILLE J. MM Pte 250219 Durham Light Infantry
McNEILLE James L. MM Sjt 482032 Royal Engineers
McNEIR George Alfred MM Sjt 10011 1st East Kent Regt KIA 1.12.17.
McNEISH James MM Cpl 98930 Machine Gun Corps
McNELLIE James S. MM+Bar Sjt 240354 1/5th King's Own Scottish Borderers
McNERLIN William MM Sjt 28399 2nd Royal Inniskilling Fusiliers
McNICHOL Archie MM Pte 50542 1/5th Suffolk Regt
McNICHOL George MM+Bar Pte 303379 1/8th Arg & Suth Highlanders DOW 11.4.18.
McNICHOLL Roderick MM L/Cpl 24107 Royal Irish Fusiliers
McNICOL Allan MM Cpl 18973 12th Highland Light Infantry
McNICOL Charles MM Pte 24 2nd Arg & Suth Highlanders
McNICOL John "DCM,MM" Cpl 254130 14 Div Sig Coy Royal Engineers
McNICOL Robert MM Pte 40092 1/5th Arg & Suth Highlanders
McNICOL Robert MM Cpl 21890 1st Royal Dublin Fusiliers KIA 30.3.18.
McNICOLL John MM Cpl 12618 Arg & Suth Highlanders
McNICOLL John W. MM+Bar Sjt 265842 Monmouthshire Regt
McNIELL Donald McI. MM L/Cpl 41982 Highland Light Infantry
McNIFFE John MM Sjt 265172 7th Liverpool Regt
McNINCH Alexander MM Cpl 8986 2nd Highland Light Infantry
McNIVEN Alexander MM+Bar 2nd Cpl 211254 2 Light Railway Const Coy Royal Engineers
McNIVEN Archel MM Sjt 315095 1/1(Lowland)Fd Amb RAMC
McNIVEN Archibald MM Pte 84449 Machine Gun Corps
McNIVEN Hugh MM Cpl S/5585 Gordon Highlanders
McNIVEN Robert MM Pte 129082 45th Royal Fusiliers
McNIVEN William MM CSM 1207 Royal Engineers
McNIVEN William MM+Bar Cpl 309 11th Highland Light Infantry
McNORTON Alfred P. MM Sjt 108520 407 Bty 96 Bde RFA
McNORTON Percy MM Cpl 45880 94 Fd Coy Royal Engineers
McNULTY Arthur "DCM,MM" Sjt 3442 2nd Gordon Highlanders
McNULTY Francis MM Sjt 6924 11th Manchester Regt
McNULTY James MM Sjt 201646 East Lancashire Regt
McNULTY John MM L/Cpl 201238 4th North Lancashire Regt
McNULTY John J. MM Pte 8078 1st Irish Guards
McNULTY John L. MM Sjt 22977 RGA
McNULTY Michael MM L/Cpl 9362 2nd Royal Irish Rifles
McNULTY Peter MM Pte 5806 1st Irish Guards
McNULTY Thomas MM Sjt 13100 1st East Lancashire Regt KIA 21.3.18
McNULTY William MM Dvr 73907 110 Bty 24 Bde RFA
McNUTT John MM L/Cpl 15897 Royal Inniskilling Fusiliers
McONIE John T. MM L/Cpl 490363 1/13th London Regt
McOUAN James MM Pte 37929 46th Bn Machine Gun Corps
McPARLAND William James MM Sjt 20195 7/8th Royal Irish Fusiliers KIA 7.6.17.
McPARTLAND Frank MM Pte 1632 6th Connaught Rangers DOW 17.9.16.
McPARTLIN Michael "DCM,MM+Bar" Sjt 21379 1st Royal Dublin Fusiliers
McPARTLIN Peter MM L/Cpl 25/1181 Northumberland Fusiliers
McPETRIE James W. MM Sjt 192 Royal Engineers
McPHAIL Alexander J. MM L/Cpl S/41893 1/6th Royal Highlanders
McPHAIL Donald MM Cpl S/16015 2nd Seaforth Highlanders
McPHAIL Frank MM Cpl 10310 2nd Gordon Highlanders
McPHAIL George MM Sjt 57498 8th Tramway Coy Royal Engineers
McPHAIL James MM Pte 24943 6th King's Own Scottish Borderers
McPHAIL John MM Pte 79 1/6th Arg & Suth Highlanders
McPHAIL John MM Sjt 40566 Royal Scots
McPHEAT Edward MM L/Cpl 41990 1/5th King's Own Scottish Borderers
McPHEE Angus MM Cpl 17695 20th Manchester Regt DOW 26.8.16.
McPHEE Archibald M. MM Pte 3524 16th Highland Light Infantry
McPHEE Douglas MM Cpl 203034 8th Seaforth Highlanders
McPHEE Hugh MM Sjt 836741 RFA
McPHEE Malcolm MM Pte 200756 5/6th Scottish Rifles
McPHEE Thomas MM Sjt 240788 1/5th Royal Scots Fusiliers
McPHEELY Alexander MM Sjt 22053 Machine Gun Corps
McPHERSON Alexander MM Pte 242035 Gordon Highlanders
McPHERSON Alexander MM Pte 202939 Royal Lancaster Regt
McPHERSON Alexander MM Pte 265332 Seaforth Highlanders
McPHERSON Alexander MM Pte 266111 Royal Highlanders
McPHERSON Archibald MM L/Cpl 186526 5 Fd Svy Bn Royal Engineers
McPHERSON Donald MM L/Cpl 243490 1/6th Highland Light Infantry
McPHERSON Douglas MM Pte 235340 Notts & Derby Regt
McPHERSON George MM L/Cpl 250676 2/6th Durham Light Infantry
McPHERSON H. MM Pte 131623 46th Royal Fusiliers
McPHERSON James MM Spr 193350 185 Tunnelling Coy Royal Engineers
McPHERSON James MM Pte S/2111 9th Seaforth Highlanders
McPHERSON James MM Pte 31386 RAMC
McPHERSON James MM Pte S/3745 9th Seaforth Highlanders
McPHERSON James MM Pte 22165 Highland Light Infantry
McPHERSON James J. MM+Bar Pte 40707 2nd Royal Scots Fusiliers
McPHERSON John MM Sjt 265454 1/4th Gordon Highlanders
McPHERSON John MM Sjt 320178 15th Suffolk Regt
McPHERSON John David MM Pte 102971 51st Bn Machine Gun Corps
McPHERSON Kenneth MM Pte 200282 1/4th Seaforth Highlanders
McPHERSON Neil MM Pte 4033 Seaforth Highlanders
McPHERSON P. MM Gnr 645147 RFA
McPHERSON Roderick "MM,MID" Sjt 43204 Royal Engineers
McPHERSON S.N. MM L/Cpl S/19956 1st Gordon Highlanders
McPHERSON William MM Pte 240399 1/5th Royal Highlanders
McPHERSON William MM Sjt 16/25903 Durham Light Infantry
McPHIE Robert MM Pte 276277 Arg & Suth Highlanders
McPHILEMY John MM Cpl 50040 1st Cheshire Regt KIA 22.8.18.
McQUADE Alexander MM Pte S/16110 10th Arg & Suth Highlanders DOW 16.10.18.
McQUADE James MM Sjt 115814 Labour Corps
McQUADE James MM Pte 106002 Machine Gun Corps
McQUADE John MM Sjt 6282 2nd Essex Regt KIA 1.7.16.
McQUADE John MM L/Cpl 12460 King's Own Scottish Borderers
McQUADE John Joseph MM Cpl 18767 Machine Gun Corps
McQUADE Joseph Francis Edward MM Pte 6943 1st Northumberland Fusiliers KIA 28.3.18.
McQUADE Peter MM Pte 25877 Royal Inniskilling Fusiliers
McQUAKER William MM Pte 30164 1st Scottish Rifles
McQUARRIE Donald MM Pte 9274 Arg & Suth Highlanders

McQUARRIE Duncan MM Pte 300619 10th Arg & Suth Highlanders
McQUARRIE William MM Sjt S/5034 11th Arg & Suth Highlanders KIA 22.8.17.
McQUAT James T. MM Pte 200294 5/6th Scottish Rifles
McQUEEN Alexander M. MM Sjt 69979 110 Bty 24 Bde RFA
McQUEEN Andrew "DCM,MM" CSM 705 9th Royal Fusiliers
McQUEEN Charles MM Cpl 26756 2nd Highland Light Infantry
McQUEEN David MM+Bar Pte 10416 11th Northumberland Fusiliers
McQUEEN Duncan "MM,MID" Sjt 248 1/7th Arg & Suth Highlanders
McQUEEN Ernest R.G. MM+Bar L/Sjt 17411 2nd Royal Scots Fusiliers
McQUEEN James William "MM,MSM,MID" Sjt 44034 30 Bde RFA
McQUEEN John MM Pte 21378 Royal Dublin Fusiliers
McQUEEN John MM Pte 42064 1/6th Seaforth Highlanders
McQUEEN John T. MM S/Sjt 67734 Royal Engineers
McQUEEN Neel B.P. MM Sjt 54240 RGA
McQUEEN Robert MM Pte S/4343 9th Royal Highlanders
McQUEEN William MM Pte 7720 15 Fd Amb RAMC
McQUIGGAN John MM Cpl 18127 12th Liverpool Regt
McQUIGGAN Lawrence MM+Bar Pte 12374 1/8th Liverpool Regt
McQUILLAN Charles MM Pte R/33196 King's Royal Rifle Corps
McQUILLAN Clarence MM Pte 10922 2nd Yorkshire Light Infantry
McQUILLAN James "DCM+Bar,MM+Bar" CSM 4804 18th Highland Light Infantry
McQUILLAN Peter MM Pte 5366 5th Connaught Rangers KIA 10.10.18.
McQUILLAN Peter MM L/Bdr 55362 37 Siege Bty RGA
McQUILLAN Thomas MM Pte 6021 1st Irish Guards
McQUILLAN William MM Sjt 15823 7th King's Own Scottish Borderers
McQUILLIAN John MM Cpl 13386 Royal Irish Fusiliers
McQUILTON Allan MM Cpl 1973 Liverpool Regt
McQUISTON William MM Sjt 43896 60 Coy Machine Gun Corps
McQUITTERS William C. MM Pte 21741 Royal West Surrey Regt
McQUITTY William C.J. MM Pte 12923 Machine Gun Corps
McRAE A. MM Sjt 131199 46th Royal Fusiliers
McRAE Donald MM+Bar L/Sjt S/12175 Seaforth Highlanders
McRAE Donald MM L/Sjt 12175 Seaforth Highlanders
McRAE Duncan A. MM Cpl 125410 Lovat's Scouts Yeomanry
McRAE John MM Pte S/22742 1st Gordon Highlanders
McRAE John M. MM Pte 267292 Seaforth Highlanders
McRAE Roderick MM Pte 315178 13th Royal Highlanders
McROBB David C. MM Pte 61263 Northumberland Fusiliers
McROBBIE Alan "DCM,MM" Pte 265214 1/7th Gordon Highlanders
McROBBIE John MM Pte 13227 Arg & Suth Highlanders
McROBERT Allan MM Pte 7142 2nd Royal Scots Fusiliers
McROBERT William MM L/Cpl 1165 1/6th Gordon Highlanders DOW 16.11.16.
McROBERTS Harold MM Pte 4649 17 Fd Amb RAMC
McROBERTS James MM Dvr Sig 176034 D/69 Bde RFA
McROBERTS John MM+Bar Sjt 303019 1/7th Royal Scots
McROBERTS Thomas MM+Bar Pte 267758 Royal Highlanders
McROBIE James MM Cpl 632665 20th London Regt
McRORIE James MM Cpl 2227 RGA
McRORY David Connell MM Pte 3/5876 2nd Arg & Suth Highlanders DOW 27.7.16.
McSEPHNEY Thomas MM Pte 310146 1/7th Royal Highlanders
McSHANE Frank MM Pte 10891 North Lancashire Regt
McSHANE George MM Gnr 7001 RFA
McSHANE Thomas MM Dvr 6522 RFA
McSKIMMING James MM+Bar Sjt 326194 110 Siege Bty RGA
McSORLEY Robert "DCM,MM" L/Cpl 13733 9th North Lancashire Regt
McSWAN Roderick MM Cpl 300502 10th Arg & Suth Highlanders DOW 28.10.18.
McSWEENEY Daniel MM Pte 681538 22nd London Regt
McSWEENEY David M. MM Sjt 15137 10th Royal Welsh Fusiliers
McSWEENEY Edward MM Sjt 800335 B/230 Bde RFA
McSWEENEY John MM Pte 8230 1st Royal Munster Fusiliers
McSWEENEY Thomas MM+Bar Pte 4/6852 2nd Royal Munster Fusiliers
McTAGGART Angus MM Sjt (MCDR) 43352 Signal Service Royal Engineers
McTAGGART Colin MM Pte 695094 22nd London Regt
McTAGGART George MM 2nd Cpl 86593 Royal Engineers
McTAGGART Henry MM Pte 9846 Arg & Suth Highlanders
McTAGGART Owen MM L/Cpl 9979 1st King's Own Scottish Borderers
McTAGGART T. MM Dvr 645325 RFA

McTAVISH Alexander MM L/Cpl 300593 1/8th Arg & Suth Highlanders
McTAVISH James MM S/Sjt SE24779 Army Veterinary Corps
McTAVISH John MM L/Cpl 11244 1st Scots Guards
McTAVISH John MM Cpl 282 2nd Gordon Highlanders
McTIGHE Henry G. MM+Bar L/Cpl 77905 10th Royal Fusiliers
McTIGHE James MM Pte 4497 2/7th Worcestershire Regt
McTIGUE Martin MM Pte 33010 2nd Yorkshire Regt
McTURK James MM Cpl 44335 Machine Gun Corps
McTURK John MM+Bar Pte 10441 RAMC
McVARISH John MM Sjt 203969 Cameron Highlanders
McVEAN James MM Pte 41712 5/6th Scottish Rifles
McVEAN James MM L/Cpl 13513 12th Durham Light Infantry
McVEE Allan MM Cpl 11472 2nd Highland Light Infantry KIA 27.4.17.
McVEE James MM Sjt 76089 8 Div Sig Coy Royal Engineers
McVEY John "MM,MID" Sjt 5864 1st Royal Highlanders
McVEY John MM Sjt 9470 11th Highland Light Infantry
McVEY William MM Pte 28925 Highland Light Infantry
McVICAR Donald MM Cpl 300186 1/7th Arg & Suth Highlanders
McVICAR Duncan MM Sjt 300269 1/8th Arg & Suth Highlanders
McVICAR H. MM Bdr 7596 RFA
McVICAR Niven MM 2nd Cpl 60682 75 Fd Coy Royal Engineers
McVICAR Robert MM Sjt 275053 11th Royal Scots
McVICKER John Henry MM Cpl 64636 121 Fd Coy Royal Engineers DOW 5.7.16.
McVIE John MM Dvr 103908 D/330 Bde RFA
McVIE Robert MM Sjt T2/015162 16 Div Train Army Service Corps
McVITTIE Alexander MM Sjt 14277 7/8th King's Own Scottish Borderers KIA 22.5.18.
McVITTIE Bertram MM Pte 241572 1/4th Royal Lancaster Regt KIA 10.5.18.
McVITTIE George MM L/Cpl 16258 3rd Coldstream Guards
McVITTIE George "DCM,MM(8285 W Yorks)" L/Sjt 45275 13th York & Lancaster Regt
McWATT William MM Sjt 277317 1/7th Arg & Suth Highlanders
McWATT William MM 2nd Cpl 412488 Royal Engineers
McWHINNIE John MM Pte S/2517 Arg & Suth Highlanders
McWHINNIE Thomas MM Spr 155591 184 Tunnelling Coy Royal Engineers
McWHIRTER Anthony MM L/Bdr 59222 RGA
McWHIRTER James "DCM,MM" Pte 15/12052 15th Royal Irish Rifles
McWILLIAM Alexander MM Gnr 127993 RGA
McWILLIAM George MM+Bar L/Sjt 266286 7th Seaforth Highlanders
McWILLIAMS Andrew MM L/Cpl 2073 Arg & Suth Highlanders
McWILLIAMS David MM Cpl 10389 5th Cameron Highlanders
McWILLIAMS James MM Sjt 93139 C/84 Bde RFA KIA 7.10.18.
McWILLIAMS John MM Sjt 330010 1/8th Royal Scots
McWILLIAMS John MM Sjt 136859 235 Siege Bty RGA
McWILLIAMS John MM L/Sjt 7351 Arg & Suth Highlanders
McWILLIAMS John MM Cpl 62815 38 Bde RFA
McWILLIAMS John MM Gnr 41209 RGA
McWILLIAMS Joseph MM Dvr 48736 B/74 Bde RFA
McWILLIAMS Robert MM Gnr 6053 RFA
McWILLIAMS William Laurence MM L/Cpl 200998 1/5th Durham Light Infantry KIA 12.4.18.
McWORTH John H. MM Sjt 63395 Royal Engineers
MEABURN John G. MM L/Cpl 13060 Yorkshire Regt
MEABY Frederick Charles MM Sjt 325686 1/1st Cambridgeshire Regt
MEACHAM Alfred G. "DCM,MM" Sjt 470722 1/12th London Regt
MEACHAM Charles MM Pte 4451 7th Royal West Surrey Regt
MEACHAM Ernest H. MM+Bar Gnr 83989 RFA
MEACHAM John MM L/Cpl 71081 54 Coy Machine Gun Corps
MEACHAM Moses MM Pte 6673 2nd Royal West Surrey Regt
MEACHEM Percy MM Dvr 75636 A/71 Bde RFA
MEACHIN George E. MM L/Cpl 63634 13th Yorkshire Regt
MEACHIN John E. MM Pte 200679 Gloucestershire Regt
MEAD Albert E. MM Pte 65397 4 Fd Amb RAMC
MEAD Albert William MM Pte 2543 1/24th London Regt
MEAD Alfred H. "MM+Bar,MID" L/Sjt A/478 King's Royal Rifle Corps
MEAD Alfred W. MM Pte 61299 11th Royal Fusiliers
MEAD Arthur Ernest Charles MM Cpl 83695 RFA
MEAD Arthur John MM CQMS 684 17th Royal Fusiliers DOW 18.10.18.
MEAD Edward S. MM Pte 1896 1/8th Liverpool Regt
MEAD Ernest R. MM Cpl 149498 Machine Gun Corps
MEAD Ernest W. MM Pte 12149 9th Essex Regt

MEAD Francis J. MM Sjt 15086 121 Heavy Bty RGA
MEAD Frederick A. MM Pte 78893 7th Royal Fusiliers
MEAD George MM Pte 30974 1st Royal West Kent Regt
MEAD George W. MM Bdr 22526 48 Heavy Bty RGA
MEAD Harold Rowland MM Pte 27952 4th Grenadier Guards
MEAD Henry G. MM CSM 28907 7th Royal Warwickshire Regt
MEAD Horace MM Pte 3792 2/20th London Regt
MEAD J.L. MM Cpl 3/2877 Essex Regt
MEAD James MM BSM 18983 182 Siege Bty RGA
MEAD James A. MM Bdr 56548 RGA
MEAD John Bulley MM Sjt 501988 Royal Engineers
MEAD Philip MM Pte 202608 2/4th Royal Berkshire Regt KIA 11.8.18.
MEAD Reginald Edward MM Cpl 202488 X/57 Med TM Bty RFA
MEAD Stanley W. "DCM,MM" CSM 15618 11th Suffolk Regt
MEAD Thomas MM+Bar Sjt 36399 2nd Royal Berkshire Regt
MEAD Thomas Joseph MM Sjt 2429 9th Rifle Brigade DOW 15.9.16.
MEAD William H. MM Sjt 70194 113 Bty 25 Bde RFA
MEAD William J. MM Cpl 103086 9th Bn Machine Gun Corps
MEAD William J. MM Pte S/2107 Rifle Brigade
MEADE George MM Pte R/5937 4th King's Royal Rifle Corps
MEADE Harry W. MM Pte 703432 23rd London Regt
MEADE Henry J. MM Pte 633010 20th London Regt
MEADE John MM Sjt 12347 8th Royal Welsh Fusiliers
MEADE John J. MM L/Cpl 243002 1/7th Middlesex Regt
MEADE Joseph F. MM Cpl 54205 25 Div Sig Coy Royal Engineers KIA 30.5.18.
MEADEN George MM Sjt 200100 2/4th Hampshire Regt
MEADEN Thomas MM L/Cpl 17546 Machine Gun Corps
MEADER Albert Frank MM Pte 350433 7th London Regt DOW 27.4.18.
MEADES Arthur E. MM Sjt 541086 Royal Engineers
MEADES William MM L/Cpl 22948 9th Notts & Derby Regt
MEADLEY George MM Gnr 10602 A/58 Bde RFA DOW 5.8.17.
MEADLEY Harry MM Sjt 151600 251 Tunnelling Coy Royal Engineers
MEADLEY Harry MM Pte 72494 Machine Gun Corps
MEADOWCROFT Edward MM Cpl 5702 3rd Bn GMGR
MEADOWCROFT Ernest F. MM Pte 228082 1st London Regt
MEADOWS Albert MM Pte 34537 Labour Corps
MEADOWS Albert Arthur MM L/Sjt 34696 1st Duke of Cornwall's LI
MEADOWS Ambrose MM Sjt 500124 50 Div Sig Coy Royal Engineers
MEADOWS Arthur MM L/Cpl 9890 6th Northamptonshire Regt DOW 30.9.18.
MEADOWS Daniel MM Sjt 148550 Royal Engineers
MEADOWS Ebenezer MM Pte 15073 9th Suffolk Regt KIA 20.11.17.
MEADOWS Ernest E. MM BQMS 12876 11 Bde RFA
MEADOWS George MM Sjt 8036 1st West Yorkshire Regt
MEADOWS George Gardiner MM+Bar Pte 14959 2nd Suffolk Regt DOW 10.10.18.
MEADOWS Harold MM Cpl 1894 1/5th Yorkshire Light Infantry
MEADOWS James "MM,MIDx2" L/Cpl 8640 1st Essex Regt
MEADOWS John MM Pte 202072 North Lancashire Regt
MEADOWS John R. MM 2nd Cpl 554147 Royal Engineers
MEADOWS John W. MM L/Cpl 13435 19th Durham Light Infantry
MEADOWS Oliver Thomas Grenville MM Cpl 28793 D/275 Bde RFA
MEADOWS Phillip "MM,MID" Cpl 23531 Royal Engineers
MEADOWS William MM Sjt 15577 Yorkshire Regt
MEADS Arthur MM Pte 241681 6th Royal Warwickshire Regt
MEADS Cecil MM Pte 13303 Royal West Kent Regt
MEADS Ephraim MM+Bar Gnr 63687 A/94 Bde RFA DOW 11.5.17.
MEADS Frederick MM Pte 18425 Northamptonshire Regt
MEADS J.A. MM Pte G/6807 Royal Fusiliers
MEAGER Daniel or David MM Pte 10804 10th Essex Regt
MEAGER Hubert J. MM Gnr 184736 53 Bty 2 Bde RFA
MEAGER Sidney A.J. MM L/Cpl 42663 9th Devonshire Regt
MEAGER William MM Pte 200765 4th Hampshire Regt
MEAGHER E. MM Cpl 18401 14th Liverpool Regt
MEAHAN John "MM,MID" Pte 18265 Scottish Rifles
MEAKER Arthur MM Pte 19755 9th Welsh Regt
MEAKIN Charles Thomas MM Sjt 19057 298 Siege Bty RGA
MEAKIN Eric Newby MM Sjt 2185 1/1st Leicestershire Yeo
MEAKIN Francis W. MM L/Cpl 22788 4th Hussars
MEAKIN Isaac MM L/Cpl 200501 Notts & Derby Regt
MEAKIN James H. MM Sjt 3302 17th Lancashire Fusiliers
MEAKIN John MM L/Sjt 240356 1/5th Leicestershire Regt
MEAKIN Joseph MM Pte 17192 2nd Coldstream Guards
MEAKIN William MM Gnr L/7868 RFA

MEAKINS William E. MM L/Cpl 639 17th Lancers
MEALEY Lawrence MM Pte 21136 2nd Royal Dublin Fusiliers
MEALING Edward MM Cpl 5142 1st Royal West Kent Regt
MEALING George Henry W. MM Bdr 33258 RFA
MEALING Harry MM Sjt 50870 5 Bde RFA
MEALING Harry R. MM Sjt 496055 475 Fd Coy Royal Engineers
MEALING William H. MM Pte 101554 77 Fd Amb RAMC
MEAN John Robert MM Sjt 18208 7th Bn Machine Gun Corps
MEANEY Thomas MM L/Sjt 10504 10th Royal Irish Rifles KIA 1.7.16.
MEANWELL Frederick Arthur MM Spr 93649 49 Div Sig Coy Royal Engineers
MEANWELL Raymond MM Sjt 200081 Lincolnshire Regt
MEANWELL Robert H. MM Cpl 175260 1/1st Yorkshire Dragoons Yeo
MEANWELL Samson G.E. MM Pte 1230 5th Lincolnshire Regt
MEAR Harry MM Pte 241218 6th North Staffordshire Regt
MEARA Michael J. MM L/Cpl 439903 Royal Engineers
MEARA William MM Cpl 10515 2nd Royal Irish Regt
MEARES Ethel Isabella Devenish MM Sister F QAIMNS
MEARING Ernest MM Gnr 1005 RFA
MEARNS John William MM Pte 36127 5th Royal Berkshire Regt
MEARNS Joseph L. MM Cpl 13263 11th Border Regt
MEARNS Patrick "MM,MSM" CSM 43417 Gordon Highlanders
MEARNS Robert Campbell MM Pte 92909 101 Fd Amb RAMC
MEARS Albert MM Pte 35085 10th Essex Regt KIA 26.4.18.
MEARS Albert E. MM Cpl 88959 RFA
MEARS Alfred H. MM Pte 1999 Royal West Surrey Regt
MEARS Alfred James MM Gnr 192710 200 Siege Bty RGA DOW 29.6.18.
MEARS C. MM CQMS 3165 6th Essex Regt
MEARS Claude A. MM Sjt 28043 301 Siege Bty RGA
MEARS Edwin G. MM L/Cpl 5499 9th Seaforth Highlanders
MEARS Fergus "MM+Bar,MID" Pte 17836 9th Cheshire Regt
MEARS Frank MM Sjt 18287 Army Cyclist Corps
MEARS Henry MM L/Cpl 58047 1st Middlesex Regt
MEARS Horace MM Spr 73927 Royal Engineers
MEARS John MM Sjt 852 25 Div Ammn Col RFA
MEARS John "DCM,MM" L/Cpl 10658 7th Duke of Cornwall's LI
MEARS Oliver Roland "MM,MID" Sjt 13820 11th Royal Welsh Fusiliers
MEARS W. MM Pte 203951 Durham Light Infantry
MEARS William H. MM L/Cpl G/4207 13th King's Royal Rifle Corps
MEARS William T. MM Pte 250506 1/5th Essex Regt
MEASDAY William MM Pte 55821 18th Bn Machine Gun Corps
MEASON James George MM Sjt 15807 2nd Royal Fusiliers
MEASURES J. MM Sjt 15449 8th Somerset Light Infantry
MEATES Charles O. MM L/Cpl 242377 2/5th Gloucestershire Regt
MEATYARD Herbert S. MM Sjt 28877 179 Bde RFA
MECHAN William MM Pte S/5337 9th Royal Highlanders
MEDCALF Fred MM Pte 40992 Cameron Highlanders
MEDCALF John MM Dvr 66168 64 Bty 5 Bde RFA
MEDCRAFT James E.G. MM CSM 11115 7th Royal Berkshire Regt
MEDDICK Albert MM Pte 144088 6th Bn Machine Gun Corps
MEDDICK William Henry MM Pte 19111 6th Somerset Light Infantry
MEDDINGS Albert Edward MM Cpl 89149 B/48 Bde RFA
MEDDINGS Frederick Charles MM L/Cpl 22129 10th Worcestershire Regt
MEDDINGS Henry C. MM+Bar Sjt 57649 16th Lancashire Fusiliers
MEDDINGS J.W.G. MM Pte 4367 1st Hampshire Regt
MEDDINGS Samuel MM L/Cpl 492378 59 Div Sig Coy Royal Engineers
MEDDOMS Percy G. MM Cpl 22612 RFA
MEDFORTH George MM Pte 15377 2nd Coldstream Guards
MEDFORTH Wilfred MM L/Bdr 700937 RFA
MEDGETT Albert MM Sjt 220 6th East Kent Regt
MEDHURST Charles F. MM Spr 1047 1/2(London)Fd Coy Royal Engineers
MEDHURST Frank MM Sjt 200867 3/4th Royal West Kent Regt
MEDLAM George MM Sjt WR/179550 Railway Troops Royal Engineers
MEDLEY Fred MM Pte 18607 2nd Royal Munster Fusiliers
MEDLEY Fred W. "DCM,MM" Sjt 58957 70 Fd Amb RAMC
MEDLEY William "MC,MM" CSM 200441 1/4th West Riding Regt AKA William MORRIS
MEDLICOTT William MM Dvr 16985 RFA
MEDLICOTT William MM L/Cpl 225432 1/3rd Monmouthshire Regt
MEDOVITCH Philip MM Gnr 147043 RFA
MEDUS William J.J. MM Sjt 517 Royal Engineers
MEDWAY Edward W. MM Sjt 931567 RFA

MEE Bert MM L/Cpl 1908 1/6th West Yorkshire Regt
MEE Charles William MM Sjt 32519 1st South Staffordshire Regt
MEE George MM Cpl 20816 18 Coy Machine Gun Corps
MEE George "MM,MID" Sjt 6281 Signal Service Royal Engineers
MEE George MM Pte 202256 5/6th Scottish Rifles
MEE Harry MM Sjt 10177 6th Leicestershire Regt
MEE Richard MM Pte 268964 4th Liverpool Regt
MEE Richard MM L/Cpl 43469 Yorkshire Light Infantry
MEE William MM+Bar Cpl 15178 11th Northumberland Fusiliers
MEECH Herbert William MM Pte S/11346 Rifle Brigade att 1/8th London Regt.KIA 31.8.18.
MEECH Walter MM L/Cpl 39966 6th Royal West Surrey Regt
MEECHAM Henry G. MM Dmr 13234 1st Middlesex Regt
MEECHAM Patrick MM Sjt 84499 RFA
MEECHAN Henry MM Pte 8629 2nd Scots Guards KIA 16.9.16.
MEECHAN William "DCM,MM" Pte 4/8858 2nd Arg & Suth Highlanders KIA 24.10.18.
MEEDS Charles MM Sjt 800246 B/230 Bde RFA
MEEHAN Arthur MM Pte 51934 65 Fd Amb RAMC
MEEHAN Felix MM Cpl 240752 1/6th Highland Light Infantry
MEEHAN J. MM CSM 13836 2nd Worcestershire Regt
MEEHAN James MM Pte 9138 2nd Royal Dublin Fusiliers KIA 16.8.17.
MEEHAN James Eustace MM Sjt 42482 RAMC
MEEHAN Michael MM Gnr 5554 A/122 Bde RFA
MEEHAN Patrick MM Cpl 4190 5th Lancers
MEEHAN Patrick MM Gnr 79711 D/110 Bde RFA
MEEHAN Thomas J. MM Bdr 70582 A/77 Bde RFA
MEEK Andrew MM L/Cpl 11822 11th Royal Scots KIA 29.9.18.
MEEK George MM L/Cpl 16481 2nd Yorkshire Regt
MEEK George E. MM Pte 6617 1/8th Durham Light Infantry
MEEK Henry MM Pte 13481 10th Gloucestershire Regt
MEEK John MM L/Cpl 330426 1/8th Royal Scots
MEEK Matthew W. MM L/Cpl 202147 Royal Highlanders
MEEK Robert MM Sjt 7427 Machine Gun Corps
MEEK William MM Pte S/8633 1st Royal Highlanders
MEEK William MM Pte S/7230 Arg & Suth Highlanders
MEEKE John MM Pte 29097 Royal Inniskilling Fusiliers
MEEKS Arthur MM Gnr 45575 187 Bde RFA
MEEKS Clarence MM Spr 482169 Royal Engineers
MEEKS Jesse MM Pte 16002 7th Bedfordshire Regt
MEEKS William MM+Bar Pte 40727 Suffolk Regt
MEEN Arthur MM Pte 2672 7th Royal West Kent Regt
MEEN Frederick G. "DCM,MM+Bar" CSM 15226 2nd Suffolk Regt
MEER Harry MM Cpl 17244 10th Notts & Derby Regt
MEER William MM Sjt 810575 RFA
MEERES Thomas MM+Bar Pte 47878 8th Northumberland Fusiliers
MEERS Thomas W. MM Pte 2065 1/7th Liverpool Regt
MEERTEN Frank MM Cpl 9970 RAMC
MEESE Albert MM Pte 19416 5th South Wales Borderers
MEESON Arthur J. MM Gnr 221642 RFA
MEESON James MM Pte 32267 69 Fd Amb RAMC
MEESON William James MM+Bar L/Sjt 9764 1st Shropshire Light Infantry
MEETEN Harry MM L/Bdr 37587 355 Siege Bty RGA
MEFFAN John S. MM Sjt S/12068 7th Cameron Highlanders
MEFFEN John MM Pte 266153 7th Scottish Rifles
MEGAHEY Robert MM+Bar L/Cpl 17212 9th Royal Inniskilling Fusiliers
MEGGINSON Albert MM L/Cpl 1695 1/4th Yorkshire Regt
MEGGITT Lorenzo MM Pte 21279 14th York & Lancaster Regt
MEGICKS Wentworth MM Pte 83044 RAMC
MEGORAN John Edward MM L/Cpl 3064 1/8th Durham Light Infantry
MEGROFF William J. MM Pte M2/184173 Army Service Corps
MEHAFFEY Alexander MM Pte 12057 15th Royal Irish Rifles
MEHARG Robert MM Pte 936 2nd Royal Irish Rifles att 107 Light TM Bty
MEHEGAN Daniel J. MM L/Sjy 6782 2nd Irish Guards
MEICHAN John MM Cpl 443 RFA
MEICHAN Thomas MM Pte 37873 Highland Light Infantry
MEIGH Thomas MM Sjt 20645 Machine Gun Corps
MEIKLE Andrew MM L/Sjt S/3145 Gordon Highlanders
MEIKLE Henry J. MM Pte 20190 Grenadier Guards
MEIKLE John MM Bdr 306093 1/1(Highland)HeavyBty RGA
MEIKLE John MM Spr 76353 Royal Engineers
MEIKLE John "VC,MM" L/Cpl 200854 1/4th Seaforth Highlanders KIA 20.7.18.
MEIKLE John MM Cpl 276795 1/7th Arg & Suth Highlanders KIA 23.3.18.
MEIKLE John D. MM Pte S/11582 Gordon Highlanders
MEIKLE William S. MM Sjt S/7368 8th Seaforth Highlanders
MEIKLEJOHN Frank MM Bdr 71438 RGA
MEIKLEJOHN George MM L/Cpl 39621 12th Royal Scots
MEIKLEJOHN John R. MM Sjt 4807 9 Coy Labour Corps
MEIKLEJOHN William M. MM Pte 295217 12th Royal Scots Fusiliers
MEIKLEJOHN William M. MM Pte 18380 Cameron Highlanders
MEIKLEM James U. MM Pte 34904 North Staffordshire Regt
MEIN James MM Gnr 55906 4 Bde RFA
MEIN William MM Pte 6527 16th Manchester Regt KIA 1.7.16.
MEIR Thomas S. "MM,MID" Cpl 64602 RAMC
MEIRE Leonard MM Sjt 66576 RAMC
MELBOURNE George MM Sjt 240706 1/5th Royal Scots Fusiliers
MELBOURNE George MM Gnr 805320 B/231 Bde RFA KIA 15.8.17.
MELBOURNE James MM Sjt 8122 2nd Leicestershire Regt
MELDRUM Alexander MM L/Cpl S/14877 1st Gordon Highlanders
MELDRUM George MM L/Cpl 634 15th West Yorkshire Regt
MELDRUM William Rollo MM L/Cpl S/8806 8th Royal Highlanders KIA 18.7.16.
MELHUISH Douglas H. MM Gnr 236749 A/152 Bde RFA
MELIA Charles MM Cpl 265986 North Lancashire Regt
MELIA James MM Cpl 306672 5th West Yorkshire Regt
MELIA John MM Pte 26396 Shropshire Light Infantry
MELIA Thomas MM Pte 10652 2nd East Lancashire Regt KIA 27.5.18.
MELLA Fred E. MM L/Cpl 307057 15th Bn Tank Corps
MELLARS John William MM Gnr 10305 26 Bde RFA
MELLERSH Harry John MM Dvr T4/065205 41 Div Train Army Service Corps
MELLETT John Arthur MM+Bar Cpl 54833 28 Bde RFA
MELLEY Edward MM Cpl 217716 4 Light Railway Op Coy Royal Engineers
MELLING James MM Pte 41931 2nd King's Own Scottish Borderers
MELLING James MM Cpl 201646 Manchester Regt
MELLING John J. MM Pte 5858 Northumberland Fusiliers
MELLING Joseph B. MM Dvr 695566 RFA
MELLINGS Richard G. MM Sjt STK/758 10th Royal Fusiliers
MELLON Henry MM L/Cpl 10610 2nd Scottish Rifles
MELLON Richard MM Pte 13274 2nd Royal Irish Rifles KIA 24.3.18.
MELLON Tom MM Bdr 111227 D/72 Bde RFA
MELLONIE Reginald Ernest MM Dvr T4/037897 Army Service Corps att 56 Fd Amb RAMC.
MELLOR Albert MM Cpl S/6458 1st Rifle Brigade DOW 10 9 18.
MELLOR Alfred MM Pte 277113 2/7th Manchester Regt
MELLOR Arthur MM Sjt 14494 7th North Staffordshire Regt
MELLOR Arthur MM Pte 380988 Liverpool Regt
MELLOR Arthur Charles Ernest MM Pte 52777 RAMC
MELLOR Charles MM Pte 203802 9th West Riding Regt
MELLOR Edmund MM Cpl 22975 10th Royal West Surrey Regt
MELLOR Edward MM Sjt 9304 2nd West Yorkshire Regt
MELLOR Frank MM Cpl 25849 10th Royal West Surrey Regt
MELLOR Frank MM Pte 21737 North Lancashire Regt
MELLOR Fred MM Pte 2756 1/7th West Riding Regt
MELLOR Harold MM Pte M2/119087 Army Service Corps
MELLOR Harold MM Cpl 785402 RFA
MELLOR James MM Cpl 48678 92 Fd Coy Royal Engineers
MELLOR James E. MM L/Cpl 30105 1st Duke of Cornwall's LI
MELLOR James W. MM Pte 95646 Liverpool Regt
MELLOR James W. MM Pte 306205 West Riding Regt
MELLOR Jodeph MM Pte 24036 13th Cheshire Regt
MELLOR John K. MM Pte 809 18th Durham Light Infantry
MELLOR John Robert MM L/Cpl 46561 25th Bn Machine Gun Corps KIA 11.4.18.
MELLOR John T. MM L/Cpl 108023 25th Liverpool Regt
MELLOR John T. MM Pte 14186 Notts & Derby Regt
MELLOR Juliet Vivian MM Senior Section Leader F BRCS
MELLOR Lambert MM(1(WR)Bde)+Bar Cpl 1079 246 Bde RFA
MELLOR Lawrence MM Pte 305147 8th West Yorkshire Regt
MELLOR Peter MM L/Cpl 80149 Royal Engineers
MELLOR Richard MM Dvr 805571 C/231 Bde RFA
MELLOR Thomas H. MM Gnr 81459 D/312 Bde RFA
MELLOR Tom K. MM L/Cpl 307454 7th West Riding Regt
MELLOR Walter MM Pte 43277 RAMC
MELLOR William MM Gnr 247695 B/51 Bde RFA
MELLOR William MM Pte 29233 Highland Light Infantry
MELLOR William MM Pte R/7569 King's Royal Rifle Corps
MELLORS Albert MM Gnr 49284 12 Bde RFA
MELLORS Robert MM Pte 32888 1st Royal Scots Fusiliers KIA 4.10.18.

MELLORS Robert MM Gnr 127616 RFA
MELLORS Walter MM Cpl 554 D/238 Bde RFA
MELLORS William MM Pnr 165878 19 Div Sig Coy Royal Engineers
MELLOWS Leslie Herbert MM L/Bdr 930702 B/291 Bde RFA
MELLS Ernest E. MM Spr 496688 Royal Engineers
MELLS Thomas Edward MM Dvr L/882 RFA att HQ 34 Div
MELROSE A. MM L/Cpl 200407 King's Own Scottish Borderers
MELROSE D.O. MM Pte 270630 East Kent Regt
MELROSE James MM+Bar L/Cpl 56233 Royal Engineers
MELROSE John MM Pte 25066 6th King's Own Scottish Borderers
MELROSE Robert MM Pte 10144 1st Scots Guards KIA 16.9.16.
MELROSE Walter William MM Sjt 80101 MGC(Motors)
MELROSE William MM Cpl 425934 Signal Service Royal Engineers
MELROSE William MM Pte 26150 12th Royal Scots
MELROSE William MM Cpl 33178 King's Own Scottish Borderers
MELSON Alfred H. MM Pte 203498 1st London Regt
MELTON Albert MM Cpl 16929 10th Worcestershire Regt
MELTON Ephraim "MM,MID" CQMS 7128 Coldstream Guards
MELTON Harry MM L/Cpl 2469 1/7th Middlesex Regt KIA 1.10.16.
MELTON Henry Edwards MM Gnr 120315 504 Bty 65 Bde RFA
MELTON Sidney A. MM Cpl 16332 6th Lincolnshire Regt
MELTON Thomas MM+Bar Cpl 200479 1/4th Seaforth Highlanders
MELVILLE Alexander MM S/Sjt Armourer 934 Army Ordnance Corps
MELVILLE Andrew Learmouth MM Gnr 187734 174 Bde RFA
MELVILLE David MM Sjt 12794 6th King's Own Scottish Borderers
MELVILLE Guthrie MM Pte 14250 10th Scottish Rifles
MELVILLE John MM Sjt 16589 Cameron Highlanders
MELVILLE John J.R. MM Pte 260071 1/7th Gordon Highlanders
MELVILLE Robert MM Pte 201058 1/8th Arg & Suth Highlanders
MELVILLE Rodney C. MM Dvr 550478 Royal Engineers
MELVILLE Thomas MM Pte S/20343 1st Gordon Highlanders
MELVIN Henry C. MM Pte 611707 2/19th London Regt
MELVIN John MM Sjt 645593 RFA
MELVIN Robert MM Spr 45862 102 Fd Coy Royal Engineers Died 31.10.18.
MELVIN Robert C. MM Sjt 92466 RFA
MELVIN Thomas MM L/Cpl 5654 Machine Gun Corps
MELVIN William MM L/Cpl 42175 58 Coy Machine Gun Corps
MEMBERY F.C. MM Cpl 12867 4th Coldstream Guards
MEMBERY George R. MM Sjt 551245 1/16th London Regt
MENADUE Simeon J. "DCM,MM" Sjt 132221 251 Tunnelling Coy Royal Engineers
MENAGHAN Thomas MM Pte 201923 1/4th West Riding Regt DOW 5.8.18.
MENDES Alfred Hubert MM Pte B/203484 1st Rifle Brigade
MENDHAM C. MM Pte 421185 London Regt
MENDON James MM Pte 22702 9th Royal Inniskilling Fusiliers Died 23.4.18.
MENDOZA Richard MM 2nd Cpl 249102 Royal Engineers
MENDS David MM Cpl 17968 16th Royal Welsh Fusiliers
MENEELY Thomas W. MM Pte 201071 Royal Lancaster Regt
MENEER Andrew MM Gnr 1491 5(London)Bde RFA
MENELAWS George MM L/Cpl S/10910 1st Gordon Highlanders
MENHAMS Jonathan MM Pte 9690 23rd Bn Machine Gun Corps
MENNELL Harold MM+Bar Pte 8337 Northumberland Fusiliers KIA 4.10.17.
MENNELL John H. "MM,MID" Cpl 755760 RFA
MENNELL William MM Pte 23997 1/7th West Riding Regt
MENNIE A. MM Sjt 90007 Labour Corps
MENPES Sydney MM Gnr 3427 RFA
MENZIES Archibald "DCM,MM+Bar,CG(F)" L/Cpl 265554 1/6th Royal Highlanders
MENZIES Archibald MM L/Cpl 350962 1/9th Royal Scots
MENZIES George MM Sjt 290295 1/7th Royal Highlanders
MENZIES J. MM L/Cpl 265523 Royal Highlanders
MENZIES J. MM Pte G/68245 4th London Regt
MENZIES John MM L/Cpl 8433 1st Scots Guards
MENZIES John MM Pte S/12493 2nd Royal Highlanders
MENZIES John MM Pte M2/047044 Army Service Corps
MENZIES John C. "MM,MID" Sjt 3/6189 8th Duke of Cornwall's LI
MENZIES Nigel A. MM Gnr 50644 RFA
MENZIES Robert MM Pte 31408 Royal Scots
MENZIES Thomas MM+Bar Sjt 332051 2nd Highland Light Infantry
MENZIES Thomas A. MM Pte 424383 10th London Regt
MENZIES William R. MM Dvr 187229 C/311 Bde RFA
MEPHAM Thomas MM Pte 201685 1/4th South Lancashire Regt
MEPSTED Sidney MM Sjt 30474 RGA
MERCER Alexander Kirkland MM L/Cpl 418076 52 Div Sig Coy Royal Engineers
MERCER Alfred William MM Cpl 230509 1/2nd London Regt
MERCER Charles MM Pte 40635 Scottish Rifles
MERCER David MM L/Cpl 41720 5/6th Scottish Rifles KIA 25.10.18.
MERCER Ernest MM Pte 201402 East Yorkshire Regt
MERCER Francis H. MM Sjt 9866 Royal Engineers
MERCER Frank MM Sjt 706063 B/331 Bde RFA
MERCER Frank D. MM Sjt 56734 RFA
MERCER Frederick G. MM Sjt 358342 162 Siege Bty RGA
MERCER Harold MM Bdr L/17274 A/49 Bde RFA DOW 22.7.16.
MERCER James MM Cpl 19728 Army Cyclist Corps
MERCER James MM L/Cpl 40719 22nd Manchester Regt KIA 17.4.17.
MERCER James A. MM Pte 40036 South Staffordshire Regt
MERCER John R. MM Pte 74980 Northumberland Fusiliers
MERCER Lawrence MM Sjt 34448 128 Coy Machine Gun Corps
MERCER Richard MM L/Cpl 61433 12th Manchester Regt
MERCER Samuel MM Gnr 8353 RFA
MERCER Walter James MM Pte 549 15th Royal Warwickshire Regt
MERCER Walter V. MM L/Cpl 3415 Machine Gun Corps
MERCER Wilfred MM Pte 242584 Yorkshire Light Infantry
MERCER William Herbert MM Bdr 29133 D/160 Bde RFA
MERCER William M. MM L/Cpl 52786 Highland Light Infantry
MERCHANT Sidney MM Sjt 61261 Machine Gun Corps
MERCHANT Sidney MM Sjt 70217 58 Coy Machine Gun Corps KIA 26.3.18.
MERCHANT Thomas MM Cpl 292610 136 Hy Bty RGA
MERCHANT Tom MM Pte 13037 1st Grenadier Guards
MEREDEW Alfred MM Pnr 444621 42 Div Sig Coy Royal Engineers
MEREDITH Albert MM Dvr 735515 RFA
MEREDITH Albert MM L/Sjt 12634 1st Grenadier Guards
MEREDITH Clifford E. MM Pte 19940 26th Royal Fusiliers
MEREDITH Edward MM Pte 306983 2/8th Royal Warwickshire Regt KIA 5.12.17.
MEREDITH Edward John MM+Bar Sjt 7831 2nd Manchester Regt DOW 5.10.18.
MEREDITH Edward L. MM Spr 267266 Royal Engineers
MEREDITH Ernest Henry MM L/Cpl 22159 1st Grenadier Guards KIA 12.10.17.
MEREDITH George MM Cpl 14689 9th Yorkshire Regt
MEREDITH George E. MM Spr 146424 130 Fd Coy Royal Engineers
MEREDITH Harry Sylvanus MM Pte 56760 74th Bn Machine Gun Corps DOW 30.9.18.
MEREDITH Henry MM Sjt 19868 C/251 Bde RFA
MEREDITH Herbert J. MM Pte 12934 6th Shropshire Light Infantry
MEREDITH James MM Sjt 200431 1/5th Royal Warwickshire Regt
MEREDITH John R. MM Gnr 45551 RGA
MEREDITH Robert MM Sjt 59627 155 Fd Coy Royal Engineers
MEREDITH Samuel MM Pte 44157 RAMC
MEREDITH Teddy MM Cpl 56759 Machine Gun Corps
MEREDITH Thomas L. MM Pte 20170 19 Fd Amb RAMC
MEREDITH Wilfred P. MM Pte 473192 RAMC
MEREDITH William MM Pte 52668 Liverpool Regt
MEREDITH William MM Bdr 558 Machine Gun Corps
MEREDITH William H. MM Cpl 8493 2nd Royal Warwickshire Regt
MEREDITH William H. MM Pte 435407 RAMC
MEREFIELD Philip MM Sjt 1078 1/1(London)Fd Coy Royal Engineers
MERKAVITCHES Pioushas MM Pte 40565 King's Own Scottish Borderers
MERNER James MM Cpl 8859 1st Royal Munster Fusiliers
MERRELL Horatio H. MM Sjt 534 1/4th London Regt
MERRELL William Henry MM Bdr 53970 'L' Bty RHA
MERRETT Charles MM Sjt 6004 1st Duke of Cornwall's LI
MERRETT F.P. MM Pte 2169 1/5th Gloucestershire Regt
MERRETT George J. MM Cpl 96125 RFA
MERRETT Henry C. MM L/Cpl 1050 Royal Engineers
MERRETT Reginald W.S. MM QMS Wheeler 558 RFA
MERRETT Richard MM L/Cpl 2380 1st Welsh Guards
MERRICK Alfred MM Gnr 141580 RGA
MERRICK Walter Percy MM L/Cpl 10436 2nd York & Lancaster Regt
MERRIFIELD Percy MM Pte 53828 37th Bn Machine Gun Corps
MERRIKIN William MM L/Bdr Sig 930634 A/281 Bde RFA
MERRILL Edwin MM Pte 1813 RAMC DOW 1.12.17.
MERRILL James A. MM Pte 375820 1/10th Manchester Regt
MERRILLS Walter MM Gnr 233014 RFA
MERRIMAN Arthur MM L/Cpl 302571 Royal Scots
MERRIMAN Douglas MM Cpl 560208 Royal Engineers
MERRIMAN George A. MM L/Cpl 546314 Royal Engineers

MERRIMAN Hedley Silverwood "DCM,MM(1/5th Bn)+Bar" Sjt 240088 2/5th West Riding Regt
MERRINGTON Thomas MM L/Cpl 7974 2nd Leinster Regt KIA 12.4.17.
MERRINGTON John "DCM,MM" L/Sjt 201129 1/4th Essex Regt
MERRINS James MM+Bar Sjt 6568 2nd Royal Dublin Fusiliers
MERRITT Charles J. MM Dvr L/22330 RFA
MERRITT Edward G. MM Sjt 28331 RFA
MERRITT Fred MM Sjt 17428 A/170 Bde RFA
MERRITT H. MM L/Cpl G/8413 Royal West Kent Regt
MERRITT Henry MM Pte 240880 Royal West Surrey Regt
MERRITT John William MM Pte 3/7982 2nd Royal Irish Regt KIA 8.10.18.
MERRITT Joseph MM Gnr 222903 RFA
MERRITT Norman B. MM Bdr 127855 RFA
MERRITT Robert Henry MM Sjt 63374 A/107 Bde RFA KIA 21.7.17.
MERRY Arthur H. MM+Bar Sjt 326285 1/1st Cambridgeshire Regt
MERRY George MM Cpl 19979 RFA
MERRY George L. MM L/Cpl 15559 Gloucestershire Regt
MERRY Jack C. MM Pte 24741 3rd Grenadier Guards
MERRY John MM Pte 252571 3rd London Regt
MERRY Stephen MM Pte 7042 2nd Royal Munster Fusiliers
MERRY Thomas MM Sjt 8610 1st Essex Regt KIA 14.4.17.
MERRYLEES Thomas MM L/Cpl 3194 Royal Scots
MERRYWEATHER Fred Hardwick MM Cpl 200034 1/5th Durham Light Infantry DOW 27.6.17.
MERRYWEATHER Sidney MM Gnr 36802 RGA
MERRYWEATHER Wilfred J. MM Sjt 96256 RFA
MERSON Frederick Charles MM Pte 356839 2/4th Hampshire Regt DOW 12.9.18.
MERTON William MM+Bar L/Cpl 1439 Northumberland Fusiliers
MERVIN Walter MM Dvr 38471 A/180 Bde RFA
MESHAM John MM Gnr Sig 685396 B/48 Bde RFA
MESKIMMON Alexander MM Sjt 200936 West Riding Regt
MESS Victor A. MM+Bar Pte S/19202 Royal Fusiliers
MESS William MM Cpl 266836 1/7th Gordon Highlanders
MESSAM Abraham Herbert MM Pte MS/1843 Army Service Corps att 18 Fd Amb RAMC
MESSENGER Albert MM Sjt 14552 9th Yorkshire Regt KIA 23.9.17.
MESSENGER Albert Edward MM Pte S/15079 13th Rifle Brigade
MESSENGER Alfred MM Pte 265401 1/1st Hertfordshire Regt
MESSENGER Frederick George MM Pte 33497 1st Devonshire Regt DOW 9.11.18.
MESSENGER Frederick J. MM Pte 105338 RAMC
MESSENGER Harold MM Pte 11233 Scottish Rifles
MESSENGER Henry MM Pte 1555 1/22nd London Regt
MESSENGER John MM Dvr 13171 Machine Gun Corps
MESSENGER Leonard William MM Cpl 55583 'L' Bty RHA
MESSENGER Oliver MM Pte 203620 Scottish Rifles
MESSENGER Rupert MM Pte M2/152379 Army Service Corps
MESSENGER Thomas MM Gnr 216081 D/18 Bde RFA
MESSER George MM L/Cpl 252 1st Welsh Guards
MESTON David Murray MM Pte 305315 60 Fd Amb RAMC
MESTON Douglas Charles MM Pte 5622 Machine Gun Corps
MESTON Joseph "DCM,MM" Sjt 418077 52 Div Sig Coy Royal Engineers
MESTON William MM Pte B/201721 2nd Rifle Brigade
METCALF Arthur T. MM Cpl 765141 RFA
METCALF Ernest MM Spr 106861 Royal Engineers
METCALF Grosvenor MM Pte 307367 West Riding Regt
METCALF Herbert MM+Bar Cpl W/5712 RFA
METCALF Horace Llewellyn MM Pte 9936 1st Cheshire Regt
METCALF John Edward MM Bdr 2580 RFA
METCALF Robert "DCM,MM" L/Cpl 12/44 12th Yorkshire Light Infantry DOW 17.4.18.
METCALF Stephen MM L/Cpl 48875 13th att 2nd Royal Welsh Fusiliers
METCALFE Arthur MM Pte 7761 2nd Royal Munster Fusiliers
METCALFE Arthur MM L/Bdr 102886 23 Siege Bty RGA
METCALFE Arthur V. MM Cpl 45400 RFA
METCALFE Austin MM L/Sjt 1780 West Yorkshire Regt
METCALFE Bertram MM Pte 358359 1/10th Liverpool Regt
METCALFE D. MM Cpl 265664 West Riding Regt
METCALFE Harold MM Pte S/35332 17th London Regt
METCALFE Harry MM Sjt 350968 1/9th Manchester Regt
METCALFE Henry MM Dvr 214197 1(Berkshire)Bty RFA
METCALFE Herbert MM Sjt 67127 59th Bn Machine Gun Corps
METCALFE Horace Clifford MM Sjt 26794 B/91 Bde RFA
METCALFE J. MM Pte 266375 West Riding Regt
METCALFE John MM Pte 30352 2nd Manchester Regt
METCALFE John MM Pte 401129 9th Essex Regt

METCALFE John MM L/Cpl 265231 West Yorkshire Regt
METCALFE John MM Gnr 28112 35 Bde RFA
METCALFE John A. MM Pte 17662 7th Royal Berkshire Regt
METCALFE John J.A. MM Sjt S/6776 Rifle Brigade
METCALFE John S. MM Sjt 9561 2nd Manchester Regt
METCALFE Joseph MM L/Cpl 65255 4th Yorkshire Light Infantry
METCALFE Leslie MM Cpl 197872 Royal Engineers
METCALFE M.M. MM Pte 10/19467 Northumberland Fusiliers
METCALFE Ned MM+Bar Pte 13526 10th West Riding Regt
METCALFE Reginald MM Gnr 262012 C/82 Bde RFA
METCALFE T. MM Spr 267772 Royal Engineers
METCALFE Thomas MM CSM 22206 38 Coy Labour Corps
METCALFE W. MM Pte 6520 West Riding Regt
METCALFE Walter Holden MM Cpl 13763 12th West Yorkshire Regt DOW 1.4.16.
METCALFE William "DCM,MM" Sjt 265600 1/7th Royal Warwickshire Regt
METCALFE William E. MM Pte 11136 12/13th Northumberland Fusiliers
METCHETTE Frank MM Sjt 48673 7/8th Royal Inniskilling Fusiliers
METHERELL Westcott G. MM Pte 24153 5th Devonshire Regt
METHERINGHAM Frank MM Cpl 46840 RFA
METHERINGHAM George Spencer Benham MM Cpl 630796 1/20th London Regt
METHUEN Thomas MM+Bar Pte 141196 51st Bn Machine Gun Corps
METHVEN George Rutherford MM L/Cpl 4485 226 Coy Machine Gun Corps
METSON George MM Spr 34587 226 Fd Coy Royal Engineers
METTAM Erneat Augustus MM Cpl 301625 13th Bn Tank Corps KIA 8.8.18.
METTAM George Laurence MM Cpl 24981 Notts & Derby Regt
MEW William MM CQMS 720219 1/24th London Regt
MEWHA David MM Pte 73030 32nd Bn Machine Gun Corps
MEYER Charles E. MM Cpl 52958 RFA
MEYRICK Edgar MM L/Cpl 4264 Royal Warwickshire Regt
MEYRICK Frederick G. "MM,MID" Pte M2/077328 Army Service Corps
MEYRICK Hugh H. MM L/Cpl 19329 2 Fd Coy Royal Engineers
MICHAEL Henry W. MM Cpl 612419 19th London Regt
MICHELSON Matthew MM L/Cpl 200936 2/4th Lincolnshire Regt
MICHIE James L. MM Cpl 18605 Royal Scots
MICKLE Frederick MM Pte 15359 6th Royal Berkshire Regt
MICKLEBOROUGH George MM S/Sjt Farrier 14101 Royal Engineers
MICKLEBURGH Albert MM Pte 43243 Suffolk Regt
MICKLEBURGH Charles MM Cpl 20219 131 Hy Bty RGA
MICKLETHWAITE George J. MM Sjt 411173 1 Fd Amb RAMC
MICKLEWAITE J. MM Cpl 1605 Yorkshire Light Infantry
MIDDLEBROOK Thomas "DCM,MM" Cpl 480673 Royal Engineers
MIDDLEDITCH Andrew G. "MM(2Y&L)+Bar,MID" Sjt 18935 16 Coy Machine Gun Corps
MIDDLEDITCH Joseph K. MM Pte G/61857 Royal Fusiliers
MIDDLEDITCH Walter MM Pte 23992 Grenadier Guards
MIDDLEHURST Joseph MM Pte 200353 1/4th East Lancashire Regt
MIDDLEMAS Charles William MM(96 Coy)+Bar Sjt 70323 9th Bn Machine Gun Corps
MIDDLEMAS Thomas MM Bdr 815 RFA
MIDDLEMAS Walter MM Pte 24323 Machine Gun Corps
MIDDLEMASS William H. MM Pte M2/032977 Army Service Corps
MIDDLETON Albert W. MM Spr 31695 Royal Engineers
MIDDLETON Anthony MM Sjt 598 4th Bn GMGR
MIDDLETON Arthur MM Pte 6879 1st Norfolk Regt
MIDDLETON Arthur H. MM Pte 632670 20th London Regt
MIDDLETON Arthur R. MM Pte 7945 Machine Gun Corps
MIDDLETON Bertie MM L/Cpl 59243 12/13th Northumberland Fusiliers
MIDDLETON C. MM Pte 290547 Gordon Highlanders
MIDDLETON Charles D. MM Sjt 18506 57 Fd Coy Royal Engineers
MIDDLETON Charles E. MM Pte 14510 12th Liverpool Regt
MIDDLETON Charles E. MM Pte 91527 8th Bn Tank Corps
MIDDLETON David MM L/Sjt 25689 Welsh Regt
MIDDLETON David MM Sjt 241032 2/6th Royal Warwickshire Regt KIA 6.12.17.
MIDDLETON David J. MM L/Cpl 30466 Royal Engineers
MIDDLETON Dimsdale T.Y. "MM,MID" Pte 2063 25 Fd Amb RAMC
MIDDLETON Ernest MM Pte 1603 RAMC
MIDDLETON Ernest MM Pte 12145 2/9th Manchester Regt KIA 21.3.18.

MIDDLETON Francis MM Cpl 14512 1/7th Gordon Highlanders
MIDDLETON Frank "DCM,MM" CSM 8930 1st North Staffordshire Regt DOW 24.10.17.
MIDDLETON Frank MM Pte 4039 Highland Light Infantry
MIDDLETON Frank C. MM Cpl 22413 Durham Light Infantry
MIDDLETON Fred MM Bdr 800688 D/230 Bde RFA
MIDDLETON Frederick MM L/Cpl 19104 Hampshire Regt
MIDDLETON Frederick H. MM Cpl 14351 4th Royal Fusiliers
MIDDLETON George MM Sjt 940467 A/152 Bde RFA
MIDDLETON George J. MM L/Cpl 44280 2/4th Royal Berkshire Regt
MIDDLETON Guy MM Sjt 50951 102 Bde RFA DOW 22.7.16
MIDDLETON Harold MM Cpl 8687 2nd Cameron Highlanders
MIDDLETON Henry Arthur MM Sjt M1/08663 9 Pontoon Park Army Service Corps
MIDDLETON Hilton MM Pte 42867 8th Yorkshire Regt
MIDDLETON J.C. MM Air Mech 2 8847 Royal Flying Corps
MIDDLETON James MM Cpl 346 1 Fd Amb RAMC
MIDDLETON James MM Cpl 1280 1st Royal Highlanders
MIDDLETON James MM Pte 1057 15th Highland Light Infantry
MIDDLETON John MM Sjt 2735 1/8th West Yorkshire Regt
MIDDLETON John MM Gnr L/4370 RFA
MIDDLETON John MM L/Cpl 19171 2nd Lancashire Fusiliers
MIDDLETON John C. MM Spr 480409 Royal Engineers
MIDDLETON Percy MM Pte 19208 Manchester Regt
MIDDLETON Percy Albert MM Gnr 75261 B/72 Bde RFA
MIDDLETON Richard Alfred "MM,CG(F)" Pte 653786 21st London Regt
MIDDLETON Sidney A. MM Pte 41461 Bedfordshire Regt att 1/1st Hertfordshire Regt.
MIDDLETON Sidney W. MM L/Cpl 14180 7th Bn Machine Gun Corps
MIDDLETON Thomas MM CQMS 8409 4th King's Royal Rifle Corps
MIDDLETON Thomas MM Pte 25751 4th Leicestershire Regt
MIDDLETON Thomas Harvey MM+Bar Sjt 2094 1/4th Royal Lancaster Regt
MIDDLETON Thomas W. MM Pte 19770 Durham Light Infantry
MIDDLETON W.G. MM Gnr 776428 RFA
MIDDLETON Wilfred MM Pte 240674 1/5th West Riding Regt
MIDDLETON William MM Spr 96783 Royal Engineers
MIDDLETON William MM Pte 20380 22nd Manchester Regt
MIDDLETON William MM Cpl C/8040 King's Royal Rifle Corps
MIDDLETON William T. MM+Bar Cpl 402314 Royal Engineers
MIDDLETON Willie MM L/Cpl 242490 1/6th West Yorkshire Regt
MIDDLEWICK William L. MM Pte 102804 1st Bn Machine Gun Corps
MIDGLEY Albert MM Sjt 266534 1/6th West Riding Regt KIA 11.10.18.
MIDGLEY Albert MM Gnr L/12174 C/161 Bde RFA
MIDGLEY Edmund MM Pte 69891 49 Fd Amb RAMC
MIDGLEY Fred MM Pte 260114 15/17th West Yorkshire Regt KIA 19.7.18.
MIDGLEY Harry B. MM+Bar L/Cpl 12137 10th Royal Fusiliers
MIDGLEY James Edward MM L/Cpl 266475 West Riding Regt
MIDGLEY Joseph MM Gnr Sig 146241 168 Siege Bty RGA
MIDGLEY Percy MM Pte R23241 8th King's Royal Rifle Corps KIA 26.12.17.
MIDGLEY Sidney MM Gnr 52301 87 Bde RFA
MIDGLEY Stanley MM Gnr L/19429 HQ 161 Bde RFA
MIDGLEY William Henry MM L/Bdr 140984 C/64 Bde RFA
MIDLANE Cecil Thomas MM Pte 204999 2nd Devonshire Regt
MIDLANE Egbert Robert MM Cpl 592 3rd Rifle Brigade KIA 22.6.16.
MIDMER Walter MM Sjt 32145 RGA
MIDWINTER Albert MM Cpl 352607 7th London Regt
MIDWINTER William MM Pte 8143 2nd Wiltshire Regt
MIGHELL Frederick MM Sjt 1682 1/1st HAC(Infantry)
MIIRON Gabrial MM Pte R/13130 4th King's Royal Rifle Corps
MILBOURN William A. MM Cpl 2183 Royal Sussex Regt
MILBOURNE Walter MM Pte 9067 2nd Suffolk Regt
MILBURN Frederick MM+Bar Sjt 23494 Machine Gun Corps
MILBURN Herbert MM Bdr 103590 200 Siege Bty RGA Died 4.1.18.
MILBURN James MM Cpl 19751 Durham Light Infantry
MILBURN John MM L/Sjt 18/120 18th Durham Light Infantry KIA 1.7.16.
MILBURN John MM Cpl 226036 311 Rd Constr Coy Royal Engineers
MILBURN William MM Pte 7064 Yorkshire Light Infantry
MILCOVICH Marino MM Sjt 301580 5th London Regt
MILDENHALL H. "MM,MID" Sjt 44719 RFA
MILDENHALL Sidney James MM Pte 14262 2nd Hampshire Regt KIA 18.10.16.

MILDOON Charles MM Dvr 100238 4 Div Ammn Col RFA
MILDRED William MM Cpl 875244 RFA
MILES Albert C. MM Pte S/10128 Rifle Brigade
MILES Albert E. MM Sjt 202159 Royal Lancaster Regt
MILES Albert J. MM L/Cpl 150 6th Royal West Kent Regt
MILES Arthur MM Cpl 7698 10th Royal West Kent Regt
MILES Cecil MM Sjt 17719 9th Royal Welsh Fusiliers
MILES Charles MM Pte 9558 Wiltshire Regt
MILES Charles A. MM Pnr 316555 21 Div Sig Coy Royal Engineers
MILES Charles F. MM Cpl 51247 Royal Fusiliers
MILES Charles L. MM+Bar L/Cpl 32830 33 Div Sig Coy Royal Engineers
MILES Charles M. MM Pte 39692 Northumberland Fusiliers
MILES Charles Richard "MM,MID" Cpl MS/1606 3 Ammn Park Army Service Corps
MILES David MM L/Cpl 7840 1st Royal Berkshire Regt
MILES Edwin MM Pte 86493 42nd Bn Machine Gun Corps
MILES Edwin Albert MM Pte 57122 24th Welsh Regt
MILES Ernest G. MM Cpl 15461 7th Royal Berkshire Regt
MILES Ernest W. MM Pte 46583 North Staffordshire Regt
MILES Frederick "MM,MID" SSM T/14121 5 Div Train Army Service Corps
MILES Frederick MM Gnr 68793 RGA
MILES Frederick MM Cpl 15485 Worcestershire Regt
MILES Frederick A. MM Pte 11020 6th Dorsetshire Regt
MILES Frederick J. MM Cpl 358102 RGA
MILES Frederick John MM Sjt 102133 230 Siege Bty RGA
MILES G.H. MM Sjt 11989 Gloucestershire Regt
MILES George MM Pte 240401 1/6th Notts & Derby Regt DOW 15.8.18.
MILES George MM Gnr 72629 34 Bde RFA
MILES George MM Cpl 28154 11th Royal Fusiliers
MILES George MM Spr 146066 178 Tunnelling Coy Royal Engineers
MILES George MM Pte 10323 Army Cyclist Corps
MILES George Albert William MM Gnr 51368 B/150 Bde RFA
MILES George E.V. MM Sjt 492319 13th London Regt
MILES George H. MM L/Cpl D/16720 7th Dragoon Guards
MILES George H. MM Pte 55159 Machine Gun Corps
MILES George William MM Pte 16873 Northamptonshire Regt
MILES Gilbert Arthur MM Pte 7587 1st Somerset Light Infantry
MILES Gordon MM Pte 1132 17th Royal Fusiliers
MILES H.M. "MM,MSM" CQMS M/24557 1 Cav Div Supply Column Army Service Corps
MILES Harry MM Pte 10163 10th Royal West Surrey Regt DOW 29.10.17.
MILES Henry H. MM Pte 7537 1st Royal Berkshire Regt
MILES Henry J. MM Cpl 10665 2nd Royal Scots Fusiliers
MILES Henry W. MM Pte 269771 1/1st Hertfordshire Regt
MILES Jack MM Pte 1327 7th East Surrey Regt
MILES James H. MM Pte 23323 RAMC
MILES John C. "DCM,MM" BQMS 25365 C/152 Bde RFA
MILES John P. MM Pte 1325 1st Royal West Kent Regt
MILES Joseph Alfred MM L/Cpl 1053 9th Royal Fusiliers KIA 30.11.17.
MILES Joseph Walter MM Sjt 5857 1st Middlesex Regt KIA 17.4.18.
MILES Leonard J. MM Cpl 16159 Suffolk Regt
MILES Lionel MM Gnr 66879 RFA
MILES Oscar A. MM Spr 140429 Royal Engineers
MILES Owen MM Cpl 28916 RFA
MILES Samuel J. MM Pte R/10895 King's Royal Rifle Corps
MILES Stanley MM+Bar Pte 7939 1st Wiltshire Regt
MILES Stanley C. MM Pte 205525 15th Hampshire Regt
MILES Sydney J. MM Sjt 2276 8th Royal West Surrey Regt
MILES Victor C.D. MM Gnr 58559 28 Bde RFA
MILES W. MM Pte 9852 2nd Oxf & Bucks Light Infantry
MILES Walter Cecil MM L/Cpl 14936 8th East Lancashire Regt
MILES Walter G. MM Cpl 351240 7th London Regt
MILES Walter L. MM Sjt 17416 6th Northamptonshire Regt
MILES William MM L/Cpl 13109 2nd Grenadier Guards
MILES William MM Sjt 3794 RFA
MILES William A. MM Pte 4863 1/17th London Regt
MILES William J. MM Pte 6684 1st Royal West Kent Regt
MILEY John "MM,CG(F)" L/Sjt 201515 12th Lancashire Fusiliers
MILFORD Auriol C.G. MM Spr 25839 Royal Engineers
MILFORD Harry MM L/Cpl 14348 Machine Gun Corps
MILFORD John MM Cpl 970259 D/18 Bde RFA
MILGATE Charles MM Pte 9839 Royal West Surrey Regt
MILGROVE Albert "DCM,MM" Sjt 12056 6th Royal Berkshire Regt
MILL Hugh MM L/Cpl 350376 Royal Highlanders

MILL William MM Pte 8894 1st East Yorkshire Regt KIA 1.7.16.
MILLAR Alexander MM Dvr T4/041046 59 Div Train Army Service Corps
MILLAR Alexander MM Cpl 275184 1/7th Arg & Suth Highlanders KIA 23.4.17.
MILLAR Alexander H. MM Pte S/42122 1/7th Royal Highlanders
MILLAR Archibald MM Pte M2/166954 35 Div MT Coy Army Service Corps
MILLAR Christie MM L/Cpl 251841 1/6th Arg & Suth Highlanders
MILLAR Christopher MM Sjt 635418 A/256 Bde RFA
MILLAR David MM Pte 9282 2nd King's Own Scottish Borderers
MILLAR David MM 2nd Cpl 47234 Royal Engineers
MILLAR David MM Pte 25248 Royal Scots
MILLAR David H. MM Pte 202039 Gordon Highlanders
MILLAR Douglas F. MM CQMS 18169 2nd Royal Scots
MILLAR Frank MM L/Cpl 139327 Royal Engineers
MILLAR Frank MM Sjt 44651 RGA
MILLAR George MM Cpl 47265 109 Fd Amb RAMC
MILLAR Harry MM L/Cpl 290993 1/7th Gordon Highlanders KIA 30.7.18.
MILLAR Hector C. MM Pte 49961 2nd Royal Scots
MILLAR Herbert MM L/Cpl 700789 23rd London Regt
MILLAR James MM L/Cpl 53419 RAMC
MILLAR James MM+Bar Sjt 67026 Royal Engineers
MILLAR James D. MM+Bar Pte 290718 Royal Highlanders
MILLAR James G. MM Spr 49692 Royal Engineers
MILLAR James McK. MM Pte 9139 Seaforth Highlanders
MILLAR John MM Sjt S/4094 9th Royal Highlanders
MILLAR John H. "MM,MSM" Pte 332392 1/9th Highland Light Infantry
MILLAR John R. MM Gnr 59876 99 Siege Bty RGA
MILLAR John S. MM Pte 41039 King's Own Scottish Borderers
MILLAR Joseph MM L/Cpl 12578 12th Royal Scots
MILLAR Robert MM Cpl 202354 6th King's Own Scottish Borderers
MILLAR Thomas MM Sjt S/4408 10th Arg & Suth Highlanders
MILLAR William MM L/Cpl 88662 33rd Bn Machine Gun Corps DOW 29.10.18.
MILLAR William MM Pte 51250 2nd Royal Scots Died 21.11.18.
MILLAR William MM L/Cpl S/13686 7th Cameron Highlanders
MILLAR William MM+Bar Pte 20813 1st Royal Scots Fusiliers
MILLAR William MM Spr 88878 Royal Engineers
MILLARD Edward MM L/Cpl 27662 8th Somerset Light Infantry
MILLARD Edward G. MM Pte 15565 10th Worcestershire Regt
MILLARD Frederick MM L/Cpl 147552 Machine Gun Corps
MILLARD Henry Albert MM Sjt 55154 38 Bde RFA DOW 16.9.16.
MILLARD J. MM L/Cpl 147473 Royal Engineers
MILLARD John "MM,MID" Sjt 14936 12th West Yorkshire Regt
MILLARD John MM Cpl 27787 1/4th Hampshire Regt
MILLARD Reginald MM Pte 201721 2/4th Royal Berkshire Regt
MILLARD Robert Arnold MM Pte 240410 1/6th Liverpool Regt KIA 31.7.17.
MILLARD William MM Pte 291440 2/10th Middlesex Regt DOW 28.12.17
MILLEN Charles V. MM L/Cpl 9041 Shropshire Light Infantry
MILLEN E.F. MM Cpl 240941 1st East Kent Regt
MILLEN Richard F.M. MM Pte 232570 2nd London Regt
MILLEN William MM Pte 22602 Royal Inniskilling Fusiliers
MILLENS F.J. MM Pte 18379 Grenadier Guards
MILLER Albert MM Gnr 32722 RFA
MILLER Albert MM Pte M2/073566 Army Service Corps
MILLER Albert E. MM L/Cpl 17755 Royal Engineers
MILLER Albert E. MM Cpl 86082 144 Labour Coy Labour Corps
MILLER Albert E. MM+Bar Pte 41496 2nd Manchester Regt
MILLER Albert Henry MM L/Cpl 7807 2nd Oxf & Bucks Light Infantry DOW 26.10.16.
MILLER Albert J. MM+Bar Sjt 19699 2 Fd Coy Royal Engineers
MILLER Albert Walter MM Pte 2662 8th Royal West Kent Regt
MILLER Alexander MM Pte 204075 8th Seaforth Highlanders
MILLER Alexander MM Cpl 12416 6/7th Royal Scots Fusiliers
MILLER Alexander "MM,MSM" Spr 113780 157 Fd Coy Royal Engineers
MILLER Alexander MM Gnr 46600 RFA
MILLER Alfred MM L/Cpl 43100 2nd Royal Irish Rifles
MILLER Alfred E. MM L/Cpl 19392 Norfolk Regt
MILLER Anthony MM Pte 30181 7th East Yorkshire Regt
MILLER Arthur Edward MM Gnr 60992 156 Siege Bty RGA
MILLER Arthur W. MM Cpl 33602 Cheshire Regt
MILLER Bertram Augustus MM Cpl 40951 Royal Engineers
MILLER C. MM Pte 14470 1st Essex Regt
MILLER Charles MM Gnr 34712 122 Heavy Bty RGA
MILLER Charles MM Pte 2338 1/17th London Regt
MILLER Charles MM Pte 15005 North Lancashire Regt
MILLER Charles Bush MM Sjt DM2/138228 63 Div Train Army Service Corps
MILLER Charles E. MM Cpl 68280 34 Bde RFA
MILLER Charles F. "MM,MID" Sjt 2605 1/4th Leicestershire Regt
MILLER Charles F. MM Pte 16183 9th Suffolk Regt
MILLER Charles Frank MM Pte 56568 74 Coy Machine Gun Corps AKA Frank SLATER.DOW 27.10.18.
MILLER Charles W. MM Cpl 71790 25 Div Ammn Col RFA
MILLER Clarence John MM Gnr 676936 B/281 Bde RFA
MILLER D. MM Pte 12146 Manchester Regt
MILLER Daniel MM Cpl 8799 5th Dragoon Guards
MILLER Daniel P. MM Pte 38906 RAMC
MILLER David MM L/Cpl S/5742 8th Seaforth Highlanders KIA 26.8.16.
MILLER David MM L/Cpl 3356 1/2nd London Regt KIA 23.11.17.
MILLER Donald William "DCM,MM" Sjt 11313 1st Middlesex Regt KIA 26.9.17.
MILLER E. MM Pte 14620 9th Gordon Highlanders
MILLER Edgar J. MM Gnr Sig 910839 337 Bde RFA
MILLER Edward MM L/Cpl 2499 1/1st Cambridgeshire Regt
MILLER Edward MM Sjt 26514 Machine Gun Corps
MILLER Edwin Foster MM Pte 79 2nd Royal Highlanders DOW 20.4.17.
MILLER Ernest MM Bdr 89358 B/85 Bde RFA
MILLER Ernest V. MM Gnr 71632 25 Bde RFA
MILLER Francis Charles MM Sjt 15726 8th Royal Lancaster Regt
MILLER Francis W.M. MM Pte 303163 5th London Regt
MILLER Frank MM Dvr 8234 HQ 83 Bde RFA
MILLER Frank Dennis MM Pte 94496 109 Coy Labour Corps
MILLER Frank J. MM L/Sjt C/12631 20th King's Royal Rifle Corps
MILLER Frederick A. MM Tpr 5704 3rd Bn GMGR
MILLER Frederick A. MM Gnr 66964 132 Siege Bty RGA
MILLER Frederick Charles MM Gnr 97090 263 Siege Bty RGA DOW 20.4.18.
MILLER Frederick G. MM Pte M2/051993 Army Service Corps
MILLER Frederick Henry MM L/Cpl 11150 Middlesex Regt
MILLER Frederick S.T. MM+Bar Pte 28039 Liverpool Regt
MILLER Garnet Harkness MM Gnr 89305 A/47 Bde RFA
MILLER George MM Sjt 82940 178 Tunnelling Coy Royal Engineers
MILLER George MM Gnr 117689 RFA
MILLER George MM Pte 238146 2nd Worcestershire Regt
MILLER George MM L/Cpl 18209 Machine Gun Corps
MILLER George MM Pte 12490 1st Scots Guards
MILLER George MM Dvr 548081 Royal Engineers
MILLER George MM Pte 240250 Devonshire Regt
MILLER George MM+Bar L/Cpl 330428 1/8th Royal Scots
MILLER George Frederick MM Pte 43201 Royal Irish Fusiliers
MILLER H.J. MM Cpl 21340 Royal Engineers
MILLER Harold MM S/Sjt 78 1/1(North Midland)Fd Amb RAMC
MILLER Harold MM Pte 4173 1/7th Liverpool Regt DOW 26.9.16.
MILLER Harold H. MM Sjt 18414 XIX Corps Cyclist Bn Army Cyclist Corps
MILLER Harry MM Pte 555 6th East Kent Regt
MILLER Harry MM L/Cpl 44064 Royal Engineers
MILLER Henry Maitland MM Sjt 290205 1/7th Royal Highlanders
MILLER Henry T. MM 2nd Cpl 500368 Royal Engineers
MILLER Herbert MM Bdr 96046 296 Siege Bty RGA
MILLER Herbert MM Sjt 44160 'Q' Special Coy Royal Engineers
MILLER Herbert Frederick MM L/Cpl 352701 7th London Regt DOW 21.4.18.
MILLER Herbert S. MM Sjt 27431 17 Fd Amb RAMC
MILLER Herman Geoffrey MM Gnr 920201 B/50 Bde RFA
MILLER J. MM Pte 24453 Northumberland Fusiliers
MILLER J.W. MM Pte 18059 13th Essex Regt
MILLER Jack MM L/Sjt 6555 8th Royal Munster Fusiliers
MILLER James MM Sjt 22178 6th Bn Machine Gun Corps
MILLER James MM Pte 54907 5th West Yorkshire Regt
MILLER James MM Cpl 203589 6th East Kent Regt
MILLER James MM Sjt WR/260613 268 Rly Const Coy Royal Engineers
MILLER James MM Pte 40060 Royal Irish Rifles
MILLER James MM Sjt 282627 RGA
MILLER James MM Pte 39636 RAMC
MILLER James MM Spr 420398 406 Fd Coy Royal Engineers
MILLER James MM Sjt 21392 Machine Gun Corps
MILLER James MM Gnr 87670 7 Bde RHA
MILLER James MM Sjt 113348 2 Special Coy Royal Engineers
MILLER James MM Cpl 7854 Machine Gun Corps

MILLER James MM Bdr 51110 RFA
MILLER James MM Pte 23815 Royal Dublin Fusiliers
MILLER James H. MM Pte 202484 Scottish Rifles
MILLER John MM Bdr 20117 26 Heavy Bty RGA
MILLER John MM Pte 17/778 15th Royal Irish Rifles
MILLER John MM Pte 39387 15th Royal Scots
MILLER John MM Pte 102672 RAMC
MILLER John MM Spr 412650 Royal Engineers
MILLER John "DCM,MM+Bar" Sjt 200293 1/4th North Lancashire Regt
MILLER John MM+Bar Pte 38887 54 Fd Amb RAMC
MILLER John MM Pte 608648 18th London Regt
MILLER John MM Sjt 240154 5/6th Scottish Rifles
MILLER John W. MM Cpl 17003 1/1st Northumberland Yeomanry
MILLER John W. MM Pte 19379 6th York & Lancaster Regt
MILLER John William MM Gnr 155722 112 Bty 24 Bde RFA
MILLER Joseph MM Sjt 48281 52nd Bn Machine Gun Corps
MILLER Kenneth MM Dvr 197400 37 Bty 27 Bde RFA
MILLER Leonard MM L/Cpl 14056 11th Northumberland Fusiliers DOW 16.8.16.
MILLER Oliver MM Sjt 330876 1/9th Highland Light Infantry
MILLER Peter MM Pte 6859 2nd Dragoons
MILLER Philip Pickess MM+Bar Sjt 22198 5 Div Ammn Col RFA
MILLER R.R. MM Cpl 10581 2nd Highland Light Infantry
MILLER Rankin MM Sjt S/40625 1st Royal Highlanders
MILLER Reginald de Hochepied Marillier MM Pte 61339 Northumberland Fusiliers DOW 27.10.18.
MILLER Reginald E. MM Pte 6683 East Surrey Regt
MILLER Reginald Hugh MM Gnr 290547 113 Siege Bty RGA
MILLER Richard MM Pte 88586 28 Fd Amb RAMC
MILLER Richard MM Cpl 23773 Machine Gun Corps
MILLER Robert MM Cpl S/15012 1/6th Royal Highlanders
MILLER Robert J. MM Gnr 129749 161 Siege Bty RGA
MILLER Samuel A. MM Spr 222011 2 Div Sig Coy Royal Engineers
MILLER Sidney G. MM Sjt M/28780 Army Service Corps
MILLER T.C.B. MM L/Cpl 244886 Royal Engineers
MILLER Thomas MM Pte 13536 8th Norfolk Regt
MILLER Thomas MM Bdr 71092 30 Bde RFA
MILLER Thomas MM Pte 44713 RAMC
MILLER Thomas MM Gnr 88156 RHA
MILLER Thomas MM Pte 36852 Gloucestershire Regt
MILLER Victor MM Dvr 15338 'O' Bty RHA
MILLER Vivian Charles MM Gnr 107772 RFA
MILLER W. "DCM,MM" Sjt 2232 London Regt
MILLER W.E. MM Air Mech 2 58471 Royal Air Force
MILLER Walter MM Pte B/2088 Rifle Brigade
MILLER William MM Spr 81185 87 Fd Coy Royal Engineers
MILLER William MM Pte 43896 Durham Light Infantry
MILLER William MM Pte 16421 7th South Lancashire Regt
MILLER William "MM,MID" L/Sjt 13872 1st Grenadier Guards
MILLER William MM+Bar CSM 1643 RAMC
MILLER William MM Pte 39554 11th Essex Regt
MILLER William MM Pte 14820 9th North Lancashire Regt
MILLER William MM Gnr Shoeing Smith 307637 RGA
MILLER William Duncan MM Cpl 240989 1/9th Liverpool Regt
MILLER William Francis MM Pte DM2/137888 645 Coy Army Service Corps
MILLER William G. MM Pte 32522 Hampshire Regt
MILLER William Gordon MM Pte 202009 1/5th Liverpool Regt
MILLER William H. MM CSM 330469 1/9th Highland Light Infantry
MILLER William Harry MM Sjt 11083 29 Siege Bty RGA
MILLER William T. "MM,MID" CQMS 5151 1st Duke of Cornwall's LI
MILLER William W. MM Pte 20364 Royal Fusiliers
MILLER Zachariah MM Sjt 14759 8th Yorkshire Regt
MILLERSHIP Bernard "DCM,MM+Bar" Pte 22707 1/5th Notts & Derby Regt
MILLERSON Alfred T. MM L/Cpl 78545 'I' Bn Tank Corps
MILLEST Charles W. MM Cpl 45227 4th Hussars
MILLET Joseph MM Pte 204193 1/5th Liverpool Regt KIA 25.3.18.
MILLETT Elijah MM Pte 95809 12th Liverpool Regt
MILLETT Frank MM Pte 242592 6th North Staffordshire Regt
MILLETT Frederick MM Pte 2479 1/6th London Regt
MILLETT Thomas J. MM Spr 132313 251 Tunnelling Coy Royal Engineers
MILLETT William MM L/Cpl 202785 Hampshire Regt
MILLGATE Albert E. MM Spr 224954 56 Div Sig Coy Royal Engineers
MILLGATE Robert MM Sjt 18442 Royal Irish Regt
MILLHAM Albert MM Bdr 14270 D/71 Bde RFA KIA 24.4.17.
MILLHOUSE Arthur MM Pte 381313 7th Liverpool Regt

MILLHOUSE Hugh MM L/Cpl 268744 Notts & Derby Regt
MILLIARD A.W. MM L/Cpl 9022 2nd Bedfordshire Regt
MILLICAN Harold W. MM Sjt 200426 1/4th Royal Berkshire Regt
MILLICAN Thomas MM Pte 23/611 23rd Northumberland Fusiliers Died 20.3.18.
MILLICHAP Philip J. "DCM,MM" Pte 1891 1/5th Gloucestershire Regt
MILLIGAN Albert M. MM L/Cpl 20289 South Lancashire Regt
MILLIGAN Alexander MM+Bar L/Cpl S/3283 Arg & Suth Highlanders
MILLIGAN Alexander MM L/Cpl 3662 8th Seaforth Highlanders
MILLIGAN Francis MM Pte 17916 19th Lancashire Fusiliers
MILLIGAN Francis S. MM Pte 2018 RAMC
MILLIGAN Frederick MM Cpl 47987 38 Bde RFA
MILLIGAN Henry J. MM Pte 352790 7th London Regt
MILLIGAN John MM Cpl 43644 19 Heavy Bty RGA
MILLIGAN John "MM,MSM" Sjt 4484 2nd Border Regt
MILLIGAN John H. MM Pte 4841 1/9th Highland Light Infantry KIA 24.8.16.
MILLIGAN Matthew Watson MM Pte 52743 1st Scottish Rifles
MILLIGAN Robert MM Sjt 16146 17th Highland Light Infantry KIA 1.12.17.
MILLIKEN Arthur Jennings MM Sjt 2681 'C' Bn Machine Gun Corps(Heavy Branch)
MILLIKEN James MM Pte 13421 2nd Scots Guards
MILLIN Duncan MM Cpl 300431 Arg & Suth Highlanders
MILLIN Frank Charles Hallam MM Sjt 6838 4th Coldstream Guards
MILLIN Frederick G. MM Pte 3616 5th Oxf & Bucks Light Infantry
MILLINER Frederick Strange James MM Pte 638 6th Royal West Kent Regt att 25 Div Sig Coy
MILLINGTON Albert MM Bdr 119180 RFA
MILLINGTON Charles MM Pte 14891 8th Royal Berkshire Regt
MILLINGTON H.J. MM L/Cpl 7897 East Kent Regt
MILLINGTON Richard MM+Bar Sjt 62579 151 Fd Coy Royal Engineers
MILLINGTON Richard H. MM Pte 370699 8th London Regt
MILLINGTON Thomas MM Pte 74277 RAMC
MILLINGTON William G. MM Pte 69252 RAMC
MILLINS William A. "MM+Bar,MID" Sjt 12143 2nd Middlesex Regt
MILLIS William J. MM Cpl 77158 45 Bde RFA
MILLMAN John W. MM+Bar L/Cpl 11688 East Lancashire Regt
MILLMORE John MM Gnr 59727 15 Bde RFA
MILLOTT Arthur Ernest MM Spr 35892 7 Cav Bde Sig Tp Royal Engineers
MILLOTT Curzon MM Bdr 46164 117 Heavy Bty RGA
MILLOY John MM Pnr 158932 Special Bde Royal Engineers
MILLRAY Frederick W. MM Pte 200111 1/5th Liverpool Regt
MILLS A.G. MM L/Cpl 39872 9th Essex Regt
MILLS Albert MM Pte 6500 1st Gloucestershire Regt
MILLS Albert MM Pte L/11861 1st Royal West Surrey Regt
MILLS Albert E. MM Pte 266771 West Riding Regt
MILLS Albert E.G. MM Sjt 42485 Royal Engineers
MILLS Albert Thomas MM L/Cpl 14676 11th Essex Regt
MILLS Alexander MM Sjt 4205 296 Coy Labour Corps
MILLS Alexander B. MM Pte 9619 5th Wiltshire Regt
MILLS Alfred MM Cpl 44454 20th Manchester Regt
MILLS Alfred MM Cpl 10676 Hampshire Regt
MILLS Andrew MM Sjt 56227 31st Bn Machine Gun Corps
MILLS Andrew MM Pte 19520 2nd Grenadier Guards
MILLS Arnold MM Pte 8614 10th Lancashire Fusiliers
MILLS Arthur MM 2nd Cpl 198625 Royal Engineers
MILLS Arthur MM Dvr 770929 RFA
MILLS Arthur "MM,MID" L/Sjt 1540 Middlesex Regt
MILLS Charles MM Sjt T2/9472 8 Reserve Park Army Service Corps
MILLS Charles E.H. MM Sjt 494117 477 Fd Coy Royal Engineers
MILLS Charles R. MM Pte 21955 2nd Coldstream Guards
MILLS Charles Richard MM L/Cpl 473414 RAMC
MILLS Charles William MM Pte 21673 Royal West Surrey Regt
MILLS Cyril MM Sjt 17113 47th Bn Machine Gun Corps
MILLS Daniel William MM Cpl 3026 1/4th Gloucestershire Regt KIA 17.7.16.
MILLS David MM Cpl 290231 1/7th Royal Highlanders
MILLS Ernest MM Spr 491960 46 Div Sig Coy Royal Engineers
MILLS Ernest P. MM Sjt 15740 Royal Inniskilling Fusiliers
MILLS F.C. MM Air Mech 1 5715 Royal Flying Corps
MILLS Frank MM Pte 8024 1st Gloucestershire Regt
MILLS Frank MM Pte 47675 Royal Fusiliers
MILLS Frank H. MM Pte 34354 Northumberland Fusiliers
MILLS Frank K. MM Bdsm 10020 2nd Devonshire Regt
MILLS Frederick Charles MM Pte 5/4902 2nd King's Royal Rifle Corps Death sentence commuted Apr 1915.

MILLS George MM Cpl 6599 1st Hampshire Regt KIA 1.7.16.
MILLS George MM L/Sjt 275742 1/7th Arg & Suth Highlanders KIA 9.4.17.
MILLS George A. MM Pte 307963 8th Liverpool Regt
MILLS George D. "DCM,MM" Sjt 84992 34 Div Sig Coy Royal Engineers
MILLS George E. MM Pte 204304 13th Liverpool Regt
MILLS George E. MM Sjt 9093 1st Middlesex Regt
MILLS George L. MM Gnr 48155 RFA
MILLS Gilbert MM+Bar Sjt 1409 2nd Royal Sussex Regt
MILLS Gordon H. MM Cpl 604076 RFA
MILLS Harold MM L/Cpl 53 Lincolnshire Regt
MILLS Harold MM Pte 5266 8th East Surrey Regt
MILLS Harry MM Pte 76945 9th Royal Fusiliers
MILLS Harry MM Pte 29565 East Lancashire Regt
MILLS Harry "DCM,MM" Sjt 5756 12th East Surrey Regt
MILLS Henry J. MM Pte 15722 8th Bedfordshire Regt
MILLS Herbert MM L/Cpl 17118 6th Royal Berkshire Regt
MILLS Horace V. MM Cpl 11236 1st Royal West Kent Regt
MILLS Hubert H. MM Pte 76243 4th London Regt
MILLS Hyram B. MM Cpl 35107 8th East Surrey Regt
MILLS Isaac MM Pnr 443927 Royal Engineers
MILLS J. MM Pte 2142 Arg & Suth Highlanders
MILLS J.E. MM SQMS 3501 15th Hussars
MILLS James MM Sjt 337042 RGA
MILLS James MM Pte 21619 Royal Irish Fusiliers
MILLS James "MM,MID" Cpl 19330 RGA
MILLS James MM Pte S/7146 Royal Highlanders
MILLS James W. MM Sjt 4711 8th Suffolk Regt
MILLS James Walter MM Pte 315146 16th Royal Sussex Regt Died 7.10.18.
MILLS John MM Sjt 6414 Royal Welsh Fusiliers
MILLS John A. MM L/Cpl 73134 11th Notts & Derby Regt
MILLS John Arthur MM Sjt 39019 4th Bn Machine Gun Corps
MILLS John Felix MM+Bar L/Cpl 320892 6th London Regt KIA 8.10.16.
MILLS John Henry "DCM,MM,CG(It)" Sjt 5579 23rd Bn Machine Gun Corps
MILLS John R. MM L/Cpl 650174 1/21st London Regt
MILLS Joseph MM Pte 14970 10th Yorkshire Regt
MILLS Joseph MM Pte 14563 9th North Lancashire Regt
MILLS Joseph A. MM Cpl 252534 6th Durham Light Infantry
MILLS Joshua MM Pte 201164 North Lancashire Regt
MILLS Leonard B. MM Sjt 17/646 Royal Irish Rifles
MILLS Percy T. MM Gnr Sig 35121 50 Siege Bty RGA
MILLS Reuben G. MM Pte 22080 1/6th Gloucestershire Regt
MILLS Richard A. MM Pte 29833 1st North Lancashire Regt
MILLS Robert MM L/Cpl 10609 5th Oxf & Bucks Light Infantry
MILLS Robert MM Spr 159916 219 Fd Coy Royal Engineers
MILLS Robert MM Pte 201164 4th York & Lancaster Regt
MILLS Robert MM Gnr 32951 5 Div Ammn Col RFA
MILLS S. MM Pte 24578 Duke of Cornwall's LI
MILLS Samuel MM Cpl 29671 East Lancashire Regt
MILLS Samuel Arthur MM Gnr 78730 C/87 Bde RFA DOW 18.4.18.
MILLS Sydney B. MM Sjt SE/1490 Army Veterinary Corps
MILLS Thomas MM Pte 350481 1/7th London Regt
MILLS Thomas MM CSM 23142 Royal Engineers
MILLS Thomas MM Pte 243697 Liverpool Regt
MILLS Thomas MM Sjt 3905 11th Royal Sussex Regt
MILLS Thomas MM Sjt 19094 Machine Gun Corps
MILLS Thomas C. MM Cpl A/543 King's Royal Rifle Corps
MILLS Tom MM 2nd Cpl 147790 Royal Engineers
MILLS Victor Thomas Benjamin MM Sjt 64375 C/74 Bde RFA
MILLS W. MM Cpl 20014 1st Essex Regt
MILLS W.R. MM Pte 40650 Yeomanry
MILLS Walter G. MM Cpl 3402 2nd Dragoon Guards
MILLS Walter P. MM Pte 24950 1st Gloucestershire Regt
MILLS Wilfred MM Pte 20769 Shropshire Light Infantry
MILLS William MM Pte 30844 1/4th Yorkshire Light Infantry KIA 13.10.18.
MILLS William MM Pte M2/100658 17 Ammn Pk Army Service Corps
MILLS William MM Gnr 725872 RFA
MILLS William C. "DCM,MM,MID" BSM 25053 116 Siege Bty RGA
MILLS William E. MM Pte 7615 21st London Regt
MILLS William H. MM Pte 3080 1st Welsh Guards
MILLS William John MM Pte 551936 12th London Regt
MILLS William P. MM Sjt 44284 18 Bde RFA
MILLS William R. MM Pte 505122 13th London Regt
MILLS William T. MM Bdr 47058 40 Bde RFA

MILLSON Harry MM Pte 265771 1/7th West Yorkshire Regt DOW 1.5.18.
MILLSON Sidney T. MM Pte 536354 RAMC
MILLSOPP William MM Cpl 3949 2 Bde RFA
MILLWARD Charles H. MM Cpl 54356 Royal Engineers
MILLWARD E. MM Pte 20470 Machine Gun Corps
MILLWARD Frank MM Pte 20405 Bedfordshire Regt
MILLWARD George MM Cpl 20986 2nd Worcestershire Regt
MILLWARD Harry MM L/Cpl 1615 Worcestershire Regt
MILLWARD Henry S. MM Pte 51252 5th Manchester Regt
MILLWARD James MM Pte 20382 4th Grenadier Guards
MILLWARD James Sinclair MM Gnr 7128 RFA
MILLWARD Joseph MM Gnr 45507 10 Siege Bty RGA
MILLWARD Ralph MM Gnr 800507 RFA
MILLWARD Thomas MM Sjt 10987 C/59 Bde RFA
MILLWARD Thomas MM Sjt 200956 1/7th Worcestershire Regt
MILLWARD Thomas MM Dvr 64897 RFA
MILLWARD Walter MM Pte 200837 1/7th Worcestershire Regt
MILLWARD William MM Pte 200991 South Staffordshire Regt
MILLWARD William Churchill MM Pte 10169 2nd South Wales Borderers KIA 1.7.16.
MILLWOOD Herbert MM Cpl 22523 164 Coy Machine Gun Corps KIA 9.8.16.
MILLYARD Richard MM L/Cpl 23369 11 Fd Coy Royal Engineers
MILMINE John W. MM Cpl 750396 RFA
MILNE Alexander MM Pte 17160 15th Royal Scots
MILNE Alexander MM Pte 16209 Arg & Suth Highlanders
MILNE Andrew MM Spr 75847 15 Div Sig Coy Royal Engineers
MILNE Andrew MM L/Cpl 265248 Seaforth Highlanders
MILNE Charles MM+Bar Pte 17161 Royal Scots
MILNE David R. "DCM,MM" Sjt 70484 37 Div Sig Coy Royal Engineers
MILNE Douglas MM L/Cpl 290890 Gordon Highlanders
MILNE Ernest MM Pte 82057 42nd Bn Machine Gun Corps
MILNE Ernest MM Sjt 10/15597 10th Royal Irish Rifles
MILNE Ferguson MM Staff SM T4/241428 51 Div Train Army Service Corps
MILNE Forbes MM Sjt 200413 1/4th Gordon Highlanders KIA 23.4.17.
MILNE Forbes James MM Sjt 303011 2(Highland)Fd Amb RAMC
MILNE George MM Pte 9638 2nd King's Own Scottish Borderers
MILNE George MM L/Cpl 11826 5th Cameron Highlanders
MILNE George Forbes MM Pte 14996 1st Scots Guards
MILNE George James MM Cpl 152853 RGA
MILNE Henry MM Pte 30708 2nd Royal Scots
MILNE Henry G. MM+Bar L/Cpl 24718 1st Royal Scots Fusiliers Died 13.11.18.
MILNE Ian MM Sjt 265629 1/6th Royal Highlanders
MILNE J. MM Cpl 200187 Gordon Highlanders
MILNE J. MM Gnr 352479 RGA
MILNE James MM Sjt 837160 RFA
MILNE James MM Cpl S/18145 1st Gordon Highlanders
MILNE James MM Pte 15534 1st Scots Guards
MILNE James MM Pte 6416 Gordon Highlanders
MILNE James MM L/Cpl 9045 14th Arg & Suth Highlanders KIA 27.3.18.
MILNE John MM Pte 41193 2nd Royal Scots Fusiliers
MILNE John MM Pte 12943 20th Manchester Regt att RE.
MILNE John MM Cpl 332437 1/9th Highland Light Infantry
MILNE Peter L. MM Pte 201628 1st King's Own Scottish Borderers
MILNE R. MM Cpl 10344 South Lancashire Regt
MILNE Robert MM Pte S/9461 9th Royal Highlanders DOW 11.9.16.
MILNE Robert J. MM Cpl 15571 Gordon Highlanders
MILNE Robert R. MM Sjt 23152 Royal West Surrey Regt
MILNE Thomas MM Pte 51779 Royal Scots
MILNE Thomas MM L/Cpl 266894 1/6th Gordon Highlanders
MILNE Thomas K. MM Spr 414793 56 Div Sig Coy Royal Engineers
MILNE Walter Scott MM Sjt 504 1/5th Royal Scots
MILNE William MM+Bar Pte M2/183733 Army Service Corps
MILNE William MM Pte 3/2125 1st Royal Highlanders KIA 20.9.18.
MILNE William MM Pte 29973 17th Royal Scots
MILNE William MM L/Cpl 240964 1/5th Gordon Highlanders
MILNE William George MM L/Cpl 8889 1/7th Highland Light Infantry
MILNER Arthur MM Pte 12/732 2/4th York & Lancaster Regt
MILNER Charles "MM,MSM" 2nd Cpl 80873 138 Army Troops Coy Royal Engineers
MILNER Ernest "DCM,MM(1564 Cpl N&D)" CSM 238047 Lincolnshire Regt
MILNER Frank MM L/Cpl 53406 13th Liverpool Regt
MILNER Fred MM+Bar Sjt 54492 11 Bde RFA

MILNER George MM Sjt 390027 3(Northumbrian)Fd Amb RAMC
MILNER Harold M. MM Pte 13987 Machine Gun Corps
MILNER Henry John MM Gnr 322605 364 Siege Bty RGA
MILNER John MM Pte 325917 Royal Scots
MILNER John MM Pte 12449 11th West Yorkshire Regt
MILNER John A. MM L/Cpl 13925 6th Dragoon Guards
MILNER John E. MM Pte 13536 9th York & Lancaster Regt
MILNER Joseph MM Sjt 375754 1/10th Manchester Regt KIA 20.10.18.
MILNER Leslie MM L/Sjt 9162 1st Scots Guards
MILNER Montgomery J. MM Pte 1831 1/15th London Regt
MILNER Norman MM L/Cpl 81256 Machine Gun Corps
MILNER Samuel Ernest MM Cpl 41292 22nd Manchester Regt
MILNER Sidney MM Pte 93044 Durham Light Infantry
MILNER Walter MM Spr 476978 121 Fd Coy Royal Engineers
MILNER William "DCM,MM" Cpl 240649 1/5th King's Own Scottish Borderers
MILNER William A. MM L/Bdr 630380 A/48 Bde RFA
MILNES Albert MM L/Cpl 13971 4th Coldstream Guards
MILNES Albert James MM L/Cpl 355957 Liverpool Regt
MILNES Charles Edward MM Pte 34951 22nd Manchester Regt KIA 4.10.17.
MILNES Eric MM Spr 75839 25 Div Sig Coy Royal Engineers
MILNES George MM L/Cpl 280667 Lancashire Fusiliers
MILNES George B. MM Sjt 33280 2nd Hampshire Regt
MILNES Lawrie MM Gnr 34143 RFA
MILNES Norman MM Dvr 775859 C/310 Bde RFA
MILROY David Harold J. MM Pte 531717 15th London Regt
MILROY Peter MM Bdr 7639 RFA
MILROY William MM L/Cpl 240249 1/5th King's Own Scottish Borderers KIA 1.8.18.
MILROY William MM Sjt 13426 Highland Light Infantry
MILSOM George W. MM Pte 15224 7th Yorkshire Light Infantry
MILSOM Henry Thomas MM Sjt 44393 421 Bty RFA
MILTON A. MM Pte L/17755 23rd Bn Royal Fusiliers
MILTON Charles MM Gnr 35971 RGA
MILTON Christopher T. MM Pte 14047 Royal Sussex Regt
MILTON Edwin MM Pte 124115 30th Bn Machine Gun Corps
MILTON Frank MM Pte 20899 10th Royal Fusiliers
MILTON Harry MM Cpl 13760 2nd Lincolnshire Regt
MILTON Herbert E. MM Pte 89030 Machine Gun Corps
MILTON John W. MM Pte 536411 RAMC
MILTON Thomas MM Gnr 17921 35 Bde RFA
MILTON William George MM Cpl L/10036 2nd Royal West Surrey Regt KIA 13.5.17.
MILTON William J. MM Pte 15594 11th Royal Sussex Regt
MILTON William John "DCM,MM" Sjt 8652 1st South Wales Borderers DOW 19.10.18.
MILUM Arthur S. MM+Bar L/Bdr 109489 D/87 Bde RFA
MILWARD Arthur G. MM Cpl PS/2961 Royal Fusiliers
MILWARD James MM+Bar Pte R/8008 7th King's Royal Rifle Corps
MIMMS George MM L/Cpl 9019 2nd Northamptonshire Regt
MINCHER Joseph E. MM Pte 62953 17th Lancashire Fusiliers
MINCHIN Charles E. "DCM,MM+Bar" Sjt 5374 5th Royal Berkshire Regt
MINCHIN William H. MM Sjt 17183 7th Lincolnshire Regt
MINDHAM Herbert J. "MM,MSM" Sjt 67941 19 Div Sig Coy Royal Engineers
MINEHAN William J. MM L/Cpl 77964 10th Royal Fusiliers
MINER Albert E. MM CQMS 1473 1st Lancashire Fusiliers
MINER William MM Pte 12531 South Staffordshire Regt
MINERS Albert MM CSM 5575 2nd Royal Welsh Fusiliers KIA 20.7.16.
MINERS Francis A. MM Pte 93616 17th Royal Welsh Fusiliers
MINERS Francis H. MM Cpl 128267 RGA
MINERS William H. MM Cpl STK762 10th Royal Fusiliers
MINERT George E. "DCM,MM" Pte 5270 8th East Surrey Regt
MINETT Alfred George MM Sjt 33182 1st Royal Warwickshire Regt
MINETT Edward G. MM L/Cpl 572476 2/17th London Regt
MINETT F.A. MM Sjt 240234 1/6th Royal Warwickshire Regt
MINETT John MM Spr 86401 Royal Engineers
MINFORD Alfred MM Pte 11/2996 12th Royal Irish Rifles
MINGAY Henry C. MM Pte 241075 1/5th Suffolk Regt
MINGO Percy MM Pte 19443 Dorsetshire Regt
MINHINNICK William MM Pte 240017 5th Devonshire Regt
MINIHAN Thomas MM Gnr 904 RFA
MINISTER Samuel MM Pte 50022 1/9th Highland Light Infantry
MINK William "DCM,MM" CSM 250981 3rd London Regt
MINNERY John "DCM,MM" Sjt 905 2nd Arg & Suth Highlanders
MINNEY Frank MM Pte 22202 5th Royal Irish Fusiliers

MINNEY John MM Pte M2/049882 14 Fd Amb Army Service Corps
MINNEY Sidney MM Sjt 60856 V/22 Heavy TM Bty RGA
MINNIKIN W.W. MM L/Cpl 32786 1st Northumberland Fusiliers
MINNIS David MM Sjt 14/15601 14th Royal Irish Rifles
MINNIS William MM Sjt 57482 122 Fd Coy Royal Engineers
MINNITT Bernard Arthur "MC,MM(35943 L/Cpl N&D)" T/2Lt 18th King's Royal Rifle Corps
MINNS C. MM Sjt 57957 RAMC
MINNS David MM Cpl 925685 RFA
MINNS Frederick MM L/Cpl 7783 2nd Essex Regt KIA 1.7.16.
MINNS Harry F.W. MM Pte 7846 1st East Kent Regt
MINNS Richard J. MM L/Cpl 13293 Bedfordshire Regt
MINNS Sidney W.R. MM Pte 232983 2nd London Regt
MINOGUE John P. MM Pte 19274 2nd Royal Dublin Fusiliers
MINORS James Hamilton MM Dvr 650419 C/86 Bde RFA KIA 20.6.17.
MINSHALL John W. MM Sjt 112630 A/159 Bde RFA
MINSHALL Lewis MM Pte 12055 9th Cheshire Regt
MINSHALL William G. MM L/Cpl 72058 Royal Engineers
MINSHULL Richard A. MM Spr 451851 Royal Engineers
MINSHULL William MM L/Cpl 49906 9th Cheshire Regt
MINTER Claude MM L/Cpl 43344 10th Essex Regt
MINTER Frederick G. MM Pte 41331 Royal Irish Rifles
MINTER William H.F. MM Pte 5575 13th Rifle Brigade
MINTO William MM L/Cpl 7051 7th Gordon Highlanders
MINTON Charles MM Cpl 24308 Shropshire Light Infantry
MINTRAM Alfred MM Cpl 7380 2nd Hampshire Regt
MINTY James E. MM Spr 268367 18 Div Sig Coy Royal Engineers
MINTY John MM Pte S/10423 8/10th Gordon Highlanders
MINTY John T. MM Cpl 3425 Royal West Surrey Regt
MIRAMS Arthur W. MM Pte 2889 8th Royal West Surrey Regt
MIRAMS William MM Cpl 51232 1st Cheshire Regt
MIREE Samuel MM L/Cpl 14/1060 14th York & Lancaster Regt
MIRRILEES Alexander MM L/Cpl 34860 8th York & Lancaster Regt KIA 7.6.17.
MIRRLEES William M. MM L/Cpl 1576 1/4th Gordon Highlanders
MISELL David MM+Bar Pte 17395 2nd South Lancashire Regt
MISKELL Thomas MM Pte 35105 Labour Corps
MISKELLA John MM L/Sjt 240562 1/5th South Lancashire Regt DOW 12.4.18.
MISKELLY Herbert MM Cpl 371014 8th London Regt
MISKIMMIN George MM Sjt 6798 Royal Irish Rifles
MISON Frederick G. MM Bdr 2428 RFA
MISSEN Ernest H. MM+Bar Pte 48562 17th London Regt
MISSEN Ernest William MM Pte 10894 2nd Wiltshire Regt KIA 9.4.17.
MISSIONS Arthur Sidney MM Cpl 354133 7th London Regt KIA 1.9.18.
MISSON William MM L/Sjt 5640 1st Duke of Cornwall's LI
MIST L. MM Pte 13569 10th Essex Regt
MITCHARD Stanley H. MM Pte 22272 1/4th Seaforth Highlanders
MITCHELHILL Andrew MM Pte 40191 1/6th Gordon Highlanders
MITCHELL A. MM L/Cpl 305031 RAMC
MITCHELL A.J. MM Sjt M2/078887 Army Service Corps
MITCHELL A.V. MM Sjt 2626 Rifle Brigade
MITCHELL Albert "MM,MID" Spr 25059 5 Div Sig Coy Royal Engineers
MITCHELL Albert MM Pte 241312 5/6th Scottish Rifles
MITCHELL Albert E.B. MM Pte 202726 Middlesex Regt
MITCHELL Alec MM Cpl 201013 1/4th West Riding Regt DOW 19.4.18.
MITCHELL Alexander MM CSM 290019 Royal Highlanders
MITCHELL Alexander MM Gnr 40610 D/126 Bde RFA
MITCHELL Alexander MM+Bar Sjt S/2503 9th Seaforth Highlanders
MITCHELL Alexander MM Gnr 1087 MGC(Motors)
MITCHELL Alexander John MM L/Cpl 65244 105 Fd Coy Royal Engineers KIA 20.7.17.
MITCHELL Alfred MM Pte 553903 16th London Regt
MITCHELL Alfred MM Sjt 8105 6th Royal West Kent Regt
MITCHELL Alfred MM+Bar L/Cpl 8077 21 Fd Amb RAMC
MITCHELL Allan C. MM Sjt 350090 1/9th Royal Scots
MITCHELL Andrew "MM,MID" Cpl 58650 152 Fd Coy Royal Engineers
MITCHELL Andrew T. MM L/Cpl S/20051 Cameron Highlanders
MITCHELL Archibald MM Pte 112667 36 Fd Amb RAMC
MITCHELL Archibald J. MM Pte 24717 Royal Dublin Fusiliers att RE.
MITCHELL Arthur MM L/Cpl 490424 Royal Engineers
MITCHELL Arthur MM Cpl 25992 Notts & Derby Regt
MITCHELL Arthur MM Gnr 67477 7 Bty 4 Bde RFA

MITCHELL Arthur MM Sjt L/13805 9th Royal Fusiliers DOW 21.11.17.
MITCHELL Arthur MM Pte 356410 1st Hampshire Regt KIA 28.3.18.
MITCHELL Arthur A. MM Pte 28539 Durham Light Infantry
MITCHELL Arthur Frederick MM+Bar Sjt 23541 33 Bty 33 Bde RFA
MITCHELL Bramwell MM Pte 201072 4th West Riding Regt
MITCHELL C.harles Frederick MM Sjt 275094 33 Siege Bty RGA
MITCHELL Cecil R. MM Pte 23147 10th Gloucestershire Regt
MITCHELL Charles MM Sjt 20315 12th Bn Machine Gun Corps
MITCHELL Charles MM Pte 91953 9th Bn Tank Corps
MITCHELL Charles MM Bdr 81870 RGA
MITCHELL Charles MM Cpl 1576 Royal Engineers
MITCHELL Charles "MM,MID" Gnr 65452 22 Bde RFA
MITCHELL Charles MM Cpl 79884 15 Bde RHA
MITCHELL Charles Alexander MM Pte 9803 2nd Scots Guards DOW 28.3.18.
MITCHELL Charles E. MM Sjt S/3036 11th Rifle Brigade
MITCHELL Charles E. MM+Bar Sjt 10119 2nd South Lancashire Regt
MITCHELL Charles H. MM+Bar Bdr 781764 5(West Riding)Bty RFA
MITCHELL Charles Napier MM+Bar Cpl 21764 13th Liverpool Regt KIA 21.8.18.
MITCHELL Charles W. MM Sjt 780366 RFA
MITCHELL Charles W.R. MM Pte 626 19th Durham Light Infantry
MITCHELL Charles William MM Spr 98194 20 Army Troops Coy Royal Engineers
MITCHELL Charlie MM Pte M2/053003 Army Service Corps
MITCHELL Charlie Young MM Sjt 279345 3rd London Regt att 4th Royal Fusiliers.KIA 31.8.18.
MITCHELL Claude MM L/Cpl 202162 West Yorkshire Regt
MITCHELL David MM Pte 22518 9th Royal Inniskilling Fusiliers
MITCHELL David MM Gnr 29400 168 Bde RFA
MITCHELL David MM L/Sjt 31364 1/4th Royal Scots
MITCHELL David MM Pte 203263 Seaforth Highlanders
MITCHELL David B. MM Pte 40940 1/5th Highland Light Infantry
MITCHELL David J. MM Cpl 686809 D/310 Bde RFA
MITCHELL David T. MM Cpl 600 Royal Engineers
MITCHELL Edward P. MM L/Sjt 9335 2nd Royal Berkshire Regt
MITCHELL Edward P. MM Pte 38603 1/4th Gloucestershire Regt
MITCHELL Edward Patrick "MM,CG(B)" Sjt 253912 Royal Engineers
MITCHELL Edward T. MM Pte S/11171 Rifle Brigade
MITCHELL Edwin MM Pte 28559 6th Yorkshire Regt KIA 29.8.17.
MITCHELL Edwin T. MM Sjt 23446 RGA
MITCHELL Eli MM L/Cpl 200688 1/4th Seaforth Highlanders
MITCHELL F.C. MM Sjt P/5524 Military Mounted Police
MITCHELL Francis MM Gnr 39200 RFA
MITCHELL Francis S. MM Pte 29411 Machine Gun Corps
MITCHELL Frank MM Pte 241971 1st Gordon Highlanders
MITCHELL Frank MM Bdr 118603 RFA
MITCHELL Frederick "DCM,MM" RSM 265405 1/6th Cheshire Regt
MITCHELL G. MM Sjt 15604 Royal Irish Rifles
MITCHELL Garner MM Cpl 16794 1/4th Yorkshire Light Infantry
MITCHELL George MM L/Sjt 705286 23rd London Regt
MITCHELL George MM Sjt 265492 Royal Warwickshire Regt
MITCHELL George MM Pte 3/2186 2nd York & Lancaster Regt
MITCHELL George MM Sjt 8890 1st Devonshire Regt
MITCHELL George MM Pte 18166 2nd Yorkshire Regt
MITCHELL George MM Gnr 22701 B/82 Bde RFA
MITCHELL George H. MM Pte 57837 6th Yorkshire Regt
MITCHELL George H. MM Pte 25073 Leicestershire Regt
MITCHELL George Herbert MM Pte 3136 1/5th West Riding Regt KIA 6.10.17.
MITCHELL H. MM Pte 17030 1st Essex Regt
MITCHELL H. "MM,MID" Cpl R/2333 King's Royal Rifle Corps
MITCHELL Harold MM Sjt 17088 2 Fd Coy Royal Engineers
MITCHELL Harold Frederick MM L/Cpl 12626 Worcestershire Regt
MITCHELL Harold W. MM Cpl 98234 Machine Gun Corps
MITCHELL Harry F. MM CQMS 10033 2nd South Wales Borderers
MITCHELL Hedley MM Sjt 91214 153 Coy Labour Corps
MITCHELL Henry MM Pte 6130 2nd Yorkshire Light Infantry
MITCHELL Herbert MM Pte 28446 8th Somerset Light Infantry
MITCHELL Herbert MM Pte 44606 1st Lincolnshire Regt DOW 17.10.18.
MITCHELL Herbert MM Pte 40313 Manchester Regt
MITCHELL Isaac MM Pte 41266 15th Lancashire Fusiliers
MITCHELL Isaac MM+Bar Sjt 20/244 West Yorkshire Regt
MITCHELL J. MM Dvr 3324 5 Div Ammn Col RFA
MITCHELL J.A. MM+Bar L/Cpl 266055 Gordon Highlanders
MITCHELL J.F. MM Pte 22983 Machine Gun Corps
MITCHELL Jack MM Pte 14068 8th Yorkshire Regt

MITCHELL James MM Cpl 26293 63 Siege Bty RGA
MITCHELL James MM L/Cpl 8172 8/10th Gordon Highlanders
MITCHELL James MM Pte M2/176139 Army Service Corps
MITCHELL James MM Cpl 73465 152 Coy Machine Gun Corps KIA 29.5.17.
MITCHELL James MM Pte 4562 18th Highland Light Infantry
MITCHELL James B MM Cpl 79596 257 Tunnelling Coy Royal Engineers KIA 21.2.17.
MITCHELL James W. MM+Bar Cpl 46909 A/18 Bde RFA
MITCHELL James William "MM,MID" Sjt 5073 Machine Gun Corps
MITCHELL John MM Pte 23985 1st Northamptonshire Regt
MITCHELL John MM Sjt 390844 9th London Regt
MITCHELL John MM Pte 202711 2/4th Hampshire Regt
MITCHELL John MM Pte 7443 1st Gordon Highlanders
MITCHELL John MM L/Cpl Y/553 King's Royal Rifle Corps
MITCHELL John MM+Bar Pte 290364 1/7th Royal Highlanders
MITCHELL John MM Gnr 10786 105 Bty 22 Bde RFA
MITCHELL John MM Sjt S/3773 11th Arg & Suth Highlanders KIA 10.7.17.
MITCHELL John MM L/Cpl S/4125 1/8th Arg & Suth Highlanders KIA 19.9.18.
MITCHELL John MM S/Sjt Fitter 56786 242 Siege Bty RGA
MITCHELL John MM+Bar Sjt 265211 1/6th Royal Highlanders
MITCHELL John MM L/Cpl 235422 Liverpool Regt
MITCHELL John "MM,MSM" Sjt S/31694 1 Div Train Army Service Corps
MITCHELL John A. MM Cpl 167150 230 Siege Bty RGA
MITCHELL John A.C. MM Dvr 227042 D/82 Bde RFA
MITCHELL John B. MM Pte 1096 1/6th Gordon Highlanders
MITCHELL John Bridgeman "MM,MID" Sjt M2/022062 Army Service Corps att 2 Fd Amb RAMC.
MITCHELL John Drew MM Pte 28424 1st Gloucestershire Regt DOW 9.9.16.
MITCHELL John E. MM+Bar Pte 1641 Royal Sussex Regt
MITCHELL John H. MM Gnr 104488 112 Bty 24 Bde RFA
MITCHELL John H.C. MM Pte 30195 5th East Lancashire Regt
MITCHELL Joseph MM Sjt 19315 Royal Inniskilling Fusiliers
MITCHELL Joseph MM Sjt 7436 2nd Leicestershire Regt
MITCHELL Joseph MM+Bar Sjt 546 2nd Gordon Highlanders
MITCHELL Joseph E. MM Pte 41183 RAMC
MITCHELL Joseph Henry MM Pte 2699 1/5th North Staffordshire Regt
MITCHELL L.E. MM Pte 457285 RAMC
MITCHELL M. MM Pte 341336 RAMC
MITCHELL Matthew MM CQMS 6914 1st East Yorkshire Regt
MITCHELL Percy MM Pte 7601 1st Lincolnshire Regt
MITCHELL Peter MM Pte 12238 Gordon Highlanders
MITCHELL Peter MM Cpl 19752 12th Durham Light Infantry KIA 1.1.17.
MITCHELL Peter MM Cpl 265498 1/6th Royal Highlanders KIA 20.11.17.
MITCHELL R. MM L/Cpl 263171 4th West Riding Regt
MITCHELL R.S. MM L/Cpl 23221 Royal Engineers
MITCHELL Ralph MM+Bar Pte 200814 1/4th Royal Berkshire Regt
MITCHELL Reuben MM Sjt 113002 2 Special Coy Royal Engineers
MITCHELL Richard MM Sjt 240950 West Riding Regt
MITCHELL Richard MM+Bar Cpl L/38362 C/186 Bde RFA
MITCHELL Robert MM Pte 22711 King's Own Scottish Borderers
MITCHELL Robert MM Pte 15747 Royal Inniskilling Fusiliers
MITCHELL Robert G. MM Sjt 17385 Machine Gun Corps
MITCHELL Robert O. MM Cpl S/7156 Rifle Brigade
MITCHELL Rowland MM L/Cpl 263113 2/4th Yorkshire Light Infantry DOW 27.9.18.
MITCHELL Rowland MM Pte 241485 Lancashire Fusiliers
MITCHELL S.C. MM Pte 17635 Royal West Kent Regt
MITCHELL Samuel MM Cpl 14299 41st Bn Machine Gun Corps
MITCHELL Sidney J. MM Pte 44043 4th Royal Berkshire Regt
MITCHELL Stewart MM+Bar Sjt 292653 1/7th Royal Highlanders
MITCHELL Sydney MM Pte 23593 Duke of Cornwall's LI
MITCHELL Thomas MM Pte 17812 Gordon Highlanders
MITCHELL Thomas MM Cpl 74562 2nd Highland Light Infantry
MITCHELL Thomas MM L/Cpl 1831 18th Hussars
MITCHELL Thomas MM L/Cpl S/4757 7th Seaforth Highlanders DOW 20.5.17.
MITCHELL Thomas MM Cpl 19714 South Lancashire Regt
MITCHELL Thomas W. MM Cpl 518727 11 Div Sig Coy Royal Engineers
MITCHELL Victor H. MM Cpl 53803 30 Bde RFA
MITCHELL Walter MM Sjt 7657 1st Royal Scots Fusiliers
MITCHELL Walter MM L/Cpl 265161 7th Royal Warwickshire Regt

MITCHELL Walter A. MM Gnr 307598 RGA
MITCHELL Walter R. MM Pte 241164 Cheshire Regt
MITCHELL William "MM,CG(F)" Pte 43664 5 Fd Amb RAMC
MITCHELL William "DCM,MM" CSM 1374 8th Royal West Kent Regt
MITCHELL William MM Pte 6668 1st Royal Irish Fusiliers
MITCHELL William MM L/Cpl 23/1339 Northumberland Fusiliers
MITCHELL William MM Gnr 167239 266 Siege Bty RGA
MITCHELL William MM Sjt 201077 Royal Highlanders
MITCHELL William "MM,MID" Spr 64427 150 Fd Coy Royal Engineers
MITCHELL William MM Pte 7541 Middlesex Regt
MITCHELL William MM Pte 275946 5/6th Royal Scots
MITCHELL William MM Cpl 275823 Arg & Suth Highlanders
MITCHELL William D. MM Sjt 275692 1/7th Arg & Suth Highlanders
MITCHELL William Francis MM Pte 30186 East Lancashire Regt
MITCHELL William H. MM Sjt 200581 1/4th West Riding Regt
MITCHELL William H. MM L/Cpl 192675 Royal Engineers
MITCHELL William H. MM CSM 3/10007 7th Norfolk Regt
MITCHELL William J. MM Sjt 14474 Royal Irish Fusiliers
MITCHELL William John MM Sjt 203225 1/4th Essex Regt
MITCHELL William K. MM L/Cpl 514134 14th London Regt
MITCHELL William T. MM Bdr 26967 5 Siege Bty RGA
MITCHELL William Taylor MM Pte S/11900 1st Royal Highlanders KIA 3.9.16.
MITCHELMORE Sydney F. MM Pte DM2/154901 Army Service Corps
MITCHELSON Peter John MM Sjt 93945 RAMC
MITCHELSON William McKenzie "MM,CG(F)" L/Sjt 46760 10th King's Own Scottish Borderers
MITCHEM Cyril J. MM Pte 54110 2nd Royal Irish Rifles
MITCHEM Fred "MC+Bar,MM(5136 Cpl 2DG)" 2Lt 7th Shropshire Light Infantry
MITCHEM Robert MM Sjt 16499 7th Royal Irish Fusiliers
MITCHENER Albert MM Pnr 560317 Royal Engineers
MITCHENER Harry MM Pte G/11238 11th Royal West Surrey Regt
MITCHESON George "MM,MID" L/Cpl 470723 Royal Engineers
MITCHINSON George R. MM Sjt 82593 29th Bn Machine Gun Corps
MITCHINSON J. MM Cpl 29678 Royal Engineers
MITCHINSON James MM Gnr 73779 D/76 Bde RFA KIA 25.8.18.
MITCHINSON William MM Sjt 34723 10th Northumberland Fusiliers
MITCHINSON William Thomas MM Gnr Shoeing Smith 750634 315 Bde RFA
MITCHISON George Albert Stanley MM Sjt 463016 50 Div Sig Coy Royal Engineers
MITCHISON John MM Sjt 57829 36 Div Sig Coy Royal Engineers
MITCHLEY Bernard A.F. MM Pte 372548 8th London Regt
MITCHLEY E.S. MM Pte 43895 1st Essex Regt
MITHAM Robinson MM Pte 44036 1/4th Suffolk Regt
MITSON David MM Sjt 5900 RHA
MITTELL Arthur Stewart MM Pte 266686 2/6th Gloucestershire Regt
MITTELL James Brett MM Sjt 54638 108 Siege Bty RGA
MITTEN John MM Pte S/40645 8th Seaforth Highlanders KIA 21.4.18.
MITTLESTRASS Henry A. MM Sjt 9245 1st West Yorkshire Regt
MITTON Arthur MM L/Cpl 20117 7th Shropshire Light Infantry
MITTON Harold MM Gnr 59510 110 Siege Bty RGA
MITTON Samuel H. MM Cpl 250816 6th Manchester Regt
MIZEN Arthur J. MM Pte 23604 5th Royal Berkshire Regt
MIZON Albert C. MM L/Cpl M2/182234 Army Service Corps
MIZON Alfred MM Pte 18/16703 18th Lancashire Fusiliers
MOAG David MM L/Cpl 18485 12th Royal Irish Rifles
MOAKES George MM L/Sjt 1541 17th Royal Fusiliers
MOAKLER Robert John MM Sjt 254 15th Royal Warwickshire Regt
MOAR Sinclair MM Pte 17025 Seaforth Highlanders
MOAT George MM L/Cpl 5555 Machine Gun Corps
MOAT George W. MM L/Cpl 21769 Cheshire Regt
MOATE John Albert George MM Pte 302757 10th Bn Tank Corps
MOATES Henry J. MM Sjt 76254 X/5 Med TM Bty RFA
MOBBS Alfred MM Sjt 17367 9th Norfolk Regt
MOBBS Christopher James MM Cpl 74189 7 Div Sig Coy Royal Engineers DOW 19.7.16.
MOBBS Reginald MM Bdr 70481 'Q' Bty RHA
MOBBS Thomas C. MM Gnr Fitter 42654 RFA
MOCHAN Thomas MM Pte 28379 5/6th Scottish Rifles
MOCK Horace M. MM Bdr 62617 RFA
MOCKFORD Alfred "See CALLAWAY,88144 RFA"
MOCKFORD William "MM,MIDx2" Sjt 50952 Royal Engineers
MOCKRIDGE William MM Pte 3464 11th Manchester Regt
MOCOCK Charles MM Gnr 5365 RFA

MODDER Veere MM Pte S/8641 Rifle Brigade
MODEN Arthur W. MM L/Sjt 242693 5th East Lancashire Regt
MODEN Percy MM L/Bdr 291046 21 Heavy Bty RGA
MOFFAT James MM Sjt S/10833 7th Cameron Highlanders
MOFFAT John MM Spr 341889 123 Fd Coy Royal Engineers
MOFFAT John MM L/Cpl 8161 2nd Royal Scots Fusiliers KIA 12.10.16.
MOFFAT John MM CQMS 13120 15th Highland Light Infantry
MOFFAT Joseph "MM,CG(F)" L/Cpl 15943 Royal Highlanders
MOFFAT Samuel MM Cpl 56371 52nd Bn Machine Gun Corps
MOFFAT Thomas MM Pte 310016 1/6th Royal Highlanders
MOFFAT William MM Pte 42833 1st Scottish Rifles
MOFFAT William MM L/Sjt 200229 1/5th Liverpool Regt
MOFFATT Arthur Clarence MM Pte 27897 9th Lancashire Fusiliers KIA 4.10.17.
MOFFATT Charles William MM Pte 25236 1st South Wales Borderers KIA 18.4.18.
MOFFATT David "MM,MID" S/Sjt 47040 RAMC
MOFFATT George MM Pte 883 6th Royal West Kent Regt
MOFFATT George MM Gnr 60879 82 Siege Bty RGA
MOFFATT John MM Cpl 200416 1/4th Cheshire Regt
MOFFATT John "DCM,MM" CSM 10145 6/7th Royal Scots Fusiliers
MOFFATT John T. MM Pte 632343 229 Empl Coy Labour Corps
MOFFATT Robert MM Cpl 10/14384 10th Northumberland Fusiliers KIA 22.9.16.
MOFFATT William MM Sjt 1878 1/7th Northumberland Fusiliers DOW 21.9.16.
MOFFATT William MM Pte 10936 King's Own Scottish Borderers
MOFFETT David MM Cpl 282590 RGA
MOGER Arthur Joseph MM L/Cpl 3586 1/4th London Regt
MOGER Herbert E. MM L/Cpl G/2355 8th Royal Sussex Regt
MOGERLEY John E. "DCM,MM" Cpl 920 1/4th Northumberland Fusiliers
MOGFORD James MM Sjt 9057 1st Essex Regt KIA 14.4.17.
MOGG Arthur George "MM,MSM,MIDx2" Sjt 506154 2(Wessex)Fd Coy Royal Engineers
MOGG Ernest MM Sjt 85489 RFA
MOGRIDGE Herbert C. MM L/Cpl 25195 1st Dorsetshire Regt
MOGRIDGE Samuel MM 2nd Cpl 164726 130 Fd Coy Royal Engineers
MOHAN Thomas J. MM Pte 45154 South Wales Borderers
MOIR A.A.L.C. MM Sjt 23232 Royal Flying Corps
MOIR Alexander MM L/Cpl 201561 Seaforth Highlanders
MOIR Alexander MM Pte 201489 1/4th Gordon Highlanders
MOIR Alexander E. MM Cpl 1416 23rd Royal Fusiliers
MOIR Allan "DCM,MM" CSM S/2916 8th Royal Highlanders
MOIR Benjamin MM Pte 292303 Gordon Highlanders
MOIR Edward D. MM Spr 178358 Royal Engineers
MOIR Francis MM L/Cpl S/42092 7th Royal Highlanders
MOIR Frederick J. MM Sjt 7187 2nd Cameron Highlanders
MOIR James G. MM Pnt 96540 Royal Engineers
MOIR John MM Pte 704 Army Cyclist Corps
MOIR Robert MM Sjt 28614 6th Somerset Light Infantry
MOIR William MM Pte 59556 RAMC
MOIST Richard MM Pte 37582 Northumberland Fusiliers
MOKES William H. MM Pte 269304 West Riding Regt
MOLD Charles MM Pte 3467 2/7th Royal Warwickshire Regt
MOLE Albert E. MM Pte S/10143 Rifle Brigade
MOLE Alfred MM Pte 14102 17th Lancashire Fusiliers
MOLE Ernest "MM,MID" Sjt 9124 7th Suffolk Regt att 1/1st Cambridgeshire Regt
MOLE Frank "MM,CG(It)" CSM 200037 1/7th Worcestershire Regt
MOLE George E. MM Sjt 200524 1st London Regt
MOLE John MM L/Sjt 14845 Royal Sussex Regt
MOLE Robert MM L/Cpl 24146 Northumberland Fusiliers
MOLE Samuel MM L/Sjt 10163 11th Royal Warwickshire Regt
MOLES W.H. MM L/Cpl 115593 Yeomanry
MOLESWORTH William MM Pte 27273 2nd Hampshire Regt
MOLLAND John MM Sjt 27095 'N' Corps Sig Coy Royal Engineers
MOLLAND Keith J. MM Sjt 372969 8th London Regt
MOLLER Charles E. MM Sjt 320121 16th Royal Sussex Regt
MOLLETT Thomas A. MM Sjt TT/03191 Army Veterinary Corps
MOLLISON Charles Stewart MM Pte 17427 19th Liverpool Regt KIA 21.3.17.
MOLLISON Norman MM Sjt 9981 RFA
MOLLON William H. MM Bdr Fitter 173297 RGA
MOLLOY A.S. MM Sjt 465 38 Bde Ammn Col RFA
MOLLOY Albert MM Pte 90967 1st Liverpool Regt
MOLLOY Albert E. MM Sjt 5105 4th Dragoon Guards
MOLLOY Edward "MM,MID" Sjt 44392 Royal Engineers

397

MOLLOY Francis MM L/Cpl 45995 13th Durham Light Infantry
MOLLOY Francis J. MM Pte 44108 RAMC
MOLLOY John George MM Pte 10896 2nd Leinster Regt
MOLLOY Joseph MM L/Cpl 7888 2nd Northumberland Fusiliers
MOLLOY Michael J. MM Gnr 70554 281 Siege Bty RGA
MOLLOY Patrick MM Sjt 4/4282 7th Leinster Regt
MOLONEY Arthur Michael MM BQMS 10995 RFA
MOLONEY John MM Cpl 3747 8th Hussars
MOLONEY Thomas MM Pte 22665 21st West Yorkshire Regt
MOLONEY Thomas MM Sjt 4/5608 7th Royal Irish Regt KIA 2.9.18.
MOLONEY Timothy MM Pte 6344 1st Royal Irish Regt
MOLONY John L. MM Pte 530587 15th London Regt
MOLSON Francis C. MM Sjt 15462 11th Notts & Derby Regt
MOLYNEAUX Charles MM Pte 201490 5th Manchester Regt
MOLYNEUX Alfred MM S/Sjt T/908 Army Ordnance Corps
MOLYNEUX Charles MM Pte 17214 7th Royal Lancaster Regt
MOLYNEUX G. "MM,MID" L/Cpl 5111 Coldstream Guards
MOLYNEUX George MM Cpl 15993 1st Cheshire Regt DOW 22.8.18.
MOLYNEUX George William MM Cpl 11002 13th Cheshire Regt KIA 10.8.17.
MOLYNEUX Peter MM+Bar Pte 323002 1/8th Durham Light Infantry
MOLYNEUX Samuel MM Pte 11994 7th York & Lancaster Regt
MOLYNEUX William H. MM Cpl 280872 Lancashire Fusiliers
MONAGHAN Adam MM Cpl 10463 2nd Wiltshire Regt
MONAGHAN Bernard MM Sjt 73913 36 Bde RFA
MONAGHAN Edward MM Sjt 71251 12 Bde RFA
MONAGHAN Francis MM Gnr 26119 RFA
MONAGHAN John "DCM,MM" CSM 19395 North Lancashire Regt
MONAGHAN Leo F. MM Gnr 352558 RGA
MONAGHAN Mark MM+Bar Spr 36305 9 Div Sig Coy Royal Engineers
MONAGHAN Patrick MM Spr 440560 97 Fd Coy Royal Engineers
MONAGHAN Robert MM Pte 1787 RAMC
MONCK Harry "DCM,MM+Bar" Sjt 351833 1/7th London Regt
MONCK William MM Cpl 8165 King's Royal Rifle Corps
MONCKTON Walter Herbert Austin MM Cpl Z/2765 13th Rifle Brigade
MONCRIEFF David MM L/Cpl 13668 7th Cameron Highlanders
MONCRIEFF William D. MM L/Cpl 23140 10th Gloucestershire Regt
MONDAY Harry MM Dvr T1/3810 Army Service Corps
MONEL Percy MM S/Sjt Farrier 22153 RFA
MONEN James MM Pte 70421 151 Coy Machine Gun Corps
MONET Elias C. MM Dvr 69597 44 Bde RFA
MONEY Clarence William MM Pte 40021 8th Lincolnshire Regt
MONEY Frederick T. MM Pte 127140 3rd Bn Machine Gun Corps
MONEY John J.H. MM+Bar Cpl 18393 5th Royal Berkshire Regt
MONEY Joseph W. "MM,MSM" Sjt 43216 2nd Royal Dublin Fusiliers
MONEY Nathaniel MM Pte S/5033 Rifle Brigade
MONEY William MM Sjt 8091 Machine Gun Corps DOW 31.7.16.
MONGER Ernest MM Pte 42053 9th Royal Inniskilling Fusiliers
MONGER Frederick W. MM Pte 116180 9th Bn Machine Gun Corps
MONGER William James MM Pte 14263 2nd Hampshire Regt DOW 19.10.16.
MONK Albert H. MM Sjt 16941 1st Bn Machine Gun Corps
MONK Alfred J. MM+Bar Sjt 47209 Northumberland Fusiliers
MONK Donald MM L/Cpl 21778 5th Cameron Highlanders KIA 22.3.18.
MONK H.J. MM Pte 16447 9th Essex Regt
MONK Harry MM L/Cpl 7596 1st Scottish Rifles KIA 8.5.18.
MONK Herbert "MM,MID" Bdr 68897 RFA
MONK Herbert Sidney MM Sjt 282189 2/4th London Regt KIA 16.6.17.
MONK John J. MM Pte 8052 13th Middlesex Regt
MONK Reuben "DCM,MM" Gnr L/406 C/158 Bde RFA
MONK Robert A. MM Sjt R/4275 13th King's Royal Rifle Corps
MONK Walter "MM,MSM" Sjt 2093 9th Royal Fusiliers
MONK William MM L/Cpl 24648 Duke of Cornwall's LI
MONK William MM+Bar CSM 18795 12th Durham Light Infantry
MONK William MM Cpl 49236 RFA
MONK William A.E. MM L/Cpl 12443 6th Bedfordshire Regt
MONK William G. MM Pte 201756 Gloucestershire Regt
MONKHOUSE Edward MM Pte 28565 6th Yorkshire Regt
MONKHOUSE John William MM Pte 68449 91 Fd Amb RAMC
MONKS Charles MM Sjt 7659 Notts & Derby Regt
MONKS Christopher MM L/Cpl R/37051 13th King's Royal Rifle Corps
MONKS Gilbert MM Pte 300855 2nd Manchester Regt
MONKS Harold L. MM Cpl 24573 1st Wiltshire Regt
MONKS Herbert MM Sjt 2137 Royal Flying Corps
MONKS James H. MM Pte 23522 12th Liverpool Regt
MONKS Richard J. MM Pte 29532 18th Lancashire Fusiliers
MONKS W. MM Sjt 280609 1/7th Lancashire Fusiliers
MONNICKENDAM Harold MM Sjt 331745 1/9th Highland Light Infantry
MONRO George MM+Bar L/Cpl 18726 36th Bn Machine Gun Corps
MONRO William "MM,MdH(F)" Spr 178255 Royal Engineers
MONTAGUE Alfred MM Gnr 83840 18 Bty 3 Bde RFA
MONTAGUE Charles MM Dvr 206576 RFA
MONTAGUE Frank MM Bdr 33226 C/50 Bde RFA KIA 2.5.17.
MONTAGUE George MM Pte 240595 9th Scottish Rifles
MONTAGUE Paul A. MM Pte 4814 1st East Surrey Regt
MONTEITH John B. MM Cpl 38473 RFA
MONTEITH William MM Sjt 56387 24 Div Sig Coy Royal Engineers
MONTGOMERIE Robert R. MM L/Cpl 204127 Liverpool Regt
MONTGOMERY David MM L/Cpl 9236 Seaforth Highlanders
MONTGOMERY David J. MM Sjt 650003 Royal Engineers
MONTGOMERY Edin MM Spr 424127 Royal Engineers
MONTGOMERY F.T. MM L/Cpl P/5063 1 Traffic Control Coy Military Foot Police
MONTGOMERY Frank MM Pte M1/6250 First Army MT Coy Army Service Corps
MONTGOMERY George MM Sjt 14/18503 14th Royal Irish Rifles
MONTGOMERY Henry MM Cpl 9315 1st East Surrey Regt KIA 29.7.16.
MONTGOMERY James MM CSM M2/205046 1015 Coy Army Service Corps
MONTGOMERY James MM Pte 333047 Highland Light Infantry
MONTGOMERY James MM L/Cpl 25087 7/8th Royal Inniskilling Fusiliers
MONTGOMERY James MM 2nd Cpl WR/278260 50 Rly Op Coy Royal Engineers
MONTGOMERY John MM Pte 14104 9th Royal Inniskilling Fusiliers
MONTGOMERY John MM Cpl 53072 15th Highland Light Infantry
MONTGOMERY John MM Pte 2280 8th Royal Lancaster Regt
MONTGOMERY John MM Pte 3353 1st Leinster Regt
MONTGOMERY Joseph MM L/Cpl 1224 1st Royal Irish Rifles
MONTGOMERY Robert MM+Bar Sjt 19124 9th Royal Inniskilling Fusiliers
MONTGOMERY Robert MM Pte 7977 1st Scots Guards
MONTGOMERY Robert MM Pte 15376 7/8th King's Own Scottish Borderers
MONTGOMERY W. MM Pte 388304 RAMC
MONTGOMERY William MM+Bar L/Cpl 14992 7/8th King's Own Scottish Borderers
MONTY Frank MM Cpl 463072 Royal Engineers
MOODIE Adam MM Sjt 290721 1/7th Royal Highlanders DOW 17.4.18.
MOODIE Alexander J. MM Bdr Sig 121789 208 Siege Bty RGA
MOODIE Charles W. MM Sjt 69903 82 Fd Coy Royal Engineers
MOODIE David "DCM,MM,MID" Sjt 46817 63 Fd Coy Royal Engineers
MOODIE George M. "DCM,MM" Sjt 20348 2nd Yorkshire Light Infantry
MOODIE James MM Dvr 7025 D/78 Bde RFA Died 11.11.18.
MOODIE James MM Pte 291526 Gordon Highlanders
MOODIE James MM 2nd Cpl 198768 Royal Engineers
MOODIE Robert MM Gnr 92530 Tank Corps
MOODNICK Barrett MM Pte 242046 7th Royal West Kent Regt
MOODY Andrew MM Spr 53099 18 Div Sig Coy Royal Engineers
MOODY Benjamin R. MM Sjt 471255 Royal Engineers
MOODY Bernard S. MM Spr 65693 107 Fd Coy Royal Engineers
MOODY Charles F. "DCM,MM,MID" Sjt 385 8th Royal Sussex Regt
MOODY David MM L/Cpl 17572 12th Northumberland Fusiliers
MOODY Ernest MM Pte 240495 5th Lincolnshire Regt
MOODY Ernest Brightmore MM Cpl 41333 8th Northumberland Fusiliers KIA 5.6.18.
MOODY Frederick MM Gnr L/19999 D/161 Bde RFA
MOODY George W. MM Dvr 755443 A/251 Bde RFA
MOODY George William "MM+Bar,CdiG(It)" Cpl 7039 2nd Border Regt
MOODY Henry J. MM L/Cpl 201824 4th Hampshire Regt
MOODY Herbert MM Pte 40145 1st Lincolnshire Regt DOW 12.4.17.
MOODY James Alfred MM Cpl 42438 West Yorkshire Regt
MOODY John E. MM Gnr 8967 RFA
MOODY John Watson MM Sjt 11692 10th West Yorkshire Regt KIA 1.7.16.
MOODY Leonard W. "MM,MID" L/Cpl 11458 9th Devonshire Regt
MOODY Sidney MM Cpl T4/042473 56 Div Train Army Service Corps

MOODY Thomas MM Pte 27098 Royal Lancaster Regt
MOODY William MM CQMS 15995 10th Durham Light Infantry DOW 29.8.16.
MOODY William R. MM L/Cpl 42633 20th Durham Light Infantry
MOOK James MM Gnr 158822 RFA
MOON Charles MM Pte 653 6th Royal West Kent Regt DOW 14.8.16.
MOON Frederick Charles MM Sjt 1441 2nd Royal Warwickshire Regt KIA 9.10.17.
MOON George "DCM,MM" L/Sjt 4549 2nd Royal Welsh Fusiliers
MOON Graham J. MM Sjt K/210 17th Royal Fusiliers
MOON Harry C. MM Pte 75915 Tank Corps
MOON Jack Frederick MM Gnr 37933 65 Siege Bty RGA DOW 21.9.18.
MOON James MM Pte 21056 14th Liverpool Regt
MOON James W. MM L/Sjt 14098 7th Wiltshire Regt
MOON L. MM L/Cpl 390919 London Regt
MOON Richard MM Pte 242087 5th East Lancashire Regt
MOON William MM Pte 4680 King's Royal Rifle Corps
MOON William MM Pte 240757 5th Royal Lancaster Regt
MOONEY Frank MM Dvr 771497 C/251 Bde RFA
MOONEY Hugh MM Pte 5409 2nd Dragoons
MOONEY James MM Dvr 77241 RFA
MOONEY John MM+Bar L/Cpl 79409 Royal Engineers
MOONEY John MM Gnr 37459 2 Siege Bty RGA
MOONEY John P. MM Pte 270877 1/1st Northumberland Yeo
MOONEY Matthew MM Sjt 35682 2 Bde RFA
MOONEY Maurice MM Pte 20243 22nd Manchester Regt
MOONEY Michael MM Sjt 6978 2nd Royal Dublin Fusiliers
MOONEY Nicholas MM L/Cpl 32474 14th Royal Warwickshire Regt KIA 2.5.18.
MOONEY Peter MM Bdr 6262 RFA
MOONEY Peter MM Sjt 192689 Special Bde Royal Engineers
MOONEY Richard "MM,MID" Pte 20697 18 Fd Amb RAMC
MOONEY Thomas MM+Bar Sjt 8671 71 Fd Amb RAMC
MOONEY William MM Dvr 49320 5 Div Ammn Col RFA
MOONEY William MM+Bar Pte 240343 5/6th Scottish Rifles
MOORCOCK Frank Cecil MM Sjt 1349 7th East Kent Regt
MOORCOCK Henry E. "DCM,MM" Pte 26318 71 Fd Amb RAMC
MOORCROFT Alfred "DCM,MM" Sjt 70745 33rd Bn Machine Gun Corps
MOORCROFT Charles MM Pte 141346 25th Machine Gun Corps KIA 4.5.18.
MOORCROFT Harold MM Pte 72464 7th Royal West Surrey Regt
MOORE A. MM Pte 7903 North Staffordshire Regt
MOORE A. MM Pte 12/18494 Royal Irish Rifles
MOORE Abraham MM Cpl 46607 12 Div Sig Coy Royal Engineers
MOORE Abraham MM Pte S/9412 Rifle Brigade
MOORE Albert MM Sjt 42068 1st South Wales Borderers
MOORE Albert E. MM Pte 39929 Royal West Surrey Regt
MOORE Albert G. MM Pte 267105 Northumberland Fusiliers
MOORE Albert J. MM Sjt 138857 RGA
MOORE Albert J. MM BSM 9053 1 Siege Bty RGA
MOORE Albert John MM Pte 21926 19th Royal Welsh Fusiliers KIA 31.1.18.
MOORE Albert W. MM L/Cpl 680550 1/22nd London Regt
MOORE Alexander MM Gnr 250611 D/110 Bde RFA
MOORE Alfred MM L/Bdr 70262 98 Bty 18 Bde RFA DOW 1.9.18.
MOORE Alfred MM Pte 280808 1/7th Lancashire Fusiliers
MOORE Alfred Charles "DCM,MM" Sjt 5/4582 1st King's Royal Rifle Corps
MOORE Alfred Charles MM CSM 5/4243 King's Royal Rifle Corps
MOORE Alfred L. MM L/Cpl 195392 14 Div Sig Coy Royal Engineers
MOORE Alfred S. MM Pte 3/6040 1st Somerset Light Infantry
MOORE Arthur MM Pte 33753 1st Border Regt Died 23.2.17.
MOORE Arthur George MM Pte 41369 2nd Bedfordshire Regt
MOORE Arthur James MM Cpl Shoeing Smith L/6269 B/156 Bde RFA
MOORE Arthur Robert MM Sjt 8364 2nd Wiltshire Regt
MOORE Bernard MM Pte 3311 Leinster Regt
MOORE Bertie MM L/Cpl 19882 Royal Inniskilling Fusiliers
MOORE Bertram E. MM Sjt 8875 Worcestershire Regt
MOORE Cecil Courtenay MM Sjt 57707 B/71 Bde RFA
MOORE Charles MM Cpl Mechanic 76072 1st Bn Tank Corps
MOORE Charles MM Sjt 16061 Duke of Cornwall's LI
MOORE Charles MM Spr 63528 Royal Engineers
MOORE Charles Edward MM Sjt 55389 196 Coy Machine Gun Corps
MOORE Charles H. MM Gnr Wheeler 34300 RGA

MOORE Charles S. MM Pte 74923 RAMC
MOORE Charles S. MM Dvr 42229 RFA
MOORE Cleave Alfred MM Cpl 57249 105 Fd Coy Royal Engineers
MOORE David MM Cpl 514097 14th London Regt
MOORE David MM+Bar Cpl 29464 13th Yorkshire Regt
MOORE David Henry MM Cpl 11061 11th Royal Warwickshire Regt
MOORE Edmund   "See MASON, Edmund, Pte 16270"
MOORE Edmund C. MM Pte R/5052 King's Royal Rifle Corps
MOORE Edward MM CSM G/61147 24th Royal Fusiliers
MOORE Edward MM Gnr 64684 RFA
MOORE Edward S. MM Cpl 15622 10th Royal Irish Rifles
MOORE Edward T. MM Pte 57091 Royal Welsh Fusiliers
MOORE Eli MM Cpl 3/6104 1st Somerset Light Infantry
MOORE Ernest MM Sjt 23183 15th Notts & Derby Regt
MOORE Ernest MM Sjt 20903 10th Notts & Derby Regt
MOORE Ernest S. MM Cpl 1657 18th Durham Light Infantry
MOORE F. MM Sjt 200520 Yorkshire Light Infantry
MOORE Frank MM Pte 240089 York & Lancaster Regt
MOORE Frank H. MM Pte 23613 7th Royal Sussex Regt
MOORE Frank P. MM Sjt 38375 RGA
MOORE Fred MM Sjt 12679 9th Essex Regt DOW 6.9.18.
MOORE Frederick MM Pte 17188 6th South Wales Borderers
MOORE Frederick MM Pte 285074 Oxf & Bucks Light Infantry
MOORE Frederick MM Pte 14012 9th Royal Fusiliers
MOORE Frederick G. MM Cpl 30240 Royal Engineers
MOORE Frederick Reginald MM L/Cpl 46046 6th Northamptonshire Regt
MOORE George MM Pte 27699 Lancashire Fusiliers
MOORE George MM L/Cpl 14041 6th Northamptonshire Regt
MOORE George MM Pte 268111 1/5th Cheshire Regt
MOORE George Adams MM Pte 3187 7th Leinster Regt
MOORE George H. MM L/Sjt 2760 1st Welsh Guards
MOORE George H. MM L/Cpl 14139 2nd Royal Munster Fusiliers
MOORE George Harwood MM Pnr 128986 'F' Special Coy Royal Engineers Died 1.9.17.
MOORE George Henry MM L/Cpl 94447 13th Liverpool Regt KIA 24.4.18.
MOORE George M. MM Cpl 26452 8th Somerset Light Infantry
MOORE George Morris MM Sjt 10517 2nd Welsh Regt
MOORE George Nicoll MM Pte 305223 3 Fd Amb RAMC
MOORE Gilbert Lawrence MM Sjt 98040 RFA
MOORE Harold MM Pte 241664 5th Lincolnshire Regt
MOORE Harry MM Pte 6281 2nd Royal Sussex Regt
MOORE Harry MM Cpl 57655 122 Fd Coy Royal Engineers
MOORE Harry MM+Bar Gnr 87466 B/63 Bde RFA
MOORE Harry D. MM L/Cpl 33304 Worcestershire Regt
MOORE Harry Jack MM Cpl 1253 London Electrical Engineers Royal Engineers att 1/3(London)Fd Coy
MOORE Harry Walter MM L/Cpl 17087 2nd Hampshire Regt KIA 13.4.18.
MOORE Henry MM Sjt 146212 157 Siege Bty RGA
MOORE Henry MM L/Cpl 201151 Royal Berkshire Regt
MOORE Henry MM Pte 11426 Army Cyclist Corps
MOORE Herbert Douglas MM Pte 61400 13th Royal Fusiliers KIA 24.10.18.
MOORE Herbert J. MM L/Sjt K/730 22nd Royal Fusiliers
MOORE Herbert William MM Pte 16772 5th Northamptonshire Regt
MOORE Horace J. MM Sjt 470778 12th London Regt
MOORE Horace L. MM Sjt 19872 21st Manchester Regt
MOORE Howarth MM Pte 19894 1st Devonshire Regt
MOORE Hugh MM Pte 24649 South Staffordshire Regt
MOORE J. MM Pte 386211 RAMC
MOORE J. MM 2nd Cpl 16451 Royal Engineers
MOORE James MM Pte 6213 11/13th Royal Irish Rifles
MOORE James MM Pte 18968 12th Durham Light Infantry
MOORE James MM Sjt 37515 RGA
MOORE James MM Pte 18804 Durham Light Infantry
MOORE James A. MM L/Cpl 46786 Northumberland Fusiliers
MOORE James G. "DCM,MM+Bar" Sjt 27523 211 Siege Bty RGA
MOORE James George "MM,MID" Sjt Bugler 2744 2nd Rifle Brigade Died 5.7.18.
MOORE James H. MM Cpl 85968 Royal Engineers
MOORE James J. MM Cpl 5980 Gloucestershire Regt
MOORE James J. MM L/Cpl 16013 East Lancashire Regt
MOORE Jesse H. MM L/Cpl 13437 6th Dorsetshire Regt
MOORE John MM L/Cpl 57778 121 Fd Coy Royal Engineers
MOORE John MM Cpl 72263 Machine Gun Corps
MOORE John MM Pte 200156 Royal Lancaster Regt
MOORE John MM Spr 64591 36 Div Sig Coy Royal Engineers
MOORE John MM Cpl 44238 RFA

MOORE John MM Pte 15612 8th Royal Lancaster Regt
MOORE John E. MM Cpl 252550 2nd Manchester Regt
MOORE John E. MM Sjt 98694 Royal Engineers
MOORE John Elsted MM Pte 337543 RAMC
MOORE John G. MM L/Cpl 201310 1/9th Durham Light Infantry
MOORE John G. MM Pte 23832 RAMC
MOORE John G. MM Pte 9712 Middlesex Regt
MOORE John Sydney MM Bdr 26278 C/70 Bde RFA KIA 31.7.17.
MOORE John W. MM Pte 325886 1/9th Durham Light Infantry
MOORE John W.V. MM Pte 242437 Royal Warwickshire Regt
MOORE Joseph MM Sjt 337159 142 Heavy Bty RGA
MOORE Joseph MM Pte 277080 12th Manchester Regt
MOORE Joseph MM Sjt 106128 'K' Special Coy Royal Engineers
MOORE Joseph MM Sjt 24066 D/177 Bde RFA DOW 8.7.17.
MOORE Kenelm F. MM Cpl 4996 12th Royal Fusiliers
MOORE Leonard MM Pte 11543 9th Royal Inniskilling Fusiliers
MOORE Llewellyn MM Pte 9177 6th Somerset Light Infantry
MOORE Louis MM Pte 9133 Royal West Surrey Regt
MOORE Martin L. MM Pte 64707 RAMC
MOORE Matthew A. MM L/Cpl 3798 Seaforth Highlanders
MOORE Michael MM Pte 62196 RAMC Died 4.5.17.
MOORE N. "MM,MID" Flt Sjt 3697 Royal Flying Corps
MOORE Nolan Davis MM Sjt 3673 East Kent Regt
MOORE Norman C. MM Pte 307340 5th London Regt
MOORE Patrick MM Pte 8272 2nd Royal Dublin Fusiliers
MOORE Patrick MM Pte 13259 13th Cheshire Regt
MOORE Percy MM Cpl 98577 Royal Engineers
MOORE Percy MM Cpl 18042 7th Northamptonshire Regt DOW 19.10.17.
MOORE Percy J. MM Pte 9992 Leicestershire Regt
MOORE Peter MM Pte 7763 Irish Guards
MOORE Peter MM+Bar Cpl S/6085 2nd Arg & Suth Highlanders
MOORE R.J. MM Cpl 10237 Royal Lancaster Regt
MOORE R.M. MM Pte 33146 11th Essex Regt
MOORE Robert MM L/Cpl 14160 8th York & Lancaster Regt
MOORE Robert J. "MM,MID" Sjt 4992 9th Lancers
MOORE Robert McConnell MM Sjt 9/15621 Royal Irish Rifles KIA 27.3.18.
MOORE Rupert J. MM+Bar Gnr 52450 RFA
MOORE Samuel MM Bdr 89644 Y/6 Med TM Bty RFA
MOORE Samuel MM Drummer 9894 1/9th Arg & Suth Highlanders
MOORE Samuel W. "DCM,MM" Sjt 200500 1/4th Royal Berkshire Regt
MOORE Sidney MM Bugler 2553 1/6th London Regt
MOORE Stanley R. MM Sjt 19978 Machine Gun Corps
MOORE T.C. MM Pte 400538 Manchester Regt
MOORE Thomas MM Sjt 200186 1/5th Notts & Derby Regt
MOORE Thomas MM Pte 202905 16th Royal Warwickshire Regt
MOORE Thomas MM Pte 14299 8th South Staffordshire Regt
MOORE Thomas MM Sjt 13400 9th North Staffordshire Regt
MOORE Thomas MM Cpl 7720 1st Shropshire Light Infantry KIA 19.9.18.
MOORE Thomas MM Sjt 9678 2nd Highland Light Infantry
MOORE Thomas MM Pte 12222 12th East Surrey Regt DOW 6.5.18.
MOORE Thomas MM Bdr 876169 D/94 Bde RFA
MOORE Thomas F. MM L/Cpl 632924 20th London Regt
MOORE Thomas J. MM Spr 192316 Signal Service Royal Engineers
MOORE Tom MM L/Cpl 2976 11th Manchester Regt
MOORE W.E. MM Sjt 29712 130 Siege Bty RGA
MOORE Walter MM L/Cpl M2/034577 Army Service Corps
MOORE Walter MM Pnr 301515 Royal Engineers
MOORE Walter H. "MM,MID" QMS S/2/14783 Army Service Corps
MOORE Walter J. MM L/Cpl 14946 4th Royal Fusiliers
MOORE Walter John MM Cpl 3482 2nd Hampshire Regt DOW 9.12.17.
MOORE William MM L/Cpl 32019 1st Border Regt
MOORE William MM Pte 235335 5th Lancashire Fusiliers
MOORE William MM Sjt 9843 1st Royal Scots
MOORE William MM Pte 10651 Royal Sussex Regt
MOORE William MM Cpl 20444 1st Royal Scots
MOORE William MM+Bar Cpl 2235 1/4th East Yorkshire Regt
MOORE William "DCM,MM" Sjt 147125 186 Tunnelling Coy Royal Engineers
MOORE William MM L/Cpl 20240 14th Durham Light Infantry KIA 27.8.17.
MOORE William MM Pte S/25735 Rifle Brigade
MOORE William MM Pte 41195 Seaforth Highlanders
MOORE William MM Sjt 275708 2/7th Manchester Regt

MOORE William Basil MM Sjt 374241 122 Siege Bty RGA KIA 6.10.18.
MOORE William C. MM Gnr 44948 RFA
MOORE William F. MM+Bar Spr 75276 Royal Engineers
MOORE William H. MM L/Cpl 9268 2nd Royal Welsh Fusiliers
MOORE William H. MM+Bar L/Cpl 69282 35 Div Sig Coy Royal Engineers
MOORE William Henry MM Sjt 113264 Royal Engineers
MOORE William Henry MM Cpl 202789 1/5th Liverpool Regt DOW 20.4.18.
MOORE William J. MM Sjt 10039 2nd Durham Light Infantry
MOORE William J. MM Sjt 59186 41 Bde RFA
MOORE William Littlefair MM Sjt 9492 5th Wiltshire Regt
MOORE William R. MM Cpl 12568 6th Border Regt
MOORE William S. MM Sjt 26744 24 Heavy Bty RGA
MOORES Albert MM Pte 41568 52 Fd Amb RAMC
MOORES Arthur MM Pte 45751 15th Cheshire Regt
Moores Bruce Samuel Kirkman Guise "MC+Bar,MID" Lt RGA
MOORES George MM Pte 52563 Royal Welsh Fusiliers
MOORES Joe MM Cpl 64699 2nd Bn Machine Gun Corps
MOORES John MM Pte 1016 2nd Lancashire Fusiliers
MOORES Joseph MM Pte 11849 16th Lancashire Fusiliers
MOORES Samuel MM Dvr 5886 RFA
MOORES T. MM Sjt 1252 RFA
MOORES William MM RQMS 290387 1/7th Cheshire Regt
MOOREY A.E. MM Pte 5692 RAMC
MOORHEAD Robert MM Pte 304862 17th Armoured Car Bn Tank Corps
MOORHEAD William MM Sjt 14482 9th Royal Irish Fusiliers
MOORHOUSE Abraham MM Sjt 35337 33rd Bn Machine Gun Corps
MOORHOUSE Albert MM Pte 28011 63 Coy Machine Gun Corps KIA 4.9.18.
MOORHOUSE Albert E. MM Pte 27895 1st Lancashire Fusiliers
MOORHOUSE Charles J. "DCM,MM" Bdr 35015 12 Bde RFA
MOORHOUSE Edwin MM L/Cpl 201353 Yorkshire Light Infantry
MOORHOUSE H. MM Gnr 66816 9 Bde RFA
MOORHOUSE Harry B. MM Pte 266997 9th West Riding Regt
MOORHOUSE James MM Pnr 376819 Labour Corps
MOORHOUSE James Raynor MM Sjt 16469 6th King's Own Scottish Borderers KIA 10.12.16.
MOORHOUSE Richard MM Pte 39679 42nd Bn Machine Gun Corps
MOORLEY Samuel James MM Cpl R/10469 7th King's Royal Rifle Corps KIA 23.3.18.
MORALEE William MM Cpl 25/435 Northumberland Fusiliers
MORAN Arthur MM Bdr 27824 34 TM Bty RGA KIA 6.2.17.
MORAN Daniel MM Pte 9733 2nd Manchester Regt
MORAN Daniel MM L/Cpl 41064 Royal Irish Fusiliers
MORAN David MM Cpl 267422 2/7th Liverpool Regt
MORAN Denis MM Cpl 11427 2nd Royal Irish Regt
MORAN Ernest M. MM Pte 435190 1 Fd Amb RAMC
MORAN Frank J. MM Pte 8452 3rd Worcestershire Regt
MORAN George W. MM Pte 200443 Shropshire Light Infantry
MORAN George W.J. MM CSM T/24579 Army Service Corps
MORAN James MM Cpl 13008 9th Royal Dublin Fusiliers
MORAN James MM Pte 49761 2nd Royal Scots
MORAN James MM Sjt 242130 4th North Lancashire Regt
MORAN James MM Sjt 21693 1st Royal Lancaster Regt
MORAN John MM Pte 8895 9th Royal Irish Fusiliers
MORAN John MM Pte 67111 96 Fd Amb RAMC
MORAN John MM Sjt 129130 46th Royal Fusiliers
MORAN John MM Sjt 49108 Liverpool Regt
MORAN John MM L/Sjt 7586 Irish Guards
MORAN Joseph MM Gnr 707451 RFA
MORAN Joseph "DCM,MM,MID" Sjt 71773 Machine Gun Corps
MORAN Keith Alan MM Pte 4045 1/5th Liverpool Regt KIA 8.8.16.
MORAN Michael MM L/Bdr 41390 250 Siege Bty RGA
MORAN Patrick MM Drummer 17052 5th West Riding Regt
MORAN Peter MM Sjt 73 West Riding Regt
MORAN Peter MM L/Cpl 4/7789 West Yorkshire Regt
MORAN Thomas MM Spr 155895 257 Tunnelling Coy Royal Engineers
MORAN Thomas MM Pte 26925 10th Royal Dublin Fusiliers
MORAN Wallace MM Pte 44130 Machine Gun Corps
MORAN William MM L/Sjt 200125 North Staffordshire Regt
MORAN William H. MM Sjt 266098 Royal Highlanders
MORBY Ernest C. MM Pte 666 Lincolnshire Regt
MORDAUNT Edward P. MM L/Cpl 131279 45th Royal Fusiliers
MORDEY Richard MM Pte 20/331 Durham Light Infantry

MORDUE Nicholas G. MM Pte 43449 West Yorkshire Regt
MORE Alexander MM Pte 267331 1/6th Seaforth Highlanders DOW 21.11.17.
MORE John MM Pte 51105 1/6th Highland Light Infantry
MORE John G. MM Pte 2819 1/4th Leicestershire Regt
MORE Robert MM+Bar Sjt 200092 1/4th Seaforth Highlanders
MOREHEN Arthur MM Pte 251195 3rd London Regt
MORELAND J. MM Pte 7575 Gordon Highlanders
MORELAND Thomas MM Cpl 55652 RFA
MORELAND Thomas E. MM Gnr Sig 258265 C/177 Bde RFA
MOREMAN S. MM Air Mech 2 94039 Royal Flying Corps
MOREMAN Wilfred MM Gnr 78754 C/62 Bde RFA
MORETON Edward MM L/Cpl 8218 2nd Royal Welsh Fusiliers
MORETON Samuel C. MM Pte 60433 RAMC
MOREY Alfred H. MM Spr 242167 Royal Engineers
MOREY E.L. MM Sjt L/7083 1st East Kent Regt
MOREY William MM L/Cpl 6755 2nd Hampshire Regt
MORFEE John J. MM Cpl 43074 Machine Gun Corps
MORFETT Henry George MM Sjt 59354 154 Fd Coy Royal Engineers KIA 22.4.17.
MORGAN A. MM Pte 508202 RAMC
MORGAN A.N. MM+Bar Sjt 337100 RAMC
MORGAN Albert MM Cpl 1131 1/6th Gordon Highlanders
MORGAN Albert F. MM Sjt 42834 Machine Gun Corps
MORGAN Alfred MM Sjt 10931 1st Middlesex Regt
MORGAN Alfred MM Gnr 82218 C/150 Bde RFA KIA 10.6.18.
MORGAN Andrew MM Pte S/20567 1/6th Gordon Highlanders
MORGAN Archibald MM Pte 76907 4th Bn Tank Corps
MORGAN Arthur S. MM Pte 5166 6th Royal West Surrey Regt
MORGAN Arthur W. MM L/Cpl 12851 8th Yorkshire Light Infantry
MORGAN B. "MM,MID" L/Cpl 34880 Royal Engineers
MORGAN Benjamin MM Pte 320351 24th Welsh Regt
MORGAN Benjamin J. MM Pte 235602 14th Royal Welsh Fusiliers
MORGAN Bertie MM Pte R/19049 21st King's Royal Rifle Corps
MORGAN Cadwaladr T. MM Gnr 43126 RGA
MORGAN Cecil A. MM Sjt 61858 2 Bde RFA
MORGAN Charles MM Pte 9581 1st South Wales Borderers
MORGAN Charles Fenton MM Sjt 200230 Tank Corps
MORGAN Charles Henry MM Sjt 9966 2nd Border Regt KIA 1.7.16.
MORGAN Charles Henry MM Pte 24092 7th Shropshire Light Infantry DOW 11.5.17.
MORGAN Charles James MM Bdr 24889 RFA
MORGAN Charles W. MM Pte 28380 Northumberland Fusiliers
MORGAN Daniel "MM,MID" Pte 28544 Welsh Regt
MORGAN Daniel T. MM Pte 77790 142 Fd Amb RAMC
MORGAN David MM Pte 200767 1/5th Royal Warwickshire Regt
MORGAN David MM Sjt 14370 5th South Wales Borderers
MORGAN David MM L/Cpl 39945 15th Cheshire Regt
MORGAN David A. MM Pte 73780 19th Royal Welsh Fusiliers
MORGAN David Evan MM Dvr W/670 312 Bde RFA
MORGAN David J. MM Sjt 35162 13th Welsh Regt
MORGAN E.J. MM Pte 57202 Welsh Regt
MORGAN Edgar MM L/Sjt 954 1st Welsh Guards
MORGAN Edgar MM Spr 24035 Royal Engineers
MORGAN Edmund G. MM L/Cpl D/20804 2nd Dragoons
MORGAN Edward MM L/Cpl M2/032555 Army Service Corps
MORGAN Edward MM Pte 44343 Welsh Regt
MORGAN Edward MM Pte 571804 1/17th London Regt
MORGAN Edward MM Pte 22355 Welsh Regt
MORGAN Edward Thomas MM Cpl W/342 A/119 Bde RFA
MORGAN Ernest W. MM Pte 12747 1st Irish Guards
MORGAN Francis F. MM Sjt 20891 Royal Welsh Fusiliers
MORGAN Francis Norman MM Cpl(MCDR) 30361 Signal Service Royal Engineers
MORGAN Frank MM Pte 22131 Royal Berkshire Regt
MORGAN Frank MM Pte 27/1421 27th Northumberland Fusiliers KIA 25.4.17.
MORGAN Frederick MM Pte 4/9698 1st South Staffordshire Regt
MORGAN Frederick MM+Bar Gnr 51601 RFA
MORGAN Frederick G. MM Cpl 840414 RFA
MORGAN Fredrick Charles MM Pte 21/1566 8th Northumberland Fusiliers KIA 27.9.18.
MORGAN George MM+Bar L/Cpl 7370 Royal Fusiliers
MORGAN George MM CSM 5232 1st Gloucestershire Regt
MORGAN George MM Pte 200610 1/5th Manchester Regt
MORGAN George MM Cpl 290288 Royal Welsh Fusiliers
MORGAN George MM Cpl 16501 9th Yorkshire Light Infantry DOW 27.4.18.
MORGAN George Beaumont MM L/Cpl 5332 7th Royal Fusiliers Died 9.12.18.
MORGAN George F. MM Pte D/5884 7th Dragoon Guards
MORGAN George H. MM Pte 14323 8th Royal Berkshire Regt
MORGAN George J.E. MM Gnr 810140 RFA
MORGAN George S. MM Pte 8320 2nd Royal Welsh Fusiliers
MORGAN George Spencer "MC,MM+Bar(718 Sjt)" T/2Lt 123 Fd Coy Royal Engineers
MORGAN Gwilym MM Pte 8/15809 8th South Wales Borderers
MORGAN Harry MM L/Cpl 58903 11th Welsh Regt
MORGAN Harry MM Gnr L/323 B/163 Bde RFA
MORGAN Harry MM Pte 13916 7th Shropshire Light Infantry
MORGAN Henry MM Pte 14644 7th Bedfordshire Regt
MORGAN Henry MM Gnr 371152 RGA
MORGAN Henry W. MM L/Sjt 2831 Royal Warwickshire Regt
MORGAN Henry W. MM Sjt 89842 128 Fd Coy Royal Engineers
MORGAN Herbert MM Cpl 16884 Northumberland Fusiliers
MORGAN Herbert L. MM Spr 95920 3 Fd Sqn Royal Engineers
MORGAN Ivor John H. MM Sjt 265024 4th Liverpool Regt
MORGAN Ivor R. MM Cpl 16233 Royal Welsh Fusiliers
MORGAN J. MM Spr 560350 Royal Engineers
MORGAN J. MM Sjt 14568 10th Essex Regt
MORGAN J.D. MM Cpl 21202 South Wales Borderers
MORGAN J.W.W. "MM,MID" Sjt 9191 1st East Kent Regt
MORGAN James MM Sjt 30401 15th Durham Light Infantry
MORGAN James George MM(Z/16MTMB)+Bar(V/7HTMB) Cpl 47026 RGA
MORGAN James H. MM Pte 28791 Northumberland Fusiliers
MORGAN James R. MM Cpl 33240 15th Hampshire Regt
MORGAN John MM L/Cpl 8889 11th Royal Fusiliers
MORGAN John MM+Bar L/Cpl 11003 Cheshire Regt
MORGAN John MM Pte 20752 Manchester Regt
MORGAN John MM+Bar Dvr 80060 D/104 Bde RFA
MORGAN John MM Pte 203273 1/4th Hampshire Regt
MORGAN John MM Gnr 42401 19 Siege Bty RGA DOW 17.8.18.
MORGAN John F. "DCM,MM" Sjt 332380 2/9th Liverpool Regt
MORGAN John H. MM L/Cpl 56549 Machine Gun Corps
MORGAN John I. MM Gnr 606175 RFA
MORGAN John Thomas MM Gnr 174140 270 Siege Bty RGA
MORGAN Joseph MM Pte 201920 1/5th Liverpool Regt KIA 24.9.17.
MORGAN L. MM Bdr 348 400 Bty 14 Bde RFA
MORGAN Lawrence MM Pte 291174 Scottish Rifles
MORGAN Leonard J. MM Cpl 43367 12 Heavy Bty RGA
MORGAN Lewis H. MM Pte 27099 Royal Lancaster Regt
MORGAN Lewis L. MM Cpl 92186 9th Bn Tank Corps
MORGAN Morgan D. MM Pte 19693 10th York & Lancaster Regt
MORGAN Morgan J. MM L/Cpl 290 1st Welsh Guards
MORGAN Mozart MM Pte 14181 1st Devonshire Regt
MORGAN Norman MM Cpl 201350 1/5th Liverpool Regt
MORGAN Percy MM Sjt 20311 15th Welsh Regt
MORGAN Peter MM Pte 2036 7th Leinster Regt
MORGAN Peter MM Sjt 132847 161 Siege Bty RGA
MORGAN R. MM Pte 14162 Shropshire Light Infantry
MORGAN R.C. MM L/Cpl 43695 Durham Light Infantry
MORGAN R.E. MM Cpl 1859 RFA
MORGAN Richard MM L/Cpl 1910 4th Bn GMGR
MORGAN Richard MM Dvr 24382 RFA
MORGAN Richard G. MM Pte 15818 9th York & Lancaster Regt
MORGAN Richard J. MM L/Cpl 23082 9 Fd Coy Royal Engineers
MORGAN Robert MM Spr 49495 Royal Engineers
MORGAN Robert MM Cpl W/8 B/62 Bde RFA KIA 11.3.18.
MORGAN Robert MM Pte 3324 11th Durham Light Infantry
MORGAN Robert MM L/Cpl 5082 XIV Corps Cyclist Bn Army Cyclist Corps
MORGAN Robert W. MM 2nd Cpl 61873 83 Fd Coy Royal Engineers
MORGAN Rufus MM Gnr 59456 RGA
MORGAN Samuel MM Pte 42894 Machine Gun Corps
MORGAN Sidney MM L/Cpl 325715 1/9th Durham Light Infantry
MORGAN Stanley MM Pte 33510 Royal Scots Fusiliers
MORGAN Thomas MM Pte 10988 8th Devonshire Regt
MORGAN Thomas MM Pte 59048 20th Middlesex Regt
MORGAN Thomas MM Pte 3076 9th Lancashire Fusiliers
MORGAN Thomas MM Cpl 9892 2nd East Lancashire Regt
MORGAN Thomas MM L/Sjt 14735 1st South Wales Borderers DOW 10.11.17.
MORGAN Thomas MM Gnr 663064 RFA
MORGAN Thomas MM Sjt 10501 Cameron Highlanders
MORGAN Thomas MM Pte 56735 Royal Welsh Fusiliers
MORGAN Thomas H. MM Pte 11408 6th Dorsetshire Regt
MORGAN Thomas P. MM Pte 20047 10th Hussars
MORGAN Thomas W. MM L/Sjt 9287 7th Norfolk Regt

MORGAN Tom Harold MM Sjt 18622 C/93 Bde RFA
MORGAN Victor "DCM,MM" L/Cpl 889 1st King Edward's Horse
MORGAN W. MM+Bar Gnr W/1857 B/119 Bde RFA
MORGAN W. MM+Bar Cpl 1611 1st Lancashire Fusiliers
MORGAN W. MM Air Mech 1 10500 Royal Flying Corps
MORGAN Walter MM Cpl 8352 10th Royal Warwickshire Regt
MORGAN Walter Henry MM Sjt 44608 12th Royal Irish Rifles
MORGAN Wilfred MM L/Cpl G/1930 7th Royal West Surrey Regt
MORGAN Wilfred Charles MM Bdr 1437 A/84 Bde RFA
MORGAN William MM Cpl 14231 Devonshire Regt
MORGAN William MM Bdr 166857 A/251 Bde RFA
MORGAN William MM L/Cpl 18100 1st Gordon Highlanders KIA 27.9.18.
MORGAN William MM Pte 22350 13th Welsh Regt
MORGAN William MM Pte 6293 19 Fd Amb RAMC
MORGAN William MM Pte 5892 Coldstream Guards
MORGAN William MM Pte 5639 12th Manchester Regt
MORGAN William MM Cpl 10352 2nd East Surrey Regt
MORGAN William MM Gnr 31812 109 Heavy Bty RGA
MORGAN William Albert MM L/Cpl 12757 8th Yorkshire Regt KIA 10.7.16.
MORGAN William Alexander MM Cpl 56725 54 Bty 15 Bde RFA
MORGAN William G. MM Pte 200207 Shropshire Light Infantry
MORGAN William H. MM Sjt 29563 RGA
MORGAN William Henry MM+Bar Cpl 33011 Yorkshire Regt KIA 27.8.18.
MORGAN William J. "MM,MID" Pte 9615 2nd South Wales Borderers
MORGAN William R. MM Pte 4297 XIV Corps Cyclist Bn Army Cyclist Corps
MORGAN William R. MM Pte 16535 Royal Fusiliers
MORGAN William T. MM Pte 17248 10th Yorkshire Light Infantry
MORGAN William W. MM Pte 66757 47th Bn Machine Gun Corps
MORGANS James William MM Cpl 74394 RFA
MORGANS John MM Spr 74007 'SX' Cable Section Royal Engineers
MORGANS Rees MM Pte 25396 Welsh Regt
MORIARTY Cornelius MM L/Sjt 25265 2nd Royal Berkshire Regt
MORIARTY John MM Pte 292271 14th Royal Welsh Fusiliers
MORIARTY John James MM Pte R/11929 10th King's Royal Rifle Corps KIA 10.8.17.
MORIARTY Michael MM Pte 5450 2nd Royal Munster Fusiliers
MORING Alfred MM Pte 241799 Royal West Kent Regt
MORING Sidney Thomas MM Pte 201234 1/4th Northamptonshire Regt
MORITZ Harold Charles MM L/Sjt 530841 15th London Regt
MORITZ W. MM L/Cpl M2/106053 Army Service Corps
MORLAND Hermon H. MM Pte 291662 Gordon Highlanders
MORLAND Robin Carlyle MM Pte 52005 2/7th Liverpool Regt KIA 1.9.18.
MORLAND William MM L/Cpl 22486 Durham Light Infantry
MORLEY Albert Edward George MM Dvr 931607 291 Bde RFA
MORLEY Albert W. MM Pte 8436 Royal West Surrey Regt
MORLEY Alfred Edward MM+Bar Sjt 200106 1/5th Liverpool Regt
MORLEY Alfred L. MM Pte 50830 Cheshire Regt
MORLEY Eric MM Pte 22368 8th Norfolk Regt
MORLEY Ernest Cyril MM Cpl 14/570 14th York & Lancaster Regt
MORLEY Ernest L. MM Cpl 84604 Royal Engineers
MORLEY Frank MM Sjt 26523 Notts & Derby Regt
MORLEY Frank L. MM Cpl 29077 Royal Fusiliers
MORLEY Frederick S. MM+Bar Pte 11716 Royal West Surrey Regt
MORLEY Frederick W. MM Pte 43883 Royal Inniskilling Fusiliers
MORLEY George N. MM CSM 14457 Suffolk Regt
MORLEY George Thomas MM Sjt 8089 Coldstream Guards KIA 24.3.18.
MORLEY Henry MM Pte 13504 10th Yorkshire Regt
MORLEY Hubert MM L/Cpl 23525 9th West Riding Regt
MORLEY James MM Pte 270108 12th Royal Scots
MORLEY John "DCM,MM" Cpl 27824 8th Royal Lancaster Regt
MORLEY Michael R. MM Spr 82769 Royal Engineers
MORLEY Oswald MM Cpl M2/034632 272 Coy Army Service Corps att RFA.
MORLEY Percy MM Gnr 37443 115 Heavy Bty RGA
MORLEY Richard W. MM Gnr 194197 RFA
MORLEY Robert William MM Pte 41102 16th Northumberland Fusiliers
MORLEY Stanley W. MM Pte 70281 Machine Gun Corps
MORLEY T.H. MM Dvr 796906 RFA
MORLEY Tom MM Sjt 201164 Notts & Derby Regt
MORLEY Victor E. MM Pte 203016 Middlesex Regt
MORLEY Walter A. MM+Bar Sjt 44252 2nd Worcestershire Regt
MORLEY William MM Sjt 3/5911 7th Duke of Cornwall's LI
MORLEY William A. MM Pte 40335 RAMC
MORLEY William G. MM Cpl 5608 RGA
MORNAN John MM L/Bdr 776494 Y/62 Med TM Bty RFA
MOROM Charles H. MM RSM 2392 Royal Warwickshire Regt
MORPETH Samuel MM Pte 25/1124 1st Northumberland Fusiliers KIA 20.11.17.
MORPETH William MM Gnr 751052 RFA
MORPHETT Ronald MM Pte 207614 10th Royal West Surrey Regt
MORRALL Harry MM CSM 241129 6th Liverpool Regt
MORRAN William MM Dvr 47413 366 Bty RFA
MORRELL Alfred A. MM Pte 8911 Shropshire Light Infantry
MORRELL C. MM Sjt P8088 Military Mounted Police
MORRELL Charles A. MM L/Cpl 34488 9th York & Lancaster Regt
MORRELL Ernest MM Gnr 138516 D/71 Bde RFA
MORRELL Fred MM Spr 175851 Tunnelling Coy Royal Engineers
MORRELL Henry MM Sjt M2/119391 611 MT Coy Army Service Corps att 46 SB RGA.Died 26.6.18.
MORRELL Joseph MM L/Cpl 200123 1/5th Notts & Derby Regt KIA 3.10.18.
MORRELL Neil MM Pte 421127 RAMC
MORRELL Robert MM L/Sjt 10125 Durham Light Infantry
MORRELL William MM Cpl 76467 Tank Corps
MORREN Andrew MM L/Cpl 202474 Gordon Highlanders
MORREY Albert MM Pnr 129654 1 Special Coy Royal Engineers DOW 8.8.18.
MORREY Albert MM Pte R/34261 11th King's Royal Rifle Corps
MORREY Arthur MM Gnr 805808 RFA
MORRICE Allen MM+Bar Dvr 650099 C/86 Bde RFA
MORRICE James G. MM Pte 290982 Gordon Highlanders
MORRILL Albert Edward MM Pte 2650 1/20th London Regt
MORRIN Thomas MM Gnr 228085 463 Bty 179 Bde RFA
MORRIS A. MM Pte 242658 7th Middlesex Regt
MORRIS A.M. MM Sjt 12640 1st Grenadier Guards
MORRIS Albert MM Pte 44482 20th Manchester Regt
MORRIS Albert MM CQMS 3886 21st Bn Machine Gun Corps
MORRIS Albert MM Sjt 150107 AA Bty RGA
MORRIS Albert MM L/Cpl 320646 6th London Regt
MORRIS Albert MM Sjt 5105 Lancashire Fusiliers
MORRIS Albert MM Pte 39451 RAMC
MORRIS Albert C. MM Sjt 618254 RFA
MORRIS Albert E. MM Cpl S/27771 1st Rifle Brigade
MORRIS Albert E. MM Pte 1438 7th Royal West Surrey Regt
MORRIS Albert Edward MM Sjt 8047 9th Bn Machine Gun Corps DOW 23.5.18.
MORRIS Albert J. MM Sjt 8481 1st Somerset Light Infantry
MORRIS Albert Thomas MM L/Cpl 46263 61st Bn Machine Gun Corps
MORRIS Alfred MM Sjt 200388 1/4th Royal Lancaster Regt
MORRIS Alfred MM Pte 201676 Lancashire Fusiliers
MORRIS Alfred John MM Pte 200220 1/1st London Regt
MORRIS Alfred William "MM,MID" Sjt 13647 C/76 Bde RFA
MORRIS Arthur MM Pte 16237 1st Coldstream Guards
MORRIS Arthur A. MM Pte M1/6826 91 MT Coy Army Service Corps
MORRIS Arthur C. MM Sjt 312712 'F'(AA)Bty RGA
MORRIS Arthur Clarence MM Dvr 810021 RFA
MORRIS Arthur W. MM Pte 10178 10th Hampshire Regt
MORRIS Arthur William MM Dvr L/7837 RFA
MORRIS Benjamin MM Pte 70914 19 Coy Machine Gun Corps DOW 19.4.18.
MORRIS Benjamin R. MM Sjt 20549 15th Welsh Regt
MORRIS Beriah MM L/Cpl 241070 9th Yorkshire Light Infantry DOW 8.9.18.
MORRIS Bert MM Sjt 41574 8 Bde RFA
MORRIS Bert K. MM L/Sjt 10474 9th Worcestershire Regt
MORRIS Cecil Ernest MM Pte 6705 Shropshire Light Infantry
MORRIS Cecil J. MM Pnr 316322 Royal Engineers
MORRIS Charles MM Pte 421155 3(North Midland)Fd Amb RAMC
MORRIS Charles MM Pte 41999 Machine Gun Corps
MORRIS Charles H. MM Gnr 71362 RGA
MORRIS Charles J. MM Pte 26650 7th East Kent Regt
MORRIS Charles R. MM Sjt 15533 2nd Bedfordshire Regt
MORRIS David MM Pte 25/1127 Northumberland Fusiliers
MORRIS Douglas G. MM Bdr 835538 RFA
MORRIS Eben MM Pte 7551 1/4th Royal Welsh Fusiliers KIA 6.4.18.
MORRIS Edward MM Pte 88367 17th Liverpool Regt
MORRIS Edward MM Pte 14105 7th Dragoon Guards
MORRIS Edward MM L/Cpl 12797 East Surrey Regt

MORRIS Edward Arnold MM Pte L/11484 Royal West Surrey Regt
MORRIS Edward G. MM+Bar Sjt 53287 RFA
MORRIS Edward H. MM Pte M/334383 620 MT Coy Army Service Corps
MORRIS Edwin James MM Sjt 9848 Machine Gun Corps
MORRIS Ernest Charles MM L/Cpl 17166 2nd South Staffordshire Regt
MORRIS Ernest J. MM L/Bdr W/4851 D/121 Bde RFA
MORRIS Ernest S. MM Sjt 432024 55 Div Sig Coy Royal Engineers
MORRIS Francis H. "DCM,MM" CSM 19840 105 Coy Machine Gun Corps
MORRIS Frank MM Pte 241237 1/5th North Lancashire Regt
MORRIS Frank "MM,MID" Cpl 15594 107 Bty 23 Bde RFA
MORRIS Frank E. MM Pte 433093 RAMC
MORRIS Fred MM Pte 7542 Coldstream Guards
MORRIS Frederick MM Cpl 50132 9th Cheshire Regt
MORRIS Frederick MM Pte 3474 8th Worcestershire Regt
MORRIS Frederick MM L/Cpl 109 7th East Surrey Regt
MORRIS Frederick S. MM L/Cpl 25251 62 Fd Coy Royal Engineers
MORRIS George MM Dvr 6349 31 Bty 35 Bde RFA
MORRIS George MM Gnr 685783 RFA
MORRIS George MM Pte 4/13108 1st South Wales Borderers KIA 8.9.16.
MORRIS George MM L/Cpl 14044 6th Northamptonshire Regt KIA 14.7.16.
MORRIS George MM L/Cpl 276020 1/7th Manchester Regt
MORRIS George F. MM+Bar L/Cpl 17424 2 Div Sig Coy Royal Engineers
MORRIS George H. MM Pte 53529 Cheshire Regt
MORRIS George H. MM+Bar Cpl 122137 25th Bn Machine Gun Corps
MORRIS George R. MM L/Cpl 1852 Royal Engineers
MORRIS George Rowland "MM,MSM" QMS 11613 7 Fd Amb RAMC
MORRIS H. MM Pte 12211 7th Duke of Cornwall's LI
MORRIS Harold MM Pte 515273 14th London Regt
MORRIS Harold MM L/Cpl 26130 Royal Lancaster Regt
MORRIS Harry MM Pte 945 14th Royal Warwickshire Regt
MORRIS Harry MM Pte 12889 6th Shropshire Light Infantry
MORRIS Henry MM Pte 227958 1st Monmouthshire Regt
MORRIS Henry J. MM Pte C/9318 King's Royal Rifle Corps
MORRIS Henry T. MM Pte 42121 4th Worcestershire Regt
MORRIS Herbert MM Gnr 131604 125 Hy Bty RGA
MORRIS Herbert M. MM Spr 72226 Royal Engineers
MORRIS Herbert W. MM Pte 14941 8th Suffolk Regt
MORRIS Hugh MM Pte 13106 7th South Lancashire Regt DOW 18.12.16.
MORRIS Hugh Tregerthen MM Sjt 43786 19 Div Sig Coy Royal Engineers DOW 29.4.18.
MORRIS Ivor R. MM Pte 25523 Welsh Regt
MORRIS J.G. MM Sjt 77982 Royal Flying Corps
MORRIS James MM Pte 591579 1/18th London Regt
MORRIS James MM Pte 18427 Royal Irish Regt
MORRIS James MM Gnr 167197 RFA
MORRIS James MM Pte 2209 Durham Light Infantry
MORRIS James MM Sjt 40199 1/1st City of London Yeo KIA 21.11.17.
MORRIS James C. MM Pte 46093 17th Royal Welsh Fusiliers
MORRIS James Henry MM L/Sjt 18204 6th Royal Lancaster Regt
MORRIS James Lawrence MM Pte 61312 5th Northumberland Fusiliers KIA 28.9.18.
MORRIS John MM Spr 360017 25 Div Sig Coy Royal Engineers
MORRIS John MM Pte 17991 1/5th Yorkshire Regt DOW 1.4.18.
MORRIS John "DCM,MM+Bar" Sjt 240197 1/6th South Staffordshire Regt
MORRIS John MM Sjt 372 Durham Light Infantry
MORRIS John MM Pte 34348 Lancashire Fusiliers
MORRIS John MM+Bar L/Cpl 43948 17 Div Sig Coy Royal Engineers
MORRIS John Oliver MM Gnr 186195 RGA
MORRIS John S. MM Pte 202605 1/6th Seaforth Highlanders
MORRIS John S. MM Cpl 59394 18th Bn Machine Gun Corps
MORRIS John T. MM Pte 6130 6th Dragoons
MORRIS John Thomp(son) MM CSM 6371 Duke of Cornwall's LI
MORRIS John W. MM Pte 32186 Lancashire Fusiliers
MORRIS John W. MM Gnr 1459 RFA
MORRIS Johnston MM Pte 31384 27 Fd Amb RAMC
MORRIS Joseph MM Cpl 51077 Royal Engineers att RGA.
MORRIS Joseph MM Pte M2/155899 Army Service Corps att 240 Siege Bty RGA.
MORRIS Joseph MM Pte 325474 1/9th Durham Light Infantry

MORRIS Joseph MM Gnr 31121 2 Bde RFA
MORRIS L.C. MM Bdr W/1032 RFA
MORRIS Lawrence MM Pte 241631 8th Worcestershire Regt
MORRIS Leonard MM Cpl 241792 5th Royal Lancaster Regt
MORRIS Leonard G. MM L/Sjt 11317 11th Hampshire Regt
MORRIS Lionel George Pattison MM Sjt 530072 2/15th London Regt
MORRIS Llewellyn MM Sjt 28843 C/88 Bde RFA
MORRIS Louis S.V. MM Pte 241420 Middlesex Regt
MORRIS Michael MM L/Cpl 27125 13th Cheshire Regt
MORRIS Morris H. MM+Bar Pte 15427 10th Royal Welsh Fusiliers
MORRIS Owen Corby MM Pte 17388 7th Royal Sussex Regt KIA 26.8.18.
MORRIS P. MM Pte 337320 RAMC
MORRIS P. MM L/Cpl 201356 North Lancashire Regt
MORRIS Percy MM Pte 31533 11th East Lancashire Regt
MORRIS Percy MM Sjt 27542 RGA
MORRIS Peter MM Cpl 7803 Royal Irish Regt
MORRIS Peter MM Sjt 12526 7th South Lancashire Regt KIA 22.7.17.
MORRIS Peter George MM Cpl 100779 111 Fd Amb RAMC DOW 1.4.18.
MORRIS Phillip MM Gnr 28743 A/113 Bde RFA
MORRIS R. MM Dvr 2407 RFA
MORRIS Reginald Albert MM Sjt R/8277 7th King's Royal Rifle Corps KIA 29.4.17.
MORRIS Richard MM L/Cpl 16075 7th Shropshire Light Infantry KIA 21.8.18.
MORRIS Richard MM Pte 18548 15th Welsh Regt
MORRIS Robert MM Pte 38710 1/7th Royal Scots
MORRIS Robert "DCM,MM" L/Cpl 331114 Liverpool Regt Att KAR.
MORRIS Robert MM Pte 240384 8th Royal West Kent Regt
MORRIS Robert Lewis MM Pte 49775 1st Cheshire Regt
MORRIS Samuel MM Pte 53065 11th Manchester Regt
MORRIS Samuel MM L/Cpl 17619 7th Shropshire Light Infantry
MORRIS Sidney MM Gnr 800999 RFA
MORRIS Sidney MM Pte 71426 Notts & Derby Regt
MORRIS Sidney MM Pte 43141 1st Royal Scots Fusiliers DOW 25.4.17.
MORRIS Stanier S. "DCM,MM" Sjt 121960 184 Tunnelling Coy Royal Engineers
MORRIS Stanley MM Pte 355143 25th Royal Welsh Fusiliers
MORRIS Stephen MM Bdr 48004 49 Bty 40 Bde RFA KIA 4.5.17.
MORRIS Stephen MM Pte 1834 RAMC
MORRIS T. MM Pte 241107 Liverpool Regt
MORRIS T.R. MM Pte 60564 23rd Middlesex Regt
MORRIS Thomas MM L/Sjt 11518 9th Royal Welsh Fusiliers
MORRIS Thomas MM Sjt 31681 337 Siege Bty RGA
MORRIS Thomas MM Cpl 8238 South Lancashire Regt
MORRIS Thomas MM+Bar L/Sjt 18988 1st Border Regt
MORRIS Thomas MM Sjt 18716 Royal Inniskilling Fusiliers
MORRIS Thomas MM Pte 14264 10th Northumberland Fusiliers
MORRIS Thomas MM Pte M2/113087 607 MT Coy Army Service Corps
MORRIS Thomas MM Pte 43109 Royal Scots Fusiliers
MORRIS Thomas Chisnall MM Pte 70210 17th Royal Welsh Fusiliers
MORRIS Thomas James MM L/Cpl 241887 6th Liverpool Regt
MORRIS Thomas William MM Dvr 542 3(Northumbrian)Bde RFA
MORRIS Tom MM Pte 73621 47 Fd Amb RAMC
MORRIS W. MM Gnr 3090 RFA
MORRIS W. MM L/Cpl 200938 Leicestershire Regt
MORRIS W. MM Pte 10295 Grenadier Guards
MORRIS W.A. MM Pte 575452 17th London Regt
MORRIS W.H. MM BSM 9636 4(Durham)Howitzer Bty RFA
MORRIS W.H. MM Sjt W/1015 119 Bde RFA
MORRIS Walter MM Dvr 249385 A/83 Bde RFA
MORRIS Walter MM Sjt 15261 19th Lancashire Fusiliers
MORRIS Walter MM Sjt 9289 1st Somerset Light Infantry
MORRIS Walter C. MM Bdr 14095 42 Bde RFA
MORRIS Walter D. MM Pte 2286 1/6th London Regt
MORRIS Walter J. MM Gnr 810211 RFA
MORRIS Wilfred MM Sjt 25656 22nd Manchester Regt
MORRIS Wilfred MM CSM 426028 Royal Engineers
MORRIS William MM Pte 142929 3rd Bn Machine Gun Corps
MORRIS William "See MEDLEY, William, CSM 200441."
MORRIS William MM Pte 29271 East Surrey Regt
MORRIS William MM Pte 12768 7th Royal Lancaster Regt
MORRIS William MM L/Cpl 18006 1st Royal Lancaster Regt KIA 4.1.18.

MORRIS William MM BQMS 23148 41 Div Ammn Col RFA
MORRIS William MM Pte 61273 Northumberland Fusiliers
MORRIS William MM Pte 18526 East Lancashire Regt
MORRIS William MM Pte 8207 1st South Wales Borderers
MORRIS William G. MM L/Sjt 5975 9th Seaforth Highlanders
MORRIS William G. MM Pte 235181 Yorkshire Regt
MORRIS William H. MM L/Cpl 37334 Royal Welsh Fusiliers
MORRIS William Herbert MM Pte 202150 2/6th Royal Warwickshire Regt KIA 1.11.18.
MORRIS William J. MM Cpl 17756 10th Notts & Derby Regt
MORRIS William J. MM 2nd Cpl 1069 Royal Engineers
MORRIS William J.P. MM Pte 4147 HAC
MORRISEY Thomas "MM,MID" L/Cpl 7218 2nd Leinster Regt
MORRISEY Thomas MM+Bar Cpl 23002 2nd Royal Dublin Fusiliers
MORRISH Ernest G. MM Pte S/3011 1st Rifle Brigade
MORRISH Frederick Arthur MM Cpl 966545 B/303 Bde RFA
MORRISH Percy V. "MM,MID" Sjt 12824 281 Army Troops Coy Royal Engineers
MORRISH William Richard "DCM,MM,MID" Sjt 2821 33 Div Sig Coy Royal Engineers
MORRISON A. MM Pte 303297 RAMC
MORRISON A. MM Pte 200274 Royal Highlanders
MORRISON Albert MM Cpl 384 8th Royal Fusiliers
MORRISON Alexander MM Pte 11010 2nd Royal Scots Fusiliers
MORRISON Alexander MM Pte 201832 1/4th Seaforth Highlanders KIA 9.4.18.
MORRISON Allan MM Pte 1801 1/4th Gordon Highlanders
MORRISON Andrew MM Cpl 200547 Seaforth Highlanders
MORRISON Andrew MM Sjt 9737 1st King's Own Scottish Borderers
MORRISON Charles MM Pte 34028 7th Scottish Rifles
MORRISON Charles Hendrie MM L/Cpl 44016 6th King's Own Scottish Borderers
MORRISON Donald MM Gnr 6772 B/240 Bde RFA
MORRISON Edward MM Pte 2817 1/9th Highland Light Infantry
MORRISON Edward "MM,MID" Sjt 406144 Royal Engineers
MORRISON Ewen "DCM,MM" Sjt 40530 2nd Seaforth Highlanders
MORRISON F. MM Sjt 202641 Gordon Highlanders
MORRISON Frederick W. MM Sjt 48158 103 Fd Coy Royal Engineers
MORRISON Garnet Robert MM Pte 2002 1/2nd London Regt
MORRISON George MM Pte 22951 Royal Scots Fusiliers
MORRISON George MM Pte 88173 RAMC
MORRISON George MM Pte S/43040 Seaforth Highlanders
MORRISON George Mackay MM Sjt 46484 Machine Gun Corps
MORRISON Harry Moore MM L/Sjt 19983 26th Royal Fusiliers
MORRISON James MM+Bar Sjt 291137 5/6th Scottish Rifles
MORRISON James MM Pte 11048 2nd Royal Scots Fusiliers
MORRISON James MM+Bar Cpl 38618 RGA
MORRISON James MM Gnr 63835 RGA
MORRISON James MM Pte 41629 Highland Light Infantry
MORRISON James A.F. MM Spr 400562 Royal Engineers
MORRISON James D. MM Bdr 78519 RFA
MORRISON James Francis MM Pte 240589 Cheshire Regt
MORRISON John MM Pte 265355 1/4th Seaforth Highlanders
MORRISON John MM Pte 8/13295 8th Royal Irish Rifles
MORRISON John MM Pte 202267 Royal Highlanders
MORRISON John MM Sjt 47672 D/71 Bde RFA
MORRISON John MM Pte 41327 9th Royal Irish Fusiliers
MORRISON John MM Cpl 106387 Royal Engineers
MORRISON John MM Pte 3/5436 1/4th Cameron Highlanders
MORRISON John "MM+Bar,MID" Pte 1772 2nd Royal Highlanders
MORRISON John "MM,MID" Cpl 3795 2(Cavalry)Fd Amb RAMC
MORRISON John MM Pte 2866 1/7th Arg & Suth Highlanders
MORRISON John MM Cpl 6896 1st Seaforth Highlanders
MORRISON John C. MM CSM 18895 Gordon Highlanders
MORRISON John P. MM Pte 29339 Machine Gun Corps
MORRISON John S. MM Pte 3184 Gordon Highlanders
MORRISON Joseph MM L/Cpl 1964 1st Irish Guards
MORRISON Joseph W. MM Pte 149192 31st Bn Machine Gun Corps
MORRISON Malcolm MM Sjt 20389 1st Bn Machine Gun Corps
MORRISON Matthew W. MM+Bar Sjt 14147 7th Cameron Highlanders
MORRISON Michael Devaney MM L/Cpl 40938 Lincolnshire Regt
MORRISON Patrick M. MM+Bar Cpl 301052 RAMC
MORRISON Peter MM L/Cpl 6485 8th Royal Highlanders
MORRISON Peter MM Pte 10667 1st King's Own Scottish Borderers
MORRISON Peter G. MM L/Cpl 252239 2/6th Manchester Regt
MORRISON Robert MM Cpl 2379 Royal Engineers
MORRISON Robert MM Pte D/10615 2nd Dragoons
MORRISON Robert MM Sjt 12603 10th Scottish Rifles
MORRISON Robert McA. MM L/Sjt 361 1/5th Seaforth Highlanders KIA 21.3.18.
MORRISON Roderick MM Pte 7501 2nd Scots Guards
MORRISON Thomas MM Pte 295172 12th Royal Scots Fusiliers
MORRISON Thomas A. MM Pte 25717 10th Royal West Surrey Regt
MORRISON Thomas R. MM Pte 16/237 16th Northumberland Fusiliers
MORRISON W. MM Pte 3/8840 1st Royal Highlanders
MORRISON Walter MM Pte 15040 5/6th Royal Scots
MORRISON Walter C. MM Pte 40300 2nd Royal Scots Fusiliers
MORRISON William MM Sjt 630307 A/255 Bde RFA
MORRISON William MM Dvr 167194 C/56 Bde RFA
MORRISON William MM Dvr 90941 Royal Engineers
MORRISON William MM Pte 15791 1st Cameron Highlanders
MORRISROE John MM Pte 3410 7th Leinster Regt
MORRISSEY James MM Pte 623 1st Welsh Guards
MORRISSEY Martin F. MM+Bar L/Sjt 10354 1st Irish Guards
MORRISSEY Patrick MM Pte 12106 6th Royal Dublin Fusiliers
MORRISSEY Patrick MM Bdr 5975 23 Heavy Artillery Group RGA
MORRISSY Thomas MM Sjt 38443 RFA
MORRITT Frederick MM Sjt 16361 2nd Scots Guards
MORRITT George MM Sjt 19801 96 Bty 19 Bde RFA
MORROUGH John J. "MM,MID" Sjt 5117 2nd Suffolk Regt
MORROW Alexander MM Pte 23312 Royal Scots Fusiliers
MORROW Arthur MM Cpl 11101 6th Royal West Kent Regt
MORROW Frederick MM Pte 2169 6th East Kent Regt
MORROW H. MM L/Cpl 8754 Royal Scots
MORROW Horace Louis MM Pte 11165 11th Hampshire Regt KIA 21.11.17.
MORROW Joseph MM L/Cpl 12/19705 12th Royal Irish Rifles
MORSE Albert Edward MM Sjt 7124 1st Gloucestershire Regt
MORSE Ernest MM Sjt 10487 15th Welsh Regt
MORSE Harold E. MM Pte 2844 1/1st Hertfordshire Regt
MORSE John H. MM Sjt 84960 Royal Engineers
MORSE William MM L/Cpl 13646 1st Scots Guards
MORT James MM Sjt 1499 Gordon Highlanders
MORTE Arthur MM Pte 241049 West Riding Regt
MORTER William John "MM,CG(F)" Spr 85698 Royal Engineers
MORTIMER Alexander MM Gnr 876510 Y/19 Med TM Bty RFA
MORTIMER E.J. MM L/Cpl 38200 9th Essex Regt
MORTIMER Ebenezer MM Pte 12774 11th West Yorkshire Regt
MORTIMER Edward MM Dmr 6885 9th Notts & Derby Regt KIA 27.2.18.
MORTIMER Francis J. MM Pte 30108 2nd Royal Dublin Fusiliers
MORTIMER Frederick G. MM Cpl 12794 1st Bedfordshire Regt
MORTIMER Gilbert MM Bdr 74727 69 Heavy Artillery Group RGA
MORTIMER H.D. MM Cpl 1551 17th Lancers
MORTIMER Henry J. "MM+Bar,MSM" Sjt 8001 1st Royal Berkshire Regt
MORTIMER Hugh Herbert MM Pte 16961 13th Hussars
MORTIMER J.W. MM Pte 34510 York & Lancaster Regt
MORTIMER James MM L/Cpl 4876 2nd Northumberland Fusiliers
MORTIMER John G. MM Cpl 21371 2nd York & Lancaster Regt
MORTIMER John Wilfred MM Gnr 149776 115 Siege Bty RGA
MORTIMER Joseph MM L/Cpl 200153 West Riding Regt
MORTIMER Peter MM Sjt 292957 1/7th Royal Highlanders KIA 26.3.18.
MORTIMER Rufus MM Pte 268661 1/7th West Yorkshire Regt KIA 15.10.18.
MORTIMER Samuel MM Sjt 52605 B/'77 Bde RFA
MORTIMER Walter MM Cpl 52433 RAMC
MORTIMER Walter James MM Sjt 9714 11th Essex Regt Died 6.4.18.
MORTIMER William MM Sjt 6475 2nd King's Royal Rifle Corps
MORTIMER William MM Pte 38088 Lancashire Fusiliers
MORTIMER William E. MM Sjt 761 9th Royal Fusiliers
MORTIMER William J. MM Pte 11790 East Surrey Regt
MORTIMER William W. MM Pte 241731 Lincolnshire Regt
MORTIMORE Alfred MM L/Cpl G/23712 10th Royal West Kent Regt
MORTLOCK G.W. MM Pte 47463 11 Fd Amb RAMC
MORTLOCK George W. MM L/Cpl 35169 Royal Warwickshire Regt
MORTLOCK Herbert MM Pte 15937 1/1st Cambridgeshire Regt
MORTON A. MM Pte 2500 York & Lancaster Regt
MORTON A.L. MM Cpl 1014 GMGR
MORTON Adam MM Pte 6978 5/6th Scottish Rifles
MORTON Albert MM Gnr 756112 RFA

MORTON Alexander MM Pte 306267 1/8th Liverpool Regt KIA 20.9.17.
MORTON Alfred MM Cpl 89263 RFA
MORTON Arthur T. MM Pte 12110 7th Norfolk Regt
MORTON Charles MM Sjt 14537 Norfolk Regt
MORTON Cyril MM Pte 24079 South Wales Borderers
MORTON David MM L/Sjt 295067 12th Royal Scots Fusiliers
MORTON Edward T. MM Pte 47737 1st Royal Irish Fusiliers
MORTON Frank "DCM,MM" Sjt 24315 1/6th Cheshire Regt
MORTON Frank S. MM Sjt 11668 8th Lincolnshire Regt
MORTON Frank W. MM Pte 235618 Lancashire Fusiliers
MORTON Fred MM L/Cpl 9966 9th Notts & Derby Regt KIA 4.10.17
MORTON G.J. MM Sjt 2173 Royal Flying Corps
MORTON George MM Pte M2/020454 Army Service Corps
MORTON George Alexander MM Gnr 255321 26 Bty 17 Bde RFA
MORTON George W. MM L/Cpl 65050 6th Yorkshire Regt
MORTON Harold MM Gnr 113619 X/38 Med TM Bty RFA DOW 1.7.18.
MORTON Henry MM Pte 8650 2nd King's Own Scottish Borderers DOW 8.9.17.
MORTON Henry Edward MM Pte 42239 Middlesex Regt
MORTON Herbert MM Pte 205720 Northumberland Fusiliers
MORTON Hugh MM Sjt 1511 8/10th Gordon Highlanders
MORTON J. MM Pte 126088 Machine Gun Corps
MORTON James MM Pte 1067 I Corps Cyclist Bn Army Cyclist Corps
MORTON James MM+Bar Pte 251021 11th Royal Scots DOW 23.10.18.
MORTON James C. MM Gnr 147806 393 Siege Bty RGA
MORTON James F. MM L/Cpl 303012 5th London Regt
MORTON John MM Cpl 28139 74 Bde RFA
MORTON John MM Sjt 41184 RAMC
MORTON John A. MM Pte 268073 6th Royal Highlanders
MORTON John Douglas MM Pte 388549 3 Fd Amb RAMC
MORTON John E. MM Dvr 262895 RFA
MORTON John William MM Pte 15577 IX Corps Cyclist Bn Army Cyclist Corps
MORTON Joseph MM Cpl 33793 D/110 Bde RFA
MORTON Joseph MM L/Cpl 30810 Seaforth Highlanders att 15 Coy MGC.KIA 14.4.17.
MORTON Joseph MM Pte 14447 9th Royal Irish Fusiliers
MORTON Mark Henderson MM 2nd Cpl 61166 283 Army Troops Coy Royal Engineers
MORTON Percy MM Gnr 30930 C/50 Bde RFA
MORTON Reuben MM Cpl 11892 Cheshire Regt
MORTON Reuben A. MM Gnr 184452 RFA
MORTON Robert J. MM Cpl 14340 10th Essex Regt
MORTON T. MM Pte 306202 West Yorkshire Regt
MORTON Thomas MM Pte 29450 7th Royal Warwickshire Regt
MORTON Thomas MM+Bar L/Cpl S/3650 8th Royal Highlanders
MORTON Thomas MM Cpl 9352 1st Royal Irish Rifles
MORTON William MM Pte 21656 2nd Grenadier Guards
MORTON William J. MM Cpl 21233 Middlesex Regt
MORTON William J. MM Sjt 17/48 Royal Irish Rifles
MORTON William J. MM Pte 50597 53 Fd Amb RAMC
MORVAN William Edward MM Pte 85714 219 Coy Machine Gun Corps
MORVILLE Fred MM Pte 25177 RAMC
MOSBY Fred MM Cpl 202115 Notts & Derby Regt
MOSCROP James MM Pte 23767 1/7th West Riding Regt
MOSCROP James W. MM Sjt TT/03077 Army Veterinary Corps
MOSCROP Robert MM L/Sjt 2249 1/7th Northumberland Fusiliers
MOSCROP Thomas MM L/Cpl 205050 2/4th Hampshire Regt KIA 20.10.18.
MOSDELL Arthur F. MM Sjt 8607 2nd Border Regt
MOSDELL Sidney MM Pte 769869 1/28th London Regt
MOSELEY Charles E. MM+Bar Cpl 31185 8/10th & 6th Gordon Highlanders
MOSELEY Ernest "DCM,MM" L/Cpl 10061 2nd York & Lancaster Regt
MOSELEY Frederick John MM L/Cpl 23850 6th Royal West Kent Regt KIA 1.7.18.
MOSELEY Frederick William MM Pte 27801 7/8th King's Own Scottish Borderers
MOSELEY Henry Thomas Harrington MM Sjt 9306 37th Bn Machine Gun Corps
MOSELEY John MM Pte 9101 11th Royal Warwickshire Regt
MOSELEY Joseph MM Sjt 8083 RFA
MOSELEY Levi MM L/Cpl 17396 Oxf & Bucks Light Infantry
MOSELEY Rachel Gertrude MM Miss F First Aid Nursing Yeomanry
MOSELEY Robert Edgar MM Sjt 57506 354 Siege Bty RGA
MOSEN Harold F. MM Cpl 17221 10th Worcestershire Regt
MOSEN Oliver M. MM Pte 242313 18th Gloucestershire Regt
MOSER Charles William Leslie "MM,MSM,MID" Cpl 17160 RGA
MOSES David MM L/Cpl 452134 Royal Engineers
MOSES George "MM,MID" Cpl 735142 RFA
MOSES George MM Dvr 7605 RFA
MOSES Joseph MM L/Cpl 17647 7th East Yorkshire Regt
MOSES Martin MM Cpl 52861 Cheshire Regt
MOSES Thomas MM L/Cpl 45675 12th Durham Light Infantry
MOSEY James R. MM L/Cpl 34688 South Wales Borderers
MOSGROVE Edward MM Cpl 14207 1/8th Notts & Derby Regt
MOSGROVE William James MM Sjt 20/1099 20th Northumberland Fusiliers
MOSIER C. MM Pte 36427 5th Yorkshire Light Infantry
MOSLEY Alan MM Pte 242462 2/5th West Yorkshire Regt
MOSLEY Charles MM Pte 405915 9th Liverpool Regt
MOSLEY H.P. MM Pte 417333 1 Fd Amb RAMC
MOSLEY Harris MM+Bar L/Cpl 307668 7th West Riding Regt
MOSLEY John G. MM L/Cpl 32721 8th York & Lancaster Regt
MOSLEY Lees "MM,MID" Pte 15312 24th Manchester Regt
MOSLEY William George MM L/Bdr 10143 Y/30 Med TM Bty RFA
MOSS A.J. MM Bdsm 8079 1st East Kent Regt
MOSS Alfred MM Sjt 10969 7th Duke of Cornwall's LI
MOSS Archie MM Pte 250441 1/6th Durham Light Infantry KIA 19.7.17.
MOSS Arthur MM Pte 23764 East Surrey Regt
MOSS Arthur J. MM L/Cpl 14687 8th Suffolk Regt
MOSS Charles James MM Gnr 96214 A/48 Bde RFA
MOSS Christmas MM Pte 38509 7th Shropshire Light Infantry
MOSS E.H. MM Pte 608851 18th London Regt
MOSS Edward MM Sjt 10326 4th Middlesex Regt
MOSS Edward Sowden MM Pte 2292 1/6th West Yorkshire Regt
MOSS Ernest MM Pte 652965 21st London Regt
MOSS Ernest E. MM Cpl 5317 13th Hussars
MOSS Frank MM Pte 87234 27 Coy Machine Gun Corps
MOSS Fred MM Pte 11993 8th East Surrey Regt
MOSS Frederick L. MM Pte 200185 1/4th Cheshire Regt
MOSS George MM Pte 269715 6th Notts & Derby Regt
MOSS George MM Pte 341337 RAMC
MOSS George MM L/Cpl 158356 Tunnelling Coy Royal Engineers
MOSS George MM+Bar L/Cpl 9122 Royal Fusiliers
MOSS George MM Pte 13626 Northumberland Fusiliers
MOSS Harry MM Pte 305286 West Yorkshire Regt
MOSS J.E. MM Pte 49993 16th King's Royal Rifle Corps
MOSS James "MM,MSM" Pte 200443 2/4th North Lancashire Regt
MOSS John B. MM Pte 35959 RAMC
MOSS John C. MM Sjt 26280 11th Notts & Derby Regt
MOSS John Henry MM Pte 21205 Liverpool Regt
MOSS John J. MM Pte 21491 King's Own Scottish Borderers
MOSS John L. MM Pte 201346 2/4th Royal West Surrey Regt
MOSS Leonard MM Pte 17845 Royal West Kent Regt
MOSS Leonard MM L/Cpl 24095 13th Cheshire Regt
MOSS M. MM Pte 7306 Royal Warwickshire Regt
MOSS Mark MM Pte 1238 5 Fd Amb RAMC DOW 4.6.17.
MOSS Oliver MM L/Sjt 230468 1/1st Dorset Yeomanry
MOSS Ralph W. MM L/Bdr 625395 HAC(Artillery)
MOSS Reuben MM Pte 13418 East Surrey Regt
MOSS Reuben MM+Bar Bdr 925339 A/280 Bde RFA
MOSS Robert MM Sjt 12647 7th North Lancashire Regt
MOSS Sam MM Sjt 14587 8th South Lancashire Regt
MOSS Samuel Foden MM Sjt 113355 'J' Special Coy Royal Engineers DOW 28.3.18.
MOSS Sydney A. MM L/Cpl 32092 Machine Gun Corps
MOSS Thomas MM Pte 14293 Bedfordshire Regt
MOSS Thomas MM Pte 3991 12th Highland Light Infantry
MOSS Thomas MM Pte 85011 25 Coy Machine Gun Corps
MOSS William MM Pte 241404 Liverpool Regt
MOSS William MM Pte 5716 1st Scots Guards KIA 15.9.16.
MOSS William MM Spr 50224 23 Div Sig Coy Royal Engineers KIA 3.10.16.
MOSS William MM Pte 14454 Northumberland Fusiliers
MOSS William MM Cpl 8283 1st Northamptonshire Regt
MOSS William G. MM Dvr T3/023911 18 Div Train Army Service Corps
MOSSES William J. MM Cpl 10323 6th Lincolnshire Regt
MOSSMAN George Edgar MM Gnr 52238 33 Siege Bty RGA
MOSSMAN Herbert Welch MM Pte 73929 18th Bn Machine Gun Corps
MOSSMAN John Y. MM Sjt 47973 Royal Engineers

MOSSMAN Victor MM L/Cpl 508067 RAMC
MOSSOM Sidney MM L/Sjt 12192 17th King's Royal Rifle Corps KIA 24.3.18.
MOSSOP Fred "DCM+Bar,MM" Sjt 25188 1st Liverpool Regt KIA 30.12.17.
MOSSOP George "DCM,MM+Bar" Sjt 2904 14 Fd Amb RAMC
MOSSOP Harry MM Sjt 24359 Machine Gun Corps
MOTE Frederick Thomas MM Pte 17491 2/4th West Riding Regt
MOTH Ernest MM Pte 241728 1/5th Royal West Surrey Regt
MOTHERSOLE Percy Edward MM+Bar Sjt 6971 2nd Suffolk Regt
MOTHERSOLE Robert G.C. MM 2nd Cpl 145098 Royal Engineers
MOTHERSOLE Thomas G. MM Pte 12090 7th Norfolk Regt
MOTION Robert MM Sjt 645584 71 Bde RFA
MOTT Arthur V. MM L/Cpl 110705 MGC(Cavalry)
MOTT C.F. MM Cpl 43588 Essex Regt
MOTT C.W. MM Sjt 2203 53 Bty 2 Bde RFA
MOTT Cecil MM Sjt 4036 2nd Royal Fusiliers
MOTT Charles V. MM Cpl 64820 109 Labour Coy Labour Corps
MOTT Edward MM L/Cpl 19351 Machine Gun Corps
MOTT Frederick G. MM Gnr 96986 RGA
MOTT Julius MM Bdr 3963 RFA
MOTT Leonard A. MM Cpl S4/072232 Army Service Corps
MOTTASHAW William Henry MM CSM 8620 7th Duke of Cornwall's LI KIA 5.10.18.
MOTTERSHEAD C. MM Sjt 290215 Cheshire Regt
MOTTERSHEAD Charles MM Cpl 238092 9th Royal Welsh Fusiliers
MOTTERSHEAD J.A. MM Pte 265414 Cheshire Regt
MOTTRAM Frank MM Pte 38670 Northumberland Fusiliers
MOTTRAM George MM Cpl 275365 Manchester Regt
MOTTRAM Henry MM Pte 350068 Liverpool Regt
MOTTRAM James Arthur "MM(23921,12th SWB)+Bar" Pte 23921 4th Bedfordshire Regt
MOTTRAM Raymond W. MM Spr 29415 'K' Cable Section Royal Engineers
MOTTRAM Samuel "MM,MID" Sjt 2365 1/7th Durham Light Infantry
MOTTS John H. MM Sjt 58005 A/59 Bde RFA
MOUAT Reginald S. MM Sjt 29750 Hampshire Regt
MOUATT Henry MM Pte 6094 2nd Northamptonshire Regt DOW 10.1.17.
MOUGHTON William MM Pte 39232 12th Liverpool Regt
MOULAND Walter E. MM L/Cpl 44398 Royal Engineers
MOULD Albert E. MM Bdr 765617 RFA
MOULD Dudley S. MM Pte 250974 2/3rd London Regt
MOULD Frederick MM Tpr 5721 3rd Bn GMGR
MOULD John MM Cpl 23/80 Northumberland Fusiliers
MOULD John Sydney MM Pte 66835 139 Fd Amb RAMC
MOULD Maurice A. MM Pte 22785 Liverpool Regt
MOULD Percy MM Pte 955 13th Middlesex Regt
MOULD Walter H. MM Sjt 82504 RGA
MOULDER Albert MM Cpl 7701 1st Gloucestershire Regt
MOULDER George F. MM Cpl 19435 8th Bedfordshire Regt
MOULDER William Frederick MM L/Cpl 21981 25th Bn Machine Gun Corps DOW 23.4.18.
MOULDING Alfred John MM Cpl 25819 2nd Grenadier Guards DOW 1.12.17.
MOULDING Edward MM+2 Bars L/Sjt 8786 1st Border Regt
MOULDING Vincent MM Cpl 63485 237 Siege Bty RGA
MOULDING William MM Sjt 307650 8th Royal Warwickshire Regt
MOULDS Edward "MM,CG(F)" Sjt 79315 Durham Light Infantry
MOULDS John MM Cpl 28213 Labour Corps
MOULDS William F. MM Dvr 42757 RFA
MOULE Albert MM Pte 123000 41st Bn Machine Gun Corps
MOULSON John MM CQMS 17779 19th Lancashire Fusiliers
MOULT Charles MM Cpl 44958 RFA
MOULTON Albert E. MM L/Sjt 45304 1/1st Surrey Yeomanry
MOULTON Alfred MM Sjt 9712 1st Grenadier Guards
MOULTON Francis T. "MM,MSM,MID" Bdr 18912 36 Bde RGA
MOULTON James MM Pte 27858 3rd Grenadier Guards
MOUNCEY Henry MM Pte 2215 Middlesex Regt
MOUNCEY William C. MM Cpl 43224 10th Essex Regt
MOUNSEY Charles E. MM Spr 478651 Royal Engineers
MOUNSEY Clifford MM L/Cpl 27090 9th Yorkshire Regt
MOUNT Ernest E. MM Sjt 19358 1st East Surrey Regt
MOUNT Ernest James MM L/Cpl 19156 2nd Oxf & Bucks Light Infantry
MOUNT Hugh MM Pte 201604 6th Liverpool Regt KIA 29.9.18.
MOUNT Lancelot MM Cpl 11368 Machine Gun Corps
MOUNT Robert John MM Sjt 61925 176 Siege Bty RGA
MOUNT W.A. MM Cpl L/10082 6th East Kent Regt
MOUNTAIN Albert MM Cpl 11539 4th Royal Fusiliers
MOUNTAIN James MM Sjt 241157 1/5th Lincolnshire Regt
MOUNTAIN William MM L/Cpl 13545 5th Dorsetshire Regt
MOUNTAIN William MM Sjt 43598 Royal Engineers
MOUNTAIN William MM L/Cpl 20871 Tunnelling Coy Royal Engineers
MOUNTBATTEN Winifred Eleanor Sarah MM Commandant F BRCS
MOUNTER Stanley William MM Sjt 925232 280 Bde RFA
MOUNTFIELD Charles MM Pte 39127 RAMC
MOUNTFORD Albert MM Pte 61185 36 Fd Amb RAMC Died 30.11.17.
MOUNTFORD Alfred MM Sjt 830709 41 Div Ammn Col RFA
MOUNTFORD Bertie MM Pte 31174 6th North Staffordshire Regt
MOUNTFORD Elijah MM Cpl 13805 2nd King's Own Scottish Borderers
MOUNTFORD Frank MM L/Cpl 3254 Machine Gun Corps
MOUNTFORD George MM Cpl 846368 155 Bde RFA
MOUNTFORD Henry MM Sjt 23410 10th Royal Welsh Fusiliers
MOUNTFORD Richard L. MM L/Cpl 242031 South Staffordshire Regt
MOUNTIER Sidney MM L/Cpl A/204075 13th King's Royal Rifle Corps
MOUNTJOY Percy Hugh MM Gnr Sig 179146 C/121 Bde RFA
MOUNTNEY Albert MM Pte C/141 16th King's Royal Rifle Corps DOW 3.5.17
MOUNTSTEPHENS Wilfred MM Spr 230674 218 Fd Coy Royal Engineers
MOUSDALE John MM Cpl 33248 29 Bde RFA
MOUSLEY Alfred Charles MM Sjt 38810 HQ 49 Bde RFA DOW 30.9.17.
MOUSLEY Joseph MM Pte 39804 Royal Welsh Fusiliers
MOUTREY Joseph MM Pte 9133 1st Border Regt
MOVERLEY James MM Sjt 1743 7th Royal West Surrey Regt
MOWAT A. MM Bdr 3826 90 Heavy Bty RGA
MOWAT Charles S. MM L/Cpl 47382 Machine Gun Corps
MOWAT David MM Pte 240622 1/6th Seaforth Highlanders
MOWAT James "DCM,MM+Bar" Sjt 240466 Seaforth Highlanders
MOWAT James R. MM Cpl 120561 Special Bde Royal Engineers
MOWATT Charles A. MM Pte 17533 7th Royal Berkshire Regt
MOWATT James A. MM Sjt 19877 Royal Scots
MOWBRAY A. MM Sjt 292388 Gordon Highlanders
MOWBRAY Harold MM Sjt 6795 Machine Gun Corps
MOWBRAY James MM RSM 28644 186 Bde RFA
MOWBRAY John W. MM Sjt 63688 21 Div Ammn Col RFA
MOWBRAY Reginald J. "DCM,MM" L/Cpl 203328 16th Royal Welsh Fusiliers
MOWBRAY William Bulman MM+Bar Cpl 755703 X/50 Med TM Bty RFA
MOWE William "MM,MSM" Sjt 423073 55 Div Sig Coy Royal Engineers
MOWER William MM Cpl 21091 6th York & Lancaster Regt
MOWFORTH Edward MM L/Cpl 10/1185 6th East Yorkshire Regt
MOWIS William MM Pte 44223 South Lancashire Regt
MOWL Albert MM Cpl 17436 10th Worcestershire Regt
MOWLE Alfred C. MM Sjt 59408 RAMC
MOWLE William MM Sjt 201975 Northumberland Fusiliers
MOWTHORPE Charles MM Pte C/12253 4th King's Royal Rifle Corps
MOXEY George Stanley MM L/Cpl 2129 1/8th London Regt
MOXHAM Edward J. MM Pte 292505 13th Middlesex Regt
MOXHAM John C.R. "MM,MID" Pte 9817 10th Hampshire Regt
MOXLEY Harold A. MM Pte 1072 Royal West Surrey Regt
MOXOM Arthur MM Dmr 201313 Dorsetshire Regt
MOXON Alfred MM Sjt 1468 1/5th York & Lancaster Regt
MOXON Ernest MM Pte 18139 6th Yorkshire Light Infantry KIA 25.4.18.
MOXON Frank W. MM Sjt 8742 17th Manchester Regt
MOXON Joseph E. MM Pte 45579 Lancashire Fusiliers
MOXON Walter C. MM Gnr Sig 185688 D/23 Bde RFA
MOY Archibald MM L/Cpl 250662 3rd London Regt
MOY Ernest R.C. MM Gnr 218869 RFA
MOY Henry Charles MM Pte 11342 2/4th Hampshire Regt KIA 26.8.18.
MOYENS John S. MM+Bar Sjt 13385 1st Coldstream Guards
MOYER Sydney G. MM Sjt 40567 2nd South Staffordshire Regt
MOYES Edgar MM Pte 20/39 West Yorkshire Regt
MOYES George H. MM Cpl 14688 8th Suffolk Regt
MOYES James MM Pte 43144 Royal Highlanders
MOYES John C. MM Pnr 418484 55 Div Sig Coy Royal Engineers
MOYES Robert McCartney MM Sjt 21299 10 Railway Coy Royal Engineers

MOYES W. MM Pte 291457 7th Royal Highlanders
MOYES William Blake MM L/Sjt 18669 8th Royal West Surrey Regt DOW 25.3.18.
MOYLAN John MM Bdr 23583 RGA
MOYLE John MM Pte 16103 Durham Light Infantry
MOYLE Stanley "DCM,MM" L/Cpl 38204 22nd Northumberland Fusiliers
MOYLE Thomas MM Cpl 11889 10th West Riding Regt DOW 5.1.17.
MOYLE William MM Cpl 23149 Durham Light Infantry
MOYLES Patrick "DCM,MM" Sjt 15051 7th Yorkshire Light Infantry att 61 Light TM Bty
MOYLES Thomas MM Pte 16024 Royal Irish Fusiliers
MOYLIN Thomas MM+Bar CSM 4761 8th Royal Lancaster Regt
MOYNAGH Thomas J. MM Pte 276202 6th Essex Regt
MOYNE Robert MM Pte 3329 1/8th London Regt
MOYNIHAN Bartholomew MM Cpl 8794 1st Leinster Regt
MOYNIHAN Thomas G. MM Sjt 807 1st Manchester Regt
MOYSE Charles "MM,MID" Sjt 25104 B/63 Bde RFA
MOYSES Joseph MM Pte 4191 55 Coy Machine Gun Corps
MOYSES S. MM Pte 15738 11th Essex Regt
MOZLEY Edward C. MM Cpl 14973 Dorsetshire Regt
MOZLEY William MM Pte 26539 11th East Lancashire Regt
MUCHMORE Charles A. MM+Bar Pte 63178 26th Royal Fusiliers
MUCKERSIE Alexander MM Sjt 635703 2(Fife)Bty RFA
MUCKETT Frank H. MM L/Cpl 15751 Hampshire Regt
MUDD Harold Edwin MM Pte S/314087 21 Div Train Army Service Corps
MUDD James MM Bdr 51214 RGA
MUDD William MM Sjt 930275 C/291 Bde RFA
MUDD William H. MM Pte 231373 Durham Light Infantry
MUDDIMAN Thomas MM Pte 238068 7th Lincolnshire Regt
MUDDLE Edward J. MM Sjt 511139 14th London Regt
MUDGE Alfred E. MM Sjt 39374 RGA
MUDGE William Henry MM Sjt 200753 1/4th Oxf & Bucks Light Infantry
MUDIE Alfred J.F. MM L/Cpl 198913 39 Div Sig Coy Royal Engineers KIA 28.3.18.
MUDIE John L. MM L/Cpl 192704 Royal Engineers
MUDIE Peter MM Sjt 92858 RFA
MUFF Albert MM L/Cpl 18161 7/8th King's Own Scottish Borderers
MUFF Fred MM Pte 2076 West Riding Regt
MUFF Sam MM Pte 28190 3rd Grenadier Guards
MUFFITT Ernest William MM Cpl 24598 RAMC
MUGFORD Richard Henry MM Sjt 855 1st King Edward's Horse
MUGFORD William J. MM Pte 10432 8th Devonshire Regt
MUGGLESTON David T. MM Sjt 122821 312 Siege Bty RGA
MUGGLESTON James MM Gnr 12765 B/95 Bde RFA
MUGGLESTONE William H. MM L/Cpl 58892 Royal Engineers
MUGGLETON Edward MM L/Cpl 1288 4th Bn GMGR
MUGGLETON Percy E. MM Sjt K/1183 24th Royal Fusiliers
MUGGLETON Stuart H. MM Pte 514324 14th London Regt
MUGGLETON William Edward MM Pte 40495 8th South Staffordshire Regt
MUHLECK Harry MM Pte 87481 62nd Bn Machine Gun Corps
MUIR Alexander MM Dvr 650414 C/86 Bde RFA DOW 23.10.17.
MUIR Andrew MM Pte 332961 Highland Light Infantry
MUIR Andrew Reid MM Bdr 44917 RGA DOW 7.11.17.
MUIR Archibald MM Spr 152518 Royal Engineers
MUIR Daniel Hastie MM Cpl S/14502 6th Cameron Highlanders KIA 7.2.17.
MUIR David MM Gnr 159183 RFA
MUIR David MM Pte 325472 1/9th Arg & Suth Highlanders
MUIR Ernest R. MM Sjt 240103 1/5th Royal Scots Fusiliers
MUIR G.L. MM Pte 350585 Royal Scots
MUIR Guy S. MM Pte 53639 2nd Royal Scots Fusiliers
MUIR Hugh MM Sjt 17988 12tth Highland Light Infantry
MUIR J. MM Pte 38454 Yorkshire Light Infantry
MUIR J. MM Sjt 22433 Machine Gun Corps
MUIR James MM Bdr 650693 RFA
MUIR James MM Pte 1121 2nd Royal Highlanders
MUIR James MM Pte 30053 18th Highland Light Infantry
MUIR John MM Cpl 280677 1/7th Highland Light Infantry
MUIR John "DCM,MM" CSM 8747 1st Scots Guards
MUIR John MM Pte 71249 34 Coy Machine Gun Corps
MUIR John MM Sjt 43605 16th Highland Light Infantry
MUIR John MM L/Cpl 33543 7th Royal Warwickshire Regt
MUIR John MM Pte 241080 Seaforth Highlanders
MUIR John MM CSM 10737 2nd King's Own Scottish Borderers
MUIR John MM Gnr 346783 RGA
MUIR Peter M. MM Pte 41466 1st Royal Scots Fusiliers
MUIR Samuel MM L/Cpl P5417 Military Mounted Police
MUIR Thomas MM Cpl 290997 1/7th Royal Highlanders
MUIR Thomas MM Pte 331239 1/9th Highland Light Infantry KIA 12.10.18.
MUIR Thomas MM Pte 53896 RAMC
MUIR Thomas "MC,MM(6416 CSM Cam H)" 2Lt 6th King's Own Scottish Borderers
MUIR Walter MM L/Cpl 14895 Royal Inniskilling Fusiliers
MUIR William Edward MM Pte 350593 1/9th Royal Scots KIA 23.4.17.
MUIR William M. MM Gnr 22260 RFA
MUIRCROFT Andrew MM L/Cpl 79575 Royal Engineers
MUIRDEN John MM Cpl 130497 'P' Special Coy Royal Engineers
MUIRHEAD Gavin MM Cpl 7083 9th Seaforth Highlanders
MUIRHEAD George L. MM Bdr 291315 RGA
MUIRHEAD Gordon Coghill "MC,MM(2118 CSM Cam H)" 2Lt 7th Gordon Highlanders
MUIRHEAD James MM Sjt 276463 Arg & Suth Highlanders
MUIRHEAD John MM Gnr Sig 62341 110 Siege Bty RGA
MUIRHEAD John MM Pte 12071 2nd Scots Guards KIA 15.11.16.
MUIRHEAD John MM L/Cpl 17954 2nd King's Own Scottish Borderers
MUIRHEAD John MM+Bar L/Sjt 275460 1/7th Arg & Suth Highlanders
MUIRHEAD Thomas MM L/Cpl 64122 RAMC
MUIRHEAD William MM Pte 79088 RAMC
MULCAHY John MM L/Cpl 9397 1st Royal Irish Regt
MULCAHY Michael MM Pte 42961 RAMC
MULDOON Alexander MM Pte 43480 Highland Light Infantry
MULDOON Ernest M. MM Cpl 115572 326 Siege Bty RGA
MULDOON Thomas MM Pte 7857 1st Royal Munster Fusiliers KIA 9.9.16.
MULDOWNEY Joseph "DCM,MM" L/Cpl 3956 17th Lancashire Fusiliers
MULFORD Hubert George MM L/Cpl 44688 1st South Wales Borderers KIA 23.10.18.
MULGREW John MM Pnr 63173 Royal Engineers
MULGREW Joseph MM Cpl 301009 1/8th Durham Light Infantry
MULHAIRE Francis MM Pte 4/7657 1st West Yorkshire Regt
MULHALL Cornelius MM Pte 7/2829 7th Leinster Regt
MULHALL Patrick MM L/Cpl 27634 6th Royal Dublin Fusiliers
MULHALL Thomas MM L/Cpl 12082 6th Royal Dublin Fusiliers
MULHEARN John F. MM Cpl 1811 1/5th Liverpool Regt
MULHEARN William MM Pte 266828 1/7th Liverpool Regt KIA 9.4.18.
MULHEIR John William MM Gnr 11932 C/168 Bde RFA
MULHERN John MM Pte 25522 1/5th Seaforth Highlanders
MULHERON James MM+Bar Pte 12323 9th Scottish Rifles
MULHOLLAND Edward J. MM Gnr 38408 'N' Bty RHA
MULHOLLAND George MM Sjt 18523 12th Royal Irish Rifles
MULHOLLAND John MM Pte 14668 8th Royal Scots Fusiliers
MULHOLLAND Peter MM Gnr 15198 11 Siege Bty RGA
MULHOLLAND William MM Pte 37371 Royal Scots
MULLALY Maurice MM L/Cpl 12199 17th Liverpool Regt
MULLAN John MM Cpl 4649 1/6th Arg & Suth Highlanders
MULLANY John T. MM Gnr 197049 RFA
MULLANY Joseph MM L/Cpl 438088 Royal Engineers
MULLARD William R. MM Pte 307554 Liverpool Regt
MULLARKEY John MM Pte 18795 West Riding Regt
MULLEN Andrew MM Sjt 15074 2nd Royal Dublin Fusiliers
MULLEN Daniel MM Gnr 51657 34 Siege Bty RGA
MULLEN David MM Pte 74 9 Fd Amb RAMC
MULLEN David Francis MM Sjt 36616 41 Bde RFA
MULLEN James MM+Bar Cpl 19779 18th Lancashire Fusiliers
MULLEN James "MM,MID" CSM 6992 1st Lancaster Regt
MULLEN James MM+Bar Sjt 11888 Royal Highlanders
MULLEN John MM Pte 235109 Royal Welsh Fusiliers
MULLEN Joseph MM Pte 28616 6th Royal Inniskilling Fusiliers
MULLEN Joseph MM Gnr 100014 X/Gds Med TM Bty RFA
MULLEN Michael MM Pte 40055 Royal Dublin Fusiliers
MULLEN Thomas MM Pte 11278 12th West Yorkshire Regt
MULLEN Thomas MM Pte 15740 RAMC
MULLENS James MM L/Bdr 58020 136 Siege Bty RGA
MULLETT Charles T. MM Dvr 17050 RFA
MULLETT Frederick Walter MM Sjt 4/8780 10th Durham Light Infantry KIA 25.3.18.
MULLETT James MM Sjt 33138 C/82 Bde RFA DOW 10.11.18.
MULLETT Wilfred H. MM Pte 242858 Royal Warwickshire Regt
MULLETT William Richard George MM Cpl 6186 13th East Surrey Regt KIA 25.3.18.

MULLEY Reginalod MM Cpl 59470 24th Royal Fusiliers
MULLIGAN A.R. MM Pte 46668 Yorkshire Light Infantry
MULLIGAN Edward MM Pte 7163 1st Royal Dublin Fusiliers
MULLIGAN Felix "DCM,MM+Bar" Pte 5834 1st Royal Dublin Fusiliers
MULLIGAN John MM Sjt 240683 1/5th Yorkshire Light Infantry
MULLIGAN Patrick MM Cpl 39505 12th Royal Scots
MULLIGAN Samuel MM Sjt 11563 6th Royal Irish Rifles
MULLIN Clement MM Pte 275704 1/7th Manchester Regt
MULLIN Henry MM Cpl 38002 Manchester Regt
MULLIN James Cecil MM Sjt 2645 1/24th London Regt
MULLIN Thomas MM Pte 12108 2nd Notts & Derby Regt
MULLIN William MM Pte 13305 X Corps Cyclist Bn Army Cyclist Corps
MULLINER George MM Cpl 12152 9th Royal Fusiliers
MULLINER John MM Sjt 6678 1st North Staffordshire Regt
MULLINGER Bertram F. MM L/Sjt 7/2625 2nd Royal Munster Fusiliers
MULLINS John MM Dvr 59698 28 Bde RFA
MULLINS John MM Cpl 971320 RFA
MULLINS L. MM Cpl 12832 9th Essex Regt
MULLINS M. MM Gnr 16939 RGA
MULLINS Patrick MM Cpl 250370 1/6th Manchester Regt KIA 21.8.18.
MULLINS Sidney W. MM Sjt 63587 RFA
MULLINS Thomas A. MM Cpl 152121 85 Motor Airline Sect Royal Engineers
MULLINS W.E. MM Cpl 650769 London Regt
MULLINS Wilfred MM Pte 41205 Yorkshire Light Infantry
MULLINS William MM Gnr 46793 57 Siege Bty RGA
MULLIS Thomas MM L/Bdr 91673 D/150 Bde RFA
MULLIS William MM Pte 17941 11th East Yorkshire Regt
MULLISS Henry R. MM L/Cpl 32194 Somerset Light Infantry
MULLOCK Stanley MM L/Cpl 4959 1/10th Liverpool Regt
MULLOOLY John Vincent MM Sjt 1400 1/5th Liverpool Regt
MULRANEY William MM Pte 7252 Connaught Rangers
MULRENAN T. MM Pte 25970 Royal Dublin Fusiliers
MULRIEN Bernard MM+Bar Cpl 12702 7th Bedfordshire Regt KIA 15.3.17.
MULROONEY Frank MM CSM 9819 2nd Manchester Regt
MULROONEY Herbert MM+Bar Sjt 235224 8th West Yorkshire Regt
MULVANEY Thomas "MM,MBC(Rm)" Pte 10959 1st Royal Scots
MULVANNY Henry MM Pte 15763 11th Manchester Regt KIA 10.10.18.
MULVEY Albert MM Bdr 58345 26 Bde RFA
MULVEY Frank MM Sjt 330156 1/9th Liverpool Regt
MULVEY Leo G. MM Pte 16913 10th Scottish Rifles
MULVIE Thomas MM CQMS 204743 1st Royal Scots Fusiliers
MULVILLE James MM Pte 18725 13th Liverpool Regt
MUMBY Douglas MM Pte 13/723 13th East Yorkshire Regt
MUMFORD Bernard MM Sjt 17657 6th Wiltshire Regt
MUMFORD Charles MM Pte 26761 Hampshire Regt
MUMFORD Jack MM Pte 26304 Grenadier Guards
MUMFORD John MM Pte 7644 11th Royal Fusiliers
MUMFORD Stephen MM Pte 4369 50th Bn Machine Gun Corps Died 6.10.18.
MUMFORD Steward C.E. MM Cpl 32967 1st Middlesex Regt
MUMFORD William MM Pte 13856 Border Regt
MUMMERY Albert Edward MM Pte 43408 1st Northamptonshire Regt
MUMMERY Sidney MM Pte 320172 15th Suffolk Regt
MUNDAY E. MM Gnr 37923 C/156 Bde RFA
MUNDAY Edward MM L/Cpl 3234 Notts & Derby Regt
MUNDAY Frederick MM+Bar Pte 4974 1st Scots Guards
MUNDAY Frederick P. MM Pte 11001 5th Royal Berkshire Regt
MUNDAY George E. MM Gnr 101349 RGA
MUNDAY George F. MM Sjt 9205 1st Scottish Rifles
MUNDAY Harold H. MM Gnr 106590 D/130 Bde RFA
MUNDAY John MM Gnr 125289 277 Siege Bty RGA
MUNDAY Thomas J. MM+Bar Cpl 10883 1st King's Royal Rifle Corps
MUNDAY William Henry MM Sjt 66866 Machine Gun Corps
MUNDAY William Henry MM Gnr 198285 C/286 Bde RFA DOW 9.11.18.
MUNDAY William J. MM Pte 3549 Middlesex Regt
MUNDAY William Thomas John "MC,MM(60845 Cpl),DSC(US)" 2Lt RFA
MUNDAY or MUNDEY Frederick A. MM Pte 632208 20th London Regt
MUNDELL Duncan "MM+Bar,CG(F)" Cpl 266367 1/6th Gordon Highlanders
MUNDEN Arthur Leonard MM(58 Div Sig Coy)+Bar Cpl 558068 9 Div Sig Coy Royal Engineers
MUNDEN Ernest C. MM Pte 48291 7/8th Royal Inniskilling Fusiliers
MUNDEN Ernest W. MM Pte 66242 RAMC
MUNDEN Frank MM L/Cpl 18700 Hampshire Regt
MUNDEN or MUNDON William MM Pte 39679 1/7th Worcestershire Regt
MUNDIE William "DCM,MM+Bar" Sjt 202630 1/7th Gordon Highlanders
MUNDY Frank E. MM Pte 2270 Gloucestershire Regt
MUNDY George E. MM L/Cpl 11916 32nd Bn Machine Gun Corps
MUNDY Herbert James MM Pte 16025 2nd Bn Machine Gun Corps
MUNDY Rupert J. MM Cpl 47066 25th Northumberland Fusiliers
MUNDY Victor MM Pte 205919 2nd Bedfordshire Regt KIA 21.9.18.
MUNN Albert MM L/Cpl 21384 3rd Grenadier Guards KIA 25.7.17.
MUNN Angus MM Cpl 10314 9th Royal Highlanders
MUNN J. MM Pte 19023 Royal Lancaster Regt
MUNN John MM Spr 18619 15 Fd Coy Royal Engineers
MUNN Richard MM Gnr 3017 C/241 Bde RFA DOW 14.10.16.
MUNN Robert MM L/Cpl 8075 5/6th Scottish Rifles
MUNN Walter F. MM Gnr 80303 RFA
MUNN William MM L/Sjt 32919 4th York & Lancaster Regt
MUNN William H. MM Pte 9030 2nd Leicestershire Regt AKA Frederick Smith
MUNNERLY Thomas MM Pte 4237 14th Liverpool Regt
MUNNERY Thomas MM Pte 66895 112 Coy Labour Corps
MUNNINGS Frank L. MM CQMS 20173 15th Cheshire Regt
MUNNINGS H.C. MM Sjt 2812 London Regt
MUNNINGS John "MM,MID" Sjt 40122 26 Bde RFA
MUNNIS James M. MM+Bar Spr 58805 Royal Engineers
MUNNOCK David Clark MM CQMS 290036 1/7th Royal Highlanders
MUNNS Archie MM+Bar L/Sjt 202345 5/6th Scottish Rifles
MUNNS Arthur MM Pte 200767 Lincolnshire Regt
MUNNS Egerton MM Gnr 66820 RFA
MUNNS John MM Sjt 1039 Yorkshire Light Infantry
MUNRO A. MM L/Cpl 266673 Seaforth Highlanders
MUNRO A. MM Pte 64010 RAMC
MUNRO Alexander J. MM Gnr 217726 RFA
MUNRO Alexander McL. MM L/Cpl 15383 2nd Highland Light Infantry
MUNRO Arthur MM Sjt 680346 RFA
MUNRO Bertie MM Cpl 28544 1/5th King's Own Scottish Borderers
MUNRO C.G. MM Sjt 290397 7th Gordon Highlanders
MUNRO Charles MM L/Cpl 6550 2nd Seaforth Highlanders
MUNRO Charles M.C. MM Bdr 169683 B/251 Bde RFA
MUNRO David MM 2nd Cpl 43209 Royal Engineers
MUNRO David Jackson MM Sjt 4201 8th Royal Highlanders
MUNRO Donald MM Sjt S/13524 Rifle Brigade
MUNRO Duncan MM Sjt 1015 1/4th Seaforth Highlanders
MUNRO Frederick S. MM Cpl 8075 1st Royal West Kent Regt
MUNRO George MM Cpl 18723 5th Cameron Highlanders
MUNRO George MM Sjt 265774 Seaforth Highlanders
MUNRO Hugh MM Pte 32341 6th King's Own Scottish Borderers
MUNRO Hugh MM Pte 238074 2nd Seaforth Highlanders
MUNRO James MM Sjt 91782 Tank Corps
MUNRO John MM Pte 300261 1/8th Arg & Suth Highlanders
MUNRO John MM Cpl 201872 1/4th Seaforth Highlanders
MUNRO John MM Pte 202516 Seaforth Highlanders
MUNRO John MM Pte 10565 Royal Scots
MUNRO John MM Pte 3/7366 2nd Arg & Suth Highlanders
MUNRO John Alexander MM CSM 300787 1/8th Arg & Suth Highlanders
MUNRO John H. MM Pte 632345 229 Div Emp Coy Labour Corps
MUNRO John J. MM Sjt 325025 1/9th Durham Light Infantry
MUNRO Kenneth J. MM Cpl S/40392 7th Seaforth Highlanders
MUNRO Murdoch MM L/Cpl 200147 1/4th Seaforth Highlanders
MUNRO Richard MM Pte 4078 Machine Gun Corps
MUNRO Robert MM Pte 242513 1/5th Gordon Highlanders KIA 17.5.17.
MUNRO Robert W. MM Pte 228441 1st London Regt
MUNRO Taylor Hall MM L/Cpl 16/601 16th Northumberland Fusiliers
MUNRO Thomas MM Sjt 5527 207 Siege Bty RGA
MUNRO Thomas MM Pte 17149 Arg & Suth Highlanders
MUNRO W. MM L/Cpl 266795 Seaforth Highlanders
MUNRO William MM Cpl 200372 Seaforth Highlanders
MUNRO William "DCM,MM" Cpl 200372 8th Seaforth Highlanders
MUNRO William MM Sjt 541 1/5th Royal Highlanders
MUNRO William MM L/Cpl 11115 1st Scottish Rifles
MUNRO William A. MM Pte M2/102835 Army Service Corps

MUNRO William Barry MM Bdr 92031 26 Heavy Bty RGA
MUNRO William J. MM Sjt 1511 7th Royal West Kent Regt
MUNROE Frank MM+Bar Sjt 12205 Liverpool Regt
MUNROE Susan Deverell MM Staff Nurse F QAIMNS
MUNSON Arthur James MM Sjt 8423 1st Essex Regt KIA 23.8.18.
MUNSON Charles E. "MM,MSM" Sjt 19472 12 Mobile Amb Convoy RAMC
MUNSON Gordon H. MM Pte 229293 7th Royal Fusiliers
MUNSON Henry George Thomas "DCM,MM" Sjt 52775 140 Fd Amb RAMC
MUNSON William "MM,MID" Pte 1817 2nd Rifle Brigade
MUNT Ernest MM Sjt 839 7th Royal Sussex Regt
MUNT Phillip E. MM Pte 82592 9th Durham Light Infantry
MUNT William G. MM Sjt 2365 1st Northumberland Fusiliers
MUNTON John Thomas MM Pte 31345 1st Northamptonshire Regt
MURAS William Arthur MM Gnr 111835 A/38 Bde RFA
MURCH Arthur M. MM Cpl 2940 Tank Corps
MURCH Cecil Elliott MM Sjt 2072 1/9th London Regt
MURCHIE Frank D. MM Sjt 22531 32nd Royal Fusiliers
MURCHISON Robert Cockburn MM Sjt 650827 C/315 Bde RFA KIA 11.6.17.
MURDEN Sidney H. "DCM,MM" Sjt 17976 15th Hampshire Regt
MURDIN Edward MM Pte 705279 23rd London Regt
MURDOCH Daniel MM Pte 44705 RAMC
MURDOCH Edward T.N. MM Pte 266586 1/4th Seaforth Highlanders
MURDOCH George MM Spr 420306 406 Fd Coy Royal Engineers
MURDOCH George MM Pte 291134 Gordon Highlanders
MURDOCH George R. MM L/Bdr Sig 346046 RGA
MURDOCH James MM Cpl 40266 1st Royal Highlanders
MURDOCH James MM Pte 53637 2nd Royal Scots Fusiliers
MURDOCH James MM+Bar Sjt 315526 13th Royal Highlanders
MURDOCH John MM CQMS 265477 7th Gordon Highlanders
MURDOCH John MM Pte 481 2nd Gordon Highlanders
MURDOCH Robert K. MM Pte 267684 Royal Highlanders
MURDOCH Thomas MM Pte 2678 11th Royal Scots DOW 30.9.18.
MURDOCH Thomas MM L/Cpl 235130 Scottish Rifles
MURDOCH Thomas "DCM,MM" L/Cpl 1724 'A' Bn Tank Corps
MURDOCH Thomas G. MM Pte 105990 7th Bn Machine Gun Corps
MURDOCH William MM Pte 2897 1/4th Royal Highlanders
MURDOCH William MM Cpl 200056 Seaforth Highlanders
MURDOCK Archibald James MM Sjt 6174 1st East Kent Regt KIA 12.9.17.
MURDOCK J. MM Sjt R/530 King's Royal Rifle Corps
MURDOCK John Ronald MM Gnr 107557 A/82 Bde RFA DOW 9.11.17.
MURDOCK William H. MM Cpl 25246 10th West Riding Regt
MURFIN George MM 2nd Cpl 44974 83 Fd Coy Royal Engineers KIA 23.3.18.
MURFIN John "DCM,MM" Sjt 21980 7/8th King's Own Scottish Borderers
MURFIN Thomas MM Sjt 200850 2/4th York & Lancaster Regt
MURFITT Roger A. MM Sjt 48546 'N' Bty RHA
MURGATROYD Alfred MM Dvr 1528 1(West Riding)Bde RFA KIA 13.5.17.
MURGATROYD Edward Thomas Aked MM Gnr 185556 D/110 Bty RFA
MURGATROYD Herbert MM L/Cpl 202214 2nd Bedfordshire Regt KIA 4.11.18.
MURGATROYD Percy MM Sjt 17630 Yorkshire Light Infantry
MURGATROYD Tom S. MM S/Sjt 352031 2 Fd Amb RAMC
MURISET Albert E. MM Pte 2143 1/9th Royal Scots
MURISON Alexander MM L/Cpl 292167 Gordon Highlanders
MURISON James MM L/Cpl 76028 Royal Engineers
MURISON William Stewart MM Cpl 43281 RAMC att HQ Guards Div.
MURISON or MURRISON Alexander J. MM Pte 2509 24th Royal Fusiliers
MURKIN Oliver Joseph MM Pte 40123 14th Royal Irish Rifles KIA 16.8.17.
MURLESS Herbert William MM L/Cpl 201322 8th Gloucestershire Regt KIA 14.6.18.
MURLEY Henry MM Pte 202674 4th Worcestershire Regt
MURNEY William MM Pte S/3115 1st Gordon Highlanders
MURPHEY J. MM Pte 265596 Cheshire Regt
MURPHY Albert MM Sjt 20943 Machine Gun Corps
MURPHY Albert G. MM Dvr 23829 3 Cav Div Sig Sqn Royal Engineers
MURPHY Alfred MM Pte 2814 1/6th London Regt
MURPHY Alfred MM Pte 26705 17th Notts & Derby Regt Died 17.6.18.
MURPHY Alfred MM Pte 472041 12th London Regt
MURPHY Andrew MM Sjt 200019 1/4th King's Own Scottish Borderers
MURPHY Andrew MM Pte B/3013 Rifle Brigade
MURPHY Andrew MM L/Cpl 242260 6th Liverpool Regt
MURPHY Andrew MM Cpl 29007 47th Bn Machine Gun Corps
MURPHY Austin MM Gnr 83525 RFA
MURPHY Austin MM Pte 140063 21st Bn Machine Gun Corps
MURPHY Bernard MM Sjt 24860 2nd Royal Irish Fusiliers
MURPHY Bernard MM L/Cpl 5611 XV Corps Cyclist Bn Army Cyclist Corps
MURPHY Bernard MM Pte 45763 114 Coy Machine Gun Corps
MURPHY Cornelius MM Pte 35055 16th Royal Welsh Fusiliers KIA 18.9.18.
MURPHY Daniel MM Pte 866 19 Fd Amb RAMC
MURPHY Daniel MM Pte 5713 Royal Irish Regt
MURPHY Daniel MM Pte 19341 Machine Gun Corps
MURPHY Edward "DCM,MM" Sjt 12351 11th & 13th Liverpool Regt
MURPHY Edward MM Sjt 16979 45 Bde RFA
MURPHY Francis MM Pte 46222 8th Scottish Rifles
MURPHY Francis T. MM L/Cpl S/10195 Rifle Brigade
MURPHY Frank MM L/Cpl 33108 12th Manchester Regt
MURPHY George MM Sjt 36786 Machine Gun Corps
MURPHY George MM Sjt 56441 Royal Engineers
MURPHY George MM+Bar Bdr 63331 8 Bde RFA
MURPHY George H. MM Sjt 103655 19th Bn Machine Gun Corps
MURPHY Harold MM Cpl 800392 RFA
MURPHY Henry MM L/Cpl 6300 Machine Gun Corps
MURPHY Henry E. MM Sjt 65685 RGA
MURPHY Hugh MM Pte G/30655 17th Royal Sussex Regt
MURPHY Isaac MM Pte 14076 2nd Royal Scots
MURPHY J. "DCM,MM+Bar" L/Cpl 10818 1st Essex Regt
MURPHY James MM Pte S/25502 2nd Seaforth Highlanders
MURPHY James MM Cpl 30452 1st Royal West Surrey Regt
MURPHY James MM Pte 15061 1st Royal Dublin Fusiliers KIA 29.9.18.
MURPHY James MM Pte 265663 Cheshire Regt
MURPHY James MM Cpl 52679 RFA
MURPHY James MM Dvr 65668 RFA
MURPHY James MM Dvr 2249 RFA
MURPHY James MM Sjt 6693 1st North Lancashire Regt
MURPHY James MM Sjt 43017 Machine Gun Corps
MURPHY Jeremiah MM+Bar Pte 10099 2nd Royal Munster Fusiliers
MURPHY John MM L/Cpl 5697 7th Royal Irish Regt
MURPHY John MM Pte 275233 17th Royal Scots
MURPHY John MM L/Cpl 34486 Machine Gun Corps
MURPHY John "MM,MSM" Sjt 227744 1/1st Monmouthshire Regt
MURPHY John MM Sjt 95397 1st Liverpool Regt
MURPHY John MM Pte 260303 13th Liverpool Regt
MURPHY John MM Pte 26136 1st Royal Dublin Fusiliers
MURPHY John MM Sjt 204684 Yorkshire Regt
MURPHY John MM Dvr 81805 52 Bde RFA
MURPHY John MM Pte 11659 1st Irish Guards
MURPHY John MM Pte 2058 1/6th Durham Light Infantry
MURPHY John MM Dvr 26272 C/109 Bde RFA
MURPHY John MM Pte 8878 1st Royal Munster Fusiliers
MURPHY John MM+Bar CSM 8576 2nd Royal Munster Fusiliers
MURPHY John MM Pte 6215 1/6th Royal Highlanders KIA 31.7.17.
MURPHY John MM Pte 21073 22nd Manchester Regt
MURPHY John MM Pte 23582 Highland Light Infantry
MURPHY John MM Sjt 11218 RGA
MURPHY John MM Sjt 21612 8th Royal Welsh Fusiliers DOW 10.8.17.
MURPHY John MM Pte 25110 Welsh Regt
MURPHY Joseph MM Gnr L/18402 B/119 Bde RFA
MURPHY Joseph MM Pte 33999 1/1st Bucks Bn Oxf & Bucks Light Infantry
MURPHY L. MM Cpl 43738 9th South Lancashire Regt
MURPHY Lawrence MM+Bar Pte 16400 2nd Royal Irish Regt
MURPHY Martin MM Pte 11447 Royal Irish Regt
MURPHY Maurice MM Gnr 696987 C/331 Bde RFA
MURPHY Michael MM Pte 775 2 Fd Amb RAMC
MURPHY Michael MM Cpl 18355 2nd Leinster Regt
MURPHY Michael MM Pte 34210 Royal Warwickshire Regt
MURPHY Michael MM Sjt 6211 2nd Irish Guards
MURPHY Michael MM Cpl 8623 1st Royal Munster Fusiliers DOW 6.9.16.
MURPHY Michael MM Gnr 52239 89 TM Bty RGA Died 20.10.17.
MURPHY Michael MM Gnr 36635 RGA
MURPHY Michael MM Pte 372301 8th London Regt KIA 25.7.18.

MURPHY Michael J. MM Pte 3213 Leinster Regt
MURPHY Michael J. "MM,MSM" Sjt 6892 2nd Irish Guards
MURPHY Mitchell "MM,CG(F)" Pte 240314 1/5th Seaforth Highlanders
MURPHY P. MM Pte 307586 Liverpool Regt
MURPHY Patrick "DCM,MM" Sjt 16298 10th Royal Welsh Fusiliers
MURPHY Patrick MM Gnr 36112 115 Heavy Bty RGA
MURPHY Patrick MM+Bar L/Cpl 8022 2nd Royal Munster Fusiliers
MURPHY Patrick MM L/Cpl 16490 10 Coy Machine Gun Corps KIA 4.10.17.
MURPHY Peter MM Pte 52671 Liverpool Regt
MURPHY Reuben MM Pte 9682 1/4th Royal Berkshire Regt
MURPHY Robert MM Gnr 1412 RFA
MURPHY Robert S. MM CQMS 16634 8th East Yorkshire Regt
MURPHY T. MM L/Cpl 390525 RAMC
MURPHY Thomas MM Pte M2/174508 Army Service Corps
MURPHY Thomas MM Pte 4140 1st Irish Guards
MURPHY Thomas MM Sjt 280837 1/7th Highland Light Infantry
MURPHY Thomas MM Pte 26458 North Lancashire Regt
MURPHY Thomas MM Cpl 300164 1/8th Durham Light Infantry
MURPHY Thomas MM Pte 36331 10th East Yorkshire Regt
MURPHY Thomas MM L/Cpl 203065 1/4th Yorkshire Regt
MURPHY Thomas MM Dvr T2/12310 8 Reserve Park Army Service Corps
MURPHY Thomas Henry MM L/Cpl 22086 1st North Lancashire Regt KIA 15.7.16.
MURPHY Thomas Joseph MM Pte S/5472 8th Rifle Brigade
MURPHY Thomas William MM Gnr 676578 D/275 Bde RFA Died 7.3.18.
MURPHY Timothy MM Pte 12724 1/5th Yorkshire Regt
MURPHY Timothy MM L/Cpl 24040 9 Fd Coy Royal Engineers
MURPHY W. MM Pte 23827 London Regt
MURPHY Walter MM Cpl 10524 2nd Royal Irish Regt
MURPHY William MM L/Cpl 40129 2nd Welsh Regt
MURPHY William MM Pte 332843 Highland Light Infantry
MURPHY William MM Pte 6188 2nd Royal Munster Fusiliers
MURPHY William MM Cpl 106816 Royal Engineers
MURPHY William MM Pte 2344 1/5th Cheshire Regt
MURPHY William MM L/Cpl 19736 Northumberland Fusiliers
MURPHY William MM L/Sjt 591734 18th London Regt
MURPHY William MM Sjt 9399 Royal Highlanders
MURPHY William F. MM Pte 31669 10th West Riding Regt
MURPHY William Francis MM(B/71 Bde)+Bar Bdr 98627 104 Bty 22 Bde RFA
MURPHY William Ouseley MM Cpl 90993 158 Bde Ammn Col RFA DOW 11.11.17.
MURR Alfred G. MM Pte 8139 4th Dragoon Guards
MURRANT Sidney MM Gnr 195953 RGA
MURRAY Albert MM Pte 6715 15th Royal Irish Rifles
MURRAY Albert MM+Bar Cpl 9206 1st Shropshire Light Infantry
MURRAY Alexander MM Pte 19963 Royal Highlanders
MURRAY Alexander MM L/Cpl 12806 Arg & Suth Highlanders
MURRAY Alexander MM L/Sjt 7101 Gordon Highlanders
MURRAY Alexander MM Pte 201466 10th Durham Light Infantry
MURRAY Alexander Gordon MM Pte 10421 8th Royal Highlanders KIA 15.6.18.
MURRAY Allan MM Sjt 8722 1st Cameron Highlanders
MURRAY Andrew "MM,MID" Cpl 9884 1st Cameron Highlanders KIA 23.11.17.
MURRAY Angus D. MM Pte 64558 RAMC
MURRAY Arthur MM Sjt 4389 2nd Dragoon Guards
MURRAY Arthur MM Cpl 28076 A/50 Bde RFA
MURRAY Arthur George MM Pte 241646 1st Royal Lancaster Regt KIA 8.8.18.
MURRAY Bernard MM Pte 26405 2nd King's Own Scottish Borderers
MURRAY Bernard T. MM Sjt 370979 8th London Regt
MURRAY Boyd MM Pte 7673 2nd Scottish Rifles KIA 28.11.17.
MURRAY Charles MM Pte 2590 6th Royal Irish Regt
MURRAY Charles H. MM L/Cpl 264 11th Hussars
MURRAY Colin MM L/Sjt 240312 1/4th Seaforth Highlanders
MURRAY Daniel MM Pte 240239 1/5th Royal Scots Fusiliers
MURRAY Daniel MM Pte 14800 Lancashire Fusiliers
MURRAY David MM L/Cpl 15389 17th Highland Light Infantry
MURRAY David MM L/Sjt 290316 Royal Highlanders
MURRAY David Martin MM L/Cpl 40888 9th Scottish Rifles KIA 18.6.17.
MURRAY Donald William MM Cpl 240065 1/5th Seaforth Highlanders
MURRAY Edward MM Sjt 19519 13th Liverpool Regt
MURRAY Edward Albert MM Bdr 950990 A/15 Bde RFA
MURRAY Ernest J. MM Sjt 591441 1/18th London Regt
MURRAY Eugene MM Bdr 800082 A/231 Bde RFA
MURRAY Francis "DCM,MM" Pte 11371 2nd Royal Dublin Fusiliers
MURRAY Francis S. MM L/Cpl 34421 Middlesex Regt
MURRAY Frank MM Pte 52758 10 Fd Amb RAMC
MURRAY Frederick MM Bdr 53336 RGA
MURRAY Frederick MM Pte 290127 Cheshire Regt
MURRAY Frederick MM Pte M2/149152 Army Service Corps
MURRAY George MM Pte 46654 6th South Staffordshire Regt
MURRAY George MM Cpl 240146 1/5th Seaforth Highlanders
MURRAY George MM Cpl 12760 7th Cameron Highlanders
MURRAY George "MM,MID" Pte 11187 6/7th Royal Scots Fusiliers
MURRAY George MM Pte 67758 213 Coy Machine Gun Corps
MURRAY George A. MM Dvr 750840 RFA
MURRAY George B. MM Pte 34972 Royal Scots Fusiliers
MURRAY Gordon R. MM Pte 5175 7th Seaforth Highlanders
MURRAY Harrison MM Sjt 11018 6th Border Regt
MURRAY Hector MM Gnr 88230 C/50 Bde RFA
MURRAY Henry E. MM BSM 147861 403 Bty RFA
MURRAY Henry Edward MM L/Cpl 7662 12th Lancers DOW 3.4.18.
MURRAY Herbert MM Sjt 26906 RFA
MURRAY Herbert E. MM Pte 57908 Royal Welsh Fusiliers
MURRAY I.L. MM Dvr 2107 RFA
MURRAY J. MM Sjt 295468 12th Royal Scots Fusiliers
MURRAY J. "MM,MID" Cpl 254185 Signal Service Royal Engineers
MURRAY J. MM Pte 27283 Scottish Rifles
MURRAY J. MM Pte 202054 Seaforth Highlanders
MURRAY James MM Pte 17074 1st Royal Dublin Fusiliers
MURRAY James MM Dvr 96873 B/157 Bde RFA
MURRAY James MM Pte 39631 10 Fd Amb RAMC
MURRAY James MM Pte 10544 Gordon Highlanders
MURRAY James MM Cpl 290870 Gordon Highlanders
MURRAY James MM Cpl 12164 6th King's Own Scottish Borderers
MURRAY James MM Pte 266556 7th Liverpool Regt
MURRAY James MM Pte 26629 Royal Dublin Fusiliers
MURRAY James Gordon MM Sjt 7739 1/7th Gordon Highlanders
MURRAY John MM L/Cpl 27979 1st Royal Dublin Fusiliers
MURRAY John MM Pte 49689 7th Bn Machine Gun Corps
MURRAY John MM L/Cpl 2905 1/4th Royal Lancaster Regt
MURRAY John MM Pte 17930 1/4th Gordon Highlanders KIA 25.7.18.
MURRAY John B.P. MM 2nd Cpl 249556 51 Div Sig Coy Royal Engineers
MURRAY John David MM Spr 69449 138 Army Troops Coy Royal Engineers
MURRAY John G. MM Bdr 37337 RFA
MURRAY John George MM Bdr 68479 52 Bty 15 Bde RFA KIA 2.9.18.
MURRAY John P. MM Sjt 23590 12th Bn Machine Gun Corps
MURRAY Kenneth MM Cpl 82863 55th Bn Machine Gun Corps
MURRAY Kenneth MM L/Cpl 40232 Seaforth Highlanders
MURRAY Michael MM+Bar Pte 10300 1st Royal Dublin Fusiliers
MURRAY Michael MM Pte 11320 6th Yorkshire Light Infantry
MURRAY Michael MM Sjt 36730 40 Bde RFA
MURRAY Murdo MM Pte 43022 2nd Seaforth Highlanders
MURRAY Murdo MM Pte 7311 Seaforth Highlanders
MURRAY P. MM L/Cpl 1851 2nd Royal Scots
MURRAY Peter MM Pte 1883 11th Highland Light Infantry
MURRAY Reginald J. MM Sjt 7440 Scots Guards
MURRAY Richard MM Pte 4321 1/17th London Regt
MURRAY Robert MM Sjt 26337 Royal Inniskilling Fusiliers
MURRAY Robert MM Cpl 42836 26 Fd Amb RAMC
MURRAY Robert MM Sjt 3802 144 Heavy Bty RGA
MURRAY Robert James "MM,MSM" Pte 40298 Tank Corps
MURRAY Robert Raymond MM Gnr 203754 276 Bde RFA
MURRAY Sam MM Sjt 11388 King's Own Scottish Borderers
MURRAY Samuel MM Cpl 2937 Durham Light Infantry
MURRAY Sylvester MM Pte 307362 15th Bn Tank Corps
MURRAY T. MM Air Mech 2 7330 Royal Flying Corps
MURRAY Thierman Bryant "DCM,MM" Sjt 100393 D/277 Bde RFA
MURRAY Thomas MM Pte 99453 41st Bn Machine Gun Corps
MURRAY Thomas MM Spr 63855 Royal Engineers
MURRAY Thomas MM L/Cpl 425456 10th London Regt
MURRAY Thomas MM Bdr 3167 RFA
MURRAY Thomas MM Pte 53186 Royal Scots
MURRAY Thomas MM Pte R/37811 King's Royal Rifle Corps
MURRAY Thomas "MM+Bar,CG(F)" Pte 22427 15th Durham Light Infantry
MURRAY Thomas MM CSM 202265 Royal Highlanders

MURRAY W. "MM,MID" Sjt 320138 3 Fd Amb RAMC
MURRAY W. MM Pte 51567 Royal Highlanders
MURRAY Walker MM L/Cpl 27373 9th Yorkshire Light Infantry KIA 26.4.18.
MURRAY Wiliam D. MM Cpl M2/020303 Army Service Corps
MURRAY William MM Pte 276207 1/7th Arg & Suth Highlanders
MURRAY William MM Sjt 62755 524 Siege Bty RGA
MURRAY William MM Pte 18811 2nd Royal Irish Fusiliers
MURRAY William MM Pte 200825 1/7th Royal Highlanders
MURRAY William MM Pte 42524 2nd Royal Scots
MURRAY William MM Sjt 201607 1/5th Arg & Suth Highlanders
MURRAY William MM L/Cpl 240332 Seaforth Highlanders
MURRAY William MM Sjt 1131 1/5th Royal Highlanders
MURRAY William MM Sjt 609 1/5th Seaforth Highlanders
MURRAY William MM Cpl 17495 33 Bde RFA
MURRAY William A.E. MM Sjt 277137 RGA
MURRAY William Alex MM Sjt 650470 RFA
MURRAY William Allan MM L/Cpl 35217 8th Royal Lancaster Regt Died 29.1.19.
MURRAY William C. MM Sjt 6416 Royal West Surrey Regt
MURRAY William H. MM Cpl 240237 1/5th Royal Scots Fusiliers
MURRAY William H. MM Pte 1603 1/4th West Riding Regt
MURRAY William M. MM+Bar L/Bdr 771592 50 Div Ammn Col RFA
MURRAY William R. MM Pte 576223 8th London Regt
MURRAY Williams MM Pte 2919 8 Fd Amb RAMC
MURRELL Augustus MM Pte 8671 112 Coy Machine Gun Corps KIA 8.10.17.
MURRELL BertieF. MM Pte 241044 Suffolk Regt
MURRELL Ernest Alfred MM L/Cpl 6885 2nd Suffolk Regt KIA 26.9.17.
MURRELL George MM Pte 241699 Middlesex Regt
MURRELL Herman T. MM L/Cpl 115 17 Fd Amb RAMC
MURRELL James H. MM Cpl 20089 2/4th Hampshire Regt
MURRELL John MM SSM 206323 1/1st Gloucestershire Yeomanry
MURRELL Samuel D. MM Sjt 1076 1st Royal Warwickshire Regt
MURRELL Stanley H. MM Cpl 56525 18th King's Royal Rifle Corps
MURRELL Thomas MM Gnr 167980 RGA
MURRELL William E.H. "MM+Bar,MID" Cpl 17882 54 Fd Coy Royal Engineers
MURRELL William Henry MM Sjt 40049 1st South Staffordshire Regt
MURRELLS Charles E. MM Pte 5591 12th Middlesex Regt
MURRILL William H. MM Pte 652561 1/21st London Regt
MURROW Ralph G. MM Cpl 1676 Liverpool Regt
MURSELL H.W.W. MM Sjt 78035 Cav Corps Sig Sqn Royal Engineers
MURT John MM Pte 34011 Cheshire Regt
MURTAGH Bernard "DCM,MM(1793 Cpl)" CSM 240214 1/5th York & Lancaster Regt
MURTAGH James MM Pte 24134 Worcestershire Regt
MURTAGH Michael MM Pte 11170 1st Royal Irish Fusiliers
MURTAGH Percy MM Pte 307510 6th Liverpool Regt
MURTHA John MM Cpl 63085 B/113 Bde RFA
MURTOCK John T. MM L/Bdr 131122 263 Siege Bty RGA
MURTON A. MM Cpl 8002 1st Essex Regt
MURTON Alfred "DCM,MM" Bdr 38953 B/290 Bde RFA
MURTON Alfred S. "DCM,MM" Cpl 63330 32nd Bn Machine Gun Corps
MURTON Hubert MM Pte 43149 2nd Manchester Regt
MURTON John T. MM Pte 20418 24th Royal Fusiliers
MUSCROFT Andrew MM Gnr 1629 A/246 Bde RFA
MUSCROFT Frederick MM Cpl 29388 335 Siege Bty RGA
MUSCROFT John H. MM Pte 14963 8th York & Lancaster Regt
MUSGRAVE Charles George MM L/Cpl 1164 Lincolnshire Regt
MUSGRAVE Clarence MM Pte 8834 20th Hussars
MUSGRAVE Henry MM Cpl 11641 Coldstream Guards
MUSGRAVE Samuel MM L/Cpl 2403 Yorkshire Light Infantry
MUSGRAVE Timothy MM Sjt 7352 Northumberland Fusiliers
MUSGROVE Frederick MM Bdr 77513 RFA
MUSGROVE George H. MM Pte 17446 Bedfordshire Regt
MUSGROVE William MM Pte 265924 1/7th West Yorkshire Regt KIA 17.11.17.
MUSGROVE William MM Pte 330923 Royal Warwickshire Regt
MUSK Alfred E. MM Pte 37781 6th Royal West Surrey Regt
MUSK James R. MM Pte 64001 13th Yorkshire Regt
MUSK William Alfred MM Sjt 278729 21 Heavy Bty RGA DOW 13.2.19.
MUSKER Charles MM Bdr 9826 169 Bde RFA
MUSKER Robert MM Pte 50553 RAMC
MUSKETT Alfred MM Gnr 92203 319 Siege Bty RGA

MUSPRATT Walter MM Pte 34878 Middlesex Regt
MUSSABINI John L.P. MM L/Cpl 1277 Royal Engineers
MUSSELBROOK Frederick Cecil MM Bdr 44012 55 Bty 33 Bde RFA
MUSSELBROOK Sidney MM Pte 242017 Notts & Derby Regt
MUSSELL Richard James "MM,MID" Pte M2/121031 Army Service Corps att 'N'(AA)Bty RGA
MUSSELWHITE Frederick MM Pte 43825 8th Royal Inniskilling Fusiliers KIA 21.3.18.
MUSSELWHITE Wyndham H. "DCM,MM" CSM 550024 1/16th London Regt
MUSSETT Frederick H. MM L/Cpl 50989 Middlesex Regt
MUSSON Ernest W. MM L/Cpl 17488 11 Fd Coy Royal Engineers
MUSSON George T. MM Pte 240691 Leicestershire Regt
MUSSON John Francis MM Sjt 5968 3rd Coldstream Guards KIA 24.11.17.
MUSTARD Joseph Lightfoot MM Cpl 22392 11th Royal Lancaster Regt
MUSTARDE G. MM Spr 410405 Royal Engineers
MUSTCHIN William MM Pte 965 7th Royal Sussex Regt
MUSTOE Edward T. MM Sjt 16002 Machine Gun Corps
MUSTOE Frederick W. MM Pte 13679 8th Gloucestershire Regt
MUSTOE James MM Cpl 7321 1st Wiltshire Regt
MUTCH George MM Pte 1562 1/6th Gordon Highlanders
MUTCH George MM Cpl 623 1st Gordon Highlanders
MUTCH J. MM Bdr 630635 255 Bde RFA
MUTCH John MM Pte 31838 38th Bn Machine Gun Corps
MUTCH Morris MM Pte 11157 Royal Fusiliers
MUTCH Walter MM Sjt 2125 South Lancashire Regt
MUTIMER Herbert A. MM Pte 473104 RAMC
MUTIMER R. MM Pte 34857 Suffolk Regt
MUTIMER Ronald MM Cpl 120334 297 Siege Bty RGA KIA 23.7.17.
MUTIMER Thomas MM+Bar Pte 16519 2nd Suffolk Regt
MUTLOW Albert E.V. MM Pte 142472 3rd Bn Machine Gun Corps
MUTRIE Henry M. MM Pte 41758 1st Royal Scots Fusiliers
MUTTER Andrew MM L/Sjt 6209 1st Cameron Highlanders
MUTTER Robert MM Dvr 71475 RFA
MUTTERS Charles William "MC,DCM,MM+Bar" CSM 1175 2nd Manchester Regt
MUTTITT William Charles MM L/Cpl 11374 17th Royal Fusiliers KIA 8.12.17.
MUTTON Albert H. MM L/Cpl 18394 Northamptonshire Regt
MUTTON J.T. MM L/Cpl 6908 East Kent Regt
MYALL Frederick MM Pte 2926 12th Royal Fusiliers
MYATT Arthur Foster William MM Pte 532791 1/15th London Regt DOW 3.12.17.
MYATT B.C. MM Cpl 57162 RFA
MYATT George MM Sjt 40565 7th Norfolk Regt
MYATT Richard MM+Bar L/Sjt 8589 11th Royal Fusiliers
MYATT Robert MM Pte 17303 3rd Coldstream Guards
MYATT Vernon MM Gnr 326374 RGA
MYATT William MM Dvr 77599 RFA
MYCOCK Frederick MM Pte 30340 1st Royal Inniskilling Fusiliers
MYCOCK John W. MM Sjt 10353 7th East Surrey Regt
MYCOCK Sam MM Sjt 1788 1/7th Notts & Derby Regt KIA 21.3.18.
MYCOCK William MM L/Sjt 12195 2nd Royal Fusiliers
MYCOE Arthur MM Pte 16260 12th Cheshire Regt
MYERS C. MM Pte 50801 Yeomanry
MYERS Cornelius Linge MM Dvr 45542 11 Bde RFA
MYERS Edgar Charles MM Pte 50007 1st Royal Irish Fusiliers DOW 3.10.18.
MYERS Fred MM Sjt 16786 8th Yorkshire Light Infantry
MYERS George Dobson MM Bdr 26077 B/15 Bde RHA
MYERS George Felix MM Pte 49769 13th Liverpool Regt
MYERS H. MM Sjt 200493 Royal Lancaster Regt
MYERS Harry MM+Bar Sjt 476717 Royal Engineers
MYERS Henry MM Pte 331094 9th Liverpool Regt
MYERS Henry MM Pte 10520 7th Gloucestershire Regt
MYERS John MM L/Cpl 48445 13th Liverpool Regt KIA 31.8.18.
MYERS John J. MM+Bar Cpl 488666 465 Fd Coy Royal Engineers
MYERS Joseph Morris MM Pte 572484 1/17th London Regt KIA 3.12.17.
MYERS Robert MM CQMS 15182 11th Northumberland Fusiliers
MYERS Samuel James MM Cpl 19798 1st Hampshire Regt
MYERS Stanley MM Pte 31826 Northumberland Fusiliers
MYERS Thomas MM Pte 8755 2nd King's Royal Rifle Corps
MYERS Walter Joseph MM Pte 3652 7th East Kent Regt
MYERSCOUGH James E. MM L/Sjt 23144 14th Royal Welsh Fusiliers
MYERSCOUGH William H. MM L/Cpl 47612 Lancashire Fusiliers
MYHILL Albert E. MM Pte 50479 54th Bn Machine Gun Corps

MYHILL Arthur William MM Cpl 267235 1/6th Gloucestershire Regt KIA 24.10.17.
MYHILL John Knighton MM Sjt 85207 A/63 Bde RFA
MYHILL Reginald F. MM(40 Bde RFA)+Bar Spr 312346 Royal Engineers
MYHILL William E. MM+Bar Gnr 371144 115 Hy Bty RGA
MYLAND James MM Sjt 14125 12th West Yorkshire Regt
MYLEHAM Walter "DCM,MM" Cpl 427 'C' Bn Tank Corps
MYLES Alfred MM Cpl 11485 2nd King's Own Scottish Borderers
MYLES Andrew MM Pte 2307 1/7th Royal Highlanders KIA 25.4.17.
MYLES Cornelius MM Pte 4286 7th Leinster Regt
MYLES Herbert William MM Dvr 44846 RFA
MYLES James MM Cpl T4/241267 51 Div Train Army Service Corps
MYLES James MM Pte 267806 1/6th Royal Highlanders
MYLIE Christopher MM L/Sjt 14994 38th Bn Machine Gun Corps
MYLITT Harold MM+Bar Cpl 3467 2nd Northumberland Fusiliers
MYLNE John W. MM Cpl 344683 7 Fd Coy Royal Engineers
MYNES James MM Sjt 17460 41st Bn Machine Gun Corps
MYNETT Arthur Harry MM Spr 55846 296 Railway Coy Royal Engineers
MYNOTT Albert MM Sjt 325816 1/1st Cambridgeshire Regt
MYNOTT Charles MM+Bar L/Cpl 11965 10th West Yorkshire Regt
MYNOTT James C. MM Pte 14256 2nd Bedfordshire Regt
MYRING George MM Pte 7472 1st Leicestershire Regt
MYRING George William MM Pte 7850 1st Lincolnshire Regt
MYTTION Frank MM Sjt R/8397 16th King's Royal Rifle Corps KIA 13.4.18.

N

NABBS Francis G. MM Cpl 10009 Seaforth Highlanders
NADEN John MM Dvr 12524 D/160 Bde RFA
NADIN Harry MM L/Cpl 50577 10th Cheshire Regt
NADIN Joseph MM Pte 240697 York & Lancaster Regt
NADIN Terence MM+Bar Cpl 48556 RGA
NADIN W. MM Pte 240961 Notts & Derby Regt
NAGEL William John MM Pte 6/1241 18th King's Royal Rifle Corps
NAIRN Alexander MM+Bar Sjt 20160 35th Bn Machine Gun Corps
NAIRN Andrew MM Pte 200586 1/4th King's Own Scottish Borderers KIA 23.11.17.
NAIRN Andrew P. MM Cpl 200980 1/4th King's Own Scottish Borderers
NAIRN Frederick MM Pte 267608 1/6th Royal Highlanders
NAIRN John MM L/Cpl 400622 461 Fd Coy Royal Engineers
NAIRN John MM Sjt 201244 1/5th Arg & Suth Highlanders
NAIRN Matthew MM Spr 359820 32 Div Sig Coy Royal Engineers
NAISBITT John MM Dvr 82549 C/88 Bde RFA
NAISH Frank Herbert MM Sjt 9346 12th Royal Fusiliers
NAISH Harold T. MM Sjt 56895 Royal Welsh Fusiliers
NAISMITH James MM+Bar Sjt 4093 Gordon Highlanders
NAISMITH Peter MM L/Cpl 42275 15th Highland Light Infantry
NAISMITH Robert MM Spr 66403 23 Div Sig Coy Royal Engineers
NALDRETT John MM CSM 67561 32nd Bn Machine Gun Corps
NALL Richard MM Pte 35427 64 Coy Machine Gun Corps
NALLY Patrick MM Dvr 67884 460 Bty 15 Bde RFA
NALTY S. MM Pte 7520 Irish Guards
NANCARROW Arthur MM Pte 18364 East Lancashire Regt
NANCE Fred MM Sjt 306662 8th Lancashire Fusiliers
NANGLE Patrick MM L/Cpl 9830 1st Royal Scots
NANSON Robert MM Sjt 43455 7th Bedfordshire Regt DOW 8.5.17
NAPIER Albert MM Dvr 7033 C/157 Bde RFA
NAPIER George MM Pte 19982 1/4th Gordon Highlanders
NAPIER George MM Sjt 9315 1st Border Regt
NAPIER James MM L/Cpl 33104 6th King's Own Scottish Borderers
NAPIER James MM+Bar Sjt 406052 51 Div Sig Coy Royal Engineers
NAPIER James Ross "MBE,MC,MM(5063 Sjt A&SH)" 2/Lt Rifle Brigade
NAPIER Richard MM Pte 3830 Liverpool Regt KIA 13.4.18.
NAPIER Robert MM Pte 291578 1/8th Scottish Rifles
NAPIER Thomas MM Cpl M2/148958 Army Service Corps
NAPIER William MM Cpl 300461 1/4(Highland)Mountain Bty RGA
NAPIER William MM Sjt 325075 1/8th Royal Scots
NAPPER Edwin MM Cpl 925253 A/280 Bde RFA
NAPPER Thomas C. MM Spr 3642 'G' Cable Section Royal Engineers
NAPPIN Edmund J. MM Spr 357393 Guards Div Sig Coy Royal Engineers
NAPPIN William Robert MM Sjt 68010 87 Bty 2 Bde RFA KIA 8.10.16.
NAPTIN George T. MM Cpl 41124 RFA
NARRACOTT Henry MM L/Cpl 22187 Liverpool Regt
NARRIE William MM Pte 24663 15th Royal Scots KIA 28.4.17.
NASH Albert E. MM Cpl 421074 10th London Regt
NASH Albert F. MM Bdr 56688 RFA
NASH Alfred H. "MM,MSM,MID" Cpl 418 9th Royal Fusiliers
NASH Allen Harrison MM Bdr 205 RFA
NASH Arthur MM L/Sjt 8620 2nd Gordon Highlanders
NASH Arthur MM 2nd Cpl 335 40 Broad Gauge Rly Coy Royal Engineers
NASH Arthur MM Pte S/27375 Rifle Brigade
NASH Arthur MM Pte 228554 1st London Regt
NASH Arthur J. "MM,MID" Sjt 26729 36 Bde RFA
NASH Arthur William MM Pte 25360 10th East Yorkshire Regt
NASH Charles B. MM L/Cpl 21267 1st Coldstream Guards
NASH Edward MM CSM 7583 4th York & Lancaster Regt
NASH Edward C. MM Pte 55729 4th York & Lancaster Regt
NASH Edward Frank MM+Bar Sjt 241986 1/5th Gloucestershire Regt KIA 10.8.18.
NASH Edward Mills MM Sjt 78480 Tank Corps
NASH Edward Robert MM L/Cpl 128960 45th Royal Fusiliers DOW 16.9.19.
NASH Edward William MM L/Cpl 40490 Lincolnshire Regt
NASH Enoch MM Sjt 21257 Yorkshire Light Infantry
NASH Ernest MM L/Cpl 5986 9th East Surrey Regt KIA 27.3.18.
NASH Ernest Nelson MM Pte 50020 1st Royal Irish Fusiliers
NASH Ernest W. MM Pte 53382 RAMC
NASH F.H. MM Pte 43592 Essex Regt
NASH Frank MM Pte 90788 29th Bn Machine Gun Corps
NASH Frank S. MM Cpl 281741 4th London Regt
NASH G.H. MM Sjt 19121 7th East Kent Regt
NASH George MM S/Sjt 39053 RGA Died 21.6.19.
NASH Harold G. MM Pte 7935 2nd Gloucestershire Regt
NASH Henry J. MM Bdr 14411 3 Div Ammn Col RFA
NASH Herbert E. MM Spr 500330 Royal Engineers
NASH Horace MM Spr 359534 406 Fd Coy Royal Engineers
NASH James MM Pte 14323 9th South Staffordshire Regt
NASH James MM Bdr 28799 B/173 Bde RFA DOW 22.9.17.
NASH Jesse MM Sub Cond 07086 Army Ordnance Corps
NASH John MM L/Cpl 16402 8th Bedfordshire Regt
NASH John MM Bdr 56596 20 Div Sig Coy Royal Engineers
NASH John Frederick MM Sjt 11351 11th Hampshire Regt KIA 23.3.18.
NASH Joseph MM Pte 1836 1/13th London Regt
NASH Joseph MM Pte 43148 7/8th Royal Inniskilling Fusiliers KIA 20.11.17.
NASH M. MM Cpl 777032 C/84 Bde RFA
NASH Percy E. MM Sjt 59062 30 Div Ammn Col RFA
NASH Percy O. MM Sjt 10246 King's Royal Rifle Corps
NASH Robert F. MM Pte 16/784 1st West Yorkshire Regt
NASH Theodore W.J. MM Pte 139738 Machine Gun Corps
NASH Walter MM Pte 1727 Welsh Regt
NASH Wilfred Henry MM Gnr 94341 69 Siege Bty RGA KIA 11.2.18.
NASH William MM Pte 203460 Durham Light Infantry
NASH William MM L/Cpl 13597 7th Shropshire Light Infantry
NASH William MM Sjt 13509 9th North Staffordshire Regt
NASH William H. MM+Bar Cpl 235429 Leicestershire Regt
NASH William Henry MM Cpl 3163 4th Oxf & Bucks Light Infantry
NASH William J. MM Pte 8742 11th Royal Warwickshire Regt
NASH William P. MM Cpl 52189 26th Royal Welsh Fusiliers
NASON Harry MM Pte 12855 9th West Riding Regt
NATHAN Leonard MM Sjt 2016 1/9th London Regt
NATTRASS Ernest MM Pte 41484 1st Leicestershire Regt
NATTRASS Ralph MM Pte 19778 Durham Light Infantry
NATTRASS Thomas MM L/Cpl 32885 2nd Durham Light Infantry
NATTRESS Joseph MM Spr 207980 248 Fd Coy Royal Engineers
NAUDÉ Reginald F. MM L/Cpl A/200154 King's Royal Rifle Corps
NAUGHTON Andrew MM Pte 49797 157 Coy Machine Gun Corps
NAUGHTON John "DCM,MM" Sjt 121612 185 Tunnelling Coy Royal Engineers
NAUGHTON John MM Pte 61199 23rd Lancashire Fusiliers
NAVEN Edwin MM Dvr 65276 RFA
NAVESEY Edward MM Cpl 19086 East Lancashire Regt
NAVIN Thomas MM Pte 24605 1st Royal Dublin Fusiliers
NAYLOR Albert MM Sjt 312071 RGA
NAYLOR Albert MM Dvr 186844 RFA
NAYLOR Benjamin MM Cpl 24083 15th Notts & Derby Regt
NAYLOR Bennett MM Sjt 206649 Yorkshire Light Infantry

NAYLOR Charles "MM,MID" Sjt S4/125649 Army Service Corps
NAYLOR Charles B. MM Bdr 775828 C/310 Bde RFA
NAYLOR Edward MM Pte 210914 York & Lancaster Regt
NAYLOR Edward "DCM,MM,MMV(It)" L/Cpl 241539 9th York & Lancaster Regt
NAYLOR Frank MM Spr 81427 Royal Engineers
NAYLOR H. MM Cpl 711738 RFA
NAYLOR Harold MM Cpl 5921 Machine Gun Corps
NAYLOR Harry MM Pte 236267 2nd West Yorkshire Regt
NAYLOR Harry MM Pte 8720 Irish Guards
NAYLOR Harry MM L/Cpl 17992 Manchester Regt
NAYLOR Horace MM L/Cpl 308056 2nd West Riding Regt KIA 15.4.18.
NAYLOR Horatio MM Sjt 32406 RAMC
NAYLOR James MM Bdr 661721 RFA
NAYLOR James MM Cpl 432074 Royal Engineers
NAYLOR James Harold MM Pte 201689 2nd West Riding Regt KIA 29.7.18.
NAYLOR Joe MM L/Cpl 35018 4th Royal Fusiliers
NAYLOR John William MM Pte 17993 20th Manchester Regt DOW 5.9.16.
NAYLOR Joseph MM Cpl 241579 1/5th South Lancashire Regt KIA 1.12.17.
NAYLOR Nicholas MM Sjt 41056 9th Royal Fusiliers
NAYLOR Robert MM+Bar Gnr 6137 34 Bde RFA
NAYLOR Samuel MM Sjt 8548 2nd Lincolnshire Regt KIA 23.10.16.
NAYLOR Septimus MM Dvr 750230 A/47 Bde RFA
NAYLOR Thomas MM Pte 21812 4th Grenadier Guards KIA 1.12.17.
NAYLOR William MM Pte 76531 19th Durham Light Infantry
NAYLOR William MM Pte 20423 2nd Yorkshire Regt KIA 8.5.18.
NAYLOR William MM Dvr 796101 150 Bde Ammn Col RFA
NAYLOR William MM Pte 4662 1/4th Yorkshire Light Infantry
NAYLOR William H. MM Pte 52230 9th West Riding Regt
NAYSMITH J.G. MM+Bar Cpl 44719 RAMC
NEAGLE Thomas F. MM Pte 10823 2nd Irish Guards
NEAIL Herbert MM L/Cpl 13737 16th Notts & Derby Regt KIA 25.3.18.
NEAL Alfred MM Pte 300300 Durham Light Infantry
NEAL Archer Bowles MM Pte 15868 Coldstream Guards KIA 15.9.16.
NEAL Charles A. MM Pte 6402 Royal Fusiliers
NEAL Fielden MM Pte 52019 8th Lincolnshire Regt
NEAL Frederick MM Pte 241360 Gloucestershire Regt
NEAL Frederick Charles MM L/Cpl 7397 2nd Hampshire Regt DOW 4.10.18.
NEAL George W. MM Pte 38908 Durham Light Infantry
NEAL Harry W. MM S/Sjt 419008 RAMC
NEAL John MM Pte 555 11 Fd Amb RAMC
NEAL John MM Sjt 723141 24th London Regt
NEAL John MM+Bar Sjt 69504 142 Army Troops Coy Royal Engineers
NEAL Percy MM Cpl 15109 4th Royal Fusiliers
NEAL Stanley MM Sjt 9691 2nd East Yorkshire Regt
NEAL W.J. MM L/Sjt 720922 London Regt
NEAL Walter MM Pte 3/6701 1st Bedfordshire Regt KIA 12.9.16.
NEAL William MM CQMS 42048 15th North Lancashire Regt
NEALE Alfred MM BSM 42729 RFA
NEALE Arthur MM Pte 7245 9th Royal Warwickshire Regt
NEALE Arthur Frederick MM Sjt M2/121502 611 MT Coy Army Service Corps
NEALE Atlee MM Sjt 44420 130 Fd Coy Royal Engineers KIA 19.6.17.
NEALE Charles MM Dvr 14122 RFA
NEALE Charles H. MM Gnr 132300 X/9 Med TM Bty RFA KIA 22.3.18.
NEALE E. MM Sjt 20845 Machine Gun Corps
NEALE Edward J. MM Pte 36073 69 Fd Amb RAMC
NEALE Edward Thomas "MM,MID" Pte 9591 1st Dorsetshire Regt
NEALE Ernest MM L/Cpl 7881 13th Manchester Regt
NEALE Ernest A. MM Pte 718166 23rd London Regt
NEALE Frank MM L/Cpl 12879 6th Royal Berkshire Regt
NEALE Frederick W. MM L/Sjt 7655 11th Royal Fusiliers
NEALE George MM+Bar L/Cpl 22/126 22nd Northumberland Fusiliers KIA 30.8.16.
NEALE Harry MM Pte 19299 Hampshire Regt
NEALE Harry MM L/Sjt 18556 16th Notts & Derby Regt KIA 20.9.17.
NEALE Henry MM Pte 18771 Royal Warwickshire Regt
NEALE Henry T. MM Cpl 4219 1st Dragoons
NEALE Herbert C. MM Pte 65772 RAMC
NEALE Herbert G. MM Pte 2111 1st Welsh Guards
NEALE John MM Gnr 166130 RGA
NEALE R. MM Cpl 13168 2nd Essex Regt
NEALE Ralph C. MM CSM 480031 457 Fd Coy Royal Engineers
NEALE Sidney Charles MM Pte 536047 1/5(London)Fd Amb RAMC
NEALE Walter MM L/Cpl 13594 2nd Grenadier Guards
NEALE Walter MM+Bar Sjt 12013 4th Worcestershire Regt DOW 20.4.18.
NEALE Walter C. MM Pte 9008 4th Hussars
NEALE Walter E. MM Pte 99396 Machine Gun Corps
NEALE Walter P. MM L/Cpl 14541 Royal West Surrey Regt
NEALE William George Victor MM L/Cpl 350390 7th London Regt KIA 25.7.18.
NEALE William H. MM Cpl 70160 6th Royal West Surrey Regt
NEALE William H. MM Cpl 423138 10th London Regt
NEALE William Robert MM Pte 4258 1/24th London Regt
NEALL Harold F. MM Pte 41181 Duke of Cornwall's LI
NEALLY James MM Cpl 40943 17th Royal Scots KIA 30.9.18.
NEALON Hubert Marshall Westcott MM Gnr Wheeler 101940 V/32 Hy TM Bty RFA
NEARY Charles F.W. MM Cpl 24094 57 Fd Coy Royal Engineers
NEARY John "DCM,MM" CSM 18655 7th East Lancashire Regt
NEARY Joseph MM Gnr 5508 X/14 Med TM Bty RGA KIA 21.4.17.
NEASHAM Charles MM Pte 1540 1/6th Durham Light Infantry
NEASHAM Frederick W. MM Cpl 16571 3rd Dragoon Guards
NEAT William E. MM Pte 240187 Seaforth Highlanders
NEATBY Ernest MM Cpl 11826 9th West Riding Regt
NEATE Alfred MM+Bar L/Cpl 28757 15th Hampshire Regt
NEATE Arthur MM Pte 36836 Royal Berkshire Regt
NEATE Egbert Lewis MM Dvr 16096 85 Bty 11 Bde RFA DOW 24.9.18.
NEATH William James MM Gnr 137208 RGA
NEAVE Charles MM Gnr 170444 Y/16 Med TM Bty RFA
NEAVE David Albert John MM Sjt 301024 89 Fd Amb RAMC
NEAVE J.E. MM Pte 7393 Rifle Brigade
NEAVE James MM Sjt 9405 1st King's Own Scottish Borderers KIA 18.8.18.
NEAVE Percy MM Dvr 44748 D/256 Bde RFA
NEAVERSON Alfred MM Bdr 44144 RGA
NEAVES Harold MM Cpl R/21883 King's Royal Rifle Corps
NEAVES Harry G. MM Pte 39445 6th Royal West Kent Regt
NEBEN William MM Sjt 351011 7th London Regt DOW 10.8.18.
NEDDERMAN Robert Moses MM Cpl 240594 2/5th West Riding Regt KIA 20.7.18.
NEED Frank MM Pte 39342 South Wales Borderers
NEED Leonard Hubert MM Pte 35655 7th Wiltshire Regt
NEEDHAM Arthur Charles MM CSM 240146 Lincolnshire Regt
NEEDHAM Edward MM L/Cpl 37912 12th Manchester Regt
NEEDHAM Eric W. MM Sjt 355197 10th Liverpool Regt
NEEDHAM Ernest H. MM L/Cpl 20192 Duke of Cornwall's LI
NEEDHAM Frederick MM Cpl 11441 2nd West Riding Regt
NEEDHAM George MM Pte 200162 1st Bn Tank Corps
NEEDHAM Henry T. MM Pte 250 4th Bn GMGR
NEEDHAM John MM Pte 200999 2nd Lincolnshire Regt
NEEDHAM Jonathan MM Pte 425681 Labour Corps
NEEDHAM Samuel Edgar MM Pte 23929 32 Fd Amb RAMC
NEEDHAM Thomas A. MM Cpl 21431 18th Durham Light Infantry
NEEDHAM William MM Pte 302926 2nd Manchester Regt
NEEDHAM William Henry MM Cpl 44695 150 Coy Machine Gun Corps
NEEDLE Percy MM Cpl 18160 Machine Gun Corps
NEEDLE Philip MM L/Cpl 41769 Royal Engineers
NEEDLE Tom James MM Pte 13857 6th Northamptonshire Regt KIA 7.8.18.
NEEDLEY Frank B. MM L/Cpl 371360 8th London Regt
NEEDS Hubert MM L/Cpl 76981 2nd Bn Tank Corps
NEEDS James Edward MM Sjt 6730 2nd Middlesex Regt KIA 24.4.18.
NEEDS Robert MM Cpl 487 1st Welsh Guards
NEELD Henry Cobus MM Gnr 1486 C/76 Bde RFA KIA 21.8.18.
NEELY Andrew MM Pte 18730 Machine Gun Corps
NEELY Samuel James Dyas MM Cpl 13114 12th Lancers
NEELY Thomas "VC,MM" L/Sjt 32827 8th Royal Lancaster Regt KIA 1.10.18.
NEESAM Fred "DCM,MM" CSM 277699 2/7th Durham Light Infantry
NEESON James MM L/Cpl 456 2nd Arg & Suth Highlanders
NEESON John MM Pte 22735 9th Royal Irish Fusiliers
NEEVES George E. MM Pte 33690 8th Royal Warwickshire Regt
NEEVES Percy MM Pte 12223 1/4th Suffolk Regt
NEGUS Arthur MM L/Cpl P/1179 Rifle Brigade

NEGUS Charles W. MM Cpl 30983 Royal Engineers
NEGUS James C. MM Pte R/12006 King's Royal Rifle Corps
NEGUS Joseph P. "DCM,MM+Bar" Sjt 20505 11th Suffolk Regt
NEHAN Walter G. MM Dvr 46144 RFA
NEIGHBOUR Alfred E. MM Cpl 392318 9th London Regt
NEIL Albert MM Gnr 227621 102 Bde RFA
NEIL Alexander MM Spr 45770 97 Fd Coy Royal Engineers KIA 20.2.18.
NEIL Arthur R. MM Sjt 470369 1/12th London Regt
NEIL James A. MM Pte 44190 12th North Staffordshire Regt
NEIL John MM Sjt 275218 1/7th Arg & Suth Highlanders
NEIL John MM L/Cpl 11441 9th Scottish Rifles
NEIL John J. "DCM,MM" Sjt 531737 1/15th London Regt
NEIL Peter MM Gnr 159374 RFA
NEIL William MM Sjt 200344 Arg & Suth Highlanders
NEIL William "MM,MID" L/Sjt 10499 1st Yorkshire Light Infantry
NEILD Charles MM Pte 18852 1st East Lancashire Regt KIA 1.7.16.
NEILD Frank MM Pte 52683 Liverpool Regt
NEILD John Henry MM Pte 20843 6th Bn Machine Gun Corps
NEILE Edward MM Sjt 7971 2nd Hampshire Regt
NEILES Thomas MM Pte 11990 Royal Lancaster Regt
NEILL Alexander MM L/Cpl 9/13355 Royal Irish Rifles
NEILL Andrew Cloakie MM Pte 43346 12th Royal Scots KIA 25.4.18.
NEILL David MM Pte 7305 Machine Gun Corps
NEILL Frederick William MM Bdr 38025 31 Heavy Bty RGA
NEILL Henry W. MM Pte 31301 41st Bn Machine Gun Corps
NEILL Jack H. MM Bdr 955761 44 Bde RFA
NEILL Joseph MM Pte 24752 Machine Gun Corps
NEILL Michael MM Sjt 29026 RGA
NEILL Richard MM Pte 14916 Royal Inniskilling Fusiliers
NEILL Robert MM Pte 200511 Royal Scots
NEILL Samuel MM Pnr 32761 Royal Engineers
NEILL Samuel MM Pte 41350 RAMC
NEILL William Atkinson MM+Bar Sjt 15369 8th Royal Lancaster Regt
NEILLY William MM Spr 146350 81 Fd Coy Royal Engineers
NEILSON Hugh "DCM,MM" CSM 412007 409 Fd Coy Royal Engineers
NEILSON Hugh MM Sjt 975 26th Middlesex Regt
NEILSON James MM Dvr 103947 B/48 Bde RFA
NEILSON John MM Pte 5817 9th Seaforth Highlanders
NEILSON John MM Pte 21053 11th Royal Scots
NEILSON Robert MM Pte 50294 15th Highland Light Infantry
NEILSON Robert MM L/Cpl 1359 1/6th Scottish Rifles
NEILSON William MM L/Cpl 4380 10th Arg & Suth Highlanders
NEISH Alexander Nimmo MM Sjt 490898 1/13th London Regt KIA 3.5.18.
NEISH John MM Sjt 4356 9th Seaforth Highlanders
NELHAMS Arthur MM Sjt 810424 C/231 Bde RFA
NELHAMS Charles MM Sjt 9878 1st Royal Berkshire Regt
NELLIST Robert MM Pte S/13219 Rifle Brigade
NELMES Charles MM Pte 21403 South Wales Borderers
NELMES David J. MM Cpl 26068 Machine Gun Corps
NELMES Edgar "MM,MID" Pte 14296 2nd Grenadier Guards
NELSEY Charles "MM,MID" Bdr 42594 9 Heavy Bty RGA
NELSON Aaron MM Pte 11169 1/7th Gordon Highlanders
NELSON Albert Ernest MM L/Cpl 6322 14th Royal Irish Rifles KIA 1.7.16.
NELSON Alfred MM Sjt 26078 8th Border Regt KIA 10.4.18.
NELSON Andrew MM Bdr 686686 RFA
NELSON Arthur MM Sjt 2311 1/6th Northumberland Fusiliers KIA 27.5.18.
NELSON Basil MM Sjt 24773 Lancashire Fusiliers
NELSON Cornelius MM L/Cpl 267185 2/7th Royal Warwickshire Regt KIA 3.12.17.
NELSON David C. MM Pte 33567 Royal Scots
NELSON Edgar James MM Bdr 940376 D/280 Bde RFA
NELSON Edwin MM Pte 42094 RAMC
NELSON Frank MM Pte 21941 18th Durham Light Infantry
NELSON Fred MM Sjt 9003 Yorkshire Regt
NELSON Frederick MM Pte 13388 7th Liverpool Regt
NELSON Frederick MM Dvr 12588 RFA
NELSON G.W. MM Air Mech 1 13230 Royal Flying Corps
NELSON George "DCM,MM,MMV(lt)" L/Cpl 302936 12th Durham Light Infantry
NELSON George A. MM Sjt 300490 1/7th Essex Regt
NELSON Gordon W. MM Pte 531040 15th London Regt
NELSON J.T. MM Cpl 19358 Yorkshire Regt
NELSON James MM Pte 9532 8th Royal Highlanders KIA 12.10.17.
NELSON James MM Bdr 34145 Y/38 Med TM Bty RFA KIA 29.10.16.
NELSON James E. MM L/Sjt 295132 12th Somerset Light Infantry
NELSON James H. MM Pte 57758 Liverpool Regt
NELSON John MM CSM 42607 72 Coy Labour Corps
NELSON John MM Pte 291226 Scottish Rifles
NELSON John MM Dvr 5050 RFA
NELSON John MM Pte Z/574 2nd Rifle Brigade KIA 31.7.17.
NELSON Joseph William MM Pte 266827 6th West Riding Regt
NELSON Leonard MM Sjt 201312 2/4th York & Lancaster Regt
NELSON Lewis "MM,MID" L/Cpl 15888 12th Notts & Derby Regt
NELSON Robert MM Pte 19/622 19th Durham Light Infantry Died 3.11.18.
NELSON Robert "DCM,MM" Sjt 13419 1st Essex Regt KIA 23.8.18.
NELSON Robert MM Pte 11706 1st Royal Scots Fusiliers
NELSON Roland MM Pte S/13321 Rifle Brigade
NELSON S. MM Pte 305579 West Riding Regt
NELSON Stanley MM Sjt 23742 2nd South Wales Borderers DOW 26.8.18.
NELSON Stewart J. MM Sjt 2962 10th Hussars
NELSON Thomas MM Pte 56032 Welsh Regt
NELSON Thomas A. MM Pte 17/2021 Royal Irish Rifles
NELSON Thomas R. MM Spr 78097 Royal Engineers
NELSON Walter MM Spr 528192 54 Div Sig Coy Royal Engineers
NELSON Walter MM Cpl 23/488 19th Durham Light Infantry
NELSON Wesley A. MM Pte 129754 63rd Bn Machine Gun Corps
NELSON William MM Gnr 10618 C/165 Bde RFA
NELSON William "DCM,MM+Bar" Sjt 121806 252 Tunnelling Coy Royal Engineers
NELSON William MM Pte S/15441 Rifle Brigade
NELSON William MM Dvr 71335 RFA
NELSON William F. MM Pte 102439 Notts & Derby Regt AKA James VANDOREN.
NELSON William L. MM Cpl 700640 RFA
NENDICK Fred MM Sjt 771515 50 Div Ammn Col RFA
NESBIT Frank MM Cpl 37304 20th Northumberland Fusiliers
NESBIT John W. MM Sjt 290792 Northumberland Fusiliers
NESBIT R. MM Pte A/202188 King's Royal Rifle Corps
NESBITT Alex "DCM,MM" Sjt 14478 9th Royal Inniskilling Fusiliers
NESBITT C.F. MM Air Mech 1 13990 Royal Flying Corps
NESBITT George MM Sjt 41198 9th Royal Irish Fusiliers
NESBITT George Robert MM L/Cpl 250491 1/6th Durham Light Infantry
NESBITT John MM Sjt 41403 A/124 Bde RFA
NESBITT Robert MM Sjt 34228 16th Royal Warwickshire Regt
NESBITT Samuel MM Pte 2967 South Lancashire Regt
NESBITT Stephen MM Pte 3/10056 18th Durham Light Infantry
NESBITT Thomas MM Cpl 12698 2nd Welsh Regt KIA 23.9.16.
NESMITH Archibald MM Pte 8682 2nd Royal Welsh Fusiliers KIA 22.6.16.
NESS Ernest R. MM Pte 6965 RAMC
NESS Thomas McL. MM L/Cpl 43110 1/4th Royal Scots Fusiliers
NESS W. MM Pte 267666 10th Northumberland Fusiliers
NESS William MM Dvr 831775 A/87 Bde RFA KIA 14.4.18.
NESS William MM Pte 2095 1/6th Seaforth Highlanders KIA 15.11.16.
NESSFIELD Richard S. MM Pte 2558 1/4th Yorkshire Regt
NESSWORTHY William R. MM Pte 14246 Durham Light Infantry
NETHERCOTT Arthur MM Pte M2/167360 Army Service Corps att RAMC
NETHERCOTT William MM Pte 17506 6th South Wales Borderers Died 14.11.18.
NETHERTON Charles Matthew MM Sjt 755279 B/251 Bde RFA
NETHERWOOD James A. MM Pte 18359 2nd Royal Scots Fusiliers
NETHEY Arthur F. "MM,MID" F/Sjt 104 Royal Flying Corps
NETTELL Arthur MM Spr 121983 177 Tunnelling Coy Royal Engineers DOW 9.1.17.
NETTLE William MM Spr 224201 Signal Service Royal Engineers
NETTLE William "MM,MIDx2" Spr 66948 Royal Engineers
NETTLETON Albert MM Dvr T4/252514 62 Div Train Army Service Corps
NETTLETON Harry MM Pte 13265 4th King's Royal Rifle Corps
NETTLETON Herbert MM Sjt 21268 East Yorkshire Regt
NETTS Henry MM Pte 10898 King's Royal Rifle Corps
NEVARD Arthur MM CSM 3229 7th East Kent Regt
NEVARD Harold MM L/Cpl 43021 Essex Regt
NEVE Albert H. MM Pte 203221 York & Lancaster Regt
NEVE Eric M. MM Pte 4939 24th London Regt
NEVE Victor George MM Sjt S/1827 Rifle Brigade
NEVE Wilfred Percy MM L/Cpl R/13222 9th King's Royal Rifle Corps
NEVILL David T. MM Dvr 123055 RFA
NEVILL Ephraim Jerome MM Dvr 6422 58 Bty 35 Bde RFA

NEVILLE Albert MM Pte 9401 1st Lincolnshire Regt
NEVILLE Arthur MM Pte 17963 1st Northamptonshire Regt
NEVILLE Bertie MM Sjt 3723 8th Hussars
NEVILLE Edward E. MM Bdr 321 MGC(Motors)
NEVILLE Frederick "DCM,MM" Pte 1038 15th Hussars
NEVILLE Frederick G. MM Sjt 24256 RGA
NEVILLE George H. MM Dvr 51716 'O' Bty RHA
NEVILLE Harry MM L/Cpl 39698 11th East Lancashire Regt
NEVILLE Henry MM Pte 202610 Royal Berkshire Regt
NEVILLE Henry William "MM,MID" Sjt 269 6th East Kent Regt
NEVILLE James MM Pte 25857 Royal Dublin Fusiliers
NEVILLE John MM Pte 376924 10th Manchester Regt
NEVILLE Joseph MM Pte 29954 Middlesex Regt
NEVILLE William "MM,MIDx2" Bdsm 7511 1st South Staffordshire Regt
NEVILLE William MM Dvr 46917 RFA
NEVILLE William F. MM Pte M/225758 Army Service Corps att RGA.
NEVIN Christopher MM Pte 5337 2nd Royal Munster Fusiliers
NEVIN Michael MM Cpl 7/6259 15th Royal Irish Rifles
NEVIN Nicholas MM Cpl 1749 2nd Royal Irish Regt
NEVIN Phillip John MM Dvr T2/015757 16 Div Train Army Service Corps att RAMC.
NEVITT George MM Pte 240252 1/5th South Lancashire Regt
NEVITT George H. MM Cpl 91299 C/161 Bde RFA
NEW Alfred Edmund MM Sjt 8867 1st Hampshire Regt KIA 1.7.16.
NEW Arthur C.H. MM Pte 11280 7th Lincolnshire Regt
NEW Charles MM Pte 303343 1/5th Arg & Suth Highlanders KIA 28.9.18.
NEW Charles E. MM Sjt 8606 Grenadier Guards
NEW George "DCM,MM" Sjt 15470 8th South Lancashire Regt
NEW Harold MM Sjt 55791 57 Bde RFA
NEW Leonard MM Pte M2/120179 566 Coy Army Service Corps
NEW William G. MM Pte 250759 2/3rd London Regt
NEW William J. MM Pte 68290 8th Royal West Surrey Regt
NEWALL Arthur A. MM Pte 15641 1st Devonshire Regt
NEWALL Donald N. MM Gnr 82103 354 Siege Bty RGA
NEWALL Frank MM Sjt 12872 Liverpool Regt
NEWALL Richard MM L/Cpl 7536 Gordon Highlanders
NEWALL Robert MM Sjt 28989 East Surrey Regt
NEWARK John MM Bdr 37788 A/83 Bde RFA
NEWBERRY David S. MM CSM 350194 1/9th Royal Scots
NEWBERRY Frederick MM Pnr 129021 Royal Engineers
NEWBERRY P.T. "MM,MID" Pte 13884 5th South Wales Borderers
NEWBERRY Thomas Henry MM Pte 2237 1/2(North Midland)Fd Amb RAMC
NEWBERRY Walter MM Pte 303090 1/7th Lancashire Fusiliers DOW 30.9.18.
NEWBERRY William Charles MM CQMS 5150 Devonshire Regt
NEWBERY Leslie MM Pte 13931 Wiltshire Regt
NEWBERY Sidney J. MM Gnr 55199 RFA
NEWBLE Percy E. MM Sjt 9581 1st East Surrey Regt
NEWBOLD Frank R. MM Sjt 2673 North Lancashire Regt
NEWBOLD Robert MM L/Cpl 72234 Royal Engineers
NEWBOLD Wilfred MM Pte 43140 Lincolnshire Regt
NEWBOLT or NEWBOULT Arnold MM Cpl 10400 Yorkshire Light Infantry
NEWBOULD Alfred MM Pte 81291 1st West Yorkshire Regt
NEWBOULD Sydney MM Cpl 26189 10th West Yorkshire Regt DOW 24.9.18.
NEWBOULD William MM Sjt 56255 RGA
NEWBROOKS John "MM,MdH(F)" Pte 5815 XVI Corps Cyclist Bn Army Cyclist Corps
NEWBURY Frederick J. MM Gnr 11641 6 Div Ammn Col RFA
NEWBURY Leonard MM Pte 240153 1/6th North Staffordshire Regt KIA 29.9.18.
NEWBY Edward MM Pte 9298 1/4th Seaforth Highlanders
NEWBY George Alfred "MM,MSM" Sjt 10153 2nd Suffolk Regt
NEWBY George E. MM Pte 17075 Durham Light Infantry
NEWBY George L. MM Pte 34223 York & Lancaster Regt
NEWBY Harry MM Gnr 20862 RGA
NEWBY Henry MM Pte 40027 Bedfordshire Regt
NEWBY Joseph MM Cpl 24179 Royal Lancaster Regt
NEWBY Myles D. MM Gnr 190884 Y/62 Med TM Bty RFA
NEWBY Richard MM L/Cpl 26483 13th Cheshire Regt
NEWBY Sidney J. MM Bdr 25872 366 Bty 117 Bde RFA
NEWBY Thomas Arthur MM Pte 248039 Durham Light Infantry
NEWBY W.J. MM Cpl 81450 Machine Gun Corps
NEWBY William Henry MM L/Cpl 96028 222 Fd Coy Royal Engineers
NEWCOMB Charles William MM Pte 351194 1/5th Manchester Regt KIA 15.8.18.
NEWCOMB George V. MM Dvr 76576 RFA
NEWCOMBE Francis J. MM L/Cpl 19314 Dorsetshire Regt
NEWCOMBE Fred MM L/Cpl 333 18th Durham Light Infantry
NEWCOMBE George Alfred MM Pte 9253 1st Duke of Cornwall's LI
NEWCOMBE James MM Dvr 428292 423 Fd Coy Royal Engineers
NEWCOMBE John MM Pte 8408 1st Border Regt DOW 24.4.17.
NEWCOMBE Sidney MM Cpl 7155 1st Leicestershire Regt
NEWCOMBE William MM+Bar Sjt 7854 1st Leicestershire Regt
NEWELL Albert V. MM Cpl 53690 Royal Engineers
NEWELL Arthur MM Pte 24219 2nd Royal Dublin Fusiliers
NEWELL Arthur Frederick MM Cpl 235246 17th Royal Welsh Fusiliers
NEWELL Bannister MM Cpl 20907 4th Grenadier Guards
NEWELL Benjamin MM+Bar Pte 17857 6th Northamptonshire Regt
NEWELL Charles W. "MM,MID" QMS 2157 RAMC
NEWELL Clifford A. MM S/Sjt Mechanician 562063 Royal Engineers
NEWELL E. MM Pte 200123 RAMC
NEWELL Frank A. MM Pte 62007 9th Royal Fusiliers
NEWELL Frederick MM Pte R/39430 1st King's Royal Rifle Corps
NEWELL Frederick George MM L/Cpl 14460 7th East Kent Regt DOW 25.10.18.
NEWELL George MM Cpl 515019 14th London Regt
NEWELL Herbert MM Pte 204851 1st Northamptonshire Regt
NEWELL Herbert MM Pte 321000 1/5th Suffolk Regt
NEWELL J.A. MM AM1 33549 Royal Flying Corps
NEWELL James MM Pte 14560 8th Royal Lancaster Regt
NEWELL James MM Pte 3/7657 Seaforth Highlanders
NEWELL John H. "DCM,MM" Sjt 151626 251 Tunnelling Coy Royal Engineers
NEWELL Owen MM Pte 265964 Oxf & Bucks Light Infantry
NEWELL Stanley MM Spr 357472 37 Div Sig Coy Royal Engineers
NEWELL William MM Cpl 1444 Royal Fusiliers
NEWELL William H.O. MM Pte 304583 5th London Regt
NEWEY Charles Henry MM Sjt 26742 38 Bde Ammn Col RFA
NEWEY Francis Arthur MM Pte 957 16th Royal Warwickshire Regt
NEWEY George W. MM Sjt 11685 1st Worcestershire Regt
NEWEY Horace MM Pte 300720 1/1st Staffordshire Yeomanry
NEWEY William George MM Cpl 2002 2(South Midland)Bde Ammn Col RFA
NEWHAM Frank G. MM Gnr 49685 RGA
NEWHAM John William MM Pte 19473 21st Manchester Regt DOW 15.7.16.
NEWHAM Leonard Percival MM Pte 6435 13th Royal Sussex Regt
NEWHOUSE Ernest Knight MM Pte C/7720 1st King's Royal Rifle Corps DOW 25.3.18.
NEWING Allan B. MM Pte 505209 18th King's Royal Rifle Corps
NEWINGTON Harry G. MM Pte 202792 4th Hampshire Regt
NEWINS Henry John "MM,CG(F)" Cpl 17976 Essex Regt
NEWIS Herbert T. MM Sjt 103080 RGA
NEWIS James MM Spr 166727 23 Fd Coy Royal Engineers
NEWIS John A. MM Pte 13849 7th Royal Berkshire Regt
NEWITT William MM Bdr 189118 24 Bty 38 Bde RFA
NEWLAND Alexander MM L/Cpl 17440 20th Manchester Regt
NEWLAND Charles MM Sjt 19675 RAMC
NEWLAND James W. MM Bdr 44729 RGA
NEWLAND Thomas C. MM L/Cpl 21309 Royal Fusiliers
NEWLANDS Alex MM Cpl 969 8th Royal Highlanders
NEWLANDS John MM Pte 52693 12th Durham Light Infantry
NEWLANDS Robert MM Pte 18240 20 Coy Machine Gun Corps
NEWLOVE Joseph A. MM Pte 201746 7th East Yorkshire Regt
NEWMAN Albert A. MM Pte 73171 29th Bn Machine Gun Corps
NEWMAN Albert H.C. MM Cpl 9744 1st Dorsetshire Regt
NEWMAN Albert W. MM Spr 519736 Royal Engineers
NEWMAN Alfred G. MM L/Cpl 34593 4th Oxf & Bucks Light Infantry
NEWMAN Alfred N. MM Sjt 700125 1/23rd London Regt
NEWMAN Arthur H. "DCM,MM" Sjt 45763 8 Bde RFA
NEWMAN Arthur J. MM CQMS 59404 17th Royal Fusiliers
NEWMAN Charles MM Pte 41030 5th Royal Lancaster Regt
NEWMAN Charles "DCM,MM" CSM 21455 59 Coy 20th Bn Machine Gun Corps
NEWMAN Charles MM Pte 300057 5th London Regt
NEWMAN Charles B. MM+Bar Sjt 1058 8th Royal Fusiliers
NEWMAN Charles S. MM Spr 33951 Royal Engineers
NEWMAN Charles V. MM Cpl 69688 26 Bty 17 Bde RFA
NEWMAN Cornelius D. MM Spr 198990 280 Army Tps Coy Royal Engineers
NEWMAN Cyril T. MM L/Cpl 390683 1/9th London Regt
NEWMAN E.G. MM Pte 393615 London Regt

NEWMAN Edward A.H. MM Pte 202787 1st London Regt
NEWMAN Edward Arthur MM Pte 15817 8th Lincolnshire Regt KIA 19.7.18.
NEWMAN Edward G. MM Pte 58487 RAMC
NEWMAN Ernest MM Sjt 281596 117 Hy Bty RGA
NEWMAN Ernest MM Pte 42250 4 Fd Amb RAMC
NEWMAN Ernest MM Sjt 23533 1 Div Sig Coy Royal Engineers
NEWMAN Ernest P. MM Sjt 19533 RAMC
NEWMAN Ernest William MM Cpl 47720 6 Squadron Machine Gun Corps(Cavalry)
NEWMAN Frank "MM,MID" Sjt 2488 1/4th Oxf & Bucks Light Infantry
NEWMAN Frank MM Cpl 58046 460 Bty 15 Bde RFA DOW 8.10.17.
NEWMAN Frederick MM L/Cpl 13905 9th Welsh Regt
NEWMAN Frederick G. MM Pte 5274 8th East Surrey Regt
NEWMAN G. MM+Bar Cpl 75319 Royal Engineers
NEWMAN George "DCM,MM" CSM 7761 2nd Royal Inniskilling Fusiliers
NEWMAN George MM+Bar Spr 48242 12 Div Sig Coy Royal Engineers DOW 30.11.17.
NEWMAN George MM Pte 43042 Arg & Suth Highlanders
NEWMAN George MM Pte 1608 2nd Middlesex Regt
NEWMAN George S. MM Cpl 20328 Yorkshire Regt
NEWMAN George S.H. MM L/Cpl 108119 Machine Gun Corps
NEWMAN Harold MM Pte 14294 2nd Grenadier Guards
NEWMAN Harry MM Pte 326587 1/1st Cambridgeshire Regt
NEWMAN Harry MM L/Cpl 352789 7th London Regt
NEWMAN Herbert V. MM Pte 325277 1/1st Cambridgeshire Regt
NEWMAN Horace MM Spr 34933 Royal Engineers
NEWMAN James MM+Bar L/Sjt 1862 1/21st London Regt
NEWMAN James Thomas MM L/Cpl 501672 IWT Royal Engineers
NEWMAN John MM Sjt T1/5092 Army Service Corps
NEWMAN John MM Pnr 357422 50 HAG Sig Sub-Section Royal Engineers
NEWMAN John Derkin MM Sjt 9592 1st King's Royal Rifle Corps KIA 8.10.18.
NEWMAN John G. MM L/Cpl 43757 6th Northamptonshire Regt
NEWMAN John Robert MM Sjt 306285 1/8th Lancashire Fusiliers DOW 7.9.18.
NEWMAN John William MM Dvr 50317 HQ 84 Bde RFA
NEWMAN Joseph MM Pte 75030 RAMC
NEWMAN Joseph "DCM,MM" Sjt 1330 1st Gloucestershire Regt KIA 17.4.18.
NEWMAN Kingsley MM Sjt 1603 Royal Sussex Regt
NEWMAN Leonard "MM,MSM" Cpl 33325 C/51 Bde RFA
NEWMAN Leonard MM Cpl 41532 68 Fd Coy Royal Engineers
NEWMAN Mark "DCM+Bar,MM" CSM 28580 Welsh Regt
NEWMAN Martin J. MM Gnr 234600 C/83 Bde RFA
NEWMAN Patrick MM Sjt 24708 321 Siege Bty RGA
NEWMAN Percy MM L/Cpl 498 6th Royal West Kent Regt
NEWMAN Percy W. MM Pte 201981 East Surrey Regt
NEWMAN Reginald P. MM Cpl 13379 26th Royal Fusiliers
NEWMAN Richard D. MM Pte 22308 5th Dorsetshire Regt
NEWMAN Richard J. "DCM,MM,MID" Sjt 480 10th Royal Fusiliers
NEWMAN Robert Thompson MM Bdr 37036 A/94 Bde RFA
NEWMAN Robert W. MM Dvr 930903 B/291 Bde RFA
NEWMAN Roy C.L. MM Sjt 78951 Royal Engineers
NEWMAN Samuel MM Pte 18/367 18th Northumberland Fusiliers
NEWMAN Samuel R. MM L/Cpl 97699 Royal Engineers
NEWMAN Sidney MM Pte 19621 Royal Sussex Regt
NEWMAN Sidney G. MM Sjt 202189 1st London Regt
NEWMAN Stanley Richard MM L/Cpl 5779 16th Royal Sussex Regt
NEWMAN T.A. MM Cpl 40459 Royal Engineers
NEWMAN Walter MM Pte 15807 9th Devonshire Regt
NEWMAN Walter John MM L/Cpl 3300 21st London Regt
NEWMAN William MM Spr 22802 1 Div Sig Coy Royal Engineers KIA 3.11.18.
NEWMAN William MM Cpl 13693 1st Royal Dublin Fusiliers Died 12.12.18.
NEWMAN William MM L/Cpl 52768 12th Durham Light Infantry
NEWMAN William Arthur MM Pte 66755 139 Fd Amb RAMC KIA 22.9.17.
NEWMAN William J. MM+Bar Sjt 21095 Machine Gun Corps
NEWNHAM Benjamin Walter Silva MM BSM 606332 B/293 Bde RFA
NEWNHAM Ernest G. MM L/Cpl 4837 1 Fd Amb RAMC
NEWNHAM George C. "MM,MID" L/Cpl 3146 Middlesex Regt
NEWNHAM Percy MM L/Cpl 2630 8th Royal Sussex Regt
NEWNHAM William MM Cpl 83688 D/86 Bde RFA
NEWNS Cecil R. MM Bdr 32723 RFA
NEWPORT Arthur Henry MM Bdr 60315 B/110 Bde RFA
NEWPORT Charles H. MM L/Cpl 56725 74th Bn Machine Gun Corps
NEWPORT Charles William MM Sjt 94671 D/50 Bde RFA
NEWPORT Ernest R. MM Sjt 10853 7th Royal Sussex Regt
NEWPORT Frederick MM Bdr 83648 X/25 Med TM Bty RFA KIA 3.9.16.
NEWPORT Frederick J. MM Sjt 18323 26 Fd Coy Royal Engineers
NEWPORT Graham MM Pte 29454 Gloucestershire Regt
NEWPORT Harold W.J. MM Pte 7684 Royal Sussex Regt
NEWPORT John MM Pte 3180 1st Welsh Guards
NEWPORT Percy MM Gnr 59185 B/265 Bde RFA
NEWPORT William H. MM Spr 558466 56 Div Sig Coy Royal Engineers
NEWRICK Isaac Charles MM Pte 57447 8th West Yorkshire Regt
NEWSHAM Alexander MM Cpl 11668 6th North Lancashire Regt
NEWSHAM George MM 2nd Cpl 26747 23 Fd Coy Royal Engineers
NEWSHAM William MM Pte 2967 1/7th Arg & Suth Highlanders KIA 23.3.18.
NEWSHOLME George MM CQMS 4506 2nd Worcestershire Regt
NEWSOME Arnold E. MM 2nd Cpl 311615 32 Div Sig Coy Royal Engineers
NEWSOME Herbert B. MM Pte 241014 5/6th Scottish Rifles
NEWSON Alfred H. MM L/Cpl 267846 West Yorkshire Regt
NEWSTEAD Cecil Robert "MM,GMV(S)" Sjt 10673 77 Coy Machine Gun Corps
NEWSTEAD Charles MM Sjt 8337 7th Norfolk Regt
NEWTON Albert MM Pte 8993 1st Cheshire Regt att Gordon Highlanders.
NEWTON Alfred E. MM 2nd Cpl 61568 150 Fd Coy Royal Engineers
NEWTON Anthony MM Pte 15593 8th Border Regt
NEWTON Arthur MM Pte 18799 2nd Notts & Derby Regt
NEWTON Arthur MM L/Sjt 11226 2nd Scots Guards
NEWTON Arthur MM Spr 153683 Royal Engineers
NEWTON Arthur W. MM Pte M2/121244 Army Service Corps
NEWTON Benjamin Watkins MM Cpl 3681 24th Royal Fusiliers
NEWTON Clarence MM Pte 1958 7th London Regt
NEWTON Edward MM Dvr 9123 RFA
NEWTON Edward MM Sjt 102259 65 Bty 28 Bde RFA
NEWTON Ernest Leonard MM Pte 66918 140 Fd Amb RAMC
NEWTON Frank MM Pte 242604 6th South Staffordshire Regt
NEWTON Frank MM+Bar CSM 9211 1st Royal Dublin Fusiliers
NEWTON Frank MM Pte 325392 1/9th Durham Light Infantry
NEWTON Frank James MM Pte M2/136060 604 MT Coy Army Service Corps
NEWTON Frederick Herbert MM Cpl 20736 9th Lancashire Fusiliers
NEWTON Frederick William MM+Bar Sjt 10783 1st Middlesex Regt
NEWTON George MM L/Cpl 51405 15th Cheshire Regt
NEWTON George MM Pte 20/110 19th Durham Light Infantry KIA 19.10.18.
NEWTON George E. "MM,MID" Pte 3748 7th York & Lancaster Regt
NEWTON Harry MM Pte 37371 8th Lancashire Fusiliers
NEWTON Harry MM+Bar Sjt 375932 1/10th Manchester Regt
NEWTON Henry MM Sjt 3036 13th York & Lancaster Regt
NEWTON Henry MM Cpl 24071 Notts & Derby Regt
NEWTON Herbert MM Pte 270426 11th Royal Scots
NEWTON James Buller MM Pte 10250 23rd Bn Machine Gun Corps
NEWTON James T. MM Cpl 201278 3rd Worcestershire Regt
NEWTON James W. MM L/Cpl 34726 10th Northumberland Fusiliers
NEWTON James W. "MM,MID" Gnr 42722 112 Bty 24 Bde RFA
NEWTON John MM L/Cpl 309457 Royal Engineers
NEWTON John MM Pte 6722 1st East Surrey Regt
NEWTON John C. MM Pte 39717 1st Wiltshire Regt
NEWTON John R. MM L/Cpl 37293 5th Gloucestershire Regt
NEWTON John Ramshaw MM Sjt 32058 17th Lancashire Fusiliers KIA 27.7.18.
NEWTON John W. MM Sjt 21264 Machine Gun Corps
NEWTON Joseph A. MM Pte 37035 East Yorkshire Regt
NEWTON Leonard MM Dvr 90862 233 Fd Coy Royal Engineers
NEWTON Maurice MM Pte 70471 Notts & Derby Regt
NEWTON Noble MM Pte 533418 15th London Regt
NEWTON Norman MM L/Cpl 81946 7th Bn Machine Gun Corps
NEWTON R.O. MM Dvr T4/158090 Army Service Corps
NEWTON Ralph E. MM L/Cpl 250137 2nd Manchester Regt
NEWTON Richard Grey MM L/Cpl 2993 7th London Regt DOW 25.4.18.
NEWTON Robert MM Sjt 46382 Special Brigade Royal Engineers
NEWTON Samuel MM Sjt 9710 21st Manchester Regt
NEWTON Thomas MM L/Cpl 632668 20th London Regt
NEWTON Thomas MM Pte 200746 Northumberland Fusiliers

NEWTON Thomas MM Pte 200673 1/4th Royal Scots
NEWTON Thomas P. MM Cpl 776122 RFA
NEWTON W.S. MM Gnr 97428 RGA
NEWTON William MM CQMS 240936 1/5th Royal Lancaster Regt
NEWTON William MM Pte 3500 Royal Fusiliers
NEWTON William MM Cpl 9288 7th Norfolk Regt KIA 12.10.16.
NEYLAND Mark L. MM Sjt 359 23rd Royal Fusiliers
NEYLON Bartholomew MM Pte 355 13th East Yorkshire Regt
NIBBS Arthur MM Cpl 307036 7th Royal Warwickshire Regt
NIBBS Frank H. "MM,MID" Pte 420371 1/10th London Regt
NIBBS Harry MM Pte 77739 17th Royal Fusiliers
NIBLETT Howard A.E. MM+Bar Pte 9125 2nd Gloucestershire Regt
NIBLETT Thomas W. "DCM,MM+Bar" Cpl 15140 B/162 Bde RFA
NIBLETT Thomas W.J. MM Sjt 265478 1/1st Bucks Bn Oxf & Bucks Light Infantry
NIBLETT William E. MM Sjt 241300 8th Gloucestershire Regt
NIBLETT William H. MM Pte 3437 Liverpool Regt
NICE A.J. MM Pte 12478 9th Essex Regt
NICE George MM Pte 17477 2nd London Regt
NICE Harry MM Pte 16472 7th Norfolk Regt KIA 26.3.18.
NICE Herbert MM L/Cpl 1184 6th Royal West Surrey Regt DOW 2.12.17.
NICE Horace A. MM Pte A/171 16th King's Royal Rifle Corps
NICE Percy Robert MM Pte 43613 Northamptonshire Regt
NICE Percy W. MM Sjt C/6809 King's Royal Rifle Corps
NICHOL C. MM Sjt 2028 Yorkshire Regt
NICHOL Charles MM Pte 46042 13th Durham Light Infantry DOW 7.10.18.
NICHOL Isjmael MM L/Cpl 15949 2nd Coldstream Guards
NICHOL J. MM Sjt 114784 Royal Air Force
NICHOL John MM L/Cpl 25115 9th Durham Light Infantry
NICHOL John J. MM Pte 17909 12th Durham Light Infantry
NICHOL Robert MM Pte 9449 4th King's Royal Rifle Corps
NICHOL T.S. MM Pte 204607 Northumberland Fusiliers
NICHOL Thomas MM Sjt 8318 Northumberland Fusiliers
NICHOL W. MM Cpl 347339 RGA
NICHOLAS Charles MM L/Cpl 34022 12th Highland Light Infantry
NICHOLAS Emlyn John MM Gnr 112268 D/159 Bde RFA
NICHOLAS Ernest MM Cpl 42520 438 Siege Bty RGA
NICHOLAS Grismond L. MM Sjt 448051 Royal Engineers
NICHOLAS Gwilym D. MM L/Cpl 34100 9th Welsh Regt
NICHOLAS John MM Pte 15574 8th Royal Lancaster Regt
NICHOLAS Percy MM Pte 24009 Notts & Derby Regt
NICHOLAS Reginald E. MM Pte 1699 1/15th London Regt
NICHOLAS Robert MM Pte 16220 Lancashire Fusiliers att RE.
NICHOLAS Trevor J. MM Pte 48559 RAMC
NICHOLAS William R. MM Pte 26520 Shropshire Light Infantry
NICHOLES Frederick MM Dvr 45149 B/190 Bde RFA
NICHOLL C. MM L/Cpl 15626 2nd Scots Guards
NICHOLL Frederick MM+Bar Pte 69868 2nd Royal Fusiliers
NICHOLL Gilbert Thompson MM L/Cpl 9906 18th Manchester Regt KIA 9.7.16.
NICHOLL N. MM Gnr 5265 41 Bde RFA
NICHOLL P.A. MM+Bar Pte 2979 Royal Sussex Regt
NICHOLL Robert MM Pte 203426 1/6th Seaforth Highlanders
NICHOLL Stanley MM Pte 36194 RAMC
NICHOLL Thomas P. MM Sjt 51665 RGA
NICHOLL William J. "DCM,MM" Cpl 15868 1st Royal Fusiliers
NICHOLLAS Reuben L. MM Bdr 200975 'O'(AA)Bty RGA
NICHOLLS Albert MM Pte 44721 RAMC
NICHOLLS Albert J. MM Cpl 325715 1/1st Worcestershire Yeomanry
NICHOLLS Alfred MM Pte 47267 4th York & Lancaster Regt
NICHOLLS Alfred H. MM Sjt 4491 Machine Gun Corps
NICHOLLS Alfred H. MM Pte 14718 8th South Lancashire Regt
NICHOLLS Arthur MM Bdr 312383 RGA
NICHOLLS Basil J. MM Bdr 1408 RFA
NICHOLLS Caryll I. MM L/Cpl 124518 17th Bn Machine Gun Corps
NICHOLLS Charles MM Gnr 616 RGA
NICHOLLS Charles A. MM Pte 147152 29th Bn Machine Gun Corps
NICHOLLS Charles J. MM L/Cpl 101621 Royal Engineers
NICHOLLS D. MM Pte 495415 RAMC
NICHOLLS Edward MM Cpl 41888 Royal Engineers
NICHOLLS Edward C. MM Pte 240713 1/4th Royal Lancaster Regt
NICHOLLS Edward G. MM BSM 26279 RGA
NICHOLLS Ernest E. MM Pte 27292 9th Bn Machine Gun Corps
NICHOLLS Frank V. MM Pte 124 7th Royal Sussex Regt
NICHOLLS Fred MM Dvr 474 RFA
NICHOLLS Frederick William A. "MM,MID" Sjt 40385 B/106 Bde RFA
NICHOLLS Geoffrey MM Sjt 7852 Machine Gun Corps
NICHOLLS Geoffrey Wharram MM Pte 33726 14th Royal Warwickshire Regt
NICHOLLS George MM L/Cpl 240501 2/8th Middlesex Regt
NICHOLLS George MM BSM 65402 465 Bty 65 Bde RFA
NICHOLLS George Horace MM L/Cpl 15/1608 Royal Warwickshire Regt
NICHOLLS Harry MM Pte 34626 2nd South Wales Borderers
NICHOLLS Henry MM L/Cpl 43443 12th Manchester Regt
NICHOLLS Jack MM Cpl 32746 Machine Gun Corps
NICHOLLS James MM Pte 15323 17th Lancashire Fusiliers
NICHOLLS James A. MM Cpl Z/2799 13th Rifle Brigade
NICHOLLS John MM Pte 298103 2nd London Regt
NICHOLLS John MM Pte 21269 1st Hampshire Regt
NICHOLLS John MM Gnr 71777 44 Bde RFA
NICHOLLS John Thomas MM Pte 18171 Northamptonshire Regt
NICHOLLS Joseph MM Sjt 5157 4th Worcestershire Regt Died 30.1.19.
NICHOLLS Phillip A. MM Pte 17480 Suffolk Regt
NICHOLLS S.H. MM Pte 3/1863 1st Essex Regt
NICHOLLS Sidney MM L/Cpl 98315 3rd Bn Machine Gun Corps
NICHOLLS Sidney MM L/Cpl 6/1102 King's Royal Rifle Corps
NICHOLLS Sidney E. MM Pte 56666 14th Welsh Regt
NICHOLLS Thomas MM Pte 203352 1/4th West Riding Regt DOW 26.4.18.
NICHOLLS Thomas MM L/Sjt 200621 1/4th Royal Welsh Fusiliers
NICHOLLS Victor William MM L/Cpl 14372 2nd Royal Fusiliers KIA 19.8.18.
NICHOLLS W. MM L/Cpl 38211 Welsh Regt
NICHOLLS Walter MM L/Cpl 11220 Royal West Surrey Regt
NICHOLLS Walter de C. "DCM,MM" CSM 7055 IX Corps Cyclist Bn Army Cyclist Corps
NICHOLLS William MM Gnr 252786 C/106 Bde RFA
NICHOLLS William MM Pte 50671 Middlesex Regt
NICHOLLS William A. MM L/Cpl 13932 3rd Dragoon Guards
NICHOLLS William H. MM+Bar L/Cpl 95412 Royal Engineers
NICHOLLS or NICKOLLS Christopher William MM Pte 1614 22nd London Regt
NICHOLS Albert MM Pte 43318 2nd Royal Irish Rifles
NICHOLS Albert J. MM Cpl 345043 16th Devonshire Regt
NICHOLS Arthur MM Pte 285382 1/1st Oxfordshire Yeomanry
NICHOLS Bertie MM Gnr 202624 RFA
NICHOLS C.W. MM Cpl 42972 10th Essex Regt
NICHOLS Charles MM L/Cpl 23080 Yorkshire Regt
NICHOLS David G. MM L/Cpl 5628 13th Royal Fusiliers
NICHOLS Ernest MM Pte 12189 9th West Riding Regt
NICHOLS Francis J. MM Pte 14627 2nd Royal Sussex Regt
NICHOLS Frank MM Cpl 309328 17th Armoured Car Bn Tank Corps
NICHOLS Fred MM Pte 33522 12th West Yorkshire Regt
NICHOLS George MM Gnr 19622 4 Bde RFA
NICHOLS George MM+Bar Pte 251685 3rd London Regt
NICHOLS George W. MM Cpl 32000 Royal Engineers
NICHOLS George William MM Pte 49245 6th Northamptonshire Regt
NICHOLS Henry MM Sjt 37809 2nd Lancashire Fusiliers
NICHOLS James Richard MM L/Cpl 242032 6th Liverpool Regt
NICHOLS John MM Pte 374038 8th London Regt
NICHOLS Robert MM Cpl 771991 A/317 Bde RFA KIA 16.9.18.
NICHOLS Sidney T. MM Sjt 120019 303 Siege Bty RGA
NICHOLS William MM Pte 14009 6th Northamptonshire Regt
NICHOLS Wright MM L/Cpl 44373 2nd Northumberland Fusiliers
NICHOLSON Albert MM+Bar Cpl 64170 122 Fd Coy Royal Engineers
NICHOLSON Albert MM Sjt 235531 Lancashire Fusiliers
NICHOLSON Albert MM Pte R/15190 11th King's Royal Rifle Corps DOW 30.11.17.
NICHOLSON Albert Cyril MM Cpl M2/205038 Army Service Corps
NICHOLSON Albert E. MM Pte 11572 7th East Yorkshire Regt
NICHOLSON Alfred "MM,MSM" Pte 419748 54 Coy Labour Corps
NICHOLSON Archie MM Pte 3/5035 5th Cameron Highlanders
NICHOLSON Arnold MM Cpl 45800 20th Durham Light Infantry
NICHOLSON Arthur MM Sjt 441 1/5th Yorkshire Regt
NICHOLSON Bert Rumney MM Gnr 53353 RGA
NICHOLSON Charles MM Pte 13046 7th East Yorkshire Regt
NICHOLSON Charles W. MM Sjt 755128 RFA
NICHOLSON Cyril MM Cpl 26800 A/94 Bde RFA
NICHOLSON David MM L/Cpl 27371 Highland Light Infantry
NICHOLSON Donald MM Gnr 42340 C/95 Bde RFA
NICHOLSON Edward Oswald MM Pte 305096 1/8th West Yorkshire Regt
NICHOLSON Ernest MM L/Bdr 240454 RFA

NICHOLSON Frederick MM Cpl 235818 Lancashire Fusiliers
NICHOLSON G. MM L/Cpl 350561 1 Fd Amb RAMC
NICHOLSON George MM Pte 58534 11th Notts & Derby Regt
NICHOLSON George MM Pte 4383 XIV Corps Cyclist Bn Army Cyclist Corps
NICHOLSON George MM Cpl 41004 2nd West Yorkshire Regt DOW 29.5.18.
NICHOLSON George W. MM Bdr 51199 14 Bde RHA
NICHOLSON Henry H. MM CSM 27603 47 Coy Labour Corps
NICHOLSON Henry William MM Sjt 3001 12th Middlesex Regt KIA 3.5.17.
NICHOLSON J.G. MM L/Cpl 16205 Royal Highlanders
NICHOLSON J.H. MM SM 345007 RAMC
NICHOLSON J.O. MM L/Sjt 240262 Border Regt
NICHOLSON James B. MM L/Cpl 13323 Yorkshire Regt
NICHOLSON James H. MM Pte 230811 10th Shropshire Light Infantry
NICHOLSON John MM Gnr 52110 37 Siege Bty RGA
NICHOLSON John MM Pte 2036 8th Seaforth Highlanders
NICHOLSON John MM Pte 21291 11th Highland Light Infantry
NICHOLSON John G. "DCM,MM" CSM 4/8872 14th Durham Light Infantry
NICHOLSON John H. MM Bdr 94794 RGA
NICHOLSON John Joseph MM Gnr 22054 250 Bde RFA Died 14.6.18.
NICHOLSON John W. MM Sjt 795443 RFA
NICHOLSON Leonard E. MM L/Cpl 30176 14th Royal Warwickshire Regt
NICHOLSON Leyster MM Cpl 54125 Royal Engineers
NICHOLSON Lionel George MM Pte 18076 12th Gloucestershire Regt DOW 23.8.18.
NICHOLSON Michael MM Pte 11413 9th Scottish Rifles KIA 6.4.17.
NICHOLSON N. MM Pte 38420 5/6th Scottish Rifles
NICHOLSON Percy "MM,MID" Sjt 7204 1st Norfolk Regt
NICHOLSON Peter Carl MM+Bar Sjt 10985 1st Royal Irish Fusiliers
NICHOLSON Robert MM Cpl 131632 235 Army Troops Coy Royal Engineers
NICHOLSON Robert Hamilton MM Sjt 850135 1086 Bty RFA
NICHOLSON Roderick D. MM Pte 40791 10th Cameron Highlanders
NICHOLSON Roland MM Cpl 700092 210 Bde RFA
NICHOLSON T. MM Sjt 17442 Manchester Regt
NICHOLSON Thomas MM L/Cpl 348014 1/9th Durham Light Infantry
NICHOLSON Thomas MM+Bar Cpl 285041 1/6th Royal Highlanders
NICHOLSON Thomas MM+Bar Sjt 300168 15th Durham Light Infantry
NICHOLSON Thomas MM Pte 12925 8th Border Regt
NICHOLSON Thomas Aitken MM Cpl 201041 5th Cameron Highlanders KIA 1.10.18.
NICHOLSON Thomas H. MM Pte 40031 Middlesex Regt
NICHOLSON Thomas J. MM Sjt 45539 8th Hussars
NICHOLSON W. MM Pte 376450 10th Manchester Regt
NICHOLSON William MM Spr 457361 Royal Engineers
NICHOLSON William MM Pte 29834 1st King's Own Scottish Borderers
NICHOLSON William MM Pte 2011 1/4th Royal Lancaster Regt
NICHOLSON William MM L/Cpl 12036 1st Border Regt KIA 23.10.16.
NICHOLSON William MM Cpl 935336 RFA
NICHOLSON William A. MM Cpl 202264 4th Leicestershire Regt
NICHOLSON William G. MM Pte 305231 1/8th Notts & Derby Regt
NICHOLSON William Pescod MM Pte 201044 1/5th Durham Light Infantry
NICKERSON George W. MM Pte 51917 2nd Lincolnshire Regt
NICKLESS Arthur MM Sjt 42463 26th Royal Welsh Fusiliers
NICKLESS Frederick C. MM Sjt 282915 4th London Regt
NICKLESS Reginald MM Cpl 242695 Royal Warwickshire Regt
NICKLIN George T. MM Spr 492388 Royal Engineers
NICKLIN John MM Sjt 241531 8th Worcestershire Regt
NICKLIN Joseph MM Sjt 16318 Lancashire Fusiliers
NICKOLLS or NICHOLLS Christopher William MM Pte 1614 22nd London Regt
NICKS George MM Pte 17576 7th South Staffordshire Regt
NICKSON Albert MM Pte 6578 Machine Gun Corps
NICOL Alexander "MM,MID" Pte 11180 Royal Highlanders
NICOL Alexander J. MM Pte 21686 Seaforth Highlanders
NICOL David MM Sjt 13266 6th Cameron Highlanders
NICOL George Cruickshank "MM,CG(B)" Sjt 301115 89 Fd Amb RAMC
NICOL James MM Cpl 406406 Royal Engineers
NICOL James "MM,MID" L/Cpl 23287 Durham Light Infantry
NICOL John MM Sjt 21679 17th Royal Scots
NICOL John MM Pte 8868 1st Scottish Rifles
NICOL Matthew MM Pte 41024 Royal Highlanders
NICOL Ralph William MM Sjt 34844 30 Fd Amb RAMC
NICOL Robert MM Sjt 241503 1st Gordon Highlanders
NICOL Thomas A. MM Cpl 43677 1st Gordon Highlanders KIA 27.9.18.
NICOL William MM Cpl 240545 Royal Highlanders
NICOL William MM Cpl 15909 Royal Inniskilling Fusiliers
NICOLE John A. MM CSM 5798 2nd Scots Guards
NICOLL Albert MM L/Cpl 23354 17th Royal Scots
NICOLL George MM Cpl 295723 12th Royal Scots Fusiliers
NICOLL John W. MM L/Cpl 250603 Royal Scots
NICOLS Robert MM Cpl 84889 Royal Engineers
NICOLSON John MM+Bar L/Cpl 292499 1st Royal Highlanders
NICOLSON John MM Sjt 399 RFA
NICOLSON John W. MM L/Cpl 200204 1/4th Cameron Highlanders
NIDDRIE Thomas MM Pte 114462 Machine Gun Corps
NIEBERG Isaac MM Pte 57538 11th Manchester Regt
NIELD Harold MM Cpl 74572 C/104 Bde RFA
NIGHTINGALE Abel MM Cpl 14199 X Corps Cyclist Bn Army Cyclist Corps
NIGHTINGALE Albert MM L/Cpl 58812 Royal Fusiliers
NIGHTINGALE Andrew MM L/Cpl 1577 24th Northumberland Fusiliers
NIGHTINGALE Arthur R. MM Cpl 676054 A/285 Bde RFA
NIGHTINGALE Basil MM Sjt 51027 15th Cheshire Regt
NIGHTINGALE Colin MM+Bar Cpl 26519 RFA
NIGHTINGALE Ernest MM Pte 27002 16th Notts & Derby Regt
NIGHTINGALE F. MM Pte 63822 139 Fd Amb RAMC
NIGHTINGALE George MM Sjt 40136 Royal Scots
NIGHTINGALE George MM L/Cpl 2386 1/1st Cambridgeshire Regt
NIGHTINGALE Harold V. MM Gnr 97553 RFA
NIGHTINGALE John MM L/Cpl 8171 47th Bn Machine Gun Corps
NIGHTINGALE John "DCM,MM+Bar" Pte 15195 11th Northumberland Fusiliers
NIGHTINGALE Noah MM Bdr 34539 RFA
NIGHTINGALE Reginald Frederick MM Pte 56836 18th Lancashire Fusiliers KIA 31.10.18.
NIGHTINGALE Samuel Thomas MM Sjt 558006 Royal Engineers
NIGHTINGALE Sydney Elton "DCM,MM" Cpl 3/2274 9th Essex Regt
NIGHTINGALE W. MM Pte 90736 RAMC
NIGHTINGALE Walter H. MM Sjt 558029 29 Div Sig Coy Royal Engineers
NIGHTINGALE William Frederick MM Pte M2/113108 607 Coy Army Service Corps
NIGHTINGALE William M. MM Pte 325098 1/1st Cambridgeshire Regt
NIKITENKO Vasiliy MM Gnr 129340 160 Siege Bty RGA
NILES Charles H. MM Sjt M2/176027 640 MT Coy Army Service Corps
NIMMO Andrew MM L/Cpl 34564 9 Fd Amb RAMC
NIMMO Bertie Thomas MM L/Cpl 325945 1/9th Durham Light Infantry
NIMMO George MM Cpl 14139 10th Arg & Suth Highlanders
NIMMO H. MM Gnr 4 RFA
NIMMO Henry MM Pte 35665 Royal Scots
NIMMO James MM L/Cpl 241155 1/5th Royal Scots Fusiliers
NIMMO John MM Pte 295409 12th Royal Scots Fusiliers DOW 19.8.18.
NIMMO John C. MM Cpl 614 2nd Seaforth Highlanders
NIMMO William MM Sjt 300802 1/7th Arg & Suth Highlanders
NIND Arthur MM Pte 44275 Manchester Regt
NIND Frank T. MM Cpl 1655 16th Royal Warwickshire Regt
NIPPRESS Ernest A. MM Pte 28485 1st East Surrey Regt
NIPPRESS Harry MM Cpl 421350 10th London Regt
NISBET Charles J. MM Pte 147641 37th Bn Machine Gun Corps
NISBET David MM L/Cpl 20355 2nd Royal Scots Fusiliers
NISBET David G. MM CQMS 330699 9th Highland Light Infantry
NISBET Harold MM+Bar Sjt 935388 C/260 Bde RFA
NISBET James MM Sjt 295020 12th Royal Scots Fusiliers
NISBET James Maltman Wilson MM Pte 14823 2nd Scots Guards
NISBET John MM Cpl M2/119582 Army Service Corps
NISBET Peter MM Bdr 22680 RGA
NISBET Robert MM Pte 295807 12th Royal Scots Fusiliers
NISBET Thomas MM Sjt 4695 9th Seaforth Highlanders
NISBET Thomas MM+Bar Cpl 290223 1/7th Royal Highlanders
NISBETT John T. MM Pte 295508 4th London Regt

NISBETT Thomas MM Pte 1041 1/5th Royal Lancaster Regt
NISILL Thomas MM Cpl 79656 RFA
NIVEN David MM Pte 38096 5/6th Scottish Rifles
NIVISON Stewart B. "MM,MSM" Sjt 12293 7/8th King's Own Scottish Borderers
NIX Alfred MM Pte 8995 1st Northamptonshire Regt
NIX Arthur MM Pte 40020 1st Wiltshire Regt
NIX Charles John MM L/Cpl 11/673 11th East Yorkshire Regt KIA 29.9.18.
NIX Ernest MM+2 Bars Sjt 47575 C/76 Bde RFA
NIX Vincent L. MM Pte 13678 2nd Royal Scots Fusiliers
NIXON Albert MM Sjt 15728 East Lancashire Regt
NIXON Alick MM Pte 240714 Royal Lancaster Regt Died 22.10.18.
NIXON Charles MM L/Bdr 318948 RGA
NIXON Charles D. MM Pte 37286 Yorkshire Light Infantry
NIXON Ernest W. MM Pte B/200245 1st Rifle Brigade
NIXON Francis John MM Sjt 28436 7th Shropshire Light Infantry
NIXON Frank "MM,MID" Cpl 47564 RFA
NIXON George MM L/Cpl 38381 Lincolnshire Regt
NIXON George MM L/Sjt R/2338 9th King's Royal Rifle Corps
NIXON George MM Sjt 2119 Durham Light Infantry
NIXON George MM Sjt 6 2(West Lancashire)Bde RFA
NIXON George MM Dvr 820686 RFA
NIXON George MM Pte 21023 Royal Scots Fusiliers
NIXON George F. MM Gnr 1377 RGA
NIXON Harry Earle MM L/Cpl 32160 Machine Gun Corps(Motors)
NIXON Henry MM Sjt 201657 RGA
NIXON James B. MM Sjt 29458 1st King's Own Scottish Borderers
NIXON John MM+Bar CSM 11551 2nd Royal Irish Regt
NIXON John MM L/Cpl 52188 1st Royal Welsh Fusiliers
NIXON John T. MM Dvr 83091 RFA
NIXON John William MM Cpl 57236 142 Army Troops Coy Royal Engineers
NIXON Percy MM Spr 198267 Royal Engineers
NIXON Ralph MM Sjt M2/102974 Army Service Corps
NIXON Robert MM Pte 1231 2nd Arg & Suth Highlanders
NIXON Robert MM Pte 20932 12th Durham Light Infantry KIA 28.10.18.
NIXON Thomas MM Cpl 805060 A/231 Bde RFA
NIXON Thomas MM+Bar Sjt 760071 RFA
NIXON W. MM Pte 275606 Royal Scots
NIXON W. MM Cpl 38980 Northumberland Fusiliers
NIXON Walter MM Pte R/6454 13th King's Royal Rifle Corps
NIXON William MM Pte 60679 23rd Lancashire Fusiliers
NIXON William Charles Percy MM Pte 390361 1/3(Northumbrian)Fd Amb RAMC
NOAD Richard T. MM Pte 203257 1st London Regt
NOAH William J. MM+Bar Sjt 16109 Liverpool Regt
NOAKE Alfred MM L/Sjt 878 10th Lincolnshire Regt
NOAKES Frederick MM Dvr 62714 RFA
NOAKES Jack "AFC,MM(4469 Sjt RFC)" Capt Royal Air Force
NOAKES Richard MM Pte 36525 North Staffordshire Regt
NOAKES S. MM Cpl 878 Royal Sussex Regt
NOAKES Stanton C. MM Pte 9907 HAC
NOAKES William E. MM Pte 7523 2nd Royal Sussex Regt
NOAKES or NOKES Thomas J. MM Gnr 16103 RFA
NOALL Simon MM Pte 200944 Duke of Cornwall's LI
NOBBS Edgar W. MM+Bar Sjt 12386 7th Norfolk Regt
NOBBS Henry E. "MM+Bar,MID" CSM 10233 14th Northumberland Fusiliers
NOBBS James C. MM Gnr 786176 RFA
NOBBS Percy MM Pte 13714 8th Norfolk Regt
NOBBS William MM S/Sjt Mechanic M/27507 1 Div Train Army Service Corps
NOBES Charles MM Pte 325658 1/9th Durham Light Infantry DOW 14.9.18.
NOBES Herbert MM Pte 2094 9th Royal Fusiliers
NOBES Walter L. MM Cpl 8127 1st Northamptonshire Regt
NOBLE Adolphus Charles MM S/Sjt Fitter 51560 RFA
NOBLE Albert Henry Francis MM Cpl 1915 1/19th London Regt KIA 2.10.16.
NOBLE Alexander MM Dvr T3/026894 Army Service Corps
NOBLE Alexander Gordon MM Sjt 16687 8th East Yorkshire Regt KIA 14.7.16.
NOBLE Alfred MM Cpl 9857 Middlesex Regt
NOBLE Arnold MM Pte 102643 10 Fd Amb RAMC
NOBLE Arthur MM Sjt 9752 1st Royal Lancaster Regt
NOBLE Arthur MM Dvr 149648 RFA
NOBLE Brophy MM Pte 34862 8th North Staffordshire Regt
NOBLE Frank Forster MM Sjt 325082 1/9th Durham Light Infantry KIA 12.9.18.
NOBLE G. MM Cpl 3833 37 Bde RFA
NOBLE George MM L/Cpl 19139 1st Wiltshire Regt KIA 7.7.16.
NOBLE George A.M. MM Pte 8328 2nd Durham Light Infantry
NOBLE Gordon H. MM Cpl Fitter 95137 A/162 Bde RFA
NOBLE Harry MM Cpl 13560 10th West Yorkshire Regt
NOBLE Harry MM Pte 27986 Royal Welsh Fusiliers
NOBLE Harry MM Cpl 16123 7th Yorkshire Regt
NOBLE Henry MM Bdr 32443 27 Bde RFA
NOBLE Herbert MM Sjt Fitter 780375 B/246 Bde RFA
NOBLE James MM Pte 40266 2nd Gordon Highlanders
NOBLE James B. MM Gnr 73200 23 Bde RFA
NOBLE John MM Pte 40794 Cameron Highlanders
NOBLE John MM Pte 36805 12th Highland Light Infantry KIA 21.4.18.
NOBLE John B. MM Pte 5793 East Lancashire Regt
NOBLE John Grainger MM Pte 201114 1/4th Royal Scots KIA 27.8.18.
NOBLE Joseph MM Pte 14251 9th Royal Inniskilling Fusiliers
NOBLE Joseph MM Pte 38385 Northumberland Fusiliers
NOBLE Matthew MM Pte 386168 1 Fd Amb RAMC
NOBLE Percy MM Pte 15940 9th Northumberland Fusiliers
NOBLE Robert MM+Bar Cpl 16172 1st Royal Scots Fusiliers
NOBLE Sidney MM CQMS 470216 52 Fd Coy Royal Engineers
NOBLE Thomas Edward "MC,MM(14477 Sjt 2nd Gren Gds)" 2Lt 9th Welsh
NOBLE Walter H. MM+Bar Sjt 11/493 East Yorkshire Regt
NOBLE William MM Sjt Wheeler T/18781 1 Div Train Army Service Corps
NOBLE William MM Sjt 1111 1st Gordon Highlanders
NOBLE William O. MM Cpl 242037 6th North Staffordshire Regt
NOBLETT Albert E. MM Sjt T2/14046 Army Service Corps
NOCK George MM Pte 61121 6th Royal West Surrey Regt
NOCK George W.H. MM Pte 15821 Shropshire Light Infantry
NOCKALL Albert H. MM SCM 4708 2nd Life Guards att GMGR.
NODDER Henry MM 2nd Cpl 494867 479 Fd Coy Royal Engineers
NODDER James MM L/Cpl 352577 1/7th London Regt KIA 10.7.17.
NODEN Frank H. MM Bdr 294525 RGA
NODEN John Richard "MM,MID" Pte 10710 Cheshire Regt
NODES William John MM Pte M/301384 641 MT Coy Army Service Corps
NOEL George W. MM L/Cpl 4126 East Surrey Regt att 1/23rd London Regt.
NOEL John William MM Gnr 72273 C/155 Bde RFA KIA 31.8.18.
NOEL William P. MM Cpl 1534 HQ 6(London)Bde RFA
NOKE Joseph W. MM Cpl 242242 6th Royal Warwickshire Regt
NOKES or NOAKES Thomas J. MM Gnr 16103 RFA
NOLAN Arthur MM Pte 36902 Royal Welsh Fusiliers
NOLAN Arthur George MM L/Cpl 8371 2nd Royal Irish Regt DOW 24.11.17.
NOLAN Augustus MM Pte 63694 Machine Gun Corps
NOLAN Charles C. MM Pte 67252 2nd London Regt
NOLAN D. MM+Bar Gnr 21606 RGA
NOLAN Edward MM Pte 18304 1st Royal Munster Fusiliers
NOLAN Frederick John MM Pte M2/082349 272 MT Coy Army Service Corps
NOLAN Harold MM Sjt 4240 10th Lancashire Fusiliers
NOLAN Herbert George MM L/Cpl 18701 Coldstream Guards
NOLAN J. MM Pte 3617 2nd Leinster Regt
NOLAN James MM Gnr 223035 A/285 Bde RFA
NOLAN James MM Pte 8225 21 Coy Machine Gun Corps KIA 24.3.18.
NOLAN James John MM Cpl 19059 15 Div Ammn Col RFA
NOLAN John MM Pte 14239 5th South Wales Borderers
NOLAN John MM Cpl 15176 49 Bty 40 Bde RFA KIA 12.10.17.
NOLAN John MM Pte 242331 8/10th Gordon Highlanders
NOLAN John Herman (or Henry) MM Cpl 6839 10th Royal Fusiliers DOW 14.5.18.
NOLAN John W. MM Gnr 59513 RGA
NOLAN Joseph "MM,MID" Sjt 3/4757 2nd West Riding Regt
NOLAN Louisa MM Miss F Civilian 16 years old. Awarded during 'Easter Rising'.
NOLAN Mathew MM Sjt 30203 RAMC
NOLAN Patrick MM Pte 19186 4th Hampshire Regt
NOLAN Patrick MM Pte 4029 1st Irish Guards
NOLAN Patrick MM Cpl 6878 2nd Dragoons
NOLAN Patrick MM Gnr 31311 RGA
NOLAN Patrick MM Gnr 40168 RGA
NOLAN Percy MM Pte 202957 5th Royal Berkshire Regt

NOLAN Peter "DCM,MM" Pte 12437 2nd Scots Guards
NOLAN Peter "MC,DCM,MM+Bar(6484 Irish Gds)" 2Lt 16th Royal Warwickshire Regt
NOLAN Stephen MM Cpl M2/081663 Army Service Corps
NOLAN William M. MM Sjt 180 1/1(West Riding)Bty RFA
NOON Herbert Ernest Walter MM Gnr 51728 40 Bde RFA
NOON John MM L/Cpl 6820 Connaught Rangers
NOON John MM Sjt 37046 Machine Gun Corps
NOON John L. MM Sjt 8281 11th Royal Warwickshire Regt
NOON John W. MM Gnr 13567 RGA
NOON Thomas A. MM Pte 8301 11th Middlesex Regt
NOON Walter MM Pte 48496 North Staffordshire Regt
NOON William MM Cpl Sig 33113 25 Siege Bty RGA
NOONAN James MM Pte 17807 3rd Coldstream Guards
NOONAN John "DCM,MM" Sjt 9437 2nd & 1st Royal Munster Fusiliers
NOONAN John C. MM Gnr 99767 RFA
NOONAN Michael MM Sjt 365 RFA
NOONAN Richard MM Cpl 201941 2/5th Royal Warwickshire Regt
NOONE Edward MM L/Cpl 9479 Royal Irish Rifles
NORBURN Frederick MM Sjt 240784 1/5th North Lancashire Regt
NORBURN William MM Cpl 770 6th Royal West Kent Regt KIA 7.10.16.
NORBURY John MM Sjt 15368 5th Yorkshire Light Infantry KIA 3.11.18.
NORBURY John Harold MM Spr 428653 478 Fd Coy Royal Engineers
NORCLIFFE Arthur MM+Bar Cpl 10378 1st Yorkshire Light Infantry
NORCOMBE John C. MM Cpl 510474 58 Div Sig Coy Royal Engineers
NORCOTT Harold MM L/Cpl 26192 2nd North Lancashire Regt
NORCROSS John MM Cpl 5635 155 Bde RFA
NORCUP John MM Pte A/3579 4th King's Royal Rifle Corps
NORCUTT William MM Pte 27136 1st Dorsetshire Regt
NORDASS George MM Spr 474453 Royal Engineers
NORFOLK Edwin MM Pte 25080 5th Yorkshire Light Infantry
NORFOLK Hugh MM Pte 11/251 11th East Yorkshire Regt
NORFOLK Leonard Alfred MM Dvr 37836 C/180 Bde RFA
NORFOLK William Alfred MM Sjt 931 245 Bde RFA
NORFOLK William V. MM L/Cpl 28774 2nd Royal Dublin Fusiliers
NORFORD William MM Cpl 350031 7th London Regt DOW 24.4.18.
NORGATE Alfred MM Pte 16415 8th Yorkshire Light Infantry
NORGATE Arthur F. MM Pte 42951 2nd South Staffordshire Regt
NORGATE Frederick James MM Cpl 46087 19th Bn Machine Gun Corps Died 22.9.19.
NORGATE Thomas MM Pte 1889 1st Welsh Guards
NORGROVE Humphrey MM Sjt 36965 8th Gloucestershire Regt
NORLEDGE Harry MM+Bar Cpl 240811 1/8th Worcestershire Regt
NORMAN Albert H. MM Sjt 40002 8th Lincolnshire Regt
NORMAN Cecil MM Cpl 235595 1st Northumberland Fusiliers KIA 23.10.18.
NORMAN Charles Percy MM L/Cpl 25535 43 Coy Labour Corps
NORMAN Charles S. MM Pte 16722 8th Royal Sussex Regt
NORMAN Charles Talbot MM Gnr 138556 138 Heavy Bty RGA
NORMAN E.C. MM Sjt 21163 RGA
NORMAN E.W. MM Pte 21929 Royal Warwickshire Regt
NORMAN Edward R. MM Pte 20896 Army Cyclist Corps
NORMAN Edward W. MM Sjt 325088 Essex Regt
NORMAN Eugene MM Sjt 29558 RGA
NORMAN Frank W. MM Pte 26254 6th Royal West Kent Regt
NORMAN Frederick W. MM Cpl 718028 23rd London Regt
NORMAN George MM Sjt 23127 1st Royal West Kent Regt
NORMAN Harry MM L/Sjt 700732 23rd London Regt
NORMAN Harry MM Sjt 203481 2nd Notts & Derby Regt
NORMAN Harry MM L/Cpl 40813 Gordon Highlanders
NORMAN Harry MM CQMS 8311 1st Bedfordshire Regt
NORMAN Henry MM Spr 26616 1 Div Sig Coy Royal Engineers
NORMAN Henry T. MM Pte 335 Royal Sussex Regt
NORMAN Herbert MM Pte S/9917 Rifle Brigade
NORMAN Herbert G. MM+Bar Sjt 17539 6th Somerset Light Infantry
NORMAN Hustler MM Cpl 81956 A/64 Bde RFA
NORMAN James A. MM Pte C/9669 13th King's Royal Rifle Corps
NORMAN John H. MM L/Cpl 266427 Royal Warwickshire Regt
NORMAN John Leonard MM Gnr 73785 D/72 Bde RFA
NORMAN John R. MM L/Cpl 9027 1st North Staffordshire Regt
NORMAN Joseph MM Dvr 43199 B/177 Bde RFA
NORMAN Lawrence MM+Bar Pte 7736 1st Scots Guards
NORMAN Myer MM Pte 8150 Labour Corps
NORMAN Ralph A. MM Pte 23969 Liverpool Regt
NORMAN Richard MM Sjt 10491 7th East Surrey Regt

NORMAN Robert MM L/Cpl 28018 1st Royal Dublin Fusiliers
NORMAN Robert "DCM,MM" Cpl 8439 1st Northamptonshire Regt
NORMAN Robert Lewis MM Cpl 7469 9th Devonshire Regt KIA 25.6.17.
NORMAN Thomas MM Pte 6137 XVII Corps Cyclist Bn Army Cyclist Corps
NORMAN Thomas Edwin MM Sjt 13/790 East Yorkshire Regt
NORMAN Thomas H. MM Sjt 12111 1st Leicestershire Regt
NORMAN W. "DCM,MM,MID" CSM 7645 Leicestershire Regt
NORMAN Wilfred H. MM Pnr 129655 Royal Engineers
NORMAN William MM L/Cpl 7514 1st King's Royal Rifle Corps
NORMAN William MM Dvr T2/10796 Army Service Corps
NORMAN William B. MM Spr 471347 Royal Engineers
NORMAN William C. MM Sjt 14848 Royal Sussex Regt
NORMAND Stark MM Pte 290213 Royal Highlanders
NORMANSELL William R. MM Spr 277195 Royal Engineers
NORMANTON Arthur MM Cpl 28091 168 Bde RFA
NORMANTON William MM+Bar Sjt 59402 Royal Engineers
NORMINTON Arthur MM CSM 14337 1st Lincolnshire Regt
NORMOYLE Michael MM Cpl 17239 9th Royal Dublin Fusiliers KIA 4.4.18.
NORNEY Thomas Joseph MM Pte 3286 7th Royal Inniskilling Fusiliers KIA 16.7.17.
NORQUAY James MM Gnr 368176 RGA
NORRIE Alexander MM Pte 8453 1st Royal Highlanders KIA 18.8.16.
NORRIE James MM+Bar Pte 240851 1/4th Gordon Highlanders
NORRIE John William McLaren MM Pte 50627 53 Fd Amb RAMC
NORRIE Richard MM+Bar Sjt 305011 RAMC
NORRINGTON Albert C. MM Sjt 55638 Machine Gun Corps
NORRINGTON Leonard Charles "MC,MM(E/3 Sjt)" T/2Lt 17th Royal Fusiliers
NORRIS Albert MM Pte 34075 4th North Lancashire Regt
NORRIS Albert E. MM Gnr 162315 RGA
NORRIS Albert H. MM Sjt 3118 Gloucestershire Regt
NORRIS Arthur D. MM Sjt 3/9662 8th Suffolk Regt
NORRIS Arthur J. MM Cpl B/2468 Rifle Brigade
NORRIS Charles C. MM+Bar Pte 11679 1st Royal West Kent Regt
NORRIS Clement MM Pte 6670 4th Middlesex Regt
NORRIS Edward E. MM Pte 116092 Machine Gun Corps
NORRIS Fred MM L/Cpl 74852 RAMC
NORRIS Fred Foster MM Sjt 85004 11 Div Ammn Col RFA
NORRIS Frederick MM L/Bdr 212094 RFA
NORRIS George MM Pte 10581 Machine Gun Corps
NORRIS George Richard Thomas MM L/Cpl P3366 Military Mounted Police
NORRIS H.C. MM Sjt 925127 RFA
NORRIS H.G.A. MM Cpl 10559 9th Essex Regt
NORRIS Herbert J. MM Pte 18646 11th Hussars
NORRIS J. MM Pte 471215 12th London Regt
NORRIS J. MM L/Cpl 325497 9th Durham Light Infantry
NORRIS Jack MM Pte 33862 North Lancashire Regt
NORRIS James MM L/Cpl 4919 16th Lancers
NORRIS James Benson MM Sjt 700507 C/330 Bde RFA DOW 4.4.18.
NORRIS James F. MM Pte 52519 13th Rifle Brigade
NORRIS John MM Dvr 114660 RHA
NORRIS John F. "DCM,MM+Bar" L/Cpl 17968 6th Northamptonshire Regt
NORRIS John T. MM Sjt 295615 4th London Regt
NORRIS Lewis Harold MM Pnr 1857 49 Div Sig Coy Royal Engineers KIA 30.3.18.
NORRIS Lindsay MM Sjt 93068 A/58 Bde RFA
NORRIS Neville MM Pte 6708 8th East Surrey Regt KIA 9.3.17.
NORRIS Norman Rupert MM Pte 594357 18tth London Regt
NORRIS Percy MM Pte 292141 Middlesex Regt
NORRIS Richard MM Sjt 21005 29th Bn Machine Gun Corps
NORRIS Robert MM Pte 23859 1st North Lancashire Regt
NORRIS Robert MM Pte 13447 9th Royal Irish Fusiliers
NORRIS Robert MM Dvr M/350347 Army Service Corps
NORRIS Samuel MM CSM 5965 2nd Hampshire Regt
NORRIS Sydney John MM Bdr 39848 82 Bde RFA
NORRIS Thomas MM Pte 24108 1st Grenadier Guards
NORRIS Thomas MM L/Cpl 7919 Royal Fusiliers
NORRIS Thomas B. MM Pte 32370 1/5th Devonshire Regt
NORRIS Tom "MM,MSM" Sjt 7209 'L' Cable Section Royal Engineers
NORRIS W. MM Pte 42280 2nd Essex Regt
NORRIS W.F.J. MM(77857 Sjt RFA)+Bar Sjt 245603 Royal Engineers

NORRIS William MM L/Cpl 11537 7th Duke of Cornwall's LI
NORRIS William A. "DCM,MM,MID" Sjt 8475 1st Cheshire Regt
NORRIS William C. MM Sjt 49902 18 Bde RFA
NORRIS William Charles Norris MM L/Sjt 265566 1/7th Royal Warwickshire Regt DOW 16.6.18.
NORTH Allen MM Pte 3451 1/5th West Riding Regt
NORTH Bernard G. MM Cpl 65325 Royal Fusiliers
NORTH Cecil W. MM L/Sjt 24175 Machine Gun Corps
NORTH Charles MM L/Cpl 2028 Royal West Surrey Regt
NORTH Charles MM Sjt 103870 154 Fd Coy Royal Engineers
NORTH Charles MM L/Sjt 26975 15th Hampshire Regt DOW 21.9.17.
NORTH Charles H. MM Sjt 9417 2nd Yorkshire Regt
NORTH Ernest Joseph MM Cpl 1022 Royal Engineers
NORTH F. MM L/Cpl 50761 Northumberland Fusiliers
NORTH Frank L. MM L/Cpl 304283 5th London Regt
NORTH Frederick MM L/Cpl 701556 23rd London Regt
NORTH Frederick MM Cpl 7606 1st South Staffordshire Regt
NORTH George MM Cpl 203371 West Riding Regt
NORTH George H. "MM+Bar,MID." Cpl 482037 62 Div Sig Coy Royal Engineers
NORTH Harry MM Pte 305968 8th West Yorkshire Regt
NORTH Harry MM Pte 5886 7th East Kent Regt
NORTH Harry James MM Sjt 9581 2nd Oxf & Bucks Light Infantry
NORTH Henry MM Cpl 482180 Royal Engineers
NORTH Herbert MM Cpl 202022 2nd York & Lancaster Regt KIA 21.3.18.
NORTH James MM L/Cpl 305229 1/8th Notts & Derby Regt
NORTH John MM Sjt 6693 1st West Yorkshire Regt
NORTH John "DCM,MM" Pte 9119 2nd Yorkshire Regt
NORTH John MM L/Sjt 20647 1st Dragoons
NORTH John Hainsworth MM Bdr 776997 A/70 Bde RFA KIA 11.4.18.
NORTH Leonard MM Sjt 11208 Machine Gun Corps
NORTH Mathew L. MM Cpl R/8125 King's Royal Rifle Corps
NORTH Mrevyn W.W. MM Pte 53991 6th Somerset Light Infantry
NORTH Sam S. MM Pte 242061 2/4th West Riding Regt
NORTH Thomas MM Pte 202669 4th West Riding Regt
NORTH Thomas MM Sjt 7042 1st Lincolnshire Regt
NORTH Tom MM Sjt 35390 RFA
NORTH William MM Pte 62177 West Yorkshire Regt
NORTH William George "MM,MSM" Sjt 12909 Leicestershire Regt
NORTHCOTE Robert J. MM L/Cpl 50092 16th King's Royal Rifle Corps
NORTHCOTE William "DCM,MM" Sjt 76087 8 Div Sig Coy Royal Engineers
NORTHCOTT Henry J. MM Sjt 315014 RGA
NORTHCOTT William H.E. MM Sjt 205260 4th Middlesex Regt
NORTHDALE William MM Cpl 23069 Welsh Regt
NORTHEND Ernest MM Pte 173 RAMC
NORTHEY William C. MM L/Cpl 20261 Durham Light Infantry
NORTHIN Cecil J. MM Pte 38737 4th Yorkshire Light Infantry
NORTHOVER Charles MM Bdr 19213 RFA
NORTHOVER Joseph G.J. MM Pte 201693 Dorsetshire Regt
NORTHROP Herbert MM Pte 13029 1/6th Cheshire Regt KIA 14.10.18.
NORTHWAY Ernest MM Pte 6/479 Rifle Brigade
NORTHWOOD William MM Pte 16334 7th Shropshire Light Infantry
NORTON A. MM Pte 40624 South Staffordshire Regt
NORTON A. MM L/Cpl 10657 Coldstream Guards att GMGR.
NORTON Albert Edwin MM Dvr 841124 D/70 Bde RFA
NORTON Albert V. MM Pte 114613 Machine Gun Corps
NORTON Arthur William MM Dvr 21272 A/112 Bde RFA
NORTON Bertram Joseph MM Pte 305163 1/8th Royal Warwickshire Regt KIA 1.7.16.
NORTON Charles MM Pte 2311 1 Fd Amb RAMC
NORTON Charles MM Pte 18816 5th Oxf & Bucks Light Infantry
NORTON Charles MM Pte 200504 1/4th Northamptonshire Regt KIA 27.11.17.
NORTON Charles J. MM Cpl 3093 58th Bn Machine Gun Corps
NORTON David MM+Bar Cpl 88989 RFA
NORTON George Robert MM+Bar Pte 7912 11th Royal Fusiliers
NORTON Gilbert H. MM Cpl 17731 9th Suffolk Regt
NORTON Harold MM Spr 41837 68 Fd Coy Royal Engineers DOW 27.6.17.
NORTON Harold T. MM Cpl 113365 Royal Engineers
NORTON Henry MM Pte 14406 4th Worcestershire Regt
NORTON Herbert MM Pte 2831 North Staffordshire Regt
NORTON Horace John MM Pte 18472 11th Royal West Kent Regt KIA 20.9.17.
NORTON J. MM L/Cpl 8604 1st Essex Regt
NORTON James MM Pte 2071 2nd Royal Highlanders
NORTON John MM Cpl 25725 Machine Gun Corps
NORTON John H. MM L/Bdr 25611 D/59 Bde RFA
NORTON John H. "MM,MSM" L/Cpl 12888 7th South Staffordshire Regt
NORTON Ralph MM Cpl S/1489 11th Rifle Brigade KIA 4.4.17.
NORTON Robert J. MM Spr 28505 Royal Engineers
NORTON S.T.E. MM Cpl 282198 4th London Regt
NORTON Thomas MM Sjt 8505 B/149 Bde RFA
NORTON Thomas MM Gnr 44851 A/187 Bde RFA
NORTON Wilfred MM Dvr 810770 RFA
NORTON William MM Gnr 63840 RFA
NORWOOD Benjamin MM Sjt 28035 119 Siege Bty RGA
NORWOOD Richard D. MM Cpl 15624 7th Norfolk Regt
NORWOOD William MM Dvr 915281 17 Bde RFA
NOTHER S.C. MM L/Sjt 6551 2nd King's Royal Rifle Corps
NOTHER William MM Sjt 10886 Royal Irish Regt
NOTKINS Ernest F. MM Pte 423674 10th London Regt
NOTLEY George MM 2nd Cpl 13854 70 Fd Coy Royal Engineers
NOTLEY Thomas Henry MM L/Cpl C/3378 17th King's Royal Rifle Corps DOW 20.4.18.
NOTMAN T. MM Sjt 292405 Gordon Highlanders
NOTMAN William MM L/Cpl 65756 128 Fd Coy Royal Engineers
NOTRIDGE Walter H. MM Pte 57055 Lancashire Fusiliers
NOTT Albert H. MM Sjt 955006 B/236 Bde RFA
NOTT Daniel G. MM Sjt 320801 24th Welsh Regt
NOTT Frederick MM Pte 65389 1st Devonshire Regt
NOTT Frederick C. MM Sjt 39214 RGA
NOTT Philip MM Pte 11888 1st Irish Guards
NOTTAGE Henry MM Cpl 57512 Machine Gun Corps
NOTTAGE Tom S. MM+Bar Sjt 22065 2nd Grenadier Guards
NOTTINGHAM James MM Pte 20855 Bedfordshire Regt
NOTTON Daniel J. MM S/Sjt Fitter 161409 RGA
NOVELL Ernest MM Sjt 34436 RGA
NOVIS Bert MM Pte 41349 1/7th Worcestershire Regt KIA 26.8.17.
NOWACK Ernest MM Gnr 99068 RFA
NOWELL Esmund "DCM,MM" L/Cpl 15961 11th East Lancashire Regt
NOWERS William A. "DCM,MM+Bar" Sjt 495412 2/2(Home Counties)Fd Amb RAMC
NOWN Frank George MM Pte 16385 15th Royal Warwickshire Regt
NOY Albert J. MM L/Cpl 49202 22nd Manchester Regt
NOYCE Frederick G. MM L/Cpl 17887 70 Fd Coy Royal Engineers
NOYCE Harold MM Pte 16811 2nd Dorsetshire Regt
NOYE Ernest G. MM Spr 130924 Royal Engineers
NOYES Ernest H. MM L/Cpl 13099 8th Royal Berkshire Regt
NUGENT Alfred Harry MM Pte 5734 1/9th London Regt KIA 9.10.16.
NUGENT Patrick MM Gnr 3607 RGA
NULTY Thomas MM+Bar Pte 13100 5th Liverpool Regt
NUME Phillip B. MM L/Cpl 58977 Machine Gun Corps
NUNAN Albert MM L/Cpl 23342 15th Hampshire Regt
NUNLEY Bert MM Pte 50150 1/1st Cambridgeshire Regt
NUNN Alfred MM Cpl 74114 'BB' Cable Section Royal Engineers
NUNN Arthur MM Sjt 280212 130 Heavy Bty RGA
NUNN C.A. MM Sjt 2819 RFA
NUNN Cecil P. MM Pte 268164 Cheshire Regt
NUNN Charles H. MM Sjt 30868 6th King's Own Scottish Borderers
NUNN Charles Thomas John MM Cpl 1101 1/3rd London Regt
NUNN Cyril E. MM Pte 41073 1/5th Duke of Cornwall's LI
NUNN Edward MM+Bar Cpl 33108 9th Yorkshire Regt
NUNN Frederick MM Cpl 65130 RAMC
NUNN Frederick MM Pte 326305 1/1st Cambridgeshire Regt
NUNN Frederick C. "DCM,MM" Sjt 45504 19th Royal Welsh Fusiliers
NUNN H.S. MM Sjt C/6942 King's Royal Rifle Corps
NUNN Harry MM Cpl 29179 8th Royal Fusiliers KIA 3.5.17.
NUNN James Thomas MM+Bar Cpl 2390 1/8th London Regt
NUNN John A. MM L/Cpl 3485 Suffolk Regt
NUNN John R. MM Spr 96679 Royal Engineers
NUNN John Robert MM Pte 3967 53 Coy Machine Gun Corps KIA 23.10.17.
NUNN Sidney G.A. MM L/Cpl 2424 1/1st Hertfordshire Regt
NUNN Thomas Edward MM L/Cpl 8372 Royal Irish Regt
NUNN W.G.F. MM L/Sjt 14730 11th Essex Regt
NUNN William J. MM Pnr 281688 9 Div Sig Coy Royal Engineers
NUNN William J. MM Pte 306854 Liverpool Regt
NUNN William James MM Pte 6540 2nd Notts & Derby Regt KIA 15.10.16.
NUNNS Edwin Arthur MM Cpl 10/115 10th East Yorkshire Regt

NURSE Albert R. MM Pte 47336 13th Welsh Regt
NURSE Frederick G. MM Pte S/19576 13th Rifle Brigade
NURSE Harry MM L/Cpl 27494 8th Middlesex Regt
NURSE Horace MM Pte 19377 Norfolk Regt
NURSE James AQ. MM Dvr 162962 106 Fd Coy Royal Engineers
NURSE Walter MM L/Cpl 512548 RAMC
NURSE William "MM,MSM" Sjt 23204 7th Border Regt
NURSER Leonard MM Pte 57987 Cheshire Regt
NUSSEY John Thomas MM Pte 267186 2/6th West Riding Regt
NUSSEY Richard P. MM+Bar Pte 13437 Leicestershire Regt
NUTBEEN John MM Pte 4851 1/3rd London Regt
NUTBROWN George Ernest MM Pte M1/09026 52 Div Train Army Service Corps
NUTLEY Frederick MM+Bar Pte 6/1282 13th King's Royal Rifle Corps
NUTMAN Mark MM Gnr 120831 RFA
NUTT Arthur MM Sjt 278485 217 Siege Bty RGA
NUTT Charles Edwin MM Pte 31542 11th East Lancashire Regt KIA 17.5.18.
NUTT Frederick MM Pte 39732 Manchester Regt
NUTT George William MM Pte 4320 1/19th London Regt
NUTT J. MM L/Cpl 10/15704 Royal Irish Rifles
NUTT Joseph MM Sjt R/15861 17th King's Royal Rifle Corps
NUTT William MM L/Sjt 25833 Somerset Light Infantry
NUTT William Henry MM Pte 5589 West Riding Regt
NUTTALL Allen "MM,MID" Sjt 222 Lincolnshire Regt
NUTTALL Arthur MM Pte 14935 Royal West Surrey Regt
NUTTALL Arthur "MM,MID" BSM 26432 4 Bde RFA
NUTTALL Ashworth MM Sjt 20762 3rd Grenadier Guards
NUTTALL Frank MM Pte B/1845 Rifle Brigade
NUTTALL Harold MM L/Cpl 268496 4th Liverpool Regt
NUTTALL Horace MM L/Sjt 11091 3rd Grenadier Guards KIA 14.9.16.
NUTTALL J.R. MM Sjt 1929 2/5th Lancashire Fusiliers
NUTTALL James H. MM Gnr 681705 A/286 Bde RFA
NUTTALL Terence A. MM Gnr 9241 RFA
NUTTALL Thomas MM L/Cpl 421294 1/3(North Midland)Fd Amb RAMC
NUTTALL Thomas MM Pte 12876 Liverpool Regt
NUTTALL W.G. MM Sjt 8806 1st Essex Regt
NUTTALL Walter MM Sjt 680070 RFA
NUTTALL Walter MM+Bar Sjt 14530 8th Royal Lancaster Regt
NUTTALL William R. MM Pte 10072 Coldstream Guards
NUTTER Frederick MM L/Sjt 202327 North Lancashire Regt
NUTTER James H. MM Sjt 64337 RAMC
NUTTER John MM+Bar Sjt 8670 Durham Light Infantry
NUTTER Richard MM+Bar Cpl 266951 West Riding Regt
NUTTER William MM Bdr 219129 C/251 Bde RFA
NUTTING James W. "MM,MID" Pte 1127 RAMC
NUTTON Ernest MM Pte 201294 2/4th West Riding Regt
NYE Clifford Hovey MM Cpl 76266 158 Bde RHA
NYE George H. MM Spr 471750 18 Div Sig Coy Royal Engineers
NYE George R. MM Sjt 60757 Royal Fusiliers
NYE James MM L/Bdr 81053 154 Siege Bty RGA
NYE James MM Pte 697 6th Royal West Kent Regt
NYE John MM L/Cpl 198022 Royal Engineers
NYE John Henry MM L/Sjt 201136 1/4th Essex Regt KIA 3.11.17.
NYE Thomas MM Pte 732227 24th London Regt
NYHAM P. MM Bdr 51206 RFA

O

OAG James MM Sjt M2/048951 8 Mobile Ambulance Column Army Service Corps
OAKENFULL Percy Walter MM Pte 11982 1st Scottish Rifles DOW 24.7.16.
OAKENFULL Perrin MM Sjt 512231 RAMC
OAKES Arthur Podmore MM Sjt 9780 1st North Staffordshire Regt
OAKES Charles B. MM Pte 23152 Worcestershire Regt
OAKES Edward MM Cpl 40405 RGA
OAKES Edward MM Gnr 37028 B/50 Bde RFA
OAKES F. MM Gnr 36228 RFA
OAKES George MM Pte 30462 1st Grenadier Guards
OAKES George MM Pte 11/874 11th East Yorkshire Regt KIA 27.3.18.
OAKES George MM L/Sjt 10810 2nd Notts & Derby Regt
OAKES Harold W. MM Sjt 14716 Grenadier Guards
OAKES J. "DCM,MM" Pte 200496 1/7th Worcestershire Regt
OAKES John F. MM Sjt T4/244089 46 Div Train Army Service Corps
OAKES Owen MM+Bar CSM 40627 Manchester Regt
OAKES Reginald A. MM L/Cpl 52330 Liverpool Regt
OAKEY Albert MM L/Cpl 650496 1/21st London Regt
OAKEY Edward C. MM Cpl 78423 Tank Corps
OAKEY Frederick G. "MM,MID" Sjt 8230 East Surrey Regt
OAKEY George MM Sjt 3298 1/7th Worcestershire Regt
OAKEY William John Alfred MM Bdr 58033 41 Bde RFA
OAKFORD Ernest F. MM Spr 131044 Royal Engineers
OAKHAM Edward MM Pte 8444 1st Somerset Light Infantry
OAKLAND Harry MM Cpl 201558 4th Yorkshire Light Infantry
OAKLAND William MM+Bar Pte 200667 4th Lincolnshire Regt
OAKLEY Albert Edward MM Gnr 76072 127 Siege Bty RGA
OAKLEY Albert James MM Pte 9551 2nd Royal Berkshire Regt KIA 16.8.17.
OAKLEY Arthur MM Pte 7712 3rd Coldstream Guards
OAKLEY Arthur David MM Bdr 24933 C/113 Bde RFA
OAKLEY Arthur W. MM Pte 265229 1/1st Hertfordshire Regt
OAKLEY Edward H. MM Sjt 10867 11th Hussars
OAKLEY Elijah MM Pte 21204 22nd Manchester Regt
OAKLEY Frank MM Pte 3422 58 Coy Machine Gun Corps DOW 2.8.17.
OAKLEY George R. MM Cpl 10177 2nd Bedfordshire Regt
OAKLEY George T. MM Sjt 281342 1/4th London Regt
OAKLEY Herbert F. MM Pte M2/032777 Army Service Corps
OAKLEY Herbert W. MM Cpl 37116 Royal Welsh Fusiliers
OAKLEY James H. MM Pte 45582 23rd Lancashire Fusiliers
OAKLEY John A. MM+Bar Cpl 17917 'N' Bty RHA
OAKLEY Joseph MM Pte 11106 6th Leicestershire Regt
OAKLEY Reginald MM Pte 33429 1st Hampshire Regt
OAKLEY Thomas H. MM L/Cpl 7358 Worcestershire Regt
OAKLEY Tom MM Pte 8325 2nd Hampshire Regt
OAKLEY W. MM Cpl 73594 26th Royal Fusiliers
OAKLEY Walter "DCM,MM+Bar" CSM C/174 16th King's Royal Rifle Corps
OAKLEY William MM Dvr 19605 39 Bde RFA
OAKLEY William E. MM Gnr 62812 RFA
OASTLER Alfred Charles MM Dvr 955189 A/236 Bde RFA
OATEN A.G. MM Pte S/4/056769 Army Service Corps
OATEN Ernest E. MM Sjt 4733 6th Royal West Kent Regt
OATES George MM Sjt C/139 16th King's Royal Rifle Corps
OATES Harry MM Sjt 13579 7th Yorkshire Light Infantry
OATES James Francis MM L/Bdr 71985 RFA
OATES John MM Cpl 14278 10th West Yorkshire Regt
OATES John J. MM Pte 9732 Royal Irish Regt
OATES Sam MM Pte 17331 2/7th West Yorkshire Regt KIA 28.11.17.
OATES Thomas MM Pte R/11733 King's Royal Rifle Corps
OATES Thomas MM Sjt 20732 123 Coy Machine Gun Corps
OATWAY William MM Pte 43952 1st Royal Irish Rifles
OBEE Archibald L. MM QMS Armourer T/447 Army Ordnance Corps
OBEE Bertie MM 2nd Cpl 23714 23 Fd Coy Royal Engineers
O'BEIRNE James P. MM L/Cpl 102882 32nd Bn Machine Gun Corps
O'BEIRNE Patrick MM Pte 15383 Royal Irish Fusiliers
OBENDORF Henry P. MM Pte 452406 11th King's Royal Rifle Corps
OBERMAN Philip MM L/Cpl 3317 Royal Fusiliers
OBEY J. MM Bdsm 3243 1st Northumberland Fusiliers
OBORNE James Thomas MM Sjt 20028 10th Hampshire Regt
O'BRIEN Alfred E. MM L/Sjt 13931 4th Coldstream Guards
O'BRIEN Andrew MM Pte 4534 1st Royal Welsh Fusiliers KIA 15.7.16.
O'BRIEN Archibald Cameron MM Pte 88374 2/1(Lowland)Fd Amb RAMC
O'BRIEN Arthur Albert MM Pte 11379 117 Coy Machine Gun Corps
O'BRIEN Benjamin MM Pte 241150 1/5th Border Regt DOW 27.3.18.
O'BRIEN Clement MM Bdr 806003 296 Bde RFA
O'BRIEN Edward MM Pte 9221 1st Lancashire Fusiliers
O'BRIEN Gordon MM L/Cpl 10435 2nd Scottish Rifles DOW 25.10.16.
O'BRIEN J. MM Pte 31235 1st Devonshire Regt
O'BRIEN J. MM Pte 41148 Lancashire Fusiliers
O'BRIEN James MM Pte 5962 2nd Royal Irish Regt KIA 21.3.18.
O'BRIEN James "DCM,MM" CSM 7989 2nd Leinster Regt
O'BRIEN James "MM,MIDx2" L/Cpl 10055 1st Royal Dublin Fusiliers
O'BRIEN James MM Sjt 18979 10th Yorkshire Regt
O'BRIEN James F. MM Bdr 56584 210 Bde RFA
O'BRIEN John MM Pte 9607 1st Leicestershire Regt
O'BRIEN John MM+Bar Spr 93894 50 Div Sig Coy Royal Engineers

O'BRIEN John MM Spr 308985 Royal Engineers
O'BRIEN John "DCM,MM+Bar" L/Sjt 9581 1st Royal Dublin Fusiliers
O'BRIEN John MM Pte 24454 11th Manchester Regt KIA 5.11.17.
O'BRIEN John MM Pte 4/9052 2nd Durham Light Infantry
O'BRIEN John MM Pte 41139 14th Royal Irish Rifles KIA 23.3.18.
O'BRIEN John J. MM Gnr 311183 RGA
O'BRIEN Joseph MM L/Sjt 19142 15th Hampshire Regt
O'BRIEN Joseph MM Cpl 278877 Arg & Suth Highlanders
O'BRIEN Joseph MM+Bar L/Cpl 6737 2nd Seaforth Highlanders DOW 13.8.18.
O'BRIEN M. MM Pte 3653 2nd Leinster Regt
O'BRIEN M. MM Pte 10437 Irish Guards
O'BRIEN Martin "MM,MIDx2" Cpl 8561 1st Royal Munster Fusiliers
O'BRIEN Michael MM Sjt 19318 1st Bn Machine Gun Corps
O'BRIEN Michael MM Pte 2727 2nd Irish Guards
O'BRIEN Michael MM Gnr 12045 5 Div Ammn Col RFA
O'BRIEN Michael MM Pte 3021 1/5th Leicestershire Regt
O'BRIEN Michael MM Pte DM2/074919 Army Service Corps
O'BRIEN Patrick MM Sjt 31903 116 Heavy Bty RGA
O'BRIEN Patrick "MM,MIDx2" L/Cpl 10924 1st Royal Dublin Fusiliers
O'BRIEN Patrick MM Cpl 17337 14th Welsh Regt KIA 22.8.17.
O'BRIEN Patrick MM Pte 9977 Northumberland Fusiliers
O'BRIEN Patrick "MM,MID" Pte 4943 1st Royal Munster Fusiliers
O'BRIEN Patrick MM Pte 9652 1st Royal Irish Regt
O'BRIEN Patrick MM Gnr 46907 X/15 Med TM Bty RGA
O'BRIEN Patrick MM L/Cpl 10217 2nd Leinster Regt KIA 31.7.17.
O'BRIEN Peter MM Dvr 101414 123 Bty 28 Bde RFA
O'BRIEN Philip MM Pte 10652 1st Royal Irish Regt
O'BRIEN Richard MM Pte 23727 1st Royal Dublin Fusiliers
O'BRIEN Richard C. MM+Bar Sjt 8386 2nd East Surrey Regt
O'BRIEN Thomas MM L/Sjt 8992 5th Dorsetshire Regt
O'BRIEN Thomas MM Gnr 40876 RGA
O'BRIEN Thomas MM Cpl 3051 2nd Lancashire Fusiliers KIA 9.10.17.
O'BRIEN Thomas MM Cpl 2529 6th Royal Irish Regt
O'BRIEN Thomas MM Bdr 77424 RFA
O'BRIEN Thomas L. MM Pte 302021 1/8th Durham Light Infantry
O'BRIEN Thomas T. MM 2nd Cpl 41647 67 Fd Coy Royal Engineers
O'BRIEN William MM Pte 37558 18th Lancashire Fusiliers
O'BRIEN William MM Cpl 1200 6th Royal Munster Fusiliers
O'BRIEN William MM Pte 11483 2nd King's Own Scottish Borderers
O'BRIEN William MM Sjt 14513 10th Essex Regt KIA 31.7.17.
O'BRIEN William MM Pte 6229 2nd Irish Guards KIA 27.11.17.
OBSTFELDER Henry Edward MM Pte 10207 1st Middlesex Regt
O'BYRNE John MM+Bar Sjt 3261 1st Irish Guards
O'BYRNE Lawrence MM Sjt 6189 1st Royal Dublin Fusiliers
O'CALLAGHAN John James MM Pte M2/203821 283 Coy Army Service Corps
O'CALLAGHAN Patrick MM Pte 12269 1st Royal Fusiliers
O'CALLAGHAN William J. MM Cpl 33236 14th Welsh Regt
OCCOMOOR A. MM Pte 26277 1st Duke of Cornwall's LI
OCKENDEN Albert MM Gnr 202509 X/57 Med TM Bty RFA
OCKENDEN Arthur E. MM Spr 24012 2 Div Sig Coy Royal Engineers
OCKENDEN James "VC,MM,CG(B)" Sjt 10605 1st Royal Dublin Fusiliers
OCKENDEN Ronald Shepherd MM L/Cpl 230804 2/2nd London Regt
OCKWELL Ernest George "MM+2 Bars,MM(F)" Sjt 61289 RFA
OCKWELL Frederick J. MM L/Cpl 30756 10th Devonshire Regt
OCKWELL Herbert Thomas MM L/Cpl 75759 14th Royal Welsh Fusiliers KIA 13.10.18.
O'CONNELL George MM L/Cpl 200119 1/5th Liverpool Regt
O'CONNELL Henry H. MM Cpl 58150 RAMC
O'CONNELL John MM Pte 947 34 Coy Labour Corps
O'CONNELL John MM Cpl 25420 Border Regt
O'CONNELL Joseph MM Spr 199918 126 Fd Coy Royal Engineers
O'CONNELL Maurice MM Sjt 5002 Scots Guards
O'CONNELL Michael W. MM L/Cpl 26174 Royal Dublin Fusiliers
O'CONNELL Patrick MM+Bar Cpl 10635 2nd Royal Irish Regt
O'CONNELL Patrick MM Cpl 20945 Machine Gun Corps
O'CONNELL Patrick MM Spr 140513 Royal Engineers
O'CONNELL Thomas MM Sjt 5540 12th Manchester Regt
O'CONNELL-BIANCONI Mollie MM Miss F First Aid Nursing Yeomanry
O'CONNOR Charles MM Pte 7819 1st Royal Munster Fusiliers
O'CONNOR Denis MM L/Cpl 8748 1st Royal Munster Fusiliers
O'CONNOR Edward MM Pte 23593 18th Liverpool Regt
O'CONNOR Hugh MM L/Sjt 12015 2nd Royal Dublin Fusiliers
O'CONNOR James MM Dvr 70359 A/83 Bde RFA
O'CONNOR James MM Cpl 22144 23rd Manchester Regt
O'CONNOR James MM L/Cpl 19704 North Lancashire Regt
O'CONNOR James MM+Bar Sjt 2365 8th Royal Munster Fusiliers
O'CONNOR James MM Pte 23308 12th Manchester Regt
O'CONNOR Jeremiah MM Spr 93814 Royal Engineers
O'CONNOR John MM Pte 2289 1st Irish Guards
O'CONNOR John MM Pte 339081 2(West Lancashire)Fd Amb RAMC
O'CONNOR Joseph MM Sjt 26019 Machine Gun Corps
O'CONNOR Martin MM Sjt 4256 1st Irish Guards
O'CONNOR Michael MM L/Cpl 14907 12th Liverpool Regt
O'CONNOR Michael John MM+Bar Sjt S/3716 13th Rifle Brigade
O'CONNOR Morgan MM Pte A/203296 16th King's Royal Rifle Corps
O'CONNOR Patrick MM Pte 8622 Royal Munster Fusiliers
O'CONNOR Patrick "DCM,MM" L/Sjt 20767 15th Cheshire Regt
O'CONNOR Peter MM+Bar Bdr 63495 22 Bde RFA
O'CONNOR Thomas H. MM Sjt 12685 7th South Staffordshire Regt
O'COURT George R. MM Pte 5719 12th Middlesex Regt
OCTON Robert R. MM Pte 20/1648 Northumberland Fusiliers
ODAM Edward MM Pte 17780 10th Notts & Derby Regt
ODAMS Frank MM L/Cpl 652742 21st London Regt
ODD Walter MM Sjt 14460 59 Fd Coy Royal Engineers
ODDIE George T. MM Pte 116559 195 Coy Labour Corps
ODDIE Harry MM L/Bdr 700791 A/320 Bde RFA
ODDIE Hugh W. MM Pte 34929 Liverpool Regt
ODDIE William T. MM Pte 16206 10th Scottish Rifles
ODDY Arthur MM Sjt 106208 178 Coy Labour Corps
ODDY Harold R. MM+Bar Cpl 15/690 15th West Yorkshire Regt
ODDY Walter MM L/Cpl 18/1380 18th West Yorkshire Regt
O'DEA Thomas MM L/Cpl 7321 Royal Highlanders
O'DEA Timothy MM L/Cpl 10251 2nd Irish Guards KIA 27.11.17.
ODELL Albert MM Cpl 201493 6th Leicestershire Regt
ODELL Albert George MM Pte B/200462 7th Rifle Brigade
ODELL E.F. MM Sjt 1232 6th East Kent Regt
ODELL Frank MM L/Cpl 55713 41st Bn Machine Gun Corps
ODELL Frederick H. MM L/Cpl 45466 RAMC
ODELL George Henry "MM,CG(It)" L/Cpl 1392 1/1st Buckinghamshire Oxf & Bucks Light Infantry
ODELL George William MM 2nd Cpl 75815 'BD' Cable Section Royal Engineers
ODELL Herbert G. MM Cpl 25992 2nd Oxf & Bucks Light Infantry
ODELL Percy J. MM Cpl 1825 1st Oxf & Bucks Light Infantry
ODELL William MM Sjt 806219 RFA
O'DELL William Henry MM Cpl 51907 22nd Durham Light Infantry
ODGERS Alex D. MM Pte 401152 RAMC
O'DOHERTY Frederick MM Pte 133 9th Royal Fusiliers KIA 6.8.16.
O'DONNELL Andrew MM Gnr 12456 B/160 Bde RFA
O'DONNELL Charles MM Sjt 80861 B/48 Bde RFA
O'DONNELL Cornelius MM L/Cpl 7124 1st Royal Dublin Fusiliers
O'DONNELL D. MM Cpl M2/103180 Army Service Corps
O'DONNELL Denis MM Pte 40022 Royal Irish Rifles
O'DONNELL Dohalty MM Pte 5269 18th Highland Light Infantry KIA 25.3.18.
O'DONNELL Ernest MM Cpl 52691 Machine Gun Corps
O'DONNELL George L. MM Sjt 62916 RFA
O'DONNELL Gordon MM+Bar L/Cpl 241126 1/6th West Yorkshire Regt
O'DONNELL Henry J. MM Sjt 42921 Machine Gun Corps
O'DONNELL Hugh MM Pte 21128 11th Royal Scots KIA 5.4.17.
O'DONNELL John MM+Bar Pte 12263 9th Scottish Rifles
O'DONNELL John "MM,MID" L/Sjt 3633 8th Seaforth Highlanders
O'DONNELL Joseph MM+Bar 2nd Cpl 63713 101 Fd Coy Royal Engineers
O'DONNELL Martin MM Gnr 295849 RGA
O'DONNELL Michael MM Pte 51541 West Yorkshire Regt
O'DONNELL Neil MM Sjt 25940 2nd Durham Light Infantry DOW 22.5.17.
O'DONNELL Richard MM Cpl 350861 1/9th Manchester Regt
O'DONNELL Thomas "DCM,MM" Cpl 49406 19 Div Sig Coy Royal Engineers
O'DONNELL William MM L/Cpl 275248 1/4th Royal Scots DOW 16.11.17.
O'DONNELL William MM Gnr 12904 A/51 Bde RFA
O'DONOGHUE Fergus MM Pte 23578 Norfolk Regt
O'DONOGHUE Geoffrey MM Pte 1167 4th Bn GMGR
O'DONOVAN Charles MM L/Cpl 24345 Liverpool Regt
O'DONOVAN J. MM L/Cpl 307581 Liverpool Regt
O'DONOVAN John A. MM Dvr 42336 HQ 99 Bde RFA

O'DRISCOLL John J. MM L/Cpl 60195 Middlesex Regt
ODROFT Arthur L. MM L/Cpl 491936 13th London Regt
O'DWYER John J. MM Pte 54545 RAMC
O'DWYER Michael MM Sjt 20604 3rd Bn Machine Gun Corps
OERTEL James E. MM Pte 86513 Machine Gun Corps
O'FARRELL John MM Pte 19491 East Lancashire Regt
O'FARRELL John A. MM Pte 11897 1st Irish Guards
OFFEN George MM Sjt 15480 10th Royal West Kent Regt
OFFILER Arthur MM L/Cpl 10899 7th Lincolnshire Regt
OFFLER John William MM Pte 2205 2nd Royal Sussex Regt KIA 31.7.17.
OFIELD James MM Sjt M2/034581 784 Coy Army Service Corps
O'FLAHERTY James MM Pte 11425 2nd Irish Guards
O'FLANAGAN Edwin Joseph MM Sjt 132288 X/9 Med TM Bty RFA
O'FLANAGAN Harold MM Pte 20007 1st Royal Irish Fusiliers
O'FLYNN William MM Pte 8810 Irish Guards
OFORD Albert MM Sjt 9290 1st Cheshire Regt
O'GARA Martin MM Pte 6781 Royal Irish Rifles
O'GARA Thomas MM L/Cpl 10458 6th Leicestershire Regt KIA 3.5.17.
OGDEN Albaert E. MM Cpl 17268 9th South Lancashire Regt
OGDEN Albert MM L/Cpl 52687 1st Liverpool Regt Died 30.4.18.
OGDEN Ernest MM Pte 20127 3rd Grenadier Guards
OGDEN Ernest A. MM Dvr 39121 RFA
OGDEN Francis MM Pte 20447 4th Liverpool Regt
OGDEN Frank MM Pte 19348 Notts & Derby Regt
OGDEN Frank MM Sjt 705819 RFA
OGDEN Fred F. MM L/Cpl 33399 12th Manchester Regt
OGDEN George MM Sjt 8598 C/150 Bde RFA
OGDEN George C. MM L/Cpl 200279 1/4th York & Lancaster Regt
OGDEN George H. "MM,MID" Sjt 240124 1/5th Cheshire Regt
OGDEN George Henry MM Pte 240515 1/5th Lincolnshire Regt KIA 1.7.17.
OGDEN Harry MM Pte DM2/134644 Army Service Corps
OGDEN James MM Pte 22747 2nd East Lancashire Regt KIA 31.7.17.
OGDEN Norman MM Pte 556566 16th London Regt
OGDEN Peter MM Sjt 147473 33rd Bn Machine Gun Corps
OGDEN Robert MM Sjt 7075 1st Lincolnshire Regt
OGDEN Robert MM Pte 37499 RAMC
OGDEN Sidney J.B. MM Cpl 35259 RHA
OGDEN William MM L/Cpl 19771 Machine Gun Corps
OGDEN William MM+Bar Sjt 67028 96 Fd Amb RAMC DOW 26.3.18.
OGDEN William H. MM Pte 45189 Lancashire Fusiliers
OGG Isaac E. MM Cpl 290135 Gordon Highlanders
OGG Thomas P. MM L/Cpl 242217 1/5th Gordon Highlanders KIA 31.7.17.
OGILVIE Charles MM Sjt 3759 9th Royal Highlanders
OGILVIE Charles R. MM Pte S/9764 Rifle Brigade
OGILVIE David MM Sjt 2965 1/4th Royal Highlanders
OGILVIE Gilbert M. MM Cpl 18884 Royal Scots
OGILVIE James MM Dvr 125758 RFA
OGILVIE John Joseph MM L/Cpl 15117 1st Scots Guards
OGILVIE S. MM Pte 1628 Dragoon Guards
OGILVIE William MM Pte 332322 1/9th Highland Light Infantry DOW 12.1.18.
OGLE Henry C. MM Sjt 203420 Yorkshire Light Infantry
OGLE Norman Armitage "MM,CG(B)" Pte 14083 18th Durham Light Infantry
OGLE William MM(44979 Gnr 45 Bde RFA)+2 Bars Cpl 253702 Royal Engineers
OGLESBY Richard MM Sjt 3/8839 9th Yorkshire Regt KIA 24.9.17.
OGLEY Herman E. MM Pte 36266 Yorkshire Light Infantry
O'GORMAN John MM Pte 8664 1st Royal Munster Fusiliers DOW 7.11.16.
O'GORMAN William MM Pte 1804 14 Fd Amb RAMC
O'GRADY Christopher MM Pte 6137 2nd Royal Irish Regt
O'GRADY Henry MM Sjt 8907 5th Oxf & Bucks Light Infantry DOW 25.8.16.
O'GRADY John MM CQMS 166247 8th Bn Machine Gun Corps
O'GRADY Martin MM Pte 2975 7th Leinster Regt
O'GRADY Patrick MM Pte 26678 Royal Inniskilling Fusiliers
OGSTON Matthew "DCM,MM" Sjt 47912 65 Fd Coy Royal Engineers
O'HAGAN Joseph H. MM Sjt 7167 2nd Irish Guards
O'HAIRE John Joseph MM Pte 241198 1/5th King's Own Scottish Borderers KIA 14.10.18.
O'HAIRE Patrick MM Pte 8598 2nd Royal Dublin Fusiliers
O'HALLORAN Martin MM Spr 97152 106 Fd Coy Royal Engineers

O'HANLON John MM Pte 13314 9th Royal Irish Fusiliers
O'HANLON Thomas MM Dvr 11095 D/148 Bde RFA
O'HARA Alexander MM Pte 241475 1/8th Scottish Rifles
O'HARA Francis MM Pte 238020 5/6th Scottish Rifles
O'HARA H.F. MM Pte 3048 Middlesex Regt
O'HARA James MM Cpl 356233 2/10th Liverpool Regt
O'HARA James MM Pte 13976 8th Royal Scots Fusiliers
O'HARA James MM Pte 201952 Lancashire Fusiliers
O'HARA John MM Sjt 14919 Royal Inniskilling Fusiliers
O'HARA John MM Pte 23477 1st Northumberland Fusiliers DOW 17.5.18.
O'HARA John MM CSM 6060 2nd East Lancashire Regt Died 13.11.18.
O'HARA John William MM Sjt 15959 12th Durham Light Infantry KIA 27.10.18.
O'HARA Joseph MM CSM 2523 Gloucestershire Regt
O'HARA Michael MM Pte 34523 York & Lancaster Regt
O'HARA Michael J. MM Pte 8821 1st Royal Munster Fusiliers
O'HARA P. "MM,MID" Sjt 7643 Royal Scots
O'HARA Patrick MM Dvr 720436 RFA
O'HARA R.P. MM Sjt B/2870 Rifle Brigade
O'HARA Robert MM L/Cpl 20607 2nd Wiltshire Regt KIA 8.8.18.
O'HARA Thomas MM Pte 36855 West Yorkshire Regt
O'HARA Thomas MM Dvr 80140 RFA
O'HARA Thomas MM Pte 14396 9th North Lancashire Regt
O'HARE Daniel MM L/Cpl 51532 13th Liverpool Regt
O'HARE Francis MM Pte 323 Highland Light Infantry
O'HARE Henry Michael "MM,MID" Cpl 51784 110 Bty 24 Bde RFA KIA 5.12.17.
O'HEA Daniel MM+Bar CSM 22264 12th Highland Light Infantry DOW 30.9.18.
O'HEA Eugene MM Cpl 43880 1st Wiltshire Regt
O'HEA M. MM Pte 11319 Hampshire Regt
O'KEEFE John MM Bdr 1373 RFA
O'KEEFE Patrick George MM Pte 3701 10th Hussars Died 7.2.17.
O'KEEFFE Cornelius MM Pte 10257 2nd Connaught Rangers
O'KEEFFE Edward W. "MM,MID" L/Cpl 20364 Machine Gun Corps
O'KEEFFE Martin MM Bdr 25408 RGA
O'KEEFFE Patrick Thomas "MM,MID" CSM 8172 North Lancashire Regt
O'KEEFFE Thomas Francis MM L/Cpl 3211 6th Royal Irish Regt
O'KELLY F.A. MM Bdsm 7682 2nd West Riding Regt
O'KELLY Francis Ernest MM Cpl 112170 189 Tunnelling Coy Royal Engineers
O'KELLY George C. MM L/Sjt 242141 York & Lancaster Regt
OLBY Alfred MM Pte 14653 8th Norfolk Regt KIA 5.10.16.
OLD Frank John Archbold "MM,MID" L/Cpl 16444 2 Fd Survey Coy Royal Engineers
OLD James MM S/Sjt Farrier 4787 4th Dragoon Guards
OLD James A. MM Sjt 459265 2 Fd Amb RAMC
OLD Reginald Henry MM Sjt 31759 1st Duke of Cornwall's LI DOW 12.7.18.
OLD William G. MM Pte 20504 1st Dorsetshire Regt
OLDBURY Richard H. MM Pte 203538 1st Worcestershire Regt
OLDER Walter MM Sjt 9639 2nd Oxf & Bucks Light Infantry
OLDER William "MM,MID" Spr 23435 1 Div Sig Coy Royal Engineers
OLDERSHAW John W. MM Sjt 13155 XVII Corps Cyclist Bn Army Cyclist Corps
OLDERSHAW Thomas "MC,MM(44964 Sjt)" 2/Lt 126 Fd Coy Royal Engineers
OLDFIELD Arthur S. MM L/Cpl 495872 Royal Engineers
OLDFIELD Edgar MM L/Cpl 26491 Machine Gun Corps KIA 29.5.18.
OLDFIELD Edward J. MM Pte 2092 1/18th London Regt
OLDFIELD Ephraim MM Sjt 14485 8th Royal Lancaster Regt
OLDFIELD Ernest MM+Bar L/Sjt 7485 11th Northumberland Fusiliers
OLDFIELD Fred MM 2nd Cpl 104389 228 Fd Coy Royal Engineers
OLDFIELD George "MM,MID,CG(B)" CSM 15394 9th York & Lancaster Regt
OLDFIELD Harold MM Gnr 775408 B/245 Bde RFA
OLDFIELD Harold MM Bdr 99214 RFA
OLDFIELD Herbert MM Cpl 202951 4th York & Lancaster Regt
OLDFIELD Herbert MM Gnr 960620 169 Bde RFA
OLDFIELD James MM Pte 18328 Manchester Regt
OLDFIELD Joe MM Pte 241938 1/6th South Staffordshire Regt
OLDFIELD Walte Georgs MM L/Sjt 3121 1/8th Notts & Derby Regt
OLDFIELD Walter MM Pte 15395 York & Lancaster Regt
OLDFIELD William MM Sjt 13720 10th West Riding Regt

OLDFIELD William A. MM L/Cpl 235168 Gloucestershire Regt
OLDFIELD William H. MM Pte 15499 1st Royal Fusiliers
OLDFIELD William Henry MM L/Cpl 15002 Coldstream Guards
OLDHAM Adam MM Pte 23528 Royal Lancaster Regt
OLDHAM Arden MM Pte 10694 1/7th Cheshire Regt
OLDHAM Edward MM Pte 20247 22nd Manchester Regt KIA 11.1.17.
OLDHAM Frank M. MM Gnr 82178 RFA
OLDHAM Henry MM Sjt 8576 A/150 Bde RFA
OLDHAM John MM Pte 4969 RAMC att RFA.
OLDHAM John W. MM L/Cpl 30455 17th Royal Sussex Regt
OLDHAM Samuel MM Pte 40690 RAMC
OLDHAM Samuel H. "DCM,MM" Bdr 2328 6 Bty MGC(Motors)
OLDHAM Sidney MM Cpl 226 MGC (Motors)
OLDHAM Walter H. MM L/Sjt 17809 Yorkshire Light Infantry
OLDHAM William MM Pte 26075 Manchester Regt
OLDHAMS Robert Lucas MM Gnr 149310 RFA
OLDING George T. MM Sjt 55588 RHA
OLDKNOW Reginald "MM,MID" Gnr 38211 Machine Gun Corps
OLDLAND Cyril MM Pte 241845 Middlesex Regt
OLDLAND Richard MM Sjt 227964 Monmouthshire Regt
OLDMAN Frederick Robert MM Pte 12439 2nd Scots Guards
OLDMAN John MM Pte 266267 Gordon Highlanders
OLDRIDGE J. MM L/Cpl 18450 Yorkshire Light Infantry
OLDROYD Alfred MM Cpl 301937 13th Bn Tank Corps
OLDROYD Arthur MM Pte 145315 1/1st Northamptonshire Yeomanry
OLDROYD Arthur MM Pte 14030 11th West Yorkshire Regt
OLDROYD Smith MM Cpl 307307 2nd West Riding Regt
OLDROYD Thomas MM Cpl 3321 Oxf & Bucks Light Infantry
OLDROYD W. MM L/Cpl 41125 Yorkshire Light Infantry
OLDROYD Willie MM Bdr 951 RFA
OLDS Richard Joseph MM Cpl 37206 A/94 Bde RFA
O'LEARY Bertie MM L/Cpl R/13761 King's Royal Rifle Corps
O'LEARY Charles John MM Pte 905 2nd Middlesex Regt KIA 23.10.16.
O'LEARY Christopher MM L/Cpl 10281 2nd Royal Munster Fusiliers KIA 21.3.18.
O'LEARY Dennis MM Spr 208853 Royal Engineers
O'LEARY Douglas St Patrick MM Sjt 11795 1st King's Royal Rifle Corps KIA 27.7.16.
O'LEARY John MM Sjt 6783 7th Shropshire Light Infantry KIA 4.5.17.
OLERENSHAW John W. MM Sjt 614189 RHA
OLFORD Arthur MM Dvr T4/251948 49 Div Train Army Service Corps DOW 24.3.18.
OLINSKI Percy J. MM Pte 282490 4th London Regt
OLIVANT Walter Edward Francis MM Pte 35505 2nd Yorkshire Regt
OLIVE Arthur MM L/Sjt 200979 2/5th Lancashire Fusiliers
OLIVER Albert E. MM Pte 57328 3rd Worcestershire Regt
OLIVER Alexander MM L/Cpl 66146 61st Bn Machine Gun Corps
OLIVER Alfred MM CSM 10996 1st East Lancashire Regt
OLIVER Alfred J. MM Sjt 8265 1st Hampshire Regt
OLIVER Alfred T. MM Sjt 2831 17th London Regt
OLIVER Archibald MM Cpl 40639 14 Div Sig Coy Royal Engineers
OLIVER Archibald MM Pte 40809 5/6th Scottish Rifles
OLIVER Arthur MM Pte 270036 1/1st Northumberland Yeo
OLIVER Arthur MM Bdr 45598 RGA
OLIVER Charles MM Gnr 72339 RFA
OLIVER Charles Fredick MM Pte 424 King Edward's Horse
OLIVER Ebenezer MM Pte 41450 2nd Middlesex Regt
OLIVER Edward MM L/Sjt 38374 Yorkshire Light Infantry
OLIVER Edward "MC,MM" CSM 13079 1st South Staffordshire Regt
OLIVER Edward MM Pte 33868 16th Royal Warwickshire Regt
OLIVER Edward W. MM Bdr 20424 RGA
OLIVER Edwin L. MM Bdr 91871 RFA
OLIVER Ernest W. MM Pte 37956 RAMC
OLIVER Francis Albert MM Gnr 70493 1/1(London)Heavy Bty RGA KIA 5.11.18.
OLIVER Frank MM Sjt 13948 8th York & Lancaster Regt KIA 1.7.16.
OLIVER Frederick James "MC,MM" CSM S/3937 13th Rifle Brigade
OLIVER Frederick James MM Cpl 72320 121 Coy Labour Corps
OLIVER Frederick W. MM 2nd Cpl 67689 132 Army Tps Coy Royal Engineers
OLIVER George A. MM Pte 860198 33rd London Regt
OLIVER George F. MM Pte 6356 Royal Sussex Regt
OLIVER H. MM Pte 17/723 West Yorkshire Regt
OLIVER Harry MM L/Cpl 1859 4th Bn GMGR
OLIVER Harry MM Pte 43177 Royal Irish Rifles
OLIVER Henry George MM Pte 15391 Royal West Kent Regt
OLIVER Henry H. MM Pte 253089 3rd London Regt
OLIVER Henry Richard MM Pte R/25884 2nd King's Royal Rifle Corps KIA 18.9.18.
OLIVER Herbert MM Sjt 43600 Royal Engineers
OLIVER J. MM Pte 860607 33rd London Regt
OLIVER J. MM Pte 3532 Royal Warwickshire Regt
OLIVER James MM Pte 10142 2nd Highland Light Infantry
OLIVER James Henry MM L/Cpl 2652 1/1st Hertfordshire Regt KIA 31.7.17.
OLIVER James Henry MM Gnr 20561 B/156 Bde RFA
OLIVER James Robert MM Sjt 17/341 17th Northumberland Fusiliers
OLIVER John MM Cpl 6233 1st East Kent Regt
OLIVER John MM Sjt 1207 2nd Gordon Highlanders
OLIVER John MM Bdr 765597 RFA
OLIVER John MM Sjt 19844 Machine Gun Corps
OLIVER John MM Sjt M2/05961 Army Service Corps
OLIVER John MM Cpl 48032 82 Fd Coy Royal Engineers KIA 5.6.17.
OLIVER John MM Pte 44788 33 Fd Amb RAMC
OLIVER John H. MM Cpl 33537 Devonshire Regt
OLIVER John R. MM Pte 14481 6th Dragoon Guards
OLIVER Joseph MM CQMS 18/209 8th West Yorkshire Regt
OLIVER Joseph MM Pte 15037 10th West Yorkshire Regt DOW 16.7.16.
OLIVER Joseph MM Pte 14708 1st Northumberland Fusiliers DOW 14.11.16.
OLIVER Joseph Archie MM Sjt 22132 A/26 Bde RFA
OLIVER Joseph E. MM Pte 13675 8th East Yorkshire Regt
OLIVER Joseph W. MM Dvr 50330 D/104 Bde RFA
OLIVER Laurence MM Cpl DM2/165736 10 Pontoon Park Army Service Corps
OLIVER Lawrence G. MM Pnr 75323 Royal Engineers
OLIVER Lewis MM Pte 16140 Northumberland Fusiliers
OLIVER Montague W. MM L/Cpl 1858 1/4th Royal Berkshire Regt
OLIVER Phillip MM Sjt 78740 157 Siege Bty RGA
OLIVER Richard MM Pte 13610 10th Devonshire Regt
OLIVER Richard MM Cpl 800340 B/230 Bde RFA
OLIVER Richard MM Pte 17514 10th Yorkshire Regt
OLIVER Robert MM Gnr 98853 D/72 Bde RFA
OLIVER Robert MM+Bar Pte 6228 Coldstream Guards
OLIVER Sydney Edward MM Pte 17271 Shropshire Light Infantry
OLIVER Thomas MM Cpl 34493 9th Yorkshire Regt
OLIVER Thomas MM L/Cpl 47425 8th Lancashire Fusiliers
OLIVER Thomas Thickens MM Pte 31652 17th Royal Welsh Fusiliers DOW 3.8.17.
OLIVER W. "MM,MID" Sjt 2227 2nd Northumberland Fusiliers
OLIVER Walter MM Pte 31804 6th York & Lancaster Regt
OLIVER Walter C. MM Pte 331027 Lancashire Fusiliers
OLIVER William MM Spr 83136 30 Div Sig Coy Royal Engineers
OLIVER William MM Pte 35768 Yorkshire Light Infantry
OLIVER William MM Pte 11285 2nd Royal Welsh Fusiliers
OLIVER William Clapperton MM Sjt 41932 Royal Engineers
OLIVER William T. MM Sjt 52310 RFA
OLLERENSHAW Daniel MM Sjt 265580 Cheshire Regt
OLLERENSHAW William MM Pte 106654 1st Bn Machine Gun Corps
OLLERTON Arthur James MM Sjt 5188 1st Coldstream Guards
OLLEY Gordan P. MM Sjt 6313 RFC
OLLIER J. MM Dvr 810392 B/232 Bde RFA
OLLIFFE Sideny MM L/Sjt 8662 5th Oxf & Bucks Light Infantry
OLLIS Harold MM Sjt 2806 17th Lancers
OLLMAN Simon MM Pte 18677 Shropshire Light Infantry
OLLSON Enoch Thomas MM Cpl 203584 1/4th Oxf & Bucks Light Infantry
OLNER William MM Spr 102102 171 Tunnelling Coy Royal Engineers
OLNEY Sidney H.G. MM Gnr 101684 RGA
OLORENSHAW George MM Spr 43644 Royal Engineers
O'LOUGHLIN Joseph MM Pte 3674 15 Fd Amb RAMC
O'LOUGHLIN Patrick MM Cpl 3855 8th Royal Munster Fusiliers
OLSEN Albert MM Pte 7847 11th Manchester Regt
OLSEN Charles MM Pte 19850 Durham Light Infantry
OLSEN Charles R. MM Pte 140811 11th Bn Machine Gun Corps
OLSEN Jack MM Cpl 241191 1/6th Highland Light Infantry
OLVER Harry V. MM Sjt 9289 Duke of Cornwall's LI
OLVER John MM Pte 323574 2/6th London Regt KIA 9.8.18.
OLVERSON Peter R. MM Sjt 52248 D/31 Bde RFA
O'MAHONEY Timothy Percival MM Sjt 29610 196 Heavy Bty RGA
O'MAHONEY or O'MAHONY Timothy MM BQMS 30676 RGA

O'MAHONY Michael MM L/Cpl 6589 Royal Munster Fusiliers
O'MALLEY Claude MM L/Cpl 22837 9th Yorkshire Light Infantry
O'MALLEY John Michael MM Pte 47 15th Royal Warwickshire Regt
O'MALLEY Michael Dermot MM Pte 32675 12th East Surrey Regt DOW 4.10.18.
O'MALLEY Tom MM Bdr 27021 RFA
OMAN William MM L/Cpl 32338 Border Regt
OMAND Donald MM Pte 9339 1/5th Seaforth Highlanders
OMAND James MM Spt 406208 51 Div Sig Coy Royal Engineers
OMAND John William MM Pte 242129 7th Seaforth Highlanders DOW 25.10.18.
O'MARA Lawrence J. MM Pte 1757 8th Royal West Surrey Regt
O'MARR Lawrence "MM,MID" Cpl 18232 7th Yorkshire Light Infantry
O'MAY Thomas MM Sjt 10369 1st Scots Guards
O'MEARA Stephen MM Pte 3303 6th Royal Irish Regt
O'MELIA J. MM Bdr 66052 11 Bde RFA
O'NEIL or O'NEILL Henry MM Sjt 715162 D/211 Bde RFA
O'NEILL Albert MM Cpl 36401 175 Bde RFA
O'NEILL Archibald Hugh "MM,MID" Bdr 34879 RGA
O'NEILL Arthur MM L/Cpl 4582 2nd Leinster Regt
O'NEILL Christopher MM Pte 2987 2nd Leinster Regt
O'NEILL Cornelius MM Pte 40318 Royal Inniskilling Fusiliers
O'NEILL E. MM Pte 21045 2nd Royal Inniskilling Fusiliers
O'NEILL Edward MM Pte 41627 1/6th Royal Highlanders
O'NEILL Frank MM L/Cpl 6828 1st King's Own Scottish Borderers
O'NEILL Frederick MM Sjt 7762 11th Lancashire Fusiliers
O'NEILL George MM Sjt 15459 7th South Wales Borderers
O'NEILL H.O. MM Pte 339278 63 Fd Amb RAMC
O'NEILL Henry MM Cpl 2211 2nd Leinster Regt
O'NEILL Hugh MM Cpl 15988 11th Royal Scots KIA 21.3.17.
O'NEILL Jack "MM,MID" Sjt M2/035222 657 Coy Army Service Corps
O'NEILL James MM Dvr 64275 73 Bty 5 Bde RFA
O'NEILL James MM+Bar L/Cpl 59852 9th Northumberland Fusiliers
O'NEILL James F. MM Sjt 10668 South Lancashire Regt
O'NEILL James P. MM Dvr 87204 RFA
O'NEILL John "VC,MM,MM(F)" L/Sjt 4119 2nd Leinster Regt
O'NEILL John MM Pte 15427 11th Welsh Regt
O'NEILL John MM Gnr 72457 38 Bde RFA
O'NEILL John MM Pte 4653 1st West Yorkshire Regt
O'NEILL John MM Cpl 14595 24th Manchester Regt
O'NEILL John MM Pte 6210 Royal Fusiliers
O'NEILL Joseph MM Pte 9346 1st Border Regt DOW 21.7.16.
O'NEILL Joseph MM Sjt 7890 1st Northumberland Fusiliers KIA 23.7.16.
O'NEILL Joseph MM Pte 8122 2nd Irish Guards
O'NEILL Justin MM Sjt 6184 2nd Irish Guards
O'NEILL Martin MM Cpl 240498 8th Yorkshire Light Infantry
O'NEILL Michael Fursey MM Pte 11702 2nd Grenadier Guards Died 5.11.18.
O'NEILL Peter MM Pte 4/8579 9th Durham Light Infantry
O'NEILL Peter MM Pte 31862 RAMC
O'NEILL Richard MM Pte 341140 3(West Lancashire)Fd Amb RAMC
O'NEILL Robert MM Pte 22641 17th Royal Scots
O'NEILL Samuel MM Pte 63925 4th Yorkshire Light Infantry
O'NEILL Terence MM Pte 29946 2nd Grenadier Guards DOW 4.11.18.
O'NEILL Thomas MM Pte 46936 Lancashire Fusiliers
O'NEILL Thomas MM Pte 9755 22 Fd Amb RAMC
O'NEILL Thomas MM Spr 56571 Royal Engineers
O'NEILL Thomas MM(21339 L/Cpl 9th R Dub Fus)+Bar Sjt 18288 2nd Royal Irish Regt
O'NEILL W. MM L/Bdr 3176 RFA
O'NEILL Wilbert MM Sjt 9643 11th Manchester Regt
O'NEILL William MM Cpl 53006 2nd Royal Scots Fusiliers
ONION Herbert MM Pte 43970 1st Royal Inniskilling Fusiliers
ONIONS Charles MM Dvr 89275 RFA
ONIONS Edward MM Cpl 39999 South Wales Borderers
ONIONS George A. MM Spr 92581 38 Div Sig Coy Royal Engineers
ONIONS T. MM Pte 204614 London Regt att MGC.
ONIONS Thomas MM+Bar Pte 22463 Royal Warwickshire Regt
ONIONS Thomas Henry MM Pte 722445 1/24th London Regt KIA 22.8.18.
ONIONS Watson H. MM L/Sjt 23694 7th Royal Sussex Regt
ONIONS William MM Sjt 7872 2nd Royal Welsh Fusiliers
ONLEY William F. MM Cpl R/31591 King's Royal Rifle Corps
OPENSHAW Albert MM Pte 42739 RAMC
OPPENHEIM Philip MM 45745 Royal Engineers
OPREY Peter J. MM Pte 2445 2nd Connaught Rangers
ORAM Alfred Samuel George MM Gnr 656259 D/276 Bde RFA
ORAM Frederick J. MM Pte 632926 20th London Regt
ORAM Robert Henry MM Pte 10849 1st Scottish Rifles
ORAM Samuel John MM L/Cpl 7394 1st Dorsetshire Regt DOW 8.10.18.
ORAM William M. MM L/Cpl 27119 Hampshire Regt
ORANGE Alfred "MC,MM(9505 Sjt 1st W Yorks)" 2/Lt 22nd Northumberland Fusiliers
ORANGE Herbert Sydney MM+Bar S/Sjt Fitter 676435 RFA
ORBELL John MM L/Cpl 18601 7th Royal West Kent Regt
ORBELL Robert MM Pte 573050 London Regt
ORBELL Walter William MM Sjt 21535 RFA
ORBINSON James A. MM L/Cpl 13/437 Royal Irish Rifles
ORCHARD Alfred C. MM Cpl 42064 6th King's Own Scottish Borderers
ORCHARD Charles MM Spr 98018 82 Fd Coy Royal Engineers
ORCHARD Charles S. MM Sjt 11427 6th Dorsetshire Regt
ORCHARD Fred MM Dvr 36330 11 Bde RFA
ORCHARD Harold "MM+Bar,MID" 2nd Cpl 58789 Royal Engineers
ORCHARD James A. MM Gnr 20756 RGA
ORCHARD John H.D. "DCM,MM" Sjt 489930 46 Div Sig Coy Royal Engineers
ORCHARD John Harold MM Pte 1580 1/16th London Regt KIA 14.8.17.
ORCHARD John L. MM Pte 306037 8th Lancashire Fusiliers
ORCHARD Sidney George MM Pte 7626 7th Royal West Surrey Regt KIA 20.4.18.
ORCHISTON John MM Pte 3/1257 1st Royal Highlanders
ORD Frederick MM Dvr 65456 45 Bde RFA DOW 19.9.18.
ORD James MM L/Cpl 12775 18th Durham Light Infantry
ORD John Robert MM Pte 41051 1 Squadron Machine Gun Corps(Cavalry)
ORD John Robert MM Pte 43012 9th Yorkshire Light Infantry DOW 5.10.17.
ORD Joseph MM L/Cpl 10699 Northumberland Fusiliers
ORD Nathaniel MM L/Cpl 23/136 Northumberland Fusiliers
ORD Robert MM L/Cpl 270734 1/1st Northumberland Yeo
ORD Sydney MM Pte 337654 148 Fd Amb RAMC
ORDISH Gilbert MM Spr 546084 50 Div Sig Coy Royal Engineers
O'REGAN John MM Sjt 17144 Machine Gun Corps
O'REGAN Patrick MM Pte 725785 24th London Regt
O'REILLY Francis J. MM L/Bdr 63172 RGA
O'REILLY George MM Pte 30120 1st Duke of Cornwall's LI
O'REILLY Joseph MM Sjt 5786 1st Irish Guards
O'REILLY Michael MM L/Cpl 121061 Royal Engineers
O'REILLY Patrick "MM+Bar,MID" Pte 17488 1st King's Own Scottish Borderers
O'REILLY Peter MM L/Cpl 276905 2/7th Manchester Regt
O'REILLY William MM Sjt 55912 41 Bde RFA
ORETON Frank MM+Bar Sjt 200983 Royal Warwickshire Regt
ORFORD James MM Bdr 31600 RFA
ORFORD Joseph MM Pte 20842 11th South Lancashire Regt
ORGAN David MM Sjt 31381 19th Welsh Regt
ORGAN Frederick "MM,MID" Sjt 8645 2nd East Lancashire Regt
ORGAN Phillip C.A. MM Pte 16171 8th Hussars
ORGAN William G. MM L/Sjt 29471 1st Duke of Cornwall's LI
ORGER Joseph C. MM Sjt B/1191 13th Rifle Brigade
ORGILL Fred MM Pte 43032 7/8th Royal Inniskilling Fusiliers KIA 25.8.18.
ORGLES John Ernest "MM,MID" Pte 41450 13th Royal Irish Rifles
ORGLES William Henry MM L/Cpl 14690 20th Middlesex Regt
ORKNEY Thomas B. MM Pte 307282 15th Bn Tank Corps
ORKNEY William MM Gnr 49742 39 Siege Bty RGA
ORME Albert MM Pte 18514 2nd Grenadier Guards
ORME Frank MM Pte 57660 16th Lancashire Fusiliers
ORME John MM Cpl 57185 23rd Royal Fusiliers
ORME Leonard R. MM Pte 48935 Liverpool Regt
ORME Richard MM Pte 6958 2nd Notts & Derby Regt
ORME William MM Pte 41444 2nd Northamptonshire Regt
ORME William H. MM Pte 27528 1st Notts & Derby Regt
ORMEROD David Halliday MM Sjt 10652 2nd Royal Lancaster Regt
ORMES Frederick James MM L/Bdr 191796 45 AA Section RGA
ORMISTON Ewan MM Sjt 126770 Lovat's Scouts Yeomanry
ORMISTON James MM L/Cpl 27349 16th Highland Light Infantry
ORMISTON Ralph MM Gnr 22192 C/82 Bde RFA KIA 18.9.18.
ORMOND Lionel MM Cpl 48064 134 Bty 32 Bde RFA
ORMROD Arthur MM Sjt 240268 1/5th South Lancashire Regt
ORMSBY Charles MM 2nd Cpl 98864 31 Div Sig Coy Royal Engineers
ORMSBY Daniel MM Pte 26773 Royal Inniskilling Fusiliers

ORMSBY Edward G. MM Pte 42604 1/6th Highland Light Infantry DOW 29.9.18.
ORMSBY Frank MM+Bar Sjt 18361 7th Shropshire Light Infantry
ORMSBY George MM Pte 401433 RAMC
ORMSBY John William "VC,MM,MID" Sjt 1836 2nd Yorkshire Light Infantry
ORMSBY William MM+Bar L/Cpl 2974 Royal Fusiliers
O'RORKE John Joseph Patrick "MM,MID" L/Cpl 9211 1st Royal Munster Fusiliers
O'RORKE Michael MM Pte 24232 13th Liverpool Regt KIA 17.8.18
O'ROURKE Andrew MM Pte 354057 3(East Lancs)Fd Amb RAMC
O'ROURKE Charles MM Pte 4/8720 2nd Durham Light Infantry
O'ROURKE Christopher MM Sjt 4849 Connaught Rangers
O'ROURKE Constantine MM Pte 19782 13th Durham Light Infantry Died 2.2.17.
O'ROURKE John MM Cpl 14781 6th East Kent Regt
O'ROURKE Michael MM Pte 123348 Machine Gun Corps
O'ROURKE Nicholas MM Pte R/12390 2nd King's Royal Rifle Corps KIA 27.9.16.
ORPIN Edward H. MM Cpl 78309 D/58 Bde RFA
ORPIN Leonard MM L/Cpl 12779 6th Bedfordshire Regt
ORPWOOD Sydney William MM Cpl 15360 7th Northamptonshire Regt KIA 23.7.18.
ORR David MM Dvr 227290 B/232 Bde RFA
ORR Graeme Campbell "MC,MM(74182 Spr RE)" 2Lt 2/10th Royal Scots
ORR Harry MM Pte 9814 11th Lancashire Fusiliers
ORR James MM Gnr 89569 D/177 Bde RFA
ORR James S. MM+Bar Sjt 3420 2 Bde RFA
ORR John A. MM Pte 3250 8/10th Gordon Highlanders
ORR John L. MM Cpl 350777 Royal Scots
ORR Robert MM+Bar L/Sjt 12288 6th & 6/7th Royal Scots Fusiliers Died 22.3.18
ORR Samuel MM Sjt 7937 18th Highland Light Infantry
ORR Thomas MM Pte 739 1st Dragoon Guards
ORR William MM Cpl 5807 10th Royal Highlanders
ORR William MM L/Cpl 10320 Liverpool Regt
ORR William MM Pte 19785 Durham Light Infantry
ORR William MM Sjt 61896 38 Bde RFA
ORRELL Edward MM Pte 13955 6th East Yorkshire Regt
ORRELL Edwin MM L/Cpl 12467 7th East Lancashire Regt
ORRELL Sidney Williams MM Sjt 17255 B/156 Bde RFA
ORRICK William MM Pte 23803 9th West Riding Regt
ORRILL Richard MM L/Cpl 7879 5th Dragoon Guards
ORRIN James MM Sjt 41724 Royal Engineers
ORRISS Charles MM Bdr 47569 236 Bde RFA
ORRISS Henry H. MM Dvr 147602 RFA
ORSGOOD James MM CSM 7766 1st Royal Berkshire Regt
ORSMOND Richard Thomas MM Gnr 40656 24 Heavy Bty RGA
ORSON Charles Alfred MM L/Cpl 240432 2/6th Royal Warwickshire Regt
ORTON Albert MM Pte 350365 1/9th Manchester Regt
ORTON Harry MM Sjt 39367 1st Border Regt
ORTON Harry MM L/Cpl 240911 5th Leicestershire Regt
ORTON Henry Bailey MM L/Bdr 696203 B/315 Bde RFA
ORTON Joseph MM Pte 13986 8th Yorkshire Regt KIA 19.10.17.
ORTON Robert G. MM Dvr 45431 26 Bty 17 Bde RFA
ORTON William MM Pte 12144 Leicestershire Regt
ORTON William J. MM Pte 766487 17th London Regt
ORWIN Alfred MM Spr 478067 456 Fd Coy Royal Engineers
ORWIN Reubin MM+Bar Sjt 241246 4th York & Lancaster Regt
OSBALDESTON James MM Cpl 2859 1/4th North Lancashire Regt
OSBORN Alfred J. MM Sjt SE/3160 Army Veterinary Corps
OSBORN Charles F. MM Sjt 96 Royal West Surrey Regt
OSBORN E. MM Cpl 12169 9th Essex Regt
OSBORN F.A. "MM,MSM,MID" RQMS 4461 1st Royal Scots Fusiliers
OSBORN Frederick J. MM Gnr 65592 RFA
OSBORN Frederick W. MM Pnr 130039 Royal Engineers
OSBORN George Albert MM Cpl 2232 7th Royal West Kent Regt
OSBORN George H. MM Cpl 9802 10th Royal Warwickshire Regt
OSBORN Henry H. MM Pte 225132 1st London Regt
OSBORN John MM 2nd Cpl 536318 104 Fd Coy Royal Engineers
OSBORN William H.M. "DCM,MM+Bar,MID" L/Sjt 6045 8th East Surrey Regt
OSBORNE A. MM L/Cpl 200565 Lincolnshire Regt
OSBORNE A.H.V. MM BSM 49101 RFA
OSBORNE Albert MM Pte M2/080551 Army Service Corps
OSBORNE Alexander Frank MM L/Cpl 10896 6th Duke of Cornwall's LI DOW 21.8.16.
OSBORNE Alfred MM Pte 40093 Worcestershire Regt
OSBORNE Arthur MM Pte 15926 South Staffordshire Regt
OSBORNE Arthur MM L/Cpl 48873 Lancashire Fusiliers
OSBORNE Arthur Gordon MM Cpl S/16175 9th Rifle Brigade DOW 5.4.18.
OSBORNE Bernard MM L/Cpl 89980 Machine Gun Corps
OSBORNE Charles MM Cpl 3351 Royal Highlanders Died 24.10.18.
OSBORNE Charles J.W. MM Spr 97974 Royal Engineers
OSBORNE Edgar MM SSM 267 1/1st Northamptonshire Yeomanry
OSBORNE Edgar W. MM Cpl 19775 Machine Gun Corps
OSBORNE Edward MM Sjt 11233 Worcestershire Regt
OSBORNE Francis J. MM Pte 43914 5th Royal Berkshire Regt
OSBORNE Frederick MM Spr 32783 Royal Engineers
OSBORNE Frederick MM Pte 10682 2nd South Wales Borderers
OSBORNE G.E. MM Pte 15465 Shropshire Light Infantry
OSBORNE G.H. MM Sjt 229602 26th Royal Fusiliers
OSBORNE George MM Sjt 13667 1st Coldstream Guards
OSBORNE George "MM,MID" Sjt 5112 2nd Coldstream Guards
OSBORNE George F. MM+Bar Sjt 10229 1st Royal West Surrey Regt
OSBORNE Henry MM Sjt 112220 Royal Engineers
OSBORNE Horace "DCM,MM" Sjt 53325 15th Durham Light Infantry DOW 26.10.18.
OSBORNE J.A. MM L/Cpl 40442 Suffolk Regt
OSBORNE J.G. MM Sjt 240499 Worcestershire Regt
OSBORNE James MM+Bar Pte 330 2nd Royal West Surrey Regt KIA 26.10.17.
OSBORNE Jesse Wilfred MM Gnr 796030 232 Bde RFA
OSBORNE John MM Pte 5860 1st Scots Guards
OSBORNE John MM Sjt 15964 17th Highland Light Infantry
OSBORNE John MM Pte 14335 Worcestershire Regt Formerly J.H.WESTLEY.
OSBORNE John E. MM Pte R/12797 King's Royal Rifle Corps
OSBORNE John S. MM Pte 202020 Duke of Cornwall's LI
OSBORNE Reuben MM Sjt 72103 9th Cheshire Regt
OSBORNE Robert Reginald MM Pte 16572 2nd Royal Fusiliers
OSBORNE Stanley MM Bdr 90291 'U' AA Bty RGA
OSBORNE Sydney D. MM Gnr 46855 RFA
OSBORNE Thomas MM L/Cpl 9001 2nd Worcestershire Regt
OSBORNE Thomas MM Pte 7960 2nd Hampshire Regt
OSBORNE Thomas MM+Bar Sjt 44393 Royal Engineers
OSBORNE Thomas E. MM L/Cpl 5874 Machine Gun Corps
OSBORNE W.G. MM Gnr 32539 7 Bty Machine Gun Corps(Motors)
OSBORNE Walter Jesse MM L/Sjt 415 7th Royal Sussex Regt DOW 24.11.17.
OSBORNE Walter R. MM Sjt 18030 8th Devonshire Regt
OSBORNE William MM Pte 241000 Duke of Cornwall's LI
OSBORNE William MM Pte S/17672 Rifle Brigade
OSBORNE William MM Cpl 84918 33rd Bn Machine Gun Corps
OSBORNE William A. MM Sjt 250358 1/5th Essex Regt
OSBORNE William Durword MM L/Cpl 18181 Royal Welsh Fusiliers
OSBORNE William McG. MM Cpl 290273 1/7th Royal Highlanders
OSBORNE William R. MM Gnr 109245 A/174 Bde RFA
OSBORNE William W.A. "MM,MID" Pte 4591 7th Dragoon Guards
OSBOURN Frederick MM Dvr 12823 RFA
OSCROFT William MM L/Cpl 18902 11th Notts & Derby Regt KIA 16.6.18.
OSEMAN Thomas A. MM Pte 281986 1st Lancashire Fusiliers
OSGOOD Frank MM Pte 49787 1st Northamptonshire Regt
OSGOOD John MM Sjt 265774 1/6th Gloucestershire Regt
O'SHAUGHNESSY James William MM Pte 203215 2/5th Royal Warwickshire Regt
O'SHAUGHNESSY Joseph MM Pte 37025 Northumberland Fusiliers
O'SHAUGHNESSY Patrick MM Pte R/10842 18th King's Royal Rifle Corps DOW 2.10.18.
O'SHAUGNESSY Charles P. MM Dvr 17387 RFA
O'SHEA Albert MM Bdr 174334 RFA
O'SHEA Charles MM Sjt 3969 1st Irish Guards
O'SHEA Henry W. MM Pte 268054 1st Bedfordshire Regt
O'SHEA James MM Sjt 8003 2nd Royal Irish Rifles
O'SHEA John MM Pte 23270 Welsh Regt
O'SHEA John Edward MM Spr 57205 105 Fd Coy Royal Engineers
O'SHEA Michael MM Pte 37163 RAMC
OSMAN John MM L/Cpl 87381 Royal Engineers
OSMAN Richard MM Sjt 655888 407 Bty 96 Bde RFA
OSMOND Albert Ernest MM Cpl 12467 6th Royal Berkshire Regt "KIA 6.11.17,"
OSMOND Cecil R. MM Cpl 42990 Machine Gun Corps
OSMOND Enoch T. MM Sjt 36888 Lancashire Fusiliers

OSMOND Gerard "MM,MSM" Cpl 87429 D/62 Bde RFA
OSMOND Jack F. MM Pte 33538 9th Devonshire Regt
OSMOND John MM Pte 44288 2/4th Royal Berkshire Regt DOW 11.8.18.
OSTLE John M. MM L/Cpl 35152 Highland Light Infantry
OSTLER John MM L/Cpl 28352 13th Cheshire Regt
O'SULLIVAN Cornelius MM Pte 7442 2nd Royal Munster Fusiliers
O'SULLIVAN Cornelius MM Cpl 704 Royal Engineers
O'SULLIVAN Cornelius MM Gnr 44918 RFA
O'SULLIVAN Frank MM Pte 282304 2/8th Lancashire Fusiliers
O'SULLIVAN James MM Pte 4767 9th Royal Munster Fusiliers KIA 30.9.18.
O'SULLIVAN John MM Pte 48243 6th Liverpool Regt
O'SULLIVAN John MM Pte 1161 4th Bn GMGR
O'SULLIVAN John MM Sjt 8859 2 Siege Bty RGA
O'SULLIVAN John Francis MM Pte 101960 29th Durham Light Infantry
O'SULLIVAN Patrick MM L/Cpl 14402 5th South Wales Borderers
O'SULLIVAN Patrick MM Pte 29294 14th Highland Light Infantry KIA 18.8.17.
O'SULLIVAN Robert MM Sjt 5433 1st Royal Munster Fusiliers
O'SULLIVAN Thomas MM Pte 7541 1st Irish Guards
OSWALD Ernest MM L/Cpl 8957 2nd Highland Light Infantry
OSWALD Robert MM Cpl 11084 2nd Highland Light Infantry
OSWALD Wilfrid MM Pte 2519 1/9th Liverpool Regt KIA 12.8.16.
OSWICK G.H. MM Sjt 2675 56 Div Ammn Col RFA
OTHEN Percy MM Cpl Fitter 775811 D/310 Bde RFA
OTHICK William MM Pte 3/8312 2nd Yorkshire Regt
OTLEY George MM Cpl S/17224 13th Rifle Brigade
OTLEY Ralph MM L/Cpl 39804 9th Durham Light Infantry
O'TOOLE Arthur J. MM Pte 208423 20th Middlesex Regt
O'TOOLE Denis MM Pte 25501 Royal Dublin Fusiliers
O'TOOLE James Daniel MM Sjt 2761 8th Royal Munster Fusiliers
O'TOOLE James E. MM Cpl 10527 2nd York & Lancaster Regt
O'TOOLE John MM Pte 45287 4th Hussars
O'TOOLE Thomas MM Spr 136417 Royal Engineers
OTTAWAY C.J. MM Pte 2506 East Kent Regt
OTTAWAY Dudley MM Pte R/37934 King's Royal Rifle Corps
OTTAWAY Frederick J. MM Spr 548802 Royal Engineers
OTTEN Harold Arthur "MM,MID,OStG(R)" Sjt 23070 56 Fd Coy Royal Engineers
OTTER Edward MM L/Cpl 9934 1st North Staffordshire Regt
OTTER Edwin Charles MM Pte 201162 1st Lincolnshire Regt
OTTERWILL Joseph J. MM S/Sjt Mechanic M1/07616 5 Mot Amb Convoy Army Service Corps
OTTEWELL Thomas J. "MM,MID" Pte 8439 2nd East Yorkshire Regt
OTTEY Samuel Thomas MM Pte 203226 1/4th Lincolnshire Regt
OTTLEY Alfred J. MM+Bar 2nd Cpl 560216 Royal Engineers
OTTLEY Percy D. MM Pte M2/272217 Army Service Corps
OTTO Edward G. MM Cpl 3831 64 Bde RFA
OTTOWAY Alfred MM+Bar L/Cpl 40446 9 Div Sig Coy Royal Engineers
OTTY Matthew MM Gnr 104923 X/23 Med TM Bty RFA
OTTY William A. MM L/Cpl 2144 Liverpool Regt
OTWAY John W. MM Cpl 17944 1st Royal West Kent Regt
OUGH Archibald MM Pte 36191 Leicestershire Regt
OUGHAM Harold Owen MM Pte A/2521 9th King's Royal Rifle Corps
OULD Ernest MM Cpl 17821 10th Essex Regt Died 9.11.18.
OUSBY George A. MM Sjt 15765 8th Border Regt
OUTEN Henry "MM,CG(F)" Pte 78092 2nd Royal Fusiliers
OUTERSON George MM Sjt 275035 Royal Scots
OUTHWAITE Albert MM Pte 201781 1/4th Seaforth Highlanders
OUTHWAITE Robert MM Pte 350410 12th Durham Light Infantry
OUTRAM Arthur MM Cpl 327169 Durham Light Infantry
OUTRAM Edward MM Cpl 17626 Machine Gun Corps
OUTRAM John W. MM Sjt 75124 1/1st Derbyshire Yeomanry
OUTRAM Percy H. MM Pte 39452 38 Fd Amb RAMC
OVEN Harold G. MM L/Cpl 482256 62 Div Sig Coy Royal Engineers
OVEN William MM L/Cpl 17/9514 Manchester Regt
OVENDEN James Percy MM L/Cpl 11026 East Surrey Regt
OVENDEN Stephen C. MM Gnr 65718 RGA
OVENDEN Thomas Henry Ernest MM Pte 40801 2nd Suffolk Regt
OVER Charles J. MM Spr 152446 Signal Service Royal Engineers
OVER Wilfred Thomas Edward MM Pte 17399 Hampshire Regt DOW 2.8.17.
OVERD Harry MM Pte 27201 12th Somerset Light Infantry
OVEREND Albert H. MM Pte 45985 Northumberland Fusiliers
OVEREND Arthur MM Pte 201647 1/5th Seaforth Highlanders
OVEREND J. MM Pte 16100 5th West Riding Regt
OVEREND Robert MM Pte 16483 2nd Royal Irish Regt
OVEREND William MM L/Cpl 201390 Seaforth Highlanders
OVERINGTON Ernest MM Pte 53481 2/7th Manchester Regt
OVERINGTON F. MM Pte 15797 1st Coldstream Guards
OVERLAND Ernest MM Pte 9781 Machine Gun Corps
OVERSBY Ernest MM Pte 266498 West Riding Regt
OVERTON Clement William MM Gnr Sig 183173 C/155 Bde RFA DOW 23.9.18.
OVERTON Ernest MM Cpl 43260 South Staffordshire Regt
OVERTON George T. MM Cpl 235321 2nd South Staffordshire Regt
OVERTON Harry Neander MM S/Sjt Fitter 88148 'U' Bty RHA
OVERTON William MM L/Cpl 242106 5th Gloucestershire Regt
OVERY Albert MM Dvr 40228 D/83 Bde RFA
OVERY Arthur Norman MM L/Cpl 13668 Scots Guards
OVERY T.G.B. MM Dvr 755413 RFA
OWDEN Rupert Jack MM Pte 42074 100 Coy Machine Gun Corps KIA 25.4.17.
OWEN A. MM Pte 341498 RAMC
OWEN Albert Victor MM Bdsm 12591 3rd Worcestershire Regt KIA 30.11.16.
OWEN Alexander MM Pte 23686 13th Hussars DOW 10.5.18.
OWEN Alexander William MM Dvr 76768 23 Bty 40 Bde RFA
OWEN Allan K. MM Cpl 54117 Royal Engineers
OWEN Arnold MM Pte 28776 2nd Royal Dublin Fusiliers
OWEN Benjamin MM Dvr 97904 V/15 Heavy TM Bty RFA
OWEN Bernard J. MM Pte 630780 20th London Regt
OWEN Cecil "DCM,MM+Bar" Sjt 3/10420 1st Northamptonshire Regt
OWEN Cecil Leonard MM Sjt 471035 2/12th London Regt KIA 26.9.17.
OWEN Charles G.A. MM Sjt 30626 B/83 Bde RFA
OWEN Charles Henry MM Pte 9878 Machine Gun Corps
OWEN Edward Foulkes MM Pte 201174 1/4th Royal Welsh Fusiliers Died 16.2.18.
OWEN Edward R. MM Pte 3417 1st Welsh Guards
OWEN Edwin MM L/Cpl 13377 IX Corps Cyclist Bn Army Cyclist Corps
OWEN Edwin MM Pte 56763 Machine Gun Corps
OWEN Evan J. MM Pte 124816 RAMC
OWEN Frank MM Pte 32701 2/7th West Riding Regt
OWEN Fred MM Sjt 10278 7th Royal West Surrey Regt
OWEN Fred MM+Bar Cpl 201385 7th Bn Tank Corps
OWEN Frederick MM Bdr 18325 RFA
OWEN Frederick MM Pte 12223 6th Shropshire Light Infantry
OWEN George MM Pte 240664 Lancashire Fusiliers
OWEN George D. MM Pte 17289 13th Royal Welsh Fusiliers
OWEN Harold MM Dvr 84099 RFA
OWEN Harry MM Bdr 840116 B/241 Bde RFA
OWEN Harry MM Cpl 70134 187 Bde RFA DOW 20.9.17.
OWEN Henry MM Sjt 3181 2nd Royal Warwickshire Regt
OWEN Henry Edward MM Pte M/300035 Army Service Corps att 96 Fd Amb RAMC.
OWEN Henry F. MM Sjt 8797 2nd Royal Welsh Fusiliers
OWEN Henry James MM Sjt 17804 8th Gloucestershire Regt
OWEN Herbert R. MM Gnr 830743 241 Bde RFA
OWEN Ivor H. MM Pte 3555 1st Welsh Guards
OWEN J. MM Pte 40019 Worcestershire Regt
OWEN J. MM Gnr 281638 RGA
OWEN J.C. MM Pte 19684 Devonshire Regt
OWEN James MM Cpl 19750 20th Lancashire Fusiliers
OWEN James MM 2nd Cpl 426014 Royal Engineers
OWEN James MM Pte 18956 Machine Gun Corps
OWEN John MM Pte 51491 7th East Yorkshire Regt
OWEN John MM Spr 154420 Special Coy Royal Engineers DOW 11.12.17.
OWEN John MM Pte 2054 1st Royal Warwickshire Regt
OWEN John MM Sjt 11243 6th Yorkshire Light Infantry
OWEN John MM Gnr 310354 RGA
OWEN John F. MM Sjt 43506 115 Heavy Bty RGA
OWEN John R. MM+Bar L/Sjt 70153 9th Royal Welsh Fusiliers
OWEN John S. MM Sjt 23765 Machine Gun Corps
OWEN John V. MM Pte 40446 8th York & Lancaster Regt
OWEN Joseph A. "MM,MID" L/Cpl 20143 15th Welsh Regt
OWEN M. MM Pte 40298 Royal Welsh Fusiliers
OWEN Morris MM L/Cpl 50734 Machine Gun Corps
OWEN Rhys Madoc MM Pte 19214 11th Lancashire Fusiliers
OWEN Richard MM Sjt 47665 Labour Corps
OWEN Richard MM Pte 47842 Welsh Regt
OWEN Richard E. MM Pte 32149 12th Manchester Regt
OWEN Robert A. MM+Bar Pte 368010 7th & 6th London Regt

OWEN Robert J. MM Pte 40095 14th Royal Welsh Fusiliers
OWEN Robert Tudor MM Pte 12/742 12th York & Lancaster Regt
OWEN Rowland G. MM Cpl 653681 21st London Regt
OWEN S. MM AM1 25960 Royal Flying Corps
OWEN Samuel MM Spr 93788 32 Div Sig Coy Royal Engineers
OWEN Samuel MM Sjt 21 1st Welsh Guards
OWEN Seth MM Pte 33036 Manchester Regt
OWEN Stanley C. MM Sjt 11218 10th Royal West Kent Regt
OWEN Stanley V. MM Cpl 132333 204 Siege Bty RGA
OWEN Thomas Charles MM Pte 200264 1/4th Shropshire Light Infantry KIA 26.3.18.
OWEN Thomas W. MM Sjt 121729 183 Tunnelling Coy Royal Engineers
OWEN W.J. MM Sjt 25499 194 Siege Bty RGA
OWEN William MM Sjt 20350 11th South Lancashire Regt
OWEN William MM Cpl 658 1st Royal Warwickshire Regt KIA 18.7.18.
OWEN William MM Pte 16143 9th North Lancashire Regt
OWEN William MM CQMS 6925 1st Royal West Surrey Regt
OWEN William MM Pte 36778 Machine Gun Corps KIA 24.8.18.
OWEN William MM+Bar RSM 28203 Welsh Regt
OWEN William MM L/Bdr 308285 RGA
OWEN William C. MM Pte 16821 8th Hussars
OWEN William Edwin MM Pte 18281 7th Lincolnshire Regt KIA 7.9.17.
OWEN William N.H. MM Pte 66033 10th Royal Scots
OWENS Alexander MM Spr 64526 36 Div Sig Coy Royal Engineers
OWENS Alexander Edwin MM L/Cpl 64525 36 Div Sig Coy Royal Engineers
OWENS Andrew MM Pte 27005 6th Royal Inniskilling Fusiliers
OWENS Arthur MM Spr 82895 Royal Engineers
OWENS B. MM Pte 16505 Machine Gun Corps
OWENS Charles Richard MM Pte 1855 1/3rd London Regt DOW 25.8.16.
OWENS David Norman MM Dvr 61163 73 Fd Coy Royal Engineers
OWENS Edward MM Sjt 31855 19th Welsh Regt
OWENS Edward A. MM Pte 266464 6th Welsh Regt
OWENS Frank MM Cpl 504019 Royal Engineers
OWENS James MM Pte 19694 South Lancashire Regt
OWENS James Temple MM Pte 200607 3rd(Light)Bn Tank Corps
OWENS John MM Sjt 11237 4th Liverpool Regt
OWENS Joseph MM Cpl 16835 Royal Welsh Fusiliers
OWENS Owen MM Sjt 23309 14 Siege Bty RGA DOW 4.7.19.
OWENS Owen MM+Bar Pte 61073 2nd Royal Welsh Fusiliers
OWENS Patrick MM+Bar Sjt 5644 2nd Royal Irish Rifles
OWENS Peter MM L/Cpl 4241 2nd Royal Inniskilling Fusiliers DOW 30.9.18.
OWENS T. MM Sjt Mechanic 27416 Royal Air Force
OWENS Thomas MM+Bar Sjt 17707 61st Bn Machine Gun Corps
OWENS Thomas "MM+Bar,MID" Sjt 11377 4th King's Royal Rifle Corps
OWENS William MM Pte 306746 8th West Yorkshire Regt
OWENS William MM Pte 11601 Liverpool Regt
OWENS William MM Sjt 36839 47th Bn Machine Gun Corps
OWENS William MM Dvr T4/069798 Army Service Corps
OWERS Frank H. MM Sjt 23185 2 Div Sig Coy Royal Engineers
OWERS George MM Spr 15340 RGA
OWERS Leonard George MM L/Cpl 75214 'B' Bn Tank Corps
OWERS Percy A. MM L/Cpl 260170 8th Worcestershire Regt
OWERS William A. MM Cpl 7144 1st East Surrey Regt
OWINS Albert P. MM Sjt M2/102166 272 Coy Army Service Corps
OWLERS William H. MM Pte 39457 RAMC
OWNSWORTH Arthur MM Cpl 98854 RFA
OWST Arthur L. MM Cpl 25801 RFA
OXBERRY George William MM Pte 12344 7th Yorkshire Regt
OXBOROUGH Harry MM L/Cpl 241064 7th Lincolnshire Regt
OXBORROW Sidney E. MM Sjt 61230 Machine Gun Corps
OXBY Ernest MM Cpl 15136 6th Lincolnshire Regt
OXBY James MM Dvr 314491 RGA
OXENHAM Fred MM Cpl 108321 6th Duke of Cornwall's LI
OXENHAM Hugh A. MM Pte 52083 Royal Fusiliers
OXENHAM William A. MM Cpl 9443 2nd Royal Fusiliers
OXENHAM William Charles MM Cpl 23489 9th Royal Fusiliers
OXFORD Albert E. MM Dvr 9544 RFA
OXFORD Fred MM L/Cpl M2/078202 Army Service Corps
OXFORD George MM Bdr 58753 RFA
OXFORD George MM Sjt 46636 Durham Light Infantry
OXFORD Patrick MM Pte 31278 RAMC
OXLEE Albert J. MM Sjt 22736 Northumberland Fusiliers
OXLEY Albert MM Cpl 12627 1st Royal Fusiliers
OXLEY Arthur Guy Herbert MM Sjt 93729 41 Div Sig Coy Royal Engineers
OXLEY Ernest E. MM Pte 34568 RAMC
OXLEY Frank MM Pte 202350 4th York & Lancaster Regt
OXLEY Percy J. MM Cpl 5612 9th Lancers
OXLEY Richard S. MM L/Cpl 3734 1/1st HAC(Infantry)
OXLEY Thomas MM Pte 352689 1/9th Royal Scots
OXSPRING Frederick Arnold MM Pte 18017 6th Leicestershire Regt
OXTABY Harold MM Pte 13/1128 13th York & Lancaster Regt
OXTOBY Thomas MM Pte 32165 West Yorkshire Regt
OYSTON Frederick MM Pte 19292 Bedfordshire Regt
OZENBROOK J.W. MM Pte 23606 East Kent Regt

P

PACE Albert E. MM Pte 612815 19th London Regt
PACE Emanuel MM Pte 24309 South Wales Borderers
PACE George MM Sjt 156 6th Royal West Kent Regt KIA 9.4.17.
PACE Victor H. "DCM,MM" Cpl 31285 28 Fd Amb RAMC
PACE Wilfred Hughes MM Gnr 352195 RGA
PACE William R. MM Sjt 13393 2nd Scots Guards
PACEY Alfred MM Bdr 34244 RGA
PACEY John MM Pte 14665 8th Lincolnshire Regt
PACEY Luis Alan MM Sjt 810566 232 Bde RFA
PACEY Richard MM Sjt 9463 7th Lincolnshire Regt DOW 12.10.17.
PACEY Tom MM Cpl 241521 7th Lincolnshire Regt
PACK Gerald A. MM Pte M2/153802 Army Service Corps att RAMC.
PACKARD Charles MM+Bar Pte 202239 Suffolk Regt
PACKER A.E. MM Bdr 318614 2/1(Lowland)Hy Bty RGA
PACKER Albert MM Gnr 146339 180 Siege Bty RGA
PACKER Albert E.G. MM L/Cpl 65873 Machine Gun Corps
PACKER Alfred MM Sjt S/1283 13th Rifle Brigade
PACKER Alfred MM Gnr 121013 RFA
PACKER Alfred E. MM Sjt 311255 Royal Engineers
PACKER Frank MM Sjt 242307 1/5th Gloucestershire Regt
PACKER Frederick J. MM L/Cpl 1771 1/9th London Regt
PACKER George MM L/Sjt 1007 Rifle Brigade
PACKER George W. MM L/Cpl 9187 Royal Fusiliers
PACKER Henry W. MM Cpl 265067 1/6th Gloucestershire Regt
PACKER John MM Sjt 72664 70 Bty 34 Bde RFA
PACKER John MM Sjt 687199 D/285 Bde RFA
PACKER Reginald William "MM,MID" CSM 9524 2nd Essex Regt
PACKER Thomas MM Cpl 265066 1/6th Gloucestershire Regt
PACKER William MM+Bar Pte 23549 1st Royal Irish Fusiliers
PACKHAM Clarence Harold MM Sjt 458 Royal Sussex Regt
PACKHAM Fred MM Cpl 16355 7th Royal Sussex Regt
PACKHAM Percy MM L/Cpl 11746 8th Royal Fusiliers
PACKHAM Walter H. MM+Bar Cpl 32570 Royal Fusiliers
PACKMAN EdwardA. MM Pte 681653 22nd London Regt
PACKMAN George MM Pte 41829 1/6th Royal Highlanders
PACKMAN Henry George MM Pte 21042 3rd Grenadier Guards
PACKMAN Horace MM Pte 18478 Royal West Kent Regt
PACKMAN Percy MM Spr 50962 70 Fd Coy Royal Engineers
PACKMAN W.J. MM Pte 201355 Gordon Highlanders
PADDEN Edward MM Gnr 148108 195 Heavy Bty RGA
PADDICK Charles MM L/Cpl R/4985 13th King's Royal Rifle Corps
PADDICK Harry MM Sjt 200406 1/4th Royal Berkshire Regt KIA 3.10.17.
PADDICK Thomas William MM Gnr Shoeing Smith 40979 118 Bty 26 Bde RFA
PADDISON Thomas MM Pte 38734 RAMC
PADDOCK Frederick MM Sjt 16555 Grenadier Guards
PADDOCK George MM L/Cpl 79405 Royal Engineers
PADDOCK Joseph MM+Bar Sjt 60040 Royal Engineers
PADDOCK William MM+Bar L/Cpl 79945 173 Tunnelling Coy Royal Engineers
PADDOCK William E. MM Pte 1867 RAMC
PADDON Arthur E. MM Sjt DM2/163144 Army Service Corps
PADDON John MM Sjt 10504 8th Devonshire Regt
PADDY William G. MM CQMS 16577 56th Bn Machine Gun Corps
PADFIELD Allan T. MM Pte 23785 Royal Fusiliers
PADFIELD Reginald MM Cpl 9264 2nd Royal Munster Fusiliers
PADFIELD Reginald MM Pte 16179 Machine Gun Corps
PADGET Thomas Richard MM Pnr 255079 Royal Engineers
PADGETT Charley MM CSM 260007 1/6th West Yorkshire Regt
PADGETT Dennis Turnbull MM Sjt 2129 1/9th Durham Light Infantry
PADGETT John MM Pte 242880 8th Yorkshire Light Infantry
PADGETT John MM L/Cpl 36929 1st West Yorkshire Regt

PADGETT John Leonard MM Gnr Shoeing Smith 1155 RFA
PADGETT Sam MM Sjt 28188 RFA
PADGETT Sam "MM,CG(B)" Pte 15499 2nd West Riding Regt KIA 23.3.18.
PADGINTON Frank A. MM Dvr 45784 RFA
PADLEY Edwin M. MM Pnr 165435 Royal Engineers
PADLEY Frederick MM L/Cpl 43582 Royal Engineers
PADLEY Harold MM Cpl 23864 8th West Riding Regt
PADLEY John MM Pte 15153 8th Royal Scots Fusiliers
PADLEY Matthew MM Pte 42276 York & Lancaster Regt
PAFFETT Albert E. MM L/Cpl 18730 15th Hampshire Regt
PAFFETT William H. MM Sjt 7968 2nd Hampshire Regt
PAFLIN Samuel MM L/Bdr 16314 64 Siege Bty RGA
PAGE Albert MM Sjt 8018 2nd Royal Scots Fusiliers
PAGE Albert Edward MM Pte 23828 4th Grenadier Guards att MG Gds.
PAGE Albert V. MM Bdr 77703 RFA
PAGE Albert W.J. MM Pte M2/114980 Army Service Corps
PAGE Alec P.E. MM Pte 265548 1/1st Hertfordshire Regt
PAGE Alfred MM Sjt 21146 Machine Gun Corps
PAGE Alfred J. MM Sjt 12298 6th Bedfordshire Regt
PAGE Alic D. MM Pte 80586 1/1st Essex Yeomanry
PAGE Arthur R. MM+Bar Sjt C/4736 King's Royal Rifle Corps
PAGE Cecil MM L/Cpl 20544 2nd York & Lancaster Regt
PAGE Charles MM L/Cpl 43014 Leicestershire Regt
PAGE Charles MM Pte 270847 1/1st Northumberland Yeo
PAGE Charles MM Sjt 11216 11th Hampshire Regt
PAGE Charles B. MM Pte H/7336 15th Hussars
PAGE Charles H. MM Dvr 344071 Royal Engineers
PAGE Charles T. MM Cpl 2591 8th Royal Sussex Regt
PAGE Cyril Morson MM Pte 1622 1/7th Royal Warwickshire Regt KIA 15.7.16.
PAGE Douglas MM Cpl 249499 9 Div Sig Coy Royal Engineers
PAGE Edward MM Dvr 780292 B/246 Bde RFA
PAGE Elijah J. MM Cpl 3613 12th Lancers
PAGE Ephraim "DCM,MM" Sjt 59042 29 Bde RFA
PAGE Ernest MM L/Bdr 56768 RGA
PAGE Ernest MM CSM 1712 59 Fd Coy Royal Engineers
PAGE Ernest Charles MM Sjt 485 1st Royal West Kent Regt
PAGE Ernest W. MM Gnr 58688 11 Bde RFA
PAGE F.W. MM Pte 10134 2nd Scottish Rifles
PAGE Frank MM Pte 24657 2nd Grenadier Guards
PAGE Frank Leslie MM Gnr 64402 133 Siege Bty RGA
PAGE Fred MM Cpl 56632 RFA
PAGE Fred MM Sjt 50136 24 Bty 38 Bde RFA
PAGE Fred G. MM+Bar Sjt 10/603 10th East Yorkshire Regt
PAGE Frederick MM+Bar Pte 7854 4th Middlesex Regt
PAGE Frederick MM CoH 832 Household Bn
PAGE Frederick MM Cpl 39386 RFA
PAGE Frederick G. MM Pte 678233 21st London Regt
PAGE Frederick J.N. MM Pte 352381 7th London Regt
PAGE Frederick Thomas MM Cpl 9934 1st East Kent Regt DOW 3.12.17.
PAGE George MM Pte 45695 6th South Wales Borderers
PAGE George MM L/Cpl 265267 1/6th West Riding Regt KIA 12.4.18.
PAGE George MM Sjt 147113 2nd Bn Special Bde Royal Engineers KIA 3.9.16.
PAGE George A. MM Sjt 9801 1st East Kent Regt
PAGE George Henry MM Bdr 755317 HQ 251 Bde RFA
PAGE George L. MM Pte 35998 Gloucestershire Regt
PAGE George W. MM Bdr 43432 RFA
PAGE Harry Alfred MM Cpl 558087 56 Div Sig Coy Royal Engineers
PAGE Harry Thomas MM Dvr 836613 C/155 Bde RFA DOW 26.10.17.
PAGE Henry MM BSM 31758 353 Siege Bty RGA
PAGE Henry MM Pte 31779 27 Fd Amb RAMC
PAGE Henry Ignatius MM Pte 203161 13th Durham Light Infantry
PAGE Henry S. MM Cpl 31210 RFA
PAGE Herbert Robert MM L/Cpl P/1125 16th Rifle Brigade KIA 27.9.17.
PAGE J. MM Cpl 265746 7th Notts & Derby Regt
PAGE J.W.G. MM Sjt 12305 Army Veterinary Corps
PAGE James MM Dvr 95417 31 Bde Ammn Col RFA
PAGE James MM Sjt Dmr 200070 1/4th Essex Regt
PAGE James A. MM Pte 64334 7th Royal Fusiliers
PAGE James T. MM Pte 3/4425 12th Hampshire Regt
PAGE Jervis MM Pte 5642 Royal Welsh Fusiliers
PAGE John MM Pte 3979 1st Royal Warwickshire Regt KIA 16.12.17.Served as John RADFORD.
PAGE John MM Pte 17151 Suffolk Regt
PAGE John MM Pte 141315 Machine Gun Corps
PAGE John MM L/Cpl S/357 12th Rifle Brigade
PAGE John T. MM+Bar Sjt 16069 Machine Gun Corps
PAGE Joseph E. MM Sjt 24754 3 Siege Bty RGA
PAGE Justin MM Pte 309395 14th Bn Tank Corps
PAGE Leonard L. MM Sjt 37048 RAMC
PAGE Lewis MM Sjt 59164 32nd Bn Machine Gun Corps
PAGE Matthew MM Pte 203268 1/4th Lincolnshire Regt
PAGE P. MM Pte 41785 5th West Yorkshire Regt
PAGE Percy Charles Emmanuel MM Pte 516914 1/14th London Regt
PAGE Percy G. MM L/Bdr 105327 RGA
PAGE Reginald Percy MM CSM 3/8190 8th Norfolk Regt KIA 21.7.16.
PAGE Richard MM L/Cpl 2291 1/1st Hertfordshire Regt
PAGE Richard John MM+Bar Sjt 27395 16th Notts & Derby Regt KIA 16.4.18.
PAGE Thomas MM Spr 447876 Royal Engineers
PAGE Thomas MM Pte 8403 RAMC
PAGE Thomas Henry MM L/Cpl 17967 Duke of Cornwall's LI
PAGE Victor Arthur MM Sjt 5428 20th Royal Fusiliers KIA 20.6.17.
PAGE Walter MM Pte 329214 1/1st Cambridgeshire Regt
PAGE Walter MM Pte 29281 10th Essex Regt KIA 12.4.18.
PAGE Walter MM Spr 526246 62 Div Sig Coy Royal Engineers
PAGE Walter MM Sjt 14928 7th South Wales Borderers
PAGE Walter Walman MM Pte 20536 Grenadier Guards
PAGE William MM Gnr 156460 82 Bde RFA
PAGE William MM Sjt 230261 Royal Engineers
PAGE William MM Pte 5000 8th Royal West Surrey Regt
PAGE William Buxton MM L/Sjt 8836 2nd Suffolk Regt
PAGE William H. MM Pte M2/050856 Army Service Corps
PAGE William Ward MM Cpl 20082 6th Dorsetshire Regt
PAGET Arthur MM Gnr 76700 RFA
PAGET Harry MM Pte 202967 West Yorkshire Regt
PAGET L.H. MM Cpl 475178 RAMC
PAGET Richard W. MM Cpl 4692 7th Dragoon Guards
PAGET Sydney A. MM Cpl Fitter 20404 25 Bde RFA
PAGETT Albert MM Dvr 676875 B/285 Bde RFA
PAGETT William MM Pte 39399 RAMC
PAGETT William A. MM Pte 302644 10th Royal Scots
PAGGETT Henry J. MM Pte 241589 8th Worcestershire Regt
PAGRAM Walter MM Cpl 2024 Gloucestershire Regt
PAICE George Thomas MM Pte 17438 2nd Wiltshire Regt
PAICE Henry Arthur MM Cpl 54536 32 Bde RFA
PAICE James J. "MM,MID" Sjt 8130 1st Hampshire Regt
PAICE William A. MM Cpl 701309 23rd London Regt
PAIGE Hazell MM+Bar Sjt 59802 36 Bde RFA
PAIGE Stephen J. MM+Bar L/Cpl 21931 Hampshire Regt
PAIGE Thomas MM Pte 26332 1st Duke of Cornwall's LI
PAIN Charles H. MM Gnr 49912 RFA
PAIN George MM Pte 22071 1st Duke of Cornwall's LI
PAIN Gilbert MM Cpl 31499 A/177 Bde RFA
PAIN Isaac MM Pte 13820 15th Durham Light Infantry KIA 29.5.18.
PAIN William MM Dvr 950647 RFA
PAINE Dennis Lello Adkins "MC,MM(1349 Sjt)" 2Lt 2/7th Royal Warwickshire Regt
PAINE Ernest A. MM Pte 23625 7th Royal Sussex Regt
PAINE Ernest F. MM Pte 590355 18th London Regt
PAINE George MM CQMS 200292 1/4th Leicestershire Regt
PAINE Henry J. MM Sjt M2/103935 Army Service Corps
PAINE John J. MM Pte 300954 Essex Regt
PAINE Marshall A. MM L/Cpl 192 10th Royal Fusiliers
PAINE Roland MM Pte 9280 2nd Somerset Light Infantry
PAINE Walter J. MM Cpl 14179 3rd Royal Fusiliers
PAINE Walter William MM Pte 7395 8th Royal West Kent Regt KIA 22.8.18.
PAINE Wilfred or William Edward MM Pte 240521 1/8th Middlesex Regt
PAINES Walter "MM,MID" Sjt 60530 23 Bde RFA
PAINTER Edward J. MM L/Cpl 4711 2/20th London Regt
PAINTER John P. MM Pte 75761 Royal Fusiliers
PAINTER Percy "MM,MID" Pte 1253 1/1st Cambridgeshire Regt
PAINTER Reginald Frank MM Gnr Wheeler 66647 109 Siege Bty RGA
PAINTER Royd Frederick MM Pte 53659 6th Bn Machine Gun Corps
PAINTER Sydney Frank MM Gnr 122607 RFA
PAINTER Thomas MM Pte 39575 RAMC
PAINTER William H. MM L/Cpl 9731 17 Coy Labour Corps

PAINTER William J. MM L/Cpl 27670 3rd Grenadier Guards
PAINTIN Harold MM Pte 12385 1st Grenadier Guards
PAINTING Arthur MM Cpl 11683 15th Hampshire Regt
PAINTING C. MM Sjt 200966 4th Hampshire Regt
PAINTING John MM Pte 10649 5th Oxf & Bucks Light Infantry
PAINTING Thomas H. MM CSM 7320 1st King's Royal Rifle Corps
PAIRPOINT Albert Victor MM L/Sjt 41020 21st Middlesex Regt KIA 23.3.18.
PAISH Frederick M. MM+Bar Sjt 12478 7th Wiltshire Regt
PAKEMAN Oscar Henry MM Cpl 320321 1/1st Wiltshire Yeomanry
PALETHORPE Joseph MM Pte 25594 Machine Gun Corps
PALETHORPE Roderigo G. MM Pte 91103 Machine Gun Corps
PALEY Edward H. MM Pte 10924 9th Royal Sussex Regt
PALEY Frank William "MC,DCM,MM(7930 Sjt 2nd Bn),MID" Capt King's Royal Rifle Corps
PALFRAMAN George MM Pte 21150 8th East Yorkshire Regt DOW 12.4.17.
PALFRAMAN John MM Pte 40804 8th West Yorkshire Regt
PALFREY Benjamin C. MM L/Cpl 149646 12th Bn Machine Gun Corps
PALFREY Charles MM Gnr 11580 RFA
PALFREY Edward George MM Cpl 12827 1st Grenadier Guards DOW 5.4.18.
PALFREY James W. MM Pte 240919 Suffolk Regt
PALFREY Walter MM Cpl 77089 129 Coy Labour Corps
PALIN Arthur MM Pte 27253 9th Cheshire Regt
PALIN Cecil MM L/Sjt S/10111 Rifle Brigade
PALIN Ernest E. MM Cpl 352521 2nd Manchester Regt
PALIN Fred MM Pte 2658 South Lancashire Regt
PALIN John MM Sjt 19226 21st Manchester Regt
PALING Joseph Henry MM Pte 70504 Notts & Derby Regt
PALLANT Edgar MM Sjt 327253 1/9th Durham Light Infantry
PALLENT Francis MM Cpl 58665 45 Bde RFA
PALLETT Albert MM Pte 33754 5th West Riding Regt
PALLETT Charles J. MM Pte 13672 1st Royal Fusiliers
PALLETT James A. MM L/Cpl 15067 Worcestershire Regt
PALLETT Robert MM Pte 240566 5th Yorkshire Light Infantry
PALLETT Roland MM Cpl 53078 Liverpool Regt
PALLETT S. MM Spr 251727 Royal Engineers
PALLISER Fred MM Pnr 126626 VII Corps Sig Coy Royal Engineers
PALLISER Fred MM Dvr 110887 C/58 Bde RFA
PALLISER Harry MM Bdr 221842 11 Bde Ammn Col RFA
PALLISTER Christopher MM Cpl 2251 West Yorkshire Regt
PALLISTER H.T. MM Pte 50204 12th Royal Irish Rifles
PALLISTER Henry MM+Bar Cpl 388452 2/2(Northumbrian)Fd Amb RAMC
PALMER Albert MM Pte 87932 147 Labour Coy Labour Corps
PALMER Albert E. MM Sjt 78007 Tank Corps
PALMER Albert Edward MM Sjt 12908 10th Yorkshire Regt
PALMER Alfred E. MM Sjt 51395 42nd Bn Machine Gun Corps
PALMER Alfred E. MM Pte 14563 9th Norfolk Regt
PALMER Alfred H. MM Cpl 59778 RFA
PALMER Arthur MM Gnr 230206 C/82 Bde RFA
PALMER Arthur MM Cpl 45172 RAMC
PALMER Arthur MM Pte 15053 9th South Staffordshire Regt
PALMER Arthur H. MM Pte 14944 7th Northamptonshire Regt
PALMER Arthur James MM Pte 14878 7th Bedfordshire Regt Died 6.9.17.
PALMER Arthur John "MM,MID" Sjt 58327 B/82 Bde RFA
PALMER Arthur Stanley MM Pte 32962 2nd Hampshire Regt KIA 13.4.18.
PALMER Arthur V. MM Sjt 241965 Notts & Derby Regt
PALMER Basil McNatty MM Cpl 1409 17 Fd Amb RAMC
PALMER Charles MM Sjt 12205 6th Dorsetshire Regt
PALMER Charles MM L/Cpl 53292 Liverpool Regt
PALMER Charles H. MM Pte 14603 1st Wiltshire Regt
PALMER Charles S. MM L/Cpl 5558 1/6th South Staffordshire Regt
PALMER D. MM Sjt 1917 A/122 Bde RFA
PALMER David W. "MM,MID" Spr 28400 Royal Engineers
PALMER E. MM Pte 461188 RAMC
PALMER Edward C. MM Cpl Z/170 Rifle Brigade
PALMER Edwin A. MM Pte 242587 Leicestershire Regt
PALMER Edwin G. MM Sjt 504321 503 Fd Coy Royal Engineers
PALMER Ernest MM Sjt 22912 1st Scottish Rifles
PALMER Ernest "MM,MID" Sjt 14769 7th Shropshire Light Infantry
PALMER Ernest MM Pte 19879 Machine Gun Corps
PALMER Ernest MM Sjt 53800 RAMC
PALMER Ernest F. MM Pte 300167 Liverpool Regt
PALMER Francis William MM Sjt 15837 6th Northamptonshire Regt KIA 18.9.18.

PALMER Frank MM Sjt 71269 42 Bde RFA
PALMER Frank MM Pte 201142 Welsh Regt
PALMER Frank "DCM,MM+Bar,MM(F)" Cpl 201108 2/5th Lancashire Fusiliers
PALMER Frank MM Cpl 3039 1/5th Gloucestershire Regt
PALMER Frank A. MM+Bar L/Cpl 4647 13th Royal Fusiliers
PALMER Frank Archibald MM Cpl 3338 1/19th London Regt
PALMER Frederick Charles MM Cpl 7697 Machine Gun Corps
PALMER Frederick E. MM Pte M2/115456 Army Service Corps
PALMER Frederick H. MM Pte 43723 Machine Gun Corps
PALMER Frederick William "VC,MM" L/Sjt 731 22nd Royal Fusiliers
PALMER George MM L/Cpl 37555 Bedfordshire Regt att 1/1st Hertfordshire Regt.
PALMER George MM Pte 65201 1st Northumberland Fusiliers DOW 21.9.18.
PALMER George MM L/Cpl 34761 2nd Yorkshire Light Infantry KIA 30.9.18.
PALMER George J. MM Pte 6319 Royal Warwickshire Regt
PALMER George S. MM Cpl 676 Middlesex Regt
PALMER Harold MM L/Cpl 7038 Manchester Regt
PALMER Harold MM+Bar Pte 678129 11th & 21st London Regt
PALMER Harry MM Sjt 11380 Oxf & Bucks Light Infantry
PALMER Henry S. MM Cpl 156935 219 Siege Bty RGA
PALMER Herbert MM Pte 241380 2/5th Gloucestershire Regt
PALMER Horace E. MM Spr 549956 Royal Engineers
PALMER J.F. MM Pte 19004 Northumberland Fusiliers
PALMER J.H. MM Pte 3537 2 Fd Amb RAMC
PALMER James MM Pte 15349 10th West Riding Regt
PALMER James F. MM Cpl 345134 16th Devonshire Regt
PALMER John MM Pte 2312 Royal Warwickshire Regt
PALMER John Charles MM Pte 1317 1st Welsh Guards
PALMER John Robert MM Sjt 21/288 Northumberland Fusiliers
PALMER John W. MM Cpl 9661 2nd Coldstream Guards
PALMER John William MM Pte 1556 RAMC Died 25.12.18.
PALMER Joseph MM Pte 39395 RAMC
PALMER L.P. MM Pte 17438 7th East Kent Regt
PALMER Lewis George MM Pte 18812 Bedfordshire Regt
PALMER Matthew MM Pte S/6411 38 Ord Ammn Sect Army Ordnance Corps
PALMER Nathaniel Charles MM Pte 41334 2 Squadron Machine Gun Corps(Cavalry)
PALMER Owen MM Pte 23560 Leicestershire Regt
PALMER Owen Henry "MM,MID" Sjt 51342 70 Fd Coy Royal Engineers
PALMER Philip S. MM Cpl 57488 3 Bty 45 Bde RFA
PALMER Reginald MM Gnr 86489 RFA
PALMER Robert MM Spr 186224 3 Fd Svy Coy Royal Engineers
PALMER Robert MM Sjt 16992 8th East Yorkshire Regt
PALMER Robert Henry MM Sjt 8983 4th Liverpool Regt KIA 7.12.17.
PALMER Roy V. MM Cpl 39660 RAMC att KOSB.
PALMER Samuel MM Pte 678 9 Fd Amb RAMC
PALMER Samuel R.H. MM Bdr 279080 RGA
PALMER Sidney Arthur MM Pte 14466 2nd Coldstream Guards
PALMER Sidney Norman MM L/Cpl 2170 1/8th Worcestershire Regt
PALMER Thomas MM Cpl 350302 1/9th Royal Scots
PALMER Thomas MM L/Sjt 331437 Hampshire Regt
PALMER Thomas Charles Herbert MM Pte 9700 1st Leicestershire Regt
PALMER Thomas Edward MM Pte M2/101380 Army Service Corps att 62 Siege Bty RGA.
PALMER Thomas G. MM Pte 10736 10th Royal Fusiliers
PALMER Thomas H. MM CQMS 470662 12th London Regt
PALMER Thomas P. "DCM,MM" Sjt 31819 V/9 Hy TM Bty & X/25 Med TM Bty RGA
PALMER Thomas William MM Sjt 95308 B/62 Bde RFA
PALMER Tom MM Spr 154515 Royal Engineers
PALMER Tom MM L/Bdr 17209 115 Bty 25 Bde RFA
PALMER Walter MM+Bar Sjt 242424 1st Middlesex Regt
PALMER Walter H. MM Pte 35962 East Surrey Regt
PALMER Walter William "DCM,MM" Sjt 13765 8th Norfolk Regt
PALMER Warren MM+Bar Sjt 5617 23rd Bn Machine Gun Corps
PALMER Wilfred Leonard "DCM,MM+Bar" Sjt 43550 7th Northamptonshire Regt
PALMER William MM L/Cpl 41096 1/2(Highland)Fd Amb RAMC
PALMER William MM Pte 24171 Welsh Regt
PALMER William Augustus MM Spr 133509 Postal Section Royal Engineers att HQ Guards Division
PALMER William G. MM Pte 43022 Norfolk Regt
PALMER William Henry MM Pte CMT/1693 2 Div Train Army Service Corps

PALMER William Henry MM Sjt 66844 139 Fd Amb RAMC
PALMER William Herbert MM Sjt 14601 9th Royal Irish Fusiliers
PALMER William J. MM Pte M/08398 Army Service Corps
PALMER William J. "DCM,MM" Bdr 36854 RGA
PALMER William J. MM Pte 1652 9th London Regt
PALMER William K. MM+Bar Sjt 17739 15 Fd Coy Royal Engineers
PALMER William L. MM L/Cpl 29793 Gloucestershire Regt
PALMER William Whyndom MM Pte 374 11th Middlesex Regt DOW 18.12.16.
PALMORE Ernest J. MM Cpl 50795 Highland Light Infantry
PALTRIDGE Alfred Stanley MM Cpl 73460 72 Coy Machine Gun Corps
PAMLEY William Arthur MM Gnr 761389 RFA
PAMMENT Charles MM+Bar L/Sjt 42393 8th West Yorkshire Regt
PANKHURST Arthur Philip MM Pte M2/022036 Army Service Corps
PANKHURST Edward James MM Sjt 36254 32 Div Sig Coy Royal Engineers
PANKHURST Ernest MM Pte 50145 36th Northumberland Fusiliers
PANKHURST Ernest J. MM+Bar Cpl S/32484 13th Rifle Brigade
PANKHURST Joseph W. MM Gnr 208489 RFA
PANKHURST Percy MM Pte 735 6th Royal West Kent Regt
PANNELL Frederick A. MM Gnr 800400 409 Bty 96 Bde RFA
PANNELL George MM Cpl S/29532 Rifle Brigade
PANNELL Jim MM Pte 24692 7th Royal West Surrey Regt KIA 21.5.18.
PANNETT Thomas MM Cpl 10385 8th Royal West Kent Regt KIA 16.5.17.
PANTER Arthur William MM Sjt 44466 196 Coy Machine Gun Corps
PANTER George F. MM Pte 50278 Suffolk Regt
PANTER John C. MM L/Cpl 14462 6th Northamptonshire Regt
PANTON Helen Elizabeth MM Staff Nurse F TFNS
PANTON Matthew MM Cpl 27448 Royal Scots
PANTON William MM L/Cpl 53803 36 Fd Amb RAMC
PANTRY Herbert MM Pte 201735 1st West Yorkshire Regt
PAPADOPOULLOS Nicholas Gavriel MM Pte 202642 2/4th Hampshire Regt KIA 1.12.17.
PAPADOURIS Gabriel MM Gnr 7647 11 Siege Bty RGA
PAPE Arnold MM Gnr 755938 RFA
PAPE William E. MM Cpl 193317 Royal Engineers
PAPPS William MM Dvr 40647 RFA
PAPWORTH Arthur MM Pte 9808 2nd West Yorkshire Regt
PAPWORTH Charles Wallace "MM,CG(F)" Cpl 3/3154 11th Essex Regt
PAPWORTH Frank Henry MM Pte 307671 10th Royal Warwickshire Regt DOW 29.10.18.
PAPWORTH Walter Charles MM Pte 21548 Duke of Cornwall's LI
PAPWORTH William MM Sjt 43407 1st Bedfordshire Regt
PAPWORTH William Henry MM Pte 29725 4th Bedfordshire Regt KIA 27.9.18.
PARADINE Harry "MM,MID" Sjt 15209 2nd Grenadier Guards
PARAGREEN Harold G. MM Cpl 42623 4th North Staffordshire Regt
PARAMOR William "DCM,MM" Sjt 36717 97 Bty 147 Bde RFA
PARDEW Frederick MM+Bar Cpl 9769 8th Devonshire Regt
PARDEY John MM Pte 26748 50 Coy Machine Gun Corps DOW 14.5.17.
PARDEY Leslie "MM,MID" Sjt 645577 RFA att ASC.
PARDINGTON John G. MM Pte 19363 Machine Gun Corps
PARDOE Donald MM SSM 325904 1/1st Worcestershire Yeomanry
PARDOE William MM Pte 41528 18th Highland Light Infantry
PARDY Alfred Herbert MM Sjt 9102 Hampshire Regt
PARDY Robert Willis "MM,MID" Sjt 17760 Special Brigade Royal Engineers
PARFETT Edward John "MM,MID" Gnr 128981 29 Bde RFA
PARFITT Frederick MM Pte 307227 15th Bn Tank Corps
PARFITT Frederick MM Spr 311000 Royal Engineers
PARFITT Geoffrey B. MM L/Cpl 16544 7th Norfolk Regt
PARFITT Henry MM Bdr 13232 RFA
PARFITT Henry Thomas MM Spr 66913 171 Tunnelling Coy Royal Engineers DOW 16.8.17.
PARFITT James H. MM Bdr 313414 RGA
PARFITT Robert James MM Pte 13969 8th Suffolk Regt KIA 31.7.17.
PARFITT Thomas J. MM Cpl 30184 RGA
PARFREMENT Walter MM Sjt 3962 RFA
PARHAM Jack MM Pte 6260 Royal Warwickshire Regt
PARIS Dawson MM Pte 39802 5/6th Scottish Rifles
PARIS Leslie W. MM Pte 1241 7th Royal West Surrey Regt
PARIS Reginald J. MM Sjt 89434 RFA
PARISH Arthur T. MM Pte 11202 2nd Scots Guards
PARISH Frank Frederick MM Pte 106745 21st Bn Machine Gun Corps KIA 19.9.18.
PARISH Henry G. MM Spr 26644 Royal Engineers
PARISH Henry H. MM Spr 310886 Signal Service Royal Engineers
PARISH Thomas MM Cpl 491376 13th London Regt KIA 25.4.18.
PARISH Walter P. MM Pte 189562 Labour Corps
PARISH William MM L/Bdr 33812 RGA
PARK Alexander MM Bdr 23637 2 Div Ammn Col RFA
PARK Archie MM Sjt 19137 6th King's Own Scottish Borderers
PARK Arthur MM Cpl 120553 4 Speial Coy Royal Engineers
PARK Cornelius Pinder MM Pte 200256 1/4th East Yorkshire Regt
PARK Daniel MM Dvr 7291 RFA
PARK David MM Pte 8422 East Kent Regt
PARK David MM Pte 139484 Machine Gun Corps
PARK Edmund J. MM Pte 24026 1st Royal Lancaster Regt
PARK George MM Pte 29744 1st Border Regt
PARK George MM Spr 79464 173 Tunnelling Coy Royal Engineers KIA 17.4.16.
PARK George S. MM Pte 34927 Royal Scots
PARK James "MM,MC(G)" Gnr Sig 650531 1 Bde RFA
PARK James MM L/Cpl 1021 Army Cyclist Corps
PARK James MM L/Cpl 134228 Royal Engineers
PARK John MM Pte 271477 5/6th Royal Scots
PARK John MM+Bar Sjt 655806 RFA
PARK John MM L/Cpl 200547 1/4th Gordon Highlanders
PARK John T. MM Pte 20377 10th Royal West Kent Regt
PARK John W. MM L/Cpl 24749 2/4th York & Lancaster Regt
PARK Peter MM+Bar Gnr 80131 D/124 Bde RFA
PARK Raymond MM Cpl 10565 7th East Surrey Regt
PARK Samuel MM Pte 5677 14th Northumberland Fusiliers
PARK Stephen C. MM Pte 39834 21 Fd Amb RAMC
PARK Thomas "DCM,MM" Pte 200782 1/4th North Lancaster Regt
PARK V.V. MM Cpl 13067 North Lancashire Regt
PARK William MM+Bar Sjt 18560 Royal Scots
PARK William MM Cpl 325262 1/9th Durham Light Infantry KIA 21.7.18.
PARK William C. MM Sjt 15600 Machine Gun Corps
PARKE Albert MM Pte 43705 Norfolk Regt KIA 18.4.18.
PARKE Edward Arnold MM+Bar Cpl 33523 2nd Yorkshire Regt
PARKE H. MM Pte 49783 1st Royal Irish Fusiliers
PARKE Herbert "DCM+Bar,MM" Sjt 14716 Norfolk Regt
PARKE Isaac John MM Pte 28727 1st East Surrey Regt
PARKE James MM Sjt 14481 11th Royal Inniskilling Fusiliers KIA 16.8.17.
PARKER A. MM Pte 201600 2/4th Hampshire Regt
PARKER A.L. MM L/Cpl 265565 ? Yeomanry
PARKER Agnes Jack MM Staff Nurse F TFNS
PARKER Albert MM L/Cpl 56827 Machine Gun Corps(Cavalry)
PARKER Albert MM Sjt 474689 Royal Engineers
PARKER Albert E. MM Gnr Sig 741649 A/112 Bde RFA
PARKER Albert E. MM Bdr 9048 RFA
PARKER Albert E. MM L/Cpl 16759 Durham Light Infantry
PARKER Albert E. MM Pte 9453 2nd Border Regt
PARKER Albert W. MM Pte 3900 Machine Gun Corps
PARKER Albert W. MM Pte 12131 10th Gloucestershire Regt
PARKER Alfred MM Cpl 12087 Royal Fusiliers
PARKER Alfred MM Sjt 7701 2nd Hampshire Regt
PARKER Alfred Abraham MM L/Cpl 15482 3rd Grenadier Guards
PARKER Alfred J. MM Pte 202847 4th West Riding Regt
PARKER Alfred J. MM Cpl 283643 4th London Regt
PARKER Archie W. MM Pte 200209 1/4th Suffolk Regt
PARKER Arthur MM Pte 24387 8th Gloucestershire Regt
PARKER Arthur MM Sjt 15632 9th Norfolk Regt
PARKER Arthur MM Bdr 785289 RFA
PARKER Arthur C. MM Pte 29341 North Lancashire Regt
PARKER Arthur C. MM Pte 402 Royal Fusiliers
PARKER Arthur E. MM Cpl 306466 West Riding Regt
PARKER Arthur J. MM Pte 110784 MGC(Cavalry)
PARKER Arthur J. MM L/Cpl 7023 1st Norfolk Regt
PARKER Arthur S. MM Pte 3454 Middlesex Regt
PARKER Bertram MM Pte 14054 6th Yorkshire Regt
PARKER C.F. MM Sjt 29469 23 Bde RFA
PARKER Cecil Charles MM Pte 76423 1/5th Notts & Derby Regt DOW 30.9.18.
PARKER Charles "DCM,MM" Sjt 10904 69 Fd Amb RAMC
PARKER Charles MM Pte 6600 7th Rifle Brigade
PARKER Charles MM L/Cpl 16961 2 Coy Machine Gun Corps KIA 16.11.17.
PARKER Charles MM Sjt 27004 Labour Corps
PARKER Charles MM Cpl 106666 Royal Engineers

PARKER Charles E. "DCM,MM+Bar" RSM 13769 10th West Riding Regt
PARKER Charles F. MM L/Cpl 555282 16th London Regt
PARKER Charles Frederick MM Cpl 241689 2/5th West Riding Regt
PARKER Charles H. MM Gnr 781100 RFA
PARKER Charles T. MM Sjt 680880 22nd London Regt
PARKER Clifford MM L/Cpl 18638 6th East Yorkshire Regt
PARKER Edward MM Pte 30194 8th Royal Lancaster Regt
PARKER Edward MM Pte 82139 Machine Gun Corps
PARKER Edward Vincent MM Cpl 2585 1/6th Royal Warwickshire Regt KIA 1.7.16.
PARKER Edwin D. MM L/Cpl 311100 Royal Engineers
PARKER Ernest MM Cpl 938 12th Yorkshire Light Infantry
PARKER Ernest H. MM Dvr 184969 C/311 Bde RFA
PARKER F.W. MM+Bar L/Cpl 498 6th East Kent Regt
PARKER Francis Charles MM Sjt 12836 3rd Grenadier Guards KIA 31.7.17.
PARKER Francis James MM Sjt 2228 1/4th Suffolk Regt KIA 15.7.16.
PARKER Frank MM Cpl 132695 197 Siege Bty RGA
PARKER Frank H. MM L/Cpl 11348 Royal West Surrey Regt
PARKER Frank J. MM Pte 29073 East Yorkshire Regt
PARKER Frederick MM Pte 25897 6th Oxf & Bucks Light Infantry
PARKER Frederick Arthur MM Cpl 49347 161 Coy Machine Gun Corps
PARKER Frederick George MM Pte 15371 7th Bedfordshire Regt
PARKER Frederick I. MM Pnr 1719 Royal Engineers
PARKER Frederick J. MM Pte 4163 Coldstream Guards
PARKER Frederick William MM Cpl 1245 38 Bde RFA
PARKER G.W. MM+Bar Sjt 225 Lincolnshire Regt
PARKER George MM Cpl 63701 13th Yorkshire Regt
PARKER George MM L/Cpl 242233 Highland Light Infantry
PARKER George MM Pte 11332 7th Leicestershire Regt
PARKER George MM CoH 1787 Royal Horse Guards
PARKER George MM+Bar Cpl 138780 41 Siege Bty RGA
PARKER George MM Sjt 275426 1/7th Manchester Regt
PARKER George H. MM Cpl 6332 RAMC
PARKER George J. "DCM,MM" Sjt 200041 8th Lincolnshire Regt
PARKER George W. MM Pte 700985 23rd London Regt
PARKER Harold MM Sjt 240877 1/5th Gloucestershire Regt
PARKER Harry MM Pnr 72088 18 Div Sig Coy Royal Engineers
PARKER Harry MM Dmr 2088 Gloucestershire Regt
PARKER Harry MM Pte 16015 2nd Bedfordshire Regt
PARKER Harry MM Pte 34667 Cheshire Regt
PARKER Harry MM Pte 41701 Northumberland Fusiliers
PARKER Harry MM Pte 9248 2nd Lincolnshire Regt
PARKER Harry MM Cpl 11726 6th Shropshire Light Infantry
PARKER Harry S. MM Pte 88463 1/7th Liverpool Regt KIA 29.9.18.
PARKER Henry MM Pte 570743 1/17th London Regt
PARKER Henry Gordon MM Sjt 528012 54 Div Sig Coy Royal Engineers
PARKER Herbert "DCM,MM" CQMS 9570 1st Royal Lancaster Regt
PARKER Irving MM Pte 11709 Machine Gun Corps
PARKER J. MM L/Cpl P/4824 Military Mounted Police
PARKER Jack MM Pte 1945 Worcestershire Regt
PARKER James MM Pte 27/587 Northumberland Fusiliers
PARKER James "MM,MID" CQMS 5109 3rd West Riding Regt
PARKER James MM+Bar Sjt 8165 1st Shropshire Light Infantry
PARKER James MM Cpl 9939 15 Div Ammn Col RFA
PARKER James MM Pte 90364 151 Coy Labour Corps
PARKER James H. MM Cpl 18626 9th Devonshire Regt
PARKER James Henry "MM,MdH(F)" Sjt 13514 9th East Lancashire Regt
PARKER James W. MM L/Cpl 325513 1/9th Durham Light Infantry
PARKER James W. MM Sjt 11787 4th Yorkshire Light Infantry
PARKER John MM Pte 43206 13th Middlesex Regt
PARKER John MM Pte 102840 8th Notts & Derby Regt
PARKER John "MM,MSM" Sjt 200496 1/4th Royal Scots Fusiliers
PARKER John Albert MM Sjt 40678 RHA
PARKER John C. MM Cpl 7766 2nd South Lancashire Regt
PARKER John F. MM Cpl 54853 48 TM Bty RGA
PARKER John G. MM Gnr 92366 C/148 Bde RFA
PARKER John G.H. MM Pte 202619 15th Royal Warwickshire Regt
PARKER John T. MM Cpl 9005 2nd Leicestershire Regt
PARKER John W. MM Cpl 204106 Northumberland Fusiliers
PARKER John W. MM Spr 474405 Royal Engineers
PARKER John William MM Sjt 12021 2nd Durham Light Infantry DOW 20.9.16.
PARKER Joseph MM Pte 18475 1st North Lancashire Regt
PARKER Joseph MM Sjt 99305 RFA
PARKER Joseph MM Cpl 36788 RGA
PARKER Joseph R. MM Sjt 14441 Suffolk Regt
PARKER L. MM Pte 40601 9th London Regt
PARKER Lawrence "MM,MID" Sjt 3461 2nd Dragoon Guards
PARKER Lawrence Henry MM Pte C/6674 18th King's Royal Rifle Corps KIA 26.10.18.
PARKER Leonard MM Sjt 305569 West Riding Regt
PARKER Lionel MM Pte 41431 Yorkshire Light Infantry
PARKER Nelson MM Cpl 2099 12th Middlesex Regt
PARKER P. MM Pte 13250 Leicestershire Regt
PARKER P. MM Sjt 277040 Royal Engineers
PARKER Percy MM L/Cpl 202740 8th Worcestershire Regt
PARKER Percy Charles MM Pte 3/6759 2nd Devonshire Regt KIA 31.5.18.
PARKER Peter MM Pte 9605 1st Liverpool Regt
PARKER R. MM Sjt 89656 7 Div Ammn Col RFA
PARKER R.H. "MM,MSM" Cpl 51919 17th Liverpool Regt
PARKER Ralph MM L/Cpl 86456 31st Bn Machine Gun Corps
PARKER Ralph MM Pte 241903 Welsh Regt
PARKER Richard MM Pte 240803 Northumberland Fusiliers
PARKER Richard MM Dvr 54879 RFA
PARKER Richard Foggo MM Sjt 70982 34th Bn Machine Gun Corps
PARKER Richard J. MM Pte 73650 RAMC
PARKER Robert MM Sjt 27518 8th Royal Lancaster Regt KIA 27.7.18.
PARKER Robert MM Pte 2208 Durham Light Infantry
PARKER Robert MM Sjt 87744 RFA
PARKER Robert MM Pte 8901 RAMC
PARKER Robert H. MM Cpl 44464 10th South Wales Borderers
PARKER S.A. "DCM,MM" Cpl 56831 HQ 16 Bde RHA
PARKER Samuel MM Pte 43293 15th Royal Irish Rifles
PARKER Samuel "MM,MSM" L/Cpl 1478 1/1st Cambridgeshire Regt
PARKER Samuel MM L/Cpl 23499 Machine Gun Corps
PARKER Samuel E. MM Gnr 675891 RFA
PARKER Sydney MM L/Cpl 10530 4th Royal Fusiliers
PARKER Thomas MM Pte 240097 5th Leicestershire Regt
PARKER Thomas MM Pte 15125 7/8th King's Own Scottish Borderers
PARKER Thomas MM Pte 7239 Royal Irish Fusiliers
PARKER Thomas MM Pte 17936 Machine Gun Corps
PARKER Thomas "MM+2 Bars,MID" Sjt 16072 Machine Gun Corps
PARKER Thomas MM Pte 28651 Royal Scots Fusiliers
PARKER Vincent G. MM Dvr 3187 A/173 Bde RFA
PARKER W.E. MM Sjt 12128 Somerset Light Infantry
PARKER Walter MM L/Cpl 29796 2nd South Wales Borderers
PARKER Walter J. MM Sjt 353118 Manchester Regt
PARKER William MM Cpl 241145 5th Royal Lancaster Regt
PARKER William MM Pte 47947 Royal Inniskilling Fusiliers
PARKER William MM L/Cpl 36479 280 Coy Machine Gun Corps
PARKER William MM L/Cpl 375144 10th Manchester Regt
PARKER William MM Cpl 55775 23 Bde RFA
PARKER William MM Pte S/26395 2 Div Train Army Service Corps
PARKER William MM Cpl 72479 2 Sig Troop Royal Engineers
PARKER William MM Pte 11653 1st Somerset Light Infantry
PARKER William MM Pte 203240 2/6th Royal Warwickshire Regt
PARKER William C. MM L/Cpl 4517 14th Liverpool Regt
PARKER William E. MM Pte 10381 2nd Yorkshire Regt
PARKER William H. MM Cpl 7954 Machine Gun Corps
PARKER William J. MM Cpl Farrier TS/1005 Army Service Corps
PARKER William J. MM Sjt 48029 RAMC
PARKER William Robert MM Pte M2/192882 729 MT Coy Army Service Corps
PARKER William T. MM Pte 75917 2nd London Regt
PARKER Willie MM Cpl 26580 2nd Yorkshire Regt
PARKES Albert MM Cpl 290782 1/7th Cheshire Regt
PARKES Albert MM L/Cpl 5985 Royal Sussex Regt
PARKES Arthur MM Pte 34757 5th West Riding Regt
PARKES Arthur Augustus MM BSM 50536 D/84 Bde RFA KIA 3.9.17.
PARKES Edward MM Pte 24905 7th Seaforth Highlanders
PARKES George MM Sjt 5133 42nd Bn Machine Gun Corps
PARKES George MM Pte 9400 Coldstream Guards
PARKES Jasper MM L/Cpl 240721 1/6th Notts & Derby Regt KIA 30.5.17.
PARKES Johan "MM,MID" L/Cpl 15054 7th North Staffordshire Regt
PARKES John Thomas MM Gnr 810321 D/232 Bde RFA KIA 30.9.17.
PARKES S.N. MM L/Cpl P/12433 Military Mounted Police
PARKES Thomas MM Sjt G/8843 4th Royal Fusiliers DOW 6.11.18.
PARKES Thomas MM Bdr 25496 36 Bde RFA

PARKES Thomas A. MM Sjt 2025 2nd Royal Warwickshire Regt
PARKES W. MM Pte 19487 Notts & Derby Regt
PARKES W.F. MM+Bar Bdr 49871 RGA
PARKES W.I. MM Pte 15621 Coldstream Guards
PARKES William "MM+Bar,CG(F),MID" Sjt 7646 RFA
PARKHILL David MM Pte 278721 1/7th Arg & Suth Highlanders
PARKHILL James MM Spr 57505 121 Fd Coy Royal Engineers
PARKIN Arthur MM L/Cpl 11617 7th East Yorkshire Regt
PARKIN Arthur C. MM Pte 733528 24th London Regt
PARKIN Charles Baden MM Pte 390150 3(Northumbrian)Fd Amb RAMC
PARKIN Ernest MM Dvr T4/252331 62 Div Train Army Service Corps
PARKIN Ernest MM L/Sjt 13145 Notts & Derby Regt
PARKIN F. MM Pte 204604 Northumberland Fusiliers
PARKIN Frank Wilson MM Gnr Sig 113400 84 Siege Bty RGA
PARKIN Fred MM Cpl 6896 XV Corps Cyclist Bn Army Cyclist Corps
PARKIN Fred MM Pte 29128 Highland Light Infantry
PARKIN George MM Pte 5615 5th Royal Berkshire Regt
PARKIN Harry MM Dvr 26805 RFA
PARKIN Isaac MM Pte 40849 7th Manchester Regt
PARKIN James MM Gnr 72380 RFA
PARKIN James MM Bdr 36389 RFA
PARKIN John E. MM Pte 305537 West Riding Regt
PARKIN John Haswell MM Pte 386540 1(Northumbrian)Fd Amb RAMC
PARKIN John Michael MM Sjt 14611 8th Yorkshire Regt
PARKIN Joseph MM Dvr 64441 19 Div Ammn Col RFA DOW 8.6.18.
PARKIN Joseph MM Sjt 19027 9th York & Lancaster Regt KIA 1.7.16.
PARKIN Joseph MM L/Sjt 20/249 Durham Light Infantry
PARKIN Leonard MM Sjt 717 1/6th Cheshire Regt
PARKIN Maurice MM L/Cpl 240832 1/8th Middlesex Regt
PARKIN Percy MM Gnr 8080 RFA
PARKIN Robert N. MM Sjt 461392 RAMC
PARKIN Samuel MM L/Cpl 7382 2nd Coldstream Guards KIA 26.9.16.
PARKIN Samuel S. MM Cpl 13901 12th Durham Light Infantry
PARKIN Sidney MM L/Cpl 108739 18th Bn Machine Gun Corps
PARKIN Thomas MM Sjt 25/535 1st Northumberland Fusiliers
PARKIN Walter MM L/Cpl 14171 2nd Lincolnshire Regt
PARKIN William MM Pte 200143 1/5th Notts & Derby Regt
PARKIN William MM Pte 13525 9th York & Lancaster Regt
PARKIN William R. MM L/Cpl 700917 1/23rd London Regt
PARKIN Willie MM+Bar L/Cpl 6136 2nd Yorkshire Regt
PARKINS Henry MM Dvr 228242 21 Div Ammn Col RFA
PARKINS John T. MM Sjt 246331 B/281 Bde RFA
PARKINSON Albert E. MM Cpl 40382 7th Bn Tank Corps
PARKINSON Arthur "DCM,MM" Sjt 265468 Royal Warwickshire Regt
PARKINSON Arthur MM Cpl 240356 1/5th Royal Lancaster Regt
PARKINSON Charles F. MM Cpl 47208 Royal Engineers
PARKINSON Clifford MM L/Sjt 200986 2/4th North Lancashire Regt KIA 28.9.18.
PARKINSON Douglas MM Cpl 10017 2nd Gordon Highlanders
PARKINSON Edward MM Dvr 26640 D/71 Bde RFA
PARKINSON Edward S. MM Pte 19421 Arg & Suth Highlanders
PARKINSON Frank MM Gnr 75015 41 Bde RFA
PARKINSON Fred MM Pte 242022 North Lancashire Regt
PARKINSON Frederick A.J. MM L/Cpl 64592 17th Worcestershire Regt
PARKINSON George MM Pte 18211 Machine Gun Corps
PARKINSON George MM Sjt 87301 RFA
PARKINSON George MM Pte 937 12th Yorkshire Light Infantry
PARKINSON George H. MM Gnr 19796 D/168 Bde RFA
PARKINSON Gilbert Vint MM Pte 251332 1/6th Manchester Regt
PARKINSON H.W. MM Cpl 79163 185 Tunnelling Coy Royal Engineers
PARKINSON Harrison MM Pte 15935 14th Hampshire Regt KIA 26.9.17.
PARKINSON Haselwood MM Gnr 55328 26 Siege Bty RGA
PARKINSON Henry MM Spr 37625 Royal Engineers
PARKINSON Herbert MM L/Cpl 12300 2nd Scots Guards
PARKINSON Isaac N. MM Pte 8404 21 Fd Amb RAMC
PARKINSON James MM Pte 13639 13th Liverpool Regt
PARKINSON James Croft MM Sjt 21128 40 Bde RFA
PARKINSON John E. MM Pte 12782 7th North Lancashire Regt
PARKINSON John H. MM Pte 200357 1/4th North Lancashire Regt
PARKINSON John Henry "MM,MID" S/Sjt Farrier T1/284 105 Coy Army Service Corps
PARKINSON John S. MM Pte 4753 1/10th Liverpool Regt
PARKINSON Joseph MM Cpl 16887 7th South Lancashire Regt KIA 18.12.17.
PARKINSON Maurice MM Pte 241014 5th York & Lancaster Regt
PARKINSON N. MM AM1 4251 Royal Flying Corps
PARKINSON Norman MM L/Cpl 44352 198 Coy Machine Gun Corps
PARKINSON Richard MM Gnr 715035 D/210 Bde RFA Killed 28.11.18.
PARKINSON Richard MM+Bar Sjt 200218 1/4th North Lancashire Regt KIA 13.10.18.
PARKINSON Robert MM Pte 16692 10th Yorkshire Regt
PARKINSON Robert W. MM Dvr 24951 11 Fd Coy Royal Engineers
PARKINSON Robinson MM Cpl 48111 2nd South Wales Borderers
PARKINSON Roland MM Bdr 20412 D/15 Bde RFA
PARKINSON Samuel T. MM Sjt 7780 7/8th King's Own Scottish Borderers
PARKINSON Thomas MM L/Cpl 15297 8th South Lancashire Regt KIA 18.2.17.
PARKINSON Thomas MM Dvr 786070 RFA
PARKINSON Thomas MM Pte 29679 1/4th North Lancashire Regt
PARKINSON William MM Pte 51570 Liverpool Regt
PARKINSON William MM Pte 18446 9th Scottish Rifles KIA 20.9.17.
PARKINSON William G. MM Cpl 99805 4th Bn Machine Gun Corps
PARKINSON William H. MM Pte M2/180798 Army Service Corps
PARKINSON William H. MM Pte 11360 15th Hampshire Regt
PARKINSON William K. MM L/Cpl 45112 1/1st Surrey Yeomanry
PARKMAN Edward John MM Cpl 14106 56 Siege Bty RGA Died 23.5.18.
PARKMAN Reginald G. MM Pte 15735 7th Royal West Surrey Regt
PARKS Alexander W. "MM+Bar,MID" Cpl 43520 1st Middlesex Regt
PARKS Charlie Raymond MM Pte 493640 2/1(Home Counties)Fd Amb RAMC
PARKS Frederick MM Cpl 10307 North Staffordshire Regt
PARKS Herbert MM Pte 18519 6th Lincolnshire Regt
PARKS Herbert James "MM,MID" CQMS 8624 2nd East Yorkshire Regt
PARKS Joseph A. MM+Bar Pte 55348 2nd Welsh Regt
PARKS Samuel MM Pte 4071 2nd Royal Irish Rifles
PARKYN James Robert Henry MM Sjt 680040 1/22nd London Regt KIA 2.89.18.
PARLE Moses MM L/Cpl 24697 South Wales Borderers
PARLETT Reginald W. "DCM,MM" Sjt 15485 9th Norfolk Regt
PARLOUR Charles MM Sjt 240461 11th East Lancashire Regt
PARMENTER Frederick MM Pte 57721 Middlesex Regt
PARMENTER George Arthur MM Spr 189972 Rly Tpt Div Royal Engineers
PARMENTER John J.E. MM Sjt 50034 123 Bty 28 Bde RFA
PARMENTER William MM Sjt 45890 28 Bde RFA
PARMLEY John MM Sjt 25505 Durham Light Infantry
PARNABY Frederick R. MM Cpl 200146 Yorkshire Regt
PARNABY Henry MM Pte 78417 Durham Light Infantry
PARNABY William MM+2 Bars Sjt 46547 37 Div Sig Coy Royal Engineers
PARNCUTT George L. MM Pte 632980 20th London Regt
PARNELL Claude H. MM L/Cpl 320237 1/6th London Regt
PARNELL Ernest MM Sjt 73388 303 Siege Bty RGA
PARNELL George H. MM Pte 35827 Wiltshire Regt
PARNELL Henry MM Sjt 200481 1/4th Royal Lancaster Regt
PARNELL James A. MM Pte 59503 West Yorkshire Regt
PARNELL John N. MM Gnr 56021 RGA
PARNELL Thomas MM Cpl 28610 1st Border Regt
PARNELL William MM Pte 30766 9th Lancashire Fusiliers KIA 4.10.17.
PARNHAM Samuel MM Sjt 1557 1st Notts & Derby Regt
PARNWELL Frank MM Pte 42952 2nd South Staffordshire Regt
PAROISSIEN Frederick E. MM L/Cpl 1209 1/21st London Regt
PARR Alexander MM Pte 242295 1/5th Seaforth Highlanders
PARR Arthur MM Pte 15325 1st Coldstream Guards DOW 5.11.18.
PARR Arthur MM Pte 24121 Leicestershire Regt
PARR Arthur "DCM,MM,CG(F)" Sjt 265509 1/6th Northumberland Fusiliers
PARR Ben MM Gnr W/2757 B/122 Bde RFA
PARR Charles H. MM Sjt 19748 4(Cavalry)Fd Amb RAMC
PARR Ernest MM Pte 142958 Machine Gun Corps Died 15.10.18.
PARR Frederick MM Pte 13695 9th Suffolk Regt
PARR George MM Sjt 786071 D/312 Bde RFA
PARR George MM Pte 15358 7th Yorkshire Light Infantry
PARR George H. MM+Bar Cpl 15780 4th Yorkshire Light Infantry
PARR Harry MM Sjt 21859 Machine Gun Corps DOW 27.10.18.

PARR John MM Sjt 476 24th Royal Fusiliers KIA 23.8.18.
PARR John MM Gnr 105886 RFA
PARR Robert MM Pte 17444 3rd Royal Fusiliers
PARR Robert E. MM Gnr 69813 RGA
PARR Sam MM CQMS 290416 1/7th Cheshire Regt
PARR Samuel MM L/Cpl 240492 Lincolnshire Regt
PARR Sydney MM Pte 33359 15th Highland Light Infantry
PARR William MM Cpl 426086 Royal Engineers
PARR William H. MM CSM 9453 2nd South Staffordshire Regt
PARR William P. MM Pte 241256 Royal Lancaster Regt
PARREN Cecil G. MM Pte 18487 Royal West Kent Regt
PARRETT William MM Pte 8777 12th Durham Light Infantry
PARRETT William Herbert MM+Bar Cpl 32062 81 Siege Btys RGA KIA 13.7.16.
PARRINGTON Frank MM Pte 36439 99 Coy Machine Gun Corps
PARRINGTON Thomas MM Pte 266451 5th West Riding Regt
PARRIS Archibald MM Pte 15916 1st Northamptonshire Regt
PARRIS Edward MM Pte 21700 2/4th Hampshire Regt KIA 20.7.18
PARRIS H. MM Pte 538267 RAMC
PARRIS Walter MM Pte 10555 1/4th Royal Berkshire Regt
PARRISH Albert F. MM Pte 472286 12th London Regt
PARRISH Alfred Henry MM Pte M2/055214 Army Service Corps att 1(Highland)Fd Amb RAMC.
PARRISH George W. MM Spr 229537 Royal Engineers
PARRISH Henry MM Sjt B/3302 9th Rifle Brigade KIA 15.9.16.
PARRISH Jacques MM S/Sjt 34571 RAMC
PARRISH John MM Pte 241082 Scottish Rifles
PARRISH Percy MM Cpl 24264 RFA
PARRISH Robert MM RQMS 31152 19th Welsh Regt
PARRISH Samuel MM Cpl 16430 15th Royal Warwickshire Regt
PARRISH Thomas W. MM Pte 12967 7th Somerset Light Infantry
PARROT George H. MM Spr 96457 Royal Engineers
PARROTT Albert G. MM Pte 16033 Royal West Kent Regt
PARROTT Albert H. MM Sjt 650373 1/21st London Regt
PARROTT Alfred E. MM Cpl 56026 42 Bde RFA
PARROTT Alva S.H. MM Pte 34303 15th Royal Warwickshire Regt
PARROTT Charles MM Sjt 200455 Tank Corps
PARROTT Charles MM Cpl 15375 8th South Lancashire Regt
PARROTT Frank L. MM Pte 4886 9th Notts & Derby Regt
PARROTT Frederick MM Pte 24136 1st Northamptonshire Regt
PARROTT George MM Sjt 12944 1st Middlesex Regt DOW 12.10.18.
PARROTT George Frederick William MM Pte G/5432 8th D Coy East Kent Regt KIA 15.6.17.
PARROTT Herbert MM Cpl 112277 RGA
PARROTT Peter Edward MM Pte S/10536 3rd Rifle Brigade KIA 11.10.18.
PARROTT Robert MM Pte 200616 1/5th Bedfordshire Regt DOW 13.5.18.
PARROTT Walter MM L/Sjt 251067 1/3rd London Regt
PARROTT William MM Pte 351869 Manchester Regt
PARROTT William MM Sjt 803 1st Lancashire Fusiliers
PARRY A.L. MM Pte 102323 Labour Corps
PARRY Albert Ernest MM Pte M1/09095 Army Service Corps
PARRY Benjamin "MM,MID" Pte 2433 1/17th London Regt
PARRY Bernard MM Pte 10760 2nd Leicestershire Regt
PARRY Daniel MM Pte 14698 1st Dorsetshire Regt DOW 11.4.18.
PARRY David Phillip MM Pte 54961 14th Royal Welsh Fusiliers KIA 24.8.18.
PARRY E.E. MM L/Sjt 350191 RAMC
PARRY Edmund MM Pte 40140 16th Royal Welsh Fusiliers
PARRY Edward MM Pte 18046 5th Shropshire Light Infantry KIA 16.9.16.
PARRY Edward O. MM Pte 331926 Liverpool Regt
PARRY Eric MM Pte 22014 4th Grenadier Guards
PARRY Evan MM Sjt 18481 Welsh Regt
PARRY Francis MM Cpl 83054 RFA
PARRY Frank MM Cpl 59695 14 Div Sig Coy Royal Engineers
PARRY Frederick MM Sjt 345251 24th Royal Welsh Fusiliers
PARRY George MM Pte 307049 Lancashire Fusiliers
PARRY George MM Pte 16753 11th Notts & Derby Regt
PARRY George MM Pte 242134 Worcestershire Regt
PARRY Henry Hugh MM Pte 40807 2nd Suffolk Regt
PARRY Humphrey MM Spr 63687 Royal Engineers
PARRY Isaac MM+Bar Pte 292473 Gordon Highlanders
PARRY James MM Pnr 161694 8 Div Sig Coy Royal Engineers
PARRY James B. MM Pte 2354 1/24th London Regt
PARRY John MM Pte 345591 24th Royal Welsh Fusiliers
PARRY John MM Bdr 74303 C/110 Bde RFA
PARRY John E. MM Pte 23695 1st Royal West Surrey Regt

PARRY John E. "MM,MID" Pte 36978 Royal Welsh Fusiliers
PARRY John H. MM Spr 471695 Royal Engineers
PARRY John O. MM Sjt 355182 25th Royal Welsh Fusiliers
PARRY Lewis MM Cpl 16424 8th North Staffordshire Regt
PARRY Morgan MM Sjt 33079 Welsh Regt
PARRY Percy MM Pte 43466 7th Bedfordshire Regt
PARRY Rex M. MM Cpl 113936 201 Bn Machine Gun Corps
PARRY Richard MM+Bar Sjt 265342 1/6th Royal Welsh Fusiliers DOW 29.12.17.
PARRY Samuel MM Pte 26642 2nd Grenadier Guards
PARRY Thomas MM Pte 240503 Northumberland Fusiliers
PARRY Thomas MM Pte 200790 Manchester Regt
PARRY Thomas J. MM+Bar Pte 28704 2nd Welsh Regt
PARRY Thomas Robert MM Pte 21831 10th Welsh Regt KIA 12.7.16.
PARRY Trevor MM Cpl 40859 16th Royal Welsh Fusiliers
PARRY Walter C. "DCM,MM" L/Sjt 40946 1/4th Suffolk Regt
PARRY Watkin MM Sjt 17109 Royal Welsh Fusiliers
PARRY William MM+Bar Cpl 714 16 Fd Amb. RAMC
PARRY William MM Pte 265549 Royal Welsh Fusiliers
PARRY William "MM,MID" CSM 10543 2nd Grenadier Guards
PARRY Wyndham P. MM Cpl 62890 124 Fd Coy Royal Engineers
PARSEY Harry E. MM L/Cpl 13941 Dorsetshire Regt
PARSLEY Charles MM Cpl 51337 86 Coy Labour Corps
PARSLOW Albert G. MM Pte 41049 7th Royal Warwickshire Regt
PARSLOW Arthur E. MM Sjt 543008 RAMC
PARSLOW Charles MM L/Cpl 266134 1/1st Hertfordshire Regt
PARSLOW Frank Douglas MM Sjt 17817 15 Fd Coy Royal Engineers
PARSLOW Reginald Ernest MM Pte 762 1/5th London Regt
PARSON Cyril MM Pte 68529 17 Fd Amb RAMC
PARSONAGE Joshua "MM,MID" Sjt 254280 Royal Engineers
PARSONS Albert MM Sjt 638 7th Royal Sussex Regt
PARSONS Albert E. MM Pte 8842 1st Royal West Kent Regt
PARSONS Alfred E. MM Sjt 51772 C/84 Bde RFA
PARSONS Alfred S. MM Pte 62715 Royal Fusiliers
PARSONS Arthur MM Pte 32910 16th Royal Warwickshire Regt
PARSONS Arthur R. MM Pte 301687 5th London Regt
PARSONS Bertie Edward MM Pte 41201 1st Worcestershire Regt
PARSONS Charles MM CSM 14910 17th Lancashire Fusiliers
PARSONS Charles C.V. MM+Bar Sjt 20365 41st Bn Machine Gun Corps
PARSONS Charles E. MM Dvr 498214 Royal Engineers
PARSONS Charles W. MM Pte 35942 2nd Wiltshire Regt
PARSONS Colin MM Sjt 795146 49 Div Ammn Col RFA
PARSONS Edward MM Pte 9639 South Staffordshire Regt
PARSONS Edward W. MM L/Sjt 19971 Grenadier Guards
PARSONS Ernest MM Sjt 6004 1st Northamptonshire Regt
PARSONS Ernest Walter MM Pte 330237 1/8th Hampshire Regt
PARSONS F.J. MM Cpl 256 Machine Gun Corps(Motors)
PARSONS Francis George MM L/Cpl 14863 5th Shropshire Light Infantry
PARSONS Frank MM Pte 4049 1/4th Lincolnshire Regt KIA 4.7.16.
PARSONS Frank MM L/Cpl 24406 10th Royal Welsh Fusiliers
PARSONS Frederick C. MM Pte 1840 16th Middlesex Regt
PARSONS G. MM Pte 202235 1/4th Hampshire Regt
PARSONS George MM Gnr 106225 RFA
PARSONS George MM Pte 8717 21 Fd Amb RAMC
PARSONS George MM Pte S/526 Rifle Brigade
PARSONS George MM Pte 8056 10th Royal Dublin Fusiliers Awarded for 'Easter Rising'.
PARSONS George Henry MM Bdr 31869 95 Siege Bty RGA
PARSONS George Robert MM Pte 26438 16th Notts & Derby Regt
PARSONS H. MM Pte 20345 23rd Middlesex Regt
PARSONS Harry MM Cpl 548152 510 Fd Coy Royal Engineers
PARSONS Harry MM Cpl 169415 Royal Engineers
PARSONS Henry MM Pte 242062 Royal West Kent Regt
PARSONS Howard MM Pte 37172 RAMC
PARSONS Isaac MM Gnr 148109 12 Mountain Bty RGA
PARSONS James MM Pte 3607 1/2nd London Regt
PARSONS James T. MM Cpl M2/151782 Army Service Corps
PARSONS John H. MM Bdr 334398 RGA
PARSONS John W. MM Cpl 102236 179 Tunnelling Coy Royal Engineers
PARSONS Joseph E. MM S/Sjt Fitter 165978 RGA
PARSONS Leonard MM L/Sjt 16530 1st Coldstream Guards
PARSONS Martin MM Pte SE/8953 Army Veterinary Corps
PARSONS Marwood MM QMS Saddler 7892 12 Bde RFA
PARSONS Nolan MM+2 Bars Pte 9738 King's Royal Rifle Corps
PARSONS Percy S. MM Pte M2/080743 Army Service Corps

PARSONS Reginald T.G. MM Pte 241889 Worcestershire Regt
PARSONS Robert MM Pte 8040 2nd Border Regt
PARSONS Robert G. MM Bdr 17306 B/99 Bde RFA
PARSONS Robert H. MM Pte 19256 Hampshire Regt
PARSONS Samuel G. "MM+Bar,MID" L/Cpl 498283 476 Fd Coy Royal Engineers
PARSONS Sidney John MM L/Cpl G/4381 1st Royal West Surrey Regt KIA 3.11.16.
PARSONS Stenson MM Sjt 20331 8th Leicestershire Regt
PARSONS Thom MM Bdr 119475 RGA
PARSONS Thomas MM Sjt 8832 Yorkshire Regt
PARSONS V.M. MM Pte 10778 1st Essex Regt
PARSONS Walter C. MM 2nd Cpl 17705 9 Fd Coy Royal Engineers
PARSONS Wilfred G. MM Pte 37120 Somerset Light Infantry
PARSONS William MM Sjt 13471 D/77 Bde RFA KIA 23.3.18.
PARSONS William H. MM Pte 14472 17th Lancashire Fusiliers
PARSONS William Henry MM Pte 23937 12th Gloucestershire Regt KIA 4.10.17.
PARSONS William Ivor MM Dvr 112403 5 Bde Ammn Col RFA
PARSONS William J. MM Pte R/22528 King's Royal Rifle Corps
PARTING Bertram MM Pte 37328 11th Lancashire Fusiliers KIA 20.4.18.
PARTINGTON Frank MM Sjt 18939 8th Scottish Rifles
PARTINGTON George MM Sjt 60455 12th Manchester Regt
PARTINGTON James MM L/Cpl 202428 5th East Lancashire Regt
PARTINGTON James MM Cpl 3336 Machine Gun Corps
PARTINGTON John MM Pte 87977 Liverpool Regt att MGC.
PARTINGTON John MM L/Sjt 23198 3rd Grenadier Guards
PARTINGTON Joseph MM Pte 202483 Lancashire Fusiliers
PARTINGTON Percy Elvin Octavius MM Spr 218722 2 Lt Rly Op Coy Royal Engineers
PARTINGTON William MM L/Cpl 22419 Grenadier Guards
PARTIS James W. MM Pte 53486 RAMC
PARTNER Walter MM Pte 24794 5th Northamptonshire Regt
PARTON Albert MM Pte 194 1st Royal West Surrey Regt KIA 1.7.16.
PARTON Gordon MM Pte 16211 9th North Staffordshire Regt DOW 15.9.18.
PARTON Harry MM+Bar L/Cpl 4/8995 1st South Staffordshire Regt
PARTON Reginald MM Gnr 70833 11 Bde RFA
PARTRIDGE Arthur MM Sjt 868 2nd Royal Warwickshire Regt
PARTRIDGE Carles H. MM L/Cpl 881505 34th London Regt
PARTRIDGE Edward MM Pte 2434 24th Royal Fusiliers
PARTRIDGE Ernest MM Sjt 5033 5th Dragoon Guards
PARTRIDGE Ernest MM+Bar Sjt 11417 South Staffordshire Regt
PARTRIDGE Ernest G. MM Spr 49300 Royal Engineers
PARTRIDGE F. MM L/Cpl 3/1496 9th Essex Regt
PARTRIDGE Frederick MM Pte 201839 Middlesex Regt
PARTRIDGE George H.A. MM Pte 45649 RAMC
PARTRIDGE George Henry MM Pte 70506 9th Notts & Derby Regt
PARTRIDGE Harry MM Pte 23847 Royal Irish Fusiliers
PARTRIDGE Heber MM Sjt 266611 West Riding Regt
PARTRIDGE Herbert MM Cpl 200708 1/5th West Yorkshire Regt
PARTRIDGE Herbert H.C. MM Bdr 38742 RFA
PARTRIDGE John MM Spr 59387 Royal Engineers
PARTRIDGE Joseph N. MM Pte 198 RAMC
PARTRIDGE Nathaniel J.C. MM CSM 37649 1st Royal Berkshire Regt
PARTRIDGE Percy MM Pte 31999 12th Suffolk Regt KIA 12.4.18.
PARTRIDGE W.C. "DCM,MM" Sjt S/26847 Rifle Brigade
PARVIN Frederick H. MM Pte 3663 Royal Sussex Regt
PARVIN Richard MM Pte 7137 8/10th Gordon Highlanders
PASCALL H.A. MM Sjt 8618 RFA
PASCOE Alfred MM Gnr 69432 Tank Corps
PASCOE Alfred J. MM Pte 4424 Royal Sussex Regt
PASCOE Alfred W. MM Pte 53091 Manchester Regt
PASCOE Arthur W. MM Pte 16245 Royal Sussex Regt
PASCOE Edward Cyril MM Pte 203688 7th North Staffordshire Regt KIA 26.8.18.
PASCOE Edward John MM Sjt 200399 1/4th Northamptonshire Regt
PASCOE Percival MM Pte R/22034 King's Royal Rifle Corps
PASCOE Robert MM Pte 27511 Somerset Light Infantry
PASCOE William George MM Sjt 8733 5th Devonshire Regt
PASCOE William H. MM Pte 51175 1/6th Cheshire Regt
PASH William J. MM Gnr 49051 RFA
PASHBY Thomas MM Sjt 201042 4th York & Lancaster Regt
PASHEN Gerald B. MM Cpl 128524 RFA
PASHLER Sydney T.W. MM Cpl 59704 Royal Engineers
PASHLEY George A. MM Pte 405434 7 Fd Amb RAMC
PASHLEY Thomas MM Spr 188032 Rly Op Div Royal Engineers
PASHLEY Walter MM Pte 294017 6th Durham Light Infantry

PASK Alexander Frederick MM Bdr 23595 B/95 Bde RFA
PASK Edwin George MM Sjt 241490 Welsh Regt
PASK John William MM Pte 51956 1st Notts & Derby Regt
PASK Thomas MM Pte 20138 South Wales Borderers
PASKELL William Frederick MM L/Cpl 9458 1st Middlesex Regt KIA 23.4.17.
PASQUILL James MM Sjt 25171 South Wales Borderers
PASS Harry MM Sjt S/782 Rifle Brigade
PASS John MM Cpl 23741 Machine Gun Corps
PASS Thomas MM Pte 54292 Labour Corps
PASS W. MM Sjt 268394 West Riding Regt
PASS William MM Pte 270586 2nd Royal Scots KIA 23.10.18.
PASSANT Llewellyn MM Cpl 226027 Monmouthshire Regt
PASSELOW George "MM,MID" Sjt 6353 Royal Scots
PASSELOW James MM L/Cpl 6236 2nd Royal Scots
PASSEY Frank L. MM Pte 10199 7th Royal West Kent Regt
PASSEY George MM Pte 27506 1st Shropshire Light Infantry
PASSEY George A. MM Cpl 240211 1/5th Cheshire Regt
PASSEY Harold MM Dvr 69549 B/123 Bde RFA
PASSMAN Joseph W. MM Dmr 11999 West Yorkshire Regt
PASSMORE Albert William MM+Bar Cpl 201973 2/7th Worcestershire Regt
PASSMORE Arthur "DCM,MM" CSM 242563 1/5th Leicestershire Regt KIA 5.9.18.
PASSMORE Edward Victor MM Sjt 9529 1st Worcestershire Regt
PASSMORE G. MM Pte 24469 12th Durham Light Infantry
PASSMORE Joseph T. MM Cpl 147684 176 Tunnelling Coy Royal Engineers
PASSMORE Richard MM 2nd Cpl 397211 Royal Engineers
PASSMORE Sidney Herbert MM Pte 200455 1st London Regt KIA 26.10.17.
PASSMORE W. MM L/Cpl 612578 London Regt
PASTERFUL William Albert MM Pte 251439 3rd London Regt KIA 8.8.18.
PATCHETT Albert MM Pte 11343 6th Yorkshire Regt
PATCHETT Edward MM Bdr 771221 Y/63 Med TM Bty RFA
PATCHETT George MM Pte 12385 7th Yorkshire Regt
PATCHETT Harry "MM308320 R Warw)+Bar,MID" Pte 52414 15th Royal Irish Rifles
PATCHETT Joseph MM Pte 201536 2/4th West Riding Regt
PATCHETT Joshua MM L/Cpl 16/1501 1st West Yorkshire Regt
PATCHETT Tom MM L/Cpl 16309 9th Northumberland Fusiliers
PATCHING Benjamin MM L/Cpl 65510 245 Coy Machine Gun Corps
PATE David J. MM L/Cpl 51080 2nd Royal Scots
PATE Robert Hall MM L/Cpl 43728 6th Lincolnshire Regt
PATE W. MM Bdr 700371 RFA
PATEFIELD Ernest MM L/Cpl 19523 Grenadier Guards
PATEFIELD William MM Pte 200507 East Lancashire Regt
PATEMAN Charles R. MM L/Cpl 76444 Tank Corps
PATEMAN Edward William MM Pte 17508 Coldstream Guards
PATEMAN George M. MM Pte 240214 1/4th Yorkshire Regt
PATEMAN Thomas "MM,MIDx2" RSM 4582 4th Hussars
PATEMAN Thomas W. MM Pte 510469 RAMC
PATERSON Adam MM Pte 275515 1/7th Arg & Suth Highlanders
PATERSON Alexander MM Pte 331943 1/9th Highland Light Infantry
PATERSON Alexander MM L/Cpl 11619 1st Scots Guards
PATERSON Alexander MM L/Cpl 5898 1st Cameron Highlanders
PATERSON Alexander MM Cpl 40501 1/5th Gordon Highlanders KIA 26.7.18.
PATERSON Alexander K. "DCM,MM" Sjt S/2574 11th Rifle Brigade
PATERSON Alister MM Cpl 200575 5/6th Scottish Rifles KIA 26.9.17.
PATERSON Andrew "MM,MSM" Pte 335733 1/8th Royal Scots
PATERSON Andrew MM Gnr 69524 RGA
PATERSON Angus MM Pte 40620 Arg & Suth Highlanders
PATERSON Charles MM Pte 201759 1/4th Gordon Highlanders KIA 25.7.18.
PATERSON David Moffat MM Pte 26699 1st Scottish Rifles
PATERSON Donald MM Spr 312908 Royal Engineers
PATERSON Duncan MM Pte 8898 RAMC
PATERSON Gavin "MM,MID" Sjt 11828 5th Cameron Highlanders
PATERSON George MM Piper 200347 1/4th Gordon Highlanders
PATERSON George "DCM,MM" Sjt 20213 61st Bn Machine Gun Corps
PATERSON George MM L/Cpl 11254 2nd King's Own Scottish Borderers
PATERSON George MM Cpl 22093 Highland Light Infantry
PATERSON Henry MM Sjt 15640 Liverpool Regt
PATERSON J. MM Pte 303176 Arg & Suth Highlanders
PATERSON J. MM Pte 265165 Liverpool Regt

PATERSON Jack MM Pte 12963 8th North Staffordshire Regt
PATERSON James MM L/Sjt 292870 1/7th Royal Highlanders
PATERSON James MM L/Bdr 171003 121 Bty 27 Bde RFA
PATERSON James MM+Bar Sjt M2/104762 Army Service Corps
PATERSON James F. MM Pte 4199 1/9th Highland Light Infantry
PATERSON James G. MM Pte 1623 1/7th Arg & Suth Highlanders
PATERSON James S. MM Sjt 35369 55 Fd Amb RAMC
PATERSON John MM Pte 89108 25th Bn Machine Gun Corps
PATERSON John MM+Bar Pte 45476 16 Fd Amb RAMC
PATERSON John MM Sjt 277698 Royal Engineers
PATERSON John MM Sjt 200018 1/4th Royal Scots
PATERSON John C. MM Sjt 51817 11th Royal Scots
PATERSON Joseph J. MM Pte 200645 2/7th Middlesex Regt
PATERSON K.M. MM Pte(1st) 19740 Royal Air Force
PATERSON M.L. MM Sjt 788 RFA
PATERSON Philip MM Spr 402976 35 Div Sig Coy Royal Engineers
PATERSON Richard W. MM Sjt 2486 Yorkshire Light Infantry
PATERSON Robert MM Sjt 7680 1st Royal Scots Fusiliers
PATERSON Robert B. MM Pte 26994 King's Own Scottish Borderers
PATERSON Thomas MM Pte 29295 1st Highland Light Infantry
PATERSON Thomas MM Sjt 2126 10th Arg & Suth Highlanders
PATERSON Thomas MM Sjt 43795 Royal Scots
PATERSON Thomas L. MM Sjt 3/7294 1st Gordon Highlanders
PATERSON W. MM Pte 23858 1/4th Seaforth Highlanders
PATERSON Walter MM Pnr 247370 Royal Engineers
PATERSON William MM Pte 281527 1/7th Highland Light Infantry
PATERSON William "MM+Bar,MID" Cpl 12297 12th Royal Scots
PATERSON William MM Sjt 16781 6th Cameron Highlanders
PATERSON William MM Pte 49496 54 Fd Amb RAMC
PATERSON William MM L/Cpl 351728 1/9th Royal Scots
PATES William MM Sjt 11008 11th Royal West Surrey Regt
PATIENCE Alexander MM L/Cpl 204453 1/5th Seaforth Highlanders
PATIENCE George "DCM,MM" Sjt 7312 6th Lincolnshire Regt
PATIENT Sidney H. MM Cpl 15907 6th Oxf & Bucks Light Infantry
PATMAN Leonard MM Pte 8492 2nd Lincolnshire Regt
PATMORE Charles J. MM Spr 24623 5 Div Sig Coy Royal Engineers
PATMORE Joseph MM Bdr 40238 RFA
PATMORE P(or R.)H. MM Pte 8446 8 Fd Amb RAMC
PATON Alexander W. MM Cpl 345440 RGA
PATON Arthur James MM L/Sjt 928 Seaforth Highlanders
PATON Herbert MM L/Cpl 13883 Royal West Surrey Regt
PATON J. MM Pte 202821 Seaforth Highlanders
PATON James W. MM Cpl 350055 1/9th Royal Scots
PATON John MM+Bar L/Cpl 325235 1/7th Arg & Suth Highlanders
PATON John MM Cpl 10832 Northumberland Fusiliers
PATON Peter F. MM Gnr 365973 RGA
PATON Robert MM Pte 40969 1/7th Royal Highlanders
PATON Robert MM L/Cpl 414103 Royal Engineers
PATON Robert MM Pte 20326 2nd Royal Scots Fusiliers DOW 6.2.18.
PATON Thomas MM Pte 14345 6th Cameron Highlanders
PATON William MM L/Cpl 251110 1/6th Arg & Suth Highlanders
PATON William MM Cpl 200950 North Staffordshire Regt
PATON William MM Pte 14271 7/8th King's Own Scottish Borderers
PATON or PATTON Gavin MM Sjt 3/4315 5th Royal Highlanders
PATRICK A. MM Cpl 6519 RGA
PATRICK Alexander MM L/Cpl 358086 32 Div SigCoy Royal Engineers
PATRICK Alfred MM L/Cpl 201239 2/4th West Riding Regt
PATRICK Arthur MM Cpl 13536 2nd Lincolnshire Regt
PATRICK Arthur James MM L/Sjt 9519 2nd Suffolk Regt KIA 1.10.18.
PATRICK Bertie MM Dvr 75901 A/83 Bde RFA
PATRICK Ernest "DCM,MM+Bar,CG(It)" Sjt 1998 22 Fd Amb RAMC
PATRICK Ernest James MM Sjt 3/10818 5th Northamptonshire Regt
PATRICK F. MM Dvr 1869 RFA
PATRICK Frank W. MM Sjt 591538 1/18th London Regt
PATRICK Frederick John MM Sjt 879 Royal Sussex Regt
PATRICK Henry Alfred MM Sjt 8749 7th Shropshire Light Infantry
PATRICK J.T. MM Pte 22/867 1st Northumberland Fusiliers
PATRICK James MM Sjt 20 1st Arg & Suth Highlanders
PATRICK James Owen MM Pte 17398 1st Northamptonshire Regt KIA 9.9.16.
PATRICK Joseph MM Pte 39312 10th Royal Warwickshire Regt
PATRICK Ralph "DCM,MM,MID" Sjt 15095 11th West Yorkshire Regt
PATRICK Stephen MM L/Cpl 7771 3rd Coldstream Guards
PATRICK Sydney Watt MM L/Sjt 20926 10th South Wales Borderers
PATRICK William MM Pte 21365 Seaforth Highlanders

PATRICK William F. MM Gnr Sig 176404 217 Siege Bty RGA
PATRICK William J. MM Pte 11995 Royal Berkshire Regt
PATRICKSON John MM Sjt 23934 6th Royal Inniskilling Fusiliers
PATRICKSON Joseph MM Pte 16/1783 11th Northumberland Fusiliers KIA 14.10.17.
PATSTON Henry Richard MM Pte 1907 1/8th London Regt
PATTEN Albert W. MM L/Cpl 20723 1st Bn Machine Gun Corps Died 8.2.19.
PATTEN Simeon MM Cpl 27123 Hampshire Regt
PATTEN William MM L/Cpl 61176 24th Royal Fusiliers Died 11.5.18.
PATTEN William T. MM Pte 27842 Suffolk Regt
PATTENDEN Edwin MM Pte 242025 2/6th Royal Warwickshire Regt KIA 21.3.18.
PATTENDEN F.A.B. MM AM2 8483 Royal Flying Corps
PATTENDEN Frank Herbert MM Cpl T3/028772 36 Div Train Army Service Corps
PATTENDEN John MM Pte 17972 12th Royal Fusiliers
PATTENDEN Kenneth MM L/Cpl 1046 1/5th Royal Sussex Regt
PATTENDEN Thomas MM Sjt 204447 5th Liverpool Regt
PATTENDEN W.T. MM Pte 1625 Royal Sussex Regt
PATTERSON A. MM Pte 20846 RAMC
PATTERSON Adam MM L/Cpl 21192 Royal Scots
PATTERSON Albert H. MM+Bar Pte 3804 1st Hampshire Regt
PATTERSON Alexander MM Bdr 38083 RFA
PATTERSON Archibald Richard Leslie MM 2nd Cpl 51517 Royal Engineers att HQ 22 Div.
PATTERSON Arthur T. MM Pte 76677 26th Royal Fusiliers
PATTERSON Duncan MM Pte 16747 Durham Light Infantry
PATTERSON Edward MM Pte 22/1381 22nd Northumberland Fusiliers KIA 14.4.18.
PATTERSON Frederick Hewitt MM Sjt Farrier 463093 50 Div Sig Coy Royal Engineers
PATTERSON Frederick J. MM Pte 423330 10th London Regt
PATTERSON George MM Pte 4395 184 Coy Labour Corps
PATTERSON Harold P. MM 2nd Cpl 95458 Royal Engineers
PATTERSON Harry Edward MM CSM S/4086 13th Rifle Brigade KIA 24.8.18.
PATTERSON Henry MM Pte 4/8571 1st West Yorkshire Regt DOW 17.9.18.
PATTERSON Henry John "MM,CG(F)" Cpl 1197 46 Div Ammn Col RFA
PATTERSON Isaac MM L/Cpl 7385 Northumberland Fusiliers
PATTERSON James MM Sjt 3688 9th Lancashire Fusiliers
PATTERSON James "DCM,MM" Sjt 15726 10th Royal Irish Rifles
PATTERSON James MM Pte 28/327 1st Northumberland Fusiliers
PATTERSON James A. MM Pte 124334 RAMC
PATTERSON James W. MM Dvr 53835 Royal Engineers
PATTERSON John B. MM Cpl 42153 Royal Engineers
PATTERSON John J.R. MM Cpl 478069 Royal Engineers
PATTERSON John W. "MM,MID" Sjt 93061 Royal Engineers
PATTERSON John W. MM Pte 8477 Coldstream Guards
PATTERSON Joseph MM Pte 18484 9th Scottish Rifles DOW 15.4.17.
PATTERSON Louis MM Pte 7000 RAMC
PATTERSON Martin MM Pte 43796 Royal Scots
PATTERSON Nathaniel MM Bdr 675466 275 Bde RFA
PATTERSON R. MM Pte 205666 Northumberland Fusiliers
PATTERSON Richard James MM Gnr 955409 A/236 Bde RFA
PATTERSON Robert MM+Bar Pte 17/1860 15th Royal Irish Rifles
PATTERSON Robert MM Pte 41191 RAMC
PATTERSON Robert B. MM Cpl 2351 Northumberland Fusiliers
PATTERSON Robert Hastie MM Pte 33111 1st Royal Warwickshire Regt
PATTERSON Samuel B. MM Sjt 305513 Royal Warwickshire Regt
PATTERSON Thomas MM CQMS 355566 10th Liverpool Regt
PATTERSON Thomas MM Pte 7048 2nd Royal Irish Rifles
PATTERSON Thomas Norman MM Cpl 22/1556 22nd Northumberland Fusiliers
PATTERSON W.J. MM L/Cpl 3799 Royal Highlanders
PATTERSON William MM Pte 270870 1/1st Northumberland Yeo
PATTERSON William MM Sjt 4068 2nd Dragoons
PATTERSON William E. MM Sjt 42569 C/147 Bde RFA
PATTERSON William Flynn MM Sjt 161472 Imperial Sig Coy East Africa Royal Engineers
PATTERSON William J. MM Cpl 6543 1st Royal Irish Rifles
PATTERSON William P. MM Pte 30501 1st Royal Dublin Fusiliers
PATTERSON William Robert MM Gnr 41754 'U' Bty RHA
PATTIE George MM Cpl 12040 35th Bn Machine Gun Corps
PATTIMORE William James "DCM,MM,MLaS(Pan)" Sjt R/45078 1st King's Royal Rifle Corps

PATTINSON Alfred H. MM+Bar L/Sjt B/2399 13th Rifle Brigade
PATTINSON Arthur MM Pte 56551 RAMC
PATTINSON George MM Spr 776 254 Tunnelling Coy Royal Engineers
PATTINSON Herbert MM Gnr 33380 RFA
PATTINSON Richard B. MM Cpl 16447 1/5th Border Regt
PATTINSON William MM Pte 35151 2nd Highland Light Infantry
PATTINSON William H. MM L/Cpl 19459 11th Border Regt
PATTISON Alfred "MM,MSM" Sjt 405051 2/3(West Riding)Fd Amb RAMC
PATTISON Charles MM Pte 201735 Manchester Regt
PATTISON Donald M.W. MM Cpl 44370 Royal Engineers
PATTISON Frederick MM Pte 12817 7th Royal Lancaster Regt
PATTISON Frederick D. MM Pte 57535 4th York & Lancaster Regt
PATTISON George MM Sjt 650394 C/86 Bde RFA
PATTISON Joseph MM L/Cpl 266022 West Riding Regt
PATTISON Samuel MM Cpl 530163 1/15th London Regt
PATTISON Thomas H. MM Cpl 15524 Durham Light Infantry
PATTISON Walter MM Pte 26599 1st North Lancashire Regt DOW 20.10.18.
PATTISON William MM Pte 2367 1/4th Yorkshire Regt
PATTISON William "MM,MSM" Cpl 19313 12th Durham Light Infantry
PATTISON William MM Gnr 6463 D/156 Bde RFA
PATTISON William Dobson MM Pte 2283 1/5th Northumberland Fusiliers KIA 11.4.18
PATTON A. MM Pte 46648 Lancashire Fusiliers
PATTON Charles E. MM Spr 95150 Royal Engineers
PATTON Edward MM L/Cpl 25547 1st Suffolk Regt
PATTON Thomas MM Pte 9565 1st Irish Guards
PATTON William MM Pte 2490 12th Royal Irish Rifles
PATTON or PATON Gavin MM Sjt 3/4315 1/5th Royal Highlanders
PATTULLO John MM Pte 24517 2nd King's Own Scottish Borderers
PATTULLO Robert MM Spr 410255 Royal Engineers
PAUER William Lambert "DCM,MM" Sjt 3/7033 2nd Royal Munster Fusiliers
PAUL Alexander MM Pte 240413 1/5th King's Own Scottish Borderers
PAUL Alexander C. MM Pte 54905 18th Scottish Rifles
PAUL Benjamin MM Pte 9002 2nd Essex Regt
PAUL Bernard Douglas MM Bdr 94188 B/64 Bde RFA KIA 18.10.17.
PAUL Charles E. MM Sjt 202715 RHA
PAUL Frederick MM Pte 32185 8th East Lancashire Regt
PAUL Frederick Charles MM Pnr 280072 332 RDCC Royal Engineers
PAUL Frederick G. MM Pte 90698 RAMC
PAUL Harry MM Cpl Sig 630621 C/255 Bde RFA
PAUL Harry MM+Bar Sjt 15038 1st Coldstream Guards
PAUL Harry "MM,MID" Sjt 496384 478 Fd Coy Royal Engineers
PAUL Hosea MM Cpl 10480 5th Oxf & Bucks Light Infantry
PAUL James MM+Bar Sjt 81136 Royal Engineers
PAUL James N. MM+Bar Pte 15867 1st Scots Guards
PAUL John MM Pte 240297 5th East Lancashire Regt
PAUL John McBain MM Bdr 45394 413 Siege Bty RGA
PAUL Joshua MM Pte 41355 9th Royal Irish Fusiliers
PAUL Percy Roy MM L/Cpl R/10181 King's Royal Rifle Corps
PAUL Reuben Stanley "DCM,MM" L/Cpl C/7740 13th King's Royal Rifle Corps DOW 26.8.16.
PAUL Silas A. MM Sjt 3145 6th Royal Irish Regt
PAUL T.G. MM Spr 602473 Royal Engineers
PAUL Thomas MM Bdr 80885 RFA
PAUL William MM Pte 41457 1st Scottish Rifles
PAUL William MM Pte 6921 1/7th Royal Highlanders
PAUL William Ernest MM L/Cpl 19543 Dorsetshire Regt
PAUL William J. MM Pte 40060 RAMC
PAULDING John MM Dvr 931574 C/291 Bde RFA
PAULEY Robert MM Cpl 8706 Machine Gun Corps
PAULIN Thomas George MM Cpl 3/4668 6th Connaught Rangers
PAULING Frederick MM Sjt 7503 1st Royal Berkshire Regt
PAULL Samuel James MM Pte R/34516 King's Royal Rifle Corps
PAULLEY Alex MM Spr 193172 Royal Engineers
PAULSON Harry K. MM Cpl 312313 1/1(Highland)Hy Bty RGA
PAVELY Alfred P. MM Sjt 46366 B/103 Bde RFA
PAVELY William C. MM L/Cpl 91736 Tank Corps
PAVEY James H. MM Pte 295336 12th Somerset Light Infantry
PAVEY William Thomas "MM,MID" Sjt 9873 2nd Middlesex Regt
PAWASS George MM Pte S/1760 12th Rifle Brigade
PAWLEY Horace J. MM Cpl 39066 7th Royal West Surrey Regt
PAWSEY Osborne MM L/Bdr 775526 B/310 Bde RFA
PAWSON John MM L/Cpl 75435 Royal Engineers

PAWSON Reginald MM Pte 15/1622 1/6th West Yorkshire Regt
PAWSON Willie MM+Bar Pte 17379 1st Royal Scots Fusiliers
PAXFORD Albert Edward MM Sjt 305887 1/8th Royal Warwickshire Regt
PAXTON Edward MM Sjt 7521 12th Middlesex Regt KIA 9.4.18.
PAXTON George James MM Sjt G/3304 12th Middlesex Regt KIA 3.5.17.
PAXTON J.N. MM Sjt 41645 12 Div Sig Coy Royal Engineers
PAXTON John S. "MM,MID" Sjt 2385 Royal Engineers
PAXTON Peter C. MM Gnr Sig 837176 307 Bde RFA
PAXTON Robert MM Sjt 1673 8th Gordon Highlanders
PAXTON Robert MM Pte 41981 Northumberland Fusiliers
PAXTON Thomas E. MM Bdr 57706 RFA
PAXTON Thomas Henry MM Pte 3095 Northumberland Fusiliers
PAXTON Walter MM Pte 631704 2/20th London Regt KIA 20.2.18.
PAXTON William C. "DCM,MM" L/Cpl 20727 1st King's Own Scottish Borderers
PAY Charles H. MM CoH 2592 2nd Life Guards
PAY Frederick G. MM Pte 23442 3rd Grenadier Guards
PAYLIS Frank William MM Pte 1962 7th Royal West Kent Regt Died 15.7.18.
PAYLOR George Henry MM Pte 38876 25th Northumberland Fusiliers KIA 23.3.18.
PAYNE Abner MM Pte 27123 10th Worcestershire Regt
PAYNE Albert MM L/Cpl 8444 11th Royal Fusiliers
PAYNE Albert E. MM Pte 65765 RAMC
PAYNE Alfred MM L/Cpl 53840 Welsh Regt
PAYNE Alfred MM Pnr 32767 18 Div Sig Coy Royal Engineers KIA 1.12.17.
PAYNE Alfred Charles MM Sjt 20545 East Yorkshire Regt
PAYNE Alfred Charles Joseph MM Sjt 8159 Royal West Kent Regt
PAYNE Alfred H. MM L/Cpl 54171 5th West Yorkshire Regt
PAYNE Arthur MM Pte 27680 2nd Royal Fusiliers
PAYNE Arthur Arnold MM L/Cpl 30864 12 Div Sig Coy Royal Engineers
PAYNE Bertie William "DCM,MM,DM(B)" Pte 6211 1st Dragoon Guards
PAYNE Bertram J. MM L/Cpl 17493 1st Grenadier Guards
PAYNE Cecil M. MM Pte 9651 Suffolk Regt
PAYNE Charles MM Bdr 30307 RFA
PAYNE Charles Frederick MM Cpl C/375 16th King's Royal Rifle Corps att RE.
PAYNE Charles H. MM Bdr 38895 35 Heavy Bty RGA
PAYNE Charles Percival MM L/Sjt 11324 10th Royal West Kent Regt
PAYNE Christopher MM Pte 13772 1st Royal Inniskilling Fusiliers
PAYNE Cyril MM L/Cpl 38823 1/5th Gloucestershire Regt
PAYNE Cyril J. MM Cpl A/200013 King's Royal Rifle Corps
PAYNE Douglas R. MM Cpl 18126 11th Worcestershire Regt
PAYNE Edward MM+Bar Cpl 38579 8th East Surrey Regt
PAYNE Edward MM Sjt 29342 4th North Lancashire Regt
PAYNE Edward "MM,MID" S/Sjt Farrier 12471 1 Fd Sqn Royal Engineers
PAYNE Edward MM Pte 372631 8th London Regt KIA 25.7.18.
PAYNE Edward James MM Pte 3461 7th East Kent Regt KIA 20.7.17.
PAYNE Edward W. MM Pte 34922 1st Duke of Cornwall's LI
PAYNE Edwin G. "MM,MSM" Cpl 93700 261 Siege Bty RGA
PAYNE Ernest MM+Bar L/Cpl 8661 1st Norfolk Regt DOW 29.9.18.
PAYNE Ernest MM Dvr 42772 RFA
PAYNE Ernest J.G. MM Sjt 242559 6th Royal Warwickshire Regt
PAYNE Ernest V. "DCM+Bar,MM+Bar" Cpl 44751 19 Div Sig Coy Royal Engineers
PAYNE Ernest W. MM Sjt 46285 A/88 Bde RFA
PAYNE Eustace MM Sjt M2/151777 Army Service Corps
PAYNE Francis C. MM Pte 95366 2nd London Regt
PAYNE Frank E. MM Cpl 4592 D/75 Bde RFA
PAYNE Frederick MM Cpl 305531 6th Bn Tank Corps
PAYNE Frederick MM S/Sjt Farrier 14645 127 Hy Bty RGA
PAYNE Frederick MM L/Cpl 3/7184 1st Bedfordshire Regt
PAYNE Frederick MM Pte 15831 7/8th King's Own Scottish Borderers KIA 18.8.16.
PAYNE Frederick Charles MM L/Cpl 538506 2 Tank Bde Sig Coy Royal Engineers
PAYNE Frederick E. MM L/Bdr 154187 RGA
PAYNE Frederick J. MM Pte 30828 Lancashire Fusiliers
PAYNE Frederick W. MM Pte M2/153804 Army Service Corps
PAYNE G. MM Pte 65762 RAMC
PAYNE George MM Pte 66400 RAMC
PAYNE George Henry MM Pte B/200465 10th Rifle Brigade KIA 30.11.17.

PAYNE George W.R. MM Pte 7222 1st East Surrey Regt
PAYNE George William Golby "MM+Bar,CG(F)" Sjt 18524 Scottish Rifles
PAYNE Gilbert F. "MM,MID" Pte 8337 2nd Oxf & Bucks Light Infantry
PAYNE Harold MM Bdr 29317 RGA
PAYNE Harold MM Sjt 41324 5 Bde RFA
PAYNE Harold C. MM Cpl 67948 Royal Engineers
PAYNE Harry MM Dvr 121416 RFA
PAYNE Harry MM Gnr 150041 RGA
PAYNE Harry MM Pte 302994 5th London Regt
PAYNE Harry MM Pte 13173 6th Shropshire Light Infantry
PAYNE Henry MM Sjt 14227 RGA
PAYNE Herbert "DCM,MM" Sjt 371575 1/8th London Regt
PAYNE Herbert MM Pte 3826 1/8th London Regt
PAYNE Herbert MM Bdr 48264 RFA
PAYNE Herbert H. MM Bdr 67084 RFA
PAYNE Jack MM(7708 Suffolk Regt)+Bar Sjt 52370 2nd Northamptonshire Regt
PAYNE James MM Spr 193363 257 Tunnelling Coy Royal Engineers
PAYNE John MM L/Bdr 10654 165 Bde RFA
PAYNE John J. MM Spr 397633 Royal Engineers
PAYNE John J. MM Sjt 29673 116 Heavy Bty RGA
PAYNE John William MM Pte 308355 1/5th Liverpool Regt KIA 17.8.18.
PAYNE Joseph MM Pnr 354225 74 Div Sig Coy Royal Engineers
PAYNE Joseph MM Pte 4261 2nd Leinster Regt
PAYNE Michael MM Pte 203469 Manchester Regt
PAYNE Mortimer James MM CSM 3427 1st Rifle Brigade KIA 11.10.17.
PAYNE Owen H. MM L/Cpl 312902 Royal Engineers
PAYNE Percy R. MM L/Sjt 17079 Coldstream Guards
PAYNE Reginald J. MM Cpl 8445 10th Hussars
PAYNE Richard Victor MM L/Bdr Sig 29114 C/92 Bde RFA
PAYNE Robert MM Sjt 28570 RGA
PAYNE Robert E. MM Dvr 80984 106 Fd Coy Royal Engineers
PAYNE Robert William MM Pte 43200 6th Northamptonshire Regt
PAYNE Samuel MM Cpl 49461 43 Bde RFA
PAYNE Stanley J. MM L/Cpl 1555 King Edward's Horse
PAYNE Sydney MM Pte R/4749 13th King's Royal Rifle Corps KIA 28.7.17.
PAYNE Thomas MM Pte 21109 4th Grenadier Guards
PAYNE Thomas F. MM Sjt 23417 6 Div Sig Coy Royal Engineers
PAYNE Tom MM Pte 265410 West Yorkshire Regt
PAYNE Walter MM Pte 26459 1st Grenadier Guards
PAYNE Walter MM Pte 59927 10th Royal West Surrey Regt
PAYNE Walter MM CQMS 267123 7th Royal Warwickshire Regt
PAYNE Walter J. MM CSM 12040 6th Royal Berkshire Regt
PAYNE William MM Pte 11049 5th Royal Berkshire Regt
PAYNE William MM+Bar L/Sjt 6238 5th Notts & Derby Regt
PAYNE William MM Pte 12229 5th Royal Irish Fusiliers
PAYNE William MM Sjt 7788 11th Lancashire Fusiliers
PAYNE William MM L/Sjt 1374 1/3rd London Regt
PAYNE William MM L/Cpl S/21286 Rifle Brigade
PAYNE William George MM Pte 4794 2/1st HAC(Infantry) KIA 9.10.17.
PAYNE William H. MM Pte 56094 Labour Corps
PAYNE William H. MM Sjt 200028 Royal Warwickshire Regt
PAYNE William H. MM Pte 439386 RAMC
PAYNTER James John MM Cpl 16145 3rd Rifle Brigade
PAYSDEN George MM Pte 14/19720 14th Royal Irish Rifles DOW 11.10.16.
PAYTEN Walter H. MM Spt 547030 51 Div Sig Coy Royal Engineers
PAYTON Henry MM Pte 326297 1/1st Cambridgeshire Regt
PAYTON John MM Pte 201596 7th Worcestershire Regt
PEABODY John F. "DCM,MM" Sjt 14767 11th West Yorkshire Regt
PEACE Edward MM Gnr 64464 RGA
PEACE Frank MM Pte 15641 8th Oxf & Bucks Light Infantry
PEACE Frank Harry MM Cpl 49561 9th Royal Fusiliers KIA 30.11.17.
PEACE Fred MM Pte 325115 8th Lancashire Fusiliers
PEACE George Peter MM Pte 10967 8th Seaforth Highlanders KIA 24.12.17.
PEACE Richard H. MM Pte 19378 6th York & Lancaster Regt
PEACEY Alfred MM Pte 360039 22nd Northumberland Fusiliers
PEACEY Harold MM Dvr 11798 RFA
PEACH Arthur MM L/Cpl 22412 East Kent Regt
PEACH Charles MM Spr 55292 Royal Engineers
PEACH Ernest A. MM+Bar Sjt C/837 16th King's Royal Rifle Corps
PEACH Ernest W. MM Tpr 1235 Household Bn
PEACH Frederick W. MM Pte 7602 East Surrey Regt
PEACH John R. MM Pte 26727 2nd Grenadier Guards
PEACH Joseph MM Bdr 38820 77 Bde RFA
PEACH Sidney "MM,MID" Sjt 13994 1st Middlesex Regt
PEACH Walter V.H. MM Dvr 125133 RFA
PEACHEY Andrew MM+Bar 2nd Cpl 26276 Royal Engineers
PEACHEY Archibald Randolph MM Cpl 511386 1/14th London Regt KIA 11.5.17.
PEACHEY Charles MM Sjt 265642 1/6th West Riding Regt KIA 11.12.17.
PEACHEY Harry O. MM BQMS 961623 C/235 Bde RFA
PEACOCK Albert MM Bdr 56877 RFA
PEACOCK Albert MM Pte 200644 1/4th Essex Regt
PEACOCK Albert Nelson MM L/Sjt 524 7th Royal Sussex Regt
PEACOCK Alexander Heim MM Pte 17578 King's Own Scottish Borderers
PEACOCK Charles MM Pte 3/5020 2nd Suffolk Regt
PEACOCK Christopher MM L/Cpl 1941 1/4th Yorkshire Regt
PEACOCK Edward MM Pte 202443 Royal Warwickshire Regt
PEACOCK Edwin E. MM Pte 47213 Northumberland Fusiliers
PEACOCK Elijah MM Sjt 17246 305 Siege Bty RGA
PEACOCK Ernest MM CSM 265479 4th West Riding Regt
PEACOCK Ernest MM Cpl 200556 1/4th Yorkshire Regt KIA 27.5.18.
PEACOCK Frank MM Pte 325249 1st West Yorkshire Regt
PEACOCK George MM+Bar Bdr 14710 105 Bty 22 Bde RFA
PEACOCK George MM Sjt 66730 38 Bde RFA
PEACOCK George E. MM Sjt 23329 Royal Engineers
PEACOCK Harry MM Pte 10342 2nd South Wales Borderers
PEACOCK Harry Patrick James "DCM,MM" Sjt 87207 204 Fd Coy Royal Engineers
PEACOCK Henry MM Gnr 751400 D/223 Bde RFA
PEACOCK Herbert MM Pte 240688 1/4th Cheshire Regt
PEACOCK J.R. MM+Bar Sjt 238 2 Div Sig Coy Royal Engineers
PEACOCK James H. MM Pte 10154 1st Border Regt
PEACOCK James S. MM L/Cpl 26256 8th Yorkshire Regt
PEACOCK John MM Sjt 751352 RFA
PEACOCK John Alfred MM Pte 29056 2nd West Yorkshire Regt KIA 27.3.18.
PEACOCK John E. MM+Bar L/Bdr 19789 D/168 Bde RFA
PEACOCK John G. MM L/Sjt 325 7th Royal Sussex Regt
PEACOCK Reginald "MM,MID" Sjt 522032 483 Fd Coy Royal Engineers
PEACOCK Robert J. "MM,MID" 2nd Cpl 75068 Royal Engineers
PEACOCK Sydney MM CSM 200219 1/7th Worcestershire Regt
PEACOCK T. MM Cpl 37506 20th Northumberland Fusiliers
PEACOCK Thomas C. MM Cpl 51532 2nd Yorkshire Light Infantry
PEACOCK Thomas R. MM Pte 51840 4th Yorkshire Light Infantry
PEACOCK Thomas W. MM L/Cpl 202073 2/4th South Lancashire Regt
PEACOCK W. MM Pte 17914 13th Essex Regt
PEACOCK Walter F. MM Pte 19280 10th Hussars
PEACOCK William MM Pte 3886 1/8th Arg & Suth Highlanders KIA 23.7.18.
PEACOCK William MM Pnr 207311 Royal Engineers
PEAD Robert D. MM Sjt 572058 1/17th London Regt
PEADON Frank MM Cpl 80115 RFA
PEAK Thomas MM Dvr 3001 RFA
PEAKE Benjamin J. "DCM,MM" CSM 14272 7th Shropshire Light Infantry
PEAKE Frederick D. MM Sjt 553031 16th London Regt
PEAKE George E.A. MM Cpl 111879 RGA
PEAKE Harry MM Cpl 4273 RFA
PEAKE Harry MM L/Cpl 58014 1/6th Cheshire Regt KIA 27.3.18.
PEAKE James MM L/Sjt 266 18th Middlesex Regt
PEAKE Leonard "DCM,MM,CG(F)" Sjt 18685 6th King's Own Scottish Borderers
PEAKE Walter MM+Bar S/Sjt 223 RAMC
PEAKE William John MM Cpl 13/19168 13th Royal Irish Rifles KIA 1.7.16.
PEAKER Thomas MM S/Sjt Fitter 158127 12 Heavy Bty RGA
PEAKER William MM L/Cpl 242093 1st King's Own Scottish Borderers KIA 11.10.18.
PEAKMAN George J. MM Pte 403249 RAMC
PEAKMAN J. MM Sjt 17812 Duke of Cornwall's LI
PEAPLE Sidney C. MM Gnr 94843 RFA
PEAR Cecil William MM Pte 21317 10th York & Lancaster Regt
PEARCE A.E. MM Sjt 11207 6th Dorsetshire Regt
PEARCE Albert MM L/Cpl 76630 Signal Service Royal Engineers
PEARCE Albert MM Cpl 44430 33 Bde RFA
PEARCE Albert E. MM Sjt 331458 9th Liverpool Regt

PEARCE Albert Edward MM Pte 32312 1st Wiltshire Regt KIA 7.6.17
PEARCE Albert Edward MM Pte 533640 15th London Regt DOW 24.3.18.
PEARCE Albert G. MM Spr 134868 Royal Engineers
PEARCE Alfred MM Dvr 82666 RFA
PEARCE Alfred MM Dvr T/33370 2 Div Train Army Service Corps
PEARCE Alfred C. MM L/Bdr 37116 41 Div Ammn Col RFA
PEARCE Archibald MM Spr 69658 122 Fd Coy Royal Engineers
PEARCE Archibald Arthur MM Cpl 950443 B/235 Bde RFA
PEARCE Arthur MM Cpl 15695 7th Shropshire Light Infantry KIA 26.9.17.
PEARCE Arthur Charles MM Cpl 57336 37 Div Sig Coy Royal Engineers
PEARCE Arthur L. MM Pte 20131 7th Wiltshire Regt
PEARCE Arthur W. MM Pte 17528 6th South Wales Borderers
PEARCE Benjamin MM Pte 4984 3rd Rifle Brigade
PEARCE Benjamin MM L/Cpl 496393 Royal Engineers
PEARCE Benjamin E. MM Sjt 36420 RAMC
PEARCE Charles A. MM Gnr Fitter 51570 147 Bty 97 Bde RFA
PEARCE Charles Gilbert MM L/Cpl 6172 1st Scots Guards
PEARCE Charles H.W. MM L/Cpl 10655 Royal Berkshire Regt
PEARCE Charles R. MM Dmr 240932 Gloucestershire Regt
PEARCE Cornelius MM Spr 224164 406 Fd Coy Royal Engineers
PEARCE David MM Pte 355932 25th Royal Welsh Fusiliers
PEARCE Edward A. MM Pte 275 1/1st Cambridgeshire Regt
PEARCE Ernest MM Cpl 64221 7 Bde RHA
PEARCE Ernest A. MM Pte 57495 11th West Yorkshire Regt
PEARCE Ernest E. MM Pte 94497 7th Notts & Derby Regt
PEARCE Ewart C. MM Spr 202475 Royal Engineers
PEARCE F. MM Sjt 15222 Grenadier Guards
PEARCE Frank H. MM Pte 16936 13th Welsh Regt
PEARCE George MM Bdr 10968 B/58 Bde RFA
PEARCE George Charles MM Cpl 912 RGA
PEARCE George W. MM Pte 242759 5th West Riding Regt
PEARCE Gilbert James MM Pte 493269 89 Fd Amb RAMC
PEARCE H. MM Spr 59525 Royal Engineers
PEARCE H.E. MM L/Bdr 776435 D/310 Bde RFA
PEARCE H.S. MM Pte 202366 6th Royal West Surrey Regt
PEARCE Harold MM Sjt G/6494 7th East Kent Regt DOW 30.9.17.
PEARCE Harold Charles MM Gnr 88973 B/174 Bde RFA KIA 11.9.17.
PEARCE Harold S. MM Pte 200749 1/4th Oxf & Bucks Light Infantry
PEARCE Harry MM L/Bdr 82111 RGA
PEARCE Henry B. MM Sjt 246326 Royal Engineers
PEARCE Henry T. MM Pte 21678 Gloucestershire Regt
PEARCE Herbert MM Pte 93050 Durham Light Infantry
PEARCE Herbert MM L/Cpl 24771 16th Royal Welsh Fusiliers DOW 24.4.18.
PEARCE Herbert Charles "DCM,MM" Sjt 12587 40th Bn Machine Gun Corps
PEARCE Herbert J. MM Pte 242431 1st Middlesex Regt
PEARCE James "DCM,MM" Sjt 9649 2nd West Yorkshire Regt Died 13.11.18.
PEARCE James MM Gnr 960373 C/236 Bde RFA
PEARCE James E. "DCM,MM" CSM 33105 1st Wiltshire Regt
PEARCE James Hales MM Spr 538448 62 Div Sig Coy Royal Engineers DOW 26.10.18.
PEARCE James V. MM Pte 48380 54th Bn Machine Gun Corps
PEARCE John MM Cpl 81530 RFA
PEARCE John MM Pte 16971 6th South Wales Borderers
PEARCE John Arthur MM Pte 15441 11th Welsh Regt
PEARCE John Edward MM L/Cpl 16819 1st Hampshire Regt
PEARCE John W. MM Cpl Fitter 149170 RGA
PEARCE Leslie Benjamin MM Cpl 42771 4th South Staffordshire Regt
PEARCE Percy E. MM Spr 508374 Royal Engineers
PEARCE Percy L.J. MM Gnr 110423 RGA
PEARCE Phillip H. MM Sjt 19728 5 Fd Svy Bn Royal Engineers
PEARCE R.W. MM Sjt 7746 Royal Fusiliers
PEARCE Ralph S. MM Sjt 2076 RAMC
PEARCE Reginald J. MM L/Cpl 22155 Dorsetshire Regt
PEARCE Richard A. MM Spr 312347 3 Div Sig Coy Royal Engineers
PEARCE Robert MM Pte 27238 Durham Light Infantry
PEARCE Robert J. MM Pte 241080 1/5th Devonshire Regt
PEARCE S.D. MM Cpl 1805 RFA
PEARCE Sidney "MC,DCM,MM+Bar,MM(F)" CSM 7427 2nd & 1st Wiltshire Regt
PEARCE Stanley MM Spr 66037 12 Div Sig Coy Royal Engineers
PEARCE Sydney Edward MM Cpl 221786 50 Div Sig Coy Royal Engineers
PEARCE Thomas MM Cpl 37631 5th Royal Berkshire Regt
PEARCE Thomas MM Cpl 23522 1 Div Sig Coy Royal Engineers
PEARCE Thomas MM Pte 84493 Machine Gun Corps
PEARCE Thomas MM Gnr 29162 RFA
PEARCE Tom MM+Bar L/Cpl 18589 2nd Bedfordshire Regt KIA 23.10.18.
PEARCE Walter MM Sjt 1223 2(South Midland)Fd Coy Royal Engineers DOW 16.8.17.
PEARCE William MM Pte 235087 5th Gloucestershire Regt
PEARCE William MM Pte 497184 104 Fd Amb RAMC
PEARCE William "DCM,MM" Sjt 2003 2/1(Wessex)Fd Amb RAMC
PEARCE William E. MM Cpl 23942 1st Norfolk Regt
PEARCE William Edgar MM Dvr 8275 D/51 Bde RFA
PEARCE William Edward MM Cpl S/1832 13th Rifle Brigade KIA 14.11.16.
PEARCE William Ernest MM Pte 23833 Gloucestershire Regt
PEARCE William G. MM 2nd Cpl 554309 513 Fd Coy Royal Engineers
PEARCE William H. MM Sjt 14683 7th Shropshire Light Infantry
PEARCE William J. MM+Bar Sjt 20446 7th Dragoon Guards
PEARCE William J. MM Sjt 41774 78 Fd Amb RAMC
PEARCY John MM L/Cpl 200715 2/4th East Lancashire Regt KIA 31.3.18.
PEARL John James MM Dvr 51406 155 Fd Coy Royal Engineers
PEARL Joseph J. MM Spr 199060 1 Div Sig Coy Royal Engineers
PEARL Percy S. MM L/Cpl 326087 1/1st Cambridgeshire Regt
PEARMAN Charles K. MM Pte 201915 Northumberland Fusiliers
PEARMAN James MM Cpl 41176 Essex Regt
PEARMINE W.V.H. MM L/Cpl 11375 Royal Berkshire Regt
PEARS Charles William MM Cpl 9578 1st Northamptonshire Regt DOW 20.4.18.
PEARS Herbert MM Pte 1241 Royal Fusiliers
PEARS John W. MM Pte 24186 RAMC
PEARSALL Albert Edward MM Pte 19603 2nd Leicestershire Regt
PEARSALL Harry MM L/Cpl 9815 2nd South Staffordshire Regt DOW 30.12.17.
PEARSALL Sydney MM Cpl 75339 RGA
PEARSE William E. MM L/Cpl 339518 2 Fd Amb RAMC
PEARSON A. MM Pte 339435 RAMC
PEARSON Albert A. MM L/Cpl 75982 8th Northumberland Fusiliers
PEARSON Albert B. MM L/Sjt 21868 2nd Grenadier Guards
PEARSON Albert G. MM Pte 26911 Royal Lancaster Regt
PEARSON Alfred MM L/Cpl 200592 1/4th Yorkshire Regt Died 14.8.18.
PEARSON Alfred MM Sjt 235775 5th West Riding Regt
PEARSON Arnold MM L/Cpl 28442 4th Grenadier Guards
PEARSON Arthur MM L/Cpl 6177 1st West Yorkshire Regt
PEARSON Arthur Henry MM Gnr 316087 RGA
PEARSON Arthur Henry MM Gnr 11635 V/33 Heavy TM Bty RFA
PEARSON Benjamin MM L/Sjt 49014 11th Cheshire Regt
PEARSON Benjamin MM Gnr 44611 25 Bde RFA
PEARSON Bertie MM Pte 323762 1/6th London Regt KIA 28.3.18.
PEARSON Bill MM Pte 201473 West Riding Regt
PEARSON C.A. MM Pte 6735 East Surrey Regt
PEARSON Charles MM Sjt 45514 194 Coy Machine Gun Corps
PEARSON Charles E. MM Sjt 587 Royal Fusiliers
PEARSON Charles J. MM Cpl 110650 MGC(Cavalry)
PEARSON Charles W. MM Pte 16962 10th Royal Fusiliers
PEARSON Cuthbert MM Bdr 453 'C' Bty Machine Gun Corps(Motors)
PEARSON David MM Pte 17234 1st Scots Guards
PEARSON Edward MM Pte 270564 1/1st Northumberland Yeo
PEARSON Edwin MM Pte 240855 11th Notts & Derby Regt
PEARSON Ernest MM Pte 40180 15/17th West Yorkshire Regt KIA 18.9.18.
PEARSON Ernest MM Pte 12326 2nd Notts & Derby Regt KIA 1.7.17.
PEARSON Ernest MM Pte 8868 2nd South Staffordshire Regt
PEARSON Ernest MM L/Cpl 7760 10th West Riding Regt KIA 27.10.18.
PEARSON Frank MM L/Cpl 88099 6th Liverpool Regt
PEARSON Frank MM Pte 41583 2nd Royal Inniskilling Fusiliers
PEARSON Frank MM L/Cpl 13746 6th Royal West Surrey Regt DOW 5.4.18.
PEARSON Frank H. MM Spr 172289 Royal Engineers
PEARSON Fred MM+Bar L/Cpl 29798 9th Northumberland Fusiliers
PEARSON Frederick MM Pte 4785 1st East Surrey Regt

PEARSON George MM Pte 203193 1/4th West Riding Regt KIA 10.4.18.
PEARSON George MM Pte 8902 12th Suffolk Regt KIA 6.1.18.
PEARSON George MM Pte 6344 11th Lancashire Fusiliers
PEARSON George MM Pte 8558 2nd East Surrey Regt
PEARSON George A. MM L/Cpl 15538 13th Liverpool Regt
PEARSON George W. MM Cpl 10463 Royal West Surrey Regt
PEARSON Harold MM L/Cpl 175822 1/1st Yorkshire Dragoons Yeo
PEARSON Harold MM Pte 241552 22nd Northumberland Fusiliers
PEARSON Harold Thomas "MM,MID" Cpl 94684 D/50 Bde RFA
PEARSON Harry MM Pte 202019 South Staffordshire Regt
PEARSON Henry MM Sjt 1426 1/7th Notts & Derby Regt KIA 1.7.16.
PEARSON Herbert A. MM Sjt 201129 West Yorkshire Regt
PEARSON Herbert E. MM Sjt 318013 1/1(London)Hy Bty RGA
PEARSON Hugh MM Pte 5980 11th Arg & Suth Highlanders
PEARSON J. MM Dvr 37389 RFA
PEARSON James MM CQMS 63102 2nd West Yorkshire Regt
PEARSON James MM L/Cpl 27267 17th Highland Light Infantry
PEARSON James A. MM Pte 43104 Scottish Rifles
PEARSON James I. MM Sjt 18609 Scottish Rifles
PEARSON James Leonard MM Gnr 31538 86 Bty 32 Bde RFA
PEARSON James T. MM Pnr 76527 Royal Engineers
PEARSON John MM Pte 275420 7th Manchester Regt
PEARSON John MM Pnr 487992 Royal Engineers
PEARSON John MM Pte 70587 Durham Light Infantry
PEARSON John MM Pte 1542 1/5th Border Regt
PEARSON John MM Gnr 151 67 TM Bty RFA
PEARSON Joseph MM Cpl 6799 54 Fd Coy Royal Engineers
PEARSON Joseph MM Sjt 16406 Durham Light Infantry
PEARSON Joseph Edward MM Pte 71283 33 Coy Machine Gun Corps
PEARSON Joseph S. MM Cpl 98272 195 Siege Bty RGA
PEARSON Leonard MM Gnr 12488 D/242 Bde RFA
PEARSON Leonard A. MM L/Cpl 631058 20th London Regt
PEARSON Maurice MM Cpl 49589 Royal Engineers
PEARSON Melville Llewellyn MM Bdr 13274 D/3 Bde RFA
PEARSON Oscar C. MM Cpl 249031 Royal Engineers
PEARSON Patrick DCM(10617 10th R Dub Fus);MM Pte 10851 Royal Munster Fusiliers
PEARSON Percy "DCM,MM" CSM 200214 1/5th Notts & Derby Regt
PEARSON Richard S. MM Pte 302117 5th London Regt
PEARSON Robert MM Pte 7914 1st Norfolk Regt
PEARSON Robert David MM Pte 65184 72 Fd Amb RAMC
PEARSON Robert Wrightson MM Pte 13732 1/6th Durham Light Infantry DOW 29.5.18.
PEARSON Stephen M. MM Dvr 761366 RFA
PEARSON Thomas MM Pte M2/082583 Army Service Corps att 153 Siege Bty Ammn Col RGA.
PEARSON Thomas MM L/Cpl 200853 1/4th Yorkshire Regt
PEARSON Thomas MM L/Sjt 13414 2nd Grenadier Guards
PEARSON Thomas MM Pnr 43493 Royal Engineers
PEARSON Thomas MM Sjt 15469 14th Durham Light Infantry KIA 9.7.17.
PEARSON Thomas MM Gnr 26987 RFA
PEARSON Thomas H. MM L/Cpl F/20 16th Middlesex Regt
PEARSON Thomas Percy MM Pte 27630 1/5th Border Regt
PEARSON Titus MM+Bar CSM 15879 10th Lancashire Fusiliers
PEARSON W. MM Cpl 18934 Machine Gun Corps
PEARSON W.H. MM Pte 7143 West Riding Regt
PEARSON Wilfred H. MM Sjt 390333 1/9th London Regt
PEARSON William MM Pte 23936 2nd Grenadier Guards
PEARSON William MM Sjt 265471 1/6th Welsh Regt
PEARSON William MM Pte 1340 2(Northumbrian)Fd Amb RAMC
PEARSON William John MM Cpl 241942 1/5th Gloucestershire Regt
PEARSON William Osborne MM Pte 50454 Royal Fusiliers
PEART Charles E. MM Sjt 12939 9th Gloucestershire Regt
PEART G.R. MM Sjt 204532 1st Essex Regt
PEART George MM+Bar Pte 2770 2nd Northumberland Fusiliers
PEART George Cuthbert MM Cpl 14/301 Royal Warwickshire Regt
PEART George R. MM Sjt 41291 Northumberland Fusiliers
PEART Harold MM Pte 203419 1/4th York & Lancaster Regt KIA 13.10.18.
PEART Herbert MM Spr 192135 Royal Engineers
PEART John MM Cpl 5140 Gordon Highlanders
PEART Joseph Vickers MM Pte 301841 1/8th Durham Light Infantry KIA 10.4.18.
PEART Walter MM Cpl 6887 1st Scottish Rifles
PEARTREE T. "DCM,MM" Sjt 13363 10th Essex Regt
PEARY Henry W. MM Bdr 149751 RGA
PEASE Albert MM Sjt 306088 1/8th Lancashire Fusiliers
PEASE Charles MM Pte 27/1175 Northumberland Fusiliers
PEASE Frederick MM Cpl 16090 6th Lincolnshire Regt
PEASE Frederick O. "DCM,MM" Cpl 558546 46 Div Sig Coy Royal Engineers
PEASEY Charles W. MM CSM Y/1865 King's Royal Rifle Corps
PEASLAND William MM Cpl 132388 257 Tunnelling Coy Royal Engineers
PEASTON James MM Cpl 59776 RGA
PEASTON Richard MM L/Cpl 7070 8/10th Gordon Highlanders
PEAT Archibald MM Sjt 240032 5/6th Scottish Rifles
PEAT Duncan MM Cpl 7838 2nd Yorkshire Regt
PEAT F. MM L/Cpl P/365 Military Foot Police
PEAT Frederick C. MM Cpl 19425 RGA
PEAT Joseph MM Cpl 34544 115 Heavy Bty RGA DOW 7.1.17.
PEAT Robert MM Sjt 12392 Gordon Highlanders
PEAT Rowland MM+Bar L/Cpl 8/4362 1st Northumberland Fusiliers KIA 23.10.18.
PEAT Sidney L. MM L/Cpl 34814 Manchester Regt
PEAT William MM Pte 240899 1/5th York & Lancaster Regt KIA 15.4.18.
PEAT William MM Pte 16757 12th Durham Light Infantry KIA 24.9.16.
PEAT William MM L/Sjt 48644 Royal Fusiliers
PEATE Edwin MM L/Cpl 10673 1st Shropshire Light Infantry KIA 25.9.16.
PEATFIELD Joseph MM Sjt 13086 7th Lincolnshire Regt KIA 5.9.18.
PEATFIELD William MM Sjt 54810 Royal Fusiliers
PEATS William F. MM Pte M2/099462 Army Service Corps
PEATTIE Frederick "MM,MID" Sjt 6470 1st East Kent Regt
PEATTIE Thomas MM Pte 291449 1/7th Royal Highlanders KIA 19.9.17.
PEATTIE William MM Pte 3193 Gordon Highlanders
PEBODY Harry MM Sjt 15607 7th Northamptonshire Regt
PECK Albert MM Pte 28454 Lincolnshire Regt
PECK Alfred George MM+Bar Pte 14576 9th Norfolk Regt KIA 15.4.18.
PECK Arthur MM Sjt 11624 11th Royal West Surrey Regt
PECK Arthur John MM Gnr 815123 D/296 Bde RFA
PECK Arthur Samuel MM Cpl 31518 34th Bn Machine Gun Corps
PECK Charles H. MM Pte 513694 14th London Regt
PECK Frank MM Pte M2/101925 Army Service Corps
PECK Frederick MM L/Cpl 2188 1/4th Suffolk Regt
PECK Frederick John MM L/Cpl 15236 Coldstream Guards
PECK George MM Pte 1625 10th Royal Fusiliers
PECK George MM Pte 1879 1/5th Yorkshire Regt
PECK George Walter MM 2nd Cpl 23950 57 Fd Coy Royal Engineers DOW 25.7.17.
PECK Henry J. MM Sjt 275671 1/6th Essex Regt
PECK James C. MM Pte 203 7th Royal Sussex Regt
PECK Joseph MM Pte 21542 1st Yorkshire Light Infantry
PECK Joseph H. MM Pte 52354 6th North Staffordshire Regt
PECK Richaed W. MM L/Cpl 11/1292 11th East Yorkshire Regt
PECK Robert MM CQMS 265402 7th Norfolk Regt
PECK Sidney B. MM Cpl 84238 D/94 Bde RFA
PECK Willie W.J. MM Cpl 56727 'H' Bty RHA
PECKET Henry C. MM L/Cpl C/12204 King's Royal Rifle Corps
PECKETT Leslie V. MM Pte 403634 1(West Riding)Fd Amb RAMC
PECKHAM Arthur MM Pte 12965 1st East Surrey Regt
PECKHAM Harold MM Pte 6803 Royal West Surrey Regt
PECKHAM Harry MM Pte 306483 Royal Warwickshire Regt
PECKHAM Henry MM Sjt 17820 RAMC
PECKOVER A.E.L. MM Pte 82718 25th Liverpool Regt
PEDDER Ben MM Pte 18325 10th West Riding Regt
PEDDER Jonathan MM Pte 4402 Royal Lancaster Regt
PEDDIE Henry MM Pte 268374 Royal Highlanders
PEDDIE J. MM Gnr 362964 RGA
PEDDIE James MM Pnr 192729 'N' Special Coy Royal Engineers
PEDDIE John MM Sjt 8026 10th Arg & Suth Highlanders
PEDDIE Peter MM Cpl 265425 1/6th Royal Highlanders
PEDDLESDEN William MM Pte 1441 7th Royal West Kent Regt KIA 3.7.16.
PEDEN James MM Bdr 92612 A/77 Bde RFA
PEDEN James MM Sjt 4501 9th Seaforth Highlanders
PEDEN James MM Cpl 4091 Machine Gun Corps
PEDLEY Alfred E. MM Gnr 326367 163 Siege Bty RGA
PEDLEY Ernest V. MM Pte 241710 6th South Staffordshire Regt
PEDLEY Harry MM Pte 1730 North Staffordshire Regt
PEDLEY Samuel MM Sjt 3/12193 2nd West Riding Regt

PEDLEY Walter MM Pte 12404 5th Northamptonshire Regt
PEDLEY William A. MM Sjt 236339 Guards Div Sig Coy Royal Engineers
PEDRICK Charles H. MM Sjt 207240 3rd Worcestershire Regt
PEDRICK James W. MM L/Cpl 24869 10th Duke of Cornwall's LI
PEDUZIE William Augustus. MM L/Cpl 74135 XIII Corps Sig Sub Sect Royal Engineers
PEDWELL H. MM L/Cpl 496242 479 Fd Coy Royal Engineers
PEE Albert MM Pte 15435 8th Northumberland Fusiliers
PEE William Henry MM Spr 81515 202 Fd Coy Royal Engineers DOW 3.5.18.
PEEBLES Ernest F. MM Pte 83272 1st Middlesex Regt
PEEL Albert MM Pte 17/1635 12th West Yorkshire Regt
PEEL Foster MM Cpl 21951 King's Own Scottish Borderers
PEEL George MM Cpl 46547 Northumberland Fusiliers
PEEL Harry MM Pte 7203 2nd Yorkshire Regt
PEEL Herbert MM+Bar Pte 34499 5th West Riding Regt
PEEL James "DSO,MM(14072 Sjt 2nd Bn)" 2Lt Royal Fusiliers
PEEL John R. MM CSM 22819 4th Yorkshire Light Infantry
PEEL Joseph MM Pte 2348 Royal Warwickshire Regt
PEEL Richard MM Sjt 240379 1/4th Royal Lancaster Regt
PEEL Robert MM Dvr 71488 RFA
PEEL Samuel MM Sjt 293659 RGA
PEEL William MM L/Cpl C/6204 King's Royal Rifle Corps
PEERLESS George Edward James MM Pte 2203 7th Royal West Kent Regt
PEERLESS Victor MM L/Cpl G/6316 6th East Kent Regt KIA 3.8.17.
PEERMAN Harold Willoughby MM Sjt 68145 126 Siege Bty RGA
PEERS Archie MM Pte 42244 9th Royal Irish Fusiliers
PEERS Austin Marshall MM Cpl 505228 13th King's Royal Rifle Corps KIA 26.10.18.
PEERS C. MM Cpl 4619 Leicestershire Regt
PEERS George MM Sjt 74952 2nd Manchester Regt
PEERS Henry William MM Gnr 137479 279 Siege Bty RGA
PEERS Herbert MM Sjt 94348 14th Royal Welsh Fusiliers
PEERS Percy G. MM Pte 15329 3rd Hussars
PEERS Robert MM Pte 339649 RAMC
PEET A. MM Pte 201880 York & Lancaster Regt
PEET Albert MM Cpl 27927 Notts & Derby Regt
PEET Frederick J. MM Pte 3098 Machine Gun Corps
PEET George Henry MM Cpl 1978 1/4th Lincolnshire Regt KIA 22.11.17.
PEET Herbert E. "DCM,MM" QMS 22316 17th Bn Machine Gun Corps
PEET James MM Dvr 137414 46 TM Bty RFA KIA 13.8.18.
PEET John Taylor MM CSM 1654 1/4th Oxf & Bucks Light Infantry KIA 23.7.16.
PEFFERS Philip MM Sjt 10751 1st King's Own Scottish Borderers
PEFFERS Robert MM L/Cpl 330027 1/8th Royal Scots
PEGG Alfred MM Pte 12218 East Surrey Regt
PEGG Arthur F. MM L/Cpl 20986 Hampshire Regt
PEGG Charles E. MM Pte 300685 1/1st Staffordshire Yeomanry
PEGG H.W. MM CQMS 1410 Royal Warwickshire Regt
PEGG Henry MM Cpl 301 1/9th Durham Light Infantry
PEGG Herbert MM Cpl 8076 Rifle Brigade
PEGG Percy MM Pte A/3682 8th King's Royal Rifle Corps
PEGG Thomas Edwin MM Pte 25863 Notts & Derby Regt
PEGG William MM Pte 22984 Machine Gun Corps
PEGGIE J. MM Cpl 267287 Royal Warwickshire Regt
PEGGS Edward George MM Cpl 22191 32nd Royal Fusiliers
PEGLER Bertie MM Pte 13773 1/5th Gloucestershire Regt KIA 6.10.18.
PEGLER Frederick Alfred MM Pte 28995 1st Royal Warwickshire Regt
PEGLER William MM Sjt 67546 Machine Gun Corps
PEGRAM Leonard S. "DCM,MM" Cpl G/7145 1st Royal Fusiliers
PEGRAM Thomas James MM Pte 295051 1/7th Durham Light Infantry KIA 29.3.18.
PEIRCE Harry George MM Sjt 17535 25th Bn Machine Gun Corps KIA 26.7.18.
PELAN McIntyre S. MM Spr 57669 Royal Engineers
PELHAM Arthur MM Pte 4073 1st Royal West Surrey Regt DOW 27.12.16.
PELHAM Edward V. MM Gnr 498 RGA
PELL Alfred MM Cpl 30627 2nd Northamptonshire Regt
PELL George R. MM Pte 93120 Tank Corps
PELL Harry MM Sjt 338 Royal Sussex Regt
PELL Jackson MM Pte 22419 20th Hussars
PELL John Frederick MM Gnr Fitter 96269 B/48 Bde RFA
PELLETT Charles MM Dvr 103449 RFA

PELLETT Horace Bertram MM Pte C/3443 17th King's Royal Rifle Corps KIA 21.3.18.
PELLING Roland W. MM Spr 398785 5 Fd Coy Royal Engineers
PELLOW James MM Pte 44790 RAMC
PEMBERTON A. MM Pte 290788 Cheshire Regt
PEMBERTON Arthur MM Sjt 200931 4th York & Lancaster Regt
PEMBERTON Edward MM Cpl 28987 9th East Surrey Regt
PEMBERTON Ernest MM Pte 102318 Labour Corps
PEMBERTON Fred MM Pte 351462 1/9th Manchester Regt
PEMBERTON George Alfred MM Pte 18525 11th Cheshire Regt KIA 10.4.18.
PEMBERTON George W. MM Pte 27503 RAMC
PEMBERTON George W. "DCM,MM" CSM 692 4th York & Lancaster Regt
PEMBERTON George William MM Sjt 1918 1/8th West Yorkshire Regt KIA 13.8.16.
PEMBERTON Harold MM Spr 45659 Royal Engineers
PEMBERTON Henry MM Pte 16391 13th Liverpool Regt KIA 21.8.18.
PEMBERTON Horace MM Pte 32957 22nd Manchester Regt KIA 26.10.17.
PEMBERTON Horace W. MM L/Cpl 370494 1/8th London Regt
PEMBERTON Nathaniel MM CSM 19389 1/4th Royal Lancaster Regt
PEMBERTON Percy MM Sjt 267955 2/5th West Riding Regt KIA 26.8.18.
PEMBERTON Reginald MM Pte 40276 1st Cheshire Regt
PEMBERTON Thomas MM L/Cpl 50007 Cheshire Regt
PEMBERTON Tom MM Cpl 15541 17th Lancashire Fusiliers
PEMBERTON William MM Pte 12999 9th Royal Welsh Fusiliers
PEMBERTON William H. MM Pte 16342 2nd Yorkshire Regt
PEMBRO Bertram T.E. MM Gnr 292615 RGA
PEMBRO Thomas J. MM Sjt 47338 Royal Engineers
PEMBROKE John A.E. MM Cpl 302119 5th London Regt
PENBERTHY Albert V. MM L/Cpl 1979 24 Fd Amb RAMC
PENBERTHY Ernest J. MM Gnr 138715 RGA
PENCOTT Thomas MM Pte 235120 1/4th Northumberland Fusiliers
PENDELL James MM Pte 35027 17th Lancashire Fusiliers
PENDER Edward "MM,MID" Dvr 90756 Royal Engineers
PENDERGAST William MM Pte 15648 5th Yorkshire Regt KIA 27.5.18.
PENDLEBURY Benjamin MM Pte 14867 1st Coldstream Guards
PENDLEBURY Robert MM Pte 3613 8th Royal Irish Regt
PENDLEBURY Thomas MM+Bar Cpl 290665 North Lancashire Regt
PENDLETON John H.D. MM Pte M2/032489 Army Service Corps
PENDLETON Leonard MM L/Cpl R/8216 9th King's Royal Rifle Corps KIA 9.4.17.
PENDLETON Samuel MM Pte 11194 Coldstream Guards
PENDLINGTON George H. MM Cpl 15676 6th Yorkshire Regt
PENDRAY Thomas W. MM L/Cpl 36603 Royal Engineers
PENDRICK C. MM+Bar L/Cpl 16055 1/1st Cambridgeshire Regt
PENDRIGH James H. MM Gnr 57795 RGA
PENDRILL Archibald J. MM Pte 57223 Machine Gun Corps
PENDRILL Ernest Ivor MM Pte 85347 228 Coy Machine Gun Corps
PENFOLD Alfred E. "MM,MID" 2nd Cpl 45051 Royal Engineers
PENFOLD Frederick MM Pte 30627 10th Royal West Kent Regt
PENFOLD George MM Sjt 8339 2nd Royal Scots
PENFOLD George Rupert MM Pte 2244 12th Middlesex Regt att 54 Coy MGC.
PENFOLD John MM Pte 51073 2nd Worcestershire Regt
PENFOLD John MM Pte 698166 22nd London Regt
PENFOLD Joseph MM Cpl 12663 6th East Kent Regt
PENFOLD Sidney J. MM Dvr 63628 1 Div Ammn Col RFA
PENFOLD William MM Sjt 2719 8th Royal Sussex Regt
PENFOLD William Frederick MM Cpl 2757 1/2(Hampshire)Army Troops Coy Royal Engineers
PENGELLEY Arthur "DCM+Bar,MM" Sjt 31649 112 Bty 24 Bde & B/83 Bde RFA
PENGILLY Alexander James MM Sjt M2/113811 Army Service Corps att 57 Fd Amb RAMC.
PENHALE Tom MM Pte 240288 Duke of Cornwall's LI
PENHALL Ernest MM Bdr 64805 RGA
PENISTON William R. "DCM,MM+2 Bars" L/Cpl A/2273 9th King's Royal Rifle Corps
PENISTONE Albert MM L/Cpl 10794 6th York & Lancaster Regt
PENKETH Harold MM Pte 66827 26th Royal Fusiliers KIA 29.9.18.
PENKETHMAN Albert MM Cpl 1913 5th Manchester Regt
PENKEYMAN William MM L/Cpl 265091 Liverpool Regt
PENLINGTON Benjamin MM Sjt 10918 9th Royal Welsh Fusiliers

PENLINGTON Edward MM Pte 355874 10th Liverpool Regt
PENLINGTON Henry MM Gnr 279445 RGA
PENLINGTON Jack MM+Bar Sjt 46787 Machine Gun Corps
PENLINGTON William MM L/Cpl 14583 Machine Gun Corps
PENMAN Alexander MM+Bar Cpl 275747 1/7th Arg & Suth Highlanders
PENMAN George MM Cpl 347365 RGA
PENMAN James MM Spr 137668 178 Tunnelling Coy Royal Engineers
PENMAN Thomas MM Cpl 139326 Royal Engineers
PENMAN Thomas MM Sjt 291020 Royal Highlanders
PENMAN William MM Pte 10031 RAMC
PENMAN William MM Pte 38299 12th Royal Scots KIA 25.4.18.
PENN Charles Comley MM Sjt 614177 RHA
PENN Charles E.J. MM L/Cpl 10392 Essex Regt
PENN Clifford Herbert MM Pte 792 10th Lincolnshire Regt
PENN Edward J. MM Pte M2/077398 Army Service Corps
PENN Frank R. MM+Bar L/Cpl 3577 18th London Regt
PENN Oscar Styles "MM,MID" Sjt 218 Machine Gun Corps(Motors)
PENN Walter MM L/Cpl 15021 8th Norfolk Regt
PENNEC Emile MM Pte 35177 Royal Warwickshire Regt
PENNELL Cyril E. MM Cpl 322134 London Regt
PENNELL George MM Sjt 8453 2nd Royal Fusiliers
PENNELL Harold MM Cpl 240460 1/6th South Staffordshire Regt
PENNELL James A. MM CSM 9798 6th Royal West Kent Regt
PENNELL Josephine MM Miss F BRSC(VAD)
PENNELL R.H. MM Sjt 18563 6th East Kent Regt
PENNELL Walter MM Pte 46037 2nd Durham Light Infantry Died 28.10.18.
PENNELLS Willie MM Pte 43094 Cameron Highlanders
PENNEY Alfred MM Sjt 786145 RFA
PENNEY Charles John MM Pte 15316 1st Middlesex Regt KIA 17.4.18.
PENNEY Frederick G. MM Pte 18767 Hampshire Regt
PENNEY W.H. MM CSM 8485 1st Hampshire Regt
PENNEY William MM Cpl 266162 1/6th Royal Highlanders
PENNIALL Henry Thomas MM Pte S/23596 1st Rifle Brigade
PENNICARD Charles David William MM Sjt 1259 1/22nd London Regt
PENNIE Alexander MM Pte 7047 1/4th Yorkshire Light Infantry DOW 26.7.17.
PENNIFOLD A. MM Pte 45493 11th Lancashire Fusiliers
PENNINGTON Arthur "DCM,MM" Sjt 6124 112 Coy & 3rd Bn Machine Gun Corps
PENNINGTON Arthur MM L/Cpl 20358 15th Welsh Regt KIA 26.8.18.
PENNINGTON Bert MM Pnr 25404 1 Div Sig Coy Royal Engineers
PENNINGTON Edwin MM Pte 23599 1st Royal Warwickshire Regt
PENNINGTON George MM Cpl 30039 5/6th Royal Scots
PENNINGTON Harold L. "MM,MID" Sjt 54209 25 Div Sig Coy Royal Engineers
PENNINGTON Harry MM Sjt 426450 Royal Engineers
PENNINGTON James MM Gnr 169078 RFA
PENNINGTON James MM L/Sjt 330073 Liverpool Regt
PENNINGTON James MM Sjt 21350 1st Lancashire Fusiliers
PENNINGTON John H. MM Sjt 1253 1/6th Liverpool Regt
PENNINGTON Joseph MM Sjt 5508 Irish Guards
PENNINGTON Norman MM Pte 72478 Liverpool Regt
PENNINGTON Orlando MM Spr 147918 Royal Engineers
PENNINGTON William MM Gnr 2011 B/246 Bde RFA
PENNINGTON William MM L/Cpl 18106 11th Durham Light Infantry
PENNINGTON William Henry MM Sjt 4684 1/6th South Staffordshire Regt
PENNOCK John MM Pte 1375 1/4th Yorkshire Regt
PENNY A. MM Cpl 202635 Gordon Highlanders
PENNY Albert C. MM Sjt 201460 7th Bn Tank Corps
PENNY Arthur MM CSM 923 173 Tunnelling Coy Royal Engineers
PENNY Charles Edward MM Cpl 13196 D/76 Bde RFA
PENNY Edward C. MM Pte 18849 Hampshire Regt
PENNY Fred Bromley MM Cpl 161600 51 Div Sig Coy Royal Engineers
PENNY Sidney Thomas MM Pte 9501 Machine Gun Corps
PENNY Sydney MM Pte 12987 2nd Coldstream Guards KIA 6.11.18.
PENNY Thomas O. MM Spr 311496 Royal Engineers
PENNY William MM Cpl 24529 15th Notts & Derby Regt KIA 25.7.18.
PENNYCOOK J. MM Pte 51719 11th Royal Scots
PENNYCOOK Thomas MM L/Cpl 47179 Bedfordshire Regt
PENNYFATHER John "DCM,MM" RSM 8407 1st Northamptonshire Regt
PENROSE Albert W. MM Cpl 472 17th Lancers
PENROSE Geneste MM Asst Administrator F QMWAAC
PENROSE James MM Cpl 1905 174 Bde RFA
PENROSE William H. MM L/Sjt 23861 Duke of Cornwall's LI
PENSON Ernest William MM Pte 2454 1/5th Royal Warwickshire Regt
PENSTONE Edward A. MM Sjt 207951 Royal West Surrey Regt
PENTICOST John MM Pte 726 Royal Sussex Regt
PENTLAND Joseph G. MM Pte 3213 Durham Light Infantry
PENTLAND Thomas MM L/Cpl 296327 12th Royal Scots Fusiliers
PENTNEY Richard MM Spr 217769 Royal Engineers
PENTNEY Thomas MM Pte 16613 7th Norfolk Regt
PENTY Kenneth MM L/Cpl 16012 9th Yorkshire Light Infantry KIA 3.10.17.
PENWARDEN Harold T. MM Cpl 240682 5th Devonshire Regt
PENWARDEN Walter F. MM Sjt 568246 9 Div Sig Coy Royal Engineers
PENZER William MM Pte 5708 8th Royal West Surrey Regt
PEOPLE William MM Pte 8047 1st Royal West Surrey Regt
PEOVER Arthur MM Pte 306632 Lancashire Fusiliers
PEOVER Samuel H. MM Cpl 20463 6th East Lancashire Regt
PEPALL George MM Cpl 48829 83 Fd Coy Royal Engineers DOW 28.3.18.
PEPLER Frederick Clifford MM CSM R/6808 King's Royal Rifle Corps
PEPPER David MM Pte 19958 1st King's Own Scottish Borderers
PEPPER Ernest MM Sjt 7470 1st Leicestershire Regt
PEPPER Ernest "MM,MID" Sjt 9544 2nd Bedfordshire Regt
PEPPER Francis H. MM Cpl 63377 RGA
PEPPER Francis W. MM Gnr 239560 RFA
PEPPER Frederick E. MM Sjt 5584 2nd Royal Fusiliers
PEPPER Frederick J. MM Pte 10208 RAMC
PEPPER George MM L/Cpl 202737 4th York & Lancaster Regt
PEPPER George MM Cpl 25495 37th Bn Machine Gun Corps
PEPPER George MM L/Cpl 727 1/7th Middlesex Regt
PEPPER Henry MM Pte 8977 2nd Northamptonshire Regt
PEPPER Herbert R. MM Pte 320552 Norfolk Regt
PEPPER John MM Pte 201441 Royal Warwickshire Regt
PEPPER John H. MM Sjt 44535 12th Manchester Regt KIA 18.9.18.
PEPPER Joseph W. MM Pte 1919 1/3rd London Regt
PEPPER Joseph William MM Pte 269766 1st Liverpool Regt
PEPPER Matthew MM Pte 12593 7th East Lancashire Regt
PEPPER Sidney MM Pte 24875 7th Royal Sussex Regt
PEPPER Walter MM Pte 8220 1st East Surrey Regt
PEPPER Walter MM Pte 18978 Royal Fusiliers
PEPPERCORN Frederick W. MM Pte 9243 Royal West Surrey Regt
PEPPERELL Allan MM L/Cpl 370211 1/8th London Regt KIA 22.3.18.
PEPPERELL Thomas MM Pte 14367 Devonshire Regt
PEPPERELL W. MM Cpl 47542 10th Essex Regt
PEPPIN Austin MM Pte 43819 1st Bn Machine Gun Corps
PEPPIN Harold MM Pte 9524 13th Royal Fusiliers
PEPPIN James B. MM CQMS 240051 Somerset Light Infantry
PEPPITT J. MM CSM 44004 7th Lincolnshire Regt KIA 29.5.18.
PERCIVAL Albert A. MM Gnr Sig 293420 136 Hy Bty RGA
PERCIVAL Albert A. MM Pnr 259155 Royal Engineers
PERCIVAL Frederick MM Cpl 29957 Somerset Light Infantry
PERCIVAL G.G. MM Cpl 18404 12/13th Northumberland Fusiliers
PERCIVAL Harold MM Pte 200625 11th Notts & Derby Regt DOW 5.11.18.
PERCIVAL Harry MM Pte 40586 Suffolk Regt
PERCIVAL Herbert MM Sjt 28683 Royal Engineers
PERCIVAL Hubert William MM Sjt 2625 1/4th Royal Lancaster Regt
PERCIVAL Jack MM Pte 9418 13th Royal Sussex Regt
PERCIVAL James MM L/Cpl 21479 11th South Lancashire Regt
PERCIVAL John MM L/Sjt 14375 Manchester Regt
PERCIVAL John T. MM Sjt 372688 8th London Regt
PERCIVAL Joseph "DCM,MM" CSM 17/1207 17th West Yorkshire Regt
PERCIVAL Leonard MM Pte 31942 1st Northumberland Fusiliers
PERCIVAL Samuel MM Cpl 32371 8th North Staffordshire Regt
PERCIVAL Ted "DCM,MM+Bar" L/Cpl 24695 7th Royal West Surrey Regt
PERCIVAL Walter "DCM,MM" CSM 11591 1st Grenadier Guards
PERCIVAL William MM Sjt 154 10th Arg & Suth Highlanders
PERCIVAL William A. MM Cpl 7296 RAMC
PERCY Foster B. MM Sjt 240642 Northumberland Fusiliers
PERCY Harold MM Cpl 701001 1/23rd London Regt

PERCY John MM Sjt 31833 2nd South Lancashire Regt
PERCY Kenneth MM Bdr 221602 RFA
PERCY Robert H. MM L/Cpl 12674 2nd Dragoon Guards
PEREIRA Francis MM Gnr Fitter 82859 'G' Bty RHA
PERFECT E. MM Sjt R/4765 King's Royal Rifle Corps
PERFECT William Robert MM Gnr 82452 X/8 Med TM Bty RFA KIA 27.5.18.
PERFITT Thomas A. "MM,MID" Sjt 9911 Royal Engineers
PERFITT Walter Frederick MM Sjt 19486 Manchester Regt
PERHAM John K. MM Bdr 109562 RFA
PERIAM Herbert MM L/Sjt 235083 1/1st Gloucestershire Yeomanry
PERIAM Robert MM Pte 11669 South Wales Borderers
PERIAM William MM Pte 225372 1/1st Monmouthshire Regt
PERKINS Albert E. MM Pte 423765 10th London Regt
PERKINS Alfred J. MM Sjt 16545 6th Somerset Light Infantry
PERKINS Arthur R. MM L/Cpl 15327 7th Royal West Surrey Regt
PERKINS Charles MM Pnr 237830 Signal Service Royal Engineers
PERKINS Charles H. MM Pte 52692 8th Lancashire Fusiliers
PERKINS Charles James MM Pte 17317 7th Bedfordshire Regt
PERKINS Cyril A. MM L/Cpl 24074 Royal Warwickshire Regt
PERKINS David John MM Pte 18125 Royal Welsh Fusiliers
PERKINS Ernest J. MM Pte 5537 17 Fd Amb RAMC
PERKINS Ernest Richard MM Cpl 60960 17th Royal Fusiliers DOW 13.8.17
PERKINS F. MM L/Cpl 13624 10th Essex Regt
PERKINS Frederick MM Sjt 76399 3rd(Light)Bn Tank Corps
PERKINS Frederick C. MM+Bar CSM 12849 6th Bedfordshire Regt
PERKINS George MM Pte 4641 Labour Corps
PERKINS George MM Sjt 701843 RFA
PERKINS Gwylym M. MM L/Bdr 13463 505 Bty 65 Bde RFA
PERKINS Harry MM Pte 40108 6th Royal West Surrey Regt
PERKINS Harry MM Cpl 115810 16 TM Bty RFA DOW 27.9.18.
PERKINS Harry A. MM Pte 54778 Manchester Regt
PERKINS Harry Bertram MM L/Sjt 16872 1st Grenadier Guards
PERKINS Henry C.A. MM Pte 40619 South Staffordshire Regt
PERKINS James P. MM Sjt 47048 5 Div Ammn Col RFA
PERKINS James Philip MM L/Cpl 20582 8th Royal Sussex Regt KIA 23.10.18.
PERKINS John "DCM,MM" Sjt 374 B/122 Bde RFA
PERKINS John C. "MM,MID" L/Cpl 3/3134 6th Yorkshire Light Infantry
PERKINS John D. MM+Bar Sjt 9348 1st Northamptonshire Regt
PERKINS Joseph B. MM S/Sjt Armourer T/1230 Army Ordnance Corps
PERKINS Lionel MM Cpl 9953 9th Royal Fusiliers
PERKINS Luke MM Gnr 100740 RFA
PERKINS Percy W.R. MM Pte 41327 1st Duke of Cornwall's LI
PERKINS Richard MM Dvr Fitter 10869 B/110 Bde RFA
PERKINS Rudolph MM L/Cpl 70 1st Royal Highlanders
PERKINS S.R. MM Cpl 8700 2nd Devonshire Regt
PERKINS Stanley Oliver Charles William MM L/Cpl 357462 37 Div Sig Coy Royal Engineers
PERKINS W. MM Pte 130440 46th Royal Fusiliers
PERKINS W.E. MM Air Mech 1 15632 Royal Flying Corps
PERKINS William MM L/Cpl 23036 2nd Lancashire Fusiliers
PERKINS William MM Pte 1826 8th Royal Sussex Regt
PERKINS William MM Sjt 53260 RFA
PERKINS William A. MM L/Cpl 200868 4th Bn Tank Corps
PERKINS William A. MM Pte 9400 Royal Fusiliers
PERKINS William George MM Pte 330357 1/9th Highland Light Infantry KIA 25.10.18.
PERKINS William H. MM Pte 38502 Royal Fusiliers
PERKS Albert MM Cpl 280213 1/1st South Notts Hussars Yeo
PERKS Alfred George MM L/Cpl 36505 2nd Royal Welsh Fusiliers DOW 31.8.18.
PERKS Charles J. MM Gnr 614019 RHA
PERKS Charles Peter MM Spr 28503 15 Fd Coy Royal Engineers
PERKS Harry MM Cpl 4236 7th Royal Irish Rifles
PERKS James MM Dvr 57288 RFA
PERKS Joseph H. MM 2nd Cpl 44067 Royal Engineers
PERKS Samuel MM Sjt 11200 Coldstream Guards
PERREN John MM L/Cpl 1942 Middlesex Regt
PERREN William G. MM Pte 3892 Machine Gun Corps
PERRETT Albert Edward MM Cpl 2431 Royal Engineers
PERRETT Charles MM+Bar Bdr 53044 RFA
PERRETT Frederick C. MM Sjt 374069 RGA
PERRIER Francis A. MM Gnr 110575 RGA
PERRIN Alfred MM Pte 869 1st Royal West Kent Regt KIA 3.10.17.
PERRIN Arthur MM Pte 47171 RAMC
PERRIN Bert MM Pte 6204 Middlesex Regt
PERRIN Fred MM Sjt 50875 Cheshire Regt
PERRIN George MM Pte 27293 East Surrey Regt
PERRIN George MM L/Cpl 98259 17 Coy Machine Gun Corps KIA 23.3.18.
PERRIN Joseph MM Cpl 96409 Royal Engineers
PERRIN Peter MM L/Cpl 263757 Royal Engineers
PERRING Norman T. MM Sjt 508301 502 Fd Coy Royal Engineers
PERRINS A.J. MM Pte 16409 6th South Wales Borderers
PERRINS Frank MM Spr 97168 Royal Engineers
PERRINS Harry MM Gnr 786458 HQ 312 Bde RFA
PERRINS Leslie G. MM L/Bdr 614394 1(Warwickshire)Bty RHA
PERRINS Wilfred J. MM Pte 305537 9th Bn Tank Corps
PERRIS Archibald MM Pte S4/039131 Army Service Corps
PERRIS Edward E. MM+Bar Spr 48908 25 Div Sig Coy Royal Engineers
PERRIS L.W. MM Pte 10286 Royal Berkshire Regt AKA James MAHONEY
PERRITT George MM Pte 31263 2nd Grenadier Guards
PERRONS Albert MM Dvr 797363 RFA
PERRONS Charles A. MM Pte 4784 24th London Regt
PERROTT J.F. MM Pte 388552 RAMC
PERROTT Nathan MM Dvr A/800 Army Service Corps
PERROTT Nathan W. MM Gnr 121860 RFA
PERROTT W.J. MM Cpl 24981 Royal Flying Corps
PERROTT William L. MM Sjt 106194 Royal Engineers
PERRY A.H. MM Cpl 435282 RAMC
PERRY Albert MM Pte 53990 Welsh Regt
PERRY Albert J. MM Pte 47033 Northumberland Fusiliers
PERRY Arthur W. MM Pte 260022 Worcestershire Regt
PERRY Benjamin MM Pte 200786 1/5th South Staffordshire Regt
PERRY Bertie MM Pte 20024 Machine Gun Corps
PERRY Caryl Henry MM+Bar Pte 5094 1/1st HAC(Infantry)
PERRY Cheistopher MM Pte 16479 6th Royal Dublin Fusiliers
PERRY Cyril Stanley MM Pte 41626 9th Norfolk Regt
PERRY Daniel MM L/Cpl 17517 10th Yorkshire Regt
PERRY Douglas G. MM Pte 81239 1/1st Essex Yeomanry
PERRY Edmund MM Pte 45483 12th Manchester Regt
PERRY Edward "MM,MID,CG(B)" CSM 73 Royal Engineers
PERRY Ernest C. MM Sjt 550218 Royal Engineers
PERRY F. MM Pte 386270 1 Fd Amb RAMC
PERRY F. MM Cpl 12468 9th Essex Regt
PERRY Frank MM Pte 33996 13th York & Lancaster Regt
PERRY Fred MM L/Sjt 12732 West Riding Regt
PERRY George MM Sjt 50615 1st East Yorkshire Regt
PERRY Harry P. MM Cpl 36552 East Surrey Regt
PERRY Henry MM L/Cpl 3198 12th Middlesex Regt
PERRY Henry MM Gnr 37078 RFA
PERRY Henry MM Pte R/16352 King's Royal Rifle Corps
PERRY Henry R. MM Pte A/201034 King's Royal Rifle Corps
PERRY Herbert MM Pte 203334 6th Wiltshire Regt
PERRY Herbert MM Pte 45474 55 Fd Amb RAMC DOW 18.10.18.
PERRY Herbert Frank MM Spr 1524 56 Div Sig Coy Royal Engineers
PERRY Horace N. MM Sjt 18321 1st Grenadier Guards
PERRY James MM Pte 25615 7th Royal West Kent Regt Died 19.10.17.
PERRY James MM Sjt 10027 9th Northumberland Fusiliers
PERRY James C. MM L/Cpl 32972 2nd Hampshire Regt
PERRY James H. MM L/Cpl 27297 North Lancashire Regt
PERRY John MM Sjt 24133 7th West Riding Regt
PERRY John C. MM+Bar L/Cpl 1084 Royal Sussex Regt
PERRY Maurice E. MM Cpl S/109 12th Rifle Brigade
PERRY Oliver Joseph MM Cpl 4905 13th Middlesex Regt KIA 18.8.16.
PERRY P. "MM,MIDx2" L/Cpl 8613 1st Essex Regt
PERRY Percy MM Cpl 1491 4th Bn GMGR
PERRY Percy Charles MM Cpl 98310 D/291 Bde RFA
PERRY Percy Robert MM L/Sjt 26524 1st Hampshire Regt Died 1.11.18.
PERRY Reginald MM L/Cpl 267931 14th Royal Welsh Fusiliers
PERRY Richard MM Cpl 2665 Rifle Brigade
PERRY Robert S. MM Cpl 57959 15th Highland Light Infantry
PERRY Sydney "MC,MM(1101 Sjt 9th Lancers)" Capt 2nd Royal West Surrey Regt KIA 7.8.18.
PERRY Thomas MM+Bar Cpl 931508 293 Bde RFA
PERRY Thomas H.A. MM Cpl 370989 8th London Regt
PERRY Thomas Stephen MM Pte 39091 Gloucestershire Regt
PERRY William H. MM Pte 95195 1st Liverpool Regt
PERRY William J. MM Pte 12522 1st Coldstream Guards
PERRYMAN Edgar MM Cpl 6867 Royal Fusiliers

PERRYMAN Fred MM Sjt 414021 Royal Engineers
PERRYMAN William Charles MM S/Sjt 534005 4(London)Fd Amb RAMC DOW 20.4.18.
PERT Walter D. MM Gnr 609 RFA
PERUSSE Adelard MM Pte 307127 8th Liverpool Regt
PESCOD Benjamin MM Cpl M2/049815 283 MT Coy Army Service Corps att X Corps HAG.KIA 28.9.18.
PESKETT Albert MM L/Cpl 21843 Royal West Surrey Regt
PESKETT George MM L/Cpl 8323 1st Royal West Kent Regt
PESTELL Edward J. MM Gnr 45756 RFA
PESTELL Frank C. MM Cpl 17658 Royal Sussex Regt
PESTER Ernest P. MM Cpl 113207 Royal Engineers
PESTER Joseph MM Cpl 19253 Royal Engineers
PETCH Charles MM Pte 203134 11th Essex Regt
PETCH Charles E. MM L/Sjt C/12525 King's Royal Rifle Corps
PETCH John A. "MM,MID" Pte 14582 8th Royal Berkshire Regt
PETCH Thomas C. MM Pte 201654 7th Middlesex Regt
PETCHEY James MM Pte 2059 22nd Royal Fusiliers KIA 22.6.17.
PETCHILL George S. MM Dvr 29095 RFA
PETERKIN George MM Pte 21937 1/4th Gordon Highlanders
PETERS A.E. MM Cpl 14311 6th Royal Dublin Fusiliers
PETERS Alexander MM Cpl 655251 75 Bde RFA
PETERS Arthur Jacob MM Pte 74154 10th Notts & Derby Regt
PETERS Arthur W. MM L/Sjt 30/253 8th Northumberland Fusiliers
PETERS Burtwell Walter MM Pte 10612 9th Essex Regt
PETERS Charles "MM,CG(F)" 2nd Cpl 11792 Royal Engineers
PETERS Charles Edward MM Sjt 2987 8th East Surrey Regt
PETERS David MM Sjt 66999 138 Fd Amb RAMC
PETERS Edward MM Gnr 82995 A/94 Bde RFA KIA 18.9.16.
PETERS Frederick MM Cpl 113435 B/178 Bde RFA
PETERS Frederick E. MM Pte 295132 4th London Regt
PETERS Frederick J. MM Sjt 1857 16th Rifle Brigade Died 13.6.17.
PETERS Frederick J. MM Gnr(SS) 14533 D/157 Bde RFA
PETERS Hamilton MM Sjt 9620 1st Border Regt
PETERS Harold C. MM Sjt 151600 104th Bn Machine Gun Corps
PETERS Henry T. MM Sjt Z/827 13th Rifle Brigade
PETERS James H. MM Pte 19151 2nd Welsh Regt
PETERS James William MM Spr 47728 21 Div Sig Coy Royal Engineers KIA 28.5.18.
PETERS John MM Pnr 85919 Royal Engineers
PETERS Joseph W. MM Pte 34720 6th Royal Warwickshire Regt
PETERS Mesheck MM Cpl 15109 11th Royal Welsh Fusiliers Died 7.9.18.
PETERS Reginald J. MM Cpl 60179 Royal Fusiliers
PETERS Thomas MM Sjt 280695 4th London Regt
PETERS Walter William MM Pte M2/155929 Army Service Corps
PETERS William MM Sjt 200492 Leicestershire Regt
PETERS William C. MM L/Cpl 122 Rifle Brigade
PETERS William F. MM Pte 26139 Notts & Derby Regt
PETERSON Arvid MM Pte 102564 Notts & Derby Regt
PETERSON Charles MM Pte 48260 Northumberland Fusiliers
PETERSON James G. MM Pte 27285 9th Royal Highlanders
PETERSON John E. MM Spr 508084 Royal Engineers
PETERSON Montague MM L/Cpl 69537 6th Bn Tank Corps
PETHERAM Robert W. MM L/Cpl 165368 101st Bn Machine Gun Corps
PETHICK Ernest C. MM Dvr 47145 41 Div Ammn Col RFA
PETHYBRIDGE Frank MM Sjt 11402 12 Fd Coy Royal Engineers
PETIT James John MM Sjt 68334 308 Siege Bty RGA
PETLEY Claude MM L/Sjt 2664 2/1st HAC(Inf)
PETO John MM Sjt 31725 RGA
PETRE William MM Pte 8112 38 Fd Amb RAMC
PETRE William J. MM+Bar Sjt 240404 Border Regt
PETRIE Alexander MM Pte 81113 RAMC
PETRIE Charles MM Pte 1286 1/5th Royal Highlanders
PETRIE Conrad E. MM Cpl 89260 1st Middlesex Regt
PETRIE Donald "DCM,MM" L/Cpl 202339 1/4th Royal Highlanders
PETRIE Edward MM Pte 13456 6/7th Royal Scots Fusiliers
PETRIE George MM Sjt 75730 145 Hy Bty RGA
PETRIE George A. MM Pte 31608 18th Highland Light Infantry
PETRIE Harold MM Dvr 966735 RFA
PETRIE Harry MM Sjt 13/727 13th East Yorkshire Regt
PETRIE James MM Sjt 23049 Machine Gun Corps
PETRIE James MM+Bar Sjt 47366 Machine Gun Corps(Cavalry)
PETRIE John MM L/Cpl 23500 6th King's Own Scottish Borderers
PETRIE John MM L/Cpl 62948 RAMC
PETRIE John Duncan MM Sjt 34 1/4th Royal Highlanders
PETRIE Joseph MM Pte 332379 9th Liverpool Regt
PETRIE Lawrence MM Pte 68259 2nd London Regt
PETRIE Louis G. MM Cpl 474616 529 Fd Coy Royal Engineers
PETRIE Robert F. MM Pte 514177 14th London Regt
PETRIE William F. MM Bdr 33414 D/50 Bde RFA
PETRIE William G. MM L/Cpl 11103 2nd Worcestershire Regt
PETRUSE Percival MM L/Sjt 47717 22nd Northumberland Fusiliers
PETT Edgar J. MM L/Cpl 531344 1/15th London Regt
PETT William MM Pte 1673 2nd Middlesex Regt att HQ 23 Inf Bde
PETTECREW Edward MM Pte 29626 16th Manchester Regt
PETTENGELL Bertie MM L/Cpl 17568 2nd Bedfordshire Regt
PETTERSEN Peter E. MM L/Cpl 146712 Royal Engineers
PETTERSON J. MM Pte 21569 Machine Gun Corps
PETTET John MM Pte 79131 10th Royal Fusiliers
PETTICAN Frank MM Pte DM2/155780 Army Service Corps
PETTICAN Harry MM Pte 26268 9th Essex Regt KIA 18.90.18.
PETTIFER Arthur MM Pte 378581 Labour Corps
PETTIFER Frank MM Pte 5855 1st Royal Munster Fusiliers
PETTIFER George MM Pte 11514 5th Royal Berkshire Regt KIA 26.8.18.
PETTIFER John W. MM Bdr 119186 RFA
PETTIFER Willie MM L/Cpl 467397 Royal Engineers
PETTIGREW Keeble MM+Bar Cpl 106427 Special Coy Royal Engineers
PETTIGREW Peter MM L/Cpl 146710 Royal Engineers
PETTIS Alfred MM Pte R/33844 2nd King's Royal Rifle Corps
PETTIT George H. MM Pte 353617 7th London Regt
PETTIT Stephen MM Pte 15622 1 Special Coy Middlesex Regt
PETTIT William A. MM L/Cpl 250014 Royal Engineers
PETTITT Ebenezer Wallace MM L/Cpl 50874 8th Royal Fusiliers
PETTITT Francis Frank MM Pte 201336 1/4th West Riding Regt KIA 26.4.18.
PETTITT Francis T. MM Cpl 201064 2/4th York & Lancaster Regt
PETTITT Frank MM Sjt 240146 1/8th Middlesex Regt
PETTITT Frederick G. MM Spr 85237 Royal Engineers
PETTITT George MM Pte 49435 Royal Fusiliers
PETTITT George E. MM Cpl 80244 1/1st Essex Yeomanry
PETTITT Harry MM Sjt 53919 A/98 Bde RFA
PETTITT Richard MM L/Sjt 14418 11th Suffolk Regt
PETTITT William A. MM Sjt 7004 2nd Royal Fusiliers
PETTITT William J. MM Dvr 36336 RFA
PETTMAN Arthur MM Cpl 469 Royal Engineers
PETTS William E. MM Gnr 181110 D/77 Bde RFA
PETTY Albert Vincent George MM Pte 50231 2nd Bedfordshire Regt KIA 19.9.18.
PETTY Amos MM L/Cpl 2854 8th Hussars
PETTY Fred MM Pte 46423 5th Yorkshire Light Infantry
PETTY Horace Edward MM Pte 28221 1st Royal Dublin Fusiliers KIA 3.4.18.
PETTY James Marshall "MC,MM,MID(51009 Sjt)" 2Lt 105 Fd Coy Royal Engineers
PETTY John Darneley MM L/Cpl 10/1099 10th East Yorkshire Regt
PETTY Joseph MM Sjt 2129 2/1st(Bucks)Bn Oxf & Bucks Light Infantry
PETTY William Fenton MM Gnr 3455 1/2(West Riding)Bde RFA
PETVIN Edward J. MM Pte 240798 Somerset Light Infantry
PEVERELL Charles MM Dvr 41460 RFA
PEVERILL Lewis W. MM Dvr 599676 28 Bty 9 Bde RFA
PEVERLEY Robinson MM Cpl 79591 RGA
PEVERLEY William H. MM Pte 41076 Lancashire Fusiliers
PEW James Robert MM Pte 19027 7th West Yorkshire Regt
PEXTON Arthur E. MM Pte 427212 10th London Regt
PEYTO William MM L/Cpl 12353 King's Royal Rifle Corps
PFOB Stanley MM Pte 13116 8th Norfolk Regt
PHAIR Robert MM Gnr 745843 C/70 Bde RFA
PHARAOH Alfred J. "DCM,MM" Pte 22938 Border Regt
PHAROAH Alfred MM L/Sjt 25110 15th Durham Light Infantry KIA 10.4.17.
PHAROAH Andrew J. MM Sjt 50670 RAMC
PHARRO Reginald MM Dvr 38641 D/83 Bde RFA
PHEAR Harold William "MM,MID" Sjt 11661 C/59 Bde RFA
PHEASANT Ernest Walter MM Pte 242080 2/5th York & Lancaster Regt
PHEASANT James A. MM Cpl 63752 RAMC
PHEASEY Harry MM Gnr 830783 5 Div Ammn Col RFA
PHEAZEY George W. MM Gnr Fitter 70006 D/147 Bde RFA
PHELAN Christopher MM Pte 7805 Royal Irish Regt
PHELAN Kevin MM Pte 21060 Machine Gun Corps
PHELAN Nelson MM Pte 3044 19th Hussars
PHELAN Sydney Francis MM L/Cpl 695090 1/22nd London Regt
PHELAN Thomas MM Pte 21375 Arg & Suth Highlanders
PHELP T.H. MM Bdr 66060 RFA
PHELPS Bert MM Sjt 771469 C/250 Bde RFA

PHELPS Charles B. MM Pte 18671 10th Worcestershire Regt
PHELPS Edward C. MM Cpl 13764 23rd Middlesex Regt
PHELPS Frank MM Pte 10477 Worcestershire Regt
PHELPS Frederick C. MM+Bar Cpl 13869 3 Div Sig Coy Royal Engineers
PHELPS Frederick George MM Gnr 102288 D/123 Bde RFA DOW 22.10.17.
PHELPS Herbert W. MM Pte 1054 Lincolnshire Regt
PHELPS John A. MM L/Cpl B/200699 Rifle Brigade
PHELPS Nelson MM Gnr 39185 30 Bde RFA
PHELPS William A. MM Sjt 720417 1/24th London Regt
PHENNAH Thomas Henry MM Cpl 276499 V/9 Heavy TM Bty RGA
PHILBEN Joseph MM Pte 201757 Seaforth Highlanders
PHILBEY Albert H. MM Pte 14186 1/5th Bedfordshire Regt
PHILBIN James MM Pte 29042 1st East Lancashire Regt
PHILBRICK Ernest G. MM Pte 8814 129 Fd Amb RAMC
PHILBY Oswald Percy MM Pte 1162 22nd London Regt KIA 5.10.16.
PHILCOX Walter G. MM Cpl T/30434 Army Service Corps
PHILIP Alfred J. MM Sjt 1456 1/7th Middlesex Regt
PHILIP D. MM+Bar Cpl 46583 5 Fd Amb RAMC
PHILIP David T. MM Gnr 201444 'G' Bn Tank Corps
PHILIP Edward MM Pte 202035 1/6th Arg & Suth Highlanders
PHILIP R. MM Pte 50560 MGC(Cavalry)
PHILIPS Herbert G. MM Cpl 54368 4th Middlesex Regt
PHILIPSON David "DCM,MM" Sjt 86412 178 Tunnelling Coy Royal Engineers
PHILIPSON Henry Livingstone MM Pte 6724 6th Northumberland Fusiliers DOW 14.2.17.
PHILIPSON Thomas Stanley MM Spr 302022 2 Div Sig Coy Royal Engineers KIA 29.9.18.
PHILLIMORE Gilbert W. MM Sjt 275079 6th Essex Regt
PHILLIMORE Percy MM Gnr 77296 RHA
PHILLINGHAM Joseph MM Cpl 3418 9th Lancashire Fusiliers
PHILLIPPE Percy A.E. MM Pte 9909 Royal West Surrey Regt
PHILLIPPS John R. MM+Bar Bdr 52008 18 Bde RFA
PHILLIPPS S.F. MM L/Cpl 15337 Lincolnshire Regt
PHILLIPS A.E. MM Cpl 63453 RAMC
PHILLIPS Albert MM Pte M2/105228 Army Service Corps
PHILLIPS Albert Frederick MM L/Cpl 15841 10th Essex Regt KIA 31.10.18.
PHILLIPS Albert P. MM Gnr 170408 RFA
PHILLIPS Alfred MM CQMS C/9167 King's Royal Rifle Corps
PHILLIPS Alfred E. MM(14th Gloucs att RWK)+Bar L/Cpl 38759 7th Royal West Kent Regt
PHILLIPS Arthur MM Sjt 30525 12th Highland Light Infantry
PHILLIPS Arthur L. MM Cpl 65747 1/5th Northumberland Fusiliers
PHILLIPS Cecil B. MM Pte 471850 12th London Regt
PHILLIPS Charles MM Cpl 10051 5th Northamptonshire Regt
PHILLIPS Charles E. MM Pte 241009 5th Devonshire Regt
PHILLIPS Charles Edward Stewart MM L/Cpl 11116 Durham Light Infantry
PHILLIPS Charles H. MM Sjt 41395 5th Royal Berkshire Regt
PHILLIPS Charles H. MM Pte 23774 Shropshire Light Infantry
PHILLIPS Daniel MM+Bar Cpl 53632 2nd Welsh Regt DOW 25.10.18.
PHILLIPS David MM Pte 9549 8/10th Gordon Highlanders
PHILLIPS David L. MM Pte 320071 24th Welsh Regt
PHILLIPS Dick MM+Bar Cpl 65788 13th Royal Fusiliers
PHILLIPS E.A. MM Pte 452771 London Regt
PHILLIPS Edgar MM Dvr 773 238 Bde RFA
PHILLIPS Edgar B. MM Spr 51640 Royal Engineers
PHILLIPS Edgar George MM Gnr 290934 126 Heavy Bty RGA DOW 24.3.18.
PHILLIPS Edward MM Pte 23087 1st Royal Inniskilling Fusiliers
PHILLIPS Edward MM Dvr 1466 D/122 Bde RFA
PHILLIPS Edward J. MM Sjt 8682 1st Gloucestershire Regt
PHILLIPS Edward J. MM CSM 201576 1st London Regt
PHILLIPS Edwin "MM,MID" L/Cpl 41272 Royal Engineers
PHILLIPS Ernest MM L/Cpl 4934 Rifle Brigade
PHILLIPS Ernest MM Pte 8077 1st Gloucestershire Regt
PHILLIPS Ernest MM Pte 17681 9th Cheshire Regt
PHILLIPS Evan D. MM L/Sjt 12668 Welsh Regt
PHILLIPS Evelyn MM Gnr 54057 RGA
PHILLIPS Francis G. MM L/Cpl T4/240803 Army Service Corps
PHILLIPS Frank MM Gnr 775647 310 Bde RFA
PHILLIPS Frank MM Sjt 5695 3 Fd Amb RAMC
PHILLIPS Frank Campbell MM Spr 96752 33 Div Sig Coy Royal Engineers
PHILLIPS Fred MM Dvr 61236 27 Bde RFA
PHILLIPS Frederick MM Cpl 11801 Shropshire Light Infantry Died 7.1.17.
PHILLIPS Frederick MM Pte 34574 Labour Corps
PHILLIPS Frederick A. MM Pte 3974 Machine Gun Corps
PHILLIPS Frederick G. MM Sjt 265813 1/1st Hertfordshire Regt
PHILLIPS G.M. MM Dvr 625687 RFA
PHILLIPS George MM Sjt 16895 7th South Staffordshire Regt
PHILLIPS George MM Sjt 687 Royal Engineers
PHILLIPS George Angus MM Dvr 740087 266 Bde RFA
PHILLIPS George B. MM Sjt 120270 47th Bn Machine Gun Corps
PHILLIPS George H. MM Pte 43613 4th Hampshire Regt
PHILLIPS George T. MM Pte 393301 9th London Regt
PHILLIPS George William MM Cpl 69415 Tank Corps KIA 8.1.18.
PHILLIPS Griffith MM L/Cpl 495895 13th London Regt
PHILLIPS Harold Llewellyn MM Pte 39068 2/8th Lancashire Fusiliers KIA 18.11.17.
PHILLIPS Harry MM Pte 22384 1st Worcestershire Regt KIA 24.1.18.
PHILLIPS Harry Howard MM Pnr 443973 42 Div Sig Coy Royal Engineers
PHILLIPS Harry L. MM Pte 41206 1/7th Royal Highlanders
PHILLIPS Henry MM Pte 27318 1st Royal Welsh Fusiliers KIA 4.5.17.
PHILLIPS Henry MM CSM 21490 88 Coy Machine Gun Corps
PHILLIPS Henry MM Cpl 47068 18 Bde RFA
PHILLIPS Henry J. MM Pte 20758 Manchester Regt
PHILLIPS Herbert MM Pte 50651 RAMC
PHILLIPS Herbert J. MM Pte 3426 Royal Sussex Regt
PHILLIPS Horace MM Gnr 54084 326 Siege Bty RGA
PHILLIPS Hubert Cecil MM Pte 81319 88 Coy Machine Gun Corps
PHILLIPS Ieuan MM Pte 48563 130 Fd Amb RAMC DOW 1.9.18.
PHILLIPS Ivor MM L/Cpl 265634 1/1st Monmouthshire Regt
PHILLIPS J. "DCM,MM" Pte 38587 Yorkshire Light Infantry
PHILLIPS Jabez MM Pte 16890 Royal Welsh Fusiliers
PHILLIPS James MM Pte 42828 4th Yorkshire Light Infantry
PHILLIPS James MM Spr 58904 106 Fd Coy Royal Engineers KIA 17.2.17.
PHILLIPS John MM Sjt 49031 4th Bedfordshire Regt
PHILLIPS John MM L/Cpl 6486 8th East Kent Regt
PHILLIPS John MM Sjt 4653 10th Royal Warwickshire Regt DOW 11.3.19.
PHILLIPS John MM Pte 242206 Worcestershire Regt
PHILLIPS John MM CQMS 6825 1st Royal West Surrey Regt
PHILLIPS John MM Pte 8116 1st East Kent Regt
PHILLIPS John "MM,MSM" Sjt 50753 Labour Corps
PHILLIPS John MM Pte 64378 RAMC
PHILLIPS John R. MM Pte 295122 4th London Regt
PHILLIPS John Sydney MM Cpl 1833 138 Heavy Bty RGA
PHILLIPS John William MM Gnr 33394 B/70 Bde RFA DOW 11.8.17.
PHILLIPS Joseph MM Cpl 12355 10th Shropshire Light Infantry
PHILLIPS Joseph MM Pte 16813 6th South Staffordshire Regt
PHILLIPS Joseph Ernest MM L/Cpl 38127 23rd Northumberland Fusiliers
PHILLIPS Joseph F. MM Pte 62769 Machine Gun Corps
PHILLIPS Josiah MM Pte 5935 9th Rifle Brigade KIA 2.6.17.
PHILLIPS L. MM Pte 593508 London Regt
PHILLIPS Lewis V. MM Pnr 172551 19 Div Sig Coy Royal Engineers
PHILLIPS Luther MM Pte 188 1st Welsh Guards
PHILLIPS Major Samuel MM CQMS 225061 1/1st Monmouthshire Regt
PHILLIPS Michael MM Pte 30152 5/6th Royal Scots
PHILLIPS Patrick "DCM,MM" Pte 278878 1/7th Arg & Suth Highlanders
PHILLIPS Percy James MM Pte 240432 1/5th Devonshire Regt DOW 15.9.18.
PHILLIPS Philip J. MM Pte 25964 Welsh Regt
PHILLIPS Phillip S. MM L/Cpl 201412 Royal Scots Fusiliers
PHILLIPS Reginald MM CSM 13148 10th Gloucestershire Regt KIA 19.8.16.
PHILLIPS Reginald G. MM Cpl 76692 RGA
PHILLIPS Richard J. MM L/Sjt 64847 9th Welsh Regt
PHILLIPS Ritchie MM Pte 490600 13th London Regt
PHILLIPS Robert MM Spr 57929 36 Div Sig Coy Royal Engineers
PHILLIPS Sidney MM Sjt 13432 Royal Welsh Fusiliers
PHILLIPS Sidney C. MM Cpl 49613 Royal Engineers
PHILLIPS Sidney George MM Pte 12298 RAMC
PHILLIPS Stanley A. MM Pte 205877 6th Royal West Kent Regt
PHILLIPS Sydney MM Pte 19471 Duke of Cornwall's LI
PHILLIPS Thomas MM L/Cpl 53739 Welsh Regt

PHILLIPS Thomas MM Pte 33175 1st Wiltshire Regt
PHILLIPS Thomas MM L/Cpl 18371 11th Notts & Derby Regt
PHILLIPS Thomas J. MM Spr 49764 Royal Engineers
PHILLIPS Thomas L. MM Gnr 371218 RGA
PHILLIPS Thomas Spencer MM Pte 5877 7th Royal Sussex Regt
PHILLIPS Walter Arthur MM Pte 1220 1st Rifle Brigade KIA 13.10.17.
PHILLIPS Walter E. MM Bdr 48593 5 Bde RFA
PHILLIPS William MM Pte 42376 12 Fd Amb RAMC
PHILLIPS William MM Pte 1320 1st Welsh Guards
PHILLIPS William MM Pte 1422 1/6th Welsh Regt
PHILLIPS William MM Pte 14345 1st South Wales Borderers
PHILLIPS William MM Spr 500069 Royal Engineers
PHILLIPS William C. MM Sjt 36153 Welsh Regt
PHILLIPS William G. MM Sjt Farrier 1844 RFA
PHILLIPS William Henry MM Pte 7372 6th Somerset Light Infantry
PHILLIPS William J. MM Spr 158326 176 Tunnelling Coy Royal Engineers
PHILLIPS William J. MM Sjt 35257 7 Bde RHA
PHILLIPSON Isaac MM Pte 241213 1/5th Royal Lancaster Regt DOW 9.12.17.
PHILLIPSON John Francis MM Sjt 12301 33rd Bn Machine Gun Corps
PHILLIPSON Leonard George MM Cpl 42646 25 Coy Machine Gun Corps KIA 24.3.18.
PHILLIPSON Thomas MM L/Sjt 33623 9th Cheshire Regt
PHILLIPSON Thomas MM Cpl H/270076 1/1st Northumberland Yeo
PHILLPOT Percy S. MM Cpl S/1857 Rifle Brigade
PHILLPOTT David MM Pte 7944 6th East Kent Regt KIA 5.10.17.
PHILP Joseph MM Gnr 45928 B/87 Bde RFA
PHILP Thomas MM Gnr 7690 RFA
PHILP Thomas Johnston MM Sjt T4/210398 6 Reserve Park Army Service Corps
PHILP W. MM Pte 473669 1/12th London Regt KIA 30.11.17.
PHILPIN James MM Pte 29081 South Wales Borderers
PHILPOT Arthur J. MM Pte 92471 Tank Corps
PHILPOT Horace D. MM Pte 204158 4th Bedfordshire Regt
PHILPOT Walter J. "DCM+Bar,MM" BSM 59343 B/123 Bde RFA
PHILPOT William E. MM Pte 124117 Machine Gun Corps
PHILPOT William J.F. MM Pte 4743 2nd Royal West Kent Regt
PHILPOTT Edward J. MM L/Cpl 18991 33 Coy Machine Gun Corps
PHILPOTT Ernest W.. MM Sjt 11178 282 Army Tps Coy Royal Engineers
PHILPOTT Frederick H. MM Sjt 438760 66 Div Sig Coy Royal Engineers
PHILPOTT George Edward MM Spr 104985 171 Tunnelling Coy Royal Engineers
PHILPOTT James E. MM Sjt 889591 D/168 Bde RFA
PHILPOTT John Charles MM Cpl 40149 Royal West Surrey Regt
PHILPOTT L.C.H. MM Sjt 21316 Northumberland Fusiliers
PHILPOTT Walter George MM Sjt 22691 80 Siege Bty RGA
PHILPOTTS Charlie A. MM L/Cpl 59800 15th Welsh Regt
PHILPOTTS Harry MM Pte 40307 4th Worcestershire Regt
PHILPOTTS William Charles MM Sjt 955086 B/236 Bde RFA
PHILPS B. MM L/Cpl 11433 2nd Royal Scots
PHILPS Ernest H. MM Bdr 78564 RFA
PHIMISTER Andrew "MM,CG(F)" L/Cpl 23828 12th Royal Scots Fusiliers
PHIMISTER Robert G. MM Pte 265749 Seaforth Highlanders
PHIPPEN Albert E. MM CQMS 17195 20th Manchester Regt
PHIPPEN Frank D. MM Sjt 23685 3 Div Sig Coy Royal Engineers
PHIPPEN Lot MM Sjt 14657 7th Somerset Light Infantry
PHIPPIN Thomas C.M. "DCM,MM" Sjt 11467 1st Grenadier Guards
PHIPPS Albert MM Dvr 86370 RFA
PHIPPS Alfred MM Pte 201898 4th Worcestershire Regt KIA 29.9.18.
PHIPPS Charles H. MM Pte 41262 1st Duke of Cornwall's LI
PHIPPS E.E. MM Cpl 74408 RFA
PHIPPS Frank J. MM Bdr 55361 RFA
PHIPPS George Henry MM Pte 11474 1st Notts & Derby Regt
PHIPPS George Henry Arthur MM Spr 103469 105 Fd Coy Royal Engineers
PHIPPS George J. MM Sjt 266783 6th Royal Warwickshire Regt
PHIPPS Herbert MM Sjt 17587 12th Gloucestershire Regt
PHIPPS John MM+Bar Cpl 282679 1/7th Lancashire Fusiliers
PHIPPS Joseph W. MM L/Bdr 236756 80 Bty 15 Bde RFA
PHIPPS Leonard MM Pte 64963 2nd Worcestershire Regt
PHIPPS William C. MM Pte 76986 2nd Bn Tank Corps
PHIPPS William Charles MM L/Sjt 9/3740 9th Royal Munster Fusiliers
PHIPPS William Henry John MM+Bar Pte 235319 2nd Suffolk Regt DOW 9.10.18.
PHIZACKLEA George T. MM 2nd Cpl 30454 Royal Engineers
PHOENIX Thomas MM Pte 55355 RAMC
PHOENIX William MM 2nd Cpl 57513 150 Fd Coy Royal Engineers DOW 30.1.17.
PHYALL Alfred MM Cpl 50848 9th Highland Light Infantry
PHYALL Edward C. MM Pte 521 6th Royal West Kent Regt
PHYALL Stephen Edward MM Pte 386 6th Royal West Kent Regt KIA 3.7.16.
PHYPERS Alfred W. MM L/Cpl 422303 10th London Regt
PHYPERS Henry T. MM Sjt 330807 1/1st Cambridgeshire Regt
PHYSICK William MM Cpl 6467 Machine Gun Corps
PHYTHIAN Albert V. MM Spr 440327 Royal Engineers
PICK Albert MM Pte 18895 Leicestershire Regt
PICK Arnold W. MM Spr 546699 Royal Engineers
PICK Ben MM 2nd Cpl 16045 Royal Engineers
PICK Walter MM Pte 62179 2nd Northumberland Fusiliers
PICKARD Aaron MM Pte 270087 12th Royal Scots
PICKARD Edwin MM Sjt 10090 2nd Scots Guards
PICKARD Frank "DCM,MM,MID" L/Cpl 8636 1st Northamptonshire Regt
PICKARD Frederick MM Pte 26136 8th Yorkshire Regt
PICKARD Frederick W. MM Gnr 7336 A/160 Bde RFA
PICKARD Harry MM Cpl 1083 7th Lincolnshire Regt
PICKARD Henry MM Pte 45673 4th Hampshire Regt
PICKARD Joseph MM Cpl 7177 IV Corps Cyclist Bn Army Cyclist Corps
PICKARD Joseph MM Cpl 12538 7th Lincolnshire Regt DOW 21.10.18.
PICKARD Nelson T. MM Pte 9404 2nd Hampshire Regt
PICKARD Percy T. MM SM 386014 RAMC
PICKARD Sidney MM Pte 41282 West Yorkshire Regt
PICKARD Wallace MM Pte 11089 5th Royal Berkshire Regt
PICKAVANCE David MM Sjt 432163 Royal Engineers
PICKAVANCE David MM L/Cpl 240449 1/5th South Lancashire Regt KIA 30.11.17.
PICKAVANCE James MM Pte 3/8676 6th Royal Irish Regt KIA 9.9.16.
PICKAVANCE James J. MM Pte 33403 Manchester Regt
PICKAVANCE Joseph MM Pte 10495 2nd South Lancashire Regt
PICKEN Ernest MM Cpl 200335 South Staffordshire Regt
PICKEN William A. MM Gnr 74462 RFA
PICKENINGS Robert Edward MM Pte 13827 1st East Lancashire Regt KIA 28.10.18.
PICKERILL Frederick MM Sjt 46778 11th Northumberland Fusiliers
PICKERILL James MM L/Cpl 281963 7th Lancashire Fusiliers
PICKERILL Thomas MM+Bar Sjt 9497 2nd South Staffordshire Regt KIA 23.8.18.
PICKERING Albert Amos MM Spr 167721 209 Fd Coy Royal Engineers
PICKERING Arthur MM Pte 388537 2/2(Northumbrian)Fd Amb RAMC
PICKERING Arthur MM S/Sjt 629 Army Ordnance Corps
PICKERING Arthur C. MM Cpl 265517 Gloucestershire Regt
PICKERING F. MM Sjt 405244 RAMC
PICKERING Francis MM Pte 8918 2nd Royal Welsh Fusiliers
PICKERING George MM Bdr 37367 36 Bde RFA
PICKERING George MM Dvr T4/084356 Army Service Corps KIA 22.3.18.
PICKERING George H. MM Spr 546793 Royal Engineers
PICKERING George T. MM Sjt 4291 9th Lancers
PICKERING George W. MM Sjt 20895 2nd York & Lancaster Regt
PICKERING Gordon MM Sjt 201286 Royal Lancaster Regt
PICKERING H. "MM,MID" Sjt 11532 2nd Durham Light Infantry
PICKERING Harry MM+Bar Pte 19129 East Kent Regt
PICKERING Herbert MM Pte 40671 Leicestershire Regt
PICKERING John MM+Bar Spr 102160 170 Tunnelling Coy Royal Engineers
PICKERING John R. MM Cpl 42499 RAMC
PICKERING John Summers MM Pte 388579 2/2(Northumbrian)Fd Amb RAMC
PICKERING John William MM L/Cpl 12782 19th Manchester Regt
PICKERING Joseph "MM,MID" Sjt 7680 Northumberland Fusiliers
PICKERING Luke MM Pte 11573 9th Royal Warwickshire Regt
PICKERING Thomas G. MM Sjt 17041 Royal Welsh Fusiliers
PICKERING Thomas W. MM+Bar Pte 9436 2nd Yorkshire Regt
PICKERING W.J. MM L/Cpl 16913 2nd Essex Regt
PICKERING Walter MM Sjt 34877 1st Royal Welsh Fusiliers KIA 4.5.17.

PICKERING William MM L/Bdr 710503 RFA
PICKERING William MM Cpl 1196 1/5th Leicestershire Regt
PICKERING William C. MM Dvr 72538 RFA
PICKERS Albert MM Sjt 69627 RHA
PICKERSGILL Arthur MM Sjt 7974 10th Hussars
PICKERSGILL David MM Spr 253357 18 Div Sig Coy Royal Engineers
PICKERSGILL Frank MM Pte 14/473 York & Lancaster Regt
PICKERSGILL Harry MM Sjt 65203 Northumberland Fusiliers
PICKERSGILL Horace MM Pte 612579 19th London Regt
PICKERSGILL Ivy MM Spr 151325 253 Tunnelling Coy Royal Engineers
PICKERSGILL John W. MM+Bar Sjt 36337 9th Royal Welsh Fusiliers
PICKERSGILL W.W. MM Pte 301694 Durham Light Infantry
PICKERSGILL Walter A. MM L/Cpl 7976 2nd Yorkshire Regt
PICKERSGILL William MM Bdr 290855 RGA
PICKETT Albert MM L/Cpl 37541 10th Essex Regt KIA 21.9.18.
PICKETT Albert E. MM CSM 9226 Royal Engineers
PICKETT Charles A. "MM,MID" Spr 34912 Royal Engineers
PICKETT Charles S. MM Pte 62387 9th Royal Fusiliers
PICKETT Cuthbert MM Cpl(SS) 937 5th Dragoon Guards
PICKETT Edwin Thomas MM Sjt 10717 Leicestershire Regt
PICKETT Francis A.F. MM Sjt M/28593 Army Service Corps
PICKETT Frederick MM RSM 79429 RGA
PICKETT Harry MM Pte 23324 12th South Wales Borderers
PICKETT John MM+Bar Pte 10709 Machine Gun Corps
PICKETT Leonard MM+Bar Sjt 64440 D/87 Bde RFA
PICKFORD Alan Norman MM Sjt 230083 1/1st Dorset Yeomanry
PICKFORD Eli MM Gnr 34438 113 Heavy Bty RGA
PICKFORD John W. MM Pte 25848 Royal Welsh Fusiliers
PICKFORD Joseph J. MM Pte 295202 12th Somerset Light Infantry
PICKFORD Percy MM Sjt 805429 C/231 Bde RFA KIA 5.10.18.
PICKFORD Raymond MM Pte 235430 17th Royal Welsh Fusiliers KIA 8.10.18.
PICKFORD Richard E. MM Pte 17441 7th East Kent Regt
PICKFORD Wilfred MM Sjt 2714 1/14th London Regt
PICKIS Sydney MM Gnr 935831 RFA
PICKLES Arnold MM Dvr 60922 80 Fd Coy Royal Engineers
PICKLES Arthur MM Pte 325151 2/7th Royal Warwickshire Regt DOW 8.4.18.
PICKLES Benjamin MM L/Cpl 15887 1/6th West Yorkshire Regt
PICKLES Edward MM Cpl 3/12442 2nd West Riding Regt
PICKLES Ernest MM Pte 936 16th West Yorkshire Regt
PICKLES Fred MM Dvr T2/12744 Army Service Corps
PICKLES Gilbert Owen MM Pte 242029 Leicestershire Regt
PICKLES Harry MM Pte 18/1288 1/5th West Yorkshire Regt KIA 29.10.18.
PICKLES Harry "MM,MID" Cpl 82170 A/50 Bde RFA
PICKLES Henry MM Pte 55003 Royal Fusiliers
PICKLES Herbert B. MM Spr 59772 Royal Engineers
PICKLES Horace E. MM Sjt 241047 West Yorkshire Regt
PICKLES John W. MM L/Cpl 207277 Royal Engineers
PICKLES Joseph MM Dvr 109970 RFA
PICKLES Percy MM L/Cpl 3176 West Yorkshire Regt
PICKLES Richard MM L/Cpl 38831 Northumberland Fusiliers
PICKLES Walter MM Gnr Sig 18134 C/170 Bde RFA
PICKRELL Albert H. MM Pte 47484 RAMC
PICKSLEY Harry MM L/Cpl 11816 7th Lincolnshire Regt
PICKTHALL William MM Pte 240750 2/6th West Yorkshire Regt KIA 3.5.17.
PICKUP Albert MM Pte 21691 18th Lancashire Fusiliers
PICKUP Cyril MM Sjt 265482 1/6th Cheshire Regt KIA 20.9.17.
PICKUP Edmund MM Pte 8086 1st East Lancashire Regt
PICKUP Harry "MM,MID" Cpl 39394 33 Bde RFA
PICKUP J. MM Sjt 281161 7th Lancashire Fusiliers
PICKUP James W. MM Pte 204716 Lancashire Fusiliers
PICKUP John MM Pte 12873 7th East Lancashire Regt
PICKUP Thomas "MM,MSM" Bdr 45595 Y/12 Med TM Bty RFA
PICKUP Thomas MM Gnr 8686 RFA
PICKUP William MM Dvr 676655 D/275 Bde RFA
PICKVANCE James MM L/Cpl 206268 1st Worcestershire Regt DOW 28.8.18.
PICKWICK William A. MM Sjt 88982 C/48 Bde RFA
PICKWORTH Frank R. MM Gnr 2676 Tank Corps
PICKWORTH Percy MM Pte 28863 Royal Lancaster Regt
PICKWORTH Robert Turner MM Bdr 64365 RGA
PICTON Bertie MM Sjt 371050 RGA
PICTON Frederick John Llewellyn MM Lt 290 Royal Sussex Regt Died 6.2.18.
PICTON John MM Pte 18021 3/5th Lancashire Fusiliers DOW 15.11.17.
PICTON Stanley Frederick MM L/Cpl 266094 8th Bedfordshire Regt
PICTON Thomas MM Pte 48440 RAMC
PIDCOCK Benjamin B. MM CQMS 206 17th Royal Fusiliers
PIDCOCK Harold MM Bdr 99598 RGA
PIDDINGTON Frank MM Pte 265670 1/1st Bucks Bn Oxf & Bucks Light Infantry
PIDGEON William J. MM Sjt 21012 Gloucestershire Regt
PIDGEON William L. MM Pte 457347 RAMC
PIDGLEY Daniel MM L/Cpl 7657 Machine Gun Corps
PIELOW John J. MM Spr 30875 Royal Engineers
PIERCE Charles E. MM Cpl 71957 RHA
PIERCE Frank "DCM,MM" Sjt R/2295 4th King's Royal Rifle Corps
PIERCE Frank MM Gnr 343 Machine Gun Corps(Motors)
PIERCE Frederick A. MM Pte 4014 Royal West Kent Regt
PIERCE Harold MM Pte 1957 7th Royal West Kent Regt KIA 12.10.17.
PIERCE James W.G. MM Sjt 34878 Royal Welsh Fusiliers
PIERCE John F. MM+Bar L/Cpl 24580 7th Royal West Surrey Regt
PIERCE John O. MM Pte 14194 10th Royal Welsh Fusiliers
PIERCE Matthew MM L/Cpl 29009 Machine Gun Corps
PIERCE Robert MM L/Bdr 706331 C/210 Bde RFA
PIERCE Robert "DCM,MM" Sjt 339017 98 Fd Amb RAMC
PIERCE Robert D. MM Pte 35358 Liverpool Regt
PIERCE Robert H. MM Cpl 1432 9th Royal Sussex Regt
PIERCE William MM Pte 345597 24th Royal Welsh Fusiliers
PIERCE William E. MM L/Cpl 25396 70 Fd Coy Royal Engineers
PIERCE William J. MM Pte 63068 9th Welsh Regt
PIERCY Edward MM Sjt 78109 15 Div Ammn Col RFA
PIERCY H. MM Sjt 18169 13th Essex Regt
PIERCY James MM Cpl 2091 1/7th Northumberland Fusiliers KIA 14.11.16.
PIERCY Thomas Victor MM Sjt 15540 7th Bedfordshire Regt DOW 7.4.18.
PIERCY William MM Sjt 1766 Royal Engineers
PIERPOINT Harry MM Pte 36938 Royal Welsh Fusiliers
PIERRE Harold S. MM Sjt 46487 127 Bty 29 Bde RFA
PIERS Thomas "MM,MSM,MID" Sjt 498187 476 Fd Coy Royal Engineers
PIERSON Joseph MM L/Cpl 23839 4 Div Sig Coy Royal Engineers
PIFF George E. MM Pte 1604 1st Northumberland Fusiliers
PIFF William MM+Bar Spr 74384 Royal Engineers
PIFF William H. MM Spr 43707 Royal Engineers
PIGG Albert Edward Wheatley MM Pte 128059 40th Bn Machine Gun Corps DOW 9.4.18.
PIGG Ernest "MM,MID" L/Sjt 824 1/1st Northumberland Yeo
PIGG Henry Charles MM Spr 58215 25 Div Sig Coy Royal Engineers
PIGG J.H. MM Sjt 61213 RAMC
PIGGIN Frank W. MM Pte 131494 17th Bn Machine Gun Corps
PIGGOTT Charles J. MM L/Cpl 3/7357 1st Dorsetshire Regt
PIGGOTT Daniel "MM,MID" Pte 9542 2nd Oxf & Bucks Light Infantry
PIGGOTT Edward C.C. MM L/Cpl 316723 62 Div Sig Coy Royal Engineers
PIGGOTT H. MM Pte 341505 RAMC
PIGGOTT Harold W. MM Sjt 71624 32 Bde RFA
PIGGOTT John George MM Pte 4172 11th Rifle Brigade KIA 20.3.18.
PIGGOTT Robert MM L/Cpl 87294 Middlesex Regt
PIGGOTT Stanley MM Spr 137918 Royal Engineers
PIGGOTT William C. MM Bdr 110810 RFA
PIGGOTT Willie MM Cpl 23271 1st Royal West Kent Regt KIA 27.9.18.
PIGGOTT or PIGOTT Arthur MM Bdr 25791 111 Heavy Bty RGA
PIGOTT Frank MM+Bar Pte 202235 7th Royal West Kent Regt KIA 19.9.18.
PIGOTT Frederick MM Pte 16156 6th Dorsetshire Regt
PIGOTT George MM L/Cpl 14598 9th Norfolk Regt
PIGOTT Harold Burton MM Sjt 39575 84 Bty 11 Bde RFA
PIGOTT Joseph M. MM L/Cpl 11317 King's Royal Rifle Corps
PIGOTT Robert MM Pte 3941 6th Royal Inniskilling Fusiliers
PIGOTT Robert MM Gnr 43635 RGA
PIGOTT or PIGGOTT Arthur MM Bdr 25791 111 Heavy Bty RGA
PIGRUM A. MM L/Cpl 14435 10th Essex Regt
PIKE A.C. "MM+Bar,MID" Sjt 44338 75 Fd Coy Royal Engineers
PIKE Arthur E. MM BSM 31921 B/75 Bde RFA
PIKE Edwin B. MM Pte 220201 Royal Berkshire Regt
PIKE Frank MM Pte 11763 5th Royal Berkshire Regt

PIKE Frederick C. MM Sjt 19884 South Wales Borderers
PIKE Frederick H. MM Sjt 45042 D/69 Bde RFA
PIKE Frederick L. MM+Bar Sjt 41891 116 Heavy Bty RGA
PIKE George MM Cpl 11492 10th Lancashire Fusiliers
PIKE George MM Cpl 35732 Royal Fusiliers
PIKE George Guy MM Pte 17997 11 Coy Machine Gun Corps KIA 9.4.17.
PIKE George P. MM SSM 2163 1/1st Gloucestershire Yeo
PIKE H. MM Sjt 267478 2nd Notts & Derby Regt
PIKE H. MM Pte 200541 Lincolnshire Regt
PIKE Henry MM L/Cpl 307502 3 Tank Supply Coy Tank Corps
PIKE Herbert MM Pte 29197 3rd Grenadier Guards
PIKE James MM Pte DM2/155364 Army Service Corps att 2/3(Home Counties)Fd Amb RAMC
PIKE Walter MM+Bar Sjt 25824 9th Devonshire Regt
PIKE William J. MM Cpl 514488 427 Fd Coy Royal Engineers
PIKE William J. MM Pte M2/175756 Army Service Corps
PIKE William John MM L/Cpl 15596 2nd Devonshire Regt KIA 24.4.18.
PIKEMAN Joseph "DCM,MM+Bar" CSM 13391 12th Royal Irish Rifles
PILBEAM Harold MM Pte 139694 Machine Gun Corps
PILBEAM Walter William Duke MM L/Cpl 532376 490 Fd Coy Royal Engineers
PILBRO Henry S. MM Cpl S/27917 Rifle Brigade
PILBROW Horace MM L/Cpl 38867 1/5th York & Lancaster Regt
PILBROW John MM L/Cpl 200429 1/4th Yorkshire Light Infantry DOW 22.4.18.
PILBROW Stanley Edward MM Pte 44340 22nd Manchester Regt KIA 15.8.17.
PILBURY William MM Pte 16356 7th Shropshire Light Infantry
PILCHER James MM L/Cpl 10952 32nd Bn Machine Gun Corps
PILCHER Rupert J. MM Pte 34989 Welsh Regt
PILCHER W. MM Sjt 22687 23 Fd Coy Royal Engineers
PILDITCH Cleverton Leonard MM L/Cpl 16/75 Royal Warwickshire Regt
PILE John P. MM Sjt 10199 West Yorkshire Regt
PILE William T. MM Sjt 9522 Devonshire Regt
PILFORD J. MM Pnr 249516 41 Div Sig Coy Royal Engineers
PILGREM Frederick G. MM Spr 134152 Royal Engineers
PILGRIM Arthur Charles MM Pte 18314 14th Royal Warwickshire Regt DOW 4.10.18.
PILGRIM Charles MM Pte 17502 Leicestershire Regt
PILGRIM David William MM Pte 58838 188 Coy Machine Gun Corps DOW 30.10.17.
PILGRIM Frederick MM Dvr 162784 64 Fd Coy Royal Engineers
PILGRIM James MM Sjt 2949 12th Middlesex Regt
PILGRIM James MM L/Sjt 7653 2nd Royal Scots Fusiliers
PILGRIM Kenneth Frere MM L/Cpl 5473 15th London Regt
PILKINGTON Albert E. MM L/Cpl 11910 Manchester Regt
PILKINGTON Edward MM Sjt 23726 319 Rd Constr Coy Royal Engineers
PILKINGTON Ernest MM S/Sjt Fitter 13692 RFA
PILKINGTON George MM Pte 13662 South Staffordshire Regt
PILKINGTON Harry MM Pte 12966 8th North Staffordshire Regt
PILKINGTON Henry MM Pte 13372 9th East Lancashire Regt
PILKINGTON J. MM Dvr 88197 'L' Bty RHA
PILKINGTON James MM Pte 240617 1/5th York & Lancaster Regt KIA 9.10.17.
PILKINGTON John MM Sjt 8133 4th King's Royal Rifle Corps
PILKINGTON John MM Pte 74654 7th Royal Fusiliers
PILKINGTON John G. MM Pte 550032 1/16th London Regt
PILKINGTON John Henry MM Pte M2/139200 Army Service Corps
PILKINGTON Linnaeus MM Pte 266599 East Yorkshire Regt
PILKINGTON Richard MM Sjt C/955 16th King's Royal Rifle Corps
PILKINGTON Thomas MM Sjt 12729 7th Border Regt KIA 8.8.16.
PILL Edward MM L/Cpl 33934 1st Royal Berkshire Regt
PILL Francis George MM Cpl 29426 19th Royal Welsh Fusiliers
PILL Stanley G. MM Pte 18910 Royal Berkshire Regt
PILLANS John MM Pte 42415 9th Scottish Rifles
PILLER William MM Pte 4451 1st Royal West Kent Regt
PILLEY Ernest C. MM Sjt 350419 1/7th London Regt
PILLING Arthur Ewart MM Dvr 188888 463 Bty 179 Bde RFA
PILLING Charles MM Pte 63565 RAMC
PILLING George MM Pte 18228 9th Scottish Rifles
PILLING George MM Pte 23811 1st Royal Welsh Fusiliers KIA 4.5.17.
PILLING John MM Pte 52515 9th Scottish Rifles
PILLING John MM Cpl 240626 1/5th North Lancashire Regt
PILLING Joseph MM Spr 44356 Royal Engineers
PILLING Sam MM+Bar Cpl 241001 1/5th North Lancashire Regt
PILLING Samuel MM Pte 243159 North Lancashire Regt
PILLING Thomas F. MM Spr 143860 59 Fd Coy Royal Engineers
PILLSWORTH William MM Pte 24586 Yorkshire Light Infantry
PILSBURY Samuel MM Pte 18917 8th South Lancashire Regt
PILSON William MM Dvr 35677 376 Bty 169 Bde RFA
PILSON William MM Spr 463193 50 Div Sig Coy Royal Engineers
PILSWORTH Charles T. MM Pte 325386 1/1st Cambridgeshire Regt
PILTON William C. MM 2nd Cpl 14822 Royal Engineers
PILTON William Henry MM Cpl 14356 2nd Lincolnshire Regt
PIM John MM L/Cpl 10410 1st Royal Dublin Fusiliers
PIMBLETT Thomas MM L/Sjt 11519 2nd Royal Fusiliers
PIMBLOTT William MM Pte 52661 11th Cheshire Regt KIA 10.8.17.
PIMLETT David MM Pte 451640 11th London Regt
PIMLEY William MM Sjt 12517 57 Div Ammn Col RFA
PIMLOTT John MM Gnr 5956 88 Bde RFA
PIMM Ernest MM Cpl 15379 6th Royal Berkshire Regt
PINCH Fred MM Sjt 45859 196 Coy Machine Gun Corps
PINCH Reginald MM L/Sjt 4798 10th Duke of Cornwall's LI DOW 25.3.18.
PINCHAM Albert MM Pte M2/076297 Army Service Corps
PINCHARD William F. MM Bdr 34674 RGA
PINCHBACK Ernest C. MM Cpl 33377 1st Hampshire Regt
PINCHBECK George William MM 2nd Cpl 313157 25 Div Sig Coy Royal Engineers
PINCHEMAIN John T. MM Pte 143386 1st Bn Machine Gun Corps
PINCHEN W.F. MM L/Cpl 90 1st Rifle Brigade
PINCHIN Arthur MM BSM 796 120 Heavy Bty RGA
PINCHIN Clement MM Pte 70785 1st Notts & Derby Regt
PINCHIN Frank MM Gnr 96299 RFA
PINCHING Arthur Richard MM Sjt 200740 1st Norfolk Regt
PINCKNEY Joseph S. MM Cpl 14821 2nd Royal Sussex Regt
PINCOTT Henry N. MM L/Cpl 198127 19 Div Sig Coy Royal Engineers DOW 30.9.17.
PINDER Albert E. MM Dvr 97090 RFA
PINDER Arthur MM Pte 017521 Army Ordnance Corps
PINDER Frank MM Cpl 31810 2nd Lincolnshire Regt
PINDER George MM Cpl 12216 7th East Yorkshire Regt
PINDER Harold F. MM Sjt 531777 15th London Regt
PINDER Henry "DCM,MM,MID" Sjt 444601 42 Div Sig Coy Royal Engineers
PINDER Herbert E. MM Pte 50960 17th Liverpool Regt
PINDER James A. MM Sjt 72365 Royal Engineers
PINDER John MM L/Sjt 241867 1/5th Border Regt
PINDER Percival MM+Bar Sjt 67429 97 Fd Amb RAMC KIA 21.3.18.
PINDER Percy MM 2nd Cpl 482202 Royal Engineers
PINDER Samuel MM Pte 15271 24th Manchester Regt
PINDRED Joseph W. MM Pte 25125 2/4th West Riding Regt
PINE Frederick MM Pte 9570 2nd South Wales Borderers KIA 11.4.18.
PINE George MM+Bar Sjt 51635 RGA
PINEL Raymond St.J. MM Cpl 28941 6th Dorsetshire Regt
PINFOLD Fred Brookes MM Pte 20998 10th Royal Warwickshire Regt
PINFOLD Wilfred MM Pte 41015 1/1st Hertfordshire Regt
PINION John MM Dvr 30535 411 Bty 126 Bde RFA KIA 17.4.18.
PINK Alfred "DCM,MM" Sjt 74935 C/50 Bde RFA
PINK Arthur MM Pte 6382 2nd Royal Sussex Regt
PINK Edward MM Pte 3/4660 1st Hampshire Regt DOW 25.10.16.
PINK Francis H. MM Pte 12883 7th Royal Fusiliers
PINK Horace Leonard MM Cpl 2437 7th Royal West Kent Regt
PINK James A. MM Cpl 312022 34 Div Sig Coy Royal Engineers
PINKERTON Robert MM Cpl 82949 RFA
PINKETT George MM Cpl R/8286 King's Royal Rifle Corps
PINKETT John H.K. MM+Bar Pte 52811 19th Durham Light Infantry
PINKHAM Stanley MM Cpl 495 1st Welsh Guards DOW 6.11.18.
PINKHAM William R. MM Pte 10093 10th Royal Fusiliers
PINKNEY Arnold J. MM Cpl 2025 1/4th Yorkshire Regt
PINKNEY George MM L/Cpl 14923 4th Coldstream Guards
PINKNEY James "DCM,MM+Bar" Bdr 71737 A/112 Bde RFA
PINKNEY John H. MM Gnr 127858 RFA
PINKNEY Thomas MM Gnr 20188 RFA
PINKNEY Thomas Smith MM Pte 24927 11th West Yorkshire Regt
PINNEGAR William C. MM Sjt 11602 8th Cheshire Regt
PINNELL Frederick MM BSM 29359 C/119 Bde RFA
PINNELL Thomas MM Pte 15864 2nd Grenadier Guards
PINNER Albert V. MM Gnr 272406 8 Bde RFA
PINNER John MM Cpl 12414 4th Worcestershire Regt KIA 23.4.17.
PINNER John William George MM Pte 472646 9th London Regt
PINNER Leonard C. MM Pte 36646 24th Royal Fusiliers

PINNICK Benjamin MM Bdr 56527 RGA
PINNIGAR William MM Pte 36893 Machine Gun Corps
PINNIGER Albert Edward MM Sjt 496465 478 Fd Coy Royal Engineers
PINNINGTON Joseph MM Bdr 681787 RFA
PINNINGTON Thomas H. MM Gnr 85328 124 Hy Bty RGA
PINNOCK Ernest J. MM L/Cpl 76966 2nd Bn Tank Corps
PINNOCK Francis A. MM Sjt 24976 336 Siege Bty RGA
PINNOCK L. "MM,MID" Sjt 2787 2nd Rifle Brigade
PINNOCK Leonard MM Gnr 91425 240 Siege Bty RGA
PINNY H.G. MM Sjt R/730 King's Royal Rifle Corps
PINSON Arthur MM Dvr 90846 RFA
PINSON Grant Murray MM Sjt M2/153057 272 MT Coy Army Service Corps KIA 16.9.18.
PIPE Clifford Herbert Joyce MM Pte 470051 12th London Regt
PIPE Edgar G. MM Pte 23673 4th Worcestershire Regt
PIPE Harry MM L/Cpl 11614 1st Liverpool Regt KIA 15.11.16.
PIPE James MM Gnr 34828 RFA
PIPE James W. MM Sjt 653098 1/21st London Regt
PIPE Lewis Harry Joyce MM L/Cpl 67920 11th Royal West Surrey Regt
PIPER Albert MM Cpl Sig 951205 A/15 Bde RFA
PIPER Arthur F. MM Pte 200897 4th Hampshire Regt
PIPER Arthur G. MM Sjt 250241 1/5th Essex Regt
PIPER Charles J. MM Pte 63303 Royal Fusiliers
PIPER Cuthbert William MM L/Cpl 14793 Yorkshire Regt
PIPER Ernest Walter MM Sjt 17539 D/189 Bde RFA KIA 13.10.18.
PIPER Fred MM Sjt 18004 4th North Lancashire Regt
PIPER Harry Ernest Langley MM Cpl 513304 2/14th London Regt
PIPER James MM+Bar L/Cpl 10126 1st Royal Berkshire Regt
PIPER James MM Sjt 13202 6th Shropshire Light Infantry
PIPER John Louis MM Pte M2/054188 277 Coy Army Service Corps
PIPER Joseph MM Pte 27913 2nd Hampshire Regt KIA 30.11.17.
PIPER S. MM Pte 282801 London Regt
PIPER William MM Cpl 20350 Hampshire Regt
PIPER William A. MM Pte 42749 Durham Light Infantry
PIPER William Henry MM L/Sjt 12145 11th West Yorkshire Regt DOW 2.10.17.
PIPER William J. MM Cpl 14267 RGA
PIPET William "MM,MIDx2" Sjt 75006 126 Coy Labour Corps
PIPKIN George MM L/Cpl 10694 Wiltshire Regt
PIPPETT John Gilbert MM Cpl 10/768 10th East Yorkshire Regt
PIQUET George Clement MM CSM 8024 East Lancashire Regt
PIRCH Charles Herbert MM Cpl 420505 10th London Regt
PIRIE Alexander MM L/Cpl 8516 9th Royal Highlanders
PIRIE Alexander MM Pte 3134 3 Fd Amb RAMC
PIRIE Alexander MM+Bar Cpl 4243 Labour Corps
PIRIE Edwin MM Sjt 21500 RGA
PIRIE James MM Pte 355661 1/10th Liverpool Regt
PIRIE James MM Dvr 635366 A/256 Bde RFA
PIRIE James B. MM Cpl 315557 13th Royal Highlanders
PIRIE John MM Pte 12423 1/4th Royal Scots Fusiliers
PIRIE Joseph B. MM Bdr 650052 RFA
PIRIE Robert MM 2nd Cpl 21768 11 Fd Coy Royal Engineers
PIRIE William MM Sjt 2414 Labour Corps
PIRIE William MM L/Cpl 41837 Machine Gun Corps
PIRIE or PIRRIE Donald MM Pte 200270 1/5th Highland Light Infantry
PIRNIE J. MM Pte 43332 Royal Highlanders
PIRRET James MM Pte 77 2nd Gordon Highlanders
PIRRET Norman McLeod MM Sjt 4415 RAMC
PIRRIE Donald MM L/Cpl 21525 Machine Gun Corps
PIRRIE James MM Pte 242002 1/5th Seaforth Highlanders KIA 21.3.18.
PIRRIE John MM Pte 2849 9th Gordon Highlanders DOW 20.8.18.
PIRRIE W. MM Pte 129675 Machine Gun Corps
PIRRIE or PIRIE Donald MM Pte 200270 1/5th Highland Light Infantry
PIRT Henry MM Dvr 109659 RFA
PITCAIRN Alex D. MM Pte 32106 5/6th Scottish Rifles
PITCHER A.A. MM L/Cpl 20963 1st Essex Regt
PITCHER A.E. MM AM2 8192 Royal Flying Corps
PITCHER Albert G. MM Sjt 73205 Notts & Derby Regt
PITCHER Charles J. MM Pte A/203036 13th King's Royal Rifle Corps
PITCHER Frederick MM Cpl 200809 1/4th North Lancashire Regt DOW 22.9.17.
PITCHER Frederick J. MM Pte 16441 6th Northamptonshire Regt
PITCHER George Henry MM Gnr 194353 194 Siege Bty RGA
PITCHER H.A. MM Sjt 590280 London Regt
PITCHER Harry George MM L/Cpl 53088 Royal Fusiliers
PITCHER Walter MM Pte 26118 9th Cheshire Regt
PITCHER Ward H. MM Cpl 482235 Royal Engineers
PITCHES G. MM Cpl 26963 9th Essex Regt
PITCHFORD Henry MM L/Cpl 102099 171 Tunnelling Coy Royal Engineers KIA 20.8.17.
PITCHFORD Nathaniel MM Pte 200470 1/1st London Regt
PITCHFORK Harry MM Pte 43674 8th Royal Berkshire Regt
PITCOCK Ernest MM L/Cpl 200577 1/5th South Staffordshire Regt
PITFIELD William P. MM Sjt 32088 RGA
PITHER Arthur MM L/Cpl 20109 Signal Service Royal Engineers
PITHER Thomas C.L. MM L/Cpl 293342 2/10th Middlesex Regt
PITHIE George Lorimer MM L/Sjt 202517 1/4th Royal Scots KIA 27.918.
PITHIE Thomas MM Gnr 121714 23 Heavy Bty RGA
PITKIN Charles Henry MM Cpl 41651 4 Squadron Machine Gun Corps(Cavalry) KIA 26.3.18.
PITMAN Albert T. MM Pte 2012 1st Gloucestershire Regt
PITMAN Francis Edwin MM Cpl S4/056787 Army Service Corps
PITMAN George MM Pte M2/139030 Army Service Corps
PITMAN John R. MM Pte 17055 12th Notts & Derby Regt
PITMAN John W. MM Pte 5486 6th Dragoons
PITMAN Joseph MM Sjt 7941 1st Somerset Light Infantry KIA 1.7.16.
PITMAN Joseph MM Sjt 54404 RFA
PITMAN William MM L/Cpl 9401 2nd Royal Irish Rifles
PITMAN William C. MM S/Sjt 457173 24 Fd Amb RAMC
PITNEY William E. MM Pte 1984 9th Lancers
PITT Ambrose MM Pte 10472 Leicestershire Regt
PITT Cecil Archie MM Pte 5468 HAC
PITT George MM Pte 40023 Worcestershire Regt
PITT George MM Sjt 11048 4th Middlesex Regt
PITT George H. MM Cpl 27809 Border Regt
PITT Gilbert E.C. MM L/Cpl 62652 RFA
PITT Horace William MM L/Cpl 16595 10tth Essex Regt DOW 31.3.18.
PITT John MM Pte 24387 Worcestershire Regt
PITT John Thomas MM Pte 18100 2nd South Staffordshire Regt
PITT Phillip W. MM Pte 49752 23rd Lancashire Fusiliers
PITT Richard J. MM Pte 45383 2nd Royal Berkshire Regt
PITT Robert William MM L/Sjt 9334 2nd Grenadier Guards
PITT Samuel MM Cpl 104984 258 Tunnelling Coy Royal Engineers
PITT Stanley MM Pte 1462 9th Welsh Regt
PITT William MM Pte 19989 1st Royal Irish Fusiliers
PITT William E. MM Pte 240065 8th Worcestershire Regt
PITT William Henry Charles MM L/Cpl 19224 116 Coy Machine Gun Corps KIA 23.9.17.
PITT William N. MM Cpl 1401 RGA
PITTARD Frederick Tristram MM Cpl 79511 RFA
PITTARD Leonard MM Sjt 21768 15th Hampshire Regt KIA 4.9.18.
PITTAWAY Charles L. MM Pte 79139 RAMC
PITTAWAY David MM Pte 240367 Worcestershire Regt
PITTAWAY John William MM CSM 8055 2nd Lincolnshire Regt
PITTENDREIGH Fred MM Sjt 1531 Northumberland Fusiliers
PITTOCK Ernest A. MM Pte 40434 Suffolk Regt
PITTOCK William John MM Pte 3032 Army Cyclist Corps
PITTOM Thomas MM Pte 108329 181 Coy Labour Corps
PITTS Bernard MM Spr 325997 62 Div Sig Coy Royal Engineers DOW 28.10.18.
PITTS Charles MM Bdr 26294 42 Bde RFA
PITTS Frederick J. MM L/Sjt 204560 Hampshire Regt
PITTS Robert Bennett MM Cpl 20239 D/153 Bde RFA DOW 25.9.18.
PITTS Thomas MM Sjt 47423 RFA
PITTS William Joshia MM L/Cpl 10758 10th Essex Regt
PIZZEY Claude Albert MM Cpl 2193 1/4th Suffolk Regt KIA 9.4.17.
PIZZEY W.R. MM L/Cpl 15803 West Riding Regt
PIZZOFERO Lorenzo MM Pte 20425 1st Dorsetshire Regt
PLACE Frank Clarke "MC,MM(54952 Pte 22nd R Fus)" 2Lt 1/4th Royal Lancaster Regt KIA 22.9.18.
PLACKETT Edward G. MM Dvr 15253 B/162 Bde RFA
PLADDYS Charles J. MM Pte 142981 Machine Gun Corps
PLADGEMAN or PLAGEMAN Ernest MM L/Cpl 419307 2nd(North Midland)Fd Amb RAMC
PLAISTER George Henry MM Pte 103564 Machine Gun Corps
PLAMPIN George MM Pte 7532 Middlesex Regt
PLANCK William MM Gnr 751077 250 Bde RFA
PLANK Charles F. MM Cpl 15306 10th Gloucestershire Regt
PLANK George "DCM+Bar,MM,MID" CSM 7950 1st Royal Berkshire Regt

PLANK George MM L/Cpl 240285 Northumberland Fusiliers
PLANK George MM Gnr 61154 28 Bde RFA
PLANT Aalbert E. MM Sjt 200075 1/5th West Yorkshire Regt
PLANT Albert MM L/Cpl 141749 42nd Bn Machine Gun Corps
PLANT Albert MM Pte 12531 Gordon Highlanders
PLANT Albert A. MM Pte 33928 7th Norfolk Regt
PLANT Albert E. MM Sjt Farrier 20209 5th Dragoon Guards
PLANT Arthur MM Dvr 1157 RFA
PLANT Arthur Ernest Biddulph MM Sjt 371217 1/8th London Regt KIA 30.11.17.
PLANT Bert MM+Bar Pte 142327 Machine Gun Corps
PLANT Edward MM Pte 51888 18th Lancashire Fusiliers
PLANT Edward MM L/Cpl 21823 18th Lancashire Fusiliers KIA 5.8.18.
PLANT Edward MM Pte 3970 53 Coy Machine Gun Corps
PLANT Edward William MM L/Cpl 1679 7th East Surrey Regt
PLANT George J. MM L/Cpl 251321 1/3rd London Regt
PLANT George John MM L/Cpl 20724 2nd Coldstream Guards DOW 27.8.18.
PLANT George W. MM L/Cpl 437283 RAMC
PLANT Harold G. MM Pte 57191 2/5th West Yorkshire Regt
PLANT Henry John MM Pte 200899 1st North Staffordshire Regt
PLANT J.W. MM Sjt 200965 Northamptonshire Regt
PLANT James Jubilee MM+Bar L/Cpl 356644 1/10th Liverpool Regt
PLANT Joseph MM Cpl 51659 1st East Yorkshire Regt
PLANT Joseph William MM Sjt 800247 RFA
PLANT Samuel Clifton MM Pte 26863 14th Hampshire Regt KIA 27.3.18.
PLANT Thomas A. MM Cpl R/645 12th King's Royal Rifle Corps
PLANT Walter MM Pte 14286 10th Notts & Derby Regt
PLANT William "MM,MID" Sjt 10850 2nd Worcestershire Regt
PLANT William MM L/Cpl 27255 Machine Gun Corps
PLANT William H. MM Sjt A/3358 King's Royal Rifle Corps
PLANT William M. MM L/Sjt 9957 19th Durham Light Infantry
PLASKETT Albert MM Pte 203490 5th Royal Berkshire Regt
PLASKETT Percy J. MM Gnr 87875 RHA
PLASTOW Henry A. MM Pte 3383 15th London Regt
PLATEL Sidney Henry MM Cpl 25362 Royal Flying Corps
PLATO Charles H. MM Pte B/203156 Rifle Brigade
PLATO F.H. MM Pte 18108 Essex Regt
PLATT Albert MM Cpl 2146 9th Manchester Regt
PLATT Amos MM L/Cpl 201909 2/4th North Lancashire Regt
PLATT Arthur MM Pte 9087 HAC
PLATT Bertie T. MM(20484 5th W Yorks)+Bar Pte 55731 4th York & Lancaster Regt
PLATT Edmund MM Dvr 54585 B/56 Bde RFA
PLATT Eric MM Pte 1340 Lincolnshire Regt
PLATT Ernest MM L/Sjt 55812 Royal Welsh Fusiliers
PLATT Forrester MM Pte 203026 4th Yorkshire Light Infantry
PLATT Frank Cuthbert MM Sjt 207429 Royal Engineers
PLATT Frederick MM Cpl 34981 X/21 Med TM Bty Royal Artillery KIA 6.10.16.
PLATT George MM Pte 204434 2nd Wiltshire Regt
PLATT George MM Sjt 31884 A/235 Bde RFA
PLATT James E. MM Gnr 122557 RFA
PLATT Joseph T. MM Cpl 43809 39 Bde RFA
PLATT Leonard MM Pte 10221 11th Royal Fusiliers
PLATT Richard MM Pte R/38319 13th King's Royal Rifle Corps
PLATT Richard MM Pte 513239 14th London Regt
PLATT Robert P. MM Sjt 20232 Machine Gun Corps
PLATT Robert William MM Pte 21455 2nd Oxf & Bucks Light Infantry
PLATT Sylvester Walker MM Sjt 242172 1/5th South Lancashire Regt
PLATT Thomas MM Spt 207577 Royal Engineers
PLATT Thomas "MM,CG(F)" Pte 6041 20th Middlesex Regt
PLATT W.J. MM Pte 47677 2nd King's Royal Rifle Corps
PLATT Wiliam MM Sjt 21157 11th South Lancashire Regt
PLATT William MM+Bar L/Cpl 9993 8th Royal Fusiliers
PLATT William H.H. MM Pte 887 18th Hussars
PLATT William Joseph MM Sjt 28684 A/153 Bde RFA
PLATTS Albert H. MM Spr 161689 37 Div Sig Coy Royal Engineers
PLATTS Alfred MM Spr 147815 179 Tunnelling Coy Royal Engineers
PLATTS Arthur MM L/Cpl 6779 1st East Kent Regt DOW 10.7.18.
PLATTS Frank MM Cpl 41339 Machine Gun Corps
PLATTS Fred MM Pte R/12807 16th King's Royal Rifle Corps
PLATTS L.A. MM Sjt 36027 Machine Gun Corps
PLATTS Tom MM Pte 19587 West Riding Regt
PLATTS William MM Cpl 11496 6th Leicestershire Regt

PLAYER Arthur MM Pte 242433 Middlesex Regt
PLAYER Charles F. MM Sjt 300576 1 Gun Carrier Coy Tank Corps
PLAYER Edward William MM Sjt 97990 D/92 Bde RFA
PLAYER George MM Pte 1650 1/1st Essex Yeomanry
PLAYER John E. MM Pte 9663 RAMC
PLAYFORD George T. MM Pte 204812 7th Middlesex Regt
PLAYLE Alfred MM Pte 166 1st Rifle Brigade
PLEACE Ernest H. MM Pte 241996 Worcestershire Regt
PLEASANCE Martin Dennis MM L/Cpl 1270 1/1st Cambridgeshire Regt
PLEDGER Albert George MM L/Sjt 7664 10th Royal Fusiliers DOW 4.10.18.
PLEDGER Charles "MM,MSM" Sjt 36503 RGA
PLEDGER John Ambrose MM L/Cpl 12098 2nd Royal Fusiliers KIA 11.5.18.
PLEECE Ernest Walter MM Pte 20305 10th South Wales Borderers KIA 27.8.17.
PLENTY Phillip MM Gnr 610325 RFA
PLENTY William J. MM Sjt 7726 1st Dorsetshire Regt
PLESTED Herbert R. MM L/Cpl 9862 1st Royal Berkshire Regt
PLESTED Robert MM Pte 32450 1st East Lancashire Regt
PLEVEY Samuel J. MM Cpl M2/050671 Army Service Corps
PLEWS Tom MM Gnr 73332 68 Bty 14 Bde RFA KIA 1.9.18.
PLIMMER A.G. MM Pte 35037 Grenadier Guards att 2nd Hampshire Regt.
PLIMMER Edward W. MM Pte 39392 RAMC
PLIMMER Enoch MM Pte 14708 93 Coy Machine Gun Corps
PLIMMER Richard MM Sjt 4197 2nd Border Regt
PLIMMER William MM Pte 14323 8th North Staffordshire Regt KIA 10.10.16.
PLINT Richard G. MM Cpl 19797 Royal Fusiliers att RE.
PLOWMAN Albert MM CQMS 4808 1st Dorsetshire Regt
PLOWMAN Frank A. MM L/Cpl 28794 10th Royal West Kent Regt
PLOWMAN H. MM Pte 22959 Yorkshire Regt
PLOWMAN John Lambert MM L/Sjt 223 10th Lincolnshire Regt KIA 28.4.17.
PLOWRIGHT Joseph MM Pte 40635 Leicestershire Regt
PLOWRIGHT Thomas MM Pte 10157 1st Northamptonshire Regt
PLOWS Bertie MM Spr 312746 Royal Engineers
PLOWS George MM L/Cpl 16135 Royal Lancaster Regt
PLUES Raymond MM Pte 33626 Welsh Regt
PLUM Fred MM L/Cpl R/13135 King's Royal Rifle Corps
PLUMB Charles MM L/Cpl 240940 1/8th Worcestershire Regt
PLUMB Francis Carter MM Pte 3700 2nd West Yorkshire Regt KIA 29.5.18.
PLUMB Frederick MM Gnr 82707 RGA
PLUMB John MM Pte 14559 11th West Yorkshire Regt
PLUMB T. MM Pte 17865 10th West Riding Regt
PLUMBRIDGE Herbert G. MM L/Cpl 178976 152 Fd Coy Royal Engineers
PLUME George MM Pte 307127 West Riding Regt
PLUME James A. MM CSM 8090 1st Northamptonshire Regt
PLUMLEY Charles MM Cpl 23301 Norfolk Regt
PLUMLEY Harry MM Sjt 71635 RFA
PLUMLEY Harry H. MM L/Cpl 240255 Hampshire Regt
PLUMLEY Harry W. MM Pte 573136 17th London Regt
PLUMLEY Robert MM Cpl 16332 9th Royal Inniskilling Fusiliers
PLUMMER Arthur E. MM Pte 80067 23rd Royal Fusiliers
PLUMMER David MM Dvr T4/240008 47 Div Train Army Service Corps
PLUMMER Donald MM Spr 47890 Royal Engineers
PLUMMER Edward John MM Pte 26013 4th Grenadier Guards DOW 28.11.17.
PLUMMER Harold MM Pte 46553 Machine Gun Corps
PLUMMER Percy George MM Pte 2540 1/8th London Regt
PLUMMER Vincent MM+Bar Sjt 1242 23rd Royal Fusiliers
PLUMMER William MM Cpl 33467 C/53 Bde RFA
PLUMPTON John MM Gnr 1830 1(South Midland)Bde RFA
PLUMRIDGE James S. MM Dvr T/2133 Army Service Corps
PLUMRIDGE Percy MM Cpl 265642 1/1st Bucks Bn Oxf & Bucks Light Infantry
PLUMRIDGE Reginald MM Pte 32959 RAMC
PLUNKETT Alfred MM Sjt 1081 1(London)Fd Coy Royal Engineers
PLUNKETT Herbert MM Sjt 2237 19th London Regt KIA 15.9.16.
PLUNKETT Michael MM+Bar Bdr 32409 116 Heavy Bty RGA
PLURIGHT Dyson MM Sjt 32415 RAMC
PLUSH Cornelius F. MM L/Cpl 49076 4th Bedfordshire Regt
PLUSH Sydney F. MM+Bar Cpl 63581 98 Fd Coy Royal Engineers
POACHER William MM L/Cpl 476307 Labour Corps
POBJOY Henry "MM,MID" Sjt 34362 118 Bde RFA

POCKETT W. MM Cpl 9612 1st Essex Regt
POCOCK Albert MM+Bar Pte 25426 12th East Surrey Regt
POCOCK Arthur P. MM Sjt 165377 101st Bn Machine Gun Corps
POCOCK Charles W. MM Pte 1403 9th East Surrey Regt
POCOCK E.J. MM Pte 200893 9th Royal Berkshire Regt
POCOCK Frederick MM(5565 Pte 1st R Berks)+Bar Spr 198115 2 Div Sig Coy Royal Engineers
POCOCK Frederick "MM,MID" Bdr 6416 RGA
POCOCK Henry MM Sjt 295120 12th Somerset Light Infantry
POCOCK Herbert C. MM Sjt 3430 Royal Sussex Regt
POCOCK M.V. MM AM1 9176 Royal Flying Corps
POCOCK S.T. MM Pte 5069 Royal Berkshire Regt
POCOCK Samuel C. "MM,MID" SM 898 26 Fd Amb RAMC
POCOCK Stephen E. MM Pte 473941 London Regt "att MGC,"
POCOCK William A. MM L/Cpl 68771 10th Royal Fusiliers
PODBERY Albert James MM Pte 285462 1/1st Oxfordshire Yeomanry KIA 5.7.17.
PODD Jeremiah MM Cpl 1703 1/4th Suffolk Regt
PODEVIN Charles E.G. MM Cpl Fitter 23897 RGA
POET Albert MM L/Cpl 23697 10th Royal West Kent Regt
POFFLEY Frank MM Pte 46668 Leicestershire Regt
POGMORE William MM Cpl 44513 8 Bde RFA
POGSON Edgar MM Pte 14134 11th Notts & Derby Regt DOW 7.10.18.
POGUE Abraham MM Sjt 3096 1st Irish Guards
POILE William MM Pte 2184 8th Royal Sussex Regt DOW 12.4.18.
POINEY Walter MM+Bar Bdr 27179 233 Bde RFA
POINTER Alfred G. MM Pte 29536 105 Fd Amb RAMC
POINTER Alfred K. MM Cpl M2/033264 Army Service Corps
POINTER Frederick James MM+Bar Cpl Sig 109818 238 Siege Bty RGA
POINTON William H. MM L/Cpl 241087 2/6th North Staffordshire Regt
POKE Ernest MM Pte R/312 King's Royal Rifle Corps
POKE John Barrett (Jack) MM Pte 300288 1/8th Manchester Regt
POKE William J.B. MM Sjt 19808 296 Siege Bty RGA
POLAND Frederick P. MM Cpl 17943 Royal Engineers
POLAND Thomas H. MM Gnr 690283 RFA
POLDEN Sidney J. MM Dvr 32823 RFA
POLDEN Stephen H. MM Dvr 79237 RFA
POLE A. MM Pte 201703 4th Leicestershire Regt
POLEY David J. MM Sjt 918 1/6th Welsh Regt
POLGLAZE Joseph Arthur MM Pte 8821 2nd South Lancashire Regt
POLGREAN Fred MM+Bar Gnr 71326 211 Siege Bty RGA
POLHILL Robert MM L/Cpl 20151 6th Dorsetshire Regt KIA 27.8.18.
POLIN Edward Arthur MM Pte 15483 10th Royal Welsh Fusiliers KIA 20.7.16.
POLINE Joseph MM+Bar Cpl 10856 15th Hampshire Regt
POLKINGHORNE John MM Spr 51120 Royal Engineers
POLKINHORN Frederick Ernest MM Cpl 925498 B/290 Bde RFA
POLLARD A.O.A. MM Sjt 15110 Royal Flying Corps
POLLARD Albert E. MM CSM 13477 6/7th Royal Scots Fusiliers KIA 31.7.17.
POLLARD Bertram G. MM Cpl M1/7446 Army Service Corps
POLLARD Cecil James MM Sjt 700535 23rd London Regt
POLLARD Charles W. MM Pte 29695 8th East Surrey Regt
POLLARD Christopher C. MM Sjt 5667 1st Norfolk Regt
POLLARD Edward MM Dvr 68553 B/74 Bde RFA
POLLARD Fred MM Cpl 786141 RFA
POLLARD Frederick "DCM,MM+Bar" Cpl 42580 6 Bty 40 Bde RFA
POLLARD Frederick MM Pte 10855 18th Hussars
POLLARD Harold Arthur MM Sjt 12276 8th Gloucestershire Regt KIA 30.7.16.
POLLARD Harry MM+Bar L/Cpl 241666 2nd London Regt
POLLARD Horace MM Pte 242286 5th Leicestershire Regt
POLLARD Horace Albert MM Pnr 495945 315 Rd Constr Coy Royal Engineers
POLLARD Ivor W. MM Sjt 17179 6th South Wales Borderers
POLLARD J.W. MM Pte R/39514 King's Royal Rifle Corps
POLLARD Joe MM Pte 5377 10th Lancashire Fusiliers
POLLARD John MM Pte 7792 11th Arg & Suth Highlanders
POLLARD John MM Spr 179294 209 Fd Coy Royal Engineers
POLLARD John E. MM Dvr 1786 1/8th London Regt
POLLARD Joseph MM L/Cpl 18913 10th North Lancashire Regt
POLLARD Joseph W. MM Pte 103908 62nd Bn Machine Gun Corps
POLLARD M.J. MM Cpl 1267 Military Foot Police
POLLARD Paul H.F. MM Pte 11167 1st Royal Scots
POLLARD Percy John Wyatt MM CQMS 13780 Bedfordshire Regt
POLLARD Sidney L. MM Pte 703871 21st London Regt
POLLARD Thomas William MM Pte 23275 Lancashire Fusiliers
POLLARD Walter MM Cpl 17145 5/6th Scottish Rifles
POLLARD Walter MM L/Sjt 12830 9th Essex Regt DOW 7.5.17.
POLLARD Walter Richard MM L/Cpl 27139 219 Coy Machine Gun Corps KIA 8.7.17.
POLLARD Wilfred MM Tpr 1828 Royal Horse Guards
POLLARD William MM Pte 419005 2 Fd Amb RAMC
POLLARD William MM Dvr 697294 RFA
POLLARD William MM Pte 9446 1/1st Cambridgeshire Regt
POLLARD William MM Spr 311601 32 Div Sig Coy Royal Engineers
POLLARD William W. MM L/Cpl 9876 2nd Oxf & Bucks Light Infantry
POLLARD Zech(ariah?) MM L/Cpl 315947 13th Royal Highlanders
POLLEN Augustus MM Pte 203649 1st London Regt
POLLEY Alfred G. MM 2nd Cpl 23136 1 Div Sig Coy Royal Engineers
POLLEY Frederick MM Cpl 304599 12th Bn Tank Corps
POLLEY Jack MM Pte 8913 2nd Essex Regt
POLLIKETT Alfred J. MM L/Cpl 2989 Middlesex Regt
POLLINGTON Arthur MM Pte 86963 62nd Bn Machine Gun Corps
POLLINGTON George H. "DCM,MM+Bar" Sjt 12059 7th Norfolk Regt
POLLINGTON Herbert MM Pte 20454 3rd Grenadier Guards
POLLITT Fred MM Pte 251785 Manchester Regt
POLLITT Harold MM Cpl 13606 9th North Lancashire Regt
POLLITT Joseph MM L/Cpl 13036 12th Cheshire Regt
POLLITT Thomas MM Pte 201545 1/4th Royal Lancaster Regt
POLLITT William MM Sjt 275421 Manchester Regt
POLLOCK Allan R. MM Pte 40735 1/7th Arg & Suth Highlanders
POLLOCK Arthur "MM,MID" Sjt 42624 Royal Engineers
POLLOCK David "MM,MID" Sjt 11301 1st Cameron Highlanders KIA 18.9.18.
POLLOCK Henry MM Pte 511514 1/14th London Regt
POLLOCK Isaac MM Pte 11783 5th Royal Irish Fusiliers
POLLOCK James MM Pte 24812 Scottish Rifles
POLLOCK James MM Sjt 29144 Royal Inniskilling Fusiliers
POLLOCK James MM Dvr 6255 RFA
POLLOCK James MM Dvr 101219 RFA
POLLOCK James J. MM Sjt 2281 6th Connaught Rangers
POLLOCK John MM Sjt 43088 7th Bn Machine Gun Corps
POLLOCK John MM Pte 12861 5th Dragoon Guards
POLLOCK John MM L/Cpl 2419 Royal Irish Rifles
POLLOCK John MM Sjt 15818 Scottish Rifles
POLLOCK John Ronald MM+2 Bars Pte 355686 1/10th Liverpool Regt
POLLOCK Peter MM Cpl 15273 6/7th Royal Scots Fusiliers KIA 22.8.17.
POLLOCK Robert MM Pte 6022 2nd Lancashire Fusiliers
POLLOCK Robert MM Sjt 13642 9th Royal Inniskilling Fusiliers DOW 27.4.18.
POLLOCK Robert P. MM L/Cpl 295142 12th Royal Scots Fusiliers
POLLOCK Thomas "MM,MSM,MIDx2" Staff SM S/18630 Army Service Corps
POLLOCK William MM Sjt 69430 138 Army Troops Coy Royal Engineers
POLMEAR William Henry MM Pte 266776 2/1st Bucks Bn Oxf & Bucks Light Infantry KIA 6.12.17.
POLSON Alexander MM CQMS 14975 1st Royal Scots Fusiliers KIA 3.10.18.
POLSON Robert J. MM Sjt 18342 6th King's Own Scottish Borderers
POLSTON George MM Cpl 13713 1st Royal Berkshire Regt
POLWIN William J. MM Pte 136591 49th Bn Machine Gun Corps
POMEROY Arthur MM Gnr 179019 RFA
POMEROY John MM Dvr 108202 C/160 Bde RFA
POMFORD Edward "DCM,MM" Pte 33307 19th & 17th Royal Welsh Fusiliers
POMFRET Albert MM Pte 4694 1st Lancashire Fusiliers
POMFRET Thomas MM Gnr 62799 RGA
POMFRET William MM L/Cpl 90913 13th Liverpool Regt
POMROY George W. MM+Bar Sjt 14577 8th Suffolk Regt
PONCIA Giovanni MM Spr 213069 Royal Engineers
POND Albert J. MM Sjt 203394 8th East Surrey Regt
POND Bob F. MM Pte 201913 Northumberland Fusiliers
POND Henry W. "DCM,MM" Cpl 58925 50th Bn Machine Gun Corps
POND Nathan J.G. MM Dvr 931028 C/291 Bde RFA
POND Robert H. MM L/Bdr 68147 37 Bde RFA
PONDER Albert MM L/Cpl 153258 Rly Ops Div Royal Engineers
PONMAN George MM L/Cpl 12230 East Surrey Regt
PONSFORD Charles W. MM Pte 6637 Royal West Surrey Regt

PONSFORD Edgar J. MM L/Cpl 695111 22nd London Regt
PONSFORD Mark MM Pte 203600 1/5th Devonshire Regt
PONT Ernest Eugene MM Pte M2/151039 Army Service Corps att 2/3(London)Fd Amb RAMC.
PONT Ernest S. MM Sjt 48445 21 Bde RFA
PONT James D. MM Bdr 346689 108 Siege Bty RGA
PONT Sydney R. MM Sjt 2502 9th Lancers
PONT William MM L/Cpl 9217 1st North Staffordshire Regt
PONTET Harold C. MM Pte 42419 Lancashire Fusiliers
PONTING Ernest MM Bdr 87517 RFA
PONTING William C. MM Pte 200194 1/4th Wiltshire Regt
PONTON Thomas V. MM Sjt 164848 100th Bn Machine Gun Corps
POOK Arthur Charles MM Pte 92216 RAMC
POOK Charles Ernest MM Pte 81569 141 Coy Machine Gun Corps
POOK Frank MM L/Sjt 240441 1/5th Devonshire Regt
POOK Walter F. MM L/Cpl 41270 1/1st Cambridgeshire Regt
POOK William Leonard "MC,MM(27628 CSM RE Postal Section),MID" Capt 7th Royal West Surrey Regt
POOL William MM L/Sjt 11/597 11th East Yorkshire Regt
POOLE Albert MM Gnr 23562 34 Div Ammn Col RFA
POOLE Albert MM+Bar Sjt 17460 1/4th Royal Scots KIA 21.9.18.
POOLE Albert W. MM Sjt 492250 Royal Engineers
POOLE Albert William MM Pte 242700 2/5th South Lancashire Regt
POOLE Alfred MM Pte 36564 Lancashire Fusiliers
POOLE Alfred J. MM Pte M2/153464 Army Service Corps
POOLE Archibald MM Pte 3482 1/17th London Regt
POOLE Arthur MM Pte 200848 9th South Staffordshire Regt
POOLE Charles Arthur MM Pte 97558 31st Bn Machine Gun Corps
POOLE Charles G.W. MM Sjt 48006 Labour Corps
POOLE Charles H. MM Pte 16903 2nd Northumberland Fusiliers
POOLE Charles H. MM Sjt 9043 2nd Royal Welsh Fusiliers
POOLE Charles R. MM Pte 30964 17th Royal Sussex Regt
POOLE Edward W. MM Pte 242202 Worcestershire Regt
POOLE Ernest G. MM L/Cpl 203512 2/4th Oxf & Bucks Light Infantry
POOLE Ernest Ward MM Pte 11374 6th Yorkshire Light Infantry KIA 13.3.17.
POOLE F. MM L/Cpl 20487 1st Essex Regt
POOLE Frederick MM Pte 9568 2nd Northumberland Fusiliers
POOLE Frederick MM Pte 9834 1st Gloucestershire Regt
POOLE Frederick MM Sjt 7035 Machine Gun Corps KIA 21.8.18.
POOLE Frederick MM CSM 46322 Machine Gun Corps
POOLE G.S. MM Sjt 16040 Oxf & Bucks Light Infantry
POOLE George MM Sjt 31379 D/130 Bde RFA
POOLE George A. MM Cpl 9582 1st Northamptonshire Regt
POOLE George E. MM Pte 200078 Manchester Regt
POOLE Hamlet MM Pte 15251 8th North Staffordshire Regt
POOLE Harry MM Pte 2319 2nd Manchester Regt
POOLE Harry MM Sjt 255182 1/1st Leicestershire Yeomanry
POOLE Harry MM Pte 39833 RAMC
POOLE J.T. "DCM,MM" CSM 9405 1st East Kent Regt
POOLE John MM Dvr T/28490 Army Service Corps
POOLE John T. MM L/Cpl 16705 Yorkshire Light Infantry
POOLE Len R. MM Gnr 614101 1/1(Warwickshire)Bty RHA
POOLE Leslie Frederick "DCM,MM" L/Sjt 59619 10th Royal Fusiliers
POOLE Lionel MM Pte 7198 Coldstream Guards
POOLE Norman MM Pte 65674 103 Fd Amb RAMC
POOLE Percy C. MM Pte 1559 Lincolnshire Regt
POOLE Philip MM Sjt 60182 121 Bty 27 Bde RFA
POOLE Reginald Frank MM Cpl 11750 Leicestershire Regt
POOLE Richard MM L/Sjt 18734 9th South Staffordshire Regt
POOLE Richard H. MM L/Cpl 200969 2/5th Lancashire Fusiliers
POOLE Richard William MM L/Cpl 9598 2nd South Wales Borderers KIA 14.4.17.
POOLE Robert MM Dvr 33402 D/50 Bde RFA
POOLE Robert MM Sjt 105761 RGA
POOLE Samuel H. MM+Bar Sjt 8647 2nd West Yorkshire Regt
POOLE Sidney W. MM L/Cpl 19152 Welsh Regt
POOLE Stanley G. MM Pte 648344 20th London Regt
POOLE Stanley R. MM Spr 24363 1 Div Sig Coy Royal Engineers
POOLE T.H. MM CSM 4485 2nd Leinster Regt
POOLE Thomas MM Gnr 4358 RFA
POOLE Thomas MM Gnr 25454 RFA
POOLE Walter MM L/Cpl 10922 15th Hussars
POOLE Walter W. MM Pte 242137 1st Royal Lancaster Regt
POOLE William MM Pte 43850 Machine Gun Corps
POOLE William D. MM L/Cpl 169214 Royal Engineers
POOLE William H. MM AM2 65519 Royal Flying Corps
POOLER James MM Pte 28652 Royal Welsh Fusiliers
POOLES Thomas MM Pte 145474 25th Bn Machine Gun Corps
POOLEY Arthur G. MM Pte 36706 Lancashire Fusiliers
POOLEY E.C. MM Pte 14821 11th Essex Regt
POOLEY G.R. MM Pte 260707 Yeomanry
POOLEY George W. MM Sjt 10115 8th Suffolk Regt
POOLEY Horace MM Spr 132930 Royal Engineers
POOLMAN Emile H. MM Cpl 8957 1st Wiltshire Regt
POOLTON E. MM Pte 25116 East Surrey Regt
POOLTON Harry MM Pte 51516 16th Manchester Regt
POOLTON Joseph MM L/Cpl 330129 6th Royal Warwickshire Regt
POORE Alfred G. MM L/Cpl 49715 Royal Engineers
POORE Edward MM Pte 63615 13th Royal Fusiliers KIA 23.4.17.
POORE Walter MM+Bar Cpl 307095 6th Liverpool Regt
POPE Albert E. MM Pte 36169 Gloucestershire Regt
POPE Alfred MM CQMS 200026 2/5th West Yorkshire Regt
POPE Arthur E. MM Cpl 54920 RFA
POPE Charles MM Pte 21328 2nd Royal West Surrey Regt
POPE Charles George MM Sjt 10832 1st Royal Irish Fusiliers KIA 16.8.17.
POPE Edward T. MM Sjt 03212 Army Ordnance Corps
POPE Ernest A. MM Pte 3592 Army Cyclist Corps
POPE Frank MM Sjt S/1422 Rifle Brigade
POPE Frank MM Sjt 8078 5th Shropshire Light Infantry
POPE Frank V. "MM,MID" Cpl 66256 42 Bde RFA
POPE Frederick MM Sjt 20992 Hampshire Regt
POPE G.E. "DCM,MM" Sjt 10455 1st Shropshire Light Infantry
POPE Herbert C. MM Sjt 12247 7th Wiltshire Regt
POPE Herbert F. MM Pte 5698 1st Royal West Kent Regt
POPE J.J. "MM,MID" Bdr 5422 4(Durham)Coy RGA
POPE James MM Sjt 203500 9th Notts & Derby Regt
POPE John MM Cpl 32867 1st Royal Berkshire Regt
POPE John MM Pte 11732 1st Coldstream Guards att MGC.
POPE Joseph C. MM L/Cpl 344031 8 Div Sig Coy Royal Engineers
POPE Joseph T. "MM,MID" Sjt M2/079938 Army Service Corps
POPE Lionel MM Sjt S/961 7th Rifle Brigade
POPE Norman J. MM Pte 229281 1/2nd London Regt
POPE Richard MM Cpl 95433 A/65 Bde RFA
POPE Robert MM Pte 82218 20th Durham Light Infantry
POPE S.R. MM Pte 45250 Essex Regt
POPE Stephen H. MM Cpl 806239 RFA
POPE Sydeny MM Sjt 9673 1st Devonshire Regt
POPE Thomas R. MM CSM 62405 105 Coy Labour Corps
POPE William S. MM Dvr Sig 940296 D/280 Bde RFA
POPE William T. MM Sjt 330537 Liverpool Regt
POPEJOY Bert Samuel MM Sjt 72 8th Rifle Brigade KIA 21.3.18.
POPKINS John H. MM Cpl 10336 D/69 Bde RFA
POPLE A. MM Bdr 6808 35 Bde RFA
POPLE George MM+Bar Sjt 14022 7th Shropshire Light Infantry
POPLE Harry MM 2nd Cpl 499937 61 Div Sig Coy Royal Engineers
POPPLEWELL Richard E.C. MM Pte S/355493 Army Service Corps
PORCH William MM Pte 45427 15th Durham Light Infantry
PORCH William J. MM L/Cpl 504470 Royal Engineers
PORDAGE Harry Mackay MM Cpl 102287 RGA
PORKER Leonard H. MM Pte 1181 22nd Royal Fusiliers
PORLEY John Arthur "DCM,MM" Cpl 23177 27 Siege Bty & Y/17 Med TM Bty RGA
PORT Alexander MM Cpl 280984 1/7th Highland Light Infantry KIA 19.9.18.
PORT Charles William MM Cpl 7851 1st East Kent Regt DOW 8.6.17.
PORTAL James MM Sjt 3236 6th Dragoon Guards
PORTAS Harry MM Pte 26806 Notts & Derby Regt
PORTCH Alec Bernard MM Spr 151784 49 Div Sig Coy Royal Engineers
PORTCH William T. MM Cpl 530385 1/15th London Regt
PORTE Albert Douglas MM Pte 62911 1/6th West Yorkshire Regt
PORTEOUS Adrian MM Pte 11487 Northumberland Fusiliers
PORTEOUS Dennis Reid MM Pte 22923 7th Royal Sussex Regt KIA 28.3.18.
PORTEOUS Edward Kallis MM Pte 316438 RAMC
PORTEOUS Harry MM L/Cpl 496983 447 Fd Coy Royal Engineers
PORTEOUS James MM Sjt 9489 7th Seaforth Highlanders KIA 12.10.17.
PORTEOUS Kenneth McK. MM Sjt 155 Royal Engineers
PORTEOUS Ronald F. MM Pte 96223 2nd Middlesex Regt
PORTEOUS Wilfred G. MM Spr 301487 'F' Corps Sig Coy Royal Engineers
PORTEOUS William MM Pte 350753 Royal Scots
PORTEOUS William MM Pte 16513 9th Scottish Rifles
PORTEOUS William S. MM Pte 7991 2nd Cameron Highlanders
PORTEOUS William S. MM Gnr 99481 RGA

PORTER A.J. MM Cpl 1562 RFA
PORTER Alfred MM Pte 78211 18th Durham Light Infantry
PORTER Arthur MM Sjt 43108 Royal Engineers
PORTER Arthur MM Cpl 42428 13th Yorkshire Regt
PORTER Arthur T. MM L/Sjt 390756 9th London Regt
PORTER Benjamin R. MM Sjt 22909 1st Grenadier Guards
PORTER Bertie MM L/Cpl 34183 Middlesex Regt
PORTER Charles L. MM L/Cpl 512864 14th London Regt
PORTER David MM Pte 324841 9th London Regt
PORTER Edward "DCM,MM" L/Cpl 65337 126 Fd Coy Royal Engineers
PORTER Edward A. MM+Bar Sjt 720127 24th London Regt
PORTER Edward C. MM Gnr 170146 331 Siege Bty RGA
PORTER Edward Clifford MM L/Cpl 43957 1st Royal Irish Rifles KIA 16.8.17.
PORTER Edward G.C. MM Cpl 223 1/4th Royal Sussex Regt
PORTER Edward S. MM Sjt 14815 Dorsetshire Regt
PORTER Edwin MM Sjt 7764 1st East Yorkshire Regt
PORTER Egbert "MM,MID" Cpl 13720 C/74 Bde RFA
PORTER Eric Henry MM Spr 558584 Royal Engineers
PORTER Ernest MM Sjt 18357 20th Manchester Regt
PORTER Ernest J. MM+Bar L/Cpl 48266 Rifle Brigade
PORTER F. MM Spr 444270 Royal Engineers
PORTER Frank A. MM L/Cpl 70357 Notts & Derby Regt
PORTER Fred MM Pte 14991 6th Oxf & Bucks Light Infantry KIA 19.7.16.
PORTER Frederick MM Sjt 255152 1/1st Leicestershire Yeomanry
PORTER Frederick J. MM+Bar L/Cpl 241455 5th Yorkshire Light Infantry
PORTER Frederick James MM Cpl 11869 10th Royal Fusiliers KIA 8.10.18.
PORTER Frederick James MM L/Cpl 2822 6th Royal Irish Regt
PORTER Frederick William "DCM,MM" Cpl 16061 Machine Gun Corps
PORTER George MM Pte 30198 Border Regt
PORTER George N.S. MM Pte 9586 3rd Royal Fusiliers
PORTER H.S. MM AM2 4882 Royal Flying Corps
PORTER Harold MM L/Cpl 265697 Liverpool Regt
PORTER Harold Walter MM+Bar Sjt 2024 4th Gloucestershire Regt
PORTER Harry MM Cpl 11974 7th York & Lancaster Regt
PORTER Harry MM Tpr 2617 Household Bn DOW 7.12.17.
PORTER Harry Charles MM L/Cpl 672 1/4th York & Lancaster Regt
PORTER Henry C. MM Sjt M2/080591 Army Service Corps
PORTER Henry Dickinson MM Pte 23/64 9th Northumberland Fusiliers KIA 24.10.18.
PORTER Henry J. MM Sjt 72331 11th Royal Fusiliers
PORTER Herbert MM Pte 203528 1/4th Yorkshire Regt
PORTER Herbert MM Cpl 18301 Norfolk Regt
PORTER Herbert J. MM S/Sjt 34858 95 Fd Amb RAMC
PORTER Herbert S. MM Spr 159237 Royal Engineers
PORTER Hugh MM Pte 3999 RAMC
PORTER James MM Sjt 82313 26th Royal Welsh Fusiliers
PORTER James Edward MM Pte 15305 8th Royal Lancaster Regt
PORTER James L. MM L/Cpl 16376 1st King's Own Scottish Borderers
PORTER James Robert MM Spr 85498 Royal Engineers
PORTER John A. MM Sjt 17339 D/175 Bde RFA
PORTER John William MM Cpl 31287 Notts & Derby Regt
PORTER Joseph MM L/Cpl 7971 Machine Gun Corps
PORTER Leslie R. MM Cpl 201681 Middlesex Regt
PORTER Matthew James MM Cpl 2702 1/4th Royal Lancaster Regt
PORTER Norman MM Pte 290887 Gordon Highlanders
PORTER Percy Richard MM Sjt 7395 11th Royal Fusiliers
PORTER Percy W. MM Dvr 263124 16 Div Ammn Col RFA
PORTER R.W. MM Pte R/38213 King's Royal Rifle Corps
PORTER Richard MM+Bar Gnr 79443 D/1 Bde RFA
PORTER Richard Edward MM Spr 548626 Royal Engineers
PORTER Sidney Thomas William MM Cpl 30833 RFA
PORTER Stanley "MM,MID" Pte 9901 2nd South Wales Borderers
PORTER Stanley L.K. MM Pte 4362 3rd Dragoon Guards
PORTER Stephen MM Pte 31795 2nd Welsh Regt DOW 23.10.18.
PORTER Sydney MM Sjt 83202 HQ 68 Bde RFA
PORTER Thomas "MM,MSM" Sjt 12362 6 Fd Amb RAMC
PORTER Victor Richard MM Spr 558495 29 Div Sig Coy Royal Engineers DOW 22.3.18.
PORTER Walter MM Pte 235936 2/4th York & Lancaster Regt DOW 7.10.18.
PORTER Walter MM Sjt 202111 1/9th Royal Scots KIA 1.8.18.
PORTER Walter J. MM+Bar Cpl 200120 1/7th Worcestershire Regt
PORTER Walter P. MM Sjt 3726 Royal Fusiliers

PORTER William MM L/Cpl 300801 15th Durham Light Infantry KIA 18.9.18.
PORTER William MM Pte 290880 Gloucestershire Regt
PORTER William MM Pte 41735 Liverpool Regt
PORTER William MM Gnr 141311 RFA
PORTER William MM Pte Z/2108 12th Rifle Brigade KIA 20.11.17.
PORTER William MM Sjt 240117 4/5th Royal Highlanders Died 29.8.17.
PORTER William George MM Pte 3032 1/5th North Lancashire Regt KIA 30.11.17.
PORTER William J. MM Dvr 65199 121 Bty 27 Bde RFA
PORTER William J. MM Sjt 10724 1st Royal Fusiliers
PORTERFIELD Victor MM Cpl 265107 1/1st Bucks Bn Oxf & Bucks Light Infantry
PORTHOUSE John MM Pte 2705 1/8th Arg & Suth Highlanders
PORTLOCK George MM Sjt 34622 York & Lancaster Regt
PORTLOCK Percival MM Pte 20827 15th Hampshire Regt KIA 20.9.17.
PORTLOCK William MM Cpl 3295 6th North Lancashire Regt
PORTMAN Arthur John MM Sjt 201432 1/7th Worcestershire Regt
PORTMAN Joseph J. MM L/Sjt 242450 Worcestershire Regt
PORTON Thomas G. MM Pte 9745 Coldstream Guards
PORTSMOUTH E. MM Sjt 102312 Labour Corps
PORTWAY Joseph MM Pte 721962 24th London Regt
POSGATE Alfred MM Spr 558750 Royal Engineers
POSKETT H. MM Sjt 25281 11th Durham Light Infantry
POSKETT Robert MM L/Cpl 325324 1/9th Durham Light Infantry KIA 26.3.18.
POSKITT George Ernest Fisher MM Pte 2512 1/4th Royal Lancaster Regt DOW 31.7.16??
POSKITT John M. MM Gnr 2292 MGC(Motors)
POST Albert MM Pte S/34075 Rifle Brigade
POST Frederick MM L/Cpl 203654 1st London Regt
POST Reginald MM Pte 25135 4th Royal Fusiliers
POST William James "MM,MC(G)" SM 42062 66 Fd Amb RAMC
POSTANCE William "MM,MID" Sjt 2176 1/6th South Staffordshire Regt
POSTANS John MM L/Cpl 29823 Wiltshire Regt
POSTINS Leonard MM Sjt 201865 1/7th Worcestershire Regt
POSTLE Frederick MM Spr 102642 176 Tunnelling Coy Royal Engineers
POSTLE Thomas MM Pte 11002 11th Northumberland Fusiliers
POSTLETHWAITE C. MM Cpl 16079 RFA
POSTLETHWAITE Henry V. MM L/Cpl 821 Royal Engineers
POSTLETHWAITE John R. MM Pte 44621 8th Lincolnshire Regt
POSTLETHWAITE John R. MM Pte 21869 13th Liverpool Regt
POSTLETHWAITE Phillip MM Pte 9092 RAMC
POSTLETHWAITE William MM L/Cpl 480538 Royal Engineers
POSTON Edward Randolph MM Pte R/28596 17th King's Royal Rifle Corps
POTE John Henry MM Sjt 321404 'R' AA Bty RGA
POTHECARY Charles MM L/Bdr 109619 RGA
POTIPHAR John E. MM Pte 17894 Royal Sussex Regt
POTT A. MM Sjt 147593 252 Tunnelling Coy Royal Engineers
POTTAGE George Ernest MM Pte 30522 11th East Yorkshire Regt KIA 8.9.18.
POTTEN Allen J. MM Sjt 925549 B/290 Bde RFA
POTTER Albert E. MM Pte 24708 Royal Inniskilling Fusiliers
POTTER Alexander MM Pte 43436 12th Royal Scots DOW 3.6.18.
POTTER Alfred Edward "MM+Bar,MSM" Sjt 806690 A/296 Bde RFA
POTTER Alfred G. MM Gnr 146298 RFA
POTTER Alfred J. MM L/Cpl 1606 7th King's Royal Rifle Corps
POTTER Alfred T.W. MM Pte 422381 10th London Regt
POTTER Arthur MM L/Sjt 235489 1st North Lancashire Regt
POTTER Arthur MM+Bar Sjt 38952 Yorkshire Light Infantry
POTTER Arthur George MM Sjt 1054 6th East Kent Regt
POTTER Arthur Samuel MM L/Cpl 202886 10th West Riding Regt DOW 17.10.17.
POTTER Charles B. MM L/Bdr 612120 19 Bde RHA
POTTER Charles G. MM Sjt 300912 5th London Regt
POTTER Charles S. MM Pte 351916 7th London Regt
POTTER Edward "DCM,MM" CSM 7963 2nd Royal Munster Fusiliers
POTTER Edwin J. MM Pte 24394 South Wales Borderers
POTTER Enos MM Dvr T/1648 Army Service Corps
POTTER Ernest MM L/Cpl 19942 Grenadier Guards
POTTER Francis Xavier MM Sjt 38968 'N' Bty RHA
POTTER Frank MM+2 Bars Cpl 9634 D/83 Bde RFA
POTTER Frank MM Pte 2425 Army Cyclist Corps
POTTER George A. MM Pte 30781 10th Royal West Kent Regt

POTTER George L. MM L/Cpl 41258 9th Royal Fusiliers
POTTER George Samuel MM Sjt 12609 Labour Corps
POTTER H. MM AM2 50120 Royal Flying Corps
POTTER Hampton MM Sjt 70130 C/246 Bde RFA
POTTER Harry MM Gnr 136493 RGA
POTTER Henry "MM,MSM" Pte 50437 15th Cheshire Regt
POTTER Henry G. MM Pte 31179 5th East Lancashire Regt
POTTER Henry M. MM Pte 49534 19th Lancashire Fusiliers
POTTER Isaac MM Pte 58430 1st Leicestershire Regt
POTTER James L. MM Bdr 981 1/1(Worcs)Bty RFA
POTTER John MM Pte 22119 3rd Grenadier Guards
POTTER John Frederick MM L/Cpl 20715 15th Durham Light Infantry KIA 10.9.18.
POTTER John T. "DCM,MM" Sjt 20368 11th & 1/4th South Lancashire Regt
POTTER Joseph MM Sjt 23533 6th Dorsetshire Regt
POTTER Joseph "MM,MID" Cpl 57201 105 Fd Coy Royal Engineers
POTTER Leonard S. MM Pte 71599 Machine Gun Corps
POTTER Lomas MM Pte 14566 9th Norfolk Regt KIA 15.4.18.
POTTER Reginald C. MM Pte R/15745 2nd King's Royal Rifle Corps
POTTER Robert E. MM Sjt 14446 7th Royal Berkshire Regt
POTTER Robert E. MM L/Cpl 421215 RAMC
POTTER Thomas MM Pte 11144 1st Coldstream Guards
POTTER Thomas H. MM Pte 242237 York & Lancaster Regt
POTTER Thomas N. MM Dvr 750549 C/250 Bde RFA
POTTER Tom MM Dvr 39736 B/107 Bde RFA
POTTER Walter G. MM Pte 235321 13th Liverpool Regt
POTTER Whiteford MM Cpl 1537 Arg & Suth Highlanders
POTTER Wilfred T. MM Pte 240324 1/5th Devonshire Regt
POTTER William MM Sjt 240521 1/5th South Lancashire Regt
POTTER William "DCM,MM,MMV(It)" Sjt 2138 1/5th South Lancashire Regt
POTTER William A. "DCM,MM" QMS 31476 RAMC
POTTER William E. MM Pte 242613 South Staffordshire Regt
POTTERELL Stewart MM Sjt 37747 'Z' Bty RHA
POTTERILL Arthur W.T. MM Pte 39315 1/5th Border Regt
POTTERTON Charles MM Pte 15150 7th Royal Lancaster Regt
POTTINGER A. MM Spr 183984 Royal Engineers
POTTINGER George MM Pte 26938 RAMC
POTTINGER H. MM Pte 27589 8th Royal Berkshire Regt
POTTINGER Maurice W. MM Pte 201929 7th Bn Tank Corps
POTTINGER William Charles MM Pte 3281 2/4th Royal Berkshire Regt
POTTINGTON P.H. MM Pte 37571 55 Fd Amb RAMC
POTTLE Richard MM Cpl 12205 2nd Dragoon Guards
POTTON Ernest MM Sjt 7936 11th Royal Fusiliers
POTTON Richard MM Sjt 65523 Machine Gun Corps
POTTON Thomas James MM L/Cpl 10908 2nd Dragoon Guards
POTTS Alexander MM Sjt 24908 South Wales Borderers
POTTS Arthur MM Cpl 251048 1/6th Manchester Regt
POTTS Arthur MM Gnr 128123 RFA
POTTS Ernest MM Sjt 15700 East Yorkshire Regt
POTTS Ernest MM Pte 2245 23rd Middlesex Regt DOW 26.6.17.
POTTS Frank MM Pte 18020 1st Shropshire Light Infantry
POTTS Gabriel R. MM Cpl 77251 6 Div Sig Coy Royal Engineers
POTTS George MM Sjt 2069 1st Royal Highlanders
POTTS George W. MM L/Cpl 18771 South Lancashire Regt
POTTS Herbert MM Sjt M2/078211 Army Service Corps
POTTS Horace MM Cpl 4197 Machine Gun Corps
POTTS J.J. MM Pte 181342 Durham Light Infantry
POTTS James MM Gnr 686772 D/312 Bde RFA DOW 12.9.18.
POTTS James MM Pte 11328 20th Hussars
POTTS John MM Spr 148556 182 Tunnelling Coy Royal Engineers
POTTS John MM Sjt 20/815 Durham Light Infantry
POTTS John MM Pte 156115 17th Bn Machine Gun Corps
POTTS John "DCM,MM+Bar" Sjt 10727 23rd Middlesex Regt
POTTS John MM Cpl 17198 20th Manchester Regt
POTTS Joseph MM Pte 387 Lancashire Fusiliers
POTTS R. MM Pte 8319 1st Liverpool Regt
POTTS Reginald "MM,MID" Sjt 10733 8th Cheshire Regt
POTTS Samuel MM Cpl 50793 1/4th Cheshire Regt
POTTS Samuel Carr MM Bdr 134686 RFA
POTTS Septimus E. MM Cpl 270736 1/1st Northumberland Yeo
POTTS Sidney MM L/Cpl 99036 Machine Gun Corps
POTTS T. MM Cpl 49847 RGA
POTTS Thomas MM Cpl 30693 RFA
POTTS Thomas MM L/Cpl 265800 1/5th Cheshire Regt
POTTS Thomas MM L/Sjt 265183 Northumberland Fusiliers
POTTS Thomas G. MM Sjt 806 1/1st Northumberland Yeo
POTTS William MM Pte 240772 1/6th North Staffordshire Regt
POTTS William MM Pte 63455 2/4th Yorkshire Light Infantry KIA 2.9.18.
POTTS William MM Cpl 270404 1/1st Northumberland Yeo
POTTS William MM Pte 20852 Grenadier Guards
POTTS William Edgar MM L/Sjt 3370 5th West Yorkshire Regt KIA 13.4.18.
POUGET William Alfred MM Pte 33276 3rd Worcestershire Regt
POULSON Alfred MM Cpl 34 RAMC
POULSON John H. MM Sjt 41382 41 Div Ammn Col RFA
POULSON Owen F. MM Pte 307422 15th Bn Tank Corps
POULTER Albert Sidney MM Pte 14/1147 14th York & Lancaster Regt
POULTER Alfred MM Sjt 15758 54 Fd Coy Royal Engineers
POULTER Arthur Henry MM Pte 66475 99 Fd Amb RAMC
POULTER Charles MM Pte 8462 8th Yorkshire Regt
POULTER Edward J. MM L/Cpl 25329 1st Grenadier Guards
POULTER George MM Pte 280199 1/4th London Regt
POULTER George W. MM Pte 57883 15/17th West Yorkshire Regt
POULTER Herbert MM Pte 78424 13th Durham Light Infantry
POULTER Smith Stevens MM Sjt 13573 11th Suffolk Regt KIA 1.7.16.
POULTON Alfred MM Sjt 235476 1/1st Herefordshire Regt
POULTON Arthur MM Pte 32022 Norfolk Regt
POULTON Charles MM L/Cpl T2/14149 8 Reserve Park Army Service Corps
POULTON Claude H. MM Pte DM2/154024 Army Service Corps
POULTON Edwin Charles MM L/Cpl 8160 Royal Irish Rifles
POULTON Ernest "MM,MSM" Sjt 79460 173 Tunnelling Coy Royal Engineers
POULTON Harry MM Pte 2306 Coldstream Guards
POULTON James MM Sjt 36903 1st Leicestershire Regt
POULTON John B. MM Pte 202244 North Lancashire Regt
POULTON John Samuel MM Sjt 15206 2/6th Royal Warwickshire Regt DOW 25.10.18.
POULTON Ralph G. MM Sjt 69670 RFA
POULTON Richard E. MM Cpl 18740 D/148 Bde RFA
POULTON Thomas MM Sjt 22/1057 Northumberland Fusiliers
POULTON Walter MM+Bar Pte 8333 10th Royal Warwickshire Regt
POULTON William MM Sjt 201070 South Staffordshire Regt
POUNCEBY William MM Pte 20086 11th South Lancashire Regt
POUND Earnest MM Bdr 33416 RFA
POUND Henry MM Pte 6/1092 8th King's Royal Rifle Corps
POUNDER Reevel MM Sjt 7714 RFA
POUNDER William Henry MM Pte 251408 1/6th Manchester Regt KIA 28.3.18.
POUNDS Walter MM L/Bdr 56258 RGA
POUNTAIN Albert L. MM Pte 20118 1st Royal West Kent Regt
POUNTAIN Harold MM Gnr Wheeler 52118 67 Siege Bty RGA
POUNTAIN Sidney MM Pte 417330 1st(North Midland)Fd Amb RAMC
POUNTNEY John W. MM L/Cpl M2/191176 'P' Siege Park Army Service Corps
POUNTNEY Thomas F. MM L/Cpl 33940 1/1st Bucks Bn Oxf & Bucks Light Infantry
POUT James F. MM Pte 45473 RAMC
POVAH Thomas MM Pte 13712 12th Manchester Regt
POVALL Joseph MM Pte 239253 1/1st Herefordshire Regt att 6th KSLI.
POVER George MM Pte 241907 6th Liverpool Regt
POVEY Albert E.P. MM Pte 46359 13th Royal Fusiliers
POVEY Alfred H. MM Sjt 9221 1st Middlesex Regt
POVEY Arthur T. MM+Bar Sjt 11071 6th Royal West Kent Regt
POVEY Benjamin MM Sjt 13904 9th Norfolk Regt KIA 15.9.16.
POVEY Bertram "DCM,MM" Cpl 25389 1/5th South Staffordshire Regt
POVEY James J.G. MM Pte 52202 Machine Gun Corps
POVEY Thomas MM Sjt 240162 1/5th South Lancashire Regt DOW 6.12.17.
POVEY W.H. MM Pte 11630 1st Royal Welsh Fusiliers
POVEY William A. MM Sjt Farrier 697485 A/83 Bde RFA
POVEY William C. MM Dvr 16663 11th Notts & Derby Regt
POW Elliot MM Sjt 42259 Scottish Rifles
POW James "MM+Bar,MID" Cpl 49207 Guards Div Sig Coy Royal Engineers
POWDITCH George "DCM,MM" Sjt 10302 1st & 2nd Notts & Derby Regt
POWDRILL Ernest Oscar MM Sjt 14755 Leicestershire Regt
POWDRILL T.B. MM Pte 202928 7th East Kent Regt
POWE Albert V. MM Gnr 75527 RFA
POWELL Albert E. MM Cpl 18012 Gloucestershire Regt

POWELL Alexander MM Sjt 10348 Worcestershire Regt
POWELL Alexander MM Pte 72068 133 Fd Amb RAMC
POWELL Alexander MM Pte 7991 1st Shropshire Light Infantry
POWELL Alfred E. MM Spr 202743 206 Fd Coy Royal Engineers
POWELL Algy MM Pte 5648 21st London Regt
POWELL Arthur MM L/Cpl 202322 12th Manchester Regt
POWELL Arthur MM Dvr 25182 71 Bde HQ RFA KIA 28.3.18.
POWELL Arthur MM Pte 463 8th Royal Fusiliers
POWELL Arthur MM Sjt 103176 32 Div Sig Coy Royal Engineers
POWELL Arthur G. MM Pte B/344 Rifle Brigade
POWELL Arthur J. MM Gnr 616436 RHA
POWELL Arthur W. MM Pte 74093 2nd Devonshire Regt
POWELL Ben MM L/Sjt 260033 6th Royal Warwickshire Regt
POWELL Bert MM Sjt 14844 7th South Staffordshire Regt
POWELL Charles MM Pte 46888 9th Royal Welsh Fusiliers
POWELL Charles MM Pte 7358 2nd Middlesex Regt
POWELL Christopher MM Pte 29085 Machine Gun Corps KIA 26.3.18.
POWELL Clifford MM Spr 450042 9 Div Sig Coy Royal Engineers
POWELL Clifford MM Spr 62490 Royal Engineers
POWELL Daniel MM Sjt 5759 2nd Worcestershire Regt
POWELL E. MM L/Cpl 16324 Lancers
POWELL Edward MM Sjt 10184 2nd East Surrey Regt
POWELL Edward MM Pte 472142 12th London Regt KIA 21.9.18.
POWELL Edward A. MM L/Cpl 1589 7th East Kent Regt
POWELL Ernest H. MM Dvr 238266 B/79 Bde RFA
POWELL Evan B. MM Pte 76468 1st Royal Welsh Fusiliers
POWELL Evan M. MM Sjt Farrier 19187 RFA
POWELL Frank MM Sjt 630662 20th London Regt
POWELL Frank Joseph "MC,DCM,MM+Bar(10633 Sjt 5th Bn)" 2Lt 8th Royal Berkshire Regt
POWELL Frederick MM Sjt 81608 137 Coy Labour Corps
POWELL Frederick MM L/Sjt 240980 1/6th West Yorkshire Regt
POWELL Frederick C. MM Sjt 12529 9th Gloucestershire Regt
POWELL Frederick G. MM Sjt 25947 118 Heavy Bty RGA
POWELL Frederick Henry MM Sjt 607 2nd Royal Fusiliers KIA 9.10.17.
POWELL Frederick W. MM Sjt 242429 Liverpool Regt
POWELL Frithjof W. MM+Bar L/Cpl 68130 11th Royal West Surrey Regt
POWELL George MM Pte 49087 1st Cheshire Regt KIA 26.6.18.
POWELL George MM Spr 75584 Royal Engineers
POWELL George MM Gnr 179584 122 Siege Bty RGA
POWELL George MM Pte 1317 1/3rd Monmouthshire Regt
POWELL George H. MM Cpl 9610 2nd Royal Irish Fusiliers
POWELL George Richard MM Sjt 906 B/241 Bde RFA
POWELL George William MM Gnr 935491 C/315 Bde RFA KIA 4.4.18.
POWELL Gordon L. MM Pte 514971 14th London Regt
POWELL H. MM Pte 3516 Royal Warwickshire Regt
POWELL Harvey MM Pte 267399 10th Gloucestershire Regt
POWELL Henry MM Gnr 102742 RGA
POWELL Henry MM 2nd Cpl 136455 251 Tunnelling Coy Royal Engineers Died 23.9.17.
POWELL Henry G. MM L/Cpl P/1458 Rifle Brigade
POWELL Henry W. MM Sjt 60407 Machine Gun Corps
POWELL Herbert H. MM L/Bdr 128236 C/173 Bde RFA
POWELL Horace MM Sjt 109639 RGA
POWELL Horace A. MM Spr 246816 Royal Engineers
POWELL Hugh R. MM L/Cpl 33085 Lancashire Fusiliers
POWELL Isaac W.M. MM Pte M2/178460 Army Service Corps att RAMC.
POWELL Jack P. MM Cpl 393 Royal Flying Corps
POWELL James "MM,MID" Sjt 276223 117 Siege Bty RGA
POWELL James MM L/Cpl 107164 40 Div Sig Coy Royal Engineers
POWELL James MM Sjt T/20236 3 Reserve Park Army Service Corps
POWELL James MM Sjt 8667 3rd Worcestershire Regt
POWELL James C. MM Pte 52787 1st Middlesex Regt
POWELL James William MM Cpl 20809 22nd Manchester Regt KIA 13.7.16.
POWELL Jesse MM Sjt 17012 1st Somerset Light Infantry KIA 4.10.17.
POWELL John MM Pte 46407 South Staffordshire Regt
POWELL John MM L/Sjt 11898 1st Notts & Derby Regt
POWELL John MM Bdr 676632 C/275 Bde RFA
POWELL John Arthur MM Pte 55626 9th Royal Welsh Fusiliers DOW 7.11.18.
POWELL John Charles "MM,MSM,MID" CSM 15543 2nd Grenadier Guards
POWELL John H. MM Gnr 109024 RGA
POWELL John P. MM L/Cpl 53882 Royal Welsh Fusiliers
POWELL John William MM Sjt 17264 8th Northumberland Fusiliers
POWELL Jonathan MM L/Cpl 23167 Liverpool Regt
POWELL Joseph MM Cpl 16611 8th East Yorkshire Regt
POWELL Joseph C. MM L/Cpl 4176 6th Royal West Surrey Regt
POWELL L. MM Pte 19221 11th Essex Regt
POWELL L.B. MM L/Sjt 33895 Royal Welsh Fusiliers
POWELL Landeg MM Cpl 79996 174 Tunnelling Coy Royal Engineers
POWELL Leo Percy MM L/Cpl 40629 Middlesex Regt
POWELL Leslie G. MM L/Cpl 1917 RAMC
POWELL Louis MM+2 Bars L/Cpl 43434 9th Essex Regt
POWELL Malcolm MM Gnr 205292 241 Bde RFA
POWELL Miles MM Pte 260280 18th Gloucestershire Regt
POWELL Oscar M. MM L/Cpl M2/203324 Army Service Corps
POWELL Owen Thomas MM Sjt T/254341 Army Service Corps
POWELL P. MM L/Cpl 30711 Machine Gun Corps
POWELL P. MM Sjt 36985 RGA
POWELL Robert Henry MM Pte 7584 1st Lincolnshire Regt DOW 9.10.18.
POWELL Robert James MM L/Cpl 266032 1/2nd Monmouthshire Regt KIA 31.7.17.
POWELL S.J. MM Bdr 1047 B/121 Bde RFA
POWELL Samuel MM Pte 78422 13th Durham Light Infantry KIA 29.10.18.
POWELL Samuel MM Pte 39541 South Staffordshire Regt
POWELL Samuel Arthur MM Sjt 103199 32 Div Sig Coy Royal Engineers DOW 17.11.16.
POWELL Samuel E. MM Gnr 32228 RHA
POWELL Sidney MM Cpl 266127 Monmouthshire Regt
POWELL Stanley G. MM Pte 265 1st Welsh Guards
POWELL Stephen R. MM Sjt 36887 16th Royal Welsh Fusiliers
POWELL T.C. MM Sjt 2898 RFA
POWELL Thomas MM Pte 18277 2nd Royal Dublin Fusiliers
POWELL Thomas MM Pte 40422 Lancashire Fusiliers
POWELL Thomas MM Pte 39584 13 Fd Amb RAMC
POWELL Thomas H. MM Pte 25392 14th Royal Warwickshire Regt
POWELL W. MM Cpl 439046 3rd(South Midland)Fd Amb RAMC
POWELL William MM Pte 706 1st Welsh Guards
POWELL William MM Pte 1517 2nd Welsh Regt
POWELL William MM Bdr 30490 122 Heavy Bty RGA
POWELL William MM Pte 243030 5th Leicestershire Regt
POWELL William MM L/Sjt 30094 16th Royal Warwickshire Regt
POWELL William MM Pte 22100 Machine Gun Corps
POWELL William "MM,MID" CSM 658 Royal Engineers
POWELL William MM Pte 46657 RAMC
POWELL William MM Pte 22181 13th Welsh Regt DOW 13.10.18.
POWELL William MM Sjt 19/348 13th Durham Light Infantry KIA 5.10.18.
POWELL William Edward MM Pte 9533 1st Royal West Surrey Regt KIA 13.4.18.
POWELL William F. MM L/Bdr 825443 A/240 Bde RFA
POWELL William H. MM Pte 13708 8th Somerset Light Infantry
POWELL William H. MM Sjt T4/241948 Army Service Corps
POWELL William T. MM Sjt Y/832 13th King's Royal Rifle Corps
POWELL William Thomas MM Cpl 595 1st Middlesex Regt KIA 23.10.18.
POWER Alfred MM Gnr 124615 A/117 Bde RFA
POWER Charles MM Pte 19830 Machine Gun Corps
POWER Edwain MM Dvr 34372 RFA
POWER Geoffrey MM Pte 10550 1st Irish Guards
POWER George MM+2 Bars Sjt 8714 2nd York & Lancaster Regt KIA 1.12.17.
POWER Herbert James MM Pte 9704 8th Royal Fusiliers
POWER John MM L/Cpl 794 9th Royal Munster Fusiliers
POWER John H. MM L/Cpl 17296 19th Lancashire Fusiliers
POWER John J. "DCM,MM,MSM" RSM 14388 HQ First Army Royal Engineers
POWER Joseph Henry MM Pte 20174 12th Yorkshire Regt
POWER Leo J.J. MM Pte 56986 10th Lancashire Fusiliers
POWER Martin MM Pte 12611 5th Lancers
POWER Michael MM Pte 102979 Machine Gun Corps
POWER Peter MM L/Cpl 50109 1/6th Cheshire Regt
POWERS Herbert E. MM Pte 2039 Middlesex Regt
POWERS Thomas MM Dvr 23666 49 Div Ammn Col RFA
POWIS Bertie MM Pte 54231 Royal Welsh Fusiliers
POWIS Frank MM+Bar Cpl 30725 1st Gloucestershire Regt
POWIS P.W. MM L/Cpl P1948 Military Foot Police
POWIS William MM Gnr 24486 RFA

POWLESLAND John William Wallington MM Pte 21563 4th Grenadier Guards KIA 25.9.16.
POWLS William MM Pte 420 9 Fd Amb RAMC
POWNALL Alfred MM Cpl 10751 2nd Notts & Derby Regt
POWNALL John MM+Bar Pte 241828 1/5th South Lancashire Regt
POWNALL William MM Spr 6973 Royal Engineers
POWNER Arthur "MM,MID" Sjt PW/1534 19th Middlesex Regt
POWNER William H. MM Pte R/37818 King's Royal Rifle Corps
POWNEY A.S. MM Pte 48441 131 Fd Amb RAMC
POWNEY Albert MM Pte 12927 South Staffordshire Regt
POWNEY George Victor MM L/Cpl 496335 Royal Engineers
POWRIE Henry MM Sjt 44209 RFA
POWSEY John "MM,MID" Pte 6278 1st Royal Berkshire Regt
POXON Christopher William MM Sjt C/241 16th King's Royal Rifle Corps
POXON Henry MM Sjt 2126 1/5th York & Lancaster Regt KIA 7.10.16.
POXON Samuel MM Pte 18315 2nd Cheshire Regt
POXON Silas MM 2nd Cpl 49540 Royal Engineers
POXON William MM Pte 27667 Notts & Derby Regt
POYNER James MM Pte 16400 18th Lancashire Fusiliers
POYNER Thomas MM Cpl 34558 58 Coy Labour Corps
POYNTER Edward MM Pte 18835 8th Royal Berkshire Regt KIA 16.11.17.
POYNTER Robert B. MM Pte(SS) 3411 7th Dragoon Guards
POYNTON James "MM,MID" Sjt 89152 RFA
POYNTON Robert MM 2nd Cpl 444169 66 Div Sig Coy Royal Engineers
POYNTS or POYNTZ William MM+Bar Cpl 44746 41 Bde RFA
POYSER Arthur MM Dvr 31814 RFA
POYSER William MM Pte 14763 Machine Gun Corps
PRAED Thomas A. MM Sjt 137727 RGA
PRAGNELL Arthur Henry MM Pte 70834 8th Bn Machine Gun Corps Died 31.5.18.
PRAGNELL Frederick J. MM Pte 1949 1/23rd London Regt
PRAGNELL Gilbert MM Cpl 11170 11th Hampshire Regt KIA 17.10.18.
PRAGNELL Harry MM Sjt 748 1/3(London)Fd Coy Royal Engineers KIA 15.9.16.
PRAGNELL Leonard Cyril MM Gnr 28593 B/174 Bde RFA
PRAGNELL Louis V. MM Pte 25002 1st Hampshire Regt
PRAGNELL William James MM Cpl 13306 1st East Kent Regt
PRALET Edward MM Cpl S/35441 17th London Regt
PRANDLE Owen MM Pte 15751 Royal Welsh Fusiliers
PRANGLE William MM Cpl 8500 1st Rifle Brigade
PRANGLEY Arthur H. MM Cpl 107693 180 Coy Labour Corps
PRANGNELL William MM Sjt 173745 202 Siege Bty RGA
PRATCHETT Sidney James MM Cpl T3/025119 194 Coy Army Service Corps DOW 16.6.17.
PRATCHETT William MM Pte 16644 Yorkshire Light Infantry
PRATER Harry E. MM Pnr 360677 18 Div Sig Coy Royal Engineers
PRATER Sidney Percy MM L/Cpl 137723 237 Fd Coy Royal Engineers
PRATLEY Alfred D. MM L/Cpl 4512 10th Royal Fusiliers
PRATLEY Leonard MM Sjt 318046 5th London Regt
PRATT Alexander M. MM Sjt 37540 A/46 Bde RFA
PRATT Alfred MM Spr 28410 Royal Engineers
PRATT Alfred MM Pte 15318 7th Bedfordshire Regt DOW 7.8.17.
PRATT Andrew MM Pte 13005 Scots Guards
PRATT C. MM L/Cpl 437359 RAMC
PRATT Charles E. MM+Bar Sjt 16207 6th Leicestershire Regt
PRATT Charles Henry MM Sjt 19810 21st Middlesex Regt DOW 13.11.18.
PRATT Charles V. MM L/Cpl M2/133337 Army Service Corps
PRATT David MM Cpl 46537 RAMC
PRATT Douglas MM Pte 305111 8th West Yorkshire Regt
PRATT Edward Broquire MM Pte 10674 9th Royal Fusiliers
PRATT Ernest MM Pte 12807 Seaforth Highlanders
PRATT Frank "MM,MID" Sjt 75576 1/1st Derbyshire Yeomanry
PRATT George C. MM Gnr 4416 RFA
PRATT George E. MM Cpl 84609 Royal Engineers
PRATT George Henry Michael MM Pte 25664 2nd Grenadier Guards
PRATT Harold Mornington MM Spr 44966 93 Fd Coy Royal Engineers
PRATT Henry MM Pte 50610 1st West Yorkshire Regt
PRATT James R. MM Cpl 34709 2nd York & Lancaster Regt
PRATT James W. MM L/Cpl 241296 Lancashire Fusiliers
PRATT John J. MM Pte 242740 15th Cheshire Regt
PRATT John W. MM Pte 200124 Leicestershire Regt
PRATT Joseph MM Sjt 12773 10th Durham Light Infantry
PRATT Joseph B. MM Pte 21708 6th York & Lancaster Regt
PRATT Norman MM Cpl 46125 307 Siege Bty RGA
PRATT Norman MM Cpl 11429 2nd Durham Light Infantry
PRATT Tom L. "MM,MID" Sjt 12796 Royal Engineers
PRATT Walter MM Cpl 131185 233 Fd Coy Royal Engineers DOW 7.8.17.
PRATT William MM Pte 201336 2nd Bedfordshire Regt
PRATT William MM Sjt 79522 Royal Engineers
PRATT William E. "MM,MSM" L/Bdr 685827 C/293 Bde RFA
PRATT William Ernest MM Pte 15918 6th Northamptonshire Regt
PRATT William F. MM Bdr 68963 5 Bde RFA
PRATT William H. MM Pte 280930 2/4th London Regt
PRATT William J. MM Pte 200877 1/5th York & Lancaster Regt
PRATT William John MM Pte 733 7th East Surrey Regt
PRATTEN Benjamin "DCM,MM" CSM 6458 1st South Wales Borderers
PRATTEN James R. "DCM,MM" Dvr 48845 9 Bde RFA
PREBBLE F.R. MM L/Cpl 659 7th East Kent Regt
PREBBLE Rupert H. MM Cpl 71671 10th Royal Fusiliers
PREBBLE William MM Pte 17020 7th Wiltshire Regt
PRECIOUS Alan Montagu MM Cpl 102862 Machine Gun Corps
PRECIOUS Fred MM Pte 18343 1st West Yorkshire Regt
PRECIOUS George MM L/Cpl 16/187 West Yorkshire Regt
PRECIOUS Henry MM Sjt 312038 RGA
PRECIOUS Hubert P. MM Sjt 352825 7th London Regt
PRECIOUS Thomas MM Pte 22447 2nd West Yorkshire Regt
PREECE Charles MM Pte 21/860 Northumberland Fusiliers
PREECE Edgar A. MM L/Cpl 26646 2nd Grenadier Guards
PREECE EdwinJ. "DCM,MM" Sjt 200037 1/4th Yorkshire Light Infantry
PREECE Frank E. MM Bdr 830029 48 Div Ammn Col RFA
PREECE Frederick M. "MM,MID" Spr 22721 Royal Engineers
PREECE George Reginald MM Sjt 25437 10th Royal Dublin Fusiliers Awarded for 'Easter Rising'.
PREECE James Henry MM Pte 42438 13th Yorkshire Regt
PREECE Jesse MM L/Sjt 265976 Welsh Regt
PREECE John W. MM Sjt 894 1/6th Welsh Regt
PREECE Sidney R. MM Pte 18633 Shropshire Light Infantry
PREECE Thomas Leonard MM Pte 75559 13th Royal Welsh Fusiliers
PREEDY Albert E. MM Pte 36890 1st Gloucestershire Regt
PREEDY George T. MM Pte 233310 2nd London Regt
PREEDY Henry Wakefield MM Sjt 11983 2nd Worcestershire Regt
PREEN Arthur MM L/Cpl 9631 1st Devonshire Regt
PRENDERGAST Edward MM Pte 13587 9th North Staffordshire Regt
PRENDERGAST John MM Sjt 240480 1/5th North Lancashire Regt
PRENDERGAST Thomas MM Dvr 131651 235 Army Troops Coy Royal Engineers
PRENDERGAST William MM L/Cpl 27140 106 Coy Machine Gun Corps
PRENDIVILLE John MM+Bar Pte 4559 1st Royal Munster Fusiliers KIA 12.9.18.
PRENTICE Adam MM Pte 7978 1/6th Royal Highlanders
PRENTICE Albert MM Sjt 3174 2/4th Oxf & Bucks Light Infantry
PRENTICE Charles MM Pte 1114 17th Middlesex Regt att MGC.
PRENTICE Edmund George MM Pte 38516 2nd Yorkshire Regt KIA 6.5.18.
PRENTICE George MM Gnr 193407 122 Bty 52 Bde RFA
PRENTICE J. MM Pnr 418139 Royal Engineers
PRENTICE Thomas MM Pte 10428 Seaforth Highlanders
PRENTICE Walter MM L/Cpl STK/800 10th Royal Fusiliers
PRENTICE William MM Pte 29566 7th Hussars
PRENTICE William MM Cpl 18893 Royal Scots
PRENTICE William MM Pte 1026 15th Hussars
PRENTICE William MM L/Cpl 43464 12th Highland Light Infantry
PRENTICE William MM Pte 65978 2nd Royal Fusiliers KIA 9.10.17.
PRENTICE William D. MM Gnr Sig 84458 213 Siege Bty RGA
PRENTIS Joseph E. MM Pte 306731 8th West Yorkshire Regt
PRENTIS Wilfred G. MM L/Cpl 6034 Royal West Surrey Regt
PRESBURY George F. MM Sjt 43482 41 Bde RFA
PRESBURY William Walter Henry MM+Bar Bdr 43481 93 Bty 18 Bde RFA
PRESCOT Harry MM Pte 23742 North Lancashire Regt
PRESCOTT Arthur E.C. MM Pte 24900 Oxf & Bucks Light Infantry
PRESCOTT Fred MM Gnr 123823 RFA
PRESCOTT George Thomas MM Pte 495329 2/2(Home Counties)Fd Amb RAMC
PRESCOTT Harold C. MM Pte 39642 RAMC

PRESCOTT Harry MM Pte 203242 2/4th North Lancashire Regt
PRESCOTT Harry MM Pte 718 Lincolnshire Regt
PRESCOTT Henry J. MM L/Cpl 241404 2/5th South Lancashire Regt
PRESCOTT Herbert Edwin MM Pte 34839 1st Essex Regt
PRESCOTT James MM Pte 235498 1st Royal Lancaster Regt
PRESCOTT James MM Pte 20377 11th South Lancashire Regt
PRESCOTT Thomas MM Spr 74428 30 Air Line Section Royal Engineers Died 30.10.17.
PRESCOTT Thomas MM Pte 4882 20th Royal Fusiliers KIA 16.4.17.
PRESCOTT Thomas MM Sjt 19303 6th South Lancashire Regt
PRESCOTT William MM Pte 20610 11th South Lancashire Regt
PRESLAND Frederick J. MM Sjt 79109 185 Tunnelling Coy Royal Engineers
PRESLY George McConnachie MM L/Cpl 357439 Signal Service Royal Engineers att 73 HAG RGA.
PRESS Sydney A. MM Pte MS/2943 40 Div MT Coy Army Service Corps
PRESS Sydney G. MM Spr 558695 Royal Engineers
PRESS Walter MM CSM 502 10th Royal Fusiliers
PRESSDEE James MM Sjt 21083 231 Coy Machine Gun Corps KIA 24.11.17.
PRESSEY Jabez H. MM Cpl 700353 1/23rd London Regt
PRESSLEY Charles MM Pte 9784 1st Northumberland Fusiliers
PRESSLEY Frank MM+Bar L/Cpl 290443 1/7th Gordon Highlanders
PRESSLEY Harold J. MM Dmr 1566 Gordon Highlanders
PRESSLEY Lewis MM Sjt Dmr 240544 1/4th Gordon Highlanders
PRESSLEY Percy MM Sjt 40890 Manchester Regt
PRESSLING Albert MM Dvr 35773 RFA
PREST Joseph MM Pte 6368 Northumberland Fusiliers
PREST Stanley E. MM Pte 36171 1st Gloucestershire Regt
PRESTAGE Ralph MM Sjt 10347 1st Royal Dublin Fusiliers KIA 5.10.17.
PRESTIDGE Leonard MM Cpl 17136 12th Notts & Derby Regt
PRESTIDGE William MM Sjt 15057 7th South Lancashire Regt
PRESTON Albert E. MM Pte 57465 12th Suffolk Regt
PRESTON Albert Edward MM Bdr 20761 49 Bty 40 Bde RFA KIA 19.10.18.
PRESTON Arthur MM Pte 2129 Royal Irish Rifles
PRESTON Bernard T. "MM,MID" Cpl 8170 RFA
PRESTON Charles MM Pte 140460 32nd Bn Machine Gun Corps
PRESTON Edward MM Pte 245180 Manchester Regt
PRESTON Edward H. MM Pte 21983 Royal Fusiliers
PRESTON Frederick Alexander Halkerston MM Cpl 22150 3 Sig Sqn Royal Engineers
PRESTON George MM Pte 16373 Lancashire Fusiliers
PRESTON George MM Sjt 95218 D/64 Bde RFA
PRESTON George B. MM Sjt 10574 1st Royal Scots
PRESTON George Henry MM Gnr 28879 D/160 Bde RFA
PRESTON George W. MM Gnr 71534 32 TM Bty RFA DOW 7.6.17
PRESTON George William MM Sjt 684 7th Royal Sussex Regt KIA 20.11.17.
PRESTON Harry MM Pte 23786 Worcestershire Regt
PRESTON Henry MM Cpl 40112 Royal Engineers
PRESTON Henry MM L/Cpl 9214 2nd Bedfordshire Regt
PRESTON Henry Spencer MM L/Cpl 352205 2/2(East Lancashire)Fd Amb RAMC
PRESTON Herbert MM L/Cpl 430264 25 Div Sig Coy Royal Engineers
PRESTON Herman MM Pte 50307 25th Northumberland Fusiliers Died 8.4.18.
PRESTON Horace Bert MM Pte B/2662 7th Rifle Brigade
PRESTON Isaac E. MM Bdr 198692 460 Bty 15 Bde RFA
PRESTON James MM Sjt 240377 1/5th King's Own Scottish Borderers
PRESTON James E. MM L/Cpl 7824 1st Royal Lancaster Regt
PRESTON James E. MM Dvr 111200 RFA
PRESTON John MM Gnr 1583 Tank Corps
PRESTON John Freeman MM Bdr 775809 C/310 Bde RFA
PRESTON John W. MM Pte 388349 2 Fd Amb RAMC
PRESTON Joseph MM L/Cpl 44207 Royal Welsh Fusiliers
PRESTON Lawrence N. MM Cpl 240742 2/8th Middlesex Regt
PRESTON Lindley MM Bdr 12130 HQ 161 Bde RFA KIA 10.7.17.
PRESTON Robert Joseph Roland MM Pte 41366 Leicestershire Regt
PRESTON Samuel MM L/Cpl 20695 Scottish Rifles
PRESTON T. MM Pte 11129 Royal Irish Rifles
PRESTON Wallace MM Sjt 780050 RFA
PRESTON Walter MM L/Cpl 26279 2nd North Lancashire Regt
PRESTON William MM Cpl 108170 Machine Gun Corps
PRESTON William MM Pte 25631 Leicestershire Regt
PRESTON William H. MM Gnr 103133 236 Hy Bty RGA
PRESTWICH James MM Sjt 43710 'O' Bty RHA
PRESTWOOD Arthur W. MM Pte 280939 Lancashire Fusiliers
PRESTWOOD Walter Marshall MM Pte 6862 1st Lincolnshire Regt KIA 8.11.17.
PRETIOUS Arthur Victor MM Pnr 193077 2 Special Coy Royal Engineers
PRETSEL John MM Cpl 43025 Royal Scots
PRETTY Felix MM Gnr 751357 D/317 Bde RFA
PRETTY Reginald H. MM+Bar Pte 46062 Worcestershire Regt
PREVAL Sidney MM Pte 2995 West Yorkshire Regt
PREW Mark MM Pte 27815 11th Royal Warwickshire Regt
PRICE Albert MM L/Cpl 10196 South Staffordshire Regt
PRICE Albert C. MM L/Bdr 182625 203 Siege Bty RGA
PRICE Albert Edward MM Pte 23464 7th Royal West Kent Regt KIA 28.3.18.
PRICE Albert J. MM Pte 15637 4th Grenadier Guards
PRICE Albert W. MM Sjt 1285 RAMC
PRICE Alfred MM Sjt 776883 245 Bde RFA
PRICE Alfred MM Dvr 40624 8 Bde RFA
PRICE Alfred J. MM Pte 43278 13th West Riding Regt
PRICE Alfred R. MM Pte 241118 Gloucestershire Regt
PRICE Arnold MM Spr 492406 Royal Engineers
PRICE Arthur MM Cpl 295017 12th Royal Scots Fusiliers DOW 3.11.18.
PRICE Arthur MM Cpl 200230 1/5th South Staffordshire Regt KIA 28.4.18.
PRICE Arthur MM Cpl 25727 X/2 Med TM Bty RFA KIA 11.6.16.
PRICE Arthur MM Sjt 15614 7th South Wales Borderers
PRICE Arthur E. MM+Bar Pte 200611 1/4th Leicestershire Regt
PRICE Bertie MM L/Cpl 14651 8th Suffolk Regt
PRICE Bromley H. MM Pte 5591 141 Fd Amb RAMC
PRICE C.W. MM Cpl 52110 28th London Regt
PRICE Caleb MM L/Sjt 8449 Royal Fusiliers
PRICE Charles MM Bdr 67156 9 Bde RFA
PRICE Charles A. MM CSM 39922 67 Coy Labour Corps
PRICE Charles A. MM Cpl 16354 8th South Wales Borderers
PRICE Charles B. MM CQMS 5268 1st Worcestershire Regt
PRICE Charles H. MM Cpl 492356 Royal Engineers
PRICE Charles J. MM Cpl 2196 1/1st London Regt KIA 7.10.16.
PRICE Charles W. MM Gnr 2346 RFA
PRICE Charles William MM Pte 34738 Royal Fusiliers
PRICE David W. "DCM,MM" L/Cpl 452577 3 Div Sig Coy Royal Engineers
PRICE Edgar MM Gnr 706064 RFA
PRICE Edmund Trevor MM Spr 126428 1 Sig Constr Coy Royal Engineers
PRICE Edward MM Bdr 45524 RFA
PRICE Edward C. MM Sjt 680179 1/22nd London Regt
PRICE Edwin MM Pte 364309 RAMC
PRICE Elias MM L/Cpl 16946 6th South Wales Borderers
PRICE Ernest MM Pte 10457 8th Devonshire Regt
PRICE Ernest MM Dvr 46538 RFA
PRICE Ernest S. "DCM,MM+Bar" Sjt 29407 33 Div Sig Coy Royal Engineers
PRICE Eustace MM Pte 55919 RAMC
PRICE F.J. MM Pte 24033 15th Royal Irish Rifles
PRICE Francis J. MM Cpl 2503 1/5th South Lancashire Regt
PRICE Frank MM Pte 3402 2 Fd Amb RAMC
PRICE Frank J. MM Pte 33015 1/4th Oxf & Bucks Light Infantry
PRICE Fred MM Pte 42579 8th York & Lancaster Regt
PRICE Fred MM Pte 28903 20th Lancashire Fusiliers
PRICE Frederick MM Cpl 41397 6th King's Own Scottish Borderers Died 29.11.18.
PRICE Frederick MM Sjt 9825 2nd South Wales Borderers
PRICE Frederick MM Spr 230775 406 Fd Coy Royal Engineers
PRICE Frederick C. MM Gnr 5340 A/174 Bde RFA
PRICE Frederick Gilbert MM Pte 6470 2nd Royal West Surrey Regt KIA 1.9.16.
PRICE Frederick Walter MM+Bar Pte 1339 VIII Corps Cyclist Bn Army Cyclist Corps
PRICE Geirge Leonard J. MM Gnr 129660 RGA
PRICE George MM Pte 137524 49th Bn Machine Gun Corps
PRICE George MM Pte 45590 5th Lancashire Fusiliers
PRICE George MM Sjt 11725 Shropshire Light Infantry
PRICE George MM Pte 9579 South Staffordshire Regt
PRICE George A. MM L/Cpl 1804 26th Royal Fusiliers
PRICE George E.T. MM L/Cpl 10857 7th Norfolk Regt
PRICE H. MM Pte 36901 1st Gloucestershire Regt

PRICE Harry MM Sjt 14689 4th Grenadier Guards
PRICE Henry MM Bdr 56592 RGA
PRICE Henry MM Pte 26059 9th Royal Dublin Fusiliers
PRICE Henry G. MM Cpl S/2058 Rifle Brigade
PRICE Henry G. MM Pte 200753 1/4th Gloucestershire Regt
PRICE Henry J. MM Cpl CMT/733 1 Cav Div Train Army Service Corps
PRICE Howell MM Pte 8495 2nd Royal Welsh Fusiliers DOW 20.7.16.
PRICE Ivor MM Pte 13737 9th Welsh Regt
PRICE James MM L/Cpl 41 12th Yorkshire Light Infantry
PRICE James MM+Bar Pte 27826 1/4th Cheshire Regt
PRICE James MM Pte 6439 22nd Northumberland Fusiliers KIA 5.6.17.
PRICE James Arthur MM Bdr 66265 RFA
PRICE James William MM Cpl 149495 119 Railway Coy Royal Engineers
PRICE John MM Pte 28553 1/4th Shropshire Light Infantry
PRICE John MM Pte 240874 1/5th Cheshire Regt
PRICE John MM Pte 19948 3rd Grenadier Guards
PRICE John MM Pte 42439 Yorkshire Regt
PRICE John MM Pte 10335 13th Gloucestershire Regt KIA 22.3.18.
PRICE John MM Pte 14433 5th South Wales Borderers DOW 4.4.18.
PRICE John MM Dvr 105631 RFA
PRICE John MM Pte 16181 8th East Lancashire Regt
PRICE John MM Pte 6287 1st Royal Welsh Fusiliers
PRICE John MM Pte 16899 6th South Wales Borderers
PRICE John MM+Bar L/Cpl 2088 2nd South Lancashire Regt
PRICE John MM Pte 10616 1st Royal Dublin Fusiliers
PRICE John MM Pte 10222 3rd Worcestershire Regt DOW 15.4.18.
PRICE John "MM,MID" L/Cpl 444445 Royal Engineers
PRICE John C. MM Sjt 200239 1/4th Cheshire Regt
PRICE John Edward "DCM,MM" Sjt 11017 2nd Hampshire Regt
PRICE John M. MM L/Cpl 15215 10th Royal Welsh Fusiliers
PRICE John W. MM Cpl 1068 6 Fd Amb RAMC
PRICE John William MM L/Cpl 9631 Machine Gun Corps
PRICE Joseph "DCM,MM" Sjt 202132 2/4th South Lancashire Regt
PRICE Joseph C. MM Cpl 110528 MGC(Cavalry)
PRICE Joseph Henry MM Pte 1863 (370347) 8th London Regt DOW 21.4.18.
PRICE Leonard "DCM,MM" Pte 13582 7th Leicestershire Regt
PRICE Leonard MM Gnr 51118 RGA
PRICE Leonard H. MM Pte M2/148629 Army Service Corps
PRICE Leonard S. MM Pte 1787 8th Royal Sussex Regt
PRICE Llewellyn MM Cpl 200702 2nd Royal Welsh Fusiliers
PRICE Morgan R. MM L/Cpl 265721 1/2nd Monmouthshire Regt
PRICE Norman MM Pte 6889 1/4th Royal Welsh Fusiliers
PRICE P. "MM,MID" Dvr 2247 D/119 Bde RFA
PRICE Peter MM Pte 17102 6th Royal Inniskilling Fusiliers
PRICE R. MM L/Cpl 240303 South Lancashire Regt
PRICE Rees MM Gnr 37654 RGA
PRICE Reginald MM Dvr 32 RFA
PRICE Reginald L. MM Pte 390848 15th London Regt
PRICE Richard MM Gnr 79721 RFA
PRICE Richard MM L/Cpl 375041 1/10th Manchester Regt
PRICE Richard MM L/Sjt 16940 7th South Staffordshire Regt DOW 7.8.17.
PRICE Robert A. MM L/Cpl 4266 1st Dragoon Guards.
PRICE Robert G. "MM,MSM" Sjt 82431 123 Fd Coy Royal Engineers
PRICE Robert H. MM Sjt 680178 1/22nd London Regt
PRICE Samuel MM Pte 3061 14 Fd Amb RAMC
PRICE Samuel MM+Bar Sjt 137629 179 Tunnelling Coy Royal Engineers
PRICE Samuel MM Bdr 131226 A/70 Bde RFA
PRICE Samuel MM Pte 29298 20th Lancashire Fusiliers
PRICE Samuel R. MM Cpl 66251 RAMC
PRICE Sidney MM Pte 10613 6th Duke of Cornwall's LI Died 8.2.17.
PRICE Stanley P. MM Gnr 56974 B/104 Bde RFA
PRICE Thomas MM Pte 53692 2nd Royal Scots Fusiliers
PRICE Thomas MM Sjt 200338 1/4th Cheshire Regt
PRICE Thomas MM Sjt 1687 1/5th Cheshire Regt
PRICE Victor W.J. MM Pte 33236 10th Shropshire Light Infantry
PRICE W. MM Pte M2/200464 Army Service Corps
PRICE W. MM Sjt 75934 Tank Corps
PRICE W.G. MM Cpl 53023 Royal Air Force
PRICE W.H.L. MM Sjt 536365 RAMC
PRICE W.J. MM Cpl 66421 100 Fd Amb RAMC
PRICE Wallace MM Bdr 75325 RGA
PRICE Walter MM Pte 9956 7th East Kent Regt
PRICE Walter Edward MM Sjt 33728 59 Bty RFA DOW 11.8.17.
PRICE Walter Henry MM Cpl 20639 1/8th Worcestershire Regt
PRICE Wesley MM Sjt 15124 7/8th King's Own Scottish Borderers KIA 18.8.18.
PRICE Wilfred C.H. MM Cpl 60237 Royal Fusiliers
PRICE William MM Pte 43876 1st Bedfordshire Regt
PRICE William MM L/Cpl 1642 4th Bn GMGR
PRICE William MM L/Cpl 473 12th Yorkshire Light Infantry
PRICE William MM Pte 9357 2nd Lancashire Fusiliers
PRICE William MM Sjt 54483 RAMC
PRICE William MM Sjt 267859 Cheshire Regt
PRICE William E. MM Cpl 56757 9th Welsh Regt
PRICE William Edward MM Sjt 1897 1/1st Gloucestershire Yeomanry KIA 21.9.18.
PRICE William G. MM Dvr 75530 113 Bty 25 Bde RFA
PRICE William J. "MM,MID" Cpl 1061 Royal Engineers
PRICE William J. MM Sjt 8673 Royal Berkshire Regt
PRICE William J. MM Pte R/6221 King's Royal Rifle Corps
PRICE William J. MM Gnr 99451 RHA
PRICE William Thomas MM L/Cpl 29986 1st Grenadier Guards
PRICKETT Wilson MM Sjt 241348 Royal Lancaster Regt
PRIDDING Arthur R. MM Sjt 201321 Liverpool Regt
PRIDDLE Albert C. MM Sjt 11899 1st Coldstream Guards
PRIDE Cyril MM Pte 10006 Royal Berkshire Regt
PRIDEAUX A. MM AM1 13896 Royal Flying Corps
PRIDGEON W.E. MM Pte R/6432 King's Royal Rifle Corps
PRIDMORE George MM Pte 9752 2nd York & Lancaster Regt
PRIDMORE John T. MM L/Cpl 9097 2nd Northamptonshire Regt
PRIESS E.C. MM Pte 29817 Hampshire Regt
PRIEST Adam MM Pte 200883 9th South Staffordshire Regt
PRIEST Alexander MM Pte 41513 Seaforth Highlanders
PRIEST Eli MM Pte 20518 Cheshire Regt
PRIEST Frederick C. MM Pte 34634 4th West Riding Regt
PRIEST Joseph MM Pte 7900 10th Royal Warwickshire Regt DOW 24.3.18.
PRIEST Sydney MM Pte 52985 12th Manchester Regt
PRIEST Thomas MM+Bar Sjt 200669 1/4th Gordon Highlanders
PRIEST Thomas MM Sjt 25462 10th Royal Dublin Fusiliers KIA 11.2.17.
PRIEST William MM Sjt 201258 4th York & Lancaster Regt
PRIEST William Joseph MM L/Cpl 11038 11th Royal Warwickshire Regt Died 29.1.17.
PRIESTLEY Albert MM+Bar Dvr 776727 RFA
PRIESTLEY Arthur MM Sjt 21440 West Yorkshire Regt
PRIESTLEY Barker MM Cpl 40128 York & Lancaster Regt
PRIESTLEY Charles H. MM Cpl 200018 Royal Engineers
PRIESTLEY Edgar MM Sjt 241414 West Riding Regt
PRIESTLEY Harold MM Sjt 15812 11th West Yorkshire Regt
PRIESTLEY Hubert Briggs MM+Bar L/Sjt 242897 West Riding Regt
PRIESTLEY J. MM L/Cpl 15728 York & Lancaster Regt
PRIESTLEY John MM L/Cpl 4548 2/8th West Yorkshire Regt KIA 22.11.17.
PRIESTLEY Sam MM Gnr 26656 26 Bty 17 Bde RFA
PRIESTLEY Thomas Walter MM L/Sjt 16250 1st Lincolnshire Regt KIA 21.3.18.
PRIESTLEY Walter MM Pte 13777 Coldstream Guards
PRIESTLY Edward MM Sjt 20/220 20th Durham Light Infantry Died 13.8.18.
PRIESTMAN Harry MM L/Cpl 2265 1/5th Yorkshire Regt
PRIESTMAN John W. MM Spr 10285 Royal Engineers
PRIESTMAN Leonard MM L/Cpl 242696 7th Royal West Surrey Regt
PRIESTNER William MM Pte 52699 Cheshire Regt
PRIGG Charles William MM Pte 13310 8th Norfolk Regt KIA 15.10.17.
PRIGG George B. MM 2nd Cpl 141551 Royal Engineers
PRIGMORE George E. MM Pte 202731 1st London Regt
PRIKE L. MM L/Sjt 302424 London Regt
PRIME Alfred MM Pte 10620 1st Royal West Surrey Regt
PRIME Claude MM Cpl 805739 A/296 Bde RFA KIA 6.11.18.
PRIME Ernest MM Sjt 5034 Machine Gun Corps
PRIME Frank H. MM Bdr 47251 RFA
PRIME Henry George MM Sjt 9425 2nd Royal Welsh Fusiliers
PRIME J. MM Pte 722914 London Regt
PRIME William MM L/Cpl 16253 Middlesex Regt
PRIMETT Harry MM Spr 69270 35 Div Sig Coy Royal Engineers
PRIMMER Frederick MM Pte 3/5312 2nd Hampshire Regt DOW 2.5.17.
PRIMMER William MM Pte 21446 15th Hussars

PRIMROSE J.G. MM L/Cpl 8974 2nd Royal Scots
PRINCE Albert MM L/Cpl 18656 Royal Scots
PRINCE Charles MM+Bar Sjt 201348 1/8th Worcestershire Regt
PRINCE Charles F. MM Gnr 149063 RFA
PRINCE Frederick MM Sjt 200533 1/5th King's Own Scottish Borderers
PRINCE George MM 2nd Cpl 137576 257 Tunnelling Coy Royal Engineers
PRINCE George Edward MM+Bar Cpl 36644 2nd Royal Fusiliers KIA 17.10.18.
PRINCE Harold MM Pte 281126 18th Lancashire Fusiliers
PRINCE Harold A.V. MM Cpl 201502 1/5th Bedfordshire Regt
PRINCE Harry Richard MM Cpl 38764 21 Bty 2 Bde RFA KIA 4.11.18.
PRINCE Ivor MM Pte 29040 6th South Wales Borderers KIA 22.10.18.
PRINCE J.E. "DCM,MM" Sjt 14017 RFA
PRINCE John MM Pte 23605 South Wales Borderers
PRINCE John R. MM Cpl 11864 20th Hussars
PRINCE John William MM Pte 7354 8th East Lancashire Regt
PRINCE Joseph MM Pte 11051 2nd Welsh Regt
PRINCE Reginald J. MM Pte 51244 4th Bedfordshire Regt
PRINCE Reginald W. MM Spr 500281 Royal Engineers
PRINCE Richard MM Cpl 18376 10th Yorkshire Regt
PRINCE William MM Sjt 48988 82 Coy Machine Gun Corps
PRINCE William MM 2nd Cpl 63373 Royal Engineers
PRINCE William Charles "MM,MID" QMS 15288 RAMC att GHQ BEF.
PRING Stephen H. MM Pte 285329 14th Welsh Regt
PRINGLE Alexander MM Pte 45785 RAMC
PRINGLE Archibald MM Sjt 145385 1/1st Northamptonshire Yeomanry
PRINGLE Frank MM L/Cpl 202962 Gloucestershire Regt
PRINGLE George G. MM L/Cpl 44189 Royal Scots
PRINGLE George P. MM Pte 95680 10th Bn Tank Corps
PRINGLE James E. MM L/Cpl 221375 Durham Light Infantry
PRINGLE Laurence MM Sjt 463129 50 Div Sig Coy Royal Engineers
PRINGLE Robert MM L/Cpl 27025 6th Cameron Highlanders
PRINGLE Thomas Henry MM Pte 24951 14th Durham Light Infantry
PRINGLE William MM Pte 19241 6/7th Royal Scots Fusiliers
PRINGLE William MM L/Cpl 285400 Seaforth Highlanders
PRINT George MM Bdr 65334 RFA
PRINT Samuel H. MM L/Cpl 76052 Tank Corps
PRIOR Albert MM Sjt Farrier 947721 RFA
PRIOR Albert C. MM Gnr 139184 RFA
PRIOR Albert H. MM Spr 538433 Signal Service Royal Engineers
PRIOR Benjamin Richard MM Spr 505662 IWT Div Royal Engineers
PRIOR C. MM L/Cpl P1411 Military Foot Police
PRIOR Charles MM Pte 40588 Royal Scots
PRIOR Harry "MM,MID" Bdr 124969 120 Bde RFA
PRIOR Harry W. MM Cpl 10930 8th West Riding Regt
PRIOR Hubert J. MM Cpl 200746 1/4th Suffolk Regt
PRIOR James MM Pte 6156 2nd Scots Guards
PRIOR John MM Pte 28520 Scottish Rifles
PRIOR John A. MM Pte 235835 Lancashire Fusiliers
PRIOR John J. MM Cpl 19340 2 Fd Coy Royal Engineers KIA 23.10.16.
PRIOR Joshua H. MM Dvr 90588 45 Bde RFA
PRIOR Stephen MM Cpl 10733 2nd Royal Berkshire Regt DOW 12.4.17.
PRIOR Sydney C. MM Sjt 201505 1/4th Royal Berkshire Regt
PRIOR Thomas B. MM+Bar Cpl 27598 Somerset Light Infantry
PRIOR William MM Pte 12978 VIII Corps Cyclist Bn Army Cyclist Corps
PRIOR William A. MM+Bar Sjt 1415 5 Fd Amb RAMC
PRIOR William Henry MM Gnr 82057 A/64 Bde RFA
PRISCOTT William MM Bdr 130218 C/87 Bde RFA
PRISLEY Charles MM Pte 1243 20th London Regt
PRISMALL William G. MM Cpl 3266 RFA
PRITCHARD Alfred G. MM Bdr 91588 RFA
PRITCHARD Alfred Jesse MM Pte 3494 24th Royal Fusiliers KIA 13.11.16.
PRITCHARD Algernon W. MM Sjt 502002 55 Div Sig Coy Royal Engineers
PRITCHARD Arthur MM Spr 5361 Royal Engineers
PRITCHARD Benjamin T. MM Pte 2523 1st Welsh Guards
PRITCHARD Charles MM Cpl 13543 17th Royal Scots
PRITCHARD Charles MM CQMS 457 1/2nd Monmouthshire Regt
PRITCHARD Edgar P.H. MM Cpl 22257 Royal Welsh Fusiliers
PRITCHARD Edward MM Sjt 166 RGA
PRITCHARD Edward MM Sjt 1480 South Staffordshire Regt
PRITCHARD Ernest MM Pte 235022 Royal Warwickshire Regt
PRITCHARD Francis MM Pte 10889 6th Royal Inniskilling Fusiliers
PRITCHARD Frank MM L/Cpl 12934 2nd Worcestershire Regt
PRITCHARD Frederick H. MM Bdr 79250 266 Siege Bty RGA
PRITCHARD George MM Pte 20756 10th South Wales Borderers
PRITCHARD George S. MM Pte 136255 58th Bn Machine Gun Corps
PRITCHARD Harry MM Pte 48794 13th Liverpool Regt
PRITCHARD James MM Pte 295177 4th London Regt
PRITCHARD James C. MM Sjt 1218 Royal West Surrey Regt
PRITCHARD John MM Spr 488430 203 Fd Coy Royal Engineers DOW 12.6.18.
PRITCHARD John MM Pte 15689 14th Royal Welsh Fusiliers DOW 2.11.16.
PRITCHARD John MM Pte 20865 16 Coy Machine Gun Corps KIA 27.6.17.
PRITCHARD John MM Pte 12064 4th Worcestershire Regt
PRITCHARD Richard MM Pte 19050 1/5th Arg & Suth Highlanders
PRITCHARD Richard MM Cpl 310101 RGA
PRITCHARD Robert MM CSM 15460 8th South Lancashire Regt
PRITCHARD Rowland MM Pte 63057 Notts & Derby Regt
PRITCHARD Samuel MM Pte 37276 Lancashire Fusiliers
PRITCHARD Stanley MM Pte 34881 1/5th Yorkshire Regt
PRITCHARD Thomas E. MM Pte 19131 Cheshire Regt
PRITCHARD Thomas E. MM Gnr 3848 RFA
PRITCHARD William MM Gnr 5085 RGA
PRITCHARD William MM Cpl 132855 RGA
PRITCHARD William J. MM Pte 242068 Notts & Derby Regt
PRITCHARD William J. MM Cpl 17097 8th East Lancashire Regt
PRITCHARD William John MM Cpl 12611 1st South Wales Borderers
PRITCHARD William R. MM L/Cpl 266478 7th Liverpool Regt
PRITCHARD Wilson MM Pte 3687 Army Cyclist Corps
PRITCHETT Alfred MM Pte 12492 6th Royal Berkshire Regt
PRITT Alan D. MM Dvr 214985 RFA
PRITTY Thomas J.C. MM Gnr 9992 RFA
PRIVETT George MM L/Cpl 241198 East Surrey Regt
PRIVETT W.H. MM Pte 39165 23rd London Regt
PROBERT David MM Sjt 13063 Machine Gun Corps
PROBERT George Llewellyn MM Pte 39318 Yorkshire Light Infantry
PROBERT Harry MM Pte 8170 1st Shropshire Light Infantry KIA 12.10.16.
PROBERT John William Moule MM Pte 4821 1st Rifle Brigade
PROBERT William MM Sjt 14329 5th South Wales Borderers
PROBERT William J. MM Cpl 48627 RAMC
PROCKTER Leonard MM Pte 1679 1/24th London Regt
PROCTER Edmund W. MM Pte R/34588 2nd King's Royal Rifle Corps
PROCTER F. MM Sjt 2939 Machine Gun Corps
PROCTER James W. MM L/Bdr 37083 2 Mountain Bty RGA
PROCTER Mason MM Gnr 108693 10 Mountain Bty RGA
PROCTER Thomas MM Pte 306873 4th West Riding Regt
PROCTER Thomas MM Pte 136805 62nd Bn Machine Gun Corps
PROCTER William MM Pte P/749 1st Rifle Brigade
PROCTER William H. MM Pte 11216 5th Royal Berkshire Regt
PROCTOR Albert J. MM Sjt 45624 45 Bde RFA
PROCTOR Alfred J. MM Pte 1592 19th London Regt
PROCTOR Arthur MM Pte 28591 East Yorkshire Regt
PROCTOR Arthur W. MM Cpl 16033 9th Northumberland Fusiliers
PROCTOR Douglas MM CoH 2875 Life Guards
PROCTOR Edwin "MM,MSM" Sjt 480070 457 Fd Coy Royal Engineers
PROCTOR Ernest MM Cpl 232853 2nd London Regt
PROCTOR Ernest Edwin MM Pte 51765 2nd Suffolk Regt Died 22.11.18.
PROCTOR F.G. MM Gnr 820368 RFA
PROCTOR Frank MM Cpl 295092 Manchester Regt
PROCTOR Frederick R. MM 2nd Cpl 500247 Royal Engineers
PROCTOR Harry MM Pte 7392 11th Royal Fusiliers
PROCTOR Herbert MM Sjt 4879 1st North Staffordshire Regt
PROCTOR John Whitehead MM Pte 16/935 1st West Yorkshire Regt DOW 4.6.18.
PROCTOR N. MM Gnr 794 RFA
PROCTOR Richard MM Pte 15746 Royal Irish Rifles
PROCTOR Samuel MM Pte 12356 Highland Light Infantry
PROCTOR Samuel MM Dvr 108172 86 Bty 32 Bde RFA KIA 31.8.18.
PROCTOR Thomas MM Gnr 800342 B/230 Bde RFA

PROCTOR Thomas A. MM Cpl 10145 2nd East Lancashire Regt
PROCTOR Thomas Edward MM Sjt 24308 A/64 Bde RFA
PROCTOR William MM Cpl 34934 225 Siege Bty RGA
PROCTOR William "DCM,MM" CQMS 10476 2nd Seaforth Highlanders
PRODERICK John MM Sjt Dmr 5205 1st South Staffordshire Regt
PRODHAM William MM L/Cpl 15954 Northumberland Fusiliers
PROFFITT Alfred MM Cpl 6545 16th Manchester Regt
PROFFITT Charles MM Sjt 15339 11th Notts & Derby Regt
PROFFITT Thomas MM Cpl 101507 RFA
PROLE Robert MM Pte 54651 110 Fd Amb RAMC
PROLL J. "MM+Bar,MID" Cpl 2622 B/148 Bde RFA
PROLL John MM L/Cpl 12901 7th Somerset Light Infantry
PRONGER Harry G. MM Pte 15961 Royal Sussex Regt
PRONGER Percy T. "DCM,MM" Cpl 9027 4 Fd Amb RAMC
PROPHET Daniel W. MM Pte 41830 1/6th Royal Highlanders
PROSPER Peter MM 2nd Cpl 87348 Royal Engineers
PROSSER Albert MM Pte 27806 18th Welsh Regt KIA 24.3.18.
PROSSER Cecil MM CQMS 13109 6th South Staffordshire Regt
PROSSER Charles L. MM Sjt 18067 16th Royal Welsh Fusiliers
PROSSER George Valentine MM+Bar Pte 64545 Machine Gun Corps
PROSSER George W.C. MM Sjt 10029 1st East Surrey Regt
PROSSER Harry E. MM Cpl 203619 1st London Regt
PROSSER John MM Pte 40885 4th Yorkshire Light Infantry
PROSSER Oliver MM Spr 63494 Royal Engineers
PROSSER Thomas Edward MM Gnr 105218 D/75 Bde RFA
PROSSER Thomas J. MM Pte 36909 Lancashire Fusiliers att RE.
PROTHERO David MM Pte M/206143 32 Div Train. Army Service Corps
PROTHERO George Richard MM Cpl 18922 16th Royal Welsh Fusiliers DOW 7.2.17.
PROTHEROE Albert MM Pte 200268 Worcestershire Regt
PROTHEROE Joseph MM Pte 12539 7th Somerset Light Infantry KIA 1.9.16.
PROUD Harold C. MM Pte 268071 Royal Warwickshire Regt
PROUD Richard P. MM Pte 93430 23rd Royal Fusiliers
PROUD Sydney MM L/Cpl 571 Army Cyclist Corps
PROUD William "DCM,MM" Sjt 9047 2nd Scots Guards
PROUDFOOT Andrew MM Pte 201124 4th North Lancashire Regt
PROUDFOOT Daniel John MM Sjt 10853 1st Royal Scots Fusiliers
PROUDFOOT Henry MM L/Cpl 16087 6th Yorkshire Regt
PROUDFOOT John L. MM Pte 25721 Scottish Rifles
PROUDFOOT Peter MM Pte 39229 5th Gloucestershire Regt
PROUDLOVE Herbert MM+Bar Cpl 55901 51st Bn Machine Gun Corps
PROUDLOVE T. MM Pte 55934 Yeomanry
PROUDLOVE William MM Pte 1316 Royal Fusiliers
PROUSE Frederick MM Cpl 6873 Devonshire Regt
PROUSE Percy MM Pte 118640 Machine Gun Corps
PROUT Alfred MM Pte 8545 Somerset Light Infantry
PROUT G.H. MM Pte 28306 10th Essex Regt
PROUT George MM L/Cpl 15205 8th Somerset Light Infantry
PROUT James MM Pte 16341 6th South Wales Borderers
PROVAN J. MM Pte 3123 Arg & Suth Highlanders
PROVAN James MM L/Cpl 273003 Royal Scots
PROVAN William MM Cpl 2330 10th Arg & Suth Highlanders
PROVEN William MM Sjt 7541 1st Scots Guards
PROVINCE Charles MM Sjt 240336 5th Devonshire Regt
PROVO Cecil J. MM Pte 60567 17th Royal Welsh Fusiliers
PROVOST Thomas V. MM Dvr 695423 D/286 Bde RFA
PROW Arthur A. MM Sjt 251766 1/8th Arg & Suth Highlanders
PROWSE Edwin Walter John MM Sjt 30460 Devonshire Regt
PROWSE Henry W. MM Pte 25393 Somerset Light Infantry
PROWSE Wilfred MM CSM 265070 1/9th Middlesex Regt
PROWSE William H. MM Sjt 800627 RFA
PRUCE Bertram MM L/Cpl 2183 1/21st London Regt
PRUDDEN Frederick MM Pte 6465 6th Bn Machine Gun Corps
PRUDEN Herbert MM Gnr 800928 2/1(North Midland)Bde RFA
PRUDENCE C. MM Pte 3199 17th Lancers
PRUDHAM Thomas MM Pte 325410 1/9th Durham Light Infantry
PRUDHOE George F. MM Cpl 95201 1st Liverpool Regt
PRUEN Philip William MM Pte 240879 2/5th Gloucestershire Regt KIA 31.3.18.
PRYCE Alexander B. MM CQMS 1738 5/6th Royal Scots
PRYCE Cecil Trevor MM Pte 399362 63 Fd Amb RAMC
PRYCE Edwin MM Pte 15163 8th Shropshire Light Infantry
PRYCE Herbert C. MM Sjt 291122 Royal Welsh Fusiliers
PRYCE Robert E. MM Cpl 355356 25th Royal Welsh Fusiliers
PRYDE James MM Pte 273165 13th Royal Scots
PRYDE James MM Cpl 11945 1st Dragoon Guards
PRYDE James A. MM Cpl 345451 24th Royal Welsh Fusiliers
PRYDE Thomas MM Sjt M2/049847 Army Service Corps att 10 Fd Amb RAMC.
PRYDE Walter MM Pte 4724 Highland Light Infantry
PRYDE William MM L/Cpl 350858 1/7th Royal Highlanders
PRYER Charles "MC,MM,MSM" CSM 7272 Norfolk Regt
PRYER George MM Cpl 11423 1st Liverpool Regt
PRYER Harry J. MM Pte 1497 7th Royal West Surrey Regt
PRYER John W. MM L/Cpl 200895 8th Cheshire Regt
PRYKE Charles W. MM Cpl 17176 Machine Gun Corps
PRYKE George MM Pte 230331 10th Shropshire Light Infantry
PRYKE William J. MM L/Cpl 201497 Yorkshire Regt
PRYOR Edward MM Sjt 546057 509 Fd Coy Royal Engineers
PRYOR Reginald H. MM L/Cpl 281130 4th London Regt
PRYOR William J. MM Cpl 70408 1/1st Berkshire Yeomanry
PRYTHERCH John T. MM Sjt 251213 113 Rly Const Coy Royal Engineers
PTOLOMEY Charles E.A. MM L/Cpl 1238 Army Cyclist Corps
PUBLICOVER Thomas Dudley MM Pte 14088 2nd Coldstream Guards
PUCKETT Henry George MM Sjt 47091 64 Fd Coy Royal Engineers
PUCKETT Percy MM Sjt 10052 1st Border Regt
PUCKEY Charles MM L/Cpl 22306 Duke of Cornwall's LI
PUDDICK P.W. MM Cpl 10890 Wiltshire Regt
PUDDIFOOT Walter MM Cpl 3835 52 Coy Machine Gun Corps KIA 10.11.17.
PUDDY George MM Sjt 81686 46 Bde RFA
PUDNER Terence MM Cpl 20869 14th Royal Welsh Fusiliers
PUDNEY Alfred MM Pte 40485 2nd Bedfordshire Regt KIA 18.9.18.
PUDNEY Arthur Leonard MM Pte 24114 Hampshire Regt
PUDNEY Cecil MM Pte 11132 7th Lincolnshire Regt KIA 6.2.17.
PUDNEY Edward J. MM Pte 31272 6th Royal Dublin Fusiliers
PUDNEY Mark B. MM L/Cpl 498343 476 Fd Coy Royal Engineers
PUDNEY Norman H. MM+Bar L/Cpl 24204 2nd Yorkshire Regt
PUDNEY Sidney George MM Cpl 12530 9th Essex Regt
PUDNEY Victor W. MM Pte 42795 4th Middlesex Regt
PUE Alexander MM L/Cpl 18642 12th Royal Irish Rifles KIA 2.9.18.
PUFFET Frederick George MM L/Cpl 48580 5th Royal Berkshire Regt
PUGH A. MM Sjt 12588 Worcestershire Regt
PUGH Alfred Edward MM Pte 18282 15th Cheshire Regt
PUGH C. MM Dvr 835916 C/311 Bde RFA
PUGH D. MM Pte 20218 Royal Lancaster Regt
PUGH D.T. MM L/Cpl 265385 Royal Welsh Fusiliers
PUGH Edward John MM Pnr 249176 42 Div Sig Coy Royal Engineers Died 2.11.18.
PUGH F.C. MM Sjt 17268 1/4th Shropshire Light Infantry
PUGH F.E. MM L/Cpl 240292 5th Gloucestershire Regt
PUGH Frederick John MM Sjt S/34490 13th Rifle Brigade
PUGH G. MM Pte 31138 8th Somerset Light Infantry
PUGH H. MM Pte 18216 Manchester Regt
PUGH H. MM Sjt 8062 Shropshire Light Infantry
PUGH H. "DCM,MM" Pte 12069 8th Gloucestershire Regt
PUGH H. MM Pte 290046 Royal Welsh Fusiliers
PUGH Horace William MM Pte 60503 7th Royal West Surrey Regt KIA 8.8.18.
PUGH I.H. MM Cpl 2645 RFA
PUGH J. MM Cpl 265434 1/7th Royal Warwickshire Regt
PUGH J. MM Sjt 10952 South Staffordshire Regt
PUGH J. MM Pte 242728 East Lancashire Regt
PUGH J.J. MM Pte 9136 Royal Fusiliers
PUGH Richard A. MM Cpl 345755 Royal Welsh Fusiliers
PUGH Richard D. MM Spr 452300 Royal Engineers
PUGH Robert Henry "MC,MM(40190 Pte)" 2Lt 19th Welsh Regt
PUGH Thomas MM Pte B/2055 Rifle Brigade
PUGH Thomas MM Pte 16566 8th Shropshire Light Infantry
PUGH Thomas Arthur MM Sjt 150837 119 Railway Coy Royal Engineers
PUGH Thomas S. MM Pte 41576 RAMC
PUGH W. "DCM+Bar,MM" Cpl S/14429 12th Rifle Brigade
PUGH William MM Pte 10645 7th North Staffordshire Regt
PUGH William MM Sjt 17191 Machine Gun Corps KIA 19.2.18.
PUGH William MM Dvr 37431 RFA
PUGH William Lewis MM L/Cpl 19273 3rd Grenadier Guards
PUGSLEY Bertie H. MM Pte 278023 3rd London Regt
PUGSLEY George "DCM,MM" Pte 12479 2nd South Lancashire Regt
PULFER George E. MM Pte 119822 Machine Gun Corps
PULFORD Arthur MM Sjt 57511 150 Fd Coy Royal Engineers

PULFORD Harold MM Spr 57512 Royal Engineers
PULHAM Frederick David MM+Bar Gnr 9815 C/153 Bde RFA
PULHAM Walter MM Spr 10981 7 Div Sig Coy Royal Engineers
PULHAM William MM Sjt 260776 264 Railway Coy Royal Engineers
PULL Ernest A. MM Cpl 24008 Durham Light Infantry
PULL Percy MM L/Cpl 14890 9th Norfolk Regt
PULLAN Fred H. MM Cpl 267752 West Yorkshire Regt
PULLAN Joseph MM Gnr 89985 68 Bty 14 Bde RFA
PULLAN Thomas Henry MM Sjt 61890 RFA
PULLAR John MM Pte 9394 8th Royal Highlanders Died 19.7.18.
PULLEN Alexander MM Sjt 34913 114 Siege Bty RGA
PULLEN Alfred E. MM Pte 204593 4th London Regt
PULLEN Arthur MM Pte 12866 10th Essex Regt KIA 23.8.18.
PULLEN Arthur Henry William MM Pte S/8057 12th Rifle Brigade
PULLEN Cecil R. MM Spr 193181 Royal Engineers
PULLEN Charles MM Spr 100503 33 Div Sig Coy Royal Engineers
PULLEN David MM L/Cpl 18578 1st South Wales Borderers
PULLEN Edwin A. MM Cpl 64535 108 Coy Labour Corps
PULLEN Ernest MM L/Sjt 12018 7th Lincolnshire Regt
PULLEN Ernest MM Pte 12546 11th West Yorkshire Regt
PULLEN Frank MM Sjt 7923 11th Hussars
PULLEN Henry G. MM Sjt 11659 1st Royal West Surrey Regt
PULLEN Percy W. MM Gnr 44005 RFA
PULLEN Thomas A. MM Pte 320041 3 Fd Amb RAMC
PULLEN Thomas James MM Pte 19160 Dorsetshire Regt
PULLEN W. MM Cpl 14976 Royal Engineers
PULLEN Walter G. MM Cpl 25238 1st Royal West Surrey Regt
PULLEY Frank MM L/Cpl 241433 Worcestershire Regt
PULLEYN William P. MM CQMS 200535 1/5th West Yorkshire Regt
PULLIN Albert V. MM Pte 12874 8th Gloucestershire Regt
PULLIN Arthur A. MM Gnr Fitter 149380 RGA
PULLIN Claud William MM Bdr 59329 RFA
PULLIN Eric James Livingstone MM Cpl 203244 Gloucestershire Regt
PULLIN Frank MM Sjt 13947 8th Gloucestershire Regt
PULLING William MM Sjt 17869 15 Fd Amb RAMC
PULLINGER Bernard C. MM Cpl 2595 1/5th Royal Sussex Regt
PULLINGER William MM Cpl 12581 1 Special Coy King's Royal Rifle Corps
PULLMAN Richard N. MM Pte 30936 Lincolnshire Regt
PULMAN Albert H. MM Spr 24907 6 Div Sig Coy Royal Engineers
PULMAN John Thomas MM Sjt 16975 Machine Gun Corps
PUMFREY William MM Sjt 299 Royal Engineers
PUMMELL Samuel George MM Cpl 12044 7th Norfolk Regt DOW 9.8.18.
PUMMERY Charles William MM Sjt 971096 B/235 Bde RFA
PUMPHREY Herbert MM Pte 27018 1st Grenadier Guards
PUNCHER Percy MM Sjt 510018 Royal Engineers
PUNSHON Ernest MM Pte 266172 2/7th Royal Warwickshire Regt
PUNTON Andrew MM Pte 40887 1/6th Royal Highlanders
PUNTON James MM Sjt 79333 181 Tunnelling Coy Royal Engineers
PUNYER Alfred MM Pte 2469 2nd Yorkshire Light Infantry KIA 21.3.18.
PURBRICK Henry MM Pte 5582 1st Royal Berkshire Regt
PURCELL Albert MM Dvr 314022 RGA
PURCELL J. MM Pte 18246 Connaught Rangers
PURCELL John "DCM,MM" L/Sjt 10500 1st Shropshire Light Infantry
PURCELL John D. MM L/Cpl 11677 Machine Gun Corps
PURCELL Reginald F. MM Bdr 34137 RFA
PURCELL Sidney MM Cpl 91466 8th Bn Tank Corps
PURCELL Sidney MM L/Cpl P/407 Rifle Brigade
PURCELL Thomas S. MM Pte 63643 RAMC
PURCELL Victor Lewis Thomas MM Gnr 139572 D/232 Bde RFA
PURCELL William MM Cpl 26262 17th Welsh Regt
PURCHASE Arthur R. MM Tptr 1180 RFA
PURCHASE Frederick William MM Pte 2311 13th Royal Fusiliers KIA 8.10.18.
PURCHASE John J. MM Pte 702670 23rd London Regt
PURCHASE Sidney H. MM Cpl 55124 2 Bde RFA
PURCHASE William George Richard MM Pte M2/020760 Army Service Corps
PURCHASE William P. MM L/Sjt 53010 11th Manchester Regt
PURCHELL Arthur James MM Pte 10254 1st Royal Berkshire Regt DOW 5.5.17.
PURDEN Robert MM+Bar L/Cpl 38846 Welsh Regt
PURDIE David MM Sjt 18242 Machine Gun Corps KIA 15.6.18.
PURDIE James MM Pte 12551 1st Royal Highlanders
PURDIE Robert MM Pte 43137 13th Royal Scots KIA 22.8.17.
PURDON Robert MM Pte 9897 2nd King's Own Scottish Borderers
PURDON Sidney MM L/Cpl 241919 Notts & Derby Regt
PURDUE William "MM+Bar,MID" Pte 8470 1/6th Hampshire Regt
PURDY Christopher S. MM Pte 84855 RAMC
PURDY MacDermott MM L/Cpl 2596 1st Irish Guards
PURDY Thomas MM L/Cpl 12987 1st Grenadier Guards
PURDY William MM Sjt 17742 Machine Gun Corps
PURGAVIE William R. MM Cpl 57350 23rd Royal Fusiliers
PURKIS Henry MM+Bar Sjt 29717 Hampshire Regt
PURKIS William Ernest MM Pte 200579 1/4th Essex Regt Died 1.5.18.
PURKISS Albert MM L/Cpl 13572 8th Norfolk Regt
PURKISS Albert Samuel MM L/Cpl 10071 10th Yorkshire Regt
PURKISS Frederick Walmer MM Pte 8630 4th Hampshire Regt
PURKISS Preston H. MM Sjt 23177 3 Div Sig Coy Royal Engineers
PURKISS Stanley MM Pte 77532 7th Royal Fusiliers
PURKISS William MM+Bar Pte 990 7th East Kent Regt
PURLING Arthur D. MM Spr 85037 Royal Engineers
PURNELL Arthur J. MM Cpl 21234 2 Siege Bty RGA
PURNELL Charles Henry "MM,MID" Sjt 3753 3rd Coldstream Guards
PURNELL John MM Pte 227975 1/1st Monmouthshire Regt
PURNELL John Silas MM Cpl 45589 13 Siege Bty RGA
PURR Alfred J. MM Pte 10114 1st East Yorkshire Regt
PURR Alfred L.C. MM Pte 313048 1/7th Gordon Highlanders
PURSELL Edgar MM Spr 249440 Royal Engineers
PURSER A.J. MM L/Sjt 15205 9th Gloucestershire Regt
PURSER Frederick MM Cpl 26585 RGA
PURSER Lawrence Albert MM Gnr 38255 306 Siege Bty RGA DOW 22.10.18.
PURSEY Percy H.G. MM Dvr T4/174172 Army Service Corps
PURSGLOVE Jos(eph?) MM Sjt 9425 Machine Gun Corps
PURSGLOVE Joseph MM Pte 241104 6th Notts & Derby Regt
PURSLOW Thomas W. MM L/Cpl 15307 Shropshire Light Infantry
PURVES George MM Sjt 3117 11th Royal Scots
PURVES James A. MM Pte 200328 1/4th Royal Scots
PURVES James W. MM Pte 131303 46th Royal Fusiliers
PURVES Robert MM Sjt 6212 2nd Dragoons
PURVES Thomas S. "DCM,MM+Bar" Sjt 6581 1st Royal Scots Fusiliers
PURVES William MM L/Cpl 38401 RAMC
PURVIS Charles MM Sjt 43616 B/197 Bde RFA
PURVIS Ernest MM L/Cpl 15010 7th Dragoon Guards
PURVIS Henry MM Pte 14240 23rd Northumberland Fusiliers KIA 9.4.17.
PURVIS J. MM Pte 290801 Middlesex Regt
PURVIS James "MM,MID" Pte 2171 1/5th Durham Light Infantry
PURVIS John C. MM Sjt 15069 10th Yorkshire Regt
PURVIS John W. MM Pte 25803 1/9th Durham Light Infantry
PURVIS Mark P. MM Gnr 771613 RFA
PURVIS Robert MM Pte 18777 Durham Light Infantry
PURVIS William MM+Bar Cpl 22938 149 Coy Machine Gun Corps KIA 26.6.17.
PUSEY Sidney Herbert MM L/Cpl F/408 17th Middlesex Regt
PUSEY Stanley E.J. MM L/Cpl 253450 3rd London Regt
PUSHMAN George J. MM Pte 201468 1st Bedfordshire Regt
PUTLAND Alfred J. MM Pte 16944 Machine Gun Corps
PUTLAND James T. MM Cpl 5751 11th Hussars
PUTMAN Thomas F. MM L/Cpl C/953 16th King's Royal Rifle Corps
PUTNAM Reginald C. MM Pte 116474 Machine Gun Corps
PUTNAM Thomas G. MM Pte 636032 20th London Regt
PUTT Beecham MM Bdr 33236 303 Siege Bty RGA
PUTT Ernest MM L/Cpl M2/201285 Army Service Corps
PUTT James W. MM Sjt 240065 1/5th Leicestershire Regt
PUTTERGILL George F. MM Pte 267885 1/6th West Riding Regt
PUTTICK Archibald MM Sjt 10011 1st East Lancashire Regt
PUTTNAM Arthur G. MM Pte 10006 5th Northamptonshire Regt
PUXTY Frederick J. MM Cpl 6327 10 Fd Amb RAMC
PUZEY Amos MM Cpl 14529 1st Royal Berkshire Regt
PYATT W. MM Pte 20936 Machine Gun Corps
PYATT William Ernest MM Pte 300530 1/7th Essex Regt KIA 2.11.17.
PYBUS Edwin MM Pte 240924 4th Yorkshire Regt KIA 12.4.18.
PYCOCK Ernest MM Spr 482313 Royal Engineers
PYCOCK Harry MM Cpl 3/9818 2nd West Yorkshire Regt DOW 5.4.18.
PYCOCK Percy Waldemar MM Sjt 37571 319 Siege Bty RGA KIA 8.5.18.
PYE Arthur George MM Pte 9337 1st East Yorkshire Regt KIA 4.10.17.
PYE Edward MM L/Cpl 43447 Royal Irish Fusiliers
PYE Frederick A. MM Pte 22237 Shropshire Light Infantry

PYE George H. "DCM,MM" Sjt 8654 1st Royal Fusiliers
PYE John MM Pte 16774 12th Durham Light Infantry KIA 7.6.17.
PYE John Thomas MM Bdr 66965 24 Bty 38 Bde RFA
PYE Robert MM Pte 38569 20th Northumberland Fusiliers Died 5.6.17.
PYE Thomas MM Cpl 32146 2nd South Lancashire Regt
PYE William Hartley MM Pte 7776 21 Fd Amb RAMC
PYE William Thomas MM Pte 19778 11th Essex Regt DOW 23.9.18.
PYETT Charles Frederick MM L/Cpl 934 2nd Royal West Surrey Regt
PYETT Herbert E. MM+Bar L/Sjt 2322 2nd Northumberland Fusiliers
PYGOTT Thomas MM Sjt 10951 1/6th Manchester Regt KIA 23.7.18.
PYKE Ernest G. MM Spr 75586 'O' Corps Sig Coy Royal Engineers
PYKE James T. MM Sjt 17955 11th Durham Light Infantry
PYM Charles H. MM Pte 52053 13th Royal Fusiliers
PYM Francis P. MM Cpl 241251 1/6th Leicestershire Regt
PYM Richard MM CSM 11913 15th Hampshire Regt
PYMAN William George MM Pnr 192732 26 Special Coy Royal Engineers
PYMM H. MM L/Cpl 20030 Highland Light Infantry
PYMM Walter T. MM L/Cpl 491177 2/15th London Regt
PYMONT Harry MM Sjt 19359 8th Somerset Light Infantry
PYNE Albert Henry MM Gnr 61505 X46 Med TM Bty RGA
PYNE Charles H. MM Sjt 67657 Royal Engineers
PYNE Frederick J. MM Gnr 35986 35 Siege Bty RGA
PYNE John H. MM Cpl 11/9 11th East Yorkshire Regt
PYNER John T. MM Pte 129464 2nd Bn Machine Gun Corps
PYOTT William Frederick MM L/Cpl 19086 9th Yorkshire Light Infantry KIA 4.10.17.
PYRAH Sydney MM Dvr 34479 RFA
PYZER William E. MM+Bar Pte 14162 1st Lincolnshire Regt

Q

QUAIFE Ernest E. MM+Bar Sjt 11086 11th Royal West Surrey Regt
QUAIFE Frederick MM Gnr 56797 RGA
QUAIL Wesley MM Pte 1750 Royal Irish Rifles DOW 3.4.18.
QUANCE Ernest John MM Cpl 882 10th Lincolnshire Regt KIA 28.4.17.
QUANCE John Edward MM Pte 7999 11th Lancashire Fusiliers DOW 15.4.18.
QUARMBY Charles W. MM Cpl 203684 1/4th Leicestershire Regt
QUARMBY Harry MM Pte 266763 Cheshire Regt
QUARRELL John MM Pte 23354 5th Cameron Highlanders
QUARTERMAIN Arthur MM Pte 21014 Royal Berkshire Regt
QUARTERMAIN Edward MM+2 Bars Sjt 13378 6th Northamptonshire Regt
QUARTERMAIN George "DCM,MM" Sjt 13937 6th Northamptonshire Regt
QUARTERMAINE George MM Pte 4787 20th Hussars
QUARTERMAN Alfred W. MM L/Cpl S/19897 Rifle Brigade
QUARTERMAN Henry MM Pte 44135 Royal Irish Rifles
QUARTERMAN Reginald Charles MM Cpl 240670 West Riding Regt
QUARTON Harry MM Pte 38916 25th Northumberland Fusiliers KIA 17.4.18.
QUAYLE Christopher Hall MM Pte 357805 10th Liverpool Regt
QUAYLE John MM Cpl 57286 RGA
QUAYLE Lawrence MM Bdsm 8831 2nd East Yorkshire Regt
QUEEN George MM Pte 40753 9th Essex Regt
QUEEN James MM Pte 43446 5/6th Scottish Rifles
QUEENAN James MM L/Cpl 40059 2nd King's Own Scottish Borderers KIA 18.9.18.
QUEENAN John F. MM Sjt 9240 1st York & Lancaster Regt
QUEENEY John MM Pte 8473 2nd Worcestershire Regt
QUELCH Arnold MM L/Cpl 615 8th East Surrey Regt
QUELCH Charles Thomas MM Pte 14335 1st Hampshire Regt DOW 27.7.17.
QUELCH Clarence MM Pte 62891 Machine Gun Corps
QUELCH Frank MM Pte 6575 1st Royal Berkshire Regt
QUELCH William C. MM Gnr 292562 RGA
QUEMBY G.H. MM Pte 16013 9th South Staffordshire Regt
QUERIPEL Cecil MM Pte 3321 6th Royal Irish Regt DOW 30.11.17.
QUERNEY D. MM Cpl 6515 RAMC
QUICK Herbert J. MM Gnr 70506 'Q' Bty RHA
QUICK John MM L/Cpl 22431 165 Coy Machine Gun Corps DOW 15.8.17.
QUICK Stanley MM L/Cpl 18452 1st Hampshire Regt
QUICK William John MM Cpl 722 RFA
QUICKENDEN Joseph James MM Sjt 38701 77 Bde RFA
QUICKFALL Alfred E. MM Pte 7256 Northumberland Fusiliers
QUICKFALL Robert MM Cpl 6199 1st Lincolnshire Regt KIA 3.7.16.
QUIGGIN John MM Cpl 310879 Royal Engineers
QUIGLEY George MM Sjt 18/492 18th West Yorkshire Regt
QUIGLEY Henry MM+Bar Pte 9583 2nd Royal Irish Rifles KIA 23.3.18.
QUIGLEY Newton MM Gnr 26147 RGA
QUIGLEY William MM Sjt 17605 Royal Irish Fusiliers
QUIGLEY William J. "MM,MSM" Cpl 99973 138 Army Troops Coy Royal Engineers
QUILLIAN William H. MM Cpl 5781 RFA
QUILTER George Sidney MM Pte 10780 1/4th Essex Regt
QUILTER John MM Pte 204937 2nd Devonshire Regt
QUIN Francis W. MM Cpl 204279 1st East Yorkshire Regt
QUIN Patrick MM Pte 275454 1/7th Arg & Suth Highlanders
QUIN Percy S. MM L/Cpl 72716 Royal Fusiliers
QUINAULT H. MM Cpl 1/7342 Royal Munster Fusiliers
QUINCE Edward MM Sjt 8765 1st Bedfordshire Regt KIA 27.7.16.
QUINCE Horace MM Pte 78900 7th Royal Fusiliers
QUINCE James W. MM Sjt 240546 Lincolnshire Regt
QUINCEY William MM L/Sjt 46616 4th North Staffordshire Regt
QUINE William Martin MM Cpl 267571 2/7th Liverpool Regt DOW 28.9.18.
QUINION Bernard Leslie MM Dvr 16865 RFA
QUINLAN Eugene H. MM L/Cpl 77976 10th Royal Fusiliers
QUINLAN Frederick Thomas MM Pte 4340 1/3rd London Regt
QUINLAN James MM Pte 11070 Royal Irish Fusiliers
QUINLAN James MM L/Cpl 21508 11th West Yorkshire Regt
QUINLAN Martin MM L/Cpl 4/8365 West Yorkshire Regt
QUINLAN Patrick MM Pte 5760 1st Royal Irish Regt
QUINN Bernard MM L/Cpl 2783 2nd Dragoon Guards
QUINN Charles "MM,MID" L/Sjt 10096 3rd Coldstream Guards
QUINN David MM Sjt 12405 2nd Royal Irish Rifles
QUINN David MM Pte 4/8021 9th West Yorkshire Regt KIA 30.11.16.
QUINN Edward "DCM,MM" Cpl 73873 83 Bty 11 Bde RFA
QUINN Edward MM L/Sjt 8430 9th Yorkshire Regt KIA 5.10.18.
QUINN Francis MM+Bar Sjt 3157 Arg & Suth Highlanders
QUINN Francis J. MM Pte 15458 7/8th King's Own Scottish Borderers
QUINN Francis P. MM Pte 301118 Manchester Regt
QUINN George MM Cpl 38280 2nd Yorkshire Regt
QUINN George A. MM Pte 245773 2nd London Regt
QUINN George John MM L/Sjt 7678 3rd Coldstream Guards
QUINN Gerard MM Pte 48521 7/8th Royal Inniskilling Fusiliers
QUINN Harold MM Gnr 675549 275 Bde RFA
QUINN J. MM Pte 46135 RAMC
QUINN J. MM Pte 17904 Seaforth Highlanders
QUINN James MM L/Cpl 6301 Royal Irish Fusiliers
QUINN James MM Gnr 112400 83 Bty 11 Bde RFA
QUINN James MM Pte 8/15102 9th Royal Dublin Fusiliers DOW 11.8.17.
QUINN James MM Pte 2494 7th Leinster Regt KIA 1.2.17.
QUINN James MM Sjt 9707 D/165 Bde RFA KIA 15.12.17.
QUINN James MM Pte 12894 9th Royal Dublin Fusiliers
QUINN James A. MM Pte 47259 RAMC
QUINN James David MM L/Cpl 23918 12th South Wales Borderers
QUINN John MM Cpl 254940 15 Div Sig Coy Royal Engineers
QUINN John MM Gnr 770434 RFA
QUINN John MM Pte 5897 1st Royal Munster Fusiliers DOW 23.2.18.
QUINN John MM Sjt 7832 2nd Leinster Regt
QUINN John MM L/Cpl 9216 1st Royal Munster Fusiliers
QUINN John MM Pte 29437 1st King's Own Scottish Borderers KIA 18.8.18.
QUINN John MM Dvr 101741 RHA
QUINN John Francis MM Pte 27912 2nd Oxf & Bucks Light Infantry
QUINN Joseph MM Pte 27242 8th Royal Inniskilling Fusiliers KIA 6.9.16.
QUINN Joseph MM+Bar Sjt 7703 RFA
QUINN Joseph MM+Bar L/Cpl 34866 8th York & Lancaster Regt DOW 16.9.17.
QUINN Leslie MM Pte 240624 1/5th York & Lancaster Regt
QUINN Matthew MM Pte 20/634 Durham Light Infantry
QUINN Michael MM Pte 16931 13th Royal Scots
QUINN Owen MM Pte 11967 1st Irish Guards
QUINN Patrick MM Pte 46625 18th Lancashire Fusiliers
QUINN Patrick MM Pte 11820 2nd South Wales Borderers KIA 1.7.16.

QUINN Peter MM+Bar Sjt 357193 Liverpool Regt
QUINN Robert MM L/Cpl 325156 1/9th Durham Light Infantry
QUINN Thomas MM Pte 53200 Royal Scots
QUINN Thomas MM Pte 17990 Royal Scots
QUINN Thomas MM Pte 21466 22nd Manchester Regt
QUINN Thomas Barry MM Cpl 10934 RFA
QUINN William MM Dvr 125412 D/47 Bde RFA
QUINN William MM Spr 127902 Fourth Army Sig Coy Royal Engineers att 158 Bde RFA.
QUINN William MM Pte 15756 9th West Yorkshire Regt
QUINN Wilson Foster "DCM,MM,CG(B)" Pte 41192 109 Fd Amb RAMC
QUINNELL Charles Robert MM Sjt 533 9th Royal Fusiliers
QUINNEY Laurence C. MM Sjt 10162 1st Duke of Cornwall's LI
QUINTON Arthur J. MM+Bar Sjt 17437 6th South Wales Borderers
QUINTON Edward MM Sjt 200283 1/4th Lincolnshire Regt
QUINTON Henry M. "DCM,MM+Bar" CSM 14954 9th Norfolk Regt
QUINTON William MM+Bar Sjt 23056 13th Royal Scots
QUIRK Henry P. MM Pte 474306 1/12th London Regt
QUIRK William Edward MM Sjt 242872 5th Yorkshire Light Infantry KIA 28.3.18.

R

RABBAGE Andrew MM Cpl 30499 46 Fd Amb RAMC KIA 28.7.17.
RABBAGE Stephen J. MM Pte 24832 10th Duke of Cornwall's LI
RABBETTS Edgar W. MM Sjt 35981 RGA
RABBIT John MM Sjt 8226 1st Royal West Kent Regt
RABBITTS Frederick J. MM L/Cpl 20004 19th Bn Machine Gun Corps
RABJOHNS Frank MM Pte 66826 138 Fd Amb RAMC
RABY Adam MM Cpl 60698 23rd Lancashire Fusiliers
RABY Alfred George MM Pte 5733 1st Leinster Regt
RABY Benjamin MM CSM 7069 7th Shropshire Light Infantry
RABY Frank MM Pte 27310 Middlesex Regt
RACE James H. MM Pte 26/601 Northumberland Fusiliers
RACE John H. MM Cpl 43554 114 Hy Bty RGA
RACE Leonard MM Pte 307080 1st West Yorkshire Regt
RACE Victor MM Pte 24198 10th West Riding Regt
RACEY Charles R. MM+Bar Pte 50613 2nd Suffolk Regt
RACEY Edward MM Sjt 8103 1st Royal Inniskilling Fusiliers KIA 9.8.16.
RACEY George W. MM+Bar Sjt 37225 7th South Staffordshire Regt
RACHAEL George Herbert MM Pte 20023 12th Gloucestershire Regt
RACHER F. MM Sjt 15020 11th Essex Regt
RACHER Roland Charles MM Pte 10547 6th Bedfordshire Regt KIA 28.4.17.
RACK William MM Spr 154517 Royal Engineers
RACKHAM Francis M. MM Pte 68333 RAMC
RACKLEY Alfred MM Pte 201508 1/4th Royal Berkshire Regt KIA 1.11.18.
RACKLEY Arthur MM Pte R/9106 13th King's Royal Rifle Corps
RADBAND Ernest T. MM Cpl 201125 West Yorkshire Regt
RADBOURN Albert MM Dvr 59867 52 Bty 15 Bde RFA
RADCLIFFE Alexander MM Sjt 16731 11th Worcestershire Regt
RADCLIFFE Ernest F. MM Spr 510381 58 Div Sig Coy Royal Engineers
RADCLIFFE F. MM L/Cpl 350185 Manchester Regt
RADCLIFFE Frank MM Sjt 200433 'C' Bn Tank Corps
RADCLIFFE Frank W. MM Sjt 18754 1/4th Gordon Highlanders
RADCLIFFE H. MM Cpl 202946 20th Durham Light Infantry
RADCLIFFE H. MM Pte 24670 Royal Welsh Fusiliers
RADCLIFFE Harry MM Pte 2721 Gordon Highlanders
RADCLIFFE Herbert MM Pte 105623 RAMC
RADCLIFFE J. MM Pte 268410 7th Liverpool Regt
RADCLIFFE J. MM Pte 268561 Liverpool Regt
RADCLIFFE John MM Sjt 17567 East Surrey Regt
RADCLIFFE Joseph William MM Pte 26664 9th Royal Inniskilling Fusiliers KIA 29.3.18.
RADCLIFFE T. MM Pte 350214 Manchester Regt
RADCLIFFE Thomas MM Cpl 42189 B/181 Bde RFA
RADCLIFFE Tudor MM Cpl 320572 24th Welsh Regt
RADCLIFFE W. MM Pte 377167 Manchester Regt
RADCLIFFE William MM Pte 302547 1/5th Manchester Regt KIA 21.10.18.
RADCLIFFE William MM Pte 9431 1st Royal Irish Fusiliers
RADFORD Albert V. MM Pte 266460 7th Liverpool Regt
RADFORD Bertram E. MM+Bar S/Sjt 41869 50 Fd Amb RAMC
RADFORD Ernest W. MM Dvr 86018 38 Bde Ammn Col RFA
RADFORD Fred MM+Bar Pte 27744 9th & 16th Lancashire Fusiliers
RADFORD Frederick John MM Sjt 56642 Royal Welsh Fusiliers
RADFORD George MM Sjt 13099 1st East Surrey Regt
RADFORD George E. MM Sjt 117038 331 Siege Bty RGA
RADFORD George John MM L/Cpl 200422 1/4th Gloucestershire Regt
RADFORD James MM Pte 325705 9th Durham Light Infantry
RADFORD John MM Pte 3979 1st Royal Warwickshire Regt KIA 16.12.17. Real name PAGE.
RADFORD Phillip MM Sjt Farrier 99123 D/187 Bde RFA
RADFORD Thomas MM Pte 28702 Notts & Derby Regt
RADFORD Vernon MM Gnr 45035 RFA
RADFORD Wilfred MM L/Cpl 43274 Lincolnshire Regt
RADLEY Harry MM Dvr 96841 18 Bde Ammn Col RFA
RADLEY Joseph W. MM Gnr Fitter 14788 2 Bde RFA
RADLEY Leonard MM+Bar CSM 14495 6th Northamptonshire Regt
RADLEY R. MM Pte 472353 London Regt
RADLEY William MM Sjt 472154 2/12th London Regt KIA 12.9.18.
RADLEY William MM Pte 8259 2nd Lincolnshire Regt
RADLEY William MM Sjt 17939 Liverpool Regt
RADMORE Thomas E. MM Pte 43234 9th Devonshire Regt
RADMORE William George MM L/Cpl 240124 1/5th Devonshire Regt
RADWELL John L. MM Pte 19668 Oxf & Bucks Light Infantry
RAE Alexander MM Sjt 24563 51st Bn Machine Gun Corps
RAE Andrew MM Sjt 8586 Highland Light Infantry
RAE Andrew MM Sjt 6413 8/10th Gordon Highlanders
RAE David MM Cpl 255 2nd Arg & Suth Highlanders
RAE Ellington MM L/Cpl 1283 1/6th Seaforth Highlanders
RAE George MM Cpl 41840 Machine Gun Corps(Cavalry)
RAE Horace MM Pte 39866 9th York & Lancaster Regt
RAE Ivy MM Pte 16347 9th Scottish Rifles
RAE James MM Sjt 36392 1st South Wales Borderers
RAE James MM Spr 246482 Royal Engineers
RAE James MM Cpl 21092 11th Royal Scots
RAE James MM L/Cpl 265428 Royal Highlanders
RAE James MM Pte 26421 12th Royal Scots
RAE James S. MM Cpl Fitter 715399 A/15 Bde RFA
RAE Robert Senier MM Pte 13924 7th Norfolk Regt
RAE William MM 2nd Cpl 18975 9 Fd Coy Royal Engineers
RAE William MM L/Cpl 1538 1st Royal Highlanders
RAE William MM L/Cpl 14549 8th Border Regt
RAE William MM Sjt 52069 23 Bde RFA
RAE William L. MM Sjt 406012 Royal Engineers
RAEBURN Archibald MM Pte 266094 Gordon Highlanders later name MITCHELL.
RAEBURN Joseph MM Pte 300262 1/7th Royal Scots
RAESIDE Matthew MM Cpl 27479 1st King's Own Scottish Borderers
RAFFAN Andrew MM Sjt 307830 13th Bn Tank Corps
RAFFAN Samuel MM Pte 241387 Gordon Highlanders
RAFFEL John MM+Bar Sjt 200515 10th Bn Tank Corps
RAFFELL Cuthbert MM Dvr 200384 Durham Light Infantry
RAFFERTY John MM Sjt 10047 7th South Staffordshire Regt
RAFFERTY Joseph MM Gnr 141898 C/67 Bde RFA
RAFFERTY Malcolm MM Cpl 7626 70 Bde RFA
RAFFERTY Owen MM L/Cpl 335848 1/8th Royal Scots
RAFFERTY P. MM Sjt 43034 Royal Irish Fusiliers
RAFFERTY Peter MM Cpl 17363 14th Welsh Regt
RAFFERTY Peter MM+Bar Bdr 6081 RFA
RAFFERTY Terence MM Bdr 67446 A/250 Bde RFA
RAFFERTY Thomas MM Pte 5274 Northumberland Fusiliers
RAFFILL Walter J. MM Pte 240153 Somerset Light Infantry
RAFFIN Charles MM Cpl 1832 RAMC
RAFTER Thomas MM Cpl 9135 1st York & Lancaster Regt
RAFTER W.J. MM Sjt 479299 45 Coy Labour Corps
RAFTERY Harry MM Pte 307234 10th Notts & Derby Regt
RAFTERY John "MM,MID" L/Sjt 200789 1/5th West Yorkshire Regt KIA 25.4.18.
RAGAN William Thomas MM Gnr 95525 D/46 Bde RFA
RAGGETT Albert L. MM Sjt 9448 1st East Yorkshire Regt
RAGGETT Alfred William MM Sjt 19405 15th Hampshire Regt
RAGGETT Arthur MM L/Cpl C/6 16th King's Royal Rifle Corps
RAGGETT David Ernest MM Sjt 40243 10th Northumberland Fusiliers Died 15.7.18.
RAGGETT William Charles MM L/Cpl 151924 I(Indian)Corps Sig Coy Royal Engineers
RAGSDALE George MM Sjt 12662 RGA

RAHILLY T. MM Pte 3/4491 2nd Royal Munster Fusiliers
RAILTON James MM Pte 13204 9th Northumberland Fusiliers
RAILTON William J. MM CQMS 246771 5 Fd Svy Bn Royal Engineers
RAINBIRD Bertie Harold MM L/Sjt 8878 2nd Gloucestershire Regt
RAINBIRD Herbert H. MM 2nd Cpl 63379 Royal Engineers
RAINBIRD William J. MM Sjt 56775 Machine Gun Corps(Cavalry)
RAINBOW Albert T. MM Gnr 24290 31 Heavy Bty RGA
RAINBOW Alfred MM L/Sjt 200699 1/4th Essex Regt
RAINBOW Arthur MM Cpl 17420 C/104 Bde RFA
RAINBOW Frank Davis MM+Bar L/Cpl 39688 55 Fd Amb RAMC KIA 25.8.18.
RAINBOW Hugh William MM Bdr 614181 2/1(Warwickshire)Bty RHA KIA 4.10.17.
RAINBOW Walter J. MM Gnr 75487 RGA
RAINBOW William MM Pte 42551 11th Essex Regt KIA 24.9.18.
RAINE Alexander MM Gnr 21936 RFA
RAINE Clifford MM L/Cpl 19751 12th West Yorkshire Regt KIA 20.11.17.
RAINE Fred MM L/Cpl 33198 1/5th Yorkshire Regt
RAINE Herbert H. MM L/Cpl 23558 Machine Gun Corps
RAINE John T.N. MM Pte 162130 23rd Bn Machine Gun Corps
RAINE John William MM Gnr 751407 D/223 Bde RFA
RAINE Philip MM Pte 16387 11th Border Regt
RAINE Robert Henry MM L/Cpl 104314 227 Fd Coy Royal Engineers
RAINE Rupert MM Sjt 10820 1st Notts & Derby Regt
RAINE S.W. MM Cpl 9649 Durham Light Infantry
RAINE Thomas MM Cpl 18286 8th Border Regt
RAINER Arthur H. MM L/Cpl 515201 14th London Regt
RAINER H.A.W. MM Pte 495335 RAMC
RAINES Charles MM Pte 304741 5th London Regt
RAINES E.A. MM Pte 18754 Royal West Kent Regt
RAINEY John MM Pte 33307 1st Devonshire Regt
RAINEY Joseph MM Cpl 13773 7th Royal Inniskilling Fusiliers
RAINEY Samuel "MM,MSM" Sjt 71343 North Irish Horse
RAINFORD George Edward MM Sjt 16957 Machine Gun Corps
RAINFORD Henry MM L/Cpl 330125 9th Liverpool Regt KIA 28.8.18.
RAINFORD J. MM Pte 30328 North Lancashire Regt
RAINFORD John MM Pte 375 6th East Kent Regt
RAINGER David J. MM L/Bdr 120483 37 Bty 27 Bde RFA
RAINGER Herbert Horace MM Pte MS/1949 4 Div Train Army Service Corps
RAINSBURY Charley MM+Bar Cpl 242321 1st East Kent Regt
RAINSDON Frank MM Sjt 265474 1/1st Hertfordshire Regt
RAINSFORD W. MM Cpl 2291 Royal Warwickshire Regt
RAINSLEY Edward MM Bdr 83589 96 Bty 19 Bde RFA
RAINTON Charles MM Sjt 14022 32 Div Ammn Col RFA
RAISEY Allen MM L/Cpl 624 1st Welsh Guards
RAISMAN Montague MM Gnr 139008 RGA
RAISTRICK Gilbert MM L/Cpl 38150 2nd Yorkshire Regt
RAISTRICK Taylor MM+Bar Pte 242439 2/5th West Riding Regt KIA 22.7.18.
RAITT David MM Pte 241911 Royal Warwickshire Regt
RAKE Frederick MM Pte 7674 11th Royal Fusiliers
RALEY Cecil MM Pte 240959 1/6th Liverpool Regt
RALEY Patrick MM Cpl 293490 136 Heavy Bty RGA DOW 3.6.18
RALLS John S. MM Spr 45258 Royal Engineers
RALLS Louis John G. MM L/Cpl 14505 10th Essex Regt
RALPH Albert Charles MM Pte 225203 1/1st Monmouthshire Regt
RALPH Daniel MM Cpl 44109 Machine Gun Corps
RALPH Donald MM Sjt 9651 1st Royal Scots Fusiliers
RALPH E. MM Pte 226536 1/1st Monmouthshire Regt
RALPH Francis E. MM Pte 1447 14th Royal Warwickshire Regt
RALPH Frederick R. MM Gnr 1163 RGA
RALPH J.J. "MM+Bar,MSM" C/Sjt 1148 Military Foot Police
RALPH John Thomas MM Gnr 94462 A/315 Bde RFA
RALPH Maurice MM Gnr 43777 9 Bty 41 Bde RFA DOW 17.8.16.
RALPH Samuel MM Sjt 450005 1/11th London Regt
RALPH William MM L/Cpl 21948 Grenadier Guards
RALPH William MM Spr 532371 510 Fd Coy Royal Engineers
RALPH William S. MM Sjt 140489 226 Fd Coy Royal Engineers
RALPH William T. MM L/Cpl 252806 1st Essex Regt
RALPHS Charles MM Cpl 31 Northumberland Fusiliers
RALPHS John MM+Bar Sjt 20233 3rd Bn Machine Gun Corps
RALPHS Joseph MM Cpl 27023 12th East Surrey Regt
RALPHS Leslie M. MM Gnr 79645 RFA
RALPHS Thomas MM Pte 14163 5th Manchester Regt
RALPHS Thomas MM Pte 50395 1/6th Manchester Regt KIA 7.4.18.

RALPHSON Arthur MM Pte 283031 5th Lancashire Fusiliers
RALSTON Hugh MM Sjt 1447 Scottish Rifles KIA 29.7.18.
RAMAGE Arthur "DCM,MM+Bar" Sjt 17641 12th Highland Light Infantry KIA 1.8.17.
RAMAGE Charles "DCM,MM" Sjt 290834 1/8th Scottish Rifles
RAMAGE James S. MM Sjt 10575 1st Royal Scots Fusiliers
RAMAGE John MM L/Sjt 2725 17th Highland Light Infantry
RAMAGE Matthew MM Sjt 151640 104th Bn Machine Gun Corps
RAMAGE William MM Sjt 52257 154 Fd Coy Royal Engineers
RAMAGE William MM L/Cpl 2080 7th Seaforth Highlanders KIA 27.3.18.
RAMAGE William Jackson MM Cpl 16973 7th Cameron Highlanders KIA 3.8.17.
RAMBERT Charles MM L/Cpl 551432 16th London Regt
RAMM Cornelius W.H. MM Sjt 85110 Royal Engineers
RAMM Geoffrey E. MM Cpl 35997 9th Norfolk Regt
RAMMELL Charles E. MM Cpl 48966 'A' Bty RHA
RAMPLING Albert MM Pnr 312349 3 Div Sig Coy Royal Engineers
RAMSAY A.H. MM Sjt 10020 King's Own Scottish Borderers
RAMSAY Alan MM L/Cpl 16213 1/7th Arg & Suth Highlanders
RAMSAY Alexander MM+Bar Sjt 1291 1st Royal Highlanders Died 18.10.18.
RAMSAY Alexander MM Pte 3505 Gordon Highlanders KIA 20.10.18.
RAMSAY Alexander MM L/Cpl 127643 40 Div Sig Coy Royal Engineers
RAMSAY Alexander C. MM Pte 266071 Gordon Highlanders
RAMSAY Andrew MM L/Cpl 200397 1/4th King's Own Scottish Borderers
RAMSAY Andrew D. MM Pte 265603 1/6th Royal Highlanders
RAMSAY Charles MM Cpl 65302 4th Royal Fusiliers KIA 21.8.18.
RAMSAY Charles MM Pnr 48048 Royal Engineers
RAMSAY Christopher B. MM Gnr 3529 RFA
RAMSAY Daniel MM Dvr 46219 RFA
RAMSAY George MM Sjt 14429 Labour Corps
RAMSAY J. MM L/Sjt 8606 2nd Royal Scots
RAMSAY J.T. MM Pte 11472 7th Yorkshire Regt
RAMSAY James MM Pte 296147 12th Royal Scots Fusiliers
RAMSAY James MM Sjt 8180 1st Scottish Rifles
RAMSAY James MM Sjt 6013 RFA
RAMSAY James MM Pte 352351 Royal Scots
RAMSAY John MM Pte 105490 4th Liverpool Regt
RAMSAY John MM L/Cpl 22172 1st Bn Machine Gun Corps
RAMSAY John MM Spr 79569 180 Tunnelling Coy Royal Engineers
RAMSAY John A. MM Cpl 636218 RFA
RAMSAY John Davie MM Cpl 347462 RGA
RAMSAY Peter MM Cpl 300682 1/7th Royal Scots
RAMSAY Richard MM Gnr 7083 RFA
RAMSAY Robert MacKay MM Sjt 3739 Royal Scots
RAMSAY Thomas MM Sjt 53119 3 Pontoon Park Royal Engineers
RAMSAY Thomas L. MM Cpl 913 A/88 Bde RFA KIA 6.6.18.
RAMSAY Thomas W. MM Pte 14121 7th Yorkshire Regt
RAMSAY Walter MM Sjt 21752 Royal Scots
RAMSAY William MM Gnr 660700 RFA
RAMSAY William MM L/Cpl 240225 1/5th Royal Highlanders
RAMSAY William MM L/Cpl 11189 6th Dorsetshire Regt
RAMSAY William MM L/Cpl 46039 Royal Engineers
RAMSAY William MM Cpl 10951 8/10th Gordon Highlanders
RAMSAY William MM Pte 17383 Gordon Highlanders
RAMSBOTHAM Allen G. MM Spr 165352 Royal Engineers
RAMSBOTHAM William L. MM L/Cpl 247023 Royal Engineers
RAMSBOTTOM Ephraim MM Gnr 686677 95 Bde RFA
RAMSBOTTOM James MM Dvr 711357 RFA
RAMSBOTTOM Thomas MM Gnr 725891 RFA
RAMSBOTTOM Thomas MM Bdr 750875 B/315 Bde RFA
RAMSDALE Fred MM Pte 5101 Notts & Derby Regt
RAMSDALE Richard MM Cpl 175838 257 Tunnelling Coy Royal Engineers
RAMSDEN Albert MM Pte 11407 6th York & Lancaster Regt
RAMSDEN Albert Edward MM Sjt 1338 West Yorkshire Regt
RAMSDEN Frank MM Pte 13650 9th Leicestershire Regt
RAMSDEN Fred MM L/Cpl 53671 12th Durham Light Infantry
RAMSDEN Herbert Edward MM Pte 16561 Royal Lancaster Regt
RAMSDEN Horace J. MM Gnr 935463 C/235 Bde RFA
RAMSDEN James MM Pte 147840 Machine Gun Corps
RAMSDEN James MM L/Cpl 18189 Durham Light Infantry
RAMSDEN John MM Sjt 3295 2nd Notts & Derby Regt
RAMSDEN John MM CSM 26524 15th Durham Light Infantry
RAMSDEN Richard MM Ptr 13349 7th Leicestershire Regt DOW 29.3.18.

RAMSDEN Walter MM L/Cpl 200826 1/4th York & Lancaster Regt
RAMSDEN Wilfred MM Pte M2/181170 641 Coy Army Service Corps att RGA.
RAMSDEN William Ewart MM Spr 148742 Signal Service Royal Engineers
RAMSEY Arthur "MM,MID" Sjt 18848 Royal Engineers
RAMSEY Charles V. MM Pte 591391 1/18th London Regt
RAMSEY Clement H. MM Gnr 112497 A/161 Bde RFA
RAMSEY Frederick MM Sjt 6444 2nd York & Lancaster Regt
RAMSEY Frederick MM Gnr(SS) 62328 RHA
RAMSEY Harry MM Pte 10191 1st Liverpool Regt
RAMSEY Henry MM Dvr 26574 RFA
RAMSEY James MM Bdr 118737 RGA
RAMSEY Leslie G.D. MM Sjt 43745 57th Bn Machine Gun Corps
RAMSEY R. MM Pte 18834 1st Royal Inniskilling Fusiliers
RAMSEY Robert MM L/Cpl 75889 Royal Engineers
RAMSEY Robert M. MM Pte 33488 West Riding Regt
RAMSEY Thomas MM Pte 39995 8th York & Lancaster Regt
RAMSEY Thomas W. MM Pte 36268 Durham Light Infantry
RAMSEY W. MM L/Cpl 10986 1st Scottish Rifles
RAMSEY William MM Pte 6848 12th Royal Irish Rifles
RAMSHAW Edward MM Pte 35810 2nd Yorkshire Light Infantry
RAMSHAW Joseph MM Gnr 65657 RGA
RAMSKILL George MM Sjt 820025 46 Div Ammn Col RFA
RAMSKILL John H. MM L/Cpl 7710 23rd Royal Fusiliers
RAMSTEAD H. MM Pte 60642 Machine Gun Corps
RANBY John T. MM Sjt 34575 RFA
RANCE Cecil H. MM Sjt 720547 1/24th London Regt
RANCE Frederick MM Cpl 7989 5th Dragoon Guards
RANCE Harry William MM Pte 40708 12th Middlesex Regt
RAND Edward P. MM Pte 31653 6th Cameron Highlanders
RAND F.C. MM Sjt 10038 2nd East Kent Regt
RAND Francis G. MM Pte 40363 Worcestershire Regt
RAND James MM Sjt 8221 7th Royal West Surrey Regt KIA 10.8.17.
RAND John MM Cpl 583 18th Durham Light Infantry
RAND Joseph MM Pte 572610 1/17th London Regt
RANDALL Archibald Edward MM L/Cpl 17410 3rd Coldstream Guards
RANDALL Arthur MM Pte 240455 5th Leicestershire Regt
RANDALL Arthur "DCM,MM+Bar" Sjt 242402 1/6th North Staffordshire Regt
RANDALL Arthur J. MM Spr 100451 Royal Engineers
RANDALL C. MM Sjt P1439 Military Foot Police
RANDALL C.S. MM Cpl 950868 RFA
RANDALL Charles R. MM Pte 24538 11th Hussars
RANDALL Charlie MM L/Cpl 200983 Royal Berkshire Regt
RANDALL Claude MM+2 Bars Sjt 235169 13th Liverpool Regt
RANDALL Clifford F. MM Pte 22583 6th Royal Warwickshire Regt
RANDALL David E. MM Pte 611958 19th London Regt
RANDALL Edward W. MM+Bar Cpl 99191 37th Bn Machine Gun Corps
RANDALL Edwin MM Pte 19149 4th Grenadier Guards
RANDALL Frederick H. MM Dvr 55197 RFA
RANDALL Frederick J. MM L/Cpl 39928 1st Wiltshire Regt
RANDALL George Edward MM Pte 7318 2nd Royal Warwickshire Regt
RANDALL George Frederick MM+Bar Cpl 52903 56 Bty 34 Bde RFA KIA 5.5.17.
RANDALL H.E.M. MM L/Cpl 32675 Royal Engineers
RANDALL Harold V. MM Sjt 281174 1/4th London Regt
RANDALL Henry F. MM Dvr 955794 RFA
RANDALL Herbert G. MM Sjt 200381 16th Bn Tank Corps
RANDALL J. MM Pte 339115 RAMC
RANDALL J.H. MM Pte 33874 2nd Essex Regt
RANDALL Jack MM Pte 4438 Royal Sussex Regt
RANDALL John C. MM Sjt 27935 Postal Section Royal Engineers
RANDALL John Edward MM Pte 31620 1st East Surrey Regt
RANDALL John S. MM Pte 73506 RAMC
RANDALL Lawrence MM Gnr 57414 RGA
RANDALL Montague Edgar MM Pte 7667 2/4th Dorsetshire Regt KIA 11.4.18.
RANDALL Percy T. MM L/Cpl 3826 23rd Royal Fusiliers
RANDALL Stanley "DCM,MM,MID" CSM 9703 East Kent Regt Died 31.12.18.
RANDALL Stanley C. MM RSM 219111 Royal Engineers
RANDALL Thomas MM Pte 202900 1/4th East Yorkshire Regt DOW 6.6.18.
RANDALL Walter A. MM Pte 44596 1/6th Seaforth Highlanders
RANDALL William MM Cpl 120590 'M' Special Coy Royal Engineers
RANDALL William MM Sjt 10298 1st Middlesex Regt
RANDALL William MM Bdr 73441 14 Bde RFA
RANDALL William Christopher MM+Bar Bdr 89222 B/48 Bde RFA
RANDALL William E. MM Sjt 8161 2nd Wiltshire Regt
RANDALL William J. MM Pte M2/178158 Army Service Corps
RANDELL Frederick C. MM Sjt DM2/117859 Army Service Corps
RANDLE Ernest MM Bdr 119224 RFA
RANDLE George Wilkins MM Cpl 34136 2/4th Oxf & Bucks Light Infantry
RANDLE Harold MM Cpl 200560 1/7th Worcestershire Regt
RANDLE Isaac MM Sjt 1915 RFA
RANDLE John MM Pte 992 15th Royal Warwickshire Regt DOW 16.10.18.
RANDLE Lionel MM+Bar Sjt R/7142 King's Royal Rifle Corps
RANDLE Raymond R.W. MM Sjt 16842 10th Worcestershire Regt
RANDLES Charles MM L/Cpl 201427 1/5th Liverpool Regt
RANDLES Edward William MM L/Cpl 26192 Royal Welsh Fusiliers
RANDLES George MM Cpl 345182 24th Royal Welsh Fusiliers
RANDLES William Thomas MM Sjt 50558 Royal Engineers
RANDS George W. MM Pte 15202 Duke of Cornwall's LI
RANDS James MM Sjt 25692 Y/23 Med TM Bty RFA
RANE Joseph MM Dvr 1427 RFA
RANGER Charles MM Cpl 10747 7th Royal Sussex Regt
RANGER Frederick MM Pte 12435 King's Royal Rifle Corps
RANGER George Henry MM Pte 6362 2nd Royal Sussex Regt KIA 17.10.18.
RANGER George T. MM+Bar Gnr 11786 B/156 Bde RFA
RANGER Norman Frederick Lewis "MM,MID" L/Sjt 41590 8th Yorkshire Regt
RANKIN Andrew MM Cpl 187552 RGA
RANKIN Frank MM Pte 21198 14th Liverpool Regt
RANKIN George MM+Bar Sjt 412003 1/1(Lowland)Fd Coy Royal Engineers
RANKIN James N. MM Cpl 11897 2nd Royal Scots Fusiliers KIA 31.7.17.
RANKIN James William MM L/Cpl 22398 7/8th King's Own Scottish Borderers
RANKIN Matthew MM Cpl 17736 29th Bn Machine Gun Corps
RANKIN Peter MM L/Sjt 300759 Arg & Suth Highlanders
RANKIN Robert "MC,MM(7334 CSM 1st Bn)" 2Lt 2nd South Staffordshire Regt
RANKIN Robert A. MM Pte 201187 1/4th Seaforth Highlanders
RANKIN Robert Neilston MM Gnr 651096 D/84 Bde RFA KIA 10.7.17.
RANKIN Robert R. MM Pte 202763 1/4th Seaforth Highlanders
RANKIN William MM Sjt 267234 13th Royal Highlanders
RANKINE John MM Cpl 11034 2nd Royal Scots
RANKINE Thomas MM Pte 201262 1/5th Royal Highlanders
RANKMORE Albert E. MM Sjt 260 Liverpool Regt
RANNER Charles E. MM+Bar Sjt 113424 Royal Engineers
RANNS Harry MM Pte 204065 Middlesex Regt
RANSCOMBE George MM L/Cpl 546933 Second Army Sig Coy Royal Engineers
RANSCOMBE Thomas MM Pte 8990 1st Royal Berkshire Regt
RANSCOMBE William MM L/Cpl 203809 1st Royal Berkshire Regt
RANSCOMBE William MM Sjt 87533 RFA
RANSHAW Tom P. MM Bdr 84942 RFA
RANSOM Frederick James "DCM,MM,CG(F)" Sjt 574 7th Royal Sussex Regt DOW 8.10.18.
RANSOM George W. "MM,MSM" Gnr 755235 A/251 Bde RFA
RANSOM J. MM Sjt 19223 6th South Wales Borderers
RANSOM John H. MM L/Sjt 719 17th Middlesex Regt DOW 9.12.17.
RANSOM William MM Sjt MS/4966 2 Ammn Park Army Service Corps
RANSOM William E. MM L/Cpl 206513 2/4th Royal West Surrey Regt
RANSOM William G. MM+Bar Pte 30458 2nd Yorkshire Regt
RANSOME Leonard MM Pte M2/174803 36 Motor Ambulance Convoy Army Service Corps
RANSOME Walter MM Pte 22/154 Durham Light Infantry
RANSOME William G. MM Sjt 57357 71 Bde RFA
RANSON Charles Walter MM Bdr 955510 5 Bde RFA
RANSON Donald MM Pte M2/191868 Army Service Corps att RAMC.
RANSON Ernest S. MM+Bar L/Sjt 22022 2nd Royal Fusiliers
RANSON Walter J. MM Pte 250262 1/5th Essex Regt
RANSON William MM Pte 22/184 Durham Light Infantry
RANSON William Arthur MM Pte 2876 1/18th London Regt
RANSTEAD Charles "DCM,MM,MSM" Sjt 1522 2nd Rifle Brigade
RAPER Alfred E. MM 2nd Cpl 37695 Third Army HQ Sig Coy Royal Engineers

RAPER David Atkinson MM Sjt 18677 1/5th Yorkshire Regt
RAPER Edward MM Pte 2317 Notts & Derby Regt
RAPER Horace P. MM Sjt 9607 2nd West Yorkshire Regt
RAPHAEL H. MM Pte 45123 9th Essex Regt
RAPLEY A. MM Cpl 229924 Royal Fusiliers
RAPLEY Alfred MM Pte 7471 Royal Sussex Regt
RAPLEY Cecil MM Sjt 317 6th Royal West Surrey Regt KIA 23.8.18.
RAPLEY Edgar MM+Bar Cpl 28638 56 Fd Coy Royal Engineers
RAPLEY Eli Gilbert MM Pte 25941 11th Royal West Kent Regt
RAPPS Frank Thomas MM L/Cpl 2191 1/15th London Regt
RAPSON William L. MM Sjt 2975 24th Royal Fusiliers
RARITY David MM Sjt 627 VI Corps Cyclist Bn Army Cyclist Corps
RASBERRY M.C. MM Cpl 350546 1/7th London Regt
RASH Arthur MM Sjt 8898 11th Suffolk Regt
RASHBROOK E.W. MM Pte 80049 18 Fd Amb RAMC
RASON Thomas MM Pte 9461 Norfolk Regt
RASPIN Walter MM Pte 52129 1st East Yorkshire Regt
RASTRICK Walter MM+Bar Sjt 21/394 5th West Yorkshire Regt
RATCLIFF A.F. MM Sjt 43602 9th Essex Regt
RATCLIFF Cecil E. MM Sjt 26204 Shropshire Light Infantry
RATCLIFF Percy MM 2nd Cpl 538239 Royal Engineers
RATCLIFFE Albert MM Cpl 24131 Royal Welsh Fusiliers
RATCLIFFE Arthur G. MM Pte 18874 4th Grenadier Guards
RATCLIFFE Brook MM Pte 101981 29th Durham Light Infantry
RATCLIFFE Charles H. MM L/Cpl 15146 Liverpool Regt
RATCLIFFE Daniel Percival MM Pte 45640 19th Royal Welsh Fusiliers
RATCLIFFE E. MM Bdr 42069 RFA
RATCLIFFE Edward Thomas "MM+Bar,CG(B)" Sjt 345601 24th Royal Welsh Fusiliers
RATCLIFFE Ernest MM L/Bdr 97877 195 Siege Bty RGA
RATCLIFFE Fred MM L/Cpl 9170 XIII Corps Cyclist Bn Army Cyclist Corps
RATCLIFFE George MM Gnr 74251 31 Div Ammn Col RFA
RATCLIFFE George W. MM Pte 142534 62nd Bn Machine Gun Corps
RATCLIFFE Herbert MM L/Cpl 42815 81 Fd Coy Royal Engineers KIA 17.4.18.
RATCLIFFE Jack MM Pte 32674 Hampshire Regt
RATCLIFFE James H. MM Cpl 9612 5 Fd Coy Royal Engineers
RATCLIFFE James H. MM Pte 22073 1st Dragoon Guards
RATCLIFFE James W. MM Sjt 3896 9th North Lancashire Regt
RATCLIFFE Jesse MM Sjt 242896 22nd Northumberland Fusiliers DOW 19.10.17.
RATCLIFFE John MM L/Cpl 3580 11th Manchester Regt
RATCLIFFE John MM Pte 6624 Army Cyclist Corps
RATCLIFFE John R. MM Pte 36809 Machine Gun Corps
RATCLIFFE John T. MM Cpl 13809 8th North Staffordshire Regt
RATCLIFFE Leonard MM L/Cpl 49479 1st Royal Inniskilling Fusiliers
RATCLIFFE Leonard "MM,DM(B)" Sjt 3354 1/5th Cheshire Regt
RATCLIFFE Neville Trend MM L/Cpl 471825 2/12th London Regt
RATCLIFFE Percy G. MM Gnr 777117 RFA
RATCLIFFE Percy John Stuart MM Gnr 199944 160 Bde RFA
RATCLIFFE Thomas MM L/Cpl 243590 Lancashire Fusiliers
RATCLIFFE Thomas MM Pte 417398 RAMC
RATCLIFFE W. MM Sjt 326 RFA
RATCLIFFE Walter MM Sjt 307335 9th Bn Tank Corps
RATCLIFFE William "VC,MM" Pte 2251 2nd South Lancashire Regt
RATCLIFFE William MM Pte 2251 2nd South Lancashire Regt
RATCLIFFE William MM Sjt 67651 Royal Engineers
RATCLIFFE William G. MM Sjt 42499 20th Bn Machine Gun Corps
RATCLIFFE William H. MM Sjt 235054 1/1st Gloucestershire Yeomanry
RATHBONE David MM Pte 12910 1/4th North Lancashire Regt KIA 19.9.17.
RATHBONE Fred MM Sjt 9774 2nd East Yorkshire Regt
RATHBONE John Wade MM Pte S4/064701 14 Div Train Army Service Corps
RATHBONE Roland MM SPnr 487981 1(North Midland)Fd Coy Royal Engineers att 59 Div Sig Coy.
RATHBONE Samuel MM L/Cpl 96924 176 Tunnelling Coy Royal Engineers
RATHBONE Thomas Smith MM Sjt 202784 1/4th Royal Lancaster Regt KIA 9.7.18.
RATHBONE Walter MM Pte 72011 Machine Gun Corps
RATLEY Thomas MM Pte 17353 Grenadier Guards
RATLIDGE John MM Sjt 13337 10th West Riding Regt
RATTEY Sidney R. MM Pte 91687 RAMC
RATTI Robert A.Gordon MM Cpl 20243 East Kent Regt
RATTIGAN Edward MM Spr 396310 Royal Engineers

RATTIGAN Martin MM Gnr 44876 81 Bty 5 Bde RFA
RATTLE Thomas "MM,MID" Sjt 19028 Welsh Regt
RATTLEY George A. MM Sjt 8547 2nd Hampshire Regt
RATTLEY Jack MM Pte PW/835 19th Middlesex Regt
RATTRAY George A. MM Pte 3327 1/24th London Regt
RATTRAY Herbert MM Bdr 25929 RFA
RATTRAY James MM L/Cpl 8453 Seaforth Highlanders
RATTRAY John MM Pte 31133 Royal Scots
RATTRAY John C. "MM,MSM" Sjt 37249 51 Fd Amb RAMC
RATTUE George MM Pte 26147 7th Wiltshire Regt
RATTY Ernest A. "DCM,MM" L/Cpl 12731 5 Fd Amb RAMC
RATTY W.H. MM Sjt 21750 RFA
RAUTH or ROUTH Albert Frederick MM Cpl 344 2nd Lancashire Fusiliers AKA Samuel RILEY
RAVEN Arthur F. "DCM+Bar,MM,MIDx2" RSM 3/10396 8th & 9th Norfolk Regt
RAVEN Cecil P. MM+Bar Pte 255360 3rd London Regt
RAVEN James Edward MM Cpl 16927 56 Fd Coy Royal Engineers
RAVEN John R. MM L/Cpl 14392 2nd Suffolk Regt att 1/1st Cambridgeshire Regt.
RAVEN John William MM Pte 38495 West Yorkshire Regt
RAVEN Reginald L. MM Pte A/200456 2nd King's Royal Rifle Corps
RAVEN Robert J. MM Bdr 78852 124 Siege Bty RGA
RAVEN Thomas MM 2nd Cpl 15542 74 Fd Coy Royal Engineers
RAVEN William MM Pte 242630 1/5th Leicestershire Regt KIA 6.1.18.
RAVENHILL Albert E. MM Pte 8389 1st South Wales Borderers
RAVENHILL Alfred MM L/Cpl 9595 1st South Wales Borderers
RAVENHILL Frank MM Cpl 280230 RGA
RAVENHILL James "DCM,MM" Sjt 56831 2nd Welsh Regt
RAVENHILL John W. MM Pte 12843 9th Devonshire Regt
RAVENHILL Thomas Henry William MM Pte S/8494 7th Rifle Brigade KIA 26.12.17.
RAVENHILL William J.T. MM Cpl 18302 11th Worcestershire Regt
RAVENSCROFT Frederick MM Cpl 1731 8th East Kent Regt
RAVENSCROFT Harold MM Pte 29959 Middlesex Regt
RAVENSCROFT William MM Sjt 8849 2nd King's Royal Rifle Corps
RAVEY John G. MM Sjt 240076 Notts & Derby Regt
RAVIE Thomas MM Sjt 302896 1/7th Royal Scots
RAW Alfred E. MM Cpl 43571 22nd Manchester Regt
RAW Arthur A. MM Cpl 13621 2nd Royal Fusiliers
RAW Frederick MM Pte 52885 1st Northumberland Fusiliers
RAW John Robert MM Cpl 42120 2/5th West Yorkshire Regt
RAW Joseph Dixon MM Pte 30709 2nd Yorkshire Regt KIA 8.5.18.
RAW Robert William MM Bdr 33515 28 Siege Bty RGA
RAWCLIFFE Frederick MM Bdr 9119 B/150 Bde RFA
RAWCLIFFE Harold MM Pte 306113 West Yorkshire Regt
RAWCLIFFE Henry MM Cpl 306540 Liverpool Regt
RAWCLIFFE John MM Pte 203530 East Lancashire Regt
RAWCLIFFE Samuel L. MM Pte 32688 4th York & Lancaster Regt
RAWDING Hubert Thomas MM Pte 54181 1/6th West Yorkshire Regt
RAWET Thomas MM Cpl 9808 Cameron Highlanders
RAWLE James G. MM Cpl 256794 1/1st Bedfordshire Yeomanry
RAWLES Everard E. MM Pte 56111 Machine Gun Corps
RAWLES Stephen MM Pte 9459 1st Somerset Light Infantry
RAWLIN Ernest MM Pnr 444351 Royal Engineers
RAWLIN Frederick A. MM Sjt 22080 10th Royal Fusiliers
RAWLING Alfred MM Cpl 444162 Royal Engineers
RAWLING Harold MM L/Cpl 10/1361 East Yorkshire Regt
RAWLING James MM Spr 228278 314 Rd Constr Coy Royal Engineers
RAWLINGS Bernard MM L/Cpl 942 1/5th Seaforth Highlanders
RAWLINGS Charles Henry MM Sjt 8822 2nd Yorkshire Light Infantry
RAWLINGS Edward MM Gnr 840023 RFA
RAWLINGS Edward J. MM Pte 38898 7th Royal West Surrey Regt
RAWLINGS Frederick MM Gnr 25008 1 Bty 45 Bde RFA KIA 1.7.16
RAWLINGS George MM Cpl 130265 51st Bn Machine Gun Corps
RAWLINGS Harry William MM Pte 3238 12th Middlesex Regt KIA 22.10.17.
RAWLINGS John W. "DCM,MM" Sjt 82213 172 Tunnelling Coy Royal Engineers
RAWLINGS R.E. MM L/Cpl 21955 Machine Gun Corps
RAWLINGS Samuel George "DCM,MM" Sjt 7276 6th Somerset Light Infantry
RAWLINGS William MM Sjt 37271 South Lancashire Regt
RAWLINGS or RAWLINS Alfred George MM Pte 17401 6th Oxf & Bucks Light Infantry
RAWLINS Alfred MM Sjt 41547 65 Fd Coy Royal Engineers
RAWLINS Arthur MM(1132 L/Sjt Mon R)+Bar Sjt 53706 Welsh Regt

RAWLINS Arthur J. MM Cpl 37895 8th Royal Berkshire Regt
RAWLINS Charles A. MM Sjt 314006 RGA
RAWLINS James S. MM Dvr 38559 RFA
RAWLINS S. MM Pte 15594 West Riding Regt
RAWLINSON Ernest MM+Bar Sjt 18263 7th Border Regt
RAWLINSON George MM L/Cpl 5469 9th Royal Fusiliers DOW 28.3.18.
RAWLINSON Joseph MM Gnr 675374 RFA
RAWLINSON Joseph MM Pte R/8519 King's Royal Rifle Corps
RAWLINSON Walter MM Spr 33968 Royal Engineers
RAWLINSON William MM Pnr 129720 2 Special Coy Royal Engineers
RAWNSLEY Granville MM Pte 43975 42 Fd Amb RAMC
RAWNSLEY Harry MM Pte 202382 West Riding Regt
RAWNSLEY Lewis H. MM Gnr 71729 RGA
RAWNSLEY Robert MM Pte 26326 21st Manchester Regt
RAWNSLEY William MM Pte 10897 10th West Riding Regt DOW 30.11.16.
RAWORTH Percy MM Gnr 2506 Machine Gun Corps(Motors) DOW 23.9.17.
RAWSON Eric MM Pte 139627 49th Bn Machine Gun Corps
RAWSON Frank MM Cpl 391618 London Regt
RAWSON George P.. MM Pte 241626 Lincolnshire Regt
RAWSON Harry MM Gnr 44765 RFA
RAWSON John H. MM Sjt 175552 1/1st Yorkshire Dragoons Yeomanry
RAWSON Robert MM Cpl 15381 7th Lincolnshire Regt KIA 26.8.18.
RAWSON William MM Bdr 8159 RFA
RAWSON William "MM,MSM,MID" BQMS 51076 123 Bty 28 Bde RFA
RAWSTHORNE John H. MM L/Cpl 3862 8th Liverpool Regt
RAWSTHORNE John T. MM Dvr T2/13083 Army Service Corps
RAWSTHORNE William Henry MM L/Sjt 27544 Liverpool Regt
RAY Albert E. MM CQMS 1650 2nd Lancashire Fusiliers
RAY Albert E. MM Pte 5400 Royal West Surrey Regt
RAY Albert W. MM Pte 44265 Royal Irish Rifles
RAY Arthur MM Pte 703121 23rd London Regt
RAY Charles "DCM,MM" Sjt 203501 2nd & 5th Notts & Derby Regt
RAY Charles Edward MM L/Sjt 305024 2/8th Royal Warwickshire Regt Died 29.10.18.
RAY Charles William MM Pnr 99777 30 Div Sig Coy Royal Engineers
RAY E. MM Pte 11118 10th Royal West Surrey Regt
RAY Edward S. MM Pnr 312351 Royal Engineers
RAY F. MM L/Cpl 232270 London Regt
RAY George MM Gnr 83767 B/47 Bde RFA
RAY George V. MM Sjt 522548 153 Fd Coy Royal Engineers
RAY Isaac MM Sjt 200269 Yorkshire Light Infantry
RAY J. MM L/Cpl 240728 North Lancashire Regt
RAY John MM Pte 251611 3rd London Regt
RAY John G. MM L/Cpl 265588 Liverpool Regt
RAY Robert MM Sjt 30575 99 Siege Bty RGA
RAY Thomas MM Pte M2/114502 Army Service Corps
RAY Tyson MM Sjt M2/077929 403 Coy Army Service Corps
RAY William MM Dvr 89438 73 Bty 5 Bde RFA
RAY William MM Sjt 10053 2nd Durham Light Infantry
RAYBOULD James R.L. MM L/Cpl 102218 Notts & Derby Regt
RAYBOULD John William MM Sjt 575 1/5th Notts & Derby Regt
RAYBOULD Sydney MM Cpl 17895 10th Worcestershire Regt
RAYBOULD Thomas MM Pte 17079 2/4th Hampshire Regt
RAYBOULD William MM Pte 435169 RAMC
RAYCRAFT Archie MM Spr 265938 Royal Engineers
RAYER John MM Pte 203517 Gloucestershire Regt
RAYMENT Albert E. MM Pte 6464 6th Royal West Surrey Regt
RAYMENT Anthony William MM Pte 151 2nd Royal Fusiliers KIA 27.10.16.
RAYMENT Bernard A. MM Pte R/29500 King's Royal Rifle Corps
RAYMENT Ernest Henry MM+Bar Sjt 17281 13th Essex Regt
RAYMENT James MM Pte 291979 2/10th Middlesex Regt
RAYMENT John W. MM L/Cpl 12460 9th Essex Regt
RAYMENT William MM+Bar Pte 70362 Notts & Derby Regt
RAYMOND Alfred James MM Cpl 764260 28th London Regt
RAYMOND Arthur MM L/Sjt 202495 Scottish Rifles
RAYMOND Oliver J. MM Pte 242544 1/5th Suffolk Regt
RAYMOND Percy R. MM Sjt 6022 1st Suffolk Regt
RAYMOND William H. MM Spr 62492 123 Fd Coy Royal Engineers
RAYMONT Daniel W. MM Sjt 201136 4th Hampshire Regt
RAYMONT W. MM Pte 3/7193 Devonshire Regt
RAYNARD Arthur MM Pte 2159 8th Royal Sussex Regt
RAYNARD John E. MM Pte 242367 5th West Riding Regt

RAYNE Henry MM L/Sjt 22852 2nd Yorkshire Light Infantry KIA 2.12.17.
RAYNE Thomas R. MM Gnr 50964 RGA
RAYNER Albert MM Pte 657747 223 Div Emp Coy Labour Corps
RAYNER Albert MM Sjt 230 C/157 Bde RFA
RAYNER Arthur Harry William MM Pte 31739 9th Essex Regt
RAYNER Charlie W. MM Pte 26120 Shropshire Light Infantry
RAYNER Edward H. MM Pte 7010 10th Royal Warwickshire Regt
RAYNER Frederick William MM L/Cpl 9320 6th East Kent Regt
RAYNER George Robert MM L/Cpl R/7105 9th King's Royal Rifle Corps KIA 10.4.17.
RAYNER H. MM Cpl 12234 9th Essex Regt
RAYNER H. MM Sjt 545702 RAMC
RAYNER H. MM Dvr 5364 35 Bde RFA
RAYNER Harold B. MM L/Cpl 10825 6th Duke of Cornwall's LI
RAYNER James B. MM Pte 374074 8th London Regt
RAYNER Kirby MM L/Cpl 474089 Royal Engineers
RAYNER Stanley G. MM Pte 1965 1/3rd London Regt
RAYNER Thomas MM Pte 201283 Tank Corps
RAYNER Thomas MM Sjt 244 18th Middlesex Regt
RAYNER William MM Pte 53706 2/5th West Yorkshire Regt
RAYNER William MM L/Sjt 17218 1st Leicestershire Regt
RAYNER William "DCM,MM" Bdr 50718 147 Bde RFA
RAYNER William MM Sjt 3549 50 Coy Machine Gun Corps
RAYNER William C. MM Pte 10910 1st South Wales Borderers
RAYNER William G.T. MM Pte 7287 Royal West Surrey Regt
RAYNES Frank Leggott MM Gnr 801120 B/295 Bde RFA
RAYNOR Alfred Ernest "MM,MID" Sjt 9290 2nd Leicestershire Regt
RAYNOR Arthur MM Pte 9086 2nd Notts & Derby Regt
RAYNOR Arthur MM Pte 512783 223 Div Emp Coy Labour Corps
RAYNOR Harry MM Pte 53660 Notts & Derby Regt
RAYNOR Harry MM Spr 311443 Royal Engineers
RAYNOR Joel MM Spr 280023 332 Rd Constr Coy Royal Engineers
RAYNOR Joseph W. MM L/Bdr 216398 255 Bde RFA
RAYNOR Leonard MM Pte R/13683 16th King's Royal Rifle Corps
RAYNOR William MM Sjt 14457 24th Manchester Regt
RAYSON James Bowden "MM,MID" 2nd Cpl 459264 447 Fd Coy Royal Engineers
RAYWOOD Eli MM+2 Bars Sjt 241315 Yorkshire Light Infantry
RAYWORTH Thomas Allen "MM,CG(B)" Pte 33407 11th East Lancashire Regt
REA A.F. MM Gnr 61772 RFA
REA Andrew MM Sjt 138243 223 Siege Bty RGA
REA Frederick C. MM Cpl 2233 1/6th Welsh Regt
REA George A. MM Pte 241515 Gloucestershire Regt
REA James MM Sjt 9090 2nd West Yorkshire Regt
REA John MM Sjt 3741 6th Connaught Rangers
REA Leonard MM Pte 201762 Royal West Surrey Regt
REACHER Fred MM Pte 42289 6th South Wales Borderers DOW 29.8.17.
READ Albert MM Cpl 6844 2nd King's Own Scottish Borderers
READ Albert Francis MM Sjt 5/4171 1st King's Royal Rifle Corps
READ Albert Lane MM Sjt 400 1/1st Northamptonshire Yeomanry
READ Albert T. MM Pte 1686 1/1st Buckinghamshire Yeomanry
READ Arthur Henry MM Sjt 2594 Royal Flying Corps
READ Arthur Robert MM Spr 34898 Signal Service Royal Engineers
READ B.A. MM Cpl 44683 A/187 Bde RFA
READ Bernard Henry MM Sjt 46292 Machine Gun Corps
READ Bertram James MM Dvr 10469 23 Bty 40 Bde RFA DOW 2.10.18.
READ Charles Edward "DCM,MM" Cpl 10444 Middlesex Regt
READ Charles S. MM Sjt 7532 1st Dorsetshire Regt
READ Charles W. MM Pte 69073 9th Royal Fusiliers
READ Ernest B. MM Sjt 10208 2nd Royal Sussex Regt
READ Ernest J. MM Sjt 67326 RAMC
READ F. MM Sjt 8876 1st Border Regt
READ Frederick Arthur MM Sjt 551077 2/16th London Regt
READ Frederick C. "DCM,MM" Sjt 325705 1/1st Cambridgeshire Regt
READ Frederick Herbert "DCM,MM" Sjt 13438 24th Royal Fusiliers KIA 16.4.18.
READ Frederick J. MM Pte 24365 1st Northamptonshire Regt
READ George Harry MM L/Cpl 84204 59th Bn Machine Gun Corps
READ George W. MM Pte 62611 6th West Yorkshire Regt
READ Grosvenor Woodhouse MM Spr 62366 62 Div Sig Coy Royal Engineers
READ Harold MM Cpl 410 Middlesex Regt
READ Harold Ambrose MM Pte 331466 12th Liverpool Regt DOW 3.7.18.
READ Harry P. MM Cpl 46590 Welsh Regt

READ Harry R. MM L/Cpl 25409 Royal Engineers
READ Henry MM 2nd Cpl 153230 Royal Engineers
READ Henry H. MM Pte 78 5th Dragoon Guards
READ Henry Walter MM 2nd Cpl 77849 29 Airline Section Royal Engineers
READ Herbert E. MM Gnr 155522 RFA
READ Herbert S. MM Pte 14161 Royal Sussex Regt
READ Horace W. MM Pte S/17665 Rifle Brigade
READ Isaac J. MM Gnr 71432 RFA
READ James MM Pte 36204 North Lancashire Regt
READ James MM Pte M2/081847 Army Service Corps
READ John MM Pte 67679 Machine Gun Corps
READ John MM Sjt 38183 Y/50 Med TM Bty RGA Died 19.12.16.
READ John MM Pte 18099 7th Northamptonshire Regt
READ John H. MM Pte 86512 23rd Bn Machine Gun Corps
READ John H. MM Pte M2/104979 Army Service Corps
READ John W. MM L/Cpl 33191 36th Northumberland Fusiliers
READ John W. MM L/Cpl 34224 142 Fd Amb RAMC
READ Louis Henry MM Sjt 19580 Essex Regt
READ Philliip T. MM Sjt 30997 RAMC
READ Ralph Hobill "MM,MSM" Spr 127861 3 Fd Svy Bn Royal Engineers
READ Reginald MM Spr 41982 Royal Engineers
READ Robert E. MM Pte 10266 5th Dorsetshire Regt
READ Robert J. MM Pte 8004 Army Cyclist Corps
READ Thomas MM Pte 19413 7th Wiltshire Regt
READ Vincent H. "MM(15,Household Bn)+Bar" Sjt 22584 1st Coldstream Guards
READ Walter MM L/Cpl 2680 3rd Middlesex Regt
READ Walter S. MM Sjt 14428 9th South Staffordshire Regt
READ Wilfred "DCM,MM" Cpl 348 16th West Yorkshire Regt
READ William MM Gnr 915690 RFA
READ William H. MM L/Cpl 18190 2nd Coldstream Guards
READ William James MM Cpl 1091 10th Royal Fusiliers
READ William L. MM+Bar Pte 17816 9th Scottish Rifles
READDY Charles MM L/Cpl 32232 8th East Lancashire Regt KIA 22.9.17.
READE Arthur MM Sjt 23994 6 Div Sig Coy Royal Engineers
READE John MM Gnr 76593 40 Bde RFA
READER Alfred MM Sjt 3/10328 11th Suffolk Regt
READER William MM Sjt 40704 2 Bde RFA
READER William MM Pte 5640 6th Royal West Kent Regt
READHEAD Winn MM Gnr 23167 34 Div Ammn Col RFA
READING Bert MM Cpl 17929 1/6th Royal Warwickshire Regt
READING George MM Cpl 44967 93 Fd Coy Royal Engineers
READING George "DCM,MM+Bar" Spr 96350 28 Div Sig Coy Royal Engineers KIA 21.10.17.
READING George Alfred MM Cpl 9641 2nd Royal Irish Rifles KIA 4.4.17.
READING James T. MM Sjt 145068 1/1st Northamptonshire Yeomanry
READING John MM S/Sjt Farrier 31723 71 Bde RFA
READING Joseph W. MM Pte 36015 1/4th Gloucestershire Regt
READSHAW Joseph N. MM L/Sjt C/12121 13th King's Royal Rifle Corps
READY A.W. MM Cpl 15735 Royal Air Force
READY Arthur Henry MM Sjt 3137 12th Middlesex Regt KIA 26.10.16.
READY Richard MM L/Cpl 66869 RAMC
READY Walter MM+Bar Pte 5947 12/13th Northumberland Fusiliers
REAL William R. MM Sjt 14248 Middlesex Regt
REANEY George H. MM Spr 26818 Royal Engineers
REANEY James MM Sjt 245911 5 Fd Svy Bn Royal Engineers
REANEY Joseph MM Gnr 4148 RFA
REANEY M. MM Pte 281152 Labour Corps
REARDON Edmond MM+Bar Sjt 1183 26th Northumberland Fusiliers
REARDON Frank MM Pte 105364 Liverpool Regt
REARDON G.C. MM Sjt 275689 Essex Regt
REARDON Matthew MM+Bar Cpl 21903 RGA
REARDON William "DCM,MM" Cpl 5011 9th Lancers
REARDON William MM Pte 10086 Royal Irish Regt
REASON Harold MM Sjt 387515 Royal Engineers
REASON Herbert J. MM 2nd Cpl 42844 Royal Engineers
REASON William O. MM Sjt 16218 RFA
REAST Arthur W. MM Sjt 7754 2 Fd Amb RAMC
REAVLEY Thomas MM+Bar Pte 18/584 19th Durham Light Infantry
REAVLEY William MM Sjt 15707 8th Somerset Light Infantry
REAY Charles W. MM 2nd Cpl 470888 Royal Engineers
REAY Frank MM+Bar Cpl 23523 4th Worcestershire Regt

REAY George J. MM Pte 18/1542 Northumberland Fusiliers
REAY James MM Pte 40086 2/4th West Riding Regt DOW 17.11.18.
REAY John MM Dvr 113232 17 Bde RHA
REAY John M. MM Pte 35477 Northumberland Fusiliers
REAY Joseph MM L/Cpl 11018 1st Royal Highlanders
REAY Robert MM Pte 14650 7th Border Regt KIA 9.8.16.
REAY Walter MM Pnr 192798 Royal Engineers
REAY William MM Cpl H/270579 1/1st Northumberland Yeomanry
REAY William David MM Dvr 771367 63 Div Ammn Col RFA
RECKIE W. MM Pte S/5859 1st Royal Highlanders
RECORD Percy Samuel MM Pte 26960 12th East Surrey Regt KIA 22.10.18.
REDALL A. MM Cpl P1716 Military Foot Police
REDDAWAY Harry MM+Bar L/Cpl 7955 Machine Gun Corps
REDDEN Albert MM Pte 27796 RAMC
REDDEN Robert MM Sjt 243008 5th Leicestershire Regt
REDDICK Gordon Philip MM Pte 2912 1/21st London Regt
REDDICK William MM Cpl 9146 2nd Royal West Surrey Regt
REDDIN Harry MM Cpl 207983 248 Fd Coy Royal Engineers
REDDING Albert J. MM Cpl 66976 112 Coy Labour Corps
REDDING Frederick C. MM Pte 52119 8th West Yorkshire Regt
REDDING Frederick W. MM L/Cpl 45384 2nd Royal Berkshire Regt
REDDING Sydney MM L/Cpl 439321 RAMC
REDDINGTON Edward MM Pte 41198 17th Highland Light Infantry
REDDINGTON Ernest MM Pte 203339 4th Middlesex Regt
REDDINGTON T. MM Pte 242762 Liverpool Regt
REDDINGTON Thomas Edward MM Pte 13163 9th Notts & Derby Regt
REDDISH Frank "DCM,MM" Cpl 28064 1/4th North Lancashire Regt
REDDY John MM Spr 93254 218 Fd Coy Royal Engineers
REDDY Robert MM Pte 5977 2nd Leinster Regt
REDDYHOFF George Berty MM Cpl 43708 9th Scottish Rifles KIA 6.8.18.
REDFEARN Albert MM Pte R/16861 King's Royal Rifle Corps
REDFEARN Edgar MM+Bar Sjt 306764 4th West Riding Regt
REDFEARN George Owen MM Bfr 80331 210 Siege Bty RGA
REDFEARN James T. MM Bdr 780246 RFA
REDFERN Bertie MM Pte 19761 Scottish Rifles
REDFERN Edward J. MM L/Cpl 64651 35th Bn Machine Gun Corps
REDFERN Ernest J. "DCM,MM" Cpl 11120 'O' Bty RHA
REDFERN Fred MM Pte 28814 RAMC
REDFERN Fred MM Cpl 14469 24th Manchester Regt
REDFERN George H. MM L/Cpl 15840 10th Northumberland Fusiliers
REDFERN Joseph MM Cpl 46567 X/18 Med TM Bty RGA
REDFERN Louis MM Pte 10/18650 Leicestershire Regt
REDFERN Robert G. MM Cpl 58843 Machine Gun Corps
REDFERN Thomas MM Pte 12321 6th Royal Berkshire Regt
REDFERN William MM Cpl 8376 13th East Yorkshire Regt KIA 27.1.18.
REDFORD Alexander MM Pte 1629 1/5th Royal Highlanders
REDFORD Frank MM Cpl 15379 8th Somerset Light Infantry
REDFORD Harold MM Cpl 15386 Shropshire Light Infantry
REDFORD James MM Pte 2257 12th Yorkshire Light Infantry
REDFORD James MM L/Sjt 10861 5th Royal Berkshire Regt
REDFORD Stanley MM Pte 321796 6th London Regt
REDGARD William MM Sjt 4822 Machine Gun Corps
REDGRAVE Charles M. MM Cpl 251599 Royal Engineers
REDGRAVE James MM Pte 32238 1st Lancashire Fusiliers
REDHEAD Edward MM Pte 9584 1st Border Regt
REDHEAD Ernest H. MM L/Cpl 702509 23rd London Regt
REDHEAD George MM+Bar Sjt 463185 50 Div Sig Coy Royal Engineers
REDHEAD Joseph S. MM Gnr 750937 RFA
REDHEAD Thomas E. MM Pte 25903 East Yorkshire Regt
REDHEAD Walter MM L/Cpl 240533 1/5th Royal Lancaster Regt
REDLEY James R. MM L/Cpl 31147 1st Royal West Kent Regt
REDLEY William MM L/Sjt 15216 7th Northamptonshire Regt DOW 1.8.17.
REDMAN Charles Bernard William MM Pte 20417 11th Royal Sussex Regt
REDMAN Clifford H. MM Sjt 450895 11th London Regt
REDMAN Edward MM Pte 10100 9th Seaforth Highlanders KIA 24.4.18.
REDMAN Ernest L. MM Cpl 1094 1/22nd London Regt
REDMAN Frederick J. MM L/Cpl 108395 Machine Gun Corps
REDMAN George MM Sjt 306830 2/4th Hampshire Regt
REDMAN John MM Cpl 27776 26 Fd Coy Royal Engineers
REDMAN John S. MM Cpl 492382 Royal Engineers
REDMAN Richard MM Bdr 308910 2/1(Lancs)Hy Bty RGA

REDMAN Robert MM Sjt 8211 2nd Hampshire Regt
REDMAN Ronald James MM+Bar Gnr Sig 961276 C/235 Bde RFA
REDMAN Walter MM Pte 18696 2nd Manchester Regt
REDMAN William Henry MM Cpl 604177 293 Bde RFA
REDMAYNE Alfred B. MM Dvr 161081 RFA
REDMAYNE Giles Blomfield MM Dvr 199 RFA Died 31.3.17.
REDMAYNE Richard H. MM L/Cpl 42272 2nd Suffolk Regt
REDMILE Alfred Bennet MM L/Sjt R/4327 12th King's Royal Rifle Corps
REDMILL Esmond MM Pte 75232 Tank Corps
REDMOND Alexander MM+Bar Sjt 120526 'B' Special Coy Royal Engineers
REDMOND Francis MM Sjt DM2/112155 Army Service Corps
REDMOND George Herbert MM L/Sjt 5140 2/4th Royal Berkshire Regt
REDMOND Joseph MM Cpl 3836 2nd Irish Guards DOW 8.9.17.
REDMOND Michael MM Pte 43026 Royal Irish Fusiliers
REDMOND Patrick MM Pte 1917 7th Royal Irish Regt
REdMOND Patrick MM Pte 11376 Machine Gun Corps
REDMOND Philip MM L/Cpl 7295 Irish Guards
REDMOND Robert "DCM,MM" L/Cpl D/2115 3rd Dragoon Guards
REDMOND Robert H. MM Sjt 9008 Royal Warwickshire Regt
REDMOND W. MM Pte 241053 Duke of Cornwall's LI
REDMOND William MM Pte 10722 1st Royal Dublin Fusiliers
REDMORE Walter MM Sjt 203293 Yorkshire Light Infantry
REDPATH Ernest MM Pte 202188 Royal Lancaster Regt
REDPATH H. "DCM,MM" CSM 106 8th Royal Highlanders
REDPATH James "DCM,MM" Pte 242274 1/4th West Riding Regt
REDPATH John MM+Bar Cpl 16632 10th East Yorkshire Regt DOW 29.9.18.
REDPATH Joseph W. MM L/Cpl 14698 Machine Gun Corps
REDPATH Samuel John MM Sjt 10437 Northumberland Fusiliers
REDPATH Walter MM Sjt 20370 Machine Gun Corps KIA 31.8.16.
REDPATH William MM Pte 13461 9th South Lancashire Regt
REDSHAW Charles MM Pte 241115 6th Notts & Derby Regt
REDSHAW Frederick William "MC,MM(23/66 Sjt 18th Nbld F)" 2Lt 1/5th York & Lancaster Regt
REDSHAW Harry Smith MM Pte 36910 36 Fd Amb RAMC
REDSHAW James MM Pte 40588 Essex Regt
REDSHAW Joseph MM Sjt 302171 Durham Light Infantry
REDSHAW William MM L/Cpl Mechanic 77383 1st Bn Tank Corps
REDWOOD Cyril J. MM Pte 242198 Leicestershire Regt
REDWOOD Frederick Robert MM L/Cpl 9336 2nd Devonshire Regt DOW 1.4.18.
REDWOOD Levi MM L/Cpl 134727 Royal Engineers
REDWOOD P.J. MM+Bar Cpl P1603 Military Foot Police
REDWORTH CliffordW. MM Gnr 83542 RGA
REE John Harry MM Pte 16845 9th Scottish Rifles KIA 23.3.18.
REECE Charles MM L/Cpl 4662 14th Liverpool Regt
REECE Charles Frederick MM L/Cpl 453071 11th London Regt
REECE Ernest "DCM,MM" Cpl 113722 202 Fd Coy Royal Engineers
REECE George MM 2nd Cpl 36113 35 Div Sig Coy Royal Engineers
REECE James A. MM Pte 30120 7th Wiltshire Regt
REECE Walter MM Pte 266926 7th Liverpool Regt
REECE William MM L/Cpl 321823 6th London Regt
REECE William MM Pte 27641 1st Liverpool Regt
REECE William H. MM Sjt M2/079279 Army Service Corps att RFA.
REED Albert C. MM L/Sjt 29720 2nd Hampshire Regt
REED Albert E. MM Cpl 9634 1st Middlesex Regt
REED Albert George MM Pte 9/15249 2/5th Leicestershire Regt KIA 5.7.17.
REED Albert R. MM Bdr 90495 1/1(London)Hy Bty RGA
REED Alfred Charles MM Pte 42744 12th Royal Irish Rifles KIA 25.10.18.
REED Arthur MM Pte 240143 Lincolnshire Regt
REED Charles MM Pte 60508 9th Royal Fusiliers KIA 3.5.17.
REED Charles I. MM Sjt 16881 1 Pontoon Park Royal Engineers
REED Charles V. MM L/Cpl 28867 Shropshire Light Infantry att 1/1st Herefordshire Regt.
REED Charles Wilson MM Sjt 15789 2nd Bedfordshire Regt
REED Douglas R. MM Bdr 72343 44 Bde RFA
REED Edward MM L/Cpl 6785 6th Royal West Kent Regt KIA 3.5.17.
REED Edwin MM Cpl 6221 Lancashire Fusiliers
REED Ernest MM Sjt 21392 Yorkshire Light Infantry
REED Ernest MM L/Cpl 48840 Royal Engineers
REED Frederick MM Gnr 168717 A/122 Bde RFA
REED Frederick MM Cpl 52537 Royal Fusiliers
REED Frederick C. MM L/Cpl 869 Army Cyclist Corps
REED Frederick J. MM L/Cpl 20222 7th Royal Sussex Regt

REED Frederick John MM Gnr 16244 RGA
REED George MM Sjt 9500 King's Royal Rifle Corps
REED George MM Sjt 3173 1/1st Duke of Lancaster's Own Yeomanry
REED George MM+Bar L/Cpl 19069 9th Essex Regt
REED George Thomas MM Sjt 42216 9 Heavy Bty RGA
REED George Wilfred MM Pte 9478 2nd Manchester Regt
REED Harry MM Gnr 17132 26 Heavy Bty RGA
REED Harry MM Sjt 2953 11th West Yorkshire Regt
REED Harry "DCM,MM" Cpl 75275 16 Div Sig Coy Royal Engineers
REED Harry E. MM Pte 10391 2nd Royal Sussex Regt
REED Henry F. MM CQMS 5705 Machine Gun Corps
REED Herbert MM Sjt 291981 132 Heavy Bty RGA
REED Herbert W. MM Dvr T/28907 Army Service Corps
REED J.B. MM Cpl 77008 RFA
REED Jacob "DCM,MM" Sjt 20825 15th & 16th Cheshire Regt
REED John MM L/Cpl 110156 10th Bn Tank Corps
REED John "MM,MID" Pte 6753 16 Fd Amb RAMC
REED John MM L/Cpl 8792 2nd North Lancashire Regt
REED John Barrett MM Pte 52910 13th Durham Light Infantry
REED John G. MM Dvr 129354 D/280 Bde RFA
REED John W. MM Pte 60475 8th West Yorkshire Regt
REED John W. MM Sjt 770684 2 Bde RFA
REED Kenneth MM Sjt 513208 14th London Regt
REED Marmaduke MM+Bar L/Cpl 20551 18 Fd Amb RAMC
REED Osborne H. MM Pte 99324 26th Royal Fusiliers
REED Samuel MM L/Cpl 18865 15th Hampshire Regt
REED Selby MM Pte 2249 8th Royal Sussex Regt
REED Simpson MM Sjt 241743 1/5th Border Regt
REED Stanley MM+Bar Pte 17645 7th Border Regt
REED Stanley R. MM+Bar 2nd Cpl 510462 Royal Engineers
REED Thomas MM Sjt 14034 2nd Durham Light Infantry
REED Thomas MM Pte 144 18th Durham Light Infantry
REED Thomas MM S/Sjt Mechanic 75671 1st Bn Tank Corps
REED Thomas MM Pte 533362 15th London Regt
REED Thomas Ernest MM Pte 1452 3rd Royal Fusiliers
REED W.G. MM CQMS 23667 9th Royal Welsh Fusiliers
REED Walter Nelson "DCM,MM" CSM 1147 7th East Kent Regt
REED William MM L/Cpl 303361 2nd Manchester Regt
REED William A. MM Pte 306705 Lancashire Fusiliers
REED William F.S. MM+Bar Cpl 33126 228 Fd Coy Royal Engineers
REED William J. MM Pte 3/6678 Somerset Light Infantry
REED William S. MM Gnr 70176 Tank Corps
REED William T. MM Bdr 13719 2 Siege Bty RGA
REED William T. MM L/Cpl 40147 Royal Scots Fusiliers
REEDAY Frank MM Sjt 65088 Royal Flying Corps
REEDER Charles Edward MM Bdr 163 C/64 Bde RFA DOW 18.7.17.
REEDER Dick MM Sjt 266791 6th West Riding Regt
REEDER John S. MM Dvr T/35049 Army Service Corps
REEDER Leonard MM Sjt 8417 2nd East Lancashire Regt
REEDER Richard Harold MM Pnr 443968 42 Div Sig Coy Royal Engineers
REEDMAN William MM Cpl 30286 7th Royal Warwickshire Regt
REEDY Nicholas MM L/Cpl 266281 2/4th West Riding Regt
REEKIE A. MM Pte 34601 Labour Corps
REEKIE Robert MM Cpl 305118 1 Fd Amb RAMC
REEKS George A. MM 2nd Cpl 278256 176 Tunnelling Coy Royal Engineers
REEKS Stanley MM Cpl P/10235 Military Mounted Police att HQ 9 Div.
REELAND George J. MM L/Cpl 470856 12th London Regt
REEN Thomas P. MM Cpl 45233 25 Bde RFA
REENAN R.W. MM Pte 9402 4th Hussars
REES Ben Percy MM Gnr 625337 HAC(Artillery)
REES Benjamin "DCM,MM+Bar" Pte 24740 17th Lancashire Fusiliers
REES C.S. MM Pte 14113 Dragoon Guards
REES Daniel MM L/Cpl 249508 9 Div Sig Coy Royal Engineers
REES David MM L/Bdr 105665 RFA
REES David John MM Pte 16442 2nd Devonshire Regt
REES Dillwyn W. MM Gnr 103341 226 Siege Bty RGA
REES E.H. MM L/Cpl 448157 Royal Engineers
REES E.J. MM Cpl 32995 Welsh Regt
REES Edgar W. MM L/Cpl 14391 5th South Wales Borderers
REES Edward A. MM Sjt 39680 RAMC
REES Edwin MM L/Cpl R/4031 13th King's Royal Rifle Corps
REES Emlyn MM Pte 42016 Welsh Regt
REES Emrys T. MM Spr 231148 Royal Engineers
REES Francis D. MM L/Cpl 22773 6th Royal West Surrey Regt

REES George William MM Pnr 487989 59 Div Sig Coy Royal Engineers
REES Gomer John MM Pte 73193 9th Royal Welsh Fusiliers
REES Gwilym Havard MM Cpl 17491 Royal Welsh Fusiliers
REES H.V. MM Pte 34473 9th Welsh Regt
REES Harold MM Pte 52064 2nd Royal Fusiliers
REES Herbert MM Sjt 13802 10th North Lancashire Regt
REES Idwal MM Pte 72067 Cheshire Regt
REES James MM Pte 49012 Royal Welsh Fusiliers
REES James MM Pte R/33710 King's Royal Rifle Corps
REES James E. MM+Bar Sjt 111771 RGA
REES John MM 2nd Cpl 67378 124 Fd Coy Royal Engineers
REES John MM L/Cpl 16428 6th South Wales Borderers Died 28.10.18.
REES John MM Gnr 80087 204 Siege Bty RGA
REES John MM Gnr 118492 RFA
REES John H. MM+Bar L/Cpl 15401 Middlesex Regt
REES John M. MM Pte 202188 Welsh Regt
REES Joseph G. MM Sjt 52051 Lancashire Fusiliers
REES Lewis Archibald MM Cpl 47597 X/50 Med TM Bty RGA
REES Percival T. MM Sjt 26126 Welsh Regt
REES Phillip Isaac MM Pte 368097 3(Welsh)Fd Amb RAMC
REES Stephen MM Pte 201034 1/4th Welsh Regt
REES Thomas MM Cpl 51552 RFA
REES Thomas Jenkin MM Pte 20182 Welsh Regt
REES Thomas W. MM Sjt 57097 14th Welsh Regt
REES William MM Pte 56514 Welsh Regt
REES William E. MM Pte 6636 10 Fd Amb RAMC
REES William M. MM Bdr 29123 RFA
REESE Albert E. MM Pte 238100 Royal Welsh Fusiliers
REESE Albert E. MM Cpl 54889 RAMC
REESON Frank MM L/Bdr 94397 B/57 Bde RFA
REEVE Arthur MM Cpl R/16879 King's Royal Rifle Corps
REEVE Arthur E. MM+Bar L/Cpl 12134 7th Norfolk Regt
REEVE Arthur G. MM Sjt 65792 RAMC
REEVE Benjamin MM Sjt 2546 2nd Northumberland Fusiliers
REEVE Ernest MM Pte 13014 9th West Riding Regt
REEVE George MM Cpl(MCDR) 54121 Guards Div Sig Coy Royal Engineers
REEVE George "MC,MM(7574 Sjt 1st Bn)" 2Lt Royal Irish Fusiliers Died 15.10.18.
REEVE George Ernest MM Pte 17389 Leicestershire Regt
REEVE Harry "DCM,MM" Sjt 70726 33rd Bn Machine Gun Corps
REEVE Herbert "DCM,MM" Sjt 8658 Norfolk Regt
REEVE Horace "MM,MID" L/Cpl 201359 2nd Bedfordshire Regt
REEVE John N. MM Cpl 18178 7th South Staffordshire Regt
REEVE Joseph William "MM,MSM" Sjt 54842 A/56 Bde RFA
REEVE Leonard J. MM Sjt 46915 RFA
REEVE Oscar MM Sjt 12822 2nd Suffolk Regt
REEVE Percy MM Pte S/6537 Rifle Brigade
REEVE Reginald Ellwood MM L/Cpl 47558 2nd Manchester Regt KIA 19.8.18.
REEVE Richard MM CSM 47805 13th Royal Inniskilling Fusiliers KIA 29.10.18.
REEVE Robert MM L/Cpl 3/10399 7th Norfolk Regt
REEVE S.B. MM Pte 43226 Essex Regt
REEVE Scarlet MM Cpl 13712 8th Norfolk Regt KIA 26.3.18.
REEVE Thomas George MM L/Cpl 10655 7th Northamptonshire Regt
REEVELL William Porritt MM Sjt R/628 11th King's Royal Rifle Corps
REEVES A.J. MM L/Cpl 20677 1st Essex Regt
REEVES Albert S. MM Pte 3432 1/22nd London Regt
REEVES Alfred MM Cpl 11920 8th Devonshire Regt
REEVES Arthur MM+Bar Spr 312468 Royal Engineers
REEVES Arthur Leslie MM Sjt 14709 5th South Wales Borderers
REEVES Basil A. MM Pte 16327 11th Suffolk Regt
REEVES Bertie MM L/Cpl 265569 1/7th Royal Warwickshire Regt
REEVES Charles R. MM Spr 165636 Royal Engineers
REEVES Clifford MM Pte M2/223120 283 Coy Army Service Corps
REEVES Douglas P. MM Sjt 67070 128 Bty 29 Bde RFA
REEVES Edward MM Cpl 13013 8tth York & Lancaster Regt
REEVES Edward MM+Bar Sjt 6532 Machine Gun Corps
REEVES Edward MM Pte 11237 19th Middlesex Regt
REEVES Ernest MM Pte 2494 1/5th North Lancashire Regt
REEVES Ernest G. MM Pte 49738 7th Manchester Regt
REEVES Frank Leonard MM Spr 239228 262 Railway Coy Royal Engineers
REEVES Frederick MM L/Cpl 33767 Border Regt
REEVES Frederick MM Sjt 9917 18th Manchester Regt
REEVES Frederick C. MM Pte 20262 Wiltshire Regt
REEVES G.A. MM Pte 22395 8th Royal Lancaster Regt
REEVES George Albert MM CSM 4817 9th Lancashire Fusiliers
REEVES George W. MM Gnr 215538 D/113 Bty RFA
REEVES Harold MM Cpl 58774 Royal Engineers
REEVES Horace M. MM Pte 1246 16th Royal Warwickshire Regt
REEVES James O. MM Pte 281172 7th Lancashire Fusiliers
REEVES John MM Pte 76426 2nd Bn Tank Corps
REEVES John MM Pte 31575 6th Leicestershire Regt
REEVES John MM+Bar Sjt 13068 7th East Kent Regt
REEVES John MM 2nd Cpl 53613 Royal Engineers
REEVES Joseph H. MM Sjt 81866 200 Fd Coy Royal Engineers
REEVES Reginald MM Sjt 102943 253 Tunnelling Coy Royal Engineers
REEVES Sydney MM Pte 2001 12th Middlesex Regt KIA 3.5.17.
REEVES Thomas "MM,MSM" Cpl 7907 2nd Wiltshire Regt
REEVES Walter MM Pte 451820 11th London Regt
REEVES William "DCM,MM" Sjt 54243 Welsh Regt
REEVES William MM L/Cpl 265656 4th Bedfordshire att 1/1st Hertfordshire Regt. KIA 6.9.18.
REGAN Charles C. MM Pte 21097 1st Royal Dublin Fusiliers
REGAN Edward MM Pte 13280 1st Royal Highlanders KIA 3.9.16.
REGAN J. MM L/Cpl 572069 London Regt
REGAN James MM Pte 24016 2nd Royal Dublin Fusiliers
REGAN James MM Pte 13916 7th East Lancashire Regt KIA 30.7.17.
REGAN James "MM,GMV(S)" Cpl 24807 7th South Wales Borderers
REGAN John MM Pte 29002 1st Welsh Regt
REGAN John MM Cpl 102397 RFA
REGAN John "MM,MSM" Sjt 3/8803 2nd West Riding Regt
REGAN John MM Cpl 232079 2nd London Regt
REGAN John MM Pte 106748 Machine Gun Corps
REGAN Owen MM Pte 304520 15th Bn Tank Corps
REGAN Patrick MM Pte 4459 1st Royal Welsh Fusiliers
REGAN Percy R. MM QMS Eng Clk 18 29(LofC)Coy Royal Engineers
REGAN Thomas MM Pte 51532 10th Cheshire Regt
REGNIER William F. MM Pte 505049 13th London Regt
REIBER John A. MM Sjt 16737 10th Arg & Suth Highlanders
REID A. MM Sjt 17103 Durham Light Infantry
REID A. MM Shoeing Smith 88558 RGA
REID Albert MM Pte 43344 1st Royal Highlanders
REID Alexander MM Pte 7593 1st Gordon Highlanders
REID Alexander MM Pte 4281 1/7th Arg & Suth Highlanders KIA 23.4.17.
REID Alfred MM Pte 265977 Gordon Highlanders
REID Archibald MM Pte 3998 2nd Dragoons
REID Arthur William MM Sjt 105593 213 Siege Bty RGA DOW 20.12.17.
REID Charles MM L/Cpl 11273 7th Seaforth Highlanders
REID Charles MM Bdr 65262 197 Siege Bty RGA
REID Charles S. "MM+Bar,MM(F)" L/Cpl 325330 1/9th Durham Light Infantry DOW 3.8.18.
REID D. MM Sjt 15419 Highland Light Infantry
REID Daniel M. MM Sjt 151639 104th Bn Machine Gun Corps
REID David MM Sjt 94014 127 Army Tps Coy Royal Engineers
REID David MM CQMS 200253 1/5th Arg & Suth Highlanders
REID David W. MM Sjt 5521 1st Gordon Highlanders
REID Donald "MM,MC(G)" L/Cpl 4572 12th Arg & Suth Highlanders KIA 18.9.18.
REID Edward MM CSM 7360 13th Royal Scots
REID Edward MM Sjt 15849 9th Royal Irish Rifles KIA 7.8.17.
REID Frank MM Spr 500432 Royal Engineers
REID Frank Campbell MM Sjt 200770 Royal West Surrey Regt
REID Fred MM Cpl R/3842 18th King's Royal Rifle Corps
REID Frederick MM Pte 39589 56 Fd Amb RAMC DOW 23.10.17.
REID G. MM Pte 13678 Highland Light Infantry
REID George MM Pte 21584 2nd Royal Dublin Fusiliers
REID George MM Cpl 3761 2nd Highland Light Infantry
REID George MM Cpl 266291 5/6th Scottish Rifles
REID George MM Pte 305116 RAMC
REID George MM L/Cpl 9952 2nd Scottish Rifles
REID George A. MM+Bar Pte 290207 Gordon Highlanders
REID George S. MM Pte 266181 1/7th Gordon Highlanders
REID Gerald Mutrie MM Pte 240779 1/5th Yorkshire Regt
REID Harry MM L/Sjt 8849 1st Scottish Rifles
REID Henry MM Cpl 23769 Machine Gun Corps
REID Henry MM Pte 8982 2nd Cameron Highlanders
REID Hugh MM Pte 42974 RAMC

REID Hugh L. MM L/Cpl 121848 Royal Engineers
REID J. MM Cpl 14398 16th Highland Light Infantry
REID J. MM Cpl 18468 2nd Royal Irish Regt
REID James MM Cpl 316364 13th Royal Highlanders
REID James MM Cpl 10398 9th Gordon Highlanders
REID James MM Pte 265863 1/7th Gordon Highlanders
REID James MM L/Sjt 240438 1/5th Royal Scots Fusiliers DOW 7.9.18.
REID James MM Spr 32835 Royal Engineers
REID James MM Cpl 630859 A/255 Bde RFA
REID James MM Pte 34726 MM+Bar York & Lancaster Regt
REID James Petrie MM Pte 943 4th Bn GMGR
REID James S. MM Cpl 14703 12th West Yorkshire Regt
REID John MM Pte 35015 5/6th Scottish Rifles
REID John MM Sjt 402743 123 Fd Coy Royal Engineers
REID John MM Pte 13453 1/5th Royal Highlanders
REID John MM Sjt 7253 1/7th Arg & Suth Highlanders
REID John MM Spr 43333 Royal Engineers
REID John MM CQMS 240465 1/5th Royal Highlanders
REID John MM Sjt 17214 Royal Scots
REID John MM Pte 240077 Seaforth Highlanders
REID John A. MM L/Cpl 15584 2nd Scots Guards
REID John B.C. MM Sjt 650457 1/21st London Regt
REID John S. MM Pte 24649 1/4th Seaforth Highlanders
REID John W. MM Pte 325902 Arg & Suth Highlanders
REID Joseph MM Pte 251446 5/6th Royal Scots
REID Louis MM Pnr 152092 Second Army Sig Coy Royal Engineers
REID Luke MM Sjt 3122 1st Irish Guards
REID Percy Howard MM Sjt 44968 Royal Irish Rifles KIA 28.3.18.
REID Peter MM Pte 241942 1/7th Gordon Highlanders
REID Peter MM Pte 8030 2nd Leinster Regt
REID Peter C. MM L/Cpl 325742 Arg & Suth Highlanders
REID R. MM Dvr 32 RFA
REID Robert Sutherland MM Pte 9275 6th Dragoons
REID Samuel MM Pte 18/1288 15th Royal Irish Rifles
REID Thomas MM L/Cpl 12628 1st Scots Guards
REID Thomas MM Cpl 325592 Arg & Suth Highlanders
REID Thomas MM Bdr 19784 2 Siege Bty RGA
REID Thomas MM L/Cpl 240911 1/5th Royal Scots Fusiliers
REID William MM Spr 522232 483 Fd Coy Royal Engineers
REID William MM Sjt 116031 260 Siege Bty RGA DOW 28.10.18.
REID William MM Pte 4340 10th Arg & Suth Highlanders
REID William MM Pte 200344 1/4th Royal Highlanders
REID William MM Pte 38504 Lancashire Fusiliers
REID William "MM,MID" Pte 17121 Royal Scots Fusiliers
REID William MM Pte 2346 Highland Light Infantry
REID William MM L/Cpl 1348 9th Royal Highlanders KIA 26.4.17.
REID William MM Spr 443 Royal Engineers
REID William MM Sjt 9776 2nd Gordon Highlanders
REID William MM Bdr 125759 332 Siege Bty RGA
REID William MM L/Cpl 290140 Gordon Highlanders
REID William MM Pte M2/099345 Army Service Corps
REID William A. MM Sjt 51045 Royal Engineers
REID William H. MM Pte 33170 RAMC
REID William J. MM Pte 17905 Seaforth Highlanders
REID William S. MM Dvr 631115 D/121 Bde RFA
REID William S. MM Pte 40314 7th Seaforth Highlanders
REIDIE William MM Pte 9497 1st King's Own Scottish Borderers
REIFFER Roy Alfred Henry MM Gnr 2684 'A' Coy Machine Gun Corps(Heavy Section)
REILLY Alfred MM Pte 4618 5th Connaught Rangers
REILLY C. MM Pte 16471 2nd Royal Irish Regt
REILLY David MM L/Cpl 10869 2nd Royal Irish Regt KIA 27.9.18.
REILLY George MM L/Cpl 7498 2nd King's Own Scottish Borderers
REILLY J. MM Pte 18540 2nd Royal Irish Regt
REILLY J.H. MM Pte 130433 46th Royal Fusiliers
REILLY James MM Pte 2666 2nd Royal Scots KIA 22.3.18.
REILLY James MM+Bar Gnr 74248 A/240 Bde RFA KIA 17.917.
REILLY John MM Dvr 20367 7 Fd Coy Royal Engineers
REILLY John MM Pte 3/1906 1st Royal Highlanders
REILLY John MM Pte 16971 Royal Irish Fusiliers
REILLY John MM Sjt 7036 2nd Royal Irish Rifles
REILLY Matthew R. MM+Bar Sjt 305647 13th Bn Tank Corps
REILLY Michael MM Pte 335835 Royal Scots
REILLY Michael MM Dvr 47715 76 Bde Ammn Col RFA
REILLY Nicholas MM Cpl 4504 2nd Leinster Regt Died 31.7.18.
REILLY Patrick MM Pte 10159 2nd Leinster Regt KIA 20.10.18.
REILLY Patrick MM L/Sjt 9042 2nd Royal Dublin Fusiliers
REILLY Robert MM Cpl 43115 Royal Irish Fusiliers
REILLY Thomas MM Pte 27045 1st Royal Dublin Fusiliers
REILLY Thomas "DCM,MM" Sjt 2506 2nd Irish Guards
REILLY Walter MM Gnr 36559 RFA
REILLY William MM Pte 218 6th Royal West Kent Regt KIA 17.7.17.
REILLY William MM L/Cpl 3/2861 2nd York & Lancaster Regt KIA 22.4.17.
REIMANN Max MM Pte 638 South Staffordshire Regt
REIP Francis G. MM Pte M2/210288 Army Service Corps
REISS Philip Julius "MC+Bar,MM(1986 CSM 18th R Fus)" Capt 2nd Bedfordshire Regt
REISSING Patrick MM Gnr 43626 113 Hy Bty RGA
REISSLAND Charles F. MM Pte 1143 King Edward's Horse
REITH David E. MM Bdr 71945 RFA
REITH David W. MM Cpl 106566 Royal Engineers
REITH Robert MM Pte 290435 Gordon Highlanders
RELF George MM Gnr 70510 RGA
RELF Matthew MM Sjt 21453 10th Royal West Surrey Regt
RELF Reginald MM L/Cpl 2321 8th Royal Sussex Regt
RELF Richard MM Pte S/32221 7th Rifle Brigade DOW 30.5.18.
RELFWEST T.F. MM Sjt 2244 Royal Sussex Regt
RELPH Alfred George MM Cpl 31890 116 Heavy Bty RGA
REMBLANCE Herbert J. MM Sjt 14653 8th Suffolk Regt
REMINGTON A. MM Sjt 58887 RAF
REMINGTON Albert E. MM Sjt A/130 King's Royal Rifle Corps
REMMINGTON Richard MM Gnr 25099 RFA
REMNANT Alfred E. MM Bdr 891218 B/270 Bde RFA Died 4.12.17.
REMNANT Charles W. MM Sjt 15964 7th Royal Sussex Regt
RENALS Robert MM Pte 345079 16th Devonshire Regt
RENANT William MM Staff SM 1st Cl T/12658 6 Div Train Army Service Corps
RENARDSON George MM Sjt 65738 13th Yorkshire Regt
RENDALL Balfour L.C. MM Pte 17842 1/6th Seaforth Highlanders
RENDALL David MM L/Cpl 241052 Seaforth Highlanders
RENDALL William H. MM Pte 2107 3rd Rifle Brigade
RENDELL Albert MM Cpl 37012 RGA
RENDER Richard MM CQMS 816 West Yorkshire Regt
RENDLE Albert E. MM Gnr 329614 113 Hy Bty RGA
RENDLE William H. MM Pte 34084 5th Yorkshire Light Infantry
RENELT George MM Pte 11652 Royal West Surrey Regt
RENFORTH James MM Pte 11061 2nd King's Own Scottish Borderers
RENFREE Thomas MM L/Cpl 32/1759 Northumberland Fusiliers
RENNER John R. MM Sjt 21/1304 21st Northumberland Fusiliers
RENNETT Thomas R. MM Pte 491017 1/13th London Regt
RENNEY Joshua MM Dvr 21999 Royal Engineers
RENNICK Harvey MM L/Cpl 49721 2nd Royal Inniskilling Fusiliers
RENNIE Alexander MM Sjt 40372 2nd Royal Scots Fusiliers
RENNIE Alexander William MM Gnr Wheeler 70206 325 Siege Bty RGA
RENNIE Donald MM Cpl 656303 RFA
RENNIE Dora MM Pte 33113 Scottish Rifles
RENNIE Ebenezer R. MM Pte 41537 5th Cameron Highlanders KIA 14.10.18.
RENNIE Francis Andrew MM Pte 3090 1/20th London Regt
RENNIE James MM Gnr 1955 'C' Bn Machine Gun Corps(Heavy Branch)
RENNIE James A. MM Pte 40042 Gordon Highlanders
RENNIE James A. "DCM,MM" Spr 76127 8 Div Sig Coy Royal Engineers
RENNIE John MM Pte 92353 6th(Light)Bn Tank Corps
RENNIE "John McG," MM Cpl 23169 13th Royal Scots
RENNIE Martin "MM,MSM" Pte M2/191823 Army Service Corps att RGA.
RENNIE William MM+2 Bars Pte 290966 Gordon Highlanders
RENNIE William MM Pte 9244 8th Royal Highlanders KIA 3.5.17.
RENNIE William MM Pte 201322 Gordon Highlanders
RENNISON A. MM Pte 28768 West Riding Regt
RENNISON Arthur MM Pte 27926 16th Lancashire Fusiliers KIA 2.10.18.
RENNISON Francis A. MM Sjt M2/032445 Army Service Corps
RENNISON S.M. MM L/Cpl 37250 Northumberland Fusiliers
RENNISON William Henry MM Pte 22168 1/4th Yorkshire Light Infantry KIA 26.4.18.
RENNOCKS William MM L/Cpl 13894 11th West Yorkshire Regt
RENNY William W. MM Sjt 8485 6th Bedfordshire Regt
RENOUF Sydney J. MM Pte 19672 Middlesex Regt
RENSHAW Arthur MM Pte 285080 2nd Welsh Regt
RENSHAW Arthur H. MM+Bar Pte 12580 King's Royal Rifle Corps
RENSHAW Eric MM Sjt 305804 Liverpool Regt
RENSHAW H. MM Pte 37516 Northumberland Fusiliers

RENSHAW Harry MM L/Cpl 17777 2/4th East Lancashire Regt KIA 21.3.18.
RENSHAW Henry "DCM,MM" Sjt 15270 9th South Staffordshire Regt
RENSHAW Herbert MM Pte 201513 York & Lancaster Regt
RENSHAW Herbert Henry MM Cpl 15777 11th Royal Sussex Regt KIA 25.9.17.
RENSHAW John MM Pte S/7957 3rd Rifle Brigade
RENSHAW John T. MM Pte 11022 2nd East Lancashire Regt
RENSHAW William R. MM L/Cpl 4923 12th Manchester Regt
RENTON Adam A.McG. MM Dvr 650045 C/315 Bde RFA
RENTON Andrew "DCM,MM" CSM 13521 12th Royal Scots
RENTON Harry MM Cpl 28386 8th Royal Lancaster Regt
RENWICK Halbert MM Pte 6586 1st Royal Scots Fusiliers
RENWICK James R. MM Pte 514282 14th London Regt
RENWICK John MM Pte 292331 Gordon Highlanders
RENWICK John MM Sjt 1356 1/9th Royal Scots
RENWICK Robert MM L/Cpl 14401 1st Scots Guards
RENWICK W. MM L/Cpl 267539 Northumberland Fusiliers
REPTON Helena Kate MM Miss F BRCS
RESTEAUX William MM Cpl G/32971 4th Royal Fusiliers
RESTELL Thomas W. MM Pte 253403 3rd London Regt
RESTRICK W.J. MM Dvr 62607 RFA
RETTIE J.C. MM Cpl 607 8/10th Gordon Highlanders KIA 19.1.17.
REUSS William H. MM Pte 540606 15th London Regt
REVEIRS George L. MM CQMS 38048 8th East Surrey Regt
REVELEY Harold G. MM+Bar Sjt 47422 9th Royal Fusiliers
REVELL Bertie MM Pte 370997 1/8th London Regt
REVELL Charles MM Sjt 49544 25 Bde RFA
REVELL Joseph MM Pte 200511 1/4th East Yorkshire Regt
REVELY John MM Sjt 90 Royal Engineers
REVELY William MM Cpl 19/1060 19th Northumberland Fusiliers
REVETT Frederick MM Cpl 783 1st Dragoon Guards
REVILL John MM Pte R/10378 King's Royal Rifle Corps
REVILL Percy MM Sjt 13503 Notts & Derby Regt
REVIS Edward MM Pte 38571 10th West Yorkshire Regt DOW 27.8.18.
REVITT Henry J. MM Pte 62254 2nd Royal Fusiliers
REX G.S.J. MM Sjt 80180 1/1st Essex Yeomanry
REX Harry MM Pte 351373 7th London Regt
REX Percy C. "MM,MID" Pte 9025 1st Royal Dublin Fusiliers
REX Samuel George MM S/Sjt 897 1/3(South Midland)Fd Amb RAMC
REYLAND William T. MM Pte 11294 Royal Sussex Regt
REYNER Arthur MM Cpl M2/051148 Army Service Corps
REYNOLDS A.W. MM+Bar Pte 2773 7th East Kent Regt
REYNOLDS Albert E.H. MM Sjt 41474 13th Middlesex Regt
REYNOLDS Alexander MM Pte 28474 Duke of Cornwall's LI
REYNOLDS Alfred T. MM L/Cpl 242287 5th Yorkshire Light Infantry
REYNOLDS Archibald MM Pte 8683 2nd Highland Light Infantry
REYNOLDS Arthur MM Pte 68243 2nd London Regt
REYNOLDS Arthur E. MM Cpl 10823 10th Royal West Surrey Regt
REYNOLDS Arthur W. MM Spr 103138 32 Div Sig Coy Royal Engineers
REYNOLDS Bertie George MM Pte 24316 1st Royal Dublin Fusiliers KIA 28.9.18.
REYNOLDS Charles MM Pte A/204175 13th King's Royal Rifle Corps
REYNOLDS Charles C. MM Pte 10/668 10th East Yorkshire Regt
REYNOLDS Charles Howard "DCM,MM" Sjt 17454 2nd Bedfordshire Regt
REYNOLDS Charles W. MM Pte 470673 12th London Regt
REYNOLDS Daniel W. MM Pte 14725 Royal Sussex Regt
REYNOLDS Edward MM CSM 31 1st Lancashire Fusiliers
REYNOLDS Edward Samuel MM Sjt 320825 1/6th London Regt DOW 27.6.18.
REYNOLDS Ernest T. MM Bdr 341115 RGA
REYNOLDS Francis MM Pte 43350 Royal Scots Fusiliers
REYNOLDS Francis J. MM L/Cpl 43782 2nd Suffolk Regt
REYNOLDS Fred MM Pte R/37954 18th King's Royal Rifle Corps
REYNOLDS Fred MM Sjt M2/152182 335 MT Coy Army Service Corps att XIII Corps HAG.DOW 27.10.18.
REYNOLDS Frederick MM Pte 9312 Seaforth Highlanders
REYNOLDS Frederick MM Sjt 32382 RAMC
REYNOLDS Frederick MM Cpl 58148 RAMC
REYNOLDS Frederick R. MM Pte M2/055151 Army Service Corps
REYNOLDS Frederick W. MM Pte 55164 1st North Staffordshire Regt
REYNOLDS G. MM Gnr 37268 RGA
REYNOLDS George A. MM L/Sjt 2865 1/1st Hertfordshire Regt
REYNOLDS George Arthur MM Pte 24784 3rd Grenadier Guards
REYNOLDS George C. MM L/Cpl 200300 1/7th Middlesex Regt
REYNOLDS George E. MM L/Cpl 701670 23rd London Regt
REYNOLDS George W. MM L/Cpl 371055 8th London Regt
REYNOLDS H. MM Spr 245968 35 Div Sig Coy Royal Engineers
REYNOLDS Harold A. MM Sjt STK/509 Royal Fusiliers
REYNOLDS Harry MM Pte 45372 15th Cheshire Regt
REYNOLDS Harry MM Pte 6577 4th King's Royal Rifle Corps
REYNOLDS Henry MM Pte 2466 8th Middlesex Regt
REYNOLDS Henry MM L/Cpl 3/10354 Durham Light Infantry
REYNOLDS Henry J. MM Pte 30005 Norfolk Regt
REYNOLDS Herbert MM Gnr Fitter 156225 RFA
REYNOLDS Herbert MM Pte 393925 9th London Regt
REYNOLDS Hubert I. MM Cpl 47221 37 Bty 27 Bde RFA
REYNOLDS J. MM Spr 229037 Royal Engineers
REYNOLDS J. MM Pte 43655 Royal Irish Rifles
REYNOLDS James MM Pte 81651 16 Fd Amb RAMC
REYNOLDS James MM Pte 3248 Northumberland Fusiliers
REYNOLDS James E. MM Gnr 128819 222 Siege Bty RGA
REYNOLDS James William MM Sjt 22279 39 Bty 19 Bde RFA
REYNOLDS Jim MM Pte 42026 Lancashire Fusiliers
REYNOLDS John MM Pte 592959 18th London Regt
REYNOLDS John MM Pte 7898 2nd Highland Light Infantry
REYNOLDS John MM L/Cpl 19643 4th Grenadier Guards KIA 1.12.17.
REYNOLDS John Charles MM 2nd Cpl 1061 1(London)Fd Coy Royal Engineers
REYNOLDS John E. MM Cpl 1481 1/7th Middlesex Regt
REYNOLDS John Edgar MM CQMS 6262 3rd Coldstream Guards
REYNOLDS John G. MM Pte M1/5917 Army Service Corps
REYNOLDS John James MM Bdr 7656 160 Bde RFA
REYNOLDS John T. MM Pte 53854 RAMC
REYNOLDS Joseph MM Pte 202063 Liverpool Regt
REYNOLDS Leonard G. MM Pte 242208 Worcestershire Regt
REYNOLDS Lowthern MM L/Cpl 43441 West Yorkshire Regt
REYNOLDS Mark MM Pte 6414 1st Northamptonshire Regt
REYNOLDS P.F. MM Cpl 15239 Royal Berkshire Regt
REYNOLDS Patrick MM Pte 2174 2nd Highland Light Infantry Died 10.6.17.
REYNOLDS Percy MM L/Cpl 58772 Royal Fusiliers
REYNOLDS Peter MM Pte 9794 1st Royal Highlanders
REYNOLDS R. "DCM,MM" Sjt 29257 10th Essex Regt
REYNOLDS Robert MM Sjt 1977 23rd Royal Fusiliers
REYNOLDS Roden MM Pte 3711 2nd Rifle Brigade
REYNOLDS Sidney MM+Bar L/Cpl 8781 1st Wiltshire Regt
REYNOLDS Sidney J. MM Pte 18114 9th Suffolk Regt
REYNOLDS T. MM AM1 6705 Royal Flying Corps
REYNOLDS T. MM Sjt 13404 South Lancashire Regt
REYNOLDS Thomas MM L/Cpl 10137 1st Gordon Highlanders
REYNOLDS Thomas J. MM+Bar Sjt 268472 Royal Warwickshire Regt
REYNOLDS Thomas W. MM Pte 250413 1/3rd London Regt
REYNOLDS Tom MM Cpl 70036 Notts & Derby Regt
REYNOLDS Victor MM Pte 35484 RAMC
REYNOLDS Walter MM Pte 203646 1st London Regt
REYNOLDS Walter MM Pte 27336 7th Worcestershire Regt
REYNOLDS Walter John MM Gnr 75292 RFA
REYNOLDS Walter L. MM Pte 37241 1/1st Cambridgeshire Regt
REYNOLDS Wilfred MM L/Cpl 22471 1st Notts & Derby Regt KIA 30.9.17.
REYNOLDS William MM Pte 377821 5th Manchester Regt
REYNOLDS William MM+Bar Sjt 560403 47 Div Sig Coy Royal Engineers
REYNOLDS William "MM,MSM" Pte 10306 6th Lincolnshire Regt
REYNOLDS William Fussell MM Sjt 22199 RGA
REYNOLDS William Henry MM Pte 9350 2nd Lincolnshire Regt
REYNOLDS William Henry MM Gnr 46665 D/51 Bde RFA DOW 23.4.17.
REYNOLDS William Herbert MM Pte 200353 1/5th Notts & Derby Regt KIA 22.9.18.
REYNOLDS William J.J. MM Pte 44458 Royal Fusiliers
REYNOLDS William T. MM Sjt 11512 Coldstream Guards
REYNOLDS William Thomas MM Pte 17529 6th South Wales Borderers DOW 9.4.18.
REZIN William W. MM Gnr 630520 RFA
RHEIMS Frederick G. MM Cpl 52999 Machine Gun Corps att RE.
RHIND Alexander MM Sjt 265929 Gordon Highlanders
RHIND William "DCM,MM" Bdr 47888 'F' Bty RHA
RHOADES Arthur MM Sjt 6232 2nd King's Royal Rifle Corps
RHODES Albert MM Pte 202161 Cheshire Regt

RHODES Albert MM Pte 46531 North Staffordshire Regt
RHODES Albert G. MM Gnr 7744 RGA
RHODES Arthur MM L/Cpl 51540 1st Cheshire Regt
RHODES Arthur MM L/Sjt 1173 London Regt
RHODES Arthur MM Pte R/29368 13th King's Royal Rifle Corps
RHODES Austin MM L/Sjt 7087 1st Scots Guards
RHODES B.C. MM AM2 402637 Royal Air Force att RGA.
RHODES Cecil MM L/Cpl 304356 17th Armoured Car Bn Tank Corps
RHODES Cecil MM L/Cpl 2106 1/6th West Riding Regt KIA 26.12.17.
RHODES Charles MM L/Cpl 241222 5th West Riding Regt
RHODES Edward MM Pte 3964 23rd London Regt
RHODES Enoch "MM,CG(B)" L/Cpl 11585 8th West Riding Regt
RHODES Ernest MM Pte C/1064 16th King's Royal Rifle Corps KIA 15.7.16.
RHODES F. "DCM+Bar,MM" CSM 14873 11th Northumberland Fusiliers
RHODES F.rederick MM Pte 202746 4th West Riding Regt
RHODES Frederick MM Cpl 444003 42 Div Sig Coy Royal Engineers
RHODES Frederick D. MM Pte 49150 RAMC
RHODES Harold MM Sjt 9390 1st North Lancashire Regt KIA 1.7.16.
RHODES Harold MM CSM 14571 1st Lancashire Fusiliers
RHODES Harold MM Gnr 79769 RFA
RHODES Harry MM Pte 15936 10th Arg & Suth Highlanders DOW 25.8.18.
RHODES John MM Pte 306310 16th Royal Warwickshire Regt
RHODES John MM Gnr(SS) 11506 D/75 Bde RFA
RHODES Joseph MM Pte 351013 2/9th Manchester Regt
RHODES Melbourne Laurie MM Pte 1024 23rd Royal Fusiliers
RHODES Michael MM Dvr 760841 RFA
RHODES Robert MM S/Sjt Fitter 12522 230 Siege Bty RGA
RHODES Robert MM Gnr 70120 B/106 Bde RFA
RHODES Robert MM Sjt 305649 West Riding Regt
RHODES Ronald Victor MM Pte 48246 16th Royal Warwickshire Regt
RHODES Sam MM Gnr 60485 87 Siege Bty RGA
RHODES Samuel C.M. MM Cpl 1591 9th East Surrey Regt
RHODES Victor Albert MM Pte 17626 York & Lancaster Regt
RHODES William MM Sjt 9394 1st East Yorkshire Regt
RHODES William "MM,MID" Sjt 10175 7th South Staffordshire Regt
RHODES William H. MM Bdr 711645 RFA
RHYMER Archibald MM Pte 64219 RAMC
RIACH Frederick MM Sjt 4860 1st Gordon Highlanders
RIACH John MM Cpl 28426 4th Bedfordshire Regt
RIAL Arthur MM Cpl 755081 RFA
RIBBANDS Charles R. MM Gnr 37708 157 Siege Bty RGA
RIBBINS Herbert Harry MM Sjt 240782 Middlesex Regt
RIBBITS Arthur W. MM L/Cpl 656178 21st London Regt
RIBBITS Charles MM Pte 291923 Northumberland Fusiliers
RIBCHESTER George MM L/Cpl 42945 72 Coy Labour Corps
RICE Albert John MM L/Bdr 118974 147 Siege Bty RGA
RICE Albert W. MM+Bar Sjt 131230 233 Fd Coy Royal Engineers
RICE Alfred MM Sjt 7347 1st East Surrey Regt
RICE Alfred A. MM Pte G11112 13th Royal Fusiliers
RICE Arthur MM L/Cpl 64051 58th Bn Machine Gun Corps
RICE Charles F. MM Pte 241790 Worcestershire Regt
RICE Charles William MM Pte 4301 1st Rifle Brigade KIA 1.7.16.
RICE Edward MM Pte 56459 Machine Gun Corps
RICE Francis MM Cpl 200157 2/4th Lincolnshire Regt
RICE Frank MM Pte 200106 1/4th Royal Sussex Regt
RICE Fred MM Sjt 10714 Labour Corps
RICE Frederick J. "DCM,MM" BSM 60735 434 Siege Bty RGA
RICE George MM Pte 1416 18th Middlesex Regt
RICE George MM Pte 2367 19th Middlesex Regt
RICE George Alfred MM Bdr 32997 RFA
RICE Henry Vincent MM Pte 16308 12th East Surrey Regt DOW 6.5.17.
RICE James MM Pte 23487 East Yorkshire Regt
RICE James E. MM CQMS 32900 Yorkshire Light Infantry
RICE John MM Pte 235182 2nd South Lancashire Regt
RICE John C. MM Sjt 352619 RGA
RICE John J. MM+Bar Pte 2504 2nd Leinster Regt
RICE John Richard MM Pte 9964 2nd South Wales Borderers KIA 11.4.18.
RICE Norman MM L/Cpl 11164 6th North Lancashire Regt
RICE Peter MM Cpl 11554 1st Liverpool Regt
RICE Reginald J. MM+Bar Cpl 825196 C/240 Bde RFA
RICE Ronald B. MM Cpl 2612 1/4th Royal Berkshire Regt
RICE Stanley G. MM Pte 320241 12th Norfolk Regt
RICE William MM+Bar Sjt 9388 2nd Royal Berkshire Regt
RICE William Bernard MM Cpl 70031 Notts & Derby Regt
RICE William F. MM Pte 2517 1/20th London Regt
RICH Albert Oriel MM L/Cpl 87009 204 Fd Coy Royal Engineers
RICH Cyril MM Pte 4835 Middlesex Regt
RICH Edward John MM L/Cpl 1123 11th Royal Sussex Regt
RICH Frederick Herbert(Frank) MM Cpl 510419 Royal Engineers Died 16.5.18.
RICH George MM+Bar Sjt 5466 Machine Gun Corps
RICH Sydney MM Cpl 28547 253 Coy Machine Gun Corps
RICH William J. MM Cpl 13256 10th Devonshire Regt
RICHARD James MM Bdr 56908 C/103 Bde RFA DOW 5.6.17.Real name James DICK.
RICHARD or RICHARDS Andrew MM Pte M2/051443 Army Service Corps
RICHARDS A. MM Sjt 1951 38 Div Ammn Col RFA
RICHARDS Albert E. MM Gnr 22468 A/162 Bde RFA
RICHARDS Albert E. MM Cpl 1722 1/20th London Regt
RICHARDS Albert Harold MM Pte 405485 3(West Riding)Fd Amb RAMC
RICHARDS Albert R. MM Pte 512360 14th London Regt
RICHARDS Alfred MM CSM 9629 2nd West Riding Regt
RICHARDS Arthur W. MM Pte 3736 HAC(Infantry)
RICHARDS B. MM Pte 050794 1023 MT Coy Army Service Corps
RICHARDS Benjamin J. MM Sjt 1876 1/6th London Regt
RICHARDS Bryant J. MM+Bar Sjt 26641 5th Bn Machine Gun Corps
RICHARDS Charles "MM,MID" Pte 28234 8th Cheshire Regt
RICHARDS Charles Henry MM Gnr 294890 113 Heavy Bty RGA
RICHARDS Charles James MM Cpl 4605 East Surrey Regt
RICHARDS Clifford T. MM Cpl 324 8th Middlesex Regt
RICHARDS Daniel MM Pte 18517 8th Yorkshire Light Infantry
RICHARDS David MM Pte 71263 21st Bn Machine Gun Corps
RICHARDS E. MM Cpl 43035 RFA
RICHARDS Edgar MM L/Cpl 12581 6th Oxf & Bucks Light Infantry
RICHARDS Edgar W. MM Bdr 56185 RGA
RICHARDS Edward William MM Sjt C/9726 King's Royal Rifle Corps
RICHARDS Edwin T. MM Cpl 137439 RGA
RICHARDS Eli MM Dvr 57164 C/50 Bde RFA
RICHARDS Ernest Harry MM Cpl 54983 15th Welsh Regt KIA 1.8.17.
RICHARDS Frank MM+Bar L/Cpl 10144 1st Shropshire Light Infantry
RICHARDS Frank MM Pte 92018 154 Labour Coy Labour Corps
RICHARDS Frank "DCM,MM" Sjt 15027 Coldstream Guards
RICHARDS Frank "DCM,MM" Pte 6584 2nd Royal Welsh Fusiliers
RICHARDS Franklyn Wallace MM Gnr 28752 C/91 Bde RFA DOW 12.3.17.
RICHARDS Fred MM Bdr 3559 RFA
RICHARDS Frederick Herbert MM Pte 24713 3rd Grenadier Guards
RICHARDS G.T. MM Cpl 6625 1st East Kent Regt
RICHARDS George MM Pte 235690 1/1st Herefordshire Regt
RICHARDS George MM Dvr 810218 D/232 Bde RFA
RICHARDS George MM Cpl 21515 Machine Gun Corps
RICHARDS George MM Cpl 101386 RFA
RICHARDS George MM Bdr 110245 RFA
RICHARDS George MM Sjt 11044 1st Notts & Derby Regt
RICHARDS George H. MM Pte 10026 1st Border Regt
RICHARDS George H. MM 2nd Cpl 42440 101 Fd Coy Royal Engineers
RICHARDS Harry MM Pte 9106 1st Worcestershire Regt
RICHARDS Harry MM Pte 100458 6 Sqn MGC(Cavalry)
RICHARDS Harry MM Sjt 9349 1st Oxf & Bucks Light Infantry
RICHARDS Harry MM Pte 14653 10th Hampshire Regt
RICHARDS Harry L. MM Sjt 146264 RGA
RICHARDS Harvey MM Pte 9607 1st Royal Berkshire Regt
RICHARDS Henry "DCM,MM" Sjt 147091 'N' Special Coy Royal Engineers
RICHARDS Henry E. MM+Bar Sjt 265895 7th Liverpool Regt
RICHARDS Henry H. MM Cpl 147136 Royal Engineers
RICHARDS J.H. MM Cpl 10478 East Kent Regt
RICHARDS James MM Cpl 18903 2nd South Wales Borderers
RICHARDS James MM L/Cpl 13481 5th Dorsetshire Regt
RICHARDS James MM Pte 701396 23rd London Regt
RICHARDS James H. MM L/Cpl 204 16th Royal Warwickshire Regt
RICHARDS James T. MM Pte 2721 1st Welsh Guards
RICHARDS John MM Sjt 740739 D/110 Bde RFA
RICHARDS John MM Sjt 30741 RAMC

RICHARDS John Samuel MM Pte 3179 Gloucestershire Regt
RICHARDS Joseph MM Pte 48179 130 Fd Amb RAMC
RICHARDS Joseph MM Pte 16759 10th York & Lancaster Regt
RICHARDS Joseph George Francis MM Sjt 18966 5th South Wales Borderers KIA 11.4.18.
RICHARDS Oswin MM Pte 38492 15th Highland Light Infantry
RICHARDS Percy MM Pte 13748 6th Royal West Surrey Regt
RICHARDS Percy MM Cpl M2/120517 14 Mot Amb Conv Army Service Corps
RICHARDS Percy Herbert MM+Bar Sjt 2457 8th Royal Fusiliers
RICHARDS Philip MM Sjt 156114 Royal Engineers
RICHARDS Rees P. MM Pte 18946 Royal Welsh Fusiliers
RICHARDS Richard MM Pte 13341 2nd Dragoon Guards
RICHARDS Richard J. MM Pte 4139 10th Hampshire Regt
RICHARDS Richard William MM Gnr 118287 43 Bty 24 Bde RFA
RICHARDS Samuel MM Cpl 39049 60 Coy Labour Corps
RICHARDS Sherman H. MM L/Cpl M2/119293 Army Service Corps
RICHARDS Sidney MM Bdr 58013 18 Bde RFA
RICHARDS Sidney J. MM Pte 17722 Welsh Regt
RICHARDS Sydney G. MM Pte 17528 Welsh Regt
RICHARDS Thomas MM Pte 9332 2nd Royal Welsh Fusiliers
RICHARDS Thomas MM Cpl 16993 18th Liverpool Regt
RICHARDS Thomas MM Spr 104930 179 Tunnelling Coy Royal Engineers
RICHARDS Timothy MM Pte 48180 130 Fd Amb RAMC
RICHARDS Vincent MM Gnr 78453 228 Siege Bty RGA
RICHARDS William MM L/Cpl 43401 9th Essex Regt
RICHARDS William MM Sjt 19592 14th Royal Welsh Fusiliers
RICHARDS William MM Pte 28539 Royal Inniskilling Fusiliers
RICHARDS William "DCM,MM" Sjt 13321 2 Fd Coy Royal Engineers
RICHARDS William MM Sjt 143051 Royal Engineers
RICHARDS William MM Pte 201786 8th Leicestershire Regt
RICHARDS William MM Sjt 281132 18 Hy Bty RGA
RICHARDS William Arthur John MM Pte 377566 9th Manchester Regt
RICHARDS William C. MM Pte 54235 9th Royal Welsh Fusiliers
RICHARDS William C.L. MM Cpl 432051 Royal Engineers
RICHARDS William D. MM Sjt 29057 6th Bn Machine Gun Corps
RICHARDS William E. MM Sjt 23981 Welsh Regt
RICHARDS William E.P. MM Pte 10283 HAC
RICHARDS William H. MM Pte 13556 4th Bn Machine Gun Corps
RICHARDS William J. MM Pte 290122 Royal Welsh Fusiliers
RICHARDS William R. MM Pte 60998 23rd Lancashire Fusiliers
RICHARDS William Reginald MM Bdr 87434 4 Div Ammn Col RFA
RICHARDSON A. MM L/Cpl 390504 3 Fd Amb RAMC
RICHARDSON A. MM Gnr 6438 RFA
RICHARDSON A. MM Pte 28263 Royal Inniskilling Fusiliers
RICHARDSON A. MM Sjt 26322 Machine Gun Corps
RICHARDSON A. "DCM,MM" Sjt 10294 1st Coldstream Guards
RICHARDSON A. MM Pte 1252 Army Cyclist Corps
RICHARDSON A.E. MM Sjt 18647 12th Durham Light Infantry
RICHARDSON Albert MM+Bar Sjt 24375 6th Northamptonshire Regt KIA 18.9.18.
RICHARDSON Albert MM Pte 20715 15th Hampshire Regt KIA 7.10.16.
RICHARDSON Albert A. MM Bdr 50611 15 Bde RFA
RICHARDSON Albert E. MM Pte 79603 6th Durham Light Infantry
RICHARDSON Albert W. MM Sjt 7669 Royal West Surrey Regt
RICHARDSON Albert W.H. MM Gnr 291903 RGA
RICHARDSON Alfred MM Pte 201452 4th Hampshire Regt
RICHARDSON Alfred MM Pte 252488 6th Durham Light Infantry
RICHARDSON Alfred MM Gnr(SS) 13231 V/48 Heavy TM Bty RGA
RICHARDSON Alfred C.T. MM Pte 200627 1/4th Royal Sussex Regt
RICHARDSON Alfred E. MM Cpl 20443 8th Royal Sussex Regt
RICHARDSON Alfred E. MM Pte 4056 17th Lancers
RICHARDSON Alfred E. MM L/Cpl 7745 1/20th London Regt
RICHARDSON Andrew MM Pte 9156 Arg & Sth Highlanders
RICHARDSON Andrew MM Pte 325152 1/8th Royal Scots
RICHARDSON Andrew MM+Bar Cpl 463071 50 Div Sig Coy Royal Engineers
RICHARDSON Arthur "DCM,MM,MID" RSM 18700 9th Northumberland Fusiliers
RICHARDSON Arthur MM Pte 65567 RAMC
RICHARDSON Arthur MM Pte 70033 Notts & Derby Regt
RICHARDSON Arthur E. MM Pte 203226 Cheshire Regt
RICHARDSON Aubrey V. MM Pte 201838 5th Notts & Derby Regt
RICHARDSON Benjamin MM Sjt 240473 1/5th Suffolk Regt
RICHARDSON Benjamin MM Gnr 25059 C/77 Bde RFA
RICHARDSON C.M.H. "MM,MID" Cpl 47213 RAMC
RICHARDSON Charles MM Sjt DM2/075520 Army Service Corps

RICHARDSON Charles MM Pte 32435 RAMC
RICHARDSON Charles H. MM Sjt 42444 2nd Hampshire Regt
RICHARDSON Charles W. MM 2nd Cpl 430042 421 Fd Coy Royal Engineers
RICHARDSON Claude MM Sjt 9885 2nd Royal Sussex Regt
RICHARDSON Cyril MM Pte 9077 Coldstream Guards
RICHARDSON David F. MM Sjt 27709 Postal Section Royal Engineers
RICHARDSON Edgar J. MM+Bar Cpl 74787 RAMC
RICHARDSON Edward MM Pte M2/052765 Army Service Corps
RICHARDSON Edward "MM,MSM" Sjt 705227 B/210 Bde RFA
RICHARDSON Edward MM Sjt 18861 Royal Engineers
RICHARDSON Edward Arthur MM BQMS 2066 192 Siege Bty RGA
RICHARDSON Edward Earle MM L/Cpl 3110 1/21st London Regt KIA 9.11.18.
RICHARDSON Edward George MM Pte 375093 8th London Regt KIA 10.10.18.
RICHARDSON Edwin MM Bdr 7941 RFA
RICHARDSON Ernest "DCM+Bar,MM" Sjt 795382 RFA
RICHARDSON Ernest H. MM Pte 306252 6th Bn Tank Corps
RICHARDSON Ernest H. MM Sjt R/719 King's Royal Rifle Corps
RICHARDSON Frank MM SM 30668 6(Cav)Fd Amb RAMC
RICHARDSON Frank MM Pte 24511 15th Notts & Derby Regt
RICHARDSON Frank MM Sjt 3110 Machine Gun Corps
RICHARDSON Fred MM Sjt 34664 2nd Yorkshire Light Infantry
RICHARDSON Fred MM Pte 24568 15/17th West Yorkshire Regt
RICHARDSON Frederick MM L/Sjt 15767 Norfolk Regt
RICHARDSON Frederick H. MM Pte 50520 West Yorkshire Regt
RICHARDSON Frederick L. MM Pte 267199 West Riding Regt
RICHARDSON George MM Sjt 23257 42nd Bn Machine Gun Corps
RICHARDSON George MM Cpl 25440 2nd Highland Light Infantry
RICHARDSON George MM Pte 20577 7th Dragoon Guards
RICHARDSON George A. "DCM,MM" CSM 265046 1/1st Bucks Bn Oxf & Bucks Light Infantry
RICHARDSON George Cartwright MM Gnr 781336 A/246 Bde RFA
RICHARDSON George H. MM Pte 26267 Yorkshire Regt
RICHARDSON George M. MM+Bar Pte 37829 Northumberland Fusiliers
RICHARDSON H.S. MM CQMS 7617 1st Essex Regt
RICHARDSON Harold MM Cpl 53973 1st Bn Machine Gun Corps
RICHARDSON Harold MM Pte 21415 23rd Manchester Regt
RICHARDSON Harold Victor MM Sjt T4/254361 66 Div Train Army Service Corps DOW 1.4.18.
RICHARDSON Harry MM Cpl 313417 2/1(North Midland)Hy Bty RGA
RICHARDSON Harry MM Pte 29239 Royal Welsh Fusiliers
RICHARDSON Harry MM L/Sjt 1352 GMGR
RICHARDSON Harry MM Pte 1245 22nd Royal Fusiliers
RICHARDSON Harry MM Slt 11363 23rd Middlesex Regt
RICHARDSON Harry "MM+Bar,MSM" Gnr 69190 29 Bty 42 Bde RFA
RICHARDSON Harry Arthur MM Cpl 202561 10th Worcestershire Regt
RICHARDSON Hector Lawrence MM Pte S/7813 9th Rifle Brigade DOW 20.9.16.
RICHARDSON Henry Charles MM Pte 9614 12th East Surrey Regt KIA 3.8.17.
RICHARDSON Hereward MM Spr 249795 21 Div Sig Coy Royal Engineers
RICHARDSON J. MM Cpl 1441 West Yorkshire Regt
RICHARDSON J.C.S. MM Cpl 1407 Royal Engineers
RICHARDSON James MM Dvr T2/01219 Army Service Corps
RICHARDSON James MM Pte 42185 2nd Royal Scots
RICHARDSON James MM+Bar Pte 3192 Durham Light Infantry
RICHARDSON James MM Pte 3239 1/5th Northumberland Fusiliers
RICHARDSON James MM L/Cpl 11562 1st Royal Fusiliers
RICHARDSON James MM+Bar Cpl 265424 1/6th Seaforth Highlanders KIA 19.10.17.
RICHARDSON James H. MM Pte 267596 West Riding Regt
RICHARDSON James H. "DCM,MM" Sjt 148474 179 Tunnelling Coy Royal Engineers
RICHARDSON James T. MM Pte 345052 2nd King's Royal Rifle Corps
RICHARDSON Jesse G. MM Cpl 33422 Hampshire Regt
RICHARDSON John MM Pnr 267748 Royal Engineers
RICHARDSON John MM Sjt 305932 8th West Yorkshire Regt
RICHARDSON John MM Pte 12631 4th Liverpool Regt
RICHARDSON John MM Pte 45299 Durham Light Infantry
RICHARDSON John MM Sjt 671444 27 Bde RFA
RICHARDSON John MM Dvr 204 C/158 Bde RFA

RICHARDSON John "MM,MID" Sjt 1261 1/7th Northumberland Fusiliers
RICHARDSON John MM Bdr 18795 118 Heavy Bty RGA
RICHARDSON John B. MM Cpl 36039 RAMC
RICHARDSON John H. MM+Bar Sjt 19432 2nd Suffolk Regt
RICHARDSON John H. MM Sjt 20419 15th Welsh Regt
RICHARDSON John R. MM Cpl 512673 14th London Regt
RICHARDSON John R. MM Pte 19299 1st South Wales Borderers
RICHARDSON John Thomas "MM,MID" Pte 7348 3rd Coldstream Guards
RICHARDSON Joseph MM Cpl 71775 135 Fd Amb RAMC
RICHARDSON Joseph MM Pte 27745 Lancashire Fusiliers
RICHARDSON Joseph MM+Bar Sjt 16700 Duke of Cornwall's LI
RICHARDSON Leonard MM Pte M2/046487 Army Service Corps
RICHARDSON Leslie W. MM Pnr 142157 Royal Engineers
RICHARDSON Mark MM Pte 8907 Army Cyclist Corps
RICHARDSON Mary MM Miss F First Aid Nursing Yeomanry
RICHARDSON Matthew MM Pte 22592 Army Cyclist Corps
RICHARDSON Norman MM Pte 350408 6th Manchester Regt
RICHARDSON Ralph MM Pte 241130 6th Notts & Derby Regt
RICHARDSON Richard MM L/Cpl 5311 2nd Coldstream Guards
RICHARDSON Richard MM+Bar L/Cpl 19204 15th Cheshire Regt
RICHARDSON Robert "MM,MID" 2nd Cpl 109289 Rly Ops Div Royal Engineers
RICHARDSON Robert MM Pte 51816 12th West Yorkshire Regt
RICHARDSON Robert MM Sjt 2045 Northumberland Fusiliers
RICHARDSON Robert N. MM L/Cpl 18855 1st Grenadier Guards
RICHARDSON Samuel MM Pte 241193 1/4th King's Own Scottish Borderers
RICHARDSON Sidney B. MM Sjt 53960 11th Notts & Derby Regt
RICHARDSON Sydney Harold MM Pte 1245 Lincolnshire Regt
RICHARDSON Thomas MM Pte 25642 10th Cheshire Regt
RICHARDSON Thomas MM Pte 78760 RAMC
RICHARDSON Thomas MM L/Cpl 1865 10th Arg & Suth Highlanders
RICHARDSON Thomas MM Pte 11/15442 11th Border Regt DOW 10.6.16.
RICHARDSON Thomas MM Pte 19709 1st East Yorkshire Regt
RICHARDSON Thomas MM L/Cpl 16899 10th North Lancashire Regt
RICHARDSON Thomas Alfred MM Pte 17458 10th Royal West Kent Regt
RICHARDSON Thomas H. MM Cpl 12095 Highland Light Infantry
RICHARDSON Thomas J. MM+Bar Sjt 100728 RFA
RICHARDSON Thomas W. "DCM,MM" Pte 20518 10th Essex Regt
RICHARDSON W. "MM,MSM" SM 10675 RAMC
RICHARDSON W.J. MM Pte 20903 Army Cyclist Corps
RICHARDSON Walter MM Pte 54263 19 Fd Amb RAMC
RICHARDSON Walter MM Pte 305674 Lancashire Fusiliers
RICHARDSON Walter William MM Pte 36280 2/3(West Riding)Fd Amb RAMC
RICHARDSON William MM L/Cpl 23924 6th East Kent Regt
RICHARDSON William MM Pte 13920 Northamptonshire Regt
RICHARDSON William MM Sjt 785533 A/312 Bde RFA
RICHARDSON William MM Pte 27902 Northumberland Fusiliers
RICHARDSON William MM Pte 78626 Tank Corps
RICHARDSON William MM Sjt 17508 2nd Grenadier Guards
RICHARDSON William MM Cpl 3496 1/24th London Regt KIA 20.5.16.
RICHARDSON William MM Pte 8089 3rd Hussars
RICHARDSON William MM Pte R/20002 King's Royal Rifle Corps
RICHARDSON William MM Pte 5259 Northumberland Fusiliers
RICHARDSON William MM Pte 8667 2nd Northamptonshire Regt KIA 16.8.17.
RICHARDSON William A. "MM+Bar,CG(F)" Sjt 240173 1/5th King's Own Scottish Borderers
RICHARDSON William C. MM Sjt 8666 1st Middlesex Regt
RICHARDSON William F. MM Pte 240420 6th South Staffordshire Regt
RICHARDSON William F. MM Spr 506597 Royal Engineers
RICHARDSON William G. MM Pte M2/082776 Army Service Corps
RICHARDSON William H. MM+Bar Sjt 37437 Machine Gun Corps
RICHARDSON William John MM Pte DM2/206724 Army Service Corps
RICHARDSON William Joseph MM Cpl 76176 'B' Bty 15 Bde RHA
RICHARDSON William O. MM Gnr 32271 D/152 Bde RFA
RICHBELL John J. MM Pte 370368 1/8th London Regt
RICHENS Harry MM Pte 8853 9th East Surrey Regt
RICHENS James W. MM Sjt 8554 2nd Wiltshire Regt
RICHER Edward Charles MM Pte 19186 11th Essex Regt KIA 26.9.16.
RICHER George R. "DCM+Bar,MM+Bar" Sjt 12071 8th Lincolnshire Regt
RICHER Walter Trowell MM Pte 28527 Durham Light Infantry
RICHES Frank MM Cpl 56485 38 Bde RFA
RICHES Frederick W.C. MM Cpl 14004 8th Suffolk Regt att 1/1st Cambridgeshire Regt.
RICHES George MM Dvr 80646 99 Fd Coy Royal Engineers Died 20.11.18.
RICHES George B. MM Spr 85721 Royal Engineers
RICHES Henry MM Gnr 122517 315 Bde RFA
RICHES Isaac MM Pte 19/1590 Northumberland Fusiliers
RICHES James William MM L/Cpl 2295 1/9th Durham Light Infantry
RICHES Joseph S. MM Pte 3/7136 1st Norfolk Regt
RICHES Lawrence J. MM Cpl 21509 15th Durham Light Infantry
RICHES Leonard Gladstone MM Pte 252386 2nd Essex Regt
RICHES William J. MM Pte 14520 8th Suffolk Regt
RICHFORD Thomas MM Pte 10272 1st Seaforth Highlanders
RICHINGS Frederick J. MM Gnr 102053 RGA
RICHLING Charles MM Pte 11100 11th Middlesex Regt
RICHMAN George Henry MM Pte 356427 1st Hampshire Regt
RICHMOND Alexander MM Sjt 6218 RFA
RICHMOND Andrew MM L/Cpl 200590 2nd Royal Scots Fusiliers
RICHMOND Charles MM Sjt 553222 16th London Regt
RICHMOND Edward J. MM+Bar Sjt 21285 Suffolk Regt
RICHMOND Frank George MM Sjt 22986 Machine Gun Corps
RICHMOND Herbert W. "DCM,MM" L/Cpl 12565 9th Yorkshire Light Infantry
RICHMOND Hugh MM Sjt 12894 D/160 Bde RFA
RICHMOND J.P. MM Sjt 29261 27 Bde RFA
RICHMOND James MM Sjt 305462 1/8th Lancashire Fusiliers
RICHMOND James MM Pte 201410 North Lancashire Regt
RICHMOND Joseph MM Pte 20125 2nd Coldstream Guards
RICHMOND Joseph MM Pte 6712 1st King's Royal Rifle Corps
RICHMOND Joseph MM Pte 5036 16th Lancers
RICHMOND Peter MM Pte 47512 Royal Scots Fusiliers
RICHMOND Richmond C. MM Sjt 6872 2nd Border Regt
RICHMOND William E. MM RQMS 200372 2/5th West Yorkshire Regt
RICHMOND William J. MM Sjt 301107 28th London Regt
RICHMOND William J. MM Pte 8160 Coldstream Guards
RICHOLD Alfred A. MM CSM 4867 7th Royal Sussex Regt
RICKABY Frank MM Dvr 75531 A/124 Bde RFA
RICKABY William MM L/Cpl 302250 1/8th Durham Light Infantry
RICKARD Frank MM Pte 19775 23rd Middlesex Regt
RICKARD George MM Sjt 240036 1/8th Middlesex Regt
RICKARD George H. "DCM,MM" Sjt 9707 2nd Bedfordshire Regt
RICKARD John E. MM Sjt 81364 RGA
RICKARD R. MM Pte A/1629 King's Royal Rifle Corps
RICKARD William MM Pte S/21648 Cameron Highlanders
RICKARD William E. MM Sjt 412 RAMC
RICKARDS Frederick MM Sjt 52207 143 Hy Bty RGA
RICKARDS James MM Pte S/2893 Rifle Brigade
RICKARDS William "DCM,MM" Sjt 3560 11th Royal Fusiliers KIA 7.8.18
RICKEARD James MM Sjt 20691 1st Dragoons
RICKELLS Walter MM Cpl 738210 24th London Regt
RICKER Ernest MM Pte 538177 RAMC
RICKERBY George MM L/Cpl 10826 1st Irish Guards
RICKETT Cyril George MM Cpl 3106 44 Coy Machine Gun Corps KIA 3.7.17.
RICKETT Percy J. MM Pte 3108 Machine Gun Corps
RICKETT Robert William MM Bdr 35650 41 Siege Bty RGA
RICKETT Thomas J.C. MM Cpl 1958 6th Dragoons
RICKETT Walter S.H. MM Sjt 7447 Machine Gun Corps
RICKETTS Frederick Thomas MM Sjt 47987 Royal Engineers
RICKETTS Henry Edward George MM Sjt 3201 1/6th Gloucestershire Regt
RICKETTS Walter "DCM+Bar,MM" CSM 17063 6th South Wales Borderers
RICKMAN Harry W. MM Dvr 17755 124 Bty 28 Bde RFA
RICKS Benjamin V. MM Pte 26600 East Surrey Regt att 23rd London Regt.
RICKS James MM Pte 27909 1st Lancashire Fusiliers
RICKWOOD Arthur MM Pte 18491 Royal West Kent Regt
RICKWOOD Edward A. MM Cpl 16262 32nd Bn Machine Gun Corps
RICKWOOD Ernest MM Pte 43699 12th Royal Irish Rifles KIA 13.10.18.
RICKWOOD Frederick G. MM+Bar L/Sjt 200058 Norfolk Regt
RICON J.W. MM Pte 58321 142 Fd Amb RAMC

RIDAL Ernest MM Dvr Fitter 785134 C/293 Bde RFA
RIDDEL James MM L/Cpl 23302 Royal Inniskilling Fusiliers
RIDDELL George MM Sjt 22/487 Northumberland Fusiliers
RIDDELL Harold W. MM Sjt 58127 5th Yorkshire Light Infantry
RIDDELL John MM Pte 39200 Royal Scots
RIDDELL John Fairbairn MM Pte 1211 1/1st Lothians & Border Horse Yeomanry
RIDDELL Norman Grey MM L/Cpl 15833 11th Northumberland Fusiliers KIA 15.6.18.
RIDDELL Walter H. MM L/Cpl 200198 1/5th Liverpool Regt
RIDDELL William MM Pte 59344 Machine Gun Corps
RIDDETTE Charles MM L/Cpl 421238 2/10th London Regt Died 21.10.18.
RIDDEX Alexander MM Pte 241475 1st Royal Scots Fusiliers
RIDDICK Robert S. MM Pte M2/132665 Army Service Corps
RIDDICK Walter Harold MM L/Cpl 6424 16th Manchester Regt
RIDDICK William J. MM Pte 22258 18th Lancashire Fusiliers
RIDDING John W. MM Cpl 72342 RFA
RIDDINGTON Fred MM Sjt 7402 1st Leicestershire Regt KIA 15.9.16.
RIDDLE Alexander W. MM L/Cpl 266303 1/6th Gordon Highlanders DOW 13.4.18.
RIDDLE Arthur MM Pte 1603 19th Durham Light Infantry
RIDDLE Charles H. MM Cpl 33598 41 Bde RFA
RIDDLE Frederick MM+Bar Sjt 42782 2nd Worcestershire Regt
RIDDLE John MM Dvr 106529 RFA
RIDDLE Nicholas J. MM Sjt 16475 1/4th Yorkshire Regt
RIDDLE Robert MM Cpl 7486 1/9th London Regt
RIDDLE Thomas MM Sjt 26089 Machine Gun Corps
RIDDLE Walter H. MM Cpl 18/1207 1st Northumberland Fusiliers
RIDDLE Wilfred Hedley MM Pte 392434 9th London Regt DOW 28.8.17
RIDDLE William Job MM Spr 136326 184 Tunnelling Coy Royal Engineers
RIDDLE William Stanley MM Pte 45779 1st Devonshire Regt
RIDDLER George MM 2nd Cpl 629 Royal Engineers
RIDDLES Arthur MM+Bar Sjt 8805 1st Cheshire Regt
RIDDOCH Alexander MM+Bar L/Cpl 265909 Gordon Highlanders
RIDDOCH John L. MM L/Cpl 60313 Machine Gun Corps
RIDDOCH William J. MM L/Cpl 23697 1st Gordon Highlanders
RIDDY Albert Ernest "DCM,MM" Sjt 681095 1/22nd London Regt KIA 15.10.18.
RIDE Sidney E. MM Pte 265245 7th East Kent Regt
RIDEALGH William MM Sjt 49630 Royal Engineers
RIDEHALGH Victor MM Cpl M2/133304 Army Service Corps
RIDEOUT Charles MM Dvr T2/13730 14 Div Train Army Service Corps
RIDER Allen MM Pte 34464 5th West Riding Regt
RIDER Benjamin J. MM Pte 27891 North Lancashire Regt
RIDER Charles MM Pte 19156 4th Grenadier Guards
RIDER Harry "DCM,MM" Sjt 776674 A/310 Bde RFA
RIDER John W. MM L/Cpl 200134 1/4th West Riding Regt
RIDER William H. MM L/Cpl 15046 Shropshire Light Infantry
RIDETT George MM Pte 38685 4th North Lancashire Regt
RIDGE Charles L. MM Pte 240937 5th Devonshire Regt
RIDGE John MM Gnr 8856 B/150 Bde RFA
RIDGE Richard MM Cpl 85146 87 Bty 2 Bde RFA
RIDGE William H. MM L/Cpl 17934 Royal Berkshire Regt
RIDGE William Henry "MM,MSM" Sjt 29929 C/114 Bde RFA
RIDGELY Sydney MM Cpl 323360 6th London Regt
RIDGEON William "DCM,MM" Sjt 40938 RGA
RIDGEWAY Arthur Thomas MM SM Mechanician M/36072 Army Service Corps
RIDGEWAY William J. MM Pte 48181 RAMC
RIDGEWELL John W. MM Sjt 83302 288 Siege Bty RGA
RIDGEWELL Walter J. MM Pte 21446 Machine Gun Corps
RIDGEWELL Walter William MM Gnr 282655 RGA
RIDGEWELL William G. MM Pte 41230 4th Bedfordshire Regt
RIDGLEY James MM Sjt 451042 9th London Regt KIA 22.9.18. AKA James SCHOOLER.
RIDGWAY Allan MM Pte 300681 12th Manchester Regt
RIDGWAY Arthur MM Cpl 24462 RAMC
RIDGWAY Arthur MM Sjt 15458 12th Bn Machine Gun Corps
RIDGWAY F. MM Dvr 201699 RFA
RIDGWAY George MM+Bar Sjt 572492 17th London Regt
RIDGWAY Herbert E. MM L/Cpl 19920 12th Liverpool Regt
RIDGWAY James MM L/Cpl 28049 1st South Staffordshire Regt
RIDGWAY Joseph S. MM Sjt 39368 RFA
RIDING Albert MM Pte 28503 Royal Warwickshire Regt
RIDING Frank MM Sjt 34581 1/6th Cheshire Regt

RIDING James MM Pte 56617 RAMC
RIDING Samuel MM Pte 11125 1st South Wales Borderers
RIDING Thomas E. MM Cpl 444598 Royal Engineers
RIDING William MM Cpl 16532 1st Scottish Rifles
RIDINGS Frank MM Pte 242948 1/5th North Lancashire Regt KIA 1.10.18.
RIDINGS G. "DCM,MM" Pte 15245 10th North Lancashire Regt
RIDINGS Joe "MM,CG(B)" Sjt 281116 Lancashire Fusiliers
RIDINGS Samuel MM Pte 67706 9th Royal Welsh Fusiliers
RIDINGS William H. MM Pte 48609 2nd Lancashire Fusiliers
RIDLER Arthur J. MM+Bar Sjt 97844 C/70 Bfe RFA
RIDLER David J. MM Cpl 725447 D/83 Bde RFA
RIDLER G.T. MM Sjt Mechanic 20243 Royal Air Force
RIDLER George MM Cpl 320563 24th Welsh Regt
RIDLEY Arthur F. MM L/Cpl 632221 20th London Regt
RIDLEY Charles MM S/Sjt Fitter 376694 RGA
RIDLEY David MM Sjt 27841 Machine Gun Corps
RIDLEY Emmerson MM+Bar Sjt 15631 7/8th King's Own Scottish Borderers
RIDLEY Ernest W. MM Pte 79741 13th Royal Fusiliers
RIDLEY Frederick MM Pte 241750 8th Scottish Rifles
RIDLEY Frederick H. MM Gnr 172540 336 Siege Bty RGA
RIDLEY George MM Cpl 27885 1st Northumberland Fusiliers DOW 24.10.18.
RIDLEY Henry MM+Bar L/Cpl 3749 2nd Royal West Surrey Regt
RIDLEY Henry M. MM Sjt 32364 Durham Light Infantry
RIDLEY James A. MM Cpl 16071 15/17th West Yorkshire Regt
RIDLEY James W. MM Spr 148387 Royal Engineers
RIDLEY John W. MM Pte 22/84 Durham Light Infantry
RIDLEY John William "MM,MID" L/Cpl 1529 1/4th Northumberland Fusiliers
RIDLEY Ralph H. MM Pte 652945 21st London Regt
RIDLEY Thomas W. MM+Bar Pte 21686 10th Royal West Surrey Regt
RIDLEY William MM Cpl 388295 2(Northumbrian)Fd Amb RAMC
RIDLEY Wilson MM Pte 19533 11th Border Regt KIA 10.7.17.
RIDOUT Arthur T. MM L/Cpl 6443 2nd Coldstream Guards
RIDOUT Clifford Charles MM Gnr 200561 'C' Bn Tank Corps
RIDOUT Ernest MM Pte 9436 1st Somerset Light Infantry
RIDOUT John E. MM+Bar Sjt 27084 1st Middlesex Regt
RIDPEATH Robert MM Sjt 292026 Northumberland Fusiliers
RIDSDAL William Iles MM Cpl 67631 41st Bn Machine Gun Corps
RIDYARD Albert "MM,MSM" CSM 265719 1/7th Liverpool Regt
RIDYARD Arthur MM Sjt 265115 1/7th Liverpool Regt
RIDYARD George MM Pte 268966 1/7th Liverpool Regt
RIEDLING Charles F. MM Pte 26850 Durham Light Infantry
RIETIKER John F. MM Sjt 201666 1st London Regt
RIGBY Bert MM L/Cpl 2885 7th Seaforth Highlanders
RIGBY Carl MM Sjt 62628 9th Yorkshire Light Infantry
RIGBY Charles John MM Cpl 165894 37 Div Sig Coy Royal Engineers
RIGBY Ernest MM Spr 184275 60 Div Sig Coy Royal Engineers
RIGBY Frank MM L/Cpl 200221 4th North Staffordshire Regt
RIGBY Frederick MM Gnr 109386 115 Hy Bty RGA
RIGBY James MM Sjt 428429 Royal Engineers
RIGBY James MM L/Bdr 186918 RGA
RIGBY James MM L/Cpl 15587 East Lancashire Regt
RIGBY James "DCM,MM" Sjt 49644 RAMC
RIGBY James MM Dvr 74117 36 Bty 33 Bde RFA
RIGBY James Douglas MM Sjt 15780 17th Liverpool Regt KIA 31.7.17.
RIGBY John MM L/Cpl 14162 17th Lancashire Fusiliers
RIGBY John "MM,MID" Pte 9410 1/6th Lancashire Fusiliers
RIGBY John MM Sjt 5234 10th Lancashire Fusiliers
RIGBY John W. MM L/Cpl 7567 4 Siege Coy Royal Monmouthshire Royal Engineers
RIGBY Joseph MM Pte 6308 6th Lancashire Fusiliers
RIGBY Joseph Charles MM Pte 48124 1st South Wales Borderers KIA 5.10.18.
RIGBY Thomas "DCM,MM" Sjt 24437 9th Royal Welsh Fusiliers
RIGBY Thomas E. MM Cpl 200888 1/5th Liverpool Regt
RIGBY Thomas W. MM Pte 40560 8th Manchester Regt
RIGBY Wallis MM Spr 45136 Royal Engineers
RIGBY William MM Pte 267706 Liverpool Regt
RIGBY William MM Pte 241736 1/5th South Lancashire Regt
RIGBY William H. MM Pte 48179 10th South Wales Borderers
RIGBY William Joseph MM Pte 245891 18th Durham Light Infantry
RIGBY William P. MM Pte 200744 1/5th Royal Warwickshire Regt
RIGDEN Jesse W. MM Sjt 72607 122 Coy Labour Corps
RIGDEN William T. MM Sjt 260015 Royal Lancaster Regt

RIGG George MM L/Sjt 10921 8th West Riding Regt
RIGG John Arnold MM Gnr 79926 125 Heavy Bty RGA
RIGG Tom MM Pte 29483 15th Hampshire Regt
RIGG Tyson MM L/Cpl 18/356 18th Durham Light Infantry KIA 28.3.18.
RIGG William MM L/Cpl 275183 1/7th Arg & Suth Highlanders
RIGGALL Alfred MM Pte 49170 15th Lancashire Fusiliers
RIGGALL Arthur MM L/Sjt 25057 7th Lincolnshire Regt
RIGGALL Harold MM L/Cpl 1264 10th Lincolnshire Regt
RIGGS Albert Charles MM Pte 10520 6th Royal West Kent Regt KIA 9.3.18.
RIGGS Eustace C.H. MM Sjt 2654 7th Royal West Surrey Regt
RIGGS Frederick MM Pte 6421 8th Royal Sussex Regt
RIGGS Frederick Charles "VC,MM" Sjt 20695 6th York & Lancaster Regt KIA 1.10.18.
RIGGS Stanley William MM Pte R/3629 King's Royal Rifle Corps
RIGGS Thomas Henry Robinson "DCM,MM" Sjt 8900 2nd Lincolnshire Regt
RIGLEY George MM Bdr 11168 RFA
RIGLEY Herbert MM Gnr 73459 A/147 Bde RFA
RIGNALL Arthur J. MM Pte 320446 15th Suffolk Regt
RIGNEY Robert J. MM 2nd Cpl 20101 4 Div Sig Coy Royal Engineers
RILETT William MM Gnr 89881 B/178 Bde RFA
RILEY Albert MM Cpl 24146 9th West Riding Regt
RILEY Albert Edward MM Cpl 14783 2nd Arg & Suth Highlanders
RILEY Arnett H. MM Pte 21281 Royal Scots
RILEY Christopher MM Sjt 9011 2nd Border Regt
RILEY Cornelius MM Sjt 10847 5th Shropshire Light Infantry KIA 24.10.17.
RILEY Edward MM Pte 9713 2nd Durham Light Infantry KIA 16.9.16.
RILEY Edward MM+Bar Sjt 8901 2nd East Lancashire Regt
RILEY Ernest MM Pte 265209 6th West Riding Regt
RILEY Fred "DCM,MM" Sjt 467735 Royal Engineers
RILEY Frederick MM L/Bdr 68998 B/15 Bde RFA
RILEY George MM Sjt 22095 9th Notts & Derby Regt
RILEY George "MM,MID" Cpl 96537 A/51 Bde RFA
RILEY Harold MM Sjt 260232 1st Cheshire Regt
RILEY Harold MM Sjt L/147 A/158 Bde RFA DOW 29.7.16.
RILEY Harold Ernest MM Dvr 9168 150 Bde RFA
RILEY Harry MM Cpl 35611 175 Bde Ammn Col RFA
RILEY Henry MM Sjt 12990 West Yorkshire Regt
RILEY J. MM L/Cpl 39217 7th Royal Warwickshire Regt
RILEY James MM Sjt 241355 1/5th East Lancashire Regt
RILEY James MM Pte 20428 Royal Irish Rifles
RILEY James MM CQMS T4/210395 11 Div Train Army Service Corps
RILEY James MM Sjt 202973 5th Lancashire Fusiliers
RILEY James MM Pte 11222 8th Cheshire Regt
RILEY James MM Sjt 35610 100 Coy Machine Gun Corps
RILEY John MM L/Cpl 21584 6th Cameron Highlanders
RILEY John MM Sjt 14424 10th North Lancashire Regt
RILEY John MM Pte 201797 1/7th Royal Warwickshire Regt
RILEY John MM Pte 25630 Machine Gun Corps KIA 22.3.18.
RILEY John Albert MM Pte 1005 15th Royal Warwickshire Regt
RILEY John G. MM Pte 276535 Manchester Regt
RILEY John H. MM Pte 17537 10th Yorkshire Regt
RILEY John T. MM Pte 242695 24th Royal Welsh Fusiliers
RILEY John W. MM+Bar L/Cpl 26537 2nd South Staffordshire Regt
RILEY Jonathan MM L/Cpl 16213 6/7th Royal Scots Fusiliers
RILEY Joseph MM CSM 305401 8th Lancashire Fusiliers
RILEY Martin MM Pte 20608 Yorkshire Regt
RILEY Michael MM Sjt 353 1st Northumberland Fusiliers
RILEY Michael J. MM Pte 305269 1/8th Liverpool Regt
RILEY Oswald Leonard MM Cpl 266385 2/7th West Yorkshire Regt
RILEY Patrick MM Pte 572611 17th London Regt
RILEY Patrick MM Pte 21/912 Northumberland Fusiliers
RILEY Robert MM Sjt 275468 1/7th Manchester Regt KIA 8.10.18.
RILEY Samuel MM Cpl 344 2nd Lancashire Fusiliers See Albert Frederick RAUTH or ROUTH
RILEY Samuel MM L/Cpl 45674 Royal Engineers
RILEY Stephen MM Sjt 20744 Royal Welsh Fusiliers
RILEY Thomas MM Pte 17553 North Lancashire Regt
RILEY Thomas MM Spr 139309 Royal Engineers
RILEY Thomas MM Pte 1994 Royal Warwickshire Regt
RILEY Thomas R. MM Sjt 3238 Liverpool Regt
RILEY Walter J. MM L/Cpl 81402 48th Bn Machine Gun Corps
RILEY William MM Pte 241394 4th York & Lancaster Regt
RILEY William MM L/Cpl 12668 7th East Lancashire Regt KIA 21.12.17.
RILEY William MM Pte 48537 7th Liverpool Regt
RILEY William MM Gnr 82498 RFA
RILEY William Arnold MM Sjt 38415 RAMC
RIMBAULT John MM Pte M2/114792 Army Service Corps
RIMER William J. MM Sjt 265788 1/6th Gloucestershire Regt
RIMINGTON William MM Pte 761168 28th London Regt
RIMMER Bertrand Joseph MM Sjt 9987 2nd South Lancashire Regt
RIMMER Edward R. MM Cpl 242508 1/5th Royal Lancaster Regt
RIMMER Ernest MM+Bar Cpl 10318 4th Liverpool Regt Died 15.11.18.
RIMMER Frank MM Sjt 20316 Manchester Regt
RIMMER George A. MM 2nd Cpl 23024 2 Fd Coy Royal Engineers
RIMMER George W. MM Cpl 23643 2nd Yorkshire Light Infantry
RIMMER James MM Pte 241740 5th South Lancashire Regt
RIMMER John MM L/Cpl 311735 Third Army Sig Coy Royal Engineers
RIMMER John MM Pte 14345 7th King's Own Scottish Borderers
RIMMER John MM Pte 30818 RAMC
RIMMER John W. MM L/Cpl 285079 2nd Welsh Regt
RIMMER Richard "DCM,MM" Pnr 43671 Signal Service Royal Engineers
RIMMER Thomas MM Gnr 693 113 Bty 25 Bde RFA
RIMMER William MM Pte 301638 8th Manchester Regt
RIMMER William J. MM L/Cpl 242222 Lancashire Fusiliers
RIMMER William M. MM Pte 21259 North Lancashire Regt
RIMMINGTON Thomas L. MM Pte 20623 2 Fd Amb RAMC
RINDER Arthur S. MM Gnr 107353 RGA
RING Frederick W. MM Pte 3010 RAMC
RING John MM Cpl 96195 17 Squadron Machine Gun Corps(Cavalry)
RING Michael H. MM Pte 012896 Army Ordnance Corps
RING William MM Cpl 284145 4th London Regt
RINGE Edward Bertie MM Spr 25222 20 Div Sig Coy Royal Engineers KIA 24.3.18.
RINGE William F. MM 2nd Cpl 560255 Royal Engineers
RINGLAND Archibald McDonald MM Spr 76494 XXI Corps Sig Coy Royal Engineers
RINGLAND James MM+Bar Sjt 11281 9th Royal Inniskilling Fusiliers
RINGROSE Albert F. MM Dvr 731119 389 Bty 37 Bde RFA
RINGROSE Jesse MM Gnr 312179 1 Hy Bty RGA
RINGROSE John William MM L/Cpl 238222 2nd West Yorkshire Regt KIA 27.5.18.
RINGROSE William J. MM L/Cpl 242457 10th Royal West Surrey Regt
RINGROSE Worley MM Cpl 301442 13th Bn Tank Corps
RINGWOOD Edward MM L/Cpl 532309 490 Fd Coy Royal Engineers
RINTOUL John MM Cpl 307025 RGA
RIOCH Thomas MM Pte 291126 Gordon Highlanders
RIPLEY Frank MM L/Cpl 250083 1/6th Durham Light Infantry
RIPLEY Harry MM Pte 7581 1st Dorsetshire Regt
RIPLEY Herbert MM Cpl 13033 10th Lancashire Fusiliers
RIPLEY Herbert Edward MM Bdr 53558 103 Siege Bty RGA
RIPLEY J. MM Pte 36543 2nd Durham Light Infantry
RIPLEY Joseph MM Pte 1547 12th Royal Sussex Regt DOW 4.11.16.
RIPLEY Joseph William MM Pte 13203 8th Leicestershire Regt
RIPPEN Horace A. MM Spr 348091 6 Div Sig Coy Royal Engineers
RIPPEN Horace H. MM L/Cpl 204983 15th Hampshire Regt
RIPPENGAL Clifford G. MM Cpl 300351 1/5th London Regt
RIPPER Clemence G. "DCM,MM" L/Sjt S/10746 Rifle Brigade
RIPPIE James MM Pte 58018 Highland Light Infantry
RIPPON Henry Wilson "MM,MID" L/Cpl 14916 1st Coldstream Guards
RIPPON J.W. MM L/Cpl 23431 2nd Royal West Surrey Regt
RISDON J.S. MM L/Cpl 7467 2nd Oxf & Bucks Light Infantry
RISDON Montague Tristram MM Sjt 760192 1/28th London Regt
RISEBOROUGH Gordon MM Gnr 21804 A/91 Bde RFA
RISEBOROUGH John MM Pte 18034 Norfolk Regt
RISELEY Frank MM Sjt 44400 Royal Engineers
RISELEY Thomas MM Pte 59589 17th Royal Welsh Fusiliers
RISHWORTH Joseph MM Pte 15295 8th Northumberland Fusiliers
RISING Frederick MM Sjt 17190 RGA
RISING Frederick Charles "DCM,MM+Bar" Sjt 84567 20 Div Sig Coy Royal Engineers
RISLEY Albert E. MM Pte 201764 9th Cheshire Regt
RISPIN Herbert MM Dvr 134689 D/149 Bde RFA
RISSLEY Arthur MM Cpl 12209 Machine Gun Corps
RISTOW Alfred MM Dvr 34725 RFA

RITCHIE Alexander MM Cpl M2/047899 Army Service Corps att 23 Siege Bty Ammn Col RGA.
RITCHIE Alexander MM L/Cpl 240125 Gordon Highlanders
RITCHIE David MM Sjt 30871 5th Royal Inniskilling Fusiliers
RITCHIE David MM Gnr 189184 C/250 Bde RFA DOW 1.9.18.
RITCHIE David F. MM Cpl 16496 9th Scottish Rifles
RITCHIE E. MM Bdr 23923 RFA
RITCHIE George MM Sjt 13397 12th Durham Light Infantry
RITCHIE Henry A. MM QMS 19320 7 Fd Amb RAMC
RITCHIE James MM Cpl 4030 7th Seaforth Highlanders
RITCHIE James MM Piper 5614 Gordon Highlanders
RITCHIE James MM Pte 949 GMGR
RITCHIE James MM L/Cpl 8492 2nd Gordon Highlanders
RITCHIE James MM Pte 16485 13th Royal Scots
RITCHIE James B. MM RQMS 528057 14th London Regt
RITCHIE James L. MM Sjt 43064 1st Gordon Highlanders
RITCHIE John MM Cpl 40139 Royal Scots
RITCHIE John T. MM Pte 19749 XIX Corps Cyclist Bn Army Cyclist Corps
RITCHIE Robert MM Spr 48249 Royal Engineers
RITCHIE Robert MM Cpl 11/13723 11th Border Regt KIA 1.7.16.
RITCHIE Robert MM Pte 202347 5/6th Scottish Rifles KIA 22.6.17.
RITCHIE Robert MM L/Cpl 43065 Royal Scots Fusiliers
RITCHIE Robert F. MM Sjt 8875 11th Lancashire Fusiliers
RITCHIE Thomas MM Pte 201193 1/4th Seaforth Highlanders
RITCHIE Thomas MM Cpl 18191 2nd South Staffordshire Regt
RITCHIE Thomas MM Sjt 15415 17th Highland Light Infantry
RITCHIE Thomas MM Sjt 365036 20 Siege Bty RGA DOW 15.9.17.
RITCHIE William MM Sjt 9724 10th Arg & Suth Highlanders
RITCHIE William MM L/Cpl 9564 1st Dragoons
RITCHIE William MM Pte 281994 Highland Light Infantry
RITCHIE William MM Gnr 44493 120 Heavy Nty RGA
RITCHIE William J. MM Pte 8853 Royal Highlanders
RITCHINGS Albert Arthur William MM L/Cpl 530974 1/15th London Regt
RITCHINGS Albert E. MM Pte 17866 11th East Lancashire Regt
RITCHINGS Stephen MM Pte 356357 2/10th Liverpool Regt
RITSON John MM Sjt 45921 Royal Engineers
RITTER Arthur E. MM L/Cpl 571656 17th London Regt
RIVA Archibald MM Gnr(SS) 157381 130 Heavy Bty RGA
RIVERS Albert E. MM Pte 32439 2/1st(Highland)Fd Amb RAMC
RIVERS Albert John MM Pte 23928 Machine Gun Corps
RIVERS Cecil MM Pte 204930 2/8th Middlesex Regt
RIVERS Francis John "MM,MM(F)" Pte 13970 7th Oxf & Bucks Light Infantry
RIVERS Frank M. MM Sjt 4493 Royal Fusiliers
RIVERS George "DCM,MM" Cpl 40406 2nd Bn Tank Corps
RIVERS Henry MM Sjt 12437 RGA
RIVERS Herbert MM Pte 201140 4th Hampshire Regt
RIVERS John MM Pte 1247 16th Royal Warwickshire Regt
RIVERS Percy F. MM Pte 27029 15th Hampshire Regt
RIVERS Thomas MM Pte 79470 9th Royal Fusiliers KIA 21.9.18.
RIVERS Walter E. "MM,MSM" Sjt M/23137 1 Cav Div Supply Col Army Service Corps
RIVETT Albert MM L/Cpl 29922 9th Norfolk Regt KIA 15.4.18.
RIVETT Francis William MM Sjt M2/051003 47 Ammn Sub Park Army Service Corps KIA 16.10.17.
RIVETT George William MM Pte 4093 54 Coy Machine Gun Corps KIA 3.5.17.
RIVETT John S. "DCM,MM" Sjt 23733 Royal Lancaster Regt
RIVETT John Thomas MM Sjt 8114 2nd Leicestershire Regt
RIVETT Leonard J. MM Sjt 39909 RFA
RIVETT Percy MM Pte 56695 17th Lancashire Fusiliers
RIVETT Robert MM Pte 43074 Middlesex Regt
RIVETT Sidney MM L/Cpl 21/965 Northumberland Fusiliers
RIVITT Arthur G. MM+Bar 2nd Cpl 154546 Royal Engineers
RIX Arthur Victor MM Pte 701301 1/23rd London Regt KIA 25.3.18.
RIX E.C. MM Cpl 29470 1st Norfolk Regt
RIX Joseph MM L/Cpl 17091 129 Bty 42 Bde RFA KIA 30.7.16.
RIX Leonard Fowler MM L/Cpl 40904 Suffolk Regt
RIX Robert H. MM Pte 25707 Welsh Regt
RIX William C. MM+Bar L/Cpl 75203 4th Royal Fusiliers
RIXON Edwin MM Cpl 201618 1/4th Oxf & Bucks Light Infantry
RIXON John MM Sjt 200530 Cheshire Regt
RIXON Leonard MM Pte 148 12th Lancers
RIXON Walter MM+Bar Sjt 3120 1/4th Royal Berkshire Regt
ROABUCK Albin "DCM,MM" Cpl 10703 1st Royal Irish Fusiliers
ROACH Frank MM Pte 230110 2nd London Regt
ROACH Frank MM L/Cpl 9/14798 9th Leicestershire Regt
ROACH Frederick C. MM S/Sjt 459025 RAMC
ROACH George Edward MM Pte 47036 6th Leicestershire Regt DOW 25.10.18.
ROACH Harold MM L/Cpl 10587 1st Scottish Rifles
ROACH James MM Pte 6/588 13th King's Royal Rifle Corps
ROACH Thomas MM L/Cpl 18768 6th York & Lancaster Regt
ROACH Wallace MM Pte 3127 Seaforth Highlanders
ROACH William MM Sjt 510001 Royal Engineers
ROACH William MM Pte 280831 5th Lancashire Fusiliers
ROACHE Adam MM Pte 5068 2nd Royal Dublin Fusiliers
ROACHE or ROCHE James MM Sjt 89435 RFA
ROADHOUSE Arnold E. MM 2nd Cpl 43771 Royal Engineers
ROADHOUSE George Henry MM Sjt 1402 1/5th York & Lancaster Regt
ROADS Stanley MM Sjt 1856 1/9th London Regt
ROADS Thomas W.G. MM L/Cpl 43877 1/8th Middlesex Regt
ROADY T.J. MM Pte 8303 2nd East Kent Regt
ROAKE Charles W. MM L/Cpl 680769 1/22nd London Regt
ROAKE Joseph E. MM L/Sjt 9037 1st East Surrey Regt
ROAKE Reginald MM+Bar Sjt 1968 Royal Fusiliers
ROANE John MM L/Cpl 200362 1/5th Liverpool Regt
ROBATHAN William C. MM Pte 41024 South Wales Borderers
ROBB Albert Victor MM Cpl 3/5746 1st Cameron Highlanders
ROBB Alexander MM Sjt 9142 1/8th Arg & Suth Highlanders
ROBB Alexander MM Pte 17955 Gordon Highlanders
ROBB Alexander MM L/Cpl 41467 Royal Scots Fusiliers
ROBB Andrew "MC,MM+Bar" CSM 89 2nd Arg & Suth Highlanders
ROBB C. MM Cpl 555057 2nd King's Royal Rifle Corps
ROBB David Thomas MM Pte 43070 12th Royal Scots KIA 3.5.17.
ROBB Gavin MM Pte 3971 12th Royal Scots
ROBB George MM Sjt 22822 18th Liverpool Regt
ROBB George M.S. MM Bdr 281967 169 Bde RFA
ROBB James MM L/Cpl 9719 2/1st HAC (Inf)
ROBB John MM Spr 217838 19 Light Railway Coy Royal Engineers
ROBB John MM Sjt 265713 1/6th Gordon Highlanders
ROBB John C. MM Pte 292 Royal Highlanders
ROBB Robert D. MM 2nd Cpl 406110 51 Div Sig Coy Royal Engineers
ROBB Ronald MM 2nd Cpl 548455 513 Fd Coy Royal Engineers
ROBB Sidney Edward MM Bdr 21051 A/26 Bde RFA
ROBB Thomas MM Pte 8368 Seaforth Highlanders
ROBB William MM Pte 3066 1/5th Gordon Highlanders DOW 23.8.16.
ROBB William MM Pte 42720 Highland Light Infantry
ROBB William Murray MM Spr 254913 66 Div Sig Coy Royal Engineers
ROBBIE Richard MM Pte 20008 RAMC
ROBBINS Albert MM Pte 985 1st Rifle Brigade
ROBBINS Arthur MM L/Cpl 37439 Machine Gun Corps
ROBBINS Augustus C.J. MM Pte 6824 RAMC
ROBBINS Charles MM Cpl 250439 4th London Regt
ROBBINS Charles David MM Pte 10982 2nd Worcestershire Regt
ROBBINS Ernest MM Pte 50660 1st Royal Berkshire Regt
ROBBINS Ernest J. MM Spr 87466 Royal Engineers
ROBBINS Francis J. MM Sjt 207794 10th Royal West Surrey Regt
ROBBINS Frank W. MM Cpl 5628 1st Gloucestershire Regt
ROBBINS George MM Pte 15065 7/8th King's Own Scottish Borderers
ROBBINS George H. MM L/Sjt 1182 Army Veterinary Corps
ROBBINS George Henry Thomas "DCM,MM" Cpl 15817 2nd Devonshire Regt att 23 Light TM Bty.
ROBBINS George W. MM L/Cpl 42435 10th Essex Regt
ROBBINS Harry Alfred MM L/Cpl 12409 Coldstream Guards
ROBBINS Herbert Edward MM Pte 202050 2/5th Manchester Regt
ROBBINS James Henry MM Sjt 22193 Royal Fusiliers
ROBBINS John MM Pte 34966 1st Essex Regt
ROBBINS John Richard MM Bdr 66241 RFA
ROBBINS John T. MM Cpl 185671 102 Siege Bty RGA
ROBBINS Leonard T. MM Pte 66682 RAMC
ROBBINS Sidney MM 2nd Cpl 94516 Guards Div Sig Coy Royal Engineers
ROBBINS Sidney John MM Sjt 560339 63 Div Sig Coy Royal Engineers
ROBBINS Stanley MM Pte 22364 10th Gloucestershire Regt
ROBBINS Walter Thomas MM L/Cpl 11909 1st Duke of Cornwall's LI KIA 23.4.17.
ROBBINS William MM Pte 300504 7th Liverpool Regt
ROBBINS William MM L/Cpl 9040 2nd South Staffordshire Regt
ROBBINS William Edward MM L/Cpl 459376 2(wessex)Fd Amb RAMC
ROBBINS William Edward MM Pte 12845 1st Coldstream Guards KIA 15.9.16.

ROBBINS William G. MM L/Cpl 266311 1/1st Bucks Bn Oxf & Bucks Light Infantry
ROBBINS William H.M. MM L/Cpl 200304 1/4th Royal Sussex Regt
ROBERSON Arthur MM+Bar Cpl 432022 Royal Engineers
ROBERTS Albert MM L/Cpl 33129 Manchester Regt
ROBERTS Albert MM L/Cpl 7024 2nd Suffolk Regt
ROBERTS Albert MM Sjt 38267 Welsh Regt
ROBERTS Albert E. MM Pte 79110 23rd Cheshire Regt
ROBERTS Alfred MM Pte 11723 2/4th Royal West Surrey Regt
ROBERTS Alfred G. MM Sjt 42862 6th South Staffordshire Regt
ROBERTS Alfred T. MM Sjt 2029 5th Royal Warwickshire Regt
ROBERTS Allen MM+Bar Pte 25610 17th Royal Welsh Fusiliers
ROBERTS Archie MM Pte 241347 6th Royal Welsh Fusiliers
ROBERTS Arnold MM Pte 10765 Liverpool Regt
ROBERTS Arthur MM Sjt 295161 206 Siege Bty RGA
ROBERTS Arthur MM Sjt 16883 11th Royal Scots KIA 9.4.17.
ROBERTS Arthur MM Dvr 31544 RFA
ROBERTS Arthur Bertram Howard MM Pte L/8935 1st East Kent Regt KIA 2.12.17.
ROBERTS Arthur E. MM Gnr 318681 RGA
ROBERTS Arthur W. MM Pte 1857 1/20th London Regt
ROBERTS Benjamin MM Cpl 9979 Durham Light Infantry
ROBERTS Bertram MM Pte 7766 11th Lancashire Fusiliers
ROBERTS Charles MM Pte 19561 6th Dorsetshire Regt
ROBERTS Charles "MM,MID" Cpl 6539 Army Cyclist Corps
ROBERTS Charles A. MM Sjt 19244 Royal West Kent Regt
ROBERTS Charles E. MM Bdr 7132 RFA
ROBERTS Charles Edward MM Sjt 8305 2nd Lincolnshire Regt DOW 10.10.16.
ROBERTS Charles Henry MM L/Bdr 124123 381 Siege Bty RGA
ROBERTS Charles William MM Pte PW/4866 19th Middlesex Regt
ROBERTS Charlie MM Dvr 105903 RHA
ROBERTS Christopher J. MM L/Cpl 10645 2/1st HAC (Inf)
ROBERTS David MM Sjt 6854 Royal Anglesey Royal Engineers
ROBERTS David MM Pte 38490 2nd South Wales Borderers
ROBERTS David MM Pte 56765 Machine Gun Corps
ROBERTS David MM Pte 8072 South Staffordshire Regt
ROBERTS David MM Pte 36967 11th Royal Welsh Fusiliers
ROBERTS David J. MM Sjt 355064 25th Royal Welsh Fusiliers
ROBERTS Duncan MM Pte 24178 21st West Yorkshire Regt
ROBERTS E. MM SM 354020 3 Fd Amb RAMC
ROBERTS E. MM Pte 417360 RAMC
ROBERTS E.T. MM Cpl 15806 Liverpool Regt
ROBERTS Edgar C. MM Pte 35490 RAMC
ROBERTS Edward MM Pte 1522 1st Welsh Guards
ROBERTS Edward MM Cpl 33249 Royal Welsh Fusiliers
ROBERTS Edward MM Pte 53117 Worcestershire Regt
ROBERTS Edward MM Dvr 805897 RFA
ROBERTS Edward MM+Bar Pte 10085 1st Border Regt AKA GISBY
ROBERTS Edward MM RSM 15313 10th Royal Welsh Fusiliers DOW 30.7.16.
ROBERTS Edward MM+Bar SSM 46311 15th Hussars
ROBERTS Edward MM Gnr 36276 GHQ Ammn Park RGA
ROBERTS Edward MM L/Cpl 22386 Machine Gun Corps
ROBERTS Edward A. MM Pte 15084 10th Royal Welsh Fusiliers
ROBERTS Edward C. MM L/Cpl 265149 Royal Welsh Fusiliers
ROBERTS Edward J. MM Cpl S/7146 13th Rifle Brigade
ROBERTS Edward J. MM Cpl 400 Machine Gun Corps(Motors)
ROBERTS Edward O. MM Sjt 43824 110 Hy Bty RGA
ROBERTS Edward S.J. MM Cpl 240492 Royal Welsh Fusiliers
ROBERTS Enoch MM Pte 45176 RAMC
ROBERTS Ernest Hiram MM Pte 3725 1/1st Duke of Lancaster's Own Yeomanry
ROBERTS Ernest W. MM Dvr 496480 Royal Engineers
ROBERTS Evan MM Cpl 745034 RFA
ROBERTS Evan MM Pte 339321 RAMC
ROBERTS Evan MM Dvr 159563 RFA
ROBERTS Evan R. MM Pte 62393 RAMC
ROBERTS Ewert T. "DCM,MM" Cpl 50997 RGA
ROBERTS F. MM Gnr 32016 Machine Gun Corps
ROBERTS Francis MM L/Cpl 15933 18th Lancashire Fusiliers
ROBERTS Frank MM Gnr 308699 13th Bn Tank Corps KIA 10.8.18.
ROBERTS Frank MM Pte 12514 Leicestershire Regt
ROBERTS Frank MM Bdr 1365 230 Bde RFA DOW 8.1.17.
ROBERTS Frank MM Pte M2/180945 Army Service Corps
ROBERTS Fred MM Cpl 67680 178 Coy Machine Gun Corps DOW 2.4.18.
ROBERTS Fred S. MM Pte 36896 Machine Gun Corps
ROBERTS Frederick MM Gnr 131495 B/92 Bde RFA DOW 9.7.18.
ROBERTS Frederick MM Pte 551952 16th London Regt
ROBERTS Frederick MM Pte 14544 8th Border Regt
ROBERTS Frederick MM Pte 11626 2nd King's Own Scottish Borderers
ROBERTS Frederick W. MM Pte 48437 North Staffordshire Regt
ROBERTS George MM Sjt 15993 35th Bn Machine Gun Corps
ROBERTS George MM L/Cpl 330874 1/4th Royal Scots KIA 27.9.18.
ROBERTS George MM Sjt 14637 5th West Riding Regt
ROBERTS George MM Pte 8365 11th Royal Welsh Fusiliers
ROBERTS George MM L/Cpl 11028 1st Scottish Rifles
ROBERTS George MM Sjt 12940 4th Royal Fusiliers
ROBERTS George MM Pte 8505 2nd Royal West Surrey Regt
ROBERTS George Alfred MM Sjt 7974 1st Leicestershire Regt KIA 21.3.18.
ROBERTS George E. MM Sjt 61395 Machine Gun Corps
ROBERTS George W. MM+Bar Spr 532214 Royal Engineers
ROBERTS Goronwy C. MM Cpl 241261 Welsh Regt
ROBERTS Guy B. MM+Bar Pte 305568 5th Bn Tank Corps
ROBERTS Gwilym MM Sjt 240285 Royal Welsh Fusiliers
ROBERTS Harry MM Sjt 11489 7th Yorkshire Light Infantry
ROBERTS Harry MM Pte 3597 7th Dragoon Guards
ROBERTS Harry MM L/Sjt 351252 1/5th Manchester Regt
ROBERTS Harry MM Bdr 59680 RGA
ROBERTS Harry MM Gnr 1272 RFA
ROBERTS Harry MM Pte 419413 1/2(North Midland)Fd Amb. RAMC
ROBERTS Harry H. MM Pte 14518 2nd Suffolk Regt
ROBERTS Henry C. MM L/Cpl 7586 2nd Oxf & Bucks Light Infantry
ROBERTS Henry G. MM Pte 632788 20th London Regt
ROBERTS Henry George William MM Pte 9705 11th Royal West Kent Regt
ROBERTS Henry William MM Cpl 290606 Royal Welsh Fusiliers
ROBERTS Herbert Harry MM Pte 12579 2nd Suffolk Regt
ROBERTS Herbert J. MM Pte 612583 19th London Regt
ROBERTS Hugh MM CQMS 173 1/4th North Lancashire Regt
ROBERTS Hugh MM Pte 39128 Royal Welsh Fusiliers
ROBERTS Hugh Lewis MM Gnr 79818 V/15 Heavy TM Bty RGA
ROBERTS Isaac Burleston "MM,MID" Bdr 490 RHA
ROBERTS Isaac Henry MM Cpl 7362 90 Coy Machine Gun Corps KIA 3.10.17.
ROBERTS Ivor MM Pte 200545 3rd(Light)Bn Tank Corps
ROBERTS Ivor MM Pte 31075 Royal Welsh Fusiliers
ROBERTS J. MM L/Cpl 5219 Royal Irish Rifles
ROBERTS J.C. MM Sjt 40022 110 Bty 24 Bde RFA
ROBERTS J.E. MM Bdr 76199 32 Bde RFA
ROBERTS J.W. MM(15396 RSF)+Bar Sjt 65366 15th Yorkshire Light Infantry
ROBERTS J.W. MM Sjt 36610 Royal Engineers
ROBERTS Jack MM Pte R/19274 13th King's Royal Rifle Corps
ROBERTS James MM Sjt 60453 Labour Corps
ROBERTS James MM L/Cpl 21636 1/5th Border Regt
ROBERTS James MM L/Bdr 78356 A/70 Bde RFA
ROBERTS James MM CSM 200075 1/4th King's Own Scottish Borderers
ROBERTS James MM Pte 2193 1/1st Monmouthshire Regt
ROBERTS James MM Pte 19763 9th Scottish Rifles KIA 9.4.17.
ROBERTS James MM Pte 22372 15th Royal Welsh Fusiliers
ROBERTS James F. MM Cpl 36717 Cheshire Regt
ROBERTS James Martin MM Cpl 48190 B/103 Bde RFA
ROBERTS John MM Pte 120135 32nd Bn Machine Gun Corps
ROBERTS John MM Cpl 14447 Royal Irish Rifles
ROBERTS John MM Sjt 17300 12th Notts & Derby Regt
ROBERTS John MM Sjt 6600 1st Hampshire Regt
ROBERTS John MM Sjt 15775 17th Highland Light Infantry
ROBERTS John MM Pte 39820 Welsh Regt Enlisted as T/33515 Samuel JONES ASC.Deserted & re-enlisted in Welsh Regt.
ROBERTS John "DCM,MM" Cpl 240326 1/5th South Lancashire Regt KIA 30.11.17.
ROBERTS John MM Sjt 12649 RGA
ROBERTS John MM Pte 28416 21st Manchester Regt
ROBERTS John B. MM Gnr 618352 RHA
ROBERTS John C. MM Pte 1452 Liverpool Regt
ROBERTS John E. MM Cpl 9309 2nd Royal Welsh Fusiliers
ROBERTS John Edward MM Pte 87393 14th Royal Welsh Fusiliers
ROBERTS John Edward MM 2nd Cpl 46984 95 Fd Coy Royal Engineers
ROBERTS John F. MM+Bar Sjt 16878 2nd Royal Dublin Fusiliers
ROBERTS John H. MM Pte 108776 37th Bn Machine Gun Corps
ROBERTS John H. MM Pte 1213 King Edward's Horse
ROBERTS John James MM Pte 232692 2nd London Regt

ROBERTS John L. MM Pte 2138 1st Welsh Guards
ROBERTS John O. MM+Bar Sjt 265293 4th Liverpool Regt
ROBERTS John P. MM L/Cpl 17223 Royal Welsh Fusiliers Died 28.11.18.
ROBERTS John R. MM Bdr 117895 RFA
ROBERTS John Richard MM Pte 21386 14th Royal Welsh Fusiliers KIA 24.2.17.
ROBERTS John Thomas MM Bdr 7319 160 Bde RFA
ROBERTS John W. MM Sjt 3315 10 Siege Bty RGA
ROBERTS Joseph MM L/Sjt 242823 1/4th South Lancashire Regt
ROBERTS Joseph Aloysius MM L/Cpl 1139 14th Royal Warwickshire Regt
ROBERTS Joseph E. MM Pte 204303 Liverpool Regt
ROBERTS Joseph F. MM Gnr 319259 RGA
ROBERTS L.C. MM AM1 19101 Royal Flying Corps
ROBERTS Leonard MM L/Cpl 19774 7th Shropshire Light Infantry DOW 3.9.16.
ROBERTS Leonard MM Cpl 39831 6 Siege Bty RGA
ROBERTS Leonard John MM L/Cpl 15592 7th Northamptonshire Regt
ROBERTS Leslie MM Pte 17057 8th East Lancashire Regt
ROBERTS Norman MM L/Sjt 13765 10th West Riding Regt
ROBERTS Norman MM Cpl 106048 Royal Engineers
ROBERTS Oscar C. MM L/Cpl 250606 Manchester Regt
ROBERTS P. MM Sjt 240625 4th Royal Welsh Fusiliers att 1/4th KAR.
ROBERTS Percy MM Cpl 31753 9th Devonshire Regt
ROBERTS Phillip N. MM Sjt 14092 D/130 Bde RFA
ROBERTS Preston Thomas MM Cpl 2187 1/24th London Regt
ROBERTS Reginald Louis MM Cpl 9987 2nd Devonshire Regt DOW 4.5.17.
ROBERTS Richard MM L/Cpl 41279 2nd Royal Scots Fusiliers
ROBERTS Richard MM Pte 1666 7th East Kent Regt KIA 6.8.17.
ROBERTS Richard E. MM Pte 25653 18th Lancashire Fusiliers
ROBERTS Richard F. MM Pte 13304 7th Shropshire Light Infantry
ROBERTS Richard J. MM L/Cpl STK/1759 10th Royal Fusiliers
ROBERTS Richard Parry MM Cpl 58358 Machine Gun Corps KIA 18.4.18.
ROBERTS Robert MM Pte 33652 1st South Wales Borderers
ROBERTS Robert MM Pte 241589 2/5th York & Lancaster Regt
ROBERTS Robert MM Cpl 31335 Royal Welsh Fusiliers
ROBERTS Robert MM Pte 6339 19th London Regt
ROBERTS Robert MM Gnr 69264 RGA
ROBERTS Robert MM Pte 17202 2nd Royal Welsh Fusiliers
ROBERTS Robert MM+Bar L/Cpl 19377 16th Royal Welsh Fusiliers Died 9.10.18.
ROBERTS Robert A. MM Pte 78233 3 Fd Amb RAMC
ROBERTS Robert Arthur MM Pte 44136 10th South Wales Borderers KIA 8.10.18.
ROBERTS Robert T. MM Spr 170477 Royal Engineers
ROBERTS Samuel MM Pte 20935 XVII Corps Cyclist Bn Army Cyclist Corps
ROBERTS Samuel MM+Bar L/Cpl 18685 12th Royal Irish Rifles
ROBERTS Sidney MM L/Cpl 11224 6th York & Lancaster Regt
ROBERTS Stanley MM Cpl 780147 246 Bde RFA
ROBERTS Stephen N. MM Pte 117482 38 Fd Amb RAMC
ROBERTS Sydney MM Sjt 18076 Shropshire Light Infantry
ROBERTS Sydney B. MM Dvr 705140 RFA
ROBERTS T.J. MM+Bar Pte 26438 17th Royal Welsh Fusiliers
ROBERTS Thomas MM L/Cpl 86366 170 Tunnelling Coy Royal Engineers
ROBERTS Thomas MM Sjt 12375 6th Shropshire Light Infantry
ROBERTS Thomas MM Cpl 8824 1st Cheshire Regt KIA 7.10.17.
ROBERTS Thomas MM L/Sjt 16898 Grenadier Guards
ROBERTS Thomas MM Pte 8818 17th Manchester Regt
ROBERTS Thomas MM+2 Bars Pte 14998 8th South Lancashire Regt
ROBERTS Thomas MM Sjt 1533 19th Middlesex Regt
ROBERTS Thomas MM L/Cpl 266235 1st Royal Lancaster Regt DOW 4.9.18.
ROBERTS Thomas MM Sjt 62291 Royal Engineers
ROBERTS Thomas Henry MM Sjt 43800 RFA
ROBERTS Thomas James MM Pte 12800 7th Somerset Light Infantry
ROBERTS Thomas M. MM+Bar Sjt 486308 468 Fd Coy Royal Engineers
ROBERTS Thomas R. MM L/Cpl 22426 11th Hussars
ROBERTS Trevor MM Pte 201256 Royal Welsh Fusiliers
ROBERTS W.H.S. MM Pte 439270 RAMC
ROBERTS Walter MM Cpl 350096 3 Fd Amb RAMC
ROBERTS Walter MM Sjt Saddler 705704 C/211 Bde RFA
ROBERTS Walter MM Sjt 20229 Machine Gun Corps
ROBERTS Walter G. MM Sjt 71891 RFA
ROBERTS Walter G.C. MM Pte 54079 5th South Lancashire Regt
ROBERTS Walter R. MM Pte 238051 11th Oxf & Bucks Light Infantry
ROBERTS Walter R. MM L/Cpl 8636 Royal West Kent Regt
ROBERTS Wilfred J. MM Pte 40884 18th Lancashire Fusiliers
ROBERTS William MM Pte 266806 26th Royal Welsh Fusiliers
ROBERTS William MM 2nd Cpl 81581 200 Fd Coy Royal Engineers
ROBERTS William MM CSM 974 Army Cyclist Corps
ROBERTS William MM Cpl 267682 1/6th Liverpool Regt
ROBERTS William "DCM,MM" Pte 23404 Yorkshire Regt
ROBERTS William MM Pte 3413 1/6th North Staffordshire Regt
ROBERTS William MM Pte 12188 Coldstream Guards
ROBERTS William MM Sjt 70297 36 Bde RFA
ROBERTS William MM Cpl 7003 1st Liverpool Regt
ROBERTS William MM Pte 241160 5th Devonshire Regt
ROBERTS William MM Gnr 19505 B/186 Bde RFA
ROBERTS William MM Gnr 76209 Machine Gun Corps(Heavy Branch)
ROBERTS William MM Pte R/19763 King's Royal Rifle Corps
ROBERTS William MM+Bar Sjt 14837 12th Liverpool Regt
ROBERTS William MM Spr 198144 Royal Engineers
ROBERTS William Albert MM Cpl 11508 A/86 Bde RFA DOW 1.11.17.
ROBERTS William E. MM Sjt 591016 1/18th London Regt
ROBERTS William Edward MM Sjt 3/8498 2nd Yorkshire Regt
ROBERTS William H. MM Pte 42483 Suffolk Regt
ROBERTS William H. MM Pte 12141 Royal Irish Fusiliers
ROBERTS William Henry MM Sjt 191 RGA
ROBERTS William J. MM Pte 10417 2nd Oxf & Bucks Light Infantry
ROBERTS William J. MM L/Cpl 203633 Royal Welsh Fusiliers
ROBERTS William J. MM Pte 13984 8th Shropshire Light Infantry
ROBERTS William L. MM Pte 200603 Royal Welsh Fusiliers
ROBERTS William P. MM Gnr 159653 RFA
ROBERTS William Robert MM Gnr 310118 RGA
ROBERTS William S. MM L/Bdr Sig 915987 A/250 Bde RFA
ROBERTS William S. MM+Bar Sjt 36963 1st Gloucestershire Regt
ROBERTS Willie MM+Bar Sjt 11575 9th West Riding Regt
ROBERTSHAW Arthur MM Dvr 25514 A/152 Bde RFA
ROBERTSHAW Fred MM L/Cpl 480118 154 Fd Coy Royal Engineers
ROBERTSHAW James W. MM Sjt 83966 Royal Engineers
ROBERTSHAW Percy MM Pte 205560 West Riding Regt
ROBERTS-MORGAN D. "DCM,MM" Sjt 9358 Royal Welsh Fusiliers
ROBERTSON A. MM Gnr 810704 A/232 Bde RFA
ROBERTSON A. MM QMS Farrier 394 RFA
ROBERTSON Adam MM Pte 40044 1/4th Gordon Highlanders
ROBERTSON Albert E. MM Sjt 493653 13th London Regt
ROBERTSON Alderman H. MM+Bar L/Sjt 24770 Grenadier Guards
ROBERTSON Alexander MM Sjt M2/132301 59 Div MT Coy Army Service Corps
ROBERTSON Alexander MM Sjt 18467 Royal Munster Fusiliers
ROBERTSON Alexander MM Pte 9171 2nd Royal Scots
ROBERTSON Alexander MM Pte 18731 Royal Highlanders
ROBERTSON Alexander MM Cpl 265218 Royal Highlanders
ROBERTSON Alexander MM Sjt 30729 C/155 Bde RFA KIA 30.10.17.
ROBERTSON Alexander MM Spr 93874 41 Div Sig Coy Royal Engineers
ROBERTSON Alexander MM Cpl 46474 40 Div Ammn Col RFA
ROBERTSON Alexander D. MM L/Cpl 514000 14th London Regt
ROBERTSON Alexander K. MM Sjt 20666 Royal Scots
ROBERTSON Alfred T. MM Cpl 3163 2nd Dragoons
ROBERTSON Allen H. MM Sjt 202582 York & Lancaster Regt
ROBERTSON Andrew MM Pte 201554 1/5th Highland Light Infantry
ROBERTSON Andrew MM Cpl 43719 Royal Scots
ROBERTSON Andrew G. MM Cpl 220299 Cameron Highlanders
ROBERTSON Bertie Harry Chalmers "DCM,MM" Sjt 15262 RFA
ROBERTSON Cecil Duncan MM Sjt 5180 Seaforth Highlanders
ROBERTSON Charles MM Pte 53443 RAMC
ROBERTSON Charles MM Bdr 26990 35 Heavy Bty RGA
ROBERTSON Charles B. MM Pte 18409 1/7th Royal Highlanders
ROBERTSON Charles Graham "VC,MM" L/Cpl 58769 10th Royal Fusiliers
ROBERTSON Daniel "MM,MID" Pte 18643 12th Highland Light Infantry
ROBERTSON David MM Spr 1004 Royal Engineers
ROBERTSON David MM Dvr 69632 38 Bde Ammn Col RFA

ROBERTSON David MM Pte 10727 Scots Guards
ROBERTSON David James MM Sjt 18219 22 Fd Amb RAMC DOW 3.11.18.
ROBERTSON Donald MM Pte 62983 10th Lancashire Fusiliers
ROBERTSON Donald MM L/Cpl 8974 Cameron Highlanders
ROBERTSON Donald Oscar Lance MM Sjt 4422 9th East Surrey Regt
ROBERTSON Douglas MM Sjt 511439 1/14th London Regt
ROBERTSON Duncan "MM,MSM" Sjt 1013 2nd Gordon Highlanders
ROBERTSON E. MM Cpl 230778 10th Shropshire Light Infantry
ROBERTSON Edward A. MM Pte 17171 1st Royal Scots
ROBERTSON Edward Marston MM L/Cpl 6413 2nd East Lancashire Regt KIA 2.4.18.
ROBERTSON Finlay MM Sjt 43978 1st Royal Irish Rifles
ROBERTSON Frederick MM L/Cpl 14721 1st Scots Guards
ROBERTSON Frederick Charles MM Sjt R/8036 King's Royal Rifle Corps
ROBERTSON Frederick G. MM Gnr 71677 RGA
ROBERTSON George MM Cpl 251847 1/6th Arg & Suth Highlanders
ROBERTSON George MM Cpl 7718 RFA
ROBERTSON George MM Pte 9564 Scots Guards
ROBERTSON George MM L/Cpl 8659 Arg & Suth Highlanders
ROBERTSON George MM Pte 200866 Gordon Highlanders
ROBERTSON George A. MM Cpl 31814 Liverpool Regt
ROBERTSON George H. MM L/Cpl 344178 55 Fd Coy Royal Engineers
ROBERTSON Harold MM Pte 243916 1/5th North Lancashire Regt
ROBERTSON Henry N. MM L/Cpl 14528 5th Cameron Highlanders
ROBERTSON Henry Thomas MM Pte 36762 4th Royal Fusiliers KIA 21.3.18.
ROBERTSON Hugh MM L/Cpl 2500 10th Arg & Suth Highlanders
ROBERTSON J. "DCM,MM" Sjt 9428 Highland Light Infantry
ROBERTSON J. MM Sjt 7029 London Regt
ROBERTSON J. "MM,MSM" Sjt 2797 1st Royal Highlanders
ROBERTSON James MM Sjt 40505 16th Highland Light Infantry
ROBERTSON James MM Pte 40696 King's Own Scottish Borderers
ROBERTSON James MM Sjt 01144 Army Ordnance Corps
ROBERTSON James MM Cpl 4033 1st Royal Highlanders
ROBERTSON James MM Pte 5642 18th Highland Light Infantry
ROBERTSON James MM Pte 6755 Seaforth Highlanders
ROBERTSON James Alexander MM L/Cpl 31021 2nd Royal Scots KIA 26.9.17.
ROBERTSON James C. MM Pnr 50104 Royal Engineers
ROBERTSON James F. MM Pnr 130244 Royal Engineers
ROBERTSON James H. MM Pte 133270 31st Bn Machine Gun Corps
ROBERTSON James M.(or W). MM Pte 16328 19th Hussars
ROBERTSON James William MM Bdr 74676 199 Siege Bty RGA
ROBERTSON John MM Pte 43650 9th Scottish Rifles
ROBERTSON John MM Pte 10130 1/4th Gordon Highlanders DOW 6.11.18.
ROBERTSON John MM Dvr 175381 A/256 Bde RFA
ROBERTSON John MM Pte 201691 1/7th Gordon Highlanders
ROBERTSON John MM L/Cpl 276409 1/7th Arg & Suth Highlanders
ROBERTSON John MM Pte 33949 13th Yorkshire Regt
ROBERTSON John MM Sjt 6392 11th Royal Scots
ROBERTSON John MM Cpl 8404 1st Cameron Highlanders DOW 4.9.16.
ROBERTSON John MM Pte 8696 1st Scots Guards KIA 15.9.16.
ROBERTSON John MM L/Cpl 22230 Scottish Rifles
ROBERTSON John MM Pte 242169 1/4th Gordon Highlanders
ROBERTSON John MM Sjt 655558 RFA
ROBERTSON John MM Pte 81587 RAMC
ROBERTSON John L. MM Pte 266675 Royal Highlanders
ROBERTSON John McD. MM CQMS 265594 1/6th Royal Highlanders
ROBERTSON John R. MM Cpl 141714 290 Siege Bty RGA
ROBERTSON John R. "DCM,MM" Sjt 13672 19th Durham Light Infantry
ROBERTSON John R.F. "DCM,MM+Bar" Sjt 14854 2nd Bedfordshire Regt
ROBERTSON John S. MM Cpl M2/114780 Army Service Corps
ROBERTSON John W. MM CSM 11701 9th West Yorkshire Regt
ROBERTSON Joseph MM Pte 240105 1/5th South Lancashire Regt
ROBERTSON Keith D. MM L/Cpl 85252 1st Bn Machine Gun Corps
ROBERTSON Leonard G. MM Cpl 29922 Highland Light Infantry
ROBERTSON Michael MM Sjt 7050 9th Seaforth Highlanders KIA 11.4.18.

ROBERTSON Neil MM Spr 47330 Royal Engineers
ROBERTSON Oliver Thomas Cunningham MM Gnr 159110 250 Siege Bty RGA
ROBERTSON P. MM L/Cpl 28057 17th Highland Light Infantry
ROBERTSON Peter "DCM,MM,MSM" RQMS 3953 8th Royal Highlanders
ROBERTSON Peter MM Pte 14562 1st Gordon Highlanders DOW 30.5.18.
ROBERTSON R. MM Pte 7103 14th Arg & Suth Highlanders
ROBERTSON R. MM Pte 5547 Gordon Highlanders
ROBERTSON R. MM Pte 3844 Gordon Highlanders
ROBERTSON R.H. MM Spr 45001 Royal Engineers
ROBERTSON Ralph MM Cpl 57953 36 Div Sig Coy Royal Engineers
ROBERTSON Rees MM Sjt 293777 141 Hy Bty RGA
ROBERTSON Robert MM Pte 6224 1st Gordon Highlanders
ROBERTSON Robert MM Sjt 8769 1st Cameron Highlanders
ROBERTSON Robert MM Pte 9315 8th Royal Highlanders KIA 3.5.17.
ROBERTSON Robert MM Pte 1855 3 12th Highland Light Infantry
ROBERTSON Robert MM L/Cpl 5411 Seaforth Highlanders
ROBERTSON Robert D. MM Pte 56439 5/6th Scottish Rifles
ROBERTSON Robert D. MM Gnr 94287 RGA
ROBERTSON Robert M. MM L/Cpl 28462 5/6th Scottish Rifles
ROBERTSON Ronald MM Pte 278585 1/7th Arg & Suth Highlanders
ROBERTSON S. MM Dvr 39295 RFA
ROBERTSON Samuel MM Cpl 13772 15th Highland Light Infantry KIA 18.11.16.
ROBERTSON Theophilus MM L/Cpl 7053 11th Lancashire Fusiliers KIA 23.3.18.
ROBERTSON Thomas MM CQMS 265072 1/6th Royal Highlanders
ROBERTSON Thomas MM L/Cpl 12471 2nd Royal Scots Fusiliers
ROBERTSON Thomas "DCM,MM" CSM 13344 Royal Scots
ROBERTSON Thomas MM Cpl 64 RAMC
ROBERTSON Thomas MM Pte 17735 13th Royal Scots KIA 19.2.18.
ROBERTSON W.J. "DCM,MM" L/Cpl P/888 Military Mounted Police
ROBERTSON William MM Pte 202613 4/5th Royal Highlanders
ROBERTSON William MM Cpl 66181 10th Royal Fusiliers
ROBERTSON William MM Pte 201687 1/4th Gordon Highlanders KIA 11.4.18.
ROBERTSON William MM Spr 412824 Royal Engineers
ROBERTSON William MM Sjt 29880 Royal Warwickshire Regt
ROBERTSON William MM L/Cpl 292794 4/5th Royal Highlanders
ROBERTSON William MM Pte 6677 8/10th Gordon Highlanders
ROBERTSON William MM Pte 16389 10th Royal West Kent Regt KIA 2.6.18.
ROBERTSON William MM+Bar Pte 5360 Royal Highlanders
ROBERTSON William MM Sjt 9171 2nd Scottish Rifles
ROBERTSON William MM Pte 201100 Gordon Highlanders
ROBERTSON William MM Sjt 40044 Royal Highlanders
ROBERTSON William MM Pte 351194 1/9th Royal Scots
ROBERTSON William John "DCM,MM" Sjt 11839 1st Cameron Highlanders
ROBERTSON William M. MM Pte M2/132304 Army Service Corps
ROBERTSON or ROBINSON E. MM RQMS 2102 1st Royal Highlanders
ROBESON Charles MM Spr 164754 Royal Engineers
ROBESON Leslie A. MM Pte 371653 8th London Regt
ROBESON Rupert MM Cpl PS/1346 16th Middlesex Regt
ROBIE John MM L/Sjt 265712 1/6th Gordon Highlanders
ROBIN Thomas R. MM Pte 841 1st Royal Guernsey LI
ROBINS Albert MM Pte 201951 1/5th South Staffordshire Regt KIA 28.6.17.
ROBINS Arthur MM Sjt 12812 89 Fd Coy Royal Engineers KIA 14.10.18.
ROBINS Edgar or Edward MM Pte 15996 1/4th Royal Berkshire Regt
ROBINS Edward MM Pte 19776 1/5th York & Lancaster Regt DOW 17.4.18.
ROBINS Edward C. MM Pte 123701 62nd Bn Machine Gun Corps
ROBINS Ernest MM L/Cpl 59692 70 Fd Coy Royal Engineers
ROBINS Ernest E. MM Cpl 3901 Machine Gun Corps
ROBINS George MM Pte 15724 Dorsetshire Regt
ROBINS George W. MM Sjt 570209 1/17th London Regt
ROBINS Herbert MM Pte 14917 2nd Coldstream Guards
ROBINS James B. MM+Bar L/Cpl 10476 5th Dorsetshire Regt
ROBINS John J. MM Cpl 51221 42 Bde RFA
ROBINS John W. MM Spr 158762 Royal Engineers
ROBINS Joseph MM Pte 32518 1st East Surrey Regt

ROBINS Thomas MM+Bar Sjt 388063 RAMC
ROBINS Walter MM Pte 18065 1st Lancashire Fusiliers
ROBINSHAW Tom MM L/Cpl 15005 9th West Riding Regt
ROBINSON A. MM Dvr T4/250886 Army Service Corps
ROBINSON A.V. MM Pte 266776 West Riding Regt
ROBINSON Abraham J. MM Pte 162 38th Royal Fusiliers
ROBINSON Adam MM CSM 30715 32nd Bn Machine Gun Corps
ROBINSON Albert MM Pte 720800 24th London Regt
ROBINSON Albert MM L/Cpl 44078 7th Lincolnshire Regt
ROBINSON Albert F.(or J.) "DCM,MM" Sjt 8759 1st Royal West Kent Regt
ROBINSON Albert Henry MM Dvr 55134 RFA
ROBINSON Albert Ingham MM Sjt 240954 2/6th West Yorkshire Regt KIA 20.11.17.
ROBINSON Albert V.H. MM L/Cpl 106662 40 Div Sig Coy Royal Engineers DOW 6.5.17.
ROBINSON Albert William MM Bdr 60516 B/112 Bde RFA
ROBINSON Alexander MM Sjt 240961 2/4th Yorkshire Light Infantry KIA 21.7.18.
ROBINSON Alexander MM Sjt 1467 1/7th Durham Light Infantry
ROBINSON Alfred MM Pte 21034 12th West Yorkshire Regt KIA 14.7.16.
ROBINSON Alfred MM Pte 8171 Border Regt
ROBINSON Alfred H. MM Pte 85308 3rd London Regt
ROBINSON Alfred Henry MM L/Cpl 12001 6th Bedfordshire Regt KIA 10.7.16.
ROBINSON Alfred Henry "MM,MID" Bdr 872 233 Bde RFA
ROBINSON Allen MM Cpl 20072 Machine Gun Corps
ROBINSON Andrew MM Pte 9203 Liverpool Regt
ROBINSON Archibald S. MM Pte 51251 4th Bedfordshire Regt
ROBINSON Archibald Stuart Clayton MM Pte 2805 1/24th London Regt
ROBINSON Archie MM Pte 5/4741 1st King's Royal Rifle Corps
ROBINSON Arthur MM L/Cpl 57888 1st West Yorkshire Regt
ROBINSON Arthur MM Pte 26765 6th Bedfordshire Regt
ROBINSON Arthur MM Gnr 780141 RFA
ROBINSON Arthur MM Sjt 805069 A/231 Bde RFA
ROBINSON Arthur MM Pte 22224 Yorkshire Light Infantry
ROBINSON Arthur MM+Bar Pte 22/734 Durham Light Infantry
ROBINSON Arthur MM Pte 283691 4th London Regt
ROBINSON Arthur E. MM Pte 15791 4th Worcestershire Regt
ROBINSON Arthur F. MM+Bar S/Sjt Fitter 174815 RGA
ROBINSON Arthur H. MM Pte 266562 Seaforth Highlanders
ROBINSON Arthur S.O. MM Cpl 31290 RAMC
ROBINSON Arthur W.F. MM Pte 27138 1st Shropshire Light Infantry
ROBINSON Asa MM Bdr 85936 66 Siege Bty RGA
ROBINSON B. MM Sjt 22831 RGA
ROBINSON Ben B. "MM,MSM" Cpl 376223 1/10th Manchester Regt
ROBINSON Benjamin MM Pte 235514 6th Leicestershire Regt
ROBINSON Benjamin MM Pte 10559 6th Lincolnshire Regt
ROBINSON Benjamin MM L/Cpl R/7250 King's Royal Rifle Corps
ROBINSON Bertram Albert MM Gnr 48649 32 Siege Bty RGA KIA 11.5.17.
ROBINSON Brooke MM L/Cpl 40571 1st Norfolk Regt
ROBINSON Charles "DCM,MM" Sjt 15739 11th Notts & Derby Regt
ROBINSON Charles MM Spr 79103 Royal Engineers
ROBINSON Charles "MM+Bar,MID" Sjt 99881 C/315 Bde RFA
ROBINSON Charles "MM,MSM" Cpl 9810 1st Royal Irish Fusiliers
ROBINSON Charles MM Pte 20615 Suffolk Regt
ROBINSON Charles MM Pte 281773 Lancashire Fusiliers
ROBINSON Charles A. MM Cpl 13980 2nd Grenadier Guards
ROBINSON Charles Duncan MM Sjt 83504 210 Siege Bty RGA
ROBINSON Charles L. MM Cpl 630925 20th London Regt
ROBINSON Charlotte Lillian Annie "MM,ARRC" Sister F QAIMNS
ROBINSON Christopher J. MM Gnr 228191 RFA
ROBINSON Christopher Richard MM Pte 42865 3rd Worcestershire Regt KIA 10.4.18.
ROBINSON Clarence William MM Gnr 22655 C/82 Bde RFA
ROBINSON Cyril MM Sjt 17985 6th Northamptonshire Regt
ROBINSON Cyril G. MM Pte 240284 Lincolnshire Regt
ROBINSON Cyril W. MM Pte 861115 33rd London Regt
ROBINSON David MM Sjt 1944 1/5th North Lancashire Regt
ROBINSON Dick MM Sjt 34047 North Lancashire Regt
ROBINSON Edward MM L/Cpl 19814 21st Manchester Regt
ROBINSON Edward MM Cpl 8488 Yorkshire Regt
ROBINSON Edward D. MM L/Cpl 143113 222 Fd Coy Royal Engineers
ROBINSON Edward J. MM Pte 18082 6th Royal West Surrey Regt
ROBINSON Edward J. MM Sjt 43294 1/1st Cambridgeshire Regt
ROBINSON Edwin MM Pte 14785 8th Border Regt
ROBINSON Ernest MM Cpl 77513 RFA
ROBINSON Ernest MM Pte 33489 8th Royal Lancaster Regt
ROBINSON Ernest MM Cpl 23298 14th Liverpool Regt
ROBINSON Ernest MM Cpl 643 12th East Yorkshire Regt
ROBINSON Ernest MM Pte 12536 11th Hampshire Regt
ROBINSON Ernest George MM Pte 200229 1/4th Royal Lancaster Regt KIA 20.11.17.
ROBINSON Ernest W. MM Gnr 705316 RFA
ROBINSON F.W. MM L/Cpl 13884 Army Cyclist Corps
ROBINSON Frank MM Sjt 16945 1st Bn Machine Gun Corps
ROBINSON Frank MM Dvr 28071 RFA
ROBINSON Frank MM Sjt 41893 Royal Engineers
ROBINSON Frank "MM+Bar,CG(It)" Sjt 2029 23 Fd Amb RAMC
ROBINSON Frank MM Sjt 50960 294 Siege Bty RGA
ROBINSON Frank MM Pte 22497 Welsh Regt
ROBINSON Frank H. MM Pte 2329 1/5th North Lancashire Regt
ROBINSON Frank P. MM Pte 74830 RAMC
ROBINSON Frank W. MM Dvr 188209 RFA
ROBINSON Fred MM Pte 305144 1/8th Lancashire Fusiliers KIA 25.3.18.
ROBINSON Fred MM Pte 11612 Yorkshire Regt
ROBINSON Fred MM Pnr 194914 11 Div Sig Coy Royal Engineers
ROBINSON Fred MM L/Cpl 11838 York & Lancaster Regt
ROBINSON Fred MM+Bar Cpl C/12765 King's Royal Rifle Corps
ROBINSON Frederick MM Pte 5654 8th East Surrey Regt
ROBINSON Frederick MM Pte 16144 5th Northamptonshire Regt
ROBINSON Frederick MM Pte 40925 2nd Suffolk Regt KIA 28.3.18.
ROBINSON Frederick MM Cpl 1225 Royal Engineers
ROBINSON Frederick MM Sjt 5389 2nd Bedfordshire Regt
ROBINSON Frederick MM Sjt B/1439 Rifle Brigade
ROBINSON Frederick MM Dvr 66979 D/110 Bde RFA
ROBINSON Frederick F. "MM,MSM" Sjt 25945 55 Fd Coy Royal Engineers
ROBINSON Frederick John MM Pte 565071 16th London Regt KIA 4.11.18.
ROBINSON Frederick L. MM Sjt 65797 85 Bty 11 Bde RFA
ROBINSON Frederick S. MM Sjt 300042 1/5th London Regt
ROBINSON Frederick T. MM L/Cpl 85941 Royal Engineers
ROBINSON Frederick W. MM Sjt DM2/162914 'K' Siege Park Army Service Corps
ROBINSON Frederick W. MM L/Cpl 14677 4th Coldstream Guards
ROBINSON Frederick W.J. MM Dmr 200905 1/4th Royal Berkshire Regt
ROBINSON G. MM Pte 20051 1st Essex Regt
ROBINSON George MM Pte 8204 11th Royal Fusiliers
ROBINSON George MM Pte 295827 12th Royal Scots Fusiliers
ROBINSON George MM Pte 201714 Worcestershire Regt
ROBINSON George MM Sjt 17093 7/8th King's Own Scottish Borderers
ROBINSON George MM Pte 2555 1st Leicestershire Regt
ROBINSON George MM Sjt 18238 RGA
ROBINSON George MM Pte 25649 Lancashire Fusiliers
ROBINSON George E. MM Pte 10170 1st Royal West Surrey Regt
ROBINSON George G. MM+Bar Cpl 241688 5th West Riding Regt
ROBINSON George J. MM Pte 124374 Machine Gun Corps
ROBINSON George T. MM Cpl 681421 35 Div Ammn Col RFA
ROBINSON George W. MM Pte 12661 5th Cameron Highlanders
ROBINSON George William MM Cpl 19963 8th Bedfordshire Regt KIA 25.9.16.
ROBINSON Gilbert MM L/Cpl 9725 1st Bedfordshire Regt
ROBINSON H. MM Sjt 435244 RAMC
ROBINSON H. MM Pte 41434 Lincolnshire Regt
ROBINSON H.E.B. MM Bdr 409 RGA
ROBINSON Harold MM L/Cpl 44546 Royal Engineers
ROBINSON Harold MM Pte 13657 7th Worcestershire Regt
ROBINSON Harold James MM Pte 403103 RAMC
ROBINSON Harry MM Pte 15062 9th West Riding Regt KIA 7.7.16.
ROBINSON Harry MM+Bar L/Cpl 235711 4th West Riding Regt
ROBINSON Harry MM Sjt 200087 5th Lancashire Fusiliers
ROBINSON Harry MM Pte 16257 6/7th Royal Scots Fusiliers
ROBINSON Harry Charles Edwin MM Pte 34743 2nd Essex Regt KIA 28.3.18.
ROBINSON Henry MM Spr 42539 Royal Engineers
ROBINSON Henry MM Pte 64474 RAMC
ROBINSON Henry MM+Bar Sjt 200017 1/4th Yorkshire Regt
ROBINSON Henry MM Sjt 106150 Royal Engineers
ROBINSON Herbert MM Spr 160683 Royal Engineers
ROBINSON Herbert MM Pte 12678 8th Cheshire Regt
ROBINSON Herbert MM Sjt 17879 12th Highland Light Infantry
ROBINSON Herbert MM Gnr 44285 291 Siege Bty RGA

ROBINSON Herbert William MM Sjt 15427 2nd Royal Fusiliers DOW 4.6.18.
ROBINSON Horace MM Sjt 200116 6th Northamptonshire Regt
ROBINSON Hubert E. MM Dvr 33527 D/50 Bde RFA
ROBINSON Hugh MM Pte 23325 Royal Inniskilling Fusiliers
ROBINSON J. MM Pte 9518 18th Lancashire Fusiliers "See DARWELL, Roger, L/Bdr 293458 RGA"
ROBINSON J.C. MM L/Cpl 52744 Cheshire Regt
ROBINSON J.R. MM Pte 354271 3 Fd Amb RAMC
ROBINSON Jack MM Sjt 8842 2nd Welsh Regt
ROBINSON Jack Courtney MM Sjt 96538 C/311 Bde RFA
ROBINSON James MM Cpl 13281 12th Cheshire Regt
ROBINSON James MM Pte 48959 17th Lancashire Fusiliers
ROBINSON James MM Gnr 326436 126 Siege Bty RGA
ROBINSON James MM Sjt 235830 9th West Yorkshire Regt
ROBINSON James MM L/Cpl 81840 520 Fd Coy Royal Engineers
ROBINSON James MM Gnr 230234 X/9 Med TM Bty RFA
ROBINSON James MM L/Cpl 23447 13th Durham Light Infantry
ROBINSON James MM Sjt 8686 2nd West Yorkshire Regt
ROBINSON James "MM,MID" Bdr 16538 RFA
ROBINSON James MM Sjt R/7145 King's Royal Rifle Corps
ROBINSON James MM Sjt 240791 2/5th York & Lancaster Regt KIA 20.11.17.
ROBINSON James MM Gnr 34428 RFA
ROBINSON James MM Sjt 35608 Duke of Cornwall's LI
ROBINSON James MM Pte 18870 2nd Royal Dublin Fusiliers
ROBINSON James A. MM Pte 13849 2nd Worcestershire Regt
ROBINSON James F. MM Sjt 200806 Northamptonshire Regt
ROBINSON James J. MM Gnr 19368 D/87 Bde RFA
ROBINSON James L. MM 2nd Cpl 83480 Royal Engineers
ROBINSON James Robert MM Sjt 8467 2nd Royal Irish Regt
ROBINSON James William MM Bdr 5520 RGA
ROBINSON Jeremiah E. MM L/Cpl 16069 9th Leicestershire Regt
ROBINSON Job MM Pte 1539 1/5th York & Lancaster Regt
ROBINSON John MM Pte 29474 3rd Grenadier Guards
ROBINSON John MM Pte 9089 8th Seaforth Highlanders
ROBINSON John MM Pte 200676 1/4th Cheshire Regt Died 3.8.18.
ROBINSON John MM Dvr 63942 RFA
ROBINSON John MM L/Cpl 3707 5th Dragoon Guards
ROBINSON John MM CSM 9627 2nd Yorkshire Regt KIA 31.8.18.
ROBINSON John MM Pte 32186 South Staffordshire Regt
ROBINSON John MM+Bar Cpl 2903 165 Bde RFA
ROBINSON John MM Pte 10951 Royal Highlanders
ROBINSON John "DCM,MM" CSM 24905 Durham Light Infantry
ROBINSON John MM+Bar Pte 305291 1/7th West Riding Regt
ROBINSON John MM+Bar Pte 20483 1/8th Notts & Derby Regt DOW 18.10.18.
ROBINSON John MM L/Cpl 11380 East Lancashire Regt
ROBINSON John MM Pte 22865 Durham Light Infantry
ROBINSON John MM Pte 11107 2nd Cheshire Regt
ROBINSON John MM Pte 1528 Royal Warwickshire Regt
ROBINSON John MM L/Sjt 14473 6th East Yorkshire Regt
ROBINSON John MM L/Sjt 201390 North Lancashire Regt
ROBINSON John Arthur MM L/Cpl R/3222 King's Royal Rifle Corps
ROBINSON John E. "DCM,MM" CSM 14798 8th Lincolnshire Regt
ROBINSON John G. MM L/Cpl 44742 42nd Bn Machine Gun Corps
ROBINSON John G. MM L/Cpl 15387 Northumberland Fusiliers
ROBINSON John Makepeace MM+Bar L/Cpl 13986 14th Durham Light Infantry DOW 3.12.17.
ROBINSON John R. MM Pte 513520 14th London Regt
ROBINSON John Richard MM Sjt 16098 10th Scottish Rifles DOW 13.8.16.
ROBINSON John Thomas MM Pte 24931 9th Yorkshire Regt
ROBINSON John V. MM+Bar Pte 21965 5th South Lancashire Regt
ROBINSON "John W," MM L/Cpl 20219 Grenadier Guards
ROBINSON John W. MM Pte 4223 15th Bn Machine Gun Corps
ROBINSON John W. MM Gnr 785751 RFA
ROBINSON John William MM Pte 27659 Notts & Derby Regt
ROBINSON Jonathan MM Pte 24640 Durham Light Infantry
ROBINSON Joseph MM Pte 96073 13th Durham Light Infantry
ROBINSON Joseph MM Pte 32563 Cheshire Regt
ROBINSON Joseph MM Dvr 127420 17 Div Sig Coy Royal Engineers
ROBINSON Joseph MM Sjt 64089 2/1st Shropshire Bty RHA
ROBINSON Joseph MM Pte 709 2nd Lancashire Fusiliers
ROBINSON Joseph "MM,MID" Cpl 2440 46 Div Sig Coy Royal Engineers
ROBINSON Joseph MM Sjt 20375 15th Durham Light Infantry KIA 23.10.18.
ROBINSON Joseph MM L/Cpl 250071 1/6th Durham Light Infantry
ROBINSON Joseph MM Cpl 305314 1/8th Liverpool Regt
ROBINSON Joseph S. MM Cpl 42395 8th West Yorkshire Regt
ROBINSON Joseph William MM Pte 10738 3rd Coldstream Guards KIA 15.9.16.
ROBINSON Kenneth F. MM Gnr 102108 RGA
ROBINSON L. MM L/Cpl P/8093 Military Mounted Police
ROBINSON Lawrence Sydney MM Spr 429751 55 Div Sig Coy Royal Engineers att RFA
ROBINSON Leonard MM Sjt 201912 4th North Lancashire Regt
ROBINSON Leslie MM L/Cpl 200505 1/7th Worcestershire Regt
ROBINSON Leslie MM Pte 7387 1st King's Royal Rifle Corps KIA 23.8.18.
ROBINSON Lyonel M. MM Gnr 33533 RFA
ROBINSON Mark MM Gnr 131194 RFA
ROBINSON Matthew MM L/Cpl 36776 Royal Berkshire Regt
ROBINSON Michael MM Pte 205131 Lancashire Fusiliers
ROBINSON Nathaniel T. MM Cpl 44204 43 Bde RFA
ROBINSON Nicholas Albany Lunn MM Cpl M/338101 Army Service Corps
ROBINSON Percy MM Gnr 62278 88 Siege Bty RGA
ROBINSON Percy MM+Bar Sjt 444409 Royal Engineers
ROBINSON Percy E. MM Gnr 294222 RGA
ROBINSON Percy F.G. MM Pte 151658 104th Bn Machine Gun Corps
ROBINSON Perrin A. MM Gnr 92536 RFA
ROBINSON Peter MM Pte 251937 3rd London Regt
ROBINSON Preston MM Pte 3/7233 7th East Yorkshire Regt
ROBINSON R. MM Sjt 240354 Border Regt
ROBINSON Ralf Hubert MM Sjt 214 10th Royal Fusiliers DOW 23.8.17.
ROBINSON Richard C. MM Cpl 28756 Royal Engineers
ROBINSON Richard H. MM Cpl 30976 RAMC
ROBINSON Robert MM Sjt 19794 15th Cheshire Regt
ROBINSON Robert MM Cpl 11473 Leicestershire Regt
ROBINSON Robert E. MM Cpl 20086 Royal Irish Fusiliers
ROBINSON Robert George MM Gnr(SS) 127940 157 Siege Bty RGA
ROBINSON Robert William George MM Spr 65525 106 Fd Coy Royal Engineers
ROBINSON Samuel MM Pte 1094 13th Cheshire Regt
ROBINSON Samuel "DCM,MM" Sjt 11271 1st South Staffordshire Regt
ROBINSON Samuel MM Pte 45613 Royal Welsh Fusiliers
ROBINSON Samuel MM L/Cpl 60190 26th Royal Fusiliers DOW 1.11.18.
ROBINSON Samuel John Jim MM Pte 26311 1st Grenadier Guards
ROBINSON Stephen John MM Sjt 59583 100 Coy Labour Corps
ROBINSON Stewart J. MM Sjt 500334 Royal Engineers
ROBINSON Thomas MM CQMS 8360 2nd Lancashire Fusiliers
ROBINSON Thomas MM Spr 144868 185 Tunnelling Coy Royal Engineers
ROBINSON Thomas MM Pte 9977 10th Gloucestershire Regt KIA 23.7.16.
ROBINSON Thomas MM Cpl 13355 1st Border Regt
ROBINSON Thomas MM+Bar Sjt 15151 4th Royal Fusiliers
ROBINSON Thomas MM Pte 27922 6th Leicestershire Regt
ROBINSON Thomas MM Sjt 201123 1/4th Royal Lancaster Regt DOW 9.6.18.
ROBINSON Thomas MM Pte 573381 17th London Regt
ROBINSON Thomas MM Pte 307067 19th Lancashire Fusiliers DOW 13.10.18.
ROBINSON Thomas MM+Bar Sjt 40820 Royal Engineers
ROBINSON Thomas MM L/Cpl 68771 91 Fd Amb RAMC KIA 15.12.17.
ROBINSON Thomas MM Pte 16490 West Riding Regt
ROBINSON Thomas MM AM2 26967 Royal Flying Corps
ROBINSON Thomas MM Pte 34169 8th Yorkshire Regt
ROBINSON Thomas MM+Bar Pte 205677 5th Yorkshire Light Infantry
ROBINSON Thomas MM Cpl 437 10th Cheshire Regt KIA 16.4.18.
ROBINSON Thomas Hendry MM Cpl 54345 95 Siege Bty RGA
ROBINSON Thomas William MM Pte 26887 4th Grenadier Guards
ROBINSON Tom MM L/Sjt 305341 7th West Riding Regt
ROBINSON Tom MM Pte 241768 5th Yorkshire Light Infantry
ROBINSON W. MM Pte 305166 West Riding Regt
ROBINSON W. MM Pte 352312 RAMC
ROBINSON W.H. MM Pte 200270 Yorkshire Regt
ROBINSON Walter MM Sjt 240231 Yorkshire Light Infantry
ROBINSON Walter MM Sjt 265278 1/6th Cheshire Regt
ROBINSON Walter MM 2nd Cpl 459093 Royal Engineers

ROBINSON Watson MM Pte 1550 RAMC
ROBINSON Wilfred E. MM Bdr 53441 RFA
ROBINSON William MM Dvr 68746 A/124 Bde RFA
ROBINSON William MM+Bar Sjt 10412 2nd Royal Irish Regt
ROBINSON William MM Pte 67969 Machine Gun Corps
ROBINSON William "MM,CG(F)" L/Cpl 10/586 10th East Yorkshire Regt
ROBINSON William MM Cpl 43109 15 Bde RFA
ROBINSON William MM L/Cpl 240650 5th Lincolnshire Regt
ROBINSON William MM Pte 13071 9th Essex Regt DOW 1.7.18.
ROBINSON William "DCM,MM" Sjt 23903 Border Regt
ROBINSON William MM L/Cpl 24798 Cheshire Regt
ROBINSON William MM Pte 24049 Royal Irish Fusiliers
ROBINSON William MM L/Cpl 21389 Yorkshire Light Infantry
ROBINSON William MM Sjt 245620 Royal Engineers
ROBINSON William A. MM Pte 26889 1st Bedfordshire Regt
ROBINSON William A. MM Dvr 37920 RFA
ROBINSON William A. MM Sjt 2780 1/8th Durham Light Infantry
ROBINSON William A. MM Sjt 12852 8th Shropshire Light Infantry
ROBINSON William Alfred MM Pte 29716 1st Cheshire Regt KIA 28.6.17.
ROBINSON William C. MM Pte 68570 RAMC
ROBINSON William E. MM Cpl 61949 8th West Yorkshire Regt
ROBINSON William E. MM Pte 40906 Lincolnshire Regt
ROBINSON William Ezra Charles MM Cpl 96756 213 Siege Bty RGA
ROBINSON William G. MM+Bar L/Sjt 51862 8th Liverpool Regt
ROBINSON William H. MM Sjt 43521 Durham Light Infantry
ROBINSON William Henry MM Pte 45692 2/4th Hampshire Regt KIA 30.9.18.
ROBINSON Willie MM Pte 11118 8th West Riding Regt
ROBINSON Willie MM Sjt 561 RFA
ROBINSON or ROBERTSON E. MM RQMS 2102 1st Royal Highlanders
ROBISON Adam MM Pte 25318 Highland Light Infantry
ROBLEY Joseph MM L/Cpl 26886 Shropshire Light Infantry
ROBLEY Nevison MM Cpl 72373 Machine Gun Corps
ROBOTTOM Walter E. MM Pte 5545 15th Royal Warwickshire Regt
ROBSHAW Henry J. MM Pte 7876 99 Fd Amb RAMC
ROBSON A.H. MM+Bar Sjt 534039 4(London)Fd Amb RAMC
ROBSON Albert MM L/Cpl 266104 22nd Northumberland Fusiliers DOW 30.3.18.
ROBSON Albert E. MM Cpl 474598 Royal Engineers
ROBSON Alfred MM Dvr 20061 D/91 Bde RFA
ROBSON Alfred MM Cpl 54979 B/76 Bde RFA KIA 9.8.17.
ROBSON Amos MM CSM 6516 12/13th Northumberland Fusiliers KIA 27.5.18.
ROBSON Andrew MM Cpl 60910 172 Siege Bty RGA
ROBSON Andrew Gilbert MM Sjt 16387 15th Durham Light Infantry KIA 29.5.18.
ROBSON Anthony MM Pte 12433 10th Durham Light Infantry
ROBSON Arthur MM Cpl 220 RFA
ROBSON Barton MM Pte 200118 1/4th King's Own Scottish Borderers
ROBSON Charles MM Spr 98246 152 Fd Coy Royal Engineers
ROBSON Charles F. "DCM,MM" Spr 48459 23 Div Sig Coy Royal Engineers
ROBSON Christopher P. MM Pte 240660 Yorkshire Regt
ROBSON Daniel MM Cpl 22881 1st Royal Inniskilling Fusiliers
ROBSON David MM Gnr 59341 RGA
ROBSON Donald MM Cpl 73592 Signal Service Royal Engineers
ROBSON Edward Morgan MM Pte 29765 East Yorkshire Regt
ROBSON Eric S.N. MM Cpl 56507 18th King's Royal Rifle Corps
ROBSON Frederick F. MM Cpl 6772 2nd Coldstream Guards
ROBSON Frederick William MM Sjt 1670 RAMC DOW 22.8.18.
ROBSON George MM Pte 4413 Northumberland Fusiliers
ROBSON George MM Pte 13516 Royal Scots
ROBSON George MM Pte 25/1415 Northumberland Fusiliers
ROBSON George MM Pte 15/1300 15th West Yorkshire Regt KIA 23.11.16.
ROBSON George MM Sjt 200505 1/4th King's Own Scottish Borderers
ROBSON George F. MM Pte 8780 1 Fd Amb RAMC
ROBSON George H. MM Pte 325097 8th Lancashire Fusiliers
ROBSON Harold MM Bdr 75095 RGA
ROBSON Harold Harland MM Gnr 68007 71 Heavy Bty RGA
ROBSON Hugh G.B. "MM,MSM" Gnr Fitter 122536 B/92 Bde RFA
ROBSON J. MM Pte 388256 RAMC
ROBSON James MM Pte 14838 1st Scots Guards
ROBSON James MM L/Cpl 25/1233 Northumberland Fusiliers
ROBSON James H. MM Pte 12984 9th Northumberland Fusiliers
ROBSON John MM Spr 459073 447 Fd Coy Royal Engineers
ROBSON John MM Pte 55070 4th Royal Fusiliers
ROBSON John MM+Bar Pte 42455 Machine Gun Corps
ROBSON John MM Pte 19/752 Northumberland Fusiliers
ROBSON John MM Sjt 21147 Durham Light Infantry
ROBSON John Henry MM Pte 76008 'A' Bn Machine Gun Corps(Heavy Branch) Died 26.6.18.
ROBSON John J. MM Pnr 252689 Royal Engineers
ROBSON John W. MM L/Cpl 270928 1/1st Northumberland Yeo
ROBSON John W. MM Sjt 1925 1/8th Durham Light Infantry
ROBSON John William MM Pte 22147 15th Durham Light Infantry DOW 21.9.16.
ROBSON Joseph MM Pte 34238 70 Coy Machine Gun Corps DOW 3.9.18.
ROBSON Joseph J. "DCM,MM" Cpl Saddler 13318 D/88 Bde RFA
ROBSON Lionel R. MM Bdr 107315 RFA
ROBSON Matthew MM Sjt 200022 1/5th Durham Light Infantry
ROBSON Nicholas MM Sjt 202194 7th Royal Lancaster Regt
ROBSON Ridley MM+Bar Pte 200329 1/4th Northumberland Fusiliers
ROBSON Robert MM Sjt 84622 A/63 Bde RFA
ROBSON Robert MM Pte 22413 Royal Inniskilling Fusiliers
ROBSON Robert A. MM Gnr 38067 A/256 Bde RFA
ROBSON T. MM Pte 300581 8th Durham Light Infantry
ROBSON Thomas MM Spr 102651 176 Tunnelling Coy Royal Engineers
ROBSON Thomas MM Bdr 36181 RFA
ROBSON Thomas C. MM Sjt 251567 5/6th Royal Scots
ROBSON Thomas W. MM L/Cpl 325833 1/9th Durham Light Infantry
ROBSON W. MM Pte 42465 Royal Scots
ROBSON Walter J. MM Pte 2745 1/5th Gordon Highlanders
ROBSON Wilfred N.O. MM Gnr 127715 RFA
ROBSON William MM Pte 62889 18th Lancashire Fusiliers
ROBSON William "MM,CG(B)" 2nd Cpl 67976 121 Fd Coy Royal Engineers
ROBSON William MM Sjt 28254 15th Hampshire Regt
ROBSON William MM Sjt 20/896 Northumberland Fusiliers
ROBSON William MM Pte 7/12650 7th Border Regt KIA 10.8.16.
ROBSON William MM Pte 13358 11th Northumberland Fusiliers DOW 9.10.16.
ROBSON William H. MM Pte 200666 1/4th Northumberland Fusiliers
ROBSON William J. MM Cpl 67396 32nd Bn Machine Gun Corps
ROBUS E.H. MM Sjt 260264 1/6th Royal Warwickshire Regt
ROBY Alfred H. MM Pte 266253 11th Somerset Light Infantry
ROBY Samuel MM Pte 34066 4th North Lancashire Regt
ROCHE Alexander G. MM Pte 93493 18 Fd Amb RAMC
ROCHE Edward MM Sjt 2178 26 Heavy Bty RGA
ROCHE Frank MM Pte 35161 142 Fd Amb RAMC
ROCHE John MM Sjt 4304 Leinster Regt
ROCHE John MM Pte 29576 14th Highland Light Infantry
ROCHE John MM Pte 19537 RAMC
ROCHE John MM L/Cpl 8938 2nd East Lancashire Regt
ROCHE John F. MM Sjt 133063 45th Royal Fusiliers
ROCHE Patrick MM Pte 776 1st Irish Guards
ROCHE Robert MM Sjt 1455 7th Leinster Regt
ROCHE or ROACHE James MM Sjt 89435 RFA
ROCHELLE T.H. MM Pte 266102 Cheshire Regt
ROCHESTER James W. MM Spr 761 Royal Engineers
ROCHESTER James William MM Pte 44365 36 Coy Machine Gun Corps
ROCHESTER Robert MM Gnr 760763 3 Bde RFA
ROCHESTER Robert MM L/Sjt 18239 6th Northamptonshire Regt
ROCHFORD James "DCM,MM+Bar" Pte 5279 1st Irish Guards
ROCHFORD Robert "MM,MID" Pte 11285 4th Hussars
ROCHFORD Thomas Alfred J. MM Pte 27094 12th East Surrey Regt
ROCK Edward D. MM Pte 25516 3rd Grenadier Guards
ROCK Henry J. MM Cpl 2266 Middlesex Regt
ROCK James L. MM Pte 39890 1/8th Worcestershire Regt
ROCK Thomas W. MM Sjt 263 RGA
ROCK William MM Pte 538099 RAMC
ROCKALL Daniel MM L/Sjt 20197 2nd Royal Munster Fusiliers KIA 14.10.18.
ROCKCLIFFE William Henry MM L/Cpl 65369 Machine Gun Corps
ROCKETT C. MM Pte 15282 Machine Gun Corps
ROCKETT F. MM Pte 11113 7th East Yorkshire Regt
ROCKLEY Arthur MM Pte 15507 2nd Grenadier Guards
ROCKLEY George MM+Bar Pte 14864 2nd Devonshire Regt

ROCKLIFFE Richard Clarke MM Gnr 11803 HQ 156 Bde RFA
RODD Neville James MM Cpl 664 216 Bde RFA
RODDAM Joseph MM Sjt 20387 14th Northumberland Fusiliers
RODDEN William MM Pte 10265 2nd Scottish Rifles
RODDIS Arthur MM Pte 15884 8th Royal Lancaster Regt
RODDIS George MM Sjt 23067 48th Bn Machine Gun Corps
RODDY Frank MM Sjt 57597 2/4th York & Lancaster Regt KIA 4.11.18.
RODDY Patrick W. MM L/Cpl 179313 204 Fd Coy Royal Engineers
RODDY Thomas MM Pte 36700 East Lancashire Regt
RODDY William MM Dvr 96282 D/51 Bde RFA
RODEN Albert MM Pte 307597 Royal Warwickshire Regt
RODEN Arthur C. MM Cpl 236301 1/1st Herefordshire Regt
RODEN Harry H. MM Pte 25551 4th Grenadier Guards
RODEN Richard MM Pte 16671 Royal Lancaster Regt
RODEN Walter Joseph MM Spr 152030 Signal Service Royal Engineers
RODER John H. MM L/Cpl 5363 Rifle Brigade
RODERICK William MM Pte 35161 Labour Corps
RODERICK Wyndham MM Gnr 105214 85 Bty 11 Bde RFA
RODGER Amery G.B. MM Bdr 645622 RFA
RODGER David Scott MM Pte 31109 5th Cameron Highlanders
RODGER Douglas MM Pte 345075 14th Royal Highlanders
RODGER George MM Pte 13944 1st Gordon Highlanders
RODGER James MM Pte 23796 King's Own Scottish Borderers
RODGER John MM Pte 14948 16th Highland Light Infantry DOW 12.7.16.
RODGER John MM Pte 51687 11th Royal Scots
RODGER John "MM,MID" Pte T4/062048 Army Service Corps
RODGER Robert W. MM L/Cpl 36818 Royal Engineers
RODGER Thomas A. MM Sjt 116780 Labour Corps
RODGER William MM L/Cpl 1756 Arg & Suth Highlanders
RODGER William MM Pte 105448 Machine Gun Corps(Cavalry)
RODGER William J. MM 2nd Cpl 48014 14 Div Sig Coy Royal Engineers
RODGER or RODGERS James MM Pte 7367 Arg & Suth Highlanders
RODGERS Albert MM Pte 58907 Machine Gun Corps
RODGERS Charles MM L/Cpl 150706 Dorsetshire Regt
RODGERS Edward "MM,MID" Cpl 2407 1/1st Glasgow Yeomanry
RODGERS Ernest "MM,MID" Sjt 1374 RFA
RODGERS Ernest MM Pte 15828 11th Northumberland Fusiliers
RODGERS F. MM Pte 7267 King's Royal Rifle Corps
RODGERS Frank MM Pte 15914 2nd Lincolnshire Regt
RODGERS Frederick D. MM+Bar Bdr 67064 15 Bde RFA
RODGERS George MM Pte 9139 9th York & Lancaster Regt "KIA 1.7.16,"
RODGERS George MM Gnr 52349 RGA
RODGERS Henry MM Cpl 253913 Royal Engineers
RODGERS Herbert MM Cpl 57511 9th Bn Machine Gun Corps
RODGERS Horace MM Pte 55580 11th Northumberland Fusiliers KIA 27.10.18.
RODGERS James MM Pte 5484 18th Highland Light Infantry KIA 25.3.18.
RODGERS James MM Pte 20353 9th Royal Irish Fusiliers
RODGERS John MM Pte 24135 4th West Riding Regt
RODGERS John A. MM Cpl(MCDR) 54213 Royal Engineers
RODGERS Patrick MM Sjt 60816 Machine Gun Corps
RODGERS Philip H. MM+Bar Cpl 19243 10th Manchester Regt
RODGERS Richard A. MM Pte 37977 RAMC
RODGERS Sidney E.J. MM Cpl 490677 13th London Regt
RODGERS Thomas F. MM Pte 92268 9th Notts & Derby Regt
RODGERS or ROGERS Thomas MM L/Cpl 4128 10th Hussars
RODLEY David MM Cpl 275177 Durham Light Infantry
RODMAN Arthur MM L/Sjt 7626 1/7th Royal Highlanders DOW 25.3.18.
RODMAN Harry R.M. "DCM,MM" S/Sjt 15289 RAMC
RODNEY F.J. MM Sjt 10261 Royal Munster Fusiliers
RODON Robert MM L/Cpl 13440 12th Royal Scots KIA 9.4.17.
RODWAY William MM L/Cpl 423139 10th London Regt
RODWAY William W. MM Sjt 240353 5th Royal Sussex Regt
RODWELL Herbert Thomas MM Pte 12912 6th Bedfordshire Regt DOW 17.4.17.
RODWELL James W. MM Pte Y/1686 1st King's Royal Rifle Corps
RODWELL John Alfred MM CSM 570234 1/17th London Regt
ROE Alfred MM Pte 14840 Notts & Derby Regt
ROE Charles William "DCM,MM" Sjt 21372 1st Royal Inniskilling Fusiliers DOW 22.10.18.
ROE H.A.T. MM Pte Z/111 Rifle Brigade
ROE Harold MM Spr 558254 56 Div Sig Coy Royal Engineers
ROE Henry MM Sjt 5163 Norfolk Regt
ROE Henry Thomas MM Gnr 725717 A/52 Bde RFA KIA 2.9.18.
ROE James MM Pte 94501 1/8th Notts & Derby Regt
ROE James MM Pte 11741 1st Lancashire Fusiliers
ROE John Henry MM Cpl 4928 1st Notts & Derby Regt KIA 31.7.17.
ROE John William MM Pnr 97088 Royal Engineers
ROE Joseph MM Cpl 21925 101 Fd Amb RAMC
ROE Patrick MM Pte 11416 2nd Royal Dublin Fusiliers
ROE Silas MM Pte 200783 Notts & Derby Regt
ROE Wilfred MM Pte 202589 East Surrey Regt
ROE William Richard "MM,MID,CG(It)" SQMS 503 1/1st Northamptonshire Yeomanry
ROEBUCK Arthur MM Cpl 305323 6th West Riding Regt
ROEBUCK Edward MM+Bar L/Cpl 276101 2nd Manchester Regt
ROEBUCK Harold MM Pte 59248 2nd Manchester Regt
ROEBUCK Harry MM Pte 28433 25th Northumberland Fusiliers KIA 17.4.18.
ROEBUCK James S. MM Pte M2/045664 Army Service Corps
ROEBUCK John Mellor MM L/Cpl 28547 2nd Royal Dublin Fusiliers
ROELINK William T. MM Pte 11945 Coldstream Guards
ROFF Arthur T. MM L/Cpl 701025 21st London Regt
ROFF Samuel A. MM L/Cpl 8955 Rifle Brigade
ROFFE Harry William MM Pte 243085 Middlesex Regt
ROFFEY Archibald F. MM L/Cpl 5665 Army Cyclist Corps
ROFFEY Horace Walter MM Pte T/201396 2/4th Royal West Surrey Regt KIA 27.12.17.
ROFFEY Spencer MM Gnr 87283 RFA
ROGAN Arthur MM Pte 31880 Royal Scots
ROGAN Daniel John MM Pte 202570 2/4th Royal Berkshire Regt KIA 12.4.18.
ROGAN Edward MM Spr 50247 Royal Engineers
ROGAN Martin MM L/Cpl 9712 11th Royal Scots
ROGAN Michael MM Pte 325155 1/8th Royal Scots
ROGERS A. MM+Bar Sjt 14316 10th Essex Regt
ROGERS Albert MM Gnr 92603 D/84 Bde RFA
ROGERS Albert MM Cpl 10911 RFA
ROGERS Albert MM Sjt 45847 RFA
ROGERS Albert E. MM L/Cpl 41079 Yorkshire Regt
ROGERS Albert George MM Pte 27002 Wiltshire Regt
ROGERS Albert George MM Pte 15281 1st Somerset Light Infantry
ROGERS Albert L.G. MM Pte 24898 1/5th Royal Warwickshire Regt
ROGERS Alfred MM Cpl 240110 8th North Staffordshire Regt
ROGERS Alfred H. MM Spr 99706 Royal Engineers
ROGERS Alfred James MM Sjt 4009 3rd Rifle Brigade Died 16.6.16.
ROGERS Andrew MM Sjt 2156 6th Connaught Rangers
ROGERS Archie MM Pte 7740 3 Fd Amb RAMC
ROGERS Arnold E. MM+Bar Sjt 13940 1st Gordon Highlanders
ROGERS Arthur MM Cpl 58421 4th York & Lancaster Regt
ROGERS Arthur MM Pte 133765 36th Bn Machine Gun Corps
ROGERS Arthur MM Cpl 35862 282 Siege Bty RGA
ROGERS Arthur H. MM Pte 48992 2nd South Wales Borderers
ROGERS Benjamin MM Pte 4100 1st Hampshire Regt
ROGERS Bertram MM Sjt 204773 Somerset Light Infantry
ROGERS C.J. MM Cpl 36040 RAMC
ROGERS Charles MM Cpl 51355 69 Fd Coy Royal Engineers
ROGERS Charles MM+Bar CSM 6365 1st Duke of Cornwall's LI
ROGERS Charles MM Bdr 3071 Z/1 Med TM Bty RGA
ROGERS Charles MM Pte M2/031902 Army Service Corps
ROGERS Charles MM Pte 345269 16th Devonshire Regt
ROGERS Charles B. MM Cpl 251431 3rd London Regt
ROGERS Charles E. MM Gnr 850297 RFA
ROGERS Charles Henry MM Pnr 96362 346 Rd Constr Coy Royal Engineers
ROGERS E.H. MM Pte 5493 1st Rifle Brigade
ROGERS Edward MM Sjt 8404 2nd Wiltshire Regt
ROGERS Edward J. MM Sjt 30597 RGA
ROGERS Elijah MM Pte 8522 9th North Staffordshire Regt
ROGERS Ernest MM Sjt 20600 7th Dragoon Guards
ROGERS F. MM Pte 200505 Northumberland Fusiliers
ROGERS Francis L. MM+Bar Cpl 105548 Royal Engineers
ROGERS Frank MM L/Cpl 26388 17th Welsh Regt KIA 25.11.17.
ROGERS Frank MM Sjt 32777 D/62 Bde RFA
ROGERS Frank A. MM Sjt 329653 RGA
ROGERS Frank Albert MM L/Cpl 16554 12th Gloucestershire Regt
ROGERS Frank C. MM+Bar Pte 23504 Royal Irish Fusiliers
ROGERS Frank L. MM Cpl 2299 1/1st Bucks Bn Oxf & Bucks Light Infantry
ROGERS Frank O. MM Pte 33936 Middlesex Regt
ROGERS Frederick MM Bdr 16550 113 Heavy Bty RGA KIA 3.10.17.

ROGERS Frederick MM Sjt 1114 1/2(Highland)Fd Amb RAMC DOW 1.8.16.
ROGERS Frederick C. MM Sjt 300407 13th Bn Tank Corps
ROGERS Frederick G. MM L/Sjt 266857 Oxf & Bucks Light Infantry
ROGERS George MM+Bar Pte 88910 6th Liverpool Regt
ROGERS George "MM,MID" CSM 14275 38th Bn Machine Gun Corps
ROGERS George MM+Bar Pte 9534 12th Royal Fusiliers
ROGERS George H. MM L/Cpl 87681 Liverpool Regt
ROGERS George H.D. MM Pte 230504 2nd London Regt
ROGERS George Thomas MM Sjt 67064 2nd Notts & Derby Regt KIA 1.7.17.
ROGERS H.E.J. MM Pte 46304 10th Essex Regt
ROGERS Harold MM Pte 26863 3rd Grenadier Guards DOW 28.3.18.
ROGERS Harold MM Pte 8827 Manchester Regt
ROGERS Harold Nuttall "MM,MSM" 2nd Cpl 78577 'W' Airline Section Royal Engineers
ROGERS Harry MM Pte 14315 11th Hampshire Regt
ROGERS Harry MM Pte 7809 1st Dorsetshire Regt
ROGERS Harry MM+Bar Cpl 265405 1st Royal Warwickshire Regt
ROGERS Henry MM Pte 87870 1/6th Liverpool Regt
ROGERS Henry James MM L/Cpl 94313 129 Fd Coy Royal Engineers KIA 25.6.17.
ROGERS Herbert "MM,MSM" Sjt 17916 6th Lincolnshire Regt
ROGERS Herbert MM Sjt 8355 2nd Hampshire Regt
ROGERS Herbert MM Spr 432141 Royal Engineers
ROGERS Herbert F. MM Bdr 37162 RGA
ROGERS Horace Llewellyn MM Pte 17292 Devonshire Regt
ROGERS Horace T. MM L/Cpl 200926 Northamptonshire Regt
ROGERS J. MM L/Cpl 90758 18th Liverpool Regt
ROGERS J. "DCM,MM" CSM 15353 13th & 9th Essex Regt
ROGERS J. "MM,MID" Sjt 1117 West Riding Regt
ROGERS James MM+Bar Cpl 17637 12th East Surrey Regt
ROGERS James MM Pte 8252 Royal Fusiliers
ROGERS James MM Pte 202182 Seaforth Highlanders
ROGERS John MM Spr 432202 55 Div Sig Coy Royal Engineers
ROGERS John MM Pnr 254711 32 Div Sig Coy Royal Engineers
ROGERS John MM Cpl 10677 5th Shropshire Light Infantry KIA 19.10.17.
ROGERS John MM Sjt 4490 2nd Essex Regt
ROGERS John MM L/Cpl 155791 253 Tunnelling Coy Royal Engineers KIA 30.3.18.
ROGERS John MM Spr 34950 Royal Engineers
ROGERS John MM Cpl 40312 Royal Dublin Fusiliers
ROGERS John J. MM Bdr 77155 RGA
ROGERS John L. MM Pte 13384 7th Oxf & Bucks Light Infantry
ROGERS John M. MM Sjt 6370 Royal Welsh Fusiliers
ROGERS John William MM L/Cpl 49219 13th Cheshire Regt
ROGERS Joseph MM Cpl 5664 RAMC
ROGERS Joseph MM Cpl 482353 62 Div Sig Coy Royal Engineers
ROGERS Lewis MM Bdr 94081 A/331 Bde RFA
ROGERS Llewellyn S. MM Pte 22354 Royal Welsh Fusiliers
ROGERS Mathew MM Sjt 200661 Royal Welsh Fusiliers
ROGERS Matthew B. MM L/Cpl 85697 Signal Service Royal Engineers
ROGERS Norman MM Pte 200726 West Yorkshire Regt
ROGERS Octavius MM Pte 308914 4 Tank Supply Coy Tank Corps
ROGERS Phillip David MM 2nd Cpl 67484 Royal Engineers
ROGERS R.A. MM QMS 434004 RAMC
ROGERS Reginald G. MM Pte R/15560 16th King's Royal Rifle Corps
ROGERS Robert MM Pte 276101 Royal Scots
ROGERS Robert G. MM Pte 38792 2nd Yorkshire Regt
ROGERS Robert J. MM Sjt 132863 161 Siege Bty RGA
ROGERS Robert Jesse MM Pnr 130462 4 Bn Special Brigade Royal Engineers
ROGERS Samuel MM L/Cpl 37937 Royal Berkshire Regt
ROGERS Samuel H. MM Pte 240730 Royal Welsh Fusiliers
ROGERS Stephen G. MM Sjt 265923 1/1st Bucks Bn Oxf & Bucks Light Infantry
ROGERS Sydney Thomas MM L/Cpl 72536 24th Royal Fusiliers
ROGERS T. MM+Bar Pte 17514 1/5th Arg & Suth Highlanders
ROGERS Thomas MM Cpl 10515 14th Royal Welsh Fusiliers
ROGERS Thomas MM Sjt 89997 RFA
ROGERS Thomas MM Sjt 17892 Machine Gun Corps
ROGERS Thomas MM Pte 1534 2nd Rifle Brigade
ROGERS Thomas H. "DCM,MM" Sjt 67540 123 Fd Coy Royal Engineers
ROGERS Thomas W. MM Cpl 27860 18th Welsh Regt
ROGERS Tom H. MM Pte 26643 North Lancashire Regt
ROGERS Tom P. MM Pte M1/09254 Army Service Corps
ROGERS V. MM Pte 495312 RAMC
ROGERS Victor MM Cpl 165795 101st Bn Machine Gun Corps
ROGERS Victor MM Pte 203245 York & Lancaster Regt
ROGERS W.H. MM BSM 739 B/119 Bde RFA
ROGERS W.T. MM Gnr 404 RFA
ROGERS Walter MM Pte 280161 Lancashire Fusiliers
ROGERS Walter MM Pte 26101 East Yorkshire Regt
ROGERS Walter Edward MM Sjt 604022 2/1st(Shropshire)Bde RHA
ROGERS Walter or William "MM,MID" Bdr 810147 A/232 Bde RFA KIA 1 6 17.
ROGERS Walter S. "MM,MSM" Sjt 3377 11th Rifle Brigade
ROGERS Wilfred A.P. MM Sjt 47048 25th Northumberland Fusiliers
ROGERS William MM Pte 9849 2nd Royal West Kent Regt
ROGERS William MM Spr 558608 Royal Engineers
ROGERS William MM Pte 22414 Worcestershire Regt
ROGERS William MM Gnr 37081 B/63 Bde RFA
ROGERS William MM Pte 46055 Worcestershire Regt
ROGERS William D. MM L/Cpl 33133 15th Hampshire Regt
ROGERS William Edward MM Gnr 880529 271 Bde RFA
ROGERS or RODGERS Thomas MM L/Cpl 4128 10th Hussars
ROGERSON Adam MM Spr 418408 Royal Engineers
ROGERSON Arthur MM Pte 75014 RAMC
ROGERSON David MM Pte 44069 8th Worcestershire Regt
ROGERSON E. MM Pte 22320 1st Northumberland Fusiliers
ROGERSON George MM Pte 22473 Machine Gun Corps
ROGERSON George W. MM Cpl 301811 1/8th Durham Light Infantry
ROGERSON Harold S. MM L/Cpl 12119 Lancashire Fusiliers
ROGERSON Jesse MM Cpl 108031 RGA
ROGERSON Joseph H. MM Pte 11672 16th Lancashire Fusiliers
ROGERSON Richard F. MM Pte 149469 Machine Gun Corps
ROGERSON Robert Henry MM Pte 1556 22nd Royal Fusiliers KIA 29.4.17.
ROGERSON Thomas MM Pte 38287 54 Fd Amb RAMC
ROGERSON William Henry MM L/Cpl 16335 18th Liverpool Regt
ROHRER Robert "DCM,MM" CSM 7882 1st & 16th Royal Welsh Fusiliers
ROLESTONE John Stanley MM Gnr 30382 D/231 Bde RFA DOW 30.9.18.
ROLFE Albert S. MM Pte 23/1639 Northumberland Fusiliers
ROLFE Charles J. MM+Bar Cpl 33789 8th Royal Warwickshire Regt
ROLFE Edward F. MM Pte 15780 1st Royal Scots Fusiliers
ROLFE Edwin James MM L/Bdr 96755 154 Siege Bty RGA
ROLFE Harold MM Sjt 3023 1/4th Hampshire Regt
ROLFE J.C. MM L/Cpl P/8099 Military Mounted Police
ROLFE John A. MM Pte 106787 61st Bn Machine Gun Corps
ROLFE Percy E.W. MM Sjt 251268 3rd London Regt
ROLFE William J. MM Cpl 1845 21st Lancers
ROLLAND James MM L/Cpl 7075 7th Seaforth Highlanders
ROLLAND William F. MM Pte 15104 2nd Scots Guards
ROLLASON William H. MM Dvr 59364 C/104 Bde RFA
ROLLASON William Percy MM L/Cpl 311257 1/1st Northumberland Yeo
ROLLES Edward MM+Bar L/Sjt 7400 1st Irish Guards
ROLLETT Charles W. MM Pte 9061 Coldstream Guards
ROLLETT Ernest MM Sjt 241760 1/4th York & Lancaster Regt
ROLLETT Thomas W. MM Cpl 302643 Durham Light Infantry
ROLLEY Harold James Joseph MM Spr 59690 Fourth Army Sig Coy Royal Engineers
ROLLIN James W. MM Pte 12376 6th East Yorkshire Regt
ROLLINGS George MM Pte 41876 Suffolk Regt att 1/1st Cambridgeshire Regt
ROLLINGS James MM Cpl 14707 Essex Regt
ROLLINGS John W. MM Pte 40421 4th Worcestershire Regt
ROLLINGS Percy MM Pte 326080 12th Royal Scots
ROLLINGS Thomas J. MM Spr 88345 Royal Engineers
ROLLINGS William G. MM Gnr 317388 25 Hy Bty RGA
ROLLINS Joseph H. MM Cpl 55980 12 Bde RFA
ROLLINS Thomas MM Bdr 25624 RFA
ROLLITT Ernest MM CSM 53484 Durham Light Infantry
ROLLO James King "DCM,MM,MM(F)" CSM 170 1st Gordon Highlanders KIA 28.9.18.
ROLLO Leonard MM Sjt 37194 RAMC
ROLLO Robert MM Pte 50562 6 Sqn MGC(Cavalry)
ROLLO Walter MM Pte 14240 10th Arg & Suth Highlanders DOW 5.4.18.
ROLLO William C. MM(1294 Cpl RFA)+Bar Cpl 489988 Royal Engineers

ROLLS Albert H. MM Cpl 27300 North Lancashire Regt
ROLLS Harry MM Pte 9883 11th East Surrey Regt
ROLLS John W. MM Gnr 58540 RGA
ROLLS Richard MM Sjt 153251 277 Railway Coy Royal Engineers
ROLLS Stanley MM Pte M2/074969 Army Service Corps att RFA.
ROLPH Arthur MM Pte 895 1/1st Essex Yeomanry
ROLPH Edward Henry MM L/Cpl 15736 1st Bedfordshire Regt
ROLPH Edward R. MM Pte 251125 3rd London Regt
ROLPH Reginald MM Pte 35917 106 Coy 35th Bn Machine Gun Corps
ROLPH W.D. MM Sjt 59804 40 Bde RFA
ROLPH William MM Cpl 773 1/1st Cambridgeshire Regt
ROLT Aubrey Frederick MM Pte B/200469 13th Rifle Brigade
ROLT Henry John MM Sjt 7442 1st Middlesex Regt
ROME John T. MM Pte 308155 Liverpool Regt
ROMERIL John MM Cpl 37894 53 Fd Amb RAMC
ROMNEY Charles MM Cpl 56656 RFA
RONALD Arnold MM Pte 243425 4/5th North Lancashire Regt
RONALD Gordon MM Pte 28194 1st Scottish Rifles
RONALD James Horsbrugh MM Cpl(MCDR) 30362 Royal Engineers
RONALDSON Donald MM Pte 265850 1/6th Royal Highlanders
RONAN Christopher MM Cpl 4277 2nd Leinster Regt
RONAN James MM Pte 6/7380 6th Royal Irish Rifles
RONEY Joseph MM+Bar Pte 10998 6th Border Regt
RONSON Fred MM Pte 241137 2/5th Royal Lancaster Regt KIA 28.9.18.
RONSON George MM Pte 16529 Cheshire Regt
RONSON George William MM L/Cpl 14401 2nd Coldstream Guards KIA 27.8.18.
RONTREE Michael MM Gnr 185167 129 Bty 42 Bde RFA KIA 18.10.18.
RONTREE Norman W. MM Pte DM2/154174 Army Service Corps
ROO James William MM Sjt 225198 10th East Yorkshire Regt KIA 15.8.18.
ROOCROFT William MM Pte 238002 North Lancashire Regt
ROOFF Charles P. MM Cpl 2737 Worcestershire Regt
ROOK Cecil G. MM Pte 62307 RAMC
ROOK Frank MM Pte 321842 2/6th London Regt
ROOK Robert MM Sjt 266132 5th Notts & Derby Regt
ROOK William Henry MM Cpl 31486 Machine Gun Corps
ROOKE Clarance MM Pte 25029 Worcestershire Regt
ROOKE Henry MM+Bar Sjt 14689 17th Lancashire Fusiliers
ROOKE James MM Pte 201009 Manchester Regt
ROOKE John G. MM Spr WR/267528 Railway Ops Div Royal Engineers
ROOKE Leonard Harry Hepple MM Pte 722412 1/24th London Regt
ROOKE William MM Cpl 11236 1st Worcestershire Regt
ROOKE William Ewart MM Sjt R/8244 9th King's Royal Rifle Corps
ROOKER Charles E.E. MM Pte 10169 4th Hussars
ROOKER Ephraim MM Pte 201816 Yorkshire Light Infantry
ROOKES Walter "DCM,MM" Sjt 106867 40 Div Sig Coy Royal Engineers
ROOKLEDGE J.W. MM AM2 10607 Royal Flying Corps
ROOM Samuel MM Pte 60081 26th Royal Fusiliers
ROOME James MM L/Cpl 17519 Notts & Derby Regt
ROONEY Andrew MM Pte 337730 63 Fd Amb RAMC
ROONEY James MM Pte 16682 Royal Welsh Fusiliers
ROONEY John MM Pte 307766 West Yorkshire Regt
ROONEY John Martin "DCM,MM" L/Sjt 13699 2nd King's Own Scottish Borderers KIA 26.8.18.
ROONEY Patrick MM Sjt 3174 45 Coy Machine Gun Corps KIA 22.8.17.
ROONEY Patrick MM Pte 51167 RAMC att 10 Rly Coy RE.
ROONEY Robert MM Pte 56541 18th King's Royal Rifle Corps
ROONEY Thomas MM Sjt 23829 Royal Irish Fusiliers
ROONEY Thomas MM L/Sjt 4739 18th Highland Light Infantry
ROONEY William MM Bdr 38062 RFA
ROONEY William MM L/Cpl 265144 4th Liverpool Regt
ROONEY William MM Pte 18347 2nd Border Regt
ROONEY William MM L/Cpl 17887 Machine Gun Corps
ROOSE Leigh Richmond MM Pte 10898 9th Royal Fusiliers KIA 7.10.16.Served as ROUSE.Welsh international soccer player.
ROOT Albert S. MM Pte 32365 10th York & Lancaster Regt
ROOT William MM CQMS 420627 10th London Regt
ROOT William MM Pte 70079 16th Notts & Derby Regt KIA 15.9.17.
ROOTE William Arthur MM L/Cpl 6323 8th Royal West Surrey Regt KIA 21.3.18.
ROOTS George MM Pte 235633 13th Yorkshire Regt
ROOTS H.W. MM Dvr 2444 RFA
ROOTS Walter E. MM Gnr 910304 222 Bde RFA
ROPER Arthur Charles MM Sjt 201015 1/4th Suffolk Regt KIA 8.8.18.
ROPER Benjamin Knox MM Cpl 151579 182 Tunnelling Coy Royal Engineers
ROPER Bertie W. MM Sjt 43033 7th Norfolk Regt
ROPER Denis MM Pte 72716 15th Bn Machine Gun Corps
ROPER Edward MM L/Sjt 13335 8th Norfolk Regt
ROPER Ernest MM+Bar Pte 8764 2nd Suffolk Regt
ROPER Ernest G. MM L/Cpl 2955 8th Royal West Surrey Regt
ROPER Frank MM Pte 65380 4th Royal Fusiliers KIA 1.9.18.
ROPER Frederick V. MM Pte 372474 8th London Regt
ROPER Herbert S. MM Sjt 326628 1/1st Cambridgeshire Regt
ROPER Laurence H. MM Cpl 201965 5th Notts & Derby Regt
ROPER Reginald T. MM Pte 7590 8th Royal West Kent Regt
ROPER Shirley MM Bdr 60901 A/113 Bde RFA
ROPER Stephen "MM,MID" Sjt M2/121597 593 MT Coy Army Service Corps
ROPER William MM Pte 81192 1/1st Essex Yeomanry
ROPER William Albert MM Pte 16243 2nd Grenadier Guards DOW 28.9.18.
ROPER William H. MM Pte 50461 6th Northamptonshire Regt
RORKE Andrew Buchan "MC,MM+Bar(44466 Sjt)" 2Lt Royal Engineers
RORKE George MM Gnr 138781 235 Siege Bty RGA DOW 20.8.17.
RORRISON Alexander MM Pte 51724 11th Royal Scots KIA 28.9.18.
ROSAM Thomas MM Sjt 10092 12th Northumberland Fusiliers KIA 16.6.17.
ROSCALEER Frederick W. MM Sjt 240624 South Lancashire Regt
ROSCOE Charles MM Pte 331583 4th Liverpool Regt
ROSCOE Ernest MM Cpl(MCDR) 444453 Signal Service Royal Engineers
ROSCOE Harold MM Pte 18647 13th Essex Regt Died 17.12.18.
ROSCOE Henry MM L/Cpl 37295 Norfolk Regt
ROSCOE Jack MM Pte 2581 2/5th Lancashire Fusiliers
ROSCOE Peter MM Pte R/8070 King's Royal Rifle Corps
ROSE A.G. MM Pte 2101 3rd Hussars
ROSE Albert E. MM Cpl 19655 Middlesex Regt
ROSE Archibald MM Sjt 645178 RFA
ROSE C. MM Spr 552953 33 Div Sig Coy Royal Engineers
ROSE Charles MM Dvr 635627 256 Bde RFA
ROSE Charles A. MM Pte 8253 2nd Royal Berkshire Regt
ROSE Daniel MM Pte 2522 1st Royal Lancaster Regt
ROSE David MM CQMS 8502 2nd Seaforth Highlanders
ROSE David MM+Bar Pte 23068 19th Highland Light Infantry
ROSE Dudley Edwin MM Cpl 340414 RGA
ROSE Edward MM Pte 4421 1/4th Yorkshire Light Infantry
ROSE Edward MM Sjt 960572 C/236 Bde RFA
ROSE Francis J.P. MM L/Cpl 2594 1/9th London Regt
ROSE Frank MM Pte 150135 102nd Bn Machine Gun Corps
ROSE Frank MM Pte 19471 5th Dorsetshire Regt
ROSE Frederick MM Pte 45304 South Staffordshire Regt
ROSE Frederick MM Pte 12676 9th Suffolk Regt KIA 26.4.17.
ROSE George MM L/Cpl 79175 2nd Northumberland Fusiliers
ROSE George MM Cpl 46486 Northumberland Fusiliers
ROSE George MM Gnr 56503 RGA
ROSE George MM Pte 422315 10th London Regt
ROSE George A. MM Sjt 16595 Machine Gun Corps
ROSE George T. MM Pte 202388 Royal Welsh Fusiliers
ROSE George W. MM Pte 23399 Suffolk Regt
ROSE George W. MM CSM 3299 2nd Rifle Brigade
ROSE Henry MM L/Cpl 4329 6th East Kent Regt
ROSE Henry MM Dvr 148558 C/112 Bde RFA
ROSE Herbert MM Gnr 16222 72 Bde RFA
ROSE Herbert S. MM Gnr 950285 RFA
ROSE Howard MM Pte DM2/195187 272 Coy Army Service Corps Died 23.10.18.
ROSE Hugh MM Dvr 45910 D/112 Bde RFA
ROSE James A. MM Cpl 20217 Somerset Light Infantry
ROSE James J. MM Pte 10965 2nd South Wales Borderers
ROSE John MM Pte 125655 39th Bn Machine Gun Corps
ROSE John MM Cpl 321717 6th London Regt
ROSE John MM Pte 23246 7th Cameron Highlanders
ROSE John William "MM,MID" Cpl 19590 Cheshire Regt
ROSE Joseph MM Sjt 80455 D/63 Bde RFA KIA 1.12.17.
ROSE Leonard George MM Sjt 13926 8th Suffolk Regt KIA 12.10.17.
ROSE Leslie V. MM Pte 29731 4th Bedfordshire Regt
ROSE Norman C.S. MM Pte M2/033961 Army Service Corps att MGC

ROSE Sidney MM Sjt SE/1390 Army Veterinary Corps
ROSE Stanley MM Pte 12053 6th Royal West Kent Regt DOW 14.7.18.
ROSE Sydney R. MM Sjt 2119 Royal Sussex Regt
ROSE T. MM Sjt P/1416 Military Foot Police
ROSE Thomas MM Pte 20684 Grenadier Guards KIA 1.8.17.
ROSE Thomas F. MM Pte 305595 13th Bn Tank Corps
ROSE Thomas Henry MM+Bar L/Cpl 16069 8th Royal Lancaster Regt
ROSE Tom MM L/Cpl 265862 1/3rd Monmouthshire Regt
ROSE William MM Pte 335185 5/6th Royal Scots
ROSE William MM Pte 250760 5/6th Royal Scots DOW 19.8.18.
ROSE William "DCM,MM" Cpl 8520 9th Suffolk Regt
ROSE William MM Pte 1082 4 Fd Amb RAMC att 34 Bde RFA.KIA 28.4.17.
ROSE "William B," MM Pte M2/077113 Army Service Corps att RAMC.
ROSE William Bertie "MM,MSM" S/Sjt Armourer T/1021 4 Ord Mobile Wksp Army Ordnance Corps
ROSE William Charles MM Cpl 4741 1st East Kent Regt
ROSE William E. MM Sjt 930807 RFA
ROSE William J. MM Gnr 340745 RGA
ROSE William T. MM Cpl 1493 17th Royal Fusiliers
ROSE William Thomas MM L/Cpl 321632 1/6th London Regt
ROSEBLADE Charles J. MM Spr 161196 Royal Engineers
ROSEBLADE Frederick MM Sjt 89629 RFA
ROSEBOOM Edward MM Cpl 40211 Highland Light Infantry
ROSEMAN Albert MM Pte 203068 1st London Regt
ROSEN Abraham MM Pte B/203654 Rifle Brigade
ROSENDALE Frederick J. MM Pte 15241 2nd Grenadier Guards
ROSER Ernest C. MM Bdr 56874 RFA
ROSER Frederick MM Sjt M2/192845 402 MT Coy Army Service Corps
ROSEWARNE Horace R. MM Gnr 107779 RGA
ROSEWEIR Fergus MM Pte 2226 1/9th Highland Light Infantry
ROSHER Albert "DCM,MM+Bar" Bdr 35313 RGA
ROSHIER Samuel William "DCM,MM,MID" Sjt 74765 3 LAC Bty Machine Gun Corps(Motors)
ROSIER Charles MM Pte 7214 1st Wiltshire Regt
ROSINDALE Richard MM CSM 3/6585 8th East Yorkshire Regt DOW 28.6.17.
ROSINDELL Ernest B. MM L/Cpl 5082 7th Royal West Surrey Regt
ROSKELL Alexander MM Pte 241613 Royal Lancaster Regt
ROSKELL Robert MM Bdr 61744 RGA KIA 25.10.17.
ROSKELL Robert W. MM+Bar Sjt 17012 1st North Lancashire Regt
ROSKILL John MM Pte 32762 1st Royal Lancaster Regt
ROSS A. MM Cpl 2955 Tank Corps
ROSS A.G. MM Sjt 2260 7th East Kent Regt
ROSS A.J. MM Cpl 300005 RAMC
ROSS Alexander MM L/Cpl 406086 51 Div Sig Coy Royal Engineers
ROSS Alexander MM BSM 26303 230 Siege Bty RGA
ROSS Alexander MM L/Cpl 200553 1/5th Highland Light Infantry
ROSS Alexander "DCM,MM" Pte 6884 1st Gordon Highlanders
ROSS Alexander MM Sjt 27216 Highland Light Infantry
ROSS Alexander MM Cpl 40399 2nd Gordon Highlanders
ROSS Alexander E. MM+Bar Cpl 13997 5th Cameron Highlanders
ROSS Alexander E.D. MM L/Cpl 43849 2nd Seaforth Highlanders
ROSS Alexander McGhee MM Pte 40322 7th Seaforth Highlanders KIA 1.10.18.
ROSS Alexander McKay MM Pte 15844 10th Gloucestershire Regt
ROSS Alexander S. MM L/Cpl 3498 Gordon Highlanders
ROSS Andrew MM Pte 59665 Royal Scots
ROSS Andrew MM Sjt 11081 King's Own Scottish Borderers
ROSS Andrew MM Sjt 200222 Seaforth Highlanders
ROSS Andrew MM Sjt 275888 Royal Scots
ROSS Angus A. MM Pte 10865 Seaforth Highlanders
ROSS Archibald Morris MM L/Sjt 17466 Royal Scots
ROSS Brian Aurias MM Pte 3128 1/4th Royal Berkshire Regt
ROSS C. MM Pte 5809 London Regt
ROSS Carl F.W. MM Pte 679 King Edward's Horse
ROSS Charles MM Cpl 32483 16th Royal Warwickshire Regt
ROSS Charles E. MM Pte 43716 21 Fd Amb RAMC
ROSS Charles F. MM Pte 7944 Royal Fusiliers
ROSS Charles Frederick MM Pte 43578 Royal Irish Rifles
ROSS Cyril MM Sjt 205686 9th Yorkshire Light Infantry
ROSS Cyril MM Dvr 186197 94 Bde RFA
ROSS D. MM Sjt 125552 Yeomanry
ROSS Daniel MM L/Sjt 325284 1/8th Royal Scots
ROSS Donald MM Spr 160999 Royal Engineers
ROSS Donald "DCM,MM" CSM 7111 1/6th Royal Highlanders
ROSS Donald Nisbet MM Pte 9207 1st Cameron Highlanders KIA 18.4.18.
ROSS Ernest MM Pte 20853 18th Lancashire Fusiliers
ROSS F.R. MM Gnr 68264 RGA
ROSS Frederick MM Sjt 15/12128 15th Royal Irish Rifles
ROSS Frederick MM Pte 292301 1/7th Gordon Highlanders
ROSS George MM Pte 223240 10th Cameron Highlanders
ROSS George MM Sjt 290368 1/7th Gordon Highlanders
ROSS George "MM,MSM" Cpl 201052 Gordon Highlanders
ROSS George MM Pte 1989 10th Arg & Suth Highlanders
ROSS George MM Cpl 43734 84 Fd Coy Royal Engineers KIA 26.3.18.
ROSS George MM L/Cpl 55394 19th Highland Light Infantry
ROSS George MM Cpl 9200 8th Royal Fusiliers DOW 30.6.17.
ROSS George A.T. MM Pte 14267 16th Highland Light Infantry
ROSS George C. MM Pte 353772 7th London Regt
ROSS George D. MM Cpl 57460 2/5th West Yorkshire Regt
ROSS George E.McD. MM Pte 201205 6th Bn Tank Corps
ROSS George M. MM Cpl 129396 RGA
ROSS Gilbert G. MM Pte 14396 Highland Light Infantry
ROSS Henry E. MM Sjt 201502 7th Bn Tank Corps
ROSS Hugh MM L/Cpl 265341 1/6th Seaforth Highlanders
ROSS Hugh MM Gnr 635723 256 Bde RFA
ROSS Hugh A. MM CQMS 21059 51st Bn Machine Gun Corps
ROSS Isaac MM L/Cpl 201014 1/5th Highland Light Infantry
ROSS J. MM Pte 41497 1/6th Gordon Highlanders
ROSS J. MM Cpl 8254 Royal Flying Corps
ROSS James MM Sjt 695654 57 Div Ammn Col RFA
ROSS James MM Sjt 265855 Royal Warwickshire Regt
ROSS James MM Spr 406418 Royal Engineers
ROSS James "DCM,MM" Sjt 265395 1/6th Gordon Highlanders
ROSS James MM Sjt 200099 1/4th Seaforth Highlanders DOW 12.5.17.
ROSS James MM Gnr(SS) 4312 B/157 Bde RFA
ROSS James MM Sjt 13810 Labour Corps
ROSS James MM L/Cpl 9090 Seaforth Highlanders
ROSS James R. MM Pte 41221 1/7th Royal Highlanders
ROSS John MM Gnr 45809 RFA
ROSS John MM Pte 245264 2nd Manchester Regt
ROSS John MM+Bar Sjt 23534 3 Div Sig Coy Royal Engineers
ROSS John MM Sjt 347 1/5th Seaforth Highlanders KIA 6.9.17.
ROSS John MM Dvr 50499 Royal Engineers
ROSS John MM Pte 241685 1/5th Gordon Highlanders KIA 27.7.18.
ROSS John MM Cpl 40328 Scottish Rifles
ROSS John MM Pte DM2/224558 Army Service Corps
ROSS John MM L/Cpl 10846 5th Cameron Highlanders
ROSS John MM Sjt 200039 1/4th Seaforth Highlanders KIA 22.10.17.
ROSS John F. MM Pte 46823 Manchester Regt
ROSS Leslie W. MM Cpl 61219 24th Royal Fusiliers
ROSS Lionel B. MM L/Cpl 60703 23rd Lancashire Fusiliers
ROSS Malcolm MM Sjt M2/032255 2 Div MT Coy Army Service Corps
ROSS Norman MM+Bar L/Cpl 200097 1/4th Seaforth Highlanders
ROSS Peter MM Pte 634963 20th London Regt
ROSS R. MM Sjt 241873 Seaforth Highlanders
ROSS Richard MM+Bar Cpl 3814 2nd Royal Highlanders
ROSS Richard G. MM Pte 126803 1st Lovat's Scouts Yeomanry
ROSS Robert MM Pte 275929 5/6th Royal Scots
ROSS Robert MM Dvr 169656 D/256 Bde RFA
ROSS Robert MM Pte 315372 5th London Regt
ROSS Robert A. MM L/Cpl 37259 RAMC
ROSS Robert H. MM Pte 242274 Seaforth Highlanders
ROSS Roderick MM Pte 40912 Cameron Highlanders
ROSS Sidney D. MM Gnr 76195 10th Bn Tank Corps
ROSS Simon MM Pte 200066 1/5th Highland Light Infantry
ROSS Thomas MM Dvr 129585 RFA
ROSS Thomas MM Cpl 40064 Lincolnshire Regt
ROSS Thomas MM L/Cpl 300038 1/8th Arg & Suth Highlanders
ROSS Thomas MM L/Cpl 14441 8th York & Lancaster Regt
ROSS Thomas B. MM L/Cpl 5642 Machine Gun Corps
ROSS Thomas Robert "MM,CG(F)" Pte 265339 4/5th Royal Highlanders KIA 19.8.18.
ROSS Thomas W. MM Cpl 8934 109 Heavy Bty RGA
ROSS William "MM,MID" Pte 25401 Border Regt
ROSS William MM Sjt 95553 RFA
ROSS William MM(9691 Sjt 8th R Berks)+Bar Pte 129640 45th Royal Fusiliers
ROSS William MM Pte 22353 12th Highland Light Infantry
ROSS William MM L/Cpl 26863 Cameron Highlanders

ROSS William S. MM Pte 21707 Seaforth Highlanders
ROSSALL William Walker MM Cpl 24540 10th West Riding Regt
ROSSER Charles MM+Bar Pte 4002 10th Lancashire Fusiliers
ROSSER Frank MM L/Cpl 21884 15th Royal Welsh Fusiliers
ROSSER Harry MM Cpl 11636 1st South Wales Borderers
ROSSER Lewis Robert MM Cpl 202123 4th Oxf & Bucks Light Infantry
ROSSER T.J. MM Sjt 2190 RFA
ROSSETER G.S. MM Cpl 1996 8th Royal Sussex Regt
ROSSI Pietro C. MM Pte 46309 9th London Regt
ROSSIN Ernest MM L/Cpl 19557 York & Lancaster Regt
ROSSINGTON George MM Pte 41218 9th Northumberland Fusiliers
ROSSINGTON George L. MM Cpl 281204 2/4th London Regt
ROSSITER Edward George MM Cpl 34526 120 Bty 27 Bde RFA DOW 24.4.17.
ROSSITER Frank J. MM Pte 28034 8th East Surrey Regt
ROSSITER George A. MM Cpl 204705 2nd London Regt
ROSSITER Luther T. MM Cpl 31116 RFA
ROSSITER Oliver MM Pte 20539 3rd Grenadier Guards KIA 28.2.18.
ROSTRON Albert MM Dvr 710404 42 Div Ammn Col RFA
ROSTRON Richard E. MM Pte 33335 RAMC
ROSTRON Samuel MM Pte 20552 8th Royal Lancaster Regt
ROTCHELL John Edward MM Cpl 19794 9th South Staffordshire Regt
ROTHAM George H. MM Pte 36036 York & Lancaster Regt
ROTHAN James MM Pte 48576 1/7th Manchester Regt
ROTHERA Cain MM Pte 24533 10th West Riding Regt KIA 27.10.18.
ROTHERAM J. MM+Bar Sjt 785429 RFA
ROTHERFORTH Edmund MM Cpl 1211 12th Yorkshire Light Infantry
ROTHERHAM George MM Pte 202814 North Lancashire Regt
ROTHERHAM John H. MM L/Cpl 68989 Royal Fusiliers
ROTHERHAM Philip MM Bdr 118550 RFA
ROTHERHAM Walter Sutton MM Bdr 63205 'A' Bty RHA
ROTHERO William J. MM Cpl 459261 RAMC
ROTHERY Albert "MC,MM(19191 Sjt 10th Yorks Regt)" 2Lt 2nd Bn Tank Corps
ROTHERY H. MM Pte 6311 Border Regt
ROTHNIE David MM L/Cpl 265754 7th Seaforth Highlanders
ROTHWELL Harold MM Pte 290795 7th Cheshire Regt
ROTHWELL Harold MM Sjt 200571 Lancashire Fusiliers
ROTHWELL Henry MM Sjt 11652 19th Manchester Regt KIA 2.12.17.
ROTHWELL J.A. MM Sjt 41026 Royal Engineers
ROTHWELL John Edward MM Pte 12225 7th North Lancashire Regt
ROTHWELL Robert "DCM,MM" Pte 29291 2nd Royal Welsh Fusiliers
ROTHWELL Thomas MM Pte 267746 2/7th Liverpool Regt
ROTHWELL Thomas H. MM Pte 49371 4th Liverpool Regt
ROTHWELL William MM Sjt SE/2853 Army Veterinary Corps
ROTTON Thomas MM L/Cpl 8187 1/5th South Staffordshire Regt
ROUCH John T. MM+Bar Pte 16535 Royal West Kent Regt
ROUD George MM Pte 46023 12th East Surrey Regt
ROUGET Wilfred H. MM Pte 10715 22 Fd Amb RAMC
ROUGH Charles E. MM L/Cpl 54179 6th West Yorkshire Regt
ROUGH Duncan MM Pte 53157 15th Highland Light Infantry
ROUGH Edward Charles MM Sjt 7325 15th Hussars KIA 22.3.18.
ROUGH James MM L/Bdr 4071 HQ 157 Bde RFA
ROUGH James E. MM L/Cpl P/4718 Military Mounted Police
ROUGH Robert "DCM,MM" Sjt 31718 165 Coy 55th Bn Machine Gun Corps
ROUGH William MM Spr 8965 Royal Engineers
ROUGH William S. MM Pte 14482 1st Middlesex Regt
ROUGHLEY Peter MM Sjt 6805 423 Fd Coy Royal Engineers
ROUGHLEY William MM Pte 17943 18th Liverpool Regt KIA 8.10.18.
ROUGHSEDGE Harold MM Pte 90147 1st Bn Machine Gun Corps
ROUGHTON Albert H. MM L/Cpl 201967 Suffolk Regt
ROUGHTON J. MM Pte 42581 Essex Regt
ROUGVIE Walter MM Pte 16906 5th Cameron Highlanders
ROUILLAULT Leslie H. MM Pte 58627 West Yorkshire Regt
ROULSTON James MM L/Sjt 15986 1st Royal Inniskilling Fusiliers DOW 5.10.18.
ROULSTON Robert MM L/Sjt 14489 11th Royal Inniskilling Fusiliers
ROULSTON William MM+Bar L/Cpl 1869 2nd South Lancashire Regt
ROUND Albert MM Pte 240888 6th Notts & Derby Regt
ROUND Edward MM Sjt 478054 237 Fd Coy Royal Engineers
ROUND Horace MM Pte 21465 4th Grenadier Guards
ROUND John MM Pte 13269 7th Royal Lancaster Regt
ROUND John MM Bdr 86299 A/86 Bde RFA KIA 22.10.17.
ROUND John T. MM Pte 200409 1/7th Worcestershire Regt
ROUND P. "MM,MID" Sjt 13 Royal Engineers
ROUND Sidney MM Cpl 31206 East Yorkshire Regt
ROUND Walter James "MM,MSM" L/Cpl 14252 Grenadier Guards
ROUNDING Jack MM Pte 307873 West Riding Regt
ROURKE John MM Pte 1539 1/6th Northumberland Fusiliers
ROURKE Joseph MM Pte 25201 North Lancashire Regt
ROURKE Thomas MM Pte 300184 1/8th Durham Light Infantry
ROURKE William MM Pte 37647 1/7th Manchester Regt
ROUSE Albert Walter MM Sjt 1084 2(South Midland)Bde RFA
ROUSE Alick MM Pte A/203161 16th King's Royal Rifle Corps
ROUSE Ernest R. MM Sjt M2/115668 Army Service Corps
ROUSE Frederick Arthur MM Pte 14645 10th Essex Regt Died 20.3.18.
ROUSE George C. MM Sjt 11952 9th West Riding Regt
ROUSE John Dracott MM Sjt 426028 RAMC
ROUSE Leigh Richmond MM Pte 10898 9th Royal Fusiliers KIA 7.10.16.Real name ROOSE.Welsh International soccer player.
ROUSE Richard MM Cpl 8969 1st Royal Munster Fusiliers
ROUSE Victor MM Pte 26207 Somerset Light Infantry
ROUSE Walter MM Pte 43899 8th Lincolnshire Regt
ROUSE William MM Pte 200946 Lancashire Fusiliers
ROUSE William S. MM Pte 22612 Leicestershire Regt att RE.
ROUSE William T. MM Spr 1188 Royal Engineers
ROUSELL Lambert T. MM Sjt 659 RAMC
ROUSTOBY John W. MM Pte 16946 8th East Yorkshire Regt
ROUT Alfred E. MM Cpl 6/504 4th Rifle Brigade
ROUT Francis W. MM Pte 350632 7th London Regt
ROUT William T. MM Pte B/372 Rifle Brigade
ROUTE Ernest MM Pte 40434 1st West Yorkshire Regt
ROUTE Paul A. MM L/Cpl 1178 Royal Sussex Regt
ROUTH Frank R. MM Pte 760797 28th London Regt
ROUTH James MM Sjt M2/076141 Army Service Corps
ROUTH John E. MM+Bar Pte 241037 9th West Riding Regt
ROUTH or RAUTH Albert Frederick MM Cpl 344 2nd Lancashire Fusiliers AKA Samuel RILEY
ROUTLEDGE Adam MM Cpl 23/759 Northumberland Fusiliers
ROUTLEDGE Albert MM Cpl 16011 7th Border Regt
ROUTLEDGE Clement MM Pte 14792 8th Border Regt
ROUTLEDGE Guy Anthony McLeod "MC,MM(1383 Bdr 1/2(Warw)Bty)" 2Lt RFA
ROUTLEDGE Herbert J. "DCM,MM" CSM 9364 1st Yorkshire Light Infantry
ROUTLEDGE John J. MM Pte 27281 Yorkshire Regt
ROUTLEDGE John R. MM Cpl 34858 RFA
ROUTLEDGE Joseph MM Sjt 5513 15th Lancashire Fusiliers KIA 14.9.17.
ROUTLEDGE Leonard W. MM Bdr 72808 125 Bty 29 Bde RFA
ROUTLEDGE Robert MM Sjt 58077 5th Yorkshire Light Infantry
ROUTLEDGE Russell MM Pte 14841 8th Suffolk Regt
ROUTLEDGE William MM Pte 63934 8th West Yorkshire Regt
ROUTLEDGE William MM+Bar Cpl 41290 Middlesex Regt
ROUTLEDGE William West MM Cpl 148592 50th Bn Machine Gun Corps DOW 25.10.18.
ROUTLIFF William MM L/Cpl 11453 6th Dorsetshire Regt
ROUVRAY Thomas W. MM Pte 205758 2nd London Regt
ROVERY Leonard MM Sjt 4199 Royal Sussex Regt
ROW Arthur H. MM+Bar Sjt 147679 173 Tunnelling Coy Royal Engineers
ROW Arthur Leslie MM Cpl 22927 Royal Engineers KIA 5.6.18.
ROW Cecil A.Richard MM Gnr 2608 Machine Gun Corps(Motors)
ROW Frederick MM Cpl 7998 6th Yorkshire Light Infantry
ROW William MM Sjt 10055 2nd Royal Irish Fusiliers
ROWAN Patrick MM Sjt 10922 1st King's Own Scottish Borderers
ROWAN William MM Cpl 12970 7th Lincolnshire Regt DOW 30.8.18
ROWANE Michael J. MM Pte 3232 1/5th Liverpool Regt
ROWATT Thomas MM Cpl 207424 Royal Engineers
ROWBERRY Edwin C. MM Cpl 92815 Tank Corps AKA Claude WESTALL.
ROWBERRY William MM Cpl 7906 10th Royal Warwickshire Regt KIA 18.11.??
ROWBOTHAM Arthur R. MM L/Cpl 49086 7th Norfolk Regt
ROWBOTHAM Edward MM Sjt 6470 6th Bn Machine Gun Corps
ROWBOTHAM George MM Pte 265434 Cheshire Regt
ROWBOTHAM Sidney MM Pte 27482 4th Grenadier Guards

ROWBOTHAM Stephen John MM Pte 24266 4th Grenadier Guards KIA 13.4.18.
ROWBOTTOM Douglas W. MM L/Cpl 22971 Machine Gun Corps
ROWBOTTOM Ernest MM Pte 67407 8th Worcestershire Regt
ROWBOTTOM Joseph A. MM L/Cpl 1758 Oxf & Bucks Light Infantry
ROWBOTTOM Miles MM 2nd Cpl 147535 252 Tunnelling Coy Royal Engineers
ROWBURY John MM L/Cpl 2848 12th Middlesex Regt
ROWCLIFFE Harold J. MM Pte 31592 8th Royal Berkshire Regt
ROWDEN William R. MM Pte 84862 2nd Bn Machine Gun Corps
ROWE Albert MM Sjt 5295 8th East Surrey Regt KIA 12.10.17.
ROWE Alfred MM Pte 7848 1st Rifle Brigade
ROWE Alfred MM Pte 69132 Royal Fusiliers
ROWE Alfred MM Bdr 10247 RFA
ROWE Alfred J. MM Pte 18434 7th Royal Berkshire Regt
ROWE Alfred Stanley MM Pte 44630 1st Essex Regt
ROWE Arthur MM Pte 351460 1/5th Manchester Regt KIA 20.10.18.
ROWE Arthur MM Cpl 8608 1st North Staffordshire Regt
ROWE Arthur George MM Pte 15522 11th Essex Regt
ROWE Bernard J. MM L/Cpl 25626 3 Div Sig Coy Royal Engineers
ROWE Charles Frederick MM Pte 49590 4 Coy Machine Gun Corps
ROWE Charles W. MM Sjt 11102 11th Hampshire Regt
ROWE Claude MM Sjt 771 1/1st HAC(Infantry)
ROWE Edward MM L/Bdr 119255 RFA
ROWE Edward MM Cpl 591163 18th London Regt
ROWE Edwin J. "MM,MID" Sjt 14068 1st Grenadier Guards
ROWE Frank MM L/Cpl 10120 9th Suffolk Regt
ROWE Frank MM Pte 3530 3rd Coldstream Guards
ROWE Frederick "MM,MSM" Staff SM S/18394 Army Service Corps
ROWE Frederick Arthur MM Cpl 44244 2nd Worcestershire Regt KIA 29.9.18.
ROWE Frederick M. MM L/Cpl 10699 7th Royal West Surrey Regt
ROWE Frederick Skinner MM Pte 461042 19 Fd Amb RAMC KIA 22.6.18.
ROWE Frederick William MM L/Cpl 33270 Hampshire Regt
ROWE Gassie J. MM Pte 12224 7th Wiltshire Regt
ROWE George J. MM CQMS 19202 Labour Corps
ROWE Harry MM Sjt 8904 2nd Hampshire Regt
ROWE Henry MM Sjt 59206 3rd Bn Machine Gun Corps
ROWE Henry James Courtney MM L/Cpl 9471 1/5th London Regt
ROWE Herbert L. MM L/Cpl 437098 RAMC
ROWE Herbert Ramsay MM Cpl 241137 1st Border Regt
ROWE Horace Hicks MM Pte 20231 1st Dorsetshire Regt
ROWE Hubert MM L/Cpl 375211 Manchester Regt
ROWE James P. MM Pte 202550 Worcestershire Regt
ROWE John MM Sjt 10136 9th North Lancashire Regt Died 18.10.18.
ROWE John W. MM Pte 63206 15th Lancashire Fusiliers
ROWE Michael MM Pte 3638 2nd Irish Guards
ROWE Mortimer MM Pte 352587 2/3(East Lancashire)Fd Amb RAMC
ROWE Norman Benjamin MM Pte 93279 RAMC
ROWE Percy S. MM L/Cpl 1231 7th Royal West Surrey Regt
ROWE R.C. MM Cpl 31116 Essex Regt
ROWE Sidney MM Cpl 612032 19 Bde RHA
ROWE Stanley John Henry MM Sjt S4/056702 29 Div Train Army Service Corps
ROWE Thomas H. MM Pte 240980 1/5th Duke of Cornwall's LI
ROWE Walter MM L/Cpl 9858 2nd Oxf & Bucks Light Infantry
ROWE Walter E. MM Pte 43663 1/7th Middlesex Regt
ROWE Walter Thomas MM Pte 304455 2/5th London Regt
ROWE Walter William MM Sjt 104408 175 Coy Labour Corps
ROWE William MM Cpl 8192 1st Royal West Surrey Regt
ROWE William Arthur MM Cpl 26145 Z/3 Med TM Bty RGA
ROWE William H. MM L/Cpl 3972 8th York & Lancaster Regt
ROWE William J. MM Sjt 94560 RFA
ROWE William R. "MM,MSM" Sjt 13658 Machine Gun Corps
ROWE William S. MM L/Cpl 44834 Durham Light Infantry
ROWE William S.C. MM Sjt 33919 16 Siege Bty RGA
ROWE William Walter MM Sjt 44331 RFA
ROWELL Charles S. MM Pte 38557 Durham Light Infantry
ROWELL George E. MM Cpl 80270 1/1st Essex Yeomanry
ROWELL Johnstone V. MM Pte 87699 33rd Bn Machine Gun Corps
ROWELL Matthew MM Pte 38403 RAMC
ROWELL Robert MM Pte 38505 Lancashire Fusiliers
ROWELL Robert W. MM Cpl 37813 Northumberland Fusiliers
ROWELL Thomas MM Spr 156148 176 Tunnelling Coy Royal Engineers
ROWELL William MM Pte 28859 Northumberland Fusiliers
ROWEN Charles MM Pte 275600 2nd Royal Scots

ROWETH Matthew MM Pte 21206 Suffolk Regt
ROWLAND Abel MM Pte M2/020355 Army Service Corps
ROWLAND Albert J. MM Dvr 82645 RFA
ROWLAND Arthur John MM CSM 5414 1st Essex Regt DOW 21.10.16.
ROWLAND Clarence MM Cpl 15674 7th East Kent Regt KIA 15.7.17.
ROWLAND Edward P. MM+Bar Sjt 5657 Royal West Surrey Regt
ROWLAND Francis William MM Cpl 85594 143 Coy Labour Corps
ROWLAND Frank MM Pte 81092 RAMC
ROWLAND Frederick MM Pte 241260 1/8th Worcestershire Regt KIA 5.10.18.
ROWLAND Frederick Harrison MM Sjt 925644 A/290 Bde RFA
ROWLAND Frederick J. MM Sjt 32109 17th Lancashire Fusiliers
ROWLAND George Charles MM L/Cpl 15625 8th Royal Berkshire Regt KIA 23.6.18.
ROWLAND George F. MM Pte 13952 2nd Middlesex Regt
ROWLAND Henry MM Sjt 340047 RGA
ROWLAND Herbert E. MM L/Cpl 16784 6th North Staffordshire Regt
ROWLAND James MM Sjt 84787 Royal Engineers
ROWLAND James MM Pte 141766 42nd Bn Machine Gun Corps
ROWLAND John R. "MM,MID" Spr 43357 Royal Engineers
ROWLAND John William MM Pte 13917 2nd Middlesex Regt KIA 23.10.16.
ROWLAND Lawrence S. MM Pte 16744 Royal Sussex Regt
ROWLAND Leonard C. MM L/Cpl 9351 1st Hampshire Regt
ROWLAND Philip MM Pte 31078 4th Somerset Light Infantry
ROWLAND Samuel Thomas MM CSM 7985 6th Northamptonshire Regt KIA 17.2.17.
ROWLAND W. MM Pte 350756 Royal Scots
ROWLAND Wallace MM Sjt R/38161 King's Royal Rifle Corps
ROWLAND William MM L/Cpl 9904 2nd Leinster Regt
ROWLAND William MM+Bar S/Sjt Farrier 755787 5(Durham)How Bty & 251 Bde RFA
ROWLAND William C. MM L/Cpl 40778 Northumberland Fusiliers
ROWLANDS Alfred MM Pte 332681 1/9th Liverpool Regt
ROWLANDS Claude R. MM Spr 78138 Royal Engineers
ROWLANDS David Lawrence MM Cpl 275906 Durham Light Infantry
ROWLANDS Edward "MM,DM(B)" Sjt 25135 Royal Welsh Fusiliers
ROWLANDS Edward D. MM Pte 2954 1st Welsh Guards
ROWLANDS Edward T. MM Pte 37042 Royal Welsh Fusiliers
ROWLANDS F. "DCM,MM" L/Cpl 437308 RAMC
ROWLANDS Harold MM Cpl 27348 1st Shropshire Light Infantry
ROWLANDS Harold MM L/Cpl 19286 Notts & Derby Regt
ROWLANDS John MM Pte 72898 Machine Gun Corps
ROWLANDS John MM Sjt 14017 7th South Wales Borderers
ROWLANDS John MM Sjt 173620 RGA
ROWLANDS Richard MM Pte 15451 13th Liverpool Regt
ROWLANDS Richard T. MM Cpl 452160 Royal Engineers
ROWLANDS Thomas MM Pte 26180 17th Royal Welsh Fusiliers
ROWLANDS Thomas MM Sjt 200304 1/4th Royal Welsh Fusiliers
ROWLANDS Thomas C. MM Cpl 358015 Royal Engineers
ROWLANDS Vivian MM+Bar Sjt 20697 6th York & Lancaster Regt
ROWLANDS W. MM Dvr 707382 RFA
ROWLANDS William MM Dvr 104928 D/162 Bde RFA
ROWLANDSON Arthur MM Pte 5958 West Riding Regt
ROWLANDSON Benjamin MM Bdr 47091 5 Div Ammn Col RFA
ROWLANDSON Richard MM L/Cpl 308572 4th Liverpool Regt
ROWLATT Edward W. MM Spr 49141 Royal Engineers
ROWLEDGE Ernest A. MM Sjt 7283 2nd South Staffordshire Regt
ROWLEDGE Reginald MM Sjt 498229 Royal Engineers
ROWLEDGE Robert A. MM Cpl 15225 Machine Gun Corps
ROWLES Arthur Herbert MM Gnr 124198 200 Siege Bty RGA DOW 23.8.18.
ROWLES Frank MM Pte 23512 17th Lancashire Fusiliers DOW 9.2.18.
ROWLES James E. MM Pte 11633 7th Somerset Light Infantry
ROWLETT H.V. MM AM1 44246 Royal Flying Corps
ROWLETT James French MM L/Sjt 19211 Grenadier Guards
ROWLETT Thomas L. MM Pte 24923 Lincolnshire Regt
ROWLEY Albert MM Pte 15386 Somerset Light Infantry
ROWLEY Albert Vering MM Dvr 4542 D/75 Bde RFA KIA 23.8.17.
ROWLEY Alfred MM Pte 43489 Royal Highlanders
ROWLEY Alfred MM L/Sjt 12363 North Staffordshire Regt
ROWLEY Archibald D. MM Bdr 120845 RFA
ROWLEY Bernard MM L/Cpl 18046 4th Hussars. KIA 30.3.18.
ROWLEY Charles MM Cpl 266167 2/4th West Riding Regt
ROWLEY Charles W. MM+Bar Spr 478250 Royal Engineers
ROWLEY Ernest MM Sjt 5320 4th Dragoon Guards

ROWLEY Ernest Gordon MM Cpl 12463 23rd Royal Fusiliers DOW 27.7.17.
ROWLEY Frank Ashley MM L/Cpl B/203044 7th Rifle Brigade
ROWLEY Frederick William MM Cpl 6535 1st Bedfordshire Regt KIA 21.8.18.
ROWLEY George MM L/Cpl 266072 5th West Riding Regt
ROWLEY George Frederick MM Sjt 13043 Essex Regt
ROWLEY George Henry MM L/Cpl 4279 1/1st Hertfordshire Regt
ROWLEY Harry A. MM Cpl R/43865 13th King's Royal Rifle Corps
ROWLEY Henry J. MM Pte 40950 Royal Inniskilling Fusiliers
ROWLEY J.H. MM L/Cpl P/5077 Military Foot Police
ROWLEY John MM L/Cpl 40033 1st South Staffordshire Regt
ROWLEY John MM Pte 72759 Machine Gun Corps
ROWLEY John G. MM 2nd Cpl 486389 468 Fd Coy Royal Engineers
ROWLEY John W. MM Pte 73692 42nd Bn Machine Gun Corps
ROWLEY Joseph MM Bdr 140760 128 Bty 29 Bde RFA
ROWLEY Reginald MM L/Cpl 11914 6th Royal Inniskilling Fusiliers
ROWLEY Sidney MM Pte 26463 9th Yorkshire Light Infantry
ROWLEY Thomas MM Pte 12363 7th South Lancashire Regt
ROWLEY W. MM Pte 20900 Grenadier Guards
ROWLEY Walter MM Sjt 104226 225 Fd Coy Royal Engineers
ROWLEY William MM Bdr 84642 RFA
ROWLEY William MM Pte 16034 8th Somerset Light Infantry
ROWLEY William B. MM Pte 26385 Liverpool Regt
ROWLEY William E. MM Spr 74425 Royal Engineers
ROWLINSON E. MM Spr 140473 Royal Engineers
ROWLINSON Samuel MM Pte 241473 5th Royal Lancaster Regt
ROWNEY George W. MM Sjt 27236 15th Durham Light Infantry
ROWNEY John MM Cpl 57794 122 Fd Coy Royal Engineers
ROWNTREE Alfred MM Bdr 755659 C/251 Bde RFA
ROWNTREE Robert MM Bdr 760681 A/317 Bde RFA
ROWNTREE Smith MM Pte 3259 1/7th Northumberland Fusiliers
ROWNTREE T. MM Pte 11615 11th Royal West Surrey Regt
ROWORTH Alan MM Sjt 45951 Machine Gun Corps
ROWSE Eric A.A. MM Pte 513938 14th London Regt
ROWSE Hawtry MM Cpl 41599 RGA
ROWSELL Albert E. MM L/Cpl 65234 9th Royal Fusiliers
ROWSELL Albert E. MM Cpl 22191 Duke of Cornwall's LI att London Regt.
ROWSELL Herbert J. MM Pte 240568 Somerset Light Infantry
ROWSELL Louis F. MM Pte 2865 2/1st HAC(Inf)
ROWSELL Walter H. MM Cpl 1506 1st Middlesex Regt
ROWSON Albert MM Dmr 2037 Royal Warwickshire Regt
ROWSON Charles F. MM Sjt 604093 C/293 Bde RFA
ROWSON George MM Pte 17014 1st Shropshire Light Infantry KIA 30.11.17.
ROWSWELL Thomas MM Pte 6862 Royal West Kent Regt
ROXBOROUGH William Henry Bowman MM Spr 211249 56 Div Sig Coy Royal Engineers
ROXBURGH Thomas MM Cpl 21993 2 Div Sig Coy Royal Engineers
ROXBURGH William Edgar MM Sjt 614014 1/1(Warwick)Bty RHA
ROXBY John W. MM Cpl 22231 Machine Gun Corps
ROXBY Jonathan MM L/Cpl 10049 Cheshire Regt
ROY Alexander MM Pte 40040 7/8th King's Own Scottish Borderers
ROY Arthur MM L/Cpl 7364 1st Northamptonshire Regt
ROY Catherine Murray MM Sister F QAIMNS
ROY Charles MM Dvr T/29921 Army Service Corps
ROY Duncan MM Sjt 316784 13th Royal Highlanders
ROY G.R. MM Pte 3929 Lincolnshire Regt
ROY George MM Pte 8824 2nd Seaforth Highlanders
ROY James MM Cpl 60777 33rd Bn Machine Gun Corps
ROY James MM Sjt 11036 Gordon Highlanders
ROY James MM Cpl 350431 1/9th Royal Scots
ROY James MM L/Cpl 28892 Durham Light Infantry
ROY James H.L. MM Pte 39706 9th Scottish Rifles
ROY John "DCM,MM" Sjt 121813 250 Tunnelling Coy Royal Engineers
ROY Percy H. MM Sjt 241610 Royal Lancaster Regt
ROY Robert G.D. MM Sjt 17910 Royal Highlanders
ROY Walter MM Pte R/32652 13th King's Royal Rifle Corps
ROYAL Walter MM Spr 48697 96 Fd Coy Royal Engineers
ROYALL Harry "MM,MSM" Pte 24121 4th Worcestershire Regt
ROYALS Sam MM Pte 1889 1/4th West Riding Regt KIA 3.9.16.
ROYCE R. MM Pte 202980 South Staffordshire Regt
ROYCE William G. MM Sjt SE/20879 Army Veterinary Corps
ROYDEN W.H. MM Pte 565104 London Regt
ROYLANCE John MM+Bar L/Cpl 26775 21st Manchester Regt
ROYLANCE William G. MM Pte 4207 15th London Regt

ROYLE Allen MM Gnr 1488 D/122 Bde RFA DOW 27.8.18.
ROYLE Arthur MM Cpl 24991 Royal Welsh Fusiliers
ROYLE Ernest MM Pte 15867 8th Royal Lancaster Regt
ROYLE Francis MM Pte 76370 Royal Fusiliers
ROYLE Frederick P. MM Sjt 27571 Suffolk Regt
ROYLE George MM Sjt 19726 18th Lancashire Fusiliers
ROYLE James W.R. MM Pte 40252 North Staffordshire Regt
ROYLE John William MM Pte 240606 1/5th Cheshire Regt
ROYLE Leonard "DCM,MM" Sjt 2502 11th Manchester Regt
ROYLE William MM Sjt 38207 250 Siege Bty RGA KIA 25.4.18.
ROYLES Arthur Edmund MM Pte 10124 15th Lancashire Fusiliers KIA 10.8.18.
ROYON William MM S/Sjt Mechanic 96799 10th Bn Tank Corps
ROYSE Stanley MM L/Sjt 241305 1/5th North Lancashire Regt
ROYSTON Charles T. MM Pte R/11883 1st King's Royal Rifle Corps
ROYSTON Francis Ronald MM Sjt 240166 1/5th York & Lancaster Regt
ROYSTON G. MM Pte 14811 8th York & Lancaster Regt
ROYSTON Herbert MM L/Cpl 70219 IX Corps Sig Coy Royal Engineers
RUAL Frederick C. MM Gnr 81449 10 Bty 147 Bde RFA
RUALD Frederick S. MM Cpl M2/052589 Army Service Corps
RUAN John MM Pte 5142 2nd York & Lancaster Regt
RUANE Thomas MM Gnr 155530 RFA
RUAUX George F. MM Pte 458 1st Royal Guernsey LI
RUBELEY Alfred E. MM L/Cpl 307569 8th Royal Warwickshire Regt
RUBENS Louis MM Pte 57996 6th Liverpool Regt
RUBERY John H. "DCM,MM" CSM 243115 1/6th Royal Warwickshire Regt
RUCASTLE William MM Gnr 308 B/158 Bde RFA
RUCKERT William MM Bdr 955024 RFA
RUCKLEY Thomas Albert MM Pte 235019 15th Hampshire Regt KIA 9.8.18.
RUCKWOOD James A.R. MM Dvr 28512 RFA
RUDA M. MM Sjt 7724 Royal Fusiliers
RUDD A.E. MM AM2 50863 Royal Flying Corps
RUDD Albert Henry MM Pte 19055 2nd Royal Warwickshire Regt
RUDD Bert J. MM Spr 458137 Signal Service Royal Engineers
RUDD Clifford "MM,MSM" Cpl 83604 210 Fd Coy Royal Engineers
RUDD Edward James MM Pte 422509 2/10th London Regt KIA 24.8.18.
RUDD Ernest MM Bdr 277818 17 Hy Bty RGA
RUDD Ernest Henry John MM L/Sjt 2643 1/8th Middlesex Regt KIA 1.7.16.
RUDD F.W. MM Sjt 1606 Lincolnshire Regt
RUDD Frederick MM L/Cpl 9306 1st Royal Berkshire Regt
RUDD Harold S. MM Sjt 204460 Royal West Kent Regt
RUDD James W. MM L/Cpl 15435 1/5th Border Regt
RUDD John MM+Bar Pte 13607 Yorkshire Regt
RUDD John E. MM Sjt 11/380 11th East Yorkshire Regt
RUDD John W. MM L/Cpl 6071 Royal Sussex Regt
RUDD Leslie MM Pte 8386 1st Suffolk Regt
RUDD Philip John MM Pte 2095 17 Fd Amb RAMC
RUDD Stewart MM Sjt 265498 Northumberland Fusiliers
RUDD Tom MM Gnr 82962 B/71 Bde RFA
RUDD Walter Edward MM Gnr(SS) 98358 42 Bty 2 Bde RFA
RUDD William MM Pte 10862 1st Royal Lancaster Regt
RUDD William MM Sjt 13072 7th East Yorkshire Regt
RUDDER James MM Cpl 307898 West Riding Regt
RUDDERHAM George A. MM Pte 476 2nd Royal Sussex Regt
RUDDERHAM Thomas H. MM Gnr 70789 RGA
RUDDICK Joseph T. MM L/Cpl 300962 10th Arg & Suth Highlanders
RUDDIMAN George MM Pte 42933 5/6th Scottish Rifles DOW 7.11.18.
RUDDLE John J. MM Pte 2432 Middlesex Regt
RUDDLE W. MM Cpl 1620 4 Div Ammn Col RFA
RUDDOCK Eli MM Pte M2/267634 894 Coy Army Service Corps
RUDDOCK Frank T. MM Pte 285059 1/1st Hertfordshire Regt
RUDDOCK William MM Pte 25372 10th West Riding Regt
RUDDY John MM Pte 1526 Northumberland Fusiliers att MGC.
RUDELHOFF Leonard E. MM Pte 423078 10th London Regt
RUDGE Albert Ernest MM Cpl 29884 Royal Engineers Died 27.5.17.
RUDGE Albert J. MM Sjt 10145 1st Royal West Surrey Regt
RUDGE Arthur E. MM Cpl 12802 2nd Worcestershire Regt
RUDGE Arthur F. MM Pte 16328 2nd Gloucestershire Regt
RUDGE Charles MM Cpl 1352 14th Royal Warwickshire Regt
RUDGE Ernest MM Cpl 465724 26 Searchlight Section Royal Engineers
RUDGE Ernest F. MM Sjt 337050 1 Fd Amb RAMC
RUDGE Frank George Herbert MM Sjt 3021 4th Rifle Brigade

RUDGE Josiah MM Pte 13018 9th Northumberland Fusiliers
RUDGE Leonard Merrick "MC,MM(15274 Sjt 3 Gren Gds)" Capt Worcestershire Regt
RUDGE Wilfred Arthur MM L/Cpl 129607 'H' Coy 2 Special Bn Royal Engineers
RUDGE William MM Spr 112817 176 Tunnelling Coy Royal Engineers
RUDKIN Edward Henry MM Pte 7720 3rd Dragoon Guards
RUDLIN Albert H. MM CSM 11852 7th Bn Machine Gun Corps
RUDLIN Harry Edward MM Sjt M/38451 HQ VII Corps MT Coy Army Service Corps
RUDLINTON Leonard F. MM Sjt 240180 North Staffordshire Regt
RUDMAN Albert MM Pte 40545 South Wales Borderers
RUDMAN John Benjamin MM Sjt 270221 10th East Kent Regt
RUDOLPH William V. MM Cpl 8423 1st Norfolk Regt
RUDRAM Alfred J. MM Pte 90065 38th Bn Machine Gun Corps
RUEL Charles Simpson MM+Bar Pte 283530 4th London Regt
RUFF Cyril MM L/Cpl 16362 Royal Berkshire Regt
RUFF Enos MM Pte 201076 Bedfordshire Regt
RUFFELL Samuel George MM Pte 321273 6th London Regt
RUFFLES Harry G. MM Sjt 5351 8th East Surrey Regt
RUFFLES Leslie MM Bdr 54258 191 Siege Bty RGA
RUFFLES William R. MM Pte 43327 Norfolk Regt
RUGG Christopher George MM Pte 202483 1/6th South Staffordshire Regt
RUGG William E. MM L/Cpl 35127 9th East Surrey Regt
RUGGLES Arthur E. MM Cpl 242536 8th Worcestershire Regt
RUGGLES George MM Pte 30292 Bedfordshire Regt
RULE Andrew Hill MM Pte 200804 1/4th King's Own Scottish Borderers KIA 17.9.18.
RULE David J. MM L/Cpl 332097 12th Highland Light Infantry
RULE Richard MM Cpl 21074 55 Fd Coy Royal Engineers
RULE Robert "DCM,MM+Bar" L/Sjt 240255 7th Border Regt
RULE William MM CSM 305928 1/8th Lancashire Fusiliers
RULE William J. MM Cpl /756 7th East Surrey Regt
RUMBLE Alfred Edward MM Gnr 79458 136 Siege Bty RGA
RUMBLE Arthur MM Cpl 11758 C/236 Bde RFA KIA 7.7.18.
RUMBLE Harry MM Pte S/28647 Rifle Brigade
RUMBLE Joseph F. MM L/Cpl 203994 East Surrey Regt
RUMBLE Percy MM Sjt 15559 5th Royal Berkshire Regt
RUMBLE Percy B.D. "DCM,MM" Sjt 10040 Royal Berkshire Regt
RUMBLE Stephen R. MM Pte 204866 11th South Lancashire Regt
RUMBLE Thomas MM Pte 4099 RAMC
RUMBLE William H. MM L/Cpl 203162 1st Dorsetshire Regt
RUMBLES W.R. MM Cpl 13300 8th Norfolk Regt
RUMBOL Thomas H.J. MM Pte 19719 6th Duke of Cornwall's LI
RUMBOLD Frederick C. MM Gnr 71129 RFA
RUMBOLD Tom MM Pte 60401 Royal Welsh Fusiliers
RUMBOLD Walter Thomas MM+Bar Sjt 26710 6th Royal West Kent Regt
RUMENS Harry MM Pte 572 8th Royal West Kent Regt
RUMMING William J. MM Sjt 9392 Coldstream Guards
RUMNEY Arthur MM Pte 11/13424 11th Border Regt
RUMP Robert S. MM Pte 25787 Norfolk Regt
RUMSEY Harry V. MM Pte 35363 Border Regt
RUMSEY Herbert "DCM,MM" L/Cpl C/6687 18th King's Royal Rifle Corps
RUMSEY Norman H. MM Sjt 18582 5 Bty 45 Bde RFA
RUMSEY Tom MM Spr 72292 Royal Engineers
RUMSEY William Maynard MM Spr 70289 4 Div Sig Coy Royal Engineers
RUNACRES William MM Cpl 14566 8th Suffolk Regt KIA 12.10.17.
RUNCORN Frederick "DCM,MM" CSM 14236 24th Royal Fusiliers
RUNDELL William John Tretheway MM Pte 24199 10th Duke of Cornwall's LI DOW 16.12.17.
RUNDLE Richard Nicholas MM L/Cpl 49092 27th Bn Machine Gun Corps
RUNDLE Sydney MM L/Cpl 550588 16th London Regt
RUNDLE Sydney Crymes MM Pte 30443 2nd Devonshire Regt KIA 24.4.18.
RUNDLE Watkin MM Sjt 240536 1/5th Royal Lancaster Regt
RUNDLE William MM Sjt 240193 Devonshire Regt
RUNHAM Albert Ellis MM Gnr 776958 Y/9 Med TM Bty RFA
RUNHAM Herbert Auther MM Pte 72102 135 Fd Amb RAMC
RUNNEGAR T. MM L/Cpl P/1835 Military Mounted Police
RUNYEARD Edgar John "MM,MID" Sjt 23324 Guards Div Sig Coy Royal Engineers DOW 20.3.16.
RUSBY Harold R. MM Gnr 338068 RGA
RUSE George Benjamin MM Pte 20370 8th East Surrey Regt KIA 18.9.18.
RUSE James MM Pte 118034 18th Bn Machine Gun Corps
RUSH Albert MM Bdr 74280 2 Bde RFA
RUSH Charles Martin "MM,MID" CSM 1151 1/6th London Regt
RUSH Ernest H. MM Bdr 651424 D/198 Bde RFA
RUSH F. MM L/Cpl 24274 20 Fd Coy Royal Engineers
RUSH Henry MM Pte 49500 72 Fd Amb RAMC DOW 16.4.17.
RUSH J. MM Pte 43979 Royal Irish Rifles
RUSH John MM L/Bdr 340166 RGA
RUSH John W. MM BSM 55799 A/74 Bde RFA
RUSH Percy J. MM Pte 82248 46th Bn Machine Gun Corps
RUSH William MM+Bar Sjt 10199 37th & 2nd Bns Machine Gun Corps
RUSHALL Richard MM Pte 145432 1/1st Northamptonshire Yeomanry
RUSHBROOK David E. MM Pte 653783 21st London Regt
RUSHBY Frank MM Pte 376985 10th Manchester Regt
RUSHBY Fred MM Dvr 2885 RFA
RUSHBY George MM Gnr(SS) 770923 RFA
RUSHFORD James MM Pte 7839 Arg & Suth Highlanders
RUSHFORD Oliver MM Pte 3803 Durham Light Infantry
RUSHFORD William L. MM Pte 104941 Machine Gun Corps
RUSHFORTH Charles MM L/Cpl 14/1312 13th York & Lancaster Regt KIA 24.10.18.
RUSHFORTH G. MM Pte 22108 Border Regt
RUSHFORTH Herbert MM Sjt 35668 59 Coy 20th Bn Machine Gun Corps
RUSHFORTH John William MM L/Cpl 17481 1st Royal Fusiliers DOW 24.3.18.
RUSHFORTH William J. MM Cpl 1360 50 Div Sig Coy Royal Engineers
RUSHTON Abraham MM Pte 16656 9th North Lancashire Regt
RUSHTON Alfred MM Cpl 705642 211 Bde RFA
RUSHTON Arthur MM Cpl 27198 Notts & Derby Regt
RUSHTON Arthur MM+Bar L/Cpl 12264 9th Cheshire Regt
RUSHTON Edward MM Pte 268668 1st West Yorkshire Regt
RUSHTON George MM Pte 66987 140 Fd Amb RAMC
RUSHTON Harold E. MM Pte 73610 RAMC
RUSHTON James MM L/Cpl 30009 1st Royal Lancaster Regt KIA 18.4.18.
RUSHTON James Henry MM Pte 19577 9th Notts & Derby Regt DOW 2.12.16.
RUSHTON Joseph MM Pte 200255 1/5th North Staffordshire Regt
RUSHTON Richard A. MM Pte 64321 RAMC
RUSHTON William MM Sjt 356589 1/10th Liverpool Regt
RUSHTON William James MM Sjt 2094 1st Lancashire Fusiliers
RUSHWORTH Albert MM Pte 38216 2/5th West Yorkshire Regt
RUSHWORTH Alec B. MM Gnr 6158 246 Bde RFA DOW 19.11.16.
RUSHWORTH George MM Pte 80048 Notts & Derby Regt
RUSHWORTH Norman MM Gnr 780525 B/311 Bde RFA
RUSK James MM Pte 8503 Arg & Suth Highlanders
RUSLING Alfred MM Cpl 800930 RFA
RUSS Edwin MM Pte 10660 9th Royal Fusiliers
RUSS Ewart Percy MM Pte 18651 7th Wiltshire Regt Died 26.10.18.
RUSS Frederick MM Pte 7803 2nd Border Regt KIA 10.5.17.
RUSS John H. MM S/Sjt 40068 RAMC
RUSS Oliver E. MM Pte 19100 Machine Gun Corps
RUSSAM Henry E. MM Cpl 29857 Worcestershire Regt
RUSSELL Alan W. MM Pte 10479 2/1st HAC(Inf)
RUSSELL Albert Edward MM Cpl 31527 6th Bn Machine Gun Corps
RUSSELL Alexander MM Sjt 10394 1st Royal Highlanders
RUSSELL Alexander "DCM,MM" Sjt 1270 1/6th Gordon Highlanders DOW 19.11.16.
RUSSELL Alfred MM Sjt 15814 RFA
RUSSELL Alfred M. "DCM,MM" Sjt 96878 177 Tunnelling Coy Royal Engineers
RUSSELL Alfred S. MM Pte 1813 1/7th Durham Light Infantry
RUSSELL Algernon F. MM Pte 51589 Machine Gun Corps
RUSSELL Arthur MM Pte 364 14th York & Lancaster Regt KIA 6.10.18.
RUSSELL Arthur MM Pte 1130 Durham Light Infantry
RUSSELL Arthur J. "DCM,MM" Sjt 32760 129 Bty 42 Bde RFA
RUSSELL Bert "MM,MID" L/Cpl 18855 Liverpool Regt
RUSSELL Bertie MM Pte 88065 6th Liverpool Regt
RUSSELL Charles MM Pte 40652 15th Highland Light Infantry
RUSSELL Charles MM L/Cpl 1584 XIX Corps Cyclist Bn Army Cyclist Corps
RUSSELL Charles MM Pte 12890 9th West Riding Regt
RUSSELL Charles A. MM L/Cpl R/13411 King's Royal Rifle Corps
RUSSELL Charles F. MM+Bar Sjt 17192 Machine Gun Corps
RUSSELL Charles H. MM Pte 8906 Machine Gun Corps

RUSSELL David MM Dvr 46620 RFA
RUSSELL E. MM Bdr 608 RGA
RUSSELL Ebenezer MM Pte 276356 1/8th Arg & Suth Highlanders KIA 23.7.18.
RUSSELL Edgar MM Pte 27503 Hampshire Regt
RUSSELL Edward MM L/Cpl 16612 South Staffordshire Regt
RUSSELL Ellen MM Miss F First Aid Nursing Yeomanry
RUSSELL Ernest MM Pte 242987 2/5th West Yorkshire Regt DOW 21.4.18.
RUSSELL Ernest Michael MM Sjt 9075 7th East Kent Regt
RUSSELL F.H. "MM,MID" Cpl 49198 RFA
RUSSELL Frank C. MM L/Cpl 25429 1st Border Regt
RUSSELL Frederick MM Sjt 49396 13th West Riding Regt
RUSSELL Frederick MM Pte 722340 24th London Regt
RUSSELL Frederick MM Cpl 306280 10th West Yorkshire Regt KIA 5.9.18.
RUSSELL Frederick George MM L/Sjt 16260 8th Bedfordshire Regt DOW 11.2.17.
RUSSELL Frederick James MM L/Cpl 58824 92 Fd Coy Royal Engineers DOW 3.7.16.
RUSSELL Frederick P. MM Cpl 9706 8th Royal Sussex Regt
RUSSELL G.A. MM Pnr 74948 Royal Engineers
RUSSELL George MM Pte 332963 Highland Light Infantry
RUSSELL George MM L/Cpl 155944 255 Tunnelling Coy Royal Engineers
RUSSELL George MM Sjt 226773 312 Rd Constr Coy Royal Engineers
RUSSELL George MM Pte 44365 Notts & Derby Regt
RUSSELL George W. MM Sjt 43440 13th Durham Light Infantry
RUSSELL George William Charles MM Pte 11325 6th Royal West Kent Regt
RUSSELL Graham MM Cpl 10231 1st Seaforth Highlanders
RUSSELL Hamilton McA. MM L/Sjt 15051 2nd Scots Guards
RUSSELL Harold H. MM L/Sjt 11982 6th Somerset Light Infantry
RUSSELL Harry A. MM Pte M/318304 Army Service Corps
RUSSELL Henry MM Pte 8565 10th Royal West Kent Regt
RUSSELL Henry MM Dvr 27299 43 Bde RFA
RUSSELL Henry MM Pte 14675 8th Suffolk Regt
RUSSELL Herbert MM Pte 201160 Seaforth Highlanders
RUSSELL J MM L/Sjt 6711 2nd Dragoons
RUSSELL J. MM Pte 25671 Yeomanry
RUSSELL Jack E.B. MM+Bar Bdr 36854 RFA
RUSSELL James MM Pte 8149 2nd Royal Inniskilling Fusiliers
RUSSELL James MM Cpl 24196 2nd Royal Inniskilling Fusiliers
RUSSELL James MM Pte 42633 4th North Staffordshire Regt
RUSSELL James MM Pte 7585 5th Cameron Highlanders
RUSSELL James MM L/Cpl 1089 8th Seaforth Highlanders DOW 25.3.18.
RUSSELL James MM Pte 203116 Manchester Regt
RUSSELL James Comyns MM Pte 132796 62nd Bn Machine Gun Corps
RUSSELL James H. MM+Bar Cpl 570777 17th London Regt
RUSSELL James T. MM Sjt 42609 RFA
RUSSELL John MM+Bar Spr 37533 59 Fd Coy Royal Engineers
RUSSELL John MM L/Cpl 2914 1/4th Yorkshire Regt
RUSSELL John E. MM Sjt 1399 1/15th London Regt
RUSSELL John H. MM Dmr 1252 4th Liverpool Regt
RUSSELL John Stanley MM Sjt 434419 1/3(South Midland)Fd Amb RAMC
RUSSELL John William "MC,DCM,MM(50323 Sjt 24 Div Sig Coy)" 2Lt Royal Engineers
RUSSELL Joseph MM L/Cpl 10664 10th Royal Warwickshire Regt
RUSSELL Lewis MM Spr 93730 228 Fd Coy Royal Engineers
RUSSELL Luther MM Dvr 508335 502 Fd Coy Royal Engineers
RUSSELL Nisbet MM Cpl 40 RAMC
RUSSELL P. MM Cpl 24151 Essex Regt
RUSSELL Peter MM Sjt 3709 8th Seaforth Highlanders KIA 31.7.17.
RUSSELL Reginald MM L/Cpl 1853 8th Royal Sussex Regt
RUSSELL Reginald MM Pte 306506 2/8th West Yorkshire Regt
RUSSELL Reginald E. MM+Bar Sjt 500226 Royal Engineers
RUSSELL Richard MM Sjt 350127 4th Liverpool Regt
RUSSELL Richard MM Pte 9310 7th Royal Irish Regt
RUSSELL Robert MM Cpl 18715 12th Royal Irish Rifles
RUSSELL Robert MM Spr 412564 409 Fd Coy Royal Engineers
RUSSELL Robert MM Cpl 252651 6th Durham Light Infantry
RUSSELL Robert MM Pte 265443 1/6th Seaforth Highlanders DOW 29.7.18.
RUSSELL Robert B. MM Pte 16233 2nd Scots Guards
RUSSELL S. MM Sjt 1498 RFA
RUSSELL Samuel MM Pte 17127 8th Royal Inniskilling Fusiliers KIA 16.8.17.
RUSSELL Sidney "MM,MID" Cpl 2107 1 Siege Coy R Monmouth RE att 56 Fd Coy
RUSSELL Stanley J. MM Pte 41584 Middlesex Regt
RUSSELL Sydney E. MM Cpl 493173 RAMC
RUSSELL Sydney E. MM Cpl 73594 48th Bn Machine Gun Corps
RUSSELL "Sydney V," MM L/Sjt 551762 16th London Regt
RUSSELL Thomas MM Pte 9229 2nd Royal Irish Regt
RUSSELL Thomas MM Pte 335125 Royal Scots
RUSSELL Thomas C. MM Spr 2471 2(Lowland)Fd Coy Royal Engineers
RUSSELL Thomas Dennis MM L/Cpl 2629 (200542) 1/4th Royal Berkshire Regt KIA 16.4.17.
RUSSELL Thomas G. MM Pte 23745 5th Northamptonshire Regt
RUSSELL Thomas J. MM Cpl 144739 266 Siege Bty RGA
RUSSELL Thomas John MM Cpl 965262 24 Bde RFA
RUSSELL Thomas L. MM Cpl 265331 9th Scottish Rifles
RUSSELL Victor John MM Sjt 17640 14th Welsh Regt KIA 10.5.18.
RUSSELL W.L. MM Dvr 14793 RFA
RUSSELL Walter MM Bdr 95482 B/62 Bde RFA DOW 20.5.18.
RUSSELL Wilfred MM L/Cpl 35061 193 Coy Machine Gun Corps
RUSSELL William MM Dvr 49647 A/104 Bde RFA
RUSSELL William MM Sjt 12692 9th West Yorkshire Regt
RUSSELL William MM Cpl 7354 A/160 Bde RFA KIA 6.2.18.
RUSSELL William E. MM Pte 33036 Royal Berkshire Regt
RUSSELL William J. MM+Bar L/Cpl 3/2968 Essex Regt
RUSSELL William J. MM Sjt 464 13th Royal Irish Rifles
RUSSELL William John MM Sjt 56633 21 Div Sig Coy Royal Engineers
RUSSELL William Lester MM Sjt Pnr 15884 9th Royal Irish Rifles
RUSSELL William Richard John "MM,MSM" CSM 10098 122 Fd Coy Royal Engineers
RUSSEN Henry B. MM Pte 345616 24th Royal Welsh Fusiliers
RUSSON Thomas "DCM,MM" Cpl 67878 30 Bde RFA
RUSSON William "DCM,MM" Sjt 12276 1st Notts & Derby Regt
RUST Bertram Edgar MM Cpl 1668 1(Northumbrian)Fd Amb RAMC
RUST Dick H. MM BQMS 30006 281 Siege Bty RGA
RUST Ernest Walter MM Pte 241624 2/5th West Riding Regt
RUST George MM Sjt 24803 121 Heavy Bty RGA
RUST George MM Bdr 7757 RFA
RUST George P. MM+Bar Sjt 11/422 East Yorkshire Regt
RUST H. MM Pte 291383 Gordon Highlanders
RUST Herbert G. MM Sjt 44281 Royal Engineers
RUST John MM Sjt 21428 Machine Gun Corps
RUST John C. MM Cpl 21504 A/157 Bde RFA
RUSTON Allan Maxwell MM Sjt 15585 7th Northamptonshire Regt KIA 23.4.18.
RUSTON George MM Pte 22577 1/4th York & Lancaster Regt DOW 15.10.18.
RUTH John MM Pte 8552 1st Irish Guards
RUTH Richard Cornelius MM Sjt 19627 7 Div Ammn Col RFA
RUTHERFORD Alexander C. MM L/Cpl 17225 Royal Scots
RUTHERFORD Alfred MM Pte 18377 Durham Light Infantry
RUTHERFORD Angus MM Pte 41114 Royal Scots
RUTHERFORD Edward Thomas MM Bdr 97806 D/124 Bde RFA
RUTHERFORD George Frederick MM Bdr 750687 315 Bde RFA
RUTHERFORD Harry "MM,MIDx2" Pte 1293 South Irish Horse Died 24.3.18.
RUTHERFORD Herbert G. MM Sjt R/4259 13th King's Royal Rifle Corps
RUTHERFORD James MM Sjt 67538 Machine Gun Corps
RUTHERFORD James MM Sjt 771513 50 Div Ammn Col RFA
RUTHERFORD John MM Pte 315084 5/6th Scottish Rifles
RUTHERFORD John MM Cpl 14729 9th Royal Inniskilling Fusiliers
RUTHERFORD Joseph J. MM Sjt 1679 2/2(London)Fd Coy Royal Engineers
RUTHERFORD Patrick J. MM CSM 1719 23rd Royal Fusiliers
RUTHERFORD Thomas MM Sjt 16117 10th Northumberland Fusiliers
RUTHERFORD Thomas S. MM Gnr Sig 250101 A/175 Bty RFA
RUTHERFORD William MM Pte 386485 1/1(Northumbrian)Fd Amb RAMC
RUTHERFORD William Andrew MM Bdr 68959 123 Siege Bty RGA
RUTHVEN Thomas MM L/Sjt 10936 5th Cameron Highlanders
RUTLAND Charles MM Dvr 44523 39 Bde RFA
RUTLAND John MM Sjt 397172 Rly Ops Div Royal Engineers
RUTLAND William MM Cpl 207999 11th Royal West Surrey Regt
RUTLEDGE Walter MM Pte 11/1358 11th East Yorkshire Regt
RUTLEDGE William MM Pte 11292 9th Scottish Rifles

RUTLEDGE William George MM L/Cpl 28728 11th Royal Inniskilling Fusiliers KIA 16.8.17.
RUTLEDGE William J.H. MM Sjt 133000 66 Siege Bty RGA
RUTT Walter V. MM Dvr 656813 RFA
RUTTER Charles MM Pte 43423 West Yorkshire Regt
RUTTER Frederick MM Cpl 8029 1st North Staffordshire Regt KIA 8.9.18.
RUTTER George "DCM,MM" Sjt 45934 24 Div Sig Coy Royal Engineers
RUTTER John MM CSM 94457 13th Liverpool Regt
RUTTER John H. MM Dvr 25257 RFA
RUTTER Joseph MM CSM 1501 1/4th Suffolk Regt
RUTTER Robert MM Spr 458757 171 Tunnelling Coy Royal Engineers
RUTTER Samuel MM Dvr 36910 190 Bde HQ RFA
RUTTER Sydney MM Pte 14652 8th Suffolk Regt
RUTTER Thomas Fenwick MM Pte 31768 1st South Staffordshire Regt
RUTTER Tom MM Pte 3996 Lancashire Fusiliers
RUTTER William Ralph MM Pte 493503 13th London Regt
RUTTERFORD Harry MM Dvr 40064 B/186 Bde RFA
RUTTY Edward C. MM Cpl R/10452 King's Royal Rifle Corps
RUTTY John MM Pte 204369 12th East Surrey Regt
RYALL Edward MM Cpl 22144 10th South Wales Borderers
RYALL Edward Walter MM Dvr 75668 RFA
RYALL Harry Edward MM Cpl 16116 1st Grenadier Guards KIA 25.9.16.
RYALL Henry MM Cpl 815 12th Lancers
RYALLS John W. MM L/Bdr 785434 B/156 Bde RFA
RYAN Alfred J. MM L/Cpl 9043 1st Royal Lancaster Regt
RYAN Christopher MM L/Cpl 11053 Royal Irish Regt
RYAN Christopher MM Pte 10560 RAMC
RYAN Connie MM Cpl 8872 1st Royal Irish Regt Died 4.11.18.
RYAN Denis MM Pte 4817 2nd Irish Guards KIA 15.9.16.
RYAN Desmond O'R. MM Sjt 3967 12th Manchester Regt
RYAN Edward MM Sjt 10672 1st South Wales Borderers
RYAN Frank MM CQMS 9240 2nd Worcestershire Regt
RYAN Frank MM L/Cpl 10652 1st Royal Irish Fusiliers
RYAN Fred MM Sjt 14153 24th Manchester Regt
RYAN Frederick C. MM Pte 4515 1/18th London Regt
RYAN George E. MM Pte 89067 4th Middlesex Regt
RYAN Harry M. MM Sub Cond 6747 Army Ordnance Corps att HQ First Army
RYAN Isaiah MM Cpl 19489 Northumberland Fusiliers
RYAN J. MM Pnr 15470 3 Div Sig Coy Royal Engineers
RYAN J.F. MM+Bar Sjt P/4816 Military Mounred Police
RYAN James MM Dvr 88700 A/48 Bde RFA
RYAN John MM Sjt 9557 2nd East Lancashire Regt
RYAN John MM Cpl 304227 13th Tank Corps
RYAN John MM Pte 4944 Royal Irish Regt
RYAN John MM Pte 21114 2nd Royal West Surrey Regt
RYAN John MM Gnr 52392 41 Bde RFA
RYAN John MM Pte 5018 2nd Leinster Regt KIA 31.7.17.
RYAN John MM Sjt 35431 RGA
RYAN John J. MM Pte 35281 RAMC
RYAN John J. MM Pte 3/3111 6th Yorkshire Light Infantry
RYAN John W. MM L/Cpl 546052 509 Fd Coy Royal Engineers
RYAN John William MM Bdr 21494 C/48 Bde RFA
RYAN John William MM Sjt 46829 105 Fd Coy Royal Engineers KIA 17.12.17.
RYAN Joseph Richard MM L/Cpl 9675 13th Royal Fusiliers
RYAN Martin MM Gnr 29098 1 Siege Bty RGA
RYAN Michael MM L/Cpl 9188 Irish Guards
RYAN Michael O. MM 2nd Cpl 14068 Royal Engineers
RYAN Patrick MM Pte 43135 6th Royal Dublin Fusiliers
RYAN Richard F. MM L/Bdr 35059 RGA
RYAN Robert MM Cpl 715212 RFA
RYAN Sydney J. MM Bdr 29693 RFA
RYAN Thomas MM+Bar Sjt 8425 1st North Lancashire Regt
RYAN Thomas MM Cpl 4118 Lancashire Fusiliers
RYAN Thomas F. MM Bdr 49468 RFA
RYAN Thomas M. MM Spr 495395 63 Div Sig Coy Royal Engineers
RYAN W. MM Pte 4581 Liverpool Regt
RYAN W.P. MM Pte 721480 London Regt
RYAN William MM Pte 80608 4th London Regt
RYAN William MM Pte 7903 2nd Leinster Regt
RYAN William MM Bdr 29415 RGA
RYAN William Stanley MM Gnr 172850 186 Siege Bty RGA
RYCRAFT Stephen MM Pte 23831 2nd Suffolk Regt

RYCROFT Benjamin Crawshaw MM Spr 1997 50 Div Sig Coy Royal Engineers
RYCROFT Eli MM Pte 17938 Machine Gun Corps
RYCROFT Harry C. MM+Bar L/Cpl 81867 Royal Engineers
RYCROFT James MM Pte 242362 2/5th East Lancashire Regt
RYCROFT John F. MM 2nd Cpl 251760 Royal Engineers
RYDEARD J. MM L/Cpl P/1308 Military Foot Police
RYDER Alfred MM Dvr 42343 RFA
RYDER Arthur MM Pte 37124 8th Northumberland Fusiliers
RYDER Arthur MM Pte 85359 188 Coy Machine Gun Corps
RYDER Bertie MM L/Cpl 13240 12th Middlesex Regt KIA 17.10.17.
RYDER Charles MM Sjt 8223 1/4th Royal Lancaster Regt
RYDER Daniel MM Cpl 98329 37th Bn Machine Gun Corps
RYDER E. MM Pte 49938 1st Essex Regt
RYDER Ernest A. MM Pte 53126 RAMC
RYDER Ernest John MM L/Cpl 240153 1/5th Gloucestershire Regt KIA 17.4.17.
RYDER Fred MM Pte 14742 2nd Grenadier Guards
RYDER Frederick MM L/Cpl 9596 2nd Durham Light Infantry
RYDER Frederick M. MM+Bar Sjt C/6539 King's Royal Rifle Corps
RYDER George MM Pte 242202 4th West Riding Regt
RYDER Horace MM Cpl 17482 Machine Gun Corps
RYDER J. MM AM1 115269 Royal Flying Corps
RYDER James MM Pte 200413 2nd Yorkshire Light Infantry
RYDER James Alfred MM Pte 303395 2/6th Manchester Regt KIA 21.3.18.
RYDER James H. MM L/Cpl 19473 2nd Grenadier Guards DOW 9.10.17.
RYDER John MM Pte 241293 5th Leicestershire Regt
RYDER John MM Pte 25794 1st Royal Dublin Fusiliers
RYDER John H. MM Pte R/582 King's Royal Rifle Corps
RYDER John T. MM Pte 359725 Liverpool Regt
RYDER John Thomas MM Sjt 21007 36 Coy Labour Corps
RYDER Joseph "DCM,MM" L/Bdr 805582 C/231 Bde RFA
RYDER Joseph A. MM S/Sjt Farrier 25181 RHA
RYDER Reuben MM Pte 226050 6th Northamptonshire Regt
RYDER Sydney MM L/Cpl 18/1393 18th Durham Light Infantry
RYDER Tom MM CSM 263012 1st Liverpool Regt
RYDER William "DCM,MM" L/Sjt 1041 1st Manchester Regt
RYDING Frank MM Pte 14137 16th Lancashire Fusiliers
RYDINGS Albert MM Sjt 112480 RGA
RYE Howard MM Pte 265850 2nd Northumberland Fusiliers
RYE Percy MM L/Cpl 201674 Royal Warwickshire Regt
RYE Richard MM Sjt 65063 130 Fd Coy Royal Engineers
RYE Richard Alfred MM Pte 103686 227 Coy Machine Gun Corps
RYE Victor MM Sjt 8398 1st East Yorkshire Regt
RYLAH Ernest MM Sjt 202045 1/4th Yorkshire Light Infantry
RYLANCE Jack MM Spr 442188 429 Fd Coy Royal Engineers
RYLAND Harold H. MM Pte 29423 1st Worcestershire Regt
RYLANDS Edward MM Pte 36711 Lancashire Fusiliers
RYLANDS Edward MM Pte 240078 1/5th North Lancashire Regt KIA 30.11.17.
RYLANDS James MM Sjt 690207 D/291 Bde RFA
RYLE James MM Gnr 66772 RFA
RYLES George MM Pte 11119 9th North Staffordshire Regt
RYLES John MM Gnr 79728 RFA
RYMAN Albert MM Sjt 7419 1st Lincolnshire Regt DOW 3.7.16.
RYMELL Thomas MM L/Cpl 61139 17th Royal Fusiliers
RYMER Leonard J. MM L/Cpl 54644 Welsh Regt
RYMER Robert MM Sjt 23498 Machine Gun Corps KIA 10.4.18.
RYMER Seymour J. MM Cpl 93252 Notts & Derby Regt
RYMER Thomas MM L/Cpl 267769 7th Liverpool Regt
RYMILL A. MM Pte 2356 Liverpool Regt
RYNN James W. MM Cpl 19482 Northumberland Fusiliers
RYNO John G. MM L/Cpl 33375 2nd Border Regt
RYRIE Frank MM Sjt 5148 Machine Gun Corps
RYRIE William MM Pte 220097 6th Cameron Highlanders KIA 25.7.18.

S

SABERI Lewis R. MM Pte 7948 1st East Surrey Regt
SABERTON Gordon E MM Sjt 982 Middlesex Regt
SABIN Horace J. MM Sjt 16153 9th Royal Warwickshire Regt
SABIN Thomas MM Gnr 614220 2/1(Warwick)Bty 126 Bde RFA DOW 12.9.17.
SABINE Augustus C. MM Sjt 45538 Royal Engineers
SACH Walter MM Bdr 126644 RHA

SACHS Charles MM L/Cpl 9771 1st Royal Scots
SACKETT A.E. MM Cpl 12375 Royal Air Force
SADDINGTON Albert MM Sjt 57333 Machine Gun Corps
SADDINGTON George Henry MM Sjt 1435 7th Royal West Kent Regt KIA 12.10.17.
SADLER Arthur J. MM Cpl 20798 2nd Coldstream Guards
SADLER Benjamin G. MM L/Cpl 701279 1/23rd London Regt
SADLER Bertie E. MM Sjt 32649 RGA
SADLER David MM Pte 8111 1st Suffolk Regt
SADLER David MM Pte 201819 1/5th Royal Warwickshire Regt
SADLER E. MM Pte 4879 Northumberland Fusiliers
SADLER Edward A. MM Sjt 7385 2nd Wiltshire Regt
SADLER Frank MM Sjt 10582 Royal West Kent Regt
SADLER Frederick Noah MM Cpl 241013 2/6th West Yorkshire Regt
SADLER George Henry MM Dvr 905372 2(Home Counties)Bde RFA
SADLER Henry Armstrong "DCM,MM" L/Cpl 870 50 Div Sig Coy Royal Engineers
SADLER Herbert MM Sjt 14171 RGA
SADLER James MM L/Cpl 321 9th Royal Fusiliers
SADLER James W. MM Sjt 11940 7th York & Lancaster Regt
SADLER Jesse MM Cpl 8505 2nd South Staffordshire Regt
SADLER John MM Sjt 919 1st Northumberland Fusiliers
SADLER John MM Pte 35949 Worcestershire Regt
SADLER John Thomas MM Sjt 22554 Machine Gun Corps
SADLER Joseph Stanley MM Pte 242692 12th East Surrey Regt
SADLER Reginald MM L/Cpl 25584 12th East Surrey Regt
SADLER Robert J. MM+Bar Pte MS/4294 Army Service Corps
SADLER Rowland Charles "MM,CG(F)" Gnr 1599 31 Div Ammn Col RFA
SADLER T.H. MM L/Cpl 203346 4th Yorkshire Light Infantry
SADLER William "DCM,MM" Sjt S/14820 6th Cameron Highlanders DOW 26.7.18.
SADLER William James MM Cpl 240077 1/8th Middlesex Regt
SADLER William Proudfoot MM Pnr 93726 41 Div Sig Coy Royal Engineers
SADLER William R. MM Pte 12676 5th Lancers
SAGAR Fred MM Sjt 13/852 York & Lancaster Regt
SAGAR H. MM Pte 653872 London Regt
SAGAR Harry MM Cpl 33631 130 Coy Machine Gun Corps
SAGAR William J. MM Gnr 200619 RFA
SAGE Cyril MM Bdr 56984 RFA
SAGE Gordon Pitt MM L/Cpl 990 Royal Engineers
SAGE H. MM Pte 31599 8th Devonshire Regt
SAGE Harry W. MM Pte 320183 1st Suffolk Regt
SAGE Henry J. MM Gnr 2351 RFA
SAGE James W. MM L/Cpl 391801 9th London Regt
SAGE Walter MM Pte 4827 7th London Regt
SAGE William Albert MM Cpl M2/137559 363 MT Coy Army Service Corps
SAGE William C. MM L/Cpl 494161 474 Fd Coy Royal Engineers
SAGE William Charles MM Pte 12715 1st East Kent Regt
SAGGS Henry W. MM Bdsm 9708 1st King's Royal Rifle Corps
SAILL Albert Edward MM Gnr 155927 B/50 Bde RFA
SAINSBURY Albert MM Gnr 23056 10 Siege Bty RGA KIA 30.10.17.
SAINSBURY Alfred MM Pte 11040 5th Royal Berkshire Regt
SAINSBURY Frederick Albert MM Sjt 650077 1/21st London Regt KIA 23.3.18.
SAINSBURY George T. MM 2nd Cpl 61625 82 Fd Coy Royal Engineers
SAINSBURY Richard H. "DCM,MM" CSM 1152 26th Royal Fusiliers
SAINSBURY Rowland W. MM Pte 439278 RAMC
SAINT George James MM Pte 34278 9th Yorkshire Regt
SAINT Harry Robert MM Pte 50592 11th Royal Scots Fusiliers DOW 1.10.18.
SAINT James MM L/Cpl 2622 Northumberland Fusiliers
SAINT James E. MM Cpl 1930 Northumberland Fusiliers
SAINTE Clemitt Harrison MM Sjt 18/933 18th Durham Light Infantry
SAINTY James E. MM L/Cpl 179361 Royal Engineers
SAIT Joseph Henry MM Pte 17231 13th Essex Regt KIA 30.7.16.
SAIT William Edward MM Sjt 8061 1st Scots Guards
SAKER Frederick John MM Sjr 2527 'C' Bn Machine Gun Corps(Heavy Branch)
SALAD Hassan MM Pte 27111 Border Regt
SALCOMBE George MM Cpl 201637 1/1st(Bucks)Bn Oxf & Bucks Light Infantry
SALE Alfred J. MM Sjt 9502 1st Bedfordshire Regt
SALE Bertram MM L/Sjt 240152 1/5th Suffolk Regt
SALE Edward MM Pte 11160 Royal West Surrey Regt
SALE Harry MM L/Cpl 12839 8th North Staffordshire Regt
SALE Robert D. MM Sjt 34793 19th Middlesex Regt
SALES Edward MM+Bar Cpl 43154 8th South Staffordshire Regt
SALES Edward J.M. MM L/Cpl 30682 7th Border Regt
SALES Frank W. MM Dvr 169035 RFA
SALES James C. MM Cpl 10695 1st Royal Scots
SALES James L. MM Spr 142648 Guards Div Sig Coy Royal Engineers
SALES John "DCM,MM" CSM 7102 2nd Border Regt
SALES John C. MM Pte 20899 Lincolnshire Regt
SALES Joseph MM Cpl 1883 6th Royal West Surrey Regt
SALES William MM Bdr 14867 110 Heavy Bty RGA
SALINGER Martin MM L/Cpl 7982 Royal Irish Rifles
SALISBURY Albert Henry George MM Cpl 241537 2/8th Worcestershire Regt KIA 13.4.18.
SALISBURY Bert Henry MM Dmr 266036 2/6th Gloucestershire Regt KIA 2.12.17.
SALISBURY Charles J. MM Dvr 620033 RHA
SALISBURY Edward A. MM CQMS 1500 1/23rd London Regt
SALISBURY Frederick John MM Pte 23834 5th Oxf & Bucks Light Infantry
SALISBURY Hubert G. "MM,OStG(R)" Pte 1624 1/12th London Regt
SALISBURY Jabez "DCM,MM" BSM 19535 284 Siege Bty RGA
SALISBURY James MM Cpl 15486 Royal Berkshire Regt
SALISBURY John S. MM Sjt 11991 6th Somerset Light Infantry
SALISBURY Thomas MM Spr 733 Royal Engineers
SALISBURY Thomas "MM,CG(B)" L/Cpl 1616 87 Fd Amb RAMC
SALISBURY Walter MM Pte 3003 2/7th Royal Warwickshire Regt
SALISBURY William MM Pte 200882 1/4th Northamptonshire Regt
SALKELD James B. MM CSM 630905 20th London Regt
SALLABANKS Harry MM Gnr 47296 16 Siege Bty RGA
SALLES Pierre M. MM Dvr 110182 C/56 Bde RFA
SALLIS Thomas Edward MM Pte 26695 14th Hampshire Regt
SALLIS Walter S. MM Cpl 1913 1/1st Cambridgeshire Regt
SALLOWS Sidney MM Pte 201376 Bedfordshire Regt
SALMON Albert MM L/Cpl 146497 61st Bn Machine Gun Corps
SALMON Alexander MM Dvr 40556 41 Div Ammn Col RFA
SALMON Andrew MM Cpl 330574 1/7th Liverpool Regt
SALMON Arthur Victor MM Pte 330587 1/8th Hampshire Regt
SALMON Charles J. MM Gnr Sig 37984 32 Bty 33 Bde RFA
SALMON David MM Sjt 1121 14th Royal Warwickshire Regt
SALMON Edward MM L/Cpl 22589 North Lancashire Regt
SALMON Edward MM Pte 14604 7th Shropshire Light Infantry
SALMON Ernest V. MM Sjt 240282 Lincolnshire Regt
SALMON Francis E. MM Sjt 19531 RGA
SALMON George C. MM Gnr 189048 RFA
SALMON George W. MM Sjt 9844 Army Veterinary Corps
SALMON Gilbert MM L/Cpl 79958 Royal Engineers
SALMON H. MM L/Sjt 14518 Yorkshire Regt
SALMON John Patrick MM+Bar BSM 55022 D/310 Bde RFA Died 25.10.18.
SALMON Mark MM Bdr 930630 A/187 Bde RFA
SALMON P. MM L/Sjt 29358 10th Essex Regt
SALMON Samuel MM Pte 350787 1/9th Royal Scots
SALMON Walter MM L/Cpl 331085 9th Liverpool Regt
SALMON Walter MM L/Cpl 200295 Durham Light Infantry
SALMON William MM L/Cpl 15534 Royal Sussex Regt
SALMON William Albert MM Sjt 11788 156 Bde RFA
SALMOND Alexander MM Pte 46570 3rd Bn Machine Gun Corps KIA 8.10.18.
SALMOND Henry MM L/Cpl 81157 206 Fd Coy Royal Engineers
SALMOND John T. MM Cpl 27470 Royal Scots
SALMOND Thomas MM Pte 12566 2nd Scots Guards
SALMONS William MM Cpl 296045 RGA
SALMONS William John MM L/Cpl 2651 Royal Warwickshire Regt
SALSBURY Frank MM L/Cpl 2111 1/5th Notts & Derby Regt KIA 1.7.16.
SALT Charles E. MM L/Cpl 40100 1st South Staffordshire Regt
SALT Elias MM Sjt 492006 46 Div Sig Coy Royal Engineers
SALT Ernest MM+Bar Pte 266396 Royal Warwickshire Regt
SALT Ernest E. MM+Bar Pte 13924 1st Royal West Surrey Regt
SALT Ernest Henry MM Cpl 75691 15 Div Ammn Col RFA
SALT Frank Reginald MM L/Cpl 96188 222 Fd Coy Royal Engineers DOW 13.4.18.
SALT Frederick W. MM Sjt 19401 1st Suffolk Regt
SALT Harold A. MM Pte 35883 4th North Staffordshire Regt
SALT John S. MM Pte 203621 North Staffordshire Regt
SALT Joseph MM Cpl 32007 RGA
SALT Joseph D. MM Sjt 3186 9 Fd Coy Royal Engineers
SALT Joseph E. MM L/Cpl 2448 Notts & Derby Regt
SALT Philip MM L/Cpl 36206 41 Coy Machine Gun Corps

SALT Richard F. MM Cpl 9989 RFA
SALT William MM Gnr 43094 RFA
SALT William H. MM Pte 1525 1st Royal Irish Rifles
SALT William H. MM Sjt 371902 8th London Regt
SALTER A. MM Sjt 9639 1st Scottish Rifles
SALTER Charles "MM,MSM" L/Cpl 15765 9th South Staffordshire Regt
SALTER Frank F. MM L/Cpl 283184 4th London Regt
SALTER Frank J. MM Sjt 741259 25th London Regt
SALTER George E. MM Sjt 47467 A/123 Bde RFA
SALTER George H. MM L/Cpl 422414 10th London Regt
SALTER George W. MM Spr 32733 25 Div Sig Coy Royal Engineers
SALTER H.W. MM L/Cpl 3631 2nd Rifle Brigade
SALTER Henry MM Pte 67383 2/5th Devonshire Regt
SALTER Henry MM Sjt 66606 RGA
SALTER Herbert MM Pte 20362 4th Worcestershire Regt
SALTER Thomas F. MM Cpl 75280 Royal Engineers
SALTER Thomas J. MM L/Cpl 265201 5th Gloucestershire Regt
SALTER Walter Stephen MM Sjt 6726 RAMC
SALTER William L. MM Pte 2557 12th Middlesex Regt
SALTMARSH Frederick MM Sjt 16916 13th Durham Light Infantry DOW 18.10.18.
SALTMARSH Frederick W. MM Sjt 9495 Royal West Surrey Regt
SALTMARSH Joseph MM Pte 40383 Durham Light Infantry
SALTON James S. MM L/Cpl 242691 171 Tunnelling Coy Royal Engineers
SALTON Walter MM Pte 40587 Royal Scots Fusiliers
SALTS Frank MM Pte 34108 15th Lancashire Fusiliers
SALVAGE Ernest Arthur MM Gnr 103693 7 Div Ammn Col RFA
SALVESON Robert Henry MM Dvr 32920 A/177 Bde RFA
SAMBROOK Harry MM L/Cpl 11723 2nd Royal Fusiliers
SAMBROOK William MM Cpl 16201 Yorkshire Light Infantry
SAMBROOKS Ernest MM L/Cpl 32897 4th West Riding Regt
SAMBROOKS James MM Bdr 751582 A/282 Bde RFA
SAMMES Carl E. MM+Bar Cpl 67978 122 Fd Coy Royal Engineers
SAMMON James MM Pte 40678 1/7th Gordon Highlanders
SAMMOND Hugh MM Sjt 22829 6th Liverpool Regt KIA 9.4.18.
SAMMONS Henry MM Pte 53242 7th Middlesex Regt
SAMMONS Lewis MM Cpl 326890 1/1st Cambridgeshire Regt
SAMMS Harold MM Gnr 102780 RFA
SAMPLE Thomas MM Pte 24952 Machine Gun Corps
SAMPSON Arthur MM Spr 95909 Royal Engineers
SAMPSON Edward A. MM+Bar Cpl 249807 Royal Engineers
SAMPSON Harry MM Cpl 3274 Gloucestershire Regt
SAMPSON J. MM Pte 337596 RAMC
SAMPSON Louis B. MM L/Cpl 6058 4th Hussars
SAMPSON Stanley MM L/Cpl 7554 5th Lancers
SAMPSON William MM Pte 17117 13th Essex Regt
SAMPSON William George MM Pte 54738 47 Fd Amb RAMC KIA 29.8.17.
SAMS Arthur D. MM Cpl 18217 11th West Yorkshire Regt
SAMSA Edgar Stanley MM Pte M2/100308 Army Service Corps
SAMSON James MM Pte 8066 Royal Highlanders
SAMSON R.C. MM Pte 5520 Gordon Highlanders
SAMSON Thomas MM Pte 5429 8th Seaforth Highlanders DOW 3.8.18.
SAMSON W. MM L/Cpl 242000 Royal Warwickshire Regt
SAMSON William MM Pte 31699 5/6th Scottish Rifles
SAMSON William Stewart MM Pte 7697 3 Fd Amb RAMC
SAMUEL David J. MM L/Cpl 48186 RAMC
SAMUEL George MM Dvr 86675 RFA
SAMUEL George E. MM Pte 14510 7th Bedfordshire Regt
SAMUEL James MM L/Bdr 646399 374 Bty 53 Bde RFA
SAMUEL Samuel MM Pte 38453 2nd Royal Lancaster Regt
SAMUEL William G. MM Pte Y/1416 13th King's Royal Rifle Corps
SAMUELS Arthur E. "DCM,MM" Pte 72474 Machine Gun Corps
SAMUELS David MM Pte 63011 Royal Fusiliers
SAMUELS Frederick J. MM L/Cpl 19214 Suffolk Regt
SAMUELS Harry C. MM Pte 19878 Machine Gun Corps
SAMUELS Harry James MM+Bar Cpl 676572 B/275 Bde RFA
SAMUELS John Edward William "DCM,MM" Sjt 45928 9 Bty 41 Bde RFA KIA 29.7.16.
SAMUELS Lewis Augustus MM Pte 43234 1st Bedfordshire Regt
SAMUELS Maurice MM Gnr 3279 121 Heavy Bty RGA
SAMUELS Michael MM Pte S/17768 1st Rifle Brigade KIA 1.9.18.
SAMUELS Rupert C. MM Cpl 676571 RFA
SAMWAYS Charles John MM Pte 10260 1st Dorsetshire Regt KIA 14.4.17.
SAMWAYS George MM Sjt M2/048045 406 MT Coy Army Service Corps
SAMWAYS George William MM Dvr 800752 D/230 Bde RFA
SAMWAYS William James MM GnrSig 16270 A/108 Bde RFA
SAN Tun MM Pte 201232 6th Bn Tank Corps AKA TUN SAN
SANCASTER George Michael MM Pte 21/1270 9th Northumberland Fusiliers DOW 28.10.18.
SANDALL Norman MM Pte 34326 York & Lancaster Regt
SANDALLS Walter R. MM Cpl 67826 Royal West Surrey Regt
SANDBROOK John G. MM Pte 32464 RAMC
SANDEL John MM Cpl 102063 177 Tunnelling Coy Royal Engineers
SANDER William Alfred Christopher MM Pte 24040 2nd Royal Dublin Fusiliers KIA 21.3.18.
SANDERCOCK John MM Pte 23991 10th Duke of Cornwall's LI
SANDERS A. MM Cpl 295017 12th Royal Scots Fusiliers
SANDERS Alfred J. MM Sjt 32443 233 Siege Bty RGA
SANDERS Alfred Wray MM Spr 65080 18 Div Sig Coy Royal Engineers
SANDERS Allen MM Gnr 202127 RFA
SANDERS C.L. MM Cpl 10431 Gloucestershire Regt
SANDERS Charles H. MM Sub Cond S/5316 Army Ordnance Corps
SANDERS Elias MM Pte 42460 9th Yorkshire Regt KIA 20.9.17.
SANDERS F.G. MM Sjt 238048 Worcestershire Regt
SANDERS Frank MM Cpl 164897 100th Bn Machine Gun Corps
SANDERS Frederick Charles MM Sjt 8889 1st Shropshire Light Infantry KIA 18.4.17.
SANDERS Frederick John MM Cpl 660 King Edward's Horse DOW 6.8.18.
SANDERS George MM L/Cpl 103654 82 Fd Coy Royal Engineers
SANDERS George Harold MM Pte 13945 2nd Northamptonshire Regt KIA 16.8.17.
SANDERS Godfrey A. MM L/Sjt 10836 1st South Wales Borderers
SANDERS H.J. MM Pte 493628 RAMC
SANDERS Henry James MM Sjt 39062 32 Coy Machine Gun Corps
SANDERS Herbert B. MM Pte 8417 Royal Fusiliers
SANDERS James MM Sjt 6829 Royal Highlanders
SANDERS James MM Pte 265162 1st Devonshire Regt
SANDERS John MM S/Sjt Armt 1092 Army Ordnance Corps
SANDERS Joseph H. MM Cpl 44837 Royal Engineers
SANDERS Josiah MM RSM 200065 1/4th Gloucestershire Regt
SANDERS Paul; MM Pte 16186 10th North Lancashire Regt
SANDERS Robert L. MM Cpl 75997 127 Coy Labour Corps
SANDERS T. MM Pte 9910 2nd Dragoon Guards
SANDERS T. MM Sjt 18527 South Lancashire Regt
SANDERS Thomas MM L/Cpl 85514 1st Liverpool Regt DOW 18.9.18.
SANDERS Thomas James MM Pte 283323 2/4th London Regt KIA 21.3.18.
SANDERS W.R.O. MM Pte 457364 RAMC
SANDERS Walter MM L/Sjt 56905 14th Royal Welsh Fusiliers
SANDERS Walter MM+2 Bars Pte 266223 Oxf & Bucks Light Infantry
SANDERS Walter J. MM Gnr 294851 147 Hy Bty RGA
SANDERS William MM Pte 103296 32nd Bn Machine Gun Corps
SANDERS William "DCM,MM+Bar" Sjt 65178 106 Fd Coy Royal Engineers
SANDERS William MM S/Sjt Farrier 28767 28 Bde RFA
SANDERS William Albert MM Sjt T1/3720 18 Div Train Army Service Corps Died 3.8.18.
SANDERS William G. MM Sjt 14341 10th Essex Regt
SANDERS William H. MM Pte 702692 23rd London Regt
SANDERS William Henry MM L/Cpl 2128 2/5th Gloucestershire Regt KIA 19.8.16.
SANDERS William K. MM L/Cpl 16103 6th York & Lancaster Regt
SANDERSON Adam MM Pte 46497 Royal Scots
SANDERSON Alonza MM Pte 26420 9th York & Lancaster Regt
SANDERSON Arnold MM Pte 19933 11th Northumberland Fusiliers KIA 15.10.17.
SANDERSON Charles MM Pte 203502 4th King's Own Scottish Borderers
SANDERSON Charles MM Sjt 390234 1/3(Northumbrian)Fd Amb RAMC
SANDERSON Charles J. MM Cpl 21/911 Northumberland Fusiliers
SANDERSON Frederick John MM Pte 270553 1/1st Hertfordshire Regt KIA 24.10.18.
SANDERSON George MM Pte 88719 1st Liverpool Regt
SANDERSON George MM Pte 275509 Manchester Regt
SANDERSON Herbert MM Cpl 20056 45 Coy Machine Gun Corps KIA 24.8.17.
SANDERSON James MM Sjt 111866 B/121 Bde RFA
SANDERSON James MM Sjt 7686 2nd Shropshire Light Infantry
SANDERSON John A. MM Sjt 99871 94 Bty 18 Bde RFA

SANDERSON John Cole MM Cpl 75800 'AT' Cable Section Royal Engineers
SANDERSON John J. MM Bdr Sig 80291 232 Siege Bty RGA
SANDERSON John R. MM Gnt 50848 RGA
SANDERSON Martin MM Cpl 326540 1/1st Cambridgeshire Regt
SANDERSON Owen MM Pte 265613 6th West Riding Regt
SANDERSON Ralph MM Pte M2/155778 Army Service Corps att RE
SANDERSON Richard A. MM Dvr 26316 RFA
SANDERSON Robert Douglas MM Pte 205435 7th East Yorkshire Regt KIA 18.9.18.
SANDERSON S. "DCM,MM" Sjt 266906 1/7th West Yorkshire Regt
SANDERSON Samuel MM Cpl 58787 33rd Bn Machine Gun Corps
SANDERSON Sidney MM Sjt 352961 Manchester Regt
SANDERSON Thomas MM Sjt 240030 1/5th Royal Lancaster Regt
SANDERSON Thomas D. MM Sjt 78295 Tank Corps
SANDERSON Thomas Henry "DCM,MM" Sjt 9204 C/71 Bde RFA DOW 17.8.17.
SANDERSON Thomas Walker MM L/Cpl B/7025 7th King's Royal Rifle Corps DOW 6.12.17.
SANDERSON Walter K. MM Cpl 1459 1/15th London Regt
SANDERSON Wilfred MM Pte 9112 2nd Lincolnshire Regt
SANDERSON William MM Sjt 470173 Royal Engineers
SANDERSON William MM Pte 106201 80 Fd Amb RAMC
SANDERSON William E. MM Sjt 54096 Durham Light Infantry
SANDERSON William M. MM 2nd Cpl 470037 226 Fd Coy Royal Engineers
SANDEVER John G. MM Pte 47703 Welsh Regt
SANDFORD H. MM Sjt 20818 South Lancashire Regt
SANDFORD Jack MM Gnr 93820 D/82 Bde RFA
SANDFORD W.G. MM L/Cpl 33233 Devonshire Regt
SANDFORD William MM Sjt 7135 Machine Gun Corps
SANDHAM Benjamin MM Sjt 268032 Cheshire Regt
SANDHAM T. MM Pte 240298 Border Regt
SANDHAM William A. MM Spr 325589 61 Div Sig Coy Royal Engineers
SANDIFORD H.W. MM Pte 679 2nd Arg & Suth Highlanders
SANDIFORD Philip MM Sjt 16597 Royal Lancaster Regt
SANDIFORD William George MM L/Cpl T4/241921 Army Service Corps
SANDILANDS A.C. MM+Bar Sjt 120508 Royal Engineers
SANDILANDS George MM+Bar L/Cpl 275461 5/6th Royal Scots
SANDISON James MM Sjt 630084 RFA
SANDISON William MM Pte 292536 Gordon Highlanders
SANDISON William MM Pte 10197 1/6th Royal Highlanders
SANDISON William MM Pte 25305 12th Highland Light Infantry
SANDISON William J.H. MM CSM 320369 6th London Regt
SANDISON William R. MM Pte 10719 1/6th Gordon Highlanders
SANDOE Lyndon "DCM+Bar,MM" CSM 627 17th Middlesex Regt
SANDREICH Lewis MM Pte S/8174 9th Rifle Brigade KIA 24.8.17.
SANDS Albert MM Pte 9698 2nd East Yorkshire Regt
SANDS Alfred James MM Dvr 38954 A/83 Bde RFA
SANDS Bertie MM L/Cpl 13783 8th Norfolk Regt
SANDS James MM Pte 3643 1st Royal Inniskilling Fusiliers
SANDS James MM L/Cpl 19479 11th Cheshire Regt KIA 2.8.17.
SANDS John MM Pte 40600 9th Scottish Rifles
SANDS John Frank MM Cpl 1001 13th Rifle Brigade Died 25.10.18.
SANDWELL Harry Eugene MM Sjt 13087 7th North Lancashire Regt
SANDWICH William Anthony MM Bdr 452 Machine Gun Corps(Motors)
SANDY Frederick W. MM Spr 508598 11 Fd Coy Royal Engineers
SANDY Vernon MM Sjt 280378 4th Hampshire Regt
SANDY William MM Cpl 16355 22nd Northumberland Fusiliers
SANDYFIRTH Norris MM Sjt 141566 143 Siege Bty RGA
SANDYS Charles E. MM Cpl 703649 23rd London Regt
SANDYS Edwin James "MM,MSM" Sjt 23548 1 Signal Troop Royal Engineers
SANDYS Ernest T. MM Sjt 391299 9th London Regt
SANDYS Henry John MM Bdr 28506 24 Siege Bty RGA KIA 13.4.17.
SANDYS William George "MM,MSM" BSM 3187 154 Siege Bty RGA
SANFORD Frank MM Pte 8780 4th Middlesex Regt
SANFORD Frank E. MM Cpl 42140 Middlesex Regt
SANFORD Sidney Walter MM Pte S/25477 2nd Rifle Brigade KIA 23.3.18.
SANFORD Wilfred MM Pte 320387 16th Royal Sussex Regt
SANGAN Frank MM Cpl 3336 6th Royal Irish Regt
SANGER Sidney MM Dvr 11756 RFA
SANGER William G. MM+Bar Pte 241755 1/8th Worcestershire Regt
SANGSTER Albert MM Sjt 2088 RGA
SANGSTER Cyril MM Gnr 935682 RFA
SANGSTER David Martin MM Sjt 915857 D/291 Bde RFA
SANGSTER Herbert B. MM L/Cpl 143335 Machine Gun Corps
SANGSTER Robert MM Sjt 9073 2nd Royal Scots
SANGWIN Sydney MM Pte 15052 7th Oxf & Bucks Light Infantry
SANKERWITCH Philip MM L/Cpl 470762 12th London Regt
SANKEY A. MM Pte 200211 Hampshire Regt
SANKEY Percy MM L/Sjt 18059 9th Cheshire Regt
SANSOM John MM Cpl 42185 10th Royal Fusiliers
SANSOM John Thomas Bob MM Sjt 16920 10th Worcestershire Regt DOW 24.9.17.
SANSOM Wilfred MM Pte 853 8th Royal Fusiliers
SANSOME Arthur J. MM Pte 270105 Manchester Regt
SANSOME Ernest John Osborne MM Cpl 1500 RFA
SANSOME Frank MM Pte 16649 9th Leicestershire Regt
SANSOME Henry MM L/Cpl 40081 4th Worcestershire Regt DOW 15.6.18.
SANSOME Percy J. MM Pte 14118 Hampshire Regt
SANSOME Walter MM L/Cpl 21735 Machine Gun Corps
SANSON Charles MM Pte R/37351 King's Royal Rifle Corps
SANSUM William H.J. MM 2nd Cpl 1289 Royal Engineers
SANTE Frank MM Cpl 202066 Lancashire Fusiliers
SANTER Albert MM Cpl 40103 RGA
SANTER Stanley M. "MM,MSM" Cpl 202868 2/4th Gloucestershire Regt
SANTHOUSE Bertram MM Pte 19820 East Yorkshire Regt
SANTOS Joseph MM L/Cpl 266561 1/7th Liverpool Regt
SANTY Willie MM L/Bdr 781487 B/311 Bde RFA
SAPCOTE Thomas A. MM Sjt M2/116682 Army Service Corps
SAPSED Albert George MM Pte 267001 1/1st Hertfordshire Regt
SAPSFORD Frederick MM Pte 14558 1st Bedfordshire Regt
SAPSTEAD William MM Dvr 85167 B/64 Bde RFA
SARA Thomas S. MM Cpl 202294 RFA
SARAH Edwin J. MM Dvr 1117 Royal Engineers
SARGANT Ernest MM Pte A/3757 King's Royal Rifle Corps
SARGANT Stanley R. MM S/Sjt 26785 1st(London)Fd Amb RAMC
SARGEANT Charles "MM,MSM" Sjt 24987 D/91 Bde RFA Died 19.7.18.
SARGEANT Edward M. MM L/Cpl 1794 1/4th Royal Berkshire Regt
SARGEANT George MM Cpl 11136 2nd Royal Scots
SARGEANT J. MM Pte 9639 2nd Essex Regt
SARGEANT Joseph John "DCM(5th Bn),MM" L/Sjt 24528 6th Royal Berkshire Regt
SARGENT Algernon J. MM Sjt 650957 21st London Regt
SARGENT Ernest MM Dvr 68125 57 Bde RFA
SARGENT Ernest John MM Sjt 3156 1st Lincolnshire Regt
SARGENT F.G. MM Pte 15525 1st Grenadier Guards
SARGENT George MM Pte 16753 6th South Wales Borderers
SARGENT George Alfred MM L/Cpl 1171 11th Royal Sussex Regt
SARGENT H.A. MM Sjt 17184 2nd Bn Machine Gun Corps
SARGENT Henry Thomas Walter MM Pte 7684 2nd Scots Guards
SARGENT Jack MM Sjt 723538 24th London Regt
SARGENT James MM Dvr 801364 B/82 Bde RFA
SARGENT John Francis MM Cpl 41584 Royal Engineers
SARGENT John J. MM Pte 40311 Tank Corps
SARGENT Richard MM Cpl 1686 8th Lincolnshire Regt
SARGENT Thomas MM Pte 18773 Royal Dublin Fusiliers
SARGENT Tom MM Cpl 631070 1/20th London Regt
SARGENT William MM Bdr 25700 RFA
SARGENT William J. MM Pte 12903 10th Gloucestershire Regt
SARGENT William James MM Sjt 55818 120 Railway Coy Royal Engineers
SARGINSON Henry MM Pte 241976 East Lancashire Regt
SARGISON Charles MM Pte 15096 6th Lincolnshire Regt KIA 22.8.17.
SARGISON Joseph MM Pte 27717 41st Bn Machine Gun Corps
SARGOOD John MM Pte 8574 1st Royal Fusiliers
SARLING Bertram MM Pte 252 9th Royal Fusiliers
SARTAIN Walter MM Pte 149594 Machine Gun Corps
SARVANT Stephen George MM Cpl 12471 12th East Surrey Regt
SASSE Charles Aubrey MM Pte 1160 6 Fd Amb RAMC KIA 29.7.18.
SATCHELL Richard MM Bdr 50607 RFA
SATCHELL William MM Cpl 11624 RFA
SATCHWELL John W. MM Sjt 16931 York & Lancaster Regt
SATCHWELL Samuel MM Cpl 240573 5th Leicestershire Regt
SATERLAY John F. MM Dvr 13184 RFA
SATHERLEY William P. MM Cpl 48010 98 Fd Coy Royal Engineers
SATTERLEY Arthur M. MM Sjt 12723 2nd Durham Light Infantry
SATTERLEY R. MM Pte 6346 2nd Royal Scots Fusiliers

SATTERTHWAITE Walter MM Sjt 36467 8th Royal Berkshire Regt
SATTLER James Sidney MM Bdr 67730 104 Bty 22 Bde RFA KIA 27.4.17.
SAUL Charles Douglas MM Pte 11811 8th Yorkshire Regt
SAUL Frank "MM,MSM" Sjt 22248 20th Liverpool Regt
SAUL George MM Cpl 713 15th Royal Warwickshire Regt
SAUL George MM Sjt 5721 8th Border Regt
SAULL Harold V. MM Cpl 53174 Royal Fusiliers
SAUNBY Harry MM Pte 203318 1/5th Lincolnshire Regt
SAUNDERS A. MM Pte 241916 Lancashire Fusiliers
SAUNDERS A.E. MM Sjt 73155 44 Bde RFA
SAUNDERS Albert MM Cpl 179 1st Royal West Kent Regt
SAUNDERS Albert H. MM Cpl 2439 1/17th London Regt
SAUNDERS Alexander MM Pte 27911 9th Notts & Derby Regt
SAUNDERS Alfred "MM,MID" Cpl 10406 2nd East Surrey Regt
SAUNDERS Alfred C. MM Pte 10978 Royal West Surrey Regt att MGC
SAUNDERS Arthur MM Sjt 13972 8th Gloucestershire Regt
SAUNDERS Arthur MM Gnr 52578 3 Bde RHA
SAUNDERS C.J. MM L/Cpl 203252 Royal Berkshire Regt
SAUNDERS Caleb George MM BQMS 32297 12 Siege Bty RGA
SAUNDERS Cecil Claude MM Cpl 23787 222 Fd Coy Royal Engineers Died 25.7.17.
SAUNDERS Cecil H. MM Sjt 33492 Border Regt
SAUNDERS Charles Henry MM Sjt 143053 Special Bde Royal Engineers Died 7.11.18.
SAUNDERS Christopher MM Pte M2/073104 (sic) Army Service Corps
SAUNDERS Edward MM Cpl 526 1st Rifle Brigade DOW 27.9.18.
SAUNDERS Edward J. MM Gnr 14877 RFA
SAUNDERS Edwin Thomas MM Cpl 2855 1/1st Hertfordshire Regt
SAUNDERS Ernest MM 2nd Cpl 21341 2 Fd Coy Royal Engineers
SAUNDERS Ernest MM Pte 16870 7th Somerset Light Infantry
SAUNDERS Ernest MM L/Cpl 116223 Machine Gun Corps
SAUNDERS Ernest George MM L/Cpl 19013 4th Grenadier Guards
SAUNDERS Ernest J. MM Pte 2413 1/1st Surrey Yeomanry
SAUNDERS Ernest W. MM Gnr 3543 RFA
SAUNDERS Firth MM 2nd Cpl 246839 Royal Engineers
SAUNDERS Frank MM Pte 13517 4th Coldstream Guards
SAUNDERS Frank MM Bdr 44765 19 Heavy Bty RGA
SAUNDERS Frederick MM Sjt 12522 Middlesex Regt
SAUNDERS Frederick G. MM Pte 20019 1st Northamptonshire Regt
SAUNDERS Frederick R. MM Pte 12420 7th Yorkshire Regt
SAUNDERS George MM Pte 2717 11th Royal West Surrey Regt
SAUNDERS George MM Bdr 131100 290 Siege Bty RGA
SAUNDERS George MM Sjt 9900 Royal Irish Regt
SAUNDERS George MM Spr 310796 Signal Service Royal Engineers
SAUNDERS George C. MM Sjt 46597 RFA
SAUNDERS George Edward MM Pte 10292 6th East Kent Regt
SAUNDERS Harold C. MM L/Cpl 325141 1/1st Cambridgeshire Regt
SAUNDERS Harold E. MM 2nd Cpl 568267 Royal Engineers
SAUNDERS Harry Sabin MM Sjt 325071 1/1st Cambridgeshire Regt KIA 26.9.17.
SAUNDERS Henry MM Gnr 5201 RFA
SAUNDERS Herbert MM Cpl 44168 1st Worcestershire Regt
SAUNDERS Herbert MM Pte 29124 1st Grenadier Guards
SAUNDERS Herbert MM L/Cpl 548253 512 Fd Coy Royal Engineers
SAUNDERS Herbert C. MM Pte 200745 1/4th Oxf & Bucks Light Infantry
SAUNDERS Herbert Sydney MM Pte 391898 9th London Regt
SAUNDERS Horace MM Pte 17456 7th East Kent Regt
SAUNDERS Isaac MM Sjt 19346 5th Dorsetshire Regt KIA 3.10.18.
SAUNDERS James MM Sjt 12015 6th Shropshire Light Infantry
SAUNDERS James MM Dvr 84129 D/223 Bde RFA
SAUNDERS James MM Pte 7842 1st Royal Dublin Fusiliers
SAUNDERS James E. MM CSM 44990 8th Royal Berkshire Regt
SAUNDERS James Henry MM L/Cpl 11614 10th Royal West Kent Regt KIA 12.2.17.
SAUNDERS James P. MM Sjt 68217 1st Cheshire Regt
SAUNDERS Job A. MM Sjt 63427 RFA
SAUNDERS John MM L/Cpl 960 7th Royal Sussex Regt
SAUNDERS John MM CQMS 1305 1st Northumberland Fusiliers
SAUNDERS John MM Bdr 52182 B/15 Bde RHA DOW 24.10.17.
SAUNDERS John MM Pte 14165 2nd Grenadier Guards KIA 25.9.16.
SAUNDERS John Ernest Albert MM Pte 1446 14th Royal Warwickshire Regt KIA 29.5.18.
SAUNDERS John L. MM Cpl 285092 1/1st Oxfordshire Yeomanry
SAUNDERS John L. MM Cpl 404383 Royal Engineers
SAUNDERS John M. MM L/Cpl 115092 63rd Bn Machine Gun Corps
SAUNDERS John T. MM Pte 2564 1/1st Cambridgeshire Regt
SAUNDERS John William Edward MM Cpl 17064 B/110 Bde RFA DOW 18.9.18.
SAUNDERS Joseph MM Pte 33689 Oxf & Bucks Light Infantry
SAUNDERS Leonard MM Dvr 94064 RFA
SAUNDERS Levi J. MM Sjt 510025 Royal Engineers
SAUNDERS Louis MM L/Sjt 11827 1st Royal Berkshire Regt KIA 10.5.17.
SAUNDERS Percy MM Gnr 6457 RFA
SAUNDERS Percy C. MM Sjt 292644 264 Siege Bty RGA
SAUNDERS R. "MM,MSM" L/Cpl 34058 1 Div Sig Coy Royal Engineers
SAUNDERS Reginald MM Cpl 545 6th Royal Munster Fusiliers
SAUNDERS Robert William MM Pte 23665 4th Grenadier Guards
SAUNDERS Samuel MM Pte 20060 Worcestershire Regt
SAUNDERS Sidney Frank MM Gnr 26270 1 Siege Bty RGA DOW 18.4.17.
SAUNDERS Sydney MM Sjt 16967 13th Middlesex Regt
SAUNDERS Thurston MM Cpl 300378 18th Liverpool Regt
SAUNDERS W.H. MM Sjt 3473 13th Rifle Brigade
SAUNDERS William "MC,MM(6829 Pte)" 2Lt 4th att 5th West Riding Regt
SAUNDERS William Frederick Leonard MM+Bar Spr 48236 12 Div Sig Coy Royal Engineers
SAUNDERS William G.F. "MM,MSM" Cpl 15510 25 Army Troops Coy Royal Engineers
SAUNDERS William George MM Sjt 7738 2nd Oxf & Bucks Light Infantry KIA 13.11.16.
SAUNDERS William H. MM Pte 235082 Leicestershire Regt
SAUNDERS William Henry MM Sjt 9388 10th Royal West Surrey Regt KIA 20.9.17.
SAUNDERS William J. MM Pte 40006 Welsh Regt
SAUNDERS William Walter MM Sjt 41478 103 Bde RFA
SAUNDERSON Herbert MM Pte 10362 6th East Yorkshire Regt
SAVAGAR James Stephen MM Cpl 30513 4th Worcestershire Regt KIA 29.9.18.
SAVAGE Alfred MM Pte 18617 Royal West Kent Regt
SAVAGE Alfred E. MM Pte M2/119962 Army Service Corps
SAVAGE Arthur MM Gnr 47171 31 Siege Bty RGA
SAVAGE Arthur William MM Sjt 8516 D/257 Bde RFA
SAVAGE Charles MM Pte 15328 2nd Scots Guards
SAVAGE David MM L/Cpl 5/5064 9th King's Royal Rifle Corps
SAVAGE E.T. MM+Bar Gnr 730444 RFA
SAVAGE Edward MM Cpl 641 Royal Irish Rifles
SAVAGE Ernest MM Pte R/29607 King's Royal Rifle Corps
SAVAGE Ernest A. MM Gnr 16288 RFA
SAVAGE Francis F. MM L/Cpl 41910 1st Norfolk Regt
SAVAGE Frank Alfred MM CSM 534 Middlesex Regt
SAVAGE Frank L. MM Pte 27979 2nd Hampshire Regt
SAVAGE Frederick MM Pte 9744 1st Royal Munster Fusiliers
SAVAGE Frederick R. MM Cpl 95378 23rd Bn Tank Corps
SAVAGE George F. MM Dvr 52389 RFA
SAVAGE George H. MM Sjt 63076 C/148 Bde RFA
SAVAGE George Henry MM L/Cpl 31365 East Surrey Regt KIA 21.10.18.
SAVAGE George T. MM Pte 104237 Machine Gun Corps
SAVAGE Henry MM Sjt 1633 19th Middlesex Regt
SAVAGE Henry MM Cpl 432221 Royal Engineers
SAVAGE Henry A. MM CSM M2/105681 Army Service Corps
SAVAGE Henry H. MM Cpl 49273 Royal Engineers
SAVAGE Hugh MM Pte 9738 2nd Irish Guards KIA 14.4.18.
SAVAGE James MM+Bar Pte 54658 110 Fd Amb RAMC
SAVAGE James MM Sjt 2717 1st King's Royal Rifle Corps KIA 8.5.18.
SAVAGE James E. MM Pte 11740 12th East Surrey Regt
SAVAGE Jesaiah J. MM Pte 21881 46th Bn Machine Gun Corps
SAVAGE John MM Cpl 490434 Royal Engineers
SAVAGE John MM Pte 6789 1st Middlesex Regt
SAVAGE John MM Pte 241193 Seaforth Highlanders
SAVAGE John Patrick "MM,CG(F),MC(G)" Sjt 9748 2nd Duke of Cornwall's LI
SAVAGE John Percival MM Sjt 376529 2nd Manchester Regt KIA 1.10.18.
SAVAGE Joseph MM+Bar Pte 240437 2nd Worcestershire Regt
SAVAGE Oswald MM Pte M2/105648 Army Service Corps
SAVAGE Reginald MM Pte 206133 6th Royal West Surrey Regt

SAVAGE Robert William MM Pte 23099 6th Royal West Kent Regt
SAVAGE T. MM Pte 116436 10th Notts & Derby Regt
SAVAGE Thomas MM Dvr 36322 43 Bde RFA
SAVAGE Thomas H. MM Pte 5174 6th Dragoons
SAVAGE Walter MM Bdr 36349 RFA
SAVAGE William MM Pte 20229 1st Royal Irish Rifles
SAVAGE William Steele MM L/Sjt 1031 XVIII Corps Cyclist Bn Army Cyclist Corps KIA 27.5.18.
SAVEALL Charles L. MM Bdsm 9983 1st Scottish Rifles
SAVERTON Joseph MM Pte 265802 8th Yorkshire Regt
SAVILL Albert J.P. MM L/Cpl 2574 1/12th London Regt
SAVILL Fred George MM L/Cpl 2592 Army Cyclist Corps
SAVILL H. MM Pte 19088 1st Essex Regt
SAVILL Wilfred C. MM Pte 80161 1/1st Essex Yeomanry
SAVILL William MM Sjt S/5876 12th Rifle Brigade
SAVILLE A.E. MM L/Cpl 19416 Royal Fusiliers
SAVILLE Albert Edward "MM,MID" Gnr 203359 2 Bty Machine Gun Corps(Motors)
SAVILLE Ernest Walter MM Dvr 179131 463 Bty 179 Bde RFA DOW 7.12.17.
SAVILLE George E.B. MM L/Cpl 8528 2nd Welsh Regt
SAVILLE Harold I. MM Sjt 127 16th West Yorkshire Regt
SAVILLE Harry MM Sjt 36982 4th North Staffordshire Regt
SAVILLE Isaac MM Pte 36782 East Lancashire Regt
SAVILLE John J. MM L/Cpl 15516 Lancashire Fusiliers
SAVILLE Norman Vivian MM+Bar Cpl 65566 16 Div Sig Coy Royal Engineers
SAVILLE Robert MM Cpl 686827 RFA
SAVIN J.William "DCM,MM" Cpl 676817 285 Bde RFA
SAVIN James MM Sjt 12532 1st Irish Guards
SAVINS J.L. "MM,MSM" Cpl 4572 RFA
SAWARD J. MM+Bar Sjt 12787 9th Essex Regt
SAWARD Sidney Carman "MC,MM(1073 Cpl 1/1(London)Fd Coy)" 2Lt Royal Engineers
SAWDON Murler? MM Pte 201467 16th Lancashire Fusiliers
SAWDYE Edward Kenneth MM L/Cpl 1288 1/4th Devonshire Regt Died 15.9.16.
SAWERS Alexander MM CSM 13759 10th Scottish Rifles
SAWFORD Samuel W. MM Cpl 10551 6th Bedfordshire Regt
SAWKINS Arthur W. MM L/Cpl 25838 56th Bn Machine Gun Corps
SAWKINS John MM Cpl 29838 2nd Bedfordshire Regt
SAWLEY Thomas MM Gnr 75129 D/242 Bde RFA
SAWYER Alfred Rutland Hayes MM Cpl 113086 2 Special Coy Royal Engineers KIA 21.10.17.
SAWYER Arthur MM Sjt 23831 31 Hy Bty RGA
SAWYER Arthur Robert MM Cpl 9349 2nd Middlesex Regt KIA 24.4.18.
SAWYER Arthur Victor MM Pte 31006 Devonshire Regt
SAWYER Charles MM Pte 53418 1st Notts & Derby Regt
SAWYER Charles Edward MM Dvr 53329 C/79 Bde RFA
SAWYER Charles Henry MM Cpl 4921 1/8th Liverpool Regt DOW 9.8.17.
SAWYER Edward MM Cpl 23056 1st Royal Warwickshire Regt
SAWYER Ernest MM Pte 265682 Liverpool Regt
SAWYER Ernest R. MM Sjt 67874 62nd Bn Machine Gun Corps
SAWYER Frederick Grant MM Sjt 89303 A/47 Bde RFA
SAWYER Galley MM Cpl 306098 8th West Yorkshire Regt
SAWYER Harry MM Sjt 16028 7/8th King's Own Scottish Borderers
SAWYER Herbert MM Dvr 131175 A/59 Bde RFA
SAWYER J. MM Gnr 291322 RGA
SAWYER James S. MM Pte 15372 8th Suffolk Regt
SAWYER John MM Pte 58915 Notts & Derby Regt
SAWYER John A. MM Pte 8455 2nd Royal Irish Regt
SAWYER Ralph MM+Bar L/Cpl 139002 Royal Engineers
SAWYER Richard John MM Sjt 22747 15th Welsh Regt KIA 13.3.18.
SAWYERS Adam MM Pte MS/1338 Army Service Corps
SAWYERS George MM Pte 5414 Royal West Surrey Regt
SAWYERS Greener MM Gnr 751185 250 Bde RFA
SAWYERS Henry J. MM Cpl 201633 7th Royal West Surrey Regt
SAWYERS William MM Bdr Sig 731315 505 Bty 65 Bde RFA
SAXBY Ernest J. MM Sjt 74729 Labour Corps
SAXBY Harold MM Pte 11467 1st Royal West Kent Regt
SAXELBY Charles MM Bdr 58846 D/251 Bde RFA
SAXON Clifford MM Pte 250560 1/6th Manchester Regt
SAXON Frederick MM Spr 471725 Royal Engineers
SAXON Martin MM L/Cpl 21420 11th South Lancashire Regt
SAXON William T. MM Sjt 21910 Machine Gun Corps
SAXTON Charles Bertram MM Sjt 34803 1st Essex Regt
SAXTON John B. MM+Bar Pte 7964 23rd Royal Fusiliers
SAXTON Joseph James MM Pte 2663 Middlesex Regt
SAXTON Walter MM Pte 17547 Yorkshire Light Infantry
SAXTON William MM Sjt 19021 B/155 Bde RFA
SAXTON Young "MM,MSM" Sjt 200824 2/5th Lancashire Fusiliers
SAY E.G. MM Cpl 5710 Lancashire Fusiliers
SAY George MM Cpl 6/696 King's Royal Rifle Corps
SAY Leonard MM Pte 27910 RAMC
SAYER Albert E. MM L/Sjt 495692 13th London Regt
SAYER Alfred MM Pte 28244 1/5th Border Regt
SAYER Alfred R. MM Cpl 27027 14th Royal Welsh Fusiliers
SAYER Henry Lansbury "DCM,MM" Pte 23394 6 Coy 2nd Bn Machine Gun Corps
SAYER J.W. MM+Bar BSM 48367 RFA
SAYER Joseph MM Pte 79505 2/3rd(West Riding)Fd Amb RAMC
SAYER Walter MM Pte 8045 Norfolk Regt
SAYER William MM L/Cpl 8846 North Lancashire Regt
SAYER William Allen MM Sjt 16240 10th West Riding Regt DOW 30.10.18.
SAYER William C. MM L/Cpl 13485 14th Arg & Suth Highlanders DOW 26.5.18.
SAYER William T. MM S/Sjt 47876 54 Fd Amb RAMC
SAYER(S) Alfred MM L/Sjt 10287 10th West Riding Regt
SAYERS Alexander MM Bdr 39948 RGA
SAYERS Basil V. MM Cpl 207603 Royal Engineers
SAYERS Charles G. MM Sjt 75417 Tank Corps
SAYERS Edward J. MM Pte 11806 1st Scots Guards
SAYERS Ernest MM Pte 37275 RAMC
SAYERS George MM Sjt 18579 19th Durham Light Infantry
SAYERS George Howard MM Spr 558120 29 Div Sig Coy Royal Engineers
SAYERS Norman MM Sjt 850 1/6th Durham Light Infantry
SAYERS Percy MM L/Cpl 2396 8th Royal Sussex Regt
SAYERS Thomas J. MM L/Sjt 8511 10th Arg & Suth Highlanders
SAYERS Walter MM CSM 1008 50 Div Sig Coy Royal Engineers
SAYERS William E. MM Pte 570983 17th London Regt
SAYLE Charles MM 2nd Cpl 56978 105 Fd Coy Royal Engineers
SAYLE Frederick Alfred MM Pte 12369 4/5th Royal Highlanders
SAYSELL Charles MM Cpl Y/1676 8th King's Royal Rifle Corps KIA 22.7.16.
SAYSELL William George MM Pte M2/131668 39 Div Train Army Service Corps
SAYWARD H.C. MM Dvr 120442 RFA
SAYWELL Leonard MM Gnr 348587 402 Siege Bty RGA
SCADDAN Robert P. MM Cpl 432207 Royal Engineers
SCAGELL E.J. MM Pte 55226 19th Bn Machine Gun Corps
SCAIFE Albert I. MM BSM 50230 63 Div Ammn Col RFA
SCAIFE Ernest MM Dvr 795169 150 Bde Ammn Col RFA
SCAIFE Samuel J. MM Bdr 687338 RFA
SCAIFE Sidney "DCM,MM,MSM" CSM 14481 10th Notts & Derby Regt
SCAIFE Stanley MM Gnr 96631 RFA
SCAIFF Edgar MM Sjt 22859 47th Bn Machine Gun Corps
SCALES Donald MM L/Cpl 13209 8th Norfolk Regt
SCALES Frank MM Cpl 203390 1/4th West Riding Regt
SCALES Frank MM Cpl 818 10th Royal Fusiliers
SCALES Frederick MM L/Cpl 28744 Machine Gun Corps
SCALES Harry MM Dvr 3653 RFA
SCALES James Jarvis MM Pte 310066 1/7th Gordon Highlanders
SCALES James W. MM Pte 250777 2/3rd London Regt
SCALES John MM Pte 34683 Yorkshire Light Infantry
SCALES Walter A. MM Cpl 470812 12th London Regt
SCALES William MM Pte 19768 9th Scottish Rifles
SCALLAN William MM Pte 19191 Royal Dublin Fusiliers
SCALLY Francis MM Pte 3272 8th Yorkshire Light Infantry
SCALLY John MM Pte 20565 Yorkshire Light Infantry
SCAMADIN Walter MM Cpl 10225 2nd York & Lancaster Regt
SCAMBLER John L. MM Sjt 145242 1/1st Sherwood Rangers Yeo
SCAMBLER Robert MM Gnr 160208 B/150 Bde RFA
SCAMBLER Thomas MM+Bar 2nd Cpl 192816 'O' Special Coy Royal Engineers
SCAMMELL Ernest A. MM L/Cpl 240731 12th Middlesex Regt
SCAMMELL John H. MM L/Sjt 7961 2nd Hampshire Regt
SCAMP Harold T. MM Pte D/4739 7th Dragoon Guards
SCANDRETT Cyril MM Pte 4569 2/1st HAC(Inf)
SCANDRETT Herbert "MM+Bar,MID" Cpl 46951 22 Fd Amb RAMC
SCANLAN J. MM Pte 51635 West Yorkshire Regt
SCANLAN Joseph MM L/Cpl 611512 19th London Regt
SCANLAN Thomas MM L/Cpl 6050 11th Royal Fusiliers
SCANLAN Thomas MM L/Cpl 75728 Tank Corps
SCANLON Andrew MM L/Bdr 49282 RGA
SCANLON Denis MM Cpl 8640 2nd Royal Munster Fusiliers

SCANLON Howell MM+Bar Pte 200930 2/1st London Regt
SCANLON J.T. MM Pte 263025 5th Gloucestershire Regt
SCANLON John Joseph MM Dvr 39746 B/177 Bde RFA KIA 10.6.17.
SCANLON Michael MM Pte 9639 1st Royal Munster Fusiliers
SCANLON Thomas MM Pte 68213 RAMC
SCANNELL Patrick MM Cpl 8602 1st Royal Munster Fusiliers
SCARBOROUGH Thomas P. MM CoH 1216 Royal Horse Guards
SCARBOROUGH William MM Pte 5618 1st Royal West Kent Regt
SCARESBROOK Matthew MM L/Cpl 42310 21st Middlesex Regt
SCARFE Alfred MM L/Cpl 36394 2nd York & Lancaster Regt
SCARFE William MM L/Cpl 39275 Royal Berkshire Regt
SCARFF James William MM L/Cpl 267892 1/6th West Riding Regt KIA 11.10.18.
SCARGILL Clifford MM Sjt 265905 2/7th Liverpool Regt KIA 27.9.18.
SCARGILL Samson MM+Bar L/Cpl 132498 Royal Engineers
SCARISBRICK Robert MM Pte R/9729 4th King's Royal Rifle Corps
SCARLL G.H. MM Pte 43795 Suffolk Regt
SCARNELL Herbert William "MM,MM(F)" Sjt 14374 Royal Flying Corps
SCARR E. MM L/Cpl 2026 1/1st Cambridgeshire Regt
SCARSBROOK George F. MM L/Cpl 570177 1/17th London Regt
SCARTERFIELD Roland C. "MM,MID" Sjt 1082 15th Hussars
SCARTH George Alexander MM L/Sjt 16683 Liverpool Regt
SCASE Cyril Walter MM Pte 14644 2nd Suffolk Regt KIA 28.3.18.
SCATCHARD Ernest MM L/Cpl 56367 Royal Engineers
SCATCHARD J. MM Pte 37966 Machine Gun Corps
SCATTERGOOD William F. MM Pte R/7915 King's Royal Rifle Corps
SCHAEFER Frederick L. MM Pte M2/153620 Army Service Corps
SCHARLACH V.G. MM L/Cpl 3850 HAC
SCHEERS George MM L/Cpl 115 9th Cheshire Regt
SCHEFFERS W.H. MM Spr 512435 122 Fd Coy Royal Engineers
SCHENK G.C. MM Pte PS/2035 Royal Fusiliers
SCHEURMIER Charles H. "DCM,MM" Sjt G/5105 12th Royal Fusiliers
SCHLENCKER John "DCM,MM+Bar" Pte 10913 4th Middlesex Regt
SCHLESS Ellis MM Pte 359442 14th Liverpool Regt
SCHMALZEN Albert P. MM L/Cpl 570567 1/17th London Regt
SCHMIDT Arthur W. MM CQMS 240890 5th Yorkshire Light Infantry
SCHNABEL Arthur J. MM L/Cpl 241562 2nd London Regt
SCHNEIDER Frederick William MM Cpl 894 1/1(London)Fd Coy Royal Engineers
SCHNEITER Karl Ernest MM Pte S/31728 12th Rifle Brigade
SCHOALES William MM Sjt 9203 2nd Leinster Regt
SCHOFIELD A. MM Pte 508271 RAMC
SCHOFIELD Albert E. MM Sjt 275963 7th Manchester Regt
SCHOFIELD Alfred MM Pte 306092 2/8th West Yorkshire Regt
SCHOFIELD Alfred MM L/Cpl 252371 9th Manchester Regt
SCHOFIELD Arthur MM 2nd Cpl 442426 432 Fd Coy Royal Engineers
SCHOFIELD Arthur MM+Bar L/Sjt 41223 9th Northumberland Fusiliers KIA 24.10.18.
SCHOFIELD Bromley MM Pte 4/8637 11th West Yorkshire Regt
SCHOFIELD Clifford MM Pte 13865 1st Scots Guards
SCHOFIELD David MM Cpl 58176 5 Bty 45 Bde RFA DOW 6.6.18.
SCHOFIELD E. MM Pte 41928 10th Northumberland Fusiliers
SCHOFIELD Edgar MM S/Sjt 485 RAMC
SCHOFIELD Edgar MM CQMS 132 18th West Yorkshire Regt
SCHOFIELD Edwin MM Dvr 18712 RFA
SCHOFIELD F.B.T. MM L/Cpl 23929 6th East Kent Regt
SCHOFIELD Frank MM Pte 17527 2nd Grenadier Guards
SCHOFIELD Fred MM 2nd Cpl 442287 432 Fd Coy Royal Engineers
SCHOFIELD George Albert MM Cpl 2201 West Riding Regt
SCHOFIELD George P. MM L/Cpl 63955 Machine Gun Corps
SCHOFIELD Harold MM Cpl 154883 Y/35 Med TM Bty RFA
SCHOFIELD Harold Hawksby MM Cpl 797096 Z/62 Med TM Bty RFA
SCHOFIELD Harry MM Sjt 705813 331 Bde RFA
SCHOFIELD Harry MM Pte 280567 1/7th Lancashire Fusiliers
SCHOFIELD Harry W. MM Spr 140217 92 Fd Coy Royal Engineers
SCHOFIELD Henry "DCM,MM" Gnr Fitter 700832 A/330 Bde RFA
SCHOFIELD Herbert MM Pte 241432 1/5th West Riding Regt
SCHOFIELD Isaac H. MM Sjt 253978 297 Rly Const Coy Royal Engineers
SCHOFIELD James MM Sjt 1500 Middlesex Regt
SCHOFIELD John MM+Bar Sjt 40058 Welsh Regt
SCHOFIELD John MM Pte 241053 Lancashire Fusiliers
SCHOFIELD John J. MM Pte 52724 Liverpool Regt
SCHOFIELD Joseph MM Pte 307729 11th West Yorkshire Regt
SCHOFIELD Joseph MM Pte 6972 Machine Gun Corps
SCHOFIELD Joseph E. MM Pte 308637 8th Liverpool Regt
SCHOFIELD Rupert MM Sjt 113420 Royal Engineers
SCHOFIELD Sam MM Cpl 97988 Machine Gun Corps
SCHOFIELD Samuel MM Pte 33627 Lancashire Fusiliers
SCHOFIELD Samuel MM Pte 1386 1/3rd Monmouthshire Regt
SCHOFIELD Stephen James MM Pte 88070 RAMC
SCHOFIELD Thomas MM Pte 28777 5th South Lancashire Regt
SCHOFIELD Thomas "DCM,MM,MID" Sjt 10451 North Lancashire Regt
SCHOFIELD Thomas MM Pte S/5 12th Rifle Brigade
SCHOFIELD Thomas E. MM Pte 38117 West Yorkshire Regt
SCHOFIELD Thomas William MM Pte 20135 2nd West Riding Regt
SCHOFIELD W.C. MM Cpl 139109 RAMC
SCHOFIELD Washington W. MM L/Cpl 266235 2/7th West Yorkshire Regt
SCHOFIELD William MM Pte 1818 1st Manchester Regt Died 7.5.18.
SCHOFIELD William MM Gnr 1100 4(West Riding)Bde RFA
SCHOFIELD William MM Pte 19418 South Lancashire Regt
SCHOFIELD William H. MM Sjt 50545 22 Bde RFA
SCHOLEFIELD Joseph MM Pte 8881 RAMC
SCHOLEFIELD Tom MM Gnr 38594 Machine Gun Corps(Motors)
SCHOLES Albert H. MM Pte 40930 15th Cheshire Regt
SCHOLES Albert Vincent MM Air Mech 1 6773 12 Wing Royal Flying Corps
SCHOLES Ernest MM Pte 63987 Machine Gun Corps
SCHOLES John MM Gnr 293433 136 Heavy Bty RGA
SCHOLES Thomas MM Pte 47867 2/3(West Riding)Fd Amb RAMC
SCHOLES Thomas MM Gnr 5930 RFA
SCHOLES William MM L/Cpl 201261 1/5th East Lancashire Regt
SCHOLEY Cornelius MM Pte 17/8875 17th Manchester Regt KIA 27.4.18.
SCHOLEY John MM L/Cpl 201517 Yorkshire Light Infantry
SCHOLFIELD Arthur MM Pte M2/121886 32 Div Train. Army Service Corps
SCHOLFIELD Thomas MM Pte 12253 13th Liverpool Regt
SCHOOLER James MM London Regt see James RIDGLEY
SCHOOLER James MM Pte 12959 2nd Dragoons
SCHOOLING Joseph William MM Pte 31452 9th Essex Regt
SCHOTTLANDER Solomon MM L/Cpl 10/664 10th East Yorkshire Regt
SCHRODER Frank W. MM L/Cpl 3852 1st Lancashire Fusiliers
SCHULTE Albert H. MM L/Cpl 14929 1st Scots Guards
SCHULTZ Francis MM Sjt 680991 RFA
SCHULTZ Herman "DCM,MM" Sjt 2662 1st North Lancashire Regt KIA 14.11.17.
SCHULTZE William A. MM L/Cpl 17089 Liverpool Regt
SCHURHOFF Fritz MM Cpl 198145 Royal Engineers
SCHWABE Henry MM Pte R/21741 17th King's Royal Rifle Corps
SCHWARZHANS Albert MM Pte 202466 2nd East Lancashire Regt
SCHWEITZER G. "MM,MID" Pte 10758 Scots Guards
SCILLITOE Edgar MM Gnr 101495 RGA
SCIPIO George E. MM Cpl 592362 18th London Regt
SCOBBIE Alexander MM L/Cpl 97790 32nd Bn Machine Gun Corps
SCOBBIE Richard MM Pte M2/113928 Army Service Corps att 26 Fd Amb RAMC.
SCOBIE John "DCM,MM" Piper 17128 1st Cameron Highlanders
SCOBIE William MM Sjt 85321 A/197 Bde RFA
SCOBIE William J. "MM+Bar,MID" Sjt 22347 Royal Fusiliers
SCOGGINS Frederick MM Dvr 885175 RFA
SCOGGINS H.R. MM CSM 1474 Suffolk Regt
SCOLEY John MM Pte 12115 King's Royal Rifle Corps
SCOLLARD James A. MM Pte M2/098049 Army Service Corps
SCOLLAY Edward Francis "MM,MSM,MID" Sjt 8292 Yorkshire Light Infantry
SCOLLAY William J. MM Pte 8367 4th Royal Fusiliers
SCONCE J.A. MM Sjt 128716 Royal Engineers
SCOON Thomas MM 2nd Cpl 422536 416 Fd Coy Royal Engineers
SCORER George MM Pte 136384 25th Bn Machine Gun Corps
SCORER Herbert G. MM Sjt 47810 141 Fd Amb RAMC
SCORER William Hunter MM Cpl 348018 1/9th Durham Light Infantry
SCORER William Stanley MM Sjt 19/86 Northumberland Fusiliers
SCOREY F. MM Pte 74811 139 Fd Amb RAMC
SCORGIE William MM Pte 1722 RAMC
SCOTHERN George MM L/Cpl 14113 8th York & Lancaster Regt
SCOTLAND Archibald MM Cpl 16559 Machine Gun Corps
SCOTLAND John MM Sjt 2621 1/7th Arg & Suth Highlanders

SCOTNEY Cecil S. MM Pte 201959 Royal Berkshire Regt
SCOTNEY Harry MM Pte 35499 RAMC
SCOTSON Robert MM Gnr Fitter 89505 RFA
SCOTT A. MM Dvr 2070 RFA
SCOTT A.T. MM Pte 3823 Northumberland Fusiliers
SCOTT Albert E. MM CSM 62627 9th Yorkshire Light Infantry
SCOTT Alexander MM Cpl 263 7th Seaforth Highlanders
SCOTT Alexander C. MM Cpl 10429 2nd Gordon Highlanders
SCOTT Alfred MM RQMS 18287 33rd Bn Machine Gun Corps
SCOTT Amon MM+Bar Cpl 205610 2/4th West Riding Regt
SCOTT Andrew MM Pte 6726 Army Cyclist Corps
SCOTT Archibald MM Cpl 337185 142 Heavy Bty RGA
SCOTT Archibald Douglas MM Pte 40734 2nd Scottish Rifles Died 20.6.18.
SCOTT Arthur "MM,MIDx2" Sjt 3866 8th Royal West Kent Regt
SCOTT Arthur MM Cpl 201737 1st London Regt
SCOTT Arthur MM L/Cpl 32916 14th Royal Warwickshire Regt
SCOTT Arthur MM Sjt 240642 Gordon Highlanders
SCOTT Arthur Ernest MM Pte 23885 6th Royal West Kent Regt KIA 7.9.18.
SCOTT Arthur Heaton MM Pte 2026 1/6th West Riding Regt KIA 20.11.16.
SCOTT Arthur S. "DCM,MM" L/Sjt 1516 11th West Yorkshire Regt
SCOTT Benjamin MM Pte C/6230 18th King's Royal Rifle Corps KIA 15.9.16.
SCOTT Benjamin E. MM Cpl 203648 1st London Regt
SCOTT C.C. MM Bdr 2640 RFA
SCOTT Charles MM Pte 4271 1/5th Royal Highlanders
SCOTT Charles MM Sjt 200036 1/4th King's Own Scottish Borderers
SCOTT Charles Bennett MM Dvr 45977 A/89 Bde RFA
SCOTT Charles Frederick MM Dvr 751314 RFA
SCOTT Charles H. MM Cpl 101189 169 Coy Labour Corps
SCOTT Charles S. MM Sjt 750307 RFA
SCOTT Charles William MM Pte 270928 10th East Kent Regt
SCOTT David MM Sjt 76406 'F' Corps Sig Coy Royal Engineers
SCOTT David MM L/Cpl C/673 16th King's Royal Rifle Corps
SCOTT David MM L/Cpl 200817 1/5th South Staffordshire Regt KIA 11.10.18.
SCOTT David MM Sjt 19/866 20th Durham Light Infantry KIA 21.10.18.
SCOTT David John Edward MM Sjt 249155 'E' Corps Sig Coy Royal Engineers
SCOTT David M. MM Cpl 40235 2nd Royal Scots
SCOTT Donald MM Gnr 125790 RFA
SCOTT E.F. MM Dvr 224804 251 Bde RFA
SCOTT Edgar MM Spr 317053 Royal Engineers
SCOTT Edgar MM Pte 2267 8th Royal Sussex Regt
SCOTT Edmund MM 2nd Cpl 426050 419 Fd Coy Royal Engineers DOW 13.4.18.
SCOTT Edward MM Pte 14375 12th West Yorkshire Regt DOW 24.7.16.
SCOTT Edward MM Sjt 515515 14th London Regt
SCOTT Edward MM Gnr 795432 RFA
SCOTT Edward MM Pte 496 13th Royal Irish Rifles
SCOTT Edward MM Pte 241185 1/4th Gordon Highlanders DOW 22.7.18.
SCOTT Edward MM Pte 15386 East Yorkshire Regt
SCOTT Edward Willans MM Pte 200529 Durham Light Infantry
SCOTT Edwin F. "MM,MID" L/Sjt 721033 1/24th London Regt
SCOTT Ernest G. MM+Bar CSM 6033 1st East Lancashire Regt
SCOTT F. MM Pte 18065 Machine Gun Corps
SCOTT Francis Gordon MM Pte 5598 Royal Fusiliers KIA 20.10.18.
SCOTT Frank MM Sjt 618 2nd Gordon Highlanders
SCOTT Frederick MM Pte 540635 15th London Regt
SCOTT Frederick MM Bdr 108556 RGA
SCOTT Frederick MM Pte 19297 2nd South Wales Borderers
SCOTT Frederick Arthur MM Sjt 211121 109 Heavy Bty RGA
SCOTT Frederick C. MM L/Cpl 25138 Hampshire Regt
SCOTT Frederick J. MM Dvr 781243 310 Bde RFA
SCOTT Frederick W. MM S/Sjt Armt 286 Army Ordnance Corps
SCOTT G. MM Pte 36619 8th Royal Lancaster Regt
SCOTT George MM 2nd Cpl 491954 46 Div Sig Coy Royal Engineers
SCOTT George MM Pte 7512 2nd Scots Guards
SCOTT George MM Sjt 7481 Arg & Suth Highlanders
SCOTT George MM Cpl 42661 Machine Gun Corps
SCOTT George MM Sjt 11492 2nd Scots Guards Died 6.6.19.
SCOTT George MM+Bar Pte 1496 11th Notts & Derby Regt
SCOTT George MM Pte 18361 9th Yorkshire Light Infantry Died 22.3.18.
SCOTT George Henry MM Pte 33017 12th Gloucestershire Regt DOW 22.8.18.
SCOTT George S. MM Pte 49234 38 Fd Amb RAMC
SCOTT George William MM L/Cpl 27305 2nd South Wales Borderers KIA 18.4.17.
SCOTT Gilbert "DCM,MM" L/Cpl 5190 2nd Arg & Suth Highlanders KIA 25.9.17.
SCOTT Gilbert P. MM Pte 253618 3rd London Regt
SCOTT H. MM Sjt 89035 RGA
SCOTT Harold MM Pte 267658 8th West Yorkshire Regt
SCOTT Harold MM Pte 25589 12th East Surrey Regt
SCOTT Harry MM Pte 270269 10th East Kent Regt
SCOTT Harry MM Sjt 108532 232 Army Troops Coy Royal Engineers
SCOTT Harry MM L/Cpl 19842 10th Northumberland Fusiliers
SCOTT Harry J. MM L/Cpl M2/052295 Army Service Corps
SCOTT Harry James MM Sjt 302814 11th Bn Tank Corps
SCOTT Harry L. MM Pte 265391 1/6th Seaforth Highlanders
SCOTT Hector MM Pte 41470 2nd Royal Scots Fusiliers
SCOTT Henry MM Cpl 10282 Durham Light Infantry
SCOTT Henry MM Cpl 2252 1/4th East Yorkshire Regt KIA 22.7.16.
SCOTT Henry Charloes MM Pte 3225 13th Royal Sussex Regt KIA 30.6.16.
SCOTT Henry G. MM(2478 12th Middx)+Bar Pnr 360855 18 Div Sig Coy Royal Engineers
SCOTT Henry W. MM L/Cpl 422437 10th London Regt
SCOTT Herbert MM Pte 242553 7th Royal West Surrey Regt
SCOTT Herbert MM Pte 52153 1st East Yorkshire Regt
SCOTT Herbert MM Pte 9288 2nd Suffolk Regt
SCOTT Horace MM Spr 75455 Royal Engineers
SCOTT Hugh MM Sjt 24385 Royal Irish Fusiliers
SCOTT J. MM Cpl 238132 4th Gordon Highlanders
SCOTT J. MM Pte 2304 West Riding Regt
SCOTT J.B. MM Gnr 279 RFA
SCOTT J.G. MM Pte 41878 13 Fd Amb RAMC
SCOTT Jack MM Sjt 20/240 10th West Yorkshire Regt
SCOTT James MM+Bar Pte 40245 10th Scottish Rifles
SCOTT James MM Spr 412238 409 Fd Coy Royal Engineers
SCOTT James MM Cpl 528016 14th London Regt KIA 31.8.18.
SCOTT James MM L/Cpl 201518 Scottish Rifles
SCOTT James MM Cpl 241226 1/5th York & Lancaster Regt
SCOTT James MM Cpl 26207 7th Royal Irish Regt DOW 31.10.18.
SCOTT James MM Sjt 23060 3rd Bn Machine Gun Corps
SCOTT James MM Sjt 21750 Machine Gun Corps
SCOTT James MM L/Cpl 14661 24th Manchester Regt
SCOTT James MM L/Cpl 7672 7th Cameron Highlanders DOW 12.5.17.
SCOTT James MM L/Sjt 2036 1/6th Seaforth Highlanders
SCOTT James MM Pte 20223 12th Royal Scots KIA 25.4.18.
SCOTT James MM Dvr 6588 RFA
SCOTT James MM Cpl 21/903 Northumberland Fusiliers
SCOTT James MM Pte 4964 18th Highland Light Infantry
SCOTT James MM Sjt 14445 10th West Riding Regt KIA 18.10.17.
SCOTT James A. MM Pte 15700 9th South Staffordshire Regt
SCOTT James Clark MM Gnr Fitter 20845 C/119 Bde RFA
SCOTT James H. MM Pte 140726 Machine Gun Corps
SCOTT James H. MM L/Cpl 26/625 Northumberland Fusiliers
SCOTT James L.M. MM L/Cpl 330273 1/8th Royal Scots
SCOTT James T. MM L/Cpl 2401 1/22nd London Regt
SCOTT James Y. MM Dvr 12603 37 Bde RFA
SCOTT John MM Cpl 18186 1st Gordon Highlanders
SCOTT John MM Sjt 397323 2 Siege Coy R Mon RE Royal Engineers
SCOTT John MM Pte 201180 1/4th King's Own Scottish Borderers
SCOTT John MM L/Sjt 13055 10th West Riding Regt
SCOTT John MM Cpl 31/127 1st Northumberland Fusiliers KIA 23.8.18.
SCOTT John MM Pte 14361 Durham Light Infantry
SCOTT John MM Cpl 202841 1/5th Arg & Suth Highlanders KIA 23.7.18.
SCOTT John MM Sjt 4934 1st Royal West Kent Regt
SCOTT John MM Sjt 8142 Royal Fusiliers
SCOTT John MM Sjt 19634 Royal Scots
SCOTT John MM Pte 200397 Royal Highlanders
SCOTT John MM L/Cpl 4015 11th Arg & Suth Highlanders
SCOTT John MM Cpl 200454 'C' Bn Tank Corps
SCOTT John MM Pte 11871 Gordon Highlanders
SCOTT John MM Pte 9384 2nd Cameron Highlanders

SCOTT John Edward MM Pte 339164 RAMC att 2/1(Lancashire)Heavy Bty RGA.
SCOTT John George MM Sjt 760397 D/78 Bde RFA
SCOTT John H. MM L/Cpl 16813 11th Royal Scots
SCOTT John H. MM L/Cpl 11318 6th Royal Inniskilling Fusiliers
SCOTT John Joseph MM Pte 359433 10th Liverpool Regt
SCOTT John Miller MM L/Cpl 28979 6th King's Own Scottish Borderers KIA 18.8.18.
SCOTT John Murdoch MM Sjt TT/03601 Army Veterinary Corps att 256 Bde RFA.
SCOTT John P. MM L/Cpl 6838 2nd Royal Irish Regt
SCOTT John P. MM Spr 12852 Royal Engineers
SCOTT John R. MM Pte 1541 3(Northumbrian)Fd Amb RAMC
SCOTT John S. MM L/Cpl 4184 18th Hussars
SCOTT John S. MM Pte 275295 1/7th Arg & Suth Highlanders
SCOTT John W. MM L/Bdr 122899 355 Siege Bty RGA
SCOTT John W. MM Pte M2/114432 32 Div Train. Army Service Corps
SCOTT John W. MM+Bar Sjt 27122 6th Leicestershire Regt
SCOTT John W. MM Sjt 155925 117 Fd Coy Royal Engineers
SCOTT Joseph MM L/Cpl 15411 2nd Grenadier Guards
SCOTT Joseph MM Pte 332932 9th Highland Light Infantry
SCOTT Joseph MM Cpl 7881 2nd Cameron Highlanders DOW 19.9.18.
SCOTT Joseph MM Cpl 8855 17th Manchester Regt
SCOTT Joseph MM Pte 14095 7th Royal Dublin Fusiliers
SCOTT Joseph MM Cpl 8461 2nd Royal Irish Fusiliers
SCOTT Leonard MM Pte 16226 1st Scots Guards
SCOTT Leonard MM Cpl 15068 6th Northamptonshire Regt
SCOTT Malcolm F. MM Sjt 750200 RFA
SCOTT Matthew MM Sjt 292478 1/7th Royal Highlanders
SCOTT Percival T. MM Pnr 288287 12 Div Sig Coy Royal Engineers
SCOTT Percy G. MM Cpl R/26825 2nd King's Royal Rifle Corps
SCOTT Percy William MM Pte 8368 7th Royal Sussex Regt
SCOTT Peter MM Sjt 281093 1/7th Highland Light Infantry
SCOTT Peter W. MM Pte 20269 14th Northumberland Fusiliers
SCOTT R. MM Pte 203447 Yorkshire Light Infantry
SCOTT Raymond MM L/Cpl 4691 14th London Regt
SCOTT Raymond P. MM Pte 235370 2nd South Staffordshire Regt
SCOTT Reuben MM L/Cpl 18004 Royal Scots
SCOTT Richard "MM,CG(B)" Pte 47398 13th Royal Inniskilling Fusiliers
SCOTT Richard MM Pte 928 Northumberland Fusiliers
SCOTT Ritchie J. MM Cpl 5951 Gloucestershire Regt
SCOTT Robert MM RSM 23380 1/5th Seaforth Highlanders
SCOTT Robert MM Cpl 750436 A/250 Bde RFA
SCOTT Robert MM Cpl 350155 13th Liverpool Regt
SCOTT Robert MM Sjt 47917 226 Fd Coy Royal Engineers
SCOTT Robert MM Pte 200539 1/4th King's Own Scottish Borderers
SCOTT Robert MM Pte 119721 Machine Gun Corps
SCOTT Robert MM Pte 240651 1/5th King's Own Scottish Borderers Died 27.4.18.
SCOTT Robert MM Pte 20984 10th Durham Light Infantry
SCOTT Robert MM L/Cpl 13/43191 Royal Irish Rifles
SCOTT Robert MM Sjt 330476 Royal Scots
SCOTT Robert MM L/Cpl 22987 Machine Gun Corps
SCOTT Robert A. MM Pte 42032 RAMC
SCOTT Robert Edward MM+Bar 2nd Cpl 463066 50 Div Sig Coy Royal Engineers
SCOTT Robert J.G. MM Pte 202624 1/7th Royal Highlanders
SCOTT Robert Redcap MM Pte 242002 22nd Northumberland Fusiliers Died 9.4.18.
SCOTT Robert Young MM Cpl 76261 'OO' Cable Section Royal Engineers
SCOTT Roland J. MM Dvr 63157 112 Bde RFA
SCOTT Rupert E. MM Cpl 110897 RGA
SCOTT S. MM Pte 7767 East Kent Regt
SCOTT Samuel MM Gnr 90324 RFA
SCOTT Samuel G. MM Dvr 235361 C/124 Bde RFA
SCOTT Stanley B. MM CQMS 200065 Essex Regt
SCOTT Sydney A. MM Pte 37825 Royal Berkshire Regt
SCOTT Thomas MM Gnr 2594 B/187 Bde RFA
SCOTT Thomas MM Sjt 22556 9th Royal Irish Fusiliers KIA 4.9.18.
SCOTT Thomas MM L/Cpl 27433 2nd Grenadier Guards
SCOTT Thomas MM Sjt 11081 2nd Durham Light Infantry
SCOTT Thomas MM Cpl 3172 2nd Dragoon Guards
SCOTT Thomas MM Sjt 1839 1/4th C Coy Northumberland Fusiliers KIA 15.9.16.
SCOTT Thomas MM+Bar Pte 7097 1st Gordon Highlanders
SCOTT Thomas MM L/Cpl 16251 Arg & Suth Highlanders
SCOTT Thomas MM Pte 43268 17th Highland Light Infantry
SCOTT Thomas C. MM Pte 12936 Machine Gun Corps
SCOTT Thomas Charles Sidney MM Sjt 5964 8th Border Regt Died 12.3.18.
SCOTT Thomas L. MM Sjt 650440 RFA
SCOTT Thomas N.G. MM Pte 7273 RAMC
SCOTT Thomas Robson MM Pte 25/625 24th Northumberland Fusiliers KIA 1.7.16.
SCOTT Thomas W. MM Pte 20736 Border Regt
SCOTT Thomas W. MM+Bar Pte 22935 6th King's Own Scottish Borderers
SCOTT Tom A. MM L/Cpl 24193 Duke of Cornwall's LI
SCOTT Victor John MM Spr 46549 31 Div Sig Coy Royal Engineers
SCOTT W.S. MM L/Cpl 325202 1/8th Royal Scots
SCOTT W.T. MM Bdr 290648 RGA
SCOTT Walter MM Cpl 15116 2nd Northumberland Fusiliers
SCOTT Walter MM Sjt 8731 RFA
SCOTT Walter MM Sjt 3650 33rd Bn Machine Gun Corps KIA 22.9.18.
SCOTT Walter MM Sjt 23/1525 Northumberland Fusiliers
SCOTT Walter S. MM Pte M1/5852 27 Mot Amb Convoy Army Service Corps
SCOTT Wilfred MM Cpl 35416 9 TM Bty RGA KIA 13.10.17.
SCOTT William MM Pte 295742 12th Royal Scots Fusiliers
SCOTT William MM L/Cpl 9554 2nd West Yorkshire Regt
SCOTT William MM Cpl 113490 'M' Special Coy Royal Engineers
SCOTT William MM Pte 61012 7th Royal Fusiliers
SCOTT William MM Pte 21325 1/7th Gordon Highlanders
SCOTT William MM Sjt 16483 1st Somerset Light Infantry
SCOTT William MM Pte 8558 2nd Yorkshire Light Infantry
SCOTT William MM Pte 16094 1st Lincolnshire Regt
SCOTT William MM Pte 22173 12th Royal Scots
SCOTT William MM L/Cpl B/203236 13th Rifle Brigade KIA 25.8.18.
SCOTT William MM Pte 318411 2(Lowland)Fd Amb RAMC
SCOTT William MM L/Cpl P7540 1 Traffic Control Coy Military Foot Police
SCOTT William MM Pte 9763 2nd Royal Irish Rifles
SCOTT William MM Sjt 71023 North Irish Horse
SCOTT William MM Sjt 20302 12th Royal Scots
SCOTT William MM Spr 79042 178 Tunnelling Coy Royal Engineers
SCOTT William MM Sjt 12864 7th Northamptonshire Regt KIA 31.7.17.
SCOTT William MM Sjt S/13664 Rifle Brigade
SCOTT William MM Cpl 13349 9th North Lancashire Regt
SCOTT William A. MM Pte 238110 5/6th Scottish Rifles
SCOTT William Arthur MM L/Cpl 17417 6th York & Lancaster Regt
SCOTT William B. MM Gnr Sig 116614 115 Hy Bty RGA
SCOTT William Dawson MM Pte 3249 9th Royal Scots
SCOTT William Edward MM CSM 590 1/7th West Yorkshire Regt KIA 1.7.16.
SCOTT William G. MM+Bar 2nd Cpl 510249 Royal Engineers
SCOTT William George MM L/Cpl 27536 9th Essex Regt
SCOTT William H. MM Pte 7412 Northumberland Fusiliers
SCOTT William Henry "DCM+Bar,MM" CSM 11348 12th Northumberland Fusiliers
SCOTT William J. "MM,MID" Sjt 1456 Royal Engineers
SCOTTOW Henry "DCM,MM(15005 Yorks Regt)" Cpl 34628 2/4th West Riding Regt
SCOUGALL George MM Pte 351130 2nd Royal Scots Died 5.11.18.
SCOULAR D. MM Pte 53403 54 Fd Amb RAMC
SCOULAR James MM Pte 68058 37th Bn Machine Gun Corps
SCOULDING A.W. MM Cpl 43295 2nd Suffolk Regt
SCOULLAR J. MM Pte 122846 Machine Gun Corps
SCOUSE Albert F. MM Pte 330855 15th Hampshire Regt
SCOVELL George W. MM Pte R/5868 11th King's Royal Rifle Corps
SCOWCROFT Richard MM Sjt 350049 1(East Lancs)Fd Amb RAMC
SCOWCROFT Thomas MM Pte 16777 10th North Lancashire Regt
SCOWCROFT Thomas MM Cpl 241246 2/5th North Lancashire Regt
SCOWCROFT Thomas H. MM Cpl 16569 8th East Lancashire Regt
SCRACE Cecil George MM Sjt 51529 2nd Royal Fusiliers KIA 13.4.18.
SCRACE Herbert MM Pte 12175 7th Royal West Kent Regt DOW 24.9.18.
SCRAFTON Christopher MM Bugler 1430 1/6th Durham Light Infantry
SCRAGG Arthur MM Pte 204293 5th Lincolnshire Regt
SCRAGG Horace Samuel MM S/Sjt 435585 64 Fd Amb RAMC KIA 9.10.17.

SCRAGGS William MM Dvr 15442 B/162 Bde RFA
SCRANNEY Thomas William "MM,MSM" Sjt 46652 D/108 Bde RFA
SCRASE A. "DCM,MM,MID" CSM 9879 1st Rifle Brigade
SCRASE E.L. MM L/Cpl 5902 Royal Munster Fusiliers
SCRASE Frederick J. MM Pte 2010 8th Royal Sussex Regt
SCRATCHER John Henry MM Cpl 24723 12th Durham Light Infantry KIA 7.6.17.
SCREECH Richard John MM Bdr 41601 122 Siege Bty RGA
SCREEN Thomas MM Pte 30237 South Staffordshire Regt
SCREEN William Oliver MM Gnr 825671 C/240 Bde RFA
SCRIBBENS or SCRIBBINS Frank G. MM Pte 66356 RAMC
SCRIMGEOUR James MM L/Cpl 12980 2nd Scots Guards
SCRIMGEOUR Thomas MM Pte 41653 1st South Staffordshire Regt
SCRIPPS Frank MM Pte 6108 2nd Bedfordshire Regt
SCRIPPS John H. MM Pte 570 6th Royal West Kent Regt
SCRIVEN Arthur E. MM Pte 60326 Royal Fusiliers
SCRIVEN C. MM Pte 32449 20th Hussars
SCRIVEN Walter MM Sjt 22927 A/186 Bde RFA DOW 27.9.18.
SCRIVEN William Thomas MM Sjt 14584 6th Northamptonshire Regt att KAR.KIA 20.9.17.
SCRIVENER Albert Charles MM Sjt 301601 13th Bn Tank Corps
SCRIVENER F. MM Pte 10105 East Kent Regt
SCRIVENER F.H. MM Sjt 229561 26th Royal Fusiliers
SCRIVENER Frederick C. MM Pte 87148 Middlesex Regt
SCRIVENER George E. MM L/Cpl 10181 2nd Bedfordshire Regt
SCRIVENER Horace MM Pte 13306 1st Bedfordshire Regt
SCRIVENER Horace Henry MM Pte 202469 1st Lincolnshire Regt
SCRIVENER James MM Sjt 6854 2nd Royal Warwickshire Regt
SCRIVENER Victor P. MM Sjt B/200893 Rifle Brigade
SCRIVENS Alfred J. MM L/Cpl 18313 Royal Berkshire Regt
SCRIVENS Charles MM Cpl 66191 'N' Bty RHA
SCRIVENS Frederick MM Sjt 240788 8th Middlesex Regt
SCRIVENS W.H. MM Pte 26261 Oxf & Bucks Light Infantry
SCRIVENS William MM Sjt 5380 10th Royal Warwickshire Regt
SCROBY Albert MM Pte 18049 Royal West Kent Regt
SCROGGIE Robert H. MM L/Cpl 267041 1/7th Royal Highlanders
SCROGGS A.H. MM Pte 15675 1st Grenadier Guards
SCROGGS Ernest James "MM,MID" CQMS A/93 7th King's Royal Rifle Corps
SCROGGS George R. MM Pte 201814 7th Middlesex Regt
SCRUBY Norman C. MM Cpl 12282 6th Bedfordshire Regt
SCRUTON William Albert MM Pte 202888 2nd West Riding Regt
SCRUTTON H.G. MM Pte 19724 Suffolk Regt
SCRUTTON P.F. MM Pte 3/3241 11th Essex Regt
SCUDAMORE Norman R.W. MM+Bar L/Cpl 703880 23rd London Regt
SCUDDER John S. MM Pte 3/11700 9th East Surrey Regt
SCUFFIL John J. MM Spr 22449 Royal Engineers
SCUFFLE Alfred MM Pte 17795 2nd Hampshire Regt
SCULL Harry J. MM Cpl 16185 Machine Gun Corps
SCULL Herbert H. MM+Bar Cpl 53266 13th Royal Fusiliers
SCULLION John MM+Bar Cpl 436 12th Royal Irish Rifles
SCULLION Patrick MM Pte 10331 9th Royal Highlanders
SCULLION William MM Pte 3588 6th Royal Irish Regt
SCULLY Frank Valentine MM Cpl 300462 1st Essex Regt
SCULLY J. MM Pte 903 7th Durham Light Infantry
SCULLY James MM L/Cpl 8096 1st Irish Guards
SCULLY John MM+Bar Pte 12209 1st Royal Dublin Fusiliers
SCULLY Joseph MM Sjt 9627 8th Royal Lancaster Regt DOW 10.6.18.
SCULLY Joseph MM Sjt 5327 Machine Gun Corps
SCULLY Stephen MM Pte 5540 1st Royal Munster Fusiliers
SCULTHORP Alfred G. MM Sjt 27580 1st Somerset Light Infantry
SCURFIELD J. MM L/Cpl P1974 Military Foot Police
SCURRAH Albert E. MM Dvr 32638 460 Bty 15 Bde RFA
SCURRAH George William "DCM,MM+Bar,MM(F)" CSM 201236 1/4th Seaforth Highlanders
SCUTCHER Frederick W. "DCM,MM" Sjt 5973 37th Bn Machine Gun Corps
SCUTCHLEY C.W. MM Bdr 53856 52 Bty 15 Bde RFA
SCUTT Douglas MM Pte 57998 RAMC
SCUTT Frederisk J. MM Pte 69742 Machine Gun Corps
SCUTT George A. MM L/Cpl 9447 2nd Royal Sussex Regt
SCUTT George T. MM Sjt 511526 14th London Regt
SCUTTS William G. MM Sjt 241339 1/4th Gloucestershire Regt
SEABORNE Osborne MM Pte 82343 Durham Light Infantry
SEABOURNE Alfred MM Gnr 37269 326 Siege Bty RGA
SEABOURNE Robert H.G. MM Pte 10581 1st South Wales Borderers

SEABRIDGE Henry E. MM Cpl 27549 North Lancashire Regt
SEABROOK A.G. MM L/Cpl 6173 York & Lancaster Regt
SEABROOK Alfred MM L/Sjt 19829 10th Hampshire Regt
SEABROOK Ernest A. MM Cpl 17108 Somerset Light Infantry
SEABROOK Gerald R. MM Pnr 358513 Royal Engineers
SEABROOK Sidney MM Pte 1505 1/1st London Regt
SEABROOK Sidney William MM Sjt 95143 A/63 Bde RFA
SEABURY Walter E. "DCM,MM" Sjt 45657 B/46 Bde RFA
SEACOMBE James MM L/Cpl 18593 East Yorkshire Regt
SEACY Charles G. MM Pte 15191 Scottish Rifles
SEACY Hugh MM Pte 34630 1/5th Royal Lancaster Regt
SEAGER Albert MM L/Cpl 14320 5th South Wales Borderers KIA 10.4.18.
SEAGER Arthur MM Pte 13038 Norfolk Regt
SEAGER Arthur Joseph MM Sjt 1129 1/4th Suffolk Regt KIA 18.8.16.
SEAGER Edwin Robert MM L/Cpl 15004 54 Fd Coy Royal Engineers KIA 14.7.16.
SEAGER Elvey MM Gnr 72047 25 Bde RFA
SEAGER George A. MM Cpl 370673 8th London Regt
SEAGER J.F. MM Pte S/4420 13th Rifle Brigade
SEAGER Joseph R. MM Pte 22581 Royal West Surrey Regt
SEAGER Leonard MM Gnr 31825 RFA
SEAGER Lewis MM Sjt 67843 101 Siege Bty RGA
SEAGER Richard MM Pte 15681 7th East Kent Regt
SEAGER Walter MM Pte 17547 Devonshire Regt
SEAGER William MM Cpl 300548 1/7th Essex Regt
SEAGO Herbert J. MM Pte 43335 Norfolk Regt
SEAGROVE Alfred E.S. MM Spr 63750 Royal Engineers
SEAKINS Horace MM L/Cpl 3217 10th Royal West Surrey Regt DOW 25.2.17.
SEAL Arthur MM Bdr 44004 RFA
SEAL Charles E. MM CSM 6326 26th Middlesex Regt
SEAL Cyril J. MM Pte 366293 RAMC
SEAL George W. MM Pte 74579 RAMC
SEAL George William "MC,MM(30549 Sjt)" 2Lt RGA
SEAL Robert MM L/Cpl 19927 3rd Dragoon Guards
SEAL Samuel J. MM Pte 5031 Northumberland Fusiliers
SEALE Thomas James MM Pte 3079 10th Royal Fusiliers DOW 22.9.18.
SEALE William MM Pte 653233 21st London Regt
SEALEY Wilfred MM L/Bdr 685285 C/175 Bde RFA
SEALL Ernest A. MM+Bar L/Cpl 500406 61 Div Sig Coy Royal Engineers
SEALLEY Joseph C. "MM,MM(F)" Pte 843 1st Royal Guernsey LI
SEALS W.F. MM L/Cpl 290460 Northumberland Fusiliers
SEALY Frederick Ernest MM Pte 8393 2nd Royal Irish Regt KIA 26.8.18.
SEAMAN Arthur O. MM Dvr 219151 175 Bde Ammn Col RFA
SEAMAN Frank H. MM Pte 22373 15th Royal Warwickshire Regt
SEAMAN George H. MM Cpl 43683 Machine Gun Corps
SEAMAN Jacob B. MM Dvr 40337 RFA
SEAMAN PercyW. MM Pte 242208 Notts & Derby Regt
SEAMAN Reginald MM Pte 2875 12th East Surrey Regt
SEAMAN Robert MM L/Cpl 129512 Royal Engineers
SEAMAN Sydney MM Cpl 34775 RFA
SEAMARK Leslie H.F. "MM,MC(G)" Cpl S/13817 4th Rifle Brigade
SEAR George J. MM Sjt 82768 RGA
SEAR Henry James MM Pte 25384 2nd Bedfordshire Regt
SEAR Henry Robert MM Pte 13810 7th Wiltshire Regt KIA 18.10.18.
SEAR Herbert W. MM L/Cpl 12528 6th Oxf & Bucks Light Infantry
SEAR Robert H. MM Pte 18811 2nd Bedfordshire Regt
SEARBY Robert W. MM Pte 16027 8th West Riding Regt
SEARCH George E. MM Sjt 12381 9th Royal Sussex Regt
SEARCH Stanley B. MM Sjt 136366 RGA
SEARCY Alfred E. MM+Bar Sjt 29346 7th East Yorkshire Regt
SEARES Joseph MM L/Cpl 5938 7th Royal West Kent Regt
SEARLE Albion "DCM,MM+Bar" L/Bdr 40422 6 Bty 40 Bde RFA
SEARLE Charles MM Sjt 8558 2nd Royal Sussex Regt
SEARLE Charles H. MM Sjt 74443 RAMC
SEARLE Christopher "DCM,MM" Cpl 2528 VIII Corps Cyclist Bn Army Cyclist Corps
SEARLE Edgar MM+Bar Pte 330844 4th Liverpool Regt
SEARLE Edwin "MM,MID" Sjt 6265 1st Gloucestershire Regt
SEARLE Frank MM Spr 510190 Royal Engineers
SEARLE George Henry MM L/Cpl G7/413 7th East Surrey Regt DOW 10.4.17.
SEARLE Harold MM Pte 330311 13th Liverpool Regt
SEARLE Henry MM+Bar Pte 15967 Suffolk Regt
SEARLE James MM L/Cpl 20178 2nd Middlesex Regt KIA 24.4.18.

SEARLE John MM Cpl R/4577 11th King's Royal Rifle Corps
SEARLE John Henry MM L/Cpl 512410 2/3(London)Fd Amb RAMC
SEARLE John T. MM Pte 2414 1/1st Cambridgeshire Regt
SEARLE Joseph Victor MM Pte 12880 1st East Kent Regt
SEARLE L.C. MM Sjt 320674 London Regt
SEARLE Reginald MM Sjt Z/1365 4th Rifle Brigade
SEARLE Robert J. MM Sjt 6944 16th Middlesex Regt
SEARLE William MM Pte 16017 6th Cameron Highlanders
SEARLE William Alfred MM Cpl 46385 46 Bde RFA DOW 3.11.16.
SEARLE William E. MM Gnr 29705 RFA
SEARLE William R. MM Pte 22611 Duke of Cornwall's LI
SEARLS Henry MM L/Sjt 302414 5th London Regt
SEARS C. MM Cpl 293571 Labour Corps
SEARS Ernest MM Pte 241668 10th Royal Warwickshire Regt KIA 23.3.18.
SEARS Ernest W. MM Cpl 58672 RAMC
SEARS Frederick MM Sjt 16533 Grenadier Guards
SEARS George C. "DCM,MM" Cpl 14822 2nd Royal Sussex Regt
SEARS Herbert Rayson MM Pte 4680 23rd Royal Fusiliers KIA 17.2.17.
SEARS Stephen John MM L/Cpl 4960 1st Royal West Kent Regt KIA 23.5.18.
SEARS William H. MM Gnr 219621 B/50 Bde RFA
SEARSON Alfred J. MM Spr 311251 37 Div Sig Coy Royal Engineers
SEARSON E. MM Air Mech 1 9387 Royal Flying Corps
SEARSON Edwin C.J. MM Cpl 108938 111 Hy Bty RGA
SEARSON Tom MM Cpl 65621 113 Siege Bty RGA
SEARSTON Albert MM L/Cpl 7181 King's Royal Rifle Corps
SEARSTON Charles Frederick MM Cpl 45181 89 Fd Coy Royal Engineers
SEATH Albert E.W. MM Sjt 18216 RGA
SEATH David Laing MM L/Sjt 10333 1st Cameron Highlanders KIA 3.9.16.
SEATH James MM Pte 11266 1st Scots Guards
SEATH Peter MM L/Cpl 3283 1st Royal Highlanders
SEATH Stephan "MM,MID" Pte 148 6th East Kent Regt
SEATON Charles Henry MM Spr 526206 17 Div Sig Coy Royal Engineers att RFA.
SEATON David MM Sjt 41942 6th King's Own Scottish Borderers
SEATON Frederick MM Pte 43350 Royal Highlanders
SEATON Herbert MM Pte 201638 Seaforth Highlanders
SEATON John MM L/Cpl 1639 1/6th Cheshire Regt
SEATON William MM CSM 265559 1/6th Cheshire Regt
SEATON William MM Gnr 660584 A/262 Bde RFA
SEATON William MM Pte 21043 11th South Lancashire Regt
SEATTER John MM Sjt 65177 9 Tramway Coy Royal Engineers
SEAVERS William MM Pte 8097 7th Royal Irish Rifles
SEAWARD Wilfred J. MM Pte 202427 4th Oxf & Bucks Light Infantry
SEAWARD William MM L/Cpl 32479 RAMC
SEAZEL James MM Sjt 42087 58 Fd Amb RAMC DOW 14.10.17.
SEBRIGHT Albert MM Sjt 26238 Y/37 Med TM Bty RFA
SEBRIGHT Archibald MM L/Cpl 2305 8th Royal West Surrey Regt
SEBRY Charles MM Cpl 5736 11 Fd Amb RAMC
SECCOMBE Samuel MM L/Cpl 20623 Northumberland Fusiliers
SECKER Reginald "MM,MID" Sjt 2918 18th Hussars
SEDDEN James E. MM L/Cpl R/13101 King's Royal Rifle Corps
SEDDON Benjamin MM Sjt 269843 4th Liverpool Regt
SEDDON Edmund MM Sjt 46974 17th Lancashire Fusiliers KIA 14.10.18.
SEDDON Fred MM L/Cpl 35000 Cheshire Regt
SEDDON Frederick MM L/Sjt 265891 4th Liverpool Regt
SEDDON Frederick Robert MM L/Cpl 16499 10th North Lancashire Regt
SEDDON George MM L/Cpl 12124 8th Border Regt KIA 9.9.17.
SEDDON George MM Pte 22177 Royal Dublin Fusiliers
SEDDON Harold MM Pte 53665 2nd West Yorkshire Regt
SEDDON Isaac MM Pte 31397 Shropshire Light Infantry
SEDDON James MM 2nd Cpl 152649 34 Div Sig Coy Royal Engineers
SEDDON John MM Pte 10931 2nd South Lancashire Regt DOW 23.10.16.
SEDDON John A. MM Cpl 63533 42nd Bn Machine Gun Corps
SEDDON John E. "MM,MSM" Sjt 65079 94 Bty 18 Bde RFA
SEDDON John Harold MM Sjt 354168 1/7th London Regt KIA 2.12.17.
SEDDON Richard W. MM Sjt 151231 255 Tunnelling Coy Royal Engineers
SEDDON Thomas MM Cpl 132653 Royal Engineers
SEDDON Thomas MM Bdr 14014 D/74 Bde RFA
SEDDON Thomas MM Pte 2188 11th Manchester Regt
SEDDON Thomas A. MM BSM 3623 51 Div Ammn Col RFA
SEDDON William MM Pte R/11517 King's Royal Rifle Corps
SEDERGREEN Henry MM Cpl 72869 RFA
SEDGLEY John T. MM L/Cpl 13341 8th South Staffordshire Regt
SEDGWICK George MM Gnr 104353 RGA
SEDWELL George MM Sjt 27085 171 Siege Bty RGA KIA 28.11.17.
SEE William J. MM Pte 55340 Machine Gun Corps
SEED Argus C. MM Pte 25 16th Middlesex Regt
SEED George A. MM Sjt 795026 49 Div Ammn Col RFA
SEED John MM Pte 200851 1/4th Royal Lancaster Regt
SEED Thomas MM L/Cpl 13640 8th North Lancashire Regt
SEED Thomas MM Pte 2313 1/4th North Lancashire Regt KIA 31.7.17.
SEED Thomas W. MM Dvr 1544 RFA
SEED Wilfred MM Gnr 67137 350 Siege Bty RGA
SEED William MM Sjt 281112 1/7th Lancashire Fusiliers KIA 27.9.18.
SEED William Cyril MM Gnr 64663 12 Siege Bty RGA KIA 23.8.18.
SEEDELL Fred W. MM Pte 29197 RAMC
SEEDHOUSE Ralph MM L/Cpl 32110 1/5th King's Own Scottish Borderers
SEEKINGS Herbert MM Pte 28215 11th Border Regt KIA 2.12.17.
SEELEY James E. MM Pte 9233 2nd East Lancashire Regt
SEELEY James Henry MM Sjt 56156 3 Pontoon Park Royal Engineers
SEELEY John T. MM L/Cpl 8394 Royal Irish Regt
SEELEY Robert MM Pte 102197 2nd Notts & Derby Regt
SEELEY William J. MM Bdr 930970 A/291 Bde RFA
SEELY Charles L. MM Sjt 200674 1/4th Royal Berkshire Regt
SEELY James W. MM Sjt 13633 7th Norfolk Regt
SEELY John MM Pte 16387 6th East Yorkshire Regt
SEELY Robert J. MM Pte 330006 1/1st Cambridgeshire Regt
SEENAN Michael MM Pte 13681 11th Royal Scots
SEEVIOUR Sidney MM Pte 202556 2/4th Hampshire Regt DOW 28.8.18.
SEFTON Herbert MM Pte 19449 West Yorkshire Regt
SEFTON James MM Gnr 242945 463 Bty 179 Bde RFA
SEFTON Lewis MM L/Cpl 20604 6th York & Lancaster Regt
SEGGIE Robert MM L/Cpl 121931 250 Tunnelling Coy Royal Engineers
SEGROVE F.A. MM Cpl M1/05598 Army Service Corps
SEGUST Walter R. MM L/Cpl 702093 23rd London Regt
SEIBERT William MM Pte 44009 1st Royal Irish Rifles
SEIBOTH Henry MM Gnr 144835 154 Siege Bty RGA
SEILES John MM Pte 376956 8th Manchester Regt
SELBY Albert Edward MM Sjt 111 7th Royal Sussex Regt KIA 8.8.18.
SELBY Arthur John MM L/Cpl 282493 2/4th London Regt KIA 16.6.17.
SELBY George MM Sjt A/3662 King's Royal Rifle Corps
SELBY George William MM Cpl 12388 7 Div Ammn Col RFA DOW 11.1.17.
SELBY James E. MM Cpl 27320 31 Div Ammn Col RFA
SELBY John E. MM Pte 359398 Liverpool Regt
SELBY Joseph J. MM 2nd Cpl 87400 Guards Div Sig Coy Royal Engineers
SELBY Samuel MM Pte 20804 Liverpool Regt
SELBY Sydney Frank MM Cpl 523 10th Royal Fusiliers
SELBY Thomas MM L/Cpl 242568 6th Notts & Derby Regt
SELBY Victor J. MM Sjt 44803 RAMC
SELBY William A. MM Pte 39548 Gloucestershire Regt
SELDEN Charles E.W. MM Pte 52027 24th Royal Fusiliers
SELDON Joseph Spiller MM Sjt 26061 2nd Devonshire Regt KIA 24.4.18.
SELDON Samuel MM Spr 551843 47 Div Sig Coy Royal Engineers
SELDON William MM Sjt 95007 Royal Engineers
SELF Arthur "MM,MID" Sjt 8878 2nd West Yorkshire Regt
SELF Rowland Amos MM Pte 21529 1/6th West Yorkshire Regt KIA 25.4.18.
SELF Walter MM Pte 200741 Norfolk Regt
SELFE William G. MM Sjt 240750 North Staffordshire Regt
SELKIRK Archibald MM L/Cpl 23026 5/6th Scottish Rifles
SELL Charles Henry MM Gnr 44860 RFA
SELL Leonard MM Pte M2/131393 Army Service Corps att 14 Fd Amb RAMC.
SELL Nathan Charles MM Pte 12491 9th Essex Regt
SELL Stanley MM L/Sjt 201431 1/4th Gloucestershire Regt
SELL William J. MM Pte 265330 1/1st Hertfordshire Regt
SELLAR Victor MM Pte 290267 Gordon Highlanders

SELLARS Alfred G. MM Pte 45697 4th Hampshire Regt
SELLARS Edgar MM L/Cpl 240105 West Yorkshire Regt
SELLARS George MM L/Cpl 145176 1/1st Northamptonshire Yeomanry
SELLARS John J. MM L/Cpl 16247 Cameron Highlanders
SELLARS Joseph MM L/Cpl 14262 8th York & Lancaster Regt KIA 1.7.16.
SELLARS Thomas Henry MM Pte 241354 1/5th Yorkshire Regt Died 2.11.18.
SELLARS William "DCM,MM+Bar" Cpl 14146 9th Leicestershire Regt
SELLENS William C.H. MM Cpl 54806 RFA
SELLER William G. MM Sjt 1217 RFA
SELLERS Alfred MM Gnr 756062 RFA
SELLERS Alfred J. MM L/Cpl 281312 1/4th London Regt
SELLERS Frank MM Pte 58626 1st Bn Machine Gun Corps
SELLERS H. MM L/Cpl 241124 West Yorkshire Regt
SELLERS Harry MM Gnr 12179 160 Bde RFA
SELLERS Harry MM Sjt 772 11th East Yorkshire Regt KIA 30.6.18.
SELLERS Jim MM Pte 6885 East Yorkshire Regt
SELLERS John Oliver MM+Bar Pte 10639 2nd Worcestershire Regt
SELLERS John W. MM Pte 2990 2nd Yorkshire Light Infantry
SELLERS Joseph MM Pte 251094 1/6th Manchester Regt
SELLERS Ronald MM L/Cpl 23127 Duke of Cornwall's LI
SELLERS Thomas A. MM Gnr 10956 RFA
SELLEY Frederick MM L/Sjt 8700 2nd Wiltshire Regt
SELLICK Albert Walter George MM Cpl 457032 24 Fd Amb RAMC
SELLICK Arthur MM Pte 30894 1st South Staffordshire Regt
SELLICK Gerald MM Pte 295146 12th Somerset Light Infantry
SELLICK John A. MM+Bar Cpl 534162 RAMC
SELLICK William MM Pte 30046 8th Somerset Light Infantry
SELLORS John Thomas MM Gnr Sig 151412 253 Siege Bty RGA
SELLORS William MM Pte C/6487 King's Royal Rifle Corps
SELLS William Leonard MM Pte M2/055332 Army Service Corps
SELLWOOD Albert E. MM Pte 15789 Royal Berkshire Regt
SELLWOOD Percy MM Pte 2035 1/4th Royal Berkshire Regt
SELSBY Joseph R. MM+Bar L/Cpl 936 8th Royal Sussex Regt
SELTH Richard E. MM Pte 72729 2nd Notts & Derby Regt
SELVEY Harry "MM,MID" Pte 8829 1st Border Regt
SELVEY Henry MM Pte 9738 1st Dorsetshire Regt
SELWAY A. MM L/Cpl 265996 Gloucestershire Regt
SELWAY Charles Stanley William MM Pte 21807 South Wales Borderers
SELWAY Frederick J. MM Pte 71863 Notts & Derby Regt
SELWAY Reginald MM Pte 457386 RAMC
SELWOOD Albert MM Dvr 1549 41 Div Ammn Col RFA
SELWOOD Henry MM Pte 230551 1/2nd London Regt
SELWYN Charles MM Pte 18953 8th Gloucestershire Regt
SELWYN Ernest T. MM Sjt 91552 RFA
SELWYN Leonard MM L/Cpl 23943 Machine Gun Corps
SEMLEY Arthur MM L/Cpl 2334 1/4th York & Lancaster Regt
SEMMENS Herbert MM Dvr 90190 Royal Engineers
SEMPLE David S. MM+Bar Sjt 40222 RAMC
SEMPLE James MM Pte 8883 1st Dorsetshire Regt
SEMPLE John L. MM Pte 18924 6th Border Regt
SEMPLE Richard MM Bdr 93493 B/58 Bde RFA
SEMPLE Robert MM Pte 27491 Royal Inniskilling Fusiliers
SEMPLE Robert "MM+Bar,MID" Sjt 10996 Royal Irish Fusiliers
SEMPLE William MM Pte 200124 5/6th Scottish Rifles
SEMPLE William MM Sjt 655554 158 Bde RFA
SENDEY Charles MM Pte 3069 1st Welsh Guards
SENEVIRATNE Dionysius B. MM Cpl 30032 10th Royal West Kent Regt
SENG Edgar MM Pte 13378 Royal West Surrey Regt
SENIOR Alexander MM Sjt 10624 2nd West Riding Regt
SENIOR Alfred MM Pte 16227 7th Norfolk Regt KIA 28.4.17.
SENIOR Arthur MM Pte 205301 1/4th East Yorkshire Regt DOW 21.4.28.
SENIOR Arthur MM Sjt 446 1/7th West Riding Regt
SENIOR Arthur Ernest MM Sjt 750 1st Rifle Brigade KIA 23.10.16.
SENIOR Clifford MM L/Cpl 205189 Royal West Kent Regt
SENIOR Frank O. MM Cpl 88626 RFA
SENIOR Frederick J. "DCM,MM" Pte 10779 2nd Leinster Regt
SENIOR Henry MM Gnr 240307 RFA
SENIOR Herbert MM Pte 242510 4th Yorkshire Light Infantry
SENIOR J. MM Pte 403234 2 Fd Amb RAMC
SENIOR James MM Pte C/4528 8th King's Royal Rifle Corps Died 19.5.18.
SENIOR Percy MM Gnr 676213 15 Bde RFA
SENIOR Ralph L. MM L/Cpl 67601 113 Coy Labour Corps
SENIOR Walter MM Pte 251525 6th Manchester Regt
SENIOR Walter MM Pte 13749 10th Cheshire Regt att 25 Div Sig Coy RE.
SENIOR William MM Cpl 54469 17th Royal Welsh Fusiliers
SENSIER Edwin H.F. MM Pte 1777 16th Middlesex Regt
SENYARD Frederick G. MM Pte 283148 4th London Regt
SERELLA James MM Pte 25893 11th Liverpool Regt
SERFF Bernard MM+Bar Sjt 681961 22nd London Regt
SERGEANT Aubrey MM L/Cpl 2216 1/4th London Regt
SERGEANT George H. MM Pte 97743 20th Royal Fusiliers
SERGEANT James MM Pte 203029 1/6th North Staffordshire Regt KIA 29.9.18.
SERGENT John MM Pte 58419 RAMC
SERGINSON William MM Pte 455 17th Northumberland Fusiliers
SERMON Charles MM+Bar Sjt 23178 142 Coy Machine Gun Corps KIA 2.12.17.
SERVANTE Leonard F. MM Pte R/34385 King's Royal Rifle Corps
SERVICE David MM Cpl 41120 RAMC
SERVICE John MM Pte 40509 1/7th Gordon Highlanders
SERVICE John R.F. MM Cpl 331001 9th Liverpool Regt
SESSIONS Frederick MM Pte 242289 Gloucestershire Regt
SETCHFIELD Albert J. MM Pte 4076 1/1st Cambridgeshire Regt
SETCHFIELD Edward MM Pte 23611 6th East Kent Regt
SETH William R. MM Pte 10040 2nd South Wales Borderers
SETON George Ronald MM Sjt 625464 HAC(Artillery)
SETTERFIELD Albert E. "MM,MID" 2nd Cpl 87513 39 Div Sig Coy Royal Engineers
SETTERFIELD Albert V. "MM,MID" L/Cpl 347 6th East Kent Regt
SETTERFIELD Horace S. MM+Bar Pte 517173 14th London Regt
SETTERFIELD John Edwin MM Pte 5456 8th East Kent Regt
SETTERFIELD W. MM+Bar Sjt 10 East Kent Regt
SETTERS F. MM S/Sjt 49520 RAMC
SETTLE Frederick MM Pte 355399 10th Liverpool Regt
SETTLE Harry MM L/Cpl 305481 West Riding Regt
SETTLE Herbert MM Pte 106175 38 Fd Amb RAMC
SETTLE Herbert MM Pte 58733 17th Welsh Regt
SETTLE Herbert Lord MM Pte 39499 11th Lancashire Fusiliers
SETTLE John MM Pte 27597 19th Lancashire Fusiliers
SETTLE Wilfred MM Pte 106174 RAMC
SETTLE William MM Pte 18752 West Riding Regt
SETTLE Willie MM Cpl 780184 62 Div Ammn Col RFA KIA 27.10.17.
SEVERN Alfred Edward MM Cpl 512106 85 Fd Amb RAMC
SEVERN David MM Gnr 38828 36 Bde RFA
SEVERN Frederick MM+Bar L/Cpl 21464 Royal Fusiliers
SEVERN Harry MM Gnr 149377 RFA
SEVERN Joseph MM L/Cpl T4/244627 Army Service Corps
SEVERN Lancelot G. MM Sjt 8282 C/152 Bde RFA
SEVERS John "MM,MSM" Sjt 101131 Royal Engineers
SEVERS John J. MM Sjt W/86 9th Cheshire Regt
SEVIER Thomas J. "MM,MSM" Sjt 439298 RAMC
SEWARD Bertram A. MM Cpl 65632 RAMC
SEWARD Edward C. MM Pte 392068 3rd London Regt
SEWARD Frederick Graham MM+Bar L/Cpl 267533 Oxf & Bucks Light Infantry
SEWARD Samuel George MM Pte 956 14th York & Lancaster Regt
SEWARDS Herbert MM Pte 3123 2nd Royal Fusiliers
SEWELL Alfred MM Pte 275117 3rd London Regt
SEWELL Alfred G. MM Pnr 129420 Royal Engineers
SEWELL Edward M. MM Sjt M1/09241 Army Service Corps
SEWELL Ernest MM Pte 15749 4th Royal Fusiliers
SEWELL George H. MM Pte 76308 24th London Regt
SEWELL Henry MM Pte 13874 8th Yorkshire Regt
SEWELL James MM Pte 74 1st Royal West Surrey Regt
SEWELL John H. MM Pte 25352 1st Lincolnshire Regt
SEWELL Jonathan MM+Bar Pte 21485 5th Border Regt
SEWELL Joseph MM+Bar Spr 19659 23 Fd Coy Royal Engineers
SEWELL Joseph S. MM Cpl 32272 Border Regt
SEWELL Richard MM Pte C/571 16th King's Royal Rifle Corps
SEWELL William MM+Bar Pte 25409 6th Northamptonshire Regt
SEXTON A.E. MM Pte 8891 1st Essex Regt
SEXTON Charles MM Pte 3/8287 1st Devonshire Regt
SEXTON Henry J. MM L/Cpl 1353 1/21st London Regt
SEXTON William George MM Cpl 650094 1/12th London Regt
SEXTON William H. MM Bdr 49110 RGA
SEY Thomas K.M. MM Gnr 35749 40 Div Ammn Col RFA
SEYBURN Thomas MM Pte 51609 Manchester Regt
SEYFERTH Charles A. MM Cpl 200897 1/4th Cheshire Regt
SEYMOUR A.E. MM Pte 266286 1/1st(Bucks)Bn Oxf & Bucks Light Infantry
SEYMOUR Albert F. MM Sjt 4158 Machine Gun Corps

SEYMOUR Alfred B. MM Spr 23012 12 Fd Coy Royal Engineers
SEYMOUR Allan MM Pte 3898 2nd Royal Sussex Regt
SEYMOUR Arthur S. MM+Bar Sjt 89281 95 Fd Coy Royal Engineers
SEYMOUR Edward George MM L/Cpl R/6470 12th King's Royal Rifle Corps DOW 2.6.16.
SEYMOUR Francis W. MM Spr 532171 404 Fd Coy Royal Engineers
SEYMOUR Frederick C. MM Sjt 26124 4th Bedfordshire Regt
SEYMOUR George MM Pte 11745 5th Dorsetshire Regt
SEYMOUR George T. MM L/Cpl 392709 9th London Regt
SEYMOUR Harry S. MM Pte 16368 Machine Gun Corps
SEYMOUR Henry Baily MM Spr 100474 33 Div Sig Coy Royal Engineers
SEYMOUR Horace Churchill MM L/Cpl 16126 1st Grenadier Guards KIA 21.9.16.
SEYMOUR John MM Spr 46832 2 Div Sig Coy Royal Engineers
SEYMOUR John MM Sjt 935644 A/168 Bde RFA
SEYMOUR John H. MM Dvr 92107 RFA
SEYMOUR Robert MM L/Bdr 30372 B/113 Bty RFA
SEYMOUR Sydney MM Pte 54888 4th Hampshire Regt
SEYMOUR W.C.E. MM Pte 36657 7th East Yorkshire Regt
SEYMOUR Walter E. MM Pte 252923 3rd London Regt
SEYMOUR Walter John MM Gnr 74384 C/88 Bde RFA
SEYMOUR William John Henry MM Sjt 12235 5th Northamptonshire Regt
SHACKCLOTH Elijah MM Pte 22266 1st East Kent Regt
SHACKCLOTH John M. MM Pte M2/202645 Army Service Corps
SHACKEL George J. MM Cpl 586 4(London)Fd Coy Royal Engineers
SHACKELL Francis J. MM+Bar Gnr 49560 RGA
SHACKLADY Arthur MM Pte 27577 1/7th Liverpool Regt DOW 9.12.18.
SHACKLADY John F. MM Pte 106926 48th Bn Machine Gun Corps
SHACKLADY Thomas MM Pte 21987 Cheshire Regt
SHACKLETON Charles W. MM L/Sjt 150629 103rd Bn Machine Gun Corps
SHACKLETON Frank MM L/Cpl P13011 4 Traffic Control Coy Military Foot Police
SHACKLETON Fred MM Pte 40218 10th Northumberland Fusiliers
SHACKLETON Harold MM Cpl 2481 West Riding Regt KIA 26.8.18.
SHACKLETON James MM L/Cpl 13750 10th West Riding Regt
SHACKLETON James William Walmsley MM Cpl 4950 24th Royal Fusiliers
SHACKLETON Jonathan MM Pte 8848 Machine Gun Corps
SHACKLETON Joseph MM Pte 36863 1st Lancashire Fusiliers
SHACKLETON Roy "MM,MID" Pte 49796 2/4th West Riding Regt
SHACKLETON Thomas MM Pte 201967 5th East Lancashire Regt
SHADBOLT Henry Thomas MM Pte 15133 1st Bedfordshire Regt
SHADBOLT Thomas MM L/Cpl 18693 1st Bedfordshire Regt
SHADBOLT William Richard MM Pte 235272 8th Lincolnshire Regt DOW 16.8.17.
SHADE Leonard C. MM Cpl 151679 104th Bn Machine Gun Corps
SHADFORTH William H. MM Bdr 949 D/250 Bde RFA
SHADLOCK John W. MM Pte 145561 1/1st Northamptonshire Yeomanry
SHAILES James "MM,CG(F)" Sjt 20972 Essex Regt
SHAINE James MM Cpl 16013 17th Liverpool Regt
SHAIRP Alexander Victor MM Pte 34260 1st Bn Machine Gun Corps
SHAKESHAFT Gordon Walter MM Pte 435443 RAMC
SHAKESHAFT Lawrence Harrison MM Gnr 138922 D/123 Bde RFA
SHAKESHAFT Stanley MM Gnr 131004 146 Siege Bty RGA
SHAKESPEARE Joseph MM Dvr 687070 RFA
SHAKESPEARE William Percy "MC,MM+Bar" CSM 200445 1/7th Worcestershire Regt
SHALE George MM+Bar Sjt 74198 Royal Engineers
SHALER Frank N. MM Pte 265068 1/7th Royal Warwickshire Regt
SHALLCROSS Ernest MM Pte 53908 3 Fd Amb RAMC
SHALLCROSS John MM S/Sjt Mechanician 12324 29 Fd Coy Royal Engineers
SHALLCROSS John J. MM Pte 331659 Liverpool Regt
SHALLOW Percy MM Sjt 43319 42 Bde RFA
SHAMBROOK Frederick W. MM L/Sjt 27665 1/7th Cheshire Regt
SHAMBROOK Reginald J. MM Pte 512561 RAMC
SHAMBROOK Walter Herbert MM Cpl 307814 15th Bn Tank Corps
SHAMBROOK William Richard MM L/Cpl 3574 1/9th London Regt KIA 15.9.16.
SHANAHAN James MM Pte 24961 Royal Inniskilling Fusiliers
SHANAHAN Joseph MM Sjt 28063 39th Bn Machine Gun Corps
SHANAHAN Patrick MM Pte 5568 2nd Royal Irish Regt KIA 10.11.18.
SHANAHAN William MM Pte 7327 Irish Guards
SHAND Alexander MM Cpl 240245 Gordon Highlanders
SHAND Alfred T. MM Sjt 76206 128 Coy Labour Corps
SHAND Charles "DCM,MM" Sjt 10743 1/6th Gordon Highlanders
SHAND George M. MM Gnr 122501 RGA
SHAND J. MM Pte 241524 Middlesex Regt
SHAND James MM Sjt 11483 1/4th Gordon Highlanders KIA 25.7.18.
SHAND James MM Pte 316366 13th Royal Highlanders
SHAND James MM Cpl 200282 2nd Bn Tank Corps
SHAND James MM L/Cpl 240316 1/5th Gordon Highlanders KIA 29.7.18.
SHAND John MM Cpl 355429 10th Highland Light Infantry
SHAND William "MM,MID" Cpl 7363 2nd Royal Scots Fusiliers
SHAND William J. MM Pte 880 1st Gordon Highlanders
SHAND William J. MM L/Cpl 265333 1/6th Seaforth Highlanders
SHANDLEY William MM Pte 44975 RAMC att RFA
SHANE William MM Pte 10733 1st Scottish Rifles
SHANKIE John MM Pte M2/020830 Army Service Corps
SHANKLAND David MM Pte 263008 Gordon Highlanders
SHANKLAND James MM Pte 3540 16th Highland Light Infantry KIA 1.7.16.
SHANKLAND James MM Pte 17268 2nd Arg & Suth Highlanders KIA 17.4.18.
SHANKLAND Robert MM Cpl 35043 6th King's Own Scottish Borderers
SHANKS Charles MM Pte 23826 Royal Irish Fusiliers
SHANKS David Hughan MM Gnr 158689 81 Siege Bty RGA
SHANKS George MM L/Cpl 16414 Yorkshire Regt
SHANKS George W. MM Pte 23/462 Northumberland Fusiliers
SHANKS John MM L/Cpl 3560 8th Seaforth Highlanders
SHANKS John MM Pte 265378 1/6th Seaforth Highlanders
SHANKS John C. MM Gnr 163236 163 Siege Bty RGA KIA 20.9.18.
SHANKS Philip MM Pte 20917 Machine Gun Corps
SHANKS Robert MM Dvr 93455 14 Div Ammn Col RFA
SHANKS Samuel MM Pte 16188 Durham Light Infantry
SHANKS Thomas W. MM Gnr 631563 B/255 Bde RFA
SHANKS William MM L/Cpl 15997 2nd Royal Inniskilling Fusiliers KIA 21.3.18.
SHANKS William MM L/Cpl 5181 6th Royal Munster Fusiliers
SHANLEY William MM Sjt 9031 Royal Irish Regt
SHANLIN Patrick MM Pte 24760 1st King's Own Scottish Borderers
SHANLY Edward MM Pte 2842 IV Corps Cyclist Bn Army Cyclist Corps
SHANLY Thomas MM Pte 592812 18th London Regt
SHANN Robert MM L/Cpl 20527 22nd Manchester Regt
SHANNON David M. "DCM,MM" Sjt 14322 1st Scots Guards
SHANNON Edward MM Cpl 44301 2nd Northumberland Fusiliers
SHANNON J. MM Pte 32999 13th East Lancashire Regt
SHANNON James MM Bdr 18522 D/74 Bde RFA
SHANNON James MM Pte 305653 7th Liverpool Regt
SHANNON James MM Pte 2334 North Lancashire Regt
SHANNON John Patrick MM Sjt 2475 6th Connaught Rangers
SHANNON Patrick MM Sjt 305192 Liverpool Regt
SHANNON Richard MM+Bar Cpl 22027 Machine Gun Corps
SHANNON Thomas H. MM Pte 6653 Irish Guards
SHANNON William MM Pte 417243 RAMC
SHAPERO Louis MM Pte 10/1371 East Yorkshire Regt
SHAPLAND William MM Sjt 19798 13th Royal Welsh Fusiliers
SHARD Henry MM Pte 341104 2/1(West Lancashire)Fd Amb RAMC
SHARDLOW William MM Pte 30247 1st Royal Lancaster Regt
SHARDLOW William R. MM Spr 140412 54 Fd Coy Royal Engineers
SHARGOOL John A. "DCM,MM" Pte 1677 17th Royal Fusiliers
SHARKEY Patrick MM Pte 8932 2nd Irish Guards
SHARLAND Cuthbert MM Sjt 32581 14 Siege Bty RGA
SHARLAND George A. MM Spr 496321 Royal Engineers
SHARLOTTE Jim MM Pte 23280 13th Yorkshire Regt
SHARMAN Albert MM Pte R/17279 King's Royal Rifle Corps
SHARMAN Arthur MM Cpl 780789 B/311 Bde RFA
SHARMAN Frank MM Cpl 11990 8th Lincolnshire Regt
SHARMAN George W. MM Sjt 69953 RGA
SHARMAN Godfrey H. MM CQMS 27849 Postal Section Royal Engineers
SHARMAN Horace C. MM Pte 7636 1st Northamptonshire Regt
SHARMAN J. MM Sjt P243 Military Foot Police
SHARMAN Joseph MM Pte 81337 108 Fd Amb RAMC
SHARMAN Joseph MM Spr 144936 251 Tunnelling Coy Royal Engineers
SHARMAN Joshua MM Cpl 18680 7th Suffolk Regt

SHARMAN Robert W. MM Sjt 12767 111 Heavy Bty RGA
SHARMAN Thomas S. MM Gnr 74281 RFA
SHARMAN Tom MM Pte 308063 2/4th West Riding Regt
SHARMAN Walter MM Pte 242629 6th South Staffordshire Regt
SHARMAN William S. MM Pte 707 14th Royal Warwickshire Regt
SHARMAN William Thomas MM Pte M2/048320 37 Div Ammn Supply Park Army Service Corps
SHARP A. "MM,MSM,MID" Staff SM 609 Military Mounted Police
SHARP A.A. MM Pte 64971 9th Yorkshire Light Infantry
SHARP Aaron MM L/Cpl 240279 1/5th Leicestershire Regt
SHARP Albert MM Gnr 168559 RGA
SHARP Arthur MM+Bar L/Cpl 242303 6th North Staffordshire Regt
SHARP Arthur J. MM L/Bdr 163187 B/86 Bde RFA
SHARP Arthur W. MM Cpl 75897 4th Bn Tank Corps
SHARP Basil C. "DCM,MM+Bar" Sjt 309845 11th Tank Corps
SHARP Charles MM Dvr 17279 RFA
SHARP Charles MM+Bar Gnr 94732 RFA
SHARP Charles MM Spr 100533 33 Div Sig Coy Royal Engineers
SHARP David MM Pte 44735 35 Fd Amb RAMC
SHARP Edmund H. MM Sjt 235816 2nd Lancashire Fusiliers
SHARP Edward J. "MM,MID" Cpl 41851 Royal Engineers
SHARP Ernest MM Pte 12078 9th West Riding Regt KIA 22.3.18.
SHARP Ernest W. MM Pte Z/2788 13th Rifle Brigade
SHARP Ernest W. MM L/Cpl 1195 7th Royal West Surrey Regt
SHARP F.E. MM Pte 27920 1st Northamptonshire Regt
SHARP Francis MM Pte 307776 8th Royal Warwickshire Regt
SHARP Frank MM Sjt 12710 6th Northamptonshire Regt
SHARP Frederick MM Pte 17249 Worcestershire Regt
SHARP Frederick L. MM Sjt 12/19267 12th Notts & Derby Regt
SHARP George MM Cpl 58758 Machine Gun Corps
SHARP George "MM,MID" Sjt 2521 10th Arg & Suth Highlanders
SHARP George "DCM,MM" Sjt 14369 2nd Grenadier Guards
SHARP George MM Pte 1456 Royal Sussex Regt
SHARP George MM Pte 203386 North Lancashire Regt
SHARP George "DCM,MM+Bar" L/Cpl 43791 19 Div Sig Coy Royal Engineers
SHARP George H. MM Sjt M2/019310 Army Service Corps
SHARP George S. MM Pte 11431 6th North Lancashire Regt
SHARP George William Hatton MM Pte 512363 1/14th London Regt
SHARP Harry MM Sjt 780029 RFA
SHARP Harry MM Pte 10207 Leicestershire Regt
SHARP Harry MM Sjt 833 10th Lincolnshire Regt
SHARP Harry Frank MM 2nd Cpl 506242 504 Fd Coy Royal Engineers
SHARP Herbert MM+Bar Pte 1251 Army Cyclist Corps
SHARP Herbert Francis MM Pte M2/049258 Army Service Corps att 1(North Midland)Fd Amb RAMC.
SHARP Hugh Joel "MM,MID" Sjt 3898 3rd Coldstream Guards
SHARP James William MM+Bar CSM 18178 6th Yorkshire Light Infantry KIA 12.5.17.
SHARP Jeremiah MM Sjt 14/99 2nd York & Lancaster Regt
SHARP John MM L/Cpl 14708 9th Royal Irish Fusiliers
SHARP John MM L/Cpl 65312 Machine Gun Corps
SHARP John Robert MM L/Cpl 10757 8th Yorkshire Regt DOW 22.9.16.
SHARP Norman MM L/Bdr 786094 D/312 Bde RFA
SHARP Richard MM Pte 307528 7th Liverpool Regt
SHARP Sydney R. MM+Bar Sjt 74141 Signal Service Royal Engineers
SHARP Thomas MM Pte G/874 6th East Kent Regt DOW 9.10.16.
SHARP Wilfred MM Pte 390074 1/3(Northumbrian)Fd Amb RAMC KIA 27.5.18.
SHARP Wilfred John MM Pte 242005 1/5th Border Regt
SHARP William MM Cpl 11309 5th Royal Berkshire Regt
SHARP William MM Pte 48458 RAMC
SHARP William D. MM Spr 67097 Royal Engineers
SHARP William J. MM Pte 26582 7th East Kent Regt
SHARP William J. MM Cpl 202615 Lancashire Fusiliers
SHARPE Albert MM Pte 10190 1st Northamptonshire Regt DOW 17.10.18.
SHARPE Arthur MM L/Cpl 2899 Gordon Highlanders
SHARPE Cecil Asknil MM Pte 77024 RAMC att RGA.
SHARPE Charles A. MM Gnr 66269 22 Bde RFA
SHARPE Ernest E. MM Pte 21779 16th Royal Sussex Regt
SHARPE Fred MM Pte 93167 19th Durham Light Infantry DOW 26.10.18.
SHARPE Fred Leslie MM Cpl 11/393 11th East Yorkshire Regt KIA 12.4.18.
SHARPE Frederick MM Pte 3265 7th Royal West Surrey Regt
SHARPE Frederick Henry MM Pte 47985 Lancashire Fusiliers
SHARPE George MM L/Cpl 9156 2nd West Yorkshire Regt
SHARPE George H. MM L/Cpl H/10164 4th Hussars
SHARPE George H. MM Pte 40592 1st Leicestershire Regt
SHARPE Harry MM Cpl 60733 X/16 Med TM Bty RGA
SHARPE Henry MM Sjt 14909 7th Border Regt
SHARPE J. MM Pte 7135 Wiltshire Regt
SHARPE John Henry MM L/Bdr 700342 D/211 Bde RFA KIA 17.0.18.
SHARPE John W. MM Pte 8451 8th Lincolnshire Regt
SHARPE Lytton S. MM+Bar Pte 12970 8th Leicestershire Regt
SHARPE Oscar Turner "DCM,MM+Bar" CSM 8166 2nd Lincolnshire Regt
SHARPE Percy MM L/Cpl 11048 1st Scots Guards
SHARPE Percy MM Pte 12244 2nd Notts & Derby Regt KIA 16.9.16.
SHARPE Reginald MM Cpl 30729 RGA
SHARPE Robert Henry Edwin MM Sjt 680137 1/22nd London Regt
SHARPE Samuel F. MM Cpl 7946 RFA
SHARPE Thomas MM Pte 6761 9th Gordon Highlanders
SHARPE W.C. MM Pte 54081 5th South Lancashire Regt
SHARPE Wallace Alfred MM L/Cpl 30359 1st Royal Lancaster Regt
SHARPE Walter F. MM Pte 44903 20th Middlesex Regt
SHARPE Walter G. MM Pte 28050 14th Royal Warwickshire Regt
SHARPE William MM L/Cpl 3543 Machine Gun Corps
SHARPE William Charles MM Cpl 45139 1st Worcestershire Regt
SHARPE Willie MM+Bar Pte Y/1594 1st King's Royal Rifle Corps
SHARPES "William B," MM Sjt 95693 17th Armoured Car Bn Tank Corps
SHARPLES Fred MM L/Cpl 17808 6th Wiltshire Regt
SHARPLES Harry Vivian MM Gnr 131269 D/189 Bde RFA
SHARPLES Herbert MM Pte 39221 59 Fd Amb RAMC KIA 17.4.18.
SHARPLES James MM Gnr Fitter 61760 290 Siege Bty RGA
SHARPLES James MM Pte 43740 37 Fd Amb RAMC
SHARPLES John "DCM,MM" Cpl 220095 V/4 Heavy TM Bty RGA
SHARPLES John MM Bdr 10967 151 Bde RFA
SHARPLES John A. MM Cpl 54201 Royal Engineers
SHARPLES Leo MM Cpl 7734 Royal Highlanders
SHARPLES Robert MM Pte 16570 7th East Lancashire Regt DOW 23.9.17.
SHARPLES Samuel Henry MM L/Sjt 2084 1/6th North Staffordshire Regt
SHARPLES William MM Cpl 36752 1st Manchester Regt
SHARPLES William MM Pte 29234 8th East Surrey Regt
SHARPLES William MM L/Cpl 27122 2nd Grenadier Guards
SHARPLES William MM L/Sjt 200237 1/4th North Lancashire Regt
SHARPLES William MM Cpl 43427 1/4th Royal Highlanders
SHARPLIN Harry L. MM L/Cpl 11053 4th Royal Fusiliers
SHARRATT Albert Arthur MM Sjt 7129 6th Royal West Kent Regt KIA 3.5.17.
SHARRATT Francis Herbert MM Pte 203241 10th Royal Warwickshire Regt
SHARRATT Herbert MM Pte 11333 1st Coldstream Guards
SHARRATT Reginald E. MM Pte 225749 1st London Regt
SHARRATT Thomas MM Pte 16178 9th North Lancashire Regt
SHARRETT William MM Pte 73792 56th Bn Machine Gun Corps
SHARROCK Charles MM Sjt 305251 1/8th Notts & Derby Regt
SHARROCK Harry MM+Bar Cpl 446873 438 Fd Coy Royal Engineers
SHARROCK I. MM Pte 36941 East Lancashire Regt
SHARROCKS John MM Pte 240339 1/5th North Lancashire Regt
SHATTOCK William G.G. MM Pte 700773 1/23rd London Regt
SHAUGHNESSY John MM Pte 4520 East Lancashire Regt
SHAUGHNESSY Thomas MM L/Cpl 2089 20th Manchester Regt
SHAUGHNESSY William MM Pte 57229 Manchester Regt
SHAVE Edgar Percy MM Pte 14295 10th Hampshire Regt DOW 6.9.18.
SHAW Albert MM Cpl 235456 1st Northumberland Fusiliers KIA 8.10.18.
SHAW Albert MM L/Bdr 77039 133 Siege Bty RGA
SHAW Alec MM Pte R/15004 7th King's Royal Rifle Corps DOW 4.5.17.
SHAW Alexander MM Pte 12728 6th Royal Inniskilling Fusiliers
SHAW Alexander MM Pte 350287 1/9th Royal Scots KIA 21.3.18.
SHAW Alexander D. MM Pte 2601 Gordon Highlanders
SHAW Alfred MM Cpl 13973 11th West Yorkshire Regt
SHAW Alfred F. MM Pte 142824 1st Bn Machine Gun Corps
SHAW Alfred J. MM Gnr 43413 RFA
SHAW Alfred Thomas MM Pte 205708 5th Yorkshire Light Infantry Died 30.11.18.
SHAW Archibald MM Pte 374 2nd Gordon Highlanders
SHAW Archibald Angus MM L/Cpl 36728 11th Royal Scots KIA 20.10.18.

SHAW Arthur MM Cpl 18848 16th Royal Welsh Fusiliers
SHAW Arthur MM+Bar L/Cpl 11882 8th West Riding Regt
SHAW Arthur MM Pte 61011 Royal Fusiliers
SHAW Arthur W. MM Sjt 538101 RAMC
SHAW Ashbourne Delaney MM Sjt 1364 C/84 Bde RFA DOW 5.10.17.
SHAW Ben MM Dvr 141040 A/181 Bde RFA
SHAW Bryan Duncan MM L/Cpl 202193 South Staffordshire Regt
SHAW Cecil W. MM Cpl 296470 153 Hy Bty RGA
SHAW Charles MM Gnr 125092 RFA
SHAW Charles MM Pte 12139 15th Royal Irish Rifles
SHAW Charles A. MM Cpl 79248 2nd Durham Light Infantry
SHAW Charles H. MM Pte 307395 Royal Warwickshire Regt
SHAW Charles Louis MM Pte 8766 2nd Wiltshire Regt
SHAW Charles S. MM Sjt R/14397 King's Royal Rifle Corps att 9th London Regt.
SHAW Charles William MM Cpl 49394 89 Fd Coy Royal Engineers
SHAW Edward MM Pte M2/167295 565 Coy Army Service Corps
SHAW Edward MM Sjt 200675 1/4th Royal Berkshire Regt
SHAW Edward John MM Pte 12019 5th Northamptonshire Regt DOW 29.8.18.
SHAW Edwin MM Pte 140492 32nd Bn Machine Gun Corps
SHAW Edwin MM Sjt 9358 2nd East Yorkshire Regt
SHAW Edwin MM L/Cpl 2195 1/4th Yorkshire Regt
SHAW Edwin A. MM L/Cpl 44092 7th Lincolnshire Regt
SHAW Ernest MM Pte 8460 7th North Staffordshire Regt
SHAW Ernest MM Sjt 13810 4th Grenadier Guards
SHAW Ernest MM Pte 13/862 13th York & Lancaster Regt
SHAW Ernest Francis MM Cpl 265575 1/6th Seaforth Highlanders
SHAW F. MM Pte 26514 East Surrey Regt
SHAW Farquhar MM Pte 41562 1st Gordon Highlanders
SHAW Frank "DCM,MM" Sjt 48152 Royal Engineers
SHAW Frank E. MM Cpl 56407 14th Royal Welsh Fusiliers
SHAW Frank Thomas MM L/Cpl 1246 1/1st Bucks Bn Oxf & Bucks Light Infantry
SHAW Fred MM Pte 290892 Cheshire Regt
SHAW Fred MM Dvr 43441 RFA
SHAW Frederick MM L/Cpl R/6889 13th King's Royal Rifle Corps
SHAW George MM Pte 44150 174 Coy Machine Gun Corps
SHAW George MM Pte 14160 12th Cheshire Regt
SHAW George MM Cpl 90823 RFA
SHAW George Frederick MM L/Bdr 8166 121 Bty 27 Bde RFA Died 10.3.19.
SHAW George J. MM L/Sjt 632603 20th London Regt
SHAW George T. MM Pte 42762 1st Royal Inniskilling Fusiliers
SHAW George W. MM Bdr 294365 RGA
SHAW George William MM Cpl 2385 1/4th Lincolnshire Regt
SHAW Harold MM Pte 44483 20th Manchester Regt
SHAW Harold MM+Bar Pte 205564 2/4th West Riding Regt
SHAW Harry MM Cpl 13530 9th Yorkshire Light Infantry
SHAW Harry MM Spr 302195 42 Div Sig Coy Royal Engineers
SHAW Harry MM L/Cpl 306037 5th West Riding Regt
SHAW Harry MM Spr 159041 Royal Engineers
SHAW Harry MM L/Cpl 63715 33rd Bn Machine Gun Corps DOW 26.10.18.
SHAW Harry MM L/Cpl C/12066 King's Royal Rifle Corps
SHAW Harry MM Pte 52914 Durham Light Infantry
SHAW Henry MM Pte 21900 King's Own Scottish Borderers
SHAW Henry MM Sjt 71919 34 Bde RFA
SHAW Herbert MM Pte 24990 Shropshire Light Infantry
SHAW Herbert Wilson MM Sjt 14016 24th Manchester Regt
SHAW Horace John Jesse MM Sjt 5433 3rd Coldstream Guards
SHAW J. MM Cpl 14270 King's Own Scottish Borderers
SHAW James MM Spr 72205 49 Div Sig Coy Royal Engineers
SHAW James MM Sjt 82469 B/117 Bde RFA
SHAW James MM Pte 200875 East Lancashire Regt
SHAW James MM Sjt 25148 South Wales Borderers
SHAW James H. MM Cpl 132703 RGA
SHAW John MM+Bar Pte S/15567 Rifle Brigade
SHAW John "See CLIFFORD,John,Sjt 20359,Northumberland Fusiliers"
SHAW John MM Sjt 1385 2nd Lancashire Fusiliers
SHAW John MM Pte 2195 West Riding Regt
SHAW John MM Sjt 11191 13th Northumberland Fusiliers
SHAW John MM Pnr 129109 Royal Engineers
SHAW John MM Sjt 4611 Machine Gun Corps
SHAW John MM Pte 32881 Manchester Regt
SHAW John A. MM Cpl 60938 9th Northumberland Fusiliers
SHAW John A. MM Gnr 116968 322 Siege Bty RGA
SHAW John Alfred MM+Bar Sjt 240179 1/6th Liverpool Regt KIA 20.9.17.
SHAW John E. MM Pte 59485 12th Manchester Regt
SHAW John G. MM Pte S/99 12th Rifle Brigade
SHAW John W. MM Sjt 800807 295 Bde RFA
SHAW Joseph MM Pte 22637 1st Grenadier Guards
SHAW Joseph MM Sjt 18299 RGA
SHAW Joseph Arthur MM Pte 3/2094 2nd York & Lancaster Regt KIA 21.3.18.
SHAW Joseph C. MM Pte 18897 Royal Berkshire Regt
SHAW Lachlan MM Gnr 227865 A/93 Bde RFA
SHAW Leonard MM Cpl 240204 5th West Riding Regt
SHAW Leonard MM Sjt 15638 9th South Staffordshire Regt
SHAW N. MM Pte 405302 3 Fd Amb RAMC
SHAW Percival J. MM Sjt 55833 B/331 Bde RFA
SHAW Percy MM+Bar Pte 44192 9th Cheshire Regt
SHAW Rennie MM Pte 20761 Machine Gun Corps
SHAW Richard MM Pnr 98719 Royal Engineers
SHAW Robert MM Pte 15109 1st Grenadier Guards
SHAW Robert MM Pte 43181 16th Highland Light Infantry
SHAW Robert MM Cpl 20190 22nd Manchester Regt
SHAW Robert Laiston MM Sjt 11089 1/6th Cheshire Regt
SHAW Robert or Rufus "MM,MID" Pte 3604 1st Dragoons
SHAW Robert W. MM Pte 68313 Royal West Surrey Regt
SHAW Robert W. MM Sjt 64092 15th Yorkshire Light Infantry
SHAW Rufus or Robert "MM,MID" Pte 3604 1st Dragoons
SHAW Sam MM Pte R/13021 18th King's Royal Rifle Corps
SHAW Stephen MM L/Cpl 51268 80 Fd Coy Royal Engineers
SHAW Sydney MM Pte 269079 West Riding Regt
SHAW Sydney Herbert Lewin MM Pte 18170 9th Notts & Derby Regt
SHAW T. MM Sjt 8040 North Staffordshire Regt
SHAW Thomas MM Pte 252513 1/6th Arg & Suth Highlanders
SHAW Thomas MM Pte 11742 9th Cheshire Regt
SHAW Thomas MM Pte 5394 8th East Kent Regt
SHAW Thomas C. MM Pte 291196 1/7th Cheshire Regt
SHAW Thomas Francis MM Cpl 50559 64 Bty 5 Bde RFA
SHAW Thomas H. "MM,MSM" Cpl 30297 RAMC
SHAW Thomas W. MM Pte 63215 5th Yorkshire Light Infantry
SHAW Tom MM Cpl 6768 Machine Gun Corps
SHAW Tom MM Cpl 24026 Leicestershire Regt
SHAW William MM Pte 19820 2nd South Staffordshire Regt
SHAW William MM Sjt 33569 B/70 Bde RFA
SHAW William MM+Bar Sjt 290730 Gordon Highlanders
SHAW William MM Sjt 38672 5/6th Scottish Rifles
SHAW William MM Gnr Wheeler 785328 RFA
SHAW William MM Bdr 69448 RGA
SHAW William C. MM Pte 3454 6th London Regt
SHAW William E.N. MM Sjt 21749 Notts & Derby Regt
SHAW William Henry MM Sjt 29118 34 Div Ammn Col RFA KIA 9.4.18.
SHAW William Henry MM Sjt 330028 Liverpool Regt
SHAWL Stanley D. MM Cpl 57734 Liverpool Regt
SHAWYER Thomas A. MM CQMS 200092 East Yorkshire Regt
SHAXTON Ernest H. MM Pte 28183 Hampshire Regt
SHAY Fred MM L/Cpl 51456 1/4th Cheshire Regt
SHAYLER John MM Pte 1545 Liverpool Regt
SHEA Anthony "DCM,MM" Pte 12637 7th East Lancashire Regt
SHEA George D. MM L/Cpl 13062 1st South Wales Borderers
SHEA George E. MM Pte 71952 138 Fd Amb RAMC
SHEA James MM Dvr 38637 RFA
SHEA Matthew MM+Bar Cpl 350269 1/6th Manchester Regt
SHEA William MM Sjt 12104 6th Leicestershire Regt
SHEAD George MM Cpl 28641 Essex Regt
SHEAF Tom MM Pte 34237 Hampshire Regt
SHEAN Patrick MM Pte 14190 3rd Royal Fusiliers
SHEAR Frederick B. MM+Bar 2nd Cpl 510446 58 Div Sig Coy Royal Engineers
SHEARD Albert MM+Bar Pte B/203522 1st Rifle Brigade
SHEARD Arthur MM L/Cpl 265948 1/7th West Yorkshire Regt
SHEARD Benjamin MM Cpl 201163 2/5th West Yorkshire Regt
SHEARD Ernest MM Pte A/201971 2nd King's Royal Rifle Corps
SHEARD Frank Hampden MM Gnr 20141 D/162 Bde RFA
SHEARD George MM Pte 6676 16th Manchester Regt KIA 23.4.17.
SHEARD Herbert N. MM L/Cpl 175413 1/1st Yorkshire Dragoons Yeo
SHEARD James S. MM L/Sjt 2413 1/4th West Riding Regt DOW 18.2.17.
SHEARD Joseph MM Bdr 775231 A/175 Bde RFA
SHEARD Leonard MM Pte M/225067 Army Service Corps att 267 Siege Bty RGA.
SHEARD Linneans MM Pte 202156 Seaforth Highlanders

SHEARD Thomas Snell MM Sjt 48495 16th Manchester Regt
SHEARD Walter MM Pte 202344 2/4th Yorkshire Light Infantry
SHEARD William Duncan MM Pte 78670 17th Armoured Car Bn Tank Corps KIA 29.9.18.
SHEARER Archie MM Gnr 13762 104 Bty 22 Bde RFA
SHEARER Charles MM Cpl 7474 A/81 Bde RFA
SHEARER David MM Sjt 290974 Gordon Highlanders
SHEARER Hugh MM+Bar Sjt 2024 7th Seaforth Highlanders
SHEARER J. MM Pte 2154 Scottish Rifles
SHEARER James K. MM Cpl 8559 Seaforth Highlanders
SHEARER James O. MM Pte 377078 10th Royal Scots
SHEARER John MM+Bar L/Cpl 11603 2nd Royal Scots
SHEARER John MM Pte 53148 West Yorkshire Regt
SHEARER Robert MM Bdr 19450 RFA
SHEARER Samuel MM Pte 2462 10th Arg & Suth Highlanders
SHEARER William MM Pte 6740 Seaforth Highlanders
SHEARING Charles MM L/Cpl 37026 2nd Welsh Regt
SHEARING Frederick J. MM Sjt 26544 D/155 Bde RFA
SHEARING William E. MM Pte 736 Royal Sussex Regt
SHEARING William H. MM Bdr 51300 88 Bty 14 Bde RFA
SHEARMAN George MM Sjt 52984 63 Fd Coy Royal Engineers
SHEARMAN John George Alfred MM Pte 53871 52nd Bn Machine Gun Corps
SHEARN Herbert MM L/Cpl 13451 10th Devonshire Regt
SHEARS Alma Edward MM L/Cpl 165914 40 Div Sig Coy Royal Engineers
SHEARS George H. MM Sjt 202912 2nd Royal Berkshire Regt
SHEARS Walter MM Pte 13180 8th Royal Berkshire Regt
SHEARSBY William H. MM Sjt 9709 2nd Royal Welsh Fusiliers
SHEARSMITH Walter MM+Bar L/Cpl 241638 2/5th West Riding Regt DOW 13.9.18.
SHEARSON Charles "MM,MID" CSM 8848 1/4th Royal Lancaster Regt
SHEARSTONE Herbert MM Pte 300823 2nd Durham Light Infantry
SHEATH Arthur J. MM Pte 202409 4th Hampshire Regt
SHEATH William George "DCM,MM,MMV(It)" Sjt 5643 23rd Bn Machine Gun Corps
SHED George MM Pte 7282 8th Bedfordshire Regt
SHEE John Thomas MM Sjt 49517 73 Fd Amb RAMC
SHEED Edwin J. MM+Bar Sjt 11176 Scottish Rifles
SHEEHAN Albert F. MM L/Cpl S/15848 Rifle Brigade
SHEEHAN Daniel MM Sjt 97386 RFA
SHEEHAN George W. MM Pte 203205 1st London Regt
SHEEHAN J. MM Spr 186285 Royal Engineers
SHEEHAN John MM Sjt 10623 2nd Connaught Rangers
SHEEHAN John E. MM Pte 351 9th Royal Fusiliers
SHEEHAN Leonard MM Sjt 945006 RFA
SHEEHAN Patrick "MM,MID" L/Cpl 4548 Irish Guards
SHEEHAN William MM Gnr 52012 130 Heavy Bty RGA
SHEEHAN William G. MM Gnr 49815 1 Div Ammn Col RFA
SHEEL Edward MM Cpl 369429 RAMC
SHEEN Amberline MM L/Cpl 9129 Wiltshire Regt
SHEEN Charles Rickard MM L/Cpl 271064 10th East Kent Regt KIA 31.10.17.
SHEEN Frederick MM Pte 55426 Machine Gun Corps
SHEEN Frederick William MM Sjt 9265 2nd Royal Scots Fusiliers DOW 7.8.16.
SHEERER George "DCM+Bar,MM" Sjt 6406 1st Border Regt
SHEERIN Alexander MM Pte 10041 1st King's Own Scottish Borderers
SHEETER Michael Harry MM Pte 397093 783 AE Coy Labour Corps
SHEFFIELD Ernest Edward MM Spr 43663 7 Div Sig Coy Royal Engineers
SHEFFIELD Fred MM L/Cpl 13242 XVII Corps Cyclist Bn Army Cyclist Corps
SHEFFIELD William MM Sjt 306021 8th Royal Warwickshire Regt
SHEFFIELD William MM Pte 13577 1st Shropshire Light Infantry
SHEFFORD Albert W. MM Sjt 263064 8th Middlesex Regt
SHEFFORD Herbert J. MM L/Cpl 550534 1/16th London Regt
SHEFFORD James "MM,MID" Pte 1523 2/2nd London Regt
SHEIL Patrick MM Pte 6860 Irish Guards
SHEILD W. MM Pte 15996 Royal Inniskilling Fusiliers
SHEILS John MM Sjt 18293 77 Fd Coy Royal Engineers
SHELBORN Percy A. MM L/Cpl 13656 8th Lincolnshire Regt
SHELDON Albert Thomas "MM,MID" Sjt 1146 Royal Warwickshire Regt
SHELDON Edwin MM+Bar Sjt 26208 15th Notts & Derby Regt
SHELDON Ernest MM Pte 28862 3rd Grenadier Guards
SHELDON Frank John "DCM,MM(Cpl RFA)" Sjt 46342 Y/5 Med TM Bty RGA
SHELDON Frederick R. MM Pte 371834 1/8th London Regt
SHELDON George MM Pte 201850 South Staffordshire Regt
SHELDON John MM L/Cpl 200 6th Dragoons
SHELDON John Henry MM Pte R/3355 18th King's Royal Rifle Corps KIA 28.3.18.
SHELDON Luther Henry MM+Bar Pte 33362 9th Yorkshire Light Infantry KIA 24.10.18.
SHELDON Martin MM Gnr 127532 B/256 Bde RFA
SHELDON R.C. MM L/Cpl P/1007 Military Mounted Police
SHELDON Robert MM Cpl 242582 South Staffordshire Regt Died 12.2.20.
SHELDON Tom MM Pte 17351 10th Notts & Derby Regt
SHELDON W. MM Pte 43596 King's Royal Rifle Corps att 1/16th London Regt.
SHELDRICK David MM Pte CHT/161 2 Pontoon Park Army Service Corps
SHELDRICK Herbert L. MM L/Cpl 325777 1/1st Cambridgeshire Regt
SHELDRICK William MM Cpl 30038 1st Northumberland Fusiliers DOW 27.9.18.
SHELFORD Reginald MM Sjt 13538 11th Suffolk Regt
SHELLARD Leonard MM Pte 10126 5th Oxf & Bucks Light Infantry KIA 14.12.17.
SHELLEY Alfred Edgar MM Pte 245250 13th Durham Light Infantry KIA 23.10.18.
SHELLEY Benjamin MM Dvr 91241 C/75 Bde RFA
SHELLEY C. MM Sjt 280745 244 Siege Bty RGA
SHELLEY C. MM Cpl 26321 1st Essex Regt
SHELLEY Charles R. MM+Bar Sjt 4029 Machine Gun Corps
SHELLEY Frederick MM Spr 34896 3 Div Sig Coy Royal Engineers
SHELLEY Herbert MM L/Cpl R/12939 King's Royal Rifle Corps
SHELLEY Herbert G. MM Sjt 73173 163 Siege Bty RGA
SHELLEY Leonard MM Pte 37698 2/4th York & Lancaster Regt
SHELLEY Percy MM L/Cpl 10483 8th Royal Sussex Regt
SHELLEY W.J. MM Sjt 240668 6th East Kent Regt
SHELLY Henry H. "MM,MID" Spr 1429 47 Div Sig Coy Royal Engineers
SHELLY Joseph MM Pte 11222 Labour Corps
SHELMERDINE Eustace Standing MM L/Cpl 29689 1st Border Regt
SHELMERDINE James MM Pre 351762 9th Manchester Regt KIA 21.3.18.
SHELMERDINE Robert MM L/Cpl 15348 8th Royal Lancaster Regt
SHELTON Arthur MM Sjt 39929 35 Bde RFA
SHELTON Frederick James "MM,MID" L/Cpl 3026 1/18th London Regt
SHELTON George MM Pte 13644 Northumberland Fusiliers
SHELTON Herbert Horace MM Cpl 201432 2/4th York & Lancaster Regt
SHELTON J. MM Sjt 325105 1/1st Cambridgeshire Regt
SHELTON James F. MM L/Cpl 426133 Royal Engineers
SHELTON John Tom MM Pte 8661 1st Lincolnshire Regt
SHELTON William MM Pte 320980 15th Suffolk Regt
SHELTON William MM Pte 37918 East Lancashire Regt
SHELTON William E. MM Cpl 44228 8th Lincolnshire Regt
SHEMELD Edward MM Pte 25023 31 Coy Machine Gun Corps KIA 30.2.18.
SHEMILT David MM Cpl 315 GMGR
SHEMMANS Frank MM Spr 253290 Royal Engineers
SHEMMING Frank H. MM Pte 206178 23rd Middlesex Regt
SHENTON Donald MM Cpl 301837 Manchester Regt
SHENTON Edward MM Pte 64918 Machine Gun Corps
SHENTON Frank MM Sjt 9936 1st Grenadier Guards
SHENTON Henry MM Pte 43898 1/8th Middlesex Regt
SHENTON James A. MM Pte 22571 Royal Warwickshire Regt
SHENTON John MM L/Cpl 79121 185 Tunnelling Coy Royal Engineers
SHENTON Thomas "MM,MID" CSM 7838 2nd Royal Scots
SHENTON Thomas MM Pte 11902 RAMC
SHENTON William MM Gnr 50980 RGA
SHEPARD F.C. MM Cpl 7415 11th Royal Fusiliers
SHEPHARD Charles H. MM Bdr 21933 RGA
SHEPHARD George MM Spr 540041 Royal Engineers
SHEPHARD Harold MM Pte 263011 2/5th Leicestershire Regt
SHEPHARD Henry MM Gnr 78671 RGA
SHEPHARD Henry A. MM Cpl 38304 RFA
SHEPHARD Henry C. MM Sjt 11358 1st Middlesex Regt
SHEPHARD John C. MM Pte 12/1327 12th East Yorkshire Regt
SHEPHARD "John T," MM Sjt 56267 24 Div Sig Coy Royal Engineers
SHEPHARD R. MM Pte 130120 45th Royal Fusiliers

SHEPHARD Walter H. MM Pte 534781 15th London Regt
SHEPHARD William MM Pte 305236 7th West Riding Regt
SHEPHEARD George F. MM Cpl 42398 6th West Yorkshire Regt
SHEPHEARD Henry T.P. MM Pte M2/204889 Army Service Corps att RGA
SHEPHERD Albert MM Pte 59354 14th Welsh Regt
SHEPHERD Albert MM Pte 8396 Royal Irish Regt
SHEPHERD Albert MM Sjt 200391 South Lancashire Regt
SHEPHERD Albert MM Sjt 17733 2nd Oxf & Bucks Light Infantry
SHEPHERD Albert E. MM Cpl 12722 2nd Worcestershire Regt
SHEPHERD Albert E. MM L/Cpl 15402 Devonshire Regt
SHEPHERD Alfred MM Pte 420056 1/10th London Regt
SHEPHERD Archibald W. MM L/Cpl 15305 14th Royal Warwickshire Regt
SHEPHERD Arthur MM Cpl 21726 Liverpool Regt
SHEPHERD Ben MM Pte 241268 4th York & Lancaster Regt
SHEPHERD Charles MM L/Cpl 49945 21st Manchester Regt
SHEPHERD Charles T. MM L/Cpl 432035 55 Div Sig Coy Royal Engineers
SHEPHERD Douglas MM L/Cpl 9607 2/1st HAC(Infantry)
SHEPHERD Edgar Charles MM L/Cpl 51002 9th Cheshire Regt
SHEPHERD Edmund MM L/Bdr 33740 RFA
SHEPHERD Ernest MM Cpl 47015 D/96 Bde RFA
SHEPHERD Ernest S. MM Cpl 78206 9th Royal Fusiliers
SHEPHERD Francis Stewart Arthur MM Cpl 46004 RFA
SHEPHERD Frank "MM,MID" BSM 645587 2/1st(Highland)Bde RFA
SHEPHERD Frank H. MM CSM 7436 1st Royal Warwickshire Regt
SHEPHERD G.W. MM Pte S/22327 9th Rifle Brigade
SHEPHERD George MM Cpl 200484 1/4th Royal Lancaster Regt
SHEPHERD George MM L/Cpl 291751 Northumberland Fusiliers
SHEPHERD George MM Pte 2001 1/5th Royal Highlanders
SHEPHERD George A. "DCM,MM" Sjt 65249 105 Fd Coy Royal Engineers
SHEPHERD George T. MM L/Cpl 51430 Cheshire Regt
SHEPHERD Guy Harold MM L/Cpl 354245 1/7th London Regt KIA 31.8.18.
SHEPHERD H. MM L/Cpl 305451 West Yorkshire Regt
SHEPHERD Harry MM Cpl 58765 1/8th West Yorkshire Regt KIA 27.9.18.
SHEPHERD Harry MM Pte 41810 Lancashire Fusiliers
SHEPHERD Harry MM L/Cpl 13/817 13th York & Lancaster Regt
SHEPHERD Henry MM Sjt 241811 6th West Yorkshire Regt
SHEPHERD Henry MM Pte 42591 1st Leicestershire Regt
SHEPHERD Henry MM Pte 7821 2nd Scottish Rifles
SHEPHERD Henry R. MM Pte 236016 8th West Yorkshire Regt
SHEPHERD James MM Cpl Shoeing Smith 636113 2556 Bde RFA
SHEPHERD James MM Pte 3359 Highland Light Infantry
SHEPHERD James MM Dvr 12927 6 Div Ammn Col RFA
SHEPHERD John A. MM L/Sjt 241113 1/7th Royal Highlanders
SHEPHERD John H. MM Pte 15286 9th Leicestershire Regt
SHEPHERD John I. MM L/Cpl 201213 2/4th Yorkshire Light Infantry
SHEPHERD John W. MM Gnr 38506 3 Siege Bty RGA
SHEPHERD John W. MM Bdr 755023 RFA
SHEPHERD Joseph MM Pte 51216 Machine Gun Corps(Cavalry)
SHEPHERD Leonard W. MM Pte 21326 9th Notts & Derby Regt
SHEPHERD Lewis MM Pte 14956 9th North Lancashire Regt KIA 22.3.18.
SHEPHERD Lindsay Vernon MM Sjt 19774 Machine Gun Corps
SHEPHERD Mark MM Sjt 2201 RFA
SHEPHERD Reginald MM Spr 42124 69 Fd Coy Royal Engineers
SHEPHERD Reginald John MM Cpl 538443 6(London)Fd Amb RAMC
SHEPHERD Richard MM L/Cpl 240656 8th Middlesex Regt
SHEPHERD Richard "DCM,MM" Sjt 60984 119 Bde RFA
SHEPHERD Robert MM Cpl 43598 Northumberland Fusiliers
SHEPHERD Robert MM Pte 251580 1/3rd London Regt
SHEPHERD Robert L. MM Sjt 39778 1/7th Worcestershire Regt
SHEPHERD Rowley G. "MM,MSM,MID" SM Armourer T/498 Army Ordnance Corps att 7 Siege Bty RGA.
SHEPHERD Samuel MM Pte 89132 RAMC
SHEPHERD Thomas MM Pte 9810 1st Royal Berkshire Regt
SHEPHERD William MM Pte 202152 West Yorkshire Regt
SHEPHERD William MM Sjt 25688 18th Lancashire Fusiliers
SHEPHERD William "DCM,MM" Pte 7808 2nd Gordon Highlanders
SHEPHERD William MM L/Cpl 1417 1/7th London Regt
SHEPHERD William MM Cpl 14182 17th Lancashire Fusiliers KIA 22.10.17.
SHEPHERD William F. MM Pte 399 25 Fd Amb RAMC
SHEPHERD William George "MM,MID" 2nd Cpl 65871 21 Div Sig Coy Royal Engineers
SHEPHERD William J. MM Slt 16757 6th South Wales Borderers
SHEPHERD William J. MM Pte 574129 17th London Regt
SHEPHERD or SHEPPARD Herbert MM Pte 845 1st Welsh Guards
SHEPHERD or SHEPPERD Edward MM Pte 24152 1st Grenadier Guards
SHEPHERD or SHEPPERD Percy J. MM Pte 1627 Middlesex Regt
SHEPHERDSON Joseph MM+Bar Cpl 203504 4th York & Lancaster Regt
SHEPLEY Harry MM Dvr 796350 18 Bty 3 Bde RFA
SHEPLEY Herbert "MC,MM(4502 Cpl 11th Manch)" 2/Lt 19th Durham Light Infantry
SHEPPARD A. MM Sjt 3229 Royal Sussex Regt
SHEPPARD Albert E. MM Pte CMT/3699 7 Ammn Park Army Service Corps
SHEPPARD Albert W. MM Cpl 266376 1/6th Gloucestershire Regt
SHEPPARD Benjamin T. MM Pte 29739 Wiltshire Regt
SHEPPARD Charles MM Sjt 15723 Royal Berkshire Regt
SHEPPARD David "DCM,MM" Sjt 325063 Durham Light Infantry
SHEPPARD David MM+Bar CSM 4537 1st East Yorkshire Regt
SHEPPARD Ellis MM L/Cpl 3127 Suffolk Regt
SHEPPARD Enoch MM Pte 11542 South Staffordshire Regt
SHEPPARD Ernest MM Pte A/423 8th King's Royal Rifle Corps KIA 15.9.16.Real name Ernest SMY.
SHEPPARD Ernest "See A/423 Pte Ernest SMY, KRRC."
SHEPPARD Ernest F. MM Pte 26920 1/4th Royal Lancaster Regt
SHEPPARD George E. MM Cpl M1/08464 Army Service Corps
SHEPPARD George J. MM+Bar Cpl 4793 13th Royal Fusiliers
SHEPPARD Jack MM Cpl 1398 2nd Rifle Brigade
SHEPPARD James MM Gnr 294413 RGA
SHEPPARD Percy Edward MM Sjt 2907 8th Royal West Surrey Regt
SHEPPARD Percy Howard "MM,MID" Bdr 68638 RGA DOW 28.5.18.
SHEPPARD Reginald V. MM Dvr T3/025134 Army Service Corps
SHEPPARD Richard P. "MM,MID" Sjt 62501 Royal Engineers
SHEPPARD Robert C. MM Pte 8693 2nd Oxf & Bucks Light Infantry
SHEPPARD Robert Wickham MM Cpl 15/1096 15th West Yorkshire Regt KIA 27.3.18.
SHEPPARD Samuel C. MM Cpl 4/6259 Bedfordshire Regt
SHEPPARD Thomas MM Sjt 201133 2/4th Oxf & Bucks Light Infantry
SHEPPARD William MM L/Cpl 33947 Oxf & Bucks Light Infantry
SHEPPARD William MM L/Cpl 355955 Royal Welsh Fusiliers
SHEPPARD William MM Bdr 56698 A/166 Bde RFA KIA 14.7.16.
SHEPPARD William Henry MM Pte 232 Royal Sussex Regt
SHEPPARD William J. MM Bdr 23770 RGA
SHEPPARD or SHEPHERD Herbert MM Pte 845 1st Welsh Guards
SHEPPERD Frederick MM 2nd Cpl 498042 476 Fd Coy Royal Engineers
SHEPPERD or SHEPHERD Edward MM Pte 24152 1st Grenadier Guards
SHEPPERD or SHEPHERD Percy J. MM Pte 1627 Middlesex Regt
SHEPPERSON Herbert MM Sjt 305183 1/8th Notts & Derby Regt
SHERATT George MM Pte 352756 Royal Scots
SHERBORNE Norman MM Gnr 114526 B/315 Bde RFA
SHERET Harry MM Cpl 38771 11th Royal Scots
SHERFIELD Rupert Fred MM L/Cpl 22297 1st Grenadier Guards att 3 Gds Bde TM Bty.
SHERGOLD Charlie MM Pte 7156 1st Wiltshire Regt
SHERGOLD Harry V. MM CSM 11327 11th Hampshire Regt
SHERGOLD Sidney H. MM L/Cpl 471653 63 Div Sig Coy Royal Engineers
SHERGOLD William MM Pte 78969 9th Bn Tank Corps KIA 24.10.18.
SHERIDAN Francis Nesbit MM L/Cpl 9996 2nd Royal Irish Rifles
SHERIDAN James MM Pte 40845 Northumberland Fusiliers
SHERIDAN John Patrick "MM,MID" Sjt 8906 1st Scots Guards
SHERIDAN Peter MM L/Cpl 12355 6th King's Own Scottish Borderers
SHERIDAN Robert MM L/Cpl 37245 1st Scottish Rifles KIA 21.6.18.
SHERIFF John W. "DCM,MM,MID" CSM 20/142 20th Durham Light Infantry
SHERIFF William MM Pte 26244 14th Worcestershire Regt
SHERINGHAM Albert V. MM Sjt 36164 115 Heavy Bty RGA
SHERLIKER Frank MM L/Cpl 18436 2nd Lancashire Fusiliers
SHERLOCK Daniel J. MM Pte 30743 Cheshire Regt
SHERLOCK Fred S. MM L/Cpl 391083 9th London Regt
SHERLOCK Frederick T. MM Pte M2/134389 611 Coy Army Service Corps
SHERLOCK H. MM Pte 83158 11th Royal Fusiliers

SHERLOCK Thomas MM L/Cpl 341576 RAMC
SHERMAN Albert MM Cpl 62301 9th Royal Fusiliers KIA 22.10.18.
SHERMAN James MM L/Cpl M2/022324 Army Service Corps att HQ V Corps
SHERMAN John "MM,MSM" Sjt 3401 2 Fd Amb RAMC
SHERMAN John William MM Sjt 47347 13th Welsh Regt
SHERMAN S. MM Pte 3975 Army Cyclist Corps
SHERRARD Sydney E. MM L/Cpl 52634 7 Sqn Machine Gun Corps(Cavalry)
SHERRATT Albert E. MM L/Cpl 18619 West Riding Regt
SHERRATT Colin R. MM+Bar Pte M2/133586 Army Service Corps
SHERRATT George William Sterndale MM Cpl 2610 7th North Staffordshire Regt
SHERRATT Herbert MM Gnr 76076 189 Bde RFA
SHERRATT James MM Sjt 15080 8th Royal Lancaster Regt DOW 3.6.18.
SHERRATT James MM Pte 422445 10th London Regt
SHERRATT Norman MM Pte 26967 Royal Lancaster Regt
SHERRATT William MM Gnr 97317 RGA
SHERRIFF Walter MM Pte S/16105 12th Rifle Brigade
SHERRIFFS Alexander MM Cpl 43409 1/7th Gordon Highlanders
SHERRIFFS G. MM Pte 201684 Gordon Highlanders
SHERRIFFS John MM+Bar Bdr 3785 RFA
SHERRIN Frank W. MM Pte 38419 54 Fd Amb RAMC
SHERRING Edward MM BSM 14225 B/155 Bde RFA
SHERRING Harold Frank "MM,MSM" Sjt 44439 B/48 Bde RFA
SHERRINGTON John Bernard MM RSM 17151 18 Bde RGA
SHERRINGTON John M. MM Sjt 18/1124 23rd Northumberland Fusiliers
SHERRINGTON Tom MM Cpl 21020 22nd Manchester Regt
SHERRINGTON Walter MM L/Cpl 52124 6th Northamptonshire Regt
SHERRINGTON William MM Gnr 128124 RFA
SHERROD Harry "MM,MSM" Sjt 69429 138 Army Troops Coy Royal Engineers
SHERRY Ernest Alfred "MM,MID" Bdr 92214 118 Siege Bty RGA
SHERRY James MM Sjt M2/099993 17 Ammn Supply Park Army Service Corps
SHERRY John W. MM Sjt 200762 20th Manchester Regt
SHERRY Leslie R. MM L/Cpl 1194 1/20th London Regt
SHERVILLE Harry MM Sjt 291435 128 Hy Bty RGA
SHERVINTON John MM Cpl 28128 11th Border Regt
SHERWEN William MM Pte 18375 2nd Coldstream Guards
SHERWIN Albert H. MM L/Sjt S/3749 13th Rifle Brigade
SHERWIN Fred MM+2 Bars Sjt 780072 B/246 Bde RFA
SHERWIN George W. MM L/Cpl 20447 8th East Surrey Regt
SHERWIN Maurice MM L/Cpl S/20413 Rifle Brigade
SHERWOOD Albert Mark MM L/Cpl 148684 'Q' Corps Sig Coy Royal Engineers
SHERWOOD Alfred MM Pte 5137 12th Royal Sussex Regt
SHERWOOD George MM L/Sjt 19493 5th Oxf & Bucks Light Infantry KIA 12.12.17.
SHERWOOD John MM Pte 17105 Northamptonshire Regt
SHERWOOD Thomas William MM Cpl 9453 2nd King's Royal Rifle Corps KIA 20.8.16.
SHEVLIN Peter MM Cpl 285087 8th Royal Highlanders
SHEW George MM Pte 633292 20th London Regt
SHEWAN Henry MM Pte 9773 1st Royal Highlanders
SHEWAN William M. MM Sjt 20188 51st Bn Machine Gun Corps
SHEWARD Alfred MM L/Bdr 950980 A/18 Bde RFA
SHEWARD William Joseph MM Dvr 113428 D/150 Bde RFA
SHEWRY Thomas G. MM L/Cpl 2909 8th Royal West Kent Regt
SHIACH James MM Cpl 202644 1/4th Seaforth Highlanders
SHIACH William MM Pte 50004 5/6th Royal Scots
SHIEL Michael MM Gnr 69059 290 Bde RFA
SHIEL Robert MM L/Cpl 58199 RAMC
SHIEL Thomas MM Gnr 120149 RFA
SHIELD F. MM Cpl 28588 1st Royal Inniskilling Fusiliers
SHIELD George MM Pte 29336 15th Durham Light Infantry
SHIELD John MM Pte 9198 7th Royal Fusiliers
SHIELD John J. MM Pte 24859 1st Border Regt
SHIELD Wilfred K. MM Sjt 337192 142 Heavy Bty RGA
SHIELDS Frank MM L/Cpl 330825 Liverpool Regt
SHIELDS G. MM Pte 38213 Yorkshire Light Infantry
SHIELDS George MM Pte 235069 2nd South Lancashire Regt
SHIELDS George MM Sjt 4/3033 Royal Inniskilling Fusiliers
SHIELDS Hugh MM Sjt 1689 RAMC
SHIELDS James MM Pte 62743 Machine Gun Corps
SHIELDS John MM L/Cpl 15944 11/13th Royal Irish Rifles
SHIELDS John MM CSM 200518 1/4th Royal Scots Fusiliers
SHIELDS John MM Sjt CMT/1292 Army Service Corps
SHIELDS John James MM Sjt 17901 9th Yorkshire Regt KIA 10.7.16.
SHIELDS John Reed MM Gnr 149778 150 Siege Bty RGA
SHIELDS John William MM Pte 12/959 12th East Yorkshire Regt DOW 22.10.17.
SHIELDS Lewis MM L/Cpl 60369 Machine Gun Corps
SHIELDS Patrick MM Pte 9672 1st Royal Irish Rifles KIA 16.8.17.
SHIELDS Philip MM Gnr 13594 D/83 Bde RFA
SHIELDS Richard Thomas MM Sjt 13274 12th Yorkshire Regt DOW 7.11.18.
SHIELDS Samuel MM Sjt 8/13588 8th Royal Irish Rifles KIA 2.7.16.
SHIELDS Thomas MM Sjt 12086 6th Royal Lancaster Regt
SHIELDS Thomas John MM L/Cpl 1031 17th Royal Fusiliers
SHIELDS Tom MM Pte 13712 6th Lincolnshire Regt
SHIELDS Wilfred A. MM Cpl 42059 6th Leicestershire Regt
SHIELDS William MM Pte 59702 11th Royal Scots Fusiliers
SHIELDS William MM Pte 304859 17th Armoured Car Bn Tank Corps
SHIELDS William M. MM Pte 11064 Scottish Rifles
SHIELL William MM Cpl 4409 12th Arg & Suth Highlanders
SHIELLS James MM Pte 4650 1/4th Seaforth Highlanders
SHIELS James "MC,DCM,MM" RSM 7586 5th Cameron Highlanders
SHIELS Matthew MM Sjt 9268 2nd Royal Irish Regt KIA 15.8.17.
SHIERS William Horace MM Cpl 19808 Middlesex Regt
SHILCO Eli MM Pte 204389 7th Royal West Kent Regt att MGC.DOW 8.11.18.
SHILCOCK Arthur N. MM Pte 720425 24th London Regt
SHILCOCK Hugh Richard MM Gnr 120995 100 Bde RFA
SHILCOCK John MM Gnr 22417 286 Bde RFA
SHILLABEER Kenneth E. MM Pte 701979 23rd London Regt
SHILLINGFORD James MM Cpl 256469 1/1st Bucks Bn Oxf & Bucks Light Infantry
SHILLINGFORD William R. MM Pte 514716 14th London Regt
SHILLINGLAW James MM Pte 37957 Highland Light Infantry
SHILLINGSFORD Bertie MM Pte 41023 1st Norfolk Regt
SHILLINGTON Robert H. MM Cpl 696850 RFA
SHILLITO Arthur MM L/Cpl 9234 Coldstream Guards
SHILLITO Johnson W. MM Pte 2688 West Yorkshire Regt
SHILLITOE Horace MM L/Cpl 4725 14th Liverpool Regt
SHILSTON Percy Samuel MM Sjt 94997 11th Bn Tank Corps
SHILTON William C. "MM,MID" CQMS 7930 1st Royal Berkshire Regt
SHILVOCK Rowland MM L/Cpl 16056 Royal Warwickshire Regt
SHIMMIN James MM Gnr 660957 RFA
SHIMMIN William H. MM Sjt 444324 42 Div Sig Coy Royal Engineers
SHIMMINGS Joseph "DCM,MM" Sjt 5432 4th Coldstream Guards
SHIMWELL Gershon MM Sjt 240584 1/6th Notts & Derby Regt
SHINE George W. MM L/Cpl 4807 5th Lancers
SHINE Michael J. MM Cpl 200221 1/1st London Regt
SHINE Nathan MM+Bar Pte 12180 5th Northamptonshire Regt
SHINE Thomas MM Pte 315248 Royal Sussex Regt
SHINGLER Leslie J. MM Pte 11239 Leicestershire Regt
SHINGLER Percy MM Sjt 64865 37 Bde RFA
SHINGLES James MM Pte M2/022176 Army Service Corps att 71 Fd Amb RAMC.
SHINGLETON Isaac MM L/Cpl 13/579 13th East Yorkshire Regt
SHINKWIN Thomas MM Cpl 8775 1st Royal Dublin Fusiliers Died 4.11.18.
SHINTON Charles B. MM Pte 140457 32nd Bn Machine Gun Corps
SHIP George Samuel MM Dvr 177008 AA Bty RHA
SHIPCOTT William J. MM Pte 224312 Labour Corps
SHIPLEY E.A. "MM+Bar,MIDx2" Cpl 44133 Royal Engineers
SHIPLEY Ernest P. MM L/Cpl 48599 5th Royal Berkshire Regt
SHIPLEY Harry MM Sjt 26274 'Z' Special Coy Royal Engineers
SHIPLEY John W. MM Cpl Sig 94960 323 Siege Bty RGA
SHIPLEY John William MM Pte 40534 10th Arg & Suth Highlanders
SHIPLEY Norman C. MM Pte 65192 5th Yorkshire Light Infantry
SHIPLEY Reginald Henry MM L/Cpl 470458 12th London Regt DOW 24.4.18.
SHIPLEY Stephen R. MM L/Sjt 265301 1/6th Northumberland Fusiliers
SHIPLEY William B. MM Sjt 5827 Northumberland Fusiliers
SHIPLEY William F. MM L/Cpl 43210 Royal Engineers
SHIPMAN Harold MM Sjt 13008 2nd Coldstream Guards
SHIPMAN Joseph T. MM Dvr 172975 RFA
SHIPP Alfred J. MM Sjt 20800 15th Hampshire Regt
SHIPP Arthur MM L/Cpl 206844 3/4th Royal West Surrey Regt

SHIPP Louis E. MM L/Cpl S/17868 Rifle Brigade
SHIPPAM Edwin MM CQMS 4706 1st Middlesex Regt
SHIPPAM Joseph MM Gnr 20394 A/115 Bde RFA Died 29.10.18.
SHIPPEN Lawrence MM Gnr 49881 RGA
SHIPPEY Richard MM L/Cpl 41203 6th West Riding Regt
SHIPTON Frederick MM L/Cpl 13451 1/4th Northamptonshire Regt KIA 27.11.17.
SHIPTON Gordon MM Gnr 781598 A/311 Bde RFA
SHIRBON Charles R. MM L/Cpl 51093 Highland Light Infantry
SHIRE Francis E. MM Pte 35190 7th Royal Warwickshire Regt
SHIRES Benjiman(sic) MM Sjt 11821 8th Yorkshire Regt
SHIRES Edward MM Pte 18851 15th Hampshire Regt
SHIRES Henry MM Cpl 781175 RFA
SHIRES Ronald MM Pnr 208923 74 Div Sig Coy Royal Engineers
SHIRLAW George MM Sjt 49967 RFA
SHIRLEY Bertram F. MM L/Cpl 56073 21st Northumberland Fusiliers
SHIRLEY Cecil R. MM Spr 49713 Royal Engineers
SHIRLEY F.A. MM Cpl 202168 Royal Lancaster Regt
SHIRLEY Frederick MM Pte 15756 11th Royal Sussex Regt KIA 21.10.16.
SHIRLEY Frederick MM Pte 5532 8th East Surrey Regt
SHIRLEY Frederick J. MM Pnr 126507 Royal Engineers
SHIRLEY Frederick James MM+Bar Pte 18295 14th Royal Warwickshire Regt
SHIRLEY H.J. MM Spr 311489 23 Div Sig Coy Royal Engineers
SHIRLEY Reuben MM+Bar L/Cpl 531599 15th London Regt
SHIRLEY Thomas MM Pte 5148 3rd Rifle Brigade
SHIRREFFS Alexander MM L/Cpl T4/241175 Army Service Corps
SHIRT Edward MM Sjt 96276 B/83 Bde RFA
SHIRT Wright MM Dvr 37128 RFA
SHOCK Charles H. MM Sjt 3259 Army Cyclist Corps
SHOEBRIDGE Herbert A. MM Sjt 58999 RAMC
SHOEMACK Edward MM L/Cpl 591789 18th London Regt
SHONE Frederick MM Pte 22830 Liverpool Regt
SHONE Henry MM CSM 9640 1st King's Royal Rifle Corps DOW 10.3.17.
SHONE Richard A. MM Pte 27159 13th Liverpool Regt
SHONE Samuel MM Pte 1870 1st Royal Highlanders
SHONE Sydney MM 2nd Cpl 311708 Royal Engineers
SHONFIELD Henry Albert MM Sjt 2 8th Royal Sussex Regt
SHOOBRIDGE Reginald MM Gnr 41271 118 Heavy Bty Royal Artillery
SHOOBRIDGE Sidney MM Pte 240806 1/8th Middlesex Regt KIA 30.11.17.
SHOOK Walter Burnell MM Sjt 41001 1 Squadron Machine Gun Corps(Cavalry)
SHOOTER William H. MM Cpl 305933 6th Bn Tank Corps
SHOPLAND A.W. "MM+Bar,MID" Sjt S/7012 Rifle Brigade
SHORE Bertie Frederick George MM Pte 12367 1st Scots Guards KIA 27.9.18.
SHORE Ernest R. MM Cpl 65810 RFA
SHORE Fred MM Pte 1905 1/4th Yorkshire Regt KIA 21.4.18.
SHORE G.G. MM Gnr 145868 RGA
SHORE Herbert MM Pte 19934 9th West Yorkshire Regt
SHORE John MM L/Cpl 266083 Liverpool Regt
SHORE John MM Spr 504099 500 Fd Coy Royal Engineers
SHORE Joseph MM Pte 11438 7th Somerset Light Infantry
SHORE William H. MM L/Bdr 63574 105 Bty 22 Bde RFA
SHORE William Irving MM Sjt 2188 7th Seaforth Highlanders
SHORER Albert James MM Cpl 26429 108 Heavy Bty RGA
SHOREY Albert W. MM Cpl 242177 1/5th Border Regt
SHORMAN Leonard Ernest MM Sjt 1201 Royal Fusiliers
SHORROCKS James MM Sjt 39687 A/150 Bde RFA
SHORROCKS T.S. MM Pte PS/7062 2nd Royal Fusiliers
SHORROCKS Thomas C. MM Pte M2/114160 Army Service Corps
SHORROCKS William MM L/Cpl 19936 32nd Bn Machine Gun Corps
SHORROCKS William MM L/Cpl 2092 4th Royal Fusiliers DOW 30.12.17.
SHORT Arthur Thomas MM L/Cpl 45643 1/5th Devonshire Regt KIA 7.11.18.
SHORT Benjamin MM Dvr 42700 RFA
SHORT Bertie James Daniel MM Sjt 44380 Royal Engineers
SHORT Edward J. MM Pte 25975 10th Royal Dublin Fusiliers
SHORT Ernest William MM Sjt 9009 2nd Essex Regt DOW 26.10.18.
SHORT Fred MM Pte 8618 1st West Riding Regt
SHORT Frederick MM Cpl 4214 7th Royal Warwickshire Regt
SHORT Frederick MM Cpl S/2444 12th Rifle Brigade
SHORT George T. MM Sjt 18114 RGA
SHORT Harry MM Dvr 47234 41 Div Ammn Col RFA
SHORT Harry MM Pte 16323 1 Special Coy Middlesex Regt
SHORT Henry MM Sjt 7415 1st East Yorkshire Regt
SHORT J. MM Pte 7122 West Riding Regt
SHORT John MM L/Cpl 265461 Liverpool Regt
SHORT John H. MM 2nd Cpl 210978 Guards Div Sig Coy Royal Engineers
SHORT Leonard MM Bdr 68168 RFA
SHORT Leonard MM Pte 3002 Army Cyclist Corps
SHORT Patrick Etherington MM Pte 7800 96 Coy Machine Gun Corps
SHORT Percy W. MM L/Sjt 13479 4th Coldstream Guards
SHORT Thomas William MM Pte 327988 1/1st Cambridgeshire Regt KIA 26.9.17.
SHORT Tom MM Pte 16698 1st Dorsetshire Regt
SHORT Walter MM Pte 47468 RAMC
SHORT Walter MM Pte 9671 9th York & Lancaster Regt
SHORT Walter Frederick MM Cpl 18794 9th Yorkshire Light Infantry att London Regt. KIA 9.9.18.
SHORT William MM Pte 2605 8th Royal Sussex Regt
SHORT William Benjamin MM Pte 8618 Royal Irish Regt
SHORT William John MM Pte 29097 17th King's Royal Rifle Corps
SHORT William John Dixon MM Bdr 25702 31 Siege Bty RGA
SHORTALL Nicholas Joseph MM Cpl 56623 17 Div Sig Coy Royal Engineers
SHORTER George F. MM Sjt 142 1/4th Royal Berkshire Regt
SHORTER John MM Spr 112553 Royal Engineers
SHORTLAND Alfred H. MM Dvr 826653 RFA
SHORTLAND William H. MM Sjt 68070 2 Div Ammn Col RFA
SHORTRIDGE Walter L. "DCM,MM" Sjt 43279 16 Div Sig Coy Royal Engineers
SHORTT John V. MM L/Cpl 356684 1/10th Liverpool Regt
SHOTTER Ernest MM+Bar Cpl 32231 6 Siege Bty RGA KIA 14.7.17.
SHOTTER Morie Ernlie MM Pnr 248694 'Z' Special Coy Royal Engineers
SHOTTER Richard MM Cpl 305849 8th Liverpool Regt
SHOTTER William MM Spr 519547 559 Army Tps Coy Royal Engineers
SHOTTER William MM Pte 17761 1/4th Royal Sussex Regt
SHOTTON George B. MM Gnr 196878 RFA
SHOTTON Wilfred MM Pte 56128 13th Royal Welsh Fusiliers KIA 22.4.18.
SHOTTON William John Adam MM Pte 88269 52nd Bn Machine Gun Corps
SHOTTON William T. MM Sjt 13419 9th Royal Welsh Fusiliers
SHOULDER Richard John MM Pte 23691 112 Coy Machine Gun Corps KIA 3.8.17.
SHOVLIN Patrick MM Gnr 144898 162 Siege Bty RGA
SHOVLIN Robert MM 2nd Cpl 192833 'J' Special Coy Royal Engineers
SHOWELL Henry Richard MM Bdr 82792 22 Heavy Bty RGA KIA 17.4.18.
SHOWELL John Michael MM+2 Bars Cpl 720575 1/24th London Regt
SHOWELL William MM Cpl 21613 2nd Bedfordshire Regt
SHOWELL William F. MM+Bar Cpl 52708 12th Durham Light Infantry
SHREEVE George MM Cpl R/32039 2nd King's Royal Rifle Corps
SHRIMPTON Charles W. MM Dvr 37927 D/82 Bde RFA
SHRIMPTON Harry MM Cpl 43364 Royal Engineers
SHRIVE Cyril MM Pte 13830 2nd Northamptonshire Regt Died 15.10.17.
SHRIVES John MM Pte 2635 Army Cyclist Corps
SHRODER Frank MM L/Cpl 19945 9th Essex Regt KIA 10.7.17.
SHROSBREE William Alfred MM Sjt 18629 13th Essex Regt
SHRUBB Arthur George "MM,MID" Sjt 473007 88 Fd Amb RAMC
SHRUBB Harold "MM,MID" L/Cpl 3904 6th Royal West Surrey Regt
SHRUBSOLE William MM Sjt 6548 2 Mountain Bty RGA
SHUFFLEBOTHAM Percival T. "DCM,MM" Cpl 82452 Y/8 Med TM Bty RFA
SHUFFLEBOTTOM Charles MM Cpl 19007 21st Manchester Regt DOW 26.3.17.
SHUFFLEBOTTOM Samuel MM Pte 242279 East Lancashire Regt
SHUGRUE George Edward MM Cpl 2776 'AD' Cable Section Royal Engineers
SHUKER Thomas MM Sjt 200160 1/5th North Staffordshire Regt
SHUKER William A. MM L/Cpl 37241 Royal Engineers
SHULMAN Simon MM Pte 77023 24th Royal Fusiliers

SHULVER Hugh MM Pte 260009 1/4th Royal Lancaster Regt
SHULVER William J. MM L/Sjt 10128 1st Welsh Regt
SHUMACKER Thomas MM L/Cpl 14032 7th Cameron Highlanders
SHURETY George Henry MM Spr 98359 Royal Engineers
SHURROCK Aubrey MM Pte 800815 2nd Royal Fusiliers
SHUSTER Richard MM S/Sjt Armt 531 Army Ordnance Corps
SHUTE Albert Henry Frederick MM Cpl 275117 1/6th Essex Regt
SHUTE Edgar J. MM Sjt 71963 9th Royal Fusiliers
SHUTE Francis H. MM Pte 265042 Gloucestershire Regt
SHUTE James MM Cpl 8154 1st Royal Inniskilling Fusiliers KIA 1.7.16.
SHUTE Sidney H. MM Sjt 279824 127 Siege Bty RGA
SHUTE William Henry MM Pte 14647 1st Devonshire Regt KIA 20.10.18.
SHUTLER Charles MM Pte 9081 1st Wiltshire Regt
SHUTT Breckon William MM Pte 203821 Yorkshire Regt
SHUTTLE Harry MM Pte 44879 2nd Lincolnshire Regt DOW 10.5.18.
SHUTTLEWOOD Wilfred MM L/Cpl 65857 13th Royal Fusiliers
SHUTTLEWORTH Dennis MM 2nd Cpl 65512 105 Fd Coy Royal Engineers
SHUTTLEWORTH Frank Graham MM L/Sjt 43957 18th Manchester Regt Died 23.5.19.
SHUTTLEWORTH Frederick MM Pte 10671 Royal Warwickshire Regt
SHUTTLEWORTH Joseph MM Pte 142490 RAMC
SHUTTLEWORTH Matthew "MM,MID" Sjt 28090 10th Lancashire Fusiliers
SHUTTLEWORTH Richard B. MM Spr 41839 12 Div Sig Coy Royal Engineers
SHUTTLEWORTH Robert MM Gnr 701157 RFA
SHUTTLEWORTH Samuel MM L/Cpl 242073 East Lancashire Regt
SHYLON John T.E. MM BSM 730041 RFA
SIBBALD Francis Victor "MM,MSM,MIDx3,CG(F)" Staff SM S/18321 1 Div Train Army Service Corps
SIBBALD Harry P. MM+Bar L/Sjt 276001 1/7th Arg & Suth Highlanders
SIBBALD Hugh MM Pte 241679 5/6th Scottish Rifles
SIBBALD James R. MM Gnr 166269 RFA
SIBLEY Albert G. MM Sjt 1709 1/8th Middlesex Regt
SIBLEY Charles MM L/Sjt 7209 1st Dorsetshire Regt
SIBLEY Charles E. MM Gnr 88835 RFA
SIBLEY F.W.J. MM Sjt 9891 Royal Air Force
SIBLEY George Edgar MM Gnr 821339 A/296 Bde RFA
SIBLEY Henry MM Pte 11415 8th Royal Fusiliers DOW 3.5.17.
SIBLEY John H. MM Pte 241772 Worcestershire Regt
SIBLEY Joseph MM Pte 240191 1/8th Middlesex Regt
SIBLEY Richard MM Pte M/284692 36 Motor Ambulance Convoy Army Service Corps
SIBLEY Thomas MM L/Cpl 13442 8th Somerset Light Infantry
SIBLEY William MM L/Cpl 9949 11th Royal Fusiliers KIA 11.11.17.
SIBSON A. MM L/Cpl 703827 London Regt
SIBSON Charles A. MM Pte 65155 Royal Fusiliers
SIBSON Joseph MM Pte 36257 13th Yorkshire Regt
SIBTHORPE Thomas MM Pte 202542 1st Essex Regt
SICKEL Joseph MM Pte 62953 Machine Gun Corps
SIDAWAY Joseph Griffiths MM L/Cpl 307394 2/8th Royal Warwickshire Regt
SIDDALL Claude MM Cpl 20976 18th Hussars
SIDDALL George MM Pte 58660 10th Notts & Derby Regt KIA 13.10.18.
SIDDALL James MM Dvr 97770 A/52 Bde RFA
SIDDALL John F. MM Pte 12205 7th East Yorkshire Regt
SIDDALL John W. MM Pte 12485 15th Cheshire Regt
SIDDALL Richard MM Cpl 14825 24th Manchester Regt
SIDDALL Robert MM Pte 267956 1/6th Cheshire Regt DOW 18.11.18.
SIDDALL William MM Cpl 438444 Royal Engineers
SIDDERS John James MM Pte 45496 37 Fd Amb RAMC KIA 4.10.16.
SIDDERS Percy MM Pte 7008 11th Hussars KIA 30.3.18.
SIDDLE Bertram Proud MM Pte 43501 10th Yorkshire Light Infantry
SIDDLE Robert B. "MM,MIDx2" Sjt S/1483 12th Rifle Brigade
SIDDLE Walter MM Pte 10996 6th South Lancashire Regt
SIDDONS George MM Dvr 805221 A/231 Bde RFA
SIDDONS James "MC,DCM,MM+Bar(11352 Sjt 4th Hussars)" 2Lt Cheshire Regt
SIDDORN Alan H. MM Pte 19995 Royal Fusiliers
SIDDORN William Arthur MM Pte 14814 9th North Lancashire Regt KIA 13.4.18.
SIDDY Albert MM+Bar Pte 275642 5/6th Royal Scots
SIDE Albert Edward MM Spr 97907 155 Fd Coy Royal Engineers
SIDEBOTHAM Harry MM Cpl 18154 20th Manchester Regt KIA 6.10.18.
SIDEBOTHAM William MM L/Cpl 301396 2/6th Manchester Regt
SIDEBOTTOM James MM Pte 12/1855 13th York & Lancaster Regt
SIDEBOTTOM William MM Gnr 1166 (800522) C/230 Bde RFA KIA 26.3.18.
SIDGWICK John MM Sjt 7081 2/4th Royal West Kent Regt
SIDLEY T. MM Pte 233833 London Regt
SIDLEY William MM Sjt 32104 A/93 Bde RFA
SIDLOW William "DCM,MM" Sjt 28073 2nd Lancashire Fusiliers
SIDNEY John MM Pte 5215 Army Cyclist Corps
SIDWELL Frank MM Pte 10660 10th East Kent Regt
SIDWELL William F. MM Cpl 266185 1/7th Royal Warwickshire Regt
SIDWICK George C.B. MM Pte 433036 RAMC
SIER Frank E. MM Pte 36544 4th North Staffordshire Regt
SIEVEWRIGHT Allan Bell MM Pte 7430 5/6th Scottish Rifles KIA 26.9.17.
SIEVEWRIGHT Charles MM L/Cpl 22470 Highland Light Infantry att MGC
SIEVEWRIGHT G. "DCM,MM" Sjt 201194 1st Royal Highlanders
SIEVEWRIGHT J. MM Pte 9958 Cameron Highlanders
SIEVWRIGHT Alexander John Norman MM Sjt 3157 12th London Regt
SIGGERS Albert E. MM Gnr 58845 94 Bty 18 Bde RFA
SIGGERS George MM Gnr 9590 A/71 Bde RFA DOW 8.2.17.
SIGGERS Henry MM Pte 114141 17th Liverpool Regt
SIGGERS Robert C. MM Cpl 30375 Royal Engineers
SIGGERS William Richard MM Pte 63581 13th Royal Fusiliers KIA 4.9.18.
SIGGINS Thomas MM L/Cpl 495625 2nd London Regt
SIGSWORTH William MM Sjt 200950 2/5th West Yorkshire Regt
SILBY Frederick "MM,MID" Sjt 432344 Royal Engineers
SILCOCK George MM Cpl 1543 17th Royal Fusiliers
SILCOCK Samuel G. MM Spr 89553 138 Army Troops Coy Royal Engineers
SILCOCK Walter MM Sjt R/985 King's Royal Rifle Corps
SILCOCK Walter George MM Sjt 97301 Royal Engineers
SILCOX Alfred Charles MM Cpl 10400 1st Royal Fusiliers KIA 31.7.17.
SILK Albert MM Pte B/200701 9th Rifle Brigade
SILK Alfred H. MM Pte 12135 2nd West Riding Regt
SILK Charles MM L/Sjt 3538 Coldstream Guards
SILK George V. MM Bdr 102537 RHA
SILK Henry George Hodder MM Cpl 5488 1st Scots Guards
SILK Thomas MM Pte 13116 South Staffordshire Regt
SILKSTONE Martin "DCM,MM" CSM 240730 2/6th & 1st West Yorkshire Regt
SILL Jack Rice "MM,MID" Spr 44877 Royal Engineers
SILLAY Leslie T. MM L/Cpl 20390 12 Fd Amb RAMC
SILLENCE Edgar Victor MM Pnr 34809 Signal Service Royal Engineers
SILLENCE James MM Sjt 7612 1st Hampshire Regt DOW 24.4.18.
SILLICK Frank S. MM Pte 695085 1/22nd London Regt
SILLITOE Joseph "MC,MM(280656 Sjt Lanc Fus)" 2Lt 1/7th Northumberland Fusiliers
SILLITOE Walter T. MM Pte 240338 1/5th Devonshire Regt
SILLS Charles A. "DCM,MM" Sjt 83963 211 Fd Coy Royal Engineers
SILSBY Bertram F. MM Pte 12827 8th Bedfordshire Regt
SILVA Thomas H. MM Sjt 5621 Royal Munster Fusiliers
SILVER Alexander McRobbie Fraser MM Pte 301417 2/1(Highland)Fd Amb RAMC
SILVER Arthur MM Sjt 9522 1st East Surrey Regt
SILVER Edward MM Bdr 61093 41 Bty 42 Bde RFA
SILVER George M. MM Sjt 12037 Duke of Cornwall's LI
SILVER Jesse MM Pte 25928 2nd Hampshire Regt
SILVER Louis MM Pte B/629 Rifle Brigade
SILVERSIDES William Henry MM Sjt 18397 12t Durham Light Infantry KIA 31.8.16.
SILVERTON Ernest George MM Sjt 37793 RFA KIA 26.7.17.
SILVERTON Thomas Septimus MM Sjt 12884 9th Northumberland Fusiliers KIA 2.8.16.
SILVERWOOD Alan "DCM,MM" L/Cpl 4359 1/6th West Yorkshire Regt DOW 11.11.17.
SILVERWOOD Hugh MM Pte 18668 Coldstream Guards
SILVERWOOD Thomas MM Pte 375399 10th Manchester Regt
SILVESTER Albert MM Pte 12/506 9th Yorkshire Light Infantry KIA 9.4.17.
SILVESTER Edwin MM Sjt 201139 1/4th Hampshire Regt

SILVESTER George MM Pte 201098 6th Tank Corps Died 1.8.18.
SILVESTER George R. MM Sjt 230187 1/2nd London Regt
SILVESTER Harold A. "DCM,MM" Sjt 651329 1/21st London Regt
SILVESTER Herbert G. MM Sjt 24509 275 Siege Bty RGA
SILVESTER John MM Pte 26926 Hampshire Regt
SILVESTER Joseph MM Spr 207642 63 Div Sig Coy Royal Engineers
SILVESTER Percy MM Gnr 9431 15 Div Ammn Col RFA
SILVEY Charles Henry MM Pte 49960 King's Royal Rifle Corps London Regt att 9th London Regt.
SIM A. MM Pte 5986 Gordon Highlanders
SIM Albert R. MM Pte 42824 134 Fd Amb RAMC
SIM Andrew MM Pte 202544 Gordon Highlanders
SIM Archibald MM Pte 2057 9th Seaforth Highlanders
SIM Cecil K. MM Sjt 1471 1/9th London Regt
SIM Charles MM Cpl 402354 Royal Engineers
SIM Clement John MM Cpl 42181 215 Siege Bty RGA
SIM David E. MM+Bar Sjt 7105 Army Cyclist Corps
SIM Edward MM Sjt M/205132 Army Service Corps
SIM George MM Sjt 47207 RAMC
SIM James MM Pte 51312 1st Cheshire Regt
SIM James D. MM Cpl 40264 Royal Highlanders
SIM John Henry Charles MM Pte 201033 5th Cameron Highlanders
SIM Peter MM+Bar Dvr 630179 A/255 Bde RFA
SIM Vincent D. MM Pte 58953 Royal Fusiliers
SIM William MM Pte 3/6268 1st Cameron Highlanders
SIM William Henry "MM,MID" Sjt 89744 9 Div Sig Coy Royal Engineers
SIM William Y. MM L/Cpl 9183 Seaforth Highlanders
SIMBLETT George MM Dvr 470533 528 Fd Coy Royal Engineers
SIMCOCK Frederick William MM Sjt 71909 137 Fd Amb RAMC
SIMCOCK George MM Pte 24650 1st Royal Welsh Fusiliers KIA 10.10.17.
SIMCOCK Joseph H. MM Pte 16480 1st Hampshire Regt
SIMCOCK Richard A. MM Cpl 202302 Royal Berkshire Regt
SIMCOE Frederick MM Pte 5523 8th East Surrey Regt KIA 7.8.17.
SIMCOX Arthur Edwin MM Sjt 4679 1st Coldstream Guards
SIMCOX Edgar MM L/Cpl 13854 8th South Staffordshire Regt
SIMCOX Ernest MM Gnr 31895 27 Bde RFA
SIMCOX Isaac MM Pte 81030 1 Fd Amb RAMC
SIMCOX John E. MM Sjt 88047 47th Bn Machine Gun Corps
SIMCOX William MM L/Cpl 5926 2nd Shropshire Light Infantry
SIME Alexander MM Pte 9657 1st Cameron Highlanders DOW 4.9.18.
SIME Joseph MM Cpl 43037 Royal Engineers
SIME Peter MM Cpl 14701 12th Royal Scots DOW 14.8.18.
SIME Thomas MM L/Cpl 92337 3rd(Light)Bn Tank Corps
SIMISTER Norman MM Pte 351043 Manchester Regt
SIMKIN Frederick Charles MM Pte 7792 1st Lincolnshire Regt
SIMKIN Samuel MM Dvr 675369 RFA
SIMKINS Benjamin E. "DCM,MM" L/Cpl 550666 520 Fd Coy Royal Engineers
SIMM John MM CSM 13882 8th Northumberland Fusiliers
SIMM John MM Pte 201351 Durham Light Infantry
SIMM Robert MM Pte 55204 Machine Gun Corps
SIMM Samuel MM Pte 243641 5th Lancashire Fusiliers
SIMM Thomas H. MM Pte 41470 1st Royal Lancaster Regt
SIMM William "MM,MID" Sjt C/186 16th King's Royal Rifle Corps
SIMMEN Lawrence J. MM Cpl 8301 9th Royal Highlanders
SIMMER William H. "DCM,MM" CSM 7095 1st Royal Irish Rifles
SIMMERS J.S. MM Air Mech 1 49993 Royal Air Force
SIMMIE Andrew C. MM Pte 11130 1st Royal Scots
SIMMONDS Albert Edwin MM Bdr 735333 RFA
SIMMONDS Arthur L. MM Cpl 7967 2nd Royal Sussex Regt
SIMMONDS Arthur William MM Spr 100465 29 Broad Gauge Op Coy Royal Engineers
SIMMONDS D.H. MM Pte 145312 1/1st Northamptonshire Yeomanry
SIMMONDS Ernest Charles MM Cpl DM2/097466 Army Service Corps att 186 Siege Bty Ammn Col RGA.Died 9.2.17.
SIMMONDS Ernest J. MM Pte 7553 5th Lancers
SIMMONDS Frank MM Pte 6/9821 2nd Rifle Brigade
SIMMONDS Frederick MM Pte 18537 15th Hampshire Regt
SIMMONDS Frederick MM L/Cpl 200176 2/4th Gloucestershire Regt
SIMMONDS George W. MM Cpl 38 1st Royal West Kent Regt
SIMMONDS Harry MM L/Bdr 286148 RGA
SIMMONDS Harry MM Pte 34034 1st Border Regt
SIMMONDS Henry W. MM Pte 28292 1st Royal Warwickshire Regt
SIMMONDS J.T. MM Cpl 37197 RGA
SIMMONDS James MM+Bar Sjt 16312 7th Royal Sussex Regt
SIMMONDS James MM Pte S/27264 Rifle Brigade att 1/8th London Regt.KIA 2.10.18.
SIMMONDS Osborn MM Cpl 38480 9th Yorkshire Light Infantry
SIMMONDS Richard MM Cpl 240082 1/6th Notts & Derby Regt
SIMMONDS Stanley William Phillip MM Pte 92180 3 Fd Amb RAMC
SIMMONDS Thomas E. MM Pte 18962 10th Worcestershire Regt
SIMMONDS Walter H. MM Pte 10832 4th Royal Fusiliers
SIMMONDS Walter H. "MM,MID" Sjt 300171 1/5th London Regt
SIMMONDS William Arthur MM Cpl 8218 11th Royal Fusiliers KIA 26.9.16.
SIMMONDS William C. MM Dvr T/32185 1 Div Train Army Service Corps
SIMMONDS William G. MM Cpl 31197 22 Bde RFA
SIMMONITE William Clarence MM Pte 12499 7th Yorkshire Regt KIA 10.5.17.
SIMMONS A.C. MM Cpl 32248 Tank Corps
SIMMONS Abel MM 2nd Cpl 85512 Royal Engineers
SIMMONS Albert MM Bdr 37792 3 Bde Ammn Col RHA
SIMMONS Albert F. MM Pte 41509 1st Leicestershire Regt
SIMMONS Arthur MM Cpl 9803 1st Royal Fusiliers KIA 7.6.17.
SIMMONS Arthur MM L/Cpl 202892 3rd Worcestershire Regt
SIMMONS Arthur Facer MM Cpl 3/10914 6th Northamptonshire Regt KIA 17.2.17.
SIMMONS Austin MM Pte 15172 3rd Coldstream Guards
SIMMONS Claude H. MM L/Bdr 915150 RFA
SIMMONS Emmanuel MM Spr 102828 179 Tunnelling Coy Royal Engineers
SIMMONS Frank MM L/Cpl T4/058548 33 Reserve Park Army Service Corps
SIMMONS Fred MM Cpl 203958 6th Royal West Kent Regt
SIMMONS Fred W. MM Gnr 795519 RFA
SIMMONS Frederick H. MM Pte 22471 12th Suffolk Regt
SIMMONS Frederick W. MM Pte 7802 1st Somerset Light Infantry
SIMMONS George MM Cpl 60027 101 Coy Labour Corps
SIMMONS George E. MM Pte R/19125 King's Royal Rifle Corps
SIMMONS George F. MM L/Cpl 11911 East Surrey Regt
SIMMONS Harry MM Cpl 11448 East Yorkshire Regt
SIMMONS Harry V. MM L/Cpl 1799 1/1st Warwickshire Yeomanry
SIMMONS Henry H. MM Pte 116844 42nd Bn Machine Gun Corps
SIMMONS Henry J. MM L/Cpl 53646 RAMC
SIMMONS James MM Pte DM2/228273 Army Service Corps att 7 Fd Svy Coy RE.
SIMMONS James MM Gnr 294586 25 Heavy Bty RGA Died 3.11.18.
SIMMONS Janes(sic) MM Dvr 53233 RFA
SIMMONS John MM Pte 202384 2/5th Gloucestershire Regt
SIMMONS John Benjamin MM Pte 16345 12th Royal Fusiliers
SIMMONS Reginald George MM Pte 7435 Royal West Kent Regt
SIMMONS Robert W. MM Pte 11635 Lincolnshire Regt
SIMMONS Sam MM Gnr Sig 656469 256 Bde RFA
SIMMONS Thomas H.H. MM Cpl 15326 Worcestershire Regt
SIMMONS Tom MM L/Sjt 13725 11th West Yorkshire Regt
SIMMONS Victor MM Sjt 251340 Essex Regt
SIMMONS William MM Sjt 47333 125 Bty 29 Bde RFA
SIMMONS William MM Sjt 534104 5 Foreway Coy Royal Engineers
SIMMONS William MM Pte 587 1st Arg & Suth Highlanders
SIMMONS William MM Bdr 132311 296 Siege Bty RGA
SIMMONS William MM Cpl 10437 2nd King's Royal Rifle Corps
SIMMONS William MM Gnr 33269 C/108 Bde RFA
SIMMONS William J. MM Pte 40324 Middlesex Regt
SIMMONS William Richard MM CSM 6712 1st Royal Irish Regt
SIMMS Charles E. MM Pte 48770 Liverpool Regt
SIMMS Cyril MM Pte 10970 2nd Royal Fusiliers KIA 14.10.18.
SIMMS Edwin MM Pte 39286 16th Royal Welsh Fusiliers
SIMMS George MM Pte 16700 Northumberland Fusiliers
SIMMS George A. MM L/Cpl 20709 Machine Gun Corps
SIMMS Henry MM Pte 21/332 21st West Yorkshire Regt
SIMMS John MM Pte 17/196 9th Royal Irish Rifles
SIMMS John W. MM L/Cpl 95315 4th Liverpool Regt
SIMMS Thomas MM Cpl 42523 Machine Gun Corps
SIMMS Walter MM+Bar Pte 17800 6th Wiltshire Regt
SIMMS William MM Pte 23767 Durham Light Infantry
SIMMS William Sisson MM Cpl 13405 16th Lancashire Fusiliers KIA 3.4.18.
SIMMS or SIMS Charles MM Pte 281027 1/7th Lancashire Fusiliers
SIMMS or SIMS Charles B. MM Pte M2/082005 Army Service Corps
SIMMS or SIMS Frederick MM L/Cpl 6857 1st Devonshire Regt
SIMMS or SIMS Ivor MM Pte 27816 1/1st Brecknockshire Bn South Wales Borderers
SIMNER William F. MM Pte 25765 Machine Gun Corps
SIMON Peter MM Pte 2866 8th East Surrey Regt KIA 29.2.17.

SIMON William Thomas MM Pte 28771 19th Royal Welsh Fusiliers
SIMONDS Ernest Hugh MM Pte 18018 13th Essex Regt
SIMONDS William MM Bdr 226 1(Warwickshire)Heavy Bty RGA DOW 20.4.17.
SIMONETT Edward MM Cpl 268658 1/6th Royal Highlanders
SIMONS Alfred MM Cpl 657001 2nd London Regt
SIMONS Arthur "DCM,MM" Cpl 71230 89 Coy 30th Bn Machine Gun Corps
SIMONS Edgar MM Pte 46481 13th Yorkshire Regt
SIMONS Ernest E. MM Cpl 227731 Royal Engineers
SIMONS Frank MM BQMS 19835 D/59 Bde RFA
SIMONS George MM Gnr 76057 C/93 Bde RFA KIA 1.5.18.
SIMONS George MM Sjt 19362 11th Royal Scots KIA 12.10.17.
SIMONS H.J. MM Pte 238046 12th Middlesex Regt
SIMONS John F. MM L/Cpl 21927 55 Fd Coy Royal Engineers
SIMONS Percy MM Sjt 370248 8th London Regt KIA 14.10.18.
SIMONS Percy MM Pte C/12681 21st King's Royal Rifle Corps DOW 10.10.16.
SIMONS Rowland Edward MM L/Cpl 105955 IWT Div Royal Engineers
SIMONS S. MM L/Cpl 13509 9th Essex Regt
SIMONS Vazie MM S/Sjt Fitter 740028 RFA
SIMONS William MM Sjt 13489 7th Oxf & Bucks Light Infantry
SIMPKIN Albert MM Sjt 54255 Royal Engineers
SIMPKIN Arthur H. MM Pte 18250 IX Corps Cyclist Bn Army Cyclist Corps
SIMPKIN Bertie J. "DCM,MM" Pte 2381 1/4th Suffolk Regt
SIMPKIN James MM Bdr 29816 C/91 Bde RFA
SIMPKIN John William Henry MM L/Sjt 591 10th Hussars DOW 12.4.17.
SIMPKINS Cecil MM Pte 10/583 10th East Yorkshire Regt
SIMPKINS Frank Ernest MM Spr 62320 Guards Div Sig Coy Royal Engineers
SIMPKINS H. MM S/Sjt Farrier 13253 3rd Dragoon Guards
SIMPKINS John MM Pte 2174 7th Royal West Kent Regt
SIMPKINS Sidney John MM Sjt 16871 10th North Lancashire Regt
SIMPSON A. "DCM,MM,MID" Sjt P/862 Military Foot Police
SIMPSON A.A. MM L/Cpl 321020 Suffolk Regt
SIMPSON A.J. MM Sjt 12366 Royal Irish Rifles
SIMPSON Adam MM Cpl 265858 1/6th Royal Highlanders KIA 10.4.18.
SIMPSON Alexander MM Sjt 14193 9th Welsh Regt
SIMPSON Alexander MM Pte 7954 1/3(South Midland)Fd Amb RAMC
SIMPSON Alexander MM Sjt 241172 1/5th Seaforth Highlanders DOW 23.12.17.
SIMPSON Alexander MM L/Cpl 3647 11th Arg & Suth Highlanders KIA 20.4.18.
SIMPSON Alexander C. MM Pte 12377 7th Suffolk Regt
SIMPSON Alfred Bernard MM Gnr 2727 'C' Coy Machine Gun Corps(Heavy Section)
SIMPSON Allan MM L/Cpl 4645 12th Arg & Suth Highlanders
SIMPSON Andrew MM Pte 23/1074 Northumberland Fusiliers
SIMPSON Andrew MM+Bar L/Sjt 14297 7th Cameron Highlanders
SIMPSON Andrew MM Pte 8449 1st Scottish Rifles
SIMPSON Anthony MM Pte 295053 1/5th Durham Light Infantry
SIMPSON Anthony MM Gnr 45566 RGA
SIMPSON Arthur MM L/Cpl 8502 1st Lincolnshire Regt KIA 4.10.17.
SIMPSON Arthur MM Dvr 775873 RFA
SIMPSON Arthur "MM,MID" Pte 27757 RAMC
SIMPSON Arthur MM L/Cpl 9605 2nd Notts & Derby Regt
SIMPSON Arthur MM Cpl 13634 Yorkshire Regt
SIMPSON Arthur MM Pte 22533 13th Liverpool Regt KIA 31.8.18.
SIMPSON Arthur MM L/Cpl 10890 2nd East Lancashire Regt
SIMPSON Arthur J. MM L/Cpl 235198 York & Lancaster Regt
SIMPSON Arthur T.H. MM Pnr 209604 Royal Engineers
SIMPSON Ben MM Cpl 10392 1st Notts & Derby Regt
SIMPSON Benjamin K. MM L/Cpl 267212 West Riding Regt
SIMPSON Benjamin P. MM Pte 11067 East Surrey Regt
SIMPSON Byron MM Pte 12332 7th Yorkshire Light Infantry
SIMPSON Charles MM Cpl 17156 14th Welsh Regt KIA 10.7.16.
SIMPSON Charles MM Pte 265887 1/6th Seaforth Highlanders KIA 28.7.18.
SIMPSON Charles MM Sjt 1108 1/20th London Regt
SIMPSON Charles MM Pte 72677 23rd Bn Machine Gun Corps
SIMPSON Charles Frederick William "MC,MM(13749 Cpl Shrop LI)" T/2Lt 26th Royal Welsh Fusiliers
SIMPSON Charles H. MM L/Cpl 4701 Royal West Surrey Regt
SIMPSON Charles T. MM+Bar Pte 16405 Gloucestershire Regt
SIMPSON David MM Pte 2464 8/10th Gordon Highlanders
SIMPSON David MM Pte 291495 Royal Highlanders
SIMPSON Edward F. MM Cpl 87097 204 Fd Coy Royal Engineers
SIMPSON Ernest MM L/Cpl 201338 2/4th Yorkshire Light Infantry KIA 27.3.18.
SIMPSON Ernest "DCM,MM" Cpl 6770 Machine Gun Corps
SIMPSON Ernest "DCM,MM" Sjt 17256 6th King's Own Scottish Borderers
SIMPSON Ernest Edward MM+Bar Cpl 6909 Machine Gun Corps
SIMPSON Ernest J. MM Bdr 154739 RGA
SIMPSON F.E. MM Sjt 15089 9th Leicestershire Regt
SIMPSON F.H. MM Pte 7264 16 Fd Amb RAMC
SIMPSON Francis MM Cpl 2626 12th Middlesex Regt
SIMPSON Francis F. MM L/Cpl 355510 16th Highland Light Infantry
SIMPSON Francis G.W. MM Pte 268614 2/7th Royal Warwickshire Regt
SIMPSON Francis J. MM L/Cpl 11745 Royal Berkshire Regt
SIMPSON Francis William MM S/Sjt 497253 2/3(Home Counties)Fd Amb RAMC KIA 28.10.17.
SIMPSON Fred MM Pte 21456 9th Northumberland Fusiliers
SIMPSON Frederick MM Pte 17073 1st Leicestershire Regt
SIMPSON Frederick G. MM Pte 15199 1st Grenadier Guards
SIMPSON Frederick S. MM Pte 16567 4th Grenadier Guards
SIMPSON George MM L/Cpl 32377 6th King's Own Scottish Borderers
SIMPSON George MM Pte 11368 2nd Arg & Suth Highlanders KIA 25.9.17.
SIMPSON George MM L/Cpl 40419 2nd Royal Scots Fusiliers
SIMPSON George MM Cpl 7055 16th Manchester Regt
SIMPSON George MM Sjt 10927 Leicestershire Regt
SIMPSON George MM Pte 21055 Seaforth Highlanders
SIMPSON George E. MM Cpl 406471 Royal Engineers
SIMPSON George Isaac MM+Bar Bdr 11336 152 Bde RFA
SIMPSON George J. MM Sjt 9617 Royal Highlanders
SIMPSON George W. MM Sjt 14252 East Surrey Regt
SIMPSON Gordon MM Pte 27791 Royal Scots
SIMPSON Harold MM Sjt T4/250935 62 Div Train Army Service Corps
SIMPSON Harold MM Pte 42682 9th Royal Inniskilling Fusiliers
SIMPSON Harold MM Gnr 307510 RGA
SIMPSON Harold H. MM Pte 31532 Liverpool Regt
SIMPSON Harry MM Sjt 7595 1st Leicestershire Regt
SIMPSON Harry MM Pte 9087 Scots Guards
SIMPSON Henry MM Cpl 267226 5th West Riding Regt
SIMPSON Henry MM Cpl 945670 Y/58 Med TM Bty RFA
SIMPSON Herbert Henry MM Spr 98024 1 Fd Sqn Royal Engineers
SIMPSON Horace Henry MM Pte 22688 2nd Notts & Derby Regt
SIMPSON Hugh MM Pte 15273 1st Scots Guards
SIMPSON J. MM Pte 330019 9th Highland Light Infantry
SIMPSON J. MM Cpl T/240824 Gordon Highlanders
SIMPSON J.A. MM Sjt 200269 Northumberland Fusiliers
SIMPSON Jack MM L/Cpl 9528 Coldstream Guards
SIMPSON James MM Pte 201476 1/4th Gordon Highlanders
SIMPSON James MM Pte 9541 2nd Arg & Suth Highlanders
SIMPSON James MM Gnr 776629 RFA
SIMPSON James MM Pte 17918 1/4th Gordon Highlanders DOW 15.10.18.
SIMPSON James MM Pte 27/667 24/27th Northumberland Fusiliers
SIMPSON James MM Pte 241663 2/5th West Riding Regt KIA 26.3.18.
SIMPSON James MM+Bar Sjt 201745 1/5th Arg & Suth Highlanders
SIMPSON James MM Pte 13833 2nd Scots Guards
SIMPSON James MM L/Cpl 57428 7th Lincolnshire Regt
SIMPSON James M. MM Spr 152284 Royal Engineers
SIMPSON James R. MM Bdr 960192 RFA
SIMPSON John MM Cpl 72384 C/83 Bde RFA
SIMPSON John MM Pte M2/167475 Army Service Corps
SIMPSON John MM S/Sjt Fitter 99104 RFA
SIMPSON John MM Spr 102502 176 Tunnelling Coy Royal Engineers
SIMPSON John MM Pte DM2/075500 Army Service Corps
SIMPSON John MM Pte 21825 11th South Lancashire Regt DOW 21.12.17.
SIMPSON John MM Pte 241463 Gordon Highlanders
SIMPSON John MM Gnr 148084 RGA
SIMPSON John E. MM Pte 10/361 10th East Yorkshire Regt
SIMPSON John Henry "MM,MID" L/Cpl 98179 207 Fd Coy Royal Engineers
SIMPSON John K. MM Pte 52013 5/6th Royal Scots
SIMPSON John Samuel MM Sjt 22337 17 Bty 41 Bde RFA
SIMPSON John W. MM Pte 204517 19th Durham Light Infantry

SIMPSON John W. MM Pte 12553 1st Gordon Highlanders
SIMPSON John William MM Bdr 19507 B/76 Bde RFA
SIMPSON Leonard Pleasant MM Pte 241313 2/5th York & Lancaster Regt
SIMPSON Leslie G. MM Pte 992 5th Royal Irish Regt
SIMPSON Lewis F. MM Pte 320969 Suffolk Regt
SIMPSON Matthew MM L/Cpl 346356 226 Div Empl Coy Labour Corps
SIMPSON Murray MM Pte 24594 18th Liverpool Regt KIA 1.7.16.
SIMPSON Percy MM Cpl 12319 10th West Riding Regt
SIMPSON Peter MM Dvr T3/023867 35 Div Train Army Service Corps
SIMPSON Peter C. MM Pte 38912 5/6th Royal Scots
SIMPSON R. MM Pte 12173 East Yorkshire Regt
SIMPSON Ralph MM L/Cpl 32467 15th Durham Light Infantry DOW 17.11.18.
SIMPSON Robert MM Pte 72265 Machine Gun Corps
SIMPSON Robert MM Pte 240213 1/5th Border Regt
SIMPSON Robert MM Cpl 13127 15th Highland Light Infantry
SIMPSON Robert W. MM Pte 13700 5th Dorsetshire Regt
SIMPSON Roderick MM Pte 30587 9th Bn Machine Gun Corps
SIMPSON Rowland MM Pte R/16954 9th King's Royal Rifle Corps KIA 17.10.17.
SIMPSON Samuel MM Pte 332153 Highland Light Infantry
SIMPSON Sidney MM Pte 75561 15 Fd Amb RAMC DOW 5.7.18.
SIMPSON Sidney MM L/Sjt 497 1/14th London Regt
SIMPSON Sidney J. MM Pte 24589 Yorkshire Light Infantry
SIMPSON Stephen Byres MM Pte 303146 1/2nd(Highland)Fd Amb RAMC DOW 30 7 18.
SIMPSON Thomas MM Sjt 686778 RFA
SIMPSON Thomas MM L/Cpl 306995 Royal Warwickshire Regt
SIMPSON Thomas MM Sjt 40886 Royal Scots
SIMPSON Thomas MM+Bar L/Cpl 7243 11th Northumberland Fusiliers
SIMPSON Thomas MM Pte 8456 2nd Scots Guards
SIMPSON Thomas MM Cpl 80769 RFA
SIMPSON Thomas MM Pte 34093 Highland Light Infantry
SIMPSON Thomas William MM L/Sjt 250523 1/6th Durham Light Infantry KIA 27.3.18.
SIMPSON Tom MM L/Sjt 201568 York & Lancaster Regt
SIMPSON Walter MM Sjt 75850 Royal Fusiliers
SIMPSON Walter MM+Bar Pte 10293 2nd Notts & Derby Regt
SIMPSON Walter MM Spr 161306 16 Div Sig Coy Royal Engineers
SIMPSON Walter MM Sjt 9850 Coldstream Guards
SIMPSON Walter A. MM Pte 5050 18th London Regt
SIMPSON William MM Cpl 15787 1/6th Royal Highlanders
SIMPSON William MM Pte 34629 2nd Worcestershire Regt
SIMPSON William MM L/Sjt 13054 1st Scots Guards
SIMPSON William MM Cpl 28598 B/76 Bde RFA
SIMPSON William MM Pte 6554 1st King's Own Scottish Borderers
SIMPSON William MM Pte 268258 1/6th Royal Highlanders KIA 24.10.18.
SIMPSON William "DCM,MM+Bar" Sjt 15667 Durham Light Infantry
SIMPSON William MM Sjt 34081 RFA
SIMPSON William MM L/Sjt 14996 9th Yorkshire Regt
SIMPSON William MM Gnr 107417 RFA
SIMPSON William Albert MM Pte 42011 53 Coy Machine Gun Corps
SIMPSON William G. MM Pte 681634 22nd London Regt
SIMPSON William George "DCM,MM" Pte 3727 1/6th West Yorkshire Regt
SIMPSON William H. MM Sjt 201944 4th Yorkshire Light Infantry
SIMPSON William Noel MM Pte 25215 10th West Riding Regt
SIMPSON William P. MM Cpl 90135 RAMC
SIMPSON William R. MM Bdr 40405 B/106 Bde RFA
SIMS Albert "MM,MSM" Sub Cond 3957 Army Ordnance Corps att HQ 23 Div.
SIMS Alfred MM L/Cpl 263 2nd Royal West Surrey Regt
SIMS Alfred "MM,MID" L/Cpl 4416 10th Hampshire Regt
SIMS Arthur MM Sjt 79035 180 Tunnelling Coy Royal Engineers DOW 15.11.18.
SIMS Arthur MM Pte 31594 53 Coy Labour Corps
SIMS Charles MM Pte 3540 2 Fd Amb RAMC KIA 9.9.16.
SIMS Charles MM Pte 18661 6th Yorkshire Light Infantry KIA 31.3.18.
SIMS Charles James MM 2nd Cpl 26119 Tunnelling Coy Royal Engineers
SIMS Charles Richard MM Pte 14965 13th Middlesex Regt DOW 11.8.16.
SIMS Edward T. MM L/Cpl 204988 4th Hampshire Regt
SIMS Ernest MM L/Bdr 296490 139 Siege Bty RGA
SIMS Ernest MM Pte 29203 3rd Grenadier Guards
SIMS Ewins Lawrence MM Cpl 25825 22nd Manchester Regt
SIMS Frederick MM Pte 5289 RAMC
SIMS G. MM Sjt 12628 A/87 Bde RFA
SIMS George MM Pte 137265 46th Bn Machine Gun Corps
SIMS George MM Sjt 2287 1/13th London Regt
SIMS George A. MM Cpl 6504 1st Northamptonshire Regt
SIMS Griffith William MM Cpl 16693 Royal Engineers
SIMS Henry "MM,MID" Cpl 508 Royal Engineers
SIMS Henry A. MM Dvr 22464 A/26 Bde RFA
SIMS John "DCM,MM" Sjt 9795 32nd Bn Machine Gun Corps
SIMS Joseph MM+2 Bars Pte 20/904 Northumberland Fusiliers
SIMS Reginald MM Gnr 196189 C/315 Bde RFA KIA 4.4.18.
SIMS Tom MM Cpl 14436 7th Shropshire Light Infantry
SIMS W. MM Dvr 87542 RFA
SIMS William MM Dvr 60226 14 Div Ammn Col RFA
SIMS or SIMMS Charles MM Pte 281027 1/7th Lancashire Fusiliers
SIMS or SIMMS Charles B. MM Pte M2/082005 Army Service Corps
SIMS or SIMMS Frederick MM L/Cpl 6857 1st Devonshire Regt
SIMS or SIMMS Ivor MM Pte 27816 1/1st Brecknockshire Bn South Wales Borderers
SINCLAIR Adam T. MM Sjt 11728 11th Royal Scots
SINCLAIR Albert MM L/Cpl 10218 Coldstream Guards
SINCLAIR Alexander "MM,MID" L/Sjt 19198 12th Royal Irish Rifles
SINCLAIR Alexander MM Pte 301352 Arg & Suth Highlanders
SINCLAIR Allan J.K. MM L/Cpl 1099 17th Royal Fusiliers
SINCLAIR Andrew MM L/Cpl 345409 14th Royal Highlanders
SINCLAIR Andrew MM CSM 7803 Coldstream Guards
SINCLAIR Andrew MM Cpl 16012 9th Royal Inniskilling Fusiliers DOW 13.9.18.
SINCLAIR Colin Connell "MM,MID" CQMS 265085 1/6th Royal Highlanders
SINCLAIR F.J. MM Sjt 265974 Oxf & Bucks Light Infantry
SINCLAIR Fred MM Cpl 12959 2nd King's Own Scottish Borderers
SINCLAIR G. MM L/Cpl 8593 Royal Irish Rifles
SINCLAIR George MM L/Cpl 13863 5 Fd Coy Royal Engineers
SINCLAIR George MM Spr 46197 86 Fd Coy Royal Engineers
SINCLAIR Harold "DCM,MM" Cpl 39835 55th Bn Machine Gun Corps
SINCLAIR J.F. MM L/Cpl 14488 10th Essex Regt
SINCLAIR James MM Cpl 267297 1/5th Seaforth Highlanders KIA 26.3.18.
SINCLAIR James "DCM,MM+Bar" Sjt 28207 1st Bedfordshire Regt KIA 12.11.17.
SINCLAIR James MM Sjt 241847 Seaforth Highlanders
SINCLAIR James MM Sjt 267790 1/6th Royal Highlanders
SINCLAIR James MM Pnr 444309 42 Div Sig Coy Royal Engineers DOW 25.3.18.
SINCLAIR James MM Pte 20167 Machine Gun Corps
SINCLAIR James William MM Pte 86668 238 Coy Machine Gun Corps DOW 23.10.17.
SINCLAIR John MM Sjt 45653 98 Fd Coy Royal Engineers
SINCLAIR John MM L/Cpl 16088 Northumberland Fusiliers
SINCLAIR John MM Pte 17/1027 17th West Yorkshire Regt
SINCLAIR John H. MM+Bar Sjt 831 Machine Gun Corps(Motors)
SINCLAIR John J. MM CSM 8871 Royal West Surrey Regt
SINCLAIR Mackay MM Sjt 240033 1/5th Seaforth Highlanders KIA 21.3.18.
SINCLAIR Richard "MC,MM(18646 Sjt Nbld Fus)" 2/Lt 9th West Riding Regt
SINCLAIR Robert "MM,MID" Spr 65492 136 Army Troops Coy Royal Engineers
SINCLAIR Ronald MM Sjt 240838 Yorkshire Regt
SINCLAIR St.Clair MM Pte 242394 1/5th Seaforth Highlanders
SINCLAIR Thomas MM Pte 3404 2nd Arg & Suth Highlanders
SINCLAIR W.H. MM L/Bdr 196870 A/162 Bde RFA
SINCLAIR William MM L/Cpl 22571 Highland Light Infantry
SINCLAIR William M. MM Pte 250082 1/6th Durham Light Infantry
SINCUP Arthur Gerald MM L/Cpl 46592 4th North Staffordshire Regt
SINDEN Edward F. MM Bdr 39878 RFA
SINDEN Frederick MM Pte 220781 5th Royal Berkshire Regt
SINDEN George MM Cpl 8891 East Kent Regt
SINDREY Albert V. MM Pte 241579 Gloucestershire Regt
SINFIELD Horace MM L/Cpl 233567 2nd London Regt
SINFIELD Reginald MM Gnr 42800 5 Bde RHA
SINGER Frederick MM Sjt 30112 RGA
SINGER Herbert M. MM Sjt 20688 1st Royal West Kent Regt
SINGER W. MM Pte 15395 1st Essex Regt
SINGLE Ellis M. MM Pte 737 Royal Sussex Regt

SINGLETON Albert MM Spr 121773 185 Tunnelling Coy (sic) Royal Engineers
SINGLETON Fred MM Gnr 198842 RFA
SINGLETON Frederick MM Pte 82363 10th Royal Fusiliers
SINGLETON George MM Pte 53576 8th Middlesex Regt
SINGLETON George MM Sjt 9620 Coldstream Guards
SINGLETON George Tilbury MM Gnr 13831 'Q' Bty RHA DOW 5.4.18.
SINGLETON H. MM Pte 42976 Labour Corps
SINGLETON Hartley MM Pte 27434 8th Border Regt
SINGLETON J. MM Sjt 204019 Lancashire Fusiliers
SINGLETON John MM L/Cpl 26941 2nd Royal Dublin Fusiliers
SINGLETON John H. MM Pte 240643 East Lancashire Regt
SINGLETON Lawrence William MM Pte 723438 24th London Regt
SINGLETON Sidney R. MM L/Cpl 99398 29th Bn Machine Gun Corps
SINGLETON Thomas R. MM+Bar Pte 341771 RAMC
SINGLETON W.H.E. MM Cpl R/4556 King's Royal Rifle Corps
SINGLETON William "DCM,MM,CG(F)" Cpl 10/1134 10th East Yorkshire Regt
SINGLETON William MM Bdr 37569 RFA
SINKINSON S. MM Pte 47321 6th West Riding Regt
SINNICK Aubrey W. MM Pte 17230 17th Royal Fusiliers
SINNICK William G. MM Pte 200943 1st Dorsetshire Regt
SINNOCK Frederick J. MM L/Cpl 2780 2nd Life Guards
SINNOTT T. MM Dvr 112535 RFA
SINNOTT Thomas MM Pte 21304 Royal Irish Fusiliers
SINTON Frederick MM Spr 36640 Royal Engineers
SINTON William MM Sjt 2134 Border Regt KIA 30.11.17.
SIPPETT Albert MM Bdr 47211 RFA
SIRETT Albert J. MM Pte 205605 5th York & Lancaster Regt
SIRETT Joseph MM Pte 8066 1st Lincolnshire Regt
SIRMAN Frederick J. MM Gnr 52964 RFA
SIRRETT Frank W. MM L/Cpl 19717 Middlesex Regt
SISSON Albert MM Cpl 121776 253 Tunnelling Coy Royal Engineers
SISSON Arthur MM Gnr 42415 C/178 Bde RFA
SISSONS Arthur William MM Sjt 9437 1st Liverpool Regt KIA 21.3.18.
SISSONS Frederick W. MM Pte 201966 York & Lancaster Regt
SISSONS James Robert MM Pte 39279 9th Yorkshire Regt DOW 10.10.18.
SITCH Victor "DCM,MM" Cpl 43130 1/8th & 2nd Arg & Suth Highlanders
SITCH William George MM Pte 375953 8th London Regt KIA 14.10.18.
SIVELL Edward James MM Pte 48299 54th Bn Machine Gun Corps
SIVELL George W. MM Sjt 7992 2nd West Riding Regt
SIVEWRIGHT William MM Pte 200242 1/4th Gordon Highlanders
SIVEYER Edwin A. MM Pte 846 16th Middlesex Regt
SIVIER Edward MM Sjt 15674 5th Royal Berkshire Regt
SIVIER Walter F. MM Bdr 68958 5 Bde RFA
SIVITER Edwin MM Pte 16652 9th Royal Welsh Fusiliers
SIVITER Eli MM Pte 8914 1st Worcestershire Regt
SIVYER C.W. MM Pte 1538 Royal West Kent Regt
SIVYER Herbert G. MM Cpl 2946 9th Royal Sussex Regt
SIXSMITH Bertie MM Pte 22254 5th Northamptonshire Regt
SIXSMITH Fred MM Sjt 16631 8th East Lancashire Regt
SIXSMITH George H. MM Cpl 83184 Royal Engineers
SIZER Edwin MM Sjt 8690 1st Lincolnshire Regt
SIZER Frederick MM Pte 11/224 7th East Yorkshire Regt
SKAE John W. MM Pte M2/079768 Army Service Corps
SKAE or SKEA John F. MM+Bar Pte 10108 Royal Highlanders
SKAKLE George MM Sjt 9309 11th Royal Scots KIA 3.5.17.
SKANTLEBURY James MM Pte 21145 1st Cameron Highlanders
SKEA or SKAE John F. MM+Bar Pte 10108 Royal Highlanders
SKEAT Sydney MM Pte 102518 19 Fd Amb RAMC
SKEATE Thomas Arthur MM Cpl 551861 16th London Regt
SKEAVINGTON Arthur MM L/Cpl 40912 East Yorkshire Regt
SKED James MM Dvr 92330 Royal Engineers
SKED William MM L/Cpl 325140 1/8th Royal Scots
SKEELES Walter Richard MM Bdr 58845 RGA
SKEELS Arthur W. MM Pte 19367 4th Bedfordshire Regt
SKEELS Ernest MM L/Cpl 34755 Essex Regt
SKEELS George W. MM Pte 3702 1/1st Cambridgeshire Regt
SKEELS H. MM Cpl 10677 Middlesex Regt
SKEER George MM Sjt 280539 222 Siege Bty RGA DOW 21.3.18.
SKEET George Victor MM Pte 12732 10th Royal West Surrey Regt KIA 18.8.17.
SKEGG Charles MM L/Sjt 14306 6th Royal Dublin Fusiliers

SKEGGS Alfred "MM,MID" Sjt 14981 11th Essex Regt
SKEGGS Joseph MM Pte 7061 2nd Royal Scots
SKEGGS Thomas W. MM Pte 7612 Middlesex Regt
SKELCHER Ernest F. MM Sjt 10994 5th Oxf & Bucks Light Infantry
SKELDING Charles Samuel MM Cpl 2664 2/7th Worcestershire Regt
SKELDON John MM 2nd Cpl 98765 Royal Engineers
SKELDON Patrick MM L/Sjt 7846 Irish Guards
SKELHORN John MM Pte 6951 11th Lancashire Fusiliers KIA 22.1.17.
SKELHORN Thomas MM L/Sjt 19937 12th Liverpool Regt KIA 7.8.16.
SKELHORNE Peter MM Sjt 12615 8th Bedfordshire Regt
SKELLAM James "MM,CG(F)" L/Cpl 20187 1st York & Lancaster Regt
SKELLEY John C. MM Pte 143973 33rd Bn Machine Gun Corps
SKELLEY William H. MM Cpl 4985 Army Cyclist Corps
SKELLY Edward MM+2 Bars Sjt 11675 2nd Royal Irish Regt
SKELLY John MM Pte 21288 Manchester Regt
SKELLY John Alexander Augustus MM Cpl 60979 'Z' Special Coy Royal Engineers
SKELLY John C. MM CQMS 41013 Middlesex Regt
SKELLY William MM Pte 5322 1st Royal Welsh Fusiliers DOW 15.11.18.
SKELSEY George MM Sjt 8721 4th Middlesex Regt
SKELSEY John MM Pte 3447 2 Fd Amb RAMC
SKELSEY John J. MM L/Sjt 10744 1st Middlesex Regt
SKELTON Albert MM Sjt 9075 4th Liverpool Regt KIA 28.10.16.
SKELTON Alfred MM L/Cpl C/983 16th King's Royal Rifle Corps
SKELTON Arthur MM L/Cpl 3423 1st Royal West Surrey Regt
SKELTON Bertie MM Pte S/13138 13th Rifle Brigade
SKELTON Charles A. MM Pte 306350 Notts & Derby Regt
SKELTON Edmund MM L/Cpl 8216 2nd Yorkshire Regt KIA 25.9.15.
SKELTON Ernest A. MM Sjt 71710 RGA
SKELTON F. MM+Bar Pte 13607 Gordon Highlanders
SKELTON Frederick MM Pte 220162 8th Royal Berkshire Regt
SKELTON George MM Sjt 305330 1/8th Notts & Derby Regt
SKELTON Henry G. "MM,MSM,MID" Sjt 2386 6th Royal West Surrey Regt
SKELTON Joseph William Francis MM Cpl 12618 7th Norfolk Regt
SKELTON Mark MM Pte 9793 2nd York & Lancaster Regt
SKELTON Robert B. MM Pte 40929 2nd South Wales Borderers
SKELTON Thomas MM L/Cpl 20708 Yorkshire Regt
SKELTON Thomas A. MM Cpl 21362 7th Royal West Kent Regt
SKELTON Walter MM L/Cpl 493784 1/13th London Regt KIA 9.8.18.
SKELTON Walter Joseph MM Dvr 951400 A/15 Bde RFA
SKELTON William MM Pte 12931 Northamptonshire Regt
SKELTON William MM+Bar Cpl 63852 RFA
SKELTON William C. MM Pte 5949 2nd Royal West Kent Regt
SKELTON William R. MM Sjt 1503 4th Royal Fusiliers
SKENE Charles MM Cpl 645607 RFA
SKENE George O. MM Cpl 347407 RGA
SKENE William MM L/Cpl 27396 2nd King's Own Scottish Borderers
SKENNERTON Thomas MM Pte 24898 3rd Grenadier Guards
SKEOCH Alexander MM Pte 295233 12th Royal Scots Fusiliers
SKERMER Harry MM Sjt 265582 Cheshire Regt
SKERRY John Nicholson MM Sjt 12654 7th Border Regt
SKERRY Phillip MM Pte 3852 8th Royal West Kent Regt
SKEVINGTON Alfred MM 2nd Cpl 34805 Royal Engineers
SKEVINGTON Arthur MM Pte 9341 22 Fd Amb RAMC
SKIDMORE Harry MM Pte 9385 1st South Staffordshire Regt
SKIDMORE James MM Cpl R/6964 8th King's Royal Rifle Corps
SKIDMORE John MM L/Cpl 30594 South Staffordshire Regt
SKIDMORE Joseph MM Gnr 85083 D/83 Bde RFA
SKIDMORE Joseph MM Pte 14023 8th York & Lancaster Regt
SKIDMORE Lewis MM Gnr 24375 D/23 Bde RFA
SKIDMORE Parker MM Pte 24745 6th Royal West Kent Regt
SKILBECK Edward MM Wheeler T2/SR/02878 Army Service Corps
SKILBECK Herbert MM Pte M2/203830 Army Service Corps att 14 LAMB MGC.KIA Iraq 26.5.19.
SKILBECK James A. MM Cpl 463300 3 Div Sig Coy Royal Engineers
SKILLICORN James H. MM Pte 12920 Coldstream Guards
SKILLICORN William MM Sjt 240072 1/5th Cheshire Regt
SKILLIN Robert MM Pte 130031 Royal Engineers
SKILLING James MM Pte 12163 6/7th Royal Scots Fusiliers
SKILLINGS Charles E.W. MM S/Sjt Farrier 34755 18 Bty 3 Bde RFA
SKILTON Ernest MM Sjt 947953 56 Div Ammn Col RFA
SKILTON Jesse Frederick MM+Bar Sjt 680705 1/22nd London Regt
SKINGLE Ernest Heritage MM Pte 241300 2/6th Notts & Derby Regt

SKINNER Abel MM Sjt 13895 11th West Yorkshire Regt
SKINNER Alec Septimus MM Spr 40678 70 Fd Coy Royal Engineers
SKINNER Alfred MM Cpl 11342 6th East Lancashire Regt
SKINNER Andrew MM Pte 202644 2nd King's Own Scottish Borderers
SKINNER Arthur MM Pte 11221 11th Hampshire Regt
SKINNER Arthur F. MM Pte 7496 2 Fd Amb RAMC
SKINNER Atkinson MM Sjt 10725 2nd Yorkshire Light Infantry KIA 18.11.16.
SKINNER Charles W. "MM,MID" Cpl 1605 9th East Surrey Regt
SKINNER Dominic Logan MM Sjt 93036 C/58 Bde RFA
SKINNER Edward G. MM Pte 10743 Royal West Surrey Regt
SKINNER Ernest MM Pte 242441 1/8th Worcestershire Regt
SKINNER Frank C. MM Cpl 533421 16th London Regt
SKINNER Frederick C. MM L/Cpl 28560 2nd Royal Dublin Fusiliers
SKINNER G. MM Sjt 31507 Hampshire Regt
SKINNER George "MM,MID" CSM 9802 6th Royal Berkshire Regt
SKINNER George MM L/Cpl 50852 Machine Gun Corps(Cavalry)
SKINNER George MM Sjt 2270 8th Royal West Surrey Regt
SKINNER George MM Pte 7754 Royal West Surrey Regt
SKINNER George A. MM Sjt 8530 11th Royal West Kent Regt
SKINNER George William MM Dvr 72933 111 Bty 24 Bde RFA DOW 22.3.18.
SKINNER Henry Edward MM 2nd Cpl 209936 2 Lt Rly Op Coy Royal Engineers
SKINNER Henry G. MM Pte DM2/168455 Army Service Corps
SKINNER Herbert H. "DCM,MM" Sjt 46785 81 Bty 5 Bde RFA
SKINNER John MM Cpl 18687 13th Northumberland Fusiliers
SKINNER Percival G. MM+Bar L/Bdr 187047 RGA
SKINNER Percy James MM Pte M2/032984 36 MAC Army Service Corps
SKINNER Percy Winn MM Sjt 22082 'J' Cable Section Royal Engineers
SKINNER Ralph MM L/Cpl 22956 7th Seaforth Highlanders
SKINNER Robert Charles "MM+Bar,CG(F)" L/Cpl 16676 11th Essex Regt
SKINNER Robert E. MM Sjt 2004 8th Royal Sussex Regt
SKINNER Thomas J. MM Cpl 260369 10th Royal Warwickshire Regt
SKINNER W. MM Pte 332789 Highland Light Infantry
SKINNER William MM Pte 315348 1/5th Devonshire Regt
SKINNER William "MM,MSM" BSM 600003 RHA att 4 Bty RFA.
SKINNER William A.C. MM Pte 40455 Royal Scots
SKINNER William H. MM Cpl 34150 Royal Welsh Fusiliers
SKINNER William Hugh MM L/Cpl 242209 1st Northumberland Fusiliers DOW 19.12.17.
SKINNS William MM Pte 9996 Lincolnshire Regt
SKIPP Alfred MM Pte 130406 56th Bn Machine Gun Corps
SKIPP Charles V. MM L/Cpl 65866 Machine Gun Corps
SKIPP James W. MM Sjt 13602 4th Middlesex Regt
SKIPP John Thomas MM Spr 77234 Signal Service Royal Engineers
SKIPP Robert MM L/Cpl 10447 1st Bedfordshire Regt
SKIPP Thomas G. MM Spr 156524 179 Tunnelling Coy Royal Engineers
SKIPPEN G.A. "DCM,MM" L/Cpl 12177 9th Essex Regt
SKIPPER Bertie William MM Sjt 21751 13 Bde RFA
SKIPPER Harry J. "MM,MID" L/Cpl 8562 11th Hussars
SKIPPER Sinclair MM+Bar Cpl 267194 2/5th Gloucestershire Regt
SKIPSEY James MM Pte 341281 1st Northumberland Fusiliers
SKIPWORTH Henry MM Dvr 89736 RFA
SKIPWORTH Victor Harry MM Sjt 7331 1st Northumberland Fusiliers
SKIRROW Ronald MM Cpl 249483 9 Div Sig Coy Royal Engineers
SKITMORE Harry J. MM L/Cpl 66455 Royal Engineers
SKITT Richard W. MM L/Cpl 3058 1/9th Royal Scots
SKITT Robert MM Cpl 37895 12th Manchester Regt
SKITTER Wilfred A. MM Pte 320388 6th London Regt
SKITTERAL Benjamin Thomas "DCM,MM" Sjt G/11310 11th Royal West Surrey Regt KIA 10.8.18.
SKOINS Albert MM Sjt 121872 173 Tunnelling Coy Royal Engineers
SKOULDING William Charles MM L/Cpl 19593 10th Scottish Rifles KIA 26.4.17.
SKOYLES Charles MM+Bar Gnr 14582 5 Siege Bty RGA
SKOYLES Stephen W. MM Sjt 92423 Notts & Derby Regt
SKUCE Albert MM Sjt 3741 2nd Royal Munster Fusiliers KIA 21.3.18.
SKUSE Frederick A. MM Cpl 265039 1/6th Cheshire Regt
SKUSE James MM Sjt 81661 RFA
SKUSE Sidney J. MM Pte 21332 2nd Wiltshire Regt

SKYRME Hugh Evan MM L/Cpl 63863 Royal Engineers
SKYRME W.E. MM Pte 50785 Labour Corps
SLACK Arthur Frederick William MM Dvr T/27550 Army Service Corps att 6 Cav Fd Amb RAMC.
SLACK Benjamin MM Sjt 36275 B/97 Bde RFA
SLACK Charles MM Pte 49584 1st Lincolnshire Regt
SLACK Charles MM Cpl 387593 Royal Engineers
SLACK Charles "DCM,MM+Bar" Pte 11366 10th Notts & Derby Regt
SLACK Frederick E. MM Pte 26979 8th Somerset Light Infantry
SLACK George W. MM Cpl 21179 132 Siege Bty RGA
SLACK James MM L/Cpl 203197 1/9th Durham Light Infantry
SLACK John MM L/Cpl 361815 Signal Service Royal Engineers
SLACK John George MM Pte 240014 1/5th York & Lancaster Regt
SLACK John Spencer MM Gnr 10159 D/74 Bde RFA KIA 3.10.18.
SLACK Thomas MM Pte 16195 11th Notts & Derby Regt KIA 29.6.18.
SLACK Thomas Petty MM Gnr 543 D/156 Bde RFA
SLADDIN Frederick MM Pte M2/082612 30 Mot Amb Convoy Army Service Corps
SLADDIN Robert MM L/Cpl 18074 2nd Lancashire Fusiliers
SLADE Albert A. MM Cpl 512031 85 Fd Amb RAMC
SLADE Albert Edward MM Sjt 6292 5/6th Scottish Rifles
SLADE Albert W. MM Pte 33229 North Lancashire Regt
SLADE Benjamin MM Sjt 10889 1st B Coy Royal Fusiliers KIA 14.1.17.
SLADE Cecil Herbert MM L/Cpl 2038 1/6th Seaforth Highlanders
SLADE F.J. MM Bdr 72474 RFA
SLADE Frederick MM Pte 14903 South Wales Borderers
SLADE George Ernest MM Spr 69118 35 Div Sig Coy Royal Engineers
SLADE George F. MM L/Cpl 10109 Royal Highlanders
SLADE Henry W. MM L/Sjt 6730 Coldstream Guards
SLADE Herbert Henry MM L/Cpl 11123 1st Wiltshire Regt DOW 30.10.16.
SLADE James MM L/Cpl 457324 RAMC
SLADE John W. MM Gnr 697039 X/55 Med TM Bty RFA
SLADE John William MM Pte 51469 16th Lancashire Fusiliers DOW 5.11.18.
SLADE Joseph MM L/Cpl 304339 5th London Regt
SLADE Leonard Charles MM L/Cpl 9442 10th Royal West Kent Regt
SLADE S.W. MM Pte 222163 Labour Corps
SLADE William MM Pte 1073 9th Lancers
SLADE William C. MM Sjt 128063 196 Coy Labour Corps
SLADE William E. MM Pte 12476 7th South Lancashire Regt
SLADER Alfred J. MM Pte 110550 MGC(Cavalry)
SLADER Frederick W. MM Sjt 242432 8th Worcestershire Regt
SLAMON Patrick MM Cpl 18505 17th Lancashire Fusiliers DOW 26.3.18.
SLANE William MM Dvr 170916 C/75 Bde RFA
SLANEY Arthur MM Spr 175445 257 Tunnelling Coy Royal Engineers
SLANEY Charles MM Cpl 34312 18 Div Ammn Col RFA
SLANN Thomas A. MM Spr 45440 1 Div Sig Coy Royal Engineers
SLARK George MM Sjt 200912 Royal Berkshire Regt
SLATER Albert MM Pte Y/938 16th King's Royal Rifle Corps
SLATER Albert MM L/Cpl T4/069684 Army Service Corps
SLATER Alfred MM Pte 12302 1st Worcestershire Regt
SLATER Bernard MM Dvr 796665 B/312 Bde RFA
SLATER Burnett MM Dvr 5847 RFA
SLATER Charles MM Bdr 32324 RFA
SLATER Charles MM Pte 201082 Durham Light Infantry
SLATER David MM Pte 325089 1/9th Durham Light Infantry
SLATER David A. MM L/Cpl 241834 1/6th South Staffordshire Regt
SLATER Edgar MM L/Cpl 8010 1st Leicestershire Regt
SLATER Edwin MM Pte 22754 11th Royal Scots
SLATER Frank MM Pte 56568 74 Coy Machine Gun Corps Real name Charles Frank MILLER.DOW 27.10.18.
SLATER Fred MM Gnr 776440 D/310 Bde RFA
SLATER Fred H. MM Sjt 401330 1 Fd Amb RAMC
SLATER Frederick MM Pte 240732 2/4th York & Lancaster Regt
SLATER George MM Cpl 12272 6/7th Royal Scots Fusiliers
SLATER George MM Pte 201084 2/4th York & Lancaster Regt
SLATER George MM Pte 15461 3rd Coldstream Guards Died 13.4.18.
SLATER George MM Gnr 63837 RFA
SLATER George A. "DCM,MM" Sjt 7170 2nd Border Regt
SLATER Harold MM Pte 241679 4th York & Lancaster Regt
SLATER Harold MM Pte 10210 2nd South Wales Borderers
SLATER Harold MM L/Cpl 29387 West Yorkshire Regt
SLATER Harry MM L/Cpl 305223 8th West Yorkshire Regt

SLATER Harry MM Pte 201318 Shropshire Light Infantry
SLATER Harry MM Pte 235092 2/5th West Riding Regt DOW 27.3.18.
SLATER Harry MM Sjt 7442 2nd Worcestershire Regt
SLATER J.H. MM Pte 3620 Lincolnshire Regt
SLATER Jack MM Pte 22396 2/4th South Lancashire Regt
SLATER James MM Cpl 488028 466 Sig Section Royal Engineers
SLATER James MM Gnr 56359 B/105 Bde RFA KIA 15.4.16.
SLATER James MM Pte 420425 10th London Regt
SLATER James MM Spr 93774 41 Div Sig Coy Royal Engineers
SLATER John MM Cpl 34245 7 Fd Amb RAMC
SLATER John MM Pte 236206 2nd East Lancashire Regt
SLATER John H. MM Pte 4937 2nd Border Regt
SLATER John H.A.G. "MM,MID" Sjt 8388 4th Hussars
SLATER John R. MM Bdr 12974 Y/25 Med TM Bty RFA
SLATER John R. MM L/Sjt 12798 1st Bedfordshire Regt
SLATER Joseph "MM,MSM" Sjt 20662 121 Hy Bty RGA
SLATER Leonard MM Pte 201882 1/7th Middlesex Regt
SLATER Obadiah R. MM L/Cpl 28/501 Northumberland Fusiliers
SLATER Richard J. MM L/Cpl 4376 24th Royal Fusiliers
SLATER Samuel MM Pte 22996 1/8th Notts & Derby Regt
SLATER Sydney MM Cpl 201007 1/8th Notts & Derby Regt
SLATER T. MM Pte 18968 Yorkshire Light Infantry
SLATER Thomas MM Dvr 715900 37 Bty 27 Bde RFA
SLATER Thomas MM Dvr 107537 RFA
SLATER Thomas E. MM Gnr 750190 RFA
SLATER Thomas R. MM Pte 22134 1st Grenadier Guards
SLATER Tom MM Pte 18917 7th Yorkshire Light Infantry KIA 30.6.16.
SLATER W.T. MM Pte 18536 2nd Royal Irish Regt
SLATER William MM Sjt 250554 1/6th Arg & Suth Highlanders
SLATER William MM(R/11279 KRRC)+Bar Cpl 92999 2nd London Regt
SLATER William "MM,MID" Bdr 76326 RFA
SLATTER Arthur C.W. MM Sjt 20638 Machine Gun Corps
SLATTER Frederick G. MM L/Cpl 9081 1st Royal Fusiliers
SLATTER George William MM Pte 7302 10th Royal Warwickshire Regt
SLATTER Percy MM Pte 5309 18th London Regt
SLATTER Sidney G. MM Pte 200661 1/4th Royal Berkshire Regt
SLATTER William A. MM Pte 202136 Oxf & Bucks Light Infantry
SLATTERY Daniel MM Gnr 73017 40 Bde RFA
SLATTERY Daniel MM Pte 12664 2nd Royal Scots Fusiliers
SLATTERY James H. MM+Bar Cpl 6599 5th Lancers
SLATTERY John F. MM 2nd Cpl 312900 Royal Engineers
SLATTERY Patrick MM Pte 6701 1st Irish Guards
SLAUGHTER Arthur W. MM Pte 2047 1/9th London Regt
SLAUGHTER Charles MM L/Cpl M2/019853 Army Service Corps
SLAUGHTER Francis J. MM Cpl 31607 C/119 Bde RFA
SLAUGHTER Frederick MM Pte 1727 7th Royal Sussex Regt
SLAUGHTER George MM Sjt 55744 16th Royal Welsh Fusiliers
SLAUGHTER Herbert S. MM Sjt 2933 4th Dragoon Guards
SLAUGHTER Horace A. MM Pte 204559 2nd London Regt
SLAUGHTER Richard A. MM Bdr 63509 RGA
SLAUGHTER William MM L/Cpl 56783 Machine Gun Corps(Cavalry)
SLAVEN Anthony MM Bdr 26666 A/86 Bde RFA
SLAVEN J. MM Pte 20617 1/5th Arg & Suth Highlanders
SLAVEN James MM Spr 424078 50 Div Sig Coy Royal Engineers DOW 12.4.18.
SLAVEN John MM Cpl 12078 6th King's Own Scottish Borderers
SLAVEN Patrick MM Pte 291104 1/8th Scottish Rifles
SLAVIN Daniel MM Dvr 60188 421 Bty RFA
SLAYMAKER Thomas George MM Pte 1224 1/5th Leicestershire Regt
SLEAP Henry A. MM Bdr 960913 C/251 Bde RFA
SLEATER George MM Pte 26179 7th Royal Irish Regt
SLEATH Albert MM Sjt 11674 Leicestershire Regt
SLEATH Victor Allen MM Cpl 810055 RFA
SLEDGE Arthur "DCM,MM" Sjt 18483 13th Durham Light Infantry
SLEDMAR George MM Dvr 26510 16 Bty 41 Bde RFA
SLEE C.H. MM Pte 59455 4th Liverpool Regt
SLEE Henry J. MM Pte 266371 Welsh Regt
SLEE John MM L/Cpl 24645 8th Border Regt DOW 23.3.18.
SLEEMAN Ralph MM Pte 16855 7th North Staffordshire Regt
SLEET Alfred M. MM Sjt 7415 2nd Northamptonshire Regt
SLEETH Thomas MM Sjt 7244 2nd Highland Light Infantry
SLEIGH Henry J. MM L/Cpl 2973 1/17th London Regt
SLEIGHT Albert "DCM,MM" Sjt 8485 6th Lincolnshire Regt
SLEIGHTHOLM Arthur MM L/Cpl 263112 4th Yorkshire Light Infantry
SLEIGHTHOLME Alfred Percival MM Sjt C/12136 21st King's Royal Rifle Corps KIA 5.8.17.
SLEIGHTHOLME James MM Pte 241698 Liverpool Regt
SLESSER Alexander K. MM Pte 203194 Seaforth Highlanders
SLIDDERS James MM Gnr 104305 336 Bty 117 Bde RFA DOW 27.9.18.
SLIDDERS John McK. MM Gnr 217666 B/124 Bde RFA
SLIDDERS William MM Cpl 759 RFA
SLIM Reginald MM Bdr 825290 B/223 Bde RFA
SLIMAN John MM L/Sjt 25440 7th Border Regt
SLIMM James MM L/Cpl 1501 Royal Warwickshire Regt
SLIMMING Alexander MM Gnr 133749 RFA
SLIMMON David MM Spr 7544 Royal Engineers
SLINGSBY Frederick N. MM F/Sjt 1145 Royal Flying Corps
SLINGSBY George MM Cpl 99636 Royal Engineers
SLINGSBY Percy MM Sjt 202470 4th York & Lancaster Regt
SLINN Harold MM Pte 17847 8th Northumberland Fusiliers
SLINN Reginald T. MM L/Bdr 626088 HAC(Artillery) att 309 Siege Bty RGA
SLOAN Edward MM Pte 19827 10th York & Lancaster Regt
SLOAN Francis N. MM Pte 266295 11th Royal Scots Fusiliers
SLOAN Frank MM Pte 34463 Royal Scots
SLOAN George MM Pte 88012 13th Liverpool Regt
SLOAN Henry T. MM+Bar L/Cpl 12357 Yorkshire Regt
SLOAN James MM Sjt 3851 8th Royal Highlanders DOW 1.2.17.
SLOAN John MM Pte 17677 1st Gordon Highlanders
SLOAN Robert MM Gnr 675156 RFA
SLOAN Robert MM Pte 238015 5/6th Scottish Rifles
SLOAN Samuel MM L/Cpl 54711 RAMC
SLOAN Thomas J. MM Pte 17/1311 17th Royal Irish Rifles
SLOANE Edward MM L/Cpl 10268 4th Hussars KIA 23.3.18.
SLOANE Frederick MM Pte 17790 8th East Lancashire Regt
SLOANE George MM Pte 363 Royal Sussex Regt
SLOANE Herbert MM Pte 18305 10th West Riding Regt
SLOANE James MM Pte 22726 9th Royal Irish Fusiliers KIA 16.8.17.
SLOCOMBE Harry MM 2nd Cpl 6364 Royal Engineers
SLOCOMBE Richard MM Bdr 9747 B/71 Bde RFA
SLOCOMBE William Arthur MM Pte 202864 Oxf & Bucks Light Infantry
SLODDEN John Frederick MM Sjt 558354 Royal Engineers
SLOMAN George MM Pte 43050 Welsh Regt
SLOMAN James H. MM Cpl 70158 Royal Welsh Fusiliers
SLOPER Albert E. MM Cpl 201069 Oxf & Bucks Light Infantry
SLOPER Arthur L. MM Sjt 233 10th Royal Fusiliers
SLOPER Frederick G. MM Sjt 1041 7th Royal Sussex Regt
SLOSS William MM Sjt 3013 1/10th Liverpool Regt
SLOUGH John MM Pte 23008 Bedfordshire Regt
SLOUGH Leonard H. MM Pte 25903 1/5th Bedfordshire Regt
SLOUGH Thomas William MM Sjt 538003 6 Fd Amb RAMC
SLOWE Arthur MM L/Cpl M1/5849 Army Service Corps
SLOWE E. MM Pte 300131 Manchester Regt
SLOWE John B. MM Gnr 47064 RFA
SLOWEY Robert J. MM Pte 13688 17th Highland Light Infantry
SLUDDEN Edward A. MM Cpl 26344 2nd Seaforth Highlanders
SLUGGETT Samuel MM Cpl 15231 10th Devonshire Regt
SLY George W. MM Pte 6479 16th Lancers
SLY Harold Frederick MM L/Cpl 765050 28th London Regt
SLY Nelson John MM Pte 13998 2nd Wiltshire Regt
SLYFIELD Charles MM Cpl 11666 10th West Yorkshire Regt
SLYFIELD Robert MM Pte 10518 Royal Berkshire Regt
SLYMAN George MM Gnr 88796 RFA
SLYTH Frederick E. MM Cpl 58996 29 Bde RFA
SMAILES John Thomas MM L/Cpl 37210 Northumberland Fusiliers
SMALE Alfred MM Pte 632583 252 Coy Labour Corps
SMALE Gilbert C. MM Cpl 311330 Royal Engineers
SMALE John MM Pte 30813 2nd Devonshire Regt KIA 16.8.17.
SMALE Richard MM Sjt 266483 6th West Riding Regt
SMALE William G. MM Pte DM2/166096 717 Coy Army Service Corps
SMALES George MM+Bar Sjt 47905 C/84 Bde RFA
SMALES Graham MM Sjt 18169 2nd King's Own Scottish Borderers
SMALES Robert MM Pte 88167 Liverpool Regt
SMALES S. MM L/Cpl 417446 1(North Midland)Fd Amb RAMC
SMALES William MM+Bar Pte 266932 West Riding Regt
SMALL Albert E. MM L/Cpl 301043 1/5th London Regt
SMALL Alexander MM Pte 4594 15th London Regt
SMALL Alfred T. MM L/Cpl 13547 13th Liverpool Regt
SMALL Arthur Cecil MM Sjt 200996 6th Leicestershire Regt
SMALL Cecil F. MM Pte M2/119947 Army Service Corps

SMALL Charles MM Pte 25182 Machine Gun Corps
SMALL David MM Bdr 38320 38 Bde RFA
SMALL David Bruce MM Sjt 275961 5/6th Royal Scots DOW 8.4.18.
SMALL F. MM Pte 13039 9th Essex Regt
SMALL Frank Gilbert Hurrell MM Sjt 3021 1/23rd London Regt
SMALL George R. MM Pte 9957 Arg & Suth Highlanders
SMALL Henry MM Pte 201213 1st London Regt
SMALL James A. MM Cpl 371503 1/8th London Regt
SMALL James Summer MM Cpl 7819 Labour Corps
SMALL John MM Sjt 290755 Royal Highlanders
SMALL John MM Pte 19622 South Wales Borderers
SMALL Joseph MM Pte 242346 York & Lancaster Regt
SMALL Percival MM Bdr 62032 39 Bde RFA
SMALL Ralph Theodore MM Pte 48562 13th Liverpool Regt KIA 1.9.18.
SMALL Robert Frederick Jones MM Sjt 12824 7th Cameron Highlanders
SMALL Samuel MM Gnr 95206 12 Heavy Bty RGA
SMALL Samuel P. MM Sjt 22863 Royal Engineers
SMALL Sidney H. MM S/8185 Rifle Brigade
SMALL Thomas M. "MM,MID" Pte 9056 1st Royal Munster Fusiliers
SMALL Wallace MM L/Sjt 1583 2nd Rifle Brigade
SMALL Wallace H. MM Sjt 61797 Royal Engineers
SMALL Wilfred J. MM Pte 304667 15th Bn Tank Corps
SMALL William MM L/Sjt 17399 1st Gordon Highlanders
SMALL William MM Cpl 320682 24th Welsh Regt
SMALLBONE Alfred S. MM Pte 20362 11th Essex Regt
SMALLBONES Charles George MM Sjt S/625 7th Royal West Surrey Regt KIA 1.7.16.
SMALLCOMBE William A. MM L/Cpl 15066 12th Gloucestershire Regt
SMALLEY Albert MM Cpl 21019 1 Bty 45 Bde RFA KIA 1.7.16.
SMALLEY Ernest MM Pte 240638 5th Lincolnshire Regt
SMALLEY Ezra James MM L/Cpl 44505 1/6th Liverpool Regt att MGC. KIA 26.9.18.
SMALLEY John MM Spr 79752 176 Tunnelling Coy Royal Engineers
SMALLEY Joseph MM Cpl 13172 11th West Yorkshire Regt
SMALLEY Samuel MM Pnr 130743 2 Special Coy Royal Engineers
SMALLEY William MM Pte 19156 6th Lancashire Fusiliers
SMALLEY or SMALLY Herbert H. MM Pte 35589 RAMC
SMALLMAN Edward J. MM Pte 1670 1/17th London Regt
SMALLMAN James MM+Bar Sjt 25793 8th Royal Lancaster Regt
SMALLMAN John MM Cpl 201947 8th Manchester Regt
SMALLMAN Samuel MM Pte 9865 16th Lancashire Fusiliers DOW 27.9.17.
SMALLMAN William T.F. MM Sjt 79949 251 Tunnelling Coy Royal Engineers
SMALLSHAW Albert E. MM Pte 240191 1/5th Royal Lancaster Regt
SMALLWOOD Benjamin MM CQMS 7557 2nd Northamptonshire Regt Died 30.7.18.
SMALLWOOD Frank MM Pte 10793 1st Notts & Derby Regt
SMALLWOOD Frank Henry MM Gnr 19040 RFA
SMALLWOOD George MM L/Cpl 53372 169 Coy Machine Gun Corps
SMALLWOOD George Baxter MM+Bar CSM 48451 2nd Royal Lancaster Regt att MGC.Died 2.11.18.
SMALLWOOD George E. MM Bdr 950769 RFA
SMALLWOOD George Edward MM CSM 83704 2nd Bn Machine Gun Corps
SMALLWOOD James MM L/Cpl 40085 9th Royal Irish Fusiliers
SMALLWOOD Thomas Albert MM Cpl 12237 6th Royal Berkshire Regt
SMALLY or SMALLEY Herbert H. MM Pte 35589 RAMC
SMART Alexander MM Sjt 4301 RFA
SMART Alfred MM Cpl 10934 1st Scottish Rifles
SMART Arthur James MM 2nd Cpl 145035 Royal Engineers
SMART Charles MM L/Cpl 312427 Fifth Army Sig Coy Royal Engineers att 126 Bde RFA.
SMART David MM Pte 37265 55 Fd Amb RAMC
SMART David "DCM,MM,MID" Pte 2607 1/5th Royal Highlanders
SMART Edmund Swapp MM Gnr 133613 505 Bty 65 Bde RFA
SMART Edward MM Sjt 52461 6 Div Ammn Col RFA
SMART Edward Charles MM L/Cpl S/31759 7th Rifle Brigade
SMART Edward J. "DCM,MM" Pte 2432 11th Royal West Kent Regt
SMART Edward John MM Cpl 30143 Z/38 Med TM Bty RGA
SMART Eugene W. MM Sjt 10533 2nd Border Regt
SMART Frank MM Sjt 11461 7th Gloucestershire Regt
SMART Frank "MM,MID" L/Cpl 1115 1st Royal Warwickshire Regt
SMART Fred MM Sjt 29000 Royal Engineers
SMART Frederick J. MM L/Bdr 3387 D/149 Bde RFA
SMART G.T. MM L/Cpl P3010 Military Mounted Police
SMART George MM Dvr 776480 D/310 Bde RFA DOW 19.5.17.
SMART George MM Pte 28467 8th Somerset Light Infantry
SMART George MM Pte 8853 2nd Suffolk Regt
SMART George MM+Bar Cpl 266326 Gordon Highlanders
SMART George C. MM L/Sjt 200703 Gordon Highlanders
SMART Gilbert C. MM Sjt 240236 8th Gloucestershire Regt
SMART Harold MM Bdr 34782 RGA
SMART Harold W. MM Sjt 505206 18th King's Royal Rifle Corps
SMART Harry MM Pte 30286 8th Gloucestershire Regt
SMART Henry MM Pte 18536 1st Duke of Cornwall's LI DOW 12.10.18.
SMART Henry MM+Bar Sjt 27699 2nd Suffolk Regt
SMART Herbert Francis MM Pte R/27618 2nd King's Royal Rifle Corps KIA 27.5.18.
SMART Herbert L. MM Cpl 93737 D/255 Bde RFA
SMART James "MM,CG(F)" Sjt 14471 7/8th King's Own Scottish Borderers
SMART John MM Pte 43161 16th Highland Light Infantry
SMART John MM Pte 51915 Royal Scots
SMART John A. MM Sjt R/5003 13th King's Royal Rifle Corps
SMART John D. MM L/Cpl 202686 Royal Warwickshire Regt
SMART John McGregor MM Sjt 66913 RGA
SMART John William MM Pte 203003 1/6th North Staffordshire Regt KIA 3.10.18.
SMART Martin G. MM Pte 240821 1/6th Highland Light Infantry
SMART Percy T. MM Gnr 3840 A/285 Bde RFA
SMART Peter MM Sjt 9036 2nd Scots Guards KIA 20.5.18.
SMART Sidney MM Sjt 12289 7th Suffolk Regt
SMART Sidney MM Sjt 63994 RFA
SMART Silas A. MM Pte 31898 10th Shropshire Light Infantry
SMART Walter Claud MM Gnr 9436 B/149 Bde RFA
SMART Walter J. MM Sjt 307329 Royal Engineers
SMART Walter T. MM Cpl 24523 29th Bn Machine Gun Corps
SMART William MM Sjt 20093 11th South Lancashire Regt
SMART William Alfred MM Pte 22325 2nd Worcestershire Regt
SMART William E. MM Pte 15504 11th Welsh Regt
SMART William Joseph MM+Bar L/Cpl 43609 7th Northamptonshire Regt
SMART William Middlemiss MM Sjt 49381 19 Div Sig Coy Royal Engineers
SMART William S. MM Pte 27764 2nd Grenadier Guards
SMARTT Reginald D. MM L/Sjt 11308 1st Royal West Kent Regt
SMEATH Ernest G. MM Cpl 25969 Norfolk Regt
SMEATHERS Albert T. MM Pte 77809 17th Royal Fusiliers
SMEATON Andrew J. MM Cpl 899 Royal Highlanders
SMEATON Arthur MM Pte 275810 1/7th Durham Light Infantry
SMEATON John MM L/Cpl 265416 Royal Highlanders
SMEDLEY Benjamin MM Sjt 24370 15th Notts & Derby Regt
SMEDLEY Hugh Lionel "MC,MM(2513 Pte 15th London Regt)" T/2Lt 11th Royal Fusiliers
SMEDLEY James MM Pte 101921 RAMC
SMEDLEY Joseph MM L/Cpl 10339 2nd York & Lancaster Regt
SMEDLEY Thomas MM Sjt 36499 256 Bde RFA
SMEDLEY Thomas H. MM Sjt 23361 2nd Yorkshire Light Infantry
SMEE Alfred George MM+Bar Pte 12461 9th Essex Regt KIA 30.11.17.
SMEE Arthur J. MM Pte M2/270137 Army Service Corps
SMEE George J. MM Sjt 275311 RGA
SMEED Frank Alfred MM Pte 536144 RAMC att 12th London Regt.DOW 9.8.18.
SMEED L. MM Cpl 490833 London Regt
SMEED William H. MM Gnr 59994 17 Siege Bty RGA
SMEETH Joseph "MM,MIDx2" CSM 1873 'L' Corps Sig Coy Royal Engineers
SMEETH William MM Pte 5820 1st East Surrey Regt
SMELE George E. MM Spr 494876 Royal Engineers
SMELLIE Fred "MM,CG(B)" L/Cpl 23328 8th East Lancashire Regt
SMELLIE Thomas MM Pte 316813 13th Royal Highlanders
SMELLIE Walter MM+Bar Pte 7460 1st Scottish Rifles
SMELT Joseph James MM Cpl 242487 1/5th York & Lancaster Regt
SMERDON Frank MM Sjt 10374 8th Devonshire Regt
SMETHURST Frank MM Cpl 201408 1/5th Lancashire Fusiliers
SMETHURST Harry Pierpoint MM Dvr 187991 250 Bde RFA
SMETHURST James MM Sjt 7613 11th Manchester Regt
SMETHURST John MM Pte 201806 6th(Light)Bn Tank Corps
SMETHURST Robert Macey MM Pte 23455 11th Manchester Regt
SMETTEN Joseph "MM,MID" Spr 42131 Royal Engineers
SMEWIN George MM Sjt 278 1/1st(Bucks)Bn Oxf & Bucks Light Infantry

SMILES Robert William MM Cpl 19831 13th Gloucestershire Regt
SMILLIE James MM L/Cpl 51514 2nd Lincolnshire Regt
SMILLIE James MM Pte 202550 Royal Warwickshire Regt
SMIRTHWAITE Benjamin MM Cpl 201075 1/5th Durham Light Infantry KIA 11.4.18.
SMIT Pieter J. MM L/Cpl 33360 Royal Welsh Fusiliers
SMITH A. MM Pte 405223 2/3rd(West Riding)Fd Amb RAMC
SMITH A. MM Pte 303254 RAMC
SMITH A. MM L/Cpl 14239 Grenadier Guards
SMITH A.A. MM Pte 8094 15th Hussars
SMITH A.B. MM Pte 252459 Manchester Regt
SMITH A.E. MM Sjt 16941 RGA
SMITH A.G. MM+Bar L/Cpl 493437 13th London Regt
SMITH A.G. MM Pte 375158 Manchester Regt
SMITH A.M. MM+Bar Pte 300281 5th London Regt
SMITH Abel J. MM Sjt 51315 11 Bde RFA
SMITH Abraham MM Pte 15784 11th Suffolk Regt KIA 19.4.18.
SMITH Adam MM Pte 81363 Machine Gun Corps
SMITH Adam MM Pte 8993 4th Dragoon Guards
SMITH Albert MM Sjt 242567 1/4th West Riding Regt KIA 11.10.18.
SMITH Albert MM Sjt 308250 8th Liverpool Regt
SMITH Albert MM Pte 25414 2nd Notts & Derby Regt KIA 19.9.18.
SMITH Albert MM Pte 2419 1/1st Cambridgeshire Regt KIA 27.9.18.
SMITH Albert "DCM,MM" Sjt 68323 A/50 Bde RFA
SMITH Albert MM+Bar Dvr 91235 56 Div Ammn Col RFA
SMITH Albert MM Gnr 2074 Machine Gun Corps(Motors)
SMITH Albert "MM,MID" Sjt 935 1/2nd London Regt
SMITH Albert MM L/Cpl 15149 10th Essex Regt KIA 22.10.17.
SMITH Albert MM Cpl 9721 1st Royal Welsh Fusiliers Died 31.3.18.
SMITH Albert MM Sjt 11478 16th Lancashire Fusiliers
SMITH Albert MM Pte 11195 8th West Riding Regt
SMITH Albert MM Pte 32267 6th York & Lancaster Regt
SMITH Albert MM Pte 19742 1st Shropshire Light Infantry DOW 25.9.18.
SMITH Albert MM Pte S/24624 Rifle Brigade
SMITH Albert MM Gnr 26466 C/155 Bde RFA
SMITH Albert MM Pte 290733 Cheshire Regt
SMITH Albert MM Pte 266635 Royal Warwickshire Regt
SMITH Albert C. MM Gnr 73430 37 Bde RFA
SMITH Albert C. MM Sjt 19211 Oxf & Bucks Light Infantry
SMITH Albert E. MM Sjt 39869 10th Lancashire Fusiliers
SMITH Albert E. MM Cpl 164928 100th Bn Machine Gun Corps
SMITH Albert E. MM Cpl 66550 10th Royal Scots
SMITH Albert E. MM Gnr 55298 RFA
SMITH Albert E. MM Cpl 12914 1st Worcestershire Regt
SMITH Albert E. "MM,MSM" Sjt 265385 1/2nd Monmouthshire Regt
SMITH Albert Edward MM Cpl 76307 'D' Bn Machine Gun Corps(Heavy Branch) KIA 23.4.17.
SMITH Albert Edward MM Pte 78945 2nd Notts & Derby Regt KIA 11.10.18.
SMITH Albert Edward MM Cpl 60489 66 Siege Bty RGA
SMITH Albert Ernest "MC,MM(28741 Sjt)" Lt 2 Siege Bty RGA
SMITH Albert F. MM L/Cpl 252156 2nd Manchester Regt
SMITH Albert G. MM Pte 90536 Machine Gun Corps
SMITH Albert G. MM Sjt 13066 1st Worcestershire Regt
SMITH Albert George MM Pte 32069 Border Regt
SMITH Albert H. MM Sjt 60545 15/17th West Yorkshire Regt
SMITH Albert H. MM L/Cpl R/19604 King's Royal Rifle Corps
SMITH Albert J. MM Pte 7314 9th Lancers
SMITH Albert S. MM 2nd Cpl 488078 466 Fd Coy Royal Engineers
SMITH Albert Thomas MM L/Cpl 241318 Worcestershire Regt
SMITH Albert V. MM Pte 300132 7th Essex Regt
SMITH Albert Watford MM Spr 522831 466 Fd Coy Royal Engineers
SMITH Aldhelm Stewart Courtney "MM,MID" Shoeing Smith 1874 1/1st Warwickshire Yeomanry DOW 4.4.17.
SMITH Alexander MM L/Cpl 27142 1st Border Regt
SMITH Alexander MM Cpl 66553 2/10th Royal Scots
SMITH Alexander MM Pte 7236 1st Cameron Highlanders
SMITH Alexander MM Cpl 8858 2nd Lincolnshire Regt
SMITH Alexander MM L/Cpl M2/183248 Army Service Corps
SMITH Alexander MM+Bar Sjt 93181 218 Fd Coy Royal Engineers
SMITH Alexander MM Sjt 10065 7th Seaforth Highlanders KIA 23.3.18.
SMITH Alexander MM Cpl(MCDR) 51774 'Y' Corps Sig Coy Royal Engineers
SMITH Alexander G. MM S/Sjt Armourer 1330 Army Ordnance Co9rps att RGA.
SMITH Alexander Heron MM Pte 260042 1/4th Yorkshire Regt
SMITH Alexander Joseph MM 2Lt 11th Royal West Surrey Regt KIA 31.7.17.
SMITH Alfred MM Pte 50877 23rd Royal Fusiliers
SMITH Alfred MM Cpl 14634 11th Royal Fusiliers
SMITH Alfred MM Pte 42113 7th Royal Highlanders
SMITH Alfred MM Pte 1542 1st Royal Fusiliers
SMITH Alfred MM L/Cpl 21211 9th Northumberland Fusiliers
SMITH Alfred MM Sjt 253860 74 Div Sig Coy Royal Engineers
SMITH Alfred MM L/Cpl 514240 14th London Regt
SMITH Alfred MM Pte 630149 1/20th London Regt
SMITH Alfred MM Sjt S/5269 11th Rifle Brigade KIA 10.2.18.
SMITH Alfred MM Sjt 19815 104 Fd Amb RAMC
SMITH Alfred MM+Bar Pte 29487 Highland Light Infantry
SMITH Alfred "DCM,MM+Bar" Sjt 8214 2nd Oxf & Bucks Light Infantry
SMITH Alfred MM Pnr 43660 7 Div Sig Coy Royal Engineers KIA 4.10.17.
SMITH Alfred MM CQMS 230 Royal Warwickshire Regt
SMITH Alfred MM+Bar L/Cpl 11473 8th Gloucestershire Regt
SMITH Alfred MM Pte 3543 20th London Regt
SMITH Alfred MM+2 Bars Cpl 7451 1st Leicestershire Regt
SMITH Alfred MM Pte 7876 7th Royal Irish Rifles
SMITH Alfred MM L/Cpl 265091 Notts & Derby Regt
SMITH Alfred A. MM Pte 22535 Liverpool Regt
SMITH Alfred C. MM Pte 15474 Royal West Surrey Regt
SMITH Alfred C. MM Farrier Sjt 810274 RFA
SMITH Alfred Charles MM Gnr 62395 234 TM Bty RFA KIA 23.10.16.
SMITH Alfred D. MM Cpl 2468 1/4th Suffolk Regt
SMITH Alfred F. MM Pte 14918 Dorsetshire Regt
SMITH Alfred George MM Sjt 8429 2nd Rifle Brigade KIA 23.3.18.
SMITH Alfred H. MM Cpl 4135 12th Lancers
SMITH Alfred Henry MM Bdr 31826 A/277 Bde RFA DOW 16.8.17.
SMITH Alfred J. MM Pte M2/201461 Army Service Corps att RGA
SMITH Alfred John MM Pte 38748 2nd Essex Regt
SMITH Alfred Tom MM Pte M2/132294 Army Service Corps att 89 Fd Amb RAMC.
SMITH Alfred V. MM Pte 16678 2nd Royal Fusiliers
SMITH Alfred W. MM+Bar Sjt 51909 12 Div Sig Coy Royal Engineers
SMITH Alfred William MM Sjt 2766 Leicestershire Regt DOW 4.10.17.
SMITH Ambrose MM Pte Y/1902 12th King's Royal Rifle Corps
SMITH Ambrose M. "MM,MID" Pte 12740 8th Leicestershire Regt
SMITH Andrew MM Sjt 45872 B/110 Bde RFA KIA 27.4.18.
SMITH Andrew MM Pte 14287 16th Highland Light Infantry
SMITH Andrew MM Sjt 18/177 Royal Irish Rifles
SMITH Andrew MM Pte 11928 19th Manchester Regt KIA 21.10.16.
SMITH Andrew MM Pte 34791 York & Lancaster Regt
SMITH Andrew MM L/Cpl 5399 Gordon Highlanders
SMITH Andrew MM L/Cpl 24248 Highland Light Infantry
SMITH Andrew James Victor MM Sjt 94963 187 Bde RFA
SMITH Andrew K. MM Cpl 106389 Royal Engineers
SMITH Anthony MM 2nd Cpl 155755 182 Tunnelling Coy Royal Engineers
SMITH Archibald MM Pte 45169 2nd Royal Inniskilling Fusiliers
SMITH Archibald MM Pte 42875 RAMC
SMITH Archibald C. MM Cpl 62800 37th Bn Machine Gun Corps
SMITH Archibald P. MM Cpl 511510 1/14th London Regt
SMITH Archie MM L/Cpl 145143 1/1st Northamptonshire Yeomanry
SMITH Arthur MM Sjt 51404 86 Coy Labour Corps
SMITH Arthur MM Pte 23689 6th Lincolnshire Regt
SMITH Arthur MM Pte 15850 7th Bedfordshire Regt KIA 24.4.18.
SMITH Arthur MM Gnr 756054 A/251 Bde RFA
SMITH Arthur MM Pte 23025 1st Notts & Derby Regt
SMITH Arthur MM Pte 19009 East Yorkshire Regt
SMITH Arthur MM+Bar Sjt 30274 8th Royal Warwickshire Regt
SMITH Arthur MM L/Cpl 63073 Royal Fusiliers
SMITH Arthur MM Sjt 265835 West Riding Regt
SMITH Arthur MM Pte 201893 Leicestershire Regt
SMITH Arthur MM Sjt 12019 16th Lancashire Fusiliers
SMITH Arthur MM Pte 13630 10th Essex Regt
SMITH Arthur MM Sjt 1422 2nd Manchester Regt KIA 28.12.17.
SMITH Arthur MM Gnr 41327 RGA
SMITH Arthur MM Gnr 34186 RGA
SMITH Arthur MM Pte 45862 South Wales Borderers
SMITH Arthur MM Spr 500377 Royal Engineers
SMITH Arthur MM+Bar L/Cpl 2108 1st Gloucestershire Regt Died 24.9.18.
SMITH Arthur Charles MM Pte 1345 5(London)Fd Amb RAMC KIA 24.12.16.
SMITH Arthur D. MM L/Bdr 132701 RGA

SMITH Arthur E. MM Sjt 241573 1/4th South Lancashire Regt
SMITH Arthur E. MM Pte 11966 Royal West Surrey Regt
SMITH Arthur E. MM S/Sjt Mechanician 29772 Royal Engineers
SMITH Arthur Edwin MM Pte 33354 50 Fd Amb RAMC
SMITH Arthur Edwin "MM,MSM" Sjt 6914 1st Duke of Cornwall's LI
SMITH Arthur Frederick MM+Bar L/Cpl 7717 1st Leicestershire Regt
SMITH Arthur G. MM CQMS 45514 Devonshire Regt
SMITH Arthur G. MM Cpl 17175 Machine Gun Corps
SMITH Arthur G. MM Dvr 50418 'A' Bty RHA
SMITH Arthur George MM Spr 548537 510 Fd Coy Royal Engineers
SMITH Arthur H. MM Gnr 38228 RFA
SMITH Arthur J. MM Pte 200108 1st Bn Tank Corps
SMITH Arthur J. MM Sjt 11498 5th Shropshire Light Infantry
SMITH Arthur L. MM Sjt 22531 A/82 Bde RFA
SMITH Arthur Lloyd "MM,BA" Pte 11129 5th Royal Berkshire Regt KIA 20.11.17.
SMITH Arthur R. MM Sjt 13093 8th Royal Berkshire Regt
SMITH Arthur Reginald MM L/Cpl 96113 17 Squadron Machine Gun Corps(Cavalry)
SMITH Arthur Sidney "MM,MID" CoH 1457 Royal Horse Guards
SMITH Arthur W. MM Cpl 4259 RFA
SMITH Arthur W. MM Pte R/12499 King's Royal Rifle Corps
SMITH Benjamin MM Spr 480443 460 Fd Coy Royal Engineers
SMITH Benjamin MM Pte 3/1137 2nd Yorkshire Light Infantry
SMITH Benjamin A.S. MM Trumpeter 3093 5th Dragoon Guards
SMITH Benjamin Fair MM Cpl 4853 2/1st Bn HAC(Inf) DOW 10.10.17.
SMITH Benjamin Thomas Birch MM Pte 16999 1st Coldstream Guards
SMITH Bernard MM Sjt M/31424 Army Service Corps
SMITH Bert MM Sjt SE/5875 Army Veterinary Corps
SMITH Bert T. MM Cpl 2145 Royal Engineers
SMITH Bertie Alfred MM Pte 43225 6th Bedfordshire Regt
SMITH Bertie Charles MM Pte 200086 1/4th Suffolk Regt KIA 25.9.17.
SMITH Bertie J.W. MM Pte 51137 7th Royal Fusiliers
SMITH Bertrand MM Cpl C/6246 King's Royal Rifle Corps
SMITH Brigg MM Pte 13193 9th West Riding Regt
SMITH C. MM+Bar L/Cpl 14635 7th East Kent Regt
SMITH C.B.L. MM Pte 4494 London Regt
SMITH C.E. MM Sjt 8904 2nd Essex Regt
SMITH C.L. MM Gnr 137959 RFA
SMITH Cameron MM Pte 325243 1/4th Royal Scots
SMITH Cecil MM Pte 22261 Scottish Rifles
SMITH Cecil Ernest MM Gnr 77754 210 Siege Bty RGA
SMITH Cecil G. MM Sjt 14288 9th Norfolk Regt
SMITH Charles MM Pte 305939 1/8th Notts & Derby Regt
SMITH Charles MM Pte 390851 9th London Regt DOW 15.9.18.
SMITH Charles "See ISITT, C., B/200346"
SMITH Charles MM Gnr 68537 331 Siege Bty RGA
SMITH Charles MM Pte 19260 Manchester Regt
SMITH Charles MM Sjt 5727 Royal Warwickshire Regt
SMITH Charles MM Pte 3506 1/6th West Yorkshire Regt
SMITH Charles MM Sjt 41256 69 Fd Coy Royal Engineers KIA 7.5.17.
SMITH Charles MM L/Cpl 887 13th East Yorkshire Regt
SMITH Charles MM Cpl 5613 1st Wiltshire Regt
SMITH Charles MM Sjt 5520 Royal West Kent Regt
SMITH Charles MM+Bar L/Cpl 37785 11th Royal Fusiliers
SMITH Charles MM Sjt 14174 8th Suffolk Regt
SMITH Charles MM L/Sjt 8983 2nd Cameron Highlanders
SMITH Charles A. MM Pte 11647 Coldstream Guards
SMITH Charles A. MM Bdr Sig 157251 544 Siege Bty RGA
SMITH Charles Andrew MM Pte 23882 51 Fd Amb RAMC
SMITH Charles Drayton MM Cpl 11015 6th Duke of Cornwall's LI KIA 18.8.16.
SMITH Charles E. MM Pte 769937 28th London Regt
SMITH Charles E. MM Pte 38778 5/6th Scottish Rifles
SMITH Charles E. "DCM,MM" L/Cpl 7658 1st North Staffordshire Regt
SMITH Charles E. MM+Bar Sjt 4080 Rifle Brigade
SMITH Charles E. MM L/Cpl 1893 7th Royal West Kent Regt
SMITH Charles E.D. MM Pte 13507 2nd Suffolk Regt
SMITH Charles Edward "MM,MSM" Cpl 15689 Royal Engineers
SMITH Charles Edward MM Sjt 39225 76 Fd Amb RAMC KIA 17.4.18.
SMITH Charles Edwin MM Gnr 22385 40 Bde RFA
SMITH Charles Ernest Edwin MM Pte 275277 1/6th Essex Regt
SMITH Charles F. MM Gnr 755138 RFA
SMITH Charles F. MM Sjt 6485 1st Somerset Light Infantry

SMITH Charles H. MM Sjt 27089 96 Fd Amb RAMC
SMITH Charles H. MM Sjt 201722 6th Royal West Surrey Regt
SMITH Charles H. MM Pte 10625 King's Royal Rifle Corps
SMITH Charles Henry MM 2nd Cpl 40450 61 Fd Coy Royal Engineers DOW 19.11.18.
SMITH Charles John MM Pte 12061 5th Northamptonshire Regt DOW 20.9.18.
SMITH Charles R. MM Gnr 70639 3 Siege Bty RGA
SMITH Charles R. MM Pte 47288 5th York & Lancaster Regt
SMITH Charles R. MM Dvr 87047 Royal Engineers
SMITH Charles S. MM Cpl 21445 7th Royal West Kent Regt
SMITH Charles T. MM Pte 148950 Machine Gun Corps
SMITH Charles T. MM Cpl 840276 411 Bty 126 Bde RFA
SMITH Charles Thomas MM Gnr 205395 X/1 Med TM Bty RFA
SMITH Charles W. MM Dvr 40594 RFA
SMITH Charles W. MM L/Cpl R/6159 12th King's Royal Rifle Corps
SMITH Charles W. MM+Bar Sjt 32982 RAMC
SMITH Charles William MM Cpl 76103 2nd Bn Tank Corps
SMITH Charley MM Sjt 11524 1st Leicestershire Regt KIA 28.6.27.
SMITH Charlie MM Cpl 632016 2/20th London Regt
SMITH Christopher MM Pte 2325 1/5th Durham Light Infantry DOW 4.11.18.
SMITH Christopher MM L/Sjt 44670 8th Royal Berkshire Regt DOW 12.11.18.
SMITH Christopher MM Pte 22566 Lancashire Fusiliers
SMITH Christopher D. MM Pte 31320 1st Devonshire Regt
SMITH Clarence MM Pte 326293 1/1st Cambridgeshire Regt
SMITH Clarence V. MM Pte 9813 Royal Highlanders
SMITH Claude E. MM S/Sjt 19849 RGA
SMITH Clement MM S/Sjt Farrier TS/8397 Army Service Corps
SMITH Clifford MM Gnr 99893 25 Bde RFA DOW 12.7.17.
SMITH Clifford MM Spr 440226 Royal Engineers
SMITH Clifford MM Pte M2/078854 Army Service Corps
SMITH Colin MM Pte 39028 2nd North Lancashire Regt
SMITH Cyril MM L/Cpl 24748 13th Yorkshire Regt
SMITH Cyril MM Sjt 320402 15th Suffolk Regt
SMITH Cyril Horton MM Pte 17230 7th Royal Berkshire Regt KIA 26.10.16.
SMITH D. MM Dvr 8150 RFA
SMITH Daniel MM Gnr 20401 D/121 Bde RFA KIA 12.9.18.
SMITH David MM L/Cpl 536352 55 Fd Coy Royal Engineers
SMITH David MM Pte 27795 5/6th Scottish Rifles
SMITH David MM Pte 43328 1st Hampshire Regt
SMITH David MM Pte 17814 9th Scottish Rifles
SMITH David MM Bdr 7411 C/241 Bde RFA
SMITH David MM Pte 29196 14th Highland Light Infantry
SMITH David MM Cpl 4742 2nd Royal Sussex Regt
SMITH David MM L/Cpl 10581 Wiltshire Regt
SMITH David MM Cpl 2756 1/6th Seaforth Highlanders
SMITH David MM Sjt 291343 RGA
SMITH David C. MM Gnr 38019 RFA
SMITH David J. MM Cpl 8242 2nd Royal Inniskilling Fusiliers
SMITH Douglas MM Cpl 11993 16th Lancashire Fusiliers
SMITH Duncan MM Sjt 200266 1/5th Highland Light Infantry
SMITH E. MM Pte 293901 Highland Light Infantry
SMITH E. MM Sjt 35685 RGA
SMITH E.F. MM Bdr 2401 RFA
SMITH Ebenezer MM L/Cpl 44459 Manchester Regt
SMITH Edgar MM Sjt 187537 RGA
SMITH Edgar MM Cpl 49839 4th West Riding Regt
SMITH Edgar A. MM Gnr 316180 RGA
SMITH Edgar J. MM Sjt 19341 1st North Lancashire Regt
SMITH Edgar Robert MM Pte 16088 8th Norfolk Regt KIA 22.10.17.
SMITH Edgar William MM L/Cpl 241902 Worcestershire Regt
SMITH Edmund MM Sjt 24819 132 Hy Bty RGA
SMITH Edward MM Pte 73169 33rd Bn Machine Gun Corps
SMITH Edward MM S/Sjt Mechanic 99585 Royal Engineers
SMITH Edward "MM,MSM" Sjt 34222 39th Bn Machine Gun Corps
SMITH Edward MM Pte 14699 Middlesex Regt
SMITH Edward MM Spr 31289 Royal Engineers
SMITH Edward A. MM Sjt 9911 9th Royal Fusiliers
SMITH Edward Bertie "DCM,MM" Sjt 18687 9th South Staffordshire Regt
SMITH Edward E. MM Sjt 201874 1/4th Suffolk Regt
SMITH Edward H. MM Sjt 43256 Gordon Highlanders
SMITH Edward Hollock MM Sjt 35070 C/153 Bde RFA KIA 13.7.17.
SMITH Edward James MM Spr 61927 82 Fd Coy Royal Engineers
SMITH Edward T. MM Cpl 198675 A/285 Bde RFA
SMITH Edward Victor MM Pte 386257 1(Northumbrian)Fd Amb RAMC

SMITH Edward W. MM L/Cpl 267259 Oxf & Bucks Light Infantry
SMITH Edward William MM Pte C/3457 12th King's Royal Rifle Corps Died 25.6.18.
SMITH Edwin MM Sjt 240937 2/6th Notts & Derby Regt DOW 28.4.17.
SMITH Edwin MM Bdr 49792 113 Bty 25 Bde RFA
SMITH Edwin MM L/Cpl 6521 17th Lancers
SMITH Edwin MM Bdr 781403 A/311 Bde RFA DOW 31.10.17.
SMITH Egerton W. MM+Bar Sjt 112970 10th Tank Corps
SMITH Eli MM Pte 11446 Leicestershire Regt
SMITH Eli MM Sjt 277602 RGA
SMITH Elias MM Dvr 13794 C/124 Bde RFA
SMITH Elias W. "DCM,MM" CSM 8191 2nd Leicestershire Regt
SMITH Eric MM Pte 22433 8th East Surrey Regt KIA 22.3.18.
SMITH Eric F. "MM,MID" Sjt 5648 RAMC
SMITH Ernest MM Pte 240532 Leicestershire Regt
SMITH Ernest MM Pte 63218 5th Yorkshire Light Infantry
SMITH Ernest MM+Bar Pte 16423 11th Notts & Derby Regt KIA 21.8.18.
SMITH Ernest MM Bdr 108718 RGA
SMITH Ernest MM Sjt 780131 246 Bde RFA
SMITH Ernest A. "DCM,MM" CSM 13428 4th Bedfordshire Regt
SMITH Ernest A. MM L/Cpl 11415 8th East Surrey Regt
SMITH Ernest A. MM Bdr 828 RFA
SMITH Ernest C. MM Pte 18168 Durham Light Infantry
SMITH Ernest George MM Cpl 201195 9th Norfolk Regt DOW 21.10.18
SMITH Ernest H. MM L/Cpl 319 4th GMGR
SMITH Ernest H. "DCM,MM" CSM 19235 6 Div & 21 Div Sig Coys Royal Engineers
SMITH Ernest Henry MM Cpl 40732 69 Fd Coy Royal Engineers
SMITH Ernest J. "DCM,MM" CSM 9104 2nd Oxf & Bucks Light Infantry
SMITH Ernest N. MM Sjt 6213 RFA
SMITH Ernest P. MM Pte 79586 Durham Light Infantry
SMITH Ernest Valentine MM Pte 26281 4th Grenadier Guards
SMITH F. MM L/Cpl 361207 3 Fd Svy Bn Royal Engineers
SMITH F. MM Cpl 47380 Hussars
SMITH F. MM Pte 128062 Machine Gun Corps
SMITH F.A. MM L/Cpl 300761 London Regt
SMITH Francis MM Pte 9954 2nd Leinster Regt KIA 1.9.16.
SMITH Francis MM Sjt 24420 15th Notts & Derby Regt
SMITH Francis MM Sjt 286206 488 Siege Bty RGA
SMITH Francis G. MM Cpl 28056 15th Hampshire Regt
SMITH Francis J. MM Pte 14525 1st Grenadier Guards
SMITH Francis J. MM Bdr 13608 B/165 Bde RFA
SMITH Francis W. MM L/Cpl 25445 Oxf & Bucks Light Infantry
SMITH Frank MM Sjt 240519 1/5th Leicestershire Regt
SMITH Frank MM Pte 203767 2nd Hampshire Regt
SMITH Frank MM Pte 352759 11th Royal Scots
SMITH Frank MM+Bar Pte 203456 11th Notts & Derby Regt Died 6.11.18.
SMITH Frank MM Bdr 60386 27 Bde RFA
SMITH Frank MM Pte 40739 1/5th South Lancashire Regt
SMITH Frank MM Gnr 39896 36 Bde RFA
SMITH Frank MM Cpl 50676 West Yorkshire Regt
SMITH Frank MM+Bar L/Cpl 2755 West Yorkshire Regt
SMITH Frank MM L/Cpl 9073 2nd Welsh Regt
SMITH Frank MM Gnr 53320 RGA
SMITH Frank MM Cpl 6832 13th King's Royal Rifle Corps KIA 8.3.18.
SMITH Frank MM Pte 437482 2/2(South Midland)Fd Amb RAMC DOW 12.4.18.
SMITH Frank Andrews MM Pte 6/621 7th Rifle Brigade KIA 7.12.17.
SMITH Frank Ernest MM Cpl 944057 A/330 Bde RFA Died 23.3.18.
SMITH Frank F. MM Cpl 241354 6th South Staffordshire Regt
SMITH Frank F. MM L/Cpl 470801 12th London Regt
SMITH Frank George MM Cpl 11690 8th Royal Berkshire Regt DOW 1.9.18.
SMITH Frank James "MM,MID" Sjt 8454 2nd Royal Berkshire Regt
SMITH Fred "MM,MID" Sjt 800074 A/230 Bde RFA
SMITH Fred MM 2nd Cpl 83595 249 Fd Coy Royal Engineers
SMITH Fred MM Pte 2518 10th Royal Fusiliers
SMITH Fred MM Pnr 359890 34 Div Sig Coy Royal Engineers
SMITH Fred MM Cpl 31254 1st Northamptonshire Regt
SMITH Fred MM L/Sjt 18478 10th Lancashire Fusiliers
SMITH Fred MM Pte 17982 11th Durham Light Infantry
SMITH Fred MM Pte 7021 2nd Border Regt
SMITH Fred MM Cpl 10344 2nd Royal Munster Fusiliers
SMITH Fred MM+Bar Pte 40697 9th Essex Regt KIA 5.4.18.
SMITH Fred MM Sjt 17816 Machine Gun Corps
SMITH Fred "MM,MID" Pte 23136 11th East Lancashire Regt
SMITH Frederick MM Pte 11590 10th Royal West Kent Regt
SMITH Frederick MM Bdr 20846 RFA
SMITH Frederick MM Pte 305829 West Riding Regt
SMITH Frederick MM Dvr 140996 C/251 Bde RFA
SMITH Frederick MM Pte 37963 58th Bn Machine Gun Corps
SMITH Frederick   "See MUNN, William H.,Pte, 9030"
SMITH Frederick MM Cpl 4211 Machine Gun Corps
SMITH Frederick MM Sjt 207207 Royal West Surrey Regt
SMITH Frederick MM Pte 11749 11th West Yorkshire Regt
SMITH Frederick "MM,MSM" Cpl 197873 19 Div Sig Coy Royal Engineers
SMITH Frederick MM Pte 235075 1/4th Suffolk Regt
SMITH Frederick MM Sjt 94319 277 Bde RFA DOW 29.3.18.
SMITH Frederick MM Pte S/2549 12th Rifle Brigade
SMITH Frederick MM Pte 15497 1st South Wales Borderers
SMITH Frederick MM L/Cpl 17016 9th Yorkshire Light Infantry
SMITH Frederick MM Pte 266266 1/1st(Bucks)Bn Oxf & Bucks Light Infantry
SMITH Frederick MM L/Cpl 17076 4th Grenadier Guards DOW 8.8.17.
SMITH Frederick MM Sjt 25919 11th Royal West Kent Regt KIA 20.9.17.
SMITH Frederick MM Gnr 781797 246 Bde RFA
SMITH Frederick MM Cpl 44912 93 Fd Coy Royal Engineers DOW 29.5.18.
SMITH Frederick A. MM SM 508059 1 Fd Amb RAMC
SMITH Frederick A. MM Cpl 463244 Royal Engineers
SMITH Frederick C. MM Dvr TS/667 7 Reserve Park Army Service Corps
SMITH Frederick C. MM L/Cpl M2/074155 Army Service Corps
SMITH Frederick C. MM Pte 7904 Scots Guards
SMITH Frederick Charles MM Cpl 1136 1/4(London)Fd Amb RAMC
SMITH Frederick Charles MM Pte 52767 Durham Light Infantry
SMITH Frederick Edward MM Bdr 31986 38 Siege Bty RGA
SMITH Frederick G. MM Bdr 27273 223 Siege Bty RGA
SMITH Frederick G. MM Pte 63097 2/4th Royal West Surrey Regt
SMITH Frederick G. MM Cpl 96037 RFA
SMITH Frederick G. MM L/Cpl 9751 10th Royal Warwickshire Regt
SMITH Frederick Gilbert MM Sjt 9752 1st Yorkshire Light Infantry KIA 17.10.18.
SMITH Frederick J. MM Pte 24949 Oxf & Bucks Light Infantry
SMITH Frederick John Lewin MM Pte 44760 5th Royal Berkshire Regt
SMITH Frederick T. MM Pte 204612 1/5th Bedfordshire Regt
SMITH Frederick T. MM Pte M2/102806 Army Service Corps
SMITH Frederick Thomas MM CQMS 22501 1/8th West Yorkshire Regt
SMITH Frederick W.C. MM Sjt 99354 26th Royal Fusiliers
SMITH Frederick William MM Sjt G/5705 7th D Coy East Kent Regt KIA 5.8.17.
SMITH G.F. MM Gnr 1285 33 Bde RFA
SMITH G.R. MM Sjt 30869 Royal Air Force
SMITH Geoffrey S. MM Cpl 75269 Royal Engineers
SMITH George MM Pte 44444 1st Royal Inniskilling Fusiliers
SMITH George MM Spr 137544 179 Tunnelling Coy Royal Engineers
SMITH George MM Sjt 22686 7th South Staffordshire Regt
SMITH George MM 2nd Cpl 408140 105 Fd Coy Royal Engineers
SMITH George MM Spr 156371 179 Tunnelling Coy Royal Engineers
SMITH George MM Sjt 139333 183 Tunnelling Coy Royal Engineers
SMITH George MM L/Sjt 4819 13th Middlesex Regt KIA 11.10.18.
SMITH George MM L/Cpl 265864 1/7th West Yorkshire Regt DOW 1.5.18.
SMITH George MM Cpl 4391 RAMC
SMITH George MM Pte 16249 Middlesex Regt
SMITH George MM L/Cpl 32527 12th East Surrey Regt
SMITH George MM Sjt 8099 4th Bedfordshire Regt
SMITH George MM Gnr 69354 RGA
SMITH George MM Pte 22966 1st Royal Irish Fusiliers
SMITH George MM S/Sjt 18418 4 Fd Amb RAMC
SMITH George MM Cpl 40354 Suffolk Regt
SMITH George MM L/Cpl 15479 7/8th King's Own Scottish Borderers
SMITH George MM Pte 22918 1st Royal Scots Died 10.10.18.
SMITH George "DCM,MM+Bar" Sjt 16237 6th King's Own Scottish Borderers

SMITH George MM Pte 1693 1/1st Cambridgeshire Regt DOW 3.11.16.
SMITH George MM Spr 132671 Royal Engineers
SMITH George MM Pte 9505 1st Royal Warwickshire Regt KIA 30.8.18.
SMITH George MM Pte 43706 8th Royal Berkshire Regt
SMITH George MM+Bar Sjt 13181 16th Highland Light Infantry
SMITH George MM L/Cpl 5206 9 Coy Labour Corps
SMITH George MM Pte 14547 10th West Riding Regt
SMITH George MM Sjt 15233 8th South Lancashire Regt
SMITH George MM Sjt 17/2154 Royal Irish Rifles
SMITH George MM Gnr Fitter 18161 X/19 TM Bty RFA DOW 18.3.18.
SMITH George MM Sjt 25453 Suffolk Regt
SMITH George MM Pte 33132 Yorkshire Regt
SMITH George MM Cpl 38851 RFA
SMITH George MM L/Cpl 43175 Seaforth Highlanders
SMITH George MM Cpl 28357 South Wales Borderers
SMITH George MM Pte 242162 Highland Light Infantry
SMITH George MM Pte 30360 East Lancashire Regt
SMITH George MM Cpl 200919 Gordon Highlanders
SMITH George MM Gnr 141647 289 Siege Bty RGA KIA 15.6.18.
SMITH George A. MM L/Cpl 663 10th East Yorkshire Regt
SMITH George A. MM Pte 633290 20th London Regt
SMITH George Arthur MM Sjt 37105 346 Siege Bty RGA DOW 19.4.18.
SMITH George Battison MM Sjt 200352 9th Scottish Rifles KIA 19.10.18.
SMITH George Clifford MM Pte 42495 2nd Suffolk Regt DOW 19.10.18.
SMITH George D. MM Cpl 9869 1st East Yorkshire Regt
SMITH George D. MM Sjt 93594 90 Fd Amb RAMC
SMITH George E. MM Cpl 41052 1/9th Durham Light Infantry
SMITH George E. MM Pte 22075 Hampshire Regt
SMITH George E. MM Pte 39949 South Wales Borderers
SMITH George E. MM Sjt 398 RAMC
SMITH George F. MM Sjt 266 1/3rd London Regt
SMITH George Gordon "DCM,MM,MM(F)" BSM 966 'I' Bty RHA
SMITH George H. MM Pte 156370 104th Bn Machine Gun Corps
SMITH George H. MM Cpl 470260 528 Fd Coy Royal Engineers
SMITH George H. MM Pte 17480 6th Somerset Light Infantry
SMITH George H. MM Spr 107162 Royal Engineers
SMITH George H. MM Pte 201311 Royal Berkshire Regt
SMITH George Henry MM L/Cpl 73020 Notts & Derby Regt
SMITH George Henry "MM,MID" L/Cpl 4758 Machine Gun Corps
SMITH George I. MM Pte 12624 Middlesex Regt
SMITH George J. MM Spr 153837 Royal Engineers
SMITH George J. MM Gnr 48537 100 Bde RFA
SMITH George K. MM Bdr 4147 RFA
SMITH George Lammin MM Cpl 9841 1st Royal Welsh Fusiliers
SMITH George Langford MM Bdr 52451 22 Bde RFA
SMITH George N.C. MM QMS S/18096 Army Service Corps
SMITH George Owen MM Pte 30276 14th Royal Warwickshire Regt
SMITH George R. MM Cpl 131548 Royal Engineers
SMITH George R. MM Spr 207589 Royal Engineers
SMITH George Samuel MM CQMS 8125 2nd Lincolnshire Regt
SMITH George T. MM Pte 16152 Northamptonshire Regt
SMITH George W. MM Pte 12613 7th Norfolk Regt
SMITH George W. MM Sjt 8596 Royal West Surrey Regt
SMITH George William MM Pte 807 13th York & Lancaster Regt
SMITH George Y. MM Pte 200153 1/4th Gordon Highlanders
SMITH Gerald MM Gnr 94386 D/63 Bde RFA
SMITH Gilbert MM Pte 30380 2nd Grenadier Guards
SMITH Gilbert MM Pte 5320 ` East Surrey Regt
SMITH Gordon MM Sjt 2069 1/7th Gordon Highlanders
SMITH Gordon J. MM Pte 709 14th Royal Warwickshire Regt
SMITH Gordon R. MM L/Cpl 270316 1/1st Northumberland Yeo
SMITH Gordon S. MM Pte 25170 1/6th Seaforth Highlanders
SMITH Griffiths "MM,MSM" Cpl 645563 Y/51 Med TM Bty RFA
SMITH H. MM Sjt 435408 1 Fd Amb RAMC
SMITH H. MM Cpl 30298 Essex Regt
SMITH H. MM Pte 25643 Manchester Regt
SMITH H. MM Pte 457034 RAMC
SMITH H. "MM,MID" Pte 10758 1st Border Regt
SMITH H. MM Pte 5098 East Surrey Regt
SMITH H. MM Sjt 1266 Royal Warwickshire Regt
SMITH H. MM Pte 7628 East Kent Regt
SMITH H.E. MM Pte A/202136 King's Royal Rifle Corps
SMITH H.FitzG. MM Sjt 40304 2nd South Wales Borderers
SMITH H.N. MM L/Cpl 15026 Labour Corps
SMITH H.W. MM Cpl 75608 Machine Gun Corps
SMITH H.W. MM Pte S/3697 13th Rifle Brigade
SMITH Harold MM Sjt 3122 2nd York & Lancaster Regt
SMITH Harold MM Pte R/4449 13th King's Royal Rifle Corps
SMITH Harold MM Pte 98898 Machine Gun Corps
SMITH Harold MM Spr 488375 79 Fd Coy Royal Engineers
SMITH Harold MM L/Cpl 20061 Machine Gun Corps
SMITH Harold MM Spr 50386 Royal Engineers
SMITH Harold "MM,MSM" Sjt 18924 12th Highland Light Infantry
SMITH Harold MM Sjt 7577 1st West Yorkshire Regt
SMITH Harold MM Gnr 65608 RFA
SMITH Harold MM Pte 40416 Manchester Regt
SMITH Harold C. MM L/Sjt 2885 1/8th Worcestershire Regt
SMITH Harold George MM L/Cpl 2948 4th London Regt
SMITH Harold V. MM Pte 10944 King's Royal Rifle Corps
SMITH Harry MM Pte 51235 2nd Royal Scots
SMITH Harry MM Cpl 775751 Y/62 Med TM Bty RFA
SMITH Harry MM Sjt 604071 1(Shropshire)Bty RHA
SMITH Harry MM Sjt 14554 10th Essex Regt
SMITH Harry MM CQMS 18727 21st Manchester Regt
SMITH Harry MM Dvr 111376 B/93 Bde RFA
SMITH Harry "MM,CG(F)" Bdr 10173 C/149 Bde RFA
SMITH Harry MM Cpl 6408 B/82 Bde RFA
SMITH Harry MM Gnr 123645 RFA
SMITH Harry MM+Bar CSM 12335 7th Wiltshire Regt
SMITH Harry MM+Bar Sjt 33899 1st Notts & Derby Regt
SMITH Harry MM L/Sjt 200604 1/4th Royal Lancaster Regt
SMITH Harry MM L/Cpl 200258 South Lancashire Regt
SMITH Harry MM Dvr T4/061584 Army Service Corps
SMITH Harry MM Pte 268037 West Yorkshire Regt
SMITH Harry MM Pte 9532 Royal Warwickshire Regt
SMITH Harry MM Pte 15818 6th Northamptonshire Regt
SMITH Harry MM Pte 306801 2/4th West Riding Regt KIA 29.9.18.
SMITH Harry MM L/Cpl 179334 Royal Engineers
SMITH Harry MM Sjt 572229 17th London Regt
SMITH Harry "DCM,MM" Sjt 775224 B/245 Bde RFA
SMITH Harry MM 2nd Cpl 1699 Royal Engineers
SMITH Harry MM Bdr 23004 166 Bde RFA
SMITH Harry MM Pte 235310 Yorkshire Regt
SMITH Harry MM Sjt 200192 West Riding Regt
SMITH Harry MM+Bar Pte 9970 2nd East Lancashire Regt
SMITH Harry MM Sjt 13151 11th Lancashire Fusiliers
SMITH Harry MM L/Cpl 21/436 West Yorkshire Regt
SMITH Harry C. MM Spr 207528 Royal Engineers
SMITH Harry Godfrey MM L/Cpl 70545 25th Bn Machine Gun Corps
SMITH Harry J. MM Sjt 63963 Machine Gun Corps
SMITH Harry Leonard MM Pte 15748 1 Special Coy Middlesex Regt
SMITH Harry Manser MM Pte 2175 17th Lancers
SMITH Harry Percy MM L/Cpl 11828 9th Cheshire Regt KIA 15.9.16.
SMITH Harry Ralph MM Pte 10189 11th Suffolk Regt
SMITH Harry Wright MM L/Cpl 13/236 13th East Yorkshire Regt
SMITH Hartley MM Cpl 51946 1st East Yorkshire Regt
SMITH Hector MM Pte 44973 17 Coy Machine Gun Corps
SMITH Henry MM Sjt 33812 'T' Bty RHA DOW 26.7.17.
SMITH Henry MM Sjt 20448 2nd Royal Munster Fusiliers
SMITH Henry "DCM,MM" Cpl 8955 4th Worcestershire Regt
SMITH Henry MM Sjt 570154 1/17th London Regt
SMITH Henry MM Pte 17592 Gloucestershire Regt
SMITH Henry MM Spr 107380 Royal Engineers
SMITH Henry MM Sjt 200657 North Lancashire Regt
SMITH Henry "DCM,MM" Sjt 8955 4th Worcestershire Regt
SMITH Henry MM Sjt 8/17006 8th Royal Irish Rifles
SMITH Henry MM Pte 12744 6th Oxf & Bucks Light Infantry
SMITH Henry "MM,MID" Sjt 5788 1st Leicestershire Regt
SMITH Henry MM Spr 83555 Royal Engineers
SMITH Henry MM Gnr 67074 112 Siege Bty RGA
SMITH Henry MM Sjt 31772 Welsh Regt
SMITH Henry MM+Bar Sjt 11278 7th Somerset Light Infantry
SMITH Henry MM Pte 17148 York & Lancaster Regt
SMITH Henry MM Pte 44110 Yorkshire Light Infantry
SMITH Henry A. MM Dvr 87782 RFA
SMITH Henry C.B. MM CSM 235661 10th Lancashire Fusiliers
SMITH Henry Cecil MM Cpl 205134 7th Shropshire Light Infantry
SMITH Henry Charles MM Cpl M2/167966 Army Service Corps att RFA
SMITH Henry D. MM Gnr 32984 RFA
SMITH Henry George MM Pnr 48446 31 Div Sig Coy Royal Engineers Died 10.11.18.
SMITH Henry J. MM CQMS 11336 11th Hampshire Regt
SMITH Henry J. MM Pte 288106 1/6th Royal Highlanders

SMITH Henry J. MM Pte 3069 9th Royal Warwickshire Regt
SMITH Henry James MM L/Cpl 63621 13th Royal Fusiliers KIA 4.9.18.
SMITH Henry James MM Cpl (MCDR) 160875 Royal Engineers att IX Corps HAG.
SMITH Henry James Moore MM Gnr 85821 283 Siege Bty RGA
SMITH Henry John "MM,CG" Pte M2/054723 Army Service Corps att 28 Fd Amb RAMC
SMITH Henry P. MM Pte 15949 2nd Hampshire Regt
SMITH Herbert MM Pte 266763 1/7th West Yorkshire Regt
SMITH Herbert MM CQMS 34394 9th Yorkshire Regt
SMITH Herbert MM Sjt 11736 A/86 Bde RFA
SMITH Herbert MM Pte 20928 5th West Yorkshire Regt
SMITH Herbert MM Pte 12010 7th Norfolk Regt
SMITH Herbert MM L/Sjt 40742 2nd Suffolk Regt
SMITH Herbert MM+Bar L/Cpl 11784 5th Oxf & Bucks Light Infantry
SMITH Herbert MM Dvr 84993 D/211 Bde RFA DOW 4.11.18.
SMITH Herbert MM Sjt 86643 173 Tunnelling Coy Royal Engineers KIA 17.11.17.
SMITH Herbert MM Pte 20024 6th Bedfordshire Regt DOW 3.4.18.
SMITH Herbert MM Pte 11837 10th West Riding Regt
SMITH Herbert D. MM Pte G/24040 7th East Kent Regt KIA 18.9.18.
SMITH Herbert E. MM Gnr 69986 Tank Corps
SMITH Herbert G. MM Spr 25632 5 Div Sig Coy Royal Engineers
SMITH Herbert J. MM Cpl M2/102670 Army Service Corps
SMITH Herbert James MM Sjt 15421 7th Oxf & Bucks Light Infantry
SMITH Herbert James MM Sjt 7130 1st Norfolk Regt KIA 27.7.16.
SMITH Herbert L. MM+Bar Pte 9211 2nd Worcestershire Regt
SMITH Herbert O. MM Sjt 328 Royal Flying Corps
SMITH Herbert R. MM L/Cpl 10146 2nd Oxf & Bucks Light Infantry
SMITH Herbert S. MM Dvr 32445 RHA
SMITH Horace E. MM+Bar Sjt 13880 11th Northumberland Fusiliers
SMITH Horace J. MM Pte 87487 13th Royal Fusiliers
SMITH Horace R. MM 2nd Cpl 25196 Royal Engineers
SMITH Horace William MM Sjt 800063 A/230 Bde RFA
SMITH Howard P. MM Cpl 915738 RFA
SMITH Hugh MM Pte 7689 1/4th Royal Scots Fusiliers
SMITH Hugh E. MM Pte 41916 Liverpool Regt
SMITH Hugh L.H. MM Cpl 39226 RGA
SMITH I. MM Pte 6584 1st Connaught Rangers
SMITH Isaac MM Pte 10659 7th Lincolnshire Regt
SMITH Isaac MM+Bar L/Cpl A/2954 13th King's Royal Rifle Corps
SMITH Isaac J. MM Sjt 1740 Royal Sussex Regt
SMITH Israel MM Pte 73015 11th Notts & Derby Regt
SMITH J. MM Cpl 8662 Northamptonshire Regt
SMITH J. MM Pte 88110 91 Fd Amb RAMC
SMITH J. MM Pte 16323 1st Devonshire Regt
SMITH J. MM Pte 290487 Gordon Highlanders
SMITH J. MM Pte 5827 Coldstream Guards
SMITH J. MM Pte S/26446 Rifle Brigade
SMITH J.G. MM Pte 301401 1 Fd Amb RAMC
SMITH J.H. MM Sjt 11899 2nd Grenadier Guards
SMITH J.H. MM Sjt 2279 London Regt
SMITH J.H. MM Gnr 3850 RFA
SMITH J.W. MM L/Cpl 241214 Liverpool Regt
SMITH Jack "DCM,MM" Pte 201202 West Yorkshire Regt
SMITH Jack MM Cpl 1013 B/245 Bde RFA
SMITH James MM Sjt R/9062 13th King's Royal Rifle Corps
SMITH James MM Pte 265093 1/7th Gordon Highlanders
SMITH James MM Pte 23582 55th Bn Machine Gun Corps
SMITH James MM Pte 232571 2nd London Regt
SMITH James MM Sjt 2959 Gordon Highlanders
SMITH James MM Pte 265042 1/7th Gordon Highlanders
SMITH James MM Pte 9986 6th North Staffordshire Regt
SMITH James MM L/Cpl 18822 2nd Royal Sussex Regt
SMITH James MM Sjt 240467 2/6th Highland Light Infantry
SMITH James MM Cpl 10721 2nd Dragoon Guards
SMITH James MM L/Cpl 325165 1/9th Durham Light Infantry
SMITH James MM+Bar Sjt 2825 12th Manchester Regt
SMITH James MM Pte 7008 2nd South Staffordshire Regt
SMITH James MM Pte 383836 Yorkshire Light Infantry
SMITH James MM Sjt 53331 28 Bde RFA
SMITH James MM Cpl 39576 10th Lancashire Fusiliers KIA 25.8.18.
SMITH James MM Pte 251386 1st Essex Regt
SMITH James MM Pte 13429 1st Notts & Derby Regt
SMITH James MM Cpl 14286 10th Scottish Rifles KIA 3.1.17.
SMITH James MM L/Sjt 12957 Durham Light Infantry
SMITH James MM Spr 132670 Royal Engineers
SMITH James MM Pte 11017 1st King's Own Scottish Borderers
SMITH James MM L/Cpl 5329 8th East Surrey Regt KIA 22.3.18.
SMITH James MM Pte 17365 7th North Lancashire Regt
SMITH James MM Pte 265509 1/6th Seaforth Highlanders
SMITH James MM Cpl 4799 2nd Dragoons
SMITH James MM Pte 19872 Royal Sussex Regt
SMITH James MM Pte 205278 Royal Scots Fusiliers
SMITH James MM Pte 27896 Northumberland Fusiliers
SMITH James MM+Bar Cpl 965338 RFA
SMITH James A. MM Pte 65164 13th Royal Fusiliers
SMITH James Arthur MM Cpl 786087 312 Bde RFA DOW 1.1.18.
SMITH James B. "DCM,MM+Bar" CSM 18729 21st Manchester Regt
SMITH James C. MM Pte 202551 Royal Warwickshire Regt
SMITH James D. MM Pte 265940 West Riding Regt
SMITH James Dickinson MM Sjt 18/851 18th Durham Light Infantry
SMITH James Douglas MM Sjt 201205 Cheshire Regt
SMITH James E. MM Sjt 7135 Northumberland Fusiliers
SMITH James Edward MM L/Cpl 252251 3rd London Regt KIA 26.8.18.
SMITH James Edward MM Pte 241811 Liverpool Regt
SMITH James Ernest MM L/Cpl 202049 2/4th Lincolnshire Regt
SMITH James F. MM Bdr 9077 HQ 108 Bde RFA
SMITH James Fraser MM Pnr 334898 198 Sig Coy Royal Engineers
SMITH James G. "DCM,MM+Bar" Sjt 11960 2nd Highland Light Infantry
SMITH James H. MM CQMS 240675 5th Yorkshire Light Infantry
SMITH James H. "DCM,MM" L/Cpl G/3961 1st East Kent Regt KIA 29.10.18.
SMITH James H. MM L/Sjt 8065 2nd Scottish Rifles
SMITH James Herbert MM Pte 19958 11th Notts & Derby Regt
SMITH James M. MM Sjt 6495 Northumberland Fusiliers
SMITH James P. MM Pte 7834 1st Somerset Light Infantry
SMITH James Patrick George MM Sjt 1224 15th Lancashire Fusiliers
SMITH James Thomas MM L/Cpl 46125 Machine Gun Corps
SMITH James W. MM Cpl 10556 7/8th King's Own Scottish Borderers
SMITH James W. MM Sjt 235347 2nd South Staffordshire Regt
SMITH James W. MM Cpl 11368 7th Duke of Cornwall's LI
SMITH James W. MM Sjt 122612 RGA
SMITH James W. MM Pte 202018 West Yorkshire Regt
SMITH James W. MM Pte 77292 5th Bn Tank Corps
SMITH James William MM Pte 7827 12th Manchester Regt KIA 10.11.17
SMITH Jarvis Henry MM Pte 16048 9th Leicestershire Regt
SMITH Jasper T. MM Spr 85094 34 Div Sig Coy Royal Engineers
SMITH Jephthah William MM Gnr 165458 C/114 Bde RFA
SMITH Joe MM Cpl Shoeing Smith 5785 C/291 Bde RFA
SMITH Joe MM Pte C/7690 13th King's Royal Rifle Corps
SMITH Joe MM Pte 72383 19 Fd Amb RAMC
SMITH John MM L/Cpl 632378 234 Div Emp Coy Labour Corps
SMITH John MM L/Cpl 295153 12th Royal Scots Fusiliers
SMITH John MM Pte 804 1st Royal Highlanders
SMITH John MM Sjt 200205 Yorkshire Light Infantry
SMITH John MM Dvr 85939 82 Bde RFA
SMITH John MM Cpl 6637 RFA
SMITH John MM Pte 14441 1st Royal Highlanders
SMITH John MM Pte 75438 101 Fd Amb RAMC
SMITH John MM Pte 300363 13th Liverpool Regt
SMITH John MM L/Cpl 2640 1st Irish Guards
SMITH John MM Sjt 240127 1/6th Highland Light Infantry
SMITH John MM Pte 9641 2nd Royal Highlanders
SMITH John MM Pte 140181 Machine Gun Corps
SMITH John MM Pte 9585 2nd Durham Light Infantry
SMITH John MM Sjt 85098 Machine Gun Corps
SMITH John MM L/Cpl 267889 1/6th West Riding Regt att MGC.
SMITH John MM+Bar CSM 11074 6th East Kent Regt
SMITH John MM L/Cpl 266246 1/4th Gordon Highlanders KIA 25.3.18.
SMITH John MM Pte 19615 East Lancashire Regt
SMITH John MM L/Cpl 200493 Tank Corps
SMITH John MM Pte 33484 West Riding Regt
SMITH John MM Pte 33423 Lancashire Fusiliers
SMITH John MM Cpl 200280 1/5th Manchester Regt
SMITH John MM Pte 281314 Lancashire Fusiliers
SMITH John MM Pte 15748 1st West Yorkshire Regt
SMITH John MM Pte 20255 13th Gloucestershire Regt
SMITH John MM Sjt 3166 Machine Gun Corps
SMITH John MM+Bar Sjt 37787 RAMC
SMITH John MM L/Cpl 8889 2nd Coldstream Guards KIA 31.7.17.
SMITH John MM Sjt 18914 Northumberland Fusiliers

SMITH John MM Pte 26784 Suffolk Regt
SMITH John MM Pte 25320 2nd Yorkshire Light Infantry
SMITH John MM Pte 13940 7th Somerset Light Infantry KIA 1.10.16.
SMITH John MM Sjt 1638 33 CCS RAMC
SMITH John MM Pte 31552 Notts & Derby Regt
SMITH John MM Sjt 15684 11th Northumberland Fusiliers
SMITH John MM Sjt 9433 2nd Royal West Surrey Regt
SMITH John MM Pte 74206 10th Notts & Derby Regt
SMITH John MM Pte 265298 1/6th Seaforth Highlanders
SMITH John MM L/Cpl 6230 1st Royal Welsh Fusiliers
SMITH John MM Pte 40627 Seaforth Highlanders
SMITH John MM+Bar Cpl 16861 13th Cheshire Regt
SMITH John MM Pte 30154 Machine Gun Corps
SMITH John MM Pte 9834 2nd Royal Dublin Fusiliers
SMITH John MM Sjt Fitter 685110 RFA
SMITH John MM Pte 16862 7th Bedfordshire Regt
SMITH John MM L/Cpl 242465 1/5th Gordon Highlanders KIA 12.4.18.
SMITH John MM Pte 15385 11th Border Regt
SMITH John MM+Bar Pte 16455 Royal Highlanders
SMITH John MM Dvr 39526 RFA
SMITH John MM+Bar Cpl 9678 Royal Highlanders
SMITH John A. MM Pte 89589 Middlesex Regt
SMITH John A. MM Pte M2/155624 Army Service Corps
SMITH John Alfred MM Pte 18450 I Corps Cyclist Bn Army Cyclist Corps
SMITH John Arthur MM Pte 12/234 11th East Yorkshire Regt KIA 6.9.18.
SMITH John Brown MM Pte 4881 9th Seaforth Highlanders DOW 11.7.17.
SMITH John C. MM Sjt 201053 RGA
SMITH John C. MM Sjt 250805 Manchester Regt
SMITH John C. MM L/Cpl 42196 Yorkshire Light Infantry
SMITH John D. MM L/Cpl 550065 1/16th London Regt
SMITH John E. MM Sjt 275310 1/1st Sherwood Rangers Yeo
SMITH John Edward MM Dvr 120853 B/95 Bde RFA DOW 23.9.17.
SMITH John Edward MM Sjt 23113 1st Royal Inniskilling Fusiliers KIA 23.4.17.
SMITH John Edward MM Gnr 86139 103 Bde RFA
SMITH John F. MM L/Cpl 242449 1st Gordon Highlanders
SMITH John F. MM Pte 10515 Royal Sussex Regt
SMITH John F. MM Pte 1067 Notts & Derby Regt
SMITH John F. MM Pte 76431 2nd Bn Tank Corps
SMITH John G. MM Dvr 90422 23 Div Sig Coy Royal Engineers
SMITH John H. "MM,MSM" Gnr 4399 RFA att HQ 157 Inf Bde.
SMITH John Henry MM L/Cpl 10114 2nd Notts & Derby Regt
SMITH John Henry MM Pte 18314 Machine Gun Corps KIA 28.8.18.
SMITH John James MM Pte 203077 1/4th Hampshire Regt
SMITH John L. MM L/Cpl 17930 9th Suffolk Regt
SMITH John Leonard MM Sjt 7869 2nd Devonshire Regt
SMITH John Nicholas MM Sjt T4/038664 98 Coy Army Service Corps KIA 14.2.17.
SMITH John P. MM Pte 251073 Royal Scots
SMITH John Percival "MM,GMV(S)" Sjt 538016 Royal Engineers
SMITH John R. MM Pte 28626 North Lancashire Regt
SMITH John R. MM Sjt 123 6th Royal West Surrey Regt
SMITH John R. MM Pte 47873 Royal Scots
SMITH John Robert MM Gnr 93986 A/187 Bde RFA
SMITH John S. MM Pte 1992 RAMC
SMITH John T. MM Pte 8894 1st Royal West Surrey Regt
SMITH John T. MM L/Cpl 73193 RAMC
SMITH John T. MM 2nd Cpl 43578 Royal Engineers
SMITH John T. MM Spr 155843 251 Tunnelling Coy Royal Engineers
SMITH John Taylor MM Sjt 13724 11th West Yorkshire Regt DOW 26.3.18.
SMITH John Thomas MM Sjt S/4939 9th Rifle Brigade
SMITH John Thomas MM Gnr 113787 253 Siege Bty RGA Died 31.10.17.
SMITH John W. MM Pte 13482 7th Leicestershire Regt
SMITH John W. MM Dvr 71662 RFA
SMITH John W. MM Bdr 5728 RFA
SMITH John W. MM Cpl 17311 1st Royal Warwickshire Regt
SMITH John W. MM Pte 65355 Northumberland Fusiliers
SMITH John W. MM Pte 2940 1/1st Warwickshire Yeomanry KIA 8.11.17.
SMITH John W. "MM,MID" Pte 2373 Royal Scots
SMITH John W. MM Pte 17192 13th Essex Regt
SMITH John W. MM Cpl 9700 A/149 Bde RFA
SMITH John W. MM L/Cpl 9263 2nd West Yorkshire Regt
SMITH John W. MM Pte 229315 Royal Fusiliers
SMITH John W.G. MM Spr 630237 1/20th London Regt
SMITH John William MM L/Cpl 24826 13th Durham Light Infantry
SMITH John William MM Gnr 751267 D/285 Bde RFA
SMITH Joseph MM L/Cpl 143472 106 Fd Coy Royal Engineers
SMITH Joseph MM Pte 52132 6th Northamptonshire Regt
SMITH Joseph MM Pte 19933 21st Manchester Regt
SMITH Joseph MM L/Cpl 13845 12th Manchester Regt KIA 7.7.16.
SMITH Joseph MM L/Cpl 202981 Royal Berkshire Regt
SMITH Joseph "MM,MID" Pte 2275 1/4th Yorkshire Light Infantry
SMITH Joseph MM Sjt 9402 8th Lincolnshire Regt KIA 12.4.17.
SMITH Joseph MM Cpl 11879 7th East Yorkshire Regt KIA 12.5.17.
SMITH Joseph MM Sjt 2558 Gordon Highlanders
SMITH Joseph MM Pte 6632 11th Manchester Regt KIA 5.10.17.
SMITH Joseph MM Cpl 18673 19th Lancashire Fusiliers
SMITH Joseph MM Gnr 99527 RGA
SMITH Joseph MM Pte 10814 6th Border Regt
SMITH Joseph MM Cpl 12748 10th West Riding Regt KIA 18.10.17.
SMITH Joseph H. "DCM,MM" Sjt 24175 2 Div Sig Coy Royal Engineers
SMITH Joseph H.W. MM+Bar Pte 22934 2nd Grenadier Guards
SMITH Joseph Henry "MM,MSM" L/Cpl 2682 1/8th Middlesex Regt
SMITH Joseph Henry MM Spr 53223 18 Div Sig Coy Royal Engineers KIA 2.10.17.
SMITH Joseph J. MM L/Cpl 350088 9th Royal Scots
SMITH Joseph Stanislaw MM Sjt 2085 24th Royal Fusiliers
SMITH Joseph Stanley "MM,MSM" Sjt 242672 1/5th North Lancashire Regt
SMITH Joseph T. MM L/Cpl 3045 Gloucestershire Regt
SMITH Joseph Thomas MM Pte 201720 1/4th York & Lancaster Regt Died 19.11.18.
SMITH Joseph W. MM Sjt 253 Liverpool Regt
SMITH Joseph Wilfred MM Pte 202138 1/5th Seaforth Highlanders DOW 26.7.18.
SMITH Josiah MM Gnr 51334 RGA
SMITH Josiah George MM L/Cpl 12218 5th Northamptonshire Regt
SMITH L. MM Pte 20537 6th Northamptonshire Regt
SMITH L. MM Cpl 3345 Gloucestershire Regt
SMITH Lancelot MM L/Cpl 2390 11th Suffolk Regt KIA 24.10.18.
SMITH Laurence E. MM Pte 42470 1st Dorsetshire Regt
SMITH Laurie MM L/Cpl 11184 1st King's Own Scottish Borderers
SMITH Lawrence MM Pte R/3655 13th King's Royal Rifle Corps
SMITH Lawrence MM Sjt 43092 Machine Gun Corps
SMITH Lawrence B.A. MM Spr 142595 Royal Engineers
SMITH Leonard MM L/Sjt 2057 8th Royal West Surrey Regt
SMITH Leonard MM L/Sjt 19/453 19th Northumberland Fusiliers
SMITH Leonard MM Pte 24701 13th Royal Scots
SMITH Leonard MM Pnr 259569 18 Div Sig Coy Royal Engineers
SMITH Leonard MM Sjt 35961 6th Bedfordshire Regt KIA 29.4.17.
SMITH Leonard Clifford MM Sjt 430 11th Royal Warwickshire Regt KIA 11.7.16.
SMITH Leonard Edward MM Cpl 32668 RAMC
SMITH Leonard G. MM Cpl 19119 1 Fd Sqn Royal Engineers
SMITH Leonard H. MM Sjt 1084 12th Lancers AKA BOWKER
SMITH Leonard Haffner MM Pte 341566 RAMC
SMITH Leonard V. MM Bdr 136861 RGA
SMITH Leslie MM Cpl 406082 Royal Engineers
SMITH Leslie G. MM L/Cpl 554888 16th London Regt
SMITH Leslie S. MM Dvr 22526 RFA
SMITH Leslie T. MM Pte 14046 7th Wiltshire Regt
SMITH Levi MM Pte 13720 8th North Staffordshire Regt KIA 18.4.18.
SMITH Lewis Henry MM Spr 218562 Rly Ops Div Royal Engineers
SMITH M. MM+Bar Sjt P2406 Military Foot Police
SMITH Mark R.E. MM S/Sjt Farrier 26737 25 Bde RFA
SMITH Mark W. MM Pte R/37827 King's Royal Rifle Corps
SMITH Marshall "DCM,MM+Bar" Sjt 16071 9th Yorkshire Regt
SMITH Matthew MM L/Cpl 14334 XIII Corps Cyclist Bn Army Cyclist Corps
SMITH Maurice A. MM Sjt M2/191903 Army Service Corps
SMITH Michael MM Pte 8145 2nd Royal Dublin Fusiliers
SMITH Montague F. MM Pte 47291 77 Fd Amb RAMC
SMITH N. MM L/Cpl 3601 West Riding Regt
SMITH Nathaniel S. MM Pte 17905 11th Notts & Derby Regt KIA 5.10.18.
SMITH Noah MM Pte 33575 Welsh Regt
SMITH Norman "MM,MID" Cpl 482204 Royal Engineers
SMITH Norman MM L/Cpl 44203 7th Lincolnshire Regt
SMITH Norman S. MM Pte 250326 Manchester Regt

SMITH Obadiah Ellis MM Sjt 13096 8th Norfolk Regt
SMITH Oliver MM Bdr 36623 RFA
SMITH Oliver S. MM L/Sjt 5011 20th Hussars ? Hussars
SMITH P. MM Pte 42378 17th Highland Light Infantry
SMITH P. "DCM,MM" Sjt 200855 South Lancashire Regt
SMITH P.J. MM+Bar Sjt 2806 RFA
SMITH P.T. MM L/Cpl 452060 London Regt
SMITH Patrick MM Pte 20/441 20th Durham Light Infantry
SMITH Percival Ernest Day MM Pte 64586 63 Coy Machine Gun Corps
SMITH Percy MM Cpl 62441 10th West Yorkshire Regt
SMITH Percy MM L/Cpl 266313 6th Gloucestershire Regt
SMITH Percy MM Pte 20378 Oxf & Bucks Light Infantry
SMITH Percy MM Pte 6475 20 Coy Machine Gun Corps KIA 26.10.17.
SMITH Percy MM Pte 1696 1/23rd London Regt KIA 14.4.18.
SMITH Percy MM Pte 495 Royal West Surrey Regt
SMITH Percy MM Sjt 102865 1st Notts & Derby Regt
SMITH Percy MM Cpl 203197 2/4th Lincolnshire Regt
SMITH Percy MM L/Cpl 4699 Seaforth Highlanders
SMITH Percy MM Cpl 18732 6th Yorkshire Light Infantry
SMITH Percy E. MM Pte 1228 RAMC
SMITH Percy H.V. MM Pte 95316 4th Middlesex Regt
SMITH Percy J. MM Sjt M1/08271 Army Service Corps
SMITH Percy Lloyd MM Cpl 72120 42 Bty 2 Bde RFA KIA 21.3.18.
SMITH Percy R. MM Sjt 25920 56th Bn Machine Gun Corps
SMITH Percy V. MM Pte 1747 7th Royal West Surrey Regt
SMITH Peter MM Pte 75214 13th Royal Fusiliers
SMITH Peter MM+Bar Pte 192209 201 Coy Machine Gun Corps
SMITH Peter MM Pte 241181 Gordon Highlanders
SMITH Peter MM Pte 20817 22nd Manchester Regt
SMITH Peter L. MM Pte 315218 13th Royal Highlanders
SMITH Philip Clarence "MM,MSM" Sjt 13310 RFA Died 22.2.19.
SMITH R. MM L/Cpl 55779 11th Northumberland Fusiliers
SMITH R.C. MM+Bar Sjt 59744 32 Bde RFA
SMITH Rabbi MM Dvr T/368136 Army Service Corps
SMITH Ralph MM L/Sjt 652821 1/21st London Regt DOW 3.9.18.
SMITH Ralph J. MM Bdr 681769 RFA
SMITH Reginald MM Pte 240409 6th Notts & Derby Regt
SMITH Reginald MM Cpl 19061 12th Bn Machine Gun Corps
SMITH Reginald MM Pte 25139 2nd West Riding Regt DOW 10.9.18.
SMITH Reginald MM Pte Z/53 2nd Rifle Brigade KIA 25.4.18.
SMITH Reginald MM Dvr 33735 RFA
SMITH Reginald C. MM Cpl 17984 Suffolk Regt
SMITH Reginald F. MM Pte 29719 12th Somerset Light Infantry
SMITH Reginald J. MM Pte 11832 3rd Grenadier Guards
SMITH Reginald R. MM Pte 33983 RAMC
SMITH Reginald W. MM L/Cpl 6420 9th Lancers
SMITH Richaed Samuel MM Pte 4246 1/5th West Riding Regt
SMITH Richard MM Dvr T2/016151 Army Service Corps
SMITH Richard MM Pte 27767 1st Bedfordshire Regt
SMITH Richard MM Sjt 630741 RFA
SMITH Richard MM Pte 17660 Royal Warwickshire Regt att MGC
SMITH Richard MM Sjt 650436 RFA
SMITH Richard MM Pte 200917 1/4th North Lancashire Regt KIA 13.10.18.
SMITH Richard MM Sjt 12440 12 Fd Amb RAMC
SMITH Richard MM Cpl 63324 45 Bde RFA
SMITH Richard E. MM Cpl 112584 14th Bn Tank Corps
SMITH Richard Edwin MM Cpl 17579 1st South Staffordshire Regt KIA 26.10.17.
SMITH Richard H. MM+Bar CSM 10475 1st King's Own Scottish Borderers
SMITH Richard H. MM Dvr 10729 Hampshire Regt
SMITH Richard J. MM Pte 701339 1/23rd London Regt
SMITH Richard Stanley MM Cpl 200590 2/5th North Staffordshire Regt KIA 21.3.18.
SMITH Robert MM L/Cpl 28822 2nd Royal Scots Fusiliers
SMITH Robert MM Cpl 295521 12th Royal Scots Fusiliers
SMITH Robert MM Gnr Fitter 122079 RFA
SMITH Robert MM Pte 41031 1st Norfolk Regt
SMITH Robert MM Pte 50809 2/6th Liverpool Regt KIA 30.8.18.
SMITH Robert MM Sjt 023182 Army Ordnance Corps
SMITH Robert MM Pte 201167 Cameron Highlanders
SMITH Robert MM Pte 14548 8th Royal Dublin Fusiliers KIA 7.9.16.
SMITH Robert MM QMS 9 1(Northumbrian)Fd Amb RAMC Died 1.8.16.
SMITH Robert MM Pte 19680 Duke of Cornwall's LI
SMITH Robert MM Cpl 545 2nd Gordon Highlanders
SMITH Robert MM Pte 17319 Royal Scots Fusiliers
SMITH Robert MM Pte 26793 5th Cameron Highlanders KIA 25.4.18.
SMITH Robert MM Pte 6635 1st Gordon Highlanders
SMITH Robert MM Pte 202802 Liverpool Regt
SMITH Robert B. MM Pte 201082 Gordon Highlanders
SMITH Robert C. MM+Bar Cpl 37378 42nd Bn Machine Gun Corps
SMITH Robert E. MM Pte 910 6th Royal West Kent Regt
SMITH Robert G. MM Pte 61170 RAMC
SMITH Robert George MM Pte 2529 1/7th Middlesex Regt
SMITH Robert Godfrey MM Gnr Fitter 94598 B/63 Bde RFA
SMITH Robert H. MM L/Cpl 6995 5th Shropshire Light Infantry
SMITH Robert L. MM+Bar Sjt 74570 14 Bde RFA
SMITH Robert S. MM Pte 5520 1/7th Middlesex Regt
SMITH Robert S. MM Sjt 18031 10th Manchester Regt
SMITH Robert Taylor MM Cpl 51442 10th West Yorkshire Regt
SMITH Robert V. MM L/Bdr 950675 A/18 Bde RFA
SMITH Robert Wray "DCM,MM+Bar" Sjt 386188 1(Northumbrian)Fd Amb RAMC
SMITH Rodney MM Pte 207899 Royal West Surrey Regt
SMITH Roger MM Pte 6683 16th Manchester Regt KIA 15.10.16.
SMITH Ronald H. MM Pte 13938 3rd Royal Fusiliers
SMITH Roy MM+Bar L/Cpl 54840 Royal Fusiliers
SMITH S. MM Pte 35871 1st Essex Regt
SMITH S. MM Sjt 13152 Royal Fusiliers
SMITH S. MM Pte 285065 Oxf & Bucks Light Infantry
SMITH Samuel MM Pte 22612 2nd Highland Light Infantry
SMITH Samuel MM L/Cpl 592699 1/18th London Regt
SMITH Samuel MM L/Cpl 51475 2nd Scottish Rifles
SMITH Samuel MM Pte 202333 2/4th West Riding Regt
SMITH Samuel MM Pte 86582 29th Bn Machine Gun Corps
SMITH Samuel MM Gnr 755544 RFA
SMITH Samuel MM Sjt 28073 4th North Staffordshire Regt KIA 29.3.18.
SMITH Samuel MM Pte 6774 1st Hampshire Regt
SMITH Samuel MM Pte 7129 1st Rifle Brigade
SMITH Samuel "MM,MID" Sjt 7046 2nd Royal Berkshire Regt
SMITH Samuel MM Pte 19651 South Lancashire Regt
SMITH Samuel MM Pte 16100 9th York & Lancaster Regt KIA 24.9.17.
SMITH Samuel A. MM Pte 201038 2nd Lincolnshire Regt
SMITH Samuel Ernest Earlean MM Cpl 13023 7 Div Ammn Col RFA
SMITH Samuel W. MM Pte 39620 7th West Yorkshire Regt
SMITH Seymour Norton MM Pte MS/3583 Army Service Corps att HQ 3 Cav Div.
SMITH Sidney MM BSM 280764 166 Siege Bty RGA
SMITH Sidney MM Pte 200948 1/4th Gloucestershire Regt KIA 23.4.17.
SMITH Sidney MM Pte 19337 9th Royal Inniskilling Fusiliers
SMITH Sidney A. MM Pte 531004 1/15th London Regt
SMITH Sidney G. MM BSM 11118 D/52 Bde RFA
SMITH Sidney H. MM Pte 6795 1st Royal West Surrey Regt
SMITH Sidney H. MM Cpl 56059 RGA
SMITH Sidney H. MM Pte 72404 15th Notts & Derby Regt
SMITH Sidney H. MM+2 Bars Pte 14270 5th Yorkshire Light Infantry
SMITH Sidney J. MM Pte 13070 8th Norfolk Regt
SMITH Sidney Oliver MM L/Cpl 9129 1st Essex Regt DOW 15.10.16.
SMITH Sidney W. MM L/Cpl R/4776 13th King's Royal Rifle Corps
SMITH Stanley MM Pte 250874 1/5th Essex Regt
SMITH Stanley MM Sjt 3/10169 9th Norfolk Regt Died 18.8.16.
SMITH Stanley "MM,MID" Pte 12060 9th Essex Regt
SMITH Stanley MM Pte DM2/162277 Army Service Corps
SMITH Stephen MM L/Cpl 149195 Royal Engineers
SMITH Stephen Alexander MM Cpl 114209 327 Siege Bty RGA
SMITH Stephen J. "MM,MSM" Sjt 7894 1st Royal Berkshire Regt
SMITH Stuart W.J. MM Pte 14707 1/5th Arg & Suth Highlanders
SMITH Sydney MM Pte 261081 13th West Riding Regt
SMITH Sydney MM Pte 22877 Cameron Highlanders
SMITH Sydney MM Pte 27060 Royal Scots
SMITH Sydney MM Bdr 64599 27 Bde RFA
SMITH Sydney B. MM Sjt 794 15th Royal Warwickshire Regt
SMITH Sydney C. MM L/Cpl 144 1/4th Royal Berkshire Regt
SMITH Sydney Edwin MM Pte 201259 1/4th East Yorkshire Regt DOW 11.4.18.
SMITH Sydney J. MM Pte 12367 7th Norfolk Regt
SMITH Sydney T. MM+Bar Sjt R/4061 13th King's Royal Rifle Corps
SMITH Sydney W. MM Gnr 801368 295 Bde RFA
SMITH Sydney W. MM Sjt 25844 10th Royal West Surrey Regt
SMITH Sylvester MM Pte 39832 South Wales Borderers

SMITH T. MM Pte 318218 2 Fd Amb RAMC
SMITH T. MM Pte 27233 Yorkshire Light Infantry
SMITH T. MM Pte 200423 Worcestershire Regt
SMITH Thomas MM Pte 306263 10th West Yorkshire Regt
SMITH Thomas MM Spr 134015 Royal Engineers
SMITH Thomas MM Cpl 71089 18th Bn Machine Gun Corps
SMITH Thomas MM L/Sjt 630022 20th London Regt
SMITH Thomas MM L/Cpl 265979 2/7th Royal Warwickshire Regt DOW 28.10.18.
SMITH Thomas MM Pte 40485 Highland Light Infantry
SMITH Thomas MM Sjt 3068 2nd Rifle Brigade
SMITH Thomas MM Pte 31753 6th Royal West Kent Regt
SMITH Thomas MM Pte 63744 1/6th Cheshire Regt
SMITH Thomas MM Spr 147699 176 Tunnelling Coy Royal Engineers
SMITH Thomas MM Cpl 59592 Welsh Regt
SMITH Thomas MM L/Cpl 17/862 17th Northumberland Fusiliers
SMITH Thomas MM+Bar Pte 17181 1st Royal Irish Fusiliers
SMITH Thomas MM Pte 202745 Gloucestershire Regt
SMITH Thomas MM Dvr 20318 RFA
SMITH Thomas MM Pte 92365 'E' Bn Tank Corps DOW 24.11.17.
SMITH Thomas MM Sjt 267466 West Yorkshire Regt
SMITH Thomas MM Pte 240083 1/5th King's Own Scottish Borderers
SMITH Thomas "DCM,MM,MID" Sjt 17850 11th Scottish Rifles
SMITH Thomas MM Pte R/9460 King's Royal Rifle Corps
SMITH Thomas MM Pte 17002 12th Notts & Derby Regt
SMITH Thomas MM Gnr 73663 D/211 Bde RFA KIA 4.11.18.
SMITH Thomas "MM,MID" Cpl 6047 Royal Scots Fusiliers
SMITH Thomas MM Pte 7273 1st Gordon Highlanders
SMITH Thomas MM Sjt 413 22nd Royal Fusiliers KIA 17.2.17.
SMITH Thomas MM Pte 19408 2nd Grenadier Guards
SMITH Thomas MM Gnr 16213 C/189 Bde RFA
SMITH Thomas MM Cpl 14511 11th West Yorkshire Regt
SMITH Thomas MM Sjt 37402 4th Liverpool Regt
SMITH Thomas MM Pte 22329 King's Own Scottish Borderers
SMITH Thomas MM Sjt 8907 9th North Staffordshire Regt
SMITH Thomas MM L/Cpl 203689 1st London Regt DOW 15.4.18.
SMITH Thomas MM Pte 24343 Grenadier Guards
SMITH Thomas MM Pte S/17871 Rifle Brigade
SMITH Thomas MM L/Cpl 10020 Royal Highlanders
SMITH Thomas "DCM,MM" Sjt 8112 7th Bedfordshire Regt
SMITH Thomas MM Pte S/9416 Rifle Brigade
SMITH Thomas MM Pte 66209 Royal Fusiliers
SMITH Thomas MM Pte 38739 Welsh Regt
SMITH Thomas A. "DCM,MM" Sjt 285016 1/1st Hertfordshire Regt
SMITH Thomas Arthur MM Gnr 124307 HQ 45 Bde RFA
SMITH Thomas C. MM Pte 65226 1st Northumberland Fusiliers
SMITH Thomas C. MM Gnr 8265 420 Bty RFA
SMITH Thomas C. MM Pte 9413 1st Royal Berkshire Regt
SMITH Thomas Charles MM+Bar Sjt 7718 1st Royal West Kent Regt
SMITH Thomas Charles "MM,MID" Sjt 50242 Machine Gun Corps
SMITH Thomas E. MM Pte 77988 10th Royal Fusiliers
SMITH Thomas Finlayson MM Sjt 350996 1/9th Royal Scots KIA 22.3.18.
SMITH Thomas Gordon MM Pte 10073 5th Cameron Highlanders KIA 12.10.17.
SMITH Thomas H. MM Sjt 75391 12th Manchester Regt
SMITH Thomas H. MM L/Cpl 24635 Grenadier Guards
SMITH Thomas Harry MM Pte 200335 1/4th Oxf & Bucks Light Infantry
SMITH Thomas Henry MM Pte 8648 1st Coldstream Guards
SMITH Thomas J. MM Pte 1391 1/5th Liverpool Regt
SMITH Thomas John MM Cpl 618345 A/298 Bde RFA DOW 22.3.18.
SMITH Thomas Noah MM Sjt 830924 306 Bde RFA
SMITH Thomas Richard MM Sjt 11962 7th Cameron Highlanders
SMITH Thomas V. MM L/Bdr 40293 108 Heavy Bty RGA
SMITH Thomas W. MM Sjt 851328 C/242 Bde RFA
SMITH Thomas W. MM Pte 14517 15/17th West Yorkshire Regt
SMITH Thomas W. MM Sjt 13987 8th Suffolk Regt
SMITH Tom MM Pte 18870 7th East Lancashire Regt
SMITH Trevor MM Spr 79728 170 Tunnelling Coy Royal Engineers DOW 23.11.17.
SMITH Vernon L.H. MM Cpl 19777 Machine Gun Corps
SMITH Vernon Samuel MM L/Cpl 1936 1/6th Notts & Derby Regt
SMITH Victor MM Cpl 96600 A/51 Bde RFA
SMITH Victor MM Sjt 18799 9 Fd Amb RAMC
SMITH W. MM Cpl 219721 147 Bde Ammn Col RFA
SMITH W. MM Pte 301500 1 Fd Amb RAMC
SMITH W. MM Pte 42747 Essex Regt
SMITH W. MM+Bar Sjt 2851 RFA
SMITH W.A. MM Pte 703474 London Regt
SMITH W.C. MM Pte 8928 1st Norfolk Regt
SMITH W.H. MM Gnr 117515 A/106 Bde RFA
SMITH W.J. MM Sjt 773 Military Mounted Police
SMITH W.T. MM Pte 17972 2nd Wiltshire Regt
SMITH W.T. "DCM,MM" Pnr 48027 14 Div Sig Coy Royal Engineers
SMITH W.W. MM Sjt 45646 Royal Engineers
SMITH Wallace MM Pte 200867 1/4th Northamptonshire Regt
SMITH Walter MM Pte 15072 2nd Scots Guards
SMITH Walter MM Cpl 240657 1/5th Lancashire Fusiliers
SMITH Walter MM Pte 18377 5th Leicestershire Regt
SMITH Walter MM Pte 202816 6th Leicestershire Regt
SMITH Walter MM Pte 265844 2/4th West Riding Regt
SMITH Walter MM L/Cpl 50301 Suffolk Regt
SMITH Walter MM Pte 290791 Cheshire Regt
SMITH Walter MM Pte 242218 North Lancashire Regt
SMITH Walter MM Cpl Saddler 13295 RFA
SMITH Walter MM Pte C/12938 King's Royal Rifle Corps
SMITH Walter MM Cpl 1319 47 Siege Bty RGA
SMITH Walter MM Sjt 18933 Machine Gun Corps
SMITH Walter MM Sjt 1386 1/4th Lincolnshire Regt
SMITH Walter MM Pte 25678 1st Bn Machine Gun Corps
SMITH Walter MM L/Bdr 38063 B/186 Bde RFA KIA 13.10.18.
SMITH Walter MM Sjt 19031 1st Essex Regt DOW 25.8.17.
SMITH Walter MM Gnr 63754 2 Bde RFA
SMITH Walter MM Gnr 42814 A/14 Bde RFA
SMITH Walter MM Pte 510035 2/2(London)Fd Amb RAMC
SMITH Walter MM L/Sjt C/1521 King's Royal Rifle Corps
SMITH Walter George MM Cpl 133469 2nd Bn Machine Gun Corps DOW 21.10.18.
SMITH Walter L. MM Sjt 46350 1205 Bty 12 Bde RFA
SMITH Walter T. MM L/Cpl 52337 8th West Yorkshire Regt
SMITH Walter T. MM Sjt Farrier 41564 39 Bde RFA
SMITH Wiilfred J. "DCM,MM" Sjt 39708 4th Worcestershire Regt
SMITH Wilfred MM Pte 54866 10th Notts & Derby Regt
SMITH Wilfred MM Cpl 73162 5th Bn Machine Gun Corps
SMITH Wilfred MM Cpl 43698 'O' Bty RHA
SMITH Wilfred MM Pte R/7669 18th King's Royal Rifle Corps DOW 29.9.18.
SMITH Wilfred A. MM+Bar Sjt 40839 8th Royal Lancaster Regt
SMITH Wilfred H. MM Gnr 200815 B/87 Bde RFA
SMITH Wilfred H. MM Pte 423076 10th London Regt
SMITH Wilfred Henry MM Cpl 26823 1st Dorsetshire Regt DOW 13.10.18.
SMITH William MM Pte 12685 17th Royal Fusiliers
SMITH William MM Pte 38639 9th Scottish Rifles KIA 20.10.18.
SMITH William MM Cpl 630051 C/255 Bty RFA
SMITH William MM Pte 144877 50th Bn Machine Gun Corps
SMITH William MM CQMS 3985 5th Royal Highlanders
SMITH William "DCM,MM" CSM 235348 2nd South Staffordshire Regt
SMITH William MM Cpl 5325 8th East Surrey Regt
SMITH William MM L/Cpl 267559 Rly Ops Div Royal Engineers
SMITH William MM Gnr 630845 C/255 Bde RFA
SMITH William MM CQMS 158934 25th Bn Machine Gun Corps
SMITH William MM Pte 14550 Durham Light Infantry
SMITH William MM L/Cpl 63657 13th Yorkshire Regt
SMITH William MM Pte 27037 6th Leicestershire Regt KIA 3.5.17.
SMITH William MM Sjt 51793 5/6th Royal Scots
SMITH William MM Sjt 11172 Royal West Surrey Regt
SMITH William MM Sjt 3152 6th Leinster Regt
SMITH William MM Cpl 23089 Oxf & Bucks Light Infantry
SMITH William MM Pte 200237 1/4th Seaforth Highlanders
SMITH William MM Pte 11534 2nd Royal Sussex Regt KIA 4.11.18.
SMITH William MM Pte 20501 15th Cheshire Regt
SMITH William MM L/Cpl 244734 15th Cheshire Regt
SMITH William MM Sjt 65777 49 Bty 40 Bde RFA
SMITH William MM Pte 23025 2nd West Riding Regt
SMITH William MM L/Cpl 4518 6th Dragoons
SMITH William MM Sjt 235648 1/4th Gordon Highlanders
SMITH William MM Pte 375772 8th London Regt
SMITH William MM Cpl 120626 'C' Special Coy Royal Engineers
SMITH William MM L/Cpl 32565 Royal Welsh Fusiliers
SMITH William MM Pte 40464 Yorkshire Regt
SMITH William MM Cpl 108579 Royal Engineers att HQ 41 Div
SMITH William MM Pte 1518 Welsh Regt
SMITH William MM L/Cpl 422567 Royal Engineers

SMITH William MM Pte 75012 Tank Corps
SMITH William MM Dvr 836000 RFA
SMITH William MM Sjt 25666 Dorsetshire Regt
SMITH William MM Cpl 21999 Middlesex Regt
SMITH William "DCM,MM" L/Sjt 66599 99 Fd Amb RAMC KIA 1.11.17.
SMITH William "MM+Bar,MID" Cpl 12344 Machine Gun Corps
SMITH William MM Pte 5570 2nd Gordon Highlanders
SMITH William MM Pte 10315 2nd Scottish Rifles
SMITH William "DCM,MM+Bar" Pte 9747 1st Cameron Highlanders
SMITH William MM L/Sjt 8700 2nd Welsh Regt
SMITH William MM Cpl 2214 1/4th East Yorkshire Regt
SMITH William MM L/Cpl 7640 1st Royal West Kent Regt
SMITH William MM Sjt R/7926 2nd King's Royal Rifle Corps
SMITH William MM Pte 3079 Royal West Surrey Regt
SMITH William MM Pte 12572 2nd Royal Scots Fusiliers
SMITH William MM Gnr 45563 13 Siege Bty Royal Artillery KIA 26.9.17.
SMITH William MM Pte B/793 12th Rifle Brigade KIA 6.6.16.
SMITH William MM 2nd Cpl 67618 129 Fd Coy Royal Engineers DOW 23.6.17.
SMITH William MM Sjt 58647 163 Siege Bty RGA
SMITH William MM Cpl 63496 C/114 Bde RFA
SMITH William MM Cpl 49998 5/6th Royal Scots
SMITH William MM Cpl 53039 1/7th Royal Scots
SMITH William MM Pte 9080 Coldstream Guards
SMITH William "MM,MID" Sjt 62362 3 Bde RHA
SMITH William MM Sjt 32133 RAMC
SMITH William MM L/Cpl 36480 Royal Berkshire Regt
SMITH William "MM,MSM" Sjt 17/52 17th Northumberland Fusiliers
SMITH William MM Sjt 43412 Royal Engineers
SMITH William MM+Bar Sjt 39193 33 Coy Machine Gun Corps
SMITH William MM Gnr 755177 RFA
SMITH William MM Pte 40355 Highland Light Infantry
SMITH William MM Pte 18236 Royal Sussex Regt
SMITH William MM Pte 26065 Liverpool Regt
SMITH William MM Cpl 128604 RFA
SMITH William MM Pte 300812 1/8th Arg & Suth Highlanders "KIA 29.7.18,"
SMITH William MM L/Sjt 325225 1/1st Cambridgeshire Regt
SMITH William MM Sjt 8140 1st East Yorkshire Regt
SMITH William A. MM 2nd Cpl 193186 Royal Engineers
SMITH William A. MM L/Cpl 528490 74 Div Sig Coy Royal Engineers
SMITH William A. MM Cpl 568055 1 Div Sig Coy Royal Engineers
SMITH William Alexander MM L/Cpl 14378 1st Lincolnshire Regt KIA 16.4.18.
SMITH William Bernard "DCM+Bar,MM" Sjt 3783 1st Notts & Derby Regt
SMITH William Brooks MM Pte 3/8894 2nd Suffolk Regt KIA 19.7.16.
SMITH William C. MM Pte 242568 Royal Warwickshire Regt
SMITH William C. MM Cpl 1969 1/4th Northumberland Fusiliers
SMITH William C. MM Pte 265626 1/1st Hertfordshire Regt
SMITH William E. MM L/Cpl 33366 East Surrey Regt
SMITH William E. "MM+Bar,MID" CSM 7593 18th King's Royal Rifle Corps
SMITH William E. MM Cpl 513735 14th London Regt
SMITH William E. MM Gnr 931200 B/291 Bde RFA
SMITH William E. MM Sjt 34384 29 Bde RFA
SMITH William E. MM Pte 10711 20th Manchester Regt
SMITH William E. MM Cpl 42554 2nd Worcestershire Regt
SMITH William E.S. MM L/Cpl 21226 Royal Engineers
SMITH William F. MM Dvr 486320 468 Fd Coy Royal Engineers
SMITH William F. MM Dvr 338325 RGA
SMITH William G. MM Sjt 37151 41 Div Ammn Col RFA
SMITH William G. MM Cpl 8174 1st Royal Berkshire Regt
SMITH William G. MM L/Cpl 9256 1st Royal Berkshire Regt
SMITH William G. MM Dvr 227836 RFA
SMITH William G. MM Pte 74018 RAMC
SMITH William G.A. MM Pte 680736 1/22nd London Regt
SMITH William H. MM Sjt 242348 8th Worcestershire Regt
SMITH William H. MM Pte 275499 1/1st South Notts Hussars Yeomanry
SMITH William H. "MM,MIDx2" Sjt 7704 2nd Wiltshire Regt
SMITH William H. MM+Bar Sjt 50398 RGA
SMITH William H. "MM,MID" CSM 6245 4th King's Royal Rifle Corps
SMITH William H. MM Pte 202051 2/4th West Riding Regt
SMITH William H. "DCM,MM" Sjt 201458 West Riding Regt
SMITH William H. MM Sjt 22611 Durham Light Infantry
SMITH William H. MM Sjt 9814 1st East Yorkshire Regt
SMITH William H. MM Cpl 294371 144 Heavy Bty RGA
SMITH William H. MM Pte 15811 9th South Staffordshire Regt
SMITH William H. MM Cpl 6270 227 Coy Machine Gun Corps
SMITH William H.J. MM Pte 17228 13th Essex Regt
SMITH William Harry MM Pte 3769 1/1st Cambridgeshire Regt
SMITH William Henry "MM,MID" Cpl Sig 62493 117 Siege Bty RGA
SMITH William Henry MM+Bar L/Sjt 265343 1/7th Notts & Derby Regt
SMITH William Henry "MM,MSM,MID" Sjt 10602 1st South Staffordshire Regt
SMITH William Henry MM Cpl 30911 11th East Yorkshire Regt DOW 1.7.18.
SMITH William J. MM Pte 7412 11th Royal Fusiliers
SMITH William J. MM Sjt 8799 1st Cheshire Regt
SMITH William J. MM Pte 17062 Machine Gun Corps
SMITH William J. MM SQMS 47500 14th Hussars
SMITH William J. MM Pte 11986 RAMC
SMITH William J. MM 2nd Cpl 36908 Royal Engineers
SMITH William John MM Sjt 534014 1/4(London)Fd Amb RAMC
SMITH William Jordan MM Sjt 5203 1st Lincolnshire Regt KIA 11.4.17.
SMITH William Joseph MM Pte 26708 4th Bedfordshire Regt KIA 23.4.17.
SMITH William Joseph MM Cpl 51261 19 Light TM Bty RGA KIA 4.7.16.
SMITH William Joseph MM Pte 14814 7th Somerset Light Infantry KIA 24.6.17.
SMITH William L. MM Dvr 630956 RFA
SMITH William L. "DCM,MM" Sjt 16512 1st Coldstream Guards
SMITH William L. MM Pte DM2/207842 Army Service Corps att RGA.Died 22.2.19.
SMITH William Michael MM Gnr 2764 B/317 Bde RFA
SMITH William Neilson MM Gnr 2720 'C' Coy Machine Gun Corps(Heavy Section)
SMITH William O. MM+Bar Sjt 12258 57 Bde RFA
SMITH William Peel MM Spr 127584 'MM' Cable Section Royal Engineers
SMITH William Perfect MM Pte 37488 2nd Royal Berkshire Regt
SMITH William R. MM Gnr 20737 RFA
SMITH William Roy MM Sjt 1467 Durham Light Infantry
SMITH William S. MM L/Cpl 27402 Durham Light Infantry
SMITH William T. MM Pte 42159 Lancashire Fusiliers
SMITH William T. MM Pte 345740 Royal Highlanders
SMITH William T. MM Sjt 240983 Lancashire Fusiliers
SMITH William Thomas MM Cpl 241987 2/6th Royal Warwickshire Regt KIA 2.11.18.
SMITH William W. MM Gnr 39966 RGA
SMITH Willie Augustus MM Cpl 66915 111 Siege Bty RGA
SMITH Wilson MM Spr 42917 Royal Engineers
SMITH or SMYTH Joseph MM Pte 6928 Royal Irish Rifles
SMITHARD Herbert MM Pte 17641 Hampshire Regt
SMITHARD Richard S. MM L/Cpl 281837 2nd Highland Light Infantry
SMITHER H. MM Spr 56133 Royal Engineers
SMITHERS E.G. MM Pte 22478 6th East Kent Regt
SMITHERS Frank MM Gnr 87404 2 Bde RFA
SMITHERS George MM Cpl 1311 Royal Engineers
SMITHERS Harold G. MM Pte 68591 7th Royal West Surrey Regt
SMITHERS William MM L/Cpl Y/125 King's Royal Rifle Corps
SMITHERS William J. MM Cpl 17512 95 Fd Coy Royal Engineers
SMITHIES David MM L/Bdr 38696 39 Bty 19 Bde RFA
SMITHIES David MM L/Cpl 20/37 West Yorkshire Regt
SMITHIES Richard MM Sjt 199 64 Bde RFA
SMITHSON Charles MM Cpl 240862 8th Yorkshire Regt
SMITHSON James MM Pte 241949 2/5th York & Lancaster Regt
SMITHSON James A. MM Sjt 1633 2nd Lancashire Fusiliers
SMITHSON John Andrew MM Pte 3438 Machine Gun Corps
SMITHSON Walter MM Sjt 2211 1/7th Liverpool Regt KIA 20.9.17.
SMITHSON William MM Pte 11445 2/3(West Riding)Fd Amb RAMC
SMITHURST Bramley MM Pte 305973 1/8th Notts & Derby Regt
SMITHWAITE S.E. MM Gnr 14815 RFA
SMOKER Walter S. MM Dvr 931224 C/291 Bde RFA
SMOKER William E. MM Pte 1914 Royal Fusiliers
SMOOTHY Fred MM Cpl 19271 Machine Gun Corps
SMTH Alexander MM Pte 19/8 Royal Irish Rifles
SMULLEN Michael MM L/Cpl 44226 7/8th Royal Inniskilling Fusiliers
SMURTHWAITE Henry MM Cpl 187066 'C' AA Bty RGA
SMURTHWAITE J.T. MM Sjt 206148 6th East Kent Regt
SMURTHWAITE Ralph MM L/Cpl C/1132 16th King's Royal Rifle Corps

SMURTHWAITE Thomas MM L/Cpl 108628 Machine Gun Corps
SMY E. MM Sjt 923 RGA
SMY Edward MM Pte 35980 9th Norfolk Regt
SMY Ernest MM Pte A/423 8th King's Royal Rifle Corps KIA 15.9.16.AKA Ernest SHEPPARD
SMY Frank "MM,MID" Sjt 1555 1/1st Essex Yeomanry
SMYLIE Cecil R. MM L/Cpl 332373 Highland Light Infantry
SMYTH Daniel MM L/Cpl 35633 East Surrey Regt
SMYTH David MM Pte 201135 1/4th Seaforth Highlanders
SMYTH F. MM Pte 53738 RAMC
SMYTH F.G. MM Air Mech 1 23611 Royal Flying Corps
SMYTH George Owen MM Sjt 13763 10th Essex Regt
SMYTH H. MM L/Sjt 25789 7th Royal Irish Regt
SMYTH J. MM Dvr 34451 94 Bty 18 Bde RFA
SMYTH James MM Pte 27802 8th Northumberland Fusiliers
SMYTH James H. MM L/Cpl 18800 1st Royal Irish Rifles
SMYTH John MM Sjt 8582 2nd Royal Irish Rifles KIA 23.3.18.
SMYTH Joseph MM Sjt 17330 9th West Riding Regt
SMYTH Joseph MM Cpl 7104 Royal Irish Rifles
SMYTH Richard "DCM,MM" Sjt 14420 11th Royal Inniskilling Fusiliers
SMYTH Richard MM Cpl 24033 197 Siege Bty RGA KIA 15.6.18.
SMYTH Thomas J.K. MM Cpl 12/484 12th Royal Irish Rifles
SMYTH William MM+Bar Pte 8487 1st Royal Irish Rifles
SMYTH William MM Pte 5762 Royal Irish Rifles
SMYTH William J. MM Gnr 60660 RFA
SMYTH William Samuel MM Cpl 1109 South Irish Horse
SMYTH or SMITH Joseph MM Pte 6928 Royal Irish Rifles
SMYTHE Albert MM Sjt 200271 1/4th Gordon Highlanders
SMYTHE Christopher MM Pte 816 7th Royal West Kent Regt KIA 7.8.17.
SMYTHE Frank MM Spr 34871 Royal Engineers
SMYTHE Henry Herbert MM Pte S/32433 Rifle Brigade
SNADDEN James MM L/Cpl 275345 1/7th Arg & Suth Highlanders
SNADDON John MM+Bar Pte 303186 Arg & Suth Highlanders
SNAITH Edward MM Dvr 20440 37 Bty 27 Bde RFA
SNAITH George MM Cpl 15836 10th Yorkshire Regt
SNAITH George F. MM Cpl 1574 1/1st Derbyshire Yeomanry
SNAITH H. MM L/Cpl 36026 Yorkshire Light Infantry
SNAITH Ralph MM L/Cpl 19098 West Yorkshire Regt KIA 15.8.18.
SNAPE Arthur MM L/Cpl 11343 2nd Royal Scots
SNAPE Fred MM+2 Bars Sjt 10521 8th Royal Lancaster Regt
SNAPE Harry D. MM Pte 12327 1 Special Coy King's Royal Rifle Corps
SNAPE Jack MM Cpl 31414 4th Bn GMGR
SNAPE John MM Cpl S/4444 13th Rifle Brigade
SNAPE Joseph MM Pte 16119 1st North Lancashire Regt
SNAPE Reginald MM L/Cpl 345179 24th Royal Welsh Fusiliers
SNAPE Stephen MM L/Cpl 71212 Royal Engineers
SNAPE Thomas MM Pte 7768 1st South Staffordshire Regt DOW 19.7.16.
SNAPES Charles MM Pte 17504 6th Northamptonshire Regt
SNARE Albert MM Spr 77320 Royal Engineers
SNAREY Walter MM+Bar Pte S/3052 Rifle Brigade
SNART Frank MM Pte 235076 1/4th Yorkshire Regt Died 15.9.18.
SNARY Thomas H. MM Sjt 78065 9th Bn Tank Corps
SNASDELL Walter MM L/Cpl A/201728 King's Royal Rifle Corps
SNASHALL Frederick J. MM Sjt 444557 1/1st Sussex Yeomanry
SNASHFOLD James F. MM Sjt 63834 9th Yorkshire Light Infantry
SNATT C.D. MM L/Cpl 12224 9th Essex Regt
SNEAD Richard Ernest MM Gnr 98150 195 Siege Bty RGA KIA 24.8.18.
SNEATH Cecil MM Pte 705745 23rd London Regt
SNEATH Ernest MM L/Cpl 40074 2nd Bn Tank Corps
SNEATH Sidney Joseph MM Pte 32998 Notts & Derby Regt
SNEDDEN Alexander K. MM Pte 38527 11th Royal Scots
SNEDDEN R. MM Spr 198056 Royal Engineers
SNEDDON Henry MM Pte 15477 1st Cameron Highlanders
SNEDDON James MM Bdr 7716 RFA
SNEDDON James MM Pte 223201 326 Coy Labour Corps
SNEDDON R. "DCM,MM" Pte 353 1st Royal Highlanders
SNEDDON Richard MM Pte 7165 2nd Royal Dublin Fusiliers KIA 4.11.18.
SNEDDON William MM Sjt 7338 RFA Died 22.2.19.
SNEE John MM Pte 4766 York & Lancaster Regt
SNELGROVE Percy Harry MM Cpl 265339 1/1st Hertfordshire Regt KIA 11.1.18.
SNELGROVE Samuel MM Gnr 19883 A/56 Bde RFA
SNELGROVE Thomas "DCM,MM" Cpl 10505 8th Royal Lancaster Regt
SNELGROVE Walter MM Sjt 6748 2nd Wiltshire Regt
SNELL Archie MM L/Cpl 22372 12 Fd Coy Royal Engineers
SNELL Arthur John MM Pte 40526 7th Bedfordshire Regt DOW 12.7.17.
SNELL C. MM Sjt 545158 RAMC
SNELL Charles MM L/Cpl 97397 50 Div Sig Coy Royal Engineers
SNELL George MM Sjt 22659 'T' Bty RHA DOW 16.3.17.
SNELL George V. MM Pte 74364 RAMC
SNELL George W. MM Pte 3861 1st Welsh Guards
SNELL Roland MM Pte 5990 2/6th Gloucestershire Regt
SNELL Thomas Henry "DCM,MM" Pte 25943 2nd Lincolnshire Regt DOW 31.8.18.
SNELL William MM L/Cpl 12341 7th East Yorkshire Regt
SNELLING Edward MM Sjt 306702 9th West Riding Regt
SNELLING Edward T. MM L/Cpl C/25 16th King's Royal Rifle Corps
SNELLING Ernest D. MM L/Cpl 13355 Machine Gun Corps
SNELLING Ernest G. MM Cpl 2908 8th Royal West Surrey Regt
SNELLING Frederick MM L/Cpl C/12415 King's Royal Rifle Corps
SNELLING Frederick C. MM Pte 17937 Northamptonshire Regt
SNELLING Gerald F. MM Dvr 114267 RFA
SNELLING R.J. MM Sjt 53356 28 Bde RFA
SNELLING Sidney T. MM L/Cpl 63323 Machine Gun Corps
SNELLING Walter MM Pte 10878 Essex Regt
SNELLING William MM Pte 532823 15th London Regt
SNELLINGS Henry MM Pte 5340 5th Dragoon Guards
SNEYD George MM+Bar Cpl 200671 1/7th Worcestershire Regt
SNODGRASS Cyril A. MM+Bar Bdr 940300 RFA
SNOOK Arthur G. MM Pte 53233 9th Cheshire Regt
SNOOK Charles MM Pte 13248 7th East Kent Regt
SNOOK Charles MM Pte 37684 RAMC
SNOOK Cyril MM Cpl 352341 RGA
SNOOK Ernest E. MM Pte 20040 12th Somerset Light Infantry
SNOOK Thomas E. MM Sjt 33323 113 Hy Bty RGA
SNOOKE Oliver MM Cpl 5150 12th Royal Fusiliers KIA 6.12.16.
SNOOKS Thomas MM Sjt 44701 15th Bn Machine Gun Corps
SNOW Charles Pinfold MM Sjt 12351 RGA
SNOW George J. MM Cpl B/603 Rifle Brigade
SNOW George Upperton MM Gnr 900652 B/337 Bde RFA
SNOW Harry B. MM L/Cpl 320444 1/6th London Regt
SNOW John W. MM Pte 22213 4th Worcestershire Regt
SNOW Sidney MM Pte 8735 Royal Fusiliers
SNOW Stanley "MM,MSM+Bar" Sjt 19617 25 Army Troops Coy Royal Engineers
SNOW Walter S. MM Bdr 33636 RFA
SNOW William G. MM Bdr 41537 RFA
SNOWBALL H.or R. "MM,MID" Sjt 6429 18th Hussars
SNOWBALL Harry "MM,MSM" Cpl 10846 19 Coy Labour Corps
SNOWBALL James "MM,CG(F)" Pte 36478 2nd North Lancashire Regt
SNOWBALL John MM Pte 52722 12th Durham Light Infantry KIA 29.10.18.
SNOWDEN Arthur B. MM Cpl 42168 23rd Royal Fusiliers
SNOWDEN Christopher MM Pte M2/079849 Army Service Corps
SNOWDEN Fred "MM,MID" Cpl T/2/14243 Army Service Corps
SNOWDEN Fred MM Pte 27148 East Lancashire Regt
SNOWDEN Harry MM+Bar Sjt 46873 Royal Engineers
SNOWDEN James William MM Pte 34552 2/5th West Riding Regt DOW 20.10.18.
SNOWDEN Jonas MM Pte 14110 9th West Riding Regt KIA 10.10.17.
SNOWDEN Reginald J. MM Gnr 141163 121 Bty 27 Bde RFA
SNOWDEN Robert MM Sjt 7486 2nd Arg & Suth Highlanders
SNOWDEN William H. MM Spr 482131 Royal Engineers
SNOWDEN William W. MM+Bar L/Cpl 506610 97 Fd Coy Royal Engineers
SNOWDON Arthur L. MM Sjt 14342 13th Manchester Regt
SNOWDON Ernest Frank MM L/Cpl 14271 3rd Coldstream Guards
SNOWDON George MM Sjt 353 Royal Engineers
SNOWDON R. "MM,MID" Pte 3128 West Riding Regt
SNOWDON Robert MM Sjt 4194 13th Northumberland Fusiliers KIA 14.4.17.
SNOWLING George MM Pte 39820 5th Gloucestershire Regt
SNOWLING Harry MM Pte 14394 9th Norfolk Regt
SNOWLING William E. MM Sjt 320558 12th Norfolk Regt
SNOXELL Frank H. MM Gnr 14933 RFA
SNYDER Joseph Louis MM Gnr 885 1/7(London)Bde RFA
SOAKELL Harry MM L/Cpl 42141 Yorkshire Light Infantry
SOAL George MM Sjt 21243 Royal Fusiliers
SOAMES Walter H. MM Pnr 19107 2 Bridging Train Royal Engineers

SOAN Samuel MM 2nd Cpl 568100 Royal Engineers
SOANE Nelson MM L/Cpl 16696 6th Royal West Kent Regt KIA 17.9.17.
SOANES Arthur MM Gnr 80863 RFA
SOANES William J. MM L/Cpl 240877 1/5th Royal Sussex Regt
SOAR John MM Pte 23681 Royal Welsh Fusiliers
SOAR Samuel MM L/Cpl 21151 14th Royal Welsh Fusiliers KIA 2.9.17.
SOCKETT John MM Sjt 28015 9th Lancashire Fusiliers
SOCKETT John W. MM Pte 435525 RAMC
SOCKETT Thomas MM(14005 1st Nbld Fus)+Bar Sjt 129964 46th Royal Fusiliers
SODEN Frederick MM Pte 103544 Machine Gun Corps
SOLE Charles MM L/Cpl 16104 23 Fd Coy Royal Engineers
SOLE Frederick J. MM Gnr 96679 RGA
SOLE Thomas J. MM L/Cpl 3530 22nd London Regt
SOLE William MM Pte 27569 Hampshire Regt
SOLLARS John Francis MM Sjt 203286 2/5th Royal Warwickshire Regt
SOLLERS Albert MM Gnr 291419 128 Heavy Bty RGA DOW 21.3.18.
SOLLEY William J. MM Pte 233269 2nd London Regt
SOLLIS Dennis B. MM Pte 307924 6th Royal Warwickshire Regt
SOLLIS Ernest MM Sjt 17293 2nd Worcestershire Regt DOW 29.12.17.
SOLLITT William MM Pte 75669 15th Durham Light Infantry
SOLLY Arthur MM Sjt 2115 16th Middlesex Regt
SOLLY Edward C. MM Pte 52062 9th Highland Light Infantry
SOLLY Herbert MM Pte 11493 Royal West Surrey Regt
SOLLY James MM Pte 6499 1st East Surrey Regt
SOLOMON Benjamin MM Sjt 16381 13th Royal Scots
SOLOMON George MM+Bar L/Cpl 371311 8th London Regt
SOLOMON Henry Ernest MM Cpl 202726 2/4th Lincolnshire Regt
SOLOMON Morris MM Pte 34268 8th York & Lancaster Regt
SOLOMONS Abraham MM Pte 44997 12th Royal Irish Rifles
SOLOMONS Judah MM Cpl 6356 2nd Middlesex Regt DOW 31.10.16.
SOLOMONS Moss MM L/Cpl 114504 17th Bn Machine Gun Corps
SOLWAY Isaac MM Pte 48938 Royal Welsh Fusiliers
SOMERFORD Herbert F. MM Pte 202334 Suffolk Regt
SOMERS Albert MM+Bar Sjt 7984 2nd Royal Irish Regt DOW 2.10.18.
SOMERS Charles MM L/Cpl 240290 1/8th Worcestershire Regt
SOMERS John MM Sjt R/2033 King's Royal Rifle Corps
SOMERS Lawrence MM Pte 8112 2nd Irish Guards DOW 28.10.16.
SOMERS Patrick J. MM L/Bdr 141669 56 Bty 34 Bde RFA
SOMERS Philip P. MM Dvr 496412 Royal Engineers
SOMERSET James MM Pte 2813 1/4th South Lancashire Regt
SOMERVILLE Alexander MM Sjt 303062 1/7th Royal Scots
SOMERVILLE Andrew MM Spr 76411 'C' Corps Sig Coy Royal Engineers
SOMERVILLE Edward MM Spr 148645 185 Tunnelling Coy Royal Engineers
SOMERVILLE Hugh MM Cpl 141672 206 Fd Coy Royal Engineers
SOMERVILLE James MM Pte 200534 1/4th King's Own Scottish Borderers
SOMERVILLE James MM L/Cpl 63850 Royal Engineers
SOMERVILLE James B. MM Pte 8639 Royal Highlanders
SOMERVILLE James Marshall MM Pte M2/073659 Army Service Corps att 1/2(West Riding)Fd Amb RAMC
SOMERVILLE John MM Cpl 250711 5/6th Royal Scots
SOMERVILLE Ralph Alfred Erskine "MC,MM(17582 Sjt)" Lt RGA
SOMERWILL Lewis W. MM L/Cpl 107404 Royal Engineers
SOMMERS Godfrey MM Sjt 21151 10th Gloucestershire Regt
SOMMERVILLE Alexander MM Pte 250809 5/6th Royal Scots
SOMMERVILLE Andrew MM Pte 42214 1/5th King's Own Scottish Borderers
SOMMERVILLE Andrew MM L/Bdr 133614 111 Bty 24 Bde RFA
SOMMERVILLE James MM Pte 10214 3 Fd Amb RAMC
SOMMERVILLE John MM L/Cpl 178 7th Dragoon Guards
SOMMERVILLE William MM Pte 260151 1/5th Seaforth Highlanders KIA 4.9.17.
SOMNER Harry A. MM Sjt 1113 2nd Royal Fusiliers
SOMNER Leonard MM Bdr 616055 1/1(Berkshire)Bty RHA
SONGHURST C.E. MM L/Sjt 18061 13th Essex Regt
SONGHURST Charles Albert MM Pte 704025 2/23rd London Regt
SONLEY George E. MM Sjt 11/1428 East Yorkshire Regt
SOOBY Charles MM Pte 15420 Middlesex Regt
SOPER Cecil E. MM Sjt 591115 18th London Regt
SOPER Frederick J. MM Pte 8025 Lincolnshire Regt
SOPER Frederick James "MM,MSM" Sjt 7950 1st Lincolnshire Regt
SOPER James MM Pte 372609 8th London Regt
SOPER John L. MM Cpl 510357 58 Div Sig Coy Royal Engineers
SORBIE Alexander MM Cpl 2667 1/9th Highland Light Infantry
SORENSEN E. MM Pnr 268494 Royal Engineers
SORENSEN Marinius H. MM Pte 20911 6th Royal West Kent Regt
SORGE Alfred V. MM Pte 732 14th Royal Warwickshire Regt
SORLEY James MM Pte 29662 Cameron Highlanders
SORREL Fred C. MM Bdr 28689 A/104 Bde RFA
SORRELL Edward MM+Bar L/Cpl 8041 2nd South Lancashire Regt KIA 12.4.18.
SORRELL John MM Pte 200235 Royal Warwickshire Regt
SORRELL Thomas Henry MM Sjt 9750 2nd Scots Guards DOW 4.12.17.
SORRIE Alexander L. MM Pte 20340 1/8th Arg & Suth Highlanders
SOULS Arthur William MM L/Cpl 21683 16th Cheshire Regt KIA 25.4.18.
SOULSBY James Collier MM Cpl 14914 6th East Kent Regt
SOULSBY Thomas MM CSM 201434 1st King's Own Scottish Borderers
SOUNDIE Richard MM Pte 31667 Liverpool Regt
SOUNDIE W.H. MM Gnr 55364 30 Bde RFA
SOURBUTTS Arthur MM Pte 11306 3rd Royal Fusiliers
SOUSTER Albert MM Pte 652863 23rd London Regt
SOUTAR George MM Sjt 240295 1/5th Royal Highlanders
SOUTAR R. MM Pte 307140 RAMC
SOUTAR or SOUTER William MM+Bar Pte 1613 1/5th Gordon Highlanders
SOUTER George MM Pte 20195 Leicestershire Regt
SOUTER John MM Sjt 8167 1st Gordon Highlanders
SOUTER John MM Cpl 7858 1st Royal Fusiliers
SOUTER T.W. MM L/Cpl 9899 1st Essex Regt
SOUTER or SOUTAR William MM+Bar Pte 1613 1/5th Gordon Highlanders
SOUTH A. MM L/Cpl P1449 Military Foot Police
SOUTH Albert W. MM L/Cpl 317 4th Bn GMGR
SOUTH Arthur J. MM L/Cpl 31253 Notts & Derby Regt
SOUTH Brinley I.T. MM Pte 235581 Royal Welsh Fusiliers
SOUTH Charles MM L/Sjt 702503 23rd London Regt
SOUTH Ernest MM Pte 24738 11th Suffolk Regt KIA 28.4.17.
SOUTH G.W. MM Cpl 31436 Welsh Regt
SOUTH Stephen William George MM Gnr 51301 C/76 Bde RFA KIA 17.8.17.
SOUTH Thomas MM Pte 42651 4th North Staffordshire Regt
SOUTH William Sydney MM Pte 18440 1st Essex Regt DOW 18.8.17.
SOUTHALL Ernest MM Cpl 10571 2nd Worcestershire Regt
SOUTHALL George MM Pte 201976 7th Worcestershire Regt
SOUTHALL Leonard Christopher MM+Bar L/Cpl 17531 12th East Surrey Regt
SOUTHALL Thomas MM Pte 41709 8th North Staffordshire Regt
SOUTHALL William E. MM Cpl R/5389 1st King's Royal Rifle Corps
SOUTHALL William James MM Pte 241484 1/5th Yorkshire Regt
SOUTHAM Edward C. MM Pte 61235 24th Royal Fusiliers
SOUTHAM George MM Pte 202951 5th Border Regt
SOUTHAM William A. MM Pte 52584 Cheshire Regt
SOUTHAM William Alfred MM Pte 28816 1st Lancashire Fusiliers KIA 4.9.18.
SOUTHAM or SOUTHAN Ben MM Dvr 810405 D/232 Bde RFA
SOUTHARD Richard William MM Pte 53120 38 Fd Amb RAMC
SOUTHBY W. MM Sjt 24151 North Staffordshire Regt
SOUTHCOMBE Reginald E. MM Sjt 1096 Royal Engineers
SOUTHERDEN Ernest W. MM Cpl 12737 2nd Bedfordshire Regt
SOUTHERN Arnold MM Spr 15104 Royal Engineers
SOUTHERN Charles MM Sjt 100480 499 Siege Bty RGA
SOUTHERN Charles William John MM Pte 101824 29th Durham Light Infantry
SOUTHERN George MM Dvr 21432 Royal Engineers
SOUTHERN Harold MM Pte 28125 18th Hussars
SOUTHERN James Henry MM Gnr 67308 111 Siege Bty RGA
SOUTHERN John MM Pte 8726 1st Cheshire Regt
SOUTHERN Norman MM Pte 12400 1st Irish Guards
SOUTHERN Reginald A. MM Pte 283652 1/4th London Regt KIA 16.3.18.
SOUTHERN Rodney C. MM Pte 240713 1/5th Devonshire Regt
SOUTHERN Sidney H. MM Pte 11049 5th Oxf & Bucks Light Infantry
SOUTHEY Thomas John MM Sjt 39492 RFA KIA 19.8.17.
SOUTHGATE Arthur MM Pte 18859 12 Coy Machine Gun Corps DOW 13.10.16.

SOUTHGATE Cecil MM Pte 27244 Royal Warwickshire Regt
SOUTHGATE Cyril T. MM Sjt 5741 HAC
SOUTHGATE Ernest MM Pte 2475 2(London)Sanitary Coy RAMC DOW 23.10.16.
SOUTHGATE Ernest Orbell MM Cpl 8934 1st Essex Regt
SOUTHGATE Frederick Samson MM Pte 326547 1/1st Cambridgeshire Regt
SOUTHGATE Herbert MM L/Sjt 266170 5th West Riding Regt
SOUTHGATE Jack G. MM Sjt 8577 2nd Northamptonshire Regt
SOUTHGATE John W. MM+Bar Sjt 15533 9th Norfolk Regt
SOUTHGATE Robert J. MM Sjt 146003 312 Siege Bty RGA
SOUTHGATE Walter MM Pte 30475 17th Royal Sussex Regt
SOUTHON George H. MM L/Cpl 8373 2nd Oxf & Bucks Light Infantry
SOUTHWARD George MM Pte 30148 8th Royal Lancaster Regt
SOUTHWARD Richard MM Pte 40613 2nd South Lancashire Regt
SOUTHWAY Arthur MM Bdr 837080 C/307 Bde RFA
SOUTHWELL Charles MM Cpl 245439 19th Durham Light Infantry
SOUTHWELL Frederick Henry MM Spr 515903 33 Lt Rly Op Coy Royal Engineers
SOUTHWELL William E. MM Spr 548813 69 Fd Coy Royal Engineers
SOUTHWOOD George W. MM Pte 698189 22nd London Regt
SOUTHWOOD William A. MM Pte 12565 East Surrey Regt
SOUTHWORTH Harry MM Pnr 427938 57 Div Sig Coy Royal Engineers
SOUTHWORTH Horace MM CQMS 37289 7th Norfolk Regt
SOUTHWORTH James MM L/Cpl 14452 9th Northumberland Fusiliers
SOUTHWORTH John MM Sjt 680548 A/286 Bde RFA
SOUTHWORTH John MM Sjt 7599 2nd Highland Light Infantry
SOUTHWORTH Percy Hugh Alexander MM Spr 29538 3 Cav Div Sig Sqn Royal Engineers
SOUTHWORTH Thomas Emmanuel MM Sjt 680841 286 Bde RFA
SOWERBUTTS Richard Henry MM Gnr 110803 RFA
SOWERBY Frederick J. MM L/Cpl 2425 1/13th London Regt
SOWERBY John MM L/Cpl 2605 1/6th Northumberland Fusiliers
SOWERBY Squire MM Pte 11690 7th Yorkshire Regt
SOWERBY William MM Sjt 260324 7th Border Regt
SOWLER Edward MM Cpl 10984 Northumberland Fusiliers
SOWLER John George MM Dvr 45896 33 Bde RFA
SOWRY Robert H. MM CSM 6069 17th Royal Welsh Fusiliers
SOWRY William Musgrave MM Sjt 776903 245 Bde RFA
SPACKMAN Frank MM Sjt 201064 RGA
SPACKMAN Thomas MM Gnr 70656 26 Bde RFA
SPACKMAN Thomas B. "DCM,MM" L/Cpl 15585 7 Div Sig Coy Royal Engineers
SPACKMAN Walter MM L/Cpl 20835 7th Wiltshire Regt
SPACKSMAN George Thomas MM Cpl 96062 222 Fd Coy Royal Engineers DOW 27.4.18.
SPAIN Harry MM Bdsm 7896 1st Worcestershire Regt
SPAIN Harry W. MM Sjt 200567 2/1st London Regt
SPAIN Herbert William MM Sjt 27612 RGA
SPALDING Alfred MM Tpr 152 Household Bn
SPALDING Alfred J. MM L/Cpl 16602 8th Bedfordshire Regt
SPALDING Charles R. "DCM,MM" Sjt 85061 207 Fd Coy Royal Engineers
SPALDING George MM Gnr 83521 D/47 Bde RFA
SPALDING George V. MM Dvr 85378 73 Bty 5 Bde RFA
SPALDING Harry K. MM Pte 268326 1st Royal Highlanders
SPALDING J. MM Cpl 266594 Northumberland Fusiliers
SPALDING James MM L/Bdr 82304 Y/8 Med TM Bty RFA
SPALDING John MM Sjt 265405 7th Liverpool Regt
SPALDING John MM Pte 201466 Royal Highlanders
SPALDING Reginald MM Pte 2778 7th East Kent Regt
SPALDING Sidney John MM Pte 10199 Royal Fusiliers
SPALDING William C. MM Dvr 39305 RFA
SPANSWICK George A. MM Pte 103010 Notts & Derby Regt
SPANTON Robert MM Pte 15107 8th Duke of Cornwall's LI
SPARE WalterC. MM Pte 18754 14th Leicestershire Regt
SPAREY Oliver F. "MM,MID" SM Armourer 435 Army Ordnance Corps
SPARGO Arthur Nicholas MM CQMS 470173 12th London Regt
SPARGO Frederick MM L/Cpl 357008 1/10th Liverpool Regt
SPARHAM Alexander G. MM Pte 532985 15th London Regt
SPARK James MM L/Sjt 316388 13th Royal Highlanders
SPARK James B. MM Pte 5809 Labour Corps
SPARK James Grant MM Sjt 13170 6th East Kent Regt
SPARK Jonathan MM Pte 34881 York & Lancaster Regt
SPARK Joseph B. MM Spr 477116 56 Div Sig Coy Royal Engineers
SPARK Robert MM L/Cpl 33738 2nd Royal Scots Fusiliers
SPARK William MM Sjt 305095 RAMC
SPARK William MM Gnr 7158 A/106 Bde RFA KIA 22.3.18.
SPARKES Alfred "MM,GMV(S)" S/Sjt 243 1/1(London)Fd Amb RAMC
SPARKES Charles MM L/Cpl 389 14th Royal Warwickshire Regt
SPARKES Ernest F. MM Sjt 16/212 Royal Warwickshire Regt
SPARKES Frederick J. MM Cpl 15297 Machine Gun Corps
SPARKES George MM Pte 320302 6th London Regt
SPARKES George A. MM Pte 8389 1st Somerset Light Infantry
SPARKES Harry B. MM 2nd Cpl 444420 Royal Engineers
SPARKES Harry T. MM L/Cpl 21521 Machine Gun Corps
SPARKES Jesse MM Bfr 33717 RFA
SPARKES Joseph A. MM L/Cpl 21914 East Surrey Regt
SPARKES Percy J. MM+Bar Pte 6953 8th Rifle Brigade
SPARKES William MM Pte 15508 Devonshire Regt
SPARKES William Harper MM Spr 64944 18 Div Sig Coy Royal Engineers
SPARKES or SPARKS William MM Pte 7087 1st Devonshire Regt
SPARKS Albert Charles MM Staff SM T/13202 7 Div Train Army Service Corps
SPARKS Albert James MM Sjt 29248 3/10th Middlesex Regt
SPARKS Edward MM Sjt 241206 2/5th Hampshire Regt KIA 9.4.18.
SPARKS ErnestW. MM Cpl 67385 C/82 Bde RFA
SPARKS Frederick J. MM Sjt 240774 1/5th Devonshire Regt
SPARKS G. MM Gnr 426 RFA
SPARKS H. MM L/Cpl 9901 2nd Essex Regt
SPARKS Harry MM Pte 18579 1st East Lancashire Regt
SPARKS Henry MM Pte 18814 4th Bn Machine Gun Corps
SPARKS Herbert MM Pte 31483 2nd Northumberland Fusiliers
SPARKS I.F. MM Air Mech 3 24970 Royal Air Force
SPARKS Richard J. MM Pte 34904 Duke of Cornwall's LI
SPARKS Robert MM Cpl 9739 1st Liverpool Regt KIA 28.4.17.
SPARKS Robert MM Pte 17971 11th Cheshire Regt
SPARKS Walter MM L/Cpl 6634 Coldstream Guards
SPARKS William H. "DCM,MM+Bar" Sjt 11701 7th Leicestershire Regt
SPARKS or SPARKES William MM Pte 7087 1st Devonshire Regt
SPARLING T.W. MM Pte 323187 London Regt
SPARROW Alexander Henry MM L/Cpl 28114 6th Bedfordshire Regt
SPARROW Ernest MM CQMS 8816 2nd Coldstream Guards KIA 16.9.16.
SPARROW G. MM L/Cpl 21589 6th Lincolnshire Regt
SPARROW George MM Pte 18628 8th Royal Berkshire Regt
SPARROW J. MM Cpl 4650 Army Cyclist Corps
SPARROW J. MM Pte 326917 1/1st Cambridgeshire Regt
SPARROW John MM Pte 40422 2nd Suffolk Regt KIA 30.8.18.
SPARROW John MM Sjt 3551 Machine Gun Corps
SPARROW Leonard MM Sjt SE/3677 Army Veterinary Corps
SPARROW Leslie F. MM Pte 44644 8th Royal Berkshire Regt
SPARROW Richard J. MM Cpl 3077 11th Royal Fusiliers
SPARROW Stanley MM Sjt 3084 Royal Fusiliers
SPARROW William A. "DCM,MM" Sjt 835636 D/242 Bde RFA
SPARROWHAWK Albert MM Pte 60911 Royal Fusiliers
SPARY Ernest MM L/Cpl 24987 23rd Middlesex Regt
SPATCHETT Robert C. MM Gnr 102922 RFA
SPAVEN John MM Cpl 27657 RFA
SPAVEN Lionel MM Pte 24684 49th Bn Machine Gun Corps
SPEAK E. MM Pte 66097 19th Bn Machine Gun Corps
SPEAK H. MM Gnr 127988 A/112 Bde RFA
SPEAK Holford MM Pte 24139 East Lancashire Regt
SPEAKMAN William MM Cpl 200341 North Lancashire Regt
SPEAR Arthur Edgar MM L/Sjt 720373 1/24th London Regt
SPEAR Bertram H. MM Cpl 372251 8th London Regt
SPEAR Edward MM Pte 9522 17th Lancashire Fusiliers
SPEAR Frederick MM Gnr 348133 RGA
SPEAR Joseph MM Sjt 478 RFA
SPEAR Norman Victor MM Sjt 3686 1/14th London Regt
SPEARMAN John MM L/Cpl 358012 1 Div Sig Coy Royal Engineers
SPEARMAN William H. MM Pte 573452 17th London Regt
SPEARS Charles MM Pte 33342 South Wales Borderers
SPEARS Henry "MM,MID" Cpl 45352 RFA
SPEARS William H. MM L/Cpl 16788 Royal Sussex Regt
SPECK Edward E. MM Pte 220026 2nd Wiltshire Regt
SPEDDING Ellis MM Pte 20439 18Fd Amb RAMC
SPEDDING William MM+Bar Pte 13271 1/8th Lancashire Fusiliers
SPEECHLEY Oswald MM Cpl 26255 RAMC
SPEED Charles MM Dvr 141497 123 Army Troops Coy Royal Engineers
SPEED David MM Sjt 3122 10th Royal Highlanders

SPEED George MM Pnr 130333 Royal Engineers
SPEED George E. MM+Bar Sjt C/12374 18th King's Royal Rifle Corps
SPEED Henry Charles MM L/Cpl 610262 19th London Regt
SPEED James MM Pte 28859 3rd Worcestershire Regt
SPEED James A. "DCM,MM+Bar" Sjt 18662 12th Durham Light Infantry
SPEED John MM Dvr 17748 A/170 Bde RFA
SPEED Joseph MM Pte 10049 2nd Durham Light Infantry
SPEED Richard H. MM Pte 18865 2nd Yorkshire Light Infantry
SPEED W. MM CQMS 14372 Cheshire Regt
SPEEDIE Finlay MM Pte 302869 Arg & Suth Highlanders
SPEER Joseph MM Sjt 16025 Royal Inniskilling Fusiliers
SPEIACHVILI Rackkmin MM Pte J/54 38th Royal Fusiliers
SPEID Robert MM Gnr 104497 A/170 Bde RFA
SPEIGHT Albert E. MM Pte 86718 8th Liverpool Regt
SPEIGHT Arthur MM Gnr 78580 Tank Corps
SPEIGHT Ebenezer MM Cpl 241718 2/6th West Yorkshire Regt
SPEIGHT Edward R. MM L/Cpl 242426 1st Middlesex Regt
SPEIGHT Ernest W. MM Cpl 15818 11th West Yorkshire Regt
SPEIGHT George MM L/Cpl 670 Lincolnshire Regt
SPEIGHT H. MM Dvr 2426 RFA
SPEIGHT John W. MM L/Sjt 12677 7th York & Lancaster Regt DOW 21.11.18.
SPEIGHT Robert MM Sjt 3881 10th York & Lancaster Regt
SPEIGHT William "MM,MID" Sjt 33684 B/70 Bde RFA
SPEIRS Andrew MM Pte 60915 RAMC
SPEIRS Hamilton MM Sjt 12135 2nd Scots Guards
SPEIRS James Hamilton MM Cpl 18170 7th Cameron Highlanders KIA 20.8.17.
SPEIRS John MM Sjt 295056 12th Royal Scots Fusiliers
SPEIRS Robert MM Gnr 7287 RFA
SPELLER Arthur Ernest Church MM Sjt S/6291 13th Rifle Brigade
SPELLER Cecil "DCM,MM+Bar" Sjt 19306 21 Fd Amb RAMC
SPELLMAN James MM+Bar Pte 12263 West Riding Regt
SPELLMAN Joseph MM Cpl 12588 1st North Lancashire Regt
SPELLMAN or SPELMAN John MM Pte 2746 6th Connaught Rangers
SPELMAN John MM Sjt 397 2nd Rifle Brigade
SPENCE Albert MM Cpl 21319 Leicestershire Regt
SPENCE Albert MM Pte 17692 2nd South Lancashire Regt
SPENCE Andrew MM Pte 2222 1/9th Highland Light Infantry
SPENCE Arthur MM Pte 103195 Notts & Derby Regt
SPENCE Charles W. MM Pte 282152 4th London Regt
SPENCE Cissy MM Sister F QAIMNS
SPENCE Frank MM+Bar L/Sjt 8143 Lincolnshire Regt
SPENCE George MM Sjt 12871 7th Cameron Highlanders
SPENCE George Ernest MM Pte 9441 8th Lincolnshire Regt
SPENCE George G. MM L/Cpl 18231 1st Border Regt
SPENCE Harry MM Pte 40609 RAMC
SPENCE Harry Turner MM Gnr 146244 168 Siege Bty RGA
SPENCE James MM L/Cpl 290062 1/7th Royal Highlanders
SPENCE James MM Pte 8900 Royal Irish Rifles
SPENCE John MM S/Sjt 318010 1/2(Lowland)Fd Amb RAMC
SPENCE John MM Pte 9035 2nd Cameron Highlanders
SPENCE John H. MM L/Bdr 213870 C/256 Bde RFA
SPENCE Joseph MM Gnr 191251 RFA
SPENCE Peter MM Pte 2432 1st Royal Highlanders
SPENCE Peter MM Pte 26551 Royal Scots
SPENCE Robert MM Dvr 126074 A/168 Bde RFA
SPENCE Robert MM Bdr 751317 D/250 Bde RFA
SPENCE Sidney T. MM Sjt 200198 1/7th Middlesex Regt
SPENCE Thomas MM L/Cpl 250777 Royal Scots
SPENCE Thomas MM L/Cpl 19828 Wiltshire Regt
SPENCE Thomas Francis MM Sjt 32731 13th East Lancashire Regt
SPENCE William MM Pte 54119 4th Middlesex Regt
SPENCE William MM Pte 373462 8th London Regt
SPENCE William Alexander "MC,MM(534 L/Cpl 10th Bn)" T/2Lt 11th Royal Fusiliers
SPENCE William Proctor MM Pte 41533 8th Royal Highlanders KIA 14.10.18.
SPENCE William R. MM Pte 8794 2nd Royal Irish Rifles
SPENCELEY F.V. MM+Bar L/Cpl 728 1st East Kent Regt
SPENCELY Ralph MM Pte 14113 1st East Yorkshire Regt
SPENCER Alban W. MM Sjt 17241 Royal Fusiliers
SPENCER Albert MM Sjt 290627 RGA
SPENCER Albert MM Pte 43899 17th Royal Welsh Fusiliers KIA 30.8.18.
SPENCER Albert MM Pte 51735 Cheshire Regt
SPENCER Albert J. MM Cpl 35263 D/112 Bde RFA
SPENCER Alfred MM Pte 36446 4th York & Lancaster Regt
SPENCER Andrew MM Pte 18203 Hampshire Regt
SPENCER Archibald MM Pte 15411 Machine Gun Corps
SPENCER Arthur MM Pte 13963 2nd West Riding Regt
SPENCER Arthur MM Cpl 18/1231 18th West Yorkshire Regt
SPENCER Arthur MM Pte 220115 East Yorkshire Regt
SPENCER Arthur MM Gnr 76496 Tank Corps
SPENCER Arthur William MM L/Cpl 44269 10th Cheshire Regt
SPENCER B.J. MM Sjt P4606 Military Mounted Police
SPENCER Charles MM Pte 64611 RAMC
SPENCER Charles W. MM Pte 1664 Lincolnshire Regt
SPENCER Cyril W. MM Pte 11315 Army Cyclist Corps
SPENCER E. MM Sjt 4769 Middlesex Regt
SPENCER Edwin MM Pte 29334 RAMC
SPENCER Francis Henry Joseph "MM,MID" Cpl 9346 1st Leicestershire Regt
SPENCER Frank MM L/Cpl 8483 1st Northamptonshire Regt
SPENCER Frank B. MM Cpl 16645 RFA
SPENCER Frank Woodward MM Pte 81889 RAMC
SPENCER Fred MM Pte 203137 2/7th Lancashire Fusiliers
SPENCER Fred MM Gnr 83978 RFA DOW 13.7.16.
SPENCER Frederick MM Pte 19713 1st Shropshire Light Infantry
SPENCER Frederick Charles MM L/Cpl 282344 4th London Regt KIA 26.10.17.
SPENCER Frederick G. MM Sjt 925036 C/280 Bde RFA
SPENCER George MM Dvr 680839 RFA
SPENCER George A. MM Pte M2/074251 Army Service Corps
SPENCER George M. MM Sjt 1129 17th Royal Fusiliers
SPENCER Gordon MM Pte 50642 1st Royal Berkshire Regt KIA 3.8.18.
SPENCER H.E. MM Cpl 3890 RFA
SPENCER Harold MM L/Cpl 7802 Machine Gun Corps
SPENCER Harry Robert MM Pte 25254 Royal Berkshire Regt
SPENCER Henry MM L/Cpl 200260 North Staffordshire Regt KIA 3.9.18.
SPENCER Henry S. MM Pte S/25283 Rifle Brigade
SPENCER Herbert MM Pte 26350 1st East Surrey Regt KIA 21.8.18.
SPENCER Hubert MM Pte 2891 12th Middlesex Regt
SPENCER Ira MM Cpl 205099 4th Hampshire Regt
SPENCER J.A. MM BQMS 2349 A/102 Bde RFA
SPENCER James MM Bdr 33690 RFA
SPENCER James MM Pte 202761 North Lancashire Regt
SPENCER James H. MM Pte 14975 6th Northamptonshire Regt
SPENCER James Harold MM L/Cpl 518 1/4th Yorkshire Regt
SPENCER John MM Sjt 3329 1st Royal Lancaster Regt
SPENCER John MM Gnr 71748 23 Bde RFA
SPENCER John MM Pte 37873 12th Northumberland Fusiliers Died 27.5.18.
SPENCER John MM L/Sjt 9887 3rd Grenadier Guards
SPENCER John "DSO,MM(24045 L/Cpl RWSurr)" Capt 17th Royal Fusiliers
SPENCER John MM Gnr 89132 RFA
SPENCER John MM Gnr 155185 251 Bde RFA
SPENCER John MM Sjt 13655 RFA
SPENCER John MM 2nd Cpl 155786 Royal Engineers
SPENCER John H. MM Cpl 8234 C/178 Bde RFA DOW 29.11.17.
SPENCER John H. MM Dvr 186354 RFA
SPENCER John Henry MM L/Cpl 31834 106 Coy Machine Gun Corps
SPENCER John Nelson MM Pte 51022 15th Cheshire Regt
SPENCER John William MM Sjt 2241 14th London Regt
SPENCER Joseph MM Pte 20690 6th King's Own Scottish Borderers
SPENCER Joseph MM Cpl 15102 8th Yorkshire Light Infantry KIA 1.7.16.
SPENCER Joseph Ewart MM Dvr 13236 HQ 153 Bde RFA
SPENCER Joseph H. MM Pte 423851 10th London Regt
SPENCER Norman F. "MM,MID" Sjt 39898 RGA
SPENCER Oscar MM Pte 18246 2nd Suffolk Regt
SPENCER Percy MM L/Sjt 10217 1st Border Regt
SPENCER Percy MM Dvr 80120 A/46 Bde RFA KIA 8.9.16.
SPENCER Randolph Churchill "MM,MIDx2" Sjt 11050 1st Scots Guards
SPENCER Reginald H. MM Cpl 482347 Royal Engineers
SPENCER Richard J. MM L/Cpl 325439 1/1st Worcestershire Yeomanry
SPENCER Robert MM Cpl 44334 75 Fd Coy Royal Engineers
SPENCER Robert A. MM Dvr T3/025675 Army Service Corps
SPENCER Robert Rufus MM Pte 12734 6th Northamptonshire Regt

SPENCER Samuel B. MM Dvr 28469 RFA
SPENCER Sidney H. MM L/Cpl 265603 1/6th Gloucestershire Regt
SPENCER Stanley G. MM Pte 144 1st Welsh Guards
SPENCER Stanley John MM Pte 267920 17th Royal Welsh Fusiliers DOW 2.9.18.
SPENCER Sydney MM Pte 44480 Machine Gun Corps
SPENCER Thomas MM Sjt 28220 Labour Corps
SPENCER Thomas Alfred MM Cpl 35601 Machine Gun Corps
SPENCER Thomas N. MM Pte 60666 RAMC
SPENCER Thomas Richard MM Pte 42409 15th Durham Light Infantry
SPENCER Thomas S. MM Sjt 14927 5th Dorsetshire Regt
SPENCER Thomas W. MM+Bar Sjt 240138 1/6th Notts & Derby Regt
SPENCER Valrose MM Pte 75825 Tank Corps
SPENCER Walter MM Gnr 781555 X/62 Med TM Bty RFA
SPENCER Walter B. MM Dvr 780643 B/246 Bde RFA
SPENCER Walter J. MM Sjt 835813 RFA
SPENCER William MM L/Cpl 39191 4th South Staffordshire Regt KIA 27.5.18.
SPENCER William MM Pte 15758 Yorkshire Regt
SPENCER William C. MM Sjt 429996 Royal Engineers
SPENCER William F.A. MM Cpl 36859 RFA
SPENCER William J. MM Pte 19627 1st Shropshire Light Infantry
SPENDER Frank MM Cpl T4/037983 18 Div Train Army Service Corps
SPENDLEY Edgar MM Bdr 7665 RFA
SPENDLOVE David W. MM Spr 66607 1 Div Sig Coy Royal Engineers
SPERINCK Henry Lewis MM L/Bdr 46041 B/112 Bde RFA
SPICE James William MM Pte 7219 10th Hussars Died 31.10.18.
SPICE Walter MM Cpl 200233 1/4th Suffolk Regt
SPICER Albert MM Pte 21519 13th Essex Regt KIA 18.2.17.
SPICER Arthur G. MM Pte 7344 2nd Border Regt
SPICER Charles B. MM Air Mech 1 87720 Royal Flying Corps
SPICER Ernest Albert MM Sjt 10042 5th Royal Berkshire Regt KIA 26.8.18.
SPICER Ernest Bernard "MC,MM(14922 CSM 2nd Bedfords)" Capt 9th Norfolk Regt
SPICER Frank MM Pte 533712 15th London Regt
SPICER Frank MM L/Cpl 19123 9th Essex Regt
SPICER Frederick MM Pte S/18546 8th Rifle Brigade
SPICER Herbert MM+Bar Sjt 325227 1/1st Cambridgeshire Regt
SPICER L. MM Air Mech 2 8853 Royal Flying Corps
SPICER Walter W. MM Pte 22730 Grenadier Guards
SPICKERNELL William MM Cpl 1777 16th Royal Sussex Regt
SPIDEN Thomas MM Pte 352218 5/6th Royal Scots
SPIER Arthur MM Cpl 132578 254 Tunnelling Coy Royal Engineers
SPIER Herbert John MM Pte 10035 1st Royal West Surrey Regt KIA 26.9.17.
SPIERS Arthur MM L/Sjt 9718 2nd Worcestershire Regt
SPIERS Emanuel MM Drummer 4314 2/5th Royal Warwickshire Regt KIA 8.8.16.
SPIERS Sidney H. MM Cpl B/98 1st Rifle Brigade
SPIERS Thomas MM Pte 241290 2/5th Yorkshire Light Infantry
SPIERS William MM Cpl 304512 15th Bn Tank Corps
SPIERS or SPIRES Arthur Wilson MM Pte 240820 1/8th Worcestershire Regt
SPIES Harold J.H. MM(Pte AIF)+Bar Cpl 133054 45th Royal Fusiliers
SPILG George MM+Bar Cpl 330390 1/9th Highland Light Infantry
SPILLANE Michael MM+Bar Pte 9746 1st Royal Munster Fusiliers
SPILLARD Charles Victor MM Pte 2964 Gloucestershire Regt
SPILLER Charles H. MM+Bar Cpl 1547 3rd Rifle Brigade
SPILLER Edward John "MM,MID" Cpl 112826 X/16 Med TM Bty RFA
SPILLER Harry I. MM Sjt 394231 1/9th London Regt
SPILLER John Gordon MM Sjt 86112 189 Siege Bty RGA
SPILLER Samuel MM Pte 8807 2nd Leicestershire Regt
SPILLER W.C. "DCM,MM" Sjt 9872 2nd East Kent Regt
SPILSBURY Harold MM Bdr 21307 RFA
SPINDLER Charles K. MM+Bar Sjt 15020 8th Suffolk Regt
SPINK Daniel MM Sjt 96803 C/156 Bde RFA
SPINK Edward L. MM L/Cpl 463258 50 Div Sig Coy Royal Engineers
SPINK Edwin MM Pte 42531 1/10th Manchester Regt
SPINK Harry MM Cpl 81819 5 Bde Ammn Col RFA
SPINK Walter MM Pte 242038 1/6th Northumberland Fusiliers
SPINKS Alfred MM L/Cpl 71584 Machine Gun Corps
SPINKS Charles MM Bdr 74039 RFA

SPINKS Edward C. MM Pte 202033 Suffolk Regt
SPINKS F.J. MM L/Cpl L/15353 Royal Fusiliers
SPINKS Harry MM Spr 56902 19 Div Sig Coy Royal Engineers
SPINKS William James MM L/Cpl 570791 17th London Regt Died 5.11.18.
SPINNER William G. MM Sjt 358005 RGA
SPIRES Charles Bertram MM Bdr 165872 RFA
SPIRES Charles H. MM Sjt 10542 Royal Munster Fusiliers
SPIRES Thomas A. MM 2nd Cpl 457206 Royal Engineers
SPIRES or SPIERS Arthur Wilson MM Pte 240820 1/8th Worcestershire Regt
SPIRET George A. MM CSM 1075 6th Royal West Surrey Regt
SPIRING Adam MM Cpl 66821 Machine Gun Corps
SPIRIT John MM+Bar Cpl 761054 Y/50 Med TM Bty RFA
SPIRLING George MM L/Cpl 9682 1st Dorsetshire Regt KIA 1.7.16.
SPIRLING William MM Cpl 5177 4 Fd Amb RAMC
SPIRRETT Herbert MM Dvr 2510 1/3(West Riding)Bde RFA
SPITTLE John MM L/Cpl 56614 RAMC
SPITTLE John T. MM Pte 87437 62nd Bn Machine Gun Corps
SPITTLE Joseph MM Pte 2071 9th Royal Fusiliers
SPITTLEHOUSE William MM Dvr 558593 56 Div Sig Coy Royal Engineers
SPIVEY Frank MM+Bar Sjt 268050 2/5th West Riding Regt DOW 15.9.18.
SPIVEY Lewis MM Pte 41748 12th West Yorkshire Regt
SPIVEY Norman MM Cpl 9603 Machine Gun Corps
SPODE William MM Bdr 7889 D/152 Bde RFA
SPOKES J.W. MM L/Cpl P4786 Military Mounted Police
SPOONER Arthur MM+Bar Cpl 10683 6th Royal West Surrey Regt
SPOONER Edward W. MM Pte 12280 6th Oxf & Bucks Light Infantry
SPOONER George Piercy MM Sjt 2175 1/2nd London Regt KIA 20-23.9.17.
SPOONER James H. MM Dvr 35787 33 Bde RFA
SPOONER John MM Cpl 12110 5th Northamptonshire Regt
SPOONER John MM L/Cpl 1251 1/21st London Regt
SPOONER Nicholas MM Pte 36583 Northumberland Fusiliers
SPOONER Robert MM Bdr 48688 RFA
SPOONER Sidney A. MM Bdr 9014 RFA
SPOONER Stanley H. MM Pte 12735 7th Norfolk Regt
SPOONER Walter A. MM Pte 461503 RAMC
SPOONER William MM Pte 19955 Notts & Derby Regt
SPOOR George MM Bdr 115644 B/82 Bde RFA
SPOORS George A. MM Pte 11445 Coldstream Guards
SPOORS John MM Pte 43580 15th Durham Light Infantry
SPOORS Joseph MM L/Sjt 10726 Northumberland Fusiliers
SPORLE Frederick MM L/Cpl 11676 2nd Middlesex Regt
SPORLE Thomas MM Sjt 62406 Labour Corps
SPORNE David C. MM Pte 12130 Leicestershire Regt
SPORTON Henry Charles MM Gnr 926167 D/290 Bde RFA
SPOTTISWOOD James MM Gnr 6734 159 Bde RFA
SPOUGE Walter "DCM,MM+Bar" Pte 16650 3rd Grenadier Guards
SPOWAGE Percy H. MM Sjt 1318 23rd Royal Fusiliers
SPOWAGE Wilfred MM L/Cpl 19383 Northamptonshire Regt
SPOWART Samuel MM Cpl 11493 1/8th Arg & Suth Highlanders
SPOWART William MM Pte 8648 10/11th Highland Light Infantry KIA 11.4.17.
SPOWART William MM Gnr 306144 RGA
SPRACKLAND Henry Richard MM Sjt 3072 2nd Rifle Brigade
SPRAGG Joseph MM L/Cpl 260400 Worcestershire Regt
SPRAGG Percy F. MM Sjt 54636 6th Durham Light Infantry
SPRAGG William A. MM Pte 24294 Gloucestershire Regt
SPRAGG William T. MM L/Cpl 12626 11th Manchester Regt KIA 27.9.18.
SPRAGG William W. MM L/Cpl A/1581 13th King's Royal Rifle Corps
SPRAGGINS Reginald John MM Pte 20594 11th Suffolk Regt
SPRAGGON John W. MM CSM 11980 14th Northumberland Fusiliers
SPRAGGS Albert W. MM Sjt 201907 1st London Regt
SPRAGGS Cecil J. MM L/Cpl 51477 West Yorkshire Regt
SPRAGUE Ernest H. MM L/Sjt 201780 4th Gloucestershire Regt
SPRAGUE William MM Sjt 5656 Coldstream Guards
SPRAKES Ernest MM Pte 372866 2/8th London Regt KIA 30.10.17.
SPRAKES Stanley MM Gnr Fitter 80617 128 Bty 29 Bde RFA
SPRANGE Sidney F. MM Pte 492517 13th London Regt
SPRATLEY John B. MM Pte C/268 16th King's Royal Rifle Corps
SPRATLEY Reginald F. MM L/Cpl 5994 7th East Surrey Regt
SPRATLEY William R. MM Pte 43337 Manchester Regt
SPRATT Charles MM Pte 266062 1st Royal Highlanders

SPRATT Edward MM+Bar Sjt 26721 Royal Dublin Fusiliers
SPRATT Herbert H. MM Pte 391663 London Regt
SPRATT Thomas E. MM S/Sjt 550230 Royal Engineers
SPRATT Thomas H. MM Pte M2/018973 Army Service Corps
SPRAY Bernard MM Sjt 755254 B/251 Bde RFA
SPRAY Charles MM Pte 35967 5th Bn Machine Gun Corps
SPREADBOROUGH Walter MM Gnr 164198 RFA
SPREADBURY James F. MM 2nd Cpl 53189 Royal Engineers
SPREDBURY Sidney J. MM Pte 881489 34th London Regt
SPRIGG or SPRIGGS William W. MM Cpl 14734 Royal Lancaster Regt
SPRIGGE Harold J. MM Pte 220000 RAMC
SPRIGGS Edwin J. "DCM,MM" Sjt 50321 90 Fd Coy Royal Engineers
SPRIGGS George John Felton MM Gnr 37978 98 Bde RFA
SPRIGGS John W. MM Pte 3912 1/1st Cambridgeshire Regt
SPRIGGS William MM Pte 9568 2nd West Riding Regt
SPRIGGS Zachariah MM Pte 33076 12th East Surrey Regt
SPRIGGS or SPRIGG William W. MM Cpl 14734 Royal Lancaster Regt
SPRING Frank MM+Bar Cpl 240168 4th West Riding Regt
SPRING Frank MM Pte 27832 Bedfordshire Regt
SPRING Frederick C. MM L/Cpl 14802 7th Bedfordshire Regt
SPRING George H.J. MM Cpl 4784 13th Royal Fusiliers
SPRING Samuel MM Pte 275236 1/1st Nottinghamshire Yeomanry(Sherwood Rangers)
SPRING Sidney MM Pte 19623 Royal Fusiliers
SPRINGALL Alfred Hayward MM Pte 420466 2/10th London Regt KIA 31.7.18.
SPRINGATE Arthur S. MM Sjt 11455 8th Leicestershire Regt
SPRINGATE John Edgar MM L/Cpl 9759 11th Royal West Surrey Regt KIA 1.10.18.
SPRINGBETT George Thomas MM Sjt 10838 11th Royal West Kent Regt DOW 17.9.16.
SPRINGER Frederick Charles MM Pte 57538 17th Worcestershire Regt
SPRINGETT Arthur J. MM Pte 20596 RAMC
SPRINGETT George MM Pte 17292 5th Northamptonshire Regt
SPRINGETT Lewis Sydney MM Pte 702501 1/23rd London Regt
SPRINGETT Reginald C. MM Pte 5092 9th East Surrey Regt
SPRINGETT Richard Thomas MM Gnr 9419 71 Bde RFA
SPRINGETT W.A. MM Pte 9402 Royal West Surrey Regt
SPRINGHAM Arthur MM Pte 244924 North Lancashire Regt
SPRINGHAM Percy David MM Pte 200147 'A' Bn Tank Corps
SPRINGLE Jack MM Pte 240515 12th Middlesex Regt
SPRINGTHORPE Charles J.T. MM Cpl R/17024 16th King's Royal Rifle Corps
SPROAT Arthur L. MM L/Cpl 1527 1/5th Gloucestershire Regt
SPROAT George MM Pte 17516 1/5th Border Regt
SPROATES Morpeth MM L/Sjt 6474 Machine Gun Corps
SPROSTON Arthur Cecil MM Cpl 74062 Signal Service Royal Engineers
SPROSTON H. MM+Bar Gnr 131148 RFA
SPROSTON Herbert Arnold MM Pte 241310 1/5th Lincolnshire Regt
SPROUL Robert MM Pte 6652 10th Arg & Suth Highlanders
SPROULE Arthur James MM Pte M2/222216 14 LAMB Army Service Corps
SPROULE Robert "MM,MID" QMS 17633 RAMC
SPRUCE George MM Pte 73376 11th Notts & Derby Regt
SPRUCE Stanley Edgar "MC,MM(136338 L/Cpl" T/Lt 254 Tunnelling Coy Royal Engineers
SPRUELS William MM Cpl 9737 5th Wiltshire Regt
SPRUNT Henry Arthur MM Pte 18846 2nd Suffolk Regt KIA 26.9.17.
SPURDON Samuel MM Pte R/27556 17th King's Royal Rifle Corps KIA 12.11.17.
SPURGEON Charles E. MM Cpl 2726 Machine Gun Corps
SPURGEON Herbert MM Pte 43463 10th Essex Regt
SPURGEON Percy C. MM L/Sjt 42695 11th Suffolk Regt
SPURIN Frederick Stanley MM Cpl R/56196 4th King's Royal Rifle Corps DOW 13.11.18.
SPURLING Thomas MM Dvr 14447 D/157 Bde RFA
SPURLOCK Ernest P. MM+Bar Sjt 506576 Royal Engineers
SPURR Alfred MM Pte 142589 62nd Bn Machine Gun Corps
SPURR Clifford MM Pte 240099 1/5th York & Lancaster Regt DOW 4.1.18.
SPURR John W. MM+Bar Pte 26394 1st Grenadier Guards
SPURR Percy MM Pte 1925 11th Yorkshire Light Infantry
SPURWAY George W. MM Pte 52471 8th West Yorkshire Regt
SPURWAY William E.J. MM L/Cpl 18993 Devonshire Regt
SPY Bruce Carstairs MM Sjt 225884 10th Cameron Highlanders

SQUIBB Albert J. MM Pte 37423 South Lancashire Regt
SQUIBB T.W. MM L/Bdr 32586 RGA
SQUIBB William F. MM Sjt 700474 24th London Regt
SQUIER Maurice Arthur MM L/Cpl 34757 11th Essex Regt KIA 28.6.17.
SQUIRE Bruce W. MM Sjt DM2/170039 Army Service Corps
SQUIRE F.H. MM Cpl 9566 Royal Flying Corps
SQUIRE Frank S. MM L/Cpl 12032 Coldstream Guards
SQUIRE Frederick James "MM,MID" Sjt 10278 RFA
SQUIRE Harold MM Sjt 200408 Northamptonshire Regt
SQUIRE John MM Pte 40717 12th West Yorkshire Regt KIA 3.5.17.
SQUIRE Joseph Samuel Maisey MM Sjt 100654 70 Fd Coy Royal Engineers
SQUIRE Thomas G. MM Cpl 28537 RGA
SQUIRE William "MM,CG(F)" Dvr 103735 72 Bty 38 Bde RFA
SQUIRES Albert MM Bdr 830836 67 Bde RFA
SQUIRES Alfred MM L/Cpl 862 7th Royal Sussex Regt
SQUIRES Alfred "MM,CG(F)" Cpl 482341 62 Div Sig Coy Royal Engineers
SQUIRES Alfred W. MM Pte 2101 1/9th London Regt
SQUIRES Allen MM Pte 240750 5th West Riding Regt
SQUIRES Charles W. MM Gnr 89991 RFA
SQUIRES Harry MM Cpl 3/7954 5th Dorsetshire Regt
SQUIRES Harry Reeves MM Pte 34163 2nd Hampshire Regt DOW 24.8.17.
SQUIRES John F. MM Pte 21480 4th Hampshire Regt
SQUIRES Norman MM Pte 30028 East Yorkshire Regt
SQUIRES Sidney Leslie MM L/Cpl 1788 1/1st HAC(Infantry)
SQUIRES Sydney MM Cpl 28928 8th Royal Lancaster Regt
SQUIRES Walter MM Sjt 376907 10th Manchester Regt
SQUIRES William MM Pte 68622 17 Coy Machine Gun Corps
SQUIRES William MM L/Cpl 200393 Lancashire Fusiliers
SQUIRES Willie MM Bdr 104105 RGA
SQUIRREL John MM Pte 93229 20th Durham Light Infantry
SQUIRRELL Stanley Aldis MM L/Cpl 22633 2nd Grenadier Guards DOW 29.4.18.
SQUIRRELL William J. MM Dvr 31530 RFA
SQUIRRELL or SQUIRRILL William Clover MM Sjt 29201 3 Bde RHA
St AUBYN Horace MM Pte 4735 4th Royal Berkshire Regt
St AUBYN Patrick E. MM Pte 15943 East Surrey Regt
St CLAIR Clarence Victor MM Pte 300102 1/7th Essex Regt
St LEDGER Benjamin MM Cpl 13086 1st South Wales Borderers
St LEDGER George Edward "DCM,MM,CG(F)" Sjt 65307 33rd Bn Machine Gun Corps
St LEDGER James MM Gnr 16367 50 Siege Bty RGA
St PIER James MM Pte 14412 Worcestershire Regt
STABLER Fred MM Dvr T4/251947 62 Div Train Army Service Corps
STABLES George "DCM,MM" Sjt 22589 6/7th Gordon Highlanders
STABLES George A. MM Pte 28140 RAMC
STABLES Harry C. MM Pte 78828 RAMC
STABLES William MM Sjt 41023 A/104 Bde RFA
STABLES Wilson "MM,MID" Pte 6952 2nd Border Regt
STACEY Albert MM Pte 8227 6th Yorkshire Regt
STACEY Albert MM Pte 7837 32nd Bn Machine Gun Corps
STACEY Arthur MM Sjt 15432 1st Royal Fusiliers
STACEY Charles MM Pte 280544 4th London Regt
STACEY Charles MM L/Sjt 1200 Rifle Brigade
STACEY Charles MM+Bar Sjt 9633 Royal Berkshire Regt
STACEY Eric MM Spr 94794 Royal Engineers
STACEY Ernest James "MM,MID" Sjt 30118 59 Siege Bty RGA
STACEY Frederick MM+2 Bars Pte 10421 7th Royal West Kent Regt
STACEY Frederick William MM Pte 41011 14th Worcestershire Regt KIA 27.7.17.
STACEY George F. MM+Bar Sjt 28019 Lancashire Fusiliers
STACEY Herbert "DCM,MM" Sjt Farrier 54650 153 Bde RFA
STACEY Herbert O. MM Gnr 330399 RGA
STACEY Horace MM Pte 20210 2nd Yorkshire Light Infantry
STACEY John Charles MM Sjt 3112 1/5th Seaforth Highlanders KIA 10.4.18.
STACEY John W. "MM+Bar,MID" Sjt 7995 1st East Surrey Regt
STACEY Reginald John MM+Bar Pte S/3826 13th Rifle Brigade KIA 4.11.18.
STACEY Richard J. MM Pte 25512 1st Wiltshire Regt
STACEY Robert G. MM Pte 203982 4th Middlesex Regt
STACEY Stanley George MM Pte 201288 2/4th Royal Berkshire Regt KIA 27.5.18.
STACEY Thomas George MM L/Cpl 53090 2nd Manchester Regt

STACKHOUSE Bert MM L/Cpl 20029 Highland Light Infantry
STADDON Ernest O. MM Pte 12007 Coldstream Guards
STADDON Frederick C. MM Pte 25614 Oxf & Bucks Light Infantry
STADELMAN William MM Sjt 48601 39 Bde RFA
STADEN Stanley Frank MM Cpl 9727 11th Suffolk Regt KIA 27.10.18.
STAFF Henry MM Pte 93445 23rd Royal Fusiliers
STAFF William Donald MM Pte 400974 10th Essex Regt
STAFFORD A.J. MM Pte 20894 1st Essex Regt
STAFFORD Frank G. MM CQMS 22295 10th Duke of Cornwall's LI
STAFFORD Fred MM Cpl 36381 11th Notts & Derby Regt
STAFFORD Fred MM Cpl 2702 17th Manchester Regt KIA 30.4.18.
STAFFORD George MM Bdr 771183 RFA
STAFFORD George E. MM Pte 3127 8th Royal West Surrey Regt
STAFFORD George William MM L/Cpl 40859 Manchester Regt
STAFFORD Harry MM Cpl R/6864 King's Royal Rifle Corps
STAFFORD Howard F.N. MM Pte 48403 4th Northamptonshire Regt
STAFFORD J.E. MM Sjt 17723 Notts & Derby Regt
STAFFORD James MM Gnr 45451 RFA
STAFFORD John "MM,CG(B)" Sjt 14787 9th Northumberland Fusiliers KIA 11.4.18.
STAFFORD John Robert MM Cpl 46806 109 Siege Bty RGA KIA 23.5.18.
STAFFORD Maurice MM Gnr 31433 A/112 Bde RFA
STAFFORD Percival Herbert "MM,MID" Sjt 452168 Royal Engineers
STAFFORD Percy Haworth MM Sjt 46118 Machine Gun Corps
STAFFORD Thomas MM Pte 69931 RAMC
STAFFORD Walter Charles MM Sjt 14739 D/242 Bde RFA
STAFFORD William Dean "DCM,MM,MSM" CSM 1618 23rd Royal Fusiliers
STAFFORD William J. MM Pte 14659 8th Border Regt
STAFFORD William M. "MM,MID" Cpl 1759 1st Northumberland Fusiliers
STAGEMAN James William MM Pte 16/683 16th West Yorkshire Regt
STAGG Anthony F.W. MM Spr 160278 476 Fd Coy Royal Engineers
STAGG George MM Cpl 2183 9th Royal Fusiliers
STAGG George P. MM Pte 8669 1st Somerset Light Infantry
STAGG Walter T. MM Spr 42813 Royal Engineers
STAGG William MM L/Cpl 14058 4th Middlesex Regt
STAHL Albert W. MM Spr 87904 Royal Engineers
STAIG Alexander J. MM L/Cpl 2580 1/8th London Regt
STAINBURN William Edward MM Pte 28566 19th Northumberland Fusiliers
STAINER Tom MM L/Cpl 5988 2nd Rifle Brigade KIA 24.3.28.
STAINES Albert C. MM Pnr 558640 Royal Engineers
STAINES D.E. MM+Bar Sjt 27053 12th East Surrey Regt
STAINES Francis A. MM Sjt 825635 A/240 Bde RFA
STAINES William A. MM Pte 2328 8th Royal Sussex Regt
STAINES William John MM Spr 58834 87 Fd Coy Royal Engineers
STAINSBY Fred MM Sjt 11188 1st East Lancashire Regt
STAINSBY William MM Cpl 490161 Royal Engineers
STAINTHORPE George W. MM Sjt 2368 Yorkshire Light Infantry
STAINTHORPE Norman T. MM Pte 32914 2/4th York & Lancaster Regt
STAINTON George MM Bdr 800447 RFA
STAINTON George MM Sjt 240424 1/5th Lincolnshire Regt
STAINTON James C. MM L/Cpl 27181 Royal Warwickshire Regt
STAINTON John W. MM Sjt 15620 9th Yorkshire Regt
STAIRMAND George MM Pte 203111 Royal Scots Fusiliers
STAIRS Arthur MM Gnr 68522 23 Bde RFA
STAIT Albert Ernest MM L/Cpl 10597 2nd Worcestershire Regt
STAIT Charles MM Pte 8078 2nd Royal Warwickshire Regt
STAITE Albert Frederick "MM,MID" Gnr 40708 A/74 Bde RFA KIA 20.10.18.
STAITE Francis G. MM+Bar Pte 242368 1/8th Worcestershire Regt
STAITE Frederick W. MM Pte 18073 1st Coldstream Guards
STAITE Herbert MM Sjt 17128 26 Bde RFA
STALEY Albert V. MM Sjt 241993 4th North Staffordshire Regt
STALEY Cyril MM Cpl 200008 North Staffordshire Regt
STALEY Daniel MM Spr 155742 182 Tunnelling Coy Royal Engineers Died 14.11.18.
STALEY W.I. MM Cpl 14018 1st Coldstream Guards
STALKER George MM Sjt 143014 Royal Engineers
STALKER James MM Sjt 695022 55 Div Ammn Col RFA
STALKER Percy MM Cpl 2488 1/4th Royal Lancaster Regt
STALLARD Albert G. MM Pte 19879 Dorsetshire Regt
STALLARD Edgar C. MM Dvr 77358 Royal Engineers
STALLARD Herbert MM Pte 9035 4 Fd Amb RAMC DOW 14.10.17.
STALLARD Percy Albert "DCM,MM+Bar" L/Cpl STK/841 10th Royal Fusiliers
STALLARD William Arthur MM Gnr 171937 A/162 Bde RFA KIA 27.9.18.
STALLEBRASS Albert MM Pte 36190 11th Notts & Derby Regt
STALLEY Charles MM Pte 14189 6th Lincolnshire Regt
STALLWOOD Charles MM Dvr 687072 A/174 Bde RFA DOW 29.5.18.
STALLWOOD Stanley R. MM Pte 139988 Machine Gun Corps
STAM Edward MM L/Cpl 12524 Liverpool Regt
STAMFORD Alan MM Pte 11/803 11th East Yorkshire Regt
STAMFORD Charles Wilfred MM L/Cpl 40089 11th Royal West Surrey Regt
STAMFORD George MM Pte 91299 8th Notts & Derby Regt
STAMMERS James W. MM L/Cpl 15010 7th Duke of Cornwall's LI
STAMMERS Thomas MM Sjt 29251 Essex Regt
STAMP Henry MM Pte 13865 2nd Grenadier Guards
STAMP Henry MM Dvr 680239 RFA
STAMP Horace J. MM Sjt 11732 Royal Berkshire Regt
STAMPER George "MM,MID" L/Cpl 14663 8th Border Regt
STAMPER Henry MM Cpl 66875 182 Tunnelling Coy Royal Engineers
STAMPER Philip A. MM CQMS 200198 Manchester Regt
STAMPER Robert H. MM L/Cpl 42685 Machine Gun Corps
STAMPS Alfred MM Gnr 866077 66 Bde RFA
STAMPS Clifford MM Cpl M2/020828 363 MT Coy Army Service Corps
STANAWAY Joseph Henry MM Pte 9145 2nd Royal Fusiliers
STANBOROUGH John "DCM,MM" L/Sjt 250177 1/3rd London Regt
STANBRIDGE Alfred MM Pte 151698 104th Bn Machine Gun Corps
STANBRIDGE Ernest A. MM Sjt 8958 2nd North Lancashire Regt
STANBRIDGE James MM Cpl 33343 5th Royal Berkshire Regt
STANBRIDGE Richard MM Pte 3168 Gloucestershire Regt
STANBURY Arnold MM Cpl 54200 Royal Engineers
STANBURY Harold J. MM L/Cpl 113448 Machine Gun Corps "att 17th Indian Div,Mesopotamia."
STANBURY William Victor MM Sjt 46830 97 Bde RFA
STANCER Joseph Harold MM L/Cpl 7811 1st Lincolnshire Regt
STANCLIFFE Ernest MM Gnr 25412 B/75 Bde RFA
STANCLIFFE Frank MM Sjt 24720 Machine Gun Corps
STANCLIFFE William MM Pte 235752 10th West Yorkshire Regt
STANDBRIDGE Charles H. MM+Bar Bdr 48605 1 Div Ammn Col RFA
STANDBRIDGE F.T. MM Cpl Shoeing Smith 51743 111 Bty 24 Bde RFA
STANDELL William Bryan MM Pte 5612 237 Coy Machine Gun Corps KIA 24.3.18.
STANDEN Alfred MM Pte 9729 2nd Royal West Surrey Regt
STANDEN Herbert MM Bdr 891250 RFA
STANDEN Sydney MM Sjt 1647 11th Hussars
STANDEN Thomas MM Pte 56547 36 Fd Amb RAMC
STANDFIELD Herbert MM Bdr 687388 28 Bde RFA
STANDING Ernest MM Pnr 254350 Royal Engineers
STANDING George William MM Sjt 4529 2nd Essex Regt
STANDING Leonard G. MM Cpl 2165 8th Royal Sussex Regt
STANDISH Alfred MM L/Cpl 300077 2/5th West Riding Regt KIA 29.3.18.
STANDLEY Ernest MM Pte 9350 2nd Worcestershire Regt KIA 16.5.15.
STANDLEY G.H. MM Dvr T4/243253 Army Service Corps
STANDRING Thomas MM L/Cpl 200742 1/4th Royal Scots
STANDRING Walter MM Cpl 376453 7th Manchester Regt
STANFIELD G. MM+Bar Pte 40810 1st Northamptonshire Regt
STANFIELD John MM Pnr 16971 11th Manchester Regt
STANFIELD Thomas A. MM Pte 337482 RAMC
STANFIELD Thomas William MM Pte 18/384 18th Durham Light Infantry KIA 23.11.17.
STANFORD Alfred MM L/Bdr 945611 D/291 Bde RFA
STANFORD Charles MM Sjt 3463 Royal Sussex Regt
STANFORD Charles MM Sjt 33470 RFA
STANFORD Francis MM Sjt 3300 2nd Rifle Brigade
STANFORD Stephen Arthur MM CSM 9452 1st Welsh Regt
STANFORD William J. MM Sjt 200397 1/7th Middlesex Regt
STANGER John W. MM L/Cpl 200842 9th West Riding Regt
STANGER Thomas MM Pte 240959 Gordon Highlanders
STANGER Thomas MM L/Sjt 64712 RAMC
STANGER William Moss MM Pte 23/265 Northumberland Fusiliers
STANGHON George MM Pte 26394 Welsh Regt
STANHOPE Ernest Chesterfield MM Gnr 90433 A/110 Bde RFA DOW 21.4.18.

STANHOPE James MM+Bar Sjt 306818 8th West Yorkshire Regt
STANHOPE James MM L/Cpl 61168 24th Royal Fusiliers
STANHOPE John MM Sjt 13881 9th West Yorkshire Regt
STANHOPE William "MM,GMV(S)" Pte 13559 Royal Lancaster Regt
STANIER Joseph Leonard MM L/Cpl 48234 12 Div Sig Coy Royal Engineers
STANIFORD Ernest Reginald MM Cpl M2/147146 594 MT Coy Army Service Corps
STANIFORD George W. MM Pte 200958 Royal Berkshire Regt
STANIFORD Samuel J. MM Pte 74593 RAMC
STANIFORTH Bert MM Sjt 1558 1/5th Leicestershire Regt
STANILAND Arthur C. MM Pte 523 RAMC
STANLEY Albert MM Pte 20202 2nd Royal Munster Fusiliers KIA 7.11.18.
STANLEY Albert MM Sjt 355588 1/10th Liverpool Regt
STANLEY Albert G. MM Gnr 850500 222 Bde RFA
STANLEY Alfred MM Pte 3/5897 1st East Yorkshire Regt
STANLEY Alfred Charles MM Gnr 18916 A/99 Bde RFA
STANLEY Arthur MM Pnr 321956 Royal Engineers
STANLEY Charles MM Sjt 19766 10th Royal West Kent Regt
STANLEY Charles Frank MM Bdr 95208 D/65 Bde RFA
STANLEY Charles H. MM L/Cpl 12285 7th Wiltshire Regt
STANLEY Charles James MM Sjt 723 7th Worcestershire Regt
STANLEY E.T. MM Cpl 39251 2nd South Wales Borderers
STANLEY Edward Joseph MM Sjt 228423 Royal Engineers
STANLEY Edwin C. MM Cpl 358111 10th Liverpool Regt
STANLEY Ernest Edward MM Pte R/4981 13th King's Royal Rifle Corps
STANLEY Frank G. MM Sjt 8557 1st Bedfordshire Regt
STANLEY Frank H. MM Pte 32625 13th Essex Regt
STANLEY Frederick MM Sjt 8535 2nd Northamptonshire Regt
STANLEY Frederick MM Spr 49430 Royal Engineers
STANLEY Frederick MM Pte 17620 9th North Lancashire Regt
STANLEY Frederick H. MM Spr 25490 Royal Engineers
STANLEY Guy MM Cpl 5944 Royal Fusiliers
STANLEY H. MM L/Cpl 18925 Royal Engineers
STANLEY H. MM Cpl 28466 Royal Scots
STANLEY Harold MM L/Cpl 288104 4 Div Sig Coy Royal Engineers
STANLEY Henry W. MM 2nd Cpl 98587 Royal Engineers
STANLEY J. MM Pte 13162 10th Cheshire Regt
STANLEY James MM Cpl 23715 15th Highland Light Infantry KIA 5.11.18.
STANLEY James J.W. MM+Bar Sjt 12594 Bedfordshire Regt att 1/1st Hertfordshire Regt.
STANLEY John MM Gnr 820400 46 Div Ammn Col RFA
STANLEY John A.W. MM L/Cpl 6775 Royal Irish Rifles
STANLEY Richard MM+Bar Sjt 6796 Royal Lancaster Regt
STANLEY Sidney D. MM Sjt 11068 188 Siege Bty RGA
STANLEY Thomas MM+Bar Pte 3765 1st Lancashire Fusiliers
STANLEY Thomas MM Pte 53121 RAMC
STANLEY Thomas MM Cpl 84165 29th Bn Machine Gun Corps
STANLEY Thomas W. MM Bdr 41790 7 Bde RHA
STANLEY Thomas Walter MM Pte 24446 4th Grenadier Guards
STANLEY William MM Spr 254045 Royal Engineers
STANLEY William MM Sjt 128190 193 Siege Bty RGA
STANLEY William C. MM Sjt 14764 7 Fd Amb RAMC
STANNARD C.W.G. MM Pte 2189 23rd Middlesex Regt
STANNARD Cecil A. MM Pte 246015 15th Durham Light Infantry
STANNARD Charles MM Gnr Sig 7046 RFA
STANNARD Frank MM Sjt 18005 8th Suffolk Regt DOW 6.3.17.
STANNARD George MM Bdr 98335 B/106 Bde RFA
STANNARD Harry MM+Bar Bdr 1193 'A' Bty RHA
STANNARD Herbert V. MM Pte 93009 6th Bn Tank Corps
STANNARD James MM Pte 2376 8th Royal Sussex Regt
STANNARD Thomas "DCM,MM" Cpl 16847 7 Div Sig Coy Royal Engineers
STANNERS George T. MM Sjt 12900 6th Royal Berkshire Regt
STANNERS Harold MM Sjt 1111 Royal West Surrey Regt
STANNETT Henry MM Pte 8674 2nd Royal Scots
STANSBRIDGE Reuben MM L/Cpl 26981 Hampshire Regt
STANSBY George Buxton MM L/Cpl 52120 6th Northamptonshire Regt KIA 21.9.18.
STANSELL Lionel Brough MM L/Cpl 19045 10th Royal West Kent Regt
STANSFIELD Arthur John MM Pte 27725 124 Coy Machine Gun Corps
STANSFIELD Clement MM Gnr 92081 8 Bty 15 Bde RFA
STANSFIELD Egbert MM Cpl 29937 B/91 Bde RFA
STANSFIELD Fred MM Cpl 26774 1st North Lancashire Regt
STANSFIELD Harold E. MM Spr 66119 19 Div Sig Coy Royal Engineers
STANSFIELD Harry MM Pte 46296 RAMC
STANSFIELD John MM L/Cpl 59980 2nd Royal Scots Fusiliers
STANSFIELD Nathan MM L/Cpl 111785 187 Coy Labour Corps
STANSFIELD Richard MM Pte 26332 Machine Gun Corps KIA 23.9.18.
STANSFIELD Sam MM Pte M2/180943 30 Mot Amb Convoy Army Service Corps
STANSFIELD Walter MM+Bar Sjt Fitter 780429 A/246 Bde RFA
STANTON Albert E. MM Spr 151649 179 Tunnelling Coy Royal Engineers
STANTON Arthur MM L/Cpl 17139 Grenadier Guards
STANTON Francis W. MM Cpl 56130 Labour Corps
STANTON George H. MM Gnr 70793 RGA
STANTON Harry MM Pte 15910 North Staffordshire Regt
STANTON John MM Pte 9029 Arg & Suth Highlanders
STANTON John MM Pte 325357 Durham Light Infantry
STANTON John MM Cpl 720314 1/24th London Regt
STANTON Leslie O. MM Sjt 265772 13th Liverpool Regt
STANTON Leslie Thomas MM Pte 38431 RAMC
STANTON Patrick MM L/Cpl 14098 13th Liverpool Regt
STANTON Percival MM Pte 22255 16th West Yorkshire Regt
STANTON Percy MM Sjt 70694 138 Siege Bty RGA
STANTON Phillip MM CSM 3893 11th Arg & Suth Highlanders
STANTON Robert MM Pte 72077 46th Bn Machine Gun Corps
STANTON Samuel E. MM Spr 55849 Royal Engineers
STANTON Thomas MM Sjt 37376 20 Bty 9 Bde RFA
STANTON Walter E. MM Sjt 1259 1/6th West Yorkshire Regt
STANTON Wilfred S. MM Pte 2918 1/15th Unknown
STANTON William MM Spr 275256 278 Rly Const Coy Royal Engineers
STANTON William S. MM L/Cpl 30527 2nd Grenadier Guards
STANWAY David MM Gnr Sig 261954 135 Bty 32 Bde RFA
STANWAY John MM+Bar L/Cpl 486137 465 Fd Coy Royal Engineers
STANYARD John MM+Bar Sjt 5203 26th Royal Fusiliers
STANYON Algernon A. MM L/Cpl 39257 Royal Berkshire Regt
STAPELEY Frank MM Cpl 10900 2nd Oxf & Bucks Light Infantry
STAPLES Bernard M. MM Sjt 27740 7th Lincolnshire Regt
STAPLES Frank MM Sjt 11587 Leicestershire Regt
STAPLES Frederick MM Cpl 29865 RGA
STAPLES G.E. MM Cpl 29405 Essex Regt
STAPLES George William MM L/Cpl 15192 9th Leicestershire Regt DOW 18.2.17.
STAPLES Gilbert "DCM,MM+Bar" S/Sjt 1407 27 Fd Amb RAMC
STAPLES James MM Sjt 8387 1st Lincolnshire Regt
STAPLES John Joseph MM Sjt 4464 2nd Notts & Derby Regt
STAPLES John W. MM Sjt 51523 2nd Yorkshire Light Infantry
STAPLES William F. MM Cpl 925180 Y/56 Med TM Bty RFA
STAPLES William J. MM Pte 29725 Hampshire Regt
STAPLETON A.J. MM Sjt 450857 London Regt
STAPLETON Alfred MM Pte 266517 1/8th Notts & Derby Regt
STAPLETON Arthur MM Cpl 3685 2 Fd Amb RAMC
STAPLETON Cecil MM Sjt 13674 Notts & Derby Regt
STAPLETON Charles MM Pte M2/034447 350 Coy Army Service Corps
STAPLETON Charles MM L/Cpl 524009 484 Fd Coy Royal Engineers
STAPLETON Edward Philip MM+2 Bars Cpl 13629 9th Norfolk Regt
STAPLETON Frederick MM Spr 113840 106 Fd Coy Royal Engineers
STAPLETON Henry MM+Bar Pte 1410 2nd Manchester Regt
STAPLETON Joseph T. MM Sjt 331206 1/9th Liverpool Regt
STAPLETON Martin MM Cpl 8239 6th Northamptonshire Regt KIA 14.7.16.
STAPLETON Percy MM Cpl 41409 2nd Highland Light Infantry
STAPLEY Albert H. MM Sjt 776403 D/310 Bde RFA
STAPLEY Benjamin J. MM+Bar Pte 203963 1st East Kent Regt
STAPLEY Bert MM Spr 17813 Royal Engineers
STAPLEY Edward MM Bdr 1376 RFA
STAPLEY George Aubrey MM Sjt 2795 8th Royal Sussex Regt
STARBUCK John H. MM Pte 14571 Arg & Suth Highlanders
STARBUCK T. MM Pte 16/1009 16th Royal Warwickshire Regt
STARBUCK Tom MM L/Cpl 241913 1/5th Leicestershire Regt
STARES William E. MM 2nd Cpl 21434 Royal Engineers
STARK Albert MM L/Bdr 37955 8 Siege Bty RGA
STARK Alfred MM L/Sjt 8708 2nd Royal Berkshire Regt KIA 28.10.16.
STARK Andrew MM Pte 290134 1/7th Royal Highlanders
STARK Francis MM Pte 200224 1/4th Royal Scots

STARK James MM Cpl 30962 Labour Corps
STARK Robert MM Sjt 325078 1/9th Durham Light Infantry
STARK Thomas E. MM Sjt 11549 19 Div Ammn Col RFA
STARK William MM Bdr Sig 92470 C/256 Bde RFA
STARK William MM Sjt 350364 Royal Scots
STARKE Sidney C. MM Pte 203872 15th Hampshire Regt
STARKEY Albert MM Cpl 50029 92 Fd Coy Royal Engineers
STARKEY Edward MM Pte 15488 11th West Yorkshire Regt
STARKEY George MM Pte 19257 Border Regt
STARKEY Harry MM Cpl 55107 Royal Engineers
STARKEY Thomas R. "DCM,MM" Sjt 7105 Border Regt
STARKEY ThomasH. MM Sjt 9532 2nd East Yorkshire Regt
STARKEY William MM Dvr 30989 37 Bde RFA
STARKEY William MM+Bar Cpl 11781 1st Cameron Highlanders
STARKIE Thomas MM Gnr 687348 RFA
STARKINGS James MM Sjt 15667 9th Norfolk Regt
STARKINGS John W. MM Sjt 53539 12th Durham Light Infantry
STARKS Fred MM Sjt 17055 9th Yorkshire Light Infantry
STARLING Albert G. MM Pte B/200899 2nd Rifle Brigade
STARLING Arthur J. MM Gnr Sig 266962 420 Bty RFA
STARLING B.J. MM Sjt 15400 10th Essex Regt
STARLING Bertie MM Pte 6044 1st Suffolk Regt
STARLING John MM Pte 8971 1st Norfolk Regt KIA 4.9.16.
STARMAN William Edward MM L/Sjt 7000 1st Norfolk Regt DOW 16.9.18.
STARNS Charles Thomas Henry MM Sjt 680069 1/22nd London Regt DOW 2.9.18.
STARR George MM L/Cpl 27031 4th Hampshire Regt
STARR George E. MM Gnr 140439 HQ 42 Bde RFA
STARR Henry MM Pte 40760 2nd South Wales Borderers KIA 15.5.18.
STARR John W. MM Pte 306301 1/8th Notts & Derby Regt
STARR Richard Lawrence MM Pte R/27328 17th King's Royal Rifle Corps
STARR Walter MM Gnr 214801 RFA
START Frank William MM Gnr 950768 18 Bde RFA
START Samuel Charles MM Pte 20738 146 Coy Machine Gun Corps
STARTIN James MM+Bar Pte 30821 28 Fd Amb RAMC
STARTUP John Henry MM Pte 18/741 1st West Yorkshire Regt DOW 3.11.18.
STATHAM Albert E.V. "DCM,MM+Bar" Cpl 85704 34 Div Sig Coy Royal Engineers
STATHAM Percy J. MM Cpl 13265 9th Notts & Derby Regt
STATHAM Selwyn MM Pte 9610 Coldstream Guards
STATHAM Thomas A. MM 2nd Cpl 51472 93 Fd Coy Royal Engineers
STATHAM W. MM Pte 240956 York & Lancaster Regt
STATHER John Norrison MM Cpl 10/205 10th East Yorkshire Regt KIA 12.4.18.
STATHERS William Robert MM Dvr 14032 32 Div Ammn Col RFA
STATON Albert MM Cpl 372532 2/8th London Regt
STATON Chares H. MM Pte 2271 RAMC
STATON Charles MM Gnr 294214 RGA
STATON Horace "MM,MSM" Sjt 33473 13th Yorkshire Regt
STATON Peter MM Pte 16763 1st Lancashire Fusiliers
STAUNTON Ernest W. MM+Bar L/Sjt 617133 1/19th London Regt
STAUNTON Henry C. MM Gnr 14123 107 Bde Royal Artillery
STAVELEY John MM Cpl 18746 Border Regt
STAYNES George MM Sjt M2/113196 51 Auxiliary Bus Coy Army Service Corps
STAYTON Edward MM Pte 25580 Northamptonshire Regt
STEAD Alfred MM Cpl 8800 2nd Hampshire Regt
STEAD Arthur MM Pnr 98791 Royal Engineers
STEAD Charles MM Sjt 295333 303 Siege Bty RGA
STEAD Clifford MM Pte 589036 17th London Regt
STEAD Ernest "DCM,MM" Sjt 15173 10th West Riding Regt
STEAD Frank MM L/Cpl 14321 9th Yorkshire Regt
STEAD Harry MM L/Cpl 34879 York & Lancaster Regt
STEAD Herbert W. MM Pte 306513 5th West Riding Regt
STEAD Hubert MM Sjt 266033 2/7th West Yorkshire Regt
STEAD John H. MM L/Cpl C/12393 King's Royal Rifle Corps
STEAD Leonard "MM,MID" Pte 2716 1/4th West Riding Regt
STEAD Mark MM Cpl 21965 6th Yorkshire Light Infantry
STEAD R.H. MM Air Mech 1 2776 Royal Flying Corps
STEAD Reginald B. MM Pte 304201 10th London Regt
STEADMAN Bernard MM L/Cpl 41176 20th Middlesex Regt
STEADMAN Charles MM Pte 240137 5th Royal Sussex Regt
STEADMAN Edward S. MM+Bar L/Sjt 56903 14th Royal Welsh Fusiliers
STEADMAN Henry MM L/Sjt 16077 Lancashire Fusiliers
STEADMAN Leonard "DCM,MM" Sjt 68600 B/110 Bde RFA
STEADMAN Sidney MM Sjt 8778 Worcestershire Regt
STEADMAN Thomas F. MM Pte 82520 6th Bn Machine Gun Corps
STEADMAN William MM Pte 24280 Worcestershire Regt
STEADMAN William Gilmour MM Cpl 6250 9th Seaforth Highlanders
STEADMAN William Thomas MM Gnr 31139 B/177 Bde RFA
STEANE Clarence Thomas MM Sjt 1531 1/5th Royal Warwickshire Regt DOW 24.8.16.
STEANE John MM L/Cpl 164878 26 Fd Coy Royal Engineers
STEARE Henry R. MM Gnr 116095 RGA
STEARMAN William MM Pte 63838 9th Yorkshire Light Infantry
STEARN Charles MM Pte 32959 6th Leicestershire Regt KIA 12.11.17.
STEARN William MM Cpl 59722 41 Bde RFA
STEARNS Harry MM Pte 202497 8th Royal Berkshire Regt
STEARS Herbert MM Pte 10422 Royal West Kent Regt
STEATHAM Thomas MM Pte 238056 5th Lancashire Fusiliers
STEBBEDS Henry Alfred MM L/Cpl 15599 7th Bedfordshire Regt
STEBBING Frank MM Sjt 5326 8th East Surrey Regt
STEBBINGS Albert W. MM Pte 26005 Somerset Light Infantry
STEBBINGS Charles S. MM 2nd Cpl 69147 35 Div Sig Coy Royal Engineers
STEBBINGS Herbert MM Pte 37160 Lancashire Fusiliers
STEBBINGS William MM Cpl 35161 D/153 Bde RFA
STEDMAN C. MM Sjt 8466 11th Essex Regt
STEDMAN Clifford S. "DCM,MM" L/Sjt 28383 6th Northamptonshire Regt
STEDMAN Jack MM Pte 12139 9th Norfolk Regt
STEDMAN Jack MM Pte M2/034808 48 Div Train Army Service Corps
STEDMAN John MM Pte 10553 8th Royal Sussex Regt
STEDMAN Stanley MM Gnr 915470 D/223 Bde RFA
STEDMAN Thomas MM Pte 30095 Royal Inniskilling Fusiliers
STEED Alfred MM Pte 597 7th East Kent Regt
STEED Charles Frank MM Gnr 201161 A/103 Bde RFA
STEED John MM Cpl 10837 1st Middlesex Regt
STEED John R. MM Pte 421358 10th London Regt
STEEDMAN Alexander MM L/Cpl 6643 Arg & Suth Highlanders
STEEDMAN Arthur MM Spr 482274 Royal Engineers
STEEDMAN William MM Pte 20919 5th Cameron Highlanders
STEEL Allan MM L/Cpl 31501 6th King's Own Scottish Borderers
STEEL Arthur MM Dvr 1519 1/7th London Regt
STEEL Arthur Augustus MM Sjt 86171 144 Coy Labour Corps
STEEL Benjamin MM Dvr 14295 RFA
STEEL C.H. "DCM,MM" Sjt 4655 18th Hussars
STEEL Edwin MM Sjt 8928 2nd West Yorkshire Regt KIA 16.8.17.
STEEL Ernest MM Gnr 1344 A/252 Bde RFA
STEEL Harold Victor MM Pte 38500 9th Yorkshire Regt KIA 7.9.18.
STEEL Horace MM Cpl 104619 222 Siege Bty RGA
STEEL Hugh J. MM Sjt 51709 Liverpool Regt
STEEL J. MM Spr 215712 Royal Engineers
STEEL James MM Pte 16152 13th Royal Scots
STEEL James B. MM Cpl 292109 1/5th Gordon Highlanders
STEEL James O. MM Pte 72199 Machine Gun Corps
STEEL John MM Cpl 277031 V/49 Heavy TM Bty RGA
STEEL John Arthur MM Pte 20464 Grenadier Guards DOW 9.11.18.
STEEL John T. MM Pte 290967 Northumberland Fusiliers
STEEL Omar MM L/Cpl 240406 1/5th Royal Lancaster Regt
STEEL Robert MM Dvr 7640 A/73 Bde RFA
STEEL Robert MM Pte 12902 Scots Guards
STEEL Robert Taylor MM Bdr 134276 RFA
STEEL Tom MM L/Cpl 95908 18 Squadron Machine Gun Corps(Cavalry)
STEEL Walter MM Gnr 77492 25 Bde RFA
STEEL William MM Pte 23134 1st Cameron Highlanders
STEEL William MM Pte 38301 Royal Scots
STEEL William MM Pte 5003 11th Arg & Suth Highlanders
STEEL William MM Sjt 201270 2/4th Lincolnshire Regt
STEEL William MM Sjt 6554 RFA
STEEL William Pollock MM Cpl 34849 8th York & Lancaster Regt
STEELE Albert J. MM Sjt 246321 C/286 Bde RFA
STEELE Alexander "DCM,MM" Sjt R/5093 12th King's Royal Rifle Corps
STEELE Alister Watt Donald MM Pte 1325 1/6th Seaforth Highlanders
STEELE Arthur MM Bdr 62856 25 Bde RFA
STEELE Bowden MM Dvr M2/116269 Army Service Corps
STEELE Charles O. MM Pte 41582 1/4th Seaforth Highlanders

STEELE Edward E. "DCM,MM" Sjt 925409 C/290 Bde RFA
STEELE Edwin MM Pte M2/229790 Army Service Corps
STEELE Edwin T. "MM,MID" Gnr 69567 RFA
STEELE F.C. MM L/Cpl 17953 Royal Engineers
STEELE Francis W. MM Pte 3/7537 6th Somerset Light Infantry
STEELE Frederick Alfred MM Pte 1483 3 Fd Amb RAMC
STEELE Fullerton MM+Bar Pte 16760 Manchester Regt
STEELE George MM Pte 22562 Royal Irish Fusiliers
STEELE George Edward MM L/Cpl 507 1/1(East Riding)Fd Coy Royal Engineers
STEELE George William MM Sjt 9843 8th North Staffordshire Regt KIA 24.3.18.
STEELE H. MM L/Cpl 7932 Bedfordshire Regt
STEELE Harold John MM Sjt 2511 1/15th London Regt KIA 7.6.17.
STEELE Horace C. MM Gnr 138936 RFA
STEELE J. MM Pte 40358 Leicestershire Regt
STEELE James MM Sjt 5952 Royal Irish Rifles
STEELE James MM+Bar Pte 241239 5th Royal Scots Fusiliers
STEELE John MM Cpl 19356 1st Royal Scots Fusiliers
STEELE L. MM Cpl 3158 4 Fd Amb RAMC
STEELE Matthew MM Sjt 41443 39 Bde RFA
STEELE Neil MM Sjt 266237 Royal Highlanders
STEELE Percy W. MM Pte 7593 3 Ambulance Train RAMC
STEELE Robert J. MM Gnr Sig 175530 407 Bty 96 Bde RFA
STEELE Robert J. MM Cpl 444335 Royal Engineers
STEELE Robert J. "DCM,MM" CSM 32461 1/5th East Lancashire Regt
STEELE Theo MM Cpl 200750 Northumberland Fusiliers
STEELE Thomas MM Spr 49217 4 Div Sig Coy Royal Engineers
STEELE W. MM L/Cpl 15970 Royal Irish Rifles
STEELE William MM Sjt 19293 Royal Engineers
STEELE William MM Pte 10662 10th Scottish Rifles KIA 31.7.17.
STEELE William C. MM+Bar Cpl 83143 3rd London Regt
STEELE William E. MM Spr 518899 Royal Engineers
STEELE William H. MM Cpl 13437 7th Royal Berkshire Regt
STEELEY Harry MM Dvr 18959 A/155 Bde RFA
STEELS William MM L/Bdr 93504 RFA
STEEN Thomas John MM Pte 11138 1st Welsh Regt
STEEN Victor J. MM Pte R/42519 18th King's Royal Rifle Corps
STEEN William MM L/Sjt 16577 2nd Coldstream Guards
STEEN William MM+Bar Pte 9864 1st Gordon Highlanders
STEENKISTE William Albert MM Cpl 67925 218 Coy Machine Gun Corps
STEENSON Robert J. MM Pte 301116 1/7th Royal Scots
STEEPLE John MM Sjt 200288 1/5th York & Lancaster Regt DOW 9.5.18.
STEEPLES Alexander MM Pte 9997 Royal Highlanders
STEER Arthur MM Sjt 34303 RGA
STEER Arthur "MM,MID" Sjt 4516 RAMC
STEER Edward W. MM Cpl 42829 Machine Gun Corps
STEER Frederick MM Pte 241865 8th Worcestershire Regt
STEER Frederick W. MM Dvr T4/060647 Army Service Corps
STEER Harry MM L/Sjt 14586 4th Coldstream Guards
STEER Herbert Graham MM Gnr 209293 RFA
STEER Leslie M. MM Cpl 24009 22 Fd Amb RAMC
STEER Samuel MM Pte 70434 5th Bn Machine Gun Corps
STEER William H. "DCM,MM" Sjt 18801 4th & 15th Hampshire Regt
STEER William H. MM Dvr 34634 'C' Bty RHA
STEGGLES Arthur MM Dvr 12460 27 Bde RFA
STEGGLES Walter MM Gnr 8177 152 Bde RFA
STEGGLES William MM Pte 13997 Royal Berkshire Regt
STEIN Fred A.B. MM Gnr 26902 RFA
STEIN William MM Sjt 8412 1st East Yorkshire Regt DOW 7.2.17.
STEINBERG Nataan MM Pte 24709 Yorkshire Light Infantry
STELFOX Charles Ernest MM Gnr 53030 RGA
STEMBRIDGE Leonard MM Pte 27575 10th Royal Welsh Fusiliers
STEMP Albert F. MM Cpl 17120 6th South Wales Borderers
STEMP Walter Henry MM Pte 2091 1/4th Royal Sussex Regt
STENDALL John T. MM L/Cpl 34514 9th Yorkshire Regt
STENHOUSE J.P. MM Pte 18717 Royal Scots
STENHOUSE Leonard MM Gnr 755587 RFA
STENHOUSE Thomas MM Pte 200444 1/4th King's Own Scottish Borderers
STENHOUSE Thomas MM Sjt 291154 Royal Highlanders
STENLAKE William MM Pte 19/1094 19th Northumberland Fusiliers
STENNER Albert Havelock MM L/Cpl 35140 Worcestershire Regt
STENNING Albert MM Pte 17252 2nd Grenadier Guards KIA 30.3.18.
STENNING Albert MM Pte 2156 8th Royal Sussex Regt
STENNING Charles H. MM CSM B/2397 9th Rifle Brigade
STENNING Ernest C. MM L/Cpl 574399 17th London Regt
STENNING Hartley MM Gnr 120168 321 Siege Bty RGA
STENSON Percy MM Gnr 87794 'N' Bty RHA
STENSON Stephan MM L/Cpl 20079 2nd Royal Munster Fusiliers
STENT Herbert C. MM Cpl 504007 65 Fd Amb RAMC
STENTON George E. MM Pte 27019 12th East Surrey Regt
STENTON Lewis MM Pte 67444 RAMC
STEPHEN Alexander MM Sjt 23677 51st Bn Machine Gun Corps
STEPHEN Arthur MM Cpl 630042 RFA
STEPHEN Charles H. MM Pte 17711 Gordon Highlanders
STEPHEN David MM Bdr 58495 22 Bde RFA
STEPHEN Donald MM Pte 240135 1/5th Seaforth Highlanders
STEPHEN Forbes MM Spr 140405 Royal Engineers
STEPHEN Francis C. MM Sjt 20489 Machine Gun Corps
STEPHEN Henry MM Pte 200229 1/4th Gordon Highlanders
STEPHEN J. MM Pte 301387 2/1st(Highland)Fd Amb RAMC
STEPHEN James MM Pte 3026 1/7th Gordon Highlanders
STEPHEN John MM Pte 3/5442 2nd Gordon Highlanders
STEPHEN John MM Pte 53779 RAMC
STEPHEN John E. MM Pte 245405 22nd Manchester Regt
STEPHEN John G. MM Pte 21842 Seaforth Highlanders
STEPHEN John I MM Sjt 240948 Royal Highlanders
STEPHEN John J. MM L/Bdr 117204 B/162 Bde RFA
STEPHEN John W. MM Gnr Fitter 4172 RFA
STEPHEN Urquhart MM Pte 377074 Labour Corps
STEPHEN William MM Pte 25762 1st Royal Highlanders
STEPHEN William MM Pte 1241 1st Gordon Highlanders
STEPHEN William Andrew MM Spr 406187 51 Div Sig Coy Royal Engineers
STEPHENS Albert Edward MM Sjt 7714 10th Cheshire Regt DOW 17.7.17.
STEPHENS Arthur MM Pte R/33216 King's Royal Rifle Corps
STEPHENS Arthur Edward MM Pte 1438 1/5th Duke of Cornwall's LI KIA 1.7.16.
STEPHENS Augustus MM L/Cpl 9617 2nd North Lancashire Regt
STEPHENS Charles Henry MM Pte 66839 RAMC
STEPHENS Edward MM L/Cpl 19767 9th Scottish Rifles
STEPHENS Fred MM Pte 241392 1/5th Devonshire Regt
STEPHENS Frederick MM L/Sjt 9599 Liverpool Regt
STEPHENS Frederick C. MM Sjt 2343 South Lancashire Regt
STEPHENS Frederick H. MM Sjt 31994 RGA
STEPHENS Frederick J. MM+Bar L/Cpl 48202 14th Royal Warwickshire Regt
STEPHENS Frederick W. MM Pte 14654 8th Royal Berkshire Regt
STEPHENS Geoffrey Ernest MM Pte 201827 'B' Bn Tank Corps
STEPHENS George MM Pte 358388 Liverpool Regt
STEPHENS George T. MM Pte 472112 12th London Regt
STEPHENS Harry MM Pte 204226 Liverpool Regt
STEPHENS Henry R. MM Pte 18492 Northumberland Fusiliers
STEPHENS John E. MM Cpl 14930 12/13th Northumberland Fusiliers
STEPHENS John E. MM Cpl 46143 14th Royal Welsh Fusiliers
STEPHENS Richard MM L/Cpl 1771 South Lancashire Regt
STEPHENS Robert W. MM Sjt 14291 7th Shropshire Light Infantry
STEPHENS Ronald Campbell MM L/Cpl 19776 Machine Gun Corps(Heavy Section)
STEPHENS Samuel MM Sgt 11931 A/93 Bde RFA KIA 11.9.17.
STEPHENS Sidney G. "DCM,MM(2761 Pte)" L/Sjt 720767 1/24th London Regt
STEPHENS Thomas "MM,MID" Cpl 2558 2/4th Gloucestershire Regt KIA 27.8.17.
STEPHENS Thomas Henry MM Spr 77495 50 Div Sig Coy Royal Engineers
STEPHENS William MM Dvr 199629 B/186 Bde RFA
STEPHENS William MM Pte 260627 7th Border Regt
STEPHENS William A. MM Sjt 240530 1/5th Gloucestershire Regt
STEPHENS William J. MM Pte 15270 Devonshire Regt
STEPHENS William L. MM L/Cpl 85705 33rd Bn Machine Gun Corps
STEPHENSON Albert MM Pte 28670 Durham Light Infantry
STEPHENSON Albert MM Sjt 680196 1/22nd London Regt
STEPHENSON Albert MM+Bar Sjt 341364 2/1(West Lancashire)Fd Amb RAMC
STEPHENSON Albert E. MM Pte 57975 6th Yorkshire Regt
STEPHENSON Alfred MM Dvr 715366 42 Div Ammn Col RFA
STEPHENSON Andrew M. MM L/Cpl 19851 15th Royal Irish Rifles
STEPHENSON Arthur MM Pte 9762 2nd Oxf & Bucks Light Infantry
STEPHENSON Arthur Lawrence "MM,MSM" L/Sjt 22/377 22nd Durham Light Infantry
STEPHENSON Benjamin MM Cpl 36291 2nd Yorkshire Regt

STEPHENSON Benjamin MM Pte 65284 4th Royal Fusiliers
STEPHENSON Cecil E. MM Sjt 730064 A/255 Bty RFA
STEPHENSON E. MM Pte 386164 RAMC
STEPHENSON Eddie MM Pte 35235 West Yorkshire Regt
STEPHENSON Edgar MM RQMS 21933 2nd South Staffordshire Regt
STEPHENSON Edward MM Pte 79611 9th Royal Fusiliers
STEPHENSON Edward MM L/Cpl 16/773 17th Northumberland Fusiliers
STEPHENSON Frank R. MM Sjt 705007 RFA
STEPHENSON Fred MM Cpl 42150 5th York & Lancaster Regt
STEPHENSON Frederick MM L/Cpl 14680 7th Yorkshire Regt
STEPHENSON Frederick MM Spr 42434 Royal Engineers
STEPHENSON Frederick MM+Bar L/Cpl 10388 Royal West Surrey Regt
STEPHENSON Frederick MM Pte 235488 4th York & Lancaster Regt
STEPHENSON Frederick Thomas Luther MM Pte 35291 2nd Yorkshire Light Infantry KIA 31.8.18.
STEPHENSON George MM Pte 79616 9th Royal Fusiliers
STEPHENSON George MM L/Sjt 23846 3rd Grenadier Guards DOW 3.9.18.
STEPHENSON George MM Sjt 630854 1/20th London Regt
STEPHENSON George MM Spr 102720 177 Tunnelling Coy Royal Engineers
STEPHENSON George MM Pte 34364 134 Coy Machine Gun Corps KIA 20.9.18.
STEPHENSON George Oswald MM Sjt 79134 112 Siege Bty RGA
STEPHENSON George P. MM Pte 45479 2nd Yorkshire Regt
STEPHENSON Harold Archibald MM Pte 6994 2/1st HAC DOW 6.4.17.
STEPHENSON Henry MM Sjt 241283 1/5th North Lancashire Regt
STEPHENSON James William MM Pte 301738 1/5th Durham Light Infantry
STEPHENSON John MM Pte 46310 11th Royal Scots
STEPHENSON John MM L/Cpl 34602 Yorkshire Light Infantry
STEPHENSON John MM Cpl 16/455 16th Northumberland Fusiliers
STEPHENSON John MM Pte 2600 24th Royal Fusiliers Died 4.11.18.
STEPHENSON John C. MM Sjt 14141 X Corps Cyclist Bn Army Cyclist Corps
STEPHENSON John Robert MM L/Cpl 2937 1/5th Yorkshire Regt
STEPHENSON John W. MM+Bar Pte 268027 6th West Riding Regt
STEPHENSON Joseph S. MM L/Bdr 114988 B/186 Bde RFA
STEPHENSON Leonard John MM Cpl 100536 33 Div Sig Coy Royal Engineers
STEPHENSON Matthew J. MM Pte 34886 2nd West Riding Regt
STEPHENSON Norman MM Pte 12213 9th Northumberland Fusiliers
STEPHENSON R. MM Pnr 127739 7 Div Sig Coy Royal Engineers
STEPHENSON Reginald H. MM L/Sjt 15985 9th Yorkshire Regt
STEPHENSON Richard MM Pte 200868 Yorkshire Regt
STEPHENSON Robert H. MM L/Cpl 681913 22nd London Regt
STEPHENSON Robert Hudson MM Gnr 116581 C/87 Bde RFA
STEPHENSON Samuel H. MM Sjt 20778 15th Welsh Regt
STEPHENSON Sidney T. MM(1st Bn)+Bar Sjt 53580 201 Coy Machine Gun Corps
STEPHENSON Thomas MM Dvr 800226 A/230 Bde RFA
STEPHENSON Thomas MM Sjt 33580 Cheshire Regt
STEPHENSON Thomas MM Pte 13873 4th Liverpool Regt
STEPHENSON Thomas MM Dvr 21376 54 Fd Coy Royal Engineers
STEPHENSON Thomas MM Pte 27/1232 Northumberland Fusiliers
STEPHENSON Thomas Frederick MM Dvr 98792 RFA
STEPHENSON Thomas W. MM Pte 77067 RAMC
STEPHENSON Tom MM Sjt 235616 7th Lincolnshire Regt KIA 4.11.18.
STEPHENSON Tom MM L/Sjt 13874 7/8th King's Own Scottish Borderers
STEPHENSON Vincent E. MM Pte 52279 23rd Middlesex Regt
STEPTOE Amos MM Pte S/7166 7th Rifle Brigade
STERLING William MM+Bar L/Cpl 325379 9th Durham Light Infantry
STERLING William MM Pte 12553 Durham Light Infantry
STERN Philip MM Pte 6817 10th Northumberland Fusiliers KIA 29.10.18.
STERNE Guthrie K. MM Sjt S/5492 Rifle Brigade
STERNE Henry Kaye MM Pte 1884 12th Middlesex Regt
STERRETT Ernest William MM+Bar Pte 41443 Lincolnshire Regt
STERRY Ernest MM Cpl 12700 6th Royal Berkshire Regt
STERRY Miles John "DCM,MM+Bar" Sjt 21501 7th Royal West Kent Regt DOW 27.10.18.
STERRY Samuel J. "DCM,MM" Pte 2193 1/9th Durham Light Infantry
STERRY Walter MM L/Cpl 19954 12th Yorkshire Regt
STERRY Walter MM Pte 3/4699 2nd Suffolk Regt
STEVEN David MM Gnr 7556 RFA
STEVEN George Stables MM Spr 48434 9 Div Sig Coy Royal Engineers
STEVEN John R.A. MM Pte 267581 Seaforth Highlanders
STEVENS A.McE. MM Cpl 3955 Gordon Highlanders
STEVENS Albert MM Pte 43219 13th Middlesex Regt
STEVENS Albert Ernest MM L/Cpl 5268 8th East Kent Regt
STEVENS Albert H. "DCM,MM" Cpl 51261 1 Squadron Machine Gun Corps(Cavalry)
STEVENS Albert V. MM Pte 20516 RAMC
STEVENS Alfred MM Pte 74412 99 Fd Amb RAMC
STEVENS Alfred D. MM Pte 17536 Devonshire Regt
STEVENS Alfred Henry MM+Bar Sjt 955424 A/236 Bde RFA
STEVENS Arthur MM Sjt 55710 11th Hampshire Regt
STEVENS Arthur MM L/Cpl 205031 Devonshire Regt
STEVENS Arthur MM Pte 8044 2nd Royal Sussex Regt
STEVENS Arthur MM Sjt 13751 2nd Grenadier Guards
STEVENS Benjamin MM Pte 13000 1st South Wales Borderers
STEVENS Bertie MM Gnr 50291 RGA
STEVENS Charles MM L/Cpl 9304 1st Royal Berkshire Regt KIA 29.11.17.
STEVENS Charles Henry "MM,MIDx2" Pte 563 RAMC att 1st Wiltshire Regt.KIA 21.3.18.
STEVENS Charles T. MM Cpl 30546 RGA
STEVENS Clement Alfred MM L/Cpl 27836 2nd Notts & Derby Regt KIA 19.9.18.
STEVENS Clifford MM Gnr 11731 D/88 Bde RFA
STEVENS Daniel MM Pte 10125 7th South Staffordshire Regt
STEVENS Daniel George MM Cpl 66623 Y/12 Med TM Bty RFA
STEVENS Donald MM CSM 8822 1st Dorsetshire Regt
STEVENS Dudley MM L/Cpl 330039 1/8th Royal Scots
STEVENS Edward MM Pte R/32488 18th King's Royal Rifle Corps
STEVENS Edwin MM Pte 42998 2nd Durham Light Infantry
STEVENS Edwin James MM Pte 65880 132 Fd Amb RAMC DOW 27.9.17.
STEVENS Ernest MM Sjt 11999 1st Royal Fusiliers
STEVENS Ernest Harry MM Sjt 11099 5th Royal Berkshire Regt KIA 19.7.17.
STEVENS Ernest O. MM Cpl 38463 109 Heavy Bty RGA
STEVENS F. MM Sjt 241 RGA
STEVENS Francis W. MM Cpl 75830 'AU' Cable Section Royal Engineers
STEVENS Frank MM Pte 14565 6th Northamptonshire Regt
STEVENS Frank A. MM L/Cpl 357322 4th Hampshire Regt
STEVENS Frank H. MM+Bar Cpl R/16521 King's Royal Rifle Corps
STEVENS Fred MM Pte 13396 Northamptonshire Regt
STEVENS Frederick MM+Bar Sjt 8097 2nd Yorkshire Light Infantry
STEVENS Frederick C. MM Spr 357475 37 Div Sig Coy Royal Engineers
STEVENS Frederick J. MM+Bar S/Sjt 90053 106 Fd Amb RAMC
STEVENS G. MM 2nd Cpl 412181 409 Fd Coy Royal Engineers
STEVENS George MM Cpl M2/221861 Army Service Corps att RGA.
STEVENS George MM Pte M2/223495 363 MT Coy Army Service Corps
STEVENS George MM Pte 14058 8th South Staffordshire Regt
STEVENS George "DCM,MM+Bar" Cpl 5087 8th Northumberland Fusiliers DOW 9.5.18.
STEVENS George MM Sjt 9003 7th Lincolnshire Regt
STEVENS George MM Pte 6942 1st Cameron Highlanders
STEVENS George MM Pte 28784 Royal Welsh Fusiliers
STEVENS George MM Sjt 330086 1/8th Royal Scots
STEVENS George MM Pte 25220 13th Gloucestershire Regt Died 23.3.18.
STEVENS George Alfred MM Gnr 18368 D/59 Bde RFA
STEVENS George Alfred MM Cpl 8070 84 Bde RFA
STEVENS George H. MM Dvr 965529 RFA
STEVENS George W. MM Pte 11388 8th Gloucestershire Regt
STEVENS George W. MM Cpl 7288 2nd Dragoon Guards
STEVENS Harold Frederick MM Pte 53408 122 Coy Machine Gun Corps
STEVENS Harry MM L/Cpl 322078 6th London Regt
STEVENS Harry MM Pte 6503 2nd Northamptonshire Regt
STEVENS Harry MM Sjt 837051 RFA
STEVENS Henry MM Pte 51232 8th Lincolnshire Regt
STEVENS Herbert MM Cpl 5297 1st East Yorkshire Regt

STEVENS Herbert MM L/Cpl 9993 2nd South Wales Borderers
STEVENS Horace MM L/Cpl 326030 1/1st Cambridgeshire Regt
STEVENS J. MM Pte 15240 1st Essex Regt
STEVENS James MM L/Bdr Sig 56430 38 Siege Bty RGA
STEVENS James MM Pte 202160 6th King's Own Scottish Borderers KIA 30.9.18.
STEVENS James MM Sjt 240069 1/5th Royal Scots Fusiliers
STEVENS James MM Pte 1696 1/17th London Regt
STEVENS John MM L/Cpl 8453 2nd West Yorkshire Regt
STEVENS John MM L/Cpl 1865 1st Gloucestershire Regt
STEVENS John MM Pte 13221 4th South Wales Borderers KIA 15.2.17
STEVENS John MM Pte 45625 6th Northamptonshire Regt DOW 31.8.18.
STEVENS John MM Sjt 13040 7th East Lancashire Regt
STEVENS John E. MM Dvr 810025 B/232 Bde RFA
STEVENS John Walker MM Cpl 47711 Royal Fusiliers
STEVENS John William MM Sjt 6028 4th Dragoon Guards
STEVENS Joseph MM Pte 242467 4/5th North Lancashire Regt
STEVENS Joseph H. MM Sjt 43583 125 Bty29 Bde RFA
STEVENS Joseph Henry MM Pte 10161 6th Northamptonshire Regt KIA 24.8.18.
STEVENS Mark MM Dvr T4/243003 Army Service Corps att 82 Fd Amb RAMC.
STEVENS Norman MM L/Sjt 308 13th Cheshire Regt
STEVENS Percival Charles MM Sjt 813 6th Royal West Surrey Regt
STEVENS Percy Frederick MM Pte 1614 RAMC
STEVENS Percy J. MM Dvr 935186 B/282 Bde RFA
STEVENS Reginald D. MM Gnr 34957 RGA
STEVENS Richard MM L/Cpl 10788 5th Oxf & Bucks Light Infantry
STEVENS Robert MM Pte 28160 9th Royal Welsh Fusiliers
STEVENS Robert MM Pte 266356 West Riding Regt
STEVENS Robert F. MM L/Cpl 2680 1/22nd London Regt
STEVENS Ronald William MM Cpl 1700 1/4th Oxf & Bucks Light Infantry DOW 31.10.17.
STEVENS Sidney MM L/Cpl 14147 8th Suffolk Regt
STEVENS Sidney Frederick MM Cpl 13393 2nd Royal Fusiliers KIA 19.9.16.
STEVENS Thomas H. MM Pte 4033 9th East Surrey Regt
STEVENS Thomas J. MM Pte O/338 13th Rifle Brigade
STEVENS Thomas W. MM Cpl R/14974 1st King's Royal Rifle Corps
STEVENS Walter A. MM Pte 20873 1st East Surrey Regt
STEVENS William MM L/Sjt 34580 4th Yorkshire Light Infantry
STEVENS William MM Dvr 9130 A/87 Bde RFA
STEVENS William MM Bdr 63828 28 Bty 9 Bde RFA
STEVENS William MM Dvr 930764 B/291 Bde RFA
STEVENS William E. MM Cpl 9610 Royal Berkshire Regt
STEVENS William E.H. MM Pte 306022 Royal Warwickshire Regt
STEVENS William F.T. MM Pte 33844 8th East Surrey Regt
STEVENS William R. MM Pte 596042 18th London Regt
STEVENSON Alexander MM Pte 200812 1/4th Royal Scots Fusiliers
STEVENSON Alfred O. MM Cpl 34989 RFA
STEVENSON Charles MM L/Cpl 18121 Machine Gun Corps
STEVENSON David G. MM Cpl 200366 1/4th Royal Scots
STEVENSON Edgar "MM,MSM" L/Cpl 320375 15th Suffolk Regt
STEVENSON Edward MM L/Cpl 26499 Scottish Rifles
STEVENSON Edward MM Dvr 6941 11th Notts & Derby Regt
STEVENSON Ernest MM Sjt 72368 Royal Engineers
STEVENSON Fletcher Herbert MM Sjt M2/114081 Army Service Corps att 24 Fd Amb RAMC.
STEVENSON Francis MM Pte 5031 10th Arg & Suth Highlanders
STEVENSON Frank MM Pte 18183 7th Shropshire Light Infantry
STEVENSON George MM Cpl 8309 C/82 Bde RFA
STEVENSON George MM Cpl 24535 8th West Yorkshire Regt
STEVENSON George MM Gnr 39900 28 Bde RFA
STEVENSON George MM Pte 201100 1/4th Seaforth Highlanders
STEVENSON George E. MM Pte 1489 8th East Kent Regt
STEVENSON George F. MM Pte 32957 5th South Staffordshire Regt
STEVENSON George R. MM Sjt 437135 RAMC
STEVENSON George Timothy MM Cpl 2664 D/230 Bde RFA
STEVENSON Henry MM L/Cpl 18817 3rd Grenadier Guards KIA 27.3.18.
STEVENSON Henry MM Cpl 58988 Machine Gun Corps DOW 20.7.18.
STEVENSON Hugh MM+Bar Cpl 412069 409 Fd Coy Royal Engineers
STEVENSON Hugh MM Dvr 656121 RFA
STEVENSON J. MM L/Cpl 202490 18th Scottish Rifles
STEVENSON James MM Spr 102085 185 Tunnelling Coy Royal Engineers
STEVENSON James MM Pte 3/7483 10th Arg & Suth Highlanders
STEVENSON James MM Sjt 10416 1/8th Arg & Suth Highlanders
STEVENSON James MM L/Cpl 14115 1st Dragoon Guards
STEVENSON James MM Sjt 11095 2nd Highland Light Infantry
STEVENSON James "DCM,MM" Sjt 19043 5 Fd Svy Bn Royal Engineers
STEVENSON James MM Cpl 11179 7th Cameron Highlanders
STEVENSON James MM Pte 7638 Machine Gun Corps
STEVENSON James Richard MM Pte 2234 1/5th Yorkshire Regt
STEVENSON John MM Sjt 44645 84 Fd Coy Royal Engineers
STEVENSON John MM L/Bdr 227916 C/290 Bde RFA
STEVENSON John MM Cpl 7423 13th Royal Fusiliers
STEVENSON John MM Pte 30306 16th Highland Light Infantry
STEVENSON John MM L/Cpl 331744 Highland Light Infantry
STEVENSON John "DCM,MM" CSM 240081 5/6th Scottish Rifles
STEVENSON John MM Pte 13485 10th Scottish Rifles KIA 22.7.17.
STEVENSON John Harold MM Pte 14538 2nd Grenadier Guards
STEVENSON John Henry "MM,CG(B)" Pte 16716 8th East Yorkshire Regt
STEVENSON Joseph MM Pte 2420 12th Royal Irish Rifles
STEVENSON Joseph MM Pnr 192862 Royal Engineers
STEVENSON Kenneth V. MM Cpl 242182 6th Liverpool Regt
STEVENSON Louis MM Pte 73000 RAMC
STEVENSON Luke MM Dvr 66767 46 Bty 39 Bde RFA
STEVENSON Major MM Pte 896 6th East Kent Regt
STEVENSON Michael MM Cpl 200504 1/5th Highland Light Infantry
STEVENSON Percy Telford MM Sjt 9318 25th Bn Machine Gun Corps
STEVENSON Peter C. MM Pte 28420 2nd Notts & Derby Regt
STEVENSON Richard MM L/Sjt 16779 6th Shropshire Light Infantry
STEVENSON Richard MM L/Cpl 4786 2nd Dragoon Guards
STEVENSON Robert MM Spr 148414 Royal Engineers
STEVENSON Robert MM Sjt 318034 2(Lowland)Fd Amb RAMC
STEVENSON Robert MM Pte 296646 12th Royal Scots Fusiliers
STEVENSON Robert MM Pte 46705 RAMC
STEVENSON Robert MM Cpl 598 12th Arg & Suth Highlanders
STEVENSON Samuel MM L/Cpl 2910 14th Royal Irish Rifles
STEVENSON Sidney Hall MM Pte 4525 10th Notts & Derby Regt KIA 16.9.17.
STEVENSON Taylor MM Pte 25702 17th Royal Welsh Fusiliers KIA 4.9.18.
STEVENSON Thomas MM Spr 121912 Royal Engineers
STEVENSON Thomas MM Cpl 2031 23rd Middlesex Regt
STEVENSON William MM Cpl 71654 1st North Irish Horse
STEVENSON William MM Sjt 70957 C/231 Bde RFA KIA 19.10.18.
STEVENSON William MM Cpl 79431 Royal Engineers
STEVENSON William "DCM,MM(30507 Sjt Scots Gds)" RSM 1 1st Welsh Guards
STEVENSON William "DCM,MM" Sjt 22217 51st Bn Machine Gun Corps
STEVENSON William "MM,MID" Pte 9668 1st Royal Inniskilling Fusiliers
STEVENSON William MM Pte 10/13650 10th Royal Irish Rifles
STEVENSON William MM L/Cpl 19535 6th Northamptonshire Regt
STEVENSON William A. MM Sjt 44279 RFA
STEVENSON William J. MM CSM 14667 9th Royal Irish Fusiliers
STEVENSON William Jennings MM Cpl 23603 148 Coy Machine Gun Corps
STEVENSON William R. MM Sjt 38001 D/18 Bde RFA
STEVENSON William W. MM Pte 21215 1/8th Hampshire Regt
STEVENSON William W. MM CQMS 67689 4th Bn Machine Gun Corps
STEVENSON William W. MM Pte 21215 8th Hampshire Regt
STEVENTON Charles MM Dvr 40823 RFA
STEVENTON Edwin J. MM Cpl 4760 Machine Gun Corps
STEVENTON Henry Herbert George MM Pte 9126 4th Royal Fusiliers DOW 15.6.18.
STEVENTON Percy C. MM Cpl 44169 RFA
STEWARD A.H.W. MM Bdr 115556 RFA
STEWARD Bernard G. MM Pte 80139 1/1st Essex Yeomanry
STEWARD Charles MM Sjt 98008 RFA
STEWARD Charles MM Bdr 64800 30 Bde RFA
STEWARD Christian MM Pte 51083 1/6th Cheshire Regt
STEWARD Frederick Herbert MM Pte 3125 12th Royal Fusiliers KIA 31.7.17.
STEWARD Frederick William MM Pte R/11104 8th King's Royal Rifle Corps DOW 3.5.17.

STEWARD G.R. MM Spr 49776 Royal Engineers
STEWARD George MM Gnr 107422 RGA
STEWARD George "MM,MID,MM(F)" Sjt 320121 12th Norfolk Regt
STEWARD Harry MM Pte 72790 2nd Notts & Derby Regt
STEWARD John MM Bdr 780902 RFA
STEWARD John MM Pte R/5219 13th King's Royal Rifle Corps DOW 27.4.18.
STEWARD Joshua MM Bdr 28566 B/162 Bde RFA
STEWARD Thomas Watson MM Pte 19534 13th Liverpool Regt KIA 31.8.18.
STEWARD Walter MM Pte 36535 Middlesex Regt
STEWARD William MM L/Cpl 38863 12th Gloucestershire Regt
STEWART A.G. MM Pte 301197 89 Fd Amb RAMC
STEWART Adam MM Sjt 22019 Machine Gun Corps
STEWART Alexander MM Cpl 5584 7th Seaforth Highlanders
STEWART Alexander MM L/Cpl 202232 1st London Regt
STEWART Alexander MM Dvr 227625 RFA
STEWART Alexander MM Pte 41136 1/8th Scottish Rifles
STEWART Alexander MM L/Cpl 300402 1/7th Royal Scots
STEWART Alexander MM Pte 23387 1/7th Gordon Highlanders
STEWART Alexander MM Sjt 254281 2 Div Sig Coy Royal Engineers
STEWART Alexander MM CQMS 7188 1st Northamptonshire Regt
STEWART Alexander MM Pte 41214 1/8th Scottish Rifles
STEWART Alexander MM Spr 19505 29 Fd Coy Royal Engineers
STEWART Andrew MM Spr 65938 227 Fd Coy Royal Engineers
STEWART Andrew MM Cpl 265423 1/6th Royal Highlanders
STEWART Andrew MM Pte 3992 Royal Scots
STEWART Archibald E. MM Pte 13621 15th Highland Light Infantry DOW 20.12.17.
STEWART Barclay James MM Pte 44655 103 Coy Machine Gun Corps
STEWART Bernard J. MM QMC Farrier 2225 2nd Life Guards
STEWART Bertie C. MM Gnr 123540 RFA
STEWART Cecil Joseph MM Sjt Y/1050 21st King's Royal Rifle Corps
STEWART Charles MM L/Cpl 203501 6th King's Own Scottish Borderers
STEWART Charles MM Pte 43218 2nd Royal Scots Fusiliers
STEWART Charles MM Pte 22224 5th Cameron Highlanders DOW 29.9.18.
STEWART Charles MM Cpl 8929 2nd West Yorkshire Regt KIA 31.7.17.
STEWART Charles MM Spr 2349 Royal Engineers
STEWART Charles MM Sjt 4659 70 Coy Machine Gun Corps
STEWART Charles MM L/Cpl 22569 17th Royal Scots
STEWART Charles Edward "MM,MID" Sjt 8537 2nd Worcestershire
STEWART Charles H. MM Cpl 46782 RFA
STEWART Charles H. MM Sjt 193385 Royal Engineers
STEWART Colin MM Pte 40605 1/6th Gordon Highlanders KIA 6.10.18.
STEWART Daniel MM Sjt 35649 2nd Royal Scots KIA 3.5.17.
STEWART David MM Spr 404349 404 Fd Coy Royal Engineers
STEWART David MM Pte 267694 1/6th Royal Highlanders
STEWART David MM Sjt 5971 1st Cameron Highlanders
STEWART David MM+Bar Pte 6663 1st Scots Guards
STEWART David Davidson MM Sjt 173320 151 Siege Bty RGA
STEWART David G. MM Pte 40914 Royal Highlanders
STEWART David R. MM L/Cpl 275700 1/7th Arg & Suth Highlanders
STEWART Donald MM Pte 266619 Royal Highlanders
STEWART Donald MM Pte 202490 Gordon Highlanders
STEWART Donald R. MM Sjt M2/200886 Army Service Corps
STEWART Duncan MM Pte 40635 1st Royal Highlanders
STEWART Duncan MM+2 Bars Pte 56413 4th Liverpool Regt
STEWART F.A. MM Pte 282607 London Regt
STEWART Francis MM Pte 201366 1/4th Gordon Highlanders Died 23.2.19.
STEWART Frederick MM L/Cpl 50060 Royal Engineers
STEWART Frederick A. MM Pte 351439 Royal Scots
STEWART George MM+Bar L/Sjt 331669 9th Highland Light Infantry
STEWART George MM Pnr 165864 Royal Engineers
STEWART George MM Spr 239992 Royal Engineers
STEWART George MM+Bar Spr 191584 Royal Engineers
STEWART George MM Sjt 22614 D/156 Bde RFA
STEWART George MM Spr 290262 12 Lt Rly Op Coy Royal Engineers
STEWART George MM Pte 11518 9th Scottish Rifles
STEWART George C. MM L/Cpl 250332 5/6th Royal Scots
STEWART George H. MM Cpl 201332 4th Hampshire Regt
STEWART George W. MM Pte 37863 RAMC
STEWART George Wyburn MM Pte 130961 Machine Gun Corps
STEWART Harry MM L/Cpl 41821 Middlesex Regt
STEWART Harry MM Sjt 37592 Gloucestershire Regt
STEWART Henry MM Sjt 296341 12th Royal Scots Fusiliers
STEWART Henry MM Dvr T/32013 2 Div Train Army Service Corps
STEWART Henry MM Pte 39652 Royal Scots
STEWART Henry S. MM Cpl Shoeing Smith 1075 10th Hussars
STEWART Herbert MM Cpl 16125 8th South Lancashire Regt KIA 18.2.17.
STEWART Hugh MM Cpl 5011 8th Royal Highlanders
STEWART Hugh MM Pte 18/1300 Royal Irish Rifles
STEWART Isaac Innes MM Cpl 200960 1/4th Seaforth Highlanders
STEWART James MM Sjt 63394 61 Siege Bty RGA
STEWART James MM Sjt 291370 8th Scottish Rifles
STEWART James MM L/Sjt 202806 1/4th Gordon Highlanders KIA 13.4.18.
STEWART James MM Pte DM2/189703 Army Service Corps
STEWART James MM Pte 32393 South Lancashire Regt
STEWART James "MM,MID" Pte 8640 Scots Guards
STEWART James MM Pte 10129 2nd Seaforth Highlanders
STEWART James MM Sjt 19422 13th Liverpool Regt
STEWART James MM Pte 1532 1/6th Royal Highlanders Died 15.7.18.
STEWART James MM Sjt 15 Royal Highlanders
STEWART James MM Gnr 104089 RFA
STEWART James MM Pte M2/078670 Army Service Corps
STEWART James MM Pte 5644 Gordon Highlanders
STEWART James G. MM L/Cpl 22951 Royal West Surrey Regt
STEWART James H. MM Sjt 72465 33rd Bn Machine Gun Corps
STEWART James V. MM Gnr 344284 RGA
STEWART James W. MM Pte 43325 14th Arg & Suth Highlanders
STEWART John MM Pte 27024 4th North Lancashire Regt
STEWART John MM Pte 52300 1st Royal Scots Fusiliers
STEWART John MM+Bar Sjt 267025 1/6th Gordon Highlanders
STEWART John MM Pte 3236 Royal Highlanders
STEWART John MM Sjt 36421 A/93 Bde RFA DOW 22.4.18.
STEWART John MM Pte 250295 5/6th Royal Scots
STEWART John "DCM,MM" Pte 39217 2nd Highland Light Infantry
STEWART John "DCM,MM" Cpl 8629 1st Highland Light Infantry
STEWART John MM Pte 20/346 20th Northumberland Fusiliers
STEWART John MM Gnr 3659 Y/21 Med TM Bty RGA KIA 28.6.16.
STEWART John MM Pte S/7288 11th Arg & Suth Highlanders KIA 21.8.16.
STEWART John MM Cpl 3739 9th Royal Munster Fusiliers
STEWART John MM Bdr 72198 24 Bde RFA
STEWART John MM L/Cpl 8643 6th Cameron Highlanders KIA 24.4.17.
STEWART John MM L/Cpl 265418 1/7th Scottish Rifles
STEWART John MM Dvr 668 B/86 Bde RFA DOW 26.3.18.
STEWART John MM Pte 13301 14th Arg & Suth Highlanders
STEWART John MM Sjt 95832 RGA
STEWART John MM Cpl 36165 Yorkshire Light Infantry
STEWART John MM Sjt 240227 5/6th Scottish Rifles KIA 13.4.18.
STEWART John A. MM Cpl 5811 Northumberland Fusiliers
STEWART John A.F. MM L/Cpl 305131 Notts & Derby Regt
STEWART John D. MM Pte 27398 14th Arg & Suth Highlanders
STEWART John F. MM Dvr 217992 RFA
STEWART John H. MM Cpl 64670 RAMC
STEWART John M. MM L/Cpl 10742 1st King's Own Scottish Borderers
STEWART John M. MM L/Cpl 266781 1st Gordon Highlanders
STEWART John M. MM Sjt 402336 Royal Engineers
STEWART John McL. MM Pte 251041 11th Royal Scots
STEWART John S. MM BSM 4152 RFA
STEWART John T. MM L/Cpl 20469 10 Fd Amb RAMC
STEWART John William MM L/Cpl 131469 234 Fd Coy Royal Engineers KIA 31.7.17.
STEWART John Y. MM 2nd Cpl 168103 Royal Engineers
STEWART Joseph MM Cpl 112277 Royal Engineers
STEWART Joseph MM Sjt M2/054727 Army Service Corps att RFA.
STEWART Kenneth "MM,MMV(It)" Cpl 92963 A/79 Bde RFA
STEWART Leslie Thomas MM Pte 1594 22nd Royal Fusiliers DOW 3.5.17.
STEWART Lewis E. MM Spr 422729 Royal Engineers
STEWART Neil MM L/Sjt 7968 8th Royal Highlanders
STEWART P. MM Pte 15810 2nd Essex Regt
STEWART Percy Douglas MM Sjt 13/880 13th York & Lancaster Regt
STEWART Peter MM Pte 42914 Machine Gun Corps

STEWART Peter MM L/Cpl 60095 Royal Fusiliers
STEWART Peter MM Piper 201307 1/4th Seaforth Highlanders
STEWART Peter Irons MM Cpl 916043 A/168 Bde RFA DOW 18.10.18.
STEWART Robert MM L/Cpl 325038 1/8th Royal Scots
STEWART Robert MM L/Cpl 4232 Labour Corps
STEWART Robert MM Piper 242347 Gordon Highlanders Died 29.12.18.
STEWART Robert MM L/Cpl 6498 1/8th Arg & Suth Highlanders DOW 14.4.18.
STEWART Robert C. MM Cpl 71511 North Irish Horse
STEWART Robert John MM Pte 241305 1/6th Highland Light Infantry
STEWART Robert K. MM Sjt 424003 19 Div Sig Coy Royal Engineers
STEWART Robert McM. MM Pte M2/187649 Army Service Corps
STEWART Ronald D. MM Pte M2/152911 Army Service Corps
STEWART T.G. MM Pte 40542 16th Highland Light Infantry
STEWART Thomas MM Pte 130 12th Royal Irish Rifles
STEWART Thomas MM Sjt 4615 7th Seaforth Highlanders
STEWART Thomas O. MM Pte 40352 Highland Light Infantry
STEWART Walter MM Pte 40697 1/9th Arg & Suth Highlanders
STEWART Walter D. MM L/Cpl 230341 1/2nd London Regt
STEWART Wilfred Garnett MM Sjt 132306 204 Siege Bty RGA
STEWART William MM Spr 57981 36 Div Sig Coy Royal Engineers
STEWART William MM CSM 20074 1st Royal Inniskilling Fusiliers DOW 20.10.18.
STEWART William MM Sjt 12080 2nd Royal Scots Fusiliers
STEWART William MM Pte 292562 1/7th Gordon Highlanders
STEWART William MM Pte 23533 2nd Royal Scots
STEWART William "MM,MBC(Rm)" Cpl 10014 1st Arg & Suth Highlanders
STEWART William MM Pte 17928 1/4th Gordon Highlanders DOW 5.8.18.
STEWART William MM Pte 16521 Royal Highlanders
STEWART William MM Pte M2/082249 Army Service Corps
STEWART William MM Pte 13947 Scots Guards
STEWART William MM Sjt 292863 13th Royal Highlanders
STEWART William MM Pte 26809 13th Royal Scots KIA 28.3.18.
STEWART William "DCM+Bar,MM" CSM 240991 Royal Highlanders
STEWART William MM Pte 19677 2nd South Lancashire Regt
STEWART William MM Pte 40287 Royal Irish Rifles
STEWART William MM Cpl 2250 6th Dragoons
STEWART William E. MM Gnr 56265 Royal Artillery
STEWART William George MM Sjt 965 1/3(South Midland)Fd Amb RAMC
STEWART William S. MM Pte 43207 1/9th Royal Scots
STEWART William South MM CQMS 15956 17th Highland Light Infantry
STEWARTSON Edward D. MM L/Sjt 45952 5/6th Royal Scots
STIBBARD George T. MM L/Cpl R/214 King's Royal Rifle Corps
STIBBONS Ernest George MM Sjt 2302 1/2nd London
STICKLAND Albert "MC,MM" RSM 938 9th Royal Fusiliers
STICKLAND Arthur F. MM Sjt 7154 10th Royal Fusiliers
STICKLEN Reginald MM Bdr 73175 18 Bde RFA
STICKLER Albert E. MM L/Cpl 23103 9th Royal Welsh Fusiliers
STICKLER George Hutching MM Pte 14459 2nd South Lancashire Regt DOW 22.8.18.
STICKLEY Ernest W.G. MM Sjt 43845 Worcestershire Regt
STICKLEY William C. MM Gnr 192001 A/102 Bde RFA
STICKNEY Robert MM Pte 207706 11th Royal West Surrey Regt
STIFF Albert Thomas MM Pte 252843 3rd London Regt
STIFF Alex J. MM L/Cpl 562577 Royal Engineers
STIFF Cecil Gasking MM Sjt 40671 Lincolnshire Regt
STIFF Ernest J.B. MM L/Cpl 37852 Welsh Regt
STIFF James F. "DCM,MM" Sjt 3/9563 2nd Suffolk Regt
STIFF William MM Pte 126104 62nd Bn Machine Gun Corps
STIFF William C. MM Gnr 73651 53 Bty 2 Bde RFA
STIGGER John William "DCM,MM" Bdr 46460 B/106 Bde RFA KIA 24.12.16.
STILE Walter R. MM Pte 457211 RAMC
STILES George MM Pte 37990 101 Fd Amb RAMC
STILES Harold Wolseley MM CSM 646 1/13th London Regt
STILES Sydney MM Pte 11788 2nd Coldstream Guards
STILES Thomas MM Cpl 18281 12th Notts & Derby Regt
STILES William John MM Sjt 52213 RFA
STILING William MM Cpl 8907 1st Devonshire Regt
STILL Albert MM Pte 22220 North Lancashire Regt
STILL Charles Robert William MM Sjt 46006 B/100 Bde RFA
STILL Ernest MM Cpl 1657 Royal Sussex Regt
STILL Frank MM Pte M2/194988 Army Service Corps att MGC(HB)
STILL John MM Sjt 406031 51 Div Sig Coy Royal Engineers
STILL Luke MM Pte 225339 1st London att 11th Royal Fusiliers.DOW 18.10.18.
STILL William MM Gnr 650891 RFA
STILLING Isaac MM Sjt 3664 Army Cyclist Corps
STILLING J.M. MM Cpl 307507 7th West Riding Regt
STILLMAN Cecil George MM Cpl 1527 Royal Engineers
STILLMAN Leslie Thomas MM Bdr 15051 B/296 Bde RFA
STILLWELL Frederick MM L/Cpl 2789 Royal West Surrey Regt
STILLWELL Herbert MM Cpl 76487 'B' Bn Tank Corps KIA 22.3.18.
STILLWELL Leonard S. MM Sjt 85236 C/62 Bde RFA
STILLWELL Percy J. MM CQMS 41840 York & Lancaster Regt
STIMPSON Bertram Charles MM L/Cpl 9569 1st Northamptonshire Regt KIA 20.8.16.
STIMPSON Ernest C. MM Sjt 54029 38 Fd Amb RAMC
STIMSON Albert Edward MM Pte 372808 2/8th London Regt Died 3.8.18.
STIMSON Frederick MM Dvr 99312 18 Div Ammn Col RFA
STIMSON John MM Sjt 306091 8th Notts & Derby Regt
STIMSON Reginald Owen MM Cpl 23011 1st Border Regt
STIMSON William H. MM Pe 14579 6th Northamptonshire Regt
STINCHCOMBE Edward S. MM Sjt CMT/1030 Army Service Corps att RAMC.
STINSON Frank MM Pte 235290 14th Royal Welsh Fusiliers
STINSON Frederick J. MM Sjt 14269 7th Yorkshire Regt
STINSON George MM Sjt 5851 1st East Lancashire Regt
STINSON William W. MM Pte M2/178558 884 Coy Army Service Corps
STINTON George W. MM Cpl 50730 8th Worcestershire Regt
STINTON James Stuart MM L/Cpl 12341 9th Devonshire Regt KIA 10.10.17.
STIRLING Charles MM Pte 119485 18th Bn Machine Gun Corps
STIRLING Charles Albert MM Sjt 21618 13th Durham Light Infantry
STIRLING Charles T. MM Pte 21012 Yorkshire Regt
STIRLING David MM Sjt 15284 17th Liverpool Regt
STIRLING George MM Pte 40530 10th Arg & Suth Highlanders
STIRLING George MM+Bar Cpl 9846 Scots Guards
STIRLING Hugh MM Spr 420209 406 Fd Coy Royal Engineers
STIRLING Hugh MM Spr 7651 1(West Lancashire)Fd Coy Royal Engineers
STIRLING James Robert MM Cpl 750089 RFA
STIRLING John MM Pte 22324 1st Scottish Rifles KIA 9.10.18.
STIRLING John E. MM+Bar L/Sjt 16/1277 11th Northumberland Fusiliers
STIRLING Robert G. MM Pte 285196 Seaforth Highlanders
STIRLING Samuel MM Cpl 15481 Gordon Highlanders
STIRLING Thomas Hewitt MM Pte 4519 9th Seaforth Highlanders
STIRLING William MM Pte 28391 2nd Royal Scots Fusiliers
STIRLING William MM Gnr 645190 RFA
STIRMAN Frederick MM S/Sjt Farrier 930366 A/281 Bde RFA
STIRRAT James MM Pte 200595 1/5th Arg & Suth Highlanders
STIRRAT Robert MM L/Cpl 9239 2nd Seaforth Highlanders KIA 3.5.17.
STIRRUPS Alfred T. MM Pte 49304 23rd Royal Fusiliers
STIRTON Allister MM Pte 4017 11th Arg & Suth Highlanders
STIRTON James MM Sjt 4/1862 36th Northumberland Fusiliers
STIRTON Robert F. MM L/Bdr 365058 100 Siege Bty RGA
STIRUPS George Richard MM Cpl 8177 B/50 Bde RFA
STIRZAKER John Robert MM Pte 7/3525 Northumberland Fusiliers
STIRZAKER John W. MM Cpl 22510 4th North Lancashire Regt
STITSON Ernest R. MM Gnr 138077 RGA
STITT Alexander MM L/Cpl 7096 8th Seaforth Highlanders
STITT James MM Cpl 8370 2nd Royal Inniskilling Fusiliers
STITT Robert MM L/Cpl 17717 2nd King's Own Scottish Borderers
STITT William MM L/Cpl 325490 1/8th Royal Scots
STOAKES Edward MM Cpl 684349 22nd London Regt
STOBART George MM Bdr 786289 RFA
STOBART Harold MM L/Cpl 270145 1/1st Northumberland Yeo
STOBART T.W. MM Pte 265341 6th East Kent Regt
STOBBART Thomas R. MM Cpl 1916 8th Royal Sussex Regt
STOBBS Alexander William MM Pte 22/1003 22nd Durham Light Infantry
STOBBS Robert S.H. MM L/Sjt 265602 1st Northumberland Fusiliers
STOBIE Hugh MM L/Cpl 2508 Royal Highlanders
STOBIE John W. MM+Bar Sjt 203417 4th Yorkshire Light Infantry
STOBIE Robert MM Gnr 119064 RGA
STOBIE Robert MM Pte 6802 10th Northumberland Fusiliers KIA 28.10.18.

STOBIE Thomas MM Pte 13552 1st Royal Scots Fusiliers KIA 23.7.18.
STOBO George D. MM Pte 510983 1/14th London Regt
STOBO John MM Pte 41910 1/6th Royal Highlanders
STOBO Joseph Waugh MM Sjt 9560 5th Cameron Highlanders DOW 26.4.18.
STOBO Robert A. MM Pte 16121 2nd Scots Guards
STOCK Clifford MM Pte 302915 5th London Regt
STOCK Ernest A. MM Cpl 23262 11 Fd Coy Royal Engineers
STOCK Ernest H. MM L/Cpl 8418 East Surrey Regt
STOCK Frank L. MM Cpl 24516 1st Dorsetshire Regt
STOCK Frederick MM(32nd Bn)+Bar Cpl 98030 38th Bn Machine Gun Corps
STOCK George "MM+Bar,MID" Sjt 17966 RGA
STOCK H. MM Cpl 3205 Royal Warwickshire Regt
STOCK Ivyston S. MM CSM 19634 13th Liverpool Regt
STOCK John Sydney MM Gnr 8449 C/174 Bde RFA KIA 1.9.18.
STOCK Percy G. MM Sjt 47068 6th Northamptonshire Regt
STOCK Peter MM Sjt 63409 RGA
STOCK Robert MM Pte 240220 Lancashire Fusiliers
STOCK William Edward MM Dvr 22582 291 Bde RFA
STOCKAN James William MM Sjt 13649 14th Arg & Suth Highlanders
STOCKBRIDGE Charles S. MM Cpl 201373 1st London Regt
STOCKBRIDGE S.C. MM Sjt 1332 Royal Sussex Regt
STOCKBRIDGE William R. MM Cpl 3794 1st Dragoon Guards
STOCKBURN Alfred MM Pte 32983 RAMC
STOCKDALE Albert MM L/Cpl 49772 Lincolnshire Regt
STOCKDALE Andrew MM Dvr 186859 RFA
STOCKDALE Arthur MM L/Cpl 42889 8th West Yorkshire Regt
STOCKDALE Arthur E. MM Pte 47817 80 Coy Labour Corps
STOCKDALE Cornelius MM Sjt 17726 Liverpool Regt
STOCKDALE E. MM Sjt 38010 Tank Corps
STOCKDALE Edgar MM Pte 50621 1st East Yorkshire Regt
STOCKDALE Frederick John MM L/Sjt 12353 2nd Grenadier Guards KIA 28.3.18.
STOCKDALE George MM Pte 2374 Lincolnshire Regt
STOCKDALE George W. "DCM,MM+Bar" Sjt 107435 20 Div Sig Coy Royal Engineers
STOCKDALE Harold MM Pte 1649 1/5th Liverpool Regt
STOCKDALE Harry MM Dvr 2502 245 Bde RFA
STOCKDALE Leonard MM Gnr 771913 C/315 Bde RFA
STOCKDALE Percy MM Cpl 242542 5th Lincolnshire Regt
STOCKDALE Robert MM L/Cpl 7708 9th Lancers
STOCKDALE William Howard MM Sjt 51124 6 Bty 40 Bde RFA
STOCKER Cyril B. MM 2nd Cpl 140705 123 Fd Coy Royal Engineers
STOCKER David S. MM L/Cpl 34527 Gloucestershire Regt
STOCKER Gerald Arthur Julian MM Cpl 683054 1/22nd London Regt KIA 6.7.17.
STOCKER Harold MM Pte 457378 RAMC
STOCKER J.H. MM Pte 6655 Royal Welsh Fusiliers
STOCKER Reginald J. MM Pte 42982 142 Fd Amb RAMC
STOCKER W.J. MM Dvr 4771 33 Bde RFA
STOCKER Willie MM Pte 13/804 York & Lancaster Regt
STOCKFORD Harry MM Sjt M2/103897 Army Service Corps
STOCKFORD Percy A. MM Cpl 285167 1/1st Oxfordshire Yeomanry
STOCKING Aaron A. MM Sjt 1571 1/22nd London Regt KIA 1.12.17.
STOCKING Alfred Edmund MM L/Cpl 41219 1st Norfolk Regt
STOCKING Bernard MM Pte 29222 11th Suffolk Regt
STOCKLEY Frank MM Sjt 6426 1st Dorsetshire Regt
STOCKLEY Hubert MM Pte 29387 7th Royal West Kent Regt
STOCKLEY John R. MM Spr 482255 Royal Engineers
STOCKLEY Percy H. MM Pte 5076 York & Lancaster Regt
STOCKLEY Victor J. MM Dvr 10285 RFA
STOCKLEY William "DCM,MM,DM(B)" L/Cpl 201968 10th Royal Warwickshire Regt
STOCKMAN William MM Sjt Mechanic 40700 238 Army Troops Coy Royal Engineers
STOCKS Andrew MM Pte 16889 1st King's Own Scottish Borderers
STOCKS Claude MM Gnr Wheeler 795357 21 Bty 2 Bde RFA
STOCKS George MM Pte 1379 1/8th West Yorkshire Regt
STOCKS Harry MM Pte 240688 1/5th Yorkshire Light Infantry
STOCKS John MM Pte 11168 Arg & Suth Highlanders
STOCKS John MM Gnr 801933 D/230 Bde RFA
STOCKS Joseph MM Cpl 1966 1/5th Liverpool Regt
STOCKS Joseph Dyson MM L/Sjt 242072 2/5th Yorkshire Light Infantry KIA 21.11.17.
STOCKS Leslie V. MM Pte 37202 Gloucestershire Regt
STOCKS Richard Joseph MM Sjt 241986 1/5th Border Regt DOW 30.3.18.
STOCKS Thomas MM Pnr 341207 50 Div Sig Coy Royal Engineers
STOCKS William MM Pte 686 8th Royal West Surrey Regt
STOCKS William MM Pte 27855 Yorkshire Light Infantry
STOCKTING Sidney H. MM Gnr 195743 228 Siege Bty RGA
STOCKTON Ernest MM Cpl 295102 Manchester Regt
STOCKTON Harry MM Sjt 291148 1/7th Cheshire Regt
STOCKTON Herbert MM Pte 29764 14th Worcestershire Regt
STOCKTON John MM Sjt 8083 2nd Yorkshire Regt
STOCKTON Thomas MM 2nd Cpl 45146 Royal Engineers
STOCKTON Wilfred MM Cpl 202052 5th East Lancashire Regt
STOCKWELL Albert E. MM Bdr 43918 7 Bde RHA
STOCKWELL Albert W. MM Spr 534665 Royal Engineers
STOCKWELL George W. MM Gnr 200851 'F'(AA)Bty RGA
STOCKWELL Percy MM Pte 9652 1st Northamptonshire Regt
STOCKWELL William Henry MM Sjt 10945 2nd Royal Welsh Fusiliers KIA 19.8.16.
STODART Frederick Adolphus Gerald MM Pte 3950 1/15th London Regt
STODDARD Edwin MM Sjt 47880 Royal Fusiliers
STODDART Alfred Donald MM Pte 364 11th Royal Fusiliers DOW 20.4.18.
STODDART Andrew MM Gnr 110799 RGA
STODDART David MM Pte 15483 Cameron Highlanders
STODDART George MM Gnr 35695 36 Bde RFA
STODDART Harry MM Sjt 10978 7th Border Regt
STODDART John MM Sjt 14444 RGA
STODDART John MM Gnr 65136 115 Heavy Bty RGA DOW 20.11.17.
STODDART John MM L/Cpl 200542 7th Cameron Highlanders
STODDART Joseph Thomas Patrick MM Pte 6921 9th Lancers
STOFER Cecil William MM Sjt 5882 233 Coy Machine Gun Corps DOW 2.10.17.
STOFFELL Ernest J. MM Cpl 2198 Royal Fusiliers
STOKER John Edward MM Sjt 12970 9th Northumberland Fusiliers KIA 24.10.18.
STOKER Norman MM L/Sjt 15480 8th Somerset Light Infantry
STOKER Norman V. MM L/Cpl 3/7692 2nd Yorkshire Regt
STOKER Robert William Young MM Sjt 751208 D/250 Bde RFA
STOKER Sidney MM+Bar Cpl 87829 13th Liverpool Regt
STOKER William MM Pte 20382 15th Durham Light Infantry
STOKER William Edward MM Sjt 28344 19th Royal Welsh Fusiliers
STOKER William P. MM Bdr 7613 RFA
STOKES A. MM Dvr 1647 B/88 Bde RFA
STOKES A. MM Sjt 265105 1/1st Bucks Bn Oxf & Bucks Light Infantry
STOKES Albert MM+Bar Sjt 553914 Royal Engineers att 293 Bde RFA.
STOKES Albert F. MM Sjt 374506 8th London Regt
STOKES Alexander MM Bdr 104335 RFA
STOKES Alfred MM Pte 10472 15th Highland Light Infantry
STOKES Alfred E. MM L/Cpl 18/167 18th Durham Light Infantry
STOKES Arthur John MM Pte 102392 6 Coy Labour Corps KIA 15.4.18.
STOKES Arthur Philip MM Dvr 39452 C/83 Bde RFA
STOKES Charles "DCM,MM" CSM 11060 1st Middlesex Regt
STOKES Charles A.H. MM Pte 16443 2nd Royal Irish Regt
STOKES Charles E. MM L/Cpl 11300 7th South Staffordshire Regt
STOKES Charles H. MM Cpl 5874 3rd Dragoon Guards
STOKES Charles W. MM Pte 300150 Lancashire Fusiliers
STOKES E. "MM,MID" Cpl 54 RFA
STOKES Edwin MM Cpl 240224 1/8th Worcestershire Regt
STOKES "Frederick W," "DCM,MM" BSM 810047 D/232 Bde RFA
STOKES George MM Pte 682834 23rd London Regt
STOKES George Henry MM Pte 16691 10th Welsh Regt
STOKES George Henry MM Cpl 48744 83 Fd Coy Royal Engineers
STOKES Harold F. MM Bdr 54497 B/115 Bde RFA
STOKES Henry G. MM Sjt 2889 1/24th London Regt
STOKES Herbert MM Sjt 56163 RFA
STOKES Herbert G. MM Cpl 17060 4th Bedfordshire Regt
STOKES Herbert H. MM Gnr 810336 RFA
STOKES Herbert R. MM Dvr 40288 RFA
STOKES John C. MM L/Cpl 49705 9th Cheshire Regt
STOKES John H. MM Pte 268318 Royal Warwickshire Regt
STOKES Joseph MM Cpl 744 1 Motorised Bde MGC(Motors)
STOKES Joseph E. MM+Bar Sjt 10293 3rd Worcestershire Regt
STOKES Percy C. MM Pte 225128 Royal Fusiliers
STOKES Percy W. MM Pte 16032 11th Notts & Derby Regt

STOKES Robert MM Sjt 2196 1/5th Royal Warwickshire Regt KIA 4.10.17.
STOKES Robert MM L/Cpl 12329 6th Bedfordshire Regt KIA 9.8.16.
STOKES Sidney Edwin MM Bde 1159 A/235 Bde RFA
STOKES Stanley D. MM Pte 7671 Royal Sussex Regt
STOKES Stephan E. MM Spr 471727 Royal Engineers
STOKES Victor W.R. MM L/Cpl R/16196 King's Royal Rifle Corps
STOKES Vivian G. MM+Bar Sjt 10983 6th York & Lancaster Regt
STOKES William MM Pte 22835 Royal West Surrey Regt
STOKES William MM Pte 10672 7th South Staffordshire Regt
STOKES William C. MM Sjt M2/114106 Army Service Corps
STOKES William F.J. MM Cpl 24362 1 Div Sig Coy Royal Engineers
STOKES William J. MM Pte 200769 1/4th Royal Berkshire Regt
STOKOE Harry MM Dvr 61412 Royal Engineers
STOKOE Joseph MM Bdr 66354 22 Bde RFA
STOKOE Norman MM Dvr 760742 B/317 Bde RFA
STOKOE Phillipson MM Cpl 29617 East Yorkshire Regt
STOKOE T. MM L/Cpl 38910 2nd Yorkshire Light Infantry
STOLTE William Gerard MM Pte 2310 1/5th Cheshire Regt
STOLWORTHY Sidney James MM Sjt 740 4 Div Ammn Col RFA
STONARD Charles MM Cpl 45798 1/1st Surrey Yeomanry
STONE Albert Arthur MM Gnr 29701 'P' Bty RHA
STONE Albert E. MM+Bar Sjt 8119 1st Royal West Surrey Regt
STONE Albert Edwin MM Sjt 5/9264 1st Rifle Brigade KIA 11.3.17.
STONE Alfred George MM Sjt 8275 2nd Essex Regt KIA 1.7.16.
STONE Algernon Percy Grimmett MM Sjt 2330 North Staffordshire Regt
STONE Arthur MM Pte 12320 9th Royal Highlanders KIA 30.12.17.
STONE Arthur Edgar MM Sjt 8231 11th Royal Fusiliers
STONE Arthur Percy MM Pte 55203 14th Welsh Regt KIA 31.7.17.
STONE Aubrey A. MM Pte Y/339 King's Royal Rifle Corps
STONE Charles MM Pte 31815 6th York & Lancaster Regt
STONE Charles MM Pte R/18752 King's Royal Rifle Corps
STONE Charles Edwin "VC,MM" Gnr 34328 C/83 Bde RFA
STONE Charles Henry MM L/Cpl 9268 1st Devonshire Regt KIA 4.9.16.
STONE Clifford MM Pte 21892 Welsh Regt
STONE David MM Sjt 10238 1st Bedfordshire Regt
STONE Edgar V. MM Pte 33428 York & Lancaster Regt
STONE Edward MM+Bar L/Cpl 200466 1/1st London Regt
STONE Edward R. MM Pte 44747 8th Royal Berkshire Regt
STONE Edwin G. MM Sjt 306511 8th Royal Warwickshire Regt
STONE Ernest MM Pte 201459 4th Hampshire Regt
STONE Ernest Edward MM Spr 46568 31 Indian Sig Coy Royal Engineers
STONE Ernest Mark MM Spr 62140 12 Div Sig Coy Royal Engineers
STONE Ernest William "MM,MID" Pte 82358 5th Bn Machine Gun Corps
STONE Francis John MM Pte DM2/154677 Army Service Corps
STONE Frank MM L/Cpl 13869 7th Wiltshire Regt
STONE Frederick MM L/Cpl 202919 6th Leicestershire Regt KIA 23.10.18.
STONE Frederick MM Sjt 2376 1/5th Royal Sussex Regt
STONE Frederick C. "DCM,MM" Sjt 7086 2nd Hampshire Regt
STONE Frederick G. MM Dvr 44744 RFA
STONE George MM Pte 266000 1/6th Gloucestershire Regt
STONE George MM Dvr 14757 130 Bde RFA
STONE George MM+Bar Pte 1152 1st Rifle Brigade
STONE George E. MM Pte 241015 1/5th Devonshire Regt
STONE H. MM Sjt 43863 1/8th Middlesex Regt
STONE Harold L. MM Bdr 45201 RFA
STONE Harry MM Pte 1017 11th Middlesex Regt
STONE Harry MM Pte 42459 Yorkshire Regt
STONE Henry F. MM L/Bdr 27154 B/162 Bde RFA
STONE Herbert MM CSM 7399 15th Hampshire Regt
STONE Herbert MM Sjt 252710 'Y' Corps Sig Coy Royal Engineers att HAG.
STONE Herbert Willis MM L/Cpl 240834 1/5th Leicestershire Regt KIA 24.9.18.
STONE Horace S. MM Dvr 614458 RHA
STONE Isaac MM+Bar L/Bdr 68644 144 Siege Bty RGA
STONE Isaac J.W. MM Pte 235124 7th Middlesex Regt
STONE J.F. MM Pte 42871 RAMC
STONE James MM Spr 201999 10 Railway Coy Royal Engineers
STONE John "MM,MdH(F)" L/Cpl 13385 3rd Oxf & Bucks Light Infantry
STONE John Alfred MM Pte 305100 5th London Regt att 1st Rifle Brigade.KIA 25.10.17.
STONE John C. MM Gnr 163083 499 Siege Bty RGA
STONE John Thomas MM Cpl 2329 1/5th Cheshire Regt
STONE Matthew MM Pte 11734 10th West Riding Regt
STONE Norman MM Pte 357827 Liverpool Regt
STONE Reginald MM Gnr 880364 270 Bde RFA
STONE Richard MM Sjt 1384 1st Rifle Brigade
STONE Samuel MM Pte 14620 5th South Staffordshire Regt
STONE Samuel MM Pte 24830 10th West Yorkshire Regt
STONE Sidney MM Pte 11112 11th Hampshire Regt
STONE Stephen MM Pte 22616 7th East Surrey Regt KIA 20.11.17.
STONE Stephen MM Cpl 266733 Oxf & Bucks Light Infantry
STONE T.G. MM Pte 203492 7th East Kent Regt
STONE Walter MM Pte Y/618 King's Royal Rifle Corps
STONE William MM Sjt 320002 12th Norfolk Regt
STONE William A. MM L/Cpl 356717 Liverpool Regt
STONE William A.V. MM Pte 19795 Royal West Kent Regt
STONE William B. MM Cpl M2/147410 Army Service Corps
STONE William F. MM Pte M2/080295 Army Service Corps
STONE William G.L. MM Gnr 318647 142 Heavy Bty RGA
STONE William J. MM L/Sjt 472 Royal Sussex Regt
STONE William R. MM Gnr Sig 334315 RGA
STONEHAM George E. MM Pte 1030 1st Northumberland Fusiliers
STONEHAM Leslie E. MM Pte M2/053901 Army Service Corps
STONEHOUSE Stanley MM Sjt 1752 1/4th East Yorkshire Regt
STONEHOUSE Thomas MM Cpl 22/683 Durham Light Infantry
STONELEY Edwin H. MM Cpl Wheeler 45758 RGA
STONEMAN James Henry Grigg MM Pte M2/226089 Army Service Corps
STONER Charles L. MM+Bar Sjt 13711 9th Worcestershire Regt
STONER H. MM L/Cpl 321268 London Regt
STONER John MM Pte 24705 7th Royal West Surrey Regt
STONER Norman MM Sjt 1335 11th Royal West Surrey Regt
STONES Cyril MM+Bar L/Cpl 38752 11th Northumberland Fusiliers
STONES Edward MM Spr 121794 Royal Engineers
STONES Fred MM Pte 25454 7th West Riding Regt
STONES John MM 2nd Cpl 476237 Royal Engineers
STONES Louis MM Pte 8145 4 Fd Amb RAMC
STONES Michael MM Cpl 66776 33rd Bn Machine Gun Corps
STONES Robert MM Pte 7744 2nd Yorkshire Light Infantry
STONEY William MM Pte 202243 16th Cheshire Regt att 7th Royal West Kent Regt.
STONIER Walter J. MM Pte 15866 1st Coldstream Guards
STONNILL Richard Hugh MM L/Cpl 9137 1/5th London Regt
STOPFORD Fred "DCM,MM" Gnr 18395 A/87 Bde RFA
STOPPARD Henry MM Sjt 240926 Notts & Derby Regt
STOPPS John MM Pte 10281 2nd West Riding Regt
STOPPS Sidney MM Cpl 13407 9th Notts & Derby Regt
STORAR John R, MM Spr 210857 3 Div Sig Coy Royal Engineers
STORE James MM Bdr 157636 RGA
STORER Arthur "MM,MID" Cpl 7005 1/1(West Lancashire)Fd Coy Royal Engineers
STORER Christopher W. MM+Bar L/Cpl B/2020 Rifle Brigade
STORER George C. MM L/Cpl 200529 1/4th Leicestershire Regt
STORER John MM Sjt 2650 1/1st Yorkshire Dragoons Yeomanry
STORER William MM L/Bdr 43050 41 Bde RFA
STOREY Alan MM Sjt 765853 RFA
STOREY Albert MM Pte DM2/112461 Army Service Corps
STOREY Albert MM+Bar Pte 70687 2nd Notts & Derby Regt KIA 13.5.18.
STOREY Cyril I. MM Pte 46712 1st Yorkshire Light Infantry
STOREY Edwin MM Pte 18/1287 Northumberland Fusiliers
STOREY Ernest MM Spr 203128 218 Fd Coy Royal Engineers
STOREY Ernest Edward MM Bdr 676728 D/150 Bde RFA
STOREY George MM Sjt 7548 2nd West Riding Regt
STOREY George MM Sjt 15712 8th Somerset Light Infantry
STOREY Henry MM Pte 12050 9th Norfolk Regt
STOREY Herbert MM L/Cpl 19207 9th Notts & Derby Regt
STOREY Horace MM Spr 107315 87 Fd Coy Royal Engineers
STOREY James MM Pte 375016 Manchester Regt
STOREY James S. MM Pte 42283 Yorkshire Light Infantry
STOREY John MM+Bar Cpl 350995 1/9th Royal Scots
STOREY John J. MM L/Cpl 250158 1/6th Durham Light Infantry
STOREY John William MM Pte 18189 6th Yorkshire Regt
STOREY R. MM BSM 8118 25 Div Ammn Col RFA
STOREY Robert MM Spr 470522 Royal Engineers
STOREY Robert Mason MM Spr 457074 446 Fd Coy Royal Engineers
STOREY Sydney MM Pte 32449 RAMC
STOREY T. MM Cpl 2679 London Regt
STOREY Thomas MM Cpl 15/12149 15th Royal Irish Rifles

STOREY Thomas Henry MM Cpl M2/08682 654 Coy Army Service Corps
STOREY Walter MM Pte 612180 19th London Regt
STOREY Walter Stephen MM Gnr 124420 A/149 Bde RFA
STOREY William MM Pte 15312 Royal Sussex Regt
STOREY William MM Pte 1884 RAMC
STOREY William MM Gnr 1072 (276072) Y/15 Med TM Bty RFA KIA 23.7.17.
STOREY William MM Sjt 325337 1/9th Durham Light Infantry
STORIE Anfrew MM Pte 12882 11th Royal Scots KIA 14.7.16.
STORIE James MM Pte 38775 5/6th Royal Scots
STORK Lewis A. MM Pte 1858 RAMC
STORKEY Albert E. MM L/Cpl 34609 North Lancashire Regt
STORMONT John G. MM Pte 45798 RAMC
STORNE J. MM Sjt 725825 24th London Regt
STORR Arthur Barrow MM L/Cpl 57896 Machine Gun Corps
STORR Percy W. MM Pte 24383 8th Yorkshire Regt
STORRAR Andrew N. MM Pte S/41911 1/6th Royal Highlanders
STORRIE James MM Pte 265739 9th Scottish Rifles
STORROW Richard MM Gr 3473 28 Bde RFA DOW 29.9.18.
STORRY Albert MM Sjt 51621 103 Fd Coy Royal Engineers
STORRY Harry MM+Bar L/Cpl 68875 RAMC
STORY Andrew MM L/Cpl 14763 Northumberland Fusiliers
STORY J. MM Pte 36818 Essex Regt
STORY Richard William MM Pte 318263 1/5th London Regt KIA 29.8.18.
STOTEN Henry William MM L/Cpl 18211 2nd Rifle Brigade KIA 2.12.17.
STOTESBURY Ralph MM Gnr 966048 C/268 Bde RFA
STOTT A.E. MM L/Cpl 20805 21st Bn Machine Gun Corps
STOTT Arthur MM Dvr T4/086497 Army Service Corps
STOTT David MM Pnr 129560 'F' Special Coy Royal Engineers
STOTT Edwin MM Spr 104148 225 Fd Coy Royal Engineers
STOTT Ernest MM Pte 95115 4th London Regt
STOTT Francis MM Pte 94742 4th Liverpool Regt
STOTT Frank MM Pte 52743 Durham Light Infantry
STOTT Fred MM Pte 241498 1/5th Lancashire Fusiliers
STOTT George A. MM Pte 71067 Durham Light Infantry
STOTT George Herbert "MM,MBC(Rm)" Sjt 113571 Royal Engineers
STOTT George S. MM Cpl 41453 RAMC att RFC.
STOTT Harvey T. MM 2nd Cpl 312332 3 Div Sig Coy Royal Engineers
STOTT Henry MM Cpl 14290 9th Royal Lancaster Regt
STOTT Herbert MM Pte 201293 1/4th Royal Lancaster Regt KIA 12.5.18.
STOTT Herbert MM Dvr 680595 RFA
STOTT J.W. "DCM,MM" Sjt S/3661 13th Rifle Brigade
STOTT James MM Sjt 104188 227 Fd Coy Royal Engineers
STOTT James R. MM Pte 25265 West Riding Regt
STOTT John MM L/Sjt 19374 2nd Northumberland Fusiliers
STOTT John MM Gnr 161624 463 Bty 179 Bde RFA
STOTT John MM Gnr 85420 12 Siege Bty RGA
STOTT John A. MM L/Cpl 260624 1/1st County of London Yeomanry
STOTT Roger Hugh MM Cpl 119157 HQ 123 Bde RFA
STOTT Rowland MM Bdr 645 C/48 Bde RFA
STOTT Walter MM Cpl 240883 1/6th West Yorkshire Regt
STOTT Wilkinson MM Pte 114943 56th Bn Machine Gun Corps
STOUT Allan MM Cpl 38853 Lancashire Fusiliers
STOUT Charles MM Gnr 36210 RFA
STOUT Ernest MM Pte 22004 5/6th Scottish Rifles KIA 10.3.18.
STOUT George MM Spr 132971 251 Tunnelling Coy Royal Engineers
STOUT James MM+Bar Sjt 200048 South Lancashire Regt
STOUT James G. MM Pte 423603 2/10th London Regt
STOUT Thomas Stephen MM Sjt 207860 Royal Engineers
STOVIN Arthur Harold MM Pte 350350 1/9th Highland Light Infantry
STOVOLD John Edward MM Cpl 63092 Machine Gun Corps
STOW Albert J. MM Gnr 935552 RFA
STOW Arthur MM L/Cpl M2/203240 594 MT Coy Army Service Corps
STOW Frederick George MM Sjt 10844 7th Lincolnshire Regt DOW 16.10.18.
STOW Harry MM Cpl 304355 5th London Regt
STOW Harry Reginald MM Gnr 950621 A/235 Bde RFA DOW 13.9.18.
STOW John MM Pte 298059 1st London Regt
STOWE Herbert Henry MM Sjt 32551 6 Bty Machine Gun Corps(Motors)
STOWE Thomas MM Pte 27687 2nd Royal Dublin Fusiliers
STOWELL Walter MM Sjt 252683 Railway Troops Royal Engineers
STRACEY Thomas John MM Sjt 43214 6th Bedfordshire Regt
STRACHAN Adam MM Gnr 82156 265 Siege Bty RGA
STRACHAN Allan MM Pte 41674 Gordon Highlanders
STRACHAN Edward MM Pte 42935 5/6th Scottish Rifles
STRACHAN Eric L. MM Sjt 266143 Gordon Highlanders
STRACHAN George Henry MM Spr 77402 Signal Service Royal Engineers
STRACHAN Harry MM Sjt 290367 Gordon Highlanders
STRACHAN James "MM,MSM" Sjt 6798 2nd Gordon Highlanders
STRACHAN James Penny MM Pte 5106 Gordon Highlanders
STRACHAN John MM L/Cpl 77457 Tank Corps
STRACHAN John Mount MM L/Cpl 8717 8th Royal Highlanders DOW 19.7.18.
STRACHAN Kenneth John MM Pte 50989 11th Cheshire Regt KIA 1.6.18.
STRACHAN Robert MM L/Cpl 203084 1/4th Seaforth Highlanders
STRACHAN Robert "DCM,MM" Cpl Fitter 635443 256 Bde RFA
STRACHAN Ronald S. MM Sjt 2845 1/14th London Regt
STRACHAN William MM Sjt 93606 B/46 Bde RFA
STRACHAN William "MM,MID" Sjt 42825 RAMC
STRACHEY Gilbert Robert Jardine MM Spr 148636 251 Tunnelling Coy Royal Engineers
STRADLING Charles H. MM+Bar Sjt 786097 D/310 Bde RFA
STRADLING Ernest MM Gnr 116531 RFA
STRADLING Philip MM Sjt 540 C/121 Bde RFA
STRAFFON Henry Victor MM Pte 3849 Machine Gun Corps
STRAFFORD Henry MM Pte 26155 Royal Welsh Fusiliers
STRAFFORD Henry R. MM Pte 5381 12th Royal Fusiliers
STRAFFORD Tom MM Pte 29495 5th West Riding Regt
STRAIN Patrick MM Pte 51173 8th Royal Scots Fusiliers
STRAIN Robert George MM Pte 84945 2/7th Liverpool Regt KIA 27.9.18.
STRAIT P.A. MM Sjt 33997 11th Essex Regt
STRAITON Andrew MM Cpl 28441 40th Bn Machine Gun Corps
STRAKER Charles R. MM Pte 238188 5th West Riding Regt
STRAKER William Austin MM Sjt 23/1370 23rd Northumberland Fusiliers
STRANG Andrew James MM Pte 12087 7th Somerset Light Infantry
STRANG John MM Cpl 280180 1/6th Highland Light Infantry
STRANG John MM Pte 371476 8th London Regt DOW 23.4.18.
STRANGE Alfred T. MM L/Sjt 01013 Army Ordnance Corps
STRANGE Arthur E. MM Spr 2873 Royal Engineers
STRANGE Frederick MM Gnr 94165 B/47 Bde RFA
STRANGE Hercules R. MM Cpl 266962 4th Oxf & Bucks Light Infantry
STRANGE Percy Thomas MM CSM 201801 1/5th King's Own Scottish Borderers
STRANGE Thomas L. MM Pte 9/26826 South Wales Borderers
STRANGE William John MM Pte M/285599 36 MAC Army Service Corps
STRANGEWAYS Edward "MM,MID" Pte 20061 RAMC
STRAPPS James H. MM Pte 11701 16th Lancashire Fusiliers
STRAPPS Robert W. MM Dvr 902067 337 Bde RFA
STRATFORD Frank MM L/Cpl 3892 Army Cyclist Corps
STRATFORD Henry J. MM+Bar CSM 12684 11th Royal Fusiliers
STRATFORD William Joseph "DCM,MM" Sjt 50867 Lucknow Sqn Machine Gun Corps(Cavalry)
STRATH William H. MM Sjt 9636 2nd Royal Scots
STRATHDEE Ernest Albert MM Pte M2/100822 342 Coy Army Service Corps
STRATHERN Alexander MM Cpl 39412 2nd Royal Scots
STRATHERN George T. MM Cpl 98446 Machine Gun Corps
STRATHERN McLean MM Sjt 10530 2nd Gordon Highlanders
STRATTON Cecil J. MM Pte M2/098061 Army Service Corps
STRATTON Frederick MM L/Cpl 199265 106 Fd Coy Royal Engineers
STRATTON Leonard E. MM Pte 7995 4th Royal Fusiliers
STRATTON Leslie Hubert MM Pte 13646 10th Essex Regt KIA 21.3.18.
STRATTON Percy MM Cpl 11431 2nd Notts & Derby Regt
STRATTON Thomas H. MM Pte 2118 1/8th Middlesex Regt att MGC.
STRATTON Walter Willis MM L/Cpl 203771 Royal Berkshire Regt
STRATTON William A. MM Sjt 40231 1st Middlesex Regt
STRAUGHAN John "MM,CG(B)" Sjt 104006 227 Fd Coy Royal Engineers
STRAUGHAN John MM L/Cpl 2272 Northumberland Fusiliers
STRAUTHER F. MM Pte 43921 10th Essex Regt

STRAW Eric S. MM Sjt 62099 10th Royal Fusiliers
STRAW James Frederick MM+Bar Sjt 201454 1/5th Notts & Derby Regt DOW 24.10.18.
STRAW Lewis MM Cpl 33742 RFA
STRAW Lewis H. MM L/Cpl 24392 Gloucestershire Regt
STRAW Samuel MM Cpl 14863 9th Devonshire Regt
STRAWBRIDGE John MM Cpl 18840 Somerset Light Infantry
STRAWBRIDGE William P. MM Pte 63940 4th Yorkshire Light Infantry
STRAWFORD Charles B. MM Dvr 841133 D/70 Bde RFA
STRAWSON Ernest E. MM Dvr 800608 C/230 Bde RFA
STRAWSON George Rupert MM Pte 612602 2/19th London Regt KIA 30.4.18.
STREAT Cyril MM Pte L/10486 7th East Kent Regt KIA 21.3.18.
STREAT Frank H. MM CSM M2/114084 Army Service Corps
STREATER Charles W. MM Sjt 92704 Royal Engineers
STREATFIELD Harry E. MM Pte 354 6th Royal West Kent Regt
STREATFIELD W.T. MM Pte 14/40126 Royal Irish Rifles
STREATHER William Alfred MM Cpl 1662 1/9th London Regt
STREET Albert Edward MM Pte 68798 2nd Devonshire Regt
STREET Alfred George MM Pte 241875 2/6th Royal Warwickshire Regt
STREET Charles H. MM Cpl 21973 Gloucestershire Regt
STREET Charles P. MM Pte 25702 4th Grenadier Guards
STREET D. MM Cpl P1099 Military Foot Police
STREET Edward MM Dvr 72209 27 Bde RFA
STREET Ernest MM Pte 3980 Royal Berkshire Regt
STREET George MM Pte 202428 2/4th Hampshire Regt
STREET Herbert MM L/Cpl 24791 1st Grenadier Guards DOW 19.4.18.
STREET Herbert MM Cpl 3121 6th Royal Munster Fusiliers DOW 24.11.18.
STREET James MM Cpl 200660 Lancashire Fusiliers
STREET John MM Sjt 2537 North Staffordshire Regt
STREET John E. MM Cpl 352171 RAMC
STREET Joshua MM L/Cpl 18506 8th East Yorkshire Regt
STREET Kenneth Marles MM Bdr 810150 A/232 Bde RFA
STREET Lewis Wareham MM L/Cpl 14384 6th Royal Dublin Fusiliers
STREET R.P. MM Pte 10418 RAMC
STREET Reginald MM Spr 48100 37 Div Sig Coy Royal Engineers
STREET Samuel A. MM Sjt 71759 Royal Engineers
STREET T. MM Spr 33114 Royal Engineers
STREET Thomas F. MM Pte 20395 Grenadier Guards
STREET Tom MM Pte 16090 Coldstream Guards
STREET W.V.D. MM Air Mech 2 43972 RFC att RFA.
STREET William MM Cpl 305595 1/8th Notts & Derby Regt KIA 19.5.17.
STREET William MM Cpl 45905 15th Durham Light Infantry
STREET William MM Sjt 16010 26 Fd Coy Royal Engineers
STREET William J. MM Pte 12949 8th Royal Berkshire Regt
STREETER Alfred Walter MM Sjt 124225 11 Labour Coy Royal Engineers
STREETER Edward T. MM L/Cpl 9367 1st Royal West Surrey Regt
STREETER John MM L/Cpl 19884 Royal Fusiliers
STREETING Robert MM L/Cpl 18687 East Kent Regt
STREETLY Walter W. MM+Bar Dvr 109967 RFA
STREETON Horace Cecil MM Cpl Z/2742 13th Rifle Brigade KIA 2.8.17.
STREFFORD Arthur James MM Pte 201150 1/4th East Yorkshire Regt
STREFFORD Herbert H. "DCM,MM" L/Cpl 332445 Highland Light Infantry
STRETCH Arthur MM L/Sjt 280331 1/7th Lancashire Fusiliers
STRETCH George MM L/Cpl 432390 Royal Engineers
STRETCH Richard MM Dvr 681058 RFA
STRETCH William MM L/Cpl 19498 7th Wiltshire Regt
STRETTLE Samuel MM L/Cpl 510385 58 Div Sig Coy Royal Engineers
STRETTON W. MM Sjt 862 1 Traffic Control Coy Military Foot Police
STREVENS Henry F. MM Pte 1614 Middlesex Regt
STRIBBLING Walter J. MM Sjt 11882 10th Devonshire Regt
STRIBLEY William A.M. MM L/Sjt 26433 Duke of Cornwall's LI
STRICKLAND Claude Stanley MM Cpl 1416 1/12th London Regt
STRICKLAND Denis Joseph MM CSM 186 1/4th Gloucestershire Regt KIA 17.7.16.
STRICKLAND Edward MM Bdr 715537 RFA
STRICKLAND Ernest MM Cpl 99892 RFA
STRICKLAND George MM L/Cpl 265311 West Yorkshire Regt
STRICKLAND George MM L/Sjt 200836 8th Royal Lancaster Regt KIA 27.9.18.
STRICKLAND J. MM Pte 66177 RAMC
STRICKLAND J.W.T. MM Pte 887 Seaforth Highlanders
STRICKLAND John MM Cpl 29747 East Lancashire Regt
STRICKLAND Peter MM Sjt 97987 RFA
STRICKLAND Richard "MM,MID" Pte 54325 RAMC
STRICKLAND William E. MM Pte 43171 RAMC
STRIDE Albert MM L/Cpl 20899 10th South Wales Borderers
STRIDE W.H. MM Cpl 138084 187 Siege Bty RGA
STRINGER Albert John MM Pte 538283 1/6(London)Fd Amb RAMC
STRINGER Edward C. MM Pte 1402 1/21st London Regt
STRINGER Ernest MM L/Cpl 9597 2nd Northamptonshire Regt KIA 7.10.17.
STRINGER Ernest MM L/Cpl 1834 8th Royal Sussex Regt KIA 14.5.18.
STRINGER Ernest J. "MM,MID" Cpl S4/199038 Army Service Corps
STRINGER Frank J. MM Pte 235287 4th North Staffordshire Regt
STRINGER Fred MM Pte 43575 2nd Royal Inniskilling Fusiliers
STRINGER George MM Pte 18416 2nd Bedfordshire Regt
STRINGER George H. MM L/Sjt 14016 17th Lancashire Fusiliers DOW 23.10.17.
STRINGER James MM Cpl 200115 Yorkshire Light Infantry
STRINGER James MM Dvr 5327 D/86 Bde RFA
STRINGER James W. MM+Bar Sjt 99007 13th Royal Fusiliers
STRINGER John MM Pte 40138 8th Bedfordshire Regt DOW 26.5.17.
STRINGER Stephen MM Cpl 245561 Royal Engineers
STRINGER Terence MM Pte 10/138 10th East Yorkshire Regt
STRINGER Thomas H. MM Pte 3415 1/5th Notts & Derby Regt KIA 29.9.18.
STRINGER Willie MM Pte 34397 Yorkshire Light Infantry
STRINGFELLOW Gilbert MM L/Cpl 35459 East Lancashire Regt
STRINGFELLOW John W. MM Pte 19672 Royal Welsh Fusiliers
STRINGFELLOW Peter MM Pte 22532 9th Scottish Rifles
STRINGFELLOW William MM Sjt 17575 1st King's Own Scottish Borderers
STRINGMAN Thomas Tunstall MM Pte 53712 15th Lancashire Fusiliers KIA 30.9.18.
STRIPP Sydney MM Sjt 229604 26th Royal Fusiliers
STRODE Geoffrey MM L/Sjt 10493 2nd Yorkshire Regt
STRODE Reginald MM L/Cpl 230358 1/2nd London Regt
STRODE Wilfred MM Bdr 19885 D/177 Bde RFA KIA 20.6.17.
STRONG Arthur MM Pte 37374 8th Royal Berkshire Regt
STRONG Cyril MM Gnr 204698 C/160 Bde RFA DOW 20.5.18.
STRONG John MM L/Cpl 11776 1st Royal Berkshire Regt KIA 3.5.17.
STRONG John Frederick MM Cpl 73325 'AR' Cable Section Royal Engineers
STRONG John H. MM Pte 14232 Leicestershire Regt
STRONG Lewis Edwin MM Sjt 6257 1st Gloucestershire Regt KIA 22.9.16.
STRONG Sidney MM Pte 110042 184 Coy Labour Corps
STRONG Thomas Richard MM L/Cpl 30540 Gloucestershire Regt
STRONG Walter D. "MM,CG(B)" Sjt 47091 RAMC
STRONG William G. MM Pte 19770 9th Scottish Rifles
STRONG William H.J. MM Pte M2/049257 Army Service Corps att 1(North Midland)Fd Amb RAMC>
STRONG William W. MM+Bar L/Cpl 240881 1st Liverpool Regt
STRONGMAN Tom E. MM Pte 43545 1/6th Royal Highlanders
STRONNER John MM+Bar L/Sjt 10543 Royal Munster Fusiliers
STROTHARD William MM Cpl 265590 1/7th West Yorkshire Regt
STROUD Albert MM Pte 7385 7th Hussars
STROUD Arthur MM Pte 21080 Royal Fusiliers
STROUD Arthur Edmund MM Sjt 36943 'B' Bty 15 Bde RHA
STROUD Bob MM Pte 266184 2/4th Oxf & Bucks Light Infantry
STROUD George H. MM Sjt 29757 RFA
STROUD Horace James MM Pte 6995 2nd Royal West Surrey Regt KIA 14.5.17.
STROUD Richard J. MM Sjt S/19903 Rifle Brigade
STROUD Richard T. MM Pte 34748 North Lancashire Regt
STROUD Sidney J. MM Sjt 35785 12 Bde RFA
STROUD Sidney O. "DCM,MM" L/Cpl 392317 9th London Regt
STROUD William MM Pte 13022 Royal West Kent Regt
STROULGER Edward "DCM,MM" Pte 8200 1st Lincolnshire Regt
STROUTHER Ernest James MM Pte 36583 2nd Notts & Derby Regt DOW 3.3.17'
STROWBRIDGE Albert E. MM Pte 102391 Labour Corps
STROWGER Robert L. MM Pte 11035 1st Royal Lancaster Regt
STROWS Thomas C. MM Pte 1332 1/3rd London Regt

STROYAN Arthur MM Cpl 2323 Notts & Derby Regt
STROYAN Charles P. MM Pte 202105 1/5th Highland Light Infantry
STRUDWICK Albert MM Sjt 9450 2nd Royal West Surrey Regt
STRUDWICK Alfred William Charles MM Sjt 20397 6th Dragoons
STRUDWICK Frank E. MM L/Bdr 160298 109 Siege Bty RGA
STRUDWICK James Field MM Gnr 49704 D/77 Bde RHA DOW 3.11.18.
STRUDWICK William H. MM Pte M2/078226 Army Service Corps
STRUDWICK William W. MM Pte 22597 East Surrey Regt
STRUEBIG Edwin Harold MM Pte 3876 2/10th London Regt KIA 8.8.18.
STRUGGLES William MM Pte 25261 2nd Grenadier Guards
STRUGNELL Eric MM Pte 531349 1/15th London Regt
STRUGNELL Leonard William MM Cpl 3284 1/23rd London Regt
STRUTHERS Charles McC. MM Sjt 43441 15th Highland Light Infantry
STRUTT William G. MM Cpl 45300 1st Bn Machine Gun Corps
STRUTTON Alfred MM Sjt 9172 1st Royal Munster Fusiliers
STUART Alexander W. MM Pte 24425 1/7th Royal Highlanders
STUART Alfred MM Pte 14222 Northumberland Fusiliers
STUART Arthur Harry "MM,MSM" Sjt 536054 6 Provisional Coy Royal Engineers
STUART Charles MM Spr 446205 439 Fd Coy Royal Engineers
STUART Edward MM Pte M/379228 Army Service Corps
STUART J.F. MM+Bar L/Sjt 10026 1st East Kent Regt
STUART John "MM,CG(F)" CSM 1033 2nd Arg & Suth Highlanders
STUART John W. MM Pte 11925 Gordon Highlanders
STUART Lachlan MM Cpl 845 10th Royal Fusiliers
STUART Richard E. MM Cpl 7896 9th Royal Sussex Regt
STUART Robert MM Sjt 51264 RFA
STUART Robert MM Pte 11574 2nd Gordon Highlanders
STUART Sydney H. MM Pte M2/052488 Army Service Corps
STUART Thomas MM Sjt 201122 1/5th Manchester Regt KIA 20.4.18.
STUART Thomas MM Gnr 31833 RFA
STUART Thomas Alexander MM Sjt 10876 4th Liverpool Regt
STUART William MM Sjt 43402 1st Gordon Highlanders
STUART William MM Pte 3273 Royal Scots
STUART William A. MM L/Cpl 15732 East Lancashire Regt
STUART William G. MM Pte 5450 10th Royal Highlanders
STUBBERFIELD Alfred MM L/Cpl 246836 Royal Engineers
STUBBINGS Charles MM Bdr 121276 RFA
STUBBINGS Francis G. MM L/Cpl 3104 Royal Fusiliers
STUBBINGS Fred "MM,MID" Sjt 3/6670 1st Bedfordshire Regt
STUBBINGS Harold T. MM Pte 15647 13th Royal Sussex Regt
STUBBINGS John W. "DCM,MM" Sjt 18195 36th Bn Machine Gun Corps
STUBBINGS M.W. MM Sjt 265703 1/1st Hertfordshire Regt
STUBBINGTON Arthur Philip MM Gnr 137056 114 Heavy Bty RGA
STUBBINGTON Fred MM Gnr 39498 115 Hy Bty RGA
STUBBINS Harry MM Pte 22261 32nd Bn Machine Gun Corps
STUBBS Alfred MM Pte 12499 4th Coldstream Guards
STUBBS Arthur MM Bdr 91572 2 Div Ammn Col RFA
STUBBS Bertram MM+Bar Pte 250612 1/6th Manchester Regt
STUBBS C. MM Cpl 61872 Royal Engineers
STUBBS Christopher J. MM Pte 52346 Middlesex Regt
STUBBS Frank Edward MM Pte 21108 18th Middlesex Regt KIA 13.4.18.
STUBBS Fred MM Gnr 60032 RGA
STUBBS George "DCM,MM" Sjt 14324 10th Yorkshire Regt
STUBBS George Harry MM Sjt 776896 A/245 Bde RFA
STUBBS Hedley B. MM Gnr 117900 RGA
STUBBS Henry MM Gnr 150074 405 Siege Bty RGA
STUBBS Herbert MM Pte 29490 2nd Yorkshire Regt
STUBBS James E. MM Sjt 41401 D/119 Bde RFA
STUBBS John MM Pte 201265 South Lancashire Regt
STUBBS John MM L/Cpl 75 Royal Fusiliers
STUBBS John J. MM Cpl 241022 Liverpool Regt
STUBBS John R. MM Pte 2231 1/5th Border Regt
STUBBS Joseph MM+Bar Cpl 66717 155 Siege Bty RGA DOW 16.4.18.
STUBBS Joseph MM L/Cpl 10801 2nd Notts & Derby Regt
STUBBS Joseph Henry MM Cpl M2/113163 607 Coy Army Service Corps
STUBBS Leonard MM Dvr 117310 RFA
STUBBS Mary MM Miss F First Aid Nursing Yeomanry
STUBBS Q.F. MM+Bar L/Cpl 4622 Royal Fusiliers
STUBBS Richard MM CSM 3019 Liverpool Regt
STUBBS Robert MM Pte 26541 Cheshire Regt
STUBBS Sam MM Sjt 52355 'N' Bty RHA
STUBBS Sidney W. MM L/Cpl 42260 Machine Gun Corps
STUBBS William MM L/Cpl 31616 2nd South Lancashire Regt
STUBBS William George MM Pte 242609 2/5th Lancashire Fusiliers DOW 3.10.18.
STUBLEY Albert Henry MM Pte 148418 33rd Bn Machine Gun Corps
STUBLEY Edward James MM Dvr 85494 RFA
STUCKES William H. MM Gnr 1977 RFA
STUCKEY E.R. MM Pte 337597 RAMC
STUCKEY George C. MM+Bar Sjt 14782 7th Bedfordshire Regt
STUCKEY Lewis S. MM Pte 30099 Oxf & Bucks Light Infantry
STUCKEY Stanley W. MM Pte 337634 RAMC
STUCKEY William MM Sjt 240140 1/6th Royal Warwickshire Regt
STUDD Frederick J. MM Gnr 32931 RGA
STUDD Frederick R. MM Pte 13254 Royal West Kent Regt
STUDD Reuben MM Sjt 17567 2nd Coldstream Guards
STUDHOLME William MM Sjt 77451 Royal Flying Corps
STUFFINS Charles MM Cpl M2/130596 272 Coy Army Service Corps
STUMP Charles H. MM Sjt 230173 1/2nd London Regt
STUMP J.J.E. MM Pte 37777 1st Essex Regt
STUNT Archibald MM Sjt 2117 8th Royal Sussex Regt
STURCH Francis Frederick MM Pte 50718 1st Royal Berkshire Regt DOW 29.8.18.
STURDY Oswald MM Cpl 13908 11th Welsh Regt
STURDY William J. MM Pte 330715 1/8th Liverpool Regt
STURGEON Alfred William MM L/Cpl 3521 Machine Gun Corps
STURGEON David MM Pte 33406 2nd Yorkshire Regt
STURGEON Ivory C.N. MM Gnr 93450 RGA
STURGEON Robert MM Cpl 10257 1st King's Own Scottish Borderers
STURGES or STURGESS Herbert J. MM Pte 8659 23 Fd Amb RAMC
STURGESS Alfred H.G. MM Cpl 201776 1/4th Royal Berkshire Regt
STURGESS Frederick MM Gnr 14455 D/159 Bde RFA
STURGESS George H. MM Bdr 91167 RFA
STURGESS John MM L/Sjt 21194 2nd Highland Light Infantry KIA 11.9.18.
STURGESS Thomas George "MC,MM(4160 Sjt)" T/2Lt 63rd Bn Machine Gun Corps KIA 10.11.18.
STURGESS Walter MM L/Bdr 148564 40 Bty 25 Bde RFA
STURGESS William MM Pte 13773 Middlesex Regt
STURGIS Edward MM Pte 228224 1st London Regt
STURLEY Frederick C. MM Cpl 35458 RGA
STURMAN Albert MM Pte 18220 Leicestershire Regt
STURMAN Frederick J. MM Pte 95133 4th Liverpool Regt
STURMAN Jack MM L/Bdr 86247 C/47 Bde RFA
STURMAN William John MM L/Cpl 43042 7th Norfolk Regt Died 1.11.18.
STURROCK Edward MM Sjt 7882 1st Cameron Highlanders
STURROCK Gilbert MM Spr 463034 50 Div Sig Coy Royal Engineers
STURROCK John MM L/Cpl 802 2nd Royal Highlanders
STURROCK Peter MM Dvr 47471 RFA
STURT Ralph H. MM Bdr 92058 RFA
STUTELEY Harold A. MM Spr 560654 Royal Engineers
STUTT William MM CSM 6066 7th East Yorkshire Regt
STUTTARD Arthur MM Sjt 6178 9th Cheshire Regt
STUTTARD Herbert MM+Bar Sjt 22/342 Northumberland Fusiliers
STUTTARD Joe MM Dvr 56116 105 Bty 22 Bde RFA
STUTTARD Percy MM Sjt 27561 RFA
STUTTARD Robert MM Pte 57218 7th Manchester Regt
STYAN Edward T. MM L/Cpl 38730 Northumberland Fusiliers
STYANTS Sidney L. MM Pte 11697 King's Royal Rifle Corps
STYCH Albert MM L/Cpl 8281 7th South Staffordshire Regt KIA 28.4.17.
STYCH Isaiah MM Cpl 8262 1st Royal Welsh Fusiliers
STYLER Harry MM Pte 240110 Worcestershire Regt
STYLER Sidney MM Pte 38448 38 Fd Amb RAMC
STYLES Albert MM Pte 5995 1st Irish Guards KIA 20.10.18.
STYLES Arthur Albert Stephen MM Pte 19461 26th Royal Fusiliers KIA 29.9.18.
STYLES D. MM Sjt 53140 Machine Gun Corps
STYLES Frederick MM Pte S/14857 Rifle Brigade
STYLES Joseph MM Dvr T/418 Army Service Corps
STYLES Lionel Dudley MM Pte R/28606 12th King's Royal Rifle Corps DOW 23.8.17.
STYLES Thomas "MM,MID" Sjt 23865 55 Fd Coy Royal Engineers
STYLES Thomas George MM Bdr 66036 824 TM Bty RFA KIA 17.11.16.

STYLES Thomas H. MM Gnr 151194 8 Bty 15 Bde RFA
STYLES Walter A. MM Dvr 911114 D/174 Bde RFA
STYLES William Henry MM Sjt 24656 16 Div Ammn Col RFA
STYMAN Henry MM Sjt 3673 King's Royal Rifle Corps
SUCH Edward T. MM Pte 35852 Royal Berkshire Regt
SUCH Henry Ernest MM Sjt 2028 1/5th Royal Warwickshire Regt
SUCH John Henry MM Pte C/6847 18th King's Royal Rifle Corps KIA 21.9.17.
SUCKLING A. MM Pte 1223 17 Fd Amb RAMC
SUDALL John MM Pte 52610 Lancashire Fusiliers
SUDDABY George Frederick Pittam MM Sjt 201516 1/5th Notts & Derby Regt
SUDDES Thomas MM Pte 17108 Durham Light Infantry
SUDDICK James MM Pte 20471 Hampshire Regt
SUDDICK Joseph MM Pte 11357 2nd South Wales Borderers Death sentence commuted.
SUDDICK Robert MM L/Cpl 23857 Hampshire Regt
SUDDICK William MM L/Cpl 21598 6th Royal Inniskilling Fusiliers
SUDWORTH John MM Sjt 20359 1st Grenadier Guards
SUFFILL John H.V. MM Sjt 11600 Highland Light Infantry
SUFFOLK John H. MM Spr 560447 Royal Engineers
SUFFOLK William H. MM Pte 39242 North Staffordshire Regt
SUGDEN Albert MM Pte 43743 West Yorkshire Regt
SUGDEN Herbert MM 2nd Cpl 479943 49 Div Sig Coy Royal Engineers
SUGDEN J. MM Dvr 34435 A/72 Bde RFA
SUGDEN J. MM Pte 40326 West Yorkshire Regt
SUGDEN John Henry "DCM,MM" Sjt 375226 Manchester Regt
SUGDEN Lawrence MM Pte 305986 1st West Yorkshire Regt
SUGDEN Leslie Herring MM Sjt 3825 1/1st HAC(Infantry)
SUGDEN William A. MM Cpl 35031 Machine Gun Corps
SUGDEN Wright MM S/Sjt Mech M2/019794 Army Service Corps
SUGG Franklin C. MM Sjt 98686 332 Siege Bty RGA
SUGGARS Archie MM Dvr 1657 A/235 Bde RFA
SUGGARS Leslie C. MM Pte 373764 8th London Regt
SUGGETT or SUGGITT Lancelot T. MM Cpl 14856 9th West Riding Regt
SUGGITT William MM Pte 12662 8th Yorkshire Regt "KIA 8.10,16."
SUITTERS Frederick J. MM Pte 17810 16 Fd Amb RAMC
SULLEY Joseph MM Pte 90922 1/8th Notts & Derby Regt KIA 3.10.18.
SULLEY William MM Pte 268856 Notts & Derby Regt
SULLINGS Edgar N. MM Sjt 570427 1/17th London Regt
SULLIVAN Albert P. MM Dvr 49655 RFA
SULLIVAN Alexander James MM Sjt 14352 RGA
SULLIVAN Beaton MM+Bar L/Cpl 200039 1/4th Gordon Highlanders DOW 30.3.18.
SULLIVAN Benjamin T. MM+Bar Sjt 37059 1/5th Devonshire Regt
SULLIVAN Bernard MM Cpl 79247 Durham Light Infantry
SULLIVAN Charles MM Dvr 31303 42 Bde RFA
SULLIVAN Daniel MM Gnr 187383 A/104 Bde RFA
SULLIVAN Daniel MM Pte 4754 9th Royal Highlanders
SULLIVAN David MM L/Cpl 8473 1st Royal Fusiliers KIA 31.7.17.
SULLIVAN Denis "DCM,MM" Sjt 25278 18th Welsh Regt
SULLIVAN Douglas MM Pte 67053 9th Royal Fusiliers KIA 26.9.17.
SULLIVAN Edward MM BSM 31030 125 Bty 29 Bde RFA
SULLIVAN Ernest E. MM Pte 630592 1/20th London Regt
SULLIVAN Eugene MM Pte 28804 1st South Wales Borderers
SULLIVAN George MM+Bar Pte 3617 6th Royal Irish Regt
SULLIVAN Gerald W. MM Pte 68152 1st Devonshire Regt
SULLIVAN Henry Daniel MM Dvr 39548 D/161 Bde RFA
SULLIVAN Herbert C. MM CSM 32008 South Lancashire Regt
SULLIVAN Herbert William MM Pte 5174 1/14th London Regt
SULLIVAN James MM Pte 28092 Durham Light Infantry
SULLIVAN James MM Pte 242186 1/5th East Lancashire Regt
SULLIVAN James MM Sjt 350712 Royal Scots
SULLIVAN John MM Gnr 62659 1 Bty 45 Bde RFA
SULLIVAN John MM Sjt 50109 2 Bde RFA
SULLIVAN John MM Gnr 32239 RGA
SULLIVAN John L. MM Gnr 114837 Y/9 Med TM Bty RFA
SULLIVAN Joseph MM Pte 266886 5th Notts & Derby Regt
SULLIVAN Maurice MM Pte 16907 2nd East Lancashire Regt
SULLIVAN Michael MM Pte 13612 3rd Coldstream Guards Died 15.9.16.
SULLIVAN Michael MM Pte 9275 3rd Worcestershire Regt
SULLIVAN Patrick MM Pte 44940 4th Hampshire Regt
SULLIVAN Patrick MM Pte R/3147 King's Royal Rifle Corps
SULLIVAN Patrick Joseph MM Pte 202700 2nd Lincolnshire Regt
SULLIVAN Samuel T. MM L/Sjt 11337 Worcestershire Regt
SULLIVAN Stephen MM Pte 43003 72 Coy Labour Corps
SULLIVAN Stephen L. MM Sjt 15156 RGA
SULLIVAN Thomas MM Sjt 10641 Northumberland Fusiliers
SULLIVAN Thomas MM Pte 18567 1st South Wales Borderers
SULLIVAN Thomas MM CQMS 20899 Machine Gun Corps
SULLIVAN Thomas A. MM+Bar Sjt 1446 6 Fd Amb RAMC
SULLIVAN Thomas A. MM Cpl 945773 RFA
SULLIVAN Thomas Bernard MM Bdr 21627 RGA
SULLIVAN Walter Leonard MM Pte 17564 7th Royal Berkshire Regt
SULLIVAN William MM Cpl 147111 'Q' Special Coy Royal Engineers
SULLIVAN William MM CSM 8277 6th Northamptonshire Regt KIA 26.9.16.
SULLIVAN William MM Sjt 7927 4th Royal Fusiliers
SULLIVAN William E. MM Cpl 47409 9th Yorkshire Light Infantry
SULLY Albert H. MM Cpl S/4357 Rifle Brigade
SULLY Arthur G. MM Pte 92 1st Welsh Guards
SULLY William A. MM Pte 452944 11th London Regt
SUMBLER George J.C. MM Spr 74952 Royal Engineers
SUMMERFIELD D.F. MM Sjt 2359 London Regt
SUMMERFIELD Frederick MM Pte 41348 Northumberland Fusiliers
SUMMERFIELD George MM L/Bdr 53642 9 Heavy Bty RGA
SUMMERHAYES Thomas R. MM Sjt 10160 6th Somerset Light Infantry
SUMMERHILL Harold S. MM Pte 203591 8th East Surrey Regt
SUMMERHILL Thomas H. MM Pte 56587 8th Scottish Rifles
SUMMERHILL William MM Pte 14059 24th Northumberland Fusiliers
SUMMERLY Michael; MM Pte 40624 Royal Inniskilling Fusiliers
SUMMERS Arthur E. MM Gnr 135078 RFA
SUMMERS C. MM Gnr 3063 RFA
SUMMERS Charles O. MM Dvr 4395 B/119 Bde RFA
SUMMERS Cyril W. MM Sjt 127478 266 Siege Bty RGA
SUMMERS Daniel MM Pte 231292 2nd London Regt
SUMMERS David MM Cpl 636096 C/256 Bde RFA
SUMMERS Edward MM Dvr 12866 D/86 Bde RFA Died 16.10.18.
SUMMERS Eric M. MM Pte 260006 4th North Lancashire Regt
SUMMERS J. MM Gnr 50085 3 Bty 45 Bde RFA
SUMMERS Jack MM L/Cpl 44479 1st Worcestershire Regt
SUMMERS James MM L/Cpl 64205 6th Bn Machine Gun Corps
SUMMERS John MM Pte 41643 1st King's Own Scottish Borderers
SUMMERS John MM Spr 232075 Signal Service Royal Engineers
SUMMERS John MM L/Cpl 46038 24 Div Sig Coy Royal Engineers
SUMMERS Robert MM Sjt 20221 42nd Bn Machine Gun Corps
SUMMERS Robert John MM Pte 241299 5th Lincolnshire Regt
SUMMERS Walter George Thomas "MC,DCM,MM(5791 Sjt 9th Bn)" T/2Lt 12th East Surrey Regt
SUMMERS Walter N. "DCM,MM" CSM 13955 8th Gloucestershire Regt
SUMMERS William MM Sjt 297930 714 Coy Labour Corps
SUMMERS William MM Pte 7744 1st Scots Guards KIA 4.8.17.
SUMMERS William MM L/Cpl 12878 7th Border Regt
SUMMERS William MM L/Cpl 79524 180 Tunnelling Coy Royal Engineers KIA 4.3.17.
SUMMERS William Edwin John MM L/Cpl P2859 Military Mounted Police att HQ XI Corps
SUMMERSBY Stanley MM Pte 309259 17th Armoured Car Bn Tank Corps
SUMMERSCALES Ernest V. MM Sjt 41149 15th Royal Irish Rifles
SUMMERSCALES George MM Pte 401160 1(West Riding)Fd Amb RAMC
SUMMERSCALES James MM Pte 21863 Grenadier Guards
SUMMERSCALES Wilkin MM Pte 14065 20th Manchester Regt Died 29.10.18.
SUMMERSGILL H. MM Cpl 47796 13th Royal Inniskilling Fusiliers
SUMMERSGILL Harry MM Sjt 201311 Lancashire Fusiliers
SUMMERSIDE William MM Pte 19/75 19th Northumberland Fusiliers
SUMMERSON Thomas MM Pte 7977 6 CCS RAMC
SUMMERVILLE James MM Pte 12364 Highland Light Infantry
SUMNER Arthur MM Pte M/301980 Army Service Corps att 16 Fd Amb RAMC.
SUMNER Edgar MM Spr 42513 76 Fd Coy Royal Engineers
SUMNER Ernest MM Sjt 20829 1st Liverpool Regt
SUMNER Harold MM CQMS 129798 226 Coy Labour Corps
SUMNER Harold MM Pte 1698 1/7th London Regt
SUMNER Isaac MM Pte 241174 5th South Lancashire Regt
SUMNER J.B. MM Pte 21238 1st Royal Inniskilling Fusiliers
SUMNER James MM+Bar Dvr 680838 D/286 Bde RFA
SUMNER John MM Pte 9215 1/9th Liverpool Regt
SUMNER John MM Sjt MS/3112 Army Service Corps att 38 Fd Amb RAMC.

SUMNER John T. MM Pte 19575 6/7th Royal Scots Fusiliers
SUMNER Peter MM Sjt 44335 75 Fd Coy Royal Engineers
SUMNER Robert E. MM Sjt 18944 1 Special Coy Middlesex Regt
SUMNER William MM Dvr 61177 106 Fd Coy Royal Engineers
SUMNER William Catchpool MM L/Cpl 161160 21 Div Sig Coy Royal Engineers
SUMPSTER William Herbert MM 2nd Cpl 69220 35 Div Sig Coy Royal Engineers
SUMPTER Benjamin MM L/Cpl 6613 Middlesex Regt
SUMPTER Herbert MM Pte 13178 6th Northamptonshire Regt
SUMPTER James A. MM Gnr 88092 343 Siege Bty RGA
SUMPTER Thomas J. MM Cpl 574784 17th London Regt
SUNDERLAND Albert MM Gnr 667 1/1(West Riding)Bde RFA
SUNDERLAND Albert MM Sjt 13/888 13th York & Lancaster Regt
SUNDERLAND Fred MM L/Cpl 243671 18th Liverpool Regt
SUNDERLAND Harold MM Pte 307446 7th West Riding Regt
SUNDERLAND J.R. MM Pte 27305 Northumberland Fusiliers
SUNDERLAND James MM Pte 78582 9th Bn Tank Corps
SUNDERLAND James William MM L/Cpl 202289 9th West Riding Regt KIA 26.8.18.
SUNDERLAND Jessie MM Pte R/6481 12th King's Royal Rifle Corps
SUNDERLAND John W. MM Pte 556578 16th London Regt
SUNDERLAND Walter MM Pte C/12892 King's Royal Rifle Corps
SUNDERLAND Wilfred MM+Bar L/Cpl 202472 2/4th West Riding Regt
SUNLEY John W. MM Pte 60129 Machine Gun Corps
SUNNERS Henry MM 2nd Cpl 1711 Royal Engineers
SUNTER John William MM L/Cpl 31072 46 Fd Amb RAMC KIA 31.7.17.
SUPPLE James MM Pte 11636 RAMC
SUPPLE John MM Sjt 34021 282 Siege Bty RGA KIA 17.12.17.
SURMAN Leslie H. MM+Bar L/Sjt 40549 Worcestershire Regt
SURR Bertie W. MM 2nd Cpl 121991 184 Tunnelling Coy Royal Engineers
SURREY C. MM L/Cpl 19292 1st Essex Regt
SURRIDGE Alfred J. MM Pte 532087 15th London Regt
SURRIDGE Alfred R. MM L/Bdr 930370 A/291 Bde RFA
SURRIDGE C.W. MM+Bar Pte 8089 2nd Essex Regt
SURRIDGE James MM Pte R/27564 King's Royal Rifle Corps
SURRIDGE William C.F. MM Cpl 14470 Royal Engineers
SURRIDGE William R. MM Pte 26566 4th Hampshire Regt
SURTEES Frank MM Pte 45307 Northumberland Fusiliers
SURTEES George MM Gnr 64049 157 Siege Bty RGA
SURTEES John W. MM Dvr T2/14671 Army Service Corps
SURTEES Thomas MM L/Cpl 300073 1/8th Durham Light Infantry
SURTEES Thomas C. MM Pte DM2/075255 Army Service Corps
SUSKINS Arthur E. MM Pte 69344 12/13th Northumberland Fusiliers
SUSSEX Arthur MM Sjt 37162 RFA
SUSSEX Harry G. MM L/Sjt 7223 2nd Irish Guards
SUTCH John J. MM Pte 25765 230 Fd Amb RAMC
SUTCH William H. MM L/Cpl 4302 5th Lancers
SUTCLIFFE Albert MM Pte 201883 1/4th West Riding Regt
SUTCLIFFE Albert MM Pte 28187 9th Yorkshire Regt
SUTCLIFFE Arthur MM Cpl 11156 1st Scottish Rifles
SUTCLIFFE Arthur E. MM Gne 292045 RGA
SUTCLIFFE Edgar MM Sjt C/1501 13th King's Royal Rifle Corps
SUTCLIFFE Edward MM L/Sjt 9630 1st Border Regt
SUTCLIFFE Fred MM Pte 36750 East Yorkshire Regt
SUTCLIFFE Harold Thomas MM Pte 37261 54 Fd Amb RAMC
SUTCLIFFE Harry MM Pte 40255 18th West Yorkshire Regt DOW 3.5.17.
SUTCLIFFE Herbert Schofield MM Pte 21/1031 11th West Yorkshire Regt
SUTCLIFFE James MM Cpl 83229 69 Fd Coy Royal Engineers
SUTCLIFFE James MM Pte 16488 10th West Riding Regt
SUTCLIFFE John R. MM Pte 11963 North Lancashire Regt
SUTCLIFFE John William MM Pte 23755 North Lancashire Regt
SUTCLIFFE Joseph MM Pte 2545 5th North Lancashire Regt
SUTCLIFFE Joseph M. MM Pte 63592 Machine Gun Corps
SUTCLIFFE Leonard MM Pte 240237 5th East Lancashire Regt
SUTCLIFFE Philip MM Pte 200882 1st London Regt
SUTCLIFFE Sam MM Pte 201325 West Riding Regt
SUTCLIFFE Sydney MM Sjt 15551 Royal Welsh Fusiliers KIA 2.10.17.
SUTCLIFFE Wallace MM L/Cpl 3301 1/6th West Yorkshire Regt
SUTCLIFFE Walter MM Pte 27415 8th Yorkshire Regt
SUTCLIFFE Whiteley MM Pte 24190 Northumberland Fusiliers
SUTCLIFFE William MM Pte 42265 RAMC
SUTCLIFFE William MM+Bar Sjt 11362 9th Scottish Rifles
SUTCLIFFE William MM L/Sjt 13745 1st Scots Guards
SUTCLIFFE Willie MM Pte 201299 West Riding Regt
SUTER James MM SM 18253 RAMC
SUTER James George MM L/Cpl 13070 2nd Scottish Rifles
SUTER Roy MM Pte 29657 South Lancashire Regt
SUTHERINGTON J.W. MM L/Cpl 23048 Lancashire Fusiliers
SUTHERLAND Albert E. MM Sjt 5257 4th Dragoon Guards
SUTHERLAND Alexander MM Pte 202372 1/7th Gordon Highlanders
SUTHERLAND Alexander MM Sjt 241112 Seaforth Highlanders
SUTHERLAND Angus MM Pte 240795 Seaforth Highlanders
SUTHERLAND Archibald MM Cpl 3050 1/1st Duke of Lancaster's Own Yeomanry
SUTHERLAND Aubrey William MM Cpl 894 2nd Arg & Suth Highlanders
SUTHERLAND Christopher MM L/Cpl 515064 245 Coy Labour Corps
SUTHERLAND Dan MM Pte 15443 2nd Scots Guards
SUTHERLAND Daniel MM Pte M/379409 Army Service Corps
SUTHERLAND Daniel MM Pte 240728 1/5th Seaforth Highlanders KIA 22.9.17.
SUTHERLAND David MM L/Cpl 204234 1/5th Seaforth Highlanders DOW 31.8.18.
SUTHERLAND David MM Bdr 12860 A/74 Bde RFA
SUTHERLAND Donald "MM,MID" Sjt 225910 10th Cameron Highlanders
SUTHERLAND Finlay MM Cpl 44640 1st Bn Machine Gun Corps
SUTHERLAND Frank MM Dvr 645961 51 Div Amn Col RFA
SUTHERLAND George MM Pte 40925 5th Cameron Highlanders
SUTHERLAND George MM Pte 242029 2nd Seaforth Highlanders
SUTHERLAND George MM L/Cpl 240153 Seaforth Highlanders
SUTHERLAND George MM Pte 240761 Seaforth Highlanders
SUTHERLAND George A. MM Sjt 122321 163 Siege Bty RGA
SUTHERLAND George Stewart MM L/Cpl 13024 7th Cameron Highlanders KIA 17.8.16.
SUTHERLAND Harry MM L/Cpl 7903 2nd Cameron Highlanders
SUTHERLAND Harry MM Pte 37145 18th Highland Light Infantry Died 24.12.17.
SUTHERLAND James MM Pte 241229 Gordon Highlanders
SUTHERLAND James MM Sjt 52423 Liverpool Regt
SUTHERLAND James MM Pte 260233 Seaforth Highlanders
SUTHERLAND James MM L/Cpl 202480 Gordon Highlanders
SUTHERLAND James C. MM Cpl 265114 1/6th Gordon Highlanders
SUTHERLAND James G. MM+Bar Sjt 418064 52 Fd Coy Royal Engineers
SUTHERLAND John MM Cpl 8911 7th Seaforth Highlanders
SUTHERLAND John MM+Bar L/Cpl 265411 1/6th Royal Highlanders
SUTHERLAND John MM Pte 28986 1/9th Highland Light Infantry KIA 29.9.18.
SUTHERLAND John "DCM,MM" Sjt 13007 7th Yorkshire Regt
SUTHERLAND John MM Pte 10844 1st Highland Light Infantry
SUTHERLAND John MM Pte 19467 Royal Scots Fusiliers
SUTHERLAND John MM+Bar Sjt 254365 14th Arg & Suth Highlanders
SUTHERLAND John A.G. MM Pte 73199 11th Notts & Derby Regt
SUTHERLAND John H. MM Gnr(SS) 706115 RFA
SUTHERLAND John W. MM Pte 301450 RAMC
SUTHERLAND John W. MM Sjt 16214 9th North Staffordshire Regt
SUTHERLAND Lawrence MM Sjt M/205136 Army Service Corps att 260 Siege Bty RGA
SUTHERLAND Robert MM L/Cpl 24147 1/5th Royal Highlanders
SUTHERLAND Robert MM Dvr 92248 A/58 Bde RFA
SUTHERLAND Septimus MM Pte 17686 1st East Yorkshire Regt
SUTHERLAND Thomas MM Sjt 200021 1/4th Seaforth Highlanders
SUTHERLAND W.McP. MM Pte 41030 8th Royal Highlanders
SUTHERLAND William MM L/Cpl 225917 10th Cameron Highlanders
SUTHERLAND William MM Pte 3461 8th Seaforth Highlanders
SUTHERLAND William MM Pte 1340 23rd Royal Fusiliers
SUTHERLAND William H. MM Pte 229478 Royal Fusiliers
SUTHERS Harcourt MM L/Cpl 58205 Machine Gun Corps
SUTHERS W. MM Pte 240308 Lancashire Fusiliers
SUTTABY A. MM Pte 40596 10th Essex Regt
SUTTERBY Daniel E. MM L/Cpl 96647 10th Bn Tank Corps
SUTTIE Robert J. MM Pte 9700 Gordon Highlanders
SUTTLE Ambrose MM L/Cpl 722974 1/24th London Regt KIA 22.8.18.
SUTTON Albert E. MM Sjt 69732 33 Bde RFA

SUTTON Alfred MM Gnr 610333 2/1(Leicester)Bty RHA
SUTTON Alfred Frederick Richard MM Sjt 6710 Devonshire Regt
SUTTON Arthur MM BSM 930372 C/104 Bde RFA
SUTTON B.A. MM Pte 17770 10th Essex Regt
SUTTON Bertie E. MM Cpl 8957 2nd Suffolk Regt
SUTTON Cecil H. MM Pte 18182 1st Royal Berkshire Regt
SUTTON Charles MM Cpl 47673 RGA
SUTTON Charles E. "DCM,MM" Cpl 72303 'EE' Cable Section Royal Engineers
SUTTON Charles W. MM Sjt 240555 Royal West Surrey Regt
SUTTON David MM Pte 26398 1st East Surrey Regt KIA 20.5.18.
SUTTON Douglas MM CQMS 8609 8th Lincolnshire Regt
SUTTON Edgar H. MM Cpl 19048 'J' Cable Section Royal Engineers
SUTTON Edward MM Gnr 45814 40 Div Ammn Col RFA Died 31.1.19.
SUTTON Edwin MM Gnr 805151 A/231 Bde RFA
SUTTON Ernest MM Pte 15603 7th Bedfordshire Regt
SUTTON Ernest W. MM Sjt 242648 1/6th Royal Warwickshire Regt
SUTTON Frank MM Pte 78030 9th Bn Tank Corps
SUTTON George MM Sjt 25298 9th Notts & Derby Regt
SUTTON George MM Sjt 7779 1st East Yorkshire Regt
SUTTON George MM Pte 73186 Notts & Derby Regt
SUTTON George Edward MM Cpl 145768 Fifth Army Sig Coy Royal Engineers Carrier Pigeon Service
SUTTON Harold MM SQMS 50501 Machine Gun Corps
SUTTON Harold Thomas MM Pte 18419 Gloucestershire Regt
SUTTON Henry James MM Pte 17541 Machine Gun Corps
SUTTON Jack MM Pte 12571 7th Suffolk Regt
SUTTON James "DCM,MM" CSM 4266 6th & 8th Royal West Kent Regt
SUTTON James N. MM L/Cpl 133032 45th Royal Fusiliers
SUTTON James William MM Pte 265543 1/6th Cheshire Regt KIA 31.7.17.
SUTTON John MM Pte 63183 Machine Gun Corps
SUTTON John MM Pte 611776 19th London Regt
SUTTON John W. MM Pte 27828 9th Notts & Derby Regt
SUTTON Joseph J. MM Pte 240456 Royal Warwickshire Regt
SUTTON Leslie John MM Spr 40004 14 Div Sig Coy Royal Engineers
SUTTON Nelson H. MM L/Bdr 129402 A/281 Bde RFA
SUTTON Percy MM Pte 306846 2/8th West Yorkshire Regt
SUTTON Reuben S. MM Sjt 235768 1/7th West Riding Regt
SUTTON Robert MM Sjt 54132 23 Div Sig Coy Royal Engineers
SUTTON Sydney MM L/Cpl 203067 Royal Warwickshire Regt
SUTTON Thomas MM L/Cpl 34518 9th Yorkshire Regt
SUTTON Thomas MM Pte 17803 7th South Staffordshire Regt KIA 14.12.17.
SUTTON Thomas MM Pte 18732 Manchester Regt
SUTTON Thomas MM L/Cpl 13828 7th East Lancashire Regt
SUTTON Thomas Edward MM L/Cpl 42987 9th Yorkshire Light Infantry DOW 6.6.17.
SUTTON Thomas H. MM L/Cpl 22738 1st Hampshire Regt
SUTTON Thomas J. MM L/Cpl 97586 Machine Gun Corps
SUTTON Walter Edward MM Cpl 554389 16th London Regt
SUTTON Walter Richard MM Sjt 66457 129 Bty 42 Bde RFA KIA 29.3.18.
SUTTON Walter Samuel MM Spr 85199 207 Fd Coy Royal Engineers
SUTTON Wilfred H. MM Pte 117000 10th Notts & Derby Regt
SUTTON William MM Pte 11095 6th Duke of Cornwall's LI KIA 18.8.16.
SUTTON William MM Pte 1909 1/1st Leicestershire Yeo
SUTTON William MM L/Cpl 8215 6th Wiltshire Regt KIA 5.6.17
SUTTON William MM Sjt 8713 1st Scottish Rifles
SUTTON William MM Pte 72114 Machine Gun Corps
SUTTON William F. MM Cpl 65086 40 Bde RFA
SUTTON William George MM Cpl 470943 12th London Regt KIA 26.4.18
SUTTON William J. MM L/Cpl 265895 Gloucestershire Regt
SUTTON William Robert James MM Sjt 8043 2nd Middlesex Regt KIA 1.7.16.
SWABEY James MM L/Cpl 59243 Royal Engineers
SWABEY Thomas MM Pte 61452 13th Royal Fusiliers
SWABY Edward MM L/Cpl 29152 East Lancashire Regt
SWAFFIELD Frederick MM Gnr 293206 140 Hy Bty RGA
SWAIN Albert MM Sjt 12658 7th Royal Lancaster Regt
SWAIN Albert J.V. MM Pte M2/176635 Army Service Corps
SWAIN Ambling MM L/Cpl R/28647 17th King's Royal Rifle Corps
SWAIN Charles MM Pte 12118 7th Norfolk Regt KIA 28.4.17.
SWAIN Charles G. MM Pte 13685 East Surrey Regt
SWAIN Charles H. MM Sjt 37100 RGA
SWAIN Daniel W. MM Pte 21751 3rd Hussars
SWAIN Edward MM Sjt 10571 10/11th Highland Light Infantry KIA 23.4.17.
SWAIN Ernest MM Spr 134011 Royal Engineers
SWAIN F.G. MM Pte 17610 8th East Kent Regt
SWAIN George "DCM,MM+Bar" L/Cpl 22868 2nd Yorkshire Light Infantry
SWAIN George Edward MM Pte 12055 4th Middlesex Regt DOW 30.6.18.
SWAIN George W. MM Bdr 232704 A/51 Bde RFA
SWAIN Henry C. MM Pte 200060 1/1st London Regt
SWAIN Henry Edward MM Pte 9717 Machine Gun Corps
SWAIN Herbert MM Pte 10762 15th Hussars
SWAIN Herbert MM Pte 202936 North Staffordshire Regt
SWAIN James Herbert MM Cpl 1897 1/15th London Regt
SWAIN Richard MM L/Cpl 18412 Devonshire Regt
SWAIN Robert MM Sjt 147163 Royal Engineers
SWAIN Sidney MM Pte 17032 1st Grenadier Guards
SWAIN Thomas Boyer MM L/Cpl 5913 1/5th North Staffordshire Regt
SWAIN Thomas John MM Bdr 12747 23 Bde RFA
SWAIN Thomas S. MM Bdr 29683 Z/33 Med TM Bty RGA
SWAIN Walter MM Pte 260318 Monmouthshire
SWAIN William MM+Bar L/Sjt 18630 4th Bedfordshire Regt
SWAIN William MM Cpl 10627 5th Dorsetshire Regt
SWAIN or SWAINE William "MM,MID" Pte 2159 1/5th West Riding Regt
SWAINBANK William G. MM Pte 11/13792 11th Border Regt
SWAINE H.F. MM+Bar Sjt 20162 1st East Kent Regt
SWAINE Willie Barker MM+Bar Sjt 34647 RFA
SWAINE or SWAIN William "MM,MID" Pte 2159 1/5th West Riding Regt
SWAINSON James MM Pte 12614 9th Royal Welsh Fusiliers
SWAINSTON G. MM Pte 472863 12th London Regt
SWAINSTON John William MM Pte 320043 19th Durham Light Infantry
SWAINSTON Joseph MM L/Cpl 31853 Northumberland Fusiliers
SWAIT Aubrey Arthur MM Pte 448 London Div Cyc Coy Army Cyclist Corps
SWALE Fred MM L/Cpl 95003 128 Fd Coy Royal Engineers
SWALE Solomon MM Pte 241184 2/5th West Riding Regt DOW 21.10.18.
SWALES Alfred MM Sjt Wheeler 785026 150 Bde RFA
SWALES J.W. MM Cpl 240273 Yorkshire Regt
SWALES John MM L/Cpl 7503 2nd Yorkshire Regt
SWALES John W. MM L/Cpl 5171 Notts & Derby Regt
SWALES Percy V. MM Pte 4/8542 Durham Light Infantry
SWALES ReginaldA. MM L/Cpl 3524 13 Fd Amb RAMC
SWALLOW Edward MM Pte 8410 5th Northamptonshire Regt KIA 1.4.18.
SWALLOW Frank MM Sjt 242536 7th West Riding Regt
SWALLOW John W. MM L/Cpl 1645 18th West Yorkshire Regt
SWALLOW Jonathan MM Pte 242502 Lancashire Fusiliers
SWALLOW Leonard MM L/Cpl 46370 Royal Engineers
SWALLOW Richard MM Pte 13485 10th West Riding Regt
SWALLOW Ronald "MM,MID" Sjt 20044 Machine Gun Corps
SWALLOW Sidney MM Cpl 34759 11th Essex Regt KIA 17.9.18.
SWALLOW Walter MM Pte 62782 9th Yorkshire Light Infantry
SWALLOW Walter S. "DCM,MM+Bar" Cpl A/2271 9th King's Royal Rifle Corps
SWALLOW William MM CSM 15588 11th East Lancashire Regt
SWALLOW William I. MM Pte 2371 8th Royal Sussex Regt
SWALLOW Willie MM Spr 136330 251 Tunnelling Coy Royal Engineers
SWALWELL Anthony MM Pte 10588 9th Royal Fusiliers
SWALWELL Archibald Joseph MM Pte 2645 1/9th Durham Light Infantry
SWAN Alfred G. MM Cpl 197769 184 Tunnelling Coy Royal Engineers KIA 3.9.18.
SWAN Andrew C. MM Pte 3137 3 Fd Amb RAMC
SWAN David MM Pte 1158 1/7th Royal Highlanders
SWAN Ernest A. MM Pte 6527 4th Hussars
SWAN George MM Sjt 19776 RAMC
SWAN George MM Cpl 14170 8th Suffolk Regt
SWAN George MM Pte S/11312 9th Rifle Brigade
SWAN Harold Victor MM Dvr T4/111107 Army Service Corps
SWAN Henry Storey MM+Bar Bdr 19424 B/94 Bde RFA
SWAN James MM Sjt 1892 10th Arg & Suth Highlanders KIA 14.4.17.

SWAN James McP. MM L/Sjt 40084 Scottish Rifles
SWAN John MM Pte 303060 Arg & Suth Highlanders
SWAN L.S. MM L/Cpl 12794 1st Grenadier Guards
SWAN Noel A. MM Pte 722850 24th London Regt
SWAN Stanley Sterry MM Pte 202409 4th Royal Welsh Fusiliers
SWAN Thomas MM Pte 1371 16th Highland Light Infantry
SWAN Thomas Dennis MM L/Cpl 15831 32nd Royal Fusiliers KIA 7.10.16.
SWAN Thomas J. MM Cpl 465730 8 AA Searchight Section Royal Engineers
SWAN William MM Pte M2/148341 Army Service Corps
SWAN William MM L/Cpl P10503 Military Mounted Police
SWANBOROUGH Arthur F. MM Cpl 240991 8th Gloucestershire Regt
SWANBOROUGH George William MM L/Cpl 14825 26th Royal Fusiliers DOW 13.3.17.
SWANBOROUGH Walter MM Pte 10453 Wiltshire Regt
SWANN Albert J. MM Sjt 240559 1/5th Royal Lancaster Regt
SWANN Charles H. MM L/Cpl 20714 Machine Gun Corps
SWANN James A. MM Sjt 29479 RGA
SWANN R. MM 2nd Cpl 312406 Royal Engineers
SWANN Richard MM L/Cpl 306058 10th Royal Warwickshire Regt
SWANN Sidney W. MM Pte 151673 104th Bn Machine Gun Corps
SWANN Sydney Herbert MM Pte 5566 8th Royal West Surrey Regt KIA 21.3.18.
SWANNELL Harry MM+2 Bars Sjt 15083 2nd Bedfordshire Regt
SWANNELL Herbert E. MM Bdr 326414 RGA
SWANNELL Sidney A.D. MM Pte 4828 16th Lancers
SWANNICK Alfred Ernest MM Pte 86054 29th Bn Machine Gun Corps
SWANSBURY Charles MM Cpl 7965 2nd Royal Fusiliers KIA 4.9.18.
SWANSBURY Tom MM Pte 22273 1/4th Seaforth Highlanders
SWANSON Alfred MM Cpl 320930 1/6th London Regt
SWANSON Donald MM Pte 240723 1/5th Seaforth Highlanders
SWANSON Donald MM Sjt 10464 1st Scots Guards
SWANSON Henry MM Pte 292563 1/7th Royal Highlanders
SWANSON John MM Pte 275343 Royal Scots
SWANSON William MM Cpl 240504 1/5th Seaforth Highlanders
SWANSTON David MM L/Cpl 12935 1/5th Seaforth Highlanders
SWANSTON David Henry MM Pte 974 GMGR
SWANSTON David S. MM Pte 40030 Royal Scots
SWANSTON Gregorio Alexander MM Sjt 9380 11 Fd Coy Royal Engineers KIA 23.8.16.
SWANTON Michael MM Pte 3973 1st Royal Munster Fusiliers KIA 28.1.17.
SWANWICK Herbert MM Sjt 132705 232 Siege Bty RGA
SWAPP George "DCM,MM" Sjt 301337 25 Fd Amb RAMC
SWARBRICK Harold MM Sjt 305213 8th West Yorkshire Regt
SWARBRICK Harry MM 2nd Cpl 427986 Royal Engineers
SWARBRICK Harry MM Sjt 17571 Scottish Rifles
SWARBRICK William MM Cpl 25409 1st North Lancashire Regt
SWARBROOK William MM L/Xpl 9798 1st Leicestershire Regt
SWARFIELD William T.G. MM Sjt 200094 Royal West Surrey Regt
SWATMAN Edward MM Cpl 200679 1/4th East Yorkshire Regt
SWATTON Ernest Arthur "MM,CG(B)" Sjt 5611 88 Fd Amb RAMC
SWATTON Walter John "MM,CG(F)" Gnr 10260 71 Bde Ammn Col RFA
SWATTRIDGE George MM L/Cpl 39315 South Wales Borderers
SWEATMAN Thomas MM Spr 121541 185 Tunnelling Coy Royal Engineers
SWEDE Joseph MM Sjt 128057 RGA
SWEENEY Alfred MM Sjt 786257 RFA
SWEENEY Bernard MM CSM 65229 1st Northumberland Fusiliers
SWEENEY Claude MM Pte 2537 1/1st Hertfordshire Regt
SWEENEY Daniel MM Spr 6064 1 Siege Coy R Monmouth RE
SWEENEY Daniel MM Pte 16929 7/8th Royal Irish Fusiliers DOW 16.8.17.
SWEENEY Daniel MM Pte 9084 Irish Guards
SWEENEY Edward MM Pnr 69060 36 Div Sig Coy Royal Engineers
SWEENEY Eugene MM Cpl 15231 23 Siege Bty RGA
SWEENEY Francis MM Gnr 42919 RGA
SWEENEY J. MM+Bar L/Cpl 11221 Royal Irish Fusiliers
SWEENEY James M. MM Spr 46738 21 Div Sig Coy Royal Engineers
SWEENEY John MM Pte 11434 18th Highland Light Infantry DOW 22.10.18.
SWEENEY John MM Pte 10192 1st Royal Inniskilling Fusiliers
SWEENEY John MM Gnr 14641 88 Bde RFA KIA 4.11.18.
SWEENEY John MM Pte 8120 1st Irish Guards KIA 9.10.17.
SWEENEY Mathew MM Cpl 241461 1/6th Highland Light Infantry
SWEENEY Michael MM Pte 28142 Royal Inniskilling Fusiliers
SWEENEY Robert MM Pte 21779 1st Royal Scots Fusiliers KIA 3.5.17.
SWEENEY Thomas MM Pte 4164 13 Fd Amb RAMC
SWEENEY William MM Dvr 19750 D/317 Bde RFA
SWEET Albert E. MM Cpl 7844 RFA AKA Leslie TOMPKINS
SWEET Cecil A. MM Cpl MS/299 1 Div Ammn Park Army Service Corps
SWEET John MM Pte 242614 1/6th West Yorkshire Regt
SWEET Reginald William MM Pte 35773 6th Wiltshire Regt
SWEET Reuben Frederick MM Sjt 1634 1/1st Monmouthshire Regt
SWEET Samuel J. MM Sjt P1467 Military Foot Police
SWEET Thomas MM Pte 3/7108 1st Dorsetshire Regt
SWEET W.H. MM Sjt 636 Military Mounted Police att HQ 18 Inf Bde
SWEET William S. MM Cpl 25299 Royal Engineers
SWEETAPPLE F. MM Pte 202073 Dorsetshire Regt
SWEETING Ernest MM Sjt 48192 RAMC
SWEETING John George MM Pte 45797 RAMC
SWEETING Joseph MM+Bar Sjt 23294 2 Div Sig Coy Royal Engineers
SWEETING Sidney MM Gnr 75090 RGA
SWEETING Thomas W. MM Pte Z/2509 Rifle Brigade
SWEETING W.C. MM L/Sjt 5188 2nd Rifle Brigade
SWEETINGHAM James MM Bdr 111624 303 Siege Bty RGA
SWEETMAN Charles MM Cpl 60961 37 Bde RFA
SWEETMAN Patrick MM Pte 290 5th Royal Irish Regt
SWEETMAN Thomas MM Cpl 10526 9th Yorkshire Regt
SWEETMAN William T. MM+2 Bars Cpl 15816 RFA
SWEETZER Charles Edward MM Bdr 616089 20 Bde RHA
SWEETZER Frederick MM Pte 16064 Machine Gun Corps
SWETMAN Richard MM Dvr 951155 B/174 Bde RFA
SWIFT Charles MM L/Cpl 306187 1/6th Notts & Derby Regt
SWIFT Charles MM Pte 4/7617 9th West Yorkshire Regt
SWIFT Charles T. MM Pte S/5639 12th Rifle Brigade
SWIFT Charles William Hayward MM Sjt 99615 221 Army Troops Coy Royal Engineers
SWIFT Clifton MM Pte 29944 2nd Notts & Derby Regt
SWIFT Dan MM Pte 39681 1/1st Oxfordshire Yeomanry DOW 6.9.18.
SWIFT Douglas MM Sjt 12259 Royal Engineers
SWIFT Edward MM Pte 5250 7th Royal West Kent Regt
SWIFT Ernest Maurice MM Gnr 3504 2(South Midland)Bde RFA
SWIFT F.R. MM Sjt 42231 Yorkshire Light Infantry
SWIFT Frederick MM L/Cpl 1898 Seaforth Highlanders
SWIFT George MM L/Cpl R/911 1st King's Royal Rifle Corps
SWIFT George MM L/Cpl 36152 Notts & Derby Regt
SWIFT George MM Sjt 6917 1st South Staffordshire Regt KIA 26.10.17.
SWIFT George T. MM Sjt 9442 RFA
SWIFT Harold MM Pte 12291 8th Gloucestershire Regt
SWIFT Harold MM Pte 8800 1st Scots Guards
SWIFT Harold B. MM Pte 3217 7th Royal West Kent Regt
SWIFT Harry MM Pte 241375 1/5th York & Lancaster Regt
SWIFT Herbert MM Spr 504415 503 Fd Coy Royal Engineers
SWIFT Herbert MM Pte 21164 22nd Manchester Regt
SWIFT James MM Sjt 240572 Leicestershire Regt
SWIFT Joseph MM Pte 38059 10th Yorkshire Regt
SWIFT Patrick MM Pte 4/4364 5th Connaught Rangers
SWIFT Richard Neville MM Pte 305078 1/8th Royal Warwickshire Regt DOW 23.10.18.
SWIFT Robert MM L/Sjt 18143 1st Coldstream Guards
SWIFT Thomas MM L/Cpl 25909 1st Grenadier Guards
SWIFT Thomas Edward MM+Bar Pte 45302 South Wales Borderers
SWIFT Walter F. MM Dvr 86912 RFA
SWIFT William MM Spr 6336 Royal Engineers
SWIFT William C. MM+Bar Cpl 29597 6th West Riding Regt
SWIFT William J. MM Pte 780035 2nd London Regt
SWINBANK George MM Spr 563 Royal Engineers
SWINBURN Charles MM Pte 16104 1st Coldstream Guards
SWINBURN Thomas H. MM Cpl 522081 483 Fd Coy Royal Engineers
SWINBURNE John MM Cpl 10713 24 Hy Bty RGA
SWINBURNE R. MM Pte 6606 West Riding Regt
SWINCHATT Phillip Charles MM Cpl 283193 4th London Regt DOW 25.1.19.
SWINDALL Alfred MM Sjt 64087 RAMC
SWINDELL Francis James MM L/Cpl 3256 7th Royal West Kent Regt KIA 13.7.16.
SWINDELL Herbert MM Pte 201086 11th Notts & Derby Regt
SWINDELL James V. MM Sjt 10806 5th Royal Berkshire Regt

SWINDELLS Arthur MM Pte 17985 Royal Lancaster Regt
SWINDELLS Frederick Arthur MM L/Cpl 43567 Manchester Regt
SWINDELLS George W. MM Cpl 16490 RFA
SWINDELLS Joseph MM Cpl 18916 9th Cheshire Regt
SWINDELLS Samuel MM Gnr 92223 24 Hy Bty RGA
SWINDELLS Samuel MM Cpl 15207 8th South Lancashire Regt
SWINDELLS William MM Gnr 97668 RGA
SWINDEN Joseph C. MM Spr 488136 Royal Engineers
SWINDLEHURST John T. MM L/Cpl 37629 Yorkshire Light Infantry
SWINHOE John Thomas MM Dvr 83991 A/156 Bde RFA Died 5.11.18.
SWINHOE Joseph MM L/Cpl 60286 8th West Yorkshire Regt
SWINHOE William M. MM Pte 44941 2nd Yorkshire Regt
SWINLEY Archibald MM+Bar Cpl 635644 RFA
SWINNERTON Albert "MM,MID" Bdr 50527 RGA
SWINNEY Peter MM Gnr 97109 RFA
SWINSCOE Ernest MM Pte 536377 RAMC
SWINSON Ernest L. MM Spr 983 Royal Engineers
SWINSON William Albert MM Dvr 65650 RFA
SWINSTEAD Edgar MM Cpl 98239 284 Siege Bty RGA
SWINTON Albert Peter MM Pte 62974 1/6th West Yorkshire Regt
SWINYARD William MM+Bar Sjt 4680 Lancashire Fusiliers
SWINYARD William Edward MM Sjt 8609 1st Royal West Kent Regt
SWIRE Edward George MM Pte 8347 15th Hussars DOW 9.8.18.
SWITHENBANK James MM+Bar Gnr 5720 RFA
SWITHINBANK Harry L. MM 2nd Cpl 479756 Royal Engineers
SWITHINBANK William MM Pte 339209 RAMC
SWITZER Albert MM Gnr 81763 RFA
SWORDS Patrick MM Pte 12518 13th `
SYCAMORE Alfred MM L/Cpl 8251 11th Essex Regt KIA 23.9.16.
SYCAMORE George MM Pte 201107 Suffolk Regt
SYCAMORE Harry W. MM CQMS 680025 1/22nd London Regt
SYE Thomas B. MM Pte 337326 RAMC
SYER George M. MM Sjt 11685 Royal West Surrey Regt
SYKES A.R. "DCM,MM" Sjt 9986 1st Scottish Rifles
SYKES Archibald H. MM L/Cpl 12032 Durham Light Infantry
SYKES Arthur MM Cpl 307755 8th West Yorkshire Regt
SYKES Arthur MM Gnr 113248 200 Siege Bty RGA
SYKES Arthur MM Gnr 608309 RHA
SYKES Charles H. MM Sjt 26/645 Northumberland Fusiliers
SYKES E. MM L/Cpl 203012 Lancashire Fusiliers
SYKES Ernest MM Pte 201333 Tank Corps
SYKES Fred MM Pte 22/505 Durham Light Infantry
SYKES Fred MM Pte 242408 1/5th West Riding Regt KIA 6.10.17.
SYKES Frederick MM Dvr 800600 C/230 Bde RFA
SYKES George E. MM Cpl C/6316 King's Royal Rifle Corps
SYKES Harry MM Cpl 306019 5th West Riding Regt
SYKES Harry MM Sjt 2512 2nd Northumberland Fusiliers
SYKES Harry MM Sjt 14781 Yorkshire Light Infantry
SYKES Herbert MM Cpl 79053 Royal Engineers
SYKES Jacob L. MM Pte 265268 Seaforth Highlanders
SYKES James MM L/Cpl 52994 15th Cheshire Regt KIA 24.3.18.
SYKES James W. MM Pte 203539 West Riding Regt
SYKES Joe Harry MM Pte 20294 26th Royal Fusiliers
SYKES John MM Pte 305944 West Riding Regt
SYKES John MM Sjt 13829 9th Yorkshire Light Infantry KIA 1.7.16.
SYKES John T. MM Pte 20/455 Durham Light Infantry
SYKES John T. MM Bdr 776338 RFA
SYKES John W. MM Pte 202481 Manchester Regt
SYKES Joseph MM Dvr 7322 RFA
SYKES Joseph MM Cpl 2791 8 Fd Amb RAMC
SYKES Samuel MM Bdr 68393 166 Siege Bty RGA
SYKES Walter J. MM Sjt 5037 5(Cav)Fd Amb RAMC
SYKES Walter P. MM Sjt 915606 4 Bde RFA
SYKES William MM Pte 38356 1/4th Yorkshire Light Infantry
SYKES William J. MM Cpl 18029 'P' Cable Section Royal Engineers
SYKES William K. MM L/Sjt 16034 10tth West Yorkshire Regt
SYLVESTER Albert G. MM Pte M2/229974 Army Service Corps
SYLVESTER Charles H. MM Sjt 265162 Royal Warwickshire Regt
SYLVESTER Ernest MM Bdr 756161 A/251 Bde RFA
SYLVESTER Frederick A. MM Sjt 14088 Machine Gun Corps
SYLVESTER John MM Pte 3/8276 1st Dorsetshire Regt
SYLVESTER Sydney MM Cpl 1129 10th Royal Fusiliers
SYLVESTER William MM L/Cpl 26823 Wiltshire Regt
SYLVESTER William MM Pte 240265 Lincolnshire Regt
SYM James MM S/Sjt Fitter 146692 RGA
SYME Alexander George MM Sjt 7460 Scots Guards
SYME David MM Sjt 290747 Royal Highlanders DOW 4.7.18.
SYME Peter MM Cpl 14242 7/8th King's Own Scottish Borderers
SYME Robert MM Pte 277406 1/7th Arg & Suth Highlanders DOW 25.7.18.

SYME Thomas MM Pte 20922 1st King's Own Scottish Borderers
SYMERS Charles MM Pte 43851 Royal Scots
SYMES Edward MM Sjt 16335 'L' Corps Sig Coy Royal Engineers
SYMES Herbert John MM Spr 257577 30 Broad Gauge Rly Coy Royal Engineers
SYMES Hubert S.O. MM L/Cpl 165640 1/1st North Somerset Yeomanry
SYMES William MM Cpl 3900 1/13th` London Regt
SYMINGTON Albert G. MM Pte 27787 1st King's Own Scottish Borderers
SYMINGTON Harold Gold MM Cpl 7256 6th Somerset Light Infantry Died 17.10.18.
SYMINGTON Joseph MM Pte 265361 1/7th Scottish Rifles
SYMINGTON Robert MM Dvr 120630 RFA
SYMKISS Frederick MM Sjt 61600 10th Royal Fusiliers
SYMMONDS Albert MM Spr 47389 6 Div Sig Coy Royal Engineers
SYMMONDS Joseph MM Sjt 26527 18 Div Ammn Col RFA
SYMMONS Leslie R. MM Pte 99119 11th Royal Fusiliers
SYMMS John T. MM Sjt 9630 10th Lancashire Fusiliers
SYMON J. MM L/Sjt 265503 6th Royal Highlanders
SYMONDS Albert E. MM Dvr 2844 3 Fd Sqn Royal Engineers
SYMONDS Charles Francis MM Cpl 121143 RGA
SYMONDS Ernest Henry MM Gnr 25011 83 Bde RFA KIA 30.10.17.
SYMONDS Frank MM Sjt 6177 14 Bde RHA
SYMONDS Frederick George "DCM,MM+Bar,MID" Sjt 15792 Norfolk Regt KIA 22.10.17.
SYMONDS Henry MM Pte 10511 2nd Coldstream Guards KIA 27.9.18.
SYMONDS John Bertram "DCM,MM" L/Cpl 235989 1/1st Herefordshire Regt KIA 23.7.18.
SYMONDS Thomas MM Sjt 16708 2nd Duke of Cornwall's LI
SYMONDS Thomas MM Pte 235716 1/1st Herefordshire Regt
SYMONDS William MM Sjt 4252 2/6th West Yorkshire Regt
SYMONDS William MM L/Cpl 45232 Machine Gun Corps
SYMONDS William MM Sjt 6137 RFA
SYMONS Ernest C. MM Pte 25461 10th Duke of Cornwall's LI
SYMONS H. MM L/Cpl 538285 RAMC
SYMONS John MM Pte 14/962 6th York & Lancaster Regt KIA 16.8.17.
SYMONS John H. MM Sjt 7751 1st Duke of Cornwall's LI
SYMONS Lawrence MM Pte 2368 2 Fd Amb RAMC
SYMONS Leslie "DCM,MM" Sjt C/7504 King's Royal Rifle Corps
SYMONS Leslie MM L/Cpl 29757 1st Wiltshire Regt
SYMONS Sidney MM Pte B/201820 2/8th London Regt
SYMONS Stanley MM Dvr 955092 C/236 Bde RFA
SYMS William MM Cpl 235099 8th Royal Lancaster Regt
SYNOTT Daniel MM L/Cpl 3622 2nd Leinster Regt KIA 23.3.18.
SYNOTT Patrick MM Pte 13329 13th Liverpool Regt
SYRETT Charles MM Pte 1738 2nd Manchester Regt KIA 4.11.18.
SYRETT Harry MM Pte 9338 2nd Royal Berkshire Regt KIA 16.8.17.
SYSON Sidney MM Gnr 38909 RGA

T

TAAFFE Lawrence MM Pte 8491 Royal Irish Regt
TAAFFE Thomas MM L/Cpl 63872 RAMC
TABBERER Edwin Mitchell MM Pte M2/139235 Army Service Corps att 'H' AA Bty RGA.
TABBERER John MM Gnr 116822 B/95 Bde RFA
TABER James MM Pte 6130 6th Royal West Kent Regt DOW 5.8.17.
TABER John E. MM L/Cpl 894 6th Royal West Kent Regt
TABERSHAM Alfred J. MM Sjt 316112 1/1(East Anglian)Hy Bty RGA
TABOR Benjamin H. MM Pte 2429 1/1st Cambridgeshire Regt
TABOR Charles David "MC,MM(46133 Bdr)" 2Lt 3 Siege Bty RGA
TABOR H.T. MM AM2 7754 Royal Flying Corps
TABOR Horace MM L/Cpl 2568 1/1st Cambridgeshire Regt
TABOR William C. MM+Bar Pte 617 17th Middlesex Regt
TABRETT Horace Edwin MM Bdr 47204 59 Siege Bty RGA Died 4.11.18.
TABRUM Cyril R. MM Pte 331020 Lancashire Fusiliers
TACE Frank "MC,MM(A/354 Sjt)" 2Lt 2nd King's Royal Rifle Corps
TACEY Wallace H. MM Pte 267352 Notts & Derby Regt
TACK Eldred William "DCM,MM" CSM 13104 6th Northamptonshire Regt KIA 18.9.18.
TACK William MM Sjt 200024 1/7th Middlesex Regt
TADGELL George A. MM Pte 30199 7th Royal West Surrey Regt
TAFFINDER Albert E. "MM,MID" L/Cpl 11232 2nd Welsh Regt

TAFFS A. MM Cpl 40429 Machine Gun Corps(Heavy Branch)
TAFT Harry MM Spr 51911 12 Div Sig Coy Royal Engineers
TAFT Norman MM Sjt 37624 1st Royal Berkshire Regt
TAFT Samuel MM Pte 267563 Northumberland Fusiliers
TAGG Arthur E. MM Gnr 26860 RGA
TAGG Edward G. MM Dmr 2149 1/6th Seaforth Highlanders
TAGG Edwin MM Pte M2/152323 7 Lt Armd Car Patrol Army Service Corps
TAGGART Albert E. MM Cpl 33769 1st Cheshire Regt
TAGGART George C. MM L/Cpl 30678 Highland Light Infantry
TAGGART J. MM Pte 4523 1/6th Arg & Suth Highlanders
TAGGART James MM Sjt 200262 5/6th Scottish Rifles
TAGGART Patrick MM Cpl 11006 2nd Highland Light Infantry
TAGGART Richard MM L/Cpl 6580 2nd South Lancashire Regt
TAGGART Thomas MM Pte 21127 7th Royal West Kent Regt
TAGGART Thomas MM Pte 6957 1st Scots Guards
TAGUE Hugh MM Pte 18191 17th Liverpool Regt
TAGUE James MM Cpl 25/1307 Northumberland Fusiliers
TAILBY William Henry MM Pte 70958 Notts & Derby Regt
TAILFORD Ralph MM Pte 271073 1/1st Worcestershire Yeo
TAINTON John W. MM L/Cpl 240285 Worcestershire Regt
TAIT Alexander Grieve MM Bdr 118670 193 Siege Bty RGA
TAIT Andrew MM Pte M2/048968 8 Motor Amb Convoy Army Service Corps
TAIT Andrew J. MM+Bar S/Sjt 58097 RAMC
TAIT Charles Herbert MM Sjt 74410 5 Bty 45 Bde RFA
TAIT George MM Dvr 1547 RFA Died 28.10.18.
TAIT George MM Pte 20284 Durham Light Infantry
TAIT George MM Pte 16224 7th Border Regt
TAIT Harry "DCM,MM" CSM 9270 7th Seaforth Highlanders
TAIT Henry MM L/Cpl 8592 2nd Dragoons
TAIT Hugh B. MM Sjt 31005 Royal Welsh Fusiliers
TAIT J.S. MM Pte 5573 Royal Highlanders
TAIT James MM Pte 250113 5/6th Royal Scots
TAIT James MM Pte 34470 Royal Scots
TAIT James MM Sjt 611 1/1st Lothian & Border Horse Yeo
TAIT James J.S. MM Pnr 126462 Royal Engineers
TAIT John MM Cpl 20526 26 Coy 9th Bn Machine Gun Corps
TAIT John "DCM,MM" CSM 13316 11th Royal Scots
TAIT John "MM,MID" Sjt 785 Royal Anglesey Royal Engineers Died 9.7.18.
TAIT John MM Pte 45887 12th Durham Light Infantry
TAIT John MM L/Cpl 4580 Machine Gun Corps
TAIT Joseph Birnie MM Sjt 19500 Royal Engineers
TAIT Mark MM+Bar Bdr 7482 Y/18 Med TM Bty RFA KIA 21.3.18.
TAIT Robert A. MM(2116 Pte London Regt)+Bar Cpl 76952 Machine Gun Corps(Heavy Branch)
TAIT Robert E. MM Sjt 20102 Northumberland Fusiliers
TAIT Thomas "DCM,MM" CSM 14613 8th Royal Dublin Fusiliers
TAIT Walter MM Dvr 635758 B/256 Bde RFA
TAIT William C. MM Cpl 11241 4th Middlesex Regt
TAIT William T. MM CSM 3/8858 9th Yorkshire Regt
TALBOT A. MM Pte 44200 7th Gordon Highlanders
TALBOT Arthur MM Sjt 30760 110 Heavy Bty RGA
TALBOT Charles R. MM Pte 51114 12th Royal Scots
TALBOT Edward MM Sjt 21692 Manchester Regt
TALBOT Frank T. MM+Bar Pte 10996 13th Royal Fusiliers
TALBOT Frederick Stephen "MM,CG(B)" Pte 31273 13th York & Lancaster Regt
TALBOT George MM Sjt 13688 5th Oxf & Bucks Light Infantry
TALBOT Harold W. MM L/Bdr 57979 RFA
TALBOT Herbert MM Sjt 8927 2nd Northamptonshire Regt
TALBOT Horace MM Pte 268178 2nd West Yorkshire Regt Died 21.10.18.
TALBOT John MM Cpl 5500 1st Dragoon Guards
TALBOT Joseph MM Pte 45857 2nd Yorkshire Regt
TALBOT Noah MM Pte 307334 5th West Riding Regt
TALBOT Samuel MM Sjt 21730 18th Lancashire Fusiliers
TALBOT Thomas MM Cpl 44 RGA
TALBOT Wilfred H. MM Pte 7759 Royal West Kent Regt
TALBOT William MM Pte 10334 1st Notts & Derby Regt
TALBOT William E. MM Pte 18108 11th Notts & Derby Regt
TALBOTT Thomas W. MM L/Cpl 14999 6th Yorkshire Regt
TALBOYS Harold L. MM Cpl 4226 1st Rifle Brigade
TALL George John MM L/Cpl 11408 5th Wiltshire Regt
TALL Stewart Joel MM Pte 240893 1/5th Devonshire Regt
TALLANTINE Sidney MM L/Sjt 14461 1st Coldstream Guards
TALLENT H.F. MM L/Cpl 43623 1st Essex Regt
TALLENTIRE Thomas MM L/Cpl 25033 Durham Light Infantry
TALLINTIRE John MM Pte 285104 Seaforth Highlanders

TALLIS Thomas MM Sjt 266504 7th Royal Warwickshire Regt
TALLIS William MM Pte 201825 1st Royal Warwickshire Regt
TALLOWIN William Edward MM+Bar Bdr 20382 Z/1 Med TM Bty RGA
TAMBLIN W.H. "DCM,MM" Cpl 957 6th East Kent Regt
TAMBLIN or TAMBLAN Reginald E.J. MM L/Sjt 8195 Devonshire Regt
TAMBLYN William E. MM Pte 202327 7th Duke of Cornwall's LI
TAME George Cecil MM Pte 285575 1/1st Oxfordshire Yeomanry
TAME George H. MM L/Sjt 240616 1/6th South Staffordshire Regt
TAME James MM Pte 34380 23rd Middlesex Regt
TAMLYN William J. MM Pte 204598 23rd Middlesex Regt
TAMPLIN Aneurin MM Pte 73209 14th Royal Welsh Fusiliers
TAMPLIN George Frederick MM+Bar Sjt 680740 1/22nd London Regt KIA 22.8.18.
TAMPLIN Thomas MM Pte 34667 3rd Worcestershire Regt
TAMPLIN William E. MM Pte 15183 1st South Wales Borderers
TAMS Frank MM Sjt 8885 1st North Staffordshire Regt
TAMS James MM Gnr 805224 A/231 Bde RFA
TAMS James MM Cpl 7360 Machine Gun Corps
TANCRED Joseph MM Pte 2859 1st Manchester Regt
TANCRED Peter MM Pte 2077 1/5th Liverpool Regt
TANDEY Henry "VC,DCM,MM,MID" Pte 34506 1/5th West Riding Regt
TANDY Charles MM Pte 4374 11th Lancashire Fusiliers KIA 25.3.18.
TANDY Frederick MM Sjt 200437 1st London Regt
TANDY John R. MM Cpl 12432 3rd Middlesex Regt
TANDY Robert MM Pte 3818 2nd Notts & Derby Regt
TANDY Stanley F. MM Sjt 940254 D/293 Bde RFA
TANDY Thomas E. MM Pte 49873 13th West Riding Regt
TANDY William A. MM Spr 492148 Royal Engineers
TANFIELD Frank MM L/Cpl 12176 7th East Yorkshire Regt
TANK Ellis M. MM Sjt 290533 Royal Welsh Fusiliers
TANK Richard MM 2nd Cpl 78643 Royal Engineers
TANKARD John William MM Gnr 6128 D/246 Bde RFA
TANKE Frederick Edmund MM Pte M2/200208 Army Service Corps att RGA.
TANN John W. "DCM,MM" Sjt 16040 Machine Gun Corps
TANN Ronald W.C. MM Sjt 43586 Machine Gun Corps
TANNAHILL Harry MM Cpl 19791 11th Royal Irish Rifles
TANNER Albert MM Pte 29749 East Yorkshire Regt
TANNER Albert E. MM Pte 9713 1st Royal Fusiliers
TANNER Andrew MM Pte 364395 RAMC
TANNER Arthur R. MM L/Sjt S/30465 Rifle Brigade
TANNER Charles H. MM Sjt 68803 23rd Bn Royal Fusiliers
TANNER Clement "MM,MID" CSM 1647 Liverpool Regt
TANNER Edward MM Pte 145 1st Welsh Guards
TANNER Edward C. "DCM,MM" L/Cpl 241535 1/6th Notts & Derby Regt KIA 5.11.18.
TANNER Frank MM L/Cpl 38682 Yorkshire Light Infantry
TANNER Frederick George MM Sjt 22183 RFA
TANNER Frederick W. MM Pte 74269 138 Fd Amb RAMC
TANNER George MM Sjt SE/11042 Army Veterinary Corps
TANNER George N. MM Pte 457407 RAMC
TANNER Henry MM Pte 30587 Welsh Regt
TANNER Henry J. MM Pte 22335 5th Royal Berkshire Regt
TANNER James T. MM+Bar L/Cpl 10987 East Lancashire Regt
TANNER John H. MM Bdr 37763 RFA
TANNER Norman R. MM Pte 356372 10th Liverpool Regt
TANNER Oscar Barrett MM L/Cpl 56583 Welsh Regt KIA 14.4.18.
TANNER Percy MM Bdr 100821 RGA
TANNER Percy Edgar MM L/Cpl 18999 37 Coy Machine Gun Corps KIA 3.5.17.
TANNER Stephen MM Gnr 101968 RGA
TANNER William G.F. MM Cpl 43690 41 Div Ammn Col RFA
TANNICK or TANNOCK Thomas Neil MM Sjt M2/048179 593 Coy Army Service Corps
TANNOCK Andrew MM Pte 53671 Royal Scots Fusiliers
TANNOCK David MM Pte 350669 18th Highland Light Infantry
TANNOCK J. MM Pte 240070 Scottish Rifles
TANSER James W. MM L/Cpl 1832 20th Hussars
TANSEY John P. MM Pte 612625 2/19th London Regt
TANSLEY Bertram Cameron MM Cpl 9743 71 Bde RFA
TANSLEY Charles MM Pte 41602 Middlesex Regt
TANSLEY Frederick W. MM Sjt 69717 195 Siege Bty RGA
TANSLEY John H. MM Sjt 625432 HAC(Arty)
TANSON Harry MM L/Cpl 21677 15th Hampshire Regt att HQ 41 Div
TANT W. "DCM,MM" Sjt 15546 11th Essex Regt
TANTON Herbert MM+Bar Pte 508435 RAMC att HAC.

TAPER Arthur John MM Sjt 240303 1/5th Duke of Cornwall's LI
TAPHOUSE George Frederick MM Sjt M2/020432 Army Service Corps
TAPLEY Elgar MM+Bar Pte 26557 7th East Kent Regt
TAPLIN Charles E. MM L/Cpl 12725 Royal Sussex Regt
TAPLIN George Henry MM L/Cpl 17981 Hampshire Regt
TAPLIN John G.M. MM Sjt 240473 5th Gloucestershire Regt
TAPLIN Walter MM Sjt 200273 1/4th Gloucestershire Regt
TAPLIN William MM Cpl 9746 2nd Royal Irish Rifles
TAPNER Arthur MM Pte 1701 2nd Royal Sussex Regt DOW 21.10.18.
TAPNER Henry G. MM Sjt 53157 B/95 Bde RFA
TAPP George MM Bdr 45685 37 Bde RFA
TAPP George MM L/Cpl 8650 1st Royal Lancaster Regt
TAPP John T. MM Sjt 2019 South Lancashire Regt
TAPP Thomas MM L/Sjt 13279 2nd Grenadier Guards
TAPP William J. MM Sjt 5450 12 Fd Amb RAMC
TAPPENDEN Fred MM Pte 202815 2/4th Hampshire Regt
TAPPENDEN William Albert MM Bdr 28522 A/109 Bde RFA
TAPPER D. MM Pte 435306 RAMC
TAPPIN Edward L.C. MM Pte 130856 45th Royal Fusiliers
TAPPIN Sidney MM Bdr 18918 B/79 Bde RFA
TAPPING William MM Sjt 265883 2nd Middlesex Regt
TAPPOLET Ernest MM Pte 6369 9 Fd Amb RAMC
TAPSELL William Algernon "DCM+Bar,MM" Sjt 8624 2nd Lincolnshire Regt DOW 18.9.18.
TAPSFIELD Walter J. MM L/Cpl 630071 20th London Regt
TARBARD Bertie MM Sjt 6601 RFA
TARBATH Albert James MM Spr 152097 11 Div Sig Coy Royal Engineers
TARBET Robert MM Sjt 41382 RAMC
TARBIN Alfred MM Cpl 15097 2nd Suffolk Regt
TARBOTTON Walter MM Pte A/204027 17th King's Royal Rifle Corps
TARBOX Albert F. MM Sjt 28482 8th Somerset Light Infantry
TARGETT Cecil F. MM+Bar Cpl 74211 56 Div Sig Coy Royal Engineers
TARLING George E. MM Gnr 73182 100 Bty 31 Bde RFA
TARLTON Albert Norman MM Sjt 55023 24th Royal Fusiliers
TARLTON Alfred Victor MM Sjt 46965 57th Bn Machine Gun Corps
TARLTON Arthur Philip MM L/Cpl 2533 13th York & Lancaster Regt
TARN George B. MM Pte 22/379 22nd Durham Light Infantry
TARNEY Patrick MM L/Sjt 419736 54 Coy Labour Corps
TARPEY Bernard James MM BSM 710 61 Div Ammn Col RFA KIA 12.9.17.
TARR Albert A. MM Pte 16694 8th Northumberland Fusiliers
TARR Charles MM L/Cpl 494470 438 Fd Coy Royal Engineers
TARR James "DCM,MM" Sjt 570065 1/17th London Regt
TARR William Robert MM L/Sjt 650659 1/21st London Regt DOW 1.9.18.
TARRAN William MM Pte 36065 Yorkshire Light Infantry
TARRANT Albert MM L/Sjt 305 Royal Sussex Regt
TARRANT Ernest E. MM Pte 321650 6th London Regt
TARRANT Frank L. MM Dmr 231815 2nd London Regt
TARRANT George MM L/Cpl 121596 179 Tunnelling Coy Royal Engineers
TARRANT George Henry MM Sjt 19155 9th Norfolk Regt KIA 28.4.17.
TARRANT John MM Sjt 240725 2/8th Worcestershire Regt KIA 3.12.17.
TARRANT Sidney J. MM Spr 28544 1 Div Sig Coy Royal Engineers
TARRANT Thomas W. MM Pte 36612 4th Worcestershire Regt
TARRIER Percy C. MM L/Cpl 97500 153 Fd Coy Royal Engineers
TARRING Frank W. MM Gnr 5078 RFA
TARRY Arthur John William MM Gnr 2256 'F' Bn Tank Corps
TARRY Frederick T. "MM+Bar,MID" Sjt 4299 6th Royal West Kent Regt
TARRY Sidney MM L/Bdr 22672 RFA
TARRY Walter MM Pte 331100 1/8th Hampshire Regt
TART Leonard MM Pte 200203 1/4th Shropshire Light Infantry
TART Richard Thomas MM Pte 14680 2nd Arg & Suth Highlanders KIA 16.4.18.
TARVER James MM Pte 6069 1st North Staffordshire Regt
TASKER Charles H. MM Pte 41825 1st Royal Irish Fusiliers
TASKER John MM Dvr 93336 129 Bty 42 Bde RFA
TASKER John MM Gnr 80153 RFA
TASKER John MM L/Cpl 26659 Machine Gun Corps
TASKER John William MM+Bar Sjt 44329 106 Coy Machine Gun Corps
TASKER Joseph Henry MM Pte 14319 2nd Bedfordshire Regt KIA 20.9.17.
TASKER Thomas W. MM Pte 14527 Royal West Kent Regt
TASKER William MM BQMS 820983 RFA
TASSART Albert MM L/Cpl 373104 8th London Regt
TATAM Alfred MM Sjt 592321 1/18th London Regt KIA 29.11.17.
TATAR Labud MM Pte 70480 9th Royal Fusiliers
TATCHELL Arthur MM Gnr 69878 RFA
TATE Arthur MM Pte M2/081147 Army Service Corps
TATE Arthur R. MM Pte 52287 Royal Fusiliers
TATE Basil MM Pte 36197 South Staffordshire Regt
TATE George MM Pte 17/1028 2nd Northumberland Fusiliers
TATE George MM Gnr 63736 RFA
TATE Henry MM Cpl 13605 RGA
TATE Henry John MM Sjt 69739 133 Army Troops Coy Royal Engineers
TATE Herbert MM Sjt 955 Royal Engineers
TATE Jack "DCM,MM" Sjt 19171 19th Bn Machine Gun Corps
TATE John MM Bdr 751546 RFA
TATE John Davey MM Sjt 2440 Army Cyclist Corps
TATE John R. MM Spr 120952 218 Fd Coy Royal Engineers
TATE Moses MM Pte 9477 69 Coy Machine Gun Corps
TATE Thomas MM Pte 44926 4th York & Lancaster Regt
TATE Victor F. MM Bdr 374389 RGA
TATESON Charles H. MM L/Cpl 42202 Yorkshire Light Infantry
TATHAM E. MM Pte 4638 Royal West Surrey Regt
TATHAM Frederick MM Cpl 238083 6th Leicestershire Regt
TATHAM William Michael MM Cpl 15613 1st Middlesex Regt
TATT Leonard MM L/Sjt S/5684 Rifle Brigade
TATTERSALL Bert MM Pte 306024 2/8th Liverpool Regt KIA 11.1.18.
TATTERSALL Charles H. "DCM,MM(425057 L?Cpl Lab C),MMV(It)" Cpl 17761 2nd Border Regt
TATTERSALL Eric MM L/Sjt 201917 1st East Lancashire Regt
TATTERSALL F.C. MM Pte 651757 London Regt
TATTERSALL George MM Pte R/14514 13th King's Royal Rifle Corps
TATTERSALL Harold MM L/Cpl 32610 5th Royal Lancaster Regt
TATTERSALL Joseph MM Cpl 25618 Border Regt
TATTERSALL Ronald C. MM Cpl 88981 41st Bn Machine Gun Corps
TATTERSALL Wright MM Dvr T/313099 18 Army Aux Horse Coy Army Service Corps
TATTERTON William MM Pte 45202 1/5th London Regt KIA 5.11.18.
TATTON Bertie MM Pte 1918 9th Royal Warwickshire Regt
TAUNT Wilfred E. MM Pte 1551 1/12th London Regt
TAUNTON Albert MM Spr 16848 1st Pontoon Park Royal Engineers
TAVANYAR Lionel A. MM Dvr 98101 A/58 Bde RFA
TAVENER Ernest J. MM Pnr 233478 47 Div Sig Coy Royal Engineers
TAVENER Wallace MM Pte 608670 18th London Regt
TAVERNER George MM Pte 345390 16th Devonshire Regt
TAVERNER Herbert G. MM Cpl 20444 Somerset Light Infantry
TAVERNER William MM Pte 7702 Royal Fusiliers
TAWSE Charles MM Pte 1436 RAMC
TAYLER A.J. MM L/Sjt 240490 Middlesex Regt
TAYLOR A. MM Pte 12209 9th Essex Regt
TAYLOR A.G.E. MM CSM 9879 4th Royal Fusiliers
TAYLOR A.H. MM Sjt P80 Military Mounted Police
TAYLOR A.J. MM Sjt 10651 9th Essex Regt
TAYLOR A.J. MM Sjt 7648 RFA
TAYLOR Albert MM L/Cpl 13633 8th West Yorkshire Regt
TAYLOR Albert MM Pte 705772 23rd London Regt
TAYLOR Albert MM L/Bdr 39677 A/150 Bde RFA
TAYLOR Albert MM Pte 22712 Worcestershire Regt
TAYLOR Albert MM Pte 7710 2nd Worcestershire Regt
TAYLOR Albert MM Pte 341371 RAMC
TAYLOR Albert MM Sjt 10224 2nd Seaforth Highlanders
TAYLOR Albert MM Dvr 92264 RFA
TAYLOR Albert Arthur MM BQMS 2735 46 Bty 39 Bde RFA
TAYLOR Albert C. MM L/Cpl 127176 37th Bn Machine Gun Corps
TAYLOR Albert C. MM Sjt 820043 RFA
TAYLOR Albert E. MM Pte 206044 5th Devonshire Regt
TAYLOR Albert Ernest MM Cpl 8485 2nd C Coy Lincolnshire Regt KIA 31.7.17.
TAYLOR Albert John MM Pte 46336 RAMC
TAYLOR Albert R. MM Bdr 57690 RFA
TAYLOR Albert Victor MM Sjt 23680 Notts & Derby Regt
TAYLOR Albert Victor MM Pte 3488 1/4th Royal Lancaster Regt DOW 16.4.18.
TAYLOR Albert W. MM Pte 21550 Royal West Surrey Regt
TAYLOR Alexander MM Pte 235191 9th Scottish Rifles

TAYLOR Alexander MM Pte 14735 Royal Inniskilling Fusiliers
TAYLOR Alexander MM Sjt 12589 10th West Yorkshire Regt KIA 23.4.17.
TAYLOR Alexander J.S. MM Dvr 218197 5 Div Ammn Col RFA
TAYLOR Alexander L. MM Pte 20217 Machine Gun Corps
TAYLOR Alexander Leighton MM L/Sjt 7265 2nd Scots Guards
TAYLOR Alfred MM Sjt 200122 1/4th Lincolnshire Regt
TAYLOR Alfred MM Pte 71513 Machine Gun Corps
TAYLOR Alfred MM Sjt 26400 13th Liverpool Regt
TAYLOR Alfred MM Gnr 54708 'N' Bty RHA
TAYLOR Alfred MM S/Sjt Fitter 51720 'L' Bty RHA KIA 15.6.17.
TAYLOR Alfred MM Dvr 88960 RFA
TAYLOR Alfred MM Dvr 750652 RFA
TAYLOR Alfred MM Pte 13/1142 13th York & Lancaster Regt
TAYLOR Alfred MM Sjt 31829 RFA
TAYLOR Alfred Cecil MM L/Sjt 1365 1/15th London Regt
TAYLOR Alfred T. MM Dvr 13517 37 Bde RFA
TAYLOR Alfred W. MM Gnr 154301 RGA
TAYLOR Allan MM Gnr 129762 113 Heavy Bty RGA
TAYLOR Andrew MM Pte 240341 1/6th Highland Light Infantry
TAYLOR Archibald MM Pte 305271 RAMC
TAYLOR Archibald MM Pte 301260 RAMC
TAYLOR Arthur MM Pte 16210 Leicestershire Regt
TAYLOR Arthur MM Gnr 190085 RFA
TAYLOR Arthur MM Pte 50392 11th Royal Scots
TAYLOR Arthur MM Pte 11789 1/5th Seaforth Highlanders
TAYLOR Arthur MM Pte 13287 X Corps Cyclist Bn Army Cyclist Corps
TAYLOR Arthur MM Cpl 53398 57th Bn Machine Gun Corps
TAYLOR Arthur MM Sjt 20416 6th Dragoon Guards
TAYLOR Arthur MM Pte 15602 9th Northumberland Fusiliers
TAYLOR Arthur MM Cpl 595 1/5th Notts & Derby Regt
TAYLOR Arthur MM Cpl 27520 Royal Berkshire Regt
TAYLOR Arthur MM Cpl 265090 1/7th Royal Warwickshire Regt
TAYLOR Arthur MM L/Bdr 98931 RFA
TAYLOR Arthur C. MM Pte 17375 Royal Sussex Regt
TAYLOR Arthur J. MM Pte 2089 9th East Surrey Regt
TAYLOR Arthur J. MM Pte 10294 2nd Worcestershire Regt
TAYLOR Arthur L. MM Pte 4670 6th London Regt
TAYLOR Arthur P. MM L/Cpl 17034 14th Royal Irish Rifles
TAYLOR Arthur Valentine "DCM,MM" Sjt 201837 122 Heavy Bty RGA
TAYLOR Arthur W. MM Sjt 61223 RAMC
TAYLOR Arthur W. MM L/Cpl 10241 1st Shropshire Light Infantry
TAYLOR Augustus R. MM+Bar Sjt 3555 D/121 Bde RFA
TAYLOR Bamford MM+Bar Cpl 282190 7th Lancashire Fusiliers
TAYLOR Ben MM Pte 18292 17th Lancashire Fusiliers KIA 14.10.18.
TAYLOR Benjamin MM Pte 19478 South Staffordshire Regt
TAYLOR Benjamin J. MM Pte 420665 10th London Regt
TAYLOR Benjamin N. MM Gnr 189806 238 Siege Bty RGA
TAYLOR Benjamin W. MM Gnr 64591 RGA
TAYLOR Bernard MM Pte 240438 1/6th Notts & Derby Regt KIA 13.8.18.
TAYLOR Bernard MM Sjt 476333 7 Foreway Coy Royal Engineers
TAYLOR Bernard A. MM Cpl 8778 2nd Royal West Surrey Regt
TAYLOR Bert MM Sjt 9534 5th Wiltshire Regt
TAYLOR Bertie MM L/Cpl 5233 1st East Kent Regt
TAYLOR Bertie T. MM Cpl 552646 16th London Regt
TAYLOR C. MM Pte 301085 89 Fd Amb RAMC
TAYLOR C.H. "MM,CG(B)" CSM 7760 2nd Essex Regt
TAYLOR Cecil A. MM Sjt 15156 Royal West Kent Regt
TAYLOR Charles MM Pte 252323 1/6th Arg & Suth Highlanders
TAYLOR Charles MM Pte 38000 Machine Gun Corps
TAYLOR Charles MM L/Cpl 27983 1st Royal Lancaster Regt DOW 3.9.18.
TAYLOR Charles MM Pte 24655 Shropshire Light Infantry
TAYLOR Charles MM Pte Z/2161 Rifle Brigade
TAYLOR Charles MM Dvr 1349 RFA
TAYLOR Charles MM Sjt 6599 47th Bn Machine Gun Corps
TAYLOR Charles MM Gnr 66619 11 Bde RFA
TAYLOR Charles A. MM+Bar L/Cpl 19517 Norfolk Regt
TAYLOR Charles F.M. MM Sjt 58470 RAMC
TAYLOR Charles H. MM L/Cpl 6746 9th Gordon Highlanders
TAYLOR Charles H. MM Sjt 25283 C/34 Bde RFA
TAYLOR Charles K. MM Dvr 59520 B/15 Bde RHA
TAYLOR Charles L. MM Sjt 85 19th Durham Light Infantry
TAYLOR Charles Percy MM L/Cpl 14481 3rd Coldstream Guards Died 13.4.18.
TAYLOR Charles R. MM Pte 53634 Welsh Regt

TAYLOR Charles S. MM Sjt 10217 1st Shropshire Light Infantry
TAYLOR Charles Samuel MM Sjt 230391 1/2nd London Regt DOW 17.9.18.
TAYLOR Charles T. MM Sjt 87413 33rd Bn Machine Gun Corps
TAYLOR Charles W. MM Sjt 204241 1/1st Hertfordshire Regt
TAYLOR Charles W. MM Pte 7619 Royal West Surrey Regt
TAYLOR Christopher MM Pte 4556 1/10th Liverpool Regt
TAYLOR Christopher A. MM+Bar RSM 8711 11 Fd Coy Royal Engineers
TAYLOR Clarence Victor MM Pte 2583 1/6th Royal Warwickshire Regt
TAYLOR Clifford MM Gnr 5630 RFA
TAYLOR Coutart-de-Butts MM Capt Royal Irish Rifles
TAYLOR Cresswell John Gilbert MM Pte A/204195 13th King's Royal Rifle Corps
TAYLOR David MM L/Cpl 242652 1/5th King's Own Scottish Borderers
TAYLOR David MM Pte 242699 Royal Welsh Fusiliers
TAYLOR Donald MM Sjt 202091 6th Highland Light Infantry
TAYLOR Dudley N. MM Cpl 251721 Signal Servise Royal Engineers
TAYLOR E.W. MM L/Sjt 40056 Leicestershire Regt
TAYLOR Ebenezer MM Pte 17866 19th Lancashire Fusiliers
TAYLOR Edgar MM Pte 226721 1/1st Monmouthshire Regt
TAYLOR Edman Charles MM+Bar Sjt 2142 12 Fd Amb RAMC
TAYLOR Edmund MM Pte 18552 Royal Lancaster Regt
TAYLOR Edward MM Gnr 295606 139 Heavy Bty RGA
TAYLOR Edward MM Sjt 692 RAMC
TAYLOR Edward MM Pte 47127 Liverpool Regt
TAYLOR Edward MM Pte 22501 Machine Gun Corps
TAYLOR Edwin MM Pte 18371 East Lancashire Regt
TAYLOR Eli MM Pte B/200876 8th Rifle Brigade
TAYLOR Eli MM(3885 Gnr 35 Bde RFA)+Bar Spr 251579 Royal Engineers
TAYLOR Ernest MM Pte 287 Royal Fusiliers
TAYLOR Ernest MM Dvr 796698 C/312 Bde RFA
TAYLOR Ernest MM Sjt 2069 2nd Manchester Regt
TAYLOR Ernest MM Pte 73611 RAMC
TAYLOR Ernest MM Pte 24/1709 Northumberland Fusiliers
TAYLOR Ernest MM Pte 19484 8th Yorkshire Light Infantry
TAYLOR Ernest MM L/Cpl 11916 10th West Yorkshire Regt
TAYLOR Ernest MM Dvr 12131 C/266 Bde RFA
TAYLOR Ernest MM L/Cpl 241287 Lancashire Fusiliers
TAYLOR Ernest B. MM Pte 86654 13th Liverpool Regt
TAYLOR Ernest C. MM Pte 38235 Royal Warwickshire Regt
TAYLOR Ernest Charles MM Pte 29143 2nd South Wales Borderers
TAYLOR Ernest E. MM L/Sjt 16271 2nd Grenadier Guards
TAYLOR Ernest M. MM Cpl 675383 RFA
TAYLOR F. MM Cpl Saddler 98589 RFA
TAYLOR F. MM L/Cpl 17743 9th Suffolk Regt
TAYLOR Flint MM+Bar Pte 241048 5th West Riding Regt
TAYLOR Francis MM Pte 51273 5th Devonshire Regt
TAYLOR Francis MM Sjt 21075 Durham Light Infantry
TAYLOR Frank MM 2nd Cpl 47327 18 Div Sig Coy Royal Engineers
TAYLOR Frank MM L/Cpl 325623 Durham Light Infantry
TAYLOR Frank "DCM,MM" Bdr 63111 'Y' Bty RHA
TAYLOR Frank Ernest MM Pte 3138 8th Royal Fusiliers KIA 5.8.16.
TAYLOR Frank J. MM Pte 353477 7th London Regt
TAYLOR Frank T. MM Sjt 756223 RFA
TAYLOR Frank William MM Sjt 54212 40 Bty 26 Bde RFA KIA 11.8.16.
TAYLOR Fred MM CQMS 25707 5th Lancashire Fusiliers
TAYLOR Fred MM Cpl 59628 1/8th Manchester Regt
TAYLOR Fred MM Pte 53072 Machine Gun Corps
TAYLOR Fred MM L/Cpl 20762 7th East Lancashire Regt
TAYLOR Fred MM Cpl 72488 40 Bde RFA
TAYLOR Fred MM Dvr 96294 A/75 Bde RFA
TAYLOR Fred Arthur MM Cpl 915686 D/223 Bde RFA
TAYLOR Fred James MM L/Cpl 108267 V Corps Sig Coy Royal Engineers
TAYLOR Frederick MM L/Cpl 11618 6th Oxf & Bucks Light Infantry
TAYLOR Frederick MM Pte 4627 1/6th South Staffordshire Regt
TAYLOR Frederick MM Bdr 21111 D/64 Bde RFA DOW 21.8.17.
TAYLOR Frederick MM Sjt 18217 8th North Staffordshire Regt DOW 16.5.18.
TAYLOR Frederick A. MM Gnr 905940 215 Bde RFA
TAYLOR Frederick A. MM Pte 41640 24th Royal Fusiliers
TAYLOR Frederick Charles MM Dvr 47069 A/121 Bde RFA Died 5.11.18.
TAYLOR Frederick Christopher MM L/Cpl S/15005 12th Rifle Brigade KIA 10.1.18.

TAYLOR Frederick Craven MM Bdr 52011 130 Heavy Bty RGA
TAYLOR Frederick Francis MM Gnr 53395 23 Siege Bty RGA
TAYLOR Frederick G. MM Pte 14796 12th Gloucestershire Regt
TAYLOR Frederick H. MM L/Bdr 9066 RFA
TAYLOR Frederick Harry MM Pte 242018 2/5th Yorkshire Light Infantry
TAYLOR Frederick J. MM Sjt 8242 11th Royal Fusiliers
TAYLOR Frederick W. MM Sjt 53440 RGA
TAYLOR George MM L/Cpl 15313 1st Gordon Highlanders
TAYLOR George MM Cpl 761094 C/87 Bde RFA
TAYLOR George MM Pte 35243 Worcestershire Regt
TAYLOR George MM+Bar L/Cpl 27988 2nd Worcestershire Regt
TAYLOR George MM CoH 2590 Royal Horse Guards
TAYLOR George MM Pte 43203 1st Royal Dublin Fusiliers
TAYLOR George MM Dvr 26949 A/123 Bde RFA
TAYLOR George MM+Bar Pte 200946 2/4th Yorkshire Light Infantry
TAYLOR George MM Sjt 293136 1/7th Cheshire Regt
TAYLOR George MM Pte 204784 1st Somerset Light Infantry
TAYLOR George MM Sjt 6944 4th Middlesex Regt
TAYLOR George MM Sjt 29583 RGA
TAYLOR George MM CQMS 4697 Royal Munster Fusiliers
TAYLOR George MM Sjt 10784 1st Grenadier Guards
TAYLOR George MM Pte 9928 South Staffordshire Regt
TAYLOR George MM Pte 5837 1st Irish Guards
TAYLOR George MM Pte 42357 33rd Bn Machine Gun Corps
TAYLOR George MM Pte 38171 9th Welsh Regt
TAYLOR George MM Sjt 93160 7th Bn Tank Corps
TAYLOR George MM Sjt M2/020833 Army Service Corps
TAYLOR George Alfred MM+Bar Cpl 40431 4th Worcestershire Regt
TAYLOR George C. MM Pte 2144 1/22nd London Regt
TAYLOR George C. MM L/Cpl 558124 56 Div Sig Coy Royal Engineers
TAYLOR George D. MM Gnr 72247 RFA
TAYLOR George Daniel MM Pte 44895 15th Royal Irish Rifles Died 22.6.18.
TAYLOR George E. MM Spr 558199 Royal Engineers
TAYLOR George E. MM Dvr T/35626 Army Service Corps
TAYLOR George F. MM Pte 119831 51st Bn Machine Gun Corps
TAYLOR George F. MM Pte 4398 1st Lancashire Fusiliers
TAYLOR George F. MM L/Cpl 10972 12th Royal Fusiliers
TAYLOR George H. MM Sjt 18571 8th Northumberland Fusiliers
TAYLOR George H. MM Pte 20/1525 Northumberland Fusiliers
TAYLOR George H. MM+2 Bars Sjt 8878 Highland Light Infantry
TAYLOR George H. MM Sjt 102327 RFA
TAYLOR George Harold MM Pte 240510 1/5th West Riding Regt
TAYLOR George Henry MM+Bar L/Bdr 94171 C/87 Bde RFA
TAYLOR George Henry MM Pte 9391 2nd Lincolnshire Regt KIA 31.7.17.
TAYLOR George Henry "MC,MM(18/70 Pte W Yorks)" 2Lt 2nd Yorkshire Light Infantry
TAYLOR George Henry MM L/Cpl 18854 6th Somerset Light Infantry
TAYLOR George Horsbrugh "DCM,MM,MM(F)" Cpl 75540 4th Bn Tank Corps
TAYLOR George John MM CSM 550575 2/16th London Regt DOW 10.12.18.
TAYLOR George M. MM Cpl CMT/53 Army Service Corps
TAYLOR George T. MM Sjt 15328 3rd Grenadier Guards
TAYLOR George W. MM Spr 74207 4 Div Sig Coy Royal Engineers
TAYLOR George W. MM Pte 63741 Machine Gun Corps
TAYLOR George W. MM Pte 57686 13th Yorkshire Regt
TAYLOR George W. MM L/Cpl 1707 West Yorkshire Regt
TAYLOR George W. MM Sjt 83822 RGA
TAYLOR Gladstone MM Sjt 39785 RFA
TAYLOR Guy Rawstron MM L/Sjt 27004 11th East Lancashire Regt KIA 5.9.18.
TAYLOR H.E. MM Spr 20197 12 Fd Coy Royal Engineers
TAYLOR H.E. MM Cpl 512795 London Regt
TAYLOR H.T. MM AM2 18030 Royal Flying Corps
TAYLOR Harold MM Pte 40333 20th Manchester Regt DOW 12.10.18.
TAYLOR Harold MM Dvr 756159 A/251 Bde RFA
TAYLOR Harold MM Pte 91906 15th Durham Light Infantry
TAYLOR Harold MM Cpl 751080 C/250 Bde RFA
TAYLOR Harold MM L/Cpl 20134 1st Royal West Kent Regt
TAYLOR Harold MM Pte 36492 Durham Light Infantry
TAYLOR Harold A. MM L/Sjt 6860 1st Dorsetshire Regt
TAYLOR Harold Edwin MM Sjt 17038 15th Royal Warwickshire Regt
TAYLOR Harold George MM L/Sjt 201405 5th Bedfordshire Regt Died 3.11.18.
TAYLOR Harry MM Bdr 835196 RFA
TAYLOR Harry MM Cpl 65740 5th Bn Machine Gun Corps
TAYLOR Harry MM L/Cpl 450229 Labour Corps
TAYLOR Harry MM Pte 8114 2nd Royal Sussex Regt
TAYLOR Harry MM Pte 19555 6th York & Lancaster Regt DOW 3.5.17.
TAYLOR Harry MM L/Cpl 7792 10th C Coy Royal Warwickshire Regt KIA 20.9.17.
TAYLOR Harry MM Pte S/5588 10th Rifle Brigade
TAYLOR Harry MM Pte 38472 RAMC
TAYLOR Harry MM Cpl Fitter 39058 130 Siege Bty RGA
TAYLOR Harry MM Sjt 16596 9th Royal Lancaster Regt
TAYLOR Harry MM Cpl 9184 1st Lincolnshire Regt
TAYLOR Harry MM Pte 370089 6 Fd Amb RAMC
TAYLOR Harry MM Pte 6145 11th Lancashire Fusiliers
TAYLOR Harry D. MM Pte 203128 20th Durham Light Infantry
TAYLOR Harry William MM Sjt 8741 2nd Suffolk Regt DOW 14.6.17.
TAYLOR Henry MM Sjt 11803 2nd Notts & Derby Regt
TAYLOR Henry "DCM,MM" Sjt 9262 1st Royal Warwickshire Regt
TAYLOR Henry MM Pte 4/9345 1st South Staffordshire Regt KIA 27.11.16.
TAYLOR Henry MM Pte C/6585 King's Royal Rifle Corps
TAYLOR Henry F. MM(C/4264 KRRC)+Bar Pte 128903 45th Royal Fusiliers
TAYLOR Herbert MM Sjt 7157 1st Royal Irish Regt
TAYLOR Herbert MM Pte 1222 2nd Royal Warwickshire Regt Died 8.11.18.
TAYLOR Herbert MM+Bar L/Sjt 10535 Coldstream Guards
TAYLOR Herbert "MM,MID" L/Bdr 296555 RGA
TAYLOR Herbert G. MM Sjt 15458 17th Highland Light Infantry KIA 1.7.16.
TAYLOR Herbert Joshua MM Pte 3733 1/1st Cambridgeshire Regt
TAYLOR Herbert R. MM Sjt 65101 5 Bde RFA
TAYLOR Herbert S. MM Pte 15759 Royal Sussex Regt
TAYLOR Herbert V. "DCM,MM" Sjt 13627 2nd Royal Fusiliers
TAYLOR Herbert W. MM Pte 40381 Lancashire Fusiliers
TAYLOR Herbert W. MM Pte SS/639 Army Service Corps
TAYLOR Hope Edward James MM Sjt 11401 33rd Bn Machine Gun Corps
TAYLOR Horace "DCM,MM,MM(F)" L/Cpl 27316 Royal Lancaster Regt
TAYLOR Horace MM Pte M2/227416 Army Service Corps
TAYLOR Isaac MM Sjt 6481 1st King's Royal Rifle Corps
TAYLOR J. MM Pte 53574 2nd Lancashire Fusiliers
TAYLOR J. MM Pte 56048 Yeomanry
TAYLOR J.E. MM Cpl 370380 London Regt
TAYLOR J.R.B. MM Pte 240882 5th Devonshire Regt
TAYLOR James MM Pte 270743 17th Royal Scots
TAYLOR James MM Sjt 635638 256 Bde RFA
TAYLOR James MM Dvr 74286 A/112 Bde RFA
TAYLOR James MM Sjt 20813 11th South Lancashire Regt
TAYLOR James MM Sjt 21275 Royal Engineers
TAYLOR James "DCM,MM" Gnr 52937 19 Heavy Bty RGA
TAYLOR James MM Cpl 12629 2nd Worcestershire Regt
TAYLOR James MM Pte 3436 22nd London Regt
TAYLOR James MM L/Cpl 50781 76 Fd Amb RAMC
TAYLOR James MM L/Cpl 1941 4/5th Royal Highlanders
TAYLOR James MM+Bar Sjt 18258 9th Royal Inniskilling Fusiliers
TAYLOR James MM L/Cpl 240315 North Lancashire Regt
TAYLOR James MM Gnr 60285 RGA
TAYLOR James MM Sjt 3384 12th Royal Scots KIA 25.4.18.
TAYLOR James A. MM Pte 56581 16th King's Royal Rifle Corps
TAYLOR James A. MM Sjt 28674 Royal Inniskilling Fusiliers
TAYLOR James D. MM Spr 406006 Royal Engineers
TAYLOR James Edwin MM Dvr 5411 B/121 Bde RFA
TAYLOR James H. MM Sjt 4013 11th Hussars
TAYLOR James R. MM Pte 240626 6th Royal Warwickshire Regt
TAYLOR James Richard MM Sjt 242062 2/6th West Yorkshire Regt
TAYLOR James William MM Pte 9732 2nd Welsh Regt
TAYLOR James William MM L/Cpl 37650 RAMC
TAYLOR Jeffrey MM Sjt 6434 8th Somerset Light Infantry KIA 28.4.17.
TAYLOR Jeremiah MM Pte 325045 1/9th Durham Light Infantry
TAYLOR Jesse MM CQMS 18734 12 Coy Machine Gun Corps KIA 1.7.16.
TAYLOR Jesse MM S/Sjt 38461 55 Fd Amb RAMC
TAYLOR John MM L/Cpl 9725 2nd Royal West Surrey Regt
TAYLOR John MM Gnr 47953 RFA
TAYLOR John MM Pte 37182 2nd Lancashire Fusiliers
TAYLOR John MM Cpl 19445 XVIII Corps Cyclist Bn Army Cyclist Corps

TAYLOR John MM Pte 8693 5th Cameron Highlanders
TAYLOR John MM Pte 240405 1/5th Yorkshire Light Infantry
TAYLOR John MM Pte 25140 2/7th West Riding Regt
TAYLOR John MM L/Cpl 203745 Liverpool Regt
TAYLOR John MM L/Cpl 332049 Liverpool Regt
TAYLOR John MM Pte 4570 1/19th London Regt
TAYLOR John "DCM,MM,MID" Sjt 67900 149 Army Troops Coy Royal Engineers
TAYLOR John MM Cpl 1486 1/16th London Regt
TAYLOR John MM Bdr 11851 70 Bty 34 Bde RFA
TAYLOR John MM Pte 12136 10th Durham Light Infantry KIA 16.9.16.
TAYLOR John MM Pte 235730 5th West Riding Regt
TAYLOR John MM Pte 16416 1st Hampshire Regt
TAYLOR John MM Pte 22823 Duke of Cornwall's LI
TAYLOR John MM Pte 12326 5th Dorsetshire Regt
TAYLOR John MM 2nd Cpl 188917 30 Broad Gauge Op Coy Royal Engineers
TAYLOR John MM Pte 1349 23rd Middlesex Regt
TAYLOR John MM L/Cpl 40341 10th South Wales Borderers KIA 29.6.18.
TAYLOR John MM Gnr 165751 D/187 Bde RFA
TAYLOR John MM+Bar Cpl 57454 24th Royal Fusiliers
TAYLOR John MM Pnr 279977 Royal Engineers
TAYLOR John MM Pte 1452 11th East Yorkshire Regt
TAYLOR John MM Gnr 73073 RFA
TAYLOR John MM Pte 16637 8th Yorkshire Light Infantry KIA 18.10.17.
TAYLOR John Amos MM Sjt 324500 2nd King's Royal Rifle Corps att 6th London Regt.KIA 17.10.18.
TAYLOR John B. MM Gnr 135968 B/285 Bde RFA
TAYLOR John E. MM Pte 533842 15th London Regt
TAYLOR John Edward MM Pte 1953 1/4th Northumberland Fusiliers KIA 26.10.17.
TAYLOR John F. MM Spr 457319 Royal Engineers
TAYLOR John H. MM Gnr 82664 RFA
TAYLOR John Henry MM Pte 5277 1st Royal Welsh Fusiliers KIA 14.5.17.
TAYLOR John J. MM S/Sjt Farrier 28802 135 Bty 32 Bde RFA
TAYLOR John L. MM Pte 14543 16th Highland Light Infantry
TAYLOR John P. MM Pte 62910 Royal Fusiliers
TAYLOR John R. MM Spr 153926 Royal Engineers
TAYLOR John Robert MM Cpl 21618 Worcestershire Regt
TAYLOR John S. MM L/Cpl 24714 16th Royal Welsh Fusiliers
TAYLOR John T. "DCM,MM" Pte 57610 42nd & 32nd Bn Machine Gun Corps
TAYLOR John W. MM Pte A/201983 2nd King's Royal Rifle Corps
TAYLOR John W. MM Pte 240514 West Riding Regt
TAYLOR John W. MM Pte 202149 1/4th West Riding Regt
TAYLOR John W. MM Sjt 240523 1/5th South Lancashire Regt
TAYLOR John W. MM Sjt Fitter 1982 RFA
TAYLOR John W. MM Cpl 20770 North Lancashire Regt
TAYLOR John Walter MM Pte 307899 18th Lancashire Fusiliers
TAYLOR John William MM Cpl 313146 25 Div Sig Coy Royal Engineers KIA 28.9.18.
TAYLOR Joseph MM Pte 23683 2nd York & Lancaster Regt att 16 Coy MGC.
TAYLOR Joseph MM Cpl 22269 Liverpool Regt
TAYLOR Joseph MM Cpl 200475 1/4th Hampshire Regt
TAYLOR Joseph MM Pte 48545 Northumberland Fusiliers
TAYLOR Joseph MM Pte 386109 1(Northumbrian)Fd Amb RAMC
TAYLOR Joseph MM Pte 141755 Machine Gun Corps
TAYLOR Joseph MM Pte 8/13307 8th Lincolnshire Regt KIA 28.4.17.
TAYLOR Joseph MM Sjt 14239 24th Manchester Regt
TAYLOR Joseph MM Sjt 245768 2 Railway Survey Coy Royal Engineers
TAYLOR Joseph MM Pte 28814 King's Own Scottish Borderers
TAYLOR Joseph C. MM Pte R/37018 16th King's Royal Rifle Corps
TAYLOR Joseph Christopher MM Pte 29577 3rd Grenadier Guards
TAYLOR Joseph E. MM Pte 119733 23rd Bn Machine Gun Corps
TAYLOR Joseph Edward MM Cpl 265611 1/1st Hertfordshire Regt KIA 31.7.17.
TAYLOR Joseph H. MM Cpl 9913 2nd South Lancashire Regt
TAYLOR Joseph W. MM L/Cpl 990 Cheshire Regt
TAYLOR Kenneth J. MM Sjt 12572 1st Liverpool Regt
TAYLOR Lawrence MM Pte 200498 1/7th Worcestershire Regt
TAYLOR Leonard MM Sjt A/3730 12th King's Royal Rifle Corps DOW 28.10.17.
TAYLOR Leonard George William MM Bdr 960079 RFA
TAYLOR Leslie MM Pte 18449 11th Royal Scots
TAYLOR Lewis MM Gnr 810159 RFA
TAYLOR Luke MM Pte 49208 13th Liverpool Regt
TAYLOR Mark MM Spr 444207 66 Div Sig Coy Royal Engineers
TAYLOR Mark MM Sjt 41586 1st Essex Regt
TAYLOR Martin MM Pte 14719 Manchester Regt
TAYLOR Matthew Vernon MM Cpl 700 4th Bn GMGR
TAYLOR Milburn MM Sjt 33821 D/70 Bde RFA
TAYLOR Nathaniel MM CSM 91891 15th Durham Light Infantry
TAYLOR Nathaniel MM Pte 21826 3rd Coldstream Guards
TAYLOR P. MM Pte 14080 Army Cyclist Corps
TAYLOR Paul "MM,MID,MC(G)" Pte 24435 8th Shropshire Light Infantry
TAYLOR Percival George Alfred MM L/Cpl 17665 23 Coy Machine Gun Corps KIA 7.10.17.
TAYLOR Percy Frederick MM Pte 10343 7th South Staffordshire Regt
TAYLOR Percy K. MM Gnr 63186 RFA
TAYLOR Percy P. MM Sjt 13074 7th East Yorkshire Regt
TAYLOR Percy W. MM Cpl 21565 7th Royal West Surrey Regt
TAYLOR Percy W. MM L/Cpl 251923 Royal Engineers
TAYLOR Peter MM Gnr 32570 4 Bty MGC(Motors)
TAYLOR Philip Sykes MM Pte 38768 9th York & Lancaster Regt
TAYLOR Phillip MM Sjt 66771 139 Fd Amb RAMC
TAYLOR Ralph MM Pte 41560 Lancashire Fusiliers
TAYLOR Ralph MM Cpl 30493 'Q' Bty RHA
TAYLOR Ratcliffe MM Pte 21702 1/4th Royal Lancaster Regt
TAYLOR Raymond MM Pte 14839 1st Scots Guards
TAYLOR Reginald MM L/Cpl R/37257 13th King's Royal Rifle Corps
TAYLOR Reginald C. MM Cpl 15/879 15/17th West Yorkshire Regt
TAYLOR Reginald D. MM Sjt 16261 8th Worcestershire Regt
TAYLOR Reginald F. MM Pte 10810 1st East Surrey Regt
TAYLOR Reginald J. MM Sjt 41027 Royal Engineers
TAYLOR Reginald Lionel MM Pnr 154840 'G' Special Coy Royal Engineers
TAYLOR Reginald Vernon Patrick MM Bdr 293039 138 Heavy Bty RGA KIA 6.10.18.
TAYLOR Reginald W. MM Pte 242563 Worcestershire Regt
TAYLOR Richard MM Pte 242067 2/5th West Riding Regt
TAYLOR Richard MM L/Bdr 69103 139 Heavy Bty RGA
TAYLOR Richard MM Cpl 305744 West Riding Regt
TAYLOR Richard MM Pte 6947 Devonshire Regt
TAYLOR Richard MM Pte 266210 Liverpool Regt
TAYLOR Richard MM Sjt 2955 1st Irish Guards
TAYLOR Richard MM Sjt 241099 2/5th East Lancashire Regt DOW 12.4.18.
TAYLOR Richard MM Pte 20761 2nd Yorkshire Light Infantry att 183 Tunnelling Coy RE.
TAYLOR Richard "MM,CG(B)" L/Cpl 26263 7th South Staffordshire Regt
TAYLOR Richard G. MM Sjt 200170 1/4th Dorsetshire Regt
TAYLOR Richard Glyndwr MM Dvr T4/037276 "1 Aux HT Coy,1 Cav Div" Army Service Corps
TAYLOR Robert MM Spr 357441 Signal Service Royal Engineers att 73 HAG
TAYLOR Robert MM L/Sjt 7622 8th Royal West Kent Regt
TAYLOR Robert MM Pte 22051 1/7th Gordon Highlanders
TAYLOR Robert MM Sjt 345386 24th Royal Welsh Fusiliers
TAYLOR Robert MM Sjt 54047 RFA
TAYLOR Robert MM Dvr 454 RFA
TAYLOR Robert MM Sjt 765342 RFA
TAYLOR Robert James MM BQMS 42765 D/87 Bde RFA
TAYLOR Robert K. MM L/Sjt 242857 Lancashire Fusiliers
TAYLOR Robert Newton MM Gnr 137042 196 Siege Bty RGA
TAYLOR Robert W. MM Pte 10175 Royal West Surrey Regt
TAYLOR Rowland S. MM L/Cpl 220213 7th East Yorkshire Regt
TAYLOR S. MM Gnr 2670 RFA
TAYLOR S.A. MM Sjt 134856 Royal Air Force
TAYLOR Samuel MM Pte 251772 1/6th Arg & Suth Highlanders
TAYLOR Samuel MM Gnr Fitter 35300 RFA
TAYLOR Samuel MM Pte 47641 Northumberland Fusiliers
TAYLOR Samuel MM Cpl 21027 22nd Manchester Regt
TAYLOR Samuel MM Sjt B/2486 Rifle Brigade
TAYLOR Samuel H. "MM,MID" CSM 8510 1st Devonshire Regt
TAYLOR Samuel R. MM Pte 72848 17th Royal Welsh Fusiliers
TAYLOR Samuel William MM Sjt 240099 1/5th Leicestershire Regt KIA 29.9.18.
TAYLOR Seth MM Sjt 11794 16th Lancashire Fusiliers
TAYLOR Sidney MM Pte 14783 20th Manchester Regt
TAYLOR Sidney MM Pte 9802 2nd Suffolk Regt

TAYLOR Sidney MM Pte 204984 15th Hampshire Regt
TAYLOR Sidney MM Sjt 240721 Royal Lancaster Regt
TAYLOR Sidney MM L/Cpl 38881 Durham Light Infantry
TAYLOR Sidney A. MM Pte 71548 Notts & Derby Regt
TAYLOR Sidney R. MM Dvr T/1152 Army Service Corps
TAYLOR Sidney V. MM Gnr 34098 C/83 Bde RFA
TAYLOR Sidney W. MM Bdr 318249 RGA
TAYLOR Silas MM Cpl 800633 D/230 Bde RFA
TAYLOR Squire "DCM,MM" Sjt 9212 1st Liverpool Regt
TAYLOR Stanley A. MM Pte 200209 1/7th Middlesex Regt
TAYLOR Sydney MM Sjt 26982 15th Notts & Derby Regt
TAYLOR T. MM+Bar L/Cpl 41667 Highland Light Infantry
TAYLOR T.L. MM Pte 388382 RAMC
TAYLOR Thomas MM Pte M2/100543 Army Service Corps att RFA.
TAYLOR Thomas MM Dvr 15916 31 Div Ammn Col RFA
TAYLOR Thomas MM Pte 235310 9th West Riding Regt
TAYLOR Thomas MM Dvr 771279 RFA
TAYLOR Thomas MM Pte 45842 Welsh Regt
TAYLOR Thomas MM Pte 244412 Cheshire Regt
TAYLOR Thomas MM Pte 18016 11th Cheshire Regt
TAYLOR Thomas MM L/Cpl R/8225 King's Royal Rifle Corps
TAYLOR Thomas MM Cpl 155 8th Royal Fusiliers
TAYLOR Thomas MM Pte 22363 North Lancashire Regt
TAYLOR Thomas MM Pte 14374 7th South Lancashire Regt
TAYLOR Thomas MM Pte 52464 11th Cheshire Regt
TAYLOR Thomas MM Pte 22636 9th Lancashire Fusiliers
TAYLOR Thomas MM Sjt 14505 1/5th South Lancashire Regt KIA 13.4.18.
TAYLOR Thomas MM Pte 200356 1/4th Leicestershire Regt
TAYLOR Thomas MM Pte 32595 7th Royal Lancaster Regt DOW 8.10.18.
TAYLOR Thomas MM Pte 72130 17 CCS RAMC
TAYLOR Thomas MM Pte 331294 Highland Light Infantry
TAYLOR Thomas MM L/Cpl 27598 Machine Gun Corps KIA 19.10.18.
TAYLOR Thomas MM Pte 240378 Northumberland Fusiliers
TAYLOR Thomas MM Pte 28013 10th Royal Warwickshire Regt
TAYLOR Thomas A. "MM,MID" L/Sjt 1657 1/21st London Regt
TAYLOR Thomas E. MM Cpl 438066 Royal Engineers
TAYLOR Thomas Edward MM Sjt 1232 1/23rd London Regt
TAYLOR Thomas Henry MM Dvr 13751 103 AA Section RFA
TAYLOR Thomas Henry MM Pte 350351 12th Highland Light Infantry att 106 Light TM Bty
TAYLOR Thomas Henry MM(1/21st London)+Bar Cpl 650182 8th East Surrey Regt
TAYLOR Thomas R. "DCM,MM" CSM 240090 1/6th South Staffordshire Regt
TAYLOR Vernon MM Pte 137429 32nd Bn Machine Gun Corps
TAYLOR Vernon Howard MM Sjt 2434 1/4th Royal Berkshire Regt DOW 18.8.16.
TAYLOR Vincent MM Sjt 201186 West Riding Regt
TAYLOR W. MM L/Cpl P/1542 Military Foot Police
TAYLOR W. MM Sjt 3/12386 Liverpool Regt
TAYLOR W. MM Dvr T4/249048 Army Service Corps
TAYLOR W. MM+Bar Pte 10948 Gloucestershire Regt
TAYLOR W.M. MM Pte 301173 RAMC
TAYLOR W.P. MM Pte 2112 24th Royal Fusiliers
TAYLOR W.T. MM Pte 4320 Royal Fusiliers
TAYLOR Wallace MM Pte 55066 15th Lancashire Fusiliers
TAYLOR Wallace Thomas MM Pte 4109 13th Royal Sussex Regt
TAYLOR Walter MM Pte 20860 Liverpool Regt
TAYLOR Walter MM Dvr 66387 RFA
TAYLOR Walter G. MM+Bar Sjt 60394 9th Royal Fusiliers
TAYLOR Walter Herbert MM L/Cpl 71742 'L' Corps Sig Coy Royal Engineers
TAYLOR Walter J. MM Dvr 960964 RFA
TAYLOR Walter Prince MM Cpl 3063 24th Royal Fusiliers KIA 29.4.17.
TAYLOR Walter T. MM Pte 49429 6th Northamptonshire Regt
TAYLOR Walter W. MM Pte 2688 1/4th Royal Lancaster Regt
TAYLOR Webley Charles MM Pte 5294 West Yorkshire Regt
TAYLOR Wilfred MM CQMS 300627 8th Manchester Regt
TAYLOR Wilfred MM Pte 40284 Leicestershire Regt
TAYLOR William MM Pte 8295 8th Devonshire Regt
TAYLOR William MM Spr 47740 Royal Engineers
TAYLOR William MM Spr 251895 Royal Engineers
TAYLOR William MM Pte 3483 Middlesex Regt
TAYLOR William MM L/Cpl 11072 1st Royal Irish Fusiliers KIA 6.7.16.
TAYLOR William MM Pte 18526 Royal West Kent Regt
TAYLOR William MM Pte 37381 10th West Yorkshire Regt
TAYLOR William MM Cpl 5931 2nd Royal Munster Fusiliers
TAYLOR William MM Pte 205718 1st Wiltshire Regt
TAYLOR William MM Sjt 235114 1/5th Royal Warwickshire Regt
TAYLOR William MM Gnr 146174 276 Siege Bty RGA
TAYLOR William MM Pte 11042 2nd King's Own Scottish Borderers
TAYLOR William MM Pte 45041 Northumberland Fusiliers
TAYLOR William MM L/Cpl 310248 1/7th Gordon Highlanders
TAYLOR William MM Pte 350776 Manchester Regt
TAYLOR William "DCM,MM" Sjt 9946 1st Gloucestershire Regt
TAYLOR William MM SSM 41413 4 Squadron Machine Gun Corps(Cavalry)
TAYLOR William MM+Bar L/Sjt 7217 Seaforth Highlanders
TAYLOR William MM Sjt 17311 Machine Gun Corps
TAYLOR William MM Sjt 7774 2nd Lancashire Fusiliers KIA 23.4.18.
TAYLOR William MM Pte 20698 6 Coy Machine Gun Corps
TAYLOR William MM+Bar Sjt 3197 2nd Northumberland Fusiliers
TAYLOR William MM Sjt 200347 1/4th Gloucestershire Regt
TAYLOR William MM Cpl 18/1152 18th Durham Light Infantry
TAYLOR William MM Pte 16438 1st Middlesex Regt KIA 18.7.18.
TAYLOR William MM Gnr 12565 160 Bde RFA
TAYLOR William MM L/Cpl 84038 Machine Gun Corps DOW 11.3.18.
TAYLOR William A. MM Bdr 1562 RFA
TAYLOR William A. MM+Bar Cpl 34869 York & Lancaster Regt
TAYLOR William A. MM L/Cpl S/14721 Rifle Brigade
TAYLOR William Andrew MM Pte 18/1068 18th Durham Light Infantry
TAYLOR William Arthur MM Pte 11647 Royal West Kent Regt
TAYLOR William B. MM Pte 20445 Royal Fusiliers
TAYLOR William Cecil MM S/Sjt Farrier 617 C/231 Bde RFA
TAYLOR William E. MM+Bar L/Cpl 265603 1/1st Hertfordshire Regt
TAYLOR William E. MM Gnr 3226 RFA
TAYLOR William Eades "MM,CG(F)" Sjt 14760 7th Royal Berkshire Regt
TAYLOR William F. MM Cpl 25075 RGA
TAYLOR William Frank MM BSM 44728 B/306 Bde RFA
TAYLOR William Frank "MM,OStG(R)" Sjt 13913 7th Royal Berkshire Regt
TAYLOR William G. MM Sjt 15527 Devonshire Regt
TAYLOR William G. MM Pte 57134 Royal Welsh Fusiliers
TAYLOR William H. MM L/Cpl 201272 Worcestershire Regt
TAYLOR William H. MM Pte 41209 Worcestershire Regt
TAYLOR William H. MM Cpl 113808 RGA
TAYLOR William H. MM Cpl 13134 10th Yorkshire Regt
TAYLOR William H. MM Pte 38874 20th London Regt
TAYLOR William H. MM Cpl 31291 4 Div Ammn Col RFA
TAYLOR William H. MM Cpl 3855 Machine Gun Corps
TAYLOR William H. MM+Bar Cpl 12595 1st Gordon Highlanders
TAYLOR William H. MM+Bar Pte 16080 Royal Sussex Regt
TAYLOR William H.J. MM Cpl 3899 7th Dragoon Guards
TAYLOR William Healey MM Cpl 22930 7th Cameron Highlanders
TAYLOR William Henry MM Bdr 785288 C/150 Bde RFA
TAYLOR William J. MM Sjt 7217 1st East Surrey Regt
TAYLOR William J. MM L/Cpl 12989 4th Royal Fusiliers
TAYLOR William Jack MM Cpl 72426 RAMC att 1st East Lancashire Regt.
TAYLOR William James MM L/Cpl 18418 Wiltshire Regt
TAYLOR William James Frederick "DCM,MM" L/Cpl 40783 171 Tunnelling Coy Royal Engineers
TAYLOR William John MM Pte 357561 2/10th Liverpool Regt
TAYLOR William L. MM Pte 37302 Lancashire Fusiliers
TAYLOR William R. MM Cpl M2/102576 Army Service Corps
TAYLOR William T. MM Sjt 300771 Essex Regt
TAYLOR William T. MM Pte 13 Royal Fusiliers
TAYLOR William T. MM Sjt 35395 RAMC
TAYLOR William Telford MM Pte 24464 10th Northumberland Fusiliers KIA 30.9.16.
TAYLOR William Thomas MM Sjt 25050 A/77 Bde RFA
TAYLORSON Harry MM Sjt 295960 151 Heavy Bty RGA DOW 13.4.18.
TAZEY George MM Pte 250373 Durham Light Infantry
TAZIKER William MM Spr 405962 Royal Engineers
TEA A.V. MM Cpl 33152 10th Essex Regt
TEAGLE Thomas MM L/Cpl 15058 2nd Grenadier Guards KIA 4.4.18.
TEAGUE Albert E. MM Pte 47651 Manchester Regt
TEAGUE David MM L/Cpl 532351 233 Fd Coy Royal Engineers
TEAGUE Harry MM Pte 7700 9th Royal Sussex Regt
TEAGUE John MM Sjt 707192 RFA

TEAGUE John MM Cpl 21/226 Northumberland Fusiliers
TEAGUE William C. MM Sjt 175443 258 Tunnelling Coy Royal Engineers
TEAKLE A. MM AM1 17991 Royal Air Force
TEAL Arnold MM Sjt 240100 York & Lancaster Regt
TEAL Harold MM Sjt 12139 5th Dorsetshire Regt
TEAL Levi MM+Bar L/Cpl 10252 1st Shropshire Light Infantry
TEAL Thomas MM L/Cpl 201708 Seaforth Highlanders
TEALE John William MM Pte 87131 Machine Gun Corps
TEALE Vyner MM+Bar Pte 41222 16th Highland Light Infantry
TEALL Reginald F. MM Cpl R/3413 12th King's Royal Rifle Corps
TEAR Charles MM Pte 22967 Machine Gun Corps
TEAR Henry J. MM Pte 370082 RAMC
TEAR Joseph MM Pte 37857 1st Gloucestershire Regt
TEAR Stanley Anige MM Cpl 28096 2nd Northamptonshire Regt
TEARCE or TEARSE James MM Pte 386046 RAMC
TEARE Arnold Maxwell MM Bdr 1441 RFA
TEARE Wilfred MM L/Cpl 305627 1/8th Notts & Derby Regt
TEARLE Albert E. MM Pte 24956 Machine Gun Corps
TEARLE Sidney MM L/Cpl 34135 Middlesex Regt
TEASDALE Frank MM Pte 28154 10th Lancashire Fusiliers
TEASDALE John MM Bdr 18611 B/93 Bde RFA
TEASDALE John Thomas MM Cpl Wheeler 750922 A/315 Bde RFA
TEASDALE Willie MM Pte 44290 58th Bn Machine Gun Corps
TEATUM William H. MM SM 461174 26 Fd Amb RAMC
TEBB James MM Pte 242371 West Riding Regt
TEBBETT Frank MM Sjt 12361 8th Lincolnshire Regt
TEBBETT Wilfred MM Cpl 240094 North Staffordshire Regt
TEBBITT Frank Jackson MM Sjt 9334 7th Royal West Kent Regt
TEBBS Fred MM Pte 202948 5/6th Scottish Rifles
TEBBS Joseph MM Pte 27467 2nd Royal Berkshire Regt
TEBBUTT Frank MM Pte 242546 2nd Lincolnshire Regt
TEBBUTT Herbert MM Pte 28017 East Yorkshire Regt
TEBBUTT Walter MM Gnr 201747 Tank Corps
TEBBY Harry MM L/Cpl 26720 10th Shropshire Light Infantry
TECTER Cyril Douthitt MM Pte 67892 7th Royal Fusiliers KIA 26.5.18.
TEDDER G. MM Cpl 1158 Royal Warwickshire Regt
TEDDER Harry G. MM+Bar L/Cpl 27722 Royal Lancaster Regt
TEDDER Neil C. MM Sjt 54974 5 Bde RFA
TEDMAN Alfred MM Dvr 38489 D/82 Bde RFA
TEDMAN Cecil John MM Pte 3022 1/16th London Regt
TEDMAN John T. "MM,MID" Pnr 32753 Royal Engineers
TEDSTILL George "MM,MID" L/Sjt 214 1st Northumberland Fusiliers
TEE Edward T. MM Sjt 248241 4 Fd Svy Bn Royal Engineers
TEECE George MM+Bar Sjt 2153 York & Lancaster Regt
TEER Robert "DCM,MM+Bar" Sjt 9685 2nd Notts & Derby Regt
TEES David MM Sjt 13849 15th Highland Light Infantry
TEESDALE Alfred MM Cpl 318058 RGA
TEHAN Alfred G. MM Cpl 3125 12th Lancers
TELFER Allan Cunningham MM Cpl 201425 Seaforth Highlanders
TELFER David M. MM L/Cpl 345116 14th Royal Highlanders
TELFER Gilbert F. MM Sjt 2361 1/9th London Regt
TELFER John MM Pte 202874 6th Border Regt
TELFER John MM Gnr 46135 26 Bde RFA
TELFER Richard MM L/Cpl 8669 2nd Seaforth Highlanders
TELFER William MM L/Cpl 46766 Northumberland Fusiliers
TELFER William MM Cpl 351253 1/9th Royal Scots
TELFORD Fred MM Gnr 701208 RFA
TELFORD George MM Pte 24891 Border Regt
TELFORD John MM Pte 60107 Machine Gun Corps
TELFORD John MM Spr 166576 219 Fd Coy Royal Engineers
TELFORD John MM(34635 Nbld F)+Bar Pte 223029 1st East Yorkshire Regt
TELFORD John MM Cpl 155731 182 Tunnelling Coy Royal Engineers
TELFORD John Thomas MM Pte 31470 Leicestershire Regt
TELFORD T. MM Sjt 63819 Royal Engineers
TELFORD William MM Cpl 20090 51st Bn Machine Gun Corps
TELFORD William MM+Bar Pte 352713 Royal Scots
TELLERY Stephen J. MM Pte 699014 22nd London Regt
TELLETT William "MM,MSM" CQMS 16799 11th Cheshire Regt
TELLING Arthur Henry MM Pte 372274 36 Fd Amb RAMC
TELLING Bertram Ernest MM L/Cpl 19356 1st Wiltshire Regt KIA 10.7.17.
TELLING O. MM Sjt 57551 38th Bn Machine Gun Corps
TELLWRIGHT William F. MM Pte 19491 8th South Wales Borderers
TEMPERTON Alfred Claud Shores MM Gnr 81586 32 Bty 33 Bde RFA
TEMPERTON Charles Edward MM Pte 1470 1/4th East Yorkshire Regt
TEMPERTON George W. MM Sjt 24164 236 Siege Bty RGA
TEMPEST Arthur MM Pte 24787 1/8th Arg & Suth Highlanders
TEMPEST Frederick William MM Bdr 140513 103 Bde RFA
TEMPEST James "DCM,MM" Pte 281655 1/7th Lancashire Fusiliers
TEMPEST Matthew MM Sjt 18638 9th Border Regt
TEMPEST William M. MM Pte 242694 Yorkshire Light Infantry
TEMPLAR Edwin C. MM CSM 320114 6th London Regt
TEMPLE Charles Richard MM Pte 1153 9th Royal Fusiliers KIA 21.9.18.
TEMPLE Frederick B. MM Pte 29983 Grenadier Guards
TEMPLE George A. "DCM,MM" Sjt 760665 A/317 Bde RFA
TEMPLE George M. MM Pte 49390 Royal Fusiliers
TEMPLE Harold "DCM,MM" Sjt 13666 1 Div Sig Coy Royal Engineers
TEMPLE Robert MM Dvr CHT/1078 Army Service Corps
TEMPLE Robert Stanley MM L/Cpl 13/541 13th East Yorkshire Regt KIA 2.5.17.
TEMPLE Robert W. "DCM,MM" Sjt 51732 18th Lancashire Fusiliers
TEMPLE T. MM Sjt 26203 Lincolnshire Regt
TEMPLEMAN George "MM,MID" Pte 10445 6th King's Own Scottish Borderers
TEMPLEMAN George W. MM Gnr 925619 RFA
TEMPLEMAN John MM Cpl M2/033008 Army Service Corps
TEMPLEMAN John T. MM Cpl 1508 1/8th Notts & Derby Regt
TEMPLETON Bertram MM Sjt 438047 427 Fd Coy Royal Engineers
TEMPLETON George MM Sjt 316846 13th Royal Highlanders
TEMPLETON James MM Sjt 4014 Machine Gun Corps
TEMPLETON John MM Sjt 266989 1/6th Seaforth Highlanders
TEMPLETON Robert MM CSM 295001 12th Royal Scots Fusiliers
TEMPLETON Robert MM Pte 49579 13th Cheshire Regt
TEMPLETON Thomas MM CQMS 265930 1/6th Seaforth Highlanders
TEMPLETON Thomas MM Pte 20563 9th Scottish Rifles
TEMPLETON William MM Pte 46786 RAMC
TENCH G.H. MM Pte 250923 2/3rd London Regt
TENCH Richard Herbert MM Gnr 205344 B/74 Bde RFA
TENNANT Alfred MM Cpl(SS) 35396 112 Bty 24 Bde RFA
TENNANT Charles MM Sjt 41455 10th East Yorkshire Regt
TENNANT Elwin MM Cpl 4030 2nd Dragoon Guards
TENNANT James MM+Bar Pte 331636 1/9th Highland Light Infantry
TENNANT James MM Pte 301570 1/8th Arg & Suth Highlanders
TENNANT James or John MM Pte 266473 Gordon Highlanders
TENNANT Joseph MM Pte 265211 1/6th Seaforth Highlanders
TENNANT Philip MM Bdr 13993 D/315 Bde RFA
TENNANT Robert MM Sjt 76217 IV Corps Sig Coy Royal Engineers
TENNANT Sidney A. MM Pte M2/074290 Army Service Corps
TENNANT William MM Dvr 22212 RFA
TENNANT William MM Cpl 15457 9th Norfolk Regt
TENNENT John M. MM L/Cpl 200781 Tank Corps
TENNUCI Charles MM SSM 547 Military Mounted Police att HQ VIII Corps.
TENNUCI Percy MM Sjt 5087 5th Dragoon Guards
TERRELL William MM L/Cpl 155182 Royal Engineers
TERRETT George A. MM Pte 59800 Machine Gun Corps
TERRETT R. MM Gnr 58172 RGA
TERRETT William Charles MM Sjt 9505 2nd South Wales Borderers
TERRINGTON Arthur W. MM Sjt 10396 1st Highland Light Infantry
TERRINGTON D.J. MM Gnr 112969 245 Bde HQ RFA
TERRINGTON Edward MM Cpl 95237 1 Tank Fd Coy Tank Corps
TERRIS Alexander "MM+Bar,MID" Sjt 16989 57 Fd Coy Royal Engineers
TERRIS James MM L/Cpl 811 2nd Arg & Suth Highlanders
TERRITT James MM+Bar Pte 10026 1st Royal Dublin Fusiliers
TERRY Albert MM Pte 260039 Liverpool Regt
TERRY Albert W. MM Gnr 35559 'K' Bty RHA
TERRY Charles M. MM Pte 42149 Lancashire Fusiliers
TERRY E. MM L/Cpl P/3446 Military Foot Police
TERRY Ernest F. MM Pte 27915 Hampshire Regt
TERRY Frank MM Gnr 148688 D/256 Bde RFA
TERRY George MM Pte 50505 Lancashire Fusiliers
TERRY Herbert MM Cpl 17786 Yorkshire Light Infantry
TERRY J.H. MM Pte 71428 15th Notts & Derby Regt KIA 28.3.18.
TERRY James H. MM Pte 265558 1/1st Hertfordshire Regt
TERRY John MM Dvr 23015 D/150 Bde RFA
TERRY Joseph MM Dvr 40853 RFA
TERRY Percy C. MM Cpl 10062 2nd Royal West Surrey Regt
TERRY Ralph MM Cpl 10/135 10th East Yorkshire Regt
TERRY Richard MM Pte 1699 1/22nd London Regt

TERRY Richard Henry MM Pte 19723 Manchester Regt
TERRY Thomas B. MM Pte 58058 Machine Gun Corps
TERRY Thomas W. MM+Bar Sjt 558156 56 Div Sig Coy Royal Engineers
TERRY William MM Dvr 122345 RFA
TERRY William C. MM Pte 267350 Gloucestershire Regt
TERRY William J. MM Pte 66309 138 Fd Amb RAMC
TERZZA Albert MM Pte R/7941 4th King's Royal Rifle Corps
TERZZA William A. MM Pte 91237 9th Bn Tank Corps
TESSEYMAN Harold S. MM Sjt 290832 RGA
TESSEYMAN Harry MM Sjt 1517 GMGR
TESSEYMAN William F. "MM,MID" Sjt 47212 RAMC
TESTER Archibald Edmund MM L/Cpl 200784 1/4th Royal Sussex Regt DOW 7.11.17.
TESTER Bertie "MM,MID" Sjt 57086 D/18 Bde RFA Died 13.2.19.
TESTER E.W. MM L/Cpl T4/044835 Army Service Corps
TESTER Ernest H. MM Pte 41327 Middlesex Regt
TESTER George D. MM Pte 7089 8 Fd Amb RAMC
TESTER Henry MM Sjt 28092 B/178 Bde RFA
TESTER John MM L/Cpl 8513 2nd Royal Sussex Regt KIA 20.8.16.
TESTER John H. MM Gnr 77806 'G' Bty RHA
TETLEY George H. MM Sjt 14234 A/75 Bde RFA
TETLEY Greenwood MM Dvr 21502 RFA
TETLEY Thomas MM Pte 240241 2/5th West Riding Regt
TETLOW Edward MM Cpl 66590 22nd London Regt
TETLOW Frank MM+Bar Sjt 14956 17th Lancashire Fusiliers
TETLOW Harold MM Cpl 16299 Machine Gun Corps
TETLOW John MM Pte 3712 2nd Lancashire Fusiliers DOW 23.6.18.
TETSILL Cornelius MM L/Cpl 21370 Machine Gun Corps
TETSILL Percy Reynold MM Cpl 201766 20th Manchester Regt
TEULON Austin MM Cpl M2/102253 Army Service Corps att 13 Fd Amb RAMC.
TEVENDALE John G. MM L/Cpl 331602 1/9th Highland Light Infantry
TEVERSHAM Arthur MM Pte 235053 Liverpool Regt
TEVERSON Harry Gordon "MC+2 Bars,MM(2478 Cpl 1/1st Cambs Regt)" 2Lt 8th att 2nd Suffolk Regt
TEW George MM Sjt 8550 5th Cameron Highlanders KIA 19.7.18.
TEW William MM BQMS 6590 D/152 Bde RFA
TEWKESBURY Thomas MM+Bar Pte 12044 1st Scots Guards
THACKER Albert C. MM Pte 47524 10th Essex Regt
THACKER Charles MM Gnr 32627 25 Bde RFA
THACKER Charles H. MM Cpl 11/784 11th East Yorkshire Regt
THACKER Herbert Lane MM Sjt MS/4471 Army Service Corps att MGC.Died 15.4.17.
THACKER Leonard K. MM Sjt 476155 Royal Engineers
THACKER Thomas Charles MM Cpl R/10974 4th King's Royal Rifle Corps KIA 7.11.18.
THACKERAY Arthur MM Pte 30321 RAMC
THACKERAY James MM Pte 28278 Yorkshire Regt
THACKERAY William H. "DCM,MM" Gnr 751409 D/223 Bde RFA
THACKRAY Frank MM Cpl 21220 10th York & Lancaster Regt
THACKRAY Fred MM L/Cpl 31052 9th Yorkshire Light Infantry KIA 22.3.18.
THACKRAY Herbert MM Bdr 780156 RFA
THACKRAY Herbert "MM,CG" Pte 73408 25th Bn Machine Gun Corps
THACKRAY Horace MM L/Cpl R/3354 King's Royal Rifle Corps
THACKRAY Joseph MM Gnr 96336 29 Div Ammn Col RFA Died 24.12.16.
THACKWAY Alfonso W. MM Pte 457139 RAMC
THACKWELL Edgar MM Pte 12921 King's Royal Rifle Corps
THACKWELL George W. MM Pte 23742 1st Grenadier Guards
THACKWRAY Harold MM Sjt 200621 2nd London Regt
THAIN Henry H. MM Pte 571397 17th London Regt
THAIN Obediah MM Sjt 15278 7th South Wales Borderers
THAIN Robert MM Pte 200338 Gordon Highlanders
THARME Sampson Frank MM L/Bdr 79511 RGA
THARRATT George MM Gnr 738 77 Siege Bty RGA
THATCHER Alfred MM Sjt 203873 1/4th Royal Berkshire Regt
THATCHER Alfred MM Spr 96404 Royal Engineers
THATCHER Alfred G. MM Pte 18809 Devonshire Regt
THATCHER Henry J. MM Pte 13442 East Surrey Regt
THATCHER William C. MM Pte 243127 8th Middlesex Regt
THAYER George W. MM Cpl 293368 2/10th Middlesex Regt
THAYER John Robert MM BQMS 58508 D/83 Bde RFA Died 28.9.18.
THEAKER Clifford MM+Bar Cpl 15293 6th York & Lancaster Regt
THEAKER George F. MM BSM 61357 D/110 Bde RFA
THEAKSTON Joseph E. MM Cpl C/796 1st King's Royal Rifle Corps
THEAR William G. MM Gnr 97973 RFA
THECKSTON Henry MM Pte 19341 9th Royal Sussex Regt
THEEDOM Ernest Robert MM L/Cpl 6097 8th East Surrey Regt KIA 22.3.18.
THELWELL John J. MM Sjt 28445 7th Shropshire Light Infantry
THELWELL Joseph "DCM,MM" Sjt 200721 1/4th Royal Welsh Fusiliers
THELWELL William MM 2nd Cpl 130079 Royal Engineers
THEOBALD G. MM L/Cpl 16468 1st Essex Regt
THEOBALD George MM Cpl 37330 8th Gloucestershire Regt
THEOBALD George MM Pte 8137 2nd York & Lancaster Regt
THEOBALD George Ellis MM Gnr 54 C/92 Bde RFA
THEOBALD Henry MM L/Sjt 512252 14th London Regt
THEOBALD Leonard MM Cpl 57908 42 Bde RFA
THEOBALD Thomas MM Pte M4/237277 Army Service Corps
THEOBALD Walter MM Pte 13286 8th Norfolk Regt
THEOBALD William J. MM Pte 201699 Royal Sussex Regt
THEOCHARIS Paul MM L/Cpl 87679 17th Royal Fusiliers
THERIN Alfred MM Pte 18202 13th Essex Regt
THEW Viveon Gordon MM Bdr 127164 RGA
THEXTON Gordon Frederick MM Pte 20707 Liverpool Regt
THEXTON John MM Sjt 874 1/1st Westmorland & Cumberland Yeomanry
THICKETT George William MM Pte 28153 1/4th York & Lancaster Regt KIA 26.4.18.
THICKETT Wilson A. MM Cpl 14103 8th York & Lancaster Regt
THIRD Charles McGilvery MM Cpl 11136 1/8th Scottish Rifles KIA 29.7.18.
THIRKELL Alfred R. MM Pte 471809 12th London Regt
THIRKELL Herbert MM Dvr 41206 RFA
THIRKELL Sidney J. MM Pte 37773 RAMC
THIRKETTLE John William MM Pte 2839 7th East Kent Regt KIA 29.9.17.
THIRLAWAY Thomas MM Cpl 200196 Durham Light Infantry
THIRLWELL Edward MM L/Bdr 337198 142 Heavy Bty RGA
THIRLWELL Peter W. MM Gnr 33803 RFA
THIRLWELL Thomas MM Cpl 751211 RFA
THIRST William MM Pte 9353 7th Royal Sussex Regt DOW 4.10.18.
THIRTLE John MM Pte 200818 Northumberland Fusiliers
THIRWELL Isaac MM Pte 240974 Border Regt
THISTLETHWAITE Leslie MM Pte 241568 1/6th West Yorkshire Regt
THISTLETHWAITE Richard MM Pte 200632 1/4th Royal Lancaster Regt
THISTLETON T.J. MM Pte 200352 North Lancashire Regt
THODAY George MM Sjt 50194 31 Bty 35 Bde RFA
THOIRS William MM Dvr 630347 255 Bde RFA
THOM Andrew MM Cpl 201285 1/6th Royal Highlanders
THOM Archibald MM L/Cpl 302103 Signal Service Royal Engineers
THOM David MM Pte 266001 2nd Royal Scots Fusiliers
THOM Hugh Barr MM Pte 200290 5/6th Scottish Rifles DOW 29.11.17.
THOM James MM Pte 301145 1 Fd Amb RAMC
THOM Robert G. MM Pte 8712 2nd Highland Light Infantry
THOM William MM Pte M2/073631 Army Service Corps att RAMC.
THOM William MM Pte 240305 Gordon Highlanders
THOM William F. MM Gnr 281301 RGA
THOMAS A.J. MM SM 675 Military Mounted Police
THOMAS Albert MM Sjt 11542 1st Royal Dublin Fusiliers
THOMAS Albert E. MM Dvr 62341 'T' Bty RHA
THOMAS Albert Edward MM L/Cpl 11007 1/8th Middlesex Regt KIA 28.3.18.
THOMAS Albert George MM Pte 798 1st Welsh Guards
THOMAS Albert J. MM L/Cpl 17567 6th South Wales Borderers
THOMAS Alfred MM Pte 4109 23rd Royal Fusiliers
THOMAS Alfred MM Pte 37562 7th Lancashire Fusiliers
THOMAS Alfred MM Pte 19833 Shropshire Light Infantry
THOMAS Alfred Clement MM Dvr 945785 58 Div Ammn Col RFA
THOMAS Alfred Francis MM Pte 25234 23rd Middlesex Regt KIA 25.3.18.
THOMAS Alfred Guy MM L/Cpl 3290 111 Coy Machine Gun Corps
THOMAS Alfred W. MM Sjt 11146 Oxf & Bucks Light Infantry
THOMAS Alwyn MM Pte 9000 2nd Welsh Regt
THOMAS Aneurin MM Sjt 40696 354 Siege Bty RGA
THOMAS Arthur MM Bdr 950878 A/15 Bde RFA
THOMAS Arthur Coke MM Pte 147 1/5th London Regt
THOMAS Arthur J. MM Pte 301677 28th London Regt
THOMAS Arthur J. MM Gnr 26285 RGA

THOMAS Benjamin MM L/Bdr 46712 B/175 Bde RFA
THOMAS Benjamin MM Gnr 675334 RFA
THOMAS Benjamin MM+Bar S/Sjt 48036 129 Fd Amb RAMC
THOMAS Bert MM L/Cpl 61398 14th Royal Welsh Fusiliers
THOMAS Bertie MM Pte 16507 7th Border Regt
THOMAS Bertram MM L/Cpl 25862 9th Scottish Rifles
THOMAS Bevan E. MM+Bar Pte 48909 RAMC
THOMAS Brinley H. MM Gnr 740882 A/266 Bde RFA
THOMAS Charles MM Bdr 12596 A/88 Bde RFA
THOMAS Charles MM Pte 69635 6th(Light)Bn Tank Corps
THOMAS Charles MM Cpl C/12619 13th King's Royal Rifle Corps
THOMAS Charles MM Pte 32123 7th South Lancashire Regt
THOMAS Charles MM Cpl 21776 Welsh Regt
THOMAS Charles MM Bdr 93386 A/81 Bde RFA
THOMAS Charles Burn MM L/Sjt 720867 24th London Regt KIA 22.8.18.
THOMAS Charles G. MM Pte 56635 Welsh Regt
THOMAS Charles H. MM Pte 281020 2/4th London Regt
THOMAS Cyril MM Pte 974 1st Welsh Guards
THOMAS D.J. MM AM2 50104 Royal Flying Corps
THOMAS Daniel MM+Bar Cpl 26794 15th Welsh Regt
THOMAS David MM L/Cpl 242770 1/6th West Yorkshire Regt
THOMAS David MM Pte 48514 RAMC
THOMAS David MM Pnr 83470 Royal Engineers
THOMAS David MM L/Cpl 14504 6th South Wales Borderers
THOMAS David A. MM Pte 48197 130 Fd Amb RAMC
THOMAS David H. MM Sjt 20250 South Wales Borderers
THOMAS David J. MM L/Cpl 21663 Seaforth Highlanders
THOMAS David J. MM L/Cpl 267053 6th Welsh Regt
THOMAS David L. MM Pte 46143 1st South Wales Borderers
THOMAS David M. MM+Bar Spr 79495 Royal Engineers
THOMAS David P. MM Cpl 74797 74th Bn Machine Gun Corps
THOMAS E. MM L/Cpl 200332 Yorkshire Regt
THOMAS Edgar MM Sjt 56908 14th Royal Welsh Fusiliers KIA 4.8.17.
THOMAS Edgar MM+Bar Sjt 6493 1st Somerset Light Infantry
THOMAS Edgar MM Cpl M2/081000 Army Service Corps att RE.
THOMAS Edmund MM Sjt 25691 Welsh Regt
THOMAS Edward MM Cpl 69919 170 Tunnelling Coy Royal Engineers
THOMAS Edward MM Bdr 102681 RGA
THOMAS Edward MM Pte 23712 1st Lancashire Fusiliers Real name Edward Thomas DOOLEY
THOMAS Edward MM Pte 3653 6th London Regt
THOMAS Edward G. MM L/Cpl 85445 Durham Light Infantry
THOMAS Edwin George MM Pte M2/130593 272 MT Coy Army Service Corps
THOMAS Eli MM Cpl 19388 1st Bn Machine Gun Corps
THOMAS Elias MM Pte 6305 2nd Royal Welsh Fusiliers
THOMAS Elvet MM Pte 200268 Welsh Regt
THOMAS Ernest E. MM Cpl 5063 4th Dragoon Guards
THOMAS Ernest William Noel MM Pte 3584 Oxf & Bucks Light Infantry KIA 20.11.17.
THOMAS Evan MM Gnr 13376 B/77 Bde RFA
THOMAS Evan MM Gnr 2134 D/174 Bde RFA
THOMAS Evan MM Cpl 4374 RFA
THOMAS Evan MM Dvr T4/173326 Army Service Corps
THOMAS Francis Joseph MM Pte 35410 8th East Lancashire Regt
THOMAS Frank MM Pte 46164 17 Fd Amb RAMC
THOMAS Frank MM Dvr 54867 29 Bde RFA
THOMAS Frank MM Sjt 6385 2nd Royal Welsh Fusiliers KIA 19.8.16.
THOMAS Frank MM+Bar Sjt 22073 Border Regt
THOMAS Frank MM Sjt 8373 6th Shropshire Light Infantry Died 2.8 18.
THOMAS Fred MM Sjt 20974 14th Royal Welsh Fusiliers
THOMAS Fred MM Pte 15833 7th South Wales Borderers
THOMAS Fred MM L/Bdr 705086 C/210 Bde RFA
THOMAS Fred MM L/Cpl 3/6076 1st Duke of Cornwall's LI KIA 8.5.17.
THOMAS Fred C. MM Pte 73893 142 Fd Amb RAMC
THOMAS Frederick MM Sjt C/7395 12th King's Royal Rifle Corps
THOMAS Frederick MM+Bar Sjt 885 13th & 6th Cheshire Regt
THOMAS Frederick Stanley MM Sjt 202667 1/5th Liverpool Regt DOW 1.12.18.
THOMAS G.F. MM Cpl 403117 2 Fd Amb RAMC
THOMAS Geoffrey MM Pte 67595 1/5th Devonshire Regt
THOMAS George MM L/Bdr Sig 30072 A/93 Bde RFA
THOMAS George MM Sjt 37733 RGA
THOMAS George MM Cpl 266188 Liverpool Regt

THOMAS George MM Cpl 355307 1/10th Liverpool Regt
THOMAS George MM+Bar Sjt 10086 2nd Welsh Regt DOW 6.6.18.
THOMAS George MM L/Cpl 18521 7th East Yorkshire Regt
THOMAS George A. MM 2nd Cpl 159507 Royal Engineers
THOMAS George A. MM Pte 164330 48th Bn Machine Gun Corps
THOMAS George Arthur MM Pte 10/21269 10th South Wales Borderers
THOMAS George David MM Pte 58458 14th Welsh Regt KIA 20.10.18.
THOMAS George Henry MM Pte 12967 8th Gloucestershire Regt DOW 30.4.18.
THOMAS George Henry MM Pte M2/191493 Army Service Corps att MGC(HS).KIA 3.5.17.
THOMAS George J. "DCM,MM" Cpl 64018 107 Coy Labour Corps
THOMAS George Percy MM Gnr 154009 2 Siege Bty RGA
THOMAS Gomer B. MM Cpl 19571 26th Royal Fusiliers
THOMAS Griffith MM Pte 11621 9th Devonshire Regt
THOMAS Guy D.W. MM Sjt SE/6928 Army Veterinary Corps
THOMAS Gwilym MM Pte 1276 1st Welsh Guards
THOMAS Gwilym MM L/Cpl 91545 Royal Engineers
THOMAS H.C. MM AM2 55961 Royal Air Force
THOMAS Harley MM Sjt 61322 RFA
THOMAS Harold MM Pte 4150 West Riding Regt
THOMAS Harry MM Pte 12162 6th Shropshire Light Infantry
THOMAS Harry MM L/Bdr 17629 C/148 Bde RFA
THOMAS Harry MM Pte 722575 24th London Regt
THOMAS Harry MM Pte B/1509 7th Rifle Brigade
THOMAS Harry MM Pte 8511 11th Lancashire Fusiliers
THOMAS Harry P. MM+Bar Cpl 240485 Liverpool Regt
THOMAS Haydn MM Cpl 25835 Welsh Regt
THOMAS Henry MM Cpl 575806 17th London Regt
THOMAS Henry MM Bdr 23464 RGA
THOMAS Henry MM Cpl 140997 5 Tramway Coy Royal Engineers DOW 13.5.18.
THOMAS Henry MM L/Cpl 21358 13th Liverpool Regt
THOMAS Henry MM Cpl 292846 3/10th Middlesex Regt
THOMAS Henry MM Sjt 139246 Royal Engineers
THOMAS Henry George MM Cpl 34946 Royal Welsh Fusiliers
THOMAS Henry George MM Cpl 567 6th Royal West Kent Regt KIA 5.8.16.
THOMAS Henry J. MM Sjt 6268 2nd Grenadier Guards
THOMAS Henry O. MM Pte 17233 2nd Worcestershire Regt
THOMAS Henry P. MM Sjt 25602 8th East Surrey Regt
THOMAS Herbert MM Spr 492172 Royal Engineers
THOMAS Herbert MM Sjt 48652 92 Fd Coy Royal Engineers
THOMAS Herbert MM Sjt 267442 Royal Warwickshire Regt
THOMAS Herbert MM Cpl 8723 1st West Yorkshire Regt
THOMAS Herbert F. MM Pte 28804 Duke of Cornwall's LI
THOMAS Hopkin Joseph MM Pte 241808 Welsh Regt DOW 22.9.18.
THOMAS Horace W. MM Cpl C/242 16th King's Royal Rifle Corps
THOMAS Howard MM L/Sjt 20084 Royal Munster Fusiliers
THOMAS Hugh MM L/Cpl 27535 Royal Lancaster Regt
THOMAS Isaac MM Cpl 229913 C/84 Bde RFA
THOMAS Isaiah MM Cpl 10543 1st Welsh Regt
THOMAS J. MM Cpl 200026 Yorkshire Regt
THOMAS James MM Pte 18469 1st Leicestershire Regt
THOMAS James MM CSM 5614 2nd Worcestershire Regt
THOMAS James MM+Bar Pte 11511 1st South Wales Borderers
THOMAS James MM Pte 26688 9th East Surrey Regt
THOMAS James MM Gnr 50497 RGA
THOMAS James "DCM,MM" Sjt 14801 2nd Grenadier Guards DOW 6.9.18.
THOMAS James MM Spr 46530 37 Div Sig Coy Royal Engineers
THOMAS James MM S/Sjt 75668 Tank Corps
THOMAS James MM Pte 306698 Lancashire Fusiliers
THOMAS James H. MM Pte(SS) 75733 1/1st Derbyshire Yeomanry
THOMAS James Henry MM Cpl 5332 103 Coy Machine Gun Corps KIA 28.4.17.
THOMAS John MM Pte 42271 19 Fd Amb RAMC
THOMAS John MM CSM 13130 9th Royal Welsh Fusiliers
THOMAS John MM Gnr 2943 RFA DOW 30.3.18.
THOMAS John MM Gnr 19617 A/75 Bde RFA
THOMAS John MM Spr 500456 61 Div Sig Coy Royal Engineers
THOMAS John MM Pte 19625 9th Welsh Regt
THOMAS John D. MM CQMS 17001 Liverpool Regt
THOMAS John E. MM Pte 265690 Royal Welsh Fusiliers
THOMAS John H. "MM,MID" L/Cpl 15530 11th Welsh Regt
THOMAS John James MM Pte 12414 9th Welsh Regt KIA 7.6.17.
THOMAS John Matthew MM Pte 22577 10th Welsh Regt

THOMAS John N. MM Pte 55515 Royal Welsh Fusiliers
THOMAS John P.L. MM Pte 30292 North Lancashire Regt
THOMAS John R. MM Pte 18750 Hampshire Regt
THOMAS John T. MM Pte 4767 Notts & Derby Regt
THOMAS John Vandersluys MM Cpl 66304 100 Fd Amb RAMC
THOMAS John W. MM Pte 202130 Royal Lancaster Regt
THOMAS John William MM Sjt 282120 2/7th Lancashire Fusiliers KIA 11.3.18.
THOMAS Joseph MM L/Cpl 26751 2nd Grenadier Guards
THOMAS Joseph MM Sjt 240772 9th Royal Welsh Fusiliers
THOMAS Joseph MM Pte 91431 Tank Corps
THOMAS Joseph MM Cpl 147881 255 Tunnelling Coy Royal Engineers
THOMAS Joseph MM Spr 108073 Royal Engineers
THOMAS Joseph "DCM,MM" Sjt 3238 2nd Royal Scots KIA 12.4.17.
THOMAS Joseph MM Pte 18025 Royal Welsh Fusiliers
THOMAS Leonard MM Cpl 38088 Royal Fusiliers
THOMAS Leonard MM+2 Bars Pte 306028 8th Notts & Derby Regt
THOMAS Lewis J. MM Pte 56962 2/2nd(West Riding)Fd Amb RAMC
THOMAS Llewellyn MM+Bar Cpl 97578 130 Fd Coy Royal Engineers
THOMAS M. MM L/Cpl 201796 1/4th Royal Berkshire Regt
THOMAS M.L. MM Cpl 241641 East Kent Regt
THOMAS Niah MM Pte 320489 Welsh Regt
THOMAS Norman MM Sjt R/3758 11th King's Royal Rifle Corps DOW 30.11.17.
THOMAS Owen Thomas MM Sjt 50016 'D' Bty RHA KIA 20.10.16.
THOMAS Percy MM Pte 8930 1st Leicestershire Regt
THOMAS Percy MM Pte 27298 22nd Manchester Regt
THOMAS Percy E. MM Cpl Sig 230403 1/1st Dorset Yeomanry
THOMAS Peter MM L/Cpl 53451 2/5th Lancashire Fusiliers KIA 25.10.18.
THOMAS Pryce MM Sjt 61374 26 Bde RFA
THOMAS Ralph MM L/Cpl 205077 1/1st Buckinghamshire Yeo DOW 21.11.17.
THOMAS Reginald MM Pte 27787 18th Welsh Regt KIA 13.4.18.
THOMAS Reginald George MM Cpl(MCDR) 32338 24 Div Sig Coy Royal Engineers
THOMAS Richard "MM,MID" Sjt B/3161 Rifle Brigade
THOMAS Richard D.T. MM L/Cpl 241697 1st East Surrey Regt
THOMAS Richard H. MM AM1 13554 Royal Flying Corps
THOMAS Richard J. MM Cpl 14095 11th Royal Welsh Fusiliers
THOMAS Robert MM L/Cpl 240915 24th Royal Welsh Fusiliers
THOMAS Robert MM L/Cpl 61068 16th Royal Welsh Fusiliers
THOMAS Robert B. MM Gnr 168189 RFA
THOMAS Robert L. MM+Bar Cpl 236079 249 Fd Coy Royal Engineers
THOMAS S. MM Pte 46909 Manchester Regt
THOMAS Samuel MM Pte 27189 8th Lincolnshire Regt
THOMAS Samuel MM Pte 17151 2nd South Staffordshire Regt
THOMAS Samuel H. MM Gnr 326976 RGA
THOMAS Sidney MM Pte 16398 2nd South Staffordshire Regt
THOMAS Stanley MM Pte 11280 1st Hampshire Regt
THOMAS Sydney MM L/Cpl 19281 21st Manchester Regt
THOMAS Sydney George Frederick MM Spr 504357 49 Div Sig Coy Royal Engineers
THOMAS Taliesin MM CQMS 47401 80 Coy Labour Corps
THOMAS Theodore F.J. MM Cpl 148356 11 Div Sig Coy Royal Engineers
THOMAS Thomas MM Pte 13705 7th Shropshire Light Infantry
THOMAS Thomas MM Sjt 25071 Welsh Regt
THOMAS Thomas MM Cpl 17116 13th Royal Welsh Fusiliers KIA 22.4.18.
THOMAS Thomas G. MM Pte 9546 11th Royal Fusiliers
THOMAS Thomas H. MM Pte 1125 1st Welsh Guards
THOMAS Thomas Henry MM Pte 291824 2/10th Middlesex Regt KIA 27.12.17.
THOMAS Thomas J. MM Pte 46916 1st South Wales Borderers
THOMAS Thomas J. MM Spr 448174 Royal Engineers
THOMAS Thomas R. MM Sjt 4154 RFA
THOMAS Thomas W. MM Pte 1296 23rd Royal Fusiliers
THOMAS Tyssul J. MM+Bar Cpl 15663 7th Shropshire Light Infantry
THOMAS Vinton E.C. MM L/Cpl 24418 26 Fd Coy Royal Engineers
THOMAS W.D. MM Dvr 436 RFA
THOMAS Walter MM Cpl 107178 947 Area Emp Coy Labour Corps
THOMAS Walter MM Pte 798 1 Fd Amb RAMC
THOMAS Walter MM Pte 203664 5th Gloucestershire Regt
THOMAS Walter MM Spr 6645 422 Fd Coy Royal Engineers KIA 20.9.17.
THOMAS Walter R. MM Sjt 109092 Royal Engineers
THOMAS Walter R. MM Pte 6769 West Riding Regt
THOMAS William MM Sjt 49033 8th Devonshire Regt
THOMAS William MM Pte 12320 17th Lancashire Fusiliers
THOMAS William MM Pte 21323 7th Shropshire Light Infantry
THOMAS William MM L/Cpl 43367 Essex Regt Died 7.11.18.
THOMAS William MM Cpl 87505 22nd Northumberland Fusiliers
THOMAS William MM Pte 17025 1st Shropshire Light Infantry
THOMAS William MM Gnr 167533 163 Siege Bty RGA
THOMAS William MM Pte 202018 1/5th Liverpool Regt
THOMAS William MM Pte 37456 Machine Gun Corps
THOMAS William MM Cpl 22973 RFA
THOMAS William MM Spr 248878 Royal Engineers
THOMAS William MM Pte 11512 5th Shropshire Light Infantry
THOMAS William "MM,MID" Pte 31172 Royal Welsh Fusiliers
THOMAS William MM Cpl(SS) 6013 19th Hussars
THOMAS William MM Sjt 14491 6th South Wales Borderers KIA 20.10.16.
THOMAS William MM Pte 15424 10th Royal Welsh Fusiliers
THOMAS William MM Bdr 36264 RFA
THOMAS William MM Sjt 23367 2nd Yorkshire Light Infantry KIA 18.11.16.
THOMAS William MM Pte 56715 2nd Royal Welsh Fusiliers
THOMAS William MM Pte 50132 RAMC
THOMAS William MM Bdr 73360 34 Bde RFA
THOMAS William MM L/Cpl 4/8291 Arg & Suth Highlanders
THOMAS William MM Spr 27184 Signal Service Royal Engineers
THOMAS William MM Pte R/35719 King's Royal Rifle Corps
THOMAS William A. MM Sjt 203268 4th York & Lancaster Regt
THOMAS William Cuthbert MM Sjt 113484 Royal Engineers
THOMAS William G. MM L/Cpl 48196 RAMC
THOMAS William H. MM Cpl 3/8916 Yorkshire Regt
THOMAS William H. "DCM,MM" L/Cpl 37096 1 Div Sig Coy Royal Engineers
THOMAS William J. MM Pte 3208 1st Welsh Guards
THOMAS William John MM L/Cpl 54058 16th Royal Welsh Fusiliers KIA 22.4.18.
THOMAS William John MM CQMS 13716 1st Grenadier Guards KIA 18.11.16.
THOMAS William Joseph MM L/Cpl 13741 9th Royal Welsh Fusiliers
THOMAS Zophar D. MM Pte 14498 5th South Wales Borderers
THOMASON Ben MM Bdr 614111 1st(Warwickshire)Bty RHA
THOMASON Ernest MM Gnr 130178 400 Bty 14 Bde RFA
THOMASON John S. MM Pte 29309 8th Royal Lancaster Regt
THOMASON William MM Cpl 240979 Royal Lancaster Regt
THOMASSON Frederick MM AM1 2551 Royal Flying Corps
THOMASSON Joseph MM Pte 203069 2/4th South Lancashire Regt
THOMLINSON Herbert MM Sjt 312009 RGA
THOMPSETT Arthur MM Pte 68097 11th Royal Fusiliers
THOMPSETT Herbert George MM+Bar L/Cpl 3029 Royal Sussex Regt
THOMPSON A. MM Cpl 16422 Royal Engineers
THOMPSON Abner MM Pte 85248 1/7th Durham Light Infantry
THOMPSON Abraham MM Sjt 4742 10th York & Lancaster Regt
THOMPSON Albert MM Pte 44824 RAMC
THOMPSON Albert MM Pte 17733 8th Duke of Cornwall's LI
THOMPSON Albert James MM Pte 8757 4th Liverpool Regt KIA 28.10.16.
THOMPSON Albert M. MM Cpl 96771 355 Siege Bty RGA
THOMPSON Albert V.N. MM Sjt 7197 East Surrey Regt
THOMPSON Alfred "DCM,MM" Sjt 201649 2/4th West Riding Regt
THOMPSON Alfred A. MM Pte 721834 24th London Regt
THOMPSON Alfred Armstrong "MM,MM(F)" Sjt 27562 Machine Gun Corps
THOMPSON Alfred J. MM Spr 40044 Royal Engineers
THOMPSON Ambrose H. MM BSM 38784 1 Hy Bty RGA
THOMPSON Andrew MM L/Cpl 151866 33rd Bn Machine Gun Corps
THOMPSON Archibald MM L/Cpl 1834 4th Dragoon Guards
THOMPSON Archibald Edward MM L/Cpl 192875 4 Special Coy Royal Engineers
THOMPSON Arthur MM Gnr 47258 RFA
THOMPSON Arthur MM Pte 15213 7th Bedfordshire Regt
THOMPSON Arthur MM Bdr 33570 RGA
THOMPSON Arthur MM Pte 12644 7th East Lancashire Regt
THOMPSON Arthur MM Pte 46625 94 Coy Machine Gun Corps Died 8.5.20.
THOMPSON Arthur George MM L/Sjt 16321 2nd Grenadier Guards
THOMPSON Arthur H. MM Pte 14093 8th Suffolk Regt

THOMPSON Arthur W. MM Pte R/32838 13th King's Royal Rifle Corps
THOMPSON Augustus W. MM Cpl 84911 Royal Engineers
THOMPSON B. MM Dvr 127298 RFA
THOMPSON Benjamin Robert MM Pte 13632 11th Suffolk Regt DOW 4.8.16.
THOMPSON Bernard William MM Pte 75635 47 Fd Amb RAMC
THOMPSON Bertie C. MM Spr 64974 6 Div Sig Coy Royal Engineers
THOMPSON C.E. MM Sjt 11071 6th Royal West Kent Regt
THOMPSON Charles MM L/Cpl 43986 1st Royal Inniskilling Fusiliers
THOMPSON Charles MM Pte 26712 Hampshire Regt
THOMPSON Charles MM L/Cpl 46665 83 Fd Coy Royal Engineers
THOMPSON Charles E. MM Pte 4834 Gloucestershire Regt
THOMPSON Charles Edward MM Sjt 9142 11th Royal Warwickshire Regt
THOMPSON Charles J. MM Cpl 15546 1st Royal Fusiliers
THOMPSON Charles Robert MM Sjt 9951 1st Notts & Derby Regt DOW 30.4.17.
THOMPSON Clement A. MM Pte 40073 Royal Irish Fusiliers
THOMPSON Costa I. MM 2nd Cpl 478150 Royal Engineers
THOMPSON Cyril A. MM Pte 13583 8th Norfolk Regt
THOMPSON David MM Pte 53089 RAMC
THOMPSON David MM Bdr 75048 44 Bde RFA
THOMPSON David MM Pte 45195 RAMC
THOMPSON David J. MM L/Cpl 25573 17th Welsh Regt
THOMPSON Edward MM Pte 14238 Coldstream Guards
THOMPSON Edward H. MM Pte 392346 8th London Regt
THOMPSON Edward Vaughan MM Pte 230744 2/2nd London Regt
THOMPSON Edwin "DCM,MM" Pte 1738 1/1st Lincolnshire Yeomanry
THOMPSON Ernest MM L/Sjt 26965 14th Worcestershire Regt
THOMPSON Ernest MM L/Cpl 108208 Royal Engineers
THOMPSON Ernest MM Pte 12511 9th Yorkshire Regt
THOMPSON Ethel Kate MM Sister F QAIMNS
THOMPSON Francis MM L/Cpl 18103 Royal Welsh Fusiliers
THOMPSON Francis B. MM Pte 30243 Durham Light Infantry
THOMPSON Francis Edwin MM Dvr 110884 C/58 Bde RFA
THOMPSON Frank MM L/Cpl 53000 12th Manchester Regt
THOMPSON Frank MM Pte 29713 2nd Manchester Regt
THOMPSON Frank MM L/Cpl 570290 2/17th London Regt KIA 29.12.17.
THOMPSON Frank MM Pte 53989 22nd Manchester Regt
THOMPSON Fred MM Sjt 30781 15th Lancashire Fusiliers
THOMPSON Fred MM Cpl 1646 1/4th East Yorkshire Regt
THOMPSON Fred "MM,MID" Sjt 12510 2 Div Sig Coy Royal Engineers
THOMPSON Frederick MM Sjt 46280 A/124 Bde RFA
THOMPSON Frederick MM Pte M2/180950 Army Service Corps
THOMPSON Frederick MM L/Cpl 53631 51st Bn Machine Gun Corps
THOMPSON Frederick MM Pte 235309 Suffolk Regt
THOMPSON Frederick MM Cpl 78437 Tank Corps
THOMPSON Frederick MM+Bar Pte 70792 Machine Gun Corps
THOMPSON Frederick MM Bdr 36919 RFA
THOMPSON Frederick John MM Gnr 11208 C/152 Bde RFA
THOMPSON George MM Cpl 275049 Durham Light Infantry
THOMPSON George MM Pte 3444 Manchester Regt
THOMPSON George "DCM,MM" CSM 52647 13th Durham Light Infantry
THOMPSON George MM Sjt 14279 7th Royal Lancaster Regt
THOMPSON George MM Dvr 76922 RFA
THOMPSON George MM Cpl 16/191 16th Northumberland Fusiliers
THOMPSON George MM Bdr 6471 RFA
THOMPSON George MM Gnr 47657 RFA
THOMPSON George MM Pte 20966 7th East Kent Regt KIA 7.8.18.
THOMPSON George MM Pte 12867 9th West Riding Regt
THOMPSON George A. MM L/Cpl 23/513 Northumberland Fusiliers
THOMPSON George Armstrong MM Gnr 29275 65 Bde RFA KIA 30.7.17.
THOMPSON George Dean MM Cpl M2/133583 8 Pontoon Park Army Service Corps
THOMPSON George E. MM Sjt 50958 83 Fd Coy Royal Engineers
THOMPSON George Edward MM Pte 275988 1/7th Durham Light Infantry
THOMPSON George H. MM Pte 13559 30th Bn Machine Gun Corps
THOMPSON George Henry MM Sjt 2850 16th Manchester Regt
THOMPSON George J. MM Pte 352285 7th London Regt
THOMPSON George J. MM Cpl 55413 9 Bde RFA
THOMPSON George R. MM Dvr T4/249467 Army Service Corps
THOMPSON George W. MM L/Sjt 16326 1st Grenadier Guards
THOMPSON H. MM L/Cpl 18117 Leicestershire Regt
THOMPSON Harold MM L/Cpl 277380 7th Manchester Regt
THOMPSON Harold MM Pte 358555 Liverpool Regt
THOMPSON Harold Victor MM Cpl 7580 Royal Monmouthshire Royal Engineers
THOMPSON Harry MM Pte 82537 11th Royal Fusiliers
THOMPSON Harry MM Pte 22852 1st North Lancashire Regt
THOMPSON Harry MM+Bar CSM 19993 13th Liverpool Regt
THOMPSON Harry MM Dvr 4644 37 Bde RFA
THOMPSON Harry MM Pte 11920 7th York & Lancaster Regt
THOMPSON Harry MM Pte 10179 1st Middlesex Regt
THOMPSON Harry MM Pte 17758 8th Duke of Cornwall's LI
THOMPSON Harry MM Dvr 800416 B/230 Bde RFA
THOMPSON Henry MM Cpl 242282 1st King's Own Scottish Borderers
THOMPSON Henry MM L/Cpl 10522 5th Dragoon Guards
THOMPSON Henry J. MM Pte 242367 Cheshire Regt
THOMPSON Henry J. MM Pte 4218 Machine Gun Corps
THOMPSON Henry Peck MM Pte 321376 1/6th London Regt KIA 30.11.17.
THOMPSON Herbert MM Dvr 179133 D/162 Bde RFA
THOMPSON Herbert MM Cpl 201696 Yorkshire Light Infantry
THOMPSON Herbert W. MM Pte 29247 Royal Fusiliers
THOMPSON Herbert W. MM L/Cpl 18/619 18th Durham Light Infantry
THOMPSON Isaac MM Pte 29406 11th East Lancashire Regt KIA 28.9.18.
THOMPSON Isaac Lewis MM L/Cpl 5/203277 1/5th South Staffordshire Regt
THOMPSON J. MM Pte 386288 RAMC
THOMPSON J. MM Pte 16640 9th Essex Regt
THOMPSON J.E. MM Pte 1427 RAMC
THOMPSON James MM Pte 1659 2nd Royal Sussex Regt
THOMPSON James MM Dvr 100830 RFA
THOMPSON James MM L/Cpl 52182 Royal Fusiliers
THOMPSON James "DCM,MM" Sjt 9089 2nd & 1st Royal Inniskilling Fusiliers DOW 28.11.16.
THOMPSON James MM AM1 11167 7/8th Royal Irish Fusiliers KIA 20.11.17.
THOMPSON James MM 2nd Cpl 07689 Army Ordnance Corps
THOMPSON James MM Pte 203162 Northumberland Fusiliers
THOMPSON James A. MM Pte 19411 2nd East Lancashire Regt
THOMPSON James E. MM Pte 49373 Machine Gun Corps
THOMPSON James Edward MM+Bar L/Cpl 22133 20th Durham Light Infantry KIA 29.9.18.
THOMPSON James F. MM Sjt 98 1/6th London Regt
THOMPSON James S. MM Dvr 765308 RFA
THOMPSON James Thomas MM Sjt 18795 3rd Grenadier Guards
THOMPSON James V. MM Pte DM2/209078 Army Service Corps
THOMPSON John MM Pte 129913 18th Bn Machine Gun Corps
THOMPSON John MM Spr 474696 18 Div Sig Coy Royal Engineers
THOMPSON John MM Pte 17/217 15th Royal Irish Rifles KIA 20.10.18.
THOMPSON John MM Cpl G/3554 7th East Kent Regt KIA 30.9.16.
THOMPSON John MM L/Cpl 22977 2nd Yorkshire Light Infantry
THOMPSON John MM Pte 551815 79 Coy Labour Corps
THOMPSON John MM Sjt 24803 Notts & Derby Regt
THOMPSON John MM Pte 8413 Royal Fusiliers
THOMPSON John MM Bdr 115387 RFA
THOMPSON John MM Cpl 201197 1/4th North Lancashire Regt
THOMPSON John B. MM Sjt 18463 5th Northamptonshire Regt
THOMPSON John B. MM Pte 19/1465 Northumberland Fusiliers
THOMPSON John Dring MM Pte 37665 9th Yorkshire Light Infantry KIA 26.4.18.
THOMPSON John E. MM L/Cpl 6602 11th Northumberland Fusiliers
THOMPSON John Gardner MM Pte 38000 RAMC
THOMPSON John H. MM Pte 55788 16th Royal Welsh Fusiliers
THOMPSON John M. MM Pte 54245 Royal Welsh Fusiliers
THOMPSON John R. MM Pte 44750 35 Fd Amb RAMC
THOMPSON John R. MM Cpl S/26471 Rifle Brigade
THOMPSON John S. MM Pte M2/019660 Army Service Corps
THOMPSON John W. MM Pte 4233 Machine Gun Corps
THOMPSON John W. MM Cpl 14310 9th South Staffordshire Regt
THOMPSON John W. MM Sjt 200049 West Yorkshire Regt
THOMPSON Joseph MM Pte 17851 2nd South Staffordshire Regt DOW 26.7.18.
THOMPSON Joseph MM Cpl 37500 D/101 Bde RFA

THOMPSON Joseph MM L/Sjt 12858 10th West Yorkshire Regt KIA 18.9.18.
THOMPSON Joseph MM 2nd Cpl 441922 Royal Engineers
THOMPSON Joseph MM Pte 17197 1st Yorkshire Light Infantry KIA 8.10.18.
THOMPSON Joseph MM Pte 6183 2nd Border Regt
THOMPSON Joseph MM AM1 12270 Royal Flying Corps
THOMPSON Joseph MM Pte 14445 9th Yorkshire Regt DOW 10.12.17.
THOMPSON Joseph B. MM Gnr 311647 115 Hy Bty RGA
THOMPSON Joshua MM Pte 32270 South Lancashire Regt
THOMPSON Lewis MM Pte 303930 1/5th London Regt
THOMPSON Mark MM Gnr 64147 B/87 Bde RFA
THOMPSON Mark MM Pte 10075 19th Durham Light Infantry KIA 31.8.17.
THOMPSON Mark Edward Butler MM L/Cpl 202031 Yorkshire Light Infantry
THOMPSON Mat Collinson MM Pte 28678 2nd Yorkshire Regt
THOMPSON Matthew MM Cpl 405 19th Durham Light Infantry
THOMPSON Maurice MM Pte 21663 6th Cameron Highlanders
THOMPSON Moxon MM Gnr 77608 RGA
THOMPSON Muriel MM Miss F First Aid Nursing Yeomanry
THOMPSON Oliver MM L/Cpl 419313 2/2(North Midland)Fd Amb RAMC
THOMPSON Oscar MM Sjt 18236 1st Royal Inniskilling Fusiliers
THOMPSON Percy MM Sjt 241997 5th Leicestershire Regt
THOMPSON Percy MM Cpl 48089 23rd Royal Fusiliers
THOMPSON Percy MM Spr 240117 Royal Engineers
THOMPSON Peter MM Pte 7761 2nd Connaught Rangers
THOMPSON Peter MM L/Cpl 44470 Royal Engineers
THOMPSON Peter MM Pte 13971 1/5th West Yorkshire Regt KIA 25.4.18.
THOMPSON Philip I.S. MM Pte 10101 2nd Royal Irish Regt
THOMPSON Ralph William George MM Sjt R/6374 7th King's Royal Rifle Corps KIA 21.3.18.
THOMPSON Reginald MM Pte 16385 York & Lancaster Regt
THOMPSON Reginald George "MM,OStA(R)" Sjt 48044 14 Div Sig Coy Royal Engineers
THOMPSON Richard MM Cpl 8930 2nd Lincolnshire Regt
THOMPSON Richard E. MM Pte 512038 14th London Regt
THOMPSON Richard J. MM Sjt 54572 117 Bty 26 Bde RFA Died 21.7.16.
THOMPSON Richard O. MM Sjt 2717 Gloucestershire Regt
THOMPSON Robert MM Cpl 315719 13th Royal Highlanders
THOMPSON Robert MM Pte 200962 5/6th Scottish Rifles KIA 3.10.18.
THOMPSON Robert MM Sjt 57590 150 Fd Coy Royal Engineers
THOMPSON Robert MM Dvr 775315 B/245 Bde RFA
THOMPSON Robert MM Sjt 2754 7/8th Royal Inniskilling Fusiliers
THOMPSON Robert A. MM Cpl 6030 Royal Irish Rifles
THOMPSON Robert A. MM Sjt 11940 54 Fd Coy Royal Engineers
THOMPSON Robert John MM Spr 51459 25 Div Sig Coy Royal Engineers Died 27.10.18.
THOMPSON Robert L. MM Pte 31692 6th King's Own Scottish Borderers
THOMPSON Robert N. MM Cpl 249579 Royal Engineers
THOMPSON Roger MM Dvr 73841 104 Bde RFA
THOMPSON Samuel MM Spr 486519 154 Fd Coy Royal Engineers
THOMPSON Samuel MM Sjt 306098 Liverpool Regt
THOMPSON Samuel MM+Bar Sjt 21706 6th King's Own Scottish Borderers
THOMPSON Samuel MM Sjt 631396 RFA
THOMPSON Samuel John MM Sjt 504252 500 Fd Coy Royal Engineers
THOMPSON Sidney MM Sjt 150173 102nd Bn Machine Gun Corps
THOMPSON Sidney MM Pte 11667 2nd South Wales Borderers
THOMPSON Sidney MM Pte 73050 Notts & Derby Regt
THOMPSON Stephen MM+Bar Pte 9595 2nd Middlesex Regt
THOMPSON Stephen MM Cpl 57603 4th York & Lancaster Regt
THOMPSON Stewart MM Pte 41134 108 Fd Amb RAMC
THOMPSON Sydney MM Pte 20321 Northamptonshire Regt
THOMPSON Sydney E. MM L/Cpl 66067 20 Div Sig Coy Royal Engineers KIA 31.3.18.
THOMPSON T.H. MM Pte M1/08743 Army Service Corps
THOMPSON Thomas MM+Bar L/Cpl 1278 16th Royal Warwickshire Regt
THOMPSON Thomas MM Pte 13385 10th West Riding Regt KIA 20.9.17.
THOMPSON Thomas MM+Bar Pte 6692 Durham Light Infantry
THOMPSON Thomas MM L/Cpl 17603 Northumberland Fusiliers
THOMPSON Thomas MM L/Cpl 15087 6th Northamptonshire Regt
THOMPSON Thomas MM Cpl 17572 8th Yorkshire Regt
THOMPSON Thomas "DCM,MM" L/Cpl 14478 9th York & Lancaster Regt
THOMPSON Thomas MM Sjt 34886 19 Fd Amb RAMC Died 4.1.18.
THOMPSON Thomas Anthony MM L/Cpl 22953 16th Northumberland Fusiliers
THOMPSON Thomas M. MM Pte 203539 York & Lancaster Regt
THOMPSON Thomas M. "DCM,MM" Sjt 84144 199 Siege Bty RGA
THOMPSON Thomas P. MM L/Cpl 160365 Royal Engineers
THOMPSON Tom MM Pte 38427 1st Northumberland Fusiliers
THOMPSON W.C. MM Pte 386033 RAMC
THOMPSON W.S. MM Pte B/200133 Rifle Brigade
THOMPSON Walter MM L/Sjt 14046 York & Lancaster Regt
THOMPSON Walter MM L/Sjt 4508 8th Northumberland Fusiliers KIA 27.11.17.
THOMPSON Walter A. MM Pte 77090 24th Royal Fusiliers
THOMPSON Walter J. MM L/Cpl 32702 East Surrey Regt
THOMPSON Wilfred MM Pte 200819 Lincolnshire Regt
THOMPSON Wilfred MM Pte 11289 7th Yorkshire Regt
THOMPSON Wilfred H. "DCM,MM" Sjt 37469 20th Northumberland Fusiliers
THOMPSON Wilfred R. MM Cpl 16936 6th Northamptonshire Regt
THOMPSON Willard MM Sjt 13014 8th West Riding Regt
THOMPSON William MM L/Cpl 41132 5 Sqn MGC(Cavalry)
THOMPSON William MM Cpl 15533 9th Notts & Derby Regt
THOMPSON William MM Pte 265351 1/9th Middlesex Regt
THOMPSON William MM Dvr 18827 B/94 Bde RFA
THOMPSON William MM Sjt 231092 2nd London Regt
THOMPSON William MM L/Cpl 71123 55 Coy Machine Gun Corps KIA 23.3.18.
THOMPSON William MM L/Cpl 240205 Notts & Derby Regt
THOMPSON William MM Sjt 15006 Labour Corps
THOMPSON William MM Pte 20194 Grenadier Guards
THOMPSON William MM Pte 3/8446 2nd` Suffolk Regt
THOMPSON William MM L/Cpl 2602 8th Liverpool Regt DOW 23.8.16.
THOMPSON William MM Gnr 9442 RFA
THOMPSON William MM Gnr 5576 RGA
THOMPSON William MM Pte 2801 1/5th Royal Lancaster Regt
THOMPSON William MM Pte 617139 2/19th London Regt
THOMPSON William MM QMS 240107 North Staffordshire Regt
THOMPSON William MM Pte 29617 16th Manchester Regt KIA 21.3.18.
THOMPSON William MM Pte 30120 Royal Inniskilling Fusiliers
THOMPSON William MM Cpl 19041 16 Fd Amb RAMC
THOMPSON William MM Dvr 806208 D/298 Bde RFA KIA 19.1.18.
THOMPSON William A. MM Sjt 10/342 10th East Yorkshire Regt
THOMPSON William Arthur MM Sjt 8367 B/150 Bde RFA
THOMPSON William Colley MM Gnr 29203 B/91 Bde RFA
THOMPSON William D. MM Gnr 680273 RFA
THOMPSON William H. MM Spr 496555 Royal Engineers
THOMPSON William H. MM Pte 37755 21 Fd Amb RAMC
THOMPSON William H. MM Bdr 294676 RGA
THOMPSON William H. MM Pte 25349 Worcestershire Regt
THOMPSON William H. MM Cpl 18124 Durham Light Infantry
THOMPSON William Herbert MM Gnr Sig 62811 84 Siege Bty RGA
THOMPSON William Robert John MM Pte 8900 2nd Royal West Kent Regt DOW 1.11.18.
THOMPSON William S. MM Pte 9721 2nd Durham Light Infantry
THOMPSON William Samuel MM Cpl R/17445 2nd King's Royal Rifle Corps DOW 8.9.18.
THOMPSON or THOMSON Adam L. MM+Bar Pte 40234 8 Fd Amb RAMC
THOMPSTONE Sydney MM Pte 21068 14th Royal Welsh Fusiliers KIA 20.10.18.
THOMS Arnold Spencer MM L/Cpl 5087 14th London Regt
THOMS Henry James MM Sjt 2872 1/14th London Regt
THOMSON A. MM Pte 2411 Royal Highlanders
THOMSON Adam MM Sjt 265027 1/6th Gordon Highlanders
THOMSON Adam MM L/Cpl 8419 8th Royal Highlanders KIA 19.7.18.
THOMSON Alexander MM Pte 265663 7th Scottish Rifles
THOMSON Alexander MM Cpl 240684 Gordon Highlanders
THOMSON Alexander MM Pte 265379 Royal Highlanders
THOMSON Alexander Bennett MM Bdr 141080 X/37 Med TM Bty RFA
THOMSON Alexander M. MM Dvr 645962 RFA
THOMSON Allan "DCM,MM" L/Cpl 240460 1/5th Gordon Highlanders KIA 28.7.18.

THOMSON Andrew E. MM Sjt 42048 Royal Engineers
THOMSON Andrew W. MM Sjt 13122 15th Highland Light Infantry
THOMSON Archibald R. MM+Bar L/Cpl 15335 1/8th Arg & Suth Highlanders
THOMSON Arthur MM Pte 1875 1/8th Arg & Suth Highlanders
THOMSON Arthur D. MM Dvr 19736 D/168 Bde RFA
THOMSON Arthur Jacob MM Gnr 10953 B/94 Bde RFA KIA 17.9.17.
THOMSON Charles A. MM Pte 304341 17th Armoured Car Bn Tank Corps
THOMSON Charles G. MM Cpl 402431 105 Fd Coy Royal Engineers
THOMSON Charles J. MM Pte 393934 1/9th London Regt
THOMSON Daniel MM Pte 14154 11th Royal Scots
THOMSON Daniel MM Sjt 7099 Arg & Suth Highlanders Died 22.10.18.
THOMSON David MM Sjt 27826 Royal Scots
THOMSON David MM Cpl 10703 2nd Gordon Highlanders
THOMSON David B. MM+Bar Pte 242456 1/5th Gordon Highlanders
THOMSON David F. MM Pte 130969 Machine Gun Corps
THOMSON Douglas J. MM L/Cpl 24556 Machine Gun Corps
THOMSON Dunbar Dyson Beck MM Gnr 936007 A/70 RFA
THOMSON Duncan MM Pte 42106 1st Scottish Rifles
THOMSON Edward MM L/Cpl 240272 5/6th Scottish Rifles
THOMSON Ernest A. MM Pte 60544 Welsh Regt
THOMSON Ernest Blair MM L/Cpl 21669 7th Cameron Highlanders KIA 28.4.17.
THOMSON Ferguson MM Pte 16204 1st Scots Guards DOW 29.9.18.
THOMSON Frank Y. MM Spr 400069 Royal Engineers
THOMSON Frederick G. MM Pte 72191 9th Notts & Derby Regt
THOMSON George MM Pte 656 Royal Highlanders
THOMSON George MM+Bar Sjt 16211 5th Bn Machine Gun Corps
THOMSON George MM Gnr 2788 Tank Corps
THOMSON George MM Pte 34882 York & Lancaster Regt
THOMSON George M. "DCM,MM" Sjt 5189 Arg & Suth Highlanders
THOMSON Harold MM Pte 6603 9th Royal Highlanders
THOMSON Henry MM L/Cpl 265290 1/6th Gordon Highlanders
THOMSON Henry George MM Sjt 860 16th Rifle Brigade DOW 3.4.18.
THOMSON Herbert MM Pte 42821 49 Fd Amb RAMC
THOMSON Hugh MM Sjt 7905 Arg & Suth Highlanders
THOMSON J.A. MM Sjt 2238 1st Royal Highlanders
THOMSON James MM Pte 7659 8th Scottish Rifles
THOMSON James MM Dvr 6354 RFA
THOMSON James MM+Bar L/Cpl 41242 1/7th Royal Highlanders
THOMSON James MM L/Sjt 86182 12th Bn Machine Gun Corps
THOMSON James MM+Bar Bdr 650604 RFA
THOMSON James MM Spr 143368 Royal Engineers
THOMSON James MM Cpl 1231 Royal Highlanders KIA 21.3.18.
THOMSON James MM Pte 200342 1/4th Royal Scots
THOMSON James MM Pte 305184 Tank Corps
THOMSON James MM L/Cpl 420239 Royal Engineers
THOMSON James C. MM Pte 9539 2nd Gordon Highlanders
THOMSON James S. MM Cpl 52783 2nd Highland Light Infantry
THOMSON James S. MM Sjt 42463 Machine Gun Corps
THOMSON John MM Pte 332837 Highland Light Infantry
THOMSON John MM Dvr 6098 RFA
THOMSON John MM 2nd Cpl 129278 Royal Engineers
THOMSON John MM Sjt 40823 RFA
THOMSON John MM Spr 49482 95 Fd Coy Royal Engineers
THOMSON John MM Pte 40075 12th Highland Light Infantry
THOMSON John MM Sjt 2619 10th Arg & Suth Highlanders KIA 12.10.17.
THOMSON John MM Pte 11869 6/7th Royal Scots Fusiliers
THOMSON John MM Pte 90223 RAMC
THOMSON John MM Cpl 44748 RAMC
THOMSON John A. MM 2nd Cpl 406389 Royal Engineers
THOMSON John A. MM L/Cpl 43074 Scottish Rifles
THOMSON John Barr MM L/Cpl 33810 10th Scottish Rifles DOW 4.1.18.
THOMSON John H. MM Gnr 165992 B/119 Bde RFA
THOMSON John P. MM Sjt 265547 11th Royal Scots Fusiliers
THOMSON John Somerville MM Pte 18509 1st King's Own Scottish Borderers
THOMSON John W. MM Pte 12823 1st Scottish Rifles
THOMSON L.I. MM Sjt 23213 RGA
THOMSON Lancelot G. MM BQMS 337724 RGA
THOMSON Lelia Helen Ann MM Sister F TFNS
THOMSON Louis MM Pte 2814 Gordon Highlanders
THOMSON Matthew MM Pte 292170 Gordon Highlanders
THOMSON Ninian MM Sjt 610381 19th London Regt
THOMSON Owen MM Sjt 29028 115 Siege Bty RGA
THOMSON Percival J. MM Sjt 3769 1/10th Liverpool Regt
THOMSON Peter MM Cpl 497 Royal Engineers
THOMSON R. MM L/Sjt 200869 Seaforth Highlanders
THOMSON Randolph MM Gnr 36763 5 Div Ammn Col RFA
THOMSON Robert MM Sjt 7360 Arg & Suth Highlanders
THOMSON Robert MM Sjt 350161 1/9th Royal Scots
THOMSON Robert Affleck MM Sjt 550239 520 Fd Coy Royal Engineers
THOMSON Robert D. MM Pte 250345 5/6th Royal Scots KIA 12.10.18.
THOMSON Robert H. MM Sjt 3873 Gordon Highlanders
THOMSON Robert J.G. MM Pte 31955 RAMC
THOMSON Robert W. MM Pte 200952 King's Own Scottish Borderers
THOMSON Roy MM Pte 240956 1/5th Gordon Highlanders
THOMSON Thomas MM Pte 12470 12th Royal Scots DOW 24.8.16.
THOMSON Thomas MM Pte 27646 Royal Scots
THOMSON Thomas B.B. MM+Bar Pte 40689 10th Scottish Rifles
THOMSON Thomas H. MM Sjt 20129 2 Fd Amb RAMC
THOMSON W. MM Gnr 56460 RFA
THOMSON Walter MM Sjt 200807 6th King's Own Scottish Borderers
THOMSON Webster MM CSM M2/048964 326 Coy (8 MAC) Army Service Corps
THOMSON William MM Pte 5369 Gordon Highlanders
THOMSON William MM Sjt 645111 RFA
THOMSON William MM Pte 43302 6th Cameron Highlanders
THOMSON William MM Pnr 48982 18 Div Sig Coy Royal Engineers KIA 23.10.17.
THOMSON William MM Pte 14492 16th Highland Light Infantry
THOMSON William MM L/Cpl 43398 5/6th Scottish Rifles
THOMSON William MM Pte 981 4th Bn GMGR
THOMSON William D. MM Pte 250251 5/6th Royal Scots
THOMSON William R. MM Bdr 75311 24 Bde RFA
THOMSON or THOMPSON Adam L. MM+Bar Pte 40234 8 Fd Amb RAMC
THORAGOOD Joseph J. MM Cpl 75632 127 Coy Labour Corps
THORBURN David MM Sjt 330614 1/9th Highland Light Infantry KIA 29.9.18.
THORBURN Henry MM Cpl 16149 17th Highland Light Infantry
THORBURN John MM Pte 201739 1/5th Arg & Suth Highlanders
THORBURN Thomas MM Spr 154715 Royal Engineers
THORBY Ernest MM Pte 15755 7th Bedfordshire Regt
THORGILSON Fred C. MM Pnr 458940 Royal Engineers
THORLBY Henry MM Pte M2/227050 Army Service Corps
THORLEY Charles J. MM L/Cpl 192882 'D' Special Coy Royal Engineers
THORLEY Ernest MM Pte 88674 2/5th Liverpool Regt KIA 29.10.17.
THORLEY Frederick "DCM,MM" Sjt 8107 2nd Royal Welsh Fusiliers
THORLEY Frederick Thomas "MM,CG(F)" Pte 202127 9th Royal Lancaster Regt
THORLEY George MM Pte 24527 9th Notts & Derby Regt
THORLEY John James MM Pte 12493 8th Royal Lancaster Regt
THORLEY Thomas E. MM Pnr 321458 63 Div Sig Coy Royal Engineers
THORN Edward Thomas MM Pte 18687 8th Devonshire Regt KIA 26.10.17.
THORN Edwin MM+Bar Pte 4/7136 2nd Bedfordshire Regt KIA 23.10.18.
THORN Frederick H.(or E.) MM Sjt 8028 2nd South Lancashire Regt
THORN Harry MM Pte 80123 1/1st Essex Yeomanry
THORN Harry MM Pte 40246 RAMC
THORN Thomas C. MM Cpl 2996 1/6th London Regt
THORNBER Louis MM Pte 20406 2nd Suffolk Regt KIA 1.10.18.
THORNBER Roland MM Gnr 781250 RFA
THORNBER Thomas MM Pte R/19983 16th King's Royal Rifle Corps
THORNBOROUGH Aalfred Edward MM Sjt 10769 1st Royal Welsh Fusiliers KIA 14.7.16.
THORNBOROUGH Harrison MM Pte 2054 11th Manchester Regt
THORNBOROUGH William MM Pte 11323 Royal Welsh Fusiliers
THORNBURN Samuel MM Pte 125054 Lovat's Scouts Yeomanry
THORNBURY William MM Cpl 321127 6th London Regt
THORNCROFT Frederick MM Tptr 3915 6th Dragoon Guards
THORNDICK George W. MM L/Cpl 6050 8th East Surrey Regt
THORNDICK William MM Pte S/20476 13th Rifle Brigade

THORNDIKE Roland MM Pte G/51395 11th Royal Fusiliers DOW 3.10.18.
THORNDYCRAFT Reginald Frank MM Pte R/966 11th King's Royal Rifle Corps KIA 3.9.16.
THORNDYKE Frederick H. "DCM,MM" CSM 320660 2/6th London Regt
THORNDYKE Frederick H. "DCM,MM" CSM 320660 2/6th London Regt
THORNDYKE Joseph R. MM Cpl(SS) 26514 27 Bde RFA
THORNE Albert J. MM Cpl 7149 15th Hussars
THORNE Alfred C. MM Gnr 146602 RFA
THORNE Arthur Edwin MM L/Cpl 242487 1/5th Gloucestershire Regt
THORNE Edward "MM,MIDx2" Cpl 16593 2 Mountain Bty RGA
THORNE Edwin Henry MM Pte 62543 9th Royal Fusiliers KIA 27.3.18.
THORNE Gerald B. MM Gnr 1601 RFA
THORNE Harry B.M. MM Pte 2112 Liverpool Regt
THORNE Thomas M. MM Cpl 37055 Royal Welsh Fusiliers
THORNE W. MM Pte 463055 RAMC
THORNE William MM Spr 230131 Royal Engineers
THORNE William T. MM L/Cpl 63949 62nd Bn Machine Gun Corps
THORNELOE Ernest MM L/Cpl 28574 Royal Engineers
THORNES John Charles Frankland MM Cpl 73261 'H' Corps Sig Coy Royal Engineers
THORNETT Charles MM Sjt 320614 1/6th London Regt KIA 18.8.18.
THORNHILL Albert MM Sjt Farrier 785083 RFA
THORNHILL Alfred MM L/Cpl 165797 2 Fd Svy Bn Royal Engineers
THORNHILL Charles H. MM Pte 16549 7th Lincolnshire Regt
THORNHILL Cyril William MM Cpl 83412 47th Bn Machine Gun Corps
THORNHILL Johnson "MM,MID" Sjt 8782 2nd Suffolk Regt
THORNHILL Robert MM Sjt 203143 1/5th West Yorkshire Regt
THORNHILL Stanley MM Sjt 354207 2/3(East Lancashire)Fd Amb RAMC
THORNHILL Victor MM Cpl 829 Seaforth Highlanders
THORNHILL William MM L/Cpl 165846 101st Bn Machine Gun Corps
THORNHILL William J. MM Pte 10665 Leicestershire Regt
THORNLEY Arthur MM L/Cpl 58666 Machine Gun Corps
THORNLEY Benjamin MM Pte 26602 Notts & Derby Regt
THORNLEY Enoch Arthur MM Pte 1690 4th Bn GMGR
THORNLEY Harry MM L/Cpl 10065 1st Notts & Derby Regt
THORNLEY Percy MM Pte 24134 13th Liverpool Regt
THORNLEY Thomas MM Pte 8081 1st North Lancashire Regt
THORNLEY Thomas MM Pte 50540 1st Cheshire Regt
THORNLEY Thomas MM Sjt 686052 C/175 Bde RFA
THORNLEY William MM Pte 14630 1/5th Gordon Highlanders DOW 29.7.18.
THORNLEY William MM Pte 375768 8th Manchester Regt
THORNS Frank A. "DCM,MM" Sjt 10713 7th Royal West Surrey Regt
THORNS Herbert J. MM L/Cpl 11876 11th Royal Fusiliers
THORNS Ronald W. MM Pte 3475 Royal Sussex Regt
THORNTON Alfred MM Pte 23667 11th Royal Scots KIA 12.10.17.
THORNTON Allan MM Pte 24294 4th Grenadier Guards
THORNTON Arthur MM Sjt 16903 8th Bedfordshire Regt
THORNTON Arthur Lewis "DCM,MM" Sjt 200201 1/4th West Riding Regt "att 147 Light TM Bty,"
THORNTON Charles MM Gnr 1114 246 Bde RFA
THORNTON Charles E. MM Sjt 14970 9th Cheshire Regt
THORNTON Daniel MM Pte 30023 North Lancashire Regt
THORNTON Edward MM Pte 405444 2/3(West Riding)Fd Amb RAMC KIA 27.11.17.
THORNTON Ernest MM Cpl 200487 3rd(Light)Bn Tank Corps
THORNTON Frederick W. MM Gnr 154325 C/310 Bde RFA
THORNTON George "MM,MID" SM 364 Royal Flying Corps
THORNTON H.G. MM+Bar Sjt P/1139 Military Mounted Police
THORNTON Harry MM Cpl 550045 Royal Engineers
THORNTON Harry E. MM Gnr 39251 RFA
THORNTON James MM Pte 306625 1/6th West Riding Regt KIA 1.11.18.
THORNTON James MM Bdr 88186 RHA
THORNTON John MM Sjt 11782 2nd King's Own Scottish Borderers
THORNTON John MM L/Cpl 15783 9th South Staffordshire Regt
THORNTON John Frederick MM Pte 18615 4th Grenadier Guards DOW 13.9.16.
THORNTON Joseph MM Cpl 23438 V/20 Heavy TM Bty RGA
THORNTON Joseph MM Spr 132931 Royal Engineers
THORNTON Julian MM Sjt 358240 10th Liverpool Regt
THORNTON Ralph MM Cpl 2216 1/1st Sherwood Rangers Yeomanry
THORNTON Samuel MM Pte 11556 7th Dragoon Guards
THORNTON Sydney MM Gnr 3037 RFA
THORNTON Sydney MM Pte 43030 Lincolnshire Regt
THORNTON T.E. MM Pte 49796 23rd Lancashire Fusiliers
THORNTON Thomas MM Sjt 305364 8th Lancashire Fusiliers
THORNTON Wilfred MM Bdr 775194 245 Bde RFA
THORNTON William MM Sjt 14662 6th Royal Inniskilling Fusiliers
THORNTON William MM Pte 19474 East Lancashire Regt
THORNTON William MM Sjt 14874 12th West Yorkshire Regt
THORNTON William E. MM Pte 62271 4th Yorkshire Light Infantry
THORNTON William J. MM Pte DM2/155015 Army Service Corps
THORNTON William Thomas MM Cpl 8543 7th Shropshire Light Infantry KIA 1.12.17.
THORNYCROFT George B. MM Sjt 12126 4th Middlesex Regt
THOROGOOD Alfred MM L/Cpl 9757 2nd Bedfordshire Regt
THOROGOOD Henry William MM L/Cpl T4/038061 10 Aux Horse Coy Army Service Corps
THOROGOOD Richard MM Pte 47433 RAMC
THOROGOOD Samuel T. MM Pte 56533 18th King's Royal Rifle Corps
THOROGOOD Wilfred MM Pte 8810 Machine Gun Corps
THORP Bertie MM L/Cpl 9355 Royal Berkshire Regt
THORP Harold MM Pte 50774 61 Fd Amb RAMC DOW 22.9.17.
THORP Ira B. MM Pte 24393 4th Grenadier Guards
THORP John MM Dvr 35704 RFA
THORP Joseph H. MM S/Sjt 339012 98 Fd Amb RAMC
THORP Leonard John MM L/Cpl 14088 1st Middlesex Regt KIA 15.7.16.
THORP William MM Pte 40619 8th Northumberland Fusiliers
THORPE Adolphus MM L/Cpl 4648 8th Royal Highlanders
THORPE Albert MM Pte 41090 Worcestershire Regt
THORPE Alfred Joseph MM Sjt 6666 8th Suffolk Regt
THORPE Arthur MM Pte 28345 East Yorkshire Regt
THORPE Bernard MM Gnr 79765 76 Bde RFA DOW 30.9.17.
THORPE Clifford MM Pte 10130 RAMC
THORPE Edward MM Pte 39289 1/4th Northamptonshire Regt
THORPE Edward MM Pte 23714 12th South Wales Borderers DOW 6.12.17.
THORPE Edward Francis MM Dvr 87037 204 Fd Coy Royal Engineers
THORPE Edward G. MM Sjt 22292 RFA
THORPE Ernest W. MM Pte 11460 17th Lancers
THORPE Francis W. MM Sjt 478450 144 Coy Labour Corps
THORPE Frank MM Pnr 480796 Royal Engineers
THORPE Frederick B. MM Pte 1655 Durham Light Infantry
THORPE George MM Sjt 46944 1st South Wales Borderers
THORPE George MM Pte 16413 9th Yorkshire Light Infantry KIA 26.4.18.
THORPE H. MM Sjt 6507 Notts & Derby Regt
THORPE Harold MM Pte S/27374 13th Rifle Brigade
THORPE Harry MM Spr 79554 180 Tunnelling Coy Royal Engineers
THORPE Horace MM Pte 276540 Manchester Regt
THORPE J. MM+Bar Pte 36569 10th London Regt
THORPE Jabez MM Sjt R/517 King's Royal Rifle Corps
THORPE James MM Sjt 5539 8/10th Gordon Highlanders
THORPE James N. MM Bdr 32628 RFA
THORPE John MM Pte 15141 1st Lincolnshire Regt
THORPE John Wilfred MM L/Cpl 200883 1/4th Lincolnshire Regt
THORPE Malcolm MM L/Cpl 245 1st Middlesex Regt
THORPE Nelson V. "DCM,MM" CSM 10563 2nd York & Lancaster Regt
THORPE Ralph MM 2nd Cpl 312148 Royal Engineers
THORPE Robert MM+Bar Cpl 281148 10th Lancashire Fusiliers
THORPE Samuel MM Pte 10365 1/4th Shropshire Light Infantry
THORPE Sidney MM Pte 4940 2nd Royal West Surrey Regt
THORPE Thomas J. MM Pte 75574 Royal Fusiliers
THORPE Walter MM L/Sjt 269754 6th Notts & Derby Regt
THORPE William MM Cpl 16767 7th Yorkshire Regt
THORPE William MM Gnr 102367 RGA
THORPE-TRACEY Reginald John Stanley MM Cpl 2723 1/6th London Regt
THOW James MM Gnr 143458 105 Bty 22 Bde RFA
THRAVES Richard MM Pte 13835 2nd Grenadier Guards
THREADFOLD H. MM Pte 41473 1st Essex Regt
THREADGOLD Francis Henry MM Cpl P/6411 Military Mounted Police

THREADGOLD George W. "MM,MID" Sjt 9735 1st York & Lancaster Regt
THREADGOULD Henry H. MM Sjt 305814 8th West Yorkshire Regt
THREADGOULD Willie MM Sjt 243878 North Lancashire Regt
THREAPLETON Bertie MM Dvr 775825 310 Bde RFA
THRELFALL Edward MM S/Sjt Farrier 13703 C/75 Bde RFA
THRELFALL Herbert MM+Bar Sjt 15005 1st Coldstream Guards
THRELFALL Nathan MM L/Sjt 18377 20th Manchester Regt DOW 29.10.18.
THRELFALL Richard H. MM Cpl 106642 Royal Engineers
THRELFALL Thomas MM Pte M2/099552 Army Service Corps
THRELFALL William MM Sjt 91206 153 Coy Labour Corps
THRESH George MM Dvr 608315 RHA
THRESHER Frank J. MM Pte 203833 4th Hampshire Regt
THRESHER Stanley W.C. MM+Bar Pte 722990 24th London Regt
THRESHIE W. MM L/Cpl 12120 8th Royal Irish Regt
THRIFT Robert B. MM L/Bdr 110289 D/11 Bde RFA
THRISTAN Owen MM Pte 45283 121 Coy Machine Gun Corps
THROSSELL Harry MM Sjt 3/6933 East Yorkshire Regt
THROSSELL William MM Sjt 13124 9th Notts & Derby Regt DOW 9.10.17.
THROWER Christmas John MM Pte 47738 2nd Welsh Regt KIA 15.9.18.
THROWER Philip James MM Spr 2251 46 Div Sig Coy Royal Engineers KIA 17.10.18.
THROWER William MM Pte 10242 6th Northamptonshire Regt KIA 22.3.18.
THRUSSELL Frederick Charles MM Cpl 33851 39 Div Ammn Col RFA
THRUSSELL Robert Frederick "MM,MID" Cpl 74769 'I' Bty Machine Gun Corps(Motors)
THUMPSTON Charles MM Pte M2/051045 Army Service Corps att RAMC.
THUMPSTON Percy E. MM Cpl 680574 22nd London Regt
THUMWOOD Frederick J. MM Pte 202260 1/4th Wiltshire Regt
THURGOOD Edward MM CQMS 7917 2nd Rifle Brigade
THURGOOD Harry MM Spr 59646 68 Fd Coy Royal Engineers DOW 17.9.18.
THURGOOD Herbert L. MM Cpl 14470 2nd Bedfordshire Regt
THURKETTLE A. MM Pte 283708 4th London Regt
THURKLE George Horace MM Cpl 2813 2nd Manchester Regt
THURLBECK George MM Cpl 98795 A/50 Bde RFA
THURLBY Jesse MM L/Cpl 201030 2/4th Lincolnshire Regt
THURLBY Thomas E. MM L/Cpl 201815 2nd Lincolnshire Regt
THURLEY Willie S. MM Bdr 4278 RFA
THURLING Alfred G. MM Sjt CMT/975 2 Div Train Army Service Corps
THURLOW Fred MM+Bar Pte 14134 8th Suffolk Regt
THURLOW John MM Pte R/8884 9th King's Royal Rifle Corps
THURLOW William MM Sjt 21731 6th Royal Dublin Fusiliers
THURLWELL Edward MM L/Cpl 13800 11th West Yorkshire Regt
THURLWELL Harold MM Pte 14796 Yorkshire Regt
THURMAN Alfred MM+Bar L/Cpl 241374 5th Leicestershire Regt
THURMAN William MM Bdr 63735 37 AA Bty RFA
THURNELL C.G. MM L/Cpl 301362 London Regt
THURRELL William Alfred Lacey MM Sjt 95738 C/47 Bde RFA
THURSFIELD Sidney John "DCM,MM" Sjt 5635 Coldstream Guards
THURSTAN Violetta MM Sister F BRCS
THURSTON Arthur Thomas MM Pte 13602 8th Gloucestershire Regt KIA 12.4.18.
THURSTON William C. MM Dvr 85140 Royal Engineers
THWAITES Albert MM Pte 17186 2nd Shropshire Light Infantry
THWAITES Albert C. MM Cpl 56507 56 Siege Bty RGA
THWAITES Arthur Dennett "MM,Md'H(F)" Spr 155675 Royal Engineers
THWAITES Arthur R. MM Cpl 54151 Royal Engineers
THWAITES Ernest Norman MM L/Cpl 13742 2nd Royal Fusiliers
THWAITES Thomas MM Dvr 33785 B/71 Bde RFA
THWAITES Thomas Sutcliffe "MM,MSM" SM Mechanic M2/055296 39 Div MT Coy Army Service Corps
THWAITES William MM Pte 242055 Border Regt
THYNE John D. MM Pte 120379 1/1st Lothian & Border Horse Yeo
TIBBETT Albert MM Pte 43255 6th Northamptonshire Regt
TIBBETT Charles MM L/Cpl 16424 10th Essex Regt
TIBBLE Albert MM Pte 452208 11th London Regt
TIBBLE Arthur Richard MM Cpl 64511 225 Coy 15th Bn Machine Gun Corps
TIBBLE George MM CSM 8900 2nd Northamptonshire Regt KIA 24.4.18.
TIBBLES William George MM Cpl 39647 A/106 Bde RFA
TIBBS Alfred MM Pte 23804 12th South Wales Borderers
TIBBS Alfred E. MM+Bar Cpl 31092 42 Bde RFA
TICKELL William L. MM Pte R/33233 King's Royal Rifle Corps
TICKLE Frank MM Pte 375438 1/10th Manchester Regt
TICKLE Fred MM Pte 108487 25th Liverpool Regt
TICKLE Frederick MM Sjt 531037 15th London Regt
TICKLE Frederick MM+Bar Gnr 17610 132 Hy Bty RGA
TICKLE J. MM Sjt 337211 RAMC
TICKLE Percy James MM Cpl 1099 1/15th London Regt
TICKLE Thomas MM Bdr 13524 D/76 Bde RFA
TICKLE William MM Cpl 2058 9th Lancashire Fusiliers
TICKNER Ethelbert James MM Pte 25622 2nd Grenadier Guards
TICKNER Frederick MM Pte 2762 82 Fd Amb RAMC
TICKNER George T. MM Dvr 48566 C/83 Bde RFA
TICKNER George William MM Pte M2/022250 42 Div MT Coy Army Service Corps
TICKNER George William MM Sjt 3125 9th Royal Sussex Regt
TICKNER Joseph MM Pte 1869 7th Royal West Surrey Regt DOW 16.6.17.
TICKNER Leonard MM Sjt M2/101886 Army Service Corps
TICKNER Mornington MM Sjt 10868 1st Coldstream Guards KIA 15.9.16.
TIDCOMBE Herbert James MM Pte 265063 10th East Kent Regt
TIDD Charles George MM Pte 1484 1st Royal West Kent Regt
TIDD George MM Sjt 8110 1st Norfolk Regt KIA 27.7.16.
TIDDEMAN Alfred A. MM L/Cpl 15622 Machine Gun Corps
TIDESWELL Ernest MM L/Cpl 20666 Machine Gun Corps
TIDESWELL Walter MM+Bar Pte 47612 5/6th Royal Scots
TIDEY John Stephen MM Pte 8988 6th East Kent Regt
TIDEY W.H. MM Sjt Farrier 5148 D/174 Bde RFA
TIDMAN Herbert G. MM Sjt 8521 2nd Middlesex Regt
TIDMAN Wilfred MM Pte 17284 8th Border Regt
TIDMAN William H. MM Sjt 1461 1/1st Monmouthshire Regt
TIDMARSH Caleb R. MM Pte 16611 Royal Fusiliers
TIDMARSH Samuel "DCM,MM+Bar,OLeo(B)" Sjt 650731 1/21st London Regt
TIDNAM John Albert MM Gnr 876113 95 Bde RFA
TIDSEY Frank MM Dvr 75525 15 Div Ammn Col RFA
TIDSWELL Fred MM Pte 29097 West Riding Regt
TIDSWELL John MM Sjt 25647 8th Royal Lancaster Regt KIA 9.4.17.
TIDSWELL Sidney MM Bdr 122847 216 Siege Bty RGA
TIDY James MM Cpl 17976 7th Royal Irish Fusiliers KIA 5.9.16.
TIER H.W. MM Sjt 2642 1st Rifle Brigade
TIERNAN John MM Pte 1644 6th Royal Irish Regt
TIERNAN Peter MM Pte 12373 7th Yorkshire Regt KIA 10.7.16.
TIERNEY John MM Cpl 44291 51st Bn Machine Gun Corps
TIERNEY Joseph MM Pte 21170 1st Royal Dublin Fusiliers
TIERNEY Michael MM Gnr 3681 219 Siege Bty RGA
TIERNEY Richard MM Cpl 40073 RAMC
TIERNEY Walter MM Pnr 316961 Special Bde Royal Engineers
TIESTEEL Issaac MM Sjt Dmr 6135 1st Royal Berkshire Regt
TIETJEN George Atwill MM Pte 471823 12th London Regt KIA 23.8.18.
TIFFEN W. MM Sjt 1425 1/5th Border Regt
TIFFIN Joseph MM Pte (sic) 14568 1st Bn Machine Gun Corps
TIFFIN William MM Pte 11743 7th Royal West Surrey Regt
TIFFIN William Baty MM Sjt 200423 1/4th Northumberland Fusiliers KIA 29.3.18.
TIFT Bert T. MM Pte 20081 Royal Lancaster Regt
TIGHE James MM Pte 285361 1/6th Seaforth Highlanders
TIGHE Paul Wynne MM Sjt 457250 24 Fd Amb RAMC
TIGWELL Henry J. MM Bdr 58036 41 Bde RFA
TIGWELL Henry L. MM Cpl M/29103 Army Service Corps att 2 Cav Fd Amb RAMC.
TILBORN Charles MM Pte B/200619 Rifle Brigade
TILBROOK Henry Charles MM Gnr 830857 306 Bde RFA
TILBROOK Herbert Arthur "MM,MID,CG(B)" Sjt M/2/031695 Army Service Corps att 34 Fd Amb RAMC.
TILBURY Albert MM+Bar Spr 48239 Signal Service Royal Engineers
TILBURY Joseph MM+Bar L/Cpl 8665 2nd Oxf & Bucks Light Infantry
TILCOCK John MM Pte 9736 1st Bedfordshire Regt
TILDSLEY J.E. MM L/Cpl 40004 South Wales Borderers
TILEY Albert MM Pte 43629 19th Durham Light Infantry
TILEY Harold Thomas MM Pte 266640 2/6th Gloucestershire Regt
TILFORD George MM L/Cpl 11450 3rd Grenadier Guards
TILL Charles W. MM Sjt 53131 3rd Worcestershire Regt
TILL Christopher J. MM+Bar Sjt 53093 24th Royal Fusiliers
TILL Edward MM Cpl 200469 3rd Bn Tank Corps

TILL Francis V. MM Pte 12895 8th North Staffordshire Regt
TILL Frederick MM Bdr 4383 RFA
TILL George MM L/Cpl 8302 King's Royal Rifle Corps
TILL J. MM L/Cpl P/4890 Military Mounted Police
TILL Robert A. MM Pte 31627 East Surrey Regt
TILL W.Cashmare(Casimir?) MM Gnr 69683 'U' Bty RHA
TILL William MM Sjt PW/1296 18th Middlesex Regt DOW 15.4.18.
TILL William R. MM CSM 290121 701 Coy Labour Corps
TILLCOCK Richard Bernard MM L/Cpl 3139 8th Royal Fusiliers
TILLER Alfred MM Sjt 9858 2nd East Lancashire Regt
TILLER Alfred MM L/Cpl 10566 Hampshire Regt
TILLER Ernest E. MM Bdr 36653 RFA
TILLER Ernest T. MM Sjt R/16812 King's Royal Rifle Corps
TILLER William James MM CSM 9543 10th Arg & Suth Highlanders
TILLETT Arthur MM Sjt 546249 509 Fd Coy Royal Engineers
TILLEY A.E. MM Gnr 46094 RGA
TILLEY Alfred George MM Bdr 16127 D/46 Bde RFA
TILLEY Charles E. MM Pte 203683 5th Notts & Derby Regt
TILLEY Edmund G. MM Pte M2/078242 Army Service Corps
TILLEY Edwin MM L/Cpl 240298 8th Gloucestershire Regt
TILLEY Eilley A. MM Cpl 40938 25 Bde RFA
TILLEY Francis Omar MM Sjt 9425 1st Leicestershire Regt DOW 14.12.17.
TILLEY Frederick R. MM Cpl 8397 2nd Hampshire Regt
TILLEY George MM+Bar Cpl 18445 6th Northamptonshire Regt KIA 5.4.18.
TILLEY Horace MM Pte 27339 2nd Worcestershire Regt
TILLEY John MM L/Cpl 240129 1/6th Liverpool Regt Died 25.6.18.
TILLEY Joseoph W. MM L/Cpl 15168 2nd Middlesex Regt
TILLEY Lewis MM Cpl 241630 1/6th Royal Warwickshire Regt KIA 4.10.17.
TILLEY Stanley J. MM Cpl 202858 1st Essex Regt
TILLEY Stephen Thomas MM Sjt 50001 Middlesex Regt
TILLEY Thomas R. MM Pte 252331 3rd London Regt
TILLEY William MM Pte 34981 Machine Gun Corps
TILLEY William H. MM Pte 31879 12th East Surrey Regt
TILLING Edwin MM Gnr 89311 B/48 Bde RFA
TILLING Ernest J. MM BQMS 935028 C/282 Bde RFA
TILLING Frederick John MM Pte 31294 6th Royal West Kent Regt
TILLING Herbert R. MM Pte 1312 7th East Surrey Regt
TILLING S.V. MM Pte 24274 East Kent Regt
TILLING William MM Sjt 22413 13th Welsh Regt
TILLOTSON Benjamin MM Pte 984 4th GMGR
TILLOTSON Harold Victor MM Pte 23476 150 Coy Machine Gun Corps
TILLOTSON John "DCM,MM" Sjt 11859 9th West Riding Regt
TILLOTSON Joseph MM Pte 301047 1 Fd Amb RAMC
TILLOTSON Samuel MM Cpl 266325 5th West Riding Regt
TILLOTSON William MM Pte 28328 11th East Yorkshire Regt
TILLS Benjamin Samuel Amos MM Spr 155770 177 Tunnelling Coy Royal Engineers
TILLSON Ernest F. MM Pte 1765 1/8th London Regt
TILLSON Leonard MM L/Cpl 201457 Royal Scots Fusiliers
TILSED Cecil F. MM Bdr 10449 RFA
TILSED Robert MM Pte 9807 5th Dorsetshire Regt
TILSLEY Bernard MM Pte 8372 1st North Staffordshire Regt
TILSON J.C. MM Pte 200846 Tank Corps
TILSON John R. "DCM,MM" CSM 200343 2/4th Hampshire Regt
TILSTON William E. MM Pte 77603 RAMC
TILT C.William "MM,MSM" Bdr 107220 217 Siege Bty RGA
TILZEY Charles MM Pte 55152 2nd Hampshire Regt
TIMBERLAKE Sidney H. MM L/Cpl 302688 10th London Regt
TIMBERLAKE William MM Dvr 4173 B/122 Bde RFA
TIMBRELL Joseph MM Sjt 6420 7th York & Lancaster Regt
TIMBY Charles A. MM Cpl 43506 7th Norfolk Regt
TIMILTY Bernard MM Sjt 30689 11th East Lancashire Regt
TIMLIN John MM Pte 265544 11th Cheshire Regt KIA 20.4.18.
TIMLIN William MM Pte 868 19th Northumberland Fusiliers
TIMM G. MM Sjt 30411 75 Fd Amb RAMC
TIMMINGS Richard James MM L/Cpl 40527 2nd Lincolnshire Regt KIA 14.8.17.
TIMMINS Arthur MM L/Cpl 9399 11th Royal Warwickshire Regt KIA 14.7.16.
TIMMINS Ernest Beardsell MM Pte 240827 1/6th West Riding Regt
TIMMINS George W. MM Bdr 200 49 Div Ammn Col RFA
TIMMINS Ivor S. "DCM,MM" Sjt 18787 7th Royal Irish Fusiliers
TIMMINS James MM Sjt 40714 1/8th Worcestershire Regt DOW 18.10.18.
TIMMINS Thomas MM Pte 36592 Worcestershire Regt
TIMMINS Walter MM Cpl 18428 10th Worcestershire Regt
TIMMINS William MM Cpl 270040 10th East Kent Regt
TIMMIS Albert MM Sjt 3345 Middlesex Regt
TIMMIS Charles H. MM Pte 4519 19th Bn Machine Gun Corps
TIMMIS George MM Pte 16736 4th Coldstream Guards
TIMMIS John MM Dvr 32093 RFA
TIMMONS Edmund MM Pte 276356 1/1st Sherwood Rangers Yeomanry
TIMMONS John MM Spr 259498 47 Div Sig Coy Royal Engineers
TIMMS Albert MM Pte 30629 1/1st Bedfordshire Yeomanry
TIMMS Alfred MM Cpl 89340 142 Army Tps Coy Royal Engineers
TIMMS Arthur MM L/Cpl 205038 1/1st Buckinghamshire Yeomanry
TIMMS Ernest MM Pte 115298 17th Bn Machine Gun Corps
TIMMS Frederick MM Pte 18100 4th Bn Machine Gun Corps Died 13.11.18.
TIMMS Frederick J. MM Bdr 68431 RHA
TIMMS Harold J. MM Cpl 3127 5th Gloucestershire Regt
TIMMS Joseph MM Pte 3115 Machine Gun Corps
TIMMS Robert W. MM Pte 62297 4th Yorkshire Light Infantry
TIMMS S. MM Pte 27315 Somerset Light Infantry
TIMMS Sidney MM L/Cpl 645067 20th London Regt
TIMMS William MM Cpl 26332 RGA
TIMOTHY Frank MM Pte 325111 1/9th Durham Light Infantry
TIMOTHY Ralph MM L/Cpl 204230 Durham Light Infantry
TIMPERLEY John MM+Bar Cpl 19978 12th Liverpool Regt
TIMPERLEY William "MM,CG(B)" CSM 16636 6th King's Own Scottish Borderers
TIMPSON James E. MM Bdr 855396 RFA
TIMSON Arthur MM Pte 9080 1st Dragoons
TIMSON Frank W. MM Pte 2097 Oxf & Bucks Light Infantry
TIMSON J.H. MM Cpl 46046 24 Div Sig Coy Royal Engineers
TIMSON Joseph MM Spr 289177 Royal Engineers
TIMSON Joseph "DCM,MM+Bar" Sjt 765514 C/233 RFA
TIMSON Samuel MM Gnr 83441 V/11 Heavy TM Bty RGA
TIMSON Walter MM Pte 24209 10th South Staffordshire Regt
TINCKLER William Austin MM CSM 26659 11th Lancashire Fusiliers KIA 31.7.17.
TINDALE George MM Sjt 79844 176 Tunnelling Coy Royal Engineers
TINDALL Arthur MM+Bar L/Cpl 39652 Yorkshire Light Infantry
TINDALL Charles MM Pte 201584 1st Royal Scots Fusiliers
TINDALL Douglas MM L/Cpl 33097 7th Wiltshire Regt
TINDALL Henry Oswald "MM,CG(B)" Cpl 9007 1st East Yorkshire Regt
TINDALL Lawrence MM L/Cpl 2145 1/5th Yorkshire Regt KIA 21.6.18.
TINDALL Walter John MM Sjt C/1021 16th King's Royal Rifle Corps DOW 17.4.18.
TINDELL John MM Pte S/15220 Rifle Brigade att MGC.
TINDILL Lawrence E. MM Gnr 755331 RFA
TINDLE Thomas MM Pte 3131 1/6th Durham Light Infantry
TING William MM Pte 7028 Royal Fusiliers
TINGAY William MM 2nd Cpl 65187 106 Fd Coy Royal Engineers
TINGEY A.R. MM Cpl 573553 17th London Regt
TINGLE Bernard Howard MM Gnr 89562 48 Bty 36 Bde RFA
TINGLE Harry MM Pte 16628 7th York & Lancaster Regt
TINGLE Leslie W. MM Pte 33393 RAMC
TINGLE Tom MM Pte A/202866 1st King's Royal Rifle Corps
TINGLE William H. MM Pte 410103 RAMC
TINHAM John Arthur Russel MM Pnr 70360 25 Div Sig Coy Royal Engineers KIA 29.4.18.
TINKER Frank Victor MM Pte 345310 24th Royal Welsh Fusiliers
TINKER George C. MM Sjt 175025 1/1st Yorkshire Dragoons Yeomanry
TINKER George Herbert MM Cpl 10464 18th Manchester Regt DOW 9.5.17.
TINKER James MM L/Cpl 476318 Royal Engineers
TINKER Percy MM Pte 17774 11th Royal Fusiliers
TINKER W. MM Cpl 53747 8th West Yorkshire Regt
TINKLER Cyril V. MM Pte 39491 6th York & Lancaster Regt
TINKLER John G. MM Pte 17850 6th East Yorkshire Regt
TINKLER Joseph "MM,MID" Gnr 53725 35 Bde RFA
TINKLER Robert MM L/Cpl 15931 7/8th King's Own Scottish Borderers
TINKLER William G. MM L/Cpl 17750 Cameron Highlanders
TINLEY Richard N. MM L/Cpl 2 Army Cyclist Corps
TINLIN James MM Gnr 656267 RFA
TINLIN John MM Pte 19906 2nd King's Own Scottish Borderers DOW 30.7.18.
TINMOUTH Frederick MM L/Cpl 5429 East Kent Regt Died 21.10.18.

TINNEY Sidney MM Pte 24213 Duke of Cornwall's LI
TINNEY William G. MM Pte 56839 Welsh Regt
TINNION Joseph MM Cpl 69021 6 Bty Machine Gun Corps(Motors)
TINNISWOOD William Arthur MM L/Cpl 355372 10th Liverpool Regt
TINNOCK John MM L/Bdr 931434 RFA
TINSEY William MM L/Cpl 989 8th Royal West Surrey Regt
TINSLEY Albert E. MM Cpl 40663 12tth Manchester Regt
TINSLEY Edward MM Pte 103154 2nd Notts & Derby Regt
TINSLEY Herbert Francis MM Cpl 201394 Leicestershire Regt
TINSLEY James Alfred "DCM,MM" Sjt 15464 8th North Lancashire Regt
TINSLEY John MM L/Cpl 16276 2nd South Lancashire Regt
TINSLEY Thomas MM Pte 73168 Notts & Derby Regt
TINSLEY William MM Pte 32076 Gloucestershire Regt
TINSON Archibald E. MM L/Cpl 23301 Oxf & Bucks Light Infantry
TINTO Hugh MM L/Cpl 27470 King's Own Scottish Borderers
TIPLADY Eric R. MM L/Cpl 2126 1/1st Cambridgeshire Regt
TIPLADY Frederick Arthur MM Pte 200937 1/4th East Yorkshire Regt KIA 25.3.18.
TIPLADY Harold MM Bdr 294674 146 Heavy Bty RGA
TIPLADY Henry MM Sjt 13000 9th Royal Fusiliers
TIPLADY Robert MM Pte 250520 1/6th Durham Light Infantry
TIPLADY Walter H. MM Pte 50114 Lancashire Fusiliers
TIPLER Frederick MM Cpl M2/099327 641 MT Coy Army Service Corps
TIPLER H.D. MM AM1 9866 Royal Flying Corps
TIPLER Harold MM Pte 28321 8th Royal West Kent Regt
TIPLER William MM Sjt 200938 1/4th Northamptonshire Regt
TIPLER William John MM Pte S/14713 12th Rifle Brigade KIA 27.3.18.
TIPPEN Arthur E. MM Pte S/14851 2nd Rifle Brigade
TIPPEN Leslie Gerald "MM,MSM" RSM 3021 8th Royal West Surrey Regt
TIPPEN Robert MM+Bar Sjt 10082 2nd Gordon Highlanders
TIPPER Alfred J. MM Sjt 22067 25 Div Sig Coy Royal Engineers
TIPPER Arthur Herbert MM Cpl 193789 2 Lt Rly Op Coy Royal Engineers
TIPPER Arthur J. MM Pte 508053 RAMC
TIPPER Fred G. MM Cpl 10263 1st Yorkshire Light Infantry
TIPPER Frederick George MM Pte 18412 North Staffordshire Regt
TIPPER Nathaniel MM Sjt 43779 33 Bde RFA
TIPPER Thomas W. "MM,MID" Sjt 8585 1st Royal West Surrey Regt
TIPPETT Christopher T. MM Pte 26304 5th West Riding Regt
TIPPING Albert William MM Pte S/24257 9th Rifle Brigade KIA 23.3.18.
TIPPING Alfred MM Pte 17710 9th Scottish Rifles KIA 22.10.16.
TIPPING Frederick MM Pte 65038 3 Fd Amb RAMC
TIPPING George A. MM Cpl 28122 Royal Welsh Fusiliers
TIPPING James MM+Bar Pte 1485 23 Fd Amb RAMC
TIPPING Joseph MM Cpl 209 58 Div Ammn Col RFA
TIPPING Robert MM Gnr 293421 14 Hy Arty Grp RGA
TIPPING Robert MM Cpl 128984 Special Bde Royal Engineers
TIPPING Thomas MM L/Cpl 266528 1/1st Bucks Bn Oxf & Bucks Light Infantry
TIPTON Timothy MM L/Sjt 350590 9th Manchester Regt KIA 21.3.18.
TIPTON William A. MM Pte 263029 West Riding Regt
TISDALL Christopher MM Sjt 35457 47 Coy 16th Bn Machine Gun Corps
TISSEMAN John MM Pte 42001 Royal Inniskilling Fusiliers
TISSIMAN John "DCM,MM" Cpl 463138 50 Div Sig Coy Royal Engineers
TISSINGTON John W. MM Sjt 19961 9th Yorkshire Light Infantry
TISSINGTON John Walter MM Pte 28458 8th North Staffordshire Regt DOW 23.4.18.
TITCHENER E.K. MM Sjt 3020 B/76 Bde RFA
TITCHENER Edward MM Pte 303634 1/7th Manchester Regt
TITCHENER Gerald G. MM Pte 8469 1st Royal Berkshire Regt
TITCHENER Joseph H. MM Sjt 30604 RFA
TITCHENER William MM Pte 25913 Wiltshire Regt
TITCHMARSH Ernest MM Cpl 202255 1st London Regt
TITCHMARSH George MM Pte 15630 11th Suffolk Regt
TITCHMARSH Norman MM Pte 32830 6th York & Lancaster Regt
TITCOMB Albert W. MM Cpl 129417 RGA
TITCOMB Alfred T. MM Sjt 31029 17th Royal Sussex Regt
TITCOMB Walter MM Pte 201337 Royal Berkshire Regt
TITCOMBE Jesse MM+Bar Cpl 48538 RGA
TITE Henry R. MM Gnr 41375 RGA
TITE John MM+Bar Sjt 12784 6th Northamptonshire Regt KIA 8.8.17.
TITE Leonard MM Pte 281195 Lancashire Fusiliers
TITE Thomas H. MM+Bar Cpl 12992 4th Royal Fusiliers
TITHERINGTON William Victor MM Dvr 60164 37 Div Sig Coy Royal Engineers
TITLEY F.H. MM L/Sjt S/13859 13th Rifle Brigade
TITLEY John MM L/Cpl 1589 1/6th Cheshire Regt
TITLEY Reginald C. MM Pte 50521 Royal Fusiliers
TITMAS Herbert MM Pte 42495 Middlesex Regt
TITMASS Alfred James Austen MM Pte 18406 East Lancashire Regt
TITMUS Albert MM+Bar Pte 602 1st Middlesex Regt
TITMUS George MM Pte 26061 2nd Bedfordshire Regt
TITMUS Walter MM Pte 260172 1/8th Notts & Derby Regt
TITT Frederick W. MM Pte 205254 1/1st Buckinghamshire Yeomanry
TITT Sidney C. MM Cpl 331438 Hampshire Regt
TITT William MM Pte 18405 1st Grenadier Guards
TITTERELL Frank A. MM Cpl 533673 15th London Regt
TITTERINGTON Harry L. MM Cpl 275883 1/7th Manchester Regt
TITTERINGTON J. MM Pte 68652 RAMC
TITTERINGTON Phillip MM+Bar Pte 15897 Liverpool Regt
TITTERINGTON Robert MM Pte 47774 13th Royal Scots
TITTERINGTON Thomas E. MM Sjt P/887 Military Mounted Police
TITTERTON Frank MM Pte 45830 15th Cheshire Regt
TITTERTON William MM Pte M2/183142 62 Div MT Coy Army Service Corps
TITTLEY Ernest S. MM Pte 9419 South Staffordshire Regt
TIVEY George "MM,MSM" Cpl 78962 46 Bty 39 Bde RFA
TIVEY Tom Brown MM Sjt 53132 2nd Leicestershire Regt
TIZZARD Lyndell MM L/Cpl 15972 7th Somerset Light Infantry DOW 25.3.18.
TOALL John MM Pte 31346 Royal Scots
TOBBELL Joseph MM Pte 10/19778 Northumberland Fusiliers
TOBIAS Woolf MM Pte 41583 7th Leicestershire Regt
TOBIASEN Trygve Bernard MM Cpl 23003 16th Welsh Regt
TOBIN Arthur MM CSM 200915 1/4th Welsh Regt
TOBIN James "DCM,MM" L/Cpl 3/5089 6th Connaught Rangers KIA 21.3.18.
TOBIN James MM Sjt 55901 15 Bde RFA
TOBIN John MM Pte 306363 8th Liverpool Regt
TOBIN Patrick MM Pte 2088 7th Leinster Regt KIA 21.3.18.
TOBY Sidney James MM Sjt 30671 119 Heavy Bty RGA
TOCHER James MM Pte 292215 Gordon Highlanders
TOCHRANE Adam W. MM L/Cpl 295921 12th Royal Scots Fusiliers
TODD A.S. MM Gnr 6057 RFA
TODD Albert C. MM Gnr 75978 Tank Corps
TODD Alexander MM Pte 385057 8th London Regt
TODD Andrew "MM+Bar,MID" Sjt 53424 74 Fd Amb RAMC
TODD Andrew MM Sjt 14582 7th East Yorkshire Regt "KIA 31.3.18,"
TODD Andrew C. MM L/Cpl 17244 Yorkshire Regt
TODD Andrew McF. MM Pte 202898 1/4th Gordon Highlanders
TODD Arnold MM Pte 50814 13th Liverpool Regt
TODD Arthur MM Pte 201339 1/4th Yorkshire Light Infantry
TODD Arthur G. MM Cpl 14951 9th Norfolk Regt
TODD Arthur Havelock MM Pte 21724 14th Hampshire Regt KIA 25.3.18.
TODD Bernard J. MM Cpl 34308 62nd Bn Machine Gun Corps
TODD Charles MM Pte 235096 2nd Notts & Derby Regt
TODD Charles O.H. MM Pte 44777 Manchester Regt
TODD Clifford G. MM Sjt 21859 'M' Cable Section Royal Engineers
TODD Constance Elizabeth MM Matron F SJAB
TODD D. MM Sjt 512974 London Regt
TODD David MM Pte 203546 Royal West Kent Regt
TODD Douglas MM L/Cpl 45615 1/1st Hertfordshire Regt
TODD Duglas MM Pte 34883 RAMC
TODD Edward MM Sjt 21812 1st Yorkshire Light Infantry
TODD Edward MM Sjt 13457 10th Durham Light Infantry KIA 22.8.17.
TODD Ernest MM L/Cpl 19/908 Northumberland Fusiliers
TODD Ernest J. MM Pte 57565 4th York & Lancaster Regt
TODD F.W. MM Sjt 18147 13th Essex Regt
TODD Frederick MM Sjt 8277 2nd East Kent Regt
TODD Frederick John MM Cpl 113119 'H' Special Coy Royal Engineers
TODD Garnett MM L/Bdr 715174 A/177 Bde RFA
TODD George G. MM Sjt 335227 1/8th Royal Scots
TODD George S. MM L/Cpl 37339 Yorkshire Light Infantry
TODD George W. MM L/Cpl S/23858 13th Rifle Brigade
TODD George W. MM L/Cpl 58627 Machine Gun Corps
TODD Harold Edwin MM Pte 33568 2nd Yorkshire Regt KIA 2.8.17.

TODD Henry "MC,DCM,MM(8232 Sjt)" 2Lt 2nd Arg & Suth Highlanders
TODD Herbert MM Sjt 203370 9th Norfolk Regt
TODD Herbert "MC,MM(12473 Sjt 7th Bn)" 2Lt 1st Royal Scots Fusiliers
TODD Hugh J. MM L/Cpl 169585 5 Fd Svy Bn Royal Engineers
TODD J. MM+Bar Pte 63916 RAMC
TODD James MM L/Cpl 352508 1/9th Royal Scots
TODD James MM Gnr 97316 A/63 Bde RFA
TODD James MM Spr 64614 124 Fd Coy Royal Engineers
TODD James MM Bdr 65502 135 Siege Bty RGA
TODD James MM Pte 4071 1/6th Royal Highlanders
TODD James W. MM Dvr 38193 24 Bde RFA
TODD John MM Pte 22536 1st Cameron Highlanders
TODD John MM Sjt 4373 8th Northumberland Fusiliers Real name RT MALLENBY
TODD John MM Sjt 655634 RFA
TODD John MM Spr 50252 Royal Engineers
TODD John MM Pte 16416 Arg & Suth Highlanders
TODD John MM+Bar Sjt 12655 11th Royal Scots KIA 26.7.18.
TODD John MM L/Cpl 20359 Army Cyclist Corps
TODD John E. MM L/Cpl 15/1226 8th West Yorkshire Regt
TODD John H. MM Pte 7259 1st King's Royal Rifle Corps
TODD Joseph Henry MM Pte M2/116536 Army Service Corps att 75 Fd Amb RAMC.
TODD Joseph W. MM Pte 292089 10th Northumberland Fusiliers
TODD M.William MM Pte 364 RAMC
TODD Nathaniel MM Sjt 20688 14 Bde RFA
TODD Percival R. MM L/Cpl 403338 RAMC
TODD Peter MM Pte 9484 2nd Arg & Suth Highlanders
TODD R.B. MM Pte 881076 34th London Regt
TODD Sydney MM Sjt R/4442 13th King's Royal Rifle Corps
TODD Thomas MM+Bar Pte 7620 1st & 9th Scottish Rifles
TODD Thomas "MM,MID" Sjt 22/94 22nd Northumberland Fusiliers
TODD Thomas Albert MM Cpl 2379 1/5th Northumberland Fusiliers KIA 3.10.16.
TODD Thomas W. "DCM,MM" Sjt 23916 2nd York & Lancaster Regt
TODD William MM Pte 295094 1/9th Durham Light Infantry
TODD William MM Pte 266492 1/1st Hertfordshire Regt
TODD William MM Pte M2/137054 65 Coy Army Service Corps
TODD William MM Pte 78300 RAMC
TODD William MM Pte 40531 Gordon Highlanders
TODD William MM Sjt 306083 1/1(Highland)Bty RGA
TODD William Arthur MM Cpl 17892 9th Norfolk Regt KIA 15.4.18.
TODHUNTER Thomas MM Cpl 10212 2nd South Lancashire Regt
TODKILL Harold MM+2 Bars Pte 203060 1st Border Regt
TODMAN John MM L/Cpl 23935 1st East Kent Regt
TODMAN John MM L/Cpl 722 7th Royal Sussex Regt
TODMAN William MM L/Cpl 9884 6th Lincolnshire Regt DOW 31.8.18.
TOE Walter Dennis MM Sjt 43254 6th Northamptonshire Regt DOW 10.11.17.
TOFF Jack MM Pte 6844 Middlesex Regt
TOFIELD Stanley Frank MM Pte 14014 5th Dorsetshire Regt
TOFT Cuthbert William MM Sjt P/1101 3 Tfc Contr Coy Military Foot Police
TOFT George Albion MM Bdr 80770 148 Siege Bty RGA
TOFT John W. MM Dvr 31867 A/76 Bde RFA
TOFT William MM Cpl 13862 8th Gloucestershire Regt
TOFTS William Henry MM Spr 69278 35 Div Sig Coy Royal Engineers
TOGHILL Noel F. MM Pte 21581 12th Somerset Light Infantry
TOGWELL Arthur E. MM Sjt 2235 55 Fd Coy Royal Engineers
TOHER Daniel MM Sjt 1725 1st Irish Guards
TOKINS Arthur "MM,MM(F)" L/Cpl P/7661 Military Mounted Police
TOLAND Robert MM Pte 27718 10th Scottish Rifles
TOLCHER George MM Pte 21903 7th Royal Irish Fusiliers
TOLERTON John MM L/Cpl 5650 8/10th Gordon Highlanders
TOLFREE Harry MM CSM 71 11th Middlesex Regt
TOLFREE William MM Gnr 75574 129 Bty 42 Bde RFA
TOLHURST Frederick MM Pte 30696 RAMC
TOLHURST James S. MM L/Cpl 21105 1st Royal West Kent Regt
TOLLER Lucie Maud Mary "MM,RRC" Matron F QAIMNS
TOLLERFIELD Reginald E. MM Cpl 1197 Royal Flying Corps
TOLLERVEY Frederick William MM BSM 35030 6 Bty 40 Bde RFA
TOLLEY Albert MM Cpl 35826 4th South Staffordshire Regt
TOLLEY Albert W. MM Pte 32046 Machine Gun Corps
TOLLEY Frank MM Sjt 47268 10th Royal Fusiliers
TOLLEY Percy G. MM Cpl 240887 Gloucestershire Regt
TOLLEY Samuel "DCM,MM" Cpl 10580 8th Yorkshire Light Infantry
TOLLEY or TOLLY Zachariah MM Pte 38443 South Staffordshire Regt
TOLLIDAY Alfred L. MM Pte 393828 London Regt
TOLLIDAY C.E. MM Pte S/8852 Rifle Brigade
TOLMAN Cyril J. MM Gnr 147194 RFA
TOLMIE David MM Pte 200421 1/6th Royal Highlanders
TOLSON Clifford MM Pte 36783 22nd Northumberland Fusiliers
TOLSON Hugh E. MM+Bar Sjt 95135 2nd London Regt
TOMALIN Arthur E. MM L/Cpl 26264 1st Norfolk Regt
TOMAN John MM Pte 51504 7th East Yorkshire Regt
TOMAN Leo MM Sjt 249546 51 Div Sig Coy Royal Engineers
TOMAN Phillip MM Pte 267011 Seaforth Highlanders
TOMBLESON Albert V. MM Pte 326901 1/1st Cambridgeshire Regt
TOMBLESON Walter James MM Sjt 470231 12th London Regt
TOMBLIN George W. MM Pte 240764 5th Leicestershire Regt
TOMBS Henry Victor MM Sjt 81205 RFA
TOMBS Victor MM Pte S/13202 13th Rifle Brigade
TOMES Benjamin MM L/Cpl 9852 2nd Arg & Suth Highlanders
TOMEY Frederick MM Pnr 558754 Royal Engineers
TOMKINS Arthur E. MM Pte 7977 11th Royal Fusiliers
TOMKINS Benjamin MM Dvr T4/145783 29 Div Train Army Service Corps
TOMKINS Charles John MM Dvr 8851 33 Bde RFA
TOMKINS Edward MM Cpl 621 21st Middlesex Regt
TOMKINS Frederick MM Sjt 52291 RFA
TOMKINS Frederick G. MM Cpl 57770 158 Siege Bty RGA
TOMKINS Henry A. MM Pte 5362 12th Royal Fusiliers
TOMKINS Thomas MM L/Sjt 11088 5th Shropshire Light Infantry
TOMKINS Thomas S. MM Pte 57553 2nd King's Royal Rifle Corps
TOMKINS W.H. MM Sjt 41945 Royal Engineers
TOMKINS Walter S. MM Spr 180889 Royal Engineers
TOMKINS William J. MM Dvr 438457 497 Fd Coy Royal Engineers
TOMKINSON Arthur MM Spr 43031 Royal Engineers
TOMKINSON Harold MM Pte 10987 North Staffordshire Regt
TOMKINSON James MM Spr 151634 251 Tunnelling Coy Royal Engineers
TOMKINSON James M. MM Spr 91835 Royal Engineers
TOMKINSON Thomas MM Pte 17129 Grenadier Guards
TOMKINSON William MM Pte 251371 Manchester Regt
TOMKISS Frank MM Pte 1825 9th Manchester Regt
TOMLIN Arthur C. MM L/Cpl 200682 1/4th Oxf & Bucks Light Infantry
TOMLIN Frederick W. MM Pte 508345 RAMC
TOMLIN Herbert G. MM BSM 915695 D/317 Bde RFA
TOMLIN Sidney W. MM L/Sjt S/27297 Rifle Brigade
TOMLIN William MM Sjt 9070 2nd Royal Welsh Fusiliers
TOMLINS Hugh MM Gnr 85554 B/63 Bde RFA
TOMLINSON Albert MM Pte 34500 10th Lancashire Fusiliers
TOMLINSON Arthur MM Sjt 268296 9th West Riding Regt
TOMLINSON Bernard MM Pte 21467 9th Notts & Derby Regt
TOMLINSON Bert MM L/Cpl 238069 7th Lincolnshire Regt
TOMLINSON Christopher MM Dvr 65547 45 Bde RFA
TOMLINSON Edward MM+Bar Spr 46898 87 Fd Coy Royal Engineers
TOMLINSON Ernest MM Sjt 28190 North Lancashire Regt
TOMLINSON Frank MM Cpl 554236 511 Fd Coy Royal Engineers
TOMLINSON Frank William MM Sjt 800842 RFA
TOMLINSON Fred "DCM,MM" L/Cpl 19641 24 Coy Machine Gun Corps KIA 2.12.17.
TOMLINSON Fred MM+Bar L/Cpl 290761 1/7th Gordon Highlanders
TOMLINSON Fred MM Gnr 67655 109 Siege Bty RGA
TOMLINSON Frederick MM Sjt 139 18th Northumberland Fusiliers
TOMLINSON Frederick A. MM+Bar Cpl 238024 1/5th West Yorkshire Regt
TOMLINSON George MM Sjt 291395 1st Cheshire Regt
TOMLINSON George MM Sjt M2/099626 971 Coy Army Service Corps
TOMLINSON George MM Pte 16254 11th Notts & Derby Regt
TOMLINSON Harold MM Dvr 113233 'A' Bty RHA
TOMLINSON Harold R. MM Spr 24991 Signal Service Royal Engineers
TOMLINSON Harry MM L/Cpl 1110 9th Lancers
TOMLINSON Harry MM Pte 5594 13th Royal Sussex Regt DOW 6.4.18.
TOMLINSON Harry MM Pte M2/181528 Army Service Corps
TOMLINSON Henry MM Pte 240299 Border Regt
TOMLINSON Herbert MM Pte 9524 1st Northumberland Fusiliers
TOMLINSON Herbert W. MM Gnr 232222 505 Bty 65 Bde RFA
TOMLINSON Horace MM L/Cpl 200517 1/4th Essex Regt
TOMLINSON James MM 2nd Cpl 015577 Army Ordnance Corps

TOMLINSON James MM L/Cpl 13769 1st Grenadier Guards
TOMLINSON James MM Sjt 14068 17th Lancashire Fusiliers
TOMLINSON John MM Gnr 200399 115 Hy Bty RGA
TOMLINSON John MM Spr 155965 182 Tunnelling Coy Royal Engineers
TOMLINSON John W. MM Pte 4697 7th Dragoon Guards
TOMLINSON John W. MM L/Sjt 41432 Lancashire Fusiliers
TOMLINSON John W. MM L/Cpl 11601 Coldstream Guards
TOMLINSON Joseph "DCM,MM+Bar" Cpl 5886 21st Bn Machine Gun Corps
TOMLINSON Ralph MM Pte 240742 5th West Riding Regt
TOMLINSON Reginald G. MM Tpr 1781 Royal Horse Guards
TOMLINSON Samson MM Pte 19733 Dorsetshire Regt
TOMLINSON Samuel MM Pte 251139 Manchester Regt
TOMLINSON Samuel T. MM Cpl Wheeler 926446 B/290 Bde RFA
TOMLINSON Sidney MM Sjt 6778 7th East Lancashire Regt
TOMLINSON Sidney H. MM Sjt 83052 A/74 Bde RFA
TOMLINSON Sidney Handforth MM Sjt 781813 246 Bde RFA
TOMLINSON Thomas W. MM Pte 15389 East Lancashire Regt
TOMLINSON W.F. MM Pte B/1666 Rifle Brigade
TOMLINSON Walter MM Pte 82338 RAMC
TOMLINSON William MM Pte 24542 10 Fd Amb RAMC
TOMLINSON William MM Cpl 675076 D/157 Bde RFA
TOMLINSON William MM Sjt 15584 RGA
TOMLINSON William A. MM Cpl CMT/174 5 Div Train Army Service Corps
TOMLINSON or TOMLISON John MM Pte 7710 2nd Arg & Suth Highlanders
TOMLISON Edward Frederick MM Sjt 3375 RFA
TOMLISON or TOMLINSON John MM Pte 7710 2nd Arg & Suth Highlanders
TOMLYN Francis E. MM Pte 12339 1st Irish Guards
TOMMEY Aldwyn MM Cpl 17599 8th South Wales Borderers
TOMNEY Squire W. MM Cpl 200267 Lancashire Fusiliers
TOMPKINS A.E. MM Bdr 168386 RGA
TOMPKINS Bert MM Gnr 198102 D/242 Bde RFA
TOMPKINS Edgar C. MM+Bar Pte 20473 2nd York & Lancaster Regt
TOMPKINS Ernest MM Sjt 265328 1/1st Hertfordshire Regt
TOMPKINS Frank MM L/Cpl 19816 2nd Dragoons
TOMPKINS Frederick George MM L/Cpl 8005 2nd Bedfordshire Regt DOW 3.8.16.
TOMPKINS George F. MM Pte 423794 10th London Regt
TOMPKINS Gerald J. MM Cpl 285391 1/1st Oxfordshire Yeomanry
TOMPKINS James MM Pte 41610 West Yorkshire Regt
TOMPKINS Leslie MM RFA "see SWEET, Albert E."
TOMPKINS Robert F. MM Sjt 250961 3rd London Regt
TOMPKINS Wesley MM Pte 9784 2nd Middlesex Regt KIA 20.9.17.
TOMPKINS Wigley L. MM Pte 33589 8th London Regt
TOMPKINS William H. MM Gnr 78296 Tank Corps
TOMPKINSON A. MM Sjt 4156 Machine Gun Corps
TOMPKINSON H. MM Bdr 28277 RFA
TOMPKINSON Henry MM Pte 38914 2nd Yorkshire Light Infantry
TOMPOFSKY Myer MM Pte 267261 1/8th West Yorkshire Regt KIA 27.9.18.
TOMPSON or THOMPSON R. MM Pte 2958 1st Rifle Brigade
TOMS Edward George MM Sjt 72740 D/256 Bde RFA
TOMS Edwin MM Sjt 200958 1st Middlesex Regt KIA 23.10.18.
TOMS Gordon P. MM Pte 60059 1st Middlesex Regt
TOMS William H. MM Sjt 27316 14th Royal Welsh Fusiliers
TOMSETT Alfred MM Pte 2519 23rd Middlesex Regt
TOMSON Harold Peake MM Pte M2/130945 Army Service Corps att 73 Fd Amb RAMC.
TONER Albert Ernest MM+Bar CQMS 200018 1/5th Liverpool Regt KIA 9.4.18.
TONER Michael Joseph MM Pte 2431 6th Connaught Rangers
TONG Ernest MM Spr 259495 Royal Engineers
TONG W.T. MM Pte 44481 2nd Essex Regt
TONGE Ernest C. MM Sjt 137057 RGA
TONGE Fred MM Pte 10047 Manchester Regt
TONGE Henry MM L/Cpl 42784 Royal Engineers
TONGE John Thomas MM Cpl 269462 2/7th Liverpool Regt
TONGE S. MM+Bar Cpl 33267 2/4th Hampshire Regt
TONGE Thomas MM Pte 7935 6th Lancashire Fusiliers
TONGE William John MM Pte 242523 Gloucestershire Regt
TONGUE Charles MM Gnr 16900 312 Siege Bty RGA
TONGUE Edwin MM Pte 40349 Scottish Rifles
TONGUE George MM Cpl 13784 10th Notts & Derby Regt
TONGUE Isaac E. MM Sjt 18547 12th Highland Light Infantry

TONGUE Walter Edward MM+Bar Cpl 14/73 14th Royal Warwickshire Regt
TONKIN Frederick A.E. MM Pte 33560 2/4th Hampshire Regt
TONKIN James MM Pte 13304 Durham Light Infantry
TONKIN James W. MM Sjt 37264 South Lancashire Regt
TONKIN Stanley MM Cpl 5254 HAC
TONKINS Thomas J. MM L/Sjt 25326 Welsh Regt
TONKINSON John I. MM L/Cpl 28438 4th Hampshire Regt
TONKS Charles S. "DCM,MM" S/Sjt 99919 155 Fd Coy Royal Engineers
TONKS George Fryer MM Cpl 23246 2nd Worcestershire Regt KIA 29.9.18.
TONKS Samuel MM Cpl 11923 6th Shropshire Light Infantry
TONKS William MM Cpl 246869 A/187 Bde RFA
TONNER H. MM L/Cpl 21237 Machine Gun Corps
TONNER James MM 2nd Cpl 91977 185 Tunnelling Coy Royal Engineers
TONNER James MM+Bar Sjt 11895 Royal Scots Fusiliers
TOOBY Arthur MM Sjt 54942 25 Bde RFA
TOOBY Walter MM Pte 242032 West Yorkshire Regt
TOOGOOD Charles W. MM Pte 11/56 11th East Yorkshire Regt
TOOGOOD Henry W. MM L/Cpl R/16330 1st King's Royal Rifle Corps
TOOGOOD J. MM Pte 202535 1/6th North Staffordshire Regt
TOOGOOD Samuel MM Cpl 12353 7th Leicestershire Regt
TOOGOOD Sidney MM L/Cpl 5649 13th Royal Sussex Regt KIA 27.9.17.
TOOHEY Walter H. MM Bdr 48698 RGA
TOOKE Ernest W. MM Sjt 54512 38 Bde RFA
TOOKE Harry MM L/Cpl 41444 Bedfordshire Regt att 1/1st Hertfordshire Regt.
TOOKE Herbert Henry Thomas MM Spr 560268 47 Div Sig Coy Royal Engineers Died 1.11.18.
TOOKE John H. MM Dvr T3/028872 32 Div Train Army Service Corps
TOOKE William E. MM Pte 27494 Somerset Light Infantry
TOOKER Douglas MM Pte 31127 1st Devonshire Regt
TOOKEY John W. MM L/Cpl 240651 Leicestershire Regt
TOOLE Edward MM Sjt 42056 15th North Lancashire Regt
TOOLE Edward Penty MM L/Cpl 242846 West Yorkshire Regt
TOOLE Francis MM Pte 200885 Lancashire Fusiliers
TOOLE James MM Pte 453307 1/11th London Regt KIA 22.12.17.
TOOLE John MM Pte 20832 11th Royal Scots
TOOLE Vincent MM Cpl 171323 246 Bde RFA
TOOLEY Francis James MM+Bar Sjt 320920 12th Norfolk Regt KIA 19.8.18.
TOOLEY George MM Pte 220010 4th Royal Berkshire Regt
TOOLEY Ralph Eric MM Bdr 800089 RFA
TOOLEY Walter F. MM+Bar Sjt 680078 1/22nd London Regt
TOOLEY William J. MM Pte 17397 Bedfordshire Regt
TOOMAY James MM Pte 22683 Royal Irish Fusiliers
TOOMER Timothy C.A. MM Pte 33770 7th West Riding Regt
TOOMER William E. MM(1287 L/Sjt R Fus)+Bar Sjt 21002 Royal West Kent Regt
TOOMEY Andrew MM Bdr 39965 B/84 Bde RFA DOW 18.8.17.
TOOMEY Daniel MM Dvr 41116 37 Bty 27 Bde RFA
TOOMEY Edward MM Pte 33024 Wiltshire Regt
TOOMEY Edward Charles MM Bdr 12103 D/74 Bde RFA
TOOMEY John MM Sjt 9456 2nd East Lancashire Regt DOW 8.7.16.
TOOMEY Michael MM Pte 9642 Royal Munster Fusiliers
TOOMEY Oliver MM Sjt 9290 12th Royal Scots KIA 15.10.18.
TOOMS Frederick John MM Sjt 5070 7th Royal Sussex Regt KIA 22.8.18.
TOON Arthur J. MM L/Cpl 5259 49th Bn Machine Gun Corps
TOON Elijah "MM,MSM" Cpl 1466 1/1st Leicestershire Yeo
TOON George Henry MM Dvr 87771 6 Bty 40 Bde RFA
TOON Harold MM L/Cpl 266461 Seaforth Highlanders
TOONE Ernest MM Pte 13792 6th Royal West Surrey Regt
TOONE John MM Pte 203287 1/5th Notts & Derby Regt
TOONE Walter Harry MM L/Cpl 11623 Leicestershire Regt
TOOP Arthur Victor MM Bdr 58924 RGA
TOOP John Richard "MM,CG(F)" L/Cpl 9206 2nd Gloucestershire Regt
TOOP Thomas MM Pte 4748 Notts & Derby Regt
TOOP Walter MM Gnr 951292 RFA
TOOTH Joel MM Pte 37977 Northumberland Fusiliers KIA 20.7.18.
TOOTH Sitnah John MM Cpl 83024 B/162 Bde RFA KIA 25.8.16.
TOOTH William Eric MM Sjt 72724 B/223 Bde RFA Died 24.3.18.
TOOTILL Joseph MM Sjt 202724 Seaforth Highlanders

TOOTILL Reginald MM Sjt 444086 66 Div Sig Coy Royal Engineers
TOOTILL William MM Pte 321662 6th London Regt KIA 26.9.17.
TOOTILL William MM CQMS 9836 2nd South Wales Borderers
TOOZE Albert E. MM L/Cpl 245341 2nd Manchester Regt
TOPE Clarence T. MM Cpl M2/135937 63 Div MT Coy Army Service Corps
TOPHAM Alfred MM Pte 10054 RAMC
TOPHAM Charles MM Spr 45525 Royal Engineers
TOPHAM John R. MM L/Cpl 11504 6th Lincolnshire Regt
TOPHAM Robert MM Pte 26626 North Staffordshire Regt
TOPHAM Thomas MM Pte 12987 13th Yorkshire Regt
TOPHAM William MM Bdr 9375 B/72 Bde RFA
TOPLEY John MM Gnr 12896 D/280 Bde RFA
TOPLIS Phillip MM L/Cpl 241361 5th Yorkshire Light Infantry
TOPLIS Wilfred MM L/Cpl 276430 7th Manchester Regt
TOPLISS John Henry MM Cpl 52995 Cheshire Regt
TOPLISS Joseph William MM Dvr 796394 49 Div Ammn Col RFA
TOPLISS William H. MM Sjt 240829 North Staffordshire Regt
TOPP Albert George MM Gnr 132483 296 Siege Bty RGA
TOPP Frank Herbert MM Pte 15325 1st Hampshire Regt DOW 24.10.18.
TOPP Harry T. MM Pte 10627 5th Royal Berkshire Regt
TOPPING Allen MM Pte 16020 15th Royal Irish Rifles KIA 28.9.18.
TOPPING Charles MM Pte 241686 North Lancashire Regt
TOPPING Charles W. "DCM,MM" Sjt 11049 4th Royal Fusiliers
TOPPING Irving G. MM Cpl 15364 11th Border Regt
TOPPING James MM Pte 48527 19th Manchester Regt
TOPPING Joe T. MM L/Cpl 202147 Lancashire Fusiliers
TOPPING Robert MM Pte 18/614 18th Durham Light Infantry
TOPPING Septimus MM CQMS 11928 10th Durham Light Infantry KIA 9.4.17.
TOPPING Thomas J. MM Sjt 53787 RFA
TOPPLE Charles A. MM Sjt 330005 1/8th Royal Scots
TORBETT Reginald MM Sjt 1521 1st London Regt
TORDOFF Herbert "DCM,MM,MSM" L/Sjt 11777 6th Yorkshire Light Infantry
TORDOFF Walter MM Sjt 43238 19th Durham Light Infantry
TORDOFF William H. MM Pte 41164 Lancashire Fusiliers
TORKINGTON Alfred J. MM Cpl 22417 Machine Gun Corps
TORKINGTON George MM Bdr 735724 B/298 Bde RFA
TORODE Thomas H. MM L/Cpl 6/3352 6th Royal Irish Regt
TORR George MM Pte S/4231 2nd King's Royal Rifle Corps
TORRANCE Alexander MM Cpl Fitter 72603 9 Bty 41 Bde RFA
TORRANCE Alexander Beggs MM Sjt 3691 1/14th London Regt KIA 1.7.16.
TORRANCE Arthur Stanley MM L/Cpl 230346 1/2nd London Regt
TORRANCE James MM Pte 202210 Royal Highlanders
TORRANCE John MM Cpl 414055 410 Fd Coy Royal Engineers
TORRANCE Oliver Albert James MM Sjt 1878 1/2nd London Regt
TORRANCE Thomas MM Pte 251106 1/6th Arg & Suth Highlanders
TORRANCE William MM+Bar Bdr 46376 A/103 Bde RFA
TORRIE James MM L/Cpl 14306 1st Scots Guards
TORRIE Lauchlan MM L/Cpl 285037 Gordon Highlanders
TORRINGTON Clifford P. MM+Bar L/Cpl 18525 15 Fd Coy Royal Engineers
TORRINGTON George MM Pte 241395 1/8th Middlesex Regt Died 6.8.18.
TOSELAND Charles W. MM L/Sjt 18302 8th Leicestershire Regt
TOSELAND James "MM,MSM" Cpl 11794 2nd Leicestershire Regt
TOSH Alexander MM Sjt 51376 5/6th Royal Scots
TOSH John MM Sjt 326010 40 Siege Bty RGA
TOSH William Cameron "MM,CG(B)" Pte 44218 12th North Staffordshire Regt
TOSSELL Wesley MM Pte 22496 1st Gloucestershire Regt
TOSTEVIN Peter MM Sjt 324458 254 Army Troops Coy Royal Engineers
TOTEN Ernest William MM L/Cpl 30689 8th East Surrey Regt KIA 7.8.17.
TOTHAM S.W. MM Pte 12505 9th Essex Regt
TOTHILL John MM Pte 57901 Machine Gun Corps
TOTMAN Cubitt MM L/Cpl 7240 5th Lancers
TOTT William MM Sjt 71128 42 Bde RFA
TOTTEN William MM Pte 52665 1st Scottish Rifles
TOTTENHAM William "MM,MID" Pte 16008 12th Royal Scots
TOTTEY Joseph MM Spr 446238 123 Fd Coy Royal Engineers
TOTTLE William Thomas MM Gnr Sig 56853 'X' Bty RHA
TOTTY James MM Sjt 40685 22nd Manchester Regt
TOUELL F. MM Pte 650125 London Regt
TOUGH George MM Sjt 241960 1/5th Seaforth Highlanders
TOUGHER George MM Pte 24015 Notts & Derby Regt

TOULSON Ephraim MM Pte 14293 11thy West Yorkshire Regt
TOURLE Harry MM Pte 10917 Royal West Surrey Regt
TOUT Arthur A. MM Pte 10683 8th Devonshire Regt
TOUT Arthur William MM Gnr 21666 157 Siege Bty RGA
TOVEE Frederick J. MM Cpl 50485 RGA
TOVEY Edmund L. MM CSM 3025 Royal West Kent Regt detached to Archangel.
TOVEY Godfrey E. MM Cpl B/709 7th Rifle Brigade
TOVEY Jesse MM Pte 133 Wiltshire Regt
TOVEY William Henry MM Sjt 930457 RFA
TOW Frederick William Edward MM Cpl 8144 2nd Lincolnshire Regt
TOWELL H. MM Cpl 7768 RFA
TOWELL Tom Dickson MM Pte 2858 7th Yorkshire Regt KIA 21.4.17.
TOWELL William MM Pte 34335 RAMC
TOWELLS Leonard H. MM Sjt 24389 153 Heavy Bty RGA
TOWER Edward S. MM Sjt P/963 Rifle Brigade
TOWERS Andrew MM Sjt 267920 1st West Yorkshire Regt
TOWERS Arthur MM Sjt 240724 5th Royal Lancaster Regt
TOWERS Charles MM Sjt 252790 6th Durham Light Infantry
TOWERS David MM Cpl 25452 17th Royal Welsh Fusiliers KIA 2.2.17.
TOWERS Ernest MM L/Cpl 44359 76 Fd Coy Royal Engineers
TOWERS George MM Gnr 176397 504 Siege Bty RGA
TOWERS Henry Quayle MM L/Cpl 200736 1/4th Royal Lancaster Regt DOW 6.4.18.
TOWERS Herbert G. MM Sjt 2275 4th Middlesex Regt
TOWERS Hugh Hayes MM Pte 103087 106 Fd Amb RAMC
TOWERS John B. MM Pte 53668 2nd Royal Scots Fusiliers
TOWERS John J. MM Gnr 32544 RGA
TOWERS John W. MM L/Cpl 260446 7th Border Regt
TOWERS Joseph MM Pte 40677 5th Lincolnshire Regt
TOWERS Richard MM L/Cpl 18860 6th Royal Lancaster Regt KIA 8.3.17.
TOWERS Thomas C. MM Pnr 197412 Royal Engineers
TOWERS Walter MM L/Cpl 13955 103 Fd Coy Royal Engineers
TOWERS Walter "DCM,MM" L/Cpl 76094 8 Div Sig Coy Royal Engineers
TOWERS William MM Pte 41658 Lincolnshire Regt
TOWERS William Alfred MM S/Sjt 426003 RAMC
TOWERSEY James Henry Thomas MM Pte 13382 6th East Kent Regt
TOWHILL Sidney R. "MM,MSM" Cpl 348065 113 Siege Bty RGA
TOWLAND James MM Pte 4975 16 Fd Amb RAMC
TOWLAND William MM Cpl 14835 10th Northumberland Fusiliers
TOWLE Charles MM Gnr 511 RFA
TOWLE Edward MM Pte 48779 Liverpool Regt
TOWLE H.F. MM Pte 245914 Durham Light Infantry
TOWLER James MM Cpl 21390 1st Royal Lancaster Regt KIA 17.6.18.
TOWLER Joseph MM Pte 11654 6th Border Regt
TOWLER Percy MM Bdr 35430 RFA
TOWLER Sidney MM Sjt M2/035144 Army Service Corps att 7 Bty MGC(Motors).
TOWLER Thomas MM Pte 14281 9th East Lancashire Regt
TOWLER Thomas G. MM S/Sjt Mechanic 92134 10th Bn Tank Corps
TOWLSON Albert John MM Cpl 1099 1/1(London)Fd Coy Royal Engineers
TOWLSON Edwaed MM Cpl 41237 Royal Engineers
TOWN Albert Harry MM L/Cpl 26234 341 Rly Const Coy Royal Engineers
TOWN Frederick Albert MM Cpl 80613 135 Coy Labour Corps
TOWN George MM Dvr 54209 32 Bde RFA
TOWN George MM+Bar Cpl S/3140 11th Rifle Brigade
TOWN Philip A. MM Sjt 224596 252 Coy Labour Corps
TOWN Walter MM L/Cpl 250425 1/5th Essex Regt
TOWN William MM Gnr 160271 D/250 Bde RFA
TOWNEND Arthur MM Pte 7639 2nd Royal Munster Fusiliers
TOWNEND Asa MM Pte 117469 38 Fd Amb RAMC
TOWNEND George O. MM L/Sjt 22267 Durham Light Infantry
TOWNEND Henry MM Sjt 2512 6th Dragoons
TOWNEND Herbert MM Sjt 35135 RFA
TOWNEND John MM Pte 7484 8th Leicestershire Regt KIA 13.4.17.
TOWNEND John Alfred MM L/Cpl R/18561 8th King's Royal Rifle Corps DOW 25.8.17.
TOWNEND John S. MM Cpl 37021 North Staffordshire Regt
TOWNEND Ralph MM Spr 82060 Royal Engineers att HQ 25 Div.
TOWNEND Walter MM Cpl 90258 B/86 Bde RFA
TOWNER Alfred H. MM Dvr 64926 A/159 Bde RFA

TOWNER Charles R. MM+Bar L/Sjt 32499 14th Royal Warwickshire Regt
TOWNER Ernest W. MM Spr 532353 Royal Engineers
TOWNER Horace MM Pte 30628 2nd Oxf & Bucks Light Infantry
TOWNER Thomas W. MM L/Cpl 1912 1/5th Royal Sussex Regt
TOWNLEY Alexander MM Gnr 4765 RFA
TOWNLEY Alfred J. MM Pte 358918 10th Liverpool Regt
TOWNLEY Arthur Eric MM CSM A/1064 7th King's Royal Rifle Corps DOW 16.9.16.
TOWNLEY Charles H. MM Pte 6248 Border Regt
TOWNLEY Harold MM Gnr 620369 2/1(Somerset)Bty RHA DOW 5.11.17.
TOWNLEY William MM Pte 21626 Manchester Regt
TOWNROW Frederick MM Sjt 14726 Lincolnshire Regt
TOWNS Alexander MM L/Cpl 267078 5/6th Scottish Rifles
TOWNS Herbert MM L/Cpl 26374 1st Grenadier Guards
TOWNS J.B. MM Pte 305066 3 Fd Amb RAMC
TOWNS James MM Pte 39156 Royal Scots
TOWNSEND Abraham MM Pte 5467 10th Royal Warwickshire Regt DOW 31.7.16.
TOWNSEND Alfred MM Sjt 940065 D/280 Bde RFA
TOWNSEND Arthur MM Dvr 202430 D/168 Bde RFA
TOWNSEND Arthur William MM Sjt 14505 7th Wiltshire Regt
TOWNSEND Benjamin MM L/Cpl 1138 Royal Fusiliers
TOWNSEND Christopher J. MM+Bar Sjt 63708 101 Fd Coy Royal Engineers
TOWNSEND E. MM Pte 4/8346 10th West Yorkshire Regt
TOWNSEND Ernest MM Sjt 20797 36 Bde RFA
TOWNSEND Ernest MM Pte 7436 11th Royal Fusiliers
TOWNSEND Ernest C. MM Pte 233196 2nd London Regt
TOWNSEND Ernest J. MM+Bar Sjt 205036 15th Hampshire Regt
TOWNSEND Ernest J. MM Gnr 91947 RFA
TOWNSEND Frank MM Pte 23657 12th South Wales Borderers
TOWNSEND Frederick MM Pte 20871 1st Dorsetshire Regt
TOWNSEND Frederick MM Sjt 210928 112 Hy Bty RGA
TOWNSEND Frederick MM Pte 25184 1st Royal Dublin Fusiliers
TOWNSEND George MM L/Cpl 21558 Machine Gun Corps
TOWNSEND H.E. MM Pte 16554 10th Essex Regt
TOWNSEND Harold MM Pte 33017 2/4th Oxf & Bucks Light Infantry
TOWNSEND Harry MM Sjt 9921 1st East Lancashire Regt AKA Harry WILSON
TOWNSEND Harry C. MM+Bar Pte 45736 15th Hampshire Regt
TOWNSEND Henry MM Gnr 169149 RFA
TOWNSEND Henry J. MM L/Cpl 323606 6th London Regt
TOWNSEND John MM L/Cpl B/1446 Rifle Brigade
TOWNSEND John C. MM Gnr 12235 'Z' Bty RHA
TOWNSEND John George MM Bdsm 8948 1st Leicestershire Regt
TOWNSEND Leonard MM Sjt 690311 278 Bde RFA
TOWNSEND Lewis MM Pte 8703 2nd East Surrey Regt
TOWNSEND Lionel MM Cpl 56548 4 Div Sig Coy Royal Engineers
TOWNSEND Oliver G. MM L/Cpl 15603 Royal West Surrey Regt
TOWNSEND Reginald F. MM Cpl 1687 1/16th London Regt
TOWNSEND Thomas MM Cpl 65576 2nd Royal Fusiliers
TOWNSEND Walter James MM Sjt 130520 5th Bn Special Bde Royal Engineers
TOWNSEND William H. MM Cpl 13717 2nd Royal Fusiliers
TOWNSEND William H. MM Gnr 78385 RFA
TOWNSEND William R. MM Sjt 8438 2nd King's Royal Rifle Corps
TOWNSEND Willie MM Gnr 25598 RFA
TOWNSHEND Harry George MM L/Cpl 16560 1st Norfolk Regt KIA 27.9.18.
TOWNSLEY David "MM,MID" L/Cpl 64097 122 Fd Coy Royal Engineers
TOWNSON A. MM Pte 22982 East Lancashire Regt
TOWNSON Dean MM+Bar Spr 448744 12 Div Sig Coy Royal Engineers
TOWNSON Francis J. MM Cpl 226 157 Bde RFA
TOWNSON Leonard MM Cpl 276800 7th Manchester Regt
TOWSE Harold MM Cpl 11038 11th East Yorkshire Regt KIA 12.7.18.
TOWSE Robert MM Gnr 801692 C/59 Bde RFA
TOWSE Sidney MM Sjt 240030 1/5th Yorkshire Regt KIA 11.4.18.
TOWSEY Frederick MM Pte 39562 Worcestershire Regt
TOY Albert MM Pte 24090 Gloucestershire Regt
TOY Reginald MM Pte 1872 RAMC
TOY William MM Pte 5622 1st Gordon Highlanders
TOY William MM Dvr 20802 112 Bde RFA
TOYER Charles MM Pte 33091 Leicestershire Regt
TOYER George MM Pte 45369 124 Coy Machine Gun Corps
TOYN George MM Sjt 8550 2nd Lincolnshire Regt KIA 9.4.18.

TOYNBEE John William MM Cpl 295340 145 Siege Bty RGA
TOYNE Albert MM Gnr 168571 403 Bty RFA
TOYNE Ernest Shep "MM,CG(F)" Cpl 28152 2nd Cheshire Regt
TOZER A.A. MM Cpl 16625 11th Essex Regt
TOZER Clifford M. MM Sjt 64840 121 Bty 27 Bde RFA
TOZER John R. MM Sjt 51506 Machine Gun Corps
TOZER Richard MM Gnr 358348 RGA
TOZER T. MM Cpl 17188 13th Essex Regt
TOZER Thomas MM Sjt 8722 2nd Shropshire Light Infantry
TOZER William MM Pte 10226 54 Fd Amb RAMC
TOZER William MM Sjt M2/020750 Army Service Corps
TOZER William Harold John MM L/Sjt 17707 10th Royal Warwickshire Regt
TRACEY Archibald MM Cpl 248219 352 Elect & Mech Coy Royal Engineers
TRACEY E. MM Sjt P/4813 Military Mounted Police
TRACEY Francis MM Sjt 41929 RFA
TRACEY G.W. MM Pte 39575 Welsh Regt
TRACEY Henry A. "DCM,MM" Sjt 10018 1st Royal West Surrey Regt
TRACEY Herbert MM Sjt 5734 Royal Munster Fusiliers
TRACEY James MM Pte 67088 62nd Bn Machine Gun Corps
TRACEY James MM L/Cpl 10311 1st East Surrey Regt DOW 10.5.17.
TRACEY John MM Pte 2278 2nd Rifle Brigade DOW 1.8.18.
TRACEY John MM Pte 37482 Machine Gun Corps
TRACEY Lewis MM+Bar Pte R/20347 King's Royal Rifle Corps
TRACEY Patrick J. MM+2 Bars CSM 681546 22nd London Regt
TRACEY Thomas MM Pte 18929 2nd Royal Dublin Fusiliers
TRACEY Thomas MM L/Cpl 244968 8 Div Sig Coy Royal Engineers
TRADEWELL William H. MM Pte 405424 RAMC
TRAFFORD Edward H. MM Sjt 1393 1/20th London Regt
TRAFFORD Edwin L. MM Pte 137431 32nd Bn Machine Gun Corps
TRAFFORD George W. MM Pte 13685 6th Lincolnshire Regt
TRAFFORD Isaac MM Dvr 21751 RFA
TRAFFORD Sidney A. MM Gnr 64502 RFA
TRAIL Hugh H. MM Sjt 161411 329 Siege Bty RGA
TRAIN George Frederick MM Cpl 9908 Machine Gun Corps
TRAIN John D. MM Pte 27579 Royal Scots
TRAIN William MM Pte 16738 7th Cameron Highlanders DOW 19.3.17.
TRAINER Albert MM Cpl 36999 62 Coy Labour Corps
TRAINER Lawrence MM+Bar L/Cpl 5275 1st Border Regt
TRAINER Thomas MM Pte 33854 1/7th Scottish Rifles
TRAINOR Patrick MM Gnr 60399 RGA
TRAINOR Thomas MM+Bar Pte 1121 99 Fd Amb RAMC Died 26.7.17.
TRALAN George Walter MM Cpl 76269 C/87 Bde RFA DOW 25.4.18.
TRAN Alexander MM L/Cpl 28718 2nd King's Own Scottish Borderers
TRANGMAR Leslie J. MM L/Cpl 15847 1st Scots Guards
TRANMER John William MM Cpl 240080 1/5th Yorkshire Regt
TRANTER Arthur L. MM Pte 235323 23rd Middlesex Regt
TRANTER Benjamin MM L/Cpl 42747 75 Fd Coy Royal Engineers
TRANTER Edward MM Sjt 72236 1st Notts & Derby Regt
TRANTER George W. MM Sjt 618 18th Middlesex Regt
TRANTER Harry MM L/Cpl 1019 16th Royal Warwickshire Regt
TRANTER J. MM Sjt 308486 5th Liverpool Regt
TRANTER Oliver Stanley MM Spr 102746 177 Tunnelling Coy Royal Engineers
TRANTER Samuel MM L/Sjt 37653 RAMC
TRANTER Wilfred E. MM Pte 22367 4th West Riding Regt
TRATT William MM Pte 17578 Devonshire Regt
TRAVELL William MM L/Cpl 13998 6th Northamptonshire Regt KIA 5.4.18.
TRAVERS James MM Pte 9555 1st Hampshire Regt
TRAVERS Patrick MM Dvr T4/241156 Army Service Corps
TRAVERS Peter "DCM,MM" Sjt 303356 Arg & Suth Highlanders
TRAVERS Thomas MM+Bar Sjt 2997 12th Middlesex Regt
TRAVERS William H. MM Pte 18606 Dorsetshire Regt
TRAVERSE Job MM Pte 242206 5th South Lancashire Regt
TRAVES James MM+Bar Sjt 7673 1st Dorsetshire Regt
TRAVIS Ernest MM Pte 304509 London Regt
TRAVIS Frank MM Pte 15159 7th Royal Lancaster Regt KIA 30.7.17.
TRAVIS George MM Sjt 202660 RGA
TRAVIS James MM Pte 52752 Liverpool Regt
TRAVIS John MM Pte 27820 Royal Lancaster Regt
TRAVIS John James MM Gnr 61762 RGA

TRAXTON Thomas C. MM Gnr 20604 B/123 Bde RFA
TRAYLER Arthur G. MM Pte 281270 1/4th London Regt
TRAYNOR John T. MM Pte 2565 11th Durham Light Infantry
TRAYNOR Joseph W. MM Pte 59185 RAMC
TRAYNOR Samuel MM Cpl 32404 45 Bde RFA
TRAYNOR William MM Dvr 4515 C/47 Bde RFA
TREACY James MM Pte 9622 Royal Dublin Fusiliers
TREADAWAY Arthur E. MM Pte 17401 7th East Kent Regt
TREADAWAY or TREADWAY James W. MM Sjt 11481 1st Middlesex Regt
TREADGOLD Charles Raymond MM+Bar L/Cpl 251464 3rd London Regt KIA 28.8.18.
TREADWELL Frank MM Gnr 75496 103 Bde RFA
TREADWELL Thomas E. MM Cpl 297089 156 Hy Bty RGA
TREADWELL Thomas H. MM Sjt 538060 RAMC
TREADWELL Walter MM L/Cpl 267478 1/6th Gloucestershire Regt
TREADWELL William E. MM Pte 60866 RAMC
TREASURE Alban Theodore MM Pte 4109 18th Bn Machine Gun Corps
TREASURE Arthur Seward MM Cpl 439139 3(South Midland)Fd Amb RAMC
TREASURE Sydney Percival MM Bdr 22377 C/93 Bde RFA
TREBELL Frederick MM Sjt 202412 Duke of Cornwall's LI
TREBILCOCK John W. MM Pte 24031 Duke of Cornwall's LI
TREBLE William MM CSM 280 6th Royal West Surrey Regt
TREBLE William T. MM Sjt 548435 513 Fd Coy Royal Engineers
TREBY Frederick A. MM Pte 19082 XIX Corps Cyclist Bn Army Cyclist Corps
TREDGETT Charles Stanley MM Sjt 755249 A/251 Bde RFA
TREDGETT Herbert MM Gnr 40025 RFA
TREDWELL Walter MM Dvr 97512 RFA
TREE George MM Sjt 114851 RFA
TREEBY Alroy MM Pte 373833 8th London Regt att MGC.
TREEBY Harry L. MM Pte 350716 1/7th Royal Highlanders
TREELOVE William A. MM Sjt 13623 23rd Royal Fusiliers
TREGAY Harry MM Pte 241816 Lancashire Fusiliers
TREGLOWN George MM Cpl 492036 46 Div Sig Coy Royal Engineers
TREGONING Arthur H. MM Pte 25460 Royal Fusiliers
TREGURTHA Charles F. MM Sjt 10931 RFA
TREHARNE David J. MM L/Cpl 54557 14th Welsh Regt
TREHARNE Gomer MM L/Cpl 13129 9th Royal Welsh Fusiliers
TREHARNE Treharne MM Pte 241130 Welsh Regt
TREHERN Frank Montague MM CSM 300086 1/5th London Regt
TREHERNE Frederick C. MM+Bar Cpl 9468 2nd Royal Scots Fusiliers
TRELEAVEN Thomas D. MM Cpl M2/183750 Army Service Corps
TRELEAVEN Vyne MM Sjt 22315 9th Royal Fusiliers
TRELOAR Ralph MM Sjt 10423 6th Duke of Cornwall's LI DOW 14.4.17.
TREMAIN Henry J. MM Spr 26469 7 Div Sig Coy Royal Engineers
TREMAIN Percy Nelson MM Pte 470619 12th London Regt
TREMAINE Richard MM Pte 52624 2nd Suffolk Regt
TREMAYNE John S. MM Dvr(Wlr) 123124 RFA
TREMBATH Daniel "MM+Bar,MID" L/Cpl 97163 11 Div Sig Coy Royal Engineers
TREMBATH W. MM Pte 49953 RAMC
TREMBATH William MM Cpl 87555 33 Div Sig Coy Royal Engineers
TREMLETT Henry MM L/Cpl 27130 Hampshire Regt
TRENCHARD Edward P.B. MM Pte 2610 24th Royal Fusiliers
TRENDALL Frank G. MM Cpl 201606 Tank Corps
TRENDALL Thomas MM+Bar L/Cpl 69073 35 Div Sig Coy Royal Engineers
TRENFIELD Charles H. MM Cpl 310925 1/1st Warwickshire Yeomanry
TRENFIELD Robert C. MM Pte 4610 16th Lancers
TRENHOLM Arthur Edwin MM L/Cpl 31534 2nd Royal Welsh Fusiliers DOW 2.7.18.
TRENHOLM John P. MM L/Cpl 29469 2nd Highland Light Infantry
TRENOUTH Thomas MM Pte 21775 Duke of Cornwall's LI
TRENT Frank MM Pte 202527 4th Hampshire Regt
TRENTER Alfred MM Pte 16555 10th Royal Fusiliers Died 27.10.18.
TRENWITH Eedward J. MM Pte S19313 Rifle Brigade
TRESARDEN William MM Cpl 321193 10th London Regt
TRESIDDER Ernest Sidney MM Sjt 58249 41 Bde RFA
TRESS William George MM Sjt 4455 7th East Kent Regt
TRETHEWEY Marshall H. MM Cpl 75596 RGA
TRETT Arthur Richard MM Cpl 24178 2 Div Sig Coy Royal Engineers
TRETT George MM Pte 29479 Duke of Cornwall's LI
TRETT John MM Pte 3/8553 2nd Northumberland Fusiliers
TRETT William G. MM Sjt 960203 C/235 Bde RFA
TREVANION Harold A.E. MM Sjt 3694 17th Lancers
TREVENA Harold MM Cpl R/9285 13th King's Royal Rifle Corps
TREVERSH Frank E. MM L/Cpl 646 9th Royal Fusiliers
TREVES Henry G. MM Sjt 531523 15th London Regt
TREVETT Frank MM Cpl S/4319 13th Rifle Brigade
TREVETT Jack MM Pte 241565 1/5th South Lancashire Regt
TREVETT John MM Gnr 19250 24 Bde RFA
TREVILLON Harry MM Pte 10729 South Staffordshire Regt
TREVITT Arthur A. MM Dvr 29502 D/178 Bde RFA
TREVIVIAN Randoplh MM Cpl 48034 Cav Corps Sig Sqn Royal Engineers
TREVOR Albert W. "DCM+Bar,MM" Sjt 1192 7th Royal Sussex Regt
TREVOR David MM Sjt Saddler 34398 8 Bde RFA
TREVOR Harold E. MM Cpl 305774 Lancashire Fusiliers
TREVOR Owen William MM+Bar Pte 11135 7th Shropshire Light Infantry
TREW Edwin Charles MM Pte 242015 1st East Kent Regt DOW 3.8.18.
TREW Frederick W. MM L/Cpl 87048 32nd Bn Machine Gun Corps
TREW George Alfred MM L/Cpl 6668 4th Middlesex Regt KIA 23.4.17.
TREW Reginald Edwin MM Cpl 265411 1/2nd Monmouthshire Regt KIA 2.12.17.
TREW W.H.A. "DCM,MM" Sjt 10300 1st Duke of Cornwall's LI
TREW William Percival Frederick MM Cpl 20460 2nd Royal Munster Fusiliers Died 4.11.18.
TREWBY Eric C. MM L/Cpl M2/076626 Army Service Corps
TREWEEK James MM Pte 5925 12th Lancers
TREWEEK Mathias MM Spr 40546 Royal Engineers
TREWIN Alfred Ernest MM Cpl 128279 RGA
TREWIN Sydney E. MM Pte 27921 1st Duke of Cornwall's LI
TRIANCE Richard T. MM Pte 232772 2nd London Regt
TRIBBLE Samuel Henry Lemilling MM Cpl 28974 7th Duke of Cornwall's LI KIA 27.9.17.
TRIBBLE William H. MM L/Cpl 241056 1/5th Devonshire Regt
TRIBE Albert Allan Wytham "DCM,MM" Cpl 233640 74 Div Sig Coy Royal Engineers
TRIBE Alfred R. MM Pte S/18655 13th Rifle Brigade
TRIBE George Holt MM Pte 43694 2nd Suffolk Regt KIA 28.3.18.
TRIBICK Frederick W. MM L/Cpl 558228 56 Div Sig Coy Royal Engineers
TRICKER Albert E. MM Cpl 17299 1 Fd Squadron Royal Engineers
TRICKETT Allan MM Spr 244216 84 Fd Coy Royal Engineers
TRICKETT Frank MM Pte C/6564 King's Royal Rifle Corps
TRICKETT John H. MM Pte 164996 100th Bn Machine Gun Corps
TRICKETT Sidney F. MM Pte 15478 15th Hampshire Regt
TRICKEY Albert E. MM Sjt 19175 Machine Gun Corps
TRICKEY Arthur MM Pte 14183 6th Northamptonshire Regt
TRICKEY Henry MM Pte 43377 Royal Irish Rifles
TRICKEY T. MM Pte 52635 Cheshire Regt
TRIESE T. MM Cpl 87808 Royal Flying Corps
TRIETLINE Frank MM Dvr 163065 422 Fd Coy Royal Engineers
TRIFFITT Edward Walter MM Dvr 1227 246 Bde RFA DOW 30.3.17.
TRIGG Alfred J. MM Pte 64060 46th Bn Machine Gun Corps
TRIGG Charles H. MM Pte S/16617 13th Rifle Brigade
TRIGG Frederick MM L/Cpl 16889 Machine Gun Corps
TRIGG James F. MM Pte 203992 1st London Regt
TRIGG Loftus D. MM Pte 240287 5th Gloucestershire Regt
TRIGG Sydney MM Pte 39160 Machine Gun Corps
TRIGG Thomas J. MM Dvr 69633 RFA
TRIGG W.J. MM Sjt 9435 1st East Kent Regt
TRIGG Walter MM Cpl 48074 130 Fd Amb RAMC
TRIGG William A. MM Cpl M2/077455 Army Service Corps
TRIGGER William MM+Bar Cpl 201649 2nd South Lancashire Regt
TRIGGS Ethelbert MM Gnr 73654 2 Bde RFA
TRIGGS S.H.G. MM AM2 8267 Royal Flying Corps
TRIGGS William MM Sjt 83751 B/48 Bde RFA
TRIGWELL George A. MM Pte 393221 9th London Regt
TRILL Alfred Ernest MM Spr 259553 Royal Engineers
TRILL Frederick J. MM L/Cpl 16944 8th Bedfordshire Regt
TRILLIAN John "DCM,MM" Sjt 34069 Signal Service Royal Engineers
TRIM Edward J. MM+Bar L/Cpl 42093 RAMC
TRIM George B. MM Sjt 46510 RAMC
TRIM John A. MM Pte R/14641 King's Royal Rifle Corps
TRIMBEY W. MM Pte 1769 Royal Fusiliers
TRIMBLE Edward MM+Bar Cpl 17818 54 Fd Coy Royal Engineers
TRIMMELL W.A. MM Gnr 70754 41 Bde RFA

TRIMMER Ernest MM Cpl 300310 1/7th Royal Scots
TRINDER Alfred John MM Pte 2425 1/5th Gloucestershire Regt KIA 27.8.26.
TRINDER Ernest MM Pte R/3372 King's Royal Rifle Corps
TRINDER George MM Sjt 12358 11th Hampshire Regt
TRINDER J. MM Sjt 37982 RGA AKA VOSE.
TRINDER Ralph J. MM Pte 67397 1/5th Devonshire Regt
TRINDER Robert MM Cpl 291391 156 Heavy Bty RGA
TRINGHAM Walter T. "MM,MSM" Sjt 15967 RAMC
TRIPLOW H. MM Gnr 82185 RFA
TRIPP Albert V.T. "DCM,MM" Cpl 9210 1st Scottish Rifles
TRIPP Herbert MM L/Cpl 13/1307 13th East Yorkshire Regt
TRIPPETT Frederick A. MM Pte 30505 Yorkshire Regt
TRISH Alfred MM L/Cpl 6099 9th East Surrey Regt
TRISTRAM Francis MM CSM 200049 1/5th Notts & Derby Regt
TRISTRAM William MM Bdr 68884 RHA
TRITTON D.McR. MM Pte 6382 2nd Dragoons
TRIVETT Frederick MM L/Cpl 2321 Manchester Regt
TRIVETT Noel MM L/Cpl 21894 11th Manchester Regt
TROAKE Daniel MM Pte 9594 2nd Northumberland Fusiliers
TRODD Edward C. MM Pte 87389 11th Royal Fusiliers
TRODD William MM Spr 46518 5 Div Sig Coy Royal Engineers
TRODDEN James "DCM,MM" Pte 45758 Royal Welsh Fusiliers
TRODDEN John MM Pte 3/6845 2nd Arg & Suth Highlanders DOW 17.4.18.
TROLL Joseph MM Gnr 69813 42 Bde RFA
TROLLEY George MM Sjt 40876 RAMC
TROLLOPE George R. MM Pte 204646 West Riding Regt
TROMAN Albert MM Pte 201899 4th South Lancashire Regt
TROMAN Ernest C. "DCM,MM" Sjt 9826 2nd Royal Welsh Fusiliers
TRON Henry MM Spr 161798 1 Div Sig Coy Royal Engineers
TROPMAN Lewis MM Pte 11997 1st Gloucestershire Regt KIA 18.4.18.
TROPP Charles J. MM Cpl 46344 RFA
TROTH George MM Sjt 240889 2/8th Worcestershire Regt KIA 5.1.17.
TROTH Walter James MM L/Bdr 67725 A/110 Bde RFA KIA 18.9.18.
TROTMAN Charles MM Pte 15792 9th South Staffordshire Regt
TROTMAN David MM Pte 22610 Welsh Regt
TROTMAN Herbert J. MM Sjt 63281 228 Siege Bty RGA
TROTT Bert MM Sjt 156553 4 Special Coy Royal Engineers
TROTT E.R. MM Pte 59137 1/6th Essex Regt
TROTT George MM L/Cpl 3/7607 7th Bedfordshire Regt KIA 3.5.17.
TROTT James MM Sjt 25051 3 Bde RHA
TROTT James MM Gnr 12305 RFA
TROTT William MM Sjt 265562 8th West Yorkshire Regt
TROTT William Charles MM L/Cpl P/2811 Military Foot Police att HQ Fifth Army.
TROTTER Anthony MM Sjt 26/675 Northumberland Fusiliers
TROTTER Beecher MM L/Bdr 151442 303 Siege Bty RGA
TROTTER Frank MM L/Cpl 5334 10th Lancashire Fusiliers
TROTTER Henry Baron MM Pte 9204 HAC DOW 10.9.18.
TROTTER Jane Elizabeth MM Sister F QAIMNS
TROTTER Joseph MM Dvr 390 RFA
TROTTER Robert MM Sjt 64260 1st Bn Machine Gun Corps
TROTTER Robert MM Pte 10343 Scots Guards
TROTTER Thomas MM L/Sjt 20016 4th Grenadier Guards
TROTTER Thomas E. MM L/Sjt 5265 Machine Gun Corps
TROTTER W. MM Sjt 200330 1/4th Royal Scots
TROUGHTON Francis E. MM Sjt 631515 20th London Regt
TROUGHTON James MM Pte S/946 10th Rifle Brigade
TROUGHTON Wilson MM L/Cpl 5854 8th Border Regt
TROUNSON Edwin MM L/Cpl 11846 10th Devonshire Regt
TROUP George MM Spr 406022 Royal Engineers
TROUP Ian MM Cpl 290383 1/7th Gordon Highlanders
TROUSDALE Albert MM Gnr 232223 A/87 Bde RFA
TROUSDALE James MM L/Cpl 240737 Royal Scots Fusiliers
TROUSDALE Thomas MM Sjt 19114 14th Liverpool Regt
TROUSDALE William "DCM,MM,DM(B)" CSM 52983 1st Royal Scots Fusiliers
TROUT George MM Pte 240579 York & Lancaster Regt
TROUT Henry E. MM Sjt 13167 XVII Corps Cyclist Bn Army Cyclist Corps
TROUT James W. MM Pte 37252 12th East Surrey Regt
TROUT Tom MM Cpl 241248 2/5th York & Lancaster Regt DOW 15.7.17.
TROWBRIDGE Arthur George MM Cpl 14115 2nd Bedfordshire Regt
TROWBRIDGE Charles H. MM 2nd Cpl 182427 Royal Engineers
TROWBRIDGE Ernest MM Pte 20995 Hampshire Regt
TROWBRIDGE F. MM Pte 556593 16th London Regt
TROWBRIDGE HenryG. MM L/Bdr 75391 24 Hy Bty RGA
TROWELL Charles H. MM Sjt 38554 RHA
TROWELL Leonard MM Sjt 37099 Bedfordshire Regt
TROWER Frederick MM Cpl 69580 9th Northumberland Fusiliers
TROWILL Bernard MM L/Cpl 11/743 11th East Yorkshire Regt
TROWSDALE Albert Frederick MM Pte 14627 8th Yorkshire Light Infantry
TROWSDALE C.R. MM CSM 7975 2nd King's Royal Rifle Corps
TROWSDALE Leslie MM+Bar Pte 1709 West Yorkshire Regt
TROY J. MM Pte 1112 4th Hussars
TROY John H. MM Pte 15792 8th Royal Sussex Regt
TROY William MM Cpl 500401 61 Div Sig Coy Royal Engineers
TROY William J. MM Pte 7381 Irish Guards
TRUBY William MM Sjt 5993 2nd South Staffordshire Regt
TRUDGILL Edgar MM L/Cpl 7671 11th Lancashire Fusiliers
TRUE Ghuznee G. "MM,MID" Sjt 282 Lincolnshire Regt
TRUELOVE William MM Cpl 1375 Royal Engineers
TRUEMAN Alwyn MM Pte 200470 1/5th Bedfordshire Regt
TRUEMAN Frank MM Cpl 17805 Machine Gun Corps
TRUEMAN George MM Pte 11840 6th Wiltshire Regt
TRUEMAN Harry MM L/Cpl 492533 Royal Engineers
TRUEMAN Henry C. MM Sjt 34496 71 Fd Amb RAMC
TRUEMAN Joseph MM Spr 251737 ? Div Sig Coy Royal Engineers
TRUEMAN Lionel E. MM Sjt 11176 20th Hussars
TRUEMAN Richard Pew MM Pte 26101 1st Grenadier Guards
TRUESDALE William MM Pte 241033 Seaforth Highlanders
TRUMAN Arthur MM Sjt 41893 7th Leicestershire Regt
TRUMAN Arthur P. MM Spr 193373 Royal Engineers
TRUMAN Edgar MM Dvr 11345 A/152 Bde RFA
TRUMAN Joseph C. MM Sjt 251646 1st London Regt
TRUMAN Percy MM Sjt 26156 16th Notts & Derby Regt
TRUMAN Thomas MM Sjt 8570 Royal Fusiliers
TRUMAN Thomas R. MM L/Cpl 2419 Notts & Derby Regt
TRUMP Thomas MM Gnr 37244 A/51 Bde RFA
TRUMP William H. MM Pte 538112 6 Fd Amb RAMC
TRUMPER George James MM Pte 2294 1/22nd London Regt
TRUMPER Harry Norman MM+Bar Pte 10547 South Staffordshire Regt
TRUMPER Thomas William Walwyn MM 2nd Cpl 26540 Royal Engineers
TRUNDELL Daniel MM L/Cpl 422792 10th London Regt
TRUNDLE Harry George MM Pte 5831 2nd Middlesex Regt DOW 16.8.17.
TRUNKS Frederick J. MM Sjt 57603 2nd Welsh Regt
TRUNLEY John MM Pte 128979 58th Bn Machine Gun Corps
TRUSCOTT Albert MM(71587 Bdr C/88 Bde RFA)+Bar L/Cpl 358158 Signal Service Royal Engineers att 277 Bde RFA.
TRUSLOVE Alibone L. MM Pte 29327 RAMC
TRUSLOW Henry T.G. MM Pte 72801 Machine Gun Corps
TRUSS Thomas Henry MM Pte 41928 Royal Irish Rifles
TRUSSELL Arthur MM Sjt 22631 Bedfordshire Regt
TRUSSELL Arthur MM Bdr 79158 RFA
TRUSSELL Ernest G. MM L/Bdr 77723 146 Siege Bty RGA
TRUSSELL John Winfield MM Spr 489931 46 Div Sig Coy Royal Engineers DOW 7.10.18.
TRUSSELL Leonard W. MM Pte 325173 1st Essex Regt
TRUSSLER Archibald "DCM,MM" Pte 32704 East Surrey Regt
TRUSSLER John P. MM L/Cpl 26179 23 Fd Coy Royal Engineers
TRUSTER Almer MM Bdr 9484 RFA
TRUSTUM Harry MM Sjt Farrier 45096 RFA
TRUTE George MM Sjt 30247 Devonshire Regt
TUBB Albert E. "DCM,MM" L/Sjt 5325 12th Northumberland Fusiliers
TUBB George MM Cpl 55093 194 Coy Machine Gun Corps KIA 21.9.17.
TUBB Herbert Bardon MM Pte 4447 13th London Regt
TUBB Horace C. MM CSM 530422 15th London Regt
TUBB Joseph MM L/Cpl 651644 21st London Regt
TUBB William H. MM L/Cpl M/29185 Army Service Corps
TUBBS Arthur E. MM L/Cpl 23500 Hampshire Regt
TUBBS William Frederick MM Pte 42375 1st East Yorkshire Regt
TUBBY Edward MM Pte 13916 10th Northumberland Fusiliers KIA 27.19.18.
TUBBY Harry MM Pte 104008 33rd Bn Machine Gun Corps
TUBBY Jacob MM+Bar Pte 71257 34 Coy Machine Gun Corps
TUCHY Michael MM Sjt 63819 RAMC
TUCK Arthur M. MM Cpl 161237 Royal Engineers
TUCK Ephraim MM CQMS 5103 10th Northumberland Fusiliers
TUCK Henry David MM Pte 23301 16th Welsh Regt
TUCK Ronald A. MM L/Cpl 10613 61st Bn Machine Gun Corps

TUCK Thomas MM Pte 27764 Northumberland Fusiliers
TUCK Thomas G. MM L/Cpl 325282 1/1st Cambridgeshire Regt
TUCK William C. MM Cpl 13909 2nd Middlesex Regt
TUCKER Albert MM Pte 6583 Royal West Surrey Regt
TUCKER Albert E. MM Sjt 64383 Machine Gun Corps
TUCKER Albert H. MM L/Cpl 231256 2nd London Regt
TUCKER Arthur "DCM,MM,MSM" Cpl 504359 503 Fd Coy Royal Engineers
TUCKER Arthur MM L/Cpl 16274 7th Somerset Light Infantry
TUCKER Arthur W. MM Sjt 165032 1/1st North Somerset Yeomanry
TUCKER Austin R. MM Gnr 293308 140 Hy Bty RGA
TUCKER Charles R. MM Pte 19641 Royal Fusiliers
TUCKER Edward MM Pte 238077 5th Liverpool Regt
TUCKER Edwin "MM,CG(B)" Cpl 9249 2nd Royal Sussex Regt
TUCKER Ernest MM L/Cpl 90125 Royal Engineers
TUCKER Ernest E.G. MM+Bar Spr 206934 Royal Engineers
TUCKER Frederick A. MM+Bar Sjt Z/452 Rifle Brigade
TUCKER George MM Pte 54025 16th Royal Welsh Fusiliers
TUCKER George B. MM L/Cpl 28600 8th South Wales Borderers
TUCKER George J.A. MM Sjt 52671 RGA
TUCKER Harry MM 2nd Cpl 506447 504 Fd Coy Royal Engineers
TUCKER Harry MM Dvr 91003 Royal Engineers
TUCKER Herbert Harold MM Sjt 54675 D/242 Bde RFA DOW 20.9.17.
TUCKER Horace Edward MM Dvr 915480 D/317 Bde RFA
TUCKER Isaac A. MM Pte 14314 10th Notts & Derby Regt KIA 8.8.16.
TUCKER John MM Gnr 40276 A/187 Bde RFA
TUCKER John H. MM Sjt 137923 173 Siege Bty RGA
TUCKER John H. MM+Bar Sjt 16117 Devonshire Regt
TUCKER Norman J. MM Sjt 202820 4th Hampshire Regt
TUCKER Oswald MM Pte 44573 16th Royal Irish Rifles
TUCKER Reginald H. MM Sjt 10446 5th Royal Berkshire Regt
TUCKER Samuel MM+Bar Sjt 14439 1st Royal West Surrey Regt
TUCKER Sidney MM Sjt 2560 16th London Regt DOW 11.8.18.
TUCKER Sydney MM Pte 18036 7th Yorkshire Regt DOW 24.4.17.
TUCKER Sydney "MM,MID" Sjt 9273 2nd Royal West Surrey Regt
TUCKER Thomas B. MM Gnr 329032 114 Heavy Bty RGA
TUCKER William H. "DCM,MM" Sjt 3/6797 2nd Yorkshire Regt
TUCKER William J. MM Cpl 40141 226 Fd Coy Royal Engineers
TUCKER William J. MM Sjt 8630 2nd Devonshire Regt
TUCKERMAN Charles MM L/Cpl 9458 9th Devonshire Regt
TUCKETT Harold MM Spr 301526 9 Div Sig Coy Royal Engineers
TUCKEY Isaac MM L/Sjt 9105 1st Duke of Cornwall's LI
TUCKEY William MM Pte 2041 Liverpool Regt
TUCKLEY Herbert MM Sjt 391728 9th London Regt
TUCKWELL Walter James MM Pte G/2022 7th Royal West Surrey Regt KIA 25.10.18.
TUDDENHAM Henry MM+Bar CSM 44852 2nd Lincolnshire Regt
TUDGE Sidney MM Pte 8631 11th Royal Warwickshire Regt
TUDGE Walter Henry MM L/Cpl 27898 2nd Worcestershire Regt
TUDOR Arthur I. MM+Bar Pte 19988 4th Royal Fusiliers
TUDOR Thomas A. MM Sjt 948 2nd Northumberland Fusiliers
TUDOR W.J. MM Sjt 79686 Royal Engineers
TUDOR William G. MM Spr 37522 Royal Engineers
TUFFERY Harold MM Cpl 8556 8th Devonshire Regt KIA 20.7.16.
TUFFIELD Harry R. MM Sjt 71005 D/5 Bde RFA
TUFFILL Stanley MM Cpl 311350 12 Div Sig Coy Royal Engineers
TUFFIN Edgar G. MM Pte 39614 Worcestershire Regt
TUFFLEY Fred MM Dvr 63417 'U' Bty RHA
TUFFLEY H. MM Dvr T/34988 62 Div Train Army Service Corps
TUFFNELL H. MM L/Cpl 69090 1/1st Gloucestershire Yeomanry
TUFFS Arthur J. MM Pte 202081 Middlesex Regt
TUFFY Peter MM Pte 10180 2nd Irish Guards
TUFTS Albert E. MM Sjt 26577 2nd Yorkshire Regt
TUGHAN Robert MM Pte 41280 Royal Irish Fusiliers
TUHILL Harry MM L/Bdr 965562 D/236 Bde RFA
TUKE Harry G. MM Pte 556759 16th London Regt
TUKE William MM Dvr 44344 RFA
TULETT William C.J. MM Sjt 780 7th Royal Sussex Regt
TULIP George W. MM L/Cpl 7734 2nd Worcestershire Regt
TULIP John O. MM Pte 18952 Royal Inniskilling Fusiliers
TULIP Sydney F. MM Pte 75676 15th Durham Light Infantry
TULITT William J. MM L/Cpl 582 7th Royal Sussex Regt
TULK Alfred George MM Pte 57074 14th Welsh Regt
TULL S. MM Sjt 10236 1st Essex Regt
TULL William MM Dvr 563 3(Durham)Bty RFA
TULLETT Ernest A. MM Sjt 33303 RGA
TULLEY Andrew MM+Bar Sjt 46515 15th Durham Light Infantry
TULLEY George Robert MM Bdr 52129 174 Siege Bty RGA
TULLEY Joseph O. MM L/Cpl 321238 2/6th London Regt
TULLEY William MM Sjt 29310 King's Own Scottish Borderers
TULLIS William MM L/Cpl 12167 5th Cameron Highlanders
TULLOCH George William MM Pte 354 1/7th Gordon Highlanders KIA 26.3.18.
TULLOCH James M. MM CQMS 8825 2nd Seaforth Highlanders KIA 23.1016.
TULLOCH John MM Pte 40292 1/4th Cameron Highlanders
TULLOCH John MM Pte 16391 2nd Cameron Highlanders
TULLOCH John R.M. MM Cpl 10897 7th Seaforth Highlanders
TULLOCH Robert M. MM Sjt 11776 Cameron Highlanders
TULLOCH William MM Spr 40354 Royal Engineers
TULLOCH William H. MM Pte 28448 South Wales Borderers
TULLY Arthur "MM,MID" L/Cpl 926 2(Home Counties)Fd Coy Royal Engineers
TULLY George MM Gnr 7297 94 Bty 18 Bde RFA
TULLY George Smith MM Spr 97478 128 Fd Coy Royal Engineers
TULLY James MM Sjt 235183 Northumberland Fusiliers
TULLY Phillip MM Pte 1059 XVII Corps Cyclist Bn Army Cyclist Corps
TULLY Thomas Edward MM Cpl 66682 270 Siege Bty RGA
TUMBER Albert MM Sjt 147106 Royal Engineers
TUMELTY Henry MM Pte 9258 1st Royal Irish Rifles
TUMILTY Dennis MM Pte 16840 10th West Riding Regt
TUMNER E.H. MM L/Sjt 365043 London Regt
TUMNER Ernest W. MM Cpl 52832 Middlesex Regt
TUN SAN MM Pte 201232 6th Bn Tank Corps "see also under SAN,Tun"
TUNBRIDGE Robert W. MM CSM 8176 2nd Oxf & Bucks Light Infantry
TUNESI Joseph P.G. MM Gnr 83534 RFA
TUNGATE Henry J. MM Pte 6700 Coldstream Guards
TUNLEY Mabel Mary MM Matron F QAIMNS
TUNNACLIFFE James MM Sjt 20115 D/156 Bde RFA
TUNNACLIFFE Walter Frederick MM Dvr 756149 251 Bde RFA
TUNNELL William MM Sjt 8596 1st Grenadier Guards
TUNNEY James MM Sjt 7252 4th Liverpool Regt
TUNNEY James MM L/Cpl 6705 6th Connaught Rangers
TUNNEY John MM Gnr 183398 280 Bde RFA
TUNNEY Nicholas MM Pte 17275 2/7th West Riding Regt
TUNNICLIFFE George MM Pte 3/8827 1st Northamptonshire Regt
TUNNY John William "MM,MSM" 2nd Cpl 175902 179 Tunnelling Coy Royal Engineers
TUNSTALL Herbert MM L/Cpl 21026 22nd Manchester Regt
TUNSTALL John MM Sjt 800258 B/230 Bde RFA
TUNSTALL John MM L/Sjt 277353 1/7th Arg & Suth Highlanders KIA 23.4.17.
TUNSTALL John MM Sjt 19400 Cheshire Regt
TUNSTALL Joseph MM Pte 15516 10th North Lancashire Regt KIA 14.7.16.
TUNSTALL Ralph MM CQMS 9508 2nd Arg & Suth Highlanders
TUNSTILL Fred MM Cpl 28876 8th Royal Lancaster Regt
TUPLIN Charles Frederick MM Pte M2/137306 Army Service Corps
TUPLIN Ernest MM Pte 241323 1/5th Lincolnshire Regt
TUPLIN Neave MM+Bar CSM 9390 1st Lincolnshire Regt
TUPMAN Edwin B. MM Pte 14658 9th York & Lancaster Regt
TUPMAN Fred MM Gnr Sig 180756 183 Siege Bty RGA
TUPPER William MM Bdr 36693 RGA
TURGOOSE William MM Sjt 12004 C/168 Bde RFA
TURK Albert Edward MM Spr 151763 84 Airline Section Royal Engineers
TURK Ernest MM Pte 72935 37 Fd Amb RAMC
TURK Frank MM Pte 202952 1st Essex Regt
TURK Richard MM Pte 5676 8th Royal West Kent Regt
TURK Thomas A. MM Pte 30389 10th Royal West Kent Regt
TURKINGTON Alfred MM Sjt 14720 9th Royal Irish Fusiliers
TURKINGTON Joseph MM Pte 14/18845 14th Royal Irish Rifles
TURLAND Charles Rudolph MM Cpl S2/016267 18 Div Train Army Service Corps
TURLEY Albert James MM Pte 3931 1st Welsh Guards
TURLEY Christopher MM L/Cpl 21790 20th Durham Light Infantry
TURLEY Frederick Christopher MM Pte 26360 14th Worcestershire Regt DOW 24.7.17.
TURLEY Thomas S. MM Pte 8103 23 Fd Amb RAMC
TURLEY William MM Pte 18724 2nd Grenadier Guards
TURNBAR Charles H.D.P. MM Sjt 39919 1 Siege Bty RGA
TURNBULL Adam MM Cpl 40632 Seaforth Highlanders
TURNBULL Albert MM Pte 202999 20th Durham Light Infantry
TURNBULL Alexander MM Sjt 116793 195 Coy Labour Corps
TURNBULL Archibald MM Pte 1547 1/9th Liverpool Regt

TURNBULL Charles H. MM Cpl 51095 Machine Gun Corps(Cavalry)
TURNBULL D. MM Pte 41607 17th Highland Light Infantry
TURNBULL E. MM Gnr 64401 RFA
TURNBULL Francis T. MM L/Cpl 203202 6th King's Own Scottish Borderers
TURNBULL Frederick MM L/Cpl C/433 16th King's Royal Rifle Corps
TURNBULL Frederick MM Spr 48467 Royal Engineers
TURNBULL George MM Pte 268619 2nd West Riding Regt
TURNBULL George MM Pte 28841 2/7th West Riding Regt
TURNBULL George MM Pte 240595 Royal Highlanders
TURNBULL George MM Cpl 32622 66 Coy Machine Gun Corps
TURNBULL Hector "MM,MID" S/Sjt Fitter 1046 236 Bde RFA
TURNBULL Henry W. MM Pte 46864 34 Fd Amb RAMC
TURNBULL Herbert MM Pte 89651 19th Bn Machine Gun Corps
TURNBULL Herbert Wettwer MM Spr 42915 29 Rly Coy Royal Engineers
TURNBULL James MM Gnr Fitter 236237 A/250 Bde RFA
TURNBULL James MM L/Cpl 200245 5/6th Scottish Rifles
TURNBULL James MM Pte 18108 Cameron Highlanders
TURNBULL James MM Dvr 14534 123 Bty 28 Bde RFA
TURNBULL James MM L/Cpl 33051 82 Fd Coy Royal Engineers DOW 13.6.18.
TURNBULL John MM L/Cpl 1948 50 Div Sig Coy Royal Engineers KIA 12.4.18.
TURNBULL John MM Gnr 97080 RFA
TURNBULL Joseph MM Cpl 102536 174 Tunnelling Coy Royal Engineers
TURNBULL Joseph Hall MM L/Cpl 18/1285 18th Durham Light Infantry
TURNBULL Peter MM Pte 290015 Royal Highlanders
TURNBULL Robert MM Pte 23032 Seaforth Highlanders
TURNBULL Robert MM Pte 23/459 9th Northumberland Fusiliers KIA 25.9.18.
TURNBULL Robert MM Cpl 13940 Yorkshire Regt
TURNBULL Robert MM Cpl(MCDR) 46729 21 Div Sig Coy Royal Engineers
TURNBULL Stephen Newton Walter MM Sjt 1344 9th Royal Fusiliers
TURNBULL Thomas MM Pte 63785 5th Yorkshire Light Infantry
TURNBULL Thomas A. MM L/Cpl 372348 8th London Regt
TURNBULL Thomas Alfred MM Pte 267910 1/7th Liverpool Regt
TURNBULL Walter MM Pte 23/432 Northumberland Fusiliers
TURNBULL William MM Dvr 34348 A/86 Bde RFA
TURNBULL William MM L/Cpl 29940 2nd King's Own Scottish Borderers DOW 3.10.18.
TURNBULL William MM+Bar Pte 22945 1st Northumberland Fusiliers
TURNBULL William MM Gnr 73097 8 Bde RFA
TURNBULL William MM Pte 2963 1/6th Durham Light Infantry
TURNBULL William MM Pte 14153 9th Yorkshire Regt
TURNBULL William H. MM Cpl 39461 Durham Light Infantry
TURNBULL William Marshall MM Cpl 353066 15th Highland Light Infantry
TURNBULL William S. MM L/Cpl 290718 9th Northumberland Fusiliers
TURNELL George Brinley MM Pte 21396 16th Cheshire Regt att 7th Royal West Kent Regt.
TURNELL Robert Douglas MM Sjt 606 1/1st Essex Yeomanry KIA 27.3.18.
TURNER A. MM(15347 N&D Regt)+Bar L/Cpl 49974 1st Essex Regt
TURNER A. MM Pte 33384 RAMC
TURNER Adam Graham MM Pte 31536 7th Lincolnshire Regt KIA 6.9.18.
TURNER Albert MM Pte 235309 4th East Lancashire Regt
TURNER Albert MM+Bar Pte 9298 2nd East Lancashire Regt
TURNER Albert MM Sjt 23371 Border Regt
TURNER Albert B. MM Pte 66583 RAMC
TURNER Albert E. MM Gnr 86018 32 Bde RFA
TURNER Albert Henry MM Pte 235408 1/5th Northumberland Fusiliers KIA 27.5.18.
TURNER Albert V. MM Gnr 83208 RGA
TURNER Alexander MM Cpl 350382 1/9th Royal Scots
TURNER Alexander N. MM Pnr 334813 Royal Engineers
TURNER Alfred MM L/Sjt 23863 3rd Grenadier Guards
TURNER Alfred MM Pte 203464 1/5th Notts & Derby Regt
TURNER Alfred MM Pte 72683 23rd Bn Machine Gun Corps
TURNER Alfred MM Gnr 777000 B/64 Bde RFA
TURNER Alfred E. MM Pte 230602 1/1st 1st County of London Yeomanry (Middlesex Hussars)

TURNER Alfred Edwin MM+Bar Pte S3/1020 7th East Surrey Regt
TURNER Alfred H. MM Pte 51754 West Yorkshire Regt
TURNER Alfred J. MM Sjt 22008 Bedfordshire Regt
TURNER Alfred Noel MM Cpl 240618 1/8th Worcestershire Regt Died 20.1.18.
TURNER Alfred R. MM Cpl(MCDR) 182077 Royal Engineers
TURNER Allan Berry MM Cpl 14691 6th Bedfordshire Regt
TURNER Andrew MM L/Cpl 350997 2nd Royal Scots
TURNER Arthur MM Sjt 201010 2/7th Worcestershire Regt
TURNER Arthur MM L/Cpl 245373 Manchester Regt
TURNER Arthur MM L/Cpl 2723 8th Royal West Kent Regt
TURNER Arthur MM Dvr 760544 A/317 Bde RFA
TURNER Arthur MM L/Cpl 6522 16th Middlesex Regt KIA 1.12.17.
TURNER Arthur MM Sjt 280896 Hampshire Regt
TURNER Arthur MM Pte C/4127 17th King's Royal Rifle Corps 16 years old.
TURNER Arthur MM Sjt 2200 1/2nd Monmouthshire Regt
TURNER Arthur C. MM Pte 28656 5th Royal Lancaster Regt
TURNER Arthur D. MM Bdr 16359 RFA
TURNER Arthur Ernest "MC,MM(734 Sjt 14th Bn)" 2Lt Royal Warwickshire Regt
TURNER Arthur G. MM L/Cpl 266762 Gloucestershire Regt
TURNER Arthur L. MM Cpl 345453 24th Royal Welsh Fusiliers
TURNER Arthur R. MM Cpl 13408 IX Corps Cyclist Bn Army Cyclist Corps
TURNER Arthur T. MM Pte 3399 1/4th Oxf & Bucks Light Infantry
TURNER Arthur William MM Pte 36970 1st Northumberland Fusiliers KIA 27.9.18.
TURNER Aubrey MM Pte 1622 1/1st Leicestershire Yeomanry
TURNER Augustus MM Pte 241627 1/5th Gordon Highlanders KIA 17.5.17.
TURNER Bartholomew L. MM Sjt 686222 22nd London Regt
TURNER Benjamin W. MM Spr 30475 Royal Engineers
TURNER Cecil Frank MM Pte 55847 28 Fd Amb RAMC
TURNER Charles MM Pte 242103 5/6th Scottish Rifles
TURNER Charles "MM,MID" Pte 9501 Royal Sussex Regt
TURNER Charles MM L/Cpl 47317 Manchester Regt
TURNER Charles "DCM,MM" BSM 23301 D/36 Bde RFA
TURNER Charles MM Pte 3371 1st Royal Munster Fusiliers KIA 28.1.17.
TURNER Charles MM Pte 12361 East Surrey Regt
TURNER Charles MM Cpl 88002 Royal Engineers
TURNER Charles A. MM L/Cpl 98276 3 Fd Sqn Royal Engineers
TURNER Charles F. MM Bdr 33544 RGA
TURNER Charles H. MM Sjt 62338 143 Siege Bty RGA
TURNER Charles J. MM Pte CMT/2736 Army Service Corps
TURNER Charles Samuel MM Sjt 175 RAMC
TURNER Charles W. MM Sjt 12317 12th East Surrey Regt
TURNER Charles William Matthew MM 2nd Cpl 459170 447 Fd Coy Royal Engineers
TURNER Christopher MM CSM 7876 1st Northumberland Fusiliers
TURNER Claude MM Pte 470395 12th London Regt
TURNER Colin "MM,VM(Rm)" Spr 155921 251 Tunnelling Coy Royal Engineers
TURNER Colin MM Sjt Pnr 14300 16th Highland Light Infantry
TURNER D.G. MM Pte 202429 Hampshire Regt
TURNER David MM Pte 240774 1st Border Regt
TURNER David "MM,MIDx2" Pte 9598 1st Border Regt
TURNER David MM Bdr 61190 A/124 Bde RFA
TURNER David B. MM+Bar Cpl 8106 8th Royal Highlanders
TURNER David W. MM Gnr 195615 RFA
TURNER E. MM Pte 201104 Yorkshire Regt
TURNER E.B. MM L/Cpl 268059 West Yorkshire Regt
TURNER Ebenezer MM Sjt 200101 West Riding Regt
TURNER Edgar MM+Bar Sjt 240817 1/8th Worcestershire Regt
TURNER Edward MM Sjt 13073 3rd Worcestershire Regt KIA 9.10.17.
TURNER Edward MM Sjt 250350 1/1st Lancashire Hussars Yeomanry
TURNER Edward D. MM Pte 201088 Royal Berkshire Regt
TURNER Edward G. MM Sjt 7263 6th Dragoon Guards
TURNER Edwin MM Gnr 185697 116 Bty 26 Bde RFA
TURNER Elias "MM,CG(B)" Pnr 444591 Royal Engineers
TURNER Emmanuel MM Sjt 279248 RGA
TURNER Eric M. MM Sjt 240671 5th Gloucestershire Regt
TURNER Ernest MM Pte 266505 7th Middlesex Regt
TURNER Ernest MM L/Cpl 3155 Royal Fusiliers
TURNER Ernest MM L/Cpl 235232 1/1st Gloucestershire Yeomanry
TURNER Ernest MM Pte 43577 Suffolk Regt
TURNER Ernest MM Sjt 985 6th Royal West Kent Regt

TURNER Ernest MM Cpl 109573 RFA
TURNER Ernest MM Cpl 10886 Royal West Surrey Regt
TURNER Ernest A. MM Cpl 9386 Middlesex Regt
TURNER Ernest A. MM Pte 135230 50 Fd Amb RAMC
TURNER Ernest Arthur MM Cpl M2/035296 19 Div Train Army Service Corps
TURNER Ernest Charles "MM+Bar,MID" BSM 24330 85 Bty 11 Bde RFA
TURNER Ernest E. MM Bdr 6092 RFA
TURNER Ernest W. MM Sjt 20708 39th Bn Machine Gun Corps
TURNER F.A. MM L/Cpl 24897 16th Royal Warwickshire Regt
TURNER Francis George MM Pte 13709 8th East Yorkshire Regt
TURNER Frank MM Pte 14800 7th Northamptonshire Regt
TURNER Frank MM Dvr CMT/111 Army Service Corps
TURNER Frank MM L/Cpl 41053 King's Own Scottish Borderers
TURNER Franklin MM Sjt 72583 Machine Gun Corps
TURNER Fred MM Pte 44234 Durham Light Infantry
TURNER Fred "MM,MSM" Sjt 200541 1/4th North Lancashire Regt
TURNER Fred C. MM Pte 20495 Army Cyclist Corps
TURNER Frederick MM Sjt 265988 6th West Riding Regt
TURNER Frederick MM Gnr Fitter 13936 115 Bty 25 Bde RFA
TURNER Frederick A. MM Sjt 201578 1st London Regt
TURNER Frederick C. MM Pte 15583 12th Hampshire Regt
TURNER Frederick E. MM Pte 36300 5th Lancashire Fusiliers
TURNER George MM Pte 26358 8th East Surrey Regt
TURNER George MM Pte 91306 Durham Light Infantry
TURNER George MM Cpl 13670 12th Hampshire Regt
TURNER George MM Pte 12257 2nd Suffolk Regt
TURNER George MM Cpl 81954 A/64 Bde RFA
TURNER George MM Sjt 5840 11th Lancashire Fusiliers KIA 10.6.18.
TURNER George B. MM BSM 5341 B/312 Bde RFA
TURNER George C. MM Pte 56267 RAMC
TURNER George H. MM Sjt 67996 12 Bde RFA
TURNER George H. MM Pte 83178 Middlesex Regt
TURNER George H. MM Gnr 947785 RFA
TURNER George W. MM Cpl 320108 15th Suffolk Regt
TURNER George W. MM Sjt 2157 1/5th Liverpool Regt
TURNER George W. MM Sjt 8608 1st Hampshire Regt
TURNER George W. MM Sjt 32178 RGA
TURNER H.G. MM Pte 630 10th Royal Fusiliers
TURNER H.H. MM L/Cpl 403550 2(West Riding)Fd Amb RAMC
TURNER H.L. MM Pte 6834 West Riding Regt
TURNER Harley L. MM Gnr 83919 RFA
TURNER Harold MM Pte 36124 16th Yorkshire Regt
TURNER Harry MM+Bar Pte 242592 1/8th Worcestershire Regt
TURNER Harry MM Pte 266893 6th Welsh Regt
TURNER Harry MM Cpl 9453 1/5th London Regt
TURNER Harry "MM,MSM" S/Sjt Armt T/389 8 Mobile Workshop Army Ordnance Corps
TURNER Harry A. MM Sjt 8303 RGA
TURNER Henry MM Sjt 100808 169 Coy Labour Corps
TURNER Henry MM Sjt 260101 1/6th South Staffordshire Regt
TURNER Henry MM Sjt 200318 1st London Regt
TURNER Henry MM L/Cpl 320117 16th Royal Sussex Regt
TURNER Henry "MC,MM(6406 Sjt 1st Bn)" 2Lt 2nd Royal Welsh Fusiliers
TURNER Henry MM Pte 2475 1st Royal Lancaster Regt KIA 12.10.17.
TURNER Henry MM Pte 8176 11th Royal Warwickshire Regt
TURNER Henry MM Sjt 10180 1st Shropshire Light Infantry
TURNER Henry C. MM L/Cpl 117508 32nd Bn Machine Gun Corps
TURNER Henry John MM Cpl 13229 8th Royal Berkshire Regt KIA 3.5.16.
TURNER Henry W. MM Cpl 250529 1/3rd London Regt
TURNER Herbert C. MM L/Cpl 202014 7th East Yorkshire Regt
TURNER Herbert S. MM Pte 3471 1st Northumberland Fusiliers
TURNER Ivan MM+Bar 2nd Cpl 50390 Royal Engineers
TURNER J.H. MM Pte 41215 Middlesex Regt
TURNER James MM Pte S/31166 13th Rifle Brigade
TURNER James MM Pte 266435 Gloucestershire Regt
TURNER James MM Sjt 18846 15th Royal Irish Rifles
TURNER James MM Gnr Sig 121829 C/123 Bde RFA
TURNER James MM Pte 12140 Gordon Highlanders
TURNER James MM Sjt 15/12159 15th Royal Irish Rifles
TURNER James "DCM,MM" L/Cpl 17525 7th South Lancashire Regt
TURNER James MM L/Cpl 1112 Royal Engineers
TURNER James MM Pte 43768 Royal Scots
TURNER James MM L/Cpl 200980 2/5th Lancashire Fusiliers
TURNER James MM Sjt 9086 10th Highland Light Infantry

TURNER James Arthur MM Cpl 11551 8th Yorkshire Regt
TURNER James Henry MM Pte 201458 Manchester Regt
TURNER James P. MM+Bar Pte 17578 Northumberland Fusiliers
TURNER James R. MM Cpl 16185 8th East Lancashire Regt
TURNER James Sidney MM Sjt M2/022072 58 Div MT Coy Army Service Corps
TURNER James W. MM Pte 8999 Suffolk Regt
TURNER John MM L/Cpl 40071 1st Royal Scots Fusiliers
TURNER John MM Cpl C/6946 18th King's Royal Rifle Corps KIA 28.7.17.
TURNER John MM Pte 45520 5th Yorkshire Light Infantry
TURNER John MM L/Cpl 10695 East Kent Regt
TURNER John MM Cpl 36053 171 Coy Machine Gun Corps
TURNER John MM Pte 43020 1st Scottish Rifles DOW 10.10.18.
TURNER John "MM,MSM" RQMS 9647 2nd Royal Irish Rifles
TURNER John MM Sjt 202213 Royal Welsh Fusiliers
TURNER John MM Cpl 19421 110 Heavy Bty RGA
TURNER John Archibald MM CSM 7971 3rd King's Royal Rifle Corps
TURNER John Frank MM Sjt 20296 8th Royal Sussex Regt KIA 21.3.18.
TURNER John G. MM Pte 283725 4th London Regt
TURNER John H. MM L/Cpl 56447 2nd King's Royal Rifle Corps
TURNER John James MM Cpl 71352 Machine Gun Corps Died 11.8.18.
TURNER John R. MM Cpl 83552 51st Bn Machine Gun Corps
TURNER John T. MM Sjt 15265 Labour Corps
TURNER John W. MM Cpl 17844 8th East Surrey Regt
TURNER John W. MM L/Cpl 45550 Durham Light Infantry
TURNER Joseph MM Dvr 3784 A/161 Bde RFA
TURNER Joseph MM Sjt 26442 108 Heavy Bty RGA
TURNER Joseph MM L/Cpl 107846 33rd Bn Machine Gun Corps
TURNER Joseph MM Cpl 13683 Yorkshire Regt
TURNER Joseph H. MM L/Cpl 129347 Royal Engineers
TURNER Lennard G. MM Cpl 67840 62nd Bn Machine Gun Corps
TURNER Leo MM Cpl 960295 RFA
TURNER Leslie John MM Bdr 99787 183 Bde RFA DOW 1.10.18.
TURNER Michael MM Pte 39096 3/5th Lancashire Fusiliers
TURNER Percy MM Pte 32135 7th South Lancashire Regt
TURNER Percy "MM,MID" Spr 430266 25 Div Sig Coy Royal Engineers
TURNER Percy MM Gnr 11752 RFA
TURNER Percy C. "MM,MSM" SSM T/18494 39 Div Train Army Service Corps
TURNER Percy W. MM L/Cpl 252010 3rd London Regt
TURNER Percy William MM L/Sjt 2779 17th London Regt KIA 30.16.16.Real name JACKSON
TURNER Ralph MM Pte 38319 2/4th York & Lancaster Regt
TURNER Richard MM Pte 59856 Royal Welsh Fusiliers
TURNER Richard H. MM Sjt 235314 2nd South Staffordshire Regt
TURNER Robert MM Sjt 15130 16th Highland Light Infantry
TURNER Robert H. MM L/Sjt 305440 Notts & Derby Regt
TURNER Robinson MM Pte 200684 Lancashire Fusiliers
TURNER Roland MM S/Sjt 1350 RAMC
TURNER Samuel MM Pte 200283 1/5th South Staffordshire Regt
TURNER Samuel D. MM Pte 59432 50th Bn Machine Gun Corps
TURNER Sefton J. "MM,MID" Pte M2/119610 Army Service Corps
TURNER Sidney MM Cpl 24347 1st West Yorkshire Regt
TURNER Sidney C.C. MM Sjt 45017 43 Bde RFA
TURNER Sidney G. MM Sjt 40973 24 Heavy Bty RGA
TURNER Stanley MM Sjt 8860 10th Royal West Kent Regt
TURNER Stanley James MM Pte 510181 2(London)Fd Amb RAMC
TURNER Sydney MM Pte 21123 7th Border Regt
TURNER T. MM+Bar L/Cpl 20124 11th West Yorkshire Regt
TURNER Thomas MM+Bar L/Sjt 19229 Machine Gun Corps
TURNER Thomas MM L/Cpl 14706 24th Manchester Regt
TURNER Thomas MM Gnr 71823 158 Siege Bty RGA
TURNER Thomas Edward Francis MM CSM 530412 1/15th London Regt
TURNER Thomas H. MM Cpl 19141 5th Dorsetshire Regt
TURNER Thomas H. MM Pte 21526 Worcestershire Regt
TURNER Thomas H. MM L/Cpl 20726 Gloucestershire Regt
TURNER Thomas William MM Bdr 61762 RFA
TURNER Thompson MM L/Sjt 45291 Rifle Brigade att 1/5th London Regt.DOW 7.11.18.
TURNER Walter MM Pte R/11675 King's Royal Rifle Corps
TURNER Walter Edward MM Pte 22243 6th Dorsetshire Regt KIA 19.9.18.
TURNER Walter G. MM L/Cpl 18501 Norfolk Regt
TURNER Wilfred Dougals MM Gnr 808 Machine Gun Corps(Motors)

TURNER William MM Pte 57594 2nd Worcestershire Regt
TURNER William MM Pte 157210 12th Bn Machine Gun Corps
TURNER William MM Sjt 63027 303 Siege Bty RGA
TURNER William MM Pte 14620 Cheshire Regt
TURNER William MM Pte 850 22nd Royal Fusiliers
TURNER William MM Pte 9891 10th Royal Warwickshire Regt
TURNER William MM Sjt 20002 3rd Dragoon Guards
TURNER William MM L/Cpl 60674 Notts & Derby Regt
TURNER William MM+Bar Sjt 20670 Northumberland Fusiliers
TURNER William MM Dvr 796242 RFA
TURNER William MM Pte 5655 Northumberland Fusiliers
TURNER William A. MM Sjt 35266 D/173 Bde RFA
TURNER William E. MM CQMS 13500 9th Gloucestershire Regt
TURNER William E. MM Pte 48967 13th Rifle Brigade
TURNER William G. MM Pte 421461 10th London Regt
TURNER William Henry MM Sjt 6148 2nd Royal Berkshire Regt
TURNER William J. MM L/Cpl 143123 Royal Engineers
TURNER William McL. MM L/Cpl 14096 15th Highland Light Infantry
TURNER William T. MM Sjt 10126 17th Lancers
TURNER Willis P. MM+Bar Spr 360265 Royal Engineers
TURNER-MOORCROFT David MM+Bar Sjt 18101 Royal Engineers
TURNEY Ernest MM Pte 1821 109 Fd Amb RAMC
TURNEY George H. MM Gnr 382424 133 Siege Bty RGA
TURNHAM Cecil E. MM Cpl 73143 3 Div Sig Coy Royal Engineers
TURNPENNY Victor Frank MM Cpl(MCDR) 73792 X Corps Sig Coy Royal Engineers
TURNPENNY Walter MM Gnr 796337 V/49 Heavy TM Bty RFA
TURP Stanley MM Pte 9744 Royal Fusiliers
TURPIE Alexander MM L/Cpl 276798 1/7th Arg & Suth Highlanders
TURPIE John MM Bdr 50366 RGA
TURPIE Lewis George MM Spr 146321 219 Fd Coy Royal Engineers
TURPIE Robert MM Pte 12604 9th Royal Warwickshire Regt
TURPIN A. MM Pte 307069 1/8th Notts & Derby Regt
TURPIN A. MM Pte 10835 9th Essex Regt
TURPIN Albert MM Pte 41714 Leicestershire Regt
TURPIN Arthur MM L/Sjt 201303 Yorkshire Light Infantry
TURPIN George MM L/Sjt 32616 13th East Lancashire Regt
TURPIN George MM Pte 122819 37th Bn Machine Gun Corps
TURPIN Harold MM Bdr 20066 C/49 Bde RFA
TURPIN Lewis Edward MM Dvr 94187 A/64 Bde RFA DOW 5.12.17.
TURRALL Joe MM Pte 9578 2/4th York & Lancaster Regt KIA 21.7.18.
TURRALL William Frank MM Sjt 11424 2nd Royal Fusiliers KIA 3.5.18.
TURRELL Charles W. MM Pte 4071 1/5th Royal Sussex Regt
TURRELL George MM Pte 7410 1st Royal Berkshire Regt
TURRELL George MM Sjt 8810 2nd Northamptonshire Regt
TURRELL James "MM,MID" Pte 33891 2nd South Wales Borderers
TURRELL John MM Pte 12324 7th Suffolk Regt att 1/1st Cambridgeshire Regt.
TURRELL Thomas "MM,MSM" Sjt 27274 129 Siege Bty RGA
TURTINGTON John MM Pte 46924 13th Royal Welsh Fusiliers KIA 30.8.18.
TURTLE John C. MM+Bar Pte 17511 York & Lancaster Regt
TURTLE William John Frederick MM Sjt 45068 Royal Engineers
TURTON Albert "DCM,MM(318 L/Cpl 7th R Sussex)" Pte 66242 2/10th Royal Scots
TURTON Albert Edward MM Sjt 13198 8th Norfolk Regt
TURTON Alfred MM Pte 31295 Machine Gun Corps
TURTON Alfred J. MM Pte 33315 Devonshire Regt
TURTON Horace MM Cpl 240143 1/6th West Yorkshire Regt
TURTON Horace V. MM Sjt 32989 RAMC
TURTON John MM Cpl 40275 6th Wiltshire Regt
TURTON John Walter MM Bdr 1511 7 Bty 3(West Riding)Bde RFA
TURTON Joseph MM Sjt 8915 2nd Durham Light Infantry KIA 21.3.18.
TURTON Joseph MM Dvr 25155 D/110 Bde RFA
TURTON Richard MM Cpl 26667 RFA
TURTON Robert MM L/Cpl R/7920 King's Royal Rifle Corps
TURTON W. MM Cpl 4151 Royal Flying Corps
TURTON Walter MM Sjt 201253 2/4th York & Lancaster Regt
TURTON William P. MM Cpl 19688 Royal Dublin Fusiliers
TURVER Edwin MM Pte 266494 2/7th West Yorkshire Regt
TURVEY Albert E. MM Cpl 141154 219 Fd Coy Royal Engineers
TURVEY Alfred J. MM Pte 203549 1/1st Hertfordshire Regt
TURVEY Arthur MM Cpl 20720 Machine Gun Corps
TURVEY George G. "DCM,MM+Bar" CSM 9332 2nd Royal Berkshire Regt
TURVEY Reginald MM Pte 262961 8th Middlesex Regt

TURVEY Stanley J. MM Spr 78413 Royal Engineers
TURVEY Thomas MM Bdr 830870 C/241 Bde RFA
TURVILLE Albert J. MM+Bar Sjt 14626 7th Bedfordshire Regt
TUSTIN Charles T. MM Pte 16078 East Surrey Regt
TUSTIN George MM L/Cpl 20842 Worcestershire Regt
TUSTIN Henry MM Sjt 153102 62nd Bn Machine Gun Corps
TUTE Thomas MM L/Cpl 332900 1/9th Highland Light Infantry
TUTIN Frederick George MM Dvr 129698 B/122 Bde RFA
TUTT Charles R. MM Pte 11656 Middlesex Regt
TUTT Henry S. MM Cpl S/14712 Rifle Brigade
TUTT John W. "DCM,MM" CSM 1958 8th Royal Sussex Regt
TUTT Richard T. MM L/Cpl 35888 1st Duke of Cornwall's LI
TUTTLE Charles F. MM Sjt 10273 8th Suffolk Regt
TUTTON Francis James MM L/Cpl 8675 10th Royal West Kent Regt
TUTTON Frederick C. MM Sjt 498321 476 Fd Coy Royal Engineers
TUTTON George MM Gnr 12445 RFA
TUTTON Samuel MM Cpl 61397 RFA
TUTTY George W. MM Pte 9595 2nd Royal Berkshire Regt
TUTUNGEAN Manuel MM Pte 54437 2nd Bn Machine Gun Corps
TUXFORD Sidney MM Sjt 608025 20 Bde RHA
TUZO Frederick S. MM Gnr 215189 RFA
TWADDLE Andrew MM L/Cpl 43232 Royal Scots
TWAITS Edward H. MM Pte 22568 Royal Fusiliers
TWEDDELL Thomas MM Dvr 750350 A/250 Bde RFA
TWEDDIE John Lawrence "MM,VM(Rm)" CSM 32500 15th Highland Light Infantry
TWEDDLE John "MM,MID" Cpl 2612 1/7th Durham Light Infantry
TWEED Albert MM Sjt 240103 1/6th North Staffordshire Regt
TWEED Albert MM Bdr 786186 RFA
TWEED James A. MM Gnr 97913 RFA
TWEED John B. MM+Bar Cpl 17481 Royal West Kent Regt
TWEED John Henry MM Gnr 344559 245 Siege Bty RGA
TWEED Lawrence MM Sjt 18289 19 Fd Amb RAMC
TWEEDALE Harry MM Sjt 20628 Royal Welsh Fusiliers
TWEEDDALE George W. MM L/Sjt 7355 1st Royal West Kent Regt
TWEEDIE Douglas S. MM Sjt 38117 Northumberland Fusiliers
TWEEDIE John MM L/Sjt 40217 7/8th King's Own Scottish Borderers KIA 23.7.18.
TWEEDIE Joseph MM+Bar Sjt 141 Royal Engineers
TWEEDIE William MM Sjt 9/13751 9th Royal Irish Rifles
TWEEDLE Frank MM Pte 358498 1/10th Liverpool Regt
TWEEDOLE T. MM Pte 266669 Liverpool Regt
TWEEDY Robert Edwin MM Cpl 39151 147 Bde RFA DOW 3.10.18.
TWEEN William MM Pte 25897 8th East Surrey Regt DOW 1.9.18.
TWEENEY R.C. MM L/Cpl 5/19414 South Wales Borderers
TWEENEY R.C. MM L/Cpl 19414 South Wales Borderers
TWELFTREE Alfred Thomas MM L/Sjt 851 1st East Kent Regt KIA 31.3.17.
TWELFTREE Harold E. MM Bdr 40188 RFA
TWELL Fred MM Pte 122968 17th Bn Machine Gun Corps
TWEMLOW John "DCM+Bar,MM,MID" Sjt 10393 1st Cheshire Regt
TWENTYMAN Richard MM+Bar Sjt 12679 7th Northamptonshire Regt
TWIDALE Albert MM Pte 301220 8th Hussars
TWIDLE Walter MM CoH 1547 Royal Horse Guards
TWIGG Charles MM L/Cpl 16249 12th Cheshire Regt
TWIGG Frederick MM L/Cpl 30470 4th North Lancashire Regt
TWIGG Thomas MM Pte 31236 1st Shropshire Light Infantry
TWIGG Thomas H. MM+Bar L/Cpl 33488 101 Fd Amb RAMC
TWIGGER Horace James MM L/Cpl 44125 10th Essex Regt
TWINBORROW George H. "DCM,MM+Bar" Sjt 13725 1st South Staffordshire Regt
TWINE Robert MM Spr 560087 47 Div Sig Coy Royal Engineers
TWINEHAM Clifford MM+Bar Pte 201221 West Yorkshire Regt
TWINN Frank W. MM Sjt 44451 Royal Engineers
TWINN Frank Wilfred MM L/Cpl 242576 1/6th Notts & Derby Regt KIA 3.10.18.
TWINN George E. MM Sjt 2167 8th Royal West Surrey Regt
TWINN Jack Escott MM Cpl B/200487 13th Rifle Brigade DOW 9.5.18.
TWISLETON George MM Spr 237937 17 Div Sig Coy Royal Engineers DOW 4.9.18.
TWISS Alfred MM Cpl 17945 10th West Yorkshire Regt
TWISS George H. MM Sjt 12213 RGA
TWISS George J. MM Pte 4512 6th Dragoon Guards
TWISS Henry R. MM Pte 352562 Manchester Regt
TWISS William MM Pte 3682 South Lancashire Regt
TWIST Frank "MC,MM(10085 L/Sjt 3DG)" 2Lt Machine Gun Corps(Cavalry)
TWIST John William MM Pte 23616 18th Lancashire Fusiliers

TWIST Thomas MM+Bar Pte 277020 7th Manchester Regt
TWIST William Thomas Francis MM Pte 81928 33rd Bn Machine Gun Corps
TWITCHELL Leonard George MM Dvr 39715 15 Div Ammn Col RFA
TWITCHEN George MM Pte 265279 1/1st Bucks Bn Oxf & Bucks Light Infantry
TWITCHEN Herbert O. MM Pte 394730 15th London Regt
TWOHIG Thomas MM Pte 6594 2nd Royal Munster Fusiliers
TWOMEY John MM Pte 9423 2nd Royal Berkshire Regt
TWOMEY Walter MM Sjt 13261 Yorkshire Light Infantry
TWYBLE William James MM Sjt 57845 36 Div Sig Coy Royal Engineers
TWYCROSS George Kean "MM,CG(B)" Sjt 93660 41 Div Sig Coy Royal Engineers
TWYFORD Bertram MM Pte 52149 6th Northamptonshire Regt
TWYMAN Stephen MM CSM 257449 Royal Engineers
TWYMAN William MM Sjt 1420 RAMC
TWYNHAM James MM Pte 2416 Royal Warwickshire Regt
TYAS Arthur MM+Bar L/Cpl 482117 49 Div Sig Coy Royal Engineers
TYAS Norman MM Dvr 42460 49 Bty 40 Bde RFA
TYAS Robert W. MM Pte 44882 12th North Staffordshire Regt
TYDEMAN William MM Sjt 3565 Machine Gun Corps
TYE Frederick MM Pte 44027 Middlesex Regt
TYE Frederick E. MM Cpl M2/119866 Army Service Corps
TYE Robert MM Sjt 32012 2nd South Lancashire Regt KIA 13.8.17.
TYERMAN Ralph MM Pte S/13386 7th Rifle Brigade KIA 17.10.17.
TYERS Arthur MM Cpl 8761 1st Leicestershire Regt KIA 23.7.17.
TYESON Charles MM Cpl 59449 11th Royal Scots Fusiliers
TYLDESLEY Edward MM Cpl 430043 461 Fd Coy Royal Engineers
TYLDESLEY Walter MM Pte 1968 1/9th Liverpool Regt KIA 25.9.16.
TYLER A.J. MM Sjt 394222 London Regt
TYLER Albert MM Pte R/10900 King's Royal Rifle Corps
TYLER Arthur MM Pte 568941 175 Coy Labour Corps
TYLER Bertie Hugh MM Spr 107335 11 Fd Coy Royal Engineers DOW 24.9.17.
TYLER Charles A. MM Cpl 22884 30 Bty 39 Bde RFA
TYLER Charles F. MM Cpl 232860 2nd London Regt
TYLER Edgar S. MM Pte 76403 67 Fd Amb RAMC
TYLER Edward Victor MM Pte G/1037 1st Royal West Surrey Regt DOW 31.5.17.
TYLER Frank MM+Bar Spr 56786 11 Div Sig Coy Royal Engineers
TYLER George MM Pte 4508 Worcestershire Regt
TYLER George H. MM 2nd Cpl 275624 Royal Engineers
TYLER George H. MM Pte M2/018668 Army Service Corps
TYLER Henry MM L/Cpl 139457 250 Tunnelling Coy Royal Engineers
TYLER Henry MM Pte 7368 Machine Gun Corps
TYLER Henry MM Pte 6969 Royal West Kent Regt
TYLER Henry Norman MM Pte 32566 8th York & Lancaster Regt
TYLER Herbert H. MM Dvr 122325 123 Bty 28 Bde RFA
TYLER James MM Pte 220803 1/7th Worcestershire Regt
TYLER James MM Sjt 8390 1st Worcestershire Regt
TYLER James MM Pte 8846 1st East Kent Regt
TYLER Joseph MM Sjt 632643 20th London Regt
TYLER Joseph Leslie MM Sjt 2687 2/8th Royal Warwickshire Regt
TYLER Leonard MM Sjt 200233 1/5th Royal Warwickshire Regt
TYLER Richard MM+2 Bars Sjt 37504 2nd Suffolk Regt
TYLER Sidney MM CSM 2376 1st King's Royal Rifle Corps
TYLER Thomas MM Sjt 513499 Labour Corps
TYLER Wilfred V. MM Cpl 191672 2 Div Sig Coy Royal Engineers
TYLER William MM L/Cpl 8546 Machine Gun Corps
TYLER William MM Pte 202544 1/4th York & Lancaster Regt Died 23.10.18.
TYLER William Harold MM Pnr 209611 'Z' Special Coy Royal Engineers
TYLOR James MM Cpl 12590 6th Royal Berkshire Regt
TYMON James MM Sjt 252702 Signal Service Royal Engineers
TYNAN Patrick MM L/Sjt 2208 1st Irish Guards
TYNAN William MM Pte 13347 Manchester Regt
TYNDALL Edward MM Gnr 89 125 Siege Bty RGA
TYPE Leonard MM Sjt 691 4th Bn GMGR
TYRER Alfred Richard MM Pte 3265 23rd Middlesex Regt
TYRER Ernest J. MM+Bar L/Cpl 201157 North Staffordshire Regt
TYRER Fred MM Sjt 307735 7th West Riding Regt
TYRER Frederick MM L/Cpl 201771 North Lancashire Regt
TYRER James MM Pte 57993 25th Bn Machine Gun Corps
TYRER John M. MM Pte 70946 Machine Gun Corps
TYRER Robert MM Pte 241409 1/5th North Lancashire Regt
TYRER Thomas MM Pte 25274 Liverpool Regt
TYRER Thomas MM Cpl 202755 5th Liverpool Regt

TYRIE Charles A. MM Sjt 680247 1/22nd London Regt
TYRRELL Archie MM Pte 20016 South Wales Borderers
TYRRELL Arthur MM+Bar Cpl G/1816 7th Royal West Surrey Regt KIA 18.11.16.
TYRRELL Arthur H. MM Pte 1498 8th Royal West Kent Regt
TYRRELL Arthur J. MM L/Cpl 13505 Royal Engineers
TYRRELL Charles Thomas MM L/Cpl T4/240995 Army Service Corps
TYRRELL Francis MM Pte 34146 1/4th Royal Berkshire Regt
TYRRELL Frank L. MM Sjt 47005 Royal Engineers
TYRRELL Frederick A. MM Sjt 558283 Royal Engineers
TYRRELL Frederick B. MM Pte 275022 3rd London Regt
TYRRELL George MM Cpl R/1481 8th King's Royal Rifle Corps
TYRRELL George MM Pte 280728 2/4th London Regt
TYRRELL Harry T. MM Pte 18148 Royal West Kent Regt
TYRRELL Henry MM Pte 26728 Royal Welsh Fusiliers
TYRRELL John MM Dvr 23483 RFA
TYRRELL Joseph MM Cpl 8308 11th Royal Warwickshire Regt
TYRRELL Michael MM Pte 18368 Royal Munster Fusiliers
TYRRELL Patrick MM L/Cpl 9927 1st Irish Guards DOW 28.9.18.
TYRRELL Patrick MM Pte 6276 2nd Royal Munster Fusiliers
TYRRELL Robert MM Pte 31342 27 Fd Amb RAMC
TYRRELL Sidney MM CSM 9112 2nd Royal Munster Fusiliers
TYRRELL William MM Cpl 301152 1/7th Arg & Suth Highlanders
TYSOE Ralph MM Sjt 22087 8th Bedfordshire Regt
TYSOM Horace MM Cpl 631605 20th London Regt
TYSON Archibald McKechnie MM Pte M2/130664 Army Service Corps att 5(London)Fd Amb RAMC.
TYSON Arthur MM Gnr 57059 RFA
TYSON David "DCM,MM" L/Sjt 9432 2nd Arg & Suth Highlanders
TYSON Frederick W. MM Cpl 12366 King's Royal Rifle Corps
TYSON George W. MM Sjt 38446 RFA
TYSON Herbert MM Spr 43654 Royal Engineers
TYSON Jackson MM Cpl 30153 8th Royal Lancaster Regt
TYSON James MM Pte 332768 9th Liverpool Regt
TYSON Reginald MM Pte 11288 1st Durham Light Infantry
TYSON Richard E.S. MM Spr 155350 54 Fd Coy Royal Engineers
TYSON William H. MM Pte 17101 1st East Yorkshire Regt
TYSON William Henry MM Gnr Fitter 67615 A/123 Bde RFA KIA 25.8.18.
TYTE Henry Brockman MM Pte 200482 12th Royal Berkshire Regt
TYTHER Thomas William MM Pte 15/9258 14th Royal Irish Rifles KIA 2.7.16.
TYTHERLEIGH Ernest A. MM Cpl 41586 2nd Northamptonshire Regt
TYTLER Alan B. MM Sjt 304789 5th London Regt
TYTLER John MM Pte 201293 1/4th Gordon Highlanders
TYZACK Eric A. MM Pte 9812 HAC

U

UDALL Frank G. MM+Bar Sjt 280292 4th London Regt
UDALL Thomas H. MM Pte 8279 1st Worcestershire Regt
UDELL Edward MM Sjt 27186 Dorsetshire Regt
UDEN Alfred Ethelbert MM Sjt 38333 RGA
UDEN William MM Sjt 60266 A/18 Bde RFA
UFFENDELL or UFFINDALE Benjamin Edward MM Cpl 4910 1/6th Seaforth Highlanders
UINGS George MM L/Cpl 253661 Royal Engineers
ULLIOTT Arthur Charles MM L/Cpl 44534 41 Coy Machine Gun Corps
ULLYATT Henry MM Sjt 36355 RAMC
ULLYOTT Dalton MM Sjt 19824 RFA
ULYATT Jim MM(1043 Pte 1st Welsh Gds)+Bar Pte 131434 46th Royal Fusiliers
UMNEY Dennis Albert MM Sjt 68580 366 Bde RFA
UMNEY Joseph MM Pte 14093 7th Leicestershire Regt
UMPHRAY Peter MM Gnr 265109 RFA
UMPLEBY A. MM L/Bdr 772063 84 Bty 11 Bde RFA
UMPLEBY Henry MM Sjt 26749 133 Siege Bty RGA
UMPLEBY James Dalton MM Pte 307506 3 Tank Carrier Coy Tank Corps
UMPLEBY Joseph MM Pte 23761 Durham Light Infantry
UMPLEBY Robert W. MM Pte 18971 West Yorkshire Regt
UNCLES Thomas H. MM Cpl 43754 RAMC att RGA
UNDERHILL Albert MM Pte M1/07981 Army Service Corps att 177 Tunnelling Coy RE.
UNDERHILL Bertram E. MM Pte 36254 Leicestershire Regt

UNDERHILL George MM L/Cpl 19517 1st South Staffordshire Regt
UNDERHILL Harry G. MM Pte 20458 Grenadier Guards
UNDERHILL Walter MM Sjt Farrier 70721 33rd Bn Machine Gun Corps
UNDERHILL Walter Stanley MM Pte 200435 Gloucestershire Regt
UNDERHILL William S. MM+Bar Sjt 25085 11th Royal West Surrey Regt
UNDERWOOD Albert E. MM Cpl 531603 15th London Regt
UNDERWOOD Albert E.G. MM Pte 19543 Bedfordshire Regt
UNDERWOOD Albert W. MM L/Cpl 9123 8th Royal Berkshire Regt
UNDERWOOD Arthur J. MM Sjt 266150 Oxf & Bucks Light Infantry
UNDERWOOD Charles H. "DCM,MM" CSM 21297 Royal Welsh Fusiliers
UNDERWOOD Charles Henry "DCM,MM" CSM 6141 2nd Northamptonshire Regt
UNDERWOOD Charles W. MM Sjt 550277 Royal Engineers
UNDERWOOD Edward G. MM Pte 532855 15th London Regt
UNDERWOOD F. MM Pte 202005 1/4th Hampshire Regt
UNDERWOOD Frank MM Pte 30916 East Yorkshire Regt
UNDERWOOD Frank MM Cpl 840 2nd Royal Warwickshire Regt
UNDERWOOD Frank MM+Bar Pte 10316 1st Notts & Derby Regt
UNDERWOOD Fred Thomas MM Pte 10312 7th Gloucestershire Regt
UNDERWOOD George Edward MM Pte 241147 10th Royal West Surrey Regt
UNDERWOOD George Joseph MM Cpl 362080 RAMC
UNDERWOOD Harold John MM L/Cpl R/6760 12th King's Royal Rifle Corps KIA 2.4.18.
UNDERWOOD Harry MM Pte 18262 6th Northamptonshire Regt DOW 30.9.18.
UNDERWOOD Herbert "DCM,MM,MSM" CSM 9224 2nd Notts & Derby Regt
UNDERWOOD Herbert Bernard MM L/Cpl 202253 Notts & Derby Regt
UNDERWOOD John F. MM L/Sjt 1128 11th Northumberland Fusiliers
UNDERWOOD Joseph MM L/Cpl 200588 Welsh Regt
UNDERWOOD Noel MM Gnr 366148 434 Siege Bty RGA
UNDERWOOD Percy MM+Bar Sjt 21240 C/77 Bde RFA
UNDERWOOD Robert E. MM Pte 53929 10th Liverpool Regt
UNDERWOOD Thomas MM Pte 22940 Leicestershire Regt
UNDERWOOD Thomas E. MM Pte 7758 6th Lincolnshire Regt
UNDERWOOD Thomas J. MM Pte 10350 King's Royal Rifle Corps
UNDERWOOD Walter MM L/Cpl 15647 11th West Yorkshire Regt
UNDERWOOD Walter F. MM Sjt 7748 1st Northamptonshire Regt
UNDERWOOD William MM Sjt 41096 4th Worcestershire Regt
UNDERWOOD William MM L/Cpl 267535 1/1st Bucks Bn Oxf & Bucks Light Infantry
UNDERWOOD William MM L/Cpl 3019 14 Fd Amb RAMC
UNDERWOOD William MM L/Cpl 268714 7th Liverpool Regt
UNDERWOOD William H. MM Cpl 14450 25 Coy Labour Corps
UNDRILL Walter J. MM Cpl 30331 17th Royal Sussex Regt
UNETT Henry James MM L/Cpl 241057 1/5th Welsh Regt
UNGERER Christian Arthur MM Pte 44891 1st King's Royal Rifle Corps DOW 37.8.18.
UNGLESS William F. MM Sjt 10615 Machine Gun Corps
UNITT Walter J.A. MM Pte 242224 Worcestershire Regt
UNSWORTH Fred MM+Bar Sjt 19285 Manchester Regt
UNSWORTH George MM Gnr 65554 RFA
UNSWORTH George C. MM Cpl 112874 RGA
UNSWORTH Harold MM L/Sjt 20540 Devonshire Regt
UNSWORTH Henry MM Sjt 7744 1st Royal Munster Fusiliers
UNSWORTH James MM Sjt 74675 123 Bde RFA
UNSWORTH John MM Pte 21286 6th Royal West Kent Regt
UNSWORTH John Robert MM Sjt 19127 13th Liverpool Regt Died 10.10.18.
UNSWORTH Leonard MM Pte 13106 5th Oxf & Bucks Light Infantry
UNSWORTH Robert MM Cpl 55942 296 Railway Coy Royal Engineers
UNSWORTH Walter or William MM Spr 48899 Royal Engineers
UNSWORTH William MM L/Cpl 350872 1/9th Royal Scots
UNWIN Alfred B. MM Sjt 72479 Machine Gun Corps
UNWIN Frederick MM Pte 5545 South Staffordshire Regt
UNWIN Frederick George MM Sjt 72274 134 Fd Amb RAMC
UNWIN James MM Sjt 10 RGA
UNWIN Matthew James MM Sjt 2230 1/6th Notts & Derby Regt
UPCHURCH William MM Pte 15110 13th Essex Regt
UPFOLD James MM L/Cpl 556596 16th London Regt
UPHILL Percy MM Pte 39105 Lancashire Fusiliers
UPHILL William F. MM Gnr 323012 336 Siege Bty RGA
UPPERTON James MM Pte 90091 2/4th London Regt
UPPINGTON Charles James MM Bdr 1115 1(South Midland)Bde RFA
UPSHALL Thomas G. MM Cpl 15320 Devonshire Regt
UPSON Alfred E. MM CSM 9886 2nd Royal Irish Regt
UPSON George H.A. MM Sjt 9413 1st Gloucestershire Regt
UPSON Harry MM+Bar Pte 34381 Middlesex Regt
UPSON Herbert H. MM Pte 235372 2nd South Staffordshire Regt
UPSON Leslie G. MM Dvr 622270 RHA
UPSTONE James MM L/Cpl 200899 1/4th Oxf & Bucks Light Infantry
UPSTONE John MM Pte 13319 5th Northamptonshire Regt
UPTON Augustus G. MM Cpl 1819 RAMC
UPTON Benjamin G. MM+Bar Pte 47088 15th Lancashire Fusiliers
UPTON Edward MM Gnr 53558 'C' Bty RHA
UPTON Edward James MM Sjt 7318 2nd Royal Sussex Regt
UPTON Frederick Charles MM Cpl 207461 63 Div Sig Coy Royal Engineers
UPTON George Humphrey MM Sjt 19007 Cameron Highlanders
UPTON H. MM Cpl 60132 Royal Engineers
UPTON Harold MM Pte 21016 7th Dragoon Guards
UPTON Irvine MM CSM 14235 9th East Lancashire Regt
UPTON John MM Pte 1674 9th Royal Munster Fusiliers
UPTON John H. MM L/Cpl 439042 RAMC
UPTON John Henry MM Pte M2/054852 Army Service Corps att 6 Fd Amb RAMC.
UPTON Robert N. MM+Bar Pte 10634 2nd Royal West Surrey Regt
UPTON William MM Pte 43570 1st Royal Inniskilling Fusiliers
UPTON William George "DCM,MM" Sjt 41719 4 Squadron Machine Gun Corps(Cavalry) DOW 29.6.18.
UPTON William H.S. MM Sjt 11571 9th East Surrey Regt
UPWARD Herbert MM Cpl 18422 B/76 Bde RFA
URCH William MM Pte 10495 1st Royal Welsh Fusiliers
URE Alexander MM L/Cpl 276044 5/6th Royal Scots
URE George R. MM Pte 85259 Durham Light Infantry
URE William "MM,MID" Cpl 1806 1st Royal Highlanders
UREN Cornelius MM L/Cpl 39510 125 Coy Machine Gun Corps
UREN Wilfred George MM Pte 15621 11th Welsh Regt KIA 18.9.18.
URINOWSKI William MM Cpl 200235 Cheshire Regt
URION George MM Sjt 11693 5th Shropshire Light Infantry Died 14.11.18.
URPETH John MM Spr 143331 82 Fd Coy Royal Engineers
URQUHART Alex MM Pte 23014 Scottish Rifles
URQUHART Alexander MM Pte M2/177136 Army Service Corps
URQUHART Christina Margaret MM Miss F First Aid Nursing Yeomanry
URQUHART David "DCM,MM" Sjt 6959 2nd Royal Scots Fusiliers
URQUHART David MM Pte 7339 Seaforth Highlanders
URQUHART Donald G. MM Dmr 10236 2nd Royal Welsh Fusiliers
URQUHART Donald George MM L/Cpl 40361 1st Gordon Highlanders KIA 15.6.18.
URQUHART George MM L/Sjt 2174 1/5th York & Lancaster Regt KIA 11.8.16.
URQUHART James "DCM,MM" Cpl 2010 1/5th Gordon Highlanders
URQUHART James "MM,MID" Sjt 16507 7/8th King's Own Scottish Borderers
URQUHART John MM L/Cpl 250268 5/6th Royal Scots KIA 11.8.18.
URQUHART John MM Gnr 69168 RGA
URQUHART John G. MM L/Cpl 350989 1/9th Royal Scots
URQUHART Lockhart MM Cpl 6611 8th Seaforth Highlanders DOW 27.8.17.
URQUHART Robert MM Sjt 11588 6th Cameron Highlanders
URQUHART William Archibald MM Sjt 3/7704 Devonshire Regt
URRY Maurice W. MM Pte 200479 1/1st London Regt
URSELL Alfred MM Cpl 9119 2nd Royal Welsh Fusiliers
URSELL Sidney W. MM L/Cpl 4/10178 1st Royal West Kent Regt
URWIN James Thomas "DCM,MM" Pte 20439 8th Northumberland Fusiliers KIA 15.5.18.
URWIN John Davison MM Spr 459300 447 Fd Coy Royal Engineers Died 27.9.18.
URWIN Thomas F. MM Dvr 761170 C/251 Bde RFA
USHER Albert MM Gnr 43811 D/27 Bde RFA
USHER Arthur C. MM Sjt 7968 1st Worcestershire Regt
USHER Ernest E. MM Sjt 45329 14 Bde RHA Died 28.5.19.
USHER Francis Harold "MM,MID" CQMS 57101 36 Div Sig Coy Royal Engineers
USHER Frederick C. MM Sjt 32494 14th Royal Warwickshire Regt
USHER Frederick G. MM Pte 232388 2nd London Regt
USHER John A. MM Pte 9047 2nd Yorkshire Light Infantry
USHER Paul H. MM+Bar Cpl 29851 D/178 Bde RFA

USHER Richard G. MM Cpl 12/1375 12th East Yorkshire Regt
USHERWOOD James H. MM Cpl 724487 24th London Regt
UTLEY Fred MM L/Cpl 1585 1/6th Cheshire Regt DOW 8.3.17.
UTTING Bertie MM Sjt 1615 1st Rifle Brigade KIA 30.10.18.
UTTING Ernest "MM,MSM" Sjt 13887 8th Norfolk Regt
UTTING Richard MM Sjt 1329 1/2nd London Regt
UTTLEY Albert E.A. MM Pte 202714 5th West Yorkshire Regt
UTTLEY Arnold Sutcliffe MM L/Cpl 7019 17th Royal Fusiliers KIA 24.3.18.
UTTLEY Fred A. MM Dvr 786245 RFA
UTTLEY Herbert "DCM,MM+Bar" Sjt 16301 2nd & 9th Notts & Derby Regt
UTTLEY James MM Cpl 53433 38 Siege Bty RGA
UTTLEY Thomas MM 2nd Cpl 97818 156 Fd Coy Royal Engineers KIA 21.1.18.
UTTLEY Walter G. MM Pte 68894 RAMC
UWINS William C. MM+Bar CSM 262 10th Royal Fusiliers
UZZELL Charles W. MM Cpl M2/182082 Army Service Corps

V

VACEY Robert MM Pte 201199 Lincolnshire Regt
VACHER Charles MM+Bar Cpl 49270 Royal Engineers
VAGE Robert MM Sjt 15153 13th Royal Scots
VAILES Albert T. MM Bdr 1404 RFA
VAINES Sydney G. MM Dvr 118159 RFA
VAISEY John Clere MM Pte 1015 22nd Royal Fusiliers
VAIZEY George R. MM L/Cpl 300648 5th London Regt
VALDER Frank MM Pte 1897 RAMC
VALE Christopher MM Pte 2642 1/1st Cambridgeshire Regt
VALE George W. MM Sjt 2028 8th Royal Sussex Regt
VALE Harold G. MM Cpl 37283 Lancashire Fusiliers
VALE James A. MM Cpl 51915 101 Fd Coy Royal Engineers
VALE John W.G. MM+Bar L/Cpl 254280 3rd London Regt
VALE Sidney F. MM Pte 11581 Royal Berkshire Regt
VALENTINE Bertie MM Cpl 290907 Gordon Highlanders
VALENTINE Christopher Arthur MM Cpl 21681 5th Cameron Highlanders KIA 3.5.17.
VALENTINE David MM Sjt 23061 51st Bn Machine Gun Corps DOW 26.10.18.
VALENTINE Harold MM Pte 39345 7th North Staffordshire Regt
VALENTINE Henry MM Pte 201148 5th Manchester Regt
VALENTINE James A. MM Cpl 2212 1/1st London Regt
VALENTINE James Wicks MM Sjt 17548 13th Essex Regt KIA 30.7.16.
VALENTINE John William James MM Pte 5657 3rd Dragoon Guards
VALENTINE Jonah MM Pte 15910 Royal Welsh Fusiliers
VALENTINE Moses Idwal MM Gnr 113108 A/59 Bde RFA
VALENTINE Norman MM L/Cpl 437184 RAMC
VALENTINE Peter MM Sjt 11163 1st Royal Dublin Fusiliers
VALENTINE Reece C. MM Pte 241771 Royal Scots Fusiliers
VALENTINE S.A. MM Miss F Hosp Ship 'Vologjanin' VAD
VALENTINE Sam MM Pte 13706 11th West Yorkshire Regt
VALENTINE William MM Sjt 65148 336 Siege Bty RGA
VALENTINE William MM Pte 102527 38 Fd Amb RAMC
VALLANCE James MM Pte 200010 Tank Corps
VALLANCE Robert MM Pte 4649 12th Arg & Suth Highlanders
VALLANCE Robert MM+Bar Pte 30485 75 Fd Amb RAMC
VALLANCE Thomas MM(11603 7th RSF)+Bar Pte 44176 10th Highland Light Infantry
VALLANS Thomas MM Pte 348038 1/9th Durham Light Infantry Died 6.12.18.
VALLENDER Charles MM Gnr 89313 251 Siege Bty RGA
VALLER Arthur MM Pte 7933 2nd Royal Sussex Regt
VAN DER VORD Charles J. MM Pte 491221 13th London Regt att 2nd KRRC.
VAN MILLINGEN Ralph Edwin Charles MM L/Cpl 4135 1/14th London Regt
VAN SCHAICK L. "DCM,MM" Cpl 2707 Royal Flying Corps
VAN ZANT Jack MM Bdr 90303 RFA
VANBIENE Bernard MM L/Cpl 3438 7th Royal Lancaster Regt
VANCE Charles Henry MM Sjt S/4951 10th Rifle Brigade
VANCE James MM Pte 47105 Lucknow Squadron Machine Gun Corps(Cavalry)
VANCE Matthew MM L/Cpl 3374 5/6th Scottish Rifles
VANCE Thomas S. MM Bdr 73817 38 Bde RFA
VANDOME Henry MM Gnr 10573 A/235 Bde RFA KIA 5.8.17.
VANDOREN James MM Pte 102439 Notts & Derby Regt AKA William F.NELSON
VANE Christopher V. MM L/Cpl 565120 16th London Regt
VANE Leslie Murray MM Bdr 2913 RFA
VANES James MM Cpl 240526 1/6th Notts & Derby Regt
VANLINT James H. MM L/Cpl 2830 1/17th London Regt
VANN Cecil MM L/Cpl 305501 1/8th Notts & Derby Regt
VANN Charles MM L/Sjt 571716 17th London Regt
VANN Edwin MM L/Bdr 84398 191 Siege Bty RGA
VANN Harry H.R. MM L/Cpl 497513 RAMC
VANNER Frank MM SSM 47426 MGC(Cavalry)
VANSTON John J. MM L/Cpl 4133 1st Irish Guards
VANSTONE Francis G. MM Dvr 83498 C/123 Bde RFA
VANT James MM Pnr 316896 Royal Engineers
VANTOLL Thomas S. MM Pte 45520 1/1st Surrey Yeomanry
VARAH Albert W. MM L/Cpl 39893 1st Wiltshire Regt
VARCOE James S. "DCM,MM" Sjt 9439 2nd Royal Welsh Fusiliers
VARDY Arthur Edward MM Pte 58667 17th Notts & Derby Regt
VARDY George MM Pte 46885 Notts & Derby Regt
VARDY Herbert MM Pte 43276 1st Lincolnshire Regt
VARDY William H. MM L/Cpl 203805 1st Notts & Derby Regt
VARLEY James W. MM L/Sjt 238031 4th West Riding Regt
VARLEY John MM Cpl 23464 1/6th West Riding Regt
VARLEY John MM Sjt 355587 25th Royal Welsh Fusiliers
VARLEY Leonard MM S/Sjt Fitter 185310 RGA
VARLEY Wilfred MM Spr 482076 Royal Engineers
VARNAM Harry MM Cpl 201411 Bedfordshire Regt
VARNDELL Frederick James MM Pte 28273 8th Somerset Light Infantry KIA 21.9.18.
VARNEY Arthur MM Cpl 32110 11th Notts & Derby Regt KIA 4.10.18.
VARNEY Frank "DCM,MM+Bar" Sjt 24045 5th Royal Berkshire Regt
VARNEY Joe MM+Bar Sjt 62012 11 Bde RFA
VARNEY Stanley MM CQMS 53342 41st Bn Machine Gun Corps
VARNEY William J. MM Pte 22953 West Riding Regt
VARNHAM or VARMAN John W. MM L/Cpl 12371 West Riding Regt
VARNON Thomas MM Pte 17910 14th Royal Warwickshire Regt
VARNS G.A. MM Bdr 2760 RFA
VARRALL Lewis Oswald MM Sjt 1325 1/1st Surrey Yeomanry
VARRIER Albert Henry MM Cpl 24696 1st Royal West Surrey Regt DOW 16.4.18.
VARROW Walter J. MM Pte 32730 East Surrey Regt
VARTY David MM Pte 7763 Durham Light Infantry
VARTY John MM L/Cpl 12724 Coldstream Guards
VARTY John MM Pte 13589 6th Border Regt
VARTY Thomas Armstrong MM Cpl 327216 1/9th Durham Light Infantry
VASEY Frederick MM L/Cpl 75114 RAMC
VASEY Henry MM Gnr 80820 64 Bty 5 Bde RFA KIA 5.5.18.
VASEY John D. MM Dvr 41696 RFA
VASEY John R. MM Cpl R/14817 King's Royal Rifle Corps
VASEY Stanley MM Pte 201726 1/4th Seaforth Highlanders
VASEY William MM Pte 27075 5th Royal Berkshire Regt
VASS Charles R. MM Pte 3445 Gloucestershire Regt
VASS George T. MM Dvr 960912 RFA
VASS James MM Pte 21005 1st Coldstream Guards
VASS Thomas Kinnear MM Pte 40757 8th Royal Highlanders KIA 3.5.17.
VASS Thomas McKenzie MM L/Cpl 25863 Scottish Rifles KIA 4.5.18.
VASSELIN Alfred A. MM CSM 3327 Rifle Brigade
VASSEY William MM Cpl 43422 1/5th Lincolnshire Regt
VAUGHAN Allen MM Sjt 15573 6th Yorkshire Light Infantry
VAUGHAN Cecil L. MM Pte 71967 Royal Fusiliers
VAUGHAN Edward Samuel MM Sjt 925486 B/290 Bde RFA
VAUGHAN Edward William MM Sjt 12802 101 Coy Machine Gun Corps
VAUGHAN F.M. MM Pte 13678 11th Essex Regt
VAUGHAN George MM+Bar Pte 8832 1st Royal West Kent Regt
VAUGHAN Henry MM Sjt 18126 Gloucestershire Regt
VAUGHAN Herbert MM 2nd Cpl 7463 Royal Monmouthshire Royal Engineers
VAUGHAN John MM Sjt 11640 8th Somerset Light Infantry
VAUGHAN John MM Cpl 201451 Royal Engineers
VAUGHAN John D. MM Pte S/38597 13th Rifle Brigade
VAUGHAN John David MM Cpl 120519 'M' Special Coy Royal Engineers
VAUGHAN John E. MM Pte 2881 1st Welsh Guards
VAUGHAN Joseph MM Sjt 1541 Royal Engineers

VAUGHAN Joseph MM Sjt 13794 8th York & Lancaster Regt Died 22.1.18.
VAUGHAN Lancelot MM Sjt 27321 RGA
VAUGHAN Maurice MM Sjt 52740 87 Fd Coy Royal Engineers
VAUGHAN R. MM L/Cpl 401194 RAMC
VAUGHAN Robert MM Dvr 67215 D/110 Bde RFA KIA 24.3.18.
VAUGHAN Thomas MM Pte 10511 7th Shropshire Light Infantry
VAUGHAN Thomas MM Dvr 168193 RFA
VAUGHAN Thomas H. MM L/Cpl 33265 Border Regt
VAUGHAN Thomas William MM Cpl 36695 South Staffordshire Regt
VAUGHAN Walter MM Pte 14140 York & Lancaster Regt
VAUGHAN William MM Sjt 9313 2nd Royal Berkshire Regt
VAUGHAN William MM Pte 25283 Shropshire Light Infantry
VAUGHAN William H. MM Cpl 675075 RFA
VAUGHAN William James MM Pte 13568 11th South Wales Borderers KIA 31.7.17.
VAUSE Geoprge E. MM Pte 37618 2/4th York & Lancaster Regt
VAUSE George A. MM Pte 29281 2nd Border Regt
VAUSE John MM Pte 350587 9th Manchester Regt
VAUSE P.J. MM Cpl 2061 RFA
VAUSE Walter MM Cpl 20169 8th Yorkshire Light Infantry
VAUX Ernest George MM Pte 8082 2nd Middlesex Regt DOW 12.7.16.
VAUZELLES Stafford E. MM Pte 368101 7th London Regt
VEACOCK Albert MM Pte 29468 Highland Light Infantry
VEACOCK Leslie MM Pnr(MCDR) 29633 Cav Sig Sqn Royal Engineers
VEAL Ernest MM Bdr 755030 RFA
VEAL Frank E. MM Cpl 23388 24th Royal Fusiliers
VEAL Frederick Frank MM Pte 11332 11th Hampshire Regt
VEAL H. MM Pte 241257 Yorkshire Regt
VEAL William MM Pte 8991 2nd Royal West Surrey Regt
VEALE Bertie R. "MM,MID" Sjt 490374 1/13th London Regt
VEALE Henry W. MM Spr 37460 Royal Engineers
VEALE William S. MM Pte S/31330 Rifle Brigade
VEALL George Frederick Wright MM Pte 77402 2nd(Light)Bn Tank Corps KIA 21.8.18.
VEARNCOMBE Frederick J. "MM,MID" Sjt 7866 1st Somerset Light Infantry
VEARS William MM Bdr 840029 RFA
VEASEY B. MM Pte 11900 Durham Light Infantry
VECK Edward MM Pte 25145 2nd Wiltshire Regt
VEDE Eugene MM Sjt 43696 6th Northamptonshire Regt
VEEVERS Robert H. MM Gnr 130267 RGA
VEEVERS Walter Craven MM Pte 359265 10th Liverpool Regt
VEIGHEY Andrew MM L/Cpl 201161 Seaforth Highlanders
VEITCH Andrew MM+2 Bars Pte 10054 2nd Royal Scots Fusiliers
VEITCH Charles Ievine MM Gnr 85191 A/82 Bde RFA DOW 14.3.17.
VEITCH David MM L/Cpl 10138 Scots Guards
VEITCH George "DCM,MM" Sjt 20693 88 Coy Machine Gun Corps
VEITCH James MM Pte 10174 8/10th Gordon Highlanders
VEITCH John MM Pte 13738 12th Royal Scots
VEITCH John MM L/Cpl 5567 1st Scots Guards
VEITCH Robert MM Pte M2/103866 Army Service Corps att RAMC.Died 6.10.18.
VEITCH Thomas MM Pte 266859 1/6th Gordon Highlanders
VEITCH William MM Pte 22812 2nd King's Own Scottish Borderers
VELASCO John MM CSM 9097 1st Border Regt
VELER John René MM Pte 12744 6th Dorsetshire Regt Died 30.10.18.
VELLA Arthur MM Pte 13632 2nd Scots Guards
VENABLES George E.R. MM Spr 478388 Royal Engineers
VENABLES James B. MM Pte 242862 Lancashire Fusiliers
VENABLES Philip MM Cpl M1/07651 5 Mot Amb Convoy Army Service Corps
VENABLES Robert MM Dvr 154588 RFA
VENABLES W.A. MM Dvr 67 RFA
VENARD Abraham MM Sjt 14740 9th Royal Irish Fusiliers
VENESS John Arthur MM Sjt 36237 V/20 Heavy TM Bty RGA Died 23.6.19.
VENEY John H. MM L/Cpl 202592 Liverpool Regt
VENN L.G. MM AM2 7255 Royal Flying Corps
VENN Sidney E. MM Pte 15813 1st Grenadier Guards
VENN William MM+Bar 2nd Cpl 46796 Royal Engineers
VENN William G. MM Sjt 53715 9th Welsh Regt
VENN William H. MM Spr 500593 Royal Engineers
VENNER Walter Edward MM Cpl 202596 114 Heavy Bty RGA
VENNING Herbert C. MM Pte 23157 9th Devonshire Regt
VENNING William E. "MM(7647 Sjt 1st Som LI)+Bar,MID" Sjt P/4881 Military Mounted Police
VENTERS Alfred MM BQMS 67157 A/190 Bde RFA
VENTHAM John Baxter MM Sjt 43530 Special Brigade Royal Engineers
VENTRESS George Ernest MM Cpl 50654 5th North Staffordshire Regt
VENTRIS Harry Leslie MM Sjt 95505 128 Fd Coy Royal Engineers
VENUS Alfred Henry MM Cpl 765489 A/88 Bde RFA
VENUS Robert MM Pte 57675 4th York & Lancaster Regt
VENUS Walter B. MM L/Cpl 5261 Leinster Regt
VERDIN Edwin MM Sjt 10473 Royal Scots
VERE Henry William MM Pte 2025 RAMC
VERGE Cecil H. MM+Bar Cpl 76808 35 Bde RFA
VERGE Edwin MM L/Cpl 22945 Border Regt
VERGE Frank MM L/Sjt 8495 2nd Royal Scots Fusiliers
VERHOEFF Cornelius MM Cpl 62307 Royal Fusiliers
VERITY Archibald MM Sjt 35431 RFA
VERITY Charles MM L/Cpl 13/267 13th East Yorkshire Regt
VERITY Frank C. MM Cpl 5053 Machine Gun Corps
VERITY Henry MM Pte 17046 12th Royal Irish Rifles
VERLANDER George T.W. MM Pte 202818 23rd Middlesex Regt
VERNEL Thomas MM Pte 23501 1/6th Highland Light Infantry
VERNEY Arthur MM Pte M2/119642 Army Service Corps att 'H' Special Coy RE.
VERNEY Arthur Charles MM Cpl 7508 1st Royal Berkshire Regt KIA 30.11.17.
VERNEY Arthur S. MM Pte 25944 7th Shropshire Light Infantry Died 13.12.18.
VERNEY Noel MM Spr 361751 2 Div Sig Coy Royal Engineers
VERNEY Robert H. MM Pte 1609 Lincolnshire Regt
VERNHAM Henry A. MM Pte 532238 15th London Regt
VERNON Alfred E. MM Pte 96657 14th Bn Tank Corps
VERNON Alfred G. MM+Bar Pte 11826 1st Worcestershire Regt
VERNON Arthur MM 2nd Cpl 96913 Royal Engineers
VERNON Ben MM Gnr 67467 176 Siege Bty RGA
VERNON Egbert A.H. MM L/Cpl 182228 Royal Engineers
VERNON Frederick H. MM Sjt 57674 26 Bde RFA
VERNON Herbert MM Cpl 63526 RGA
VERNON James MM Pte 305812 Royal Warwickshire Regt
VERNON John MM L/Cpl 112504 Royal Engineers
VERNON Karl MM Sjt 528198 RAMC
VERNON Percy H. MM Pte 530860 15th London Regt
VERNON William MM Sjt 703489 1/23rd London Regt
VERNOUN Percy J. MM Cpl 202140 1/4th Royal Lancaster Regt
VERNUM Alfred MM Pte 19660 6th Duke of Cornwall's LI DOW 18.12.17.
VERO Ernest MM Pte 17/733 West Yorkshire Regt
VERON Archibald MM Pte 6249 1/4th York & Lancaster Regt
VERSEY Alfred C. MM Bdr 3225 RFA
VERSEY Harry T. MM Sjt 58800 RFA
VERTIGAN Basil MM Cpl 42169 9th Essex Regt
VERWYMEREN Joseph MM L/Cpl 4612 8th Royal West Surrey Regt KIA 21.8.16.
VESSEY Frank Court "MC,MM(33465 Sjt)" 2Lt 353 Siege Bty RGA Died 25.10.18.
VESSEY Harry MM L/Sjt 1358 Army Cyclist Corps
VEST Anthony R. MM Pte 386252 RAMC
VEVERS Charles L. MM Pte 4906 1st Dragoon Guards
VEVERS John MM L/Cpl 39080 42nd Bn Machine Gun Corps
VEZEY Thomas "MM,MID" Sjt 3292 Gloucestershire Regt
VICARY George E. MM Sjt 10273 2nd Royal Sussex Regt
VICARY Thomas C. MM L/Cpl 68754 22nd London Regt
VICCARS William James MM Sjt 24257 10th Royal West Kent Regt
VICK Albert H. MM Cpl 16468 23 Fd Coy Royal Engineers
VICK Arthur MM Pte 439032 RAMC
VICK Arthur J. MM Pte 16035 Royal West Kent Regt
VICK Charles H. MM Pte 352400 7th London Regt
VICK John W. MM Cpl 104 Cheshire Fd Coy Royal Engineers
VICK Thomas MM Cpl 52430 26th Royal Fusiliers DOW 29.9.18.
VICKERMAN Frank MM Spr 199091 257 Tunnelling Coy Royal Engineers
VICKERMAN John MM Sjt 25194 464 Bty 179 Bde RFA
VICKERS Albert E. MM Sjt S/2703 Rifle Brigade
VICKERS Alfred A. MM Pte 33946 6th West Riding Regt
VICKERS Alfred John MM Pte 25612 17th Royal Welsh Fusiliers
VICKERS Arthur S. MM Sjt 15493 Arg & Suth Highlanders
VICKERS Charles Edgar MM Sjt 129129 Royal Engineers
VICKERS Charles Ernest MM Pte 30241 10th East Yorkshire Regt KIA 29.9.18.

VICKERS Edward Roger "DCM,MM" Sjt 8049 9th King's Royal Rifle Corps
VICKERS Ernest James MM Cpl 69641 89 Fd Coy Royal Engineers
VICKERS Harry "DCM,MM(275855 Cpl Manch Regt)" Sjt 236148 2nd East Lancashire Regt KIA 14.10.18.
VICKERS James MM Pte 126464 25th Bn Machine Gun Corps
VICKERS James MM Sjt 372479 294 AE Coy Labour Corps
VICKERS Joe MM Pte 18969 Yorkshire Light Infantry
VICKERS John W. MM L/Cpl 242537 Worcestershire Regt
VICKERS Joseph MM Pte 18231 Cameron Highlanders
VICKERS Joseph MM Sjt 19/1126 13th Northumberland Fusiliers KIA 20.9.17.
VICKERS Joseph C. MM Pte 4212 Royal Irish Rifles
VICKERS Robert MM Gnr 710720 C/330 Bde RFA
VICKERS Robert W. MM Pte M2/076159 Army Service Corps
VICKERS Rupert Alfred Wentworth MM L/Cpl 1350 1st King Edward's Horse
VICKERS Sidney MM Cpl 1178 2nd Lincolnshire Regt KIA 21.3.18.
VICKERS Sydney MM Pte 12/1118 York & Lancaster Regt
VICKERS Thomas MM Pte 1835 Durham Light Infantry
VICKERS Thomas Kendal MM Cpl 241157 1/5th Border Regt
VICKERS Walter MM 2nd Cpl 36648 89 Fd Coy Royal Engineers
VICKERS William MM Pte 9904 1st King's Own Scottish Borderers
VICKERS William MM Gnr 185632 C/293 Bde RFA
VICKERSON Vincent George MM Dvr 1468 RFA
VICKERSTAFF Thomas MM Sjt S4/197673 Army Service Corps
VICKERSTAFFE Ernest MM Sjt 9969 Leicestershire Regt
VICKERY Arthur MM L/Bdr 19126 D/72 Bde RFA
VICKERY Charles S. MM Bdr 826487 RFA
VICKERY George MM L/Cpl 8052 2nd Northamptonshire Regt
VICKERY Richard MM Pte 62545 2nd Royal Fusiliers
VICKERY Thomas W. MM+Bar S/Sjt 363006 7 Cavalry Fd Amb RAMC
VICKERY Thomas William MM Sjt 889 232 Bde RFA DOW 24.4.17.
VICKERY William MM Pte DM2/170705 402 MT Coy Army Service Corps DOW 6.9.18.
VICKERY William MM Pte 10061 7th Somerset Light Infantry DOW 28.9.17.
VICTOR Louis MM Pte 17844 South Lancashire Regt
VICTORY Patrick MM Sjt 9737 1st Royal Munster Fusiliers
VIDGEN Arthur E. MM Pte 84010 2nd London Regt
VIDGEN George MM Gnr 61042 RFA
VIDLER Felix A. MM L/Cpl 55162 2nd Hampshire Regt
VIDLER Harry MM Gnr 27712 24 Siege Bty RGA KIA 1.10.18.
VIDLER Victor MM L/Cpl 534673 491 Fd Coy Royal Engineers
VIDLER William George MM Pte 3039 11th Royal Sussex Regt
VIEWEG Charles A. MM Bdr 140418 RGA
VIGAR Arthur L.J. MM Pte 320287 16th Royal Sussex Regt
VIGAR Frederick J. MM Pte 1464 2nd Royal Sussex Regt
VIGAR Thomas MM Pte 52971 8th Lancashire Fusiliers
VIGG John MM Pte 267286 9th Devonshire Regt
VIGGARS Benjamin MM Pte 51082 RAMC
VIGGERS John MM Sjt 6163 1st East Kent Regt KIA 12.5.16.
VIGOR James MM L/Sjt 2194 8th Royal Sussex Regt
VIGOR John A. MM Sjt 25981 10th Royal West Kent Regt
VIGOR Walter MM L/Cpl 60102 Royal Fusiliers
VIGURS Joseph H. MM Bdr 77316 RHA
VIGURS Walter J. MM L/Cpl 33876 1st Oxf & Bucks Light Infantry
VILE Frank A. MM Pte 42448 Royal Irish Rifles
VILLAGE William MM Sjt 23714 Royal Warwickshire Regt
VILLIERS Henry G. MM Cpl 14558 18th Hussars
VILLIS Charles MM L/Cpl 17215 7th Somerset Light Infantry
VINALL Arthur MM Sjt 8300 2nd Wiltshire Regt
VINALL Harry F. MM+Bar Pte 321364 6th London Regt
VINCE Alfred E. MM Cpl 36891 Royal Welsh Fusiliers
VINCE Frank MM+Bar Sjt 350449 9th Essex Regt
VINCE Frederick MM L/Cpl 2313 West Yorkshire Regt
VINCE Frederick MM Sjt 51184 RHA
VINCE Frederick J.S. MM Cpl 5392 6th Dragoons
VINCE John MM+Bar Gnr 110454 X/11 Med TM Bty RFA
VINCE John MM+Bar Pte 3185 2nd Rifle Brigade
VINCE William J. "MM,MID" Cpl 700368 1/23rd London Regt
VINCENT Ambaces C. MM Pte 28714 4th Hampshire Regt
VINCENT Arthur MM Pte 9592 1st Gloucestershire Regt
VINCENT Arthur MM L/Cpl 10242 2nd Royal Scots Fusiliers
VINCENT Ben L. MM Pte S/27364 13th Rifle Brigade
VINCENT Bruce MM Sjt 19545 251 Siege Bty RGA
VINCENT David MM Cpl 200955 12th Middlesex Regt
VINCENT Edgar J. MM Pte 27147 2nd Suffolk Regt
VINCENT Edward MM Gnr 57217 5 Bde RFA
VINCENT Ernest MM Cpl 10030 Gloucestershire Regt
VINCENT Francis MM Bdr 120919 260 Siege Bty RGA
VINCENT Frank MM Gnr 83738 48 Bde RFA
VINCENT Frederick MM Cpl 12518 A/160 Bde RFA
VINCENT Frederick Godwyn MM Pte 439455 2/3(South Midland)Fd Amb RAMC
VINCENT Frederick W. MM Spr 70678 2 Div Sig Coy Royal Engineers
VINCENT Harry "MM,MID" Pte 4607 4th Rifle Brigade
VINCENT Henry "DCM,MM" Sjt 231746 2nd London Regt
VINCENT Henry MM Pte 353290 7th London Regt KIA 25.4.17.
VINCENT Henry John MM Sjt 55307 57th Bn Machine Gun Corps
VINCENT Horace Samuel MM Pte 68432 41st Bn Machine Gun Corps DOW 3.4.18.
VINCENT James "MM,CG(F)" Pte 4881 12th Arg & Suth Highlanders
VINCENT John J. MM Sjt 13460 161 Bde RFA
VINCENT Jonathan Herren MM Gnr 1532 35 Bde RFA
VINCENT Leonard MM Spr 71494 Royal Engineers
VINCENT Phil MM Pte 17275 2/4th Oxf & Bucks Light Infantry
VINCENT R.C. MM L/Cpl P/1483 Military Foot Police
VINCENT Robert B. MM S/Sjt 33588 RAMC
VINCENT Tom W. MM L/Cpl 2217 1/1st Bucks Bn Oxf & Bucks Light Infantry
VINCENT William J. MM Spr 504687 Royal Engineers
VINCER P.A. "DCM,MM,MID" CSM 7967 1st East Kent Regt
VINDIN Thomas E. MM Pte 201637 10th Lancashire Fusiliers
VINE Albert MM Pte 70269 7th Royal West Surrey Regt
VINE Albert MM Sjt 7579 1st Leicestershire Regt
VINE Alfred MM Pte 33948 6th West Riding Regt
VINE Charles MM Sjt 52569 1st West Yorkshire Regt KIA 27.5.18.
VINE Frank A. MM+Bar Sjt 8118 2nd Hampshire Regt
VINE Herbert Chares MM Pte 15549 7th South Wales Borderers DOW 12.12.17.
VINE J. MM L/Sjt 330416 1/9th Highland Light Infantry
VINE Percival MM+Bar Bdr 24502 Y/15 Med TM Bty RGA KIA 31.10.16.
VINE Percy MM Pte 5547 Leinster Regt
VINE Thomas W. MM L/Cpl 229320 10th Royal Fusiliers
VINER Frederick MM L/Cpl 4491 13th Hussars
VINER Frederick William Thornton MM Sjt 85597 'Y' AA Bty RGA
VINER Harry MM Pte 4785 3rd Royal Fusiliers
VINER Stanley MM Pte 12411 9th King's Royal Rifle Corps
VINEY Cecil MM Pte 33591 RAMC
VINEY Percy Clifford MM L/Cpl 27754 1st Shropshire Light Infantry DOW 23 9 18.
VINEY Reginald C.R. MM L/Cpl R/9601 King's Royal Rifle Corps
VINING Sidney MM Sjt 2188 Middlesex Regt
VINING William Harold MM Pte 5692 1st Royal Munster Fusiliers DOW 15.10.16.
VINNEY Sidney MM Dvr 84528 RFA
VINNICOMBE James W. MM Dvr M2/047271 Army Service Corps
VINNICOMBE Robert MM Pte 5469 9th Royal Warwickshire Regt
VINSON Frederick Thomas MM L/Sjt 1828 18th London Regt KIA 15.9.16.
VINTER Charles George MM Pte 40632 10th Essex Regt DOW 23.8.18.
VINTER Henry G MM+Bar Cpl 253811 Royal Engineers
VINTON Alfred J. MM Dvr 36293 RFA
VINUE Stephen MM L/Cpl 12589 13th Liverpool Regt
VINYCOMB(E) Alexander R.D. MM Sjt 94094 Royal Engineers
VIPOND James William MM L/Cpl 1416 1/5th Liverpool Regt KIA 8.8.16.
VIPOND John Elliott MM Pte 16429 13th Durham Light Infantry DOW 14.10.16.
VIPOND Joseph MM Pte 94554 1/8th Notts & Derby Regt
VIRGO Howard MM Pte 27908 Gloucestershire Regt
VIRGO Thomas MM+Bar Pte 22989 1st Lancashire Fusiliers
VIRGO Thomas H.C. MM Pte 240172 7th Worcestershire Regt
VIRTUE Archibald MM Cpl 346714 70 Siege Bty RGA
VIRTUE Samuel MM Dvr 8211 120 Bty 27 Bde RFA
VISICK Arthur Robert MM S/Sjt Fitter 315356 111 Hy Bty RGA DOW 5.10.18.
VIVASH Naylass James MM Pte 111721 8th Bn Tank Corps
VIVIAN Ernest MM Pte 353465 7th London Regt
VIVIAN William L. MM Pte 28532 Duke of Cornwall's LI
VIZARD Albert T. MM Pte 309132 732 Coy Labour Corps
VIZOR Austin William "MM,MID" Sjt 8807 2nd South Staffordshire Regt
VOADEN John MM Pte 241969 Worcestershire Regt

VOCE George MM+Bar Pte 16539 3rd Grenadier Guards
VOCE James Ernest MM Bdr 11979 126 Bty 29 Bde RFA
VOCKINS Frederick J. "MM,MID" CQMS 6323 2nd Royal Berkshire Regt
VOCKINS Sidney MM L/Cpl 372057 8th London Regt KIA 23.3.18.
VOCKUICH Thomas Richard MM Pte 18/981 18th Durham Light Infantry KIA 28.9.17.
VOGAN Henry MM L/Cpl 11095 2nd King's Own Scottish Borderers
VOGAN Robert MM Pte 49848 1st Royal Irish Fusiliers
VOGAN Robert MM Pte 18521 2nd Royal Irish Regt KIA 27.9.18.
VOGEL Ernest MM Sjt 3334 225 Coy Machine Gun Corps
VOGT Richard B. MM Pte 718279 23rd London Regt
VOICE Ernest S. MM Cpl 8492 D/64 Bde RFA
VOICE John F. MM Gnr 177673 RGA
VOICE W. MM L/Cpl 15538 Royal West Surrey Regt
VOISEY William "DCM,MM,CG(B)" Sjt 10534 B/187 Bde RFA
VOKES Alfred MM Pte 253435 3rd London Regt
VOKINS George L. MM Sjt 7226 6th Dragoon Guards
VOKINS Henry Almond MM Bdr 75275 11 Bty 1 Bde RFA
VOLK Edward MM Pte DM2/208388 Army Service Corps
VOLLANS Harold MM L/Cpl 1537 1st Yorkshire Light Infantry
VOLLENS James Reginald MM L/Cpl 15490 1st West Yorkshire Regt DOW 27.9.16.
VOLLER Harry MM Pte 15344 Gloucestershire Regt
VOLLER Richard W. MM Sjt 101005 RGA
VOLLER William Alfred MM Cpl 62311 16 Siege Bty RGA
VOLLMAR Hans MM L/Cpl 40140 York & Lancaster Regt
VOSE Herbert MM L/Cpl 9909 1st East Lancashire Regt KIA 21.3.18.
VOSE J. MM Sjt 37982 RGA AKA TRINDER.
VOSE Thomas "DCM,MM" CSM 241248 South Lancashire Regt
VOSPER Frank Leonard MM Dvr T/28744 Army Service Corps
VOSPER William MM Cpl 240163 5th Gloucestershire Regt
VOWELL Arthur MM Bdr 72395 C/83 Bde RFA
VOWELS Frank W. MM CQMS 7451 2nd Lancashire Fusiliers
VOWLES Dennis MM L/Cpl 8558 11th Royal Warwickshire Regt
VOWLES Edward MM Sjt 203232 11th Essex Regt
VOWLES Edwin MM Pte 301266 Labour Corps
VOWLES Francis James MM Pte 371 1st Welsh Guards
VOWLES Percy MM Pte 165259 1/1st North Somerset Yeomanry
VOYCE Caleb "MM,MSM" Sjt 258627 277 Rly Const Coy Royal Engineers
VOYCE William MM Cpl 241445 8th Gloucestershire Regt
VOYCE William MM L/Cpl 25135 Grenadier Guards
VOYLE Abraham J. "DCM,MM" Sjt 26692 13th Welsh Regt
VOYLE James H. MM L/Cpl 242440 East Kent Regt
VOZZA Michael MM Spr 311173 5 Fd Svy Bn Royal Engineers
VYSE Herbert Ramsay MM Pte 242511 9th York & Lancaster Regt
VYSE Maurice MM Bdsm 10344 2nd Royal Welsh Fusiliers DOW 20.7.16.
VYSE Thomas Winn MM Pte 28080 East Yorkshire Regt
VYVYAN Frank G. "DCM,MM" Cpl 2749 Machine Gun Corps(Heavy Branch)

W

WABY R.W. "DCM,MM" Sjt 3424 1st East Kent Regt
WACEY Thomas E. MM Pte 380074 Liverpool Regt
WACKETT Frank MM Dvr 24 2 Bde RFA
WACKETT Herbert MM Pte 47470 RAMC
WACKFORD Sidney MM Cpl 863 2nd Royal Sussex Regt
WADDELL Alexander "DCM,MM" Sjt 8804 2nd Arg & Suth Highlanders
WADDELL Arthur Oliver "MM,MID" CQMS 1046 1st Northumberland Fusiliers
WADDELL Charles D. MM Gnr 202618 RFA
WADDELL David MM Cpl 28436 Royal Engineers
WADDELL Ernest MM Pte 15936 2nd Royal Scots Fusiliers
WADDELL James MM L/Cpl 38677 5th Royal Berkshire Regt
WADDELL John MM L/Cpl 12551 Scots Guards
WADDELL John B. MM Pte 307949 15th Bn Tank Corps
WADDELL Thomas L. MM Pte 203122 5th Cameron Highlanders
WADDELL William MM Pte 9516 Gordon Highlanders
WADDICOR Jim "MM,MID" Bdr Sig 63193 124 Siege Bty RGA
WADDIE John Norman MM Pte 40427 16th Royal Scots KIA 11.4.18.
WADDILOVE Elijah MM Cpl 9984 1st North Lancashire Regt
WADDINGHAM Arthur MM Sjt 12142 7th East Yorkshire Regt
WADDINGHAM Sydney J. MM L/Cpl 22415 12th East Surrey Regt
WADDINGTON Arthur D. "MM,MSM" Sjt R/4775 13th King's Royal Rifle Corps
WADDINGTON Edward MM L/Cpl 8738 King's Royal Rifle Corps
WADDINGTON Frank MM L/Cpl 305589 7th West Riding Regt
WADDINGTON George "DCM,MM" Sjt 14306 10th Scottish Rifles
WADDINGTON Guy MM L/Cpl 76888 2nd Bn Tank Corps
WADDINGTON Harry "MM,MID" Sjt 29599 RGA
WADDINGTON Herbert H. MM Gnr 346856 258 Siege Bty RGA
WADDINGTON J.R. MM Cpl 14452 8th Lincolnshire Regt
WADDINGTON John MM Pte 241912 1/5th York & Lancaster Regt KIA 15.4.18.
WADDINGTON John "MM,MID" Pte 7625 3rd Coldstream Guards
WADDINGTON John MM Pte 9432 XIV Corps Cyclist Bn Army Cyclist Corps
WADDINGTON Obadiah F. "DCM+Bar,MM" L/Sjt 2259 1st Welsh Guards
WADDINGTON Richard MM Bdr 710247 A/211 Bde RFA KIA 28.9.17.
WADDINGTON William MM Sjt 11/13652 11th Border Regt KIA 1.7.16.
WADDINGTON William MM Cpl 45054 RGA
WADDLE Thomas MM Cpl 21442 Durham Light Infantry
WADDOUPS George F. MM Spr 121582 185 Tunnelling Coy Royal Engineers
WADDY John William MM L/Cpl 167481 Royal Engineers
WADE Arthur William MM Pte 304392 5th London Regt Died 17.10.18.
WADE B. MM Cpl 280037 Yeomanry
WADE Bernard MM L/Cpl M2/046519 Army Service Corps
WADE Bidwell MM Pte 269087 13th Liverpool Regt
WADE Burt MM Cpl 10238 1st Royal Scots
WADE Cyril Archibald MM Pte 4801 16th Lancers
WADE Daniel MM L/Cpl 1603 1st Seaforth Highlanders
WADE Edward MM Pte 12090 2nd North Lancashire Regt
WADE Ernest W. MM+Bar Cpl 9316 2nd Royal Sussex Regt
WADE Frederick D. MM Cpl 5897 Machine Gun Corps
WADE George MM Cpl 48871 RGA
WADE George MM Pte 315360 5th London Regt
WADE George T. MM L/Cpl 8980 1st East Surrey Regt
WADE Harold B. MM Sjt 1446 12th Yorkshire Light Infantry
WADE Henry "MM,MID" L/Sjt 320039 1/6th London Regt
WADE Herbert J. MM Sjt 13867 8th Suffolk Regt
WADE James MM Sjt 9240 1st Royal Dublin Fusiliers
WADE John MM Pte 15521 10th Yorkshire Regt
WADE John D. MM Sjt 10095 15th Lancashire Fusiliers
WADE John E. MM Pte 10034 3rd Worcestershire Regt
WADE Josiah MM L/Sjt 21/362 21st West Yorkshire Regt
WADE Richard MM L/Cpl 43050 7th Norfolk Regt KIA 8.8.18.
WADE Richard William MM Spr 166399 23 Fd Coy Royal Engineers
WADE Robert MM Gnr 66450 D/152 Bde RFA
WADE Thomas Stanley Dudley MM CSM 19195 10th Yorkshire Regt
WADE Thomas W. MM Gnr 3614 RFA
WADE Walter Gilliham Tankerville MM Bdr 24808 51 Div Ammn Col RFA
WADE William A. MM Cpl 142255 38 Heavy Bty RGA
WADEY Ezra MM Bdr 188897 D/77 Bde RFA
WADGE Albert E. MM Sjt 13124 2nd Scots Guards
WADHAM Benjamin MM Pte 12075 10th Hampshire Regt
WADLEY Harry MM Pte 46058 Worcestershire Regt
WADLEY Reginald E. MM L/Cpl 250668 3rd London Regt
WADLING William MM Pte 700313 1/23rd London Regt
WADLOW Frederick MM Spr 265648 Royal Engineers
WADSWORTH Charles MM Pte 11796 1st Worcestershire Regt
WADSWORTH Edward MM Bdr 65480 127 Bty 29 Bde RFA
WADSWORTH Frank MM Pte 202215 4th Yorkshire Light Infantry
WADSWORTH Harry MM L/Cpl 20275 1st Coldstream Guards
WADSWORTH John G. MM Pte 9373 Royal Fusiliers
WADSWORTH Joseph MM Gnr 9510 D/79 Bde RFA KIA 3.5.17.
WADSWORTH Robert MM Pte 240468 1/5th Royal Lancaster Regt
WADSWORTH William J. MM L/Cpl 67456 1st Cheshire Regt
WADY Arthur F. MM+Bar L/Cpl 17005 Royal Lancaster Regt
WAGER Tom MM Pte 27707 12th West Yorkshire Regt
WAGERFIELD Ernest James MM Gnr 125208 X/19 Med TM Bty RFA
WAGG Albert MM Bdr 805690 D/232 Bde RFA
WAGG John W. "DCM,MM+Bar" Sjt 417018 1/1(North Midland)Fd Amb RAMC
WAGG R.B. MM Sjt 240083 Suffolk Regt

WAGGOTT George MM Pte 11934 10th Durham Light Infantry
WAGHORN Clarence L. MM Sjt 1989 7th Royal West Kent Regt
WAGHORN Edward MM Pte 7545 1st Royal West Kent Regt DOW 17.6.18.
WAGHORN John MM Pnr 343265 Royal Engineers
WAGHORN Thomas C. MM Pte 23675 7th Royal Sussex Regt
WAGHORNE John A. MM L/Bdr 374356 RGA
WAGHORNE William MM Gnr 31114 2 Siege Bty RGA
WAGLAND Percival MM Pte 1363 Royal Fusiliers
WAGNER C. MM Cpl 232946 London Regt
WAGNER William MM Pte 266710 1/7th Liverpool Regt DOW 9.4.18.
WAGSTAFF Albert MM Pte 21483 9th Notts & Derby Regt
WAGSTAFF Arnold Clifford MM L/Cpl 17783 20th Manchester Regt KIA 29.8.16.
WAGSTAFF Cecil Percy MM L/Cpl 200514 Oxf & Bucks Light Infantry
WAGSTAFF Harry B. MM Pte 2044 10th Royal Warwickshire Regt
WAGSTAFF John Sharwell MM Sjt 200320 2nd Yorkshire Regt
WAGSTAFF Joseph MM Pte 202503 5th Notts & Derby Regt
WAGSTAFF Ralph MM Cpl 17544 1st Cheshire Regt
WAGSTAFF Wilfred B. MM Pte 2039 Royal Berkshire Regt
WAGSTAFF or WAGSTAFFE Arthur MM Sjt 20130 Manchester Regt
WAGSTAFFE Elias "MM,MID" Sjt 267574 Monmouthshire Regt
WAGSTAFFE Hubert MM Pte 529 17th Royal Fusiliers
WAGSTAFFE Stanley MM Pte 242958 6th West Yorkshire Regt
WAIDE Edward H. MM Sjt 775542 RFA
WAIGHT James MM Sjt 51740 24 Bde RFA
WAILES Henry MM Cpl 23443 2nd Royal West Surrey Regt
WAILES John R. MM Sjt 414 Yorkshire Light Infantry
WAILES Robert H. MM Pte 880611 34th London Regt
WAILES Thomas William MM Pte 34192 8th York & Lancaster Regt DOW 30.9.16.
WAILING Sydney "MM,MID" Sjt 432009 Royal Engineers
WAIN Cyril MM Cpl 99570 1/1(Welsh)Hy Bty RGA
WAIN George Henry MM Sjt 6800 9th North Staffordshire Regt DOW 26.5.18.
WAIN Gilbert C. MM L/Cpl 201545 North Staffordshire Regt
WAIN James W. MM Dvr 54622 11 Bde RFA
WAIN Robert MM Pte 240082 6th North Staffordshire Regt
WAIN Robert J. MM Pte M2/191862 Army Service Corps
WAIN William MM Sjt 230588 10th Shropshire Light Infantry KIA 18.9.18.
WAINE Albert F. MM Cpl 20088 Royal Munster Fusiliers
WAINE Alexander MM Pte 13042 1st Scots Guards
WAINE Sydney MM Sjt 1705 1/1st Oxfordshire Yeomanry
WAINMAN Benjamin MM Cpl 432280 Royal Engineers
WAINMAN George MM Pte 11/28278 11th Border Regt KIA 25.11.17.
WAINMAN Irvine MM+Bar Sjt 5854 11th Lancashire Fusiliers DOW 25.3.18.
WAINWRIGHT Arthur MM Pte 13574 11th West Yorkshire Regt
WAINWRIGHT Arthur R. MM Pte 202772 8th Worcestershire Regt
WAINWRIGHT Harry MM Sjt 3102 1/8th Liverpool Regt
WAINWRIGHT Herman MM Cpl 200204 1/4th West Riding Regt
WAINWRIGHT Horace MM Dvr 785368 RFA
WAINWRIGHT James MM L/Cpl 7857 1st North Staffordshire Regt
WAINWRIGHT James MM Pte 11524 4th Worcestershire Regt
WAINWRIGHT John MM 2nd Cpl 78416 Royal Engineers
WAINWRIGHT John MM Sjt 78416 Royal Engineers
WAINWRIGHT Joseph MM L/Cpl 1868 11th Manchester Regt KIA 26.9.16.
WAINWRIGHT Matthew L. MM L/Bdr 671121 RFA
WAINWRIGHT Reginald MM L/Cpl 266228 2/8th West Yorkshire Regt
WAINWRIGHT Stanley MM Cpl 47245 59 Coy Labour Corps
WAINWRIGHT William MM Pte 238153 19th Lancashire Fusiliers
WAINWRIGHT William MM Pte 36298 Yorkshire Light Infantry
WAINWRIGHT William MM L/Sjt 23199 3rd Grenadier Guards
WAISTELL Thomas MM(12th Bn)+Bar(15th Bn) L/Cpl 14823 Durham Light Infantry
WAISTELL William Henry MM Sjt 295785 151 Heavy Bty RGA
WAIT Albert Edward MM Cpl P2796 3 Traffic Control Coy Military Foot Police
WAITE Albert Victor MM Pte 40746 23rd Northumberland Fusiliers DOW 12.2.17.
WAITE Alfred "DCM,MM" CSM 10573 Royal Berkshire Regt
WAITE Arthur MM Pte 25003 13th Liverpool Regt
WAITE Arthur G. MM L/Cpl 15052 4th Worcestershire Regt
WAITE Charles MM Gnr 128611 RFA
WAITE Charles MM Sjt 20146 Leicestershire Regt
WAITE Charles V. MM+Bar Pte C/12243 King's Royal Rifle Corps att RE.
WAITE George MM Pte 10713 8th West Riding Regt
WAITE George W. "DCM,MM+Bar" CSM 3446 50th Bn Machine Gun Corps
WAITE Henry MM Pte 21222 10th Royal West Kent Regt
WAITE Herbert L. MM Bdr 622422 RHA
WAITE Joe MM Pte 16483 1st Middlesex Regt
WAITE John T. MM Cpl 11349 20th Hussars
WAITE Joseph J. MM Pte 265951 Royal Warwickshire Regt
WAITE Norman G. MM Sjt 21119 Machine Gun Corps
WAITE Samuel MM Pte 4989 Royal West Surrey Regt
WAITE Walter MM Cpl 15414 2nd Notts & Derby Regt
WAITE William MM Cpl 39557 10th West Yorkshire Regt
WAITE William T. MM Gnr 300434 Tank Corps
WAITES Elijah MM Pte 51052 Liverpool Regt
WAITES James H. MM Bdr 75610 RFA
WAITES John G. MM Pte 16871 11th Durham Light Infantry
WAITSON John MM Pte 1777 1st Royal Lancaster Regt
WAITT Christopher W. MM Sjt 1196 Royal Flying Corps
WAITT Joseph MM+Bar Pte 325217 1/9th Durham Light Infantry
WAKE Arthur MM+Bar L/Cpl 203362 6th Northamptonshire Regt
WAKE Frederick L. MM Pte 21485 Machine Gun Corps
WAKE H. MM Sjt 6687 Dragoons
WAKE Joseph MM Pte 200162 West Yorkshire Regt
WAKE Leonard MM Bdr 128355 D/124 Bty RFA
WAKE R.H. MM Bdr 35757 35 Heavy Bty RGA
WAKE Thomas J. MM L/Sjt 19376 12th Bn Machine Gun Corps
WAKE Tom MM Cpl 6722 4th Dragoon Guards
WAKE William MM Cpl 62289 42 Bde RFA
WAKEFIELD Albert W. MM Pte 29991 7th Royal West Kent Regt
WAKEFIELD Charles R. MM Pte 13020 8th Gloucestershire Regt
WAKEFIELD David T. MM Sjt 415072 9th London Regt
WAKEFIELD Edward MM+Bar Cpl 653322 21st London Regt
WAKEFIELD Frank H. MM Sjt M2/138667 Army Service Corps
WAKEFIELD G. MM Pte 201182 Royal Lancaster Regt
WAKEFIELD George E. MM Sjt 786188 B/312 Bde RFA
WAKEFIELD George F. MM Sjt 19093 5th Dorsetshire Regt
WAKEFIELD H. "MM,MID" Pte 266575 Gloucestershire Regt
WAKEFIELD Henry MM Pte 791 7th Royal West Surrey Regt
WAKEFIELD James MM Cpl 92889 2nd(Garr) Liverpool Regt
WAKEFIELD Peter MM Pte 17379 8th East Lancashire Regt KIA 25.6.18.
WAKEFIELD Reginald MM Pte M2/047458 Army Service Corps
WAKEFIELD William A. MM Cpl 681418 RFA
WAKEFORD Alfred N. MM Sjt 114 1st Dragoon Guards
WAKEFORD Arthur MM Spr 222952 Royal Engineers
WAKEFORD Henry MM L/Cpl A/3114 King's Royal Rifle Corps
WAKEFORD Henry T.B. MM Pte 105457 15th Bn Machine Gun Corps
WAKEHAM A. MM Sjt 321387 RGA
WAKEHAM Charles "MC,DCM,MM,MID" CSM 24258 10th Durham Light Infantry
WAKEHAM Charles W. MM L/Cpl 8868 2nd Devonshire Regt
WAKEHAM George MM+Bar L/Cpl 9794 2nd Duke of Cornwall's LI
WAKEHAM Norman G. "DCM,MM" Sjt 22375 10th Duke of Cornwall's LI
WAKELEY Percival John MM L/Cpl 17071 10th Worcestershire Regt
WAKELIN Arthur W. MM Gnr 18526 23 Heavy Bty RGA
WAKELIN Charles MM L/Cpl 17/1215 17th Northumberland Fusiliers
WAKELIN Joseph MM Pte 2275 North Staffordshire Regt
WAKELIN Stephen J. MM Bdr 90497 RHA
WAKELIN Walter J. MM Pte 91325 13th Liverpool Regt
WAKELING Harold MM Pte 5636 Machine Gun Corps
WAKEM Arthur MM+Bar Sjt 5110 RFA
WAKEM Frederick W. MM Pte 202132 Duke of Cornwall's LI
WAKEMAN Leonard C. MM BQMS 30492 7 Siege Bty RGA
WAKEMAN S.W. MM L/Cpl 673 7th East Kent Regt
WAKEMAN Thomas MM Pte 8016 7th Royal Fusiliers
WAKEN T. MM Sjt 11008 East Surrey Regt
WAKENSHAW Thomas MM Pte 1176 1/7th Northumberland Fusiliers
WAKLEY Ernest MM Pte 11027 6th Duke of Cornwall's LI
WAKLEY Herbert MM Pte 8490 2nd Coldstream Guards
WALBY Sidney MM Sjt 15023 2nd Bedfordshire Regt KIA 21.9.18.
WALCH M. MM L/Cpl P4870 Military Mounted Police
WALCHESTER Edwin MM Pte 40832 8th Royal Lancaster Regt
WALDEN Cecil J. MM Gnr 182659 RFA
WALDEN Frederick William MM Cpl 30990 Northamptonshire Regt

WALDEN George A. MM L/Cpl 6/3358 6th Royal Irish Regt
WALDEN Harry MM Pte 202137 1st Lancashire Fusiliers
WALDEN William MM L/Cpl 10913 2/1st HAC(Inf)
WALDEN or WALDON George MM Sjt 58132 44 Bde RFA
WALDER Percy Warden MM Sjt 1379 7th Royal West Surrey Regt
WALDER Roderick Jesse MM+Bar Cpl 55928 9th Machine Gun Corps
WALDING Edward MM Sjt 1209 3rd Rifle Brigade KIA 31.7.17.
WALDOCK Charles MM Pte 14051 Bedfordshire Regt
WALDOCK Frederick MM L/Cpl 12190 6th Bedfordshire Regt
WALDON or WALDEN George MM Sjt 58132 44 Bde RFA
WALDRAM Leonard J. MM Sjt 19945 Durham Light Infantry
WALDRAM Samuel MM Pte 27566 2/5th Lancashire Fusiliers KIA 26.8.18.
WALDREN or WALDRON William T. MM+Bar Sjt 4286 Machine Gun Corps
WALDRON C.W. MM Pte 593689 London Regt
WALDRON Charles MM L/Cpl S/3175 Rifle Brigade
WALDRON Charles E. MM L/Cpl 26909 Worcestershire Regt
WALDRON Ernest Granville MM Sjt 12004 2nd Notts & Derby Regt
WALDRON George MM Cpl 293495 Labour Corps
WALDRON Harry W. MM Cpl 15857 Lancashire Fusiliers
WALDRON James Joseph "DCM,MM" Cpl 18786 2/4th York & Lancaster Regt
WALDRON John MM Cpl 5971 2nd Royal Munster Fusiliers
WALDRON John E. MM Pte 74833 RAMC
WALDRON John T. MM Pte 21725 Royal West Surrey Regt
WALDRON Leonard Victor "MM,MID" Cpl 1202 RFA
WALDRON Owen William "MC,MM(21760 MGC)" 2?lt 12th Gloucestershire Regt
WALDRON Patrick MM Pte 6508 1st Irish Guards
WALDRON Wilfred MM+Bar Sjt 20904 Machine Gun Corps
WALDRON William Herbert MM L/Cpl 3503 13th Royal Sussex Regt DOW 1.8.17.
WALDRON or WALDREN William T. MM+Bar Sjt 4286 Machine Gun Corps
WALE Alfred MM Pte 9671 2nd Coldstream Guards
WALE Arthur MM Pte 12271 Royal Berkshire Regt
WALE Ernest MM Sjt 192978 Royal Engineers
WALE Joseph MM Pte 4885 56 Coy Machine Gun Corps KIA 31.7.17.
WALE William W. MM Pte 41650 2nd Bedfordshire Regt
WALES Alfred E. MM Pte 39250 1st Yorkshire Light Infantry
WALES Edwin E. MM Pte 51441 1st Northumberland Fusiliers
WALES George C. MM Pte 14532 13th Yorkshire Regt
WALES John MM Bdr 1307 50 Div Ammn Col RFA
WALES Thomas MM Pte 51495 2nd Royal Scots
WALES William MM Cpl 87489 25 Div Sig Coy Royal Engineers
WALES William MM Pte 2142 6th Dragoon Guards
WALFORD Dennis MM Dvr 925308 A/280 Bde RFA
WALFORD Frederick George MM Cpl 1674 23rd Royal Fusiliers
WALFORD Frederick James "MM,MSM,MID" Sjt 56000 63 Fd Coy Royal Engineers
WALFORD John MM Pte 202017 2/4th West Riding Regt
WALFORD Leonard O. MM Cpl 45389 RAMC
WALGATE Charles MM Pte 19431 8th Leicestershire Regt KIA 21.3.18.
WALGATE George MM Pte 265714 2/7th West Yorkshire Regt
WALKDEN Fred MM Sjt 50158 17 Div Sig Coy Royal Engineers
WALKDEN George MM+Bar Cpl 242181 1/5th Border Regt
WALKDEN Gilbert MM L/Bdr 24642 RHA
WALKDEN James MM Sjt 18512 RAMC
WALKDEN James G. MM Sjt Drummer 200905 East Lancashire Regt
WALKDEN Joseph MM Pte 860689 33rd London Regt
WALKDEN Peter MM Cpl 78829 4th Liverpool Regt
WALKER A. MM Pte 267121 West Yorkshire Regt
WALKER Albert MM Sjt 6442 16th Manchester Regt DOW 8.4.18.
WALKER Albert MM Pte 49597 Liverpool Regt
WALKER Albert MM Pte 201335 Lancashire Fusiliers
WALKER Albert MM+2 Bars Cpl 5113 8th East Surrey Regt
WALKER Albert B.C. MM Sjt 24196 33rd Bn Machine Gun Corps
WALKER Albert E. MM Spr 1085 Royal Engineers
WALKER Albert Edward MM L/Cpl 4076 6th East Kent Regt
WALKER Albert Edward MM Cpl 106883 229 Fd Coy Royal Engineers
WALKER Albert Frederick Austin MM CSM 45949 204 Coy Machine Gun Corps
WALKER Alexander MM Sjt 332209 1/9th Highland Light Infantry
WALKER Alexander MM Cpl 49918 2nd Durham Light Infantry

WALKER Alexander MM L/Cpl 62591 93 Fd Amb RAMC
WALKER Alexander H. MM Pte 3532 16th Highland Light Infantry
WALKER Alfred MM L/Cpl 204417 5th South Staffordshire Regt
WALKER Alfred MM L/Cpl 301307 1/8th Manchester Regt
WALKER Alfred MM Pte 50707 11th Cheshire Regt DOW 22.4.18.
WALKER Alfred MM Sjt 13478 11tth Border Regt KIA 23.4.18.
WALKER Alfred MM Pte 203261 2/1st(Bucks)Bn Oxf & Bucks Light Infantry
WALKER Alfred MM Pte 38478 Yorkshire Regt
WALKER Alfred E. MM Gnr 224392 D/186 Bde RFA
WALKER Alfred J. MM Pte 283418 3rd London Regt
WALKER Alfred Percy MM Pte 19344 2nd Northamptonshire Regt
WALKER Andrew McL. MM Spr 252722 Royal Engineers att 11 HAG Sig Sub-Section
WALKER Anthony J. MM Pte 45817 5th Royal Berkshire Regt
WALKER Archibald MM Cpl 241443 5/6th Scottish Rifles
WALKER Arthur MM Pte 62802 9th Yorkshire Light Infantry
WALKER Arthur MM+Bar Pte 33763 1st Middlesex Regt
WALKER Arthur MM Cpl 1794 20th Manchester Regt
WALKER Arthur Charles MM Pte 4739 Notts & Derby Regt
WALKER Arthur J. MM Cpl 203285 1/5th South Staffordshire Regt
WALKER Arthur J. "MM,MID" Sjt 13323 4th Middlesex Regt
WALKER Arthur M. MM Pte 470332 12th London Regt
WALKER B. MM Pte 421081 RAMC
WALKER Ben MM+Bar CSM 26842 Notts & Derby Regt
WALKER Ben R. MM+Bar Sjt 9431 2nd East Yorkshire Regt
WALKER Bernard MM Cpl MS/1671 3 Cav Div Supp Col Army Service Corps
WALKER Charles MM Gnr 8157 RFA
WALKER Charles MM L/Cpl B/203255 13th Rifle Brigade
WALKER Charles MM Pte 350622 1/9th Highland Light Infantry
WALKER Charles MM Sjt 240060 Gordon Highlanders
WALKER Charles Anton MM Pte 6623 2nd Royal Welsh Fusiliers KIA 26.9.17.
WALKER Charles E. MM CSM 19951 9th West Riding Regt
WALKER Charles E. MM Gnr 51890 9 Bde RFA
WALKER Charles E. MM Pte 23340 Worcestershire Regt
WALKER Charles H. "DCM,MM" L/Cpl 15/12170 15th Royal Irish Rifles
WALKER Charles Henry MM L/Cpl 551762 4 Fd Svy Coy Royal Engineers KIA 14.8.18.
WALKER Charles Henry MM Spr 102492 252 Tunnelling Coy Royal Engineers
WALKER Charles W. MM Pte C/1563 King's Royal Rifle Corps
WALKER Clifford MM Pte 14632 9th Seaforth Highlanders
WALKER David "DCM,MM" CSM 350317 1/9th Royal Scots
WALKER David MM 2nd Cpl 40183 Royal Engineers
WALKER David D. MM Cpl 240832 Gordon Highlanders
WALKER Douglas MM Pte M2/131647 Army Service Corps
WALKER E.H. MM Gnr 4364 RFA
WALKER Edmund MM Cpl 305546 2nd West Riding Regt
WALKER Edward MM Pte 77091 24th Royal Fusiliers
WALKER Edward MM Pte 36310 6th Yorkshire Light Infantry
WALKER Edward "MM,MID" Sjt 4296 3rd Hussars
WALKER Edward Lionel MM Gnr 123633 D/64 Bde RFA
WALKER Edward McKendry MM Pte 3753 2nd Royal Irish Rifles KIA 6.9.18.
WALKER Edwin MM Sjt 19047 Cheshire Regt
WALKER Edwin MM+Bar Sjt 46107 14 Bde RFA
WALKER Eneas MM Pte 52206 Royal Welsh Fusiliers
WALKER Enos E. MM Pte 40778 1/7th Cheshire Regt
WALKER Ernest MM Pte 268768 1st West Yorkshire Regt
WALKER Ernest MM L/Sjt 11359 7th Leicestershire Regt
WALKER Ernest MM L/Cpl 38471 Northumberland Fusiliers
WALKER Francis MM L/Cpl 9016 2nd Scots Guards
WALKER Francis H. MM Sjt 26177 15th Notts & Derby Regt
WALKER Francis J. MM Cpl 11734 King's Royal Rifle Corps
WALKER Frank MM Pte C/12313 King's Royal Rifle Corps
WALKER Fred MM L/Cpl 15431 9th York & Lancaster Regt
WALKER Fred "DCM,MM" Pte 139630 49th Bn Machine Gun Corps
WALKER Fred Morton MM L/Cpl 267936 6th West Riding Regt
WALKER Frederick MM Pte 20551 8th Royal Lancaster Regt
WALKER Frederick MM Pte 12188 10th Hussars DOW 13.3.18.
WALKER Frederick MM Pte 359338 Liverpool Regt
WALKER Frederick MM Pte 16524 1/7th West Riding Regt KIA 29.4.18.
WALKER Frederick MM Spr 102939 Royal Engineers
WALKER Frederick MM Sjt 13596 Durham Light Infantry
WALKER Frederick C. MM Cpl 200499 1/4th Norfolk Regt

WALKER Frederick Harry MM+Bar L/Cpl 550691 1/16th London Regt KIA 28.9.18.
WALKER Frederick William MM Cpl 12595 9th Yorkshire Regt
WALKER Garnet MM Pte 76125 1/1st Derbyshire Yeomanry
WALKER George MM Sjt 277158 RGA
WALKER George MM L/Sjt 43404 9th Scottish Rifles KIA 25.10.18.
WALKER George MM Cpl 265742 1/4th Seaforth Highlanders
WALKER George MM Pte 49500 2nd Lincolnshire Regt
WALKER George MM Dvr 56198 72 Bty 38 Bde RFA
WALKER George MM L/Sjt 201591 7th Worcestershire Regt
WALKER George MM+Bar L/Cpl 21829 23rd Manchester Regt
WALKER George MM Sjt 11951 Royal Berkshire Regt
WALKER George MM Pte 40034 Royal Irish Fusiliers
WALKER George MM Pte 267016 1st Liverpool Regt
WALKER George MM Pte 12578 6th King's Own Scottish Borderers
WALKER George MM Cpl 1206 2nd Yorkshire Light Infantry
WALKER George MM Pte 15896 1/5th South Staffordshire Regt DOW 29.4.18.
WALKER George MM Sjt 15378 8th Royal Lancaster Regt
WALKER George A. MM L/Cpl 24595 Machine Gun Corps
WALKER George Benedict MM Pte 15456 2nd Leinster Regt
WALKER George E. MM CQMS 231722 2nd London Regt
WALKER George Edwin MM Sjt 19065 2nd Yorkshire Regt KIA 22.3.18.
WALKER George G. MM Cpl 5954 Machine Gun Corps
WALKER George H. MM Pte 32251 Notts & Derby Regt
WALKER George R. MM L/Sjt 18282 1st Grenadier Guards
WALKER George R. MM Cpl 270766 1/1st Northumberland Yeo
WALKER George W. MM Cpl 2527 1/4th East Yorkshire Regt
WALKER George William MM Cpl 9119 2nd Yorkshire Regt KIA 8.5.18.
WALKER Harold MM Dvr 776585 RFA
WALKER Harold J. MM S/Sjt Armourer T/987 Army Ordnance Corps
WALKER Harry MM Sjt 236169 248 Fd Coy Royal Engineers
WALKER Harry MM Cpl 871 1 Corps Cyclist Bn Army Cyclist Corps
WALKER Harry MM Pte 304521 15th Bn Tank Corps
WALKER Harry MM L/Cpl 243742 1/6th Cheshire Regt
WALKER Harry MM Pte 18747 21st Manchester Regt
WALKER Harry MM+Bar Pte 40726 1st Royal Dublin Fusiliers
WALKER Harry MM Pte 34561 5th West Riding Regt
WALKER Harry MM Pte 44893 RAMC
WALKER Harry "DCM,MM+Bar" Sjt 707 4th Bn GMGR KIA 20.10.18.
WALKER Harry MM Gnr 45136 42 Bde RFA
WALKER Harry MM Pte 9253 1st Royal Fusiliers
WALKER Harry "MM,MID" Sjt 11834 7th York & Lancaster Regt
WALKER Harry MM Pte 225221 East Yorkshire Regt
WALKER Harry A. MM Pte 34293 West Yorkshire Regt
WALKER Harry Mortimer MM Pte 21184 12th Yorkshire Regt
WALKER Harry W. MM Pte 40893 Rifle Brigade
WALKER Henry MM Bdr 632 B/156 Bde RFA
WALKER Henry MM L/Cpl 10989 6th Leicestershire Regt
WALKER Henry MM Pte 36402 Yorkshire Regt
WALKER Henry MM Gnr 91887 A/47 Bde RFA KIA 6.5.18.
WALKER Henry MM Pte 5097 12th Royal Fusiliers KIA 31.7.17.
WALKER Henry J. MM Sjt 21653 74 Div Ammn Col RFA
WALKER Herbert MM Pte A/202005 2nd King's Royal Rifle Corps
WALKER Herbert MM L/Sjt 15469 8th Somerset Light Infantry
WALKER Herbert W. MM Pte 354538 8th Middlesex Regt
WALKER J. MM Pte 301335 89 Fd Amb RAMC
WALKER J.W. MM Gnr 2282 Tank Corps
WALKER Jack MM Dvr 489996 Royal Engineers att RFA.
WALKER James MM Pte 32123 Lancashire Fusiliers
WALKER James MM Pte 23323 7th Seaforth Highlanders
WALKER James MM Pte 333959 9th Highland Light Infantry
WALKER James "DCM,MM+Bar" Sjt 13710 10th West Riding Regt
WALKER James MM Pte 7816 11th Lancashire Fusiliers
WALKER James MM Gnr 44869 D/104 Bde RFA KIA 6.8.16.
WALKER James MM Gnr 96681 D/157 Bde RFA KIA 29.9.18.
WALKER James MM Pte 37406 Lancashire Fusiliers
WALKER James MM Pte 34130 1st Worcestershire Regt
WALKER James B. MM L/Cpl 13358 11th Border Regt
WALKER James C. MM Gnr 125344 312 Bde RFA
WALKER James D. MM Pte 251001 1/6th Arg & Suth Highlanders
WALKER James Mitchell MM Gnr 46588 X/9 Med TM Bty RGA
WALKER James W. MM Cpl 63194 RFA
WALKER James William MM Gnr 93999 RFA
WALKER Jesse MM Gnr 312482 2/1(North Midland)Hy Bty RGA
WALKER John MM Gnr 203919 464 Bty 179 Bde RFA
WALKER John MM Pte 26511 5th Border Regt
WALKER John MM Pte 13938 Royal Highlanders
WALKER John MM Sjt 229605 Royal Fusiliers
WALKER John MM Pte 240910 1/6th West Yorkshire Regt KIA 25.4.18.
WALKER John MM Sjt T/576 Army Service Corps
WALKER John MM Pte 10116 2nd York & Lancaster Regt
WALKER John MM Pte 17640 8th Somerset Light Infantry
WALKER John MM Pte 1453 Royal Highlanders
WALKER John MM Pte 13450 Royal Scots
WALKER John "MM,MID" Sjt 7625 RFA
WALKER John "MM,MID" Pte 2190 Connaught Rangers
WALKER John MM L/Cpl 241671 Gordon Highlanders
WALKER John A. MM Pte 200673 Royal Sussex Regt
WALKER John Benson MM Gnr 46134 13 Siege Bty RGA
WALKER John Charles MM CSM 2164 1/4th West Riding Regt KIA 3.9.16.
WALKER John Ernest Frederick MM Sjt 767 1/1st Essex Yeomanry
WALKER John H. MM Pte 26320 Yorkshire Regt
WALKER John James MM Sjt 15195 1/4th Cheshire Regt
WALKER John S. MM Pte 27677 5th Notts & Derby Regt
WALKER John Thomas MM Gnr 751416 4(Northumbrian)Bde RFA
WALKER John W. MM Sjt 316376 13th Royal Highlanders
WALKER John W. MM S/Sjt Fitter 291400 RGA
WALKER John W. MM Pte 267274 West Yorkshire Regt
WALKER John W. MM Pte C/7077 King's Royal Rifle Corps
WALKER John W. MM Dvr 32824 RFA
WALKER Johnstone MM Cpl 5041 2nd Dragoons
WALKER Joseph MM Pte B/1979 Rifle Brigade
WALKER Joseph MM Pte 28740 Durham Light Infantry
WALKER Joseph MM L/Cpl 14259 12th Cheshire Regt
WALKER Joseph MM Cpl 919 B/233 Bde RFA KIA 20.9.17.
WALKER Joseph MM Cpl 3745 8th York & Lancaster Regt KIA 17.9.17.
WALKER Joseph MM L/Cpl C/371 King's Royal Rifle Corps
WALKER Joseph "DCM,MM" Sjt 11630 Yorkshire Regt
WALKER Joseph MM Dvr 76402 RFA
WALKER Joseph Alexander MM Pte 723497 24th London Regt DOW 6.4.18.
WALKER Joseph Harold MM Cpl 23202 152 Bde RFA
WALKER Joseph J. MM Sjt 1243 Royal Fusiliers
WALKER Joseph W. MM Pte 203202 Manchester Regt
WALKER Joseph William MM L/Cpl 204130 5th Shropshire Light Infantry
WALKER Laurence L.B. MM L/Cpl 88835 Royal Engineers
WALKER Lawrence MM Dvr 82915 RFA
WALKER Lawrence John MM Spr 496540 478 Fd Coy Royal Engineers
WALKER Leonard MM Pte 10486 1st Royal Welsh Fusiliers
WALKER Lewis "DCM,MM" Cpl 3491 11th Rifle Brigade
WALKER Lewis F. MM Sjt 54185 25th Royal Welsh Fusiliers
WALKER Lot MM Pte 42915 19th Durham Light Infantry
WALKER Maxwell N. MM Cpl 38438 Royal Scots
WALKER Nathaniel G. MM Pte 200339 1/4th Royal Scots
WALKER Newman "DCM,MM,MIDx2" Bdr 160820 504 Bty 65 Bde RFA
WALKER Norman MM L/Cpl 11855 2nd Seaforth Highlanders
WALKER Percy A.T. MM Sjt 13919 8th Bedfordshire Regt
WALKER Percy Charles MM+Bar Sjt 21964 Machine Gun Corps
WALKER Percy T. MM Pte 16584 6th Oxf & Bucks Light Infantry
WALKER Peter Handley MM Sjt 841036 RFA
WALKER Peter S. MM Pte 353038 Highland Light Infantry
WALKER Phillip MM Pte 12404 5th Dorsetshire Regt
WALKER Ralph MM Pte 51768 18 Fd Amb RAMC
WALKER Reginald A. MM Cpl 106753 Royal Engineers
WALKER Reginald R. MM Spr 97655 Royal Engineers
WALKER Robert MM Pte 22583 6th Royal West Surrey Regt
WALKER Robert MM L/Cpl 42000 16th Highland Light Infantry
WALKER Robert MM Pte 240651 5/6th Scottish Rifles
WALKER Robert MM Pte 31089 2nd York & Lancaster Regt
WALKER Robert MM Sjt 414256 413 Fd Coy Royal Engineers
WALKER Robert MM Sjt 39685 42nd Bn Machine Gun Corps
WALKER Robert MM Sjt 8479 1st Royal Lancaster Regt
WALKER Robert MM Sjt 8825 2nd Royal West Surrey Regt
WALKER Robert MM L/Sjt 43418 2nd Gordon Highlanders KIA 26.10.17.
WALKER Robert MM Sjt 15202 11th Scottish Rifles
WALKER Robert A. MM L/Cpl 101187 Royal Engineers
WALKER Robert D. MM+Bar Sjt 330504 1/7th Liverpool Regt
WALKER Robert David MM Sjt 297931 714 Coy Labour Corps

WALKER Robert F. MM Pte 240880 1/6th Highland Light Infantry DOW 25.8.18.
WALKER Robert Purvis MM L/Cpl 3066 1/9th Durham Light Infantry
WALKER Robert Thomas MM Pte 266066 1/6th Royal Highlanders KIA 21.3.18.
WALKER Roderick Stewart MM Sjt 17766 15th Royal Scots
WALKER Roscoe Ernest MM Pte 333001 1/9th Liverpool Regt
WALKER S. MM Cpl 20730 Cheshire Regt
WALKER Samuel MM Pte 16214 9th Royal Inniskilling Fusiliers
WALKER Samuel MM Sjt 25871 B/168 Bde RFA
WALKER Samuel Clifford MM Sjt 2353 1/7th Liverpool Regt
WALKER Samuel J. MM CSM 207101 2nd Royal West Surrey Regt
WALKER Samuel J. MM Pte 270090 Durham Light Infantry
WALKER Saville MM Pte 73724 8 Fd Amb RAMC KIA 1.10.18.
WALKER Scott MM Cpl 34495 York & Lancaster Regt
WALKER Sidney William George MM Sjt 12087 7th Duke of Cornwall's LI
WALKER Stanley Fred Howard "MM,MSM" Sjt 921 Military Foot Police
WALKER Stephen MM Bdr 45690 11 Bde RFA
WALKER Stuart MM Sjt 10651 1st Royal Scots Fusiliers
WALKER Sydney MM+2 Bars Pte 18928 13th Liverpool Regt
WALKER Thomas MM Pte 101364 110 Fd Amb RAMC
WALKER Thomas MM Pte R/9118 2nd King's Royal Rifle Corps
WALKER Thomas MM Cpl 2854 1st Welsh Guards
WALKER Thomas MM L/Cpl 308103 Liverpool Regt
WALKER Thomas MM L/Cpl 10/11508 South Staffordshire Regt
WALKER Thomas MM CQMS 7056 1st Scottish Rifles
WALKER Thomas MM Sjt 28125 First Army Sig Coy Royal Engineers
WALKER Thomas Bernard MM+Bar L/Cpl 2569 1/1st HAC(Inf) KIA 18.4.17.
WALKER Thomas C. MM Cpl 485 RFA
WALKER Thomas F. MM Cpl 13305 11th Border Regt
WALKER Thomas H. MM L/Cpl 22815 15 Fd Coy Royal Engineers
WALKER Thomas H. MM Pte 13728 7th Leicestershire Regt
WALKER Thomas L. MM Pte 90917 Machine Gun Corps
WALKER Thomas P. MM Sjt 28130 31 Heavy Bty RGA
WALKER Thomas W. MM Pte 30698 East Lancashire Regt
WALKER Tom MM Pte 58953 RAMC
WALKER Vernon Dudley "DSO,MM(1427 L/Cpl 24th R Fus)" T/2Lt 34th Bn Machine Gun Corps
WALKER W. MM Dvr 6167 RFA
WALKER W. MM Pte 13791 1st Royal Scots
WALKER Walter MM+Bar Drummer 265782 5th West Riding Regt
WALKER Walter "DCM,MM" CSM 1140 1/4th A Coy Suffolk Regt KIA 15.7.16.
WALKER Walter MM Pte 3134 44 Coy Machine Gun Corps KIA 28.3.18.
WALKER Walter Herrick MM Pte 29231 Somerset Light Infantry
WALKER William MM Pte 24098 1st Gordon Highlanders
WALKER William MM Pte 46633 4th North Staffordshire Regt
WALKER William MM Cpl 14393 6th Lincolnshire Regt
WALKER William MM Pte 34976 16th Lancashire Fusiliers
WALKER William MM L/Cpl 155452 12th Bn Machine Gun Corps
WALKER William MM Sjt T4/043305 Army Service Corps
WALKER William MM Pte 15/9266 Royal Irish Rifles
WALKER William MM Pte 20/684 20th Northumberland Fusiliers KIA 1.7.16
WALKER William MM+Bar Cpl 2849 1/8th Durham Light Infantry
WALKER William MM Pte 38054 25th Northumberland Fusiliers KIA 28.3.18.
WALKER William MM Pte 6679 12th Middlesex Regt
WALKER William MM Sjt 16710 1st Leicestershire Regt
WALKER William MM Pte S/11485 1st Rifle Brigade
WALKER William MM L/Cpl 27637 109 Coy Machine Gun Corps
WALKER William MM Pte 16204 11th Durham Light Infantry
WALKER William MM Pte 9606 2nd Royal Scots
WALKER William A. MM Pte 345173 24th Royal Welsh Fusiliers
WALKER William A. MM Pte 69031 1st Devonshire Regt
WALKER William A. MM Sjt 106640 Royal Engineers
WALKER William Frederick MM Pte R/27473 13th King's Royal Rifle Corps DOW 10.3.18.
WALKER William G. MM Pte 201034 Shropshire Light Infantry
WALKER William H. MM Cpl 32267 8th Somerset Light Infantry
WALKER William H. MM Pte R/2387 11th King's Royal Rifle Corps
WALKER William H. MM Sjt 705885 RFA
WALKER William H. MM Pte 50019 1/6th Cheshire Regt
WALKER William H. MM+Bar L/Cpl 13138 6th Northamptonshire Regt
WALKER William H. MM Gnr 32981 A/177 Bde RFA Died 4.4.18.
WALKER William Henry MM Pte 12462 9th Royal Fusiliers
WALKER William Henry MM Sjt 15189 8th Royal Lancaster Regt
WALKER William J. MM L/Bdr 750839 RFA
WALKER William J. MM Pte 42820 6th Leicestershire Regt
WALKER William K. MM Gnr 154772 RGA
WALKER William Lindsay MM Gnr 93364 RFA
WALKER William S. MM Pte 19276 Royal Irish Rifles
WALKER William Walter MM Pte 53198 11th Royal Fusiliers KIA 18.9.18.
WALKER Wilson W. MM Dvr 48704 RFA
WALKINGSHAW John MM Pte 18/1062 12th Royal Irish Rifles
WALKINGTON Frederick J. MM Sjt 22591 RGA
WALKINGTON George R. MM Sjt 14891 23 Hy Bty RGA
WALKLAND Harry Bernard William MM Pte M2/053990 Army Service Corps att RAMC.
WALKLATE Joseph MM Sjt 14201 8th North Staffordshire Regt
WALKLEY Arthur F. MM Sjt 8898 2nd Gloucestershire Regt
WALL A.E. MM Spr 161431 Royal Engineers
WALL Alexander MM+Bar Cpl 34005 4th West Riding Regt
WALL Arthur MM L/Cpl 12704 2nd Grenadier Guards KIA 1.12.17.
WALL Edward MM Cpl 202763 2nd Worcestershire Regt
WALL Frederick C. MM L/Cpl 14454 10th Essex Regt
WALL Frederick J. MM Pte 41147 South Wales Borderers
WALL George MM Sjt 18905 Machine Gun Corps
WALL George H. MM Spr 30910 Royal Engineers
WALL George Meynell MM Cpl 39853 RFA
WALL Henry William MM Pte 3043 2/6th Gloucestershire Regt KIA 28.8.16
WALL James MM Bdr 39597 A/106 Bde RFA
WALL James H. MM Sjt 12581 228 Siege Bty RGA
WALL Joseph J. "MM,MSM" Sjt 9069 1st Scottish Rifles
WALL Lawrence MM CSM 72280 1/4th Cheshire Regt
WALL Leonard J. MM Pte 205039 Royal West Surrey Regt
WALL Lewis Harold MM Cpl R/3210 11th King's Royal Rifle Corps DOW 30.11.17.
WALL Matthew "MM,MID" Cpl 48586 99 Fd Coy Royal Engineers
WALL Percy MM 2nd Cpl 246833 1 Fd Svy Coy Royal Engineers
WALL Peter MM Pte 26623 Royal Inniskilling Fusiliers
WALL Richard MM Gnr 48541 391 Siege Bty RGA
WALL Richard MM CSM 8853 8th Shropshire Light Infantry KIA 18.9.18.
WALL Stanley G. MM Spr 87018 152 Fd Coy Royal Engineers
WALL Thomas E. MM Cpl 3102 2/1st HAC(Inf)
WALL Thomas Frederick MM Pte 1693 1/5th Northumberland Fusiliers
WALL W.J. "MM,MID" Cpl 260 East Kent Regt
WALL William MM Cpl B/1365 13th Rifle Brigade
WALL William MM Pte 146364 46th Bn Machine Gun Corps
WALL William MM Pte 15376 7th Bedfordshire Regt
WALL William MM+Bar Pte 12525 6th King's Own Scottish Borderers
WALL William J. MM Pte M2/099490 31 Div MT Coy Army Service Corps
WALL William John Henry MM Pte 25072 3rd Grenadier Guards
WALL William Owen MM Pte 27854 Royal Welsh Fusiliers
WALLACE Albert MM L/Cpl 482301 62 Div Sig Coy Royal Engineers DOW 21.10.18.
WALLACE Alexander MM Pte 20617 2nd Royal Scots DOW 3.9.18.
WALLACE Alexander MM Pte 11495 2nd Royal Scots
WALLACE Alexander MM L/Cpl 253862 Royal Engineers
WALLACE Alezander MM Cpl 22739 West Riding Regt
WALLACE Alfred MM CSM 240144 1/6th West Yorkshire Regt
WALLACE Archibald MM+Bar Sjt 202283 Royal Highlanders
WALLACE Archie MM L/Cpl 1676 1/5th Notts & Derby Regt
WALLACE Arthur MM Pte 70 RAMC
WALLACE Arthur R. MM 2nd Cpl 40952 Royal Engineers
WALLACE Charles MM Sjt 252087 1/6th Arg & Suth Highlanders
WALLACE Charles MM Sjt 223 2nd Gordon Highlanders
WALLACE Charles Claude "MC,MM(5031 Sjt 2DG),MID" 2Lt 1st East Yorkshire Regt
WALLACE Charles Henry MM Sjt 50808 Royal Warwickshire Regt
WALLACE Claude N. MM Sjt 6642 2nd Royal Dublin Fusiliers
WALLACE David MM Pte 4362 9th Royal Highlanders
WALLACE David John MM Pte 19283 2nd South Wales Borderers Real name Cyril Arthur FISHER.KIA 1.7.16.
WALLACE Edwin M. MM Cpl 19966 King's Own Scottish Borderers
WALLACE Frank MM L/Cpl 15005 8th Border Regt
WALLACE George MM L/Cpl 26936 Royal Scots
WALLACE George MM Pte 22833 9th Royal Inniskilling Fusiliers

WALLACE George MM L/Cpl 203391 9th Durham Light Infantry
WALLACE George MM Cpl M2/048977 21 Mot Amb Convoy Army Service Corps
WALLACE George Archibald MM L/Cpl 139677 Royal Engineers
WALLACE George Nicol MM Pte 43101 Highland Light Infantry
WALLACE Gordon MM Gnr 72283 RFA
WALLACE Henry "MM,MID" L/Sjt 1966 9th Seaforth Highlanders
WALLACE Henry Edward MM Cpl 27174 11th West Yorkshire Regt KIA 11.10.17.
WALLACE Henry Ewart MM Sjt 82081 Tunnelling Coy Royal Engineers
WALLACE Henry J. MM Bdr 44501 'N' Bty RHA
WALLACE Herbert J. MM Pte 308435 4 Tank Supply Coy Tank Corps
WALLACE Hubert J.H. MM Pte MS/244 Army Service Corps att HQ III Corps.
WALLACE J. MM Pte 16993 5th Royal Irish Fusiliers
WALLACE J. MM Pte 265812 1/6th Seaforth Highlanders
WALLACE James MM L/Cpl 10210 1st Scots Guards
WALLACE James MM Cpl 41252 38 Bde RFA
WALLACE James MM L/Cpl 1873 1/6th Royal Highlanders
WALLACE James MM L/Cpl 1676 9th Highland Light Infantry KIA 15.7.16.
WALLACE James MM Sjt 530035 15th London Regt
WALLACE James MM Pte M2/080908 Army Service Corps
WALLACE James R. MM Pte 859 1st Welsh Guards
WALLACE John MM Pte 11498 5th Cameron Highlanders
WALLACE John MM L/Cpl 325 2nd Gordon Highlanders
WALLACE John MM Pte 1929 8th Seaforth Highlanders
WALLACE John MM+Bar BSM 40845 B/88 Bde RFA
WALLACE John MM Pte 24715 12th Highland Light Infantry
WALLACE John MM Cpl 18436 Royal Scots
WALLACE John D. MM Sjt 25881 Machine Gun Corps
WALLACE John J. MM L/Sjt 17/754 17th Northumberland Fusiliers
WALLACE John Leo Casares Smith MM Cpl 3728 1/10th Liverpool Regt
WALLACE John Ronald "MM,CG(B)" Gnr 6846 RFA
WALLACE John S. MM Cpl 7269 Arg & Suth Highlanders
WALLACE Michael MM Sjt 77115 403 Bty RFA
WALLACE Michael "DCM,MM" BSM 771561 50 Div Ammn Col RFA
WALLACE Michael MM Sjt 12187 RFA
WALLACE N. MM Bdr 125902 RFA
WALLACE Percy Arnott MM L/Cpl 146427 'E' Special Coy Royal Engineers
WALLACE Robert MM Cpl 88259 51st Bn Machine Gun Corps
WALLACE Robert MM+Bar L/Sjt 2186 Royal Highlanders
WALLACE Robert MM Cpl 265417 1/7th Scottish Rifles
WALLACE Robert MM Cpl 59449 11th Royal Scots
WALLACE Robert MM L/Sjt 25149 6th East Kent Regt
WALLACE Robert MM Pte 39203 Royal Scots
WALLACE Robert G. MM Pte 24743 1st Scottish Rifles
WALLACE Thomas MM Gnr 10117 RFA
WALLACE Thomas MM Spr 43589 Royal Engineers
WALLACE Thomas S. MM Sjt 265178 1/6th Gordon Highlanders
WALLACE Walter MM+Bar Sjt 482138 62 Div Sig Coy Royal Engineers
WALLACE Walter M. "DCM,MM" Pte 20795 18 Fd Amb RAMC
WALLACE William MM L/Cpl 330185 1/8th Royal Scots
WALLACE William MM Pte 19739 1/4th Gordon Highlanders
WALLACE William MM+Bar Sjt 82442 40th Bn Machine Gun Corps
WALLACE William MM Pte 202263 1/5th Lancashire Fusiliers
WALLACE William MM Pte 7791 1st Scots Guards
WALLACE William L. MM Spr 29473 Royal Engineers
WALLACE William N. MM Sjt 6886 10th Northumberland Fusiliers
WALLAND Joseph "MM,MID" Pte 5762 11th Hussars
WALLARD Thomas MM Pte 204246 Liverpool Regt
WALLBANK Reginald D. MM Pte 25653 1st South Wales Borderers
WALLDER Henry W. MM Cpl 280714 2/4th London Regt
WALLEN A. MM Sjt 62375 69 Bty 179 Bde RFA
WALLEN Henry William "MM+Bar,CG(B)" CSM 40981 9th Royal Inniskilling Fusiliers
WALLEN John C. MM Pte 10544 Royal West Kent Regt
WALLER Alfred MM Pte 64636 108 Coy Labour Corps
WALLER Dennis "DCM,MM" L/Cpl 24989 2nd West Riding Regt DOW 22.10.18.
WALLER Edward James MM Dvr 950728 B/235 Bde RFA
WALLER Fred MM L/Cpl 20962 Manchester Regt
WALLER Frederick MM L/Cpl 265643 1/1st Hertfordshire Regt
WALLER Frederick J. MM Pte 60599 Royal Fusiliers
WALLER Frederick W. MM L/Cpl 27808 7th Shropshire Light Infantry
WALLER Frederick W. "MM,MID" Cpl 549974 Royal Engineers
WALLER George "MM,MID" Sjt 18472 RAMC
WALLER George William MM Pte S/7065 13th Rifle Brigade
WALLER Herbert MM Pte 11766 Lincolnshire Regt
WALLER Herbert MM+Bar L/Cpl 45497 Royal Engineers
WALLER Herbert "MM,MID" Sjt 9153 2nd West Riding Regt
WALLER Herbert J. MM Bdr 341111 RGA
WALLER J.H. "DCM,MM" Sjt 5800 25 Sqn Royal Flying Corps
WALLER James MM Pte 16514 2nd Grenadier Guards
WALLER James MM Pte 200700 Yorkshire Regt
WALLER James William MM Cpl Fitter 755318 251 Bde RFA Died 21.5.18.
WALLER John MM BQMS 35145 'G' Bty RHA
WALLER Percy MM 2nd Cpl 440281 Royal Engineers
WALLER R.C. MM Pte 41727 2nd Suffolk Regt
WALLER Reginald MM L/Cpl 25168 Royal West Surrey Regt att MGC.
WALLER Thomas MM Pte Shoeing Smith TS/10337 34 Div Train Army Service Corps
WALLER Walter MM Pte 330769 1/9th Highland Light Infantry
WALLER William H. "MM,MID" Cpl 10465 1st Royal Fusiliers
WALLER William J. MM+Bar Pte 10846 6th Royal West Kent Regt
WALLEY Albert MM+Bar L/Cpl 36311 East Yorkshire Regt
WALLEY Arthur MM Pte 15633 12th Cheshire Regt
WALLEY Frank MM Cpl 33180 16 Fd Amb RAMC att Shropshire LI. KIA 18.9.18.
WALLEY George MM Cpl 28891 130 Fd Amb RAMC
WALLEY George Arthur MM Pte 240604 1/5th York & Lancaster Regt
WALLEY Philip "MM,MID" L/Cpl 11249 7th Shropshire Light Infantry
WALLHEAD George MM Pte 2445 1/1st Lincolnshire Yeomanry DOW 7.4.18.
WALLHEAD Walter MM Spr 159968 Royal Engineers
WALLINGTON Arthur J. MM L/Cpl 28239 Somerset Light Infantry
WALLINGTON David James MM Pte 9961 1st Middlesex Regt Died 24.6.18.
WALLINGTON George MM+Bar Sjt 265292 1st Oxf & Bucks Light Infantry
WALLINGTON John Charles MM Pte 4606 2nd Royal West Surrey Regt
WALLINGTON William "MM,MIDx2" Cpl 7612 2nd East Lancashire Regt
WALLIS Albert MM+Bar Cpl 7126 12th Middlesex Regt
WALLIS Albert MM Pte 18226 1st Coldstream Guards
WALLIS Alfred MM L/Cpl A/3064 9th King's Royal Rifle Corps
WALLIS Alfred G. MM Pte 63750 10th Royal West Surrey Regt
WALLIS Arthur MM L/Cpl 204 1st Royal Fusiliers
WALLIS Arthur MM Spr 10299 Royal Engineers
WALLIS Charles MM Sjt 8138 6th Lincolnshire Regt
WALLIS Edgar S. MM Cpl 315090 5th London Regt
WALLIS Ernest MM Sjt 8506 1st Royal Berkshire Regt
WALLIS Ernest "MM,MID" Sjt 43526 Royal Engineers
WALLIS Frederick Charles MM Pte 241358 1/4th North Lancashire Regt KIA 3.5.18.
WALLIS George MM Pte 21069 6th Dragoons
WALLIS George C. MM Gnr 109628 RGA
WALLIS George T. MM Cpl 92049 154 Coy Labour Corps
WALLIS Harold Robert "MC,MM(8773 Cpl London Regt)" 2Lt 5th att 2nd South Staffordshire Regt
WALLIS Harry Collier MM+Bar Cpl 72446 4th Royal Fusiliers KIA 24.10.18.
WALLIS Harry L. MM Pte 205348 7th Royal West Surrey Regt
WALLIS John E. MM Pte CMT/1656 2 Div Train Army Service Corps
WALLIS Michael George MM+Bar Bdr 46075 C/88 Bde RFA DOW 8.10.17.
WALLIS Percy MM Cpl 10148 Royal West Kent Regt
WALLIS Robert MM Pte 60639 8th Royal Fusiliers KIA 30.11.17.
WALLIS Robert MM Sjt 19/178 Durham Light Infantry
WALLIS Robert E. MM Pte R/2102 11th King's Royal Rifle Corps
WALLIS Thomas H. MM Pte 3079 Middlesex Regt
WALLIS Tom MM L/Sjt 306209 8th West Yorkshire Regt
WALLIS William MM Pte 291612 1/8th Scottish Rifles
WALLIS William MM Sjt 124917 Royal Engineers
WALLIS William MM Cpl 15665 7th Duke of Cornwall's LI
WALLIS William A.C. MM Cpl 18238 Oxf & Bucks Light Infantry
WALLIS William D. MM L/Cpl 12423 1st Grenadier Guards
WALLIS William J. MM Sjt 32290 4th North Staffordshire Regt
WALLOND Alfred MM Pte 11137 7th Royal West Kent Regt

WALLS Charles MM Spr 42968 Royal Engineers
WALLS David MM Cpl 48383 43 Bde RFA
WALLS Fred MM Sjt 13008 5th Dorsetshire Regt
WALLS George Henry MM Pte 49247 13th Cheshire Regt DOW 13.8.17.
WALLS George Henry MM Pte 6569 1st East Surrey Regt
WALLS James MM+Bar Sjt 12137 1st Royal Dublin Fusiliers
WALLS John MM Piper 4374 Arg & Suth Highlanders
WALLS Peter MM L/Cpl 1501 1/7th Arg & Suth Highlanders
WALLS Walter J. "DCM,MM" CSM 9905 8th Royal Sussex Regt
WALLSGROVE John "DCM+Bar,MM" CSM 9650 1st & 14th Royal Welsh Fusiliers
WALLWORK Arthur MM Cpl 254422 Royal Engineers att RFA.
WALLWORK Harold MM Sjt 61419 114 Siege Bty RGA
WALLWORK John W. MM Sjt 97157 RFA
WALLWORK Samuel MM Sjt 16328 7th Shropshire Light Infantry KIA 14.7.16.
WALLWORK Thomas MM Pte 15698 1st North Lancashire Regt DOW 15.7.17.
WALLWORTH Harry MM Pte 277636 2nd Manchester Regt
WALMSLEY Allen MM Cpl 15872 V/30 Heavy TM Bty RFA
WALMSLEY Anthony MM Sjt TT/02598 Army Veterinary Corps
WALMSLEY David C. MM Sjt 200055 1/5th Arg & Suth Highlanders
WALMSLEY Edward MM Gnr 116800 RFA
WALMSLEY Edwin MM Pte 68056 RAMC
WALMSLEY F. MM L/Sjt 19912 7th South Staffordshire Regt
WALMSLEY Gillies E. MM Cpl 202633 1/7th Royal Highlanders
WALMSLEY Harold MM Cpl 761443 28th London Regt
WALMSLEY Henry MM Pte 332785 Liverpool Regt att MGC.
WALMSLEY Herbert MM Sjt 16466 8th East Lancashire Regt
WALMSLEY Horace MM Dvr 26832 C/90 Bde RFA
WALMSLEY J. MM Pte 32633 Essex Regt
WALMSLEY John MM Sjt 37871 2nd Lancashire Fusiliers
WALMSLEY John MM L/Cpl 201521 1/4th North Lancashire Regt KIA 20.9.17.
WALMSLEY John W. MM Gnr 5285 RFA
WALMSLEY Joseph MM Pte 92098 11th Notts & Derby Regt
WALMSLEY Ralph MM L/Sjt R/13100 11th King's Royal Rifle Corps DOW 30.11.17.
WALMSLEY Richard MM Gnr 800531 C/230 Bde RFA
WALMSLEY Robert MM Cpl 29485 11th East Lancashire Regt KIA 28.9.18.
WALMSLEY Sydney "DCM,MM,MSM" Bdr 81995 D/173 Bde RFA
WALMSLEY William MM Pte 83114 55 Fd Amb RAMC DOW 28.11.17.
WALMSLEY William Rigby MM L/Cpl 241967 1/6th South Staffordshire Regt
WALNE Richard MM Pte 252232 Lancashire Fusiliers
WALPOLE Charles H. MM Sjt 16599 1st Northamptonshire Regt
WALPOLE Ernest E. MM Pte 3/7188 1st Norfolk Regt
WALPOLE Herbert MM Pte 39161 11th Bn Machine Gun Corps
WALPOLE Hubert MM Sjt 240665 Leicestershire Regt
WALPOLE John W. MM Pte 201993 Middlesex Regt
WALPOLE Thomas MM Pte 62191 RAMC
WALROND George H. MM L/Cpl 9127 Manchester Regt
WALSH Abraham MM Pte 10/1308 10th East Yorkshire Regt
WALSH Abraham MM Pte 16501 5/6th Scottish Rifles
WALSH Arthur MM+Bar Cpl 165861 RGA
WALSH Benjamin C. MM Pte 37093 RAMC
WALSH Bernard E. MM Bdr 881126 65 Bde RFA
WALSH Cecil MM Pte 200320 West Riding Regt
WALSH Daniel MM Sjt 25693 11th Royal West Surrey Regt
WALSH David MM Cpl 266631 Liverpool Regt
WALSH Edmund MM Pte 73303 RAMC
WALSH Edward MM Pte 48240 13th Royal Inniskilling Fusiliers
WALSH Edward A. MM Sjt 52533 Machine Gun Corps(Cavalry)
WALSH Ernest MM Pte 467798 1/7th Liverpool Regt
WALSH Ernest J. MM Pte 11765 1st Irish Guards
WALSH Frank MM Pte 73308 RAMC
WALSH Harry MM Pte 23968 9th Lancashire Fusiliers DOW 31.10.17.
WALSH Henry Joseph MM Pte M/020656 16 Div MT Coy Army Service Corps
WALSH Herbert MM Spr 17306 98 Fd Coy Royal Engineers KIA 2.11.18.
WALSH Herbert James MM Pte 4481 1/8th Notts & Derby Regt
WALSH James MM Pte 12046 16th Lancashire Fusiliers
WALSH James MM Pte 41477 15th West Yorkshire Regt KIA 27.3.18.
WALSH James MM Cpl M2/081082 51 Div Train Army Service Corps
WALSH James MM Sjt 14421 7th East Lancashire Regt
WALSH James MM Cpl 6819 RAMC
WALSH James MM Pte 8549 1st Royal Munster Fusiliers
WALSH James MM L/Cpl 7724 2nd Border Regt
WALSH James MM Spr 444371 42 Div Sig Coy Royal Engineers KIA 7.7.17.
WALSH James "MM,MSM" L/Cpl P4596 Military Mounted Police
WALSH James MM Sjt 9927 1st Royal Irish Rifles
WALSH James MM Pte 275590 1/7th Manchester Regt
WALSH James H. MM Pte 37150 12th Manchester Regt
WALSH James W. MM Bdr 92881 111 Hy Bty RGA
WALSH John MM L/Sjt 5571 1st Middlesex Regt
WALSH John MM Pte 27172 13th Welsh Regt
WALSH John MM Pte 242096 1/5th Seaforth Highlanders
WALSH John MM Pte 202760 5th Liverpool Regt
WALSH John MM L/Cpl 23285 104 Coy 35th Bn Machine Gun Corps
WALSH John MM Spr 27260 2 Div Sig Coy Royal Engineers
WALSH John MM Cpl 18169 8th Royal Lancaster Regt
WALSH John MM Sjt 9889 1st Royal Irish Rifles
WALSH John MM Pte 1506 9th Royal Munster Fusiliers DOW 12.2.19.
WALSH John MM Pte 13269 2nd Royal Dublin Fusiliers
WALSH John MM Pte 18724 1st East Lancashire Regt KIA 11.4.18.
WALSH John Henry MM Cpl 57860 36 Div Sig Coy Royal Engineers
WALSH John Henry "MM,DM(B)" Cpl 11302 1st Devonshire Regt
WALSH John J. MM Pte 52317 Liverpool Regt
WALSH John T. MM L/Bdr 293641 136 Hy Bty RGA
WALSH Joseph MM+Bar Pte 22119 6th Northamptonshire Regt KIA 24.4.18.
WALSH Joseph MM Pte 11312 6th Border Regt
WALSH Joseph MM Pte 44634 Manchester Regt
WALSH Joseph Gerald MM L/Cpl 246052 'C' Corps Sig Coy Royal Engineers DOW 26.4.18.
WALSH Martin MM Sjt 6745 2nd Royal Dublin Fusiliers KIA 1.6.17.
WALSH Maurice MM Pte 14386 5th South Wales Borderers
WALSH Michael "MM,MID" Cpl 8495 50 Siege Bty RGA
WALSH Michael MM Dvr 37714 RFA
WALSH Michael MM Gnr 81806 B/54 Bde RFA
WALSH Michael MM Bdsm 8043 2nd Royal Welsh Fusiliers
WALSH Patrick MM L/Sjt 19488 3rd Grenadier Guards KIA 23.8.18.
WALSH Patrick MM Pte 37733 10th Yorkshire Light Infantry KIA 26.10.17.
WALSH Percival Henry MM Gnr 836121 RFA
WALSH Percy MM CQMS 7340 1st Scots Guards
WALSH Peter MM Pte 88236 Liverpool Regt
WALSH Peter MM Pte 18886 7 Fd Amb RAMC
WALSH Peter MM Cpl 15111 16th Lancashire Fusiliers
WALSH Richard MM Pte 11102 6th Royal Irish Regt DOW 3.9.16.
WALSH Richard MM Gnr 63273 45 Bty 42 Bde RFA
WALSH Robert MM Pte 200775 1st Lancashire Fusiliers
WALSH Rupert Sharpe "DSO,MM(1322 Sjt)" Lt 4th Gordon Highlanders
WALSH S. MM L/Sjt 200256 Manchester Regt
WALSH Shaw MM Pte 15993 6th North Lancashire Regt
WALSH Stanley F. MM Pte 9469 Suffolk Regt
WALSH Stephen MM Pte 300956 1/7th Arg & Suth Highlanders
WALSH Thomas MM Pte 15749 2nd York & Lancaster Regt DOW 24.10.18.
WALSH Thomas MM Cpl 14223 8th South Staffordshire Regt
WALSH Thomas MM L/Cpl 11804 9th Cheshire Regt
WALSH Thomas MM Pte 72812 Machine Gun Corps
WALSH Thomas Francis MM Pte 38698 9th York & Lancaster Regt
WALSH William MM Pte 202228 Royal Welsh Fusiliers
WALSH William E. MM Cpl 64809 35 Bde RFA
WALSH William J. MM Bdr 202604 RGA
WALSH William P. MM CSM 200069 2/4th Hampshire Regt
WALSHAM George A. MM Sjt 42321 12th Manchester Regt
WALSHAM James R.M. "MM,MID" Sjt 11699 2nd Scottish Rifles
WALSHAW James C. MM Gnr Shoeing Smith 760802 27 Bty 32 Bde RFA
WALSHAW Norman MM Sjt 14729 10th Yorkshire Regt KIA 1.7.16.
WALSHE Patrick MM Cpl 10758 2nd Royal Irish Regt KIA 14.7.16.
WALSHE Thomas F. MM L/Cpl 147635 37th Bn Machine Gun Corps
WALSTER A. MM Sjt 275025 Yeomanry
WALSTER John Thomas MM Sjt 23207 34 Div Ammn Col RFA
WALSTER Richard H. MM Bdr 38179 6 Siege Bty RGA
WALSTOW Herbert MM Sjt 75742 24th Royal Fusiliers

WALSTOW William Henry MM L/Cpl 15646 23 Fd Cdoy Royal Engineers DOW 20.5.18.
WALTER Arthur MM Sjt 4924 18th Hussars KIA 21.3.18.
WALTER Arthur Denzil "DCM,MM" Sjt 9830 1st Royal Berkshire Regt
WALTER Charles MM Bdr 73266 32 Bde RFA
WALTER Claud MM Pte 2269 7th East Kent Regt
WALTER Ernest W. MM Sjt MS/1601 704 Coy Army Service Corps
WALTER H. MM L/Cpl 12693 West Riding Regt
WALTER Henry William MM Sjt 630737 1/20th London Regt
WALTER John W. MM CSM T/18657 3 Div Train Army Service Corps
WALTER Justinian Hodson MM Sjt 31745 RAMC
WALTER Lewis MM Cpl 94243 C/62 Bde RFA
WALTER Percy Edward MM Pte 555341 16th London Regt
WALTER Robert MM Pte 10652 8th Cheshire Regt
WALTER Thomas Richard MM Pte 11960 7th Oxf & Bucks Light Infantry Died 9.7.17.
WALTERS A. MM Cpl 94042 Royal Flying Corps
WALTERS Albert MM Gnr 244444 RFA
WALTERS Albert L. MM Sjt 250225 1/6th Durham Light Infantry
WALTERS Albert William MM Gnr 97998 B/48 Bde RFA
WALTERS Arthur E. MM L/Cpl 92750 Royal Engineers
WALTERS Ernest Alfred MM Sjt 51434 RFA
WALTERS Evan MM Pte 73757 21 Coy Machine Gun Corps
WALTERS Francis MM Pte 656 12th Lancers
WALTERS Fred MM Pte 407123 25th Liverpool Regt
WALTERS Frederick J. MM Pte 7778 1st Devonshire Regt
WALTERS Frederick Thomas MM Pte 17240 2nd Worcestershire Regt KIA 10.4.18.
WALTERS George MM Spr 155853 Royal Engineers
WALTERS George MM L/Cpl 241557 Royal Lancaster Regt
WALTERS H. MM Pte 15942 Royal West Surrey Regt
WALTERS Harold MM Pte 14568 1st East Kent Regt
WALTERS Henry MM Pte B/203129 9th Rifle Brigade KIA 20.8.17.
WALTERS Henry Samuel MM Pte 25277 Grenadier Guards
WALTERS Herbert MM Pte 28113 10th Royal Warwickshire Regt
WALTERS Howard J.P. MM Pte 57043 24th Welsh Regt
WALTERS Ivor R. MM Cpl 203244 11th Essex Regt
WALTERS John MM Dvr 37938 RFA
WALTERS John MM Pte 336 1st Welsh Guards
WALTERS John MM Pte 24495 Royal Welsh Fusiliers
WALTERS John A. MM Cpl 241182 5th Devonshire Regt
WALTERS Joseph MM Pte 10185 Royal Fusiliers
WALTERS Sam MM Pte 83585 30th Bn Machine Gun Corps
WALTERS Stanley G. MM Sjt 10109 8th Devonshire Regt
WALTERS Thomas MM Pte 43570 16 Fd Amb RAMC
WALTERS Thomas MM Sjt 5826 1 Siege Coy R Monmouth RE
WALTERS Thomas Francis MM L/Cpl 240466 1/8th Worcestershire Regt KIA 9.10.17.
WALTERS Tom S. MM L/Cpl 4114 23rd Royal Fusiliers
WALTERS Walter G. MM Gnr 128667 'O' Bty RHA
WALTERS William MM Sjt T/28835 Army Service Corps
WALTERS William MM Pte 40687 Lincolnshire Regt
WALTERS William E. MM Gnr 281175 34 Siege Bty RGA
WALTERS William H. MM+Bar Pte R/3082 13th King's Royal Rifle Corps
WALTERS William Henry MM CQMS 104410 Labour Corps
WALTON A. MM Pte 54309 141 Fd Amb. RAMC
WALTON Adam MM Pte 203992 Durham Light Infantry
WALTON Albert Bertie MM Sjt R/3871 King's Royal Rifle Corps DOW 16.9.18.
WALTON Andrew MM L/Cpl 43311 Royal Highlanders
WALTON Arnold MM Pte 1330 1/6th Cheshire Regt
WALTON Arnold MM+Bar Sjt 1099 7 Fd Amb RAMC DOW 23.8.18.
WALTON B. MM Pte 341378 64 Fd Amb RAMC
WALTON Barker MM Sjt 444440 Royal Engineers
WALTON Bertie MM Sjt 14892 2nd Grenadier Guards KIA 1.12.17.
WALTON Brooks MM Pte 99079 10th Royal Fusiliers
WALTON Cecil MM Pte 73312 RAMC
WALTON Charles MM Sjt 61100 RFA
WALTON Charles MM Sjt 24499 11th Cheshire Regt
WALTON Charles W. MM Sjt 350787 2/7th London Regt
WALTON Edward MM Pte 242651 5th West Riding Regt
WALTON Edward "MM,MID" Pte 9024 RAMC
WALTON Ernest MM Pte 10515 7th East Surrey Regt
WALTON Ernest P.L. MM L/Cpl 44715 Welsh Regt
WALTON Francis J. MM Pte 20236 Bedfordshire Regt
WALTON Fred MM CSM 2538 2nd King's Royal Rifle Corps KIA 15.9.16
WALTON Frederick G. "MM,MID" Sjt 8780 2nd Northamptonshire Regt
WALTON Frederick G. MM Pte 275604 1/7th Manchester Regt
WALTON Frederick William "MM,MSM" Cpl 69350 33 TM Bty RFA
WALTON George MM L/Cpl 703408 1/23rd London Regt KIA 5.4.18.
WALTON George MM Cpl 305852 West Riding Regt
WALTON George MM Sjt 8379 2/6th Lancashire Fusiliers KIA 6.9.17.
WALTON George MM Sjt 51274 RGA
WALTON George A. MM Cpl 42591 Yorkshire Regt
WALTON Harold MM L/Cpl 102568 Machine Gun Corps
WALTON Harry MM Pte 242484 8th Royal Lancaster Regt
WALTON Harry MM Pte 2349 West Yorkshire Regt
WALTON Henry MM Pte 13630 Rifle Brigade
WALTON Herbert MM+Bar Sjt 42452 18th Bn Machine Gun Corps
WALTON Isaac Bell MM Sjt 18/1488 13th Durham Light Infantry
WALTON J. MM Pte 43731 Machine Gun Corps
WALTON James MM Cpl 21276 9th West Yorkshire Regt
WALTON John MM Sjt 31770 37 Siege Bty RGA KIA 26.7.18.
WALTON John MM Gnr 1340 RFA
WALTON John MM L/Cpl 21107 2nd Royal West Surrey Regt
WALTON John MM Gnr 79983 46 Siege Bty RGA
WALTON John F. MM Pte 44462 Machine Gun Corps
WALTON John M. MM Pte S/3644 Rifle Brigade
WALTON John Uriah MM Pte 33905 North Lancashire Regt
WALTON John William MM Cpl 67858 105 Siege Bty RGA
WALTON John William MM L/Sjt 242009 Northumberland Fusiliers
WALTON Joseph MM Sjt 17632 10th Yorkshire Regt KIA 11.4.17.
WALTON Joseph MM Sjt 17207 8th East Yorkshire Regt
WALTON Maurice Arthur MM Spr 36533 5 Fd Coy Royal Engineers
WALTON Norman MM Cpl 28778 Durham Light Infantry
WALTON Percy MM Pte 229365 Royal Fusiliers
WALTON Robert A. MM Sjt 2459 1/5th Cheshire Regt
WALTON Robert Allen MM Sjt 37 C/48 Bde RFA
WALTON Robert E. MM L/Cpl 123589 6th Bn Machine Gun Corps
WALTON Robert P. MM Pte 232918 2nd London Regt
WALTON Stanley MM Pte 235398 8th Middlesex Regt
WALTON Thomas Newton MM Pte 21/321 Durham Light Infantry
WALTON William MM Sjt 45582 4th North Staffordshire Regt
WALTON William "MM,MID" Cpl 12781 6 Fd Amb RAMC
WALTON William G. MM L/Cpl 26258 Royal Engineers
WALTON William E. MM Pte 1294 16 Fd Amb RAMC
WALWYK Ernest MM CSM 4859 3rd Rifle Brigade
WALWYN Henry MM Pte 302336 Manchester Regt
WAMBACH George MM Pte R/17859 2nd King's Royal Rifle Corps KIA 8.11.17.
WANE Thomas MM Dvr 56769 RFA
WANLESS A. MM Pte 37204 11th Royal West Surrey Regt
WANLESS Richard MM Pte 290837 Royal Highlanders
WANLESS Thomas MM Pte 25091 Royal West Surrey Regt
WANLESS Thomas William MM Gnr 46558 X/25 Med TM Bty RGA
WANLEY John MM Pte 21064 Northumberland Fusiliers
WANN Edward M. MM Dvr 755541 B/251 Bde RFA
WANNELL George "DCM,MM" Cpl 11958 1st & 2nd South Wales Borderers
WANSBON Rowland MM Cpl Shoeing Smith 60787 73 Bty 5 Bde RFA
WANSTALL Isaac MM Sjt 9195 2nd Middlesex Regt KIA 1.7.16.
WANT Ernest MM Pte 200417 2nd South Staffordshire Regt
WAPLES Albert G. MM Pte 18264 Northamptonshire Regt
WARBOYS Ernest MM Spr 197854 181 Tunnelling Coy Royal Engineers
WARBRICK Charles MM Pte 241013 5th Royal Lancaster Regt
WARBRICK George William MM Cpl 16626 Royal Lancaster Regt
WARBURTON Fred MM+Bar Sjt 53676 19th Durham Light Infantry
WARBURTON Fred MM Pte 20012 Yorkshire Light Infantry
WARBURTON George A. MM Sjt 42092 1st South Wales Borderers
WARBURTON Herbert MM Pte 251963 1/6th Manchester Regt DOW 2.10.18.
WARBURTON J. MM Pte 32641 Liverpool Regt
WARBURTON James MM Pte 201286 South Lancashire Regt
WARBURTON John MM L/Cpl 18261 XIX Corps Cyclist Bn Army Cyclist Corps
WARBURTON Joseph MM Pte M2/193659 402 MT Coy Army Service Corps DOW 6.9.18.
WARBURTON Joseph MM Cpl 12555 9th Cheshire Regt
WARBURTON Joseph MM Bdr 690430 RFA
WARBURTON Richard MM Sjt 13015 7th North Lancashire Regt
WARBURTON Samuel MM Pte 34941 19th Lancashire Fusiliers

WARBURTON Sidney Ernest "MC,MM(2187 L/Sjt)" 2Lt 1/4th York & Lancaster Regt
WARBURTON Thomas E. MM Pte 201247 Royal Lancaster Regt
WARBURTON Thomas P. MM Pte 201411 1/4th Northamptonshire Regt
WARBURTON William MM Pte 1842 7th Hussars
WARBURTON William H. MM Spr 41759 Royal Engineers
WARD A.L. MM Pte 290828 Middlesex Regt
WARD Albert MM Sjt 15135 8th Royal Irish Fusiliers
WARD Albert MM L/Sjt 9728 1st West Yorkshire Regt
WARD Albert A. MM Pte 12810 8th Leicestershire Regt
WARD Albert E. MM Sjt 34219 Labour Corps
WARD Albert F. MM Pte S/14543 Rifle Brigade
WARD Albert G. MM Pte 64391 15th Yorkshire Light Infantry
WARD Albert H. MM Spr 19509 17 Fd Coy Royal Engineers
WARD Albert T. MM Pte 24413 North Lancashire Regt
WARD Alfred MM Cpl 12821 8th Lincolnshire Regt
WARD Alfred F. MM Pte 2091 1/21st London Regt
WARD Arnold MM L/Cpl 17/1095 West Yorkshire Regt
WARD Arnold R. MM Pte 300054 5th London Regt
WARD Artemus MM Pte 26635 70 Coy Machine Gun Corps
WARD Arthur MM Pte 281599 18th Lancashire Fusiliers
WARD Arthur MM Gnr 72758 RFA
WARD Arthur MM Pte 240441 Lincolnshire Regt
WARD Arthur MM Pte B/200704 9th Rifle Brigade
WARD Arthur Jackson "MC+Bar,MM(6107 L/Sjt 10H)" 2Lt West Yorkshire Regt
WARD Cecil MM L/Cpl 240387 East Lancashire Regt
WARD Charles MM Pte 241215 Royal Scots Fusiliers
WARD Charles MM Sjt 157 18th Middlesex Regt
WARD Charles MM L/Cpl 18409 Royal Inniskilling Fusiliers
WARD Charles MM Sjt 17532 8th East Lancashire Regt
WARD Charles E. MM Dvr 50113 43 Bde RFA
WARD Charles William MM Pte 200912 1/4th Suffolk Regt Died 29.4.18.
WARD Clarence MM Bdr 4184 RFA
WARD Edgar George Capelhorn MM Sjt 530452 2/15th London Regt
WARD Edward MM Bdr 60520 A/87 Bde RFA
WARD Edward MM Cpl MS/164 1 Div Train Army Service Corps
WARD Edward MM Sjt 1335 1/17th London Regt
WARD Edward MM Sjt 75716 28 Bde RFA
WARD Edward G. MM Sjt 118964 147 Siege Bty RGA
WARD Edwin James MM Cpl 70919 'RR' Cable Section Royal Engineers Died 5.11.18.
WARD Ernest A. MM L/Cpl 4397 Machine Gun Corps
WARD Ernest G. MM Pte 3366 1st Welsh Guards
WARD Ernest G. MM Pte 12484 19th Manchester Regt
WARD Francis C. MM Pte 265994 4th Oxf & Bucks Light Infantry
WARD Francis Joseph Harrison MM L/Cpl 21867 32nd Bn Machine Gun Corps
WARD Frank MM Pte 421083 RAMC
WARD Frank MM L/Cpl P11908 Military Foot Police
WARD Frank MM Pte 64180 RAMC
WARD Fred MM Pte 66430 RAMC
WARD Frederick A. MM Gnr 80263 RGA
WARD Frederick C. MM L/Cpl 90030 Machine Gun Corps
WARD Frederick C.F. MM Pte 14181 Norfolk Regt
WARD Frederick G. MM Pte 8039 3rd Hussars
WARD Frederick J. MM Pte 1865 8th Royal Sussex Regt
WARD G. MM Sjt 241506 Lancashire Fusiliers
WARD George MM Pte 16742 1st Coldstream Guards
WARD George MM Pte 17975 Shropshire Light Infantry
WARD George MM Pte 15504 5th Northamptonshire Regt
WARD George MM Sjt 15627 17th Liverpool Regt KIA 12.10.16.
WARD George MM Pte M2/194750 Army Service Corps att 2/3(HC)Fd Amb RAMC.
WARD George Albert MM L/Cpl 548381 510 Fd Coy Royal Engineers
WARD George E. MM Bdr 211628 RGA
WARD George E. MM Pte 200240 Shropshire Light Infantry
WARD George E. MM Dvr 154656 RFA
WARD H. MM Gnr 21042 RGA
WARD H.J. MM Cpl 17768 10th Essex Regt
WARD Harold MM Pte 21482 11th Royal West Surrey Regt
WARD Harold MM Cpl 235921 1/1st Herefordshire Regt
WARD Harold G. MM+Bar Sjt 28364 East Yorkshire Regt
WARD Harold Wilson MM L/Cpl 13524 Notts & Derby Regt
WARD Harry MM Cpl 119456 260 Siege Bty RGA
WARD Harry MM L/Cpl 558 12th Yorkshire Light Infantry
WARD Harry "DCM,MM" CSM 1825 2nd Royal Warwickshire Regt
WARD Harry MM L/Cpl 13789 2nd Grenadier Guards KIA 1.12.17.
WARD Henry MM Sjt 220185 RGA
WARD Henry MM Pte 3380 16th Lancashire Fusiliers
WARD Henry MM Pte 13/735 13th York & Lancaster Regt
WARD Henry MM Sjt 40271 Norfolk Regt
WARD Henry MM Spr 89232 Royal Engineers
WARD Henry MM Cpl 39667 42nd Bn Machine Gun Corps
WARD Henry C. MM Pte 34688 Suffolk Regt
WARD Henry G. MM Pte M2/188237 Army Service Corps
WARD Herbert MM Pte 201817 4th Yorkshire Light Infantry
WARD Herbert MM Pte 41323 2nd Suffolk Regt
WARD Herbert MM Pte 473108 London Regt
WARD Herbert MM Pte 17682 7th South Staffordshire Regt
WARD Herbert Edward MM Gnr 610 C/64 Bde RFA
WARD Horace MM Sjt 15844 Lancashire Fusiliers
WARD Horace S.G. MM Pte 701828 23rd London Regt
WARD J. MM L/Cpl P/2996 Military Mounted Police
WARD Jack Havelock "DCM,MM+Bar" Cpl 200186 1/7th Middlesex Regt
WARD James MM Sjt 156288 182 Tunnelling Coy Royal Engineers
WARD James MM Cpl 201437 1/4th Lincolnshire Regt
WARD James MM L/Sjt S/3290 12th Rifle Brigade
WARD James Alexander or John MM Dvr 6293 RFA
WARD James Frederick MM Cpl 74150 35 Bde RFA
WARD James H. MM Cpl 200218 1/4th Cheshire Regt
WARD James H. MM+Bar Sjt 12464 24th & 1st Royal Fusiliers
WARD James H. MM Pte 32791 Border Regt
WARD James Pailing MM Pte 20536 8th Gloucestershire Regt KIA 18.4.18.
WARD James R.G. MM Cpl R/14244 King's Royal Rifle Corps
WARD James William "MM,MID" Pte M2/054822 Army Service Corps att 1/3(Highland)Fd Amb RAMC.
WARD John MM L/Cpl 10/1335 East Yorkshire Regt
WARD John MM Pte 202213 16th Lancashire Fusiliers
WARD John MM+Bar Sjt 11430 2nd Scots Guards
WARD John MM Pte 9913 2nd Royal Irish Regt DOW 27.9.18.
WARD John MM Pte 14134 7th Cameron Highlanders
WARD John MM L/Cpl 18803 9th Suffolk Regt
WARD John MM Pte 202874 Royal Scots
WARD John MM Pte 38446 Gloucestershire Regt
WARD John A. MM 2nd Cpl 127273 25 Div Sig Coy Royal Engineers
WARD John D. MM L/Bdr 70242 63 Div Ammn Col RFA
WARD John D. MM Pte 49024 13th Rifle Brigade
WARD John E. "DCM,MM" Pte 301 2nd Manchester Regt
WARD John E. MM Pte 202179 King's Own Scottish Borderers
WARD John H. MM Sjt 23707 8th North Staffordshire Regt
WARD John J.S. MM Cpl 2213 RAMC
WARD John W. MM Pte 15093 9th West Riding Regt
WARD John W. MM Pte 71538 Machine Gun Corps
WARD Joseph MM Sjt 29619 East Yorkshire Regt
WARD Joseph MM Pte 9065 1st South Staffordshire Regt
WARD Joseph MM Cpl 2672 2nd Life Guards
WARD Joseph MM Pte 23864 East Lancashire Regt
WARD Joseph MM Dvr T4/065326 292 Coy Army Service Corps
WARD Joseph MM Pte 15313 7th South Staffordshire Regt
WARD Joseph P. MM L/Cpl 3692 1/5th Lancashire Fusiliers
WARD Lambert MM L/Sjt 12869 Royal West Surrey Regt
WARD Leonard MM Pte 90783 29th Bn Machine Gun Corps
WARD Leonard MM Sjt 95190 420 Bty RFA
WARD Leonard MM L/Cpl 6631 12th Lancers
WARD Leonard C. MM Spr 312092 Royal Engineers
WARD Leonard W. MM Pte 73918 Notts & Derby Regt
WARD Michael MM+Bar Sjt 31198 RFA
WARD Norman MM Dvr 751685 A/250 Bde RFA
WARD Patrick MM L/Cpl 8442 1st Irish Guards
WARD Reginald MM Pte K/1577 22nd Royal Fusiliers
WARD Richard MM Pte 20458 11 Fd Amb RAMC
WARD Richard MM Pte 44484 20th Manchester Regt
WARD Richard Alexander MM Pte 72601 55 Coy Machine Gun Corps KIA 10.10.17.
WARD Richard B. MM Pte 74565 10th Manchester Regt
WARD Robert MM Pte 38919 2nd Yorkshire Light Infantry
WARD Robert MM Sjt 10449 East Yorkshire Regt
WARD Robert George MM Pte 13559 2nd Grenadier Guards KIA 26.5.18.
WARD Sidney MM+Bar Sjt 18820 Machine Gun Corps
WARD Sidney A.A. MM Pte 9478 Royal Berkshire Regt
WARD Stanley MM L/Cpl 29833 Wiltshire Regt

WARD Stephen MM Sjt 12467 South Staffordshire Regt
WARD Sydney MM Gnr 19764 RFA
WARD Sydney T.G. MM Pte 15686 6th Duke of Cornwall's LI
WARD Tedd MM Sjt 205674 9th Essex Regt
WARD Thomas MM Pte M2/188893 'P' Siege Park Army Service Corps
WARD Thomas MM Pte 241070 1/4th Leicestershire Regt KIA 24.9.18.
WARD Thomas MM Sjt 18202 Liverpool Regt
WARD Thomas MM Pte 11113 2nd South Staffordshire Regt
WARD Thomas MM Cpl 30783 9th Royal Inniskilling Fusiliers
WARD Thomas MM Pte 235653 5th West Riding Regt
WARD Thomas MM Spr 57847 36 Div Sig Coy Royal Engineers
WARD Thomas "MM,CG(It)" Pte 3637 1/4th Oxf & Bucks Light Infantry
WARD Thomas MM Pte 9995 Royal Highlanders
WARD Thomas MM+Bar Gnr 35089 RFA
WARD Thomas MM Pte 201886 7th Seaforth Highlanders KIA 21.7.18.
WARD Thomas E. MM+Bar Spr 231978 19 Div Sig Coy Royal Engineers
WARD Thomas Henry MM Gnr 204400 A/158 Bde RFA DOW 3.11.18.
WARD Thomas R. MM Spr 422118 Royal Engineers
WARD Tom MM Pte 18343 20th Manchester Regt KIA 4.10.18.
WARD W.A. MM Cpl 19930 Royal Flying Corps
WARD W.E. MM Pte 439050 RAMC
WARD Walter MM Pte 10681 HAC
WARD Walter James MM Pte 279154 2nd London Regt DOW 2.9.18.
WARD Wilfred Percy MM Sjt 87924 45 Coy Machine Gun Corps
WARD William MM Pte 250550 1/6th Durham Light Infantry KIA 5.10.18.
WARD William MM Pte 18/469 Northumberland Fusiliers
WARD William MM Spr 26133 Royal Engineers
WARD William "MM,MID" Sjt 11904 115 Coy Machine Gun Corps
WARD William MM Sjt 8728 1st Yorkshire Light Infantry
WARD William MM Sjt 41442 10th East Yorkshire Regt KIA 4.9.18.
WARD William MM Cpl 63955 RGA
WARD William MM Sjt 14371 2nd Grenadier Guards
WARD William MM Cpl 17846 1st King's Own Scottish Borderers KIA 16.8.17.
WARD William MM Cpl 377 8th Rifle Brigade
WARD William MM Pte 16461 Northamptonshire Regt
WARD William MM Sjt 80171 D/149 Bde RFA
WARD William MM Sjt 11904 West Yorkshire Regt
WARD William MM Sjt 13670 RFA KIA 29.7.18.
WARD William MM Cpl 15776 11th West Yorkshire Regt
WARD William MM Pte 61190 Royal Fusiliers
WARD William Charles MM Bdr 88111 RGA
WARD William E. MM Pte 40950 Royal Lancaster Regt
WARD William George MM Sjt 147102 Royal Engineers
WARD William Henry MM L/Cpl 66219 22 Div Sig Coy Royal Engineers
WARD William J. MM Pte 45716 4th Hampshire Regt
WARD William L. MM Dvr 7997 RFA
WARD William W. MM L/Cpl 3694 Suffolk Regt
WARDALE Harold MM Cpl 305449 11th Notts & Derby Regt
WARDALE William MM Pte 40308 1st Norfolk Regt
WARDALL Leonard E. MM Cpl 165860 101st Bn Machine Gun Corps
WARDELL Edward E. MM F/Sjt 26712 RFC/RAF
WARDELL Henry W. MM 2nd Cpl 24166 Royal Engineers
WARDELL J. MM Pte 386401 RAMC
WARDELL Walter MM Pte 52146 8th West Yorkshire Regt
WARDEN A. MM Pte 301128 2 Fd Amb RAMC
WARDEN Frederick H. MM Pte 87706 RAMC
WARDEN H.A. MM Pte 12171 Leicestershire Regt
WARDEN Harry MM+Bar Pte B/683 Rifle Brigade
WARDEN William MM Pte 341 7 Fd Amb RAMC
WARDER John T. MM Sjt SE/5265 Army Veterinary Corps
WARDHAUGH Alfred John MM Pnr 281988 Fifth Army Sig Coy Royal Engineers Died 5.5.18.
WARDHAUGH Ed MM Cpl 770538 RFA
WARDLAW James MM Sjt 50952 RFA
WARDLAW John MM Pte 22339 5th Cameron Highlanders
WARDLAW Robert H. MM Pte 20/689 8th Northumberland Fusiliers
WARDLE Alfred R. MM L/Cpl 134983 Royal Engineers
WARDLE Arthur MM Cpl 202675 South Lancashire Regt
WARDLE Arthur "DCM,MM+2 Bars" Sjt 5702 1st King's Royal Rifle Corps

WARDLE Herbert MM Pnr 131539 234 Fd Coy Royal Engineers KIA 31.7.17.
WARDLE Hugh MM L/Cpl 21758 50th Bn Machine Gun Corps
WARDLE J.W. MM L/Sjt 19/951 Northumberland Fusiliers
WARDLE John J. MM Pte 118238 11th Notts & Derby Regt
WARDLE John W. MM L/Cpl R/4085 4th King's Royal Rifle Corps
WARDLE Lawrence MM Pte 7908 1st Northumberland Fusiliers
WARDLE Samuel MM Bdr 64099 RGA
WARDLE Samuel Garth MM Cpl 242174 2/5th Yorkshire Light Infantry
WARDLE William MM Cpl 243366 1/5th North Lancashire Regt
WARDLE William J. MM Gnr 57065 B/116 Bde RFA
WARDMAN John "DCM,MM" Sjt 11888 10th West Riding Regt
WARDMAN Thomas MM Spr 551142 474 Fd Coy Royal Engineers
WARDMAN Walter "MM,MID" L/Cpl 3/1860 2nd Yorkshire Light Infantry
WARDROP Robert G. "DCM,MM" Sjt 32509 27 Fd Amb RAMC
WARDROPE James MM Sjt 335774 Royal Scots
WARDROPPER George W.P. MM L/Sjt 201299 1/4th Norfolk Regt
WARE Alfred P. "MM,MSM" Cpl 18644 4 Div Sig Coy Royal Engineers
WARE Archibald Bryant MM L/Cpl 27333 2nd Suffolk Regt KIA 8.10.18.
WARE Arthur Stephen MM Sjt 26769 Hampshire Regt
WARE Frank MM Pte G/187 1st Royal West Surrey Regt KIA 25.9.17.
WARE Frederick S. MM Pte 49929 9th Royal Irish Fusiliers
WARE George A.W. MM Sjt 240156 5th West Riding Regt
WARE George H. MM Pte M2/053443 Army Service Corps
WARE Henry S. MM Sjt 275943 1/6th Essex Regt
WARE James MM Dvr 57318 RFA
WARE Percival J. MM Sjt 32828 RGA
WARE Reginald "MM,MID" Sjt 7130 5th Lancers
WARE Thomas MM L/Cpl 9518 1st Scottish Rifles
WARE Thomas H.L. MM L/Cpl 8454 2nd Devonshire Regt
WARE W. MM Pte 18353 Hampshire Regt
WAREHAM Alfred W. MM Pte 242103 7th Royal West Kent Regt
WAREHAM E. MM Pte 320342 24th Welsh Regt
WAREHAM Edward MM Sjt 16298 6th Dorsetshire Regt
WAREHAM George E. MM Pte 51107 1/7th Cheshire Regt
WAREHAM Harold "DCM,MM,MIDx2" Sjt 74771 Machine Gun Corps(Cavalry)
WAREHAM James "DCM,MM" Pte 50974 13th Royal Fusiliers
WAREHAM Louis W. MM Sjt 103043 19th Bn Machine Gun Corps
WAREING George MM Pte 18990 1st East Lancashire Regt
WAREING Hugh MM L/Cpl 428318 423 Fd Coy Royal Engineers
WAREING James MM L/Cpl 27824 6th Liverpool Regt
WAREING Ralph MM Sjt 14128 22nd Manchester Regt
WAREING Thomas MM L/Sjt 200785 North Lancashire Regt
WAREING William MM Pte 8605 2nd Lancashire Fusiliers
WAREING William MM+Bar Sjt 61379 252 Siege Bty RGA
WAREN William W. MM L/Cpl 8550 1st Worcestershire Regt
WARFIELD James MM Bdr 1590 RFA
WARFORD Henry G. MM Cpl 10702 Royal West Kent Regt
WARHAM Albert MM Sjt 47254 Royal Engineers
WARHAM David MM L/Cpl 12059 18th Hussars
WARHURST A. MM L/Cpl 205530 5th Lancashire Fusiliers
WARHURST William MM Pte 17180 Royal Welsh Fusiliers
WARING Arthur MM Pte 31088 Cheshire Regt
WARING F. MM Gnr 291674 RGA
WARING George MM Sjt 19172 Cheshire Regt
WARING Harry MM Sjt 35016 5th Border Regt
WARING Harry MM L/Cpl 15955 7/8th King's Own Scottish Borderers
WARING Henry A. "MM,MSM" Pte 20297 12/13th Northumberland Fusiliers
WARING J. "DCM,MM" Sjt 228391 1st London Regt
WARING James H. "DCM,MM" L/Cpl 40183 15/17th West Yorkshire Regt
WARING John MM Sjt 307448 9th West Riding Regt
WARING Robert MM Sjt 5525 161 Bde RFA DOW 21.10.17.
WARING Samuel MM Cpl 61727 75 Fd Coy Royal Engineers
WARING William Herbert "VC,MM" L/Sjt 355014 25th Royal Welsh Fusiliers DOW 8.10.18.
WARINGTON E.F. MM Pte 13476 6th Royal West Surrey Regt
WARK John MM Pte 200790 5/6th Scottish Rifles
WARLOW Washington MM Pte 302461 Manchester Regt
WARMAN Albert S. MM Sjt 54264 29 Bde RFA
WARMER Charles A. MM CSM 10831 1st Notts & Derby Regt
WARMINGTON Alfred S. MM Sjt 12214 8th Gloucestershire Regt

WARMINGTON Reginald Walter William MM L/Bdr 841053 D/70 Bde RFA
WARN Herbert MM L/Sjt 97418 103 Coy Labour Corps
WARN Walter R. MM Pte S/18183 Rifle Brigade
WARNE A.E. MM Pte 42277 1/1st Hertfordshire Regt
WARNE Albert MM L/Cpl 11521 Devonshire Regt
WARNE Henry T. MM Pte 208026 Royal West Surrey Regt
WARNE William A. MM Dvr 208722 RFA
WARNE William T. MM Pte 241324 Royal West Kent Regt
WARNER Albert E. "MM,MSM,MID" Staff SM T/19558 15 Reserve Park Army Service Corps
WARNER Albert E. MM Tpr 538 Household Bn
WARNER Alfred S. MM Cpl 10400 Leicestershire Regt
WARNER Arthur G. MM Cpl 75063 'N' Corps Sig Coy Royal Engineers
WARNER Catherine MM Sister F SJAB
WARNER Charles F. MM Pte 46481 36 Fd Amb RAMC
WARNER Charles S. MM Bugler 1478 1/21st London Regt
WARNER Charles W. MM Pte 15997 8th East Surrey Regt
WARNER Ernest G. MM Cpl 58003 Middlesex Regt
WARNER Ernest J. MM L/Bdr 52004 23 Heavy Bty RGA
WARNER Frank MM L/Cpl 18353 1st Dorsetshire Regt
WARNER Frank MM+Bar Pte 14007 2nd Grenadier Guards
WARNER Frederick E. MM Cpl 20385 55 Fd Coy Royal Engineers
WARNER George MM Dvr 92887 RFA
WARNER George Andrew MM+Bar Sjt 5504 11th Royal Fusiliers
WARNER Henry R. MM Sjt 12353 7th Norfolk Regt
WARNER Herbert J. MM L/Cpl 22836 Yorkshire Light Infantry
WARNER Horace MM L/Sjt B/203313 13th Rifle Brigade KIA 31.5.17.
WARNER Howard MM Pte 255471 1/1st Leicestershire Yeomanry
WARNER Hugh Geoffrey MM Cpl 8011 11th Royal Fusiliers KIA 7.8.18.
WARNER Leslie F. MM Sjt 33768 391 Siege Bty RGA
WARNER Oscar "DCM,MM" Sjt 9567 2nd Coldstream Guards
WARNER Tam MM L/Cpl 405305 2/3(West Riding)Fd Amb RAMC
WARNER Thomas MM Pte 330614 5th Notts & Derby Regt
WARNER Thomas MM Sjt 22544 164 Coy Machine Gun Corps KIA 9.8.16.
WARNER Thomas George Ferguson MM Sjt 54504 47 Coy Machine Gun Corps
WARNER Walter MM Dvr 765535 2 Bde RFA
WARNER Walter MM Sjt 7975 1st Lincolnshire Regt
WARNER William MM Pte 41399 Suffolk Regt att 1/1st Cambs Regt.
WARNER William F. MM Pte S/18969 Rifle Brigade
WARNER William John MM L/Cpl 10482 East Kent Regt
WARNES Charles A. MM L/Cpl 98569 1st Middlesex Regt
WARNES Clarence MM Pte 202241 Gloucestershire Regt
WARNETT John "MM,MID" Gnr 62769 43 Bde RFA
WARNOCK James MM Pte 13817 1st Royal Irish Rifles
WARNOCK Terence MM Cpl 6582 RAMC
WARR Frank MM Cpl 8286 1st Dorsetshire Regt
WARR John N. MM Pte 66603 RAMC
WARR Joseph MM Dvr 31565 RFA
WARRANT Bertie MM Pte 421963 10th London Regt
WARRE William Walter John MM Sjt 10612 6th Dorsetshire Regt
WARREN Albert MM Pte 20641 Leicestershire Regt
WARREN Albert E. MM Pte 33195 9 Fd Amb RAMC
WARREN Alfred MM Cpl 16066 Machine Gun Corps
WARREN Alfred MM Pte 2984 1/6th London Regt
WARREN Arthur MM Pte 60246 10th Royal Fusiliers
WARREN Arthur MM Pte 39791 7th Royal Berkshire Regt
WARREN Arthur Stanhope MM Cpl 20948 1st Royal Lancaster Regt DOW 12.8.18.
WARREN C.E. MM Pte 703125 London Regt
WARREN Charles MM Cpl 388466 RAMC
WARREN Charles S. MM Sjt 738020 24th London Regt
WARREN Claud Rowland MM Pte 49382 161 Coy Machine Gun Corps
WARREN Clement MM Cpl 242221 6th Liverpool Regt
WARREN D.W.L. MM Pte 51534 Machine Gun Corps
WARREN Edward F. MM Sjt 51275 5 Bde RFA
WARREN Edwin John MM Cpl 14435 1/4th Gloucestershire Regt KIA 29.3.18.
WARREN Ernest MM Sjt 14969 56 Fd Coy Royal Engineers
WARREN Ernest MM Cpl 50277 Royal Fusiliers
WARREN Ernest T. MM+Bar Pte M2/167773 61 Div Train Army Service Corps
WARREN Francis Robson "MC,MM(12/95 Sjt E Yorks)" T/2Lt 16th Royal Welsh Fusiliers
WARREN Frank MM S/Sjt Farrier 36791 RFA
WARREN Frank MM Gnr 58992 RFA
WARREN Fred MM+Bar Sjt 240216 Lincolnshire Regt
WARREN Frederick MM+Bar Bdr 180186 C/124 Bde RFA
WARREN Frederick "DCM,MM" Pte 7322 8th Royal Fusiliers
WARREN Frederick MM Cpl 93066 218 Fd Coy Royal Engineers
WARREN Frederick MM Cpl 310125 RGA
WARREN Frederick J. MM Pte 38659 7th Royal West Kent Regt
WARREN George MM Cpl 491565 13th London Regt
WARREN George MM Dvr 119142 460 Bty 15 Bde RFA
WARREN George MM Pte 9876 4th Royal Fusiliers
WARREN George Leonard MM Pte 200279 1st London Regt att 2/2nd London Regt.KIA 18.9.18.
WARREN George W. MM Cpl 240621 Norfolk Regt
WARREN Gilbert A. MM Pte 200796 Northamptonshire Regt
WARREN H. MM Sjt 64517 RFA
WARREN Harold V. MM Cpl M2/118949 Army Service Corps att XI Corps HAG RGA.Died 15.11.18.
WARREN Harry MM Dvr 61901 19 Bty 9 Bde RFA
WARREN Henry MM Sjt 10582 RFA
WARREN Henry C. MM L/Cpl 59380 Royal Engineers
WARREN Henry J.A. MM Cpl 25 RGA
WARREN Herbert James MM Sjt 2519 1/18th London Regt
WARREN Horace MM Sjt 283947 235 Lt Rly Coy Royal Engineers
WARREN Horace MM Gnr 114186 RFA
WARREN Horace William MM Pte 9868 10th Royal West Kent Regt
WARREN J.W. MM Sjt 4050 2 Div Ammn Col RFA
WARREN James F. MM Cpl 22017 RFA
WARREN John MM Cpl 39179 1/4th Gloucestershire Regt
WARREN John MM Pte 82704 2nd London Regt
WARREN John E. MM Sjt 201986 York & Lancaster Regt
WARREN John Stanley MM 2nd Cpl 275509 21 Lt Rly Op Coy Royal Engineers
WARREN Joseph MM Sjt 20476 Royal Inniskilling Fusiliers
WARREN P. MM Sjt 1805 1st Essex Regt
WARREN Percival D. MM Pte 6416 7th London Regt
WARREN Richard W. MM L/Bdr 65322 115 Hy Bty RGA
WARREN Robert MM Spr 79964 Royal Engineers
WARREN Robert H. MM Sjt 10450 1st East Lancashire Regt
WARREN Robert H. MM Sjt 241191 Worcestershire Regt
WARREN Robert Moberey MM Sjt 45269 50th Bn Machine Gun Corps
WARREN Stanley MM Gnr 889626 RFA
WARREN Thomas MM Pte 260115 11th West Yorkshire Regt
WARREN Thomas MM L/Cpl 24590 Royal Welsh Fusiliers
WARREN Walter MM Pte 240223 5th Devonshire Regt
WARREN Walter MM Pte 41210 Royal Lancaster Regt
WARREN Walter MM Pte 90005 RAMC
WARREN Walter MM Pte 38700 13th Royal Welsh Fusiliers KIA 22.4.18.
WARREN Walter H. MM L/Cpl 3010 24th Royal Fusiliers
WARREN William MM 2nd Cpl 15787 75 Div Sig Coy Royal Engineers
WARRENDER Benjamin F. MM Pte 23292 1/6th Cheshire Regt
WARRENDER Ernest J. MM L/Cpl 11236 7th Duke of Cornwall's LI
WARRENDER William MM L/Cpl 17882 Grenadier Guards
WARRENER Anderson MM Bdr 8841 RFA
WARRICK Henry T. MM Pte 42233 Middlesex Regt
WARRILLOW Samuel J. MM Pte B/203251 Rifle Brigade
WARRILOW Frank MM+Bar Sjt 203180 1/5th North Staffordshire Regt
WARRINER Percy Edwin MM Gnr 148849 100 HAG RGA
WARRINER Richard MM Cpl 7838 4th Worcestershire Regt
WARRINGTON Archibald MM Cpl 11787 9th Cheshire Regt
WARRINGTON Arthur A. MM Dvr 73023 RFA
WARRINGTON Edwin MM Cpl SE/20150 Army Veterinary Corps
WARRINGTON Ernest MM Sjt M2/132932 Army Service Corps
WARRINGTON George MM Pte 21915 10th Duke of Cornwall's LI KIA 28.10.18.
WARRINGTON George MM Pte 22367 17th Notts & Derby Regt
WARRINGTON Harry MM Sjt M1/5022 Army Service Corps
WARRINGTON Stephen MM Pte 45489 Northumberland Fusiliers
WARRINGTON Thomas MM Cpl 15010 7th Yorkshire Light Infantry
WARRINGTON Wilfred MM Pte 275646 1/7th Manchester Regt
WARRY Fred MM Pte 6003 Royal Munster Fusiliers
WARWICK A. MM Cpl 19218 10th Essex Regt
WARWICK Albert Edward MM+Bar L/Cpl 73700 2nd Bn Machine Gun Corps
WARWICK Alfred Henry MM Dvr T2/015933 Army Service Corps att 56 Fd Amb RAMC.

WARWICK Alfred W. MM L/Cpl 32476 1st Devonshire Regt
WARWICK Ernest A. MM Sjt 63207 Machine Gun Corps
WARWICK Frederick G. MM CQMS 4413 Machine Gun Corps
WARWICK George MM Sjt 417 1/7th West Riding Regt Died 22.7.16.
WARWICK George John MM Sjt 191073 'R'(AA)Bty RGA
WARWICK Harold S. MM Pte 92053 RAMC
WARWICK Luther MM Pte 1447 Royal Fusiliers
WARWICK Sidney Douglas MM Sjt B/19271 King's Royal Rifle Corps
WARWICK Soloman MM L/Cpl 12720 7th Lincolnshire Regt
WARWICK Thomas MM+Bar Sjt 25516 6th King's Own Scottish Borderers
WARWICK Thomas W. MM Pte 8812 South Lancashire Regt
WARWICK Thomas W. MM Pte 386253 1/1(Northumbrian)Fd Amb RAMC
WARWICK William A. MM Pte 5097 Middlesex Regt
WARWICK William David MM Pte 123 RAMC
WASEY E. MM Pte 6822 West Riding Regt
WASH Weymouth George MM Pte 300498 1/8th Durham Light Infantry
WASHBOURNE Arthur F. MM L/Cpl 4800 8 Fd Amb RAMC
WASHBOURNE William Phillip MM Cpl 2726 1/5th Gloucestershire Regt
WASHER Levi MM Pte 51993 RAMC
WASHFORD Sydney Albert MM Sjt 358140 RGA
WASHINGTON Edward MM Cpl 304241 13th Bn Tank Corps
WASHINGTON George Henry MM Pte 14524 7th Wiltshire Regt
WASHINGTON Richard J. MM Pte 17239 Worcestershire Regt
WASHINGTON Robert MM+Bar Sjt 240603 6th North Staffordshire Regt
WASHINGTON William James MM Sjt 2129 1/6th South Staffordshire Regt
WASLEY Albert MM Gnr 16826 31 Div Ammn Col RFA
WASLEY Edgar MM Pte 9504 2nd South Wales Borderers
WASON William Munn MM 2nd Cpl 2563 52 Div Sig Coy Royal Engineers
WASS George MM Pte 4754 9th Notts & Derby Regt
WASS H. MM L/Cpl P8853 Military Foot Police
WASS John MM+Bar Cpl 5874 1st King's Royal Rifle Corps
WASS Matthew Ellis MM L/Cpl 24088 9th North Lancashire Regt DOW 9.6.18.
WASS Wilfred G. MM Cpl 204963 Royal Engineers
WASS William MM L/Sjt 22763 15th Notts & Derby Regt
WASS Willie MM Pte 15231 Labour Corps
WASSELL Frederick J. MM Pte 1871 Worcestershire Regt
WASSELL George MM Cpl 16832 11th Worcestershire Regt
WASSELL Joseph A. "DCM,MM" CSM 16274 37 Div Sig Coy Royal Engineers
WASSELL Oliver T. "MM,MSM" Bdr 6572 B/73 Bde RFA
WASSELL Samuel MM Pte 27544 1st Shropshire Light Infantry
WASSELL Thomas MM Sjt 240795 Middlesex Regt
WASSON Samuel MM Pte 41414 9th Royal Irish Fusiliers
WATCHMAN Samuel MM Pte 15207 2nd Border Regt
WATCHORN Arthur MM Sjt 235104 Lincolnshire Regt
WATCHORN Reginald M. "DCM,MM,MID" Sjt 1790 3(Welsh)Fd Amb RAMC
WATCHORN Roy MM L/Cpl 51687 7 Sqn Machine Gun Corps(Cavalry)
WATERFIELD Albert E. MM Gnr 121631 C/170 Bde RFA
WATERFIELD Charles J. MM Pte 50232 142 Fd Amb RAMC
WATERFIELD Cyril MM Pte 202115 2/4th West Riding Regt
WATERFIELD Frank MM Gnr 175945 RGA
WATERFIELD Frederick MM Pte 3164 4 Fd Amb RAMC
WATERFIELD Frederick MM L/Cpl 3866 Royal West Surrey Regt
WATERFIELD Harry MM Gnr 174185 88 Bty 14 Bde RFA
WATERFIELD James MM Pte 419342 2/2(North Midland)Fd Amb RAMC
WATERFIELD Lewis S. MM Pte 26356 9th Royal Fusiliers
WATERFIELD William H. MM Pte 8646 Machine Gun Corps
WATERHOUSE Alfred James MM Sjt 401 1/6th Notts & Derby Regt
WATERHOUSE Clifford MM Pte 41461 1st Notts & Derby Regt KIA 15.4.18.
WATERHOUSE David MM Sjt 8040 Worcestershire Regt
WATERHOUSE Edward MM L/Cpl 19026 7th Royal West Kent Regt
WATERHOUSE Frank MM Pte 1482 West Riding Regt
WATERHOUSE George A. MM Pte 42041 1st Royal Inniskilling Fusiliers
WATERHOUSE George L. MM Dvr 656392 RFA
WATERHOUSE Harry MM Pte 44486 20th Manchester Regt
WATERHOUSE Harry MM Pte 38807 25th Northumberland Fusiliers Died 21.3.18.
WATERHOUSE Harry MM Gnr 8652 RFA
WATERHOUSE Jack MM Pte 34820 2nd Oxf & Bucks Light Infantry
WATERHOUSE James MM Gnr 56566 RFA
WATERHOUSE John E. MM L/Cpl 50660 5th Lancashire Fusiliers
WATERHOUSE Reginald Valentine MM L/Cpl 20284 26th Royal Fusiliers
WATERHOUSE Robert N. MM Gnr 95032 RGA
WATERHOUSE William MM L/Cpl 277745 Manchester Regt
WATERIDGE Albert S. MM L/Cpl 75071 Machine Gun Corps(HB)
WATERIDGE Herbert MM Pte 16430 Royal Lancaster Regt
WATERMAN Arthur C. MM L/Cpl 9048 1/4th Gordon Highlanders
WATERMAN Charles MM Sjt 17225 13th Essex Regt KIA 30.7.16.
WATERMAN Frederick Francis MM Pte 6606 6th East Surrey Regt KIA 10.4.17.
WATERMAN George A. MM Pte 57008 RAMC
WATERMAN George Thomas MM Sjt 203555 1/4th Oxf & Bucks Light Infantry DOW 22.6.18.
WATERMAN Thomas "DCM,MM+Bar" L/Sjt 6434 15 Fd Amb RAMC
WATERMAN Thomas MM Spr 2738 Royal Engineers
WATERS Albert George "MM,MID" Bdr 321355 546 Siege Bty RGA
WATERS Albert H. MM Sjt 22418 Machine Gun Corps
WATERS Alexander MM Pte 14602 10th Arg & Suth Highlanders
WATERS Alfred W. MM Pte 21053 2nd Bedfordshire Regt
WATERS Arthur MM Cpl 16306 York & Lancaster Regt
WATERS Charles W. MM+Bar Cpl 9545 2nd Royal Berkshire Regt
WATERS Edgar MM Pte 39294 Northamptonshire Regt
WATERS Edwin H. MM L/Cpl 19757 Royal Fusiliers
WATERS Ernest C. MM+2 Bars Bdr 40990 D/124 Bde RFA
WATERS Ernest P. MM Pte 12847 Hampshire Regt
WATERS Frederick MM Cpl 4941 Notts & Derby Regt
WATERS Frederick G. MM Sjt 3878 2nd Rifle Brigade
WATERS Frederick William MM Cpl 265202 1/1st Hertfordshire Regt KIA 31.7.17.
WATERS George C.F. MM Cpl 16390 Royal Sussex Regt
WATERS George F. MM Dvr 876105 35 Div Ammn Col RFA
WATERS Harry V. MM Sjt 28276 A/124 Bde RFA
WATERS Harry W. MM Cpl 75950 154 Siege Bty RGA
WATERS Henry MM Cpl 3702 RFA
WATERS Herbert MM Sjt 27930 37 Div Ammn Col RFA
WATERS Herbert James MM Spr 131106 233 Fd Coy Royal Engineers
WATERS Ivor A. MM L/Cpl 51744 Suffolk Regt
WATERS Jack S. MM Pte 3409 9th Royal Sussex Regt
WATERS John MM Cpl 15734 8th Somerset Light Infantry
WATERS John Eustice MM Gnr 157132 19 Siege Bty RGA
WATERS Jonathan Robert MM Cpl 19397 Yorkshire Regt
WATERS Leonard MM L/Cpl S/19389 Rifle Brigade
WATERS Robert MM Sjt 9150 Coldstream Guards
WATERS Samuel MM Pte 17080 6th South Wales Borderers
WATERS Samuel MM Pte 1590 1/1(West Riding)Fd Amb RAMC
WATERS Thomas MM L/Cpl 325617 1/9th Durham Light Infantry
WATERS Thomas H. MM Cpl 266899 1/1st Bucks Bn Oxf & Bucks Light Infantry
WATERS W. MM Dvr 770832 RFA
WATERS William MM Pte 10733 7th Wiltshire Regt
WATERS William G. MM Gnr 1595 RFA
WATERS William Henry MM Sjt 278895 61 Siege Bty RGA KIA 29.4.18.
WATERS William J. MM Bdr 1208 14(London)Bty RFA
WATERS William Joseph MM Sjt 8418 Northumberland Fusiliers
WATERS William W.G. MM Sjt 39083 32 Coy Machine Gun Corps
WATERS William Wilson MM Cpl 26129 Y/18 Med TM Bty RFA
WATERSON Frank MM Bdr 661080 RFA
WATERSON Joseph Henry MM Sjt 36189 25th Bn Machine Gun Corps
WATERSON Robert F. "DCM,MM" Sjt 54625 C/286 Bde RFA
WATERSTON Alexander MM Pte 3043 8th London Regt
WATERSTON Christopher MM Cpl 10369 1st King's Own Scottish Borderers
WATERSTON David MM Pte 34734 York & Lancaster Regt
WATERTON Alexander Douglas "MM,CG(F)" L/Cpl 42399 Essex Regt
WATERTON Ernest MM Pte 266017 1/1st Hertfordshire Regt
WATERWORTH Albert "MM,MdH(F)" Sjt 39448 11th Bn Machine Gun Corps
WATERWORTH Eli MM Pte 40863 23rd Northumberland Fusiliers Died 23.3.18.

WATERWORTH John W. MM L/Cpl 325784 1/9th Durham Light Infantry
WATERWORTH Robert George William MM Pte 573690 1/17th London Regt
WATERWORTH Thomas MM Pte 9128 1st Royal Inniskilling Fusiliers KIA 1.7.16.
WATERWORTH Thomas MM Pte 21764 Grenadier Guards
WATES Frank H. MM+Bar Pte 4545 9th Lancers
WATFORD Walter MM Sjt 8486 5th Northamptonshire Regt DOW 30.7.16.
WATHEN Trevor MM Cpl 3387 228 Fd Coy Royal Engineers
WATKIN Ernest MM Pte 45067 11th Suffolk Regt
WATKIN Ernest W. MM Pte 11409 5th Shropshire Light Infantry
WATKIN Frederick MM Sjt 57940 55 Stationary Hosp RAMC
WATKIN John W. MM Pte 236366 7th West Yorkshire Regt
WATKIN Thomas MM Pte 28/79 Northumberland Fusiliers
WATKIN William J. MM Pte 15208 8th South Lancashire Regt
WATKINS A.J. MM Cpl 364041 RAMC
WATKINS A.L. MM CQMS 13680 Welsh Regt
WATKINS Albert MM Pte 703 9th Royal Fusiliers
WATKINS Albert G. MM Cpl 14632 7th Shropshire Light Infantry
WATKINS Alfred MM+Bar Pte 22951 2nd Suffolk Regt
WATKINS Alfred Francis MM Sjt 55560 Machine Gun Corps
WATKINS Archar G. MM Spr 30439 23 Fd Coy Royal Engineers
WATKINS Arthur MM Pte 339272 63 Fd Amb RAMC
WATKINS Ernest F.C. MM Pte 721103 London Regt
WATKINS Ethel Frances MM Sister F QAIMNS
WATKINS Francis Edwin MM Cpl 12/548 12th York & Lancaster Regt KIA 1.7.16.
WATKINS Francis G. MM L/Cpl 233074 2nd London Regt
WATKINS Garfield MM Pte 48862 Lancashire Fusiliers
WATKINS George MM Pte 251974 1/6th Arg & Suth Highlanders
WATKINS Harold A. MM Dvr 960575 C/235 Bde RFA
WATKINS Harold W. MM Spr 486826 Royal Engineers
WATKINS Iorwerth MM L/Cpl 19408 12th Gloucestershire Regt
WATKINS J. MM Pte 814 East Kent Regt
WATKINS James W. MM Pte 19092 Army Cyclist Corps
WATKINS John MM Pte 69237 2nd Devonshire Regt
WATKINS John MM Gnr 4194 RFA
WATKINS John H. MM Cpl 6272 Shropshire Light Infantry
WATKINS Joseph MM L/Sjt 6728 2nd Welsh Regt
WATKINS Kingsley H.K. MM Sjt 75339 14th Royal Welsh Fusiliers
WATKINS Laurence A. MM L/Cpl 650926 1/21st London Regt
WATKINS Lindsay Gilbert MM Pte 288034 2/6th Gloucestershire Regt Died 6.12.17.
WATKINS Reginald C. MM Sjt 235078 1/1st Herefordshire Regt
WATKINS Richard John MM L/Sjt 11158 4th Grenadier Guards KIA 1.12.17.
WATKINS Sidney MM Gnr 109514 RFA
WATKINS Sidney MM Pte 20444 South Wales Borderers
WATKINS Thomas MM Pte 17514 6th South Wales Borderers
WATKINS Thomas P. MM L/Cpl 11769 Royal West Surrey Regt
WATKINS Trevor Frank MM Bdr 46060 38 Bde RFA
WATKINS W.A. MM S/Sjt 512228 3(London)Fd Amb RAMC
WATKINS Watkin W. MM BSM 33655 A/148 Bde RFA
WATKINS William MM Pte 24776 10th Royal West Kent Regt
WATKINS William A. MM Cpl M2/132655 Army Service Corps
WATKINS William B. MM L/Sjt 4501 1/14th London Regt
WATKINS William C. MM Gnr 79941 RFA
WATKINS William Charles "MC,MM,MID" CSM 8/9711 8th Border Regt KIA 3.7.16.
WATKINS William James MM Pte 36764 Machine Gun Corps
WATKINSON Carlton P. MM L/Cpl 201143 4th Leicestershire Regt
WATKINSON F. MM L/Cpl 403528 RAMC
WATKINSON Hammond N. MM Dvr 42133 RFA
WATKINSON Henry MM Pte 7983 1st Royal Berkshire Regt KIA 24.9.17.
WATKINSON John W. MM Spr 325465 Royal Engineers
WATKINSON Richard MM+Bar Cpl 308534 1/8th Liverpool Regt
WATKINSON Robert W. "DCM,MM" Sjt C/12699 9th King's Royal Rifle Corps
WATKINSON Thomas MM Pte 8347 22 Fd Amb RAMC
WATKINSON Tom MM Pte 28125 2nd Yorkshire Regt
WATKINSON Wilfred MM Pte 352771 7th London Regt
WATKISS Frederick E. MM Gnr 170067 RGA
WATKISS John MM Pte 7436 1st Shropshire Light Infantry
WATKISS Thomas E. MM Pte 41567 Essex Regt
WATLER Stanley C. MM L/Cpl P/795 Rifle Brigade
WATLING Albert MM Dvr 52274 33 Bde RFA
WATLING Frank MM Pte 34108 Royal Berkshire Regt

WATLING George M. MM Sjt 715028 23rd Bn London Regt
WATLING Herbert MM+Bar Sjt 11793 5th Royal Berkshire Regt
WATLING James R. MM Sjt 242135 8th North Staffordshire Regt
WATLING Ruben MM L/Cpl 52712 Machine Gun Corps(Cavalry)
WATMOUGH Alfred MM+Bar Sjt 69311 C/156 Bde RFA
WATMOUGH Edward MM Pte 65027 6th Yorkshire Regt
WATMOUGH John H. MM L/Cpl 1071 Lincolnshire Regt
WATSON Abraham "MC,MM" RSM R/1955 9th King's Royal Rifle Corps
WATSON Albert MM Pte C/363 16th King's Royal Rifle Corps KIA 13.8.16.
WATSON Albert E. MM 2nd Cpl 249533 Royal Engineers
WATSON Albert Edward MM Cpl 235757 9th Northumberland Fusiliers
WATSON Albert H. MM Pte 5407 Northumberland Fusiliers
WATSON Albert J. MM Pte 230074 1/2nd London Regt
WATSON Alexander MM Sjt 41045 Royal Highlanders
WATSON Alexander MM+Bar Sjt 240251 5/6th Scottish Rifles
WATSON Alexander MM Pte 5941 RAMC
WATSON Alexander MM Sjt 15938 17th Highland Light Infantry
WATSON Alexander MM L/Bdr 46852 RGA
WATSON Alexander MM Gnr 104682 81 Bty 5 Bde RFA KIA 27.9.17.
WATSON Alexander Harry MM Pte 41011 7/8th Royal Inniskilling Fusiliers KIA 16.8.17.
WATSON Alfred MM Pte 235156 16th Royal Welsh Fusiliers
WATSON Alfred MM Pte 240206 1/5th York & Lancaster Regt
WATSON Alfred MM Cpl 3285 3rd Dragoon Guards
WATSON Alfred MM Pte 11/1054 11th East Yorkshire Regt
WATSON Alfred MM Bdr 76114 RFA
WATSON Alfred H. MM Cpl 820466 RFA
WATSON Alfred W. "MM,MID" Pte 3187 8th Royal West Kent Regt
WATSON Andrew MM Pte 18775 Machine Gun Corps
WATSON Andrew "MM,MID" Cpl 23313 Royal Engineers
WATSON Archibald MM Sjt 44103 234 Coy Machine Gun Corps
WATSON Arnold MM L/Bdr 22946 A/51 Bde RFA
WATSON Arthur MM Sjt 1276 2/5th Lancashire Fusiliers
WATSON Arthur MM Pte M2/116987 Army Service Corps
WATSON Arthur MM Spr 156333 258 Tunnelling Coy Royal Engineers
WATSON Arthur A. MM+Bar L/Cpl 301903 Tank Corps
WATSON Cameron MM Pte 9637 1/1st HAC(Inf)
WATSON Cecil MM Cpl 267368 1/4th Seaforth Highlanders
WATSON Charles "MM,MID" QMS Eng Clk 428 Royal Engineers
WATSON Charles "MM,MID" CQMS 1146 1/16th London Regt
WATSON Charles MM Sjt 265801 2/7th Notts & Derby Regt KIA 21.3.18.
WATSON Charles MM L/Cpl 266143 Bedfordshire Regt att 1/1st Hertfordshire Regt
WATSON Charles F. "DCM,MM+Bar" Bdr 78543 59 Bty RFA
WATSON Charles F. MM Cpl 325312 1/1st Cambridgeshire Regt
WATSON Charles Henry MM Pte 270176 2/7th West Yorkshire Regt
WATSON Charles K. MM Pte 30560 1st Norfolk Regt
WATSON Cyril G. MM Sjt 5343 23rd Middlesex Regt
WATSON David MM L/Cpl 268274 1/6th Royal Highlanders
WATSON David "DCM,MM+Bar" Sjt 18004 2nd Royal Irish Regt
WATSON David MM Cpl 267211 13th Royal Highlanders
WATSON David MM Pte M2/149115 Army Service Corps
WATSON David MM Dvr 87309 RFA
WATSON David C. MM Pte 50638 Machine Gun Corps(Cavalry)
WATSON Davidson MM Gnr 93436 C/180 Bde RFA
WATSON Donald S. MM Pte 200879 2/4th Royal West Kent Regt
WATSON Ebenezer Thomas MM Pte 7527 2nd Lincolnshire Regt
WATSON Edgar John MM+2 Bars Cpl R/12590 2nd & 7th King's Royal Rifle Corps
WATSON Edward MM Dvr 680303 RFA
WATSON Edward MM Sjt 14952 6th Lincolnshire Regt
WATSON Edwin MM L/Cpl 62549 7th Lancashire Fusiliers
WATSON Ernest Arthur MM Sjt 12955 11th West Yorkshire Regt KIA 7.6.17.
WATSON Frank MM Cpl 97298 RFA
WATSON Frank W. MM Pte 28714 1st Lancashire Fusiliers
WATSON Fred MM Cpl 143567 212 Fd Coy Royal Engineers
WATSON Fred MM Pte 11281 Labour Corps
WATSON Fred MM Pte 1385 1/5th Yorkshire Regt KIA 28.10.17.
WATSON Fred Norman MM Pte 16/599 19tth Northumberland Fusiliers KIA 19.10.18.
WATSON Frederick MM Pte 3495 1/21st London Regt
WATSON Frederick MM Dvr 31563 RFA
WATSON Frederick G. MM 2nd Cpl 85262 Royal Engineers

WATSON Frederick J. MM Gnr 51866 RGA
WATSON Frederick J. MM Gnr 284074 RGA
WATSON Frederick James MM Cpl 48514 4th Liverpool Regt DOW 12.10.18.
WATSON Frederick T. MM CSM 1434 12/13th Northumberland Fusiliers
WATSON Frederick W. MM+Bar L/Cpl 147605 177 Tunnelling Coy Royal Engineers
WATSON George MM Spr 463105 50 Div Sig Coy Royal Engineers
WATSON George MM Sjt 30385 46 Fd Amb RAMC DOW 29.4.17.
WATSON George MM 2nd Cpl 80117 Royal Engineers
WATSON George B. MM Pte 27118 2nd King's Own Scottish Borderers
WATSON George D. MM Pte 241870 Northumberland Fusiliers
WATSON George F. MM Sjt 79768 401 Bty 4 Bde RFA
WATSON George Frederick "DCM,MM" L/Cpl 240230 4/5th Royal Highlanders
WATSON George Herbert MM Sjt 202161 1/4th Royal Lancaster Regt KIA 8.6.18.
WATSON George L.G. MM Air Mech 2 8237 Royal Flying Corps
WATSON George William MM Sjt 24838 11th West Yorkshire Regt
WATSON H. MM Cpl 492040 2 Fd Amb RAMC
WATSON H. MM Pte 386145 RAMC
WATSON Harry MM Bdr 680984 RFA
WATSON Harry MM Sjt 10648 4th Worcestershire Regt KIA 6.7.16.
WATSON Harry MM Pte 4906 2nd Bn GMGR
WATSON Harry MM AM1 65385 Royal Flying Corps
WATSON Henry MM Pte 19659 1 Special Coy Middlesex Regt
WATSON Henry Charles MM Pte 9199 13th Middlesex Regt KIA 31.8.16.
WATSON Henry Ernest MM Pte 12255 2nd Notts & Derby Regt
WATSON Henry G. MM Pte 240531 Gordon Highlanders
WATSON Henry S. MM Pte M2/184229 Army Service Corps
WATSON Herbert MM Cpl 305721 6th Notts & Derby Regt
WATSON Herbert MM Pte 13920 7th Norfolk Regt
WATSON Herbert MM L/Cpl 2014 2/1(West Lancashire)Fd Amb RAMC
WATSON Houston MM Pte 73732 51st Bn Machine Gun Corps DOW 3.9.18.
WATSON Hugh H. MM Pte 5337 Northumberland Fusiliers
WATSON J. MM L/Cpl 266099 Seaforth Highlanders
WATSON J.F. MM Pte 25245 Border Regt
WATSON Jack MM Pte 18060 King's Own Scottish Borderers
WATSON Jack James Leslie MM Pte 30854 8th East Surrey Regt
WATSON James MM L/Cpl 44504 8th Seaforth Highlanders
WATSON James MM Sjt 715247 RFA
WATSON James MM Pte 3744 15th Highland Light Infantry
WATSON James MM Dvr 46639 D/94 Bde RFA KIA 22.9.18.
WATSON James MM L/Cpl 240481 4/5th Royal Highlanders KIA 3.5.18.
WATSON James MM Sjt 5057 3rd Rifle Brigade
WATSON James MM Sjt 1560 1/6th West Riding Regt
WATSON James MM Pte 1931 5/6th Royal Scots
WATSON James MM Pte 670 Gordon Highlanders
WATSON James MM Cpl 400053 Royal Engineers
WATSON James MM Spr 56706 101 Fd Coy Royal Engineers
WATSON James MM+Bar Pte 352436 Royal Scots
WATSON James MM Pte 25757 7th North Lancashire Regt KIA 31.7.17.
WATSON James A. MM Cpl 421089 10th London Regt
WATSON James B. MM L/Cpl 22686 Lincolnshire Regt
WATSON James C. MM L/Cpl C/12634 King's Royal Rifle Corps
WATSON James D. MM L/Cpl 7329 2nd South Staffordshire Regt
WATSON James Gordon MM Sjt 2186 1/12th London Regt
WATSON James Henry MM S/Sjt Armourer 557 Army Ordnance Corps att 36 Siege Bty RGA.
WATSON James L. MM Sjt 16358 10th Durham Light Infantry
WATSON James Leonard MM Pte 49583 1/6th Cheshire Regt KIA 26.9.17.
WATSON James M. MM Pte 355684 10th Liverpool Regt
WATSON James M. MM Cpl 38996 Royal Engineers
WATSON John MM Cpl 63554 2nd West Yorkshire Regt
WATSON John MM Pte 241473 1/5th Border Regt
WATSON John MM L/Cpl 24138 North Lancashire Regt
WATSON John MM Pte 42544 Royal Scots
WATSON John MM Pte R/3329 9th King's Royal Rifle Corps DOW 24.8.16.
WATSON John MM L/Cpl 204873 North Lancashire Regt
WATSON John MM Pte 22319 2nd Highland Light Infantry
WATSON John MM Pte 8714 10th Scottish Rifles
WATSON John MM Pte 21/593 23rd Northumberland Fusiliers KIA 10.1.17.
WATSON John MM Gnr 16669 RFA
WATSON John MM Pte 28286 1st Border Regt
WATSON John MM Gnr Fitter 148729 RGA
WATSON John MM Pte 241311 Gordon Highlanders
WATSON John MM Sjt 12711 7th Lincolnshire Regt KIA 26.8.18.
WATSON John "MM,MID" Sjt 18628 Durham Light Infantry
WATSON John E. MM Sjt 1916 Royal Sussex Regt
WATSON John F. MM L/Cpl 23752 8th Durham Light Infantry
WATSON John H. MM Sjt 24228 46th Bn Machine Gun Corps
WATSON John H. MM Pte 41004 Royal Dublin Fusiliers
WATSON John Keith MM Gnr 61412 172 Siege Bty RGA
WATSON John R. MM+Bar Spr 492102 46 Div Sig Coy Royal Engineers
WATSON John W. MM Sjt 38121 Royal Fusiliers
WATSON John W. MM Pte 33491 Machine Gun Corps
WATSON Joseph MM Cpl 24207 1st Royal Inniskilling Fusiliers KIA 2.12.17.
WATSON Joseph H.C. MM Sjt 6601 2nd Royal Sussex Regt
WATSON Joseph W. MM Gnr 34058 RFA
WATSON Lawrence MM 2nd Cpl 193098 2 Special Coy Royal Engineers KIA 25.5.18.
WATSON Leslie MM CQMS 59284 Labour Corps
WATSON Martin MM Pte 19350 Border Regt
WATSON Matthew "DCM,MM" CSM 200390 1/5th Liverpool Regt
WATSON Nicholas W. MM Cpl 50875 RGA
WATSON Oswald Eric MM L/Cpl 926 16th Royal Warwickshire Regt
WATSON Percy MM Pte 290066 1st Norfolk Regt
WATSON Peter MM Pte 4682 1/7th Arg & Suth Highlanders KIA 9.4.17.
WATSON Peter D. MM Sjt 16139 Highland Light Infantry
WATSON R.B. MM Air Mech 1 8609 Royal Air Force
WATSON Reginald MM Pte 15144 7th Norfolk Regt
WATSON Reginald A. MM Bdr 76057 127 Siege Bty RGA
WATSON Robert MM Spr 244153 209 Fd Coy Royal Engineers
WATSON Robert MM+Bar L/Cpl 16946 6th Northamptonshire Regt
WATSON Robert MM Spr 61614 73 Fd Coy Royal Engineers
WATSON Robert MM Pte 16675 11th Royal Scots
WATSON Robert MM Pte 15252 12th West Yorkshire Regt
WATSON Robert MM Pte 4022 9th Seaforth Highlanders KIA 27.3.18.
WATSON Robert Henry MM Pte 475351 88 Fd Amb RAMC KIA 2.10.18.
WATSON Robert McLean MM Pte 15818 17th Highland Light Infantry
WATSON Robert T. "DCM,MM" Sjt 11062 1st Scottish Rifles
WATSON Ronald Alexander "DCM,MM" Sjt 2611 1/9th Highland Light Infantry
WATSON Samuel MM Pte 38504 1/5th Yorkshire Regt
WATSON Samuel MM L/Cpl 7808 2nd Scots Guards
WATSON Samuel MM Cpl 9570 2nd Cheshire Regt
WATSON Sidney C. MM Dvr 35377 B/174 Bde RFA
WATSON Simon S. MM Pte 23/629 Northumberland Fusiliers
WATSON Stafford Frank MM L/Cpl 1200 1/16th London Regt DOW 15.8.16.
WATSON Stanley E. MM Pte 41808 South Staffordshire Regt
WATSON Stanley L. MM Sjt 387652 6 Siege Coy Royal Engineers
WATSON Stephen Gibbon MM Pte 13388 8th Yorkshire Regt
WATSON Thomas MM L/Bdr 100 D/168 Bde RFA
WATSON Thomas MM Pte 555419 16th London Regt
WATSON Thomas MM L/Sjt 19479 Machine Gun Corps
WATSON Thomas MM Pte 201663 5th Liverpool Regt
WATSON Thomas "MM,MSM" Sjt 18869 10th Scottish Rifles
WATSON Thomas MM Cpl 457503 Royal Engineers
WATSON Thomas MM Cpl 75947 Signal Service Royal Engineers
WATSON Thomas MM Pte 6005 2nd Dragoons
WATSON Thomas MM Pte S/4008(6?) 11th Arg & Suth Highlanders KIA 28.8.16.
WATSON Thomas MM 2nd Cpl 45948 25 Div Sig Coy Royal Engineers KIA 15.6.17.
WATSON Thomas MM Pte 1518 7th Seaforth Highlanders KIA 16.4.18.
WATSON Thomas C. MM Pte 271043 1/1st Northumberland Yeo
WATSON Thomas Hunter May MM Cpl 805522 231 Bty RFA KIA 28.5.18.
WATSON Thomas M. MM+Bar Sjt 24287 Machine Gun Corps
WATSON Thomas Sydney "MM,MID" 2nd Cpl 101124 225 Fd Coy Royal Engineers

WATSON Tom MM L/Cpl PS/7248 11th Royal Fusiliers DOW 25.10.17.
WATSON Urban MM L/Cpl 909 1st Royal Warwickshire Regt
WATSON Vernon V. MM Sjt M2/081642 Army Service Corps att RGA.
WATSON W. MM Sjt 75158 Machine Gun Corps
WATSON W. MM(28463 E Yorks)+Bar Sjt 238058 Lincolnshire Regt
WATSON W.H. MM Pte 393657 London Regt
WATSON Walter MM+Bar Pte 240888 5th & 2/6th West Yorkshire Regt
WATSON Walter Ballentyne MM L/Cpl 18627 12th Durham Light Infantry
WATSON Walter J. MM Pte 15034 Machine Gun Corps
WATSON William MM Bdr 631128 A/255 Bde RFA
WATSON William MM Spr 63919 69 Fd Coy Royal Engineers
WATSON William MM Cpl 9663 2nd Arg & Suth Highlanders
WATSON William MM Pte 202743 2nd Royal Scots Fusiliers
WATSON William MM Sjt 14551 13th Royal Scots
WATSON William MM Cpl 1252 2nd Arg & Suth Highlanders
WATSON William MM L/Cpl 2829 1/4th Royal Highlanders
WATSON William MM+Bar L/Sjt 276658 Arg & Suth Highlanders
WATSON William MM Cpl 240297 1/5th Royal Highlanders
WATSON William MM Pte 268279 1/6th Royal Highlanders DOW 8.8.17.
WATSON William MM Pte 22/1115 Durham Light Infantry
WATSON William A. MM L/Cpl 18327 Shropshire Light Infantry
WATSON William Cecil MM L/Bdr 31632 RFA
WATSON William E. MM Sjt 25764 28 Bty 9 Bde RFA
WATSON William Gilbert MM Bdr 110059 RGA
WATSON William J. MM Pte 371543 8th London Regt
WATSON William K. MM Pte 25559 Durham Light Infantry
WATSON William M. MM Pte 23977 1/6th Seaforth Highlanders
WATSON William Sidney MM CSM 5948 2nd Coldstream Guards KIA 16.9.16.
WATSON William T. MM Cpl 40154 RGA
WATSON William T. MM Bdr 77833 'K' Bty RHA
WATT Alec MM Pte 7231 2nd West Riding Regt
WATT Alexander S. MM Pte 266399 Gordon Highlanders
WATT Andrew MM Pte 6146 1st Cameron Highlanders
WATT Arthur MM Pte 34386 RAMC
WATT Charles W. MM Pte 514962 14th London Regt
WATT David MM Sjt 630579 RFA
WATT Duncan Samuel MM Pte 28734 Border Regt
WATT Edward MM Pte 47765 1st Royal Scots Fusiliers
WATT Francis MM+Bar Pte 292580 1/7th Gordon Highlanders
WATT George MM Cpl 200529 5/6th Scottish Rifles
WATT George MM Pte 265908 1/5th Gordon Highlanders
WATT George MM Sjt 27745 20 Fd Coy Royal Engineers
WATT George MM Gnr Fitter 656334 RFA
WATT J.B. MM Cpl 463046 Royal Engineers
WATT James MM Pte 40530 17th Highland Light Infantry
WATT James MM Pte 11290 1st Royal Scots Fusiliers KIA 28.4.17.
WATT James MM Sjt 7419 Gordon Highlanders
WATT James MM Pte 1607 Seaforth Highlanders
WATT James MM Pte 266442 Gordon Highlanders
WATT James MM Sjt 4330 RFA
WATT James M. MM Sjt 265052 1/6th Gordon Highlanders
WATT James W. MM Sjt 406008 Royal Engineers
WATT John MM Cpl 13790 5/6th Royal Scots
WATT John MM+Bar Sjt 200967 1/4th Gordon Highlanders
WATT John MM Sjt 200189 5/6th Scottish Rifles
WATT Matthew MM Pte 12110 6th King's Own Scottish Borderers
WATT Peter MM Pte 21287 Cameron Highlanders
WATT Peter MM Pte 2652 1/7th Gordon Highlanders KIA 13.11.16.
WATT Peter MM L/Cpl 21252 16th Royal Scots
WATT Robert L. "MM,MID" Pte 320108 3 Fd Amb RAMC
WATT Thomas MM Pte S/7610 13th Rifle Brigade
WATT Thomas MM Pte 11226 10th Royal Inniskilling Fusiliers
WATT Thomas A. MM Spr 50167 Royal Engineers
WATT Thomas Russell MM Sjt 7398 D/48 Bde RFA
WATT William MM Sjt 290504 1/7th Gordon Highlanders KIA 4.7.17.
WATT William MM Pte 1001 North Irish Horse
WATT William Henry MM Sjt 913 RFA
WATTERS David "MM+2 Bars,CG(B)" Cpl 359954 3 Div Sig Coy Royal Engineers
WATTERS Robert MM Pte 10/16087 15th Royal Irish Rifles
WATTERS T. MM Pte 21797 Welsh Regt
WATTERS Thomas MM Pte 235176 4th North Lancashire Regt
WATTERS W. MM Sjt 444007 42 Div Sig Coy Royal Engineers
WATTERSON Edward S. MM Cpl 10733 12th Manchester Regt

WATTON Alfred MM Pte 37778 1st Northumberland Fusiliers
WATTON Frederick MM Sjt 12545 2nd Worcestershire Regt
WATTON Frederick G. MM Pnr 221657 62 Div Sig Coy Royal Engineers
WATTON Percy MM Cpl 19920 2nd Worcestershire Regt
WATTON Thomas MM Gnr 36947 C/82 Bde RFA
WATTS A.J. MM L/Cpl 64481 RAMC
WATTS Albert MM Pte 40075 11th Royal West Surrey Regt
WATTS Albert MM Sjt 200177 1/4th Northamptonshire Regt
WATTS Albert E. MM Gnr Sig 618243 298 Bde RFA
WATTS Albert Henry MM Pte 25390 Shropshire Light Infantry
WATTS Albert J. MM Pte 320639 12th Norfolk Regt
WATTS Alfred MM Pte 1783 19th Middlesex Regt
WATTS Alfred J. MM+Bar Pte 43640 1/7th Middlesex Regt
WATTS Arthur MM L/Sjt 2978 12th Middlesex Regt
WATTS Arthur Ernest MM Pte G8/4790 8th East Surrey Regt KIA 13.7.16.
WATTS Arthur S. "DCM,MM" Sjt 13353 3rd Grenadier Guards
WATTS Benjamin H. MM Sjt 7898 8th Northumberland Fusiliers
WATTS Brien G. MM Spr 487285 9 Div Sig Coy Royal Engineers
WATTS Cecil N. MM Gnr 245762 434 Bty RFA
WATTS Charles "MM,MID" Pte 2771 1st Gloucestershire Regt
WATTS Charles H. MM Spr 63157 Royal Engineers
WATTS Charles Robert MM Pte 24805 1/4th Suffolk Regt
WATTS Clarence E. MM Sjt 70911 5 Bde RFA
WATTS Clement Frank "MM,CG(It)" Cpl 21819 8th Devonshire Regt KIA 27.10.18.
WATTS Cyril Russell "MM,MID" Sjt 22682 Machine Gun Corps
WATTS David Jesse MM L/Cpl 10914 1st Worcestershire Regt DOW 1.12.17.
WATTS Edward H. MM Sjt 9640 1st Royal Scots
WATTS Elijah MM Pte MS/4947 Guards Div Train Army Service Corps
WATTS Ernest Albert MM Sjt Fitter 79398 37 Bty 27 Bde RFA
WATTS F.G. MM Cpl 8717 1st East Kent Regt
WATTS Francis Cornforth MM L/Cpl 650451 1/21st London Regt
WATTS Frank MM Pte 70538 11th Notts & Derby Regt
WATTS Frank "DCM,MM" Cpl 25593 19 Fd Amb RAMC
WATTS Frank E. MM 2nd Cpl 59265 Royal Engineers
WATTS Frank J. MM Pte 700446 1/23rd London Regt
WATTS George MM Sjt 6849 1st Somerset Light Infantry
WATTS H.D. MM L/Cpl 512303 RAMC
WATTS Harry MM Cpl 23416 6 Div Sig Coy Royal Engineers
WATTS Harry MM Pte 8267 2nd South Staffordshire Regt
WATTS Herbert MM L/Cpl 23206 4th Grenadier Guards
WATTS Herbert Horace MM Cpl B/2502 7th Rifle Brigade
WATTS James MM Cpl 31494 115 Hy Bty RGA
WATTS James MM Pte 325493 1/9th Durham Light Infantry
WATTS James W. "DCM,MM" Sjt 486259 468 Fd Coy Royal Engineers
WATTS John MM Pte 305614 7th Royal Warwickshire Regt
WATTS John B. MM Pte 267434 Royal Warwickshire Regt
WATTS John T. MM Spr 96919 Royal Engineers
WATTS Leonard MM Sjt 251402 1/3rd London Regt KIA 9.10.18.
WATTS Merlin R. MM Pte 260373 Gloucestershire Regt
WATTS Oliver Frederick MM Air Mech 1 2073 18 Squadron Royal Flying Corps Killed 27.11.16.
WATTS Oswald MM Bdr 66523 RFA
WATTS Percy MM Dvr 16198 RFA
WATTS R.F. MM+Bar Cpl 34597 11th Essex Regt
WATTS Reginald MM Cpl 8424 2nd Royal Irish Regt
WATTS Richard MM Cpl 28205 12th East Surrey Regt
WATTS Richard Henry MM Sjt 34219 'L' Bty RHA
WATTS Robert "DCM,MM" 2nd Cpl 24077 2 Div Sig Coy Royal Engineers
WATTS Rowland MM Sjt 38978 RAMC
WATTS Thomas Henry "MM,MSM,MID" S/Sjt Mechanician MS/451 32 Div MT Coy Army Service Corps
WATTS Thomas Percival "MM,MID" SSM 245 1/1st North Somerset Yeo
WATTS Victor B. MM Pte 4919 Middlesex Regt
WATTS Walter MM Pte 238154 1st Worcestershire Regt
WATTS Walter MM L/Cpl 27803 12th Suffolk Regt KIA 12.4.18.
WATTS William MM Pte 90270 Machine Gun Corps
WATTS William MM Pte 5047 Notts & Derby Regt
WATTS William F. MM Cpl 498167 476 Fd Coy Royal Engineers
WATTS William G. MM Pte 89600 32nd Bn Machine Gun Corps
WATTS William H. MM Pte 29576 Northumberland Fusiliers
WATTS William Henry MM Cpl 15859 10th Essex Regt KIA 2.9.18.
WATTS William James MM 2nd Cpl 524200 484 Fd Coy Royal Engineers

WATTS William P. MM Sjt 31416 6th Royal West Kent Regt
WATTS William R. MM Pte M2/080515 Army Service Corps
WAUGH Alexander MM Pte 2864 RAMC
WAUGH Alexander MM Pte 202263 2nd Royal Scots KIA 27.9.18.
WAUGH Alexander MM Sjt 6567 2nd Royal Highlanders
WAUGH Andrew McKinnon MM Spr 58033 106 Fd Coy Royal Engineers
WAUGH Charles MM L/Cpl 10175 15th Durham Light Infantry
WAUGH Ernest MM Sjt 325182 Durham Light Infantry
WAUGH Fred MM Bdr 21506 B/91 Bde RFA
WAUGH Henry MM Pte 43455 21st West Yorkshire Regt KIA 1.5.17.
WAUGH Ian MM Pte M2/132070 Army Service Corps att 88 Fd Amb RAMC.
WAUGH Isaac MM Pte 37480 20th Northumberland Fusiliers KIA 9.4.17.
WAUGH James MM Pte 16574 33rd Bn Machine Gun Corps
WAUGH John MM L/Cpl 40196 King's Own Scottish Borderers
WAUGH Joseph MM Sjt 4738 9th Seaforth Highlanders
WAUGH Richard MM Pte 6003 Scots Guards
WAUGH Samuel M. MM Pte 553 2nd Lancashire Fusiliers
WAUGH Walter MM Spr 69160 35 Div Sig Coy Royal Engineers
WAUGH William "DCM,MM" Cpl 47678 RFA
WAUGH William Robert MM Spr 46978 Signal Service Royal Engineers Died 8.12.17.
WAXTER G. MM Pte 43020 1st Essex Regt
WAY Frank MM Sjt 8648 2nd Devonshire Regt
WAY Harry J.P. MM L/Cpl 265622 1/1st Bucks Bn Oxf & Bucks Light Infantry
WAY Stanley H. MM Gnr 91723 Tank Corps
WAY Stanley J. MM Pte 9409 12th Middlesex Regt
WAY Walter D. MM Pte 43782 18 Fd Amb RAMC
WAY Walter G. MM Spr 510443 Royal Engineers
WAY William MM Sjt 13258 10th Devonshire Regt
WAY William Thomas John MM Bdr 371186 114 Siege Bty RGA
WAYBURN John MM+Bar Sjt 8886 8th Devonshire Regt
WAYLAN Sidney MM Cpl 98178 155 Fd Coy Royal Engineers DOW 25.3.18.
WAYMARK William Victor MM Pte 6173 7th Rifle Brigade DOW 27.8.17.
WAYNE Frank MM Pte 6445 1st Manchester Regt
WAYNE George "MM,MID" Bdr 132171 RGA
WAYT Henry V. MM+Bar Sjt 203581 1st London Regt
WEAKE Harry MM Pte 8967 2nd West Riding Regt AKA Harry HAGGER
WEAKFORD Henry G. MM Sjt 70468 1/1st Berkshire Yeomanry
WEAKFORD Thomas R. MM Sjt 34598 11th Essex Regt
WEAL John Henry MM Sjt 528106 54 Div Sig Coy Royal Engineers
WEALE Edward Gerald Douglas MM Pte 203670 14th Gloucestershire Regt
WEALL John A. MM Pte 121 Lincolnshire Regt
WEALL William MM Gnr 63198 D/112 Bde RFA
WEALLEANS Joshua P. MM BSM 36806 C/59 Bde RFA
WEAR Robert David MM L/Sjt 21/565 21st Northumberland Fusiliers DOW 9.7.16.
WEARE M. MM F/Sjt 276 Royal Flying Corps
WEARING Cyril Murray MM Cpl 106064 187 Tunnelling Coy Royal Engineers
WEARING John MM L/Cpl 35891 East Surrey Regt
WEARMOUTH Isaac MM+Bar Pte 23/415 Northumberland Fusiliers
WEARN Charles E. MM L/Cpl 531648 15th London Regt
WEARN Percy "DCM,MM" L/Cpl 9352 6th Wiltshire Regt
WEARNE Thomas MM Pte 33644 Duke of Cornwall's LI
WEARY Abel MM Pte 204881 2nd Devonshire Regt
WEATE Joseph MM Sjt 20483 18 Fd Amb RAMC
WEATHERALL Albert MM Pte 26325 8th Royal Inniskilling Fusiliers KIA 16.8.17.
WEATHERALL Joseph MM Dvr 64706 5 Div Ammn Col RFA
WEATHERHEAD Edmund L. MM Pte 17309 2nd Royal Scots Fusiliers
WEATHERHEAD Ernest MM Pte 1030 16th Lancers
WEATHERHEAD Frederick W. MM Pte 45613 Lancashire Fusiliers
WEATHERHEAD Harry MM L/Cpl 13612 Cameron Highlanders att KAR.
WEATHERHEAD L.B. MM Pte 1010 GMGR
WEATHERHEAD Maurice MM Pte 43981 2nd Durham Light Infantry
WEATHERILL Thomas MM Cpl 66286 15 Bde RFA
WEATHERILL William MM L/Cpl S/12566 14th Arg & Suth Highlanders KIA 24.4.17.
WEATHERITT John MM Sjt 64965 33 Bde RFA

WEATHERLEY J.H. MM Cpl M1/6774 Army Service Corps att 24 Fd Amb RAMC.
WEATHERLEY John Henry Thomas MM Gnr 94773 D/276 Bde RFA
WEATHERLY Edward William Sprot MM Pte 200259 2nd Bn Tank Corps
WEATHERSTONE James MM Sjt 144998 Royal Engineers
WEATHERSTONE John MM Sjt M2/081170 Army Service Corps
WEATHERUP William MM Cpl 14/6725 Royal Irish Rifles
WEAVER A. MM Cpl 186 RFA
WEAVER A.A. MM Sjt 497309 RAMC
WEAVER Arthur MM Pte 681675 1/22nd London Regt KIA 2.9.18
WEAVER Arthur L. MM Cpl M2/051554 Army Service Corps
WEAVER Edgar Frank MM Gnr 32741 RFA
WEAVER Edward H. "DCM,MM" Sjt 67599 RFA
WEAVER Ernest MM Spr 104490 233 Fd Coy Royal Engineers KIA 13.8.17.
WEAVER Francis C. MM Pte 241178 Gloucestershire Regt
WEAVER Harry O. MM Cpl 12954 RGA
WEAVER Henry Isaac MM Gnr 38881 26 Bde RFA
WEAVER Herbert MM Pte 53942 8th Liverpool Regt
WEAVER Joseph MM Pte 8359 1st North Staffordshire Regt
WEAVER Robert E. MM Cpl 269722 1/1st Hertfordshire Regt
WEAVER Thomas George C. MM Sjt 74032 10th Notts & Derby Regt
WEAVER W. MM Pte 269723 Hertfordshire Regt
WEAVER William Davies MM+Bar Cpl 18780 C/87 Bde RFA
WEAVER William T. MM Gnr 604142 RHA
WEAVING Arthur Charles MM Pte 3147 2/6th Royal Warwickshire Regt
WEAVING Edwin MM+Bar L/Cpl 13027 8th Gloucestershire Regt DOW 13.11.16.
WEBB A. MM Pte 17224 9th Essex Regt
WEBB Albert MM Cpl 20089 2nd Royal Munster Fusiliers
WEBB Albert MM Sjt 305689 1/8th Liverpool Regt
WEBB Albert MM Dvr 935559 RFA
WEBB Albert E. MM Pte 26347 Norfolk Regt
WEBB Albert E. MM Pte M2/132608 Army Service Corps att RAMC.
WEBB Albert Laurence MM Pte 72040 132 Fd Amb RAMC
WEBB Albert W. MM Pte 24369 1st Northamptonshire Regt
WEBB Alfred MM Pte 8321 6th Royal West Kent Regt
WEBB Alfred T. MM+Bar Pte 305057 Royal Warwickshire Regt
WEBB Alfred Wilson MM Cpl 1646 1 Cav Div Supply Col Army Service Corps
WEBB Arthur MM Pte 10021 10th Royal West Kent Regt
WEBB Arthur MM L/Cpl 1423 12th Lancers
WEBB Arthur MM Spr 103101 Royal Engineers
WEBB Arthur MM Pte 9909 11th Royal West Kent Regt
WEBB Arthur MM Pte 34793 Durham Light Infantry
WEBB Arthur C. MM+Bar Sjt 34198 26 & 31 Heavy Btys RGA
WEBB Arthur Edward William MM Pte M2/022041 Army Service Corps att 1 Fd Amb RAMC.
WEBB Arthur H. MM Sjt 17987 9th South Staffordshire Regt
WEBB Augustus H. MM Pte 7058 13th Royal Fusiliers
WEBB Austin Arthur MM Sjt 15518 11th Suffolk Regt KIA 8.4.17.
WEBB Bertie MM L/Cpl 43408 1st Norfolk Regt DOW 8.11.17.
WEBB C.J. MM L/Cpl 21452 Machine Gun Corps
WEBB C.J. MM Cpl 9168 1st Essex Regt
WEBB Caleb MM+Bar Gnr 37339 354 Siege Bty RGA
WEBB Cecil H. MM Pnr 26524 1 Div Sig Coy Royal Engineers
WEBB Charles MM Pte 9353 7th Suffolk Regt
WEBB Charles "MM,MID" L/Cpl 8455 Coldstream Guards
WEBB Charles J. MM Pte 13443 10th Gloucestershire Regt
WEBB Charles W. MM L/Cpl 7401 1st Royal Berkshire Regt
WEBB Clifford MM+Bar Sjt 61810 'AP' Cable Section Royal Engineers
WEBB Cyril MM L/Cpl 496911 97 Fd Coy Royal Engineers
WEBB Edward MM L/Cpl 307706 1/5th West Yorkshire Regt
WEBB Edward A. MM Dvr 49097 B/123 Bde RFA DOW 12.9.18.
WEBB Edward Percy MM Pte 25918 10th West Riding Regt Died 26.8.18.
WEBB Edwin F. MM Gnr 30856 24 Bde RFA
WEBB Ernest MM 2nd Cpl 230127 Royal Engineers
WEBB Ernest MM Cpl 19061 13th Liverpool Regt
WEBB Ernest C. MM Cpl 65611 106 Fd Coy Royal Engineers
WEBB Ernest G. MM Cpl 27767 35 Div Ammn Col RFA
WEBB Ernest R. MM Spr 534734 23 Div Sig Coy Royal Engineers
WEBB Felix W. MM CQMS 2196 7th Royal West Surrey Regt
WEBB Francis Handel MM Sjt 2521 1/8th Royal Warwickshire Regt
WEBB Frank MM Pte 241339 Worcestershire Regt
WEBB Frank MM Spr 218200 10 Railway Coy Royal Engineers

WEBB Fred MM Pte 240699 1/5th Suffolk Regt
WEBB Frederick MM CSM 7851 1st South Staffordshire Regt
WEBB Frederick MM L/Cpl 41780 Royal Engineers
WEBB Frederick A. MM Cpl 29189 RGA
WEBB Frederick Arthur MM Pte 42333 1st Middlesex Regt KIA 6.12.17.
WEBB Frederick G. MM Sjt 10083 2nd North Lancashire Regt DOW 16.6.18.
WEBB Frederick J. MM+Bar Cpl 12635 2nd Grenadier Guards
WEBB Frederick William MM Cpl R/5127 10th King's Royal Rifle Corps Died 2.11.16.
WEBB G.A. MM Pte S/26278 Rifle Brigade
WEBB George MM L/Cpl 148842 46th Bn Machine Gun Corps
WEBB George MM Pte 54496 19th Middlesex Regt
WEBB George MM L/Cpl 235402 14th Royal Welsh Fusiliers KIA 8.10.18.
WEBB George A. MM Pte 200760 1/5th Liverpool Regt
WEBB George H. MM CSM 240666 5th Royal Lancaster Regt
WEBB Glenlivet MM L/Cpl 1574 1/4th Suffolk Regt KIA 20.7.16.
WEBB Gordon MM Sjt 56116 11 Bde RFA
WEBB H.C. MM Cpl 2476 9th Essex Regt
WEBB H.T. MM Pte 473305 RAMC
WEBB Harold J. MM Spr 568425 25 Div Sig Coy Royal Engineers
WEBB Harold Sidney MM Sjt 21965 118 Coy Machine Gun Corps KIA 14.11.17.
WEBB Harry MM L/Cpl 39555 West Yorkshire Regt
WEBB Harry B. MM L/Cpl 48849 Royal Engineers
WEBB Henry MM Gnr 22864 A/70 Bde RFA
WEBB Henry MM Sjt 8260 RGA
WEBB Henry Steohen MM Sjt 9285 1st South Staffordshire Regt KIA 4.10.17.
WEBB Herbert MM Pte 22145 Machine Gun Corps
WEBB Horace Reginad MM Cpl 270814 10th East Kent Regt
WEBB Horace Stanley MM L/Cpl 13099 12th Suffolk Regt
WEBB Jack MM Pte M2/020115 17 Div MT Coy Army Service Corps
WEBB James MM Cpl 45240 53 Coy Machine Gun Corps
WEBB James MM Pte 200787 1/5th Manchester Regt
WEBB James MM Sjt 26223 40 Bde RFA
WEBB James E. MM Pte 38189 RAMC
WEBB James Edward MM Sjt 1577 1/4th South Lancashire Regt
WEBB James H. "MM,MID" Sjt 71594 36 Bde RFA
WEBB James W. MM L/Cpl 17415 4th Royal Fusiliers
WEBB John MM L/Cpl 22129 1st North Lancashire Regt KIA 1.7.16.
WEBB John MM Sjt 1680 1/5th North Staffordshire Regt
WEBB John MM Pte 9072 2nd Royal Dublin Fusiliers
WEBB John C. MM Sjt 24436 9th Royal Welsh Fusiliers
WEBB John E. MM Pte 28134 2nd Wiltshire Regt
WEBB John James MM L/Cpl 2799 1/8th West Yorkshire Regt
WEBB John L. "MM+Bar,MSM" CSM 12709 7th Norfolk Regt
WEBB John P. MM Cpl 75533 4th Bn Tank Corps
WEBB Joseph "DCM,MM" Sjt 2244 1st Royal Warwickshire Regt
WEBB Joseph MM Pte 10797 5th Oxf & Bucks Light Infantry
WEBB Joseph Giles MM Pte 419420 1/3(North Midland)Fd Amb RAMC
WEBB Joseph H. MM L/Cpl 202055 North Staffordshire Regt
WEBB Leonard Inch MM L/Cpl 142693 34 Div Sig Coy Royal Engineers DOW 3.8.18.
WEBB Leonard R. MM L/Cpl 3579 1/4th London Regt
WEBB Leslie Malcolm MM Pte 493544 2/1(Home Counties)Fd Amb RAMC
WEBB P.J.B. MM Pte 11429 6 Fd Amb RAMC
WEBB Percy MM Bdr 76899 RGA
WEBB Percy W. MM Spr 71316 Royal Engineers
WEBB Reginald A. MM Cpl 38993 Royal Engineers
WEBB Reginald Arthur MM Dvr 1725 240 Bde RFA
WEBB Reginald S.B. MM Sjt 48853 Royal Engineers
WEBB Richard R. MM Cpl 28295 Royal Engineers
WEBB Robert MM Pte 240326 5/6th Scottish Rifles
WEBB Robert Owen MM L/Cpl 3055 1/5th Northumberland Fusiliers KIA 14.11.16.
WEBB Robert W.S. MM L/Cpl 426010 10th London Regt
WEBB Samuel "MM,MID" Pte 10473 2nd King's Own Scottish Borderers
WEBB Sideny W. MM Cpl 200530 1/5th Bedfordshire Regt
WEBB Sydney "MM,MIDx2" Sjt 47127 94 Fd Coy Royal Engineers
WEBB Thomas L. MM Sjt 13317 12th Hampshire Regt
WEBB Tom Ernest MM Pte 1515 1/1st Monmouthshire Regt DOW 14.10.16.
WEBB Walter E. "MM,MID" L/Cpl 11143 1st Duke of Cornwall's LI
WEBB Walter F. MM Pte 22880 Liverpool Regt
WEBB Walter Frederick MM Gnr 86557 410 Bty 90 Bde RFA
WEBB Walter Frost MM L/Cpl 9946 18th Manchester Regt att APM 30 Div.
WEBB Walter Hinton MM Sjt 201015 8th Worcestershire Regt
WEBB Walter L. MM Sjt 39894 10th Lancashire Fusiliers
WEBB William MM L/Cpl 28518 9th Scottish Rifles
WEBB William MM Pte 15069 2nd Leinster Regt
WEBB William MM Cpl 12691 A/147 Bde RFA
WEBB William MM Pte 1324 16th Royal Warwickshire Regt
WEBB William MM Pte M2/136543 Army Service Corps
WEBB William MM Sjt 23000 RGA
WEBB William MM Pte 24011 Durham Light Infantry
WEBB William MM Pte S/5632 12th Rifle Brigade
WEBB William MM Sjt 7015 1st Dorsetshire Regt
WEBB William "MC,MM" SSM 50864 Machine Gun Corps(Cavalry)
WEBB William MM Cpl 291928 RGA
WEBB William H. MM S/Sjt Mechanic 21724 Royal Engineers
WEBB William Henry MM Gnr 480 RFA
WEBB William R. MM+Bar Pte 15078 9th West Riding Regt
WEBB William V. MM Bdr 44911 22 Bde RFA
WEBB William W. MM Pte M2/080120 Army Service Corps
WEBBER Albert Edward MM L/Cpl 22213 12th Suffolk Regt
WEBBER Alfred C. MM Pte 29747 1st Somerset Light Infantry
WEBBER Alfred James MM Sjt 1254 1/15th London Regt
WEBBER Arthur Dunn MM Pte 12907 9th Devonshire Regt KIA 10.10.18.
WEBBER Frank MM Pte MS/3399 Army Service Corps att 107 Fd Amb RAMC.
WEBBER Frederick D. MM L/Cpl 5719 1st South Wales Borderers
WEBBER Frederick W. MM Pte 242530 5th Gloucestershire Regt
WEBBER George MM Pte S/14729 Rifle Brigade
WEBBER H. MM Pte 58558 20th Middlesex Regt
WEBBER Harry MM Pte 309807 14th Bn Tank Corps
WEBBER Harry MM Gnr 75512 30 Bde RFA
WEBBER Harry MM Cpl 16082 Welsh Regt
WEBBER Horace Edward MM Bdr 19201 15 Div Ammn Col RFA KIA 28.3.18.
WEBBER James "DCM,MM,MID" Sjt 355626 25th Royal Welsh Fusiliers
WEBBER John MM+Bar Pte 204571 15th Hampshire Regt
WEBBER Mark G. MM Cpl 23925 1st Devonshire Regt
WEBBER Percy V. MM Pte C/6645 18th King's Royal Rifle Corps
WEBBER Reginald H. MM Cpl 358002 1 Div Sig Coy Royal Engineers
WEBBER Richard MM Sjt 39777 Worcestershire Regt
WEBBER Thomas MM Sjt 19029 Welsh Regt
WEBBER William A. MM Pte 17659 1st Dorsetshire Regt
WEBBER William C. MM L/Cpl 9465 2nd Royal Welsh Fusiliers
WEBBER William Charles MM Pte 9347 2nd Devonshire Regt DOW 19.10.16.
WEBBERLEY Frederick MM Pte 14614 7th Royal West Kent Regt
WEBB-TALBOT Frederick W. MM Dvr 20303 Royal Engineers
WEBER John MM+Bar Cpl 10429 1st Border Regt
WEBLEY Frank MM Sjt 9324 1st Gloucestershire Regt
WEBSTER A. MM Cpl 2364 Royal Warwickshire Regt
WEBSTER A. MM Pte 5553 Gordon Highlanders
WEBSTER Albert MM 2nd Cpl 95597 203 Fd Coy Royal Engineers KIA 7.6.18.
WEBSTER Albert Thomas MM Sjt 14883 10th Cheshire Regt
WEBSTER Alfred "MM,MID" Sjt 6801 20th Hussars
WEBSTER Alfred John MM Pte 28250 8th Cheshire Regt
WEBSTER Andrew Norman Sewell MM L/Cpl 511187 1/14th London Regt
WEBSTER Arthur MM Sjt 23736 Royal Lancaster Regt
WEBSTER Benjamin MM L/Cpl 39862 9th Yorkshire Light Infantry
WEBSTER Benjamin MM Cpl 56670 RHA att D/187 Bde RFA.DOW 29.11.17.
WEBSTER Charles Douglas MM Pte 266112 2/7th Notts & Derby Regt KIA 21.3.18.
WEBSTER Charles O. MM Spr 207564 Royal Engineers
WEBSTER Edmund C.H. MM Spr 38807 2 Div Sig Coy Royal Engineers
WEBSTER Edward MM Pte 45532 Durham Light Infantry
WEBSTER Edward MM Sjt 28905 East Yorkshire Regt
WEBSTER Ernest MM CSM 5054 2nd Royal Inniskilling Fusiliers
WEBSTER Frank MM+Bar Sjt 305726 1/8th West Yorkshire Regt
WEBSTER Frank MM Pte 10625 8th Lincolnshire Regt
WEBSTER Frank MM 2nd Cpl 253840 Royal Engineers
WEBSTER Frank MM Spr 1336 2/1(West Riding)Fd Coy Royal Engineers

WEBSTER Frank MM Gnr 81152 B/90 Bde RFA
WEBSTER Fred "DCM,MM" Cpl 107212 40 Div Sig Coy Royal Engineers
WEBSTER Frederick C. MM Gnr 71101 RGA
WEBSTER Frederick S. MM Sjt 337702 41 Siege Bty RGA
WEBSTER Frederick W. MM Sjt 82827 RGA
WEBSTER G. MM Pte 43308 Essex Regt
WEBSTER George "DCM,MM" CSM 200911 1/5th Liverpool Regt
WEBSTER George H. MM Pte 33597 RAMC
WEBSTER Harold MM Cpl 235273 1st West Yorkshire Regt
WEBSTER Harry MM Cpl 113959 238 Coy Machine Gun Corps
WEBSTER Harry MM Pte 14174 Scots Guards
WEBSTER Henry MM Sjt 7554 1/16th Lancashire Fusiliers
WEBSTER James MM L/Cpl 7218 1st Royal Scots Fusiliers
WEBSTER James MM Pte 21716 Manchester Regt
WEBSTER James C. MM Dmr 267687 7th Liverpool Regt
WEBSTER James Francis MM Pte 6565 1st Scots Guards
WEBSTER James H. MM Pte 55354 Royal Fusiliers
WEBSTER Jeremiah MM L/Cpl 20052 1st Royal West Kent Regt Died 21.2.19.
WEBSTER John MM Pte 201163 Scottish Rifles
WEBSTER John MM L/Cpl 61951 83 Fd Coy Royal Engineers
WEBSTER John MM Dvr 47672 40 Bde RFA
WEBSTER John MM Pte 33241 Royal Welsh Fusiliers
WEBSTER John MM Gnr 34069 B/88 Bde RFA KIA 25.4.18.
WEBSTER John MM Sjt 32 1/6th West Riding Regt
WEBSTER John MM Pte W/1080 13th Cheshire Regt KIA 16.7.16.
WEBSTER John "DCM,MM" L/Cpl 3289 2nd Rifle Brigade
WEBSTER John MM Piper 201290 Gordon Highlanders
WEBSTER John Edward MM Sjt 16840 9th Yorkshire Light Infantry KIA 16.9.16.
WEBSTER Joseph MM Pte 15836 62nd Bn Machine Gun Corps
WEBSTER Joseph T. MM Cpl 9072 10th Lancashire Fusiliers
WEBSTER Joseph W. MM L/Cpl 1321 2nd Lancashire Fusiliers
WEBSTER Kenneth "MC,MM(R/6523 Cpl KRRC)" 2Lt 4th att 7th East Yorkshire Regt
WEBSTER Maurice MM Pte 34007 4th West Riding Regt
WEBSTER P. MM Pte 44501 Manchester Regt
WEBSTER Percy J. MM Spr 359533 446 Fd Coy Royal Engineers
WEBSTER Ralph MM Pte 9520 South Staffordshire Regt
WEBSTER Reginald J. MM Gnr 55331 RHA
WEBSTER Richard MM Pnr 199066 3 Div Sig Coy Royal Engineers KIA 25.4.17.
WEBSTER Richard G. MM+Bar Sjt 8376 23rd Royal Fusiliers
WEBSTER Richard O. MM Sjt 60893 Machine Gun Corps
WEBSTER Robert MM Pte 576624 17th London Regt
WEBSTER Robert G. MM Spr 457978 Royal Engineers
WEBSTER Samuel H. MM Pte 714 RAMC
WEBSTER Sidney MM Pte 53066 4th Royal Fusiliers
WEBSTER Thomas MM Pte 46940 26th Royal Welsh Fusiliers
WEBSTER Thomas MM Cpl 47346 8 Div Ammn Col RFA
WEBSTER Thomas MM Sjt 39533 57 Div Sig Coy Royal Engineers
WEBSTER W. MM Pte 29299 Lancashire Fusiliers
WEBSTER Waddington MM Pte 17137 Durham Light Infantry
WEBSTER Walter "DCM,MM" Sjt 86530 176 Tunnelling Coy Royal Engineers
WEBSTER Walter MM Pte 200455 Royal Warwickshire Regt
WEBSTER Walter H. MM Cpl 43057 Royal Engineers
WEBSTER William MM Pte 5834 Middlesex Regt
WEBSTER William MM L/Cpl 240468 18th Liverpool Regt
WEBSTER William MM Cpl 56514 RGA
WEBSTER William MM L/Cpl 15047 Yorkshire Regt
WEBSTER William MM Cpl 889 RFA
WEBSTER William MM Pte 358008 Liverpool Regt
WEBSTER William F. MM Sjt 10839 5th Royal Berkshire Regt
WEBSTER William Harry MM Sjt SE/10313 Army Veterinary Corps att 23 Bty 24 Bde RFA.DOW 5.11.18.
WEBSTER William R. MM Cpl 35781 12/13th Northumberland Fusiliers
WEBSTER Willie MM L/Bdr 45482 5 Bty 45 Bde RFA
WEDDELL Albert L. MM Cpl 16722 2nd Northumberland Fusiliers
WEDDELL Alexander MM Spr 423967 Royal Engineers
WEDDELL Douglas MM Sjt 725924 39 Bty 169 Bde RFA
WEDDELL George MM Sjt 5022 315 Bde RFA
WEDDELL James MM Cpl 290168 10th Northumberland Fusiliers
WEDDELL John MM Sjt 270373 1/1st Northumberland Yeo
WEDDELL Philip MM Pte 14829 Yorkshire Regt
WEDGBURY Edmund "DSO,MC,DCM,MM,MID(1426 Sjt Worcs Regt)" 2Lt Gloucestershire Regt att 1/8th Worcs Regt.
WEDGE Arthur MM Pte 240136 5th Leicestershire Regt
WEDGE Frederick James MM Sjt B/2350 Rifle Brigade
WEDGE John H. "MM,MID" Sjt 4527 Machine Gun Corps
WEDGWOOD Ernest MM+Bar Sjt 329 8th Royal Fusiliers
WEDGWOOD John MM Pte 8/5968 8th Border Regt KIA 30.7.16.
WEEBER Frank MM Spr 143759 26 Fd Coy Royal Engineers
WEED Edward J. MM Pte 682485 22nd London Regt
WEEDEN Percy L. "DCM,MM" Pte 2152 2nd Royal Sussex Regt
WEEDON Frederick J. MM+Bar Sjt 11956 3rd Royal Fusiliers
WEEDON George MM Sjt 5730 12th Middlesex Regt
WEEDON Stanley MM Sjt 965542 D/236 Bde RFA
WEEDON Sydney "DCM,MM" Sjt 46383 97 Fd Coy Royal Engineers
WEEDON Victor MM Dvr 72552 B/50 Bde RFA
WEEDON William E. MM Sjt 2759 2nd Irish Guards
WEEDS William MM Pte 62796 Labour Corps
WEEDY Thomas MM Dvr 18898 B/88 Bde RFA
WEEKES Percy MM Cpl 947971 X/56 Med TM Bty RFA
WEEKS Alfred C. "DCM,MM" Sjt 36990 63 Fd Coy Royal Engineers
WEEKS Edgar G. MM L/Bdr 78288 11 Div Ammn Col RFA
WEEKS F.J. MM Pte 371821 London Regt
WEEKS Frank Douglas MM Sjt 14194 12th Gloucestershire Regt
WEEKS Frederick MM Pte 15703 9th Royal Welsh Fusiliers DOW 20.10.18.
WEEKS James MM Sjt 18731 RGA
WEEKS John MM Pte 65238 9th Royal Fusiliers
WEEKS Joshua MM Sjt 76860 Machine Gun Corps(Heavy Branch) KIA 22.8.17.
WEEKS Lawrence MM Cpl 439211 RAMC
WEEKS Reginald Frederick MM L/Sjt 1542 Middlesex Regt
WEEKS Richard H. MM Pte 13582 Royal Sussex Regt
WEEKS Sidney J. MM Bdr 46223 RFA
WEEKS Thomas MM Cpl 510367 Royal Engineers
WEEKS Walter MM Pte 14684 11th Cheshire Regt
WEEKS William R. MM L/Cpl 17830 6th Wiltshire Regt
WEEKS William S. "DCM,MM,MIDx2" SSM 10344 2 Div Sig Coy Royal Engineers
WEEKS-PEARSON E.E. MM Cpl 18000 Royal Sussex Regt
WEETMAN John A. MM Sjt 22/66 Northumberland Fusiliers
WEGG Frank "MM,MdH(F)" L/Cpl 345640 24th Royal Welsh Fusiliers
WEGG George F.J. MM Pte 41388 15th Royal Irish Rifles
WEIGHT George Harry MM L/Cpl 17991 6th Wiltshire Regt KIA 23.7.16.
WEIGHTMAN Arthur MM Bdr 89379 RGA
WEIGHTMAN Ernest MM L/Cpl 55690 15/17th West Yorkshire Regt
WEIGHTMAN George MM Pte 205017 5th Lancashire Fusiliers
WEIGHTMAN John R. MM Pte 13358 10th West Riding Regt
WEIKERT Charles D. MM Pnr 560448 Royal Engineers
WEIL Fred MM Cpl 28137 48 Heavy Bty RGA
WEILDING Charles MM Cpl 280175 1/7th Lancashire Fusiliers
WEILDING John Henry MM BQMS 9425 RFA
WEIR Adam "DCM,MM" L/Cpl 352979 1/9th Royal Scots
WEIR Alexander MM Pte 14479 7/8th King's Own Scottish Borderers
WEIR Andrew MM Pte 105981 30th Bn Machine Gun Corps
WEIR Annie MM Nurse F BRCS(VAD)
WEIR C. MM Cpl 321822 London Regt
WEIR Charles R. MM Pte 721099 1/24th London Regt
WEIR Daniel MM Gnr 96893 276 Siege Bty RGA
WEIR Duncan MM Dvr 645039 RFA Died 3.6.19.
WEIR George MM+Bar Pte 275329 1/7th Arg & Suth Highlanders
WEIR Harold T. MM L/Cpl 3532 Gloucestershire Regt
WEIR Henry Mervyn MM CQMS CMT/2211 1 Cav Div Ammn Park ASC
WEIR J. MM Pte 241338 1/5th Royal Scots Fusiliers
WEIR J.M.C. MM Sjt 18041 King's Own Scottish Borderers
WEIR John MM Pte 266802 Scottish Rifles
WEIR John MM Sjt 20485 14th Liverpool Regt
WEIR John MM 2nd Cpl 93632 219 Fd Coy Royal Engineers
WEIR "John B," MM Cpl 1962 2nd Royal Highlanders
WEIR William MM Gnr 50375 33 Bde RFA
WEIR William MM Spr 93833 Royal Engineers
WEIR William Edward MM+Bar Sjt 24365 Cheshire Regt
WEIR William H. MM Pte 22811 Royal Inniskilling Fusiliers
WEIRBRICK Michael MM L/Cpl 249611 34 Div Sig Coy Royal Engineers
WEISBERG Thomas MM+Bar Pte 678174 11th & 21st London Regt
WELBON George MM Sjt 35651 RFA
WELBORN George "DCM,MM" Sjt 16589 2nd Middlesex Regt
WELBORN Percy MM Sjt 57611 Liverpool Regt
WELBOURN A. MM Bdr 21071 108 Heavy Bty RGA

WELBOURN C. MM Pte 307539 1/8th Notts & Derby Regt
WELBURN John MM Pte 175756 1/1st Yorkshire Dragoons Yeo
WELBY John MM Sjt 705061 RFA
WELCH A.J.S. MM Pte C/1347 King's Royal Rifle Corps
WELCH Arthur H. MM Cpl 50096 18 Bde RFA
WELCH C.E. MM L/Cpl P2860 Military Mounted Police
WELCH Charles William MM Sjt 7012 62 Coy Machine Gun Corps KIA 2.4.17.
WELCH Edward W. MM L/Cpl 23112 'L' Cable Section Royal Engineers
WELCH Edwin A. MM L/Cpl 23084 Machine Gun Corps
WELCH George P. MM Sjt 34273 RAMC
WELCH Gordon L. MM Sjt 720486 1/24th London Regt
WELCH Harold MM Pte 45514 Northumberland Fusiliers
WELCH Harry "MM,MID" L/Cpl 148957 Royal Engineers
WELCH Harry W. MM Spr 471636 Royal Engineers
WELCH Jack MM L/Cpl 2587 1/1st Hertfordshire Regt
WELCH James MM Cpl 241323 Somerset Light Infantry
WELCH James MM L/Cpl 1511 1st Gloucestershire Regt
WELCH James MM Pte S/7111 Rifle Brigade
WELCH John MM L/Cpl 11667 16th Lancashire Fusiliers
WELCH John E.P. MM Pte 680140 22nd London Regt
WELCH John Frederick "MM,MSM" Sjt 450235 823 Coy Labour Corps
WELCH Joseph H. MM Sjt 22164 42 Army Troops Coy Royal Engineers
WELCH Josiah T. MM Spr 281643 Signal Service Royal Engineers
WELCH M. MM Cpl 177 Northumberland Fusiliers
WELCH Percy W. MM+Bar Pte 66829 RAMC
WELCH S. MM L/Sjt 201056 Bedfordshire Regt
WELCH T. MM Cpl 7223 Gloucestershire Regt
WELCH William MM Pte 267450 7th Liverpool Regt
WELCH William MM Dvr 94614 71 Bde RFA
WELCH Wylan MM Bdr 1139 RFA
WELD Bertram G. MM Gnr 239301 RFA
WELDEN Harold MM Pte 280894 Lancashire Fusiliers
WELDING John MM Gnr 686026 RFA
WELDON Clifford "DCM,MM" Sjt 17733 9th Yorkshire Light Infantry
WELDON Foster Thomas MM Pte 3663 1st Northumberland Fusiliers KIA 23.12.16.
WELDON Walter MM Sjt 21186 6th Dragoons
WELDRAKE George MM Pte 20293 1st Royal West Kent Regt
WELHAM Arthur G. MM L/Cpl 91892 8th Bn Tank Corps
WELHAM Clifford John MM Pte 473141 88 Fd Amb RAMC DOW 23.11.17.
WELHAM Henry C. MM Cpl 200447 1/4th Suffolk Regt
WELHAM Henry William MM Gnr 950473 B/235 Bde RFA
WELHAM Victor MM Cpl R/9609 13th King's Royal Rifle Corps KIA 23.8.18.
WELLARD Eric Henry "MM,MIDx2" Bdr 58289 330 Bde RFA
WELLBELOVE Albert W. MM CSM M/32252 Army Service Corps
WELLBELOVE George MM Gnr 31083 RGA
WELLBELOVE Harry MM Sjt 4234 'C' Bty RHA
WELLBURN John Oswald MM L/Cpl 23397 1st Yorkshire Light Infantry
WELLDEN George T.S. MM Pte 240504 Northumberland Fusiliers
WELLENS Harry MM Pte 6289 7th Shropshire Light Infantry DOW 5.9.16.
WELLER A.G. MM Cpl 18247 Royal Sussex Regt
WELLER Alfred MM Gnr 110978 RHA
WELLER Arthur Frederick MM L/Bdr 8149 B/112 Bde RFA
WELLER B. MM Gnr 9342 RFA
WELLER Charles MM L/Sjt 12315 2nd Royal Fusiliers
WELLER David MM Pte 12011 6th Royal West Kent Regt
WELLER Edward MM Pte 391371 11th London Regt
WELLER Ernest MM Pte 5888 8th Rifle Brigade KIA 4.4.18.
WELLER Ernest J. MM Pte 6800 6th Royal West Surrey Regt
WELLER Frederick C. MM L/Cpl 7260 1st East Surrey Regt
WELLER G. MM Pte 31104 Worcestershire Regt
WELLER George MM Cpl 113645 'G' Corps Sig Coy Pigeon Service Royal Engineers
WELLER J. MM Pte 70419 RAMC
WELLER Oliver H. MM L/Cpl 38916 1st Duke of Cornwall's LI
WELLER Percivel MM Sjt 2131 7th Royal West Kent Regt
WELLER Raymond MM L/Cpl 74429 Royal Engineers
WELLER Robert C. MM+Bar CSM 631650 1/20th London Regt
WELLER William MM Spr 541035 504 Fd Coy Royal Engineers
WELLINGS Alfred J. MM Pte 3580 1st Welsh Guards
WELLINGS Charles J. MM+Bar Cpl 8040 4th Royal Fusiliers
WELLINGS Thomas MM Spr 56512 102 Fd Coy Royal Engineers
WELLINGTON Charles MM Pte 13196 4th South Wales Borderers
WELLINGTON George MM Sjt 35989 4th York & Lancaster Regt
WELLINGTON Herbert H. MM Cpl 66507 5th West Yorkshire Regt
WELLINGTON John MM Sjt 8301 1st Shropshire Light Infantry KIA 7.9 17.
WELLINGTON Reginald H. MM Pte 33584 1/1st Bucks Bn Oxf & Bucks Light Infantry
WELLINGTON Stanley MM Dvr 87035 RFA
WELLMAN Arthur S. "MM,MID" Pte M2/055079 Army Service Corps
WELLMAN Victor MM Cpl 97534 155 Fd Coy Royal Engineers
WELLOCK William MM L/Bdr 675499 RFA
WELLON Walter J. MM L/Cpl 29237 4th Shropshire Light Infantry
WELLS Albert MM Sjt 247899 Royal Engineers
WELLS Albert E. MM Pte 11228 7th South Staffordshire Regt
WELLS Albert H. MM Tpr 285717 1/1st Oxfordshire Yeomanry
WELLS Albert Victor MM L/Cpl 11341 2/8th Worcestershire Regt KIA 21.3.18.
WELLS Alfred T. MM Sjt 28810 5th Bn Machine Gun Corps
WELLS Archibald MM Pte 5164 Royal Sussex Regt
WELLS Arthur MM Pte 25969 11th Royal West Surrey Regt
WELLS Arthur "DCM,MM" Sjt 17669 8th East Lancashire Regt KIA 27.3.18.
WELLS Arthur MM Pte L/10685 2nd Royal West Surrey Regt KIA 5.10.17.
WELLS Arthur MM L/Cpl 34534 2/4th Oxf & Bucks Light Infantry
WELLS Charles MM Dvr 27465 32 Bde RFA
WELLS Charles H. MM L/Cpl 2369 RAMC
WELLS Charles Hyron MM Pte 2092 7th East Surrey Regt
WELLS Clement MM L/Cpl 8429 11th Royal West Kent Regt DOW 22.4.17.
WELLS Edward W. MM Gnr 730415 RFA
WELLS Ernest Hinvis "MM,MID" Cpl 2074 7th Royal West Kent Regt
WELLS Ernest L. MM Cpl 26626 7th Royal Irish Regt
WELLS Frank MM Pte 8104 1st Coldstream Guards
WELLS Frederick MM Sjt 20 1/20th London Regt
WELLS Frederick G. MM Pte 474283 15th London Regt
WELLS Frederick Robert MM Sjt 15636 7th Duke of Cornwall's LI KIA 3.7.18.
WELLS Frederick T. MM Spr 20754 Royal Engineers
WELLS George MM L/Cpl 6245 1st Dorsetshire Regt
WELLS George MM Pte 17930 8th Shropshire Light Infantry
WELLS George "DCM,MM" Sjt 90232 C/51 Bde RFA
WELLS George MM Pte 4547 6th Royal West Kent Regt
WELLS George "MM,MID" Pte 161 1st Seaforth Highlanders
WELLS George MM L/Cpl 2683 (720730) 24th London Regt KIA 16.7.17.
WELLS George MM Sjt 69163 26 Bde RFA
WELLS George C. MM Pte 14882 6/7th Royal Scots Fusiliers
WELLS George Walter MM Pte 265941 10th West Yorkshire Regt KIA 18.9.18.
WELLS Harry MM Sjt 9223 1st Shropshire Light Infantry
WELLS Harry MM Spr 86253 179 Tunnelling Coy Royal Engineers
WELLS Harry MM 2nd Cpl 554115 511 Fd Coy Royal Engineers
WELLS Harry MM Sjt SE/2958 Army Veterinary Corps att RGA.
WELLS Harry MM L/Sjt 220438 1st Royal Berkshire Regt KIA 24.8.18.
WELLS Henry MM Pte 10865 East Surrey Regt
WELLS Herbert MM Pte 39028 1st Leicestershire Regt
WELLS Horace MM L/Cpl 1559 Royal Sussex Regt
WELLS J.G. MM L/Cpl 388455 RAMC
WELLS James MM Pte 32275 Bedfordshire Regt att 1/1st Hertfordshire Regt.
WELLS James W. MM Pte 23346 6th Yorkshire Regt
WELLS John A. MM Cpl 5416 Royal Sussex Regt
WELLS John R. MM+Bar L/Cpl 3782 2 Fd Amb RAMC
WELLS John W. MM Spr 43665 Royal Engineers
WELLS Laurence MM L/Cpl M2/098836 Army Service Corps
WELLS Leonard "DCM,MM" Sjt 610824 1/19th London Regt
WELLS Leonard MM L/Cpl 204544 1st Essex Regt
WELLS Lewis J. MM Cpl 2723 1/22nd London Regt
WELLS Nimrod MM Pte 23800 Machine Gun Corps
WELLS Percy MM Cpl 242248 Hampshire Regt
WELLS Percy John MM Sjt 616353 RHA att 158 Bde RFA
WELLS Percy Sewards MM Cpl 3767 1/4th Lincolnshire Regt
WELLS Richmond MM Pte 11449 3rd Coldstream Guards
WELLS Ridgill H. "DCM,MM" CSM 202247 1/4th Royal Welsh Fusiliers
WELLS Robert MM L/Cpl 12190 2nd Royal Irish Regt
WELLS Robert J. MM Pte 4/6838 2nd Bedfordshire Regt
WELLS S.F. MM Pte 240197 Suffolk Regt

WELLS Samuel R. MM Sjt 305257 Notts & Derby Regt
WELLS Sidney MM Pte 15306 16th Royal Welsh Fusiliers
WELLS Stanley MM+Bar 2nd Cpl 51465 25 Div Sig Coy Royal Engineers
WELLS Stephen G. MM Pte 7597 Royal West Kent Regt
WELLS Thomas "DCM,MM+Bar" Sjt 267110 2/7th West Yorkshire Regt
WELLS Thomas MM Pte 99381 5th Liverpool Regt
WELLS Thomas E. MM Pte 202895 4th Leicestershire Regt
WELLS Thomas G. "MM+Bar,MID" Sjt 7151 2 Fd Coy Royal Engineers
WELLS Thomas William Maurice MM Sjt 8796 2nd Essex Regt KIA 1.7.16.
WELLS Walter H. MM Pte 20613 7th York & Lancaster Regt
WELLS Walter W. MM Cpl 14636 Royal Engineers
WELLS Wilfred MM Cpl 92089 2nd Durham Light Infantry
WELLS William MM L/Cpl 412176 409 Fd Coy Royal Engineers
WELLS William MM Pte 45057 15th Highland Light Infantry
WELLS William MM Pte 50989 8th Manchester Regt
WELLS William MM Pte 9579 Oxf & Bucks Light Infantry
WELLS William MM Pte 42241 6th South Wales Borderers
WELLS William MM Pte 267081 2/6th Gloucestershire Regt Died 2.12.17.
WELLS William P. MM Pte 204146 Seaforth Highlanders
WELLS William Robert MM Sjt 55515 112 Railway Coy Royal Engineers
WELLSTEED Arthur MM Pte 13801 7th Wiltshire Regt
WELLUM Claude R. MM Sjt 534297 RAMC
WELLUM William H. MM Pte 721902 24th London Regt
WELMAN William E. MM Pte 10267 1st Middlesex Regt
WELSBY William MM Sjt 19954 15th Welsh Regt
WELSBY William "MM,MID" Pte 242067 East Lancashire Regt
WELSFORD George Cyril MM Bdr 138616 117 Siege Bty RGA
WELSH Cuthbert "DCM,MM" Sjt 250303 1/6th Durham Light Infantry
WELSH Edward MM Sjt 139026 180 Tunnelling Coy Royal Engineers
WELSH Ernest MM Sjt 8509 6th Border Regt
WELSH George MM Cpl 92964 Y/17 Med TM Bty RFA
WELSH George MM Sjt 25597 Royal West Surrey Regt
WELSH George MM Sjt SE/12331 Army Veterinary Corps att RFA.
WELSH Henry Thomas MM Pte 534295 4(London)Fd Amb RAMC
WELSH J.W. MM Pte 240536 Royal Welsh Fusiliers
WELSH James MM Pte 59622 11th Royal Scots Fusiliers
WELSH James MM Pte 9520 14th Arg & Suth Highlanders
WELSH John MM Gnr 109298 28 Bty 9 Bde RFA
WELSH John MM Pte 29385 2nd King's Own Scottish Borderers DOW 15.11.17.
WELSH John MM Gnr 21723 113 Bde RFA
WELSH John MM Pte 352288 1/9th Royal Scots DOW 23.12.17.
WELSH Matthew MM Dvr 64353 RFA
WELSH Patrick MM Pte 37423 West Yorkshire Regt
WELSH Patrick MM Pte 4/8660 2nd Arg & Suth Highlanders
WELSH Phares MM Pnr 312543 Royal Engineers
WELSH R. MM Pte 405445 1(West Riding)Fd Amb RAMC
WELSH Thomas MM Pte 14205 10th North Lancashire Regt
WELSH W. MM Pte 37250 Essex Regt
WELSH William MM Pte 1750 X Corps Cyclist Bn Army Cyclist Corps
WELSH William MM Pte 9943 8th Royal Highlanders KIA 14.10.18.
WELSH William J. MM Pte 630207 1/20th London Regt
WELSMAN Arthur J. MM+Bar Bdr 25730 Y/50 Med TM Bty RFA
WELSTEAD John MM Pte 30254 RAMC
WELSTEAD Reginald Arthur MM L/Sjt 3779 1/1st HAC(Inf)
WELTON Frank MM Cpl 421508 1/10th London Regt
WELTON Fred MM Pte 35431 12/13th Northumberland Fusiliers
WELTON G. MM Dvr 4908 55 Bty 33 Bde RFA
WELTON William MM Pte 202114 2/4th Royal West Surrey Regt KIA 27.12.17.
WEMBRIDGE Charles MM Pte 47506 RAMC
WEMYSS William MM L/Cpl 5775 Gordon Highlanders
WEMYSS William Marks MM Gnr 821845 RFA
WENBAN Albert W. MM 2nd Cpl 532670 Royal Engineers
WENBAN Charles MM Sjt M2/167943 Army Service Corps
WENDROP Ernest MM+Bar Dvr 26073 RFA
WENHAM Frederick W. MM L/Cpl 95749 123 Fd Coy Royal Engineers
WENLOCK William H. MM Pte 37974 Northumberland Fusiliers
WENMAN Albert Thomas MM L/Cpl M2/130584 594 Coy Army Service Corps
WENSLEY Victor J. MM Pte 34615 2/4th Oxf & Bucks Light Infantry

WENT Charles MM Pte 15883 Scots Guards
WENT G. MM Pte 131074 46th Royal Fusiliers
WENTFORD Thomas MM+Bar Sjt 43530 Norfolk Regt
WENTWORTH Charles A. MM+Bar Pte 3/9873 7th Suffolk Regt
WENTWORTH Ernest John MM Pte 2361 1/8th Arg & Suth Highlanders
WENTWORTH John William MM Cpl 209966 64 Broad Gauge Coy Royal Engineers
WENTWORTH William Henry MM Sjt 15491 3rd Grenadier Guards DOW 28.11.17.
WEPENER John H.L. MM Pte 11655 17th Lancers
WERNER Alfred MM Pte 36266 2nd Yorkshire Regt
WERNER Frederick Stephen MM Cpl 4248 1/2nd London Regt KIA 1.7.16.
WERNHAM Harold MM Pte 4968 1/4th Royal Berkshire Regt
WERNHAM Samuel E.C. MM Pte 5254 10th Royal West Surrey Regt
WERRILL Allan MM Cpl 810427 RFA
WERRITT Samuel MM Pte 241306 Royal Lancaster Regt
WERRY Albert V. MM Gnr 146461 RGA
WESLEY Arthur H. MM Sjt 8148 2nd Hampshire Regt
WESLEY B.A. MM Pte 2144 Royal West Kent Regt
WESLEY Charles Thomas MM Pte 2382 10th Royal Warwickshire Regt
WESLEY George H. "DCM,MM" Pte 306422 1/8th Notts & Derby Regt
WESSON Ernest MM Pte 34377 RAMC
WESSON Herbert J. MM Cpl 1940 4th Liverpool Regt
WESSON James MM Bdr 38907 D/83 Bde RFA
WESSON William MM Pte 58101 2nd Northumberland Fusiliers
WEST Albert MM Sjt 17492 A/77 Bde RFA
WEST Albert MM CSM 984 8th Royal West Surrey Regt
WEST Albert MM Sjt 39191 RFA
WEST Albert W. MM Sjt 551984 47 Div Sig Coy Royal Engineers
WEST Alexander MM Pte 1181 1/6th Gordon Highlanders
WEST Alfred E. MM Sjt 8034 2nd Oxf & Bucks Light Infantry
WEST Alfred James MM Pte 200446 1/5th Durham Light Infantry
WEST Anthony A. MM Pte 758 1st Welsh Guards
WEST Arthur MM Spr 121506 252 Tunnelling Coy Royal Engineers
WEST Arthur MM Pte 19888 Machine Gun Corps
WEST Arthur H. MM L/Cpl 12513 90 Fd Amb RAMC
WEST Arthur J. MM Pte 722845 24th London Regt
WEST Arthur W. MM Cpl 8787 2 Fd Coy Royal Engineers
WEST Bert MM L/Cpl 13664 11th Suffolk Regt
WEST Charles MM Pte 18348 4th Bedfordshire Regt
WEST Charles MM L/Sjt 17910 10th Worcestershire Regt
WEST Charles A. MM Sjt 60906 45 Bde RFA
WEST Charles F. "DCM,MM" Sjt 3147 7th Royal Sussex Regt
WEST Charles W. MM Spr 43676 4 Foreway Coy Royal Engineers
WEST Charles Wyndham MM Sjt 1080 13th Middlesex Regt KIA 18.8.16.
WEST Claude James John "MM,MSM,MID" Cpl 58567 68 Bty 14 Bde RFA DOW 21.3.19.
WEST D.J. MM Sjt 687582 RFA
WEST Daniel McWilliams MM L/Cpl 199095 185 Tunnelling Coy Royal Engineers
WEST Edward MM L/Cpl 13306 Royal West Surrey Regt
WEST Edward J. "DCM,MM" Sjt R/7339 6th King's Royal Rifle Corps
WEST Eric C. MM L/Sjt 242740 12th East Surrey Regt
WEST Ernest J. MM Gnr 1353 RGA
WEST Ernest M. MM Cpl 710 Royal Fusiliers
WEST F.S. MM Sjt 204060 11th Essex Regt
WEST Forbes MM Pte 40166 Gordon Highlanders
WEST Francis F. MM Sjt 23109 2 Div Sig Coy Royal Engineers
WEST Francis W. MM Pte 350084 2 Fd Amb RAMC
WEST Frank MM Pte 493859 13th London Regt
WEST Frank O. MM Sjt 44195 Royal Fusiliers
WEST Fred MM Pte 15307 24th Manchester Regt
WEST Frederick MM Sjt 68497 28 Bde RFA
WEST Frederick C. MM Pte 13010 1st Dorsetshire Regt
WEST Frederick J.R. MM Pte 452254 11th London Regt
WEST Frederick T. MM Cpl 30317 London Yeomanry
WEST George MM Cpl 27383 12th Suffolk Regt
WEST George MM Pte 4145 Royal Highlanders DOW 24.6.16.
WEST George MM Cpl 565 Northumberland Fusiliers
WEST George A. MM Cpl 154263 RGA
WEST George E. MM L/Cpl 324043 6th London Regt
WEST George W. MM+Bar Cpl 33 6th Royal West Kent Regt
WEST Gordon MM Sjt 325615 1/1st Cambridgeshire Regt KIA 22.8.18.

WEST Harold A. MM Cpl 2137 4th Rifle Brigade
WEST Harold Charles MM Pte M2/193232 Army Service Corps att 1/6(London)Fd Amb RAMC.
WEST Harry MM Pte 8999 2nd Royal West Surrey Regt
WEST Harry MM Sjt 20181 5th Dragoon Guards
WEST Harry MM Sjt 1740 7th Royal Sussex Regt
WEST Harry G. MM Dvr T/32801 4 Div Train Army Service Corps
WEST Henry T. MM Sjt 242478 6th Notts & Derby Regt
WEST Herbert J. MM L/Cpl 20084 Royal Engineers
WEST James MM Sjt 265615 1/6th Gordon Highlanders
WEST James E. MM Spr 432164 Royal Engineers
WEST John MM L/Cpl 15/13839 Royal Irish Rifles
WEST John MM Cpl 266045 1/1st Bucks Bn Oxf & Bucks Light Infantry
WEST John MM L/Cpl 17068 York & Lancaster Regt
WEST John A. MM Cpl 935395 C/282 RFA
WEST John E. MM Spr 502177 Royal Engineers
WEST John E. MM Gnr 32443 RFA
WEST John F. MM Sjt 19909 7/8th King's Own Scottish Borderers
WEST John Frederick MM Bdr 831622 Y/61 Med TM Bty RFA
WEST John R. MM Pte 200032 RAMC
WEST John Thomas MM Sjt Fitter 58083 RGA
WEST Joseph T. MM Pte 20016 Coldstream Guards
WEST Leonard MM Pte 2819 13th Royal Sussex Regt KIA 31.7.17.
WEST Leroy MM Pte 203453 1/4th Northamptonshire Regt
WEST Percy MM Bdr 74554 B/232 RFA
WEST Percy Frank MM Pte 19748 8th Bedfordshire Regt KIA 31.12.17.
WEST Percy Goodenough MM Pte 201825 2/4th Hampshire Regt
WEST Ralph Edwin MM L/Cpl 1049 South Irish Horse
WEST Robert MM Pte 9172 4th Dragoon Guards
WEST Samuel L. MM Pte 13822 Machine Gun Corps
WEST Sidney Millard MM Bdr 59524 40 Bde RFA
WEST Sydney H. MM Spr 91806 216 Army Tps Coy Royal Engineers
WEST Thomas MM Pte 241737 7th Border Regt DOW 19.9.18.
WEST Thomas William MM L/Sjt 4805 1st Lincolnshire Regt
WEST Walter MM Sjt 66227 10th Royal Scots
WEST Walter MM Pte 14737 7th Northamptonshire Regt Died 3.11.17.
WEST Walter E. MM Cpl M2/150027 Army Service Corps
WEST Walter E. MM Pte 10452 1st Liverpool Regt
WEST William MM L/Cpl 6848 1st East Yorkshire Regt
WEST William Bruce MM L/Sjt 15/1744 8th West Yorkshire Regt
WEST William F. MM Cpl 9115 31 Heavy Bty RGA
WEST William J. MM Pte M2/032148 Army Service Corps
WESTACOTT HerbertC. MM Gnr 68593 RFA
WESTALL Alfred John MM Cpl 55390 Machine Gun Corps
WESTALL Arthur J. MM Pte 633040 20th London Regt
WESTALL Claude MM Cpl 92815 Tank Corps AKA Edwin C.ROWBERRY.
WESTALL Edward Albert MM Sjt 9031 1st Scottish Rifles
WESTALL James MM Sjt 230039 1/2nd London Regt
WESTALL Sidney Thomas "MM,MID" Pte 8382 1st Duke of Cornwall's LI
WESTAWAY Arthur J. MM CSM 7921 1st Devonshire Regt
WESTAWAY Richard MM Dvr 82587 123 Fd Coy Royal Engineers
WESTBROOK A. MM L/Cpl 553 Household Bn
WESTBROOK Edward MM Pte A/203177 16th King's Royal Rifle Corps
WESTBROOK Ernest MM Cpl 7792 4th Middlesex Regt
WESTBROOK Ernest J. MM Gnr Sig 115328 306 Siege Bty RGA
WESTBROOK Fred MM Pte 11186 11th Hampshire Regt
WESTBROOK Frederick MM Sjt 4215 8th Royal Sussex Regt
WESTBURY Albert MM Cpl 5925 Machine Gun Corps
WESTBURY Alfred W. MM Sjt 3819 8th Royal West Kent Regt
WESTBY Harold MM Gnr 23412 C/152 Bde RFA DOW 14.5.18.
WESTBY Leo MM L/Sjt 19146 1st East Lancashire Regt
WESTCOMBE George MM Pte 48976 13th Rifle Brigade
WESTCOTT Albert MM Pte 295261 4th London Regt
WESTCOTT Charles A. MM Cpl 42549 4th Worcestershire Regt
WESTCOTT Edwin G. MM Pte 445 8th Royal West Surrey Regt
WESTCOTT William James MM Sjt A/203107 1st King's Royal Rifle Corps KIA 29.9 18.
WESTERBY Victor MM Cpl 64944 23 Bde RFA
WESTERDALE Frederick Charles MM Cpl 200833 1/1st London Regt DOW 18.2.18.
WESTERMAN Albert Watson MM L/Sjt 241246 2/6th West Yorkshire Regt
WESTERMAN Alfred Parkinson MM Pte 32686 West Yorkshire Regt
WESTERMAN Dennis MM Pte 305477 8th West Yorkshire Regt
WESTERMAN Frederick MM Dvr 800420 B/230 RFA
WESTERN Thomas W. MM Pte 76294 RAMC
WESTERN William P. MM Pte 3141 24th Royal Fusiliers
WESTFIELD Henry B. MM L/Cpl 11267 5th Royal Berkshire Regt
WESTGARTH Harrison MM L/Cpl 292219 Northumberland Fusiliers
WESTGARTH James Wall MM Sjt 4739 8th Northumberland Fusiliers
WESTGATE Albert O. "DCM,MM" Sjt 9546 1st Coldstream Guards
WESTGATE M. MM L/Cpl 10541 9th Essex Regt
WESTGATE Richard W. MM Sjt 41038 Royal Inniskilling Fusiliers
WESTINGTON Abraham MM Spr 43356 81 Fd Coy Royal Engineers KIA 24.3.18.
WESTLAKE Francis A. MM Sjt 240043 1/5th Yorkshire Light Infantry
WESTLAKE George MM Pte 350882 7th London Regt
WESTLAKE Reginald Frank MM Cpl M2/116576 25 Div Train Army Service Corps
WESTLAKE Richard Edward MM Sjt 11257 33 Bde RFA
WESTLAKE Samuel MM Sjt SE/11505 Army Veterinary Corps
WESTLAKE Thomas Richard MM Pte 14940 7th Bedfordshire Regt KIA 1.7.16.
WESTLAKE William MM Cpl 5828 11th Arg & Suth Highlanders
WESTLE John T. MM Cpl 11992 Northumberland Fusiliers
WESTLEY Francis Michael MM Cpl 43529 10th Lincolnshire Regt
WESTLEY J.H. MM Pte 14335 Worcestershire Regt See 14335 John OSBORNE.
WESTLEY Wilfred "MM,CG(F)" Sjt 43292 10th Essex Regt
WESTMACOTT Frederick R. MM Sjt 895 2nd Royal Warwickshire Regt
WESTMACOTT Harry R. MM Pte 14391 10th Scottish Rifles
WESTMACOTT Percival C. MM Pte 11357 6th Royal Berkshire Regt
WESTMORELAND Arthur MM Spr 482220 Royal Engineers
WESTMORELAND Marshall MM L/Cpl 20178 3rd Grenadier Guards KIA 27.11.17.
WESTMORELAND William MM S/Sjt Fitter 149526 RGA
WESTNEY Bertram MM Pte 8786 12th Middlesex Regt
WESTNEY Philip Edward "DCM,MM" Cpl 29558 123 Bty 28 Bde RFA
WESTNIDGE William H. MM Pte 305144 1/8th Notts & Derby Regt
WESTOBY Sydney MM Pte 203515 5th Yorkshire Light Infantry
WESTON Albert MM Spr 48633 95 Fd Coy Royal Engineers
WESTON Albert P. MM L/Cpl 60918 23rd Royal Fusiliers
WESTON Alfred MM Pte 15136 6th Royal Berkshire Regt
WESTON Alfred MM Pte 240083 Worcestershire Regt
WESTON Arthur MM Pte 22280 3rd Worcestershire Regt
WESTON Charles MM Pte 450636 1/11th London Regt
WESTON Charles MM L/Cpl 33606 Devonshire Regt
WESTON Clarence P. MM Pte 40459 Middlesex Regt
WESTON Clayton T. MM+Bar Gnr 2338 RFA
WESTON Cyril J. MM L/Cpl 301854 5th London Regt
WESTON Francis J. MM CQMS 498110 Royal Engineers
WESTON Frederick MM CSM 7041 Worcestershire Regt
WESTON Frederick MM Sjt 1981 7th Dragoon Guards
WESTON Frederick G. MM Pte 11109 Royal Fusiliers
WESTON G.J. MM+Bar Spr 107351 4 Div Sig Coy Royal Engineers
WESTON George MM Pte 16976 2nd South Staffordshire Regt
WESTON George MM Gnr 97677 RFA
WESTON George E. MM Pte 29826 8th Somerset Light Infantry
WESTON George F. MM Sjt 8927 1st Royal West Kent Regt
WESTON H. MM Cpl 252727 9th Essex Regt
WESTON Harold MM Spr 25424 3 Fd Coy Royal Engineers
WESTON Herbert H. MM L/Cpl 9507 2nd Royal West Kent Regt
WESTON J. MM Pte 258057 Labour Corps
WESTON John MM L/Sjt 11901 11th West Yorkshire Regt
WESTON John Leslie MM L/Cpl 82463 34th Bn Machine Gun Corps
WESTON Joseph MM Sjt 7060 1st Scots Guards
WESTON Joseph Edwin "MM+Bar,MID" Sjt 85769 187 Bde RFA
WESTON Lewis H. MM Gnr 209642 B/121 Bde RFA
WESTON Maurice Hubert MM Sjt 87925 226 Coy 30th Bn Machine Gun Corps
WESTON Michael MM Bdr 788 D/121 Bde RFA
WESTON Raymond MM Pte 4784 21st Bn Machine Gun Corps
WESTON Raymond MM L/Cpl 41777 4 Squadron Machine Gun Corps(Cavalry)
WESTON Richard Walter MM Gnr 62169 112 Siege Bty RGA
WESTON Robert MM Pte 91434 9th Bn Tank Corps
WESTON Stanley Valentine MM L/Cpl 2568 1/14th London Regt Died 18.2.19.
WESTON T. MM Sjt 113305 Royal Engineers
WESTON Thomas MM Pte 375070 10th Manchester Regt

WESTON Walter J. MM Sjt 14366 10th Essex Regt
WESTON William MM L/Cpl 9209 2nd Worcestershire Regt
WESTON William G. MM Cpl 18722 Wiltshire Regt
WESTON William Henry MM Cpl 61905 73 Fd Coy Royal Engineers
WESTRIP Edward B. MM Pte 41696 Leicestershire Regt
WESTROP Herbert MM Pte 5791 Rifle Brigade
WESTROP J.W. MM L/Cpl P/825 Military Mounted Police
WESTWATER William MM Sjt 76742 16th Bn Tank Corps
WESTWELL William MM Cpl 202369 2/5th Royal Warwickshire Regt KIA 25.3.18.
WESTWOOD Albert MM 2nd Cpl 476311 Royal Engineers
WESTWOOD Alexander Lawrence MM Pte 2993 1/9th Royal Scots
WESTWOOD Alfred MM Sjt 40151 6th York & Lancaster Regt
WESTWOOD Arthur J. "MM,MID" Sjt 21400 55 Fd Coy Royal Engineers
WESTWOOD Benjamin J. MM Gnr 64919 RGA
WESTWOOD Edward MM+Bar Sjt 24315 Royal Welsh Fusiliers
WESTWOOD Frederick MM Pte 241425 5th South Staffordshire Regt
WESTWOOD George C. MM Pte 200441 1/4th Royal Highlanders
WESTWOOD George Edward MM Sjt M2/114997 661 Coy Army Service Corps
WESTWOOD Harry A.E. MM Pte 34137 Middlesex Regt
WESTWOOD Harry Arthur MM Pte 201618 Middlesex Regt
WESTWOOD Herbert MM L/Cpl 423528 10th London Regt
WESTWOOD James MM Gnr 103856 RGA
WESTWOOD James G. "MM,MSM" L/Cpl 17068 7th Duke of Cornwall's LI
WESTWOOD John MM Pte 10779 12th West Yorkshire Regt
WESTWOOD John P. MM L/Cpl 332779 Liverpool Regt
WESTWOOD Joseph MM Cpl A/1371 King's Royal Rifle Corps
WESTWOOD Joseph W. MM Pte 28579 Royal Warwickshire Regt
WESTWOOD Leonard MM Sjt 9381 2nd Royal Fusiliers
WESTWOOD Lewis Henry George MM Gnr 13637 109 Bty 281 Bde RFA KIA 15.3.17.
WESTWOOD Percy MM Pte 2117 Royal Irish Rifles
WESTWOOD Robert MM Sjt 111509 2 Lab Bn Royal Engineers
WESTWOOD Thomas Edward "MM,MIDx2" Sjt 11795 1st Worcestershire Regt
WESTWOOD William MM Dvr 810232 A/232 Bde RFA
WESTWOOD William F. MM Pte 325296 1/1st Cambridgeshire Regt
WESTWOOD William H. MM Bdr 100741 RFA
WESTWORTH William S. MM Dvr 120563 RFA
WETHERALL Edward Victor MM Gnr 120836 130 Bde RFA
WETHERELL Arthur W. MM L/Cpl 325536 1/1st Cambridgeshire Regt
WETHERELL Bryan MM Pte 18082 15th Durham Light Infantry KIA 29.5.18
WETHERELL William MM Sjt 202988 Durham Light Infantry
WETHERELL William Frederick MM Pte 31021 East Yorkshire Regt
WETHERILL Herbert Edward MM Pte A/203376 17th King's Royal Rifle Corps DOW 3.9.18.
WETHERTON James MM Pte 16152 Coldstream Guards
WETTON Arthur MM+Bar CSM 11421 446 Fd Coy Royal Engineers
WEYERS Victor C. MM L/Cpl 32997 Royal Fusiliers
WEYLEY J. MM Pte 20940 10th Scottish Rifles
WEYMAN Richard C. MM L/Cpl S/9240 Rifle Brigade
WEYMOUTH Horace W. MM S/Sjt Fitter 89550 RFA
WHADCOCK James T. MM Pte 14852 12th West Yorkshire Regt
WHAITES Frank MM+2 Bars Pte 205401 10th Royal West Kent Regt
WHALE Alfred J. MM Bdr 36015 36 Bde RFA
WHALE Charles E. MM Sjt 25621 121 Hy Bty RGA
WHALE Edgar G. MM L/Cpl 37314 1st Gloucestershire Regt
WHALE Ernest H. MM 2nd Cpl 10973 56 Fd Coy Royal Engineers
WHALE Frederick MM Pte 32566 16th Notts & Derby Regt KIA 21.3.18.
WHALE Frederick Charles MM Pte M2/103962 Army Service Corps att 69 Fd Amb RAMC.
WHALE Mark MM Pte 22536 116 Coy Machine Gun Corps KIA 26.10.17.
WHALE Stanley V. "DCM,MM" Sjt 2403 12th Middlesex Regt
WHALEY Jim MM Cpl 38654 2nd Yorkshire Light Infantry
WHALL Robert MM L/Cpl 2779 7th East Kent Regt
WHALLEY Albert MM+Bar Gnr 42875 RFA
WHALLEY Alfred MM Pte 26730 9th West Riding Regt
WHALLEY Cyril E. MM Cpl 46444 23rd Manchester Regt
WHALLEY George MM Sjt 20332 5th Royal Lancaster Regt
WHALLEY George William MM Sjt 100480 33 Div Sig Coy Royal Engineers
WHALLEY Harold MM Pte 40603 21st Manchester Regt DOW 9.10.18.
WHALLEY Harold MM Pte M2/227644 Army Service Corps
WHALLEY Harry MM Sjt 8853 B/150 Bde RFA
WHALLEY James MM Bdr 8473 A/311 Bde RFA
WHALLEY James MM Pte 53879 90 Coy Labour Corps
WHALLEY John MM Pte 4538 1st Liverpool Regt
WHALLEY John MM Bdr 8824 RFA
WHALLEY John A. MM Cpl 33396 Border Regt
WHALLEY John B. MM Sjt TT/01717 Army Veterinary Corps
WHALLEY Ralph MM Pte 15285 8th South Lancashire Regt KIA 13.6.17.
WHALLEY Thomas MM Pnr 125202 Royal Engineers
WHALLEY Thomas W. MM Pte 200249 South Lancashire Regt att RE.
WHAMMOND John "MC(2Lt Lovat's Scouts),DCM,MM" Sjt 129318 46th Royal Fusiliers Resigned commission and re-enlisted.
WHANT Henry George MM Sjt 66237 RFA
WHAPPLES C. MM Pte 12144 Royal Warwickshire Regt
WHARE George Stapleton William MM Cpl 9701 1st Royal Fusiliers
WHARF Ernest MM Pte 40388 1st Royal Dublin Fusiliers
WHARF William Russell MM Sjt 1630 1/3(Nortumbrian)Fd Amb RAMC
WHARFE Harry "DCM,MM" Sjt 8538 15/17th West Yorkshire Regt
WHARFE Noah MM Sjt 7679 2nd West Riding Regt
WHARMBY Herbert MM+Bar Sjt 14353 1st Grenadier Guards
WHARTON Alfred MM Sjt 4960 2nd York & Lancaster Regt
WHARTON Bertram MM Sjt 463207 50 Div Sig Coy Royal Engineers
WHARTON Charles MM Cpl 20020 6th York & Lancaster Regt
WHARTON Charles E. MM L/Cpl 5511 Leinster Regt
WHARTON George H. "MM,MSM,MID" CSM 16993 7(Horsed)Pontoon Park Royal Engineers
WHARTON Harry MM Spr 957 50 Div Sig Coy Royal Engineers
WHARTON Henry MM L/Cpl 320134 12th Norfolk Regt
WHARTON Herbert MM Pte 442 22nd Royal Fusiliers att MGC.KIA 28.7.16.
WHARTON James MM Pte 4788 13th Royal Fusiliers
WHARTON John MM Pte 8185 6th Royal Irish Rifles
WHARTON John MM Pte 60545 Welsh Regt
WHARTON Joseph MM+Bar L/Cpl 24464 Durham Light Infantry
WHARTON Joseph W. MM L/Cpl 22210 2nd Coldstream Guards
WHARTON W.J. MM L/Cpl 39666 Worcestershire Regt
WHARTON William MM Cpl S/3348 10th Rifle Brigade KIA 30.11.17.
WHARTON William MM Pte 31679 Notts & Derby Regt
WHATES Charles Septimus MM Pte 571918 17th London Regt
WHATLEY Bernard MM Sjt 1637 C/83 Bde RFA
WHATLEY John MM Pte 60376 2nd West Yorkshire Regt
WHATLEY John MM Pte 15557 12th Hampshire Regt
WHATLEY Spencer MM Cpl 51920 Royal Fusiliers
WHATMORE George MM Sjt 9249 Yorkshire Light Infantry
WHATMOUGH Arthur "DCM,MM" CSM 11532 2nd King's Own Scottish Borderers
WHATMOUGH Harry MM Spr 79618 176 Tunnelling Coy Royal Engineers
WHATMOUGH Robert MM Pte 201944 5th Lancashire Fusiliers
WHATNALL Herbert MM Gnr 110147 10th Bn Tank Corps
WHAYLING Charles F. MM Sjt 10796 5th Royal Berkshire Regt
WHEADON Ernest G. MM Pte 17171 Dorsetshire Regt
WHEADON Frederick J. MM Pte 18932 Grenadier Guards
WHEAR John MM Sjt 1803 5th Dragoon Guards
WHEAR Sidney MM+Bar Cpl 240387 5th Duke of Cornwall's LI
WHEAR William John MM Cpl 10977 RFA
WHEARE Arthur Joseph MM Pte 71118 20 Coy Machine Gun Corps KIA 23.3.18.
WHEARTY John MM Pte 3494 1st Irish Guards
WHEATCROFT Frederick H. MM Pte 11981 Manchester Regt
WHEATCROFT George MM Cpl 18958 Machine Gun Corps
WHEATCROFT George H.S. MM Sjt 494432 Royal Engineers
WHEATCROFT Thomas MM Pte 240194 1/6th Notts & Derby Regt
WHEATER Claude MM Cpl 24405 20th Liverpool Regt
WHEATER Thomas Walter MM Gnr 795469 62 Div Ammn Col RFA
WHEATLEY Amos "DCM,MM" Sjt 9264 1st South Staffordshire Regt
WHEATLEY Arthur MM Sjt 18/1439 16th West Yorkshire Regt DOW 8.5.18.
WHEATLEY Edward MM Cpl 290146 Labour Corps
WHEATLEY Edward J. MM L/Cpl 235 1st Welsh Guards
WHEATLEY Ernest MM Cpl 335415 11th Royal Scots
WHEATLEY Ernest E. MM Pte 28946 1st Gloucestershire Regt
WHEATLEY George MM Dvr 785652 RFA

WHEATLEY George MM Spr 602439 Royal Engineers
WHEATLEY George MM Pte 40773 Scottish Rifles
WHEATLEY Henry "MM,MID" Pte 8550 South Staffordshire Regt
WHEATLEY Hugh A. MM Sjt 61780 79 Fd Coy Royal Engineers
WHEATLEY Jacob MM+Bar L/Sjt 9204 2nd East Lancashire Regt KIA 16.8.17.
WHEATLEY James Harold MM Pte 235102 South Lancashire Regt
WHEATLEY Robert MM Bdr 760827 B/317 Bde RFA
WHEATLEY Robert H. MM Pte 34567 5/6th Scottish Rifles
WHEATLEY Sidney MM Cpl 14748 HQ 73 Bde RFA
WHEATLEY Thomas MM Pte 9865 1st Royal Highlanders KIA 17.9.18.
WHEATLEY Tom Newman MM Pte 28763 12th West Yorkshire Regt
WHEATLEY Utrick MM Cpl 1731 1/9th Durham Light Infantry
WHEATLEY William MM Pte 240439 1/6th Notts & Derby Regt
WHEATLEY William K. "DCM,MM" L/Sjt 36687 6th East Yorkshire Regt
WHEATLEY William S. MM L/Cpl 19924 1st Dorsetshire Regt
WHEATON Albert MM Sjt 4761 2nd Devonshire Regt
WHEATON Henry MM Pte 43281 Northamptonshire Regt
WHEATON William MM Cpl 265778 1/6th Gloucestershire Regt
WHEAVER William J. MM Cpl 160765 Royal Engineers
WHEELAN John MM Pte 29887 12th Royal Scots Fusiliers
WHEELDON Aandrew W.J. MM Gnr 64253 RGA
WHEELDON Frederick MM Pte 240578 1/5th North Lancashire Regt
WHEELDON Hubert Horace "DCM,MM" Sjt 305820 1/8th Royal Warwickshire Regt KIA 27.8.17.
WHEELDON John Wesley MM Sjt 801398 D/295 Bde RFA
WHEELDON Thomas Harold MM Gnr 20082 RFA
WHEELDON William MM L/Cpl 7929 12th Lancashire Fusiliers
WHEELER Albert B. MM Sjt 330307 1/8th Hampshire Regt
WHEELER Albert C. MM L/Cpl 1986 1/1st Gloucestershire Yeo
WHEELER Albert E.G. MM Spr 141630 Royal Engineers
WHEELER Albert H. MM Cpl 22290 11 Fd Coy Royal Engineers
WHEELER Albert H. MM Spr 73930 Royal Engineers
WHEELER Albert J. MM Pte 17909 Royal West Kent Regt
WHEELER Alfred MM Sjt 9300 10th Royal West Kent Regt DOW 10.6.17.
WHEELER Algernon Maxwell MM Cpl 33219 2nd Middlesex Regt
WHEELER Arthur James MM Sjt 317 1/6th London Regt
WHEELER Arthur W. MM Pte 2357 8th Royal Sussex Regt
WHEELER Dennis William MM Pte M2/114120 5 Div Train Army Service Corps DOW 27.5.18.
WHEELER Edward MM Cpl 18143 9th Lancashire Fusiliers
WHEELER Edward W. MM Sjt 201659 2/4th Royal Berkshire Regt
WHEELER Edwin R. MM Pte 5973 RAMC
WHEELER Ernest James MM Pte 6749 10th Royal West Surrey Regt KIA 20.9.17.
WHEELER Francis E. MM+Bar Bdr 36740 50 Siege Bty RGA
WHEELER Frank MM Pte 6938 Royal West Surrey Regt
WHEELER Frederick A. MM Pte 78957 9th Bn Tank Corps
WHEELER Frederick Parker MM Sjt 7395 91 Coy Machine Gun Corps
WHEELER George W. MM Pte R/13533 2nd King's Royal Rifle Corps
WHEELER George W. MM CSM 306197 8th West Yorkshire Regt
WHEELER Harry MM Cpl 99250 C/58 Bde RFA
WHEELER Harry Edward MM Pte 32814 2nd Lincolnshire Regt KIA 27.5.18.
WHEELER Henry J. MM Pte 1317 8th Royal West Kent Regt
WHEELER Henry James "DCM,MM" S/Sjt 45684 56 Fd Amb RAMC KIA 2.11.18.
WHEELER Henry Roland MM Cpl 7990 11th Royal Fusiliers KIA 26.9.16.
WHEELER Herbert Charles MM Sjt Y/1059 13th King's Royal Rifle Corps
WHEELER James MM Pte 51159 1/6th Cheshire Regt
WHEELER James John "MM+Bar,MID" Sjt 11732 C/70 Bde RFA
WHEELER James R. MM Pte 17543 Hampshire Regt
WHEELER James W. MM Cpl 19914 Royal Berkshire Regt
WHEELER John MM Dvr 40408 B/187 Bde RFA
WHEELER John MM Pte 11318 1 Special Coy King's Royal Rifle Corps
WHEELER John "MM,MSM" Sjt 9283 2nd Bedfordshire Regt
WHEELER John MM Pte 240326 1/8th Middlesex Regt
WHEELER John L. MM Cpl 2655 8th Royal Sussex Regt
WHEELER Joseph MM Sjt 45852 5 Div Ammn Col RFA
WHEELER Joseph F. MM Sjt 68026 D/170 Bde RFA
WHEELER Luther J.R. MM Pte 43050 Labour Corps
WHEELER Nehemiah Albert MM Sjt 510255 RAMC
WHEELER Percy W. MM Gnr 79640 A/123 Bde RFA
WHEELER Ralph MM Gnr 42054 'O' Bty RHA
WHEELER Ronald D. MM L/Sjt 17436 6th South Wales Borderers
WHEELER Thomas D. MM Sjt 50419 D/82 Bde RFA
WHEELER Thomas John MM Spr 1520 29 Div Sig Coy Royal Engineers
WHEELER Vernon MM Bdr 73329 23 Bde RFA
WHEELER W. MM Spr 254439 Royal Engineers
WHEELER Walter H. MM Sjt 1173 Middlesex Regt
WHEELER William Arthur MM Sjt 9912 5th Oxf & Bucks Light Infantry DOW 22.3.18.
WHEELER William C. MM Spr 201448 Royal Engineers
WHEELER William H. MM L/Cpl 235849 1/1st Herefordshire Regt
WHEELER William Henry MM Spr 521933 144 Army Troops Coy Royal Engineers
WHEELER William John MM Dvr T4/038051 Army Service Corps att 3 Fd Amb RAMC.
WHEELER William T. "DCM,MM" Sjt 26521 1st Middlesex Regt
WHEELHOUSE Edwin MM Sjt 31849 50th Bn Machine Gun Corps
WHEELHOUSE Fred MM Gnr 135206 RFA
WHEELHOUSE Thomas H. MM L/Cpl 116818 Labour Corps
WHEELIKER George MM CSM 16888 York & Lancaster Regt
WHEELTON Edward MM L/Cpl 33405 11th Border Regt
WHEELWRIGHT Henry MM Gnr 166554 194 Siege Bty RGA
WHEILDON Joseph H. MM Sjt 325041 1/1st Worcestershire Yeomanry
WHELAN Daniel P. MM Sjt 13910 7th Royal Berkshire Regt
WHELAN Frank Burnelle George MM Sjt 925628 A/290 Bde RFA DOW 26.4.18.
WHELAN James MM 2nd Cpl 64110 121 Fd Coy Royal Engineers
WHELAN John MM Pte 20610 32nd Bn Machine Gun Corps
WHELAN John MM Gnr 31353 HQ 106 Bde RFA
WHELAN John MM Cpl 6722 Royal Engineers
WHELAN John MM Pte 42740 Machine Gun Corps
WHELAN John MM Sjt 6720 2nd Royal Irish Rifles
WHELAN John C. MM Cpl 5975 8th Royal Munster Fusiliers
WHELAN Joseph MM Sjt 680159 276 Bde RFA
WHELAN Matthew "DCM,MM" Cpl 26/1297 26th Northumberland Fusiliers KIA 2.9.17.
WHELAN Michael MM Sjt 27988 Postal Section Royal Engineers
WHELAN Michael MM Spr 444434 Royal Engineers
WHELAN Robert Selkirk "MC,MM" CSM 10/16093 10th Royal Irish Rifles KIA 29.8.17.
WHELAN Thomas MM Pte 58051 13th Royal Welsh Fusiliers
WHELAN Thomas MM Sjt 7476 1st Royal Warwickshire Regt DOW 1.7.16.
WHELAN Thomas MM Sjt 26644 8th Royal Inniskilling Fusiliers
WHELAN William MM Pte 35879 Liverpool Regt
WHELDRAKE Alfred MM L/Cpl 20419 8th Yorkshire Light Infantry
WHELLER William C. "MM,MSM" Sjt 87545 39 Div Sig Coy Royal Engineers
WHELPTON James MM Spr 480261 Royal Engineers
WHENT W. MM Pte 40258 10th Essex Regt
WHERBY Richard C. MM CSM 22/715 Durham Light Infantry
WHERLEY Albert Victor MM Pte M2/132300 Army Service Corps
WHERRY Harry MM Sjt 34455 Liverpool Regt
WHETREN Percy MM Pte 22350 Dorsetshire Regt
WHETSTONE Charles Walter MM Gnr 2749 B/58 Bde RFA KIA 22.9.17.
WHETSTONE Jarvis Albert MM Cpl 810248 232 Bde RFA KIA 21.4.17.
WHETSTONE Stuart MM L/Cpl 50967 Middlesex Regt
WHETTER Arthur J. MM CSM 53205 19th Durham Light Infantry
WHETTER John Henry Pearce MM Pnr 165603 56 Div Sig Coy Royal Engineers
WHETTINGSTEEL Harry A. MM Cpl 20807 1st Devonshire Regt
WHETTON Daniel Thomas MM L/Sjt 19072 2nd Yorkshire Regt KIA 25.4.18.
WHETTON Frederick MM Pte 240981 North Staffordshire Regt
WHETTON George MM Pte 16858 1st Grenadier Guards
WHEWAY George Andrew MM Pte 12816 7th York & Lancaster Regt KIA 27.8.17.
WHEWELL Reginald C. "DCM,MM" Pte 22998 12th Royal Scots
WHIBLEY Frank Oliver MM Pte G/4940 7th Royal West Surrey Regt KIA 27.2.17.
WHICHELLO Frederick W.G. MM Sjt 42446 C/99 Bde RFA
WHICKER William James MM Cpl M2/055232 Army Service Corps att 2/1(Highland)Fd Amb RAMC.
WHIDDETT Alfred G. MM Cpl 58937 6th Northamptonshire Regt

WHIDDETT Alfred G. MM L/Sjt 12401 2nd Middlesex Regt
WHIDDETT George MM Pte 4929 1st East Kent Regt
WHILES George MM L/Cpl 267508 Notts & Derby Regt
WHILES William MM Sjt 21861 RFA
WHILEY Albert MM Sjt 12502 9th South Staffordshire Regt
WHILEY Reginald MM Pte 240194 Worcestershire Regt
WHILLANS John MM Cpl 200086 1/4th King's Own Scottish Borderers
WHINCUP Sam MM+Bar Sjt 24339 10th West Yorkshire Regt
WHINES Henry C. MM L/Cpl 552309 16th London Regt
WHINHAM John W. MM Cpl 41862 12th Highland Light Infantry KIA 24.3.18.
WHINN Robert MM L/Cpl 240103 1/5th Border Regt DOW 21.8.18.
WHIPP Frederick MM L/Cpl 60488 Machine Gun Corps
WHIPP John MM Bdr 156509 D/52 Bde RFA
WHIPP Roland MM L/Sjt 54943 22nd Royal Fusiliers
WHIPPS Albert E. MM Pte 27181 2nd Suffolk Regt
WHIPPS Alfred MM Sjt G/3569 7th East Kent Regt KIA 1.7.16.
WHISKER Harry MM L/Cpl 12/698 11th East Yorkshire Regt KIA 26.3.18.
WHISKIN Charles W. MM Sjt Pnr 6511 Coldstream Guards
WHISKIN Ernest William MM Pte 6031 1st East Kent Regt
WHISTLECROFT John MM Bdr 39146 RGA
WHISTON Charles B.H. MM Sjt 7556 1st Somerset Light Infantry
WHISTON Thomas MM Pte 39227 RAMC
WHITAKER Arthur MM Sjt 200753 West Riding Regt
WHITAKER Arthur MM CSM 10934 13th Royal Fusiliers
WHITAKER Arthur MM Pte 175760 1/1st Yorkshire Dragoons Yeo
WHITAKER Charles E. MM Bdr 296941 RGA
WHITAKER Edward MM Pte R/19421 King's Royal Rifle Corps
WHITAKER Ernest MM Bdr 780304 B/246 Bde RFA
WHITAKER Fred MM Pte 13204 Machine Gun Corps
WHITAKER Frederick E. MM Gnr 101453 9 Hy Bty RGA
WHITAKER Harold William MM Sjt 15623 13th Royal Sussex Regt
WHITAKER Henry W. MM Cpl 51009 Machine Gun Corps(Cavalry)
WHITAKER John MM Gnr 780783 B/311 Bde RFA
WHITAKER Joseph W. "MM,MSM" Sjt 240318 2/5th York & Lancaster Regt
WHITAKER Rennie MM Pte S/11488 Rifle Brigade
WHITAKER Ronald MM Pte 538075 6 Fd Amb RAMC
WHITAKER Sam MM Dvr 786247 RFA
WHITAKER Sam MM Pte 325786 1/9th Durham Light Infantry
WHITAKER Thomas MM L/Cpl 201622 Notts & Derby Regt
WHITAKER Whalley Thomas MM Gnr 671976 377 Bty RFA
WHITAKER Wilfred MM Pte 14553 Machine Gun Corps
WHITAKER William "MM,MID" L/Bdr 951281 A/235 Bde RFA
WHITAKER William George MM Pte 11873 6th Royal West Kent Regt KIA 30.11.17.
WHITBOURN Gilbert W. MM L/Cpl SS/1053 Army Service Corps
WHITBREAD Andrew G. MM Pte 9260 5th Wiltshire Regt
WHITBREAD Arthur J. MM Cpl 10461 1st Yorkshire Light Infantry
WHITBREAD Edward G. MM Cpl 101 7th Royal Sussex Regt
WHITBREAD Ernest MM Pte 73753 116 Coy Machine Gun Corps
WHITBREAD Frank MM+Bar Sjt 200707 4th West Riding Regt
WHITBREAD James H. MM Pte 44081 Middlesex Regt
WHITBREAD Leonard MM L/Cpl 8287 2nd West Riding Regt
WHITBREAD Thomas Alfred "MM,MID" Sjt 13077 7th Royal Berkshire Regt
WHITBREAD William "DCM,MM" CSM 10677 1st Royal Welsh Fusiliers KIA 14.5.17.
WHITBROOK Charles Henry MM Pte 13522 1st Coldstream Guards
WHITBY Frederick MM Pte 20600 2nd Suffolk Regt KIA 1.10.18.
WHITBY Harold MM Pte 44270 1st Cheshire Regt
WHITBY Thomas E. MM Sjt 378003 Liverpool Regt
WHITCHER Lionel MM Cpl 546 Royal Sussex Regt
WHITCHER Sidney G. MM Sjt 89258 Middlesex Regt
WHITCHER W. MM+Bar Cpl 29562 Hampshire Regt
WHITCOMBE Alfred MM Sjt 13687 35th Bn Machine Gun Corps
WHITCOMBE Thomas "MM,MID" Pte 14289 4th South Wales Borderers
WHITCROFT Joseph MM Gnr 58233 RFA
WHITE A.J. MM Sjt 108567 Royal Engineers
WHITE A.T. MM L/Cpl P4947 Military Foot Police
WHITE Aaron MM Pte 24159 15th Cheshire Regt DOW 4.2.18.
WHITE Adam MM 2nd Cpl 50165 Royal Engineers
WHITE Albert MM Dvr 118863 A/42 Bde RFA
WHITE Albert MM Pte 22385 2nd Wiltshire Regt KIA 5.11.18.
WHITE Albert E. MM Pte 242364 6th Liverpool Regt
WHITE Albert Edward Thomas MM Pte 10243 Oxf & Bucks Light Infantry
WHITE Albert J. MM Pte 36869 Royal Berkshire Regt
WHITE Albert R. MM Pte 385155 London Regt
WHITE Albert V. MM+Bar Sjt 40126 10th West Yorkshire Regt
WHITE Alex MM Bdr 960613 RFA
WHITE Alexander MM Pte 333059 1/9th Highland Light Infantry
WHITE Alexander Glenorchy MM Cpl 9716 2nd Royal Scots DOW 28.5.18.
WHITE Alfred S. MM L/Cpl 27349 9th Cheshire Regt
WHITE Ambrose MM Pte 933 18th Hussars
WHITE Andrew "MC,MM" CSM 16093 Royal Inniskilling Fusiliers
WHITE Andrew MM Gnr Fitter 147434 174 Bde RFA
WHITE Andrew J. MM Pte 14177 4th Royal Fusiliers
WHITE Angus MM L/Cpl 60194 20th Bn Machine Gun Corps
WHITE Archibald MM Pte 8786 1st Scots Guards KIA 4.11.18.
WHITE Archibald MM Cpl 785682 D/312 Bde RFA
WHITE Archibald McK. MM L/Sjt 59615 Royal Scots
WHITE Arnold MM Sjt 21972 D/46 Bde RFA
WHITE Arthur MM Sjt 18927 XIX Corps Cyclist Bn Army Cyclist Corps
WHITE Arthur MM Sjt 24518 'R' Corps Sig Coy Royal Engineers
WHITE Arthur MM Pte 46499 North Staffordshire Regt
WHITE Arthur MM Pte 8341 1/5th South Staffordshire Regt
WHITE Arthur MM L/Cpl 46659 Northumberland Fusiliers
WHITE Arthur MM L/Cpl 8194 1st Northamptonshire Regt
WHITE Arthur E. MM L/Cpl 18910 Northamptonshire Regt
WHITE Arthur Goodwin MM L/Cpl 2588 1/4th Royal Lancaster Regt
WHITE Arthur John MM Bdr 151589 426 Siege Bty RGA
WHITE Arthur P. MM Cpl 204739 8th Northumberland Fusiliers
WHITE Arthur Sharpin MM Sjt 538005 1/6(London)Fd Amb RAMC
WHITE Arthur William MM Pte 36956 1st Gloucestershire Regt KIA 29.9.18.
WHITE Arthur Yirrell MM L/Cpl 301644 2/5th London Regt KIA 20.9.17.
WHITE Benjamin A. MM Cpl 421060 3 Fd Amb RAMC
WHITE Bernard MM L/Cpl 9400 1st South Staffordshire Regt
WHITE C. MM Bdr 27988 RGA
WHITE Cecil W. MM+Bar Pte 240244 1/5th Devonshire Regt
WHITE Charles MM Sjt 6076 2nd Coldstream Guards
WHITE Charles MM Pte 40613 Royal Highlanders
WHITE Charles MM L/Cpl 15122 Royal Fusiliers att MGC.
WHITE Charles MM L/Cpl 9240 2nd Arg & Suth Highlanders
WHITE Charles MM+Bar L/Cpl 5745 9th Royal Welsh Fusiliers
WHITE Charles MM Pte 49479 23rd Royal Fusiliers
WHITE Charles E. MM Sjt 571141 1/17th London Regt
WHITE Charles F. MM Pte 536457 1st(London)Fd Amb. RAMC
WHITE Charles H. MM Pte R/8370 12th King's Royal Rifle Corps
WHITE Clarence Ashton MM Sjt 19151 1st Royal West Kent Regt KIA 27.9.18.
WHITE Clifford Charles "MM,MID" Bdr 8 48 Div Amn Col RFA
WHITE David J. MM Pte 1909 RAMC
WHITE Douglas Thomas MM Pte 72638 2/10th Middlesex Regt
WHITE E.G. MM Sjt 55157 Royal Welsh Fusiliers
WHITE Edgar MM Pte 265475 6th West Riding Regt
WHITE Edward "DCM,MM+Bar" Cpl 240244 1/6th Notts & Derby Regt
WHITE Edward "MM,MID" Sjt 251337 1st Essex Regt
WHITE Edward G. MM 2nd Cpl 249421 18 Div Sig Coy Royal Engineers
WHITE Edward R. MM Sjt 2438 Royal Fusiliers
WHITE Edwin S. MM Gnr 135087 RFA
WHITE Eli MM Sjt 200095 Durham Light Infantry
WHITE Eric H. MM Pte C/1102 16th King's Royal Rifle Corps
WHITE Ernest MM Pte 57651 4th York & Lancaster Regt
WHITE Ernest B. MM Sjt 3122 Manchester Regt
WHITE Ernest J. MM Pte 42271 4th King's Own Scottish Borderers
WHITE Ernest James William MM Spr 48444 69 Fd Coy Royal Engineers
WHITE F. MM Pte 51881 West Yorkshire Regt
WHITE F. MM L/Cpl 75039 Machine Gun Corps
WHITE F.J. MM Sjt 38921 41 Bde RFA
WHITE Felix A. MM L/Cpl 494298 Royal Engineers
WHITE Francis C. MM Gnr 30230 B/173 Bde RFA
WHITE Frank MM Pte 18090 Royal Berkshire Regt
WHITE Frank MM Pte 59458 RAMC
WHITE Frank MM Bdr 614 Machine Gun Corps(Motors)
WHITE Frank MM Pte 351220 9th Manchester Regt
WHITE Frank C. MM Pte 34555 Royal Welsh Fusiliers
WHITE Fred MM Pte 126041 62nd Bn Machine Gun Corps
WHITE Fred MM Sjt 14433 25 Coy Labour Corps
WHITE Fred MM Pte 80071 Notts & Derby Regt

WHITE Frederick MM Pte 4/7274 2nd Bedfordshire Regt
WHITE Frederick Charles MM Pte 30457 1/1st Bedfordshire Yeomanry
WHITE Frederick Edward MM Cpl 608 17th Middlesex Regt KIA 28.4.17.
WHITE Frederick G. MM L/Cpl 9205 2nd Shropshire Light Infantry
WHITE Frederick G. MM L/Bdr 78329 45 Bde RFA
WHITE Frederick G. MM Cpl 45304 Durham Light Infantry
WHITE Frederick G. MM Pte 513009 14th London Regt
WHITE Frederick J. MM Pte 81218 24th Royal Fusiliers
WHITE Frederick T.G. MM Pte 533321 15th London Regt
WHITE Frederick Victor "MC,MM(49890 Sjt)" 2Lt RFA
WHITE G. MM Pte S/10277 13th Rifle Brigade
WHITE G.W. MM Pte 17132 9th York & Lancaster Regt
WHITE George MM Pte 33897 North Lancashire Regt
WHITE George "DCM,MM" Sjt 7314 8th Lincolnshire Regt
WHITE George MM Pte 2606 5/6th Royal Scots KIA 24.10.17
WHITE George A. MM Pte A/2983 12th King's Royal Rifle Corps
WHITE George A. MM L/Cpl S/8739 Rifle Brigade
WHITE George E. MM L/Cpl 201469 1st Royal Scots Fusiliers
WHITE George E. MM L/Cpl 43338 West Yorkshire Regt
WHITE George E. MM Gnr 99377 RHA
WHITE George F. MM Pte 243095 Middlesex Regt
WHITE George F. MM Dvr 96774 RFA
WHITE George H. MM Pte 534034 RAMC
WHITE George H. MM Pte 201204 1/4th Royal Highlanders
WHITE George M. MM Sjt 290153 2nd Devonshire Regt
WHITE George Thomas MM L/Cpl 12584 5th Oxf & Bucks Light Infantry
WHITE H.E. MM Pte 29498 Essex Regt
WHITE Harold MM Gnr 800167 52 Bty 15 Bde RFA
WHITE Harold MM Pte 44376 Manchester Regt att MGC.
WHITE Harold G. MM Sjt 200846 1/4th Royal Berkshire Regt
WHITE Harold P. MM Pte 21538 9th East Surrey Regt
WHITE Harry MM L/Cpl 38092 9th Devonshire Regt
WHITE Harry MM Pte 72516 76 Fd Amb RAMC
WHITE Harry MM Pte 3/6887 5th Dorsetshire Regt
WHITE Harry MM Cpl 297950 714 Coy Labour Corps
WHITE Harry J. MM Pte 235722 5th West Riding Regt
WHITE Harry J. MM L/Cpl 55721 Machine Gun Corps
WHITE Harry Voss MM Cpl 19215 2nd South Wales Borderers
WHITE Henry MM L/Cpl 9980 2nd Royal Dublin Fusiliers KIA 21.3.18.
WHITE Henry MM Spr 14234 2 Fd Squadron Royal Engineers
WHITE Henry A. MM L/Bdr 98165 12 Hy Bty RGA
WHITE Henry C. MM Gnr 71689 26 Bde RFA
WHITE Henry George "MM,MSM" Sjt 120683 'P' Special Coy Royal Engineers
WHITE Henry J. "MM,MID" Sjt 12417 6th Royal Berkshire Regt
WHITE Henry T. MM Cpl 22908 Wiltshire Regt
WHITE Henry William MM 2nd Cpl 56614 17 Div Sig Coy Royal Engineers Died 21.11.17.
WHITE Herbert MM L/Sjt 56119 74th Bn Machine Gun Corps
WHITE Herbert J. MM Sjt 500050 Royal Engineers
WHITE Herbert Percy Thomas MM Pte 60751 23rd Lancashire Fusiliers
WHITE Herbert W. MM Gnr 72624 RFA
WHITE Herbert Walter MM Cpl 35337 31 Heavy Bty RGA
WHITE Hiram Thomas Wesley MM L/Bdr 315277 31 Bde Ammn Col RGA
WHITE Horace MM L/Cpl 17652 Shropshire Light Infantry
WHITE Horace A. MM+Bar Cpl 39941 1st Wiltshire Regt
WHITE Horace G. MM Cpl 47200 1st Welsh Regt
WHITE Hubert C. MM Pte 18111 11th Worcestershire Regt
WHITE Hugh H. MM Sjt 4382 1st Irish Guards
WHITE Hugh N. MM Dvr 109167 RFA
WHITE James MM Pte 157714 2nd Bn Machine Gun Corps
WHITE James MM L/Cpl 3/7611 15th Royal Irish Rifles
WHITE James MM Pte 16795 6th Lincolnshire Regt
WHITE James MM Bdr 42109 RFA
WHITE James E. MM Sjt 8331 8th Royal Berkshire Regt
WHITE James H. MM Cpl 200436 West Yorkshire Regt
WHITE James W. MM Pte 18480 8th Royal Berkshire Regt
WHITE James William MM Pte 26/1445 Northumberland Fusiliers
WHITE Jeffrey R. MM L/Cpl 701816 23rd London Regt
WHITE Jesse MM Sjt 14282 9th Norfolk Regt
WHITE John MM Cpl 412092 409 Fd Coy Royal Engineers
WHITE John MM Pte 66637 101 Fd Amb RAMC
WHITE John MM Dvr 800235 A/230 Bde RFA
WHITE John MM Pte 200362 Wiltshire Regt
WHITE John MM L/Cpl 11715 6th King's Own Scottish Borderers KIA 9.4.17.
WHITE John MM Pte 2695 1st Irish Guards KIA 10.10.17.
WHITE John MM Sjt 43646 RFA
WHITE John Edward Forbes MM Sjt 5424 3 Fd Coy Royal Engineers
WHITE John Henry MM Sjt 9615 1st Oxf & Bucks Light Infantry KIA 26.6.19.
WHITE John Herbert Charles MM Pte 2433 (240552?) 1/5th Gloucestershire Regt KIA 16.8.17
WHITE John James MM L/Cpl 1589 17th Middlesex Regt
WHITE John Samuel "MC,MM(45458 Sjt)" 2Lt Royal Engineers
WHITE John T. MM Pte 200482 1/4th Oxf & Bucks Light Infantry
WHITE John W. MM Gnr 18227 RFA
WHITE Joseph MM Pte 81659 15th Durham Light Infantry
WHITE Joseph MM Pte 2554 1/5th Yorkshire Light Infantry KIA 28.8.16.
WHITE Joseph MM L/Cpl 352498 Royal Scots
WHITE Joseph H. MM Pte 64027 5th Yorkshire Light Infantry
WHITE Joseph William MM Sjt 14750 Yorkshire Regt
WHITE Leonard MM Pte 573836 1/17th London Regt KIA 22.8.18.
WHITE Leonard G. MM Bdr 78962 D/73 Bde RFA
WHITE Louis MM Pte 377878 2/10th Manchester Regt
WHITE Martin MM Cpl 10203 1st East Lancashire Regt
WHITE Maurice T.J. MM Bdr 71170 34 Bde RFA
WHITE Michael MM Pte 73053 South Irish Horse
WHITE Milson "DCM,MM" Sjt 21128 8th Yorkshire Light Infantry
WHITE Nicholas MM Gnr 37007 50 Siege Bty RGA
WHITE Norman MM Cpl 6760 6th East Yorkshire Regt
WHITE Norman B. MM Cpl 37317 1/4th Royal Berkshire Regt
WHITE Oliver Charles MM 2nd Cpl 48302 61 Fd Coy Royal Engineers KIA 15.10.17.
WHITE Patrick MM L/Cpl 8373 1st Royal Munster Fusiliers
WHITE Percy MM Pte 25318 4th Worcestershire Regt
WHITE Percy MM Gnr 31081 15 Bty 36 Bde RFA
WHITE Percy MM Sjt 11324 6th York & Lancaster Regt
WHITE Percy A.C. MM Pte 725 7th Royal Sussex Regt
WHITE Peter R. MM Pte 30398 2nd Devonshire Regt
WHITE R. MM Pte 50981 Highland Light Infantry
WHITE Richard MM Bdr 39849 RFA
WHITE Richard MM L/Cpl 10761 13th Northumberland Fusiliers
WHITE Richard MM+Bar Pte 451928 11th London Regt
WHITE Richard J. MM Pte 47375 Royal Welsh Fusiliers
WHITE Richard Robinson MM+Bar Sjt 1950 50 Div Sig Coy Royal Engineers
WHITE Richard S. MM Spr 164937 Royal Engineers
WHITE Robert MM Pte 200994 Leicestershire Regt
WHITE Robert MM Sjt 15500 10th Royal Welsh Fusiliers
WHITE Robert MM Bdr 200182 RFA
WHITE Robert MM Dvr 105301 73 Bty 5 Bde RFA
WHITE Robert Bransby MM Sjt 22023 13th Durham Light Infantry KIA 20.9.17.
WHITE Robert Leslie MM Pte 538292 6(London)Fd Amb RAMC
WHITE Rupert MM Sjt 220384 Royal Berkshire Regt
WHITE Samuel MM Bdr 110458 RGA
WHITE Samuel MM Pte Z/2145 Rifle Brigade
WHITE Samuel J. MM Sjt 191376 'T'(AA)Bty RGA
WHITE Sidney MM L/Cpl 1465 1st Welsh Guards
WHITE Sidney George MM Sjt 8485 2nd Devonshire Regt Died 9.6.17.
WHITE Sidney J. MM L/Cpl 16193 2nd Royal Irish Regt
WHITE Sidney James MM L/Cpl 506065 504 Fd Coy Royal Engineers
WHITE Stanley Curson MM L/Cpl 14301 9th Norfolk Regt KIA 9.7.17.
WHITE Stanley J. MM Gnr 87243 D/240 Bde RFA
WHITE Stephen MM Bdr 67161 111 Siege Bty RGA
WHITE Stephen MM Pte 17528 20th Manchester Regt
WHITE Sydney Reginald MM Gnr 86737 C/63 Bde RFA
WHITE Sydney S. "DCM(1426 Gnr HQ 2(WR)Bde RFA)+Bar,MM" L/Cpl 479952 49 Div Sig Coy Royal Engineers
WHITE Thomas MM Sjt 88202 23 Heavy Bty RGA
WHITE Thomas MM Pte 23537 9th Highland Light Infantry
WHITE Thomas MM Cpl 71602 47th Bn Machine Gun Corps
WHITE Thomas MM Pte 60109 2nd Royal Fusiliers DOW 5.9.18.
WHITE Thomas MM Sjt 46644 RFA
WHITE Thomas MM Sjt 83929 RFA
WHITE Thomas MM Cpl 59285 Z/34 Med TM Bty RGA DOW 16.3.17.
WHITE Thomas MM Pte 36509 11th East Yorkshire Regt KIA 19.7.17.

WHITE Thomas MM+Bar Sjt 13435 12th & 11th Royal Scots
WHITE Thomas MM Dvr 20675 45 Bde RFA
WHITE Thomas A. MM Gnr 1051 9(West Riding)Bty RFA
WHITE Thomas C. MM Gnr 59775 69 Bty 31 Bde RFA
WHITE Thomas Frederick MM Pte 12401 RAMC
WHITE Thomas Henry MM L/Cpl 9758 5th Royal Berkshire Regt
WHITE Thomas Herbert MM Sjt 13441 D/180 Bde RFA
WHITE Thomas S. MM Spr 495254 Royal Engineers
WHITE Thomas William MM Sjt 16603 8th West Riding Regt KIA 29.9.16.
WHITE Thomas William MM+Bar Pte 8740 1st Royal West Kent Regt KIA 4.10.17.
WHITE Thomas William MM Sjt 17155 11th Essex Regt KIA 8.8.18.
WHITE Victor MM Pte S/33323 Rifle Brigade
WHITE Victor Charles Thomas MM Pte 200986 1/4th Royal Berkshire Regt KIA 20.10.18.
WHITE Vincent MM Sjt 23995 Liverpool Regt
WHITE Walter MM Bdr 78026 45 Bde RFA
WHITE Walter MM Pte 23447 2nd Wiltshire Regt DOW 15.6.18.
WHITE Walter F. MM Cpl 19 Army Cyclist Corps
WHITE Walter H. MM Pte 9585 1st Somerset Light Infantry
WHITE Walter J. MM Sjt 2416 8th Royal Sussex Regt
WHITE Walter William MM CSM 812 9th East Surrey Regt KIA 3.9.16.
WHITE Wilfred MM L/Cpl 16201 11th East Lancashire Regt KIA 28.6.18.
WHITE William MM Spr 144869 257 Tunnelling Coy Royal Engineers
WHITE William MM L/Cpl 632034 20th London Regt
WHITE William MM L/Cpl 99315 10th Royal Fusiliers
WHITE William MM Pte G/9089 10th Royal West Surrey Regt KIA 18.8.17.
WHITE William MM Pte 203256 South Staffordshire Regt
WHITE William MM Pte 11234 6th York & Lancaster Regt
WHITE William MM L/Sjt 9806 2nd Leinster Regt KIA 4.9.18.
WHITE William MM Sjt 7859 6tth Royal Irish Rifles
WHITE William MM Sjt 14158 15 Div Ammn Col RFA
WHITE William MM L/Cpl 4616 1/6th West Yorkshire Regt
WHITE William MM Spr 18659 'L' Cable Section Royal Engineers
WHITE William MM Cpl M2/098716 Guards Div MT Coy Army Service Corps
WHITE William MM Bdr 69881 RFA
WHITE William MM L/Sjt 300996 1/8th Manchester Regt
WHITE William MM Gnr 165820 RGA
WHITE William MM L/Cpl 99300 Royal Engineers
WHITE William Albert MM L/Cpl 2248 7th East Kent Regt
WHITE William D. MM Sjt 23544 6 Div Sig Coy Royal Engineers
WHITE William George MM Pte 253851 3rd London Regt
WHITE William H. MM L/Cpl 70686 49th Bn Machine Gun Corps
WHITE William H. MM Sjt 97641 RFA
WHITE William Hartley MM Pte 5772 12th Royal Sussex Regt
WHITE William Henry MM Pte 569 23rd Royal Fusiliers DOW 26.11.16.
WHITE William J. MM Pte M2/050687 Army Service Corps
WHITE William J. MM Sjt 54817 Royal Fusiliers
WHITE William J. MM Cpl 30759 RGA
WHITE Woodruff Negus MM Pte 541 17th Royal Fusiliers
WHITEAKER David MM 2nd Cpl 550384 Royal Engineers
WHITECROSS Alexander MM Sjt 10071 1st Royal Scots Fusiliers DOW 21.8.18.
WHITECROSS David MM Pte 40204 1st Royal Highlanders
WHITEFIELD Albert F. MM Gnr 16808 HQ 109 Bde RFA
WHITEFIELD John MM Pte 40583 9th Scottish Rifles KIA 23.3.18.
WHITEFORD Edward MM L/Cpl 350339 1/9th Highland Light Infantry
WHITEFORD James MM Pte 296034 12th Royal Scots Fusiliers
WHITEFORD James G. MM Sjt 332198 1/9th Highland Light Infantry
WHITEFORD John MM Cpl 7108 A/109 Bde RFA
WHITEFORD Robert MM Sjt 40682 12th Royal Scots
WHITEHALL Isaac MM Pte M/281419 Army Service Corps att 1/3(East Lancashire)Fd Amb RAMC.
WHITEHALL John MM Gnr 41842 RGA
WHITEHAND David MM Pte 9529 2nd Suffolk Regt
WHITEHART Arthur MM Bdr 209377 RFA
WHITEHEAD Albert "DCM,MM" Sjt 31704 17 Div Sig Coy Royal Engineers
WHITEHEAD Alex MM Pte 6628 19th Middlesex Regt
WHITEHEAD Alfred MM L/Cpl 241941 8th West Yorkshire Regt
WHITEHEAD Alfred "DCM,MM" Sjt 91955 8th Bn Tank Corps

WHITEHEAD Alfred MM Pte 22729 Machine Gun Corps
WHITEHEAD Alfred James MM Spr 43880 Royal Engineers
WHITEHEAD Arthur C. MM Pte 1465 West Yorkshire Regt
WHITEHEAD Cecil William MM L/Cpl 2130 1/19th London Regt
WHITEHEAD Charles M. MM Pte 200529 King's Own Scottish Borderers
WHITEHEAD E.B. MM Cpl 492023 RAMC
WHITEHEAD Edward MM Pte 376467 6th Manchester Regt
WHITEHEAD Ernest Edward MM Sjt 18615 East Lancashire Regt
WHITEHEAD Ernest G. MM L/Cpl M2/115025 13 Lt Armd Mot Bty Army Service Corps
WHITEHEAD Frank Holt MM Gnr 1910 A/276 Bty RFA
WHITEHEAD Fred "DCM,MM,MSM,MID" Sjt 45858 18 Div Sig Coy Royal Engineers
WHITEHEAD Frederick MM Pte 57308 1/8th Royal Warwickshire Regt
WHITEHEAD George W. MM Sjt 5152 1st Gordon Highlanders
WHITEHEAD Harold "DCM,MM" Sjt 14178 2/9th Manchester Regt
WHITEHEAD Harry MM Pte 23928 Yorkshire Regt
WHITEHEAD Harry MM Pte 42629 RAMC
WHITEHEAD Henry MM Pte 3130 2/4th London Regt
WHITEHEAD J. MM Pte 201734 London Regt
WHITEHEAD J. MM Pte 268497 Liverpool Regt
WHITEHEAD James MM Pte 351450 5th Manchester Regt
WHITEHEAD James G. MM L/Cpl 17110 Royal Fusiliers
WHITEHEAD John R. MM+Bar Sjt 476392 461 Fd Coy Royal Engineers
WHITEHEAD John W. MM Pte 33805 Border Regt
WHITEHEAD John W. MM Pte 11911 1st North Lancashire Regt
WHITEHEAD Joseph MM L/Cpl 26461 East Lancashire Regt
WHITEHEAD Joseph Frederick James MM Sjt 61061 112 Bty 24 Bde RFA KIA 21.3.18.
WHITEHEAD Joseph W. MM Pte 69581 RAMC
WHITEHEAD Philip MM Sjt 1373 21st London Regt KIA 13.9.16.
WHITEHEAD Philip Thomas MM+Bar Cpl F/823 23rd Middlesex Regt DOW 14.9.17.
WHITEHEAD Robert MM Pte 26804 1st Somerset Light Infantry
WHITEHEAD Thomas MM Pte 15499 11th Border Regt
WHITEHEAD Thomas "DCM+Bar,MM" Sjt 280506 X/18 Med TM Bty RGA
WHITEHEAD Thomas MM Sjt 38485 Yorkshire Light Infantry
WHITEHEAD Thomas H. MM L/Cpl 240890 1/5th Gloucestershire Regt
WHITEHEAD Walter "DCM,MM" CQMS 40904 Northumberland Fusiliers
WHITEHEAD William "DCM,MM" CSM 25592 2/7th Notts & Derby Regt KIA 21.3.18.
WHITEHEAD William MM Cpl 112229 Royal Engineers
WHITEHEAD William MM Gnr 188632 A/52 Bde RFA
WHITEHORN Alfred Charles MM Pte TT/0710 Army Veterinary Corps
WHITEHORN Newland B. MM Cpl 2606 1st Life Guards
WHITEHORN Roland Taylor MM+Bar Spr 51884 11 Div Sig Coy Royal Engineers
WHITEHOUSE Arthur MM Spr 486582 69 Fd Coy Royal Engineers
WHITEHOUSE Arthur George J. MM Air Mech 1 78563 Royal Flying Corps
WHITEHOUSE Arthur V. MM Cpl 69573 39 Bde RFA
WHITEHOUSE Charles A. MM Cpl 7684 1st Dorsetshire Regt
WHITEHOUSE Edgar C. MM 2nd Cpl 63738 Royal Engineers
WHITEHOUSE Ernest MM Pte 41484 1st Norfolk Regt
WHITEHOUSE Frank MM Pte R/14048 8th King's Royal Rifle Corps
WHITEHOUSE Frank MM Pte 240976 South Staffordshire Regt
WHITEHOUSE Harold MM Pte 308095 2/4th West Riding Regt
WHITEHOUSE Henry "MM,MID" Sjt 13601 11th West Yorkshire Regt
WHITEHOUSE Henry Bernard MM Sjt S/942 13th Royal Fusiliers DOW 21.8.16.
WHITEHOUSE Herbert H. MM+Bar Spr 49690 23 Div Sig Coy Royal Engineers
WHITEHOUSE Howard L. MM Cpl 57236 42 Bty 2 Bde RFA
WHITEHOUSE John MM L/Cpl 95735 15th Bn Tank Corps
WHITEHOUSE John J. MM Sjt 17169 6th South Wales Borderers
WHITEHOUSE John W. MM Spr 102062 171 Tunnelling Coy Royal Engineers
WHITEHOUSE John W. MM Bdr 75919 C/124 Bde RFA
WHITEHOUSE Joseph Charles MM Cpl 8449 2nd Royal Warwickshire Regt KIA 8.10.17.
WHITEHOUSE Moses George MM Pte 35728 54 Coy Machine Gun

Corps KIA 10.8.17.
WHITEHOUSE Percy MM Bdr 71794 8 Bde RFA
WHITEHURST George "MM,MID" Cpl 1818 49 Div Sig Coy Royal Engineers
WHITEHURST Walter H.J. MM L/Cpl 63986 Royal Engineers
WHITELAND William MM Cpl 8417 2nd Hampshire Regt
WHITELAW Cornelius MM L/Cpl 34886 York & Lancaster Regt
WHITELAW Harry MM Bdr 663255 RFA
WHITELAW James MM L/Cpl 10010 X Corps Cyclist Bn Army Cyclist Corps
WHITELEGG John R. MM Gnr Sig 925709 C/280 RFA
WHITELEY Benjamin MM Pte 60418 93 Fd Amb RAMC
WHITELEY Charles MM Pte 12732 11th West Yorkshire Regt
WHITELEY Clement MM L/Cpl 14148 X Corps Cyclist Bn Army Cyclist Corps
WHITELEY George Ernest MM Pte 41592 Lincolnshire Regt
WHITELEY Harry MM Pte 201288 4th Yorkshire Light Infantry
WHITELEY Harry MM+Bar Pte 200529 4th West Riding Regt
WHITELEY Herbert "DCM,MM" Sjt 96358 D/86 Bde RFA DOW 30.3.18.
WHITELEY James MM L/Sjt 3/9113 2nd Yorkshire Regt KIA 10.7.17.
WHITELEY James MM Pte 21284 Cheshire Regt
WHITELEY James H. MM Sjt 266131 West Riding Regt
WHITELEY John T. MM Pte 43629 West Yorkshire Regt
WHITELEY Louis G. MM Dvr 1510 RFA
WHITELEY Louis I. MM Sjt 1434 West Riding Regt
WHITELEY Stuart MM Cpl 29831 D/178 Bde RFA
WHITELEY William MM Sjt 27829 9th Lancashire Fusiliers KIA 4.10.17.
WHITELEY William Wilfred MM Gnr 110308 C/82 Bde RFA DOW 24.9.18.
WHITELOCK Albert E. MM Sjt 5721 2nd Dragoon Guards
WHITELOCK Lawson MM L/Sjt 21886 1/5th Border Regt
WHITELOCK Thomas MM L/Cpl 23736 Welsh Regt
WHITELOW Edward MM(41611 Pte W Yorks)+Bar Sjt 51242 1st East Yorkshire Regt
WHITEMAN ArthurG. MM Sjt 20293 Royal Sussex Regt
WHITEMAN Charles Frederick "MC,MM(2436 Sjt)" 2Lt 3rd Rifle Brigade
WHITEMAN Charles S. MM L/Cpl 56655 1st Royal Welsh Fusiliers
WHITEMAN Donald MM Cpl 41283 33 Bde RFA
WHITEMAN Henry MM 2nd Cpl 489993 Royal Engineers att RFA.
WHITEOAK Henry MM Pte 41556 Northumberland Fusiliers
WHITEROD Albert Ernest MM+Bar Dmr 7189 2nd Suffolk Regt DOW 1.10.17.
WHITESIDE George Stephen MM L/Sjt 23788 2nd Grenadier Guards
WHITESIDE John MM Cpl 16991 13th Royal Scots
WHITESIDE John J.F.A. MM Gnr 66325 94 Bty 18 Bde RFA
WHITESIDE Owen Edward Preston MM Cpl 7730 16th King's Royal Rifle Corps
WHITESIDE Samuel MM Cpl 14748 9th Royal Irish Fusiliers
WHITESIDE Thomas MM Spr 241700 218 Fd Coy Royal Engineers
WHITESIDE William T. MM Sjt 200734 1/4th Royal Lancaster Regt
WHITEWAY Walter MM Gnr 86285 111 Bty 24 Bde RFA
WHITFIELD Andrew MM Sjt 8931 Border Regt
WHITFIELD Frank MM Pte 742 5th York & Lancaster Regt
WHITFIELD Fred MM Pte 116603 Labour Corps
WHITFIELD Henry MM Cpl 201648 Liverpool Regt
WHITFIELD James MM Sjt 290655 1/7th Cheshire Regt
WHITFIELD John MM Sjt 24190 B/119 Bde RFA
WHITFIELD John J. MM 2nd Cpl 45526 Royal Engineers
WHITFIELD John W. MM Sjt 62764 RGA
WHITFIELD Stanley McKnight MM Pte 47889 1/8th Manchester Regt
WHITFIELD Thomas MM Pte 21133 Royal Irish Fusiliers
WHITFORD Howard MM Cpl 2244 RFA
WHITHAM Albert E. MM L/Cpl 300156 7th Lancashire Fusiliers
WHITHAM George MM Spr 149101 Royal Engineers
WHITHAM John S. MM Pte 266187 2/5th West Riding Regt
WHITHAM Percy MM Spr 47599 50 Div Sig Coy Royal Engineers
WHITHAM Richard MM Pte 3263 1/1st Duke of Lancaster's Own Yeomanry
WHITHAM William MM Cpl 91835 Labour Corps
WHITHORN Tom MM Pte 2496 1(South Midland)Fd Amb RAMC
WHITING Edward A. "DCM+Bar,MM" Pte 8491 2nd Coldstream Guards
WHITING Frank MM Cpl 18633 7th East Yorkshire Regt
WHITING Frederick "MM,MID" Pte 5752 1st Cheshire Regt
WHITING Frederick Charles MM Sjt 621 RFA

WHITING George MM+Bar L/Cpl 1766 1/4th Suffolk Regt KIA 25.4.18.
WHITING George B. MM L/Cpl 8427 2nd Wiltshire Regt
WHITING George J. MM Pte 10033 Gloucestershire Regt
WHITING Harold E. MM Pte 67407 7th Royal West Surrey Regt
WHITING Harry William MM Pte 72118 104 Fd Amb RAMC
WHITING Horace MM Pte 12354 Leicestershire Regt
WHITING James George MM L/Cpl 7080 2nd Wiltshire Regt KIA 9.4.17.
WHITING John MM L/Cpl 4819 Rifle Brigade
WHITING John W. MM L/Cpl 260410 7th Border Regt
WHITING Robert S. MM Sjt 200346 1/4th Royal Sussex Regt
WHITING S. MM+Bar Sjt 21993 33rd Bn Machine Gun Corps
WHITING Samuel Henry MM Sjt 9517 RFA
WHITING Sidney MM Pte S/4229 Rifle Brigade
WHITING Stanley Victor MM Pte 10689 9th York & Lancaster Regt Died 24.11.18.
WHITING Valentine "MM,MID" Pte M2/046575 Army Service Corps
WHITING William MM L/Cpl 241330 West Riding Regt
WHITING William MM Sjt 24157 2nd South Wales Borderers
WHITING William MM Pte S/18203 Rifle Brigade
WHITINGTON Frank MM Cpl 5433 13th Hussars
WHITINGTON John MM Pte 5286 Machine Gun Corps
WHITLA James "MM,MID" Pte 16/582 Royal Irish Rifles
WHITLAM Walter MM L/Cpl 241555 2nd Lancashire Fusiliers
WHITLAM William MM L/Sjt 18061 20th Manchester Regt
WHITLAW Charles Young Myles MM Cpl 143007 'C' Special Coy Royal Engineers DOW 23.7.18.
WHITLEY Ernest MM Pte 18619 East Lancashire Regt
WHITLEY John MM Dvr 85804 RFA
WHITLEY William MM Pte 61981 RAMC
WHITLIE Robert Christopher MM Cpl 459278 447 Fd Coy Royal Engineers
WHITLING Harry MM Bdr 66137 RFA
WHITLOCK Albert Eli MM L/Cpl 902 23rd Royal Fusiliers KIA 30.10.16.
WHITLOCK Arthur Ernest MM Sjt 5943 9th Royal Sussex Regt DOW 4.11.18.
WHITLOCK Frederick "MM,MID" Sjt 9697 2nd Yorkshire Regt
WHITLOCK George Charles MM+Bar Pte 92104 11th Notts & Derby Regt KIA 24.10.18.
WHITLOCK George Henry MM L/Cpl 14304 4th Middlesex Regt
WHITLOCK Harry MM Sjt 36991 33rd Bn Machine Gun Corps
WHITLOCK James MM Pte 204877 1st Northamptonshire Regt
WHITLOCK Robert MM L/Cpl 14892 7th Somerset Light Infantry
WHITLOCK William MM Cpl 202574 5th Liverpool Regt
WHITLOW Archie MM Cpl 47292 RAMC
WHITMAN Alfred E. MM Pte 2601 North Lancashire Regt
WHITMARSH Edwin MM+Bar L/Cpl 34657 Middlesex Regt
WHITMARSH Henry H. MM Dvr 32188 RFA
WHITMARSH John R. MM L/Cpl 75276 1st Northumberland Fusiliers
WHITMARSH W.H. MM Cpl 275596 Essex Regt
WHITMEE William MM L/Cpl 15753 18 Fd Amb RAMC
WHITMORE Alfred MM Pte 40769 8th Somerset Light Infantry
WHITMORE Charles MM L/Cpl 12082 7th Duke of Cornwall's LI
WHITMORE Henry MM Sjt 8871 2nd Royal Irish Regt KIA 5.7.16.
WHITMORE John MM Pte 14736 10th York & Lancaster Regt
WHITMORE John MM Sjt S/2498 Rifle Brigade
WHITMORE John MM+Bar Pte 15625 10th Worcestershire Regt
WHITMORE Joseph MM Pte 290697 1/7th Cheshire Regt
WHITMORE Leonard William MM BSM 462 6(London)Bde RFA
WHITMORE Marcus Walton MM L/Cpl 31781 47 Div Sig Coy Royal Engineers
WHITMORE Martin E. MM Pte 2693 1/22nd London Regt
WHITMORE Robert MM Pte 241460 Leicestershire Regt
WHITMORE Walter G. MM S/Sjt Fitter 308906 RGA
WHITNELL Henry MM Pte 202547 1/4th Gloucestershire Regt
WHITNEY Daniel MM Pte 91105 8th Liverpool Regt
WHITNEY Frederick MM Cpl 20646 Machine Gun Corps
WHITNEY John "DCM,MM" Sjt 21337 C/122 Bde RFA
WHITNEY Percy MM Sjt 10403 Royal West Surrey Regt
WHITNEY Thomas MM Pte 91095 25th Bn Machine Gun Corps
WHITNEY William "DCM,MM" Sjt 10099 1st Shropshire Light Infantry
WHITSON Wilfred G. MM L/Cpl 4190 13th Royal Fusiliers
WHITSTONE William MM Pte 17150 Suffolk Regt
WHITTAKER Abraham MM Sjt 32464 1/5th East Lancashire Regt
WHITTAKER Alfred N. MM Sjt 77789 RFA

WHITTAKER Arthur E. MM L/Cpl 504409 503 Fd Coy Royal Engineers
WHITTAKER Charles MM L/Cpl 110776 MGC(Cavalry)
WHITTAKER Charles MM L/Cpl 277359 Manchester Regt
WHITTAKER Ernest MM Pte 44998 RAMC
WHITTAKER F. MM Pte 13583 Worcestershire Regt
WHITTAKER Fred MM Sjt 32554 Machine Gun Corps(Motors)
WHITTAKER Fred MM+2 Bars Cpl 15452 24th Manchester Regt
WHITTAKER Frederick Albert MM Gnr 1443 C/77 Bde RFA
WHITTAKER George Edward Harris MM Pte 71280 33 Coy Machine Gun Corps
WHITTAKER George H. "MM,MID" Cpl 13333 Leicestershire Regt
WHITTAKER Harry MM Pte 350485 10th Manchester Regt
WHITTAKER Harry MM L/Cpl 40494 Norfolk Regt
WHITTAKER James MM Pte 201297 Notts & Derby Regt
WHITTAKER John MM Sjt 200060 South Staffordshire Regt
WHITTAKER John MM Pte 33336 Border Regt
WHITTAKER John "MM,MID" Sjt 79715 Royal Engineers
WHITTAKER John W. MM Pte 68111 RAMC
WHITTAKER Joseph MM Sjt 42486 22nd Northumberland Fusiliers
WHITTAKER Joseph MM L/Cpl 40602 21st Manchester Regt KIA 24.6.17.
WHITTAKER Leo "MM,MID" Sjt 9709 Royal Dublin Fusiliers KIA 26.3.18.
WHITTAKER Owen MM Cpl 251836 6th Manchester Regt
WHITTAKER Smith Stephenson MM Pte 22827 10th West Riding Regt
WHITTAKER Soloman MM Pte 19034 North Staffordshire Regt
WHITTAKER Stanley MM Pte 55639 Royal Welsh Fusiliers
WHITTAKER Thomas MM Pte 9/26065 South Wales Borderers
WHITTAKER Thomas Henry MM Pte 50090 2nd Lincolnshire Regt KIA 18.10.18.
WHITTAKER Thomas Stafford "MM,MSM" Sjt 6975 4 Div Sig Coy Royal Engineers
WHITTAKER Thomas W. MM Gnr 68464 111 Bty 24 Bde RFA
WHITTAKER William MM Pte 13077 1st East Lancashire Regt
WHITTAKER William MM Pte 376848 10th Manchester Regt
WHITTAKER William Henry MM Pte 3866 1st Lancashire Fusiliers KIA 30.5.17.
WHITTAKER William J. MM Pte 55005 RAMC
WHITTAKER William L. MM Sjt 1932 25 Fd Amb RAMC
WHITTAKER William R.(or B.) MM(20588 12th N&D)+Bar Pte 72706 Royal West Surrey Regt
WHITTALL George MM Pte 4704 1st North Lancashire Regt
WHITTAMORE William George MM CQMS 13468 2nd King's Own Scottish Borderers
WHITTEMORE Frederick Arthur MM+Bar Pte 14877 7th Royal Sussex Regt KIA 26.8.18.
WHITTERN Harry "MM,CG(F)" Sjt 9387 2nd Gloucestershire Regt
WHITTERON William Henry MM Cpl 242106 1/5th West Riding Regt
WHITTET David MM Pte 43165 16th Highland Light Infantry
WHITTEY Charles MM Cpl 242649 1/6th Royal Warwickshire Regt
WHITTING Robert MM Cpl 18128 Royal Engineers
WHITTING William H. MM Sjt T4/213003 51 Div Train Army Service Corps
WHITTINGHAM Frank MM Spr 108790 202 Fd Coy Royal Engineers
WHITTINGHAM George L. MM Sjt 19911 16th Royal Welsh Fusiliers
WHITTINGHAM Harry MM Cpl 15301 Leicestershire Regt
WHITTINGHAM Sydney MM Cpl 238025 4th Worcestershire Regt
WHITTINGHAM William MM Cpl 24364 1 Div Sig Coy Royal Engineers
WHITTINGSTALL Alfred J. MM Cpl 470125 528 Fd Coy Royal Engineers
WHITTINGTON Ernest MM Sjt 6123 2nd King's Royal Rifle Corps
WHITTINGTON George H. MM Pte 19674 Machine Gun Corps
WHITTINGTON George Henry MM Sjt 12247 11th Royal Fusiliers KIA 22.3.18.
WHITTINGTON Oliver F. MM Pte 331227 1/8th Hampshire Regt
WHITTINGTON William MM Pte 43528 11th Suffolk Regt DOW 30.4.17.
WHITTINGTON William G.. MM L/Bdr 318640 RGA
WHITTLE Arthur MM Gnr 47421 D/58 Bde RFA KIA 26.9.17.
WHITTLE Arthur G. MM L/Cpl 25171 1st Royal West Surrey Regt
WHITTLE Charles MM Pte 40064 1/1st Dorset Yeomanry
WHITTLE Frank MM Pte 275257 3rd London Regt
WHITTLE Fred MM Sjt 14642 9th North Lancashire Regt
WHITTLE Harry MM Sjt 17617 148 Bde RFA
WHITTLE Herbert MM Pte 7554 1st Leicestershire Regt
WHITTLE James MM+Bar Sjt 300101 1/8th Durham Light Infantry
WHITTLE James R. MM Pte 50817 RAMC
WHITTLE Joseph MM Pte 30025 North Lancashire Regt
WHITTLE Leonard MM L/Cpl 5747 1st East Lancashire Regt
WHITTLE S. MM Pte 870 Royal Fusiliers
WHITTLE Thomas MM Cpl 20782 RAMC
WHITTLE W. MM Sjt 441035 RAMC
WHITTLE Walter G. MM Sjt 267369 Royal Engineers
WHITTLE Wilfred MM L/Cpl 201592 Manchester Regt
WHITTLE William MM Pte 45500 12th Highland Light Infantry
WHITTLES Thomas MM L/Bdr 123615 366 Siege Bty RGA
WHITTON Anfrew MM Cpl 357 2 Fd Amb RAMC
WHITTON Charles MM Sjt 761393 RFA
WHITTON Charles MM Pte 36608 Northumberland Fusiliers
WHITTON Frank "MM,CG(F)" L/Cpl 14827 1st East Yorkshire Regt
WHITTON John MM Sjt 42333 69 Coy Machine Gun Corps DOW 7.10.16.
WHITTON Matthew MM Dmr 1532 1/7th Arg & Suth Highlanders
WHITTON P.H. MM Pte 373 Royal Sussex Regt
WHITTY Albert Edward "MM,MID" CSM 9607 1st Devonshire Regt
WHITTY Robert MM L/Cpl 33330 11th Border Regt
WHITTY Thomas MM Sjt 608576 18th London Regt
WHITWAM A. MM Pte 201925 28th London Regt
WHITWAM John A. MM+Bar Pte 21504 Lancashire Fusiliers
WHITWAM Willie MM Pte 38163 2nd Lancashire Fusiliers
WHITWOOD Edward MM L/Cpl 15231 7th Norfolk Regt
WHITWORTH Charles MM Gnr 175063 194 Siege Bty RGA
WHITWORTH Charles F. MM Cpl 710013 RFA
WHITWORTH Frederick MM Pte 2968 1/24th London Regt
WHITWORTH George MM Cpl 3834 Notts & Derby Regt
WHITWORTH Harry MM Pte 40551 Lincolnshire Regt
WHITWORTH John James MM Pte 5690 12th Manchester Regt
WHITWORTH Leonard MM L/Cpl 156064 104th Bn Machine Gun Corps
WHITWORTH Percy MM Cpl 10833 2nd Bedfordshire Regt
WHITWORTH Percy C. MM L/Sjt 22332 Dorsetshire Regt
WHITWORTH Roger MM Pte 11838 7th Yorkshire Light Infantry
WHITWORTH Thomas "DCM,MM" Pte 2173 1/5th York & Lancaster Regt
WHOLTON William MM Cpl 10945 Leicestershire Regt
WHOMERSLEY George MM Sjt 7471 Yorkshire Regt
WHOMERSLEY George William MM Pte 235152 1/4th York & Lancaster Regt
WHOMES Henry MM Pte 680321 1/22nd London Regt
WHORTON William Frederick MM Pte 241229 1/4th York & Lancaster Regt
WHOTTON Harry MM Spr 252042 Royal Engineers
WHY Arthur W. MM L/Cpl 50262 Machine Gun Corps
WHY William MM Sjt 252114 Essex Regt
WHYATT Albert Herbert MM Pte 3497 7th Royal West Kent Regt DOW 6.5.17.
WHYATT Joseph Walter "MM,CG(F)" Pte 204393 2/4th York & Lancaster Regt
WHYATT William George . "See DRAKE, George,29918 RFA"
WHYBORN W.J. MM L/Cpl C/6046 King's Royal Rifle Corps
WHYBREW Percy Charles MM Pte M2/136150 13 LAMB Army Service Corps
WHYBROW Frederick Charles Erwin MM L/Cpl 304253 18th Bn Tank Corps
WHYBROW Geoffrey H.R. MM Pte 137277 62nd Bn Machine Gun Corps
WHYBROW James MM L/Cpl 3749 1st Northumberland Fusiliers
WHYBROW William John MM Cpl 55666 Royal Engineers
WHYLD Sidney S. MM Pte 45716 South Wales Borderers
WHYLD Walter F. MM L/Sjt 20670 9th Royal Fusiliers
WHYLEY W. MM Pte 201346 Leicestershire Regt
WHYMAN Ambrose MM Pte 10292 Royal West Kent Regt
WHYMAN Fred MM+Bar Cpl 26831 C/83 Bde RFA
WHYMAN Frederick MM+Bar Pte 10297 1st Northamptonshire Regt
WHYMAN George "DCM,MM" CSM 200824 2/4th York & Lancaster Regt
WHYMAN Jack MM L/Bdr 85932 C/83 Bde RFA
WHYMAN John MM Pte 9711 15th Royal Warwickshire Regt
WHYMAN Richard MM Pte 8440 34 Fd Amb RAMC
WHYMAN William MM Gnr 59690 RGA
WHYMAN William MM L/Cpl 9362 2nd West Yorkshire Regt
WHYMAN William H. MM Sjt 201509 Bedfordshire Regt
WHYMARK Frederick MM Pte 17463 1st Suffolk Regt
WHYMARK George A. MM Pte 5103 17th Lancers

WHYMARK Harry James MM Pte 22304 4th Middlesex Regt
WHYTE Andrew MM L/Cpl 2424 1/9th Arg & Suth Highlanders
WHYTE Bernard MM Pte 525 11th Cheshire Regt
WHYTE Charles MM Pte 125077 Lovat's Scouts Yeomanry KIA 22.5.17.
WHYTE Daniel MM Sjt 25953 RGA
WHYTE Ernest MM Cpl 143061 Royal Engineers
WHYTE George MM Sjt 32813 8th Royal Lancaster Regt
WHYTE George "MM,MIDx2" Pte 9602 1st Royal Munster Fusiliers
WHYTE H. MM Pte 43112 Arg & Suth Highlanders
WHYTE J. MM Dvr 720621 RFA
WHYTE James MM L/Cpl 240979 1st Gordon Highlanders KIA 1.10.18.
WHYTE James MM Pte 6261 Arg & Suth Highlanders
WHYTE James S. MM+Bar Pte 23791 2nd & 1st Royal Scots Fusiliers
WHYTE Jean Strachan MM Staff Nurse F TFNS
WHYTE William "MM,MSM,MID" S/Sjt 12302 5 Fd Amb RAMC
WHYTOCK Edwin MM Spr 498537 Royal Engineers
WHYTOCK James C. MM+Bar Pte 40794 Royal Scots
WIBREW Arthur H. MM Sjt 358148 RGA
WIBREW Sidney A. MM Sjt 9720 X/15 Med TM Bty RFA
WICKEN Percy Charles MM Pte 12941 1st East Kent Regt
WICKENDEN Harold MM Pte 275216 3rd London Regt KIA 11.8.18.
WICKENDEN Reginald C. MM Pte 53060 2nd Royal Fusiliers
WICKENS Frederick J.N. MM Cpl 133092 45th Royal Fusiliers
WICKENS J.T. MM Cpl 1240 Military Foot Police
WICKENS James MM Pte 295223 21st London Regt
WICKENS Leslie MM Pte 21232 Hampshire Regt
WICKENS Reuben J.E. MM Pte 730 4th Bn GMGR
WICKENS Richard Alfred MM Sjt 445 1/4th Royal Berkshire Regt
WICKES Frederick MM Sjt R/31579 13th King's Royal Rifle Corps
WICKES William C.H. MM L/Cpl 11784 King's Royal Rifle Corps
WICKES William H. MM Pte 25110 Royal West Surrey Regt
WICKETT Sidney MM L/Cpl 13991 6th East Kent Regt
WICKETTS George F. MM Pte A/631 King's Royal Rifle Corps
WICKHAM Andrew W. MM Sjt 19572 226 Fd Coy Royal Engineers
WICKHAM Frederick Henry MM Cpl 70629 Royal Engineers att 27 Bde RGA.
WICKHAM Harry MM Cpl 428 1st Royal West Kent Regt
WICKHAM Harry T. MM+Bar Spr 87382 Royal Engineers
WICKHAM Patrick MM L/Cpl 10474 1st Royal Irish Regt
WICKHAM Thomas MM Pte 292047 2nd Devonshire Regt
WICKHAM Wilfred MM L/Cpl 165402 1/1st North Somerset Yeomanry
WICKINGTON H.G. "DCM,MM,MID" CQMS G/1300 7th East Kent Regt
WICKS Albert Edward MM Bdr 45907 25 Bde RFA
WICKS Arthur A. MM Cpl 24854 7th Royal West Surrey Regt
WICKS Edward Victor MM Sjt 643 11th Middlesex Regt KIA 4.10.16.
WICKS Percevale MM L/Cpl 567942 Royal Engineers
WICKS William MM Pte 13313 1st East Surrey Regt
WICKS William H. MM Pte 8092 2nd Royal Berkshire Regt
WICKSTEAD Richard MM Pte 21339 Shropshire Light Infantry
WIDD Thomas "DCM+Bar,MM,MID" CSM 2515 1/4th South Lancashire Regt
WIDDOP James MM Sjt 16075 4th West Riding Regt
WIDDOP Thomas MM+Bar Cpl 59689 RGA
WIDDOWS George MM L/Cpl 305048 1/7th Liverpool Regt DOW 22.3.18.
WIDDOWS Harry MM Pte 52495 Cheshire Regt
WIDDOWS Percy MM CSM 39505 6th York & Lancaster Regt
WIDDUP Frank MM L/Cpl 58550 Royal Engineers
WIDOCKS Edward John MM CQMS 1714 South Lancashire Regt
WIEDHOFT Ernest A. MM Spr 268263 Royal Engineers
WIER J. MM L/Cpl 19309 Royal Irish Rifles
WIFFEN William MM Spr 181150 Royal Engineers
WIGG Cyril G. MM Pte 493325 13th London Regt
WIGG Sydney Charles MM Pte S/17209 13th Rifle Brigade Died 19.3.17.
WIGG William Edward MM Pte 2514 9th East Surrey Regt
WIGGANS William "DCM,MM" Pte 60482 10th Cheshire Regt
WIGGETT Alfred MM Sjt 25934 Notts & Derby Regt
WIGGETT Charles MM+Bar CSM 3/9995 2nd Suffolk Regt
WIGGIN James MM Cpl 22117 7/8th King's Own Scottish Borderers
WIGGINS Albert Henry MM 2nd Cpl 49753 24 Div Sig Coy Royal Engineers KIA 31.7.17.
WIGGINS Alfred C.H. MM L/Sjt 201049 1/4th Oxf & Bucks Light Infantry
WIGGINS Bertram MM CSM 240610 6th Royal Warwickshire Regt
WIGGINS Charles W. MM Pte 203862 1/4th Royal Berkshire Regt
WIGGINS Frederick C. MM Sjt 43729 'K' Bty RHA
WIGGINS Henry J. MM Sjt 10404 4th Royal Berkshire Regt
WIGGINS Herbert MM Pte 74000 1st Bn Machine Gun Corps
WIGGINS John R. MM Pte 435391 1(South Midland)Fd Amb RAMC
WIGGINS Robert Henry MM Pte 20341 2nd Bedfordshire Regt DOW 5.11.18.
WIGGINS W.G. MM Spr 87477 Royal Engineers
WIGGLESWORTH Charles F. MM Sjt 2174 1/19th London Regt
WIGGLESWORTH Harold T. MM Pte C/385 16th King's Royal Rifle Corps
WIGGLESWORTH Richard MM Pte 18863 9th Yorkshire Light Infantry
WIGGLESWORTH Thomas H. MM L/Cpl 35631 4th York & Lancaster Regt
WIGGLESWORTH William MM Pte 17891 10th West Riding Regt
WIGHAM Allan MM Pte 116752 195 Coy Labour Corps
WIGHAM Hugh MM Pte 25096 1st Royal Scots Fusiliers
WIGHAM James MM L/Sjt 22/760 Durham Light Infantry
WIGHAM John James MM Pte 19786 2nd Yorkshire Regt KIA 31.7.17.
WIGHAM Jonathan MM L/Cpl 14533 10th Yorkshire Regt
WIGHAM L. MM Pte 291674 Northumberland Fusiliers
WIGHAM Robert R. MM Sjt 760398 408 Bty 96 Bde RFA
WIGHT Graham MM Cpl 217041 A/14 Bde RFA
WIGHT James L. MM Sjt C/6146 King's Royal Rifle Corps
WIGHT Peter C. MM Sjt 110036 10th Bn Tank Corps
WIGHTMAN Edward W. MM L/Cpl 267425 1/6th Northumberland Fusiliers
WIGHTMAN Frederick Harold MM Pte 14761 6th Bedfordshire Regt KIA 23.4.17.
WIGHTMAN James MM Pte 1418 16th Highland Light Infantry
WIGHTMAN Kenneth Charles MM Gnr 955105 A/236 Bde RFA
WIGHTMAN Walter MM Pte 273219 12th Royal Scots
WIGHTMAN William "DCM,MM" Cpl 202791 5/6th Scottish Rifles
WIGHTON John C. MM Pte 61796 10th West Yorkshire Regt
WIGHTON William MM Pte 532875 5th London Regt
WIGHTWICK Percy MM Bdr 105361 RGA
WIGLEY Ernest MM Pte 6039 6th Dragoon Guards
WIGLEY H.B. MM Cpl 32342 Machine Gun Corps
WIGLEY J. MM Pte 19698 5/6th Scottish Rifles
WIGLEY John David MM L/Cpl 5016 10th Hussars
WIGMORE George H. MM Bdr 1590 RFA
WIGNALL John MM Cpl 32523 RAMC
WIGSTON John MM Pte 280379 1/7th Highland Light Infantry
WIGTON Andrew MM L/Cpl 3863 11th Royal Scots KIA 16.9.17.
WILBER Ernest William MM Spr 156286 180 Tunnelling Coy Royal Engineers DOW 15.11.18.
WILBERFORCE William MM Gnr 89409 RFA
WILBOR Thomas MM L/Cpl 34711 9th Yorkshire Light Infantry
WILBRAHAM George Henry "MM,MID" Sjt 1610 Machine Gun Corps
WILBRAHAM Henry P. MM Pte 36985 16th Royal Welsh Fusiliers
WILBUR Arthur MM Gnr 123326 RGA
WILBUR Charles MM Bdr 47967 Z/1 Med TM Bty RFA
WILBY Albert MM L/Cpl 15421 Yorkshire Light Infantry
WILBY Arthur MM Pte 306218 2/8th West Yorkshire Regt
WILBY Ernest MM Pte 594 Durham Light Infantry
WILBY Frederick MM L/Cpl 10155 10th Royal West Kent Regt
WILBY George MM Pte 3/7133 1st Bedfordshire Regt
WILBY James H. MM+Bar Pte 11454 7th York & Lancaster Regt
WILBY John H. MM L/Sjt 15961 King's Own Scottish Borderers
WILCOCK Albert MM Pte 85565 55th Bn Machine Gun Corps
WILCOCK Cyril Joseph MM L/Cpl 12966 Royal Sussex Regt
WILCOCK Ellis MM Pte 19563 9th York & Lancaster Regt
WILCOCK Herbert MM L/Cpl 31213 1/5th King's Own Scottish Borderers
WILCOCK James MM Sjt 240728 Royal Lancaster Regt
WILCOCK John MM Pte 48675 RAMC
WILCOCK John MM L/Cpl 202785 1/5th Liverpool Regt
WILCOCK Joseph MM L/Cpl 36968 68 Fd Coy Royal Engineers
WILCOCK Joseph S. MM Pte 200846 Yorkshire Light Infantry
WILCOCK Reuben "MM,CG(F)" Pte 14386 7th Royal Lancaster Regt
WILCOCK Robert MM Sjt 8358 Lancashire Fusiliers
WILCOCK Robert MM Bdr 710176 RFA
WILCOCK Tom MM L/Cpl 3331 1st King's Royal Rifle Corps
WILCOCK William MM+Bar Cpl 5440 Northumberland Fusiliers
WILCOX A.H. MM Pte 354447 London Regt
WILCOX Albert L. MM L/Cpl 43838 Yorkshire Light Infantry

WILCOX Alfred W. MM Sjt 51051 42 Bde RFA
WILCOX Clement A. MM Sjt 267467 Gloucestershire Regt
WILCOX George T. MM Pte M2/183159 328 Coy Army Service Corps
WILCOX John MM Pte 50633 1st Royal Berkshire Regt
WILCOX John MM Gnr 805645 RFA
WILCOX John E. MM+Bar L/Cpl 19505 10th North Lancashire Regt
WILCOX John R. "MM,MSM" CSM 200870 1/4th Gloucestershire Regt
WILCOX Joseph MM Pte 42029 Machine Gun Corps
WILCOX Joseph MM L/Cpl 19151 Royal Welsh Fusiliers
WILCOX Rutherford F. MM L/Cpl 15979 Royal Engineers
WILCOX Sidney MM Pte 16704 11th Cheshire Regt
WILCOX Thomas MM Sjt 1202 B/78 Bde RFA
WILCOX William MM Pte 22307 Devonshire Regt
WILCOX William H. MM L/Cpl 14612 1/7th Liverpool Regt
WILCOX William Thomas MM L/Cpl 37293 50th Bn Machine Gun Corps Died 20.10.18.
WILCOXON Arthur Henry MM Pte 67150 1/5th Devonshire Regt
WILD Albert MM Pte R/45337 1st King's Royal Rifle Corps
WILD Arnold MM Cpl 27616 South Wales Borderers
WILD Arthur MM Pte 25558 Scottish Rifles
WILD E. MM Pte 52770 Liverpool Regt
WILD Frank MM L/Sjt 13302 Coldstream Guards
WILD Frank P. MM Spr 33845 Royal Engineers
WILD Frederick C. MM Pte 24997 2nd Oxf & Bucks Light Infantry
WILD Garvin MM CQMS 26/1310 Northumberland Fusiliers
WILD George MM+Bar Sjt 6823 1st Royal Lancaster Regt
WILD Harold V. MM Bdr Sig 806164 C/296 Bde RFA
WILD James MM Pte 474596 12th London Regt
WILD James Josephus MM Gnr 960559 RFA
WILD John MM Cpl 53503 8th Middlesex Regt
WILD John MM Pte 43769 11th West Yorkshire Regt KIA 20.9.17.
WILD John J. MM Sjt 40030 67 Coy Labour Corps
WILD John Thomas MM Pte 201667 1/4th Royal Lancaster Regt KIA 20.11.17.
WILD John William MM Pte 281454 Lancashire Fusiliers
WILD Peter MM Cpl 37891 6th Leicestershire Regt KIA 6.11.18.
WILD Reginald E. MM Cpl 320193 16th Royal Sussex Regt
WILD Robert E. MM CQMS 272201 Railway Troops Royal Engineers
WILD Samuel MM Cpl 34110 RFA
WILD Thomas MM Sjt 90174 D/76 Bde RFA
WILD Thomas Henry MM Pte 57282 Machine Gun Corps KIA 31.8.18
WILD Thomas Leonard MM L/Cpl 203767 7th Shropshire Light Infantry
WILD Walter MM Cpl 20562 East Lancashire Regt
WILDE Cornelius MM Cpl 66471 Machine Gun Corps
WILDE F. MM L/Cpl 331319 2nd Hampshire Regt
WILDE Fred MM Cpl 34510 2/5th West Riding Regt KIA 28.9.18
WILDE Gordon Leonard MM Cpl 940253 RFA
WILDE Harold MM Pte 19199 Royal Welsh Fusiliers KIA 3.9.18.
WILDE Harry MM Spr 546911 526 Fd Coy Royal Engineers
WILDE Henry MM Pte 232643 2nd London Regt
WILDE James "DCM,MM" Sjt 1275 4th Bn GMGR
WILDE John MM Pte 28837 9th Royal Welsh Fusiliers
WILDE John "MM,MID" Pte 2317 1/5th York & Lancaster Regt
WILDE Thomas MM Bdr 55058 84 Bty 11 Bde RFA DOW 2.11.17.
WILDE Thomas Abbott MM Cpl 25089 11th East Yorkshire Regt DOW 30.2.18.
WILDE Wilfred T. MM Sjt 113088 Royal Engineers
WILDE William MM Pte 351825 5th Manchester Regt
WILDER Frederick S. MM Pte 353079 1/9th Highland Light Infantry
WILDERS S. MM Bdr 44341 B/15 Bde RFA
WILDERSPIN Charles G. MM Spr 179633 89 Fd Coy Royal Engineers
WILDERSPIN Harry Oliver MM Sjt 295248 2/4th London Regt
WILDGOOSE E. MM Dvr 507 RFA
WILDGOOSE George H. MM L/Cpl 40295 1st Leicestershire Regt
WILDGOOSE Harry MM Cpl 285586 13th Welsh Regt
WILDGOOSE Harry MM Pte 417400 RAMC
WILDGOOSE John MM Sjt 52507 Cheshire Regt
WILDGOOSE Walter J. MM 2nd Cpl 478536 Royal Engineers
WILDING Edward C. MM Bdr 292682 RGA
WILDING Edward William MM Pte 17951 13th Essex Regt
WILDING Ernest G. MM Sjt 39167 52 Fd Amb RAMC
WILDING Frederick C. MM Cpl 78004 10th Royal Fusiliers
WILDING G.H. MM Pte 32966 Royal Warwickshire Regt
WILDING George H. MM+Bar Cpl 16638 11th Suffolk Regt
WILDING Harry Ernest MM Sjt 49459 160 Coy Machine Gun Corps
WILDING Harry T. MM+Bar Pte 15564 2nd Grenadier Guards
WILDING Philip MM Gnr 107946 RFA
WILDING Ralph MM Pte 25119 1st Cheshire Regt
WILDING Thomas MM Pte 14674 8th Royal Lancaster Regt
WILDING Walter MM Cpl 6056 1st Worcestershire Regt
WILDING William S. MM Spr 63780 Royal Engineers
WILDISH John MM L/Cpl 912 Durham Light Infantry
WILDMAN Bernard William MM Pte 45967 13th Rifle Brigade
WILDRIDGE Alfred MM Cpl 63750 RFA
WILDRIDGE Charles Isaac MM Pte 44958 6th Bn Machine Gun Corps
WILDS John A. MM Cpl 75309 Royal Engineers
WILDSMITH Gersham MM Pte 306454 1/8th Notts & Derby Regt KIA 17.10.18.
WILDSMITH John Ferguson MM Cpl 16525 12th Durham Light Infantry KIA 28.10.18.
WILEMAN Arthur Harold MM Sjt 19825 11th Royal Sussex Regt KIA 28.4.18.
WILEMAN Edward MM Pte 18832 Gordon Highlanders
WILEMAN John T. MM Pte 38263 5th Gloucestershire Regt
WILEMAN Thomas W. MM Pte 14798 8th Border Regt
WILES Alfred MM Pte 43832 4th Bedfordshire Regt KIA 27.9.18.
WILES Alfred L. MM+Bar Cpl 18532 Royal West Kent Regt
WILES Edward Henry MM Pte 19845 4th Bedfordshire Regt DOW 3.5.17.
WILES Ernest MM Sjt 51606 28 Bde RFA
WILES Ernest F. MM Cpl 17936 8th Royal Berkshire Regt
WILES George Albert MM Pte 270212 10th East Kent Regt
WILES George B. MM Sjt 1056 22nd Royal Fusiliers
WILES Harry MM L/Cpl 45 RAMC
WILES Henry W. MM L/Cpl 52695 11th West Yorkshire Regt
WILES Percy George MM Cpl 5884 Gloucestershire Regt
WILES Robert MM Pte 31012 1st Northamptonshire Regt
WILEY James MM Pte 10638 5th Oxf & Bucks Light Infantry
WILEY Thomas MM+Bar Sjt 67014 B/93 Bde RFA
WILFORD William Frederick Shirley MM Pte 27075 Leicestershire Regt DOW 25.10.18.
WILKERSON Wilfred E. MM Sjt 320934 Norfolk Regt
WILKES Charles E. MM Sjt 49316 21 Div Sig Coy Royal Engineers
WILKES Charles H. MM Bdr 11674 RFA
WILKES Charles Henry MM Spr 40243 103 Fd Coy Royal Engineers
WILKES Edwin MM L/Cpl 8902 Worcestershire Regt
WILKES George MM Sjt 305490 11th Notts & Derby Regt
WILKES George MM Gnr 29464 181 Bde RFA
WILKES James MM Sjt 25203 Machine Gun Corps
WILKES John C. MM Pte 12317 4th Worcestershire Regt
WILKES John Thomas MM Sjt 17786 B/170 Bde RFA
WILKES Richard MM Cpl 9092 7th South Staffordshire Regt
WILKES Samuel MM L/Sjt 34509 2nd Manchester Regt
WILKES Thomas MM Spr 158400 257 Tunnelling Coy Royal Engineers
WILKES Thomas MM Sjt 6062 2nd South Staffordshire Regt KIA 29.7.16.
WILKES William MM Pte 13621 7th Shropshire Light Infantry
WILKIE Alexander MM L/Cpl 11019 1st Scottish Rifles
WILKIE Alexander MM Cpl 266159 Royal Highlanders
WILKIE Daniel MM Pte 253963 1/6th Arg & Suth Highlanders
WILKIE Duncan MM Pte 14306 16th Highland Light Infantry
WILKIE George MM Pte 46403 17th Lancashire Fusiliers
WILKIE James MM Dvr 63887 18 Bde Ammn Col RFA
WILKIE James MM L/Sjt 1121 6th Dragoon Guards
WILKIE James MM Pte M/377833 Army Service Corps
WILKIE James MM Pte 352010 1/9th Royal Scots
WILKIE James L. MM Gnr 59112 RGA
WILKIE James S. MM+Bar Pte 24192 Highland Light Infantry
WILKIE John K. MM Pte 250281 5/6th Royal Scots
WILKIE John Selkirk MM 2nd Cpl 76445 'AP' Cable Section Royal Engineers
WILKIE Peter MM Gnr 45772 D/110 Bde RFA
WILKIE R. MM Pte 331973 9th Highland Light Infantry
WILKIE Robert MM Cpl 33468 Border Regt
WILKIE Robert MM+Bar L/Cpl 242202 1/5th Gordon Highlanders
WILKIE William MM Cpl 44677 20th Durham Light Infantry
WILKIE William MM Sjt 92494 231 Siege Bty RGA
WILKIE William MM Pte 44679 20th Durham Light Infantry KIA 4.9.18
WILKIE William A. MM Gnr 650120 RFA
WILKIE William H. MM Sjt 51333 'E' Bty RHA

WILKIN John MM Cpl 98647 RFA
WILKIN John W. MM Cpl 59858 9th Northumberland Fusiliers
WILKIN Thomas MM Pte 143479 Machine Gun Corps
WILKIN Thomas MM Cpl 85661 143 Coy Labour Corps
WILKIN Thomas Alexander MM Cpl 16098 Royal Highlanders
WILKIN Tom MM Bdr 47046 135 Bty 32 Bde RFA
WILKIN W. MM Pte 204916 16th London Regt
WILKIN William MM Spr 236090 Royal Engineers
WILKINS Albert E. MM Pte 3/8016 2nd Yorkshire Regt
WILKINS Albert E. MM Pte 15016 1st Notts & Derby Regt
WILKINS Alfred MM Sjt 7924 2nd South Staffordshire Regt
WILKINS Alfred Charles MM Pte 13446 Worcestershire Regt
WILKINS Arthur MM Gnr 95000 RFA
WILKINS Arthur W.W. MM Cpl 915 2nd Royal Warwickshire Regt
WILKINS Charles E. MM L/Cpl 9211 7th Shropshire Light Infantry
WILKINS Edgar MM+Bar Sjt 225987 1/1st Monmouthshire Regt
WILKINS Ernest MM Gnr 104724 230 Siege Bty RGA
WILKINS Ernest Alfred MM Pte 14071 9th Devonshire Regt KIA 3.10.17.
WILKINS F.J. MM Cpl 1887 15 Bty 36 Bde RFA
WILKINS Frederick MM Pte 8905 Worcestershire Regt
WILKINS Frederick MM Sjt 2299 Liverpool Regt
WILKINS George MM Pte 15838 East Surrey Regt
WILKINS H.A. MM Sjt 439350 RAMC
WILKINS James MM Sjt 30214 C/160 Bde RFA
WILKINS John W. MM Pte 40300 Worcestershire Regt
WILKINS M.E. MM Pte 423681 London Regt
WILKINS Robert F.C. MM Pte PS/2063 Middlesex Regt
WILKINS Ronald MM Cpl 204552 1st Essex Regt
WILKINS Rowland MM Pte 75123 12/13th Northumberland Fusiliers
WILKINS Russell W. MM BSM 61948 A/119 Bde RFA
WILKINS Thomas MM Sjt 10255 4th Middlesex Regt KIA 2.7.16.
WILKINS Thomas MM Gnr 371167 RGA
WILKINS Tom MM Pte 204461 4th Oxf & Bucks Light Infantry
WILKINS Vernon L. MM Pte 200329 1/4th Welsh Regt
WILKINS Walter MM Spr 255129 Signal Service Royal Engineers att 11 Bde RFA.
WILKINS William Fitts MM L/Cpl 8344 1st Norfolk Regt
WILKINS William Henry Victor MM L/Cpl 283660 1/4th London Regt KIA 28.3.18.
WILKINSON A. MM Cpl 481 RFA
WILKINSON A.R. MM Pte 121822 18th Bn Machine Gun Corps
WILKINSON Albert MM Sjt 300219 13th Bn Tank Corps
WILKINSON Albert MM L/Cpl 26880 Hampshire Regt
WILKINSON Albert MM Pte 332782 1/9th Liverpool Regt
WILKINSON Alfred MM Spr 72288 Royal Engineers
WILKINSON Alfred MM Gnr 26064 RFA
WILKINSON Alfred MM L/Cpl 265266 Royal Welsh Fusiliers
WILKINSON Alfred MM Pte 37398 RAMC
WILKINSON Alfred MM Cpl 16090 7th South Staffordshire Regt
WILKINSON Alfred W. MM Pte 22/1683 Northumberland Fusiliers
WILKINSON Arthur MM Pte 8976 17th Manchester Regt DOW 25.4.17.
WILKINSON Arthur MM Pte 37396 56 Fd Amb RAMC DOW 4.6.17.
WILKINSON Arthur MM Sjt 785377 RFA
WILKINSON Arthur E. MM Sjt 4180 2nd Rifle Brigade
WILKINSON Arthur F. MM Sjt 29289 Middlesex Regt
WILKINSON Arthur W. MM Pte 534255 15th London Regt att MGC.
WILKINSON Arthur William MM Sjt 290222 1/1st Hertfordshire Regt
WILKINSON Benjamin Caswell MM Pte 12/822 12th York & Lancaster Regt KIA 1.7.16.
WILKINSON Charles MM+Bar Sjt 19297 21st Manchester Regt
WILKINSON Charles E. MM Gnr 88436 RHA
WILKINSON Charles F. MM Cpl 31058 183 Siege Bty RGA
WILKINSON Charles George MM Sjt 10016 2nd Royal Scots Fusiliers
WILKINSON Charles George MM Sjt 6241 Royal Munster Fusiliers
WILKINSON Charles Henry "MM,CG(F)" Pte 12540 5th Northamptonshire Regt
WILKINSON Charles W. MM Sjt 11/154 11th East Yorkshire Regt
WILKINSON Christopher MM Pte 28725 1st Somerset Light Infantry
WILKINSON Clarence MM CSM 16/351 16th West Yorkshire Regt
WILKINSON David MM Pte 41161 1st Bedfordshire Regt
WILKINSON David MM L/Cpl 248556 Royal Engineers
WILKINSON E. MM Sjt 32929 RFA
WILKINSON Edward MM Cpl 25042 335 Road Const Coy Royal Engineers
WILKINSON Edward MM L/Cpl 205355 2/5th West Riding Regt
WILKINSON Edward MM Pte 6810 16th Northumberland Fusiliers KIA 7.8.17.
WILKINSON Edward MM Sjt 18050 Durham Light Infantry
WILKINSON Ellis MM Pte 7901 Lancashire Fusiliers
WILKINSON Ernest MM Pte 374807 17th London Regt
WILKINSON Ernest MM+Bar Sjt 706029 A/331 Bde RFA DOW 23.5.18.
WILKINSON Ernest MM Sjt 403067 RAMC
WILKINSON Ernest MM Gnr 781256 D/311 Bde RFA
WILKINSON Ernest MM Sjt 9363 10th York & Lancaster Regt KIA 21.4.17.
WILKINSON Ernest MM Sjt 14799 8th Border Regt
WILKINSON Ernest G. MM Sjt T4/243729 Army Service Corps
WILKINSON Ernest W. MM Pte 75022 Tank Corps
WILKINSON F.W.W. MM Sjt 20938 Cheshire Regt
WILKINSON Fletcher Frederick MM Sjt 301156 Arg & Suth Highlanders
WILKINSON Francis H. MM L/Cpl 20742 6th King's Own Scottish Borderers
WILKINSON Francis Leslie MM Sjt 296039 152 Heavy Bty RGA DOW 12.10.18.
WILKINSON Francis W. MM Sjt 35035 24th Bn Machine Gun Corps
WILKINSON Frank MM Pte M2/114908 Army Service Corps
WILKINSON Frederick MM L/Cpl 22485 York & Lancaster Regt
WILKINSON Frederick MM Sjt 8634 12th Lancashire Fusiliers
WILKINSON Frederick MM Pte 13186 10th Cheshire Regt KIA 7.6.17.
WILKINSON Frederick F. MM Gnr 965454 RFA
WILKINSON George MM Pte 240686 1/6th North Staffordshire Regt
WILKINSON George MM Pte 306303 1/8th Liverpool Regt
WILKINSON George MM L/Cpl 39234 6th South Staffordshire Regt
WILKINSON George MM Pte 13508 1/5th Yorkshire Regt
WILKINSON George MM L/Cpl 327220 1/9th Durham Light Infantry KIA 23.7.18.
WILKINSON George E. MM L/Cpl 15343 56 Fd Coy Royal Engineers
WILKINSON George Emsley MM Cpl 240112 2/5th West Riding Regt DOW 26.7.18.
WILKINSON George Herman MM Sjt 15267 9th Yorkshire Regt KIA 20.9.16.
WILKINSON H. MM Pte 275632 Manchester Regt
WILKINSON Harold "MM,CG(F)" L/Cpl 201227 11th East Lancashire Regt
WILKINSON Harold V. MM+Bar Pte 1330 22nd Royal Fusiliers
WILKINSON Harry MM L/Cpl 34388 4th Yorkshire Light Infantry
WILKINSON Harry MM Pte 31033 17 Coy Machine Gun Corps
WILKINSON Harry E. "DCM,MM(67486 Gnr 5 Bde RFA)" Spr 310870 Signal Service Royal Engineers att 5 Bde RFA.
WILKINSON Henry MM Cpl 463295 3 Div Sig Coy Royal Engineers
WILKINSON Henry MM Pte 325821 1/9th Durham Light Infantry KIA 16.6.18.
WILKINSON Henry Sydney MM Sjt 751 11th Royal Sussex Regt KIA 30.10.16.
WILKINSON Herbert MM Sjt 30327 RAMC
WILKINSON Herbert MM Gnr 165187 RFA
WILKINSON Herbert J. MM Sjt 101310 Royal Engineers
WILKINSON Hilton MM Cpl 307861 West Riding Regt
WILKINSON Isaac MM Pte 243047 5th Yorkshire Light Infantry
WILKINSON James MM Sjt 795696 49 Div Ammn Col RFA
WILKINSON James MM Sjt 31514 D/180 Bde RFA
WILKINSON James MM Bdr 18208 D/170 Bde RFA
WILKINSON James MM Cpl 21965 7th Border Regt
WILKINSON James MM Pte 9/17589 9th Cheshire Regt DOW 5.2.18.
WILKINSON James MM Sjt 87304 D/64 Bde RFA
WILKINSON James MM Pte 8759 2nd Arg & Suth Highlanders
WILKINSON James E. MM Spr 398791 123 Fd Coy Royal Engineers
WILKINSON James K. MM+Bar L/Cpl 3/6910 1st Gordon Highlanders KIA 28.3.18.
WILKINSON James W. MM Pte 270732 5/6th Royal Scots
WILKINSON Jesse J. MM Cpl 51625 7th Manchester Regt
WILKINSON John MM Cpl 12109 11th Durham Light Infantry
WILKINSON John MM Pte 4538 1/5th Lincolnshire Regt KIA 21.4.17.
WILKINSON John MM Pte 14/1050 2nd York & Lancaster Regt
WILKINSON John MM Pte 15262 1st Coldstream Guards
WILKINSON John MM Sjt 12431 16th Lancashire Fusiliers
WILKINSON John MM Spr 482539 Royal Engineers
WILKINSON John MM Cpl 10066 1st East Lancashire Regt KIA 1.7.18.
WILKINSON John E. MM Sjt 11905 Leicestershire Regt

617

WILKINSON John E. MM Gnr 771594 RFA
WILKINSON John Frederick MM Pte 17184 13th Essex Regt
WILKINSON John H. MM Sjt 106293 RGA
WILKINSON John Henry MM Pte 10/1038 10th East Yorkshire Regt DOW 2.6.17.
WILKINSON John Joseph MM Pte 17809 13th Durham Light Infantry KIA 20.9.17.
WILKINSON John T. MM Pte 14062 8th Yorkshire Regt
WILKINSON John W. MM Sjt 382072 146 Siege Bty RGA
WILKINSON John William MM Pte 51054 11th East Yorkshire Regt KIA 8.9.18.
WILKINSON Joseph MM Sjt 40270 RAMC
WILKINSON Joseph MM+Bar Pte 12901 6th Lincolnshire Regt
WILKINSON Joseph MM Pte 4491 11th Royal Warwickshire Regt
WILKINSON Kay MM CQMS 201101 2/5th Lancashire Fusiliers
WILKINSON Louisa Alice MM Sister F QAIMNS
WILKINSON Mathew M. MM Sjt 12572 A/102 Bde RFA
WILKINSON Oswald MM Gnr 760700 A/317 Bde RFA
WILKINSON Ralph A. MM Pte 60071 14th Royal Welsh Fusiliers
WILKINSON Richard MM Cpl 240935 8th Border Regt
WILKINSON Robert MM Pte 3171 1/8th Liverpool Regt
WILKINSON Robert MM Pte 16873 9th North Lancashire Regt
WILKINSON Robert MM Cpl 12765 9th Northumberland Fusiliers Died 22.3.18.
WILKINSON Samuel MM Sjt 203533 1st London Regt
WILKINSON Samuel B. MM Pte 18458 Manchester Regt
WILKINSON Sidney "DCM,MM" Sjt 22586 2nd Worcestershire Regt
WILKINSON Sidney MM Sjt 1137 1st Northumberland Fusiliers
WILKINSON Sydney F. MM L/Cpl 16762 16th Royal Sussex Regt
WILKINSON Thomas MM Pte 19115 1st Royal Dublin Fusiliers
WILKINSON Thomas MM Pte 305173 6th West Yorkshire Regt
WILKINSON Thomas MM Sjt 240629 22nd Northumberland Fusiliers
WILKINSON Thomas MM Pte 307254 8th West Yorkshire Regt
WILKINSON Thomas MM Sjt 337938 RGA
WILKINSON Thomas MM+Bar L/Cpl 839 Royal West Surrey Regt
WILKINSON Thomas A. MM Sjt M1/08424 Army Service Corps
WILKINSON Thomas F. MM Bdr 28663 RGA
WILKINSON Thomas Francis MM Cpl 200251 5/6th Scottish Rifles
WILKINSON Thomas Harry MM Pte 2503 1st Royal Lancaster Regt
WILKINSON Thomas Neal "MM,MdH(F)" L/Cpl 3/5994 2nd East Yorkshire Regt
WILKINSON Tom MM Gnr Sig 59283 109 Siege Bty RGA
WILKINSON Ulric Charles MM Pte 19026 3/5th Lancashire Fusiliers
WILKINSON Wallace D. MM L/Cpl 21048 36 Coy Labour Corps
WILKINSON Will Harry Bridge MM Gnr 17056 D/170 Bde RFA
WILKINSON William MM Sjt S/15638 13th Rifle Brigade
WILKINSON William MM Sjt 8470 9th Yorkshire Regt
WILKINSON William MM Sjt 15482 2nd South Lancashire Regt KIA 12.4.18.
WILKINSON William MM Pte 300983 1/8th Durham Light Infantry
WILKINSON William MM BSM 25393 1(Shropshire)Bty RHA
WILKINSON William MM Pte 14152 2nd Dragoon Guards
WILKINSON William MM L/Cpl 2293 RAMC
WILKINSON William B. MM Pte 350574 1st Essex Regt
WILKINSON William Edward MM Pte 15356 2nd Grenadier Guards
WILKINSON William G. MM Sjt 36265 RGA
WILKINSON William Henry MM Gnr 53794 123 Heavy Bty RGA
WILKINSON William Henry Adolphus MM Sjt M2/131725 34 Div Train Army Service Corps
WILKINSON William J. MM Pte 22593 1st Coldstream Guards
WILKINSON William S. MM Cpl 20364 Army Cyclist Corps
WILKS Ernest MM Pte 75066 RAMC
WILKS Ernest Luke MM Pte 1795 23rd Royal Fusiliers
WILKS George Henry Walter MM Cpl 70771 68 Bty 14 Bde RFA KIA 21.3.18.
WILKS Harry MM Sjt 9328 3rd Worcestershire Regt KIA 3.9.16.
WILKS Harry W. MM Dvr 43562 2 Div Ammn Col RFA
WILKS John T. MM Pte 12213 8th Gloucestershire Regt
WILKS Sidney William MM L/Cpl 203418 1/4th Oxf & Bucks Light Infantry
WILKS William G. "MM+Bar,MM(F)" Cpl 10103 10th Arg & Suth Highlanders
WILL George MM Pte 241050 1/5th Gordon Highlanders KIA 2.4.18.
WILL Harry MM Pte 3952 1/20th London Regt
WILL John MM Dvr T/27485 Army Service Corps att 13 Fd Amb RAMC.
WILL Joseph MM CSM 6610 6th Royal West Kent Regt
WILL Matthew MM Pte 136578 36th Bn Machine Gun Corps
WILL William MM Pte 266529 Gordon Highlanders
WILL William J. MM Spr 121259 Royal Engineers
WILLACY James MM L/Cpl 49663 2nd Royal Inniskilling Fusiliers
WILLACY Robert MM Sjt 43263 7th Bedfordshire Regt KIA 13.3.17.
WILLANS John MM CSM 114263 221 Coy Machine Gun Corps
WILLARD Edward Thomas MM Cpl 5489 Y/21 Med TM Bty RGA
WILLARD William J. MM Sjt 9109 1st Middlesex Regt
WILLATT Charles MM Cpl 12150 3rd Coldstream Guards KIA 13.4.18.
WILLATT James MM Cpl 8193 1st Royal Irish Rifles
WILLATT William MM Dvr 185398 B/168 Bde RFA
WILLBOND Edward George MM Pte 30481 7th East Yorkshire Regt
WILLBOURNE Thomas William MM Pte 29398 Essex Regt
WILLBY Henry E. MM Sjt 12484 1st East Surrey Regt
WILLCOCK Edgar D. MM Pte M/337649 Army Service Corps
WILLCOCK George B.S. MM Sjt 76653 'S' Corps Sig Coy Royal Engineers
WILLCOCKS George J. MM Pte 508437 2 Fd Amb RAMC
WILLCOCKS J. MM Pte 13100 10th Lancashire Fusiliers
WILLCOCKS P.R. MM Pte 421 East Kent Regt
WILLCOX Albert E. MM Dmr 8800 2nd Worcestershire Regt
WILLCOX Ernest MM Cpl 17012 B/99 Bde RFA
WILLCOX Samuel MM Dvr T4/083224 Army Service Corps
WILLCOX Stanley W. MM Cpl 11019 11th Royal West Surrey Regt
WILLDEN Ernest MM L/Cpl 12188 2nd Oxf & Bucks Light Infantry
WILLERTON David S. MM Pte 11/1221 11th East Yorkshire Regt
WILLERTON George William MM+Bar Cpl 11/730 11th East Yorkshire Regt
WILLERTON Robert T. MM L/Cpl 39512 Bedfordshire Regt
WILLERTON Sam W. MM Sjt 1959 Lincolnshire Regt
WILLETT Alfred William "MM,MID" Sjt 548150 510 Fd Coy Royal Engineers
WILLETT Arthur MM Pte 204405 York & Lancaster Regt
WILLETT Charles H. MM Pte 3548 1st Welsh Guards
WILLETT Charles J. MM Pte 41135 7th Northamptonshire Regt
WILLETT George MM Pte 242564 6th South Staffordshire Regt
WILLETT Robert MM L/Cpl 68428 33rd Bn Machine Gun Corps
WILLETT Robert MM Dvr 66720 RFA
WILLETT William A. MM Bdr 13405 RFA
WILLETTS Benjamin MM Pte 240696 1/5th South Lancashire Regt DOW 1.8.17.
WILLETTS Edward MM Sjt 7389 1st Somerset Light Infantry
WILLETTS Enoch MM Pte 18259 6th Yorkshire Light Infantry
WILLETTS Frederick W. MM Pte 9822 Royal Highlanders
WILLETTS Joseph MM Pte 12601 4th Worcestershire Regt
WILLETTS Joseph MM 2nd Cpl 1046 Royal Engineers
WILLETTS Joseph MM Gnr 8941 RFA
WILLEY Frederick W. MM Bdr 68138 120 Siege Bty RGA
WILLEY George MM Cpl 202826 8th Somerset Light Infantry
WILLEY George MM Spr 146309 254 Tunnelling Coy Royal Engineers
WILLEY George N. MM Cpl 38933 2nd Yorkshire Light Infantry
WILLEY Harold A.F. MM L/Cpl 27911 Welsh Regt
WILLEY Herbert MM Sjt 78639 Royal Engineers
WILLEY James MM Pte 15746 2nd Coldstream Guards
WILLEY Joseph MM Pte 3/1830 2nd Yorkshire Light Infantry
WILLEY Reginald Fryer MM Sjt 24143 9th York & Lancaster Regt
WILLEY Thomas MM Pte 28821 East Yorkshire Regt
WILLEY William MM Cpl 801205 11th Royal Fusiliers
WILLIAM A. MM Pte 32502 Cheshire Regt
WILLIAMES Arthur William MM+Bar Sjt 277 Royal Fusiliers
WILLIAMS A. MM Pte 364082 3 Fd Amb RAMC
WILLIAMS A. MM AM1 12660 Royal Air Force
WILLIAMS A.E. MM L/Cpl 6541 Notts & Derby Regt
WILLIAMS A.T. MM 2nd Cpl 506322 Royal Engineers
WILLIAMS Abel James MM Cpl 16287 Royal Welsh Fusiliers
WILLIAMS Abram M. MM L/Cpl 56857 Royal Welsh Fusiliers
WILLIAMS Albert MM+Bar Cpl 56843 16th Royal Welsh Fusiliers
WILLIAMS Albert MM Sjt 16329 6th South Wales Borderers KIA 4.8.17.
WILLIAMS Albert MM Pte 9741 6th Wiltshire Regt
WILLIAMS Albert MM Sjt 11808 9th Yorkshire Regt
WILLIAMS Albert MM Cpl 84055 20 Div Ammn Col RFA
WILLIAMS Albert MM Pte 17649 5th South Wales Borderers
WILLIAMS Albert MM Pte 30930 8th Gloucestershire Regt
WILLIAMS Albert MM L/Cpl 10992 18th King's Royal Rifle Corps KIA 3.10.18.
WILLIAMS Albert E. MM Pte 42311 2nd Yorkshire Light Infantry
WILLIAMS Albert E. MM Sjt 753 5th Dragoon Guards
WILLIAMS Albert H. MM Sjt 41142 19 Siege Bty RGA
WILLIAMS Albert H. MM Pte 18146 Royal Highlanders

WILLIAMS Albert J. MM Pte 232252 2nd London Regt
WILLIAMS Alfred MM Pte 10666 6th Leicestershire Regt
WILLIAMS Alfred MM Sjt R/10562 2nd King's Royal Rifle Corps
WILLIAMS Alfred MM L/Cpl 19091 Yorkshire Light Infantry
WILLIAMS Alfred "DCM,MM" Sjt 202609 2/4th Hampshire Regt
WILLIAMS Alfred MM Pte 887 East Surrey Regt
WILLIAMS Alfred MM L/Cpl Z/1531 1st Rifle Brigade
WILLIAMS Alfred E. MM Pte 7527 HAC
WILLIAMS Alfred Edward "MM,MID" Sjt 1579 1st London Regt
WILLIAMS Alfred H. MM Pte 30345 RAMC
WILLIAMS Alfred J. MM Pte 494076 13th London Regt
WILLIAMS Alfred J. "DCM,MM" Sjt 37655 52 Bty 15 Bde RFA
WILLIAMS Alfred J. MM Pte S/28829 Rifle Brigade
WILLIAMS Alfred James MM Cpl 17653 Royal Welsh Fusiliers
WILLIAMS Archibald MM Pte 15213 1st Cameron Highlanders
WILLIAMS Arthur MM Pte 33630 8th Royal Warwickshire Regt
WILLIAMS Arthur MM Pte 18236 Royal Irish Regt
WILLIAMS Arthur MM Pte 15728 10th Royal Welsh Fusiliers
WILLIAMS Arthur MM Gnr 34194 RGA
WILLIAMS Arthur MM Pte 8271 4th Liverpool Regt
WILLIAMS Arthur MM Pte 5922 Seaforth Highlanders
WILLIAMS Arthur E. MM Pte 63410 6th Royal West Surrey Regt
WILLIAMS Arthur E. MM Gnr Sig 606136 1(Glamorgan)Bty RHA
WILLIAMS Arthur E. MM Pte 34742 Middlesex Regt
WILLIAMS Arthur H. MM Cpl 17153 6th South Wales Borderers
WILLIAMS Arthur H. MM L/Sjt 18904 Grenadier Guards
WILLIAMS Arthur Henry MM L/Bdr 110925 16 Bde RFA
WILLIAMS Arthur Joseph MM Pte 27820 11th Royal Warwickshire Regt DOW 29.4.17.
WILLIAMS Arthur L. MM Cpl 240734 12th Middlesex Regt
WILLIAMS Arthur Trestain MM L/Cpl 45793 9th B Coy Devonshire Regt KIA 26.10.17.
WILLIAMS Aubrey MM Cpl 15966 8th Somerset Light Infantry KIA 25.4.18.
WILLIAMS Aubrey Phillip MM Bdr 13860 C/75 Bde RFA
WILLIAMS B. MM Bdr W/1074 RFA
WILLIAMS Benjamin MM Gnr 156071 154 Heavy Bty RGA
WILLIAMS Benjamin MM+Bar Dvr 11505 B/88 Bde RFA
WILLIAMS Benjamin MM Cpl 21138 50th Bn Machine Gun Corps
WILLIAMS Beresford Leslie MM Cpl 23806 Machine Gun Corps
WILLIAMS Bert MM Pte S/5596 10th Rifle Brigade
WILLIAMS Bert MM Pte 33331 9th Royal Welsh Fusiliers Died 14.10.18.
WILLIAMS Bertram A. MM S/Sjt 538004 6 Fd Amb RAMC
WILLIAMS Brindley MM Dvr 4222 B/122 Bde RFA
WILLIAMS C. "MM,MID" Cpl 28766 Royal Engineers
WILLIAMS Charles MM L/Cpl 59782 Machine Gun Corps
WILLIAMS Charles MM Cpl 28610 26 Siege Bty RGA
WILLIAMS Charles "DCM,MM" Cpl 34075 1/5th Notts & Derby Regt
WILLIAMS Charles MM Cpl DM2/165077 Army Service Corps
WILLIAMS Charles MM Sjt 41006 Royal Engineers
WILLIAMS Charles MM Pte 14319 11th Hampshire Regt
WILLIAMS Charles A. MM Pte 24176 Worcestershire Regt
WILLIAMS Charles B. MM Pte 24326 Royal West Surrey Regt
WILLIAMS Charles B. MM Sjt 159303 RFA
WILLIAMS Charles C. MM Sjt 16638 Royal Welsh Fusiliers
WILLIAMS Charles Dixon MM Sjt 9279 8th Royal West Kent Regt
WILLIAMS Charles E. MM Sjt M2/032305 Army Service Corps
WILLIAMS Charles H. MM L/Cpl 220344 1st Berkshire Regt
WILLIAMS Charles H. MM+Bar Sjt 13606 9th Royal Fusiliers
WILLIAMS Charles J. MM Pte 345212 24th Royal Welsh Fusiliers
WILLIAMS Charles Oswald "DCM,MM" Cpl 16259 12th Royal Sussex Regt
WILLIAMS Charles W. MM Sjt 10123 2nd Welsh Regt
WILLIAMS Claude L. MM Pte 279017 3rd London Regt
WILLIAMS Cuthbert MM Sjt 13733 RFA
WILLIAMS Daniel MM Pte 22530 2nd South Wales Borderers
WILLIAMS Daniel MM Pte S/6465 13th Rifle Brigade KIA 4.11.18.
WILLIAMS Daniel Beattie MM L/Cpl 11/15368 11th Border Regt KIA 1.7.16.
WILLIAMS Daniel John "MC,MM(2203 Pte 1/2nd London Regt)" 2Lt 3rd Bn Machine Gun Corps KIA 5.10.17.
WILLIAMS David MM Sjt 53887 Royal Welsh Fusiliers
WILLIAMS David MM Pte 811 2nd Royal Munster Fusiliers
WILLIAMS David MM Pte 2529 1/10th Liverpool Regt
WILLIAMS David MM Sjt 6572 Shropshire Light Infantry
WILLIAMS David Daniel MM Pte 12753 2nd Devonshire Regt KIA 25.3.18.
WILLIAMS David Edward MM(5676 Sjt R Mun Fus)+Bar Sjt 57286 13th Welsh Regt KIA 8.11.17.
WILLIAMS David G. MM Pte S/2506 Rifle Brigade
WILLIAMS David Owen MM Sjt 14445 Royal Welsh Fusiliers
WILLIAMS David W. MM+Bar L/Cpl 18429 13th Welsh Regt
WILLIAMS Dick MM Pte 19479 Shropshire Light Infantry
WILLIAMS E.A. MM Cpl 20111 12 Fd Amb RAMC
WILLIAMS E.J. MM L/Cpl 200550 London Regt
WILLIAMS Edward MM Pte 235821 14th Royal Welsh Fusiliers
WILLIAMS Edward "DCM,MM" Pte 15177 South Wales Borderers
WILLIAMS Edward MM+Bar L/Sjt 10638 2nd Scottish Rifles
WILLIAMS Edward MM Pte 38275 RAMC
WILLIAMS Edward MM Spr 62595 Royal Engineers
WILLIAMS Edward MM Pte 200284 1/4th Royal Welsh Fusiliers
WILLIAMS Edward H. MM Cpl 26411 RGA
WILLIAMS Edward J. MM Cpl 448162 Royal Engineers
WILLIAMS Edward N. MM Cpl 19418 Royal Welsh Fusiliers
WILLIAMS Edward S. MM Dvr 837105 RFA
WILLIAMS Edwin MM Cpl 61481 7th Middlesex Regt
WILLIAMS Edwin John Thomas MM Pte 13420 Army Cyclist Corps
WILLIAMS Eli MM Cpl 19638 18th Lancashire Fusiliers
WILLIAMS Emlyn MM L/Sjt 15835 13th Royal Welsh Fusiliers
WILLIAMS Enoch MM L/Cpl 13042 Royal Welsh Fusiliers
WILLIAMS Eric MM Bdr 940077 RFA
WILLIAMS Eric Brook MM Cpl 15390 RFA
WILLIAMS Eric C. MM Dvr 29520 RFA
WILLIAMS Ernest MM Pte 12253 6th Shropshire Light Infantry
WILLIAMS Ernest MM Pte 12198 King's Royal Rifle Corps
WILLIAMS Ernest MM L/Cpl 24829 Royal Scots
WILLIAMS Ernest G. MM Sjt 43669 RGA
WILLIAMS Ernest Thomas "MC,MM(9440 CSM)" 2Lt 10th Shropshire Light Infantry
WILLIAMS Evan MM Pte 265900 24th Royal Welsh Fusiliers
WILLIAMS Evan MM Sjt 52996 78 Coy Machine Gun Corps
WILLIAMS Evan Edward MM Pte 16124 12th East Surrey Regt DOW 3.4.18.
WILLIAMS Evan S. MM L/Cpl 195965 Royal Engineers
WILLIAMS F. MM L/Cpl 554493 16th London Regt
WILLIAMS F. MM L/Cpl 11589 2nd Oxf & Bucks Light Infantry
WILLIAMS F.B. MM Cpl 106244 255 Siege Bty RGA
WILLIAMS F.C. MM Gnr 652012 RFA
WILLIAMS F.H. MM Cpl 265268 6th Gloucestershire Regt
WILLIAMS F.J. MM Cpl 10246 6th East Kent Regt
WILLIAMS F.J.B. MM Pte 240589 Devonshire Regt
WILLIAMS F.O. MM Gnr 56971 RFA
WILLIAMS F.W. MM Cpl 63388 13th Royal Fusiliers
WILLIAMS Florence MM Miss F Civilian Awarded for 'Easter Rising'.
WILLIAMS Francis MM L/Cpl 265799 1/2nd Monmouthshire Regt KIA 23.4.17.
WILLIAMS Francis MM Pte 16696 Royal Welsh Fusiliers
WILLIAMS Frank MM Pte 10704 7th Shropshire Light Infantry DOW 10.4.17.
WILLIAMS Frank MM Gnr 604366 2/1st(Shropshire)Bty RHA
WILLIAMS Fred MM Sjt 8350 6th East Lancashire Regt
WILLIAMS Fred MM Pte 40308 Royal Welsh Fusiliers
WILLIAMS Frederick MM Cpl 280206 1/7th Lancashire Fusiliers
WILLIAMS Frederick MM Cpl 17913 10th Worcestershire Regt
WILLIAMS Frederick MM L/Cpl 241551 Gloucestershire Regt
WILLIAMS Frederick MM+Bar Cpl 4836 1/4th Royal Welsh Fusiliers
WILLIAMS Frederick Charles Bertie MM Cpl 4049 10th Rifle Brigade DOW 24.9.17.
WILLIAMS Frederick David MM Sjt 36646 B/296 Bde RFA DOW 1.5.18.
WILLIAMS Frederick Francis MM Pte 10094 1st Royal West Kent Regt
WILLIAMS G. MM Pte 89016 25th Bn Machine Gun Corps
WILLIAMS G. MM L/Cpl 92880 8th Bn Tank Corps
WILLIAMS G. MM Pte 25993 1st South Wales Borderers
WILLIAMS G. MM Pte 65760 Machine Gun Corps
WILLIAMS G. MM Cpl 10662 Welsh Regt
WILLIAMS G. MM Pte 242133 Worcestershire Regt
WILLIAMS G. MM Pte 39930 Notts & Derby Regt
WILLIAMS G. MM L/Cpl C/12787 King's Royal Rifle Corps
WILLIAMS G. MM Pte 265889 Liverpool Regt
WILLIAMS G.P. MM Sjt 68474 7th Royal West Surrey Regt
WILLIAMS Geoffrey R. MM L/Cpl 197907 Royal Engineers
WILLIAMS George MM Sjt 63009 11th Notts & Derby Regt KIA 5.10.18.
WILLIAMS George "DCM,MM" Cpl 4940 1st Lincolnshire Regt
WILLIAMS George MM Pte 1/13760 1st South Wales Borderers
WILLIAMS George MM Pnr 192966 'P' Special Coy Royal Engineers KIA 10.6.17.

WILLIAMS George A. MM CSM 9428 1st Royal Irish Fusiliers
WILLIAMS George E. MM Sjt 3580 2nd Lancashire Fusiliers
WILLIAMS George E. MM Dvr 51853 11 Bde RFA
WILLIAMS George Edward MM Sjt 9593 2nd Oxf & Bucks Light Infantry
WILLIAMS George F. MM Gnr 785758 RFA
WILLIAMS George G. MM Pte 9624 10th Lancashire Fusiliers
WILLIAMS George Henry MM Sjt 443 1/5th Royal Warwickshire Regt KIA 18.7.16.
WILLIAMS George Mervyn MM Pte 16859 7th Leicestershire Regt Died 22.3.18.
WILLIAMS George T. MM Pte 30365 RAMC
WILLIAMS George T. MM Pte 210937 Liverpool Regt
WILLIAMS George William MM L/Sjt 12139 King's Royal Rifle Corps
WILLIAMS Gerald A. MM+Bar Gnr 810165 A/232 Bde RFA
WILLIAMS Gilbert C. MM Pte M2/104876 306 Coy Army Service Corps
WILLIAMS Glyn T. MM Pte 54019 Welsh Regt
WILLIAMS Griffith T. MM L/Cpl 794 1st Welsh Guards
WILLIAMS Gwilym MM L/Cpl 7131 2nd Welsh Regt KIA 21.8.16.
WILLIAMS H. MM Pte 36412 Yorkshire Regt
WILLIAMS H. MM Cpl 1274 Military Foot Police
WILLIAMS H. MM Sjt 18953 12th Cheshire Regt
WILLIAMS H. MM Cpl 40032 2nd Royal Irish Rifles
WILLIAMS Harold MM Pte 12296 8th East Lancashire Regt
WILLIAMS Harold MM Sjt 5689 2nd Worcestershire Regt
WILLIAMS Harold Glyn MM Pte B/20003 26th Royal Fusiliers
WILLIAMS Harold H. MM Pte 90083 2/4th London Regt
WILLIAMS Harold Hugh MM Gnr 44283 29 Siege Bty RGA
WILLIAMS Harry "DCM,MM" L/Sjt 2428 1st Royal Warwickshire Regt KIA 21.6.17.
WILLIAMS Harry MM Sjt 9426 2nd Grenadier Guards KIA 31.7.17.
WILLIAMS Harry MM Sjt 4492 Liverpool Regt
WILLIAMS Harry MM+Bar Sjt 465 1st Royal Warwickshire Regt
WILLIAMS Harry MM Pte C/8051 King's Royal Rifle Corps
WILLIAMS Harry Edgar MM 2nd Cpl 69432 138 Army Troops Coy Royal Engineers
WILLIAMS Harry V. MM Bdr 326870 RGA
WILLIAMS Henry MM Cpl 51198 154 Fd Coy Royal Engineers
WILLIAMS Henry MM Pte 4000 7th Royal Lancaster Regt
WILLIAMS Henry A. MM Pte 42612 6th Gordon Highlanders
WILLIAMS Henry E. MM+Bar Pte 20143 Essex Regt
WILLIAMS Henry E. MM Sjt 681408 C/286 Bde RFA
WILLIAMS Henry E. MM+Bar Pte R/12511 King's Royal Rifle Corps
WILLIAMS Henry G. MM Pte 6239 Royal Irish Fusiliers
WILLIAMS Henry J. MM Pte 24594 5th Devonshire Regt
WILLIAMS Henry Samuel "MM,MID" Sjt 14355 1st Grenadier Guards
WILLIAMS Herbert MM Gnr 116428 A/285 Bde RFA
WILLIAMS Herbert MM Sjt 49589 74th Bn Machine Gun Corps
WILLIAMS Herbert MM Pte 136 14th Royal Warwickshire Regt
WILLIAMS Herbert George MM Cpl 42157 9th Royal Irish Fusiliers KIA 3.10.18.
WILLIAMS Herbert L. MM Gnr 161468 RGA
WILLIAMS Herbert T. MM Sjt 142371 12 Heavy Bty RGA
WILLIAMS Herrick MM 2nd Cpl 1202 Royal Engineers
WILLIAMS Horace MM Gnr 676981 B/285 Bde RFA
WILLIAMS Horace MM L/Cpl 304940 15th Bn Tank Corps
WILLIAMS Horace MM Pte 53264 7(Indian)Div MG Bn Machine Gun Corps
WILLIAMS Horace MM Pte 8018 1st Lancashire Fusiliers
WILLIAMS Horace Ernest MM CSM 5005 1st Scots Guards
WILLIAMS Howell "DCM,MM+Bar" Cpl 8969 2nd & 9th Welsh Regt
WILLIAMS Hugh MM Sjt 128198 RGA
WILLIAMS Hugh H. MM Gnr 742 RFA
WILLIAMS Hugh Owen MM Sjt 820 RFA
WILLIAMS Hugh T. MM Pte 25294 Royal Welsh Fusiliers
WILLIAMS Idwal MM Cpl 21522 Royal Welsh Fusiliers
WILLIAMS Illtyd MM Sjt 4568 13th Rifle Brigade KIA 13.11.16.
WILLIAMS Isaac Leonard MM Sjt 9152 2nd South Staffordshire Regt KIA 29.7.16.
WILLIAMS Ivor MM Gnr 66141 21 Heavy Bty RGA
WILLIAMS J. MM Pte 308741 13th Bn Tank Corps
WILLIAMS J. MM Sjt 203896 5th Lancashire Fusiliers
WILLIAMS J. MM Sjt 474 38 Div Ammn Col RFA
WILLIAMS J. MM Pte 265507 Royal Welsh Fusiliers
WILLIAMS J. MM Cpl P1829 Military Foot Police
WILLIAMS J. MM Sjt 320166 Welsh Regt
WILLIAMS J. MM+Bar Pnr 449920 Royal Engineers
WILLIAMS J.A. MM Pte 55624 2nd Royal Welsh Fusiliers
WILLIAMS J.E. MM Pte 14090 1st East Surrey Regt
WILLIAMS J.J. MM L/Cpl 267550 Monmouthshire Regt
WILLIAMS J.J. MM Spr 151397 Royal Engineers
WILLIAMS J.J. MM Cpl 17055 11th Essex Regt
WILLIAMS J.P. "MM,MID" Cpl 151222 Royal Engineers
WILLIAMS J.T. MM Sjt 40682 68 Coy Labour Corps
WILLIAMS Jack MM Pte 10760 6th Shropshire Light Infantry DOW 18.5.18.
WILLIAMS James MM+Bar Pte 266835 7th West Riding Regt
WILLIAMS James MM L/Cpl 240234 6th South Staffordshire Regt
WILLIAMS James MM Pte 3955 6th London Regt
WILLIAMS James "MM,MID" L/Sjt 16243 7th South Wales Borderers
WILLIAMS James "MC,MM" CSM 22276 13th Welsh Regt
WILLIAMS James MM L/Cpl 1798 Lincolnshire Regt
WILLIAMS James MM Cpl 83300 Royal Engineers
WILLIAMS James MM Cpl 42894 RGA
WILLIAMS James MM Sjt 240227 South Lancashire Regt
WILLIAMS James MM L/Cpl 421035 10th London Regt
WILLIAMS James C. MM+Bar Sjt 500091 Royal Engineers
WILLIAMS James E. MM Cpl 45594 25 Bde RFA
WILLIAMS James E. MM Sjt 6900 1/4th Royal Welsh Fusiliers
WILLIAMS James H. MM Pte 82527 15th Durham Light Infantry
WILLIAMS James Norman "DCM,MM" Sjt 15722 9th Devonshire Regt KIA 5.10.18.
WILLIAMS Job MM Sjt 38020 15th Welsh Regt DOW 5.11.18.
WILLIAMS Joe MM Sjt 10728 15th Cheshire Regt KIA 24.3.18.
WILLIAMS John MM Cpl 19303 21st Manchester Regt
WILLIAMS John MM Pte 10517 1st East Surrey Regt
WILLIAMS John MM Cpl 28470 13th Royal Welsh Fusiliers
WILLIAMS John MM Cpl 486262 468 Fd Coy Royal Engineers
WILLIAMS John MM Pte 355943 25th Royal Welsh Fusiliers
WILLIAMS John MM Pte 350995 9th Essex Regt
WILLIAMS John MM Pte 20878 1/8th Durham Light Infantry
WILLIAMS John MM Sjt 20663 15th Welsh Regt
WILLIAMS John MM Pte 21464 6th East Kent Regt
WILLIAMS John MM Pte 2163 1st Welsh Guards
WILLIAMS John MM Pte 24312 10th Duke of Cornwall's LI KIA 22.10.17.
WILLIAMS John MM L/Cpl 400879 2/7th Manchester Regt
WILLIAMS John MM Sjt 6443 1/5th South Staffordshire Regt
WILLIAMS John MM L/Cpl 2120 1st Lancashire Fusiliers
WILLIAMS John MM Bdr 1176 1(Northumbrian)Bde RFA
WILLIAMS John MM Sjt 15601 12th West Yorkshire Regt
WILLIAMS John "MM,MdH(F)" Sjt 10169 1st Scottish Rifles
WILLIAMS John MM L/Cpl 26152 Royal Welsh Fusiliers
WILLIAMS John MM Pte 81931 RAMC
WILLIAMS John MM Dvr 686480 RFA
WILLIAMS John A. MM Cpl 5905 RFA
WILLIAMS John Clifford MM Pte 56636 10th Welsh Regt
WILLIAMS John F. MM Sjt 240207 York & Lancaster Regt
WILLIAMS John F. MM Sjt 7079 13 Fd Amb. RAMC
WILLIAMS John G. MM CQMS 200633 1/4th Shropshire Light Infantry
WILLIAMS John H. MM Spr 502848 Royal Engineers
WILLIAMS John Henry "VC,DCM,MM+Bar,MM(F)" CSM 20408 10th South Wales Borderers
WILLIAMS John J. MM Sjt 106073 35th Bn Machine Gun Corps
WILLIAMS John J. MM+Bar Pte C/138 16th King's Royal Rifle Corps
WILLIAMS John J. MM Pte 18021 7th Yorkshire Regt
WILLIAMS John Norton Bailey MM Gnr 62329 117 Siege Bty RGA
WILLIAMS John P. MM Pte MS/3466 63 Div MT Coy Army Service Corps
WILLIAMS John R. MM Sjt 12911 4th South Wales Borderers
WILLIAMS John R. MM Pte 69711 RAMC
WILLIAMS John Richard MM L/Cpl 15/1483 1st West Yorkshire Regt
WILLIAMS John T. MM Pte 40997 2nd South Staffordshire Regt
WILLIAMS John Thomas MM Cpl 200980 1/7th Worcestershire Regt
WILLIAMS John William "DCM,MM(642 L/Cpl Nbld Fus)" Cpl 60985 23rd Lancashire Fusiliers
WILLIAMS John William MM L/Sjt 20203 1/4th South Lancashire Regt Died 1.11.18.
WILLIAMS Joseph MM Pte 201491 16th Lancashire Fusiliers
WILLIAMS Joseph MM Sjt 87615 147 Coy Labour Corps
WILLIAMS Joseph MM Pte 53983 Royal Welsh Fusiliers
WILLIAMS Joseph MM Pte 20299 South Wales Borderers
WILLIAMS Joseph MM L/Bdr 56982 C/103 Bde RFA
WILLIAMS Joseph MM Sjt R/2344 King's Royal Rifle Corps
WILLIAMS Joseph I. MM Sjt G10/8118 10th East Surrey Regt
WILLIAMS Joseph W. MM Pte 205373 1st Lancashire Fusiliers

WILLIAMS L. MM Air Mech 2 8191 Royal Flying Corps
WILLIAMS Laurence Allan MM L/Cpl 10787 1st Wiltshire Regt DOW 29.3.18.
WILLIAMS Lawrence MM L/Sjt 265095 6th West Riding Regt
WILLIAMS Leonard MM Sjt 420058 1/10th London Regt
WILLIAMS Llewellyn MM Sjt 485 1st Welsh Guards
WILLIAMS Montague Arthur MM+Bar L/Cpl 259377 62 Div Sig Coy Royal Engineers
WILLIAMS Morgan MM L/Cpl R/894 King's Royal Rifle Corps
WILLIAMS Morgan William MM Dvr 11867 7 Div Ammn Col RFA
WILLIAMS Moses MM Pte M2/193468 10 Siege Park Army Service Corps
WILLIAMS Myrddin MM Pte 13676 11th Welsh Regt
WILLIAMS Noel Pryce MM Pte 11882 2nd Coldstream Guards
WILLIAMS Owen MM Gnr 230442 122 Bty 52 Bde RFA
WILLIAMS Owen MM Pte 22160 Lancashire Fusiliers
WILLIAMS Owen MM Pte 13106 9th Royal Welsh Fusiliers
WILLIAMS Owen MM Gnr 63041 RGA
WILLIAMS P. MM Sjt 200073 Royal Welsh Fusiliers
WILLIAMS Percival L. MM Pte 7449 XVII Corps Cyclist Bn Army Cyclist Corps
WILLIAMS Percy MM L/Cpl 19961 51st Bn Machine Gun Corps
WILLIAMS Percy MM Pte 14885 1/6th Cheshire Regt KIA 24.9.17.
WILLIAMS Percy George MM Cpl 71968 137 Fd Amb RAMC
WILLIAMS Percy J. MM Sjt 63290 RGA
WILLIAMS Peter MM L/Cpl 47145 Liverpool Regt
WILLIAMS Peter Emrys MM Pte 341636 RAMC
WILLIAMS Peter J. MM Pte 8951 1st Hampshire Regt
WILLIAMS R. MM Cpl 312360 Signal Service Royal Engineers
WILLIAMS R.J. MM+Bar Cpl 444 Machine Gun Corps(Motors)
WILLIAMS R.O. MM Pte 37658 Royal Welsh Fusiliers
WILLIAMS Rayal G. MM Gnr 58249 RGA
WILLIAMS Reginald C. MM Sjt 24954 25 Hy Bty RGA
WILLIAMS Reginald D. MM L/Cpl 250325 1/6th Manchester Regt
WILLIAMS Richard MM Sjt T1/673 Army Service Corps
WILLIAMS Richard MM Sjt 492 RFA
WILLIAMS Richard MM Sjt 23164 3 Div Ammn Col RFA
WILLIAMS Richard MM Dvr 805523 RFA
WILLIAMS Richard B. MM L/Cpl 351061 7th London Regt
WILLIAMS Richard Croft MM Dvr 74288 110 Bde RFA
WILLIAMS Richard J. MM L/Cpl 366238 RAMC att RWF.
WILLIAMS Robert MM Pte 15696 5th Royal Lancaster Regt
WILLIAMS Robert MM Pte 32211 1/4th North Lancashire Regt DOW 23.10.18.
WILLIAMS Robert MM L/Cpl 32140 17th Lancashire Fusiliers KIA 7.4.18.
WILLIAMS Robert MM Sjt 14799 8th Somerset Light Infantry
WILLIAMS Robert MM+Bar Cpl 27629 1/9th Durham Light Infantry
WILLIAMS Robert Einion MM Pte 54311 61 Fd Amb RAMC KIA 19.9.18.
WILLIAMS Robert G. MM Cpl 26049 Royal Engineers
WILLIAMS Robert George MM+Bar Sjt R/4953 13th King's Royal Rifle Corps KIA 4.11.18.
WILLIAMS Robert H. MM L/Cpl 43926 5th Royal Berkshire Regt
WILLIAMS Robert John "DCM,MM,MID" Sjt 62867 84 Bty 11 Bde RFA
WILLIAMS Robert L. MM Gnr 2255 RFA
WILLIAMS Robert Maurice MM L/Cpl 14633 8th Norfolk Regt DOW 5.5.18
WILLIAMS Robert T. "DCM,MM" CSM 25391 17th Royal Welsh Fusiliers
WILLIAMS S. MM 2nd Cpl 86584 172 Tunnelling Coy Royal Engineers
WILLIAMS S. MM L/Cpl 650063 London Regt
WILLIAMS S. MM Pte 10501 2nd Border Regt
WILLIAMS S. MM Sjt 705100 RFA
WILLIAMS S.H. MM Pte 20707 4th London Regt
WILLIAMS Samuel MM Cpl 7478 20th Manchester Regt
WILLIAMS Samuel MM Pte 17148 13th Durham Light Infantry
WILLIAMS Samuel MM Pte 14374 East Lancashire Regt
WILLIAMS Samuel MM CSM 39228 Northumberland Fusiliers
WILLIAMS Samuel E. "DCM,MM" Sjt 16883 18th Liverpool Regt
WILLIAMS Sidney MM Pte 570633 1/17th London Regt
WILLIAMS Sidney MM Pte 3/8697 Dorsetshire Regt
WILLIAMS Sidney MM Cpl 653324 21st London Regt
WILLIAMS Simpson MM Gnr 44982 RGA
WILLIAMS Stanley Benjamin MM L/Cpl 16749 6th Dragoon Guards KIA 26.8.18.
WILLIAMS Stanley E.P. MM Cpl 1898 1/2nd London Regt
WILLIAMS Stephen MM Cpl 2109 9th East Surrey Regt KIA 3.12.17.
WILLIAMS Stephen MM L/Cpl R/7262 13th King's Royal Rifle Corps KIA 23.10.18.
WILLIAMS Stuart T. MM Pte 36498 Royal Berkshire Regt
WILLIAMS Sydney T. MM Sjt 22024 Royal Welsh Fusiliers
WILLIAMS T.C. MM Pte 75437 Machine Gun Corps
WILLIAMS T.J. MM Bdr 2620 RFA
WILLIAMS Thomas MM Pte 41448 1/6th Seaforth Highlanders
WILLIAMS Thomas MM Pte 203742 16th Royal Welsh Fusiliers
WILLIAMS Thomas MM Pte 23582 14th Royal Welsh Fusiliers
WILLIAMS Thomas MM Pte 42431 2nd Royal Berkshire Regt KIA 29.11.18.
WILLIAMS Thomas MM Sjt 3701 9th Bn Machine Gun Corps
WILLIAMS Thomas MM Cpl 27855 2nd Manchester Regt
WILLIAMS Thomas "MM,CG(F)" Gnr 92128 B/251 Bde RFA
WILLIAMS Thomas MM Pte 102170 21st Bn Machine Gun Corps
WILLIAMS Thomas MM Pte 13201 1st Royal Inniskilling Fusiliers KIA 30.11.17.
WILLIAMS Thomas MM L/Cpl 11146 2nd Royal Welsh Fusiliers KIA 22.6.16.
WILLIAMS Thomas MM Sjt 10522 5th Shropshire Light Infantry
WILLIAMS Thomas MM Sjt 53897 Royal Engineers
WILLIAMS Thomas MM Spr 79620 Royal Engineers
WILLIAMS Thomas MM Pte 17898 1st Royal Scots Fusiliers Died 26.9.17.
WILLIAMS Thomas MM Dvr 87654 9 Div Ammn Col RFA
WILLIAMS Thomas MM Sjt 200611 Yorkshire Regt
WILLIAMS Thomas MM Pte 20846 10th South Wales Borderers
WILLIAMS Thomas MM Bdr 71415 RFA
WILLIAMS Thomas MM Cpl 12110 8th Yorkshire Regt KIA 29.9.17.
WILLIAMS Thomas MM Dvr 656213 RFA
WILLIAMS Thomas MM Cpl 325171 Durham Light Infantry
WILLIAMS Thomas Albert. MM Sjt 6881 Machine Gun Corps
WILLIAMS Thomas E. MM Pte 276887 7th Manchester Regt
WILLIAMS Thomas Edward MM CSM 2745 Royal Warwickshire Regt
WILLIAMS Thomas F. MM Sjt 52627 26th Royal Fusiliers
WILLIAMS Thomas F. MM Pte 250915 5/6th Royal Scots KIA 6.6.18.
WILLIAMS Thomas G. MM+Bar L/Cpl 87455 Royal Engineers
WILLIAMS Thomas George MM Pte 11421 10th North Lancashire Regt
WILLIAMS Thomas H. MM Gnr Sig 626053 HAC(Artillery) att 309 Siege Bty RGA.
WILLIAMS Thomas J. MM Cpl 21055 2nd Bedfordshire Regt
WILLIAMS Thomas John MM Sjt 325155 2/7th Royal Warwickshire Regt KIA 24.10.18.
WILLIAMS Thomas Joseph MM Gnr 13602 B/74 Bde RFA
WILLIAMS Thomas O. MM Spr 397332 Royal Engineers
WILLIAMS Thomas P. MM+Bar Pte 260297 5th Gloucestershire Regt
WILLIAMS Thomas Richard MM Dvr 105408 7 Div Ammn Col RFA
WILLIAMS Thomas W. MM Sjt 56220 25 Div Sig Coy Royal Engineers
WILLIAMS Tom MM+Bar L/Cpl 1142 14th Royal Warwickshire Regt
WILLIAMS Vincent MM Pte 57105 Royal Welsh Fusiliers
WILLIAMS W. MM Cpl 305764 17th Lancashire Fusiliers
WILLIAMS W. MM Gnr 2198 Machine Gun Corps
WILLIAMS W. MM Cpl 15435 Machine Gun Corps
WILLIAMS W. "DCM,MM" L/Cpl 14356 2nd Grenadier Guards
WILLIAMS W.A. MM Pte 553807 London Regt
WILLIAMS W.G. MM Pte 1834 1/9th Liverpool Regt
WILLIAMS W.T. MM Pte 366261 RAMC
WILLIAMS Wallace MM Pte 65451 RAMC
WILLIAMS Walter MM Pte 7/15134 7th South Wales Borderers
WILLIAMS Walter MM Dvr 13189 42 Bde RFA
WILLIAMS Walter MM Pte 241661 Worcestershire Regt
WILLIAMS Walter MM L/Cpl 16016 2nd Coldstream Guards
WILLIAMS Walter H. MM Cpl 24872 14th Royal Welsh Fusiliers
WILLIAMS Warren W. MM Pte 302737 5th London Regt
WILLIAMS Wilfred "DCM,MM" Cpl 444610 42 Div Sig Coy Royal Engineers
WILLIAMS Wilfred A. MM Cpl 532269 15th London Regt
WILLIAMS William MM Sjt 19374 1st Bn Machine Gun Corps
WILLIAMS William MM Pte 27040 5 Fd Amb RAMC
WILLIAMS William MM Cpl 331743 Liverpool Regt
WILLIAMS William MM Pte 39228 South Wales Borderers
WILLIAMS William MM Sjt 1914 1/2nd Monmouthshire Regt
WILLIAMS William MM L/Sjt 58663 92 Fd Amb RAMC
WILLIAMS William MM Gnr 169833 331 Siege Bty RGA
WILLIAMS William MM Dvr 52627 92 Fd Coy Royal Engineers
WILLIAMS William MM Cpl 95040 7th Liverpool Regt

WILLIAMS William MM L/Cpl 244781 North Lancashire Regt
WILLIAMS William MM Pte 32575 16th Welsh Regt
WILLIAMS William MM Pte 28268 Welsh Regt
WILLIAMS William "DCM,MM" Sjt 4787 13th King's Royal Rifle Corps
WILLIAMS William "DCM,MM,CG(F)" Sjt 265363 1/2nd Monmouthshire Regt
WILLIAMS William MM Cpl 47010 Z/49 Med TM Bty RGA
WILLIAMS William MM Cpl L/15692 1st Royal Fusiliers KIA 21.8.16.
WILLIAMS William MM Pte 7874 2nd Royal Welsh Fusiliers
WILLIAMS William MM Gnr 310046 RGA
WILLIAMS William MM L/Cpl 18849 Welsh Regt
WILLIAMS William MM Sjt 710190 RFA
WILLIAMS William A. MM Gnr 38000 RFA
WILLIAMS William A. MM Bdr 1793 RFA
WILLIAMS William A. MM L/Bdr 108747 RFA
WILLIAMS William E. MM Pte 337150 6(Cavalry)Fd Amb RAMC att RHA.
WILLIAMS William Edward MM Pte 119879 33rd Bn Machine Gun Corps
WILLIAMS William G. MM+Bar L/Cpl 40211 Worcestershire Regt
WILLIAMS William George MM Pte 4024 1/6th Liverpool Regt
WILLIAMS William H. MM Pte 345655 24th Royal Welsh Fusiliers
WILLIAMS William H. MM L/Cpl 178090 153 Fd Coy Royal Engineers
WILLIAMS William H. MM Cpl 2140 2nd Middlesex Regt
WILLIAMS William H. "DCM,MM" Sjt 1397 Lincolnshire Regt
WILLIAMS William H. MM L/Cpl 16813 Duke of Cornwall's LI
WILLIAMS William Henry MM Pte 14682 5th South Wales Borderers KIA 30.7.16.
WILLIAMS William Henry MM Pte 7190 1/7th West Riding Regt KIA 28.2.17.
WILLIAMS William Henry MM Cpl 253236 1/3rd London Regt KIA 24.3.18.
WILLIAMS William Henry MM L/Cpl 126930 Guards Div Sig Coy Royal Engineers
WILLIAMS William J. MM BQMS 32581 A/168 Bde RFA
WILLIAMS William J. MM Gnr 310160 RGA
WILLIAMS William J. MM Sjt 58642 112 Bty 24 Bde RFA
WILLIAMS William John MM Pte 27463 2nd King's Own Scottish Borderers
WILLIAMS William John MM Dvr 66991 A/110 Bde RFA
WILLIAMS William M. MM L/Cpl 15318 2nd Royal Welsh Fusiliers
WILLIAMS William Percy MM Sjt 13495 Royal Lancaster Regt
WILLIAMS William Phillip MM Pte 40362 1st Somerset Light Infantry DOW 17.8.18.
WILLIAMS William R. MM Sjt 320529 24th Welsh Regt
WILLIAMS William R. MM Pte M2/227220 Army Service Corps
WILLIAMS William T. MM Cpl 4894 13th Middlesex Regt
WILLIAMS William Thomas "MM,MSM" Sjt 35593 50 Fd Amb RAMC Died 24.4.17.
WILLIAMSON A. MM Pte 401489 1 Fd Amb RAMC
WILLIAMSON A. MM L/Cpl 30897 Lancashire Fusiliers
WILLIAMSON Albert MM Pte 202313 4th Yorkshire Light Infantry
WILLIAMSON Alexander MM Sjt 4204 Labour Corps
WILLIAMSON Alfred S. MM+Bar Bdr 48722 RGA
WILLIAMSON Arthur MM Gnr 935643 C/280 Bde RFA
WILLIAMSON Charles MM Pte 7257 2nd Cameron Highlanders
WILLIAMSON Claude H. MM Pte 23511 11th Leicestershire Regt
WILLIAMSON David MM Pte 25903 1/4th Seaforth Highlanders
WILLIAMSON David Stewart MM Pte 30722 13th Royal Scots
WILLIAMSON E. MM L/Cpl 3/9356 1st Essex Regt
WILLIAMSON Edward MM Pte 81487 RAMC
WILLIAMSON Edwin MM Pte 9215 1st Border Regt
WILLIAMSON Elijah MM Pte 8988 13th Royal Fusiliers
WILLIAMSON Eric MM Sjt 18764 Manchester Regt
WILLIAMSON Ernest MM Pte 235757 9th West Yorkshire Regt
WILLIAMSON Ernest A. "MM,MID" Dvr 52893 26 Bde RFA
WILLIAMSON Ernest Edward MM Cpl 22219 1st Norfolk Regt
WILLIAMSON Ernest J. MM L/Cpl 7673 Norfolk Regt
WILLIAMSON Frederick MM Gnr 280643 RGA
WILLIAMSON G.A. MM Pte 145910 1/1st Northamptonshire Yeomanry
WILLIAMSON George MM Gnr 168032 187 Siege Bty RGA
WILLIAMSON George MM L/Cpl 253852 2nd Arg & Suth Highlanders KIA 24.10.18.
WILLIAMSON George MM Pte 53842 Notts & Derby Regt
WILLIAMSON George R. MM+Bar Pte 10790 9th Northumberland Fusiliers
WILLIAMSON George William MM Pte 11943 1st Coldstream Guards att GMGR.
WILLIAMSON H. MM Pte 275172 Arg & Suth Highlanders
WILLIAMSON Herbert Davey MM Pte 1245 2nd Lincolnshire Regt DOW 9.8.18.
WILLIAMSON J. MM Pte 52155 6th Northamptonshire Regt
WILLIAMSON J. "DCM,MM+Bar" Sjt 11052 8th Royal Lancaster Regt
WILLIAMSON James MM Spr 430367 427 Fd Coy Royal Engineers
WILLIAMSON James MM Pte 2557 1/17th London Regt
WILLIAMSON James MM Pte 2730 1/9th Highland Light Infantry
WILLIAMSON James MM Cpl 53356 RAMC
WILLIAMSON James R. MM+Bar Sjt 23535 9th Bn Machine Gun Corps
WILLIAMSON James S. MM L/Sjt 242351 1/5th Gordon Highlanders DOW 19.5.17.
WILLIAMSON James T. MM L/Cpl 200317 Scottish Rifles
WILLIAMSON John MM 2nd Cpl 81041 206 Fd Coy Royal Engineers
WILLIAMSON John MM Cpl 41272 108 Fd Amb RAMC
WILLIAMSON John MM Sjt 16298 9th Scottish Rifles
WILLIAMSON John MM Sjt 1732 1/7th Royal Highlanders KIA 24.10.18.
WILLIAMSON John "DCM,MM" BQMS 34679 83 Bty 11 Bde RFA
WILLIAMSON John H. MM Pte 325915 1/9th Durham Light Infantry
WILLIAMSON John William MM Pte 93125 2nd Durham Light Infantry DOW 24.10.18.
WILLIAMSON John William MM Cpl 3178 1/7th Liverpool Regt KIA 28.6.16.
WILLIAMSON Joseph MM L/Cpl 16098 1st Royal Inniskilling Fusiliers
WILLIAMSON Joseph MM Pte 38870 2nd Yorkshire Regt
WILLIAMSON Joseph MM Cpl 10914 1st Scottish Rifles KIA 20.7.16.
WILLIAMSON Joseph MM Cpl 4694 12th Manchester Regt
WILLIAMSON Leonard MM L/Cpl 2/9020 9th Leicestershire Regt
WILLIAMSON Leonard Sidney MM Pte 18289 10th Royal Warwickshire Regt
WILLIAMSON Pierre de L. MM Spr 406122 Royal Engineers
WILLIAMSON R. MM Pte 25846 8th Yorkshire Regt
WILLIAMSON Reed A.T. MM Pte 43339 13th West Riding Regt
WILLIAMSON Robert MM Pte 225970 10th Cameron Highlanders
WILLIAMSON Robert MM Cpl 96662 8 Div Ammn Col RFA
WILLIAMSON Roland J. MM Dvr 146870 RFA
WILLIAMSON Sidney MM Sjt 40740 137 Siege Bty RGA Died 2.11.18.
WILLIAMSON Sydney "MM,MID" L/Cpl 305199 8th Royal Warwickshire Regt
WILLIAMSON Thomas MM Spr 37417 23 Fd Coy Royal Engineers
WILLIAMSON Thomas MM+Bar Cpl 63246 5th Yorkshire Light Infantry
WILLIAMSON Thomas MM Pte 71964 26th Royal Welsh Fusiliers
WILLIAMSON Thomas MM Gnr 931412 C/291 Bde RFA
WILLIAMSON Thomas MM Pte 17614 6/7th Royal Scots Fusiliers
WILLIAMSON Thomas Henry MM Sjt 33738 200 Siege Bty RGA
WILLIAMSON Thomas John MM L/Cpl 19450 9th Royal Inniskilling Fusiliers Died 21.5.18.
WILLIAMSON Tom MM Pte 38321 5th York & Lancaster Regt
WILLIAMSON W. MM Pte 12359 9th Essex Regt
WILLIAMSON W. MM L/Cpl 43110 Scottish Rifles
WILLIAMSON William MM Pte 31708 9th Scottish Rifles
WILLIAMSON William MM Pte 235758 9th West Yorkshire Regt
WILLIAMSON William MM Sjt 330663 1/9th Highland Light Infantry
WILLIAMSON William MM L/Cpl R/9706 King's Royal Rifle Corps
WILLIAMSON William J. MM Sjt 50348 A/153 Bde RFA
WILLIE Herbert MM Gnr 25868 65 Siege Bty RGA
WILLINGHAM Frank MM Cpl 8475 1st Lincolnshire Regt KIA 4.10.17.
WILLINGHAM Herbert MM Cpl 266595 Oxf & Bucks Light Infantry
WILLINGHAM John George MM Sjt 200982 East Yorkshire Regt
WILLIS Albert MM 2nd Cpl 24381 3 Div Sig Coy Royal Engineers
WILLIS Albert E. MM Sjt 583 RAMC
WILLIS Albert E. MM Cpl 58493 Liverpool Regt
WILLIS Albert Samuel "MM,MSM" QMS 12185 5(Cavalry)Fd Amb RAMC
WILLIS Albert Walter MM Pte 270872 10th East Kent Regt
WILLIS Alexander Wreford MM L/Cpl 1978 Gloucestershire Regt
WILLIS Alfred MM Pte 46050 Northumberland Fusiliers
WILLIS Arthur MM Sjt 200610 West Yorkshire Regt
WILLIS Arthur MM L/Sjt 14905 6th North Lancashire Regt

WILLIS Arthur H. MM Sjt T/19949 6 Reserve Park Army Service Corps
WILLIS Arthur T. MM Gnr 58272 23 Siege Bty RGA
WILLIS Arthur T. MM Pte 265218 Oxf & Bucks Light Infantry
WILLIS Charles MM+Bar CSM 15503 Shropshire Light Infantry
WILLIS Clifford H. "MM,MID" Bdr 825087 C/240 Bde RFA
WILLIS Edward J. MM L/Cpl 240176 1/5th Devonshire Regt
WILLIS Edwin Ernest MM SM 527708 RAMC
WILLIS Ernest G. MM Sjt 12835 7th Norfolk Regt
WILLIS Ernest H. MM Pte 52355 10th Royal Fusiliers
WILLIS Ernest William MM Sjt M2/150337 594 MT Coy Army Service Corps
WILLIS F. MM Cpl 220098 RAMC
WILLIS Frederick MM L/Cpl 27078 18th Durham Light Infantry
WILLIS Frederick A. MM Dvr 89056 C/82 Bde RFA
WILLIS Frederick C.D. MM Pte 420830 1/10th London Regt
WILLIS Frederick J. MM Sjt 203703 6th Royal West Surrey Regt
WILLIS Frederick W. MM Gnr 34402 RFA
WILLIS George MM Pte 15914 8th Somerset Light Infantry
WILLIS George Edward MM Pte 20/958 Northumberland Fusiliers
WILLIS Henry MM Cpl 266993 Northumberland Fusiliers
WILLIS Henry MM L/Cpl 201211 1/4th Essex Regt
WILLIS Henry James MM L/Cpl 33051 1st Royal Warwickshire Regt
WILLIS Herbert MM Pte 81329 70 Coy Machine Gun Corps
WILLIS Isaac MM Bdr 1435 C/242 Bde RFA DOW 19.10.17.
WILLIS John MM Cpl 16737 8th East Lancashire Regt
WILLIS John Charles MM Pte 28754 1st Leicestershire Regt
WILLIS Joseph MM Pte 64651 RAMC
WILLIS Joseph J. MM Gnr 1833 RFA
WILLIS W. MM Dvr 216899 A/312 Bde RFA
WILLIS W. MM Pte 26929 Essex Regt
WILLIS W.E. MM L/Cpl 13328 10th Essex Regt
WILLIS Walter George MM Cpl 293772 1/7th Middlesex Regt KIA 31.8.18.
WILLIS Walter T. "MM,MID" Sjt 10266 2nd Highland Light Infantry
WILLIS William MM Sjt 53650 8 Div Ammn Col RFA
WILLIS William MM Gnr 112291 X/41 Med TM Bty RFA
WILLIS William MM Pte 39162 Machine Gun Corps
WILLIS William MM L/Cpl 5092 8th East Kent Regt
WILLIS William C. MM Bdr 11289 3Bde RHA
WILLIS William Charles MM S/Sjt Armourer 1073 Army Ordnance Corps KIA 2.3.17.
WILLIS William R. MM Gnr 96882 RFA
WILLIS William T. MM Pte 7184 2nd Hampshire Regt
WILLIS William T.H. MM L/Sjt 351142 7th London Regt
WILLISCROFT Thomas C. MM Pte 44761 RAMC
WILLISFORD Herbert MM Gnr 70782 RFA
WILLISFORD John MM Gnr 49336 323 Siege Bty RGA KIA 6.10.17.
WILLISON Ernest MM Sjt 3/11605 Durham Light Infantry
WILLISON James S. MM Sjt 57558 52 Bty 15 Bde RFA
WILLISON William MM Pte 3683 6th Royal West Kent Regt
WILLITT Arthur Dore MM L/Bdr 292550 135 Hy Bty RGA
WILLITTS Arthur M. MM BQMS 220 RFA
WILLITTS William MM Sjt Fitter 20892 RGA
WILLMENT George Frederick MM Sjt 11961 'K' Bty RHA KIA 11.4.17.
WILLMER Harry MM Pte 325999 1/1st Cambridgeshire Regt
WILLMER John William MM Pte 593054 18th London Regt
WILLMER Reginald MM Pte 275952 1/7th Manchester Regt
WILLMER Robert C.W MM Sjt 320027 16th Royal Sussex Regt
WILLMORE George MM L/Cpl 12590 6th Bedfordshire Regt att 1/1st Hertfordshire Regt.KIA 23.8.18.
WILLMORE Henry J. MM Pte 4555 1/17th London Regt
WILLMORE Vivian MM Pte 425183 Labour Corps
WILLMOT Frederick MM Gnr 51775 RGA
WILLMOTT Alfred E. MM L/Cpl 30004 2nd Grenadier Guards
WILLMOTT Charles "MM,MID" Cpl 73044 Signal Service Royal Engineers att V Corps HAG.
WILLMOTT G.H. MM Cpl 147115 Royal Engineers
WILLMOTT George MM L/Cpl 23795 5th Gloucestershire Regt
WILLMOTT Graham J. MM Sjt 15675 9th Norfolk Regt
WILLMOTT Percy E. MM Cpl 18337 Royal Fusiliers
WILLMOTT Reginald H. MM L/Cpl 9671 2nd Royal West Surrey Regt
WILLMOTT W. MM Pte 202023 Northumberland Fusiliers
WILLMOTT William A. MM Pte 283808 4th London Regt
WILLOCKS John Simpson MM CSM 350039 1/9th Royal Scots KIA 25.5.17.
WILLOCKS William MM CSM 23050 51st Bn Machine Gun Corps
WILLOTT Samuel MM CSM 14603 11th West Yorkshire Regt KIA 7.6.17.

WILLOUGHBY Charles V. MM Sjt 703458 23rd London Regt
WILLOUGHBY Ernest Charles MM Pte 508136 RAMC
WILLOUGHBY Horace MM Sjt 20166 111 Heavy Bty RGA
WILLOUGHBY John H. MM Pte 241444 8th West Yorkshire Regt
WILLOUGHBY John J. MM Pte 32988 Durham Light Infantry
WILLOUGHBY Norman D. MM Cpl 54357 Signal Service Royal Engineers
WILLOUGHBY Raymond R. MM Spr 249620 Royal Engineers
WILLOUGHBY Thomas MM Pte 64663 108 Coy Labour Corps
WILLOUGHBY Thomas MM Pte 7725 11th Royal Fusiliers
WILLOWS Fred MM Pte 11687 8th Lincolnshire Regt
WILLOWS George Albert MM Spr 103582 152 Fd Coy Royal Engineers
WILLOWS Percy MM Pte 325929 1/1st Cambridgeshire Regt
WILLOWS William Henry MM 2nd Cpl 89388 128 Fd Coy Royal Engineers
WILLS Albert E. MM Pte 15423 6th Northamptonshire Regt
WILLS Alfred MM Cpl 38629 5th Royal Berkshire Regt
WILLS Allan MM Spr 44905 Royal Engineers
WILLS Arthur MM Sjt 38546 Yorkshire Light Infantry
WILLS Arthur H. MM Sjt Mechanic 205035 2 Carrier Coy Tank Corps
WILLS C.W. MM Pte 34326 1st Essex Regt
WILLS Charles MM Cpl SR/7 Royal Flying Corps
WILLS George MM Pte 13706 1st Scots Guards
WILLS George A. "DCM,MM" CSM 13868 4 Div Sig Coy Royal Engineers
WILLS Harry Burden MM+Bar 2nd Cpl 28496 128 Fd Coy Royal Engineers KIA 26.10.18.
WILLS Henry MM Pte 292011 Northumberland Fusiliers
WILLS John MM Sjt MS/3416 Army Service Corps
WILLS John "MM+Bar,MID." Cpl 5758 2nd Royal Munster Fusiliers
WILLS John MM Bdr 930631 A/291 Bde RFA
WILLS Merlin MM Sjt 77238 RHA
WILLS Robert MM Pte 36674 Northumberland Fusiliers
WILLS Robert Dixon MM Cpl 2538 13th London Regt KIA 23.4.17.
WILLS Robert George "MC,MM(452152 Sjt)" 2Lt Sig Svce Royal Engineers Died 3.12.18.
WILLS W. MM Pte 31157 1st Devonshire Regt
WILLS Walter Alfred MM Pte 11957 13th East Surrey Regt
WILLS William MM Pte 66510 130 Fd Amb RAMC
WILLS William Joseph MM Pte 10624 5th Oxf & Bucks Light Infantry
WILLSHER Cecil V. MM Sjt 79916 29th Durham Light Infantry
WILLSHER Edmund W. MM Gnr 59991 9 Bde RFA
WILLSHIRE Arthur Eric MM Pte 39850 5th South Wales Borderers KIA 8.5.18.
WILLSHIRE B. MM Sjt 15426 6th Royal West Surrey Regt
WILLSON Alfred MM L/Sjt 201557 1/5th Lincolnshire Regt
WILLSON Alfred MM Pte S/19818 13th Rifle Brigade
WILLSON Alfred Percy MM Pte 32686 9 Fd Amb RAMC
WILLSON Charles T. MM Pte 12198 47th Bn Machine Gun Corps
WILLSON George Jesse MM Pte 6639 6th Royal West Kent Regt
WILLSON Gerald Nathaniel "MM,MM(P)" Spr 71737 Royal Engineers
WILLY George James MM Spr 64962 18 Div Sig Coy Royal Engineers
WILMAN Charles MM Cpl 11099 West Riding Regt
WILMER Harold MM Pte 6956 8th Royal Fusiliers
WILMOT George MM CSM 13060 7/8th Royal Inniskilling Fusiliers
WILMOT George MM Pte 30399 13 Fd Amb RAMC
WILMOT Henry Walter MM Sjt 41138 C/123 Bde RFA
WILMOT James MM Pte 12959 32nd Bn Machine Gun Corps
WILMOT James MM Pte S/17202 Rifle Brigade
WILMOT John J. MM Sjt 27385 Royal Inniskilling Fusiliers
WILMOT John W. MM Sjt 490077 467 Fd Coy Royal Engineers
WILMOT Thomas C. MM Cpl 337751 RGA
WILMOT William J. MM Gnr 120334 RFA
WILMOTT Alfred George MM Pte 10954 7th Somerset Light Infantry
WILMOTT Charles A. MM Sjt 1519 1/7th Middlesex Regt
WILMOTT Edgar T. MM Spr 121477 430 Fd Coy Royal Engineers
WILMOTT Henry MM Pte 10192 8th Royal Berkshire Regt
WILMOTT Herbert Charles MM Bdr 620080 1/1(Somerset)Bty RHA
WILMSHURST Cecil Arthur MM Sjt 225 1/5th Royal Sussex Regt KIA 5.4.18.
WILMSHURST Jack W. MM Pte 10237 7th Royal Sussex Regt
WILMSHURST James MM Sjt 8513 1st Somerset Light Infantry
WILMSHURST Thomas MM Pte 1664 Royal Sussex Regt
WILSDON Harry MM L/Cpl 22902 145 Coy Machine Gun Corps DOW 29.4.17.
WILSEA Benjamin C. MM Sjt 98212 6th Notts & Derby Regt
WILSHAW Arthur MM Sjt 200636 1st North Staffordshire Regt

WILSHAW John MM Pte 41573 2nd Manchester Regt
WILSHAW John MM L/Sjt 2116 19th Middlesex Regt
WILSHER Charles MM Pte 17514 7th Bedfordshire Regt KIA 2.5.16.
WILSON A. MM CQMS 909 East Lancashire Regt
WILSON A. MM Pte 9/4040 Royal Irish Rifles
WILSON A. MM Pte 13380 Dragoon Guards
WILSON A.E. MM Cpl 1386 RAMC
WILSON A.E. MM S/Sjt 437548 2 Fd Amb RAMC
WILSON A.J. MM Sjt 388423 2 Fd Amb RAMC
WILSON Aaron MM L/Cpl 38083 7th Lincolnshire Regt DOW 5.11.18.
WILSON Albert MM Pte 23698 1/6th West Riding Regt KIA 1.11.18.
WILSON Albert MM Pte 240630 5th Royal Lancaster Regt
WILSON Albert MM Bdr 49840 RFA
WILSON Albert MM Pte 35220 234 Coy Machine Gun Corps
WILSON Albert C. MM Pte 14040 York & Lancaster Regt
WILSON Albert E. MM L/Cpl 36799 Northumberland Fusiliers
WILSON Albert Edward MM Pte 203194 1st London Regt KIA 26.10.17.
WILSON Albert W. MM Pte 27735 Royal Fusiliers
WILSON Alexander MM Cpl 18100 1st Grenadier Guards KIA 25.8.18.
WILSON Alexander MM Dvr 646184 255 Bde RFA
WILSON Alexander MM L/Cpl 1645 1/6th Arg & Suth Highlanders
WILSON Alexander MM Pte 10/16076 10th Northumberland Fusiliers
WILSON Alexander MM Cpl 13793 1st Royal Scots
WILSON Alexander J. MM Bdr 1041 RFA
WILSON Alexander L. MM Dvr 402894 404 Fd Coy Royal Engineers
WILSON Alexander M. MM Pte 7760 2nd Highland Light Infantry
WILSON Alfred MM L/Cpl 75564 26th Royal Fusiliers
WILSON Alfred MM Cpl 28082 Welsh Regt
WILSON Alfred MM Pte 8086 East Surrey Regt
WILSON Alfred MM CSM 3135 1/8th Liverpool Regt
WILSON Alfred MM Cpl 21534 2nd York & Lancaster Regt
WILSON Alfred MM Pte 8411 2nd Scots Guards
WILSON Alfred G. MM Gnr 74527 B/123 Bde RFA
WILSON Allan MM Sjt 290423 Royal Highlanders
WILSON Allan Black MM Gnr 1780 Y/55 Med TM Bty RFA Died 26.8.18.
WILSON Allan McL. MM Sjt 90134 RAMC
WILSON Ambrose MM Pte 11080 Middlesex Regt
WILSON Ambrose Norris MM Gnr 755958 D/246 Bde RFA KIA 11.10.18.
WILSON Andrew MM Sjt 255083 Signal Service Royal Engineers
WILSON Andrew MM L/Cpl 3019 1/6th Arg & Suth Highlanders
WILSON Andrew MM L/Sjt 1034 RAMC
WILSON Andrew MM Pte 7557 8/10th Gordon Highlanders
WILSON Andrew MM L/Cpl 7744 2nd Royal Scots
WILSON Andrew C. MM Sjt 201128 Scottish Rifles
WILSON Archie MM Gnr 138331 RFA
WILSON Arnold MM Cpl 240371 1/6th Lancashire Fusiliers
WILSON Arthur MM Pte 59080 5th West Yorkshire Regt
WILSON Arthur MM Pte 41278 8th North Staffordshire Regt
WILSON Arthur MM L/Bdr 12171 C/161 Bde RFA DOW 26.10.18.
WILSON Arthur MM Pte 230864 Shropshire Light Infantry
WILSON Arthur MM Pte 24261 Grenadier Guards
WILSON Arthur J. MM CQMS 2896 1/9th London Regt
WILSON Arthur R. MM Pte 1677 1/5th Royal Sussex Regt
WILSON Arthur Snowden MM L/Cpl 18/1436 18th West Yorkshire Regt DOW 4.7.17.
WILSON Arthur T. MM Pte 241327 4th North Staffordshire Regt
WILSON Arthur W. MM Dvr 42095 B/58 Bde RFA
WILSON Arthur W. MM Pte 267003 Northumberland Fusiliers
WILSON Benjamin MM Pte 18972 2nd Royal Sussex Regt
WILSON Bertie MM Sjt 9500 2nd Hampshire Regt
WILSON Bertie S. MM Cpl 11964 1st King's Royal Rifle Corps
WILSON Bertram MM Cpl 201795 West Riding Regt
WILSON Campbell William MM Pte 90816 RAMC
WILSON Charles MM L/Cpl 265385 Seaforth Highlanders
WILSON Charles MM Pte 43689 9th Royal Inniskilling Fusiliers
WILSON Charles MM Gnr 45179 RGA
WILSON Charles A. MM Pte 15333 1st Grenadier Guards
WILSON Charles D. MM Pte 20383 1/7th Gordon Highlanders
WILSON Charles E. MM+Bar Sjt 29333 2nd Yorkshire Light Infantry
WILSON Charles H. MM Pte 530165 15th London Regt
WILSON Charles J. "DCM,MM" Cpl 50223 4th Liverpool Regt
WILSON Charles Robert MM Pte 267569 1/2nd Monmouthshire Regt DOW 23.10.17.
WILSON Charles T. MM Pnr 84266 Royal Engineers
WILSON Charles W. "DCM,MM,MID" Sjt 11286 1st Royal Warwickshire Regt
WILSON Charles Walter MM Pte 46985 RAMC
WILSON Christopher MM L/Cpl 250305 1/6th Durham Light Infantry KIA 27.5.18.
WILSON Claude D. MM Pte 513539 14th London Regt
WILSON D.V. MM 2nd Cpl 85519 Royal Engineers
WILSON D.W.R. MM Pnr 195928 Royal Engineers
WILSON Daniel MM Sjt M2/053851 Army Service Corps
WILSON Daniel MM Sjt 9740 2nd Gordon Highlanders
WILSON David MM Cpl 76480 'GQ' Cable Section Royal Engineers
WILSON David MM L/Cpl B/21250 2nd Highland Light Infantry KIA 23.8.18.
WILSON David H. MM Pte 1738 Liverpool Regt
WILSON David W. "MM,MID" L/Cpl 5927 1st Royal Highlanders
WILSON Denton MM Sjt 25965 1st Cameron Highlanders
WILSON Duke E. "MM,MID" Gnr 63905 RFA
WILSON Duncan MM Pte 12410 10th Durham Light Infantry
WILSON Edgar MM Cpl 217701 6 Light Rly Op Coy Royal Engineers
WILSON Edmund MM L/Cpl 162782 61 Fd Coy Royal Engineers
WILSON Edward MM Gnr 160893 105 Bty 22 Bde RFA
WILSON Edward C. MM Spr 42602 105 Fd Coy Royal Engineers
WILSON Edward C.C. MM Pte 235052 Liverpool Regt
WILSON Ernest "MM,MID" 2nd Cpl 498457 461 Fd Coy Royal Engineers
WILSON Ernest MM Pte 15064 8th York & Lancaster Regt KIA 1.7.16.
WILSON Ernest MM Pte 304882 15th Bn Tank Corps
WILSON Ernest A. MM Pte P/213 13th Rifle Brigade
WILSON Ernest Arthur MM Pte M2/055336 Army Service Corps att 129 Fd Amb RAMC.
WILSON Ernest F. MM L/Cpl 33141 147 Army Tps Coy Royal Engineers
WILSON Ernest W. MM Sjt 150164 102nd Bn Machine Gun Corps
WILSON Francis J. "MM+Bar,MID" S/Sjt Fitter 44971 140 Siege Bty RGA
WILSON Frank MM Cpl 9373 Worcestershire Regt
WILSON Frank MM Pte 16169 2nd Suffolk Regt KIA 20.7.16.
WILSON Frank MM+Bar Cpl 46597 Royal Engineers
WILSON Frank MM Gnr 39168 RGA
WILSON Frank Robertshaw MM Cpl 7587 2nd Yorkshire Regt
WILSON Fred MM Pte 95122 15th Durham Light Infantry
WILSON Fred MM Bdr 174555 17 Bde RFA
WILSON Fred MM Pte 66540 138 Fd Amb RAMC
WILSON Frederick MM Pte 241403 6th South Staffordshire Regt
WILSON Frederick MM Pte 18514 3rd Royal Fusiliers
WILSON Frederick MM Sjt 16924 6th King's Own Scottish Borderers
WILSON Frederick MM Gnr 20330 C/173 Bde RFA
WILSON Frederick MM L/Cpl 4196 11th Royal Warwickshire Regt
WILSON Frederick MM Pte 5245 7th Royal West Kent Regt
WILSON Frederick A. MM L/Cpl 232733 2nd London Regt
WILSON Frederick G. MM L/Cpl 200461 1/4th Oxf & Bucks Light Infantry
WILSON Frederick M. MM Gnr 47113 RFA
WILSON Frederick William Deyes "MM+Bar,MM(F)" Sjt 47378 Royal Engineers
WILSON Gavin Murgh Head MM Cpl 11450 2nd King's Royal Rifle Corps DOW 20.10.18.
WILSON George MM Sjt 9335 1/7th Royal Highlanders
WILSON George MM Cpl 86531 258 Tunnelling Coy Royal Engineers
WILSON George MM Pte 200598 1/5th Durham Light Infantry KIA 18.5.18.
WILSON George MM Sjt 64018 RAMC
WILSON George MM+Bar L/Cpl 10205 Royal West Surrey Regt
WILSON George "MM,MID" Sjt 64405 150 Fd Coy Royal Engineers
WILSON George MM L/Cpl 24284 5th Royal Scots Fusiliers
WILSON George MM Pte 325457 1/1st Cambridgeshire Regt KIA 22.8.18.
WILSON George MM Sjt 303326 Arg & Suth Highlanders
WILSON George MM Dvr 706097 RFA
WILSON George MM Spr 218625 Rly Op Div Royal Engineers KIA 18.8.18.
WILSON George MM Gnr 1892 RFA
WILSON George MM Sjt M/36397 Army Service Corps
WILSON George MM L/Cpl 11070 East Lancashire Regt
WILSON George MM Pte 8521 1st Lincolnshire Regt
WILSON George MM Pte 4/9545 12th Arg & Suth Highlanders
WILSON George MM Sjt 51208 9 Bty 41 Bde RFA KIA 8.5.17.

WILSON George "MM,MID" Sjt 9675 2nd Bedfordshire Regt
WILSON George MM+Bar Sjt 55627 112 Railway Coy Royal Engineers
WILSON George MM L/Cpl 248965 Signal Service Royal Engineers
WILSON George MM Sjt 27/1285 Northumberland Fusiliers
WILSON George MM Bdr 4265 RFA
WILSON George MM Pte 301278 12th Durham Light Infantry
WILSON George MM Sjt 200235 1/5th Liverpool Regt
WILSON George H. MM Pte 14195 Grenadier Guards
WILSON George J. MM CQMS 242172 5th Yorkshire Light Infantry
WILSON George James "DCM,MM,MID" Sjt 10683 2nd Notts & Derby Regt
WILSON George M. MM Pte 11817 Devonshire Regt
WILSON George R. MM Pte 13/665 13th East Yorkshire Regt
WILSON George W. MM Gnr 294651 RGA
WILSON Gerald MM Pte 17112 5th West Riding Regt
WILSON Gilbert MM L/Cpl 230714 10th Shropshire Light Infantry
WILSON Guy MM Pte 755 1/5th Border Regt
WILSON H. MM Pte 301334 RAMC
WILSON H. MM L/Cpl 201790 Suffolk Regt
WILSON H. MM Pte 1598 6th Connaught Rangers
WILSON Harold MM Spr 479989 62 Div Sig Coy Royal Engineers
WILSON Harold MM L/Cpl 201172 West Yorkshire Regt
WILSON Harold MM Cpl 27587 RFA
WILSON Harold MM Pte 8991 1st Norfolk Regt
WILSON Harold MM Sjt 15466 8th Suffolk Regt
WILSON Harold Bertram MM Pte 251512 6th Manchester Regt
WILSON Harry MM Pte 18932 1st North Lancashire Regt
WILSON Harry MM L/Cpl 178050 Royal Engineers
WILSON Harry MM Pte 8955 4th King's Royal Rifle Corps
WILSON Harry MM Cpl 11005 Royal Fusiliers
WILSON Harry MM Sjt 9921 1st East Lancashire Regt AKA Harry TOWNSEND
WILSON Harry MM Spr 31009 1(Indian)Fd Sqn Royal Engineers
WILSON Harry MM S/Sjt Armt 1736 Army Ordnance Corps
WILSON Harry MM Sjt 6397 11th Arg & Suth Highlanders
WILSON Hector MM Sjt 201964 Norfolk Regt
WILSON Henry MM Dvr 751128 A/331 Bde RFA
WILSON Henry MM Cpl 8617 1st Coldstream Guards
WILSON Henry MM L/Cpl 52763 Durham Light Infantry
WILSON Henry MM Pte 17149 Durham Light Infantry
WILSON Henry MM Pte 19506 Machine Gun Corps
WILSON Henry MM Sjt 23/514 Northumberland Fusiliers
WILSON Henry M. MM Cpl 12581 B/160 Bde RFA
WILSON Henry Noah MM Sjt 15336 2nd Middlesex Regt DOW 16.10.18.
WILSON Herbert MM Pte 12048 7th York & Lancaster Regt
WILSON Herbert MM Gnr 751032 B/250 Bde RFA
WILSON Herbert MM Dvr 11281 D/152 Bde RFA
WILSON Herbert MM Pte 11610 Coldstream Guards
WILSON Herbert Walter MM 2nd Cpl 74126 'SX' Cable Section Royal Engineers
WILSON Horace MM L/Cpl 20644 Worcestershire Regt
WILSON Horace John MM Pte 20893 1st Dorsetshire Regt
WILSON Hugh MM Pte 53733 138 Fd Amb RAMC
WILSON Hugh MM Pte 376054 Royal Scots
WILSON Hugh MM L/Cpl 8461 2nd York & Lancaster Regt
WILSON Hugh MM Cpl 2117 1/13th London Regt
WILSON Hugh MM Pte 8/13888 8th Royal Irish Rifles
WILSON Hugh C. MM+Bar Pte 14547 5th Cameron Highlanders
WILSON Hugh H. MM L/Cpl 32456 King's Own Scottish Borderers
WILSON Hugh M. MM L/Cpl 22832 7th Seaforth Highlanders
WILSON Irving N. MM Pte 46573 15th Durham Light Infantry
WILSON Isaac MM Bdr 23601 RGA
WILSON Isaac MM Sjt 14860 11th West Yorkshire Regt
WILSON J.A. MM Pte 13203 Machine Gun Corps
WILSON J.A. MM L/Cpl 352974 London Regt
WILSON J.A. MM Sjt 191245 RGA
WILSON James MM Pte 30910 11th Royal Scots
WILSON James MM Pte 267069 1/4th Seaforth Highlanders
WILSON James MM Cpl 42060 8th Royal Highlanders
WILSON James MM Spr 459119 447 Fd Coy Royal Engineers
WILSON James MM Pte 115783 Machine Gun Corps
WILSON James MM Bdr 12416 RFA
WILSON James MM L/Sjt 7136 1st Liverpool Regt
WILSON James MM Pte 11266 62nd Bn Machine Gun Corps
WILSON James MM Sjt 675011 RFA
WILSON James MM Pte 6620 2nd Middlesex Regt
WILSON James "MM,CG(B)" CSM 240757 1st King's Own Scottish Borderers
WILSON James MM Sjt 33786 2 Siege Bty RGA
WILSON James MM Pte 307570 West Riding Regt
WILSON James MM Pte 240429 East Lancashire Regt
WILSON James MM Sjt 4461 9th Seaforth Highlanders
WILSON James MM+Bar Cpl 457062 Royal Engineers
WILSON James MM+Bar Bdr 25994 A/56 Bde RFA
WILSON James MM Pte 267508 Seaforth Highlanders
WILSON James MM Sjt 30354 9th Scottish Rifles KIA 3.5.17.
WILSON James Douglas MM Pte 4575 1st Royal Welsh Fusiliers
WILSON James H. "DCM,MM" Sjt 950424 B/235 Bde RFA
WILSON James H. MM Sjt 15901 Royal Dublin Fusiliers
WILSON James H. MM Pte 65072 Northumberland Fusiliers
WILSON James L. MM L/Cpl 34853 York & Lancaster Regt
WILSON James Morrison MM Cpl 57982 36 Div Sig Coy Royal Engineers
WILSON James Ralph "MC,MM(10668 L/Sjt)" 2Lt 1st East Surrey Regt
WILSON James W. MM L/Cpl 41630 Lincolnshire Regt
WILSON Jim MM L/Cpl 241553 6th West Yorkshire Regt
WILSON John MM Sjt 295690 12th Royal Scots Fusiliers
WILSON John MM Gnr 671244 C/256 Bde RFA DOW 27.8.18.
WILSON John "MM,MID" Sjt 23110 3 Div Sig Coy Royal Engineers
WILSON John MM L/Cpl 235684 4th Gordon Highlanders
WILSON John MM Sjt 7650 RGA
WILSON John MM L/Cpl 87206 Machine Gun Corps
WILSON John MM Pte R/19753 King's Royal Rifle Corps
WILSON John MM+Bar Dvr 81287 39 Div Ammn Col RFA
WILSON John MM Sjt 43385 5/6th Scottish Rifles
WILSON John MM Gnr 58809 RGA
WILSON John MM Bdr 24069 'A' Bty RHA KIA 2.9.18.
WILSON John "DCM,MM" Sjt 44560 D/84 Bde & C/75 Bde RFA
WILSON John MM Pte 1944 1st Royal Highlanders
WILSON John MM 2nd Cpl 97459 23 Div Sig Coy Royal Engineers
WILSON John MM Spr 46934 95 Fd Coy Royal Engineers
WILSON John MM Dvr T/975 Army Service Corps
WILSON John MM L/Cpl 9165 1st North Staffordshire Regt
WILSON John MM Sjt Piper 20/290 Northumberland Fusiliers
WILSON John MM Pte 15/13878 15th Royal Irish Rifles KIA 7.6.17.
WILSON John MM Spr 46198 Royal Engineers
WILSON John MM Pte 4/6413 11th Arg & Suth Highlanders KIA 22.8.17.
WILSON John MM Cpl 55820 18th Scottish Rifles
WILSON John MM+2 Bars L/Cpl 1330 7 Fd Amb RAMC
WILSON John MM Cpl 15755 Yorkshire Regt
WILSON John MM Spr 61896 84 Fd Coy Royal Engineers
WILSON John MM Sjt 63574 Royal Engineers
WILSON John MM Pte 27302 Machine Gun Corps
WILSON John MM Cpl 3407 8th Seaforth Highlanders DOW 25.7.18.
WILSON John MM Pte 24679 13th Yorkshire Regt
WILSON John A. MM Pte 309029 5th Bn Tank Corps
WILSON John Bennett "MC,DCM,MM" CSM 13/297 13th East Yorkshire Regt
WILSON John H. MM Sjt 40619 6th Lincolnshire Regt
WILSON John J. MM Sjt 40928 1st Royal Irish Rifles
WILSON John J. MM Sjt Farrier 52631 RFA
WILSON John L. MM Pte M2/082059 Army Service Corps
WILSON John M. MM Cpl 3232 7th Seaforth Highlanders
WILSON John McD. MM Pte 40935 Cameron Highlanders
WILSON John R. MM Pte 203426 York & Lancaster Regt
WILSON John Richard MM Pte 24697 2nd Oxf & Bucks Light Infantry
WILSON John Seaton MM Pte 265630 1/6th Seaforth Highlanders DOW 1.8.17.
WILSON John T. "MM,MSM" Sjt 16941 6th King's Own Scottish Borderers
WILSON John T. MM Sjt 39175 1st South Wales Borderers
WILSON John T. MM Sjt 345 2nd Lancashire Fusiliers
WILSON John W. MM Bdr 72587 355 Siege Bty RGA
WILSON John W. MM Spr 102963 Royal Engineers
WILSON John W. MM Pte 203134 West Yorkshire Regt
WILSON John W. MM Sjt 13/1416 East Yorkshire Regt
WILSON John William MM Cpl 2169 1/8th Notts & Derby Regt KIA 21.3.18.
WILSON Jonathan "MM,MID" Sjt 2346 1/4th West Riding Regt
WILSON Joseph MM Cpl 760565 3 Bde RFA
WILSON Joseph MM Cpl 204443 5th York & Lancaster Regt
WILSON Joseph MM Sjt 305960 2/8th West Yorkshire Regt
WILSON Joseph MM Gnr 76459 39 Bde RFA
WILSON Joseph "DCM,MM" Sjt 705245 1(East Lancashire)Bde & 2 Bde RFA

WILSON Joseph MM+Bar Pte 322 7th Royal Sussex Regt
WILSON Joseph MM L/Sjt 12281 7th Yorkshire Light Infantry
WILSON Joseph MM L/Cpl 266154 1/6th Seaforth Highlanders KIA 25.10.18.
WILSON Joseph Harry Bernard MM Gnr 895189 855 TM Bty RFA DOW 24.8.18.
WILSON Joseph R. MM Spr 46567 7 Div Sig Coy Royal Engineers
WILSON L. MM Pte 437458 RAMC
WILSON Leonard MM Sjt M1/5857 Army Service Corps
WILSON Leonard MM Sjt 498062 Royal Engineers
WILSON Leonard "DCM,MM" Sjt 307341 1/7th West Riding Regt
WILSON Leonard J. MM Pte 25756 7th Somerset Light Infantry
WILSON Leslie MM Pte DM2/207831 Army Service Corps
WILSON Luke MM Gnr 67162 D/232 Bde RFA
WILSON Mark MM Spr 101445 26 Fd Coy Royal Engineers
WILSON Matthew MM Pte 64905 RAMC
WILSON Matthew Henry MM CQMS 52 1st Northumberland Fusiliers
WILSON Norman MM Pte 12826 19th Manchester Regt KIA 31.7.17.
WILSON Norman J.S. MM Pte 200856 Gordon Highlanders
WILSON Ogilvie "MM,MLaS(Pan)" L/Cpl 30560 1st Royal Scots
WILSON Paul MM L/Cpl 12424 2nd King's Own Scottish Borderers
WILSON Percival H. MM Pte 20687 1st Dorsetshire Regt
WILSON Percy MM Pte 201777 Yorkshire Light Infantry
WILSON Peter MM L/Cpl 42407 1st Gordon Highlanders KIA 1.10.18.
WILSON Peter MM Sjt 301624 5th London Regt
WILSON R. MM Pte 10862 1st Royal Munster Fusiliers
WILSON R. MM Pte 337351 RAMC
WILSON Reuben MM Sjt 41976 43 Bde RFA
WILSON Reuben Parker MM L/Cpl 23554 4th Bedfordshire Regt
WILSON Richard MM Gnr 16986 RFA
WILSON Robert MM Pte 25250 5th Border Regt
WILSON Robert MM Bdr Sig 141626 355 Siege Bty RGA
WILSON Robert MM Pte 12283 2nd Scots Guards
WILSON Robert MM Pte 25958 10th West Riding Regt
WILSON Robert MM Pte 12/825 12th York & Lancaster Regt KIA 30.6.17.
WILSON Robert "MM,MID" CQMS 9811 2nd East Lancashire Regt
WILSON Robert MM Sjt 1142 Royal Engineers
WILSON Robert MM Cpl 240141 Gordon Highlanders
WILSON Robert MM Bdr 63966 39 Bde RFA
WILSON Robert MM Pte 25137 Highland Light Infantry
WILSON Robert MM L/Cpl 3598 11th Arg & Suth Highlanders
WILSON Robert A. MM Spr 463139 50 Div Sig Coy Royal Engineers
WILSON Robert V. MM Pte 513706 14th London Regt
WILSON Roy MM Gnr 137544 RGA
WILSON Samuel MM Pte 146845 57th Bn Machine Gun Corps
WILSON Samuel MM Cpl 2844 1/6th Gordon Highlanders
WILSON Samuel MM Sjt 6364 2nd King's Royal Rifle Corps
WILSON Samuel J. "DCM,MM" Sjt 39540 52 Bty 15 Bde RFA KIA 4.11.18.
WILSON Sidney MM Pte 9109 2nd Oxf & Bucks Light Infantry
WILSON Sidney Charles MM L/Cpl 3/6448 1st Bedfordshire Regt KIA 2.7.17.
WILSON Sidney G. MM Pte 73694 35 Fd Amb RAMC
WILSON Sidney H. MM Spr 448534 Royal Engineers
WILSON Sidney Thomas MM L/Cpl 24491 3rd Grenadier Guards
WILSON Stanley MM Sjt 33112 Bedfordshire Regt att 1/1st Hertfordshire Regt.
WILSON Stanley MM Pte 201032 Duke of Cornwall's LI
WILSON Stanley "DCM,MM+Bar" L/Cpl 8827 1st East Kent Regt DOW 22.3.18.
WILSON Sydney H. MM Pte 129948 31st Bn Machine Gun Corps
WILSON Sydney J. "DCM,MM" Pte 202337 1st London Regt
WILSON T.T.W. MM Pte 62004 RAMC
WILSON Thomas MM Sjt 202817 5th West Yorkshire Regt
WILSON Thomas MM Cpl 1710 Middlesex Regt
WILSON Thomas MM Dvr 107235 A/173 Bde RFA
WILSON Thomas MM Cpl 295277 120 Heavy Bty RGA
WILSON Thomas MM+Bar Sjt 103989 D/162 Bde RFA
WILSON Thomas MM Pte 200966 King's Own Scottish Borderers
WILSON Thomas "MM,MID" Pte 28251 8th Cheshire Regt
WILSON Thomas MM Sjt 49804 109 Fd Amb. RAMC
WILSON Thomas MM L/Cpl 70736 98 Coy Machine Gun Corps
WILSON Thomas MM Cpl 83342 88 Bde RFA DOW 25.4.18.
WILSON Thomas A. MM Pte 13617 West Yorkshire Regt
WILSON Thomas E. MM Pte 93194 2nd Durham Light Infantry
WILSON Thomas Fletcher MM Sjt 67027 96 Fd Amb RAMC
WILSON Thomas G. MM Pte 75733 24th Royal Fusiliers
WILSON Thomas H. MM Sjt 28617 18th Hussars
WILSON Thomas H. MM Pte 73300 RAMC
WILSON Thomas H. MM Gnr 42771 RGA
WILSON Thomas J. MM L/Cpl 488175 Royal Engineers
WILSON Thomas James MM Sjt 82472 140 Siege Bty RGA KIA 7.9.17.
WILSON Thomas John MM Cpl 7124 13th Middlesex Regt KIA 15.4.17.
WILSON Thomas S. MM Pte 27821 Royal Scots
WILSON Tom S.Urton MM Pte 41772 7th Royal Irish Rifles
WILSON W. MM Sjt 8483 Essex Regt
WILSON W. "DCM,MM" Sjt 21818 11th Essex Regt
WILSON W. "DCM,MM" Sjt 201115 1/4th Royal Berkshire Regt
WILSON W.B. MM Cpl 981 Cameron Highlanders
WILSON W.H. MM Pte 201370 Leicestershire Regt
WILSON W.S. MM L/Cpl 130323 45th Royal Fusiliers
WILSON Wallace MM L/Cpl 3/8747 2nd Suffolk Regt
WILSON Walter MM Sjt 240570 1/5th King's Own Scottish Borderers
WILSON Walter MM Pte 33343 13th East Lancashire Regt
WILSON Walter MM Cpl 444164 Royal Engineers
WILSON Walter W. MM Sjt 18320 Machine Gun Corps
WILSON William MM Pte 200975 1/4th Royal Scots Fusiliers
WILSON William MM Cpl 34778 8th North Staffordshire Regt
WILSON William MM Sjt 322644 203 Siege Bty RGA
WILSON William MM Pte 57078 12th Manchester Regt KIA 9.9.18.
WILSON William MM L/Cpl 87182 62nd Bn Machine Gun Corps
WILSON William MM Pte 8884 2nd Royal Scots
WILSON William MM Pte 23877 King's Own Scottish Borderers
WILSON William MM Sjt 20/566 20th Durham Light Infantry KIA 25.3.18.
WILSON William MM Pte 16133 1st Scots Guards
WILSON William MM L/Cpl 406011 Royal Engineers
WILSON William MM Pte 2426 1/5th Border Regt
WILSON William "DCM,MM" BSM 12326 C/112 Bde RFA
WILSON William MM Pte 18727 6th King's Own Scottish Borderers
WILSON William MM Cpl 23546 5 Div Sig Coy Royal Engineers
WILSON William MM Pte 43256 Royal Scots Fusiliers
WILSON William MM Sjt 1490 2nd Royal Highlanders
WILSON William MM L/Cpl 5692 East Lancashire Regt
WILSON William MM+2 Bars Sjt 40186 Highland Light Infantry
WILSON William MM L/Cpl 16592 13th Royal Scots
WILSON William MM Sjt 16281 1st King's Own Scottish Borderers
WILSON William MM Pte 17586 10th Yorkshire Regt
WILSON William MM Pte 383661 Highland Light Infantry
WILSON William MM L/Cpl 72680 69 Coy Machine Gun Corps
WILSON William Brown MM Spr 66005 19 Div Sig Coy Royal Engineers
WILSON William F. MM Dvr 1526 RFA
WILSON William G. MM Pte 87676 13th Liverpool Regt
WILSON William G. MM Sjt 16909 Somerset Light Infantry
WILSON William H. MM L/Cpl 43882 5th South Lancashire Regt
WILSON William H. MM Pte 13958 15th Highland Light Infantry
WILSON William H. MM Pte 14/1076 2nd York & Lancaster Regt
WILSON William H. MM Bdr 72250 B/82 Bde RFA
WILSON William H. MM Bdr 751320 D/250 Bde RFA DOW 26.8.17.
WILSON William J. MM Cpl 172078 Royal Engineers
WILSON William J. MM Sjt 17338 7th Royal Berkshire Regt
WILSON William J. MM Spr 94709 Royal Engineers
WILSON William J.H. MM L/Sjt 325006 1/9th Durham Light Infantry
WILSON William James MM Sjt 240503 8th South Lancashire Regt
WILSON William Linn MM Gnr 83982 RFA
WILSON William S. MM+Bar Pte 40154 14th Royal Irish Rifles KIA 27.4.18.
WILSON William Stewart MM Pte 2955 1/5th Border Regt
WILSON William V. MM Pte 241687 5th York & Lancaster Regt
WILTHEW Leicester MM Gnr Shoeing Smith 866267 RFA
WILTON Arthur MM Pte 202163 2nd Royal Sussex Regt
WILTON Christopher G. MM Pte 8322 2nd Northamptonshire Regt
WILTON Ernest J. "MM,MID" CQMS 3409 2nd King's Royal Rifle Corps att Nigeria Regt WAFF.
WILTON Frederick MM Cpl 12045 9th Leicestershire Regt
WILTON Herbert MM L/Sjt 200591 1/5th Liverpool Regt
WILTON Humphrey W. MM Gnr 37362 71 Heavy Bty RGA
WILTON Sydney MM Pte 88026 Machine Gun Corps
WILTON William Francis MM Cpl 3264 A/89 Bde RFA
WILTSHIRE Albert W. MM Gnr 239369 RFA
WILTSHIRE Charles Henry MM CQMS 1413 1/7th Middlesex Regt
WILTSHIRE Frank MM L/Cpl 10542 Wiltshire Regt

WILTSHIRE Frank G. MM L/Bdr 618059 20 Bde RHA
WILTSHIRE Frederick MM L/Cpl 4820 6th Dragoons KIA 1.12.17.
WILTSHIRE Harold George MM Pte 29771 Wiltshire Regt
WILTSHIRE Harry MM Pte 272 17th Royal Fusiliers KIA 24.5.17.
WILTSHIRE James MM Sjt 18091 Royal Munster Fusiliers
WILTSHIRE Walter "MM,CG(F)" Sjt 265560 8th Royal Highlanders
WILTSHIRE William Alfred MM Cpl 13938 14th Hampshire Regt DOW 30.9.18.
WILTSHIRE William Harry MM Pte 470428 1/12th London Regt
WILTSHIRE William Henry MM L/Sjt 13171 3rd Coldstream Guards
WILTSHIRE William J. MM Pte 7303 1st Wiltshire Regt
WILTSHIRE William J. "MM,MID" Sjt 17108 Machine Gun Corps
WIMBLETT Harry MM+Bar Cpl 265961 1/6th West Riding Regt
WIMBORN Reginald MM L/Cpl 1721 Royal Sussex Regt
WIMPENEY Harold MM Sjt 398206 Royal Engineers
WIMPENNY Harry MM Sjt 21/249 21st West Yorkshire Regt
WIMPEY Ernest William MM L/Cpl 66106 20 Div Sig Coy Royal Engineers
WIMPORY Harry MM+Bar Spr 87372 9 Div Sig Coy Royal Engineers
WINCH John Orbell MM Pte A/200796 18th King's Royal Rifle Corps DOW 28.3.18.
WINCH Maurice MM Pte 13045 1st Bedfordshire Regt KIA 23.4.17.
WINCH Sidney John MM Pte 14931 7th Bedfordshire Regt
WINCH Walter MM Pte 25989 Welsh Regt
WINCHESTER Cecil Fowler MM Gnr 930806 RFA
WINCHESTER Christopher B. MM Cpl 161035 A/251 Bde RFA
WINCHESTER Ernest "MM,MIDx2" Dmr 8549 1st South Staffordshire Regt
WINCKLES Leonard F. MM CQMS 2158 1/23rd London Regt
WINCUP Henry MM Pte 46283 RAMC
WINDAS Arthur W. MM Pte 25063 East Yorkshire Regt
WINDEBANK Albert MM Pte 15655 Royal Sussex Regt
WINDEBANK Arthur MM Sjt 14080 12 Fd Coy Royal Engineers
WINDEBANK Edward J. MM L/Cpl 8807 1st Royal Inniskilling Fusiliers
WINDEBANK George MM L/Cpl 19025 15th Hampshire Regt
WINDEBANK W.J.F. MM Gnr 158379 RGA
WINDEBANK William MM Cpl Mechanic 104631 Royal Air Force
WINDER Francis E. MM Pte 3347 Middlesex Regt
WINDER Frederick G. MM Cpl 214786 Labour Corps
WINDER Herbert MM Pte 51481 Cheshire Regt
WINDER Horace Edward MM L/Cpl 60571 15/17th West Yorkshire Regt
WINDER John MM Bdr 102680 RGA
WINDER Louis MM Gnr 223463 RFA
WINDER Percy W. MM Cpl 37594 7 Siege Bty RGA
WINDER Robert MM Cpl 37498 13th Royal Welsh Fusiliers
WINDER William MM Cpl 24168 Royal Lancaster Regt
WINDLE Parker MM Bdr 700579 210 Bde RFA
WINDLEY James William MM Spr 165786 34 Div Sig Coy Royal Engineers
WINDMILL Clifford MM Sjt 2799 Royal Warwickshire Regt
WINDMILL Joseph MM Cpl 1741 8th Royal Sussex Regt
WINDOWS Alfred MM Cpl 1276 Royal Engineers
WINDRIDGE T. MM Sjt 971 Royal Warwickshire Regt
WINDROSS Albert MM Gnr 68488 RGA
WINDSOR Albert B. MM Bdr 66927 RGA
WINDSOR C. MM Sjt 267788 16th Royal Warwickshire Regt
WINDSOR Edward MM Cpl 266272 2/1st Bucks Bn Oxf & Bucks Light Infantry
WINDSOR Herbert Thierry MM Cpl 137722 237 Fd Coy Royal Engineers
WINDSOR R. MM L/Cpl 266273 1/1st Bucks Bn Oxf & Bucks Light Infantry
WINDY Charles H. MM L/Cpl 27076 1/7th Royal Warwickshire Regt
WINDYBANK Frederick G. MM Pte 82290 113 Fd Amb RAMC
WINDYBANK Percy Charles MM Pte 21488 88 Coy Machine Gun Corps KIA 23.4.17.
WINEARLS Arthur MM L/Cpl 16170 8th East Surrey Regt
WINFIELD Arthur MM Sjt 41165 11th Manchester Regt
WINFIELD Charles MM Sjt 266076 1/6th Gloucestershire Regt
WINFIELD Charles MM+Bar Cpl 7152 Middlesex Regt
WINFIELD Charles H. MM Pte 8750 2nd South Staffordshire Regt
WINFIELD Edward MM Pte 9955 1st Yorkshire Light Infantry
WINFIELD Frederick MM L/Cpl 39331 Machine Gun Corps
WINFIELD Henry S. MM Cpl 9469 1st South Wales Borderers
WINFIELD Samuel MM L/Cpl 16604 8th Northumberland Fusiliers
WINFIELD William MM Pte 374512 17th London Regt
WINFIELD William A. MM Pte 50667 Royal Berkshire Regt
WING Arthur MM Pte 24032 1/5th York & Lancaster Regt
WING George MM L/Cpl 8148 8th East Surrey Regt KIA 22.8.18.
WING George MM L/Sjt 19789 11th Royal Scots Fusiliers
WING George H. MM Pte 16534 33rd Bn Machine Gun Corps
WING Henry Charles MM CSM 4860 13th Royal Fusiliers KIA 4.9.18.
WING Richard MM Pte 328062 1/1st Cambridgeshire Regt DOW 28.9.18.
WING Stanley MM Cpl 1239 2nd Royal Warwickshire Regt
WING William J. MM Spr 87501 Royal Engineers
WINGATE Charles A. MM Pte 20757 Hampshire Regt
WINGATE Eric J. MM Sjt 320137 1/6th London Regt
WINGATE George MM Pte 6523 Border Regt
WINGATE Henry B. MM Cpl 419971 Labour Corps
WINGATE James "DCM,MM+Bar" Pte 43615 2nd Gordon Highlanders
WINGATE Thomas Charles MM Cpl 186 23rd Royal Fusiliers KIA 23.3.18.
WINGFIELD Arthur Mark "MM,MIDx2" Pte 2390 1/16th London Regt
WINGFIELD George E. MM L/Cpl R/39323 13th King's Royal Rifle Corps
WINGFIELD H.A. "DCM,MM" Cpl 13287 Essex Regt
WINGHAM George V. MM Sjt 11224 5th Cameron Highlanders
WINGHAM John A. MM Cpl 30402 Royal Engineers
WINGROVE Albert Arthur MM Sjt R/19338 16th King's Royal Rifle Corps KIA 24.9.18.
WINGROVE Alfred T. "MM,MID" Sjt 290272 2/10th Middlesex Regt
WINGROVE Arthur J. MM Pte 471270 1/12th London Regt
WINGROVE Christopher MM Sjt 8661 2nd Royal West Surrey Regt
WINGROVE Ernest W. MM Sjt 8699 2nd Oxf & Bucks Light Infantry
WINGROVE Frederick MM Pte 15648 1 Special Coy Middlesex Regt
WINGROVE Frederick George MM Gnr 78500 'D' Bn Tank Corps
WINGROVE George E. MM Cpl 3201 1/17th London Regt
WINGROVE Walter George "MM,MID" 2nd Cpl 100258 226 Fd Coy Royal Engineers
WINKLE Harry MM L/Cpl 148 1/1(North Midland)Fd Coy Royal Engineers
WINKLE James MM Pte 230986 10th Shropshire Light Infantry KIA 2.9.18.
WINKLE John MM Spr 28364 Royal Engineers
WINKLEY William MM Gnr 55761 RFA
WINKWORTH James MM L/Cpl 9742 1st Royal Berkshire Regt
WINN Albert R. MM Gnr 19458 101 Bde RFA
WINN Charles George MM Sjt 7769 1st Essex Regt
WINN E.D. MM L/Cpl 34571 Liverpool Regt
WINN James MM CQMS 9775 Liverpool Regt
WINN James MM Pte 204630 Hampshire Regt
WINN James Percy MM Gnr 67528 140 Siege Bty RGA
WINN John William MM Cpl(MCDR) 211071 8 Div Sig Coy Royal Engineers
WINN Robert A. MM Sjt 12668 46 Siege Bty RGA
WINN William MM L/Cpl 265746 2/8th West Yorkshire Regt
WINN William Joseph MM Cpl 10627 1st South Wales Borderers KIA 18.4.18.
WINNALL Thomas H. MM Sjt 941 RFA
WINNING David MM L/Cpl 17098 1st Cameron Highlanders
WINNING James MM Pte 11860 9th Scottish Rifles
WINNING Percy MM Bdr 940088 RFA
WINNY William MM CQMS 9259 1st Middlesex Regt
WINPENNY George A. MM L/Cpl 201432 4th Yorkshire Light Infantry
WINROW Frederick MM Pte 4627 1/9th Liverpool Regt
WINROW James MM CQMS 44720 1st Liverpool Regt
WINSBORROW Albert J. MM+Bar CSM 240068 1/5th Devonshire Regt
WINSER Leonard George Odger MM Pte 5/4792 1st King's Royal Rifle Corps
WINSHIP William MM Cpl 21234 9th Northumberland Fusiliers
WINSKILL James MM Cpl 99629 4th Liverpool Regt
WINSLADE G. MM L/Cpl 47521 10th Essex Regt
WINSLADE Tom MM Pte 204700 13th York & Lancaster Regt
WINSLOW Edward William MM Pte 11363 3rd Coldstream Guards
WINSON A. MM Sjt 307579 1/8th Notts & Derby Regt
WINSON John MM Dvr 800759 D/230 Bde RFA
WINSOR John "DCM,MM" CSM 9123 2nd Devonshire Regt
WINSOR William George Hill MM Pte 351582 2/7th London Regt
WINSPER Joseph MM Pte 2527 1st North Lancashire Regt
WINSTANLEY Albert MM Cpl 430005 Royal Engineers

WINSTANLEY Charles MM Pte 592038 1/18th London Regt KIA 26.3.18.
WINSTANLEY Charles B. MM L/Cpl 241072 Liverpool Regt
WINSTANLEY Isaac MM L/Cpl 34531 17th Lancashire Fusiliers
WINSTANLEY John Edward MM Pte 23770 2nd Lancashire Fusiliers KIA 7.5.17.
WINSTANLEY John Thomas MM Pte 358330 10th Liverpool Regt KIA 31.7.17.
WINSTANLEY John Thomas MM Cpl 81652 Royal Engineers
WINSTANLEY Leigh MM Pte 200069 Manchester Regt
WINSTANLEY Walter MM Pte 28794 Cheshire Regt
WINSTON Harry P. MM S/Sjt 95074 10th Bn Tank Corps
WINSTONE Frank MM L/Cpl 117295 Machine Gun Corps
WINSTONE Harry Jacques MM Gnr 18199 40 Siege Bty RGA KIA 19.10.17.
WINSTONE Lionel MM L/Cpl 24255 Gloucestershire Regt
WINTER A.J. MM AM1 33801 Royal Air Force
WINTER Albert MM Gnr 35835 RFA
WINTER Albert W. MM Cpl 38872 RGA
WINTER Alfred MM+Bar Sjt 26729 1st Somerset Light Infantry
WINTER Charles MM Pte 28873 1/4th Royal Scots
WINTER Christopher James MM Pte 15809 11th Middlesex Regt DOW 12.4.17.
WINTER Edward MM L/Sjt 20/502 20th Durham Light Infantry KIA 24.2.17.
WINTER Ernest MM Cpl 352523 7th London Regt
WINTER Frederick "MM,MSM" Sjt 496 1st Welsh Guards
WINTER Frederick W. MM Sjt 16365 1st Devonshire Regt
WINTER George MM L/Cpl 776 1st Welsh Guards
WINTER George MM L/Cpl 78036 Tank Corps
WINTER Glyndwr MM Dvr 29358 366 Bty 117 Bde RFA
WINTER Griffiths A. MM Pte 551545 16th London Regt
WINTER Harry MM Pte 265845 1/1st Hertfordshire Regt
WINTER Harry MM Pte 2089 Middlesex Regt
WINTER Harry E. MM Pte 47632 RAMC
WINTER Henry N. MM L/Cpl 420653 10th London Regt
WINTER Herbert MM CSM 7947 8th West Yorkshire Regt
WINTER Herbert MM Pte 425201 66 Coy Labour Corps
WINTER Herbert W. MM Pte 54317 13th Durham Light Infantry
WINTER Hugh J. MM Sjt 201357 5th Gloucestershire Regt
WINTER J. MM Pte 17512 King's Own Scottish Borderers
WINTER James MM Sjt 16612 39 Bde RFA
WINTER James Allen "MM,GMV(S)" Sjt 518482 Royal Engineers
WINTER John H. MM 2nd Cpl 128817 Royal Engineers
WINTER John S. MM Spr 207518 Royal Engineers
WINTER Leonard MM Cpl 420460 10th London Regt
WINTER Maurice MM Pte 230333 1/2nd London Regt
WINTER Richard MM Pte 14/877 1/4th York & Lancaster Regt
WINTER Richard J. MM L/Bdr 49286 RFA
WINTER Richard W. MM L/Cpl 241915 Worcestershire Regt
WINTER Robert "DCM,MM,MID" CSM 7410 1st Leinster Regt
WINTER Robert C. MM Pte 23692 2nd Highland Light Infantry
WINTER Robert J. MM Sjt 358044 RGA
WINTER Sidney MM Pte 10130 7th Leicestershire Regt KIA 22.3.18.
WINTER Thomas MM Pte 202271 2/4th Somerset Light Infantry
WINTER Thomas MM Sjt 64831 109 Coy Labour Corps
WINTER Thomas MM Sjt 17149 8th Royal Lancaster Regt
WINTER Thomas MM Pte 9313 1st Coldstream Guards
WINTER Victor John MM Cpl 2136 RFA DOW 16.10.17.
WINTER W.H. MM Sjt 256 Liverpool Regt
WINTER Watson MM Gnr 201818 RFA
WINTER William MM Pte 29937 11th Royal Fusiliers
WINTER William C. MM Pte 353646 7th London Regt
WINTER William H.V. MM Sjt 10/1262 East Yorkshire Regt
WINTER William Hewitt MM Sjt 9474 2nd Worcestershire Regt KIA 15.7.16.
WINTER Wilson MM Cpl 17410 D/256 Bde RFA
WINTERBOTTOM A. MM L/Cpl 35524 7th Lancashire Fusiliers
WINTERBOTTOM Alfred "MM,MSM,MID" CSM 9226 2nd Manchester Regt
WINTERBOTTOM Benjamin MM Pte 241655 10th North Lancashire Regt
WINTERBOTTOM Ernest MM L/Cpl 202239 4th York & Lancaster Regt
WINTERBOTTOM Irvine MM L/Sjt 30356 9th Manchester Regt
WINTERBOTTOM James MM Pte 240409 1/5th North Lancashire Regt KIA 30.11.17.
WINTERBOTTOM Joseph H. MM Sjt 86681 Royal Engineers
WINTERBOURNE James MM Pte 15553 7th Bedfordshire Regt KIA 3.5.17.
WINTERBURN J. MM Bdr 44788 RFA
WINTERBURN John MM Pnr 98671 Royal Engineers
WINTERBURY Harold C. MM Pte 231730 2nd London Regt
WINTERFLOOD Charles Edward MM Sjt 471826 1/12tth London Regt KIA 20.9.17.
WINTERHALDER William MM Dvr 961500 C/235 Bde RFA
WINTERS Burnaby MM L/Cpl 240181 Lincolnshire Regt
WINTERS Francis W. MM Sjt 1931 RFA
WINTERS Frank MM Bdr 73086 9 Bty 41 Bde RFA
WINTERS Herbert S. MM Cpl 71098 18th Bn Machine Gun Corps
WINTERS Sydney MM Pte 204957 1st Devonshire Regt
WINTERSON John W. MM Pte 5836 Royal Munster Fusiliers
WINTERSON Thomas W. MM Pte 16535 2nd Scots Guards
WINTLE A.H. "MM,MID" Sjt 2742 1/5th Gloucestershire Regt
WINTLE Francis E. MM Sjt 240388 Worcestershire Regt
WINTON Arthur John MM L/Cpl 700718 23rd London Regt
WINTON David MM Sjt 6616 1/6th Gordon Highlanders
WINTON Francis MM Pte 13433 1st Scots Guards
WINTON Harold MM L/Cpl 534117 Royal Engineers
WINTON James MM Pte 12279 12th Royal Scots
WINTON William MM L/Cpl 290122 1/7th Royal Highlanders
WINTOUR Harold MM Sjt 2130 16th Middlesex Regt KIA 1.12.17.
WINTRIP James MM Pte 57533 1st Lincolnshire Regt
WINZER Walter "DCM,MM+Bar" Cpl 24373 4 Div Sig Coy Royal Engineers
WIPER George E. MM Pte 43732 Scottish Rifles
WIRDNAM Walter J. MM Sjt 241294 Middlesex Regt
WIRE Herbert MM L/Cpl 15714 East Kent Regt
WISCOMBE William MM Gnr 926252 D/290 Bde RFA
WISDELL Alfred J. MM Pte 42927 Liverpool Regt
WISDEN Albert MM Pte 10733 1st King's Royal Rifle Corps
WISDOM Frederick MM L/Cpl 548768 419 Fd Coy Royal Engineers
WISDOM George MM+Bar L/Cpl 241284 8th Worcestershire Regt
WISDOM Harry MM Cpl 9815 Machine Gun Corps
WISDOM Walter MM+Bar Pte 917 7th Royal West Surrey Regt Died 3.11.18.
WISDOM Walter J. MM Spr 34958 Royal Engineers
WISE Arthur MM Sjt 781038 D/246 Bde RFA KIA 3.11.17.
WISE Duncan William MM L/Cpl 3710 1st East Kent Regt KIA 8.10.18.
WISE Francis George MM Sjt 93159 A/82 Bde RFA KIA 4.11.18.
WISE Harry Frank MM Sjt 1814 1/1st Oxfordshire Yeomanry
WISE Henry Charles MM Cpl 21036 8th Border Regt KIA 22.3.18.
WISE Theodore H. MM Dvr M2/018606 Army Service Corps
WISE Thomas Harold MM Spr 534679 Signal Service Royal Engineers att 35 Bde RGA.
WISE W. MM Pte 2504 6th East Kent Regt
WISE William MM L/Cpl 305209 8th West Yorkshire Regt
WISE William Edward MM Pte 1831 1/5th Royal Warwickshire Regt
WISE William Frederick Mason MM Sjt 12722 6th Oxf & Bucks Light Infantry
WISELY George MM Pte 266400 1/7th Gordon Highlanders
WISEMAN Albert H. MM L/Sjt 22574 Royal Fusiliers
WISEMAN Alfred MM Dvr 14740 D/157 Bde RFA
WISEMAN Andrew MM Pte 201048 1/4th Royal Scots
WISEMAN Gavin MM Pte 203642 10th Scottish Rifles KIA 19.8.18.
WISEMAN George MM Sjt 31052 Machine Gun Corps
WISEMAN Harry MM Pte 375495 9th Durham Light Infantry
WISEMAN Joseph Henry MM Sjt 31099 C/177 Bde RFA
WISEMAN Stanley Thomas MM BSM 39568 27 Bde RFA
WISEMAN William MM Pte S/41925 1/6th Royal Highlanders
WISEMAN William MM Pte 23067 Border Regt
WISEMAN William MM L/Cpl 265370 1/6th Seaforth Highlanders
WISEMAN William E. MM L/Cpl 879033 33rd London Regt
WISEMAN William J. MM Sjt 18194 6 Div Sig Coy Royal Engineers
WISER Frank MM Gnr Shoeing Smith 292027 RGA
WISHART David G. MM Sjt 59012 RAMC
WISHART Emmerson MM Pte 22737 Durham Light Infantry
WISHART James MM Cpl 2557 Royal Highlanders
WISHART Peter MM Dvr T/29964 Army Service Corps
WISHART Robert MM Sjt 29879 D/150 Bde RFA DOW 3.12.17.
WISHART William MM Pte 325091 1/9th Durham Light Infantry
WISKEN Alec MM Pte 276635 1/7th Manchester Regt DOW 22.8.18.
WISKER Francis MM Cpl 240150 Suffolk Regt
WISTANCE Walter MM Cpl 65619 V/19 Heavy TM Bty RGA
WITCHELL Albert William MM Gnr 15145 C/162 Bde RFA DOW 24.10.17.
WITCHELL M.E. MM Cpl 3/1913 10th Essex Regt
WITCHELL Norman G. MM Pte 235438 1/1st Gloucestershire Yeomanry

WITCHELL Percival A. MM L/Bdr 107373 296 Siege Bty RGA
WITCHELL Percy MM Gnr 66521 X/46 Med TM Bty RGA
WITCHER Edward MM+Bar Cpl 30004 8th East Surrey Regt
WITCHER Sidney William MM Sjt 17788 1st Hampshire Regt
WITCUTT Ernest MM Spr 86339 Royal Engineers
WITHAM Alfred MM Pte 14363 12th West Yorkshire Regt
WITHAM Ernest A.G. MM L/Sjt 14992 2nd Arg & Suth Highlanders
WITHAM G. MM S/Sjt 510182 RAMC
WITHAMS John MM Pte 3206 Royal Fusiliers
WITHAMS Leonard Cecil MM Gnr 23755 D/232 Bde RFA KIA 12.10.17.
WITHAMS William Robert MM Gnr 69320 113 Bty 25 Bde RFA
WITHERDEN Arthur MM Sjt R/577 12th King's Royal Rifle Corps
WITHERDEN John T. MM L/Cpl 416 6th Royal West Kent Regt
WITHERELL Alfred MM Pte 23404 South Wales Borderers
WITHERS Arthur V. MM Cpl 200356 1/4th Royal Berkshire Regt
WITHERS Charles D. MM Gnr 173308 RFA
WITHERS Charles H. MM CQMS 240676 Royal West Kent Regt
WITHERS Charles James MM Sjt 392633 1/9th London Regt
WITHERS Edward MM+Bar Pte 22144 10th Northumberland Fusiliers
WITHERS George MM Pte 18748 2nd Coldstream Guards
WITHERS George C. MM BQMS 46960 139 Hy Bty RGA
WITHERS George H. MM L/Cpl 1461 13th Royal Fusiliers
WITHERS R.V. MM Pte 5487 13th Rifle Brigade
WITHERS Thomas MM Cpl 11225 Royal West Surrey Regt
WITHERS Thomas MM Pte 202307 Gloucestershire Regt
WITHERS William H. MM Cpl 228329 330 Rd Constr Coy Royal Engineers
WITHEY Albert MM Cpl 108167 87 Fd Coy Royal Engineers
WITHEY E.W. MM L/Cpl 25889 Royal Engineers
WITHEY Harold Bertram MM Pte 202137 1/8th Worcestershire Regt
WITHEY Tom MM Pte 267725 Monmouthshire Regt
WITHINGTON George MM Gnr 8705 RFA
WITHINSHAW J. MM Sjt 751688 RFA
WITHRINGTON Albert E. MM Pte 203166 1st London Regt
WITHYCOMBE John H. MM Pte R/3346 King's Royal Rifle Corps
WITNEY John J. MM CSM 8572 4th Royal Fusiliers
WITT Reginald J. MM Pte 32325 Wiltshire Regt
WITT Robert MM Cpl 461173 RAMC
WITT Stephen MM Pte 539 6th Royal West Kent Regt
WITT William P.R. "MM,MID" Cpl 8904 15th Hussars
WITTE Wilfred MM Bdr 41476 RFA
WITTER Ernest J. MM L/Sjt 19894 1/6th Royal Highlanders
WITTS Albert MM Cpl 7832 1st Wiltshire Regt
WITTS Albert MM Gnr 35931 RGA
WITTS Joseph E. MM Sjt 10518 Durham Light Infantry
WITTS Thomas MM Pte 11045 2nd Worcestershire Regt
WITTS William F. MM Pte 235120 West Riding Regt
WITTY Henry MM Cpl 25957 Royal Engineers
WITTY John A. MM L/Cpl 200637 3rd Light Bn Tank Corps
WIX Cecil MM Dvr 110319 RFA
WIXCEY or WIXEY Charles MM Pte 14864 South Lancashire Regt
WIXEY Henry J. MM Pte 235451 Liverpool Regt
WIXEY William Albert George MM Pte 34718 2nd Oxf & Bucks Light Infantry KIA 23.10.18.
WIXON Charles MM Dvr 676922 B/285 Bde RFA
WIXON Charles Edward MM Gnr 60865 41 Div Ammn Col RFA
WOFFENDALE A. MM Cpl 795029 RFA
WOGIN John W. MM+2 Bars L/Cpl 248612 Royal Engineers
WOLBOLD Christian F. MM+Bar Cpl 74138 Royal Engineers
WOLFE George H. MM Sjt 7920 RFA
WOLFE Leslie J. MM L/Cpl 33361 6th King's Own Scottish Borderers
WOLFE Richard John MM L/Sjt 18609 9th Royal Irish Fusiliers KIA 16.8.17.
WOLFE Stanley MM+Bar L/Cpl 30080 1st East Yorkshire Regt
WOLFE William James MM Cpl 58236 20 Div Sig Coy Royal Engineers
WOLFENDALE James MM Pte 17786 9th North Lancashire Regt
WOLFENDEN Charles MM Pte 8004 1/1st Bn HAC(Infantry)
WOLFENDEN J. MM Spr 342332 209 Fd Coy Royal Engineers
WOLFENDEN Joseph Whittaker MM Dvr 9190 150 Bde RFA
WOLFENDEN R. MM Pte 5969 Royal Fusiliers
WOLFENDEN Thomas MM Pte 39461 12th Royal Scots DOW 26.10.18.
WOLFENDEN W.E. MM Gnr Sig 222137 86 Bty 32 Bde RFA
WOLFF Harold MM Gnr 36476 RGA
WOLITER William MM Pte A/203752 18th King's Royal Rifle Corps
WOLLACOTT Archie MM Cpl 203535 1st Dorsetshire Regt
WOLLAN Percy MM Gnr 740380 RFA
WOLLAS George Herbert MM Pte 12/1526 12th East Yorkshire Regt KIA 13.11.16.
WOLLEDGE Archibald P. MM Dvr 39668 D/83 Bde RFA
WOLLEN Edwin J. MM Pte 54880 Machine Gun Corps
WOLLIN Thomas Louis MM+Bar Pte 205605 1st Essex Regt
WOLSEY George MM Cpl 6840 21 Div Cyclist Coy Army Cyclist Corps
WOLSTENCROFT Albert MM Cpl 205387 1st Notts & Derby Regt
WOLSTENCROFT Edward MM Pte 21070 22nd Manchester Regt KIA 14.3.17.
WOLSTENCROFT George MM Pte 38378 55 Fd Amb RAMC
WOLSTENCROFT Harry MM CQMS 240249 18th Lancashire Fusiliers
WOLSTENCROFT Samuel MM Pte 26990 Royal Lancaster Regt
WOLSTENHOLME Albert MM L/Cpl 31966 33 Coy Machine Gun Corps DOW 22.8.18
WOLSTENHOLME Henry MM Pte 12990 7th Royal Lancaster Regt
WOLSTENHOLME Irving MM Cpl 47688 6 Mobile Ambulance Column RAMC
WOLSTENHOLME James MM Cpl 204281 Liverpool Regt
WOLSTENHOLME Joseph K. MM Cpl 438409 430 Fd Coy Royal Engineers
WOLSTENHOLME Sam MM L/Cpl 2470 Cheshire Regt
WOLSTENHOLME William MM+Bar Sjt 7732 2nd Royal Scots Fusiliers
WOLTON Ernest F.E. MM L/Cpl 702613 23rd London Regt
WOMACK Frank P. MM Pte 4978 Royal Fusiliers
WOMACK Thomas Hedley MM L/Cpl 14756 1/4th Suffolk Regt KIA 23.3.18.
WOMBWELL Harry MM Gnr 66233 11 Bde RFA
WOMERSLEY A. MM L/Cpl P5158 Military Foot Police
WOMERSLEY Albert MM Sjt 22894 Northumberland Fusiliers
WOMERSLEY Edgar MM L/Cpl 201823 5th West Riding Regt
WOMERSLEY Frank MM Dvr 766013 49 Div Ammn Col RFA
WOMERSLEY Harold Walker MM Gnr 780719 B/311 Bde RFA
WOMERSLEY Harry MM Pte 235096 Yorkshire Light Infantry
WOMERSLEY James MM Pte 71064 102 Coy Machine Gun Corps
WOOD Abraham MM Pte 19963 3rd Grenadier Guards
WOOD Albert MM Gnr 29111 152 Bde RFA
WOOD Albert Archer "MM,MID" Sjt 6943 82 Bde RFA
WOOD Albert Edward MM+Bar Pte 17031 2nd Hampshire Regt
WOOD Alexander MM Pte 13899 5th Dorsetshire Regt
WOOD Alexander MM Pte 2321 1/6th Seaforth Highlanders
WOOD Alexander MM+Bar Pte 265762 Gordon Highlanders
WOOD Alexander MM Sjt 76443 Signal Service Royal Engineers att 64 Bde RFA.
WOOD Alexander F. MM Sjt 2620 24th Royal Fusiliers
WOOD Alexander Ritchie "MC,DCM,MM(6751 CSM 1/7th Bn)" Capt 1/4th Royal Highlanders
WOOD Alfred MM Pte 290008 Gloucestershire Regt
WOOD Alfred MM Pte 12323 7th East Lancashire Regt
WOOD Alfred MM RSM 4402 HQ 123 Bde RFA
WOOD Alfred MM Gnr 105272 RGA
WOOD Alfred MM Bdr 53038 35 Bde RFA
WOOD Alfred MM Sjt L/9817 6th East Kent Regt KIA 11.7.17.
WOOD Alfred Ernest MM Pte 3240 12th Royal Fusiliers KIA 31.7.17.
WOOD Allen Stanley MM Sjt 106225 6th Bn Machine Gun Corps
WOOD Andrew MM L/Cpl M2/153183 Army Service Corps
WOOD Andrew MM Pte 12951 1st Bedfordshire Regt KIA 31.11.17.
WOOD Andrew MM Pte 18491 2nd Gordon Highlanders
WOOD Arthur MM CQMS 200770 West Riding Regt
WOOD Arthur MM Cpl 11974 1st Royal Lancaster Regt
WOOD Arthur MM L/Cpl 308261 Liverpool Regt
WOOD Arthur "MM,MID" L/Cpl 1517 1/6th Cheshire Regt
WOOD Arthur "MM+Bar,MID" L/Sjt 426 7th East Surrey Regt KIA 19.11.16.
WOOD Arthur MM Gnr 200800 Tank Corps
WOOD Arthur Edward MM Sjt 15/1008 15th West Yorkshire Regt DOW 15.4.18.
WOOD Arthur H. MM Pte 42575 Worcestershire Regt
WOOD Arthur J. MM Cpl 240458 1/8th Worcestershire Regt
WOOD Arthur R. MM Pte 75941 55 Fd Amb RAMC
WOOD Basil MM Gnr 100753 RGA
WOOD Bertie A. MM L/Cpl 9516 1st Royal Fusiliers
WOOD Bertram C. MM Pte 18046 Royal Scots
WOOD Birkby "DCM,MM" L/Cpl 327247 1/9th Durham Light Infantry
WOOD C. MM Cpl 9045 Yorkshire Light Infantry
WOOD C. MM Pte 41685 2nd Northumberland Fusiliers
WOOD Cecil MM Pte 350981 1/9th Durham Light Infantry

WOOD Charles MM Pte 14518 10th Notts & Derby Regt
WOOD Charles MM Pte 33000 RAMC
WOOD Charles MM Dvr 134043 12 Bty 24 Bde RFA
WOOD Charles Frederick MM Sjt M2/152435 Army Service Corps
WOOD Charles Henry MM L/Cpl T2/02309 47 Div Train Army Service Corps
WOOD Charles S. MM Pte 34935 East Lancashire Regt
WOOD Charles S.D. MM Pte 22564 1/6th Seaforth Highlanders
WOOD Charles W. MM Sjt 53808 4th Liverpool Regt
WOOD Charley MM Gnr 77841 RGA
WOOD Claude H. MM Sjt 238150 9th Yorkshire Light Infantry
WOOD D.A. MM Air Mech 3 134709 Royal Air Force
WOOD Douglas J. MM(38311 Yorks Regt)+Bar Sjt 72480 2nd West Yorkshire Regt
WOOD E. MM Air Mech 2 61869 Royal Flying Corps
WOOD E.C. MM L/Cpl 10059 1st East Kent Regt
WOOD E.S. MM L/Cpl 14121 Essex Regt
WOOD Edgar MM Cpl 28130 C/93 Bde RFA DOW 12.11.16.
WOOD Edmund MM Cpl 28713 33rd Bn Machine Gun Corps
WOOD Edward MM Cpl 200291 Lancashire Fusiliers
WOOD Edward MM Spr 13968 Royal Engineers
WOOD Edward MM Pte 10486 Coldstream Guards
WOOD Edward R. MM Pte 34544 8th East Surrey Regt
WOOD Edwin MM L/Bdr 85172 200 Siege Bty RGA
WOOD Ernest MM Pte 1616 1/7th West Riding Regt DOW 23.9.16.
WOOD Ernest S. MM CQMS 31782 4th Yorkshire Light Infantry
WOOD Evelyn H. MM CQMS 8167 2nd Suffolk Regt
WOOD Francis J. MM Pte 9210 2nd Worcestershire Regt
WOOD Frank MM L/Cpl 242102 2nd Yorkshire Light Infantry KIA 4.11.18.
WOOD Frank MM Pte 42430 4th Hampshire Regt
WOOD Frank MM Sjt 1025 15th Hussars
WOOD Frank MM+Bar Pte 241719 8th Worcestershire Regt
WOOD Frank MM L/Cpl 16217 8th West Riding Regt
WOOD Frank L. MM Pnr 549980 Royal Engineers
WOOD Frank W. MM Sjt 16539 20th York & Lancaster Regt
WOOD Fred MM Pte 16563 7th North Staffordshire Regt
WOOD Fred MM Pte C/22 16th King's Royal Rifle Corps
WOOD Fred MM Sjt 15532 9th North Lancashire Regt
WOOD Fred "DCM,MM" CSM 201191 1/4th West Riding Regt
WOOD Frederick MM Pte 66848 140 Fd Amb RAMC
WOOD Frederick MM Pte 13849 10th Cheshire Regt DOW 5.8.17.
WOOD Frederick Archie MM Sjt 14935 9th Leicestershire Regt
WOOD Frederick Charles John MM Sjt 930425 A/281 Bde RFA
WOOD Frederick D. MM Sjt 348112 RGA
WOOD Frederick G.H. MM Pte 29481 Duke of Cornwall's LI
WOOD Frederick George MM Sjt 13814 9th Devonshire Regt
WOOD Frederick Harold MM Sjt 965293 35 Bty 22 Bde RFA
WOOD Frederick T. MM Pte 4179 2nd Dragoon Guards
WOOD Frederick William MM Dvr 806214 147 Bde RFA
WOOD G. MM Pte 303288 RAMC
WOOD G.H. MM Pte 401033 1(West Riding)Fd Amb RAMC
WOOD G.W.A. MM Dvr 59678 3 Div Ammn Col RFA
WOOD George MM Pte M2/200713 Army Service Corps
WOOD George MM Pte 1303 1/8th West Yorkshire Regt
WOOD George MM Pte 7589 Coldstream Guards
WOOD George MM Pte 39188 56 Fd Amb RAMC DOW 21.10.17.
WOOD George MM Pte 201122 1/4th South Lancashire Regt KIA 20.9.17.
WOOD George MM Sjt 240541 1/5th Gordon Highlanders KIA 24.7.18.
WOOD George MM Sjt 6466 1st Wiltshire Regt
WOOD George E. MM L/Cpl 4092 1st Welsh Guards
WOOD George Fleming MM Pte 14770 1st Northumberland Fusiliers DOW 29.4.18.
WOOD George H. MM Sjt 11325 9th Cheshire Regt
WOOD George Richard MM Sjt 7218 East Surrey Regt
WOOD George W. MM L/Cpl 5539 3rd Dragoon Guards
WOOD Gilbert MM Pte 10372 9th Devonshire Regt DOW 4.10.17.
WOOD H. MM Cpl 240291 Worcestershire Regt
WOOD H. MM L/Cpl 260002 Royal Lancaster Regt
WOOD H.W. MM Pte 420764 London Regt
WOOD Harold MM Pte 43646 21st Manchester Regt
WOOD Harold MM Cpl 388056 2 Fd Amb RAMC
WOOD Harold P. MM L/Cpl 19276 Machine Gun Corps
WOOD Harold Vernon MM Cpl 48646 57 Bty 45 Bde RFA KIA 24.6.17.
WOOD Harry MM Cpl 35355 8th Bn Machine Gun Corps
WOOD Harry MM Cpl 11803 10th West Riding Regt
WOOD Harry MM L/Sjt 15411 3rd Coldstream Guards Died 13.4.18.
WOOD Harry MM Pte 114987 242 Coy Machine Gun Corps
WOOD Harry "MM,MID" S/Sjt Farrier T/50 50 Div Train Army Service Corps
WOOD Harry MM Sjt 10483 Cheshire Regt
WOOD Harry MM+Bar Pte 23414 Worcestershire Regt
WOOD Harry MM Bdr 775953 C/245 Bde RFA
WOOD Harry A. MM S/Sjt Fitter 285873 445 Siege Bty RGA
WOOD Harry B. MM Sjt 17080 12th West Yorkshire Regt
WOOD Harry Blanshard "VC,MM" L/Sjt 16444 2nd Scots Guards
WOOD Harry Edwin MM L/Cpl 24093 1st South Staffordshire Regt
WOOD Harry G. MM Pte 11376 2nd Wiltshire Regt
WOOD Harry P. MM Sjt 12924 Army Cyclist Corps
WOOD Harry W. MM Pte 5825 6th Royal West Kent Regt
WOOD Henry MM Bdr 38237 RFA
WOOD Henry MM L/Cpl 352998 Royal Scots
WOOD Henry MM Pte 9359 2nd South Staffordshire Regt
WOOD Henry Edward MM Sjt 11982 6th Dorsetshire Regt
WOOD Herbert MM Pte M/283050 Army Service Corps
WOOD Herbert MM Pte S/7377 1st Rifle Brigade KIA 6.7.15.
WOOD Herbert Edward MM Pte 23970 Essex Regt
WOOD Herbert Henry MM+Bar L/Cpl 11670 6th East Kent Regt
WOOD Horace MM Sjt 27831 9th Lancashire Fusiliers
WOOD Horace MM Pte 7930 1st Leicestershire Regt
WOOD Horace Alfred MM Pte 13216 7th Bedfordshire Regt DOW 25.10.17.
WOOD J.Charlton MM Cpl 64066 RAMC
WOOD J.T. MM Sjt 44955 Royal Engineers
WOOD James MM Cpl 36466 49th Bn Machine Gun Corps
WOOD James MM+Bar Cpl 10956 15th Lancashire Fusiliers
WOOD James MM Pte 2445 3rd Coldstream Guards KIA 15.9.16.
WOOD James MM Dvr 1086 12 Bty 5(London)Bde RFA
WOOD James MM Pte 15521 2nd Scots Guards KIA 27.3.18.
WOOD James MM Pte 25414 Royal Inniskilling Fusiliers
WOOD James Abram MM L/Sjt 19041 1st Grenadier Guards KIA 10.9.16.
WOOD James Frederick MM Pte 348042 8th Manchester Regt
WOOD James H. MM L/Bdr 103905 RGA
WOOD Jesse MM L/Cpl 24566 13th Liverpool Regt
WOOD John MM Pte 265703 1/6th Royal Highlanders
WOOD John MM Cpl 8696 Gordon Highlanders
WOOD John MM Pte 22976 2nd Royal Scots Fusiliers
WOOD John MM Gnr 68847 RGA
WOOD John MM L/Cpl 275297 5/6th Royal Scots DOW 21.7.18.
WOOD John MM Dvr 751219 250 Bde RFA Died 29.9.18.
WOOD John "DCM+Bar,MM" Sjt 8090 1st Liverpool Regt
WOOD John MM Pte T4/085379 Army Service Corps
WOOD John MM Cpl 16897 10th North Lancashire Regt
WOOD John MM Pte 23706 12th South Wales Borderers DOW 16.7.17.
WOOD John MM Cpl 21674 RGA
WOOD John MM Gnr 221270 RFA
WOOD John MM 2nd Cpl 197922 Royal Engineers
WOOD John MM Pte 5463 Machine Gun Corps
WOOD John A. MM Sjt 6871 2nd Durham Light Infantry
WOOD John F. MM Pte 6619 1st Royal Lancaster Regt
WOOD John George MM 2nd Cpl 67913 145 Army Troops Coy Royal Engineers
WOOD John H. MM Pte 571456 17th London Regt
WOOD John Henry MM L/Cpl 38162 15th Lancashire Fusiliers KIA 20.3.18.
WOOD John R. MM S/Sjt 96868 11th Bn Tank Corps
WOOD John T. MM Pte 27126 8th East Surrey Regt
WOOD John T. MM Gnr 57392 V/37 Heavy TM Bty RFA
WOOD John W. MM Pte 47672 8th Lancashire Fusiliers
WOOD John W. MM+Bar Cpl 18332 8th Yorkshire Regt
WOOD John William MM L/Cpl 20516 XVIII Corps Cyclist Bn Army Cyclist Corps KIA 27.3.18.
WOOD Joseph MM Pte M2/148604 Army Service Corps att 'N'(AA)Bty RGA.
WOOD Joseph MM+Bar Pte 9408 1st Scottish Rifles
WOOD Joseph MM L/Sjt 15403 24th Manchester Regt
WOOD Joseph MM+Bar Pte 51766 19 Fd Amb RAMC
WOOD Joseph W. "DCM,MM" Sjt 82129 170 Tunnelling Coy Royal Engineers
WOOD Lawrence J. MM Pte 493017 13th London Regt
WOOD Leonard MM Pte 13097 1st Grenadier Guards
WOOD Leonard William MM Pte M2/054953 Army Service Corps att 2/2(Northumbrian)Fd Amb.Died 29.10.18.
WOOD Leslie MM Cpl 1849 1/5th Northumberland Fusiliers KIA 11.9.16.

WOOD Leslie Giilbert Milford MM Pte B/200393 13th Rifle Brigade KIA 20.7.18.
WOOD Leslie R. MM Pte 14757 8th Suffolk Regt
WOOD Lewis H. MM Pte 137375 62nd Bn Machine Gun Corps
WOOD Mark MM Pte 8608 4th King's Royal Rifle Corps
WOOD Martin E. MM L/Cpl 40813 West Yorkshire Regt
WOOD Matthew MM L/Sjt 44710 2nd Northumberland Fusiliers
WOOD Matthew MM Cpl 23926 Highland Light Infantry
WOOD Minnie MM Sister F QAIMNS
WOOD Norman MM Pte 5410 Royal West Surrey Regt
WOOD P. MM 2nd Cpl 86311 172 Tunnelling Coy Royal Engineers
WOOD Percy MM Dvr 776659 RFA
WOOD Percy MM Spr 700 Royal Engineers
WOOD Percy G. MM+Bar L/Sjt 33898 RAMC
WOOD Percy W. "MM,MID" Sjt 906 3rd Rifle Brigade
WOOD Radcliffe MM L/Sjt B/234 13th Rifle Brigade
WOOD Ralph MM Pte 12536 2nd West Riding Regt KIA 2.10.18.
WOOD Reginald MM Dvr T4/199968 Army Service Corps
WOOD Richard MM Pte 13248 3rd Worcestershire Regt
WOOD Richard MM Cpl 2255 1/4th Royal Highlanders
WOOD Richard C. MM Sjt T/29050 Army Service Corps
WOOD Richard T. "DCM,MM(1/6th Bn)" Sjt 265555 6/7th Gordon Highlanders
WOOD Robert MM Pte 266909 1/7th Gordon Highlanders KIA 25.10.18.
WOOD Robert L. MM Sjt 76343 RGA
WOOD Robert M. MM Sjt 305811 Royal Warwickshire Regt
WOOD Sidney J.M. MM Sjt 916038 RFA
WOOD Stanley MM Dmr 45167 2nd Lancashire Fusiliers KIA 2.9.18.
WOOD Stanley R. MM S/Sjt 153 25 Fd Amb RAMC
WOOD Stuart Comber MM L/Bdr 88476 171 Siege Bty RGA
WOOD Sylvester MM Pte 12797 8th West Riding Regt
WOOD Thomas MM Cpl 26284 1st Gloucestershire Regt
WOOD Thomas MM Pte 265791 2/4th West Riding Regt
WOOD Thomas MM Pte 122674 Machine Gun Corps
WOOD Thomas MM Sjt 480057 Royal Engineers
WOOD Thomas MM+Bar Sjt 57780 RAMC
WOOD Thomas MM Dvr 444284 58 Div Sig Coy Royal Engineers
WOOD Thomas Collier MM L/Cpl 16846 7th Leicestershire Regt
WOOD Thomas E. MM Cpl 12112 8th East Surrey Regt
WOOD Thomas E. MM L/Cpl 471164 12th London Regt
WOOD Thomas H. MM Dvr 34766 RFA
WOOD Thomas H. MM Pte 13064 Labour Corps
WOOD Thomas Irvin MM Pte 20189 10th West Riding Regt
WOOD Thomas McDougall MM Sjt 9893 1st Scots Guards
WOOD Thomas S. MM Pte 20929 Army Cyclist Corps
WOOD Thomas William "MM,MID" Pte M2/054734 Army Service Corps att 54 Fd Amb RAMC.
WOOD W. MM Dvr 107127 RFA
WOOD W. MM Sjt 108037 25th Liverpool Regt
WOOD W. MM Pte 36391 1st Essex Regt
WOOD Walter MM Bdr 24414 RFA
WOOD Walter Charles MM Sjt 5910 11 Coy Machine Gun Corps DOW 4.8.17.
WOOD Walter Leonard MM Cpl 82222 23rd Royal Fusiliers Died 1.11.18.
WOOD Wilfred MM(200119 Pte 5th DLI)+Bar Cpl 235937 4th York & Lancaster Regt
WOOD Wilfred Harry MM Pte 47519 2(Cavalry)Fd Amb RAMC DOW 30.11.17.
WOOD Wilfred T. MM Bdr 561 RFA
WOOD William MM CSM 200485 1/4th York & Lancaster Regt
WOOD William MM Pte 260140 6th South Staffordshire Regt
WOOD William MM Pte 365124 7th London Regt
WOOD William MM Cpl 491995 46 Div Sig Coy Royal Engineers
WOOD William MM Cpl 14039 Gordon Highlanders
WOOD William MM Pte 29399 2nd Manchester Regt
WOOD William MM Pte 5867 6th Dragoons DOW 26.6.18.
WOOD William MM Pte R/2428 King's Royal Rifle Corps
WOOD William MM+Bar L/Cpl 6122 1st Middlesex Regt
WOOD William A.H. MM L/Cpl 1146 17th Royal Fusiliers
WOOD William Ainsworth MM Pte M2/103571 Army Service Corps
WOOD William Arthur MM Pte 49109 1st Cheshire Regt
WOOD William E. MM Pte 24844 Royal Warwickshire Regt
WOOD William F. MM L/Sjt 41561 12th Royal Scots
WOOD William Francis MM Pte 1886 23rd Royal Fusiliers KIA 10.4.18.
WOOD William H. MM+Bar Pnr 611851 30 Div Sig Coy Royal Engineers
WOOD William H. "MM,MSM,MID" Sjt 7688 2nd Leinster Regt
WOOD William Henry MM Gnr 68213 RHA
WOOD William Henry MM+Bar Cpl 9098 1st Royal Irish Rifles
WOOD William J. MM Sjt 14392 9th Royal Fusiliers
WOOD William J. MM L/Cpl 50306 Royal Engineers
WOOD William Owen MM Cpl 34514 1/1(London)Heavy Bty RGA
WOODACRE Henry "MM,MID" Sjt 59209 42 Bde RFA
WOODALL Clement MM Cpl 15209 Cheshire Regt
WOODALL Harry MM L/Cpl 52796 Durham Light Infantry
WOODALL John J. MM Pte 41907 4th Bedfordshire Regt
WOODALL John William MM Pte 241508 5th Yorkshire Light Infantry KIA 30.9.18.
WOODALL T.W. MM Pte 43464 King's Royal Rifle Corps
WOODALL William J. MM L/Sjt 41113 18th Lancashire Fusiliers
WOODARD Arthur T. MM Pte 53179 RAMC
WOODARD Jack MM Sjt 1531 1/4th Suffolk Regt
WOODARD Thomas A. MM Pte 6574 Royal West Surrey Regt
WOODARDS J. MM Pte M2/081827 Army Service Corps att RFA.
WOODBINE John MM Pte 19848 21st Manchester Regt
WOODBOURNE Harold MM Sjt 15242 Border Regt
WOODBURN Douglas C. MM Pte 4696 11th Arg & Suth Highlanders
WOODBURN Edward MM Bdr 36499 RFA
WOODBURN James MM Bdr 69392 270 Siege Bty RGA
WOODBURY Joseph MM Cpl 28571 Manchester Regt
WOODCOCK Albert E.A. MM Pte B/2770 Rifle Brigade
WOODCOCK Ernest MM Pte 266897 1/7th West Yorkshire Regt DOW 19.10.18.
WOODCOCK F. MM Cpl 625392 RGA
WOODCOCK Frank MM CSM 8227 2nd Leicestershire Regt
WOODCOCK George W. MM Gnr 94106 RFA
WOODCOCK H. MM Pte 42498 9th Norfolk Regt
WOODCOCK Harold A.L. MM Pte 14516 7th Wiltshire Regt
WOODCOCK Harry MM Sjt 23915 RFA
WOODCOCK Harry MM Pte 241876 North Lancashire Regt
WOODCOCK Harry Ernest MM L/Cpl 204543 1st Essex Regt DOW 4.11.18.
WOODCOCK James "MM,MID" Sjt 2066 1/1st Sherwood Rangers Yeo
WOODCOCK James E. MM+Bar Sjt 46596 4th North Staffordshire Regt
WOODCOCK Jesse MM Pte 42 6th East Kent Regt
WOODCOCK John MM L/Cpl 17101 1/4th North Lancashire Regt KIA 31.7.17.
WOODCOCK John Thomas MM Pte 14866 9th York & Lancaster Regt KIA 10.10.17.
WOODCOCK Joseph MM Pte 7824 1st Manchester Regt
WOODCOCK Richard MM Pte 240521 1/5th West Riding Regt
WOODCOCK Richard E. MM Pte 7992 1st Royal West Kent Regt
WOODCOCK Sidney MM Cpl 1163 East Surrey Regt
WOODCOCK Sidney Alfred MM Sjt M2/131155 641 MT Coy Army Service Corps att RFA.
WOODCOCK Stephen Henry MM Gnr 80187 B/52 Bde RFA
WOODCOCK Sydney E. MM Pte 350973 7th London Regt
WOODCOCK Tom MM Pte 7040 2/1st HAC(Infantry)
WOODCOCK W. MM Pte 23907 Norfolk Regt
WOODCOCK William MM Pte 68234 2nd London Regt
WOODCOCK William "MM,MID" Sjt 7707 2nd Oxf & Bucks Light Infantry
WOODCOCK William J. MM Pte 24849 7th Royal West Kent Regt
WOODCRAFT George MM Pte 29766 Worcestershire Regt
WOODEND James Daniel MM Pte M/301977 406 MT Coy Army Service Corps
WOODEND Leslie H. MM Pte 11012 5th Shropshire Light Infantry
WOODEND Reginald MM Cpl 16958 18th Lancashire Fusiliers DOW 3.11.17.
WOODEND Robert MM Pte 13438 1/7th Gordon Highlanders
WOODERSON Charles MM Pte 6048 12 Fd Amb RAMC
WOODFALL R.B. MM Cpl 25833 Liverpool Regt
WOODFIELD Frederick MM Spr 71753 Royal Engineers
WOODFIELD Harry MM Pte 242310 6th Royal Warwickshire Regt
WOODFIELD Hubert MM L/Cpl 15750 7th Duke of Cornwall's LI DOW 11.2.17.
WOODFIELD John J. MM Sjt 14851 8th Royal Berkshire Regt
WOODFORD Charles King MM L/Cpl 22348 54 Fd Coy Royal Engineers KIA 22.10.17.
WOODFORD Frederick J. MM L/Cpl 277347 1/6th Essex Regt
WOODFORD George MM Spr 476972 464 Fd Coy Royal Engineers DOW 6.5.18.
WOODFORD George H. MM Cpl 478667 511 Fd Coy Royal Engineers
WOODFORD Jonah MM L/Sjt 9116 Oxf & Bucks Light Infantry

WOODGATE Arthur MM Pte 5345 8th East Surrey Regt
WOODGATE Arthur F. MM Pte 515248 14th London Regt
WOODGATE Reginald MM Pte 1875 24 Fd Amb. RAMC
WOODGATE Walter Roan "MM,MID" Cpl 21804 15 Fd Coy Royal Engineers KIA 31.1.17.
WOODGATES Ernest MM L/Cpl 8061 3rd Rifle Brigade
WOODGER James Henry MM Pte 241194 5th Yorkshire Regt
WOODGER Walter Thomas Stanley MM Sjt 44208 62 Fd Coy Royal Engineers KIA 21.3.18.
WOODHALL Charles V. MM Pte 203360 Yorkshire Light Infantry
WOODHALL John MM Sjt 66301 27 Fd Amb RAMC
WOODHALL John W. MM Pte 235076 Royal Lancaster Regt
WOODHAM A. MM C/Sjt 1064 Military Foot Police
WOODHAM Samuel T.H. MM Sjt 265405 Oxf & Bucks Light Infantry
WOODHAM William A. MM Sjt 92137 Royal Engineers
WOODHAM William Frederick MM Sjt 11579 11th Hampshire Regt
WOODHAMS Arthur MM Pte 15853 1st Scots Guards
WOODHAMS William T. MM Spr 541848 Royal Engineers
WOODHEAD Albert Edward MM L/Cpl 81463 16th Bn Machine Gun Corps
WOODHEAD Ambler MM Pte 201540 2/4th West Riding Regt KIA 30.8.18.
WOODHEAD Cecil Keswick MM CSM 10849 11th Royal West Surrey Regt
WOODHEAD Edmund C. MM Sjt 75976 RGA
WOODHEAD Frank MM+Bar Sjt 2452 1/7th Liverpool Regt
WOODHEAD Frederick MM Pte 265322 1/6th Cheshire Regt
WOODHEAD George MM Dvr T2/01881 5 Cav Reserve Park Army Service Corps
WOODHEAD Harry MM Pte 202227 4th West Riding Regt
WOODHEAD James A. MM Sjt 200191 6th West Riding Regt
WOODHEAD John J. MM Gnr 780755 B/311 Bde RFA
WOODHEAD John W. MM Pte 16252 8th Border Regt Died 23.11.18.
WOODHEAD Norman MM Pte 24575 ' Machine Gun Corps
WOODHEAD Thomas MM L/Cpl 46686 18th Lancashire Fusiliers
WOODHEAD Thomas MM Pte 27861 2nd Grenadier Guards
WOODHEAD William "MM,CG(It)" L/Cpl 15421 12th Durham Light Infantry
WOODHEAD William MM Pte 5736 1st King's Royal Rifle Corps
WOODHOUSE Albert MM Pte 15071 2nd West Riding Regt
WOODHOUSE Arthur MM L/Cpl 49792 Durham Light Infantry
WOODHOUSE Edward MM Cpl 421660 1/10th London Regt
WOODHOUSE Frank MM Gnr 680472 RFA
WOODHOUSE George MM Pte 6091 1/17th London Regt KIA 1.10.16.
WOODHOUSE Godfrey MM Cpl 58941 Notts & Derby Regt
WOODHOUSE Herbert Allen "MM,MSM" Sjt 876137 B/95 Bde RFA
WOODHOUSE Ivan E.F. MM Spr 558419 Royal Engineers
WOODHOUSE John MM L/Cpl 10617 19th Durham Light Infantry
WOODHOUSE Lawrence MM Sjt S/1805 Rifle Brigade
WOODHOUSE Sidney MM Pte 325486 1/1st Cambridgeshire Regt
WOODHOUSE Thomas John MM Pte 31398 6th King's Own Scottish Borderers
WOODHOUSE William MM Pte 12047 7th King's Royal Rifle Corps
WOODHOUSE William MM Sjt 7646 8th York & Lancaster Regt DOW 4.7.17.
WOODHOUSE William H. MM L/Cpl 72746 Royal Engineers
WOODING Charles H. MM L/Cpl 14634 Royal Engineers
WOODING John F. MM Cpl 21498 2nd South Wales Borderers
WOODINGTON Arthur H. MM Cpl(MCDR) 28176 3 Div Sig Coy Royal Engineers
WOODINGTON Frederick H.L. MM Pte 202809 1/6th Arg & Suth Highlanders
WOODIWISS Ellison MM Pte 240787 1/6th West Yorkshire Regt
WOODLAND Herbert William MM+Bar Sjt 151585 182 Tunnelling Coy Royal Engineers
WOODLAND James B. MM L/Cpl 692 1/9th London Regt
WOODLAND Richard J. MM Pte 202207 Somerset Light Infantry
WOODLAND Robert George MM L/Cpl 17618 1st East Surrey Regt
WOODLAND Sam MM L/Cpl 2098 1/2nd Monmouthshire Regt
WOODLEY Alfred E. MM Gnr 26897 50 Div TM Bty RFA
WOODLEY Edward MM Sjt 10291 5th Royal Berkshire Regt
WOODLEY Frank W.C. MM Sjt 117053 291 Siege Bty RGA
WOODLEY George H. MM Sjt 40628 1st Royal Scots
WOODLEY Walter MM L/Cpl 17842 8th Royal Berkshire Regt KIA 20.3.18.
WOODLIFFE William Robert MM Dvr 800424 230 Bde RFA
WOODMAN Alfred MM Bdr 39590 420 Heavy Bty RGA DOW 18.4.17.

WOODMAN Dennis MM Pte 40627 9th North Staffordshire Regt
WOODMAN Edwin George MM Pte 58524 17th Welsh Regt KIA 25.11.17.
WOODMAN John MM Pte 242356 5th Gloucestershire Regt
WOODMAN Robert MM Sjt 10991 1st Scottish Rifles KIA 26.11.17.
WOODMAN William A. MM Sjt 9044 1st East Surrey Regt
WOODMORE William "MM,MID" Pte 330088 1/8th Hampshire Regt
WOODROFFE Frederick MM Gnr 8889 46 Bty 39 Bde RFA
WOODROOFFE Frederick E. MM Pte 15179 1 Special Coy Middlesex Regt
WOODROW Alfred Frank MM Sjt 5901 Machine Gun Corps
WOODROW Charles Edward MM Pte 35110 12th Suffolk Regt "DOW 11.4.18,"
WOODROW Charles W. MM Cpl 18994 2/4th Royal West Kent Regt
WOODROW Robert W. MM Pte 31885 8th Northumberland Fusiliers
WOODROW William J. MM Pte 3889 7th Dragoon Guards
WOODRUFF John Thomas MM Pte 22/1014 13th Durham Light Infantry
WOODRUFF William MM Pte 41678 1st Royal Irish Rifles
WOODRUFF William John "MM,MM(F)" Sjt 49917 85 Coy Machine Gun Corps
WOODRUFFE Walter MM Pte 29170 East Lancashire Regt
WOODS Albert E. MM Pte 240986 Lincolnshire Regt
WOODS Arthur MM Gnr 80988 RGA
WOODS Arthur MM Sjt 9885 2nd Royal Irish Regt
WOODS Arthur J. MM Sjt 1086 6th Royal West Surrey Regt
WOODS Arthur R. MM Pte 2012 1/6th Seaforth Highlanders
WOODS Arthur Vincent MM Cpl 72938 'K' Corps Sig Coy Royal Engineers
WOODS Augustus R. MM Pte 6676 7 Fd Amb RAMC
WOODS C.W. MM Pte 5264 3rd Rifle Brigade
WOODS C.W. MM Sjt 9123 1st Scottish Rifles
WOODS Cedric MM Cpl 5002 10th Northumberland Fusiliers
WOODS Charles MM Gnr 155782 RFA
WOODS Charles E.V. MM Pte 235393 2nd South Staffordshire Regt
WOODS Charles Ernest "MM,MSM" QMS 1378 Scots Guards
WOODS Charles R. MM Cpl 11456 8th East Surrey Regt
WOODS Cyril G. "DCM,MM" L/Cpl 27206 2/7th Royal Warwickshire Regt
WOODS Ernest MM Pte 36345 Leicestershire Regt
WOODS Ernest Alfred MM Cpl 2987 2/6th Royal Warwickshire Regt
WOODS Ernest G. MM Bdr 56298 14 Bde RFA
WOODS Ernest V. MM Sjt 55503 36 Bde RFA
WOODS Fred MM S/Sjt Mechanician M2/200564 Army Service Corps
WOODS Fred MM Sjt 8349 2nd West Yorkshire Regt
WOODS Frederick Charles MM L/Sjt 22778 East Lancashire Regt
WOODS Frederick T. MM Pte R/39975 1st King's Royal Rifle Corps
WOODS Frederick Thomas MM Pte 22229 10th Royal Fusiliers DOW 14.5.18.
WOODS George MM L/Cpl 56601 2nd Hampshire Regt
WOODS George F. MM L/Cpl 121111 Royal Engineers
WOODS George H. MM Sjt 64456 RGA
WOODS George William "MM,SMV(S)" Pte 3/26916 9th East Lancashire Regt
WOODS Herbert MM Cpl 2107 7th Leinster Regt
WOODS Herbert E. MM Sjt R/34447 2nd King's Royal Rifle Corps
WOODS Horace MM Cpl 721807 1/24th London Regt
WOODS James MM Sjt 8136 2nd York & Lancaster Regt KIA 21.3.18.
WOODS James Leo MM Gnr 188417 A/87 Bde RFA KIA 23.9.18.
WOODS Jesse MM Sjt 16754 Machine Gun Corps
WOODS John MM Pte 8430 Royal West Kent Regt
WOODS John MM Sjt 13668 6th Lincolnshire Regt
WOODS John Charles MM Pte M2/077129 Army Service Corps
WOODS John William MM Pte 36332 231 Coy Machine Gun Corps
WOODS Joseph MM Pte 32959 11th Royal Lancaster Regt
WOODS Joseph MM L/Cpl 10280 2nd Leinster Regt
WOODS Joseph MM Spr 46484 Royal Engineers
WOODS Joseph H. MM Cpl 10274 King's Royal Rifle Corps
WOODS Lewis S. MM Cpl 38128 RGA
WOODS Malcolm MM Pte 24308 1st West Yorkshire Regt
WOODS Patrick MM Cpl 29765 Yorkshire Regt
WOODS Rennie MM Pte 39794 2nd Lancashire Fusiliers
WOODS Richard Anders MM Pte 2065 Liverpool Regt
WOODS Robert MM Pte 240721 11th Suffolk Regt
WOODS S.J. MM Sjt S/9751 13th Rifle Brigade
WOODS Seymour V. MM Pte M2/077919 Army Service Corps
WOODS Thomas MM Pte 15518 Lancashire Fusiliers
WOODS Thomas MM Sjt 13005 7th Lincolnshire Regt

WOODS Victor Cecil Walter MM Cpl 513615 1/14th London Regt
WOODS Walter "MM,MSM,MC(G)" Cpl 6119 12th Hampshire Regt
WOODS Walter MM Pte 16773 10th North Lancashire Regt KIA 28.4.17.
WOODS William MM Sjt 265045 1/6th West Riding Regt
WOODS William MM L/Cpl 7661 95 Coy Machine Gun Corps KIA 15.4.18.
WOODS William MM Pte 8431 6th Dragoon Guards
WOODS William MM+Bar 2nd Cpl 436009 Royal Engineers
WOODS William C. MM Sjt 42544 30 Bde RFA
WOODS William J. MM Pte 570463 1/17th London Regt
WOODS William R. MM L/Cpl 11580 1st Gloucestershire Regt
WOODSIDE Sydney MM L/Cpl 10564 2nd Royal Irish Rifles
WOODSIDE William John MM Cpl 14/6905 14th Royal Irish Rifles
WOODSTOCK Ernest A. MM L/Cpl 253812 18 Div Sig Coy Royal Engineers
WOODTHORPE Leonard Guy MM Sjt 810425 D/231 Bde RFA
WOODVINE John H. MM Pte 14198 7th North Staffordshire Regt
WOODWARD Albert MM Dvr 50523 37 Div Sig Coy Royal Engineers
WOODWARD Albert MM Cpl 6760 12th Lancashire Fusiliers
WOODWARD Arthur C. MM L/Cpl 31947 West Yorkshire Regt
WOODWARD Charles E. MM Spr 42411 Royal Engineers Died 26.6.19
WOODWARD Charles Edgar MM Gnr 78845 156 Siege Bty RGA
WOODWARD Charles Frederick MM Pte 18596 1st Notts & Derby Regt
WOODWARD Charles William MM Cpl 1879 1/18th London Regt
WOODWARD Christopher MM Pte 18011 12th Durham Light Infantry
WOODWARD Edward "DCM,MM" Sjt 1441 Royal Fusiliers
WOODWARD Edward A. MM Cpl 32044 Royal Engineers
WOODWARD F. MM Cpl 79004 Royal Flying Corps
WOODWARD Frank MM Dvr 80126 A/113 Bde RFA
WOODWARD Frank MM 2nd Cpl 52069 82 Fd Coy Royal Engineers
WOODWARD George L. MM Sjt 701448 RFA
WOODWARD George T. MM Pte 6410 16th King's Royal Rifle Corps
WOODWARD George William MM Pte 43188 12th Royal Irish Rifles
WOODWARD Gerald F. MM Pte 18807 7th Gloucestershire Regt
WOODWARD Harold "MC,MM(2891 Pte 1/5th Bn)" Lt 5th att 4th North Staffordshire Regt
WOODWARD Harry MM Pte 24611 18th Liverpool Regt
WOODWARD Henry MM L/Cpl 23297 10th Royal Welsh Fusiliers
WOODWARD Herbert MM Pte 8/40537 8th South Staffordshire Regt
WOODWARD Herbert E. MM Gnr 291372 RGA
WOODWARD Horace A. MM Dvr 14962 86 Bty 32 Bde RFA
WOODWARD James H. MM Cpl 91456 9th Bn Tank Corps
WOODWARD James W. MM L/Cpl 290658 1/7th Royal Highlanders
WOODWARD John MM Sjt 65895 11th Bn Machine Gun Corps DOW 11.9.18.
WOODWARD John MM Pte 59635 Notts & Derby Regt att MGC.
WOODWARD John G.H. MM Cpl 310791 Royal Engineers
WOODWARD John H. MM Sjt 640 1st Royal Warwickshire Regt
WOODWARD John H. MM Pte 20514 18 Fd Amb RAMC
WOODWARD Martin E. MM Sjt 49877 Royal Fusiliers
WOODWARD Pearce MM Pte 137578 33rd Bn Machine Gun Corps
WOODWARD Percy MM L/Cpl 265644 Royal Warwickshire Regt
WOODWARD Peter H. MM L/Cpl 36784 East Lancashire Regt
WOODWARD Sidney MM Pte 17858 9th Cheshire Regt
WOODWARD Stanley MM Pte 242881 Liverpool Regt
WOODWARD Sydney Forest MM L/Sjt 19291 Cheshire Regt DOW 19.10.18.
WOODWARD Thomas A. MM 2nd Cpl 308968 Royal Engineers
WOODWARD Walter MM Sjt 12910 16th Royal Warwickshire Regt
WOODWARD William MM Sjt Y/872 King's Royal Rifle Corps
WOODWARD William MM Sjt 201538 South Lancashire Regt
WOODWARD William Burrill MM Cpl 426180 419 Fd Coy Royal Engineers
WOODWARD William C. MM Cpl 13818 7th Wiltshire Regt
WOODWARD William J. "DCM,MM" Pte 16958 7th North Staffordshire Regt
WOODWORTH Christopher MM Gnr 4130 RFA
WOODWORTH Thomas William MM Cpl 17516 Liverpool Regt
WOOF Joseph MM Dvr 24588 RFA
WOOF Thomas MM Sjt 1248 13th Rifle Brigade KIA 13.9.18.
WOOFFINDIN Vincent MM Gnr 60421 114 Siege Bty RGA
WOOKEY George MM Cpl 10575 Royal West Kent Regt
WOOKEY Percy S. MM Gnr 66271 RGA

WOOLACOTT Noah James MM Pte 9438 2nd Devonshire Regt
WOOLARD Harold MM+Bar Sjt 12400 2nd Scots Guards
WOOLASS Wilfred MM Pte 15987 1st Lincolnshire Regt
WOOLCOCK Alfred MM Spr 19965 23 Fd Coy Royal Engineers DOW 5.11.18.
WOOLCOCK John MM Bdr 128286 RGA
WOOLCOTT Israel MM Sjt 15428 9th York & Lancaster Regt
WOOLCOTT Lewis W. MM Sjt 240070 5th Devonshire Regt
WOOLCOTT Walter G. MM Gnr 28403 RFA
WOOLDRIDGE Bertam MM Dvr 219484 30 Div Ammn Col RFA
WOOLDRIDGE Dick MM Pte 11998 1st Grenadier Guards
WOOLDRIDGE Edmund James MM Pte 24013 2nd Lancashire Fusiliers
WOOLDRIDGE F.G. MM L/Cpl 18848 Essex Regt
WOOLDRIDGE Frederick W. MM Pte 3466 9th Lancers
WOOLDRIDGE George MM L/Sjt 3454 50th Bn Machine Gun Corps
WOOLDRIDGE John H. MM Pte 20292 2nd Worcestershire Regt
WOOLDRIDGE Joseph MM Dvr 92486 Royal Engineers
WOOLERSON Albert George MM Pte 201516 7th Bedfordshire Regt
WOOLEY George F. MM Sjt 5559 19th Hussars
WOOLEY William E. MM Pte 242425 North Staffordshire Regt
WOOLF David MM Pte 630043 20th London Regt
WOOLF Henry Richard MM Pte 8056 2nd Lincolnshire Regt
WOOLF James MM Pte 40491 Essex Regt
WOOLFORD Arthur MM Pte 22201 Yorkshire Light Infantry
WOOLFORD Charles H. MM Gnr 98047 RFA
WOOLFORD Henry J. MM L/Sjt 18042 Gloucestershire Regt
WOOLFORD Herbert T. MM Cpl 24559 Wiltshire Regt
WOOLFORD Phillip MM Sjt 86950 178 Tunnelling Coy Royal Engineers DOW 2.10.16.
WOOLFSON Frank MM Sjt 30289 RFA
WOOLFSON Paul MM Pte 22884 Royal Scots Fusiliers
WOOLGAR Arthur E. MM Pte R/10160 9th King's Royal Rifle Corps
WOOLGAR George MM Cpl 592048 18th London Regt
WOOLGAR George MM Pte 2621 8th Royal Sussex Regt
WOOLGAR George MM Pte 25355 11th Royal West Kent Regt
WOOLGAR William MM Gnr 66436 3 Bde RHA
WOOLHAM Harold MM L/Cpl 240737 1/6th West Yorkshire Regt
WOOLLAM Arthur S. MM Pte 1510 Royal Sussex Regt
WOOLLAM Thomas MM Pte 90945 4th Liverpool Regt
WOOLLANDS Harry MM Dvr 75911 B/94 Bde RFA
WOOLLARD Arthur W. MM L/Cpl 21255 Royal West Surrey Regt
WOOLLARD Bernard MM Sjt 50504 D/3 Bde RHA
WOOLLARD Bertie E. MM Cpl 2470 Suffolk Regt
WOOLLARD Cyril MM Pte 14899 13th Royal Sussex Regt
WOOLLARD Frederick Benjamin MM Sjt 260193 1/8th Worcestershire Regt
WOOLLARD John MM Sjt 3199 11th Royal Fusiliers
WOOLLAS John William MM L/Cpl 36947 Royal Berkshire Regt
WOOLLATT Percy MM Sjt 7761 1st East Yorkshire Regt KIA 28.5.18.
WOOLLER Arthur H. MM+Bar L/Sjt 361679 9th & 34th London Regt
WOOLLERSON Frank E. MM Spr 86687 Royal Engineers
WOOLLETT Charles MM Sjt 165 23rd Royal Fusiliers
WOOLLETT H. MM Bdr 358114 RGA
WOOLLEY Arthur MM Sjt 800432 C/230 Bde RFA
WOOLLEY C.W. MM Sjt 1450 Notts & Derby Regt
WOOLLEY Charles MM Pte 10472 Royal Sussex Regt
WOOLLEY Charles Robert "MC,MM+Bar(8508 Sjt 2nd Bn),MID" 2Lt 2nd South Staffordshire Regt
WOOLLEY Claude MM Cpl 3394 Notts & Derby Regt
WOOLLEY Ernest MM Dvr 75929 153 Bde RFA
WOOLLEY Ernest MM Pte 51627 22nd Manchester Regt
WOOLLEY Ernest R. MM Cpl 57146 69 Bde RFA
WOOLLEY Frank MM Sjt 45376 B/102 Bde RFA
WOOLLEY George Laurence "DCM,MM" CSM 6392 Leicestershire Regt
WOOLLEY John MM L/Cpl 4091 1/2nd London Regt
WOOLLEY John W. MM+Bar Pte 17580 2nd Royal Sussex Regt
WOOLLEY R.T. MM Cpl 840120 D/241 Bde RFA
WOOLLEY Robert MM+Bar Cpl 7302 West Riding Regt
WOOLLEY Samuel MM L/Cpl 61725 Rly Ops Div Royal Engineers
WOOLLEY Thomas MM Pte 23036 Manchester Regt
WOOLLEY Victor MM Cpl 240591 1/5th Leicestershire Regt
WOOLLEY Walter MM Cpl 12482 8th Shropshire Light Infantry
WOOLMER Frederick C. MM L/Sjt 20992 1st Coldstream Guards
WOOLNER Charles H. MM 2nd Cpl 550767 517 Fd Coy Royal Engineers
WOOLNOUGH Arthur MM Sjt 14136 8th Suffolk Regt Died 12.10.17.

WOOLNOUGH George MM Pte 10206 1st Royal West Surrey Regt
WOOLNOUGH James Trower MM Sjt 2292 1/4th Oxf & Bucks Light Infantry
WOOLNOUGH Wilfred C. MM Gnr 75918 RGA
WOOLRICH Harry "MM,MID" Bdr 13084 B/74 Bde RFA KIA 26.11.17.
WOOLRIDGE Ernest George MM Cpl 267847 D/83 Bde RFA KIA 3.9.18.
WOOLSEY Abbott L. MM QMS 168 Royal Flying Corps
WOOLSEY Bertie MM L/Cpl 4582 19th Hussars
WOOLSEY James S. MM Pte 32497 14th Royal Warwickshire Regt
WOOLSGROVE Thomas G. MM Pte 13966 1st East Surrey Regt
WOOLSTON Albert S. MM Pte 39059 11th Bn Machine Gun Corps
WOOLSTON Arthur MM Pte R/19874 20th King's Royal Rifle Corps DOW 4.3.17.
WOOLTORTON Frederick MM Pte 18955 Royal West Kent Regt
WOOLVEN Albert G. MM Cpl 200484 1/4th Royal Sussex Regt
WOOLVEN George F. MM L/Cpl 17926 7th Royal Sussex Regt
WOOLVERIDGE Percy MM Pte 281595 2nd London Regt
WOOLVIN Sidney MM Pte 495703 13th London Regt
WOOMBS Arthur H. MM Pte 101857 29th Durham Light Infantry
WOOMBS Arthur Joseph MM Pte A/203359 1st King's Royal Rifle Corps
WOOSNAM Ernest J. MM Sjt 13535 7th Shropshire Light Infantry
WOOSNAM Stanley James MM Pte 201467 1/4th Shropshire Light Infantry KIA 19.4.18.
WOOSTER Harold C. MM Pte 41812 2nd Worcestershire Regt
WOOTON Arthur H. MM Sjt 1671 1/4th Oxf & Bucks Light Infantry
WOOTON James W. MM Cpl 9388 6th Yorkshire Regt
WOOTON Malcolm George MM L/Cpl 51552 37 Div Sig Coy Royal Engineers
WOOTTEN Leonard MM Pte 12297 7th Wiltshire Regt
WOOTTEN Lionel MM CSM 12490 7th Wiltshire Regt
WOOTTEN W.H. MM Pte 204421 6th South Staffordshire Regt
WOOTTEN William Charles MM Cpl 280703 14 Heavy Bty RGA
WOOTTON Charles Thomas MM Pte S/12031 9th Rifle Brigade KIA 6.11.16
WOOTTON Clarence MM Dvr 23658 C/152 Bde RFA
WOOTTON Frederick MM+Bar Sjt 307788 8th Royal Warwickshire Regt
WOOTTON H. MM Dvr 624 RFA
WOOTTON Harry MM Cpl 11453 11th Royal Fusiliers KIA 10.8./17.
WOOTTON Herbert MM Sjt 241014 1/4th Yorkshire Light Infantry
WOOTTON Herbert J. MM CoH 1591 Royal Horse Guards
WOOTTON John H. MM Pte 17642 South Staffordshire Regt
WOOTTON Joseph Isaiah MM L/Cpl 132394 180 Tunnelling Coy Royal Engineers KIA 22.9.18.
WOOTTON Leonard MM Pte R/14962 7th King's Royal Rifle Corps
WOOZLEY John Eaton MM Cpl 71514 255 Siege Bty RGA
WORBOY Albert "DCM,MM" Cpl 202601 1st London Regt
WORBOYS Albert MM Pte M/285928 Army Service Corps
WORBOYS Arthur Allen MM Dvr 46068 RFA
WORBOYS Charles MM Cpl 14112 1st Bedfordshire Regt
WORBOYS Charles H. MM Sjt 41401 5th Royal Berkshire Regt
WORBOYS George W. MM Pte 13332 1st Bedfordshire Regt
WORBY Claude H. MM Gnr 876335 30 Bde RFA
WORBY William MM Dvr 546099 509 Fd Coy Royal Engineers
WORCESTER Ernest MM L/Cpl 5345 2nd Royal Sussex Regt
WORCESTER Frederick MM Pte 10666 4th Worcestershire Regt
WORDIE P. "DCM,MM" Sjt 34805 8th York & Lancaster Regt
WORDLEY Ernest S. MM Dvr 219615 150 Fd Coy Royal Engineers
WORDLEY Frank James Carter "DCM,MM" CSM 3394 2/1st HAC(Infantry)
WORDLEY George MM Pte 17419 East Yorkshire Regt
WORDLEY Stanley MM Pte 331028 1/1st Cambridgeshire Regt
WORDSWORTH Ambrose C. MM L/Cpl 482222 Royal Engineers
WORDSWORTH Austin MM Pnr 357959 5 Fd Svy Bn Royal Engineers
WORDSWORTH George MM Pte 6822 16th Manchester Regt
WORDSWORTH Henry A. MM Gnr 80143 RFA
WORGAN Reginald F. MM Cpl 2282 1/6th Gloucestershire Regt KIA 14.8.17.
WORGAN William MM Pte 42801 1st Scottish Rifles
WORKER Wilfred MM Sjt 13481 8th South Staffordshire Regt
WORKMAN Alfred MM Pte 241751 4th Worcestershire Regt
WORKMAN Archie MM Sjt 10886 2nd Royal Welsh Fusiliers
WORKMAN Arthur J. MM Spr 82183 38 Div Sig Coy Royal Engineers
WORKMAN Charles "DCM,MM" BSM 352080 270 Siege Bty RGA
WORKMAN George MM L/Cpl 42095 4th Worcestershire Regt
WORKMAN James H. MM Pte M2/100192 Army Service Corps
WORKMAN John H. MM Pte 106735 19th Durham Light Infantry
WORKMAN Percy MM Cpl 12193 2nd Worcestershire Regt
WORKMAN Thomas A. MM Gnr 64784 143 Siege Bty RGA
WORKMAN Wilfred MM Gnr 960094 RFA
WORKMAN William MM Pte 18/954 12th Royal Irish Rifles KIA 21.3.18.
WORLAND Albert W. MM Pte 202654 1st Royal West Surrey Regt
WORLEY Brooke MM Pte 10483 7th Royal Fusiliers
WORLEY Frank MM Pte 18780 Northamptonshire Regt
WORLEY Frank F. MM Cpl 50233 RFA
WORLING Albert MM Pte 267542 1/1st Bucks Bn Oxf & Bucks Light Infantry
WORLOCK Edward George MM Pte 364325 19 Fd Amb RAMC
WORMALD Clarence MM Cpl 98597 449 Siege Bty RGA
WORMALD Francis J. MM Sjt M2/147629 Army Service Corps
WORMALD Joseph MM Sjt 21220 1st Northumberland Fusiliers KIA 20.11.17.
WORMALD Samuel MM Sjt 4 1/7th West Yorkshire Regt
WORMALD Stanley MM Cpl 64109 RAMC
WORMALD Wilfred MM Sjt 25798 A/161 Bde RFA
WORMALL Joseph MM Cpl 12231 8th Lincolnshire Regt
WORMAN George W. MM Pte 200336 1/7th Middlesex Regt
WORMLEIGHTON William MM Gnr Sig 155217 479 Siege Bty RGA
WORMS Edwards William "MM,MSM" Dvr 44645 41 Div Ammn Col RFA
WORMWALD George William MM L/Cpl 202900 West Riding Regt
WORRALL Albert MM Spr 447946 Royal Engineers
WORRALL Charles A. MM+Bar Pte 46491 51st Bn Machine Gun Corps
WORRALL Charles L. MM Pte 306703 8th West Yorkshire Regt
WORRALL Clarence MM Bdr 736277 C/101 Bde RFA
WORRALL Edward Sydney MM Pte 48314 162 Coy Machine Gun Corps
WORRALL Frederick MM Pte 9688 South Staffordshire Regt
WORRALL Henry Edward Thomas MM Sjt 11884 South Staffordshire Regt
WORRALL Jack MM Pte 331302 15th Notts & Derby Regt
WORRALL James MM Pte 66113 15th Lancashire Fusiliers
WORRALL Jesse MM Gnr 172703 RFA
WORRALL John MM Spr 42981 Royal Engineers
WORRALL John MM L/Cpl 39624 5th Lancashire Fusiliers
WORRALL Joseph H. MM Cpl 18103 XIX Corps Cyclist Bn Army Cyclist Corps
WORRALL Richard E. MM Sjt 4966 4th Dragoon Guards
WORRALL Thomas MM Cpl 305103 Royal Warwickshire Regt
WORRALL Thomas Stanley MM CQMS 15352 10th Cheshire Regt
WORRALL Walter MM Spr 47083 Royal Engineers
WORRALL William MM Sjt 15242 7th Northamptonshire Regt
WORRALL William E. MM Sjt 321047 2/6th London Regt
WORRALL William H. MM Gnr 48597 RGA
WORRALL William H. MM Sjt 7927 South Staffordshire Regt
WORRELL Harry MM Pte 26582 1/5th Somerset Light Infantry Died 5.6.18.
WORRELL James Charles MM Pte 11719 3rd Coldstream Guards
WORRELL W. MM Gnr 168753 RGA
WORRELL Walter MM Pte 13119 8th Royal Dublin Fusiliers
WORROW David A.J. MM Pte 31734 Bedfordshire Regt
WORSDALL Charles A. MM Pte 15486 Leicestershire Regt
WORSDALL W.G. MM Air Mech 2 43691 Royal Flying Corps
WORSDELL Charles MM Cpl 24557 57 Fd Coy Royal Engineers
WORSDELL Frederick W. MM L/Cpl 51011 Machine Gun Corps(Cavalry)
WORSELL John MM Pte 62290 2nd Royal Fusiliers KIA 5.9.18.
WORSEY William MM Spr 1034 Royal Engineers
WORSFOLD Arthur MM Cpl 249431 Royal Engineers
WORSFOLD Charles F. MM Bdr 63677 109 Bty 283 Bde RFA
WORSFOLD Eric MM Pte 945 Royal West Surrey Regt
WORSFOLD F. MM L/Cpl 16796 Royal Engineers
WORSFOLD George MM L/Cpl 733 17th Royal Fusiliers
WORSFOLD James W. MM Gnr 92057 RFA
WORSFOLD John MM+Bar Pte 200556 1/1st London Regt
WORSFOLD John MM+Bar Pte 15375 5th Royal Berkshire Regt
WORSLEY Alfred Thomas "MM,MID" Sjt 52145 79 Fd Coy Royal Engineers
WORSLEY Edward MM+Bar Cpl 18181 7th Royal West Kent Regt
WORSLEY James MM Pte 241514 1/5th South Lancashire Regt
WORSLEY James Thomas MM Pte 204258 1st Lancashire Fusiliers KIA 11.4.18.
WORSLEY Sidney MM Gnr 18968 8 Siege Bty RGA

WORSNIP Harold MM Pte 76650 93 Fd Amb RAMC
WORSNOP Charley MM Cpl 796714 D/312 Bde RFA KIA 5.9.18.
WORSNOP Robert Samuel MM Cpl 131455 234 Fd Coy Royal Engineers
WORSNOP Samuel MM Gnr 777071 106 Bty 22 Bde RFA KIA 26.10.17.
WORSNUP Harold MM Sjt 10751 15th Lancashire Fusiliers
WORSTER James MM L/Cpl 13053 11th Royal West Surrey Regt
WORSWICK Herbert MM Pte 58308 RAMC
WORT Thomas MM L/Cpl 14954 8th Royal Berkshire Regt KIA 1.9.16.
WORTH Albert MM Sjt 165054 6th Bn Machine Gun Corps
WORTH Ernest V. MM+Bar 2nd Cpl 32751 4 Div Sig Coy Royal Engineers
WORTH Frederick J. "MM,MID" L/Cpl 5356 1st Duke of Cornwall's LI
WORTH George Thomas MM Bdr 27572 A/155 Bde RFA KIA 10.9.18.
WORTH Henry MM Pte 19300 Dorsetshire Regt
WORTH S. MM L/Cpl P1790 Military Mounted Police
WORTH Thomas H. MM Pte 25796 9th Cheshire Regt
WORTH Thomas W.S. MM Sjt 200550 1/4th Leicestershire Regt
WORTHINGTON Albert E. MM Pte 200390 North Staffordshire Regt
WORTHINGTON Alfred MM Dvr 457102 Royal Engineers
WORTHINGTON Charles H. MM Bdr 44056 RFA
WORTHINGTON Francis Noel MM Pte 8935 17th Manchester Regt
WORTHINGTON Frank MM Pte 73064 RAMC
WORTHINGTON George Richard MM Pte 3141 9th York & Lancaster Regt
WORTHINGTON Joseph MM Sjt 12888 1st King's Own Scottish Borderers
WORTHINGTON Thomas MM(3752 N&D)+Bar Pte 49987 1st Essex Regt
WORTHINGTON Thomas MM Dvr 676433 RFA
WORTHINGTON Thomas MM+Bar Pte 9125 Liverpool Regt
WORTHINGTON Tom MM Gnr 84989 252 Siege Bty RGA
WORTHINGTON William MM Pte 21270 Liverpool Regt
WORTHINGTON William Lydney MM Pte 31104 15th Lancashire Fusiliers DOW 11.11.18.
WORTLEY Edward J. MM Pte R/40259 18th King's Royal Rifle Corps
WORTLEY J.H. MM Sjt 31784 D/84 Bde RFA
WORTON George R. MM Sjt 98411 35th Bn Machine Gun Corps
WORTON Harry "DCM,MM" Sjt 12498 1st Grenadier Guards
WORTON William J. MM Sjt 1154 Royal Warwickshire Regt
WOSKET Thomas Harold MM Pte 202765 1/6th Royal Warwickshire Regt
WOTHERSPOON Alexander "DCM,MM+Bar" Sjt 4583 9th Seaforth Highlanders
WOTHERSPOON Alexander MM Gnr 7396 94 Bty 18 Bde RFA
WOTHERSPOON John I. MM Pte 53085 5/6th Scottish Rifles
WOTTON Ernest J. MM Cpl 51396 Machine Gun Corps(Cavalry)
WOTTON George MM Pte 240823 5th Devonshire Regt
WOTTON James MM Cpl R/4539 13th King's Royal Rifle Corps
WOTTON William J.L. MM Pte 296300 12th Royal Scots Fusiliers
WOULDS Harry MM Cpl 442496 432 Fd Coy Royal Engineers
WOULIDGE Leonard Benjamin MM+Bar Sjt 45870 123 Coy 41st Bn Machine Gun Corps
WOX Albert B. MM Sjt 9853 1st East Yorkshire Regt
WRAGG Cornelius MM Pte R/8448 King's Royal Rifle Corps
WRAGG Ernest "MM,MID" Pte C/588 16th King's Royal Rifle Corps
WRAGG Frederick MM CSM 407117 25th Liverpool Regt
WRAGG George MM 2nd Cpl 309022 33 Lt Rly Op Coy Royal Engineers
WRAGG Henry MM Pte 12088 2nd Notts & Derby Regt
WRAGG Horace Clarence MM Sjt 9787 1st Leicestershire Regt
WRAGG John Robert MM Gnr 150404 411 Siege Bty RGA
WRAGG Reuben MM Pte 11371 1/5th York & Lancaster Regt KIA 13.10.18.
WRAGG William MM Cpl 74216 Royal Engineers
WRAIGHT Frank C. MM Spr 528252 37 Div Sig Coy Royal Engineers
WRAIGHT Horace MM Pte 2509 7th East Kent Regt
WRAIGHT Sidney Arthur MM Cpl 24870 RFA
WRAITH Robert MM Bdr 307639 312 Siege Bty RGA
WRATTEN Edward A. MM Cpl 33248 North Lancashire Regt
WRATTEN G. MM Pte 50046 1st Rifle Brigade
WRATTEN George A. MM Pte 1962 Royal Sussex Regt
WRATTEN Herbert E. MM Cpl 153304 Royal Engineers
WRATTEN John MM Spr 534680 33 Div Sig Coy Royal Engineers
WRATTEN Sydney MM Pte 395 23rd Royal Fusiliers
WRATTEN William George MM Bdr 940341 V/58 Heavy TM Bty RFA
WRAY Alfred P. MM Gnr 87237 RFA
WRAY Andrew MM Sjt 242717 North Lancashire Regt
WRAY Archibald MM Gnr 671916 158 Bde RFA
WRAY Charles MM Pte 18279 11th Royal Inniskilling Fusiliers KIA 15.9.16.
WRAY E. MM Pte 16091 Scottish Rifles
WRAY Edward G. MM Pte 242466 5th West Riding Regt
WRAY Frank J. MM Gnr 109509 152 Hy Bty RGA
WRAY Frederick Alexander MM Bdr 950697 RFA
WRAY George MM Sjt 20114 Signal Service Royal Engineers
WRAY Harold MM L/Cpl 24839 West Yorkshire Regt
WRAY Percy MM Pte 10/40486 1/4th York & Lancaster Regt KIA 2.11.18.
WRAY Robert MM L/Cpl 43525 Suffolk Regt
WRAY Saunders MM Gnr 127079 270 Siege Bty RGA
WRAY William MM Cpl 111832 A/108 Bde RFA
WREAKS Alfred Ernest MM Pte 354330 1/1(East Lancashire)Fd Amb RAMC
WREFORD Bertie MM Pte 265393 1/6th Gloucestershire Regt
WREFORD Walter H.A. MM L/Cpl 13528 6th Northamptonshire Regt
WREN Alan James MM Pte 6277 2/6th South Staffordshire Regt
WREN B. MM Pte 201945 Royal Warwickshire Regt
WREN Charles H. MM Sjt 43 1st Welsh Guards
WREN Fred MM Pte 46998 25th Northumberland Fusiliers
WREN Frederick C. MM Cpl 2103 1/24th London Regt
WREN Frederick C. MM Sjt 277907 7 Siege Bty RGA
WREN H. MM Sjt 1925 12th Lancers
WREN H.G. MM Cpl 14681 Royal Fusiliers
WREN J. MM Pte 5783 XIII Corps Cyclist Bn Army Cyclist Corps
WREN Louis Henry MM Sjt 265551 1/1st Hertfordshire Regt
WREN Luther J. MM Pte 15033 9th York & Lancaster Regt
WREN Thomas J.F. MM L/Cpl 9884 6th Somerset Light Infantry
WREN W.H. "MM,MID" Cpl 6635 1st East Kent Regt
WRENCH Albert MM Pte R/13063 King's Royal Rifle Corps
WRENCH Arthur MM Pte 16026 10th Cheshire Regt KIA 26.4.18.
WRENCH Joseph MM Pte 5457 1st Lincolnshire Regt
WRENCH William MM Pte 266449 2/7th West Yorkshire Regt
WRENCH William R.L. MM Spr 87559 Royal Engineers
WRENN William MM L/Cpl 10285 1st Bedfordshire Regt
WRIDE John E. MM Sjt 59112 93 Fd Coy Royal Engineers
WRIGGLESWORTH Tom MM L/Cpl 132008 Tunnelling Company Royal Engineers
WRIGGLESWORTH Walter MM Spr 40748 Signal Service Royal Engineers
WRIGGLESWORTH William H. MM Cpl 305172 1/8th Notts & Derby Regt
WRIGHT A. MM Pte 17111 1st Essex Regt
WRIGHT A. MM Pte 263131 10th South Wales Borderers
WRIGHT A. MM Pte 201200 Gloucestershire Regt
WRIGHT A. MM Sjt 432 Royal Engineers
WRIGHT A.H. MM Spr 32708 Royal Engineers
WRIGHT Albert MM+Bar L/Cpl 18014 8th Suffolk Regt
WRIGHT Albert MM Pte C/6182 King's Royal Rifle Corps
WRIGHT Albert Alfred MM Pte 4970 1/17th London Regt KIA 29.11.17.
WRIGHT Albert J. MM Sjt 240947 Royal Warwickshire Regt
WRIGHT Albert W. MM Sjt 250298 1/3rd London Regt
WRIGHT Alexander MM Spr 131512 234 Fd Coy Royal Engineers
WRIGHT Alexander MM Pte 8/13798 8th Royal Irish Rifles
WRIGHT Alexander W. "DCM,MM" Sjt S/3639 7th Seaforth Highlanders DOW 20.4.18.
WRIGHT Alfred MM Pte 49514 1st Royal Inniskilling Fusiliers
WRIGHT Alfred MM Sjt 152524 B/155 Bde RFA
WRIGHT Alfred MM Pte 306624 West Yorkshire Regt
WRIGHT Alfred E. MM Sjt 50193 274 Siege Bty RGA
WRIGHT Alfred E. MM+Bar Sjt 23403 107 Bde Ammn Col RFA
WRIGHT Alfred W. "DCM,MM" Pte 23826 1st Gloucestershire Regt
WRIGHT Allen MM Pte A/203617 King's Royal Rifle Corps
WRIGHT Amos MM L/Cpl 956 Yorkshire Light Infantry
WRIGHT Anthony MM Cpl 200217 1/4th Royal Scots Fusiliers
WRIGHT Anthony MM L/Sjt S/5555 Rifle Brigade
WRIGHT Archibald MM Pte 10475 2nd Northamptonshire Regt DOW 13.6.18.
WRIGHT Arthur MM Pte 15915 7th Leicestershire Regt
WRIGHT Arthur MM Pte 27327 8th Royal Lancaster Regt
WRIGHT Arthur MM Pte 31573 East Yorkshire Regt

WRIGHT Arthur MM L/Cpl S/6649 13th Rifle Brigade
WRIGHT Arthur MM Sjt 50814 32 Bde RFA
WRIGHT Arthur A. MM L/Sjt 12349 6th Bedfordshire Regt att 1/1st Hertfordshire Regt.
WRIGHT Arthur H. MM Sjt 201138 5th West Yorkshire Regt
WRIGHT Arthur Ivatt MM Sjt 10383 2nd Suffolk Regt
WRIGHT Arthur J. MM Pte 147965 Machine Gun Corps
WRIGHT Arthur L. MM Pte 722716 24th London Regt
WRIGHT Arthur Oliver MM Spr 47217 93 Fd Coy Royal Engineers KIA 31.8.18.
WRIGHT Benjamin MM L/Sjt 15113 2nd Grenadier Guards
WRIGHT Benjamin MM Spr 95672 130 Fd Coy Royal Engineers DOW 18.6.17.
WRIGHT Bernard MM Pte 92581 RAMC
WRIGHT Bertie MM Pte 376 8th Royal Fusiliers KIA 7.8.16.
WRIGHT Cecil John MM Pte 21646 18th Liverpool Regt KIA 8.10.18.
WRIGHT Cecil Walter "MC,MM(29854 Gnr)" 2Lt B/51 Bde RFA
WRIGHT Charles MM Sjt 328010 Liverpool Regt
WRIGHT Charles MM Sjt 16575 1st South Staffordshire Regt
WRIGHT Charles Arthur "MM,CG(F)" Cpl 18531 2nd East Yorkshire Regt
WRIGHT Charles Ernest MM Sjt 87303 319 Siege Bty RGA
WRIGHT Charles J.R. MM Sjt 1679 3rd Middlesex Regt
WRIGHT Charles V. MM Pte 403330 2 Fd Amb RAMC
WRIGHT D. MM Pte 14666 Lancashire Fusiliers
WRIGHT D. MM L/Cpl 31605 12th Highland Light Infantry
WRIGHT David E.R. MM Sjt 6/2511 1/6th Northumberland Fusiliers
WRIGHT David J. "MM,MID" Sjt 5469 1st Oxf & Bucks Light Infantry
WRIGHT Douglas Alexander MM Cpl 14329 2nd Arg & Suth Highlanders
WRIGHT Edgar MM Pnr 166154 62 Div Sig Coy Royal Engineers
WRIGHT Edward MM Pte 15570 9th Gloucestershire Regt
WRIGHT Edward MM Sjt 45713 23 Div Sig Coy Royal Engineers
WRIGHT Edward F. MM Gnr 76291 RFA
WRIGHT Edward S. MM Gnr 209004 RFA
WRIGHT Edward V. MM Pte 42182 9th Notts & Derby Regt
WRIGHT Edwin MM Gnr 173868 RFA
WRIGHT Edwin MM Pte 2965 1/5th Yorkshire Regt KIA 23.4.17.
WRIGHT Edwin B. "MM,MID" BSM 770581 63 Div Ammn Col RFA
WRIGHT Eric J. MM Pte 40259 RAMC
WRIGHT Ernest MM Cpl 501 6th Royal West Surrey Regt
WRIGHT Ernest MM Pte 203350 Seaforth Highlanders
WRIGHT Ernest MM Pte 357909 Liverpool Regt
WRIGHT Ernest MM L/Cpl 10360 Bedfordshire Regt
WRIGHT Ernest MM Pte 17204 Lancashire Fusiliers
WRIGHT Ernest MM Pte 12530 Coldstream Guards
WRIGHT Ernest MM Pte 61173 11th Royal Fusiliers KIA 18.9.18.
WRIGHT Ernest L. MM Sjt M2/080678 Army Service Corps
WRIGHT F.J. MM Sjt 45764 Royal Welsh Fusiliers
WRIGHT Francis H. MM Pte 71430 5th Notts & Derby Regt
WRIGHT Francis J. MM L/Cpl 241549 Suffolk Regt
WRIGHT Francis M. MM Gnr 60523 RFA
WRIGHT Frank MM Gnr 96571 A/51 Bde RFA
WRIGHT Frank MM Gnr 5504 D/122 Bde RFA
WRIGHT Frank MM Spr 179555 Royal Engineers
WRIGHT Frank MM Pte 22377 11th Royal Lancaster Regt
WRIGHT Frank MM Sjt 13508 12tth Gloucestershire Regt DOW 22.8.18.
WRIGHT Frank MM L/Cpl 23877 Oxf & Bucks Light Infantry
WRIGHT Frank W. MM Pte 235139 Notts & Derby Regt
WRIGHT Fred MM L/Cpl 240286 1/6th Notts & Derby Regt
WRIGHT Fred "MM,MSM" Sjt 755814 D/251 Bde RFA
WRIGHT Frederick MM L/Cpl 36874 1st Gloucestershire Regt
WRIGHT Frederick A. MM Pte 81720 1/9th Durham Light Infantry
WRIGHT Frederick J. MM Sjt 3184 10th Royal Fusiliers
WRIGHT Frederick R. MM Gnr 348184 96 Siege Bty RGA
WRIGHT Frederick V. MM Pte 72661 2nd Royal Fusiliers
WRIGHT G.J. MM Pte 21761 Essex Regt
WRIGHT George MM Cpl 13081 13th King's Royal Rifle Corps
WRIGHT George MM Pte 20179 1st East Kent Regt
WRIGHT George MM Cpl 9357 12th Manchester Regt
WRIGHT George MM Gnr 75832 71 Bty 36 Bde RFA
WRIGHT George MM Sjt 6522 5th Dorsetshire Regt
WRIGHT George MM Cpl 22339 39th Bn Machine Gun Corps
WRIGHT George "DCM,MM+2 Bars" Sjt 4/7856 11th West Yorkshire Regt
WRIGHT George MM Sjt 21424 Machine Gun Corps
WRIGHT George "MM,MM(F)" Sjt 41289 13th East Lancashire Regt
WRIGHT George MM Pte 205965 1/1st Buckinghamshire Yeomanry
WRIGHT George MM Sjt 8435 9th Royal Highlanders KIA 28.3.18.
WRIGHT George MM Pte 43529 7th Northamptonshire Regt KIA 28.9.17.
WRIGHT George MM Bdr 78202 RGA
WRIGHT George MM Pte 265872 Gordon Highlanders
WRIGHT George A. MM Sjt 200194 1/5th Liverpool Regt
WRIGHT George E. MM Pte 40885 Manchester Regt
WRIGHT George F. MM L/Cpl 1123 1/4th Leicestershire Regt
WRIGHT George Frederick Elliott MM Sjt G/12521 1st East Kent Regt DOW 21.3.18.
WRIGHT George H. MM Pte 24456 Royal Warwickshire Regt
WRIGHT George Horace MM+Bar Pte 24191 8th Norfolk Regt KIA 24.4.18.
WRIGHT George W. MM Cpl 18027 7th Royal Sussex Regt
WRIGHT George W. MM CQMS 164 1/4th Gloucestershire Regt
WRIGHT George William "MM,MSM" Sjt 386030 1(Northumbrian)Fd Amb. RAMC
WRIGHT Gilbert MM+Bar Spr 152677 18 Div Sig Coy Royal Engineers
WRIGHT H.G. MM L/Cpl P/5177 1 Traffic Control Coy Military Foot Police
WRIGHT H.P. MM Pte 508372 RAMC
WRIGHT Harold MM Sjt 9976 1st East Yorkshire Regt
WRIGHT Harold MM Pte 275898 1/1st Sherwood Rangers Yeo
WRIGHT Harold MM Cpl 87811 33rd Bn Machine Gun Corps
WRIGHT Harold MM Sjt 48639 22 Bde RFA
WRIGHT Harold MM Pte 38787 Yorkshire Light Infantry
WRIGHT Harold F. MM Sjt 530337 15th London Regt
WRIGHT Harold J. MM Sjt 358591 32 Siege Bty RGA
WRIGHT Harold J. MM Pte 18534 Royal West Kent Regt
WRIGHT Harry MM Pte 266993 6th West Riding Regt
WRIGHT Harry MM Cpl 240710 6th North Staffordshire Regt
WRIGHT Harry MM L/Cpl 5150 2nd Hampshire Regt
WRIGHT Harry MM Pte 265904 West Yorkshire Regt
WRIGHT Harry MM L/Cpl 46057 Royal Engineers
WRIGHT Harry MM L/Cpl 12557 7th Lincolnshire Regt
WRIGHT Harry MM Pte 1216 West Riding Regt
WRIGHT Harry MM Sjt 12656 South Staffordshire Regt
WRIGHT Harry MM Pte 11488 1st Shropshire Light Infantry DOW 5.4.18.
WRIGHT Hector D.E. MM Pte 28010 Royal Scots
WRIGHT Henry John MM Cpl 11044 1st South Wales Borderers KIA 28.8.16.
WRIGHT Herbert MM Pte 26513 Hampshire Regt
WRIGHT Herbert MM L/Cpl 2408 1st North Lancashire Regt
WRIGHT Herbert MM Pte 6975 Royal West Surrey Regt
WRIGHT Herbert A. MM Sjt 47064 42 Fd Amb RAMC
WRIGHT Herbert A. MM Pte 13589 Army Cyclist Corps
WRIGHT Herbert F. MM Spr 185775 Royal Engineers
WRIGHT Herbert O. MM Spr 528191 54 Div Sig Coy Royal Engineers
WRIGHT Herbert W. MM Pte M2/073569 Army Service Corps
WRIGHT Horace W. MM Pte 14251 Lincolnshire Regt
WRIGHT Hugh MM Pte 34011 1/1st Bucks Bn Oxf & Bucks Light Infantry
WRIGHT Hugh MM Pte 265712 Seaforth Highlanders
WRIGHT Hugh Edgson MM Sjt Wheeler 624808 19 Bde RHA
WRIGHT Isaac Scott MM Sjt 6769 Arg & Suth Highlanders
WRIGHT J. MM L/Cpl 43983 Royal Engineers
WRIGHT J.E.T. MM Pte 6498 1/24th London Regt
WRIGHT J.J. MM L/Cpl P/10970 Military Mounted Police
WRIGHT Jack A. MM+Bar L/Cpl 15632 Machine Gun Corps
WRIGHT James MM Cpl 39404 5th South Wales Borderers
WRIGHT James MM L/Sjt 91191 22nd Durham Light Infantry
WRIGHT James MM Sjt 24208 57 Fd Coy Royal Engineers
WRIGHT James MM Dvr 49822 13 Bde RFA
WRIGHT James MM Pte 202191 Gordon Highlanders
WRIGHT James MM L/Cpl 13939 8th York & Lancaster Regt
WRIGHT James "MM,MID" Sjt 81434 Royal Engineers
WRIGHT James MM Cpl 12845 B/87 Bde RFA DOW 3.11.16.
WRIGHT James MM L/Cpl 4217 9th Lancers
WRIGHT James MM Pte 290465 1/7th Cheshire Regt KIA 14.10.18.
WRIGHT James MM L/Cpl 265961 Liverpool Regt
WRIGHT James D. MM L/Cpl 3572 Arg & Suth Highlanders
WRIGHT James F. MM L/Cpl 78432 Royal Engineers
WRIGHT James H. MM Gnr 231773 RFA
WRIGHT James W. MM Pte 47765 Welsh Regt
WRIGHT John MM Bdr 835067 256 Bde RFA
WRIGHT John MM RSM 71197 North Irish Horse
WRIGHT John MM RSM 8466 11th Worcestershire Regt

WRIGHT John MM Cpl 14470 14th Arg & Suth Highlanders
WRIGHT John MM Cpl 305960 1/8th Notts & Derby Regt
WRIGHT John MM Pte 46682 18th Lancashire Fusiliers
WRIGHT John MM Pte 18424 8th Northumberland Fusiliers
WRIGHT John MM Pte 14675 2nd Grenadier Guards
WRIGHT John MM+Bar Cpl 241633 1/5th Royal Lancaster Regt
WRIGHT John MM Pte 1657 East Surrey Regt
WRIGHT John MM L/Cpl 18517 Middlesex Regt
WRIGHT John MM Sjt 19141 220 Coy Machine Gun Corps DOW 6.11.17.
WRIGHT John MM Sjt 3193 9th Lancashire Fusiliers
WRIGHT John MM Gnr 104911 D/5 Bde RFA
WRIGHT John H. MM 2nd Cpl 46596 12 Div Sig Coy Royal Engineers
WRIGHT John Henry Doxey "MM,MID" Sjt 75031 1/1st Derbyshire Yeomanry
WRIGHT John J. MM+2 Bars Sjt 24152 4th & 8th Royal Lancaster Regt
WRIGHT John Joseph MM 2nd Cpl 128775 'N' Special Coy Royal Engineers
WRIGHT John L. MM Pte 14325 Royal Fusiliers
WRIGHT John N. MM Pte 290472 Cheshire Regt att Royal West Kent Regt.
WRIGHT John R. MM Sjt 590 1/5th Royal Lancaster Regt
WRIGHT John W. MM Bdr 308007 113 Heavy Bty RGA
WRIGHT John W. MM Pte P700 Rifle Brigade
WRIGHT John W. MM Sjt 54692 Machine Gun Corps
WRIGHT John William MM Sjt 10073 2nd Oxf & Bucks Light Infantry
WRIGHT John William MM Cpl T4/250624 Army Service Corps
WRIGHT John William MM Pte 201658 2nd Lincolnshire Regt Died 30.9.18.
WRIGHT Joseph MM Sjt 240592 5th Yorkshire Light Infantry
WRIGHT Joseph MM L/Cpl 19630 15th Hampshire Regt DOW 16.5.18.
WRIGHT Joseph MM+Bar L/Cpl 6329 1st East Kent Regt
WRIGHT Joseph MM Pte 266470 Liverpool Regt
WRIGHT Joseph MM L/Cpl 27506 15th Hampshire Regt KIA 1.8.17.
WRIGHT Joseph E. MM Pte 551299 6th London Regt
WRIGHT Joseph H. MM Pte 105155 35 Fd Amb RAMC
WRIGHT Lancelot H. MM Pte 2513 Durham Light Infantry
WRIGHT Leonard MM Pnr 210742 Royal Engineers
WRIGHT Leslie Francis MM Sjt 22904 48th Bn Machine Gun Corps
WRIGHT Leslie W. MM Cpl 8955 17th Manchester Regt
WRIGHT Louis R. MM Sjt 265928 7th Liverpool Regt
WRIGHT Norman L. MM Pte 30514 17th Royal Sussex Regt
WRIGHT Oliver MM L/Cpl 15793 9th South Staffordshire Regt
WRIGHT Percy MM+Bar Cpl 12/1947 9th Yorkshire Light Infantry
WRIGHT Percy Frederick MM Bdr 40272 RFA Died 30.3.18.
WRIGHT Percy J. MM Pte 510077 RAMC
WRIGHT Ralph MM Spr 44693 Royal Engineers
WRIGHT Reginald "MM+Bar,CG(F)" Gnr 91944 Tank Corps
WRIGHT Richard MM Pte 50352 2nd Suffolk Regt
WRIGHT Richard MM Sjt 18 2nd Seaforth Highlanders
WRIGHT Richard MM Pte 11017 7th Lincolnshire Regt
WRIGHT Richard E. MM+Bar L/Cpl 85663 34 Div Sig Coy Royal Engineers
WRIGHT Robert MM Pte 388361 2 Fd Amb RAMC
WRIGHT Robert MM Sjt Pnr 10577 1st Cheshire Regt
WRIGHT S.A. MM Pte 43396 Norfolk Regt
WRIGHT Samuel "DCM,MM" Gnr 58275 104 Bty 22 Bde RFA
WRIGHT Samuel MM CSM 14364 7th East Yorkshire Regt
WRIGHT Samuel J. MM Pte 230025 2/2nd London Regt
WRIGHT Samuel W. MM Pte 267124 Northumberland Fusiliers
WRIGHT Sidney Ernest MM Sjt 8001 11th Royal Fusiliers
WRIGHT Sidney H. MM Cpl 211 22nd Royal Fusiliers
WRIGHT Simeon H. MM Gnr 109767 D/186 Bde RFA
WRIGHT Simpson MM+2 Bars Pte 21581 Border Regt
WRIGHT Stanley MM Cpl 235259 17th Royal Welsh Fusiliers
WRIGHT Sydney MM Sjt 9351 Machine Gun Corps
WRIGHT Sydney G. MM Sjt 10810 7th Shropshire Light Infantry
WRIGHT T.E. MM Pte 140570 Machine Gun Corps
WRIGHT Thomas MM Sjt 147693 179 Tunnelling Coy Royal Engineers
WRIGHT Thomas MM Pte 51618 Royal Fusiliers
WRIGHT Thomas MM Sjt 23992 7th Cameron Highlanders
WRIGHT Thomas MM+Bar Cpl 63210 D/18 Bde RFA
WRIGHT Thomas MM L/Cpl 11138 Gordon Highlanders
WRIGHT Thomas MM Sjt 24538 RGA
WRIGHT Thomas MM Pte 5007 Royal Fusiliers
WRIGHT Thomas MM Pte 14044 Notts & Derby Regt
WRIGHT Thomas "DCM,MM" Pte 40336 7/8th King's Own Scottish Borderers
WRIGHT Thomas MM L/Sjt 200878 1/4th Royal Lancaster Regt
WRIGHT Thomas Grederick MM Pte 301491 2/5th London Regt KIA 13.7.17.
WRIGHT Thomas R. MM Pte 201675 1/1st Cambridgeshire Regt
WRIGHT Thomas Richardson McRae MM Cpl 67767 RFA
WRIGHT Victor Claude MM Sjt 281076 2/5th Lancashire Fusiliers KIA 20.6.18.
WRIGHT W. MM Spr 231685 Royal Engineers
WRIGHT W.G. MM Sjt Farrier 92925 RFA
WRIGHT Walter MM Pte 34677 1/7th Royal Warwickshire Regt
WRIGHT Walter MM Pte 18162 11th Royal West Kent Regt
WRIGHT Walter C. MM Pte 28357 1st Northamptonshire Regt
WRIGHT Walter S. MM Sjt 66727 32nd Bn Machine Gun Corps
WRIGHT Walter T. MM Sjt 548 Royal West Surrey Regt
WRIGHT Wilfred MM Bdr 775321 A/245 Bde RFA
WRIGHT Wiliam J. MM Cpl 87671 'G' Bty RHA
WRIGHT William MM+Bar Pte 128963 2nd & 45th Royal Fusiliers
WRIGHT William MM Sjt 200693 5th Notts & Derby Regt
WRIGHT William MM Sjt 27294 B/119 Bde RFA
WRIGHT William MM Cpl R/11876 13th King's Royal Rifle Corps
WRIGHT William MM Pte 49785 1st Royal Irish Fusiliers
WRIGHT William MM Sjt 41281 Duke of Cornwall's LI
WRIGHT William MM L/Cpl 16158 Leicestershire Regt
WRIGHT William MM Dvr 1714 Royal Engineers
WRIGHT William MM 2nd Cpl 41781 Royal Engineers
WRIGHT William MM L/Cpl 268094 9th Cheshire Regt
WRIGHT William MM Sjt 19297 Lincolnshire Regt
WRIGHT William MM Pte 276544 1/7th Arg & Suth Highlanders KIA 27.8.18.
WRIGHT William MM L/Cpl 16484 6th Bedfordshire Regt
WRIGHT William MM Spr 42497 37 Div Sig Coy Royal Engineers
WRIGHT William Alfred MM Pte 372547 8th London Regt KIA 10.8.18.
WRIGHT William C. MM CSM 303929 17th London Regt
WRIGHT William E. MM Cpl 550039 1/16th London Regt
WRIGHT William H. MM Spr 86267 Royal Engineers
WRIGHT William H. MM Spr 83556 Royal Engineers
WRIGHT William H. MM L/Cpl S/14174 Rifle Brigade
WRIGHT William L.R. "MM,MSM" Sjt SE/4070 Army Veterinary Corps att A/63 Bde RFA.
WRIGHT William N. MM L/Cpl 83236 Royal Engineers
WRIGHT William O. MM Pte 28215 6th Dorsetshire Regt
WRIGHT William R. MM BQMS 36426 C/6 Bde RHA
WRIGHT William S. MM Pte 534358 15th London Regt
WRIGHT William T. MM+Bar L/Cpl 20104 Notts & Derby Regt
WRIGHT William Thomas MM Pte 19141 Welsh Regt
WRIGHTSON Henry MM Pte 33770 West Yorkshire Regt
WRIGHTSON Robert MM Sjt 102327 175 Tunnelling Coy Royal Engineers
WRIGHTWORTH William MM Pte 53181 19th Bn Machine Gun Corps
WRIGLEY Fred MM Pte 30574 Lancashire Fusiliers
WRIGLEY George MM Pte 25425 1st Border Regt KIA 4.10.17.
WRIGLEY George H. MM Cpl 46182 Royal Welsh Fusiliers
WRIGLEY Harold MM Sjt S4/072087 Army Service Corps
WRIGLEY Harry MM Pte 40467 5th Cameron Highlanders
WRIGLEY Horace MM+Bar L/Cpl 19310 21st Manchester Regt
WRIGLEY Joseph MM Pte 47471 11th Manchester Regt
WRIGLEY Oscar MM Dvr 98815 B/173 Bde RFA
WRINGE Richard MM Pte M2/104308 Army Service Corps
WRITER Frank Thomas MM L/Cpl 290 10th Royal Fusiliers KIA 15.7.16.
WRIXON Wilfred A. MM Sjt 240528 1/8th Middlesex Regt
WROATH Stanley MM L/Cpl 265955 6th Gloucestershire Regt
WROE James MM Sjt 5723 Machine Gun Corps
WYARTT Mark MM Pte 9516 1st Suffolk Regt
WYATT Archibald W.J. MM Sjt 435586 3 Fd Amb RAMC
WYATT Arthur MM Cpl 107494 109 Siege Bty RGA
WYATT Arthur J. MM Pte 15336 Coldstream Guards
WYATT Bernard John MM Sjt 75558 49 Bty 40 Bde RFA
WYATT Carrington MM+Bar Spr 71561 Royal Engineers
WYATT David G. MM Sjt 1929 4th Rifle Brigade
WYATT E.C. MM+Bar L/Cpl 42611 10th Royal Fusiliers
WYATT Edward Richard MM Pte C/3432 17th King's Royal Rifle Corps
WYATT Ernest MM Cpl 590887 2/18th London Regt
WYATT Ernest Herbert MM L/Cpl 202164 1/4th Oxf & Bucks Light Infantry

WYATT Francis G. MM+Bar Sjt 297144 RGA
WYATT Frank D. "MM,MID" Sjt 7321 5th Lancers
WYATT Frederick "DCM,MM" Sjt 24434 5 Bty 45 Bde RFA
WYATT G.W. MM Pte 70486 Yeomanry
WYATT Gordon MM Pte M2/153435 Army Service Corps
WYATT Harold F. MM Sjt 51744 20 Bty 9 Bde RFA
WYATT Herbert Sydney MM Sjt 10651 1st Scottish Rifles KIA 20.7.16.
WYATT James William MM Pte 10108 8th Devonshire Regt Died 20.7.18.
WYATT John MM Cpl 19275 11th Notts & Derby Regt
WYATT John George MM Sjt 21597 South Wales Borderers
WYATT Joseph MM Cpl 53887 13th Welsh Regt
WYATT Luke MM Cpl 25048 2nd Bn Machine Gun Corps
WYATT R. MM Pte 241521 Worcestershire Regt
WYATT Reginald MM Sjt 38202 Welsh Regt
WYATT Stanley R. MM Pte 62253 76 Fd Amb RAMC
WYATT Thomas MM L/Cpl 7244 1st Devonshire Regt
WYATT Trevor Cecil MM Sjt 68031 1/24th London Regt
WYATT Walker J. MM Pte 202822 Hampshire Regt
WYATT William MM Pte 39115 South Wales Borderers
WYATT William H. MM Cpl 1559 11 Fd Amb RAMC
WYATT William J. MM Pte 5210 Royal Fusiliers
WYBER Victor E. MM L/Cpl L/8814 1st Royal West Surrey Regt
WYBER William MM+Bar Pte 16730 Royal Scots
WYBER William J. MM Pte 6205 2nd Royal Scots
WYBROW Alfred E. MM Pte 15432 10th West Riding Regt
WYBROW Thomas MM Gnr 97219 RGA
WYCH Alan MM Sjt 139338 37th Bn Machine Gun Corps
WYCH John MM Cpl 22232 23rd Manchester Regt
WYCHERLEY John MM Pte 3456 Machine Gun Corps
WYE Herbert MM Cpl 24280 9th Royal Fusiliers
WYER Francis Arthur MM Pte 27973 2nd Worcestershire Regt KIA 14.4.18.
WYERS Herbert MM+Bar Pte 33037 Manchester Regt
WYERS Walter M. MM Pte 241375 Worcestershire Regt
WYKES Andrew J. MM Bdr 57147 43 Bty 24 Bde RFA
WYKES Frederick Harold "MM,CG(F)" L/Cpl 5587 2nd East Kent Regt
WYKES George MM Cpl 15585 Leicestershire Regt
WYKES George L. MM Bdr 74482 132 Hy Bty RGA
WYKES William Ernest MM Pte 31804 44 Fd Amb RAMC
WYLD Stanley MM Pte 24274 Machine Gun Corps
WYLDER Henry MM+Bar L/Cpl 7873 2nd Middlesex Regt KIA 24.4.18.
WYLES James C. MM Dvr 105795 RFA
WYLIE Alexander MM L/Cpl 205153 16th Middlesex Regt
WYLIE Andrew MM Pte 14808 6/7th Royal Scots Fusiliers
WYLIE James D. MM Pte 266617 Royal Highlanders
WYLIE James S. MM Gnr 193410 RFA
WYLIE John MM Bdr 1804 42 Siege Bty RGA
WYLIE John MM Pte A/202699 11th King's Royal Rifle Corps
WYLIE John McK. MM Sjt 12073 11th Royal Scots
WYLIE Robert MM Cpl 14315 16th Highland Light Infantry
WYLIE Robert MM Sjt 291026 1/8th Scottish Rifles
WYLIE Robert G. MM+Bar Sjt 422227 Royal Engineers
WYLIE Thomas MM Cpl 17897 2nd King's Own Scottish Borderers
WYLIE Walter MM Cpl 76106 8 Div Sig Coy Royal Engineers
WYLLIE James MM Pte 5317 2nd Royal Welsh Fusiliers KIA 22.6.16.
WYLLIE Marcus W. MM Cpl 305202 Tank Corps
WYLLIE Millar MM Sjt 265225 6th Seaforth Highlanders
WYLLYAMS Frederick A. MM Pte 74694 RAMC
WYMANT David MM Sjt 86552 RFA
WYMER Cecil Willie MM Pte 220464 1st East Yorkshire Regt
WYNES William MM L/Cpl 421379 10th London Regt
WYNESS Alexander MM Pte 24094 Royal Scots
WYNESS John Nesbit MM Dvr 47343 C/46 Bde RFA
WYNN Gerald E. MM Cpl 2183 1/1st Warwickshire Yeo
WYNN Harold E. MM CQMS 17384 9th Yorkshire Light Infantry
WYNN John E. MM Pte 24287 Worcestershire Regt
WYNN Joseph MM+Bar Sjt 71841 4th Royal Fusiliers
WYNN William MM+Bar Pte 1583 RAMC
WYNN William John MM Pte 11975 19th Manchester Regt KIA 31.7.17.
WYNNE Arthur MM Pte 10760 East Kent Regt
WYNNE Charles MM CSM 18434 16th Royal Welsh Fusiliers
WYNNE Edward MM Dvr 100529 RFA
WYNNE Ernest MM+Bar Sjt 50584 11th Notts & Derby Regt
WYNNE George William MM Cpl 240375 1/5th Yorkshire Regt KIA 28.10.17.
WYNNE J.D. MM Air Mech 1 5075 Royal Flying Corps att RFA.
WYNNE Jesse MM Pte 13631 9th Royal Welsh Fusiliers
WYNNE Reginald B. MM Pte 41237 13th East Lancashire Regt
WYNNE Robert MM Pte 41066 1st Royal Irish Fusiliers
WYNNE Robert Albert MM Pte 4697 10th Royal Welsh Fusiliers KIA 20.7.16.
WYNNE Stephen MM Pte 29418 1st Duke of Cornwall's LI
WYNNE Thomas William MM Sjt 10652 6th East Kent Regt
WYNNE Tom F. MM Sjt 200157 1/4th Oxf & Bucks Light Infantry
WYNNE William W. MM+Bar CSM 53372 2nd Suffolk Regt
WYNNE-TIGHE Paul MM Sjt 457250 24 Fd Amb RAMC
WYNNE-WILLIAMS T.H. MM Pte 302186 5th London Regt
WYNTER Harold W.S. MM Pte 2429 1/9th London Regt
WYNYARD William Charles Brain MM Pte 15658 2nd Royal Fusiliers
WYRE Patrick MM+Bar Pte 202099 North Lancashire Regt
WYRILL George A. MM L/Cpl 420189 1/10th London Regt
WYSE David MM L/Cpl 235695 Gordon Highlanders
WYSE William E. MM Cpl 4585 14th Liverpool Regt
WYVILL Edward Christopher MM Cpl 60910 X/25 Med TM Bty RFA

Y

YABSLEY Frederick John MM L/Cpl 504762 76 Bde RGA Sig Sect Royal Engineers
YACOMENI William McEwan MM L/Cpl 14440 12th Gloucestershire Regt
YALDEN Leonard MM Pte 24848 2nd South Wales Borderers KIA 1.7.16.
YALDEN Walter J. MM Gnr 47888 RFA
YALLOP Edward C. MM Sjt 55689 93 Coy Labour Corps
YALLOP George MM Dvr 12971 14 Bde RFA
YALLOP John MM Staff SM T/16471 Army Service Corps
YALLOP Sidney S. MM L/Sjt 100667 2nd York & Lancaster Regt
YANDLE Frederick MM Cpl 295152 4th London Regt
YAPP Edwin "MM,MSM" Cpl 200231 1/7th Worcestershire Regt
YAPP George W. MM Sjt H/285394 1/1st Oxfordshire Yeomanry
YAPP Henry Samuel MM Cpl 29974 377 Bde RFA
YAPP Samuel MM Sjt 240584 Worcestershire Regt
YAPP William Ernest MM L/Cpl 1723 2nd Royal Warwickshire Regt
YARDLEY Alfred George MM Sjt 6288 Worcestershire Regt
YARDLEY Edmund W. "DCM,MM" Pte 19970 1st West Yorkshire Regt
YARDLEY Richard MM Sjt 8996 Highland Light Infantry
YARDLEY Samuel MM Pte 129737 46th Royal Fusiliers
YARDLEY Walter "DCM,MM,CG(B)" L/Cpl 40615 1st Royal Irish Rifles
YARDLEY William H. MM Pte 18492 7th Royal Lancaster Regt
YARDLEY William John MM Pte 307843 Royal Warwickshire Regt
YARDY John MM L/Cpl 23429 Suffolk Regt
YARE George MM Gnr Sig 232297 D/242 Bde RFA
YARE John MM L/Cpl 632801 20th London Regt
YARE Thomas MM Sjt 33807 Machine Gun Corps
YARNALL John T. MM BSM 72528 499 Siege Bty RGA
YARNOLD Daniel MM+Bar Cpl 59407 2nd Royal Fusiliers
YARNOLD Edward "MM+Bar,MID" Sjt 550456 1/16th London Regt
YARNOLD Horace MM L/Bdr 77972 RGA
YARNOLD Reginald Harry MM Dvr T4/249140 Army Service Corps att 2/3(South Midland)Fd Amb RAMC.
YARROW David MM L/Cpl 240594 1/7th Royal Highlanders
YARROW Douglas MM L/Cpl 14276 Lincolnshire Regt
YARROW Edward MM L/Cpl 14633 7th Border Regt
YARWOOD Samuel MM Pte M2/187176 594 Coy Army Service Corps
YATES Albert MM Pte S/9807 12th Rifle Brigade DOW 2.6.17.
YATES Albert Edward MM Cpl 226947 334 Rd Constr Coy Royal Engineers
YATES Alfred E. MM Sjt 4505 6th Dragoon Guards
YATES Alfred F. MM Sjt 317461 26 Siege Bty RGA
YATES Ambrose "MM,MID" CQMS 13247 11th Cheshire Regt
YATES Arthur MM Cpl 100233 RFA
YATES Arthur E. MM+Bar L/Cpl 3247 26th Royal Fusiliers
YATES Arthur H. MM Sjt 200020 1/5th Liverpool Regt
YATES Aubrey MM+Bar Pte 15263 8th Royal West Kent Regt
YATES Bertram MM Pte 3840 Army Cyclist Corps
YATES Cyril MM+Bar Pte 403491 2/3(West Riding)Fd Amb RAMC

YATES Edward MM+Bar Sjt 52406 1st Middlesex Regt
YATES Ernest MM Gnr 49580 RGA
YATES Ernest MM L/Cpl 16566 7th South Staffordshire Regt KIA 20.12.17.
YATES Frank MM L/Cpl 266165 2/7th West Yorkshire Regt
YATES Frederick Thomas MM Pte 23648 7th Bedfordshire Regt
YATES George MM Pte 17236 6th South Wales Borderers
YATES George A. MM Pte 57885 Liverpool Regt
YATES Harold MM Cpl 46728 Royal Welsh Fusiliers
YATES Harrick MM Bdr 80213 156 Siege Bty RGA
YATES Harry MM S/Sjt Farrier 19282 128 Bty 29 Bde RFA
YATES Harry MM L/Cpl 22791 2nd Yorkshire Light Infantry
YATES Harry MM Sjt 5074 Machine Gun Corps
YATES Harry I. "DCM,MM" Pte 200848 4th Bn Tank Corps
YATES Henry MM Spr 127050 37 Div Sig Coy Royal Engineers
YATES Henry MM Pte 3/2509 2nd York & Lancaster Regt
YATES Henry E. MM Pte 51729 West Yorkshire Regt
YATES Hubert MM Pte 14/1601 York & Lancaster Regt
YATES J. MM Pte 439406 RAMC
YATES J. MM Sjt 265538 Liverpool Regt
YATES James MM Sjt 82908 RFA
YATES James MM Pte 12918 7th South Lancashire Regt
YATES John MM Pte 242804 5th East Lancashire Regt
YATES John MM+Bar Sjt 492107 46 Div Sig Coy Royal Engineers
YATES John MM Pte 25474 Durham Light Infantry
YATES John E. MM CSM 235524 1/4th West Riding Regt
YATES John G. MM Bdr 56303 RFA
YATES John R. MM Sjt 32896 Yorkshire Light Infantry
YATES Joseph MM Gnr 76880 150 Heavy Bty RGA DOW 22.12.17.
YATES Joseph R. "MM,MID" L/Cpl 18567 7th South Staffordshire Regt
YATES Leonard MM L/Cpl 58112 5th Yorkshire Light Infantry
YATES Moses MM Pte 16463 8th East Lancashire Regt
YATES Norman Daniel MM L/Sjt 48460 232 Coy Machine Gun Corps
YATES Ralph T. MM Sjt 200090 1/4th North Lancashire Regt
YATES Richard MM L/Cpl 203128 1/4th Royal Scots Fusiliers
YATES Richard "MM,CG(F)" Pte 40648 9th Scottish Rifles
YATES Richard Sydney MC.MM(47516 Sjt) 2Lt RFA
YATES Robert MM Pte 32382 North Lancashire Regt
YATES Robert MM Pte 332521 9th Liverpool Regt
YATES Samuel MM Pte 5415 10th Lancashire Fusiliers
YATES Squire MM Gnr 56008 62 Bty 3 Bde RFA
YATES Stephen Frank MM Pte 8219 2nd Scots Guards Died 2.11.18.
YATES Thomas MM Bdr 35335 RFA
YATES Thomas MM L/Cpl 4345 10th Lancashire Fusiliers
YATES Thomas MM Sjt 4876 11th Royal Warwickshire Regt KIA 9.7.16.
YATES Walter "DCM,MM" Pte 18567 8th Royal Berkshire Regt
YATES Wilfred MM Pte 25523 1st North Lancashire Regt
YATES William MM Pte 1601 13th Royal Fusiliers
YATES William MM Pte DM2/112983 Army Service Corps
YATES William MM Pte 241039 North Staffordshire Regt
YATES William MM Gnr 107804 RGA
YATES William MM Pte 202967 North Lancashire Regt
YATES William MM L/Cpl 13424 9th Royal Lancaster Regt
YATES William C. MM+Bar Pte 13787 9th South Staffordshire Regt
YATES William H. MM CSM 267818 8th Royal Warwickshire Regt
YATES William James MM Sjt 22377 A/38 Bde RFA
YAXLEY Frederick J. MM Pte 2978 1/1st Cambridgeshire Regt
YAXLEY Isaac MM Pte 240268 1/5th Yorkshire Regt KIA 19.7.17.
YAXLEY Robert J. MM Pte 242498 West Riding Regt
YAXLEY William J. MM L/Sjt 14788 9th Northumberland Fusiliers
YEA William MM Pte 16820 RAMC
YEADON E. MM L/Cpl 47899 4th Royal Fusiliers
YEADON Leslie W. MM Cpl 482375 62 Div Sig Coy Royal Engineers
YEAGERS Cecil H. MM Pte 610 1st Royal Guernsey LI
YEAMAN Peter MM Pte 42688 Middlesex Regt
YEAMAN William James MM L/Cpl 18/1174 Royal Irish Rifles
YEANDLE William A. MM Pte 295243 12th Somerset Light Infantry
YEARDLEY George W. MM Pte 42563 2nd South Staffordshire Regt
YEATES Albert Edward MM Pte 267008 1/1st Hertfordshire Regt
YEATES Alfred E. MM Pte M2/149776 Army Service Corps
YEATES James O. MM Pte 15662 10th Worcestershire Regt
YEATES William "DCM,MM" L/Cpl 13905 15th Royal Irish Rifles
YEATMAN John J. MM Pte 52827 1st Middlesex Regt
YEATS Arthur U. MM Spr 471057 103 Fd Coy Royal Engineers
YEATS James H. MM Pte 240434 Gordon Highlanders
YEATS Peter MM Spr 76447 'GQ' Cable Section Royal Engineers
YEGLISS Harry MM+Bar Pte 202767 5th East Lancashire Regt
YELDHAM Arthur E. MM Cpl 27920 50 Siege Bty RGA
YELDHAM Harry H. MM Bdr 6184 RFA
YELDON Reginald C. MM L/Cpl 510391 Royal Engineers
YELL Archibald MM Cpl 406488 Royal Engineers
YELLAND Frederick MM Sjt 321101 2/6th London Regt
YELLAND Richard Henry MM L/Cpl 3774 1/8th London Regt KIA 15.9.16.
YELTON William MM Pte 8/20043 Border Regt KIA 11.8.18.
YENDALL Albert William MM Cpl 1857 C/88 Bde RFA
YENDALL George E. MM Pte 7784 Royal Welsh Fusiliers
YENDALL Wilfred MM Pte 332078 Liverpool Regt
YENDALL William MM Cpl 3609 11th Royal Irish Rifles
YENSON George William MM Sjt 47117 D/94 Bde RFA
YEO David John MM Pte 63131 14th Welsh Regt KIA 4.11.18.
YEO Frederick Charles MM Sjt 21312 156 Fd Coy Royal Engineers
YEO John Waldron MM+Bar Spr 218840 2 Lt Rly Op Coy Royal Engineers
YEO William MM Sjt 8164 1st Devonshire Regt
YEO William H. MM Cpl R/9508 13th King's Royal Rifle Corps
YEOMAN Alfred John MM+Bar Gnr 86684 A/110 Bde RFA KIA 24.4.18.
YEOMAN Charles Frank MM Cpl 24793 7th Royal West Kent Regt
YEOMAN Clarence C. MM L/Cpl 41642 Machine Gun Corps(Cavalry)
YEOMAN F.G. MM Bdsm 6841 12th Royal Fusiliers DOW 1 3 17.
YEOMAN J. MM S/Sjt Wheeler T4/241466 51 Div Train Army Service Corps
YEOMAN John MM Gnr 82414 RGA
YEOMAN Joseph T. MM L/Cpl 24571 Duke of Cornwall's LI
YEOMANS Albert H. MM L/Cpl 12461 8th Shropshire Light Infantry
YEOMANS Alfred John MM Gnr 875456 272 Bde RFA
YEOMANS Bert MM Sjt 59746 RGA
YEOMANS Frank Edgar MM Pte 241434 5th Lincolnshire Regt
YEOMANS George S. MM L/Cpl 265953 11th West Yorkshire Regt
YEOMANS Thomas MM Pte 42575 Durham Light Infantry
YEOWARD Eric MM Sjt 64656 B/77 Bde RFA
YEOWELL William J. MM Sjt Y/874 9th King's Royal Rifle Corps DOW 28.5.17.
YEUBREY Thomas MM Pte 40143 Manchester Regt
YEULETT Henry H. MM Pte 60995 West Yorkshire Regt
YEWLETT Smith MM Pte 203949 West Riding Regt
YIRRELL Charles William MM Spr 61618 103 Fd Coy Royal Engineers
YOLLAND John H. MM+Bar Cpl 240075 5th Devonshire Regt
YORK Albert MM Dvr T4/041290 Army Service Corps
YORK Alfred MM Pte S/30593 Rifle Brigade
YORK Alfred W. MM Sjt 4333 5 Div Sig Coy Royal Engineers
YORK Arthur MM Sjt 60846 154 Hy Bty RGA
YORK Charles G. MM Sjt 15554 9th Norfolk Regt
YORK Charles H. MM Staff SM T/17543 41 Div Train Army Service Corps
YORK Charles Thompson MM+Bar L/Sjt 13315 1/4th York & Lancaster Regt
YORK Dennis MM Sjt 3148 Machine Gun Corps
YORK Edwin H. MM Sjt 61821 'E' Bty RHA
YORK Frank Herbert MM Gnr 168876 B/93 Bde RFA
YORK Harry Younger MM L/Cpl 18318 3rd Coldstream Guards
YORK John B. MM Spr 502158 52 Div Sig Coy Royal Engineers
YORK John W. MM L/Sjt 270774 1/1st Northumberland Yeo
YORK Roland J. MM Cpl 22971 Royal West Surrey Regt
YORK Samuel James "DCM,MM,MID" Sjt 8364 1st Lincolnshire Regt
YORK Thomas MM Pte 16290 South Staffordshire Regt
YORK William MM Pte 21410 Lincolnshire Regt
YORK William Thomas MM Pte 49803 2nd Bedfordshire Regt KIA 24.10.18.
YORKE Alfred MM Pte 20365 Duke of Cornwall's LI
YORKE Guy MM L/Cpl 200572 13th Yorkshire Regt
YORKE Robert MM CSM 325012 5/6th Royal Scots
YORKE Thomas MM Pte 19/991 Northumberland Fusiliers
YOUARD William H. MM Pnr 310513 9 Div Sig Coy Royal Engineers
YOUD William MM Pte 14637 58th Bn Machine Gun Corps
YOUDELL Joseph MM L/Cpl 25787 2nd Border Regt KIA 26.10.17.
YOUDLE William MM Pte 406 Somerset Light Infantry
YOUDS George MM L/Cpl 59163 8th West Yorkshire Regt
YOUENS John G. MM Sjt 33945 D/100 Bde RFA
YOULES James Albert MM Dvr 86066 B/82 Bde RFA

YOUNG Albert MM L/Cpl 266078 1/1st Bucks Bn Oxf & Bucks Light Infantry
YOUNG Albert MM Pte 6481 2nd Cameron Highlanders
YOUNG Albert "MM,MSM,MID" Cpl 1912 7th Rifle Brigade
YOUNG Albert Edward MM Gnr 64205 Y/41 Med TM Bty RFA
YOUNG Albert Victor MM Sjt 12349 11th Hampshire Regt
YOUNG Alexander MM Pte 240755 1/6th Royal Highlanders
YOUNG Alexander MM Sjt 173330 151 Siege Bty RGA
YOUNG Alexander MM Pte 36729 2nd Highland Light Infantry
YOUNG Alexander Deuchar MM Spr 64839 17 Div Sig Coy Royal Engineers
YOUNG Alexander King "DCM,MM" Sjt 47243 25 Div Sig Coy Royal Engineers
YOUNG Alexander M. MM Pte 30235 16th Highland Light Infantry
YOUNG Alfred MM 2nd Cpl 112453 447 Fd Coy Royal Engineers
YOUNG Alfred MM Pte M2/175917 Army Service Corps
YOUNG Alfred MM Sjt 14921 9th South Staffordshire Regt
YOUNG Alfred MM Sjt 630851 RFA
YOUNG Alfred T.A. MM L/Cpl 1113 1/1st Lothians & Border Horse Yeomanry
YOUNG Allan MM Spr 108886 55 Fd Coy Royal Engineers
YOUNG Andrew MM L/Cpl 7008 8th Royal Sussex Regt
YOUNG Andrew MM Spr 175619 175 Tunnelling Coy Royal Engineers
YOUNG Andrew MM L/Cpl 41062 Royal Scots Fusiliers
YOUNG Archibald MM L/Cpl 13143 1st Scots Guards
YOUNG Archibald MM L/Cpl 290765 Royal Highlanders
YOUNG Archibald B. MM Cpl 325290 1/9th Arg & Suth Highlanders
YOUNG Archibald George "MM,MID" Sjt 10105 4th Dragoon Guards Died 2.5.17.
YOUNG Arthur MM Spr 177379 Rly Op Division Royal Engineers
YOUNG Arthur MM Bdr 629 RFA
YOUNG Arthur MM Sjt 1483 2nd Royal Sussex Regt KIA 9.9.16.
YOUNG Arthur MM Dvr 810925 RFA
YOUNG Augustus J. MM Pte M/321534 Army Service Corps
YOUNG Benjamin MM L/Cpl Y/1883 4th King's Royal Rifle Corps
YOUNG Bertram J. MM Pte M2/191650 Army Service Corps att MGC(HS)
YOUNG Cecil V. MM Pte 7214 HAC
YOUNG Charles Harold Augustus MM Sjt 502 6th Royal West Kent Regt KIA 2.12.16.
YOUNG Charles McK. MM Pte 353551 Royal Scots
YOUNG Christopher MM Pte 202689 2/4th Royal West Kent Regt
YOUNG Cyril C. "MM,MID" Sjt 13166 XVII Corps Cyclist Bn Army Cyclist Corps
YOUNG David MM Bdr 43922 RGA
YOUNG David MM Sjt 16234 2nd Royal Scots
YOUNG Donald MM Sjt 365283 RGA
YOUNG Edgar MM Cpl 276411 Arg & Suth Highlanders
YOUNG Edgar William MM Sjt 370478 1/8th London Regt
YOUNG Edney "MM,MID" Cpl 16237 5 Div Sig Coy Royal Engineers
YOUNG Edward MM Sjt 16068 Machine Gun Corps
YOUNG Edward MM Sjt M2/020659 Army Service Corps
YOUNG Edward "DCM,MM" Sjt 7934 2nd Royal Scots Fusiliers DOW 26.10.18.
YOUNG Edward MM Sjt 265117 6th Gloucestershire Regt
YOUNG Edwin MM Pte 2054 1/1st Monmouthshire Regt
YOUNG Eli John MM Pte M2/120327 Army Service Corps
YOUNG Ernest MM Gnr 4747 RFA
YOUNG Ernest MM L/Cpl 18213 11th Worcestershire Regt
YOUNG Ernest G. MM Pte 36011 16th Royal Warwickshire Regt
YOUNG Francis H. MM S/Sjt Fitter 56771 RGA
YOUNG Francis Joseph MM Pte 22434 2nd Royal Irish Fusiliers DOW 30.8.36.
YOUNG Frank A.C. MM QMS(Eng Clk) 22576 12 Fd Coy Royal Engineers
YOUNG Frank Reuben MM Cpl 3749 9th Royal Fusiliers KIA 3.5.17.
YOUNG Frederick MM Sjt 20134 Devonshire Regt
YOUNG Frederick MM Gnr 1729 RFA
YOUNG Frederick W. MM Pte 40157 Norfolk Regt
YOUNG G. "MM,MID" Sjt 645637 51 Div Ammn Col RFA
YOUNG G.E. MM Sjt 14465 2nd Hampshire Regt
YOUNG Gavin MM L/Cpl 24600 1/6th Royal Highlanders
YOUNG George MM Pte 39952 9th West Riding Regt
YOUNG George MM Cpl 305018 14th Bn Tank Corps
YOUNG George MM Spr 48902 25 Div Sig Coy Royal Engineers
YOUNG George MM Pte 73718 58th Bn Machine Gun Corps
YOUNG George MM Pte 7971 2nd Royal Munster Fusiliers
YOUNG George MM Pte 44767 RAMC
YOUNG George MM Pte 9748 7th Seaforth Highlanders KIA 12.10.16.
YOUNG George MM Sjt 9195 9th North Staffordshire Regt DOW 14.8.16.
YOUNG George MM Bdr 40079 RGA
YOUNG George MM Pte 35217 Northumberland Fusiliers KIA 21.3.17.
YOUNG George C. MM Spr 94115 3 Div Sig Coy Royal Engineers
YOUNG George Herbert MM Pte 12900 9th Leicestershire Regt KIA 3.5.17.
YOUNG George J. MM L/Cpl 17303 Machine Gun Corps
YOUNG George Shepherd MM Sjt 202322 1/4th Royal Highlanders
YOUNG George Thomas MM Sjt 1599 2nd Royal Sussex Regt KIA 9.9.16.
YOUNG George Thomas MM Pte 422376 2/10th London Regt
YOUNG George William MM Gnr 44585 A/117 Bde RFA
YOUNG Graeme E.J. MM Sjt 39171 RFA
YOUNG Harold MM Cpl 73242 RFA
YOUNG Harold William MM Sjt 3397 1/4th Leicestershire Regt DOW 13.8.16.
YOUNG Harry MM Pte 76455 3rd(Light)Bn Tank Corps
YOUNG Harry MM Cpl 840522 RFA
YOUNG Harry MM Pte 8002 1/7th Manchester Regt KIA 27.9.18.
YOUNG Harry E. MM SM 512196 3rd(London)Fd Amb RAMC
YOUNG Harry H. MM Pte 241425 Gordon Highlanders
YOUNG Henry MM Pte 43901 17th Middlesex Regt
YOUNG Henry G. MM Dvr T4/036668 Army Service Corps
YOUNG Herbert MM Pte 50813 1/1st East Riding of Yorkshire Yeomanry
YOUNG Herbert D. MM Pte M2/073417 Army Service Corps
YOUNG Horace Alpin MM Dvr 1411 RFA
YOUNG J. MM Cpl 240731 1/5th Royal Scots Fusiliers
YOUNG J.L. "See IRISH, D.A.,3385 Cpl."
YOUNG Jack MM L/Cpl 150440 102nd Bn Machine Gun Corps
YOUNG James MM Pte 200750 4th Bn Tank Corps
YOUNG James MM Pte 718382 23rd London Regt
YOUNG James MM Pte 44734 20th Durham Light Infantry
YOUNG James MM Pte 330064 1/8th Royal Scots
YOUNG James MM Cpl 40599 40 Bde RFA
YOUNG James MM L/Sjt 12532 1st Scottish Rifles KIA 13.4.18.
YOUNG James MM L/Cpl 16244 8th East Yorkshire Regt KIA 14.7.16.
YOUNG James MM 2nd Cpl 23188 5 Div Sig Coy Royal Engineers
YOUNG James Learmouth "MC,DCM,MM(1432 L/Sjt 1/9th Bn)" 2Lt 16th Highland Light Infantry
YOUNG James M. MM Bdr 42045 B/181 Bde RFA
YOUNG James William MM Sjt 1657 2nd Manchester Regt
YOUNG John MM Pte 26271 4th West Riding Regt
YOUNG John MM Cpl 306306 13th Bn Tank Corps
YOUNG John MM Cpl 40745 10th Cameron Highlanders
YOUNG John MM L/Sjt 335761 1/8th Royal Scots
YOUNG John MM L/Cpl 53164 4th Worcestershire Regt
YOUNG John MM Dvr 34011 RFA
YOUNG John MM Pte 49785 157 Coy Machine Gun Corps
YOUNG John MM Pte 24193 2nd West Yorkshire Regt
YOUNG John B. MM Sjt 39940 1st Wiltshire Regt
YOUNG John Bertram MM Sjt 3416 17th London Regt
YOUNG John C. MM Pte 14680 8th Royal Scots Fusiliers
YOUNG John Daniel MM Dvr 60355 RFA
YOUNG John Fotheringham MM L/Cpl S/3637 8th Royal Highlanders DOW 19.5.16.
YOUNG John Frederick MM CSM 3702 12th Royal Fusiliers
YOUNG John G. MM Pte 20439 10th Royal West Kent Regt
YOUNG John G. MM L/Cpl 32426 20th Durham Light Infantry KIA 25.10.18.
YOUNG John George MM Bdr 760103 C/242 Bde RFA
YOUNG John H. MM Sjt 1377 2nd Royal Highlanders
YOUNG John Robert Grey MM Gnr 80786 123 Bde RFA
YOUNG John W. MM Pte 65876 Machine Gun Corps
YOUNG Joseph MM L/Cpl 5002 10th Notts & Derby Regt
YOUNG Joseph MM L/Cpl 988 2nd Royal Warwickshire Regt
YOUNG Joseph H. MM L/Cpl 18827 Yorkshire Light Infantry
YOUNG Leonard MM Pte 38058 West Yorkshire Regt
YOUNG Leonard MM Sjt 9302 Leinster Regt
YOUNG Leslie Percy MM L/Cpl 493580 2/1(Home Counties)Fd Amb RAMC
YOUNG Llewellyn MM Pte 17353 6th South Wales Borderers KIA 28.5.18.
YOUNG Matthew MM Pte 23/1308 23rd Northumberland Fusiliers

YOUNG Neil A. MM+Bar Sjt 255041 49 Div Sig Coy Royal Engineers
YOUNG Oliver MM Pte 48221 RAMC
YOUNG P. MM Sjt 57870 Liverpool Regt
YOUNG Percy "DCM,MM" Sjt 9298 11th Royal Warwickshire Regt
YOUNG Peter MM L/Cpl 27799 1st Scottish Rifles
YOUNG Peter "DCM,MM" Cpl 53688 Royal Engineers
YOUNG Philip MM Pte 50553 West Yorkshire Regt
YOUNG Reginald A.B. MM Sjt 12851 6th King's Own Scottish Borderers
YOUNG Richard MM Sjt 37704 66 Div Sig Coy Royal Engineers
YOUNG Robert MM Cpl 7910 10th Arg & Suth Highlanders
YOUNG Robert MM Gnr 18086 D/106 Bde RFA KIA 4.6.17.
YOUNG Robert MM L/Cpl 14140 7th Cameron Highlanders
YOUNG Robert MM Sjt 5666 Royal Inniskilling Fusiliers
YOUNG Robert A. MM Pte 2793 12th Middlesex Regt
YOUNG Robert G. MM Cpl 40304 Lancashire Fusiliers
YOUNG Robert T. MM Sjt 18/1517 Durham Light Infantry
YOUNG Samuel MM Gnr 92637 Tank Corps
YOUNG Samuel MM Pte 17/869 2nd Royal Irish Rifles KIA 24.3.18.
YOUNG Sidney MM+Bar L/Cpl R/6456 1st King's Royal Rifle Corps
YOUNG Sidney F. MM Pte 44691 12th King's Royal Rifle Corps
YOUNG Sydney B. MM Pte 21909 16th Royal Warwickshire Regt
YOUNG Thomas "MM,MID" Bdr Sig 935963 256 Bde RFA
YOUNG Thomas MM 2nd Cpl 312658 Signal Service Royal Engineers
YOUNG Thomas MM L/Cpl 743 4th GMGR
YOUNG Thomas MM Gnr 187310 68 Bty 14 Bde RFA
YOUNG Thomas MM Spr 197760 Royal Engineers
YOUNG Thomas MM Sjt 9/706 9th Royal Irish Rifles
YOUNG Thomas MM L/Cpl 39263 57 Coy Machine Gun Corps DOW 26.3.18.
YOUNG Thomas MM Cpl 16739 8th Yorkshire Regt
YOUNG Thomas H. MM Gnr 30534 RGA
YOUNG Thomas James MM Pte 17430 12th East Surrey Regt
YOUNG W. MM Pte 1921 Highland Light Infantry
YOUNG W.J. MM Pte 439074 RAMC
YOUNG Walter MM Sjt 11517 6th Dorsetshire Regt
YOUNG Walter E. MM Pte 370124 1/8th London Regt
YOUNG Walter J. MM Pte 41034 1/5th Duke of Cornwall's LI
YOUNG Walter T. MM Cpl 5225 RAMC
YOUNG William MM L/Sjt 117102 35th Bn Machine Gun Corps
YOUNG William MM L/Cpl 71117 Royal Engineers
YOUNG William MM Pte 40360 7th Seaforth Highlanders
YOUNG William MM Cpl 151864 33rd Bn Machine Gun Corps
YOUNG William MM Dvr 930450 A/281 Bde RFA
YOUNG William MM Pte 1740 10th Arg & Suth Highlanders
YOUNG William MM Sjt 48382 162 Coy Machine Gun Corps
YOUNG William MM Sjt 1655 1/4th Yorkshire Regt
YOUNG William MM Spr 43552 Royal Engineers
YOUNG William MM CQMS 9246 2nd Cheshire Regt
YOUNG William MM CSM 7179 11th Lancashire Fusiliers
YOUNG William Calderwood "MC,MM(5241 Pte HLI)" 2Lt 4th att 2nd Royal Scots Fusiliers
YOUNG William H. MM CSM 300584 1/8th Manchester Regt
YOUNG William H. MM+Bar Sjt 45031 41 Bde RFA
YOUNG William Henry MM Cpl 18489 1st North Lancashire Regt
YOUNG William J. MM Pte 55687 Machine Gun Corps
YOUNG William J.W. MM L/Cpl 31038 Devonshire Regt
YOUNG William L. MM+Bar Bdr 34012 RFA
YOUNG William McKay MM Cpl 7172 9th Scottish Rifles
YOUNG William Richard MM Cpl 696 1/2(Northumbrian)Fd Coy Royal Engineers
YOUNG William T. MM Pte 376064 8th London Regt
YOUNGE George MM Pte 202741 1st London Regt
YOUNGE Richard MM Sjt 9108 1st Leinster Regt
YOUNGER Alexander MM+Bar Cpl 10202 2nd Royal Irish Fusiliers
YOUNGER Andrew MM Pte 40736 Northamptonshire Regt
YOUNGER John MM Sjt 250985 1/6th Durham Light Infantry
YOUNGER Jonathan MM Pte 22486 Suffolk Regt
YOUNGER Thomas MM L/Bdr 59654 80 Bty 15 Bde RFA
YOUNGER William MM+Bar CSM 39396 7th Royal West Surrey Regt
YOUNGHUSBAND Thomas S. MM Pte 8535 Royal Fusiliers
YOUNGMAN Ernest W. MM Cpl 332927 1/9th Highland Light Infantry
YOUNGMAN Harry MM L/Cpl 14947 8th Suffolk Regt
YOUNGMAN Richard A. MM Spr 16799 1 Fd Squadron Royal Engineers
YOUNGMAN Thomas MM Sjt 13669 8th B Coy Norfolk Regt KIA 31.10.16.
YOUNGS Arthur Leslie MM Pte 1697 1/4(London)Fd Amb RAMC
YOUNGS Herbert MM Sjt 457182 Royal Engineers
YOUNGS Reginald MM Sjt 203482 9th Norfolk Regt
YOUNGSON Harold MM Sjt 10/589 10th East Yorkshire Regt
YOUNGSON Peter MM Cpl 200924 Gordon Highlanders
YOUNGSON Robert MM Cpl 403959 314 Rd Constr Coy Royal Engineers
YOUNIE Thomas MM CQMS 9500 2nd Seaforth Highlanders
YOXALL James George MM Pte 3/7853 1st Lincolnshire Regt
YOXALL John MM Pte 245910 Durham Light Infantry
YOXALL William MM Pte 39945 East Lancashire Regt
YUILE James "MM,MSM" Sjt 30531 72 Bty 38 Bde RFA
YUILE Peter MM Pte 200762 Scottish Rifles
YUILL John MM Bdr 10485 HQ 159 Bde RFA
YUILLE John MM L/Cpl 20780 Royal Scots Fusiliers
YULE A. MM Pte 68641 8th Royal West Surrey Regt
YULE Hugh MM Pte 290447 Royal Highlanders
YULE James MM+Bar Cpl 12437 1/6th Seaforth Highlanders
YULE Peter MM Pte 27261 Royal Scots

Z

ZEECK Alfred John MM Pte 281319 2/4th London Regt KIA 25.4.18.
ZELLY Walter MM L/Cpl 265980 12th Royal Lancaster Regt
ZIGGLES Harry Lewis MM Pte 49271 6th Northamptonshire Regt
ZOLOWSKI Ephraim MM L/Cpl 73055 9th Notts & Derby Regt KIA 4.11.18.